Congressional Quarterly's

POLITICS IN AMERICA 1994

THE 103rd CONGRESS

By CQ's Political Staff
Phil Duncan, Editor

A division of
CONGRESSIONAL QUARTERLY INC.
1414 22nd Street N.W., Washington D.C. 20037

Printed in the United States of America

Library of Congress Cataloging in Publication Data

Congressional Quarterly's Politics in America: 1994, the 103rd Congress / by CQ's political staff: Phil Duncan, editor.
p. cm.

Includes index

1. United States. Congress — Biography. 2. United States. Congress — Committees. 3. United States. Congress — Election districts — Handbooks, manuals, etc. 4. Election districts — United States — Handbooks, manuals, etc. I. Duncan, Phil. II. Congressional Quarterly Inc. III. Title: Politics in America.

Library of Congress Number: 93-11559
ISBN 0 87187-774-0 (hard)
ISBN 0 87187-775-9 (paper)

Politics in America • 1994 • The 103rd Congress

Editor
Phil Duncan

Managing Editor
Colette Gergely

Contributing Editors
Ronald D. Elving
Mark Willen

Principal Writers
John R. Cranford
Ceci Connolly
Kitty Cunningham
Dave Kaplan
Bob Benenson
Thomas H. Moore

Contributing Writers
Charles Mahtesian, Claude R. Marx, Rhodes Cook, Jeffrey L. Katz, Susan C. Phillips, Keith Glover, Ines Pinto Alicea, Susan Kellam, Nadine Cohodas, Beth Donovan, Stephen Gettinger, Elizabeth A. Palmer, Kristine A. Imherr, Jeanne Kislitzin, Phillip Marwill, Paul Nyhan, Jennifer S. Thomas, Ilyse J. Veron, Brad Wong

Principal Researchers
Sam Kaplan Heather C. Hill Sharon Grace Berry Lisa Wirthman

Copy Editors
Susan Carroll, Virginia Cope, Sandra Graziano, Will Heyniger, Stephen F. Langley, Marileen C. Maher, Melinda W. Nahmias, Charles Southwell

Cover Design
Ben Santora
Patt Chisholm

Photographer
R. Michael Jenkins

Phil Duncan came to Congressional Quarterly in 1979 and joined the politics staff of CQ's Weekly Report magazine in 1980. He is a senior writer and contributing columnist for the Weekly Report; he was a writer for the first four editions of "Politics in America" and has edited the book since 1989. Born in Knoxville, Tenn., Duncan graduated from Davidson College in 1979 and worked for The Charlotte Observer and The Knoxville News-Sentinel before joining CQ. He lives in Falls Church, Va., with his wife Leslie and daughter Meredyth.

Colette Gergely came to Congressional Quarterly in 1989 as copy desk chief for the Weekly Report. In 1992, she became deputy political editor for the Weekly Report and managing editor of "Politics in America." Born in Huntington, W.Va. Gergely graduated from Marshall University in 1984 and worked for the Daily Mail in Charleston, W.Va., The News and Observer in Raleigh, N.C., and The Washington Post before joining CQ. She lives in Falls Church, Va., with her husband Kevin and their two dogs.

The chief editorial contributors to "Politics in America" are current members of the Weekly Report's staff. Ronald D. Elving is political editor; Bob Benenson, Ceci Connolly, Kitty Cunningham and Dave Kaplan are politics reporters. John R. Cranford is a CQ reporter; Thomas H. Moore is a reporter/researcher on the politics staff.

TABLE OF CONTENTS

ILLINOIS

INDIANA

IOWA

KANSAS

KENTUCKY

LOUISIANA

MAINE

MARYLAND

Explanation of Statistics

Committees

Standing and select committees and subcommittees are listed for Senate and House members, as are joint committees. Seniority ranking is as of publication date. House seniority rankings include non-voting delegates and the resident commissioner, where applicable.

Elections

House

General-election returns are given for House members for 1990 and 1992. Returns do not necessarily include candidates receiving less than 5 percent of the vote. Primary returns are given for House members for 1992. No primary results are listed if a candidate ran unopposed or was nominated by caucus or convention. Because percentages have been rounded, election totals do not always add up to 100 percent.

Senate

Primary- and general-election returns are given for each senator's most recent election. No primary results are given if a candidate ran unopposed or was nominated by caucus or convention. For senators with previous service in the House, elections to the House are indicated with a footnote.

Key to Party Abbreviations

ACP - A Connecticut Party
AKI - Alaskan Independence
AM - American
AMGA - American Grassroots Alternative
AMI - American Independent
BES - Better Eastside
C - Conservative
CC - Concerned Citizens
CHGC - Change Congress Party
CIL - Conservative Party of Illinois
COLIBERT - Colorado Libertarian
COM - Communist
COP - Colorado Prohibition
COPOP - Colorado Populist
COPP - Concerns of People
CPL - Christian Pro-life
CSP - Common Sense
CUC - Clean Up Congress
D - Democratic
DCSTATE - DC Statehood
ECR - Economic Recovery
FFL - Freedom for LaRouche
FTP - For the People
GR - Grassroots
GREEN - Green
I - Independent
IA - Independent American
ICONG - Independent Congressional
IFC - Independents for Change
IFP - Independents for Perot
ILSOL - Illinois Solidarity
INF - Independent Fusion
INN - Independent Neighbors
IP - Independent Party
IPPN - Independent People's Network
IT - Independent Thinking
IV - Independent Voters
L - Liberal
LIBERT - Libertarian
LIF - Long Island First
LP - Louanner Peters
LU - Liberty Union
MFC - Magerman for Congress
NA - New Alliance
NEW I - New Independent
NL - Natural Law
NNG - No Nonsense Government
NP - New Progressive
PCP - Perot Choice
PDR - Pro-Democracy Reform
PFP - Peace and Freedom
PH - Pride and Honesty
PI - Perot's Independents
PJJ - Peace Jobs Justice
PLPFVET - Pro-Life Pro-Family Veteran
POP - Populist
R - Republican
RPI - Ross Perot Independent
RTL - Right to Life
STI - Stop Tax Increases
SW - Socialist Worker
TCP-LI - Tax Cut Party-Long Island
TFC - Time for Change
TIC - Tisch Independent Citizens
TLC - Term Limits Candidate
VR - Voter Rights
WW - Workers World
WWW - World Without War

Previous Winning Percentages

Winning election percentages are given for each member's congressional career. If no percentage is given, the member either did not run or lost the election. Percentages are included for general elections and special elections.

District Vote for President

The vote presidential candidates received in the congressional district is given for 1992. The tabulations are for the area within each current district, taking into account redistricting for the 1990s.

Data for the district vote for president were compiled by Polidata, Lake Ridge, Va., with the assistance of Congressional Quarterly. The data are estimates of the 1992 presidential election based upon the best information available at the local level, as allocated, aggregated and analyzed by Polidata.

In the statistics that accompany each profile, district vote for president was calculated using data only for the three major candidates: George Bush, Bill Clinton and Ross Perot.

County election results were computed by Congressional Quarterly using state and county election agencies' official results. Some district totals will not correlate with state totals due to variances in tabulating absentee ballots by county election officials.

Campaign Finance

Figures are given for all members of Congress and their general-election challengers, if they filed reports with the Federal Election Commission (FEC). If no figures are listed, the candidate either did not file a report (reports are not required if receipts and expenditures are less than $5,000) or the reports listed receipts and expenditures of zero.

For House members, figures are given for the 1990 and 1992 elections. For senators, figures are given for the most recent election.

Campaign finance data cover the receipts and expenditures of each candidate during the two-year election cycle ending on Dec. 31 of the year the election was held. Data for 1990 cover the period Jan. 1, 1989 - Dec. 31, 1990. Data for 1992 cover the period Jan. 1, 1991 - Dec. 31, 1992. The data for 1992 used in "Politics in America" were compiled from Federal Election Commission reports. Excluded are reports by candidate committees that exist solely to collect money for current or prior campaign debts.

Other candidate transactions, such as contributions to other campaigns, loan repayments, purchase and redemption of certificates of deposit, and debts owed to or by the campaign committees at the end of the election year, were not subtracted from the receipts and expenditures totals.

The figures for political action committee (PAC) receipts are based on the FEC summary report for each candidate. Amounts designated include contributions from both PACs and candidate committees. PAC contributions received by a candidate but returned within 10 days are not reflected in the FEC compilation. In cases where CQ was able to determine that a member does not accept PAC contributions, a zero appears in the column for PAC contributions.

Key Votes

A series of significant votes has been selected from the roll call votes taken during the 102nd Congress, as well as several taken during the 103rd. The following captions give the bill number, the major sponsor, a brief description of the bill, a vote breakdown, the date of the vote and the president's position on the issue (if he took one). The following symbols are used:

Y voted for (yea)
N — voted against (nay)
— paired for
+ — announced for
X — paired against
— — announced against
P — voted "present"
C — voted "present" to avoid possible conflict of interest
? — did not vote or otherwise make a position known

SENATE KEY VOTES

1993

S 5. Family and Medical Leave/Homosexuals in Military. Mitchell, D-Maine, motion to table the Dole, R-Kan., amendment to the Dole amendment, as amended by the Mitchell amendment, to suspend all executive orders on homosexuals in the military since Jan. 1, 1993, until a thorough review of all executive orders on homosexuals in the military is conducted by July 15, 1993, and to require that all changes to the policy be approved by Congress. Motion agreed to 62-37: R 7-35; D 55-2 (ND 42-0, SD 13-2), Feb. 4, 1993. (Subsequently, the Dole amendment, as amended by the Mitchell amendment, was adopted by voice vote.)

HR 1. Family and Medical Leave/Passage. Passage of the bill to require employers of more than 50 employees to provide 12 weeks of unpaid leave for an illness or to care for a new child or sick family member. Passed 71-27: R 16-25; D 55-2 (ND 42-0, SD 13-2), Feb. 4, 1993. (Before passage, the Senate struck all after the enacting clause and inserted the text of S 5, as amended.) A "yea" was a vote in support of the president's position.

HR 2. National 'Motor Voter' Registration/Passage. Passage of the bill to require states to allow citizens to register to vote while applying for or renewing driver's licenses or through the mail. The bill would allow states the option of registering people at other public agencies. Passed 62-37: R 5-37; D 57-0 (ND 42-0, SD 15-0), March 17, 1993. (Before passage, the Senate struck all after the enacting clause and inserted the text of S 460 as amended.) A "yea" was a vote in support of the president's position.

H Con Res 64. Fiscal 1994 Budget Resolution/Adoption. Adoption of the concurrent resolution to set binding budget levels for the fiscal year ending Sept. 30, 1994: budget authority, $1.505 trillion; outlays, $1.498 trillion; revenues, $1.251 trillion; deficit, $247.5 billion. The resolution incorporates the guidelines of the administration's economic package plus approximately $62 billion in additional deficit reduction. (Before adoption the Senate struck all after the resolving clause and inserted the text of S Con Res 18 as amended). Adopted 54-45: R 0-43; D 54-2 (ND 41-0, SD 13-2), March 25, 1993. A "yea" was a vote in support of the president's position.

1992

S 2. Elementary and Secondary Education/School Choice. Hatch, R-Utah, amendment to authorize $30 million for six demonstration projects to give low-income parents money to pay for enrolling a child at the public or private school of their choice, including religiously affiliated schools. Rejected 36-57: R 33-6; D 3-51 (ND 2-35, SD 1-16), Jan. 23, 1992. A "yea" was a vote in support of the president's position.

S 3114. Fiscal 1993 Defense Authorization/Strategic Defense Initiative. Warner, R-Va., motion to table (kill) the Sasser, D-Tenn., amendment to cut the Strategic Defense Initiative by $1 billion from the committee level of $4.3 billion. Motion rejected 43-49: R 34-5; D 9-44 (ND 4-33, SD 5-11), Aug. 7, 1992. A "yea" was a vote in support of the president's position.

S 2399. Eliminate Budget Fire Walls/Cloture. Mitchell, D-Maine, motion to invoke cloture (thus limiting debate) on the motion to proceed to the bill to modify the 1990 Budget Enforcement Act to knock down the walls that prohibit shifting funds between defense and domestic appropriations. Motion rejected 50-48: R 3-40; D 47-8 (ND 35-3, SD 12-5), March 26, 1992. A three-fifths majority vote (60) of the total Senate is required to invoke cloture. A "nay" was a vote in support of the president's position.

1991

S J Res 2. Use of Force Against Iraq/Passage. Passage of the joint resolution to authorize military force if Iraq has not withdrawn from Kuwait and complied with U.N. Security Council resolutions by Jan. 15. The resolution authorizes using force and expending funds under the War Powers Act. Passed 52-47: R 42-2; D 10-45 (ND 3-35, SD 7-10), Jan. 12, 1991. A "yea" was a vote supporting the president's position.

S 1241. Crime Bill/Handgun Waiting Period. Dole, R-Kan., amendment to require a waiting period of five business days before handgun purchases, during which time a mandatory background check of the prospective handgun buyers would be conducted, and to require the attorney general within six months of enactment to select a system and computer software for a National Instant Check system that within five years would be able to provide a record of criminal activity. Adopted 67-32: R 19-24; D 48-8 (ND 37-3, SD 11-5), June 28, 1991.

HR 2506. Fiscal 1992 Legislative Branch Appropriations/Pay Raise. Byrd, D-W.Va., amendment to raise senators' pay from $101,900 to $125,100, ban senators' honoraria and limit outside earned income to 15 percent of a senator's base pay. Adopted 53-45: R 25-18; D 28-27 (ND 22-18, SD 6-9), July 17, 1991.

Thomas Nomination/Confirmation. Confirmation of President Bush's nomination of Clarence Thomas of Georgia to be an associate justice of the U.S. Supreme Court. Confirmed 52-48: R 41-2; D 11-46 (ND 3-37, SD 8-9), Oct. 15, 1991. A "yea" was a vote supporting the president's position.

HOUSE KEY VOTES

1993

HR 1. Family and Medical Leave/Passage. Passage of the bill to require employers of more than 50 employees to provide 12 weeks of unpaid leave for an illness or to care for a new child or sick family member. Passed 265-163: R 40-134; D 224-29 (ND 162-8, SD 62-21); I 1-0, Feb. 3, 1993. A "yea" was a vote in support of the president's position.

HR 2. National Motor-Voter Registration/Passage. Passage of the bill to require states to allow citizens to register to vote while applying for or renewing a driver's license or other public certificates. Passed 259-160: R 21-146; D 237-14 (ND 165-4, SD 72-10); I 1-0, Feb. 4, 1993. A "yea" was a vote in support of the president's position.

H Con Res 64. Fiscal 1994 Budget Resolution/Adoption. Adoption of the concurrent resolution to set binding budget levels for the fiscal year ending Sept. 30, 1994: budget authority, $1.506 trillion; outlays, $1.495 trillion; revenues, $1.242 trillion; deficit, $253.5

billion. The resolution incorporates the guidelines of the administration's economic package plus an additional $63 billion in spending cuts. Adopted 243-183: R 0-172; D 242-11 (ND 164-6, SD 78-5); I 1-0, March 18, 1993. A "yea" was a vote in support of the president's position.

HR 1335. Fiscal 1993 Supplemental Appropriations/Passage. Passage of the bill to provide $16.3 billion in new budget authority and approve $3.4 billion in trust fund spending to implement the administration's stimulus package to help the economy recover. Specifically, the bill provides approximately $4.2 billion for transportation, $4.9 billion for construction and maintenance work, $4 billion for unemployment benefits, $3.4 billion for education, $900 million for business and technology programs, $700 million for summer youth jobs, $1.5 billion for other social programs, and other funding. The funds would be designated as emergency spending and thus be exempt from the spending caps of the 1990 budget agreement. Passed 235-190: R 3-168; D 231-22 (ND 164-6, SD 67-16); I 1-0, March 19, 1993 (in the session that began and the Congressional Record dated March 18). A "yea" was a vote in support of the president's position.

HR 670. Family Planning Amendments/Motion to Recommit Parental Notice. Bliley, R-Va., motion to recommit to the House Energy and Commerce Committee the bill with instructions to report it back with an amendment to federally funded Title X clinics to give parents 48 hours' notice before performing an abortion on a minor. Motion rejected 179-243: R 138-34; D 41-208 (ND 26-141, SD 15-67); I 0-1, March 25, 1993. A "nay" was a vote in support of the president's position.

1992

HR 3732. Eliminate Budget Walls/Passage. Passage of the bill to modify the 1990 Budget Enforcement Act to knock down the walls that prohibit shifting funds between defense, international and domestic appropriations. Rejected 187-238: R 0-162; D 186-76 (ND 151-28, SD 35-48); I 1-0, March 31, 1992. A "nay" was a vote in support of the president's position.

HJ Res 290. Balanced-Budget Constitutional Amendment/Passage. Passage of the joint resolution to propose a constitutional amendment that would prohibit deficit spending unless a three-fifths majority of both chambers of Congress approved a specific deficit amount or there was a declaration of war (or national military emergency) enacted into law; require the president to submit a balanced budget each fiscal year; and require a three-fifths majority of both chambers of Congress to increase the public debt. The amendment would take effect in fiscal 1998 or the second year after ratification, whichever is later. Rejected 280-153: R 164-2; D 116-150 (ND 52-130, SD 64-20); I 0-1, June 11, 1992. A two-thirds majority of those present and voting of both chambers (289 in this case) is required to propose an amendment to the Constitution. A "yea" was a vote in support of the president's position.

HR 5679. Fiscal 1993 VA, Housing and Urban Development, Independent Agencies Appropriations/Space Station Cuts. Traxler, D-Mich., amendment to cut $1.2 billion of the $1.73 billion in the bill for NASA's space station *Freedom*, leaving $525 million to close down the program. Rejected 181-237: R 38-127; D 142-110 (ND 115-59, SD 27-51); I 1-0, July 29, 1992. A "nay" was a vote in support of the president's position.

HR 4547. Russian Aid/Passage. Passage of the bill to provide aid to the former republics of the Soviet Union. The bill also increases the U.S. contribution to the International Monetary Fund by $12.3 billion and includes numerous other measures to boost aid to the former republics. Passed 255-164: R 94-68; D 161-95 (ND 115-63, SD 46-32); I 0-1, Aug. 6, 1992. A "yea" was a vote in support of the president's position.

1991

H J Res 77. Use of Force Against Iraq/Passage. Passage of the joint resolution to authorize the use of military force if Iraq has not withdrawn from Kuwait and complied with U.N. Security Council resolutions by Jan. 15. The resolution authorizes the use of force and the expenditure of funds under the War Powers Act. Passed 250-183: R 164-3; D 86-179 (ND 33-147, SD 53-32); I 0-1, Jan. 12, 1991. A "yea" was a vote supporting the president's position.

HR 7. Handgun Waiting Period/Passage. Passage of the bill to require a seven-day waiting period for handgun purchases, allowing local law enforcement authorities to check the background of prospective buyers to determine whether they have a criminal record. The waiting period requirement would end when a national computer system for instant checks became operational. Passed 239-186: R 60-102; D 179-83 (ND 138-41, SD 41-42); I 0-1, May 8, 1991.

HR 3040. Unemployment Benefits Extension/Passage. Passage of the bill to permanently extend unemployment benefits to long-term unemployed workers for up to 20 additional weeks at an estimated cost of $6.3 billion through fiscal 1996. The bill automatically declares the benefits to be emergency spending and would not require a presidential declaration to be exempt from the spending requirements of last year's budget agreement. Passed 283-125: R 48-107; D 234-18 (ND 172-2, SD 62-16); I 1-0, Sept. 17, 1991. A "nay" was a vote supporting the president's position.

Voting Studies

Voting studies prepared by Congressional Quarterly for the years since 1981 (97th Congress) indicate members' scores. The scores represent the percentage of the time a member of Congress has supported or opposed a given position. The votes are listed under two columns — S for support, O for opposition. For example, a score of 25 under the S column in the presidential support study would indicate that the member supported the president on 25 percent of the votes that were used in the study.

In cases where a "†" is used, the full footnote should be "not eligible for all recorded votes or voted 'present' to avoid a possible conflict of interest."

An explanation of the voting studies on roll call votes follows.

Presidential Support

CQ tries to determine what the president personally, as distinct from other administration officials, wants in the way of legislative action. This is done by analyzing his messages to Congress, news conference remarks and other public statements and documents.

Occasionally, important measures are so extensively amended that it is impossible to characterize final passage as a victory or defeat for the president. These votes have been excluded from the study.

Presidential support is determined by the position of the president at the time of a vote, even though that position may be different from an earlier one or may have been reversed after the vote was taken.

Votes on motions to recommit, to reconsider or to table often are key tests that govern the legislative outcome. Such votes are included in the presidential support tabulations. Failure to vote lowers both support and opposition scores equally. All presidential-issue votes have equal statistical weight in the analysis.

Party Unity

Party unity votes are defined as votes in the Senate and House that split the parties, a majority of voting Democrats opposing a majority of voting Republicans. Votes on which either party divides evenly are excluded.

Party unity scores represent the percentage of party unity votes on which a member voted "yea" or "nay" in agreement with a majority of his party. Failure to vote, even if a member announced his stand, lowers his score.

Opposition-to-party scores represent the percentage of party unity votes on which a member voted "yea" or "nay" in disagreement with a majority of his party. A member's party unity and opposition-to-party scores add up to 100 percent only if he participated on all party unity votes.

Conservative Coalition

As used in this study, the term "conservative coalition" means a voting alliance of Republicans and Southern Democrats against the non-Southern Democrats in Congress. This meaning, rather than any philosophical definition of the "conservative" position, provides the basis for CQ's selection of votes.

A conservative coalition vote is any vote in the Senate or House on which a majority of voting Southern Democrats and a majority of voting Republicans oppose the stand taken by a majority of voting non-Southern Democrats. Votes on which there is an even division within the ranks of voting non-Southern Democrats, Southern Democrats or Republicans are not included.

The Southern states are defined as Alabama, Arkansas, Florida, Georgia, Kentucky, Louisiana, Mississippi, North Carolina, Oklahoma, South Carolina, Tennessee, Texas and Virginia.

The conservative coalition support score represents the percentage of conservative coalition votes on which a member voted "yea" or "nay" in agreement with the position of the conservative coalition. Failure to vote, even if a member announced a stand, lowers the score.

The conservative coalition opposition score represents the percentage of conservative coalition votes on which a member voted "yea" or "nay" in disagreement with the position of the conservative coalition.

Interest Group Ratings

Ratings of members of Congress by four interest groups are given for the years since 1981 (97th Congress). The groups were chosen to represent liberal, conservative, business and labor viewpoints. Following is a description of each group, along with notes regarding their ratings for particular years.

Americans for Democratic Action (ADA)

Americans for Democratic Action was founded in 1947 by a group of liberal Democrats that included Sen. Hubert H. Humphrey and Eleanor Roosevelt. In 1993 the president was Democratic Sen. Paul Wellstone of Minnesota.

American Federation of Labor-Congress of Industrial Organizations (AFL-CIO)

The AFL-CIO was formed when the American Federation of Labor and the Congress of Industrial Organizations merged in 1955. With affiliates claiming more than 13 million members, the AFL-CIO accounts for approximately three-quarters of national union membership. In 1993 the president was Lane Kirkland.

Chamber of Commerce of the United States (CCUS)

The Chamber of Commerce of the United States represents local, regional and state chambers of commerce as well as trade and professional organizations. It was founded in 1912 to be "a voice for organized business." In 1993 the president was Richard L. Lesher.

American Conservative Union (ACU)

The American Conservative Union was founded in 1964 "to mobilize resources of responsible conservative thought across the country and further the general cause of conservatism." The organization intends to provide education in political activity, "prejudice in the press," foreign and military policy, domestic economic policy, the arts, professions and sciences. In 1993 the chairman was David Keene.

Other Statistics and Maps

Each state profile contains figures on the population, area, presidential election vote and composition of the legislature. The U.S. congressional delegations reflect status as of June 1993, and the membership of the state legislatures indicates status as of April 1993. These numbers do not reflect later changes. Information on the makeup of the state legislatures was obtained from the National Conference of State Legislatures. Vacancies in the state legislatures were not included in the numbers used for the breakdown of the membership.

The references to term limits for state offices generally applies to state legislative offices. The state data at the top of the pages deals with any limits on the top executive branch offices. In states where term lists for federal offices are listed, the constitutionality of those limits is unresolved.

Information on urban statistics was obtained from 1990 census materials and from CQ's 1992-93 edition of "Washington Information Directory." Party affiliation is given where possible. N-P indicates a nonpartisan position.

Data on presidential vote were calculated based on the vote for all the presidential candidates. Due to rounding and the exclusion of some minor candidates, percentages may not add to 100.

The demographic breakdowns on population, ethnic and racial makeup, settlement patterns, birth, ages, income and area were obtained from 1990 census materials and from U.S. Department of Commerce information. Some people are classified as both black and Hispanic, and some Hispanics are not classified by the Census Bureau as either black or white. Numbers are not intended to add to 100 percent.

Each House district description contains statistics about the population, background and age of residents. Statistics are given for white, black and Hispanic origin. The "other" category includes American Indian, Eskimo or Aleut; Asian or Pacific Islander; and other races. Some persons are classified as both black and Hispanic, and some Hispanics are not classified by the Census Bureau as either black or white.

All demographic data in the congressional district descriptions are based on the 1990 census; percentages were calculated by Congressional Quarterly and may not add to 100 due to rounding.

Maps for all states and selected urban areas were prepared by InContext Inc., using Census Bureau maps as a base. County names appear in capital letters. City names appear in upper and lower case.

Congress by the Numbers

Throughout this book, CQ frequently refers to a congressional session by its number. Following is a list of what years are covered within a session.

	Years Covered	Election Year		Years Covered	Election Year
96th Congress	1979-81	1978	100th Congress	1987-89	1986
97th Congress	1981-83	1980	101st Congress	1989-91	1988
98th Congress	1983-85	1982	102nd Congress	1991-93	1990
99th Congress	1985-87	1984	103rd Congress	1993-95	1992

Addenda

Campaign finance statistics: Because of 1993 elections, five members' campaign finance figures extend into 1993:

p. 156: Rep. Sam Farr, D-Calif. — figures are through May 28, 1993
p. 848: Rep. Bennie Thompson, D-Miss. — figures are through May 28, 1993
p. 1180: Rep. Rob Portman, R-Ohio — figures are through May 25, 1993
p. 1444: Sen. Kay Bailey Hutchison, R-Texas — figures are through May 28, 1993
p. 1662: Rep. Peter Barca, D-Wis. — figures are through May 25, 1993

Late committee additions: Following is a list of House committee changes that were too late to get into the statistics of individual members even though they are reflected in the committee listings beginning on p. 1712. Because of the late additions, some members' positions on committees changed, and those changes may not be reflected in the individual's statistics.

Agriculture: Terry Everett of Alabama becomes the 18th of 19 Republicans (p. 24); Nick Smith of Michigan is the 19th of 19 Republicans (p. 774).

Merchant Marines & Fisheries: Bennie Thompson of Mississippi becomes the 26th of 29 Republicans (p. 847); Helen Delich Bentley of Maryland becomes the 17th of 19 Republicans (p. 688); Charles H. Taylor of North Carolina becomes the 18th of 19 Republicans (p. 1151); and Peter G. Torkildsen of Massachusetts becomes the 19th of 19 Republicans (p. 731).

Veterans' Affairs: Peter T. King of New York becomes the 14th of 14 Republicans (p. 1030). He also will be on the Compensation Subcommittee.

Health update: On June 14, 1993, Pennsylvania Gov. Robert P. Casey underwent a heart-liver transplant. He transferred the powers of his office to the lieutenant governor. On the same day, Sen. Arlen Specter, R-Pa., underwent surgery to remove a benign brain tumor.

Maps: To clarify the Rhode Island map, p. 1349, New Shoreham is an island, not a county, as its capital letters suggest.

Rep. James Bilbray, D-Nev.: To clarify Rep. James Bilbray's military service, p. 932: He served in the Army in 1955-56, then did stints in either the National Guard or reserve in 1957-63.

Library of Congress Catalog in Publication Data: At press time, the complete catalog number for the 1994 edition of PIA was unavailable.

Introduction

Political Scorecard (as of June 15, 1993)	D	R	I
House	258	176	1
Senate	56	44	
Governors	31	17	2

After the November 1992 election, Democratic partisans and many media analysts fostered a misimpression of how Washington works by pronouncing that with Democrats holding the White House as well as majorities in the House and the Senate, the demon of legislative "gridlock" was slain. The picture they painted was of a Washington where the work of government would proceed at a snappier pace and with a clearer focus than during George Bush's tenure as president.

In very little time, of course, this picture has proved to be a fantasy.

All too often this is the pattern of American political discourse: During the campaign season, voters and even political professionals develop exaggerated expectations about what the winners will be able to accomplish in Washington. Once settled in, the officeholders realize that it is a task of staggering complexity to enact policies that balance the legitimate and often conflicting interests in our society. America is hundreds of constituencies with different economic, ethnic, racial, cultural and political characteristics that translate into a mind-numbing array of cross-pressures on decision-makers.

This panoply of political forces is now bedeviling the 103rd Congress, as lawmakers strive to give specific legislative shape to the general call for a change in national direction that voters expressed in 1992.

As this edition of "Politics in America" goes to press, we are not yet midway through 1993 — too soon to assess whether legislation of great significance will be achieved by this new Congress and its ambitious, innovative and erratic presidential partner, Bill Clinton.

But whether this Congress will be remarkable for what it does, it already has a place of significance in history for what it is. It is the most diverse collection of people ever to serve in the national legislature, and it is the first Congress in a dozen years controlled by the party that occupies the White House.

For the bulk of its 204 years, Congress has been the province of white males. Changes in society's attitudes about race and gender have reverberated in congressional voting for some time, but only with the tumultuous 1992 election did women, blacks and Hispanics definitively break from a past in which their numbers in Congress were tokenistic.

In the 103rd Congress, there are 38 black House members; as recently as 1971, there were only 12. There are 17 Hispanics in the House, more than three times the handful sitting in 1971. And there are 47 women representatives, almost quadruple the number present in the 92nd Congress. The Senate in the 92nd had one woman member. Today seven women are senators — five of them freshmen in the 103rd.

Beyond its more diverse demography, the 103rd Congress is noteworthy as part of an atypical phenomenon in recent American politics: one-party control of the federal government. Of the 24 Congresses that have convened in the post-World War II era, this is just the 10th in which the legislature's majority party also has held the presidency.

This is a momentous opportunity for the Democratic Party, but also a weighty responsibility. Voters felt they were acting in 1992 to change the status quo; now they demand results.

Competition and Turnover

Heading into the 1992 campaign cycle, there was grumbling in the land that the American political system had lost its capacity for renewal: Low-turnover elections in the late 1980s fostered a public perception of Congress as a perpetual incumbency club, one whose privileged members could gorge themselves on special interest cash and wage lavishly funded campaigns that nearly always flattened challengers.

But instead of ossification, the story of the 1992 congressional campaign was competition and turnover. Redistricting, the decennial scrambler of House politics, dramatically reshaped hundreds of constituencies, prodding many members into retirement and forcing others to run on unfamiliar turf they could not hold. Voters deeply anxious about jobs and health care were roused by reports of lax management and overdrafted checks at the House bank, and by frustration and weariness with the poor relationship between President George Bush and Democrats in Congress — who by 1992 could scarcely speak without laying blame and pointing fingers.

In congressional voting, all this agitation translated into 110 people winning their first House terms in November 1992, an influx of newcomers exceeding anything official Washington had seen in more than 40 years. In the postwar era, only one House freshman class was larger — the 118 newcomers to the 81st Congress in 1949. And no freshman class ever had so many women (25) and so many stripes of America's ethnic rainbow, counting in its ranks 16 African-Americans, eight Hispanics (including those of Mexican, Cuban and Puerto Rican heritage) and a Korean-American.

Elections for the Senate also changed the face of that previously all-white and nearly all-male club. The Senate freshman class of the 103rd Congress is the largest since 1981, with nine men and five women, including the chamber's first black woman (Democrat Carol Moseley-Braun of Illinois) and its first American Indian (Democrat Ben Nighthorse Campbell of Colorado) since Charles Curtis, a Republican from Kansas, stepped down in 1929 to become vice president under Herbert Hoover.

The Main Event

In the eyes of the media and the voters, even interesting congressional election years are a sideshow to the competition for the presidency. The

Cross-Cut Politics I: Democratic Seats

Following are districts where a Democrat won the 1992 House race and Republican George Bush ran first in presidential voting.

District	Member and winning percentage		Clinton Vote	Bush Vote	Perot Vote
Ala. 3	Glen Browder	60.3	42%	48%	11%
Ala. 4	Tom Bevill	68.5	44%	45%	12%
Ala. 5	Robert E. "Bud" Cramer	65.6	41%	44%	15%
Ariz. 1	Sam Coppersmith	51.3	34%	40%	26%
Ariz. 6	Karan English	53.0	38%	38%	24%
Calif. 19	Richard H. Lehman	47.1	38%	44%	18%
Fla. 1	Earl Hutto	52.0	26%	51%	23%
Fla. 15	Jim Bacchus	50.7	31%	43%	26%
Ga. 7	George "Buddy" Darden	57.3	38%	47%	15%
Ga. 8	J. Roy Rowland	55.7	40%	45%	15%
Ga. 9	Nathan Deal	59.2	35%	49%	16%
Ga. 10	Don Johnson	53.8	39%	46%	14%
Idaho 1	Larry LaRocco	58.1	31%	42%	28%
Ind. 2	Philip R. Sharp	57.1	35%	43%	22%
Ind. 3	Tim Roemer	57.4	38%	43%	19%
Ind. 4	Jill L. Long	62.1	31%	46%	22%
Kan. 2	Jim Slattery	56.2	36%	36%	28%
Kan. 4	Dan Glickman	51.7	33%	40%	27%
Ky. 2	William H. Natcher	61.4	41%	45%	14%
Ky. 6	Scotty Baesler	60.7	41%	43%	16%
Mich. 10	David E. Bonior	53.1	36%	42%	22%
Mo. 4	Ike Skelton	70.4	37%	38%	25%
Miss. 1	Jamie L. Whitten	59.5	41%	50%	9%
Miss. 3	G.V. "Sonny" Montgomery	81.2	34%	58%	8%
Miss. 4	Mike Parker	67.3	41%	50%	8%
Miss. 5	Gene Taylor	63.2	32%	54%	14%
N.C. 2	Tim Valentine	53.7	40%	46%	14%
N.C. 3	H. Martin Lancaster	54.4	39%	46%	15%
N.C. 5	Stephen L. Neal	52.7	43%	44%	13%
N.C. 8	W. G. "Bill" Hefner	59.3	42%	44%	14%
N.D. AL	Earl Pomeroy	56.8	32%	44%	23%
Neb. 2	Peter Hoagland	51.2	32%	48%	20%
N.Y. 1	George J. Hochbrueckner	51.7	38%	40%	21%
Ohio 6	Ted Strickland	50.7	40%	40%	20%
Okla. 4	Dave McCurdy	70.7	33%	42%	25%
Okla. 6	Glenn English	67.8	34%	43%	23%
Pa. 6	Tim Holden	52.1	36%	41%	23%
S.C. 3	Butler Derrick	61.2	35%	52%	13%
S.C. 5	John M. Spratt Jr.	61.3	43%	45%	12%
S.D. AL	Tim Johnson	69.1	37%	41%	22%
Tenn. 3	Marilyn Lloyd	48.8	44%	44%	12%
Texas 4	Ralph M. Hall	58.1	28%	41%	30%
Texas 11	Chet Edwards	67.4	36%	41%	23%
Texas 13	Bill Sarpalius	60.3	36%	43%	20%
Texas 14	Greg Laughlin	68.1	37%	41%	22%
Texas 17	Charles W. Stenholm	66.1	34%	40%	26%
Utah 2	Karen Shepherd	50.5	31%	39%	29%
Utah 3	Bill Orton	59.5	24%	49%	27%
Va. 2	Owen B. Pickett	56.1	35%	48%	17%
Va. 4	Norman Sisisky	68.4	40%	47%	14%
Va. 5	Lewis F. Payne Jr.	68.9	41%	47%	12%
Va. 11	Leslie L. Byrne	50.0	43%	43%	14%
Wash. 4	Jay Inslee	50.8	35%	43%	22%

House and Senate contests of 1992 produced an abundance of commotion and turnover, but the extraordinary spectacle of a scrap for the White House among three well-funded candidates was one of the more gripping dramas in American political history.

A writer of fiction could not have produced a campaign plot with more twists: the fall of a president who through the summer of 1991 had looked unassailable; the emergence of a challenger who won nomination after enduring intense questioning of his morality and integrity, then moved up from third place to first by marketing himself skillfully as a new-generation agent of change; the on-, then off-, then on-again independent bid of billionaire populist Ross Perot, whose stunning final tally — nearly one-fifth of the total vote — showed that journalists and major-party leaders had considerably underestimated the appeal of his plain-talk assault on the political and media establishment.

Public interest in the Bush-Clinton-Perot debates was high, and turnout in November exceeded 100 million, a first in American presidential voting. While these were encouraging signs of an electorate more engaged than alienated, there is a downside to the quadrennial ritual of intensely focusing on the single question of who will occupy the Oval Office: Among the huge number of Americans who pay only casual and infrequent attention to the workings of the political process, it creates a false picture of the presidency as so important and powerful a position that its occupant can readily bring to heel others in Washington who have competing policy priorities.

Divided Democrats

Instead, what Democrats discovered in the early months of 1993 was that even when the same party controls the party and the presidency, bad luck and wrenching disputes within the majority party itself can stand in the way of developing legislative proposals to offer for enactment.

The new administration lurched through its opening months; there were some misfires on Cabinet and sub-Cabinet nominees, clumsy handling of personnel in the White House travel office and a costly coiffure of Clinton by celebrity stylist Cristophe.

All that, though, was minor and transitory compared with the challenge Clinton faced in Congress: scrambling madly to cope with "friendly fire" — Democratic defectors in the House and Senate who threatened to derail his economic program. A round-the-clock frenzy of White House lobbying and deal-cutting in late May produced just two more votes than the minimum needed to pass Clinton's budget-and-tax package in the House, even though the chamber then had 80 more Democrats than Republicans.

Then, in early June, when it seemed clear that opposition from moderate Democrat David L. Boren of Oklahoma and other centrists would stall Clinton's budget package in the Senate, the president acceded to seeing the

Cross-Cut Politics II: GOP Seats

Following are districts where a Republican won the 1992 House race and Democrat Bill Clinton ran first in presidential voting.

District	Member and winning percentage		Clinton Vote	Bush Vote	Perot Vote
Ark. 3	Tim Hutchinson	50.2	43%	43%	14%
Ark. 4	Jay Dickey	52.3	58%	32%	10%
Ariz. 5	Jim Kolbe	66.5	42%	38%	20%
Calif. 10	Bill Baker	52.0	42%	36%	22%
Calif. 11	Richard W. Pombo	47.6	41%	38%	21%
Calif. 22	Michael Huffington	52.5	41%	35%	23%
Calif. 23	Elton Gallegly	54.3	38%	34%	27%
Calif. 27	Carlos J. Moorhead	49.7	44%	37%	19%
Calif. 38	Steve Horn	48.6	45%	33%	22%
Calif. 44	Al McCandless	54.2	41%	36%	24%
Colo. 3	Scott McInnis	54.7	40%	35%	25%
Conn. 6	Nancy L. Johnson	69.7	40%	36%	24%
Del. AL	Michael N. Castle	55.4	44%	36%	21%
Fla. 10	C.W. Bill Young	56.6	40%	36%	24%
Fla. 22	E. Clay Shaw Jr.	52.0	45%	38%	17%
Iowa 1	Jim Leach	68.1	46%	34%	19%
Iowa 2	Jim Nussle	50.2	44%	35%	20%
Iowa 3	Jim Ross Lightfoot	48.9	46%	37%	18%
Ill. 15	Thomas W. Ewing	59.3	43%	39%	19%
Ill. 18	Robert H. Michel	57.8	42%	41%	17%
Kan. 3	Jan Meyers	58.0	38%	37%	25%
Ky. 5	Harold Rogers	54.6	48%	42%	10%
Mass. 3	Peter I. Blute	50.4	45%	31%	23%
Mass. 6	Peter G. Torkildsen	54.8	44%	32%	25%
Md. 8	Constance A. Morella	72.5	53%	35%	12%
Maine 2	Olympia J. Snowe	49.1	38%	29%	33%
Mich. 4	Dave Camp	62.5	38%	37%	25%
Mich. 6	Fred Upton	61.8	40%	38%	22%
Mich. 7	Nick Smith	87.6	38%	38%	24%
Minn. 3	Jim Ramstad	63.6	39%	36%	24%
Minn. 6	Rod Grams	44.4	40%	33%	27%
Mo. 8	Bill Emerson	63.0	46%	37%	17%
N.C. 11	Charles H. Taylor	54.7	43%	43%	14%
N.J. 3	H. James Saxton	59.2	40%	40%	19%
N.M. 1	Steven H. Schiff	62.6	46%	39%	16%
N.M. 2	Joe Skeen	56.4	41%	40%	19%
N.Y. 3	Peter T. King	49.6	44%	42%	14%
N.Y. 4	David A. Levy	50.2	47%	41%	12%
N.Y. 20	Benjamin A. Gilman	66.1	45%	41%	14%
N.Y. 25	James T. Walsh	55.7	41%	36%	22%
N.Y. 30	Jack Quinn	51.7	46%	26%	28%
Ohio 10	Martin R. Hoke	56.8	42%	36%	22%
Pa. 8	James C. Greenwood	51.9	40%	39%	22%
Pa. 18	Rick Santorum	60.6	52%	30%	18%
Pa. 21	Tom Ridge	68.0	45%	35%	20%
R.I. 1	Ronald K. Machtley	70.1	50%	28%	22%
Texas 23	Henry Bonilla	59.1	42%	41%	17%
Wash. 8	Jennifer Dunn	60.4	38%	34%	27%
Wis. 2	Scott L. Klug	62.6	50%	32%	18%
Wis. 3	Steve Gunderson	56.4	43%	33%	24%

House-passed plan altered in the Senate to include more spending cuts and a revised energy tax component.

These conflicts between a Democratic president and Democrats in Congress quickly helped sour a public that seemed upbeat when Clinton and the 103rd Congress came to Washington. In January 1993, a CBS News poll found that 56 percent of respondents felt Clinton could be "trusted to deal with problems," while 35 percent thought he "might make serious mistakes." In a poll released June 1, the numbers virtually had flipped. The same poll showed that 61 percent of respondents disapproved of Congress' performance.

Focus on Members, Districts

Such wild mood swings stem from an incomplete understanding of how complex a business it is to make laws for a nation of 250 million people. Our book aims to shed light on the multidimensional challenge of governing America by looking at the 535 individuals of the House and Senate who work as advocates for the districts and states that elect them. We examine the motivations of those whose ambitions take them to Congress and the desires of the Americans who send them there.

In writing our profiles, we do not try to decide what members ought to be for or against; our goal is to explain how members go about expressing their views and to assess how effective they are at it.

This edition of "Politics in America" is the first to appear since the 1992 round of congressional redistricting fundamentally reshaped the country's political landscape. Forty-two states revised their districts' boundaries for the 1990s, many of them extensively. (Maine redistricts in 1993, and seven other states have single at-large districts.)

Redistricting caused the most upheaval in 13 states where mapmakers responded to judicial and Justice Department mandates to maximize minority representation wherever possible. In nearly every instance, minority group candidates (typically liberal Democrats) did in fact win the new districts crafted for them. But the process of pulling together often widely scattered pockets of black or Hispanic voters into "majority minority" districts usually left surrounding districts whiter and more conservative, and that was a benefit to Republican candidates. In Georgia, for instance, the House delegation before redistricting had nine Democrats (one a black) and one Republican. After redistricting, voters elected seven Democrats (three of them black) and four Republicans.

Because redistricting so often brought these kinds of marked shifts in the political currents, we have devoted special attention in this book to explaining the characteristics of the 435 House districts.

In each district description we focus on factors that shape how residents vote: What do the people do for a living? Are they city dwellers, suburbanites, townsfolk or farmers? Did their communities grow or shrink during the

1980s? Are their partisan allegiances strong or weak? What do they ask from the federal government?

Diverse Constituencies, Divided Goals

No one who spends some time examining the variety of individuals in Congress and the diverse constituencies they represent will ever be surprised that the process of making policy in Washington is often slow and tortured. What one member might see as a "special interest" with nefarious influence in the legislative process is the industry that another member regards as absolutely vital to his constituents' economic well-being. In Congress' work on issues such as health-care policy and campaign finance law, contrasting visions emerge of what a capitalistic society is all about. One side contends that obtaining health care and seeking public office should not be a function of affluence; the other side sees medicine and politics as components of a capitalistic system in which those with more money always have enjoyed more options.

And when Congress tackles issues such as the federal government's posture toward abortion, strongly held convictions about morality and personal freedom inevitably will clash.

The arguments and delays that arise when Congress grapples with itself and with the president make Washington an easy target for critics such as Perot, whose pithy pokes portray politicians as a class of people who would flop in business because they will not set priorities and make tough decisions.

But for all the popular appeal of Perot's vision that politics should be a more clear-cut business, a look at the electoral behavior of the districts and states shows that the voters themselves often act in a way that sends mixed and even conflicting signals to Washington.

In November 1992, more than 100 House districts — 24 percent of the total — registered a split decision in House and presidential voting. Fifty-three districts elected a Democrat to the House but at the same time went for Bush in presidential voting. In 50 other districts, Clinton prevailed in the presidential vote, but a Republican won the House seat. *(Split districts, charts, pp. 2, 4)*

In five states that Bush carried for president in November, voters simultaneously elected Democrats to the Senate. Half of the 18 states Bush won are represented by at least one Democrat in the Senate, and three of those — Alabama, Nebraska and North Dakota — have two Democratic senators.

Similarly, in seven states where Clinton ran first in presidential balloting, voters elected Republican senators. Overall, of the 32 states that Clinton carried in 1992, 14 have one GOP senator, and three more — Missouri, Oregon and New Hampshire — are represented by two Republicans in the Senate. *(Election tally, chart, p. 7)*

Cross-Cut Politics III: The States

In the chart below, the states Bill Clinton carried in 1992 are listed, followed by the states George Bush carried. The senators for each state are listed; those in **bold** type are up for election in 1994.

States Clinton Won

State	Clinton	Bush	Perot	Others	Senators
D.C.	84.6	9.1	4.3	2.0	
Ark.	53.2	35.5	10.4	0.9	Bumpers, D; Pryor, D
Md.	49.8	35.6	14.2	0.4	**Sarbanes, D**; Mikulski, D
N.Y.	49.7	33.9	15.7	0.6	**Moynihan, D**; D'Amato, R
Ill.	48.6	34.3	16.6	0.4	Simon, D; Moseley-Braun, D
W.Va.	48.4	35.4	15.9	0.3	**Byrd, D**; Rockefeller, D
Hawaii	48.1	36.7	14.2	1.0	Inouye, D; **Akaka, D**
Mass.	47.5	29.0	22.7	0.7	**Kennedy, D**; Kerry, D
Tenn.	47.1	42.4	10.1	0.4	**Sasser, D**; **Mathews, D** [1]
R.I.	47.0	29.0	23.2	0.8	Pell, D; **Chafee, R**
Vt.	46.1	30.4	22.8	0.7	Leahy, D; **Jeffords, R**
Calif.	46.0	32.6	20.6	0.8	**Feinstein, D**; Boxer, D
N.M.	45.9	37.3	16.1	0.6	Domenici, R; **Bingaman, D**
La.	45.6	41.0	11.8	1.6	Johnston, D; Breaux, D
Pa.	45.1	36.1	18.2	0.5	Specter, R; **Wofford, D**
Ky.	44.6	41.3	13.7	0.4	Ford, D; McConnell, R
Mo.	44.1	33.9	21.7	0.3	Bond, R; **Danforth, R**
Mich.	43.8	36.4	19.3	0.6	Levin, D; **Riegle, D**
Del.	43.5	35.3	20.4	0.7	Biden, D; **Roth, R**
Minn.	43.5	31.9	24.0	0.7	**Durenberger, R**; Wellstone, D
Ga.	43.5	42.9	13.3	0.3	Nunn, D; Coverdell, R
Wash.	43.4	32.0	23.7	1.0	**Gorton, R**; Murray, D
Iowa	43.3	37.3	18.7	0.7	Grassley, R; Harkin, D
N.J.	43.0	40.6	15.6	0.9	Bradley, D; **Lautenberg, D**
Ore.	42.5	32.5	24.2	0.8	Hatfield, R; Packwood, R
Conn.	42.2	35.8	21.6	0.4	Dodd, D; **Lieberman, D**
Wis.	41.1	36.8	21.5	0.6	**Kohl, D**; Feingold, D
Ohio	40.2	38.3	21.0	0.5	Glenn, D; **Metzenbaum, D**
Colo.	40.1	35.9	23.3	0.7	Brown, R; Campbell, D
N.H.	38.9	37.6	22.6	0.9	Smith, R; Gregg, R
Maine	38.8	30.4	30.4	0.4	Cohen, R; **Mitchell, D**
Mont.	37.6	35.1	26.1	1.1	Baucus, D; **Burns, R**
Nev.	37.4	34.7	26.2	1.7	Reid, D; **Bryan, D**

States Bush Won

State	Bush	Clinton	Perot	Others	Senators
Miss.	49.7	40.8	8.7	0.8	Cochran, R; **Lott, R**
S.C.	48.0	39.9	11.5	0.6	Thurmond, R; Hollings, D
Ala.	47.6	40.9	10.8	0.6	Heflin, D; Shelby, D
Neb.	46.6	29.4	23.6	0.4	Exon, D; **Kerrey, D**
Va.	45.0	40.6	13.6	0.8	Warner, R; **Robb, D**
N.D.	44.2	32.2	23.1	0.5	Dorgan, D; **Conrad, D**
N.C.	43.4	42.7	13.7	0.2	Helms, R; Faircloth, R
Utah	43.4	24.7	27.3	4.6	**Hatch, R**; Bennett, R
Ind.	42.9	36.8	19.8	0.5	Coats, R; **Lugar, R**
Okla.	42.6	34.0	23.0	0.3	Boren, D; Nickles, R
Idaho	42.0	28.4	27.0	2.5	Craig, R; Kempthorne, R
Fla.	40.9	39.0	19.8	0.3	Graham, D; **Mack, R**
S.D.	40.7	37.1	21.8	0.4	Daschle, D; Pressler, R
Texas	40.6	37.1	22.0	0.3	Gramm, R; **Hutchison, R**
Wyo.	39.6	34.0	25.6	0.9	Simpson, R; **Wallop, R**
Alaska	39.5	30.3	28.4	1.8	Stevens, R; Murkowski, R
Kan.	38.9	33.7	27.0	0.4	Dole, R; Kassebaum, R
Ariz.	38.5	36.5	23.8	1.2	**DeConcini, D**; McCain, R

[1] *Mathews was appointed to take the seat of Al Gore, who resigned Jan. 2, 1993, to become vice president. An election will be held in 1994 to fill the last two years of Gore's Senate term.*

Split Ballots, Split Accountability

This kind of mixed-mind behavior at the polls translates directly into the sort of legislative activity in Washington that voters purport to abhor: time-consuming horse-trading aimed at luring members who are torn between loyalty to party and loyalty to constituency. When Clinton barely won the May budget battle in the House, he lost the votes of 20 Democrats from districts that backed Bush for president. Boren, the Democratic nemesis of the president's energy tax proposal, comes from a state where Clinton won just barely one-third of the presidential vote in 1992. In April, as Clinton was grappling with united Republican opposition in the Senate to his $16.3 billion economic stimulus package, the GOP offered a stripped-down alternative. In a vote that boded ill for Clinton' plan, four Democrats sided with the GOP proposal. They were: Bob Kerrey and Jim Exon of Nebraska, where Clinton won a puny 29 percent of the presidential vote; Richard C. Shelby of Alabama, which was Bush's third-best state, giving him 48 percent; and Sam Nunn of Georgia, who in November had seen a GOP surge in his state that ousted his Democratic colleague Wyche Fowler Jr. from the Senate.

Voters say they want politicians in Washington to have a "buck stops here" kind of accountability for their actions, but they make that difficult when they refuse to put one party or the other clearly in charge. Voters' habit of splitting ballots between the parties tends to slow the legislative debate, push it toward the center and produce middle-ground compromises in which no one gets everything he or she wants, but everyone gets something. Some call that "gridlock," or "politics as usual," but really it is the normal functioning of a system that daily is compelled to resolve seemingly irreconcilable differences.

Until and unless voters break the ticket-splitting habit, it seems undemocratic to suggest that the more independent-minded members of Congress — centrist Democrats and moderate Republicans — march in lockstep with their president or their party's majority just for the sake of efficiency.

Methodology and Features of PIA

In this biennial edition of "Politics in America," as in the six preceding it, we have made our assessments of senators and representatives by watching them in action, by conducting interviews with their peers and by researching the public record. Numerous members and key staff people — a cross section of ideology, region and legislative interest — shared with us their observations about Congress. We have drawn heavily upon the collective expertise of Congressional Quarterly's reporters and editors, whose knowledge of Capitol Hill is unmatched. We also asked each member of the House and Senate to provide written information about his or her own work, and many were kind enough to do so.

Perot's Strongest Districts

	Perot %	House Member	%
Maine 2	33	Olympia J. Snowe (R)	49.1
Texas 26	32	Dick Armey (R)	73.1
Texas 3	30	Sam Johnson (R)	86.1
Texas 6	30	Joe L. Barton (R)	71.9
Texas 4	30	Ralph M. Hall (D)	58.1
Kan. 1	29	Pat Roberts (R)	68.3
Utah 1	29	James V. Hansen (R)	65.3
Calif. 52	29	Duncan Hunter (R)	52.9
Alaska AL	29	Don Young (R)	46.8
Utah 2	29	Karen Shepherd (D)	50.5
Idaho 1	28	Larry LaRocco (D)	58.1
N.Y. 30	28	Jack Quinn (R)	51.7
Texas 12	28	Pete Geren (D)	62.8
Maine 1	28	Thomas H. Andrews (D)	65.0
Minn. 2	28	David Minge (D)	47.8
Kan. 2	28	Jim Slattery (D)	56.2
Idaho 2	28	Michael D. Crapo (R)	60.8
Minn. 1	27	Timothy J. Penny (D)	73.9
Wash. 1	27	Maria Cantwell (D)	54.9
Conn. 2	27	Sam Gejdenson (D)	50.8
Calif. 51	27	Randy "Duke" Cunningham (R)	56.1
Calif. 48	27	Ron Packard (R)	61.1
N.Y. 29	27	John J. LaFalce (D)	54.5
Calif. 23	27	Elton Gallegly (R)	54.3
Ohio 13	27	Sherrod Brown (D)	53.3
Wash. 8	27	Jennifer Dunn (R)	60.4
Mo. 6	27	Pat Danner (D)	55.4
Minn. 6	27	Rod Grams (R)	44.4
Kan. 4	27	Dan Glickman (D)	51.7
Utah 3	27	Bill Orton (D)	58.9
Neb. 3	27	Bill Barrett (R)	71.7
Ariz. 3	27	Bob Stump (R)	61.5
Ore. 2	27	Bob Smith (R)	67.1
Ariz. 1	26	Sam Coppersmith (D)	51.3
Mass. 5	26	Martin T. Meehan (D)	52.2
Wyo. AL	26	Craig Thomas (R)	57.8
Mont. AL	26	Pat Williams (D)	50.5
N.Y. 31	26	Amo Houghton (R)	70.6
Texas 24	26	Martin Frost (D)	59.8
Texas 17	26	Charles W. Stenholm (D)	66.1
Fla. 15	26	Jim Bacchus (D)	50.7
Mass. 10	26	Gerry E. Studds (D)	60.8
Wash. 9	26	Mike Kreidler (D)	52.1
Texas 5	26	John Bryant (D)	58.9
Ore. 4	26	Peter A. DeFazio (D)	71.4
Ariz. 4	26	Jon Kyl (R)	59.2
Wash. 2	26	Al Swift (D)	52.1
Calif. 2	26	Wally Herger (R)	65.2
Mass. 1	25	John W. Olver (D)	51.5
Okla. 3	25	Bill Brewster (D)	75.1
Kan. 3	25	Jan Meyers (R)	58.0
Wash. 6	25	Norm Dicks (D)	64.2
Colo. 6	25	Dan Schaefer (R)	60.9
Ore. 5	25	Mike Kopetski (D)	63.9
Ohio 5	25	Paul E. Gillmor (R)	100.0
Okla. 4	25	Dave McCurdy (D)	70.7
Mo. 4	25	Ike Skelton (D)	70.4
Mich. 4	25	Dave Camp (R)	62.5
Colo. 4	25	Wayne Allard (R)	57.8
Calif. 4	25	John T. Doolittle (R)	49.8
Calif. 49	25	Lynn Schenk (D)	51.1
Calif. 45	25	Dana Rohrabacher (R)	54.5
Calif. 40	25	Jerry Lewis (R)	63.1
N.Y. 27	25	Bill Paxon (R)	63.5
Calif. 25	25	Howard P. "Buck" McKeon (R)	51.9
Fla. 16	25	Tom Lewis (R)	60.8
Fla. 9	25	Michael Bilirakis (R)	58.9
Mass. 6	25	Peter G. Torkildsen (R)	54.8
Wash. 3	25	Jolene Unsoeld (D)	56.0
Colo. 3	25	Scott McInnis (R)	54.7
R.I. 2	25	Jack Reed (D)	70.7
Mass. 2	25	Richard E. Neal (D)	53.1
Nev. 1	25	James Bilbray (D)	57.9

While there is considerable legislative information in these pages, this is primarily a book about people, so legislative detail is often truncated. We cannot know all there is to know about each member, but many people at Congressional Quarterly have worked hard to make our book thorough, balanced and fair. Still, assessing members of Congress is an undeniably subjective process, and we take responsibility for all the judgments contained herein.

In addition to the expanded descriptions of House districts, this edition of

Senate Term Expiration Years

— 1994 —

(34 Senators: 21 Democrats, 13 Republicans)

Akaka, Daniel K., D-Hawaii
Bingaman, Jeff, D-N.M.
Bryan, Richard H., D-Nev.
Burns, Conrad, R-Mont.
Byrd, Robert C., D-W.Va.
Chafee, John H., R-R.I.
Conrad, Kent, D-N.D.
Danforth, John C., R-Mo.
DeConcini, Dennis, D-Ariz.
Durenberger, Dave, R-Minn.
Feinstein, Dianne, D-Calif.
Gorton, Slade, R-Wash.
Hatch, Orrin G., R-Utah
Hutchison, Kay Bailey, R-Texas
Jeffords, James M., R-Vt.
Kennedy, Edward M., D-Mass.
Kerrey, Bob, D-Neb.
Kohl, Herb, D-Wis.
Lautenberg, Frank R., D-N.J.
Lieberman, Joseph I., D-Conn.
Lott, Trent, R-Miss.
Lugar, Richard G., R-Ind.
Mack, Connie, R-Fla.
Mathews, Harlan, D-Tenn. [1]
Metzenbaum, Howard M., D-Ohio
Mitchell, George J., D-Maine
Moynihan, Daniel Patrick, D-N.Y.
Riegle, Donald W. Jr., D-Mich.
Robb, Charles S., D-Va.
Roth, William V. Jr., R-Del.
Sarbanes, Paul S., D-Md.
Sasser, Jim, D-Tenn.
Wallop, Malcolm, R-Wyo.
Wofford, Harris, D-Pa.

— 1996 —

(33 Senators: 16 Democrats, 16 Republicans, 1 undetermined)

Baucus, Max, D-Mont.
Biden, Joseph R. Jr., D-Del.
Boren, David L., D-Okla.
Bradley, Bill, D-N.J.
Brown, Hank, R-Colo.
Cochran, Thad, R-Miss.
Cohen, William S., R-Maine
Craig, Larry E., R-Idaho
Domenici, Pete V., R-N.M.
Exon, Jim, D-Neb.
Gramm, Phil, R-Texas
Harkin, Tom, D-Iowa
Hatfield, Mark O., R-Ore.
Heflin, Howell, D-Ala.
Helms, Jesse, R-N.C.
Johnston, J. Bennett, D-La.
Kassebaum, Nancy Landon, R-Kan.
Kerry, John, D-Mass.
Levin, Carl, D-Mich.
McConnell, Mitch, R-Ky.
Nunn, Sam, D-Ga.
Pell, Claiborne, D-R.I.
Pressler, Larry, R-S.D.
Pryor, David, D-Ark.
Rockefeller, John D. IV, D-W.Va.
Simon, Paul, D-Ill.
Simpson, Alan K., R-Wyo.
Smith, Robert C., R-N.H.
Stevens, Ted, R-Alaska
Thurmond, Strom, R-S.C.
Warner, John W., R-Va.
Wellstone, Paul, D-Minn.
Tennessee seat [1]

— 1998 —

(34 Senators: 19 Democrats, 15 Republicans)

Bennett, Robert F., R-Utah
Bond, Christopher S., R-Mo.
Boxer, Barbara, D-Calif.
Breaux, John B., D-La.
Bumpers, Dale, D-Ark.
Campbell, Ben Nighthorse, D-Colo.
Coats, Daniel R., R-Ind.
Coverdell, Paul, R-Ga.
D'Amato, Alfonse M., R-N.Y.
Daschle, Tom, D-S.D.
Dodd, Christopher J., D-Conn.
Dole, Bob, R-Kan.
Dorgan, Byron L., D-N.D.
Faircloth, Lauch, R-N.C.
Feingold, Russell D., D-Wis.
Ford, Wendell H., D-Ky.
Glenn, John, D-Ohio
Graham, Bob, D-Fla.
Grassley, Charles E., R-Iowa
Gregg, Judd, R-N.H.
Hollings, Ernest F., D-S.C.
Inouye, Daniel K., D-Hawaii
Kempthorne, Dirk, R-Idaho
Leahy, Patrick J., D-Vt.
McCain, John, R-Ariz.
Mikulski, Barbara A., D-Md.
Moseley-Braun, Carol, D-Ill.
Murkowski, Frank H., R-Alaska
Murray, Patty, D-Wash.
Nickles, Don, R-Okla.
Packwood, Bob, R-Ore.
Reid, Harry, D-Nev.
Shelby, Richard C., D-Ala.
Specter, Arlen, R-Pa.

[1] *Mathews was appointed to take the seat of Al Gore, who resigned Jan. 2, 1993, to become vice president. An election will be held in 1994 to fill the last two years of Gore's Senate term.*

Governors

Listed below are the governors of the 50 states and the year in which the next election for each office is to be held. States in **bold** will hold elections in 1993 or 1994.

A dagger (†) indicates that the current governor is ineligible to run in the next election.

Alabama — James E. Folsom Jr. (D) 1994
Alaska — Walter J. Hickel (I) 1994
Arizona — Fife Symington (R) 1994
Arkansas — Jim Guy Tucker (D) 1994
California — Pete Wilson (R) 1994
Colorado — Roy Romer (D) 1994 †
Connecticut — Lowell P. Weicker Jr. (I) 1994
Delaware — Thomas R. Carper (D) 1996
Florida — Lawton Chiles (D) 1994
Georgia — Zell Miller (D) 1994
Hawaii — John Waihee III (D) 1994
Idaho — Cecil D. Andrus (D) 1994
Illinois — Jim Edgar (R) 1994
Indiana — Evan Bayh (D) 1996
Iowa — Terry E. Branstad (R) 1994
Kansas — Joan Finney (D) 1994
Kentucky — Brereton Jones (D) 1995 †
Louisiana — Edwin W. Edwards (D) 1995
Maine — John R. McKernan Jr. (R) 1994 †
Maryland — William Donald Schaefer (D) 1994 †
Massachusetts — William F. Weld (R) 1994
Michigan — John Engler (R) 1994
Minnesota — Arne Carlson (R) 1994
Mississippi — Kirk Fordice (R) 1995
Missouri — Mel Carnahan (D) 1996
Montana — Marc Racicot (R) 1996
Nebraska — Ben Nelson (D) 1994
Nevada — Bob Miller (D) 1994
New Hampshire — Steve Merrill (R) 1994
New Jersey — James J. Florio (D) 1993
New Mexico — Bruce King (D) 1994
New York — Mario M. Cuomo (D) 1994
North Carolina — James B. Hunt Jr. (D) 1996
North Dakota — Edward T. Schafer (R) 1996
Ohio — George V. Voinovich (R) 1994
Oklahoma — David Walters (D) 1994
Oregon — Barbara Roberts (D) 1994
Pennsylvania — Robert P. Casey (D) 1994 † *
Rhode Island — Bruce Sundlun (D) 1994
South Carolina — Carroll A. Campbell Jr. (R) 1994 †
South Dakota — Walter D. Miller (R) 1994
Tennessee — Ned McWherter (D) 1994 †
Texas — Ann W. Richards (D) 1994
Utah — Mike Leavitt (R) 1996
Vermont — Howard Dean (D) 1994
Virginia — L. Douglas Wilder (D) 1993 †
Washington — Mike Lowry (D) 1996
West Virginia — Gaston Caperton (D) 1996 †
Wisconsin — Tommy G. Thompson (R) 1994
Wyoming — Mike Sullivan (D) 1994 †

* *Early in June 1993, Casey, who underwent a heart-liver transplant, transferred the powers of his office to the lieutenant governor.*

"Politics in America" includes other new information and features we hope readers will find useful. The introductory page for each state contains more information on the governor and additional political and demographic data. All the state maps reflect the new congressional district boundaries, and we have added 10 maps of selected metropolitan areas where the House lines are particularly serpentine. We have computed the 1992 presidential vote within each House district; that data appears in the statistics section for each representative. And, of course, we have rewritten all the members' profiles to take into account the vast changes wrought by the 1992 election, which gave scores of members new places in the congressional committee system and changed the focus of many on the Hill who spent the past dozen years working with or against a Republican White House.

Phil Duncan
June 15, 1993

Alabama

STATE DATA

Governor:
James E. Folsom Jr. (D)
(Sworn in as governor after his predecessor, GOP Gov. Guy Hunt, was removed from office in April 1993 upon conviction on charges of misusing campaign funds)

Length of term: 4 years
Term expires: 1/95
Salary: $81,151
Term limit: 2 terms
Phone: (205) 242-7100
Born: May 14, 1949; Montgomery, Ala.
Education: Jacksonville State U., B.A. 1974
Occupation: Public official
Family: Wife, Marsha Guthrie; two children
Religion: Episcopal
Political Career: Alabama Public Service Commission, 1979-87; Democratic nominee for U.S. Senate, 1980; Ala. lieutenant governor, 1987-93

No current lieutenant governor

State election official: (205) 242-7210
Democratic headquarters: (205) 326-3366
Republican headquarters: (205) 324-1990

REDISTRICTING

Alabama retained its seven House seats in reapportionment. Map issued by federal court Jan. 27, 1992, became law March 27, after a map passed by the legislature was rejected by the Justice Department.

STATE LEGISLATURE

Bicameral legislature. Meets annually; limited to 30 legislative days within 105 calendar days; special sessions common.

Senate: 35 members, 4-year terms
1992 breakdown: 27D, 8R; 34 men, 1 woman; 30 whites, 5 blacks
Salary: $10/day plus $40/day expenses while Legislature in session; $2,280 per month living expenses.
Phone: (205) 242-7800

House of Representatives: 105 members, 4-year terms
1992 breakdown: 81 D; 23 R; 1 vacancy; 97 men, 7 women; 85 whites, 19 blacks
Salary: $10/day plus $40/day expenses while Legislature in session; $2,280 per month living expenses.
Phone: (205) 242-7600

URBAN STATISTICS

City	Pop.
Birmingham Mayor Richard Arrington Jr., D	265,965
Mobile Mayor Michael Dow, I	196,278
Montgomery Mayor Emory Folmar, R	187,543

U.S. CONGRESS

Senate: 2 D, 0 R
House: 4 D, 3 R

TERM LIMITS

For Congress: No
For state offices: No

ELECTIONS

1992 Presidential Vote

Bill Clinton	40.9%
George Bush	47.6%
Ross Perot	10.8%

1988 Presidential Vote

George Bush	59%
Michael S. Dukakis	40%

1984 Presidential Vote

Ronald Reagan	61%
Walter F. Mondale	38%

POPULATION

1990 population		4,040,587
1980 population		3,893,888
Percent change		+38%
Rank among states:		22
White		73%
Black		25%
Hispanic		1%
Asian or Pacific islander		1%
Urban		60%
Rural		40%
Born in state		76%
Foreign-born		1%
Under age 18	1,058,788	26%
Ages 18-64	2,458,810	61%
65 and older	522,289	13%
Median age		33

MISCELLANEOUS

Capital: Montgomery
Number of counties: 67
Per capita income: $15,569 (1991)
Rank among states: 41
Total area: 51,705 sq. miles
Rank among states: 29

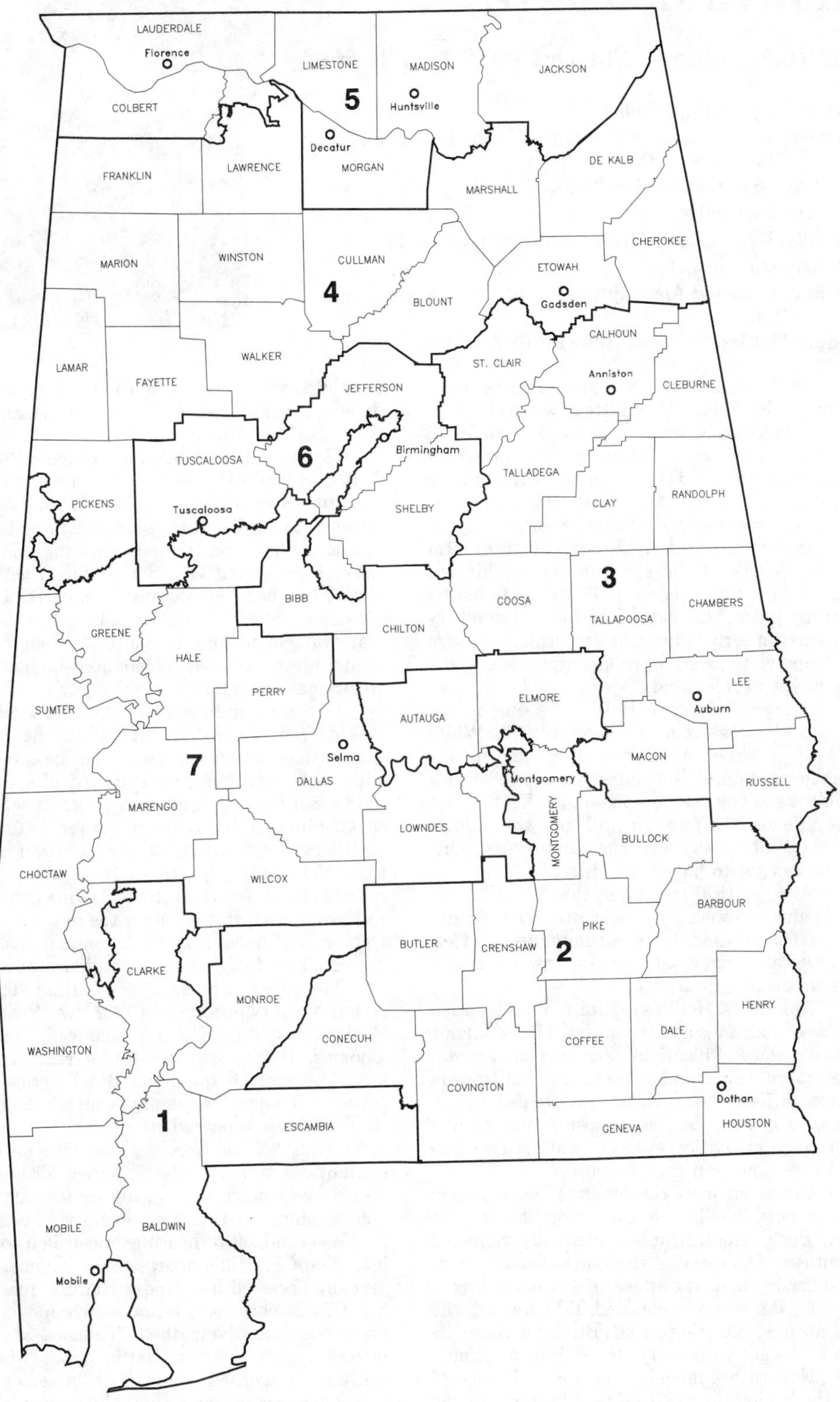
LAUDERDALE
Florence
LIMESTONE
MADISON
JACKSON
5
Huntsville
COLBERT
Decatur
LAWRENCE
MORGAN
FRANKLIN
DE KALB
MARSHALL
CHEROKEE
MARION
WINSTON
CULLMAN
ETOWAH
4
Gadsden
BLOUNT
CALHOUN
LAMAR
FAYETTE
WALKER
ST. CLAIR
Anniston
JEFFERSON
CLEBURNE
Birmingham
TUSCALOOSA
6
TALLADEGA
PICKENS
Tuscaloosa
SHELBY
CLAY
RANDOLPH
3
BIBB
COOSA
CHAMBERS
GREENE
CHILTON
TALLAPOOSA
HALE
LEE
PERRY
ELMORE
SUMTER
AUTAUGA
Auburn
7
Selma
MACON
DALLAS
Montgomery
RUSSELL
MARENGO
LOWNDES
MONTGOMERY
BULLOCK
CHOCTAW
WILCOX
BARBOUR
PIKE
BUTLER
CRENSHAW
2
CLARKE
HENRY
MONROE
DALE
CONECUH
COFFEE
WASHINGTON
COVINGTON
Dothan
1
ESCAMBIA
GENEVA
HOUSTON
MOBILE
BALDWIN
Mobile

Howell Heflin (D)

Of Tuscumbia — Elected 1978; 3rd Term

Born: June 19, 1921, Poulan, Ga.
Education: Birmingham-Southern College, B.A. 1942; U. of Alabama, J.D. 1948.
Military Service: Marine Corps, 1942-46.
Occupation: Judge; lawyer.
Family: Wife, Elizabeth Ann Carmichael; one child.
Religion: Methodist.
Political Career: Ala. Supreme Court chief justice, 1971-77.
Capitol Office: 728 Hart Bldg. 20510; 224-4124.

In Washington: Though no longer chairman of the Ethics Committee, where he presided as either chairman or vice chairman for 12 years, Heflin is ever "the Judge," his preferred title from earlier days as chief justice of the Alabama Supreme Court (and the way he is known to members, staff and reporters).

In fact, now midway through his third term in the Senate, Heflin continues to see himself that way, not as a senator: "I just try to be the country judge," he said in late 1987. "I don't try to reach an early opinion on something. A judge is supposed to listen to the last argument before he makes up his mind."

A favorite story of Heflin's — one he has told audiences from Alabama to the White House — serves to illustrate his lot in the Senate: A hunter is trapped in a tree with a wildcat and begs his companion to shoot it. But the friend is afraid he will hit the hunter instead. "Shoot anyway," the hunter begs. "One of us has got to have some relief!"

As a political metaphor, that treed hunter is Heflin, trapped by one controversy or another. On questions large or commonplace, Heflin typically anguishes over the arguments and resists making decisions.

As a result, Heflin's reputation has teetered between judicious and indecisive. His nickname has lost some of its original, respectful connotation; it is not uncommon now to hear it uttered in sarcasm. Even his jowlish, pear-shaped frame, generously described as imposing, makes him appear in his critics' eyes as a caricature of an old-time Southern courthouse pol.

One of the more conservative Democrats in the Senate, Heflin's votes during the Reagan and Bush administrations generally reflected Southern Democrats' allegiance to the commander in chief, regardless of his party label.

"If I'm sort of undecided, I'll vote with the Democrats," he said in 1991. But on defense, he said, "I went with every Republican position."

Now with a moderate to liberal Democrat in the White House, Heflin's allegiance to the commander in chief will be tested as President Clinton seeks support for his efforts to cut the defense budget and to allow homosexuals to serve in the military.

Heflin and his Alabama colleague, Richard C. Shelby, were the only Democrats to support Minority Leader Bob Dole's February 1993 effort to block Clinton's plan to eliminate prohibitions on homosexuals in the military through an executive order in July 1993. And Heflin has been a consistent supporter of the Strategic Defense Initiative, a target for Democratic budget cutting. In the 102nd Congress, he joined efforts to pass a balanced-budget constitutional amendment.

Heflin's ponderous approach to decision-making may have been suited to the Ethics Committee, where as chairman he presided with all the deliberation expected of a former judge. But that approach can frustrate senators seeking hints of his views on matters before the Judiciary Committee, where partisan splits arise frequently, particularly when judicial nominees are screened. Still, Heflin continues to have a great influence on the votes of other Democrats on controversial nominations, and he remains a bellwether of Southern members.

The most publicized nomination fight in recent memory occurred in 1991 over President Bush's Supreme Court nominee, Clarence Thomas. Heflin said his initial reaction was that Thomas was qualified. But he grew frustrated at Thomas' testimony, which he said was riddled with contradictions and "outright disavowals" of his previous positions on some contentious subjects. Heflin joined all but one Judiciary Democrat in voting against a favorable recommendation; the panel's vote was 7-7.

A second set of hearings was called to look into Anita F. Hill's charges that Thomas had sexually harassed her. Under Heflin's questioning, Hill denied any ulterior motive for making public her complaint about Thomas. She dismissed questions from Heflin about whether she was "a scorned woman" or "a zealot civil rights believer . . . [who thinks] progress will be turned back" if Thomas is confirmed. Heflin's inquiries (as well as his accent and girth) were lampooned in a sketch on TV's "Saturday Night Live." But while his questions may have appeared provocative or obtuse, Heflin was engaging in a technique judges often employ to cut to the essence of a matter by asking questions on many jurors' minds. Thomas was confirmed 52-48, the closest margin of any high court nominee in more than a century.

Heflin scored a big win in the 102nd Congress when the Senate voted to confirm Bush's nomination of Edward E. Carnes Jr. of Alabama to the 11th U.S. Circuit Court of Appeals. Heflin was Carnes' primary backer on the committee and in the Senate, and he worked to rebut objections from key Democrats and the nation's leading civil rights groups who were upset over the nominee's role as a national advocate for the death penalty. But a handful of black politicians and lawyers and one prominent Alabama civil rights lawyer said Carnes had fought for racial fairness. After months of wrangling, the Senate confirmed Carnes, 62-36.

Heflin was a pivotal swing voter on the Judiciary Committee for the six years the GOP controlled the Senate, before Democrats regained a majority in the 1986 elections. He frequently allied with Chairman Strom Thurmond of South Carolina and other GOP conservatives on major issues. Once, when Thurmond failed to notice Heflin among Democrats during a head count, Massachusetts Sen. Edward M. Kennedy protested, "I believe Mr. Heflin is a Democrat." Thurmond replied: "I always thought he was one of us."

Heflin's reputation as a bellwether suffered some over his unwillingness to reach a decision during the 1987 showdown over confirmation of Ronald Reagan's Supreme Court nominee Robert H. Bork.

As usual in controversial matters, Judiciary was split along party lines on Bork, with three undecided swing voters — Heflin, conservative Democrat Dennis DeConcini of Arizona and liberal Republican Arlen Specter of Pennsylvania — holding both the balance of power and the media's attention. Heflin seemed to relish the attention most and appeared regularly on the Sunday TV talk shows.

Bork opponents and some commentators suggested that Heflin ultimately would lead other Southerners in voting against the conservative judge — out of concern that Bork would try to reverse landmark civil rights rulings. Instead, Heflin stayed on the fence while a parade of Southern Democrats, including Shelby, went to the Senate floor to state their opposition.

Reagan called Heflin to the White House (where the senator told his "treed hunter" tale), but Heflin remained undecided. But already he and the committee were irrelevant; vote counts showed that Bork would lose on the floor. All but ignored, the senator voted against confirmation.

Regard for his probity earned Heflin a spot in 1987 on the special Senate committee investigating the Reagan administration's Iran-contra scandal. But he remained a backbencher and a clumsy interrogator throughout the three-month televised hearings. Perhaps his most memorable moment was outside the hearing room, when Heflin told reporters that former White House aide Lt. Col. Oliver L. North's secretary Fawn Hall had smuggled documents from the White House in her brassiere. "She's supposedly got some pretty good capacity to carry the documents," he said. Hall snapped that Heflin was sexist but later testified that she did smuggle papers — in her back waistband and boots.

Though Judiciary's province includes many of the legal issues Heflin knows best, he has rarely been a leading participant, unless the subject deals with improvement of judicial operations, a favorite topic of his. Generally, Heflin seems uncomfortable with the legislative pace. Though coy when Republicans floated his name as a potential Supreme Court nominee in 1987, Heflin did express longing for the judiciary's more deliberative, thorough style.

Because of his background, Heflin was appointed Ethics Committee chairman in 1979, the first freshman senator to head a committee since 1910. Heflin and GOP Vice Chairman Warren B. Rudman of New Hampshire handled complaints against colleagues with informal bipartisanship.

Though Heflin had to forfeit the chair in 1981 after Democrats lost their Senate majority, he was tapped to head the committee's investigation of New Jersey Democrat Harrison A. Williams Jr., who was caught in the FBI's Abscam bribery sting. In early 1982, Heflin took the Senate floor to present the committee's recommendation that Williams be expelled. After Heflin's eloquent denunciation made an expulsion vote all but certain, Williams resigned.

The Ethics Committee put in long hours in the 101st Congress on two cases. One, against Minnesota Republican Dave Durenberger, produced the first Senate disciplinary action in a decade. The other, the Keating Five scandal, focused nationwide attention on the integrity of Congress.

One of the more popular members of the clubby Senate, Durenberger was "denounced" for financial improprieties. He was also ordered to pay more than $120,000 restitution for accepting speaking fees and housing reimbursements in violation of Senate rules.

The Keating Five affair stemmed from the collapse of the savings and loan industry in the late 1980s. Many failures were attributed to risky investments and fraudulent activities by high-flying thrift executives. One of the more notorious was Charles H. Keating Jr., chairman of American Continental Corp. in Phoenix, which owned the failed Lincoln Savings and Loan Association in Irvine, Calif.

Keating and his associates raised or contributed $1.5 million to the campaign committees and other political causes of five senators: Republican John McCain of Arizona and Democrats Alan Cranston of California, DeConcini, John Glenn of Ohio and Donald W. Riegle Jr. of Michigan. The senators were under scrutiny for intervening with federal thrift regulators in Keating's behalf. At issue was whether Keating's fundraising prompted their action and whether their intervention with regulators was undue political pressure.

Though he directed penetrating questions to several witnesses as well as the five senators, Heflin provided little indication of his own view of the affair throughout the hearings. He and Rudman in early 1991 issued the committee's findings — that Cranston likely violated the Senate standard against improper behavior and that the other four were guilty of poor judgment. The committee recommended that further action be taken only against Cranston.

The committee ultimately decided that Cranston be "reprimanded" by the Senate. As his last act as an Ethics member, Heflin read the panel's resolution and a lengthy statement to the full Senate slowly and deliberately. He took 35 minutes.

The burden of sitting in judgment of his brethren for more than a decade finally took its toll on Heflin. After the completion of Cranston's case, Heflin left the Ethics Committee.

On the Agriculture Committee, Heflin confronts much easier choices. He is for cotton and whatever else grows in the South. So protective is he of the federal peanut subsidy program that Heflin has boasted that he is the third senator from Georgia. He espoused a new subsidy program for Southern soybean farmers.

Heflin is an eager player in the committee's commodity-trading approach to legislation, in which members from one region ally with those from other regions to support subsidies for each other's products.

Frequently at odds with environmentalists back home, Heflin in 1988 joined with Republican Jesse Helms of North Carolina to oppose a pesticide regulation bill that was supported by environmentalists and cosponsored by Agriculture Committee Chairman Patrick J. Leahy of Vermont and ranking Republican Richard G. Lugar of Indiana.

Heflin's record on environmental issues led Leahy to leave Heflin off the House-Senate conference on the 1990 farm bill. The chairman sought allies for his "circle of poison" proposal barring the export of pesticides proscribed for domestic use. Instead of choosing Heflin, fourth in seniority on the committee, Leahy picked the most junior Democrat, Nebraskan Bob Kerrey.

In the 102nd Congress, Heflin sponsored a bill to make it a federal crime to vandalize animal research laboratories. The legislation, which came in response to a sharp increase in attacks by animal rights extremists, was signed by Bush in 1992.

Outside his committee assignments, Heflin is a leader in efforts to increase funding for NASA, along with other senators from states with NASA contractors and facilities.

At times, Heflin's public soul-searching is a self-parody. When the Senate in 1985 considered a bill naming the rose as the national flower, Heflin wavered between the rose, Alabama's marigold and its state flower, the camellia, in the longest speech of the day. "Roses are red, violets are blue, why must I choose between these two?" he asked. He finally chose the rose.

At Home: Alabama Republicans had hoped in 1990 that Heflin had passed his prime, both as a campaigner and as a popular political figure. But the avuncular "country judge" proved to be as formidable as ever, winning a third Senate term with 61 percent of the vote.

His GOP challenger, state Sen. Bill Cabaniss, ran a scrappy campaign that tried to portray Heflin as soft on the environment, weak on ethics and wrong on his support for the 1990 civil rights bill, which Cabaniss labeled a "quota" bill. But Cabaniss lacked the resources to challenge Heflin dollar for dollar, and his swanky suburban Birmingham address and summertime vacations near George Bush's seacoast compound in Maine left Cabaniss open to charges of being a "country club" Republican.

The result: He carried only four of Alabama's 67 counties and failed to make a dent in Heflin's rural and small-town base that the incumbent had assiduously courted over the years by presenting himself as an honest, open, approachable public figure.

Cabaniss' showing was not much better than a more ideological challenger, former GOP Rep. Albert Lee Smith, made against Heflin in 1984. Smith had lost his Birmingham-based House seat in 1982 and was expected to try a House comeback. But he opted instead for the chance to spread his conservative message before a larger audience.

Known in the House as a zealous promoter of the New Right social agenda, Smith switched gears a little in his Senate campaign, talking more about economics and accusing Heflin of frustrating the Reagan agenda of tax and spending cuts. Heflin responded by calling himself an "independent, conservative to moderate" Democrat who backed Ronald Reagan more often than he had backed Jimmy Carter. Presidential coattails helped hold Heflin to 63 percent of the vote.

Heflin's first campaign for the Senate was not much more suspenseful than his second. When Democratic Sen. John J. Sparkman announced his retirement in 1978, Gov. George C. Wallace was poised to replace him. But while the governor campaigned unofficially throughout 1977, he never announced, and for good reason. Polls showed Heflin far ahead.

One Democrat who did run against Heflin and came to regret it was Walter Flowers, a five-term U.S. House member. In a primary runoff that turned angry and unpleasant, Heflin took all but five counties in the state. Better organized and financed than the congressman, he blasted Flowers for being "part of the Washington crowd." The general election was a formality; the GOP had no candidate.

In his younger days, as a trial lawyer in the northern Alabama town of Tuscumbia, Heflin was known as one of the best. He could cajole a jury with down-home stories, cry with them over his client's plight or delight them with an unexpected move. Once he lay down on the counsel's table to show the improbability of an alleged assault victim's story.

Heflin's reputation as a lawyer led to his election as chief justice of the Alabama Supreme Court, where he streamlined the state judicial system, which had been hampered by a huge case backlog. To accomplish the task, he needed adoption of a state constitutional amendment, and the voters gave it to him. When political opponents criticized him because the amendment made him eligible for a $30,000 annual pension, Heflin pointed out that he could not receive the money if he served in the Senate or practiced law.

Heflin's uncle, "Cotton Tom" Heflin, served in the Senate from 1920 to 1931. He was an ardent segregationist and anti-Catholic who bolted the Democratic Party when Al Smith was nominated for president in 1928. Fifty-one years later, Howell Heflin made a speech welcoming Pope John Paul II to the United States.

Committees

Agriculture, Nutrition & Forestry (4th of 10 Democrats)
Rural Development & Rural Electrification (chairman); Agricultural Production & Stabilization of Prices; Domestic & Foreign Marketing & Product Promotion

Judiciary (6th of 10 Democrats)
Courts & Administrative Practice (chairman); Antitrust, Monopolies & Business Rights; Patents, Copyrights & Trademarks

Small Business (9th of 12 Democrats)
Innovation, Manufacturing & Technology; Rural Economy & Family Farming

Elections

1990 General		
Howell Heflin (D)	717,814	(61%)
Bill Cabaniss (R)	467,190	(39%)
1990 Primary		
Howell Heflin (D)	540,876	(81%)
Mrs. Frank Ross Stewart (D)	123,508	(19%)

Previous Winning Percentages: **1984** (63%) **1978** (94%)

Campaign Finance

	Receipts	Receipts from PACs		Expend-itures
1990				
Heflin (D)	$3,422,129	$1,320,755	(39%)	$3,204,160
Cabaniss (R)	$1,757,312	$77,246	(4%)	$1,853,869

Key Votes

1993	
Require unpaid family and medical leave	N
Approve national "motor voter" registration bill	Y
Approve budget increasing taxes and reducing deficit	Y
Support president's right to lift military gay ban	N
1992	
Approve school-choice pilot program	N
Allow shifting funds from defense to domestic programs	N
Oppose deeper cuts in spending for SDI	Y
1991	
Approve waiting period for handgun purchases	N
Raise senators' pay and ban honoraria	N
Authorize use of force in Persian Gulf	Y
Confirm Clarence Thomas to Supreme Court	N

Voting Studies

	Presidential Support		Party Unity		Conservative Coalition	
Year	**S**	**O**	**S**	**O**	**S**	**O**
1992	53	47	52	48	89	11
1991	73	26	49	50	88	10
1990	60	39	53	46	95	5
1989	71	29	39	61	92	8
1988	73	27	52	47	97	3
1987	54	46	50	50	94	6
1986	76	24	42	57	84	16
1985	54	45	56	43	88	12
1984	75	21	36	59	89	11
1983	42	52	57	41	77 †	16 †
1982	61	39	57	42	79	17
1981	68	30	64	34	81	15

† Not eligible for all recorded votes.

Interest Group Ratings

Year	**ADA**	**AFL-CIO**	**CCUS**	**ACU**
1992	40	75	40	48
1991	35	67	40	57
1990	28	78	64	55
1989	25	90	63	75
1988	30	64	50	58
1987	35	80	50	46
1986	25	53	58	65
1985	25	67	45	74
1984	20	45	67	91
1983	40	65	44	72
1982	25	65	75	75
1981	35	58	61	54

Richard C. Shelby (D)

Of Tuscaloosa — Elected 1986; 2nd Term

Born: May 6, 1934, Birmingham, Ala.
Education: U. of Alabama, A.B. 1957, LL.B. 1963.
Occupation: Lawyer.
Family: Wife, Annette Nevin; two children.
Religion: Presbyterian.
Political Career: Ala. Senate, 1971-79; U.S. House, 1979-87.
Capitol Office: 509 Hart Bldg. 20510; 224-5744.

In Washington: No one was much surprised when Shelby became the earliest and most visible Democratic defector from the party line emanating from the Clinton White House. Through four House terms and now into in his second in the Senate, Shelby has made a career of speaking and voting as much like a Republican as a Democrat.

In that regard, Shelby is not noticeably different from his Alabama colleague Howell Heflin. But in the early days of Bill Clinton's presidency, even as Heflin and a few other Senate Democrats found themselves establishing a measure of distance from the new president, Shelby cast himself in a most singular role: He became the foil for Clinton's efforts at party discipline.

Someone had to set the limit for apostasy, and Shelby did so in the most visible way possible. As a network television crew filmed a visit by Vice President Al Gore to seek Shelby's support for Clinton's budget plan, Shelby launched into a critical attack on it. He then cosponsored a Republican substitute. Later still, he joined a GOP filibuster of Clinton's $16.3 billion economic stimulus package — helping to stall it to death.

Even Heflin found his way to voting for Clinton's budget and voting to block the filibuster on the stimulus bill.

It was no wonder that the White House let it be known that behavior such as Shelby's would not be tolerated. Shortly after Shelby embarrassed Gore on TV, the administration announced it would shift 90 jobs from the Marshall Space Flight Center in Huntsville, Ala., to Texas.

During his years in the Senate, Shelby has departed from the party line on economic and social issues. But he has toed that line when the issue was civil rights — reflecting his heightened sensitivity to the black voters who were crucial to his 1986 upset of GOP Sen. Jeremiah Denton.

Shelby's independence has had other costs.

Democratic Banking Chairman Donald W. Riegle Jr. of Michigan forced a realignment of subcommittees at the start of the 103rd Congress, when it appeared the pro-bank Shelby might gain control of the Consumer and Regulatory Affairs Subcommittee. Instead, Shelby became chairman of a new Subcommittee on Economic Stabilization and Rural Development.

Shelby's bid for a seat on the Appropriations Committee in the 101st Congress was squashed by Democratic leaders who were sympathetic to his need to break ranks occasionally but saw no reason to reward someone who strays so often.

Nor did he endear himself by his stance in the 1988 contest to succeed Majority Leader Robert C. Byrd of West Virginia. Though widely expected to support the conservative Southern candidate, J. Bennett Johnston of Louisiana, Shelby demurred until days before the vote, and then joined the bandwagon for Maine liberal George J. Mitchell. In hesitating, Shelby angered the Johnston camp, gained little favor in Mitchell's and burnished a reputation for being occasionally opportunistic.

But although his wayward ways have won Shelby few friends in the cloakroom, the folks back home were entranced enough by his public feud with Clinton to win him an editorial encouragement to "Hang in There," and to spark rumors of Shelby's switching parties and running for governor as a Republican in 1994. Shelby vigorously denied those reports.

On occasion Shelby redeems himself with party leaders. Early in the 101st Congress he did so by opposing former Sen. John Tower's nomination as Defense secretary. Republicans had hoped for Shelby's support, so his surprise announcement just before voting in the Armed Services Committee presaged Tower's ultimate rejection on the Senate floor. Shelby's decision may not have been all that difficult for him: He was concurring with Sam Nunn of Georgia, the Armed Services chairman he greatly admires, and in Alabama, Bible Belt concern over Tower's alleged drunkenness and womanizing was perceptible.

With the Cold War thawing and enthusiasm waning for expensive weapons systems to combat the Soviet threat, Shelby (along with Democrat Jeff Bingaman of New Mexico) aided a Nunn-inspired effort to redirect the administration's plans for a space-based anti-ballistic missile system, and to increase the emphasis on ground-based interceptor missiles. The Senate adopted Bingaman and Shelby's amendment to the defense authorization bill, 54-44. Not only did that raise Shelby's stock with Nunn, the focus on a ground-based defense was helpful to the rocket industry in Huntsville.

And at the close of the 102nd, as the abortion debate cast a pall on Bush's waning campaign, Shelby stayed within the party fold and voted to override the president's veto of a bill that would have reversed a ban on abortion counseling in federally financed family planning clinics.

Shelby was active elsewhere in the 102nd. Motivated by the Capitol Hill shooting death in January 1992 of his legislative aide, Thomas Barnes, Shelby jumped into the debate on the fiscal 1993 District of Columbia appropriations bill with an amendment to make murder in the District a capital offense. He worked with his colleagues to develop a compromise. Both chambers finally accepted a provision requiring D.C. voters to choose whether to allow the death penalty for first-degree murder convictions. The required referendum was defeated in November.

Shelby also argued law-and-order to try to crack down on "deadbeat dads." A bill he sponsored that was signed into law at the close of the 102nd Congress made it a federal crime for out-of-state parents to avoid paying child support. He reasoned that going after delinquent parents would save the federal government millions of dollars in welfare costs.

In 1991, Shelby was one of 10 Senate Democrats who voted to authorize President Bush to use force against Iraq. After the war ended, he worried that Democrats could suffer politically from the partisan breakdown of the vote. "This is not a party vote," he said. "If it is seen as a party vote, we're in deep trouble."

Shelby's stand with his party in support of civil rights issues marks a break from the pattern of his early congressional career. In 1987, he voted against the confirmation of Robert H. Bork, President Ronald Reagan's Supreme Court nominee, whose defeat was a top priority for civil rights groups. In 1988, Shelby joined all Democrats in voting to override Reagan's veto of a bill to overturn a Supreme Court decision limiting enforcement of four key civil rights laws. In 1990, he voted to override Bush's veto of a civil rights bill that Bush and other Republicans said would mandate racial hiring quotas.

In 1991, he became one of 11 Democrats, mostly Southern, to vote to seat Clarence Thomas on the Supreme Court after Anita F. Hill went public with allegations that Thomas had sexually harassed her. As a black conservative, Thomas' nomination effectively split the minority community and made it difficult for liberal groups to drum up the necessary support to oppose him. However, the Thomas-Hill hearings so intensified gender and racial politics that a compromise civil rights bill emerged from White House-Senate negotiations that countered the effects of nine Supreme Court decisions and made it easier for victims of bias to bring lawsuits. Shelby voted yes; only five Republicans opposed it.

As a House member, Shelby devoted much time to the Energy and Commerce Committee. House Democratic leaders gave him a seat on the prestigious panel when he arrived in 1979, believing Shelby to be a moderate. They came to regret their decision when he proved to be a reliable vote for the GOP and pro-industry positions. In the 102nd Congress, he replaced Heflin on the Senate Energy and Natural Resources Committee.

At Home: Shelby was one of four Southern Democrats who were narrowly elected to the Senate in 1986 on the strength of an historically high turnout of black voters in their states. When they ran for re-election in 1992, two lost — Wyche Fowler Jr. of Georgia and Terry Sanford of North Carolina. But Shelby and Louisiana's John B. Breaux not only won second terms, but they won in landslides. In fact, neither Shelby nor Breaux drew a credible Republican challenger.

Shelby's march to re-election did encounter one obstacle, however, when Jefferson County Commissioner Chris McNair, a black Democrat from Birmingham, filed at the last minute to run in the Democratic primary. McNair, who had lost to Shelby in a 1978 House runoff, sought to attract the votes of liberal Democrats who had never warmed to the conservative Shelby.

Although he had a long and respected record of public service in the state's most-populous city, McNair was not widely known across the state, and he could not compete with Shelby's huge campaign treasury. Nor could McNair rely on the backing of Alabama's two influential black political organizations. The New South Coalition and the Alabama Democratic Conference endorsed both Shelby and McNair. McNair carried Jefferson County by a wide margin, but he only won one other county in the state.

Alabama Republicans failed to recruit a major candidate to take on Shelby. Businessman Richard Sellers was the only Republican to file. Largely ignored by state and national party figures and with a campaign treasury a fraction of Shelby's, Sellers lost 2-to-1.

Shelby's 1986 race against Denton was not nearly as smooth. Denton led in public-opinion polls throughout the campaign. He had a following among advocates of his staunchly conservative, pro-Reagan politics and those who viewed the former naval officer and longtime Vietnam prisoner of war as a national hero.

But in the Senate, Denton spent much time pursuing goals such as promoting chastity among teenagers — an agenda without strong appeal to the many voters concerned about economic issues. He was frequently ridiculed for being loose with his words (about spousal rape, for instance, he said, "Damn it, when you get married, you kind of expect you're going to get a little sex"). Denton, not skilled at personal politicking, was criticized for not keeping in touch with his constituency.

But Shelby had problems of his own, caused by his cool relationship with Democratic liberals. He won just 51 percent in the primary, barely avoiding a runoff.

On the same day, Lt. Gov. William J. Baxley and state Attorney General Charles Graddick finished one-two in the Democratic gubernatorial primary, setting up a runoff. After a bitter campaign, the runoff tally showed Graddick winning by 7,000 votes. But Baxley, a moderate, argued that Graddick, a conservative former Republican, had illegally recruited GOP voters to support him in the runoff. After a federal court agreed, a state party committee gave Baxley the nomination. Eventually, many angry conservative Democrats helped elect Republican Guy Hunt as governor over Baxley.

The schism prompted Shelby to lay low for a time, but when it became clear the storm would not blow over, he started stumping and made up ground quickly. He won with a strong boost from his 7th District base, taking Tuscaloosa County with 64 percent and carrying several rural Black Belt counties by 3-to-1 margins. He also did well in traditionally Democratic counties in northwest and south-central Alabama.

Shelby's first election to the House was much less trying. In 1978, his former Tuscaloosa law partner, Democratic Rep. Walter Flowers, gave up the 7th for what turned out to be an unsuccessful Senate primary campaign. Shelby, whose support for such issues as the Equal Rights Amendment had typed him as a progressive Democrat during eight years in the state Legislature, went for Flowers' open seat.

Shelby's strong base in Tuscaloosa, where he had served as a prosecutor, helped him win 48 percent in the primary. In the runoff, he defeated McNair — then a state representative — by a 3-to-2 margin, in a campaign free of racial tensions. He easily won that November and never faced significant GOP opposition. He beat back a concerted primary effort from the left in 1982 by a margin of nearly 2-to-1.

Committees

Armed Services (7th of 11 Democrats)
Force Requirements & Personnel (chairman); Coalition Defense & Reinforcing Forces; Military Readiness & Defense Infrastructure

Banking, Housing & Urban Affairs (5th of 11 Democrats)
Economic Stabilization & Rural Development (chairman); Securities

Energy & Natural Resources (7th of 11 Democrats)
Energy Research & Development (vice chairman); Public Lands, National Parks & Forestsy; Renewable Energy

Special Aging (6th of 11 Democrats)

Elections

1992 General		
Richard C. Shelby (D)	1,022,698	(65%)
Richard Sellers (R)	522,015	(33%)
Jerome Shockley (LIBERT)	31,811	(2%)
1992 Primary		
Richard C. Shelby (D)	304,957	(61%)
Chris McNair (D)	136,836	(28%)
Bob Miller (D)	28,432	(6%)
Mrs. Frank Ross Stewart (D)	25,956	(5%)

Previous Winning Percentages: **1986** (50%) **1984 *** (97%) **1982 *** (97%) **1980 *** (73%) **1978 *** (94%)

** House elections.*

Campaign Finance

	Receipts	Receipts from PACs		Expend-itures
1992				
Shelby (D)	$2,816,778	$1,258,166	(45%)	$2,451,191
Sellers (R)	$149,603	0		$149,578

Key Votes

1993	
Require unpaid family and medical leave	Y
Approve national "motor voter" registration bill	Y
Approve budget increasing taxes and reducing deficit	N
Support president's right to lift military gay ban	N
1992	
Approve school-choice pilot program	N
Allow shifting funds from defense to domestic programs	N
Oppose deeper cuts in spending for SDI	Y
1991	
Approve waiting period for handgun purchases	N
Raise senators' pay and ban honoraria	N
Authorize use of force in Persian Gulf	Y
Confirm Clarence Thomas to Supreme Court	Y

Voting Studies

	Presidential Support		Party Unity		Conservative Coalition	
Year	**S**	**O**	**S**	**O**	**S**	**O**
1992	65	35	45	55	89	11
1991	69	31	54	46	83	18
1990	55	45	59	41	95	5
1989	68	32	46	54	95	5
1988	57	43	56	43	92	5
1987	47	50	61	36	75	16
House Service:						
1986	44	49	58	33	84	8
1985	52	41	60	31	85	13
1984	43	45	44	45	78	12
1983	54	44	43	54	76	20
1982	60	40	35	63	86	10
1981	76	21	25	71	93	4

Interest Group Ratings

Year	**ADA**	**AFL-CIO**	**CCUS**	**ACU**
1992	30	58	60	63
1991	35	67	40	76
1990	33	78	50	48
1989	25	90	63	57
1988	35	71	57	60
1987	50	90	50	43
House Service:				
1986	40	93	39	55
1985	25	50	57	67
1984	15	50	46	57
1983	25	53	55	74
1982	10	35	67	73
1981	0	27	89	93

1 Sonny Callahan (R)

Of Mobile — Elected 1984; 5th Term

Born: Sept. 11, 1932, Mobile, Ala.
Education: Graduated from McGill H.S., 1950.
Military Service: Navy, 1952-54.
Occupation: Moving and storage company executive.
Family: Wife, Karen Reed; six children.
Religion: Roman Catholic.
Political Career: Ala. House, 1971-79, served as a Democrat; Ala. Senate, 1979-83, served as a Democrat; sought Democratic nomination for lieutenant governor, 1982.
Capitol Office: 2418 Rayburn Bldg. 20515; 225-4931.

In Washington: Still "Sonny" after all these years, the middle-aged Callahan is a gregarious, good-natured Southerner at ease with the personal give-and-take of the political process. He is the GOP version of a character type abundant in his region — the Democratic courthouse politician. That is not surprising, because Callahan himself was once a Democrat.

Today, though, Callahan is a reliable pro-business Republican. Not known as a legislative activist, he concentrates solidly on local matters and is a consistent vote against Democratic fiscal policies. In early 1993, he voted against President Clinton's economic stimulus package and the House budget resolution.

Callahan has shown a knack for cultivating key friendships and contacts that have proved invaluable in propelling him into important positions quickly.

He has moved from good to progressively better spots, beginning with an assignment to the Public Works Committee his freshman year. In the 100th Congress he moved onto the Energy and Commerce Committee, which has a broad legislative reach, and onto the Merchant Marine Committee, an important assignment for a member whose district is dominated by a port city like Mobile and whose major industry is shipbuilding.

Then in the 103rd Congress, he won the big prize, getting a seat on the Appropriations Committee. Callahan was assigned to the panel's Military Construction Subcommittee, which considers spending proposals on base realignment and closure. The timing couldn't have been better; it came just as the Mobile Naval Station reappeared on the Pentagon's list of bases targeted for closure.

The Mobile station, which employs 650 people, serves as a naval reserve training facility, which Callahan argued should be spared because the nation's military forces have in recent years begun to rely more heavily on the reserve units. Active-duty ships also dock at the base, and Navy units use them for training maneuvers.

The base, which was financed partly with state and local dollars, has been a mixed blessing for Callahan since he took office. His predecessor, GOP Rep. Jack Edwards, worked for years to get Mobile included in the Navy's homeporting force-dispersal strategy. Ground was finally broken for the facility in 1988, giving Callahan a well-timed publicity boost. In 1990, however, the Pentagon ordered a construction freeze on a number of homeports. Construction continued on the one in Mobile, pending an April 1991 decision. Finally, when the base was operational and "99 percent" completed, it was again placed on the chopping block.

Callahan also serves on the Appropriations Subcommittee on Foreign Operations, where he is likely to be a skeptic on foreign aid. During a subcommittee hearing on aid to the former Soviet republics at the start of the 103rd, he told Secretary of State Warren M. Christopher that he needed something to tell his Alabama constituents "who have financial needs of their own" and wonder why Russia needs more aid. "I've not been able to come up with a suitable explanation for them," Callahan said.

In the 102nd Congress, Callahan sponsored legislation that would give federal recognition to the Mowa Band of Choctaw Indians in Washington County. Federally recognized status would make the band eligible for federal money. Callahan and Alabama Sen. Richard C. Shelby had pushed for recognition after the band was unsuccessful on its own. The bill was passed by the Senate as the 102nd was closing, and time ran out before the House could give its final approval. Callahan reintroduced the bill again in the 103rd.

Serving a district with forests covering much of its rural areas, Callahan touts his sponsorship of the Forest Stewardship Program, enacted as part of the 1990 farm bill. The program reauthorized and created several programs to encourage better management of private forests and offers financial assistance for

Alabama 1

Southwest — Mobile

The proud, history-steeped city of Mobile dominates the 1st. Since Mobile was founded in 1702, the French, British, Spanish and Confederate flags have flown over the city, lending it a cosmopolitan heritage distinct from other Alabama cities. Mobile compares itself with New Orleans; indeed, it claims to celebrate the oldest Mardi Gras festival in the United States.

The 1st backs Republicans for most statewide and federal races, but it is no GOP monolith. Democratic strength lies in the rural counties in the northern part of the district, which have sizable black populations, and in Prichard, a suburb of Mobile with a 79 percent black population. George Bush carried the 1st with 63 percent in 1988. Four years later, he easily won it again. However, former GOP Gov. Guy Hunt received only 51 percent in his 1990 re-election. And 1st District voters that year gave Democratic Sen. Howell Heflin 55 percent of the vote and backed the Democratic nominee for lieutenant governor.

The city of Mobile, with just under 200,000 people, lost population during the 1980s. But Mobile County as a whole grew by a modest 4 percent, while Baldwin County, to the east across Mobile Bay, grew by 25 percent, second-fastest in the state. The small Baldwin County city of Daphne, for example, more than tripled in size, growing from 3,400 to 11,300. Independent Ross Perot's government-reform message resonated among Baldwin's mostly white, suburban voters; he received 16 percent of the vote in Baldwin in the 1992 presidential race.

Mobile is Alabama's only port city. While the commercial shipbuilding industry has been stagnant for several years, the ship repair business has thrived, keeping Mobile's shipyards busy. The 1985 completion of the Tennessee-Tombigbee Waterway, which connects Mobile Bay and the Tennessee River, was promoted as a tool to allow Mobile's port to compete with New Orleans in trade volume, but trade on the massive waterway has yet to live up to expectations.

Continued federal involvement in port development was assured with the 1988 groundbreaking for Mobile's Navy homeport. But future plans were called into question in 1993 when the Mobile Naval Station appeared on the latest base-closing list.

Timber and textiles also fuel the 1st's economy. Paper companies dot the district, farming trees from the forests that cover much of the district's rural counties. Alabama River Pulp's new $1.1 billion pulp mill near Claiborne (Monroe County) is the largest single industrial expansion in the history of Alabama. The racial climate in Monroeville, the county seat, inspired the 1960 novel "To Kill a Mockingbird," but tensions have eased since then. Now, two of the six city council members are black.

Wedged between Mississippi and Florida, the 1st contains all of Alabama's tiny coastline. Along the Gulf of Mexico, fisherman trawl for shrimp. Each October, the National Shrimp Festival at Gulf Shores draws more than 200,000 visitors.

1990 Population: 577,226. White 403,193 (70%), Black 164,448 (28%), Other 9,585 (2%). Hispanic origin 4,585 (<1%). 18 and over 414,476 (72%), 62 and over 88,450 (15%). Median age: 33.

timber and conservation activities.

Appropriate for a member whose district is dependent on shipbuilding, Callahan announced at the end of 1990 that he was moving out of his $1,300-a-month apartment in the Virginia suburbs to a 63-foot, three-bedroom, custom-built (in his district) houseboat anchored on the Potomac — his attempt to beat the Washington area's high cost of living.

At Home: When Edwards announced his retirement in late 1983, his endorsement went to Callahan. The only suspense in the race was over which party Callahan would choose. Elected to the Legislature as a Democrat, Callahan moved right. He formally joined the GOP in February 1984, and, confident of victory, waged a lackadaisical House campaign. Callahan's primary foe, Mobile lawyer Billy Stoudenmire, attacked him as a Democratic interloper. Callahan drew enough conservative Democrats across party lines to win the primary by a 60 percent to 40 percent margin. But his weakness rekindled hope among Democrats, who nominated Frank McRight, a Mobile trial lawyer.

McRight won his primary by attacking local government corruption. Then in the November campaign it was reported that Callahan had received an illegal campaign contribution two years earlier from a city official later indicted on other charges. In October, Callahan finally responded to the challenge. He reminded voters that McRight had twice been the Carter-Mondale campaign chairman in Mobile, and he repeatedly asked how McRight would vote for president in 1984. In the end, though, Callahan owed much of his narrow margin to

Ronald Reagan's smashing triumph in the 1st.

In 1986 and 1990, Democrats conceded without a fight. But in 1988, they recruited John M. Tyson Jr., a high-profile member of the state school board and member of a well-known political family. Tyson had the markings of a contender, but he ran a poorly organized, underfunded campaign and never seriously threatened the incumbent.

Callahan's biggest worry in 1992 was that redistricting might significantly reshape his territory. But the final plan left the 1st virtually untouched, and Democrats did not try to wage a serious challenge against Callahan. Callahan easily defeated William A. Brewer, a retired judge from Mobile.

Committee

Appropriations (17th of 23 Republicans)
Foreign Operations, Export Financing & Related Programs; Military Construction

Elections

1992 General

Sonny Callahan (R)	128,874	(60%)
William A. Brewer (D)	78,742	(37%)
John R. Garrett (LIBERT)	6,548	(3%)

1990 General

Sonny Callahan (R)	82,185	(100%)

Previous Winning Percentages: **1988** (59%) **1986** (100%) **1984** (51%)

District Vote for President

1992

D 84,202 (37%)
R 118,421 (52%)
I 26,797 (12%)

Campaign Finance

	Receipts	Receipts from PACs	Expend-itures
1992			
Callahan (R)	$376,087	$214,808 (57%)	$383,760
Brewer (D)	$13,500	0	$13,297
1990			
Callahan (R)	$318,680	$169,350 (53%)	$183,910

Key Votes

1993

Require parental notification of minors' abortions	Y
Require unpaid family and medical leave	N
Approve national "motor voter" registration bill	N
Approve budget increasing taxes and reducing deficit	N
Approve economic stimulus plan	N

1992

Approve balanced-budget constitutional amendment	Y
Close down space station program	N
Approve U.S. aid for former Soviet Union	N
Allow shifting funds from defense to domestic programs	N

1991

Extend unemployment benefits using deficit financing	N
Approve waiting period for handgun purchases	N
Authorize use of force in Persian Gulf	Y

Voting Studies

	Presidential Support		Party Unity		Conservative Coalition	
Year	S	O	S	O	S	O
1992	82	16	83	12	96	0
1991	65	25	72	15	70	3
1990	63	32	73 †	20 †	96	0
1989	73	21	73	23	100	0
1988	63	37	79	17	100	0
1987	68	32	79	16	93	5
1986	73	21	75	21	98	0
1985	74	26	82	16	96	4

† Not eligible for all recorded votes.

Interest Group Ratings

Year	ADA	AFL-CIO	CCUS	ACU
1992	5	27	75	96
1991	0	17	90	100
1990	6	17	92	87
1989	0	9	100	93
1988	10	29	93	96
1987	4	19	87	78
1986	0	29	89	95
1985	0	12	86	86

2 Terry Everett (R)

Of Enterprise — Elected 1992; 1st Term

Born: Feb. 15, 1937, Dothan, Ala.
Education: Enterprise State Junior College.
Military Service: Air Force, 1955-59.
Occupation: Newspaper executive; construction company owner; farm owner; real estate developer.
Family: Wife, Barbara Pitts.
Religion: Baptist.
Political Career: No previous office.
Capitol Office: 208 Cannon Bldg. 20515; 225-2901.

The Path to Washington: Everett, a wealthy businessman who had never held office, ran as an anti-politician and managed to narrowly defeat a scion of the Alabama establishment. But he quickly showed that he has a politician's knack for self-preservation.

Everett won a seat on the Armed Services Committee, replacing his predecessor, Republican Bill Dickinson, who rose to become the panel's ranking member during his 28 years representing the 2nd. Voters had nearly ousted Dickinson in 1990 after reports of his personal financial dealings became news, and he decided to retire after his 14th term.

Everett's slot on Armed Services leaves him well-positioned to look out for the area's numerous military bases and defense contractors during a time of shrinking Pentagon budgets. To help save local jobs, Everett wants to consolidate all Navy helicopter training at Fort Rucker, which employs more than 13,000 people. And in addition to Armed Services, Everett will serve on the Veterans' Affairs Committee.

But Everett owed his victory more to his outsider image than to promises about what he could deliver once in office.

He began the race a virtual unknown and ended it by defeating a man with arguably the most famous name in Alabama politics — state Treasurer George C. Wallace Jr., son of the former governor and presidential candidate. An insurgent within his own party, Everett claimed the GOP nomination by defeating a state senator who was the choice of the party establishment.

Everett proved to have a winning combination of message and means. A home builder and newspaper owner who began life in poverty, he spent hundreds of thousands of dollars of his own money blanketing the district in billboards and radio and TV ads blaring: "Send a message, not a politician." Everett renounced contributions from political action committees, vowing to work to do away with PACs once in office.

In rhetoric that echoed that of independent presidential candidate Ross Perot, Everett denounced gridlock in Washington, pointed to his own success building businesses, and appealed to voters for support "for the sake of your children." Citing concerns about the deficit, Everett, like many freshmen, says he intends to work for a balanced-budget amendment to the Constitution and the line-item veto. Early in the 103rd Congress, he voted against a Democratic bill to give the president limited line-item veto authority, in favor of an even stronger GOP substitute amendment. While most GOP freshmen chose to vote for both, Everett was one of only 12 GOP freshmen to support only the substitute.

As state treasurer, Wallace had established himself as a likable moderate and an effective if unspectacular officeholder. But Everett denounced him as a representative of the Old Guard who was weaned in the corridors of power.

To distinguish himself further, Everett said that instead of accepting a recent congressional pay raise, he would donate the money to local high school seniors to help them pay for college.

But he was careful not to go too far in his attacks on the Wallace legacy. The name still commands loyalty, especially in rural sections of the district, which were once the elder Wallace's home base. When Wallace suspended his campaign for two weeks to tend to his hospitalized father, Everett also canceled his campaign events.

In the end, Everett won by fewer than 4,000 votes. Wallace won his home county of Barbour and made a strong showing in rural areas, but he lost in two more populous urban centers at opposite ends of the district, Houston County (Dothan) and the city of Montgomery.

Everett's promise to change the way Washington operates does not extend to the controversial federal quota system for peanuts. His district grows more peanuts than almost any other in the country, but growers face an uncertain future because the peanut program, which severely limits foreign imports, is being challenged in international trade negotiations.

In wooing the farm vote, Everett touted his own experience as the owner of a 400-acre farm. He also made a trip to Moscow during the campaign to discuss export opportunities for Alabama peanut farmers.

Alabama 2

Southeast — Part of Montgomery; Dothan

Defense and agriculture fuel the economy of the 2nd.

The substantial defense presence stands as testament to the influence of Bill Dickinson, who represented the 2nd from 1965 to 1993 and rose to become ranking Republican on the House Armed Services Committee.

Maxwell and Gunter Air Force bases, on the edge of Montgomery, employ about 10,000 people, contributing $754 million annually to the 2nd's economy; Gunter was annexed by Maxwell in March 1992. Fort Rucker, northwest of Dothan, is where many Army and Air Force helicopter pilots and crews train. More than 13,000 military and civilian personnel work at Fort Rucker, whose annual economic impact is $969 million. Martin Marietta is building a new missile factory in Troy (Pike County).

Southeastern Alabama is known as the Wiregrass region for the wiry roots of its native grass. The soil was first tilled for cotton, but in the early part of the century, the boll weevil wiped out more than two-thirds of the cotton crop. Now the sparsely populated area grows more peanuts than almost any other part of the country. The Coffee County town of Enterprise (Rep. Everett's hometown) erected a monument to the boll weevil as a tribute to the insect whose destruction of the cotton crop persuaded farmers to switch to peanuts.

Although redistricting for the 1990s split the city of Montgomery between the 2nd and the new black-majority 7th District, it is still the 2nd's largest city. Montgomery has long been a national GOP stronghold, voting for Republican presidential candidates as far back as 1956. The other sizable city in the 2nd is Dothan (population 54,000), at the southeastern corner of the district in Houston County, near the Florida and Georgia borders.

George Bush carried Houston County with 74 percent in 1988 and 58 percent in 1992. The huge margins Everett ran up in Montgomery (19 percentage points) and Houston (20 points) enabled him to withstand losses in 10 of the district's 13 other counties to win his 1992 election over George C. Wallace Jr.

Originally a cotton and peanut market town, Dothan has grown and diversified by attracting new industries, including large plants run by Michelin and Sony. Sony manufactures and exports audio and video tapes and computer disks here. Largely non-union, Dothan's plants represent most of the 2nd's large industry, although Elmore County has some textile plants.

Rural Barbour and Bullock counties were the original home base for former Gov. and presidential candidate George C. Wallace. They have large black populations (Bullock is majority-black) and are loyally Democratic. Wallace's son received 66 percent in Barbour and 77 percent in Bullock. Bill Clinton received two-thirds of Bullock's vote.

Elmore and Autauga counties grew during the 1980s as people who work in Montgomery moved out of the city. Elmore grew by 13 percent, Autauga by 6 percent; they vote Republican. Bush ran up large margins in both counties in 1988 and 1992.

1990 Population: 577,227. White 431,639 (75%), Black 139,265 (24%), Other 6,323 (1%). Hispanic origin 4,765 (<1%). 18 and over 423,324 (73%), 62 and over 90,554 (16%). Median age: 33.

Committees

Armed Services (21st of 22 Republicans)
Military Installations & Facilities; Oversight & Investigations

Veterans' Affairs (8th of 14 Republicans)
Compensation, Pension & Insurance; Hospitals & Health Care; Oversight & Investigations

Campaign Finance

	Receipts	Receipts from PACs		Expend-itures
1992				
Everett (R)	$1,047,897	0		$1,016,189
Wallace (D)	$639,142	$247,409	(39%)	$637,773

Key Votes

1993

Require parental notification of minors' abortions	Y
Require unpaid family and medical leave	N
Approve national "motor voter" registration bill	N
Approve budget increasing taxes and reducing deficit	N
Approve economic stimulus plan	N

Elections

1992 General		
Terry Everett (R)	112,906	(49%)
George C. Wallace Jr. (D)	109,335	(48%)
Glynn Reeves (LIBERT)	3,150	(1%)
1992 Primary		
Terry Everett (R)	9,619	(58%)
Larry Dixon (R)	6,883	(42%)

District Vote for President

	1992	
D	82,550	(35%)
R	124,272	(53%)
I	27,377	(12%)

3 Glen Browder (D)

Of Jacksonville — Elected 1989; 2nd Full Term

Born: Jan. 15, 1943, Sumter, S.C.
Education: Presbyterian College, B.A. 1965; Emory U., M.A. 1971, Ph.D. 1971.
Occupation: Professor.
Family: Wife, Rebecca Moore; one child.
Religion: Methodist.
Political Career: Ala. House, 1983-87; Ala. secretary of state, 1987-89.
Capitol Office: 1221 Longworth Bldg. 20515; 225-3261.

In Washington: Browder has focused much legislative attention on two issues, one with direct impact on his district — the fate of Fort McClellan in Anniston — and another of primary interest to "good government" reformers — changing campaign finance regulations.

Like his predecessor in the 3rd, Democrat Bill Nichols, Browder has a seat on Armed Services. But while Nichols made a name for himself redesigning the structure of the military, Browder has been preoccupied with the more parochial priority of fighting off attempts to close Fort McClellan, a chemical warfare training facility in the 3rd District.

The first threat to Fort McClellan came before Browder had been in Congress a year. In April 1991 Defense Secretary Dick Cheney released a list of military bases to be closed that included the facility.

In response, Browder cofounded the "Fairness Network," a coalition of members whose districts would be affected by the base-closing plan. He complained that the plan's choices were based not on the military's strategic needs but on partisan considerations. Noting that most of the targeted bases were in Democratic-held districts, Browder said, "This is no time to risk America's capacity to protect her vital interests for partisan politics."

Though he usually comes across as a soft-spoken political scientist, Browder knows how to make his way in the rough-and-tumble of politics. On Armed Services he quickly established a rapport with Democratic Chairman Les Aspin of Wisconsin, another academic turned politician. Browder got a seat on the Military Installations Subcommittee, where he pursued the base-closing issue. Thanks to the appeals that he and community leaders in Anniston made to the base-closing commission, Fort McClellan survived the Bush administration.

But there is no rest for Browder. With continuing retrenchment in defense spending, the Pentagon — now with Aspin at the helm — issued another base-closing list in early 1993, and Fort Anniston was on it.

When the House Democratic leadership was pushing in the 102nd Congress to overhaul campaign finance laws, Browder led a successful effort to remove a provision calling for public financing. Browder — who worked in the area campaign regulation when he was Alabama secretary of state — proposed allowing tax credits for individual political contributions of $50 or less. He said that would increase the role of small-dollar givers in campaigns.

As that episode illustrates, Browder from time to time finds himself to the right of his party's leadership. He is a member and strong supporter of the Democratic Leadership Council, which he sees as moving the party back to its centrist roots and away from "the traditional liberal orthodoxy associated with our party."

Browder supports a balanced-budget constitutional amendment and he opposed requiring employers to provide unpaid family and medical leave. However, on matters such as backing the Civil Rights Act and overturning the ban on abortion counseling at federally funded clinics, he has sided with the majority of his party colleagues.

When President Clinton put forward an economic stimulus package in early 1993, Browder initially expressed reservations about its cost. But in the end, he backed it.

At Home: Browder's special election victory in April 1989 was one of the year's most important, since it put to rest any GOP hopes of galloping realignment in the rural South. In a district that George Bush had won in 1988 with 60 percent, Browder beat GOP state Sen. John Rice by nearly 2-to-1. In 1990 and 1992, Republicans offered only token opposition.

Browder came slowly to politics. After graduating from Presbyterian College in South Carolina in 1965, he moved to Atlanta, first working as a sportswriter for the Atlanta Journal and then as an investigator for the U.S. Civil Service Commission. But it was not long before Browder returned to college, earning his doctorate in political science at Emory University. With that, he landed a job on the faculty at Jacksonville State University in Alabama, where he found time to dabble in polling,

Alabama 3

East — Anniston; Auburn

A 14-county amalgam of defense facilities, high-tech businesses, universities, textile mills and poor rural communities, the 3rd lacks a single defining characteristic. Politically, it is conservative Democratic territory that is prone to support Republicans for governor and president.

Anniston, the Calhoun County seat and one of the largest cities in the district with a population of 26,600, is home to two huge military facilities: Fort McClellan and the Anniston Army Depot. Fort McClellan, which houses the Chemical Decontamination Training Facility, was on the 1991 list of defense bases recommended for closure, but it received a reprieve when its champions convinced the base-closing commission of its unique status as the only place where the United States and its allies can train soldiers using active but non-lethal chemical weapons.

Fort McClellan was again targeted for closure in 1993, threatening some 8,000 military and civilian jobs. It was the only large base the Army proposed to close.

Calhoun County has not staked its future on the perpetual presence of Fort McClellan. Area business and civic leaders in 1982 joined to form Forward Calhoun County, an economic development program aimed at promoting diversification by attracting new industry to help the area survive if Fort McClellan closes.

More than half the 3rd's population is contained in its four most-populous counties: Calhoun, Lee, Talladega and St. Clair. George Bush carried all four easily in 1988 and 1992. Auburn (Lee County) is home to Auburn University, the state's largest, with 21,800 students. The first Sunday in May, racing fans flock to the Talladega Superspeedway for the Winston 500.

St. Clair grew by 21 percent during the 1980s, swelled by people who work in Birmingham as well as Calhoun County. St. Clair is Republican terrain; Rep. Browder's unheralded GOP opponent carried it in 1992.

The 3rd still contains a thriving textile industry. The Russell Corp., with headquarters in Alexander City (Tallapoosa County), makes uniforms for professional football teams. The cotton and dairy industries have waned as farmers have turned to growing pine trees on their farmland and supplementing their income by raising poultry and catfish.

Macon, the only county in the 3rd with a black majority (86 percent), has had a long history of racial and economic troubles. The county seat, Tuskegee, was at the center of a 1960 landmark Supreme Court ruling striking down a racial gerrymander (*Gomillion v. Lightfoot*). Tuskegee University, founded in 1881 through the efforts of Booker T. Washington, was one of the nation's first black colleges. Today, it has 3,700 students and is a leader in research, science and engineering. Macon traditionally ranks among the most Democratic counties in the country. In the 1992 presidential race, Bill Clinton won 83 percent of the Macon County vote.

1990 Population: 577,227. White 422,187 (73%), Black 149,922 (26%), Other 5,118 (1%). Hispanic origin 3,442 (<1%). 18 and over 429,511 (74%), 62 and over 89,951 (16%). Median age: 32.

---

research and political consulting.

In 1982, Browder ran for an open seat in the Alabama House, emerging victorious from a crowded primary field.

He stayed four years, gaining attention for a controversial "career ladder" teacher pay and evaluation plan he promoted. The measure became law but drew criticism for being too costly and time-consuming to administer; it was soon repealed.

In 1986 Browder ran for secretary of state against Annie Laurie Gunter, a George Wallace ally and the outgoing state treasurer. Out-organizing his better-known rival, Browder won the pivotal Democratic primary.

Once in office, he successfully lobbied the Legislature for stricter campaign finance disclosure, which required candidates to make pre-election reports of campaign contributions.

When veteran Rep. Nichols died of a heart attack in December 1988, Browder was well-positioned to run for his seat.

The lone statewide official in the race, he had high name recognition across the rural, 13-county district.

Browder's biggest test was how to defeat his eight challengers in the Democratic primary; with support from organized labor and help from an "attack" ad that portrayed his chief conservative rivals as proponents of big tax increases, he ran first with 25 percent of the vote.

After that, Browder had few problems, easily winning a placid runoff against Tuskegee's black mayor, Johnny Ford, and the special election against Rice.

Committees

Armed Services (18th of 34 Democrats)
Military Installations & Facilities; Oversight & Investigations; Readiness

Budget (25th of 26 Democrats)

Elections

1992 General

Glen Browder (D)	119,175	(60%)
Don Sledge (R)	73,800	(37%)
Rodric D. Templeton (LIBERT)	4,570	(2%)

1990 General

Glen Browder (D)	101,923	(74%)
Don Sledge (R)	36,317	(26%)

Previous Winning Percentages: **1989 †** (65%)

† Special election.

District Vote for President

1992

D 92,142 (42%)
R 105,034 (48%)
I 23,772 (11%)

Campaign Finance

	Receipts	Receipts from PACs		Expend-itures
1992				
Browder (D)	$231,325	$105,550	(46%)	$108,814
Sledge (R)	$22,390	$27	(0%)	$22,160
1990				
Browder (D)	$280,234	$190,058	(68%)	$176,550
Sledge (R)	$22,990	$100	(0%)	$22,989

Key Votes

1993

Require parental notification of minors' abortions	N
Require unpaid family and medical leave	N
Approve national "motor voter" registration bill	N
Approve budget increasing taxes and reducing deficit	Y
Approve economic stimulus plan	Y
1992	
Approve balanced-budget constitutional amendment	Y
Close down space station program	N
Approve U.S. aid for former Soviet Union	Y
Allow shifting funds from defense to domestic programs	N
1991	
Extend unemployment benefits using deficit financing	Y
Approve waiting period for handgun purchases	N
Authorize use of force in Persian Gulf	Y

Voting Studies

	Presidential Support		Party Unity		Conservative Coalition	
Year	**S**	**O**	**S**	**O**	**S**	**O**
1992	43	53	75	23	83	13
1991	41	58	74	23	92	5
1990	41	59	74	25	93	7
1989	54 †	44 †	68 †	30 †	89 †	11 †

† Not eligible for all recorded votes.

Interest Group Ratings

Year	ADA	AFL-CIO	CCUS	ACU
1992	45	58	50	48
1991	30	82	56	50
1990	33	50	71	58
1989	44	63	70	58

4 Tom Bevill (D)

Of Jasper — Elected 1966; 14th Term

Born: March 27, 1921, Townley, Ala.
Education: U. of Alabama, B.S. 1943, LL.B. 1948.
Military Service: Army, 1943-46.
Occupation: Lawyer.
Family: Wife, Lou Betts; three children.
Religion: Baptist.
Political Career: Ala. House, 1959-67; sought Democratic nomination for U.S. House, 1964.
Capitol Office: 2302 Rayburn Bldg. 20515; 225-4876.

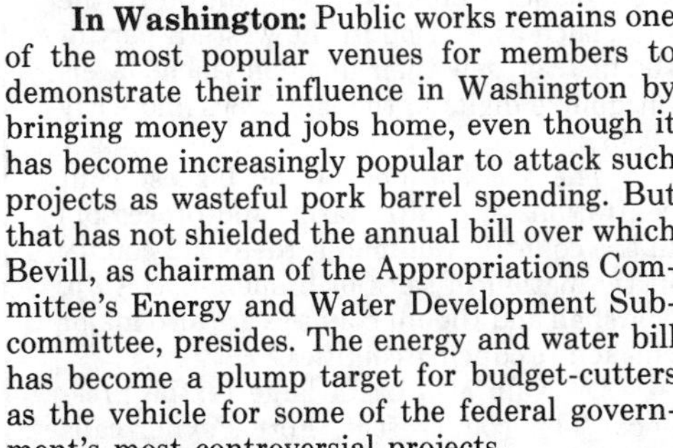

In Washington: Public works remains one of the most popular venues for members to demonstrate their influence in Washington by bringing money and jobs home, even though it has become increasingly popular to attack such projects as wasteful pork barrel spending. But that has not shielded the annual bill over which Bevill, as chairman of the Appropriations Committee's Energy and Water Development Subcommittee, presides. The energy and water bill has become a plump target for budget-cutters as the vehicle for some of the federal government's most controversial projects.

Bevill takes pride in being able to move his bill through the House with a minimum of resistance; his is usually the first of the 13 appropriations bills the House passes. But he does not have the luxury of shepherding a bill with such immensely popular yet relatively small-dollar pet-project areas as highway spending. Rather, the energy and water appropriations bill bears such unwieldy, large-ticket items as the superconducting super collider and the nation's nuclear weapons programs, as well as huge regional water and energy projects that date from the Depression era.

Bevill has always treated public works as a personal creed. That is understandable, since much of north Alabama was brought to economic health during the Depression by Tennessee Valley Authority projects. Even before the Clinton era, Bevill had mastered the vocabulary of framing his programs as "investments." "There is no question," Bevill says, "that water-resources projects have helped develop the nation." He says every dollar invested in flood control has reaped benefits many times over.

Nowadays, however, Bevill is constrained to speak in terms of having to squeeze savings from his bill. After producing the fiscal 1993 bill, which included no new building projects and cut some program funding, he commented, "The goal was to make sure everyone was a little unhappy — and we did that."

When a new national issue seizes the public consciousness, Bevill looks for ways to tie it to the need for water projects. Usually he finds some, as he has in the case of trade. He talks about how important waterways and ports are to the nation's trading capacity.

However, Bevill has shown as chairman that he is more than a business-as-usual pork-barreler, taking a strong interest in the high-tech projects that fall under his jurisdiction. His appropriations bill includes one of the most controversial projects, the $8 billion-plus superconducting super collider being built in Texas.

Bevill was initially reluctant to begin building the giant atom smasher, which scientists want so they can study the building blocks of matter.

But he became a supporter after the administration assured him that foreign investors would help pay for its construction. Bevill's backing may also have been linked to an understanding with President Bush that his administration would not block new water projects members were seeking, although Bevill has denied that there was any quid pro quo.

His support provided important momentum for the project at a critical stage, while Bevill was able to help direct some of the super collider research to the University of Alabama.

Concerns about the project's mounting price tag and the paucity of foreign investors crystallized in 1992, when the House voted to kill the project. The 232-181 vote to cut virtually all of the next fiscal year's funding for the atom smasher stunned supporters. But Senate appropriators restored funding and staved off a vote to kill it. The House agreed to the conference report that included $517 million for the project in fiscal 1993.

The fiscal 1993 energy and water bill also included a ban on all nuclear explosions after Sept. 30, 1996. Bevill was loath to incorporate an amendment on his bill that might trigger a veto. But after the Senate attached a test ban to the bill, Speaker Thomas S. Foley of Washington met with Bevill, Majority Leader Richard A. Gephardt of Missouri, key Armed Services Committee members Les Aspin of Wisconsin (the chairman) and John M. Spratt Jr. of South

Alabama 4

North Central — Gadsden

With fewer blacks and more unionized workers, the 4th has a different character from districts farther south. The 14-county stripe across northern Alabama has mine workers in the west, light and heavy industry in the east, and poultry farms throughout.

The 4th has a long populist Democratic heritage; the only district with a more reliably Democratic vote is the majority-black 7th. The "common man" rhetoric of former Gov. James E. Folsom Sr. (who grew up in the 4th's Cullman County) always played well in this region. Independent presidential candidate Ross Perot's anti-establishment message resonated in some of the 4th's counties in 1992. His 14 percent showings in Cullman, Marshall and Lawrence counties outpaced his statewide percentage.

There is a GOP presence in the 4th dating back to the Civil War. Winston County actually seceded briefly from Alabama when the state seceded from the Union and became the "free state of Winston." George Bush received 55 percent in Winston in 1992; in 1988, he got 68 percent.

The district's only sizable city is Gadsden, an industrial center of 42,500 people in Etowah County. Gadsden's once-thriving textile and heavy industries have suffered setbacks in recent years. Gulf State Steel's smokestacks still belch fumes over the city and Goodyear Tire and Rubber Co. still turns out tires, but both companies have had significant layoffs. Gadsden's other major industrial employers, Mid-South Industries and its subsidiary, Emco, turn out a diverse range of products, including toasters, fryers, and handguns as well as components for mines, bombs and torpedoes.

In and around Gadsden is the largest concentration of Democrats in the district. Bill Clinton carried Etowah with 48 percent of the vote. Bush won it by only 66 votes in 1988. Gadsden has a 28 percent black population.

The textile and apparel industries have been in decline for several years throughout the South, afflicted by cheap imports and financially weak companies. The effect has been felt across the 4th as companies such as Health-tex and Munsingwear have closed their plants. Counties dependent on textile jobs, such as Marion in the western part of the district, saw their unemployment levels hit double digits in the late 1980s and early 1990s.

The 4th has one of the biggest concentrations of poultry farms and processors in the country. Cullman is the No. 2 county in the nation in sales of broilers. De Kalb, Marshall and Blount counties are also major chicken-producing counties.

De Kalb also has a large textile presence. The county seat, Fort Payne, calls itself the "Sock Capital of the World." It says that its nearly three dozen hosiery mills make 65 percent of the world's socks.

Coal has been mined in the western part of the 4th for generations, and the United Mine Workers exerts a strong influence for Democratic candidates. In 1992, Clinton carried six of the district's eight westernmost counties.

1990 Population: 577,227. White 534,038 (93%), Black 38,020 (7%), Other 5,169 (1%). Hispanic origin 2,188 (<1%). 18 and over 432,149 (75%) 62 and over 102,196 (18%). Median age: 35.

Carolina, and test-ban sponsor Mike Kopetski of Oregon. The group decided to press ahead with the Senate-passed restrictions on the energy bill, gambling — correctly — that Bush would not veto the bill because it included funding for the super collider.

The energy and water appropriations bill also includes most of the Energy Department's budget, which came under renewed scrutiny in the 102nd due to energy concerns generated by the Persian Gulf War.

Here too, Bevill's home interests are evident; he supports federal programs to promote the use of coal, which is mined in his district. Bevill has also advocated more federal research in renewable energy sources such as solar, wind and geothermal power.

Bevill's success is not too surprising, given the nature of his legislation, which touches districts all around the country. Bevill is as gentlemanly as anyone in the House and not the type to make open threats of retaliation against opponents, but many members are aware of the power that he has to deny funds that might otherwise come their way; his reputation for wielding that power is legendary.

White Houses both Democratic and Republican have witnessed this power. In 1977, when the Carter administration tried to cancel 18 projects it said were too expensive and environmentally damaging, Bevill and his committee agreed to kill only one project and took the battle to the floor.

President Jimmy Carter eventually did stop funding for some of the least popular projects. But in the long run, Bevill won. The fight cost Carter enough political capital to cause any president to think hard about slashing the public works budget.

Although President Ronald Reagan was consistent in his efforts to reduce water-project funding, he was never willing to go to war with Congress over it.

Bevill has become inured to the accusations that he is an advocate of pork barrel legislation, but he is sensitive to the criticism. He changed the name of his subcommittee several years ago from "Public Works" to "Energy and Water Development" because the original name had such unpopular connotations.

"Energy was very popular. We thought we could pick up a few votes that way," Bevill said. "It worked. But I still like the term 'public works.' "

An Appropriations member a few years ago privately said, "You don't want to get Tom Bevill mad at you." Bevill still keeps track of members who take him on. Members who show up on the list kept by his staff often find that their projects disappear during a House-Senate conference. However, at age 72, he is seen by some as slowing down, and more members may be becoming emboldened to take on the chairman over some of the politically unappealing items in his bills, particularly as dollars become scarcer because of budget constraints and public scrutiny over government spending intensifies.

Bevill recognizes that the more restrained budgetary climate will affect his bill. Looking ahead at the end of 1991, he could see little room for new initiatives and said that his subcommittee would have to focus primarily on finishing ongoing projects. That year, the stringent spending caps of the 1990 budget pact forced Bevill's subcommittee to pass a bill with no new water projects. The final bill, however, had 14 new water construction projects added in the Senate.

The money woes appropriators faced were epitomized by a genial tussle between Bevill and fellow "cardinal" Sidney R. Yates of Illinois, chairman of the Interior Subcommittee, who wrangled during a committee meeting in 1991. Yates wanted $43.5 million to upgrade a new particle collider ring at a national laboratory near Chicago. But Bevill said it would unravel the subcommittee's pact not to fund any new construction projects.

The dispute was largely gentlemanly and good-natured. Yates quoted Shakespeare, and Bevill responded with disarming, pointed wit: "Lord, if you'll protect me from my friends, I can handle my enemies all right. This is my friend."

In the end, Yates came out on the short end of an 11-32 show-of-hands vote, and the committee had sent a message: If a veteran subcommittee chairman such as Yates cannot get money for a home-state project, things must be tough. Yates later settled for $10 million.

In 1988, Bevill had to labor to repress members' desires to build new projects, and he produced a bill that provided funding just for ongoing projects. "This has been the most difficult appropriations bill we have put together," Bevill said of the legislation, which was billed as the most austere energy and water bill in memory. With $17.8 billion in funding, it was also the biggest in memory.

Bevill has had to fend off repeated attacks on the Appalachian Regional Commission (ARC). Only 82 members voted to cut $110 million from highways and projects under the ARC, a remnant of the 1960s "War on Poverty" that has long pumped funds into the 4th District. A new highway linking Birmingham and Memphis that will run through the 4th began its funding through the ARC.

Bevill keeps an eye on his district's interests even when his subcommittee does not have jurisdiction. During the 1990 debate on the defense spending bill, for example, Bevill persuaded the House to spend $99 million for an anti-aircraft missile to be built in the 4th; the funding had been omitted from an earlier, more austere defense bill.

At the end of the 102nd Congress, Bush signed into law Bevill's bill creating the 14,000-acre Little River Canyon National Preserve in northeast Alabama.

Bevill's most cherished project has probably been the Tennessee-Tombigbee, a massive barge canal that cuts through Alabama on its way to the Gulf of Mexico. Bevill was an emotional defender of the $3 billion waterway, which finally opened in 1985 after years of controversy.

Funding the canal demanded Bevill's eternal vigilance; opponents offered numerous amendments to delete money for the "Tenn-Tom." In 1980, an amendment to cancel funding for the project lost by 20 votes on the House floor; the next year it was 10 votes.

Tennessee-Tombigbee ultimately survived thanks to a trade-off with the embattled Clinch River nuclear breeder reactor in Tennessee, which Bevill long supported. For much of 1982, Bevill and his allies managed to stall floor votes on either project. Late in the year, however, the Bevill side agreed to a vote on Clinch River, and in return environmentalists did not press for one on Tennessee-Tombigbee. The House voted to block funding for Clinch River.

At Home: It was not a smooth political road that led Bevill to Congress, but he has been on easy street since arriving: Only in his first election in 1966 did he fall below two-thirds of the vote.

Bevill was elected to the Alabama Legislature in 1958 and served as a floor leader, first for Gov. John Patterson and then for Gov. George C. Wallace. But he lost his first congressional race in 1964, when incumbent Carl Elliott defeated him in the Democratic primary by more than 3-to-2.

Two years later, the district was open. Republican James D. Martin, who had defeated Elliott in November 1964, was running for governor. Bevill entered a four-way Democratic primary that included a popular state representative, Gary Burns, and a former Wallace press secretary, Bill Jones. Bevill led the first round with 36 percent of the vote, and his strength in the western part of the district gave him a runoff victory over Burns with 56 percent.

The general election was much simpler. Bevill beat Republican Wayman Sherrer, the little-known Blount County solicitor, by nearly 2-to-1 — a margin similar to the one by which Martin was losing the governorship to Lurleen B. Wallace.

Since then, Bevill has won every Democratic primary with at least 80 percent of the vote. Generally, his opposition has come from political novices. His only prominent challenger was Jim Folsom Jr., now the governor, who made his political debut in 1976 by opposing Bevill for renomination. It was a flop. Bevill drew more than 80 percent.

Committee

Appropriations (7th of 37 Democrats)
Energy & Water Development (chairman); Interior; Treasury, Postal Service & General Government

Elections

1992 General		
Tom Bevill (D)	157,907	(68%)
Martha "Mickey" Strickland (R)	66,934	(29%)
Robert P. King (LIBERT)	5,646	(2%)
1990 General		
Tom Bevill (D)	129,872	(100%)

Previous Winning Percentages: **1988** (96%) **1986** (78%) **1984** (100%) **1982** (100%) **1980** (98%) **1978** (100%) **1976** (80%) **1974** (100%) **1972** (70%) **1970** (100%) **1968** (76%) **1966** (64%)

District Vote for President

1992
D 104,557 (44%)
R 107,087 (45%)
I 28,565 (12%)

Campaign Finance

	Receipts	Receipts from PACs	Expend-itures
1992			
Bevill (D)	$318,198	$110,675 (35%)	$519,416
Strickland (R)	$20,114	$2,500 (12%)	$20,117
1990			
Bevill (D)	$220,907	$106,550 (48%)	$168,054

Key Votes

1993	
Require parental notification of minors' abortions	N
Require unpaid family and medical leave	Y
Approve national "motor voter" registration bill	N
Approve budget increasing taxes and reducing deficit	Y
Approve economic stimulus plan	Y
1992	
Approve balanced-budget constitutional amendment	Y
Close down space station program	N
Approve U.S. aid for former Soviet Union	?
Allow shifting funds from defense to domestic programs	Y
1991	
Extend unemployment benefits using deficit financing	Y
Approve waiting period for handgun purchases	N
Authorize use of force in Persian Gulf	Y

Voting Studies

	Presidential Support		Party Unity		Conservative Coalition	
Year	**S**	**O**	**S**	**O**	**S**	**O**
1992	38	53	78	17	81	13
1991	42	55	73	23	92	8
1990	42	56	71	23	85	11
1989	52	45	70	28	78	22
1988	31	58	71	19	71	11
1987	39	46	71	19	74	16
1986	40	58	67	26	82	18
1985	54	39	66	22	80	15
1984	53	35	55	29	83	7
1983	37	54	62	31	80	17
1982	55	44	70	26	75	19
1981	54	42	54	42	79	11

Interest Group Ratings

Year	ADA	AFL-CIO	CCUS	ACU
1992	55	67	38	32
1991	35	92	30	42
1990	22	50	57	58
1989	40	70	44	39
1988	45	100	46	50
1987	36	75	40	41
1986	40	79	29	50
1985	25	53	35	57
1984	35	58	43	50
1983	55	88	32	43
1982	20	74	47	59
1981	25	71	28	40

5 Robert E. "Bud" Cramer (D)

Of Huntsville — Elected 1990; 2nd Term

Born: Aug. 22, 1947, Huntsville, Ala.
Education: U. of Alabama, B.A. 1969, J.D. 1972.
Military Service: Army, 1972; Army Reserve, 1976-78.
Occupation: Lawyer.
Family: Widowed; one child.
Religion: Methodist.
Political Career: Madison County district attorney, 1981-91.
Capitol Office: 1318 Longworth Bldg. 20515; 225-4801.

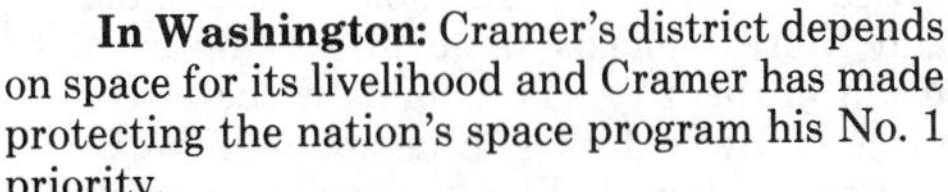

In Washington: Cramer's district depends on space for its livelihood and Cramer has made protecting the nation's space program his No. 1 priority.

In his freshman year, initial House budget plans called for eliminating $2 billion in proposed funding for the space station *Freedom*, and Cramer faced the prospect of losing as many as 3,000 jobs in his district. Cramer shook off his freshman anonymity to lobby friends and foes of the space program in Congress.

Cramer met with Vice President Dan Quayle, head of the National Space Council, and teamed up with fellow Alabama Democrat Tom Bevill, a member of the Appropriations Committee, to urge Appropriations Chairman Jamie L. Whitten, D-Miss., to restore the funds.

In June 1991, Cramer delivered a floor speech in defense of the space station. "This issue of deleting funding for the space station is not merely one of changing our space priorities," Cramer said. "It is a complete shift away from any space program.... We are talking about abandoning this vital field to the competition."

In the end, funding was restored, with Whitten's support. The following year, Cramer returned the favor when he helped avert a showdown between the Science, Space and Technology Committee and Appropriations by offering a successful compromise amendment in the space program spending bill to guarantee funding for a solid-rocket motor project in Whitten's district.

Outer space will remain the center of Cramer's congressional universe for the foreseeable future.

While President Clinton has promised to keep the space station alive, he has also said the scope of the $31 billion project must be trimmed. NASA is under orders from the White House to cut spending by about $15 billion over the next five years and to shift attention from the expensive challenges of putting human beings in space toward greater use of robotic science.

Given the heavy dependence of Huntsville, the core of Cramer's district and home to the Marshall Space Flight Center, on space and defense spending, Cramer was a natural choice for his freshman appointment to the Science, Space and Technology Committee.

Cramer also came to Congress with a strong interest in working to protect abused children, and he took a seat on the now-defunct Select Committee on Children, Youth and Families.

He sponsored a bill providing grants to states to establish child abuse intervention and treatment programs, which was included in the juvenile justice reauthorization.

The grants will fund the creation of programs modeled on the Children's Advocacy Center that Cramer established in Huntsville during his tenure as a prosecuting attorney in Madison County. The center, long recognized as a national model, offers shelter and counseling to abused children.

On the Public Works and Transportation Committee, Cramer worked to ensure that funding for a Memphis-Huntsville-Atlanta superhighway was included in the highway bill.

Cramer supported Clinton with votes for the Family and Medical Leave Act and the fiscal 1994 budget resolution and economic stimulus package. However, he was one of 14 Democrats, 10 of them Southerners, to oppose the so-called motor-voter legislation, which requires states to allow residents to register to vote while applying for or renewing driver's licenses or other documents.

In the 103rd, Cramer will have an opportunity to broaden his portfolio. He was appointed to the Select Committee on Intelligence.

At Home: When seven-term Democratic Rep. Ronnie G. Flippo indicated his intention to run for governor in 1990, Cramer was well-positioned to run for the open 5th.

Alabama 5

North — Huntsville

Space- and defense-related growth radiating from Huntsville has spurred the boom that made the 5th the fastest-growing district in the state during the 1980s, with a nearly 10 percent population gain. The Defense Department, NASA and the Tennessee Valley Authority (TVA) have helped cushion the 5th's economy from recession. The federal government is the district's largest employer.

With just under 160,000 people, Huntsville, the seat of Madison County, is the state's fourth-largest city. It went from cotton town to boom town during World War II when the Army built the Redstone Arsenal to produce chemical-warfare materiel. After the Soviet Union launched Sputnik in October 1957, Wernher von Braun headed the Marshall Space Flight Center to perform the principal research for the fledgling NASA.

Companies that built plants here — Boeing, IBM and General Electric among them — stayed and diversified when the high-tech government contracts dwindled; other industries moved in. Computer giant Intergraph Corp. has its headquarters here. Chrysler employs about 3,000 at an assembly plant.

As Huntsville has grown, businesses and people have moved out of the city and into surrounding Madison County; Intergraph has built a facility in Madison. The city of Madison's population more than tripled during the 1980s, spurting to 14,800. Madison County grew by 21 percent, fourth-fastest in the state.

Huntsville's federal installations and active labor unions in the metals, automobile and chemical plants along the Tennessee River lend the 5th a solid Democratic presence. In 1992, Bill Clinton carried three of the six counties entirely within the district. But the GOP has picked up strength as Madison County has grown. Madison went for George Bush by wide margins in 1988 and 1992. Independent Ross Perot scored well in the 5th; three of his top four counties in the state — Morgan, Limestone and Madison — are in the 5th. Morgan (Decatur) was his best county; he won more than 17 percent.

Downstream from Huntsville along the Tennessee, blue-collar jobs begin to predominate. Towns such as Decatur, a chemical manufacturing center, and the Quad Cities of Florence, Sheffield, Tuscumbia and Muscle Shoals came into being as a result of the TVA. Tuscumbia is the birthplace of Helen Keller. Blues pioneer W. C. Handy was born in Florence; an annual jazz and blues festival celebrates Florence's native son. Logging dominates in the rural eastern part of the district.

The TVA has two huge nuclear complexes in the 5th — Browns Ferry at Athens and Bellefonte at Scottsboro. Before Three Mile Island, a 1975 fire at Browns Ferry had been considered the nation's worst nuclear accident. The plant was closed from 1975 to 1977, and again in 1985. After a six-year shutdown, one of Browns Ferry's three reactors began operation again in 1991. Bellefonte's construction has been delayed indefinitely.

1990 Population: 577,227. White 481,509 (83%), Black 85,945 (15%), Other 9,773 (2%). Hispanic origin 4,549 (<1%). 18 and over 433,310 (75%), 62 and over 79,672 (14%). Median age: 33.

With Huntsville television stations reaching virtually every voter in the seven-county district, Cramer had high name identification and a favorable image as a "champion of the victim." That stemmed not just from his work on child abuse but from programs his office instituted to prosecute bad-check cases and spousal abuse.

Coupled with his strong base in the district's most populous county and an ample campaign treasury, Cramer ran far ahead of the crowded Democratic primary field, taking 44 percent of the vote.

In the runoff, state Public Service Commissioner Lynn Greer tried to paint Cramer as an upscale city slicker and liberal "national Democrat," but he was trounced 3-to-2 by Cramer.

In the fall campaign, Cramer had the added advantage of being a Democrat in a district that had not elected a Republican this century. His GOP opponent was Albert McDonald, the state commissioner of agriculture and industries, who had switched parties earlier in the year. McDonald proved slow to raise money, and he was never able to find an issue that would woo voters from their historic Democratic bias.

Like Greer, McDonald sought to court support outside Huntsville with a "just folks" manner that contrasted with Cramer's more urbane deportment. He tried to portray Cramer as a liberal by focusing on the abortion issue. But Cramer mollified many anti-abortion voters by explaining his pro-abortion rights position in terms of his personal experience. As his late wife battled cancer several years ago, she needed an abortion to prolong her life.

In any case, voters in the 5th have usually been less concerned with ideology than with the flow of federal dollars into the district. Cramer won more than two of every three votes and swept every county in the district. He posted similar results two years later.

Cramer is the district's first representative from Huntsville since Democrat John J. Sparkman held the seat from 1937 to 1946, when he was elected to the Senate.

Committees

Public Works & Transportation (21st of 39 Democrats)
Aviation; Surface Transportation

Science, Space & Technology (16th of 33 Democrats)
Energy; Space

Select Intelligence (11th of 12 Democrats)
Legislation; Program & Budget Authorization

Elections

1992 General		
Robert E. "Bud" Cramer (D)	160,060	(66%)
Terry Smith (R)	77,951	(32%)
C. Michael Seibert (LIBERT)	6,006	(2%)
1990 General		
Robert E. "Bud" Cramer (D)	113,047	(67%)
Albert McDonald (R)	55,326	(33%)

District Vote for President

1992

D	102,124 (41%)
R	110,256 (44%)
I	36,918 (15%)

Campaign Finance

	Receipts	Receipts from PACs		Expend-itures
1992				
Cramer (D)	$400,693	$223,075	(56%)	$389,349
Smith (R)	$28,545	$1,523	(5%)	$28,225
1990				
Cramer (D)	$662,457	$246,932	(37%)	$638,361
McDonald (R)	$184,089	$27,200	(15%)	$184,188

Key Votes

1993	
Require parental notification of minors' abortions	N
Require unpaid family and medical leave	Y
Approve national "motor voter" registration bill	N
Approve budget increasing taxes and reducing deficit	Y
Approve economic stimulus plan	Y
1992	
Approve balanced-budget constitutional amendment	Y
Close down space station program	N
Approve U.S. aid for former Soviet Union	Y
Allow shifting funds from defense to domestic programs	Y
1991	
Extend unemployment benefits using deficit financing	Y
Approve waiting period for handgun purchases	N
Authorize use of force in Persian Gulf	Y

Voting Studies

	Presidential Support		Party Unity		Conservative Coalition	
Year	S	O	S	O	S	O
1992	39	58	75	23	81	15
1991	38	61	77	22	89	11

Interest Group Ratings

Year	ADA	AFL-CIO	CCUS	ACU
1992	55	58	50	44
1991	40	83	40	40

6 Spencer Bachus (R)

Of Birmingham — Elected 1992; 1st Term

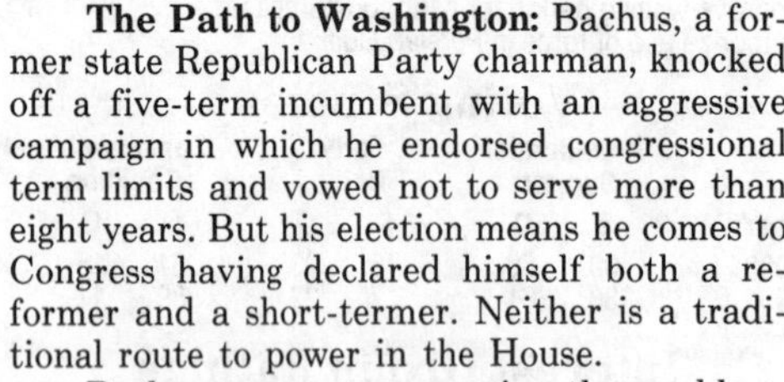

Born: Dec. 28, 1947, Birmingham, Ala.

Education: Auburn U., B.A. 1969; U. of Alabama, J.D. 1972.

Military Service: National Guard, 1969-71.

Occupation: Lawyer; manufacturer.

Family: Divorced; three children.

Religion: Baptist.

Political Career: Ala. Senate, 1983; Ala. House, 1983-87; Ala. Board of Education, 1987-91; candidate for Ala. attorney general, 1990; Ala. GOP Party chairman, 1991-92.

Capitol Office: 216 Cannon Bldg. 20515; 225-4921.

The Path to Washington: Bachus, a former state Republican Party chairman, knocked off a five-term incumbent with an aggressive campaign in which he endorsed congressional term limits and vowed not to serve more than eight years. But his election means he comes to Congress having declared himself both a reformer and a short-termer. Neither is a traditional route to power in the House.

Bachus seems to recognize the problem. After running a slashing, partisan campaign against Democrat Ben Erdreich, Bachus' tone changed after the election: He began espousing the need for cooperation between Democrats and Republicans on economic issues, health-care legislation and congressional reform.

During a decade-long apprenticeship as a state legislator and party official, Bachus may have absorbed the unwritten rules of the Alabama congressional delegation: Vote a relatively conservative line, work behind the scenes and wait your turn for a position of influence.

Following Erdreich's example, Bachus took a seat on the Banking Committee. He also will serve on Veterans' Affairs.

As one of six GOP freshmen on Banking's Financial Institutions subcommittee, however, he showed an ability to work with Democrats when he and fellow freshman Thomas M. Barrett of Wisconsin successfully pushed for language in the 1993 thrift bailout bill to severely restrict bonuses paid to Resolution Trust Corporation executives.

Despite his pledge to serve only four terms, the 6th District is so solidly Republican that it seems tailor-made to shield Bachus from serious Democratic competition.

The district was the Republicans' prize for outplaying the Democrats in redistricting. A three-judge panel adopted an Alabama map that strongly resembled one drawn by a GOP state official. The plan carved heavily Democratic neighborhoods in Birmingham out of Erdreich's old district, establishing a neighboring district with a majority-black population and transforming the 6th into one of the most Republican districts in the country.

Bachus' victory may have owed as much to the new lines of his district as to his strategy of painting Erdreich as too liberal.

Erdreich, a popular moderate with close ties to Birmingham's banking and business communities, had compiled a moderate voting record during his decade in Congress. But Bachus contended that his own views were more in line with those of voters in the newly drawn district.

He lambasted Erdreich for his vote to fund the National Endowment for the Arts. Erdreich responded by accusing Bachus of missing more than 3,000 votes while in the state Legislature.

Bachus staked out conservative positions on most issues. He is against abortion, except in cases when the woman's life is in danger.

To spark the economy, Bachus favors cutting taxes and reducing federal spending, although he opposes reductions in Medicare. He opposes affirmative action and gun control measures. He came out in favor of universal health insurance for full-time workers. Besides term limits, Bachus endorsed a GOP campaign finance reform proposal, which would curtail donations by political action committees and limit personal use of campaign funds.

Forced into a runoff in the contest for the GOP nomination in the 6th District, Bachus trounced a one-time colleague at state GOP headquarters, Marty Connors, the party's former executive director. Bachus won about 60 percent of the vote in Jefferson and Shelby counties, where all but 506 of the 33,970 votes were cast.

Bachus depleted his campaign treasury in the primary contest, leaving him at a sizable financial disadvantage against Erdreich. But the banking community did not remain entirely in Erdreich's camp. And Bachus' campaign received a significant boost when The Birmingham News, the largest-circulation newspaper in the district, enthusiastically endorsed him.

Alabama 6

Part of Birmingham and suburbs

Republicans controlled 1990s redistricting in Alabama, and they claimed the 6th as their trophy. After placing most of the black voters of Birmingham in the new, majority-black 7th, they designed a district that distilled GOP voting strength to near purity. The resulting 6th is 90 percent white and one of the most Republican districts in the country. The makeup enabled Bachus to unseat a 10-year Democratic incumbent, Ben Erdreich.

The intensity of the district's GOP vote is striking. In 1988, George Bush won the areas that make up the 6th with 76 percent — a mark topped by only one other district in the country: Bush's home in Houston. Former Republican Gov. Guy Hunt got nearly 71 percent of the vote within the 6th in his 1990 re-election — more than 18 percentage points above his statewide mark. (Hunt was found guilty of using his office for personal gain and removed from office in April 1993.) In 1992, Bush won here with more than 60 percent.

The largest portion of the 6th's population is in Jefferson County (Birmingham). Birmingham is moving away from its image as a declining steel town toward one as a financial center. AmSouth, Central Bank of the South and Southtrust are among the large banks with headquarters in Birmingham. Most of the city of Birmingham was placed in the 7th, although the city's symbol, the cast-iron statue of Vulcan, the Roman god of fire and metalworking, is in the 6th, on the summit of Red Mountain. The 55-foot-tall statue, one of the world's largest iron figures, is a monument to the city's iron industry.

Jefferson County's well-to-do, almost exclusively white bedroom communities such as Homewood, Mountain Brook and Hoover are home to people who work in Birmingham's business district.

According to the 1990 census, Mountain Brook, a city of 19,810, had 38 blacks. Nearly all of the Jefferson County suburbs in the 6th have white populations of 90 percent or more. Hoover (95 percent white) and Trussville (99 percent) were the fastest-growing cities in the Birmingham metropolitan area during the 1980s; both more than doubled their population.

South of Jefferson County is Shelby County, the most Republican county in the state — and the fastest-growing. Shelby's population spurted by 50 percent in the 1980s as Birmingham commuters moved into cities such as Alabaster (which grew by 108 percent during the 1980s) and Pelham (39 percent growth). Shelby was Bush's best Alabama county in 1988 (79 percent) and 1992 (68 percent), and Hunt's best county in 1986 (77 percent) and 1990 (73 percent).

Democratic votes can be tilled from the portion of Tuscaloosa County in the 6th. The city of Tuscaloosa (population 77,800) is split between the 6th and 7th districts. It has an industrial base that includes manufacturers of chemicals, fertilizer and rubber products, but it is more often identified as the home of the University of Alabama (19,800 students), whose campus is in the 6th. Erdreich carried the Tuscaloosa County portion of the 6th against Bachus with 61 percent.

1990 Population: 577,226. White 517,777 (90%), Black 53,309 (9%), Other 6,140 (1%). Hispanic origin 3,211 (<1%). 18 and over 441,662 (77%), 62 and over 85,223 (15%). Median age: 34.

Committees

Banking, Finance & Urban Affairs (17th of 20 Republicans)
Consumer Credit & Insurance; Financial Institutions Supervision, Regulation & Deposit Insurance; Housing & Community Development

Veterans' Affairs (11th of 14 Republicans)
Oversight & Investigations

Campaign Finance

	Receipts	Receipts from PACs		Expend-itures
1992				
Bachus (R)	$527,406	$150,307	(28%)	$502,793
Erdreich (D)	$677,829	$414,200	(61%)	$1,015,731

Key Votes

1993

Require parental notification of minors' abortions	Y
Require unpaid family and medical leave	N
Approve national "motor voter" registration bill	N
Approve budget increasing taxes and reducing deficit	N
Approve economic stimulus plan	N

Elections

1992 General		
Spencer Bachus (R)	146,599	(52%)
Ben Erdreich (D)	126,062	(45%)
Carla Cloum (I)	4,521	(2%)
Mark Bodenhausen (LIBERT)	2,836	(1%)
1992 Primary Runoff		
Spencer Bachus (R)	20,114	(59%)
Marty Connors (R)	13,856	(41%)
1992 Primary		
Spencer Bachus (R)	26,843	(37%)
Marty Connors (R)	26,221	(36%)
Jim Gunter (R)	11,190	(15%)
Mike King (R)	7,075	(10%)

District Vote for President

	1992	
D	77,506	(27%)
R	180,798	(64%)
I	26,235	(9%)

7 Earl F. Hilliard (D)

Of Birmingham — Elected 1992; 1st Term

Born: April 9, 1942, Birmingham, Ala.
Education: Morehouse College, B.A. 1964; Howard U., J.D. 1967; Atlanta U., M.B.A. 1970.
Occupation: Lawyer; insurance broker.
Family: Wife, Mary Franklin; two children.
Religion: Baptist.
Political Career: Ala. House, 1975-81; Ala. Senate, 1981-93.
Capitol Office: 1007 Longworth Bldg. 20515; 225-2665.

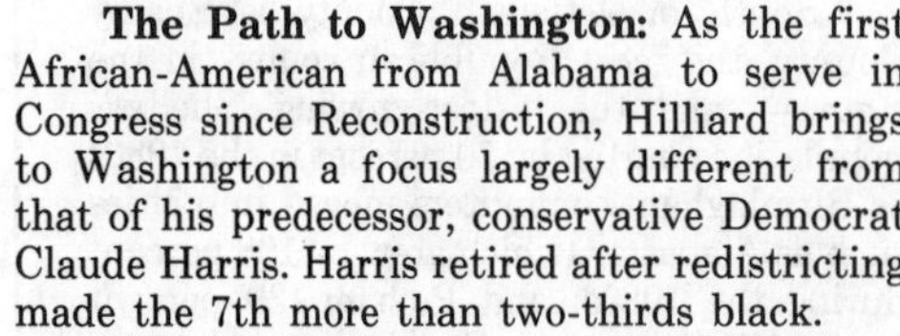

The Path to Washington: As the first African-American from Alabama to serve in Congress since Reconstruction, Hilliard brings to Washington a focus largely different from that of his predecessor, conservative Democrat Claude Harris. Harris retired after redistricting made the 7th more than two-thirds black.

Hilliard won the seat after winning a bitter primary and runoff that pitted him against state Sen. Hank Sanders, a black activist and lawyer.

During his three terms, Harris broadened his base by reaching out to blacks and labor, which helped repair relationships strained under Democratic Sen. Richard C. Shelby, who served in the 7th before him. However, Hilliard's legislative agenda will be decidedly more liberal. Hilliard has made it clear that he takes the symbolism of his election seriously. While he has vowed to represent the interests of all his constituents, he also plans to focus primarily on black voters' concerns.

Nevertheless, his priorities sound much like those of many other members elected under the banner of change. Near the top of Hilliard's list is the reallocation of federal funds from foreign to domestic aid, including cutting dollars spent for the defense of other nations, particularly Japan. With these cuts, Hilliard wants to reduce the federal deficit. He also favors a national health-care system and abortion rights.

However, unlike Harris, Hilliard opposes the death penalty and supports the distribution of contraceptives in public schools.

Early in the 103rd, Hilliard showed an animosity toward the FBI, which he thinks intimidates racial, ethnic and religious minorities. Calling the agency "a traitor to democracy," Hilliard was one of only six members to vote against giving the FBI authority to obtain unlisted phone numbers without a warrant in terrorism or espionage cases.

As a state legislator, Hilliard worked to establish urban enterprise zones and a tax-abatement program, which he said spurred the growth of small businesses and kept jobs in Birmingham. In general, he has not favored tax increases, and he voted against a 5-cent hike in the state gasoline tax and an increase in the disposal fee for toxic waste.

Years of steady political maneuvering preceded his arrival in Washington. An 18-year veteran of the Alabama Legislature, Hilliard is no political novice. He has a reputation for hardball political gamesmanship for using such tactics as slipping in legislation while opponents were out of the chamber — a move not unheard of in Congress. And despite of allegations of unethical conduct, Hilliard was able to win.

The Birmingham News endorsed Sanders, Hilliard's opponent in the Democratic primary and runoff, and Kervin Jones, his Republican rival, in the general election. The News blasted Hilliard for what it termed ethical lapses, including his use of more than $50,000 in state Senate campaign funds for his business in 1990.

Hilliard had the backing of longtime Birmingham Mayor Richard Arrington, one of the state's most powerful black politicians. Arrington's support was crucial in the fight against Sanders, who through his longtime work as a civil rights activist had a large following of his own in the black community.

Sanders' attempts to make an issue of Hilliard's ethics ultimately failed. However, Sanders' own past as an activist hurt him with white voters. In 1990, Sanders and his wife, Rose, staged protests after the Selma school board voted not to extend the contract for the city's first black superintendent. Hank Sanders called for a student boycott that resulted in a weeklong school shutdown.

Arrington's organization, the Jefferson County Citizen's Coalition, helped Hilliard carry the 7th's most populous county by nearly 9,800 votes in the runoff. With that advantage, he withstood Sanders' near-sweep of the remainder of the counties and won by 670 votes.

From there, Hilliard fairly breezed into office from the heavily Democratic district, trouncing Jones in November with 69 percent of the vote.

Hilliard got slots on the Agriculture and Small Business committees.

Alabama 7

West Central — Parts of Birmingham, Montgomery and Tuscaloosa

The majority-black 7th is the product of the Voting Rights Act's mandate to increase minority-group representation in the House. In Rep. Hilliard, Alabama has its first black member of Congress since Reconstruction.

The district sprawls over all or part of 14 counties, but it is anchored by two population centers: Birmingham and Montgomery. In between are the rural counties of the Black Belt, one of the most economically deprived regions in the nation.

The 7th extends a finger into southwestern Jefferson County (Birmingham), scooping out downtown Birmingham and the majority-black cities of Bessemer and Fairfield. Half the district's black population — and 45 percent of its total population — is in Jefferson County.

Reminders of the civil rights struggle that led to the 7th's creation dot the district; it is chronicled at Birmingham's Civil Rights Institute, which opened in November 1992. Four black girls died on Sept. 15, 1963, when the Sixteenth Street Baptist Church in downtown Birmingham was bombed. In March 1965, Selma (Dallas County) was the site of a bloody confrontation between civil rights demonstrators and police when the Rev. Dr. Martin Luther King Jr. led marchers across the Edmund Pettus Bridge. The Civil Rights Memorial in Montgomery, designed by Vietnam Veterans Memorial architect Maya Lin, commemorates the 40 Americans who died while fighting for civil rights in the 1950s and 1960s.

There are ironies within the confines of the majority-black 7th. The portion of Montgomery within the district contains the state Capitol, which doubled as the Confederate Capitol from February 1861 to July 1861.

While the term Black Belt is said to refer not to the racial composition but to the rich, cotton-growing soil in rural, west-central Alabama, all but one of the rural counties in the Black Belt portion of the district have black-majority populations. This area is in a perpetual state of poverty; it has not known prosperity since before the Civil War, when cotton plantation owners made fortunes from slave labor. Seven of the eight counties with the highest poverty rates in Alabama are in the Black Belt portion of the 7th. The poverty rate in Greene, Wilcox and Perry counties was more than 40 percent, according to the 1990 census; the others had rates above 30 percent.

Politically, the 7th is every bit as Democratic as the 6th is Republican. Michael S. Dukakis won 69 percent in his 1988 presidential race. In 1990, losing Democratic gubernatorial nominee Paul Hubbert carried the 7th with 72 percent of the vote, 20 percentage points above his statewide tally.

Democrats further down the ticket draw even bigger margins. In his successful 1990 reelection for lieutenant governor, James E. Folsom Jr. (now the governor after the 1993 conviction and removal of GOP Gov. Guy Hunt) received 84 percent in the 7th.

1990 Population: 577,227. White 185,454 (32%), Black 389,796 (68%), Other 1,977 (<1%). Hispanic origin 1,909 (<1%). 18 and over 407,367 (71%), 62 and over 96,220 (17%). Median age: 32.

Committees

Agriculture (17th of 28 Democrats)
Environment, Credit & Rural Development; Livestock

Small Business (23rd of 27 Democrats)
Minority Enterprise, Finance & Urban Development; Procurement, Taxation & Tourism; Rural Enterprises, Exports & the Environment

Campaign Finance

	Receipts	Receipts from PACs		Expenditures
1992				
Hilliard (D)	$348,669	$106,331	(30%)	$341,737
Jones (R)	$13,281	$75	(1%)	$11,963

Key Votes

1993

Require parental notification of minors' abortions	N
Require unpaid family and medical leave	Y
Approve national "motor voter" registration bill	Y
Approve budget increasing taxes and reducing deficit	Y
Approve economic stimulus plan	Y

Elections

1992 General		
Earl F. Hilliard (D)	144,320	(69%)
Kervin Jones (R)	36,086	(17%)
James M. Lewis (I)	12,461	(6%)
James Chambliss (I)	11,466	(6%)
Michael Todd Mayer (LIBERT)	2,135	(1%)
1992 Primary Runoff		
Earl F. Hilliard (D)	35,914	(50%)
Hank Sanders (D)	35,244	(50%)
1992 Primary		
Earl F. Hilliard (D)	36,005	(30%)
Hank Sanders (D)	28,156	(24%)
John Knight (D)	23,385	(20%)
Sam Taylor (D)	13,595	(12%)
Edward B. McClain (D)	8,317	(7%)
James Louis Thomas (D)	6,364	(5%)

District Vote for President

	1992	
D	137,518	(71%)
R	46,205	(24%)
I	8,691	(5%)

Alaska

STATE DATA

Governor: Walter J. Hickel (I)
First elected: 1990 *
Length of term: 4 years
Term expires: 12/94
Salary: $81,648
Term limit: 2 consecutive terms
Phone: (907) 465-3500
Born: Aug. 18, 1919; Claflin, Kan.
Education: Graduated from Claflin H.S., 1936
Occupation: Business executive
Family: Wife, Ermalee Strutz; six children
Religion: Roman Catholic
Political Career: Republican National Committee, 1954-64; * governor, 1966-69; U.S. secretary of the Interior, 1969-70; sought Republican nomination for governor, 1974, 1978, 1986

Lt. Gov.: John B. (Jack) Coghill (I)
First elected: 1990
Length of term: 4 years
Term expires: 12/94
Salary: $76,188
Phone: (907) 465-3520

State election official: (907) 465-4611
Democratic headquarters: (907) 258-3050
Republican headquarters: (907) 276-4467

STATE LEGISLATURE

Bicameral Legislature. Meets January-mid-May, with a limit of 120 calendar days.

Senate: 20 members, 4-year terms
1992 breakdown: 10R, 9D, 1I; 16 men, 4 women; 16 whites, 4 others
Salary: $24,012 per year
Phone: (907) 465-3701

House of Representatives: 40 members, 2-year terms
1992 breakdown: 20 D, 18 R, 2 I; 31 men, 9 women; 33 whites, 1 black, 6 others
Salary: $24,012 per year
Phone: (907) 465-3725

URBAN STATISTICS

City	Pop.
Anchorage	226,338
Mayor Tom Fink, R	
Fairbanks	30,843
Mayor James Hayes, D	
Juneau	26,751
Mayor Jamie Parsons, D	

U.S. CONGRESS

Senate: 0 D, 2 R
House: 0 D, 1 R

TERM LIMITS

For Congress: No
For state offices: No

ELECTIONS

1992 Presidential Vote

George Bush	39.5%
Bill Clinton	30.3%
Ross Perot	28.4%

1988 Presidential Vote

George Bush	60%
Michael S. Dukakis	36%

1984 Presidential Vote

Ronald Reagan	67%
Walter F. Mondale	30%

POPULATION

1990 population		550,043
1980 population		401,851
Percent change		+ 37%
Rank among states:		49
White		76%
Black		4%
Hispanic		3%
Asian or Pacific islander		4%
Urban		67%
Rural		33%
Born in state		34%
Foreign-born		5%
Under age 18	172,344	31%
Ages 18-64	335,330	65%
65 and older	22,369	4%
Median age		29.4

MISCELLANEOUS

Capital: Juneau
Number of counties: 25 divisions
Per capital income: $21,932 (1991)
Rank among states: 6
Total area: 591,000 sq. miles
Rank among states: 1

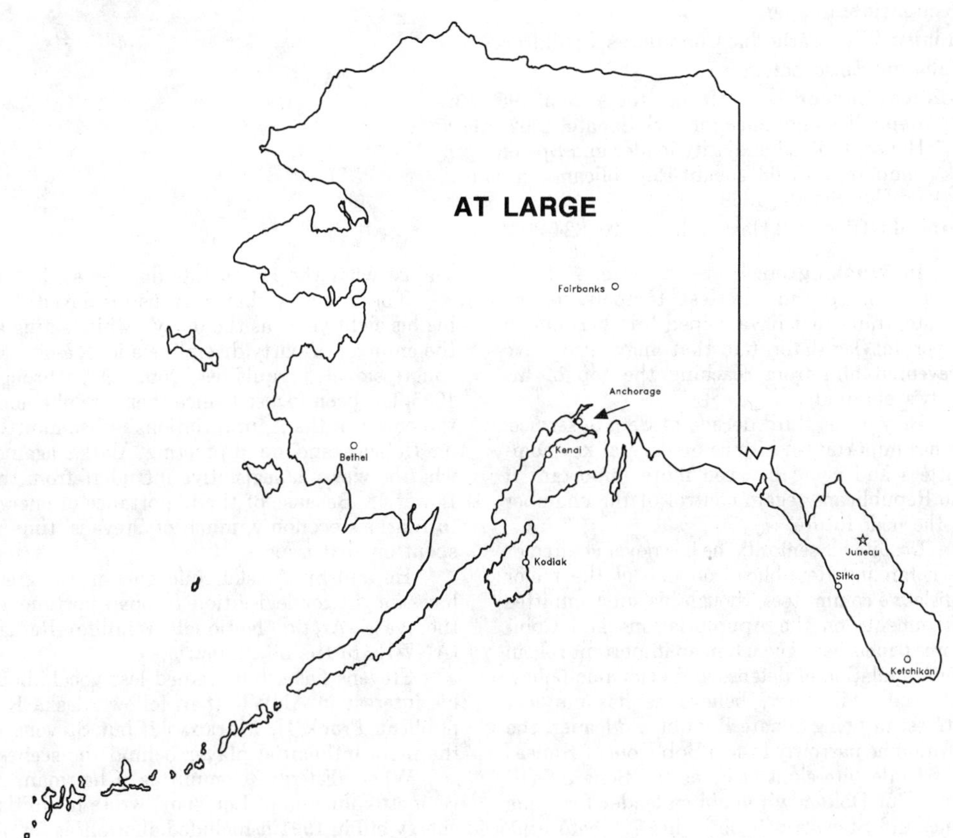
AT LARGE
Fairbanks
Anchorage
Kenai
Bethel
Kodiak
Juneau
Sitka
Ketchikan

Alaska - Senior Senator

Ted Stevens (R)

Of Girdwood — Elected 1970; 4th Full Term

Appointed to the Senate in December 1968.

Born: Nov. 18, 1923, Indianapolis, Ind.
Education: U. of California, Los Angeles, B.A. 1947; Harvard U., LL.B. 1950.
Military Service: Army Air Corps, 1943-46.
Occupation: Lawyer.
Family: Wife, Catherine Chandler; six children.
Religion: Episcopalian.
Political Career: U.S. attorney for Alaska, 1953-56; Republican nominee for U.S. Senate, 1962; Alaska House, 1965-68, majority leader and Speaker pro tempore, 1967-68; sought Republican nomination for U.S. Senate, 1968.
Capitol Office: 522 Hart Bldg. 20510; 224-3004.

In Washington: Stevens has one of the sharpest minds and hottest tempers in the Senate, traits that have helped him become an important legislator but that may also have prevented him from reaching the top of his party's pyramid.

Now in his third decade of Senate service, he has important positions on several key committees and could be even more important if the Republicans regain control of the chamber in the near future.

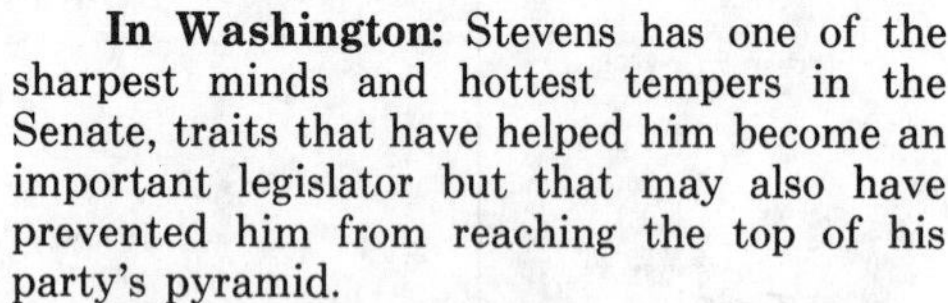

Despite his seniority, he has never chaired or been ranking Republican on one of the major legislative committees, though his subcommittee assignments on the Appropriations and Commerce panels have given him an important role in the formulation of defense and economic policy.

And while many believe he has not lost interest in being Senate Republican leader, the position he narrowly lost to Bob Dole of Kansas in 1984 despite eight years as the Senate GOP whip. But Dole may remain as leader for some time, and Stevens will be in his 70s before he gets another shot at the leadership.

More promising, perhaps, is Stevens' positioning on his two main committees. He is one seat away from being the top Republican on Appropriations and Governmental Affairs, and that could translate into a chairmanship if the Republicans regain control of the Senate in the next few years.

In the meantime, Stevens continues to apply his unique style to a range of issues. He can be cranky and combative — especially when Alaskan interests are at stake — yet he is pragmatic enough to rise above simple obstructionism.

When Stevens participated in a weekend retreat in March 1990 where GOP senators plotted strategy on campaign finance legislation, his comment on the issue in many ways summed up his approach as a leader. "We need to stand on the positive side rather than just be against what the Democrats do," he said.

The intensity that Stevens displayed during his eight years as the party's whip, acting as the enforcer of party discipline and defender of congressional perquisites from 1977 through 1985, has been focused since then on enhancing the power of the Appropriations Subcommittee on Defense and on protecting Alaska against what he views as legislative intruders from the Lower 48. Because of the importance of energy to Alaska's economy, much of Stevens' time is spent on that issue.

He and his Alaska colleagues in Congress have fought for legislation to open portions of the vast Arctic National Wildlife Refuge (ANWR) to the oil industry.

Stevens has often seemed less vocal about his interest in ANWR than fellow Alaska Republican Frank H. Murkowski, but Stevens is the more influential player behind the scenes.

When Energy Committee Chairman J. Bennett Johnston of Louisiana wrote his initial energy bill in 1991 it included allowances for oil drilling in ANWR. But Democrats who disliked the allowances protested and resented Johnston's failure to consult with them. The provision was dropped in subsequent versions, including that which ultimately passed Congress.

In early 1991 he said he might oppose the measure unless the state and federal governments could settle a multibillion-dollar disagreement over how revenues derived from drilling in the refuge should be shared. Current law gives Alaska 90 percent of the revenues and the federal government 10 percent; the Bush administration and Congress preferred a 50-50 split.

Stevens also played a role during congressional passage of oil-spill liability and cleanup legislation in the wake of the *Exxon Valdez* oil spill in March 1992. He specifically backed some Alaska-related provisions, including the authorization of the Prince William Sound Oil Spill

Recovery Institute at Cordova. He fought a provision in the measure, however, requiring congressional approval of the disbursement of funds from the $1 billion compensation fund. "An oil spill is like a fire," said Stevens, in opposing the time-consuming procedure. "Once it occurs, money has to be made available immediately."

In 1990, Stevens and Murkowski were forced to accept a compromise in their efforts to maintain a steady supply of cheap timber for mills in southeastern Alaska. Such a supply had long flowed from the 16.7 million-acre Tongass National Forest, where conservationists wanted to restrict logging. The struggle between timber and conservation had continued for nearly two decades, and the delegation seemed more relieved than angered when a bill designating more than 1 million acres off-limits was finally enacted. "After 19 years, we deserve a little peace," Stevens said.

On the issue of forcing automakers to boost the fuel efficiency of passenger vehicles, Stevens brought the Alaska angle to the debate. After opposing such a bill in 1990, Stevens got bill sponsor Democrat Richard H. Bryan of Nevada to agree to an amendment that could relax fuel standards for four-wheel-drive vehicles — common on Alaska's rugged terrain. With this addition, Stevens voted for the bill.

He broke with some conservatives on another issue important to Alaska, funding for public broadcasting. Because of the state's sparse population, public radio is an important community bulletin board there and Stevens said that superseded ideological concerns about the liberal leanings of public radio. He criticized public broadcasting for "testing the limits of public acceptance," but he was also something of a mediator on the subject — explaining that "The people who need this system are not extreme."

Ever-sensitive about the federal government trampling over the rights of less-populous states such as Alaska, Stevens can strike a defensive pose. He criticized the "motor voter" bill passed in 1993 as an unfunded federal mandate that ignores the concerns of local officials who complained about the added costs of expanding voter registration.

He also went to bat for Alaska and successfully persuaded the Bush administration to exempt the state from rules that require restoring or creating new wetlands to replace those that are damaged. Environmentalists argued that the exemption would encourage excessive economic development and place all wetland ecosystems at risk. But Stevens said the state was in a unique position, considering that some 70 percent of its territory could be characterized as wetlands.

The exemption, which will last as long as less than 1 percent of the state's wetlands have been developed, will "give Alaskan communities the opportunity to grow without ignoring the importance of wetlands."

Stevens underwent surgery for prostate cancer in August 1991, and he helped push through legislation establishing a prostate cancer research center within the National Cancer Institute.

As subcommittee chairman in the 99th Congress and as ranking Republican on Defense Appropriations now, Stevens has been determined to establish the panel as an independent voice on military programs, rather than merely a bursar for the programs authorized by the Armed Services Committee. In doing so, he has faced opposition both from Armed Services and from the subcommittee's traditionally more powerful House counterpart.

As a World War II veteran and ardent hawk, he has resisted the deeper cuts into defense spending in the post Cold War era. In 1992, for example, Stevens fought for the proposed $3.8 billion in funding for the Strategic Defense Initiative (SDI).

As ranking Republican on the Rules Committee, he has been an important player on the issue of campaign finance reform. Like most of his Republicans, he has been adamant in opposing most of the Democrats' plans, which usually include some form of public financing.

"Our side of the aisle just cannot accept paying for campaigns out of the Treasury," said Stevens in a debate during the 102nd Congress.

But all his service and loyalty did not pay off as he had hoped they would in December 1984, when he came up short in his bid to be leader. Most Senate observers actually thought Stevens an unlikely successor to Majority Leader Howard H. Baker Jr. of Tennessee, whom he had served as chief lieutenant. Yet Stevens outpolled three other contenders and survived to the final ballot, where he lost to Dole by just three votes (28-25).

That narrow defeat reflected the widespread ambivalence about Stevens. He is easily enraged and often confrontational. Yet many Republicans felt his militancy might be needed to restore order to a Senate that had fallen into some disarray under Baker's stewardship. Moreover, they could forgive a lot in a man known as "Mr. Perk," who fought so unabashedly and tenaciously for the benefits they wanted but were afraid to pursue openly.

But in the end, Stevens could not overcome the simple fact that too many colleagues consider him a very difficult person to work with. Nevertheless, he seemed to take encouragement from the closeness of the outcome. Early on, he freely acknowledged that he would seek the seat again if Dole gave it up.

From his first week in the chamber in 1969, when he tangled with Democrats over President Richard M. Nixon's nomination of Alaska Gov. Walter J. Hickel as Interior secretary, colleagues have known that debate with Stevens can quickly degenerate into a shouting match.

But for all his pugnaciousness, Stevens generally is not one to simmer and harbor grudges. His temper typically flares and just as quickly disappears. A moderate by GOP ideological standards, Stevens can deal effectively with Democrats as well as Republicans. He gets along fine in the collegial, horse-trading culture of Appropriations, where success can be measured by his catch for Alaska; an Anchorage paper in 1989 called Stevens "the six billion dollar man," estimating he has been worth at least that much to the state in federal largess.

Members in both parties appreciate his work for increased congressional salaries and benefits. While most members scurry for cover when the subject of pay raises comes up, Stevens brashly proclaims that Congress is underpaid.

Over his years as whip, Stevens pushed a variety of schemes to make congressional life more rewarding. The list of measures passed includes pay raises, a tax break for members' Washington, D.C., living expenses, expanded free mailing privileges, an end to limits on senators' outside income and an increased allowance for honoraria.

During the 101st Congress, Stevens fought to preserve mass mailings, defending them as an essential tool for members whose rural constituencies lack access to sophisticated media outlets. He worked out a proposal with Kentucky Democrat Wendell H. Ford to provide a 50 percent increase in the Senate's mail budget in fiscal 1991. Before final passage of the appropriations bill, the Senate adopted an amendment to reduce the amount included for Senate mail from the $35.5 million recommended by the Appropriations Committee to $30 million. Amendment sponsors initially sought a deeper cut — to $24 million — but compromised in the face of vigorous objections from Stevens.

His unflagging support for federal workers, an important constituency in Alaska, has made Stevens popular with public employee unions. In fact, he is one of the few Senate Republicans to draw sizable campaign help from organized labor. As chairman of the Civil Service, Post Office and General Services Subcommittee at Governmental Affairs until 1987, he was ideally positioned to look out for federal workers.

He was once a federal employee himself, in the top ranks of the Interior Department in the 1950s, and he fights regularly against caps on federal pay raises, arguing that government workers should not have to suffer from inflation.

In 1990, Stevens was one of just 10 Republicans in the Senate who voted to override President Bush's veto of a measure to revise the Hatch Act, which prohibits federal employees from engaging in political activities. The override effort fell two votes short.

At Home: Stevens' careful defense of Alaska interests has made him invulnerable at the polls. Although he has not had his way on every issue, he always seems to have the right political approach — stubborn but pragmatic.

However, not everyone in Alaska is a Stevens fan. There are those who say his long years in the Senate have made him a remote figure to the average Alaskan and part of the "Washington crowd." Despite his record as a GOP loyalist, Stevens' focus on the economy and defense policy and lack of zeal on social issues has alienated some of the staunch conservatives — including a number of religious fundamentalists — who dominate the Alaska Republican Party. This mild dissent explains the sound but relatively modest victory margins Steven ran up in the 1990 primary and general elections.

Stevens, who had been majority leader in the Alaska House, got to Washington by appointment when Democratic Sen. E. L. Bartlett died in 1968. The appointment came from Hickel, who was then the state's GOP governor (and who became governor again in 1990, this time as an independent). Stevens would soon be in the Senate arguing for Hickel's confirmation as secretary of the Interior under President Nixon.

Stevens had begun his pursuit of a Senate seat not long after Alaska became a state in 1959. He got the party's nomination for the job in 1962 but managed just 41 percent of the vote against Democrat Ernest J. Gruening that fall. He tried for the nomination again in 1968 but was defeated in the primary. The party's nominee, however, lost that November to Democrat Mike Gravel, and when Bartlett died in December, Hickel turned to Stevens.

Once in Washington, Stevens began digging in politically. In the 1970 contest to fill the final two years of Bartlett's term, he won with almost 60 percent (even as the GOP was losing the governorship). In that campaign, against liberal Democrat Wendell P. Kay, Stevens favored greater oil and mineral development; Kay was a firm conservationist.

Seeking a full term in 1972, Stevens crushed Democrat Gene Guess, the state House Speaker, whom he linked to presidential nominee George McGovern. By 1978 Stevens had been elected to the Senate Republican leadership and no prominent Democrat even considered a serious campaign against him, so the party nominated an electrical contractor who received less than one-fourth of the vote against Stevens.

Stevens has had no real problems within his own party, but some of its social-agenda conservatives regard him as something of a moderate. He was denied the chairmanship of the Alaska delegation to the 1980 Republican National Convention. After compiling a strongly pro-Reagan voting record before the 1984 convention, he was named delegation chairman; but he did not hold that title in 1988 or 1992.

Meanwhile, Stevens has continued to cruise to re-election. In 1984, John E. Havelock, a lawyer who had served as the state's attorney general in the early 1970s, tried to convince voters that the incumbent was more interested in pursuing his own Senate ambitions than in Alaskan affairs. But Stevens paid his challenger little heed. Armed with a massive campaign treasury, he spent much of the time stumping for other GOP senators in pursuit of his party's Senate leader post. He crushed Havelock with 71 percent of the vote.

Stevens' electoral strength daunted prominent Democrats, who took a pass on the 1990 Senate campaign. But the fact that he was practically unchallenged did not stop the minority of Alaskans who had a gripe with Stevens from voting for his obscure challengers. In the primary, Robert M. Bird, a teacher and anti-abortion activist, took 30 percent of the Republican vote against Stevens.

And in the general election, Stevens' 66 percent share of the vote was actually smaller than it had been in 1984. This was notable mainly because his Democratic opponent was Democrat Michael Beasley, a political gadfly who had run in Democratic statewide primaries without ever receiving more than 4 percent of the vote. But in 1990, he filed and won almost by default: His only primary opponent was an advocate of Alaskan secession from the United States.

Committees

Rules & Administration (Ranking)

Joint Printing (Ranking)

Appropriations (2nd of 13 Republicans)
Defense (ranking); Commerce, Justice, State & Judiciary; Interior; Labor, Health & Human Services & Education; Military Construction

Commerce, Science & Transportation (4th of 9 Republicans)
National Ocean Policy Study (ranking); Aviation; Communications; Merchant Marine

Governmental Affairs (2nd of 5 Republicans)
Federal Services, Post Office & Civil Service (ranking); General Services, Federalism & the District of Columbia; Oversight of Government Management; Permanent Subcommittee on Investigations

Select Ethics (2nd of 3 Republicans)

Select Intelligence (6th of 8 Republicans)

Joint Library

Joint Organization of Congress

Elections

1990 General		
Ted Stevens (R)	125,806	(66%)
Michael Beasley (D)	61,152	(32%)
1990 Primary †		
Ted Stevens (R)	81,968	(59%)
Robert M. Bird (R)	34,824	(25%)
Michael Beasley (D)	12,371	(9%)
Tom Taggart (D)	9,329	(7%)

† In Alaska's "jungle primary," candidates of all parties are listed on one ballot.

Previous Winning Percentages: **1984** (71%) **1978** (76%) **1972** (77%) **1970 *** (60%)

** Special election. Stevens was appointed in 1968 to fill the vacancy caused by the death of Sen. E.L. Bartlett. The 1970 election was to fill the remainder of Bartlett's term.*

Campaign Finance

	Receipts	Receipts from PACs	Expend-itures
1990			
Stevens (R)	$1,380,780	$751,450 (54%)	$1,273,954
Beasley (D)	$1,000	0	$445

Key Votes

1993	
Require unpaid family and medical leave	Y
Approve national "motor voter" registration bill	N
Approve budget increasing taxes and reducing deficit	N
Support president's right to lift military gay ban	N
1992	
Approve school-choice pilot program	Y
Allow shifting funds from defense to domestic programs	N
Oppose deeper cuts in spending for SDI	Y
1991	
Approve waiting period for handgun purchases	N
Raise senators' pay and ban honoraria	Y
Authorize use of force in Persian Gulf	Y
Confirm Clarence Thomas to Supreme Court	Y

Voting Studies

	Presidential Support		Party Unity		Conservative Coalition	
Year	**S**	**O**	**S**	**O**	**S**	**O**
1992	78	20	80	18	84	11
1991	83	14	78	20	85	10
1990	72	23	66	31	84	5
1989	87	13	73	27	87	13
1988	67	30	71	27	78	19
1987	65	26	64	27	81	19
1986	83	11	83 †	15 †	88	9
1985	75	16	71	21	90	3
1984	84	12	85	8	94	4
1983	92	5	80	17	77	16
1982	74	18	85	8	90	4
1981	76	14	81	10	79	13

† Not eligible for all recorded votes.

Interest Group Ratings

Year	ADA	AFL-CIO	CCUS	ACU
1992	20	33	80	74
1991	10	42	60	76
1990	33	67	64	65
1989	20	40	75	64
1988	25	36	69	64
1987	25	60	67	65
1986	15	33	74	71
1985	10	25	78	64
1984	20	22	76	67
1983	15	13	74	44
1982	15	35	76	50
1981	15	17	100	53

Frank H. Murkowski (R)

Of Fairbanks — Elected 1980; 3rd Term

Born: March 28, 1933, Seattle, Wash.
Education: U. of Santa Clara, 1951-53; Seattle U., B.A. 1955.
Military Service: Coast Guard, 1955-56.
Occupation: Banker.
Family: Wife, Nancy Gore; six children.
Religion: Roman Catholic.
Political Career: Alaska commissioner of economic development, 1966-70; GOP nominee for U.S. House, 1970.
Capitol Office: 706 Hart Bldg. 20510; 224-6665.

In Washington: As he begins his third term in the Senate, Murkowski sees himself as an Alaskan version of Horatius at the bridge, ever striving to hold off the federal government, environmentalists, South Korean fishermen and anyone else who would like to tell the state how to run its business.

Murkowski has occasionally surfaced to participate in foreign policy debates, and he takes an interest in energy and veterans' affairs.

He also has shown some signs of wanting to broaden his role within the Senate: In November 1992 he ran for the post of Senate Republican Conference secretary and finished third in the three-way race with five votes. It was his first try for leadership since he unsuccessfully challenged incumbent Sen. John H. Chafee of Rhode Island for the largely honorary chair of the GOP Conference four years earlier.

But Murkowski is unlikely to take such setbacks too seriously. A generally amiable creature of the Senate's middle rank, he devotes himself primarily to Alaskan issues. He is a dogged advocate of tapping the state's vast oil and timber reserves, and he has teamed up with Senate colleague Ted Stevens and Rep. Don Young in seeking to open up the coastal plain of Alaska's Arctic National Wildlife Refuge (ANWR) to oil exploration.

Early on in the preparation of the major energy bill passed in the 102nd Congress, it appeared that the Alaskan delegation might get its wish on ANWR. Senate Energy Committee Chairman J. Bennett Johnston of Louisiana included allowances for drilling the ANWR in the first version of the bill. That version passed the committee with Republican support, which angered Democrats who opposed the drilling provision — out of environmental concerns — and who had not been consulted.

After 44 senators joined to block floor consideration of the bill, Johnston went back to the drawing board and came up with a proposal that did not have an ANWR provision. It was this later version that ultimately passed the Senate and was enacted into law in 1992.

"Politics have overtaken policy," Murkowski said in protest of the provision's removal.

This was not the first time Alaskans have been frustrated on this issue. They experienced a setback after the 1989 *Exxon Valdez* oil spill in Prince William Sound, but they gained new momentum after 1990 passage of a comprehensive oil-spill bill and renewed concern about crude oil supplies caused by the Persian Gulf War.

Murkowski also has economic interests in his state in mind when he opposes efforts to increase royalty fees to be paid by mining operations on public lands. As ranking Republican on the Public Lands subcommittee, he argues that higher fees on gross profits would not raise additional revenues because they would kill the mining industry.

In May 1993, a bill favored by Murkowski and the mining industry passed the Energy Committee with a 2 percent net royalty. Advocates of higher fees expect to do better with lawmakers on the House side, so the issue will almost certainly return when the Senate and House take the bill to conference.

Murkowski has been known to rage against what he calls the "radical preservation ethic" of environmentalists who, he says, seek to treat Alaska as a national park for the enjoyment of the 49 other states. During a 1991 speech at a conference of the Wilderness Society, Murkowski argued that less than 1 percent of ANWR would be affected if restrictions were lifted. Quipped one environmental advocate: "OK, I'll take 1 percent of the Mona Lisa — the smile. Some places need to be preserved." When the audience laughed and applauded, Murkowski walked out in protest.

But he managed to catch environmentalists off guard in the 101st Congress when he attached a rider to a defense authorization bill that requires the president to list high-potential oil fields if imports hit 50 percent of U.S. oil use. By joint resolution, Congress could then permit the president to proceed with drilling without regard to endangered species or wilderness laws.

In 1992, Murkowski supported a Bush administration proposal that would have exempted Alaska from the general rule that developers restore or create new wetlands to compensate for those they destroy. Alaska sought exemption, arguing that less than 1 percent of its wetlands had been filled in. Murkowski said it was a "common sense solution that is vital for property owners."

In 1990, Murkowski and Stevens were forced to accept a compromise in their effort to prevent the end of an arrangement that guaranteed a steady supply of cheap timber from the 16.7 million-acre Tongass National Forest for mills in southeastern Alaska. Both senators seemed more relieved than angered when the 19-year battle was finally over, resulting in protection of more than 1 million acres.

"While this legislation errs too far on the side of preservation . . . we have received assurances that it should bring some finality to the Tongass issue," Murkowski said.

His interest in foreign policy thrust him into the spotlight in 1990 because of a meeting he and four Senate colleagues had with Saddam Hussein less than four months before Iraq invaded Kuwait. The group sought to end Iraq's isolation, and some came away impressed with Saddam. During a May 1990 floor debate on a measure to impose sanctions against Iraq, Murkowski urged colleagues to give Saddam time to respond to diplomatic overtures and participate in a Middle East peace settlement.

Murkowski's main leadership role thus far in the Senate has been on the Veterans' Affairs Committee, where he served as chairman while still in his first term and where he has served as ranking Republican since 1987. He has used this post in a way that might surprise politicians in the Lower 48: He continually blocks construction of a VA hospital.

This is quintessential Alaskan politics, a decision dictated by the state's sprawling size and sparse population. If there were a VA hospital in the state, veterans would have to go there. They prefer to visit their local doctor and bill the government the way they do now.

Murkowski was active in establishing the Department of Veterans Affairs. He initially opposed, but ultimately supported, compensation for Vietnam War veterans exposed to the chemical defoliant Agent Orange.

Expanding Alaskan trade with the Far East is perhaps his chief pursuit as ranking member on the Foreign Relations Subcommittee on East Asian and Pacific Affairs, a panel he once chaired. He regularly leads trade delegations to Pacific Rim countries, encouraging them to buy more Alaskan coal, timber and other products.

In the 102nd Congress, he sponsored legislation calling for the lifting of the trade embargo against Vietnam, a change in policy long sought by the oil industry. The proposal passed the Foreign Relations Committee but was modified on the floor at the suggestion of Arizona Sen. John McCain, a former POW. The Senate ultimately passed a resolution urging the United States to move toward normalization but linking the pace of such moves to Vietnam's cooperation in resolving MIA cases and ending the war in Cambodia.

In 1990, he sought to address growing concerns about foreign investment in the U.S. by removing a ban on the sharing of ownership data between the Bureau of Economic Analysis and the Census Bureau.

Another barrier to Murkowski's efforts comes from this side of the Pacific: the ban on export of Alaskan crude oil. Murkowski has pushed hard for years to end that export prohibition, but with very limited success, in part because U.S. maritime interests worry that the oil would be transported in foreign ships.

At Home: Murkowski has never given Alaskans much reason to love or hate him. But his attention to home-state concerns has helped dissuade big-name Democrats who might otherwise have taken him on. The net result has been a remarkably consistent share of the vote for candidate Murkowski: 54 percent in both 1980 and 1986 and 53 percent in 1992.

Murkowski's latest re-election was a testament to modern campaigning and incumbency. Expecting a tough race, Murkowski raised and spent nearly twice what his Democratic opponent did. His challenger, former state commerce commissioner Tony Smith, all but disappeared beneath the weight of Murkowski's advertising.

Even before Smith emerged from the nasty Democratic primary, Murkowski had been targeting him in his ads. Virtually ignoring his own primary opponent, Murkowski ran ads that talked about Smith's various claims and showed a farmer pushing a wheelbarrow of manure to characterize Smith's proposals.

The Democrats had been at a loss for an opponent to Murkowski in 1986, finally settling on a political unknown, Glenn Olds, president of Alaska Pacific University.

Olds sought to overcome his political anonymity by arguing that Murkowski had done little to stem the then-precipitous slide of Alaska's energy-based economy. But if voters were angry over the oil price slump, most did not vent their frustrations on Murkowski. The incumbent, aided by his connections to the local banking industry, amassed a substantial treasury, touted his efforts to remove a ban on exports of North Slope oil — and stayed 10 percentage points ahead of Olds.

Except for four years in state government and one failed campaign for the House, Murkowski had spent his entire adult life in banking before he announced for the Senate in June 1980.

His status as a relative newcomer to politics hardly seemed an advantage against Democrat Clark S. Gruening, a popular two-term state legislator and grandson of the legendary Ernest Gruening, a former Alaska senator and governor. But Democratic disunity and the Reagan tide enabled Murkowski to win with unexpected ease.

To win the Democratic nomination, Gruening had to get past two-term incumbent Sen. Mike Gravel. It was a matter of revenge for Gruening; Gravel had ousted Gruening's grandfather from the Senate 12 years before.

In the general election, Murkowski kept attention focused on Gruening's record in the Legislature. Accusing him of being too liberal for the state's electorate, Murkowski claimed the Democrat had supported the legalization of marijuana. He also tied Gruening to the environmentalist Sierra Club, anathema to pro-development Alaskans.

A Seattle native who moved to Alaska while in high school, Murkowski got his first taste of elective politics in 1970. That year he defeated a member of the John Birch Society in a Republican primary for Alaska's at-large House seat. He lost the general election to Democratic state Sen. Nick Begich, but the experience whetted his appetite. After nine years as a bank president in Fairbanks, he announced for the Senate.

Committees

Veterans' Affairs (Ranking)

Energy & Natural Resources (4th of 9 Republicans)
Public Lands, National Parks & Forests (ranking); Mineral Resources Development & Production; Renewable Energy

Foreign Relations (5th of 8 Republicans)
East Asian & Pacific Affairs (ranking); International Economic Policy, Trade, Oceans & Environment; Terrorism, Narcotics & International Operations

Indian Affairs (2nd of 8 Republicans)

Elections

1992 General		
Frank H. Murkowski (R)	127,163	(53%)
Tony Smith (D)	92,065	(38%)
Mary E. Jordan (GREEN)	20,019	(8%)
1992 Primary		
Frank H. Murkowski (R)	37,486	(81%)
Jed Whittaker (R)	9,065	(19%)

Previous Winning Percentages: 1986 (54%) **1980** (54%)

Campaign Finance

	Receipts	Receipts from PACs		Expend-itures
1992				
Murkowski (R)	$1,657,932	$680,013	(41%)	$1,663,865
Smith (D)	$913,975	$246,996	(27%)	$910,138

Key Votes

1993	
Require unpaid family and medical leave	Y
Approve national "motor voter" registration bill	N
Approve budget increasing taxes and reducing deficit	N
Support president's right to lift military gay ban	N
1992	
Approve school-choice pilot program	Y
Allow shifting funds from defense to domestic programs	N
Oppose deeper cuts in spending for SDI	Y
1991	
Approve waiting period for handgun purchases	N
Raise senators' pay and ban honoraria	Y
Authorize use of force in Persian Gulf	Y
Confirm Clarence Thomas to Supreme Court	Y

Voting Studies

	Presidential Support		Party Unity		Conservative Coalition	
Year	**S**	**O**	**S**	**O**	**S**	**O**
1992	72	27	82	11	82	13
1991	89	11	88	10	90	10
1990	75	22	85	14	92	0
1989	85	10	87	11	92	3
1988	65	18	81	7	89	3
1987	62	35	76	15	84	6
1986	80	17	81	15	88	5
1985	82	11	78	14	90	2
1984	84	12	90	5	94	2
1983	69	14	73	8	80	0
1982	79	11	91	5	89	1
1981	82	11	83	11	85	9

Interest Group Ratings

Year	ADA	AFL-CIO	CCUS	ACU
1992	25	30	100	70
1991	5	42	60	86
1990	11	44	83	76
1989	5	10	75	81
1988	15	23	85	79
1987	5	40	80	76
1986	20	36	65	78
1985	0	26	84	82
1984	10	18	88	86
1983	0	6	75	72
1982	10	24	70	63
1981	15	24	93	79

AL Don Young (R)

Of Fort Yukon — Elected 1973; 10th Full Term

Born: June 9, 1933, Meridian, Calif.

Education: Yuba Junior College, A.A. 1952; California State U., Chico, B.A. 1958.

Military Service: Army, 1955-57.

Occupation: Elementary school teacher; riverboat captain.

Family: Wife, Lula Fredson; two children.

Religion: Episcopalian.

Political Career: Fort Yukon City Council, 1960-64; mayor of Fort Yukon, 1964-68; Alaska House, 1967-71; Alaska Senate, 1971-73; GOP nominee for U.S. House, 1972.

Capitol Office: 2331 Rayburn Bldg. 20515; 225-5765.

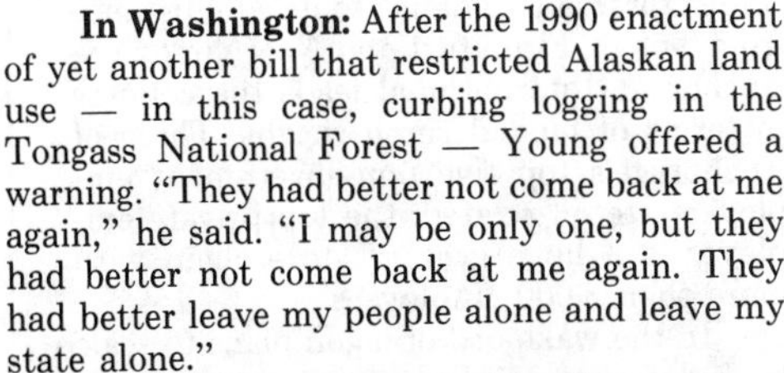

In Washington: After the 1990 enactment of yet another bill that restricted Alaskan land use — in this case, curbing logging in the Tongass National Forest — Young offered a warning. "They had better not come back at me again," he said. "I may be only one, but they had better not come back at me again. They had better leave my people alone and leave my state alone."

A former riverboat captain, Young is an individualist who regularly demands — often in angry outbursts — that Washington stay out of his state's way. But throughout his House career, Young's colleagues have done anything but respect his wishes for his gargantuan district, the state of Alaska.

Since he came to the House in 1973 as an advocate of the trans-Alaska oil pipeline, Young has fought many a losing battle against "outsiders" from the Lower 48 who want to preserve much of Alaska's unspoiled wilds from the miners, loggers, drillers and developers whose interests Young tenaciously promotes.

But he never loses his sense of outrage. At one subcommittee hearing in the 100th Congress, Young so berated New York Democratic Rep. Robert J. Mrazek, sponsor of the bill to protect the Tongass, that acting Chairman Sam Gejdenson of Connecticut recessed the panel and took Young aside to cool off. Later, on the House floor, Young erupted at Mrazek again, threatening political retribution while stabbing the air with his ever-present Buck knife.

Young has held the ranking GOP spot on the Natural Resources Committee (formerly the Interior Committee) since 1985, positioning himself well to resist environmentalist legislation. Under former Chairman Morris K. Udall of Arizona, he often operated as a broker who represented the interests of panel Republicans, who are mostly partisan, pro-development Westerners like him.

But things have changed. The committee has not only a new name but also a new chairman, California Democrat George Miller. A colleague describes Young's political relationship with Miller as "just this side of violence." (Personally, they claim to get along fine.)

If it were not for his wish to parry environmentalist Miller, Young might be tempted to move over to the ranking GOP spot on the Merchant Marine and Fisheries Committee, which also has jurisdiction over issues of interest to Alaskans. Merchant Marine's chairman, Massachusetts Democrat Gerry E. Studds, while no closer ideologically to Young than Miller is, is nonetheless one of Young's closest friends on Capitol Hill.

The friction between Young and Miller calls to mind that between the Education and Labor Committee's chairman, Democrat William D. Ford of Michigan, and its most vocal Republican member, Texan Dick Armey. But while Armey has said he remains on Education and Labor just to annoy Ford, Young is deadly serious about the issues before Natural Resources. He simply does not trust Miller enough to leave the committee in his hands.

Young is aggressively partisan, even though he is a product of Alaska's free-for-all, weak-party politics. As a member of the panel that makes House Republicans' committee assignments, Young has been known to grill applicants on party loyalty before supporting them for a Natural Resources seat. His bluster is often tactical, used to intimidate foes, but Young's combativeness can complicate his dealings with fellow members, especially the Democratic majority on Natural Resources.

Young may never stop seething about passage of a 1980 Alaska lands bill that reserved large portions of the state as federal wilderness. In his three-year fight against that bill, Young whittled down its wilderness acreage considerably and won provisions for development.

But when the bill was passed in the House

Alaska

At large

The March 1989 crash of the *Exxon Valdez* supertanker was a trauma for all of Alaska. The spilling of 10 million gallons of Alaskan crude into the waters of the Prince William Sound focused attention on the environmental risks of oil development. Oil revenues have done a lot for Alaska, but after the spill, more residents wondered what oil might do *to* the state.

The pro-oil majority that controlled the state Legislature during the 1980s — associated with the GOP majority — saw its influence threatened; within months of the wreck, the Legislature passed a spate of environmental protection measures.

And in Congress, environmental activists used publicity about the spill to dampen interest in what was already a controversial Alaskan oil exploration proposal: to allow drilling for oil on the coastal plain of the Arctic National Wildlife Refuge (ANWR), on Alaska's North Slope. When the 102nd Congress passed an energy policy bill, it declined to allow drilling in ANWR. The Clinton administration opposes drilling in ANWR.

But in Alaska, as time has passed since the *Valdez* spill, attention has come to focus more and more on this reality: The state is heavily dependent on the oil industry to provide jobs, and 85 percent of state revenues come from the industry. Due to declining production at Alaska's main oil fields at Prudhoe Bay, there are concerns that unless new sources are tapped, a budget crisis looms.

Pro-development forces enjoyed a resurgence in 1992 state legislative elections. And the potential for state revenue shortfalls and other economic trouble is rekindling the resentment many Alaskans harbor toward the federal government — which controls about 60 percent of the state's land — and toward "outsiders" who seek to restrain development.

From this longstanding sentiment springs the state's maverick political tradition, characterized by iconoclasm with a decidedly conservative bent. In 1992, independent presidential candidate Ross Perot won 29 percent of the vote in Alaska, his second-best showing among the states and almost enough to pull him into second place ahead of Bill Clinton, who got 31 percent. The current governor, Walter J. Hickel, belongs to the Alaskan Independence Party, a group that advocates secession from the United States, though Hickel does not.

George Bush, who took 60 percent of Alaska's presidential vote in 1988, dropped 20 points in 1992, but still carried the state; Alaska has voted Democratic for president only once since statehood, in 1964. Since 1981, the GOP has held all three of the state's seats in Congress.

The nation's largest state in land area, Alaska ranks 49th in population, with just over 550,000 residents. Despite Alaska's permafrost reputation, residents enjoy the state's breathtaking natural beauty and warm summers. Still, it takes a hardy type to live this far north in the winter.

The state's population nexus is Anchorage, with slightly more than 226,000 residents. Its international airport is a key trade crossroads. Thanks to its equidistance from Tokyo, Frankfurt and New York City, Anchorage International leads the country in terms of landed cargo weight. Three of Anchorage's top five non-government employers are oil-related; the top private employer is a huge grocery store chain with more than 3,000 employees.

In the wake of Pentagon plans to scale back defense spending, Anchorage is bracing for cuts. But neither Elmendorf Air Force Base nor the Army's Fort Richardson appeared on the 1993 base-closure list.

With revenues from the oil industry uncertain, efforts have intensified to diversify the economy. A promising alternative is tourism, which recently has been growing rapidly.

Fishing is already big business. Alaska fishing accounted for more than 50 percent of U.S. production in 1990 and employs about a quarter of the state's workforce. Bristol Bay, off the southwest coast, is the world's largest producer of red salmon.

About 350 miles north of Anchorage is Fairbanks (population 31,000), the traditional trading center for the villages of inland Alaska. The city grew as the supply center for the Alaska oil pipeline (which runs north from here to Prudhoe Bay).

Southeast Alaska is separated from the rest of the state by the St. Elias Mountains and the Gulf of Alaska. Juneau, the state capital, is inaccessible by land.

Alaska's vast "bush" region is dotted with mostly tiny towns. Native Indians and Eskimos predominate in remote Alaska.

1990 Population: 550,043. White 415,492 (76%), Black 22,451 (4%), Other 112,100 (20%). Hispanic origin 17,803 (3%). 18 and over 377,699 (69%), 62 and over 29,577 (5%). Median age: 29.

in 1979, he complained, "People can sit on this floor and say it is all right to take what is already the people's of Alaska. That is immoral. . . . None of you has to go home to unemployment created by national legislation." Then he broke down in tears.

The latest Alaska battle has been fought over whether to open the Arctic National Wildlife Refuge (ANWR) to oil and gas drilling along its coastal plain. Opponents contend that would threaten caribou, musk oxen, snow geese and polar bears. They were able to prevent bills from reaching the floor in either chamber during the 100th Congress. Young's bill was blocked in Interior by Udall, who countered with legislation to make the entire refuge a permanent wilderness. Young had somewhat better luck in the Merchant Marine Committee, where members are sympathetic to the shippers that would transport any new oil from ANWR.

But all efforts to pass an ANWR bill were suspended in the 101st Congress in response to public furor over the disastrous oil spill of the tanker *Exxon Valdez* off Alaska in early 1989.

The Persian Gulf War provoked a new spate of interest in domestic oil production. President Bush in 1991 made the opening of ANWR a centerpiece of his proposed energy strategy, and Senate Energy Committee Chairman J. Bennett Johnston of Louisiana included such a provision in his comprehensive energy bill. But the drilling proposal enraged environmentalists, whose allies in the Senate blocked the bill over the issue. By 1992, when the energy measure was revived, the ANWR provisions were gone.

In the 101st Congress, Young took a satirical approach to highlight what he perceives as liberals' interference in Western land matters. Young was peeved when then-Rep. Jim Jontz, D-Ind., introduced legislation to curb logging in ancient Northwestern forests, which are the habitat of the threatened northern spotted owl. So Young introduced a bill to establish a 1.3 million-acre national forest in northwestern Indiana, which is Jontz's habitat.

Among Young's bill's "findings" was that "the establishment of a national forest in northwestern Indiana would improve the environment and provide for weekend recreational opportunities for residents of Chicago and Indianapolis."

"Don's a funny guy," Jontz said. Young introduced the bill again in the 102nd Congress.

On Merchant Marine, Young has cooperated with Studds to protect fishermen's interests and the Coast Guard's budget. He worked with Studds on a bill in the 101st Congress increasing oil spillers' federal liability limits.

Young, who claims to be the only trapper in Congress, has fought off repeated attempts to impose a ban on steel-jaw leghold traps, a move sought by animal rights groups. Once, while testifying before Merchant Marine, he made his point by leaving his hand in a trap until his fingers turned blue.

On broader issues, Young fits the conservative label he claims. But like Ted Stevens, Alaska's senior Republican senator, he knows how to leaven his voting record with support for the construction unions and other labor interests important in state affairs.

At Home: Whatever the national issues at stake, each of Young's House campaigns turns into a debate over his personality. The contests seem to turn on whether Alaskans accept Young's portrayal of himself as a rough-hewn defender of home-state interests or see him as an obnoxious obstructionist who does more harm than good to Alaska.

Young thought he provided a definitive answer in 1988, when he defeated a highly touted Democratic challenger, former state prosecutor Peter Gruenstein, with 62 percent of the vote.

But after unimpressive wins in 1990 and 1992, Young's electoral strength remains shaky.

In 1990, Young barely held off college president and former Valdez Mayor John E. Devens with 52 percent. Two years later, Devens returned for a rematch, better-financed and better-known. He held Young below the 50 percent mark in a four-candidate field but could not oust the cantankerous Republican.

A co-founder of Prince William Sound Community College, Devens made his name during the *Exxon Valdez* disaster in 1989. As Valdez mayor, Devens coordinated the city's response to the oil spill, appeared on national news shows and testified before congressional committees. He also set the stage for his first House campaign, faulting Young for not quickly returning home to oversee the cleanup.

Throughout the 1990 race, Devens struggled to raise money to campaign in the enormous state. He saved his sparse dollars for a late TV ad blitz; in one spot, he appeared with mariners to underline his endorsement from the United Fishermen of Alaska, the state's largest commercial fishing organization. Devens' closing rush narrowed the gap, but Young prevailed.

Saddled with 57 overdrafts at the House bank, Young seemed even more vulnerable in 1992. His low tally in a new closed GOP primary — drawing fewer votes than the top two Democrats — fueled speculation he would not survive.

But late in the fall, Young was praised at home for putting business interests ahead of "liberal East Coast" environmentalists, as one editorial put it. He also picked up the endorsement of his primary opponent, a female state senator who supported abortion rights.

Perhaps most significant, Young conceded in advertising that voters found him "abrasive" and "arrogant." He apologized but promised to continue fighting for Alaskan interests.

Democrats may need a better-known challenger or a more potent issue than Young's personality to knock him out of office.

Born in California, Young moved to Alaska to teach, then became a licensed riverboat captain and a member of the Dog Mushers Association.

Young has lost only one election in his political career: his first, in 1972. His opponent, freshman Democratic Rep. Nick Begich, disappeared without a trace along with House Majority Leader Hale Boggs during an October airplane flight from Anchorage to Juneau. However, the missing Begich was re-elected over Young by almost 12,000 votes.

With his strong base in the Alaska "bush," Young rebounded quickly from his 1972 setback. He had hardly ended campaigning when Begich's seat was declared vacant in December. In the 1973 special election, Young edged out Emil Notti, the former state Democratic chairman. In 1974, Young weathered a vigorous challenge from state Sen. William L. Hensley. He won by comfortable margins in the next several elections.

Young then faced Pegge Begich, a former Democratic national committeewoman for Alaska and Nick Begich's widow. Begich criticized Young's attendance record, but Young brushed off the attacks, winning with 55 percent in 1984 and 57 percent in 1986.

In 1988, Gruenstein entered the House race with the positive publicity from prosecuting several well-publicized murder cases.

But Young took the luster off that reputation by suggesting that the Democrat might have received "laundered money" from environmental groups. Trumpeting his tireless work on crusades such as opening ANWR, Young even outpaced George Bush's strong Alaska performance that year. Sued by Gruenstein for slander following the election, Young was ordered in October 1990 to stand trial. (In January 1991, the two settled out of court.)

Committees

Natural Resources (Ranking)
Native American Affairs

Merchant Marine & Fisheries (2nd of 18 Republicans)
Fisheries Management (ranking); Environment & Natural Resources

Post Office & Civil Service (3rd of 9 Republicans)
Postal Operations & Services (ranking); Compensation & Employee Benefits

Elections

1992 General		
Don Young (R)	111,849	(47%)
John S. Devens (D)	102,378	(43%)
Michael A. States (AKI)	15,049	(6%)
Mike Milligan (GREEN)	9,529	(4%)
1992 Primary		
Don Young (R)	24,869	(53%)
Virginia Collins (R)	19,774	(42%)
William L. Holton (R)	1,671	(4%)
Larry A. Seip (R)	630	(1%)
1990 General		
Don Young (R)	99,003	(52%)
John E. Devens (D)	91,677	(48%)

Previous Winning Percentages: **1988** (62%) **1986** (57%) **1984** (55%) **1982** (71%) **1980** (74%) **1978** (55%) **1976** (71%) **1974** (54%) **1973 *** (51%)

* *Special election.*

District Vote for President

	1992	
D	78,294	(31%)
R	102,000	(40%)
I	73,481	(29%)

Campaign Finance

	Receipts	Receipts from PACs		Expend-itures
1992				
Young (R)	$867,848	$377,335	(43%)	$873,486
Devens (D)	$468,027	$98,851	(21%)	$469,738
States (AKI)	$6,920	0		$6,835
1990				
Young (R)	$560,908	$277,725	(50%)	$564,759
Devens (D)	$168,038	$13,150	(8%)	$164,732

Key Votes

1993	
Require parental notification of minors' abortions	Y
Require unpaid family and medical leave	Y
Approve national "motor voter" registration bill	N
Approve budget increasing taxes and reducing deficit	N
Approve economic stimulus plan	N
1992	
Approve balanced-budget constitutional amendment	Y
Close down space station program	N
Approve U.S. aid for former Soviet Union	Y
Allow shifting funds from defense to domestic programs	N
1991	
Extend unemployment benefits using deficit financing	Y
Approve waiting period for handgun purchases	N
Authorize use of force in Persian Gulf	Y

Voting Studies

	Presidential Support		Party Unity		Conservative Coalition	
Year	**S**	**O**	**S**	**O**	**S**	**O**
1992	75	22	73	19	85	10
1991	66	26	66	24	86	11
1990	56	38	60	25	78	15
1989	70	27	71	21	78	17
1988	49	42	64	29	71	16
1987	52	37	58	30	81	16
1986	61	33	63	31	90	4
1985	51	46	62	32	82	18
1984	55	43	60	39	88	10
1983	52	34	57	21	78	7
1982	45	26	50	25	66	15
1981	67	17	61	14	89	1

Interest Group Ratings

Year	ADA	AFL-CIO	CCUS	ACU
1992	25	67	88	84
1991	10	55	67	67
1990	33	33	64	67
1989	15	50	60	77
1988	30	64	69	63
1987	16	50	57	63
1986	20	62	56	65
1985	30	53	45	62
1984	25	50	69	57
1983	20	50	56	52
1982	10	25	57	73
1981	10	36	88	92

Arizona

STATE DATA

Governor:
Fife Symington (R)
First elected: 1991
Length of term: 4 years
Term expires: 1/95
Salary: $75,000
Term limit: 2 terms
Phone: (602) 542-4331
Born: Aug. 12, 1945; New York, N.Y.
Education: Harvard U., B.A. 1968
Military Service: Air Force, 1968-71
Occupation: Real estate developer
Family: Wife, Ann Pritzlaff; five children
Religion: Episcopalian
Political Career: No previous office

No lieutenant governor

State election official: (602) 542-8683
Democratic headquarters: (602) 257-9136
Republican headquarters: (602) 957-7770

REDISTRICTING

Arizona gained one House seat in reapportionment, increasing from five districts to six. Map issued by federal court May 6, 1992.

STATE LEGISLATURE

Legislature. Meets January to April, with a limit of 107 calendar days.

Senate: 30 members, 2-year terms
1992 breakdown: 18R, 12D; 21 men, 9 women; 25 whites, 1 black, 3 Hispanics, 1 other
Salary: $15,000
Phone: (602) 542-3559

House of Representatives: 60 members, 2-year terms
1992 breakdown: 35R, 25D; 37 men, 23 women; 52 whites, 2 blacks, 5 Hispanics, 1 other
Salary: $15,000
Phone: (602) 542-4221

URBAN STATISTICS

City	Pop.
Phoenix Mayor Paul Johnson, D	983,403
Tucson Mayor George Miller, D	405,390
Mesa Mayor Willie Wong, N-P	288,091
Glendale Mayor Elaine Scruggs, N-P	148,134
Tempe Mayor Harry E. Mitchell, D	141,865

U.S. CONGRESS

Senate: 1 D, 1 R
House: 3 D, 3 R

TERM LIMITS

For Congress: Yes
  Senate: 2 terms
  House: 3 terms
For state offices: Yes
  Senate: 4 consecutive terms
  House: 4 consecutive terms

ELECTIONS

1992 Presidential Vote

Bill Clinton	36.5%
George Bush	38.5%
Ross Perot	23.8%

1988 Presidential Vote

George Bush	60%
Michael S. Dukakis	39%

1984 Presidential Vote

Ronald Reagan	66%
Walter F. Mondale	33%

POPULATION

1990 population		3,665,228
1980 population		2,718,215
Percent change		+35%
Rank among states:		24
White		81%
Black		3%
Hispanic		19%
Asian or Pacific islander		2%
Urban		88%
Rural		12%
Born in state		34%
Foreign-born		8%
Under age 18	981,119	27%
Ages 18-64	2,205,335	60%
65 and older	478,774	13%
Median age		32.2

MISCELLANEOUS

Capital: Phoenix
Number of counties: 15
Per capita income: $16,401 (1991)
  Rank among states: 35
Total area: 114,000 sq. miles
  Rank among states: 6

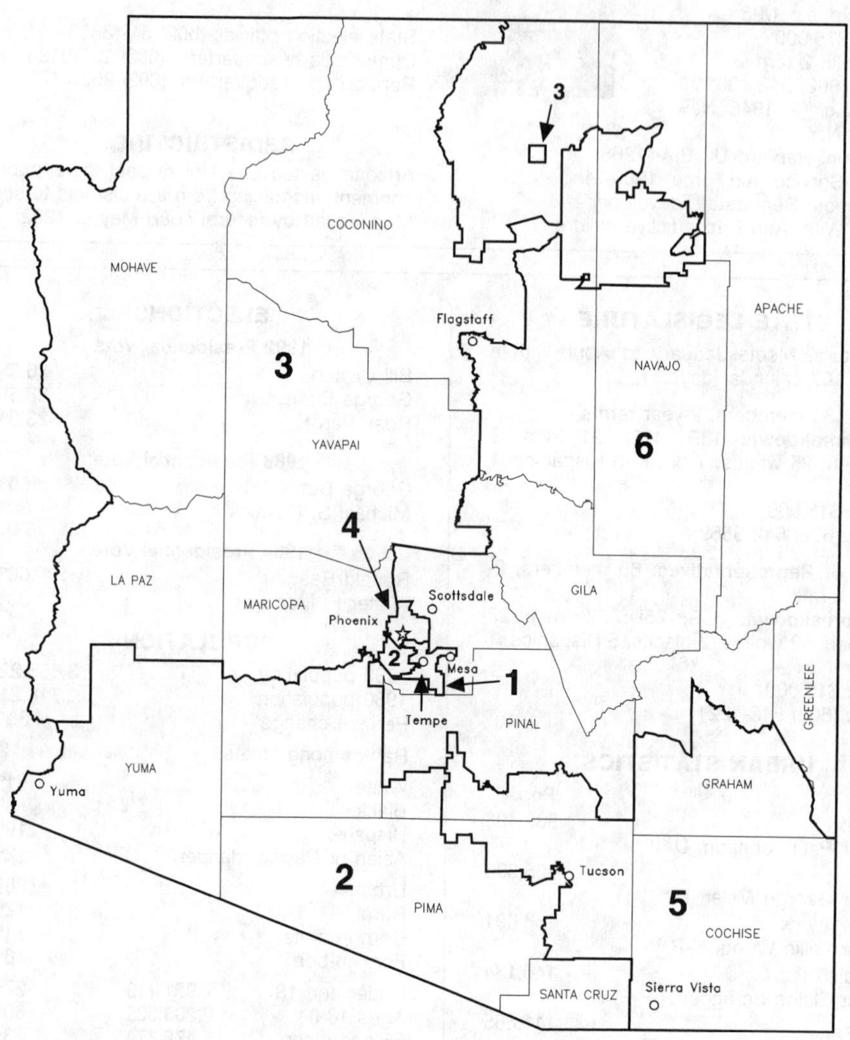
3
COCONINO
MOHAVE
APACHE
Flagstaff
NAVAJO
3
YAVAPAI
6
4
LA PAZ
GILA
Scottsdale
MARICOPA
Phoenix
2
Mesa
1
Tempe
PINAL
GREENLEE
YUMA
Yuma
GRAHAM
Tucson
2
PIMA
5
COCHISE
SANTA CRUZ
Sierra Vista

Dennis DeConcini (D)

Of Tucson — Elected 1976; 3rd Term

Born: May 8, 1937, Tucson, Ariz.
Education: U. of Arizona, B.A. 1959, LL.B. 1963.
Military Service: Army, 1959-60; Army Reserve, 1960-67.
Occupation: Lawyer.
Family: Separated; three children.
Religion: Roman Catholic.
Political Career: Pima County attorney, 1973-77.
Capitol Office: 328 Hart Bldg. 20510; 224-4521.

In Washington: DeConcini tried to dismiss questions about his ethics by describing his role in the Keating Five affair as constituent services. But that incident, and other elements of his record, make DeConcini one of the senators whose 1994 re-election campaign will be most closely watched.

The Keating scandal brought DeConcini an Ethics Committee rebuke, and it is the cloud that hangs most heavily over the moderate Arizona Democrat. But there are plenty of other reasons to encourage prospective challengers.

There is DeConcini's mystifying role in the Supreme Court nomination hearings of Clarence Thomas, alternately siding with the nominee and his accuser. There is his mixed record on free trade with Mexico and potential environmental dangers to his own constituents. And while his anti-abortion stance may help attract some crucial GOP votes, it frequently spells trouble in his own party.

But DeConcini won't go quietly and his independent, pro-business, law-and-order image still seems broadly suitable to conservative Arizona.

Of the five senators investigated in the Keating Five case, DeConcini was perhaps the most militant in behalf of savings and loan magnate Charles H. Keating Jr., and the most combative in defending himself.

He brazenly brushed off the ethics rebuke, saying in early 1991: "Aggressiveness has always been my hallmark."

Throughout the 14-month investigation, DeConcini was unapologetic for his efforts to get federal regulators to expedite their investigation of Lincoln Savings, and for his acceptance of $85,000 in campaign contributions raised by Keating.

"There is no improper conduct standard that says you cannot intervene for someone . . . who made a campaign contribution," he said as the 26-day televised hearing opened.

DeConcini took the investigating committee's recommendation that he not be punished as a full exoneration, and he did his utmost to make a virtue of the assertive posture that placed him at the heart of the Keating affair.

DeConcini is nothing if not blunt about his mission as a senator. "It's our job to get things done for our constituents," he said in 1989, defending earmarks in the bill approved by the Appropriations Subcommittee on Treasury, Postal Service and General Government, which he chairs.

When the television cameras turned on Capitol Hill again, several months after the Keating investigation concluded, DeConcini was back in the spotlight as a member of the all-white, all-male panel screening nominee Thomas.

The only Democrat on the Judiciary Committee to initially back Thomas, DeConcini left some observers wondering if he would switch when Professor Anita Hill's allegations of sexual harassment surfaced.

Democrats had reason to be encouraged when DeConcini recounted how his mother had been harassed in the workplace decades earlier.

"When she was 22 years old, she lost her job because she rejected her boss' sexual advances," he said. "Is that something you ever forget when your mother tells you that as a boy?"

But in the end DeConcini found Hill less than credible. "If you're sexually harassed, you ought to get mad about it, and you ought to do something about it.... I mean where is the gumption?" he said.

Instead of backing away from Thomas, he expressed sympathy, observing that they both knew what it was like to suffer under the intense glare of the media spotlight. As Thomas bitterly complained that the hearings had robbed him of his integrity, DeConcini chimed in: "I know exactly how you feel."

DeConcini brings a decidedly pro-business orientation to his Senate work. When House Democrats moved to eliminate the budget for Vice President Dan Quayle's Council on Competitiveness, DeConcini declined a chance to do the same in the Senate.

"If the dispute is how the council operates,

then the solution should be to change the way the executive branch reviews regulations," said DeConcini, whose Treasury-Postal Subcommittee had jurisdiction over the council.

The 103rd Congress marks a new legislative challenge for DeConcini, who moved to the top of the Intelligence panel.

Before ascending to the chair, DeConcini helped spearhead a successful effort to cut national intelligence programs by about 5 percent. With little background in the issues facing the committee, DeConcini said in early 1993 he would wait for President Clinton's spending proposals before making any moves himself.

Early in the 103rd Congress, DeConcini and a handful of other Western lawmakers went up against Clinton — and won — in the debate over grazing fees for ranchers. After initially taking a strong stand on higher fees, Clinton was forced to back off. Although DeConcini touts his deficit-cutting agenda, he says Western ranchers need the federally subsidized grazing lands to survive.

DeConcini came to the Senate after serving as the administrator of the Arizona Drug Control District. Drug trafficking has become a bigger problem for Arizona, he says, because importers of Latin American narcotics have shifted their primary routes from Florida to the West. As vice chairman of the Senate Drug Enforcement Caucus, DeConcini was active in the 1986 movement to pressure foreign governments to curb the drug trade at its source. In the 101st Congress, he helped enact a pay increase for federal law enforcement officials.

In the 102nd, DeConcini and New Mexico Republican Pete V. Domenici, then ranking member on DeConcini's Treasury-Postal Appropriations panel, put $1 billion for drug interdiction in the fiscal 1992 spending bill.

DeConcini seems unbothered by the perception that his votes are often open to negotiation. He is a willing horsetrader and has a talent for negotiating practical solutions.

In one Treasury-Postal conference, DeConcini wasted no time debating the merits of the various issues that separated the House and Senate versions. He simply proposed splitting everything down the middle.

In 1990, after Ohio Sen. Howard M. Metzenbaum dropped his effort to block DeConcini's bill to reform the federal racketeering statute known as RICO, DeConcini gave Metzenbaum the deciding vote on the Judiciary Committee for the Ohioan's vertical price-fixing bill, even as DeConcini said he opposed it.

DeConcini's desire to push RICO reform in the midst of the Keating hearing raised eyebrows since the law was being widely used to bring charges against executives of failed S&Ls.

DeConcini's admirers saw his effort as a positive sign that his aggressive nature was unbent by the scandal. But his motivation was questioned at one 1989 Judiciary Committee meeting at which as much time was spent defending him as debating his bill. "I think everyone has entered this debate with clean hands," said Chairman Joseph R. Biden Jr. of Delaware.

DeConcini's original bill to narrow RICO's reach limited the triple damages allowed under current law, even though the government was seeking them to recoup a share of the S&L funds lost. His bill had supporters from President Bush to several Senate liberals. But the idea of weakening RICO during the S&L crisis made members queasy.

DeConcini's 1989 amendment to block the sale of certain military style assault weapons met a similar fate, but if that effort was also controversial, at least it had a wider audience of enthusiasts.

At the outset, DeConcini was torn between allies in the National Rifle Association, who opposed any restriction on weapons sales, and allies in law enforcement, who backed a far-reaching ban offered by Metzenbaum. DeConcini tried to split the difference with an amendment banning the sale of nine assault weapons, half as many as the Metzenbaum bill. But he wound up infuriating the NRA, which launched a brief recall drive against him.

With a gun-control advocate in the White House and new concern arising from the Branch Davidian cult deaths in Waco, Texas, in April 1993, DeConcini was more optimistic about winning a ban in the 103rd Congress. "The new political climate has changed substantially," he said as he reintroduced his bill.

On some social issues, such as abortion, and many budget-related matters, DeConcini often parts company with his party. But he rarely casts the vote that denies them a victory on an issue truly dear to them.

In 1990, after Majority Leader George J. Mitchell of Maine was defeated by three votes on a key clean air issue, he personally appealed to DeConcini to help him reverse the outcome. DeConcini had opposed Mitchell on that vote, as well as in the leadership race a year earlier. But he agreed to withhold his vote that day, pairing with an absent senator who supported Mitchell and helping the majority leader score an important victory.

In 1992, he voted with Democrats to override Bush's veto of the family leave bill. (Clinton later signed it into law.)

DeConcini's political position makes him a pivotal vote on judicial confirmation hearings. At the start of the 102nd, he was the last member of the Judiciary Committee to announce his opposition to Bush's nomination of Kenneth L. Ryskamp to the federal appeals court; Ryskamp was rejected on a 7-6 vote. He similarly waited until the very end to announce his opposition to Reagan nominee Robert H. Bork.

But regardless of what else DeConcini has

done or may accomplish in the 103rd, it is the Keating affair that will be the lasting mark on his congressional career.

The $2 billion price tag on the failure of Keating's Lincoln Savings and Loan of California coupled with the Senate scandal emerged as emblems of the debacle. The Keating Five also included Democratic Sens. Alan Cranston of California, Donald W. Riegle Jr. of Michigan and John Glenn of Ohio, along with Arizona Republican John McCain.

The case against the five senators hung on the nexus between their intervention and the political contributions they collected from Keating. DeConcini was forced to defend himself against charges that he acted more as a negotiator in Keating's behalf than as a senator asking legitimate questions.

From his days as Pima County prosecutor in the mid-1970s, DeConcini knew of Keating as a GOP anti-pornography crusader and prominent businessman. The two met at a country club in 1981, the same year DeConcini unsuccessfully lobbied President Reagan to nominate Keating to be ambassador to the Bahamas.

Beginning in 1987, it was DeConcini who called and ran more than one meeting between bank regulators and the senators. In late 1988, DeConcini allegedly urged state and federal regulators not to seize Lincoln but to allow Keating to sell it.

But on April 13, 1989, American Continental filed for bankruptcy. The following day federal regulators seized Lincoln. That fall, the government sued Keating and American Continental, alleging among other things that Lincoln's money had been siphoned off into campaign contributions. With that action, DeConcini returned the contributions raised by Keating for his 1982 and 1988 campaigns.

In the end, the Ethics Committee rebuked DeConcini and Riegle for the appearance of improper behavior but did not issue harsher sanctions, saying that the rules governing appearances of impropriety are unclear. In the cases of Glenn and McCain, the committee faulted their poor judgment, but did not find the appearance of wrongdoing. They both won re-election in 1992. In Cranston's case, the panel said he may have engaged in improper conduct and ordered further investigation. He retired, rather than face voters at the polls.

At Home: The only Democrat to win a Senate election in Arizona in nearly 30 years, DeConcini puts considerable effort into securing himself against a conservative challenge at home. Coupled with a bit of luck — local GOP warfare in 1976 and 1988 and a good Democratic year in 1982 — his efforts have kept him from ever being seriously threatened.

But the dynamics have changed as he tries for a fourth term in 1994. Haunted by his ties to the now-convicted Keating, DeConcini seems ripe for the picking, and top challengers in both parties are already gunning for him.

On the Republican side, Rep. Jon Kyl is making the rounds in Arizona to increase his name recognition and raise money to add to the nearly $500,000 he has left in his House treasury. Kyl has already had big-name conservatives such as former HUD Secretary Jack F. Kemp visit Arizona in his behalf.

But DeConcini may have to fend off a challenge within the Democratic Party before he faces Kyl or some other Republican in the 1994 general election. Secretary of State Dick Mahoney is a possible Democratic opponent.

DeConcini will have two advantages shared by all incumbents: money and name recognition. Both have aided him in previous campaigns.

In the two years leading up to his 1988 re-election, DeConcini stockpiled campaign funds and reinforced his well-regarded organization. The GOP, meanwhile, was caught up in a bitter feud sparked by Evan Mecham's election to the governorship. After a stormy 15-month tenure, a messy impeachment fight and a threatened recall election, the GOP-controlled Legislature threw Mecham out of office in April 1988.

Virtually alone, 39-year-old businessman Keith DeGreen made scant progress against DeConcini, until he raised questions about the incumbent's personal finances; that issue prompted the National Republican Senatorial Committee to fund a $212,000 October TV advertising blitz on DeGreen's behalf.

In 1979, DeConcini — a multimillionaire with vast real estate holdings — together with his family bought 320 acres of land for $400,000. Before the purchase, the federal Bureau of Reclamation had been publicly considering part of the area as a possible route for a continuation of the Central Arizona Project (CAP), a massive aqueduct. The government chose the site in 1981 and five years later reached a $1.4 million settlement for 136 acres.

DeConcini also made a 1983 investment in a development group that was involved in a similar deal. Land purchased by the partnership for $13,000 per acre was condemned by the federal government in 1984 for construction of the New Waddell Dam, which is part of CAP. In a 1987 settlement, the partnership ceded about half of its original purchase for $20,000 per acre. DeConcini divested his 3.1 percent share of the partnership before the settlement when the U.S. attorney ruled that his involvement in a negotiated water rights settlement would violate a federal law barring contracts between the government and members of Congress. The senator gave his share to his siblings, though the U.S. attorney's decision in the case was subsequently overruled.

DeConcini said he had no privileged knowledge of the government's plans in either deal. He accused DeGreen of dirty campaign tactics and lashed out at McCain for tacitly condoning them. The episode added some drama to what was expected to be a walkaway win; some polls in the campaign's final weeks showed considerable volatility in the electorate. But most voters knew too little of DeGreen to switch to him. DeConcini won with a comfortable, if not spectacular, 57 percent.

In his 1982 campaign, GOP challenger Pete Dunn, a three-term state legislator, used DeConcini's vote in favor of the Panama Canal treaties as part of his argument that DeConcini was a labor-backed liberal who "talks like Ronald Reagan in Arizona and votes like Ted Kennedy in Washington." But by then, DeConcini had compiled a record that made it difficult to brand him a liberal. He won re-election with 57 percent.

DeConcini campaigned for the Senate as a conservative in 1976, when he defeated GOP Rep. Sam Steiger. Stressing his law enforcement background as Pima County district attorney, he called for a crackdown on organized crime in Arizona. As it happened, neither crime nor any other policy issue had as much to do with the November outcome as a vicious Republican primary between Steiger and fellow Rep. John Conlan, longtime personal enemies.

Supporters of Steiger, a Jew, accused Conlan of pandering to anti-Semitism in a pitch for fundamentalist Christian votes. When Steiger won the primary, Conlan refused to endorse him, and Democrats rallied behind DeConcini in anticipation of a rare statewide victory.

Committees

Select Intelligence (Chairman)

Appropriations (7th of 16 Democrats)
Treasury, Postal Service & General Government (chairman); Defense; Energy & Water Development; Foreign Operations; Interior

Indian Affairs (2nd of 10 Democrats)

Judiciary (4th of 10 Democrats)
Patents, Copyrights & Trademarks (chairman); Antitrust, Monopolies & Business Rights; Constitution

Rules & Administration (5th of 9 Democrats)

Veterans' Affairs (2nd of 7 Democrats)

Joint Library

Joint Printing

Elections

1988 General

Dennis DeConcini (D)	660,403	(57%)
Keith DeGreen (R)	478,060	(41%)

Previous Winning Percentages: 1982 (57%) 1976 (54%)

Campaign Finance

1988	Receipts	Receipts from PACs		Expend-itures
DeConcini (D)	$2,818,427	$968,495	(34%)	$2,640,650
DeGreen (R)	$244,971	$20,350	(8%)	$238,369

Key Votes

1993	
Require unpaid family and medical leave	Y
Approve national "motor voter" registration bill	Y
Approve budget increasing taxes and reducing deficit	Y
Support president's right to lift military gay ban	Y
1992	
Approve school-choice pilot program	?
Allow shifting funds from defense to domestic programs	Y
Oppose deeper cuts in spending for SDI	N
1991	
Approve waiting period for handgun purchases	N
Raise senators' pay and ban honoraria	N
Authorize use of force in Persian Gulf	N
Confirm Clarence Thomas to Supreme Court	Y

Voting Studies

	Presidential Support		Party Unity		Conservative Coalition	
Year	**S**	**O**	**S**	**O**	**S**	**O**
1992	28	67	68	29	50	45
1991	41	54	75	23	48	45
1990	40	57	74	21	35	59
1989	61	38	64	35	55	45
1988	52	36	61	30	65	30
1987	46	51	73	26	34	59
1986	43	53	62	35	61	37
1985	45	49	62	31	63	28
1984	42	39	50 †	24 †	45	21
1983	32	47	55	31	52	32
1982	61	34	52	36	74	20
1981	51 †	38 †	59 †	24 †	63 †	24 †

† Not eligible for all recorded votes.

Interest Group Ratings

Year	ADA	AFL-CIO	CCUS	ACU
1992	75	64	10	20
1991	50	67	20	45
1990	61	56	50	20
1989	60	80	50	32
1988	55	92	21	33
1987	60	80	33	27
1986	45	60	35	52
1985	45	62	45	38
1984	60	75	38	38
1983	45	60	41	43
1982	45	82	53	60
1981	45	50	53	57

John McCain (R)

Of Phoenix — Elected 1986; 2nd Term

Born: Aug. 29, 1936, Panama Canal Zone.
Education: U.S. Naval Academy, B.S. 1958; National War College, 1973-74.
Military Service: Navy, 1958-81.
Occupation: Navy officer; Senate Navy liaison; beer distributor.
Family: Wife, Cindy Lou Hensley; six children.
Religion: Episcopalian.
Political Career: U.S. House, 1983-87.
Capitol Office: 111 Russell Bldg. 20510; 224-2235.

In Washington: McCain's Senate career survived his involvement in the Keating Five affair, in which he interceded with federal regulators on behalf of savings and loan operator Charles H. Keating Jr., who was ultimately jailed.

A protracted ethics investigation ended with a mild rebuke of McCain in February 1991. His popularity tarnished but not corroded, McCain drew weak opposition in 1992 and won easily.

The Keating Five affair seemed to temporarily limit what had been a skyrocketing political career. A war hero who spent several years in a Vietnamese POW camp, McCain had been mentioned as a Republican vice presidential possibility in 1988. There was little talk of that after the Keating affair.

But McCain shows signs of bouncing back. With his conservative but pragmatic style, he has managed to regain the light in which he would rather be seen: as a serious legislator and authority on military affairs.

McCain benefited during the 102nd Congress from a renewed focus on the fate of more than 2,000 Americans who remained listed as missing in action during the U.S. involvement in Vietnam. Spurred by rumors that some prisoners of war might still be alive in captivity, the Senate established a Select Committee on POW-MIA Affairs, of which McCain was a member.

In October 1992, McCain took a weekend off from his re-election campaign and journeyed to Hanoi with retired Gen. John Vessey, a special emissary on POW-MIA matters: Their mission resulted in Vietnam's release of long-withheld records on missing and captured Americans. The next month, Vietnamese officials turned over to another delegation of select committee members an item of symbolic portent: The helmet McCain was wearing when his plane was shot down.

Vietnam is seeking normalization and resumed economic ties with the United States; so far, many senators have been guided by McCain's cautious approach. "I look to see what John's position is," said Democratic Sen. Christopher J. Dodd of Connecticut in a 1991 interview.

McCain says Congress might consider rewarding Vietnam for its more forthcoming efforts on the POW-MIA issue by authorizing business contacts and low-level diplomatic relations. But he has doubts about a more rapid normalization favored by members — including some Republicans — who worry that the United States may miss out on a lucrative market as Vietnam reopens itself to the West.

McCain's middle ground approach makes him suspect to some conservatives who will be forever hostile to Vietnam. And McCain, who is skeptical of the claims of "live" POW sightings, has faced criticism from groups representing families of the missing soldiers.

At a hearing of the POW panel on Veterans Day 1992, the chairman of one such group accused McCain of "discrediting" evidence that POWs were still alive. McCain, usually mild-mannered but given to an explosive temper, reacted angrily. "I do not denigrate your efforts and your patriotism and your beliefs," he said, "and I am sick and tired of you denigrating mine and many other people's who happen to have different views than yours." McCain agreed with the panel's final report in January 1993, which said there was "no compelling evidence" to suggest that any American prisoners are alive in Southeast Asia.

Emotions concerning Vietnam are not far from McCain's surface. He was tortured as a POW from 1967 to 1973. Sybil Stockdale — wife of Ross Perot's 1992 vice presidential nominee, retired Navy admiral and former POW James Stockdale — testified before the committee that a number of POW-MIA families paid money to con artists for rescue missions that never happened. "There is a very special place in hell for the people who did this to you," McCain said.

McCain is adamant that he does not let the trauma of Vietnam dominate his thinking on military issues. "I know people who are defined by the Vietnam experience. They never left, and everything they've done since somehow gets back to it," McCain told The Washington Post in March 1993. "That's not true in my case. I think you will find that I very seldom, if ever, talk about it.... I don't have headaches. I don't have nightmares. I don't have flashbacks."

Yet McCain's views on the U.S. military's role in the world appear strongly influenced by his perspective on what went wrong in Vietnam.

A member of the Armed Services Committee and the son and grandson of renowned Navy admirals, McCain is a "hawk": He supported the "peace through strength" defense spending policies of Presidents Ronald Reagan and George Bush and opposes the pace of defense cuts prescribed by President Clinton for the post-Cold War era. He also supported U.S. interventions — in Grenada, Panama and the Persian Gulf — in which the goals were clear and the weight of U.S. force provided for rapid victory.

But McCain has been sharply critical of U.S. "peacekeeping" forays that place American troops between warring parties and create the potential for long and risky troop deployments. As a House member in 1983, he took issue with the deployment of Marines between Israeli and Arab troops in Lebanon, which ended following a catastrophic terrorist bombing of a U.S. barracks.

A decade later, as a senator, McCain was a leading voice in opposition to Clinton's proposed intervention in the civil war between the Serbian and Muslim populations in Bosnia.

During confirmation hearings on Clinton's appointment of Les Aspin as Defense secretary in January 1993, McCain asked, "What do we do . . . if we launch these airstrikes and then we find ourselves with several American pilots being held captive somewhere in Serbia?"

Despite alleged Serbian atrocities that some supporters of U.S. intervention described as a "holocaust," McCain consistently warned of a Vietnam-like "quagmire" in the fragmented and mountainous republics of the former Yugoslavia.

McCain argued that some intervention advocates were taking a cavalier approach to the possibility that use of U.S. force might not get the Serbs to back down. "It smacks of total irresponsibility to say, 'Just go ahead and bomb and if that fails ... we'll have to escalate,' or as the other argument goes, if it fails, we're no worse off than we were before," he told the Post. "We're the world's superpower. The situation would be worse if we failed — in my view, considerably worse."

McCain also questioned the credibility of Clinton, who avoided military service during the Vietnam War, to lead the nation into battle. When Clinton, as president, raised a storm of controversy by trying to lift the ban on homosexuals serving in the military, McCain said, "I think his lack of military service emphasizes his need to consult on matters he knows nothing about."

Yet that issue illustrated McCain's modulated approach. The ranking Republican on the Armed Services Subcommittee on Military Readiness and Defense Infrastructure, McCain urged members in February 1993 to "come to the debate with an open mind." Eschewing the anti-homosexual rhetoric espoused by some conservatives, McCain said he opposed an outright lifting of the ban because the military "should not be used for . . . social experiments." But he voiced support for a compromise that would prevent recruiters from asking volunteers whether they were gay.

McCain took a similarly moderate approach on another social policy issue affecting the military. The solid performance of women soldiers in the Persian Gulf War — including some who flew aircraft over combat zones — spurred a strong movement to lift the legal prohibition on women in combat roles. At a June 1991 Armed Services subcommittee hearing, McCain said a "blanket denial of combat roles" for women was unfair.

However, as the move for an outright repeal of the bans picked up unexpected steam, McCain joined with Democratic Sen. John Glenn of Ohio (the chairman of the Armed Services subcommittee for which McCain was the ranking Republican) in an attempt to slow the momentum. In July 1991, their amendment authorizing the secretary of Defense to waive some combat-exclusion laws for women on a trial basis (rather than immediately repealing the laws) was adopted by the Senate on a 96-3 vote.

Their teamwork on the issue pointed up the close working relationship between McCain and Glenn, who flew combat missions for the Marine Corps during the Korean War before gaining fame as an astronaut. The two are also paired on the Governmental Affairs Committee, which Glenn chairs, and they shared the misfortune of getting caught up in the Keating Five scandal.

On broader defense-budget issues, McCain champions burden-sharing, a concept that calls on U.S. allies to increase spending for international security. He brought the issue close to home in February 1992 as he argued to cut the U.S. troop commitment in foreign countries. "A politician finds it very difficult, when Williams Air Force Base in Arizona is being closed [under a 1991 base-closing law], to explain the rationale for keeping bases overseas," McCain said.

In 1990, the Senate adopted his amendment to a defense appropriations bill requiring a quarterly report by the president to Congress on contributions made by other countries to the military deployment against Iraq.

While McCain might find the current pace of defense spending reductions too rapid, he does not oppose the overall concept as the nation adjusts to the collapse of the Soviet Union. During the 102nd Congress, he spearheaded efforts to cancel production of the *Seawolf*, an expensive high-tech submarine intended to counter a Soviet naval threat that had greatly diminished. But McCain was thwarted by an intense lobbying effort by members from New

England, where the *Seawolf* is built.

Such actions are in keeping with McCain's efforts to promote fiscal conservatism. He has proposed legislation creating a line-item veto that would allow the president to delete individual items from appropriations bills.

There is one group, though, to which McCain has sought to expand federal benefits: elderly Americans, of which there are large numbers in Arizona.

McCain — who once had to apologize for a reference to the Leisure World retirement community as "Seizure World" — has made amends. Since the 102nd Congress, he has led the fight in the Senate to lift the limit on income that retirees can obtain while receiving full Social Security benefits.

In 1989, he was one of the leaders in efforts to roll back a catastrophic health-care law that was undone by senior citizens' opposition to an income tax surcharge used to finance benefits. Initially, he and Utah Republican Orrin G. Hatch sponsored an amendment to delay implementing the program.

Unable to win with that proposal, and with calls mounting to repeal the entire catastrophic program, McCain offered a bill to repeal the surtax but keep unlimited coverage of hospital bills while eliminating most of the law's new benefits. The Senate passed it 99-0.

But the House voted overwhelmingly to repeal all but the law's extended coverage for the poor. After weeks of contentious wrangling between the two chambers, the House position prevailed. McCain first vowed to filibuster the conference agreement, but he later retracted that threat when repeal looked inevitable. "I'm not Jesse Helms," he said. "That's not my style."

McCain has also worked for home-state interests in a variety of areas. A member of the Commerce, Science and Transportation Committee (he is the ranking GOP member on the Surface Transportation Subcommittee), McCain has tried to expand landing rights for smaller airlines — including Phoenix-based America West — at the nation's largest airports. He is also senior Republican on the Indian Affairs Committee; American Indians make up about 5.5 percent of Arizona's population.

Beginning in the 101st Congress, McCain sponsored bills to protect Arizona's Grand Canyon from damage caused by excessive fluctuations in the amounts of water released from the Glen Canyon Dam farther up the Colorado River. He met success at the end of the 102nd Congress, when his measure was attached to an omnibus water projects bill that President Bush signed in October 1992.

McCain strongly opposes efforts, mainly by members from non-Western states, to rapidly raise the fees paid by ranchers who graze their cattle on federally owned lands. "These people are small family farmers, and what [this legislation] is going to do is drive them out of business," said McCain during debate on a fee-raising proposal in September 1991.

But there was one constituent whose cause McCain wishes he had never taken up: Charles H. Keating Jr. As the Keating Five scandal unfolded, McCain said he got involved to protect the jobs of Arizonans employed by Keating's American Continental Corporation (ACC).

McCain and Keating, a World War II pilot, met in 1981 and hit it off. Their families vacationed together at Keating's private resort in the Bahamas. McCain and his family often flew on planes owned or hired by ACC. Keating, his family and associates contributed about $112,000 to McCain's 1982 and 1984 House campaigns and his 1986 Senate run.

When Keating complained in early 1987 that Federal Home Loan Bank Board regulators were harassing him in their examination of ACC-owned Lincoln Savings and Loan, McCain lent an ear. But when McCain refused to negotiate with the regulators on Keating's behalf, Keating told Arizona Democratic Sen. Dennis DeConcini that McCain was a "wimp." McCain abruptly ended his friendship with the banker.

McCain went ahead and discussed Keating's complaint with regulators, along with Democratic Sens. DeConcini, Glenn, Alan Cranston of California and Donald W. Riegle Jr. of Michigan, whose constituents, because of Keating's far-flung business interests, were also affected. Fortunately for McCain, evidence showed that he was the most reluctant participant, expressing qualms about the propriety of the senators' intervention.

The Ethics Committee concluded that McCain "exercised poor judgment" but that his actions "were not improper" and did not require further discipline.

At Home: From the time Sen. Barry Goldwater announced plans not to run again in 1986, McCain was widely regarded as his likely successor.

McCain started with a strong pool of political capital. He had impressed Republican activists by winning election to the House in 1982, soon after his 1981 arrival in the state. Subsequent trips around Arizona as a member of Reagan's 1984 steering committee boosted his visibility. He became such a hot property that potential intraparty rivals backed away.

Democrats, too, were wary of his stature. Gov. Bruce Babbitt decided he would rather risk a run at the presidency than tangle with McCain for the Senate. After a host of other Democrats also passed up the race, party leaders were relieved when ex-state Sen. Richard Kimball, then a member of the Corporation Commission, declared his candidacy.

But Kimball never hit stride as a Senate candidate. He spent months holed up to research his stands on issues, which did not enhance his visibility. McCain swept all but three counties.

John McCain, R-Ariz.

McCain was not in the Senate long before he found himself embroiled in the Keating Five scandal. Although he was given only a mild rebuke, the scandal appeared to leave the freshman vulnerable to a Democratic challenge in 1992.

But Arizona Democrats failed to recruit any big-name contenders, in part because McCain's approval ratings remained at or near the 50 percent level in 1991. Neither of the two Democrats who joined the race — Retired Air Force Lt. Gen. Truman Spangrud and community activist Claire Sargent — had any political experience.

Sargent handily won the Democratic primary, but she lacked the money and name recognition to present a serious threat to McCain in the fall. Even the entrance of impeached GOP Gov. Evan Mecham into the race as an independent did little to help her cause. McCain outdistanced Sargent by more than 20 percentage points.

McCain's initial opening came in 1982, when GOP Rep. John J. Rhodes decided to give up his 1st District seat. McCain won nomination by convincing voters that his experience as Navy liaison to the Senate gave him a knowledge of "how Washington works."

When rivals charged that he was a carpetbagger who would forget Arizona once in Washington, McCain said, "I went to Hanoi and I didn't forget about the United States of America."

There was never much question McCain would be a Navy man; his father commanded U.S. forces in the Pacific during the Vietnam War, and his grandfather was a Pacific aircraft carrier commander in World War II. In a Hanoi prison camp, his captors sarcastically called him the U.S. Navy's "crown prince."

The roots of McCain's political successes lie in his long ordeal in Vietnam, the years he spent tortured and in solitary confinement in Hanoi-area camps after his plane was shot down in 1967. At the 1988 GOP convention, McCain recounted his experiences for a prime-time national TV audience.

Committees

Indian Affairs (Ranking)

Armed Services (4th of 9 Republicans)
Military Readiness & Defense Infrastructure (ranking); Force Requirements & Personnel; Regional Defense & Contingency Forces

Commerce, Science & Transportation (5th of 9 Republicans)
Surface Transportation (ranking); Aviation; Communications; Consumer

Governmental Affairs (5th of 5 Republicans)
General Services, Federalism & the District of Columbia (ranking); Oversight of Government Management; Permanent Subcommittee on Investigations Regulation & Government Information

Special Aging (6th of 10 Republicans)

Elections

1992 General

John McCain (R)	771,395	(56%)
Claire Sargent (D)	436,321	(32%)
Evan Mecham (I)	145,361	(11%)
Kiana Delamare (LIBERT)	22,613	(2%)

Previous Winning Percentages: **1986** (61%) **1984 *** (78%) **1982 *** (66%)

* House elections.

Campaign Finance

	Receipts	Receipts from PACs		Expend-itures
1992				
McCain (R)	$3,344,311	$1,196,056	(36%)	$3,481,915
Sargent (D)	$288,413	$40,770	(14%)	$287,682
Mecham (I)	$89,910	0		$86,433

Key Votes

1993

Require unpaid family and medical leave	Y
Approve national "motor voter" registration bill	N
Approve budget increasing taxes and reducing deficit	N
Support president's right to lift military gay ban	N

1992

Approve school-choice pilot program	Y
Allow shifting funds from defense to domestic programs	N
Oppose deeper cuts in spending for SDI	Y

1991

Approve waiting period for handgun purchases	N
Raise senators' pay and ban honoraria	N
Authorize use of force in Persian Gulf	Y
Confirm Clarence Thomas to Supreme Court	Y

Voting Studies

	Presidential Support		Party Unity		Conservative Coalition	
Year	**S**	**O**	**S**	**O**	**S**	**O**
1992	75	25	84	13	82	13
1991	86	14	87	11	90	8
1990	74	25	78	19	76	22
1989	91	9	85	13	84	13
1988	70	23	84	13	78	16
1987	65	24	84	11	69	25
House Service:						
1986	68	29	67	25	76	18
1985	68	25	81	13	84	13
1984	64	27	74 †	13 †	83	8
1983	80	17	83	9	90	7

† Not eligible for all recorded votes.

Interest Group Ratings

Year	ADA	AFL-CIO	CCUS	ACU
1992	20	33	90	85
1991	5	17	70	86
1990	11	22	83	87
1989	5	0	88	93
1988	10	14	64	80
1987	15	20	100	91
House Service:				
1986	10	14	60	73
1985	5	18	91	81
1984	10	31	93	86
1983	10	6	85	96

1 Sam Coppersmith (D)

Of Phoenix — Elected 1992; 1st Term

Born: May 22, 1955, Johnstown, Pa.
Education: Harvard U., A.B. 1976; Yale U., J.D. 1982.
Occupation: Lawyer; foreign service officer.
Family: Wife, Beth Schermer; three children.
Religion: Jewish.
Political Career: No previous office.
Capitol Office: 1607 Longworth Bldg. 20515; 225-2635.

The Path to Washington: Like so many elected officials, Coppersmith was exposed to politics at a young age: As a teenager, he spent much of his spare time working on his father's state Senate campaigns in Pennsylvania.

Coppersmith maintained his fondness for politics when he moved to Arizona in 1982 after completing his legal education at Yale University. He played an active role in Democrat Terry Goddard's successful 1983 Phoenix mayoral campaign.

But Coppersmith had given little thought to a congressional bid before 1992. Instead, he had been seriously considering a 1994 bid for Phoenix City Council. Not until a federal court in Arizona finished drawing the lines for the state's new congressional districts did Coppersmith decide to run for Congress.

At the urging of top Democrats in the state, who saw an opportunity to upset GOP Rep. John J. Rhodes III, Coppersmith joined the race just one week before the primary filing deadline.

His campaign sparked little attention until after the primaries. Republicans hold a solid voter registration advantage over Democrats in the 1st District, and most political observers wrote off the Democratic Party in 1992.

But a poor performance by Rhodes in the Republican primary — he won only 33 percent of the vote in a five-candidate race and defeated his nearest competitor by only 1,500 votes — and a solid victory by Coppersmith in the Democratic contest changed the dynamics.

By Election Day, officials in both parties had taken to calling the race a toss-up, and Coppersmith ended up with 51 percent of the vote to Rhodes' 45 percent.

This was in part because redistricting moved the 1st toward the center of the political spectrum. Mapmakers replaced the most conservative Republicans in the district with more moderate GOP voters, making it more competitive for a Democrat like Coppersmith.

Coppersmith also benefited from anti-incumbent sentiment as he managed to convince voters that Rhodes was out of touch.

Coppersmith leans to the left on some social issues: He was president of Planned Parenthood in central and northern Arizona before entering the race and is a strong advocate of abortion rights. But he also espouses conservative economic views in line with those held by most voters in the district.

In the campaign, Coppersmith said he would support a balanced-budget amendment and a line-item veto for the president. He called for cuts in discretionary spending and entitlements and cautioned against excessive defense cuts.

In March of 1993, he was one of only three Democratic freshmen to vote against President Clinton's proposed $16.3 billion economic stimulus package.

And while he argued that Congress must address the health-care crisis, he said that giving the government complete control would be a mistake; he favors a system of "managed competition" that encourages health-care providers to shift their emphasis to preventive medicine.

One of 15 freshman Democrats on the Public Works Committee, Coppersmith said he would try to limit discretionary spending on infrastructure programs that must be authorized by the committee, a position that could put him at odds with the Democratic leadership and Bill Clinton, who campaigned on a pledge to spark the economy with an infusion of federal public works spending. Coppersmith also won a seat on the Science, Space and Technology panel.

Coppersmith argued that the federal deficit is the root of the country's economic problems and that lawmakers should focus on deficit reduction as the long-term solution to economic woes.

The first Democrat to win election in the Phoenix-based 1st District since 1950, Coppersmith is likely to be among be among the most vulnerable freshmen in 1994.

With his slim margin of victory, he expects to be a top target of the Arizona Republican Party in his first re-election bid. "The votes weren't even fully counted yet before the exploratory committees were being formed," Coppersmith joked just weeks after the election. But, he says, "if I do a good job, that's my best case for re-election. And if I don't, I will deserve my fate."

Arizona 1

Southeastern Phoenix — Tempe; Mesa

Coppersmith's unexpected House victory in 1992 was in part an outgrowth of a redistricting plan that shifted some of the Phoenix area's most conservative Republicans into the newly created 6th District.

Mapmakers put East Mesa in the 6th, a step that gives the 1st a more centrist electorate. Remaining in the district are more moderate Republican voters in West Mesa, Tempe, Chandler and parts of Phoenix. Under certain circumstances they will consider voting for a Democratic candidate, and the business-oriented Coppersmith added enough of them to the district's Democratic minority to win with 51 percent of the vote.

Still, on paper this looks like it should be a Republican district. Nearly 53 percent of its voters are registered Republicans. The 1992 remap removed some Democratic areas from the 1st: Hispanic neighborhoods surrounding Sky Harbor Airport and the Gila River Indian reservation just south of Phoenix. Voters in those areas are now located in districts with larger minority populations.

In the 1992 presidential contest, George Bush came out on top in the 1st with 40 percent of the vote. Bill Clinton got 34 percent, and the independent streak that runs through many of the voters here showed up in a 26 percent tally for Ross Perot.

The 1st encompasses most of Mesa, where population exploded by almost 90 percent during the 1980s, exceeding 288,000. The district's other suburban pillars are Tempe (population 142,000) and Chandler (population 90,500).

Electronics and high-technology companies have thrived here in recent years, spawning a sizable class of well-to-do managers and technicians. They generally have conservative political instincts, as do the thousands of retirees who have settled in the area.

Mesa was founded by Mormons in 1878; it still has a politically active Mormon community and is the site of Arizona's Mormon temple. Mesa is home to eight manufacturing companies on the Fortune 500 list, and it is the spring-training base for two professional baseball teams, the Chicago Cubs and California Angels.

Tempe, just to the west, was developed around a flour mill in 1871; today it is primarily a manufacturing city, with more than 200 businesses producing a range of goods, from clothing to electronics. The city usually votes Republican in state and local elections, but Arizona State University's 43,000 students and 1,800 faculty provide Tempe with a significant Democratic presence.

The district also takes in a politically diverse portion of southeastern Phoenix, a tabletop-flat area of the "Valley of the Sun" that includes some upper-middle-class neighborhoods with a distinctly Republican bent.

Another new addition to the 1st in redistricting — a small, southern portion of Scottsdale — also could add to Republican strength in the district.

1990 Population: 610,872. White 530,941 (87%), Black 19,280 (3%), Other 60,651 (10%). Hispanic origin 80,350 (13%). 18 and over 457,975 (75%), 62 and over 67,266 (11%). Median age: 30.

Committees

Public Works & Transportation (26th of 39 Democrats)
Aviation; Economic Development

Science, Space & Technology (24th of 33 Democrats)
Energy; Investigations & Oversight; Technology, Environment & Aviation

Campaign Finance

1992	Receipts	Receipts from PACs	Expend-itures
Coppersmith (D)	$247,608	$66,183 (27%)	$244,633
Rhodes (R)	$455,154	$184,405 (41%)	$336,768

Key Votes

1993

Require parental notification of minors' abortions	N
Require unpaid family and medical leave	Y
Approve national "motor voter" registration bill	Y
Approve budget increasing taxes and reducing deficit	Y
Approve economic stimulus plan	N

Elections

1992 General		
Sam Coppersmith (D)	130,715	(51%)
John J. Rhodes III (R)	113,613	(45%)
Ted Goldstein (NL)	10,461	(4%)
1992 Primary		
Sam Coppersmith (D)	17,420	(74%)
David J. Sanson III (D)	6,269	(26%)

District Vote for President

1992

D 88,247 (34%)
R 105,784 (40%)
I 68,143 (26%)

2 Ed Pastor (D)

Of Phoenix — Elected 1991; 1st Full Term

Born: June 28, 1943, Claypool, Ariz.
Education: Arizona State U., B.S. 1966, J.D. 1974.
Occupation: Teacher; legal aide executive; public policy consultant.
Family: Wife, Verma Mendez; two children.
Religion: Roman Catholic.
Political Career: Maricopa County Board of Supervisors, 1977-91.
Capitol Office: 408 Cannon Bldg. 20515; 225-4065.

In Washington: Pastor, who in September 1991 became Arizona's first Hispanic congressman after winning a special election to replace veteran Democratic Rep. Morris K. Udall, benefited handsomely from the flood of House freshmen who were elected more than a year later, in November 1992.

When the huge House class of 1992 hit Washington, the 63 Democratic first-termers let party leaders know of their strong feeling that "prestige" committees, which are normally reserved for more senior members, should reflect the influx of newcomers (including women and minorities) into the House. Pastor, though not a true freshman, was considered part of the class of 1992 for organizational purposes, and he won a spot on the influential Appropriations Committee. A second "newcomer" seat went to Democrat John W. Olver of Massachusetts (who, like Pastor, won a 1991 special election). One genuine rookie got on Appropriations: black Democrat Carrie Meek of Florida.

Despite Pastor's quick grab of a coveted committee assignment, he has a long way to go to build up the kind of clout and respect earned by his predecessor Udall, who rose to become chairman of the Interior Committee and was a presidential contender in 1976. Udall, weakened by his long battle with Parkinson's disease, resigned from Congress in May 1991.

Pastor's voting record is that of a reliable Democratic loyalist. In the opening months of the 103rd Congress, he was a faithful backer of the Clinton administration's legislative priorities, supporting unpaid family and medical leave, the "motor voter" registration bill and the president's budget plan and economic stimulus package. The House leadership has given him a seat on the Steering and Policy Committee, which makes decisions about committee assignments.

On Appropriations, Pastor has seats on two subcommittees that fit nicely with the needs of his state: Agriculture, Rural Development and Related Agencies, and Energy and Water Development. He is the only Western Democrat on the Agriculture Subcommittee and one of two Western Democrats on Energy and Water. From that post, he can lobby for money for flood-control programs and for the Central Arizona Project (a longtime priority of Udall's), which brings water to Phoenix and other areas.

Pastor has joined his other Arizona House colleagues in sponsoring amendments to the Southern Arizona Water Rights legislation, which tries to solve the state's unusual water problem: plenty of water in one part of the state, but too little elsewhere.

Pastor's strong liberal instincts are evident in his actions in the area of health-care policy. He has sponsored a resolution saying that access to health care is a "fundamental human right" and said that the "day of health care as a 'fringe benefit' must go." Pastor said in a letter to his colleagues that health care needs to be a "basic right on equal footing with the right to a fair trial and to free speech."

The 1992 election had another beneficial impact on Pastor: giving him partisan company in the Arizona House delegation. Before the election, he was the state's only Democrat in the House; now three of the state's six districts are in Democratic hands.

At Home: Hispanics began making preparations to contend for the 2nd not long after the 1990 election; Udall had announced that he would retire at the end of the 102nd Congress. But the transition came sooner than expected, after Udall chose to relinquish his seat.

In addition to Pastor, four other Democrats and five Republicans entered the race to succeed Udall.

The Democratic primary preceding the September special election was Pastor's biggest hurdle. (Democrats have a wide registration advantage in the 2nd.) And Tom Volgy, mayor of Tucson (Pima County), the largest city in the district, was his principal opponent.

The five-candidate primary came down to a turf battle between Pastor and Volgy. Pima County residents had long considered the district theirs, and Pastor's electoral base was in Maricopa County (Phoenix), where he had served on the Board of Supervisors for four terms.

Arizona 2

Southwest — Southwestern Tucson; southern Phoenix; Yuma

The 2nd is Arizona's most Hispanic and most Democratic district. Redistricting in 1992 gave the 2nd a bare Hispanic-majority population: 50 percent, up from 36 percent in the 1980s. Hispanics make up 45 percent of the voting-age population.

Some Hispanic activists lobbied map-makers for a heavier minority concentration, but Rep. Pastor had no trouble winning his first re-election, taking two-thirds of the vote as Bill Clinton won a majority in presidential balloting. Clinton's 51 percent tally in the 2nd was easily his best showing in any Arizona district.

The Maricopa County (Phoenix) portion of the 2nd casts the district's largest share of votes, nearly 40 percent. Most of the Maricopa vote comes out of Hispanic areas. The south side of Phoenix, included in the 2nd, traditionally has been the city's poorest economically and most faithfully Democratic. Remapping strengthened the Democratic slant by including the minority neighborhoods near Sky Harbor Airport, which had been in the 1st District.

To the southeast, Pima County (Tucson) accounts for 35 percent of the district vote. Here also Democrats are strong in Hispanic neighborhoods, and in the community surrounding the University of Arizona. With 35,000 students and 10,000 workers, it is the biggest single factor in Tucson's economy.

Just south of Tucson, the copper-mining town of Ajo and the San Xavier and Papago Indian reservations also favor Democrats.

Tucson has begun to see the same influx of retirees and people attracted by high-tech companies that has transformed politics in other parts of Arizona. But Tucson's long Democratic tradition is still strong; Clinton won 59 percent in the Pima County part of the 2nd, well above his district average.

Though the bulk of Pima County's land area lies within the boundaries of the 2nd, most of the county's residents live in eastern Tucson in the 5th District.

The most Republican part of the 2nd is on the district's western edge, in Yuma County. It casts about one-fifth of the total district vote, and in 1992 not only gave George Bush a first-place finish with 42 percent, but also backed Pastor's GOP challenger, who was crushed districtwide.

Incorporated as Arizona City in 1871 and renamed two years later, Yuma, the county seat, lies south of California on the Colorado River; it continues in its traditional role as a regional commercial crossroads. Interstate 8 running through the city heads west to San Diego. Yuma County's economic base is agricultural, but two military bases — the Marine Corps Air Station and Yuma Proving Grounds — contribute significantly to the economy.

Rounding out the 2nd is Santa Cruz County, where the heavily Hispanic border town of Nogales and its Mexican sister city of the same name are a major crossing point between the two countries. Clinton won Santa Cruz in 1992, but ran several points below his district average.

1990 population: 610,871. White 367,125 (60%), Black 41,578 (7%), Other 202,168 (33%). Hispanic origin 308,256 (50%). 18 and over 414,281 (68%), 62 and over 72554 (12%). Median age: 28.

Pastor emphasized his 15 years of public service: He was an aide to former Democratic Gov. Raul Castro before being elected to the Board of Supervisors.

Pastor emerged as the choice of the establishment, winning the endorsements of leading officeholders, both Hispanic and Anglo, in the primary. He also enjoyed a fundraising edge — he began the campaign with $70,000 left over from his last supervisor's race — that permitted him to run ads on television and radio.

Volgy ran well in his home county of Pima, but he finished a distant third in Pastor's base in Maricopa County. Pastor won the Aug. 13 primary with 37 percent of the vote; Volgy finished with 32 percent; and Virginia Yrun, with 27 percent.

In the Sept. 24 special election, Pastor faced Republican Pat Conner, a Yuma County supervisor. Hhe criticized Pastor for accepting $2,800 in campaign contributions from thrift executive Charles H. Keating Jr. in 1988 and for accepting a $1,000 set of golf clubs from a lobbyist later indicted in a state corruption investigation.

But the charges didn't stick: Pastor had given the money from Keating to the Internal Revenue Service in 1988, and he had also returned the golf clubs.

Although Pastor did not win the seat by the large margins that Udall had — Udall topped 65 percent in his last five elections — he easily defeated Connor, winning 56 percent of the vote.

Pastor's election ended Tucson's grip on the district. Candidates who called Tucson home had controlled the seat since 1949.

Redistricting in 1992 boosted the percentage of Hispanics in the district, and Pastor worked hard to firm up the Democratic base. He drew no primary opposition and won two-thirds of the vote in November.

Committees

Appropriations (36th of 37 Democrats)
Agriculture, Rural Development & Related Agencies; Energy & Water Development

Elections

1992 General

Ed Pastor (D)	90,693	(66%)
Don Shooter (R)	41,257	(30%)
Dan Detaranto (LIBERT)	5,423	(4%)

1991 Special

Ed Pastor (D)	32,289	(56%)
Pat Conner (R)	25,814	(44%)

District Vote for President

1992

D	74,588 (51%)
R	41,757 (29%)
I	28,767 (20%)

Campaign Finance

	Receipts	Receipts from PACs		Expend-itures
1992				
Pastor (D)	$281,008	$137,122	(49%)	$266,660
Shooter (R)	$28,858	0		$27,260

Key Votes

1993

Require parental notification of minors' abortions	N
Require unpaid family and medical leave	Y
Approve national "motor voter" registration bill	Y
Approve budget increasing taxes and reducing deficit	Y
Approve economic stimulus plan	Y

1992

Approve balanced-budget constitutional amendment	N
Close down space station program	Y
Approve U.S. aid for former Soviet Union	N
Allow shifting funds from defense to domestic programs	Y

Voting Studies

	Presidential Support		Party Unity		Conservative Coalition	
Year	**S**	**O**	**S**	**O**	**S**	**O**
1992	20	75	89	9	25	73
1991	33 †	67 †	92 †	7 †	24 †	76 †

† Not eligible for all recorded votes.

Interest Group Ratings

Year	ADA	AFL-CIO	CCUS	ACU
1992	85	83	13	12
1991	83	100	25	0

3 Bob Stump (R)

Of Tolleson — Elected 1976; 9th Term

Born: April 4, 1927, Phoenix, Ariz.
Education: Arizona State U., B.S. 1951.
Military Service: Navy, 1943-46.
Occupation: Cotton farmer.
Family: Divorced; three children.
Religion: Seventh-day Adventist.
Political Career: Ariz. House, 1959-67; Ariz. Senate, 1967-77, president, 1975-77.
Capitol Office: 211 Cannon Bldg. 20515; 225-4576.

In Washington: For most veteran House members, the events of 1981 are but remote memories, footnotes of long careers spent in the spotlight. But for Stump, one of Congress' surpassingly low-profile figures, that year stands out as the one in which he did something highly uncharacteristic: He made news.

It was in 1981 when Stump, then one of the most conservative House Democrats, switched to the Republican Party. His conversion placed him in the national headlines for the first and possibly the last time.

In the years since, as before his switch, Stump has had little use for news conferences. Although he nearly always shows up on the House floor to vote — his attendance record in the 102nd Congress was near-perfect — he rarely stops by a microphone to speak while he is there. He simply tends to his legislative business, which centers on his advocacy of defense and veterans' programs.

Stump's consistently strong conservative views are the hallmark of his House career. He was annually among the members who were most supportive of Reagan and Bush administration policies. Though overall congressional support for President Bush's positions sank with his popularity ratings in 1992, Stump stuck with the president on 85 percent of the House votes on which Bush had taken a stand.

Stump jumped parties in 1981 because he believed he would be more comfortable — both politically and personally — in the conservative Republican caucus than on the liberal-dominated Democratic side. Like many of his rural constituents, Stump, a cotton farmer, was raised as a "pinto Democrat," whose conservative philosophy closely matched that of the traditional Democrats of the South.

The rise of President Ronald Reagan had led GOP strategists in the early 1980s to boldly — if misguidedly — tout an incipient "partisan realignment." Although this did not come to pass, Stump today is enjoying the rewards of his adopted party's gratitude.

Stump immediately got a GOP seat on the Armed Services Committee with no loss in seniority; his seniority also was guaranteed on Veterans' Affairs. In the 103rd Congress, Stump is in his third term as the ranking Republican on Veterans' Affairs; he is second in GOP seniority on Armed Services and is ranking Republican on the Research and Technology Subcommittee.

That subcommittee is chaired by Colorado Democrat Patricia Schroeder. The combination of Schroeder and Stump is one of the oddest pairings at the top of any House panel. Schroeder is an effusive urban liberal, while Stump is a taciturn rural conservative.

The two will undoubtedly find much on which to disagree. Stump avidly supported Reagan's military buildup in the 1980s and has warned against a rapid decline in post-Cold War defense spending. Schroeder, who consistently favored much lower defense spending levels than Reagan and Bush, supports President Clinton's proposals to reorient much of the nation's high-tech research from defense to civilian purposes.

Outside of defense, Stump takes a mainly tight-fisted approach on fiscal issues. When he does speak up, his words often have a sharp edge aimed at liberals. After proposing a constitutional amendment to give the president a line-item appropriations veto in January 1991, Stump said, "It is said that old habits die hard; this is particularly true of the tax-and-spend habit of the liberals — their unrestrained desire to spend what we do not have and take from the taxpayers what they cannot afford."

Stump can also show a temper, as he did in November 1991, when outspoken Democratic Rep. Maxine Waters of California criticized the Veterans' Affairs Committee leadership for hiring few minority-group staffers. "I'll make you a deal," Stump fired back. "I won't tell you who to hire on your staff and you don't tell me who to hire on my staff."

Fortunately for Stump, ideology and partisanship play little role on Veterans' Affairs; there is usually bipartisan consensus for the veterans' programs, and Stump works well with the chairman, conservative Democratic Rep. G. V. "Sonny" Montgomery of Mississippi.

Stump's fiscal conservatism does not pre-

Arizona 3

North and West — Glendale; part of Phoenix; Hopi reservation

The most eye-catching feature of the 3rd is the oddly shaped appendage on its northeastern edge. That cartographic flight stems from a decision by federal judges who drew Arizona's House lines to put the reservations of the Hopi and Navajo Indians — two tribes whose land disputes reach back generations — into separate congressional districts.

Redistricting, however, did little to change the fundamental political personality of the 3rd.

Once dominated by "pinto Democrats" — ranchers and other conservative rural landowners — the 3rd has become prime GOP turf over the years. And remapping in 1992 only hastened the Republican shift by moving Flagstaff and its Democratic loyalties into the 6th.

Voter registration in the 3rd is now 53 percent Republican. George Bush ran first here in 1992, taking 41 percent of the vote.

More than 55 percent of the district's vote is cast in the Maricopa County suburbs west of Phoenix. In Glendale, which produces wide GOP margins, population grew by more than 52 percent in the 1980s. Glendale's economy, once grounded in agriculture, has diversified to include manufacturing jobs in the aerospace, electronics, communications and chemical industries.

In nearby Sun City, an affluent and largely GOP retirement community, the politically active residents typically turn out for elections at an 80 percent or better rate.

The district moves west out of Phoenix, following I-10 into La Paz County, which was created in 1982 by a ballot initiative that split Yuma County, to La Paz's south. The La Paz community of Quartzsite swells during the winter, as travelers flock to take advantage of its warm climate and see its rock and mineral shows.

Mohave County, in Arizona's northwest corner, is home to three groups in constant political tension: Indians, pinto Democrats in Kingman and Republican retirees in Lake Havasu City. Mohave's 1992 presidential verdict shows how easy it is to get a political argument going in the county: Bush got 35 percent, Bill Clinton 33 percent and Ross Perot 32 percent.

Coconino County, where partisan sentiments are mixed, is now split between the 3rd and 6th districts. Most of "the Arizona strip," which includes a heavily Mormon region with strong GOP ties, remains in the 3rd. Sedona, a Republican bastion in the southern part of the county, also remains in the 3rd.

Just north of Flagstaff, the 3rd includes a narrow arm that reaches east to pick up the Hopi reservation, which lies in Coconino and Navajo counties. The court went to great lengths to separate the Navajo from the Hopi, who bitterly complain that the Navajo have long been encroaching on land designated by the federal government as Hopi. The mapmakers even went so far as to include in the 3rd the tiny Hopi village of Moenkopi, which is completely surrounded by Navajo lands that are in the 6th. Moenkopi is connected to the 3rd by an uninhabited stretch of state Route 264.

1990 Population: 610,871. White 534,991 (88%), Black 11,849 (2%), Other 64,031 (10%). Hispanic origin 72,113 (12%). 18 and over 457,293 (75%), 62 and over 140,889 (23%). Median age: 36.

vent him from fighting for educational, medical and other benefit programs that he thinks military veterans deserve. But he takes a cautious approach to creating new benefit programs.

For four years, Stump helped Montgomery block an effort, led by Illinois Democratic Rep. Lane Evans, to provide compensation for Vietnam veterans who said their exposure to the herbicide Agent Orange had caused them to develop cancer. Stump argued that studies had proved no definitive link between certain cancers and Agent Orange. But Evans persisted and pushed through a compromise bill in January 1991, which Stump supported.

Stump has been a member of Veterans' Affairs throughout his House career, except for the period of 1983 to 1987, when he took a leave to serve on the Select Intelligence Committee.

At Home: Secure after his first election to this northern Arizona seat in 1976, Stump had plenty of time to contemplate his party switch. When he finally filed on the Republican side in 1982, it caused barely a ripple at home.

Stump said his decision would not cost him any significant support in either party. He was right, at least initially. Conservative rural Democrats proved willing to move with him, while many of the retirees who had flocked to the region had brought GOP voting habits with them. Stump coasted to victory with 63 percent of the vote. His subsequent re-elections were uneventful until 1990, when a virtual unknown, Roger Hartstone, garnered 43 percent of the vote. A commercial photographer and self-described environmentalist, the Democrat launched a write-in effort after Stump successfully challenged his nomination petitions.

Hartstone ran an effective grass-roots campaign, searing Stump as "the phantom of Congress" who rarely returned to the district. Hartstone attacked Stump's record on environmental and fiscal matters. Stump was also criticized for missing four important budget votes on a weekend when he attended an Arizona State football game; Stump said he had been assured by the House leadership that no crucial votes would occur.

In 1992, Hartstone won the Democratic nomination to oppose Stump. He rehashed the same campaign themes as in 1990, but voters seemed less impressed the second time around. Stump was re-elected by a wide margin.

Stump served 18 years in the state Legislature and rose to the presidency of the state Senate during the 1975-76 session. When GOP Rep. Sam Steiger tried for the U.S. Senate in 1976, Stump ran for his House seat.

In the 1976 Democratic primary, he defeated a more liberal, free-spending opponent, Sid Rosen, a former state assistant attorney general. Stump drew 31 percent to Rosen's 25 percent, with the rest scattered among three others. In the fall campaign, Stump's GOP opponent was fellow state Sen. Fred Koory, the Senate minority leader. Stump wooed conservative Democrats by criticizing his party's vice presidential nominee, Walter F. Mondale. He was also helped by the candidacy of state Sen. Bill McCune, a Republican who ran as an independent and drained GOP votes from Koory.

Committees

Veterans' Affairs (Ranking)
Education, Training & Employment; Hospitals & Health Care

Armed Services (2nd of 22 Republicans)
Research & Technology (ranking); Military Installations & Facilities

Elections

1992 General		
Bob Stump (R)	158,906	(61%)
Roger Hartstone (D)	88,830	(34%)
Pamela Volponi (NL)	10,767	(4%)
1992 Primary		
Bob Stump (R)	38,634	(67%)
Barbara Keough (R)	18,603	(33%)
1990 General		
Bob Stump (R)	134,279	(57%)
Roger Hartstone (D)	103,018	(43%)

Previous Winning Percentages: **1988** (69%) **1986** (100%) **1984** (72%) **1982** (63%) **1980 *** (64%) **1978 *** (85%) **1976 *** (48%)

** Stump was elected as a Democrat in 1976-80.*

District Vote for President

1992

D 86,060 (32%)
R 109,840 (41%)
I 73,356 (27%)

Campaign Finance

	Receipts	Receipts from PACs		Expend-itures
1992				
Stump (R)	$233,476	$136,092	(58%)	$303,208
Hartstone (D)	$101,976	$82,800	(81%)	$99,133
1990				
Stump (R)	$231,127	$132,850	(57%)	$225,149
Hartstone (D)	$9,735	$2,650	(27%)	$9,353

Key Votes

1993	
Require parental notification of minors' abortions	Y
Require unpaid family and medical leave	N
Approve national "motor voter" registration bill	N
Approve budget increasing taxes and reducing deficit	N
Approve economic stimulus plan	N
1992	
Approve balanced-budget constitutional amendment	Y
Close down space station program	N
Approve U.S. aid for former Soviet Union	N
Allow shifting funds from defense to domestic programs	N
1991	
Extend unemployment benefits using deficit financing	N
Approve waiting period for handgun purchases	N
Authorize use of force in Persian Gulf	Y

Voting Studies

	Presidential Support		Party Unity		Conservative Coalition	
Year	**S**	**O**	**S**	**O**	**S**	**O**
1992	85	15	98	1	94	6
1991	78	22	97	3	97	3
1990	73 †	12 †	79	3	85 †	2 †
1989	72	27	96	2	90	5
1988	84	13	95	3	100	0
1987	81	19	95	3	98	2
1986	88	11	92	6	92	6
1985	84	16	93	6	96	4
1984	67	27	84	7	86	7
1983	77	18	91	6	92	7
1982	82	13	3	93	96	0
1981	74	18	17	81	97	0

† Not eligible for all recorded votes.

Interest Group Ratings

Year	ADA	AFL-CIO	CCUS	ACU
1992	0	8	75	100
1991	0	0	90	100
1990	6	9	80	100
1989	0	0	100	96
1988	0	0	85	100
1987	4	6	100	100
1986	0	8	100	100
1985	0	0	95	100
1984	5	17	79	86
1983	0	6	79	100
1982	0	0	89	100
1981	0	13	95	93

4 Jon Kyl (R)

Of Phoenix — Elected 1986; 4th Term

Born: April 25, 1942, Oakland, Neb.
Education: U. of Arizona, B.A. 1964, LL.B. 1966.
Occupation: Lawyer.
Family: Wife, Caryll Collins; two children.
Religion: Presbyterian.
Political Career: No previous office.
Capitol Office: 2440 Rayburn Bldg. 20515; 225-3361.

In Washington: During his short House tenure, Kyl has established a presence as an opponent of deep, rapid cuts in defense programs. He is a leader of the Conservative Opportunity Society, a caucus of GOP activists founded by Minority Whip Newt Gingrich of Georgia. A member of the ethics committee, Kyl helped spark the 1991 congressional reform movement with his efforts to expose the House bank scandal.

Kyl's fast ride to relative prominence now brings him to a fork in the road. Kyl is regarded as the strongest GOP prospect to run in 1994 for the Senate seat held by Arizona Democrat Dennis DeConcini. But if he gambles on a statewide campaign, Kyl will forsake a role in shaping the House Republicans' response to the policies of the Democrats who — with Bill Clinton's election as president in 1992 — have control of the federal government.

He will also have to forgo a position of House seniority: In just his fourth term, Kyl is ranking Republican on the Armed Services Military Forces Personnel Subcommittee.

Kyl's freshman appointment to Armed Services in 1987 gave him an immediate role. The "old guard" Republican committee leaders were well-suited to sign off on President Ronald Reagan's military buildup in the early 1980s. They were less suited for the tough debate over how far and fast to cut defense in the emerging post-Cold War era.

That job fell to such activist junior members as Kyl and GOP Rep. John R. Kasich of Ohio (now ranking member of the House Budget Committee), who quickly became spokesmen for conservative Republicans' defense priorities.

Kyl has been particularly involved in an often frustrating effort to preserve funding for the Strategic Defense Initiative (SDI), the anti-ballistic missile program first proposed by Reagan in 1983. Despite recent legislative setbacks, Kyl remains committed to deploying defensive weapons in space.

From its inception, critics had scoffed at the technical feasibility of the costly "star wars" program. By the end of Reagan's presidency — and the beginning of Kyl's tenure — momentum was building to limit the program.

During annual budget debates, Kyl advocated full funding of SDI budget requests by Presidents Reagan and George Bush, while liberals sought to deeply cut funding. The final dollar amount usually wound up somewhere in the middle. In 1990, Kyl lobbied Bush to veto a defense authorization bill because SDI funding was 40 percent below the administration's request, but Bush signed it, citing other priorities.

Kyl also fought unsuccessfully to block efforts to reorient SDI from a broad space "shield" to a more limited ground-based defensive system. Advocates of the latter approach said it would be less expensive and more feasible for near-term implementation. They also insisted that SDI conform to the 1972 U.S.-Soviet ABM Treaty, which they said would bar deployment of anti-missile weapons in space.

As the Soviet Union crumbled, Senate Armed Services Committee Chairman Sam Nunn of Georgia developed a plan. SDI would get substantial funding, but most of the money would be targeted to research on ground-based, not space-based, weapons.

Kyl and other SDI advocates saw an opening in early 1991 after the Persian Gulf War, when they pointed to Iraq's use of offensive Scud missiles as evidence of the continued threat of ballistic weapons. But Nunn and House Armed Services Committee Chairman Les Aspin of Wisconsin emphasized that the Patriot missiles used to shoot down the Scuds were ground-based. A March 1991 amendment by Kyl, which would have called on Bush to renegotiate the ABM treaty to allow deployment of SDI space weapons, was defeated by a 145-281 vote.

Kyl — who also pursues his interest in defense-related issues as a member of the Government Operations Subcommittee on Legislation and National Security — is nonetheless undeterred in his arguments to keep up the nation's guard, despite the seeming decline of the Cold War threat.

Kyl, along with Kasich and Republican Duncan Hunter of California, managed in 1992 to block final passage of a bill to reauthorize the

Arizona 4

Northern Phoenix; Scottsdale

Thanks to rapid growth in northern Phoenix and its suburbs during the 1980s, the 4th today is only a fraction of its former self in territory. The sparsely populated northeastern part of the state that made up most of the old 4th was shifted to the 6th in 1992 redistricting. But the electorate of the 4th remains virtually unchanged. This is Arizona's least minority-influenced district — 92 percent of its residents are white — and arguably its most conservative.

Previously in the 4th, most of the vote was cast in the comfortable confines of northern Phoenix and its Maricopa County suburbs. Now, the district is entirely within Maricopa, making it one of Arizona's two all-urban districts.

The 4th is one of four Arizona districts centered in Phoenix, incorporated in 1881 and currently the ninth-largest city in the nation. As both the state capital and Maricopa County seat, Phoenix is understandably the hub of activity in the state, although it is constantly battling Tucson to retain its pre-eminence in the eyes of employers relocating to Arizona. More than 3,200 manufacturing companies, employing more than 127,000 people, are in the Phoenix metropolitan area.

Northern Phoenix's white-collar population provides generous support for Republican candidates, as do similarly upscale residents in Scottsdale and other Maricopa County suburbs. In the 1992 presidential contest, the 4th was George Bush's best district in Arizona, giving him 43 percent of the vote to Bill Clinton's 31 percent and Ross Perot's 26 percent.

In remapping, the district extended farther west into Maricopa County, picking up several bedroom communities that add to Republican strength in the 4th.

Several high-technology firms have made their home in the 4th District. Honeywell has two plants in the district, and a number of residents work in Motorola's Government Tactical Electronics and Communications Division in Scottsdale.

The tourism industry adds to the economic base in the district. Scottsdale is an affluent resort community that attracts visitors with its warm, sunny climate, myriad golf courses and fashionable shops. Scottsdale grew by more than 46 percent in the past decade and is now home to about 130,000 people.

Many here are retirees; others commute to work at the management level in Phoenix corporations. In addition to Motorola Inc. and Honeywell, aerospace manufacturer Allied-Signal Co., American Express Travel Related Services Co. and US West Communications are among the largest employers in Phoenix. Community names such as Paradise Valley and Carefree bespeak the lifestyle ideal.

Democrats have a base of support in the southern part of the 4th, where the district stretches into downtown Phoenix. But only about one-third of the voters in the 4th are registered Democratic, compared with about 52 percent who call themselves Republicans.

1990 Population: 610,871. White 562,888 (92%), Black 11,434 (2%), Other 36,549 (6%). Hispanic origin 47,468 (8%). 18 and over 464,379 (76%), 62 and over 83,823 (14%). Median age: 34.

Export Administration Act. Kyl argued that the bill went too far in easing restrictions on U.S. exports of high-tech goods with potential military applications.

Although he has been mainly talking into the wind on defense issues, Kyl took a lead in placing the Democratic leadership on the defensive over its management of the now-defunct House bank and other institutional functions.

In late 1991, Kyl was a leading advocate of a House ethics committee investigation of evidence that many House members had been allowed penalty-free overdrafts at the House bank. When the committee in March 1992 voted to release only the names of the worst abusers of the bank, Kyl was one of four Republicans who insisted on releasing the names of all members who had overdrafts.

After a public outcry, the House voted to disclose the names of all members with overdrafts. Later in 1992, Kyl was appointed to a panel to investigate allegations of mismanagement, and possible misuse by some House members, of the House Post Office.

Even before Kyl grabbed a role as a reformer, his move to the ethics committee at the start of the 102nd Congress was considered shrewd. DeConcini, his potential 1994 Senate foe, had faced withering criticism for his ties to Charles H. Keating Jr., one of the savings and loan scandal's most prominent figures.

But the dogs of political reform have been known to turn on their handlers; Kyl has been nipped but not badly injured. A public interest group survey of House members in 1992 showed Kyl with the second-highest amount of office expenses. (Kyl explained that he had to provide constituent services for a then-expansive House district, which has since been shrunk in redistricting.) And in early 1993 — after the failure of Zoë Baird's nomination for attorney general made the ethics of household employment a major issue — Kyl had to deal with news reports that he may have neglected to pay required employer taxes for his part-time housekeeper. (He subsequently disproved them).

The chairman of the Conservative Opportunity Society during his second House term, Kyl has not neglected a fiscal agenda. In 1992, his proposed constitutional amendment to require a balanced budget and to limit federal spending to 19 percent of the gross national product was defeated by a 170-258 vote.

At Home: Launching a House campaign against a well-known former incumbent can be daunting. But for Kyl, the reputation of ex-GOP Rep. John Conlan, his 1986 primary foe, was a blessing. Conlan was the longtime nemesis of Arizona's GOP establishment, which backed Kyl. After dispatching Conlan, Kyl had little trouble thrashing a well-financed Democratic foe in this traditionally GOP district. In 1988, Democrats did not field a candidate.

The 1986 campaign was Kyl's first, but he was no newcomer to politics. The son of former GOP Rep. John H. Kyl of Iowa, he had been active in party affairs and lobbied the Arizona Legislature in behalf of highways, shopping centers and a local water project. A business-oriented attorney and former president of the Phoenix Chamber of Commerce, he won strong support from the corporate establishment.

But Kyl's success also depended on the specter of Conlan. An energetic and abrasive conservative religious activist, Conlan had alienated many Republicans in an acrimonious 1976 Senate primary. After losing that primary, Conlan refused to back nominee Sam Steiger, who then lost the general election.

Buttressed by endorsements from a string of Republicans, Kyl trounced Conlan by a 2-to-1 margin and easily won the right to succeed retiring GOP Rep. Eldon Rudd.

In 1990, Kyl further enhanced his reputation as a political comer in the state by easily defeating Mark Ivey, a doctor who was a former president of the Arizona Medical Association. In 1992, Kyl outlasted Democratic lawyer Walter Mybeck II and two other candidates.

Committees

Armed Services (8th of 22 Republicans)
Military Forces & Personnel (ranking); Oversight & Investigations

Government Operations (4th of 16 Republicans)
Legislation & National Security

Standards of Official Conduct (4th of 7 Republicans)

Elections

1992 General		
Jon Kyl (R)	156,330	(59%)
Walter R. Mybeck II (D)	70,572	(27%)
Debbie Collings (I)	25,553	(10%)
Tim McDermott (LIBERT)	11,611	(4%)
1990 General		
Jon Kyl (R)	141,843	(61%)
Mark Ivey Jr. (D)	89,395	(39%)

Previous Winning Percentages: **1988** (87%) **1986** (65%)

District Vote for President

1992
D 86,922 (31%)
R 118,927 (43%)
I 70,682 (26%)

Campaign Finance

	Receipts	Receipts from PACs		Expend-itures
1992				
Kyl (R)	$616,410	$163,168	(26%)	$458,358
McDermott (LIBERT)	$45	0		$35
Collings (I)	$18,356	0		$14,744
1990				
Kyl (R)	$588,180	$171,389	(29%)	$442,366
Ivey (D)	$39,515	$4,500	(11%)	$38,851

Key Votes

1993	
Require parental notification of minors' abortions	Y
Require unpaid family and medical leave	N
Approve national "motor voter" registration bill	N
Approve budget increasing taxes and reducing deficit	N
Approve economic stimulus plan	N
1992	
Approve balanced-budget constitutional amendment	Y
Close down space station program	N
Approve U.S. aid for former Soviet Union	N
Allow shifting funds from defense to domestic programs	N
1991	
Extend unemployment benefits using deficit financing	N
Approve waiting period for handgun purchases	N
Authorize use of force in Persian Gulf	Y

Voting Studies

	Presidential Support		Party Unity		Conservative Coalition	
Year	**S**	**O**	**S**	**O**	**S**	**O**
1992	90	10	95	4	96	4
1991	81	19	95	5	97	3
1990	79	19	94	4	96	4
1989	80	20	96	3	95	5
1988	78	19	93	3	97	0
1987	76	24	94	3	98	2

Interest Group Ratings

Year	ADA	AFL-CIO	CCUS	ACU
1992	5	33	75	92
1991	5	8	90	100
1990	6	0	86	92
1989	0	8	100	96
1988	0	8	93	100
1987	0	0	93	96

5 Jim Kolbe (R)

Of Tucson — Elected 1984; 5th Term

Born: June 28, 1942, Evanston, Ill.
Education: Northwestern U., B.A. 1965; Stanford U., M.B.A. 1967.
Military Service: Navy, 1968-69.
Occupation: Real estate consultant.
Family: Divorced.
Religion: Methodist.
Political Career: Ariz. Senate, 1977-83; Republican nominee for U.S. House, 1982.
Capitol Office: 405 Cannon Bldg. 20515; 225-2542.

In Washington: Energetic and voluble, Kolbe is not a natural fit for the reserved and tradition-bound Appropriations Committee. But that may not matter much because Kolbe appears as interested in advancing himself at home as influencing legislation in Washington.

Ambitious and positioned to channel projects to Arizona while championing budget reductions elsewhere, Kolbe is worth watching. Although he passed on a 1990 gubernatorial bid, he is often mentioned as a strong contender for higher office.

On Appropriations, Kolbe primarily promotes projects important to Arizona, but in committee and on the floor he is a loyal supporter of the GOP line, which helped him land a seat on the Budget Committee in the 102nd Congress. Like four of the five veteran Republicans appointed to the panel in 1991, he supported the 1990 budget summit agreement.

Despite his consistently high party-unity scores — he votes with the GOP more than 80 percent of the time — Kolbe has aligned himself with the "big tent" wing of the GOP, which aims to embrace more liberal-leaning members of the party. And during the 102nd, he entered that tent, voting to overturn the so-called "gag rule" prohibiting abortion counseling at federally funded clinics.

He also teamed up with then-Housing Secretary Jack F. Kemp to promote the Homeownership and Opportunity for People Everywhere program, known as HOPE. Kolbe's amendment tried to shift nearly $800 million in previously approved housing money to the program, which helps public housing tenants buy their units.

He opposed the B-2 bomber and also voted against the proposed constitutional amendment to ban flag desecration in 1990.

Kolbe is best known for his support of a free-trade agreement with Mexico, which shares a 100-mile border with his district. In 1992, Kolbe joined President George Bush and other administration officials in negotiations on the North American Free Trade Agreement and attended the Oct. 7 signing ceremony in San Antonio.

But with Bush out of the White House and Democrats considering revisions of the agreement, it is unclear how influential Kolbe will be in the ongoing debate.

Earlier, he was one of Congress' most vocal advocates for the *maquiladora* assembly plant arrangement, by which U.S. companies manufacture components, then ship the items to Mexico, where they are assembled. Because of Mexico's lower labor costs and the favorable tariff provisions, goods produced under this arrangement can be sold at prices that are competitive with Asian-produced goods, Kolbe says. Critics of the "twin plant" method say it encourages U.S. companies to close their domestic manufacturing plants and transfer manufacturing to cheap-wage Mexico.

Kolbe diligently watches over Arizona interests on Capitol Hill. In the 102nd Congress, he argued against increasing the fees charged ranchers who use federal lands for grazing, a controversial topic that resurfaced early in the Clinton administration. And each year he files a steady stream of bills aimed at protecting, preserving or opening a variety of Arizona parks, canyons, forests or ancient ruins.

One of two Arizonans on Appropriations, Kolbe often speaks out for funds aimed at flood control solutions, and for the Central Arizona Project, a massive system that brings water to Phoenix and other areas of the state.

In 1987, when the House debated the Energy and Water appropriations bill, Kolbe offered a successful floor amendment that barred construction of Cliff Dam, which environmentalists opposed. In return, an environmental coalition dropped a lawsuit opposing other parts of the project.

Kolbe's first term was spent on the Banking Committee, where then-Chairman Fernand J. St Germain of Rhode Island blocked him on a number of measures. But Kolbe did have some success with full-court legislative presses on the floor. He won passage of one amendment tight-

Arizona 5

Southeast — Tucson

Registered Democrats outnumber Republicans in the 5th, but the numerical advantage — less than 2 percent — is insignificant, especially considering that many of those who call themselves Democrats are of the rural, conservative, "pinto" variety. Thirteen percent of the district's voters are registered as independents.

At election time, this mix of swing voters and independents typically yields an advantage for Republican candidates in elections for higher office. The areas within the district have regularly backed Republican nominees in past presidential elections. But in the 1992 three-way race for the White House, Democrat Bill Clinton finished first in the 5th, taking 42 percent of the vote. GOP Rep. Kolbe was re-elected with 67 percent of the vote.

The 5th takes in the northeastern corner of Pima County, which includes most of Tucson. The only part of the city that is not in the 5th — its Hispanic neighborhoods — is strongly Democratic.

Redistricting by federal judges in 1992 put that southern part of the city into the 2nd District to help ensure the election of a Hispanic there.

Tucson, once Arizona's territorial capital, was the state's most populous city until it was surpassed by Phoenix in 1920. Largely a college town and resort center in the 1950s, Tucson today hosts an impressive number of high-technology companies.

Tucson and Prescott, in the northern part of the state, battled for the claim to be the territorial capital in the 1860s and 1870s.

The dispute was settled in 1889 by making Phoenix, located about halfway between the two cities, the permanent capital.

Hughes Aircraft is the largest private-sector employer in Tucson, and an IBM plant is on Tucson's southern outskirts. White-collar professional communities with firm Republican ties dominate the city's burgeoning east side.

Wealthy residents of the Santa Catalina foothills and retirees who worked at Davis-Monthan Air Force Base add to the Republican strength in the district. Green Valley, an outlying Pima County town that rivals Sun City among Arizona's largest retirement communities, also has become a major GOP force.

Democratic candidates get some help in the Tucson part of the 5th from voters in the residential area around the University of Arizona. (The campus itself is in the 2nd.) Although the university's student body of 35,000 leans conservative, the faculty and staff retain a Democratic allegiance, and they are more likely to vote than are students.

Outside Pima County, the 5th is largely desert.

The Old West county of Cochise, anchoring southeastern Arizona, is the home of Tombstone, "the town too tough to die." Notorious for its boomtown lawlessness in the late 1800s, Tombstone still mines some silver, but now its economy relies mainly on the tourist trade.

1990 Population: 610,871. White 537,525 (88%), Black 18,172 (3%), Other 55,174 (9%). Hispanic origin 100,874 (17%). 18 and over 465,370 (76%), 62 and over 107,977 (18%). Median age: 34.

ening training requirements for military procurement officers, and another cutting off aid to Lebanon until U.S. hostages were released.

Citing deficit-reduction as a priority, Kolbe refiled a bill in the 103rd Congress to manufacture a $1 coin. The Federal Reserve says using coins could save up to $500 million a year. "It won't solve the deficit, but it will be one of the less painful ways to save money."

At Home: Kolbe's 1984 victory did more than just avenge his narrow loss to Democrat James F. McNulty Jr. in 1982. It proved Kolbe had successfully convinced some rural 5th District residents that he was not as much a city slicker as they had thought.

Polished, articulate and brimming with nervous energy, Kolbe does not evoke the laid-back image associated with the rural Southwest. He seems more comfortable with the bustle of high-growth Tucson than with the slower pace of the district's desert and mountain towns.

In the 1982 GOP primary, he devoted much attention to Republican-rich Tucson and surrounding Pima County to win a tight three-way nomination contest. For rural residents, that linked him firmly with the city. Democrat McNulty, a plain-spoken man with a folksy air, pulled enough support from them for a 2,407-vote edge in November.

In gearing up for the rematch, Kolbe was determined not to fall into the same trap. Free of any primary opposition, Kolbe canvassed the 5th's desert and mountain counties. He aired TV advertisements showing him traversing the state on a horse. Kolbe reminded voters that he had spent much of his boyhood on a cattle ranch near the town of Sonoita — while McNulty was born and bred in Boston.

Kolbe's strategy paid off. Aided by a much better showing in the counties outside Pima, Kolbe ended with a 6,204-vote lead.

Kolbe's comeback also owed much to a change in the prevailing political conditions in the 5th. In 1982, McNulty had the advantage of running with two popular statewide Democrats at the top of the ticket. In 1984, Ronald Reagan's popularity helped Kolbe.

McNulty decided against a 1986 rematch, and local Democrats could not find a nominee of stature. Kolbe won with 65 percent.

In January 1988, Kolbe opened the door to a conservative primary challenge when he became the first Republican in Arizona's congressional delegation to call on embattled GOP Gov. Evan Mecham to resign. Mecham ultimately was removed from office by the GOP-controlled Legislature, but his conservative backers vowed revenge against Kolbe. Two Mecham supporters ran in the 5th's GOP primary; but most of the former governor's activists were bent on defeating state legislators — seven veterans were upset. Kolbe easily won both the primary and general election.

The far right threat may have enhanced Kolbe's position with independents. Their votes would be critical if Kolbe decides to seek a statewide office.

In 1990, potential legitimate Democratic candidates backed off to await the outcome of 1992 redistricting. As a result, Kolbe was blessed with an opponent whose major campaign splash occurred when he was jailed during the campaign on a charge of theft involving a purchase of a motor scooter. Chuck Phillips, a former social worker, had suffered previous clashes with the law, including serving three months for non-payment of child support. His campaign rejoinder: at least he had never been convicted of a felony.

Redistricting did not help Democrats in the 5th: In 1992, Kolbe easily defeated Jim Toevs, a former banker who moved to Tucson in 1990.

During his six years in the Arizona Senate, Kolbe was known as a member of the state GOP's moderate-to-liberal wing and frustrated some of his more conservative colleagues, with whom he clashed on social service issues.

Committees

Appropriations (12th of 23 Republicans)
Commerce, Justice, State & Judiciary; Interior

Budget (3rd of 17 Republicans)

Elections

1992 General		
Jim Kolbe (R)	172,867	(67%)
Jim Toevs (D)	77,256	(30%)
Perry Willis (LIBERT)	9,690	(4%)
1992 Primary		
Jim Kolbe (R)	37,140	(65%)
Mike Beehler (R)	19,921	(35%)
1990 General		
Jim Kolbe (R)	138,975	(65%)
Chuck Phillips (D)	75,642	(35%)

Previous Winning Percentages: **1988** (68%) **1986** (65%) **1984** (51%)

District Vote for President

1992

D 115,986 (42%)
R 104,301 (38%)
I 56,425 (20%)

Campaign Finance

	Receipts	Receipts from PACs	Expend-itures
1992			
Kolbe (R)	$409,883	$143,400 (35%)	$469,053
Toevs (D)	$104,313	$26,000 (25%)	$103,589
1990			
Kolbe (R)	$325,457	$133,605 (41%)	$250,642

Key Votes

1993	
Require parental notification of minors' abortions	N
Require unpaid family and medical leave	N
Approve national "motor voter" registration bill	N
Approve budget increasing taxes and reducing deficit	N
Approve economic stimulus plan	N
1992	
Approve balanced-budget constitutional amendment	Y
Close down space station program	Y
Approve U.S. aid for former Soviet Union	Y
Allow shifting funds from defense to domestic programs	N
1991	
Extend unemployment benefits using deficit financing	N
Approve waiting period for handgun purchases	N
Authorize use of force in Persian Gulf	Y

Voting Studies

	Presidential Support		Party Unity		Conservative Coalition	
Year	**S**	**O**	**S**	**O**	**S**	**O**
1992	77	21	84	13	81	19
1991	76	21	83	15	89	11
1990	64	31	82	14	87	11
1989	69	28	81	17	85	15
1988	58	38	88	10	89	3
1987	67	31	84	13	93	7
1986	69	29	84	13	88	8
1985	78	23	86	11	91	9

Interest Group Ratings

Year	ADA	AFL-CIO	CCUS	ACU
1992	25	25	88	76
1991	10	17	100	80
1990	22	8	86	61
1989	15	0	100	85
1988	20	14	93	80
1987	8	6	93	87
1986	20	7	88	73
1985	0	6	95	76

6 Karan English (D)

Of Flagstaff — Elected 1992; 1st Term

Born: March 23, 1949, Berkeley, Calif.
Education: U. of Arizona, B.A. 1973.
Occupation: Public official.
Family: Husband, Rob Elliot; two children; three stepchildren.
Religion: Unspecified.
Political Career: Coconino County Board of Supervisors, 1981-87, chairman, 1983-87; Ariz. House, 1987-91; Ariz. Senate, 1991-93.
Capitol Office: 1024 Longworth Bldg. 20515; 225-2190.

The Path to Washington: Fate may have played a role in English's victory.

She had intended to seek the Democratic nomination to oppose Republican Rep. Bob Stump in the 3rd District. But when three federal judges, who assumed the redistricting task after state lawmakers deadlocked, included English's Flagstaff home in the newly created 6th District, she decided to seek that seat instead.

The decision appears to have been a wise one. The absence of strongly Democratic Flagstaff in the 3rd strengthened Stump's position; he was easily re-elected to a ninth term. And English, a moderate Democrat who supports a constitutional balanced-budget amendment and the line-item veto, ended up opposing conservative Republican Doug Wead.

The demographics of the 6th were more conducive to a middle-of-the-road candidacy like English's: Democrats hold a registration advantage of about 4 percentage points over Republicans, and English's conservative economic views and more liberal social views — she favors abortion rights and stronger environmental protection — appealed to Democrats and Republicans alike.

Early in the 103rd Congress, she voted for a bill codifying the president's lifting of the so-called gag rule, which prohibited staff at federally funded family planning clinics from discussing abortion. She also voted for a bill in April 1993 to give the president modified line-item veto authority, though she voted against a more potent GOP substitute.

Local environmental concerns prompted English's initial foray into politics. While fighting to resolve water and sewer issues as a member of a neighborhood property owners association in Flagstaff, she was urged to seek a post on the Coconino County Board of Supervisors. She won election to the board in 1980 and four years later became its chairman.

English was elected to the state House in 1986 and to the state Senate in 1990. She chaired the state Senate Environment Committee as a freshman. Among the legislation that she pushed through were measures requiring environmental education in the state's elementary and high schools and establishing broad regulations for the handling of hazardous wastes.

English's support of stronger environmental regulations seems to run counter to the interests of the mining, ranching and logging industries central to the 6th's economy, but she argues that better management of natural resources can be economically beneficial. She will have a ready platform to achieve that goal — she won a seat on the Natural Resources Committee. She also has a seat on the Education and Labor Committee.

English had proved her vote-getting ability in her three state legislative races. She was elected to both the state House and Senate in GOP-dominated districts. In the Democratic congressional primary, English easily defeated state Senate Majority Leader Alan Stephens.

In the fall, English benefited from Wead's political baggage. Although Wead had won conservative friends by successfully spearheading a statewide initiative to require a two-thirds vote of the state Legislature to increase taxes, many voters questioned his motives because he had been in the state only two years before launching his congressional bid.

English made an issue of Wead's strong ties to religious activists. He was a minister of the Assemblies of God for nearly 20 years and frequent guest on, and sometimes host of, Jim Bakker's "PTL Club."

Not unexpectedly, English won the endorsement of the League of Conservation Voters. A number of women's groups, including the National Organization for Women and the National Women's Political Caucus, also backed her.

But in a surprising development, she also won the support of 1964 presidential contender and former Arizona Sen. Barry Goldwater, patriarch of the state GOP. (Goldwater's endorsement so irked some Republicans that, after the election, they considered removing his name from state GOP headquarters.)

In the end, voters gave English a 12-point margin of victory over Wead.

Arizona 6

Northeast — Flagstaff; Navajo reservation

The newly created 6th rivals the western 3rd in size, and American Indian reservations occupy much of its territory. Nearly 22 percent of the district's population — and about 18 percent of its voting-age population — is Indian.

From the expansive Navajo reservation, which occupies all of the northeastern corner of the state except for the Hopi reservation, the district runs southward through the San Carlos and Fort Apache reservations, then takes in Greenlee County and parts of Graham and Pinal counties. The eastern border of the 6th is the Arizona-New Mexico line; the western side of the district includes the cities of Gilbert and part of Mesa, in the Phoenix suburbs, as well as the Gila reservation south of Phoenix and the Salt River and Fort McDowell reservations north of the city.

By design, rural voters have a substantial voice in this district. The federal court that drew the new congressional boundaries excluded most of the Phoenix area (Maricopa County) from the 6th. The judges included the city of Flagstaff "to balance out the interests of Maricopa County."

With about 46,000 people, Flagstaff, the seat of Coconino County, is the district's largest city. Two interstate highways — I-40 and I-17 — intersect in Flagstaff, making it the commercial center of northern Arizona. Thanks to its proximity to the Grand Canyon, Flagstaff sees a lot of tourist traffic; other leading industries in the city are lumbering and mining. Flagstaff also is home to the Lowell Observatory, where astronomers in 1930 discovered the planet Pluto.

Voters in East Mesa and Gilbert add a conservative flavor to the centrist 6th. Many of the residents there work in the numerous manufacturing companies in Mesa. Maricopa County is losing one of its longtime economic pillars with the closure of Williams Air Force Base. The base, more than 50 years old, was the training ground for more Air Force pilots than any other U.S. base since World War II.

Despite English's rather easy victory in the 1992 House race here, it has the potential to be a politically competitive district. Democrats have a registration advantage of about 4 percentage points over Republicans, but nearly 9 percent of the district's registered voters claim no major-party affiliation.

Democrats are strongest in Flagstaff, where more than 15 percent of the residents are Hispanic, and in the northern part of the 6th, where the population is concentrated in mining towns and reservations.

The Navajos show a particular affinity for the Democratic Party. In Apache County, where the Navajo influence is most pronounced, Democrats outnumber Republicans by almost 4-1, and Terry Goddard won many precincts by margins of 10-1 in 1990 as the Democrats' unsuccessful gubernatorial nominee.

In 1992, George Bush squeaked out a narrow 230-vote victory over Bill Clinton, with Ross Perot finishing a distant third.

1990 Population: 610,872. White 429,716 (64%), Black 8,211 (1%), Other 172,945 (28%). Hispanic origin 79,277 (13%). 18 and over 424,811 (70%), 62 and over 99,143 (16%). Median age: 31.

Committees

Education & Labor (23rd of 28 Democrats)
Elementary, Secondary & Vocational Education; Legislation & National Security; Postsecondary Education

Natural Resources (19th of 28 Democrats)
National Parks, Forests & Public Lands; Native American Affairs; Oversight & Investigations

Campaign Finance

	Receipts	Receipts from PACs		Expend-itures
1992				
English (D)	$385,373	$127,937	(33%)	$391,015
Wead (R)	$669,568	$43,795	(7%)	$667,960

Key Votes

1993

Require parental notification of minors' abortions	N
Require unpaid family and medical leave	Y
Approve national "motor voter" registration bill	Y
Approve budget increasing taxes and reducing deficit	Y
Approve economic stimulus plan	Y

Elections

1992 General		
Karan English (D)	124,251	(53%)
Doug Wead (R)	97,074	(41%)
Sarah Stannard (I)	13,047	(6%)
1992 Primary		
Karan English (D)	23,389	(44%)
Alan Stephens (D)	15,710	(30%)
Albert Hale (D)	14,102	(27%)

District Vote for President

	1992	
D	91,247	(38%)
R	91,477	(38%)
I	56,368	(24%)

Arkansas

STATE DATA

Governor:
Jim Guy Tucker (D)

First elected: Replaced Bill Clinton; sworn in 12/12/92
Length of term: 4 years
Term expires: 1/95
Salary: $60,000
Term limit: 2 terms
Phone: (501) 682-2345
Born: June 13, 1943; Oklahoma City, Okla.
Education: Harvard U., B.A. 1964; U. of Arkansas, J.D. 1968
Military Service: Marine Corps Reserve, 1962-64
Occupation: Lawyer
Family: Wife, Betty Allen; four children
Religion: Presbyterian
Political Career: Ark. attorney general, 1973-77; U.S. House, 1977-79; sought Democratic nomination for U.S. Senate, 1978; sought Democratic nomination for governor, 1982; lieutenant governor, 1991-92

Lieutenant governor: Special election scheduled for July 1993

State election official: (501) 682-5070
Democratic headquarters: (501) 374-2361
Republican headquarters: (501) 372-7301

REDISTRICTING

Arkansas retained its four House seats in reapportionment. The legislature passed the new map March 26, 1991; the governor signed it April 10. Federal court upheld map Nov. 15; Supreme Court upheld map June 1, 1992.

STATE LEGISLATURE

General Assembly. Meets 60 calendar days, January-March, in odd-numbered years.

Senate: 35 members, 4-year terms
1992 breakdown: 30D, 5R; 34 men, 1 woman; 32 whites, 3 blacks
Salary: $12,500
Phone: (501) 682-6107

House of Representatives: 100 members, 2-year terms
1992 breakdown: 88R, 10D, 1I, 1 vacancy; 87 men, 12 women; 89 whites, 10 blacks
Salary: $12,500
Phone: (501) 375-7771

URBAN STATISTICS

City	Pop.
Little Rock	175,727
Mayor Jim Dailey, N-P	
Fort Smith	72,798
Mayor Ray Baker, N-P	
North Little Rock	61,829
Mayor Patrick Hays, D	
Pine Bluff	57,140
Mayor Jerry Taylor, I	

U.S. CONGRESS

Senate: 2 D, 0 R
House: 2 D, 2 R

TERM LIMITS

For Congress: Yes
Senate: 2 terms
House: 3 terms
For state offices: Yes
Senate: 2 terms
House: 3 terms

ELECTIONS

1992 Presidential Vote

Bill Clinton	53.2%
George Bush	35.5%
Ross Perot	10.4%

1988 Presidential Vote

George Bush	56%
Michael S. Dukakis	42%

1984 Presidential Vote

Ronald Reagan	61%
Walter F. Mondale	38%

POPULATION

1990 population		2,350,725
1980 population		2,286,435
Percent change		+3%
Rank among states:		33
White		83%
Black		16%
Hispanic		1%
Asian or Pacific islander		1%
Urban		54%
Rural		46%
Born in state		67%
Foreign-born		1%
Under age 18	621,131	26%
Ages 18-64	1,379,536	59%
65 and older	350,058	15%
Median age		33.8

MISCELLANEOUS

Capital: Little Rock
Number of counties: 75
Per capita income: $14,753 (1991)
Rank among states: 47
Total area: 53,187
Rank among states: 27

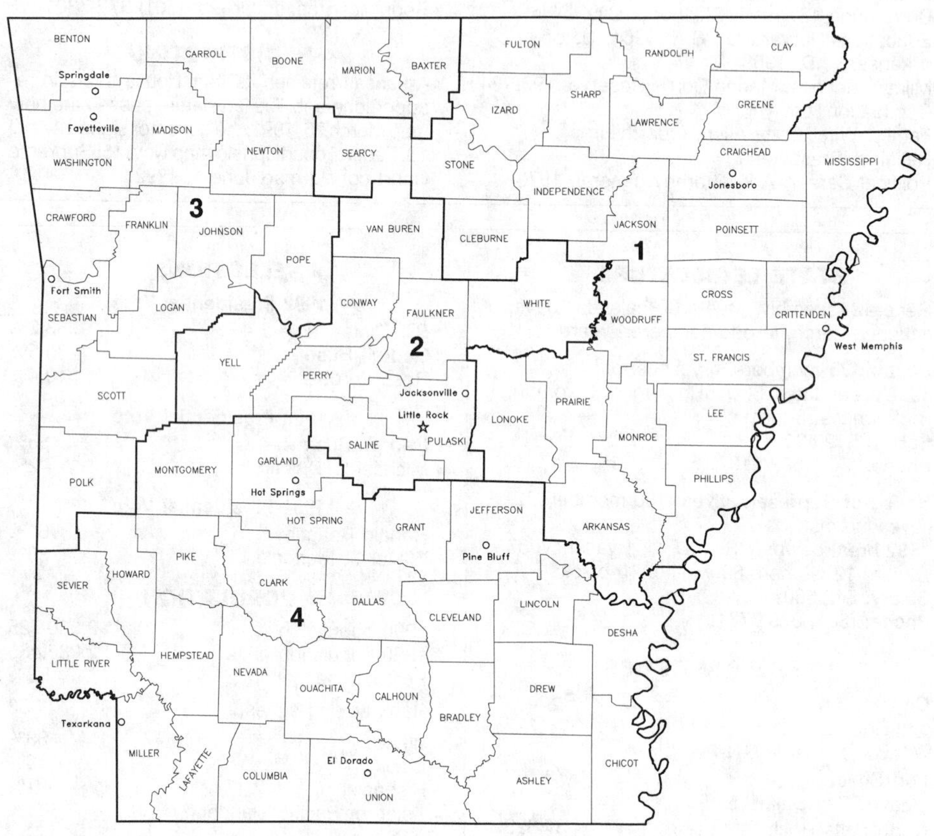
BENTON
CARROLL
BOONE
MARION
BAXTER
FULTON
RANDOLPH
CLAY
Springdale
Fayetteville
MADISON
WASHINGTON
NEWTON
SEARCY
IZARD
SHARP
LAWRENCE
GREENE
STONE
CRAIGHEAD
Jonesboro
MISSISSIPPI
INDEPENDENCE
CRAWFORD
3
FRANKLIN
JOHNSON
VAN BUREN
CLEBURNE
JACKSON
POINSETT
1
POPE
Fort Smith
SEBASTIAN
LOGAN
CONWAY
FAULKNER
WHITE
WOODRUFF
CROSS
CRITTENDEN
West Memphis
2
YELL
PERRY
ST. FRANCIS
SCOTT
Jacksonville
Little Rock
PULASKI
LONOKE
PRAIRIE
LEE
SALINE
MONROE
MONTGOMERY
GARLAND
Hot Springs
POLK
PHILLIPS
HOT SPRING
GRANT
JEFFERSON
Pine Bluff
ARKANSAS
PIKE
HOWARD
SEVIER
CLARK
DALLAS
CLEVELAND
LINCOLN
4
DESHA
LITTLE RIVER
HEMPSTEAD
NEVADA
OUACHITA
CALHOUN
DREW
BRADLEY
Texarkana
MILLER
LAFAYETTE
COLUMBIA
El Dorado
UNION
CHICOT
ASHLEY

Dale Bumpers (D)

Of Charleston — Elected 1974; 4th Term

Born: Aug. 12, 1925, Charleston, Ark.
Education: U. of Arkansas, 1946-48; Northwestern U., J.D. 1951.
Military Service: Marine Corps, 1943-46.
Occupation: Lawyer; farmer; hardware company executive.
Family: Wife, Betty Flanagan; three children.
Religion: Methodist.
Political Career: Governor, 1971-75.
Capitol Office: 229 Dirksen Bldg. 20510; 224-4843.

In Washington: The election of a fellow Arkansan as president is something of a mixed blessing for Bumpers. It probably eliminated whatever faint prospect he might have had ever to occupy the White House himself. Still, the home-state connection could boost Bumpers' stature and influence on Capitol Hill, where, despite his seniority, he is neither part of the leadership nor chairman of a major committee.

Bumpers and Clinton talk regularly. They generally work well together and share the same liberal-to-moderate philosophy. But it is David Pryor, the state's junior senator, who has always been closer to Clinton and will be his primary eyes and ears in the Senate. One former state Democratic official described the relationship between Clinton and Bumpers as one of "mutual respect." In 1990, there was even speculation among some observers that Clinton was thinking of challenging Bumpers in 1992. As it happened, Clinton took aim at a bigger target. And Bumpers, busy with his own primary and general-election challenges, had little time to campaign for Clinton.

Bumpers won his seat in 1974 by defeating the legendary Sen. J. William Fulbright, for whom Clinton worked during college, and that chilled relations with Clinton at the time.

In many ways Bumpers — who preceded both Pryor and Clinton as governor of Arkansas — paved the way for Clinton. He modernized the state's government and moved its politics to the left on issues such as education and race relations. Both as governor and as senator, Bumpers has had no trouble winning voter acceptance, despite his state's conservative tendencies. His eloquent oratory and amiable manner have overcome whatever reservations the voters might harbor about his liberalism.

When Quentin N. Burdick died at the end of the 102nd Congress, Bumpers took over the Appropriations Subcommittee on Agriculture. That should allow him to channel much-needed federal funds to Arkansas, which is heavily dependent on agriculture.

On Appropriations, Bumpers has used his various subcommittee posts to promote health programs for the poor, aid for rural areas and the rice subsidies important to his state. At the start of the 101st Congress, he traded his chairmanship of the Legislative Branch Subcommittee — a housekeeping panel unsuited to a man focused on national and international issues — for a seat on the Defense Subcommittee, where he could pursue his interests in arms control.

Bumpers also is chairman of the Small Business Committee, a panel that offers a forum for his populist creed, but not one that he has used to shape major areas of public policy.

Bumpers' distinctive style suits the individualist Senate and its permissive rules, but it does not always sit well with fellow senators. He is not quarrelsome, but he takes pleasure in argument. The fewer allies he has, the more likely he is to be on his feet at his back-of-the-chamber desk, extemporaneously weaving facts, figures and anecdotes to explain to absent colleagues why an action they are about to take is senseless.

A natural iconoclast, Bumpers is rarely deterred by an empty chamber. He delivers orations on topics from nuclear missiles to the rights of satellite-dish owners that can be dazzling to hear, if tiresome to those who work with him regularly. Calm, patient and engaging in private, Bumpers can seem downright obstreperous when he gets going in public.

A regular subject of these speeches is the 1872 Mining Act, which Bumpers wants to revamp to charge royalties for mining on public lands. Since the fall of 1988, Bumpers has introduced three bills to update the mining law and has also tried to accomplish his aims through riders on appropriations bills. So far, he has been blocked each time by Western senators whose states depend heavily on mining. Clinton embraced Bumpers' position in his budget, but after Western Democrats threatened to withhold support for his economic package, Clinton backed off. He said he still wanted mining reform and increased grazing fees on public lands, but would press them through separate legislation.

Bumpers' interest in mining law reform goes

hand in hand with his zealousness on reducing the budget deficit. Even 12 years after the fact, Bumpers still brags that his votes on the Reagan economic package — in favor of the spending cuts but against the tax cuts — would have prevented the rise in the deficit during the 1980s. He has long been an opponent of the space station and superconducting super collider because of what he sees as their excessive price tags.

"It would be nice to know the origin of matter," Bumpers said in a 1991 discussion on the super collider. "It would also be nice to have a balanced budget."

On the Energy Committee, Bumpers' streak of populism and his environmentalist stance have put him in repeated conflict with oil and mining interests. He joined other liberals in the late 1970s in fighting deregulation of oil and natural gas prices, and favored a stiff windfall-profits tax on the oil companies.

In the 100th Congress, Bumpers finally won an eight-year struggle to reform the system of leasing oil and gas drilling rights on federal lands — a campaign that began when he found that land in Arkansas near hundreds of producing wells was leased for $1 an acre.

Bumpers is a critic of nuclear power, though he has failed in his effort to bar utilities from passing on to consumers the costs of closing nuclear power plants. Bumpers was the most vociferous Senate opponent of the Clinch River breeder reactor in Tennessee. He came within one vote of killing the expensive project in 1982, and finally won in 1984.

In the 1980s, Bumpers was perhaps best known as one of the Senate's most outspoken supporters of arms control. With the Cold War over, he has tried to combine his zeal for budget cutting with his desire to limit the military.

In 1992, he sponsored an amendment to the defense appropriations bill that would have cut $1 billion for national intelligence programs; it was rejected 35-57. He withdrew another amendment to the same bill that would have stopped purchase of the Trident II missile at a savings of $900 million the first year. He was successful in requiring the Pentagon to study the merit of refurbishing the Trident I missile.

For Bumpers, who once accused President Ronald Reagan of not wanting "to spend money on anything that does not explode," the MX missile was a special target. He offered repeated amendments in the 1980s to kill the MX, which finally was capped at 50 in a 1985 compromise.

Bumpers has also been a major opponent of the Strategic Defense Initiative. While he was successful in getting Congress to vote to slow development of the SDI program, he failed in 1990 to pass an amendment to the defense authorization bill to cut overall spending on the program by $600 million.

During consideration of the defense bill in 1990, Bumpers unsuccessfully targeted Navy battleships and military base closings. His amendment to retire one of the two remaining *Iowa*-class ships equipped with cruise missiles fell by 11 votes. His amendment to nullify the secretary of Defense's list of bases to be closed suffered the same fate; among the bases slated for closure was Eaker Air Force Base in Blytheville, Ark., shut down in 1991.

As liberal as much of his work makes Bumpers sound, his iconoclasm makes him difficult to label. In 1978 he was the only senator to vote against popular "sunset" legislation for periodic reviews of all federal agencies. In 1987, as Small Business chairman, he allied with then-Sen. Dan Quayle of Indiana to oppose Labor Committee Chairman Edward M. Kennedy's bill requiring all employers to provide health insurance. In 1988, he clashed with liberal House members over revamping the scandal-plagued program that reserves federal contracts for minority-owned firms. House negotiators felt Bumpers' bill was too tough on minority firms. And in 1992, Bumpers and Pryor were among the five Southern Democrats who joined Republicans in blocking Senate action on legislation to bar the permanent replacement of striking workers.

At Home: "A smile and a shoeshine" was the phrase Winthrop Rockefeller used to describe the political phenomenon that removed him from the Arkansas governorship in 1970. It was a slur on Bumpers' intellectual substance, but it was not a bad description of the campaign that lifted him from a small-town law practice to the state Capitol in a remarkably short time.

Rockefeller had made Bumpers' accession possible by discrediting and retiring most of the segregationist "old guard" that had dominated the Democratic Party in Arkansas over the previous two decades. After four years of Republican rule under Rockefeller, the state was ready to go Democratic again under a modern leader. Bumpers was so clearly the right man that a smile, a shoeshine and a sophisticated set of TV ads were more than enough to give him a victory over the legendary race-baiter Orval E. Faubus in a Democratic primary runoff and an easy win over Rockefeller in the fall. Issues were beside the point.

Bumpers' gubernatorial campaign was so vague that the state had little reason to know what it was getting when he took office in January 1971. In fact, it was getting a man with a fair degree of liberal Yankee influence, a graduate of Northwestern University law school and a longtime admirer of Adlai E. Stevenson, who was governor of Illinois when Bumpers got his law degree. Bumpers came to the governorship without any political experience beyond the School Board in Charleston, Ark., but with a clear sense of where he was going.

During four years in office, Bumpers presided over a modernization of state government, closing down many of the bureaucratic fiefdoms that old-guard Democrats had controlled. By early 1974, he was ready for national politics. State Democrats braced themselves for a titanic struggle between the governor and Fulbright, who had helped raise money for Bumpers in 1970.

As it turned out, the struggle failed to live up to its advance billing. Bumpers decided to run only after political consultant Deloss Walker showed him polls guaranteeing he could not lose. Bumpers defeated Fulbright by nearly 2-to-1 in the Democratic primary without offering a critical word or a divisive issue.

The 1980 election was nothing to worry about either. While other Arkansas Democrats were finally paying the price for a decade of too-easy liberal politics, Bumpers was winning a second term by 150,000 votes.

In 1986, Republicans nominated an aggressive challenger in Asa Hutchinson, who had served as U.S. attorney in Little Rock under the Reagan administration. Bumpers took nothing for granted, turning up at hundreds of barbecues, fish-fries and other gatherings, re-establishing his roots by using the down-home style that had first vaulted him to success. Bumpers improved on his 1980 showing.

In the 1992 election, the Republicans came up with another plausible candidate, Mike Huckabee, a Baptist minister. Huckabee was showcased at the GOP National Convention but his challenge was hopeless in a year when the state's favorite son, Clinton, was at the top of the ticket.

Committees

Small Business (Chairman)
Export Expansion & Agricultural Development; Innovation, Manufacturing & Technology; Rural Economy & Family Farming

Appropriations (8th of 16 Democrats)
Agriculture, Rural Development & Related Agencies (chairman); Commerce, Justice, State & Judiciary; Defense; Interior; Labor, Health & Human Services & Education

Energy & Natural Resources (2nd of 11 Democrats)
Public Lands, National Parks & Forests (chairman); Energy Research & Development; Mineral Resources Development & Production

Elections

1992 General		
Dale Bumpers (D)	553,635	(60%)
Mike Huckabee (R)	366,373	(40%)
1992 Primary		
Dale Bumpers (D)	322,458	(65%)
Julia Hughes Jones (D)	177,273	(35%)

Previous Winning Percentages: **1986** (62%) **1980** (59%) **1974** (85%)

Campaign Finance

	Receipts	Receipts from PACs		Expenditures
1992				
Bumpers (D)	$1,940,691	$652,385	(34%)	$1,878,472
Huckabee (R)	$905,215	$13,119	(1%)	$910,212

Key Votes

1993	
Require unpaid family and medical leave	Y
Approve national "motor voter" registration bill	Y
Approve budget increasing taxes and reducing deficit	Y
Support president's right to lift military gay ban	Y
1992	
Approve school-choice pilot program	N
Allow shifting funds from defense to domestic programs	Y
Oppose deeper cuts in spending for SDI	N
1991	
Approve waiting period for handgun purchases	Y
Raise senators' pay and ban honoraria	N
Authorize use of force in Persian Gulf	N
Confirm Clarence Thomas to Supreme Court	N

Voting Studies

	Presidential Support		Party Unity		Conservative Coalition	
Year	**S**	**O**	**S**	**O**	**S**	**O**
1992	28	72	69	29	71	29
1991	40	59	82	16	70	30
1990	35	62	84	14	57	43
1989	50	50	87	12	26	71
1988	44	50	84	7	41	57
1987	38	58	89	11	38	59
1986	39	59	77	20	49	47
1985	32	62	79	17	52	45
1984	36	53	76	14	45	51
1983	32	56	85	10	41	45
1982	30	63	86	11	20	74
1981	39	52	81	8	20	69

Interest Group Ratings

Year	ADA	AFL-CIO	CCUS	ACU
1992	90	75	10	15
1991	70	67	20	24
1990	72	56	33	23
1989	90	90	25	21
1988	80	79	33	12
1987	85	70	35	8
1986	70	64	47	22
1985	70	71	45	13
1984	75	60	42	18
1983	75	82	17	17
1982	85	81	21	26
1981	95	84	24	13

David Pryor (D)

Of Little Rock — Elected 1978; 3rd Term

Born: Aug. 29, 1934, Camden, Ark.
Education: U. of Arkansas, B.A. 1957, LL.B. 1964.
Occupation: Lawyer; newspaper publisher.
Family: Wife, Barbara Lunsford; three children.
Religion: Presbyterian.
Political Career: Ark. House, 1961-67; U.S. House, 1967-73; sought Democratic nomination for U.S. Senate, 1972; governor, 1975-79.
Capitol Office: 267 Russell Bldg. 20510; 224-2353.

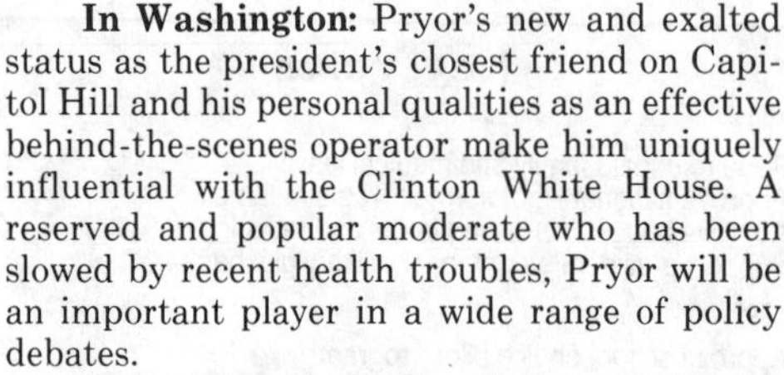

In Washington: Pryor's new and exalted status as the president's closest friend on Capitol Hill and his personal qualities as an effective behind-the-scenes operator make him uniquely influential with the Clinton White House. A reserved and popular moderate who has been slowed by recent health troubles, Pryor will be an important player in a wide range of policy debates.

Pryor suffered a heart attack in April 1991 and spent the spring and summer in Arkansas recuperating; in November 1992, he underwent heart bypass surgery. At a time when Bill Clinton would love to have Pryor vigorously promoting his legislative agenda, Pryor must pace himself. (He will, for example, have to forgo Clinton's renowned midnight bull-and-pizza sessions.)

Still, he remains an active force in the Senate. Indeed, even as he was recovering from the heart attack in Arkansas, he continued to vote on key bills, casting proxy votes on such matters before the Finance Committee as unemployment compensation and renewal of most-favored-nation status for China.

Pryor's doctors called the heart attack moderate and counseled him to cut back his activities. He had been serving on five committees, as well as holding the No. 3 party leadership position as secretary of the Democratic Caucus.

Few were surprised when Pryor responded to the medical advice by resigning from the Senate Ethics Committee, on which he had served 11 years. Ethics is always a thankless task, even by this dutiful senator's standards.

Pryor's tour of duty on Ethics had been especially stressful in 1990 and early 1991 as the committee weighed charges that five senators had used their influence to help savings and loan executive Charles H. Keating Jr., a major fundraiser.

Pryor's statements and questions during the proceedings suggested that he leaned toward relatively lenient treatment of his colleagues. In February, the committee decided that only Democrat Alan Cranston of California should be subject to further punishment by the full Senate; the other four received mild rebukes.

Pryor's heart attack indirectly delayed the case for months even though he had resigned from the panel. His replacement on Ethics, New Mexico Democrat Jeff Bingaman, recused himself from the Keating case after discovering a potential conflict of interest. As a result, Pryor was reassigned to the committee to help make the long-delayed decision about whether to punish Cranston. In November 1991, the Ethics Committee "strongly and severely" reprimanded Cranston.

After years of relatively low-profile labors and middling success, Pryor began the 101st Congress not only as conference secretary but also as chairman of the Special Committee on Aging.

He had won the leadership post when Daniel K. Inouye of Hawaii left it to run unsuccessfully for majority leader. Pryor was elected easily in the same closed-door balloting that elected George J. Mitchell of Maine majority leader in November 1988.

Some of Pryor's colleagues indicated that, as the only Southerner on the new leadership team, he had won at least in part because of the regional and philosophical balance he lent to Mitchell and Cranston, the Democratic whip. But Pryor also seemed to have been more personally popular with his colleagues than his rival for conference secretary, Patrick J. Leahy of Vermont. Pryor seemed especially well-regarded by younger members who admired his longstanding crusade against filibusters, dilatory floor tactics, quorum calls and extended roll call votes.

Pryor has long been one of the members most disturbed by the unreasonable demands the Senate schedule often puts on family life. He organized an informal panel of six senators who began pushing for changes aimed at restoring some measure of discipline to the way the Senate conducts its business. In 1985, his efforts helped produce an informal package of time-saving rules, such as limiting most votes to

15 minutes. The group's recommendation that the Senate work three weeks, then take a week off, has become the standard calendar. In 1992, he was named to the bipartisan Joint Committee on the Organization of Congress, which looked at ways to reform how Congress operates.

The chair of the Aging panel fell to Pryor when predecessor John Melcher met unexpected defeat in Montana in 1988. Pryor has since set about re-establishing himself as a leader on the issue that helped vault him into prominence. As a young legislator in Little Rock in the 1960s, he showed an inspired knack for attracting public attention to the concerns of the elderly. Later, while serving in the House, Pryor ran a kind of rogue subcommittee on the needs of the elderly, operating out of trailers parked near the House office buildings. With the House's decision to abolish its Select Aging Committee in the 103rd Congress, Pryor becomes Congress' premier figure on issues affecting the elderly.

Pryor has garnered national attention from his Aging Committee post as an outspoken critic of the prices pharmaceutical companies charge for prescription drugs.

The drug industry has been a particular target for Pryor since 1989 when, he says, pharmaceutical companies helped spawn a rebellion by senior citizens against the 1988 law that gave catastrophic health insurance to Medicare beneficiaries.

In 1990, he helped push through requirements that drug companies give the same or similar price breaks to state-federal Medicaid programs for the poor as they were providing to other bulk-drug purchasers, such as hospitals and the Department of Veterans Affairs.

But when drug companies responded by raising prices for other buyers instead of lowering them for Medicaid, Pryor upped the ante. In the 102nd Congress, he and William S. Cohen of Maine, the Aging Committee's ranking Republican, cosponsored a bill that would have punished drug companies that increased prices by more than inflation by reducing by a comparable amount the tax break they received for basing their operations in Puerto Rico. Pryor offered a slightly altered version of the legislation to a fast-track tax bill in 1992. The Senate killed it on a 61-36 vote.

The issue took on heightened prominence in the 103rd Congress as Clinton and first lady Hillary Rodham Clinton, who chaired the administration's Health Care Reform Task Force, took the drug industry to task over the high price of prescription drugs.

Melcher's upset also raised Pryor to the No. 2 Democratic slot on the Agriculture Committee, behind Leahy. Here he had already proved an effective member, helping to create a new "marketing loan" program for cotton and rice growers in the 1985 farm bill and protecting Southern soybean growers from a price-formula change in 1988.

On the 1990 farm bill, he worked with Republican Thad Cochran of Mississippi, a kindred spirit with whom he shared an interest in rice, cotton, soybeans and bipartisan cooperation. One aide who worked on the bill described the two working together "like brothers," but they could not match the success they had achieved for soybean producers five years earlier. Pryor complained that the fiscal squeeze was being misplaced. "It's hard for soybeans to contribute to deficit reduction when they don't contribute to the deficit," he said.

When it comes to Arkansas agriculture, Pryor will even reach for some of the procedural tools he generally decries. When a bill cutting federal farm price supports came to the Senate floor in 1984, he and Arkansas colleague Dale Bumpers worried that the measure would harm their rice farmers. To delay action on the time-sensitive bill, they began to read their favorite rice recipes into the Congressional Record. "I think I know of about 1,000 dishes with rice in them," Pryor said, to the delight of the galleries and the chagrin of the leadership.

Pryor has been less active on the Finance Committee. He took a rather hands-off attitude toward most of the tax-reform upheaval of the 99th Congress. But as chairman of the subcommittee with Internal Revenue Service oversight, he has been a critic of the agency's "fearsome" powers and a voice for "taxpayers' rights" legislation. In the 100th Congress, he wrote a "taxpayer bill of rights," which offered new protections against alleged IRS harassment. It became law as part of a 1988 tax technical corrections bill.

Pryor also has taken an interest in defense spending. In 1988, he amended the defense appropriations bill to require all consultants hired by the Pentagon to disclose their other clients. Passed by voice vote in the midst of publicity over alleged procurement fraud, Pryor's amendment was Congress' first response to the perceived scandal. But in the fall, House and Senate conferees quietly dropped it.

The military budget had previously attracted Pryor's eye, even before reports that the Pentagon had spent $600 for a toilet seat. But Pryor has had limited success with his efforts to impose stringent controls. One of his prime targets has been "sole source" defense contracts, by which the Pentagon certifies that only one company is qualified to produce a particular weapon. Pryor advocates competitive bidding to award contracts.

Pryor has been a longtime critic of a radar jammer designated ASPJ, intended for Navy fighter planes. Under development since the mid-1970s, the ASPJ repeatedly has failed to perform up to specification in tests. The Senate adopted Pryor's amendment in 1992 to bar any expenditures for ASPJ.

A longtime advocate of direct elections for president, Pryor's call for abolishing the Electoral College received greater attention in 1992 with the prospect that independent candidate Ross Perot could cause a deadlocked election. A Judiciary subcommittee held hearings on his constitutional amendment to provide for direct elections for president.

At Home: An impressive 1984 re-election performance and a foundering state GOP combined to ensure Pryor's re-election in 1990. His bid for a third Senate term was locked up when the GOP failed even to field a challenger. With his only opposition coming from an independent write-in candidate, Pryor was free to help former Democratic Rep. Ray Thornton, a onetime rival who was seeking a comeback by running for the open 2nd District seat. Thornton won.

In 1984, in a convincing demonstration of the personal popularity he had built up over 21 years in office, Pryor easily defeated the strongest possible GOP challenger even as Arkansas went decisively for President Ronald Reagan.

Pryor's 1983 voting record — he opposed Reagan's positions more often than any other senator — encouraged national GOP officials to believe he could be turned out in a Reagan landslide, and they urged Arkansas Rep. Ed Bethune to make the race. Throughout the campaign, Bethune predicted that 1984 would bring a revolutionary change in Arkansas politics as traditional Democrats came to realize that the Democratic Party had been "taken over by the liberals."

But Pryor was well-positioned to blunt Bethune's efforts at casting the race in ideological terms. In the eyes of most Arkansans, Pryor was not a liberal ogre who had "gone Washington"; he was a personable moderate who kept in touch with a large network of friends he had gained as a state legislator, congressman, governor and senator.

Pryor stressed the more conservative and populist aspects of his record, reminding voters of his support for a balanced-budget constitutional amendment and defense of the Rural Electrification Administration (REA) against Bethune's proposal to abolish the low-rate federal loans the REA grants to utility cooperatives.

Reagan campaigned in Arkansas the weekend before the election, but his presence was no aid to Bethune. Pryor won 57 percent, nearly matching Bumpers' 1980 re-election tally over a much weaker Republican foe.

Pryor has always had a talent for picking issues that bring favorable exposure in Arkansas. He was still in his 20s, struggling and outnumbered against the segregationist "Old Guard" in the state General Assembly, when he began investigating abuses in nursing homes. That issue helped him win a House seat in 1966, when the 4th District was left vacant with the departure of veteran Democrat Oren Harris. Once settled in Washington, Pryor ran unopposed in 1968 and 1970.

In 1972 Pryor took on a challenge that virtually every Democrat in the state told him he could not win: a primary campaign against the venerable senior senator, John L. McClellan. Pryor was determined, and he campaigned intensely all over the state for months, raising the issue of McClellan's age, which was 76. When he held the senator to 44 percent in the initial primary in May, forcing a runoff, Arkansas' startled Democrats assumed that Pryor had McClellan cornered. That was the second wrong assumption of the spring. The veteran fought back with surprising vigor in the runoff, seizing on Pryor's labor support to argue that union bosses wanted to get even for past McClellan corruption probes. On runoff night, Pryor lost by 18,000 votes.

Two years after his defeat, Pryor was elected governor, spoiling a comeback effort by Gov. Orval E. Faubus in that year's runoff. Faubus' once-vaunted political power had faded, along with the race issue that had fueled it, and his allies in the Arkansas business establishment deserted him for Pryor. Faubus called Pryor the "candidate of 52 millionaires" seeking to influence state policy, but the result was not even close. Pryor had no trouble winning the general election that fall, or a second two-year term in 1976.

Late in 1977, McClellan died. Pryor appointed Kaneaster Hodges to fill out the late senator's term. Under state law, Hodges was ineligible to succeed himself, and Pryor moved in on the seat in 1978.

This time he was no longer fighting the Old Guard. His competition in the primary came from two moderate representatives, Jim Guy Tucker of Little Rock and Thornton, who had succeeded Pryor in the 4th District House seat.

Pryor's pro-labor image had long since faded. As governor, he lost union support by sending in the National Guard to replace striking Pine Bluff firefighters. In the two-man runoff, Tucker got the labor endorsement; Pryor made an issue of it.

Pryor won the runoff by a surprising 47,000 votes, picking up much of the southern Arkansas support that had gone at first to Thornton, a close third in the initial primary. The general election against Republican Thomas Kelly was easy; Pryor won by more than 3-to-1.

Committees

Conference Secretary

Special Aging (Chairman)

Agriculture, Nutrition & Forestry (2nd of 10 Democrats)
Agricultural Production & Stabilization of Prices (chairman); Domestic & Foreign Marketing & Product Promotion; Nutrition & Investigations

Finance (6th of 11 Democrats)
Private Retirement Plans & Oversight of the Internal Revenue Service (chairman); Medicare & Long Term Care; Taxation

Governmental Affairs (5th of 8 Democrats)
Federal Services, Post Office & Civil Service (chairman); Oversight of Government Management; Permanent Subcommittee on Investigations

Joint Organization of Congress

Elections

1990 General

David Pryor (D)	493,910	(100%)

Previous Winning Percentages: **1984** (57%) **1978** (77%) **1970** *(100%) **1968** *(100%) **1966** * (65%)

** House elections.*

Campaign Finance

	Receipts	Receipts from PACs	Expend-itures
1990			
Pryor (D)	$1,228,545	$485,067 (39%)	$368,579

Key Votes

1993

Require unpaid family and medical leave	Y
Approve national "motor voter" registration bill	Y
Approve budget increasing taxes and reducing deficit	Y
Support president's right to lift military gay ban	Y

1992

Approve school-choice pilot program	N
Allow shifting funds from defense to domestic programs	Y
Oppose deeper cuts in spending for SDI	N

1991

Approve waiting period for handgun purchases	?
Raise senators' pay and ban honoraria	#
Authorize use of force in Persian Gulf	N
Confirm Clarence Thomas to Supreme Court	N

Voting Studies

	Presidential Support		Party Unity		Conservative Coalition	
Year	**S**	**O**	**S**	**O**	**S**	**O**
1992	27	73	76	22	61	32
1991	19	31	33	7	28	8
1990	34	62	85	13	65	32
1989	53	45	80	18	42	55
1988	48	47	85	11	49	43
1987	32	59	87	7	47	41
1986	35	60	70	24	55	38
1985	32	66	79	15	50	42
1984	45	47	60	25	72	23
1983	27	71	78	14	57	34
1982	45	49	73	23	56	35
1981	47	48	80	15	54	42

Interest Group Ratings

Year	ADA	AFL-CIO	CCUS	ACU
1992	90	75	30	15
1991	30	80	50	11
1990	67	56	25	18
1989	80	89	25	27
1988	75	79	43	16
1987	75	67	47	15
1986	60	40	53	33
1985	80	76	41	4
1984	55	60	50	38
1983	70	71	33	28
1982	70	69	45	55
1981	75	47	53	21

1 Blanche Lambert (D)

Of Helena — Elected 1992; 1st Term

Born: Sept. 30, 1960, Helena, Ark.
Education: Randolph-Macon Woman's College, B.A. 1982.
Occupation: Government affairs specialist; congressional aide.
Family: Single.
Religion: Episcopalian.
Political Career: No previous office.
Capitol Office: 1204 Longworth Bldg. 20515; 225-4076.

The Path to Washington: Just 32 years old, with no experience in elective office, Lambert might not seem likely to be a major mover in a freshman class that is mostly made up of seasoned political pros. But this ambitious farmer's daughter is not to be underestimated.

At home, she came from nowhere to unseat a veteran incumbent in the primary. In Washington, with the help of Mike Synar of Oklahoma, she wrested a seat on the Energy and Commerce Committee from Michigan's Bart Stupak, Chairman John D. Dingell's preferred choice. Not bad for a novice.

From her committee position, she spoke out in favor of legislation to give the Federal Trade Commission authority to fight interstate telemarketing fraud. The bill passed the House in March 1993.

Lambert left her hometown of Helena on the Mississippi Delta after graduating from high school.

In the years that followed, Lambert graduated from Randolph-Macon Woman's College, did stints at the University of Arkansas and the University of London, considered going after a career in medicine and worked briefly at Sotheby's tony auction house in New York City — all by her 23rd birthday. Then she headed to Washington for a career in government.

In 1983, she landed a job as a receptionist for the man she would unseat less than a decade later — Rep. Bill Alexander, D-Ark.

She left his office after two years for a series of research positions with lobbying firms, ending at the Pagonis & Donnelly Group Inc.

Lambert says late in 1991 that she was talking to a friend about what she thought was wrong with the system when she decided that she ought to go home and run.

Over the years, Alexander had lost the luster he once had as a promising young star. Bad publicity from a $50,000 solo fact-finding trip to Brazil in 1985 made him vulnerable in past primaries, and it appeared he would be vulnerable in 1992 because of questions raised in the media about his financial ties to businessmen whose company had received earmarked federal funds.

Lambert returned to the family farm, which is now run by her brother, to set up her campaign, and she was already out on the hustings when the news that would make her campaign broke: With 487 overdrafts, Alexander was among the top 10 abusers at the House bank.

Until then, Lambert had been something of a curiosity — a self-described Southern lady and avowed duck hunter touring the rural 1st District in her red Jeep in search of voters, followed by a gaggle of young male volunteers and an uncle as escort.

But with the bank scandal, everything she had been saying about Alexander being out of touch sounded prescient, and she appeared eminently sensible. She walloped him in the primary, 61 percent to 39 percent.

In this overwhelmingly Democratic district, which is nearly 20 percent black, her stunning primary victory was a ticket to Washington. In November she had little trouble dispatching Republican Terry Hayes, a real estate developer, by a 70 percent to 30 percent margin.

But it was much more than the House bank scandal and a Democratic district that allowed Lambert to return to Washington to sign the mail she once opened.

Lambert connected with rural voters with her understanding of farm life and talk of rural enterprise zones and rural health-care needs, of fiscal responsibility and the jobs needed to keep young people at home in the small towns that dot the district.

Her no-nonsense style also clicked.

When one farmer looked at her skeptically a few weeks before the primary, she put her hands on her hips, cocked her head and smiled — an oft-repeated pose Washington will soon be familiar with — and sprightly asked in her flatlander twang, "Now, you don't have a problem with a woman serving in Congress, do you?" according to a local newspaper account.

If being a woman required a bit of extra personal persuasion with some Arkansas voters, it also enabled Lambert to tap a fundraising base that kept her campaign flush.

Arkansas 1

Northeast — Jonesboro; West Memphis

Covering most of the eastern third of the state, the 1st divides into three geographic regions: the hilly northwest, the Mississippi River Delta, and, between them, the alluvial plain. Though soybeans flourish on the fertile bottomland along the river, and rice thrives on the plain, the 1st is the state's poorest district, and the one with the strongest Old South flavor. In keeping with a tradition that goes back to the Civil War, most of the white voters here still support Democratic candidates.

The large corporate farms in this area, like the cotton plantations that preceded them, sprawl over tens of thousands of acres and coexist with poor, largely black communities. Farm employment has declined annually since the 1940s. Until the 1980s, there was some work in small mills along the river, but many of those jobs went overseas, exacerbating generations-old poverty. In late 1992, about half of the district's 25 counties had double-digit unemployment.

The Delta counties along the Mississippi River have large black populations and are solidly Democratic. Though all the counties lost population during the 1980s, the Delta still accounts for about one-quarter of the district vote.

The largest city in the Delta is West Memphis (Crittenden County), with just over 28,000 people; it is a trucking center and bedroom community for Memphis, Tenn. North of there is the somewhat smaller city of Blytheville (Mississippi County). In 1988, Blytheville attracted 500 new jobs with the opening of Nucor-Yamato Steel Co., a U.S.-Japan venture, and in 1992 Nucor opened another plant on its own. But the city suffered a blow in 1992 when Blytheville Air Force Base closed, eliminating 3,000 military and 600 civilian jobs.

The Ozark Mountain counties in the northwestern part of the 1st are culturally distant from the Delta. Home to annual fiddle contests and outhouse races, most of these counties grew during the 1980s with an influx of retirees, many of them from the North. These newcomers diluted the area's traditional Democratic vote and helped put the 1st in the Republican column for president in 1984 and 1988. Searcy County, at the western edge of the 1st, did not even support Bill Clinton for president in 1992; it was the only county in the district he failed to carry.

The other pocket of growth in the 1st, Lonoke County, is also becoming more Republican. The growth is concentrated in suburban Cabot. Outside Cabot, Lonoke County is much like the rest of the alluvial plain, with its conservative Democratic tradition and huge rice farms. The lakes and rivers in and around Arkansas County lure fishermen and duck hunters.

Jonesboro is the district's largest city, with 46,500 people. It has a fairly stable economy built around Arkansas State University (9,700 students) and industrial enterprises engaged in die casting, tool making, printing and conveyor-belt production. Jonesboro and outlying communities in Craighead County cast nearly 10 percent of the vote in the 1st; the area is reliably, though not hugely, Democratic.

1990 Population: 588,588. White 478,761 (81%), Black 105,199 (18%), Other 4,628 (1%). Hispanic origin 3,652 (1%). 18 and over 425,369 (72%), 62 and over 106,287 (18%). Median age: 34.

Committees

Agriculture (27th of 27 Democrats)
Department Operations

Energy & Commerce (27th of 27 Democrats)
Energy & Power; Transportation & Hazardous Materials

Merchant Marine & Fisheries (22nd of 28 Democrats)
Coast Guard & Navigation; Environment & Natural Resources

Campaign Finance

	Receipts	Receipts from PACs		Expend-itures
1992				
Lambert (D)	$439,343	$176,400	(40%)	$327,100
Hayes (R)	$38,015	$2,500	(7%)	$30,571

Key Votes

1993

Require parental notification of minors' abortions	N
Require unpaid family and medical leave	Y
Approve national "motor voter" registration bill	Y
Approve budget increasing taxes and reducing deficit	Y
Approve economic stimulus plan	Y

Elections

1992 General		
Blanche Lambert (D)	149,558	(70%)
Terry Hayes (R)	64,618	(30%)
1992 Primary		
Blanche Lambert (D)	86,142	(61%)
Bill Alexander (D)	54,686	(39%)

District Vote for President

	1992	
D	131,585	(59%)
R	71,160	(32%)
I	20,116	(9%)

2 Ray Thornton (D)

Of Little Rock — Elected 1990; 5th Term

Also served 1973-79.

Born: July 16, 1928, Conway, Ark.

Education: Yale U., B.A. 1950; U. of Arkansas, J.D. 1956.

Military Service: Navy, 1951-54.

Occupation: Lawyer.

Family: Wife, Betty Jo Mann; three children.

Religion: Church of Christ.

Political Career: Ark. attorney general, 1971-73; U.S. House, 1973-79; sought Democratic nomination for U.S. Senate, 1978.

Capitol Office: 1214 Longworth Bldg. 20515; 225-2506.

In Washington: Though only in the second term of his current congressional career, Thornton is the dean of what is now a key House delegation, has an important committee assignment and is so well regarded by peers and leaders that he has the potential to be a major player among the junior members of the House. His ties to President Clinton, though not especially close, certainly will not hurt.

Thornton began the 103rd Congress by taking a seat on the Appropriations Committee, where he will undoubtedly watch out for Arkansas interests. As a member of the Agriculture Subcommittee, he can help take care of an industry that is vital to the state's economy. On the Veterans' Affairs and HUD Subcommittee, he can help Little Rock, not only the capital and largest city in the state and his district but also the economic, political and cultural center of Arkansas. Little Rock is also the site of a VA Hospital.

By seeking a spot on Appropriations and putting more emphasis on at-home interests, Thornton appears to have chosen a different path than during his first House career — he represented southern Arkansas' 4th District for three terms from 1973 to 1979. During that time, he was something of a policy expert, and in only his second term he was chosen to chair a Science, Space and Technology subcommittee. He was also on the Judiciary Committee while it considered impeachment of President Richard M. Nixon and part of a seven-person coalition of Republicans and southern Democrats who drafted the articles of impeachment and formed the impeachment strategy.

During his second stint in Washington, Thornton has declined to outline a grand policy agenda, and some reporters covering his campaigns have criticized him for being long on rhetoric and short on specifics.

An example is his outspoken support for a domestic Marshall Plan that would fund infrastructure and education improvements in this country along the lines of what the United States helped finance in Europe after World War II. Though Thornton got support for the idea from colleagues in both parties during the 102nd Congress, no legislation was enacted.

With a like-minded Arkansas Democrat in the White House, Thornton's ideas may have more chance of being implemented in the 103rd, but he has no plans to be a key player in moving legislation. He told The New York Times he is "trying to give it away" to more senior members.

Clinton embraced some of Thornton's ideas in his campaign and his initial policy proposals.

Relatively speaking, Thornton should be comfortable ideologically in Clinton's Washington. He generally backs the Democratic leadership and supported legislation mandating family leave and banning employers from hiring permanent replacements for striking workers.

But Thornton often parts ways with liberal Democrats. He opposes federal funding for abortions, a ban on semiautomatic weapons and the Brady bill to establish a waiting period before the purchase of a handgun. He was the only Democrat in Arkansas' congressional delegation to vote to give President Bush the authority to go to war in the Persian Gulf.

During the 102nd Congress, Thornton got back his seat on the Science, Space and Technology Committee, where he maintained support for science research. He voted for funding for both the space station and the superconducting super collider. Thornton's fellow Arkansan, Sen. Dale Bumpers, has repeatedly sponsored amendments to kill the super collider.

At Home: A series of unexpected events in the 1992 election season helped make Thornton one of the most powerful House sophomores in any state delegation. Thornton became the most senior member of the four-member Arkansas delegation after two veteran members,

Arkansas 2

Central — Little Rock

The political and commercial capital of Arkansas, Little Rock dominates the 2nd. The city and surrounding Pulaski County have a combined population of almost 350,000 — nearly 60 percent of the district's total — and their political weight is usually enough to determine the outcome of the 2nd's elections.

With a population one-third black and a well-organized labor community, Little Rock is a Democratic stronghold. The suburbs along the Arkansas River bluffs are home to a large managerial and professional community that prefers to vote Republican, but it will support moderate, business-minded Democrats. In 1992, Rep. Thornton carried Pulaski County with 75 percent of the vote, and Bill Clinton got 58 percent of the county's presidential vote, several points above his statewide average. (Four years earlier, Pulaski went comfortably for George Bush.)

Little Rock did not experience anything like the boom felt by other Sun Belt cities during the 1980s, but the city's 10 percent growth was more than triple that of the state as a whole. Together with North Little Rock — a much smaller, separately incorporated city just across the Arkansas River — Little Rock is more insulated from economic downturns than other parts of Arkansas because of the state government presence, as well as the legal and service industries that support it. Little Rock is also home to a large branch of the University of Arkansas (11,800 students) and to five major hospitals that serve the metropolitan area and outlying rural communities. There is also a military component in the economy: Little Rock Air Force Base, in northeastern Pulaski County near the town of Jacksonville, has 6,000 active-duty personnel.

Once a symbol of the resistance to desegregating public schools in the South, Little Rock today has shed much of its racial tension, and in 1990 the city electorate approved a local tax increase to boost funding for the school system.

Downtown Little Rock has a spruced-up business corridor and convention center, but the retail trade has moved to the western suburbs, home to the more affluent residents. Poor and working-class blacks live in east Little Rock.

Many whites have left the city for the once-rural counties that surround Pulaski. While the 20 percent growth in Saline and Faulkner counties during the 1980s weakened their Democratic traditions, the GOP lacks organization here. And Democrats still find a hospitable union movement in the aluminum industry in Saline, the nation's prime domestic source of bauxite.

Republicans have a longer tradition in rural White County, to the east. The GOP has perhaps its strongest organization in the state here, bolstered by the firmly conservative intellectual direction from the academic community at Harding University (3,400 students), an institution affiliated with the Church of Christ. Rural Conway, Yell and Perry counties are more confirmed in their Democratic habits.

1990 Population: 587,412. White 476,858 (81%), Black 103,436 (18%), Other 7,118 (1%). Hispanic origin 4,731 (1%). 18 and over 434,184 (74%), 62 and over 87,011 (15%). Median age: 33.

Democrats Bill Alexander and Beryl Anthony Jr., lost their re-election bids and a third member, Republican John Paul Hammerschmidt, retired.

Thornton has the political experience to lead the delegation. He has been a statewide presence for two decades. After serving a two-year term as state attorney general, Thornton in 1972 won the House seat vacated by Democrat David Pryor, who failed in a challenge to Democratic Sen. John L. McClellan. In 1978, Pryor, then governor, ran against Thornton and then-Rep. Jim Guy Tucker in the Democratic Senate primary. Thornton came in a close third, splitting votes with Pryor. (Pryor won the runoff and the general election.)

In 1990, Pryor, running unopposed for a new Senate term, was Thornton's House campaign chairman.

That first House race for Thornton in more than a decade showed that voters still held Thornton's image for integrity and honesty in the highest regard. After Tucker ended his flirtation with challenging Thornton in the primary, Thornton had the nomination to himself. (Tucker instead ran for lieutenant governor and won.)

State Rep. Ron Fuller appeared to be the only Republican willing to take on the popular Democrat, but he inspired little enthusiasm among Republicans and decided to drop out of the race.

Freshman state Rep. Jim Keet took Fuller's place. A fast-food restaurant entrepreneur regarded as a rising star in the state GOP, Keet was widely seen as running for the House to gain experience for future campaigns. Keet largely avoided attacking Thornton, and the statewide newspapers paid little attention to the open-seat race. Thornton reclaimed the 2nd for the Democrats with 60 percent of the vote.

In 1992, Thornton solidified his grip, drawing no primary opposition and capturing just under 75 percent of the vote in the general election against Republican Dennis Scott, a residential contractor.

Committee

Appropriations (30th of 37 Democrats)
Agriculture, Rural Development, FDA & Related Agencies; Veterans Affairs, Housing & Urban Development & Independent Agencies

Elections

1992 General

Ray Thornton (D)	154,946	(74%)
Dennis Scott (R)	53,978	(26%)

1990 General

Ray Thornton (D)	103,471	(60%)
Jim Keet (R)	67,800	(40%)

Previous Winning Percentages: **1976** (100%) **1974** (100%) **1972** (100%)

District Vote for President

1992
D 130,435 (56%)
R 84,922 (36%)
I 19,348 (8%)

Campaign Finance

	Receipts	Receipts from PACs		Expend-itures
1992				
Thornton (D)	$303,430	$141,550	(47%)	$206,328
Scott (R)	$5,724	$500	(9%)	$6,212
1990				
Thornton (D)	$697,067	$242,900	(35%)	$678,429
Keet (R)	$436,883	$24,157	(6%)	$430,932

Key Votes

1993	
Require parental notification of minors' abortions	N
Require unpaid family and medical leave	Y
Approve national "motor voter" registration bill	Y
Approve budget increasing taxes and reducing deficit	Y
Approve economic stimulus plan	Y
1992	
Approve balanced-budget constitutional amendment	N
Close down space station program	N
Approve U.S. aid for former Soviet Union	Y
Allow shifting funds from defense to domestic programs	Y
1991	
Extend unemployment benefits using deficit financing	Y
Approve waiting period for handgun purchases	N
Authorize use of force in Persian Gulf	Y

Voting Studies

	Presidential Support		Party Unity		Conservative Coalition	
Year	**S**	**O**	**S**	**O**	**S**	**O**
1992	34	62	85	11	67	23
1991	35	61	84	12	65	30

Interest Group Ratings

Year	ADA	AFL-CIO	CCUS	ACU
1992	85	91	38	8
1991	40	92	50	15

3 Tim Hutchinson (R)

Of Bentonville — Elected 1992; 1st Term

Born: Aug. 11, 1949, Bentonville, Ark.
Education: Bob Jones U., B.A. 1971; U. of Arkansas, M.A. 1990.
Occupation: Minister; college instructor; radio station executive.
Family: Wife, Donna Jean King; three children.
Religion: Baptist.
Political Career: Ark. House, 1985-93.
Capitol Office: 1541 Longworth Bldg. 20515; 225-4301.

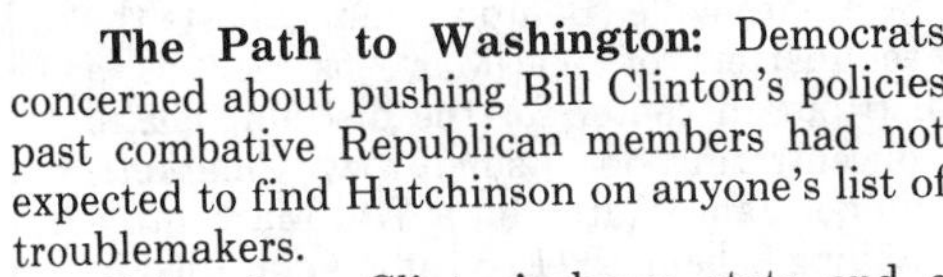

The Path to Washington: Democrats concerned about pushing Bill Clinton's policies past combative Republican members had not expected to find Hutchinson on anyone's list of troublemakers.

Being from Clinton's home state and a district that voted for Clinton in 1992, Hutchinson, a Baptist minister and educator, was feeling cooperative early on. "My position will be that where I think Bill Clinton is offering policies that will be beneficial to Arkansas and the nation," he said, "I'll support it regardless of what the leadership may say on that."

But early in the 103rd Congress, Hutchinson opposed Clinton at nearly every turn, voting against the president's budget and stimulus package, family leave legislation, and the "motor voter" bill.

As the short-lived era of good feelings ends, the GOP can only benefit from Hutchinson's special knowledge accrued as the only member of the House to have served in the Arkansas legislature while Clinton was governor.

No newcomer to politics, Hutchinson is used to stepping into the shoes of veteran legislators. He launched his run for the 3rd District after Republican incumbent John Paul Hammerschmidt announced that he would retire after 26 years in the House. And to win his first seat in the state legislature, Hutchinson beat a 12-year incumbent, Clayton Little.

With strong ties to the conservative religious community, a well-known name, a track record from serving in the state House since 1985 and Hammerschmidt's endorsement, Hutchinson was well-positioned to succeed him. In addition, Hutchinson had police support (he was twice named representative of the year by the Arkansas Association of Chiefs of Police).

Redistricting for the 1990s also helped give him an edge by making the already Republican-leaning district even more so by removing some southern counties with Democratic tendencies.

His brother, Asa, is a former U.S. attorney who ran a failed campaign in 1986 to unseat Sen. Dale Bumpers. Asa Hutchinson ran his brother's campaign for Congress. In the primary, the Hutchinson campaign was a low-budget effort that drew on grass-roots support. The organization remained much the same for the November election.

As the campaign for the general election got under way, Hutchinson appeared to be in better financial shape than Democrat John VanWinkle, a Fort Smith lawyer, who had gotten a slow start in fundraising.

However, VanWinkle received thousands of dollars during the final weeks of the campaign from labor organizations, including the AFL-CIO, and from out-of-state political action committees.

VanWinkle, who resigned a judgeship to run for Congress, outspent Hutchinson by about $100,000, but the money was not enough to wrest the seat from Republican hands. Hutchinson squeaked past VanWinkle, winning 50 percent to 47 percent.

Like so many other freshmen, Hutchinson campaigned on a pledge to seek changes in the way Congress operates. He wants to cut staff and the number of committees. He also supports a 12-year term limit for members.

Hutchinson favors a constitutional amendment that would require a balanced federal budget and a line-item veto for the president. Like many other members, Hutchinson argues that the changes would cut the federal debt and help prevent deficit spending.

While Hutchinson supports change, he also plans to safeguard his state's interests by following in Hammerschmidt's footsteps.

He sought and received assignments on the two committees on which the veteran legislator served — Veterans' Affairs and Public Works and Transportation (where Hammerschmidt was ranking member).

From a seat on Public Works, Hutchinson wants to push through projects to build up his state's underdeveloped infrastructure.

Arkansas 3

Northwest — Fort Smith; Fayetteville

The hilly 3rd, Arkansas' most reliably Republican constituency, has roots of GOP allegiance dating back to the Civil War. That conflict struck many of the small-scale farmers here as one fought mostly in behalf of the wealthy slaveholding plantations in the flatter parts of Arkansas. In 1988, George Bush won two-thirds of the district's presidential vote; even in 1992, Arkansan Bill Clinton lost four of the district's 16 counties. And in the counties Clinton won, he typically got less than 50 percent.

Back in 1974, this is where Clinton cut his teeth in electoral politics. As a 28-year-old law professor at the University of Arkansas in Fayetteville, Clinton challenged GOP Rep. John Paul Hammerschmidt and held him to 52 percent; it was the only time Hammerschmidt ever won re-election with less than two-thirds of the vote.

Carroll County (once home to Prohibitionist Carry Nation) conveys the conservative, Bible Belt character of the nearly all-white 3rd in the tourist attractions it offers: The area hosts year-round performances of The Great Passion Play, depicting Christ's last days on Earth; it has the Bible Museum; the huge Christ of the Ozarks statue; and the Inspirational Wood Carvings Gallery. The warm baths at Eureka Springs are a more earthly attraction.

For generations, the rough terrain here made for a struggling economy dependent on relatively unproductive farmland. Vast pine forests in the Ouachita Mountains provide jobs in sawmills scattered through the rural counties. The large livestock business in the western portion of the 3rd gives a distinctly Western feel to the area around Fort Smith, on the Oklahoma border.

In recent years, the economy has been boosted by retirees and two home-grown national corporations, Tyson Foods Inc. and Wal-Mart. Arkansas is the nation's leading broiler producer, and Tyson is the state's poultry industry leader. The company also has moved into hogs, a growth industry along Arkansas' western border. In the 1980s, Tyson's headquarters city, Springdale (Washington County), grew about 20 percent, to almost 30,000.

Bentonville (Benton County) hosts the headquarters of Wal-Mart, as well as a distribution center for the discount chain. Concentrating on small-town markets, founder Sam Walton built Wal-Mart into a retailing behemoth (1,853 stores); he died in 1992 as one of the nation's wealthiest men.

The Ozark economy also has benefited from an influx of retirees. The area's mild climate and natural assets — Beaver Lake and Bull Shoals Lake, the Buffalo River and two national forests — have drawn people to newly developed planned communities.

The 3rd's population centers are the manufacturing and livestock city of Fort Smith (Sebastian County), the state's second-largest city with 72,800 residents, and the university city of Fayetteville (Washington County), with just over 42,000 residents. Both cities typically support GOP candidates. In 1992, Clinton won Washington County narrowly, but Bush took Sebastian.

1990 Population: 589,523. White 565,293 (96%), Black 9,675 (2%), Other 14,555 (2%). Hispanic origin 6,753 (1%). 18 and over 440,403 (75%), 62 and over 109,410 (19%). Median age: 35.

Committees

Public Works & Transportation (13th of 24 Republicans)
Economic Development; Surface Transportation; Water Resources and the Environment

Veterans' Affairs (7th of 14 Republicans)
Education, Training & Employment (ranking); Hospitals & Health Care

Campaign Finance

1992	Receipts	Receipts from PACs		Expend-itures
Hutchinson (R)	$370,665	$120,266	(32%)	$366,419
VanWinkle (D)	$495,863	$160,362	(32%)	$489,833
Forbes (I)	$9,754	0		$9,746

Key Votes

1993

Require parental notification of minors' abortions	Y
Require unpaid family and medical leave	N
Approve national "motor voter" registration bill	N
Approve budget increasing taxes and reducing deficit	N
Approve economic stimulus plan	N

Elections

1992 General		
Tim Hutchinson (R)	125,295	(50%)
John VanWinkle (D)	117,775	(47%)
Ralph P. Forbes (I)	6,329	(3%)
1992 Primary		
Tim Hutchinson (R)	17,380	(53%)
Dick Barclay (R)	10,534	(32%)
Dryden Pence (R)	4,879	(15%)

District Vote for President

	1992
D	109,111 (43%)
R	107,351 (43%)
I	35,991 (14%)

4 Jay Dickey (R)

Of Pine Bluff — Elected 1992; 1st Term

Born: Dec. 14, 1939, Pine Bluff, Ark.
Education: U. of Arkansas, B.A. 1961, J.D. 1963.
Occupation: Lawyer; restaurateur.
Family: Divorced; four children.
Religion: Methodist.
Political Career: Pine Bluff city attorney, 1968-70.
Capitol Office: 1338 Longworth Bldg. 20515; 225-3772.

The Path to Washington: For Dickey, switching his party registration from Democratic to Republican to run for the House was a simple matter of pragmatism.

"I didn't want to go up there and have two battles — one against the bureaucracy and one against my own party," Dickey said at the time.

As a Republican, Dickey stands shoulder-to-shoulder with those on the right in his party. He supports a constitutional amendment to balance the budget and the aggressive use of the military in a war against drugs; he opposes any form of gun control and opposes abortion except in cases of rape and when the woman's life is in danger.

A businessman-cum-politician, Dickey owns two Taco Bell franchises, a commercial sign company and a travel agency, and runs an active law practice — all in the Pine Bluff area. He joins GOP loyalists who oppose federal intervention in business decisions and support a tax structure more favorable to small businesses, including a capital gains tax cut.

"Yellow dog" Democrats who traditionally dominate politics in this southern Arkansas district share many of those positions, but no previous Republican House candidate had persuaded them to abandon their party — in large part because the business community that might have funded such a campaign was cozy with veteran Rep. Beryl Anthony Jr.

From a family prominent in forestry and lumber, cornerstones of southern Arkansas' economy, Anthony likely would have had little trouble keeping his business backers aboard come the general election, but a fierce primary and runoff did him in before then.

With the House bank scandal (Anthony had to explain 109 overdrafts), his relatively liberal voting record and his past leadership position (he served as Democratic Congressional Campaign Committee chairman for the 1988 and 1990 elections), Anthony's record in Congress became a liability in the primary for the first time since he was elected in 1978.

Democratic Secretary of State W. J. "Bill" McCuen went after Anthony guns ablaze, calling him a liberal and an out-of-touch incumbent.

(Dickey later echoed his criticism of congressional obliviousness in testimony before the Joint Committee on the Organization of Congress. "Voters are fed up with us being treated like some type of royalty up here," he told the panel in early February.)

A product of the Garland County (Hot Springs) courthouse, McCuen earned notoriety for taking a 1990 motorcycle trip on state business with two female assistants. He also was criticized for accepting a $324,000 no-bid contract for computers that turned out to be worthless.

These and other controversies might have kept McCuen from winning the Democratic line were it not for a massive, last-minute infusion of anti-Anthony advertising by the National Rifle Association.

With McCuen as the Democratic standard-bearer, Dickey and the GOP knew the stakes had changed. Business leaders, including a cousin of Anthony's, came out for Dickey and saw to it that the Republican's campaign was financially competitive despite Dickey's pledge not to accept political action committee money.

The funding allowed Dickey to contend that the differences between him and McCuen were more stylistic than substantive.

The Democrat's viciously negative campaign — McCuen hinted that incest was a cause of Dickey's divorce, something Dickey, his wife and his children denied — only worked to push McCuen outside the Democratic mainstream. Dickey won with 52 percent of the vote.

During his first term in Washington, Dickey's challenge will be to keep his converts in the business community on his side. Toward that end, he secured posts on the Agriculture and Small Business committees. He also will serve on the Natural Resources Committee, where he says he will work to balance the needs of the economy and the environment.

With a Republican or another Democrat in the White House, Dickey might have somewhat less trouble holding on in the staunchly Democratic 4th. But with a native son as his foil, Dickey will be closely watched by Democrats who feel this seat is rightfully theirs.

Arkansas 4

South — Pine Bluff, Hot Springs

Though now in Republican hands, the 4th traditionally has been staunchly Democratic; in the three decades before 1992, the GOP offered a House candidate here only six times. Dickey prevailed narrowly, capitalizing on a bruising Democratic primary.

A recent convert to the GOP, Dickey won by capturing the votes of the many Democrats disaffected with their nominee and by squeezing out every possible vote in the parts of the 4th where Republicans have some presence: around the urban centers of Pine Bluff and Hot Springs and along southern Arkansas' "El Dorado fringe."

The 4th stretches from the Texas border on the west to the Mississippi River on the east; it has the most blacks (27 percent of the population) of any Arkansas district, and most of its white voters retain a Civil War-era allegiance to the Democratic Party in elections for local office. In presidential voting, Jimmy Carter in 1976 and Bill Clinton in 1992 carried the district.

The 4th's economy depends on agriculture. Scores of paper and plywood mills, most owned by Georgia Pacific and International Paper, dot the district. Rice and soybeans are grown in the Delta counties, and hogs have become an important industry on the western fringe.

With 57,000 people, Pine Bluff (Jefferson County) is the district's largest city and Dickey's hometown. It has a 53 percent black population and casts the highest minority vote of any city in Arkansas. Like the rest of the 4th, Pine Bluff is heavily dependent on the timber industry. International Paper employs about 2,000 people here.

The Pine Bluff Arsenal, which once produced the nation's entire supply of biological weapons, no longer manufactures them. Instead, the arsenal, with 1,500 military and civilian personnel, tests and refurbishes gas masks, including many used in Operation Desert Storm in early 1991.

The district is home to two other military facilities — the Red River Arsenal in Miller County and the Camden Ordnance Plant in Ouachita County.

The district's second-largest city, with 32,000 people, is Hot Springs (Garland County), a popular resort for more than a century. This is where Clinton grew up, after leaving his birthplace in the southwestern Arkansas town of Hope (Hempstead County). The bathhouses and spas of Hot Springs National Park are the center of a tourist economy and a haven for retirees. Garland County's population grew by 5 percent in the 1980s, helping make Hot Springs more Republican.

Farther south is the "El Dorado fringe," Arkansas' narrow "oil band" running along the bottom of the state from Texarkana, on the Texas border, through El Dorado. El Dorado and surrounding Union County are the site of several oil refineries and chemical plants; politically active, conservative oil operators make the area a pocket of Republican strength. In 1992, Dickey won Union County and two other southern-border counties, Miller and Columbia.

1990 Population: 585,202. White 423,832 (72%), Black 155,602 (27%), Other 5,768 (1%). Hispanic origin 4,740 (1%). 18 and over 429,638 (73%), 62 and over 113,139 (19%). Median age: 35.

Committees

Agriculture (15th of 18 Republicans)
Environment, Credit & Rural Development; General Farm Commodities; Specialty Crops and Natural Resources

Natural Resources (15th of 15 Republicans)
National Parks, Forests & Public Lands; Oversight & Investigations

Small Business (14th of 18 Republicans)
Minority Enterprise, Finance and Urban Development; Regulation, Business Opportunities and Technology

Campaign Finance

1992	Receipts	Receipts from PACs		Expend-itures
Dickey (R)	$412,465	0	(0%)	$397,841
McCuen (D)	$373,085	$184,150	(49%)	$357,911

Key Votes

1993

Require parental notification of minors' abortions	Y
Require unpaid family and medical leave	N
Approve national "motor voter" registration bill	N
Approve budget increasing taxes and reducing deficit	N
Approve economic stimulus plan	N

Elections

1992 General

Jay Dickey (R)	113,009	(52%)
W.J. "Bill" McCuen (D)	102,918	(48%)

District Vote for President

1992

D	134,692 (58%)
R	73,891 (32%)
I	23,677 (10%)

California

STATE DATA

Governor: Pete Wilson (R)
First elected: 1990
Length of term: 4 years
Term expires: 1/95
Salary: $120,000; 5% pay cut per year until fiscal crisis is resolved
Term limit: 2 terms
Phone: (916) 445-2841
Born: Aug. 23, 1933; Lake Forest, Ill.
Education: Yale U., B.A. 1955; U. of California, Berkeley, J.D. 1962
Military Service: Marine Corps, 1955-58
Occupation: Lawyer
Family: Wife, Gayle Edlund
Religion: Presbyterian
Political Career: Calif. Assembly, 1967-71; mayor of San Diego, 1971-83; U.S. Senate, 1983-91

Lt. Gov.: Leo T. McCarthy (D)
First elected: 1982
Length of term: 4 years
Term expires: 1/95
Salary: $90,000
Phone: (916) 445-8994

State election official: (916) 445-0820
Democratic headquarters: (916) 442-5707
Republican headquarters: (818) 841-5210

REDISTRICTING

California gained 7 House seats in reapportionment, increasing from 45 districts to 52. Map drawn by special panel was approved by state Supreme Court Jan. 27, 1992; federal court Jan. 28 rejected effort to block use of map in 1992 pending appeal. Federal appeals court March 3 dismissed challenge to the map.

STATE LEGISLATURE

Bicameral Legislature. Two-year session meets year-round, with recess.

Senate: 40 members, 4-year terms
1992 breakdown: 22D, 15R, 2I, 1 vacancy; 35 men, 4 women; 34 whites, 2 blacks, 3 Hispanics
Salary: $52,500
Phone: (916) 445-4251

Assembly: 80 members, 2-year terms
1992 breakdown: 48D, 31R, 1 vacancy; 57 men, 22 women; 63 whites, 7 blacks, 8 Hispanics, 1 other
Salary: $52,500
Phone: (916) 445-3614

URBAN STATISTICS

City	Pop.
Los Angeles	3,458,398
Mayor Richard Riordan,* N-P	
San Diego	1,110,554
Mayor Susan Golding, N-P	
San Jose	782,248
Mayor Susan Hammer, N-P	

* *To be sworn in July 1*

U.S. CONGRESS

Senate: 2 D, 0 R
House: 30 D, 22 R

TERM LIMITS

For Congress: Yes
Senate: 12 years in 17-year period
House: 6 years in 11-year period
For state offices: Yes
Senate: 2 terms
Assembly: 3 terms

ELECTIONS

1992 Presidential Vote

Bill Clinton	46.0%
George Bush	32.6%
Ross Perot	20.6%

1988 Presidential Vote

George Bush	51%
Michael S. Dukakis	48%

1984 Presidential Vote

Ronald Reagan	58%
Walter F. Mondale	41%

POPULATION

1990 population		29,760,021
1980 population		23,667,902
Percent change		+26%
Rank among states:		1
White		69%
Black		7%
Hispanic		26%
Asian or Pacific islander		10%
Urban		93%
Rural		7%
Born in state		46%
Foreign-born		22%
Under age 18	7,750,725	26%
Ages 18-64	18,873,744	63%
65 and older	3,135,552	11%
Median age		31.5

MISCELLANEOUS

Capital: Sacramento
Number of counties: 58
Per capita income: $20,952 (1991)
Rank among states: 8
Total area: 158,706 sq. miles
Rank among states: 3

California - Congressional Districts

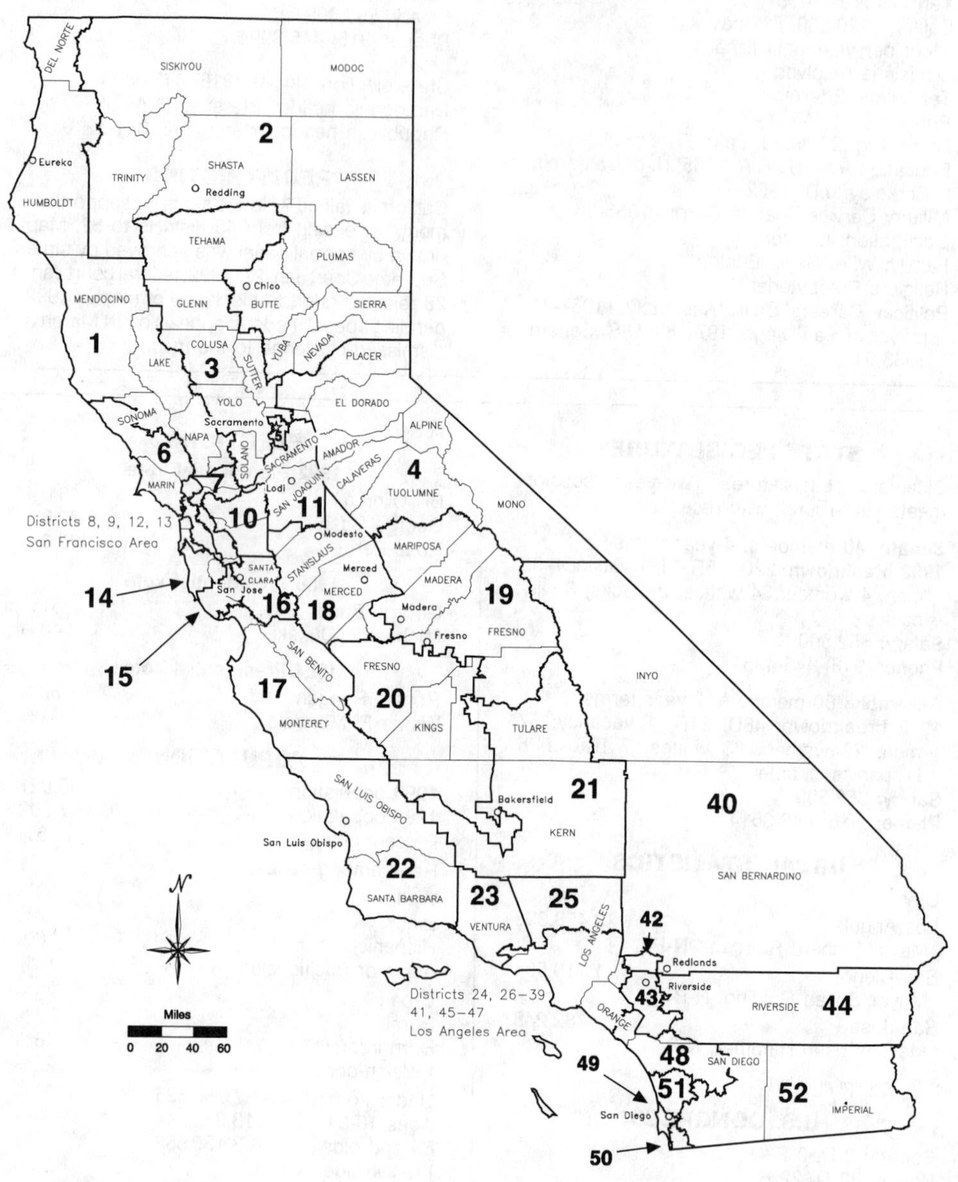

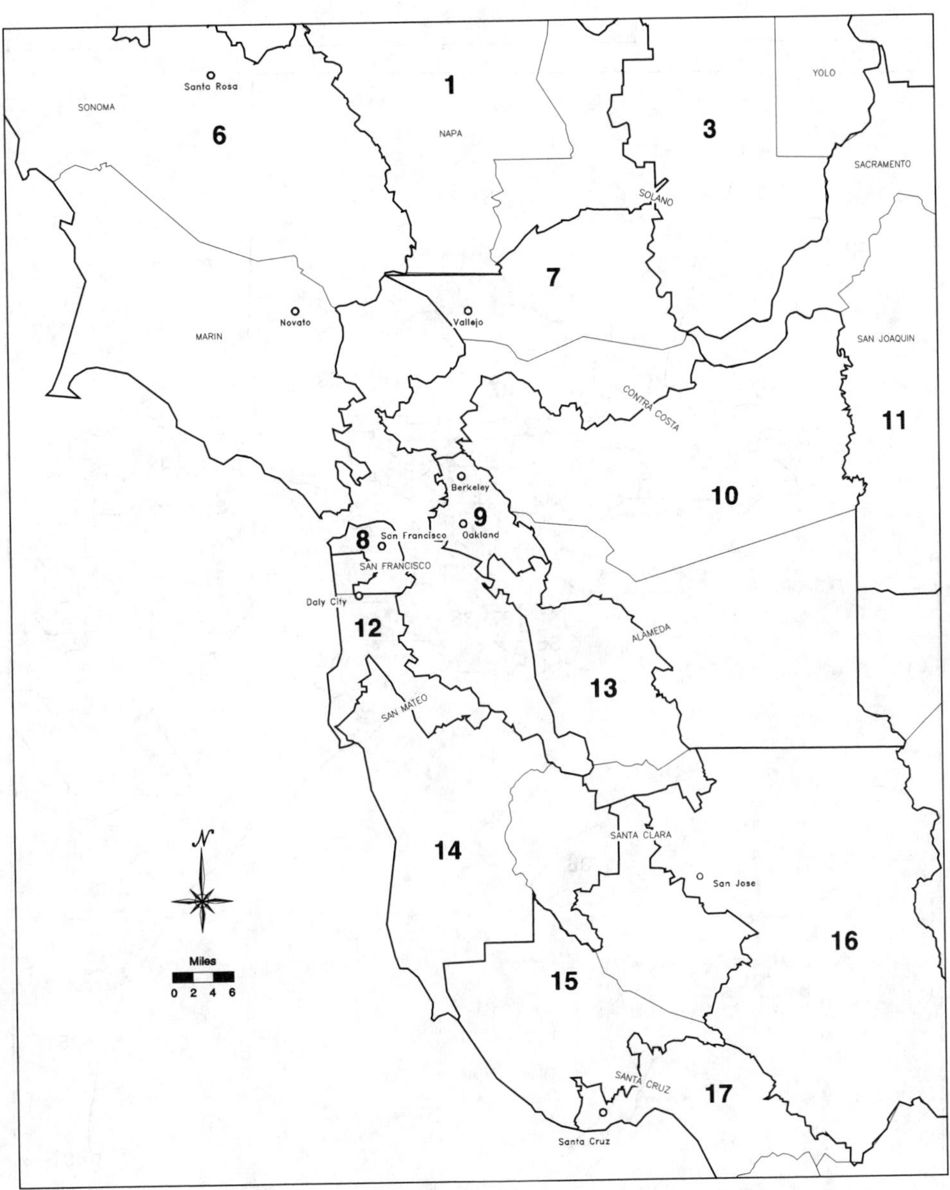
Santa Rosa
SONOMA
6
1
NAPA
3
YOLO
SACRAMENTO
SOLANO
7
MARIN
Novato
Vallejo
SAN JOAQUIN
CONTRA COSTA
11
10
Berkeley
9
Oakland
8
San Francisco
SAN FRANCISCO
Daly City
12
ALAMEDA
13
SAN MATEO
SANTA CLARA
14
San Jose
16
Miles
0 2 4 6
15
SANTA CRUZ
17
Santa Cruz

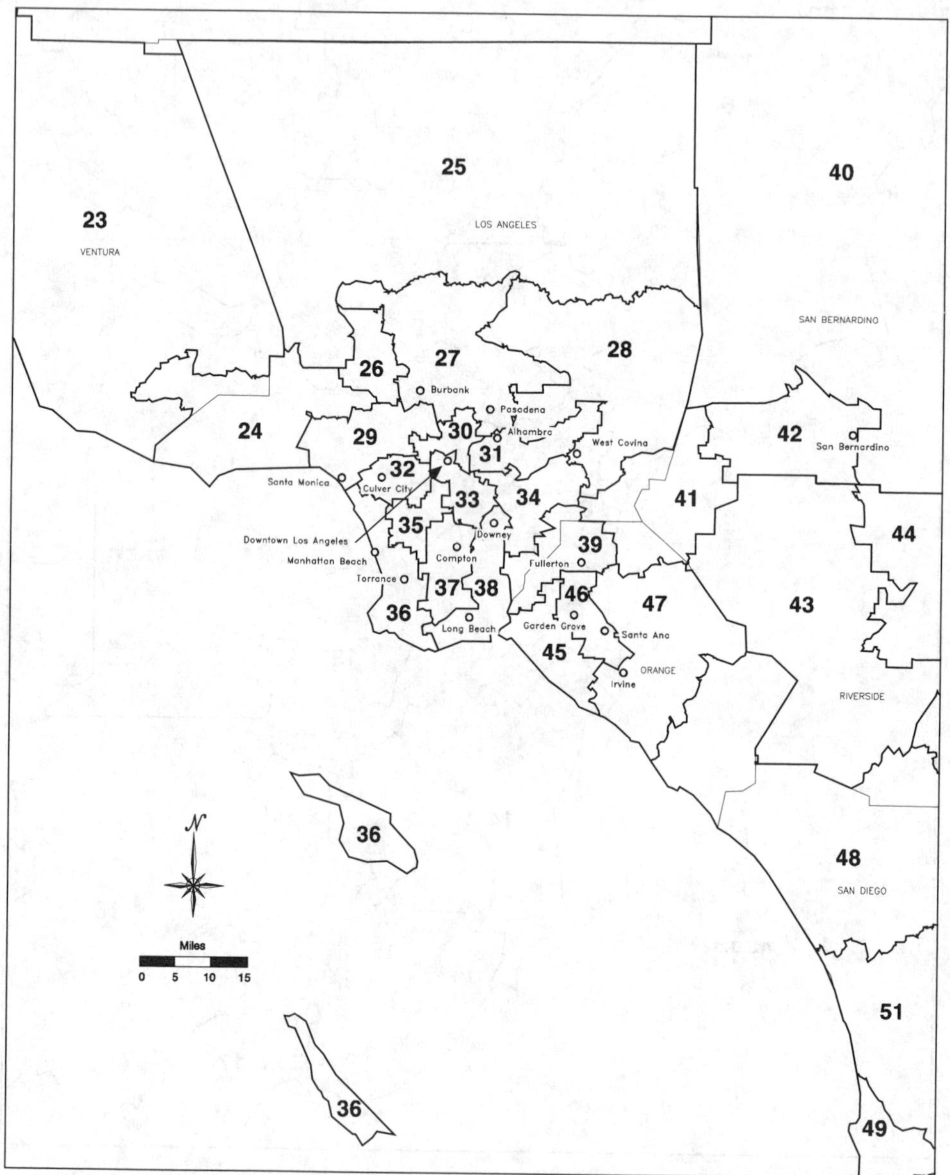

25
40
23
VENTURA
LOS ANGELES
SAN BERNARDINO
27
28
26
Burbank
Pasadena
24
29
30
Alhambra
31
West Covina
42
San Bernardino
32
Santa Monica
Culver City
33
34
41
35
Downtown Los Angeles
Downey
44
39
Manhattan Beach
Compton
Fullerton
Torrance
37
38
46
47
43
36
Long Beach
Garden Grove
Santa Ana
45
ORANGE
Irvine
RIVERSIDE
36
48
SAN DIEGO
Miles
0
5
10
15
51
36
49

Dianne Feinstein (D)

Of San Francisco — Elected 1992; 1st Term

Born: June 22, 1933, San Francisco, Calif.
Education: Stanford U., A.B. 1955.
Occupation: Public official.
Family: Husband, Richard Blum; one child, three stepchildren.
Religion: Jewish.
Political Career: San Francisco Board of Supervisors, 1970-78, president, 1970-71, 1974-75, 1978; mayor of San Francisco, 1978-89; Democratic nominee for governor, 1990.
Capitol Office: 331 Hart Bldg. 20510; 224-3841.

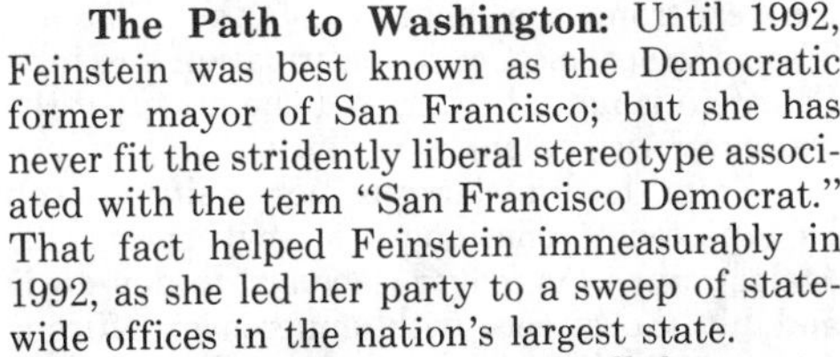

The Path to Washington: Until 1992, Feinstein was best known as the Democratic former mayor of San Francisco; but she has never fit the stridently liberal stereotype associated with the term "San Francisco Democrat." That fact helped Feinstein immeasurably in 1992, as she led her party to a sweep of statewide offices in the nation's largest state.

Her 1992 Senate victory was all the sweeter because the seat she won had previously belonged to Republican Pete Wilson, to whom she lost the 1990 gubernatorial election. After beating Feinstein, Wilson resigned from the Senate and appointed John Seymour in his place. By ousting Seymour, Feinstein won the right to serve the remaining two years of Wilson's term. She will have to run for a full six-year term of her own in 1994.

But Feinstein looks ready. In the political hurricane of 1992, while other candidates rose and fell, Feinstein honed in like a smart bomb. She began the year a little above 55 percent in the polls and won her primary with about 57 percent. Entering the fall campaign with similar standing in the polls, she won her race with about 54 percent.

Her ability to appeal to moderates and independents will be critical in determining whether Feinstein can hold her seat in a midterm election against what will doubtless be a concerted counterattack from her state's GOP. But if she can survive in the Senate, as a statewide winner in the gargantuan state of California she bids fair to become the next woman on a national ticket.

Throughout her Senate campaign, Feinstein stressed many of the same themes that Bill Clinton was using in his campaign. She proposed a $135 billion "Invest in America" program to improve the nation's schools, transportation system and technology base. The program would be funded by cuts in the defense budget, mostly by scaling back the U.S. military presence in Europe and Asia.

But she leavened her support for traditional liberal themes — such as environmental protection and abortion rights — with support for the death penalty and for a beefed-up Border Patrol to stem illegal immigration from Mexico. These positions generated some hostility from the liberal wing of the California Democratic Party, as did her support for a balanced-budget constitutional amendment and a presidential line-item veto.

But Feinstein, not unlike Clinton, used that intraparty heat to strengthen her credentials with the general electorate. That has been her pattern during more than two decades in California politics. Throughout her nine-year tenure as the mayor of fractious San Francisco, Feinstein frequently said her guiding principle was to "govern from the center."

When Feinstein ran for governor in 1990, Democratic Rep. Barbara Boxer criticized her for not backing some high-profile positions sought by feminists; Boxer even called Feinstein's primary rival, state Attorney General John Van de Kamp, "the best feminist" in the race.

But today Boxer serves alongside Feinstein in the Senate, and Feinstein can take some credit for both of them being there. The two campaigned together in 1992, enabling Boxer to temper her liberal image against her hard-charging conservative Republican opponent.

During the general-election campaign, Feinstein promised that she and Boxer would combine to form a hard-hitting "Thelma and Louise" team of California senators. But despite their tandem campaigning and conspicuous cooperation in the Senate, they are far from being political soulmates.

Feinstein is considered a coalition-builder who seeks workable solutions, while Boxer is "more like [Sen. Edward M.] Kennedy in terms of pushing the envelope of social legislation," said an adviser to both women.

Feinstein became mayor of San Francisco in 1979, when her predecessor, George Moscone, was assassinated. She first gained national note in 1984 when Walter F. Mondale, the Democratic presidential nominee, put her on his short list of vice presidential candidates. The nomination eventually went to then-Rep. Geraldine A. Ferraro of New York.

But Feinstein's later years as mayor were troubled, and when she began her 1990 gubernatorial campaign she seemed to be taking a last stab at reviving her fading career. She had the financing she needed, largely thanks to her financier husband and his extensive connections. Midway into her run against Van de Kamp, she unleashed a series of TV ads that revised voters' image of her, bringing her less liberal side to light and reversing her fortunes in the polls. Van de Kamp never recovered and was soundly beaten.

In the general election, Feinstein and Wilson at times seemed to struggle to find distinguishing issues. Both favored abortion rights, the death penalty and environmental protection. Wilson projected a solid if unexciting image of experience; Feinstein offered a more dramatic personality and personal history. Ultimately, Wilson had more money and a better party organization and slipped by with less than a majority: 49 percent to 46 percent.

Some thought that was the end for Feinstein, but Wilson's appointment of the little-known Seymour, his friend and political ally, created the perfect foil for her comeback. She began campaigning almost immediately, and the only Democrat of note who chose to challenge her was state Controller Gray Davis. Once thought a strong contender for statewide office, Davis could make no headway against Feinstein — even after he ran stunningly personal attacks relating to the financing of her 1990 gubernatorial campaign.

(The California Fair Political Practices Commission sued Feinstein and Wilson for irregularities in their 1990 campaign accounts. Feinstein eventually agreed to pay $190,000 in fines to settle the matter; Wilson paid $100,000.)

Seymour, meanwhile, was almost an invisible senator. In a Los Angeles Times poll in September, 51 percent said they did not know enough about him to judge him. Where Seymour had made an impression, it was often a negative one. He was well-known among anti-abortion activists because he switched positions to support abortion rights. He also angered many environmentalists by opposing a California desert-protection bill.

Arguably the biggest drag on Seymour, though, was the state budget crisis, which dropped Wilson's approval rating to the 20 percent range. While Seymour aired tough ads near the end, Feinstein was never threatened. She topped Seymour by more than 1.7 million votes, even winning (or managing virtual ties) in Southern California's affluent white suburbs.

Feinstein was recruited for a seat on the Judiciary Committee, which was still trying to recover from the debacle of the Clarence Thomas Supreme Court confirmation hearings. Feinstein is not a lawyer, and she accepted the Judiciary assignment reluctantly.

From the Judiciary position, Feinstein can be expected to continue her longtime crusade against crime. As mayor, she used to don a wig and hit the streets with undercover officers. And while she indicated she will introduce tough anti-crime measures, she also vowed to shake up the male-dominated committee.

"We sat back and we criticized during Anita Hill and Clarence Thomas," she said in a TV interview. "Now it's time to do something about it, and we've got to step up to the line."

In return for taking the Judiciary assignment, she received a far more enviable slot on Appropriations, where she will find her views on the line-item veto are anathema to the committee's chairman, West Virginia Democrat Robert C. Byrd.

Feinstein has already found out what Byrd can do. Although Feinstein outranks other freshmen — she won a special election and so was sworn in early — Byrd requested and got seniority on his committee for Washington's newly elected Democratic Sen. Patty Murray.

Committees

Appropriations (16th of 16 Democrats)
Agriculture, Rural Development & Related Agencies; District of Columbia; Foreign Operations; VA, HUD and Independent Agencies

Judiciary (9th of 10 Democrats)
Patents, Copyrights & Trademarks; Technology & the Law

Rules & Administration (8th of 9 Democrats)

Campaign Finance

	Receipts	Receipts from PACs		Expenditures
1992				
Feinstein (D)	$8,114,867	$941,048	(12%)	$8,054,222
Seymour (R)	$6,908,617	$1,388,708	(20%)	$6,849,805

Key Votes

1993

Require unpaid family and medical leave	Y
Approve national "motor voter" registration bill	Y
Approve budget increasing taxes and reducing deficit	Y
Support president's right to lift military gay ban	Y

Elections

1992 Special		
Dianne Feinstein (D)	5,853,621	(54%)
John Seymour (R)	4,093,488	(38%)
Gerald Horne (PFP)	305,699	(3%)
Paul Meeuwenberg (AMI)	281,972	(3%)
Richard B. Boddie (LIBERT)	247,799	(2%)
1992 Special Primary		
Dianne Feinstein (D)	1,775,730	(58%)
Gray Davis (D)	1,009,761	(33%)
David Kearns (D)	149,918	(5%)
Joseph M. Alioto (D)	139,410	(5%)

Barbara Boxer (D)

Of Greenbrae — Elected 1992; 1st Term

Born: Nov. 11, 1940, Brooklyn, N.Y.
Education: Brooklyn College, B.A. 1962.
Occupation: Congressional aide; journalist; stockbroker.
Family: Husband, Stewart Boxer; two children.
Religion: Jewish.
Political Career: Marin County Board of Supervisors, 1977-83; U.S. House, 1983-93; candidate for Marin County Board of Supervisors, 1972.
Capitol Office: 112 Hart Bldg. 20510; 224-3553.

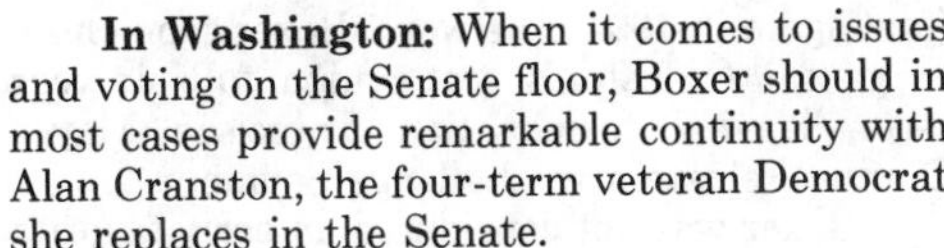

In Washington: When it comes to issues and voting on the Senate floor, Boxer should in most cases provide remarkable continuity with Alan Cranston, the four-term veteran Democrat she replaces in the Senate.

But Boxer is far more extroverted than Cranston, more of an activist and a crusader who knows and uses the media. She also pushes the parameters of liberalism, unyielding in her efforts to cut defense and boost domestic spending. By contrast, Cranston was closely allied with California business interests (an aspect of his political operation that may have contributed to his eventual downfall). He adjusted his antiwar fervor in recognition of his state's reliance on defense industries.

More generally, Cranston was well-versed in compromise, able to build bridges to moderates and even to conservatives. As a result, he had countless legislative accomplishments, not least of which was a major rewrite of federal housing policy in 1990. Boxer has been less inclined to deal, and in a decade of House service she was only modestly successful in bringing her ideas to fruition.

Boxer's determined style causes her to operate most often on the perimeter of the legislative arena — she will, for instance, offer amendments that obviously do not have a chance of adoption, rather than engaging in the work and horse-trading necessary to build coalitions for their passage.

But that does not mean she is ineffective. Boxer was one of seven House women who marched on the Senate in October 1991 to urge a delay in the vote on the nomination of Clarence Thomas to the Supreme Court until sexual harassment charges against him could be examined.

The resulting hearings, which rocked the nation and the Senate, undoubtedly had an effect on the body politic and may have directly contributed to the election of unprecedented numbers of women in 1992 (including Boxer herself). She has shown no sign of relenting since entering the Senate club. When Oregon Republican Sen. Bob Packwood was charged by some former staff members with sexual harassment in late 1992, Boxer said he should resign immediately.

If Boxer puts some people off with her unremitting assertiveness, her nature was crucial to her come-from-behind victory in the Democratic senatorial primary of 1992 and to her survival in November, when she held off a late charge by the GOP nominee, conservative TV commentator Bruce Herschensohn. Boxer also spent $10.4 million, making her No. 1 among all candidates for the Senate in 1992.

Boxer's new committee assignments suggest the possibility that she will make a more concerted legislative effort in the Senate, devoting her time to broad fiscal policy questions, environmental concerns and economic revival measures for her home state, where military cutbacks are hitting hard.

On the Budget Committee, she can continue pressing for defense cuts, but she will be better placed to champion the health-care, child-care and education issues close to her heart, much as she did before on the House Budget Committee.

As a member of the Banking and Environment and Public Works committees she can address other issues meaningful to California's strained resources, infrastructure and economy. Banking, for instance, has a role in aiding the conversion of defense industries to domestic uses. It is hard to imagine a more crucial issue for California, where military operations of all kinds face closure and aerospace and other contractors see their orders dwindling.

Her focus on defense cuts notwithstanding, Boxer has been involved with trying to mitigate proposed base closings before, as she was at the start of the 103rd Congress.

Boxer teamed with her Bay Area colleague and fellow Democrat Nancy Pelosi in the 101st Congress to resist the closing of the Presidio in San Francisco (as recommended by a commission). They said that the commission had overlooked the high costs of making the site environmentally safe and of transferring it to the Interior Department, as required by law. But they were unable to block the plan to close the Presidio.

In early 1993, Boxer and other California representatives met with President Clinton to avert what they feared would be a statewide calamity if all the rumored closings were carried out. When the Pentagon list was released, a few of the said-to-be-threatened sites were not on it.

While in the House, Boxer spent her time chiefly on Armed Services, where her attacks on Republican defense spending proposals put her in a small group out on the committee's left wing.

In 1990, she unsuccessfully sought to cut defense by $6 billion, with the savings to be split between deficit reduction and domestic spending. In 1992, she and fellow Democrat Ronald V. Dellums, another Bay Area colleague, teamed up on an amendment to cut spending on anti-missile systems by about $2 billion and eliminate the Strategic Defense Initiative organization. Their amendment was rejected, 117-248. In May 1993, however, the new Clinton administration officially eliminated the SDI office; and by then, Dellums had acceded to the Armed Services chairmanship.

Even as a House freshman, Boxer had been a caustic critic of Defense Department procurement policies, including overpayments for spare parts and other military equipment.

During the Persian Gulf War, Boxer led unsuccessful efforts aimed at passing legislation to allow one spouse in a military couple or a single parent the option of obtaining a combat exemption. Boxer drew publicity when she wrote a letter reminding Defense Secretary Dick Cheney that he got a draft deferral during the Vietnam War on the grounds that he was about to become a father.

Despite the time she has spent on defense matters, it was in the social-issue arena that Boxer made her clearest legislative mark, helping orchestrate a major victory for abortion rights advocates in 1989. During consideration of an appropriations bill, the House adopted Boxer's amendment to allow federal financing of abortions in cases involving rape and incest. Though the amendment was hailed as historic and would have reversed a decade-old policy, it provoked a veto that Congress could not override.

Boxer also served on House Government Operations, where in the 102nd Congress she assumed the chairmanship of the Subcommittee on Government Activities and Transportation. In her oversight capacity, she was among the harshest critics of the space station during floor debate in May 1991.

Though Boxer clearly has strongly held opinions, her colleagues were still startled by the stridency of her statements in support of the controversial 51 percent congressional payraise proposal in early 1989. But after all the strong language, Boxer surprised her colleagues once more, joining in the overwhelming House vote to kill the raise.

At Home: Boxer's Senate ambitions were common knowledge in California in the late 1980s, but her route to that office seemed blocked by strong incumbents and a plethora of well-situated rivals.

But in 1990, California's Republican senator, Pete Wilson, was elected governor. Two days later, Cranston, who had become embroiled in the downfall of savings-and-loan financier Charles H. Keating Jr. (who had helped bankroll his campaign in 1986), announced that he would not seek re-election in 1992.

Suddenly, Boxer had two seats to aim at, because Wilson's appointed successor, John Seymour, would have to face the voters in 1992 (and again in 1994 if he won). Boxer soon chose to go for Cranston's seat and a full six-year term, leaving former San Francisco Mayor Dianne Feinstein to challenge Seymour.

Boxer was not considered an early favorite in her race. Fellow House Democrat Mel Levine was thought better capable of raising money and organizing Southern California; and Lt. Gov. Leo T. McCarthy was also in the chase and well known statewide. Beyond that, the GOP seemed likely to nominate Rep. Tom Campbell, a moderate with ties to some state conservatives despite his support for abortion rights. Moreover, as the campaign unreeled, Boxer had to defend her 143 overdrafts and other stories of shoddy office practices and missed votes in the House.

But Boxer was missing votes because she was raising money and campaigning furiously from one end of the state to the other. Levine meanwhile, relied almost entirely on TV ads that proved disappointing; and McCarthy failed to ignite enthusiasm beyond his base among labor and traditional liberals. Boxer's numbers kept rising right up to the June primary, and she won it going away.

Thereafter, her sailing should have been smooth. Campbell had been frustrated in the primary when Sonny Bono, the former entertainer and mayor of Palm Springs, cut into his vote in Southern California and allowed Herschensohn to win the nomination with less than 40 percent of the GOP vote.

Herschensohn, however, overcame a shaky summer to run a tough and effective campaign in the fall and all but overtake Boxer, whose organization sputtered after the primary.

In the end, Boxer survived and won by about 5 percentage points. She benefited from a late barrage of ads depicting Herschensohn as a right-wing extremist and from a late story about Herschensohn visiting a nightclub featuring adult entertainment. She also got a boost from the national ticket and from the dynamism of her pairing with Feinstein. The two women often campaigned together, an ironic rebuke to all the political pros who had said California would never elect one liberal Jewish woman from the Bay Area — let alone two.

In fact, Boxer and Feinstein had not been close politically or personally before 1992. But with Feinstein running well ahead of Seymour, the alliance was clearly a plus for Boxer. And the two extended their cooperation into the Senate itself, with Boxer ceding much of the limelight to Feinstein (who must run again in 1994 for the right to the rest of Wilson's term).

Boxer had entered the House as the unintended beneficiary of one of the decade's more creative acts of district line-drawing. The 6th District was the keystone of California's 1981 redistricting plan, drawn to shore up Democratic Rep. John Burton after his close 1980 reelection contest. It was a gift from his brother, Rep. Phillip Burton, who designed the California congressional map.

But three days before the filing deadline in 1982, John Burton decided to forgo another term in office. Boxer, then a Marin County supervisor who had worked for Burton in the mid-1970s, stepped up to take his place.

Her opponent in the primary was San Francisco Supervisor Louise Renne, who had the backing of then-Mayor Feinstein. Boxer moved quickly to secure her Democratic base in Marin, and with Burton's backing, lined up the support of San Francisco's liberal activists and the politically powerful gay community. That was enough for Boxer to edge Renne out for the nomination.

In the general election, Boxer ran against Republican Dennis McQuaid, who had made a strong showing against John Burton two years before. But Phillip Burton's lines did the trick for Boxer. She won overwhelmingly in the San Francisco portion of the 6th and ran up comfortable margins in outlying blue-collar communities, countering McQuaid's majority in Marin.

The district lines were modified slightly after the 1982 election, but with no negative impact on Boxer. In 1984, she easily defeated her Republican opponent, and by 1986 she was up to 74 percent of the vote. She nearly duplicated that showing in 1988. Within days of the 1990 election (which she won with 68 percent), she announced her candidacy for the Senate.

Committees

Banking, Housing & Urban Affairs (8th of 11 Democrats)
Housing & Urban Affairs; International Finance & Monetary Policy

Budget (11th of 12 Democrats)

Environment & Public Works (10th of 10 Democrats)
Superfund, Recycling & Solid Waste Management; Toxic Substances, Environmental Oversight, Research & Development; Water Resources, Transportation, Public Buildings & Economic Development

Elections

1992 General		
Barbara Boxer (D)	5,173,443	(48%)
Bruce Herschensohn (R)	4,644,139	(43%)
Genevieve Torres (PFP)	372,816	(3%)
Jerome McCready (AMI)	372,780	(3%)
June R. Genis (LIBERT)	235,918	(2%)
1992 Primary		
Barbara Boxer (D)	1,339,126	(44%)
Leo T. McCarthy (D)	935,209	(31%)
Mel Levine (D)	667,359	(22%)
Charles Greene (D)	122,954	(4%)

Previous Winning Percentages: **1990 *** (68%) **1988 *** (73%) **1986 *** (74%) **1984 *** (68%) **1982 *** (52%)

** House elections.*

Campaign Finance

	Receipts	Receipts from PACs		Expend-itures
1992				
Boxer (D)	$10,349,048	$896,683	(9%)	$10,368,600
Herschensohn (R)	$7,915,259	$627,158	(8%)	$7,859,072

Key Votes

1993	
Require unpaid family and medical leave	Y
Approve national "motor voter" registration bill	Y
Approve budget increasing taxes and reducing deficit	Y
Support president's right to lift military gay ban	Y
House Service:	
1992	
Approve balanced-budget constitutional amendment	N
Close down space station program	?
Approve U.S. aid for former Soviet Union	N
Allow shifting funds from defense to domestic programs	#
1991	
Extend unemployment benefits using deficit financing	Y
Approve waiting period for handgun purchases	Y
Authorize use of force in Persian Gulf	N

Voting Studies

	Presidential Support		Party Unity		Conservative Coalition	
Year	**S**	**O**	**S**	**O**	**S**	**O**
House Service:						
1992	5	51	50	4	8	50
1991	21	66	76	1	8	73
1990	14	81	86	4	11	83
1989	26	72	95	2	5	93
1988	17	69	86	5	8	87
1987	12	84	88	3	2	93
1986	13	78	84	4	12	82
1985	11	86	88	3	2	93
1984	20	68	86	3	2	92
1983	15	84	94	3	4	92

Interest Group Ratings

Year	ADA	AFL-CIO	CCUS	ACU
House Service:				
1992	60	100	0	0
1991	80	100	25	0
1990	94	83	8	4
1989	100	91	30	0
1988	80	93	27	5
1987	92	93	7	0
1986	90	100	13	5
1985	95	100	19	5
1984	95	92	46	0
1983	95	100	20	0

1 Dan Hamburg (D)

Of Ukiah — Elected 1992; 1st Term

Born: Oct. 6, 1948, St. Louis.
Education: Stanford U., A.B. 1970; California Institute of Integral Studies, M.A. 1992.
Occupation: Teacher.
Family: Wife, Carrie; four children.
Religion: Jewish.
Political Career: Ukiah Planning Commission, 1976-80; Mendocino County Board of Supervisors, 1981-85.
Capitol Office: 114 Cannon Bldg. 20515; 225-3311.

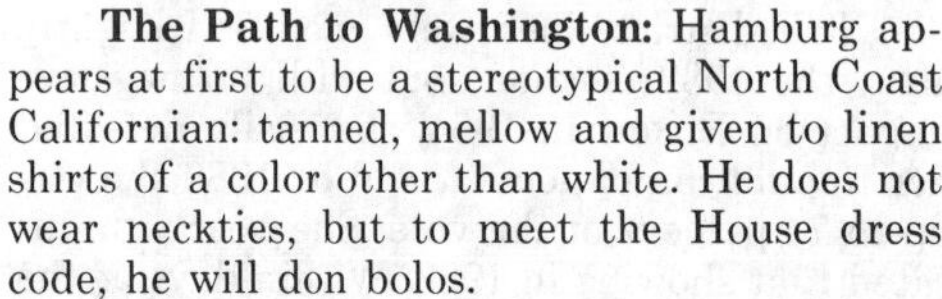

The Path to Washington: Hamburg appears at first to be a stereotypical North Coast Californian: tanned, mellow and given to linen shirts of a color other than white. He does not wear neckties, but to meet the House dress code, he will don bolos.

An easygoing product of the '60s, Hamburg still carries with him the anti-authoritarian spirit of the decade. He was one of only four members to vote against authorizing money to establish a national DNA database to track convicted criminals and one of only six to vote against giving the FBI authority to obtain unlisted phone numbers without a warrant in cases of terrorism or espionage. Hamburg also seemingly retains a fondness for other aspects of the '60s: In 1992, he told a California newspaper that he favors "growing your own."

But he brings to Congress accomplishments as a small-business operator and one-term Mendocino County supervisor, where he was credited with trying to unite the environmental and logging interests that are constantly at odds.

Hamburg is obviously simpatico with the pro-environment faction, and from his perch on the Merchant Marine and Fisheries Committee he can be counted on to look out for the 1st's 250 miles of pristine Pacific coastline.

But he took pains in the campaign to focus on economic issues. Hamburg hopes to use his seat on the Public Works and Transportation Committee to bring infrastructure improvements to the 1st to generate growth in rural industries. And he talks about economic conversion for the military in a time of post-Cold War downsizing (Travis Air Force Base is in the 1st; Mare Island Naval Shipyard, with 4,000 jobs, is just across the line in the 7th and is likely to be closed).

Hamburg extends his conversion arguments to the timber industry, which faces hard times even without pressure on the environmental front. He offers proposals for limiting logging to a rate that will sustain forest regeneration, ensure maximum protection for old-growth forests and guarantee that the benefits of logging accrue principally to the people of the 1st.

Having defeated one-term incumbent Republican Frank Riggs with less than a majority, Hamburg now must do what Riggs could not: solidify his support in this divided, if nominally Democratic district.

Riggs, a member of the "Gang of Seven" freshmen Republicans in the 102nd Congress, had tormented House Democratic leaders about members' perquisites and helped force disclosure of names and details in the House bank scandal. All seven freshmen were on the Democrats' hit list; only Hamburg managed to knock one off.

From the day he was elected, Riggs was in trouble. He defeated four-term incumbent Douglas H. Bosco, a Democrat, with only 43 percent of the vote. Bosco had fallen into the jobs-vs.-environment trap and had other liabilities as well. A Peace and Freedom Party candidate served as spoiler in the race, taking 15 percent, and Bosco lost by 3,300 votes.

Riggs, a Sonoma County developer and former police officer, appealed to more traditional voters in the district's far reaches. But he stung himself just after taking office when he backed off a campaign pledge not to accept a previously approved congressional pay raise.

Hamburg got started early, quitting his job 15 months before the election to campaign full time, crisscrossing the 350 miles from Del Norte County to Solano. He got the party nod when neither Bosco nor state Sen. Mike Thompson agreed to get in the race. Unchallenged in the primary, Hamburg was able to concentrate both on getting out his message and challenging Riggs for much of the year.

About 40 percent of the voters are new to the 1st, even though most of its territory is the same after redistricting — a testament to the rural character of most of the North Coast. The district retained a Democratic majority, which for Riggs was the biggest threat to winning re-election.

But Hamburg edged Riggs 48 percent to 45 percent, carrying only three counties. Two minor-party candidates shared 7 percent of the vote, but this time, left-leaning voters were less inclined to abandon the Democrat, and Riggs was denied a second fluke victory.

California 1

Northern Coast — Eureka

With all the changes overtaking California's political landscape in 1992, relatively little notice was paid to the reshaping of the 1st. As in the past, it stretches along the Pacific Coast from the Oregon line almost to metropolitan San Francisco. It still includes the big coastal counties of Mendocino, Humboldt and Del Norte, with their breathtaking forests and ocean waves crashing on boulders and beaches. But while these counties dominate the 1st's image, they have less than one-third of the people. Practically their only population center is the port city of Eureka in Humboldt County, the lone port for hundreds of miles, which earns its feast-or-famine living by shipping the region's world-class logs.

Just east of Mendocino, Lake County's mix of ranch, farm and tourism economy remain in the 1st. But south of Mendocino, redistricting altered the 1st. Most of Sonoma County was transferred to the 6th, which shed its city section to become wholly suburban. Included in the shift was Santa Rosa, which grew by 37 percent in the 1980s to become the largest city in the old 1st. Sonoma as a whole cast about half the total district vote in 1990. In 1992, after redistricting, the part of the county remaining in the 1st accounted for less than 10 percent of the district vote.

The new 1st still includes much of Sonoma County's prime wine-producing country. And it has added even more distinction in this arena by annexing all of neighboring Napa County. Wineries, large and small, line Highway 29 throughout the scenic Napa Valley, the source for much of the most prestigious wine in the Western Hemisphere.

Farther east, the 1st also expanded what had been a toehold in the southwestern corner of Solano County, where its holdings now spread north and east to enfold the cities of Fairfield and Vacaville. In the 1980s, the combined population of these two communities rose by roughly 50 percent to more than 150,000. In the 1992 elections, about 40 percent of the 1st's total vote came from Napa and Solano counties.

The politics of coastal Northern California have long required balancing the union sentiments of lumberjacks and other laborers with the Republican stands of timber owners, ranchers and retirees. Travis Air Force Base, at the district's southeastern extreme, has been a counterweight to the waves of "ecotopian" immigrants arriving in search of lifestyle nirvana in the coastal highlands to the north. But Travis' future is uncertain.

In partisan terms, losing Sonoma County was expected to hurt the Democrats — especially because the compensating territory in Napa and Solano counties had been relatively more Republican. But 1992 was an unusually ripe year for Democrats in California. Bill Clinton and Democratic Senate nominees Dianne Feinstein and Barbara Boxer almost achieved a triple sweep of all seven counties in the 1st (Boxer lost one: Del Norte). The Democrats' little-known House candidate, Hamburg, also held on to win, carrying Humboldt, Mendocino and Solano with just enough margin to survive losing the other four counties.

1990 Population: 573,082. White 487,230 (85%), Black 22,602 (4%), Other 63,250 (11%). Hispanic origin 64,233 (11%). 18 and over 423,418 (74%), 62 and over 87,396 (15%). Median age: 34.

Committees

Merchant Marine & Fisheries (21st of 28 Democrats)
Environment & Natural Resources; Fisheries Management

Public Works & Transportation (36th of 39 Democrats)
Economic Development; Surface Transportation; Water Resources and the Environment

Campaign Finance

	Receipts	Receipts from PACs		Expend-itures
1992				
Hamburg (D)	$652,592	$185,507	(28%)	$647,532
Riggs (R)	$729,819	$218,125	(30%)	$716,401
Baldwin (PFP)	$10,813	0		$10,588

Key Votes

1993

Require parental notification of minors' abortions	N
Require unpaid family and medical leave	Y
Approve national "motor voter" registration bill	Y
Approve budget increasing taxes and reducing deficit	Y
Approve economic stimulus plan	Y

Elections

1992 General

Dan Hamburg (D)	119,676	(48%)
Frank Riggs (R)	113,266	(45%)
Phil Baldwin (PFP)	10,764	(4%)
Matthew L. Howard (LIBERT)	7,500	(3%)

District Vote for President

1992

D 119,491 (47%)
R 74,597 (29%)
I 61,160 (24%)

2 Wally Herger (R)

Of Marysville — Elected 1986; 4th Term

Born: May 20, 1945, Sutter County, Calif.
Education: American River College, A.A. 1967; California State U., 1968-69.
Occupation: Rancher; gas company executive.
Family: Wife, Pamela Sargent; eight children.
Religion: Mormon.
Political Career: Calif. Assembly, 1981-87.
Capitol Office: 2433 Rayburn Bldg. 20515; 225-3076.

In Washington: Herger is a conservative Northern California rancher whose friendly style helps explain the ease with which he captured — and has since held — a district that was Democratic when the 1980s began.

Herger became vice president of his freshman Republican class, an early sign that his personality would wear well among his colleagues, too. His ascension to the Ways and Means and Budget committees at the beginning of the 103rd Congress confirmed his credentials as well as his career trajectory.

Like many another junior member, Herger had been campaigning for a Ways and Means slot since shortly after winning his first House election. Late in 1992, he beat out one of his California Republican colleagues, C. Christopher Cox, for the honor (Cox's consolation prize was a spot on the Budget Committee).

No one in the House suffers much suspense when Herger approaches the electronic voting device for key floor votes; in 1992, he supported the Republican Party on nine of 10 votes, and his consistently conservative line has earned him a series of perfect (or nearly so) scores from the American Conservative Union.

In order to join Ways and Means, Herger had to drop off the Agriculture Committee and the Merchant Marine Committee. Voters have been known to punish such career moves in the past, particularly where they diminish a member's power over crucial resources. But Herger will likely find ways to continue his efforts to protect farmers (his district's many fruit and nut growers were a focus for his years on Agriculture) as well as on Budget. The Budget Committee slot he landed is one of two seats reserved for members of Ways and Means.

On Agriculture, Herger's interest in averting a trade war with Europe stemmed from the threat of a European retaliatory tariff on U.S. walnuts. During consideration of the 1990 farm bill, Herger was especially keen on seeing the continuation of the Targeted Export Assistance program, which promotes exports of district products such as almonds and kiwi fruit.

From his seat on Agriculture's Forests Subcommittee, Herger also fended for his district's loggers. He bristled at the Fish and Wildlife Service's 1990 decision to list the northern spotted owl as a threatened species, which would curtail lumbering in ancient forests in the Pacific Northwest.

In June he asked Interior Secretary Manuel Lujan Jr. to exempt Northern California from the listing, arguing that the service had ignored "important biological evidence." "Once again," Herger said, "we see that prudence and common sense have been sacrificed to appease the extremists."

Following the outcry over the federal government's "let burn" policy toward fires that swept Yellowstone National Park and other public and private lands, Herger proposed a bill establishing a commission to recommend improvements in the government's management of wildfires. In May 1990, President Bush signed Herger's bill into law.

Herger has taken to the floor several times to decry alleged human rights abuses committed by the government of India against the Sikh minority in Punjab state. Members of the small Sikh community in Yuba City had told Herger of their concern for their relatives in the Punjab. Herger tried to amend the 1989 foreign aid authorization to bar development aid to India unless the president certified that India had prosecuted those responsible for several reported attacks on women in the Punjab in April 1989. His amendment lost 204-212.

Herger kept an eye on India as well in the 102nd Congress and introduced a bill to deny that country full trading status in June 1991.

Another assignment Herger dropped to join Ways and Means was the Select Narcotics Abuse and Control Committee (which was axed anyway, early in the 103rd Congress). In August 1992, Herger strongly supported a bill that would have cracked down on illegal methamphetamine labs, a large number of which are scattered across Herger's rural 2nd District.

The labs cause headaches for local authorities, who are forced to pay for cleaning the chemically laden sites once they are discovered

California 2

North and East — Chico; Redding

Redistricting can end a politician's career by shifting a single square mile of political turf. It can also switch broad swatches of territory and leave an incumbent unscathed. The new 2nd demonstrates the latter. The 1992 map tore away enough of the 2nd to encompass several New England states, while adding enough new real estate to make the district even bigger than before. It became California's least densely populated district, and its least racially diverse. The 2nd combines the northern portions of the old 2nd and the old 14th, consolidating much of the state's northern, rural Mormon population in the process.

The territorial changes, however, scarcely alter the 2nd's political coloration. Though GOP registration is slightly lower (down from 44 percent in the 1980s to 42 percent), Rep. Herger's re-election tally in 1992 inched up to 65 percent.

In the 1980s, the 2nd was a north-central inland district extending hundreds of miles south from the Oregon line to the outskirts of the Sacramento area. Its asphalt spine was Interstate 5 (which runs from Canada to Mexico), and its central feature was the mighty Mount Shasta.

The population was widely dispersed through the mountainous forests and rangelands, except for population centers in Redding (a 120-year-old mining and timber town on I-5) and Chico (home to a campus of California State University with 15,700 students).

Remapping cut deep into the 2nd's southern portion while pushing the district's eastern boundary all the way to the Nevada line. The northern timber counties of Siskiyou, Trinity and Shasta remain, but the agricultural counties of Tehama, Glenn, Colusa and Sutter were removed (along with the southwestern tip of Butte County).

The 2nd added new lands by expanding eastward to Nevada, embracing the three vast and remote counties of California's far northeastern corner (Modoc, Lassen and Plumas). These three lean to the GOP in most statewide elections, but with a combined registration of about 31,000 voters, they have little effect.

The 2nd also picked up all of Sierra and Nevada counties, named for the mountain range that marches through them. Descending from these heights on Interstate 80, travelers pass Donner Lake (named for the ill-fated pioneer party that largely perished there). Sierra County is sparsely populated, but just north and west of I-80 lie Nevada City and Grass Valley, which help make Nevada County the third-richest cache of votes in the 2nd (and the most decidedly Republican by registration). A few miles over the Yuba County line are Beale Air Force Base and Marysville, the latter at the confluence of the Feather and Yuba rivers.

But most of the 2nd's vote still comes from Butte (Chico) and Shasta (Redding) counties. Butte cast about one-third of the total vote in 1992 and gave Herger a 2-to-1 victory. Shasta cast more than one-fourth the district vote, favoring Republicans and giving Herger a 3-to-1 salute.

1990 Population: 573,322. White 525,091 (92%), Black 8,716 (2%), Other 39,515 (7%). Hispanic origin 34,425 (6%). 18 and over 424,975 (74%), 62 and over 105,763 (18%). Median age: 35.

and shut down. The bill would shift the burden onto the operators of the labs.

At Home: Expected to face tough Democratic competition for the open 2nd District in 1986, Herger won by a wide margin. He has had little difficulty in his three elections since.

The north-central California district had been Democrat Harold T. Johnson's for 22 years before Republican Gene Chappie upset him in 1980. When Chappie decided to retire in 1986, a GOP succession was in doubt. District Democrats touted the chances of Shasta County Supervisor Stephen C. Swendiman.

However, Swendiman stumbled in the Democratic primary and barely held off a challenge from rancher Wayne Meyer.

Herger, on the other hand, got a boost for the general election with his easy GOP primary victory.

Herger, who was in his third term in the state Assembly, came in with a voter base that comprised nearly half the 2nd District, and complemented that asset with superior organizing and fundraising. He spent most of the fall campaign on the offensive, linking himself to President Ronald Reagan and Gov. George Deukmejian and calling Swendiman a "tax-and-spend Democrat." When Swendiman portrayed him as a "back bencher" in the Legislature, Herger highlighted his support of popular measures such as workfare and tougher sentencing for criminals. Herger beat Swendiman in all 12 counties and took a solid 58 percent of the vote overall.

Most Democratic prospects declined to tackle Herger in 1988. Meyer, the runner-up from the 1986 Democratic primary, got the nomination unopposed. But he found it tough to raise money against Herger, who again won rather comfortably.

Democrats made even less of an effort in 1990, and Herger breezed past retired federal worker Erwin E. "Bill" Rush by a ratio of 2 to 1.

In 1992, redistricting removed from the 2nd all or part of five counties that Herger had represented, substituting all or part of five other counties. Vast as this land swap was, it scarcely altered the close ratio between the parties. The newly added territory was even more sparsely populated and mountainous than Herger's old district. It contained much of the state's rural Mormon population, and its last two congressmen (Norman Shumway and John T. Doolittle) had been, like Herger, conservative Republicans and Mormons. So it was not surprising that Herger not only won again but added a percentage point to his 1990 vote share and took a solid 65 percent.

Committees

Budget (6th of 17 Republicans)

Ways & Means (10th of 14 Republicans)
Oversight

Elections

1992 General		
Wally Herger (R)	167,247	(65%)
Elliot Roy Freedman (D)	71,780	(28%)
Harry H. Pendery (LIBERT)	17,529	(7%)
1992 Primary		
Wally Herger (R)	67,389	(89%)
Steve Kunelis (R)	8,467	(11%)
1990 General		
Wally Herger (R)	133,315	(64%)
Erwin E. "Bill" Rush (D)	65,333	(31%)
Ross Crain (LIBERT)	10,753	(5%)

Previous Winning Percentages: 1988 (59%) **1986** (58%)

District Vote for President

1992

D	93,823 (36%)
R	101,505 (39%)
I	67,298 (26%)

Campaign Finance

	Receipts	Receipts from PACs		Expend-itures
1992				
Herger (R)	$644,763	$225,289	(35%)	$533,861
Freedman (D)	$6,982	0		$4,947
Pendery (LIBERT)	$5,900	0		$5,900
1990				
Herger (R)	$616,075	$212,749	(35%)	$515,020
Rush (D)	$6,118	$2,000	(33%)	$5,951

Key Votes

1993	
Require parental notification of minors' abortions	Y
Require unpaid family and medical leave	N
Approve national "motor voter" registration bill	N
Approve budget increasing taxes and reducing deficit	N
Approve economic stimulus plan	N
1992	
Approve balanced-budget constitutional amendment	Y
Close down space station program	N
Approve U.S. aid for former Soviet Union	N
Allow shifting funds from defense to domestic programs	N
1991	
Extend unemployment benefits using deficit financing	?
Approve waiting period for handgun purchases	N
Authorize use of force in Persian Gulf	Y

Voting Studies

	Presidential Support		Party Unity		Conservative Coalition	
Year	S	O	S	O	S	O
1992	73	16	90	4	81	8
1991	68	30	86	8	95	3
1990	69	30	94	4	94	6
1989	76	24	91	8	88	12
1988	68	32	91	8	92	5
1987	74	24	89	9	93	7

Interest Group Ratings

Year	ADA	AFL-CIO	CCUS	ACU
1992	5	25	75	95
1991	5	18	89	100
1990	6	8	79	96
1989	10	25	100	100
1988	0	29	93	92
1987	12	13	100	100

3 Vic Fazio (D)

Of West Sacramento — Elected 1978; 8th Term

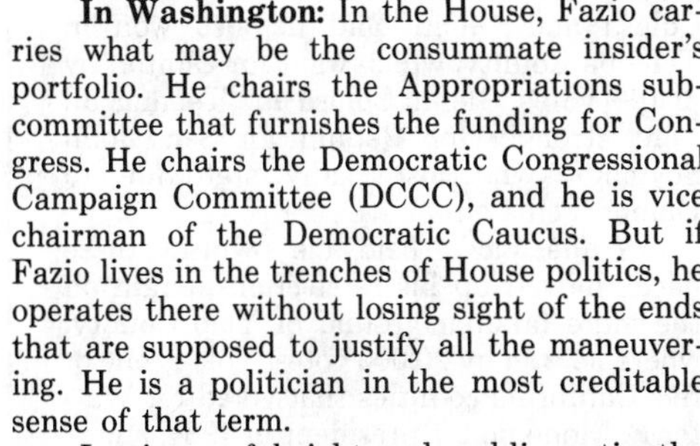

Born: Oct. 11, 1942, Winchester, Mass.
Education: Union College, B.A. 1965.
Occupation: Journalist; congressional and legislative consultant.
Family: Wife, Judy Kern; four children.
Religion: Episcopalian.
Political Career: Calif. Assembly, 1975-79.
Capitol Office: 2113 Rayburn Bldg. 20515; 225-5716.

In Washington: In the House, Fazio carries what may be the consummate insider's portfolio. He chairs the Appropriations subcommittee that furnishes the funding for Congress. He chairs the Democratic Congressional Campaign Committee (DCCC), and he is vice chairman of the Democratic Caucus. But if Fazio lives in the trenches of House politics, he operates there without losing sight of the ends that are supposed to justify all the maneuvering. He is a politician in the most creditable sense of that term.

In times of heightened public antipathy toward Congress, all these responsibilities come with a price. In 1992 he was hurt by redistricting and challenged by a hard-charging Republican who, with the help of a third-party candidate, held Fazio to a career-low 51 percent. Had it been less of a Democratic year, or if his GOP opponent had been less controversial, Fazio might not have been so fortunate.

But he survived, and in doing so he emerged as the highest-ranking member of the leadership from the largest delegation in Congress. If he can somehow secure his district and unite his state colleagues behind him, he could become the first Californian to be Speaker.

For now, Fazio is part of the younger generation of leaders that is coming into its own on Appropriations. He is one of the 13 subcommittee chairmen (known as the "college of cardinals"), but his panel, the Legislative Branch Subcommittee, is the most politically thankless of any of the Appropriations chairs. It handles the money Congress spends on itself, and members have never been so sensitized to criticism that they waste taxpayers' money by treating themselves too well.

But Fazio has never shrunk from unpleasant housekeeping chores, such as defending congressional pay raises and office budgets. "Let's face it," he says, "the Legislative [subcommittee] doesn't do much for you at home politically." But his willingness to bear that burden has won him the respect and gratitude of members from across the ideological spectrum who are glad to have someone else take the heat for what they want.

His colleagues rewarded him by electing him vice chairman of the Democratic Caucus in mid-1989, when the party leadership was rebuilt after Speaker Jim Wright's resignation. The following year, they added the chairmanship of the campaign committee to his workload.

Fazio had campaigned for the DCCC post during Wright's tenure, but he was cool at first when the job came open again. He indicated that he wanted to spend more time with his family. (Fazio in 1990 publicly acknowledged that his teenage daughter has leukemia.)

But the Californian had already established formidable campaign credentials as head of IMPAC 2000, a leadership-sponsored group designed to advance Democratic prospects in upcoming redistricting. The organizing and fundraising prowess he demonstrated there, along with his overall reputation for getting things done, made him the strong consensus pick for the job.

Fazio's task in 1992 was daunting: Hold the line in a year when redrawn districts and a presidential election coincided with a mood of impatience among voters. A postwar-record number of retirements further complicated matters. Yet Fazio and the party fared rather well. Although they lost ground in the House, dire forecasts of losses in the dozens of seats proved ill-founded. Republicans gained just 10 seats, and Fazio re-upped for a second cycle as chairman.

A strong partisan, Fazio is unapologetic about the politics of politics. "We are ... a country not served by government but by parties," he has said.

Discussing the possibility that Democrats were deliberately loading pet projects onto a funding bill that included one of President Bush's favorite projects, Fazio commented, "I wouldn't say there's a direct correlation, but if the administration is going to remain as committed as they are [to the super collider], obviously there's going to be some give-and-take."

Remarking on members' unwillingness to

California 3

North Central Valley

The 3rd bears little resemblance to the district so designated before 1992. The old 3rd had comprised much of Sacramento and some of its suburbs to the east, but now the 3rd scalps only the northwestern corner of Sacramento County before running far away to the north, west and south to incorporate tracts from the old 2nd and 4th districts.

The 3rd includes all of Yolo County and the eastern portion of Solano County, which were in the old 4th. This accounts for the 3rd's ready-made incumbent, Fazio, who had represented Yolo and eastern Solano counties as well as that portion of Sacramento's suburbs now included in the 3rd.

Now, however, Fazio has far fewer Solano County residents than he did in the 1980s. After a decade of intense growth, Solano was casting 30 percent of the vote in Fazio's old district. In 1992, the Solano precincts cast only 10 percent of the total vote in the new 3rd.

Remapping gave the 3rd the spacious northern county of Tehama, which serves as a bridge between the flat agricultural lands of the upper Sacramento River Valley and the timber-rich highlands of the Trinity-Shasta region to the north. The 3rd also picked up the farm-oriented counties of Glenn, Colusa and Sutter, the northern terminus of the state's richly productive Central Valley region.

Despite its vast new lands, however, the 3rd's most populous county is still Sacramento. Even though only the northwestern corner of the county remains, it accounted for about 40 percent of the total district vote in 1992. This corner includes McClellan Air Force Base (just outside the city limits of Sacramento) and a chunk of well-populated suburbs south of Interstate 80 and north of the American River. Residents here work in aerospace and other high-tech industry as well as in Sacramento's main business — state government.

In this vote-rich enclave, George Bush prevailed narrowly over Bill Clinton; but Fazio came up a winner by more than 7,000 votes. Fazio was able to carry two other counties in the 3rd that went for Bush, Colusa and Glenn, and he also won in Tehama County, which went for Clinton by just 89 votes. Glenn, Colusa and Tehama all went strongly for Republican Sen. John Seymour, who lost badly statewide to Dianne Feinstein.

While Fazio held his own in these parts, he ran up his re-election margin on the more familiar ground of Yolo County, where he won by 20,000 votes. Yolo is one of five California counties that voted for Walter F. Mondale for president in 1984, and it includes the college community of Davis, home of a sprawling University of California campus, which has a student population of 23,300.

Fazio lost in the small portion of Butte County that lies in the 3rd, and also in solidly Republican Sutter County (the only one of California's 58 counties to give Bush an outright majority in 1992).

1990 Population: 571,374. White 469,595 (82%), Black 18,339 (3%), Other 83,440 (15%). Hispanic origin 81,213 (14%). 18 and over 417,336 (73%), 62 and over 76,236 (13%). Median age: 31.

call attention to projects affecting their districts in one bill, Fazio said, "Most of us ... do not want to identify how successful we may have been in this legislation."

But Fazio is also sensitive to public perceptions of Congress and its possible excesses. In the past he has defended congressional mailing privileges, but during the 101st Congress, faced with perceived abuse of the system, Fazio moved for substantial reforms. His proposal was sharply attacked by some Democratic colleagues as too drastic, but members did ultimately approve some new restrictions in late 1990.

Much of Congress' institutional dirty work has fallen to Fazio because he is chairman of the Legislative Branch panel. Fazio has joked bitterly that one of the unstated purposes of the annual bill his panel produces is to "train freshman Republicans" by offering them targets to shoot at and prove their independence from the entrenched establishment.

"We'll forever be the place for freshman Republicans to cut their teeth," he has said. Of his bill's critics, he has said: "They think the only way we can save Congress is to destroy it."

Fazio was waist-deep in controversial issues — congressional pay, perks and ethics — throughout the 101st Congress. Fazio was generally admired for having defended a pay raise that many of his colleagues publicly denounced but privately coveted.

In another measure of the leadership's trust in his ability and willingness to take thankless jobs, Fazio was put in charge of a bipartisan task force to review House ethics standards.

Because of Fazio's close ties to the leadership, Republicans viewed with suspicion his role in the House ethics committee's investigation of Wright. Fazio was ranking Democrat on the ethics committee during that 1988-89 inquiry. Early in the investigation, the GOP passed a resolution calling on Fazio to disqualify himself because he invited Wright to a party fundraiser held in California after the ethics investigation had begun.

But Fazio remained in place, and while he was not as critical of Wright as some committee Democrats, neither was he an automatic pro-Wright vote. On several split committee votes, Fazio joined with committee Republicans in voting a tough anti-Wright line.

Fazio is one of the House's leading strategists on the issue of abortion rights. This brings him into conflict with another of the "cardinals," the fearsome chairman of the Labor, Health and Human Services Subcommittee, William H. Natcher of Kentucky. A staunch abortion foe known for exacting retribution on those who cross him, Natcher is now also chairman of the full Appropriations Committee.

During the years Republicans were in the White House, Fazio and other abortion rights supporters regularly sought to overturn federal anti-abortion policies by amending Natcher's Labor-HHS appropriations bill. In 1992, Fazio and Oregon Democrat Les AuCoin — another abortion rights leader on Appropriations — had hoped that Natcher would not object if they added their amendment blocking implementation of regulations barring abortion counseling in federally funded family planning clinics — the so-called "gag rule."

But Natcher gave a thunderous warning in committee that he wanted no such encumbrance on his bill, since it would invite a veto from President Bush. Bush had vetoed the previous year's bill because it included such a temporary block of the gag rule.

With Natcher newly installed atop the full committee and a separate family-planning bill available as an alternative vehicle, members deferred to the chairman and declined to add the gag rule language to his bill.

In addition to giving him leverage over the internal workings of Congress, Fazio's subcommittee chairmanship allows him to leave his mark on a variety of appropriations bills, and he has done so to help the California delegation on issues such as protecting the coastline against offshore oil drilling and pushing for a fund to clean up toxic wastes at military installations, including several in the Sacramento area.

Water is a constant concern for the farmers in Fazio's district. A wide-ranging water projects bill in the 102nd Congress revamped the operations of the nation's largest federal water program, California's Central Valley Project, which controls about 20 percent of the state's water. Fazio helped negotiate the final agreement, which made fish and wildlife preservation a central goal of the water project.

He has been less successful in an endeavor he and fellow California Democrat Robert T. Matsui have championed for the past half-dozen years: the proposed Auburn Dam, a $698 million project that proponents say would protect 300,000 Sacramento-area residents from rare but potentially deadly floods. Despite a personal appeal from Fazio, the House voted 273-140 to strike authorization for the Auburn Dam from a 1992 bill reauthorizing the U.S. Army Corps of Engineers.

At Home: Fazio's re-election fight in 1992 was the most dramatic of his career and one of the season's more notable struggles for any House incumbent. Fazio raised nearly $2 million and spent $1.9 million to garner just 51 percent of the vote. It was the biggest campaign budget for a House race in California (except the $5 million extravaganza bankrolled personally by GOP challenger Michael Huffington in the 22nd District).

Fazio was up and running early for 1992, heeding the alarm he heard in his lowered vote share in 1990 (55 percent). Voters then had seemed to be punishing him for his Mr. Insider role in the House, as well as for his defense of pay increases for Congress in the 101st Congress. That situation scarcely eased for Fazio in the 102nd Congress, with the House bank scandal and other institutional embarrassments.

Worse yet, the redistricting of 1992 reconfigured Fazio's district radically. He still represented suburban Sacramento, but he lost the exurban corridor running south toward San Francisco and found himself yanked to the north to run in four farm counties that were largely terra incognita for him.

The scenario helped attract a well-known and well-heeled challenger, former state Sen. H. L. Richardson, who had represented an Orange County district for 22 years ending in 1988. A founder of Gun Owners of America and a champion of the religious right, Richardson was able to raise more money than any California challenger except Huffington and press the attack vigorously against Fazio. But the former legislator also presented Fazio with what he needed: a target for counterattack.

Fazio accused Richardson of missing thousands of votes as a legislator and painted him as both a carpetbagger and an extremist. Richardson had lived in the state capital region for many years but remained widely identified with Southern California. The success of Fazio's attacking defense was visible in the vote cast for a Libertarian candidate, whose 9 percent share kept Richardson at just 40 percent.

Nonetheless, Fazio can no longer count on 60 percent vote shares. Nor can he count on the GOP to nominate challengers with Richardson's baggage. The district's Democratic registration is now below 50 percent, and any further erosion in that number could render Fazio's predicament acute.

Fazio has come far in not many years. Raised and educated in the East, he came to California as a journalist who covered and then worked for the state Assembly. He won a seat in that body in a 1975 special election and was re-elected easily in 1976. In 1978, he was the only Democrat ready to run for Congress when his area's embattled Democratic incumbent, Robert Leggett, suddenly retired. Fazio's Republican opponent that year was a former aide to Ronald Reagan who ran well in rural areas, but Fazio raised more money and claimed the seat. In 1980, Fazio defied Reagan's landslide in winning a second term with nearly two-thirds of the vote.

Redistricting in 1981 weakened Fazio slightly, but he won his next term easily because his opponent, political consultant Roger Canfield, did not receive the financial support he had hoped to get from, among others, the conservative network run by Richardson. Fazio walked off with better than 60 percent in each of the district's counties.

In 1984, Fazio's support for that year's congressional pay increase was supposed to make him vulnerable. But the Republicans again nominated Canfield and again shrank from making a major financial investment.

Committee

Caucus Vice Chairman

Appropriations (13th of 37 Democrats)
Legislative Branch (chairman); Energy & Water Development; Military Construction

Elections

1992 General		
Vic Fazio (D)	122,149	(51%)
H.L. "Bill" Richardson (R)	96,092	(40%)
Ross Crain (LIBERT)	20,444	(9%)
1990 General		
Vic Fazio (D)	115,090	(55%)
Mark Baughman (R)	82,738	(39%)
Bryce Bigwood (LIBERT)	12,626	(6%)

Previous Winning Percentages: **1988** (99%) **1986** (70%) **1984** (61%) **1982** (64%) **1980** (65%) **1978** (55%)

District Vote for President

1992
D 99,781 (41%)
R 90,799 (37%)
I 53,323 (22%)

Campaign Finance

	Receipts	Receipts from PACs		Expend-itures
1992				
Fazio (D)	$1,994,284	$1,148,438	(58%)	$1,906,584
Richardson (R)	$856,853	$76,661	(9%)	$853,730
1990				
Fazio (D)	$845,622	$451,245	(53%)	$1,029,304
Baughman (R)	$40,439	$3,500	(9%)	$40,040

Key Votes

1993	
Require parental notification of minors' abortions	N
Require unpaid family and medical leave	Y
Approve national "motor voter" registration bill	Y
Approve budget increasing taxes and reducing deficit	Y
Approve economic stimulus plan	Y
1992	
Approve balanced-budget constitutional amendment	N
Close down space station program	N
Approve U.S. aid for former Soviet Union	Y
Allow shifting funds from defense to domestic programs	Y
1991	
Extend unemployment benefits using deficit financing	Y
Approve waiting period for handgun purchases	Y
Authorize use of force in Persian Gulf	N

Voting Studies

	Presidential Support		Party Unity		Conservative Coalition	
Year	**S**	**O**	**S**	**O**	**S**	**O**
1992	28	68	88	9	44	48
1991	34	61	87	9	24	68
1990	19	81	91	5	26	72
1989	35	64	95	4	24	76
1988	19	73	92	2	16	74
1987	23	75	92	3	35	63
1986	20	80	93	5	30	64
1985	26	65	90	6	35	65
1984	31	64	88	8	25	68
1983	28	68	91	6	24	72
1982	36	58	92	7	29	67
1981	41	57	81	17	33	64

Interest Group Ratings

Year	ADA	AFL-CIO	CCUS	ACU
1992	90	75	50	8
1991	75	83	30	0
1990	89	100	21	4
1989	80	100	20	4
1988	85	100	29	0
1987	84	94	14	0
1986	80	93	24	9
1985	75	82	32	14
1984	75	85	38	4
1983	80	100	26	9
1982	80	90	14	5
1981	80	87	17	0

4 John T. Doolittle (R)

Of Rocklin — Elected 1990; 2nd Term

Born: Oct. 30, 1950, Glendale, Calif.
Education: U. of California, Santa Cruz, B.A. 1972; U. of the Pacific, J.D. 1978.
Occupation: Lawyer.
Family: Wife, Julia Harlow; two children.
Religion: Mormon.
Political Career: Calif. Senate, 1981-91.
Capitol Office: 1524 Longworth Bldg. 20515; 225-2511.

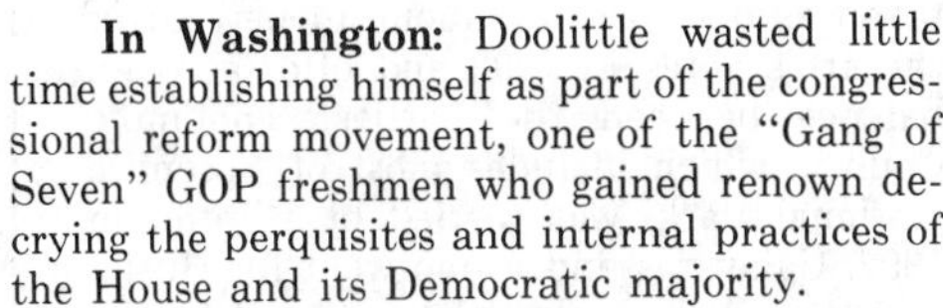

In Washington: Doolittle wasted little time establishing himself as part of the congressional reform movement, one of the "Gang of Seven" GOP freshmen who gained renown decrying the perquisites and internal practices of the House and its Democratic majority.

Doolittle and his compatriots (Frank Riggs of California, Jim Nussle of Iowa, Scott L. Klug of Wisconsin, John A. Boehner of Ohio, Rick Santorum of Pennsylvania and Charles H. Taylor of North Carolina) were instrumental in forcing full disclosure of the names of all those who had overdrafts at the House bank.

But some of the sting went out of Doolittle's attacks after a California newspaper revealed a letter sent jointly by Doolittle and Democratic Rep. Maxine Waters of California urging the House Administration Committee to adopt some of the perks they had found useful as California state legislators. These included phones, meals, moving expenses and the use of government cars.

Doolittle also raised eyebrows as the House's top user of franked mail in the 102nd Congress. His millions of mailings included substantial amounts that went outside what was then his district, a practice since abolished by the House.

An ardent spokesman for conservative causes during a 10-year tenure in the California Senate, Doolittle has fervent supporters who view him as a future leader of the Republican Party. But Doolittle has always had detractors, both inside and outside his party, who see him as an ideologue and a hardball politician.

One of his moments of note as a House freshman resulted from his somewhat surprising alliance with some environmentalists in opposition to the proposed Auburn Dam on California's American River. The dam was supported by Rep. Vic Fazio, a senior California Democrat, whose down-river constituents have long sought protection from periodic flooding. But some national environmental groups argued that the dam would inundate 34 miles of the river's pristine canyon and destroy its last free-flowing section.

For his part, Doolittle wanted to build a bigger, multipurpose dam on the site that could provide water and power to the area population as well as flood control. After some preliminary negotiations with Fazio, Doolittle decided to oppose building any dam for now and go after his own plan later. That put him in temporary alliance with the no-dam environmentalists.

During the 102nd Congress, Doolittle directed considerable energy back home in the fight to draw California's congressional districts. He got a seat at the table by beating out veteran Rep. Bill Thomas in the race to chair the California delegation's redistricting committee. Thomas, a political scientist, was the reigning expert on district mapping after a decade of battling over it in the courts and on the ballot. But some in the delegation saw Thomas as too interested in maximizing competitive districts — where Republicans could possibly win — rather than safeguarding GOP districts where they could not possibly lose.

There were no such doubts about Doolittle, who was also thought well-positioned to lobby the Legislature after serving there throughout the 1980s. As the delegation's point man, Doolittle not only went after the Democrats in Washington and Sacramento but weighed in against California's GOP Gov. Pete Wilson. Doolittle saw Wilson's plans diluting the party's strength in its strongholds for the sake of electing a few more Republicans — most likely moderates in Wilson's mold — in marginal districts. He argued for districts drawn to be Republican enough to elect strong conservatives.

In the end, Doolittle made common cause with Democrats in the California Legislature who liked his idea of bedrock Republican districts. When these Democrats passed a plan, Wilson vetoed it. And despite the union of left and right, there were not enough votes to override. A panel of three retired judges was appointed by the state Supreme Court and drew up a plan that the high court accepted (and that federal courts refused to overturn).

The court-approved map paid attention to

California 4

Northeast Central

The number is new, and six of its counties were removed in 1992 redistricting, but the 4th is still at heart the district that elected Doolittle in 1990 (when it was designated the 14th). The 4th is one of just two districts in Northern California that voted for George Bush in 1992, and one of just two with a Republican registration plurality (45 percent). The 4th is also one of just three districts in all of California where racial minorities constitute less than 15 percent of the population.

This is not to say the district has not changed with redistricting. Gone are the Republican-leaning northern counties of Modoc, Lassen, Plumas and Sierra. Republicans may also miss Nevada County, where nearly 55,000 voters registered in 1992 and a plurality identified themselves with the GOP. Democrats in the district were sorry to see San Joaquin County become part of the 11th District. San Joaquin included Democratic-voting Lodi and a portion of Stockton.

Left intact at the center of the district were the old core counties of Placer, El Dorado, Amador and tiny Alpine (733 registered voters). Placer and El Dorado were the second- and third-largest contributors to the old 14th District vote (after San Joaquin). Now they rank No. 1 and No. 3, respectively. Together, they cast 54 percent of the district vote in 1992, giving pluralities to Bush and bare majorities to Doolittle. Alpine and Amador were closer contests, with independent candidate Ross Perot running a close third behind Bill Clinton.

Amador and El Dorado counties triggered the great California gold rush of the mid-19th century (Placerville, the El Dorado county seat, was once among the state's largest cities). Far more recently, the natural beauty of the area (which includes Lake Tahoe) has spawned a more sustainable boom: Amador, Placer and El Dorado were among the eight fastest-growing counties in the state in the 1980s.

Immediately to the south, redistricting brought in three highland counties (Calaveras, Tuolumne and Mono) that, taken as one, provide about 14 percent of the 4th's votes in 1992 and offer a rough balance between the parties. Tuolumne County, which includes most of Yosemite National Park, was carried by Clinton in 1992; Calaveras and Mono went for Bush.

Remapping also gave the 4th the northeastern corner of Sacramento County, where the immediate suburbs of the state capital have grown out to meet the town of Folsom. Once known only for its prison (immortalized in song by Johnny Cash), Folsom is now home to Aerojet, the source of space shuttle technology. Folsom grew by a stunning 171 percent in the 1980s but has since been hit hard by layoffs at Aerojet.

Sacramento County as a whole votes Democratic, but the portions bordering Placer and El Dorado counties behave more like their upland neighbors. Doolittle actually ran slightly ahead of his districtwide margin here in 1992.

1990 Population: 571,033. White 529,202 (93%), Black 10,059 (2%), Other 31,772 (6%). Hispanic origin 42,424 (7%). 18 and over 426,723 (75%), 62 and over 84,051 (15%). Median age: 35.

compactness and community of interest and made no overt effort to favor either party. It was more to Wilson's and Thomas' liking than Doolittle's, but the first-termer could console himself with the knowledge that his own district became marginally more secure.

At Home: Democrats entered 1992 with high hopes of bagging Doolittle and at least four other members of the Gang of Seven. In the end, they got only Riggs, and the most frustrating of the failures may have come in California's 4th District. Although he slipped below half the vote, Doolittle survived against a challenger who could not bring herself to mount an effective attack.

In 1990, Doolittle inherited what had been a safe district for his six-term predecessor, Norman D. Shumway, another Mormon who defined the delegation's right flank. Doolittle also inherited Shumway's 1988 Democratic challenger, Patricia Malberg, a former junior college teacher from Lincoln, a small town in western Placer County. Malberg had run a spunky if quixotic campaign against Shumway and managed an almost respectable 37 percent. Malberg had never stopped running, however, and she was to give the young state senator fits in November.

Malberg offered a sharp contrast on the issues, strongly opposing Doolittle's own agenda of the death penalty, nuclear power, the Human Life Amendment, offshore oil drilling and the construction of the big-dam option at Auburn. All this clash seemed to favor the Republican in a district inclined to social as well as economic conservatism. But Malberg also stressed her outsider status to advantage, contrasting her old-fashioned campaign with Doolittle's big-dollar, high-power, PAC-financed effort.

Doolittle contributed to the closeness of the 1990 race with controversies of his own making. He created a stir with his first campaign TV ad. Calling for a constitutional ban on flag-burning, Doolittle said the American flag has been honored from "the Fourth of July parade to a place called Vietnam."

This angered some Vietnam veterans, who noted that Doolittle during the war had taken a student deferment, then served as a Mormon missionary in Argentina. However, several veterans' groups, which had supported Doolittle's previous campaigns, came to his defense.

In the end, Doolittle had just enough in his base and his operation to win the seat with 51 percent. That obviously encouraged Malberg to stretch her political career out another two years and hope for help from the redistricting process.

What happened instead was that Doolittle shed some of his more Democratic precincts in San Joaquin County, giving him an outright Republican plurality for the first time. This revised 4th would give George Bush a better share of the 1992 presidential vote than any other district in Northern California (40.7 percent).

Nonetheless, some observers saw Malberg catching the brass ring in 1992, the "Year of the Woman." Much of the district was new not only to the challenger but to the incumbent as well. And Doolittle had to slog through a primary against a political neophyte who dwelt on old controversies surrounding Doolittle's campaign tactics (some of which had brought a fine from the state's Fair Political Practices Commission).

The neophyte stuck around for the fall campaign as a write-in candidate, and Doolittle looked likely to lose even more conservative votes to Libertarian contender Patrick Lee McHargue. Near the end of the 1992 campaign, Doolittle's luck seemed to have run out with the exposure of his joint letter about perks. But Malberg was unable to take full advantage of the opening. The local organizing that had been the genius of her earlier campaigns was not geared to attacking Doolittle, and neither was her modest broadcast ad effort. In the end, Malberg slipped several points below her 1990 showing, while McHargue's 4 percent share was only enough to keep Doolittle from reaching a majority.

Committees

Agriculture (12th of 18 Republicans)
Foreign Agriculture & Hunger; General Farm Commodities; Specialty Crops & Natural Resources

Natural Resources (9th of 15 Republicans)
Energy & Mineral Resources; National Parks, Forests & Public Lands; Oversight & Investigations

Elections

1992 General		
John T. Doolittle (R)	141,155	(50%)
Patricia Malberg (D)	129,489	(46%)
Patrick Lee McHargue (LIBERT)	12,705	(4%)
1992 Primary		
John T. Doolittle (R)	57,631	(71%)
Don Brooksher (R)	23,404	(29%)
1990 General		
John T. Doolittle (R)	128,039	(51%)
Patricia Malberg (D)	120,742	(49%)

District Vote for President

1992

D 97,501 (34%)
R 117,155 (41%)
I 73,060 (25%)

Campaign Finance

	Receipts	Receipts from PACs		Expend-itures
1992				
Doolittle (R)	$610,104	$249,095	(41%)	$622,071
Malberg (D)	$385,906	$121,357	(31%)	$376,190
1990				
Doolittle (R)	$529,813	$234,764	(44%)	$517,668
Malberg (D)	$222,011	$45,911	(21%)	$220,379

Key Votes

1993	
Require parental notification of minors' abortions	Y
Require unpaid family and medical leave	N
Approve national "motor voter" registration bill	N
Approve budget increasing taxes and reducing deficit	N
Approve economic stimulus plan	N
1992	
Approve balanced-budget constitutional amendment	Y
Close down space station program	Y
Approve U.S. aid for former Soviet Union	N
Allow shifting funds from defense to domestic programs	N
1991	
Extend unemployment benefits using deficit financing	X
Approve waiting period for handgun purchases	N
Authorize use of force in Persian Gulf	Y

Voting Studies

	Presidential Support		Party Unity		Conservative Coalition	
Year	S	O	S	O	S	O
1992	81	19	97	3	96	4
1991	73	22	89	5	95	0

Interest Group Ratings

Year	ADA	AFL-CIO	CCUS	ACU
1992	5	17	75	100
1991	5	9	78	100

5 Robert T. Matsui (D)

Of Sacramento — Elected 1978; 8th Term

Born: Sept. 17, 1941, Sacramento, Calif.
Education: U. of California, Berkeley, A.B. 1963, J.D. 1966.
Occupation: Lawyer.
Family: Wife, Doris Okada; one child.
Religion: Methodist.
Political Career: Sacramento City Council, 1971-78.
Capitol Office: 2311 Rayburn Bldg. 20515; 225-7163.

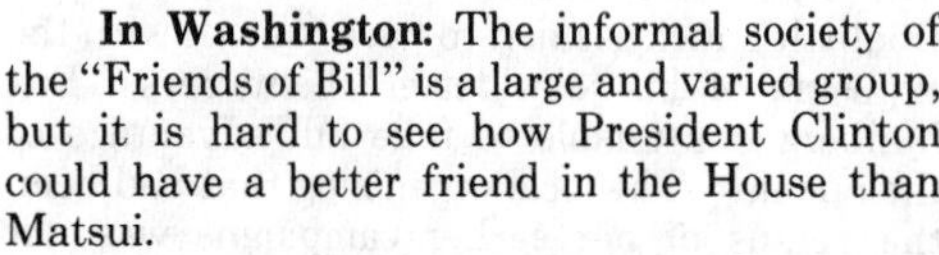

In Washington: The informal society of the "Friends of Bill" is a large and varied group, but it is hard to see how President Clinton could have a better friend in the House than Matsui.

As a senior and respected member of the Ways and Means Committee, Matsui is in a position to offer aid and comfort to the president at crucial times, as when he called upon Democrats to unite behind Clinton's economic plan in early 1993. "Bill Clinton's success is our success; his failure is our failure," Matsui said.

The political connections go deeper: Doris Matsui, his wife, served as a member of Clinton's transition team board of directors and is now a special assistant to the president. Matsui himself, a noted fundraiser, is treasurer of the Democratic National Committee.

In March 1993, Matsui used his access to lobby against the closure of several military bases in California. Sacramento's own McClellan Air Force Base had been targeted for closing, but after Matsui and others visited with Clinton, McClellan was dropped from one list (it popped up on an additional list in May).

Matsui's connections may help salve his disappointment at having to shelve his own statewide ambitions in 1992 — for the third time. After deciding the time was not right for statewide campaigns in 1988 and 1990, Matsui declared for the Senate early in the 1992 cycle. But he withdrew within weeks after learning that his father was dying of cancer.

Matsui has always been known for his energy, driving himself and his staff hard from day to day and from issue to issue. He has also generally enjoyed the good will of the news media, who find him among the most accessible and quotable members. In the 101st Congress, Matsui also added his first important leadership credential, ascending to the Democratic Steering and Policy Committee midway through 1989.

For three months at the start of the 103rd, Matsui's seniority on Ways and Means made him the acting chairman of the Human Resources Subcommittee, with jurisdiction over welfare programs. But Rep. Harold E. Ford of Tennessee, who had been the chairman prior to his indictment on long-pending fraud charges, was acquitted in April and restored to his full privileges on the committee.

Through eight terms in the House, seven of them on the Ways and Means Committee, Matsui has been remarkable in his ability to combine a thoughtful, generally liberal approach to tax policy with an intense interest in serving California business. While liberals can count on his votes on social-policy issues, Matsui has increasingly applied his capacity for hard work to the business side of the committee's ledger, especially where West Coast industries are concerned.

During debate on the mammoth 1986 overhaul of the tax code, Matsui tried to preserve the tax-exempt status of municipal bonds used to finance private development. He succeeded in wearing away room in the bill for a few exemptions, including one for an urban redevelopment bond popular in California.

Some have connected this solicitousness to Matsui's ambition: running statewide in California now requires funding in seven or eight digits. Of course, Matsui also is seen as currying public favor when he weighs in on behalf of consumers. And sometimes he seems to have played to both business and consumers on a single issue.

In 1989 he went after a provision in the 1986 tax overhaul that had allowed utilities to collect more tax-reserve money from customers than needed. This meant utilities could amass capital, avoid new debt for new plants and so hold down rates. But the extra withholding piled up embarrassingly fast, yielding a $19 billion windfall for utilities nationally by the midpoint of 1989. With Democratic Rep. Byron L. Dorgan of North Dakota, Matsui sought immediate repeal of the provision and a rebate of the reserves. Their effort failed in committee on a vote of 13-22.

On trade matters, Matsui generally has supported a free market across international borders. He argues that trade spurs growth, serving American interests as much as those of

California 5

Sacramento

No incumbent likes to see his district renumbered, a happenstance that confuses constituents, supporters and journalists alike. But for Rep. Matsui, the 14-year incumbent from Sacramento whose 3rd District was redesignated the 5th in the 1992 redistricting, there was little else to regret in the new map.

Matsui's geographical base continues to shrink as the Sacramento metropolitan area grows. Population in the city of Sacramento grew 34 percent during the 1980s, to 369,000. So even though the map drawn in 1992 was generally Republican-friendly, Matsui got a district more concentrated in Sacramento and more Democratic. The 5th has a Democratic registration of 59 percent, up four percentage points from 1990.

Despite the big Democratic numbers, the old 3rd had been a swing district in statewide elections. Republicans George Bush and Ronald Reagan carried it in the presidential elections of the 1980s, and GOP Gov. Pete Wilson won it in the 1990 gubernatorial contest. But in 1992, with some of its more affluent suburban territory pared away, the district went for Democrat Bill Clinton, giving him an outright majority of 51 percent. The 5th also gave generous victory margins to the campaigns of Democratic Senate nominees Dianne Feinstein and Barbara Boxer.

On paper, the city of Sacramento has several reasons to be reliably Democratic. Labor is better organized here than in all but a few other counties in California. The dominant newspaper is The Sacramento Bee, the flagship of the McClatchy chain and a decidedly liberal voice. The city also has a strong admixture of blacks and Hispanics, who constitute more than one-fourth of the district population. There are more than 72,000 Asian-Americans in the 5th, placing it 11th in that category (although three-fourths of those old enough to vote were not registered in 1992).

But the bedrock of Sacramento politics is the presence of the state government, the source of about 50,000 jobs and a natural pro-government attitude. Years of recession have drained the state treasury and successive Republican governors have sought to limit government spending, but the wellspring of well-being in Sacramento is unlikely to change anytime soon.

There is another Sacramento, of course, that reads The Sacramento Union and makes its living in financial services, agribusiness or in the high-tech industries that have sprung up in Sacramento County in recent years. But this sector of the local economy is no longer as robust as in the early 1980s, either. Cutbacks in defense spending have clouded the future, just as base-closing plans have cast shadows over the Sacramento Army Depot (slated to close in 1997) and, east of the city in Rancho Cordova, Mather Air Force Base (scheduled to close late in 1993).

In any event, most of the political impact of this other Sacramento is felt in the county's suburbs and exurban areas, most of which have now been apportioned among three adjoining districts.

1990 Population: 573,684. White 376,389 (66%), Black 73,567 (13%), Other 123,728 (22%). Hispanic origin 84,426 (15%). 18 and over 421,787 (74%), 62 and over 78,443 (14%). Median age: 32.

other nations. In the 102nd Congress, Matsui pressed for language stiffening enforcement of bilateral trade agreements, such as that requiring Japanese companies to buy more U.S.-made computer chips. His amendment was part of a trade bill that passed the House but died in the Senate.

In the 100th Congress, with Democratic Rep. Norman Y. Mineta of California, Matsui was an important force behind passage of legislation to provide federal redress to the surviving Japanese-Americans who were interned during World War II.

In 1942, when he was 6 months old, Matsui and his family were ousted from their Sacramento home and sent to a detention camp, where they lived for more than three years.

The legislation, passed in 1987, formally apologized to those interned, and established a $1.25 billion fund to give $20,000 to each of the estimated 60,000 surviving victims (half the total number interned). Former detainees who accept the settlement agree to drop further claims against the government.

At Home: When he looks back on what might have been, Matsui may rue most the 1992 statewide race he had to abandon. Such a year of political opportunity is not likely to be duplicated soon. Two Senate seats were open, and both were won by Democrats. Had he run, Matsui could have looked to a solid base in Sacramento, the state capital and one of California's booming growth areas. His business contacts and proven fundraising ability also would have benefited him in a year in which the sources of political money were stretched thin.

Matsui's political career began on the local level. His experience in a World War II internment camp helped him establish a bond with Sacramento's large Asian community, and he won two elections for the City Council. In 1972, the year after Matsui joined the council, he chaired U.S. Rep. John E. Moss' re-election campaign. His fundraising skills helped Moss win easily that year, and again in 1974 and 1976.

In 1978 Matsui was preparing to run for the county Board of Supervisors when Moss announced his retirement after 26 years. Matsui filed for Congress, along with two other prominent Sacramento Democrats, but his $225,000 primary campaign budget gave him a clear advantage. He ran television commercials identifying himself as "Citizen Matsui," setting himself apart from his rivals, both of whom had been heavily involved in state politics.

Matsui won the primary and then took the general election comfortably against Republican Sandy Smoley, considered the Sacramento GOP's strongest candidate to run for the House in many years. Republicans have made no similar effort to capture the district since. His 1992 challenger was a former bookstore owner and eccentric intellectual who ran 5 percentage points below the Republican registration for the district.

Committee

Ways & Means (8th of 24 Democrats)
Human Resources; Trade

Elections

1992 General		
Robert T. Matsui (D)	158,250	(69%)
Robert S. Dinsmore (R)	58,698	(25%)
Gordon D. Mors (AMI)	4,745	(2%)
Chris Rufer (LIBERT)	4,547	(2%)
Tian Harter (GREEN)	4,316	(2%)
1990 General		
Robert T. Matsui (D)	132,143	(60%)
Lowell P. Landowski (R)	76,148	(35%)
David M. McCann (LIBERT)	10,797	(5%)

Previous Winning Percentages: **1988** (71%) **1986** (76%) **1984** (100%) **1982** (90%) **1980** (71%) **1978** (53%)

District Vote for President

1992
D 120,577 (51%)
R 73,562 (31%)
I 42,566 (18%)

Campaign Finance

	Receipts	Receipts from PACs		Expend-itures
1992				
Matsui (D)	$656,875	$365,100	(56%)	$1,421,123
Dinsmore (R)	$30,093	$16	(0%)	$32,826
Harter (GREEN)	$4,771	$375	(8%)	$4,730
1990				
Matsui (D)	$1,207,843	$582,964	(48%)	$734,005
Landowski (R)	$4,545	$250	(6%)	$4,628

Key Votes

1993	
Require parental notification of minors' abortions	N
Require unpaid family and medical leave	Y
Approve national "motor voter" registration bill	Y
Approve budget increasing taxes and reducing deficit	Y
Approve economic stimulus plan	Y
1992	
Approve balanced-budget constitutional amendment	N
Close down space station program	N
Approve U.S. aid for former Soviet Union	Y
Allow shifting funds from defense to domestic programs	Y
1991	
Extend unemployment benefits using deficit financing	Y
Approve waiting period for handgun purchases	Y
Authorize use of force in Persian Gulf	N

Voting Studies

	Presidential Support		Party Unity		Conservative Coalition	
Year	S	O	S	O	S	O
1992	26	71	88	6	29	67
1991	28	60	78	5	16	62
1990	21	75	89	5	17	76
1989	33	66	94	3	15	85
1988	20	75	88	2	16	79
1987	20	80	95	2	14	79
1986	20	80	94	3	18	82
1985	20	80	94	2	9	89
1984	32	65	94	3	12	88
1983	32	67	93	6	24	76
1982	40	60	93	5	19	81
1981	45	53	80	17	32	63

Interest Group Ratings

Year	ADA	AFL-CIO	CCUS	ACU
1992	80	55	29	8
1991	70	80	25	0
1990	94	92	21	0
1989	95	92	10	4
1988	90	86	36	4
1987	92	87	20	9
1986	95	79	17	5
1985	90	94	18	5
1984	80	92	38	0
1983	85	94	25	4
1982	85	95	14	5
1981	70	87	17	0

6 Lynn Woolsey (D)

Of Petaluma — Elected 1992; 1st Term

Born: Nov. 3, 1937, Seattle, Wash.
Education: U. of Washington, 1955-57; U. of San Francisco, B.S. 1980.
Occupation: Personnel service owner.
Family: Husband, David Woolsey; four children.
Religion: Presbyterian.
Political Career: Petaluma City Council, 1984-93.
Capitol Office: 439 Cannon Bldg. 20515; 225-5161.

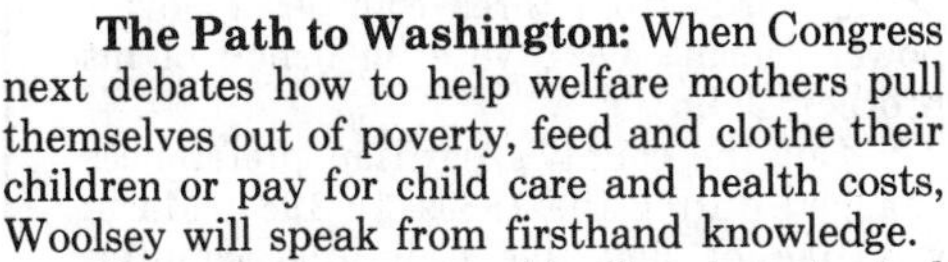

The Path to Washington: When Congress next debates how to help welfare mothers pull themselves out of poverty, feed and clothe their children or pay for child care and health costs, Woolsey will speak from firsthand knowledge.

Hers may not resemble the stereotypical portrait, but her route to the welfare lines is classic: She was 29 and had little work experience when she divorced her successful stockbroker husband and found herself with no house, no job skills and three small children.

After lying about her circumstances to land her first job, and surviving for three years on various forms of government aid that supplemented her meager wages, Woolsey remarried and left the assistance rolls. She went back to college, completed her bachelor's degree at age 42 and the same year started a temporary employment service that she still owns.

She was elected to the Petaluma City Council in 1984 and served eight years before being elected to the 6th, a liberal suburban San Francisco district anchored by Marin County.

Woolsey's firm liberal views fit the district well. She is outspoken on environmental concerns, opposing offshore drilling and exploration in the Arctic National Wildlife Refuge. She wants the defense budget cut by 50 percent over five years, supported sending U.S. troops to Somalia and wants foreign aid linked to environment standards.

Woolsey supports universal health-care coverage, abortion rights and — drawing from her own experience — increased federal aid to low-income persons for higher education and child care, a goal she can pursue from her seat on the Education and Labor Committee.

She also hopes to push for creation of a federal council on women that would report on issues of concern to women and evaluate the impact of federal policies on women's lives, particularly on child care and medical research.

Woolsey broke new ground early in the 103rd Congress when she became the first woman ever to play basketball for a congressional team. She attributed her failure to score against the Georgetown Law School faculty to her team-oriented style of play.

The race for the 6th opened when incumbent Democrat Barbara Boxer filed for the Senate seat being vacated by Democrat Alan Cranston. Woolsey was never the favorite, and she overcame a field of eight other Democrats by virtue of her geography and her gender. She was the best-known woman on the House ballot in a year when two women were at the top of the ticket running for Senate, one of whom previously represented the district.

Woolsey was one of only two candidates from Sonoma and led the balloting there over former county Supervisor Eric J. Koenigshofer. She finished second in Marin, close behind former county Supervisor Denis Rice. Sonoma voters cast more than half the ballots, assuring Woolsey's victory.

The main competition was expected to come from J. Bennett Johnston III, son of Louisiana's senior senator, a full-time environmentalist and a mirror image of his father on a subject of premier importance to the 6th's voters — offshore drilling. But Johnston never overcame the taint of charges that oil and gas money had fueled his considerable campaign treasury, and he finished fourth.

The general election was expected to be a real test for Woolsey. Her GOP opponent, Bill Filante, was the favorite. Known in the Legislature as "the last liberal Republican," he was repeatedly re-elected from a Democratic district.

By June, he had raised almost twice as much money as Woolsey. Then tragedy struck the popular, 14-year state legislator.

In early August Filante underwent emergency brain surgery, and later it was disclosed that only part of a cancerous tumor had been removed. Filante became so ill that he was forced to suspend his campaign in mid-September, but it was too late under California law to replace him on the ballot.

Republicans urged Filante's supporters to vote for him anyway and force a special election. But Woolsey swept to a 65 percent to 34 percent victory. Filante died a month after the November election.

California 6

Northern Bay area; Sonoma and Marin counties

Once a seriocomic example of partisan gerrymandering, the 6th is now a model of compactness and community of interest. It includes all of high-profile Marin County; but instead of reaching in multiple directions for additional votes as it once did, the 6th now weds Marin to the most populous portions of neighboring Sonoma County.

The Marin identity notwithstanding, most of the district's votes are now cast in Sonoma County, where the 6th hugs the Pacific Coast from scenic Bodega Bay north to the Mendocino County line and reaches inland for the county's fast-growing population centers such as Santa Rosa. Once a service town for farmers, Santa Rosa has attracted corporate as well as individual refugees from the congestion of metropolitan San Francisco. It grew by more than one-third in the 1980s, and it is the largest city in the 6th. A few miles down state Highway 12 is Sonoma, a rustic town enlivened by a campus of the California State University system. Fifteen miles to the west on the Sonoma-Marin county line sits the unpretentious city of Petaluma, which once proclaimed itself the "chicken-plucking capital of the world."

To the south, Marin County is home to the city of San Rafael, the famed prison at San Quentin and a small host of commuter suburbs such as Kentfield, Ross, San Anselmo and Fairfax. It has marvelous scenery: Mount Tamalpais, Stinson Beach and the Point Reyes National Seashore. But it is best known for its one-time artist colonies and more affluent suburbs that cling to San Francisco Bay (Sausalito, Tiburon) or nestle deep in the hills between the ocean and the bay (Larkspur, Mill Valley).

To mention some of these names is to evoke wistful sighs from former residents, visitors and "California dreamers" who know the area only through song lyrics and other myths of the counterculture. In the past decade, the politics of this social and cultural matrix have supplanted Marin's older GOP pattern. Marin had voted for Republican Gerald R. Ford for president in 1976 and for Ronald Reagan in 1980. When Phillip Burton masterminded the state's redistricting in 1981, he borrowed Democratic wards from three counties to overpower Marin's GOP vote (in behalf of his brother, John).

But the county's partisan preferences changed during the 1980s. In 1984, Marin was one of just five California counties voting for Walter F. Mondale. By 1992, GOP registration in the county (as well as in the 6th generally) was down to 30 percent. That figure is remarkably low, considering the 6th is overwhelmingly white (only two of the state's 52 congressional districts have fewer minorities). In 1992, Bill Clinton carried Marin by a more than 2-to-1 ratio over George Bush.

Marin's liberal activists in 1992 also elevated one of their own, five-term Rep. Barbara Boxer, into the Senate and delivered her House seat to another Democratic woman, Woolsey. But she is a graduate of the City Council in Petaluma, signaling the ascendance of Sonoma County in the 6th.

1990 Population: 571,227. White 513,914 (90%), Black 13,280 (2%), Other 43,783 (8%). Hispanic origin 51,030 (9%). 18 and over 443,956 (78%), 62 and over 88,219 (15%). Median age: 36.

Committees

Budget (26th of 26 Democrats)

Education & Labor (20th of 28 Democrats)
Elementary, Secondary & Vocational Education; Human Resources; Labor-Management Relations

Government Operations (24th of 25 Democrats)
Government Information, Justice, Transportation & Agriculture

Campaign Finance

1992	Receipts	Receipts from PACs		Expend-itures
Woolsey (D)	$598,664	$186,853	(31%)	$584,913
Filante (R)	$437,590	$120,606	(28%)	$436,752

Key Votes

1993

Require parental notification of minors' abortions	-
Require unpaid family and medical leave	Y
Approve national "motor voter" registration bill	Y
Approve budget increasing taxes and reducing deficit	Y
Approve economic stimulus plan	Y

Elections

1992 General		
Lynn Woolsey (D)	190,322	(65%)
Bill Filante (R)	98,171	(34%)
Claude Heater (write-in)	3,141	(1%)
1992 Primary		
Lynn Woolsey (D)	25,484	(26%)
Eric J. Koenigshofer (D)	18,090	(19%)
Denis Rice (D)	16,979	(17%)
Bennett Johnston (D)	13,202	(14%)
Anna Nevenic (D)	7,872	(8%)
David N. Strand (D)	5,666	(6%)
William Harrison Morrison (D)	4,140	(4%)
Joe Nation (D)	3,772	(4%)
Howell Hurst (D)	2,565	(3%)

District Vote for President

	1992	
D	169,301	(56%)
R	71,564	(24%)
I	60,920	(20%)

7 George Miller (D)

Of Martinez — Elected 1974; 10th Term

Born: May 17, 1945, Richmond, Calif.
Education: San Francisco State U., B.A. 1968; U. of California, Davis, J.D. 1972.
Occupation: Lawyer; legislative aide.
Family: Wife, Cynthia Caccavo; two children.
Religion: Roman Catholic.
Political Career: Democratic nominee for Calif. Senate, 1969.
Capitol Office: 2205 Rayburn Bldg. 20515; 225-2095.

In Washington: Now that Miller's expansive legislative ambitions are coming to some fulfillment, they seem increasingly to be matched by his own personal aspirations.

Not long after the big-shouldered Bay Area congressman finally had become chairman of the Interior and Insular Affairs (now Natural Resources) Committee in 1991, he aggressively began positioning himself to succeed Missouri Democrat Richard A. Gephardt as majority leader if Gephardt were to run for president in 1992.

A few short months later, Miller was among those who decried House Speaker Thomas S. Foley's handling of the House bank. When Miller suggested that he could play point man on the issue, some members were not sure if he was suggesting himself as a replacement for Foley on one issue or more generally.

But Miller was hardly consumed with trying to hop up the leadership ladder in the 102nd Congress. Most of his time was devoted to moving the Western water bill down the trail from bill to law, and he managed to get a few good licks in on the energy bill as well.

And at the beginning of the 103rd Congress, in case there was any question who was in charge, Miller put his personal stamp on his committee by scrambling its subcommittees according to his priorities and renaming it.

The new handle reflects the new course Miller wants to set with respect to the government's lands and all that flows from them. And that puts farmers and developers on edge.

"You have to start from the fundamental principle that these are the people's resources," he says. "This is not the farmer's water; it's the people's water."

This credo was the guiding principle behind the omnibus Western water bill that passed late in 1992. The bill began life as a popular, biennial reauthorization of the dam and irrigation construction projects run by the Bureau of Reclamation, an arm of the Interior Department with vast authority in the West. But by the time the measure left Congress, it had been festooned with 40 titles and bore projects and studies affecting every Western state.

Keeping in mind the nearly irresistible momentum the bill had gained from the plethora of projects attached, Miller and Democratic Sen. Bill Bradley of New Jersey tacked on yet another bill — one that overhauled the nation's largest federal water project, the Central Valley Project in California.

The bill made environmental and wildlife preservation an official purpose of the project for the first time. It closed a series of loopholes, including one through which farmers with farms too large to receive water subsidies could subdivide them and qualify for the subsidy anyway.

The energy bill was more of a challenge, if only because it was primarily the province of Energy and Commerce Committee Chairman John D. Dingell of Michigan. The redoubtable Dingell managed to move the bill smoothly through all the necessary committees but Miller's. Miller saw the energy bill as an opportunity to reclaim committee turf that he felt had slipped away over the years. In the end, Miller's success in influencing the bill was limited, but he won a few small battles from Dingell, who does not lose many.

Miller's version of the energy bill was far more partisan than Dingell's bill, which had delicate compromises woven throughout. Miller took his case to the Rules Committee, which allowed him to add some features to the bill and to offer others as floor amendments.

Bans on offshore oil drilling were included; left out were provisions allowing the federal government to bypass state laws in building a nuclear dump in Nevada. But on a subsequent floor vote, Dingell was able to restore the nuclear dump provisions.

Three bills — energy, Western water and one dealing with another nuclear dump in New Mexico — went to conference simultaneously, with many of the same conferees appearing on each. That served to keep the delicate agreements between the several chairmen in place.

After resisting efforts to weaken the drilling ban and extracting promises that the issue

California 7

Northeastern Bay Area

California Republicans were generally pleased with the court-fashioned redistricting plan, which seemed to level the state's political playing field for 1992. But there were exceptions. Some in the GOP had hoped that the new map would enable them to go after 18-year House veteran Miller, the chairman of the House Natural Resources Committee (formerly Interior and Insular Affairs) and the scourge of Western Republicans on water and environmental issues. But the new map raised Democratic registration in the 7th to 62 percent, making Miller safer than ever.

The 7th has long been based in Contra Costa County, which begins at San Pablo Bay, heads south over the San Pablo Mountains and spreads inland well to the east of Berkeley and Oakland. Since World War II, the county has seen its population swell from 100,000 to 800,000. In response, the map for the 1990s confines the 7th to those northernmost portions of the county where the growth is oldest.

The new 7th still includes the shore of San Pablo Bay, studded with industrial cities such as Richmond, San Pablo, Pinole and Martinez. Here, oil terminals, factories and warehouses stretch for miles, belying the region's reputation for natural beauty. In 1988, sensitive wetlands in Martinez were soiled by an oil spill. Less than two years later, an explosion at the Shell Oil refinery rattled windows seven miles away. In this part of the 7th, residents are multiracial (Richmond is nearly one-half black), predominantly blue collar and heavily Democratic.

Historically, this Democratic vote was diluted by Republican influence in the suburbs to the south and east — on the sunny side of the San Pablo ridge. Concord, currently a terminus for rapid transit trains, became the county's biggest city and passed the 100,000 mark in the 1970s. The unrelenting suburban expansion began altering the political balance. Jimmy Carter had carried the 7th easily in 1976, but it went for Ronald Reagan in 1980 and 1984. Slowly, Miller too was feeling the center of gravity shift. His vote share in 1990 was his lowest since 1974.

But the trend was reversed in 1992. The court-appointed "special masters" decided that the bayside residents of the 7th had more in common with their neighbors to the west (in El Cerrito, on the Alameda County line) and to the north (across San Pablo Bay and Suisun Bay in Solano County). So they drew into the 7th the cities of Vallejo, Benicia (site of an early state capital), Cordelia and Suisun City. These communities, home to farm-support services and industry, are traditionally Democratic. Although new to Miller in 1992, they gave him roughly a 2-to-1 edge over a Republican challenger from Solano County.

At its new southern limit, the 7th still includes Concord. But nearly all the other suburban territory has been removed and added to the 10th District, dropping the Republican share of registered voters in the 7th from 34 percent in 1990 to 24 percent in 1992.

1990 Population: 572,773. White 358,843 (63%), Black 95,091 (17%), Other 118,839 (21%). Hispanic origin 76,154 (13%). 18 and over 421,122 (74%), 62 and over 71,416 (12%). Median age: 32.

would be addressed in the 103rd Congress, Miller suggested during the energy conference that the ban be removed altogether to avoid a veto from President Bush.

Miller's penchant for hardball already had transformed life on his committee before he changed the name. His predecessor, longtime Chairman Morris K. Udall of Arizona, was a conciliator who never sought retribution against committee members who crossed him. Miller is a gruff partisan whose stewardship produces plenty of fireworks with the panel's aggressive Western Republicans, who have little use for Miller's environmentalist bent. Miller's relationship with ranking GOP Rep. Don Young of Alaska has been described by a colleague as "just this side of violence."

Republicans stalked out of a committee hearing one day a few years ago when they got the impression that Democrats were voting against GOP amendments without considering them on their merits. One Republican remarked on his way out the door that committee Democrats probably would "be more comfortable if the Sierra Club occupied our chairs on this side." Snapped Miller: "That's for damn sure."

Still, opponents have noted that Miller can be a pragmatic negotiator. And Miller does not view himself as a throwback to the autocratic chairmen of earlier generations, such as those who lost their jobs when Miller's "Watergate Baby" Class of 1974 arrived. "There's a difference between being a strong chairman and being a dictator, which is what we had back then," he says. "I also want to be open to new ideas and new agendas."

Since the 100th Congress, Miller had been regarded as heir apparent to the Natural Resources chair once Udall retired. But Udall, already suffering from Parkinson's disease, was injured in early 1991 when he fell in his home. In January, the Democratic Caucus elected Miller vice chairman of the panel, with all the duties of the chairman. Udall resigned May 4; Miller was elected chairman May 9.

Miller was never bashful about his imminent chairmanship: His office said he had become Udall's stand-in for much of the 101st Congress because of Udall's illness. When he was named vice chairman, he moved quickly to put his own stamp on the committee, replacing the panel's top two staff members. Miller, still in his 40s, is apt to have a long time to imprint environmental legislation with his unusual combination of liberal passion and pay-as-you-go pragmatism.

He is a most unlikely Westerner to lead Natural Resources. Representing a water-rich, urban-suburban district, he approaches water-policy debates from a perspective starkly different from that of colleagues — including Udall — from more arid Western areas.

But like Udall, Miller is a liberal with strong environmental proclivities. His assertiveness is far more likely to rankle members of the GOP contingent, most of whom are driven by "Sagebrush Rebellion" antipathy toward federal land and water policy.

Miller does not always opt for confrontation. In the 100th Congress, debate over whether to limit logging in Alaska's Tongass National Forest allowed him to demonstrate his skill at attaining compromise. He shaved just enough off the conservationists' proposal to soften Young's criticism. This produced a lopsided House victory on the controversial legislation, but the bill died in the Senate.

When the Tongass bill came up again in the 101st Congress, Young protested Miller's substitute amendment, which changed the original bill to allow the Forest Service to take competitive bids on short contracts to log enough timber to meet market demand. The bill canceled two long-term, federally subsidized pulp-mill contracts and abolished mandatory timber-sales quotas in the Tongass. Young fought to no avail in Interior, which adopted Miller's plan by voice vote, and on the floor, where the House adopted it 356-60 and rejected a Young-backed alternative from the Agriculture Committee. But a House-Senate conference reduced the acreage protected in the bill and required the government to renegotiate, not cancel, the pulp-mill contracts. It became law in 1990.

In the 100th Congress, Udall delegated to Miller responsibility for legislation to permit oil drilling in the Arctic National Wildlife Refuge (ANWR). Conservationists adamantly opposed ANWR drilling, and when the measure cleared the Merchant Marine Committee in 1988, Miller balked. He stalled on the bill, arguing the need for further study. In the wake of the 1989 *Exxon Valdez* oil spill, the bill was laid aside.

The *Valdez* disaster cleared the way for enactment of a bill increasing the federal liability limits of oil spillers. Miller joined senior Merchant Marine Democrat Gerry E. Studds of Massachusetts (now that committee's chairman), who sponsored such a bill in 1975, to push for tougher environmental amendments. The bill would compensate those harmed economically by accidents, enhance cleanup efforts and attempt to prevent spills.

Outside Natural Resources, Miller had a high-visibility platform for advocating his social services agenda as chairman of the Select Committee on Children, Youth and Families. Miller ceded the chairmanship of the Children's panel in the 102nd Congress when he was named Interior vice chairman.

Miller can be quick to express his frustration at those who do not see the urgency of social problems the way he does. He was outraged at President Ronald Reagan's approach to domestic policy and only slightly gentler toward Democrats who showed an interest in compromising with the White House. He has been a prominent advocate for abortion rights.

In the 101st Congress, he and a colleague co-authored legislation to increase federal aid for child care. Their plan competed with one approved by the Education and Labor Committee, leading to jurisdictional battles throughout most of the Congress over how to finance it — by entitlement (as recommended by Miller) or by authorization. The final bill included some of both plans, adding a five-year, $1.5 billion entitlement program to help provide care for low-income families not quite poor enough to qualify for welfare.

During his tenure on the Budget Committee, Miller was one of the strongest union supporters in Congress. He also developed the pay-as-you-go budget-freeze concept. The 1990 budget agreement imposed strict pay-as-you-go limits on entitlement spending.

In the subcommittee shuffle at the beginning of the 103rd Congress, Miller dissolved the Water, Power and Offshore Energy Resources panel, which he had chaired, and took over the revamped Oversight and Investigations Subcommittee. He also created the Native American Affairs Subcommittee and handed off his own responsibility on those issues — he had successfully shepherded an Indian health bill through Congress in the 102nd Congress — to Democratic Rep. Bill Richardson of New Mexico.

Issues likely to come into Miller's sights in the 103rd Congress are mining and grazing fees, ancient forests, clean water and endangered species and offshore drilling once again.

At Home: Not only is Miller a third-generation resident of his Northern California county — a fact that sets him apart in the state's mobile culture — he is also the third George Miller in his family to earn a living in government.

Miller's grandfather, George Sr., was the assistant civil engineer in Richmond. His father, George Jr., represented the area in the state Senate for 20 years. George Miller III was a first-year law student in 1969 when his father died. Only 23, Miller won the Democratic nomination to succeed his father but lost later in the year to Republican John Nejedly.

Miller went to work as a legislative aide to state Sen. George Moscone, the Democratic floor leader. In 1974, when Democratic Rep. Jerome Waldie decided to run for governor, Miller sought Waldie's seat in Congress, challenging a local labor leader and the mayor of Concord, the largest city in the district.

Miller was reinforced by the strong support of Assemblyman John T. Knox in Richmond, the district's second-largest city. Miller won the primary with 38 percent. In the general election, against moderate Republican Gary Fernandez, Miller exploited Watergate, disclosing his campaign finances twice a month and chiding his opponent for not doing likewise. He won 56 percent of the vote and has been a safe re-election bet since.

His usual two-thirds of the vote dropped to three-fifths in 1990. But the 1992 redistricting plan removed enough of Miller's Republican-leaning suburban constituents to put him out of reach for the foreseeable future. He won again in 1992 with 70 percent.

Committees

Natural Resources (Chairman)
Oversight & Investigations (chairman); Insular & International Affairs

Education & Labor (3rd of 28 Democrats)
Elementary, Secondary & Vocational Education; Labor-Management Relations; Labor Standards, Occupational Health and Safety

Elections

1992 General		
George Miller (D)	153,320	(70%)
Dave Scholl (R)	54,822	(25%)
David L. Franklin (PFP)	9,840	(5%)
1990 General		
George Miller (D)	121,080	(61%)
Roger A. Payton (R)	79,031	(39%)

Previous Winning Percentages: **1988** (68%) **1986** (67%) **1984** (66%) **1982** (67%) **1980** (63%) **1978** (63%) **1976** (75%) **1974** (56%)

District Vote for President

1992
D 140,159 (61%)
R 51,356 (22%)
I 39,038 (17%)

Campaign Finance

	Receipts	Receipts from PACs		Expend-itures
1992				
Miller (D)	$542,532	$261,790	(48%)	$651,360
Scholl (R)	$66,731	$3,500	(5%)	$62,047
1990				
Miller (D)	$469,400	$262,657	(56%)	$448,026
Payton (R)	$47,918	$1,150	(2%)	$47,912

Key Votes

1993	
Require parental notification of minors' abortions	N
Require unpaid family and medical leave	Y
Approve national "motor voter" registration bill	Y
Approve budget increasing taxes and reducing deficit	Y
Approve economic stimulus plan	Y
1992	
Approve balanced-budget constitutional amendment	N
Close down space station program	Y
Approve U.S. aid for former Soviet Union	N
Allow shifting funds from defense to domestic programs	Y
1991	
Extend unemployment benefits using deficit financing	Y
Approve waiting period for handgun purchases	Y
Authorize use of force in Persian Gulf	N

Voting Studies

	Presidential Support		Party Unity		Conservative Coalition	
Year	S	O	S	O	S	O
1992	14	77	88	6	13	77
1991	23	73	92	3	3	89
1990	16	81	89	6	6	93
1989	22	76	89	4	5	95
1988	18	69	85	6	5	82
1987	15	81	88	5	5	95
1986	14	80	84	4	8	80
1985	16	76	84	5	9	84
1984	22	69	85	6	7	86
1983	11	78	83	8	13	75
1982	26	71	92	4	7	90
1981	28	70	89	8	0	93

Interest Group Ratings

Year	ADA	AFL-CIO	CCUS	ACU
1992	85	92	25	0
1991	95	100	20	0
1990	100	83	21	4
1989	100	91	20	0
1988	95	93	31	4
1987	96	88	20	13
1986	90	91	15	6
1985	95	80	19	10
1984	100	85	31	4
1983	90	94	16	4
1982	95	95	20	0
1981	100	87	11	0

8 Nancy Pelosi (D)

Of San Francisco — Elected 1987; 3rd Full Term

Born: March 26, 1940, Baltimore, Md.
Education: Trinity College, A.B. 1962.
Occupation: Public relations consultant.
Family: Husband, Paul Pelosi; five children.
Religion: Roman Catholic.
Political Career: Calif. Democratic Party chairman, 1981-83.
Capitol Office: 240 Cannon Bldg. 20515; 225-4965.

In Washington: Pelosi has all the self-assurance one would expect from a woman born into the business, and it has not gone unnoticed. Her savvy has earned her the affection and trust of many of her Democratic colleagues, as evidenced by her committee assignments and high-profile party responsibilities.

Pelosi did not hold public office before coming to Congress in 1987. But her father, Thomas J. D'Alesandro Jr., was a House member during the New Deal and then mayor of Baltimore. She made her own way, however, having moved to the West Coast and served as California Democratic Party chairman and finance chairman of the Democratic Senatorial Campaign Committee.

Her background has given her a feel for the levers of power in Washington that compensates for her lack of legislative experience. On at least one occasion, when she appeared before the Rules Committee to make a request, her wishes were quickly granted because she had already made her case effectively behind the scenes.

Her ascent into the ranks of the respected continued at the start of the 102nd Congress when Pelosi won a seat on the powerful Appropriations Committee (where her father had once served).

House leaders also drafted Pelosi in 1991 to sit on the House Committee on Standards of Official Conduct, where she joined with other institutional loyalists who appear inclined to retain the ethics panel's historically cautious approach. In 1992, she replaced scandal-plagued Mary Rose Oakar as co-chairman of the Platform Committee for the Democratic National Convention.

After the 1992 elections, she joined Speaker Thomas S. Foley, Majority Leader Richard A. Gephardt and other members of the leadership on a three-city post-election tour to meet and try to bond with nearly all of the 63 Democratic freshmen. For the 103rd Congress, she sought and won assignment to the Intelligence Committee.

Despite impressive committee assignments and the initial respect she has earned from the party faithful, Pelosi does not play to unanimous rave reviews. She is a liberal Democrat from one of the nation's most liberal districts, so more conservative Democrats tend to view her more skeptically — and she always runs the risk of being positioned on the political fringe.

Pelosi raised some eyebrows when she devoted a speech against war in the Persian Gulf to the environmental impact of the conflict. "While we are gravely concerned about the loss of life from combat in the Persian Gulf War, environmental consequences of the war are as important to the people there as the air they breathe and the water they drink," said Pelosi, as she circulated a letter among her colleagues asking the U.N. environmental agency to investigate the issue. Considered offbeat at the time, Pelosi's focus seemed prescient when pollution from oil well fires darkened the sky in the region after the fighting had ended.

During the 101st and 102nd Congresses, Pelosi, whose San Francisco district includes thousands of Chinese-Americans, set her sights on China. In 1989, she sponsored a bill to allow Chinese students caught in the United States at the time of the Chinese government's June massacre of pro-democracy forces in Tiananmen Square to seek permanent residency here without returning home first. Congress cleared the measure, but President Bush vetoed the bill, and the Senate sustained the veto early in 1990. Pelosi, then on the Banking Committee, devoted considerable effort in 1990 to restricting World Bank loans to China.

In both the 101st and 102nd Congresses, Pelosi was a leading critic of most-favored-nation (MFN) trade status for China. Her bill would have made MFN approval contingent on Beijing's release of political prisoners arrested during the protests in Tiananmen Square and "significant progress" in other human rights areas.

Her efforts picked up supporters in 1991, despite the opposition of powerful Ways and Means Chairman Dan Rostenkowski. Eventually, Rostenkowski pushed for a compromise

California 8

San Francisco

San Francisco (natives call it "The City") has been romanticized for generations by writers, artists, visitors and residents. Overrun with adventurers during the gold rush era, it kept its reputation as a rough-and-tumble port city long thereafter. More recently, it has hosted successive waves of counterculturalism, notably the beats of the 1950s and the hippies of the 1960s.

Racially, San Francisco is the second most diverse county in the nation, after Queens, N.Y. In the past two decades, the city's well-established homosexual community has grown larger and more visible, wielding greater influence over the city's politics (the gay vote is estimated at one-fifth of the electorate). There has been some backlash in recent years, particularly among working-class families and white ethnic minorities. In 1991, disenchantment with the cutting edge helped replace liberal mayor Art Agnos with former police chief Frank Jordan.

But whatever their local disagreements, San Franciscans have little trouble choosing sides in federal elections. In 1992, San Francisco County (which is coterminous with the city) gave 76 percent of its vote to Bill Clinton, who turned out to be the weakling of the ticket. Senate nominees Barbara Boxer and Dianne Feinstein got 76 percent and 81 percent, respectively, in the county while Rep. Pelosi collected 82 percent in the 8th.

Seeing both Feinstein and Boxer elected was a point of special satisfaction: Feinstein is a former mayor of San Francisco, and Boxer represented part of the city throughout her decade in the House.

The 8th resembles the old 5th, except that it comes even closer to encompassing all of San Francisco within a single congressional district.

The old 5th had to give up the city's far northwest (including the bridgehead of the Golden Gate Bridge) to the 6th (centered in Marin County at the other end of the bridge). This comprised roughly one-fifth of the city's population.

But the map adopted in 1992 reclaimed these sections of the city (including Seacliff, Park Presidio and environs north of Golden Gate Park). Sacrificed instead (this time to the 12th District that adjoins to the south) were the neighborhoods south of Golden Gate Park and west of Twin Peaks (including the Sunset, Parkside and Forest Hill districts).

The shift adds nearly 50,000 more city residents to the newly renumbered San Francisco district, reducing the previous Democratic share of registered voters by just 1 percentage point, to 64 percent. But the removal of the southwestern neighborhoods does affect the district's racial mix. Whites had accounted for 59 percent of the old 5th; they constitute 52 percent in the 8th. In some future Democratic primary, the nomination may well be contested by a candidate from one of the minority communities — the largest of which, Asian-Americans, is nearing 30 percent as the Chinese and Japanese are joined by increasing numbers of Koreans, Filipinos and Southeast Asians.

1990 Population: 573,247. White 298,038 (52%), Black 73,310 (13%), Other 201,899 (35%). Hispanic origin 89,908 (16%). 18 and over 481,160 (84%), 62 and over 92,882 (16%). Median age: 35.

among Pelosi, Ways and Means Democrat Don J. Pease (a previous administration backer on MFN) and New York Democrat Stephen J. Solarz. After Congress cleared the measure, Bush, as expected, vetoed it. The Senate again failed to override.

Later in 1992, Pelosi, Pease and Senate Majority Leader George J. Mitchell sponsored a bill that would have removed MFN eligibility from Chinese state-owned industries, absent improvements in China's record on human rights, trade and weapons proliferation. But it, too, succumbed to a Bush veto.

In September 1991, Pelosi and two other House members traveled to China to urge the government to release political prisoners. While there, they paid an unsanctioned visit to Tiananmen Square, accompanied by American TV network crews. Chinese security guards scuffled with the lawmakers and the TV reporters when Georgia Democrat Ben Jones laid a white flower at the foot of a monument.

Pelosi has been particularly active in promoting legislation to fight AIDS, a serious problem in her district. In 1992, she and Edward R. Roybal, chairman of Appropriations' Treasury-Postal Service Subcommittee, won a $2.5 million earmark for a special "drug war account." The money went to the San Francisco Department of Health for its fight against the drug-related AIDS epidemic.

As the 101st Congress began, Pelosi was involved in a far different fight: She teamed with California Democrat Barbara Boxer in an unsuccessful try to reverse a recommendation by a military base-closing commission that the

Presidio in San Francisco be shut. The issue resurfaced with a fresh round of base closings in 1993, and the fate of the Presidio remains unresolved.

At Home: When she began her first House campaign, Pelosi was more familiar to national Democratic activists than to San Francisco voters. But the financial and political contacts she had developed over years of party service provided Pelosi with a critical edge in the special Democratic primary to succeed Democratic Rep. Sala Burton, who died in February 1987.

Winning that primary was tantamount to election for Pelosi. The 5th District is one of the Democrats' most loyal congressional districts.

Pelosi entered the contest backed by much of the city and state party establishment. Pelosi also had powerful friends in the national Democratic hierarchy. While chairing the state party, she helped attract the 1984 Democratic National Convention to San Francisco. She lost a bid for national party chairman in 1985 but then directed money-raising efforts for the party's successful 1986 effort to retake the Senate.

The most important support for Pelosi was delivered, in dramatic fashion, just before the seat became vacant. Burton indicated several days prior to her death of cancer that she wanted Pelosi to be her successor. That backing was crucial because the 5th had long been dominated by the organization loyal to Sala Burton and her late husband, Rep. Phillip Burton.

Pelosi's last real hurdle was a vigorous challenge from San Francisco Supervisor Harry Britt, a Democrat and a leading homosexual politician. In a district where the gay vote was roughly one-fifth of the electorate, Britt started with a large base. He also aimed his campaign at a wider audience, citing his efforts on rent control and his opposition to new real estate development.

But Pelosi was energetic and cool under fire. She fell short of 50 percent of the vote in the April ballot but took her GOP foe easily in a June runoff.

Pelosi then established the district as her own, winning re-election in 1988 with 76 percent and again in 1990, when anti-incumbent sentiment was widespread, with 77 percent.

In 1992, redistricting altered Pelosi's district slightly but left the Democratic registration about where it was: just shy of two-thirds. The Democratic ticket romped in the district, and Pelosi led the ticket with an 82 percent performance.

Committees

Appropriations (24th of 37 Democrats)
District of Columbia; Foreign Operations, Export Financing & Related Programs; Labor, Health & Human Services, Education & Related Agencies

Select Intelligence (9th of 12 Democrats)
Legislation; Oversight & Evaluation

Standards of Official Conduct (4th of 7 Democrats)

Elections

1992 General		
Nancy Pelosi (D)	191,906	(82%)
Marc Wolin (R)	25,693	(11%)
Cesar G. Cadabes (PFP)	7,572	(3%)
James R. Elwood (LIBERT)	7,511	(3%)
1990 General		
Nancy Pelosi (D)	120,633	(77%)
Alan Nichols (R)	35,671	(23%)

Previous Winning Percentages: 1988 (76%) 1987 * (63%)

** Special election.*

District Vote for President

1992

D 187,201 (76%)
R 39,396 (16%)
I 21,180 (9%)

Campaign Finance

	Receipts	Receipts from PACs		Expend-itures
1992				
Pelosi (D)	$417,254	$204,689	(49%)	$443,238
Wolin (R)	$49,256	$500	(1%)	$49,566
1990				
Pelosi (D)	$462,664	$262,900	(57%)	$440,973
Nichols (R)	$153,947	$5,190	(3%)	$154,858

Key Votes

1993	
Require parental notification of minors' abortions	N
Require unpaid family and medical leave	Y
Approve national "motor voter" registration bill	Y
Approve budget increasing taxes and reducing deficit	Y
Approve economic stimulus plan	Y
1992	
Approve balanced-budget constitutional amendment	N
Close down space station program	Y
Approve U.S. aid for former Soviet Union	Y
Allow shifting funds from defense to domestic programs	Y
1991	
Extend unemployment benefits using deficit financing	Y
Approve waiting period for handgun purchases	Y
Authorize use of force in Persian Gulf	N

Voting Studies

	Presidential Support		Party Unity		Conservative Coalition	
Year	**S**	**O**	**S**	**O**	**S**	**O**
1992	12	80	91	1	2	90
1991	24	69	89	4	3	86
1990	15	84	92	3	4	96
1989	26	70	93	1	0	98
1988	20	79	95	3	3	97
1987	15†	84†	90†	3†	0†	88†

† Not eligible for all recorded votes.

Interest Group Ratings

Year	ADA	AFL-CIO	CCUS	ACU
1992	90	92	25	0
1991	90	92	20	0
1990	100	92	15	4
1989	95	100	20	0
1988	100	93	21	0
1987	93	100	9	0

9 Ronald V. Dellums (D)

Of Oakland — Elected 1970; 12th Term

Born: Nov. 24, 1935, Oakland, Calif.
Education: San Francisco State U., B.A. 1960; U. of California, Berkeley, M.S.W. 1962.
Military Service: Marine Corps, 1954-56.
Occupation: Psychiatric social worker.
Family: Wife, Leola "Roscoe" Higgs; three children.
Religion: Protestant.
Political Career: Berkeley City Council, 1967-71.
Capitol Office: 2108 Rayburn Bldg. 20515; 225-2661.

In Washington: The almost routine atmosphere that attended Dellums' election as House Armed Services Committee chairman in January 1993 was a striking sign of the times. Had seniority raised this fiery liberal activist to that position just a few years earlier, the halls of Congress likely would have echoed with cries of opposition from pro-defense conservatives.

Dellums was carried to Congress by his opposition to the Vietnam War, and he fiercely opposed every ensuing U.S. military intervention right through the 1991 Persian Gulf conflict with Iraq.

During the 1980s, President Ronald Reagan called for major increases in military spending. His successor, George Bush, fought to preserve large defense expenditures. Through it all, Dellums argued for deep spending cuts — not to lower the burden on taxpayers but to divert the money to domestic programs for the underprivileged.

But by the time Dellums stepped up to succeed Armed Services Chairman Les Aspin — the Democratic centrist chosen by President Clinton as secretary of Defense — at the start of the 103rd Congress, the landscape had shifted. The collapse of the Soviet Union, combined with excessive federal budget deficits, had already set the defense budget on a downward track. Dellums still advocated more severe cuts than did Bush or Clinton; but he no longer seemed quite so out of tune with the times.

Moreover, during a decade as chairman of various subcommittees on Armed Services, Dellums already had proved himself to be far more flexible than his critics could have foreseen. Despite his strong views, Dellums was praised for his fairness to those with opposing viewpoints.

Typically, Dellums would hold open debates on the portions of the annual defense authorization bills that came before his subcommittee. After shaping a consensus bill, he would vote against it as spending too much on the military. He would do the same in full committee; on the floor, he would help Aspin manage the bill, even as he spoke eloquently against its passage.

During his first months as full committee chairman, Dellums had not made it clear whether he would continue this approach.

There are some who see a contradiction in Dellums' efforts to craft legislation that he so strongly opposes on moral and fiscal grounds. But Dellums says this seeming anomaly is the mark of his devotion to a democratic process, a process that promises no one that his views will prevail.

"It must be that pundits who worry aloud about how a 'dove' could come to this position or who have imputed dire national consequences to such an event have failed to understand me, my commitment to democratic principles and my belief that collegiality is essential to the effective functioning of our national legislature," Dellums said after the 198-10 vote in the House Democratic Caucus made his chairmanship official.

Even some conservative Republicans who oppose him on almost every issue vouch for his evenhandedness. "You have always been a most fair and gentlemanly chairman," said Rep. Robert K. Dornan of California at Dellums' first meeting as Armed Services chairman.

Dellums' assumption of a national security policy role was previewed in 1991, when he obtained a seat on the Select Intelligence Committee. Some conservative hard-liners implied that Dellums, a frequent critic of U.S. intelligence agencies, could not be trusted to keep classified information secret.

Dellums angrily rejected such assertions and found a defender in Minority Whip Newt Gingrich. The conservative GOP leader criticized Dellums for opposing most covert actions but described him as an "honorable" member "who has kept secrets for years."

Dellums tempers his ideological approach with a courtly manner and a dapper style. He long has tried to bury the "personally painful" perception that he is a '60s-style bomb-thrower. "I deliberately walked into the House well-groomed," he once said. "If they can relate to me and my clothes, they can relate to my ideas."

California 9

Alameda County — Oakland; Berkeley

The 1992 court-ordered district map in California made the old 8th District far more compact, compressing it into Alameda County and renumbering it the 9th. Gone are the old district lines reaching clear across Contra Costa County and the eastern reaches of Alameda County to the Central Valley.

The 9th consists of Oakland and Berkeley, and a few subsidiaries: the bayside industrial sites of Emeryville and Alameda and the bedroom suburbs of Albany (north of Berkeley) and Piedmont (an independent enclave in the Oakland hills).

The removal of the old district's inland suburbs left Dellums safer than ever in an Oakland-Berkeley based constituency. Dellums won his last election in the old district with 61 percent — roughly his career average. In 1992, in the new 9th, he walked off with 72 percent. The politics of the 9th are more complex than these numbers suggest, but Dellums has long since mastered the complexities. A liberal and a dove, he also knew how important the Alameda Naval Air Station was to the district — and how vital the Navy in general was to the Bay Area.

However, three of the district's Navy facilities showed up on the 1993 recommendations for base closures: the Alameda air station, the Naval Aviation Depot in Alameda and the Oakland Naval Supply Center.

Dellums is a native of Oakland, which dominates the district, and a product of the deep-rooted African-American community that dominates Oakland. Nearly 45 percent of the city is black, and Oakland's historic tensions between blacks and police gave birth in the 1960s to the Black Panther Party. Overall, the 9th is about one-third black; Asians and Hispanics together account for more than one-fourth of the people.

More recently, Oakland has been better known nationally for hosting three consecutive World Series (1988-90), one of which was interrupted by a deadly earthquake. The city also has always had wealthy, mostly white neighborhoods in the hills overlooking the Bay (made famous in 1991 by wildfires that obliterated scores of homes).

Berkeley, Oakland's northern neighbor, was founded at about the same time in the mid-1800s. But while Oakland has always been a port, Berkeley (population 103,000) has always been a college town. As the home of the first and foremost campus of the world-renowned University of California, Berkeley is one of those places everyone thinks they know about whether they have been there or not.

Berkeley symbolizes radicalism. But in the 1990s, the reality of life here is more removed from the passions of political and social liberation. The recession and the state's budget crises have hurt the university, and interest in activism has waned somewhat.

This is not likely to matter much in federal elections, in which the 9th is a reliable cache of support for Democrats. Bill Clinton's 78.7 percent vote share here was his best in any California district, and George Bush's 12.4 percent was his worst.

1990 Population: 573,458. White 260,128 (45%), Black 182,159 (32%), Other 131,171 (23%). Hispanic origin 68,775 (12%). 18 and over 446,911 (78%), 62 and over 80,221 (14%). Median age: 33.

Dellums was elegance personified in October 1990, when he took to the House floor during an unusual Saturday session to call for a vote on a much-debated (and ultimately unsuccessful) effort to override Bush's veto of a budget resolution. Dressed in a tuxedo, Dellums was on his way to his son's wedding. "We know how we are going to vote," Dellums said. "Let us override this veto and let me love my son." His colleagues responded with a rousing round of applause.

But Dellums remains a liberal activist to his core. Since his arrival in 1971, he has expressed the outrage of the left on the House floor, combining eloquent visions of world peace and angry charges of racism.

There is no artifice in Dellums' passion. Few who have watched him were surprised at reading in The Washington Post that when Dellums first heard news reports of the U.S. bombing of Iraq in January 1991, he sat on his bed and cried.

As early as October 1990, Dellums had lined up 83 House colleagues to sign a statement to Bush opposing offensive military action against Iraq.

In January, Dellums made a typically impassioned statement against a resolution authorizing Bush to use military force. The resolution passed, and Bush used the authority days later to launch the air war. While nearly all House members — including many who had opposed the "war resolution" — rushed to back a resolution supporting Bush and the U.S. troops, Dellums voted "present."

Dellums' efforts to cut the defense budget

to provide programs for the poor have mainly met with frustration. In February 1992, during debate on the first budget resolution following the disintegration of the Soviet Union, Dellums called for a $50 billion cut in Bush's $280 billion defense request. "This is a historic moment we should seize," he said. But the House backed a much smaller cut. That June, he and Democratic colleague Maxine Waters, also of California, proposed an amendment to cut defense spending by 10 percent, or about $27 billion; it got just 90 votes.

The decline of the Soviet threat and the pressures of budget deficits did enable Dellums to get out in front of one defense-cutting movement that had some success: the effort to limit production of the B-2 stealth bomber. Dellums formed an unexpected coalition with Republican Rep. John R. Kasich of Ohio, a pro-defense but budget-conscious conservative activist.

Dellums and Kasich fell short in their first shot at the B-2 in 1989. But in 1990, they picked up a key ally in Aspin, who had grown wary of the Bush administration's plans to build at least 75 of the ultra-expensive planes. By 1991, a 15-plane limit sought by Dellums and others was enacted; the next year, an apparently final cap of 20 planes was negotiated with the Bush administration.

In an exception to his opposition to U.S. military engagements, Dellums supported the deployment of U.S. troops — begun in late 1992 by Bush and continued by Clinton — on a mission to alleviate a hunger crisis in Somalia. This was in keeping with Dellums' abiding interest in African affairs.

Dellums' landmark legislative achievement was his effort to impose sanctions against the apartheid regime of South Africa. In 1986, 15 years after his first sanctions proposal, the House embraced his call for a trade cutoff and disinvestment by U.S. firms in that country.

The sanctions were lifted by Bush in 1991 in response to the South African government's declaration of an end to apartheid. But Dellums objected to the move. "Clearly the purpose of the [sanctions] act has not been met as apartheid continues, and the black majority of South Africans cannot vote and cannot hold office," Dellums said.

When he took the Armed Services chairmanship, Dellums gave up his chairmanship on the House District of Columbia Committee, which he had held since 1979, though he remains on the committee. In that position, Dellums is an advocate for the District, which has limited voting congressional representation and a resident population that is primarily black.

At Home: In the 102nd Congress, the House bank scandal found Dellums to have written 851 overdrafts, one of the highest totals in the chamber. But in 1992, he pushed his share of the vote over the 70 percent threshold for the first time.

In the 103rd Congress, despite his elevated status on Armed Services, Dellums could not prevent the proposed closing of several large military facilities in his district — with the attendant loss of thousands of jobs. Yet he is considered all but literally unchallengeable in the next election cycle.

Part of the explanation comes from Dellums' still-rising status in the House; this trajectory and the strong support of his mainly liberal constituency protected him in the House bank controversy. The rest of the explanation comes from redistricting. Dellums has long been a hero in the dominant Alameda County part of his district, which includes the mainly black precincts of Oakland and the liberal university community in Berkeley. But he had struggled for votes in Contra Costa County, the suburban, white, largely affluent and conservative portion of his district.

The court-drawn 1992 map extended Dellums' renumbered district (the 8th became the 9th) slightly to the south in Alameda County while excising its Contra Costa portion. The GOP registration dropped below 15 percent.

Dellums once wanted to be a professional baseball pitcher, but he has said that encounters with racial prejudice spoiled that dream, leaving him with little ambition after high school. Following two years in the Marines, he went to college with the help of the GI Bill and six years later took a degree in psychiatric social work.

He was a social worker in San Francisco, managing federally assisted poverty programs, when friends persuaded him to pursue his ideas about poverty and discrimination by running for the Berkeley City Council in 1967. He has since won every time he has run for office.

In 1970, when Dellums launched a primary challenge to six-term Democratic Rep. Jeffery Cohelan, the East Bay region was in a state of turmoil. Student protest over the war in Vietnam was becoming increasingly intense, and the Black Panther movement was gaining strength in Oakland's ghettos. Although his credentials as a liberal were solid, Cohelan was considered old-fashioned in his approach to politics. Dellums, by contrast, was usually described in the press as "angry and articulate" or "radical and militant."

Dellums put together a coalition of blacks, students and left-leaning intellectuals that has been the core of his support ever since. His major issue was Cohelan's tardiness in opposing the Vietnam War. Dellums registered nearly 15,000 new voters in the district and easily ousted Cohelan with 55 percent.

Attacks by Republican Vice President Spiro T. Agnew only brought out more support for Dellums among the district's Democrats. He easily defeated a 25-year-old political neophyte in the general election.

That victory ushered in a decade of political quiet in the district, in which Dellums rarely encountered more than minor opposition in either party. After a little-noticed Republican opponent held Dellums to 55 percent in 1980, however, the GOP put more effort into its attacks on him.

In 1982, Claude B. Hutchison Jr., a former bank president and the son of an ex-Berkeley mayor, launched a well-funded effort using campaign contributions from former business associates to help finance his campaign. The Republican pulled in more than $250,000 from donors eager to see Dellums retired.

With support among Republicans virtually guaranteed, Hutchison tried to win over moderate Democrats. He minimized his GOP ties and took positions similar to Dellums' in favor of funding for public education and against tuition tax credits for private schools.

Dellums fought back. Attacking "the madness of Reagan and Reaganomics," he drew on an impressive array of support from the national left to swamp Hutchison in raising funds.

In the end, the results were like those of previous years. While Hutchison easily won the Contra Costa County portion of the 8th, Dellums more than made up the deficit in Oakland and Berkeley, winning with 56 percent.

In 1984, Eldridge Cleaver, the former Black Panther leader turned political conservative, announced that he would challenge Dellums as an independent. Republicans put up a black banker, Charles Connor, hoping that Cleaver, despite his ideological metamorphosis, would take enough votes from Dellums to elect Connor. But Cleaver dropped out of the contest at the end of the summer. Left on his own, Connor suffered from having to run in one of the few districts in the country where Reagan's coattails would be a liability. Dellums won 60 percent, a tally he matched two years later when his GOP foe was Piedmont City Councilman Steve Eigenberg.

In 1988, Dellums won 67 percent, but he was down to just 61 percent in 1990 as his share of the vote in Contra Costa County slid to 34 percent.

Committees

Armed Services (Chairman)
Military Acquisition (chairman)

District of Columbia (2nd of 8 Democrats)

Elections

1992 General		
Ronald V. Dellums (D)	164,265	(72%)
G. William Hunter (R)	53,707	(24%)
Dave Linn (PFP)	10,472	(5%)
1990 General		
Ronald V. Dellums (D)	119,645	(61%)
Barbara Galewski (R)	75,544	(39%)

Previous Winning Percentages: **1988** (67%) **1986** (60%) **1984** (60%) **1982** (56%) **1980** (55%) **1978** (57%) **1976** (62%) **1974** (57%) **1972** (56%) **1970** (57%)

District Vote for President

	1992	
D	186,714	(79%)
R	29,394	(12%)
I	21,207	(9%)

Campaign Finance

	Receipts	Receipts from PACs		Expend-itures
1992				
Dellums (D)	$854,478	$78,437	(9%)	$921,771
Hunter (R)	$76,530	$2,200	(3%)	$73,659
1990				
Dellums (D)	$790,386	$71,935	(9%)	$840,029

Key Votes

1993	
Require parental notification of minors' abortions	N
Require unpaid family and medical leave	Y
Approve national "motor voter" registration bill	Y
Approve budget increasing taxes and reducing deficit	Y
Approve economic stimulus plan	Y
1992	
Approve balanced-budget constitutional amendment	N
Close down space station program	Y
Approve U.S. aid for former Soviet Union	N
Allow shifting funds from defense to domestic programs	Y
1991	
Extend unemployment benefits using deficit financing	Y
Approve waiting period for handgun purchases	Y
Authorize use of force in Persian Gulf	N

Voting Studies

	Presidential Support		Party Unity		Conservative Coalition	
Year	**S**	**O**	**S**	**O**	**S**	**O**
1992	12	86	89	4	4	94
1991	25	69	90	3	3	92
1990	15	85	87	5	4	96
1989	23	76	93	2	0	100
1988	19	78	88	4	0	95
1987	10	86	91	2	5	95
1986	12	86	89	4	2	92
1985	16	83	91	3	5	91
1984	21	78	89	6	0	100
1983	7	83	82	7	2	91
1982	17	81	90	5	4	96
1981	21	66	83	6	8	87

Interest Group Ratings

Year	**ADA**	**AFL-CIO**	**CCUS**	**ACU**
1992	95	92	25	0
1991	90	100	20	0
1990	100	100	29	4
1989	100	100	20	0
1988	100	100	23	0
1987	100	100	0	0
1986	100	86	12	0
1985	95	100	19	5
1984	100	85	31	4
1983	95	94	22	5
1982	85	95	18	14
1981	95	80	0	7

10 Bill Baker (R)

Of Danville — Elected 1992; 1st Term

Born: June 14, 1940, Oakland, Calif.
Education: San Jose State U., B.S. 1963.
Military Service: Coast Guard Reserve, 1957-65.
Occupation: Budget analyst.
Family: Wife, Joanne Atack; four children.
Religion: Roman Catholic.
Political Career: Calif. Assembly, 1981-93.
Capitol Office: 1724 Longworth Bldg. 20515; 225-1880.

The Path to Washington: In a district where the slight GOP edge in registration would usually translate into a big edge at the polls, Baker's 52 percent electoral majority looks thin.

The closeness reflects the fact that Baker's archconservative views on social issues do not quite sit well with his moderate constituents. But his intellectual prowess and strong record on fiscal matters during 12 years in the state Assembly counted with the mostly white, upper-middle-class suburban voters.

And he obviously appealed more to them than did Democrat Wendell H. Williams, for whom running against Baker has become something of an avocation. Baker beat Williams twice before in races for the state Assembly, in 1988 and 1990.

This newly drawn district spans eastern Contra Costa and Alameda counties, inland from the more liberal enclaves of the East Bay, such as Oakland and Hayward. The 10th is only slightly larger than Baker's old state Assembly district, and with six prior campaigns under his belt, most of the district's voters knew him well.

Baker's seat on the Science, Space and Technology Committee will benefit his district, particularly because the 10th includes the Alameda towns of Livermore and Pleasanton, which are home to numerous high-tech companies. Baker should be an ally for fellow Californian Rep. George E. Brown, the Science Committee chairman. Brown would like the Lawrence Livermore nuclear weapons laboratory converted to civilian technology development — a role coveted by all three government nuclear labs.

It is less certain that Baker will use his seat on the Public Works and Transportation Committee to boost California's parochial interests. Public Works is chaired by another Bay Area Democrat, Rep. Norman Y. Mineta, who thinks the state has been shortchanged. But Baker made his name in the state Assembly as a budget expert, with a sharp pencil for what he perceives as wasteful government spending. Public Works is the perfect target for an anti-pork crusader.

Baker voted early in the 103rd Congress against a Democratic bill giving the president limited line-item veto authority; he supported an even stronger GOP substitute amendment. While most GOP freshmen chose to vote for both, Baker was one of only 12 GOP freshmen to support only the substitute amendment.

Baker served seven years as vice chairman of the Assembly's budget-writing Ways and Means Committee. He is a former official with the Contra Costa Taxpayers Association and once wrote a regular newspaper column called "The Angry Taxpayer." He played a central role in California's 1992 budget impasse and helped GOP Gov. Pete Wilson prevent a tax increase to cover the shortfall, insisting on spending cuts.

Baker won easily against his primary opponent, Dave Williams, a consulting engineer with a string of losing campaigns under his belt.

But Wendell Williams, the eventual Democratic nominee, had trouble arranging a rematch. Ayn Weiskamp, a former teacher and 12-year member of the Livermore City Council, pushed him in the primary. Casting herself as a moderate who had boosted Wilson's gubernatorial candidacy, Weiskamp helped highlight Williams' weaknesses.

In the general-election campaign, Williams tried to portray Baker as excessively conservative for the 10th — in particular for his strident opposition to abortion and his sometimes less-than-sensitive views about women.

Baker's own tendency to shoot from the lip gave Williams plenty of ammunition. Baker once apologized for introducing a group of high school students to the state Assembly as "17 survivors of abortion," a comment that he contended was funny at the time. And for years he has had to answer for calling some welfare recipients "breeders" who should not be subsidized by the government. The remark was made to a local newspaper during his first Assembly race, and Baker complained that it was taken out of context. But the newspaper ran a transcript to refute his arguments.

Baker dismissed Williams as having no record. In the end, Baker's aggressive campaign style and superior fundraising ability gave him an unbeatable edge.

California 10

Eastern Contra Costa and Alameda counties

The 10th stands as a monument to the objectives and methods of California's redistricting in 1992.

The end product is a district that straddles two counties but unites the affected portions of both in a community of interest. For the residents of the 10th are primarily suburbanites living on the sunrise (and sunny) side of the inland ridge east of San Francisco Bay. The landscape here features hills and hidden valleys, and the long dry months of the year leave the slopes golden brown.

More than two-thirds of the district's people live in Contra Costa County, the rest in Alameda County.

For decades, in election after election, scores of thousands of GOP votes from the Bay ridges and eastward have been swamped in the tide of Democratic ballots cast in the cities that hug the East Bay shoreline: Oakland and Berkeley in Alameda County, Richmond and Martinez and others in Contra Costa.

But since the Bay Area Rapid Transit (BART) system took hold in the 1970s, the growth in once-sleepy towns such as Orinda, Pleasant Hill, Walnut Creek and Antioch has been so great that its political ramifications could no longer be denied when new district lines were drawn.

Most of this growth has been in Contra Costa County, but Alameda communities such as Castro Valley, Dublin, Pleasanton and Livermore have been on the move as well. Livermore is the site of the Lawrence Livermore Laboratory, one of the nation's leading facilities for experimental physics. But high-tech growth has been generalized through the area: Pleasanton's population grew by 44 percent in the 1980s.

By cutting a new and separate district for these voters, the court-appointed cartographers created something that suggests a harp in shape and looks like a solid Republican district in demographics. The proportion of racial minorities in the 10th (less than 18 percent) is the fourth lowest in the state. But in the process of creating this community of interest, the mappers also confirmed the partisan character of surrounding districts. Six districts border or adjoin the 10th, and five of them elected Democrats to the House in 1992.

At the same time, it would be a mistake to view the 10th as a Northern California version of Orange County. Some of the residents here represent white flight from Oakland that is now generations old. But many of the newer commuters are younger and may still identify with San Francisco or Berkeley. While concerned with taxes, crime, schools and drugs, many hold more liberal views on other social and economic questions.

Bill Clinton carried both the Alameda and Contra Costa portions of the 10th in 1992, in both cases receiving about 42 percent of the vote (or about the same as he got nationwide). And while Republican Baker did well enough in Contra Costa to win the 10th by four percentage points, he failed to carry the Alameda part of the district.

1990 Population: 572,008. White 502,626 (88%), Black 13,220 (2%), Other 56,162 (10%). Hispanic origin 49,985 (9%). 18 and over 431,405 (75%), 62 and over 72,800 (13%). Median age: 35.

Committees

Public Works & Transportation (14th of 24 Republicans)
Economic Development; Investigations & Oversight; Surface Transportation

Science, Space & Technology (21st of 22 Republicans)
Energy

Campaign Finance

	Receipts	Receipts from PACs		Expend-itures
1992				
Baker (R)	$699,687	$178,550	(26%)	$697,982
Williams (D)	$228,847	$102,626	(45%)	$238,906

Key Votes

1993

Require parental notification of minors' abortions	Y
Require unpaid family and medical leave	N
Approve national "motor voter" registration bill	N
Approve budget increasing taxes and reducing deficit	N
Approve economic stimulus plan	N

Elections

1992 General		
Bill Baker (R)	145,702	(52%)
Wendell H. Williams (D)	134,635	(48%)
1992 Primary		
Bill Baker (R)	46,786	(64%)
Dave Williams (R)	26,387	(36%)

District Vote for President

1992

D 127,450 (42%)
R 107,191 (36%)
I 66,180 (22%)

11 Richard W. Pombo (R)

Of Tracy — Elected 1992; 1st Term

Born: Jan. 8, 1961, Tracy, Calif.
Education: California State Polytechnic U., Pomona, 1979-81.
Occupation: Rancher.
Family: Wife, Annette Rena; two children.
Religion: Roman Catholic.
Political Career: Tracy City Council, 1990-93.
Capitol Office: 1519 Longworth Bldg. 20515; 225-1947.

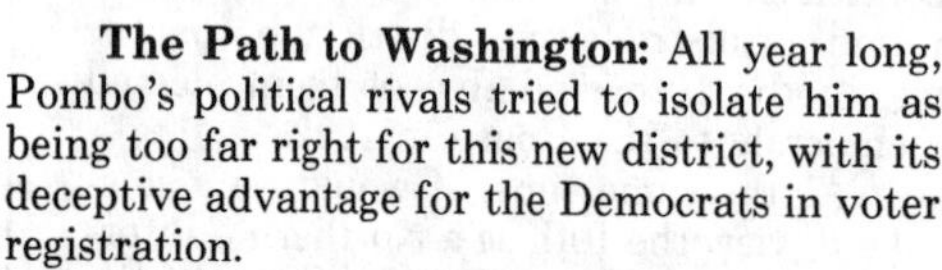

The Path to Washington: All year long, Pombo's political rivals tried to isolate him as being too far right for this new district, with its deceptive advantage for the Democrats in voter registration.

Pombo's chief adversary in the Republican primary and his Democratic opponent attacked him for holding to a line that was staunchly anti-abortion and in support of traditional values. Instead of shirking the label, however, Pombo wore it proudly, using his position on social issues to define himself and to fire back that his attackers were too far to the left and out of touch.

Having won close votes in both the primary and general elections, it would appear that Pombo could be vulnerable to a challenge from a moderate Republican or conservative Democrat. But he started as a dark horse in 1992 and will be well-positioned to appeal to 11th District voters on issues that hit much closer to home — property rights and water.

Pombo's view is that the federal and state governments have their hands too deeply into economic matters that should be strictly of local or personal concern.

He can use his seats on both the Natural Resources and Agriculture committees to press his points. And both assignments also put him in the middle of the never-ending fight over local control of central California water resources.

His vote on Natural Resources will add to the number of supporters of the controversial, long-planned multipurpose Auburn Dam, north of Sacramento, that is intended to provide crucial backup water for his San Joaquin Valley constituents, who live farther south.

Pombo served notice early in the 103rd Congress that he intends to be a thorn in the Democrats' side. During a closed-door markup of the 1993 tax bill, Pombo, accompanied by other GOP freshmen, held a news conference outside the Ways and Means committee hearing room to slam the committee's practice of closing markups to the public. To make the point, the group unveiled a sign that read "DO NOT DISTURB!!! DEMOCRATS RAISING TAXES!!!."

The 11th was carved out of portions of several districts to reward the San Joaquin area for its rapid growth. Given the chance to control a district, San Joaquin voters seized it.

The Republican primary was supposed to be dominated by Sacramento County Supervisor Sandra Smoley. A nurse with 20 years on the county board, Smoley had the backing of Gov. Pete Wilson and the Howard Jarvis Taxpayers Association.

Pombo was fairly new to campaigning, having been elected to the Tracy City Council in 1990. But he came from nowhere to upset Smoley by 4,000 votes in a five-way race. Pombo branded her a liberal for her abortion rights stand and her support for a bill banning discrimination against homosexuals. It did not help at all that Smoley was not from San Joaquin. Jack A. Sieglock, who worked for years as a district aide to former GOP Rep. Norman D. Shumway, ran third.

In the Democratic primary, Patricia Garamendi — one-half of a power couple that included state Insurance Commissioner John Garamendi — easily won the nomination, if for no other reason than she was well-known, having lost special elections in 1990 for a state Senate seat her husband was giving up, and in 1991 for the state Assembly.

Though Smoley would have been the favorite in the fall against Garamendi, Pombo's conservatism made him the underdog. Garamendi, who was known in national Democratic circles, was much better financed and had strong support from women's groups and organized labor.

Both candidates relied heavily on television attack ads: She called Pombo an extremist tool of the Christian right. He countered that she was another ambitious politician, while he was just a fourth-generation San Joaquin rancher out to defend his neighbors.

Garamendi's three consecutive negative campaigns began to backfire, and voters were left with a sour taste about her. That enabled Pombo to edge her by 2 percentage points — about 4,000 votes. Libertarian Christine Roberts, who was also in the race, pulled 7 percent and kept Pombo from winning a majority.

California 11

Parts of San Joaquin and Sacramento counties; Stockton; Lodi

In 1992 redistricting, Sacramento County was divided among four congressional districts so different from each other that their meeting point at the outskirts of the state capital is all that unites them. Most of the voters in the county live in the 5th District. But most of the county's square mileage is in the 11th, which incorporates the eastern and southern two-thirds of Sacramento County and aggregates them with nearly all of San Joaquin County to the south.

Many of the 11th District's residents still look to the state's capital city for their income, activities and media. But the city of Sacramento itself is entirely outside the district, which wraps itself around the city to the east and south. Even the sizable suburb of Elk Grove (population 17,500) sits on the district line but votes in the 5th.

So the biggest single source of votes in the 11th is the city of Stockton, 45 miles to the south on Interstate 5. Fifteen minutes north of Stockton on the same road is Lodi (population 51,900). The farms, orchards and ranches in this part of the vast Central Valley grow asparagus, avocados, walnuts, artichokes, peaches and apricots — much of which is processed through Lodi. But the small city remains best known for the Creedence Clearwater Revival song by the same name in which the refrain repeats: "Oh Lord, stuck in Lodi, again."

The 11th has regular borders on the west and east, following the county lines for Sacramento and San Joaquin counties in both cases. On the south end, the district takes in the towns of Tracy, Lathrop and Manteca and extends at some points to the Stanislaus County line (excepting the town of Ripon). The district's southern limit is defined west of Lathrop by the tracks of the old Union Pacific Railroad — a reminder of that entity's historic role throughout the state.

Stockton, however, is the district's center, not just because it is the county seat of San Joaquin (where three-fourths of the district vote is cast) but because it has stood on its own economically for more than a century. The inland waterways that snake into the Central Valley from San Francisco Bay have their southern terminus here, making Stockton an important port. In the 1980s, the city grew by more than one-third and now approaches 211,000 residents.

On paper, the farmworkers of the valley and the laborers of Lodi and Stockton make the 11th a Democratic district. But there are enough suburban voters in Sacramento County — and enough conservative Democrats in both counties — to make almost every race a tussle. Registration favors the Democrats (52 percent), but Bill Clinton carried the 11th by just two percentage points over George Bush — and he lost to Bush in the Sacramento County part of the district.

In 1992 House voting, Republican Pombo was narrowly elected over a favored Democratic candidate. Pombo carried both the counties but prevailed in San Joaquin by just 1,532 votes.

1990 Population: 571,772. White 428,076 (75%), Black 33,137 (6%), Other 110,559 (19%). Hispanic origin 120,755 (21%). 18 and over 404,673 (71%), 62 and over 74,685 (13%). Median age: 31.

Committees

Agriculture (16th of 18 Republicans)
Environment, Credit & Rural Development; Livestock; Specialty Crops and Natural Resources

Merchant Marine & Fisheries (16th of 18 Republicans)
Coast Guard & Navigation

Natural Resources (14th of 15 Republicans)
Energy & Mineral Resources; Oversight & Investigations

Campaign Finance

	Receipts	Receipts from PACs		Expend-itures
1992				
Pombo (R)	$532,902	$152,486	(29%)	$528,989
Garamendi (D)	$864,475	$338,905	(39%)	$864,411

Key Votes

1993	
Require parental notification of minors' abortions	Y
Require unpaid family and medical leave	N
Approve national "motor voter" registration bill	N
Approve budget increasing taxes and reducing deficit	N
Approve economic stimulus plan	N

Elections

1992 General		
Richard W. Pombo (R)	94,453	(48%)
Patricia Garamendi (D)	90,539	(46%)
Christine Roberts (LIBERT)	13,498	(7%)
1992 Primary		
Richard W. Pombo (R)	16,704	(36%)
Sandra Smoley (R)	12,482	(27%)
Jack A. Sieglock (R)	11,029	(24%)
Frank W. Hauck (R)	4,455	(10%)
Cleo Nichol Robinson (R)	1,703	(4%)

District Vote for President

1992		
D	79,432	(41%)
R	75,319	(38%)
I	41,006	(21%)

12 Tom Lantos (D)

Of San Mateo — Elected 1980; 7th Term

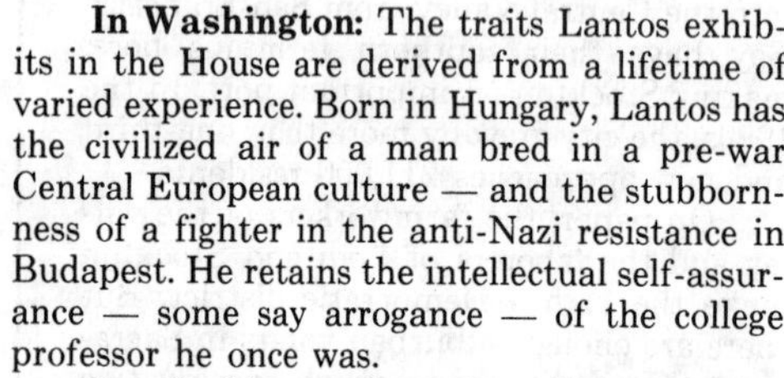

Born: Feb. 1, 1928, Budapest, Hungary.

Education: U. of Washington, B.A. 1949, M.A. 1950; U. of California, Berkeley, Ph.D. 1953.

Occupation: Professor.

Family: Wife, Annette Tillemann; two children.

Religion: Jewish.

Political Career: Millbrae Board of Education, 1958-66.

Capitol Office: 2182 Rayburn Bldg. 20515; 225-3531.

In Washington: The traits Lantos exhibits in the House are derived from a lifetime of varied experience. Born in Hungary, Lantos has the civilized air of a man bred in a pre-war Central European culture — and the stubbornness of a fighter in the anti-Nazi resistance in Budapest. He retains the intellectual self-assurance — some say arrogance — of the college professor he once was.

Despite his courtly manner, Lantos brings an assertive and sometimes confrontational approach to his roles on the Foreign Affairs Committee — he chairs its Subcommittee on International Security, International Organizations and Human Rights — and the Government Operations Committee.

At a March 1991 Foreign Affairs hearing, former U.S. Ambassador to Iraq April Glaspie was subjected to Lantos' wrath. Glaspie tried to counter criticism of her meeting with Iraqi President Saddam Hussein just prior to Iraq's August 1990 invasion of Kuwait; she said the Bush administration had made Saddam aware that the United States would react forcefully to Iraqi aggression.

But Lantos — who had for years criticized the Reagan and Bush administrations for courting an alliance with Iraq's totalitarian regime — blasted as "simply absurd" Glaspie's contention that Saddam was warned. "There was the persistent theme in the State Department that [Saddam] could be dealt with," Lantos retorted.

In the wake of the Persian Gulf War victory, a number of Democrats criticized Bush's pre-war Iraq policy; Bush scoffed that many were trying to make up for voting against the resolution permitting use of force against Iraq. But he had no such leverage with Lantos, who voted for the resolution and demanded war crimes trials for Saddam Hussein and other Iraqi leaders.

Lantos' sense of righteous anger was also on national display during the 101st Congress, when Lantos — then the chairman of the Government Operations Subcommittee on Employment and Housing — held hearings on alleged corruption at the Department of Housing and Urban Development.

One witness was former Reagan administration Interior Secretary James Watt, who defended efforts by well-connected Republican consultants to obtain HUD subsidies for housing developers. Lantos laced into Watt, one of the most staunchly conservative members of the Reagan "movement."

"What I find most obnoxious so far is the unmitigated hypocrisy of people like James Watt who exude unction, piety and noble motives, who carry on a crusade to destroy these programs and at the same time shamelessly milk them," Lantos said. The hearings helped persuade Congress to pass legislation placing new restrictions on HUD operating procedures.

Lantos does not have an extensive record of passing legislation. But he is well-suited for service on two committees that often act more as debating societies than policy-making bodies. He has shown a knack for getting ahead of issues and a zeal for publicity that raises their place on the national agenda.

He was one of the first members to call for a tough U.S. response to what he called Serbia's aggression against the other former Yugoslavian republics of Croatia and Bosnia-Herzegovina. In November 1991, after a Serb attack on Croatian civilians, Lantos excoriated Bush and other Western leaders for failing to act. "The leadership of Western Europe and our own administration have flunked dismally the first test of the new world order," Lantos said.

Early in 1992, he criticized Bush again for not recognizing Bosnia.

Lantos, who is Jewish, is an enthusiastic supporter of Israel and a critic of its Arab adversaries. And as a survivor of the Nazi Holocaust, Lantos also says devotion to human rights should drive U.S. foreign policy.

He has been highly critical of China since its government's brutal crackdown on pro-democracy demonstrators in Tiananmen Square in June 1989, and urged canceling favorable tariff treatment for Chinese exports to the United States. Even before that, Lantos was a leading critic of China's treatment of the people

California 12

Most of San Mateo County; southwest San Francisco

Not too long ago, San Francisco supplied the vote for two congressional districts that were often split between the city's eastern and western halves. But as it now takes more than 570,000 inhabitants to make a district in California, San Francisco musters just one whole district and about one-fourth of another. The whole one is now the 8th, while the remaining city population is in the 12th.

The city portion of the 12th consists of the Twin Peaks area and the Sunset District south of Golden Gate Park. The nearby presence of the Pacific is palpable here, as clouds and fog often enshroud the area. The district's city portion also includes Lake Merced, the city zoo and a California State University campus (locally still called San Francisco State).

The city portion of the district is Democratic (64 percent for Bill Clinton in 1992), but it is somewhat unfamiliar territory for Rep. Lantos. The Sunset District is increasingly Chinese, and the 12th is 16 percent Asian. Lantos' old district in San Mateo County was 10 percent Asian.

More than 70 percent of the 12th District residents live south of the San Francisco city limit in San Mateo County, and many of them live just over the city limit. The first suburb is Daly City, where spines of close-set homes appeared on the rocky hillsides after World War II and inspired folksinger Pete Seeger's song "Little Boxes." Hard by the sea itself is Pacifica, harder to reach and blessed in good weather with magnificent views. Across the peninsula on the bay side lies South San Francisco, proclaimed "The Industrial City" by a Hollywood-style sign inscribed in a hillside. "South City," as locals call it, lies between the San Francisco International Airport and Candlestick Park, home of football's 49ers and baseball's Giants.

The center portion of the northern peninsula is occupied by a huge state fish and game refuge. To the west are steep coastal mountains, to the east are heavily populated suburbs. Two freeways carry city commuters south along the eastern portion of the peninsula at night: the Junipero Serra Freeway (I-280) glides along the sparsely populated western route, while the Bayshore Freeway (U.S. 101) plows through the often smoggy, always crowded bayside suburbs. Halfway between the two freeways is another north-south arterial, El Camino Real. This one-time route of Spanish soldiers and priests is now an endless procession of overnight lodgings, restaurants and video stores.

Principal among the Bayshore communities are Brisbane, San Bruno, Millbrae and Burlingame (which pass by before the southbound commuter reaches the county seat of San Mateo) and Foster City to the east. Farther into the peninsula's highlands lies Hillsborough, one of the most exclusive estate communities on the West Coast.

San Mateo County has been somewhat less reliably Democratic than others around the bay. Lantos' district voted for Ronald Reagan in 1980 and 1984 before switching to support Michael S. Dukakis in 1988. San Mateo portions of the new 12th gave 55 percent to Clinton in 1992.

1990 Population: 571,535. White 372,572 (65%), Black 23,649 (4%), Other 175,314 (31%). Hispanic origin 81,606 (14%). 18 and over 455,454 (80%), 62 and over 95,211 (17%). Median age: 36.

of Tibet, which it controls as a province. When Chinese Premier Deng Xiaoping in 1987 referred to his Tibetan stand as "ignorant" and "arrogant," the self-assured Lantos took it as a compliment.

Lantos is not always an angry man. His regal bearing and droll intellectualism often leave his colleagues amused, or at least bemused.

During a Foreign Affairs subcommittee hearing on Yugoslavia in March 1993, a witness said the Balkan republics lacked the infrastructure for conflict resolution that exists in the United States, from legislative forums to condominium associations. Lantos interjected that "condominium" was an applicable term for the Yugoslavian region. He was referring to the word's original meaning: a territory over which two or more nations share sovereignty.

If Lantos' manner puts off some of his colleagues, he has one sure ally in the House: his son-in-law, Democratic Rep. Dick Swett of New Hampshire, who was first elected in 1990.

At Home: It took Lantos two difficult and expensive elections before he could settle securely into his district. But his efforts since have given him an enviable comfort level.

He was working on Capitol Hill as a consultant to the Senate Foreign Relations Committee when Republican Bill Royer won a 1979 special election to replace Democrat Leo J. Ryan, who had been assassinated the year before in Jonestown, Guyana. Ryan's assassination brought out a host of Democrats who claimed to be his logical political heir, and by the time the primary was finished, the party was badly splintered. Royer picked his way through the Democratic debris to win the seat for the GOP.

But Lantos, well-known within local Democratic circles, left his job right after Royer's victory and began preparing a challenge for 1980. The one-time economics professor at San Francisco State University had held elective office only as a School Board president in suburban Millbrae. But he had been active in party efforts and had built up name recognition as a foreign affairs commentator for a Bay Area TV station.

Royer, who had been a city councilman and county supervisor for 23 years before moving on to Congress, went into the contest with a solid political foundation. He had tried to strengthen it over his term in office by taking a highly visible role in the investigation of the events surrounding Ryan's death.

Yet Lantos, who had held himself apart from the 1979 Democratic feuding, was able to unite his party around him for 1980. Although Lantos was less well-known than Royer and was short of campaign funds, he was politically astute and took advantage of the incumbent's overconfidence. In the final weeks of the campaign, the Democrat filled the airwaves with advertising, while Royer, believing the election was his, yanked his own ads as an economy move. Lantos won by 3 percentage points.

Royer made it clear that he would be back two years later, and Lantos began raising money early. With typical single-mindedness, he pursued it not only at home, but within Jewish communities in the districts of other members — a habit that led initially to some hard feelings among his colleagues. By 1982, he was among the best-funded House candidates in the country. He dismissed Royer's comeback attempt easily.

In 1986, 1988 and 1990, Lantos faced Republican G.M. "Bill" Quraishi, a nuclear and electrical engineer whose share of the vote never reached 30 percent. The Republicans found another nominee in 1992, but the result was no better. Changes in the district lines gave Lantos some San Francisco constituents but scarcely altered the partisan makeup. The latest GOP challenger could not muster one-fourth of the vote.

Committees

Foreign Affairs (3rd of 27 Democrats)
International Security, International Organizations & Human Rights (chairman); Europe & the Middle East; International Operations

Government Operations (7th of 25 Democrats)
Employment, Housing & Aviation; Legislation & National Security

Elections

1992 General		
Tom Lantos (D)	157,205	(69%)
Jim Tomlin (R)	53,278	(23%)
Mary Weldon (PFP)	10,142	(4%)
George L. O'Brien (LIBERT)	7,782	(3%)
1992 Primary		
Tom Lantos (D)	62,397	(82%)
Glenn Tenney (D)	8,200	(11%)
Jim Dunlap (D)	5,696	(7%)
1990 General		
Tom Lantos (D)	105,029	(66%)
G.M. "Bill" Quraishi (R)	45,818	(29%)
June R. Genis (LIBERT)	8,518	(5%)

Previous Winning Percentages: **1988** (71%) **1986** (74%) **1984** (70%) **1982** (57%) **1980** (46%)

District Vote for President

1992
D 139,244 (57%)
R 64,967 (27%)
I 38,125 (16%)

Campaign Finance

	Receipts	Receipts from PACs	Expend-itures
1992			
Lantos (D)	$499,867	$112,850 (23%)	$600,656
Tomlin (R)	$2,815	$2,000 (71%)	$5,554
1990			
Lantos (D)	$788,298	$120,550 (15%)	$620,782
Quraishi (R)	$97,638	$6,300 (6%)	$97,030

Key Votes

1993	
Require parental notification of minors' abortions	N
Require unpaid family and medical leave	Y
Approve national "motor voter" registration bill	Y
Approve budget increasing taxes and reducing deficit	Y
Approve economic stimulus plan	Y
1992	
Approve balanced-budget constitutional amendment	N
Close down space station program	Y
Approve U.S. aid for former Soviet Union	Y
Allow shifting funds from defense to domestic programs	Y
1991	
Extend unemployment benefits using deficit financing	#
Approve waiting period for handgun purchases	Y
Authorize use of force in Persian Gulf	Y

Voting Studies

	Presidential Support		Party Unity		Conservative Coalition	
Year	S	O	S	O	S	O
1992	19	81	90	6	31	69
1991	30	65	89	6	35	62
1990	26	74	89	6	30	70
1989	31	62	90	4	34	63
1988	27	71	89	6	42	55
1987	21	75	90	5	49	49
1986	23	76	89	5	40	60
1985	19	70	88	4	27	71
1984	27	69	83	4	14	81
1983	21	73	91	5	20	76
1982	31	57	87	4	29	66
1981	46	50	69	14	39	53

Interest Group Ratings

Year	ADA	AFL-CIO	CCUS	ACU
1992	95	92	25	8
1991	75	100	11	11
1990	78	92	21	17
1989	80	100	40	0
1988	85	100	31	8
1987	84	100	20	0
1986	70	100	31	18
1985	70	94	22	5
1984	85	100	43	5
1983	85	100	25	2
1982	80	89	11	10
1981	70	71	24	7

13 Pete Stark (D)

Of Hayward — Elected 1972; 11th Term

Born: Nov. 11, 1931, Milwaukee, Wis.
Education: Massachusetts Institute of Technology, B.S. 1953; U. of California, Berkeley, M.B.A. 1960.
Military Service: Air Force, 1955-57.
Occupation: Banker.
Family: Wife, Deborah Roderick; four children.
Religion: Unitarian.
Political Career: Sought Democratic nomination for Calif. Senate, 1969.
Capitol Office: 239 Cannon Bldg. 20515; 225-5065.

In Washington: Beginning his fifth term as chairman of the Ways and Means Subcommittee on Health in the 103rd Congress, Stark faces an opportunity and a challenge. Universal health care has now become a priority not only for Stark and like-minded colleagues in Congress but for the White House as well.

At the same time, on the subcommittee, Stark is matched up against a new ranking Republican, fellow Californian Bill Thomas, whose ego and intellect rival his own.

The combination has combustible potential, particularly given their opposite ideological views. Thomas is a classic conservative. Stark is a man of personal sophistication and proven business sense (he made a fortune in banking by the time he was 40), but he has become a significant player on the Ways and Means Committee by making a decidedly liberal mark on both tax and health policy.

In the debate over national health insurance, Stark laid down his marker on the left early in 1993, ignoring the request of President Clinton to wait for an administration proposal. Stark jumped in with a plan to expand Medicare and Medicaid, to impose cost controls principally through a national health-care budget and to simplify access to insurance.

When the Clinton administration's budget called for inflation adjustments to Medicare payments for physicians and hospitals, Stark pushed his subcommittee to adopt a freeze instead.

Down the road, Stark has still more ideas. He has suggested imposing a windfall profits tax on drugs designed to treat rare diseases, in the event they become more profitable than anticipated. He has proposed creating a board to regulate prescription drug prices. And, for the perfect-world coup de grâce, Stark even proffered a constitutional amendment guaranteeing a right to health care.

But for all that horizon-gazing, over the years he has generally satisfied himself with incremental measures improving health services and insurance for those without coverage. His aptitude for translating liberal goals into pragmatic legislation contrasts with another side of Stark's persona: the confrontational, outraged liberal who sometimes speeds beyond the reach of his headlights.

Some House members still remember Stark's quixotic effort to join the Congressional Black Caucus in 1975. Stark argued that although he was white, his constituency and personal sympathies made him eligible. The caucus said it had to "respectfully decline" the request.

Stark's barbed tongue more than once has caused him to retreat. At an August 1990 news conference, Stark erupted at the mention of Health and Human Services Secretary Louis W. Sullivan. Stark said Sullivan, who is black, "comes about as close to being a disgrace to his profession and his race as anyone I've ever seen."

Sullivan demanded an apology. "I don't live on Pete Stark's plantation," he said in a statement. But at first, Stark was unrepentant. "He's right, he doesn't live on my plantation," Stark said. "He lives on John Sununu's," referring to the White House chief of staff. But after House Republicans rose to Sullivan's defense and denounced Stark for his remarks, Stark apologized — sort of.

"To the secretary, I have to say I blew it," Stark told the House. "I should not have brought into the discussion his race, because it obscures the fact that he is carrying a bankrupt policy for an administration which has been impacting the poor and the minorities of this country. . . . And I apologize for obscuring that." Republicans hooted Stark; Democrats cheered. A few days later, though, Stark sent Sullivan a formal letter of apology.

In January 1991, The Alameda Journal, a small semiweekly newspaper, reported that Stark criticized Democrats Stephen J. Solarz of New York and Tom Lantos of California for their support of military action in the Persian Gulf. The papers said Stark had called them "hostile, militant guys" and referred to Solarz as "Field Marshal Solarz."

California 13

East Bay — Oakland; Hayward; Santa Clara

The 13th is a renumbered version of the old 9th, which had been sending Pete Stark to the House for 20 years. Although somewhat altered in 1992 redistricting, the constituency is 58 percent Democratic by registration, exactly the same as the old 9th.

The old 9th began at Hayward, a city of 111,000 on the shore of San Francisco Bay. It then ran inland over the San Leandro Hills to take in the agricultural southeastern portions of Alameda County. The 1980s transformed these environs, as high-tech industry accelerated population growth. So great was the growth that remapping moved eastern Alameda County en masse into another district (the 10th) with suburban Contra Costa County.

Now Stark's district begins in Oakland, on the bay side of the Bay Area Rapid Transit (BART) tracks just south of San Leandro Bay. Here the 13th takes in the Oakland Coliseum, home of the baseball Athletics and once home of the football Raiders, and Oakland International Airport. Despite the landmarks, there is relatively little of Oakland's residential population here. The bayshore is dominated by the freeway, miles of warehouses and older factories — many of which no longer function.

The first suburb south of Oakland proper is San Leandro, an old Portuguese enclave with a strong blue-collar vote. Once attracted to Ronald Reagan, the area has returned to the Democratic fold — one of many such venues that account for the turnaround in California's presidential preferences.

Hayward has a large campus of the California State University system and mixes business and professionals' office complexes with the usual East Bay commerce. Farther south along the multilane traffic crunch of I-880 is Newark, followed by Fremont — the East Bay southern terminus for BART and site of the last operating auto plant in California, a joint venture of General Motors and Toyota. The district line coincides with the eastern limits of these cities, as it does those of San Leandro and Hayward. In each case, the limit is reached in the highlands. The district no longer reaches into the suburb-dotted interior beyond the ridges.

At its southern extreme, the 13th crosses the county line into Santa Clara County and takes in the alluvial mud flats at the southern end of San Francisco Bay. This is home to a little less than 10 percent of the 13th's residents. At the southwestern extreme, the district takes in a slice of the old Moffett Field Air Station, once home to government-operated dirigibles (the hangars are still visible from the Bayshore Freeway). The southeastern extreme reaches through the industrial city of Milpitas and appropriates a section of San Jose.

By shedding the eastern reaches of Alameda County, Stark's district lowered the non-Latino white share of population from 64 percent in 1990 to 55 percent in 1992. The black community remains small and mostly concentrated in Oakland. But in 1992, nearly two residents in five were either Latino or Asian-American.

1990 Population: 572,441. White 367,553 (64%), Black 42,228 (7%), Other 162,660 (28%). Hispanic origin 105,225 (18%). 18 and over 426,316 (74%), 62 and over 66,786 (12%). Median age: 32.

Stark said the newspaper took his remarks at a town meeting out of context and apologized to the regional Anti-Defamation League of B'nai B'rith.

While Stark's ill-considered remarks and other idiosyncrasies may strain his relationships with some members, he remains an effective chairman of the Health Subcommittee. The 102nd Congress was hardly his most productive, however, as members sparred over the idea of wholesale health-care reform but never got down to the details.

And the 101st Congress dealt Stark a supreme disappointment: It repealed virtually all of a landmark expansion of the Medicare program that had been enacted less than 17 months earlier. Stark and his colleague Bill Gradison of Ohio (then the subcommittee's ranking Republican; he has since retired) had co-authored the catastrophic coverage bill, which aimed to limit the amount for which beneficiaries could be held liable for Medicare-covered hospital and physician bills.

In winning passage in the 100th Congress, Stark and Gradison fended off attempts to derail it by a senior citizens lobbying group and by prescription-drug manufacturers. The White House balked for a while, but President Ronald Reagan signed the bill, saying that the measure would "remove a terrible threat" from seniors' lives.

Many Medicare beneficiaries, however, did not believe they were at risk. Senior citizens lobbying groups angrily protested that seniors were being forced to pay the entire costs of the new benefits. The complaints drowned out the explanations of those who put the program together, and by the end of 1989, catastrophic coverage was repealed.

Stark teamed with Gradison and California Democrat Henry A. Waxman, chairman of Energy and Commerce's Health Subcommittee, to make a last-ditch attempt to salvage a handful of the law's provisions. But Stark's amendment was rejected 156-269. "We are being stampeded by . . . a small group of the wealthiest seniors to deny needed benefits to a majority of seniors," Stark said, echoing comments of other erstwhile champions of catastrophic coverage.

Despite the coverage repeal, Stark still could point to some legislative successes in the 101st Congress. Over the strong objections of the American Medical Association (AMA), Congress overhauled the way Medicare paid doctors. The Health Subcommittee approved on an 11-3 vote Stark's package creating a national fee schedule for physician services that takes into account the time, training and skill required to perform a given service.

A controversial portion of the bill set targets for overall Medicare spending on doctor bills each year; breaching the targets in one year would result in smaller inflation increases in the following year. After a grueling House-Senate conference, the bill, with its spending targets on doctor bills, was attached to the fiscal 1990 budget-reconciliation bill.

The physician payment reform battle produced another installment in one of Capitol Hill's more entertaining sideshows: the ongoing feud between Stark and the AMA. It is one in which Stark has usually maintained the upper hand; the organization tried unsuccessfully in the 100th Congress to oust Stark from his subcommittee chair.

From his subcommittee post, Stark is well positioned to reshape a variety of programs in the massive reconciliation bills, omnibus measures that make spending cuts dictated by the budget. When the budget calls for substantial reductions in Medicare, Stark is a major force in structuring the cuts and can quietly slip in changes in health policy.

Stark used the fiscal 1991 reconciliation bill to tighten significantly federal regulation of so-called Medigap insurance — private insurance plans sold to supplement Medicare coverage. Stark was one of the authors of the bill, which put teeth into a 1980 law to clamp down on reported abuse in the sales and marketing of Medigap policies.

Stark's experience with one of the most complex areas of tax law — dealing with insurance companies — assured him an influential role as Ways and Means sat down to overhaul the tax code in the 99th Congress. Stark earned the gratitude of Chairman Dan Rostenkowski of Illinois for his work on insurance issues and was a staunch enough loyalist that he was included in the circle of committee members handpicked to be conferees on the tax-overhaul bill.

Stark has the opportunity to pursue another item on his eclectic liberal agenda, having ascended to chairman of the District of Columbia Committee in the 103rd Congress. Long a member of this backwater panel whose main task is to oversee the internal affairs of the federal city, Stark would like Congress to abandon its role as colonial overseer by granting statehood to the District. That is not a popular position on Capitol Hill and ranks with other of Stark's underdog causes.

At Home: When Stark put an 8-foot neon peace symbol atop his bank in conservative Walnut Creek in the 1960s, people knew he was no ordinary banker. Ordinary California bankers did not protest the war in Vietnam or join the consumer movement. But Stark, who left Wisconsin to go to business school in California, relished his role as a maverick. And having founded his second bank at age 31, he had the money to play it.

Stark made his first political move in 1969, running for the state Senate in a special election. He finished third in the primary, losing the nomination to George Miller, a young law school graduate with whom he would later serve in the House. Three years later, Stark decided to take on another George Miller — this one a crusty old-school conservative who had represented Oakland in Congress as a Democrat for 28 years. Stark spent his money generously and used one of the state's top political consultants to convince the voters they did not "have to settle for the 81-year-old Congressman George P. Miller anymore," as a campaign brochure put it. Miller's support for the Vietnam War was a major issue in the primary, and Stark swept him aside, winning by 11,000 votes. The November election was narrow, as Republicans were dominating most of the races that fall. But Stark managed 53 percent and took office.

Only once since then has Stark had a close call. Lulled by years of easy re-election, he prepared only a token effort in 1980. But conservative Republican William J. Kennedy, a tireless campaigner, galvanized a host of volunteers. Helped by the Republican turnout Ronald Reagan inspired that fall, Kennedy held Stark to 55 percent.

Kennedy never stopped campaigning after that. He kept his campaign office open and used his credentials from the 1980 contest to persuade donors and national GOP officials to support him more extensively in 1982. Stark, however, was ready for the rematch. He kept a high profile in the district, holding frequent meetings with constituents, and he took advantage of the area's rising unemployment in that year of recession to woo back Democrats who had turned out for Reagan two years earlier.

After it was discovered that Kennedy had misrepresented his political background — telling audiences he had voted for a 1978 tax-cutting measure when he had not even been registered to vote — Stark's victory was sealed. He took 61 percent.

The flap over his rash criticism of Sullivan may have cost Stark some votes in 1990, when he carried the district easily against Republican real estate agent Victor Romero but saw his share of the vote drop by 15 percentage points.

In 1992, remapping changed Stark's district dramatically but left the Democratic registration at 58 percent, right where it had been in 1990. Stark was opposed by a foster-care home operator Verne Teyler and prevailed easily with 60 percent.

Committees

District of Columbia (Chairman)
Government Operations & Metropolitan Affairs; Judiciary & Education

Ways & Means (5th of 24 Democrats)
Health (chairman)

Joint Economic

Elections

1992 General		
Pete Stark (D)	123,795	(60%)
Verne Teyler (R)	64,953	(32%)
Roslyn A. Allen (PFP)	16,768	(8%)
1990 General		
Pete Stark (D)	94,739	(58%)
Victor Romero (R)	67,412	(42%)

Previous Winning Percentages: **1988** (73%) **1986** (70%) **1984** (70%) **1982** (61%) **1980** (55%) **1978** (65%) **1976** (71%) **1974** (71%) **1972** (53%)

District Vote for President

1992
D 116,829 (54%)
R 55,100 (26%)
I 43,026 (20%)

Campaign Finance

	Receipts	Receipts from PACs		Expend-itures
1992				
Stark (D)	$634,994	$349,444	(55%)	$589,500
Teyler (R)	$47,360	$1,250	(3%)	$43,435
1990				
Stark (D)	$525,271	$270,170	(51%)	$300,996
Romero (R)	$206,798	$1,000	(0%)	$210,089

Key Votes

1993	
Require parental notification of minors' abortions	?
Require unpaid family and medical leave	Y
Approve national "motor voter" registration bill	Y
Approve budget increasing taxes and reducing deficit	Y
Approve economic stimulus plan	Y
1992	
Approve balanced-budget constitutional amendment	N
Close down space station program	Y
Approve U.S. aid for former Soviet Union	N
Allow shifting funds from defense to domestic programs	Y
1991	
Extend unemployment benefits using deficit financing	Y
Approve waiting period for handgun purchases	Y
Authorize use of force in Persian Gulf	N

Voting Studies

	Presidential Support		Party Unity		Conservative Coalition	
Year	**S**	**O**	**S**	**O**	**S**	**O**
1992	14	80	81	6	4	83
1991	24	71	87	3	8	86
1990	16	82	88	5	6	89
1989	24	73	90	3	2	93
1988	15	67	78	5	5	68
1987	12	81	86	4	2	88
1986	18	77	86	4	4	92
1985	18	73	89	3	2	91
1984	25	56	78	4	3	83
1983	21	72	83	7	12	83
1982	23	64	85	4	5	88
1981	29	64	84	8	11	83

Interest Group Ratings

Year	**ADA**	**AFL-CIO**	**CCUS**	**ACU**
1992	95	83	13	4
1991	100	100	20	0
1990	100	83	23	4
1989	95	100	20	0
1988	90	85	42	0
1987	96	88	20	13
1986	95	77	12	5
1985	90	94	14	11
1984	90	77	25	0
1983	90	93	26	9
1982	95	100	11	0
1981	95	87	11	13

14 Anna G. Eshoo (D)

Of Atherton — Elected 1992; 1st Term

Born: Dec. 13, 1942, New Britain, Conn.
Education: Canada College, A.A. 1975.
Occupation: Legislative aide.
Family: Divorced; two children.
Religion: Roman Catholic.
Political Career: Democratic National Committee, 1980-92; San Mateo County Board of Supervisors, 1983-93; Democratic nominee for U.S. House, 1988.
Capitol Office: 1505 Longworth Bldg. 20515; 225-8104.

The Path to Washington: The second time was the charm for Eshoo, who parlayed experience, an aggressive style and a couple of breaks into a victory in this Silicon Valley district.

Though local voters have a reputation for sending moderate Republicans to Washington, Eshoo seems destined to hang on to the seat. She capitalized on Californians' seeming desire in 1992 to elect candidates other than white men at almost every opportunity. Moreover, she offers an ideological profile not particularly distinct from that of her predecessor, Rep. Tom Campbell, who consistently bucked party orthodoxy more than other state Republicans.

Reflecting her upscale, high-tech district, Eshoo opposes tax increases for the wealthy. Because the downsizing of the computer industry and defense cutbacks have cost the district thousands of jobs, she wants government incentives to encourage new entrepreneurs. She favors a capital gains tax cut that is narrowly targeted to benefit small businesses and start-up companies, and permanent extension of the research and development tax credit.

To reduce the federal deficit, she would cut defense spending in half over five years — using some of the savings to pay for additional health-care benefits and business incentives. Because she once was head of a local hospital board, she favors a managed-care approach to universal health care that uses existing private insurance providers.

Eshoo's seat on the Science, Space and Technology Committee is a natural given the 14th's employment base. She emerged as one of the notable supporters of the space station *Freedom* at the start of the 103rd Congress.

Her seat on the Merchant Marine and Fisheries Committee will allow her to continue opposing offshore drilling and to pursue other environmental concerns. Eshoo was also one of eight first-term members named to the House Democratic whip structure.

A San Mateo County supervisor since 1982, Eshoo ran unsuccessfully in 1988 against Campbell, coming within 15,000 votes of winning (the district was then the 12th). Eshoo prevailed this time, aided by Campbell's decision to run for Senate and give up the seat he held for four years. It did not hurt that redistricting had increased the Democrats' nominal edge in registration.

Eshoo was joined in the Democratic primary by six male candidates, two of whom mounted serious campaigns. Ted Lempert, serving his second two-year term in the state Assembly, and fellow San Mateo County Supervisor Tom Nolan recognized Eshoo's built-in advantage from having run before. They attacked her record and credibility, and her strategy of making her gender an issue.

Late in the campaign, Lempert accused Eshoo in radio ads of having accepted contributions from a garbage disposal company and implied that she had a role in awarding the company a contract. The implication turned out to be false. The ad backfired on Lempert, who was reprimanded by two county AFL-CIO union councils for running a dirty campaign.

For her part, Eshoo campaigned like a front-runner, refusing to attack her opponents, and distributing a 58-page book called "First Things First" to counter requests for sound-bite responses on difficult issues. It outlined her positions on such issues as foreign policy, competitiveness and family values. She managed a 3,000-vote win in the primary over Lempert, with Nolan well back.

Meanwhile, Tom Huening, another San Mateo County supervisor, had a much easier time securing the GOP nomination, winning 43 percent in a five-way primary. Huening made a name for himself by calling for congressional reform and attempting to organize a post-election meeting of all House freshmen in Omaha, Neb.

Huening cast himself in the mold of Campbell and another popular former GOP House member from Silicon Valley, Ed Zschau. He supported deeper spending cuts than Eshoo — except for defense — and took a firm stand against tax increases of any kind.

Both candidates kept to the high road throughout, and Eshoo ran away with a 57 percent majority to Huening's 39 percent. Two minor candidates were not factors.

California 14

Southern San Mateo and northern Santa Clara counties

Sustained population growth in the San Francisco Peninsula enabled map-drawers in 1992 to fashion a full district from suburbs south of the San Mateo Bridge and north of San Jose. In the main, the 14th resembles the old 12th District. But on the north it has annexed more of San Mateo County, including Belmont, San Carlos and Redwood City, where 66,000 residents make it the district's second-largest city. About 40 percent of the district population is now in San Mateo County, the rest in Santa Clara County.

At its southern end, the district has lost the long tail that had dangled all the way to rural Gilroy and taken in some remote Santa Cruz County turf along the way. The 14th is more compact, with its center in the affluent suburbs on either side of the San Mateo and Santa Clara county line. Some of these communities have existed for more than a century, preserving their individual character despite waves of population growth. Working hardest to do so are the exclusive enclaves of Atherton, Woodside and Portola Valley. But Palo Alto, too, has stabilized its growth and sustained much of its leafy, small-town charm. Its population of 56,000 does not include the students, faculty and staff who live on the sprawling, adjacent campus of Stanford University.

Farther south, change has been more overwhelming in Mountain View, Sunnyvale, Los Altos and Cupertino. Miles of fruit groves have given way to high-tech factories: Hewlett-Packard, Apple Computer and Ford Aerospace are all in the area; Lockheed is nearby. With the rise of microprocessing, this corridor has come to be known worldwide as Silicon Valley. Sunnyvale, its informal capital, grew slowly in the 1980s; but with 117,000 residents it is easily the most populous city in the 14th.

The lure of comfy suburbs so close to jobs has kept peninsula land values climbing for decades. Million-dollar homes are commonplace, and even ramshackle units come with high price tags in East Palo Alto and other low-income communities along the Bayshore Freeway. The old 12th had the highest median real estate values of any California district in the 1980s.

With its wealth, old and new, this was the Bay Area's one Republican district in past years, favoring five GOP presidential candidates in a row. It also sent a succession of Republicans to Congress, although it preferred the moderate-to-liberal models such as Paul N. McCloskey Jr., Ed Zschau and Tom Campbell. But the 14th is different enough, and 1992 was lopsided enough, that no one is likely to call this district Republican again soon.

Population shifts and redistricting lowered the percentage of whites from 86 percent to 78 percent. GOP registration dipped accordingly, from 42 percent to 35 percent. Bill Clinton won the 14th by a ratio of 2-to-1, receiving nearly identical percentages in both counties. And yet his percentages were exceeded by Eshoo and by both of the Democrats' Senate nominees.

1990 Population: 571,131. White 445,884 (78%), Black 28,237 (5%), Other 97,010 (17%). Hispanic origin 77,305 (14%). 18 and over 456,226 (80%), 62 and over 78,985 (14%). Median age: 34.

Committees

Merchant Marine & Fisheries (23rd of 29 Democrats)
Environment & Natural Resources; Oceanography, Gulf of Mexico & the Outer Continental Shelf

Science, Space & Technology (25th of 33 Democrats)
Science; Space; Technology, Environment & Aviation

Campaign Finance

1992	**Receipts**	**Receipts from PACs**	**Expend-itures**
Eshoo (D)	$917,346	$296,322 (32%)	$909,604
Huening (R)	$673,082	$149,383 (22%)	$670,277
Wald (PFP)	$125	0	$124

Key Votes

1993

Require parental notification of minors' abortions	N
Require unpaid family and medical leave	Y
Approve national "motor voter" registration bill	Y
Approve budget increasing taxes and reducing deficit	Y
Approve economic stimulus plan	Y

Elections

1992 General

Anna G. Eshoo (D)	146,873	(57%)
Tom Huening (R)	101,202	(39%)
Chuck Olson (LIBERT)	7,220	(3%)
David Wald (PFP)	3,912	(2%)

1992 Primary

Anna G. Eshoo (D)	32,001	(40%)
Ted Lempert (D)	28,858	(36%)
Tom Nolan (D)	11,574	(15%)
Thomas Roy Harney (D)	1,800	(2%)
Gerry B. Andeen (D)	1,655	(2%)
Robert Palmer (D)	1,445	(2%)
Gary Bond (D)	1,242	(2%)

District Vote for President

1992

D	143,802	(54%)
R	71,771	(27%)
I	53,051	(20%)

15 Norman Y. Mineta (D)

Of San Jose — Elected 1974; 10th Term

Born: Nov. 12, 1931, San Jose, Calif.
Education: U. of California, Berkeley, B.S. 1953.
Military Service: Army, 1953-56.
Occupation: Insurance executive.
Family: Wife, Danealia Brantner; two children, two stepchildren.
Religion: Methodist.
Political Career: San Jose City Council, 1967-71; mayor of San Jose, 1971-74.
Capitol Office: 2221 Rayburn Bldg. 20515; 225-2631.

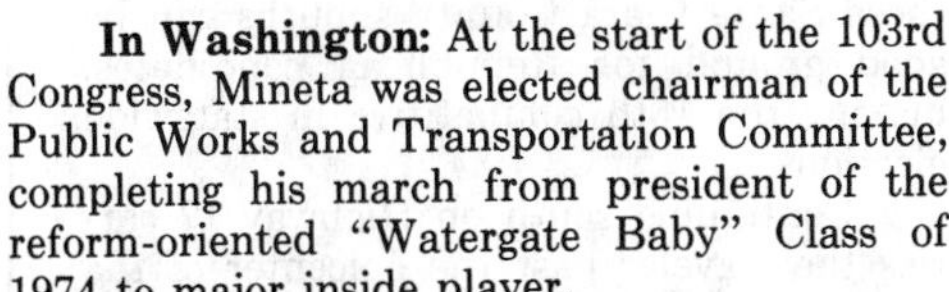

In Washington: At the start of the 103rd Congress, Mineta was elected chairman of the Public Works and Transportation Committee, completing his march from president of the reform-oriented "Watergate Baby" Class of 1974 to major inside player.

The event must have been a sweet victory for Mineta, who had tried for the job two years earlier in an end run around the seniority system. Frustrated by the lack of leadership on the Public Works and Transportation Committee and spurred on by a cabal of younger members, Mineta took on 77-year-old Chairman Glenn M. Anderson of California. Anderson went down, but the Democratic Caucus gave the chairmanship not to Mineta but to Robert A. Roe of New Jersey, the Democrat who ranked second in seniority to Anderson.

But Roe turned 68 in 1992 and chose to make the 102nd Congress his last. So when President-elect Clinton sounded out Mineta about becoming secretary of Transportation after the 1992 election, Mineta said he preferred to remain in Congress where he could realize his goal of chairing the Public Works Committee and work on a wider range of issues as well.

Public Works is not considered an elite address on the Hill, but it is certainly a desirable one — especially for members whose districts depend most on federal projects. Mineta goes to bat for his district, too, but he has long displayed an interest in the committee's larger responsibility: maintaining and improving the national infrastructure.

When the 102nd Congress passed a six-year $151 billion highway bill, Mineta, as chairman of the Subcommittee on Surface Transportation, was the principal author of the bill and the lead shepherd for its passage. But the bill's progress revealed the strains in Mineta's relations with Roe, who upstaged Mineta at certain points in the process. Roe was a gruff politician of the old school who often rode herd on his subcommittee chairmen. And Mineta, who had challenged him for the chair in defiance of the seniority system, was not among his favorites.

Although less than a decade younger, Mineta is associated with an entirely different generation of post-Vietnam and post-Watergate politicians. He is detail-oriented and familiar with the mechanics of transportation policy, but he is less inclined than Roe to micromanage the workings of each subcommittee. Calling the 1991 bill a "blueprint for rebuilding America," Mineta argued that it would provide some of the stimulus needed to end the recession — creating 300,000 jobs over six years in California alone. He made sure that the Bay area was not forgotten, including $630 million in specific highway and mass transportation funds and 16,000 new jobs for his home region.

The legislation passed overwhelmingly (372-47) in November 1991 with bipartisan support, but Mineta and other Democrats initially were skeptical of the Bush administration's resolve on this issue. Eventually, President Bush decided to sign the bill rather than appear to be discouraging recovery.

In the 102nd Congress, Mineta was the ninth-ranking member of the Science, Space and Technology Committee and used his position to obtain government funding for high-technology projects, many of which are in or near his district. In 1991, Mineta pushed through an amendment transferring $10 million from a technology grant program to provide loans to help companies commercialize emerging technologies in the electronics and computer fields.

He also accused the Bush administration of politicizing the National Aeronautics and Space Administration and making it a "public relations tool for the rehabilitation of Dan Quayle."

A keen interest in protecting labor rights has been a hallmark of Mineta's work. In the 100th Congress, he championed a measure requiring airline carriers to pay benefits to workers hurt by mergers. The "labor-protection" provisions (LPPs) cleared the House as part of the transportation appropriations bill, but a veto threat knocked them off the bill in confer-

California 15

Santa Clara County — San Jose

Two decades ago, when he was mayor of San Jose, Mineta might not have been surprised to hear that his growing city would be the state's third largest in 1992. But Mineta would have been stunned to learn that when San Jose was bigger than San Francisco, he would have a House district that included half of seaside Santa Cruz County.

But that is what redistricting can do. After 18 years in the House as the member for San Jose and a few adjoining suburbs, Mineta in 1992 got a district where the population is 40 percent new to him — a district in which heavily trafficked state Highway 17 is the spinal column.

The 15th has its northern extreme at the Great America theme park between the Bayshore Freeway (Highway 101) and the southern tip of the San Francisco Bay. The park is in the city of Santa Clara, which lies at the south end of Silicon Valley but retains some of the character of an old college town in the midst of high-tech plants and proliferating subdivisions. (The University of Santa Clara was founded here by Jesuits in 1851.)

With 94,000 people, Santa Clara is the largest city wholly within the 15th. It has usually been Democratic — although not as decidedly so as San Jose — and it helps keep Democratic registration in the 15th close to half (46 percent).

At the southeastern end of Santa Clara is an imposing interchange where Interstates 880 and 280 cross. Southeast of this landmark, the 15th has San Jose's western neighborhoods, including recent developments that spread out on either side of the Almaden Expressway (which shares its name with a giant nearby winery). Also proceeding south from the intersection of the interstates is Highway 17, which then runs all the way to the Pacific Ocean — with the district following it nearly all the way.

Some of the exit ramps from 17 lead to growing middle-class suburbs such as Campbell and Monte Sereno.

Other off-ramps lead to more affluent communities in the hills — Los Gatos and Saratoga — where some of the better-paid professionals of Silicon Valley live. All of these Santa Clara County suburbs can be good ground for Republican candidates, making the 15th competitive in statewide elections.

Continuing south on Highway 17 carries the traveler past the epicenter of the 1989 Loma Prieta earthquake, the area's worst since 1906. Not far away, the road and the district cross into Santa Cruz County, a demarcation surrounded by hillsides heavy with redwoods. Heading down the slope, the 15th takes in Scotts Valley and Felton.

Racing toward the sea, the district even reaches into the city of Santa Cruz. All told, Santa Cruz County contributes only about 10 percent of the district population. But it should help Democrats: Bill Clinton carried the 15th, but he received an outright majority only in its Santa Cruz County portions.

1990 Population: 572,485. White 470,821 (82%), Black 12,957 (2%), Other 88,707 (15%). Hispanic origin 61,884 (11%). 18 and over 444,446 (78%), 62 and over 67,179 (12%). Median age: 34.

ence.

Mineta advocated a consumer-protection bill that included the LPPs as well as provisions requiring airlines to make extensive public disclosures about flight delays and lost baggage. After both chambers passed legislation in 1987, the Department of Transportation issued rules requiring on-time disclosure. After that was accomplished, the bill got bogged down in debate over the LPPs and random drug testing of transportation workers, which Mineta vigorously opposed.

During the 100th Congress, he also pushed legislation to provide protection for aviation whistleblowers who called attention to safety violations. While the measure cruised through the House, it died in the Senate. Some suggested that Mineta's counterpart there, Aviation Subcommittee Chairman Wendell H. Ford of Kentucky, blocked the measure because he felt Mineta was foot-dragging on efforts to make the Federal Aviation Administration an independent agency. Mineta expressed concern that without the backing of the Department of Transportation, the FAA would lack the political clout to promote aviation needs.

In the 101st Congress, Mineta opposed Bush's proposal to assess airline travelers a user fee to help pay for airport improvements, arguing that it amounted to double taxation, since a portion of ticket prices goes to a trust fund that Mineta says should be used for airport improvements.

Perhaps Mineta's most significant accomplishment of recent years, however, had nothing to do with public works. He was a driving force behind passage of legislation to compensate Japanese-Americans interned by the U.S. government during World War II.

He described the internment as "an act born of racism," and the issue had topped his agenda for more than a decade. In 1978, he won passage of a bill to grant retirement benefits to interned Japanese-American civil servants. "Injustice does not dim with time," he said of the long wait for the 1987 bill.

After the Persian Gulf War began, Mineta urged federal law enforcement officials not to make the same mistakes of discrimination against Arab-Americans as had occurred against Japanese-Americans during World War II.

"Today, I am concerned that mistaken assumptions about national security have been made and may be implemented without properly protecting the rights of individuals," he said. "As these (government) agencies fight terrorism, they must never put expedience ahead of constitutional safeguards."

The issue hits Mineta close to home because half a century earlier, Mineta and his family had been sent from their San Jose home to an internment camp in Wyoming, where they lived during the war. "Some say the internment was for our own good," he said. "But even as a boy of 10, I could see that the machine guns and the barbed wire faced inward."

When Congress passed legislation to provide a formal apology and $20,000 to each of the 60,000 surviving victims, Mineta signed the bill in behalf of the House.

In the 102nd Congress, Mineta also pushed through legislation authorizing a memorial in Washington honoring the patriotism of Japanese-Americans who have served in the military.

In the 101st Congress, he also helped pass the Americans With Disabilities Act, which prohibits discrimination against the handicapped and requires increased accessibility to facilities for them.

Previously, Mineta chaired the Aviation Subcommittee, where he opposed Bush administration actions allowing foreign interests to own larger percentages of domestic U.S. airlines. In this job, Mineta showed his mettle on such irksome issues as the transfer of Dulles and National airports in suburban Virginia from federal ownership to control by a regional authority. Although the transfer had been recommended by various experts for more than 30 years, members of Congress had balked at losing control of the airports they use to travel to and from their home districts.

To mollify numerous House critics, Mineta proposed leasing the airports for 50 years, rather than selling them, and creating a federal review board consisting of members of Congress to monitor the regional authority. That allowed a transfer bill to reach the House floor, and it eventually became law.

Mineta also spent three terms on the Budget Committee, and when he rotated off the panel in 1983, he left behind a significant contribution: the concept of credit accounting. The procedure created the first formal accounting of the money the federal government spends guaranteeing private loans.

At Home: San Jose's small but cohesive Japanese-American community was the springboard to Mineta's political career. Running an insurance business with his father in the 1960s, he became active in the city's Japanese-American Citizens League. That led him to San Jose's Human Relations Commission, then on to the city's housing authority, the city council and, in 1971, the mayor's office.

The San Jose area was experiencing unprecedented suburban growth during Mineta's years as mayor, and he allied himself with those who called for some limits.

In 1974, the 13th District came open upon the retirement of GOP Rep. Charles Gubser, the incumbent for more than two decades. The district had, in fact, gone Republican in congressional elections consistently since World War II.

But with the demographic changes sweeping the Bay area in general, the 13th was younger and less settled. Mineta, who had been extremely popular as mayor, had no trouble winning the Democratic primary.

His GOP opponent was former state Rep. George W. Milias, who had lost an earlier primary for California secretary of state and gone on to work for the Defense Department in the administration of President Richard M. Nixon. Tested in the primary by more conservative opponents, Milias had only squeaked through to his nomination.

Milias was able to finance his campaign, in part by tapping the sources that had supported Gubser. But as a GOP candidate in 1974, he was impaled on the horns of dilemma. He had to remind his own party's conservatives of his loyal service to Nixon, who had resigned the presidency in August of that year. But he also had to distance himself from the Watergate scandal that had driven Nixon from the White House. Milias' absence from the district in the years prior to the election also hampered him.

In the end, Mineta's strength in San Jose and the travails attending Milias were just enough to give the Democrat a majority (53 percent). Thereafter, however, Mineta was able to prevail by fatter margins — even after Democratic registration in the district slipped below 50 percent.

But after topping out at 70 percent in 1986, Mineta suffered the trend affecting most House incumbents in 1990 and slipped a bit (58 percent). Of course, even that year's vote share, his lowest in a dozen years, was still enough to outdistance Republican David E. Smith.

In 1992, the challenge of re-election took a

new form. The California Supreme Court adopted a new map for the state's 52 congressional districts that reconfigured the southern Bay Area rather radically.

The former mayor of San Jose now represents only a slice of his old city, while his new district includes vast swatches of territory in which he had never run.

So, with the Public Works chair within sight and all that new territory to conquer, Mineta in 1992 ran one of his most vigorous campaigns ever — spending more than $1 million in the process. The GOP failed to field a proven candidate, nominating an engineering consultant who spent $63,000 and would capture less than one-third of the vote. But Mineta kept the heat on, determined not be caught napping and apparently resolved to send a message to potential challengers in future election cycles.

Committee

Public Works & Transportation (Chairman)

Elections

1992 General		
Norman Y. Mineta (D)	168,617	(64%)
Robert Wick (R)	82,875	(31%)
Duggan Dieterly (LIBERT)	13,293	(5%)
1990 General		
Norman Y. Mineta (D)	97,286	(58%)
David E. Smith (R)	59,773	(36%)
John H. Webster (LIBERT)	10,587	(6%)

Previous Winning Percentages: **1988** (67%) **1986** (70%) **1984** (65%) **1982** (66%) **1980** (59%) **1978** (57%) **1976** (67%) **1974** (53%)

District Vote for President

1992	
D	127,060 (46%)
R	83,301 (30%)
I	64,192 (23%)

Campaign Finance

	Receipts	Receipts from PACs		Expend-itures
1992				
Mineta (D)	$967,049	$546,295	(56%)	$1,112,414
Wick (R)	$62,391	$3,260	(5%)	$62,961
1990				
Mineta (D)	$666,915	$361,274	(54%)	$644,962
Smith (R)	$670	0		$624

Key Votes

1993	
Require parental notification of minors' abortions	N
Require unpaid family and medical leave	Y
Approve national "motor voter" registration bill	Y
Approve budget increasing taxes and reducing deficit	Y
Approve economic stimulus plan	Y
1992	
Approve balanced-budget constitutional amendment	N
Close down space station program	N
Approve U.S. aid for former Soviet Union	Y
Allow shifting funds from defense to domestic programs	Y
1991	
Extend unemployment benefits using deficit financing	Y
Approve waiting period for handgun purchases	Y
Authorize use of force in Persian Gulf	N

Voting Studies

	Presidential Support		Party Unity		Conservative Coalition	
Year	S	O	S	O	S	O
1992	16	81	93	5	19	81
1991	30	68	92	4	5	92
1990	16	83	92	2	11	89
1989	29	64	93	2	7	93
1988	20	78	92	2	11	89
1987	13 †	83 †	93 †	4 †	12 †	79 †
1986	22	76	95	5	20	80
1985	21	76	95	3	13	85
1984	26	74	97	1	3	97
1983	16	84	95	4	8	88
1982	40	60	91	8	32	67
1981	50	47	84	13	25	71

† Not eligible for all recorded votes.

Interest Group Ratings

Year	ADA	AFL-CIO	CCUS	ACU
1992	100	92	25	0
1991	90	100	20	0
1990	94	92	15	0
1989	95	91	50	11
1988	95	93	31	4
1987	92	100	7	0
1986	95	79	18	5
1985	80	94	18	5
1984	90	100	38	0
1983	95	100	20	0
1982	80	90	23	0
1981	80	93	32	0

16 Don Edwards (D)

Of San Jose — Elected 1962; 16th Term

Born: Jan. 6, 1915, San Jose, Calif.
Education: Stanford U., A.B. 1936, 1936-38.
Military Service: Navy, 1942-45.
Occupation: Title company executive; lawyer; FBI agent.
Family: Wife, Edith Wilkie; five children.
Religion: Unitarian.
Political Career: No previous office.
Capitol Office: 2307 Rayburn Bldg. 20515; 225-3072.

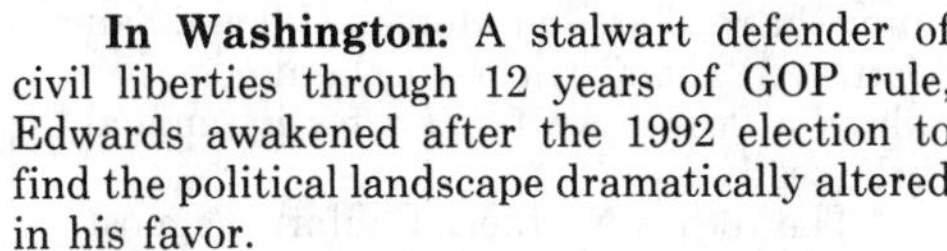

In Washington: A stalwart defender of civil liberties through 12 years of GOP rule, Edwards awakened after the 1992 election to find the political landscape dramatically altered in his favor.

With the simple stroke of a pen, newly elected President Clinton would enact some of the core abortion rights protections Edwards had struggled for years to achieve. And with the Republican veto threat eliminated, there exists even greater potential in the 103rd Congress for Edwards to see more of his liberal agenda come to fruition, particularly in the areas of abortion and the environment.

His evenhanded and personable approach has earned Edwards the respect even of those who split with him ideologically.

Republican Henry J. Hyde of Illinois, a frequent conservative foe, had complimentary words about Edwards after the wars of the Reagan years: "He's a gentleman, he's honorable, he's extremely able.... He's not arrogant or overbearing. He doesn't abuse the power he has."

As dean of the enormous California delegation, Edwards is trying to use some of his personal currency to unify a group historically subdivided by region, race, party, ideology and competing ambitions. At the start of the 102nd, Edwards was instrumental in forming the California Institute, a privately funded think tank dedicated to promoting his home state's interests on the federal level. He and the delegation's Republican dean, Carlos J. Moorhead, initiated bipartisan delegation meetings in the 103rd to focus on common state issues, including military base closures and the social-support costs for illegal immigrants.

Edwards long has been instrumental in securing money for the San Francisco Bay National Wildlife Refuge and is a reliable protector of two major California industries, computers and movies.

But California matters take a back seat to Edwards' first love: social change. Though self-doubt has afflicted other House liberals, Edwards continues to push with the same passion he brought to the House three decades ago. With him, there is no hesitation, no retrenchment. "We're absolutely right, you know," he has said.

For Edwards, liberalism means civil rights and civil liberties for everyone, including blacks, Mexican-Americans, women, children and dissenters of all kinds. He is a liberal first and a Democrat second; he has no qualms about opposing his party's leaders on what he considers a moral issue, be it Vietnam or the death penalty.

Even after his two-year quest for civil rights legislation ended somewhat successfully with a compromise bill, Edwards boycotted the Rose Garden signing ceremony, saying he doubted the Bush administration would abandon its efforts to kill affirmative action.

That signing ceremony would have been a bittersweet tableau for Edwards, the lead House sponsor of the bill reversing Supreme Court decisions that made it more difficult to challenge discrimination in the workplace. To win sufficient support on the Hill, and to prevent a second presidential veto, the bill was watered down significantly. And just hours before President Bush signed the bill into law, a draft memo was released showing that the White House intended to curtail the government's affirmative action programs. Bush cut the language, and Sen. Edward M. Kennedy, D-Mass., appeared at the Rose Garden saying he was willing to give the president the benefit of the doubt; Edwards was not.

The greatest legislative opportunities for Edwards in the 103rd lie in the area of abortion rights. Expecting the Supreme Court to overturn the landmark *Roe v. Wade* decision legalizing abortion, Edwards thought he would have the necessary lightning bolt to ignite support in the 102nd for his Freedom of Choice Act. But the court instead issued a clutch of muddled rulings, and Edwards watched as his party's leaders backed off the controversial election-year issue.

He refiled his bill codifying *Roe* on the first day of the 103rd, and it made its way predictably through House and Senate committees.

California 16

Santa Clara County

Fast-growing Santa Clara County, at the southern end of San Francisco Bay, added another 200,000 residents in the 1980s and now sprawls across four congressional districts. The 16th, however contains about two-thirds of the county's land and more than one-third of its 1.5 million residents. Most of the district consists of most of San Jose, whose 782,000 residents in 1990 ranked it the 11th-largest city in the nation. In California, only Los Angeles and San Diego are larger.

The 16th takes in the heart of San Jose, including the recently renovated downtown civic center and a large urban campus of the California State University that is still known locally as San Jose State.

San Jose dates to 1777, when the Spanish founded it as a way station between the missions of San Francisco and Monterey. It also served briefly as the capital in the early days after California's annexation by the United States. Thereafter, however, it languished in the shadow of San Francisco and Oakland. But the migration of industry southward from Oakland (45 miles to the north) and from the San Francisco peninsula has gradually reoriented San Jose to the north and away from the agricultural valleys to the south, east and west.

Now, even as other parts of the Bay Area have reached a steady state, San Jose has continued to grow, expanding by nearly one-fourth just in the 1980s. Some of the new residents were drawn by jobs in the high-tech sector. Per capita income in the city itself nearly doubled in the 1980s and was about $4,000 higher than the statewide average in 1991.

But with the growth has come strain and some resistance. In 1992, local voters were asked to approve a bond issue for a baseball stadium that was supposed to lure the baseball Giants down from San Francisco. But residents raised questions about how the stadium would affect their everyday lives, and the bond issue failed.

Passing out of the city to the south, Highway 101 winds through the scenic countryside, vineyards and wineries of the Santa Clara Valley — with tasting rooms lining the road around Morgan Hill and San Martin. At the district's southern edge lies Gilroy, a farm town famous for its annual garlic festival.

The 16th is Northern California's most Hispanic district, at 37 percent. Twenty percent of its residents are Asian-Americans. The recent-immigrant presence in the population is reflected in the low number of votes cast relative to the population. Fewer than 165,000 votes were cast for president in the 16th in 1992. This was the lowest number for any House district in Northern California (in the adjacent 10th, more than 300,000 votes were cast for president).

Veteran House member Edwards won his 16th term in 1992 with fewer than 97,000 votes. His opponent had under 50,000. The 16th gave Bill Clinton an absolute majority and held George Bush 2 percentage points below GOP registration for the district.

1990 Population: 571,551. White 315,049 (55%), Black 29,659 (5%), Other 226,843 (40%). Hispanic origin 210,463 (37%). 18 and over 409,054 (72%), 62 and over 49,967 (9%). Median age: 29.

But the bill's fate on the floor is by no means assured, as elements of the Democratic Caucus have made it clear they expect to have a chance to vote on restrictive amendments such as parental notification. Should the legislation be passed, however, Edwards finally has a president in Bill Clinton who has said he will sign it.

Edwards has long been the congressional watchdog of defendants' rights.

When the Judiciary Committee was reorganizing for the 102nd, Edwards had a chance to take the chairmanship of a new subcommittee, but no one was surprised when he stayed on at the helm of the Civil and Constitutional Rights Subcommittee, which perfectly suits his agenda. In the shuffle, however, Edwards picked up jurisdiction over death row inmate appeals.

In the debate on the omnibus crime bill, he worked to add language to further his cause: guaranteeing death row inmates competent legal counsel and restoring the chance to use new court rulings as the basis for appeal. Edwards acknowledged that it was "unique" for the Judiciary Committee to have attached the provisions to an anti-crime bill that included sweeping capital punishment provisions.

The bill never passed, but Edwards has promised to use similar tactics to preserve defendants' right of habeas corpus and their right to appeal if convicted.

Edwards' ardent liberalism can leave him outside the inner circle of House Democrats, a crusader rather than an operator. But he is not uncompromising. In fact, Edwards likes to play the facilitator, as long as he can remain true to his fundamental principles.

In 1988, Edwards shepherded into law two of the most far-reaching civil rights bills since the 1960s, and he was instrumental in defusing the furor over flag desecration.

The flag debate in the 101st saw Edwards at his best. A staunch foe of a constitutional amendment banning desecration, Edwards first worked to develop and enact a limited statute on the subject. Voting for this legislation gave cover to pressured Democrats. Meanwhile, Edwards worked behind the scenes with liberal colleagues to develop a successor strategy in the event the courts struck down the statute.

By the time the Supreme Court declared the statute unconstitutional, the task force had laid down a foundation of skepticism about further action. Political interest in the matter had waned, and the amendment died.

Edwards in the 1980s also showed himself adept at getting around the Reagan administration's opposition to civil rights legislation. In this instance, it was his gift for compromise that carried the day. Congress passed legislation that not only overturned the Supreme Court's 1984 *Grove City* decision limiting the scope of four landmark civil rights laws but actually expanded the original statutes. Reagan vetoed that bill, but Edwards helped put together enough votes to override that veto by persuading civil rights activists to accept a provision in the bill that dealt with abortion. The contested abortion language specified that the law did not require hospitals to perform abortions just because they receive federal funds.

Edwards turned next to an even longer-lived stalemate, a 20-year-old fight to put teeth in the 1968 fair housing law. To appease the housing industry at the time, that law had left federal authorities virtually powerless to be anything more than mediators in discrimination disputes. Edwards wanted new administrative law judges at the Department of Housing and Urban Development, empowered to levy fines and issue injunctions; Realtors and their Republican allies insisted on the option of a full jury trial.

After intense negotiations, a compromise was reached incorporating the housing representatives' demand for a trial option, and the agreement passed both the House and Senate overwhelmingly.

Edwards, however, is not always on the same side as his Democratic colleagues. He split with liberal ally Barney Frank of Massachusetts in the 100th Congress over Frank's ethics bill to limit lobbying by former lawmakers and senior staff. One of the few to oppose its passage, Edwards argued, "Lobbying Congress and the executive branch is an activity protected by the First Amendment. Getting paid for it doesn't make it any less protected."

When other Judiciary Democrats balked at pushing legislation to repeal insurance companies' antitrust exemption, complaining that too little time remained in the 100th Congress, Edwards lectured: "It shows how powerful a monopoly is in this country when it can intimidate Democrats into saying, 'Well, we have to be careful.' We've taken on a Goliath here, and this is what we get paid to do."

In the past, Republicans have cooperated with Edwards to move bills they oppose out of his subcommittee, trusting his word that they will have an opportunity later to kill or amend them.

Edwards' role as the House's self-appointed guardian of constitutional rights overlaps with another — overseer of the FBI, his one-time employer. Infuriated that the FBI's Abscam sting may have amounted to entrapment of seven members of Congress, Edwards chaired a subcommittee investigation of FBI undercover operations. Its 1984 report found "widespread deviation from avowed standards" resulting in "substantial harm to individuals and public institutions," and it recommended advance judicial approval of undercover activities. Later, he used his subcommittee to probe both the FBI's two-year surveillance of citizens' groups opposed to U.S. military aid to Central America and allegations of racism victimizing black and Hispanic agents.

In the ongoing debate over the independent counsel law, which expired in December 1992 and allowed for outside investigators to pursue allegations against high-level administrators, Edwards advocated reauthorization.

At Home: Stories about Edwards inevitably emphasize his FBI background, citing it as rather unusual preparation for a career as a civil libertarian. Actually, Edwards was not only an FBI agent as a young man — he also was a Republican. He did not join the Democratic Party until he was 35 and on his way to a fortune as owner of the Valley Title Insurance Co. in San Jose.

Wealth only seemed to make Edwards more liberal. He said he gave up on Republicans because they did not seem interested in the international agreements needed to preserve peace.

At the time, Edwards was beginning his long journey into activism. He joined the United World Federalists, the National Association for the Advancement of Colored People, the American Civil Liberties Union and the Americans for Democratic Action (ADA). He was national ADA chairman in 1965.

Most people in Edwards' district seem to care little about the causes that have preoccupied him all his life. What matters to them is that he is a friendly, open man whose staff takes care of their problems. With that combination, Edwards has been able to overcome a long string of challengers, candidates who have questioned his patriotism and warned voters he is too liberal for them.

Edwards had never sought office before 1962, devoting most of his time to his business. But when a new district was drawn that year to include part of his home city of San Jose, Edwards decided to run.

His two major opponents for the Democratic nomination both had more political experience but less personal charm. They fought bitterly with each other, and Edwards won the Democratic primary by 726 votes, edging Fremont Mayor John Stevenson. It was an overwhelmingly Democratic district, and Edwards easily won in the fall.

Edwards' outspoken support for Eugene J. McCarthy's presidential campaign and early reports of his possible retirement gave him a difficult time in 1968. He faced two Santa Clara city councilmen, one in the Democratic primary and one in the general election. But Edwards still won both elections comfortably.

He has had no trouble since then. In 1982 and 1984, Republican candidate Bob Herriott, an airline pilot from his party's conservative wing, received a substantial amount of funding from GOP sources but was unable to make a dent in Edwards' standing.

Edwards won his 1986 contest with 71 percent of the vote. In 1988, the GOP did not lift a finger against Edwards; his only opponents were a Hispanic challenger in the primary and a Libertarian in the general election. While his 1990 re-election contest was not quite so effortless, Edwards defeated Republican Mark Patrosso with 63 percent, a figure that was consistent with his totals in the early 1980s.

Redistricting in 1992 gave Edwards a district more than one-third Hispanic, and at some point in the not-too-distant future, Democrats will likely nominate Hispanic candidates in the 16th. But so long as Edwards remains interested, this seat will be his. Democratic registration slipped a few percentage points in 1992, but the incumbent's share of the vote scarcely budged.

Committees

Foreign Affairs (24th of 27 Democrats)
Africa; International Operations

Judiciary (2nd of 21 Democrats)
Civil & Constitutional Rights (chairman); Intellectual Property & Judicial Administration; Crime and Criminal Justice

Veterans' Affairs (2nd of 21 Democrats)

Elections

1992 General		
Don Edwards (D)	96,661	(62%)
Ted Bundesen (R)	49,843	(32%)
Amani S. Kuumba (PFP)	9,370	(6%)
1992 Primary		
Don Edwards (D)	37,833	(71%)
Edward R. Dykes (D)	15,105	(29%)
1990 General		
Don Edwards (D)	81,875	(63%)
Mark Patrosso (R)	48,747	(37%)

Previous Winning Percentages: **1988** (86%) **1986** (71%) **1984** (62%) **1982** (63%) **1980** (62%) **1978** (67%) **1976** (72%) **1974** (77%) **1972** (72%) **1970** (69%) **1968** (57%) **1966** (63%) **1964** (70%) **1962** (66%)

District Vote for President

1992
D 86,418 (52%)
R 44,693 (27%)
I 33,882 (21%)

Campaign Finance

	Receipts	Receipts from PACs	Expend-itures
1992			
Edwards (D)	$249,478	$182,700 (73%)	$291,251
Bundesen (R)	$445	0	$505
1990			
Edwards (D)	$224,999	$171,050 (76%)	$209,243
Patrosso (R)	$2,702	0	$2,581

Key Votes

1993	
Require parental notification of minors' abortions	N
Require unpaid family and medical leave	Y
Approve national "motor voter" registration bill	Y
Approve budget increasing taxes and reducing deficit	Y
Approve economic stimulus plan	Y
1992	
Approve balanced-budget constitutional amendment	N
Close down space station program	N
Approve U.S. aid for former Soviet Union	Y
Allow shifting funds from defense to domestic programs	Y
1991	
Extend unemployment benefits using deficit financing	Y
Approve waiting period for handgun purchases	Y
Authorize use of force in Persian Gulf	N

Voting Studies

	Presidential Support		Party Unity		Conservative Coalition	
Year	**S**	**O**	**S**	**O**	**S**	**O**
1992	12	85	92	3	10	90
1991	26	71	92	6	8	89
1990	17	82	92	3	7	89
1989	27	69	93	1	0	95
1988	18	80	94	3	5	87
1987	11	85	92	2	2	95
1986	16	84	95	3	4†	94†
1985	20	80	97	2	7	93
1984	24	75	94	5	2	98
1983	15	84	94	3	7	89
1982	27	68	93	4	7	93
1981	29	63	88	5	3	95

† Not eligible for all recorded votes.

Interest Group Ratings

Year	ADA	AFL-CIO	CCUS	ACU
1992	100	92	25	0
1991	95	100	10	0
1990	100	100	21	4
1989	100	100	20	0
1988	100	100	23	0
1987	100	100	0	0
1986	100	93	12	0
1985	100	100	18	0
1984	100	85	31	0
1983	100	100	20	0
1982	100	95	9	0
1981	95	93	12	0

17 Sam Farr (D)

Of Carmel — Elected 1993; 1st Term

Born: July 4, 1941, San Francisco, Calif.
Education: Willamette U., B.S. 1963.
Occupation: State legislative aide.
Family: Wife, Shary Baldwin; one child.
Religion: Episcopalian.
Political Career: Monterey County Board of Supervisors, 1975-80; Calif. Assembly, 1981-93.
Capitol Office: 1216 Longworth Bldg. 20515; 225-2861

The Path to Washington: Farr will have some adjusting to do when he encounters the ways of Washington, but his constituents have already drawn him a clear portrait of the kind of congressman they want: It looks just like the man Farr is replacing, former Democratic Rep. Leon E. Panetta.

Just about everyone running in the special election for this seat in the spring of 1993 paid homage to Panetta, the moderate eight-termer who left the House earlier in the year to become director of the Office of Management and Budget.

Once an official in the Nixon administration, Panetta had represented the central coast district since 1977, winning his last seven elections with 70 percent or more of the vote.

But if everyone was reaching for the mantle, Farr wound up wearing it. In the initial round of voting in April, Farr got 26 percent in a field of more than two dozen candidates. In the June runoff, he beat back his Republican opponent — along with three minor-party candidates and two independents — with 52 percent of the vote.

Farr, a 12-year veteran of the California Assembly, left 10 other Democrats behind in the initial balloting by mastering a turnout technique that is increasingly important in California House elections: voting by mail.

Farr actually trailed by about 1,600 votes at the polls on the day of the election, but he pulled well ahead when officials tallied up the 10,600 absentee ballots cast for him.

In the runoff, Farr's Republican opponent was Pebble Beach lawyer Bill McCampbell, who had lost badly to Panetta in 1992. McCampbell had not been the GOP's first choice to contest the vacant seat, but he beat back nine rivals in the initial GOP balloting to win a shot at Farr.

But the nomination did not translate into significant fundraising for McCampbell, whose advertising was limited by lack of money.

Farr was a strong candidate in a district already heavily Democratic. The 17th District is 52 percent Democratic and 31 percent Republican by registration. Moreover, the district that Farr represented in the California Assembly included more than half the territory within Panetta's congressional district.

Before his 1980 election to the Legislature (where his father had also served), Farr was a Monterey County supervisor.

During the campaign, Farr expressed support for the Freedom of Choice Act, gun control and an increased emphasis on women's health issues. He emphasized the need to protect the district's coast and farmers.

He also pledged to work with the Clinton administration to help manage the conversion of the Army's Fort Ord to civilian use after its scheduled closing in 1994.

Farr was highly rated by women's groups during his time in the California Assembly and he won their strong support during the campaign. Farr had been named the first male member of the Sacramento League of Women Voters in the early 1970s for his work in removing gender-specific language from the California state Constitution.

Farr hammered McCampbell for working as a lobbyist for Transkei, a black South African homeland. Farr's campaign literature labeled McCampbell "pro-apartheid." McCampbell responded by slapping Farr with a $10 million defamation and libel suit.

Farr's campaign was aided by a parade of Clinton administration officials who made the trip out to the West Coast to stump for him. Panetta appeared at a campaign event, Housing and Urban Development Secretary Henry G. Cisneros toured, spoke and raised funds with Farr, and Agriculture Secretary Mike Espy darted around the district with Farr at the campaign's conclusion.

California 17

Monterey and San Benito counties

Although it now belongs to Sam Farr, the 17th was for 16 years the political base of Leon E. Panetta, who became director of President Clinton's Office of Management and Budget in 1993. Just before his appointment, Panetta had been re-elected in the redrawn and renumbered district in 1992, running 20 points ahead of Democratic registration.

The district had changed little with the new map, which removed the less-populated half of Santa Cruz County at one end and snipped off the district's old appendix (a coastal section of San Luis Obispo County) at the other. In Santa Cruz County, the 17th keeps all the significant population centers, including the namesake city (population 50,000), the University of California at Santa Cruz and several sizable seaside communities such as Soquel, Aptos and Capitola.

Also intact within the new district are Monterey and San Benito counties. San Benito, with about 37,000 people, is ranching country and swings little weight in district elections. Santa Cruz and Monterey counties had cast about 80 percent of the vote in the old 16th; they cast nearly 95 percent in the 17th in 1992.

The district includes Monterey Peninsula with its fabulous 17-mile drive, legendary golf courses and chic colonies such as Carmel (where Clint Eastwood was mayor for a time). The city of Monterey itself (population 32,000) remains a charming village with a fishing fleet and a small canning industry. Another dominant element on the map is the vast military preserve at Fort Ord, which is slated to close in 1994. Farther down coastal Highway 1 is Big Sur, yet another retreat for artists and the affluent.

Despite these magnets for tourists and retirees, the central enterprise in the 17th remains the agriculture that has sustained the area for centuries. The inland area's capital is Salinas (population 109,000), the county seat of Monterey County and a marketing center for the avocados, artichokes and other trademark truck-farm crops. This is also the focal point for the Hispanics who constitute nearly one-third of the district population. Other farming centers in the district include Watsonville, Hollister and King City.

Panetta had dominated this district, sweeping all the counties in fair political weather and foul. But with Panetta gone, the district was more competitive in the June 1993 special election that chose Farr as his successor. And despite a 52 percent Democratic registration, the district has been a question mark in statewide voting.

In 1992, Democratic Senate nominee Barbara Boxer lost in San Benito County and had only a plurality in Monterey County; but she carried the 17th by piling up a big vote in Santa Cruz County. Clinton managed a majority districtwide, but he too did it by trouncing his GOP opponent in Santa Cruz County (where he won 3-to-1 over George Bush). Clinton managed a plurality in the other two counties.

1990 Population: 570,981. White 396,687 (69%), Black 25,342 (4%), Other 148,952 (26%). Hispanic origin 180,572 (32%). 18 and over 419,952 (74%), 62 and over 71,674 (13%). Median age: 31.

Committees

New member — assignments to be determined

Campaign Finance ‡

	Receipts	Receipts from PACs		Expend-itures
1993				
Farr (D)	$241,921	$126,650	(52%)	$203,366
McCampbell (R)	$21,121	0		$19,309

‡ Figures through May 28, 1993

Elections

1993 Special Runoff *		
Sam Farr (D)	51,764	(52%)
Bill McCampbell (R)	42,841	(43%)
Jerome McCready (AMI)	1,645	(2%)
Kevin Gary Clark (GREEN)	1,179	(1%)
1993 Special		
Sam Farr (D)	23,600	(26%)
Bill McCampbell (R)	10,911	(12%)
Bill Monning (D)	17,050	(19%)
Barbara Shipnuck (D)	12,982	(14%)
Jess Brown (R)	9,360	(10%)
Bob Ernst (R)	5,126	(6%)
Martin Vonnegut (D)	2,985	(3%)
Barbara Honegger (R)	1,855	(2%)
Lancelot C. McClair (D)	1,413	(2%)
John J. Shaw (R)	927	(1%)

** Nearly complete, unofficial returns.*

District Vote for President

	1992	
D	111,937	(53%)
R	57,990	(27%)
I	42,317	(20%)

18 Gary A. Condit (D)

Of Ceres — Elected 1989; 2nd Full Term

Born: April 21, 1948, Salina, Okla.
Education: California State College, Stanislaus, B.A. 1972.
Occupation: Public official.
Family: Wife, Carolyn Berry; two children.
Religion: Baptist.
Political Career: Ceres City Council, 1972-76, mayor, 1974-76; Stanislaus County Board of Supervisors, 1976-82, chairman, 1980; Calif. Assembly, 1983-89.
Capitol Office: 1123 Longworth Bldg. 20515; 225-6131.

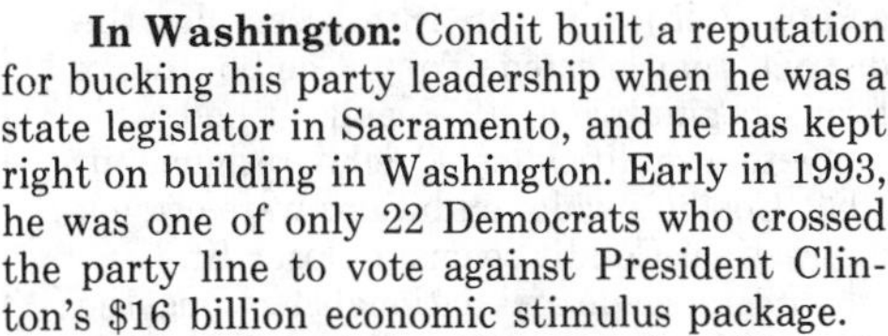

In Washington: Condit built a reputation for bucking his party leadership when he was a state legislator in Sacramento, and he has kept right on building in Washington. Early in 1993, he was one of only 22 Democrats who crossed the party line to vote against President Clinton's $16 billion economic stimulus package.

And although he did vote for Clinton's budget, he did so only after voting for an earlier, Republican plan that would have sought more than $425 billion in deficit reduction through spending cuts. Only three Democrats voted for that plan.

Such votes are hardly surprising, given that Condit voted with the Republicans and against a majority of Democrats on about one-third of 305 party-unity recorded votes in 1992.

But if he is out of step with his party colleagues, he seems to be in synch with his hometown constituents. The Democratic national ticket carried Condit's district in 1992, but it was one of the few Democratic districts in the state where the presidential voting was close. Clinton's 41 percent plurality barely eclipsed George Bush's 37 percent. And independent Ross Perot collected 22 percent.

Condit, meanwhile, was cruising to re-election with 85 percent of the vote (his only challenger was a Libertarian candidate). Dating back to his years in the California state Assembly, when he challenged the power of the Democratic speaker, Condit has found that a weak standing with legislative leaders need not harm his standing with voters.

On Capitol Hill, he has been quietly active in a group led by Minnesota Democrat Timothy J. Penny that offers cost-cutting amendments to the annual appropriations bills. While Condit does not offer the amendments, he does vote for them. In 1992, he was one of only 30 Democrats who voted for an amendment trimming about $58 million in agriculture research projects that critics decried as pork-barrel programs for members' home districts.

But then, voting against agricultural programs of any kind is not an easy choice for a man who represents one of the most productive farm districts in the country. The economy of California's Central Valley is dominated by agriculture, especially by the growing of fruits and vegetables. And Condit surprised no one by heading straight for the Agriculture Committee after winning a special election in 1989.

Condit has yet to play a prominent role on Agriculture, especially in contrast to his predecessor in the district and on the panel, former Rep. Tony Coelho. After just four terms in the House, Coelho had risen to become majority whip, the No. 3 post in the House Democratic hierarchy. And he was always an effective defender of the Central Valley's dairy and water interests both on Agriculture and beyond. But faced with questions about his personal finances, Coelho resigned his seat in 1989.

Condit seems unlikely to ever enjoy Coelho's clout. And the contrast was palpable when the Agriculture Committee considered the 1990 farm bill. Livestock and Dairy Subcommittee leaders availed themselves of their newfound opportunity to skewer California's dairy industry and barred a generous subsidy that had been available only in California. Coelho had repelled similar attacks during the 1985 farm bill, but in 1990, Condit's objections were dismissed.

Condit has registered greater success on other fronts. His proposal to add seven miles of the Merced River to the federal Wild and Scenic River program became law in the 102nd Congress. During consideration of a federal job-training program in 1990, Condit offered an amendment to increase the participation of migrant and seasonal farmworkers in the Job Training Partnership Act. The amendment was adopted by voice vote, but the bill perished in the Senate.

At Home: While Coelho's downfall led to a dramatic change in the House leadership, the succession in the 15th District was almost routine. Condit, a popular state legislator, was a logical choice for district Democrats and an easy winner in the September 1989 special election.

Candidates rarely have the best wishes of

California 18

Central Valley — Modesto; Merced

Conceived in 1870, Modesto took nine decades to reach a population of about 37,000. In the decade that followed, its population nearly doubled. In the 1970s, its population rose by more than one-half to exceed 100,000. By 1990, it had risen by more than one-half again, nearing 165,000 — a total growth of more than 300 percent in 30 years.

Part of this expansion was spurred by businesses fleeing the congestion and land prices of California's coastal cities. Modesto, the Stanislaus County seat, lies near the midpoint of the state on the north bank of the Tuolumne River. Highway 99 passes through, and Interstate 5, the only other major artery through the Central Valley, passes a few miles to the west.

But most of the growth came from growing things — the Valley's phenomenally successful agricultural industry. Modesto bottles, cans, packs and processes the extraordinary variety of fruits, vegetables, grains, fibers and wines produced in the Valley. The Gallo winery here is responsible for about one-third of all the wine bottled in California.

Booming Modesto helped drive the Stanislaus County population from 266,000 to 370,000 in the 1980s, more than the population of better-known counties such as Monterey and Santa Barbara. In essence, the 18th consists of Stanislaus and Merced County, where the city of Merced (56,000) has attracted large numbers of Southeast Asian immigrants and grew by 20,000 in the 1980s. Stanislaus and Merced counties cast 72 percent and 24 percent of the 18th District vote, respectively, in the 1992 House election.

The 18th also takes in the southwest corners of San Joaquin County (the city of Ripon) and Madera County (stopping short of Chowchilla). It also slices off the northeastern tip of Fresno County. But these are sparsely populated areas; all three together cast less than 5 percent of the district vote for president in 1992.

Farmers prosper or fail on the weather, the cost of water and the market price — and government is responsible for two out of three. So farm districts need a member's attention, and this one has been accustomed to getting it from savvy insider Democrats. Politically, the 18th resembles the district that elected Tony Coelho to six terms beginning in 1978 and turned willingly to Condit when Coelho resigned in 1989. Coelho's wider ambitions were often a distraction; Condit seems a closer fit.

In statewide and national elections, the 18th is highly competitive. It voted Republican for president throughout the 1980s. Bill Clinton struggled here, as elsewhere in the Central Valley. Though many Valley residents are Hispanic and growing numbers are Asian (26 and 6 percent, respectively, in the 18th), they have yet to exercise commensurate influence in the voting booths. Clinton's association with environmental activism and other liberal causes kept his vote share far below the Democratic registration in the district (which slipped by 2 percentage points with redistricting, to 53 percent).

1990 Population: 571,393. White 432,658 (76%), Black 16,206 (3%), Other 122,529 (21%). Hispanic origin 148,329 (26%). 18 and over 391,176 (68%), 62 and over 70,670 (12%). Median age: 30.

their political adversaries when they seek higher office. However, Democratic state Assembly Speaker Willie L. Brown Jr. was glad to see Condit go to Washington.

Condit was a member of the "Gang of Five," a group of moderate-to-conservative Assembly Democrats who bridled at the liberal Brown's ironhanded rule. In May 1988, the five launched an effort to remove Brown as Speaker. But the move failed, and the rebels found themselves stripped of leadership positions, choice committee assignments and other perks.

Brown's retaliation appeared to short-circuit Condit's political rise. An Oklahoma native and the son of a Baptist preacher, Condit was first elected to local office in his conservative, farm-oriented home base at age 24, and served six years on the Stanislaus County Board of Supervisors prior to his 1982 election to the Assembly. By the end of his first term, Condit was named assistant Assembly majority leader; two years later, he became chairman of the Government Organization Committee.

The "Gang of Five" debacle cost Condit with the Assembly Democratic Caucus — but not in his conservative, mainly white Central Valley district. Condit ran unopposed for the Assembly in 1988 and was the consensus front-runner when Coelho's House seat opened up the following year.

There were seven other contenders in the open-ballot, all-party special election. But Condit's hold on Democrats was strengthened by support from Coelho, who remained locally popular despite his ethics problems. His main rival was Clare Berryhill, one of three Republicans on the ballot. A district farmer, former state legislator and a one-time director of the state Food and Agriculture Department, Berryhill tried to appeal to the district's farm constituency. But his efforts were blunted by the strength of Condit's personal base: The Democrat defeated Berryhill by 57 percent to 35 percent.

Condit's strong showing deterred Republicans from putting up much of an effort in 1990, and they put up no effort at all in 1992.

The reconfiguration of Condit's district in 1992 may have cost him a few percentage points in terms of Democratic registration. But registered Republicans remain well below 40 percent — and many of them appear to be voting for Condit anyway. This is one of the few districts in California that has both a solid Anglo-majority (about 65 percent) and a Democratic representative who can feel secure in the House for the rest of the decade.

Committees

Agriculture (12th of 28 Democrats)
General Farm Commodities; Livestock; Specialty Crops and Natural Resources

Government Operations (11th of 25 Democrats)
Government Information, Justice, Transportation & Agriculture (chairman)

Elections

1992 General		
Gary A. Condit (D)	139,704	(85%)
Kim R. Almstrom (LIBERT)	25,307	(15%)
1990 General		
Gary A. Condit (D)	97,147	(66%)
Cliff Burris (R)	49,634	(34%)

Previous Winning Percentage: **1989** * (57%)

** Special election.*

District Vote for President

1992	
D	74,357 (41%)
R	67,948 (37%)
I	39,645 (22%)

Campaign Finance

	Receipts	Receipts from PACs		Expend-itures
1992				
Condit (D)	$362,490	$155,645	(43%)	$311,000
1990				
Condit (D)	$234,423	$74,970	(32%)	$212,430
Burris (R)	$31,920	0		$30,963

Key Votes

1993	
Require parental notification of minors' abortions	N
Require unpaid family and medical leave	Y
Approve national "motor voter" registration bill	N
Approve budget increasing taxes and reducing deficit	Y
Approve economic stimulus plan	N
1992	
Approve balanced-budget constitutional amendment	Y
Close down space station program	Y
Approve U.S. aid for former Soviet Union	N
Allow shifting funds from defense to domestic programs	N
1991	
Extend unemployment benefits using deficit financing	Y
Approve waiting period for handgun purchases	N
Authorize use of force in Persian Gulf	Y

Voting Studies

	Presidential Support		Party Unity		Conservative Coalition	
Year	S	O	S	O	S	O
1992	38	62	61	36	58	42
1991	36	61	62	33	73	27
1990	25	70	70	24	54	44
1989	35 †	65 †	83 †	10 †	25 †	75 †

† Not eligible for all recorded votes.

Interest Group Ratings

Year	ADA	AFL-CIO	CCUS	ACU
1992	55	83	75	48
1991	60	92	40	58
1990	56	67	36	29
1989	--	100	50	33

19 Richard H. Lehman (D)

Of North Fork — Elected 1982; 6th Term

Born: July 20, 1948, Sanger, Calif.
Education: Fresno City College, A.A. 1968; California State U., Fresno, 1969; U. of California, Santa Cruz, B.A. 1970.
Military Service: National Guard, 1970-76.
Occupation: Legislative aide.
Family: Divorced.
Religion: Lutheran.
Political Career: Calif. Assembly, 1977-83.
Capitol Office: 1226 Longworth Bldg. 20515; 225-4540.

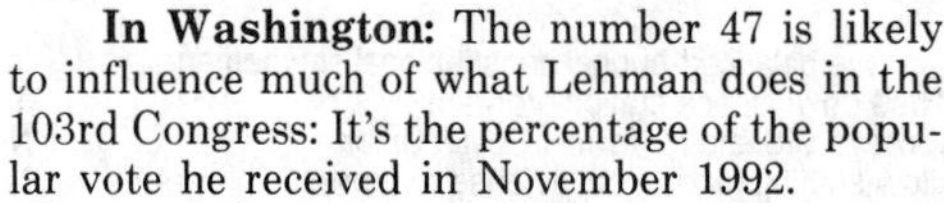

In Washington: The number 47 is likely to influence much of what Lehman does in the 103rd Congress: It's the percentage of the popular vote he received in November 1992.

Lehman's 1,030-vote victory over fresh-faced Republican Tal L. Cloud (and two minor candidates who split about 7 percent of the vote between them) will almost certainly redouble his attention on his district, much of which is new — and Republican — territory.

Lehman has a pretty good track record in this area. He knew his old district from the ground up, and it was apparent in the way he represented it. He came to Washington after six years in the California Assembly, and continued the pursuit of farm and water issues that had marked his career in Sacramento.

Lehman has also worked himself into a good position to look out for his district's interests. In the 102nd Congress, he relinquished a Banking subcommittee chairmanship to take a seat on the powerful Energy and Commerce Committee, specifically on the core Energy and Power Subcommittee. But even more important was his move into a subcommittee chair on the Natural Resources (formerly Interior) Committee.

Lehman had already been using his seat on the Interior Committee to advance legislation protecting his district's huge stretches of farmland and wilderness. He has proved adept at balancing the interests of growers and developers against those of farm workers and environmentalists.

But as the new chairman of the General Oversight and California Desert Lands Subcommittee in the 102nd Congress, he rode herd on a bill that would protect vast swaths of California desert. It passed the House in 1991, but was blocked in the Senate in 1992 by California Republican John Seymour.

With Seymour gone in the 103rd Congress, Lehman is ready to revisit the measure from the vantage point of his revamped Natural Resources subcommittee, now called Energy and Mineral Resources.

Usually an ally of Natural Resources Chairman George Miller, Lehman locked horns several times during the 102nd with his fellow California Democrat. One occasion arose with Lehman's bill to extend drought aid for another year. Miller enraged Lehman by making a last-minute change to the bill — which involved capping new water contracts at three years rather than the traditional 40-year term. Lehman succeeded in stripping it from the final version.

Lehman was also able to throw his weight around on the omnibus Western water bill. Farm operations larger than 960 acres have been barred from receiving federally subsidized irrigation water since 1982. But there has been a loophole used by larger operations that subdivide into tracts of less than 960 acres and thus qualify for the subsidy money.

Miller tried to close that loophole in the Western water bill, but Lehman successfully negotiated a compromise that exempted large farms run by families.

On the Banking Committee, Lehman allied himself with the activist liberal, mid-tier committee Democrats who frequently clashed with Chairman Henry B. Gonzalez of Texas.

When the Financial Institutions Subcommittee considered a bill in 1989 to bail out and restructure the savings and loan industry, Lehman offered an amendment that would have preserved the rights of some 31 S&Ls to convert into banks and switch to the banks' insurance fund. It was rejected, 17-28.

He and Wisconsin Democrat Gerald D. Kleczka introduced a deposit-insurance reform bill that would have limited insurance coverage to 100 percent of the first $50,000 put on deposit by an individual and 90 percent of the next $50,000. They reintroduced their bill in the 102nd Congress.

As chairman of the Consumer Affairs and Coinage Subcommittee in the 101st Congress, he pursued one of his favorite projects: the Truth in Savings Act. The bill, which would set more stringent requirements on financial institutions to disclosure interest rates on savings

California 19

Central Valley — Fresno; Madera

At its core, the 19th resembles the old 18th. They have in common all of Madera County (including the cities of Madera and Chowchilla) and most of the city of Fresno. The 19th also has inherited Rep. Lehman, the old 18th's incumbent. At the same time, the 19th has so many new constituents that it is easy to see why Lehman barely survived his first test on his new turf. After running unopposed in 1990, Lehman got just 47 percent of the vote in his 19th District debut.

Gone are the three high-elevation counties (Calaveras, Tuolumne and Mono) that usually voted Republican. But gone too is that populous portion of Stockton (in San Joaquin County) that helped Lehman win his first five House elections. New in the district are Mariposa County, the eastern half of rural Fresno County and the northern third of Tulare County. Losing Tuolumne County means Lehman no longer represents the wild northern half of Yosemite National Park; but the addition of Mariposa County (population 14,000) gives the new district more of the park's most visited areas.

The old 18th did not occupy much more of Fresno County than the city itself, which forms the knot in what resembles a bow tie. The rest of the county unfurls in either direction, approaching San Benito Mountain on the west and embracing Kings Canyon National Park on the east. In between lie thousands of square miles of San Joaquin Valley desert, crisscrossed by irrigation canals and patterned with farms, groves, vineyards and ranches. Fresno County produces about $2.9 billion in agricultural products a year, more than any other county in the United States.

The 19th enfolds the eastern half of this county. It misses downtown Fresno, but includes all of the city north of Belmont Avenue and all parts east of Chestnut Avenue. It includes the California State University campus and its 20,000 students.

The city is an older agribusiness center, saddled with fearsome summer heat and a workaday image. Despite its civic center, symphony orchestra and 10-block downtown mall, one mid-1980s survey called Fresno the least desirable place to live in America (and a satirical TV miniseries named for the city added insult to injury).

Yet Fresno continues to grow impressively. Its population (354,000) increased by 63 percent in the 1980s. Many of the newest arrivals are Central Americans and Southeast Asians who have enlivened and diversified the culture.

But 1992 redistricting gave the district a more rural tilt and dropped Democratic registration from 59 percent to 47 percent. Lehman would not have survived, except that Fresno County still casts 74 percent of the vote for the House (and most of that came from the city). Lehman had to run far ahead of Bill Clinton to win, as the 19th gave George Bush one of his best showings in the state. Bush carried every county but Mariposa and even enjoyed an outright majority in Tulare.

1990 Population: 573,043. White 421,138 (73%), Black 18,859 (3%), Other 133,046 (23%). Hispanic origin 135,408 (24%). 18 and over 404,642 (71%), 62 and over 77,591 (14%). Median age: 31.

accounts, passed the House in 1990.

Also in the 101st Congress, Lehman opposed a move to redesign the back sides of the nation's coins.

Even after he dropped the coinage subcommittee when he dropped Banking, Lehman wielded some influence on the issue and blocked similar coin redesign attempts in the 102nd Congress.

At Home: Lehman's political rise was propelled by shrewd instincts worthy of a politician with twice his experience. During his years in the California Assembly, he showed the same ability to maneuver among competing interests that he has demonstrated in the House.

Lehman's style drew criticism: The California Journal once commented that he had "learned well the fine points of political one-upmanship, and thrives on its practice."

But his political agility also earned him the respect of his Democratic colleagues.

Lehman had been working for a Fresno-area state senator in 1975 when he joined with a small group of young political activists to run the successful Fresno City Council campaign of Dan Whitehurst. The following year, Lehman won his first of three state Assembly terms. He soon was marked as a comer for Congress.

The late Democratic Rep. Phillip Burton, who recast California's congressional map in 1981, drew one district with Lehman in mind — not so much because Lehman was a pal or a sure ally, but because he would have been hard to stop.

Fueled by funding from local agribusiness, labor and education interests, and boasting an

80 percent approval rating from the California Farm Bureau, Lehman escaped even minor competition in the 1982 Democratic primary. He won easily that fall and for years thereafter. While other California House members worried about an "anti-incumbent" mood in 1990, Lehman was unopposed for re-election.

But in 1992, the redrawn California map had big surprises in store for Lehman. No longer drawn to reach out to Democrats from far-flung towns on the San Joaquin Valley floor, Lehman's new base (renumbered from 18 to 19) had less of Fresno and lots more of the small towns and farms and highlands to the north and east. The Democratic registration dropped more than 10 points, no longer constituting a majority.

Lehman spent more than $900,000 to overcome redistricting and blunt the outsider appeal of the youthful Cloud. In the end, he was helped by the Democratic tide of 1992, as well as by a business error that left payroll taxes unpaid at Cloud's paper company and cost Cloud some of his momentum.

Lehman was able to go to the bank of good will he had built up with the agribusiness community, both for funding and for political support. But while these assets should continue to assist him in holding the district, Lehman will be on the GOP target list for at least several cycles to come — and he may not be able to withstand a substantial shift in voter sentiment against his party.

Committees

Energy & Commerce (20th of 27 Democrats)
Commerce, Consumer Protection & Competitiveness; Energy & Power; Telecommunications & Finance

Natural Resources (10th of 28 Democrats)
Energy & Mineral Resources (chairman); Oversight & Investigations

Elections

1992 General		
Richard H. Lehman (D)	101,620	(47%)
Tal L. Cloud (R)	100,590	(46%)
Dorothy L. Wells (PFP)	13,334	(6%)
1992 Primary		
Richard H. Lehman (D)	39,846	(76%)
Curtis Youngs (D)	12,728	(24%)
1990 General		
Richard H. Lehman (D)	98,804	(100%)

Previous Winning Percentages: **1988** (70%) **1986** (71%) **1984** (67%) **1982** (59%)

District Vote for President

1992
D 85,049 (38%)
R 97,124 (44%)
I 41,052 (18%)

Campaign Finance

	Receipts	Receipts from PACs		Expend-itures
1992				
Lehman (D)	$832,532	$526,845	(63%)	$915,504
Cloud (R)	$157,053	$32,975	(21%)	$153,784
1990				
Lehman (D)	$302,473	$201,780	(67%)	$299,728

Key Votes

1993	
Require parental notification of minors' abortions	N
Require unpaid family and medical leave	Y
Approve national "motor voter" registration bill	Y
Approve budget increasing taxes and reducing deficit	Y
Approve economic stimulus plan	Y
1992	
Approve balanced-budget constitutional amendment	N
Close down space station program	Y
Approve U.S. aid for former Soviet Union	N
Allow shifting funds from defense to domestic programs	Y
1991	
Extend unemployment benefits using deficit financing	Y
Approve waiting period for handgun purchases	Y
Authorize use of force in Persian Gulf	Y

Voting Studies

	Presidential Support		Party Unity		Conservative Coalition	
Year	**S**	**O**	**S**	**O**	**S**	**O**
1992	26	58	72	17	58	25
1991	38	59	84	11	46	51
1990	19	81	89	6	31	65
1989	29	63	92	3	12	83
1988	20	73	89	3	26	63
1987	16	83	91	3	19	79
1986	20	76	87	4	26	68
1985	16	74	83	3	20	71
1984	23	64	81	7	20	71
1983	22	76	91	4	15	79

Interest Group Ratings

Year	ADA	AFL-CIO	CCUS	ACU
1992	60	83	50	19
1991	60	100	30	25
1990	94	83	15	4
1989	90	100	40	0
1988	85	100	25	9
1987	92	94	7	0
1986	75	100	25	10
1985	80	88	15	0
1984	85	77	50	0
1983	80	100	30	0

20 Cal Dooley (D)

Of Visalia — Elected 1990; 2nd Term

Born: Jan. 11, 1954, Visalia, Calif.
Education: U. of California, Davis, B.S. 1977; Stanford U., M.A. 1987.
Occupation: Farmer.
Family: Wife, Linda Phillips; two children.
Religion: Protestant.
Political Career: No previous office.
Capitol Office: 1227 Longworth Bldg. 20515; 225-3341.

In Washington: Dooley's family has been farming in California's Central Valley for four generations, growing everything from alfalfa to cotton to walnuts. And though he has moved all the way to Washington, Dooley's eyes remain fixed on his ancestral land. From his perches on the Agriculture and Natural Resources committees, Dooley has oversight over almost all things of interest to the valley's farmers.

In 1990, well before committee assignments were made — before the elections, even — the moderate Californian knew his assignments would include Agriculture. Dooley got that assurance from no less a source than Speaker Thomas S. Foley, a man who knows firsthand how such a seat can help a Democrat hold a rural, Republican district. Dooley made considerable use of that promise in his first campaign, and he has since done the same with the seat.

Within the California delegation, Dooley is seen as a middle-of-the-road Democrat who is not expected to take a leadership role within the delegation. He is the only Californian to belong to the Conservative Democratic Forum, a body of primarily Southern members.

But his Agriculture colleagues praise his knowledge of the committee's issues, and they view him as an up-and-comer. He declined to take a high profile on the committee in his first Congress, but his colleagues know he had no legislative experience before coming to Congress and they feel he has time to develop his own lawmaking style.

During the 102nd Congress, Dooley added more muscle to his district-serving capability by taking a seat on Natural Resources (formerly Interior), the panel with jurisdiction over life-and-death water issues in the Central Valley. He is one of four Californians among the 28 Democrats on the committee; Dooley and Rep. Richard H. Lehman, who represents the adjoining 19th District, have already butted heads with chairman George Miller (whose Bay area constituents do not share the valley's passion for spreading millions of acre-feet of water over farmland). They clashed over the 1992 omnibus water bill, and they will likely do so again in the 103rd Congress.

At Home: The 1992 redistricting map in California was seen as unfavorable to Democrats generally, but not to Dooley. By consolidating his renumbered district around southern Fresno County and sliding in more of Dooley's own Tulare County (and a leg of Kern County as well), the state Supreme Court may have guaranteed Dooley at least a decade in the House.

Trying out his new lines for the first time in 1992, Dooley was characteristically cautious. He raised and spent more than $450,000 despite the absence of a first-tier challenger. Sure enough, he pushed his 1990 winning percentage of 55 percent up by about 10 percentage points.

Although he sometimes suggests a flatland version of the cinematic Mr. Smith, Dooley is far from a rube. Well before he decided on 1990 as his year to seek elective office, his brother and sister-in-law had become senior aides to former Gov. Edmund G. "Jerry" Brown Jr. The family name has become familiar, as Dooley's brother and parents have served on public boards and party committees.

Dooley had another important connection in politics as a former aide to state Sen. Rose Ann Vuich, a Fresno Democrat legendary for her constituent service. The Vuich persona helped Dooley overcome the more liberal flavor of his relatives' politics, particularly their ties to Brown and Rose Bird, the former chief justice of the California Supreme Court whom voters ousted in 1986.

In 1990, Dooley sidestepped not only his personal associations with party liberals but also the issue at the heart of the coastal liberals' agenda: the "Big Green" environmental initiative. Dooley opposed the sweeping conservation measure, preferring the farmers' alternative that permitted wider use of pesticides.

Still, no one would have confused Dooley's campaign with that of a Republican. He regularly put forward the sociological sorrows of rural Tulare and Fresno counties, where even in good times the rates of unemployment, crime, pregnancy and disease run far ahead of state-

California 20

Parts of Kern, Kings and Fresno counties

Many Democrats were complaining after the California Supreme Court handed down the 1992 congressional district map, but not Rep. Dooley, who got a good deal in the redraw. This district is descended from the old 17th, which Dooley seized from a troubled Republican incumbent in 1990. But while that district was, for all practical purposes, a Republican one, the 1992 map trimmed away much of the GOP vote.

The 20th reaches from Fresno to Bakersfield (in Kern County). But it has far less of the latter than the old 17th had; moreover, its share of Fresno comes from that city's southeastern neighborhoods, which are home to many blacks and Hispanics who reliably support Democratic candidates.

More generally, the new district represents a dramatic shift to the west, away from the upland portions of Fresno and Tulare counties and toward the the portions of Fresno, Kings and Kern counties known as the Westlands. Here, federal water projects have spawned vast farms with battalions of workers. Motorists on Interstate 5 see nary a town while they pass fields filled with virtually every fruit, nut, vegetable, fiber and livestock animal known in the Temperate Zone. Fresno County's annual $2.9 billion agricultural output ranks No. 1 in the nation.

Democratic registration in the old 17th had been an iffy 48 percent (with the GOP at 43 percent). But in the 20th, Democratic registration stands at 61 percent, more than twice the GOP's 29 percent. The district also bears much of the burden of the Valley's urban and rural poor. The rates of unemployment, crime, teen pregnancy and disease far outstrip statewide averages.

East of the city of Fresno, the 20th takes in the towns of Sanger, Reedley, Parlier, Dinuba, Orange Cove and Kingsburg — each with its own ethnic flavor and history.

Kingsburg, where Sun Maid raisins and Del Monte peaches are processed, still adorns its main street with Swedish Dala horses. The Scandinavians who came here a century ago have largely turned Republican, as have waves of Armenians, Japanese and migrants from the Dust Bowl, who first were farmworkers.

But where crops must be picked by hand, there will always be new immigrants. In recent generations, the new arrivals have been from Mexico and Central America. Delano, site of the famous farmworkers strike in the 1960s, is in the Kern County portion of the 20th.

Hispanics constitute a 55 percent majority in the 20th; blacks and Asians together are 11 percent. But these groups, restrained by low rates of voter registration and turnout, have yet to play a significant role in primaries or general elections.

Dooley, a relatively conservative, farm-oriented Democrat, got huge margins in all four counties of the 20th in 1992. But "national Democrats" are viewed with suspicion. Bill Clinton managed to carry the district despite winning only its Fresno portion.

1990 Population: 573,282. White 279,140 (49%), Black 36,933 (6%), Other 257,209 (45%). Hispanic origin 317,372 (55%). 18 and over 373,560 (65%), 62 and over 61,308 (11%). Median age: 27.

wide averages.

With all due respect to his family, Vuich and Foley, the man who helped Dooley most in 1990 was the incumbent he defeated, Charles "Chip" Pashayan Jr. The six-termer from Fresno committed two classic errors, and Dooley showed strong instincts in exploiting his openings on both.

Pashayan's first misstep followed his 71 percent victory in 1988. At last confident that he would not face major opposition for reelection, Pashayan left the Interior Committee, where he had been a mainstay of the subcommittee in charge of water projects critical to farming in the Central Valley.

Second, and far worse, Pashayan responded in low-key, "let it blow over" fashion to the festering savings and loan scandal in 1989. Instead of blowing over, the scandal blew up, and Pashayan's own limited involvement was made to look deep and damning.

Dooley made an issue of Pashayan's $26,000 in contributions from S&L kingpin Charles H. Keating Jr. and his family and associates. He made an issue of Pashayan's efforts to loosen regulations affecting a Keating institution. But the clinching factor may have been Pashayan's own less-than-complete explanations of his connections to Keating and efforts in his behalf.

Even with the overarching significance of the Keating matter, Dooley's victory owed much to basic campaigning. He concentrated on rural Tulare and Fresno counties, stressing his roots in the soil and his agribusiness degree. But he also presented himself well as a sophisticated alternative to Pashayan among the upwardly mobile swing voters of Fresno's more affluent neighborhoods, stressing his study at the Stanford Graduate School of Business.

Committees

Agriculture (14th of 28 Democrats)
Department Operations; General Farm Commodities; Livestock

Banking, Finance & Urban Affairs (28th of 30 Democrats)
Economic Growth

Natural Resources (17th of 28 Democrats)
Oversight & Investigations

Elections

1992 General		
Cal Dooley (D)	72,679	(65%)
Ed Hunt (R)	39,388	(35%)
1990 General		
Cal Dooley (D)	82,611	(55%)
Charles "Chip" Pashayan Jr. (R)	68,848	(45%)

District Vote for President

	1992
D	55,942 (47%)
R	44,624 (37%)
I	18,568 (16%)

Campaign Finance

	Receipts	Receipts from PACs	Expend-itures
1992			
Dooley (D)	$496,485	$242,583 (49%)	$504,352
Hunt (R)	$176,878	$40,597 (23%)	$173,744
1990			
Dooley (D)	$547,763	$171,185 (31%)	$538,354
Pashayan (R)	$557,949	$283,684 (51%)	$622,184

Key Votes

1993	
Require parental notification of minors' abortions	N
Require unpaid family and medical leave	Y
Approve national "motor voter" registration bill	Y
Approve budget increasing taxes and reducing deficit	Y
Approve economic stimulus plan	Y
1992	
Approve balanced-budget constitutional amendment	Y
Close down space station program	Y
Approve U.S. aid for former Soviet Union	N
Allow shifting funds from defense to domestic programs	N
1991	
Extend unemployment benefits using deficit financing	Y
Approve waiting period for handgun purchases	Y
Authorize use of force in Persian Gulf	N

Voting Studies

	Presidential Support		Party Unity		Conservative Coalition	
Year	S	O	S	O	S	O
1992	30	65	77	18	56	42
1991	38	62	84	16	62	38

Interest Group Ratings

Year	ADA	AFL-CIO	CCUS	ACU
1992	75	75	50	20
1991	60	75	50	10

21 Bill Thomas (R)

Of Bakersfield — Elected 1978; 8th Term

Born: Dec. 6, 1941, Wallace, Idaho.
Education: San Francisco State U., B.A. 1963, M.A. 1965.
Occupation: Professor.
Family: Wife, Sharon Lynn Hamilton; two children.
Religion: Baptist.
Political Career: Calif. Assembly, 1975-79.
Capitol Office: 2209 Rayburn Bldg. 20515; 225-2915.

In Washington: Through seven terms, Thomas was a virtuoso in the House Republican's ensemble. But as he began his 15th year in Congress, he found himself hard-pressed to convince the new wave of junior GOP conservatives that he could sing their tune.

Thomas relishes the role of partisan strategist: He is one of the best in the House at watching a floor debate or a committee meeting and taking in all the political implications. He has long employed his combative style to advantage, not just on the floor but also in the Ways and Means Committee — where other Republicans have preferred to avoid public confrontations.

Thomas' style does not suit all tastes. He can be snide to slower-witted colleagues of either party and quick to anger when he does not get his way. Those traits, combined with the feeling that Thomas had been too accommodating as ranking Republican on the House Administration Committee, led to an effort to strip him of that post.

The attempted coup took place in December 1992, when conservative members of the House Republican Conference tried to install Paul E. Gillmor of Ohio as the committee's ranking Republican. They fell 12 votes shy, and Thomas was reinstated. Nonetheless, this intraparty scrape may mean Thomas will be using his sharp tongue more exclusively on the Democrats.

An irony to this targeting of Thomas was that it appeared to pit him against Newt Gingrich of Georgia, the GOP whip, who helped spur the insurgence. Thomas had supported Gingrich for whip in 1989. Roommates when they arrived in Washington a decade earlier, they are among the several former college professors who have risen in Congress as acerbic conservatives.

Thomas has also served as his party's point man on highly political issues. He led the GOP effort on campaign finance reform in 1990, 1991 and 1992, stressing a $1,000 limit on donations from political action committees (PACs) and a requirement that more than half of any member's funding come from his own constituents.

In 1992, assisted by a federal appeals court, he had a hand in getting House Democratic leaders to bar members from sending franked mass mailings to potential constituents whose votes they might need after redistricting.

The watershed experience on House Administration that helped shape Thomas' attitude came early in the 99th Congress. Thomas was the lone GOP member of a task force that seated Democrat Frank McCloskey, declaring him the winner by four votes in the 8th District of Indiana. Thomas furiously opposed the task force report, calling it a "rape" and "an arrogant use of raw power."

Nonetheless, Thomas has also shown his more pragmatic side on House Administration. He worked with Washington Democrat Al Swift on a bill to prevent the TV networks from using election returns from Eastern states to forecast presidential winners before polls closed in the West. Their uniform poll-closing time for presidential elections passed the House twice but died in the Senate.

In 1990 Thomas worked with Swift on a "motor voter" bill allowing voters to register to vote as they applied for a driver's license, a hunting permit or even a welfare check. Most Republicans opposed the idea, and in 1992 the bill was changed in ways that Thomas said would favor Democrats and could lead to fraud. He opposed the new bill then and in early 1993, when it was enacted.

From the 100th to 102nd Congresses, he served on Budget. He is now the third-ranking Republican on Ways and Means, where he is ranking Republican on the Health Subcommittee.

On legislation, Thomas' partisan style can help rally the troops, but it sometimes hampers his influence. Even though the massive tax-revision bill of the Reagan years was the Republican president's initiative, Thomas seemed to regard it largely as an example of misbehavior on the part of the House majority. Despite Thomas' clear mastery of the subject, his emotional speeches against the bill restricted his chance to alter it.

As a member of Ways and Means' Subcommittee on Trade, he often tilts with its free-

California 21

Kern and Tulare counties — Bakersfield

One aim of the court-ordered California redistricting of 1992 was to create more districts in which both parties could be competitive. But where that goal conflicted with other priorities, such as compactness and community of interest, it was shelved.

A case in point is the 21st, which is a model of compactness and community of interest, especially alongside the old, Bakersfield-based 20th District (also represented by Thomas), which shared a border with Nevada and still offered beachfront on the Pacific. Beginning high in the Sierras, it took in all of Inyo County, most of Kern County, a swath of Los Angeles County and most of San Luis Obispo County on the coast.

By comparison, the 21st looks sensible enough to be an Iowa district. About three-fourths of its vote is in Kern County (overall population 543,000). The rest comes from new territory pulled in from Tulare County to the north (overall population 312,000).

Tulare County brings into the district the magnificence of the Sequoia National Forest and the western slope of Mount Whitney, which at 14,495 feet is the tallest peak in the United States outside of Alaska. It also brings a flock of small towns. The county seat is Visalia, a farming city of 76,000 on Highway 99, straddling the line with the 20th. Running south through Tulare County just east of Highway 99, the district's lines are drawn to include the towns of Tulare, Farmersville, Porterville and Lindsay. This was one of the fastest-growing metropolitan areas in the 1980s; population expanded 27 percent.

South of Shafter, the southern appendage of the 20th District cuts into the Bakersfield metro area along Interstate 5. Farther west, the 21st resumes and picks up the towns of Maricopa and Taft.

But the district's heart beats in Bakersfield, a city the size of Little Rock, Ark., (about 175,000). Bakersfield was brought to life by a gold rush in 1885 and again by an oil strike in 1899. Farmers from the Southwest came in force during the 1930s Dust Bowl years, and the city boomed yet again in the 1980s — when its growth rate of nearly 66 percent ranked ninth among U.S. cities.

The predominance of cotton, other crops and oil hereabouts can still make a Texan feel at home, even if the Texan came to work in the defense-related industries tied to nearby China Lake Naval Air Weapons Station or Edwards Air Force Base (in Kern's southeast corner). Edwards is a frequent landing site for space shuttles because of its seven-mile landing strip in Rogers Dry Lake.

The 21st is actually slightly less white and less Republican than the old 20th (GOP registration is down 3 percentage points to 46 percent). But the Democratic registration has not risen commensurately, and when Republicans have a registration plurality they almost always win big at the polls. George Bush carried both the Tulare and Kern sections of the 21st in 1992.

1990 Population: 571,300. White 443,958 (78%), Black 23,106 (4%), Other 104,236 (18%). Hispanic origin 115,954 (20%). 18 and over 398,248 (70%), 62 and over 74,387 (13%). Median age: 31.

trade bloc, working to protect California vintners and his district's pistachio growers from imports. When talk intensified of a free trade agreement linking Mexico and Canada with the United States, Thomas wanted to know how it would affect California farmers. He endorsed the pact when President Bush unveiled it in September 1992, saying that many of his state's agricultural interests were generally satisfied.

At Home: Thomas has often described himself as a pragmatic conservative, a formula that has worked for him at the polls. Recently, some Republican hard-liners have come to view Thomas as more committed to pragmatism than conservatism. He faced a 1990 primary challenge from the right. Thomas won easily, but it was noted that he gave up 27 percent to swimming-pool repairman Rod Gregory. In the 1990 general election, Thomas' 60 percent was his lowest since his first House election in 1978.

In 1992, Thomas again faced an opponent in the primary: Financial consultant Carlos Murillo got more than one-third of the Republican vote. Once nominated, however, Thomas was more secure than ever in his newly drawn district and won with 71 percent.

Thomas had begun his career in 1974, leaving academia to run for the state Assembly as a staunch conservative (support for the death penalty was his central issue). But in 1978, when GOP Rep. William Ketchum died after the June primary and left the nomination open, Thomas positioned himself as the moderate Republican candidate. He was the ranking GOP legislator in the area, but it took him seven ballots at a party nominating convention to defeat two more conservative opponents.

Thomas and Ketchum had had some differences (Thomas backed Gerald R. Ford in the California primary in 1976 and Ketchum supported Ronald Reagan), but Thomas got a general-election endorsement from Ketchum's widow and easily defeated Democrat Bob Sogge, a former state Senate aide.

Established on this turf, Thomas spent much of his political energy in the 1980s trying to overturn the congressional redistricting maps drawn by state Democrats after the 1980 census. These artful plans helped increase Democratic strength in Sacramento and Washington, and Thomas attacked them with state ballot initiatives and lawsuits. But the last appeal was turned down by the U.S. Supreme Court in 1989, and a version of the gerrymander endured throughout the decade.

When the new cycle of redistricting began in 1991, Thomas once again pressed for more districts in which both parties could be competitive. He was opposed by some Republicans who preferred that their districts be made highly secure. In the end, GOP Gov. Pete Wilson sided with Thomas and vetoed maps drawn by the state Legislature that packed Republican votes into relatively few districts.

That threw the issue to the California Supreme Court, which produced a map emphasizing community of interest within districts and generally disregarding partisan voting patterns. It made some incumbents more secure, some less. Although it did not deliver a GOP majority in 1992, it is expected to help the party claim more seats as the 1990s continue.

Committees

House Administration (Ranking)
Administrative Oversight (ranking); Contested Elections

Ways & Means (3rd of 14 Republicans)
Health (ranking); Trade

Elections

1992 General		
Bill Thomas (R)	127,758	(65%)
Deborah A. Vollmer (D)	68,058	(35%)
1992 Primary		
Bill Thomas (R)	37,657	(66%)
Carlos Murillo (R)	19,684	(34%)
1990 General		
Bill Thomas (R)	112,962	(60%)
Michael A. Thomas (D)	65,101	(34%)
William H. Dilbeck (LIBERT)	10,555	(6%)

Previous Winning Percentages: **1988** (71%) **1986** (73%) **1984** (71%) **1982** (68%) **1980** (71%) **1978** (59%)

District Vote for President

1992
D 66,284 (32%)
R 94,727 (46%)
I 43,016 (21%)

Campaign Finance

	Receipts	Receipts from PACs		Expend-itures
1992				
Thomas (R)	$598,669	$277,436	(46%)	$615,587
Vollmer (D)	$28,803	$2,150	(7%)	$28,487
1990				
Thomas (R)	$430,525	$235,447	(55%)	$496,845
Thomas (D)	$696	0		$690

Key Votes

1993	
Require parental notification of minors' abortions	N
Require unpaid family and medical leave	N
Approve national "motor voter" registration bill	N
Approve budget increasing taxes and reducing deficit	N
Approve economic stimulus plan	N
1992	
Approve balanced-budget constitutional amendment	Y
Close down space station program	N
Approve U.S. aid for former Soviet Union	Y
Allow shifting funds from defense to domestic programs	N
1991	
Extend unemployment benefits using deficit financing	X
Approve waiting period for handgun purchases	Y
Authorize use of force in Persian Gulf	Y

Voting Studies

	Presidential Support		Party Unity		Conservative Coalition	
Year	**S**	**O**	**S**	**O**	**S**	**O**
1992	66	17	77	8	79	8
1991	72	22	80	12	95	3
1990	54	35	74	11	83	7
1989	72	28	81	15	90	7
1988	60	36	81	15	87	8
1987	64	25	81	8	88	9
1986	76	19	82	10	84	12
1985	61	33	79	15	84	11
1984	64	28	71	17	78	12
1983	74	21	81 †	10 †	84	10
1982	79	10	71	8	84	7
1981	76	14	69	11	75	11

† Not eligible for all recorded votes.

Interest Group Ratings

Year	**ADA**	**AFL-CIO**	**CCUS**	**ACU**
1992	15	10	88	90
1991	10	18	100	79
1990	17	9	91	74
1989	15	8	90	78
1988	25	43	100	78
1987	4	13	92	70
1986	10	21	93	85
1985	10	13	95	86
1984	15	9	82	64
1983	15	12	89	62
1982	5	0	85	86
1981	5	8	100	83

22 Michael Huffington (R)

Of Santa Barbara — Elected 1992; 1st Term

Born: Sept. 3, 1947, Dallas, Texas.
Education: Stanford U., A.B., B.S. 1970; Harvard U., M.B.A. 1972.
Occupation: Film production executive.
Family: Wife, Arianna; two children.
Religion: Episcopalian.
Political Career: No previous office.
Capitol Office: 113 Cannon Bldg. 20515; 225-3601.

The Path to Washington: Some people come to Washington to change the world. Huffington, who spent more than $5.4 million, mostly of his own money, to win this seat, comes with a much more modest agenda. He merely wants to turn Congress on its head.

It is not quite accurate to describe the independent-minded Huffington as Ross Perot without the big ears and flip charts. But that picture is not far from wrong, either.

He is wealthy (he will not disclose how wealthy); he thinks the system is broken; and he thinks he is just the person who can fix it.

Upsetting 18-year incumbent Robert J. Lagomarsino in the GOP primary, Huffington was one of only three GOP freshmen to oust incumbents in primaries. He then outspent and easily outpolled Democrat Gloria Ochoa and Green Party candidate Mindy Lorenz in November. He won 53 percent, despite a bare GOP plurality among registered voters in the 22nd District.

He calls himself a conservative who believes strongly in Republican values. Ronald Reagan has been his hero since 1968. He interned in George Bush's congressional office in 1968. But he is, he insists, his own man. As if to prove it, he voted with only 39 other Republicans for mandatory family leave legislation in 1993.

Huffington is hardly a mainstream Republican — except on money issues. He opposed the war in Vietnam while a student at Stanford University (though he did not publicly profess his views). He supports abortion rights, a position that he used to good effect in defeating the vigorously anti-abortion Lagomarsino. He voted for the measure to lift the so-called gag rule that prohibited staff at federally funded family planning clinics from discussing abortions.

He also opposes oil and gas drilling off the California coast (though his family's money came from overseas oil and gas exploration). He supports gay rights, and attacked the tobacco lobby during his House campaign. He accepted no PAC funds in the 1992 election cycle.

As a Republican, Huffington subscribes to a non-specific call for shrinking government, cutting taxes and spending. His real agenda involves wholesale reform of Congress.

He wants to end the accumulated power of entrenched politicians. He would like to eliminate seniority as a factor in deciding committee rankings. He favors cutting the number of committees and reducing congressional staff.

He supports 12-year limits for both House members and senators, and promises to serve no more than eight years in the House. Now in his 40s, Huffington will not rule out a Senate run after that, however.

Huffington is a relative newcomer to Santa Barbara; he bought a house there in 1988. He decided to enter the GOP primary for the 22nd when it appeared that redistricting would carve up Lagomarsino's old territory in a way that would leave the seat open. Instead, Lagomarsino had to choose between a challenge from Huffington or a head-to-head meeting with Rep. Elton Gallegly, another GOP incumbent who was running in the new 23rd.

Lagomarsino decided on the 22nd, and the GOP hierarchy tried to talk Huffington out of the race. George Bush and Dan Quayle endorsed Lagomarsino. Huffington refused to back out and launched a vigorous TV campaign both to make himself visible and to tarnish Lagomarsino.

Abortion was a key factor, as many Republican women flocked to Huffington, promising that an abortion rights candidate would win — either Huffington or Ochoa, the Democrat.

Huffington attacked Lagomarsino for accepting political action committee contributions, for having claimed no involvement in the House bank scandal — he had three bad checks — and for supporting a Santa Barbara company's efforts to sell surveillance cameras to the Chinese government after the June 1989 Tiananmen Square massacre.

Lagomarsino countered that Huffington was either a carpetbagger or had avoided paying California income taxes for the years 1988-90 by maintaining a home in Texas. But Huffington said that until 1990 he was still managing the family oil business. He added that his wife had paid income taxes in California since 1989 and that their children were born in Santa Barbara.

California 22

Santa Barbara; Santa Maria; San Luis Obispo

Santa Barbara County, with about 370,000 residents, was the mainstay of the old 19th District. It was connected to the Los Angeles area to the south by Ventura County, which had most of its land (though not most of its people) in the 19th. The two neighboring counties shared the calm waters of the Santa Barbara Channel and the rugged grandeur of Los Padres National Forest, a 1.7-million acre preserve spread over several small mountain ranges running parallel to the coast.

The 1992 redistricting separated these two counties, combining Santa Barbara with San Luis Obispo, its coastline neighbor to the north. The two counties are topographically similar, separated only by the Cuyama River that runs down from the Sierra Madre Mountains to the Pacific.

The 22nd takes in all of both counties, except for the coastal town of Carpinteria just south of Santa Barbara and adjacent acreage on the Ventura County line. Thrown in for good measure are four islands offshore in the Santa Barbara Channel: San Miguel, Santa Rosa, Santa Cruz and Santa Barbara (but not Anacapa Islands).

San Luis Obispo includes its namesake city (home to the California Polytechnic State University and about one-fifth of the county's 217,000 residents) and the northern end of the Los Padres forest. North of the city, Highway 101 angles inland to Atascadero, Paso Robles and San Miguel. Alternatively, the tourist can take the breathtaking Highway 1, which continues to hug the coast on its way to memorable Morro Bay and then to San Simeon — the fabled mansion of media magnate William Randolph Hearst.

About 60 percent of the district's vote is still cast in Santa Barbara County, the population centers of which include Vandenberg Air Force Base and the small cities of Lompoc and Santa Maria. The city of Santa Barbara was founded 200 years ago by the Spanish on a natural harbor discovered 250 years before that by the Portuguese.

More than most of contemporary California, Santa Barbara has striven to maintain some of its Iberian charm — in part with a measured pace of life. A major campus (19,000 students) of the University of California is just outside of town. Many of the city's nearly 86,000 residents are retirees; others have settled here less to make money than to make the most of the money they had.

The old 19th had a slight Democratic tilt in registration (45 percent to the GOP's 41 percent) but it generally voted Republican. In the 22nd the two parties are about even in registration, yet GOP candidates other than Huffington had to scramble here in 1992. Both counties preferred Democrats Bill Clinton for president and Dianne Feinstein for the Senate. The contest for the other Senate seat split the district, with Republican Bruce Herschensohn winning San Luis Obispo County and Barbara Boxer winning Santa Barbara.

1990 Population: 572,891. White 467,841 (82%), Black 16,024 (3%), Other 89,026 (16%). Hispanic origin 122,020 (21%). 18 and over 442,869 (77%), 62 and over 88,765 (15%). Median age: 32.

Committees

Banking, Finance & Urban Affairs (18th of 20 Republicans)
Financial Institutions Supervision, Regulation & Insurance; International Development, Finance, Trade & Monetary Policy

Small Business (11th of 18 Republicans)
Regulation, Business Opportunities and Technology; SBA Legislation and the General Economy

Campaign Finance

1992	Receipts	Receipts from PACs		Expend-itures
Huffington (R)	$5,443,247	0		$5,435,177
Ochoa (D)	$657,375	$152,663	(23%)	$663,027
Lorenz (GREEN)	$18,811	0		$18,707

Key Votes

1993

Require parental notification of minors' abortions	N
Require unpaid family and medical leave	Y
Approve national "motor voter" registration bill	N
Approve budget increasing taxes and reducing deficit	N
Approve economic stimulus plan	N

Elections

1992 General		
Michael Huffington (R)	131,242	(53%)
Gloria Ochoa (D)	87,328	(35%)
Mindy Lorenz (GREEN)	23,699	(9%)
W. Howard Dilbeck (LIBERT)	7,553	(3%)
1992 Primary		
Michael Huffington (R)	38,406	(49%)
Robert J. Lagomarsino (R)	33,844	(43%)
Gordon Klemm (R)	5,570	(7%)
Dick Pauly (R)	1,292	(2%)

District Vote for President

	1992
D	106,815 (41%)
R	92,045 (35%)
I	61,030 (23%)

23 Elton Gallegly (R)

Of Simi Valley — Elected 1986; 4th Term

Born: March 7, 1944, Huntington Park, Calif.
Education: California State U., Los Angeles, 1962-63.
Occupation: Real estate broker.
Family: Wife, Janice Shrader; four children.
Religion: Protestant.
Political Career: Simi Valley City Council, 1979-80; mayor of Simi Valley, 1980-86.
Capitol Office: 2441 Rayburn Bldg. 20515; 225-5811.

In Washington: Gallegly has emerged as the House's most aggressive GOP voice on immigration and illegal aliens. He introduced a small blizzard of attention-getting proposals on these subjects, as well as on crime, in the 102nd and 103rd Congresses.

None of the bills may have stood any chance of enactment, of course, but they serve to lay down a hard-liner's marker. And they reflect the views of a number of Gallegly's Ventura County constituents, many of whom fled north to their current homes to avoid the changes they saw happening in Los Angeles.

The immigration and illegal alien bills included proposals to hire more Border Patrol agents (an idea that also would provide employment for soldiers displaced by military cutbacks); to deny federal welfare and unemployment benefits to illegal aliens; to improve enforcement of sanctions against employers who hire illegal aliens; and to change the cards used by aliens to make them more difficult to forge.

In the 102nd Congress, Gallegly also introduced a resolution calling for a constitutional amendment to deny citizenship to those born in the United States unless their mothers were citizens or legal residents. He sponsored a bill with the same ends.

Gallegly's crime proposals included making drive-by shootings a federal offense and instituting mandatory minimum sentences for drug crimes involving children. As a member of a GOP task force on drugs, Gallegly talked tough on crime and advocated user accountability. After a Drug Enforcement Administration officer from Simi Valley was killed, Gallegly introduced legislation in the 101st Congress to reinstate a federal death penalty for anyone convicted of murdering a federal law enforcement officer. He reintroduced it in the 102nd Congress.

Although personally unassuming, Gallegly's unwavering loyalty has helped him gain his leadership's attention. His reward came in the 101st Congress with a seat on Foreign Affairs. He also picked up a third committee at the beginning of the 103rd Congress — Judiciary — an ideal forum for a member with his interest in crime and immigration law. He is the only non-lawyer on the panel. He was able to keep his spot on Natural Resources after ranking Republican Don Young of Alaska asked him to remain.

He was a leading hawk in congressional efforts to give President Bush authority to use force against Iraq. He made national headlines in December 1990 when, after a White House meeting, he quoted Bush referring to Iraqi President Saddam Hussein and saying: "If we get into an armed situation, he's going to get his ass kicked." He introduced legislation in 1991 to cut off federal funds to states or cities offering sanctuary to members of the armed forces who were absent without official leave.

Gallegly again drew notice in March 1991 when he and 11 other members who backed Bush's war policy ignored Speaker Thomas S. Foley's objections and visited Kuwait at the invitation of the Kuwaiti ambassador. The trip was paid by a company seeking business in Kuwait.

In July 1987, Gallegly made a high-profile venture into foreign policy, joining three other House members on the Capitol lawn to bash Toshiba products with sledgehammers. The Japanese firm had acknowledged selling restricted technology to the Soviet Union.

At Home: Few incumbents seeking reelection in 1992 could have failed to see the danger signals ahead, and Gallegly was among the best-warned in the nation. Although he had been re-elected without suspense in 1990, his vote share had dropped by 11 percentage points from 1988. Then, early in 1992, redistricting put him in a district with another incumbent, Robert J. Lagomarsino, who was six terms more senior and considered one of the delegation's toughest survivors.

But Lagomarsino, who hailed from Ventura, was persuaded to move north up the coast to Santa Barbara and run in a district that stretched north all the way to San Luis Obispo (and where he would lose in the primary to

California 23

Most of Ventura County; Oxnard; Ventura; Simi Valley

Gallegly began his political career as a local officeholder in Simi Valley, a burgeoning Ventura County suburb of about 100,000 residents. Until recently, those who had heard of Simi Valley were most likely to associate it with a winery. But in the spring of 1992, a jury with no blacks in this suburb acquitted four white police officers from Los Angeles in the beating of a black motorist named Rodney King, who had been apprehended after a high-speed chase. The verdict ignited the worst rioting in Los Angeles in nearly 30 years.

Simi Valley accounts for little more than one-sixth of the 23rd District, but it is not atypical of the district (blacks constitute only 3 percent of the 23rd's population). Some call it a haven for families and middle-class values, others call it flight from the Los Angeles Basin's cauldron of racial distrust. Either way, Simi Valley and Ventura County have lost their anonymity and become a touchstone for racial tension in the region.

Ventura County as a whole came into its own with the redistricting of 1992. Another decade of rapid growth (26 percent in the 1980s) had lifted its population to 669,000 — more than enough for a full district. The lines of the 23rd District are nearly identical to those of Ventura County.

There are two small exceptions, at the southwest and northeast corners, and one large exception in the southeast near the Los Angeles County line. Here, the city of Thousand Oaks (with 104,000 people the second-largest in the county) was drawn into the Los Angeles-based 24th District.

The 23rd still comprises more than 80 percent of Ventura County, including the cities of Ventura, Oxnard, Simi Valley, Camarillo and Santa Paula. About 97 percent of the district vote was cast by county residents in 1992 (the rest was cast in Carpinteria and neighboring precincts just across the Santa Barbara County line).

Republican registration in the 23rd is 42 percent, roughly equal to Democratic registration.

In most years in most districts, that margin would be enough for Republicans to win with ease. But 1992 was not a Republican year in California, especially in recent-vintage suburbs where high-wage jobs in aerospace and other defense industries were disappearing.

George Bush got just a fraction over 35 percent of the vote in Ventura County, which was carried by Bill Clinton with 37 percent (Ross Perot got 27 percent, 6 points better than his statewide percentage).

The news was better for the Republican candidates for the Senate, both of whom carried the county.

But appointed Republican Sen. John Seymour won here by fewer than 3,000 votes; conservative commentator Bruce Herschensohn, running for the other seat, managed a bare majority. Gallegly, meanwhile, managed to hold off a spirited challenger, but he dropped 4 percentage points from the 58 percent share of the vote he had won in 1990.

1990 Population: 571,483. White 439,346 (77%), Black 14,432 (3%), Other 117,705 (21%). Hispanic origin 171,722 (30%). 18 and over 412,637 (72%), 62 and over 66,068 (12%). Median age: 31.

Republican multimillionaire Michael Huffington).

Gallegly, meanwhile, had little trouble in the primary before facing what was widely considered a tough challenge from Anita Perez Ferguson, a former teacher who had run respectably well against Lagomarsino in 1990. Ferguson tapped into the "Year of the Woman" theme in California and attracted money from across the country en route to a half-million-dollar campaign. But Gallegly was even better financed. And he did not shrink from going after the Democrat.

Racial issues were especially sensitive locally in 1992, and Gallegly himself hails from Simi Valley, where the jury sat that acquitted the Los Angeles police officers of beating Rodney King (touching off the worst riots seen in the United States in more than two decades). But Gallegly took a dig at Ferguson for not always using her middle name in her campaign, and feelings were often raw in both camps.

In the end, the matchup may have been oversold. Gallegly was held to 54 percent, his lowest vote share ever, but Ferguson was never really close to winning. A Libertarian candidate picked up 4 percent.

Gallegly first got a shot at this House seat in 1986, when Republican Rep. Bobbi Fiedler embarked on an unsuccessful bid for the GOP Senate nomination. But Gallegly had to fend off a primary opponent with some celebrity.

Tony Hope, son of comedian Bob Hope, had returned to the area after a 10-year stay in Washington, D.C., with seeming access to unlimited Hollywood money and glitter. But concerned that he would be viewed as an election-buying carpetbagger, he played down his celebrity contacts and raised far less money than he might have.

Setting out to prove that he was not just "a pile of money from a distant planet," Hope stressed his background, including work for an accounting firm in Washington and service on the Grace commission on government waste.

Casting Hope as an interloper, Gallegly touted his record as mayor. He was well-known for having boosted economic development in Simi Valley, once derided in some parts as "Slimy Valley." Gallegly also pointed out that Hope had not even registered to vote during his sojourn in Washington and had registered outside the district when he returned to California. Hope responded that Gallegly had switched his own registration from Republican to independent in 1974, abandoning the party in the midst of Watergate. But party regulars backed Gallegly.

Gallegly did face the issue of heavy financial support from local real estate developers. Some of their projects needed approval by the City Council on which he sat. Hope wanted to raise questions of propriety and also tap anti-development sentiment in the district.

But Hope's campaign organization was weaker than Gallegly's, and he neutralized his most important potential asset — money — with his squeamishness about using it. Gallegly, relatively unknown outside Simi Valley when the campaign began, effectively used direct mail to spread his name and message across the populous San Fernando Valley portion of the district, resulting in an easy win.

Committees

Foreign Affairs (11th of 18 Republicans)
Europe & the Middle East; Western Hemisphere Affairs

Judiciary (11th of 14 Republicans)
Economic & Commercial Law; International Law, Immigration & Refugees

Natural Resources (4th of 15 Republicans)
Insular & International Affairs (ranking)

Elections

1992 General		
Elton Gallegly (R)	115,504	(54%)
Anita Perez Ferguson (D)	88,225	(41%)
Jay C. Wood (LIBERT)	9,091	(4%)
1992 Primary		
Elton Gallegly (R)	34,666	(63%)
Daphne Becker (R)	15,518	(28%)
Robert Shakman (R)	4,597	(8%)
1990 General		
Elton Gallegly (R)	118,326	(58%)
Richard D. Freiman (D)	68,921	(34%)
Peggy Christensen (LIBERT)	15,364	(8%)

Previous Winning Percentages: **1988** (69%) **1986** (68%)

District Vote for President

1992

D	82,613 (38%)
R	74,106 (34%)
I	58,177 (27%)

Campaign Finance

	Receipts	Receipts from PACs		Expend-itures
1992				
Gallegly (R)	$679,886	$195,705	(29%)	$862,061
Ferguson (D)	$572,372	$254,300	(44%)	$543,116
1990				
Gallegly (R)	$599,454	$156,861	(26%)	$449,668
Freiman (D)	$13,706	$50	(0%)	$13,147

Key Votes

1993	
Require parental notification of minors' abortions	Y
Require unpaid family and medical leave	N
Approve national "motor voter" registration bill	N
Approve budget increasing taxes and reducing deficit	N
Approve economic stimulus plan	N
1992	
Approve balanced-budget constitutional amendment	Y
Close down space station program	N
Approve U.S. aid for former Soviet Union	N
Allow shifting funds from defense to domestic programs	N
1991	
Extend unemployment benefits using deficit financing	N
Approve waiting period for handgun purchases	Y
Authorize use of force in Persian Gulf	Y

Voting Studies

	Presidential Support		Party Unity		Conservative Coalition	
Year	S	O	S	O	S	O
1992	80	19	91	7	96	4
1991	81	18	94	3	95	3
1990	70	29	91	6	96	4
1989	76	24	90	8	93	7
1988	68	28	94	2	95	3
1987	71	29	94	5	88	12

Interest Group Ratings

Year	ADA	AFL-CIO	CCUS	ACU
1992	15	50	75	84
1991	10	8	90	85
1990	11	0	86	92
1989	5	18	100	89
1988	15	21	100	96
1987	4	6	100	96

24 Anthony C. Beilenson (D)

Of Woodland Hills — Elected 1976; 9th Term

Born: Oct. 26, 1932, New Rochelle, N.Y.
Education: Harvard U., B.A. 1954, LL.B. 1957.
Occupation: Lawyer.
Family: Wife, Dolores Martin; three children.
Religion: Jewish.
Political Career: Calif. Assembly, 1963-67; Calif. Senate, 1967-77; sought Democratic nomination for U.S. Senate, 1968.
Capitol Office: 2465 Rayburn Bldg. 20515; 225-5911.

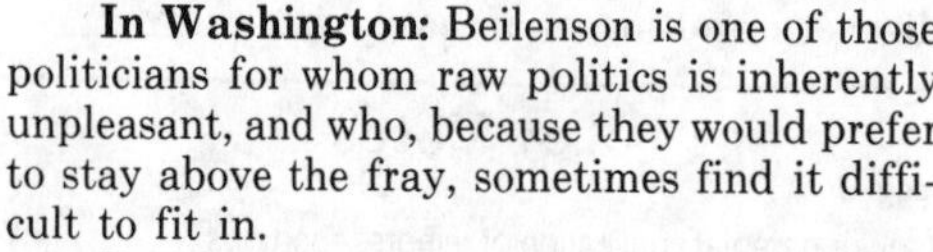

In Washington: Beilenson is one of those politicians for whom raw politics is inherently unpleasant, and who, because they would prefer to stay above the fray, sometimes find it difficult to fit in.

Despite this characteristic — or perhaps because of it — Beilenson continues to be re-elected as a liberal Democrat in a marginal district. But although he holds key positions on two important committees — including the No. 3 Democratic spot on Rules — he is too independent-minded and iconoclastic to be a true insider in the party leadership's power structure. And while Beilenson's less than partisan approach wins him respect on both sides of the aisle, it also earns him occasional reproof, from Democrats and Republicans.

It is not that he does not vote like a good Democrat — he does so more often than the average party member. On Rules, too, he generally votes with his party; but he is not an easy man for the leadership to persuade when he wants to go his own way. And while Beilenson is perhaps the panel's most independent Democrat, he often disappoints Republicans on the panel who think his heart is with them on occasions when his vote is not.

As a sign of his bipartisanship, Beilenson joined with Republican Jim Leach of Iowa in 1993 to offer a comprehensive campaign financing bill that combined limits on contributions and spending with public financing of House elections and a ban on political action committees.

Beilenson has a strong distaste for what he sees as wasteful government spending and parochial legislating, and for years he has complained that Congress has failed to gain control of the federal budget. He voted against both the Republican and Democratic versions of a tax cut bill in February 1992, in essence because each would have added to the federal deficit. And he has voted to cut deeply into spending on the space station, the superconducting super collider and the Strategic Defense Initiative.

Beilenson's frugal tendencies occasionally war with his liberalism: In 1992, he favored tearing down walls that separated defense and domestic spending to allow deeper defense cuts to finance increased spending on social needs. Other deficit hawks preferred to keep the walls intact, so that defense cuts would reduce the deficit.

And Beilenson continues to eschew what he considers gimmicks — constitutional amendments to require a balanced budget or to give the president a line-item veto, for instance. He chaired a 1984 House Rules task force on the budget process, but House leaders declined to consider its proposals for procedural reforms and spending controls. Congress instead enacted the more drastic Gramm-Rudman anti-deficit law that Beilenson criticizes for encouraging phony budgeting.

In the 101st Congress, he took a seat on the Budget Committee, a position he used to continue to speak out on the federal debt. At the start of the 103rd Congress, when Budget Chairman Leon E. Panetta resigned to join the Clinton administration, Beilenson considered seeking the chairmanship. But he changed his mind when it became clear he did not have the votes.

On Rules, Beilenson has few opportunities to affect legislation. In the 101st, however, he served as chairman of the Select Intelligence Committee, responsible for annual multibillion-dollar authorizing legislation for the CIA and other intelligence agencies.

Committee members from both parties thought Beilenson had done well, praising his deliberate style and avoidance of partisan confrontation. Although he had already served on the panel longer than the maximum six years, Beilenson expressed some interest in staying on as chairman. Three former Intelligence Committee chairmen joined him in requesting a rules change to increase tenure on the committee to eight years and to allow chairmen to serve more than one term. But Speaker Thomas S. Foley, who had already granted Beilenson a reprieve to stay on for a seventh year to complete one full term as chairman, never acted on the proposal. Beilenson left the panel at the start of the 102nd Congress.

California 24

Northwest Los Angeles County suburbs

Redistricting in 1992 seemed to toss Rep. Beilenson a hard bone to chew when it put Ventura County's conservative Thousand Oaks into his constituency. The city has three registered Republicans for every Democrat.

But the dynamics of an election year that produced unusually lopsided Democratic successes in California gave Beilenson a break.

While Beilenson took only 39 percent in Thousand Oaks — not bad considering that he was running against a Thousand Oaks-based Republican — he received 60 percent in the Los Angeles County portion of the 24th.

This gave him a comfortable 17-point margin of victory and made him the first Democrat to represent any part of Ventura County in the House since 1948.

The eastern end of the 24th District begins in the San Fernando Valley, in Van Nuys and Encino. Its main artery, the Ventura Freeway, splits the valley and heads west. This area is thoroughly suburban. Its industries tend to be service-oriented; traditional heavy industry is limited to a few struggling aerospace contractors.

A few miles west of Encino is Tarzana, envisioned by "Tarzan" author Edgar Rice Burroughs as 550 acres of sanctuary from civilization. But just six years after he bought the land in 1919, Burroughs divvied it up into tracts; the resulting community is just another subdivision along the Ventura Freeway.

The 24th's commercial districts are found about a mile south of Route 101 along Ventura Boulevard.

There are miles of suburban fast-food outlets and strip-mall stores, and while there are some high-rise office towers, they tend to house branch offices of banks, not their headquarters. Transportation issues dominate in the valley; concerns about further development are centered on how growth will affect the already-strangling traffic congestion.

As Highway 101 heads west toward Thousand Oaks, development thins. The valley narrows, with the Santa Monica Mountains National Recreation Area to the south and the Santa Susana Mountains to the north. Any industry out here is likely to be of the "clean" variety, such as the biotechnology company Amgen Inc. Beyond the recreation area lie Malibu and the Santa Monica Bay.

Malibu is reached most easily by the Pacific Coast Highway, with canyon roads wandering off to connect smaller communities in the hills. Malibu tends to be less Democratic than other towns this side of the mountains; many of its wealthy residents live inside gated developments.

Development is sparse by design; Malibu has seen the fate of its built-up southeastern neighbor, Santa Monica, and opted instead for controlled residential construction on its beaches and hillsides. While many in the San Fernando Valley are tearing their hair out over its traffic, many in Malibu are free to focus instead on the environment.

1990 Population: 572,563. White 484,496 (85%), Black 11,845 (2%), Other 76,222 (13%). Hispanic origin 72,221 (13%). 18 and over 450,849 (79%), 62 and over 78,094 (14%). Median age: 35.

Beilenson's reputation for thoughtful, bipartisan reflection makes him a regular choice for consultative positions. He was appointed by President Bush to co-chair the commission that monitored the Nicaraguan elections in March 1990; he was one of 18 members of Congress chosen to consult with Bush on the crisis in the Persian Gulf while Congress was out of session late in 1990; and he traveled to the region in December 1990 as part of an official leadership delegation. Beilenson, once a peace candidate for a Senate seat, spoke out strongly against military action in the gulf and later voted against it.

An avid environmentalist, Beilenson helped create the Santa Monica Mountains National Recreation Area in 1978 and doggedly seeks more funding for it. In the 100th Congress, he succeeded in adding language to the Endangered Species Act to ban importation of ivory from African countries that do not have effective elephant-conservation programs. And in the 102nd Congress he co-authored the Wild Bird Conservation Act, which bars import of threatened exotic birds.

At Home: Beilenson was one of the Democrats everyone thought would be in trouble after the 1992 redistricting. After he spent eight terms representing the San Fernando Valley, Malibu and Beverly Hills, the new map moved him inland and northward and gave him new territory in the conservative suburbs of Ventura County. His Democratic registration dropped from 54 percent in 1990 to 46 percent in 1992, the difference between relative security and life at the margin.

But the GOP proceeded to nominate a go-for-broke opponent in state Rep. Tom McClintock, a legislative Young Turk renowned for his clashes with moderate GOP Gov. Pete Wilson. Beilenson tended his own district politicking in the methodical way he always has. McClintock's hard-edged conservatism played poorly in a generally Democratic year, and he finished with a share of the vote slightly smaller than GOP registration for the district. Beilenson, by contrast, ran nearly 10 percentage points ahead of his party's registration.

Beilenson began his congressional career when Democratic Rep. Thomas M. Rees announced his retirement from Congress in 1976. The House district, which included some of the most liberal and heavily Jewish parts of Los Angeles, was ideal for Beilenson, who had served 14 years in the state Legislature.

Beilenson's one major obstacle was cleared away when Howard L. Berman, then the Assembly's majority leader, chose to remain in the Legislature in 1976. Beilenson dominated a field of five Democratic primary candidates and got 58 percent in the primary. He was elected with 60 percent in the general, and he did that well or better in each of his next seven contests. His only nervous moments before 1992 came during the redistricting of 1982, when his district shifted and the GOP nominated an anti-busing expert. Beilenson won with 60 percent.

Committees

Budget (4th of 26 Democrats)

Rules (3rd of 9 Democrats)
Rules of the House (chairman)

Elections

1992 General

Anthony C. Beilenson (D)	141,742	(56%)
Tom McClintock (R)	99,835	(39%)
John Paul Lindblad (PFP)	13,690	(5%)

1990 General

Anthony C. Beilenson (D)	103,141	(62%)
Jim Salomon (R)	57,118	(34%)
John Honigsfeld (PFP)	6,834	(4%)

Previous Winning Percentages: **1988** (63%) **1986** (66%) **1984** (62%) **1982** (60%) **1980** (63%) **1978** (66%) **1976** (60%)

District Vote for President

1992

D 128,572 (48%)
R 79,728 (30%)
I 57,625 (22%)

Campaign Finance

	Receipts	Receipts from PACs		Expend-itures
1992				
Beilenson (D)	$753,415	0		$786,463
McClintock (R)	$412,815	$180,735	(44%)	$469,714
1990				
Beilenson (D)	$231,386	0		$201,404
Salomon (R)	$358,367	$15,100	(4%)	$360,389

Key Votes

1993

Require parental notification of minors' abortions	N
Require unpaid family and medical leave	Y
Approve national "motor voter" registration bill	N
Approve budget increasing taxes and reducing deficit	Y
Approve economic stimulus plan	Y
1992	
Approve balanced-budget constitutional amendment	N
Close down space station program	Y
Approve U.S. aid for former Soviet Union	Y
Allow shifting funds from defense to domestic programs	Y
1991	
Extend unemployment benefits using deficit financing	Y
Approve waiting period for handgun purchases	Y
Authorize use of force in Persian Gulf	N

Voting Studies

	Presidential Support		Party Unity		Conservative Coalition	
Year	S	O	S	O	S	O
1992	26	67	84	10	15	75
1991	32	66	84	12	16	84
1990	26	71	89	8	15	81
1989	33	64	84	9	17	80
1988	26	65	89	5	11	89
1987	23	72	86	6	5	84
1986	18	81	89	7	20	80
1985	23	69	88	4	11	84
1984	34	65	87	10	12	88
1983	29	66	91	7	16	84
1982	38	53	81	5	11	82
1981	30	64	79	8	8	80

Interest Group Ratings

Year	ADA	AFL-CIO	CCUS	ACU
1992	85	75	38	9
1991	80	67	30	0
1990	83	75	8	8
1989	85	67	30	4
1988	95	77	50	8
1987	84	63	20	13
1986	80	50	18	9
1985	95	88	24	5
1984	90	62	38	9
1983	85	76	40	9
1982	95	84	19	5
1981	90	80	6	0

25 Howard P. "Buck" McKeon (R)

Of Santa Clarita — Elected 1992; 1st Term

Born: Sept. 9, 1939, Los Angeles, Calif.
Education: Brigham Young U., B.S. 1985.
Occupation: Clothing store owner.
Family: Wife, Patricia Kunz; six children.
Religion: Mormon.
Political Career: William S. Hart School Board, 1978-87; Santa Clarita City Council, 1987-92, mayor, 1987-88.
Capitol Office: 307 Cannon Bldg. 20515; 225-1956.

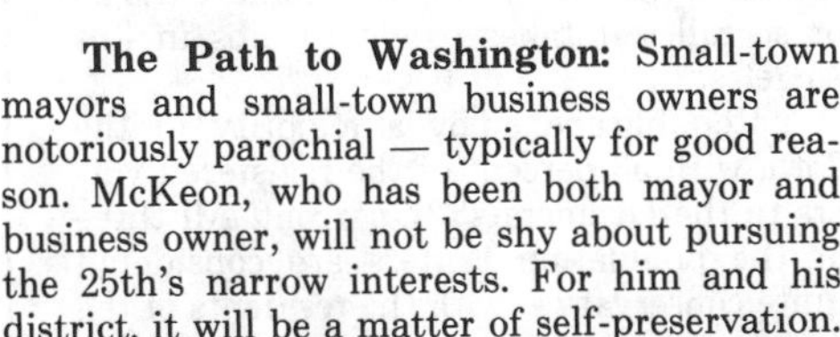

The Path to Washington: Small-town mayors and small-town business owners are notoriously parochial — typically for good reason. McKeon, who has been both mayor and business owner, will not be shy about pursuing the 25th's narrow interests. For him and his district, it will be a matter of self-preservation.

After getting past a difficult primary, McKeon did not have to work hard to win in this dramatically conservative Republican territory. He will, however, have to work hard in Washington if he is to win the jobs, roads and other accouterments that will help preserve the 25th's economic vitality.

Nothing epitomizes the district's economic concerns more than the decision to cap construction of the B-2 stealth bomber, assembled by thousands of workers at the Palmdale plant of Northrop Corp. It may take several years to start phasing out those jobs, but there is no similar big-ticket airplane ready to take its place on the Palmdale line.

McKeon does not absolutely oppose cutting back the defense budget. But he wants a big share of the savings devoted to two areas: infrastructure, chiefly roads, and worker retraining. He has acquired committee assignments that will be key to both goals: Public Works and Transportation, and Education and Labor.

Beyond trying to preserve the district's job base or entice new employers, McKeon also has promised to enlist Congress to stop a proposed landfill that Los Angeles and Los Angeles County want to build in the heart of the Angeles National Forest. He has opposed the landfill for years and regards it as a threat to the health and quality of life in the Santa Clarita Valley, particularly because of the inordinate amount of commercial traffic it would generate.

In addition, as president of the 47-member class of GOP freshmen, McKeon will have other responsibilities that transcend his significant parochial concerns.

The real race for this seat was in the GOP primary, which McKeon won by a slim 705 votes out of a relatively large turnout of nearly 62,000. McKeon finished just ahead of Phillip D. Wyman, a 14-year state Assembly veteran.

Each tried to outdo the other with endorsements to prove his conservative bona fides, in particular his aversion to taxes. Wyman, who moved into the district to run (though he had represented a major portion of it in the Assembly), called on former White House aide Oliver L. North to put in an appearance. McKeon got the support of Rep. Bill Thomas, whose previous district included much of what is now the 25th.

In the end, Wyman held most of his north county base in the Antelope Valley around Palmdale. But McKeon prevailed by scoring well in Santa Clarita, where he served as the first mayor in 1987-88.

McKeon cast himself as a businessman first, with skills that he said would make government more efficient. He proudly pointed to his family's successful chain of Western-wear stores that thrived even in the midst of the 1990 recession and its aftermath.

Well back in the pack of four other Republican hopefuls was former Rep. John H. Rousselot (1961-63, 1970-83), whose comeback was repudiated by the voters. He won only 7 percent.

The general election was something of an anticlimax, though the Democrat, James H. "Gil" Gilmartin, a lawyer and rancher, and independent Rick Pamplin, a screenwriter who tied his campaign to the presidential effort of Ross Perot, tried to make a race of it. Gilmartin hoped his background as a Navy flier would appeal to the district's defense workers. But McKeon greatly outspent him. And voter registration so overwhelmingly favors the GOP that there was little opportunity for Gilmartin or Pamplin.

The final outcome closely corresponded with registration figures: McKeon took 52 percent, Gilmartin 33 percent and Pamplin 6 percent. The rest of the votes were divided among three minor-party candidates.

California 25

Northern Los Angeles County; Lancaster; Palmdale

The 25th encompasses northern Los Angeles County, running to the borders of Ventura County to the west, Kern County to the north and San Bernardino County to the east. Much of the land area of this district is consumed by the San Gabriel Mountains in the Angeles National Forest and other lands controlled by the federal Bureau of Land Management. The district's southwest end reaches down into the city of Los Angeles.

This district is a mix of rural and suburban areas, with three roughly equally sized pockets of population separated by the federal lands: the Antelope Valley in the northeast, the Santa Clarita Valley in the west and L.A.'s upper San Fernando Valley in the far southwest.

The northwest part of the San Fernando Valley in the 25th is primarily residential, as is most of the valley, with electronics and aerospace manufacturing to the west side.

The Santa Clarita Valley, just north of the San Fernando Valley, is also primarily composed of Los Angeles suburbs, but along with its vast tracts of new homes it is attracting a lot of new manufacturing that cannot afford to locate in Los Angeles proper. Santa Clarita, a city of 111,000 created in 1987 when the communities of Valencia, Canyon Country, Saugus and Newhall merged, features one large industrial park with another in the works. McKeon was the new city's first mayor.

Up in the high desert past the national forest is the Antelope Valley, the fastest-growing area of the three. It consists of a lot of desert, a little of Edwards Air Force Base and two cities, Lancaster (population 97,000) and Palmdale (population 69,000). This rapidly growing area's economy revolves around aerospace; it is home to about 80 percent of Edwards' 15,000 workers.

Palmdale is the home of Plant 42, also known as the Flight Test Center, which runs a whole range of aircraft through their paces, including the space shuttle and the SR-71.

The Antelope Valley is not nearly as dependent on Los Angeles as are the Santa Clarita and San Fernando valleys, but over the past decade it has been attracting some residents who are willing to commute the 50 or so miles it takes to get to jobs in Los Angeles.

Republicans enjoy a majority in the 25th, with 53 percent of the registered voters to the Democrats' 37 percent. All three of the population centers are considered quite conservative, with the residents of the Antelope Valley the most conservative, followed by those in the San Fernando and Santa Clarita valleys. Santa Claritans' heightened concern over environmental issues tips the political balance of the area toward the center.

Sixteen percent of the district's residents are Hispanic, 6 percent are Asian and 4 percent are black. George Bush won the 25th in 1992, taking 39 percent of the vote to Bill Clinton's 36 percent and Ross Perot's 25 percent.

1990 Population: 573,105. White 458,364 (80%), Black 25,724 (4%), Other 89,017 (16%). Hispanic origin 94,172 (16%). 18 and over 414,953 (72%), 62 and over 54,250 (9%). Median age: 31.

Committees

Education & Labor (14th of 15 Republicans)
Elementary, Secondary & Vocational Education; Labor-Management Relations; Postsecondary Education

Public Works & Transportation (21st of 24 Republicans)
Aviation; Surface Transportation

Campaign Finance

1992	Receipts	Receipts from PACs		Expend-itures
McKeon (R)	$457,650	$96,775	(21%)	$452,792
Gilmartin (D)	$169,218	0		$168,319
Wilken (GREEN)	$1,170	0		$886

Key Votes

1993

Require parental notification of minors' abortions	Y
Require unpaid family and medical leave	N
Approve national "motor voter" registration bill	N
Approve budget increasing taxes and reducing deficit	N
Approve economic stimulus plan	N

Elections

1992 General		
Howard P. "Buck" McKeon (R)	113,611	(52%)
James H. "Gil" Gilmartin (D)	72,233	(33%)
Rick Pamplin (I)	13,930	(6%)
Peggy Christensen (LIBERT)	6,932	(3%)
Charles Wilken (GREEN)	6,919	(3%)
Nancy Lawrence (PFP)	5,090	(2%)
1992 Primary		
Howard P. "Buck" McKeon (R)	24,509	(40%)
Phillip D. Wyman (R)	23,804	(38%)
Larry Logsdon (R)	4,568	(7%)
John H. Rousselot (R)	4,438	(7%)
John J. Lynch (R)	3,366	(5%)
Tom McVarish (R)	1,242	(2%)

District Vote for President

	1992	
D	83,305	(36%)
R	89,987	(39%)
I	57,398	(25%)

26 Howard L. Berman (D)

Of Panorama City — Elected 1982; 6th Term

Born: April 15, 1941, Los Angeles
Education: U. of California, Los Angeles, B.A. 1962, LL.B. 1965.
Occupation: Lawyer.
Family: Wife, Janis Schwartz; one child, one stepchild.
Religion: Jewish.
Political Career: Calif. Assembly, 1973-83.
Capitol Office: 2201 Rayburn Bldg. 20515; 225-4695.

In Washington: Having earned a reputation as a serious-minded legislator during his first decade in the House, Berman is proving his range as well. A member of the Foreign Affairs, Judiciary and Budget committees, he gained a fourth assignment, on Natural Resources, at the start of the 103rd Congress.

Berman's busy agenda places him in hearing rooms more often than in television studios. This approach has limited Berman's profile nationally and even in California.

But it has earned him the respect of many Democrats and even some Republicans who disagree with his liberal views on most issues. The chairman of the Foreign Affairs Subcommittee on International Operations (which oversees State Department and other U.S. diplomatic functions), he usually cooperates with the ranking Republican, Olympia J. Snowe of Maine.

Berman's interest in foreign policy drove much of his legislative output through the 102nd Congress. Spurred by his concern and support for Israel, he was an early and outspoken opponent of Saddam Hussein's regime in Iraq.

As far back as 1983, Berman was questioning the Reagan administration's tilt toward Iraq in its war with the openly anti-American nation of Iran. He actively opposed the administration's decision to remove Iraq from a list of terrorist nations subject to U.S. embargoes, citing evidence that Iraq was continuing to harbor terrorists.

Berman stepped up his efforts to isolate Saddam in 1988, when Iraq's troops used poison gas against that nation's Kurdish minority. But his efforts to pass a bill enacting economic sanctions were parried by the Reagan and Bush administrations, which continued to view Iraq as a bulwark against Iran. Not until 1990, when Iraq had made clear its aggressive intentions, did the bill gain momentum. It was reported to the full House by the Foreign Affairs Committee on Aug. 1, 1990; the next day, Iraqi troops overran Kuwait.

The following January, Berman supported the resolution authorizing U.S. force against Iraq. But he held the Bush administration "partially responsible" for what he called Saddam Hussein's "miscalculation ... that the United States would tolerate any behavior by Iraq."

Although Berman called for an era of arms restraint after the Persian Gulf War, arms sales to the Middle East soon resumed at their prewar levels. In September 1992, he tried to block the sale of fighter jets and other weapons to Saudi Arabia, which he said would "affirm our role as premier arms peddler to the world." This position was also in keeping with his stand against arming Arab nations that are hostile to Israel.

Berman in the 102nd Congress did push through a measure mandating sanctions against nations and individuals that sell goods of potential military utility to Iraq or Iran. Working with Republican Rep. Henry J. Hyde of Illinois, Berman gained passage during the 101st Congress of a bill barring U.S. aid and arms sales to countries that the secretary of State has determined to be supporters of terrorism.

Although the federal budget deficit and domestic economic problems have made foreign aid programs increasingly unattractive politically, Berman remains staunch in his support. In late October 1991, he criticized Democratic and Republican members alike for succumbing to political pressure in killing a foreign aid authorization bill.

He said it was the wrong mindset to think that "the antidote for George Bush's [domestic] mistakes is a return to isolationism." Berman pursues this perspective as one of two Foreign Affairs Democrats on the Budget Committee.

On the Foreign Affairs subcommittee that he chairs, Berman is a leading advocate for bankrolling United Nations peacekeeping efforts. He worked well with Snowe during the 102nd Congress — his first as chairman — in producing State Department authorization bills.

However, the two crossed swords on one issue: the fate of the "bugged" U.S. Embassy building in Moscow. After it was revealed in

California 26

San Fernando Valley

The 26th is the heart of the San Fernando Valley. The district begins at the Angeles National Forest and drops south through the valley down to the Ventura Freeway.

This part of the valley has undergone striking demographic changes. Areas such as Pacomia and Van Nuys that had only a small minority presence 20 years ago are now heavily Hispanic.

Also new are the small clusters of black families that have appeared throughout this district. While the number of blacks in downtown Los Angeles has dropped over the past 10 years, it has risen in the county overall — and areas like this are where they are going: middle-class suburbs where blacks did not live 10 years ago.

A variety of manufacturing facilities are spread throughout the 26th, but the heaviest concentration of the heaviest industry is toward the north, in Pacomia and Sylmar.

The area is desperately searching for a replacement for its lucrative but dying aerospace industry. Defense conversion issues are a primary concern, with an eye toward getting the area's aerospace contractors into advanced transportation, such as magnetic-levitation trains, instead. General Motors, which had been the district's largest employer, closed up shop in Van Nuys in August 1992, putting a squeeze on a city already reeling from the loss of the Lockheed plant in neighboring Burbank in the 27th District.

Van Nuys is trying to avoid having the GM plant site cut up into shopping malls and is struggling to attract another large manufacturer to the area. The city has tried to sell it as a site to build electric cars; California's stringent clean air rules will soon be heavily favoring them and other alternatively fueled vehicles.

The 26th is a good district for a Democrat, though it is much less affluent, much less Jewish and has fewer voters than the district Rep. Berman is used to. Voter registration levels in the area's Hispanic communities are dramatically lower than in Berman's old district. Berman drew support fairly evenly across the 26th in 1992, and received 61 percent of the vote, the same as in 1990.

The open spaces of Sylmar, rare for the Los Angeles area, have made this community at the district's northern edge one of the fastest-growing areas in the city.

Just south of Sylmar is San Fernando, an independent city embedded within Los Angeles; 83 percent of its 22,600 middle-class residents classify themselves as Hispanic.

On the 26th's eastern edge is Sun Valley, distinctive within the district in that it is made up primarily of an Anglo working class with relatively few Hispanics. North Hollywood, along the Ventura Freeway, is a mix, its east side heavily Hispanic and its west side much less so. Much of the district's Jewish population lives toward the west.

Bill Clinton took 57 percent of the district vote in 1992, trailing Berman's performance by 4 points. George Bush received 24 percent of the vote, and Ross Perot received 19 percent.

1990 Population: 571,523. White 305,795 (54%), Black 35,611 (6%), Other 230,117 (40%). Hispanic origin 184,925 (32%). 18 and over 410,112 (72%), 62 and over 55,596 (10%). Median age: 29.

1987 that Soviet authorities had riddled the unfinished building with listening devices, Snowe had tried to get the building torn down and replaced. But by 1991, the Bush administration decided to seek less expensive options, and Berman agreed. When Snowe proposed that year to mandate the "tear down" option, Berman trumped her with an amendment leaving the decision to the State Department.

As a member of the Judiciary Committee, Berman has been active on such issues as immigration law and protection of workers' pension rights. It is on Judiciary that Berman's liberal instincts show. Berman is a strong supporter of abortion rights and has proposed to ban the sale of assault rifles and pistols.

Berman's new position on the Natural Resources Committee will enable him to work on issues affecting the Los Angeles area, which suffers from chronic air pollution. He is an advocate of developing electric cars and expanding the use of mass transit.

The cofounder, with California Rep. Henry A. Waxman, of a highly successful Democratic political organization in western Los Angeles County, Berman also keeps a hand in partisan affairs back home. In 1991, he and Democratic colleague Vic Fazio represented the Democrats in California's House delegation during that state's redistricting process.

Fazio and Berman played lead roles in drawing the Democrat-friendly redistricting plans passed that September by the state Legislature. But the legislation was vetoed by Republican Gov. Pete Wilson, sending the matter to the California Supreme Court.

At Home: The "Berman-Waxman" organization dominates the West Los Angeles political scene. It is less a "machine" than a network of like-minded politicians who pool resources to back candidates — expected to be legislative allies — with money, organization, computer technology and the skills of Berman's brother, Michael, a political consultant.

Howard Berman's influence in Democratic politics stretches back to the late 1960s, when he and Waxman, students at UCLA, were involved in the Federation of Young Democrats. Berman succeeded Waxman in the presidency of the federation in 1967 and helped him win a seat in the state Assembly the following year.

In 1972, it was Berman's turn. He challenged a veteran GOP member of the Assembly in a traditionally Republican district that had grown more Democratic. Pulling in funds from his contacts and mobilizing Young Democrats and students and recent migrants from the inner city, Berman won. In Sacramento he built up a cadre of followers in the Legislature and allied himself with Speaker Leo T. McCarthy and Gov. Edmund G. "Jerry" Brown Jr. He was a consummate facilitator and tactician, with a relaxed style that allowed even his opponents to regard him as approachable.

In 1980, Berman bet his career chips on a challenge to McCarthy, who had been his ally. The clash ended badly for both men: their rivalry opened the door for a third candidate, Willie L. Brown Jr., to become Speaker (a job he would hold into the 1990s). Soon thereafter, Brown helped pass a congressional redistricting plan that included a perfect district for Berman. Still, Berman had to work for it when the GOP nominated a wealthy auto dealer who had strong financial backing. Berman walked precincts and, with his brother's help, ran an extensive direct-mail campaign. He won with 60 percent of the vote and has had little trouble since. He topped out at 70 percent in 1988 before slipping to a more typical 61 percent in 1990. The 1992 redistricting map was nearly as kind to him as its predecessors had been, and in November he received 61 percent of the vote once again.

Committees

Budget (5th of 26 Democrats)

Foreign Affairs (5th of 27 Democrats)
International Operations (chairman); International Security, International Organizations & Human Rights

Judiciary (11th of 21 Democrats)
Administrative Law & Governmental Relations; Intellectual Property & Judicial Administration; Economic & Commercial Law

Natural Resources (25th of 28 Democrats)

Elections

1992 General		
Howard L. Berman (D)	73,807	(61%)
Gary Forsch (R)	36,453	(30%)
Margery Hinds (PFP)	7,180	(6%)
Bernard Zimring (LIBERT)	3,468	(3%)
1990 General		
Howard L. Berman (D)	78,031	(61%)
Roy Dahlson (R)	44,492	(35%)
Bernard Zimring (LIBERT)	5,268	(4%)

Previous Winning Percentages: **1988** (70%) **1986** (65%) **1984** (63%) **1982** (60%)

District Vote for President

1992
D 72,673 (57%)
R 31,013 (24%)
I 24,167 (19%)

Campaign Finance

	Receipts	Receipts from PACs		Expend-itures
1992				
Berman (D)	$548,212	$216,350	(39%)	$722,606
Forsch (R)	$76,578	$2,525	(3%)	$76,667
1990				
Berman (D)	$510,538	$181,500	(36%)	$450,401
Dahlson (R)	$83,775	$250	(0%)	$82,453

Key Votes

1993	
Require parental notification of minors' abortions	N
Require unpaid family and medical leave	Y
Approve national "motor voter" registration bill	Y
Approve budget increasing taxes and reducing deficit	Y
Approve economic stimulus plan	Y
1992	
Approve balanced-budget constitutional amendment	N
Close down space station program	N
Approve U.S. aid for former Soviet Union	Y
Allow shifting funds from defense to domestic programs	Y
1991	
Extend unemployment benefits using deficit financing	?
Approve waiting period for handgun purchases	Y
Authorize use of force in Persian Gulf	Y

Voting Studies

	Presidential Support		Party Unity		Conservative Coalition	
Year	S	O	S	O	S	O
1992	21	78	89	5	17	79
1991	32	63	83	7	14	81
1990	20	77	93	3	7	93
1989	31	63	90	3	10	90
1988	23	66	90	4	5	84
1987	14	84	89	3	5	93
1986	18	80	89	5	12	82
1985	24	68	91	3	9	85
1984	29	62	84	6	7	88
1983	24	67	85	5	10	88

Interest Group Ratings

Year	ADA	AFL-CIO	CCUS	ACU
1992	85	73	25	8
1991	85	82	22	11
1990	100	92	23	4
1989	95	100	30	4
1988	95	85	36	4
1987	88	88	13	0
1986	95	92	19	5
1985	100	94	24	10
1984	95	77	43	9
1983	95	88	25	0

27 Carlos J. Moorhead (R)

Of Glendale — Elected 1972; 11th Term

Born: May 6, 1922, Long Beach, Calif.

Education: U. of California, Los Angeles, B.A. 1943; U. of Southern California, J.D. 1949.

Military Service: Army, 1942-45; Army Reserve, 1945-82.

Occupation: Lawyer.

Family: Wife, Valery Joan Tyler; five children.

Religion: Presbyterian.

Political Career: Calif. Assembly, 1967-73.

Capitol Office: 2346 Rayburn Bldg. 20515; 225-4176.

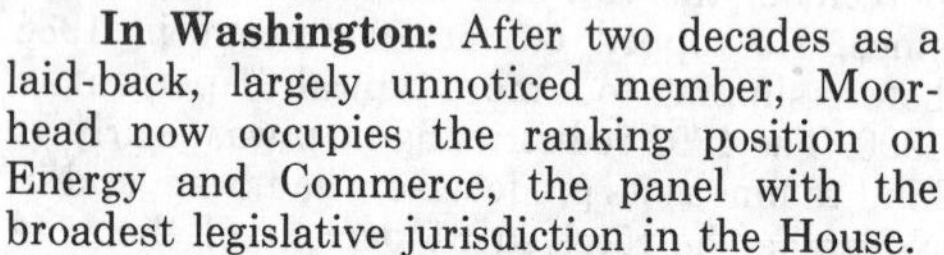

In Washington: After two decades as a laid-back, largely unnoticed member, Moorhead now occupies the ranking position on Energy and Commerce, the panel with the broadest legislative jurisdiction in the House.

At a glance, the unassertive Moorhead seems mismatched against one of the chamber's all-time heavyweights, Energy Chairman John D. Dingell of Michigan. Whereas Moorhead is soft-spoken and genial, Dingell is brusque, short-tempered and jealous of his fearsome reputation. Moorhead depends on cue cards for virtually every comment he makes in public, while Dingell runs his meetings with confidence and authority.

The matchup appeared so lopsided that House Republicans discussed pushing Moorhead aside at the start of the 103rd Congress in favor of the more forceful Thomas J. Bliley Jr. of Virginia.

Moorhead, however, assured his colleagues that he was up to the task.

"I'm willing to fight when fighting can accomplish something. I fight to win," he said before the voting. "Sometimes you can do it by yelling and screaming, and sometimes you do it by building a coalition that can win."

While it appears all but certain Moorhead will not challenge Dingell directly, his non-threatening approach has brought him legislative achievements in the past — and it is at least as likely as any approach to produce results with this chairman. The developing minuet between the pudgy, mild-mannered Moorhead and the bearish Dingell should be one of the more interesting to watch in the 103rd.

Each man has a home-state industry that often dictates his priorities. If Dingell is known as the guardian angel of Detroit's auto industry, Moorhead is Hollywood's protector on Capitol Hill. In the 102nd, Moorhead switched his vote to "no" when the cable reregulation bill sought to compensate broadcasters — rather than Hollywood — for over-the-air programs retransmitted by cable operators. Moorhead, whose district includes Disney studios and Time Warner Inc., complained: "Broadcasters hijacked this bill."

Moorhead sticks with his party, supporting the GOP and President Bush in more than 80 percent of the House votes where the president took a position in 1991 and 1992. If he joins forces with Democrats, it is likely to be on issues that relate to California. Savvy Democrats use Moorhead's amiable personality to draw him in on less partisan issues.

He has teamed up with Philip R. Sharp, chairman of the Energy and Power Subcommittee, to develop new safety standards for oil and natural gas pipelines. Moorhead supported the legislation because he said it would reduce pipeline leaks in Santa Monica Bay next to his district.

During the 101st Congress, Sharp and Moorhead successfully defied Bush administration objections to back creation of a federal reserve of refined petroleum products. They were also part of a congressional push to increase spending to help low-income families save energy by weatherizing their homes.

During deliberations over the 1990 Clean Air Act, Moorhead joined with Democrat Edward J. Markey of Massachusetts to sponsor an amendment that would reward utilities for conservation or for using renewable energy sources.

When it comes to nuclear power, however, Moorhead has been more in tune with Republican administrations.

In the 100th Congress, he continued to represent the interests of the power industry; he pushed for renewal of the Price-Anderson nuclear insurance law, which protects nuclear power producers from the financial consequences of serious nuclear disasters. Moorhead also opposed an unsuccessful effort by liberals to bar the Nuclear Regulatory Commission from relaxing its rules to allow the Shoreham (N.Y.) and Seabrook (N.H.) nuclear power plants to open.

On the Judiciary Committee, Moorhead typically has been a reliable vote for Republican administrations and business interests.

On civil rights legislation Moorhead has

California 27

Northeastern Los Angeles County; Pasadena; Burbank

Set in the rolling San Gabriel Mountains, the 27th is dominated on the north by the Angeles National Forest and spread evenly with suburbs through the south.

The district is a mirror of the demographic changes that California has seen in the past decade. Immigration has transformed formerly WASPy areas into rainbows of ethnicity. This development, along with new areas the 27th gained in redistricting, make Rep. Moorhead's once reliably Republican seat much more competitive. After years of routinely winning re-election by huge margins, Moorhead drew only 50 percent of the vote in 1992.

The major cities of the 27th are Burbank, Glendale and Pasadena.

Burbank, a city of 94,000 with a sizable share of conservative-minded Democrats, took a big hit in 1990 when Lockheed began closing its 64-year-old plant and moving or laying off the 12,000 workers there. The area is still heavily blue-collar, but it now relies more on its entertainment industry, including the NBC and Disney studios. Burbank's City Council has been active in trying to fill the void left by Lockheed. Economic pain has served to moderate the city's traditional bias against growth: One idea floated has been to build an arena on the Lockheed site to lure the L.A. Clippers basketball team.

Glendale, with 180,000 residents, is the largest city in the district and the third largest in Los Angeles County after L.A. proper and Long Beach. A decade or so ago, it was a sleepy, WASPy bedroom community, but no more. There has been an influx of about 35,000 Soviet Armenians since 1985, and large numbers of Filipinos, Koreans and Hispanics have settled here; now, less than half of Glendale's public school students speak English as a first language. The Soviet Armenians are joining a small, much wealthier, Iranian Armenian community that has lived in Glendale since the shah lost his grip on power in the late 1970s.

These changes have taken their toll on the city's onetime habit of supporting the GOP: In 1992, Bill Clinton won the city by about 100 votes — unthinkable just a few years ago. Moorhead carried the city by a reasonably comfortable 9,200 votes.

While Burbank and Glendale are less than 2 percent black, 19 percent of Pasadena's 132,000 residents are black; it is the heavily black and Hispanic half of Pasadena that Moorhead gained in 1992 redistricting. The only part of Pasadena outside Moorhead's district is a heavily Republican sliver to the east, in Rep. David Dreier's 28th District. The city includes many engineering firms that have flocked to CalTech and its Jet Propulsion Laboratory, which is a bit to the northwest in La Cañada.

Pasadena is flanked by the working-class suburbs of Altadena on the north and South Pasadena to the southwest, and by the very wealthy community of San Marino to the southeast. Altadena is 39 percent black and overwhelmingly Democratic, while South Pasadena is only 3 percent black and has always tended toward Republicans. San Marino is a GOP mainstay.

1990 Population: 572,594. White 406,235 (71%), Black 47,493 (8%), Other 118,866 (21%). Hispanic origin 56,154 (10%). 18 and over 445,260 (78%), 62 and over 88,053 (15%). Median age: 34.

striven to limit the scope and timing of discrimination suits by employees, arguing that the federal system is overloaded.

Moorhead is the ranking Republican on Judiciary's Subcommittee on Intellectual Property and Judicial Administration, which oversees patent, trademark and copyright law.

During the 100th Congress, Moorhead sponsored the administration version of legislation to implement the Berne Convention, an international agreement protecting artists' intellectual property rights.

At the start of the 103rd, Moorhead filed bills authorizing the Immigration and Naturalization Service to accept volunteers and appropriating money for several thousand more Border Patrol personnel.

Early in his career, he had an opportunity to be in the spotlight as the Judiciary Committee debated the impeachment of President Richard Nixon in 1974. But he played only a minor role. Moorhead backed Nixon on every impeachment count, changing his mind only with the release of the "smoking gun" tape.

At Home: Since entering the political arena in 1966, Moorhead has never lost an election. But the 1990s show signs of being his toughest decade to date. Although he won comfortably with 60 percent of the vote in 1990, it was his lowest vote share since 1974. And in 1992, redistricting moved his Glendale-Burbank-Pasadena district somewhat to the south, leaving some of his most Republican neighborhoods behind.

As a result, Moorhead dropped to 50 percent of the vote for the first time. His share was still more than 10 percentage points greater than that of Democrat Doug Kahn, who ran a spirited race but was underfinanced from start to finish. Democrats will be hard pressed to find a more favorable year in California than 1992, but Moorhead is likely to continue to attract active challengers.

Born in Southern California, Moorhead was reared in Glendale and worked as a lawyer there for 15 years before entering the Legislature. After three terms in Sacramento, he set his sights on Congress. When eight-term Republican Rep. H. Allen Smith decided to retire from Congress in 1972, nine candidates entered the GOP primary.

The contest quickly narrowed to two: Moorhead and Dr. Bill McColl, a Covina surgeon who once had played end for Stanford University and the Chicago Bears. Moorhead, who had carried the west side of the district in state Legislature elections, was the favorite of the local party officials. McColl had narrowly lost a primary to John H. Rousselot in the neighboring 24th District in 1970. The result was an easy nomination for Moorhead and an even easier general election.

Moorhead's one moment of political concern came in 1982. After that year's redistricting plan dissolved Rousselot's neighboring district, giving part of it to Moorhead, Rousselot toyed with the idea of challenging Moorhead in a primary. Rousselot was dean of the California Republican delegation and had a nationwide network of loyal conservative supporters. But he decided instead to run in the heavily Democratic 30th, where he eventually lost. Moorhead survived to become dean of the state's GOP delegation himself.

Committees

Energy & Commerce (Ranking)
Oversight & Investigations

Judiciary (2nd of 14 Republicans)
Intellectual Property & Judicial Administration (ranking); Economic & Commercial Law

Elections

1992 General		
Carlos J. Moorhead (R)	105,521	(50%)
Doug Kahn (D)	83,805	(39%)
Jesse A. Moorman (GREEN)	11,003	(5%)
Margaret L. Edwards (PFP)	7,329	(3%)
Dennis Decherd (LIBERT)	4,790	(2%)
1992 Primary		
Carlos J. Moorhead (R)	37,172	(62%)
Louis Morelli (R)	10,354	(17%)
Barry L. Hatch (R)	6,622	(11%)
Lionel Allen Jr. (R)	6,141	(10%)
1990 General		
Carlos J. Moorhead (R)	108,634	(60%)
David Bayer (D)	61,630	(34%)
William H. Wilson (LIBERT)	6,702	(4%)
Jan B. Tucker (PFP)	3,963	(2%)

Previous Winning Percentages: **1988** (70%) **1986** (74%) **1984** (85%) **1982** (74%) **1980** (64%) **1978** (65%) **1976** (63%) **1974** (56%) **1972** (57%)

District Vote for President

1992
D 98,057 (44%)
R 80,986 (37%)
I 42,071 (19%)

Campaign Finance

	Receipts	Receipts from PACs		Expend-itures
1992				
Moorhead (R)	$448,791	$260,025	(58%)	$705,814
Kahn (D)	$151,792	$26,465	(17%)	$167,898
Moorman (GREEN)	$12,076	0		$10,097
1990				
Moorhead (R)	$444,157	$231,350	(52%)	$400,109
Bayer (D)	$40,872	$1,975	(5%)	$40,303

Key Votes

1993	
Require parental notification of minors' abortions	Y
Require unpaid family and medical leave	N
Approve national "motor voter" registration bill	N
Approve budget increasing taxes and reducing deficit	N
Approve economic stimulus plan	N
1992	
Approve balanced-budget constitutional amendment	Y
Close down space station program	N
Approve U.S. aid for former Soviet Union	N
Allow shifting funds from defense to domestic programs	N
1991	
Extend unemployment benefits using deficit financing	N
Approve waiting period for handgun purchases	N
Authorize use of force in Persian Gulf	Y

Voting Studies

	Presidential Support		Party Unity		Conservative Coalition	
Year	**S**	**O**	**S**	**O**	**S**	**O**
1992	85	14	97	2	98	2
1991	82	15	95	3	95	0
1990	74	26	93	6	98	2
1989	72	24	88	10	95	2
1988	73	24	98	1	97	0
1987	71	27	91	6	86	12
1986	82	17	92	7	96	4
1985	80	20	96	3	93	5
1984	67	28	91	7	90	7
1983	78	16	92	3	96	2
1982	78	21	92	5	96	3
1981	75	18	91	4	92	4

Interest Group Ratings

Year	ADA	AFL-CIO	CCUS	ACU
1992	5	25	75	100
1991	5	8	90	100
1990	6	8	86	96
1989	0	0	100	93
1988	10	7	100	96
1987	4	0	100	96
1986	0	7	100	95
1985	5	0	95	90
1984	0	15	87	100
1983	0	0	85	100
1982	0	0	90	96
1981	5	0	94	100

28 David Dreier (R)

Of Claremont — Elected 1980; 7th Term

Born: July 5, 1952, Kansas City, Mo.
Education: Claremont McKenna College, B.A. 1975; The Claremont Graduate School, M.A. 1976.
Occupation: Real estate manager and developer.
Family: Single.
Religion: Christian Scientist.
Political Career: GOP nominee for U.S. House, 1978.
Capitol Office: 411 Cannon Bldg. 20515; 225-2305.

In Washington: After a dozen years in the House, Dreier is identified with no particular legislative cause beyond the baseline conservative agenda. But he seems perfectly suited to the role he has assumed as a Republican on the Rules Committee, the role of opposition scold.

He was swept into Congress on the same tide that brought Ronald Reagan to the White House. Over time he used his verbal skills to win the confidence of his GOP colleagues and their trust in him to present the party line. He was appointed to Rules at the start of the 102nd Congress, where his anti-government philosophy meshed well with the confrontational conservatism of the new ranking Republican on Rules, Gerald B. H. Solomon of New York.

Early in 1993, Dreier also became ranking House Republican on a special Joint Committee on the Organization of Congress, where he quickly used his position to berate Speaker Thomas S. Foley for what he perceived to be general Democratic arrogance.

Dreier has had to battle the perception among some colleagues — especially Democrats — that he spends too much time in the sun. But given his age, should he choose to stay in the House he could be a central player in the Republican hierarchy for years to come.

To his benefit, Dreier has married his strong conservative philosophy to an affable demeanor that softens his regular complaints about Democrats abusing their majority power. He has a style that would appear almost courtly, were he not so youthful. On the floor, he identifies colleagues of either party not only by state but hometown. His newsletters to constituents are one- or two-page, hand-printed missives, often drafted on plane flights home from Washington to Southern California. And he has a habit of sending handwritten notes to just about anyone who catches his interest, even journalists he sees on local television.

Dreier manages to express his disgust at the latest Democratic Party outrage without visibly losing his temper. It is part of his job to object when the Democrats use the Rules Committee to impose sharp restrictions on floor amendments, but he tries to be both deft and emphatic in his efforts to embarrass the majority. In June 1992, Democrats crafted a restrictive rule for a "motor voter" bill requiring states to register people to vote when they applied for a driver's permit or welfare. "It's the height of irony that the Democratic leadership, in a half-hearted attempt to bring to the floor a bill to expand voting rights and democracy, does so under a tyrannical rule," Dreier complained.

Dreier is nothing if not persistent on Rules. He energetically makes the Republicans' case to allow floor amendments, even when he knows he will lose. And sometimes, he wins. Over the objections of Rules Committee Chairman Joe Moakley of Massachusetts, the committee went along with Dreier on a 6-5 vote to permit a Republican amendment to a fiscal 1992 appropriations bill. The amendment would have increased spending on a pet project of Jack F. Kemp, then the secretary of Housing and Urban Development, that was intended to boost home ownership by public housing tenants.

It was the rarest of events for a Republican to roll a Democratic Rules chairman, given the 9-4 Democratic margin on the committee. To win, Dreier had to persuade two Democrats — Butler Derrick of South Carolina and Alan Wheat of Missouri — to vote with the four Republicans. Both voted against the amendment on the floor.

Prior to joining Rules, Dreier used his positions on the Banking and Small Business committees to promote the privatization of government services and elimination of federal agencies he deems unnecessary — the Small Business Administration, for instance. Dreier brought his distaste for bureaucracy to the 1988 debate over aid for the homeless. "We are creating a permanent homeless infrastructure in this country," he said. "What we essentially created is another grass-roots lobby that Congress will be unable to say 'no' to in the future."

He remains a strong proponent of unfettered banking, advocating removal of barriers that he contends restrain credit and unnecessarily pro-

California 28

Northeastern Los Angeles suburbs

The Angeles National Forest and its mountains run through the northern half of the 28th District. The 210 Freeway, also known as the Foothill Freeway, runs through the lower half, an area spread evenly with Los Angeles bedroom communities.

From west to east along the 210, the district takes in a sliver of eastern Pasadena and the cities of Sierra Madre, Arcadia, Monrovia, Covina and San Dimas. La Verne and Claremont lie farther east. Temple City is south of Arcadia, and West Covina and Walnut are to the south of Covina.

Much of the development here arrived right after World War II, and many of the people who arrived then are still here. In large part, these are people whose parents grew up nearby and whose children are now populating Orange County and San Bernardino.

The development here is the comfortable suburbia typical of Southern California — "Little mountains and little shrubberies," according to a resident.

Arcadia, a city of 48,000 with a 1989 per capita income of more than $25,000, boasts of its "beautiful homes, tree-lined streets, magnificent gardens and its more than 3,489 private swimming pools."

Driving through the district, it is hard to tell when one city has been left behind and another entered. The district just misses some much less wealthy areas, such as El Monte, southeast of Temple City. The industry that does exist here is confined to small defense subcontractors and service industries.

The city of Duarte, south of Monrovia, is known for its City of Hope National Medical Center, a nonprofit treatment and research hospital specializing in rare medical problems that treats its patients for free. Bradbury, a town of about 800 residents set in the hills just north of Duarte, had a per capita income of $46,361 in 1989.

While the residents of the 28th primarily identify themselves as citizens of the separate towns in which they live, they also identify as residents of the San Gabriel Valley. Although many of them commute to downtown Los Angeles for work, they do not consider themselves part of that city — so much so that residents have agitated unsuccessfully for years to declare the San Gabriel Valley a county of its own. The cities within the valley work closely together on such issues as transportation and water. A light rail line stops in Covina and continues west into Los Angeles.

Politically, the district is spread as evenly as its buildings. Republican Rep. Dreier won in 1992 by a steady margin across the district. Like in many of Los Angeles' suburbs, residents here tend to be socially moderate and economically conservative.

Dreier's strength in the district provided coattails for George Bush in 1992. He pulled 17 percentage points more support than Bush did, helping Bush win the district that year with 41 percent of the vote to Bill Clinton's 38 percent and Ross Perot's 21 percent.

1990 Population: 572,927. White 406,342 (71%), Black 32,778 (6 %), Other 133,807 (23%). Hispanic origin 56,398 (10%). 18 and over 423,910 (74%), 62 and over 77,009 (13%). Median age: 33.

tect the market positions of some financial institutions at the expense of banks. While on the Banking Committee, Dreier supported allowing banks to sell and underwrite insurance, a position that now puts him in conflict on Rules with Solomon, a big supporter of preserving the insurance industry's status quo.

Though he made little headway with those proposals, Dreier has been extraordinarily successful in another area of politics: fundraising. During the 1980s, contributions from banking interests helped him rank as one of the top money raisers in the House. Nor was his campaign-financing ability diminished by his move to Rules. He ended the 1991-92 election cycle with more than $2 million cash on hand, second only to Democrat Charles E. Schumer of New York. Dreier does not talk of aspirations beyond the House, but the size of his treasury fuels speculation that he has in mind a statewide bid if his current career becomes tiresome.

At Home: Dreier has piled up so much cash not only by raising money aggressively but by spending modestly in his routine re-elections. After a narrow victory over a Democratic incumbent in 1980, Dreier got a safe seat in redistricting. A decade later, a new redistricting plan left Dreier to run in a different but almost equally compatible district. Despite a general weakening of the Republican vote in the state, Dreier won in 1992 with 58 percent — running 12 points over GOP registration in the 28th District and 17 percentage points ahead of George Bush. Should he decide to stay in the House, Dreier should find the going easier as the decade progresses.

Dreier first came to Congress after waging a four-year campaign against Democratic Rep. Jim Lloyd. Using the influential GOP establishment linked to the Claremont Colleges as his springboard, Dreier started in 1978. Underfinanced and only 26 years old, Dreier still came within 12,000 votes of Lloyd. Dreier's 1980 bid showed greater maturity and more effort to discuss issues. He followed much of the national GOP agenda, supporting the Kemp-Roth tax cut and Reagan's presidential candidacy.

National GOP sources, rating Lloyd the most vulnerable Democratic incumbent in the state, helped Dreier outspend him by almost 2- to-1 and brought in Reagan to campaign for him. This time the 12,000-vote margin had Dreier on top.

Dreier ended up in another fight two years later — with a fellow Republican. Redistricting had moved his Pomona political base out of the 35th, where he had won in 1980, into the neighboring 33rd. But the 33rd was also home to GOP Rep. Wayne Grisham.

The primary pitted a sedate, casual Grisham against an aggressive, dynamic Dreier. With voters offered different personalities, not different ideologies, Dreier's organization and fundraising brought him a solid victory.

After averaging about 70 percent of the vote from 1984 to 1988, he slipped slightly to 64 percent in 1990.

Committees

Joint Organization of Congress (Co-Vice Chairman)

Rules (3rd of 4 Republicans)
Rules of the House (ranking)

Elections

1992 General		
David Dreier (R)	122,353	(58%)
Al Wachtel (D)	76,525	(37%)
Walter Sheasby (GREEN)	6,233	(3%)
Thomas J. Dominy (LIBERT)	4,271	(2%)
1990 General		
David Dreier (R)	101,336	(64%)
Georgia Houston Webb (D)	49,981	(31%)
Gail Lightfoot (LIBERT)	7,840	(5%)

Previous Winning Percentages: **1988** (69%) **1986** (72%) **1984** (71%) **1982** (65%) **1980** (52%)

District Vote for President

1992

D	82,958 (38%)
R	90,644 (41%)
I	45,623 (21%)

Campaign Finance

	Receipts	Receipts from PACs		Expenditures
1992				
Dreier (R)	$646,323	$131,350	(20%)	$290,128
Wachtel (D)	$23,564	$2,000	(8%)	$25,261
1990				
Dreier (R)	$591,313	$100,276	(17%)	$172,451
Webb (D)	$29,612	$2,950	(10%)	$29,177

Key Votes

1993	
Require parental notification of minors' abortions	?
Require unpaid family and medical leave	N
Approve national "motor voter" registration bill	N
Approve budget increasing taxes and reducing deficit	N
Approve economic stimulus plan	N
1992	
Approve balanced-budget constitutional amendment	Y
Close down space station program	N
Approve U.S. aid for former Soviet Union	N
Allow shifting funds from defense to domestic programs	N
1991	
Extend unemployment benefits using deficit financing	N
Approve waiting period for handgun purchases	N
Authorize use of force in Persian Gulf	Y

Voting Studies

	Presidential Support		Party Unity		Conservative Coalition	
Year	**S**	**O**	**S**	**O**	**S**	**O**
1992	84	13	90	8	98	0
1991	84	15	89	10	100	0
1990	73	27	94	6	94	6
1989	76	24	77	21	83	17
1988	76	18	89	4	89	5
1987	80	18	95	5	91	9
1986	83	16	95	4	94	2
1985	84	14	92	4	91	9
1984	73	25	95	4	88	8
1983	85	15	97	2	97	2
1982	78	17	87	2	95	1
1981	78	21	95	5	93	7

Interest Group Ratings

Year	ADA	AFL-CIO	CCUS	ACU
1992	0	8	75	100
1991	0	0	90	100
1990	17	8	79	83
1989	0	0	100	96
1988	5	0	92	100
1987	4	0	100	96
1986	0	0	100	95
1985	10	0	95	90
1984	5	8	81	92
1983	0	0	84	100
1982	0	0	95	100
1981	5	0	95	100

29 Henry A. Waxman (D)

Of Los Angeles — Elected 1974; 10th Term

Born: Sept. 12, 1939, Los Angeles, Calif.
Education: U. of California, Los Angeles, B.A. 1961, J.D. 1964.
Occupation: Lawyer.
Family: Wife, Janet Kessler; one child, one stepchild.
Religion: Jewish.
Political Career: Calif. Assembly, 1969-75.
Capitol Office: 2408 Rayburn Bldg. 20515; 225-3976.

In Washington: Through 12 years of Republican rule in the White House, Waxman counseled patience, saying, "My time has not yet arrived." With the 103rd Congress, however, the alarm clock is ringing; and Waxman knows this may be the moment for him to achieve his goal: universal health insurance.

With Democrat Bill Clinton now in the White House and also promoting an expansive health-care agenda, Waxman has never looked better positioned as chairman of the Energy and Commerce Subcommittee on Health and the Environment. All this opportunity, of course, poses a new kind of challenge and makes the legislative process harder for one subcommittee chairman to control. Still, he has to wonder: If not now, when?

"God never meant liberals to be stupid," Waxman once said, and he lives to be proof of that. He sets such ambitious policy aims that colleagues might consider him a pie-in-the-sky fool if they were not by now so familiar with his technique of taking a small slice at a time until years later he is holding the whole pie — even in the face of spending retrenchment. Persistence and patience are his strengths, and he uses both to outflank both his adversaries and his presumed allies, such as California Democrat Pete Stark, who chairs the rival Ways and Means Subcommittee on Health.

On the matter of air pollution, a critical issue in his smog-plagued district, the 101st Congress was Waxman's time. After nearly a decade of delay, Congress finally passed sweeping clean air legislation that achieved many of Waxman's long-held goals.

A monumental accomplishment, the revitalized Clean Air Act was just one of Waxman's triumphs in the 101st. He also passed bills to expand Medicaid coverage for poor women and children; to provide money for AIDS treatment; and to mandate nutrition labeling. But there was also a major disappointment: the repeal of an earlier Waxman effort, catastrophic health insurance for the elderly.

In the 102nd Congress, he was instrumental in getting provisions into a broad housing bill to cut down on lead poisoning from paint and other sources. He also pushed to enactment new standards for mammograms and the renewal, with a one-third increase in its authorized spending level, of a preventive-health block grant to states. He also suffered a loss at the hands of President Bush, who vetoed Waxman's bill to repeal an administration ban on fetal tissue research.

But while he took his share of lumps, Waxman bided his time. Like his California mentor, the late Phillip Burton, Waxman believes that power exists to be used and that changing policy, rather than mere self-expression, is the ultimate liberal goal.

Unlike Burton, he does not have the kind of explosive temper that alienates as many members as can be cultivated through personal favors. Waxman is privately passionate about his issues, and in pursuing them he takes on some of Congress' most formidable and exasperating members, such as GOP Sen. Jesse Helms of North Carolina or House Energy and Commerce Chairman John D. Dingell, Democrat of Michigan. Yet publicly, he is all but unflappable.

Waxman has chaired Energy and Commerce's Health and the Environment Subcommittee since 1979. From there he fended off Reagan-era attacks on the health budget and waged war for cleaner air. In so doing, he won a raft of small victories, despite the pressures of huge budget deficits and public skepticism about social welfare spending.

Throughout the 12 years of the Reagan and Bush administrations, Waxman was a key force in dramatically expanding Medicaid, succeeding mostly by tucking health-care provisions for poor women and infants into the massive "reconciliation" bills that are regularly part of Congress' budget-cutting routine. Such bills — by their size, importance and special protection under congressional rules — offer Waxman's initiatives safety from filibusters, killer amendments and vetoes.

In the 101st Congress, aided by some Senate Democrats, Waxman again used the budget bill to expand Medicaid coverage. One change raised from 6 to 18 the age to which states must

California 29

West Los Angeles County; Santa Monica; West Hollywood

The 29th begins at the coast in Santa Monica and curves northeast to take in some of California's best-known areas: West Los Angeles, Beverly Hills, West Hollywood, most of Hollywood, the Hollywood Hills and just a bit of the San Fernando Valley.

This affluent, predominantly white district is heavily Democratic. Rep. Waxman ran well throughout the 29th in 1992, racking up 57 percent of the vote in Santa Monica, 65 percent in Beverly Hills and 68 percent in West Hollywood.

The city of Santa Monica is strikingly more liberal than its coastal counterparts south of Los Angeles. The city gave 55 percent of its vote to Walter F. Mondale in 1984, 65 percent to Michael S. Dukakis in 1988 and 63 percent to Bill Clinton in 1992. George Bush and Ross Perot took 21 percent and 15 percent, respectively.

Santa Monica voters in 1988 supported a proposition — which was soundly defeated statewide — to use fines paid by violators of housing and restaurant codes to increase funding for the hungry and the homeless.

Although Santa Monica's 87,000 residents are mostly affluent, the city has a large renter population; 75 percent of the city's housing units are occupied by renters, who have brought about very strict rent-control laws over the years. It boasts substantially more commercial activity than Malibu, its northern neighbor, with several very successful commercial-industrial parks, shopping malls and regular street fairs.

The city and its environs grew steadily in the 1980s; Pacific Palisades, just north of Santa Monica right on the coast, has some large new developments, but because so much of the area is already fully developed, much of the new construction consists of knocking down existing structures and replacing them.

Heading out of the city on Santa Monica Boulevard, the flat land turns to the rolling foothills of the Santa Monica Mountains. Set onto the hills' southern slopes are Westwood, home to the University of California-Los Angeles (with 36,400 students), and Bel Air, the retirement home of the Reagans.

Just past Westwood is Beverly Hills, with its fabulously elaborate homes north of Sunset Boulevard and low-rise (but high-rent) apartment buildings south of it.

A key to Waxman's success here is the heavily Jewish area of Fairfax, just east of Beverly Hills. Its residents have supported him devotedly for 10 straight elections.

Further east along the boulevard is West Hollywood, a city of 36,000 residents that incorporated in 1984. It has a large, politically well-organized homosexual population and a high concentration of senior citizens.

Before reapportionment, many of the motion-picture industry's heavyweights were packed into one district. Now they are split between two: the 29th retains the bulk of the Hollywood area and all of Universal City to the north, but the 30th District pokes up just enough to take in the Paramount Studios lot and the southeastern side of Hollywood — including the eastern half of the intersection of Hollywood Boulevard and Vine Street, the symbolic center of the movie industry.

1990 Population: 571,566. White 478,696 (84%), Black 19,931 (3%), Other 72,939 (13%). Hispanic origin 75,315 (13%). 18 and over 495,536 (87%), 62 and over 106,905 (19%). Median age: 37.

cover all poor children. At Waxman's insistence, Medicaid coverage beginning in 1995 will also be expanded to cover people just above the official poverty line.

Waxman has seen his share of defeats. In late 1987, when he declared that he was not bound by health spending limits in a budget-summit agreement between President Ronald Reagan and Congress, House Democratic leaders bridled him into submission. The next month, in a budget conference, opponents swamped his far-reaching proposals to stem infant mortality.

The following year, he helped write the law providing the elderly with Medicare coverage against catastrophic illnesses. Waxman was largely responsible for major provisions such as granting first-time coverage for outpatient prescription drugs. But senior citizens soon wailed in protest over the new law, which increased premiums and imposed a surtax on wealthier recipients. Early in the 101st Congress, Waxman helped thwart an effort in his subcommittee to repeal the law's controversial surtax. The repeal movement grew more insistent, however. After a failed attempt to salvage portions of the law, Waxman, too, backed repeal rather than accept a replacement measure.

Many of Waxman's successes in the conservative climate of recent years have been defensive. But even on defense, Waxman is more interested in results than debating points. In 1985, he vehemently opposed the Gramm-Rudman anti-deficit law but did not waste time trying to kill a bill sure to pass. Instead, he worked in the House and in conference with the

Senate to exempt his favorite health programs from the law's threatened cuts.

During the later years of the Bush administration, Waxman repeatedly blasted the White House Council on Competitiveness, chaired by Vice President Dan Quayle, for its role — deemed illegal by Waxman — in blocking congressionally mandated health and environmental regulations.

In recent years, Waxman has led the House effort against AIDS, but it is a fight that taxes his usual legislative patience, given the deadliness of the disease. He is stymied not only by budget constraints but also by objections from conservatives such as Helms. Waxman outlasted one nemesis, California Rep. William E. Dannemeyer, ranking Republican on Waxman's subcommittee in the 102nd, who left the House to run, unsuccessfully, for the Senate.

Waxman engineered passage in the 100th Congress of the first comprehensive AIDS bill, authorizing money for education, testing and treatment. But to achieve that, he had to drop two priorities — confidentiality for AIDS tests and a ban on discrimination against victims.

When Congress sits down to write a health bill, Waxman and his occasional adversary Dingell may well be in near-lockstep on its terms. That was not the case with the 1990 Clean Air Act. Its passage culminated a perennial battle between the two: Waxman sought tougher measures against acid rain and urban smog; Dingell represented the interests of Detroit's auto industry and, to a lesser extent, Midwestern states with coal-burning power plants.

Their tussle dated back to 1982, when the law was up for renewal. Dingell — along with the Reagan administration, utilities and heavy industry — sought to relax emission standards. But Waxman shrewdly prolonged his subcommittee's work and repeated his stalling tactics after the bill finally reached full committee. Later, Dingell employed a similar strategy to thwart Waxman's efforts to move tougher air pollution rules.

As the 1980s progressed, however, Waxman took hope from growing voter concern about the environment. Political pressure for new air pollution laws mounted when Bush proposed legislation to the 101st Congress. With passage of some new clean air bill looking increasingly certain, Dingell began to engage Waxman in a contest to shape the coming law.

There was competition — and some collaboration — on many levels. While many Democrats on committee walked on eggshells with Dingell, Waxman would gavel him down if, during subcommittee deliberations, Dingell spoke beyond the fixed time limit. Waxman skillfully picked off members to build winning coalitions on several motor-vehicle provisions Dingell opposed.

Waxman suffered some defeats at Dingell's hand but did not make a religion of opposing him. Both men stunned fellow committee members when, in October 1989, they reached a deal on auto emissions standards.

Waxman was thought to have a better chance of winning a floor vote. But he gave ground, recognizing the uncertainty and the value of having Dingell on board. The end result was weaker than Waxman would have liked in areas such as alternative fuels for automobiles, but it was still considered landmark environmental legislation, tougher on pollution than the administration had proposed.

Waxman originally won his subcommittee chairmanship in 1979 with hardball politics. He pioneered a practice that has since become routine in leadership contests, raising money from his wealthy campaign supporters and distributing it to Energy and Commerce Democrats who would choose the subcommittee chairmen. He was accused of trying to buy the chair, but he prevailed over highly respected Richardson Preyer of North Carolina, 15-12.

With his own re-election campaigns mere formalities, Waxman has built political influence by helping others win elections. In 1982, the Los Angeles-based organization he cofounded with Rep. Howard L. Berman aided six of the California House delegation's eight new Democrats (including Berman).

At Home: The 1992 round of redistricting in California was all about creating districts with compactness and community of interest. That exercise inconvenienced some members, but not Waxman. The new 29th is only marginally different from his comfortable old berth (previously numbered the 24th). It is still concentrated in the western reaches and suburbs of Los Angeles County, and it has always had community of interest to spare. The electorate here is largely Jewish, primarily liberal and attached (emotionally if not always economically) to the entertainment industry. Perhaps the biggest change over the years in which Waxman has represented the district is the rise of gay activism.

Not only are Waxman's constituents politically involved, they are frequently wealthy. And that has enabled him to build not only an impregnable position for himself (his constituents are 58 percent Democratic, and he got 61 percent in the 1992 election) but also an impressive apparatus for extending his political influence far and wide. Waxman's political machinations have long been a joint venture with Berman, a college chum who joined him in the House in 1982.

The Waxman-Berman alliance was originally forged at UCLA, when the two budding politicians became active in the state's Federation of Young Democrats. Their first visible success came in 1968, when Waxman challenged Democratic Assemblyman Lester McMillan in a primary.

McMillan had been in office 26 years and was nearing retirement. Rather than waiting until the seat opened up, Waxman decided to take on the incumbent. With massive volunteer help, much of it recruited from the ranks of the Young Democrats, Waxman beat McMillan with 64 percent of the vote.

That election saw the beginning of what has since become a Waxman-Berman trademark — computerized mailings. Each voter is identified by a variety of sociopolitical characteristics and given a campaign pitch specifically tailored to his or her interests.

The "machine" label was affixed in 1972, when Waxman, then a two-term assemblyman, lent his muscle to help Berman win an Assembly seat. By 1974, the operation was functioning so smoothly that Waxman had little trouble winning a new U.S. House seat created with him in mind. He has had even less trouble retaining it.

In 1984, Waxman had political worries of a different sort. Ever since 1981, California Republicans had been trying to find a way to undo the redistricting plan drawn by Democratic Rep. Burton, which gave Democrats 28 California seats in the House. The GOP efforts in 1984 centered on a ballot initiative put forward by Republican Gov. George Deukmejian to dissolve the existing map before the 1986 elections and place the task of drawing new lines in the hands of a commission of retired judges.

The Democratic campaign against the measure was largely financed through the efforts of Waxman and his west Los Angeles House allies Berman and Mel Levine.

The battle was revisited in 1990, when state Republicans backed a pair of initiatives aimed at restricting the influence of the Democratic-controlled Legislature in the post-1990 round of redistricting. Waxman again helped raise money for the Democrats' anti-initiative efforts, and both ballot proposals went down to resounding defeats.

But the team lost on another front in 1990 when it failed to derail another statewide initiative setting term limits for legislators. The initiative passed and was upheld by the courts, spawning a successor initiative in 1992 that extended the limits to members of Congress.

Committees

Energy & Commerce (2nd of 27 Democrats)
Health & the Environment (chairman); Oversight & Investigations

Government Operations (4th of 25 Democrats)
Human Resources & Intergovernmental Relations

Elections

1992 General		
Henry A. Waxman (D)	160,312	(61%)
Mark A. Robbins (R)	67,141	(26%)
David Davis (I)	15,445	(6%)
Susan C. Davies (PFP)	13,888	(5%)
Felix Tsvi Rogin (LIBERT)	4,699	(2%)
1992 Primary		
Henry A. Waxman (D)	72,283	(84%)
Scott M. Gaulke (D)	13,350	(16%)
1990 General		
Henry A. Waxman (D)	71,562	(69%)
John N. Cowles (R)	26,607	(26%)
Maggie Phair (PFP)	5,706	(5%)

Previous Winning Percentages: **1988** (72%) **1986** (88%) **1984** (63%) **1982** (65%) **1980** (64%) **1978** (63%) **1976** (68%) **1974** (64%)

District Vote for President

	1992	
D	183,233	(66%)
R	55,924	(20%)
I	37,217	(13%)

Campaign Finance

	Receipts	Receipts from PACs		Expend-itures
1992				
Waxman (D)	$682,214	$402,915	(59%)	$718,695
Robbins (R)	$148,419	$1,643	(1%)	$148,274
1990				
Waxman (D)	$500,847	$315,400	(63%)	$287,505
Cowles (R)	$1,835	0		$1,830

Key Votes

1993	
Require parental notification of minors' abortions	N
Require unpaid family and medical leave	Y
Approve national "motor voter" registration bill	Y
Approve budget increasing taxes and reducing deficit	Y
Approve economic stimulus plan	Y
1992	
Approve balanced-budget constitutional amendment	N
Close down space station program	N
Approve U.S. aid for former Soviet Union	Y
Allow shifting funds from defense to domestic programs	Y
1991	
Extend unemployment benefits using deficit financing	Y
Approve waiting period for handgun purchases	Y
Authorize use of force in Persian Gulf	N

Voting Studies

	Presidential Support		Party Unity		Conservative Coalition	
Year	**S**	**O**	**S**	**O**	**S**	**O**
1992	16	81	90	5	13	85
1991	27	63	84	6	14	70
1990	20	75	90	4	6	93
1989	28	63	88	2	5	85
1988	21	66	79	4	11	71
1987	18	74	84	3	9	84
1986	12	86	87	4	2	92
1985	28	71	86	3	11	84
1984	25	66	80	5	5	93
1983	22	71	84	3	6	85
1982	36	58	87	7	12	86
1981	25	63	79	5	4	88

Interest Group Ratings

Year	ADA	AFL-CIO	CCUS	ACU
1992	95	82	25	0
1991	90	83	10	0
1990	100	92	21	4
1989	100	100	30	4
1988	90	93	21	0
1987	92	79	17	10
1986	95	92	20	5
1985	95	94	27	16
1984	100	77	42	10
1983	95	94	25	5
1982	95	90	14	5
1981	85	77	11	0

30 Xavier Becerra (D)

Of Los Angeles — Elected 1992; 1st Term

Born: Jan. 26, 1958, Sacramento, Calif.
Education: Stanford U., A.B. 1980, J.D. 1984.
Occupation: Lawyer.
Family: Wife, Carolina Reyes.
Religion: Roman Catholic.
Political Career: Calif. Assembly, 1990-92.
Capitol Office: 1710 Longworth Bldg. 20515; 225-6235.

The Path to Washington: Elected to Congress at age 34, Becerra is brash and confident, and has all the attributes of a young man in a hurry. Despite the impatience of his rapid rise, he has yet to stumble along the road to success.

In 1990, Becerra left Sacramento, where he had been a state deputy attorney general and legislative aide, and moved into the Los Angeles community of Monterey Park to win election to the California Assembly. He was not content to finish his first term in the Legislature before launching a campaign for this open House seat, once again in a district not his home.

Becerra was recruited to serve this newly drawn, overwhelmingly Hispanic district by retiring Democrat Edward R. Roybal, who represented a major part of it for 30 years.

Becerra comes to Congress determined to be a player, bringing a decidedly liberal and ambitious agenda. Early on, he threw in with a handful of other Democrats in the Class of '92 who were determined not to be made backbenchers by the seniority system or the traditional lack of seats for freshmen on favored committees. When the 103rd organized, Democratic freshmen were given more choice seats, but Becerra was unable to take advantage.

Becerra had hoped to parlay his interest in dramatically overhauling the nation's health-care system into a seat on the Energy and Commerce Committee. But two California Democrats already held prized spots on that panel, including Health Subcommittee Chairman Henry A. Waxman, whose Los Angeles district abuts Becerra's on its western edge.

Instead, Becerra was given seats on the Judiciary Committee and the Education and Labor Committee, where he impressed observers early in the 103rd. Both he and fellow freshman Gene Green of Texas have shown interest in reforming Chapter 1, a federal program for educating disadvantaged children, which critics say deprives states with high population growth of their fair share of funding.

Becerra campaigned in favor of a more sweeping program of universal health insurance than that proffered during 1992 by Bill Clinton. Becerra, for instance, would establish the federal government as the sole payer, while Clinton's early plans called for an amalgam of government and private insurance.

Drawing on his experience, Becerra called for vastly increasing the federal role in education, particularly to promote early childhood development and to reverse high dropout rates. That same focus on prevention led him to promote a higher level of community policing as a means to combat urban crime.

And he was not timid about advocating a national industrial policy for job creation — not merely federal coordination of conversion of the defense industry to peacetime pursuits.

To pay for all this, Becerra called for dramatic defense cuts, particularly in personnel devoted to the protection of Europe and Japan.

Becerra spent heavily to win his seat, dragging a $100,000 deficit from a hard-fought primary into the general election, in which he had little difficulty. As a consequence of his own experience, he became even more enamored of campaign spending caps, linked to public financing of congressional elections.

Although drafted by Roybal for the 30th, Becerra was not his first choice. Henry Lozano, Roybal's top district aide, was deemed heir apparent. (Roybal's daughter, Lucille Roybal-Allard, was anointed for the adjoining 33rd, which includes another major portion of Roybal's old constituency.) But Lozano was not interested in a competitive race. He dropped out, and Becerra got Roybal's support.

He outran nine other candidates in the primary — including school board member Leticia Quezada, another popular rising star in the Latino community. Becerra won with not quite a third of the vote. Thanks to the backing of Roybal and other Latino leaders, Becerra was able to shrug off the carpetbagger label that some of his opponents tried to saddle him with. Typical for heavily Hispanic districts, and the 30th's precincts in particular, turnout was extremely low — only about 33,000 ballots cast. Becerra won the general election with 58 percent of the vote.

California 30

Central, East and Southeast Los Angeles

This very densely populated district starts just west of downtown Los Angeles, swings up and around, and comes down on downtown's eastern side. The western side of the 30th — East Hollywood, the mid-Wilshire area and especially Koreatown — was hit hard by the May 1992 riots.

Koreatown is in an extremely compact corner in the 30th's southwest region. More than 100,000 Koreans live here. The area sustained some of the worst damage in the city. Rioters torched more than 300 businesses, and damage was estimated at $200 million, according to local media reports.

Voter registration is low in the 30th, and even lower in Koreatown, described as a "transitional area," with many recent arrivals who are either illegal or applying for residency. The community itself is in transition; Koreans are just now beginning to flex their political muscle. Koreatown tends to look inward and does not rely on tourism as heavily as do Chinatown and Little Tokyo.

Just north of Koreatown is the mid-Wilshire area, with high-rise office buildings along Wilshire Boulevard and apartment buildings everywhere else. Farther north is East Hollywood, less dense and less affluent than the mid-Wilshire area. It is a lower-middle-class community; the homes get bigger and more expensive to the west, in the 29th District. These areas also suffered in the riots, but not nearly as much as Koreatown.

Dodger Stadium, north of downtown in Elysian Park, serves as the 30th's centerpiece. Elysian Park is a blue-collar neighborhood, with a moderate number of Hispanics. Directly west of Elysian Park are the communities of Silver Lake (half of which is in the 29th, half in the 30th) and Echo Park, which have strong reputations for community activism and liberal voting patterns. The areas are troubled by some gang activity and "tagging" — the local term for graffiti. An estimated one-fourth of their residents are homosexual.

On the northeastern end of the district is the bedroom community of Eagle Rock, a hilly, middle-class pocket of relative affluence that votes Democratic, but whose leanings are more toward the center than other parts of the 30th. Dropping down the eastern side leads to Highland Park, a heavily Hispanic, blue-collar area with a significant Mexican immigrant presence.

Across the Pasadena Freeway from Highland Park is Lincoln Heights, and on the district's southeastern tip, Boyle Heights. Both are more than 80 percent Hispanic, according to some estimates.

Between Boyle Heights and Lincoln Heights is tiny Mount Washington, the 30th's most affluent section, with great views of the city and a reputation for social activism.

The district is overwhelmingly Democratic, although it showed some of the strongest support in California for third-party candidates in 1992 House voting. Green Party and Peace and Freedom Party candidates scored 8 percent and 7 percent, respectively. Bill Clinton drew 63 percent in the 30th, far ahead of George Bush's 24 percent and Ross Perot's 13 percent.

1990 Population: 572,538. White 249,412 (44%), Black 20,039 (4%), Other 303,087 (53%). Hispanic origin 351,876 (61%). 18 and over 415,463 (73%), 62 and over 56,090 (10%). Median age: 29.

Committees

Education & Labor (17th of 28 Democrats)
Elementary, Secondary & Vocational Education; Labor-Management Relations; Postsecondary Education

Judiciary (21st of 21 Democrats)
Intellectual Property & Judicial Administration; International Law, Immigration & Refugees

Science, Space & Technology (31st of 33 Democrats)
Technology, Environment & Aviation

Campaign Finance

	Receipts	Receipts from PACs		Expend-itures
1992				
Becerra (D)	$387,385	$97,450	(25%)	$373,551
Waksberg (R)	$58,197	$2,150	(4%)	$57,063
Bonpane (GREEN)	$52,275	0		$40,115

Key Votes

1993	
Require parental notification of minors' abortions	N
Require unpaid family and medical leave	Y
Approve national "motor voter" registration bill	Y
Approve budget increasing taxes and reducing deficit	Y
Approve economic stimulus plan	Y

Elections

1992 General		
Xavier Becerra (D)	48,800	(58%)
Morry Waksberg (R)	20,034	(24%)
Blase Bonpane (GREEN)	6,315	(8%)
Elizabeth A. Nakano (PFP)	6,173	(7%)
Andrew Consalvo (LIBERT)	2,221	(3%)
1992 Primary		
Xavier Becerra (D)	10,417	(32%)
Leticia Quezada (D)	7,089	(22%)
Albert C. Lum (D)	5,128	(16%)
Jeff J. Penichet (D)	4,136	(13%)
Gonzalo Molina (D)	2,320	(7%)
Helen Hernandez (D)	1,908	(6%)
Roland R. Mora (D)	611	(2%)
Esca W. Smith (D)	444	(1%)
Mark Calney (D)	336	(1%)

District Vote for President

	1992	
D	56,378	(63%)
R	21,750	(24%)
I	11,842	(13%)

31 Matthew G. Martinez (D)

Of Monterey Park — Elected 1982; 6th Full Term

Born: Feb. 14, 1929, Walsenburg, Colo.
Education: Los Angeles Trade-Technical College, 1959.
Military Service: Marine Corps, 1947-50.
Occupation: Upholstery company owner.
Family: Wife, Elvira Yorba; five children.
Religion: Roman Catholic.
Political Career: Monterey Park City Council, 1974-80, mayor, 1974-75; Calif. Assembly, 1981-82.
Capitol Office: 2231 Rayburn Bldg. 20515; 225-5464.

In Washington: After more than a decade, Martinez is still struggling to lengthen the shadow he casts in the House.

A number of Democrats in the large class of 1982 have become prominent players on hot issues and key committees, but the amiable Martinez is not among them. He took over the Education and Labor Subcommittee on Employment Opportunities in 1985 but has failed to show the legislative acumen needed to inspire confidence in his leadership. He moved to the chair of the Human Resources panel in the 102nd. Even those who are his ideological allies do not view Martinez as the kind of legislator who can strategically guide major legislation through to passage. However, Martinez is a loyal partisan who has seen some bills enacted to benefit children.

In the 102nd Congress, Martinez sponsored bills authorizing drug abuse education and delinquency prevention programs — as well as programs aimed at youth gangs and at runaway and homeless young people. Another Martinez-sponsored bill in the 102nd allowed Head Start agencies to purchase their facilities and required literacy and child development training for parents of children in the program.

Rarely has Martinez had to battle in a major political arena. However, a minor controversy developed in the 102nd over a reauthorization of the Older Americans Act, which Martinez sponsored and moved to the full committee. The bill, which would reauthorize funding for such programs as Meals on Wheels, drew a veto threat from the Bush administration because one provision would have required the administration to hold a National Conference on Aging in 1993.

The White House said this impinged on executive branch prerogatives and unnecessarily politicized the problems of the elderly. Martinez charged that the Bush administration was dragging its feet to avoid facing criticism of recent cuts in programs and services for the elderly. Eventually, the bill became law, passing the House without dissent — but not before Martinez had proposed several amendments — including one that renamed the event the White House Conference on Aging.

Some of Martinez's other legislative experiences have been more trying. After he gained the Employment Opportunities Subcommittee chairmanship, Martinez struggled with the arcane language and complex programs of the Job Training Partnership Act (JTPA), one of the laws under the panel's jurisdiction.

In 1990, during a full Education Committee markup of a bill to amend JTPA, Martinez was grilled repeatedly about details of the proposal by one of the panel's Republicans (former Rep. Steve Bartlett). Clearly unnerved, Martinez had to rely on staff to hand him the answers to Bartlett's queries.

Martinez's trouble with the measure began at the subcommittee level. During his panel's markup, he called for a vote and reported out the bill. But the chairman had failed to notice that a quorum was not present.

Though the JTPA bill died, Martinez was able to push through a measure to provide job training and counseling for displaced homemakers.

At Home: Martinez's low profile has emboldened Republicans to make several forays against him. None has succeeded.

Martinez has a place of some prominence within the Hispanic population of the Los Angeles area. After winning re-election to the House in 1990, Martinez considered but declined a January 1991 run for the Los Angeles County Board of Supervisors from a district designed, under a court-ordered plan, to favor a Hispanic.

A former Republican, Martinez got his start on the Monterey Park City Council and served as mayor. He served briefly in the state Assembly after defeating veteran incumbent Jack R. Fenton in a 1980 Democratic primary.

In 1982, Democratic Rep. George E. Danielson resigned to accept a judgeship, and Martinez took a plurality in a special election to fill the vacancy. But he then barely survived a runoff with Republican business consultant Ralph Ramirez, who held him to 51 percent.

Seeking a full House term later that year, Martinez met GOP Rep. John H. Rousselot,

California 31

Eastern Los Angeles County; El Monte; Alhambra; Azusa

The middle-income, blue-collar 31st takes in the southern San Gabriel Valley heading west from its section of East Los Angeles to Azusa, including along the way a fistful of good-size, independent cities. The influx of Hispanics to the area is turning even the district's Republican areas Democratic.

Hispanics make up 59 percent of the district's population but just 42 percent of its voters; Asians are 23 percent of the 31st but just 10 percent of its voters. This pattern of low minority registration is seen throughout Los Angeles.

Like many members of newly arrived immigrant groups, the district's Hispanics and Asians identify strongly with the Democratic Party despite cultural patterns that might otherwise tag them as conservatives. In the 31st, 59 percent of the residents register Democratic and 28 percent register Republican.

A number of engineers live here and work for small employers in the district or head south toward Long Beach. Many Los Angeles municipal and county employees call the 31st home as well.

The East Los Angeles section of the 31st is the residential section of that lower-income community; its business neighborhoods are south, in the 34th.

Monterey Park and San Gabriel are the relatively wealthy areas of the district. Almost 60 percent of Monterey Park's 61,000 residents are Asian, and more than 30 percent are Hispanic. San Gabriel is now about one-third Asian and one-third Hispanic. Less than 1 percent of each city's residents are black. Republicans used to be able to count on San Gabriel's residents, but Democratic Rep. Martinez won the city in 1992.

In the middle of the district are Rosemead, South El Monte and El Monte. Half of Rosemead's 52,000 residents are Hispanic, 85 percent of South El Monte's population of 21,000 is and nearly three-fourths of El Monte's 106,000 inhabitants are.

Baldwin Park resembles the East Los Angeles part of the 31st; its residents' incomes range from the middle of the spectrum to the poverty level.

Most of the business in the district is small and midsize. Irwindale has a few exceptions, such as a Miller Brewing Co. facility, one of the district's largest employers. Many of the city's rock quarries have been converted into industrial parks. Heavy industry exists only outside the district, in such nearby areas as Vernon.

Farthest to the east, Azusa is another former Republican stronghold that now supports Martinez. The city has been able to attract a concentration of high-tech companies.

The San Gabriel Valley is said to be more moderate than L.A.'s east side, and less likely than other parts of Los Angeles County to stick to partisan lines, but the 31st stuck pretty close to those lines in 1992. Bill Clinton won the 31st with 52 percent of the vote, above his statewide average.

1990 Population: 572,643. White 276,310 (48%), Black 9,561 (2%), Other 286,772 (50%). Hispanic origin 335,086 (59%). 18 and over 403,689 (70%), 62 and over 62,671 (11%). Median age: 28.

whose vocal brand of conservatism had earned him a national following. Rousselot's district had been dismembered in redistricting, and he decided to run in the heavily Hispanic 30th rather than challenge another GOP incumbent.

Appealing to voters' conservative social instincts and to their ethnicity, Rousselot used $1,500 in campaign funds for Spanish lessons for his wife and appeared in a Mexican Independence Day parade. But the demographics were too tough; Martinez won with 54 percent.

In 1984, Martinez sank most of his campaign funding into a primary battle with Gladys C. Danielson, the wife of his Democratic predecessor. While her challenge fell far short, it did soften up Martinez for his GOP opponent, lawyer Richard Gomez, who attacked him for poor constituent service and sought a base in the district's growing Asian-American population. Martinez ended up taking 52 percent of the vote.

After this series of close calls, Martinez in 1986 drew a non-Hispanic opponent and finally topped 60 percent.

In 1988, Martinez crushed what had been seen as a tough primary challenge from former Monterey Park Mayor Lily Chen, then in November deflected a comeback attempt by Republican Ramirez, this time taking 60 percent of the vote.

In 1990, Martinez's percentage dropped slightly against 30-year-old Republican Reuben D. Franco, an account executive.

In 1992, with his base relatively undisturbed by redistricting, Martinez pushed his share of the vote back up to 63 percent.

Committees

Education & Labor (7th of 28 Democrats)
Human Resources (chairman); Labor-Management Relations

Foreign Affairs (12th of 27 Democrats)
Asia & the Pacific; International Operations; International Security, International Organizations & Human Rights

Elections

1992 General		
Matthew G. Martinez (D)	68,324	(63%)
Reuben D. Franco (R)	40,873	(37%)
1992 Primary		
Matthew G. Martinez (D)	20,248	(57%)
Bonifacio "Bonny" Garcia (D)	8,678	(25%)
Louis A.M. Ritchie (D)	3,188	(9%)
A. Gus Hernandez (D)	3,136	(9%)
1990 General		
Matthew G. Martinez (D)	45,456	(58%)
Reuben D. Franco (R)	28,914	(37%)
G. Curtis Feger (LIBERT)	3,713	(5%)

Previous Winning Percentages: **1988** (60%) **1986** (63%) **1984** (52%) **1982** (54%) **1982 †** (51%)

† Special House election.

District Vote for President

1992	
D	59,616 (52%)
R	37,250 (32%)
I	18,449 (16%)

Campaign Finance

	Receipts	Receipts from PACs		Expend-itures
1992				
Martinez (D)	$119,807	$77,450	(65%)	$149,441
Franco (R)	$54,776	$8,291	(15%)	$54,817
1990				
Martinez (D)	$209,495	$93,803	(45%)	$186,130
Franco (R)	$72,572	$15,950	(22%)	$72,867

Key Votes

1993	
Require parental notification of minors' abortions	N
Require unpaid family and medical leave	Y
Approve national "motor voter" registration bill	Y
Approve budget increasing taxes and reducing deficit	Y
Approve economic stimulus plan	Y
1992	
Approve balanced-budget constitutional amendment	N
Close down space station program	N
Approve U.S. aid for former Soviet Union	Y
Allow shifting funds from defense to domestic programs	Y
1991	
Extend unemployment benefits using deficit financing	Y
Approve waiting period for handgun purchases	Y
Authorize use of force in Persian Gulf	N

Voting Studies

	Presidential Support		Party Unity		Conservative Coalition	
Year	**S**	**O**	**S**	**O**	**S**	**O**
1992	16	79	87	6	31	58
1991	31	52	71	10	30	43
1990	18	79	81	6	31	63
1989	34	60	86	6	22	68
1988	14	72	90	2	13	74
1987	22	72	89	5	33	58
1986	18	76	82	5	16	70
1985	19	75	88	2	15	76
1984	27	71	93	5	10	85
1983	10	59	65	2	7	73
1982	32 †	55 †	82 †	6 †	10 †	73 †

† Not eligible for all recorded votes.

Interest Group Ratings

Year	ADA	AFL-CIO	CCUS	ACU
1992	95	91	25	4
1991	65	100	20	11
1990	78	92	38	9
1989	75	91	50	11
1988	90	100	23	0
1987	80	100	8	0
1986	85	100	7	10
1985	80	100	19	5
1984	95	92	38	9
1983	70	100	20	0
1982	80	100	24	19

32 Julian C. Dixon (D)

Of Culver City — Elected 1978; 8th Term

Born: Aug. 8, 1934, Washington, D.C.
Education: California State U., Los Angeles, B.S. 1962; Southwestern U., LL.B. 1967.
Military Service: Army, 1957-60.
Occupation: Legislative aide; lawyer.
Family: Wife, Betty Lee; one child.
Religion: Episcopalian.
Political Career: Calif. Assembly, 1973-79.
Capitol Office: 2400 Rayburn Bldg. 20515; 225-7084.

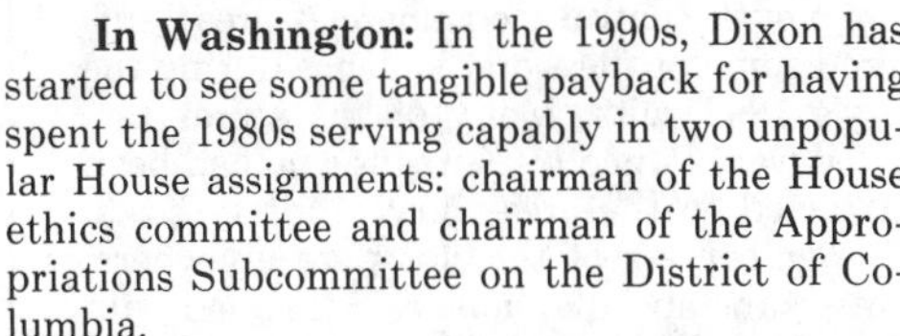

In Washington: In the 1990s, Dixon has started to see some tangible payback for having spent the 1980s serving capably in two unpopular House assignments: chairman of the House ethics committee and chairman of the Appropriations Subcommittee on the District of Columbia.

At the beginning of the 103rd Congress, he was elected by California's Democratic delegation to represent the region on the House Steering and Policy Committee, which makes committee assignments. Two months later, he was appointed to the House Intelligence Committee, where he ranks fourth. Dixon will retain his position on the House Appropriations Subcommittee on Defense, which he gained in 1989, as well as the D.C. Appropriations chair.

Although Dixon is a well-liked insider — known for his hard work and diplomacy — he has remained consistently low-profile. Even with new challenges, Dixon is not expected to make a move toward the forefront.

He is probably best known for his six years as chairman of the House ethics committee. When he joined the committee in 1983 and became its chairman in 1985, Dixon expected to serve the usual two-term rotation. However, he was asked by the Democratic leadership to stay on for a third term to handle an investigation of the Democratic leadership. Dixon had secured a reputation as a reliable, low-key loyalist who could be counted on not to be a "hanging judge."

These qualities led conservative Republicans — who were trying to make corruption an albatross issue for the Democratic Party — to complain in advance that Speaker Jim Wright of Texas, as well as others whose financial transactions were under scrutiny, would get off lightly.

In the end, however, Dixon's judicious conduct of the Wright case gave no one cause to fault his impartiality. When the turning point came, Dixon voted to pursue most of the charges against Wright. And when Wright accused the committee's special counsel Richard J. Phelan of "a lack of professionalism" and "distortion," Dixon called the Speaker's remarks "totally inaccurate, totally wrong, an exercise in bad judgment."

Wright resigned from the House in May 1989, obviating any need for a final judgment from the ethics committee. Although Dixon was praised for his handling of the affair, it was an experience he would not want to repeat. Earlier in 1989, Dixon had said, "You get burned out.... I've had it."

Dixon avoided a potentially bloody partisan battle when a committee counsel recommended in August 1989 against pursuing an investigation of House Minority Whip Newt Gingrich of Georgia on charges stemming from a book-financing deal.

However, there was more to come. The committee had to settle the case of Massachusetts Democrat Barney Frank, who had admitted to a past relationship with a male prostitute, Steven Gobie, whom Frank had once hired as a personal assistant.

The committee investigation, while finding Frank guilty of such transgressions as fixing parking tickets, concluded he was blameless on more serious allegations, including permitting Gobie to use his residence for prostitution. After weeks of partisan wrangling, the committee voted in July 1990 for the relatively mild punishment of a House reprimand.

Members seeking to again raise the charges against Frank made a motion to expel him. The usually mild-mannered Dixon furiously debunked the charges as "edited, selective garbage." Dixon also turned the debate into a referendum on his and the committee's integrity, stating, "This case boils down to, really, who do you trust?"

The House trusted Dixon. The effort to expel Frank was defeated by a 30-390 vote.

Caught in the turmoil of the 101st Congress, Dixon found no haven in his chairmanship of the D.C. Appropriations Subcommittee. Social-issue activists, using their leverage over the federal city's finances to advance their agendas, turned the debate on the routine funding bill into a battle over abortion. Such fights

California 32

West Los Angeles; Culver City

This compact, diverse district begins about a mile inland from Venice Beach, runs east through Culver City and ends up in south-central Los Angeles. Sandwiched between these areas are dozens of distinct ethnic neighborhoods.

Economically, the 32nd runs the gamut, taking in very wealthy neighborhoods such as Rancho Park in the north, middle- and upper-middle-income suburbs in the west and very poor sections of south-central Los Angeles in the east.

This area is undergoing its second demographic sea change in 30 years. A generation ago, its Jewish population migrated toward the district's northwest end, and the center of the district became predominantly black.

Now there is a new wave of immigrants: Hispanics. Blacks are still the district's largest racial group, but their dominance is slipping as more blacks migrate toward Los Angeles' suburbs. Forty percent of the district's residents are black, 30 percent are Hispanic and 8 percent are Asian.

Despite vast differences between the district's neighborhoods — the Baldwin Hills area actually features operating oil wells — a huge majority of the people in the 32nd vote Democratic: Three-fourths of the district's registered voters are Democrats; only 15 percent are Republicans. In 1992, Bill Clinton won his highest level of support in Southern California here, taking 78 percent of the vote. George Bush got only 13 percent.

The eastern end of the 32nd is a black working-class area; moving north, the concentration of Hispanics increases. The northeast, near Pico Union, has considerable multifamily housing; to the southeast there are more single-family homes and higher levels of home ownership.

While south-central Los Angeles could be described as "blighted," it's not the type of blight typically found in the very poor areas of Chicago or New York. South-central's blight shows itself in its commercial districts rather than in its residential areas; its residents actually live in fairly well-maintained, older single-family homes.

South-central's commercial areas suffered some of the worst violence during the city's 1992 riots. Many of the stores targeted were owned by Koreans who had been attracted to the area's low property costs. The epicenters of the riot were elsewhere, but substantial violence traveled up Crenshaw Boulevard from Inglewood and down Western Avenue from Koreatown.

Curiously, none of this area used to be known as south-central Los Angeles. South-central traditionally has been thought of as being farther east, but post-riot media coverage has widened the term's scope. "Apparently, anywhere blacks live is now south-central," says an observer.

On the issues, people living on the 32nd's eastern side tend to have crime and economic concerns uppermost in mind, while residents on the western side of the district tend to mirror the coast's high level of environmental concern.

1990 Population: 572,595. White 184,266 (32%), Black 230,872 (40%), Other 157,457 (27%). Hispanic origin 173,076 (30%). 18 and over 435,038 (76%), 62 and over 78,322 (14%). Median age: 32.

were especially frustrating to Dixon when the White House was in Republican hands. President George Bush vetoed the city's appropriations bills twice over abortion language.

Dixon's many distractions prevented him from playing a major role during his first term on the Defense Appropriations Subcommittee.

Although Dixon's move from the Appropriations Foreign Operations Subcommittee to Defense was hailed even by some Republicans in the California delegation, some may wish he was a stronger Pentagon backer, especially now when defense cuts have struck the state so hard. Dixon is a longtime supporter of arms control efforts; he also opposed the January 1991 resolution authorizing use of force against Iraq. The chairman of the Congressional Black Caucus during the 98th Congress, Dixon has supported the caucus' budget alternatives that would have diverted defense dollars to domestic programs.

From his Appropriations post, Dixon has helped gain federal money for construction of the Los Angeles Metro Rail project. He also pushes greater access to the subway system for inner-city residents.

In the 103rd, he reintroduced legislation that would allow unemployed persons with individual retirement accounts to withdraw funds from the accounts without penalty if they have exhausted all unemployment benefits. The bill is aimed at his home state and others with high unemployment rates.

He now supports funding of defense conversion efforts.

Although his district was not as heavily damaged in the 1992 riots as other parts of inner-city Los Angeles, Dixon introduced a supplemental appropriations bill as a member of the Appropriations Committee to provide money to rebuild the neighborhoods hardest hit. However, he was not a key player in the negotiations. He also was appointed by House Speaker Thomas S. Foley of Washington to a bipartisan congressional Urban Task Force charged with devising an urban aid package with the Bush administration.

At Home: Dixon followed a political path blazed by Yvonne Brathwaite Burke, a prominent black official of the 1960s and '70s. When she first ran for the House in 1972, Dixon resigned as an aide to state Sen. Mervyn M. Dymally — who went on to Congress and retired from the House at the end of the 102nd — and captured her open Assembly seat. In 1978, when Burke left to run what would be an unsuccessful bid for state attorney general, Dixon beat eight Democratic primary foes to win her House seat.

The primary was a power struggle among political brokers in Los Angeles' black community. Dixon's closest competitor, state Sen. Nate Holden, was backed by Kenneth Hahn, a white Los Angeles County supervisor with considerable popularity in the black areas of South Los Angeles. Another rival, City Councilman David S. Cunningham, was supported by Mayor Tom Bradley. Dixon was the choice of Rep. Henry A. Waxman and then-state Rep. Howard L. Berman (now a House member).

The Waxman-Berman machine helped Dixon win the primary. Dixon ran unopposed that November and regularly collected more than three-fourths of the district vote in each re-election bid thereafter until 1990, when he "slipped" to a mere 73 percent. Redistricting in 1992 did little to alter his situation, and he had only minor-party opposition in November.

Committees

Appropriations (12th of 37 Democrats)
District of Columbia (chairman); Defense; Military Construction

Select Intelligence (4th of 12 Democrats)
Program & Budget Authorization

Elections

1992 General		
Julian C. Dixon (D)	150,644	(87%)
Bob Weber (LIBERT)	12,384	(7%)
William R. Williams (PFP)	9,782	(6%)
1990 General		
Julian C. Dixon (D)	69,482	(73%)
George Z. Adams (R)	21,245	(22%)
William R. Williams (PFP)	2,723	(3%)
Bob Weber (LIBERT)	2,150	(2%)

Previous Winning Percentages: **1988** (76%) **1986** (76%) **1984** (76%) **1982** (79%) **1980** (79%) **1978** (100%)

District Vote for President

1992
D 147,623 (78%)
R 23,956 (13%)
I 17,561 (9%)

Campaign Finance

	Receipts	Receipts from PACs		Expend-itures
1992				
Dixon (D)	$83,583	$54,750	(66%)	$140,461
1990				
Dixon (D)	$161,900	$124,145	(77%)	$113,669
Adams (R)	$6,600	0		$3,799

Key Votes

1993	
Require parental notification of minors' abortions	N
Require unpaid family and medical leave	Y
Approve national "motor voter" registration bill	Y
Approve budget increasing taxes and reducing deficit	Y
Approve economic stimulus plan	Y
1992	
Approve balanced-budget constitutional amendment	N
Close down space station program	N
Approve U.S. aid for former Soviet Union	N
Allow shifting funds from defense to domestic programs	Y
1991	
Extend unemployment benefits using deficit financing	Y
Approve waiting period for handgun purchases	Y
Authorize use of force in Persian Gulf	N

Voting Studies

	Presidential Support		Party Unity		Conservative Coalition	
Year	**S**	**O**	**S**	**O**	**S**	**O**
1992	18	77	85	6	23	71
1991	26	66	88	4	14	84
1990	20	78	89	3	17	83
1989	29	63	87	2	17	76
1988	17	71	85	0	3	92
1987	15	83	81	1	7	79
1986	13	74	80	2	12	70
1985	18	75	84	1	11	67
1984	25	61	79	4	12	75
1983	13	71	81	1	8	80
1982	32	55	79	7	15	73
1981	37	54	85	5	11	71

Interest Group Ratings

Year	ADA	AFL-CIO	CCUS	ACU
1992	80	75	13	4
1991	85	100	20	0
1990	100	100	23	4
1989	85	100	40	0
1988	85	100	25	0
1987	96	100	7	0
1986	85	100	25	0
1985	80	100	15	0
1984	95	83	38	5
1983	90	100	20	0
1982	85	100	32	20
1981	80	100	16	0

33 Lucille Roybal-Allard (D)

Of Bell Gardens — Elected 1992; 1st Term

Born: June 12, 1941, Los Angeles, Calif.
Education: California State U., Los Angeles, B.A. 1965.
Occupation: Non-profit worker.
Family: Husband, Edward Allard; two children, two stepchildren.
Religion: Roman Catholic.
Political Career: Calif. Assembly, 1987-93.
Capitol Office: 324 Cannon Bldg. 20515; 225-1766.

The Path to Washington: Overcoming the broad expectation and resulting complacency that Roybal-Allard would naturally succeed her father in his House seat may have been the biggest obstacle to her election.

Democratic Rep. Edward R. Roybal had been a fixture in Congress for 30 years and had the best-known name in state Hispanic politics, having previously served four terms on the Los Angeles City Council. He retired from the House in 1992 as chairman of an Appropriations subcommittee and the Select Committee on Aging.

His daughter, who had begun making her own name in local politics, aspired to the seat and won it handily, facing insubstantial opposition in the Democratic primary and the November general election. She won 74 percent in the primary, holding developer Frank Fernandez to 17 percent. In the general election, she garnered 63 percent, while Republican Robert Guzman, an education consultant, won 30 percent.

But for Roybal-Allard, victory was not a foregone conclusion. Two other famous daughters sought election to the House from Los Angeles in 1992: Democrat Lynn V. Dymally in the 37th (territory represented for 12 years by Mervyn M. Dymally, who was retiring), and Republican Maureen Reagan in the 36th (whose father, former President Ronald Reagan, campaigned for her). Both lost in their primaries.

Leaving nothing to chance, Roybal-Allard spent more than $250,000 on the primary and general elections combined. She countered objections to her vigorous fundraising by saying she did not want to take her election or her future constituents for granted.

In addition to the benefits of her name, Roybal-Allard can attribute her success to having been active in the community. She served three terms in the state House, beginning with a special election in 1987, and all her wins were by wide margins.

She also scored points locally for galvanizing grass-roots opposition to a toxic-waste incinerator proposed for Vernon, which is in both her state legislative district and the 33rd.

That five-year battle was successful. And Roybal-Allard parlayed the experience into enactment of a bill requiring environmental impact reports for such facilities.

Redistricting split Roybal's old district in half (the northern end falling into the new 30th). But when Hispanic neighborhoods from adjoining districts were added to the 33rd, the result was a Latino population of 84 percent. The shift makes the 33rd the district with the largest Hispanic majority in the nation.

This area is troubled by poverty, unemployment, gangs and political apathy. But it also benefits from neighborhoods with bustling shops and large families trying to pull themselves into the middle class. It includes the heart of downtown Los Angeles, the barrios of East Los Angeles and several small towns in between.

Citizenship is a key problem. The Pico Union area is the landing point for many, if not most, immigrants from Central and South America. Less than 25 percent of the district's voting-age residents are registered to vote — a statistic that underscores both the sizable number of noncitizens (a large share of them illegal aliens) and the reluctance of many to enter the bureaucratic maze that citizenship applications entail.

Roybal-Allard hopes to tear down some barriers with workshops. And she will continue to press issues that she concentrated on in the Legislature: the environment and women's rights. But her main focus will be on economic issues. She supports efforts to reduce the deficit but wants to see savings from defense channeled into health care, education, housing and jobs. From seats on the Small Business and Banking, Finance and Urban Affairs committees, she hopes to stimulate flows of aid and capital to the businesses that provide most of the jobs in the 33rd. She supports streamlining regulations, provided the integrity of the laws they are intended to enforce is not compromised.

The 33rd, despite its middle-class neighborhoods, also suffers from a shortage of affordable housing; many of its residents live in converted garages. Roybal-Allard hopes to encourage growth in the affordable stock from her seat on the Housing subcommittee.

California 33

East-Central Los Angeles

The 33rd is a poor, densely populated and heavily Hispanic area that avoided further economic trouble by being just east of Los Angeles' worst May 1992 rioting.

The section of south-central in the 33rd is mostly residential and was hit less by the riots than south-central's business districts.

The northwest corner of the 33rd, the downtown area, is composed primarily of office buildings. It is laced with Los Angeles' legendary crowded expressways. Some residents live in single-room occupancy hotels and shelters for homeless families and women, but the bulk of this area's people live just north and south of downtown in Pico Union and Chinatown. Stores in Pico Union's downtown area were looted in the riots, but the wholesale destruction seen in most of south-central did not occur.

Two cities in the district's midsection, Commerce and Vernon, house much of the 33rd's industry, with facilities including food processing plants and metal-plating operations. The district depends less on military contractors than much of the rest of Los Angeles, so neither the defense industry's 1980s boom nor its early 1990s problems played much of a role in the economy here.

Economic development is a perennial issue in the economically struggling 33rd. Bright spots include "green" industries, such as recycling companies, that are opening.

The southeast areas of the district, including Cudahy, Maywood, Bell and Bell Gardens, are very poor, very densely populated and primarily residential, tending to have more single-family homes than apartment buildings.

The development in the district's southern region is very even; it is difficult to distinguish one community from another without a map. Most of the housing stock here was built in the 1960s and 1970s. It is different from the development found on the east side and downtown, where the bulk of the housing is 30 to 40 years older.

South Gate lies just south of Cudahy. This city has successfully converted itself over the past several years from heavy industries to small businesses and light manufacturing. It is not as Democratic as the rest of the district; it voted Republican for president throughout the 1980s.

Los Angeles' new Red Line subway, opened in January 1993 inside the 33rd, holds the promise of creating economic development, as does the Blue Line commuter train that runs from Long Beach to downtown through much of the district.

The 33rd tops the state in two areas: It is 84 percent Hispanic, and 92 percent of its residents are members of minority groups. But fewer voters are registered in this district than in any other in the state — just 86,991. No other district has fewer than 100,000 registered voters.

In 1992, turnout here was so low that Bill Clinton's 63 percent of the vote translated to only 33,642 votes — the smallest number cast for Clinton in any California district.

1990 Population: 570,943. White 203,891 (36%), Black 25,473 (4%), Other 341,579 (60%). Hispanic origin 477,975 (84%). 18 and over 384,158 (67%), 62 and over 44,759 (8%). Median age: 26.

Committees

Banking, Finance & Urban Affairs (20th of 30 Democrats)
Consumer Credit & Insurance; Housing & Community Development

Small Business (22nd of 27 Democrats)
Minority Enterprise, Finance and Urban Development; SBA Legislation and the General Economy

Campaign Finance

1992	Receipts	Receipts from PACs		Expenditures
Roybal-Allard (D)	$283,770	$133,587	(47%)	$264,755
Guzman (R)	$182,103	$4,598	(3%)	$166,756

Key Votes

1993

Require parental notification of minors' abortions	N
Require unpaid family and medical leave	Y
Approve national "motor voter" registration bill	Y
Approve budget increasing taxes and reducing deficit	Y
Approve economic stimulus plan	Y

Elections

1992 General		
Lucille Roybal-Allard (D)	32,010	(63%)
Robert Guzman (R)	15,428	(30%)
Tim Delia (PFP)	2,135	(4%)
Dale S. Olvera (LIBERT)	1,206	(2%)
1992 Primary		
Lucille Roybal-Allard (D)	14,112	(75%)
Frank Fernandez (D)	3,138	(17%)
Lucy F. Kihm (D)	1,685	(9%)

District Vote for President

	1992	
D	33,642	(63%)
R	12,607	(24%)
I	7,149	(13%)

34 Esteban E. Torres (D)

Of West Covina — Elected 1982; 6th Term

Born: Jan. 27, 1930, Miami, Ariz.
Education: East Los Angeles College, 1959-63; California State U., Los Angeles, 1963-64; U. of Maryland, 1965; American U., 1966.
Military Service: Army, 1949-53.
Occupation: International trade executive; autoworker; labor official.

Family: Wife, Arcy Sanchez; five children.
Religion: Unspecified.
Political Career: Sought Democratic nomination for U.S. House, 1974; UNESCO ambassador, 1977-79.
Capitol Office: 1740 Longworth Bldg. 20515; 225-5256.

In Washington: A former assembly-line welder who sometimes shows off the tattoos on his hands from his days as a street-gang member, Torres brings a grittier edge to Appropriations, the consummate insider's committee that he joined at the start of the 103rd Congress.

Still, Torres, the former ambassador to UNESCO, bears the insignia of an insider as well. In five terms as a backbencher he stayed in his role and voted the party line reliably. In the 102nd Congress, he became a deputy whip. Although his background and personal passion could make him a high-profile leader among Hispanics in Congress, he has opted for a quiet role in all his activities: on the Banking Committee, on Small Business and as chairman of the Congressional Hispanic Caucus in the 100th Congress.

On Banking, where he served through the 102nd, Torres was generally comfortable with the legislative agenda of the activist liberal Democrats who called the shots. Where he could, he worked as a conciliator, smoothing out the rough edges of members' personal and philosophical conflicts to help keep legislation moving. He was also one of a dwindling group of Democrats who remained on good terms with Chairman Henry B. Gonzalez. Both of these characteristics have helped advance his interests. In the 101st Congress, for example, despite Torres' relatively light participation in the overhaul of federal housing programs, Gonzalez selected him to serve on the bill's House-Senate conference committee. The bill included a Torres provision establishing a disaster-assistance program for people with low or moderate incomes.

In the 102nd Congress, Torres assumed the often thankless chair of the Consumer Affairs and Coinage Subcommittee, registering some successes amid the inevitable setbacks.

The most contentious battle he took on was an attempt to strengthen federal regulation of the nation's credit reporting industry. Torres' bill would have given consumers greater access to their credit histories and made it easier for them to correct errors. It enjoyed wide support, but credit bureaus and their congressional allies succeeded in attaching a provision blocking state governments from imposing stricter regulations on the industry. Torres said that the language pre-empting stricter state laws fatally weakened the bill. He and Gonzalez tried to remove it, but after losing in committee and on the House floor (on a seesaw 203-207 vote), they pulled the bill. Torres and Gonzalez reintroduced it in the 103rd Congress.

Torres had greater success overseeing an effort to require straightforward disclosure of interest rates and conditions on savings accounts. The Truth-in-Savings Act, which had been passed in the House and Senate repeatedly since 1985, finally became law as part of the 1991 banking regulation overhaul bill.

In 1992, Torres pushed to ban the use of the so-called "Rule of 78s" — an accounting method for calculating unearned interest on consumer loans with terms longer than five years. He called the method unfair and outdated. His legislation became law as part of a housing reauthorization bill.

Early in the 102nd Congress, as the House debated a bill to provide an additional $30 billion to bail out savings and loan institutions, Torres clashed with the committee's ranking Republican, Chalmers P. Wylie of Ohio. Wylie contended that the bill's minority-contracting provisions constituted mandatory minority hiring quotas; Torres rejected Wylie's contention as "ludicrous," saying they were merely hiring goals.

In 1990, as the Banking Committee grappled with how to stop narcotics traffickers from using the wire-transfer system to launder drug money, Torres proposed requiring banks to maintain wire-transfer records. But he ran into opposition from several lawmakers who argued that such extensive recordkeeping would be too

California 34

East Los Angeles County suburbs; West Covina

The 34th is emerging as a middle-class Hispanic district that likes to vote Democratic; it is an almost ideal place for someone like Torres to run. It begins with more than a third of East Los Angeles, goes east through Montebello and Pico Rivera, goes up north a bit for La Puente, and drops down to pick up most of Whittier and all of Santa Fe Springs and Norwalk.

The section of East Los Angeles contained in the 34th is the heart of East L.A.'s business district. The stores are well-kept, and owned or operated by Hispanics. The area just to the north, around the 60 Freeway, is populated by what some call "Muppies," or Mexican yuppies, who have come in and fixed up many of the area's old homes.

Montebello is an upper-middle-class Hispanic area, with a lot of home-grown residents who have never lived anywhere else. The area has many white-collar workers; it is bordered by four freeways, making it a convenient area for commuters. Montebello is heavily Democratic: Torres took 68 percent of its vote in 1992, the first time he ran here.

Pico Rivera has been described as pure middle America, Hispanic-style. "The values that people have, the outlook on life, what they want for their kids — it is Peoria, Ill.," says a resident. The biggest employer in the city is Northrop, which builds part of the B-2 bomber here. This area was also very supportive of Torres; he got 73 percent of Pico Rivera's vote.

Up in the district's northeastern corner past Rose Hills Memorial Park (one of the country's largest cemeteries) is La Puente, a working-class, heavily Hispanic city with 37,000 residents and a Democratic registration of 67 percent.

Down south a bit, the district includes most of Whittier, the 34th's most Republican area (a 2-point GOP voter registration advantage). The city is still recovering from being the epicenter of an October 1987 earthquake. Some houses damaged in the quake have been repaired, but vacant lots are not uncommon. Multifamily homes are mixed closely with single-family homes in some areas, but not in the part of Whittier just outside the district, where half-million-dollar houses (and the GOP) dominate.

Farther south is Santa Fe Springs, a healthy industrial area featuring light manufacturing and oil wells. Two-thirds of the city's 15,500 residents are Hispanic, but they have not flexed their political muscles here as they have elsewhere.

At the southern end of the 34th is Norwalk, the district's largest city with 94,000 residents. It has close to a majority of Hispanics and a majority of Democrats; they tend to be conservative-minded in presidential voting, though Norwalk went heavily for Bill Clinton in 1992. The city is bounded by three freeways and a fourth is coming when the Glenn Anderson Freeway opens fully in late 1993. Los Angeles' Green Line light rail is scheduled to open in 1994, which will give the area a further economic boost.

In 1992, Bill Clinton carried 51 percent of the 34th's vote to George Bush's 31 percent and Ross Perot's 18 percent.

1990 Population: 573,047. White 325,099 (57%), Black 11,060 (2%), Other 236,888 (41%). Hispanic origin 357,143 (62%). 18 and over 402,266 (70%), 62 and over 64,984 (11%). Median age: 29.

cumbersome and costly for banks.

The committee watered down his amendment to give the Treasury Department discretion over wire-transfer requirements. When Torres offered a House floor amendment to require Treasury to conduct a one-year pilot program, it was rejected, 127-283.

Torres has taken an interest in the problem of gangs. The crime bill that died in the 102nd Congress included his amendment making gang-related crimes punishable under federal law.

At Home: Torres was an assembly-line welder in Los Angeles during the 1950s and became active in the United Auto Workers. In the 1960s, he was tapped by UAW President Walter Reuther to start a community action project in heavily Hispanic East Los Angeles. In 1968, Torres founded The East Los Angeles Community Union (TELACU), which grew into one of the country's largest anti-poverty agencies.

Torres developed Democratic contacts as an activist, but he lost a 1974 primary in his initial bid for the House. Soon thereafter, however, he found his way into the Carter administration as an adviser on Hispanic affairs and later was named ambassador to UNESCO. Thus, when he made his second bid for Congress in 1982, Torres billed his campaign as "Autoworker to Ambassador, the American Dream."

Torres' second try for Congress proved far easier than his first. He was running in an open 34th District created by redistricting, and he had help from the political organizations of

Democrats Henry A. Waxman and Howard L. Berman. In the primary, he held off former Democratic Rep. Jim Lloyd (who had lost his seat in a neighboring district in 1980 to Republican David Dreier). In the general election Torres prevailed with 57 percent.

Since then, he has regularly maintained a vote share of 60 percent or better. Redistricting in 1992 changed his district little geographically and not at all politically. The Democratic registration figure remained at 61 percent, and Torres won again with 61 percent.

While cruising to re-election every two years, Torres has kept an eye on Los Angeles politics. In 1990, he hinted at a run for the Los Angeles County Board of Supervisors. But Republican incumbent Pete Schabarum, instead of announcing that he would step down, simply failed to file as a candidate by the March 1990 deadline. By that time, Torres had filed to run again for the House: He defeated former Reagan administration official John Eastman with 61 percent.

Committee

Appropriations (27th of 37 Democrats)
Foreign Operations, Export Financing & Related Programs; Veterans Affairs, Housing & Urban Development & Independent Agencies

Elections

1992 General		
Esteban E. Torres (D)	91,738	(61%)
J. "Jay" Hernandez (R)	50,907	(34%)
Carl M. "Marty" Swinney (LIBERT)	7,072	(5%)
1990 General		
Esteban E. Torres (D)	55,646	(61%)
John Eastman (R)	36,024	(39%)

Previous Winning Percentages: **1988** (63%) **1986** (60%) **1984** (60%) **1982** (57%)

District Vote for President

1992
D 78,889 (51%)
R 48,181 (31%)
I 27,944 (18%)

Campaign Finance

	Receipts	Receipts from PACs		Expend-itures
1992				
Torres (D)	$169,451	$49,300	(29%)	$254,092
Hernandez (R)	$129,919	$1,750	(1%)	$131,271
1990				
Torres (D)	$241,635	$87,788	(36%)	$217,810
Eastman (R)	$75,581	$11,050	(15%)	$75,123

Key Votes

1993	
Require parental notification of minors' abortions	N
Require unpaid family and medical leave	Y
Approve national "motor voter" registration bill	Y
Approve budget increasing taxes and reducing deficit	Y
Approve economic stimulus plan	Y
1992	
Approve balanced-budget constitutional amendment	N
Close down space station program	N
Approve U.S. aid for former Soviet Union	Y
Allow shifting funds from defense to domestic programs	Y
1991	
Extend unemployment benefits using deficit financing	Y
Approve waiting period for handgun purchases	Y
Authorize use of force in Persian Gulf	N

Voting Studies

	Presidential Support		Party Unity		Conservative Coalition	
Year	**S**	**O**	**S**	**O**	**S**	**O**
1992	20	70	84	5	19	73
1991	25	70	94	3	14	84
1990	17	81	94	2	20	78
1989	29	69	90	1	10	85
1988	16	76	90	2	11	76
1987	10	79	85	3	12	70
1986	18	80	91	2	10	84
1985	18	75	90	1	11	82
1984	26	73	94	2	5	95
1983	21	77	88	4	12	85

Interest Group Ratings

Year	ADA	AFL-CIO	CCUS	ACU
1992	85	92	29	4
1991	80	92	20	5
1990	89	100	21	0
1989	95	100	40	0
1988	90	100	23	0
1987	96	100	7	0
1986	90	93	18	5
1985	75	94	24	10
1984	95	100	38	0
1983	90	100	30	0

35 Maxine Waters (D)

Of Los Angeles — Elected 1990; 2nd Term

Born: Aug. 15, 1938, St. Louis, Mo.
Education: California State U., Los Angeles, B.A. 1970.
Occupation: Head Start official.
Family: Husband, Sidney Williams; two children.
Religion: Christian.
Political Career: Calif. Assembly, 1977-91.
Capitol Office: 1207 Longworth Bldg. 20515; 225-2201.

In Washington: No one was surprised when Waters crashed a White House meeting between President Bush and congressional leaders to discuss the aftermath of riots that had devastated her south-central Los Angeles district in the spring of 1992.

Waters had a reputation in the California Assembly for being outspoken and hard-nosed in pursuing her objectives, a reputation that preceded her to Washington. She had angered many of her Assembly colleagues at one point or another, but she also had achieved respect for her determination. And she has made a similarly singular impression on colleagues in the House.

Drawing on insider skills honed in the Assembly, Waters in her first term proved equally nimble on the national political stage. She had been a leading supporter of Jesse Jackson's 1984 and 1988 bids for the Democratic presidential nomination (casting the lone vote against the 1988 party platform at the final drafting session). But in early 1992, she sensed that Bill Clinton had the best shot at the White House among Democrats, and she signed onto his campaign with little hesitation. Despite a sharp difference in agendas — and several episodes during which Clinton seemed to be deliberately slighting Jackson — Waters and the future president maintained an uneasy alliance that carried over to the 103rd Congress.

Whether that alliance will hold is another matter. Waters is not at all reluctant to confront her adversaries, high or low, inside the party or out. When colleagues at the beginning of her first term referred to her in public as Maxine — a form of address she considered disrespectful — she corrected them on the spot.

In November 1991, the Veterans' Affairs Committee was marking up a bill to create a position at the Department of Veterans Affairs to oversee minority assistance programs. In the middle of the session, Waters attacked Chairman G. V. "Sonny" Montgomery of Mississippi over the committee's hiring practices, declaring it "unconscionable" that the panel had but one black staffer. It was just the first of a series of public confrontations between the two.

On the House floor in July 1992, she denounced a pet project of Housing Secretary Jack F. Kemp to enable public housing tenants to buy their units. She called the program a sham and urged her colleagues instead to support government spending to produce jobs: "And guess what, Mr. Speaker, if we do that, maybe the same people would want to buy a home next door to Jack Kemp instead of [in] the housing project."

Waters is firmly planted on the left fringe of House Democrats: For her, the burning and looting that ravaged her district in the spring of 1992 was a "rebellion," not a "riot." The disorder followed the acquittal of several Los Angeles police officers in the beating of Rodney King, who had tried to elude police in a high-speed chase. In the violence that followed the verdict, a white truck driver named Reginald Denny was pulled from his vehicle at a major intersection and beaten nearly to death in full view of TV cameras. When four young black men were charged with the crime, Waters was among those championing their defense, calling them "The L.A. 4."

Waters also joined Vermont socialist Bernard Sanders and several of the most liberal members of the Democratic Caucus in forming the House Progressive Forum. As a member of the Banking Committee, she allies regularly with Joseph P. Kennedy II of Massachusetts; and as a member of Veterans' Affairs, she sides most often with Kennedy and Lane Evans of Illinois, rivals of Montgomery.

Waters' legislative endeavors have focused almost exclusively on the plight of inner cities. On the Banking Committee, she succeeded in attaching amendments to a major housing reauthorization bill in 1992 to increase the stock of low-income and moderate-income housing in her district, to prevent a decline in the stock of low-income rental housing generally, and to expand assistance programs targeted to public housing tenants.

During debate on a broad banking bill in 1991, Waters was one of several liberal mem-

California 35

South-central Los Angeles

This very poor, very heavily minority district is home to what many consider the flash point of April 1992's rioting, the intersection of Normandie and Florence avenues where a white truck driver, Reginald Denny, was dragged from his vehicle and beaten by a group of blacks.

The incident serves to emphasize the home-grown nature of the riots: All of those arrested in the beating case lived within six blocks of the intersection. The rioters tended to torch their own neighborhoods, which in the 35th includes part of south-central Los Angeles and three independent cities: Inglewood, Hawthorne and Gardena.

The eastern edge of the district is the most desperately poor. As one heads west toward Inglewood, relative affluence increases. The commercial districts in this area along Vermont and Manchester (and to a lesser extent Western) avenues were devastated by looting and burning.

To the west of south-central is Inglewood, whose police force was able to keep much of the rioting there under control. Inglewood suffered some damage but was spared the wholesale destruction found in south-central. Inglewood is a historically white city that has changed dramatically; now, more than half its 110,000 residents are black. The city is home to the Hollywood Park racetrack and the L.A. Lakers, who play in the Great Western Forum. Several shipping companies have set up shop here to take advantage of its location due east of the Los Angeles International Airport.

Hawthorne, with 71,000 residents, is about 10 percent Asian with the rest split almost equally among Hispanics, whites and blacks. Its political power, however, is largely concentrated among its whites because they tend to register to vote at higher levels than the other groups.

Hawthorne was the birthplace of Northrop Corp., a major defense contractor that still has its manufacturing headquarters here. The city is alone in the district in having allowed large apartment buildings to be built.

For years, Gardena (population 50,000) received a strong revenue stream from being the only city in Los Angeles County that allowed poker parlors; their contributions made up about 15 percent of the city's budget. The extra money allowed the city to save a substantial sum, part of which it used to start a municipal insurance company to keep its costs down.

The southern part of the city is heavily Japanese; they are about a quarter of the city's total population. The community has been influential for some time; the city elected California's first Japanese mayor in 1972. Honda has its U.S. headquarters here.

Overall, the district is 43 percent black (the highest proportion of blacks in the state), 43 percent Hispanic and 6 percent Asian — a full 90 percent minority.

Politically, the 35th is overwhelmingly Democratic, the most Democratic district in California: 80 percent of its voters are registered Democrats. Bill Clinton won 78 percent here in 1992.

1990 Population: 570,882. White 121,505 (21%), Black 243,848 (43%), Other 205,529 (36%). Hispanic origin 246,201 (43%). 18 and over 389,470 (68%), 62 and over 51,632 (9%). Median age: 27.

bers on the panel to insist on changes to stiffen enforcement of the Community Reinvestment Act, the principal federal anti-redlining law. When it appeared that conservatives might have the votes to exempt many banks from coverage under the existing law, Waters engineered a compromise in committee that blocked amendments either to strengthen or weaken the law.

On the Veterans' Affairs Committee, she concentrated on boosting aid to homeless veterans, and winning additional rights of courtroom representation for vets who claim they have been discriminated against.

Waters also discovered that legislating in Washington has its pitfalls. In August 1992, she and other members of the Black Caucus hoped to win a procedural fight and amend a Russian aid bill to authorize $10 billion in loan guarantees to U.S. communities. But in a remarkable miscalculation, they called a news conference just at the moment that the vote was to be held, leaving no one on the floor to demand a roll-call vote. The procedural matter was disposed of with a voice vote, and Waters was not allowed to offer her amendment. "Chalk this one up," she said afterward, conceding her tactical mistake.

At Home: As expected, Waters had no problem being re-elected in her newly drawn 35th District, which is built on Watts and other black and Hispanic neighborhoods in the south-central portion of Los Angeles. Even after the latest redistricting, Waters' territory resembled at its heart the Assembly district she had represented for 14 years in Sacramento. It is still hers: She was returned to Congress in 1992 with 83 percent of the vote.

Waters got her chance to move up in 1990, with the retirement of 28-year veteran Rep. Augustus F. Hawkins, who retired as chairman of the House Education and Labor Committee.

Though she gave up some clout to come to Washington, it was a move for which she had been preparing for years. During legislative debates over redistricting in 1982, Waters maneuvered to remove from what was then Hawkins' district a blue-collar, mainly white suburban community, which she saw as unfriendly territory (and once referred to as "rednecky").

Although her legislative career and her marriage to a luxury automobile dealer have made Waters financially comfortable, she is no limousine liberal. She comes to her empathy for poor and working-class blacks from personal experience. Waters was born in St. Louis as one of 13 children in a welfare family and was raised in public housing projects. As a teenager, she bused tables in a segregated restaurant. Married just after high school, Waters moved in 1961 with her first husband and two children to Los Angeles, where she worked in a clothing factory and for the telephone company.

Waters' public career began in 1966, when she volunteered as an assistant teacher in the new Head Start program while pursuing a college degree. Her involvement in Head Start led Waters into other community-organizing activities and then into politics. After working as a volunteer and a consultant to several candidates, Waters ran and won an upset victory for a state Assembly seat in 1976.

Making her presence felt immediately, Waters, who had also emerged as a feminist spokeswoman, pushed to have the gender-neutral term "assembly member" replace the official title of "assemblyman." Despite the derision of some male colleagues, Waters argued her case and won.

Waters sponsored much successful legislation, including measures requiring state agencies to set minimum goals for awarding contracts to minority- and women-owned businesses; barring strip searches for those accused of non-violent misdemeanors; and creating a state child abuse prevention training program. During her House campaign, Waters touted her sponsorship of the Imperial Courts Learning Center, California's first public school within a public housing project.

Waters' most difficult legislative victory came in 1986. After a seven-year struggle, she persuaded the legislature to pass a provision requiring state pension funds to divest stocks in companies doing business with South Africa.

Waters' election to the House was never in doubt. Running in a district that has an overwhelming Democratic majority, Waters defeated Republican Bill De Witt, a former South Gate City Council member, with 79 percent.

Committees

Banking, Finance & Urban Affairs (11th of 30 Democrats)
Consumer Credit & Insurance; Financial Institutions Supervision, Regulation & Insurance; Housing & Community Development; International Development, Finance, Trade & Monetary Policy

Small Business (26th of 27 Democrats)

Veterans' Affairs (12th of 21 Democrats)
Oversight & Investigations

Elections

1992 General		
Maxine Waters (D)	102,941	(83%)
Nate Truman (R)	17,417	(14%)
Alice Mae Miles (PFP)	2,797	(2%)
Carin Rogers (LIBERT)	1,618	(1%)
1992 Primary		
Maxine Waters (D)	51,534	(89%)
Roger A. Young (D)	6,252	(11%)
1990 General		
Maxine Waters (D)	51,350	(79%)
Bill DeWitt (R)	12,054	(19%)
Waheed R. Boctor (LIBERT)	1,268	(2%)

District Vote for President

	1992	
D	100,432	(78%)
R	16,685	(13%)
I	11,950	(9%)

Campaign Finance

	Receipts	Receipts from PACs		Expend-itures
1992				
Waters (D)	$191,510	$91,890	(48%)	$207,954
Truman (R)	$7,643	0		$7,143
1990				
Waters (D)	$740,793	$211,172	(29%)	$759,538

Key Votes

1993	
Require parental notification of minors' abortions	N
Require unpaid family and medical leave	Y
Approve national "motor voter" registration bill	Y
Approve budget increasing taxes and reducing deficit	Y
Approve economic stimulus plan	Y
1992	
Approve balanced-budget constitutional amendment	N
Close down space station program	N
Approve U.S. aid for former Soviet Union	N
Allow shifting funds from defense to domestic programs	Y
1991	
Extend unemployment benefits using deficit financing	Y
Approve waiting period for handgun purchases	Y
Authorize use of force in Persian Gulf	N

Voting Studies

	Presidential Support		Party Unity		Conservative Coalition	
Year	S	O	S	O	S	O
1992	11	77	82	4	10	88
1991	23	70	85	3	5	84

Interest Group Ratings

Year	ADA	AFL-CIO	CCUS	ACU
1992	95	92	13	0
1991	90	100	11	0

36 Jane Harman (D)

Of Marina del Rey — Elected 1992; 1st Term

Born: June 28, 1945, New York, N.Y.
Education: Smith College, B.A. 1966; Harvard U., J.D. 1969.
Occupation: Lawyer; White House aide; congressional aide.
Family: Husband, Sidney Harman; four children.
Religion: Jewish.
Political Career: No previous office.
Capitol Office: 325 Cannon Bldg. 20515; 225-8220.

The Path to Washington: Abortion and the economy — which could both be one-time issues — played prominent roles in helping Harman to an upset victory in this nominally Republican district.

Harman won by a comfortable 16,000 votes over Joan Milke Flores, a well-known Los Angeles City Council member. But that earned Harman only a thin 48 percent plurality to Flores' 42 percent. (Three minor party candidates split the balance.) Harman may have to struggle to hold on to the seat, because the GOP is not likely to let her keep it without a fight.

Harman coupled her moderate-to-liberal views (including support for both national health insurance and a balanced budget) to a call for reform. Harman's campaign materials promised: "This woman will clean House."

She made her absolute support for abortion rights the centerpiece of her campaign against Flores, who opposes abortion except in cases of rape, incest or when a woman's life is endangered by her pregnancy.

And Harman also focused on the double whammy of recession and defense cuts in the aerospace industry, which employs — or employed — tens of thousands in the district's South Bay area. She called for continued defense cuts, coupled with concerted efforts at retraining workers and wholesale reorientation for defense industry contractors.

She sought and landed two committee assignments that should help her shore up support among this key constituency — Armed Services, and Science, Space and Technology. Not only can she work to ensure that there are no precipitous cuts that severely disrupt the district, but she also can pursue her aim of bringing in new, high-technology jobs.

Against a Republican who supports abortion rights, however, Harman would appear to have less of an advantage. And focusing on the economy presents a high-risk strategy, should conditions not improve over the next two years.

The fact is that redistricting aimed to put this coastal Los Angeles district back in the Republican column, where it was prior to 1982. California's mapmakers took away the liberal bastion of Santa Monica and added the affluent Palos Verdes peninsula (which previously had been part of the district).

That turned the old, Democratic-leaning 27th into the new, more Republican 36th.

And though the Republicans here tend to be more moderate than their counterparts in Orange County, they have elected their share of die-hard conservative congressmen. In a prior incarnation this district was represented by Republican Robert K. Dornan. For the past four years, the South Bay was represented by Republican Dana Rohrabacher.

During the 1992 campaign, however, Democrats made strong inroads in registration. When the year began, registration favored Republicans 46 percent to 41 percent. By September, the spread had narrowed to 2 percentage points.

Harman, who is married to the founder of Harman International, a leading manufacturer of audio equipment, moved into the district in 1991 from Washington. There she had held a variety of congressional, political and legal jobs after college and law school, including several staff jobs with former California Sen. John V. Tunney and in the Carter administration.

She withstood complaints that she was a carpetbagger — and worse, a political insider who raised much of her money from outside the district. In fact, she put almost $250,000 of her own money into the primary and finished the general-election cycle with the largest campaign debt of anyone running in an open House seat, almost $1 million. Overall, she spent $2.3 million to win the seat, the third most of any House candidate in 1992.

Harman easily captured her primary with 45 percent of the vote atop a seven-person field.

Flores, meanwhile, narrowly beat Maureen Reagan in a 12-person GOP primary. Reagan, daughter of the former president and one-time head of the Republican National Committee, tried to capitalize on her father's name. She tried to position herself more to the center than Flores, who won endorsements from both Dornan and Rohrabacher.

California 36

West Los Angeles County; Manhattan Beach; Torrance

The 36th hugs the Pacific coast, running south from Venice Beach to San Pedro and the port of Los Angeles. Along the way, it takes in some of California's most Democratic and Republican areas.

The 36th's economic core is along the ocean and the Pacific Coast Highway. Its main industry — aerospace — is found in the upper third of the district in El Segundo, home of Hughes Aircraft, Lockheed and TRW plants. Shrinking spending in both the military and civilian sectors of the aerospace business has been devastating; it is not unusual to see people with doctorates collecting unemployment compensation.

The northern end of the district is anchored by Venice, a "very, very crunchy, nuts-and-berries kind of place," as one local observer put it; Venice is widely regarded as the most liberal place in California outside Berkeley. Designed by Abbot Kinney to duplicate the Italian city, Venice opened in 1904 complete with canals and gondolas. Its heyday was short; by 1958 the city had fallen into such disrepair that Orson Welles used it as the location for the seedy town in the film "Touch of Evil." The area has been revitalized by wealthy full-time residents and weekenders drawn to the town's beautiful location and funky reputation.

Just south of Venice and Marina Del Ray lies the Los Angeles International Airport, which stretches all the way to the 405 Freeway, the eastern border of the district. The airport's expansion during the 1980s is expected to meet air traffic demands until another terminal is built at the end of the 1990s. The airport is not expected to receive much public works money in the meantime, although plans are proceeding to bring a light-rail extension of Los Angeles' new rapid-transit system here in this decade.

The land is fairly flat continuing down the coast, past El Segundo and through some of the wealthiest ocean suburbs in the region, including Manhattan, Hermosa and Redondo beaches.

The land and the incomes take a steep rise at the Palos Verdes Peninsula, where the bulk of the district's Republicans live. Nearly three-fourths of the peninsula's 90,000 residents are white. The area is almost uniformly upscale, and some communities qualify as havens of the truly wealthy: For instance, the per capita income of the 1,900 residents in Rolling Hills is $85,000.

In the 1992 House race, the peninsula's brand of social moderation and fiscal conservatism did not fit comfortably with the anti-abortion profile of the GOP nominee, Joan Milke Flores. Though Flores carried the peninsula, it did not embrace her as warmly as it had Republican candidates in the past.

A voter-registration surge in the months before the 1992 elections turned a 15,000-vote GOP margin into a slight Democratic plurality; that shift helped produce Harman's 16,000-vote victory.

The surge helped Bill Clinton, who also won this district in 1992 by about 15,000 votes; he took 41 percent to George Bush's 36 percent and Ross Perot's 23 percent.

1990 Population: 573,663. White 446,003 (78%), Black 18,392 (3%), Other 109,268 (19%). Hispanic origin 85,277 (15%). 18 and over 462,022 (81%), 62 and over 74,844 (13%). Median age: 35.

Committees

Armed Services (29th of 34 Democrats)
Oversight & Investigations; Military Forces & Personnel; Research & Technology

Science, Space & Technology (22nd of 33 Democrats)
Space; Technology, Environment & Aviation

Campaign Finance

	Receipts	Receipts from PACs		Expend-itures
1992				
Harman (D)	$2,301,376	$199,208	(9%)	$2,285,356
Flores (R)	$812,022	$267,429	(33%)	$811,592

Key Votes

1993

Require parental notification of minors' abortions	N
Require unpaid family and medical leave	Y
Approve national "motor voter" registration bill	Y
Approve budget increasing taxes and reducing deficit	Y
Approve economic stimulus plan	Y

Elections

1992 General		
Jane Harman (D)	125,751	(48%)
Joan Milke Flores (R)	109,684	(42%)
Richard H. Greene (GREEN)	13,297	(5%)
Owen Staley (PFP)	5,519	(2%)
Marc F. Denny (LIBERT)	5,504	(2%)
1992 Primary		
Jane Harman (D)	26,812	(45%)
Ada Unruh (D)	9,216	(16%)
Charlene A. Richards (D)	6,952	(12%)
Bryan W. Stevens (D)	5,200	(9%)
Paul P. Kamm (D)	4,107	(7%)
Gregory Stock (D)	4,027	(7%)
Colin Kilpatrick O'Brien (D)	2,940	(5%)

District Vote for President

1992

D 111,014 (41%)
R 95,646 (36%)
I 62,458 (23%)

37 Walter R. Tucker III (D)

Of Compton — Elected 1992; 1st Term

Born: May 28, 1957, Compton, Calif.
Education: Princeton U., 1974-76; U. of Southern California, B.A. 1978; Georgetown U., J.D. 1981.
Occupation: Lawyer.
Family: Wife, Robin Smith; two children.
Religion: Baptist.
Political Career: Mayor of Compton, 1991-93.
Capitol Office: 419 Cannon Bldg. 20515; 225-7924.

The Path to Washington: In an era when congressional pork has fallen out of favor (at least in some circles), Tucker faces the task of fashioning a silk purse in which to carry home goodies for his economically depressed district.

Tucker's agenda for this partly working-class, partly decaying slice of Los Angeles is long on increasing federal spending to satisfy urban wants and short on concern for more suburban issues, such as the size of the federal deficit.

He has a wish list that includes tax incentives for businesses that locate in designated enterprise zones; tax cuts for low- and moderate-income workers; federally financed inner-city health centers, including mobile clinics; and sweeping reallocation of the defense budget to public works projects and spending on the homeless, the elderly, drug abusers and single parents.

Tucker succeeded in landing a seat on the Public Works and Transportation Committee to pursue some of these goals.

Early in the 103rd Congress, citing the February 1993 shooting deaths of two police officers in the Compton area of his district, Tucker also called for passage of the so-called Brady bill, which would require a waiting period for handgun purchases.

Tucker's call for federal aid to cities comes straight out of his view of how best to solve the problems that plague his constituents daily.

The district is centered in Compton, a mostly black and Latino working-class enclave within Los Angeles, where Tucker became mayor in 1991. The 37th has perhaps the highest unemployment rate in the state and includes a large segment of south-central Los Angeles, the scene of days of riots, looting and arson in May 1992.

During the unrest, Tucker was a visible presence in the streets. He was frequently shown on television, attempting to ease the tension alongside the Rev. Jesse Jackson and vigorously pressing GOP Gov. Pete Wilson to call out the National Guard to restore order.

Tucker won this seat in something of an upset, narrowly defeating the early front-runner, Compton School Board member Lynn V. Dymally, in a bitter primary battle. Dymally's father, Democrat Mervyn M. Dymally, represented Compton and a large portion of the 37th for 12 years before deciding to retire after 1992. The popular elder Dymally hoped to hand the seat to his daughter.

But Tucker, who was born in the district and comes from a political dynasty of sorts himself, had no inclination to yield. Tucker's father was Compton's mayor before him; the younger Tucker was elected to that office in 1991, six months after his father's unexpected death.

The bruising primary focused not so much on issues as the involvement of a local political action group, Truth in Politics. Made up mostly of local college students, the group was advised by and had other ties to Mervyn Dymally.

The group made a practice of targeting opponents of Dymally-backed candidates. And it made Tucker a focus of its negative campaign efforts, repeatedly attacking his character and ambition. The group purchased newspaper advertisements and mailed fliers to district residents questioning whether Tucker used a Compton city car to campaign and accusing him of being a convicted felon.

The latter charge was based on Tucker's 1986 dismissal from the Los Angeles County district attorney's office after he changed the date on some photographs that were evidence in a drug case he was prosecuting. He was charged with preparing false evidence, a felony, but pleaded no contest to altering an official document, a misdemeanor. Tucker secured a court order blocking the group from repeating the felony allegation.

With Democratic registration exceeding 75 percent, the primary was the crucial contest. Tucker prevailed with 39 percent of the vote, outpolling Dymally by 1,103 votes.

In the general election Tucker easily overcame his only opponent, black activist B. Kwaku Duren, capturing 86 percent of the vote to win his first term in Congress.

California 37

Southern Los Angeles County; Compton; Carson

The 37th includes some of Los Angeles' poorest and most overwhelmingly Democratic communities, taking in the Carson, Compton and Lynwood areas of the city.

Residents of the 37th have quite a stake in efforts aimed at post-Cold War adjustments to the nation's defense industries. The scheduled closings of the Long Beach shipyard and naval station just south of the district are likely to squeeze the area anew. Long Beach's port area draws many of its blue-collar workers from the district (the naval station alone employs more than 10,000 civilian and military personnel), and many others in the 37th work in small businesses that support the port. Military contractors concentrated in the district's southern end also are suffering.

Carson, just north of the port, is a blue-collar city of 84,000, with its population split almost evenly among Hispanics, blacks, whites and Asians. This area was largely spared in the rioting of May 1992, even though it is sandwiched between Long Beach and Compton, which both suffered fairly heavy damage.

Scores of Compton's businesses went up in the smoke of 135 separate fires. California's recession had been hurting the already-poor area, and many of the surviving jobs were lost as businesses damaged in the riot closed. Few of the destroyed businesses have rebuilt. The lots with burned buildings and debris have been cleared, leaving them vacant — and hard to distinguish from the many vacant lots the city had before the riots.

Compton's Hispanic community has grown tremendously in the past decade. Forty-four percent of the city's 90,000 residents are Hispanic and 53 percent are black.

At the north end of the district is Lynwood, 70 percent of whose 62,000 residents are Hispanic and 21 percent of whom are black. The area sustained some damage during the riots, with more than 60 fires reported and 138 arrests.

One ray of light for the district is the Alameda Corridor project, an attempt to create a smooth conduit for goods to enter California through Long Beach without the traffic hassles of the Long Beach Freeway. The project runs the length of the district up Alameda Street and includes rail and road transportation improvements.

Another addition to the district is the 105 Freeway, known for years as the Century Freeway, which gave rise to a local joke that the road, planned since the middle part of this century, would not be completed until the next. But it bears a new name — retired Democratic Rep. Glenn Anderson's — and new hope for completion. The very eastern end near Norwalk is slated to open in late 1993, and the freeway's last legs are expected to be finished in about three years, finally fully connecting the area to the metropolitan area's freeway grid.

The 37th's representative, Tucker, was one of only three in the state who did not draw major-party opposition in 1992, and Bill Clinton received 74 percent of the district's presidential vote.

1990 Population: 572,049. White 149,689 (26%), Black 192,420 (34%), Other 229,940 (40%). Hispanic origin 258,278 (45%). 18 and over 375,216 (66%), 62 and over 49,338 (9%). Median age: 26.

Committees

Public Works & Transportation (38th of 39 Democrats)
Public Buildings & Grounds; Surface Transportation; Water Resources & the Environment

Small Business (20th of 27 Democrats)
Minority Enterprise, Finance and Urban Development; Regulation, Business Opportunities and Technology

Campaign Finance

1992	Receipts	Receipts from PACs	Expend-itures
Tucker (D)	$283,230	$65,100 (23%)	$277,586
Duren (PFP)	$4,129	0	$4,129

Key Votes

1993

Require parental notification of minors' abortions	N
Require unpaid family and medical leave	Y
Approve national "motor voter" registration bill	Y
Approve budget increasing taxes and reducing deficit	Y
Approve economic stimulus plan	Y

Elections

1992 General		
Walter R. Tucker III (D)	97,159	(86%)
B. Kwaku Duren (PFP)	16,178	(14%)
1992 Primary		
Walter R. Tucker III (D)	22,536	(39%)
Lynn Dymally (D)	21,433	(37%)
Vera Robles DeWitt (D)	6,491	(11%)
Joe Mendez Jr. (D)	4,804	(8%)
Lawrence A. Grigsby (D)	2,307	(4%)

District Vote for President

	1992	
D	90,523	(74%)
R	19,299	(16%)
I	12,905	(11%)

38 Steve Horn (R)

Of Long Beach — Elected 1992; 1st Term

Born: May 31, 1931, San Juan Batista, Calif.
Education: Stanford U., A.B. 1953; Harvard U., M.P.A. 1955; Stanford U., Ph.D. 1958.
Military Service: Army Reserve, 1954-62.
Occupation: Professor; college president.
Family: Wife, Nini Moore; two children.
Religion: Protestant.
Political Career: U.S. Commission on Civil Rights vice chairman/member, 1969-82; sought GOP nomination for U.S. House, 1988.
Capitol Office: 1023 Longworth Bldg. 20515; 225-6676.

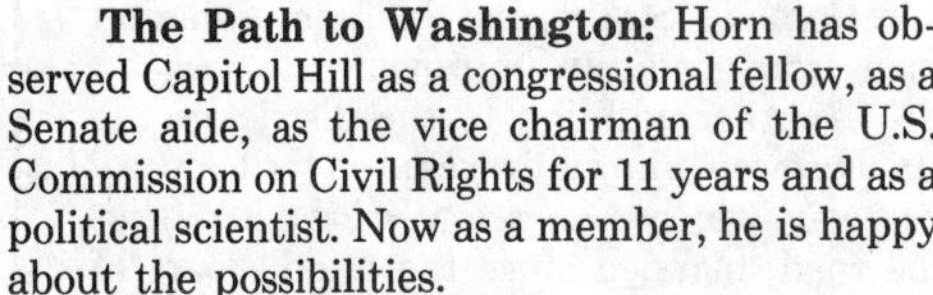

The Path to Washington: Horn has observed Capitol Hill as a congressional fellow, as a Senate aide, as the vice chairman of the U.S. Commission on Civil Rights for 11 years and as a political scientist. Now as a member, he is happy about the possibilities.

Horn is a moderate Republican who favors abortion rights and a freeze on federal spending, except for Social Security, Medicare and Head Start. His district stands to suffer from defense cutbacks, and he would like to see surplus military personnel detailed to local communities as police officers — with a five-year phaseout of federal aid for their salaries.

He was one of only 40 Republicans to vote for mandatory unpaid family leave legislation that Bill Clinton signed into law in February 1993.

From his position on the Public Works and Transportation Committee, Horn can watch over two of the nation's largest seaports — Los Angeles and Long Beach. Both are in his district and until this year were the protectorate of retired Democrat Glenn M. Anderson, who represented a large chunk of what is now the 38th for 24 years. Anderson had been chairman of the Public Works Committee from 1988 to 1991, when a cabal of dissatisfied younger members stripped him of the chairmanship. Horn will also serve on the Government Operations Committee.

Redistricting also may have played a small role in Horn's election: Some Republicans were added to try to make the district more diverse, but registration is still about 50 percent Democratic.

Horn's interest in Congress dates to his college years. His doctoral dissertation considered the constitutional issue of instituting a formal "question time" in which members of the president's Cabinet could be queried on the floors of the House and Senate — much as is done in parliamentary systems.

He later wrote books about the Senate Appropriations Committee and about ethics and campaign finance. Since then, he has taught political science at California State University at Long Beach, where he also served as president from 1970 to 1988.

Given his background, it is not surprising that Horn believes government and Congress can be progressive institutions. Nor is he deterred by being a Republican and consigned for now to the minority. He harks back to his experiences as an aide in the Senate; he served at a time during which Republicans were in the minority but still played crucial roles in civil rights. It was Republicans who provided needed assistance to break a Southern Democratic filibuster of the Civil Rights Act of 1964. And as an aide to Sen. Thomas H. Kuchel, R-Calif. (1953-69), Horn was one of a handful of aides who drafted the Voting Rights Act of 1965 in the office of Minority Leader Everett McKinley Dirksen, R-Ill. (1951-1969).

But Horn is worried that Congress has become strikingly more partisan. He thinks the House Democratic leadership is out of control, and he denounced as "claptrap" and a "constitutional disgrace" Democratic efforts to grant some floor voting privileges to delegates from the District of Columbia, Puerto Rico, American Samoa, Guam and the Virgin Islands.

Horn ran for the House once before, in 1988, in the old 42nd, just south of the current district. He fell to Dana Rohrabacher, who had more money and the campaign help of former White House aide Oliver L. North. Horn won this time by outlasting a field of seven other Republicans in the primary.

In the general election, Horn faced an uphill challenge against Long Beach City Council member Evan Anderson Braude, stepson of the retiring 12-term incumbent. Beyond the financial clout of the Anderson-Braude camp, Horn was handicapped by a 12-point Democratic edge in voter registration and a refusal to take political action committee contributions.

Despite a last-minute negative assault by Braude — including the insinuation that Horn was somehow a foreign agent for having consulted with the University of the United Arab Emirates — Horn won by nearly 10,000 votes.

California 38

Long Beach; Downey; Lakewood

Though there is a working-class Democratic tradition in the 38th (and a seven-point Democratic registration advantage), blue-collar conservatism often will shift the area toward Republican candidates. Horn beat his Democratic opponent 49 percent to 43 percent in 1992. But Bill Clinton managed to beat George Bush here 45 percent to 33 percent.

Long Beach, along the coast, is the world's second-largest port and by far the largest city in the district with 429,000 residents. All but the western end is contained within the 38th. About a quarter of the city's residents are Hispanic, and more than half are white non-Hispanics. The remaining quarter are a rainbow of ethnicities: 49 languages are spoken in the Long Beach Unified School District's schools. Overall, the district is about a quarter Hispanic, 9 percent Asian and 8 percent black.

The southwestern side of Long Beach was hard hit by the April 1992 riots that ripped through the Los Angeles area. More than 400 fires were reported, more than 300 people were injured and at least one person was killed. Much of the damage was along the Pacific Coast Highway and the city's Cambodian area along Anaheim Street.

The beautiful *Queen Mary* is docked here, but the fight to keep the Long Beach Naval Shipyard open has diverted the eyes of most residents. The shipyard employs thousands across Southern California; any move to close it is serious trouble for the area. (The shipyard made the mid-1993 list of military facilities targeted for closure.) While important, the shipyard is just part of the 38th's industrial landscape. Aerospace plants extend along the flat, brown land, sharing space with fuel tanks and oil wells. In the older homes of Long Beach are the descendants of the fishermen and sailors of many European nationalities who settled here.

Downey, a middle- to upper-middle-income city of 91,000 at the district's northern tip, has a Republican lean. The city houses Rockwell's huge aerospace plant (where the space shuttle is manufactured) on its south end, as well as many of the high-tech workers who are employed there. While Rockwell is still a major employer, levels have dropped off dramatically from their peaks of yesteryear.

Just south of Downey is Paramount, a very blue-collar city of 48,000. About 60 percent of Paramount's residents are Hispanic, far higher levels than are found elsewhere in the 38th. The city has high unemployment and high crime rates.

Directly east of Paramount is Bellflower, a quiet bedroom city of 62,000 that is similar to Downey. It has no industry that compares with Rockwell.

More than half of Lakewood's 74,000 residents are in the 38th. This community, just south of Bellflower, was built all at once after World War II to house veterans and other workers who came to the area to work in the aerospace industry and decided to stay. One of the city's claims to fame is the Lakewood Center Mall, one of America's first shopping malls.

1990 Population: 572,657. White 396,372 (69%), Black 44,337 (8%), Other 131,948 (23%). Hispanic origin 146,899 (26%). 18 and over 435,049 (76%), 62 and over 80,792 (14%). Median age: 31.

Committees

Government Operations (14th of 16 Republicans)
Government Information, Justice, Transportation & Agriculture; Human Resources & Intergovernmental Relations

Public Works & Transportation (18th of 24 Republicans)
Aviation; Water Resources and the Environment

Campaign Finance

	Receipts	Receipts from PACs		Expend-itures
1992				
Horn (R)	$441,693	$3,000	(1%)	$441,198
Braude (D)	$514,459	$168,745	(33%)	$514,381

Key Votes

1993

Require parental notification of minors' abortions	N
Require unpaid family and medical leave	Y
Approve national "motor voter" registration bill	N
Approve budget increasing taxes and reducing deficit	N
Approve economic stimulus plan	N

Elections

1992 General		
Steve Horn (R)	92,038	(49%)
Evan Anderson Braude (D)	82,108	(43%)
Paul Burton (PFP)	8,391	(4%)
Blake Ashley (LIBERT)	6,756	(4%)
1992 Primary		
Steve Horn (R)	13,423	(30%)
Dennis Brown (R)	13,318	(30%)
Tom Poe (R)	5,747	(13%)
Andrew J. Hopwood (R)	4,556	(10%)
William A. Ward (R)	3,418	(8%)
Jerry Bakke (R)	2,177	(5%)
Sanford W. Kahn (R)	1,428	(3%)
John Carl Brogdon (R)	1,032	(2%)

District Vote for President

	1992
D	88,728 (45%)
R	66,647 (33%)
I	43,596 (22%)

39 Ed Royce (R)

Of Fullerton — Elected 1992; 1st Term

Born: Oct. 12, 1951, Los Angeles, Calif.
Education: California State U., Fullerton, B.A. 1977.
Occupation: Tax manager.
Family: Wife, Marie Terese Porter.
Religion: Roman Catholic.
Political Career: Calif. Senate, 1983-93.
Capitol Office: 1404 Longworth Bldg. 20515; 225-4111.

The Path to Washington: With 10 years under his belt in Sacramento — and a couple of big notches on it — Royce was ready this year to move to the national stage. The door opened when Republican Rep. William E. Dannemeyer decided to seek the Senate seat held by fellow Republican John Seymour.

Although redistricting somewhat altered the 39th's borders (it lost Anaheim and, with it, Disneyland), it was substantially the same Republican Orange County that had sent the legendary Dannemeyer to the House every two years since 1978 by wide electoral margins.

Royce's voting record probably will closely resemble Dannemeyer's. The 39th has perhaps the most conservative constituency in the country, and Royce reflects that in his strong anti-tax, pro-free enterprise, pro-interventionist stance.

He displayed his proclivities early in the 103rd Congress when he voted with only 37 other members against a bill to require companies to place warning labels on toys that pose choking risks to small children in addition to instructing the Consumer Product Safety Commission to develop federal bicycle helmet safety standards.

He is, however, not likely to pick up Dannemeyer's staff and lead the charge on such issues as abortion and AIDS. Nor is he likely to push for House floor votes on amendments to require the United States to return to the gold standard — as Dannemeyer did for years. Instead, his chief concerns are crime and more mainstream economic matters, such as the federal budget deficit.

Royce made his name in the state Senate pushing anti-crime bills. He won enactment of a bill that makes it a felony to stalk and threaten someone with injury — giving the police recourse when the stalker has not yet attacked his intended victim. A score of other states have picked up this idea, and Royce intends to offer a similar bill in the House.

He failed to persuade the Legislature to enact a series of comprehensive changes to the state's criminal code, including giving victims the right to object to frivolous continuances and to insist on a speedy trial, enhancing the powers of grand juries curtailed by the state Supreme Court and ending jury shopping. But when the Legislature balked, Royce worked to get the changes on the ballot as Proposition 115 in 1990, where it passed overwhelmingly.

Royce made a bid for the Judiciary Committee, so he could continue his anti-crime crusade, but he failed to land the seat. But he secured a spot on the Science, Space and Technology Committee, a crucial venue for issues of interest to Orange County's aerospace industry. And he will serve on the Foreign Affairs Committee, where he can pursue his goal of pushing the United States to take a harder line with socialist and totalitarian countries. Like Dannemeyer, he supports tough trade sanctions against China.

Royce may have inherited Dannemeyer's mantle, but he did not act as if he did in the campaign.

He was positioned well enough — having represented a sizable slice of the 39th's territory in the Senate — to gain a bye in the primary. But he campaigned hard for the general election, spent slightly more than $500,000 and brought in heavyweights such as Housing and Urban Development Secretary Jack F. Kemp for fundraisers.

His Democratic opponent, Molly McClanahan, was regarded as an effective member of the Fullerton City Council. But she proved too liberal for this bastion of Orange County conservatism.

Where Royce campaigned in favor of a balanced-budget amendment and some form of line-item veto or enhanced rescission power to give the president a tool to reduce spending, McClanahan downplayed the deficit. She argued that deficits caused by government investment were not inherently bad.

McClanahan managed a respectable 38 percent, roughly equivalent to the district's Democratic registration. But she had little money — barely 20 percent of Royce's total — and could thus do little to maximize the relatively thin Democratic vote in Orange County. Though his 57 percent was well below Dannemeyer's average percentage, Royce should have little difficulty hanging onto this seat.

California 39

Parts of Orange and Los Angeles counties — Fullerton

This district straddles the line between Orange and Los Angeles counties. It is where the more-affluent parts of Los Angeles County's suburbs meet the less-affluent sections of Orange County; it is a seamless fit.

From all appearances, and spiritually speaking, this is an Orange County district. Its L.A. County portion looks like what many think of when they envision Orange County: bedroom communities, small commercial areas and regional malls. Its residents tend to vote Republican, hold conservative economic views and not identify themselves as Los Angelenos. Residents throughout the 39th typically work at jobs inside the district's borders. About three-fifths of the people are non-Hispanic whites, but there is a sizable presence of Hispanics (almost 25 percent) and Asians (14 percent).

The job situation is the top concern here, as it is throughout Southern California, but next on the list is crime. There is not a lot of violent crime or gang activity within the borders of the 39th, but this problem exists just across the line in Anaheim and in Santa Ana, and it is creeping this way.

Most of the terrain here is flat, with some hills in Fullerton and La Habra Heights. Though the cities in the district are largely residential, many have an industrial area: Machine shops, plastic injection-molding facilities, aerospace subcontractors and food manufacturers are among the installations.

Fullerton, the 39th's largest city, is upper-middle class, a label that applies to much of the district. Fullerton is home to a variety of industries and the district's largest employers, including Hughes Aircraft's ground systems division, which employs 7,000 workers who design and manufacture such things as radar, communications equipment and air traffic control equipment. Other major employers are Beckman Instruments, where 2,100 workers manufacture scientific equipment, and Hunt-Wesson, which employs 1,100 in its food plants making ketchup and other foodstuffs.

There is little variation among the communities inside the 39th. One of the only interruptions in the thoroughly developed area is Knott's Berry Farm, a major amusement park in Buena Park toward the south. Especially affluent areas include La Habra Heights, and the eastern, more Republican half of Whittier, both of which are in the 39th's northern region in L.A. County.

On the flip side, Hawaiian Gardens in L.A. County is more working-class and more Democratic than is the norm in the 39th. The district also picks up an industrial portion of Anaheim to the east.

Though this is a district landlocked in freeways, its southwestern corner reaches down to within four miles of the Pacific Ocean.

Republicans hold a 51 percent to 39 percent edge in the 39th, and Republican candidates did correspondingly well in 1992. Royce beat his opponent by 19 points across the district. In the presidential race, George Bush received 44 percent; Bill Clinton, 34 percent; and Ross Perot, 22 percent.

1990 Population: 573,574. White 417,689 (73%), Black 15,095 (3%), Other 140,790 (25%). Hispanic origin 130,920 (23%). 18 and over 430,089 (75%), 62 and over 68,307 (12%). Median age: 32.

Committees

Foreign Affairs (18th of 18 Republicans)
Africa; Asia & the Pacific

Science, Space & Technology (16th of 22 Republicans)
Space; Technology, Environment & Aviation

Campaign Finance

1992	Receipts	Receipts from PACs		Expend-itures
Royce (R)	$498,264	$199,562	(40%)	$529,196
McClanahan (D)	$99,729	$23,181	(23%)	$92,510

Key Votes

1993	
Require parental notification of minors' abortions	Y
Require unpaid family and medical leave	N
Approve national "motor voter" registration bill	N
Approve budget increasing taxes and reducing deficit	N
Approve economic stimulus plan	N

Elections

1992 General		
Ed Royce (R)	122,472	(57%)
Molly McClanahan (D)	81,728	(38%)
Jack Dean (LIBERT)	9,484	(4%)

District Vote for President

	1992
D	78,305 (34%)
R	100,669 (44%)
I	50,834 (22%)

40 Jerry Lewis (R)

Of Redlands — Elected 1978; 8th Term

Born: Oct. 21, 1934, Seattle, Wash.
Education: U. of California, Los Angeles, B.A. 1956.
Occupation: Insurance executive.
Family: Wife, Arlene Willis; four children, three stepchildren.
Religion: Presbyterian.
Political Career: San Bernardino School Board, 1965-68; Calif. Assembly, 1969-79; GOP nominee for Calif. Senate, 1973.
Capitol Office: 2312 Rayburn Bldg. 20515; 225-5861.

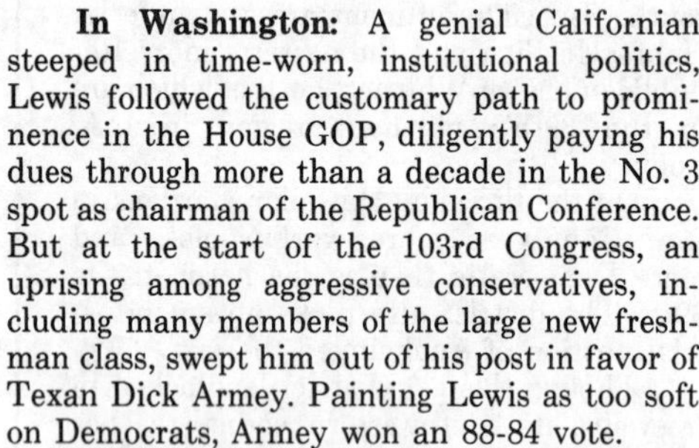

In Washington: A genial Californian steeped in time-worn, institutional politics, Lewis followed the customary path to prominence in the House GOP, diligently paying his dues through more than a decade in the No. 3 spot as chairman of the Republican Conference. But at the start of the 103rd Congress, an uprising among aggressive conservatives, including many members of the large new freshman class, swept him out of his post in favor of Texan Dick Armey. Painting Lewis as too soft on Democrats, Armey won an 88-84 vote.

If the traditional process by which GOP House leaders were chosen had prevailed, Lewis would have been able to maintain his leadership position and perhaps even use it as an eventual springboard to succeed Robert H. Michel of Illinois as minority leader. But Republicans no longer pick their leaders the old-fashioned way. The sentiment to move the GOP Conference into a more assertive mode enabled Armey, an issue-oriented, quick-thinking partisan, to topple Lewis, a likable, old-style politician.

Lewis, a member of the Appropriations Committee since his second term, has given paramount importance to having Republicans work with Democrats to achieve mutually beneficial results. Armey's approach is diametrically different: "The politics of confrontation works and the politics of appeasement fails," he said.

"This was not the year for diversity in Republican politics," Lewis said in a terse, three-paragraph statement issued after the balloting. The statement's plaintive conclusion suggested a reliance on bygone rules of camaraderie and regional loyalty. "The results ... confirm one critical fact: In times of important decisions relating to the economic and political future of our states, Texans stick together and Californians do not. Texas' solid backing and a divided California delegation was the difference in this race."

Questions about Lewis' longevity in the leadership arose as early as 1989, when Georgia's Newt Gingrich stepped over Lewis to take the party's No. 2 job as minority whip. Late in 1990, Gingrich backed a challenge to Lewis' reelection as conference chairman by Michigan's Carl Pursell. Lewis won, 98-64, but his position in the leadership seemed weaker for having been challenged. Shortly thereafter, in early 1991, Lewis lost one of his power bases by losing his seat on the House GOP panel that makes the party's committee assignments. California's seat on the Committee on Committees went instead to Ron Packard, who had two terms' less seniority than Lewis but a higher standing with conservatives in their state's House delegation.

Lewis' legislative career has been a mixture of institutional pragmatism and, in recent years, greater partisanship. Freed now from the leadership obligation, he may choose to settle into a behind-the-scenes role and use his senior position on the Appropriations Committee to channel more money back to his district.

Lewis is still the sixth-ranking Republican on Appropriations, where he oversees a wide array of spending programs. Here, too, his energies are being reoriented now that he no longer runs on the leadership track. He has given up serving as the ranking Republican on the Legislative Branch Subcommittee in favor of the same position on the VA-HUD panel, where he served prior to the 102nd Congress. The subcommittee administers funding for housing and veterans programs as well as the Environmental Protection Agency, NASA and other independent agencies.

On Appropriations, Lewis has long played the earmark game successfully, and in 1989 he was among those criticizing HUD Secretary Jack F. Kemp for his rebuke of the process. After Kemp balked at 40 projects earmarked in the housing appropriation bill — including $500,000 for a shelter for battered women in Lewis' district — Lewis implied that Kemp had better go along with Appropriations' wishes if he wanted a sympathetic hearing for his own budget requests.

Although Lewis has expressed some qualms about the pork barrel aspect of water

California 40

San Bernardino County — Redlands

The 40th is a desert district of massive proportions. It takes in most of San Bernardino County's 20,000 square miles and all of Inyo County's 10,000. San Bernardino County is the largest in the nation; between it and Inyo, the 40th covers almost one-fifth of California.

Most of the district's residents are packed into the far southwest corner in three areas: the Inland Empire, the Victor Valley region and the Morongo Basin.

The Inland Empire section of the district's south includes just a few eastern areas in the city of San Bernardino and such cities as Highland and Redlands, largely bedroom communities with many retirees from Norton Air Force Base. Yucaipa, a bit farther east, has an especially high number of retirees. Loma Linda, just west of Redlands, is a Seventh-Day Adventist community and home to the Loma Linda University Medical Center, best-known for its infant heart transplant program (including the 1984 "Baby Fay" case, in which an infant was given a baboon's heart.)

Victor Valley, north of San Bernardino, has grown by leaps and bounds. It includes the cities of Victorville, Hesperia, Apple Valley and Adelanto. It is an area that used to look to the military for support, but that presence is diminishing — George Air Force Base has closed and Norton Air Force Base in San Bernardino is slated to do so in March 1994.

Victor Valley's growth over the past 10 years has been fueled by Los Angeles workers looking for affordable housing. From the Victor Valley, they head south on the 15 Freeway through the San Bernardino Mountains' Cajon Pass — "down the hill," as they put it — and two hours later they are in downtown Los Angeles.

The Morongo Basin, east of the Inland Empire along the southern border with Riverside County, is the smallest of the three population centers, taking in cities such as Yucca Valley, Joshua Tree and Twentynine Palms. These are just north of the Joshua Tree National Monument and depend heavily on the nearby military presence, which includes the massive Twentynine Palms Marine Corps base.

The district also includes Fort Irwin, where the Army trained Desert Storm's troops for desert maneuvers, and the China Lake Naval Weapons Center. About 60,000 troops a year train at Fort Irwin.

The rest of the 40th is barren. It includes most of the Death Valley National Monument (some of which is in Nevada), whose tourists drive the economy of many of the area's small, scattered towns, such as Lone Pine, Independence and Bishop.

Lewis drew strong support across the district in 1992, beating his opponent by more than 2-to-1. Victorville gave him almost 60 percent of its vote, Redlands, 63 percent and Yucca Valley, 70 percent. This is traditionally Reagan Democrat country that went for George Bush in 1988. Bush won here again in 1992, though less impressively. He took 40 percent of the vote to Bill Clinton's 35 percent and Ross Perot's 25 percent.

1990 Population: 573,625. White 470,785 (82%), Black 31,210 (5%), Other 71,630 (12%). Hispanic origin 92,180 (16%). 18 and over 407,236 (71%), 62 and over 81,470 (14%). Median age: 31.

projects, he does his job when it comes to bringing water to his desert-dominated district. In 1986, he sponsored the successful Lower Colorado Water Supply Act, which improved access to water for small desert communities. In 1990, the House approved $65 million for the Santa Ana flood control project. In 1992, the project got $90.8 million.

Lewis also has a strong interest in earthquake research and has worked on Appropriations to steer money to the Cajon Pass earthquake research site in California. In 1992, he won approval for $6.55 million to repair damage from a series of earthquakes that hit San Bernardino County.

Among the funding he secured during the 102nd Congress was: $48.7 million to begin a five-year, $150 million Interstate highway improvement project; $10 million to build a research institute at the Loma Linda University Medical Center; $5 million to establish a National Medical Technology Testbed at the medical center; $3.2 million for improvements at Ontario International Airport (he also helped direct $2 million in Transportation Department grant funding for soundproofing homes affected by noise from the airport); and $1 million for the East Mojave National Scenic Area.

From his position on the Defense Subcommittee, Lewis looks out for the military bases in the area. Norton and George Air Force bases are slated to close. In 1992, he worked to restore $5.96 million that had been stripped from the defense spending bill to maintain the Ballistic Missile Organization at Norton. In 1991, he obtained $22 million for construction of a school at Fort Irwin.

In 1992, two organizations cited Lewis for his fiscal vigilance. Watchdogs of the Treasury Inc. gave him its Golden Bulldog Award for his deficit-cutting voting record (his sixth Bulldog award, according to his news release). And the Free Congress Foundation selected him as recipient of its 1992 Sound Dollar Award, presented to members "who support responsible legislation relating to limiting government spending and reducing the federal budget deficit."

While somewhat more politically conservative than moderate, Lewis is nonetheless identified with the accommodationist wing of the House GOP — a position clearly displayed in late 1990, when he was one of just two members of the House GOP leadership voting with Michel for the bipartisan budget-summit agreement that included tax increases.

But with pressure from the GOP's activist conservative wing intensifying, Lewis seemed to mitigate his reputation for accommodation. For instance, he showed signs in recent years of downplaying his cordial legislative relationship with the Legislative Branch panel's chairman, Vic Fazio, a California colleague and friend.

In the 101st Congress, Lewis and Fazio split on the issue of congressional mailing. Many GOP conservatives consider the frank an unfair advantage for incumbents and an obstacle to their mission of gaining a House majority. But when Lewis pushed the issue — proposing a reduction from six to two districtwide mailings (including town meeting announcements) — he was too far in front of his troops. Some Republicans resisted Lewis' plan, allowing Fazio to set a cap of four mailings with no limits on town meeting notices.

In the 102nd Congress, Lewis sought to strike $41.7 million in "excess funds" that he argued amounted to a "Speaker's slush fund" controlled by House Speaker Thomas S. Foley of Washington. But his amendment was defeated in committee by voice vote. He also led the call to disclose the names of all members with overdrafts at the House bank.

But the pragmatist in Lewis has also been evident. Early in the 101st Congress he was visible as one of four members of a bipartisan leadership task force, which crafted legislation banning honoraria and developed tactics for promoting a congressional pay raise. The 51 percent pay raise became extremely controversial, and ultimately Lewis was among the overwhelming majority voting against it. Later, a smaller pay increase was approved.

Lewis joined other Republicans in the 102nd Congress who were attacking the General Accounting Office (GAO), Congress' investigatory arm, as having a partisan slant. But in 1991, he split from most Republicans, voting against an amendment to the fiscal 1992 legislative appropriations bill by California Republican C. Christopher Cox to slash the GAO budget by 25 percent and then voting for the final bill.

A year later, in the face of Armey's challenge, he was more vocal in his partisan indignation. "The GAO has demonstrated itself, in more than one instance, to be in the employment of the Democratic majority," he said during committee consideration of the fiscal 1993 bill. This time, he voted for Cox's 25 percent GAO budget cut; but he was also one of 32 Republicans to vote to pass the bill.

Like most Southern Californians, Lewis favors stringent controls on automobile emissions. In the 101st Congress, he and Democrat Henry A. Waxman introduced a clean air bill that won praise from environmentalists. The full House approved a Waxman-Lewis amendment providing for an EPA-administered pilot program in California promoting widespread commercial use of clean fuels and low-polluting cars.

Lewis parts ways with environmental advocates on the issue of wilderness designation for the California desert. While he calls the desert "one of the crown jewels of America's public lands," he offered legislation in the 101st Congress to provide wilderness designation for 2.1 million acres, compared with the 9 million acres environmentalists want to protect. Lewis' proposal also permits grazing and motor-vehicle access in certain areas. No agreement was reached in the 101st Congress. In the 102nd, the House approved a bill to protect 8 million acres after rejecting Lewis' amendment to reduce the amount to 2.3 million acres. The bill died in the Senate.

At Home: Lewis' rise to the Republican Conference chairmanship raised his profile in California, leading to speculation that he might aim for a Senate seat in 1992.

Yet in 1990, Lewis learned the unease that sometimes visits members of the leadership — especially when the electorate is feeling hostile toward Congress. While Lewis was never seriously threatened, he did face a primary challenge and a falloff from his normal general-election tally.

In the primary, lawyer and political neophyte Mark I. Blankenship ran as an outsider. Unabashedly ambitious — he told a reporter he had his eye on the White House — Blankenship received a spate of publicity: To highlight the effect on Republican candidates if President Bush backed off his "no new taxes" pledge, The New York Times ran a feature story focusing on Blankenship's challenge to Lewis. The incumbent won easily, although Blankenship pulled off a fifth of the GOP vote.

Lewis was expected to have little trouble with Democrat Barry Norton, a welder: Stuck in Washington for most of the fall, Lewis applied part of his limited campaign time to the unsuccessful bid by Republican Bob Hammock to unseat Democratic Rep. George E. Brown Jr.

in the neighboring 36th District.

However, Lewis faced a backlash after he publicly supported the unpopular budget summit agreement in October. Although he won comfortably, his 61 percent tally was his lowest since his first contest in 1978.

Redistricting in 1992 cut Lewis's territory (which had seen its population nearly double in the 1980s) and also cut into the number of Republicans, dropping GOP registration 5 percentage points. But what remained was largely the core of Lewis' San Bernardino County district and still reliably Republican: Lewis actually improved on his 1990 showing by 2 percentage points.

A successful insurance broker, Lewis entered GOP politics in the early 1960s and won a seat on the San Bernardino School Board. After three years there, he sought a state Assembly seat in 1968 and won the first of five terms.

With an Assembly constituency that covered more than half the 37th Congressional District, Lewis was an obvious choice for Republicans in 1978 when GOP Rep. Shirley N. Pettis retired. Earlier in his career, Lewis had worked as a field representative for Jerry Pettis, Shirley's husband, who represented the district for eight years before his death in a plane crash in 1975. Declaring himself a candidate in the "Pettis tradition," Lewis won the five-candidate GOP primary with 55 percent of the vote, then won the general election handily.

He had his pick of two districts after the 1982 redistricting and chose the one that, while less Republican, included his home (then numbered the 35th). He soon established dominance, winning with at least 70 percent or more three times in the 1980s.

Committees

Appropriations (6th of 23 Republicans)
Veterans Affairs, Housing & Urban Development & Independent Agencies (ranking); Defense

Select Intelligence (7th of 7 Republicans)
Legislation; Program & Budget Authorization

Elections

1992 General		
Jerry Lewis (R)	129,563	(63%)
Donald M. Rusk (D)	63,881	(31%)
Margie Akin (PFP)	11,839	(6%)
1990 General		
Jerry Lewis (R)	121,602	(61%)
Barry Norton (D)	66,100	(33%)
Jerry Johnson (LIBERT)	13,020	(6%)

Previous Winning Percentages: **1988** (70%) **1986** (77%) **1984** (85%) **1982** (68%) **1980** (72%) **1978** (61%)

District Vote for President

1992

D 76,363 (35%)
R 86,453 (40%)
I 53,955 (25%)

Campaign Finance

	Receipts	Receipts from PACs		Expend-itures
1992				
Lewis (R)	$471,956	$358,045	(76%)	$546,541
Rusk (D)	$21,840	0		$21,555
1990				
Lewis (R)	$452,381	$292,014	(65%)	$211,940
Norton (D)	$2,266	0		$2,371

Key Votes

1993	
Require parental notification of minors' abortions	Y
Require unpaid family and medical leave	N
Approve national "motor voter" registration bill	N
Approve budget increasing taxes and reducing deficit	N
Approve economic stimulus plan	N
1992	
Approve balanced-budget constitutional amendment	Y
Close down space station program	N
Approve U.S. aid for former Soviet Union	Y
Allow shifting funds from defense to domestic programs	?
1991	
Extend unemployment benefits using deficit financing	X
Approve waiting period for handgun purchases	N
Authorize use of force in Persian Gulf	Y

Voting Studies

	Presidential Support		Party Unity		Conservative Coalition	
Year	S	O	S	O	S	O
1992	77	14	77	17	85	6
1991	81	16	78	16	84	5
1990	65	26	70	19	89	7
1989	78	21	80	17	83	17
1988	44	24	67	12	55	11
1987	68	30	81	12	91	2
1986	63	21	63	14	56	16
1985	65	28	75	18	84	11
1984	71	22	72	18	83	10
1983	70	20	74	17	74	8
1982	81	16	84	13	89	10
1981	72	20	75	15	81	15

Interest Group Ratings

Year	ADA	AFL-CIO	CCUS	ACU
1992	10	17	86	83
1991	0	18	100	83
1990	6	0	58	76
1989	10	25	78	79
1988	5	22	67	90
1987	8	13	93	83
1986	0	15	64	88
1985	10	27	62	76
1984	10	17	81	86
1983	5	13	89	88
1982	5	5	100	91
1981	5	0	100	79

41 Jay C. Kim (R)

Of Diamond Bar — Elected 1992; 1st Term

Born: March 27, 1939, Seoul, Korea.
Education: U. of Southern California, B.S. 1967, M.S. 1973; California State U., Los Angeles, M.S. 1980.
Occupation: Civil engineer.
Family: Wife, June Kim; three children.
Religion: Methodist.
Political Career: Diamond Bar City Council, 1990-91; mayor of Diamond Bar, 1991-93.
Capitol Office: 502 Cannon Bldg. 20515; 225-3201.

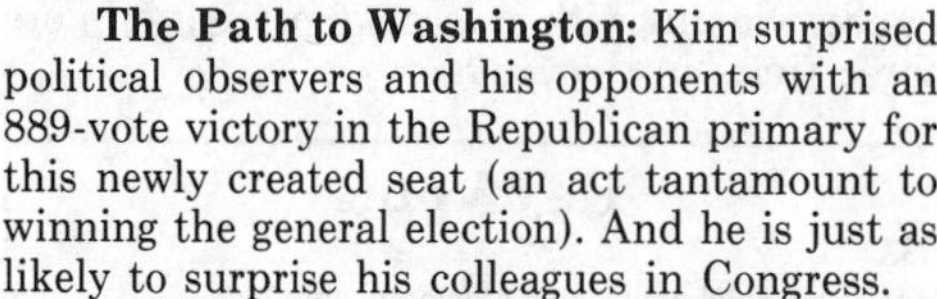

The Path to Washington: Kim surprised political observers and his opponents with an 889-vote victory in the Republican primary for this newly created seat (an act tantamount to winning the general election). And he is just as likely to surprise his colleagues in Congress.

Though mayor of the town of Diamond Bar in eastern Los Angeles County, Kim is anything but a government insider. His no-nonsense view that there is too much waste and unnecessary spending by the government may give his colleagues heartburn. That is especially likely on the Public Works and Transportation Committee, for which Kim campaigned successfully.

Most members who seek seats on Public Works have particular projects they want to see financed. Not Kim. He is coming to Public Works on a mission to cut out the pork. He also won a seat on the Small Business Committee.

Kim is a civil engineer and made his fortune through Jaykim Engineers Inc., which he founded in 1976. Jaykim concentrated on building roads and water reclamation projects and is one of five minority-owned companies hired to demolish buildings damaged in the 1992 L.A. riots.

Kim took to the floor more than the average freshman early in the 103rd Congress as a staunch opponent of deficit spending, higher taxes and government mandates. He criticized ing the president's economic plan, the Family and Medical Leave Act, infrastructure spending, and an increase in the debt limit (without which the country would default on previously incurred obligations).

He departs from the national party on abortion, essentially taking a libertarian stance and arguing that such decisions are none of the government's business. The position is consistent with Kim's hands-off economic view that government constrains many business decisions.

He also takes issue with the GOP's call for school vouchers, but not on philosophical grounds. He fears that to manage such a program would require an enormous bureaucracy — again, too much government. Kim's solution is to provide tax credits for families who pay private school tuition. That position reflects Kim's basic anti-tax conviction that a tax credit does not cost the government anything, because the money does not belong to the government.

Kim moved to California from South Korea in 1961 at age 22, fresh out of the South Korean army. After a series of menial jobs, he earned his degrees, adopted the United States as home and legally changed his given name from Chang Joon to Jay. Despite his years here, his speech remains accented and is neither polished nor glib. To the contrary, Kim is given to an honest bluntness — which may have served to his advantage in a campaign that featured him as an alternative to professional politicians.

The six-way GOP primary was the race that mattered in this demonstrably Republican district, newly drawn to accommodate the fast-growing suburbs where Los Angeles, Orange and San Bernardino counties meet.

The presumed front-runners were former Pomona Mayor Charles W. Bader and conservative businessman James V. Lacy from Yorba Linda. But Kim, who originally endorsed Bader, was approached to run as an alternative: Bader was seen as a 20-year insider. And Lacy was a Washington, D.C., lawyer who had just moved back to the area to make the race.

Kim's entrepreneurial success appealed to voters, and Bader's complaint that he was a wealthy government contractor fell flat. (Kim is selling his business to avoid any appearance of conflict of interest.) Kim out-hustled his opponents, energizing both the 10 percent of the district that is Asian-American and his Diamond Bar constituency. And his general support for abortion rights distinguished Kim from the flock of anti-abortion Republicans on the ballot.

In the general election, Kim easily outdistanced — and outspent — opponent Bob Baker, an intelligence analyst and Vietnam veteran. Baker may have benefited from a surge in Democratic registration during 1992. But the near 50 percent GOP registration in the 41st is a big cushion in a region where even registered Democrats are prone to vote Republican.

California 41

Parts of Orange, Los Angeles and San Bernardino counties

One goal of California's court-ordered reapportionment was to create as many districts as possible that follow county and city borders. The suburban 41st was not one of the successes: It splits three counties and runs up against a fourth. Its center is the intersection of Orange, Los Angeles and San Bernardino counties, and it reaches east to the northwestern border of Riverside County.

Primarily, this district consists of bedrooms for Los Angeles and the rest of Orange County. Some people in the eastern end of the district head farther east to work in the factories in Fontana.

About half the district's voters are in San Bernardino County, 20 percent in Orange County and 30 percent in Los Angeles County. In Orange County, the 41st includes Yorba Linda, part of Anaheim Hills and bits of Brea and Placentia. In Los Angeles County, it takes in Diamond Bar, a little bit of Walnut and a big bit of Pomona. In San Bernardino County, it includes Chino, Chino Hills, Montclair, Upland and Ontario.

The Orange County section of the 41st is a representative slice of the county: It is white-collar, conservative and affluent. Republicans outnumber Democrats here. In 1992, Kim found his strongest support in Orange County — 70 percent. He received 55 percent in Los Angeles County, 58 percent in San Bernardino County and 60 percent overall.

The section of San Bernardino County in the 41st is called the Inland Empire's West End. Real estate prices are relatively low, and many of its residents head south down the Carbon Canyon to work in Orange County.

Chino Hills' 28,000 residents are among the 41st's most conservative and affluent. Just north is Chino, a middle-income area whose 60,000 residents are almost evenly registered in both the parties.

North of Chino is the largest city in the district, Ontario, with 133,000 residents split between the 41st and the 42nd, which has the Democratic eastern side. The city's burgeoning airport — increasingly a passenger and cargo gateway into Los Angeles — is one of the area's primary growth engines. The airport's ability to bring passengers in and send goods out has spawned hotels, restaurants and distribution facilities nearby.

Upland, in the northern corner of the district, resembles its eastern neighbor, Rancho Cucamonga, in the 42nd. It is another conservative, wealthy area.

The economics begin to shift downward moving southwest to Montclair and into Los Angeles County, with the 41st's piece of Pomona. Montclair lacks the retailing and manufacturing activity that supports Ontario. Just south of Pomona is Diamond Bar, a more affluent suburb where Kim served as mayor before entering Congress.

George Bush won the 41st in 1992, taking 43 percent of the vote in the three-way race. It was one of Bush's relatively few California bright spots in what turned out to be a tough year for him statewide.

1990 Population: 572,663. White 389,458 (68%), Black 39,205 (7%), Other 144,000 (25%). Hispanic origin 180,331 (31%). 18 and over 400,070 (70%), 62 and over 43,038 (8%). Median age: 30.

Committees

Public Works & Transportation (16th of 24 Republicans)
Aviation; Economic Development; Surface Transportation

Small Business (15th of 18 Republicans)
Regulation, Business Opportunities and Technology

Campaign Finance

	Receipts	Receipts from PACs	Expend-itures
1992			
Kim (R)	$791,483	$91,900 (12%)	$764,895
Noonan (PFP)	$35	0	$35

Key Votes

1993

Require parental notification of minors' abortions	Y
Require unpaid family and medical leave	N
Approve national "motor voter" registration bill	N
Approve budget increasing taxes and reducing deficit	N
Approve economic stimulus plan	N

Elections

1992 General		
Jay C. Kim (R)	101,753	(60%)
Bob Baker (D)	58,777	(34%)
Mike Noonan (PFP)	10,136	(6%)
1992 Primary		
Jay C. Kim (R)	13,399	(30%)
Charles W. Bader (R)	12,510	(28%)
James V. Lacy (R)	12,070	(27%)
George Henry Margolis (R)	2,966	(7%)
John Hoover (R)	1,868	(4%)
James Todhunter (R)	1,753	(4%)

District Vote for President

1992

D 64,666 (35%)
R 78,902 (43%)
I 41,112 (22%)

42 George E. Brown Jr. (D)

Of Riverside — Elected 1962; 15th Term

Did not serve 1971-73.

Born: March 6, 1920, Holtville, Calif.
Education: El Centro Junior College, 1938; U. of California, Los Angeles, B.A. 1946.
Military Service: Army, 1942-46.
Occupation: Management consultant; physicist.
Family: Wife, Marta Macias; four children, three stepchildren.
Religion: Methodist.
Political Career: Monterey Park City Council, 1954-55; mayor of Monterey Park, 1955-58; Calif. Assembly, 1959-63; sought Democratic nomination for U.S. Senate, 1970.
Capitol Office: 2300 Rayburn Bldg. 20515; 225-6161.

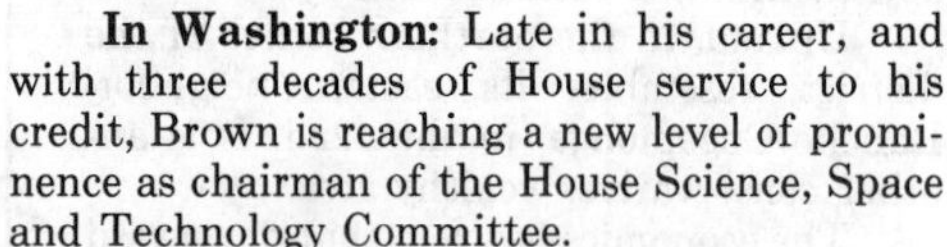

In Washington: Late in his career, and with three decades of House service to his credit, Brown is reaching a new level of prominence as chairman of the House Science, Space and Technology Committee.

Taking over the reins at Science at the beginning of the 102nd, Brown made a good start on plans to reinvigorate the committee and restore clout that dwindled under the previous chairman, Robert A. Roe of New Jersey.

Unlike Roe, Brown pushed through the annual authorization bill for NASA early enough to set the agenda for appropriations decisions.

Brown the affable cigar smoker and patient listener has mellowed considerably from the spirited anti-war crusader first elected in 1962. He now organizes district conferences on economic development and brings his reformist energies to bear on inside-baseball issues such as the imbalance of power between authorizing committees (such as Science) and appropriating committees.

But throughout his House career, broken by a one-term absence after a failed Senate bid in 1970, Brown has been consistent in a number of areas, including opposition to nuclear war and the militarization of space, and support for environmental protection efforts.

Economic changes, both domestic and global, have conspired to give the Science Committee a higher profile, making it a sought-after assignment for members who see high-tech industries as important to their districts.

Big-ticket projects such as the space station and the superconducting super collider, which enjoy only lukewarm support from the Clinton administration, will undoubtedly combine to keep Brown busy in the 103rd.

As Science chairman, Brown fought hard to keep the money flowing for the space station in the 102nd, despite his own reservations. "The space station is not the world's greatest science project," he said after winning a 1991 battle to preserve funding for the station. "But it happens to be a part of NASA's budget. And you don't go into an argument like that looking halfhearted."

Following an even tougher funding fight in 1992, Brown breathed a sigh of relief and said, perhaps prematurely: "We think this will put the issue behind us." Brown was optimistic in part because leading space station opponent Bob Traxler, who chaired the appropriations subcommittee overseeing NASA spending, was retiring at the end of the 102nd.

Ironically, however, the departure of another space station skeptic, former Rep. Leon E. Panetta of California, has led to renewed headaches for Brown. Panetta left the House to become Clinton's budget director, taking his doubts about the project to a powerful new level.

But Brown, a wily political survivor — witness his string of electoral victories in a district grown increasingly Republican — does have some chips he can call in with Clinton. In September 1992, Brown handed Clinton an effective tool in his campaign efforts to portray President Bush as unresponsive to the country's economic pain.

It was a study indicating that a program run by the U.S. Agency for International Development was spending millions of tax dollars encouraging firms to move manufacturing jobs from the U.S. to low-wage countries. The Bush administration denied it, but the charge raised eyebrows.

When Brown returned to the House in 1973, U.S. involvement in Vietnam had ended. He settled quietly into the Science and Agriculture committees and followed his issues, thoughtful but detached. On Agriculture, Brown has concentrated on issues of pesticide

California 42

San Bernardino County — San Bernardino

This is the heart of the "Inland Empire," composed of blue-collar bedrooms for Orange County and Los Angeles employers and a small manufacturing base.

San Bernardino (most of whose 164,000 people are in the 42nd) is an older community that grew about 40 percent during the 1980s; as brisk as that growth rate sounds, it was far outpaced by the population explosion in cities west of San Bernardino, such as Rancho Cucamonga and Ontario. Each of these now has upward of 100,000 residents.

San Bernardino is one of the last havens of affordably priced housing within tolerable commuting reach of Los Angeles; many who live here drive the 90 minutes it takes to get to jobs in L.A. Local leaders are trying to attract more industry to the area to spare residents from the treadmill of daily long-distance driving.

The San Bernardino area was a fruit-packing center in the 1930s. Today, its citrus industry shares space with electronics and aerospace firms. But the city is bracing for the 1994 closing of Norton Air Force Base. Studies are under way to determine what new use the base should be put to; options include an airport. One complicating factor is the need to clean up hazardous wastes at the facility.

Colton, a town of about 40,000 just southwest of San Bernardino, is about half Hispanic, 37 percent white, 8 percent black and 4 percent Asian. Many of its residents head a few miles west to work in Fontana's factories.

Fontana (population 88,000) is the area's factory town. It has a bit of a tough reputation: The Ku Klux Klan has been active here, and it is home to one of the world's largest Hell's Angels chapters.

The city's industry has been suffering. Kaiser Steel's Fontana works employed 9,000 in its heyday, but the company began slipping in the late 1970s, declared bankruptcy in 1983 and closed and sold the Fontana plant. The buyer, California Steel Industries, has 950 employees producing coiled steel, but the raw steel for that work has to come from elsewhere; the old Fontana blast furnace is being dismantled and shipped to China.

The western part of the 42nd rejects the "Inland Empire" label. Many of Rancho Cucamonga's 100,000 residents instead identify with Los Angeles, a half-hour to the west, and they cover their relatively high cost of living by commuting on the 10 Freeway to jobs in the city. Rancho Cucamonga is almost 70 percent white, 20 percent Hispanic and about five percent each black and Asian.

The city of San Bernardino, pulled by its large minority population, consistently votes Democratic in presidential elections. Much of the rest of the district, led by such areas as Rancho Cucamonga, votes Republican. Overall, voter registration in the 42nd is 53 percent Democratic to 47 percent Republican. In 1992 presidential voting, this mix yielded a solid showing for Bill Clinton: He won 46 percent of the district's vote.

1990 Population: 571,844. White 377,500 (66%), Black 63,239 (11%), Other 131,105 (23%). Hispanic origin 196,418 (34%). 18 and over 381,173 (67%), 62 and over 50,749 (9%). Median age: 28.

regulation and environmental protection.

The old peace advocate in Brown (a Quaker by upbringing) still surfaces in debates, particularly on space-based military programs. Brown voted against the January 1991 resolution authorizing the use of force against Iraq. And he was an early and outspoken foe of the Strategic Defense Initiative, supporting efforts to cut its funding.

In fact, Brown's efforts to curb the military's role in space research and policy may have hobbled his career in the 1980s. In November 1987 he resigned from the Intelligence Committee, saying he was stepping down in protest of Reagan administration policies on classifying information. But he was also under pressure from conservative Democrats who agreed with the administration's contention that Brown had divulged classified information on U.S. military satellite capabilities. Brown said he had relied only on published material.

In 1985 and 1987, Brown saw the chairmanship of the important Science Subcommittee on Space Science go to a colleague with far less seniority, Bill Nelson of Florida. Brown's strong opinions about the use of space funds may have alienated members who believe virtually any space expenditure is a good one.

Also in 1985, dispirited by a contentious battle over pesticide regulations, Brown gave up the chairmanship of the Agriculture subcommittee that oversaw the USDA's operations and research.

However, in the 100th Congress Brown regained that chairmanship and steered a more modest pesticide bill into law.

While Brown generally casts the liberal votes one would expect of him, creeping pragmatism has led him to cast some pro-defense votes he once might have denounced. In the 101st Congress, he unsuccessfully fought the recommendation of a blue-ribbon commission to close Norton Air Force Base in his district, though he was able to keep a ballistic missile section of the base from being relocated.

In 1980, he began voting for the B-1 bomber, a California product. "If the B-1 was being built in some other state and I didn't have two Air Force bases and a lot of retired military people who feel strongly about the B-1, I'd probably have voted the other way," Brown explained.

Brown became a peace advocate as a scientist and fought for his cause from the start of his first term. In 1963, he cast one of three votes against the extension of the draft. He voted against civil defense money, saying it "created a climate in which nuclear war becomes more credible."

By the spring of 1965, he already had begun speaking out against the Vietnam War, accusing President Lyndon B. Johnson of pretending "that the peace of mankind can be won by the slaughter of peasants in Vietnam." For five years, he refused to vote for any military spending.

Brown acquired a national reputation for his anti-war work during those years, but much of his legislative time was devoted to environmental issues. He supported a ban on offshore oil drilling along the California coast, backed federal land-use planning and proposed to outlaw production of internal combustion engines.

At Home: The 1992 redistricting in California left Brown surrounded by Republican districts that are likely to remain so indefinitely. The districts are numbered geographically, and Brown's 42nd District is the only one between 37 and 49 that sends a Democrat to the House. The remap also removed the Riverside portion of Brown's San Bernardino County district, stripping away one source of Democratic votes around the Riverside campus of the University of California and helping to account for a slippage in Democratic registration.

But the new map also left Brown with the city of San Bernardino and the nearby blue-collar suburbs of Fontana and Colton. The Hispanics and working-class whites who live there have been Brown's base in recent years (his first district was located far to the west, in Los Angeles County). And Brown continued to work his remarkable political magic, carrying the district against a challenger who was to make up for a lack of high-dollar financing with high-tech glamour.

That opponent was Dick Rutan, famous for having flown a lightweight aircraft around the world on one tank of fuel in 1986. Rutan had not run for office before, but he struck many observers as perfect for the anti-politician mood of 1992. The race drew national press coverage, but reporters who visited the district found Rutan was often ill at ease with the public. And the challenger was able to raise only half the money Brown had.

In the end, with Democrats winning nearly every winnable district and office in the state, Brown made it look less than close. A Libertarian candidate got more than 5 percent, helping to reduce Brown's share of the vote to a bare majority (a virtual tie with his all-time low of 51 percent in 1966). But Rutan managed only 44 percent, losing by just about the same percentage margin as Bob Hammock lost to Brown by in 1990.

Hammock's challenge, like Rutan's, was touted by national Republicans as the long-awaited end of Brown's run. Hammock had been a San Bernardino County supervisor for years and was believed to have broad bipartisan appeal.

It was not a friendly campaign. After Hammock won the June Republican primary, Brown sent a "congratulatory" telegram that also called on the real estate developer to release his business records. A mass mailing followed, detailing published allegations of potential Hammock conflicts of interest during his service on the county board. Hammock responded with a broadside about Brown's campaign fundraising from political action committees and his acceptance of honoraria.

After years of attacking Brown from the far right, GOP strategists hoped Hammock's moderate image would enable him to topple the liberal Brown. While taking anti-tax, anti-crime and strong-defense positions typical of Republican candidates, Hammock portrayed himself as an environmentalist and noted the strong support he had received at the local level from San Bernardino's Hispanic community.

However, Brown parried Hammock at every turn. He received endorsements from the League of Conservation Voters and the Sierra Club and held most of the Hispanic vote that is a crucial element of the Democratic base in the district. While Hammock tried to blame the closure of Norton Air Force Base on Brown's record of arms control and anti-war activism, Brown touted his efforts, albeit unsuccessful, to save the base and his subsequent work to convert it to useful purposes.

Prior to the Hammock bid in 1990, the Republican challenger to Brown in four of the previous five cycles was John Paul Stark — a hard-right Republican with a base among religious fundamentalists. Stark always kept Brown under 60 percent, but he never managed to bring him below 53 percent (1980).

Brown has persevered through more turbulent political seas than that. After serving as a local official and state assemblyman from a near-in Los Angeles suburb, Brown won a

House seat in 1962 and held it for four terms. But he gave it up in 1970 for a Democratic Senate primary campaign that would deal him his only defeat.

The 1970 primary boiled down to Brown and Rep. John V. Tunney, son of former boxing champion Gene Tunney. Brown's opposition to the Vietnam War gave him an initial advantage: After American troops invaded Cambodia that spring, polls began to show Brown — who had called for the impeachment of President Richard M. Nixon because of the invasion — in front of Tunney, who had been much less outspoken against the war.

But Tunney then turned the tables on Brown, accusing him of being a radical and advocating student violence. Brown attempted to deflect what he termed Tunney's "dirty" tactics, but failed and lost by a 9 percentage point margin.

Although Tunney went on to win the Senate seat, Brown exacted a revenge of sorts. His description of Tunney as the "lightweight son of the heavyweight champ" became part of California political folklore and helped end Tunney's career in 1976.

After the Senate race disappointment, Brown bounced back quickly. In 1972, he moved to a newly created district in the San Bernardino-Riverside area and won an eight-candidate primary with 28 percent of the vote. Running in a district with a strong Democratic registration advantage, Brown won easily in November. Brown then topped 60 percent in three consecutive elections before his close call against Stark in 1980.

Committees

Science, Space & Technology (Chairman)

Agriculture (2nd of 28 Democrats)
Department Operations; Specialty Crops and Natural Resources

Elections

1992 General

George E. Brown Jr. (D)	79,780	(51%)
Dick Rutan (R)	69,251	(44%)
Fritz R. Ward (LIBERT)	8,424	(5%)

1990 General

George E. Brown Jr. (D)	72,409	(53%)
Bob Hammock (R)	64,961	(47%)

Previous Winning Percentages: **1988** (54%) **1986** (57%) **1984** (57%) **1982** (54%) **1980** (53%) **1978** (63%) **1976** (62%) **1974** (63%) **1972** (56%) **1968** (52%) **1966** (51%) **1964** (59%) **1962** (56%)

District Vote for President

1992

D 76,964 (46%)
R 54,978 (33%)
I 35,828 (21%)

Campaign Finance

	Receipts	Receipts from PACs		Expend-itures
1992				
Brown (D)	$905,857	$502,920	(56%)	$916,137
Rutan (R)	$468,862	$69,065	(15%)	$443,272
1990				
Brown (D)	$818,181	$454,935	(56%)	$822,686
Hammock (R)	$538,381	$104,035	(19%)	$538,156

Key Votes

1993	
Require parental notification of minors' abortions	N
Require unpaid family and medical leave	Y
Approve national "motor voter" registration bill	Y
Approve budget increasing taxes and reducing deficit	Y
Approve economic stimulus plan	Y
1992	
Approve balanced-budget constitutional amendment	N
Close down space station program	N
Approve U.S. aid for former Soviet Union	Y
Allow shifting funds from defense to domestic programs	Y
1991	
Extend unemployment benefits using deficit financing	Y
Approve waiting period for handgun purchases	Y
Authorize use of force in Persian Gulf	N

Voting Studies

	Presidential Support		Party Unity		Conservative Coalition	
Year	**S**	**O**	**S**	**O**	**S**	**O**
1992	19	71	88	5	27	63
1991	38	59	83	7	30	65
1990	19	76	79	5	31	61
1989	31	55	87	4	22	73
1988	13	65	80	3	8	76
1987	18	70	78	5	21	65
1986	18	71	82	3	16	76
1985	20	68	84	5	9	76
1984	27	69	91	5	12	81
1983	16	77	84	5	11	82
1982	32	51	85	5	12	79
1981	38	57	77	10	19	75

Interest Group Ratings

Year	ADA	AFL-CIO	CCUS	ACU
1992	95	91	25	5
1991	70	92	20	15
1990	89	83	31	4
1989	75	100	40	0
1988	80	100	25	5
1987	76	86	7	10
1986	95	92	21	0
1985	85	93	28	6
1984	95	82	33	0
1983	90	100	25	0
1982	75	94	29	5
1981	85	86	12	13

43 Ken Calvert (R)

Of Riverside — Elected 1992; 1st Term

Born: June 8, 1953, Corona, Calif.
Education: Chaffey College, A.A. 1973; San Diego State U., B.A. 1975.
Occupation: Real estate executive.
Family: Wife, Robin L. Moore.
Religion: Protestant.
Political Career: Sought GOP nomination for U.S. House, 1982.
Capitol Office: 1523 Longworth Bldg. 20515; 225-1986.

The Path to Washington: In 1982, Calvert lost a close primary election for the House. That loss taught him a lesson that often has eluded other California politicians: Absentee voters can make a big difference in this state where ballots can either be mailed or carried into the polls on Election Day.

In 1992, Calvert concentrated on getting ballots to potential absentees. The tactic worked, earning him the distinction of winning not only the closest House contest but also the only one in which the outcome was reversed after Election Day. It was only after 17,000 "walk-in" absentee ballots were counted that Calvert's apparent 1,200-vote loss to Democrat Mark A. Takano turned into a 519-vote win.

The race should not have been that close, which raises doubts about Calvert's future. This western Riverside County district has a marginal GOP edge in registration and a tendency to vote Republican.

Several factors prevented Calvert from running away with the election. A weakened economy and a 12 percent unemployment rate had voters in an unhappy, if not angry, mood. Calvert ran a relatively lackluster campaign compared with Takano's tireless efforts. Takano also hurt Calvert, a commercial real estate developer, with charges that too-rapid growth was contributing to the economic woes.

Calvert promises to be a mainstream Republican, departing from party orthodoxy only on the issue of abortion rights, which he supports.

Calvert felt the pull of conflicting loyalties early in the 103rd Congress. He missed a vote related to granting the president modified line-item veto authority, which Calvert supports, to testify before the base-closure commission in behalf of March Air Force Base, a major employer in his district. The base is on the 1993 list to be converted to a reserve facility, a move that could cost the district thousands of jobs.

Calvert indicated that had he been present for the vote, he would have voted for both the Democratic bill, which the House passed in April and for an even more potent GOP substitute.

He will try to use his seat on the Science, Space and Technology Committee to benefit the district's high-tech employment base — some of which is defense-related and jeopardized by cutbacks. Calvert opposes the superconducting super collider, under construction in Texas, and will be a sought-after vote on that and other big-science issues.

And his seat on the Natural Resources Committee may prove helpful, given the region's water needs.

The campaign attracted no major officeholders, though seven Republicans and seven Democrats vied for the open seat in the primaries.

Neither Calvert nor Takano were seasoned politicians, but they were the closest to that on either ballot. Calvert had been active in county GOP circles, running the local party in the mid-1980s and helping to run campaigns for two prominent statewide Republicans, Gov. Pete Wilson and former Gov. George Deukmejian. Takano, a junior high school English and history teacher, was a member of the elected board of trustees of Riverside Community College.

Takano won his low-key primary with 29 percent and a margin of almost 3,200 votes. Calvert had more trouble. Two far more conservative candidates targeted him for his abortion rights position. And S. Joseph Khoury, a college professor, ran a high-profile and expensive campaign against Calvert. Together the attacks forced him to spend nearly $200,000.

But with the right wing split, Calvert managed to win 28 percent and lead Khoury by more than 2,500 votes.

The general election turned out to be gentlemanly, despite Takano's assault on Calvert's developer background. Calvert emphasized his business acumen and endorsement from the U.S. Chamber of Commerce. He called for campaign finance reform, urging that candidates be required to collect half their contributions locally to cut down on special interest influences. Yet, he relied heavily on national political action committees to build his campaign treasury, sending an urgent fundraising letter in mid-September.

California 43

Riverside County — Western suburbs

California gained seven House seats in the 1990 reapportionment, and this district is part of that bounty.

The old 37th District grew so much during the 1980s that by the time redistricting rolled around, there were enough people in it to fill up two complete districts: the 43rd, which takes in Riverside County's western edge, and the 44th, the county's eastern expanse.

To a great extent the 43rd serves as a bedroom district for three California regions. Its southern edge is just close enough to San Diego to house people who work in that city; immediately west of the 43rd lies Orange County and its aerospace industries and scattered small businesses; and beyond that — a full two- or three-hour drive for marathon commuters in the 43rd — are the office towers of downtown Los Angeles.

But in addition to its bedrooms, the district contains some of the largest avocado and citrus producers in the state, dairy ranchers to the west and March Air Force Base to the southeast of Riverside.

The largest city in the 43rd is Riverside, the county's seat, which was established as a silkworm-breeding center around 1870 and soon after jumped into the business of growing navel oranges. After decades of steady growth, the city's population began to take off in the 1950s.

Since this period of explosive growth started, Riverside city has been shifted in and out of the Riverside County district. In the 1960s, it was completely included; in the '70s, it was completely removed; in the '80s, it was split, but in a manner beneficial to the already-dominant GOP.

Now the city, with a population of 227,000, can anchor a district by itself. The 43rd has all of Riverside, including the city's more Democratic northern neighborhoods, its blue-collar communities and the area around the University of California at Riverside (8,900 students).

Despite the addition of Riverside's Democratic areas, Republicans retain a slight voter registration advantage over Democrats in the 43rd — 46 percent to 42 percent. The GOP's edge is bolstered by such fast-growing Riverside suburbs as Corona and Norco (populations 76,000 and 23,000, respectively). About 80,000 live in unincorporated county territory. The district is about one-quarter Hispanic, 6 percent black and 4 percent Asian.

The 1992 House race was tight all over the district. Calvert's razor-thin victory turned on the count of about 34,000 absentee ballots.

That number of absentee ballots, which would be extraordinary in other places, is more common in California's bedroom community districts: "If you leave for work at 5 in the morning and don't get home until 8 at night, you've got to vote absentee; the polls are closed," one local observer notes.

The district's 1992 presidential race was similarly close. George Bush beat Bill Clinton by only 797 votes out of about 200,000 cast.

1990 Population: 571,231. White 432,614 (76%), Black 33,851 (6%), Other 104,766 (18%). Hispanic origin 142,785 (25%). 18 and over 401,020 (70%), 62 and over 59,365 (10%). Median age: 30.

Committees

Natural Resources (12th of 15 Republicans)
National Parks, Forests & Public Lands; Native American Affairs; Oversight & Investigations

Science, Space & Technology (13th of 22 Republicans)
Space; Technology, Environment & Aviation

Campaign Finance

	Receipts	Receipts from PACs		Expend-itures
1992				
Calvert (R)	$423,001	$138,485	(33%)	$422,717
Takano (D)	$344,361	$156,537	(45%)	$303,691
Odom (AMI)	$7,987	$126	(2%)	$7,866

Key Votes

1993

Require parental notification of minors' abortions	Y
Require unpaid family and medical leave	N
Approve national "motor voter" registration bill	N
Approve budget increasing taxes and reducing deficit	N
Approve economic stimulus plan	N

Elections

1992 General		
Ken Calvert (R)	88,987	(47%)
Mark A. Takano (D)	88,468	(46%)
Gary R. Odom (AMI)	6,095	(3%)
Gene L. Berkman (LIBERT)	4,989	(3%)
John Schwab (write-in)	2,100	(1%)
1992 Primary		
Ken Calvert (R)	13,387	(28%)
S. Joseph Khoury (R)	10,624	(22%)
Bob Lynn (R)	8,784	(18%)
Larry P. Arnn (R)	8,750	(18%)
Bill Franklin (R)	2,694	(6%)
Daniel Hantman (R)	2,270	(5%)
William E. Jones (R)	1,958	(4%)

District Vote for President

	1992	
D	76,040	(38%)
R	76,837	(38%)
I	48,197	(24%)

44 Al McCandless (R)

Of La Quinta — Elected 1982; 6th Term

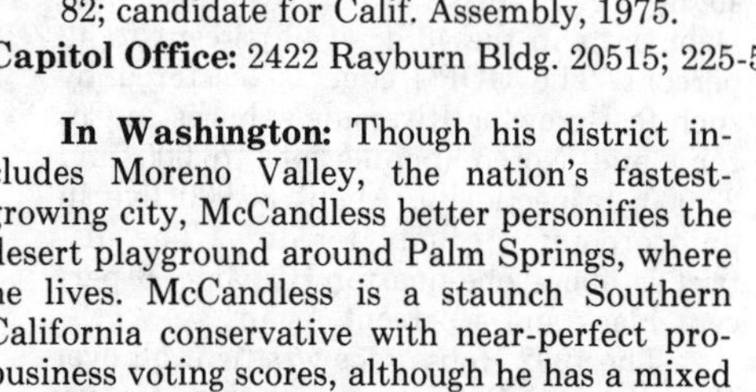

Born: July 23, 1927, Brawley, Calif.
Education: U. of California, Los Angeles, B.A. 1951.
Military Service: Marine Corps, 1945-46, 1950-52.
Occupation: Automobile dealer.
Family: Wife, Gail Walmsley Glass; five children.
Religion: Protestant.
Political Career: Riverside County supervisor, 1970-82; candidate for Calif. Assembly, 1975.
Capitol Office: 2422 Rayburn Bldg. 20515; 225-5330.

In Washington: Though his district includes Moreno Valley, the nation's fastest-growing city, McCandless better personifies the desert playground around Palm Springs, where he lives. McCandless is a staunch Southern California conservative with near-perfect pro-business voting scores, although he has a mixed record on social issues, such as abortion.

He was 55 before he came to Congress, but McCandless is now in his sixth term and, with attrition, has risen to the senior ranks on the Banking and Government Operations committees. His participation has often been at the margins, but his age (he is the second-oldest Republican on Banking) and business experience have lent weight to his views on government and free enterprise.

He regularly draws upon his past as a car dealer to bring a special perspective to policy debates. Once, when arguing against a nuclear-weapons freeze on the grounds that U.S. weaponry was inferior, he said: "We have Model Ts, and they have Thunderbirds."

McCandless' abiding resentment of federal regulation is so strong that it often limits his ability to play a consensus-building role when disputes are being thrashed out. Even some conservative Republicans say he can be too opinionated to play a significant role in shaping legislation. That could handicap McCandless in the 103rd Congress, as the Banking Committee — and its Consumer Credit Subcommittee, where he sits as ranking Republican — have become much more liberal and urban-oriented.

In the 102nd Congress, McCandless played a key role in blocking a bill to impose new federal regulations on credit reporting agencies. Consumer advocates said those businesses were all but unregulated in many states and that they ran roughshod over potential borrowers. The advocates said borrowers often had difficulty correcting erroneous reports of unpaid bills and could not get a copy of their own credit reports without paying high fees.

McCandless expressed sympathy with the goals of the bill's sponsors but complained that it would be too costly and difficult to implement. Allied with Georgia Democrat Doug Barnard Jr., McCandless not only fought against amendments intended to strengthen the proposed federal law but also insisted that any federal law pre-empt the states from imposing even tougher measures, if they chose.

McCandless prevailed on the pre-emption issue in committee and on the House floor, and as a consequence Democratic sponsors withdrew the bill from consideration.

McCandless also erected a formidable roadblock in a much less partisan fight over redesigning the nation's circulating coins.

He was generally supportive of Bush administration banking initiatives, such as the savings and loan bailout and proposals in 1991 to make wholesale changes in the nation's banking laws. He strongly supported such administration initiatives as curtailing deposit insurance coverage and allowing banks to expand into other businesses and open branches in different states. Those ideas so upset smaller California banks that they briefly tried to recruit the president of a local bank with ties to McCandless to run against him.

One cause McCandless has pursued for much of his House career is protecting the Social Security system. He has proposed removing the Social Security trust funds from calculations of the federal deficit and making the Social Security Administration an independent agency. In each of the past three Congresses, he has introduced bills to repeal the limit on how much Social Security recipients can earn without penalty. He calls the limitation "an unnecessary burden on the elderly."

If he has been rock steady on pocketbook issues, McCandless has had moments of ambivalence in his social conservatism. In 1991 he voted against allowing privately financed abortions in military hospitals overseas. But in 1990 and 1992 he voted to allow the practice.

McCandless has also been known to come to the defense of a federal program. For instance, he favors the mortgage guarantee programs of the Federal Housing Administration. And in 1992 he won inclusion of a $10 million

California 44

Eastern Riverside County

The 44th looks similar to the district McCandless represented in the 1980s, but remapping lopped off more than 500,000 people who had been on the western side of his turf. The old 37th saw more population growth during the past decade than any other district in the country. Census-takers in 1990 found that McCandless had enough constituents to fill two districts. In redistricting, he kept much of the land he had represented, but lost half the people.

Population in Moreno Valley, which is just east of Riverside and has 119,000 residents, is exploding. Before growth restrictions and the recession put on the brakes, it was picking up an additional 10,000 families a year. The city anchors the western side of the 44th, with cities such as Beaumont and Perris nearby.

The eastern portion of the district's population lives in the Coachella Valley, through which runs the 10 Freeway on its way out to Blythe and the Arizona border.

Out here, the leisure class of the oasis resorts of Rancho Mirage and Palm Springs contribute their ample wealth to the local economies. Although former President Gerald R. Ford has made his home in the area, it is better known for its Hollywood set.

Although one-quarter of Palm Springs' residents are 65 or older, the city is a bit younger than it used to be; the median age of its residents dropped 3 years during the 1980s. The city expanded from 32,000 residents in 1980 to 40,000 in 1990 — a 25 percent growth rate (which is positively sluggish by the high standards of this booming area).

A few miles southeast of Palm Springs is Palm Desert, where the population almost doubled in the 1980s, to 23,000. Here the older set became more dominant: The 65-and-over population went up almost 150 percent.

While this area is famed as a retirement destination, and while the number of older residents did grow rapidly, overall in Riverside County their influx was overshadowed by a larger immigration of younger people. The percentage of residents 65 and older in the county dropped from 15 percent to 13 percent during the 1980s.

Despite the growth of the district's suburbs and resorts, farmers continue to play a major role in the economy and politics of the 44th. Irrigation ditches knife across Riverside County, and cotton, date and livestock producers battle to keep their scarce water resources from being diverted to the urbanized areas. Riverside was originally a trade center for the citrus ranches of the Santa Ana River basin; the first domestic navel orange was grown here in the 1870s. Now the farming centers around Blythe, a burg of 8,000 reached by taking the 10 Freeway 80 miles east through the desert.

This is traditionally a very Republican district — the GOP's 3-point registration advantage understates the point — but Bill Clinton did very well here in 1992, taking 41 percent of the vote, 5 points more than George Bush.

1990 Population: 571,583. White 437,286 (77%), Black 29,354 (5%), Other 104,943 (18%). Hispanic origin 160,696 (28%). 18 and over 417,411 (73%), 62 and over 121,465 (21%). Median age: 34.

study of how to reduce the salinity of the inland Salton Sea as part of a sweeping water projects bill.

At Home: Redistricting added an extra degree of excitement to McCandless' political life, separating him from much of his old base and decreasing the Republican tilt in the district. Indeed, the GOP dropped from a 7-percentage-point advantage to a 1-point deficit in party registration. George Bush, who had carried McCandless' old district by 64,500 votes in 1988, lost McCandless' new district by 10,000 votes in 1992.

McCandless was more fortunate. While redistricting took away his affluent sections of Riverside and its immediate environs, he was just as comfortable in the exurban, desert portions of the 44th (there was plenty of the old district to go around, as its 86 percent population growth rate was the highest in the nation in the 1980s). Moreover, Democratic challenger Georgia Smith's campaign fund did not break $8,000. McCandless received 54 percent of the vote, his second-lowest victory margin ever.

Two years earlier, McCandless' low profile had nearly cost him his seat when the district's outnumbered Democrats put up the well-known actor Ralph Waite as their candidate. Waite had played the stalwart father of a rural Depression-era family in the long-running TV series "The Waltons." He was more familiar than McCandless to many voters, especially the thousands of new residents who had flooded Riverside County in recent years.

To reinforce his local base, first-time candidate Waite emphasized his community activities, including his work with an alcohol-and-drug rehabilitation center he helped found. The thrust of Waite's campaign, though, was an effort to tie McCandless' membership on the Banking Committee to the savings and loan crisis. While not accusing the incumbent of direct ethics violations, Waite said McCandless stood idly by while the scandal unfolded. McCandless countered that he had supported the 1987 industry-financed bailout of the Federal Savings and Loan Insurance Corporation.

McCandless, who had never had to run a big-money House campaign, was somewhat slow to organize for the contest. But when polls showed Waite moving up, McCandless tapped the network of affluent Republicans in the district's desert communities: Former President Gerald R. Ford and comedian Bob Hope were among those who came to his aid.

McCandless hung on to win with a plurality of just under 50 percent, to 45 percent for Waite. That close call ended a string of three consecutive elections in which McCandless had taken 64 percent.

Although McCandless, a longtime Riverside County supervisor, was little known outside his Palm Springs area base when he embarked on his 1982 House bid, he emerged atop a multi-candidate Republican primary field with 25 percent of the vote. Running in a newly created district with a strong Republican tilt, McCandless easily got by the Democratic nominee in the fall with 59 percent.

Committees

Banking, Finance & Urban Affairs (7th of 20 Republicans)
Consumer Credit & Insurance (ranking); International Development, Finance, Trade & Monetary Policy

Government Operations (2nd of 16 Republicans)
Legislation & National Security (ranking)

Elections

1992 General		
Al McCandless (R)	110,333	(54%)
Georgia Smith (D)	81,693	(40%)
Phil Turner (LIBERT)	11,515	(6%)
1992 Primary		
Al McCandless (R)	33,738	(61%)
Bud Mathewson (R)	11,323	(21%)
Lewis A. Silva (R)	10,113	(18%)
1990 General		
Al McCandless (R)	115,469	(50%)
Ralph Waite (D)	103,961	(45%)
Gary R. Odom (AMI)	6,474	(3%)
Bonnie Flickinger (LIBERT)	6,178	(3%)

Previous Winning Percentages: **1988** (64%) **1986** (64%) **1984** (64%) **1982** (59%)

District Vote for President

	1992
D	87,180 (41%)
R	76,772 (36%)
I	50,867 (24%)

Campaign Finance

	Receipts	Receipts from PACs		Expend-itures
1992				
McCandless (R)	$318,312	$195,137	(61%)	$278,880
Smith (D)	$7,693	$1,448	(19%)	$5,748
1990				
McCandless (R)	$551,789	$179,600	(33%)	$602,444
Waite (D)	$622,159	$149,266	(24%)	$624,560
Flickinger (LIBERT)	$2,318	0		$2,318

Key Votes

1993	
Require parental notification of minors' abortions	Y
Require unpaid family and medical leave	N
Approve national "motor voter" registration bill	N
Approve budget increasing taxes and reducing deficit	N
Approve economic stimulus plan	N
1992	
Approve balanced-budget constitutional amendment	Y
Close down space station program	N
Approve U.S. aid for former Soviet Union	N
Allow shifting funds from defense to domestic programs	N
1991	
Extend unemployment benefits using deficit financing	N
Approve waiting period for handgun purchases	N
Authorize use of force in Persian Gulf	Y

Voting Studies

	Presidential Support		Party Unity		Conservative Coalition	
Year	**S**	**O**	**S**	**O**	**S**	**O**
1992	78	22	90	9	96	4
1991	85	14	94	6	97	0
1990	71	29	92	7	98	2
1989	77	19	86	6	93	2
1988	67	27	84	5	95	3
1987	67	26	83	6	86	9
1986	77	18	84	11	94	6
1985	74	21	89	4	98	0
1984	71	27	90	8	92	8
1983	90	10	86	10	85	11

Interest Group Ratings

Year	ADA	AFL-CIO	CCUS	ACU
1992	10	17	75	88
1991	5	8	90	90
1990	6	8	79	92
1989	0	0	100	88
1988	10	0	92	95
1987	8	7	93	82
1986	5	7	94	95
1985	5	0	91	86
1984	5	0	71	92
1983	5	0	95	87

45 Dana Rohrabacher (R)

Of Huntington Beach — Elected 1988; 3rd Term

Born: June 21, 1947, Coronado, Calif.
Education: Los Angeles Harbor College, 1965-67; California State U., Long Beach, B.A. 1969; U. of Southern California, M.A. 1971.
Occupation: White House speechwriter; journalist.
Family: Single.
Religion: Baptist.
Political Career: No previous office.
Capitol Office: 1027 Longworth Bldg. 20515; 225-2415.

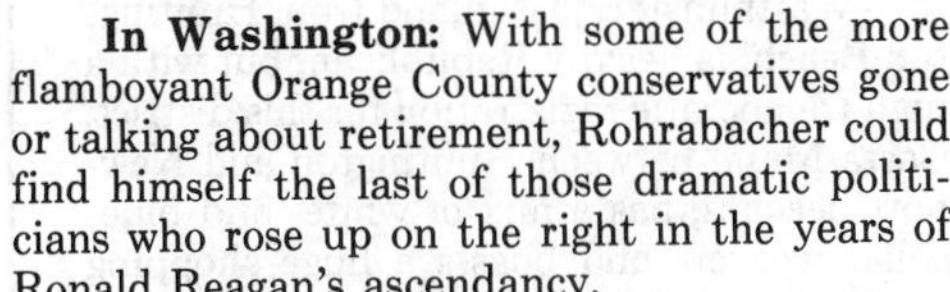

In Washington: With some of the more flamboyant Orange County conservatives gone or talking about retirement, Rohrabacher could find himself the last of those dramatic politicians who rose up on the right in the years of Ronald Reagan's ascendancy.

Most of the Republicans elected in the last few cycles from the suburbs of the Los Angeles Basin have been lawyers and businessmen — conservatives not only in substance but in style. Rohrabacher, as if to make a virtue of contrast, is bearded and single, counts heavy-metal rocker Sammy Hagar as a friend and says John Wayne taught him how to drink tequila. He has said he patterns his life on that of Ernest Hemingway, a man's man. And when the rest of his freshman class was going through orientation, Rohrabacher was off to Afghanistan to make contact with the Mujahedeen.

Rohrabacher once persuaded Reagan (then a candidate for governor) not to disband an organization of young campaign workers by camping out overnight on Reagan's front lawn. Later, after a stint as a fire-and-crime reporter and another writing editorials for the conservative Orange County Register, Rohrabacher became a speechwriter in Reagan's White House. He also served as assistant press secretary for Reagan's 1976 and 1980 presidential campaigns.

Once in Congress, Rohrabacher became known as Sen. Jesse Helms' House-side partner in the battle against the National Endowment for the Arts and the funding of works some found profane or obscene.

More recently, though, perhaps for reasons not unrelated to the change in personality-type among his colleagues, Rohrabacher has been visible on such local issues as saving the Long Beach Naval Shipyard and the proposed space station. The shipyard employs many of Rohrabacher's constituents, and some of the controversial space station is being built in his district.

Early in 1993, Rohrabacher was part of the team of Californians lobbying hard to keep the Long Beach facility off the Pentagon's list of suggested base closings. When the list was released in March 1993, it was not slated for closing (although the commission itself could still kill the facility).

During debates on the space station in the Science, Space and Technology Committee and in the full House, Rohrabacher has criticized NASA management as the source of most of the cost overruns and other problems with the project. He called for a "revolutionary reform" in the way NASA is run and defended the work on the project done by people in his district.

Rohrabacher won a round by keeping funding for the Single-Stage-To-Orbit (SSTO) vehicle from being eliminated in the 102nd Congress. He was, however, unable to prevent the halving of $175 million in funding for a National Aerospace Plane, a long-discussed craft that would fly 25 times the speed of sound. Both projects would have been built by companies in or near his district.

He was also unable to make much difference with his crusade against public funding of art, ultimately moving the House to approve only the most minimal restrictions. Rohrabacher said in 1989 that "censorship is not the solution; the answer is getting the government out of the arts."

At Home: Rohrabacher's high profile on the arts issue was bound to provoke criticism. But the only glitch in his otherwise routine 1990 re-election campaign was a magazine article that portrayed him as a hypocrite.

In its issue dated Nov. 5, The New Republic published an article titled "The Dope on Dana." The story said that although Rohrabacher had been a conservative Republican in his youth, he also experimented with drugs. Rohrabacher was also said to have declared himself an "anarchist" after his libertarian views cost him the chairmanship of a Young Americans for Freedom chapter.

Rohrabacher responded angrily, calling the article "character assassination." He said the magazine had timed its publication just prior to the election to punish him for his efforts against federal funding of obscene art. Its effect is hard to gauge precisely. He had a rematch that

California 45

Coastal Orange County

There are two distinct flavors of communities in the 45th — coastal and interior — but they both taste Republican.

Seal Beach anchors the coastal section. A quarter of its 25,000 residents live in a seniors-only community, which makes for quite a gray city: 37 percent of Seal Beach's residents are over 65, 22 percent are over 75 and 7 percent are over 85. Ninety percent of its residents are non-Hispanic whites.

Heading southeast down the coast is Huntington Beach, whose permanent population of 182,000 — mostly young aerospace and other high-tech workers and their families — is supplemented in the summer by those eager to "shred" some waves in surfing competitions, hence its nickname "Surf City." Huntington Harbor is an affluent section of the city, with such accoutrements as backyard boat slips. The rest of the city consists of huge housing tracts with a few small business districts sprinkled in.

Huntington Beach also has a McDonnell Douglas plant that is the prime design and manufacturing facility for the space station *Freedom*. It employs 7,500 people, which so far has cushioned the 45th from the worst of Southern California's recession, but the district obviously has a lot of eggs in the space station basket. As the Clinton administration seeks to cut the costs of the program, this area could be pinched.

Newport Beach resembles the other coastal communities — more bedrooms for aerospace white-collar workers — but looks a little different: Its terrain lifts into some rolling hills and Newport Bay runs right up its middle.

Compared with the coast, the 45th's interior areas tend to be more blue collar and less affluent, and they have a higher Democratic registration. But they are conservative and they vote Republican: "If there's a place where there are Reagan Democrats, it's Westminster, Garden Grove [in the 46th] and Stanton," a local GOP observer says reverently.

The blue collar of the interior is sky blue, with many working for aerospace companies within the district or commuting to those in Anaheim, Torrance or Long Beach.

Westminster, just inland from Huntington Beach, is heavily Republican, but with a high Democratic registration for this district. Costa Mesa, between Huntington and Newport beaches, has a mix of white- and blue-collar workers and boasts a huge shopping mall — South Coast Plaza, which is placed on maps of the region.

The district reaches north between Cypress and Garden Grove to take in Stanton. Democrats here have a seven-point registration advantage, a figure much higher than elsewhere in the district. The city (population 30,000) is not as wealthy as others in the 45th; 15 percent of its housing units are either mobile homes or trailers. To the north, the district takes in a small residential slice of Anaheim.

George Bush won this district in 1992 with 42 percent of its vote, compared with 32 percent for Bill Clinton and 25 percent for Ross Perot.

1990 Population: 570,874. White 468,855 (82%), Black 7,110 (1%), Other 94,909 (17%). Hispanic origin 84,684 (15%). 18 and over 450,058 (79%), 62 and over 70,820 (12%). Median age: 33.

November with Democratic college professor Guy C. Kimbrough and won with just 5 percentage points less in his vote share than he had received against Kimbrough in 1988.

The 1988 race was Rohrabacher's first try for elective office. He took the plunge when 42nd District GOP Rep. Daniel E. Lungren announced he was leaving to become state treasurer (denied confirmation for that office, Lungren won election as state attorney general in 1990).

Rohrabacher was at first regarded as an underdog in a tough GOP primary field that included an Orange County supervisor who had Lungren's support and university president Steve Horn (who would run and win in a neighboring district in 1992). Despite the competition, Rohrabacher found his way. A campaign fundraiser featuring former Marine Lt. Col. Oliver L. North raised Rohrabacher's standing among conservatives while adding $100,000 to his coffers. He ended up with 35 percent of the primary vote, well ahead of his nearest rival.

Republicans in Orange County are not supposed to worry about re-election or redistricting. But in 1992, Rohrabacher paid close attention to both. The new map may have slightly reduced the GOP majority in his redrawn base, but the percentage of Democrats did not rise, indicating some voter dissatisfaction with both parties. Rohrabacher outspent his Democratic opponent, accountant Patricia McCabe, by 10-to-1. But his share of the vote dropped roughly another 4 percentage points, leaving him at the 55 percent mark.

Committees

District of Columbia (2nd of 4 Republicans)
Judiciary & Education (ranking); Government Operations & Metropolitan Affairs

Foreign Affairs (14th of 18 Republicans)
Asia & the Pacific; Economic Policy, Trade & the Environment

Science, Space & Technology (8th of 22 Republicans)
Space; Technology, Environment & Aviation

Elections

1992 General		
Dana Rohrabacher (R)	123,731	(55%)
Patricia McCabe (D)	88,508	(39%)
Gary D. Copeland (LIBERT)	14,777	(7%)
1992 Primary		
Dana Rohrabacher (R)	30,649	(48%)
Peter Buffa (R)	17,748	(28%)
Peter Green (R)	15,592	(24%)
1990 General		
Dana Rohrabacher (R)	109,353	(59%)
Guy C. Kimbrough (D)	67,189	(36%)
Richard Gibb Martin (LIBERT)	7,744	(4%)

Previous Winning Percentage: **1988** (64%)

District Vote for President

1992
D 80,646 (32%)
R 105,893 (42%)
I 63,609 (25%)

Campaign Finance

	Receipts	Receipts from PACs		Expend-itures
1992				
Rohrabacher (R)	$323,608	$108,926	(34%)	$321,912
McCabe (D)	$32,944	$8,298	(25%)	$32,473
1990				
Rohrabacher (R)	$423,924	$119,075	(28%)	$398,963
Kimbrough (D)	$29,555	$7,950	(27%)	$28,350

Key Votes

1993	
Require parental notification of minors' abortions	Y
Require unpaid family and medical leave	N
Approve national "motor voter" registration bill	N
Approve budget increasing taxes and reducing deficit	N
Approve economic stimulus plan	N
1992	
Approve balanced-budget constitutional amendment	Y
Close down space station program	N
Approve U.S. aid for former Soviet Union	N
Allow shifting funds from defense to domestic programs	N
1991	
Extend unemployment benefits using deficit financing	N
Approve waiting period for handgun purchases	N
Authorize use of force in Persian Gulf	Y

Voting Studies

	Presidential Support		Party Unity		Conservative Coalition	
Year	**S**	**O**	**S**	**O**	**S**	**O**
1992	74	26	93	5	88	13
1991	70	30	91	8	89	11
1990	74	25	90	10	80	20
1989	70	29	82	15	93	7

Interest Group Ratings

Year	ADA	AFL-CIO	CCUS	ACU
1992	20	25	75	96
1991	15	17	90	100
1990	6	8	86	96
1989	10	9	90	96

46 Robert K. Dornan (R)

Of Garden Grove — Elected 1976; 8th Term

Did not serve 1983-85.

Born: April 3, 1933, New York, N.Y.
Education: Loyola U. (Los Angeles, Calif.), 1950-53.
Military Service: Air Force, 1953-58; Air Force Reserve, Air National Guard, 1958-75.
Occupation: Broadcast journalist and producer.
Family: Wife, Sallie Hansen; five children.
Religion: Roman Catholic.
Political Career: Candidate for mayor of Los Angeles, 1973; sought Republican nomination for U.S. Senate, 1982.
Capitol Office: 2402 Rayburn Bldg. 20515; 225-2965.

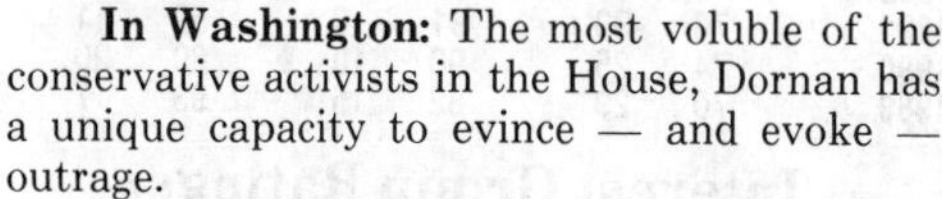

In Washington: The most voluble of the conservative activists in the House, Dornan has a unique capacity to evince — and evoke — outrage.

An Air Force pilot in the 1950s and a lifetime hawk, Dornan is also known as an advocate of strict morality. He said in 1992 that he was "nauseated" by the Democrats' nomination of Bill Clinton, who had faced allegations of draft evasion and marital infidelity. As it became evident that President George Bush — a friend and a man Dornan greatly admired — could lose to Clinton, Dornan's rhetoric escalated until it reached fever pitch.

During a one-minute speech on the House floor in August 1992, Dornan described Clinton as a "womanizer-adulterer" and "disgraced draft dodger." North Carolina Democratic Rep. W. G. "Bill" Hefner stepped in as Dornan's minute expired and demanded that the Speaker cut Dornan off. Dornan then engaged Hefner in an argument, and they nearly came to blows.

It was the kind of event that rallies fans — those who see Dornan as a conservative crusader for truths too often soft-pedaled by others. Indeed, the former actor and TV talk-show host has a national constituency that follows his fiery speeches and his appearances on TV and radio shows. That following is one reason the eight-term veteran has spoken of running for president himself in 1996, although his only previous contest above the House level was a failed bid for the Senate in 1982 (he finished fourth in the primary with 8 percent of the vote). But if Dornan's bluster and bravado attract attention, they also attract derision from critics, who belittle him as a hotheaded ideologue. Clinton told reporters late in the 1992 campaign, "Every time I see Dornan, he looks like he needs a rabies shot."

Dornan spent hours during the last weeks of the 102nd Congress in nighttime floor speeches in which he suggested a link between Clinton's anti-Vietnam War activities and a tourist trip Clinton took in 1969 to Moscow. After a White House meeting in which Dornan and others argued that the issue would destroy Clinton, Bush himself publicly questioned the Moscow trip.

But the strategy backfired. Voters who were mainly worried about the economy viewed the Moscow issue as the sort of negative campaigning for which they had little tolerance in 1992. Newspaper editorials accused Bush of tactics similar to those of redbaiting Sen. Joseph R. McCarthy of the 1950s.

With Clinton in the White House, Dornan seems destined to be an implacable opponent. A member of the Armed Services and Select Intelligence committees, Dornan strongly opposes most defense budget cuts Clinton has proposed.

Dornan can become personally identified with defense programs he advocates. His support during the 1980s for the B-1 bomber earned him the lasting nickname of "B-1 Bob."

But Dornan is best-known for his activism on social policy. His opposition to abortion is unsurpassed in the House: The author of a proposed constitutional amendment to ban most abortions, Dornan has brought models of fetuses to the House floor and sent members a video purporting to show a fetus "sucking its thumb and fighting the abortion."

Dornan's interests in military and social issues merged in his opposition to Clinton's plan to allow homosexuals to serve in the military. Dornan proposed a bill to codify the ban, saying he represented "brave men and women in uniform ... who, because Bill Clinton is their commander in chief, have no voice in Washington."

Among the few issues on which Dornan and Clinton agree is the establishment of a "police corps." A Dornan amendment, approved by the House in 1991, would have authorized funding of scholarships to students who pledge to perform police service after graduation; however, the crime bill to which the provision was attached was not enacted. Dornan resubmitted the proposal in the 103rd Congress.

At Home: For those who enjoy watching

California 46

Part of Orange County; Santa Ana; Garden Grove

The 46th is a blue-collar district, full of older suburban homes and younger families. Its defense subcontractors are the backbone of the region's large defense and aerospace companies. But with the defense and aerospace industries flat on their backs, the 46th is hurting.

Most of the district's population is contained within two cities, Santa Ana in the south and Garden Grove in the north.

Santa Ana, with 294,000 residents, is the area's hub and the seat of Orange County. It has the crime and gang problems typical of many California cities, and these problems are spilling into Garden Grove and adjacent districts. (Garden Grove is struggling with Asian gangs that have cropped up in recent years.)

Garden Grove is a more residential area than Santa Ana. It divides roughly into three sections: the western, more affluent part; the center, which is a mix of Vietnamese, Koreans and Hispanics; and the eastern, very heavily Hispanic part. Little Saigon sits just south of the district in Westminster.

Garden Grove is probably best known for the "positive thinking" television ministry of Robert Schuller and his Crystal Cathedral.

In recent years, there has been an influx of Indochinese refugees into Garden Grove, spurring a conservative backlash from some of its white, blue-collar workers.

Garden Grove is now 20 percent Asian, 23 percent Hispanic and 1 percent black. On the whole, the district is half Hispanic, 12 percent Asian and 2 percent black.

The northern part of the 46th includes the southern part of Anaheim, a chunk that has the look and feel of Garden Grove, which it borders.

The 46th does not include the wealthier area of Anaheim off to the east known as Anaheim Hills, which is split between the 41st and 47th districts. The part of Anaheim that is in the 46th does include Disneyland, many of whose employees come from the district. The park employs about 9,000 in the winter and 12,000 in the summer. Thousands of jobs at a variety of hotels and other supporting businesses depend on the park.

Other than Disneyland, there is no one employer within the 46th that drives its economy; the district is dotted with defense subcontractors and small businesses. Some residents head an hour west to the shipyard in Long Beach, but most scatter to companies all over Orange County.

The Democratic Party has a slight registration advantage over the GOP here, 46 to 45 percent, but most of the Democrats are conservative and the district votes Republican.

In 1992, George Bush won here and Dornan beat his Democratic opponent by 9 points. Bush took 40 percent of the vote, compared with 37 percent for Bill Clinton and 23 percent for Ross Perot. Still, Bush's tally here was more than 20 percentage points below his 1988 showing in the old 38th, a district with similar lines.

1990 Population: 571,380. White 380,053 (67%), Black 14,226 (2%), Other 177,101 (31%). Hispanic origin 285,529 (50%). 18 and over 405,602 (71%), 62 and over 49,393 (9%). Median age: 27.

Dornan, either as a soul mate or as entertainment, time may be running short. Whether he runs for national or statewide office, Dornan said in April 1993 that he was contemplating retirement from the House at the end of the 103rd Congress. An advocate of term limits, Dornan has proposed legislation that would restrict each House and Senate member to a maximum of 12 years' tenure.

He was in no mood to retire in 1992, however. Although his district was not as badly dismembered as it had been in the 1982 remapping (which drove him into his ill-starred Senate race), it took on a slightly more Democratic tilt. Moreover, Dorgan was challenged in the primary by Judith M. Ryan, a retired Superior Court judge who favored abortion rights.

The Dornan-Ryan primary received national press attention but drew only about 27,000 GOP voters, three-fifths of whom wanted to stick with the incumbent. The November race figured to be something of an anticlimax. But Democrat Robert John Banuelos and a Libertarian candidate ran well enough to hold Dornan to 50 percent.

Turnout in the 46th remains low, reflecting the nascent political status of its large Hispanic and Asian populations. But this is swiftly becoming a swing district, adding one more element to Dornan's calculations about his future.

Dornan could sense trouble even in 1990. Although his share of the vote that year dropped just 2 percentage points from the 60 percent he got in 1988, the vote was less an election than a referendum: The Democratic nominee had dropped out of the race months earlier.

Dornan first entered politics after an eclectic

career that included five years as an Air Force pilot, various journalism jobs, parts in TV dramas and several years as a TV talk-show host. He spent much time on the road, registering black voters in Alabama in the 1960s and trying to ban objectionable textbooks in West Virginia in the 1970s. He also raised the visibility of the prisoner-of-war issue and invented the POW bracelet.

Dornan's first political bid was a losing race for mayor of Los Angeles in 1973. But three years later, a vacancy occurred in the Republican-held 27th District. Running against two other Republicans Dornan solidified his conservative support base and won the GOP primary.

In the general election, Dornan called his opponent, Democratic businessman Gary Familian, a "warmed-over McGovernite," and he fended off Familian's efforts to link him to the John Birch Society and the Ku Klux Klan. Dornan won 55 percent of the vote.

Dornan then faced two tough contests against Democrat Carey Peck, the son of actor Gregory Peck. Although Dornan dismissed Peck as a rich political hobbyist, he won just 51 percent in 1978, then needed to spend nearly $2 million to achieve the same percentage in 1980.

A redistricting process controlled by state Democrats delivered a crueler blow to Dornan, stripping his district of its most Republican areas. Rather than run in a Democratic-oriented district or against another GOP incumbent, Dornan set out on his ill-fated Senate bid.

However, his hiatus from the House lasted just two years. In 1984, he moved from his previous base in Santa Monica to Orange County to make his House comeback.

Changing demographics in the 38th had made Democratic Rep. Jerry M. Patterson more vulnerable, and Dornan's national conservative credentials guaranteed him plenty of money.

The two fought fiercely. Patterson called Dornan "a far-right extremist" and "nearly a lunatic"; Dornan called him a "sneaky little dirt-bag." Dornan benefited from the unhappiness of the 38th's conservative electorate with the national Democratic ticket headed by Walter F. Mondale, winning with 53 percent.

Two years later, Dornan held on against a scrappy attack from state Assemblyman Richard Robinson, who accused Dornan of ignoring Orange County while pursuing his obsession with foreign policy. Responding to accusations that he had falsified his military record, Dornan denied having done so and then charged that Robinson had misrepresented his own service in Vietnam.

Committees

Armed Services (10th of 22 Republicans)
Military Acquisition; Oversight & Investigations; Readiness

Select Intelligence (3rd of 7 Republicans)
Program & Budget Authorization

Elections

1992 General		
Robert K. Dornan (R)	55,659	(50%)
Robert John Banuelos (D)	45,435	(41%)
Richard G. Newhouse (LIBERT)	9,712	(9%)
1992 Primary		
Robert K. Dornan (R)	17,558	(60%)
Judith M. Ryan (R)	11,893	(40%)
1990 General		
Robert K. Dornan (R)	60,561	(58%)
Barbara Jackson (D)	43,693	(42%)

Previous Winning Percentages: **1988** (60%) **1986** (55%) **1984** (53%) **1980** (51%) **1978** (51%) **1976** (55%)

District Vote for President

	1992	
D	44,352	(37%)
R	47,689	(40%)
I	27,542	(23%)

Campaign Finance

	Receipts	Receipts from PACs		Expend-itures
1992				
Dornan (R)	$1,443,564	$75,978	(5%)	$1,581,503
1990				
Dornan (R)	$1,615,282	$35,234	(2%)	$1,445,577

Key Votes

1993	
Require parental notification of minors' abortions	Y
Require unpaid family and medical leave	N
Approve national "motor voter" registration bill	N
Approve budget increasing taxes and reducing deficit	N
Approve economic stimulus plan	N
1992	
Approve balanced-budget constitutional amendment	Y
Close down space station program	N
Approve U.S. aid for former Soviet Union	N
Allow shifting funds from defense to domestic programs	X
1991	
Extend unemployment benefits using deficit financing	N
Approve waiting period for handgun purchases	Y
Authorize use of force in Persian Gulf	Y

Voting Studies

	Presidential Support		Party Unity		Conservative Coalition	
Year	**S**	**O**	**S**	**O**	**S**	**O**
1992	79	14	88	4	96	0
1991	76	17	87	5	95	5
1990	68	27	83	6	87	7
1989	70	23	81	9	85	12
1988	65	26	84	6	84	5
1987	73	21	82	8	88	9
1986	80	13	82	10	88	12
1985	80	16	79	10	82	13
1982	61	5	68	5	73	4
1981	57	26	67	9	63	8

Interest Group Ratings

Year	ADA	AFL-CIO	CCUS	ACU
1992	5	17	71	100
1991	10	18	88	95
1990	6	18	79	91
1989	0	10	100	96
1988	0	7	91	100
1987	0	7	100	100
1986	5	8	81	95
1985	10	12	81	95
1982	5	0	85	87
1981	10	8	93	93

47 C. Christopher Cox (R)

Of Newport Beach — Elected 1988; 3rd Term

Born: Oct. 16, 1952, St. Paul, Minn.
Education: U. of Southern California, B.A. 1973; Harvard U., M.B.A., J.D. 1977.
Occupation: White House counsel.
Family: Wife, Rebecca Gernhardt.
Religion: Roman Catholic.
Political Career: No previous office.
Capitol Office: 206 Cannon Bldg. 20515; 225-5611.

In Washington: Now in his third House term and just past 40, Cox has established himself as a thoughtful conservative who generally operates more quietly than the more confrontational conservative Republicans who are numerous in the California House delegation. But if this Harvard-trained former White House counsel is usually cool and erudite, from time to time he has shown a taste for getting involved in issues that set Republicans and Democrats at each other's throats.

During organizing for the 103rd Congress, Cox enlisted in the GOP effort to prevent the House Democratic majority from giving a vote on the floor to the previously non-voting delegates of the District of Columbia, the Virgin Islands, Guam and American Samoa, and to the Puerto Rican resident commissioner. Republicans argued that the Democrats' proposed rules change was unconstitutional, but it passed anyway.

Cox also has been an active proponent of another idea with broad appeal among Republicans: congressional term limits. In 1991, he forced a yes-or-no vote on whether Congress should allow individual states to decide for themselves whether their representatives should be subject to term limits. The "nays" won.

In 1992, Cox and fellow Republicans tried to trim money from the appropriations bill that funds the operations of the House. They were hoping to put Democrats in the bad spot of resisting operational cuts at a time of anti-Congress fervor fanned by scandals at the House bank and the House Post Office. The effort fell short.

Cox also unsuccessfully attempted to slash the budget for the General Accounting Office by 25 percent. Republicans have long complained that GAO investigations and reports are biased in favor of Democrats.

Cox reserves his deepest thought and longest hours to questions of controlling and reforming the federal budget. Before coming to Congress, he worked in the White House as senior associate counsel to President Ronald Reagan. His duties included drafting reform proposals for the federal budget process, and Cox has carried on his interest in that area, first serving as co-chairman of the GOP Task Force on Budget Process Reform and then, at the start of the 103rd Congress, taking a seat on the Budget Committee.

On the Budget panel in early 1993, Cox was quick to criticize President Clinton's economic plans. He argued that while the administration claimed it had avoided budget gimmickry, its program misclassified an increase in Social Security taxes for well-off retirees as a spending cut. He disputed the administration's claim that its proposed tax increases would not put a damper on economic growth.

Cox's interest in reforming the federal budget process is longstanding. In the 103rd, he again introduced legislation that would direct Congress and the president to approve a legally binding federal budget. Under the plan, Congress would have to set a firm budget first and appropriate afterward. While currently each Appropriations subcommittee begins with spending guidelines, Cox argues that appropriators and Congress too often do not regard the budget as binding.

While Cox is critical of excessive federal spending, when the budget ax falls close to home, he can rush to protect the 47th.

In 1993, when the Pentagon released its hit list of military bases it was recommending for closure, El Toro Marine Corps Air Station in Orange County, the heart of the 47th, was on it.

Cox launched a lobbying effort to save El Toro, and was joined by unlikely ally Sen. Dianne Feinstein. He even attempted unsuccessfully to see Defense Secretary Les Aspin to argue his case.

Some area Republicans charged that the new Democratic administration was targeting Republican Orange County, but Cox disagreed, damning the president with faint praise.

"Do I think Clinton is doing anything to hurt the Republicans in Orange County? Absolutely not," Cox told the Orange County Register. "Clinton is so ignorant about military bases.

California 47

Coastal — Central Orange County; Irvine

The 47th is very, very safe GOP territory. It boasts the highest proportion of registered Republicans in the state, with 60 percent to the Democrats' 29 percent. It gave George Bush the strongest support he got in California in 1992, 46 percent of the vote, compared with Bill Clinton's 31 percent and Ross Perot's 23 percent.

It is difficult for candidates to be too conservative for the voters here. John G. Schmitz, who represented part of this region for a term in the early 1970s, was later removed from the executive council of the John Birch Society for extremism.

The 47th sports several different kinds of coast. To the north is part of Newport Beach, a wealthy enclave noted for its beautiful sandy beaches and luxurious housing. To the south, rocky Laguna Beach attracts more scuba divers than swimmers. Between them is the Crystal Cove State Park, which covers about half of the district's coastline.

Laguna Beach's 23,000 residents are considered more liberal than those in Newport Beach, and the city is renowned as "the arts community." The city also has Orange County's highest AIDS rate.

While much of Southern California can be characterized by random suburban sprawl, Irvine's 110,000 residents live in a city whose main streets meet at right angles and whose corporate and residential areas are meticulously planned.

The University of California at Irvine is building housing for some of its 16,900 students and faculty to try to shed its image as a commuter school. The campus concentrates on engineering and other technical fields and has drawn a number of technology companies to the area, including the computer manufacturer AST Research Inc., a division of Rockwell International and Rogerson Aircraft Corp.

Just north of Irvine on the 5 Freeway is Tustin, a city of 51,000 divided into two areas: The south has this city's business district and its lower- to middle-income residents; the north, into the hills a bit, is its high-income area.

Farther north on the freeway is Orange, one of the county's oldest cities. There are 111,000 residents here, Victorian-style homes in the downtown area, affluent suburbs to the west near Anaheim and lower-income areas off to the east. The east also includes some farms.

Villa Park is Orange County's smallest city and is likely to remain that way: It is completely surrounded by Anaheim and Orange and has nowhere to go to grow. The city forbids more than two houses per acre within much of its borders, which has kept crowding down (only 6,300 people live here), the skyline low and the house prices high.

The 47th also has a lot of unincorporated county land out to the east. Silverado Canyon was a bustling silver mining area in the early 1920s and is now a secluded farming area. Much of the district's eastern end is grassy, hilly land that large development companies, with an eye on potential future growth, have snatched up.

1990 Population: 571,518. White 477,665 (84%), Black 10,495 (2%), Other 83,358 (15%). Hispanic origin 74,700 (13%). 18 and over 441,680 (77%), 62 and over 73,898 (13%). Median age: 34.

... He wouldn't even think to do that."

Cox's free-market bent showed up in 1989 when Congress looked into a rash of airline takeover bids. On the Public Works and Transportation Committee, Cox unsuccessfully offered amendments to weaken a measure designed to give the secretary of Transportation additional power to disapprove takeovers financed by leveraged buyouts. Cox said the open market should determine the financial affairs of airlines. In response to the bitter Eastern Airlines strike, Cox tried to amend the Railway Labor Act to close what he said was a loophole enjoyed by airline and railway unions that permitted them to shut down businesses of neutral third parties.

At Home: Many on Capitol Hill dream of moving down Pennsylvania Avenue to the White House. Cox spent 1988 making his move the other way — up that street to Congress.

Cox was working for Reagan in 1988 when 40th District GOP Rep. Robert E. Badham announced his plans to retire. Cox was no stranger to the Orange County district. A University of Southern California alumnus, he had signed on as a partner with a Newport Beach law firm following his graduation from Harvard and a clerkship with the U.S. Court of Appeals in San Francisco.

The odds of Cox winning to succeed Badham initially looked long: The 40th seemed likely to go to one of the well-known state legislators in the area. But when the prime prospects declined to run, Cox resigned from his White House job and joined a field of GOP primary candidates that eventually grew to 14.

The departing Badham had endorsed another Republican, Irvine city councilman Dave Baker. But Cox managed to enlist significant help from members of Orange County's prominent Irvine family.

More important to Cox's success, though, were his Washington connections. His literature pictured him with Reagan and then-Vice President George Bush in the White House. He got endorsements from 18 conservative members of Congress, and he benefited from campaign appearances by Robert H. Bork, Reagan's unsuccessful Supreme Court nominee, and former National Security Council aide Oliver L. North.

Cox pulled away from the field, winning 18 of the district's 20 municipalities in the primary. In November, he took 67 percent of the vote. Cox won with similar ease in 1990 and 1992, when he emerged unscathed in redistricting.

Cox may be the first (and only) person who published *Pravda* before coming to Congress. Cox, then working for the Newport Beach law firm, and his father (a retired publisher) produced an English-language version of the official Soviet newspaper to show how the Soviet government propagandizes its own people. The project was based in St. Paul, Minn., where Cox grew up, but the paper eventually folded after Cox turned his attention to running for Congress.

Committees

Budget (9th of 17 Republicans)

Government Operations (7th of 16 Republicans)
Commerce, Consumer & Monetary Affairs (ranking)

Joint Economic

Elections

1992 General		
C. Christopher Cox (R)	165,004	(65%)
John F. Anwiler (D)	76,924	(30%)
Maxine B. Quirk (PFP)	12,297	(5%)
1992 Primary		
C. Christopher Cox (R)	53,628	(68%)
Robert L. Moore (R)	15,633	(20%)
Steven J. Frogue (R)	9,873	(12%)
1990 General		
C. Christopher Cox (R)	142,299	(68%)
Eugene C. Gratz (D)	68,087	(32%)

Previous Winning Percentage: **1988** (67%)

District Vote for President

1992
D 86,279 (31%)
R 127,700 (46%)
I 64,227 (23%)

Campaign Finance

	Receipts	Receipts from PACs		Expend-itures
1992				
Cox (R)	$515,754	$155,500	(30%)	$402,198
1990				
Cox (R)	$688,836	$179,516	(26%)	$682,365
Gratz (D)	$43,277	$600	(1%)	$36,124

Key Votes

1993	
Require parental notification of minors' abortions	Y
Require unpaid family and medical leave	N
Approve national "motor voter" registration bill	N
Approve budget increasing taxes and reducing deficit	N
Approve economic stimulus plan	N
1992	
Approve balanced-budget constitutional amendment	Y
Close down space station program	N
Approve U.S. aid for former Soviet Union	N
Allow shifting funds from defense to domestic programs	N
1991	
Extend unemployment benefits using deficit financing	N
Approve waiting period for handgun purchases	N
Authorize use of force in Persian Gulf	Y

Voting Studies

	Presidential Support		Party Unity		Conservative Coalition	
Year	S	O	S	O	S	O
1992	78	15	85	6	94	0
1991	77	23	85	10	89	8
1990	75	24	86	8	83	13
1989	71	26	85	12	85	12

Interest Group Ratings

Year	ADA	AFL-CIO	CCUS	ACU
1992	5	17	75	100
1991	10	8	80	100
1990	11	0	85	88
1989	5	8	90	96

48 Ron Packard (R)

Of Oceanside — Elected 1982; 6th Term

Born: Jan. 19, 1931, Meridian, Idaho.
Education: Brigham Young U., 1948-50; Portland State U., 1952-53; U. of Oregon, D.M.D. 1957.
Military Service: Navy Dental Corps, 1957-59.
Occupation: Dentist.
Family: Wife, Roma Jean Sorenson; seven children.
Religion: Mormon.
Political Career: Carlsbad School Board, 1962-74; Carlsbad City Council, 1976-78; mayor of Carlsbad, 1978-82.
Capitol Office: 2162 Rayburn Bldg. 20515; 225-3906.

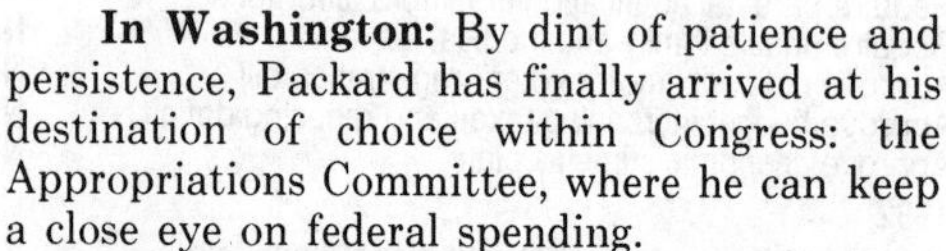

In Washington: By dint of patience and persistence, Packard has finally arrived at his destination of choice within Congress: the Appropriations Committee, where he can keep a close eye on federal spending.

Packard came to Congress with the smiling geniality of a neighborhood dentist and with firm Mormon convictions that inform his sense of right and wrong. At the start of the 102nd Congress, he was installed as his state's representative on the GOP panel that makes committee assignments for all party members (the Committee on Committees).

And by the start of the 103rd, he had parlayed that post (and 10 years of House seniority) into a seat on the Appropriations Committee. A conservative who counts deficit reduction among his highest priorities, Packard opposed many of the big bills presented to the 102nd Congress; he even joined his Orange County brethren in voting against emergency relief for areas in Los Angeles hit by riots.

Early in the 103rd, Packard offered an amendment to President Clinton's emergency stimulus package that would force roughly $12 billion in cuts elsewhere in the budget to pay for the bill's programs. The amendment became part of a larger motion that was defeated, 244-181.

He also objected to that bill's designation as "emergency" spending, which would have allowed Congress to circumvent restrictions in the 1990 budget agreement. "Not a single witness who testified before my committee as we considered the emergency spending bill could explain to me why this ... qualified as an 'emergency,'" Packard said.

For Packard, holding government spending in check translates into lower taxes in the long run. Bills he introduced in the 102nd were aimed at restoring the deductibility of Individual Retirement Accounts and repealing the taxation of Social Security benefits.

One area where Packard refuses to skimp and save, however, is in solving Southern California's water shortage. In 1992, he used his seat on Science, Space and Technology to win passage of legislation directing the National Science Foundation to spend $2.5 million for research on water desalinization. Two of Packard's water reuse bills were signed by President Bush.

Packard also evinces an interest in immigration, not surprising given the 48th's proximity to the Mexican border. The federal government requires California to provide services such as health, education and welfare to immigrants at its own expense. In the 103rd, Packard says he hopes to find more effective ways to stop illegal immigration and cut these costs.

In conjunction with GOP Rep. Al McCandless, who represents an adjoining California district, Packard also called two hearings to investigate high-speed car chases by the Border Patrol. The hearings accompanied the Senate adoption of an amendment that would require the Border Patrol to use helicopters in its high-speed pursuits. Six people died in a June 1992 car chase in Temecula, a city in the 48th District.

During his 10 years on the Public Works Committee, Packard gained skill in the old-fashioned art of horse-trading. By the 102nd Congress, he routinely put that skill to work for his state, bringing home $15 billion in funding in the 1991 Highway Act and including language in the bill making it possible to expand the Tollways Corridor Projects in Orange County.

In 1987, Packard was able to add language to that year's omnibus highway bill providing $15 million to widen a 12-mile stretch of Highway 78 in his district. He also gained an amendment to the 1986 clean water act authorizing filtering systems to defend against sewage seeping across the border from Mexico on the Tijuana River, and he worked to secure authorization for $1.1 billion for Santa Ana River flood control.

In the 100th Congress, Packard used his seat on the Aviation Subcommittee to help lead

California 48

Part of Orange, San Diego and Riverside counties

Like many of Southern California's coastal districts, the 48th is firmly in the Republican column. The party has a 58 percent to 29 percent registration advantage over the Democrats, a level surpassed in California only by the 47th District just up the coast.

As one observer put it, residents are "conservative, upper-middle class, well-educated, [and have] 2.5 kids [and] two cars."

Each of the 48th's three counties gave George Bush strong support in 1992. Overall, he won 44 percent of the 48th's vote in 1992, compared with 29 percent for Bill Clinton and 27 percent for Ross Perot. Forty-nine percent of the district's vote is cast in Orange County, 45 percent is from San Diego County and 4 percent is cast in Riverside County.

Heading down the Pacific Coast Highway, the 48th takes in some of Laguna Beach and all of Dana Point and San Clemente in Orange County, and Camp Pendleton Marine Corps Base and Oceanside in San Diego County.

The coastal area relies heavily on tourism dollars. The economies of Oceanside, and to a lesser extent San Clemente, also depend on the Marine base. Camp Pendleton supplied many of the personnel for Desert Shield/Desert Storm in 1990-91; Oceanside, the 48th's largest city with 128,000 residents, suffered the loss of retail business and the loss of the soldiers' part-time labor in area businesses.

The district breaks into Riverside County to the north only to pick up Temecula, a newer, pro-business, pro-growth community whose 27,000 residents live in the wine-producing Temecula Valley. Other new cities such as Dana Point and Laguna Niguel have incorporated in the past several years. Laguna Niguel is a centrally planned community due east from Laguna Beach.

San Marcos, in San Diego County, has burgeoned; its population more than tripled in the 1970s and grew by 123 percent in the 1980s to 39,000.

Even the town of San Juan Capistrano, famous for the swallows that flock to its ancient Spanish mission each spring, is being transformed. But the town's historic nature remains unscathed; artifacts of California's mission period were unearthed here recently.

The 48th has escaped some of the economic suffering felt throughout the rest of Southern California. Its economy relies more on service industries and on tourism, and not as much on aerospace and military contracts as does the neighboring 47th's. A steady stream of visitors to the 48th District's beach communities provides a cushion for the economy.

While this area may have been considered "lily white" in the late 1970s, there has been steady, though slow, growth in its minority populations. Now, 17 percent of its residents are Hispanic, 5 percent are Asian and 4 percent are black. The area also has a growing number of military retirees.

1990 Population: 572,928. White 476,994 (83%), Black 23,164 (4%), Other 72,770 (13%). Hispanic origin 98,746 (17%). 18 and over 426,279 (74%), 62 and over 71,638 (13%). Median age: 31.

the successful effort to require passenger aircraft to install collision-avoidance equipment. But he has opposed legislation limiting leveraged buyouts of airlines, trusting the market to determine the industry's financial affairs.

In the 102nd Congress, Packard cosponsored a bill to repeal the Social Security earnings test created during the Depression to discourage senior citizens from working.

On social issues, Packard often sides with the most conservative wing within the GOP. In his first term, when Education and Labor (on which he was sitting at the time) took up the bill granting student religious groups "equal access" to school facilities, Packard talked of giving children moral and religious values. That worried other committee Republicans, who wanted to sell the bill merely as a device to protect free expression.

During the 1987 debate over legislation to pay Japanese-Americans interned during World War II, Packard endorsed a federal apology but opposed compensation. He said that he was one of 17 children raised on an Idaho farm, and when the family was about to lose its property, his father went to work for a government contractor in the South Pacific. Within days of the Japanese attack on Pearl Harbor, his father was taken prisoner, leaving his family destitute during the war. Giving money to the internees, Packard said, "would demean a time when our family learned to work together, pull together and pray together."

At Home: No matter how long Packard serves in Congress, nothing in his electoral career is likely to match the tumult of the contest that brought him to Congress and made him one of the few members ever elected as a write-in candidate.

When GOP Rep. Clair W. Burgener announced his retirement in 1982, Packard and 17 other Republicans filed for the primary. Packard, a veteran of Carlsbad city politics, emerged as a front-runner. But he found himself in a pitched battle with recreational vehicle tycoon Johnnie Crean.

A political neophyte, Crean sank close to $1 million into his bid, which consisted largely of personal attacks on his rivals, some wildly inaccurate. Afterward, Crean blamed his campaign's conduct on his consultants, whom he fired the day after the primary. Crean earned the abiding scorn of many Republicans but won the nomination over Packard by 92 votes.

Many GOP partisans were unhappy with the outcome, and they helped persuade Packard to enter the general election as a write-in candidate. Crean tried to mend fences and reform his image. He argued that Republicans choosing Packard would split the GOP vote, electing the Democratic nominee, Roy Pat Archer, a professor of government. Party officials came out for Crean, and Packard's funding dried up.

But Packard was still strong at the grass-roots level. While press coverage kept the Crean controversy fresh, Packard sent out 350,000 pieces of mail proclaiming himself the legitimate GOP alternative. On Election Day, his poll workers handed out pencils with Packard's name, urging their use. Packard edged Archer by 8,000 votes. Crean ran third.

Packard has not been seriously challenged since and most recently won re-election by a 2-1 ratio. But there was one interesting aspect of his 1990 House contest: Although district Democrats did not field a candidate, Packard got 68 percent of the vote, with 18 percent going to the nominee of the leftist Peace and Freedom Party and 14 percent to the Libertarian candidate.

Committee

Appropriations (16th of 23 Republicans)
Interior; Legislative Branch

Elections

1992 General		
Ron Packard (R)	140,935	(61%)
Michael Farber (D)	67,415	(29%)
Donna White (PFP)	13,396	(6%)
Ted Lowe (LIBERT)	8,749	(4%)
1992 Primary		
Ron Packard (R)	45,217	(64%)
Stephen Todd (R)	13,632	(19%)
Ed Mayerhofer (R)	12,077	(17%)
1990 General		
Ron Packard (R)	151,206	(68%)
Doug Hansen (PFP)	40,212	(18%)
Richard L. Arnold (LIBERT)	30,720	(14%)

Previous Winning Percentages: 1988 (72%) **1986** (73%) **1984** (74%) **1982*** (37%)

** Write-in candidate.*

District Vote for President

1992
D 71,621 (29%)
R 108,581 (44%)
I 65,980 (27%)

Campaign Finance

	Receipts	Receipts from PACs		Expend-itures
1992				
Packard (R)	$292,021	$191,832	(66%)	$363,341
Farber (D)	$66,495	$500	(1%)	$65,944
1990				
Packard (R)	$167,017	$99,716	(60%)	$147,249

Key Votes

1993	
Require parental notification of minors' abortions	Y
Require unpaid family and medical leave	N
Approve national "motor voter" registration bill	N
Approve budget increasing taxes and reducing deficit	N
Approve economic stimulus plan	N
1992	
Approve balanced-budget constitutional amendment	Y
Close down space station program	N
Approve U.S. aid for former Soviet Union	N
Allow shifting funds from defense to domestic programs	N
1991	
Extend unemployment benefits using deficit financing	N
Approve waiting period for handgun purchases	Y
Authorize use of force in Persian Gulf	Y

Voting Studies

Year	Presidential Support S	Presidential Support O	Party Unity S	Party Unity O	Conservative Coalition S	Conservative Coalition O
1992	81	13	85	10	90	2
1991	83	17	84	12	92	5
1990	71	26	82	13	98	2
1989	81	15	69	27	93	7
1988	66	26	76	14	87	0
1987	70	27	81	14	88	12
1986	83	16	79	18	88	8
1985	75	24	85	10	91	9
1984	69	28	89	8	95	5
1983	83 †	16 †	92 †	5 †	91	2

† Not eligible for all recorded votes.

Interest Group Ratings

Year	ADA	AFL-CIO	CCUS	ACU
1992	0	8	71	100
1991	5	8	90	95
1990	11	8	93	88
1989	0	9	100	93
1988	5	15	92	100
1987	4	6	93	86
1986	5	7	94	91
1985	10	6	95	86
1984	0	8	75	83
1983	0	0	83	96

49 Lynn Schenk (D)

Of San Diego — Elected 1992; 1st Term

Born: Jan. 5, 1945, New York, N.Y.

Education: U. of California, Los Angeles, B.A. 1967; U. of San Diego, J.D. 1970; London School of Economics, 1970-71.

Occupation: Lawyer.

Family: Husband, Hugh Friedman; three stepchildren.

Religion: Jewish.

Political Career: Calif. secretary of business, transportation and housing, 1980-83; candidate for San Diego Board of Supervisors, 1984; San Diego Unified Port Commission, 1990-93.

Capitol Office: 315 Cannon Bldg. 20515; 225-2040.

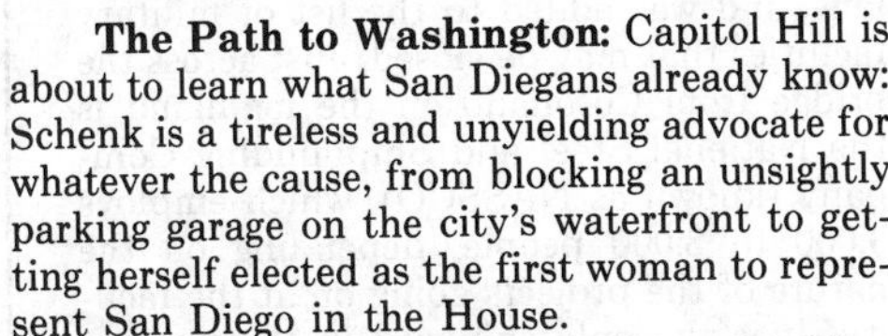

The Path to Washington: Capitol Hill is about to learn what San Diegans already know: Schenk is a tireless and unyielding advocate for whatever the cause, from blocking an unsightly parking garage on the city's waterfront to getting herself elected as the first woman to represent San Diego in the House.

Though she campaigned as an outsider, Schenk is anything but a political novice. From 1980-83, she served in former Gov. Edmund G. "Jerry" Brown Jr.'s Cabinet as the first female secretary of business, transportation and housing. There she developed a reputation as a pro-business Democrat, a species once hard to find.

She also has impeccable liberal credentials. The daughter of Hungarian Holocaust survivors who emigrated just before she was born in 1945, she grew up in a union household in the Bronx. She is a vigorous advocate of abortion rights and of women's rights generally: She helped force the University of San Diego Law School to build a women's restroom; she and others opened the doors of a male-dominated downtown club; and she helped found a bank owned by women and a free legal service for poor women.

Schenk brought strong environmental credentials to her House campaign and called for strict enforcement of the Clean Air Act and increased spending to clean up toxic waste sites.

She will be able to pursue her environmental agenda from both her committee seats: Energy and Commerce, and Merchant Marine and Fisheries. Her experience as an in-house attorney for a utility company may prove useful on Energy and Commerce. However, her views on the Clean Air Act could bring her into conflict with Democratic Chairman John D. Dingell of Michigan.

Schenk also showed herself early in the 103rd Congress to be a supporter of a strong line-item veto. She supported a Democratic version that the House passed in April 1993 and was one of only 33 Democrats to support the more potent GOP substitute.

Though San Diego has a reputation as a Republican town, the 49th proved very hospitable to Schenk. It is a new district, drawn in much the same place as the old 41st, which Republican Bill Lowery represented from 1981 to 1993.

Registration still favors the GOP, 43 percent to 39 percent. However the district is filled with independent-minded voters. Lowery chose to run elsewhere (and eventually retired, having 300 overdrafts at the House bank). That left the seat open to all comers.

Ten candidates filed for the GOP nomination, and four Democrats chose to challenge Schenk — most of them political newcomers. Schenk easily outdistanced the Democratic field, winning more than 53 percent.

Critical-care nurse Judy Jarvis was the surprise winner of the Republican primary. Though she is not related to the late anti-tax celebrity Howard Jarvis, her name undoubtedly helped her win, as did her abortion rights stand and the fact that she was the only woman on the GOP ballot. An energetic, door-to-door campaign earned Jarvis 21 percent and a 2,000-vote margin.

Both Schenk and Jarvis argued similar lines on taxes and the need for economic growth. Both favored tax incentives for business investment, including a cut in the tax on capital gains income.

Taxes also helped distinguish the two. Schenk made much of the fact that Jarvis had toyed with the idea of both a national sales tax and a flat income tax — though Jarvis was conditional in her support.

Schenk, too, embraced controversial tax ideas, including a limit on business deductions for executive salaries and fringe benefits. And, she said, if spending cuts and economic growth do not help reduce the deficit, she might support increasing taxes on the wealthy.

Schenk's superior fundraising ability and experience enabled her to defeat Jarvis by 51 percent to 43 percent, leaving two third-party candidates in the dust.

California 49

North San Diego; Coronado; Imperial Beach

The coastal 49th is the engine that drives the surrounding districts. It includes San Diego's downtown, most of its military bases, most of its other large employers and most of its coast. The 51st and the 50th districts to the north and south of the 49th, respectively, are packed with the area's bedrooms.

The district begins just south of Del Mar and includes La Jolla, Point Loma and northern and downtown San Diego. It then skips through the San Diego Bay to Imperial Beach, and swings north up the slender Silver Strand Boulevard to take in Coronado, a peninsula that reaches up to the mouth of the bay. The northern and southern parts of the district are not connected by any land. Though this is an urban district, traffic is manageable here; it is possible to hop on the 5 Freeway in La Jolla and arrive in Imperial Beach in just 20 minutes.

Compared with the south side of the city, the 49th is relatively homogeneous. Only 13 percent of its residents are Hispanic, compared with 41 percent in the 50th district; only 7 percent of the 49th's residents are Asian, and 5 percent are black, compared with 15 and 14 percent, respectively, in the 50th.

The 49th is also a lot more Republican than southern San Diego: The GOP has a three-point registration edge here, compared with a 16-point deficit in the 50th District. Despite the registration numbers, Bill Clinton won the 49th in 1992 with 43 percent of the vote; George Bush got a feeble 32 percent and Ross Perot 25 percent.

In 1992, Schenk was able to win support in many of San Diego's moderate, middle-income neighborhoods, including Clairemont, downtown, Mission Hills and the predominantly gay area of Hillcrest. She also ran well on the 49th's southern end, in the lower-income area of Imperial Beach. She narrowly won La Jolla, one of the city's wealthier areas. She did not fare so well in Coronado and Point Loma, among the district's most Republican and conservative areas.

The beautiful community of Coronado is home to 27,000 residents, many of them retired Navy officers. Thirteen percent of its population is 65 or older.

Also in Coronado is the North Island Naval Air Station, which employs almost 18,000 military personnel and 6,500 civilians, and was added to the list of military facilities that may be closed. Just across the bridge from Coronado on the mainland is the National Steel and Shipbuilding Company (known as NASSCO), which employs 3,000 to 8,000 people, depending on the nature of the projects going on at the facility. It is the only shipyard in the western United States that still builds large ocean-going ships. It has been owned by its employees since 1989.

Though the area is heavily dependent on the military — one-sixth of San Diego's gross product depends directly on military procurement, retirement benefits and salaries — the economy is diversifying a bit. A number of biotechnology and biomedical firms have set up shop in the valley just north of La Jolla.

1990 Population: 573,362. White 470,562 (82%), Black 30,408 (5%), Other 72,392 (13%). Hispanic origin 73,210 (13%). 18 and over 480,143 (84%), 62 and over 84,971 (15%). Median age: 32.

Committees

Energy & Commerce (23rd of 27 Democrats)
Telecommunications & Finance; Transportation & Hazardous Materials

Merchant Marine & Fisheries (18th of 29 Democrats)
Coast Guard & Navigation; Merchant Marine; Oceanography, Gulf of Mexico & the Outer Continental Shelf

Campaign Finance

1992	Receipts	Receipts from PACs		Expenditures
Schenk (D)	$1,154,531	$300,129	(26%)	$1,131,021
Jarvis (R)	$433,861	$149,993	(35%)	$433,649
Wallner (LIBERT)	$8,154	0		$8,153

Key Votes

1993

Require parental notification of minors' abortions	N
Require unpaid family and medical leave	Y
Approve national "motor voter" registration bill	Y
Approve budget increasing taxes and reducing deficit	Y
Approve economic stimulus plan	Y

Elections

1992 General		
Lynn Schenk (D)	127,280	(51%)
Judy Jarvis (R)	106,170	(43%)
John Wallner (LIBERT)	10,706	(4%)
Milton Zaslow (PFP)	4,738	(2%)
1992 Primary		
Lynn Schenk (D)	32,303	(53%)
Byron Georgiou (D)	14,879	(25%)
Bill Winston (D)	6,811	(11%)
Carol Lucke (D)	4,594	(8%)
Troy X. Kelley (D)	2,066	(3%)

District Vote for President

1992		
D	114,081	(43%)
R	82,834	(32%)
I	65,856	(25%)

50 Bob Filner (D)

Of San Diego — Elected 1992; 1st Term

Born: Sept. 4, 1942, Pittsburgh, Pa.

Education: Cornell U., B.A. 1963; U. of Delaware, M.A. 1969; Cornell U., Ph.D. 1973.

Occupation: Public official; college professor.

Family: Wife, Jane Merrill; two children.

Religion: Jewish.

Political Career: San Diego School Board, 1979-83, president, 1982; candidate for San Diego City Council, 1983; San Diego City Council, 1987-92, deputy mayor, 1991.

Capitol Office: 504 Cannon Bldg. 20515; 225-8045.

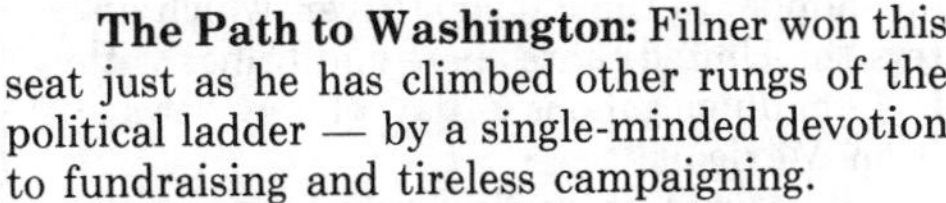

The Path to Washington: Filner won this seat just as he has climbed other rungs of the political ladder — by a single-minded devotion to fundraising and tireless campaigning.

His formula for success helped him win re-election to the San Diego City Council in 1991 with more than 70 percent of the vote in a district where he had no guarantee of winning. And it allowed him to overcome five adversaries in the Democratic primary for this House seat.

The same single-mindedness is likely to be a hallmark of Filner's congressional career. He is determined to be a player. His chief desire is to have a role in reshaping the nation's military-industrial complex. Defense conversion may be a buzzword in Washington and unintelligible jargon in many parts of the country. But for Filner's San Diego constituency, the downsizing of the military is stark reality.

More than 20 percent of the San Diego economy is directly tied to the defense industry, about half in military and civilian payrolls and half in contracts, including those to the cream of the defense establishment: General Dynamics, Hughes Aircraft and Teledyne.

Federal defense cuts in the past few years already have begun to bite, and Filner early on saw a need to protect San Diego's economy. He wrote a conversion plan for the city that incorporated planning and other assistance with local government incentives for defense-oriented companies that modernized. And in concept at least, Filner has advocated requiring the federal government to return dollar for dollar whatever is lost to local economies due to defense cuts. The aid, in Filner's view, should be for job training, health care, crime prevention and construction of public infrastructure.

His years on the city council have focused Filner on other joint local-federal concerns that he will try to address on Capitol Hill. He wants to expedite construction of a federally financed sewage plant to handle flows from Tijuana that San Diego is currently paying to treat. And he wants to break a bureaucratic logjam involving the Navy and other agencies that has held up construction of a new airport for two decades.

He currently opposes the North American Free Trade Agreement, calling it "a trickle-down treaty designed to benefit big corporations and exploit our continent's resources — both human and environmental." He was one of the founders of the congressional anti-NAFTA caucus.

By some calculations, an Anglo like Filner never should have been elected to a majority-minority district like the 50th. The district was created because of San Diego's emergence as the second-largest city in the state, and it reflects the region's diverse nature.

The 50th's registration is nominally Democratic, however, which virtually assured that the winner of the primary would prevail in November. Filner squeaked to victory in the six-way primary, upsetting longtime state Sen. Wadie P. Deddeh and former Rep. Jim Bates.

Bates was trying to return to Congress. Republican Randy "Duke" Cunningham ousted him in 1990 after the House ethics committee reproved him for sexually harassing aides on his Capitol Hill staff.

Deddeh, a real estate developer and member of the Legislature since the 1960s, had his own problems. He assumed the mantle of front-runner as Bates faltered. But Filner attacked him for his opposition to abortion and his apparent failure to make timely payments on property taxes.

Filner had the strong support of labor and women's groups. And he made a broad appeal to minority voters, despite the presence of a Latino and a black activist on the ballot. Filner's credentials were enhanced considerably by his history as an early Freedom Rider (he was imprisoned for a time after sitting in at a Mississippi lunch counter in 1960) and his years as an activist on the San Diego school board.

Filner, who moved to California from New York in 1970 to teach at San Diego State University, had little difficulty dispatching Republican Tony Valencia in the general election, winning 57 percent of the vote.

California 50

Central and south San Diego; Chula Vista; National City

This ethnic, blue-collar urban-suburban district is a world apart from the districts that surround it. It is far more diverse: 41 percent of its residents are Hispanic, 15 percent are Asian and 14 percent are black. It is also as Democratic as the others are Republican. Fifty-three percent of its registered voters are Democrats and only 35 percent are Republicans.

The northern part of the district, just south of San Diego's downtown, houses the worst of San Diego's urban problems: its highest crime rates, its most serious gang activity and so on. It is built up with rows of two-story apartment complexes, and, while certain parts are being gentrified by "urban pioneers," much of the area is downtrodden.

Farther south, the booming suburb of Chula Vista splits the city of San Diego in two; even more southern areas of San Diego such as San Ysidro and Otay Mesa are contiguous only by a legal line that extends through the bay. Residents of the southern region, cut off geographically from the rest of San Diego, sometimes feel cut off politically as well.

Chula Vista has a large number of military personnel and tends to be more Republican than the rest of the 50th. On Chula Vista's east end is East Lake, one of the largest developments in the county.

Any new housing growth the 50th experiences is likely to be here; much of the rest of the district is either stagnant or built out.

Otay Mesa is an industrial area south of Chula Vista that represents the last opportunity for expansion of San Diego's large-scale manufacturing. The area is heavily developed between the 5 and 805 freeways, but farther east is mostly empty land zoned for industry. Much of the existing industry is in the form of *maquiladoras*, factories that finish and ship goods that were partially manufactured in sibling factories in Mexico. It is unclear how the North American Free Trade Agreement might affect this area's economic potential.

The San Diego-Tijuana border crossing at San Ysidro is the world's busiest. The area's problems stem not so much from the number of immigrants, but from criminals who prey on them. One controversial border-hopper is the Tijuana River, which enters the United States here and brings with it 13 million gallons a day of raw sewage from Mexico.

The area is reeling from the deconstruction of General Dynamics over the past several years. GD had been the district's (and the county's) largest private-sector employer for years, but it is down to a fraction of its former size. In spring 1992, the company sold its Tomahawk missile manufacturing operations to Hughes, which closed the San Diego plant and moved manufacturing to Arizona.

Bill Clinton won 49 percent of the 50th District's vote in 1992 to 30 percent for George Bush and 21 percent for Ross Perot. Clinton's big margin in the district — 26,716 votes — was pivotal in helping swing San Diego County into his column.

1990 Population: 573,463. White 266,652 (46%), Black 82,735 (14%), Other 224,076 (39%). Hispanic origin 232,660 (41%). 18 and over 398,704 (70%), 62 and over 59,801 (10%). Median age: 28.

Committees

Public Works & Transportation (37th of 39 Democrats)
Economic Development; Investigations & Oversight; Water Resources and the Environment

Veterans' Affairs (14th of 21 Democrats)
Hospitals & Health Care; Oversight & Investigations

Campaign Finance

1992	Receipts	Receipts from PACs	Expenditures
Filner (D)	$856,869	$267,797 (31%)	$856,046
Valencia (R)	$63,504	0	$69,936
Hutchinson (LIBERT)	$19,154	0	$19,534

Key Votes

1993	
Require parental notification of minors' abortions	N
Require unpaid family and medical leave	Y
Approve national "motor voter" registration bill	Y
Approve budget increasing taxes and reducing deficit	Y
Approve economic stimulus plan	Y

Elections

1992 General		
Bob Filner (D)	77,293	(57%)
Tony Valencia (R)	39,531	(29%)
Barbara Hutchinson (LIBERT)	15,489	(11%)
Roger B. Batchelder (PFP)	4,250	(3%)
1992 Primary		
Bob Filner (D)	10,932	(26%)
Wadie P. Deddeh (D)	9,846	(23%)
Jim Bates (D)	8,416	(20%)
Juan Carlos Vargas (D)	7,868	(19%)
Greg Akili (D)	4,120	(10%)
Lincoln Pickard (D)	843	(2%)

District Vote for President

	1992	
D	69,546	(49%)
R	42,830	(30%)
I	30,267	(21%)

51 Randy "Duke" Cunningham (R)

Of San Diego — Elected 1990; 2nd Term

Born: Dec. 8, 1941, Los Angeles, Calif.
Education: U. of Missouri, B.A. 1964, M.A. 1967; National U., M.B.A. 1985.
Military Service: Navy, 1967-87.
Occupation: Computer software executive.
Family: Wife, Nancy Jones; three children.
Religion: Christian.
Political Career: No previous office.
Capitol Office: 117 Cannon Bldg. 20515; 225-5452.

In Washington: Cunningham brought the confidence of a combat pilot to his first congressional campaign in 1990, and the former "Top Gun" flight instructor has exhibited no lack of bravado since.

For Cunningham, being a conservative comes first and being a Republican is a close second. That meant some discomfort in the 102nd Congress: When the White House urged continued financing of the savings and loan bailout in both 1991 and 1992, Cunningham said no.

No such ambivalence will plague Cunningham in the 103rd, however, as he has had President Clinton in his sights for some time. During the fall 1992 campaign, Cunningham and two California Republican colleagues, Duncan Hunter and Robert K. Dornan, trained their fire on Clinton's activities during the Vietnam War — including insinuations of "sinister" activities on a 1969 student trip to Moscow. "Tokyo Rose has nothing on Bill Clinton," Cunningham was quoted as saying in The (Baltimore) Sun.

A new committee assignment on Education and Labor gives Cunningham a ready selection of government programs to target in the 103rd Congress. Even before joining the committee he had introduced a bill in 1992 that would have waived needy students' $65 fee for the Advanced Placement Test for college credit. That measure was ultimately tacked onto the giant Higher Education Reauthorization bill signed by President Bush.

He also introduced the Responsible Welfare Act of 1993 to deny aid to recipients during any period that they may be gainfully employed or receive education.

Cunningham still retains committee seats on Armed Services, where he knows the territory intimately, and Merchant Marine and Fisheries, where he quickly learned the ropes on subsidies and daily haul limits on tuna — key industries in his district.

A former air combat instructor with two Silver Stars and 10 Air Medals, Cunningham often speaks admiringly of the late actor John Wayne — another "Duke."

Born in Los Angeles the day after Pearl Harbor, Cunningham joined the Navy, trained as a fighter pilot and flew combat missions over Vietnam. On one such mission, his aircraft was disabled by a surface-to-air missile. He and his copilot ejected and were rescued at sea. Back in the United States, he turned to training new pilots at the Miramar Naval Air Station, the advanced training facility featured in the movie "Top Gun" (for which he was an adviser).

While still a naval officer, Cunningham received a business degree from National University, a small school in San Diego. After retiring from the Navy, he became dean of National's school of aviation. Later, he became a marketing specialist for the university. In the meantime, he sold flying instruction videos and computer software from his home and gave speeches across the country. "I've been a success at everything I've ever done," Cunningham often said.

Recently, Cunningham has also been lucky. Major military installations in his district were spared in the 1993 base-closure cycle. Elsewhere in California, a total of 16 military sites were among those proposed in mid-1993 for closure or realignment as the Pentagon moves to cut costs.

It is hard to overstate the dependence of San Diego on military bases. If the Marine Corps Recruit Depot and the Naval Training Center were to close, he estimates, 12,000 military and civilian jobs would be lost and the area economy would take a loss of more than $300 million.

Like most members whose districts are near the Mexican border, Cunningham has a keen interest in bills to control drug trafficking and illegal immigration. He is a member of the Republican Research Committee Task Force on Drugs and, in March 1993, he introduced the California-Mexico Border Drug Trafficking Reduction Act.

He also wants federal funds used to stem the flow of people crossing illegally into the

California 51

San Diego area — Northern county suburbs

The 51st reverses the pattern found throughout much of Southern California: As one moves inland from the coast, the political mood becomes more conservative, in part because of many coastal residents' emphasis on environmental issues.

This group of San Diego suburbs constitutes a very Republican district: Registered Republicans outnumber Democrats 54 percent to 31 percent.

The 15 Freeway runs north through the 51st's conservative areas like a spine, passing the Miramar Naval Air Station, Poway, Rancho Bernardo and Escondido. To the west, the 5 Freeway heads north along the district's coastal communities: Del Mar, Encinitas and Carlsbad.

Del Mar is a small beach community, an overwhelming proportion of whose 5,000 residents are white non-Hispanics — 93 percent. Carlsbad, a city of 63,000 residents, grows and distributes most of the West Coast's fresh-cut flowers.

The 51st's beach communities have more permanent residents than others in the area. San Diego's primary tourist beaches are to the south, in the 49th District.

Moving inland, the Miramar Naval Air Station anchors the district's southern border. Home to the Navy Fighter Weapons School — popularly known as the "Top Gun" pilot school — and former employer of Navy ace Rep. Cunningham (he was an instructor here), it employs 2,000 civilians and 13,000 military personnel. Miramar was added in May 1993 to the list of military facilities that may close. Many of those who have long eyed the base's demise want the site to serve as an alternative to San Diego's crowded downtown Lindbergh Field airport.

Up the 15 is Poway, an independent city of 44,000 surrounded by the city of San Diego. It has more of a rural, horsy feel to it than the surrounding suburban sprawl.

Just north of Poway is an expanse of evenly developed suburbs that includes Rancho Bernardo, an area within San Diego's city limits that has attracted many retirees.

San Diego's relentless spread across the county has caught up to the old city of Escondido, farther north. With 109,000 residents, it is larger than some of the bedroom communities closer to San Diego, but its age gave it a head start on growth.

East and north of Escondido are avocado and citrus orchards and a lot of land that speculators have bought with the idea of settling San Diego's next population spasm here.

In 1992, George Bush took 40 percent of the district's presidential vote to Bill Clinton's 32 percent and Ross Perot's 27 percent. The 51st was Bush's largest pocket of support in the county: He beat Clinton by 21,600 votes here.

Overall, however, Bush lost San Diego County by slightly more than 15,000 votes, making him the first Republican presidential candidate in four decades to lose the county. Bush won the county by nearly 200,000 votes in 1988.

1990 Population: 572,982. White 484,704 (85%), Black 10,225 (2%), Other 78,053 (14%). Hispanic origin 78,053 (14%). 18 and over 431,928 (75%), 62 and over 77,087 (13%). Median age: 33.

United States. It irks him that Californians pay heavily for services such as health care, schools and law enforcement that benefit those who are not U.S. taxpayers.

Although deft at most manuevers, Cunningham blundered early in his Washington career on a foreign aid authorization bill. He inadvertently weakened an amendment during a June 20, 1991, vote that would have terminated all aid for Jordan.

Trying to be helpful, he inserted a clause allowing the president to waive the provision if he determined it to be in the national interest. But Cunningham actually favored the aid cutoff and later tried unsuccessfully to withdraw his amendment, which was approved, 315-105.

At Home: Cunningham was elected to Congress in his first try for public office, having already been a career military officer, an educator and a businessman. It was GOP Rep. Duncan Hunter, who represented an adjoining district, who recruited Cunningham to challenge Democratic veteran Rep. Jim Bates in 1990, a year in which Bates was battling primary challengers and charges of having sexually harassed women on his staff.

The old 44th District comprised most of San Diego proper, including the central city, and Cunningham did not even live in it when he decided to run. But he left his beach home in exclusive Del Mar and bought a home in the older, middle-class suburb of Chula Vista so he could take a shot at Bates. Although a novice, Cunningham lined up party regulars and bankrollers (with Hunter's help) and beat four rivals in the primary.

Meanwhile, Bates was still taking a bruising in the sexual harassment case, which in 1989 led the House ethics committee to issue a reproval (the mildest form of disciplinary action). He proceeded to deplete his campaign treasury in the primary, apparently convinced that he could handle anyone the GOP nominated in the fall.

Indeed, despite the appeal of his military credentials in the Navy-oriented precincts of the 44th, Cunningham appeared too conservative for a district with just 34 percent GOP registration and most of the minority voters in the San Diego area.

But Bates' problems appeared to suppress turnout within his coalition — particularly among women. And he had trouble campaigning during the 1990 fall budget crisis in Washington. Cunningham also showed surprising savvy.

He targeted both evangelical Christians and older, conservative Democrats to transcend the district's base GOP vote. He de-emphasized his stands against abortion and gun control, and highlighted his profile as a family man of personal integrity. His literature and broadcast ads spoke of "Christian family values" and "a congressman we can be proud of."

It all worked just well enough to ease him past Bates by fewer than 2,000 votes.

In 1992, redistricting renumbered the 44th as the 50th and left it almost as Democratic as before. At the same time, the new map had three solidly Republican districts in the San Diego area, one of which, the 51st, included Cunningham's old home in Del Mar. The problem was that the new 51st also included Rep. Bill Lowery, a GOP colleague of Cunningham's.

Although he had a decade of seniority on Cunningham, Lowery also had some political liabilities. He had fallen below 50 percent of the vote in 1990, and that was before revelations that he had written 300 overdrafts at the House bank.

So once Cunningham made it clear he was planning to seek a new base in his old stomping grounds, Lowery retired. Cunningham won the nomination and the November election in his new district with little trouble.

Committees

Armed Services (14th of 22 Republicans)
Military Acquisition; Readiness

Education & Labor (12th of 15 Republicans)
Elementary, Secondary & Vocational Education; Postsecondary Education

Merchant Marine & Fisheries (10th of 18 Republicans)
Environment & Natural Resources; Merchant Marine

Elections

1992 General		
Randy "Duke" Cunningham (R)	141,890	(56%)
Bea Herbert (D)	85,148	(34%)
Bill Holmes (LIBERT)	10,309	(4%)
Miriam E. Clark (PFP)	10,307	(4%)
Richard L. Roe (GREEN)	5,328	(2%)
1992 Primary		
Randy "Duke" Cunningham (R)	40,645	(52%)
William Davis (R)	14,514	(19%)
Bill Lowery (R)	12,039	(15%)
Michael Perdue (R)	6,227	(8%)
Adelito M. Gale (R)	5,003	(6%)
1990 General		
Randy "Duke" Cunningham (R)	50,377	(46%)
Jim Bates (D)	48,712	(45%)
Donna White (PFP)	5,237	(5%)
John Wallner (LIBERT)	4,385	(4%)

District Vote for President

	1992
D	86,870 (32%)
R	108,470 (40%)
I	73,580 (27%)

Campaign Finance

	Receipts	Receipts from PACs		Expend-itures
1992				
Cunningham (R)	$967,013	$283,367	(29%)	$972,606
Herbert (D)	$23,315	$949	(4%)	$23,315
1990				
Cunningham (R)	$539,721	$214,547	(40%)	$534,167
Bates (D)	$773,364	$360,800	(47%)	$744,463

Key Votes

1993	
Require parental notification of minors' abortions	Y
Require unpaid family and medical leave	N
Approve national "motor voter" registration bill	N
Approve budget increasing taxes and reducing deficit	N
Approve economic stimulus plan	N
1992	
Approve balanced-budget constitutional amendment	Y
Close down space station program	N
Approve U.S. aid for former Soviet Union	N
Allow shifting funds from defense to domestic programs	N
1991	
Extend unemployment benefits using deficit financing	N
Approve waiting period for handgun purchases	N
Authorize use of force in Persian Gulf	Y

Voting Studies

	Presidential Support		Party Unity		Conservative Coalition	
Year	S	O	S	O	S	O
1992	82	13	91	4	96	2
1991	78	22	89	9	97	3

Interest Group Ratings

Year	ADA	AFL-CIO	CCUS	ACU
1992	5	17	75	96
1991	5	17	90	95

52 Duncan Hunter (R)

Of El Cajon — Elected 1980; 7th Term

Born: May 31, 1948, Riverside, Calif.
Education: U. of Montana, 1966-67; U. of California, Santa Barbara, 1967-68; Western State U., B.S.L., J.D. 1976.
Military Service: Army, 1969-71.
Occupation: Lawyer.
Family: Wife, Lynne Layh; two children.
Religion: Baptist.
Political Career: No previous office.
Capitol Office: 133 Cannon Bldg. 20515; 225-5672.

In Washington: Hunter's conservative activism moved him into the Republican hierarchy after less than a decade in the House. A leader of the Conservative Opportunity Society (COS), founded by Georgia Rep. Newt Gingrich, Hunter was elected chairman of the House Republican Research Committee in 1989 — the same year Gingrich became whip.

But the two conservative allies differ greatly in approach. Gingrich's intellectual ardor and aggressive partisan crusading have cemented his leadership position, even though he irks many colleagues with his nettlesome manner. Hunter, on the other hand, has gone far with an affable personality, gaining him support even from those who doubt his intellectual depth.

It surprised few that Hunter ran unopposed for re-election as Research Committee chairman, the fifth-highest GOP position, in December 1992. Yet he finds himself being upstaged at times by less senior (but more dynamic) spokesmen for the conservative cause.

As House Republicans organized for the 103rd Congress, Texas Republican Dick Armey, a fiery former economics professor, jumped past Hunter into the third-ranking Republican leadership post, chairman of the House Republican Conference. Armey defeated California Rep. Jerry Lewis, whose pragmatism allowed him to occasionally compromise with Democrats.

During the 100th Congress, it was Hunter, then regarded as a fast-rising GOP star, who narrowly lost a challenge to Lewis, who was then chairman of the Republican Policy Committee.

Although Hunter made no effort to move up in the 103rd, his forward movement may have been slowed in any case by political difficulties in 1992. That year, it was revealed that Hunter had run up 399 overdrafts at the scandal-plagued House bank. Hunter was not helped by having released earlier estimates that understated his involvement or by being named among the heaviest users of the congressional frank to send newsletters to constituents.

Nothing has happened, however, to dampen Hunter's zeal for taking the fight to the Democrats, who after the 1992 elections control the White House and both houses of Congress for the first time in Hunter's House career.

Hunter's strongest focus is on issues affecting national security. A member of the Armed Services Committee since his arrival in 1981, he is now ranking Republican on its Military Installations and Facilities Subcommittee.

As a junior House member in the early 1980s, Hunter was a steadfast supporter of President Ronald Reagan's military buildup. The Cold War thaw of the 1980s, followed by the collapse of the Soviet Union, did not shake Hunter's support for maintaining high defense-funding levels.

Hunter also urged against hasty post-Cold War efforts to ease restrictions on U.S. exports of high-technology equipment. During the November 1991 debate on reauthorizing the Export Administration Act (EAA), Hunter tried but failed to attach amendments to allow the secretary of Defense to review and, in some cases, veto the export of high-tech civilian goods that potentially could be converted to military use. But at the end of the 102nd Congress, Hunter — along with Republican allies John R. Kasich of Ohio and Jon Kyl of Arizona — used delaying tactics to block enactment of the EAA bill.

It is on trade issues that Hunter veers farthest from current Republican orthodoxy. Citing the party's legacy of industrial protectionism during the late 19th century, Hunter has opposed Republican presidents' advocacy of free trade. He has frequently called for tough measures to reduce the United States' trade imbalance with Japan. And, although his district takes in most of California's border with Mexico, Hunter is against the North American Free Trade Agreement.

Hunter favors stepped-up efforts to collect taxes owed by foreign corporations operating in the United States — one of the few issues on which he would agree with President Clinton,

California 52

Inland San Diego and Imperial counties

The 52nd is California's far southeastern corner, including the whole of Imperial County and about half of San Diego County's land area. A vast barren area in the middle of the district divides its two main population concentrations — a suburban west and an agricultural east.

The bulk of the district's San Diego County residents are in three suburban cities on the western edge of the 52nd: El Cajon is the largest of the three with 89,000 residents, La Mesa's population is 53,000 and Spring Valley's is 55,000. Economically, La Mesa is a bit better off than the other two, and votes a bit more Democratic, but otherwise the three cities are very similar.

These suburbs have a mix of blue and white collars, with many defense workers and a lot of military personnel; the important role of the military-industrial complex in San Diego's economy contributes significantly to the conservative tenor of the area.

East along the 8 Freeway out of El Cajon are mountains, followed by a different type of mountains that consist mostly of boulders piled on boulders. This area is the Anza-Borrego Desert State Park, which looks to the casual observer less like a nature refuge than a rock refuge.

The huge Salton Sea just east of the park used to be a terrific fishing and recreational area, but agricultural runoff has increased the sea's salinity level above that of the Pacific Ocean, and that has killed most of the fish.

Beyond the park, the land flattens into desert. The district's agricultural sector begins a few miles before El Centro, Imperial County's largest city with 31,000 residents. Everything east is agriculture.

This is the Imperial Valley — known as the "salad bowl of the country" — and it lives and dies on farming.

Lately, it has been dying: It has the nation's highest unemployment rate — 26 percent in December 1992, down from a high of 33 percent.

The area has had more than its share of tough luck lately: A plague of white flies devastated crops in the early 1990s, then there were floods, followed by more flies.

The region depends on the Colorado River for its lifeblood: water. The river defines the California-Arizona border on the district's eastern edge, and water issues dominate the farmers' political attention. The importance of irrigation is vividly evident here; along some roads, stark desert lies on one side while plush alfalfa fields flank the other.

The 52nd is heavily Republican: 46 percent of its registered voters are Republicans; 39 percent are Democrats. The district is over one-fifth Hispanic, and about 3 percent each black and Asian.

George Bush won the 52nd in 1992 with 37 percent of the vote to Bill Clinton's 34 percent and Ross Perot's 29 percent. Clinton actually won Imperial County with 44 percent of the vote, to Bush's 39 percent and Perot's 17 percent, but the effect was muted; San Diego County casts almost 90 percent of the district's ballots.

1990 Population: 573,203. White 479,206 (84%), Black 17,788 (3%), Other 76,209 (13%). Hispanic origin 129,771 (23%). 18 and over 415,866 (73%), 62 and over 75,381 (13%). Median age: 31.

who took the same stand during his 1992 campaign.

Hunter is no "Friend of Bill," however. A decorated Vietnam War veteran, Hunter joined in the effort led by Republican Rep. Robert K. Dornan of California to make a campaign issue of Clinton's trip to the Soviet Union as a college student in 1969.

Hunter's conservative views on social issues inform his work on Armed Services. His 1988 amendment authorized the use of U.S. military forces to interdict illegal drug traffic. He spoke out against Clinton's efforts in early 1993 to end the ban on gays in the military. "Lifting the ban would destroy the military as we know it and would have a tremendous impact on our defensive readiness," he said.

At Home: Hunter has an unusual background for a conservative Republican. For the three years before his initial House campaign, he lived and worked in the Hispanic section of San Diego. Running his own storefront law office, Hunter often gave free legal advice to poor people. When President Reagan called for abolition of the Legal Services Corporation, Hunter was one of the dissenters.

Hunter's work in the usually Democratic inner city was one of the reasons for his 1980 upset victory over Democrat Lionel Van Deerlin, a nine-term House veteran.

Another reason was Hunter's ceaseless campaigning. He made endless rounds of the compact district, popping up at defense plants and on street corners, shaking 1,000 hands every day while Van Deerlin remained in Washington, assuming he would score a comfortable victory.

Hunter, who won a Bronze Star for participating in 25 helicopter combat assaults in Vietnam, blasted away at what he called Van Deerlin's "anti-defense" voting record. He promised his own pro-Pentagon stance would keep jobs in the San Diego area, which boasts the nation's largest naval base and numerous defense industries. "In San Diego," he said, "defense means jobs." The message worked well enough for a stunning 53 percent majority.

Before Democrats had a chance to prove that win a fluke, the new redistricting plan for 1982 gave Hunter a safely Republican district. He won re-election with 69 percent that year and did better yet through the remainder of the decade. District Democrats did not even field a candidate in 1990.

Life got more complicated in 1992. The latest round of redistricting made Hunter move his home, but it left his base relatively intact (his district lost its coastline but still starts in metropolitan San Diego and runs east all the way to Arizona). GOP registration slipped to 46 percent, but California Republicans rarely lose a district where their registration is higher than 40 percent. Hunter's real problems stemmed from his 399 overdrafts at the House bank. Janet Gastil, a former school board member, got the Democratic nomination unopposed. Armed with the built-in overdrafts issue, the relatively underfunded challenger kept the incumbent on the defensive all fall and held him to 53 percent.

Committee

Armed Services (3rd of 22 Republicans)
Military Installations & Facilities (ranking); Research & Technology

Elections

1992 General		
Duncan Hunter (R)	112,995	(53%)
Janet M. Gastil (D)	88,076	(41%)
Joe Shea (LIBERT)	6,977	(3%)
Dennis P. Gretsinger (PFP)	5,734	(3%)
1992 Primary		
Duncan Hunter (R)	35,681	(60%)
Eric Epifano (R)	13,604	(23%)
Robert E. Krysak (R)	10,337	(17%)
1990 General		
Duncan Hunter (R)	123,591	(73%)
Joe Shea (LIBERT)	46,068	(27%)

Previous Winning Percentages: **1988** (74%) **1986** (77%) **1984** (75%) **1982** (69%) **1980** (53%)

District Vote for President

1992
D 74,913 (34%)
R 81,421 (37%)
I 63,176 (29%)

Campaign Finance

	Receipts	Receipts from PACs		Expend-itures
1992				
Hunter (R)	$561,203	$201,107	(36%)	$559,970
Gastil (D)	$161,428	$41,535	(26%)	$164,480
1990				
Hunter (R)	$368,560	$110,465	(30%)	$376,408

Key Votes

1993	
Require parental notification of minors' abortions	Y
Require unpaid family and medical leave	N
Approve national "motor voter" registration bill	N
Approve budget increasing taxes and reducing deficit	N
Approve economic stimulus plan	N
1992	
Approve balanced-budget constitutional amendment	Y
Close down space station program	N
Approve U.S. aid for former Soviet Union	Y
Allow shifting funds from defense to domestic programs	N
1991	
Extend unemployment benefits using deficit financing	?
Approve waiting period for handgun purchases	N
Authorize use of force in Persian Gulf	Y

Voting Studies

	Presidential Support		Party Unity		Conservative Coalition	
Year	**S**	**O**	**S**	**O**	**S**	**O**
1992	80	19	90	6	98	2
1991	80	16	84	6	92	5
1990	69	28	84	11	87	9
1989	76	22	85	7	90	7
1988	65	30	89	5	95	3
1987	72	22	86	6	88	7
1986	78	20	85	11	90	8
1985	74	20	75	12	87	11
1984	73	24	80	15	90	8
1983	74	24	88	10	93	7
1982	83	14	84	10	90	5
1981	74	25	89	11	95	5

Interest Group Ratings

Year	ADA	AFL-CIO	CCUS	ACU
1992	15	27	88	100
1991	5	27	78	100
1990	6	17	86	96
1989	10	18	100	96
1988	0	15	77	100
1987	4	13	93	91
1986	0	29	100	82
1985	10	19	76	86
1984	5	42	81	91
1983	15	12	80	91
1982	5	21	82	84
1981	10	27	89	100

Colorado

STATE DATA

Governor: Roy Romer (D)
First elected: 1986
Length of term: 4 years
Term expires: 1/95
Salary: $70,000
Term limit: 2 terms
Phone: (303) 866-2471
Born: Oct. 31, 1928; Garden City, Kan.
Education: Colorado State U., B.S. 1950; U. of Colorado, LL.B. 1952; Yale U., 1954
Military Service: Air Force, 1952-53
Occupation: Lawyer
Family: Wife, Bea Miller; seven children
Religion: Presbyterian
Political Career: Colo. House, 1959-63; Colo. Senate, 1963-67; Democratic nominee for U.S. Senate, 1966; Colo. commissioner of agriculture, 1975; chief of staff to Gov. Richard Lamm, 1975-77; Colo. treasurer, 1977-87

Lt. Gov.: C. Michael Callihan (D)
First elected: 1986
Length of term: 4 years
Term expires: 1/95
Salary: $48,500
Phone: (303) 866-2087

State election official: (303) 894-2211
Democratic headquarters: (303) 830-8989
Republican headquarters: (303) 893-1776

REDISTRICTING

Colorado retained its six House seats in reapportionment. The legislature passed the new map March 19, 1992; the governor signed it March 24.

STATE LEGISLATURE

General Assembly. Meets January-May.

Senate: 35 members, 4-year terms
1992 breakdown: 19R, 17D; 27 men, 8 women; 31 whites, 1 black, 3 Hispanics
Salary: $17,500
Phone: (303) 866-2316

House of Representatives: 65 members, 2-year terms
1992 breakdown: 34R, 31D; 39 men, 26 women; 56 whites, 3 blacks, 6 Hispanics
Salary: $17,500
Phone: (303) 866-2904

URBAN STATISTICS

City	Pop.
Denver Mayor Wellington E. Webb, D	467,610
Colorado Springs Mayor Robert M. Isaac, R	281,140
Aurora Mayor Paul E. Taver, N-P	222,103
Lakewood Mayor Linda Morton, N-P	126,481

U.S. CONGRESS

Senate: 1 D, 1 R
House: 2 D, 4 R

TERM LIMITS

For Congress: Yes
Senate: 2 consecutive terms, effective 1991
House: 6 consecutive terms, effective 1991
For state offices: Yes
Senate: 2 consecutive terms, effective 1991
House: 4 consecutive terms, effective 1991

ELECTIONS

1992 Presidential Vote

Bill Clinton	40.1%
George Bush	35.9%
Ross Perot	23.3%

1988 Presidential Vote

George Bush	53%
Michael S. Dukakis	45%

1984 Presidential Vote

Ronald Reagan	63%
Walter F. Mondale	35%

POPULATION

1990 population		3,294,394
1980 population		2,889,964
Percent change		+14%
Rank among states:		26
White		88%
Black		4%
Hispanic		13%
Asian or Pacific islander		2%
Urban		82%
Rural		18%
Born in state		43%
Foreign-born		4%
Under age 18	861,266	26%
Ages 18-64	2,103,685	64%
65 and older	329,443	10%
Median age		32.5

MISCELLANEOUS

Capital: Denver
Number of counties: 63
Per capita income: $19,440 (1991)
Rank among states: 14
Total area: 104,091 sq. miles
Rank among states: 8

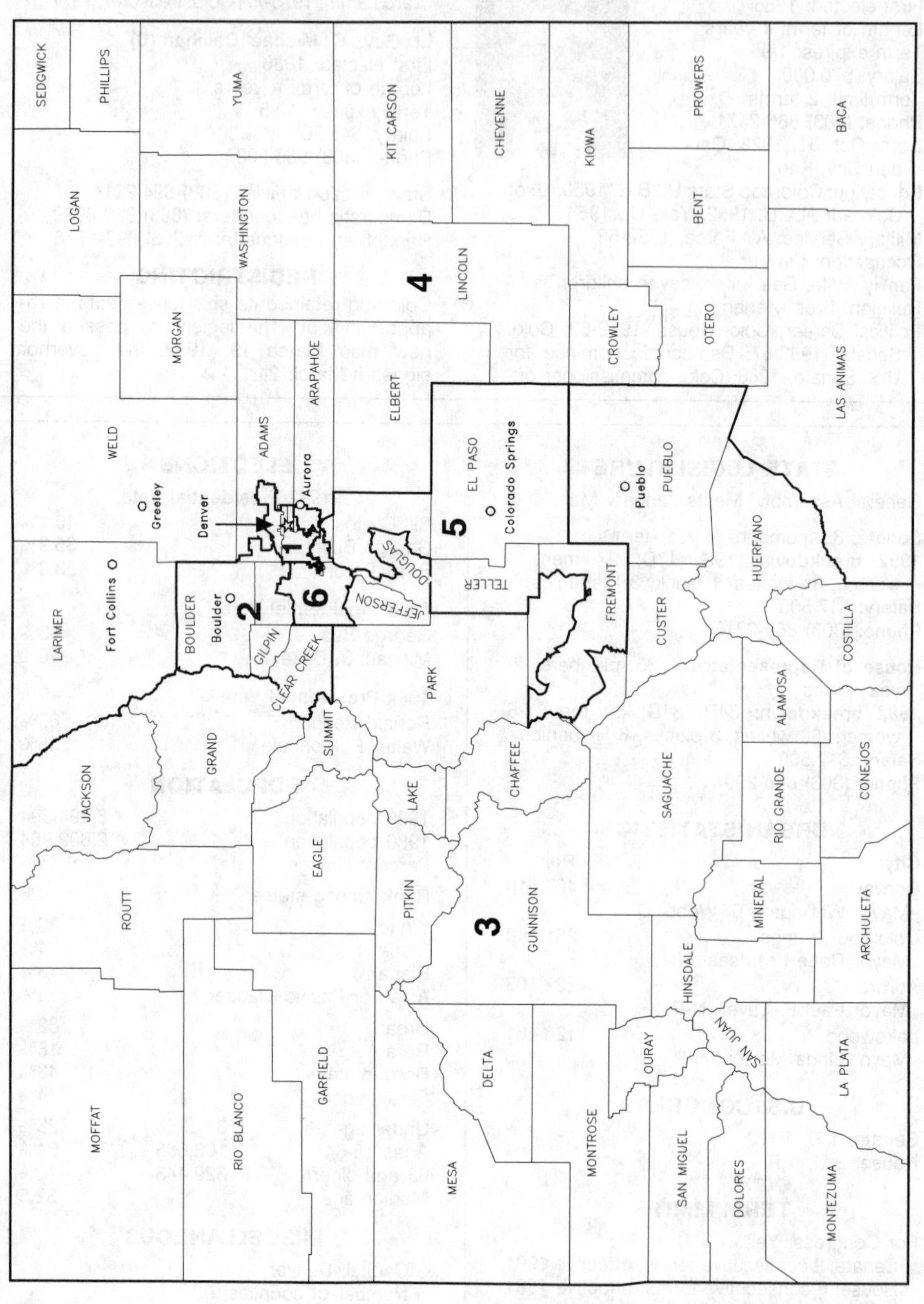

SEDGWICK
PHILLIPS
YUMA
KIT CARSON
CHEYENNE
KIOWA
PROWERS
BACA
LOGAN
WASHINGTON
BENT
LINCOLN
4
MORGAN
ARAPAHOE
CROWLEY
OTERO
ELBERT
LAS ANIMAS
WELD
ADAMS
EL PASO
Colorado Springs
PUEBLO
Pueblo
Greeley
Denver
Aurora
5
1
DOUGLAS
HUERFANO
Fort Collins
Boulder
6
2
JEFFERSON
TELLER
FREMONT
LARIMER
BOULDER
GILPIN
CLEAR CREEK
PARK
CUSTER
COSTILLA
ALAMOSA
JACKSON
GRAND
SUMMIT
CHAFFEE
SAGUACHE
RIO GRANDE
CONEJOS
LAKE
EAGLE
ROUTT
PITKIN
GUNNISON
3
MINERAL
ARCHULETA
HINSDALE
SAN JUAN
OURAY
LA PLATA
DELTA
MOFFAT
RIO BLANCO
GARFIELD
MESA
MONTROSE
SAN MIGUEL
DOLORES
MONTEZUMA

Hank Brown (R)

Of Greeley — Elected 1990; 1st Term

Born: Feb. 12, 1940, Denver, Colo.
Education: U. of Colorado, B.S. 1961, J.D. 1969; George Washington U., LL.M. 1986.
Military Service: Navy, 1962-66.
Occupation: Tax accountant; meatpacking company executive; lawyer.
Family: Wife, Nan Morrison; three children.
Religion: Congregationalist.
Political Career: Colo. Senate, 1973-77; GOP nominee for lieutenant governor, 1978; U.S. House, 1981-91.
Capitol Office: 716 Hart Bldg. 20510; 224-5941.

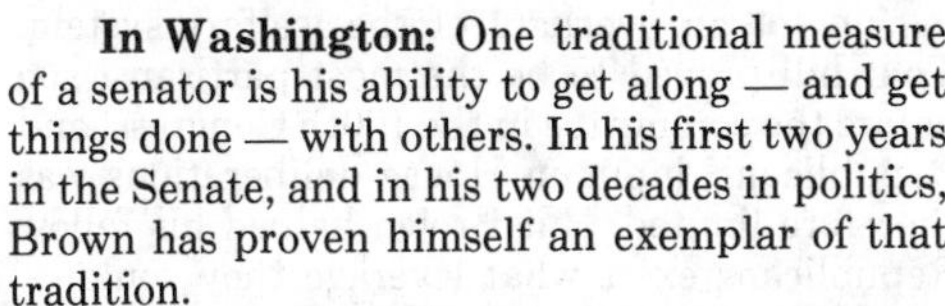

In Washington: One traditional measure of a senator is his ability to get along — and get things done — with others. In his first two years in the Senate, and in his two decades in politics, Brown has proven himself an exemplar of that tradition.

Through five terms in the House, Brown worked well with each of Colorado's senators. He agreed on budget and defense issues with his fellow Republican, William L. Armstrong, but he showed himself able to deal with Democrat Gary Hart (and successor Democrat Tim Wirth) on environmental issues.

In 1991, he joined Wirth in the Senate, and the two combined forces to solve an old and knotty issue: water rights in lands reserved for wilderness designation. Although the deal disappointed some water users and some environmentalists (who wanted an absolute water right for the wilderness areas), it broke the logjam that had prevented wilderness designations for a decade.

Brown has an undeniably pleasant manner and an open mind, traits often missing in contemporary politics. These attributes, along with his classic mix of conservatism and Western iconoclasm, have vouchsafed Brown a career of almost unbroken electoral success (he lost a race for lieutenant governor in 1978).

In the House, his reputation for independence earned him the respect of both parties. Willing to do the dirty work required of junior members — he served two terms on the House ethics panel — Brown has had little trouble transferring that respect to the Senate, where he has become a constant voice against deficit spending.

Brown is also a supporter of abortion rights, describing his stand as classic conservatism — minimizing the federal government's role in private citizens' lives.

Criticism of Brown focuses on his being perhaps too much of a gentleman, and some wondered if he would be tough enough for a rough Senate bid. While the Senate race never became close enough to test his mettle, part of the reason Brown won so comfortably was his emphasis on popular political issues during his last two years in the House: He was a leading foe of the congressional pay raise and defender of Social Security.

Brown won a seat on the Senate Budget Committee at the start of the 102nd Congress. In October 1990, he was among those who opposed the budget-summit agreement. Unlike many conservatives, however, his interest in cutting the deficit extends at times to cuts in defense.

Early in his tenure on the Senate Budget Committee, Brown teamed up with ranking Republican Pete V. Domenici of New Mexico to offer an amendment designed to limit tax increases. Conservatives on the Budget Committee wanted to eliminate provisions that allow other committees to make changes in entitlements and taxes on a pay-as-you-go basis.

When that failed, Brown and Domenici offered an amendment to prohibit tax increases from funding program expansions unless three-fifths of the Senate concurred. While the Senate went along with the idea, the House balked.

During the 1991 debate on the budget, he also resumed a longtime fight against the honey price-support program, which he calls "one of the silliest programs ever thought up in this nation or any nation in the history of the world." The Senate, however, defeated his measure to kill the program 57-38.

Brown tried again in 1992, this time offering an amendment to the fiscal 1993 agriculture appropriations to cut the honey program. But this effort was also rejected 56-41. On the same bill, Brown sided with Nevada Democrat Richard H. Bryan, who tried unsuccessfully to eliminate a market promotion program from the bill. It provided grants to private companies to promote U.S. products overseas.

When supporters argued that the program was necessary to help American companies compete worldwide, Brown countered that American products "sell because of their attributes and because they are competitive," and not because of government advertising subsidies.

Still trying to trim agriculture programs, Brown offered an amendment in the Budget Committee to the fiscal 1993 budget to bar agriculture subsidies to producers with incomes of more than $120,000 a year. But the proposal was rejected 6-15.

Brown has been willing to raise budget questions even on the sensitive issue of unemployment. In 1991, he was one of only two senators — North Dakota Democrat Kent Conrad was the other — who voted against a House-passed unemployment extension. President Bush had agreed to sign the measure after vetoing a previous measure. When another unemployment bill came through the Senate early in 1992, Brown raised a point of order against it because it would add to the deficit and thus violate the budget law's pay-as-you-go requirement. The Senate decided to waive the budget act by an overwhelming 88-8 vote.

On a more successful note, Brown in the 102nd Congress sponsored a bill aimed at encouraging unemployed Soviet scientists to bring their knowledge to America. The president signed the bill in October 1992.

A Vietnam War veteran, Brown was a member of the select committee investigating whether any Americans remained in Vietnam. He joined the panel's unanimous conclusion that there was "no compelling evidence" to suggest that American prisoners were alive in Southeast Asia almost 20 years after the Vietnam War ended. Brown agreed with some others on the panel that Vietnam should be rewarded for its cooperation with the United States, but he cautioned against giving trade incentives to the country. The ongoing trade embargo, Brown said, was the "one trump card" that needed to be retained.

Early in the 103rd Congress, Brown staunchly opposed President Clinton's plan to lift the ban on gays in the military. Citing Clinton's lack of military experience, Brown said he did not think "Clinton knows what he's talking about." Brown said the issue was one of privacy and that the military "is not currently organized to provide even minimal privacy standards for people of the same sex."

Though not generally known as a grandstander, Brown was a frequent critic of ethics enforcement in the House, and in 1990 he became a leading foe of the pay raise. In August 1990, he held a high-visibility press conference with Ralph Nader and a coalition of self-described citizens' organizations to propose rolling back congressional salaries to the 1989 level and repealing the 1990 pay increase. At the time, Brown noted that it would be easier to accomplish this in the Senate, where amendments can be offered to unrelated legislation.

His critique of Congress as an institution goes further. Brown has tried to end Congress' practice of exempting itself from civil rights and other laws it imposes on others — a cause he can champion as a member of the Senate Judiciary Committee. He has made several attempts over the years to cut funding for members' perks such as franked mail, elevator operators and leadership staff.

But when the House bank scandal broke, Brown was among the 325 sitting and former members found to have had overdrafts at the bank between July 1, 1988, and Oct. 3, 1991. Brown had 18.

When Brown won a coveted seat on the Ways and Means Committee in 1987, he was thrust immediately into a leadership role as ranking minority member of the Public Assistance Subcommittee just as Congress was gearing up for an overhaul of the welfare system. That bill proved to be the most partisan issue before the committee in the 100th Congress, and Republicans' input in House deliberations was therefore limited. But Brown helped his fellow Republicans exert what leverage they could.

He put together a GOP alternative that struck a middle ground between a Democratic-drafted bill they deemed too costly and a Reagan administration proposal that would have focused not on new federal money and mandates, but on allowing states to experiment with new welfare approaches.

Brown's efforts to mold the bill in committee fell victim to immovable party lines. And the Republican alternative did little better on the House floor, even though the Democratic leadership had a hard time holding on to its conservative flank.

But once the Senate passed a welfare bill with a lower cost and a more stringent work requirement for welfare recipients, Brown had an opening. Republicans won a rare victory when the House approved a Brown motion instructing its conferees to accept the Senate's price tag. Although the cost ultimately exceeded that, Brown's move helped pressure the House negotiators to move closer to the Senate position.

At Home: Few members of the Senate have had a smoother ascent in politics than Brown. He won election to the state Senate in 1972 and with a single exception has been winning ever since.

Within two years in the state Senate, he was assistant majority leader; in 1980, he was elected to the House, capturing the 4th District seat of retiring GOP Rep. Jim Johnson, whose campaign Brown had once managed. Brown won re-election throughout the 1980s with at least 70 percent of the vote. In 1990, he took the Senate seat being vacated by Armstrong with a comfortable 56 percent.

While Brown flirted with, but then shied away from, a run for governor in 1986, he jumped quickly into the 1990 Senate race.

Barely a week after Armstrong indicated in early 1989 that he would not seek re-election, Brown announced his own candidacy.

He turned out to be a wire-to-wire leader in the polls. While Republicans quickly coalesced behind him, Democrats had to endure a bruising nominating battle among candidates who could ill afford the cost in money or stature.

Three of the state's most prominent Democrats — former Gov. Richard D. Lamm and Reps. Ben Nighthorse Campbell and David E. Skaggs — all skipped the 1990 race. With ardent support from environmentalists and feminists, former Boulder County Commissioner Josie Heath emerged as the Democratic nominee, but only after weathering a primary against lawyer Carlos Lucero, who was able to generate reams of free publicity by employing an investigative team to look into the collapse of the Colorado-based Silverado Banking, Savings and Loan Association.

Democrats tried to use the same issue to undermine Brown. President Bush came to a lucrative Brown fundraiser in December 1989 that was chaired by a controversial Denver developer with ties to Silverado. Democrats challenged Brown to return the money, which he declined to do. And with his image of personal rectitude, he was able to ride out the criticism.

With few other issues to take advantage of, Heath was unable to offset Brown's long head start, his aura of quasi-incumbency and a feeling among many Colorado voters that one senator from the trendy college town of Boulder (which was Wirth's home) was enough. Heath carried Boulder and Democratic Denver and Pueblo counties; Brown trounced her virtually everywhere else.

Committees

Budget (7th of 9 Republicans)

Foreign Relations (6th of 8 Republicans)
Near Eastern & South Asian Affairs (ranking); European Affairs; International Economic Policy, Trade, Oceans & Environment

Judiciary (6th of 8 Republicans)
Constitution (ranking); Patents, Copyrights & Trademarks

Elections

1990 General

Hank Brown (R)	569,048	(56%)
Josie Heath (D)	425,746	(42%)
John Heckman (COPP)	15,432	(2%)
Earl F. Dodge (COP)	11,801	(1%)

Previous Winning Percentages: **1988** * (73%) **1986** * (70%) **1984** * (71%) **1982** * (70%) **1980** * (68%)

** House elections.*

Campaign Finance

	Receipts	Receipts from PACs		Expend-itures
1990				
Brown (R)	$4,179,746	$1,389,784	(33%)	$3,723,911
Heath (D)	$1,953,120	$314,413	(16%)	$1,943,422

Key Votes

1993

Require unpaid family and medical leave	N
Approve national "motor voter" registration bill	N
Approve budget increasing taxes and reducing deficit	N
Support president's right to lift military gay ban	N

1992

Approve school-choice pilot program	Y
Allow shifting funds from defense to domestic programs	N
Oppose deeper cuts in spending for SDI	Y

1991

Approve waiting period for handgun purchases	N
Raise senators' pay and ban honoraria	N
Authorize use of force in Persian Gulf	Y
Confirm Clarence Thomas to Supreme Court	Y

Voting Studies

	Presidential Support		Party Unity		Conservative Coalition	
Year	S	O	S	O	S	O
1992	75	25	93	5	92	8
1991	75	23	85	14	85	13
House Service:						
1990	70	29	87	11	87	13
1989	63	35	84	15	83	17
1988	68	29	85	12	87	11
1987	58	39	84	11	77	14
1986	67	32	92	7	84	16
1985	70	29	87	11	82	18
1984	65	35	85	15	83	17
1983	67	33	82	18	75	25
1982	68	32	89	11	75	25
1981	66	34	77	23	71	29

Interest Group Ratings

Year	ADA	AFL-CIO	CCUS	ACU
1992	20	25	100	89
1991	10	17	80	90
House Service:				
1990	11	0	79	83
1989	20	17	100	86
1988	30	21	100	72
1987	16	19	85	73
1986	10	0	94	77
1985	30	12	82	67
1984	10	8	75	83
1983	25	12	90	61
1982	20	0	91	86
1981	20	13	89	100

Ben Nighthorse Campbell (D)

Of Ignacio — Elected 1992; 1st Term

Born: April 13, 1933, Auburn, Calif.

Education: San Jose State U., B.A. 1957; Meiji U. (Tokyo, Japan), 1960-64.

Military Service: Air Force, 1951-53.

Occupation: Jewelry designer; rancher; horse trainer; teacher.

Family: Wife, Linda Price; two children.

Religion: Unspecified.

Political Career: Colo. House, 1983-87; U.S. House, 1987-93.

Capitol Office: 380 Russell Bldg. 20510; 224-5852.

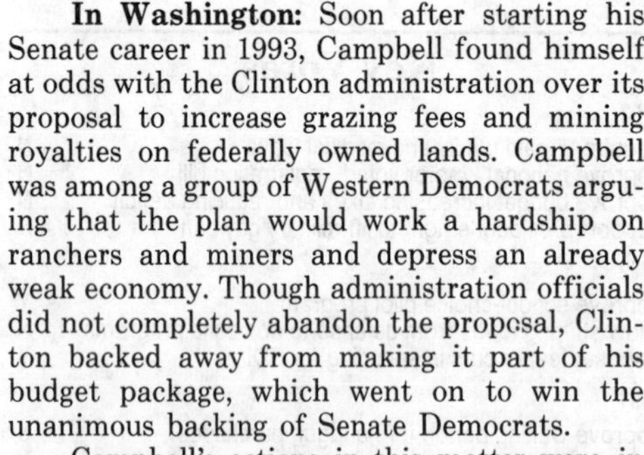

In Washington: Soon after starting his Senate career in 1993, Campbell found himself at odds with the Clinton administration over its proposal to increase grazing fees and mining royalties on federally owned lands. Campbell was among a group of Western Democrats arguing that the plan would work a hardship on ranchers and miners and depress an already weak economy. Though administration officials did not completely abandon the proposal, Clinton backed away from making it part of his budget package, which went on to win the unanimous backing of Senate Democrats.

Campbell's actions in this matter were in keeping with the pattern he had established during six years in the House: Though generally supporting the Democratic line, he was not shy about marching to his own drummer — especially where home-state interests were concerned.

Although Campbell's victory to succeed the retiring Tim Wirth kept this Senate seat in Democratic hands, the styles of the two men could not be more different. Wirth, groomed at Harvard and Stanford universities and holder of a doctorate, looked every inch the modern telegenic pol. Campbell, by contrast, cuts an unconventional figure: a one-time high school dropout, part-American Indian, former Olympic athlete and jewelry designer, he wears his hair in a ponytail and got special permission to wear his trademark bolo tie on the House floor instead of the customary necktie.

During three House terms, Campbell was strongly supportive of the ranching and mining interests of his largely rural and mountainous western Colorado district. Environmentalists eventually supported his Senate bid, but only after he took the Democratic nomination over two rivals whom environmentalists would have preferred. Campbell casts himself as a social liberal but a fiscal conservative.

Upon entering the Senate, Campbell won seats on the Banking, Energy, Indian Affairs and Veterans' Affairs committees, assignments that give him an opportunity to range over a variety of issues and broaden his reputation as a legislator. In the House, he kept a fairly low legislative profile and tended mostly to local issues.

He sponsored successful legislation that implemented a settlement of Colorado Ute Indian water rights and paved the way for the construction of the Animas-La Plata water project. He also worked unsuccessfully to achieve a compromise in the long-standing dispute over how much land should be set aside for wilderness in Colorado.

However, early in the 103rd Congress, Campbell joined his GOP Senate colleague Hank Brown in offering a bill to set aside more than 766,000 acres in Colorado as wilderness.

Campbell's unique personality showed through in an early 1991 encounter with a mugger near his Capitol Hill residence. Campbell had noticed a man following him for several blocks; when the mugger closed in and said he had a gun, Campbell demanded to see the weapon, then scuffled with the thief, who ran away. Campbell was slightly injured.

At Home: Campbell won the Democratic Senate nomination in 1992 by handily dispatching two formidable rivals, former three-term Gov. Richard D. Lamm and former Boulder County Commissioner Josie Heath, the 1990 Senate nominee who lost to Republican Brown.

Campbell entered the general-election race with a wide lead over GOP nominee Terry Considine, 45, a successful businessman and a former state senator who had built his statewide reputation by championing a term-limits ballot initiative that Coloradans passed overwhelmingly in 1990. In a campaign some called the nastiest in modern Colorado history, Considine narrowed the gap with attack ads that criticized Campbell's low voting attendance record in congressional committees and highlighted a trip Campbell and his wife took to Alaska, paid for by Chevron Oil.

Campbell struck back with attacks of his own, airing TV spots that questioned Considine's dealings with the failed Silverado

Banking, Savings & Loan Association. But the witheringly negative campaign sometimes got under the volatile Campbell's skin. At one forum, according to news accounts, the congressman testily suggested that questioners were shilling for Considine; the forum was made up of middle and high school students.

Both candidates ran afoul of previous statements on their military service records, but Campbell's misstep seemed particularly embarrassing. In mid-campaign, he had to correct a statement in his campaign literature that said he had been trapped behind enemy lines in Korea for five weeks. That never happened, he explained, noting that during his tour in Korea as a member of the Air Force police he never got closer to enemy lines than nine miles away.

Though the two candidates tangled over fiscal matters and Campbell's congressional record, the core of Campbell's campaign was his compelling life story. The son of a Northern Cheyenne, he is half American Indian. His father was an alcoholic, and his mother suffered from tuberculosis. He dropped out of high school, served in the Air Force and worked his way through college driving a truck before finding success as an Olympian — he was on the U.S. judo team at the 1964 games — a craftsman of contemporary Indian jewelry and a cattle rancher in southwest Colorado.

Considine managed to run well ahead of George Bush, who lost Colorado, but Campbell prevailed by 9 percentage points.

Campbell began his political career in 1982, winning a conservative-minded state House district. During four years in the legislature, he was a dependable vote for farmers and ranchers on water rights. Though he occasionally sided with environmentalists, Campbell's views put him among conservatives in the Democratic Caucus.

That positioned Campbell well for his 1986 challenge to GOP Rep. Mike Strang. "People are sick and tired of plastic politicians — professional politicians who have done nothing else with their lives," Campbell said in the campaign. To win his House seat, Campbell had to draw a big vote in blue-collar Pueblo, then hold his own on the conservative Western Slope.

Campbell quickly established himself and won in 1988 with 78 percent of the vote, a record for a Colorado Democratic House member. He was seriously discussed as a candidate for the Senate in 1990, but he declined to run.

Campbell's House vote fell just a shade in 1990, partly because of his opposition to the Nucla-Naturita Prairie Dog Shoot that summer. Many voters in western Montrose County, site of the event, began calling the incumbent "Ben Nightmare Campbell," and the precincts that included the tiny towns were the only ones in the district to vote against him.

Committees

Banking, Housing & Urban Affairs (9th of 11 Democrats)
Economic Stabilization & Rural Development; International Finance & Monetary Policy

Energy & Natural Resources (9th of 11 Democrats)
Public Lands, National Parks & Forests (vice chairman); Mineral Resources Development & Production; Water & Power

Indian Affairs (10th of 10 Democrats)

Veterans' Affairs (7th of 7 Democrats)

Elections

1992 General		
Ben Nighthorse Campbell (D)	803,725	(52%)
Terry Considine (R)	662,893	(43%)
Richard O. Grimes (PI)	42,455	(3%)
Matt Noah (CPL)	22,846	(1%)
Dan Winters (I)	20,347	(1%)
1992 Primary		
Ben Nighthorse Campbell (D)	117,634	(45%)
Richard D. Lamm (D)	93,599	(36%)
Josie Heath (D)	47,418	(18%)

Previous Winning Percentages: **1990** * (70%) **1988** * (78%) **1986** * (52%)

** House elections.*

Campaign Finance

	Receipts	Receipts from PACs	Expend- itures
1992			
Campbell (D)	$1,594,544	$741,686 (47%)	$1,561,347
Considine (R)	$2,704,514	$428,319 (16%)	$2,645,791

Key Votes

1993	
Require unpaid family and medical leave	Y
Approve national "motor voter" registration bill	Y
Approve budget increasing taxes and reducing deficit	Y
Support president's right to lift military gay ban	Y
House Service:	
1992	
Approve balanced-budget constitutional amendment	Y
Close down space station program	?
Approve U.S. aid for former Soviet Union	N
Allow shifting funds from defense to domestic programs	N
1991	
Extend unemployment benefits using deficit financing	Y
Approve waiting period for handgun purchases	N
Authorize use of force in Persian Gulf	Y

Voting Studies

	Presidential Support		Party Unity		Conservative Coalition	
Year	**S**	**O**	**S**	**O**	**S**	**O**
House Service:						
1992	27	45	57	15	42	17
1991	34	56	75	21	62	24
1990	35	64	72	23	67	31
1989	45	50	70	25	66	32
1988	26	65	85	11	47	45
1987	34	66	78	18	65	33

Interest Group Ratings

Year	ADA	AFL-CIO	CCUS	ACU
House Service:				
1992	55	71	0	38
1991	55	92	40	45
1990	56	67	77	33
1989	50	64	60	36
1988	65	92	43	21
1987	64	88	40	9

1 Patricia Schroeder (D)

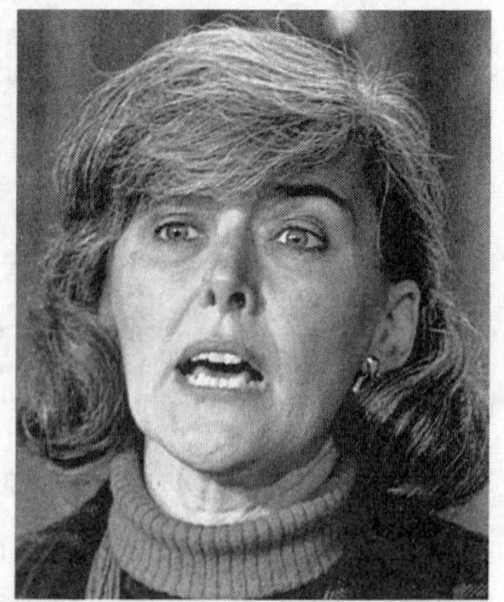

Of Denver — Elected 1972; 11th Term

Born: July 30, 1940, Portland, Ore.
Education: U. of Minnesota, B.A. 1961; Harvard U., J.D. 1964.
Occupation: Lawyer; law instructor.
Family: Husband, James Schroeder; two children.
Religion: United Church of Christ.
Political Career: No previous office.
Capitol Office: 2208 Rayburn Bldg. 20515; 225-4431.

In Washington: One of the few House members with household-name status, Schroeder may be reaching a turning point in her long congressional career. Her public persona is that of a liberal, feminist activist. Yet she is seeing some of the issues with which she is most closely identified — family leave, combat roles for women, protection against sexual harassment — move to the mainstream.

The huge freshman class of 1992, with its many new women members, symbolizes the extent to which society and Congress have evolved since Schroeder's election in 1972, often in ways that she advocated. She has joked about feeling like "a den mother" for all the new women members. But the longest-serving woman in the House may also find her star less prominent in this larger and more diverse constellation.

With the elimination of the House Select Committee on Children, Youth and Families, which she chaired, Schroeder has lost a platform for her views. Yet as the No. 2 Democrat on both the Armed Services and Post Office committees, and a senior member of Judiciary as well, she is in a better position than ever before to shape policy and legislation, should she choose to do so.

But Schroeder, who contemplated running for president in 1988, has never demonstrated much appetite for the the constant compromising that is a part of crafting major legislation and pushing it through Congress. "I think that's why some people are so frustrated with the institution, because of all this compromise and equivocating," Schroeder has said. "We sound like we have mush dribbling out of our mouths." She readily acknowledges that her style is too aggressive and confrontational to bring her to the top ranks of leadership.

Irreverence and wit are key to Schroeder's popularity, yet sometimes her sharp tongue cuts too deeply, alienating allies and violating the clubhouse rules of Congress. She won points from fellow Democrats for handing Ronald Reagan the only derogatory label that ever stuck — "Teflon president" — but angered many colleagues when she told Newsweek magazine in 1989 that "Everyone here checks their spines in the cloakroom."

Nor has she spared President Clinton. Criticizing the slow pace of appointments to the Defense Department, Schroeder noted in February 1993 that Defense Secretary Les Aspin had "fewer people at the Pentagon than Custer had at Little Bighorn."

Colleagues concede that Schroeder is bright, as might be expected of a Harvard law classmate of Attorney General Janet Reno. But some label Schroeder a flake. Others argue that she simultaneously demands to be treated as an equal, while seeking special treatment as a woman.

Her attention to her own agenda sometimes leads Schroeder to overlook the political costs to others. Early in the 103rd she pushed Clinton to move quickly to lift the ban on gays in the military, as he had promised during his campaign. Clinton indicated he would do so, touching off a potentially damaging uproar that contributed to perceptions of early disarray in the administration.

With Ronald V. Dellums of California as chairman and Schroeder ranking second, the top ranks of Armed Services are now occupied by two people who faced opposition and suspicion from what was a white male preserve. Dellums, a liberal "dove" like Schroeder, is nonetheless now seen as an insider, a respecter of Congressional mores. Schroeder remains the grenade-tossing outsider.

When she first joined Armed Services as an antiwar activist in 1973, Schroeder was practically ostracized by a dominant, conservative "old guard" that could justifiably be described as sexist. The committee's membership moderated and became more accepting of women's participation: Schroeder gained the chairmanship of the Military Installations and Facilities Subcommittee at the start of the 101st Congress, and in the 103rd, she heads the new Research and Technology Subcommittee, with jurisdiction over defense conversion efforts.

It is a post from which Schroeder could take a leading role in efforts to ease the eco-

Colorado 1

Denver

With nearly 468,000 people, Colorado's capital city of Denver anchors the 1st and is the starting point for Democratic victories in the state.

In 1992, Bill Clinton swept Denver by nearly 67,000 votes; he won the rest of Colorado by just 288 votes. At the same time, Colorado's controversial gay rights ban, approved statewide by more than 100,000 votes, was defeated in Denver by a margin of nearly 40,000 votes. Passage of the measure has threatened existing anti-gay discrimination ordinances in Denver, Boulder and Aspen.

Denver's liberal cast is due in no small part to its large minority population — nearly one-quarter Hispanic and 13 percent black. Denver's last two mayors have been from the minority community — Federico F. Peña (now Clinton's Transportation secretary) and Wellington Webb, Denver's first black mayor.

Peña put so much emphasis on major building projects — including a new airport, a new convention center and a 40,000-seat baseball stadium — that one critic accused him of having an "edifice complex."

Yet Peña's building spree was the latest example of Denver's ability to roll with the punches. It was founded on the eve of the Civil War in response to rumors of gold in Cherry Creek (a stream that flows near downtown). By 1908, when Democrats assembled in Denver to nominate William Jennings Bryan a third time for president, it was a thriving cow town. By the 1970s, Denver had established itself as headquarters for large-scale energy operations in the Rockies.

Now, a boom and bust cycle later, the economy of Colorado's largest city is more diversified. And Denver is expecting millions of dollars in revenue from its new major league baseball franchise, the Colorado Rockies, fielding its first team in 1993.

But Denver's economic future is far from secure. Much of its recent recovery has been due to fixed-life construction projects. The largest, the new $2.7-billion Denver International Airport, is to open in late 1993. The facility, about 25 miles northeast of the city, covers 53 square miles and is billed as the world's largest airport site.

Redistricting did little to change the 1st's political complexion. Denver lost 5 percent of its population during the 1980s, so the district has moved north and east into Adams and Arapahoe counties to pick up much of Commerce City and the northern chunk of the city of Aurora. The 1st also regained several neighborhoods in the southwest corner of the city that had been in the 6th District and picked up one household in Jefferson County.

Yet 85 percent of the district's population still lives in Denver, and the additions are largely blue-collar neighborhoods that swell Democratic majorities.

Much of the new land the 1st takes in is part of the vast Rocky Mountain Arsenal near Commerce City, formerly a chemical weapons storage site that is being converted into a wildlife preserve. The large vacant slice of real estate is home to myriad eagles, foxes, deer and prairie dogs, but no voters.

1990 Population: 549,068. White 400,581 (73%), Black 70,961 (13%), Other 77,526 (14%). Hispanic origin 120,506 (22%). 18 and over 424,133 (77%), 62 and over 87,184 (16%). Median age: 34.

nomic pain caused by a downsized military. The subcommittee also has jurisdiction over basic research, while remaining one step removed from the nitty-gritty issues of weapons procurement — no doubt to the relief of the Pentagon. Schroeder has in the past voted to slice funding for the Strategic Defense Initiative and the B-2 bomber. She was a proponent of nuclear test-ban laws and fought to end the development of the MX missile and other nuclear weapons systems. She supported a 1989 list of base closings, though in 1991 she opposed the inclusion of Denver's Lowry Air Force Base on a second such list.

Schroeder's never-easy relationship with the military establishment reached a high-profile low point in 1992, when she harshly criticized the Navy's initial response to sexual harassment at the 1991 Tailhook Association convention. A more complete investigation followed, revealing that 83 women and seven men were assaulted during the three-day event. The scandal resulted in the resignation of Navy Secretary H. Lawrence Garrett. More than 100 officers faced possible criminal proceedings.

While the end result may be a military culture that is less hostile to women, Schroeder became the target of hate mail and vulgar skits by pilots at an elite Navy training facility. She made an attempt at fence-mending in early 1993 with a visit to the Naval Air Station at Miramar, Calif., where the skits were staged. But Schroeder remains deeply resented by some for her history of votes against defense spending and for her championship of lifting the gay ban.

Still, Aspin's decision in early 1993 to allow women aviators to fly combat missions illustrates the extent to which the establishment has caught up to Schroeder, a longtime advocate of combat roles for women soldiers. The decision has sparked little early controversy.

Schroeder cleared the way for Aspin's decision in 1991, when she proposed an amendment to the fiscal 1992 defense authorization bill allowing women to fly combat missions. With the support of Democrat Beverly B. Byron of Maryland, the conservative chairman of the Military Personnel Subcommittee and a past opponent of women in combat, the amendment passed.

Similarly, Schroeder's long battle to win passage of the Family and Medical Leave Act, which she first introduced in the mid-1980s, ended successfully when Clinton signed the bill early in 1993.

Early signs are mixed for the rest of Schroeder's agenda.

The elimination of the Select Committee on Children, Youth and Families stripped Schroeder of her committee chairmanship, the only one held by a woman. In the 102nd, Schroeder used the committee to gain attention for a Democratic family agenda, part of a campaign to wrest the "pro-family" banner from conservative Republicans.

Schroeder is now pushing for the creation of a new standing committee on human resources, a potentially difficult battle at a time when Congress is trying for a leaner look.

"As a nation, we could be held guilty of criminal neglect of children," Schroeder said, in acknowledging the demise of her committee. "Everyone loves them to death, until we get to the funding door."

The loss of the committee may be partially offset by the rising stock of another organization: the Congressional Caucus for Women's Issues, a bipartisan group chaired by Schroeder and Republican Olympia J. Snowe of Maine. Founded in 1977, the caucus has in the past been something of a backwater. But a February 1993 visit by Hillary Rodham Clinton, the first working meeting between the caucus and an influential White House insider, could signal growing political clout. Clinton met with the caucus to discuss health-care reform. The last time a first lady visited the caucus, it was Nancy Reagan, and all talk about issues was barred.

With a new administration committed to abortion rights, Schroeder may be able to make good on her 1989 pledge to codify the 1973 *Roe v. Wade* decision that legalized abortion, through passage of a new federal law.

On the Post Office and Civil Service Committee, Schroeder is a longtime supporter of legislation easing restrictions on the political rights of federal workers.

The bill revising the 1939 Hatch Act, which passed twice during the Bush administration only to face a veto, passed the House early in the 103rd on its way to Clinton's expected approval.

In the 103rd Congress, Schroeder has reintroduced a bill that would amend the 1964 Civil Rights Act to prohibit bias against homosexuals. She argues that a controversial Colorado law prohibiting special anti-bias protection for gays and lesbians proves the need for a federal standard. Schroeder and others have pushed gay civil rights proposals since 1975, but supporters acknowledge that support in Congress is weak.

The Gender Equity in Education Act sponsored by Schroeder would target dropout prevention programs at girls who are pregnant or parents, train teachers to treat boys and girls equally in the classroom, and train female teachers for math and science. It would also fund research in sexual harassment in schools.

Schroeder has teamed with New York Democrat Charles E. Schumer to introduce legislation to protect women confronted by protesters blockading abortion clinics. The bill is intended to counter a Supreme Court decision barring federal judges from stopping clinic blockades through injunctions.

At Home: Schroeder was in the vanguard of the Democratic resurgence in Colorado in the early 1970s, scoring upset victories in the 1972 primary and general election to wrest the Denver House seat from Republican control.

Although she had been a practicing lawyer and women's rights activist, Schroeder was a political neophyte. She was encouraged to make the race by her lawyer husband, who had unsuccessfully sought a state House seat in 1970.

Cultivating support from liberals in Denver and feminists and environmentalists at the national level, Schroeder put together a strong grass-roots organization. She drew 55 percent of the vote against state Senate Minority Leader Arch Decker in the primary, and 52 percent in the fall against GOP Rep. James "Mike" McKevitt.

The GOP has fielded a variety of candidates against Schroeder since 1972, including an anti-busing leader, a veteran state legislator, a wealthy political newcomer, a prominent ex-Democrat, and for four consecutive elections from 1984 through 1990, a succession of women candidates.

The legislator, state Rep. Don Friedman, came the closest, in 1976. He sharply criticized Schroeder's liberal voting record and collected a campaign treasury that exceeded hers. He held her to 53 percent.

Since then, the Republican threat has subsided. Redistricting and population changes have tilted the district toward minority voters, and Schroeder draws on a coalition of liberals, young professionals, blacks and Hispanics.

Committees

Armed Services (3rd of 34 Democrats)
Research & Technology (chairman)

Judiciary (7th of 21 Democrats)
Civil & Constitutional Rights; Economic & Commercial Law

Post Office & Civil Service (2nd of 15 Democrats)
Civil Service

Elections

1992 General		
Patricia Schroeder (D)	156,629	(69%)
Raymond Diaz Aragon (R)	70,902	(31%)
1990 General		
Patricia Schroeder (D)	82,176	(64%)
Gloria Gonzales Roemer (R)	46,802	(36%)

Previous Winning Percentages: **1988** (70%) **1986** (68%) **1984** (62%) **1982** (60%) **1980** (60%) **1978** (62%) **1976** (53%) **1974** (59%) **1972** (52%)

District Vote for President

1992
D 135,639 (56%)
R 63,315 (26%)
I 43,294 (18%)

Campaign Finance

	Receipts	Receipts from PACs		Expend-itures
1992				
Schroeder (D)	$361,845	$134,147	(37%)	$398,749
1990				
Schroeder (D)	$441,609	$113,588	(26%)	$521,500
Roemer (R)	$162,502	$15,200	(9%)	$161,266

Key Votes

1993	
Require parental notification of minors' abortions	N
Require unpaid family and medical leave	Y
Approve national "motor voter" registration bill	Y
Approve budget increasing taxes and reducing deficit	Y
Approve economic stimulus plan	Y
1992	
Approve balanced-budget constitutional amendment	N
Close down space station program	Y
Approve U.S. aid for former Soviet Union	Y
Allow shifting funds from defense to domestic programs	Y
1991	
Extend unemployment benefits using deficit financing	Y
Approve waiting period for handgun purchases	Y
Authorize use of force in Persian Gulf	N

Voting Studies

	Presidential Support		Party Unity		Conservative Coalition	
Year	**S**	**O**	**S**	**O**	**S**	**O**
1992	20	76	76	22	29	69
1991	18	81	80	18	11	89
1990	18	81	72	27	13	83
1989	19	79	67	31	17	80
1988	20	77	70	25	29	68
1987	13	81	68	25	23	70
1986	19	78	66	28	14	82
1985	30	69	58	39	24	76
1984	28	68	73	23	17	81
1983	11	84	81	16	18	78
1982	29	65	75	19	16	82
1981	29	70	76	21	12	85

Interest Group Ratings

Year	ADA	AFL-CIO	CCUS	ACU
1992	95	80	50	4
1991	90	83	30	0
1990	100	92	21	13
1989	100	92	40	11
1988	95	100	31	0
1987	76	64	27	9
1986	95	86	29	5
1985	80	71	55	19
1984	90	62	53	23
1983	85	76	20	17
1982	90	94	25	20
1981	95	80	6	13

2 David E. Skaggs (D)

Of Boulder — Elected 1986; 4th Term

Born: Feb. 22, 1943, Cincinnati, Ohio.

Education: Wesleyan U., B.A. 1964; Yale U., LL.B. 1967.

Military Service: Marine Corps, 1968-71; Marine Corps Reserve, 1971-77.

Occupation: Lawyer; congressional aide.

Family: Wife, Laura Locher; one child, two stepchildren.

Religion: Congregationalist.

Political Career: Colo. House, 1981-87, minority leader, 1983-85.

Capitol Office: 1124 Longworth Bldg. 20515; 225-2161.

In Washington: A former Marine, Skaggs has a straightforward and conservative bearing; his approach to legislation is orderly and deliberate. His style has gotten him off to a good start in Congress and especially at the polls, where he has solidified his hold on a politically marginal district despite his relatively liberal voting record.

Having demonstrated considerable loyalty to the Democratic leadership, Skaggs snagged a plum in the 101st Congress — a seat on the Appropriations Committee. In the 103rd, he added a seat on the Intelligence Committee.

Skaggs has supported Democratic leaders with his stands in favor of a seven-day waiting period for purchasing handguns, against a constitutional amendment banning physical desecration of the flag, and against the use of force in the Persian Gulf.

He also drew the notice of senior Democrats with two high-profile roles in 1992: eliminating Vice President Dan Quayle's Council on Competitiveness and proposing the compromise amendment on granting House floor voting privileges to non-voting delegates.

The Competitiveness Council, a regulatory review panel, had come under attack for delaying or reversing regulations issued by Cabinet departments and other agencies; critics maintained that the council was effectively circumventing the will of Congress. During consideration of the annual spending bill for the White House, Skaggs offered an amendment to cut $86,000 from White House operations — the amount Quayle requested for the salaries of two staff members on the council. Skaggs called the council activities "at best improper and probably illegal," pointing to council efforts to delay regulations on Clean Air Act amendments and on those protecting workers exposed to formaldehyde. The committee adopted it on a 30-18 vote.

But a Senate Appropriations subcommittee refused to go along with that attack, and fearing a veto, House conferees ultimately conceded in the House-Senate conference, leaving the council's budget unscathed. Skaggs argued into the night for his wording, but to little avail. He finally agreed to a "manager's statement," which has no statutory effect, that included extensive language requesting that all council activities "be made available for public review." For Skaggs, though, the defeat was blessedly short-lived: In his first days in office, President Clinton disbanded the council.

As the Democratic Caucus organized for the 103rd Congress, Eleanor Holmes Norton, the District of Columbia's non-voting delegate, pressed to grant privileges to the non-voting delegates from D.C., American Samoa, Guam and the Virgin Islands, and the resident commissioner from Puerto Rico, seeking to allow them to vote in the Committee of the Whole House, where the House does most of its legislative work.

For Republicans, the move reeked of politics: All five non-voting members were Democrats, and by adding them, Democrats would halve the 10-seat gain Republicans had realized in the November elections. Several Democrats also had problems with the change, but few wanted to go on record against it and Norton.

Skaggs offered a weakening amendment that would require the House to re-vote if an issue is decided by delegate votes in the Committee of the Whole. "Many members of the caucus have constitutional and political difficulties with this," he said. His amendment eventually won approval, and it enabled the change to survive a court challenge: A federal judge ruled in 1993 that the rule was constitutional, but only because the re-vote requirement rendered the delegates' votes "meaningless."

Skaggs' district includes the Energy Department's troubled Rocky Flats compound, a plutonium-processing facility that has stopped production because of safety problems.

In 1990, he worked to delay funding for plutonium processing at the nuclear weapons plant pending a Department of Energy plan to improve safety. Environmentalists locally had backed a failed effort by Democrat Patricia

Colorado 2

Northwest Denver suburbs; Boulder

The 2nd is almost equal parts suburbs and mountains, but it is probably defined most in the national mind by the college town of Boulder, the largest community in the 2nd, with slightly more than 83,000 people.

Lying at the base of the Front Range of the Rockies, Boulder is a sort of Berkeley East. It was best known in the 1970s as the setting for comedian Robin Williams' television series, "Mork and Mindy," and since then as the headquarters of Celestial Seasonings, the herbal tea producer.

The large academic community at the University of Colorado (25,600 students), augmented by many young professionals drawn to the area's scenery and outdoorsy lifestyle, give Boulder's politics a decidedly liberal hue.

The rest of Boulder County is less so, with the old farming center of Longmont anchoring the northern end of the county and suburbs such as Lafayette, Louisville and Broomfield clustered in the south. Boulder County pulsates with government research facilities such as the National Oceanic and Atmospheric Administration and related scientific and high-tech companies.

For years, the county was comfortable voting GOP for president. When it went for Michael S. Dukakis in 1988, it was the first time since 1964 that Boulder County had backed a Democrat for president. Since then, it has veered left with a vengeance. In 1992, former California Gov. Edmund G. "Jerry" Brown Jr. easily swept the county in the Democratic presidential primary, taking 43 percent of the vote.

In November, Bill Clinton swamped George Bush in Boulder County by 2-to-1. At the same time, the successful statewide ballot measure to gut local gay rights ordinances in cities such as Boulder was rejected by nearly 60 percent of the county's voters.

Slightly more than 40 percent of the district's people live in Boulder County. Most of the rest live closer to Denver in portions of two suburban counties, Adams and Jefferson; each has nearly 30 percent of the people in the 2nd. Adams has a more blue-collar flavor; Jefferson is historically Republican. Redistricting in 1992 shifted some of Adams out of the 2nd and added turf in Jefferson, but that caused Rep. Skaggs no trouble. Bush carried Jefferson County by less than 2,000 votes in 1992, while Skaggs and Democratic Senate candidate Ben Nighthorse Campbell both won it by more than 10,000 votes.

Nearly half the district's land area (but only 2 percent of its voters) is a short drive west in the mountain counties of Clear Creek and Gilpin. To help lure tourist dollars, Gilpin County's 19th century mining towns of Central City and Black Hawk have legalized gambling.

Less of a tourist draw but more vital to the district economy is the controversial Rocky Flats plutonium plant near the Boulder-Jefferson county line. An erstwhile manufacturer of triggers for nuclear weapons, the plant is in the environmental cleanup phase.

1990 Population: 549,072. White 508,752 (93%), Black 4,606 (<1%), Other 35,714 (7%). Hispanic origin 51,896 (9%). 18 and over 407,402 (74%), 62 and over 52,988 (10%). Median age: 32.

Schroeder to cut funding outright.

As a member of the Energy and Water Subcommittee in 1991, he tried to force more study before the Bush administration could reopen Rocky Flats, but he was blocked by Senate appropriators. In December 1991, he called for the government to halt Rocky Flats' weapons production facilities and to put Rocky Flats on standby in case a national security need arose before a replacement facility was ready.

But Skaggs also pushed to keep jobs from being moved out of the complex. In 1992, he persuaded members of the Energy and Water Subcommittee to block the Energy Department's proposed consolidation of hundreds of production jobs until the department could prove that it would save money. The move would have transferred some 800 non-nuclear jobs to Kansas City. He also sponsored a "bill of rights" for nuclear defense workers to require the government to guarantee certain health insurance costs linked to radiation-related diseases.

Before joining Appropriations, Skaggs served on the Public Works and the Science, Space and Technology committees. On Public Works' Aviation Subcommittee, Skaggs was the point man in the House for Denver's proposed new airport, which is being built just outside his district. In the 100th Congress, he helped negotiate a deal allowing the city to sell some federally controlled land to help finance the project. He is also an advocate for building an annex of the Smithsonian Air and Space Museum on the site of Denver's Stapleton Airport, which is scheduled to close in 1993.

At Home: After barely winning his first

term in 1986, Skaggs has regularly won re-election since then with more than 60 percent of the vote. Besides his own political skill, he has benefited from weak GOP opposition.

In 1988 Skaggs faced GOP state Rep. David Bath, a conservative Christian activist and former Democrat; in 1990, Jason Lewis, a self-described "William F. Buckley Republican" best known as the husband of a Denver TV anchorwoman; and in 1992, Bryan Day, a conservative minister.

GOP foes have sought to pillory Skaggs as too liberal for the swing district's political mainstream. But as a Vietnam veteran, Skaggs has had considerable latitude in positioning himself, particularly on patriotic issues. He was the only member of the state House delegation to join Schroeder in opposing the proposed constitutional amendment banning flag desecration in 1990, and in opposing the use of military force in the Persian Gulf in January 1991.

Skaggs, though, appeared to be vulnerable in 1992 when it was disclosed he had 57 overdrafts at the House bank, a total that exceeded the combined overdraft count of all the other members of the Colorado congressional delegation.

But Skaggs waged an aggressive campaign that portrayed Day as outside the political mainstream of the suburban district. Skaggs, who supports abortion rights, charged that Day was part of a Christian coalition trying to force conservative religious views on the rest of the nation. Day denied his campaign was so narrowly focused, but his effort was strapped for funds and Skaggs triumphed easily at the ballot box.

Skaggs got into politics after moving to Colorado in 1971, becoming a precinct committeeman and then Democratic district chairman. That led him to Washington as the chief aide to Democratic Rep. Tim Wirth after the 1974 election. After a term, he moved back to Colorado and won a seat in the state House in 1980.

Skaggs' ties to Wirth and his high profile in the Boulder area made him a logical successor when Wirth ran for the Senate in 1986. He won the Democratic nomination handily but was the underdog in the general election against Republican Mike Norton, who had held Wirth to 53 percent of the vote in 1984 and had campaigned almost non-stop since.

While quietly building an organization, Skaggs emulated Wirth's centrist approach to issues. In the fall he ran TV ads accusing Norton of inconsistency, gaining enough of a jump in the polls to help finance his final push.

After Wirth's surprise announcement in 1992 that he would not seek re-election, Skaggs ruled out seeking the Democratic nomination to succeed him in the Senate.

Committees

Appropriations (22nd of 37 Democrats)
Commerce, Justice, State & Judiciary; District of Columbia; Interior

Select Intelligence (7th of 12 Democrats)
Oversight & Evaluation; Program & Budget Authorization

Elections

1992 General		
David E. Skaggs (D)	164,790	(61%)
Bryan Day (R)	88,470	(33%)
Vern Tharp (AMGA)	18,101	(7%)
1992 Primary		
David E. Skaggs (D)	35,248	(79%)
James L. "Flash" Harrington (D)	9,164	(21%)
1990 General		
David E. Skaggs (D)	105,248	(61%)
Jason Lewis (R)	68,226	(39%)

Previous Winning Percentages: 1988 (63%) **1986** (51%)

District Vote for President

1992
D 122,907 (45%)
R 83,164 (30%)
I 66,648 (24%)

Campaign Finance

	Receipts	Receipts from PACs		Expend-itures
1992				
Skaggs (D)	$659,719	$316,637	(48%)	$673,887
Day (R)	$93,846	$2,225	(2%)	$93,577
1990				
Skaggs (D)	$415,235	$242,070	(58%)	$396,017
Lewis (R)	$49,679	$5,900	(12%)	$49,080

Key Votes

1993	
Require parental notification of minors' abortions	N
Require unpaid family and medical leave	Y
Approve national "motor voter" registration bill	Y
Approve budget increasing taxes and reducing deficit	Y
Approve economic stimulus plan	Y
1992	
Approve balanced-budget constitutional amendment	N
Close down space station program	Y
Approve U.S. aid for former Soviet Union	Y
Allow shifting funds from defense to domestic programs	Y
1991	
Extend unemployment benefits using deficit financing	Y
Approve waiting period for handgun purchases	Y
Authorize use of force in Persian Gulf	N

Voting Studies

	Presidential Support		Party Unity		Conservative Coalition	
Year	S	O	S	O	S	O
1992	30	70	88	10	38	63
1991	36	63	91	8	24	76
1990	21	79	93	6	19	81
1989	35	65	94	6	22	78
1988	29	70	81	16	47	53
1987	24	76	91	9	35	65

Interest Group Ratings

Year	ADA	AFL-CIO	CCUS	ACU
1992	90	82	38	8
1991	85	75	40	0
1990	89	83	21	8
1989	85	83	30	7
1988	95	86	57	16
1987	84	81	33	9

3 Scott McInnis (R)

Of Glenwood Springs — Elected 1992; 1st Term

Born: May 9, 1953, Glenwood Springs, Colo.
Education: Fort Lewis College, B.A. 1975; St. Mary's U. of San Antonio, J.D. 1980.
Occupation: Lawyer.
Family: Wife, Lori Smith; three children.
Religion: Roman Catholic.
Political Career: Colo. House, 1983-93, majority leader, 1991-93.
Capitol Office: 512 Cannon Bldg. 20515; 225-4761.

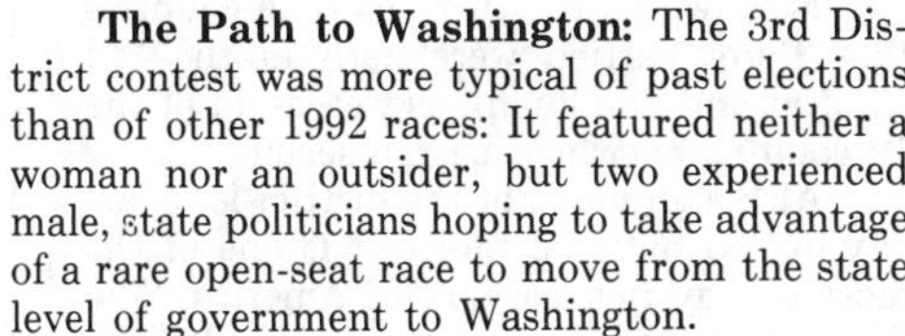

The Path to Washington: The 3rd District contest was more typical of past elections than of other 1992 races: It featured neither a woman nor an outsider, but two experienced male, state politicians hoping to take advantage of a rare open-seat race to move from the state level of government to Washington.

McInnis, a five-term Republican state lawmaker and majority leader of the state House since 1991, battled Democratic Lt. Gov. Mike Callihan for the right to succeed Democratic Rep. Ben Nighthorse Campbell, who had retired to run for an open Senate seat. Neither McInnis nor Callihan had primary opposition.

Although Democrats had virtually uninterrupted control of the district since 1964 — GOP Rep. Mike Strang was elected in 1984 only to be defeated by Campbell two years later — the demographics make it competitive for both parties. Democrats usually rack up wide victory margins in Pueblo and the San Luis Valley, while voters in the western portion of the district, particularly the northwest corner, usually favor Republican candidates.

Callihan appeared to have an edge going into the race: In his role as lieutenant governor, he had become known to far more voters in the vast, rural district than McInnis, whose legislative district included only a small portion of the congressional district.

But organizational problems plagued Callihan's campaign from the start.

The national Democratic Party eventually sent in one of its field operatives to manage the campaign. Callihan also tended to talk at length with a few voters while campaigning rather than chat briefly with more people. Many wondered whether he was "too nice a guy" to oppose the combative McInnis.

McInnis, because he was unfamiliar to so many voters, adopted a frantic campaign style and seemed to benefit from it. He tried to make time in every day to stop at a street corner somewhere, sometimes with his family by his side, to wave at passers-by.

McInnis touted his legislative experience and mocked the ceremonial nature of the lieutenant governor's office to highlight the differences between Callihan and himself.

He said that as state House majority leader he had been "the first one out of the foxhole" on controversial issues. McInnis said he had also fought to protect the district's interests while serving as chairman of the Agriculture, Livestock and Natural Resources Committee.

Callihan, a former state senator, defended his tenure as lieutenant governor, arguing that he had effectively helped create several noteworthy programs, including one that encouraged the study of math and science.

The two candidates shared similar stands on the issues. Both advocated abortion rights and argued against gun control. And like most voters in this district that depends on natural resources for much of its economic output, McInnis and Callihan opposed strict environmental regulations.

McInnis distinguished himself from Callihan by adopting a hard line on deficit reduction. In addition to calling for a constitutional balanced-budget amendment and line-item veto for the president, he told voters that he would have voted to cut federal spending even if it affected the 3rd District.

McInnis promised to start the cutbacks by streamlining his district office staff. He said he would have "one of the smallest paid staffs in Washington" and vowed not to send out any mass mailings. McInnes held true to the first promise, hiring only 12 staffers total for his district and Washington offices.

But tough talk on the deficit proved to be an effective strategy, and McInnis defeated Callihan by more than 10 percentage points.

McInnis, who won slots on the Natural Resources and Small Business committees, quickly established himself as an unpredictable legislator.

In apparent abandonment of his campaign promise to support a compromise Colorado Wilderness Act, he cosponsored a more conservative bill written by fellow Coloradan Republican Joel Hefley. He later recommitted himself to the compromise bill.

Colorado 3

Western Slope; Pueblo

This expansive district captures much of the vast spectrum of Colorado: the rural poor, the resort rich, the old steel-mill town of Pueblo and the isolated Hispanic counties of southern Colorado. Taken together, the 3rd is probably the most politically competitive district in the state.

Most of its voters live on the Western Slope of the Rockies — an area that features two different lifestyles, two different sets of voting habits.

Upscale ski resorts anchor the "granola belt," a swath of terrain that extends west and south from Boulder to include the communities of Aspen (Pitkin County), Vail (Eagle), Breckinridge (Summit), Steamboat Springs (Routt), Crested Butte (Gunnison), Telluride (San Miguel) and Durango (La Plata).

The granola belt is about as liberal as any stretch of real estate in the country. It was integral to former California Gov. Edmund G. "Jerry" Brown Jr.'s victory in the first-ever Colorado Democratic presidential primary in March 1992 (13 of 21 counties he carried were entirely in the 3rd). It also was a cornerstone of opposition to the anti-gay rights ballot measure in November 1992 (11 of 15 counties that voted "no" were in the 3rd). In addition, the granola belt was firmly in Bill Clinton's corner in November.

Juxtaposed to it are rural counties as conservative in their politics and social attitudes as other parts of the ranching West. In 1992, they tended to support both George Bush and the anti-gay rights measure.

What united the two different sectors politically in 1992 was strong support for the Senate bid of the district's three-term representative, Democrat Ben Nighthorse Campbell, and significant interest in the independent presidential candidacy of Ross Perot. Each in his own way, the American Indian jewelry maker and the Dallas billionaire reflected the frontier ethic that permeates the 3rd.

Campbell almost scored a clean sweep of the district. Of the 36 counties totally or partially within the 3rd, he won all but three on the district's eastern fringe.

Meanwhile, the two Colorado counties that Perot carried were both in the 3rd (Moffat and San Juan), as well as 14 of the 19 counties in which he ran second.

Although much of the district is federally owned national forest, it is one of the most energy-rich corners of America. The Western Slope is a prime source of oil shale, uranium, zinc and a number of other minerals, as well as the source of the Colorado River, which provides water for much of the Front Range and Southern California.

Yet the boom-and-bust cycles of the extractive industries have led many towns in the 3rd to look for more stable employment from smaller businesses. This is the case in Pueblo, the district's largest city with almost 100,000 people, where the decline of the local steel industry has led many members of the heavily unionized work force to accept non-union jobs from an array of smaller employers.

1990 Population: 549,062. White 503,752 (92%), Black 3,613 (<1%), Other 41,697 (8%). Hispanic origin 95,372 (17%). 18 and over 403,933 (74%), 62 and over 83,990 (15%). Median age: 34.

Committees

Natural Resources (13th of 15 Republicans)
Energy & Mineral Resources

Small Business (10th of 18 Republicans)

Campaign Finance

1992	Receipts	Receipts from PACs		Expend-itures
McInnis (R)	$438,090	$144,614	(33%)	$434,449
Callihan (D)	$353,489	$191,600	(54%)	$326,185

Key Votes

1993

Require parental notification of minors' abortions	N
Require unpaid family and medical leave	N
Approve national "motor voter" registration bill	N
Approve budget increasing taxes and reducing deficit	N
Approve economic stimulus plan	N

Elections

1992 General

Scott McInnis (R)	143,293	(55%)
Mike Callihan (D)	114,480	(44%)
Ki R. Nelson (COPOP)	4,189	(2%)

District Vote for President

	1992
D	107,330 (40%)
R	92,314 (35%)
I	67,201 (25%)

4 Wayne Allard (R)

Of Loveland — Elected 1990; 2nd Term

Born: Dec. 2, 1943, Fort Collins, Colo.
Education: Colorado State U., D.V.M. 1968.
Occupation: Veterinarian.
Family: Wife, Joan Malcolm; two children.
Religion: Protestant.
Political Career: Colo. Senate, 1983-91.
Capitol Office: 422 Cannon Bldg. 20515; 225-4676.

In Washington: Allard impressed fellow Republicans in his freshman term as a promising lawmaker and a fairly consistent vote for the party. As a reward, he begins the 103rd Congress with a new seat on the Budget Committee and a chance to expand his influence as a member of the GOP's own assignment-making Committee on Committees.

Allard will also be a member of the Joint Committee on the Organization of Congress, a special panel handling proposals for reforming the institution itself.

Allard is not a clone of Sen. Hank Brown, whom he succeeded in the 4th District, but his representation is similar. Both are fairly conservative legislators — Allard a bit more so than Brown — but both display moderate temperaments. They share a common forte of quiet consensus-building rather than forceful presentation of issues.

Both Brown and Allard started their political careers in the Colorado Senate, and it did not take long for either man to climb the legislative ladder. Two years after Brown was elected to that body, he was its assistant majority leader. Two years after Allard took office, he was the GOP Senate caucus chairman (generally regarded as the No. 3 post in the party leadership).

As caucus chairman, Allard quietly marshaled support for party positions. But he was rarely out front on controversial issues himself. One of the few high-profile issues he championed in the state Senate was a constitutional amendment to limit legislative sessions to 120 days. It was later approved by Colorado voters in a referendum.

Throughout his career, Allard has been publicly consistent in his doubts about government and his efforts to rein it in — from trimming regulations on small businesses to imposing term limits on legislators.

In his first term in Washington, Allard sat quietly on the Agriculture, Interior and Small Business committees.

But he worked independently to get the Rocky Mountain Arsenal designated as a wildlife refuge. Under his plan, cleanup for the arsenal, one of the state's most polluted sites, would still be the Army's responsibility.

The bill provided "an opportunity to turn problem lands into an educational and wildlife showcase," he said. "It is absolutely the best use for these lands."

One interesting bill sponsored by Allard, a veterinarian, was the Voluntary National Tuberculosis Insurance for Elk Act of 1992, which would have set up an insurance fund to compensate elk owners forced to destroy their tubercular elk. The bill was sent to the Agriculture Committee and never emerged.

Toward the end of the 102nd Congress, Allard was named to the Joint Committee on the Organization of Congress, which was created in the wake of scandals that rocked Congress throughout the 101st and 102nd Congresses.

The committee is made up of 28 members split evenly between the parties and between the houses of Congress. Its mission is to create a plan to change how Congress does business. The plan is scheduled to be released in September 1993. Similar panels convened in 1946 and 1970 produced significant change.

One of Allard's priorities in the 103rd Congress is the passage of a line-item veto. He sponsored a joint resolution calling for a constitutional amendment to that effect in the waning hours of the 102nd Congress.

At Home: After eight years dividing his time between the Colorado Senate and his Loveland veterinarian practice, Allard appeared ready to at least temporarily retire from politics in 1990.

The situation changed, though, when Republican Hank Brown decided to risk his safe House seat for a run at the Senate. Allard had managed Brown's House re-election campaigns in 1984 and 1986 and was eager to run for Congress himself. He was well-positioned for a House campaign.

Allard had the advantage of geography. He had a strong base in populous Larimer County (Fort Collins), home to approximately one-

Colorado 4

North and east — Fort Collins; Greeley

Cows, colleges and conservatives abound in the 4th, which covers the agricultural breadbasket of Colorado, the eastern third of the state.

Usually, the district votes Republican. But it is not a knee-jerk Republicanism; the most populous county in the 4th (Larimer) is comparatively liberal and is growing quickly, by a 25 percent rate in the 1980s.

Larimer's politics have been leavened in recent years by some of the same forces that have made neighboring Boulder one of the Rockies' most liberal counties. The largest of nine colleges in the district (Colorado State University) is in the county seat of Fort Collins (population 87,800), and there has been a steady influx of newcomers to the area drawn by jobs in high-tech companies such as Hewlett-Packard.

In 1992, Bill Clinton became the first Democratic presidential candidate to carry Larimer County since 1964. Earlier in the year, Larimer had voted for former California Gov. Edmund G. "Jerry" Brown Jr. in the Democratic presidential primary. (Brown carried only one other county in the district.)

Yet it is hard to see Fort Collins and its environs ever becoming another Boulder. Colorado State (21,000 students) is a land-grant college focused on agricultural research. Ranching is still a major income producer in much of the county and across the 4th.

One-third of the district's residents live in Larimer County; one-fourth live in neighboring Weld, where the economy is more dependent on agriculture. For years Greeley (with almost 61,000 people) has been known as the home of Montfort of Colorado, one of the largest feed lots and packing plants in the country. The facility is now operated by Omaha-based ConAgra.

Remapping in 1992 altered district boundaries slightly around the Denver suburbs, although the city's far northern and eastern suburbs in Adams and Arapahoe counties still make up roughly 15 percent of the 4th's population. The rest of the voters live on the Eastern Plains, a vast agricultural region of cattle, corn and wheat covering the terrain between Denver and the Kansas border.

Some of the most Republican counties in Colorado are on the Eastern Plains. Elbert County, which was added to the 4th by redistricting, is the only Colorado county that voted for Alfred M. Landon in 1936, Barry Goldwater in 1964 and George Bush in 1992. The county is close enough to Denver to be home for many "weekend cowboys," white-collar workers who own ranches they visit on weekends.

While Elbert County grew 41 percent in the 1980s, most counties on the Plains have been losing population for decades. One of them, Baca County in southeast Colorado, has been a center of agrarian ferment; the American Agricultural Movement was born there in the mid-1970s.

South toward the New Mexico border the Hispanic population tends to increase, along with the residents' willingness to vote Democratic.

1990 Population: 549,070. White 501,555 (91%), Black 3,839 (<1%), Other 43,676 (8%). Hispanic origin 80,971 (15%). 18 and over 396,906 (72%), 62 and over 72,519 (13%). Median age: 32.

third of the district population.

He could appeal for votes in the far-flung rural areas of the district by pointing to his upbringing on a ranch, involvement in 4-H and service on the state Senate's Agriculture Committee. And he stressed his fifth-generation Colorado roots and links to the popular Brown.

Still, Allard did not have an easy time winning the seat.

In the primary he faced state Sen. Jim Brandon, a farmer and rancher, who portrayed himself as a feisty legislative activist who would rattle some cages in Washington; he had strong support from a number of his legislative colleagues.

In the fall campaign Allard faced state Rep. Dick Bond, a professional biologist and former president of the University of Northern Colorado in Greeley, who was strongly backed by the state and national Democratic parties.

In both contests, the clearest difference between Allard and his opponents came on the abortion issue. Brandon and Bond both defended abortion rights; Allard maintained that abortion should be allowed only in cases of rape or incest or when the woman's life was at risk.

That stance won Allard the support of anti-abortion activists, although he won neither the primary nor general election with more than 56 percent of the vote.

Allard's modest showing in 1990 encouraged the Democrats to make a concerted effort to unseat him in 1992. They found an energetic young candidate in state Rep. Tom Redder, who combined an abortion rights stance with a litany of fiscally conservative positions, including support for a balanced-budget amendment and a line-item veto.

A former advance man in Jimmy Carter's White House, the well-connected Redder raised more money than any other 1992 House challenger in the Rocky Mountain region. Yet in the GOP-leaning district, he came no closer to beating Allard than Bond did in 1990.

Committees

Agriculture (7th of 18 Republicans)
Foreign Agriculture & Hunger (ranking); Department Operations; Environment, Credit & Rural Development

Budget (10th of 17 Republicans)

Natural Resources (10th of 15 Republicans)
Energy & Mineral Resources; Oversight & Investigations

Joint Organization of Congress

Elections

1992 General		
Wayne Allard (R)	139,884	(58%)
Tom Redder (D)	101,957	(42%)
1990 General		
Wayne Allard (R)	89,285	(54%)
Dick Bond (D)	75,901	(46%)

District Vote for President

	1992
D	94,089 (37%)
R	96,781 (38%)
I	63,254 (25%)

Campaign Finance

	Receipts	Receipts from PACs	Expend-itures
1992			
Allard (R)	$565,311	$266,115 (47%)	$551,110
Redder (D)	$384,648	$163,449 (42%)	$378,655
1990			
Allard (R)	$363,633	$174,550 (48%)	$360,206
Bond (D)	$486,762	$255,580 (53%)	$481,666

Key Votes

1993	
Require parental notification of minors' abortions	Y
Require unpaid family and medical leave	N
Approve national "motor voter" registration bill	N
Approve budget increasing taxes and reducing deficit	N
Approve economic stimulus plan	N
1992	
Approve balanced-budget constitutional amendment	Y
Close down space station program	N
Approve U.S. aid for former Soviet Union	Y
Allow shifting funds from defense to domestic programs	N
1991	
Extend unemployment benefits using deficit financing	N
Approve waiting period for handgun purchases	N
Authorize use of force in Persian Gulf	Y

Voting Studies

	Presidential Support		Party Unity		Conservative Coalition	
Year	S	O	S	O	S	O
1992	84	14	92	4	83	17
1991	80	20	94	6	95	5

Interest Group Ratings

Year	ADA	AFL-CIO	CCUS	ACU
1992	5	10	75	92
1991	0	0	100	95

5 Joel Hefley (R)

Of Colorado Springs — Elected 1986; 4th Term

Born: April 18, 1935, Ardmore, Okla.
Education: Oklahoma Baptist U., B.A. 1957; Oklahoma State U., M.S. 1962.
Occupation: Community planner; management consultant.
Family: Wife, Lynn Christian; three children.
Religion: Presbyterian.
Political Career: Colo. House, 1977-79; Colo. Senate, 1979-87.
Capitol Office: 2442 Rayburn Bldg. 20515; 225-4422.

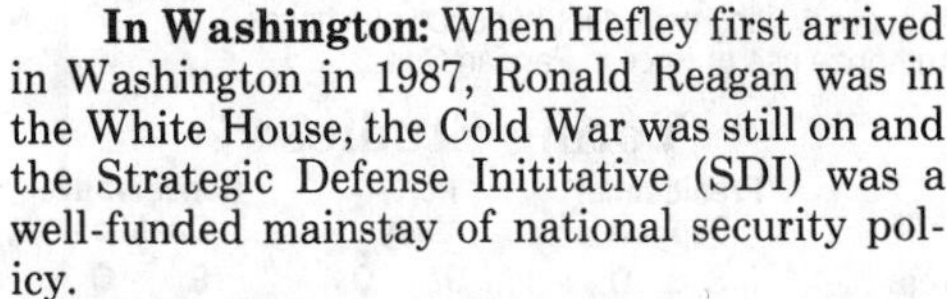

In Washington: When Hefley first arrived in Washington in 1987, Ronald Reagan was in the White House, the Cold War was still on and the Strategic Defense Inititative (SDI) was a well-funded mainstay of national security policy.

Now, none of the above is true. As Hefley enters the second half of his House career — he has said he will serve no more than 12 years there — he finds himself scrambling to ward off cutbacks instead of working toward expanding his district's military programs.

Hefley's district includes the Air Force Academy, NORAD (the North American Air Defense Command), various SDI research facilities and other underpinnings of the "military-industrial complex." But when the budget mission becomes cutting spending, few districts are so target-rich.

Hefley moved from the Science Committee to Armed Services in the 101st Congress, where he has tried to hold the line for his district and his state. But as a relatively junior Republican on the committee, his impact is hard to discern — and hard to separate from that of Colorado colleague Patricia Schroeder, the committee's third-ranking Democrat.

Hefley received some notice as a freshman for his enthusiastic support of SDI. He helped restore $65 million to the National Testing Facility at Falcon Air Force Station (in his district) after the House had killed President Reagan's $100 million request for the project.

Hefley was outspoken in support of the United States' war with Iraq. He voted for the January 1991 resolution authorizing President Bush to use force to end Iraq's occupation of Kuwait. And when the House Democratic leadership, after the outbreak of war, moved a resolution to support Bush and the U.S. troops in the Persian Gulf region, Hefley denounced them for using "a gimmick ... to save their backsides because the majority of them failed to support the president" on the war resolution.

Hefley got on the Interior Committee (the name has since been changed to Natural Resources) in the 102nd Congress, at least in part to pursue a specific objective. Hefley went after federal money to pay for the treatment of water runoff from the Leadville Mine Drainage Tunnel, which had been found to contain such heavy metals as lead and iron. Money for treatment was folded into the omnibus western water bill that Bush signed into law in October 1992.

On occasion, Hefley's conservative views on social issues get a public airing. Following the 1989 massacre of pro-democracy protesters in Beijing, the House debated a bill lifting visa restrictions on Chinese students who wanted to remain in the United States. Although the measure was aimed at democracy movement activists, Hefley pushed through an amendment extending protections to students who were affected by China's "one child" policies, which at times require abortion.

Hefley was once an outspoken advocate of statutory limits on congressional terms, and he still vows to stay in the House for no more than six terms himself. But after watching GOP Sen. Bill Armstrong of Colorado leave Congress in 1990, Hefley reconsidered. He now calls strict limits on tenure "un-American," adding: "I came here to give Americans more freedom, not less."

Hefley's overall voting record is conservative (he sides with a majority of his GOP colleagues on about nine of 10 votes) and similar to that of his GOP predecessor, Ken Kramer, who left the House for an unsuccessful 1986 Senate campaign. But in personal terms, the men are quite unalike: Kramer could be wearing and abrasive, while Hefley is regarded as genteel and approachable by colleagues in both parties.

At Home: A business-oriented legislator who lists calf-roping as one of his hobbies, Hefley seems a good fit for the 5th, which combines affluent white-collar suburbs with cattle-ranching areas and mountain communities. But unlike Kramer, Hefley is not known as a "movement conservative," and that caused him some difficulty when he first sought this seat.

Colorado 5

South Central — Colorado Springs

As Colorado's fastest-growing district in the 1980s, the 5th had to jettison nearly 100,000 residents in remapping to reach population parity with the state's five other districts. Pared away were three counties on the mountainous western side of the 5th, its large slice of suburban Jefferson County, a sliver of neighboring Douglas County on the north and all of rural Elbert County on the east. District lines also were redrawn in suburban Arapahoe and mountainous Fremont counties.

While substantial, the changes did not alter the essence of the 5th. It is an overwhelmingly Republican district that revolves around Colorado Springs. With more than 281,000 people, the city is the second largest in the state and the southern anchor of the rapidly growing Front Range. Population in El Paso County, which Colorado Springs dominates, grew 28 percent in the 1980s, double the statewide growth rate.

With its sunny climate, nearby springs and Pikes Peak looming in the distance, Colorado Springs began as a resort. Tourism remains an economic mainstay. But since World War II, Colorado Springs has become one of the nation's premier military centers. North of the city is the Air Force Academy; east is Peterson Air Force Base (headquarters of the U.S. Space Command); south is Fort Carson; and deep in a mountain to the west is NORAD (the North American Air Defense Command), maintaining a round-the-clock alert for an enemy attack, even in this post-Cold War era.

Colorado Springs is nervous about its future but so far has not been significantly affected by defense cutbacks. The economy has diversified beyond defense-related companies; employers now range from the U.S. Olympic Committee (with its training complex) to more than two dozen evangelical organizations, including Focus on the Family, which brought nearly 1,000 jobs to the area when it moved from California.

One aspect of Colorado Springs, though, has remained constant: its conservative politics. Only in the worst of GOP years does El Paso County stray into the Democratic column, and 1992 did not qualify as one of them. Although George Bush and GOP Senate candidate Terry Considine lost statewide, both swept El Paso County. Districtwide, Bush won nearly half the vote, by far his best showing in the state.

The Democrats have no reliable source of votes elsewhere in the 5th to act as a counterweight. The portions of suburban Arapahoe and Douglas counties in the 5th are firmly Republican, as are the mountain precincts in Teller County and the portion of Fremont County in the 5th.

Douglas County, which provides moderately priced exurban housing for Denver commuters, had the highest growth rate of any county in Colorado in the 1980s, more than doubling its population. Teller County, which includes the old gold mining town of Cripple Creek (which has legal gambling), grew by 55 percent. Bill Clinton ran third in both counties in 1992, trailing Bush and independent Ross Perot.

1990 Population: 549,066. White 487,334 (89%), Black 30,672 (6%), Other 31,060 (6%). Hispanic origin 40,459 (7%). 18 and over 394,039 (72%), 62 and over 49,724 (9%). Median age: 31.

Hefley entered the 1986 contest as the front-runner. After 10 years in the Legislature, he was widely known in his Colorado Springs base. But while his legislative record satisfied his mainly conservative constituency, Hefley generally avoided lining up with the Legislature's ideological right. His display of what some considered "moderate tendencies" prompted a primary challenge from millionaire Harold A. Krause, a Republican national committeeman from the several Denver suburbs that were then part of the district. Hefley tried to portray himself as the candidate with "proven experience" and Krause as a novice "who's trying to buy his way to the top." But he found his years of experience being used against him. Krause maintained that if legislative experience alone could solve the country's problems, "we'd already have a balanced budget and no trade deficit."

Krause had the money to wage a serious TV campaign in Colorado Springs, while the high cost of media in Denver made it difficult for Hefley to raid Krause's suburban base. In the end, though, money was not enough. Hefley hit pay dirt by appealing to the parochialism of El Paso County voters, reminding them that electing Krause would give the Denver area four House members. In November, Hefley had no trouble with Democratic businessman Bill Story.

In 1988, Kramer threatened to stage a comeback, complaining that Hefley was not a strong enough advocate of SDI. But Krause was persuaded to drop his challenge and offered a political appointment in the Department of the Army. Hefley was re-elected handily that year and again in 1990 and 1992.

Committees

Armed Services (11th of 22 Republicans)
Military Acquisition; Oversight & Investigations

Natural Resources (8th of 15 Republicans)
National Parks, Forests & Public Lands

Small Business (4th of 18 Republicans)
Rural Enterprises, Exports & the Environment (ranking)

Elections

1992 General		
Joel Hefley (R)	173,096	(71%)
Charles A. Oriez (D)	62,550	(26%)
Keith L. Hamburger (COLIBERT)	7,769	(3%)
1990 General		
Joel Hefley (R)	127,740	(66%)
Cal Johnston (D)	57,776	(30%)
Keith L. Hamburger (LIBERT)	6,761	(4%)

Previous Winning Percentages: 1988 (75%) 1986 (70%)

District Vote for President

1992
D 70,671 (28%)
R 125,664 (50%)
I 57,450 (23%)

Campaign Finance

	Receipts	Receipts from PACs		Expend-itures
1992				
Hefley (R)	$137,757	$99,515	(72%)	$162,718
Oriez (D)	$14,817	$2,310	(16%)	$14,613
1990				
Hefley (R)	$135,707	$114,981	(85%)	$111,435
Johnston (D)	$15,313	$6,143	(40%)	$15,288

Key Votes

1993	
Require parental notification of minors' abortions	Y
Require unpaid family and medical leave	N
Approve national "motor voter" registration bill	N
Approve budget increasing taxes and reducing deficit	N
Approve economic stimulus plan	N
1992	
Approve balanced-budget constitutional amendment	Y
Close down space station program	N
Approve U.S. aid for former Soviet Union	N
Allow shifting funds from defense to domestic programs	N
1991	
Extend unemployment benefits using deficit financing	N
Approve waiting period for handgun purchases	N
Authorize use of force in Persian Gulf	Y

Voting Studies

	Presidential Support		Party Unity		Conservative Coalition	
Year	**S**	**O**	**S**	**O**	**S**	**O**
1992	74	25	92	5	90	8
1991	71	29	88	9	95	5
1990	71	29	90	6	91	9
1989	65	31	89	9	90	5
1988	60	35	91	8	92	3
1987	71	29	85	12	81	14

Interest Group Ratings

Year	ADA	AFL-CIO	CCUS	ACU
1992	20	27	88	92
1991	10	25	90	100
1990	6	0	79	92
1989	5	17	100	93
1988	5	7	100	100
1987	4	6	100	96

6 Dan Schaefer (R)

Of Lakewood — Elected 1983; 5th Full Term

Born: Jan. 25, 1936, Guttenberg, Iowa.
Education: Niagara U., B.A. 1961; State U. of New York, Potsdam, 1961-64.
Military Service: Marine Corps, 1955-57.
Occupation: Public relations consultant.
Family: Wife, Mary Lenney; four children.
Religion: Roman Catholic.
Political Career: Colo. House, 1977-79; Colo. Senate, 1979-83, president pro tempore, 1981-83.
Capitol Office: 2448 Rayburn Bldg. 20515; 225-7882.

In Washington: If not one to garner headlines, Schaefer has raised his activity level to the point that he finds himself in the middle of a handful of important debates each session. The pattern is simple: If the issue involves Colorado, Schaefer will be in the thick of it.

At the start of the 103rd, Schaefer became ranking member on the Oversight and Investigations Subcommittee of the far-reaching Energy and Commerce Committee. The post, which pits him against Chairman John D. Dingell of Michigan and second-in-command Sherrod Brown of Ohio, should increase Schaefer's visibility and test his negotiating skills.

For several years, Schaefer has been associated most closely with efforts to stop the cable television reregulation bill, which became law with the October 1992 override of President Bush's veto. The new law orders the Federal Communications Commission to limit cable rates and set standards for service. It also orders cable vendors to deal fairly with competitors such as satellite dish owners.

Schaefer's district includes headquarters for several national cable operators; that, plus the urging of the Bush administration, led him to act.

In the 101st Congress, Schaefer had warned that it was "clearly not in the public interest to reshackle this important source of information and entertainment." It came as no surprise that he was a staunch industry defender, although colleagues were impressed by his more moderate approach in the 102nd, when he acknowledged that there were some problems in the system.

Unlike in the Reagan and Bush years when Schaefer at least had a veto threat as some leverage on Capitol Hill, he finds himself increasingly paddling upstream in the Clinton era. On his other Energy subcommittee, Telecommunications and Finance, he and Chairman Edward J. Markey, D-Mass., are at odds over the future of the so-called Baby Bells. Schaefer advocates opening a wide range of technology markets to the regional phone companies, which contrasts with Markey's attempts to restrict the Bells' activity in new markets.

Schaefer has a reputation as a party loyalist, if a rather diffident one. Home-state politics, however, routinely force him to part with the GOP.

In late 1991 he voted to block controversial Bush administration regulations regarding state payments for Medicaid. The administration wanted to bar federal Medicaid matching payments for state funds raised through voluntary donations by health-care providers. The Republicans opposing the change argued that it would cost their states too much money.

Schaefer has also been active on environmental issues. Late in 1988 he gave a rare speech on the House floor urging his colleagues to act on the Clean Air Act and stressing the "need for a strong federal role in improving the environment." Poor air quality is a severe problem in the Denver metropolitan area, and Schaefer backed alternative automotive fuels. In 1990, he was able to get language included in the bill to extend alternative fuel mandates for commercial fleet vehicles to Denver and other high-altitude cities.

At the start of the 103rd, Schaefer filed legislation aimed at ensuring that federal agencies comply with the clean water act.

The delegation experienced a rift early in the 103rd when the state's two senators, Hank Brown and Ben Nighthorse Campbell, complained that the House members had filed a wilderness protection bill identical to legislation the House killed in the 102nd. "Instead of working for a bill that can be passed, they introduced a bill that has no chance," Campbell said.

Schaefer has also supported bills to provide for the safe transportation of hazardous waste materials and to permit states to levy penalties against federal facilities that violate solid waste disposal laws.

With the other Denver-area House members, Schaefer also pushed for continued federal funding for the C-470 beltway being built

Colorado 6

Denver suburbs — Aurora; Lakewood

The 6th connects the eastern, southern and western suburbs of Denver. Generally white-collar and Republican-oriented, they have an added link in the early 1990s — a concern about their economic future.

Like others across the country whose prosperity has been closely tied to military and aerospace spending, many residents of the 6th are not sure how they will fare during the nation's economic transition.

Denver's Lowry Air Force Base, which employs a number of workers in the Arapahoe County suburbs on the 6th's eastern side, is slated for closure, as is Denver's nearby Stapleton Airport, which is to be replaced in December 1993 by a more distant facility. Martin Marietta, the aerospace company, which has a large plant near Littleton in the southern suburbs, has been laying off workers.

The 6th has enough economic diversity to provide a safety net of sorts. Many of the federal government's regional facilities have headquarters in the Denver Federal Center in Lakewood, just west of Denver. The Coors brewery and the National Renewable Energy Lab are in nearby Golden.

Golden is in a portion of western Jefferson County added by redistricting. Jefferson also includes the affluent communities of Evergreen and Conifer and mountain homes hidden in the foothills of the Rockies.

But with a 20 percent population growth in the 1980s, the 6th had to lose more people than it gained. Pared away were a few neighborhoods in southwest Denver as well as the northern portion of the city of Aurora on the eastern side of the district. The 6th, which in the 1980s included portions of Adams, Arapahoe, Denver and Jefferson counties, now is limited to portions of only Arapahoe and Jefferson. The district population is almost evenly divided between the two.

The portion of Aurora that was lost includes the "Colfax Corridor," a strip of small businesses on the main boulevard extending east from Denver, and the Fitzsimons Army Medical Center, where President Dwight D. Eisenhower spent more than six weeks in 1955 recuperating from a heart attack.

But the district retains other pieces of Americana. In the affluent community of Cherry Hills Village just south of Denver is the Cherry Hills Country Club, site of a number of professional golf tournaments including the 1960 U.S. Open, won by a young Arnold Palmer. Near Golden is the grave of the legendary frontiersman and showman, William F. "Buffalo Bill" Cody. Not far from Evergreen is the notorious Troublesome Gulch, where the media staked out Gary Hart's home in the dying days of his campaign for the Democratic presidential nomination in May 1987.

In general, GOP candidates enjoy a long head start in the 6th, thanks to the moderate to affluent bedroom communities. But the large number of registered independents will occasionally look at other options. In 1992, with Ross Perot drawing 25.4 percent of the three-way vote (his best showing in any Colorado district), George Bush carried the 6th by fewer than 3,000 votes.

1990 Population: 549,056. White 503,500 (92%), Black 19,455 (4%), Other 26,101 (5%). Hispanic origin 35,098 (6%). 18 and over 406,715 (74%), 62 and over 54,741 (10%). Median age: 33.

around Denver. The 26-mile project was completed in October 1990 after Congress cleared the final $9.1 million in funding.

The 1988 collapse of Silverado, a Denver-based savings and loan, focused attention on the state's delegation. In a decision aimed at distancing himself from S&L contributions and bolstering public confidence, Schaefer donated $3,600 in campaign funds to the federal government's debt-reduction fund.

At Home: Schaefer's lack of star quality and a short list of legislative accomplishments prompted The Denver Post to editorialize in 1992 that his career was an argument for congressional term limits.

But he has proved a good fit for his suburban constituency. The 6th was a new district in 1982, added as a result of reapportionment and carved for a Republican. Though interested, Schaefer deferred to Jack Swigert, the popular former Apollo astronaut. Swigert won but died of cancer before he was sworn in.

When Schaefer entered the special election to fill the vacancy, his biggest hurdle was the Republican nomination. Aided by national conservative GOP leaders, Schaefer won a fourth-ballot victory at a district convention in January 1983 and has won re-election ever since.

In 1988, the Democrats recruited a candidate they thought could wrest the 6th from Schaefer: former GOP state Sen. Martha Ezzard. A fiscal conservative, she was also known as an outspoken environmentalist and feminist. This appealed to her affluent Cherry Hills district but not to the legislature's conservative GOP hierarchy, causing her to quit the party and the legislature in 1987.

Against Schaefer, Ezzard quickly proved her prowess as a fundraiser and won headlines by dubbing the incumbent "the invisible congressman." Schaefer defended his style as "quietly effective," championed his efforts to secure federal funds for local programs and said Ezzard would raise taxes. Ezzard badly underestimated the GOP loyalty of the district's voters and the draw of Schaefer's parochial focus; she lost by 60,000 votes. Since then, he has had only token Democratic opposition.

Schaefer came late to politics. The Iowa-born son of a construction worker, he was raised in North Dakota and educated in New York. After several years as a high school history teacher, he moved to Colorado and opened a public relations firm. Schaefer assisted the campaigns of other local GOP candidates and then successfully ran for the state House in 1976. Two years later he moved up to the state Senate. Personable and unflappable, he became its president pro tem in 1981. When he ran for Congress, he was assistant Senate majority leader.

Committee

Energy & Commerce (6th of 17 Republicans)
Oversight & Investigations (ranking); Telecommunications & Finance; Transportation & Hazardous Materials

Elections

1992 General		
Dan Schaefer (R)	142,021	(61%)
Tom Kolbe (D)	91,073	(39%)
1990 General		
Dan Schaefer (R)	105,312	(65%)
Don Jarrett (D)	57,961	(35%)

Previous Winning Percentages: **1988** (63%) **1986** (65%) **1984** (89%) **1983** * (63%)

** Special election.*

District Vote for President

1992

D 99,045 (37%)
R 101,613 (38%)
I 68,165 (25%)

Campaign Finance

	Receipts	Receipts from PACs		Expend-itures
1992				
Schaefer (R)	$357,020	$269,984	(76%)	$332,317
Kolbe (D)	$10,316	$500	(5%)	$9,794
1990				
Schaefer (R)	$375,683	$229,103	(61%)	$280,103
Jarrett (D)	$2,295	0		$2,958

Key Votes

1993	
Require parental notification of minors' abortions	Y
Require unpaid family and medical leave	N
Approve national "motor voter" registration bill	N
Approve budget increasing taxes and reducing deficit	N
Approve economic stimulus plan	N
1992	
Approve balanced-budget constitutional amendment	Y
Close down space station program	N
Approve U.S. aid for former Soviet Union	N
Allow shifting funds from defense to domestic programs	N
1991	
Extend unemployment benefits using deficit financing	N
Approve waiting period for handgun purchases	N
Authorize use of force in Persian Gulf	Y

Voting Studies

	Presidential Support		Party Unity		Conservative Coalition	
Year	S	O	S	O	S	O
1992	82	17	95	3	96	2
1991	71	27	90	9	92	5
1990	64	36	88	11	89	9
1989	69	29	84	12	88	2
1988	56	41	82	17	87	8
1987	65	27	89	7	79	12
1986	76	21	84	11	90	4
1985	76	20	84	10	91	4
1984	70	30	93	6	95	5
1983	74 †	20 †	93 †	5 †	92 †	7 †

† Not eligible for all recorded votes.

Interest Group Ratings

Year	ADA	AFL-CIO	CCUS	ACU
1992	5	27	75	88
1991	5	17	90	95
1990	11	25	79	79
1989	5	25	90	89
1988	15	50	71	83
1987	8	19	86	87
1986	0	15	88	95
1985	10	13	91	80
1984	10	8	81	92
1983	0	7	76	100

Connecticut

STATE DATA

Governor:
Lowell P. Weicker Jr. (I)
First elected: 1990
Length of term: 4 years
Term expires: 1/95
Salary: $78,000
Term limit: No
Phone: (203) 566-4840
Born: May 16, 1931; Paris.
Education: Yale U., B.A. 1953; U. of Virginia, LL.B. 1958
Military Service: Army, 1953-55; Army Reserve, 1958-64
Occupation: Lawyer
Family: Wife, Claudia Testa Ingram; seven children
Religion: Episcopalian
Political Career: Conn. House, 1963-69; Greenwich Board of Selectmen, 1964-68; U.S. House, 1969-71; U.S. Senate, 1971-89

Lt. Gov.: Eunice S. Groark (I)
First elected: 1990
Length of term: 4 years
Term expires: 1/95
Salary: $55,000
Phone: (203) 566-2614

State election official: (203) 566-3106
Democratic headquarters: (203) 278-6080
Republican headquarters: (203) 547-0589

REDISTRICTING

Connecticut retained its six House seats in reapportionment. Redistricting commission filed the map with secretary of state Nov. 27, 1991; governor's signature was not required.

STATE LEGISLATURE

Bicameral General Assembly. Meets January-June.

Senate: 36 members, 2-year terms.
1992 breakdown: 19D, 17R; 28 men, 8 women; 33 whites, 3 blacks
Salary: $16,760
Phone: (203) 240-0500

House of Representatives: 151 members, 2-year terms
1992 breakdown: 87D, 64R; 112 men, 39 women; 142 whites, 9 blacks
Salary: $16,760
Phone: (203) 240-0400

URBAN STATISTICS

City	Pop.
Bridgeport	141,686
Mayor Joseph Ganim, D	
Hartford	139,739
Mayor Carrie S. Perry, D	
New Haven	130,474
Mayor John Daniels, D	
Waterbury	108,961
Mayor Edward D. Bergin, D	
Stamford	108,056
Mayor Stanley Esposito, R	

U.S. CONGRESS

Senate: 2 D, 0 R
House: 3 D, 3 R

TERM LIMITS

For Congress: No
For state offices: No

ELECTIONS

1992 Presidential Vote

Bill Clinton	42.2%
George Bush	35.8%
Ross Perot	21.6%

1988 Presidential Vote

George Bush	52%
Michael S. Dukakis	47%

1984 Presidential Vote

Ronald Reagan	61%
Walter F. Mondale	39%

POPULATION

1990 population		3,287,116
1980 population		3,107,576
Percent change		+6%
Rank among states:		27
White		87%
Black		8%
Hispanic		6%
Asian or Pacific islander		2%
Urban		79%
Rural		21%
Born in state		57%
Foreign-born		8%
Under age 18	749,581	23%
Ages 18-64	2,091,628	64%
65 and older	445,907	14%
Median age		34.4

MISCELLANEOUS

Capital: Hartford
Number of counties: 8
Per capita income: $25,881 (1991)
Rank among states: 1
Total area: 5,018 sq. miles
Rank among states: 48

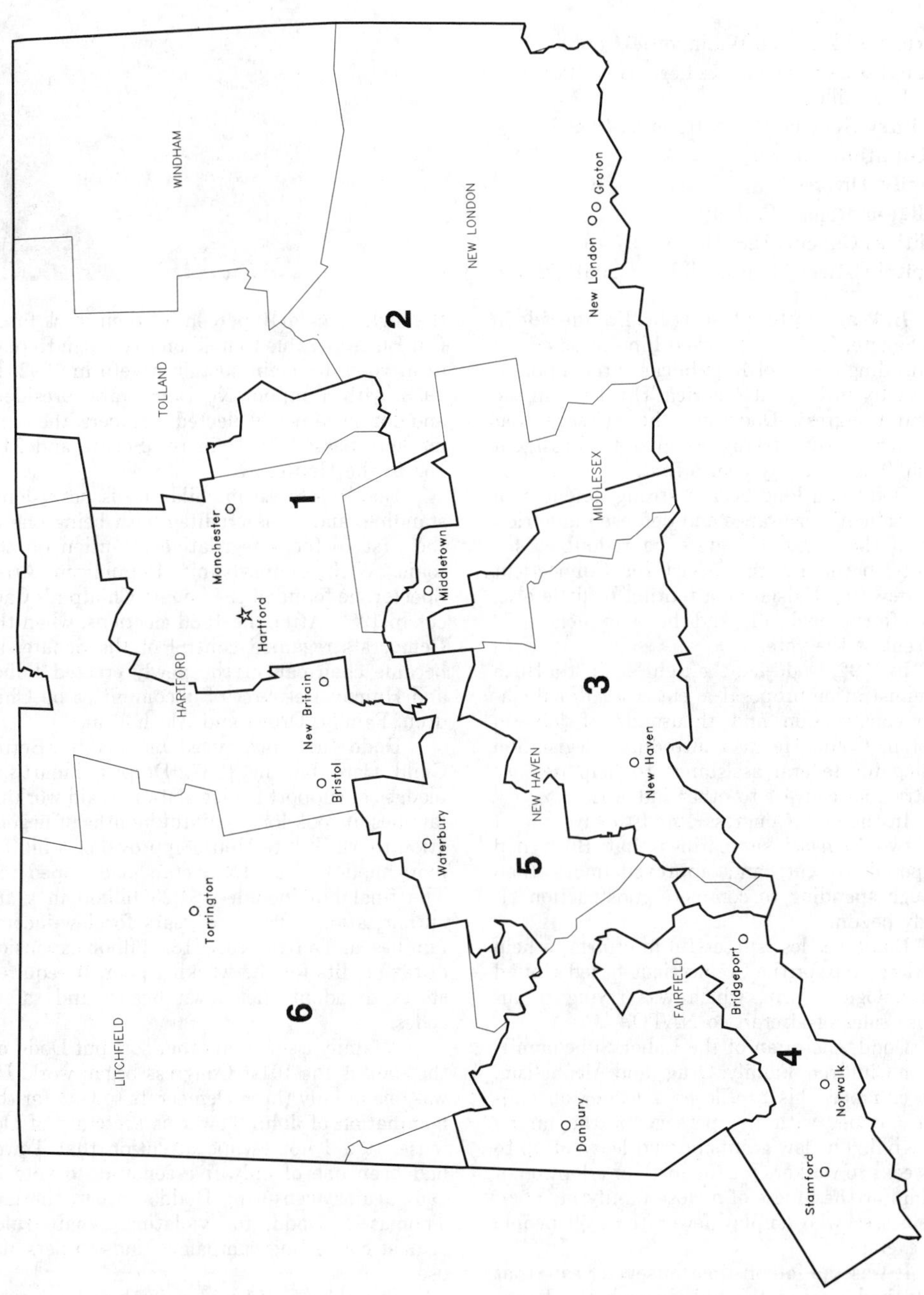
WINDHAM
NEW LONDON
New London
Groton
TOLLAND
2
1
Manchester
Hartford
MIDDLESEX
Middletown
HARTFORD
New Britain
3
Bristol
NEW HAVEN
New Haven
Waterbury
5
Torrington
FAIRFIELD
Bridgeport
6
LITCHFIELD
4
Norwalk
Danbury
Stamford

Christopher J. Dodd (D)

Of East Haddam — Elected 1980; 3rd Term

Born: May 27, 1944, Willimantic, Conn.
Education: Providence College, B.A. 1966; U. of Louisville, J.D. 1972.
Military Service: Army Reserve, 1969-75.
Occupation: Lawyer.
Family: Divorced.
Religion: Roman Catholic.
Political Career: U.S. House, 1975-81.
Capitol Office: 444 Russell Bldg. 20510; 224-2823.

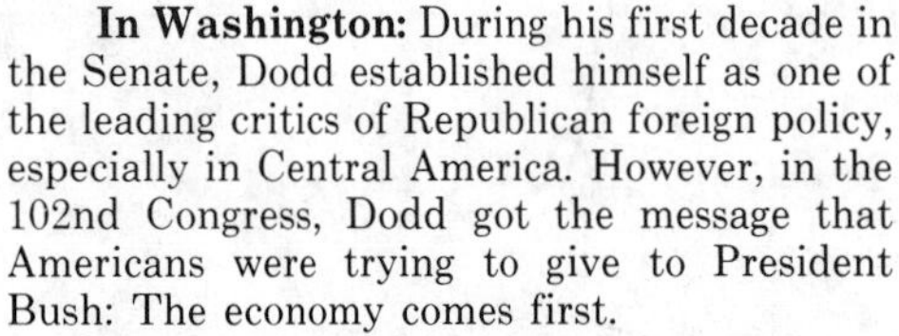

In Washington: During his first decade in the Senate, Dodd established himself as one of the leading critics of Republican foreign policy, especially in Central America. However, in the 102nd Congress, Dodd got the message that Americans were trying to give to President Bush: The economy comes first.

Dodd had long been a strong defender of Connecticut's insurance and defense industries, but in the 102nd Congress he redoubled his efforts, becoming an activist for Connecticut and devoting legislative attention to little else. His efforts paid off, and he won nearly 60 percent of the vote.

In 1992, Dodd led the fight against a Bush administration proposal to cut *Seawolf* submarine construction and thousands of jobs in Groton, Conn. He also introduced legislation calling for federal assistance to help defense contractors convert to other industries.

In the end, Congress opted to save one of the two *Seawolf* submarines that Bush had proposed to cut, and approved more than enough spending to complete construction already begun.

Dodd was less successful in efforts to help legislate help for the Connecticut-based United Technologies Corp., which was trying to increase sales of aircraft to NATO.

Dodd, chairman of the Labor Subcommittee on Children, Family, Drugs and Alcoholism, also enhanced his profile as a leader on children's issues with the passage of the family leave bill. The law grants unpaid leave of up to 12 weeks to workers for the birth or adoption of a child or the illness of a close family member. Businesses who employ fewer than 50 people are exempt.

It was the fourth time in seven years that Dodd had steered the bill through the Labor Committee. The measure was scaled back over the years to win over enough Republicans to override a veto. After Bush vetoed the bill in 1990 and Congress sustained the veto, Democrats revised the bill to limit eligibility to those employees who had worked 1,250 hours in the previous year and to allow businesses to exempt the highest-paid 10 percent of their work force. But Bush was able to hold on to enough Republican votes to again sustain a veto in 1992. In 1993, with a supportive Democratic president and dozens of newly elected members, the same measure passed 71-27 in the Senate and 247-152 in the House.

Dodd's interest in children's issues is longstanding, and he is credited with being one of the first to focus legislative attention on the topic. With Pennsylvania Republican Arlen Specter, he founded the Senate Children's Caucus in 1983. After the 1986 elections, when the Democrats regained control of the Senate, he became chairman of the newly created Labor and Human Resources Subcommittee on Children, Family, Drugs and Alcoholism.

Dodd first introduced his Act for Better Child Care bill in 1987. Despite bipartisan pledges of support for legislation to aid working families, it took long, painful months of negotiation to win White House approval of a bill far more modest than Democrats had hoped for. The final bill included $4.25 billion in grant authorizations over five years for low-income families, and a five-year, $18.3 billion expansion of tax credits for the working poor. It required states to adopt their own health and safety codes.

A family issue of another sort put Dodd on the spot as the 101st Congress began work. He was one of only three Democrats to vote for the nomination of John Tower as secretary of Defense. It did not escape attention that Tower had been one of only five senators to vote in 1967 against censuring Dodd's father, the late Thomas J. Dodd, for violating Senate rules against converting campaign funds to personal use.

The elder Dodd was a tough-talking, two-term senator who was among his party's most virulent anti-communists. When the younger Dodd took his Senate seat in 1981, his siblings gave him his father's pocket watch and chain. He hung a picture of his father in his office. And when he got the chance, he moved into office quarters that include part of his father's old office.

As Dodd enters his second decade in the Senate, he appears to be moving beyond his recognized role as a thoughtful liberal spokesman to become a full-fledged player in policymaking. His strategy has been one of high-profile mediation between the White House and congressional Democrats, but in his efforts to be more conciliatory and statesmanlike, he has often yielded considerable ground in his policy objectives.

Early in his Senate career, Dodd was a leading and often strident spokesman against what he saw as U.S. adventurism in Central America, and for federal efforts to improve the lives of children. A constant critic of the Reagan administration, he opposed military aid to Central America and introduced some of the most far-reaching legislation to aid families with young children.

Dodd began to tone down his confrontational approach in early 1989, when Bush became president and offered the prospect of a less ideological White House. That year, Dodd played a key role in Bush's victory on providing U.S. military aid to El Salvador and began negotiating toward passage of "pro-family" legislation.

But he never got the upper hand on either front: By the end of 1990, continued human rights violations in El Salvador pushed Dodd back to his opposition role on the issue; he had seen Bush veto a parental leave bill; and to win enactment of a child-care bill, Dodd stripped it of numerous provisions that were important to child-care advocates.

Whatever leadership style Dodd chooses to employ, one thing about his work is consistent: He is a purposeful legislator who masters the details of issues important to him. That trait has helped minimize negative fallout stemming from his reputation as something of a playboy: Dodd became widely known on Capitol Hill for his after-hours merrymaking with Massachusetts Sen. Edward M. Kennedy before Kennedy's second marriage in 1992.

Dodd's interest in Central America dates back to his days as a Peace Corps volunteer in the Dominican Republic, where he learned to speak Spanish fluently. But his effort to find a middle ground on aid to El Salvador in the 101st Congress was a marked departure from his previous staunch opposition to U.S. involvement in the civil war there. In 1981, his first year in the Senate, he was the chief author of a law stipulating that the president could not continue aid to El Salvador unless he certified that the country was achieving social, economic and political reforms.

But when Bush needed an ally to block congressional Democrats from restricting military aid to newly elected Salvadoran President Alfredo Cristiani in 1989, Dodd, chairman of the Foreign Relations Subcommittee on the Western Hemisphere, was there. "To me the aid is a tactical question," he explained. "The strategic question is ending the conflict."

With a critical push from Dodd, Appropriations Committee language sponsored by Democratic Sen. Patrick J. Leahy of Vermont to limit military aid was defeated by a lopsided margin. Passed in its place was an amendment increasing funds without detailed conditions, which was co-authored by Dodd and Republican Bob Kasten of Wisconsin. While publicly expressing hope that the aid would be an incentive for both sides to end human rights violations and negotiate an end to the war, Dodd called Cristiani from the Senate cloakroom to let him know of the victory.

Weeks later, in mid-November, six Jesuit priests were murdered on a campus that was under the control of government security forces. While the incident put Dodd under intense pressure to break from his stance in favor of aid for the Cristiani government, he again opposed legislation to limit aid and instead backed a resolution warning the government to make a good-faith effort to find and prosecute those responsible for the killings.

But that would be the last time Dodd supported the administration on the issue. By mid-1990, with the investigation into the murders being criticized as badly flawed, Dodd came full circle, joining with Leahy to author an amendment adding complex restrictions to military aid to El Salvador. The measure was approved over strenuous Bush administration objections.

In the 102nd, Dodd put aside most of his foreign affairs efforts to focus on home-state issues, but in 1991, he did unsuccessfully sponsor a committee amendment to restrict funding to El Salvador. Dodd wanted to hold back half of the aid requested by the Bush administration in an effort to encourage both sides, the guerrillas and the government, to continue negotiations. However, opponents argued that withholding the money would be a blow to Cristiani.

During the Reagan administration, Dodd was known for intensely critical rhetoric that at times got him into trouble. In 1983, when he was selected to respond to a speech by President Reagan on Central America, Dodd delivered a blistering attack on what he called the president's "formula for failure," accusing Reagan of condoning Salvadoran police who murder "gangland style — the victim on bended knee, thumbs wired behind the back, a bullet through the brain."

The speech angered many Democrats, who thought Dodd had gone far beyond any party consensus on the issue. That reaction proved an important lesson to Dodd, who conceded that he alienated some people with his stridency. "You yourself can become the issue, and I did," he said.

Once, Dodd was dressed down by Secretary

of State George P. Shultz for intruding in U.S. policy in an untoward manner; Shultz complained after Dodd requested a meeting with a Central American head of state that excluded the U.S. ambassador, a violation of protocol that Shultz said contributed to foreigners' confusion about policy.

Dodd uses his post on the Banking Committee, where he chairs the Securities Subcommittee, to keep an eye on home-state matters. In the 100th Congress, Dodd played hardball politics to protect Connecticut insurance companies during markup sessions on legislation to deregulate the financial services industries, which pitted banks against insurers. He threatened to force votes on issues that senators did not want to take stands on unless the committee met his demands. After an intense day and a half, he apologized, but defended his right to protect his state's large insurance industry: "It's like hogs in Iowa," he said.

In even more dramatic fashion, Dodd temporarily joined with Republicans to kill a public housing measure in 1990 in order to persuade the chairman of the House Banking Committee to support a Dodd amendment allowing the Export-Import Bank to fund defense sales to NATO and Japan. That amendment was important to Dodd, because Sikorsky Aircraft wanted to sell its Connecticut-made helicopters to Greece and Turkey. The proposal was never funded.

Dodd tried and failed again in 1991 to convince his colleagues to support another variation of the idea, this time with a proposed amendment to the State Department's authorization bill on the Senate floor.

His colleagues argued that the plan would create more defense industry jobs rather than beginning defense conversion, and would make the world more dangerous.

But Dodd responded that "the hard realities of life" dictated that "there will be defense articles made and produced in Europe and elsewhere around the globe. It is an important industry in this country. And it is our industry that is suffering."

During his tenure in the House from 1975-1981, Dodd was more liberal than most of his colleagues in the Democratic class of 1974, but he reflected his class' general distrust of bureaucracy and its interest in "good government" issues.

At Home: Once considered one of the most vulnerable Senate Democrats up for reelection in 1992, Dodd seems to have put to rest any doubts about his vote-getting abilities. With his solid defeat of millionaire Brook Johnson, Dodd has positioned himself as a true and lasting force in Connecticut politics.

That did not seem likely in early 1991. Dodd's opposition to the Gulf War and his reluctance to oppose Gov. Lowell P. Weicker Jr.'s state income tax reverberated through Connecticut. More than half the people polled in a survey that year said they wouldn't vote for him again; many felt he had lost touch with home-state concerns.

But Dodd took the warning signs to heart, pumped up his campaign coffers and increased his visibility at home. In the campaign, he stressed his efforts to save one *Seawolf* nuclear submarine and his work on family leave legislation. Johnson, although flush with his own cash, could not stop Dodd.

The Dodd name has been a household word in Connecticut politics for three decades.

From the day Democratic Sen. Abraham A. Ribicoff declared his retirement in 1979, Dodd was viewed as his heir apparent. Dodd was overwhelmingly popular in his 2nd District, and his father was still revered by many voters, despite his 1967 Senate censure for personal use of campaign funds.

Dodd's only potential obstacle on the road to the Democratic Senate nomination was his fellow House member, Toby Moffett. When Moffett agreed to wait until 1982 to run for statewide office, Dodd's path was clear.

His Republican opponent was former New York Sen. James L. Buckley, who carried the standard of the state Republican Party's newly resurgent conservative wing. The millionaire brother of columnist William F. Buckley Jr., James Buckley argued that his previous experience and national reputation would make him a significant force for conservatism in the Senate. With a strong constituency in Republican Fairfield County, he hoped to emulate Reagan by making inroads in normally Democratic blue-collar cities and towns to the east.

But Buckley's patrician style did not play well in those areas, and Dodd proved an exuberant campaigner, slipping into crowds with the comfort of a born politician, conversing both in English and fluent Spanish. He attacked Buckley as a conservative ideologue who, as a senator, had neglected the needs of the poor.

Dodd made only gentle references to Buckley's carpetbagging, quipping that the Constitution mandates two senators for each state, not two states for each senator.

Dodd easily outdistanced Buckley, pulling votes from liberal Democrats on an issue basis and from older ethnic voters on the strength of their traditional Democratic habits. He earned a larger plurality than his father did in winning his first Senate term in 1958.

By 1984, Dodd felt politically secure enough at home to endorse the presidential candidacy of Colorado Sen. Gary Hart. The rest of Connecticut's Democratic establishment, including Gov. William A. O'Neill, backed Walter F. Mondale. As a reward for his loyalty, Dodd placed Hart's name in nomination at the national convention in San Francisco.

Dodd's reputation as a rising star was

enhanced by his landslide 1986 re-election. Initial Republican hopes of threatening Dodd were deflated by the refusal of high-profile personalities to challenge him. The GOP eventually awarded its nomination to 66-year-old Roger W. Eddy, a party national committeeman and former state representative.

Eddy, inventor of the widely used Audubon birdcall, had an image as a "gentleman farmer," but his campaign style turned out to be surprisingly hard-hitting. He attacked Dodd's Central America stands, describing him as "the senator from communist Nicaragua" and told members of the state AFL-CIO that "Japan is sucking us dry."

Dodd brushed off the attacks as "disappointing" and went on to amass the largest Senate vote percentage in state history.

Dodd grew up with Connecticut politics, and he went after public office himself at age 30. He was practicing law in New London in 1974 when Republican Rep. Robert H. Steele left his secure 2nd District seat to run for governor. Dodd attached himself to the camp of Democratic gubernatorial candidate Ella T. Grasso early in the spring and began lining up delegate support.

By the time of the convention, he was the clear favorite over John M. Bailey Jr. — son of the state party chairman — and Douglas Bennet, a one-time aide to Ribicoff. He locked up the party's endorsement on the first round of convention balloting, and went on to an easy victory in the general election.

Committees

Banking, Housing & Urban Affairs (3rd of 11 Democrats)
Securities (chairman); Economic Stabilization & Rural Development; Housing & Urban Affairs

Budget (9th of 12 Democrats)

Foreign Relations (4th of 11 Democrats)
Western Hemisphere & Peace Corps Affairs (chairman); International Economic Policy, Trade, Oceans & Environment; Terrorism, Narcotics & International Operations

Labor & Human Resources (4th of 10 Democrats)
Children, Families, Drugs & Alcoholism (chairman); Aging; Education, Arts & Humanities; Labor

Rules & Administration (7th of 9 Democrats)

Elections

1992 General

Christopher J. Dodd (D, ACP)	882,569	(59%)
Brook Johnson (R)	572,036	(38%)
Richard D. Gregory (CC)	35,315	(2%)

Previous Winning Percentages: **1986** (65%) **1980** (56%) **1978 *** (70%) **1976 *** (65%) **1974 *** (59%)

** House elections.*

Campaign Finance

	Receipts	Receipts from PACs		Expend-itures
1992				
Dodd (D)	$3,827,475	$1,337,814	(35%)	$4,122,268
Johnson (R)	$2,400,715	0		$2,395,262

Key Votes

1993	
Require unpaid family and medical leave	Y
Approve national "motor voter" registration bill	Y
Approve budget increasing taxes and reducing deficit	Y
Support president's right to lift military gay ban	Y
1992	
Approve school-choice pilot program	N
Allow shifting funds from defense to domestic programs	N
Oppose deeper cuts in spending for SDI	N
1991	
Approve waiting period for handgun purchases	Y
Raise senators' pay and ban honoraria	N
Authorize use of force in Persian Gulf	N
Confirm Clarence Thomas to Supreme Court	N

Voting Studies

	Presidential Support		Party Unity		Conservative Coalition	
Year	**S**	**O**	**S**	**O**	**S**	**O**
1992	32	68	83	17	34	66
1991	49	49	83	16	43	58
1990	39	58	89	8	30	65
1989	54	45	89	9	32	66
1988	49	40	86	9	38	54
1987	29	56	80	11	28	59
1986	25	73	71	28	29	70
1985	34	64	83	14	27	73
1984	32	61	85	8	6	89
1983	41	53	67	17	14	64
1982	35	61	82	12	5	85
1981	33	59	80	8	3	85

Interest Group Ratings

Year	ADA	AFL-CIO	CCUS	ACU
1992	75	92	30	11
1991	75	92	20	24
1990	61	78	9	9
1989	65	100	50	22
1988	85	86	36	8
1987	65	100	13	0
1986	85	73	44	17
1985	85	95	41	4
1984	100	91	42	10
1983	80	100	24	8
1982	100	96	16	8
1981	90	100	0	7

Joseph I. Lieberman (D)

Of New Haven — Elected 1988; 1st Term

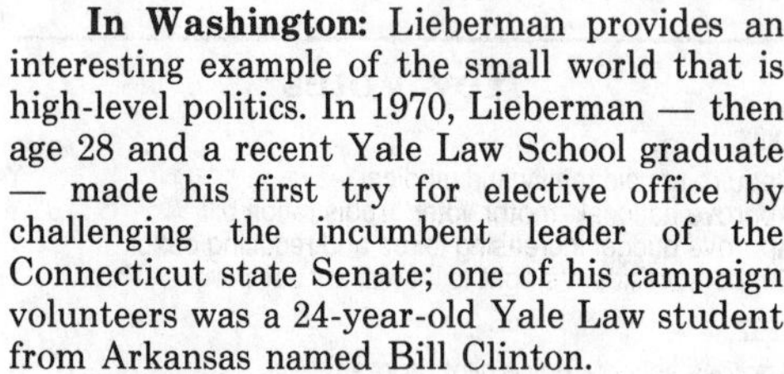

Born: Feb. 24, 1942, Stamford, Conn.
Education: Yale U., B.A. 1964, LL.B. 1967.
Occupation: Lawyer.
Family: Wife, Hadassah Freilich; four children.
Religion: Jewish.
Political Career: Conn. Senate, 1971-81, majority leader, 1975-81; Democratic nominee for U.S. House, 1980; Conn. attorney general, 1983-89.
Capitol Office: 316 Hart Bldg. 20510; 224-4041.

In Washington: Lieberman provides an interesting example of the small world that is high-level politics. In 1970, Lieberman — then age 28 and a recent Yale Law School graduate — made his first try for elective office by challenging the incumbent leader of the Connecticut state Senate; one of his campaign volunteers was a 24-year-old Yale Law student from Arkansas named Bill Clinton.

In 1992, Lieberman, by then halfway through his freshman term in the U.S. Senate, returned the favor to then-Arkansas Gov. Clinton: He was the first senator from outside Arkansas to endorse Clinton's campaign to unseat President Bush.

Even before 1992, Lieberman had re-established ties to Clinton through their work on the Democratic Leadership Council. One of the more moderate Northern Democrats in the Senate, Lieberman is a vice chairman of the DLC, which aims to draw the liberal-leaning national Democratic Party to the political center.

Well before Clinton's election as president, Lieberman had garnered a legislative stature unusual for a freshman member. Though he had defeated incumbent Republican Sen. Lowell P. Weicker Jr. in 1988 by just 1 percentage point, Lieberman quickly impressed colleagues on both sides of the aisle with his thoughtful manner and independent approach on policy issues.

Lieberman does not discourage descriptions of him as a moderate-to-conservative Democrat — a political plus in Connecticut, which tends to swing between the two major parties. It has also been widely noted that Lieberman brings in a personally conservative perspective as an Orthodox Jew (he will not campaign during the Jewish high holy days and rarely participates in Senate sessions held on Friday night or Saturday, the Jewish Sabbath).

This center-right posture caused an early rift between Lieberman and Clinton. In May 1993, Lieberman spoke on the Senate floor and criticized Clinton's enterprise zone tax-credit plan for the inner cities, which was more limited than the one they had jointly supported in the DLC.

Yet Lieberman's Senate voting record is not that far from the Democratic norm. In fact, his opposition to Bush's positions on Senate votes in the 102nd Congress trailed slightly that of his home-state Democratic colleague, Christopher J. Dodd, who is widely regarded as a staunch liberal.

Lieberman has reinforced his centrist image by breaking with his party's majority on high-profile issues. A supporter of an activist U.S. foreign policy, Lieberman joined with Republican Sen. John W. Warner of Virginia in January 1991 to author the resolution that authorized Bush to use military force against Iraq; most Democratic senators voted against it. A member from the state with the highest per capita income in 1991, Lieberman favors capital gains tax breaks and is wary of "soak the rich" tax plans favored by some of the more liberal Democrats.

On overall economic policy, Lieberman is one of the Democratic advocates of "industrial policy." Like Clinton, Lieberman — who chairs the Small Business Subcommittee on Competitiveness, Capital Formation and Economic Opportunity — envisions an aggressive federal government role in promoting economic growth, particularly in the cutting-edge high-technology industries.

"We're in a global economic war, and we've been losing ground to our competitors. The main reason why is that our government, until now, has been reluctant to get involved in helping American businesses compete," Lieberman said in February 1993. "We now have a president... who understands why it's important for government to get involved."

Lieberman also is in line with Clinton, Vice President Al Gore and much of his party in his zeal for regulations to protect the environment and consumers: These were his trademark issues during his tenure as state attorney general. Much of the legislation Lieberman has proposed has been on environment-related issues. During the 101st Congress, his first as a senator, Lieberman was active in shaping the extension of the Clear Air Act.

In 1992, he was among the Democrats who fought to strip funding from the Bush administration's Council for Competitiveness (headed by Vice President Dan Quayle), which had worked to soften the impact on businesses of some clean air regulations. In the 103rd Congress, Lieberman took over as chairman of the Environment and Public Works Subcommittee on Clean Air and Nuclear Regulation and the Governmental Affairs Subcommittee on Regulation and Government Information.

Lieberman, who played a key role in crafting oil-spill liability legislation that was enacted in 1990, opposed Bush's energy policy package in the 102nd Congress as too skewed toward production over conservation. He was outspoken against Bush's proposal to open the Arctic National Wildlife Refuge in Alaska to drilling. A participant in the Democratic threat of a filibuster that resulted in the removal of the provision, Lieberman said, "We have drawn a line in the tundra."

Still, there will likely be more areas in which Lieberman will veer from Clinton and the majority of his Senate Democrats. He worries that some tax increases proposed by Clinton may staunch the business investments they both desire. A member from a state in which defense-related industry plays a huge economic role, Lieberman also expresses concerns about the rate of defense spending cuts.

Lieberman, who joined the Armed Services Committee in the 103rd Congress, says members "speak pretty loosely ... about a peace dividend" without measuring the economic impacts of defense plant closures. During the 102nd Congress, Lieberman and Dodd helped fight off Bush's budget-related efforts to scrap the *Seawolf* submarine, built by the Electric Boat Co., one of Connecticut's largest employers.

Lieberman is also a leading advocate of federal support of economic diversification efforts by defense-reliant communities and employers, including the retraining of dislocated workers.

Lieberman's support for Connecticut's defense industrial base conforms with his support for the assertive use of U.S. forces overseas. In a speech supporting the Persian Gulf War resolution in January 1991, Lieberman quoted the Greek historian Herodotus: "To have peace you must prepare for war." Lieberman's hard line against the Iraqi regime of Saddam Hussein is consistent with his stalwart support of Israel, an Iraq adversary.

Jewish history was clearly on Lieberman's mind in 1992 when he called for forceful action to end brutalities committed in the name of "ethnic cleansing" by ethnic Serbs against Muslims and Croats in the former Yugoslav republic of Bosnia. In Bosnia, he said, "We hear ... echoes of conflicts in Europe little more than 50 years ago."

Some observers see the independent-minded Lieberman as something of a Democratic version of Weicker, the Republican he replaced. One of the more liberal members on the GOP side, Weicker developed a reputation as a political maverick during the presidency of Ronald Reagan, often bolting his party on social and economic issues.

But Weicker was a political outsider; this was borne out in 1990, when he made a comeback by winning for governor of Connecticut as an independent candidate. Lieberman is a Democratic loyalist and an ally of Senate Majority Leader George J. Mitchell of Maine.

Weicker also made plenty of enemies, including among Republicans, with his blustery style, while the quietly engaging Lieberman has many friends in both parties. His accessibility has earned him plaudits.

A glowing column by Washington Post writer David Broder in December 1992 described Lieberman's encounter with James J. Zogby, an Arab-American activist. Although Zogby, an advocate of Palestinian rights, has deep disagreements with Lieberman, the two had a rancorless discussion on a TV talk show in 1992. When Zogby, a Democrat, sensed he was being stonewalled by Clinton campaign operatives who were sensitive to alienating Jewish supporters, he turned to Lieberman. The senator used his contacts in the campaign to open the way for Zogby's participation.

Broder included Lieberman's own description of his approach. "I believe in dialogue.... to me, one of the things I like about this business of politics and this place, the Senate, is the range of people and of ideas you get exposed to," he said.

There are those, however, who are more cynical about Lieberman. They note his long-term shifts from Vietnam War critic to proponent of U.S. military interventions and from opponent to supporter of capital punishment. They also cite actions such as his switch on Bush's nomination of Clarence Thomas to the Supreme Court.

Lieberman originally endorsed Thomas, a black conservative and Yale Law alumnus. However, his support was weakened by the testimony of Anita Hill, who accused the nominee of sexual misconduct.

At the last minute, Lieberman decided to vote against Thomas. He said he came to that decision after much agonizing because of the gravity of Hill's sexual harassment charges. But skeptics said that Lieberman's switch came too late to influence other wavering senators: Thomas was confirmed by a 52-47 vote.

At Home: Lieberman was given little chance of ousting 18-year GOP Senate veteran Weicker in the 1988 race, but he wound up scoring the only Democratic upset of that year's Senate elections.

All year long, Lieberman had argued that it was a myth that Connecticut benefited from Weicker's maverick reputation. But the electoral appeal of the Republican's go-it-alone style had seemed impenetrable.

After months of trailing in opinion polls, Lieberman launched a series of animated ads late in the campaign that portrayed Weicker as a sleeping bear, dozing through important votes but waking loud and ornery when personally piqued. The imagery of the bear ads clicked, and their appearance in the closing weeks of a yearlong campaign was perfectly timed. With Lieberman peaking late, Weicker did not have a chance to counterpunch.

The challenger began the campaign well-known from prior political service. Earlier in his career, he had ended a 10-year stint in the state Senate (and his job there as majority leader) for an unsuccessful U.S. House bid. But two years later, he bounced back, becoming the top state vote-getter in his 1982 election to attorney general.

His visibility on these issues did not endear him to the "Old Guard" in Connecticut's Democratic Party, but his efforts had the liberal lilt needed to woo traditionally Democratic voters, and the party elected to unite behind him in his challenge to Weicker. Lieberman also raised doubts about Weicker's commitment to Social Security, a Democratic touchstone issue.

At the same time, Lieberman's profile also enabled him to court crossover voters. His demeanor is far more restrained than Weicker's; where the Republican campaigned with his sleeves rolled up and jacket slung over his shoulder, Lieberman seemed reluctant to loosen his tie. He stressed a family-man image, and is known as an Orthodox Jew whose avoidance of Saturday campaigning precluded him from attending even the convention that nominated him.

Lieberman also held the conservative ground on a few select issues. He supported allowing military involvement in drug interdiction, and backed the 1983 invasion of Grenada, both of which Weicker opposed. Lieberman also backed a moment of silence in schools, which may be used for prayer.

This combination won him an endorsement from noted conservative William F. Buckley Jr., who had long disdained Weicker for his social liberalism. Some conservatives concluded that a Lieberman victory would be no great catastrophe, so they sat out the Senate race. That deprived Weicker of crucial GOP support on Election Day, while Lieberman held his Democratic base and won enough independent votes to eke out a narrow victory.

While Democrats were pleased with his success, some liberals felt a twinge of remorse over the departure of Weicker, who so often had championed their causes in the Senate and in the national GOP. Some observers credit that voter guilt with helping Weicker in his successful 1990 bid, as an independent, for governor.

Although no big-name challengers had set their sights on Lieberman's seat by early 1993, he was busily tending to electoral concerns. Early breaks with the Clinton administration helped to re-establish Lieberman's independent bona fides.

Committees

Armed Services (11th of 11 Democrats)
Defense Technology, Acquisition & Industrial Base; Force Requirements & Personnel; Regional Defense & Contingency Forces

Environment & Public Works (7th of 10 Democrats)
Clean Air & Nuclear Regulation (chairman); Clean Water, Fisheries & Wildlife; Toxic Substances, Environmental Oversight, Research & Development

Governmental Affairs (6th of 8 Democrats)
Regulation & Government Information (chairman); General Services, Federalism & the District of Columbia; Oversight of Government Management; Permanent Subcommitte on Investigations

Small Business (6th of 12 Democrats)
Competitiveness, Capital Formation & Economic Opportunity (chairman); Government Contracting & Paperwork Reduction

Elections

1988 General

Joseph I. Lieberman (D)	688,499	(50%)
Lowell P. Weicker Jr. (R)	678,454	(49%)

Campaign Finance

1988	Receipts	Receipts from PACs		Expend-itures
Lieberman (D)	$2,647,603	$175,566	(7%)	$2,570,799
Weicker (R)	$2,519,961	$947,116	(38%)	$2,609,902

Key Votes

1993

Require unpaid family and medical leave	Y
Approve national "motor voter" registration bill	Y
Approve budget increasing taxes and reducing deficit	Y
Support president's right to lift military gay ban	Y

1992

Approve school-choice pilot program	Y
Allow shifting funds from defense to domestic programs	N
Oppose deeper cuts in spending for SDI	N

1991

Approve waiting period for handgun purchases	Y
Raise senators' pay and ban honoraria	Y
Authorize use of force in Persian Gulf	Y
Confirm Clarence Thomas to Supreme Court	N

Voting Studies

	Presidential Support		Party Unity		Conservative Coalition	
Year	S	O	S	O	S	O
1992	37	63	77	23	37	63
1991	49	46	80	19	38	63
1990	37	62	86	13	22	78
1989	56	44	81	19	32	68

Interest Group Ratings

Year	ADA	AFL-CIO	CCUS	ACU
1992	70	83	50	22
1991	65	83	30	25
1990	83	78	17	22
1989	75	90	38	32

1 Barbara B. Kennelly (D)

Of Hartford — Elected 1982; 6th Full Term

Born: July 10, 1936, Hartford, Conn.
Education: Trinity College (Washington, D.C.), B.A. 1958; Trinity College (Hartford, Conn.), M.A. 1973.
Occupation: Public official.
Family: Husband, James J. Kennelly; four children.
Religion: Roman Catholic.
Political Career: Hartford Court of Common Council, 1975-79; Conn. secretary of state, 1979-82.
Capitol Office: 201 Cannon Bldg. 20515; 225-2265.

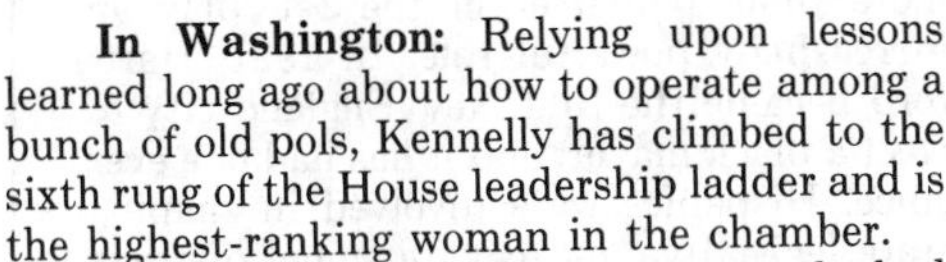

In Washington: Relying upon lessons learned long ago about how to operate among a bunch of old pols, Kennelly has climbed to the sixth rung of the House leadership ladder and is the highest-ranking woman in the chamber.

In less than a decade in the House, she had worked quietly, behind the scenes, to blaze a trail for women. Then, just as pundits began talking up the notion of 1992 being "the Year of the Woman" in politics, she became a beneficiary of those efforts and burst into a more visible role. Now one of four chief deputy whips, Kennelly remains someone to watch as additional leadership opportunities for women ripen in the 1990s.

Kennelly's knack for getting along with the male-dominated leadership showed early. She had been in the chamber less than a year when she won a seat on the prestigious Ways and Means Committee. And in December 1984 she was appointed to the Steering and Policy Committee. In the June 1989 Democratic leadership shake-up that followed Jim Wright's resignation as Speaker, Kennelly made a long-shot bid for the open post of caucus chairman. She lost to Steny H. Hoyer of Maryland, who had been the caucus vice chairman.

Her chance came in August 1991, when David E. Bonior of Michigan moved up to whip from the position of chief deputy. Speaker Thomas S. Foley of Washington, under pressure from women, blacks and Southern conservatives, all of whom felt excluded from party decision-making, decided that the time had come to make the leadership a bit more diverse. Kennelly was tapped as one of three chief deputy whips.

She played a central role in leadership efforts in the 102nd Congress to derail a balanced-budget constitutional amendment that appeared headed for passage like a locomotive with a full head of steam.

Kennelly sponsored a bill to institute a statutory requirement for a balanced budget. It was derided by some members as a transparent attempt to provide cover to members who voted against the constitutional change, and she was somewhat embarrassed when her measure failed 199-220. But it may have served its purpose. The constitutional amendment fell nine votes short of two-thirds majority necessary for passage, and 121 Democrats who voted against it had earlier voted for Kennelly's bill.

In the 103rd Congress, she further cemented her insider status by joining the Budget and House Administration committees. To do so, she gave up her assignment to the Intelligence Committee.

It is not surprising Kennelly feels at ease around old-fashioned Democrats. She grew up with them; her father was John Bailey, the legendary Connecticut party boss and chairman of the Democratic National Committee under Presidents John F. Kennedy and Lyndon B. Johnson. But Kennelly made the most of her opportunities by finding ways to fit in — notably by reviving her golf game. One way to crack any "old boy" network is to mix in socially, and the place Kennelly has mixed with members of Ways and Means is on the fairways and putting greens.

Meanwhile, back at the office, Kennelly has moved up to the top tier of the Ways and Means dias and occasionally commands the spotlight. By dint of Hartford's importance to the insurance industry, she has been typecast as an expert on the taxation of that industry. Widely respected for her erudition on the subject, she may also sense herself held back by it. As a result she picks her targets carefully for maximum success.

She is the prime sponsor of periodic bills to continue the tax-free treatment of income earned on mortgage-revenue bonds, a controversial, if wildly popular, tax subsidy that finances below-market mortgages for first-time home buyers who meet income eligibility standards. A major energy policy bill enacted in 1992 contained Kennelly's provisions increasing to $60 a month the limit on tax-free, employer-paid mass transit subsidies and permitting utilities to make tax-free rebates to customers who install energy-efficient lights, appliances and other equipment.

In working on legislation to overhaul the tax code in the 99th Congress, Kennelly specialized in the complex provisions affecting property- and casualty-insurance companies. In the 100th Con-

Connecticut 1

Central — Hartford

With Hartford as the hub and 19 surrounding communities as its spokes, the 1st is a classic example of a core urban center with interdependent suburbs. Many of the 1st's 548,000 residents work in Hartford.

Situated 100 miles southwest of Boston and 110 miles northeast of New York, Hartford is well-positioned to remain a regional commerce center. Companies such as Aetna, The Travelers and CIGNA helped earn Hartford the moniker "insurance capital of the world." But the city is also the state capital and a major financial center.

During the 1980s, banks, insurance companies and related businesses flourished, creating pockets of extreme wealth in the bedroom communities outside Hartford. But when the stock market plummeted, real estate sagged and defense contracts began to dwindle; Hartford caught the brunt of it all.

The situation appeared to stabilize in 1992 as unemployment leveled off and the aerospace industry targeted commercial customers to replace lost military contracts. Like much of Connecticut, the 1st is watching anxiously to see how defense-related companies weather the post-Cold War downsizing.

United Technologies, the state's largest private employer with headquarters in Hartford, plans more than 5,300 layoffs in the district by 1995. The state government, Hartford's largest employer, has been in a similar belt-tightening mode under independent Gov. Lowell P. Weicker Jr. And the city remains the nation's eighth-poorest.

Once the domain of the Democratic political czar John Bailey, the 1st now belongs to his daughter, Rep. Kennelly. In her past four elections, Kennelly has garnered an average of 72 percent of the vote; political security has given her latitude to become an inside player on Capitol Hill. She is now chief deputy majority whip.

During his three decades as party boss, Bailey personally selected nearly every representative for his home district. He also ran the Democratic National Committee under Presidents Kennedy and Johnson after helping orchestrate Kennedy's victory in 1960.

Minorities, which make up slightly more than a quarter of the 1st, play an increasingly powerful role. In 1981, Hartford became the first New England city to elect a black mayor, and it has had one ever since. Hispanics were involved in shaping state legislative and congressional districts in 1992 and have put up candidates for several local offices.

Registered Democrats far outnumber Republicans in the 1st — 144,000 to 69,000. In 1988, Democrat Michael S. Dukakis won the old 1st District, thanks primarily to Hartford's large black community, and four years later Bill Clinton carried every community in the 1st. The 81,000 unaffiliated voters are expected to be a key swing group in future national and statewide elections.

The district has a rich literary history. Mark Twain and Harriet Beecher Stowe both hailed from Hartford. And The Hartford Courant, founded in 1764, is the nation's oldest newspaper in continuous circulation.

1990 Population: 548,016. White 429,116 (78%), Black 77,824 (14%), Other 41,076 (7%). Hispanic origin 55,179 (10%). 18 and over 423,317 (77%), 62 and over 93,458 (17%). Median age: 35.

---

gress, Kennelly displayed her legislative savvy by winning a surprising victory for the insurance industry. She and her allies on the committee managed an end run of Chairman Dan Rostenkowski of Illinois when he tried to impose stiffer limits on the use of certain life insurance policies to shelter more income from taxation than the industry was willing to accept. In the 98th, she helped shape a major revision of insurance tax laws, reducing the industry's tax burden.

Kennelly is a latecomer to feminist issues; she says her three daughters persuaded her to become active. But she does not hold back on big issues or small ones. In 1991, hers was a loud voice expressing outrage that the Senate wanted to vote on Clarence Thomas' nomination to the Supreme Court without hearing from Professor Anita F. Hill about allegations of sexual harassment. And when invitations for congressional leaders to lunch with President Clinton on Inauguration Day stopped with Bonior, she argued persuasively that a president who campaigned on diversity might like to have a woman in the room.

One of her first accomplishments was winning passage in 1984 of a law to encourage payment of child support. It required states to see that money is withheld from the paychecks of parents who are delinquent in meeting court-ordered child-support payments.

At Home: Despite a slow start getting into politics herself, Kennelly has proved she learned well at her father's knee. Whether battling Republicans or working the angles inside her own party, Kennelly has shown real political savvy and longevity.

Her first political job came in 1975. Nearly 40 years old, the former social service director was appointed to the Hartford City Council and later won a full term on her own.

It took a strikingly independent move to win her next office. Gloria Schaffer, the Democratic secretary of state, decided to step down from her post in 1978. Party protocol called for replacing her with another Jewish woman to balance the ethnic makeup of the statewide ticket. Kennelly ignored precedent. At the party convention she pieced together an organization that prompted comparisons with her father; she finagled the nomination from the party favorites and won easily in November.

In 1981, two weeks after six-term Democratic Rep. William R. Cotter died of cancer, Kennelly announced her candidacy to replace him. Other Democrats dropped out, and she was nominated by acclamation.

Kennelly had little trouble in the subsequent special election against GOP nominee Ann P. Uccello, a former mayor of Hartford. Running in a Democratic stronghold, Kennelly had a huge financial lead that scared off the national Republican Party. The GOP wrote off Uccello, and Kennelly won with nearly 60 percent.

Since then, Kennelly has rolled up huge tallies in each of her six re-election campaigns, never falling below 62 percent.

Even a taped television report in 1990 showing Kennelly and other members of the Ways and Means Committee romping on the beach during a taxpayer-paid trip to Barbados was not enough to hurt her seriously. She defeated Republican nominee James P. Garvey with 71 percent of the vote.

In 1992, despite a weakened state economy and general distrust of incumbents, Kennelly quashed a challenge from Philip L. Steele.

Kennelly shows no signs of tiring of the political life, although she has expressed interest in moving up a rung to statewide office. She was discussed as a possible candidate for governor in 1990 when Democratic incumbent William A. O'Neill announced his retirement, but she decided against making that race.

Committees

Chief Deputy Whip

Budget (14th of 26 Democrats)

House Administration (11th of 12 Democrats)
Accounts; Libraries & Memorials; Office Systems

Ways & Means (9th of 24 Democrats)
Trade

Elections

1992 General		
Barbara B. Kennelly (D, ACP)	164,735	(67%)
Philip L. Steele (R)	75,113	(31%)
Gary R. Garneau (CC)	5,577	(2%)
1990 General		
Barbara B. Kennelly (D)	126,566	(71%)
James P. Garvey (R)	50,690	(29%)

Previous Winning Percentages: **1988** (77%) **1986** (74%) **1984** (62%) **1982** (68%) **1982** * (59%)

** Special election.*

District Vote for President

1992	
D	133,686 (50%)
R	82,086 (31%)
I	52,154 (19%)

Campaign Finance

	Receipts	Receipts from PACs		Expend-itures
1992				
Kennelly (D)	$523,025	$336,281	(64%)	$572,841
Steele (R)	$5,927	0		$3,612
1990				
Kennelly (D)	$483,041	$297,700	(62%)	$406,138

Key Votes

1993	
Require parental notification of minors' abortions	N
Require unpaid family and medical leave	Y
Approve national "motor voter" registration bill	Y
Approve budget increasing taxes and reducing deficit	Y
Approve economic stimulus plan	Y
1992	
Approve balanced-budget constitutional amendment	N
Close down space station program	N
Approve U.S. aid for former Soviet Union	Y
Allow shifting funds from defense to domestic programs	Y
1991	
Extend unemployment benefits using deficit financing	Y
Approve waiting period for handgun purchases	Y
Authorize use of force in Persian Gulf	N

Voting Studies

	Presidential Support		Party Unity		Conservative Coalition	
Year	**S**	**O**	**S**	**O**	**S**	**O**
1992	22	77	92	6	29	71
1991	30	70	94	6	24	76
1990	22	78	92	6	17	83
1989	28	67	93	5	27	71
1988	28	71	92	6	32	68
1987	22	75	89	5	37	60
1986	20	78	91	4	20	74
1985	23	78	91	5	22	78
1984	31	65	88	7	15	78
1983	16	80	95	3	12	83
1982	34	66	92	8	26	74

Interest Group Ratings

Year	ADA	AFL-CIO	CCUS	ACU
1992	100	92	25	4
1991	80	83	20	0
1990	83	92	14	8
1989	95	92	30	7
1988	90	100	36	8
1987	84	88	21	0
1986	85	93	35	0
1985	90	94	27	10
1984	85	77	38	0
1983	90	94	25	4
1982	95	85	27	0

2 Sam Gejdenson (D)

Of Bozrah — Elected 1980; 7th Term

Born: May 20, 1948, Eschwege, Germany.
Education: Mitchell College, A.S. 1968; U. of Connecticut, B.A. 1970.
Occupation: Dairy farmer.
Family: Wife, Karen Fleming; two children.
Religion: Jewish.
Political Career: Conn. House, 1975-79.
Capitol Office: 2416 Rayburn Bldg. 20515; 225-2076.

In Washington: Gejdenson, known to his colleagues both for his irreverent wit and his seriousness as a legislator, has become an increasingly important asset to the Democratic leadership. Unfortunately for Gejdenson, his constituents of late have not seemed unduly impressed by the ease with which he navigates the inner circles of the House; Gejdenson barely won a seventh term in 1992. So he devotes as much time as possible to promoting Connecticut's defense- and export-oriented economy.

At the start of the 103rd Congress, Gejdenson moved into the No. 2 Democratic seat on the Foreign Affairs Committee. Though it is potentially a position of some influence, Gejdenson has not spent an inordinate amount of time on the largely hortatory endeavor of congressional foreign policy input.

Instead, he has concentrated his efforts on the Foreign Affairs Subcommittee on Economic Policy, Trade and the Environment, which he has chaired since 1989. From there, he has spent the better part of the past two Congresses — and will devote himself in the 103rd — to rewriting the Export Administration Act.

Written in 1979 and last revised in 1985, the law strictly limits the export to communist nations of industrial goods and materials that have possible military applications — computers and machine tools, for instance.

Times have changed, with Boris N. Yeltsin's Russia now more ally than adversary. Yet even before the Cold War ended with the disintegration of the Soviet Union, Gejdenson attempted to let the United States take advantage of new export markets in Soviet bloc countries. Those markets already were being tapped by entrepreneurs in other countries, particularly Taiwan and Singapore, not a part of the Western export-control alliance known as Cocom.

Gejdenson's effort to relax controls on many sophisticated bits of technology that have dual civilian and military uses reflects his eagerness to open overseas trading doors for Connecticut's businesses, without in his view compromising national security. He also emphasized reorganizing the export licensing process to cut bureaucratic red tape.

In the 101st, the bill breezed through both houses of Congress. But President Bush complained about the bill, especially a Senate provision mandating sanctions against countries and companies involved in the international trade of chemical and biological weapons. Stating that the sanctions clause would "unduly interfere with the president's responsibility for carrying out foreign policy," Bush killed the bill in November 1990 with a pocket veto.

In the 102nd, with the offending sanctions language dropped, the bill was nearly enacted. But on the last day of the session three House Republicans erected a procedural blockade, claiming that the bill would too greatly limit the Defense Department's authority to block exports that might have a military application.

Gejdenson's role in the House is enhanced not only by his quick humor, but also by a boundless energy that helps him stay active in many arenas. In this respect, Gejdenson resembles other younger House overachievers, such as New York's Charles E. Schumer and California's George Miller, with whom he shares a house on Capitol Hill.

He moved into the ranks of the leadership in 1989, gaining a seat on the Democratic Steering and Policy Committee. In 1991, Speaker Thomas S. Foley tapped him to head a House Administration Committee task force on congressional campaign finance reform. Gejdenson produced a bill that passed the House in 1991; a compromise that would have limited expenditures and provided some public financing cleared the House and Senate in 1992. But Bush vetoed the bill, and his veto was easily sustained in the Senate. In May 1993, the Clinton administration unveiled campaign finance legislation with many of the features of the earlier failed measure.

At the start of the 103rd, Gejdenson proved his loyalty to Foley by heading his drive to be re-elected Speaker. Though Foley had drawn some intraparty criticism in the first half of 1992 for his handling of the House bank scandal, by 1993 his re-election was a cinch.

Connecticut 2

East — New London

The fate of the nuclear attack submarine *Seawolf* may shape the economic and political future of the 2nd more than any other factor. A region once devastated by the death of a single industry (the wool mills) is again faced with the prospect of seeing its economic lifeblood drain away.

In the 1980s, more than half the jobs in the district — particularly those along the seacoast — were provided by defense-related companies. But with the Pentagon budget shrinking in the post-Cold War era, the 2nd is virtually guaranteed ongoing job losses.

Entering the 1990s, about 15,000 people worked at the region's largest employer, Groton-based Electric Boat Co. A division of General Dynamics, EB expects to deliver its last submarine on order in 1997. High hopes for building dozens of *Seawolf* subs were sunk in 1992 when President Bush recommended scrapping the program.

After lobbying by the state's bipartisan delegation, Congress and the administration agreed to spend $1.5 billion on one *Seawolf* and set aside $376 million for possible future subs. The decision saved jobs in the short run, but by the end of the decade, it seems likely that EB's current work force will be cut in half.

Voters in the 2nd demonstrated a predilection for voting Republican in presidential contests of the 1980s, but in 1992 they embraced Democrat Bill Clinton. Still, the balloting appeared to be more of an anti-status quo vote than an endorsement of the Democratic Party. Rep. Gejdenson met unexpectedly stiff GOP resistance in his bid for re-election; it took nearly a week for vote-counters to declare him the winner of a seventh term.

The largest district in the state geographically and considered rural by East Coast standards, the 2nd includes some of Connecticut's poorest villages and towns. Unemployment hovered around 12 percent in the early 1990s, compared with a state average of about 7.5 percent.

Unlike Lowell, in neighboring Massachusetts, the communities along the Quinnebaug and Shetucket rivers never really recovered from the wool mills' departures in the 1960s. After several decades of economic stagnation, an effort is now under way to designate the former mill towns as a National Heritage Corridor, complete with museums and recreational opportunities.

The corridor plan fits in well with southeastern Connecticut's strategy to rejuvenate the economy with tourism. In 1989, tourism was credited with generating $435 million in revenue and $50 million in taxes in New London County. Mystic, with its historic seaport, museums, aquarium and other attractions, is the biggest success story, bringing in more than $165 million in tourist revenue annually.

Another lure for visitors is the Foxwoods casino in Ledyard. Run by the Mashantucket Pequot tribe, the casino was drawing about 8,000 people a day just a few months after its winter 1992 opening. The numbers are expected to swell as the tribe builds hotels, a golf course and convention center.

1990 Population: 548,041. White 511,184 (93%), Black 20,209 (4%), Other 16,648 (3%). Hispanic origin 16,394 (3%). 18 and over 421,044 (77%), 62 and over 78,188 (14%). Median age: 33.

Gejdenson has faced one major quandary throughout a House career in which he has mainly voted a liberal line. He opposed much of the 1980s military buildup and voted against the January 1991 resolution authorizing Bush to use military force against Iraq. Yet his state's economy relies heavily on defense contractors, including Electric Boat Co., which builds nuclear submarines in his district.

Gejdenson takes a two-pronged approach. He lobbies hard in behalf of the Navy submarine program, calling it "the most proven and effective component of our national security strategy." But he also has promoted efforts to diversify his district's economy, such as helping establish the Southeast Area Technology Development Center (SEATECH) in 1987.

Gejdenson's busy agenda is rounded out by his assignment to the Natural Resources Committee.

At Home: Gejdenson's ascent on Capitol Hill has coincided with a marked decline in Connecticut's economy, and that has helped cause problems for him at the polls. In 1992, a little-known and underfunded GOP state senator, Edward Munster, held Gejdenson to his lowest-ever tally, 51 percent.

The 2nd has some of Connecticut's more conservative voters, and it was not until his fourth House campaign that Gejdenson won with more than 56 percent of the vote. But he posted percentages in the 60s in the 1986, 1988 and 1990 elections, so the 1992 slump was a dramatic one. And Munster got no help from George Bush, who won only 30 percent of the presidential vote in the 2nd, nearly losing to independent Ross Perot in the district.

In his first bid for Congress in 1980, Gejdenson thought he would coast after defeating John N. Dempsey Jr., the son of a former governor, in the Democratic primary. But GOP nominee Tony Guglielmo benefited from Ronald Reagan's big victory in the district, and Gejdenson got just 53 percent.

Guglielmo was back in 1982, but that year's economic downturn put him on the defensive, and Gejdenson won with 56 percent.

In 1984, Gejdenson was nearly caught off guard by lightly regarded botany professor Roberta Koontz. Bolstered by Reagan's landslide in the 2nd and capitalizing on voters' concerns about Gejdenson's liberalism, Koontz held Gejdenson to 54 percent.

In 1986, Francis M. "Bud" Mullen, a former director of the federal Drug Enforcement Administration, complained that Gejdenson would not take a seat on Armed Services and had opposed some Reagan defense programs. But Gejdenson countered with evidence that he had helped bring billions of dollars in ship- and submarine-building contracts to the 2nd. He mauled Mullen, then won comfortably in the next two elections.

In 1992, Gejdenson faced GOP charges that he was more concerned with his national image than local matters. Munster, a former college professor who won the Republican primary in an upset, used Gejdenson's 51 overdrafts at the House bank as evidence that the incumbent had "gone Washington." With a little more money and time, Munster might have prevailed.

Gejdenson grew up on an eastern Connecticut dairy farm owned by his parents, Lithuanian Jews who survived the World War II Holocaust. Gejdenson himself was born in the displaced persons' camp in Germany from which his family emigrated to America.

Committees

Foreign Affairs (2nd of 27 Democrats)
Economic Policy, Trade & the Environment (chairman)

House Administration (4th of 12 Democrats)
Office Systems (chairman); Accounts

Natural Resources (9th of 28 Democrats)
Native American Affairs; Oversight & Investigations

Joint Organization of Congress

Joint Printing

Elections

1992 General		
Sam Gejdenson (D, ACP)	123,291	(51%)
Edward W. Munster (R)	119,416	(49%)
1990 General		
Sam Gejdenson (D)	105,085	(60%)
John M. Ragsdale (R)	70,922	(40%)

Previous Winning Percentages: **1988** (64%) **1986** (67%) **1984** (54%) **1982** (56%) **1980** (53%)

District Vote for President

1992

D 113,553 (43%)
R 79,110 (30%)
I 72,782 (27%)

Campaign Finance

	Receipts	Receipts from PACs		Expend-itures
1992				
Gejdenson (D)	$1,024,091	$336,601	(33%)	$1,019,417
Munster (R)	$140,416	$13,891	(10%)	$140,139
1990				
Gejdenson (D)	$458,980	$185,950	(41%)	$464,500
Ragsdale (R)	$113,024	0		$112,881

Key Votes

1993	
Require parental notification of minors' abortions	N
Require unpaid family and medical leave	Y
Approve national "motor voter" registration bill	Y
Approve budget increasing taxes and reducing deficit	Y
Approve economic stimulus plan	Y
1992	
Approve balanced-budget constitutional amendment	N
Close down space station program	N
Approve U.S. aid for former Soviet Union	Y
Allow shifting funds from defense to domestic programs	N
1991	
Extend unemployment benefits using deficit financing	Y
Approve waiting period for handgun purchases	Y
Authorize use of force in Persian Gulf	N

Voting Studies

	Presidential Support		Party Unity		Conservative Coalition	
Year	**S**	**O**	**S**	**O**	**S**	**O**
1992	16	84	96	4	17	81
1991	23	77	96	3	11	89
1990	19	81	95	4	7	89
1989	26	74	96	3	12	88
1988	19	78	93	3	8	92
1987	15	84	92	4	19	81
1986	13	87	96	3	12	88
1985	23	78	92	4	7	89
1984	27	69	91	7	5	95
1983	20	79	95	3	9	90
1982	36	60	92	4	15	82
1981	22	76	92	7	8	92

Interest Group Ratings

Year	ADA	AFL-CIO	CCUS	ACU
1992	90	92	38	12
1991	95	100	20	0
1990	94	100	14	4
1989	100	100	30	0
1988	95	92	29	0
1987	92	100	20	0
1986	95	100	41	0
1985	90	94	23	10
1984	95	100	50	0
1983	90	100	25	0
1982	100	95	23	0
1981	95	80	5	0

3 Rosa DeLauro (D)

Of New Haven — Elected 1990; 2nd Term

Born: March 2, 1943, New Haven, Conn.
Education: London School of Economics, 1962-63; Marymount College, B.A. 1964; Columbia U., M.A. 1966.
Occupation: Political activist.
Family: Husband, Stanley Greenberg; three stepchildren.
Religion: Roman Catholic.
Political Career: No previous office.
Capitol Office: 327 Cannon Bldg. 20515; 225-3661.

In Washington: With an agenda attuned to that of President Clinton, powerful connections in the Democratic Party and political street smarts, DeLauro has quickly become one of Congress' upwardly mobile members.

By the end of her first term, House officials already had bestowed upon her the first symbolic trappings of success: the No. 2 slot on a Public Works subcommittee and membership in the majority leader's "message group," which meets regularly to coordinate media presentations. A more tangible indication of the respect she has earned came in the 103rd Congress, when she won a seat on the Appropriations Committee.

DeLauro's political instincts are rooted in her upbringing in Wooster Square, a tightknit Italian neighborhood of New Haven. Her father was an Italian immigrant and her mother a factory worker. Both parents served as alders in New Haven, and her mother, Louisa DeLauro, is the longest-serving board member.

As a child, DeLauro frequently tagged along to political gatherings. When she grew up, she married within the business. Her husband, Stanley Greenberg, is President Clinton's pollster, making the DeLauro-Greenbergs one of Washington's true power couples: During the campaign they rarely saw each other except for such rendezvous as the Democratic National Convention in New York.

Before becoming a candidate, DeLauro compiled an impressive résumé of Hill experience. She spent seven years as the chief of staff to Democratic Sen. Christopher Dodd of Connecticut, then moved through stints as a lobbyist against aid to the Nicaraguan contras and as director of EMILY's List, an organization that raises funds for women candidates.

As a result, DeLauro was able to fulfill every freshman's promise to hit the ground running, developing a reputation as a committed, energetic lawmaker. At the same time, she made herself useful to the party elders, working well on whip teams and voting with the party majority roughly 95 percent of the time during her first term.

Often eschewing the usual power suits in favor of earth-tone clothes and funky jewelry, DeLauro is rarely mistaken for a conformist. And in the issues she has chosen to support, she is hard to pigeonhole. Although associated with many liberal causes since the 1960s, she refers to herself as a "progressive moderate." If the phrase strikes some as an oxymoron, it nonetheless describes her eclectic ideology.

She supports the death penalty for more than 50 federal crimes and opposes tax hikes. She was the only Democrat on Public Works to vote against the 5-cent-a-gallon gas tax increase in the 102nd Congress. These positions have helped her survive in her district, which is more centrist than liberal.

Having won her first term by beating Thomas Scott, the chief opponent of independent Gov. Lowell P. Weicker Jr.'s state income tax, she quickly sought to establish herself in the House as a friend of the middle class. She sponsored two middle-class tax relief bills in the 102nd and 103rd Congresses. However, she overcame her dislike of middle-class taxes to support Clinton's budget plan, a testament of her loyalty to the party and to the administration.

After working for years to restrict both military intervention and the purchase of weapons systems, DeLauro bowed to political expediency in advocating the *Seawolf*-class nuclear submarine. Although she supports cuts in most big-ticket defense programs, including the B-2 bomber and the Strategic Defense Initiative, she and the rest of the Connecticut delegation fought for the *Seawolf* when the Bush administration proposed killing it in early 1992. Electric Boat, the parent of the *Seawolf*, employs more than 13,000 workers in the district next to hers.

More in keeping with her political history — she voted against authorizing the use of force in the Persian Gulf — DeLauro crafted provisions in a defense diversification bill aimed at helping defense-related businesses move into commercial markets. Even as the Persian Gulf

Connecticut 3

South — New Haven

To the outside world, New Haven is synonymous with Yale University. The prestigious Ivy League school with its famous theater, renowned academics and rich history is a symbol of top-drawer higher education. But while Yale has been a fixture in New Haven since the 18th century, the prosperous academic community has little in common with the poorer white ethnics and minorities who dominate the city.

New Haven is a busy port along Long Island Sound with a substantial population of blue-collar workers; one-third of its 130,000 residents are black. But sizable swaths of the community are economically impoverished; one-fifth of New Haven's people have incomes below the poverty level. Most of the national headlines the city has garnered in recent years have been about racial tensions, violent crime and the infant mortality rate, which is the highest among small American cities.

There has long been tension between the upscale and intellectual Yalies and the townfolk around them. Many residents believe that their tax burden is unduly heavy because the university — the city's largest landowner — is not required to pay taxes on property it uses for academic purposes. Yale often is pilloried as an enclave for the elite that cares little about the city as a whole.

The university has tried to mend fences, promising $50 million for city projects over a 10-year period. School officials are widely credited with helping persuade Macy's department store not to abandon downtown New Haven. The store is symbolically important; in the 1950s, it was a key component in helping New Haven earn a reputation as a national leader in urban renewal. Yale also continues to be the largest employer in the city, with 8,800 workers.

One thing the Yalies and the townies agree on: They like Democrats. In 1992, Democrats on every level amassed huge margins in New Haven.

Districtwide, defense manufacturers and hundreds of related subcontractors employ the most people, particularly in suburbs such as West Haven, Hamden and Wallingford. They seem likely to face continued uncertainty in the years ahead as military budgets are trimmed.

Italian-Americans dominated House elections in the 3rd from 1952 through 1980, and they re-emerged as a force in 1990 with the election of Rep. DeLauro, daughter of an Italian immigrant. The 3rd went Republican in 1980 but reverted to the Democrats two years later. The Democratic bent of New Haven's blacks and its white ethnics makes the 3rd tough turf for the GOP in House elections; DeLauro won two-thirds of the vote in 1992.

Still, migration from the city to the suburbs has diminished the city's clout in the 3rd and made it possible for the GOP to carry the district in contests for higher office. The 3rd supported Hubert H. Humphrey for president in 1968 but then did not back another Democrat for the White House until 1992, when Bill Clinton won the district.

1990 Population: 547,765. White 460,918 (84%), Black 65,293 (12%), Other 21,554 (4%). Hispanic origin 27,023 (5%). 18 and over 426,557 (78%), 62 and over 95,287 (17%). Median age: 35.

crisis got under way, DeLauro campaigned for cutting defense costs and channeling that money toward retraining defense workers and domestic programs.

DeLauro studied international politics as a graduate student and handled foreign policy issues for Dodd, but she focused on domestic legislation during the 102nd Congress. Perhaps by coincidence, her efforts there presaged some of the issues Clinton would highlight in his 1992 campaign: health-care reform, family and medical leave, an anti-recession jobs package, and the creation of a jobs corps, among others. Close ties with the Clinton administration could bode well for legislative success in the 103rd.

In her first term, DeLauro also started to etch a reputation as a leader on women's issues. Her style has been relatively quiet: DeLauro was not among the women who stormed the Senate during the hearings to review sexual harassment charges by law professor Anita F. Hill against Supreme Court nominee Clarence Thomas. But she has invested herself in women's health research and in helping victims of the pregnancy drug DES. A survivor of ovarian cancer, she fought to ensure that Taxol, a drug synthesized from the Pacific yew tree and used to treat ovarian cancer, remains available. The yew grows in the same old-growth forests prized by both loggers and wildlife enthusiasts.

At Home: After a surprisingly close election in 1990, DeLauro expected to face anti-tax activist Scott again in 1992. So while working to amass a record on taxes and jobs, she also raised an impressive amount of money for the rematch.

When the showdown arrived, political circumstances nationally and locally had shifted in her favor. Anti-tax fervor in Connecticut also had subsided somewhat, depriving Scott of his best issue (he also opposes gun control and abortion rights). DeLauro was not only able to put away Scott for a second time, she also easily outran Clinton in every corner of the 3rd.

In both races Scott, a former state senator, portrayed DeLauro as a far-left radical out of synch with the working-class ethnic voters of the 3rd. He pulled close to DeLauro in their first race by highlighting her image as a Washington insider.

Both contests produced plenty of sparks. A radio announcer was forced to pull the plug on the two candidates during one particularly heated debate in their first go-around.

In 1992, Scott labeled DeLauro a hypocrite for running ads with her First Communion photograph while taking an abortion rights position. The attack had little impact, since DeLauro stopped running the spot in 1990. Relying heavily on donations from political action committees (PACS), DeLauro overwhelmed Scott with an expensive advertising blitz. This time she won every town in her district.

Committee

Appropriations (32nd of 37 Democrats)
Agriculture, Rural Development, FDA & Related Agencies; Labor, Health & Human Services, Education & Related Agencies

Elections

1992 General		
Rosa DeLauro (D, ACP)	162,568	(66%)
Tom Scott (R)	84,952	(34%)
1990 General		
Rosa DeLauro (D)	90,772	(52%)
Thomas Scott (R)	83,440	(48%)

District Vote for President

1992

D	121,163 (45%)
R	96,085 (35%)
I	54,147 (20%)

Campaign Finance

	Receipts	Receipts from PACs		Expend-itures
1992				
DeLauro (D)	$1,026,034	$494,781	(48%)	$1,022,131
Scott (R)	$207,430	$48,088	(23%)	$219,786
1990				
DeLauro (D)	$973,625	$401,805	(41%)	$957,982
Scott (R)	$311,727	$64,937	(21%)	$304,258

Key Votes

1993	
Require parental notification of minors' abortions	N
Require unpaid family and medical leave	Y
Approve national "motor voter" registration bill	Y
Approve budget increasing taxes and reducing deficit	Y
Approve economic stimulus plan	Y
1992	
Approve balanced-budget constitutional amendment	N
Close down space station program	N
Approve U.S. aid for former Soviet Union	N
Allow shifting funds from defense to domestic programs	Y
1991	
Extend unemployment benefits using deficit financing	Y
Approve waiting period for handgun purchases	Y
Authorize use of force in Persian Gulf	N

Voting Studies

	Presidential Support		Party Unity		Conservative Coalition	
Year	S	O	S	O	S	O
1992	17	82	94	6	25	73
1991	26	72	95	5	19	78

Interest Group Ratings

Year	ADA	AFL-CIO	CCUS	ACU
1992	90	92	13	4
1991	95	92	20	0

4 Christopher Shays (R)

Of Stamford — Elected 1987; 3rd Full Term

Born: Oct. 18, 1945, Stamford, Conn.
Education: Principia College, B.A. 1968; New York U., M.B.A. 1974, M.P.A. 1978.
Occupation: Real estate broker; public official.
Family: Wife, Betsi de Raismes; one child.
Religion: Christian Scientist.
Political Career: Conn. House, 1975-87; GOP candidate for mayor of Stamford, 1983.
Capitol Office: 1034 Longworth Bldg. 20515; 225-5541.

In Washington: Unlike most of his GOP colleagues, Shays has a primarily urban constituency, and that helps make him one of the House's rarest breeds — a liberal Republican. In floor votes during 1992, Shays voted 60 percent of the time against the positions supported by President George Bush — the highest opposition score of any Republican.

As founder and co-chair of the Congressional Urban Caucus, Shays has joined with Congressional Black Caucus Chairman Kweisi Mfume, D-Md., to push what they call an "Urban Marshall Plan" aimed at rebuilding American cities.

The initiative is an effort to bring businesses back to urban areas and create jobs. It is a package of bills promoting enterprise zones, welfare reform, affordable housing, education improvements and minority small-business development.

Mfume and Shays would pay for their plan by making cuts in military spending and agricultural subsidies, eliminating big-ticket projects such as the superconducting super collider and possibly increasing the gasoline tax. Shays says that federal investment in the Urban Marshall Plan would more than pay for itself, cutting the deficit by one-third.

In proposing funding sources for the plan and emphasizing the claim that it would pay its own way, Shays reveals an important facet of his own self-image: He feels that on matters of federal spending, he is a more consistent fiscal conservative than many in his party, including some hard-right Republicans who grumble that he is not a loyal soldier. These so-called conservatives, says Shays, continue to support high spending on the military and other federal activities they endorse but offer no realistic proposals for funding them without running up the deficit. Shays was successful enough at portraying himself as fiscally prudent to win a seat on the Budget Committee at the start of the 102nd Congress.

During the 102nd, Shays was at times critical of Democrats on spending matters, and at other times cooperative with them. He urged Bush to veto every Democratic-drafted appropriations bill that did not adhere to a spending freeze. But he also teamed up with Barney Frank, D-Mass., to pass an amendment to cut $3.5 billion from the defense authorization bill. The measure, approved 220-185, cut funds earmarked to station U.S. forces in Europe, Japan and South Korea.

But Shays' cooperation with Democrats has its bounds. When President Clinton put forward his budget and economic stimulus plans in early 1993, Shays voted against them both.

And in another area of controversy during the 102nd, Shays also was singing from the GOP hymnal. As the House bank scandal unfolded, Shays strongly urged the Democratic leadership to order a full disclosure of bank records. Anything less, he argued, would be a cover-up reminiscent of Watergate.

"The bottom line is, Congress isn't any more above the law than Nixon was," Shays said. The House voted 347-64 to approve a Republican-sponsored resolution to turn over the bank records to the Justice Department.

Still, Shays' independent streak probably will continue to unsettle GOP leaders from time to time, as it did in the 101st Congress. As a member of the Government Operations subcommittee investigating Reagan-era misdeeds at the Department of Housing and Urban Development, Shays was among the first Republicans to suggest that the scandal might warrant a special prosecutor. The hearings were led by Democrat Tom Lantos of California, and while Shays was less pointed and dramatic than Lantos in his questioning, he nevertheless was diligent and determined — too diligent, some GOP partisans thought — in grilling HUD officials.

Also, Shays' stance on social issues — such as support for abortion rights and for mandatory parental leave — puts him at odds with current GOP orthodoxy.

At Home: In the 1987 special election held after veteran GOP Rep. Stewart B. McKinney died, Shays' personable style helped him overcome obstacles on his left and right. Campaign-

Connecticut 4

Southwest — Stamford; Bridgeport

On a recent trip home to the 4th, Rep. Shays started the day in Bridgeport. He met a prostitute with AIDS, her teeth falling out, her body badly deformed. The woman's troubles seem to parallel the hard times of Shay's native city, a decaying former whaling community that earned notoriety in 1991 when then-Mayor Mary Moran tried to have the city declared bankrupt.

Then Shays climbed in his car and drove 32 miles to attend a polo-match fundraiser in Greenwich, where he rubbed elbows with some of the wealthiest people in America.

The contrast highlights the split personality of the 4th. The district includes the affluent white-collar communities of Connecticut's "Gold Coast," along Long Island Sound, but it also has Bridgeport, a city plagued by poverty, where one neighborhood was dubbed Mount Trashmore because of its three-story garbage pile. (The eyesore was finally removed in late 1992 after dominating the area for two decades).

Taking in Bridgeport as well as better-off Stamford and Norwalk, the 4th has the largest urban population of any Connecticut district. Bridgeport produced one-quarter of all munitions used by the Allied forces in World War II; its strategic importance made it one of two Connecticut cities to be protected by Nike missile bases in the 1950s and early 1960s.

But as the missiles shielded Bridgeport from external enemies, the city deteriorated from within; population shrank in the 1970s and remained static in the 1980s. The 142,000 people who live in Bridgeport now are among the neediest in Connecticut; 15 percent of the city's residents fall below the poverty line.

The city's economy could get a boost with the resuscitation of the University of Bridgeport. Its enrollment dropped from about 8,000 to 2,000 in the 1980s, but then the institution was bought by the Unification Church, headed by the Rev. Sun Myung Moon. While grateful for the bailout, some locals are wary of what the church has in mind for its new acquisition.

Voting and unemployment data reflect the contrasts in the 4th. Bridgeport voted overwhelmingly for Democrat Bill Clinton in the 1992 presidential contest, although George Bush carried most of the other communities in the 10th. Jobless rates in Stamford and Norwalk have frequently fallen below the state average, while Bridgeport's unemployment (near double digits through much of 1992) has routinely led Connecticut.

The dominant political force in the district are the Republican-minded upper-crust towns along the coast, which are a short drive or train-ride from New York City. Most of the towns have GOP mayors, and together they host dozens of corporate headquarters and their officers. Stamford has the third-largest concentration of corporate headquarters in the nation, including well-known names such as Pitney Bowes, GTE, Champion International and Xerox.

1990 Population: 547,765. White 438,475 (80%), Black 71,944 (13%), Other 37,346 (7%). Hispanic origin 61,014 (11%). 18 and over 426,140 (78%), 62 and over 92,570 (17%). Median age: 35.

ing from the center, Shays was positioned for success in the 4th, long a bastion of moderate Republicanism. He won the special election with a solid 57 percent of the vote and has not been seriously challenged since. Shays' ability to move easily between the worlds of extreme wealth and poverty present in the 4th has held him in good stead.

Shays stepped up to Congress from the state Legislature, where he had a reputation as a stubbornly principled moderate-to-liberal. In 1985, after criticizing what he said were lax ethical standards in Connecticut's judicial system, Shays attempted to make a courtroom statement criticizing a judge for reducing charges against a lawyer who was accused of tampering with a will. Shays was slapped with a contempt citation and a short jail sentence, but he received plenty of favorable publicity.

Though that episode helped Shays expand his cadre of loyalists, it made some local Republicans wary. At the GOP nominating convention for the House special election, Shays initially was denied a line on the ballot and qualified for the primary only after last-minute maneuvering. Nonetheless, with an extensive grass-roots network and tireless campaigning, Shays won nomination with a 38 percent plurality.

In the general election, Shays proved to be a more personally appealing candidate than Democrat Christine M. Niedermeier, who was widely known because she had run a strong 1986 campaign against McKinney. Seeking out voters at supermarkets, train stations and in movie theater queues, Shays prevailed by a comfortable margin.

Committees

Budget (4th of 17 Republicans)

Government Operations (5th of 16 Republicans)
Commerce, Consumer & Monetary Affairs; Employment, Housing & Aviation

Elections

1992 General		
Christopher Shays (R)	147,816	(67%)
Dave Schropfer (D)	58,666	(27%)
Al Smith (ACP)	11,679	(5%)
1990 General		
Christopher Shays (R)	105,682	(77%)
Al Smith (D)	32,352	(23%)

Previous Winning Percentages: **1988** (72%) **1987** * (57%)

** Special election.*

District Vote for President

1992

D 109,122 (42%)
R 110,072 (42%)
I 40,802 (16%)

Campaign Finance

	Receipts	Receipts from PACs	Expend-itures
1992			
Shays (R)	$402,100	$56,800 (14%)	$383,207
Schropfer (D)	$29,443	0	$29,162
Smith (ACP)	$24,972	0	$24,518
1990			
Shays (R)	$447,077	$58,000 (13%)	$395,892
Smith (D)	$90,780	$1,000 (1%)	$90,634

Key Votes

1993	
Require parental notification of minors' abortions	N
Require unpaid family and medical leave	Y
Approve national "motor voter" registration bill	Y
Approve budget increasing taxes and reducing deficit	N
Approve economic stimulus plan	N
1992	
Approve balanced-budget constitutional amendment	Y
Close down space station program	Y
Approve U.S. aid for former Soviet Union	Y
Allow shifting funds from defense to domestic programs	N
1991	
Extend unemployment benefits using deficit financing	N
Approve waiting period for handgun purchases	Y
Authorize use of force in Persian Gulf	Y

Voting Studies

	Presidential Support		Party Unity		Conservative Coalition	
Year	S	O	S	O	S	O
1992	40	60	62	38	42	58
1991	58	42	65	35	57	43
1990	34	66	60	40	41	59
1989	36	64	54	46	46	54
1988	42	58	59	41	61	39
1987	32 †	68 †	53 †	47 †	25 †	75 †

† Not eligible for all recorded votes.

Interest Group Ratings

Year	ADA	AFL-CIO	CCUS	ACU
1992	65	67	38	40
1991	60	42	70	50
1990	72	50	36	25
1989	85	67	70	29
1988	90	64	57	24
1987	89	78	40	67

5 Gary A. Franks (R)

Of Waterbury — Elected 1990; 2nd Term

Born: Feb. 9, 1953, Waterbury, Conn.
Education: Yale U., B.A. 1975.
Occupation: Real estate investor.
Family: Wife, Donna Williams; one child, one stepchild.
Religion: Baptist.
Political Career: Candidate for Conn. comptroller, 1986; Waterbury Board of Aldermen, 1986-90.
Capitol Office: 435 Cannon Bldg. 20515; 225-3822.

In Washington: Despite a limited legislative record in his first term, Franks received a coveted spot on the powerful Energy and Commerce Committee at the beginning of his second. His success further evinced the GOP's determination to showcase its first and only black in the House since 1935.

With appearances on national television news shows, a prime-time speaking slot at the Republican convention introducing House Minority Leader Robert H. Michel of Illinois, visits to the White House, and 1992 campaign visits from the president, vice president and Cabinet members, Franks was one of the most visible members of the freshman class.

Franks' ideological stands did not disappoint, as he quickly established himself as the lone conservative in the Congressional Black Caucus (CBC). He was the only member of the CBC to vote for the use of force in the Persian Gulf and the only member to announce his support for Clarence Thomas' nomination to the Supreme Court. In his brief introduction of Michel, Franks highlighted traditional Republican themes of individualism and self-help, while also emphasizing his disadvantaged background.

Franks' support of Thomas was touted by the GOP. When Republican Dick Armey of Texas decided to send a letter to Senate Judiciary Committee Chairman Joseph R. Biden Jr. of Delaware espousing the nomination, he enlisted Franks as his first cosigner.

At the beginning of the 103rd Congress, Franks was chosen to serve as chairman of the House GOP task force on welfare reform.

Though few on the Democratic side of the aisle agree with Franks' conservative agenda, Democrat Edolphus Towns of New York, a former chairman of the CBC, at least appreciates the coherence of Franks' views. "The thing I respect about him is at least his opinions are something that are thought out," Towns told The Washington Times.

Yet high visibility and a coherent conservative agenda did not translate into Franks' earning a reputation as a nuts-and-bolts legislator during his first term. And his relationship with the media in Connecticut contrasted sharply with the basically favorable publicity he received nationwide. For every national television appearance, there seemed to be a local story casting Franks in a less than favorable light.

In early 1992, The Hartford Courant reported that Franks had been sued by a credit card company over a delinquent bill and by a Naugatuck savings and loan that said he had defaulted on a $471,600 loan. Both suits were withdrawn after a repayment plan was agreed upon. The paper also reported that Franks' financial disclosure form revealed unsecured loans totaling more than $70,000.

Also widely reported was the rapid turnover of Franks' staff over a three-month period beginning in late 1991. Franks said that his turnover was no worse than that of any other New England office and that he was being unfairly singled out for criticism.

In addition, Franks' constituent service record drew criticism. Colt company executives discovered in the middle of a news conference called to announce the securing of a major M-16 contract that they had lost the contract. Some Colt officials contended that Franks had led them to believe they would win the contract and that it was because of Franks' statements that they had called the news conference. Franks said the executives had misunderstood him and added that he helped them to secure a smaller contract.

The coup de grâce to Franks' local media image was in an August 1992 story. It was reported that Franks switched his seating placard with that of the mayor of Ansonia so that Franks could sit next to President Bush at a reception in Connecticut. Franks countered that the White House and the Secret Service instructed him to sit next to Bush.

As a result of his troubles, Franks faced an unexpectedly challenging re-election contest. The Courant endorsed Franks' Democratic opponent, saying Franks' constituent service record "left something to be desired." Only the presence of a third candidate, who split the

Connecticut 5

West — Waterbury; Danbury

Three of Connecticut's 10 largest cities are in the 5th — Waterbury, Danbury and Meriden — but any Democratic tendencies in those urban areas are counterbalanced by two dozen smaller towns where Republican candidates usually run well among middle-class voters, and by a number of Fortune 500 companies whose headquarters employ a substantial white-collar work force.

Registered Democrats outnumber Republicans almost 3-to-2 in the 5th. But many of the nominal Democrats — especially those in the working-class Naugatuck Valley — feel the national party has become too liberal. That helps explain why a Democratic presidential candidate has not carried the 5th since 1968.

In Connecticut's heated three-way 1990 gubernatorial election, Waterbury and Danbury voted for Republican John G. Rowland (who had represented the 5th since 1985); Meriden split between Rowland and Lowell P. Weicker Jr., who won election as the state's first independent governor.

In Waterbury, the 5th's largest city with 109,000 people, Democrats have had some trouble retaining a dominant position even in local politics. Waterbury had a Republican mayor from 1985 to 1991. Rowland, a Waterbury native, ran well in the city in his three House campaigns, and Rep. Franks, also born in Waterbury, has made enough of a dent in Waterbury's usual Democratic margin to win two House elections. In both of those contests Franks also benefited from campaign visits by George Bush and other high-level Republicans, who were eager to help one of their party's few high-level black politicians. (Blacks make up only 5 percent of the district's population.)

Franks gets his strongest electoral support from a number of smaller, wealthier towns in the district, places filled with white-collar business people who commute to corporate jobs in Danbury and other venues closer to New York City.

Danbury, in Fairfield County, is home to some of the 5th's most affluent residents. The median family income in Danbury tops $51,000, and its public school system is among the nation's finest. Located in the media and cultural orbit of New York, Danbury boasts several corporate headquarters, including Union Carbide and Hughes Optical, the district's two largest employers. The city also draws visitors to the Danbury Fair Mall, New England's largest shopping center.

But the wealth has not spread to the district's two other cities.

Downtown Waterbury was sprucing up in the mid-1980s, but when New England fell into recession in the late 1980s, renewal stalled as unemployment soared. Waterbury once was hailed as the "brass capital of the world" and known for the watches it made. But those industries are no more, and the city is searching for ways to fill the void. Two hospitals are the city's major employers. Just to the east is Meriden. Once the region's silversmithing capital, Meriden remains a mostly blue-collar community, with many residents working for defense contractors located outside the district.

1990 Population: 547,764. White 499,448 (91%), Black 26,455 (5%), Other 21,861 (4%). Hispanic origin 34,132 (6%). 18 and over 416,643 (76%), 62 and over 84,175 (15%). Median age: 34.

anti-Franks vote, allowed him to survive.

Sobered by his unimpressive showing in 1992, Franks now shows some signs of pulling back from the national part that the GOP has scripted for him in favor of a more district-focused approach to his job.

In early 1992, Franks hired his close friend and district director, who had no previous Capitol Hill experience, to run his Washington and district offices. He announced that the move represented a shift to a more "district driven" office. And he speaks of his new Energy and Commerce slot almost entirely in terms of what it will allow him to do for his district.

At Home: Considering his mixed record in Washington and proclivity for gaining bad publicity at home, Franks is lucky to be serving a second term. Under normal circumstances his paltry 1992 re-election tally of 44 percent would not have been enough to win. But thanks to a bitter Democratic primary that spawned the third-party candidacy of Lynn H. Taborsak, Franks survived.

Still, his long-term political future remains uncertain at best.

Franks is a living realization of the political ideals of hard work and self-reliance. His father came north from North Carolina to work in the Waterbury brass mills, and his mother worked as a dietary aide at one of the city hospitals.

Though active in Republican politics since the early 1980s, he did not have a particularly high political profile statewide when he ran for the seat being vacated by John G. Rowland. He had served as a Waterbury alderman from 1986 to 1990 and had made an unsuccessful run for state comptroller.

During the campaign, Democrat Toby Moffett faulted Franks for missing meetings and dubbed him "Phantom Franks." Waterbury politicians sprang to Franks' defense, but his low-key style made it easy to wonder about his agenda.

In fact, Franks probably owes his first victory to his likability. One of five candidates competing at the July GOP district convention, Franks culled votes as the acceptable second choice of nearly all his rivals' partisans.

In his fall race, however, Franks did expend some of his "nice guy" capital to scuff up his opponent. He attacked Moffett (who had represented the 6th District and lived in the 3rd before moving to the 5th) as a liberal carpetbagger.

With his narrow margin in 1990, Franks seemed an easy target two years later. Not only did two Democrats enter the fray, but several fringe candidates challenged him.

Taborsak, a Democratic state representative and plumber, won the most attention in the early going. Her earthy language garnered headlines, and her vast connections produced donations from women's and labor organizations. But the liberal Taborsak seemed too extreme for many in the working-class 5th, and a mild-mannered probate judge named James J. Lawlor won the primary.

Taborsak stayed in the fall race, with the backing of Gov. Lowell P. Weicker Jr.'s A Connecticut Party. But her role became that of spoiler, and few doubt that her 22 percent could have put Lawlor over the top.

Franks received more than his share of negative coverage during the campaign. National and hometown media chronicled the luncheon seating swap, his financial and staffing problems and his last-minute cancellation of a meeting with Connecticut delegates to the Republican National Convention in Houston.

With the Democrats in control of the White House, Franks enters the next election cycle more alone than ever. Unlike 1990 and 1992, there will be no president or Cabinet members to stump with him.

Committee

Energy & Commerce (15th of 17 Republicans)
Energy & Power; Health & the Environment

Elections

1992 General		
Gary A. Franks (R)	104,891	(44%)
James J. Lawlor (D)	74,791	(31%)
Lynn H. Taborsak (ACP)	54,022	(22%)
Rosita Rodriguez (CC)	5,090	(2%)
1990 General		
Gary A. Franks (R)	93,912	(52%)
Toby Moffett (D)	85,803	(47%)
William G. Hare (Liberty)	1,888	(1%)

District Vote for President

1992

D 93,966 (35%)
R 111,327 (42%)
I 60,891 (23%)

Campaign Finance

	Receipts	Receipts from PACs		Expend-itures
1992				
Franks (R)	$644,632	$293,259	(45%)	$631,851
Lawlor (D)	$352,779	$61,200	(17%)	$345,164
Taborsak (ACP)	$497,680	$128,767	(26%)	$493,563
1990				
Franks (R)	$587,045	$177,927	(30%)	$581,625
Moffett (D)	$880,726	$411,188	(47%)	$877,116

Key Votes

1993	
Require parental notification of minors' abortions	Y
Require unpaid family and medical leave	N
Approve national "motor voter" registration bill	N
Approve budget increasing taxes and reducing deficit	N
Approve economic stimulus plan	N
1992	
Approve balanced-budget constitutional amendment	Y
Close down space station program	N
Approve U.S. aid for former Soviet Union	Y
Allow shifting funds from defense to domestic programs	N
1991	
Extend unemployment benefits using deficit financing	Y
Approve waiting period for handgun purchases	N
Authorize use of force in Persian Gulf	Y

Voting Studies

	Presidential Support		Party Unity		Conservative Coalition	
Year	S	O	S	O	S	O
1992	73	25	84	14	83	15
1991	74	24	87	12	97	3

Interest Group Ratings

Year	ADA	AFL-CIO	CCUS	ACU
1992	20	25	88	88
1991	15	25	100	85

6 Nancy L. Johnson (R)

Of New Britain — Elected 1982; 6th Term

Born: Jan. 5, 1935, Chicago, Ill.
Education: Radcliffe College, B.A. 1957; U. of London, 1957-58.
Occupation: Civic leader.
Family: Husband, Theodore Johnson; three children.
Religion: Unitarian.
Political Career: GOP candidate for New Britain Common Council, 1975; Conn. Senate, 1977-83.
Capitol Office: 343 Cannon Bldg. 20515; 225-4476.

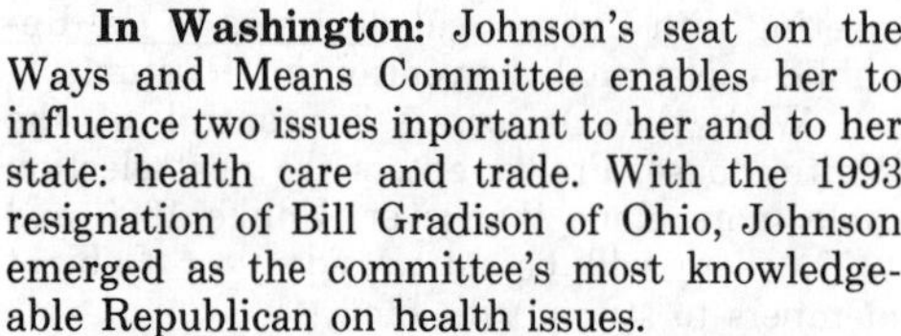

In Washington: Johnson's seat on the Ways and Means Committee enables her to influence two issues inportant to her and to her state: health care and trade. With the 1993 resignation of Bill Gradison of Ohio, Johnson emerged as the committee's most knowledgeable Republican on health issues.

But if the new Congress elevated Johnson's committee standing, it also brought frustration to her desire for a larger role in her party. Denied the rung she sought on the GOP House leadership ladder, she may now view a gubernatorial campaign in 1994 as a more felicitous career move than the continued accumulation of seniority on Ways and Means.

A decided moderate on social issues, she has publicly challenged the party's position on abortion at two successive national conventions. She also has voted with liberals on such social questions as mandated family leave and a waiting period for handgun purchases. On fiscal matters, she generally comes down against spending. In early 1993, despite Connecticut's high unemployment rate, Johnson joined with other Ways and Means Republicans in strenuous opposition to extending unemployment benefits via additional deficit spending by the federal treasury. In 1991 and 1992, she supported initiatives to terminate construction of the superconducting super collider. On the other hand, in both years she supported spending on the space-based anti-missile system (the Strategic Defense Initiative).

A degree of independence has always characterized Johnson's voting, and she has long preached the need for diversity in the party. She votes with her GOP colleagues only a little more than half the time on controversial issues. Yet Johnson can also be angrily partisan. She helped conservative firebrand Newt Gingrich of Georgia become House GOP whip in 1989, and on the first day of the 1991 session she spoke so passionately against a perceived Democratic subterfuge on the budget that she ignored the Speaker's gavel and was threatened with removal by the House sergeant at arms.

Nonetheless, her pleas for accommodation in recent years have probably cost her whatever chance she had to join the leadership. Prior to the start of the 103rd Congress, Johnson was soundly defeated when she challenged conservative Bill McCollum of Florida for the post of vice chair of the Republican Conference.

Johnson had endured frustrations in the committee assignment process during her first several years in Congress, losing bids to get on Armed Services, Energy and Commerce, and Ways and Means. She took a halfway step by winning a seat on Budget in the 100th Congress, but it was not until the 101st Congress that she won her Ways and Means assignment and established herself in the big leagues. In 1991, she was also appointed to the ethics committee, an assignment often coupled with a seat on an elite committee.

In her first two years on Ways and Means, she encountered predictable problems influencing its direction as the most junior member of the minority party. But by picking her spots on issues such as trade, Medicare, health and child care, she has made her voice heard.

In Connecticut, trade has become an increasingly sensitive issue as heavy industries have been battered by cheaper goods produced abroad. Johnson has been outspoken on a number of trade initiatives, and some of her concerns had been incorporated into trade legislation even before she joined the committee. Johnson is co-chairman of the Congressional Bearing Caucus, which looks out for the interests of the machine-tool, ball-bearing and roller-bearing industry, an important employer in Connecticut. One of her efforts has been to speed governmental review of petitions brought by domestic industries seeking relief from imports on national security grounds. The ball-bearing and roller-bearing industry has sought such protections in recent years. She has also been instrumental in winning voluntary limits on imported machine tools and a requirement that the Department of Defense buy American-made bearings.

But Johnson is wary of some measures aimed at trade competitors. She was opposed to the Gephardt "fair trade" amendment that was

Connecticut 6

Northwest — New Britain

The 6th blends the pastoral and peaceful — villages and small towns, dairy farms and nurseries — with more modern influences: hundreds of defense subcontractors. The Litchfield Hills, at the foot of the Berkshires, have attracted escapees from New York, such as actresses Jane Curtin and Susan St. James.

But for many other residents of the 6th, downsizing in the defense industry may mean hard times ahead.

United Technologies Corp. plans to reduce its Connecticut work force by more than 6,000 by 1995, and thousands of those layoffs will occur at divisions spread throughout the 6th, including Hamilton Standard in Windsor Locks, Pratt & Whitney in Southington, and Otis elevators and Carrier air conditioning, both in Farmington. When Pratt & Whitney announced it was scaling back, the Shop Rite grocery store in Southington said it too would shut down. Similar stories of retrenchment are often heard at the 300 defense subcontractors in the 6th.

Nowhere are economic problems more evident than in New Britain, the largest city in the 6th and one hit particularly hard by industrial decline. Since the Fafnir ball-bearing plant closed in the late 1980s, the city of 72,500 people has seen a number of its businesses fold or move.

Take a walk down one of New Britain's two main thoroughfares, Arch or Broad streets, and the struggle is obvious. The sidewalks and roads are crumbling; much of the housing is archaic. A city once filled with Polish immigrants is now a melting pot of blacks, Asians, Hispanics, Italians and Poles straining to get along.

The city's largest employer, tool manufacturer Stanley Works, has enabled New Britain to retain its longtime moniker "Hardware City."

Smaller communities in the district are not immune from bigger-city problems. Many retail stores have abandoned Main Street locales in favor of shopping malls. A 4.5 percent state income tax imposed in 1991 is putting an extra pinch on middle-income families struggling to get through recessionary times.

In a state where most people have been accustomed to comfortable lifestyles, unemployment is bringing difficulties normally associated with inner cities, such as drug abuse and homelessness. Officials are wrestling with questions about where to build homeless shelters, how to set up community health clinics and finding money for drug treatment centers.

Residents of the 6th supported Republican presidential candidates in the good-times 1980s, but the dramatically different economic climate of 1992 helped Bill Clinton score a comfortable victory in the district.

The House seat switched from Democratic to Republican control with Johnson's narrow open-seat victory in 1982. Since then, her moderate-to-liberal House voting record has well satisfied the voters; even in 1992, Johnson won overwhelmingly.

1990 Population: 547,765. White 520,212 (95%), Black 12,544 (2%), Other 15,009 (3%). Hispanic origin 19,374 (4%). 18 and over 423,834 (77%), 62 and over 91,007 (17%). Median age: 35.

intended to force reductions in certain foreign trade surpluses. She warned that such an amendment would spark a trade war and ultimately hurt Connecticut.

Johnson was also an outspoken supporter of the Caribbean Basin Initiative, a program of lower tariffs begun in 1983 and renewed in 1990 to benefit Latin American economies. And in 1991 she supported an extension of "fast track" negotiating authority for the president to pursue the North American Free Trade Agreement.

Johnson, the first Republican woman ever to serve on Ways and Means, has received some attention for her efforts to craft a comprehensive package on child care. Some business groups and The Washington Post praised her idea for giving families vouchers to pay for fees at licensed day-care centers and financing them by restricting child-care tax credits for higher-income families.

At Home: Johnson was a rarity in 1982, a Republican winning an open district dominated by blue-collar Democrats. But for her, that sort of victory was nothing new. In 1977 she had become the first Republican in 30 years to represent the industrial city of New Britain in the state Senate, and she was re-elected easily.

Johnson's casual style gives her an appeal across class and party lines. "She can belly up to the toughest bar in town and captivate the customers," a local political reporter once wrote, "just as effectively as she can balance the teacups with totally proper ladies at any church social." That is just the right combination for the 6th, which encompasses both the lunch-bucket bastion of New Britain and the Yankee towns of Litchfield County.

The wife of an obstetrician, Johnson was a longtime activist in New Britain community affairs. When the Republican town chairman asked her in 1976 to run for the state Senate, she agreed, and went on to defeat Democrat Paul S. Amenta by 150 votes.

When Democratic Rep. Toby Moffett announced at the end of 1981 that he was giving up the 6th to challenge incumbent Lowell P. Weicker Jr., R, for the Senate, Johnson moved eagerly to take his place. She quickly captured the backing of the party establishment and influential GOP donors, opening an early lead over her primary opponent, conservative Nicholas Schaus.

Johnson's Democratic opponent in the general election was a colleague from the state Senate, William E. Curry Jr. A liberal in the Moffett mold, Curry had won a hard-fought primary battle by putting together an impressive grass-roots organization with the support of labor, environmentalists and consumer groups. But he was badly underfunded.

Most of Curry's campaigning was in New Britain, which he did carry by 3,000 votes. But his concentrated effort cost him, shrinking the margin by which he carried the district's other Democratic communities and leaving him well short of the numbers Moffett had enjoyed.

In 1984, Johnson supported President Ronald Reagan's re-election but complained about the administration's defense spending levels, its cutbacks in education programs and its progress on arms control. The formula worked: Johnson got 64 percent of the vote.

In 1986, Johnson again faced Amenta, whom she had narrowly beaten in her first state Senate race. This time, Johnson won easily. Two years later, Democrats put scant effort into the 6th, and Johnson won big. Her 66 percent vote share that year has kept serious competitors away since.

Committees

Standards of Official Conduct (2nd of 7 Republicans)

Ways & Means (6th of 14 Republicans)
Health; Trade

Elections

1992 General		
Nancy L. Johnson (R)	166,967	(70%)
Eugene F. Slason (D)	60,373	(25%)
Daniel W. Plawecki (CC)	9,544	(4%)
1990 General		
Nancy L. Johnson (R)	141,105	(74%)
Paul Kulas (D)	48,628	(26%)

Previous Winning Percentages: **1988** (66%) **1986** (64%) **1984** (64%) **1982** (52%)

District Vote for President

1992

D 110,828 (40%)
R 99,633 (36%)
I 67,995 (24%)

Campaign Finance

	Receipts	Receipts from PACs		Expend-itures
1992				
Johnson (R)	$596,412	$339,312	(57%)	$570,046
Slason (D)	$39,706	$6,000	(15%)	$38,968
1990				
Johnson (R)	$517,724	$252,737	(49%)	$556,718
Kulas (D)	$22,475	$4,000	(18%)	$22,211

Key Votes

1993	
Require parental notification of minors' abortions	N
Require unpaid family and medical leave	Y
Approve national "motor voter" registration bill	?
Approve budget increasing taxes and reducing deficit	N
Approve economic stimulus plan	N
1992	
Approve balanced-budget constitutional amendment	Y
Close down space station program	N
Approve U.S. aid for former Soviet Union	Y
Allow shifting funds from defense to domestic programs	N
1991	
Extend unemployment benefits using deficit financing	Y
Approve waiting period for handgun purchases	Y
Authorize use of force in Persian Gulf	Y

Voting Studies

	Presidential Support		Party Unity		Conservative Coalition	
Year	S	O	S	O	S	O
1992	62	37	66	32	75	23
1991	63	35	53	46	68	32
1990	52	46	54	43	65	31
1989	60	38	43	53	71	27
1988	44	50	52	44	68	24
1987	47	52	53	42	65	28
1986	52	43	38	58	68	32
1985	50	50	45	51	67	33
1984	52	44	48	47	51	42
1983	51	46	43	49	54	46

Interest Group Ratings

Year	ADA	AFL-CIO	CCUS	ACU
1992	40	42	75	58
1991	35	42	70	55
1990	44	33	57	50
1989	30	33	80	50
1988	50	71	69	56
1987	48	50	73	35
1986	40	79	72	55
1985	40	47	64	48
1984	50	38	56	29
1983	45	44	50	26

Delaware

STATE DATA

Governor:
Thomas R. Carper (D)
First elected: 1992
Length of term: 4 years
Term expires: 1/97
Salary: $95,000
Term limit: 2 terms
Phone: (302) 739-4101
Born: Jan. 23, 1947; Beckley, W.Va.
Education: Ohio State U., B.A. 1968; U. of Delaware, M.B.A. 1975
Military Service: Navy, 1968-73; Naval Reserve 1973-92
Occupation: Public official
Family: Wife, Martha Ann Stacy; two children
Religion: Presbyterian
Political Career: Del. treasurer, 1977-83; U.S. House, 1983-93

Lt. Gov: Ruth Ann Minner (D)
First elected: 1992
Length of term: 4 years
Term expires: 1/97
Salary: $37,500
Phone number: (302) 577-3017

State election official: (302) 739-4277
Democratic headquarters: (302) 996-9458
Republican headquarters: (302) 651-0260

STATE LEGISLATURE

General Assembly. Meets January-June.

Senate: 21 members, 4-year terms
1992 breakdown: 15D, 6R; 18 men, 3 women; 20 whites, 1 black
Salary: $25,000
Phone: (302) 739-5086

House of Representatives: 41 members, 2-year terms
1992 breakdown: 23R, 18D; 35 men, 6 women; 39 whites, 2 blacks
Salary: $25,000
Phone: (302) 739-4087

URBAN STATISTICS

City	Pop.
Wilmington	71,529
Mayor Jim Sills, D	
Dover	27,630
Mayor Aaron Knopf, I	
Newark	26,371
Mayor Ron Gardner, I	
Brookside	15,307
County Executive Dennis E. Greenhouse	
Pike Creek	10,163
County Executive Dennis E. Greenhouse	

U.S. CONGRESS

Senate: 1 D, 1 R
House: 0 D, 1 R

TERM LIMITS

For Congress: No
For state offices: No

ELECTIONS

1992 Presidential Vote

Bill Clinton	43.8%
George Bush	35.6%
Ross Perot	20.6%

1988 Presidential Vote

George Bush	56%
Michael S. Dukakis	43%

1984 Presidential Vote

Ronald Reagan	60%
Walter F. Mondale	40%

POPULATION

1990 population		666,168
1980 population		594,338
Percent change		+12%
Rank among states:		46
White		80%
Black		17%
Hispanic		2%
Asian or Pacific islander		1%
Urban		73%
Rural		27%
Born in state		50%
Foreign-born		3%
Under age 18	163,341	25%
Ages 18-64	422,092	63%
65 and older	80,735	12%
Median age		32.9

MISCELLANEOUS

Capital: Dover
Number of counties: 3
Per capital income: $20,349 (1991)
Rank among states: 11
Total area: 2,045 sq. miles
Rank among states: 49

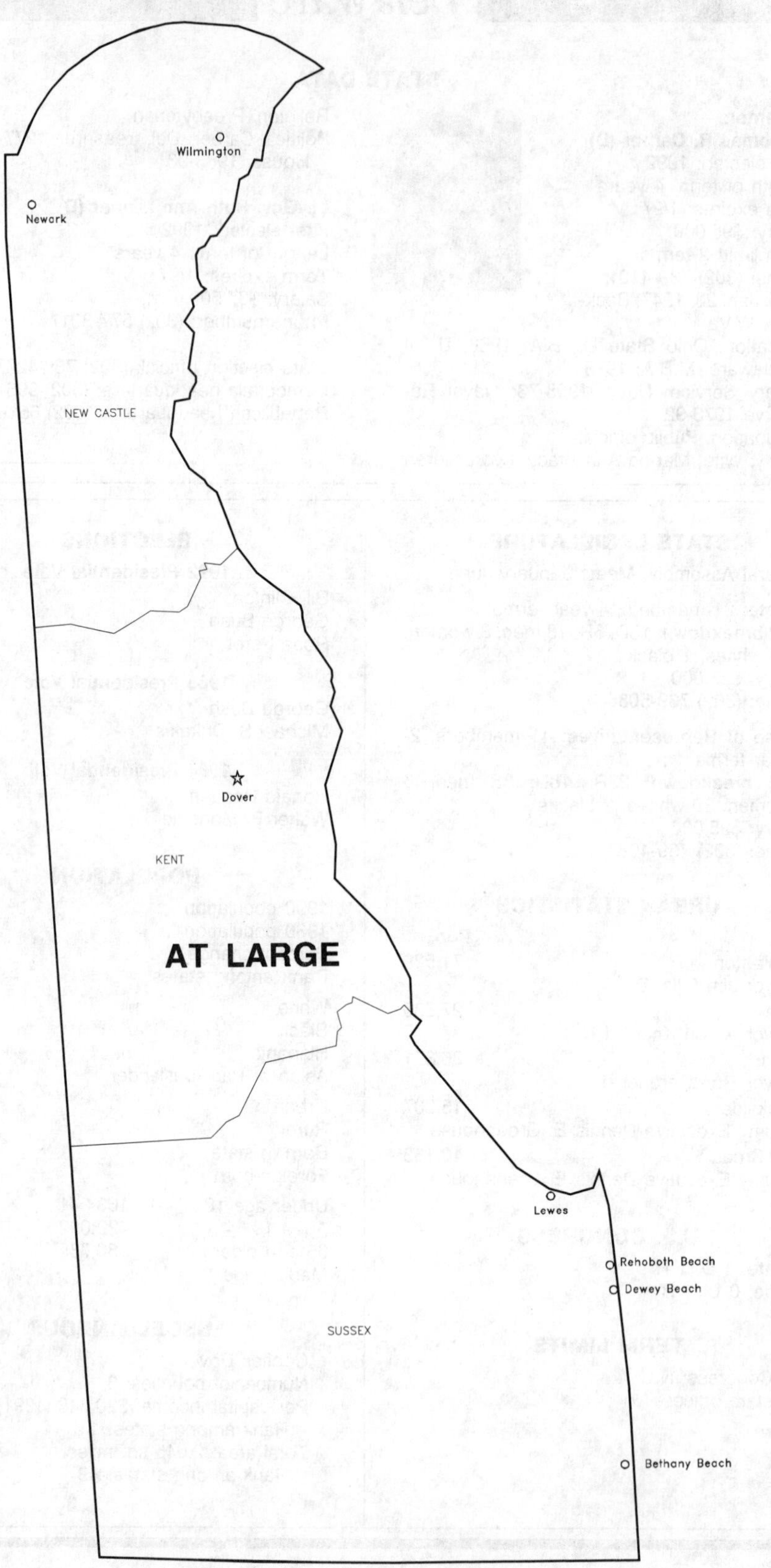
Wilmington
Newark
NEW CASTLE
Dover
KENT
AT LARGE
Lewes
Rehoboth Beach
Dewey Beach
SUSSEX
Bethany Beach

William V. Roth Jr. (R)

Of Wilmington — Elected 1970; 4th Term

Born: July 22, 1921, Great Falls, Mont.
Education: U. of Oregon, B.A. 1944; Harvard U., M.B.A. 1947, LL.B. 1949.
Military Service: Army, 1943-46.
Occupation: Lawyer.
Family: Wife, Jane Richards; two children.
Religion: Episcopalian.
Political Career: Republican nominee for lieutenant governor, 1960; U.S. House, 1967-71.
Capitol Office: 104 Hart Bldg. 20510; 224-2441.

In Washington: Roth is a legislator who likes grand ideas — massive tax cuts, huge new savings plans, sweeping revisions of government agencies. He has devoted most of his Senate career to drumming up support for such schemes, but after a quarter century in Congress, he sometimes has trouble making an impact.

In the late 1980s and early 1990s, Roth found himself in a defensive legislative posture — working to preserve the tax exemption for state and local bonds, to protect individual retirement accounts (IRAs), to guard Delaware's franchise as a haven for corporate charters as the Congress examines the corporate takeover game, and to prevent the repeal of the Hatch Act, which prohibits federal workers from engaging in political activities.

Ironically, however, with a Democrat as president, Roth may be in a better position to push a proposal he has promoted for over a decade.

Bill Clinton campaigned on the idea of changing the way government operates to make it more efficient and less costly, an idea Roth has long championed from his position as ranking Republican on the Governmental Affairs Committee. The day after Clinton's inaugural address, Roth introduced legislation aimed at reforming government by cutting government waste. Roth's proposals would consolidate agencies, reduce the size of the federal work force through attrition, maximize worker productivity and reward employee excellence.

Roth would be the first to admit that he spends a healthy block of his time looking out for Delaware. In the 102nd Congress, he worked to protect the ability of Delaware banks to sell insurance across state lines and continue to underwrite insurance.

In 1992, he held up unemployment legislation until he was satisfied that the funding formula applied equally to all states.

In 1991, a $5.4 billion bill to extend unemployment benefits was cleared and signed by President Bush. It was a victory for Democrats who portrayed Bush as more interested in foreign affairs than the economy. However, it was Roth who forced the Bush administration to provide even more generous payments to the unemployed in a second bill. An extra $400 million was included in a most-favored-nation trade status bill for Czechoslovakia and Hungary.

Roth planned to continue in the 103rd to push for legislation to restore and expand IRAs. The importance of personal savings has been a recurring theme throughout Roth's career.

When the Senate Finance Committee geared up in 1986 to produce a bill overhauling the federal tax code, Roth proposed a kind of value-added tax on gross business receipts to raise up to $115 billion over five years. Roth wanted to use that revenue to, among other things, pay for letting taxpayers establish tax-sheltered "Super Saver Accounts." The plan was not successful, but Roth kept trying. In 1989, during budget negotiations, Roth attached another major IRA savings plan to Bush's push for a capital gains tax cut. Savers would have been able to make limited withdrawals for a first home, college education or catastrophic medical expenses.

This GOP tax plan — Roth's proposal plus a capital gains tax cut offered by then-GOP Finance Chairman Bob Packwood of Oregon — was opposed by Democrats as a revenue loser. Although the Congressional Budget Office said the plan would end up costing money, Roth and Packwood disagreed.

"My IRA is exactly what the economy needs for long-term growth," he said.

Despite having Bush's backing, a near-solid phalanx of GOP Senate support and some influential Democratic backers, the plan died.

Roth introduced a less-ambitious plan in 1990 to allow families to save up to $5,000 per year with tax-free withdrawal after seven years. And, early in the 102nd Congress, Roth joined Finance Committee Chairman Lloyd Bentsen of Texas in introducing a bill to restore the deductibility of deposits in IRAs and — like the

1989 Super IRA plan — allow non-penalized withdrawals for certain expenses.

An apparently visceral distaste for high taxes and excessive government spending put Roth in a new position in the 101st Congress — that of legislative naysayer. On a number of high-profile and high-cost issues, Roth voted against final passage, often being one of a mere handful of senators to do so.

Roth was the only senator to vote against the major overhaul of housing programs that Congress passed in 1990. He was joined by just three colleagues in opposing an emergency AIDS-relief measure and by just five in voting against an anti-crime initiative. Roth also voted against final passage of the farm bill and campaign finance revisions — measures the Senate approved handily.

Roth did have a season in the national spotlight as an original co-author of President Ronald Reagan's 1981 tax cut — 25 percent across the board — with Jack F. Kemp, then a GOP House member from New York.

On Governmental Affairs, Roth can be a stubborn opponent to the easygoing, cerebral chairman, John Glenn of Ohio. In 1991, Roth asked Glenn to postpone a markup of legislation to require the administration's Office of Management and Budget and Council on Competitiveness to make public their review of federal agencies' proposed regulations. The measure was anathema to Roth, who argued that Republicans needed more time to study the measure. When Glenn declined, he was confronted with a boycott by Roth and every committee Republican. Glenn ultimately prevailed, but not until Roth had made his point by delaying action.

Roth has long been active in federal pay and procurement issues. He was a sponsor in 1990 of a federal pay-overhaul proposal and also supported locality-based raises for federal workers living in cities with a higher cost of living, a provision included in the final legislation and a significant change in the General Scale pay system.

Roth also has successfully taken the lead each year in opposing efforts to revise the Hatch Act. He continued that battle in the 103rd, although with Clinton supporting the plan, Roth's string of victories seemed likely to come to an end. Roth argues against tampering with the 1939 law, insisting that the act provides protection for federal workers against political coercion and other abuses of the civil service system. "We can hardly afford further erosion of public confidence in our civil servants," he has said.

In the 102nd Congress, Roth stepped out in front to sponsor legislation with Democrat Edward M. Kennedy of Massachusetts that would repeal rules excluding women pilots from combat.

"They flew behind enemy lines and transported troops into enemy territory [during the 1991 Persian Gulf War]," Roth said. "We owe our victory, in part, to the superb performance of these women pilots."

The Roth-Kennedy measure was blocked by the Armed Services Committee, but early in 1993 Clinton repealed the exclusion.

Concern about the changing global economy has at times led Roth to turn his attention beyond the domestic agenda. He narrowly lost a bid in December 1990 to become president of the North Atlantic Assembly, the legislative body of the North Atlantic Treaty Organization (NATO).

At Home: A mild-mannered man, Roth has never been able to generate a great deal of emotion among Delaware voters. But he has been doggedly attentive to state interests, and he has been rewarded for that service with victories in six statewide elections — two for the House and four for the Senate.

Born in Montana and educated at Harvard, Roth came to Delaware to work as a lawyer for a chemical firm and got involved in politics. After narrowly losing a 1960 bid for lieutenant governor, he became state Republican chairman.

In 1966, Roth entered the race for Delaware's at-large U.S. House seat against veteran Democrat Harris B. McDowell Jr. He talked about Vietnam — backing U.S. efforts but berating the Johnson administration for not explaining the situation more fully — and about open-housing legislation (he opposed it but was willing to endorse state GOP convention language favoring it). Riding the coattails of GOP Sen. J. Caleb Boggs and a national Republican wave that carried 47 GOP freshmen to the House in 1966, Roth pulled off an upset.

McDowell tried for a comeback two years later. But he had alienated members of the state Democratic hierarchy by deploring their "old and tired leadership." Buoyed by his first-term record of strong constituent service, Roth pushed his margin of victory to nearly 60 percent of the statewide vote.

With the retirement of GOP Sen. John J. Williams in 1970, Roth became the uncontested choice of his party against the Democratic state House leader, Jacob W. Zimmerman. A Vietnam dove, Zimmerman had little money or statewide name recognition, and the contest was never much in doubt.

In 1976, Roth had a strong Democratic challenger — Wilmington Mayor Thomas C. Maloney. But Roth's efforts against busing had given him an excellent issue to run on, and Maloney was hurt by the coolness of organized labor. Roth's margin was down from 1970, but he was too strong in the suburbs for Maloney to have any chance to beat him.

Running for a third term in 1982, Roth faced his most difficult Senate test. As cosponsor of the supply-side tax cut, he was a visible target for complaints about the then-flagging economy: Like other industrial states, Delaware had felt the effects of recession.

David N. Levinson, Roth's hard-charging Democratic opponent, encouraged voters to link Roth to Reagan's economic policies and the woes he claimed they had produced. Parodying John Steinbeck's novel about the Great Depression, Levinson branded the administration's economic blueprint "The Grapes of Roth."

The incumbent did not hide his tax legislation; billboards advertising his candidacy read, "Bill Roth, the Taxpayer's Best Friend." But he was careful to evince his concern for Frost Belt economic needs, voting against 1981 reductions in three programs important to Delaware: Conrail, trade adjustment assistance to unemployed workers and energy subsidies for the poor.

Levinson campaigned for the seat for more than two years; he got endorsements from labor and most of the other important groups Democrats need to be competitive statewide. But that was not enough. Roth focused on Levinson's out-of-state background, suggesting the Democrat had come into the state just to challenge him. Though he lost Wilmington, Roth more than made up the difference in suburban New Castle County and rural territory to the south.

In 1988, Roth aimed to become the first Delaware senator to win a fourth term since Williams was re-elected in 1964. National Democratic officials called him vulnerable, noting that he had never reached the 60 percent mark denoting electoral security. In preparation for a tough campaign, Roth amassed a huge treasury.

But Democrats' grandest designs were deflated when Rep. Thomas R. Carper declined to challenge Roth. State party leaders scurried to the side of Samuel S. Beard, a wealthy civic activist and party fundraiser. But maverick Lt. Gov. S. B. Woo spoiled their plans for a smooth nomination. Woo, whose ties to the far-flung Chinese-American community guaranteed him a healthy campaign budget, defeated Beard by 71 votes in a bitter primary battle.

While Woo and Beard were slicing up each other, Roth was stressing his political assets, running a media campaign on his record of steering federal money to Delaware and his vaunted dedication to constituent service.

Because of Delaware's September primary date, Woo had little time to prepare for the general election. Roth surpassed 60 percent for the first time in his long career.

Committees

Governmental Affairs (Ranking)
Permanent Subcommittee on Investigations (ranking)

Banking, Housing & Urban Affairs (7th of 8 Republicans)
Housing & Urban Affairs; International Finance & Monetary Policy; Securities

Finance (3rd of 9 Republicans)
Taxation (ranking); Health for Families & the Uninsured; International Trade

Joint Economic

Elections

1988 General		
William V. Roth Jr. (R)	151,115	(62%)
S.B. Woo (D)	92,378	(38%)

Previous Winning Percentages: **1982** (55%) **1976** (56%) **1970** (59%) **1968 *** (59%) **1966 *** (56%)

** House elections.*

Campaign Finance

	Receipts	Receipts from PACs		Expend-itures
1988				
Roth (R)	$1,887,995	$794,191	(42%)	$1,942,119
Woo (D)	$2,409,188	$91,810	(4%)	$2,385,414

Key Votes

1993	
Require unpaid family and medical leave	Y
Approve national "motor voter" registration bill	N
Approve budget increasing taxes and reducing deficit	N
Support president's right to lift military gay ban	N
1992	
Approve school-choice pilot program	Y
Allow shifting funds from defense to domestic programs	N
Oppose deeper cuts in spending for SDI	Y
1991	
Approve waiting period for handgun purchases	Y
Raise senators' pay and ban honoraria	Y
Authorize use of force in Persian Gulf	Y
Confirm Clarence Thomas to Supreme Court	Y

Voting Studies

	Presidential Support		Party Unity		Conservative Coalition	
Year	**S**	**O**	**S**	**O**	**S**	**O**
1992	67	22	79	14	79	18
1991	83	16	78	20	68	28
1990	72	28	80	20	76	24
1989	94	5	85	14	89	8
1988	72	27	51	47	70	30
1987	65 †	31 †	76 †	20 †	88 †	13 †
1986	83	16	83	13	80	17
1985	84	16	81	19	72	27
1984	74	18	85	10	83	15
1983	76	22	80	18	77	20
1982	77	20	76	22	83	16
1981	75	24	72	26	75	24

† Not eligible for all recorded votes.

Interest Group Ratings

Year	ADA	AFL-CIO	CCUS	ACU
1992	25	27	100	75
1991	20	25	60	81
1990	22	33	67	87
1989	0	0	88	81
1988	20	43	57	60
1987	20	50	94	80
1986	15	13	82	78
1985	20	14	83	70
1984	10	10	83	73
1983	30	13	50	56
1982	50	27	67	47
1981	20	32	78	67

Joseph R. Biden Jr. (D)

Of Wilmington — Elected 1972; 4th Term

Born: Nov. 20, 1942, Scranton, Pa.
Education: U. of Delaware, B.A. 1965; Syracuse U., J.D. 1968.
Occupation: Lawyer.
Family: Wife, Jill Jacobs; three children.
Religion: Roman Catholic.
Political Career: New Castle County Council, 1970-72.
Capitol Office: 221 Russell Bldg. 20510; 224-5042.

In Washington: Unwittingly and unwillingly, Biden and his Judiciary Committee were the catalysts for dramatic changes in the American political landscape of the 1990s. Faulted for their handling of the 1991 nomination of Clarence Thomas to the Supreme Court, they unleashed forces that led to greater diversity in Congress and the undermining of President Bush's popularity.

The nationally televised hearings in which University of Oklahoma law Professor Anita F. Hill accused Thomas of sexually harassing her were an acute embarrassment to Biden, whose committee had failed to conduct more than a cursory investigation of Hill's charges until after they leaked to the news media. But he saw good in the ultimate results. Inspired — or enraged — by the image of the all-white, all-male committee interrogating a black woman, record numbers of women and minorities sought and won seats in Congress.

As the 103rd Congress began, Biden focused on rehabilitating his committee's scarred reputation. When California Rep. Barbara Boxer won a Democratic primary on her way to a Senate victory, Biden hand-delivered a dozen red roses with an invitation to join Judiciary. She turned him down, but Biden kept looking. "Come hell or high water, there will be women on that committee," he said in January 1993. After extensive lobbying, and receiving permission to enlarge his committee by two, Biden recruited Democrats Dianne Feinstein of California and Carol Moseley-Braun of Illinois, the Senate's first black woman.

When Biden first arrived in the Senate more than 20 years ago, he struck observers as a man destined for big things, with the talent and charisma to be an influential Democrat for decades to come. He is personable, conciliatory and an impressive orator. Yet a central question remains unanswered: Does he radiate more heat than light?

His handling of the Thomas hearings disappointed many. Certainly the hearings would have been an extraordinary challenge for anyone to control, but Biden's tendency to be cordial in the extreme did not serve his party well. He made little attempt to curtail endless questioning about pubic hairs on soda cans, pornographic films or Hill's "proclivities."

Biden's chatty, deferential approach to Thomas did nothing to inspire fellow Democrats on the panel and did not begin to counter the hard-edged attack on Hill mounted by Pennsylvania Republican Arlen Specter and other GOP senators. Still, it was hardly surprising coming from a chairman who a year earlier had told Bush's first Supreme Court nominee, David H. Souter, "You are free to refuse to answer any questions you deem to be improper."

When Judiciary was thrust back into the limelight early in the 103rd Congress, Biden struck a more assertive pose. He refused to schedule the speedy hearing President Clinton requested for his attorney general nominee, Zoë Baird, saying he would wait until he had Baird's background check in hand. And when a firestorm began building over Baird's hiring of two illegal aliens for domestic work and her failure to pay their Social Security taxes, Biden was quick to demonstrate that this time he understood what the public was upset about.

"There are tens of thousands, millions of Americans out there who have trouble taking care of their children, both couples required to work or single parents, with one-fiftieth the income that you and your husband have, and they do not violate the law," he said to the nominee.

Biden was forthright in explaining his more aggressive posture. "Because I've been down this road before, from bitter experience, we take the investigative side seriously," he told The New Yorker.

It took Clinton three tries to find an attorney general who could survive the scrutiny of the news media and the Judiciary Committee. When Janet Reno was finally confirmed in mid-March, Biden spoke for most of his colleagues: "What you're hearing up here is a collective sigh of relief."

His performances early in the 103rd may hint at a maturing of the man known early in his career as someone whose mouth frequently outran his mind, who was impatient with the details and the sustained labor of legislating.

An Irish Catholic middle-class son of a Scranton, Pa., auto dealer, Biden had always exhibited a quick intelligence and considerable eloquence. He often speaks with a self-deprecation that is part of his charm, reminding witnesses before the Judiciary Committee that they did better in law school than he did. But he still talks too much. When members are given five minutes for opening remarks, Chairman Biden often takes 20 or 30.

Elected at 29 and sworn in at age 30, the constitutional minimum, Biden is now one of the Senate's most senior members (No. 8 among Democrats), even though he is barely into his 50s. If his health holds up, he seems likely to enjoy one of the longest careers in the institution's history.

Biden became chairman of the Judiciary Committee after the Democrats regained the Senate majority in the 1986 election, and in that role has maintained a warm rapport with South Carolina Republican Strom Thurmond, the previous chairman. "My Henry Clay," Thurmond liked to call Biden, in recognition of his skill at bipartisan compromises. "Mr. Chairman," Biden still calls Thurmond, long after that has ceased to be true.

At the start of the 103rd Congress, Thurmond moved to the ranking post on the Armed Services Committee, making Orrin G. Hatch of Utah ranking Republican on Judiciary. That is likely to change the tone in Judiciary somewhat; Hatch and Biden sparred during the Thomas-Hill hearings. And although Hatch, as ranking Republican on Labor and Human Resources, frequently cooperated and compromised with Chairman Edward M. Kennedy of Massachusetts, he is less inclined to give ground on the issues handled by the Judiciary Committee.

Judiciary will have its hands full in the 103rd, as Clinton moves to fill at least one opening on the Supreme Court and more than 100 federal judgeships.

In addition, Biden has promised to try once again to move a comprehensive anti-crime package; the last version died in a partisan standoff in the 102nd Congress after passing both chambers and emerging from conference. Biden backs proposals to limit death row appeals, make more crimes eligible for the death penalty and require a waiting period for handgun purchases.

In recent years, Biden has focused increasingly on crimes against women. During the 102nd Congress, he pressed legislation that would make it easier for victims of sexual assaults to bring civil suits against their attackers, increase criminal penalties for attacks on women, and authorize special aid to states for law enforcement efforts to fight sex crimes. The measure got entangled with the broader anti-crime package and did not clear. In January 1993, Biden reintroduced it.

When liberal dogma and public opinion collide, as they did in the 1989-90 flag desecration debate, few are as skilled as Biden at giving voice to the competing concerns. But in that instance, Biden's efforts to balance the competing forces ultimately came to naught.

After the Supreme Court in 1989 struck down as unconstitutional a Texas law prohibiting flag burning, Biden sponsored a bill intended to outlaw flag desecration by statute. His goal was to prohibit conduct that infuriated most Americans without resorting to a constitutional amendment, which was sought by Bush but opposed by liberals. Biden rounded up a number of legal scholars to help him draft the bill. The legislation moved quickly through both the House and Senate and was cleared in October 1989, three months after the court's ruling.

But the federal statute was struck down by the Supreme Court in June 1990, just as its state predecessor had been. While Biden came back to the table with a narrowly drawn constitutional amendment, key House liberals were working behind the scenes to fundamentally alter the debate. Ultimately, they succeeded: The public and politicians lost interest in the matter, the House defeated a constitutional amendment, and Biden glumly apologized for "wasting the taxpayers' money . . . in discussing something that is going nowhere."

One of Biden's most significant legislative achievements was his role in the 1984 passage of legislation rewriting federal criminal statutes. The culmination of an 11-year effort, the legislation revised sentencing procedures to reduce disparity in punishments and allowed pretrial detention of some dangerous suspects. Biden was the Democratic floor manager of the bill and negotiated a deal with House leaders at the close of the 98th Congress.

Two years later, in 1986, he was a guiding force behind enactment of tough new legislation against illegal drugs. His most important contribution came when the bill was deadlocked in conference, largely over a provision imposing the death penalty for certain drug crimes. Biden helped arrange the informal negotiations that cleared the way for final passage.

The drug bill's passage illustrates the two sides of Biden. He is a talented eleventh-hour mediator, riding in to save the day. But as legislation unfolds in all its mind-numbing details and slowly makes its way through a balky process, Biden often is hardly a presence. With his glib tongue and preference for action, his strength is at the podium, not the bill-drafting table.

During the 1980s, drug bills and anti-crime packages became hardy perennials as lawmakers from both parties competed for the title of toughest on crime. By 1989, however, Biden was growing weary of the game. When Bush outlined a big anti-drug plan in September, Biden gave it a decidedly cold shoulder, saying the government should fund the programs already in place. "It's time to pay off on our promises to fight drugs, and to keep paying until the job is done," he said. "That means immediately finding the full $1.8 billion we need to pay for last year's drug bill."

Biden, who sponsored the legislation that created the office of "drug czar" in 1988, releases a report each year on the status of federal drug programs. His April 1993 assessment concluded that the country must concentrate more of its attention and resources on tackling the problems of an estimated 900,000 hard-core drug addicts who do not have access to treatment.

Biden had combined his interest in foreign affairs and illegal drug trafficking with far-reaching proposals to provide debt relief to drug-producing Andean nations. In 1989, Congress approved a small piece of the program, forgiving $125 million in debts held by the U.S. government in exchange for drug eradication efforts by Bolivia, Columbia and Peru.

While it is Judiciary that has given him the clout of a committee chairmanship, Biden sees the international stage as his true calling. In June 1992, he delivered an address titled "On the Threshold of a New World Order." The wide-ranging speech proposed a four-part agenda for moving beyond the Cold War. It had the air of a presidential address, evoking memories of his failed 1988 bid.

The No. 2 Democrat on Foreign Relations behind the septuagenarian Claiborne Pell of Rhode Island, Biden has made no secret of his desire to take over the chairmanship. In early 1993, Pell relinquished some legislative authority to Biden and the other subcommittee chairmen, but he has given no indications he plans to step down. Nonetheless, Biden is still young, and he is likely to inherit Pell's mantle eventually.

Biden has been consistently liberal on foreign policy issues in the past. As a member of the Foreign Relations Committee — and of the Intelligence Committee until 1985 — he has pressed for arms control agreements, opposed the use of military force in the Persian Gulf and insisted that Congress be a full partner with the White House in decisions to send U.S. forces to hostile areas.

At the start of the 103rd, Biden, chairman of the European Affairs Subcommittee, shifted toward a more hawkish stance, urging Clinton to consider airstrikes against the artillery positions of Bosnian Serbs.

Part of what makes Biden such a compelling political figure, and what commands such attention to his personal development, are the tragedies and dramas of his public life.

Just weeks after his 1972 Senate election, Biden's wife and infant daughter were killed and his two sons seriously injured in an automobile accident. Biden said at first that he did not want to take the oath of office. Persuaded by Majority Leader Mike Mansfield to assume his seat, Biden was sworn in at his son's bedside.

After spending more than a decade rebuilding his life and career, Biden launched a long-awaited presidential campaign in June 1987. But in a season focused on candidates' character, he fell under the weight of reports that he had plagiarized passages in his speeches and a 1965 law school paper, and finally, that he had exaggerated his résumé. He withdrew from the race in September.

No sooner did the uncomfortable episode fade from public view than a brush with death put Biden back in the news. In February 1988, he had the first of two operations for a near-fatal brain aneurysm. By early 1989, Biden was back in action. But he still returns home to his family in Delaware each night regardless of how late the Senate is in.

At Home: The collapse of Biden's 1988 presidential campaign amid allegations of plagiarism raised questions about his political future — not only his hopes for the White House, but also his future in the Senate.

With a number of his constituents admitting to some embarrassment over his campaign debacle, Biden looked potentially vulnerable to a Republican challenge in 1990. Conservatives were eager to avenge the 1987 defeat of the Supreme Court nomination of Robert H. Bork, and GOP officials began to shop for potential candidates.

However, Biden's home-state downturn did not last long. His triumph over life-threatening health problems in 1988 helped revive the affections of supporters who had grown skeptical of him. His victory over deputy state attorney general M. Jane Brady with 63 percent of the vote restored him to a position of dominance in Delaware politics.

Biden was in the underdog role himself when, at age 29, he made an audacious bid to unseat GOP Sen. J. Caleb Boggs. With service on the New Castle County Council his only electoral credential, Biden seemed a sure loser. But his celebrated brashness helped Biden pull off a major upset.

Biden ran hard on a dovish Vietnam platform and accused the Republican of being a do-nothing senator. He called for more spending on mass transit and health-care services. The Biden campaign was essentially a family operation, without state-of-the-art media management, but it was sophisticated enough to cover a state with an electorate as small as Delaware's. Boggs awoke to the threat too late, and his "safe" seat disappeared by 3,162 votes.

Delaware Democratic leaders, certain that a challenge to Boggs was hopeless, had given Biden little support in 1972. He gave them little attention in return for most of his first term. At the 1976 Democratic National Convention in New York City, he stayed in one hotel, and the state delegation in another.

By 1978, Biden had made up with the state party. Of greater importance in his re-election bid that year, however, was his opposition to busing. As he ran for re-election, a long-disputed busing plan was taking effect in New Castle County, outraging voters in suburban Wilmington.

With this anti-busing position offsetting his liberalism on some other social issues, Biden seemed unbeatable in 1978, and big-name Delaware Republicans refrained from taking him on. The task fell to an obscure southern Delaware poultry farmer, James H. Baxter, who gamely tried to paint the Democrat as too far left for the state. Biden easily beat him.

For a time, it appeared as though Biden might be seriously threatened in 1984. Republican Gov. Pierre S. "Pete" du Pont IV, ineligible to seek a third consecutive term, was pressured to challenge the incumbent by President Ronald Reagan and Senate Majority Leader Howard H. Baker Jr. But du Pont chose not to run.

The Republican who eventually emerged was John M. Burris, a businessman and former Republican leader of the Delaware House who spent most of his time trying to brand Biden a fiscal profligate, echoing themes from Baxter's 1978 campaign. Burris chastised the incumbent for voting against Reagan's proposal for a constitutional amendment to balance the budget and sought to remind voters of his own role in helping to enact a state balanced-budget amendment under du Pont.

Burris succeeded in keeping the focus of the campaign on economic issues; Biden dwelt heavily on his "budget freeze" proposal. But that was the Republican's sole consolation. Biden crushed him in New Castle County and carried Delaware's two downstate counties en route to a 60 percent to 40 percent win.

Committees

Judiciary (Chairman)
Juvenile Justice

Foreign Relations (2nd of 11 Democrats)
European Affairs (chairman); East Asian & Pacific Affairs; International Economic Policy, Trade, Oceans & Environment

Elections

1990 General

Joseph R. Biden Jr. (D)	112,918	(63%)
M. Jane Brady (R)	64,554	(36%)
Lee Rosenbaum (LIBERT)	2,680	(1%)

Previous Winning Percentages: **1984** (60%) **1978** (58%) **1972** (50%)

Campaign Finance

	Receipts	Receipts from PACs		Expenditures
1990				
Biden (D)	$1,898,297	$690,816	(36%)	$1,888,146
Brady (R)	$244,788	0		$240,669

Key Votes

1993

Require unpaid family and medical leave	Y
Approve national "motor voter" registration bill	Y
Approve budget increasing taxes and reducing deficit	Y
Support president's right to lift military gay ban	Y

1992

Approve school-choice pilot program	N
Allow shifting funds from defense to domestic programs	Y
Oppose deeper cuts in spending for SDI	N

1991

Approve waiting period for handgun purchases	Y
Raise senators' pay and ban honoraria	Y
Authorize use of force in Persian Gulf	N
Confirm Clarence Thomas to Supreme Court	N

Voting Studies

	Presidential Support		Party Unity		Conservative Coalition	
Year	**S**	**O**	**S**	**O**	**S**	**O**
1992	28	70	90	8	18	79
1991	33	65	88	8	10	85
1990	33	67	83	16	16	84
1989	50	48	81	18	26	68
1988	13	3	13	1	3	5
1987	27	41	60	6	6	56
1986	27	67	83	12	25	71
1985	31	64	77	16	18	75
1984	35	65	79	21	28	72
1983	38	60	82	12	23	68
1982	34	61	79	17	28	67
1981	44	54	84	12	24	74

Interest Group Ratings

Year	ADA	AFL-CIO	CCUS	ACU
1992	100	100	20	0
1991	90	83	20	5
1990	83	67	36	17
1989	90	100	29	14
1988	15	80	67	0
1987	70	100	17	0
1986	80	87	38	5
1985	75	81	37	10
1984	85	82	44	18
1983	85	88	22	8
1982	80	84	38	32
1981	80	84	28	20

AL Michael N. Castle (R)

Of Wilmington — Elected 1992; 1st Term

Born: July 2, 1939, Wilmington, Del.

Education: Hamilton College, B.A. 1961; Georgetown U., LL.B. 1964.

Occupation: Lawyer.

Family: Wife, Jane DiSabatino.

Religion: Roman Catholic.

Political Career: Del. deputy attorney general, 1965-66; Del. House, 1967-69; Del. Senate, 1969-77, minority leader, 1976-77; lieutenant governor, 1981-85; governor, 1985-93.

Capitol Office: 1205 Longworth Bldg. 20515; 225-4165.

The Path to Washington: In 1988, the governors of two of the nation's smallest states became close allies in an effort to overhaul the federal welfare system.

In November 1992, one of them, Castle, was elected to the House. The other, Arkansas Gov. Bill Clinton, became president.

Castle likes to tell how he sent a note to Clinton shortly after the election joking that it didn't seem quite fair that he was a mere freshman member of the House minority while Clinton was headed for the Oval Office.

But Castle may be unduly modest about his influence during a Clinton administration: He is just the kind of moderate Republican that Clinton could be relying on for crucial support if he wants to enact a centrist legislative agenda.

The men share a number of political and policy views, not the least of which is their predisposition toward bipartisan governing. In fact, Castle's biggest differences could come with his own Republican House colleagues, many of whom have said they plan to take a more confrontational than cooperative stance with the new administration.

Castle says he is proud of his record of bipartisanship during two terms as governor, and he vowed in his campaign to bring some of that attitude to a Congress that he blasted as ineffective and out of touch.

Castle and Clinton also agree on the need to reduce the federal deficit by containing the growing costs of entitlement programs, reducing defense spending and giving the president the line-item veto.

In April 1993, during consideration of a measure to give the president a limited line-item veto, Castle offered a stronger substitute that would have made it more difficult for Congress to defeat the president's proposed rescissions. The Castle substitute failed, 198-219, with 33 Democrats voting for it and only four Republicans voting against it.

Castle advocates finding public policy solutions that involve the public and private sectors. One of his most notable achievements as governor was the establishment of universal health-care coverage for the state's children. With funding from the private Nemours Foundation, about a dozen clinics are being set up statewide that will make services available to the state's 24,000 uninsured children.

But while Clinton has made health-care reform a key component of his economic strategy, Castle says he has yet to see a federal health-care proposal that is an improvement over the existing system. Instead, he thinks states should be allowed to experiment longer on innovative health-care programs to see whether a better solution can be found. Castle, the only ex-governor in the House, believes in general that states should be given more flexibility in carrying out federal programs.

Although a lawyer by training, Castle has spent most of his adult life in politics and government. He became the state's deputy attorney general in 1965 when he was 26, and began a 10-year career in the Delaware General Assembly two years later. He served as lieutenant governor from 1981-85 before being elected governor. He was re-elected in 1988 with 71 percent of the vote, the highest tally ever for a statewide official.

But in the year of the political outsider, Castle got more of a run for his money. In the GOP primary, he picked up 56 percent of the vote in a four-way contest. He won the general election with 55 percent after a vigorous challenge from his former lieutenant governor, Democrat S. B. Woo.

Under state law, Castle was not allowed to seek a third term as governor and had little choice but to seek the state's one at-large House seat if he wanted to remain in politics.

Castle switched places with the state's former representative, Democrat Thomas R. Carper, who is now governor. He also took over Carper's seat on the Banking Committee, an important position for a state with a large corporate constituency.

Delaware

At large

Delaware is a bellwether in national elections — it has supported the winning presidential ticket eleven times in a row — and pursues ticket-splitting with rare relish in the elections within its borders.

The state's four major statewide office-holders — its governor, two senators and U.S. representative — are evenly split between the parties. Delaware voted in 1992 to send a Democrat to the White House, its Republican governor to the U.S. House and its Democratic House member to the governor's mansion.

Delaware's split-ticket mania is sometimes attributed to the compactness of the state. Personal campaigning is more important than party identification. Voters expect to see their candidates, and over the course of a campaign, candidates are able to meet a large part of the electorate. The absence of a commercial statewide television station accentuates the importance of grassroots campaigning.

Despite its track record of voting for presidential winners, Delaware has had trouble producing any of its own. No president has ever been elected from Delaware, and neither of the two candidates emerging from the state in 1988, former Republican Gov. Pierre S. "Pete" du Pont IV and Democratic Sen. Joseph R. Biden Jr., traveled far on the road to the White House.

Up in the small but relatively dense area north of the Chesapeake and Delaware Canal, Democrats are strong in Wilmington, the state's largest city. Fifty years ago, almost half the state's people resided in Wilmington, but the city's 72,000 residents now cast only about 11 percent of Delaware's vote. As the city has shrunk, its suburbs have grown; New Castle County, which encompasses them both, casts a full 68 percent of the state's total vote.

The GOP's strength lies in Wilmington's suburbs and down south of the canal, in the poultry farms and coastal marshes of the Delmarva peninsula, whose name is an amalgam of its ingredients: Delaware and the eastern ends of Maryland and Virginia.

Thanks to its liberal business incorporation rules, Delaware is the on-paper home to about half the Fortune 500 and over 200,000 smaller corporations. Wilmington is the very real home to the Du Pont Co., which with 20,000 employees is Delaware's largest employer. It employs 125,000 worldwide. The recession has hit even Du Pont; it shed 3,500 workers in 1991 and braced for another wave of reductions in mid-1993.

Dover, Delaware's capital, is set in the state's mid-section, in Kent County. It, too, has a strong Democratic constituency. A few miles south of the city is Dover Air Force Base, the East Coast's largest. The base employs nearly 9,000 military and civilian personnel who played a critical role in transporting cargo to the Middle East during the Persian Gulf War. But it has also brought something of a grim image to the city; its huge mortuary has received thousands of dead servicemen over the past three decades, including Persian Gulf casualties. Other major Dover employers include General Foods, Playtex, Scott Paper and a variety of chemical corporations.

Down at the southern end of the state is Sussex County, Delaware at its most rural. Sussex produces more poultry than any other county in the country, along with sorghum, corn and soybeans.

Tourism also has its place in this county, at its far southeast end. A string of beach resorts from the mouth of the Delaware Bay down the peninsula to Fenwick Island draw thousands of oceangoers each year. A series of storms that have battered the coast have washed away a series of beach rebuilding projects.

Rehoboth Beach is a popular summer resort whose sizable gay population has lately become a permanent fixture, raising tensions with the community's more-traditional visitors and older residents.

The increasing number of retirees residing in the beach communities have made Sussex the fastest-growing county in the state; they add to the county's already conservative tenor.

Ronald Reagan and George Bush won consistently in Sussex throughout the 1980s. But in 1992, Bush managed just 39 percent, 1,300 votes more than Bill Clinton.

A new bypass that leads to the beach may forever change the character of the southern counties. Relief Route 1 promises to cut the travel time between northern and southern Delaware and is expected to boost the local economies. But it is expected to do so by attracting city and suburban folks from New Castle County as new residents, a prospect that concerns the area's farmers.

1990 Population: 666,168. White 535,094 (80%), Black 112,460 (17%), Other 18,614 (3%). Hispanic origin 15,820 (2%). 18 and over 502,827 (75%), 62 and over 98,658 (15%). Median age: 33.

Committees

Banking, Finance & Urban Affairs (19th of 20 Republicans)
Consumer Credit & Insurance; Housing & Community Development; International Development, Finance, Trade & Monetary Policy

Merchant Marine & Fisheries (13th of 18 Republicans)
Coast Guard & Navigation; Environment & Natural Resources

Elections

1992 General		
Michael N. Castle (R)	153,037	(55%)
S.B. Woo (D)	117,426	(43%)
Peggy Schmitt (LIBERT)	5,661	(2%)
1992 Primary		
Michael N. Castle (R)	18,377	(56%)
Janet C. Rzewnicki (R)	9,812	(30%)
Bryant L. Richardson (R)	4,411	(13%)
James R. Withrow (R)	441	(1%)

District Vote for President

1992

D 126,054 (44%)
R 102,313 (36%)
I 59,213 (21%)

Campaign Finance

	Receipts	Receipts from PACs		Expend-itures
1992				
Castle (R)	$708,671	$206,868	(29%)	$690,740
Woo (D)	$1,018,360	$37,600	(4%)	$1,017,598

Key Votes

1993

Require parental notification of minors' abortions	Y
Require unpaid family and medical leave	Y
Approve national "motor voter" registration bill	N
Approve budget increasing taxes and reducing deficit	N
Approve economic stimulus plan	N

Florida

STATE DATA

Governor: Lawton Chiles (D)
First elected: 1990
Length of term: 4 years
Term expires: 1/95
Salary: $95,000
Term limit: 2 terms
Phone: (904) 488-4441
Born: April 3, 1930; Lakeland, Fla.
Education: U. of Florida, B.S. 1952, LL.B. 1955
Military Service: Army, 1953-54
Occupation: Lawyer
Family: Wife, Rhea May Grafton; four children
Religion: Presbyterian
Political Career: Fla. House, 1959-67; Fla. Senate, 1967-71; U.S. Senate, 1971-89

Lt. Gov.: Kenneth "Buddy" MacKay (D)
First elected: 1990
Length of term: 4 years
Term expires: 1/95
Salary: $91,000
Phone: (904) 488-4711

State election official: (904) 488-7690
Democratic headquarters: (904) 222-3411
Republican headquarters: (904) 222-7920

REDISTRICTING

Florida gained four House seats in reapportionment, increasing from 19 districts to 23. Federal court approved map May 29, 1992.

STATE LEGISLATURE

Legislature. Meets February-April; session often extended.

Senate: 40 members, 4-year terms
1992 breakdown: 20D, 20R; 34 men, 6 women; 32 whites, 5 blacks, 3 Hispanics
Salary: $22,560
Phone: (904) 487-5270

House of Representatives: 120 members, 2-year terms
1992 breakdown: 71D, 49R; 98 men, 22 women; 96 whites, 14 blacks, 10 Hispanics
Salary: $22,560
Phone: (904) 488-1157

URBAN STATISTICS

City	Pop.
Jacksonville Mayor Edward Austin, D	635,230
Miami Mayor Xavier Suarez, I	358,648
Tampa Mayor Sandra W. Freedman, I	280,015
St. Petersburg Mayor David J. Fischer, N-P	240,348

U.S. CONGRESS

Senate: 1 D, 1 R
House: 10 D, 13 R

TERM LIMITS

For Congress: Yes
Senate: 2 terms, effective 1994
House: 4 terms, effective 1994
For state offices: Yes
Senate: 2 terms, effective 1994
House: 4 terms, effective 1994

ELECTIONS

1992 Presidential Vote

George Bush	40.9%
Bill Clinton	39.0%
Ross Perot	19.8%

1988 Presidential Vote

George Bush	61%
Michael S. Dukakis	39%

1984 Presidential Vote

Ronald Reagan	65%
Walter F. Mondale	35%

POPULATION

1990 population		12,937,926
1980 population		9,746,324
Percent change		+33%
Rank among states:		4
White		83%
Black		14%
Hispanic		12%
Asian or Pacific islander		1%
Urban		85%
Rural		15%
Born in state		30%
Foreign-born		13%
Under age 18	2,866,237	22%
Ages 18-64	7,702,258	60%
65 and older	2,369,431	18%
Median age		36.4

MISCELLANEOUS

Capital: Tallahassee
Number of counties: 67
Per capita income: $18,880 (1991)
Rank among states: 18
Total area: 58,664 sq. miles
Rank among states: 22

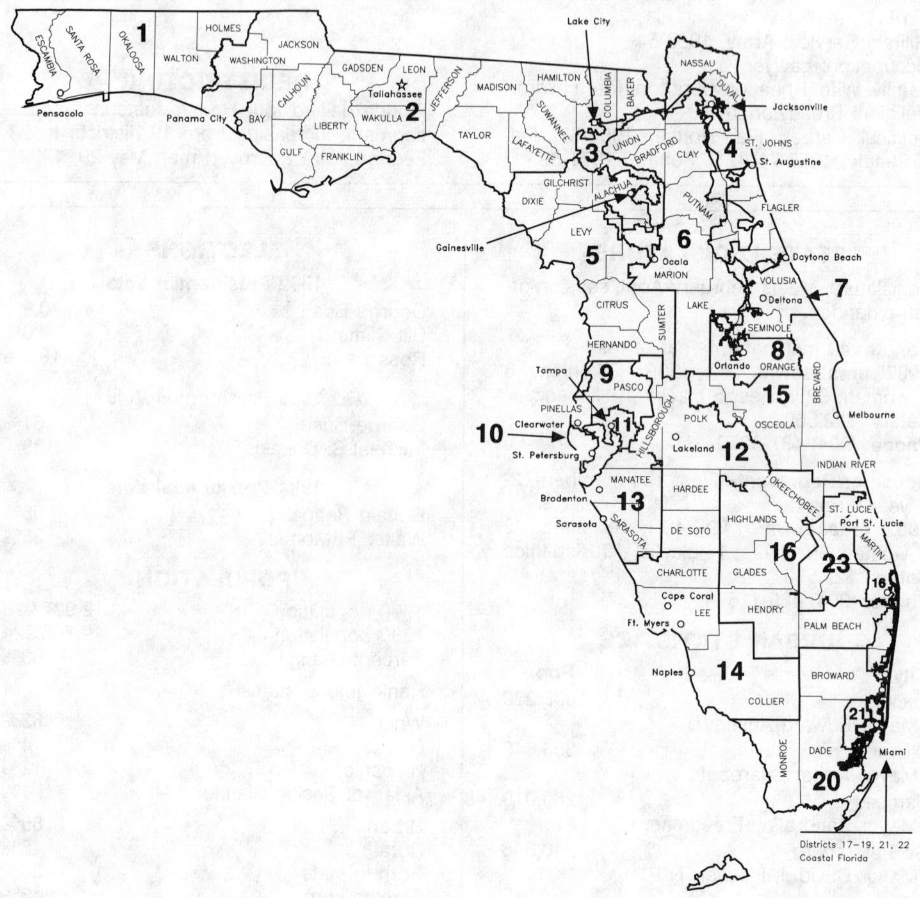

1
ESCAMBIA
SANTA ROSA
OKALOOSA
WALTON
HOLMES
WASHINGTON
JACKSON
CALHOUN
BAY
GULF
LIBERTY
FRANKLIN
GADSDEN
LEON
Tallahassee
WAKULLA
2
JEFFERSON
MADISON
TAYLOR
HAMILTON
SUWANNEE
LAFAYETTE
COLUMBIA
BAKER
Lake City
UNION
BRADFORD
3
NASSAU
DUVAL
Jacksonville
ST. JOHNS
St. Augustine
CLAY
4
Pensacola
Panama City
GILCHRIST
ALACHUA
DIXIE
LEVY
Gainesville
5
PUTNAM
FLAGLER
6
Ocala
MARION
Daytona Beach
VOLUSIA
Deltona
7
CITRUS
SUMTER
LAKE
SEMINOLE
8
HERNANDO
Orlando
ORANGE
BREVARD
Tampa
9
PASCO
PINELLAS
15
Clearwater
11
OSCEOLA
Melbourne
10
St. Petersburg
POLK
HILLSBOROUGH
Lakeland
12
INDIAN RIVER
MANATEE
HARDEE
Bradenton
13
OKEECHOBEE
Sarasota
SARASOTA
DE SOTO
HIGHLANDS
ST. LUCIE
Port St. Lucie
MARTIN
16
23
CHARLOTTE
GLADES
16
Cape Coral
LEE
HENDRY
Ft. Myers
PALM BEACH
Naples
14
BROWARD
COLLIER
21
MONROE
DADE
Miami
20
Districts 17–19, 21, 22
Coastal Florida

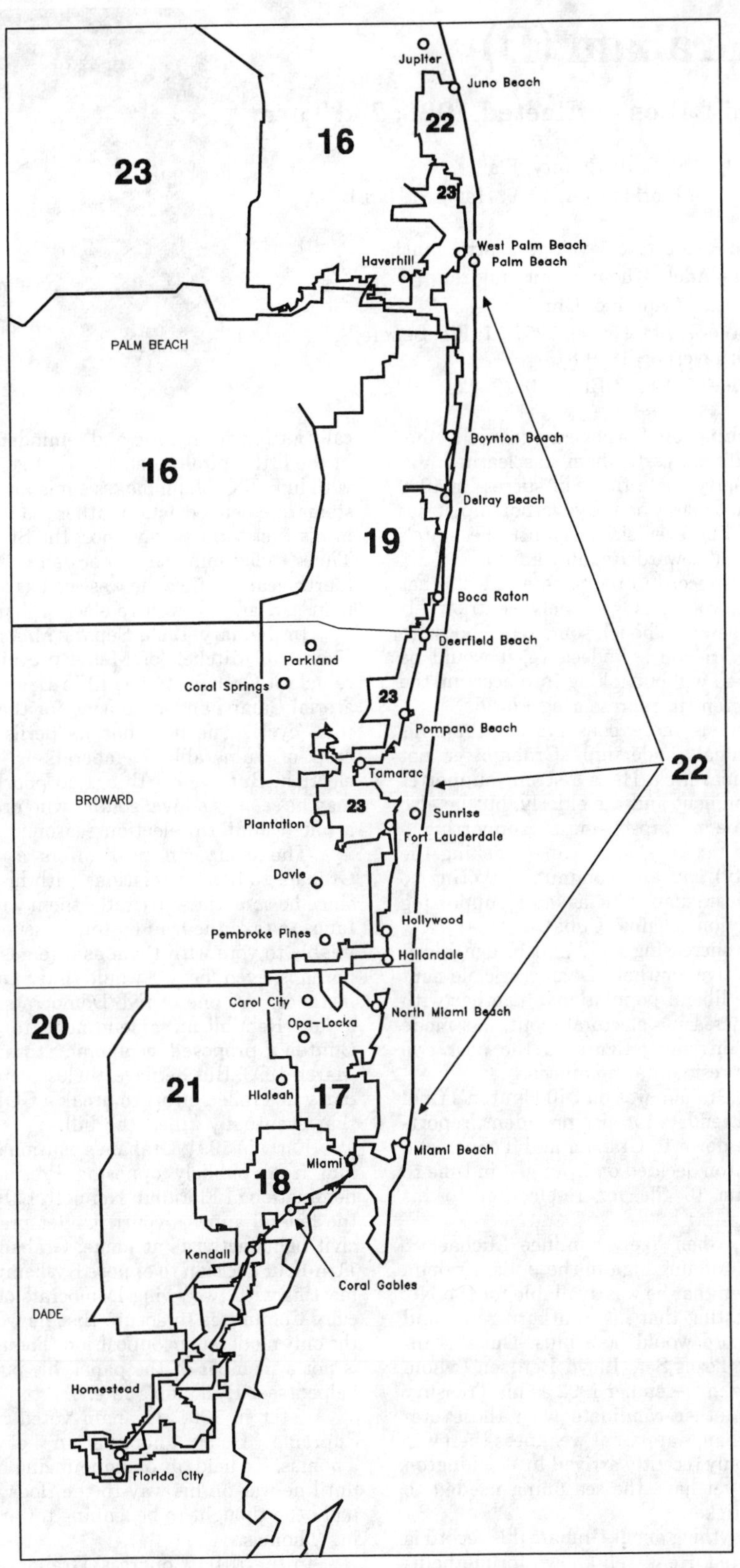
Jupiter
Juno Beach
22
16
23
23
West Palm Beach
Palm Beach
Haverhill
PALM BEACH
16
Boynton Beach
Delray Beach
19
Boca Raton
Deerfield Beach
Parkland
Coral Springs
23
Pompano Beach
22
Tamarac
BROWARD
23
Sunrise
Plantation
Fort Lauderdale
Davie
Hollywood
Pembroke Pines
Hallandale
Carol City
North Miami Beach
20
Opa-Locka
21
Hialeah
17
Miami Beach
Miami
18
Kendall
Coral Gables
DADE
Homestead
Florida City

Bob Graham (D)

Of Miami Lakes — Elected 1986; 2nd Term

Born: Nov. 9, 1936, Dade County, Fla.
Education: U. of Florida, B.A. 1959; Harvard U., LL.B. 1962.
Occupation: Real estate developer; cattle rancher.
Family: Wife, Adele Khoury; four children.
Religion: United Church of Christ.
Political Career: Fla. House, 1967-71; Fla. Senate, 1971-79; governor, 1979-87.
Capitol Office: 524 Hart Bldg. 20510; 224-3041.

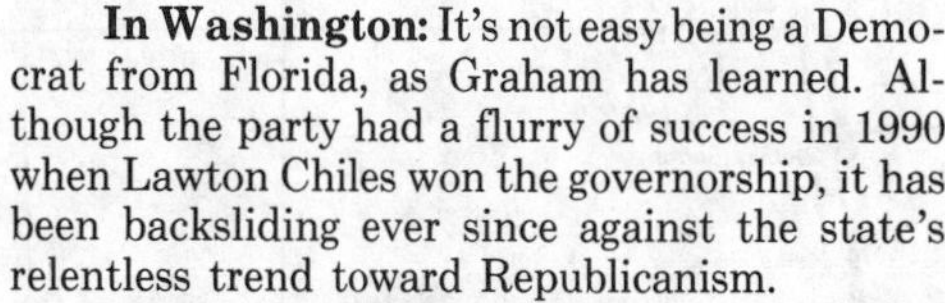

In Washington: It's not easy being a Democrat from Florida, as Graham has learned. Although the party had a flurry of success in 1990 when Lawton Chiles won the governorship, it has been backsliding ever since against the state's relentless trend toward Republicanism.

Graham's record in the Senate reflects that struggle. His voting is genuinely centrist; his method, deliberate. Though some may choose to characterize Graham as indecisive, it would be unfair to do so without taking into account the tensions inherent in representing Florida.

While he is more conservative than his party's national leadership, Graham is not viewed as a maverick. He is a strong supporter of the environment and the elderly, but he also strikes a pose as pro-business (supporting a capital gains tax cut), anti-crime (backing the death penalty) and anti-communist (voting to help the Nicaraguan contras and supporting tougher sanctions against Cuba).

And his increasing ability to bridge Florida's conservative Southern Democratic element and its more liberal populations, together with the state's increasing electoral clout, has made Graham an intriguing figure to the past two Democratic presidential nominees.

In 1992, Graham was on Bill Clinton's final list of six contenders for vice president; reportedly, it came down to Graham and Tennessean Al Gore. Clinton decided on Gore just in time to allow Graham to file for re-election to his Senate seat.

In 1988, when likely nominee Michael S. Dukakis was running high in the polls, Graham let it be known that he was available for the No. 2 spot, suggesting that his Southern roots and moderate record would be a plus. Dukakis instead picked Texas Sen. Lloyd Bentsen (whom Clinton chose in December 1992 as his Treasury secretary), another candidate with those credentials. Graham's apparent weakness then was that he had only recently arrived in Washington and did not yet have the seasoning needed to balance the ticket.

Like everything about Graham, his record is carefully crafted. He is well-known for methodically jotting down notes and reminders to himself in the little spiral notebooks that go everywhere with him. If Graham makes a mistake, it is apt to stem from belated action rather than haste. Early in his first term as governor, the St. Petersburg Times called him "Governor Jell-O." But by his fourth year in office, he was seen as a competent manager, and he won re-election handily.

In January 1993, Senate Majority Leader George J. Mitchell of Maine prevailed upon a reluctant Graham to head the Democratic Senatorial Campaign Committee for the 1994 electoral cycle. The post has its perils — a large crop of vulnerable Democrats is up for re-election. But even if things go poorly, Graham may be seen as a loyal soldier who presided over a tough midterm election season.

The campaign post offers a chance for Graham to bolster relations with his colleagues since he sometimes irritates them with his hesitance to take the lead on tough issues, and he is unable to vote with them as often as they — or perhaps even he — would like. Graham, for instance, was one of five Democrats to support a key Republican amendment to pare back Clinton's proposed economic stimulus bill in March 1993. But he nevertheless voted with his party in a failed effort to break a GOP filibuster that eventually killed the bill.

Early in 1991, Graham's caution nearly kept him from publicly opposing President Bush's nomination of Floridian Kenneth L. Ryskamp to the federal appeals court. Under pressure from civil rights activists at home, Graham made his 11th-hour decision to oppose Ryskamp only after meeting with two swing Democrats on the Judiciary Committee to ensure that he would not be the only moderate in opposition. Though Graham is not a member of the panel, his public stance helped seal Ryskamp's fate.

Later in 1991, Graham voted against the Supreme Court nomination of Clarence Thomas. He held off on announcing his position until he was on his way to the floor to vote; he had been thought to be leaning toward confirming Thomas.

In the 101st Congress, Graham stayed out

of the spotlight during the hotly contested nominations of Robert H. Bork to the Supreme Court in 1987 and John Tower for Defense secretary in 1989. Graham came down on the opposition side — but only after others had made the outcome clear.

When Mitchell of Maine was wrestling with J. Bennett Johnston of Louisiana for Southern votes in the 1988 contest for majority leader, Graham's endorsement of Mitchell came late, doing him little good with either man.

Likewise, his efforts to stake out middle ground on the Persian Gulf War wound up pleasing no one. In the 102nd Congress, during debate on the Persian Gulf conflict, Graham helped draft the resolution urging reliance on economic sanctions against Iraq. But as talks with Iraq fell apart and Bush moved the country toward war, Graham became uncomfortable opposing the president. He met with key supporters of the sanctions resolution — Armed Services Chairman Sam Nunn of Georgia and Mitchell — in an effort to redraft it so senators could justify backing sanctions and also authorizing use of force. The idea was coolly received. In the end, Graham voted against sanctions and was one of 10 Democrats voting to authorize Bush to use military force.

One issue on which Graham has been anything but wavering is the death penalty. While in the Florida statehouse, he earned the sobriquet "the killingest governor," and he carried his pro-death penalty stand to the Senate. He authored a successful amendment to strip from a 1990 crime bill provisions that would have allowed death-row inmates to appeal their sentences using claims of racial disparity in capital punishment decisions. The Senate bill would have also broadened the application of the death penalty in federal cases, but in a House-Senate conference, all the capital punishment provisions were dropped.

As a member of the Banking Committee in the 101st Congress, Graham pushed for a floor vote on a proposal by Chairman Donald W. Riegle Jr., D-Mich., to put the financing for the savings and loan bailout on the federal books. Riegle had not wanted a floor showdown, and the Bush administration wanted to keep the cost from counting as part of the deficit, but Graham was unusually insistent. He fell well short of the votes needed for a procedural waiver. Graham gave up his Banking assignment for Armed Services in the 103rd Congress.

On his other major committee, Environment and Public Works, Graham is a fairly reliable green vote. While working on an omnibus energy bill in 1992, he won a fight to include Florida's coast in a list of areas where new offshore drilling was to be banned. Those provisions were dropped in conference in the face of a veto threat, but offshore drilling foes promised to revisit the issue in the 103rd Congress.

At Home: By the time Graham sought reelection in 1992, he was the state's most popular politician. He was also the subject of a flurry of national attention during the summer when 1992 Democratic presidential nominee Clinton considered him as a running mate.

Back home, the GOP exhibited little interest in attracting a top-flight opponent against Graham. Republicans settled on former Rep. Bill Grant, defeated for re-election in 1990 after he had switched parties to join the GOP. Grant had been hounded more recently by disclosures that he had 106 overdrafts at the House bank. Graham captured nearly two-thirds of the votes.

In his 1986 challenge to GOP Sen. Paula Hawkins, Graham began the year substantially ahead, and he never lost his lead.

Graham had all the vital advantages. Though Hawkins was highly rated in voter surveys, he ranked higher. The governor maintained an image of vigor by performing muscular tasks as part of his "workdays" program, while Hawkins had to have surgery during the campaign to relieve painful back problems.

More important, Graham had an image of competence built on a record of accomplishment on environmental, economic and social issues. Hawkins was an early Senate advocate of action against drug trafficking and child abuse, but she had not played a visible role on major economic, foreign policy or defense issues. And she had committed several embarrassing and widely reported gaffes. This issue of substance was probably the decisive factor in Graham's comfortable 55 percent victory.

Graham inherited an interest in politics from his father, a wealthy dairy farmer who was a state senator in the 1930s and '40s and an unsuccessful candidate for governor in 1944. After graduating from the University of Florida and Harvard Law School, Graham joined his father in the real estate business. His projects, including development of the new town of Miami Lakes, helped him amass a fortune.

Graham was eased into politics by his half-brother Phil, publisher of The Washington Post. Before his suicide in 1963, Phil Graham had introduced his half-brother to many influential Democrats, including Lyndon B. Johnson, for whom Bob Graham worked at the 1960 Democratic National Convention.

Graham's victory in a 1966 state House campaign began his unbroken string of electoral successes. He moved up to the state Senate in 1970. Though Graham was popular in his own base, he was little known elsewhere when he entered the 1978 contest to succeed Democratic Gov. Reubin Askew. Regarded as rather bland, Graham was thought to have little chance in a field of bigger-name contenders.

But Graham came up with the "workdays" gimmick that became his trademark. He spent 100 days working at average, often menial, jobs in various regions of Florida; these efforts drew enormous publicity and gave the wealthy candidate a "common man" appeal. Graham finished a strong second in the primary, then raced past state Attorney General Robert L. Shevin in the runoff, gaining momentum for the general election. He defeated GOP drugstore magnate Jack M. Eckerd with 56 percent.

Graham was not overwhelmingly popular in his early years as governor. His support for capital punishment earned him conservative backing, but it also made him a target for anti-death penalty protesters. On other issues, Graham's caution and attention to detail gave rise to the "Governor Jell-O" nickname.

But beginning in 1982, Graham became more assertive. He hired staff members who promoted his agenda to the Legislature. He pushed his environmental initiatives, including the Save Our Rivers and Save Our Coasts projects. His high profile helped him sweep to re-election that year over GOP Rep. L. A. "Skip" Bafalis.

Graham's stature grew during his second term. He pushed for a balance between development and land-use planning to preserve the environment. Faced with a crime wave, Graham bolstered state law enforcement efforts and promoted an assault on illegal drug trafficking. He backed several tax increases, each one earmarked for a specific purpose, such as education or transportation.

By 1985, it was evident Graham would be a formidable challenger to Hawkins. Though she was known as a champion of family-oriented causes, her critics referred to her as a "lightweight." From her early Senate days, when she hosted a sirloin steak luncheon to announce a plan to jail food stamp cheaters, Hawkins had a reputation for eccentricity.

Hawkins' campaign was put on hold for weeks after her April back surgery. When it resumed, the candidates largely ignored each other, running image-building TV ads produced by Bob Squier (Graham) and Robert Goodman (Hawkins). Goodman presented emotional tales of constituents rescued from serious trouble with the government by Hawkins' intervention. Graham was pictured riding with state police in a helicopter to spot drug smugglers.

Though Graham maintained his substantial lead in opinion polls, his advisers feared Hawkins' emotional ads might earn her a sentimental vote. So in October, Graham went on the offensive, accusing Hawkins of exaggerating her anti-drug record and of "miniaturizing" the office of senator.

The Democrat's strategy succeeded in forcing Hawkins into an issues debate she could not win. She stirred up negative reactions with a pair of comments, one alleging that Graham had communist support, and another, in an appeal for Cuban-American support, that questioned the patriotism of Mexican-Americans. Graham scored a sweeping victory.

Committees

Armed Services (9th of 11 Democrats)
Coalition Defense & Reinforcing Forces; Defense Technology, Acquisition & Industrial Base; Regional Defense & Contingency Forces

Environment & Public Works (6th of 10 Democrats)
Clean Water, Fisheries & Wildlife (chairman); Clean Air & Nuclear Regulation; Superfund, Recycling & Solid Waste Management

Select Intelligence (6th of 9 Democrats)

Special Aging (8th of 11 Democrats)

Veterans' Affairs (4th of 7 Democrats)

Elections

1992 General

Bob Graham (D)	3,244,299	(65%)
Bill Grant (R)	1,715,156	(35%)

1992 Primary

Bob Graham (D)	968,618	(84%)
Jim Mahorner (D)	180,405	(16%)

Previous Winning Percentage: 1986 (55%)

Campaign Finance

1992	Receipts	Receipts from PACs		Expend-itures
Graham (D)	$3,026,137	$905,596	(30%)	$2,979,552
Grant (R)	$248,228	$19,050	(8%)	$242,251

Key Votes

1993

Require unpaid family and medical leave	Y
Approve national "motor voter" registration bill	Y
Approve budget increasing taxes and reducing deficit	Y
Support president's right to lift military gay ban	Y

1992

Approve school-choice pilot program	N
Allow shifting funds from defense to domestic programs	Y
Oppose deeper cuts in spending for SDI	N

1991

Approve waiting period for handgun purchases	Y
Raise senators' pay and ban honoraria	N
Authorize use of force in Persian Gulf	Y
Confirm Clarence Thomas to Supreme Court	N

Voting Studies

	Presidential Support		Party Unity		Conservative Coalition	
Year	S	O	S	O	S	O
1992	35	65	73	27	53	47
1991	47	51	80	18	60	40
1990	53	47	76	23	59	41
1989	64	36	68	32	71	29
1988	60	40	83	16	65	35
1987	46	53	82	18	56	44

Interest Group Ratings

Year	ADA	AFL-CIO	CCUS	ACU
1992	75	75	20	15
1991	65	75	20	38
1990	67	44	36	30
1989	50	100	38	36
1988	55	71	38	28
1987	60	100	28	23

Connie Mack (R)

Of Cape Coral — Elected 1988; 1st Term

Born: Oct. 29, 1940, Philadelphia, Pa.
Education: U. of Florida, B.S. 1966.
Occupation: Banker.
Family: Wife, Priscilla Hobbs; two children.
Religion: Roman Catholic.
Political Career: U.S. House, 1983-89.
Capitol Office: 517 Hart Bldg. 20510; 224-5274.

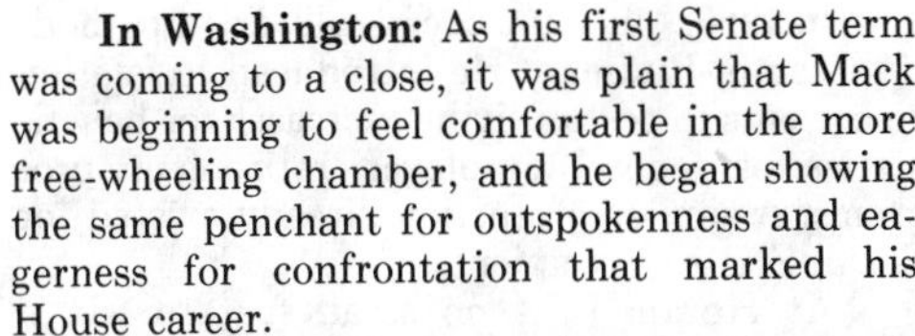

In Washington: As his first Senate term was coming to a close, it was plain that Mack was beginning to feel comfortable in the more free-wheeling chamber, and he began showing the same penchant for outspokenness and eagerness for confrontation that marked his House career.

Particularly on economic issues, he made his voice heard. In February 1992, as George Bush's re-election campaign was in full cry against a challenge from Patrick J. Buchanan on the right, Mack fired a shot at one of the president's closest and most trusted aides. In a letter to Bush followed up by a speech on the Senate floor, Mack denounced Treasury Secretary Nicholas F. Brady for giving Bush "bad economic advice" and called on him to resign.

At a scheduled appearance before the Banking Committee a day after Mack's floor speech, Brady had to listen to Mack lecture him for allowing the economy to fail.

Brady dismissed the episode as political gamesmanship, but for Mack it was not the first time he had challenged Bush over a departure from Republican economic orthodoxy. A staunch fiscal conservative, Mack was one of the most disappointed Republicans when Bush broke his no-new-taxes pledge in 1990. Within hours of Bush's announcement, Mack led a number of conservative Republicans in holding a news conference urging the president not to retreat from his promise. A consistent supply-sider, Mack also fought hard, and unsuccessfully, for inclusion of a capital gains tax cut in the budget legislation approved in 1990.

Mack did not leave a long legislative trail on his way to the Senate, but he did leave a mark. In the House, he made his reputation as an outspoken member of a group of Republicans with an aggressive approach to the Democratic majority. Like many younger-generation Republicans, he was far more prone to castigate the Democratic majority than to look for ways to cooperate with it. "In politics, you gain energy from confrontation," Mack once said, capsulizing the philosophy of the Conservative Opportunity Society, in which he was active.

His first term in the Senate has shown Mack to be an ever-stalwart conservative, although a somewhat less strident and less obviously ambitious one than he was in the House. He votes far more often than his GOP colleagues with the conservative coalition of Republicans and Southern Democrats that occasionally still allies against Northern Democrats.

But there are signs that Mack is willing to trim his sails in adjusting to the political realities of the Senate and in preparing for re-election.

Mack is one of a small core of conservative Senate Republicans — including Jesse Helms of North Carolina and Malcolm Wallop of Wyoming — who have supported revoking normalized trade with China unless that country demonstrates an increased devotion to protecting the human rights of its citizens.

And in early 1991, he was among those to raise their voices over events in the then-disintegrating Soviet Union. Equating the movement of Soviet tanks into Lithuania with the Chinese crackdown on demonstrators in Tiananmen Square, Mack wanted the United States to respond. "The Soviets correctly could have concluded as a result of what occurred after Tiananmen Square ... that while there may be some condemnation, the bottom line [is that] things will work out fine."

But as a sign of his tempered judgment, a year and a half later — after the Soviet collapse — Mack supported a Bush administration request for aid to Russia and other former Soviet republics. And Mack opposed an effort by Arizona Democrat Dennis DeConcini and South Dakota Republican Larry Pressler to suspend aid until the president certified that Russia was making substantial progress in removing troops from the Baltic States.

Also, in early 1992, Mack broke with the Bush administration over the controversial use of fetal tissue for medical research. The possibility that such research might provide new treatments or even cures for degenerative ailments such as diabetes, Parkinson's disease and Alzheimer's disease, was of obvious interest to Florida's large population of retirees.

The administration had imposed a ban on fetal tissue research, which Congress was moving to repeal. Mack voted against an administration-backed compromise that would have established a registry of fetal tissue from miscarriages. Scientists said the registry was unlikely to supply a sufficient quantity of usable tissue.

Narrowly elected to the Senate in 1988 over a well-respected Democratic opponent, Mack faced a skeptical reception upon his entry into the chamber. He made his way to the Banking and Foreign Relations committees. The former gave him an opportunity to put to use his professional background — he was a bank president at age 35 — and the latter provided him a forum to air his hawkish views on the United States' role in world affairs. When Panama became engulfed in a political and economic crisis in early 1989, Mack introduced a resolution calling for an abrogation of the Panama Canal treaties. "We should not take one step further toward the transfer of the canal," he said.

After serving on Foreign Relations during his first two years, he relinquished the seat for one on Armed Services for the 102nd Congress; he used both panels to highlight his conservative views. He successfully pushed legislation in 1990 and 1991 tightening the economic embargo on Cuba — a position likely to curry favor with the large anti-Castro segment of the Florida electorate. He also led the Senate's call on Bush to suspend talks with the Palestine Liberation Organization — a popular stand in Florida's sizable Jewish community.

More than three months before Iraq invaded Kuwait in August 1990, Mack joined two Republican Senate colleagues in calling for the imposition of economic sanctions on that nation in hope of curtailing its chemical weapons capabilities. The Bush administration, however, opposed the efforts.

In the 103rd Congress, Mack continued his game of musical chairs. He left Armed Services for a coveted seat on the Appropriations Committee, where he could continue his efforts to revise the allocation formulas for federal programs to account for Florida's large and growing population of refugees. Mack has introduced multiple bills to have federal aid apportioned on the basis of adjusted census data, which employ mathematical formulas to account for illegal aliens and others not picked up in the formal census count.

On Banking, Housing and Urban Affairs, Mack got involved in the effort to address the crisis in the savings and loan industry. When the Senate in early 1989 passed a bill overhauling the savings and loan regulatory structure, it adopted a Mack amendment requiring national standards for the selection of auditors by thrift institutions and for the conduct of such audits.

During debate on a major banking overhaul bill in 1991, Mack positioned himself as a key roadblock to enactment of provisions that would have required banks to cash government checks and to provide consumers low-cost checking accounts.

Mack also used his position on Banking to play a role in cleaning up the scandal-ridden Department of Housing and Urban Development; he was ranking Republican on the HUD investigative subcommittee.

In the House, Mack worked hard to identify himself with the 1985 Gramm-Rudman anti-deficit law. He became its chief GOP sponsor and promoter in the House. Though he was not noticeably involved in drafting it and did not play a significant role in the process by which members worked out their own language for conference with the Senate, his press releases referred to the Gramm-Rudman-Hollings-Mack law.

In 1986, Mack unsuccessfully tried to modify Gramm-Rudman. He introduced legislation to bar cuts in cost of living increases for beneficiaries of federal employee retirement programs. A similar protection already existed for Social Security recipients.

At Home: It is no small feat to win a Senate seat in a state as large and diverse as Florida, but if Mack's victory in 1988 had impressive elements, it was still a little surprising that the contest was so close given the factors working in his favor. Despite a significant head start, a financial advantage, Democratic infighting and an extremely strong GOP tide at the presidential level, Mack's victory was so narrow that the outcome was settled only by the count of absentee ballots.

Mack, a telegenic candidate in a state where media is extremely important, seemed to be charmed for much of the Senate contest. He entered the Senate race as an underdog against Democratic Sen. Lawton Chiles, but Chiles, who is now governor, surprised his party by announcing his retirement in late 1987. That boosted Mack, who had already nailed down enough Republican support to ward off a serious primary challenger. But it still did not make him the favorite; popular former Democratic Gov. Reubin Askew decided to make a comeback and was considered a likely winner. But then Askew got skittish and backed out, which helped create a Democratic nomination fight that lasted until a month before the general election. The winner, Democratic Rep. Buddy MacKay, emerged bruised, although with a degree of momentum.

While Mack avoided stiff primary competition, he did suffer some barbs from an aggressive Republican opponent, former U.S. Attorney Robert Merkle, who attacked him as a "packaged product." Merkle ran better than had been expected and refused to endorse Mack afterward.

Throughout the campaign — whether he was facing Chiles, Askew or MacKay — Mack framed the voters' choice as one between a conservative and a liberal. He maintained a theme of "less taxing, less spending, less government and more freedom." Even before the

October runoff was settled, he ran ads with the tag line: "Hey Buddy, you're liberal."

But even some Republicans considered Mack's message too simplistic and narrow. MacKay was highly regarded among political insiders for his legislative work, both in the House and previously in the state Legislature, and his voting record put him closer to the center of the political spectrum than to the left. Some prominent environmentalists in the Republican Party said they could not support Mack because he had not addressed environmental issues crucial to fast-growing Florida. In his campaign, MacKay said the choice was "mainstream vs. extreme."

On election night and for a few days following, the race was too close to call, but absentee ballots ultimately put Mack over the top. MacKay considered challenging the results, suggesting that the state's computerized voting system might have failed in some key counties, but he soon abandoned that plan. Two years later, MacKay was elected lieutenant governor.

Mack may have inherited his desire to serve in Congress. His great-grandfather, John L. Sheppard, was a Democratic House member from Texas; his grandfather, Morris Sheppard, also served in the House, then moved on to a 28-year tenure in the Senate. Mack's step-grandfather, Tom Connally, also served Texas in the Senate, from 1929 to 1953.

But it was another forebear who provided Mack with enviable name recognition when he got into politics: His paternal grandfather was the original Connie Mack, the legendary owner and manager of the Philadelphia Athletics baseball team. Like his grandfather, Mack uses the familiar rather than the given version of his name: Cornelius McGillicuddy III. (Mack's baseball past and his free-market beliefs came together in early 1993, when he embraced an end to the national pastime's congressional exemption from antitrust laws.)

After Republican Rep. L. A. "Skip" Bafalis decided to run for governor in 1982, Mack's name gave him a winning edge over four GOP primary opponents for the 13th District House seat. Once nominated, he was guaranteed election and re-election in the solidly Republican constituency.

Committees

Appropriations (12th of 13 Republicans)
Legislative Branch (ranking); District of Columbia; Foreign Operations; Labor, Health & Human Services & Education

Banking, Housing & Urban Affairs (4th of 8 Republicans)
International Finance & Monetary Policy (ranking); Economic Stabilization & Rural Development; Housing & Urban Affairs

Small Business (5th of 9 Republicans)
Competitiveness, Capital Formation & Economic Opportunity (ranking); Urban & Minority-Owned Business Development

Joint Economic

Elections

1988 General		
Connie Mack (R)	2,051,071	(50%)
Buddy MacKay (D)	2,016,553	(50%)
1988 Primary		
Connie Mack (R)	405,296	(62%)
Robert W. Merkle (R)	250,730	(38%)

Previous Winning Percentages: **1986** * (75%) **1984** * (100%) **1982** * (65%)

** House elections.*

Campaign Finance

	Receipts	Receipts from PACs		Expend-itures
1988				
Mack (R)	$5,224,061	$1,018,745	(20%)	$5,181,639
MacKay (D)	$3,622,831	$899,385	(25%)	$3,714,852

Key Votes

1993	
Require unpaid family and medical leave	N
Approve national "motor voter" registration bill	N
Approve budget increasing taxes and reducing deficit	N
Support president's right to lift military gay ban	N
1992	
Approve school-choice pilot program	Y
Allow shifting funds from defense to domestic programs	N
Oppose deeper cuts in spending for SDI	Y
1991	
Approve waiting period for handgun purchases	N
Raise senators' pay and ban honoraria	N
Authorize use of force in Persian Gulf	Y
Confirm Clarence Thomas to Supreme Court	Y

Voting Studies

	Presidential Support		Party Unity		Conservative Coalition	
Year	**S**	**O**	**S**	**O**	**S**	**O**
1992	83 †	16 †	91 †	8 †	82	13
1991	86	14	88	11	90	8
1990	88	12	86	14	95	5
1989	86	14	90	10	82	18
House Service:						
1988	33	11	35	1	37	0
1987	77	19	91	3	91	5
1986	86	12	94	4	98	0
1985	85	15	91	7	91	9
1984	76	21	94	4	92	8
1983	77	20	94	4	92	6

† Not eligible for all recorded votes.

Interest Group Ratings

Year	ADA	AFL-CIO	CCUS	ACU
1992	10	18	100	96
1991	15	50	70	90
1990	0	11	100	96
1989	5	10	88	96
House Service:				
1988	0	0	86	100
1987	0	6	93	95
1986	0	7	100	100
1985	10	18	86	95
1984	5	15	94	96
1983	15	6	89	86

1 Earl Hutto (D)

Of Pensacola — Elected 1978; 8th Term

Born: May 12, 1926, Midland City, Ala.
Education: Troy State U., B.S. 1949; Northwestern U., 1951.
Military Service: Navy, 1944-46.
Occupation: Advertising and broadcasting executive; high school teacher; sportscaster.
Family: Wife, Nancy Myers; two children.
Religion: Baptist.
Political Career: Fla. House, 1973-79.
Capitol Office: 2435 Rayburn Bldg. 20515; 225-4136.

In Washington: Since coming to Congress in 1979, Hutto saw the voting tendencies of his Florida Panhandle district shift from Southern Democratic to mainly Republican in contests for major office. But that caused little consternation for Hutto, a conservative who was one of the leading Democratic supporters of the policies of Republican Presidents Ronald Reagan and George Bush.

Through the 1980s, GOP officials who were promoting partisan "realignment" hoped that Hutto might even switch parties. But he stayed with the Democrats, choosing to pursue seniority within the majority party. Having gained an Armed Services subcommittee chairmanship that relates to his district's economy — and having survived tough GOP efforts to claim the 1st District in the 1990 and 1992 elections — Hutto is unlikely to consider changing his party label now.

But the Democrats' recapture of the White House in 1992 is unlikely to have a marked impact on Hutto's voting behavior. As a conservative on defense, social and most fiscal issues, Hutto will find plenty of reason to disagree with President Clinton, and he is unlikely to conceal it. He proved this early on, in March 1993, when he was one of 22 House Democrats to vote against Clinton's $16.3 billion "economic stimulus" program.

If they care about maintaining the Democratic hold on Florida's 1st District, Clinton legislative strategists probably will have to tolerate some deviation on Hutto's part. A more liberal voting record would be a poor fit for Hutto personally and for the Panhandle district politically.

Hutto will have to continue to win on his conservative record, because he hardly wows the voters with his personal flair. Although Hutto was once a local sportscaster, his reserve as a House member makes it hard to imagine him as the Dick Vitale of western Florida.

Hutto's political strong suits are his positions on Armed Services and as the chairman of its Readiness subcommittee. His district has several large military facilities, including the Navy base at Pensacola; Hurlburt Field is a base for Special Operations Forces, such as the Green Berets and Delta Force, over which the Readiness Subcommittee has jurisdiction.

Hutto is a member of a once-dominant but now declining Democratic species on Armed Services, the pro-Pentagon "Old Guard." While many Democrats cite the demise of Eastern European communism and the collapse of the Soviet Union in calling for deep cutbacks in military spending, Hutto counsels caution.

In February 1991, Hutto warned that even the Bush administration's post-Cold War plan to reduce military spending by 25 percent over five years might be too risky. Hutto — who that January had supported the resolution authorizing Bush to use military force to end Iraq's occupation of Kuwait — said the cutback plan should be reconsidered so that the United States "will not be vulnerable to the future Saddam Husseins of this world."

Hutto maintained this line after the election of Clinton, who advocates even deeper military reductions than did Bush. "As the United States continues to draw down our military, I will be a voice for caution," Hutto says. "We must maintain a strong defense, and we must not reduce the military too quickly or severely."

Hutto puts emphasis on his major legislative focus, military readiness: He says the rapid U.S. deployments to the Persian Gulf region in late 1990 and to Somalia in late 1992 proved that "you can't skimp" on training, equipment and provisions for American troops.

Hutto will be keeping an especially close eye on one issue being examined by the Pentagon in its effort to streamline the services' "roles and missions." Hutto, whose district has a Navy helicopter training facility, would likely oppose a proposal under discussion to consolidate all military helicopter training at Fort Rucker in Alabama.

Also a member of the Merchant Marine and Fisheries Committee, Hutto pursues his interests in military issues as a member of its

Florida 1

Panhandle — Pensacola; Fort Walton Beach

Two enterprises dominate the westernmost part of Florida's Panhandle — military bases and tourism. Tourists are attracted to the soft, white-sand beaches along the Gulf Coast. The military bases are partly an outgrowth of work by Hutto's predecessor in the House, Robert L. F. Sikes.

The huge Eglin Air Force Base primarily develops and tests weapons systems and hosts combat-ready fighter wings. Pensacola's Naval Air Station features a naval education and training center. Among the district's other bases are those involved in naval research and development, the Air Force Special Operations Command, and a Navy helicopter training center. (But one facility, the Naval Aviation Depot, showed up on the 1993 base-closure list.)

The strong military presence helps give the 1st a right-of-center political complexion. Its Democrats, such as Hutto, tend to be conservative, and in statewide elections, GOP candidates usually fare well.

In Pensacola, the district's largest city, the military's contribution to the economy is complemented by manufacturing of chemicals, plastics, textiles and paper. Despite its large natural harbor, Pensacola's potential as a trading port is restricted somewhat because nearby Mobile and New Orleans have much of the gulf trade.

The 100-mile stretch of beach from Pensacola to Panama City, dubbed the "Miracle Strip" by boosters, also has been called the "Redneck Riviera" because it attracts visitors from Georgia, Alabama and other Southeastern states. Along the coastal strip, military retirees have settled in Fort Walton Beach and Destin, both in Okaloosa County, just a few miles from Eglin Air Force Base.

Inland, the sparsely settled rural area is occupied mostly by soybeans, corn, tomatoes, cantaloupes, cattle and pine trees.

The district was not particularly hard hit by the recent recession. Many of its tourists arrive by car for relatively low-cost vacations. And the local military bases did not suffer major job reductions in 1991, a matter Hutto stressed throughout the 1992 campaign.

Local politics are shaped largely by the bases' influence. They provide numerous civilian jobs, and many enlisted personnel remain in the area after leaving the service.

Although Democrats retain a registration edge in the 1st, voters districtwide feel little kinship with the national party. In 1988, George Bush drew 72 percent of the presidential vote and Connie Mack 63 percent in the Senate race, their best showings in the state. Bush swept the district again in 1992.

Escambia County (Pensacola), which accounts for nearly half the district's population, has voted Republican in the past six presidential elections.

But many voters here still feel some guilt when they desert Old South traditions of voting Democratic. Hutto's conservatism suits them just fine, and in 1992 he was able to overcome having lost almost all of Panama City, his home and political base, in redistricting. The GOP trend is strong in Okaloosa County, which is less diversified than Escambia and more reliant on the military.

1990 Population: 562,518. White 472,474 (84%), Black 72,083 (13%), Other 17,961 (3%). Hispanic origin 11,588 (2%). 18 and over 419,490 (75%), 62 and over 78,983 (14%). Median age: 33.

Coast Guard and Navigation Subcommittee, which he once chaired. In that position, Hutto advocated expanded use of the Coast Guard in interdicting illegal drug traffic.

At Home: After a string of easy wins, Hutto got the scare of his congressional career on Election Day 1990, when his aggressive Republican challenger, Terry Ketchel, came within 7,566 votes of unseating him. Hutto appeared to be a marked man for 1992, especially since a presidential election was expected to draw more GOP votes. But Hutto widened his winning margin in a rematch.

Ketchel, a Fort Walton Beach lawyer, had strong party ties by virtue of being a former legislative aide to then-Rep. Guy Vander Jagt of Michigan. Ketchel won a 1992 GOP primary against state Rep. Tom Banjanin, then charged hard at Hutto. He said the incumbent was not conservative enough, citing Hutto's vote in favor of a waiting period for handgun purchases. He accused Hutto of lacking energy in his support for the district's many military bases. And he said Hutto lacked appreciation for the district's vast coastline by not backing a 100-mile ban on offshore drilling.

Hutto, who until 1990 had never received less than 61 percent of the vote, seemed unprepared for Ketchel's initial challenge, but he was more engaged in the rematch. He touted the value of his Armed Services Committee seat, noting that he was Florida's only member on that committee seeking re-election. Ketchel's protests aside, the district's military bases had not been hit with major job losses.

Hutto was not helped by redistricting,

which removed almost all of Panama City, his home and political base. But he ran strongly in Escambia County (Pensacola) and nearly matched Ketchel in Okaloosa County, which again went heavily for Bush and includes Ketchel's hometown of Fort Walton Beach.

Before his election to the state Legislature in 1972, Hutto was a television sportscaster in both Panama City and Pensacola, at opposite ends of the 1st. So when he began his 1978 congressional campaign, aiming to succeed the retiring Democratic Rep. Robert L. F. Sikes, his face was familiar to much of the district.

That was an enormous help to him in the Democratic primary. Rated no higher than third out of four candidates before the voting, Hutto finished a comfortable first in the initial primary, then won easily in the runoff.

With Sikes out of the picture, Republicans were optimistic that their candidate, former Pensacola Mayor Warren Briggs, could take the district in the fall. But Hutto gave Briggs no opening on the right. He promised to protect the 1st's military facilities — which had been well-tended by Armed Services Committee member Sikes — and stressed law enforcement and economy in government.

Hutto's involvement in Baptist church affairs was of special help in the district's rural areas, where Briggs' identification with Pensacola business interests was not an advantage. Hutto won 63 percent of the vote.

Briggs tried again in 1980, but Hutto was untouchable. Even though Reagan won the district's presidential vote, Briggs barely improved on his 1978 showing. Hutto then won easily for reelection, until Ketchel caught him by surprise in 1990.

Committees

Armed Services (4th of 34 Democrats)
Readiness (chairman); Research & Technology

Merchant Marine & Fisheries (3rd of 29 Democrats)
Coast Guard & Navigation; Environment & Natural Resources; Fisheries Management

Elections

1992 General		
Earl Hutto (D)	118,753	(52%)
Terry Ketchel (R)	100,136	(44%)
Barbara Ann Rodgers-Hendricks (GREEN)	9,320	(4%)
1992 Primary		
Earl Hutto (D)	60,346	(68%)
Ernie Padgett (D)	17,373	(20%)
Harry Keller (D)	10,411	(12%)
1990 General		
Earl Hutto (D)	88,416	(52%)
Terry Ketchel (R)	80,851	(48%)

Previous Winning Percentages: **1988** (67%) **1986** (64%) **1984** (100%) **1982** (74%) **1980** (61%) **1978** (63%)

District Vote for President

1992
D 59,247 (26%)
R 117,712 (51%)
I 53,286 (23%)

Campaign Finance

	Receipts	Receipts from PACs		Expend-itures
1992				
Hutto (D)	$298,700	$144,704	(48%)	$297,989
Ketchel (R)	$164,581	$27,786	(17%)	$166,762
1990				
Hutto (D)	$184,405	$95,307	(52%)	$158,280
Ketchel (R)	$184,650	$8,198	(4%)	$182,229

Key Votes

1993	
Require parental notification of minors' abortions	Y
Require unpaid family and medical leave	N
Approve national "motor voter" registration bill	N
Approve budget increasing taxes and reducing deficit	Y
Approve economic stimulus plan	N
1992	
Approve balanced-budget constitutional amendment	Y
Close down space station program	Y
Approve U.S. aid for former Soviet Union	N
Allow shifting funds from defense to domestic programs	N
1991	
Extend unemployment benefits using deficit financing	N
Approve waiting period for handgun purchases	Y
Authorize use of force in Persian Gulf	Y

Voting Studies

	Presidential Support		Party Unity		Conservative Coalition	
Year	**S**	**O**	**S**	**O**	**S**	**O**
1992	66	31	44	51	90	8
1991	59	40	50	46	92	5
1990	54	45	51	44	94	4
1989	70	29	54	43	93	7
1988	41	53	56	41	97	0
1987	53	46	55	40	91	7
1986	57	40	51	45	92	8
1985	56	43	56	40	93	7
1984	57	40	51	46	95	3
1983	61	37	45	51	96	2
1982	62	34	54	43	89	10
1981	74	25	46	53	93	5

Interest Group Ratings

Year	ADA	AFL-CIO	CCUS	ACU
1992	15	36	88	83
1991	15	33	90	80
1990	28	50	77	78
1989	10	45	100	85
1988	20	57	69	76
1987	24	27	64	68
1986	5	29	89	82
1985	15	25	86	76
1984	20	46	46	57
1983	10	24	75	91
1982	10	32	71	71
1981	10	40	78	93

2 Pete Peterson (D)

Of Marianna — Elected 1990; 2nd Term

Born: June 26, 1935, Omaha, Neb.
Education: U. of Tampa, B.S. 1976; U. of Central Michigan, 1977.
Military Service: Air Force, 1954-80.
Occupation: Educational administrator.
Family: Wife, Carlotta Ann Neal; three children.
Religion: Roman Catholic.
Political Career: No previous office.
Capitol Office: 426 Cannon Bldg. 20515; 225-5235.

In Washington: Peterson made an impression on his House colleagues less than a month after he arrived in Washington. Because of his credentials as a Vietnam War hero and former prisoner of war, members took notice when Peterson took the floor during the January 1991 debate on the use of military force in the Persian Gulf.

With the calls for intervention echoing through the chamber, Peterson urged members to vote against sending American troops to the Persian Gulf.

"I vowed when I sat in Hanoi that I would never commit troops to battle without the support of the American people," he said.

Born in Nebraska, Peterson joined the Air Force just a year after finishing high school, rising to the rank of colonel. During his 27-year military career, he volunteered for duty in Vietnam, where he was shot down and spent 6½ years as a prisoner of war.

With his impassioned speech, Peterson made it clear that he was not afraid to take a personal stand on tough issues. His voting record paints a picture of a moderate Democrat, and Peterson has shown a willingness to compromise. But he is equally willing to go his own way on what he regards as a matter of principle. On party-line votes in 1992, he voted with his fellow Democrats only about 76 percent of the time. Even before he was elected, he had a history of independent voting. Although he describes himself as a lifelong Democrat, he says he voted for George Bush in 1988.

Peterson's views sometimes put him at odds with his conservative district. Early in the 103rd, he supported the Family and Medical Leave Act. In the 102nd, he voted for legislation that included provisions to overturn President Bush's ban on abortion counseling at federally funded family planning clinics. However, he also voted against gun control legislation that called for a waiting period for handgun purchases.

With the strength of his personality, some thoughtful legislative efforts and votes on difficult issues, Peterson made enough of an impression on the party leadership to land a position on the powerful Appropriations Committee in the 103rd Congress. He sits on the subcommittees on Agriculture and Energy and Water.

During his first term, Peterson served on the Public Works and Transportation Committee, which allowed him to score important points back home. He successfully pushed for a $4.7 billion authorization for highway and other construction for Florida. Peterson said the bill would authorize more than 100,000 jobs for the state. In addition, the measure includes a $2.4 million authorization to construct a bridge over Mosquito Creek in Chattahoochee, Fla.

Peterson's military history made him a logical candidate for the Veterans' Affairs Committee, where he was active during the 102nd Congress. He introduced a bill that would make soldiers eligible for a Purple Heart if they were wounded in action by friendly fire. He also sponsored legislation that would call for the minting of coins to commemorate American prisoners of war.

Peterson also got involved on issues unrelated to his committee assignments. He offered a substitute amendment to striker replacement legislation aimed at attracting moderate members who could not support the version of the bill reported by the Education and Labor Committee. The substitute would have required that a majority of workers file for recognition with the National Labor Relations Board at least 30 days before a strike in order to get protection from permanent replacement.

He explained that the business community in his district believed that the original language was too ambiguous. "They were concerned that perhaps any two of their employees could form themselves into a unit, walk off and, therefore, shut down that business," he said.

While other members wanted faster action from the Bush administration, Peterson supported President Bush's policy of moving slowly to normalize trade relations with Vietnam. Bush offered to take steps toward resuming normal relations provided that Hanoi support a U.N.-sponsored peace settlement in neighboring Cambodia.

Florida 2

Panhandle — Tallahassee; part of Panama City

A Florida adage has it that the farther north you go from Miami, the farther South you get. Natives consider North Florida to be the "real Florida," but some city dwellers outside the district regard the 2nd as a land of "rednecks" and "crackers."

1992 remapping made the sprawling 2nd more compact. The district shed some counties to the south and east while adding much of Bay County (Panama City) to the west. About 34 percent of the district's residents live in Leon County (Tallahassee). The rest are scattered in 17 other counties; except for Panama City, none of them has a town with even 15,000 residents. The boundary shifts did little to alter the district's conservative Democratic nature.

Two major interstates — I-75 and I-10 — intersect in Columbia County (Lake City). But this is just a passing-through point for most motorists headed for beaches and tourist attractions elsewhere. The bulk of the 2nd has just begun to see hints of the kind of development that has transformed much of Florida.

Tallahassee, the capital, is economically sustained by state government and two universities, Florida State and Florida A&M, with a combined total of about 38,000 students. These institutions, along with health care, high technology and publishing industries, help make Leon County more diverse than the rural areas surrounding it. But Tallahassee's elegant antebellum homes and flower gardens symbolize a Deep South strain in its personality that persists in the face of development and rapid population growth.

The addition of Panama City to the 2nd gives it a major military installation — Tyndall Air Force Base, an air defense training facility. Panama City also has some industry and burgeoning retirement communities that attract military veterans and others who value the proximity to beaches.

The "Big Bend" Gulf Coast is mostly undeveloped. Pine trees stretch for miles, sustaining companies making paper, tobacco, pulp and chemicals. Prime agricultural products include peanuts, cotton, corn and honey. There is a local seafood industry, but its future is clouded by concerns about overfishing and environmental degradation.

Gadsden County is making a transition from tobacco crops to vegetables. The change has been tough; Gadsden was one of only two Florida counties to lose population in the 1980s. Gadsden, which is majority black, is the only Florida county to vote Democratic in the last three presidential elections. It helps give the district the state's fourth-highest percentage of black residents.

The district's Democratic presidential vote slid from 53 percent in 1980 to 40 percent in 1988 before rebounding slightly in 1992. GOP registration has increased, and conservative church groups have gotten active in anti-abortion politics. But Democratic loyalties that were forged a century ago are still strong locally. By recapturing the 2nd District seat in 1990, Democrats showed that incumbent Bill Grant had overestimated the district's drift toward the GOP when he switched to become a Republican in 1989.

1990 Population: 562,519. White 421,088 (75%), Black 130,419 (23%), Other 11,012 (2%). Hispanic origin 10,990 (2%). 18 and over 419,703 (75%), 62 and over 79,437 (14%). Median age: 32.

"My family didn't know whether I was alive or dead for three years," he said. "It's not a question of get back, it's just that we know them; we lived with them."

Peterson has said he will not support full normalization of relations until Hanoi makes a complete accounting on POW-MIA issues.

Peterson also paid close attention to the 2nd District, holding more than 50 town hall meetings during his freshman term.

At Home: Peterson's 1990 victory was due partly to the shortcomings of the incumbent, Republican Rep. Bill Grant. Though voter registration in the 2nd is heavily Democratic, Grant converted to the GOP four months after winning re-election in 1988 as a Democrat.

Grant's defection enraged Democrats, who nonetheless had trouble recruiting a well-known challenger. They settled on Peterson, whose political activity was limited to a seat on the Jackson County Democratic Executive Committee.

After Peterson finished his military career in 1980, he settled in Florida, starting a couple of businesses. He was also headmaster of the Dozier School for Boys, a state institution for male juvenile offenders.

Trying to save money, GOP Gov. Bob Martinez in 1988 sought to close the school. Peterson began a fierce and ultimately successful lobbying effort to keep the school open. That experience opened Peterson's eyes to the importance of political involvement, and it won him the support of some education groups.

Peterson's reserved manner was not ideal for a political campaign, but his background was perfect to carry the integrity banner against Grant. He chastised Grant for not resigning after his conversion to the GOP and then standing for office again as a Republican.

His military background became an asset in the general election campaign, as concerns over the Persian Gulf crisis focused attention on foreign policy and military matters. Those strengths enabled the little-known Peterson to best Grant, despite the incumbent's financial edge and support from Bush and other administration officials.

Peterson's re-election was never in doubt. He took more than 70 percent of the vote.

Committee

Appropriations (34th of 37 Democrats)
Agriculture, Rural Development, FDA & Related Agencies; Energy & Water Development

Elections

1992 General		
Pete Peterson (D)	167,151	(73%)
Ray Wagner (R)	60,378	(27%)
1992 Primary		
Pete Peterson (D)	96,909	(69%)
Buster Smith (D)	43,891	(31%)
1990 General		
Pete Peterson (D)	103,032	(57%)
Bill Grant (R)	77,939	(43%)

District Vote for President

	1992
D	98,175 (42%)
R	88,576 (38%)
I	45,206 (19%)

Campaign Finance

	Receipts	Receipts from PACs		Expend-itures
1992				
Peterson (D)	$401,747	$272,350	(68%)	$378,424
Wagner (R)	$23,425	0		$25,724
1990				
Peterson (D)	$306,429	$133,170	(43%)	$306,104
Grant (R)	$801,238	$305,253	(38%)	$839,764

Key Votes

1993	
Require parental notification of minors' abortions	N
Require unpaid family and medical leave	Y
Approve national "motor voter" registration bill	Y
Approve budget increasing taxes and reducing deficit	Y
Approve economic stimulus plan	Y
1992	
Approve balanced-budget constitutional amendment	Y
Close down space station program	N
Approve U.S. aid for former Soviet Union	Y
Allow shifting funds from defense to domestic programs	Y
1991	
Extend unemployment benefits using deficit financing	Y
Approve waiting period for handgun purchases	N
Authorize use of force in Persian Gulf	N

Voting Studies

	Presidential Support		Party Unity		Conservative Coalition	
Year	**S**	**O**	**S**	**O**	**S**	**O**
1992	27	69	76	15	65	25
1991	37	63	84	15	73	27

Interest Group Ratings

Year	ADA	AFL-CIO	CCUS	ACU
1992	75	64	38	19
1991	55	75	40	15

3 Corrine Brown (D)

Of Jacksonville — Elected 1992; 1st Term

Born: Nov. 11, 1946, Jacksonville, Fla.

Education: Florida A&M U., B.S. 1969; U. of Florida, Ed.S. 1974.

Occupation: College guidance counselor; travel agency owner.

Family: Divorced; one child.

Religion: Baptist.

Political Career: Candidate for Fla. House, 1980; Fla. House, 1983-93.

Capitol Office: 1037 Longworth Bldg. 20515; 225-0123.

The Path to Washington: In order to get to Congress, Brown had to work her way around what many call Florida's ugliest congressional district and survive one of its nastier primaries.

The 3rd District, variously described as a wishbone or horseshoe, winds its way through 14 North Florida counties, from Orlando to Jacksonville to Ocala, to bring a number of predominantly black communities together and achieve a 50.1 percent black voting-age population.

In the primary, Brown clearly out-hustled another black legislator in the race, state Sen. Arnett E. Girardeau, which forced her into a runoff with former state Rep. Andrew E. Johnson, the only white candidate. Johnson made a big issue of the district's unusual shape and frequently criticized Brown and Girardeau for having supported the creative cartography that went into drawing the 3rd.

During the campaign, Johnson, who said he was "the blackest candidate in the race" because of his position on issues, attacked Brown's integrity, claimed that she did not live in the district and filed charges with the Florida Ethics Commission that she had violated campaign finance rules. She retorted that "he's an absolute nut. It's just attack, attack, attack. He can't talk about what he's going to do."

Brown talked, promising to be an advocate for the poor and underprivileged, and won the runoff with 64 percent of the vote.

Still, Brown had not seen the last of Johnson's accusations. Though the state panel dismissed three of the charges filed in the 1992 election cycle, a local paper reported, it called in April 1993 for hearings into an allegation that Brown had used employees from her state representative's office in her private travel business.

In the general election, Brown was considered a favorite over Don Weidner, in part because of the Democratic bent of the district. She won with 59 percent of the vote.

Though Brown served as a member of the Finance and Taxation committees in the state Legislature, she sought and received a position on the Public Works and Transportation Committee. Her reasons were simple: First, her diverse district needs better transportation alternatives for congested Orlando and flood-control improvements. Second, public works projects mean jobs.

And from her position on the Veterans' Affairs Committee, Brown can keep an eye on defense policy: There are several military installations in her North Florida district.

She does not oppose scaling down the military in general but wants to see what she calls a "productive change" that would focus less on new technology and more on human resources, which she defines as the better training of military personnel. She also considers the military a place where families, particularly poor families, can find opportunities and learn self-discipline.

Brown acknowledges her debt to other women legislators — her predecessors and the women who helped her this time around. Her mentor was Gwendolyn Sawyer Cherry, the first black Florida state representative, and a sorority sister at Florida A&M University. Cherry encouraged her friend to get into politics, and though Brown lost her first state House race in 1980, Cherry kept after her to try again. Brown won a state House seat in 1982.

When Brown decided to run for Congress, the women's organizations offered financial and organizational support. After she won the primary, she triumphantly declared, "This is the year of the woman, so get out of the way, men."

Brown supports abortion rights and has been a strong supporter of programs that assist parents with child care. She plans to continue her advocacy in the House, particularly for "Healthy Start," a program that emphasizes early, preventive health care for young children. She also supports increased funding for Head Start, the federal education program for young children, and more money for student aid and loans.

Though many incoming members support a constitutional amendment to balance the budget, Brown does not. She also opposes the cap on damages recoverable by women, the disabled and religious minorities, which was enacted as part of the 1991 civil rights bill.

Florida 3

North — Parts of Jacksonville, Orlando, Daytona Beach, Gainesville

Nothing is more remarkable about the 3rd than its shape. On a map, the district looks something like a jagged horseshoe or gnawed wishbone.

Florida gained four House seats in 1990 reapportionment, and mapmakers seeking to increase minority representation drew three new majority-minority districts in South Florida and this one in the north.

The 3rd meanders about 250 miles through 14 counties, taking in nearly every black neighborhood from Orlando north to the Georgia state line, linking them with white working-class areas.

Starting at its southeastern point in Orlando, the district heads north to Jacksonville, jutting toward the Atlantic to grab black neighborhoods in Daytona Beach and St. Augustine. After reaching Jacksonville, the district turns west to Lake City before dropping south to Gainesville and Ocala.

The result of all these twists and turns is a district in which blacks make up 55 percent of the total population. Three of four registered voters are Democrats.

Jacksonville is the district's cartographic and demographic apex; about 45 percent of the 3rd's population lives here, and in 1992, both parties' House primaries were dominated by candidates from Jacksonville. Orange County (Orlando) is home to one-fifth of the people in the 3rd.

Unlike Florida cities farther south that are oriented toward leisure activities and have many northern-state transplants, Jacksonville is a workaday city with a Southern feel. Some neighborhoods are integrated, but basically the city's black and white populations live apart, even though the military, long a vital component of Jacksonville's economy, has provided middle-class means to many blacks as well as whites in the area.

The retiree population of the 3rd is significant, if not as large as that seen in many other Florida districts. The seniors in the Jacksonville area tend to be middle-income types — former teachers, former military personnel and the like — who have lived locally for much of their lives. In that respect the typical retiree-filled high-rise here is different from those farther south in Florida, whose residents are often later-in-life arrivals to the Sunshine State.

Tourism accounts for more than 40 percent of the jobs in metropolitan Orlando (Orange County), home of Disney World and other attractions. There is a large blue-collar work force in service-oriented businesses.

In Gainesville (Alachua County), the University of Florida, though not in the 3rd District, is the largest employer.

Statistics reveal the tough economic plight of many in the 3rd. It is the second-poorest district in the state, and both its poverty rate (over 25 percent) and its incidence of single-woman households are nearly double the state average.

The district has some splinters of white conservatism, in such areas as suburban Clay County, the wealthiest area in the 3rd, and Palatka in Putnam County. But GOP votes from these areas are outweighed by big Democratic margins elsewhere.

1990 Population: 562,519. White 242,516 (43%), Black 309,396 (55%), Other 10,607 (2%). Hispanic origin 15,511 (3%). 18 and over 400,759 (71%), 62 and over 82,776 (15%). Median age: 31.

Committees

Government Operations (22nd of 25 Democrats)
Legislation & National Security

Public Works & Transportation (33rd of 39 Democrats)
Aviation; Economic Development; Water Resources & the Environment

Veterans' Affairs (21st of 21 Democrats)
Hospitals & Health Care; Housing & Memorial Affairs

Campaign Finance

	Receipts	Receipts from PACs		Expenditures
1992				
Brown (D)	$289,260	$147,363	(51%)	$275,705
Weidner (R)	$258,431	$24,500	(9%)	$258,394

Key Votes

1993

Require parental notification of minors' abortions	N
Require unpaid family and medical leave	Y
Approve national "motor voter" registration bill	Y
Approve budget increasing taxes and reducing deficit	Y
Approve economic stimulus plan	Y

Elections

1992 General		
Corrine Brown (D)	91,877	(59%)
Don Weidner (R)	63,070	(41%)
1992 Primary Runoff		
Corrine Brown (D)	29,006	(64%)
Andrew E. Johnson (D)	16,427	(36%)
1992 Primary		
Corrine Brown (D)	25,374	(43%)
Andrew E. Johnson (D)	18,209	(31%)
Arnett E. Girardeau (D)	10,746	(18%)
Glennie Mills (D)	4,383	(7%)

District Vote for President

	1992	
D	93,384	(57%)
R	49,288	(30%)
I	20,255	(12%)

4 Tillie Fowler (R)

Of Jacksonville — Elected 1992; 1st Term

Born: Dec. 23, 1942, Milledgeville, Ga.
Education: Emory U., A.B. 1964, J.D. 1967.
Occupation: White House aide; congressional aide; lawyer.
Family: Husband, L. Buck Fowler; two children.
Religion: Episcopalian.
Political Career: Jacksonville City Council, 1985-92, president, 1989-90.
Capitol Office: 413 Cannon Bldg. 20515; 225-2501.

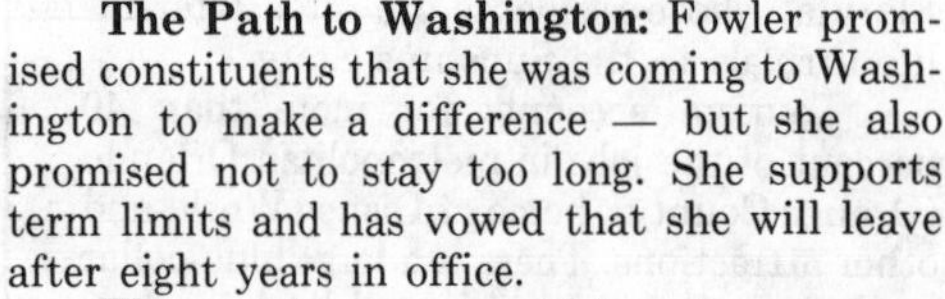

The Path to Washington: Fowler promised constituents that she was coming to Washington to make a difference — but she also promised not to stay too long. She supports term limits and has vowed that she will leave after eight years in office.

Those eight years would be a far cry from the tenure of the area's previous representative — Democrat Charles E. Bennett, who announced in 1992 that he would not seek a 23rd term.

And, much as Bennett took care of his constituents for nearly 50 years, Fowler will be looking out for her district. She made good on her campaign pledge to secure a seat on the Armed Services Committee so that she could watch over Jacksonville's Mayport Naval Air Station, which has lost about half its jobs.

In an era in which tough defense cutbacks seem inevitable, Fowler may find some guidance in the committee room, named for Carl Vinson, a family friend who represented Fowler's hometown in Georgia from 1914 to 1965. "Mr. Carl" might be surprised to see a woman serving on his old panel and a Southern Republican at that — a far cry from when almost all members of Congress were men and most Southerners were Democrats.

As an experienced local politician with two stints in Washington behind her, Fowler wants to be both consensus-builder and leader in her freshman class.

She believes her past experiences will serve her well. She was the first woman and first Republican — out of only three Republicans on the 19-member Jacksonville City Council — to be elected council president. Later she chaired the Finance Committee and worked successfully with the panel's Democrats.

But Fowler, who considers herself a negotiator, does not want anyone to mistake her willingness to forge consensus for a lack of resolve. One local newspaper dubbed her a "killer bee" because she was part of a group of council members who fought regularly to kill legislation they opposed. And she voiced no regrets when, as council leader, she ordered the arrest and return of three council members who tried to walk out of an important meeting in 1989.

Like many of her freshman colleagues, Fowler campaigned against the current Congress, calling them "timid, shell-bound career politicians." She believes the seniority system needs to be modified to allow newer members to have more influence.

Fowler announced her candidacy early in June, when incumbent Bennett, a senior member of Armed Services, had said he was going to run again. But Bennett changed his mind, and Fowler found herself facing Mattox Hair, a former state legislator and judge.

Though both were experienced politicians, Fowler repeatedly tagged Hair as standing with "the good old boys" in the Florida Legislature who she said favored legislative pay raises, "slush funds" and billion-dollar tax increases.

Fowler's early entry into the race gave her a fundraising jump, and she also lined up bipartisan support. By the time Hair announced, 22 friends who had supported his 1984 state Senate bid already had signed on to help Fowler.

In addition to supporting term limits — a popular cause among members of the 1992 class — she favors a balanced-budget constitutional amendment and abortion rights.

Fowler, who has two children and a husband who runs a small business, said she would have voted against the family leave bill that President Bush vetoed in 1992 because it would unfairly burden small businesses. She supports the concept but urges flexibility in any leave policy to accommodate businesses of all sizes.

She remained true to her stance in the early part of the 103rd Congress and voted against the family leave legislation, which President Clinton signed into law in February 1993.

Before coming to Congress, Fowler had worked in Washington as a legislative assistant for Rep. Robert G. Stephens Jr., a Georgia Democrat who served from 1961 to 1977, and as general counsel in the White House Office of Consumer Affairs during the Nixon administration.

Florida 4

Northeast — Part of Jacksonville; northern Volusia County

The 4th includes much of eastern Jacksonville and the Atlantic coastal communities from the Georgia state line to part of Daytona Beach. Democrats retain a voter-registration edge here, but it seems attributable to habit and a desire to have a say in local Democratic primaries.

These conservative Democrats — combined with a GOP trend and the transfer of black neighborhoods from the 4th to the 3rd in redistricting — should make the 4th reliably Republican at the top of the ticket. George Bush received 70 percent of the presidential vote in 1988. The 4th also gave Bob Martinez his highest voting percentage in his unsuccessful 1990 gubernatorial reelection bid, and Sen. Connie Mack got his second highest percentage vote here in 1988.

Jacksonville, which accounts for about half the district's population, is the state's most populous city and the nation's largest in land mass, thanks to its consolidation in 1969 with surrounding Duval County. The city's business and political leaders have generally preferred steady if unspectacular economic expansion based on the city's traditional economic foundations of shipping, insurance, banking and defense.

The strategy has paid dividends at the port along the St. Johns River, one of the world's few northerly flowing rivers. By touting its fine harbor and ready access to rail lines and roads that lead to dealers in the lucrative Southeastern market, Jacksonville has become the leading East Coast port of entry for foreign vehicles.

Workers who handle cargo and build and repair ships form much of Jacksonville's blue-collar community. Prudential, Independent Life and American Heritage insurance companies are among the largest white-collar employers in the city, as are AT&T/Universal Card, Winn-Dixie supermarkets, Blue Cross & Blue Shield and Barnett Banks.

Military installations include the Naval Aviation Depot, which repairs and maintains naval aeronautic equipment, and Mayport Naval Air Station, home base of the *Saratoga* aircraft carrier. Because several other ships based at Mayport have either been decommissioned or moved, civic leaders are seeking to have the base designated as capable of handling nuclear-powered ships.

The city's increasingly important medical industry includes a Mayo Clinic branch in southeast Jacksonville, a growing area that affords easy access to nearby beaches.

Northeast Florida markets itself as "Florida's First Coast," a reference to Ponce de Leon being the first European to set foot on Florida soil in the 16th century. He landed near what is now Ponte Vedra, current home of the Professional Golfers Association and the Association of Tennis Professionals.

Continuing south, Flagler County was the state's fastest growing county during the 1980s, with a population increase of 163 percent. Much of the boom was fed by an influx of retirees to the Palm Coast area.

The district extends into northern Volusia and Daytona Beach. This southernmost part of the district may be the 4th's most reliably Democratic region.

1990 Population: 562,518. White 513,579 (91%), Black 32,374 (6%), Other 16,565 (3%). Hispanic origin 17,662 (3%). 18 and over 436,058 (78%), 62 and over 95,744 (17%). Median age: 35.

Committees

Armed Services (18th of 22 Republicans)
Military Installations & Facilities; Military Forces & Personnel

Merchant Marine & Fisheries (12th of 18 Republicans)
Coast Guard & Navigation; Merchant Marine

Campaign Finance

	Receipts	Receipts from PACs		Expend-itures
1992				
Fowler (R)	$524,951	$115,350	(22%)	$512,267
Hair (D)	$428,706	$144,050	(34%)	$427,480

Key Votes

1993

Require parental notification of minors' abortions	N
Require unpaid family and medical leave	N
Approve national "motor voter" registration bill	N
Approve budget increasing taxes and reducing deficit	N
Approve economic stimulus plan	N

Elections

1992 General

Tillie Fowler (R)	135,772	(57%)
Mattox Hair (D)	103,484	(43%)

District Vote for President

1992

D 75,323 (30%)
R 131,930 (53%)
I 41,115 (17%)

5 Karen L. Thurman (D)

Of Dunnellon — Elected 1992; 1st Term

Born: Jan. 12, 1951, Rapid City, S.D.
Education: Santa Fe Community College, A.A. 1971; U. of Florida, B.A. 1973.
Occupation: Teacher.
Family: Husband, John Thurman; two children.
Religion: Episcopalian.
Political Career: Dunnellon City Council, 1975-83, mayor, 1979-81; Fla. Senate, 1983-93.
Capitol Office: 130 Cannon Bldg. 20515; 225-1002.

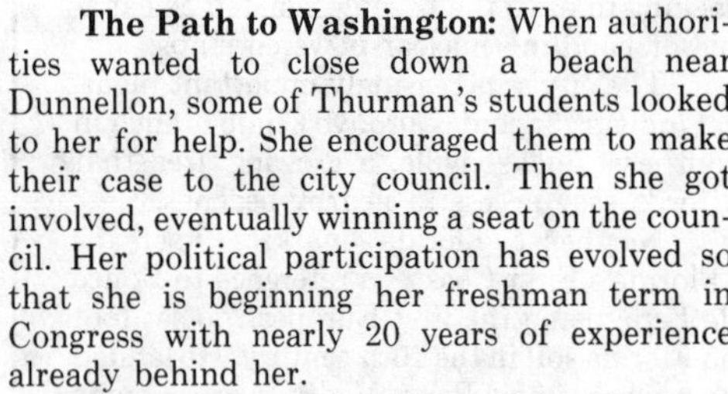

The Path to Washington: When authorities wanted to close down a beach near Dunnellon, some of Thurman's students looked to her for help. She encouraged them to make their case to the city council. Then she got involved, eventually winning a seat on the council. Her political participation has evolved so that she is beginning her freshman term in Congress with nearly 20 years of experience already behind her.

A middle school math teacher, Thurman continued teaching while she was on the city council and during a stint as mayor. She gave up the classroom when she was elected to the Florida Senate in 1982.

She built a reputation as an astute, hard-working legislator identified with such issues as education, consumer protection and the environment.

On Earth Day 1993, Thurman delivered a floor speech calling for greater use of renewable energy sources, particularly solar power. She said greater support for alternative fuels could create hundreds of thousands of jobs, save homeowners money, reduce U.S. dependence on foreign oil and cut pollution.

Among her other environmental efforts were work on legislation to clean up leaky underground petroleum tanks, protect Florida's drinking water and preserve wetlands.

For her work, Thurman has collected awards from agriculture and fisheries groups, education organizations, the Florida Sheriffs' Association, and the Veterans of Foreign Wars, which named her Outstanding Legislator for the 1989-90 legislative year. She attributes her success as a legislator to the fact that she focused on issues and sought common ground with colleagues without worrying about party labels.

In what could be considered a stroke of luck, her most recent Senate responsibilities included chairing the Subcommittee on Congressional Reapportionment as the state was redrawing its district lines.

Critics griped that she carved out a new congressional district for herself that included much of her state Senate district and preserved her strongest bases of support. Even some of her backers criticized her for participating in closed-door, private sessions where redistricting was discussed and for opposing extension of an open-meetings law to state officials.

Along with the criticism of supporters came the barbs of her primary opponent, who tried to paint her as a member of the entrenched political elite who needed to be removed from office.

Her general-election opponent, Republican Tom Hogan, a former prosecutor and now a lawyer in private practice, portrayed Thurman as a "professional, big-money politician."

Hogan, whom Thurman beat in the 1990 state Senate race, ran on a fiscally conservative platform that appealed to some of the 5th's retirees and veterans. But Thurman prevailed with 49 percent of the vote.

Thurman campaigned against Congress, criticizing gridlock and talking about reform.

But her position as a veteran lawmaker tempered her tone in discussions of term limits. Rather than seeking to limit the time a member can serve in Congress, she supports limits on the years a representative can serve on committees and in chairmanships. She also supports limiting the Speaker's term.

Thurman got a place on the Government Operations Committee, but it is her slot on the Agriculture Committee that may have been a higher priority.

The 5th is heavily agricultural, with citrus and peanut crops that compete directly with Mexican goods. And because of what is perceived as a threat to jobs in her district, she has been an outspoken opponent of the North American Free Trade Agreement.

On other issues, Thurman supports abortion rights and wants to broaden traditional "women's issues" to areas beyond health care and jobs.

She would reduce the budget deficit by cutting outmoded military projects and increasing taxes on foreign corporations and the wealthy. She supports tax incentives for companies that create jobs.

Florida 5

Northern West Coast — Parts of Alachua and Pasco counties; Hernando County

The 5th collects all or parts of nine counties as it comes around the "Big Bend" Gulf Coast from Dixie to Pasco counties. It includes several distinct regions.

About 57 percent of district residents live in Hernando, Citrus and western Pasco counties north of Tampa-St. Petersburg, where retirees have spurred rapid growth along the coast. About 25 percent live in parts of Alachua County, which is noted mainly for the presence of the University of Florida (35,000 students). Most of the remaining district residents live in lightly populated rural counties.

Democrats have wide registration leads in Alachua County and most of the rural areas, while Republicans are more competitive in the retirement areas. But except for Alachua, most of the Democrats are conservative and can be swayed to vote for Republicans at the top of the ticket. Democrat Bill Clinton won most of the counties in the 5th, but with the exception of Alachua County, his margins were quite small. Similarly, Thurman swept all nine counties in her three-candidate race, though she rarely drew more than 50 percent in them.

Western Pasco County, which was carved from GOP Rep. Michael Bilirakis' district in 1992 redistricting, has retirees and military veterans, as do Citrus and Hernando counties, which were transferred from Republican Rep. Cliff Stearns' district. These retirees from the Midwest and Northeast generally have modest incomes. They include former blue-collar workers who retain allegiance to the United Auto Workers, which has a presence here, and to such civic groups as Italian-American and Polish-American clubs.

The area has an abundance of recreational opportunities, including gulf beaches, the Withlacoochee State Forest and Weeki Wachee Spring. Manatees, which are endangered mammals, frequent the Crystal River. The health-care industry is a leading local employer, and there are two nuclear power plants.

The district includes most of Alachua County and Gainesville. Although minority neighborhoods are part of the adjacent 3rd, the presence of the University of Florida puts this area to the left of conservative Democrats who predominate in most of north Florida. Gainesville is a medical center for the northern interior of the state, and the university attracts high-tech companies. Agriculture — including peanuts, watermelon and dairy products — dominates elsewhere in the county.

The other counties in the 5th are quite rural. The parts of Marion County in the district include Rainbow Springs; some thoroughbred horses are raised here. Sumter County is at the confluence of Florida's Turnpike and Interstate 75. Dixie, Gilchrist and Levy counties have large forested areas and commercial fishing entities. The Cedar Key archipelago, off the coast of Levy County, once boasted a prosperous port and pencil-making industry, but fishing and tourism now dominate. Cedar Key resists development and resembles Key West circa 1930.

1990 Population: 562,518. White 520,393 (93%), Black 31,488 (6%), Other 10,677 (2%). Hispanic origin 15,810 (3%). 18 and over 460,123 (82%), 62 and over 168,755 (30%). Median age: 41.

Committees

Agriculture (24th of 28 Democrats)
Environment, Credit & Rural Development; Foreign Agriculture & Hunger; Livestock; Specialty Crops & Natural Resources

Government Operations (13th of 25 Democrats)
Employment, Housing & Aviation; Environment, Energy & Natural Resources; Government Information, Justice, Transportation & Agriculture

Campaign Finance

	Receipts	Receipts from PACs		Expend-itures
1992				
Thurman (D)	$340,159	$208,501	(61%)	$352,607
Hogan (R)	$145,470	$4,423	(3%)	$144,613

Key Votes

1993

Require parental notification of minors' abortions	N
Require unpaid family and medical leave	Y
Approve national "motor voter" registration bill	Y
Approve budget increasing taxes and reducing deficit	Y
Approve economic stimulus plan	Y

Elections

1992 General		
Karen L. Thurman (D)	129,678	(49%)
Tom Hogan (R)	114,331	(43%)
Cindy Munkittrick (I)	19,459	(7%)
1992 Primary		
Karen L. Thurman (D)	60,144	(76%)
Mario F. Rivera (D)	19,141	(24%)

District Vote for President

	1992	
D	113,371	(42%)
R	92,124	(34%)
I	65,303	(24%)

6 Cliff Stearns (R)

Of Ocala — Elected 1988; 3rd Term

Born: April 16, 1941, Washington, D.C.
Education: George Washington U., B.S. 1963.
Military Service: Air Force, 1963-67.
Occupation: Hotel executive.
Family: Wife, Joan Moore; three children.
Religion: Presbyterian.
Political Career: No previous office.
Capitol Office: 332 Cannon Bldg. 20515; 225-5744.

In Washington: Stearns, who came to Congress in 1989 with no political experience, has moved quickly into the front ranks of activist conservatives in the House GOP, establishing himself as a prominent voice for conservative social values. When matters such as abortion, homosexuality and pornography are under discussion in the House, Stearns is sure to be out front, arguing against Democratic policies that he sees as wrong for America.

His pursuits and his personality evidently have made a good impression on the Republican leadership: At the beginning of the 103rd Congress, Stearns got a seat on the Energy and Commerce Committee, whose broad jurisdiction should enable him to get involved in a variety of issues. He is ranking Republican on the Commerce, Consumer Protection and Competitiveness Subcommittee.

Stearns got off to a fast start in Washington, winning his freshman class' spot on the GOP Committee on Committees, which plays an influential insider role because it parcels out committee assignments to Republican members.

Now, with Democrats in charge of the White House, Stearns' profile as an advocate of cultural conservatism could well increase. Just a month after Bill Clinton won the presidency in November 1992, Stearns joined with California Republican Reps. William E. Dannemeyer and Robert K. Dornan to pre-emptively strike at Clinton's plan to lift the ban on homosexuals in the military. (Dannemeyer, who had been Congress' leading critic of homosexuals, left the House at the end of the 102nd after failing in a bid for the Senate.)

Stearns has a formal party post from which to pursue this issue: He is chairman of the Republican Research Committee's Military Personnel Task Force.

Stearns also pounced on the Clinton administration's plans to reverse the federal government's policy of not paying for abortions; the "Hyde amendment" ban, in place since 1976, was a staple of the GOP's White House tenure. But in his budget proposal, Clinton removed the ban, setting the stage for a bitter fight in Congress.

"Apparently [Clinton] believes that taxing all Americans to pay for abortions is one of our nation's top priorities," Stearns said.

Also in 1993, Stearns criticized proposals to allow immigrants infected with HIV, the AIDS virus, to settle in the United States. "Before we open up our doors to just anyone, wouldn't it be sound public policy to take care of our own citizens?" Stearns said during a House debate that ended with a 356-58 vote to continue barring the infected.

Since his early days in the House, Stearns has been involved in debate over government funding for the National Endowment for the Arts. In 1989, lawmakers agreed to cut funding for the NEA by $45,000 — the amount of two controversial grants that went to fund projects many found offensive. Despite the compromise, Stearns pushed for further cuts in the agency's budget. The House overwhelmingly rejected his proposal to cut its funding by 5 percent.

In 1991, he tried unsuccessfully to cut $7.4 million from the NEA. "I think some of the projects and productions in the arts that were funded recently . . . have made a lot of members uneasy, particularly the one that was titled, 'By Poison,' " Stearns said, referring to a documentary depicting homosexual themes.

In 1992, Stearns had better luck, winning House approval of an amendment to freeze fiscal 1993 funding for the NEA at the fiscal 1992 level.

In other work that reflects his social-issue conservatism, Stearns has proposed a National Pornography Victims Awareness Week, and he supports allowing schools to observe a moment of silence for prayer.

Before joining Energy and Commerce, Stearns was a member of the Banking and Veterans' Affairs committees. He worked to get funding for two Gainesville projects — a new psychiatric wing at a veterans hospital and a biotechnology center at the University of Florida. He also has spoken up for the Cecil Field Naval Air Station in Duval County. The base appeared on a

Florida 6

North Central — Lake and Marion counties; part of Jacksonville

The 6th spans the interior of Northeast and Central Florida.

Democrats could once consider this friendly territory, but 1992 remapping has sharpened the district's focus more on conservative rural areas that are increasingly receptive to the GOP. The 6th shed Gainesville and the Gulf Coast retirement meccas of Citrus and Hernando, nudging the district north and east into part of Jacksonville.

Democrats vying for state offices can still run competitively in the district's southernmost counties, Lake and Marion, which together account for about half of the 6th's population.

Lake County features citrus groves and about 1,400 lakes along its rolling landscape. Watermelons and berries are grown around Leesburg. Besides the citrus industry, leading employers include metal fabrication, concrete and mobile home construction.

Some of central Florida's high-technology companies have expanded operations into Ocala (Marion County), including Martin Marietta and Microdine Corp., which makes telemetry and satellite receivers. Other major employers include Emergency One, makers of fire engine equipment, and Mark III van conversions. Among the area's tourist attractions are Silver Springs and the Ocala National Forest. The county's limestone-based soil also has made it a good place to breed and raise race horses.

Both Lake and Marion counties attract retirees from the Northeast and Midwest. Marion grew by 59 percent in the 1980s, while Lake County grew by 45 percent. Although the newcomers to Marion County tend to vote Republican, most of its rural residents are traditional Southern Democrats. Those groups were closely matched in 1976, when Jimmy Carter barely carried the county, but Republicans have carried the county in subsequent presidential elections.

Southeast of Union is Putnam County, adjacent to the St. Johns River. Bass fishing is popular there, and cabbages and watermelon are common crops.

This is also the district's most Democratic area. In GOP Rep. Stearns' easy 1992 re-election bid, he barely carried Putnam County. He also barely won Bradford County in the district's northwest reaches, and he lost Union County, the state's smallest county in land area.

Clay County nearly doubled in population in the 1980s, attributable partly to the proximity of Duval County (Jacksonville) to the north and the popularity of recreation in adjacent St. Johns County.

The 6th also extends into southwest Jacksonville. North of Interstate 10, many of the residents are middle-class, blue-collar workers. South of the interstate, the residents are predominantly professionals. Many in the community work in nearby Cecil Field, a naval air base providing strategic defense.

The Jacksonville portion of the district, along with Clay County, provides Republicans with some of their best percentages in the 6th.

1990 Population: 562,518. White 508,335 (90%), Black 41,520 (7%), Other 12,663 (2%). Hispanic origin 16,532 (3%). 18 and over 427,389 (76%), 62 and over 120,541 (21%). Median age: 37.

1993 Pentagon list of facilities slated for closure. In June 1993, Stearns got a special waiver from the GOP Conference to return to Veterans' Affairs.

At Home: As a neophyte campaigner in a district that had never sent a Republican to Congress, Stearns in 1988 looked to have an uphill fight. But his limited political background gave him a salient, populist theme, and he rode it to victory over a favored Democrat.

From the outset, Stearns cast the 1988 election in the 6th as a choice not between himself and a particular politician, but between himself and the entire concept of a politician. A heavy underdog to state House Speaker Jon Mills, the Democratic nominee, Stearns stressed that "the time has come for a 'citizen' congressman."

Stearns had developed some valuable contacts in the process of turning an investment in a dilapidated motel into a successful local motel and restaurant management company (called the House of Stearns). He was a director of the local chamber of commerce (where he was active in tourism development), served on the board of a major local hospital and was involved in church and civic groups. With those alliances and instinctive political savvy, Stearns was able to beat two better-connected candidates for the GOP nomination, and he went on to out-hustle Mills.

While Stearns campaigned tirelessly, an overconfident Mills spent time in Washington getting to know Democratic House leaders. Some Mills supporters had last-minute premonitions that the race was tightening, but none expected the shock they got on Election Day when Stearns won handily, aided by George

Bush's strong showing in the 6th.

Democrats began 1990 optimistic about regaining the 6th, but they failed to recruit a strong challenger.

Art Johnson, a Gainesville lawyer, won the nomination in a lightly attended primary. In his low-budget challenge, Johnson argued that Stearns' staunch conservatism was out of sync with the district.

But Stearns drew on a solid record in his first term, including obtaining funds for the Gainesville veterans psychiatric hospital and holding frequent town meetings. Stearns won with 59 percent of the vote.

Redistricting in 1992 did him no harm, and in November he moved up to 65 percent of the vote against Democratic nominee Phil Denton, owner of a diaper service.

Committees

Energy & Commerce (11th of 17 Republicans)
Commerce, Consumer Protection & Competitiveness (ranking); Energy & Power

Veterans' Affairs (13th of 14 Republicans)
Compensation, Pension & Insurance

Elections

1992 General		
Cliff Stearns (R)	144,120	(65%)
Phil Denton (D)	76,396	(35%)
1990 General		
Cliff Stearns (R)	138,588	(59%)
Art Johnson (D)	95,421	(41%)

Previous Winning Percentage: 1988 (53%)

District Vote for President

1992

D 74,349 (31%)
R 113,029 (47%)
I 51,266 (21%)

Campaign Finance

	Receipts	Receipts from PACs		Expend-itures
1992				
Stearns (R)	$374,016	$171,239	(46%)	$309,532
Denton (D)	$1,535	0		$2,333
1990				
Stearns (R)	$497,703	$200,346	(40%)	$462,925
Johnson (D)	$27,844	0		$26,443

Key Votes

1993	
Require parental notification of minors' abortions	Y
Require unpaid family and medical leave	N
Approve national "motor voter" registration bill	N
Approve budget increasing taxes and reducing deficit	N
Approve economic stimulus plan	N
1992	
Approve balanced-budget constitutional amendment	Y
Close down space station program	N
Approve U.S. aid for former Soviet Union	N
Allow shifting funds from defense to domestic programs	N
1991	
Extend unemployment benefits using deficit financing	Y
Approve waiting period for handgun purchases	Y
Authorize use of force in Persian Gulf	Y

Voting Studies

	Presidential Support		Party Unity		Conservative Coalition	
Year	**S**	**O**	**S**	**O**	**S**	**O**
1992	79	19	92	4	94	6
1991	71	29	88	10	95	5
1990	71	29	89	10	91	7
1989	78	22	85	15	95	5

Interest Group Ratings

Year	ADA	AFL-CIO	CCUS	ACU
1992	5	11	75	92
1991	25	33	70	90
1990	17	8	71	83
1989	0	0	100	93

7 John L. Mica (R)

Of Winter Park — Elected 1992; 1st Term

Born: Jan. 27, 1943, Binghamton, N.Y.
Education: Miami-Dade Community College, A.A. 1965; U. of Florida, B.A. 1967.
Occupation: Government consultant.
Family: Wife, Pat Szymanek; two children.
Religion: Episcopalian.
Political Career: Fla. House, 1977-81; GOP nominee for Fla. Senate, 1980.
Capitol Office: 427 Cannon Bldg. 20515; 225-4035.

The Path to Washington: One of the first things Mica wants to do in Congress is find a niche among the House Republicans.

"I have the inclination of Newt Gingrich," he said, referring to the sharp-tongued minority whip from Georgia. "But I hope I have the political wisdom of [Minority Leader] Bob Michel.... You want to get things done, but sometimes you need to throw bombs."

Bomb-throwers sometimes face a tough road in the minority party, but getting comfortable on the Hill may be easy for Mica because of his past political experience and his family traditions.

Mica is the brother of Daniel A. Mica, a Democrat who represented Florida from 1979 to 1989. Another Mica brother serves as an aide to Democratic Gov. Lawton Chiles. However, John became a Republican in his high school days, when he was a member of "Youth for Nixon."

And like several other freshmen, including those in the Florida delegation, Mica has considerable past political experience. He served in the state Legislature in 1977-81 and as chief of staff and administrative assistant for former U.S. Sen. Paula Hawkins, R-Fla., in 1981-85.

Despite these past political jobs, however, Mica operates with a businessman's perspective, honed from successes he found in consulting work, lobbying and real estate ventures. He also has led trade missions for private companies to Lithuania, China and the former East Bloc.

His primary goal is to create more jobs for Florida, and he supports tax credits for industries that create new employment because he believes it is the private sector, rather than the government, that can create the most jobs. His slot on the Public Works and Transportation Committee may provide him the avenue he seeks for his new GOP-leaning district.

He has little patience for those who believe the deficit can be cut by raising taxes on the wealthy. The flaw in that, he contends, is that it reduces the amount of capital available to expand the economy: "People without money don't create jobs."

He believes that government expenses can be cut and has singled out the departments of Labor, Health and Human Services, and Education for administrative trimming.

Mica demonstrated his pro-business bent early in the 103rd Congress when he, along with only 37 other members, voted against a bill to require warning labels on toys that pose choking risks to children and to instruct the Consumer Product Safety Commission to develop federal bicycle helmet safety standards.

Mica also sees his personal wealth as an asset in serving constituents. "I've made a lot of money," Mica said when he announced for the congressional seat. "I don't need the salary, and I don't need the title." He started out his quest for a seat by lending his campaign $100,000. (He raised another $100,000 in 10 days.)

Some of his other legislative concerns include supporting a constitutional balanced-budget amendment, a presidential line-item veto and a reduction in the capital gains tax. He also strongly supports Head Start.

Mica won an impressive, hard-fought victory in a three-way Republican primary before turning his attention to Dan Webster, a Democratic lawyer, in the general election. Webster was on the attack from the word go. He tried to use Mica's extensive lobbying activities against him, calling him "the epitome of the professional politician" and warning that he might owe more favors to business clients than to constituents.

But Mica refused to be thrown on the defensive, retorting that all members are lobbyists for their districts. He said most of his lobbying was in behalf of local clients, citing the help he had provided to Daytona Beach Airport — whose status was upgraded from regional to international a month before the election — to Orlando International Airport and to the Central Florida Research Park.

Abortion was an issue in the campaign because of the clear contrast between the candidates: Webster supports abortion rights; Mica favors abortion only in cases of rape, incest or when the woman's life is in danger.

Besides the Public Works position, Mica also won a seat on the Government Operations Committee, a key watchdog panel.

Florida 7

Central — Southern Seminole and Volusia counties; Deltona; Port Orange

The 7th is an overwhelmingly suburban district created in 1992 redistricting as a result of robust growth in the Orlando area.

Although the district likely will be reliably Republican in presidential and congressional elections, GOP support is not uniform across the 7th. Republicans seem firmly entrenched in Seminole County, which accounts for nearly half the district's population, and in the piece of Orange County that makes up about 10 percent of the district. But Democrats at the top of the ticket are competitive in Volusia County.

Interstate 4 transverses the district from Daytona Beach to Orlando; it is a familiar roadway to residents of Seminole County, which grew by 60 percent during the 1980s, mainly because of its convenient location directly north of Orlando. Many county residents hop onto I-4 to commute south to such Orlando institutions as Disney World, Martin Marietta, the University of Central Florida and Orlando International Airport. So many residents clog the interstate that freshman Rep. Mica sought and secured a seat on the Public Works and Transportation Committee to try to get funding for more alternate routes into the city.

Altamonte Springs and Casselberry, just north of the Orange County line, are Republican, upper-middle-class bedroom communities predominated by professionals. North along the interstate is affluent Heathrow. Sanford is the southern terminus of Amtrak's Virginia-to-Florida auto train.

Heading into Volusia County, unincorporated Deltona is the district's largest community, with 50,000 residents. It has a mixture of retirees and young working couples, as well as a growing Hispanic contigent. The district's next largest area, Port Orange, directly south of Daytona Beach, also has some light industry and business, and some blue-collar retirees who help give it a Democratic cast.

The 7th includes about one-third of Daytona Beach. As Florida's population began to boom in the 1950s, Daytona became the most popular resort on the state's east coast for vacationers who do not want to make a longer trip down the peninsula. The city woos winter visitors from Canada, and the Daytona International Speedway schedules its Daytona 500 auto race in February to lure tourists.

However, the boardwalk and some of the city's motels are reaching middle age, and competition from neighboring beaches and inland attractions has increased. Daytona's success at attracting new jobs has been modest compared with neighboring Orlando and Jacksonville. Leading private employers include those involved in medical supplies, electronics and transportation.

Although both Seminole and Volusia counties went for George Bush in 1988, the 7th revealed its split personality in 1992. Seminole County went strongly for Bush and Mica, while Volusia County gave a slight edge to Democrats in the presidential and House contests.

1990 Population: 562,518. White 524,479 (93%), Black 22,410 (4%), Other 15,629 (3%). Hispanic origin 31,198 (6%). 18 and over 435,985 (78%), 62 and over 106,020 (19%). Median age: 36.

Committees

Government Operations (16th of 16 Republicans)
Environment, Energy & Natural Resources; Human Resources & Intergovernmental Relations

Public Works & Transportation (22nd of 24 Republicans)
Aviation; Economic Development

Campaign Finance

1992	Receipts	Receipts from PACs		Expend-itures
Mica (R)	$465,407	$145,700	(31%)	$459,135
Webster (D)	$310,201	$133,595	(43%)	$307,857

Key Votes

1993

Require parental notification of minors' abortions	Y
Require unpaid family and medical leave	N
Approve national "motor voter" registration bill	N
Approve budget increasing taxes and reducing deficit	N
Approve economic stimulus plan	N

Elections

1992 General		
John L. Mica (R)	125,790	(56%)
Dan Webster (D)	96,926	(43%)
1992 Primary		
John L. Mica (R)	24,350	(53%)
Dick Graham (R)	15,768	(34%)
Vaughn S. Forrest (R)	6,073	(13%)

District Vote for President

	1992	
D	81,312	(34%)
R	105,263	(45%)
I	49,582	(21%)

8 Bill McCollum (R)

Of Longwood — Elected 1980; 7th Term

Born: July 12, 1944, Brooksville, Fla.
Education: U. of Florida, B.A. 1965, J.D. 1968.
Military Service: Navy, 1969-72; Naval Reserve, 1972-93.
Occupation: Lawyer.
Family: Wife, Ingrid Seebohm; three children.
Religion: Episcopalian.
Political Career: Seminole County GOP Executive Committee chairman, 1976-80.
Capitol Office: 2266 Rayburn Bldg. 20515; 225-2176.

In Washington: As the Republican leadership in the House has moved to the right, McCollum's mix of personal loyalty and conservative credentials has secured his place in the hierarchy. But as his stature has grown, he has acquired more of a partisan edge and put his longstanding image as a Boy Scout at risk.

Chosen co-chairman of the platform committee at the 1992 Republican National Convention, McCollum was at the center of struggles over abortion and other divisive issues. One of his opponents in those fights, Nancy Johnson of Connecticut, would later challenge McCollum's re-election as vice chairman of the House Republican Conference. Johnson called for greater "diversity" in the party's leadership; McCollum won easily.

On the Banking Committee, the 103rd Congress saw McCollum rise to the No. 2 Republican slot. He was by far the most senior conservative, sandwiched between ranking Republican Jim Leach of Iowa and third-ranking Marge Roukema of New Jersey, both moderates by comparison. McCollum was also the ranking Republican on the Financial Institutions Subcommittee, an ideal position from which to press his agenda: relaxing regulations on how banks operate and paring away consumer protection rules he believes burden lenders unfairly.

Even before his most recent move up on Banking, McCollum's persistent nature and growing stature enabled him to block passage of major legislation — specifically the bill providing additional money for the savings and loan bailout in 1992. McCollum wanted the federal government to buy up an intangible asset known as "good will" that some thrift institutions carried on their books. His insistence on this point shut down the bailout, irritating the Bush administration and many Democrats and Republicans in Congress who thought McCollum's position wrong and his tactics needlessly costly to taxpayers. But he held out with the backing of a core group of Republicans whose votes were necessary for enactment.

McCollum did not initially stand out among the Republican freshmen who came to Washington with Ronald Reagan in 1981. Neither his political background nor his physical presence was imposing. A lawyer who had never held public office, his appearance and manner suggested a college debater on first meeting. But his election as conference vice chairman in 1988 proved that he had quietly established himself as one of the more influential survivors of that historic class of Republicans.

Legislatively, McCollum's beachhead was the Judiciary Subcommittee on Crime. After serving as ranking Republican there for six years, however, he was bumped out in the 102nd Congress by the movements of more senior members and shifted instead to the ranking post on Immigration.

The influx of refugees in Florida made this an important assignment, however, and McCollum became a vocal advocate for stemming the flow of illegal aliens. "We cannot accept all of those who seek to come to this country," he said in 1989, when he led opposition to a bill protecting undocumented Nicaraguans and Salvadorans from deportation.

In early 1993, McCollum took the lead among House Republicans in challenging President Clinton's proposal to lift a 6-year-old ban that barred AIDS-infected foreigners from entering the United States. McCollum argued that the health risk and potential cost of caring for an influx of AIDS patients were extreme.

For all his visibility on immigration, McCollum may be better known for his role in shaping the nation's gun laws. In 1988 he developed a key weapon against the Brady bill (a seven-day waiting period for handgun purchases). It was a counterproposal directing the Justice Department to develop an instant background check to prevent felons from purchasing handguns. McCollum maximizes his effectiveness on this issue by varying his tactics. In the 1980s, he worked with Crime Subcommittee Chairman William J. Hughes of New Jersey to ban for 10 years the production, importation, sale or delivery of non-detectable firearms (made mostly of plastic).

Florida 8

Central — Orange County; part of Orlando

In a state famous for its coastline, Orlando is the only one of Florida's four large metropolitan areas without one. But that has not been a hindrance to economic development or population growth in and around the city. In fact, metropolitan Orlando has a more diversified economic base than many of Florida's beach meccas, where the economy is skewed toward tourism, construction and real estate speculation.

This is not to underestimate the impact of tourism. Walt Disney is still Orange County's leading private employer; Disney World and Epcot are joined by other attractions such as Sea World and Universal Studios, which is just across the 3rd District line. Orlando boasts that its hotel-room supply rivals that in many bigger cities.

Disney has been a major catalyst for growth in metropolitan Orlando. The tourists it helps attract provide a strong and steady flow of traffic through Orlando's airport, which has taken on international flights and become a hub for adjacent warehousing and distribution facilities. Thanks to Disney and Universal, there is work in the movie- and television-production business.

Also in Orlando is the world headquarters of Westinghouse's power generation unit, and Minute Maid has a processing plant for oranges. The University of Central Florida (21,150 students) is growing on the city's east side. Its emphasis on high-tech fields such as lasers fits in well with the area's numerous aerospace and defense contractors working on missiles and aircraft-control systems. Orlando's Naval Training Center, which showed up on the 1993 base-closure list, provides simulators and training for the military.

When McCollum first won election to the House in 1980, his district stretched from the gulf almost to the Atlantic. Population growth has led the district to be whittled down in successive redistricting rounds. It now includes only parts of Orange County plus the Kissimmee area in Osceola County.

Growth has brought its share of problems to the Orlando area. Demand for water has increased dramatically, and sinkholes occasionally open up as the water table drops. More frequent problems occur with congested highways and overcrowded schools.

The parts of Orlando in the 8th contain a mixture of residents, many of them retirees and young families. North and east of the city are the affluent Orange County communities of Winter Park and Maitland. Home to Orlando's older, established elite, they strongly support the GOP. To the west, near Lake Apopka, lie Ocoee and Winter Garden. Fresh vegetables grow along the lake, while the foliage industry (growing houseplants, shrubbery and the like) has a presence in the city of Apopka.

Hispanics, especially Puerto Ricans, account for a significant minority of residents in Buena Ventura Lakes, near Kissimmee, and in Kissimmee itself. Kissimmee, which promotes itself as a centrally situated base for tourists visiting local attractions, is competitive territory politically.

1990 Population: 562,518. White 499,776 (89%), Black 29,433 (5%), Other 33,309 (6%). Hispanic origin 63,997 (11%). 18 and over 436,210 (78%), 62 and over 76,727 (14%). Median age: 32.

McCollum combines his assignments on Judiciary and Banking when it comes to legislation making it difficult for criminals to convert illegal profits into usable cash. In 1986, he and Hughes co-authored a bill that breezed through the House to make such money laundering a federal crime.

In the 100th Congress, McCollum served as one of six House Republicans on the committee investigating the Iran-contra affair. Although a staunch defender of Reagan's pro-contra policies who questioned the need for the hearings, he made news in June 1987 when he said that the testimony of a Justice Department lawyer showed that three central figures in the affair — William J. Casey, Rear Adm. John M. Poindexter and Lt. Col. Oliver L. North — had engaged in "criminal" behavior. He also said the three had committed "one of the most treacherous" acts ever against a president. But McCollum did not raise the subject of treachery when North and Poindexter testified before the committee.

At Home: The newly drawn 8th contains less than half of the 5th District McCollum previously represented, stretching south and east from Orlando instead of north and west. The new district map placed many of the city's black neighborhoods in an adjacent district, thereby enhancing the Republican nature of the 8th.

McCollum got his start in the old 5th shortly after his predecessor, Republican Rep. Richard Kelly, suffered a near-defeat in 1978. McCollum was already a candidate in the 1980 primary against Kelly when the FBI snared the incumbent in its Abscam investigation.

McCollum, a former Seminole County GOP chairman, was making his first bid for public office. But his early start helped him organize a stronger campaign than either Kelly or state Sen. Vince Fechtel, who joined the field later. Few issue differences separated the men, but McCollum successfully marketed his own image as a morally upstanding family man qualified to fill a "leadership vacuum."

McCollum got 43 percent of the primary vote, running first in Seminole County and in the Orange County suburbs of Orlando, and also carrying the Gulf Coast GOP strongholds of Pasco and Pinellas counties. Kelly ran a poor third. In the runoff, McCollum again brought his organizational strength to bear against Fechtel, carrying six of the district's eight counties and winning 54 percent.

Democrats chose lawyer David Best, the same candidate who had polled 49 percent against Kelly in 1978. McCollum, clearly more conservative than Best, caught the district's prevailing mood and was elected with 56 percent.

In 1982, McCollum's Democratic opponent was Dick Batchelor, a popular Orange County state representative considered a formidable, although underfunded, campaigner. Fearful of being dragged down by voter discontent with Reaganomics or concern over Social Security, McCollum did not emphasize his party label. Instead, he reprised the family-man theme from his 1980 campaign (compared with the unmarried Batchelor) who had "restored integrity" to the district. He won 59 percent of the vote, and local Democrats did not challenge him again until 1990, when McCollum again prevailed with about 60 percent of the vote.

McCollum's 1992 opponent, Democrat Chuck Kovaleski, was an insurance executive and a spokesman for a term-limit initiative. Kovaleski criticized McCollum for pushing six-term limits for all and then seeking a seventh term for himself. But more than two-thirds of the voters felt that McCollum had earned it.

Committees

Conference Vice Chairman

Banking, Finance & Urban Affairs (2nd of 20 Republicans)
Financial Institutions Supervision, Regulation & Deposit Insurance (ranking); Economic Growth; International Development, Finance, Trade & Monetary Policy

Judiciary (5th of 14 Republicans)
International Law, Immigration & Refugees (ranking); Intellectual Property & Judicial Administration

Elections

1992 General		
Bill McCollum (R)	141,925	(69%)
Chuck Kovaleski (D)	65,132	(31%)
1992 Primary		
Bill McCollum (R)	33,482	(80%)
Lew Oliver (R)	8,621	(20%)
1990 General		
Bill McCollum (R)	94,453	(60%)
Bob Fletcher (D)	63,253	(40%)

Previous Winning Percentages: **1988** (100%) **1986** (100%) **1984** (100%) **1982** (59%) **1980** (56%)

District Vote for President

1992

D 67,724 (32%)
R 102,514 (48%)
I 43,472 (20%)

Campaign Finance

	Receipts	Receipts from PACs		Expend-itures
1992				
McCollum (R)	$642,785	$301,830	(47%)	$675,211
Kovaleski (D)	$174,941	0		$174,940
1990				
McCollum (R)	$427,325	$148,050	(35%)	$564,994
Fletcher (D)	$22,560	$2,371	(11%)	$18,635

Key Votes

1993	
Require parental notification of minors' abortions	Y
Require unpaid family and medical leave	N
Approve national "motor voter" registration bill	N
Approve budget increasing taxes and reducing deficit	N
Approve economic stimulus plan	N
1992	
Approve balanced-budget constitutional amendment	Y
Close down space station program	N
Approve U.S. aid for former Soviet Union	Y
Allow shifting funds from defense to domestic programs	N
1991	
Extend unemployment benefits using deficit financing	N
Approve waiting period for handgun purchases	N
Authorize use of force in Persian Gulf	Y

Voting Studies

	Presidential Support		Party Unity		Conservative Coalition	
Year	**S**	**O**	**S**	**O**	**S**	**O**
1992	73	22	89	8	92	2
1991	76	21	81	13	86	3
1990	74	23	83	15	91	9
1989	72	26	76	19	90	5
1988	66	24	82	10	97	0
1987	69	26	82	12	95	2
1986	84	14	81	16	96	4
1985	80	19	82	13	91	9
1984	66	33	85	11	93	7
1983	78	17	89	6	94	3
1982	78	17	91	8	93	7
1981	67	28	83	14	85	12

Interest Group Ratings

Year	ADA	AFL-CIO	CCUS	ACU
1992	15	25	86	92
1991	10	18	89	90
1990	17	8	71	88
1989	0	9	100	96
1988	0	17	75	100
1987	4	0	100	87
1986	0	7	82	82
1985	5	6	90	90
1984	10	8	88	78
1983	0	0	89	100
1982	10	10	82	82
1981	0	13	94	93

9 Michael Bilirakis (R)

Of Palm Harbor — Elected 1982; 6th Term

Born: July 16, 1930, Tarpon Springs, Fla.
Education: U. of Pittsburgh, B.S. 1959; George Washington U., 1959-60; U. of Florida, J.D. 1963.
Military Service: Air Force, 1951-55.
Occupation: Lawyer; restaurateur.
Family: Wife, Evelyn Miaoulis; two children.
Religion: Greek Orthodox.
Political Career: No previous office.
Capitol Office: 2240 Rayburn Bldg. 20515; 225-5755.

In Washington: An unfailingly friendly, conscientious representative, Bilirakis defines his job in terms of his constituency. His activity on Capitol Hill is primarily limited to seeking programs and dollars for his district and quietly casting votes that otherwise toe the party line.

His geniality has enabled Bilirakis to establish cordial relations with key Democrats. But it has put him at odds with an increasingly aggressive group of Florida Republicans and with the more confrontational generation of GOP House leaders.

Overall, Bilirakis votes reliably Republican. But on Florida issues, he is willing to break with the traditional conservative view of limited government involvement and advocate a more activist, spending-oriented posture.

Of the 17 bills he filed in the first three months of 1993, 10 dealt with veterans or active military personnel. Much of the legislation, refiled from previous years, would grant special benefits to veterans' spouses, offer tax breaks for companies that hire reservists and guarantee 1994 cost of living increases for veterans. (In 1991, as a member of the Veterans' Affairs Committee, Bilirakis was among those who successfully fought for cost of living increases for disabled veterans.)

From his position on the Energy and Commerce Committee, Bilirakis is able to keep an eye on environmental issues — particularly in trying to protect his state's water supply. In the 102nd Congress, he successfully lobbied Edward J. Markey of Massachusetts to add conservation standards — for electric energy and plumbing fixtures — to the National Energy Security Act. And after several years of lobbying, Bilirakis won an amendment to the Federal Facilities Compliance Act that requires all fines for government facilities violating environmental laws to be put into accounts for future environmental compliance.

He also secured two $500,000 federal grants for Florida health-care centers that specialize in prenatal and pediatric care.

And Bilirakis latched onto a new home-state subject in 1992: baseball. He and GOP Sen. Connie Mack have taken the lead in trying to curtail baseball's exemption from federal antitrust laws, a special standing that allows team owners to operate monopolies. At least partly behind their uphill battle is the desire to bring a professional team to the Tampa Bay area for more than just spring training.

On the Energy Committee (where in the 103rd, Bilirakis is ranking member of the Energy and Power Subcommittee), he works cooperatively with liberal Health Subcommittee Chairman Henry A. Waxman of California when it serves his district. In the 101st, Bilirakis served as a conferee on the Clean Air Act.

In the 99th, Bilirakis had collaborated with Waxman to get five Medicare demonstration projects for victims of Alzheimer's disease included in a budget-reconciliation measure. In 1990, Congress passed a measure reauthorizing some of the programs — after adopting a Bilirakis amendment that set aside 10 percent of the funds for the very elderly.

But there are indications that Bilirakis sees the danger in being too closely associated with such a prominent liberal. In a letter summarizing his achievements in the 102nd, Bilirakis noted that he "successfully countered Chairman Waxman on the floor of the House regarding mental health funding for Florida" after realizing the original legislation did not include the money. Bilirakis managed to have the bill returned to conference. Ultimately, he lost the money. "However, winning two of three votes against Chairman Waxman can be viewed as an accomplishment," his legislative summary stated.

Bilirakis supported the GOP alternative to the catastrophic health insurance bill in the 100th, but then it was rejected on a party-line vote. Bilirakis was one of 61 House Republicans willing to vote for the Democrats' version (ignoring the president's veto threat). In 1989, he tried unsuccessfully to get Congress to slow the phase-in of a new plan for paying physicians under Medicare, fearing that some doctors in his district might simply stop treating Medicare

Florida 9

West — Northern Pinellas and Hillsborough counties; central Pasco County; Clearwater

The 9th sits above Tampa and St. Petersburg, patching together pieces of three counties. North Pinellas County accounts for about half the district's population; the rest is split between north Hillsborough and central Pasco counties.

Although the 9th looks like a Republican district, Democrats can be competitive here.

Lawton Chiles carried the areas within the 9th in the 1990 gubernatorial race, and Buddy MacKay held a slight edge in his unsuccessful 1988 Senate race. Rep. Bilirakis has gotten less than 60 percent of the vote in his past two re-election bids.

The parts of Pinellas County in the district are solidly Republican. Democrats running for state and federal office are lucky to win 45 percent of the Pinellas vote.

Clearwater, historically a beach resort, has benefited from the arrival of high-technology industry to metropolitan St. Petersburg. Honeywell, much of which is just south of the district in the 10th, is a significant employer in the area, as is Sperry.

Light industry, services and a tourism trade, some of it associated with the gulf beaches, all have a role in the county's economy.

Real estate development is also important; the area has attracted middle- to upper-middle-class retirees.

North of Clearwater is Palm Harbor, the district's second-largest city, which features more boat docks than beaches. Many residents here still commute into Tampa-St. Petersburg.

Continuing north, a substantial Greek community lives in Tarpon Springs, a century after their ancestors first came to harvest the offshore sponge beds.

Democrats are more competitive in Pasco County. Many of the retirees who have settled in the county in recent years come from working-class backgrounds in the Northeast and Midwest and cling to Democratic voting habits, particularly in contests for local office.

Even so, Bilirakis was dismayed that 1992 redistricting stripped the 9th of western Pasco County, an area filled with retirees and military veterans whose interests he worked hard to promote.

The 9th still includes some residents in areas of west Pasco. Many of the retirees also recently relocated to the area in communities such as Zephyrhills. Some are former union members who carry their conservative Democratic orientation with them.

The growth of development in Pasco County has generally been from west to east, moving into rolling hills containing dairying and some citrus. Redistricting also cost the 9th the easternmost part of Pasco County, near Dade City.

Hillsborough County accounts for about one-fifth of the district's population. One development of note is Carrollwood Village, a bedroom community for Tampa. Democrats can also be competitive here, though liberal candidates do not fare well.

1990 Population: 562,518. White 532,324 (95%), Black 19,245 (3%), Other 10,949 (2%). Hispanic origin 22,946 (4%). 18 and over 447,843 (80%), 62 and over 142,351 (25%). Median age: 39.

patients.

At Home: Bilirakis was an underdog in the GOP primary when he first campaigned for the 9th in 1982. Once nominated and elected, he quickly became entrenched. His hold on the district was demonstrated again in 1992, when he beat primary- and general-election challengers after redistricting for the 1990s cost him part of the district that had been particularly friendly territory for him.

The piece Bilirakis regretted losing — western Pasco County — is filled with retirees and military veterans, two groups whose interests he worked hard to promote. But the rest of the district proved to be equally supportive.

Bilirakis was challenged in the GOP primary by state Rep. Patricia A. "Trish" Muscarella of Clearwater. She criticized him for opposing abortion rights and for seeking a sixth term despite supporting congressional term limits. Bilirakis tried to finesse the term limit issue by saying he believed in 12-year limits and thus would not seek re-election in 1994 unless he was involved in major legislation at the time. She also portrayed Bilirakis as out of touch with the district, a characterization that did not seem to fit. He won all three counties in the district by wide margins.

That set up a rematch against Democrat Cheryl Davis Knapp, a liberal nurse from Safety Harbor. Knapp ran an unheralded, unfunded campaign in 1990, accusing Bilirakis of doing too little for the environment, the homeless and women's rights. She held Bilirakis to 58 percent. Two years later she drew more money and attention and used some of the same campaign themes, with similar results.

When Bilirakis announced plans to make his first political campaign in 1982, local GOP leaders were slightly bemused. But Bilirakis surprised the media, the party hierarchy and most supposed experts on Florida politics, turning innocence into a virtue and winning the newly created 9th.

A Democrat until 1970, Bilirakis had switched parties to back Rep. L. A. "Skip" Bafalis' bid for governor. Although he was intermittently active in local GOP campaigns during the next decade, he never considered running for office until 1982. "I found myself out of challenges," he said.

In the GOP primary, Bilirakis was an underdog to state House Republican leader Curt Kiser. But while Kiser was taking his nomination for granted, Bilirakis was blanketing the district with signs saying that his was "a hard name to spell but an easy one to remember."

Using his own resources and contributions from the Tarpon Springs Greek community, Bilirakis flooded the airwaves with ads stressing his service to the area, as a judge in county and municipal courts, and as president of several community organizations. Bilirakis finished well ahead of Kiser and Clearwater Mayor Charles LeCher and beat Kiser in the runoff.

Bilirakis emphasized his personality in his general-election campaign against Democratic state Rep. George Sheldon. When he did speak out on issues, he espoused conservative positions — defending President Ronald Reagan's economic program and arguing for a constitutional ban on abortions — and he attacked Sheldon's more liberal voting record. Bilirakis won by 4,320 votes. It got easier: In 1984 and 1986, he boosted his performance to more than 70 percent; in 1988, he was unopposed.

Committees

Energy & Commerce (5th of 17 Republicans)
Energy & Power (ranking); Health & the Environment

Veterans' Affairs (4th of 14 Republicans)
Compensation, Pension & Insurance (ranking); Hospitals & Health Care

Elections

1992 General		
Michael Bilirakis (R)	157,822	(59%)
Cheryl Davis Knapp (D)	110,023	(41%)
1992 Primary		
Michael Bilirakis (R)	34,593	(67%)
Patricia A. Muscarella (R)	17,295	(33%)
1990 General		
Michael Bilirakis (R)	142,163	(58%)
Cheryl Davis Knapp (D)	102,503	(42%)

Previous Winning Percentages: **1988** (100%) **1986** (71%) **1984** (79%) **1982** (51%)

District Vote for President

1992
D 93,626 (34%)
R 112,832 (41%)
I 67,379 (25%)

Campaign Finance

	Receipts	Receipts from PACs		Expend-itures
1992				
Bilirakis (R)	$779,124	$313,210	(40%)	$779,818
Knapp (D)	$271,378	$115,659	(43%)	$269,617
1990				
Bilirakis (R)	$600,670	$234,430	(39%)	$815,366
Knapp (D)	$90,307	$36,915	(41%)	$89,852

Key Votes

1993	
Require parental notification of minors' abortions	Y
Require unpaid family and medical leave	N
Approve national "motor voter" registration bill	Y
Approve budget increasing taxes and reducing deficit	N
Approve economic stimulus plan	N
1992	
Approve balanced-budget constitutional amendment	Y
Close down space station program	Y
Approve U.S. aid for former Soviet Union	N
Allow shifting funds from defense to domestic programs	N
1991	
Extend unemployment benefits using deficit financing	N
Approve waiting period for handgun purchases	Y
Authorize use of force in Persian Gulf	Y

Voting Studies

	Presidential Support		Party Unity		Conservative Coalition	
Year	**S**	**O**	**S**	**O**	**S**	**O**
1992	64	34	86	12	85	15
1991	78	19	81	14	78	14
1990	51	29	70	13	81	4
1989	60	36	86	11	85	12
1988	67	29	87	8	89	5
1987	66	32	86	10	91	9
1986	77	21	88	9	96	4
1985	75	24	84	10	87	11
1984	63	34	86	14	90	10
1983	79	20	90	9	93	4

Interest Group Ratings

Year	ADA	AFL-CIO	CCUS	ACU
1992	20	42	75	80
1991	15	8	80	89
1990	17	9	85	80
1989	10	25	100	86
1988	10	14	93	96
1987	16	13	87	78
1986	15	29	67	86
1985	10	29	77	71
1984	10	31	80	88
1983	10	18	85	87

10 C.W. Bill Young (R)

Of Indian Rocks Beach — Elected 1970; 12th Term

Born: Dec. 16, 1930, Harmarville, Pa.
Education: Attended Pennsylvania public schools.
Military Service: National Guard, 1948-57.
Occupation: Insurance executive; public official.
Family: Wife, Beverly F. Angelo; three children.
Religion: Methodist.
Political Career: Fla. Senate, 1961-71, minority leader, 1967-71.
Capitol Office: 2407 Rayburn Bldg. 20515; 225-5961.

In Washington: Young's thinning, blow-dried pompadour sometimes makes him look like a refugee from a country band, but in reality he is one of the House's more serious and effective conservatives.

While Young plays his most substantive role as a GOP stalwart on the Appropriations Subcommittee on Defense, he gained an honorary title of symbolic significance early in the 101st Congress: dean of the majority party in Florida's House delegation, which now has 13 Republicans and 10 Democrats.

Though Young is a moderate-to-conservative Republican in the tradition of Minority Leader Robert H. Michel of Illinois, most of Florida's GOP freshmen seem to favor the more confrontational approach of House Minority Leader Newt Gingrich of Georgia.

When Young was elected to the state Senate in 1960, he was its only Republican. A decade later, when he won a seat in the U.S. House, he was one of just three Republicans in the 12-member delegation. In the years since, Florida's House contingent and its Republican component have grown, but the GOP did not have a majority of House members until Rep. Bill Grant switched parties in February 1989. His change made it 10-9 for the GOP. "I have to admit," Young said, "this is the first time ever in my political career I'm in any kind of majority status."

Young is best-known for expanding the purview of the Defense Appropriations Subcommittee. He has become the leading congressional advocate of the National Bone Marrow Donor Registry and has worked to fund it through the defense budget.

The money initially found its way into a defense funding bill in 1986, when then-Sen. Paul Laxalt of Nevada slipped it in. That same year, Laxalt announced his retirement, and Young came into contact with a 10-year-old girl from his district who had cancer and could not find a bone marrow donor. Since then, Young has guarded the registry's funding, and in the 102nd Congress, he put $20 million in the Navy budget for bone marrow research.

In the 101st Congress, Young secured $37 million for the program in four different appropriations bills, including the 1990 supplemental to fund Operation Desert Shield. He argued that the threat of biological weapons increased the potential need for marrow transplants.

After years of championing this cause, Young learned in late 1990 that his eldest daughter had developed a form of leukemia treatable only through a marrow transplant. She received a transplant and is in remission.

While Young says the registry is his proudest achievement, he first made his mark as an advocate of the 1980s defense buildup. He is the defense subcommittee's second-ranking Republican and could ascend to the ranking position depending on the outcome of the case against Joseph M. McDade of Pennsylvania, who is under federal indictment for bribery.

Though Young supported nearly all of President Ronald Reagan's individual defense initiatives, his seriousness and willingness to work with Democrats earned him bipartisan respect. He can be counted as a voice of caution in the debate on President Clinton's plans to reduce Pentagon spending. He will also have a say on defense policy from his seat on the Select Committee on Intelligence.

Young has suggested that his unyielding stance on some issues is just a strategy to offset the zeal of liberals bent on cutting defense. "I have become one of those who is the counterbalance on the right that makes it possible to compromise in the middle," he once said.

Young's 1989 support for denying funding for the Air Force's advanced tactical fighter plane was seen as a sign of the times. "Money is getting tighter," he said. "We're more attentive to money issues, and this is a program with a lot of unanswered questions."

During his previous tenure on Intelligence, Young charted an independent course on some matters. He supported aid for anti-communist insurgents, but he was critical of the agency after disclosures that it helped elect Salvadoran President José Napoleón Duarte. "The CIA is not the place to run political campaigns," Young said.

Young also plays a role in a number of

Florida 10

West — Southern Pinellas County; St. Petersburg

The modern era of Florida politics began in this St. Petersburg-based district four decades ago.

In 1954, the district made William C. Cramer the state's first Republican House member in the 20th century. Cramer owed his election to the influence of conservative retirees. Other GOP candidates prospered later as the retirees' influence expanded elsewhere in Florida.

Today, the retirees are still crucial in the politics of the 10th, but no candidate can afford to ignore the growing numbers of young people drawn by its steadily diversifying economy. The young newcomers, like their peers moving into other parts of Florida, also tend to identify with the GOP.

Not too long ago, St. Petersburg was known almost exclusively as a retirement haven. The retirees who settled there — many of them storekeepers, office workers and civil servants from small towns in the Midwest — brought their Republican preferences with them. The economy was mostly service-oriented, geared to the needs of tourists and elderly residents. The morning rush hour saw many younger workers from St. Petersburg driving to jobs in Tampa, which provided employment in a greater variety of fields and offered a faster pace of life.

But St. Petersburg has broadened its economic base by stressing that it offers a good climate for business investment. Where the Shuffleboard Hall of Fame was once the big attraction, visitors are drawn to the Salvador Dali Museum and Sunken Gardens. The Women's Tennis Association is here. The search for a major league baseball team prompted the construction of the Florida Suncoast Dome.

St. Petersburg and Pinellas County companies such as Honeywell, Paradyne, E-Systems and Martin Marietta are busy with research, development, production and marketing of computers, communications equipment and other high-tech items.

A number of the major employers and subcontractors are engaged in defense-related work. Defense cuts and nervousness about the economy throughout the area undercut George Bush's support in 1992. After Bush won the district with 56 percent in 1988, defections to Ross Perot four years later enabled Bill Clinton to carry the 10th. But statewide GOP candidates are still more likely to campaign here than in the Tampa-based 11th. Republicans outnumber Democrats and most local officials identify with the GOP.

Although the median age of Pinellas County has dropped over the years, as younger residents have replaced retirees, the southern part of the county is already so crowded that it is growing much more slowly than the state as a whole.

Elsewhere, Pinellas Park is generally a blue-collar, lower-middle-class community, with some residents living in mobile home parks. Largo includes a large concentration of retirees. Residents of the adjacent gulf beaches are generally less affluent than those who live along the Sarasota or Miami-Fort Lauderdale coasts.

1990 Population: 562,518. White 498,333 (89%), Black 53,001 (9%), Other 11,184 (2%). Hispanic origin 13,017 (2%). 18 and over 462,536 (82%), 62 and over 167,505 (30%). Median age: 42.

domestic issues closer to home. Together with Florida Democrat William Lehman, Young led the charge in the Appropriations Committee against lifting a moratorium on offshore oil drilling in the Gulf of Mexico. When an amendment challenging the drilling ban was offered, the panel turned it back. In the 101st Congress, he supported an amendment allowing states to enforce tougher oil liability laws than those on the federal books.

Young, who notes that his St. Petersburg-based district contains a significant number of Social Security recipients, goes to considerable lengths to help them. In 1989, he was one of the 44 Republican House members to reverse his earlier support for the catastrophic health-care bill, and he helped repeal the act.

In 1985, he proposed a bill to prohibit employers from setting any mandatory retirement age; a similar measure became law in 1986. A member of the Appropriations subcommittee that sets spending levels for the Department of Health and Human Services, he has called for more expeditious health-care payments to Medicare recipients and has proposed legislation guaranteeing that the cost of living adjustments for Social Security beneficiaries could not be cut back or eliminated.

At Home: A high school dropout from a Pennsylvania mining town, Young worked his way to success in the insurance business before going into politics in 1960. Ten years later, he inherited Florida's most dependable Republican seat from William C. Cramer, who left it when he ran for the U.S. Senate in 1970.

Young had met Cramer in 1955, and he

worked in his 1956 campaign and as his district aide in 1957. In 1960 the Pinellas County GOP urged Young to challenge a veteran Democratic state senator. He won, and became the only Republican in the state Senate. By 1967, there were 20 others, and Young was minority leader.

When Cramer ran for the Senate in 1970, there was little question who would replace him. Young won 76 percent of the primary vote and 67 percent in the general election. During the 1980s, he drew Democratic opposition only twice.

Young's stiffest general-election challenge came in 1992. His Democratic opponent was Karen Moffitt, an associate professor in education and medicine. She had never held elected office and had just moved to the district from Tampa. But Moffitt was well-known, partly because her ex-husband, Lee Moffitt, was a former state House Speaker and a campaign supporter.

Karen Moffitt combined some of the outsider's credo — support for term limits, a line-item veto and cuts in congressional staffs — with typical Democratic positions favoring abortion rights and national health care.

Young took some licks in the campaign, especially for making defense contractors a major source of his campaign funding, and, until recently, a steady source of honoraria.

But the district still leans Republican at the top of the ticket, and Young retained an edge in campaign funds. Even so, Young's 12th general-election victory was his narrowest.

Committees

Appropriations (3rd of 23 Republicans)
Legislative Branch (ranking); Defense; Labor, Health & Human Services, Education & Related Agencies

Select Intelligence (4th of 7 Republicans)
Oversight & Evaluation (ranking)

Elections

1992 General		
C.W. Bill Young (R)	149,347	(57%)
Karen Moffitt (D)	114,637	(43%)
1990 General		
C. W. Bill Young (R)	Unopposed	

Previous Winning Percentages:				**1988**	(73%)	**1986**	(100%)
1984	(80%)	**1982**	(100%)	**1980**	(100%)	**1978**	(79%)
1976	(65%)	**1974**	(76%)	**1972**	(76%)	**1970**	(67%)

District Vote for President

1992
D 107,685 (40%)
R 97,492 (36%)
I 64,280 (24%)

Campaign Finance

	Receipts	Receipts from PACs		Expend-itures
1992				
Young (R)	$274,122	$165,250	(60%)	$459,861
Moffitt (D)	$202,132	$102,711	(51%)	$202,000
1990				
Young (R)	$231,400	$132,900	(57%)	$201,188

Key Votes

1993	
Require parental notification of minors' abortions	Y
Require unpaid family and medical leave	Y
Approve national "motor voter" registration bill	N
Approve budget increasing taxes and reducing deficit	N
Approve economic stimulus plan	N
1992	
Approve balanced-budget constitutional amendment	Y
Close down space station program	N
Approve U.S. aid for former Soviet Union	N
Allow shifting funds from defense to domestic programs	N
1991	
Extend unemployment benefits using deficit financing	Y
Approve waiting period for handgun purchases	Y
Authorize use of force in Persian Gulf	Y

Voting Studies

	Presidential Support		Party Unity		Conservative Coalition	
Year	**S**	**O**	**S**	**O**	**S**	**O**
1992	65	34	81	16	90	8
1991	73	23	72	22	78	16
1990	68	30	74	21	93	6
1989	71	26	83	13	95	2
1988	59	36	86	8	97	3
1987	59	36	76	17	84	9
1986	72	26	75	18	84	14
1985	74	25	80	14	87	9
1984	54	38	68	24	85	8
1983	74	23	77	18	87	11
1982	74	16	74 †	17 †	84	5
1981	72	24	83	12	88	7

† Not eligible for all recorded votes.

Interest Group Ratings

Year	ADA	AFL-CIO	CCUS	ACU
1992	15	42	63	76
1991	30	8	80	85
1990	17	8	57	79
1989	10	9	89	86
1988	10	36	79	88
1987	12	6	93	87
1986	5	8	67	95
1985	5	24	76	71
1984	25	15	60	58
1983	5	6	75	96
1982	10	5	80	86
1981	5	7	94	100

11 Sam M. Gibbons (D)

Of Tampa — Elected 1962; 16th Term

Born: Jan. 20, 1920, Tampa, Fla.
Education: U. of Florida, 1938-41, J.D. 1947.
Military Service: Army, 1941-45.
Occupation: Lawyer.
Family: Wife, Martha Hanley; three children.
Religion: Presbyterian.
Political Career: Fla. House, 1953-59; Fla. Senate, 1959-63.
Capitol Office: 2204 Rayburn Bldg. 20515; 225-3376.

In Washington: Gibbons has now spent three decades in Congress — often in the action on big issues, but nearly always at least one step removed from the epicenter of power and authority. Even now, in his 70s, he waits to learn whether his longevity will at last elevate him to the chairmanship of Ways and Means after 12 years in the No. 2 spot.

Chairman Dan Rostenkowski of Illinois began the 103rd Congress under cloud of an investigation into alleged fraud involving several members' transactions at the House Post Office. Should that result in an indictment, Rostenkowski would have to step down temporarily, and under Democratic Caucus rules Gibbons would automatically take the chair. That also might be Gibbons' best shot. Should Rostenkowski retire, there is no certainty that the Democratic caucus would choose Gibbons over other senior members more attuned to the views of the majority.

When still a junior member in the mid-1960s, Gibbons was tapped as floor manager of much of the Great Society program of President Lyndon B. Johnson, including Project Head Start. In those days, he was at once a Florida liberal and a product of the Old South, a member who could vote for Great Society social programs and the Voting Rights Act of 1965 while opposing busing and the Civil Rights acts of 1964 and 1968.

In the generation that has passed since, Gibbons has figuratively moved to the New South, and he has made the transition more easily than most. He has gone from opposing civil rights bills to cosponsoring the Civil Rights Restoration bill of 1990. A veteran of the legendary 101st Airborne Division in World War II, he has come to regret his backing of the Vietnam War and he voted against authorizing the use of military force in the Persian Gulf in 1991 — giving a moving speech on the subject on the House floor.

Along the way, Gibbons has flirted with real power: as a marginal candidate for leadership posts, a subcommittee chairman on Ways and Means and as an heir apparent for the full committee chair. He also has emerged as one of Congress' leading spokesmen for an often unpopular principle: free trade.

Since the mid-1980s, Gibbons has used his position as Trade Subcommittee chairman to resist and often moderate the forces that favor more aggressive trade policy. He has even carried to passage some modest improvements in the trade climate. In the 100th Congress, there was the free trade agreement with Canada. In the 101st, Gibbons won permanent extension of the Caribbean Basin Initiative, a 1983 program giving products of that region favored access to U.S. markets. In the 102nd, following Gibbons' lead, Congress agreed to continue the administration's so-called fast-track negotiating authority that ultimately led to the December 1992 signing of a North American Free Trade Agreement (including the United States, Mexico and Canada). Approval of that pact remained in doubt at the start of the 103rd Congress, as did the outcome of worldwide trade talks under the auspices of General Agreement on Tariffs and Trade.

Gibbons' devotion to trade has not always helped him make friends in the House. In fact, it led colleagues to snub him when the subcommittee chairmanship first became available to him. But for Gibbons, free trade is not just a political slogan; it is his creed. Raised in the Depression, and battle-scarred by world war, he is convinced that both catastrophes were born of the trade barriers nations had thrown up. "World War II had a tremendous impact on me," he has said. "I felt one reason it started was people didn't know how to work together.... My grand global goal is to make friends through commerce."

Over time, he has developed the skill of bending without breaking. In 1990, he acceded to a middle-course bill on China's trade status in the wake of the Tiananmen Square massacre. Gibbons helped strike a compromise between the Bush administration's desire for a free hand and House members' eagerness to cast Beijing's regime into the high-tariff darkness. The House passed the bill, but not before Gibbons and

Florida 11

West — Southern Hillsborough County; Tampa

Ever since a Key West cigar factory moved to Tampa in 1886, this has been a city with a blue-collar orientation. Cubans came to work in the cigar business, and they were joined later by Georgians, Alabamans and other Southerners looking for jobs in factories around the harbor.

Tampa's cigar industry is greatly diminished. But other traditional industries are still strong, among them brewing, commercial fishing, steel-making and ship construction. The city is also a major port; much of the phosphate mined from adjacent Polk County is shipped from here. That gives it an interest in international markets that coincides with Rep. Gibbons' free-trade politics.

The large working-class community makes Tampa the Florida city that most closely approximates Northern industrial cities. But the Democratic tendency this Tampa-based district historically has shown in state and national elections has been waning. There were not enough Democratic votes in the city to prevent George Bush from carrying surrounding Hillsborough County in 1992 with suburban GOP support.

Unlike many Northern industrial cities, however, Tampa has diversified to compete for the lucrative tourist trade. Busch Gardens, which started as a brewery tour, has been expanded into a 300-acre amusement park that is a leading Florida tourist attraction.

Tampa has a growing financial sector; Salomon Brothers and Citicorp recently moved some operations here. Tampa International Airport is a major employer, as is GTE Florida. The University of South Florida, one of the state's largest with about 33,000 students, is on the city's northern end.

The university's presence, combined with MacDill Air Force Base, has helped attract some high-technology industries. There have been some questions about MacDill's future, however. The base is scheduled to lose its F-16 training facility, and the continued operation of its runway is in doubt. Local officials hope that the recent relocation of the National Oceanic and Atmospheric Administration at the base will stabilize matters. The base also continues to serve as Special Operations Command and Central Command; Gen. H. Norman Schwarzkopf was based here before the Persian Gulf War, and he retired in the 11th after the conflict.

The district is 14 percent Hispanic. The influence of Cuban and Spanish culture is most pronounced in Ybor City, a long-established community in southeast Tampa named after the man who brought the cigar factory here from Key West. Although relatively few people still live in Ybor City — Hispanics are more prevalent in West Tampa and the community of Town and Country — the area is undergoing a commercial resurgence.

Blacks, who account for 17 percent of the district's population, live mostly in inner-city Tampa. Racial incidents occasionally occur. In early 1993, three white men were arrested in what authorities called the racially motivated burning of a black New York tourist whom the men kidnapped in Valrico, east of Tampa.

1990 Population: 562,519. White 442,900 (79%), Black 96,872 (17%), Other 22,747 (4%). Hispanic origin 78,295 (14%). 18 and over 430,766 (77%), 62 and over 81,578 (15%). Median age: 33.

Rostenkowski had slowed it down and adjournment had precluded Senate consideration.

The China issue re-emerged in the 102nd Congress, with even fewer members willing to defend that nation. Twice more, Congress sent bills to the White House calling for improvements in China's record on human rights, trade and weapons proliferation. Both were vetoed and both vetoes were sustained by the Senate.

While Gibbons generally opposes using trade as a weapon, he does make exceptions. When Iraq occupied Kuwait in August 1990, Gibbons authored a measure empowering the president to bar imports from countries that continued to trade with Iraq. It passed the House by unanimous consent. And in both the 99th and 100th Congresses, his panel approved legislation from the Foreign Affairs Committee imposing trade sanctions on the apartheid regime of South Africa.

And, despite a stubborn streak, Gibbons reluctantly and perhaps unavoidably accepted the need for some congressional effort to get tough with U.S. trading partners. Beginning in 1985, he cooperated with Rostenkowski to help produce what became, three years later, the most far-reaching trade law in years.

Yet even as his subcommittee prepared to draft a bill early in the 100th Congress, Gibbons was ever mindful of perhaps the most famous trade law in history, the 1930 Smoot-Hawley Act, which dramatically boosted tariffs and contributed to the ensuing global Depression. Vowing a complete reversal of that approach, Gibbons fended off a variety of industry-specific protections.

Speaker Jim Wright and other House leaders preferred a tougher measure, however, and they got their wish on the floor: The House narrowly approved a controversial amendment by Missouri Democrat Richard A. Gephardt to mandate limits on imports from nations such as Japan that maintain big surplus trade balances with the United States. Gibbons admitted he found the amended bill "a tough one to vote for," but he did so anyway, saying, "This is a bicameral organization, and there is hope that we can work out an acceptable bill before we are at the end of all this."

Other than the Gephardt amendment, the House bill contained little that Gibbons found objectionable. With the exception of telecommunications, it did not single out any industries for special treatment. And though it contained some threatening language, it still left the president considerable leeway on most trade matters. In the end, Gephardt's presidential campaign faltered and his trade amendment was dropped in House-Senate negotiations on the final bill.

Frequently in recent years, Gibbons has had the more nettlesome role of presiding over bills he wanted no part of — among them measures targeting Japanese trade surpluses and others limiting textile and apparel imports. When he could, Gibbons held objectionable amendments out of these bills until they reached the House floor. Still, he did not use his position to kill them.

In the 102nd Congress, Gibbons was unable to prevent House passage of a sweeping bill that would have required negotiations with Japan to limit Japanese auto exports to the United States and to require a higher percentage of U.S.-made parts in cars produced in the United States by Japanese-owned companies. Nor could he stop the House from passing a measure increasing tenfold the tariff on Japanese minivans — from 2.5 percent to 25 percent.

And three times in five years, he allowed textile quota bills to reach the floor, only to see them die under a presidential veto. Occasionally, Gibbons promised a free ride in committee to the textile bill's sponsors if they would agree not to support floor amendments that could broaden their coalition. When each time the House vote on passage fell short of a two-thirds majority, presaging a successful veto, Gibbons could claim a species of victory.

Gibbons' willingness not to block trade bills has brought him moderately closer to the House Democratic mainstream. That is where he would want to be should Rostenkowski leave and Gibbons attempt to move into the Ways and Means chair.

Gibbons has some experience with succession struggles. In 1977, his views probably prevented him from becoming chairman of the Trade Subcommittee. The chair was vacant then; he was the panel's senior Democrat and expected to inherit it. But his prospective leadership disturbed many committee Democrats, and Charles A. Vanik of Ohio, who had not even been on the Trade panel, exercised his full-committee seniority and snatched the chair.

By 1981, Gibbons was No. 2 on Ways and Means, and there was nobody to block him when the spot opened again.

In fact, he was poised to assume the full committee chairmanship that year. Retirements and surprise defeats left only Rostenkowski ahead of him, and Rostenkowski was more interested in being majority whip. But Speaker Thomas P. "Tip" O'Neill Jr., a past rival of Gibbons, urged Rostenkowski to take the Ways and Means chair, preferring not to have Gibbons in it. In 1973, after the death of Majority Leader Hale Boggs, Gibbons had launched a brief and futile campaign for the job. The overwhelming front-runner was O'Neill, who assumed that as majority whip he had the edge. O'Neill and Gibbons had been allies, so Gibbons' challenge was a curious one. He dropped out before the voting and O'Neill won unopposed, but the damage was done.

Gibbons' relations with Rostenkowski were strained in the 99th Congress when Gibbons emerged as a vocal critic of the committee's centerpiece legislation, a major revision of the tax code. On one occasion, he presided in the chairman's absence and lambasted the bill, prompting staffers to track down their boss, who returned fuming.

In the late 1960s, Gibbons had espoused the very reforms the bill was aimed at — lower rates, fewer loopholes and simplicity. But in the midst of Rostenkowski's reform effort, Gibbons argued that increasing business taxes to offset lower individual rates would hurt U.S. firms struggling to compete in world trade. In the end, Gibbons voted for the bill, but Rostenkowski ignored his seniority and kept him off the House-Senate conference committee.

Gibbons is an affable man, but he can be volatile. During the tax bill deliberations, he would launch into tirades against the Ways and Means staff. That reflected not only his own quick temper, but also a general frustration among panel members with the sway Rostenkowski allows his professional minions.

At Home: Gibbons, now in his 16th House term, is the only representative his Tampa-based district has ever had. He defeated a conservative Democrat to win it in 1962, the year it was created, then in 1968 held off another primary challenge from the right.

Gibbons' general election tally has only fallen below 60 percent twice — in 1984 and then again in 1992.

When Gibbons garnered 59 percent in the strong Republican year of 1984, that spurred talk of a serious challenge in the next election. He reinvigorated his campaign machinery, emphasized fundraising and hired a big-name consultant. He spent hundreds of thousands of dollars, but as it turned out, he was unopposed in 1986 and 1988 and only nominally challenged in 1990.

Redistricting enhanced the Democratic leanings of the district, peeling off some communities on the outskirts of Tampa. But Republicans thought they had an outside chance of upending Gibbons with Mark Sharpe, a former Naval Intelligence Officer who was born at the MacDill Air Force Base hospital in Tampa.

Sharpe beat a better-funded opponent in the primary, then ran an aggressive and generally positive campaign in the fall. Sharpe ran as a fiscal conservative emphasizing a pragmatic approach to domestic issues and reorienting the military budget to the post-Cold War era. He carved into Gibbons' support, but not enough to win.

Before he came to Congress, Gibbons served 10 years in the Legislature, where he drafted his state's first successful urban-renewal measure and fought the "Pork Chop Gang" that wanted to preserve rural overrepresentation in legislative reapportionment.

Gibbons finished first in the five-way 1962 Democratic House primary, then faced a runoff with retired National Guard Lt. Gen. Sumter L. Lowry, a fervid segregationist and anti-communist. Lowry got contributions from wealthy conservatives all over the South, but Gibbons picked up the support of the moderate Democratic candidates who had failed to make the runoff. He defeated Lowry and won the general election handily.

Committees

Ways & Means (2nd of 24 Democrats)
Trade (chairman)

Joint Taxation

Elections

1992 General		
Sam M. Gibbons (D)	100,962	(53%)
Mark Sharpe (R)	77,625	(41%)
Joe De Minico (I)	12,729	(7%)
1990 General		
Sam M. Gibbons (D)	99,464	(68%)
Charles D. Prout (R)	47,765	(32%)

Previous Winning Percentages: **1988** (100%) **1986** (100%)
1984 (59%) **1982** (74%) **1980** (72%) **1978** (100%)
1976 (66%) **1974** (100%) **1972** (68%) **1970** (72%)
1968 (62%) **1966** (100%) **1964** (100%) **1962** (71%)

District Vote for President

1992
D 82,898 (41%)
R 79,126 (39%)
I 39,796 (20%)

Campaign Finance

	Receipts	Receipts from PACs		Expend-itures
1992				
Gibbons (D)	$722,678	$427,161	(59%)	$960,511
Sharpe (R)	$51,952	$750	(1%)	$51,393
1990				
Gibbons (D)	$492,517	$316,125	(64%)	$825,795

Key Votes

1993	
Require parental notification of minors' abortions	N
Require unpaid family and medical leave	Y
Approve national "motor voter" registration bill	Y
Approve budget increasing taxes and reducing deficit	Y
Approve economic stimulus plan	Y
1992	
Approve balanced-budget constitutional amendment	Y
Close down space station program	N
Approve U.S. aid for former Soviet Union	Y
Allow shifting funds from defense to domestic programs	Y
1991	
Extend unemployment benefits using deficit financing	Y
Approve waiting period for handgun purchases	Y
Authorize use of force in Persian Gulf	N

Voting Studies

	Presidential Support		Party Unity		Conservative Coalition	
Year	**S**	**O**	**S**	**O**	**S**	**O**
1992	29	62	80	14	58	35
1991	41	59	82	15	49	51
1990	32	66	82	14	48	52
1989	37	53	78	13	49	51
1988	35	54	74	20	55	32
1987	29	67	82	12	49	47
1986	33	62	71	19	56	34
1985	50	45	69	20	49	45
1984	45	47	59	24	51	36
1983	45	50	68	23	38	55
1982	65	29	62	35	64	32
1981	62	34	46	45	80	15

Interest Group Ratings

Year	ADA	AFL-CIO	CCUS	ACU
1992	65	50	25	22
1991	60	58	30	16
1990	61	55	31	27
1989	80	70	40	19
1988	60	71	64	35
1987	56	69	33	32
1986	50	31	57	45
1985	40	53	50	38
1984	35	33	25	29
1983	60	53	55	22
1982	50	40	48	41
1981	30	40	50	38

12 Charles T. Canady (R)

Of Lakeland — Elected 1992; 1st Term

Born: June 22, 1954, Lakeland, Fla.
Education: Haverford College, B.A. 1976; Yale U., J.D. 1979.
Occupation: Lawyer.
Family: Single.
Religion: Presbyterian.
Political Career: Fla. House, 1985-91, majority whip 1987-89; GOP nominee for Fla. Senate, 1990.
Capitol Office: 1107 Longworth Bldg. 20515; 225-1252.

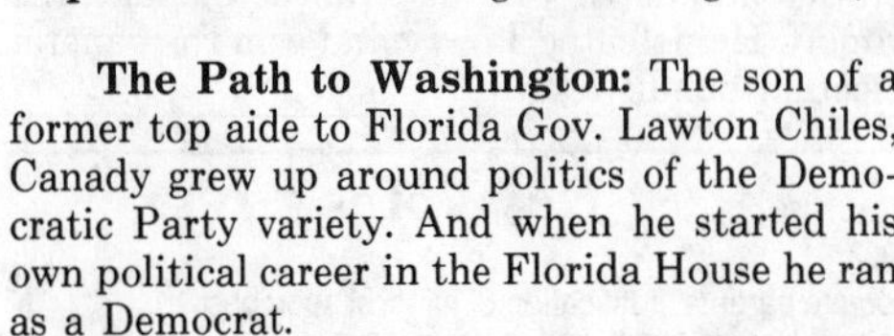

The Path to Washington: The son of a former top aide to Florida Gov. Lawton Chiles, Canady grew up around politics of the Democratic Party variety. And when he started his own political career in the Florida House he ran as a Democrat.

But Canady always has considered himself a conservative, and one term into his state legislative career, he felt that the fit between him and his party was not a good one.

When Michael S. Dukakis became the Democrats' presidential nominee in 1988, Canady started to think seriously about switching to the Republican Party.

During his re-election campaign that year, Canady's friends asked how he could run on the same ticket as Dukakis. "I never could give them a satisfactory answer," he explains. "We had basic philosophical differences across the whole spectrum."

When the state Legislature finished its work in the summer of 1989, Canady announced that he was becoming a Republican. The next year he ran for the state Senate on the GOP ticket but did not win. (His father, Charles E. Canady, who ran his son's congressional campaign, became a Republican in 1991.)

Canady welcomed George Bush's help during the 1992 election campaign, and he believes that Bush's visit toward the end of the campaign helped bring out GOP voters in a district in which the Democratic registration is 61 percent.

Canady also believes that he helped counter his opponent's partisan advantage by an intensive grass-roots effort.

The effort allowed him to defeat his Democratic opponent, state Rep. Tom Mims, 52 percent to 48 percent.

Canady is among the many new members who favor term limits. He promises not to serve more than four terms in the House.

He also supports cutting members' perquisites, asserting that "congressmen accustomed to such special privileges too often forget the needs of working Americans." Canady also would like to cut congressional staff by 50 percent.

Like many other new members, Canady also supports a constitutional balanced-budget amendment even though he concedes that the amendment, by itself, would not solve economic problems. But he believes it is "the only way we can force the hard decisions." He also supports a presidential line-item veto.

In late April 1993, Canady seemed so concerned with enacting some form of a line-item veto that he was one of only two Republicans to oppose GOP attempts to use a "vote-no" strategy on a key procedural vote to get Democrats to bring a stronger line-item veto bill to the floor. The Democrats' version ultimately passed with the support of about half the Republican caucus.

An appellate lawyer in a Lakeland law firm, Canady is used to the give-and-take of the courtroom as well as the legislative hall. He says he found that his political career and legal work have complemented each other, particularly because in both there is so much talking and thinking on one's feet.

As a Democratic and then Republican state legislator Canady was comfortable working both sides of the aisle. He has developed what he believes is an accommodating rather than a partisan style. But he is not afraid to play hardball. "When confrontation and disagreement is called for," he says, "that's what you do."

Much of Canady's time in the Florida House was spent working on state criminal justice matters, and he intends to work on these issues at the federal level from his seat on the Judiciary Committee.

Because of the importance of agriculture to the 12th District, Canady also sought and won a seat on the House Agriculture Committee.

During the campaign, he promised to work to eliminate what he calls "unnecessary, unfair and counterproductive government regulation" and to ensure that Florida growers are "not victimized by unfair foreign trade practices."

Canady also has called for retooling the welfare system to require recipients to work for their benefits. He opposes abortion except in cases of rape, incest or when the woman's life is in danger.

Florida 12

Central — Polk County; Lakeland; parts of Hillsborough County

Across much of Florida, land once devoted to agriculture is being eaten away by shopping centers, motels and condominiums. But in Polk County, centerpiece of the 12th District, citrus is still a major force.

Thousands of jobs are connected with the growing, picking, packing, processing and loading of oranges, orange concentrate and grapefruit. Besides Minute Maid, there are many smaller growers whose efforts combine to make the 12th among the nation's foremost citrus-producing districts.

However, Polk County's citrus industry has hit bumpy times in recent years, and periodic freezes have prompted some growers to move farther south. Also moving south are elements of the county's other leading industry, phosphate mining. The removal and processing of phosphate, the raw material of fertilizer, has fluctuated in recent years because of uneven demand for the product and the county's dwindling supply. IMC Fertilizer remains a leading private employer, however.

Food processing is also important in Polk County; Pepperidge Farms and BG Shrimp are leading employers. Lakeland, the county seat, is also headquarters for Publix supermarkets, the largest private employer in the state. But the county lost another leading employer in the 1980s when Piper Aircraft closed.

Tourists are drawn to Cypress Gardens, a botanical and water-show attraction in Winter Haven, just east of Lakeland.

The county grew by 26 percent in the 1980s, partly due to an influx of retirees. In the main, these retirees are less affluent than others who settle to the west along the Gulf Coast; some of them settle into mobile home parks. Large fundamentalist churches are commonplace in the district, and their parishioners contribute to the area's conservative leanings, especially on social issues.

The Dixie roots of the new arrivals are also apparent in the Democratic Party's decided registration edge in the district, 61 percent to 36 percent. But here as elsewhere, Southern Democrats often vote across party lines, and Republicans are making inroads in county offices. Ronald Reagan and George Bush carried the district by a 2-to-1 margin in the 1980s, while Democrat Buddy MacKay held a slim edge in the close 1988 Senate race.

The shaky economy held down Bush's margin in the district in 1992. It also made for the state's most competitive open-seat House race, with Canady squeezing by Democrat Tom Mims. Canady gained an 8,000-vote edge districtwide by earning 4,000-vote margins both in Polk County and in the relatively small part of Hillsborough County that is in the 12th.

The part of eastern Hillsborough County within the district includes Plant City, noted for its annual strawberry festival. Agriculture is a key here, with citrus and winter vegetables of some importance. The 12th also has part of Brandon, a Tampa suburb. Also in the district are De Soto and Hardee counties and part of Polk County.

1990 Population: 562,519. White 473,311 (84%), Black 71,083 (13%), Other 18,125 (3%). Hispanic origin 34,550 (6%). 18 and over 419,836 (75%), 62 and over 115,006 (20%). Median age: 35.

Committees

Agriculture (17th of 18 Republicans)
Department Operations; Foreign Agriculture & Hunger

Judiciary (12th of 14 Republicans)
Civil & Constitutional Rights; Economic & Commercial Law; International Law, Immigration & Refugees

Campaign Finance

1992	Receipts	Receipts from PACs		Expend- itures
Canady (R)	$158,777	$53,311	(34%)	$156,984
Mims (D)	$351,200	$96,195	(27%)	$349,895

Key Votes

1993

Require parental notification of minors' abortions	Y
Require unpaid family and medical leave	N
Approve national "motor voter" registration bill	N
Approve budget increasing taxes and reducing deficit	N
Approve economic stimulus plan	N

Elections

1992 General

Charles T. Canady (R)	100,468	(52%)
Tom Mims (D)	92,333	(48%)

District Vote for President

1992

D 67,661 (34%)
R 89,405 (46%)
I 39,171 (20%)

13 Dan Miller (R)

Of Bradenton — Elected 1992; 1st Term

Born: May 30, 1942, Highland Park, Mich.
Education: U. of Florida, B.S. 1964; Emory U., M.B.A. 1965; Louisiana State U., Ph.D. 1970.
Occupation: Businessman.
Family: Wife, Glenda Darsey; two children.
Religion: Episcopalian.
Political Career: No previous office.
Capitol Office: 510 Cannon Bldg. 20515; 225-5015.

The Path to Washington: Miller's script for turning inexperience to his advantage: Paint his opponent (in this case, Rand Snell, a former aide to Democratic Gov. Lawton Chiles) as a government insider who was part of the problem; portray himself as a fresh voice ready to work on reforming Congress.

Toss in a substantial boost from the fact that the 13th has the second-highest percentage of registered Republicans in the state and 69,000 more Republicans than Democrats, and voilà, Miller has his first shot at elective office.

A former college professor and businessman, Miller helped run a family-owned enterprise that included a restaurant, nursing homes and retirement residences.

Realizing that many incumbents were not returning — including Republican Andy Ireland, who since 1977 had represented part of what became the 13th — Miller believed that a large freshman class would offer substantial opportunities for reform.

Given the GOP advantage in registration, Miller's biggest hurdle was the primary.

The five-candidate GOP field was paced by businessman Brad Baker and Miller. Baker had a heavy presence in the district with TV ads, billboards and direct mail. Miller could boast of an endorsement from Ireland.

Miller prevailed in the runoff with 53 percent of the vote by clobbering Baker in Manatee County, where Miller had been strongest in the primary.

Miller was well-known because of his business endeavors and involvement in community affairs. He had been chairman of the local Chamber of Commerce, headed the hospital board and the local economic development council, and was on the board of numerous other organizations including the Manatee County Mental Health Center, the county Council on Aging and the local symphony.

Miller calls himself a fiscal conservative and an opponent of big government: "The federal government does not need to solve all our problems."

He supports a constitutional amendment to balance the budget as a first step for deficit reduction, but he concedes that merely passing the proposal would not solve any problems and could lead to pressure to raise taxes.

Like so many incoming freshmen, Miller supports term limits, but through a constitutional amendment. He believes House members should serve no more than 12 years.

He considers himself middle-of-the-road on abortion. He generally supports abortion rights, but he also supports "reasonable" state restrictions.

This stance pleased neither side of the issue during the campaign. Anti-abortion forces criticized him for being too liberal, and abortion rights supporters were dismayed by the limits he would place on abortions.

He was one of 51 Republicans to vote in March 1993 to codify President Clinton's lifting of the so-called "gag rule" that prohibited staff at federally funded family planning clinics from discussing abortion.

But Miller has said he could not support the Freedom of Choice Act if it would pre-empt states from enacting such abortion restrictions as parental consent and waiting periods.

Miller has a particular interest in health issues and would like to see a cap on malpractice awards as means of reducing health-care costs. He acknowledges that it is not the only solution, and he would like to curb what he calls "defensive medicine" — doctors performing unnecessary and costly procedures to protect themselves against charges of negligence. He also believes in encouraging preventive health care, noting that it makes economic sense and helps individuals.

He will be keeping an eye on these issues from the Budget and the Education and Labor committees.

Miller has special ties to two of Florida's other freshmen. Republican John L. Mica was his "big brother" in their fraternity at the University of Florida in the early 1960s, and Republican Tillie Fowler was in his wife's class at Emory University, where both lived in the same dormitory their freshman year.

Florida 13

Southwest — Sarasota and Manatee counties; Sarasota; Bradenton

When redistricting and retirements created 10 open seats in Florida in 1992, Republicans knew they had little to worry about in the newly designed 13th. The district's 56 percent GOP registration is the second highest in the state, barely below that of the adjacent 14th.

Sarasota County accounts for slightly less than half the 13th's population, and Manatee County represents just under 40 percent. The remainder live in parts of Charlotte and Hillsborough counties. More populous Sarasota was expected to have the upper hand in district politics, but in the 1992 GOP House runoff, Miller, who is from Manatee County, beat Brad Baker of Sarasota County.

George Bush ran stronger in Sarasota and Manatee than he did in the state as a whole in 1992, but the 43 percent he garnered in both counties was not overwhelming.

The political personality of the 13th is most influenced by retirees from suburbs and small towns of the Midwest. These people changed their addresses but not their party registration, and they contribute to the burgeoning strength of the GOP in Florida.

Although they closely identify with the GOP, residents of the 13th are not necessarily conservative on social issues. The 1992 House race, for example, was dominated by candidates who supported abortion rights. The proximity to gulf beaches, barrier islands and a large state park also makes the environment a bipartisan concern, with residents attuned to the problems of beach erosion and the effects of rapid population growth.

Sarasota County cultivates a refined image with its art museums, theaters and symphony performances. It generally draws a more highly educated and wealthier class of retirees than most other west coast communities in Florida. Leading private employers include tourism, retailing, health care and banking. The city of Sarasota includes some minorities and retirees who are not quite as affluent as those on the barrier islands of Longboat Key, Siesta Key and Casey Key.

Sarasota County grew by 37 percent in the 1980s. The area poised for the next growth spurt is immediately south of the city, down the coast along Route 41 to Venice. The residents of Venice itself tend to be a little older and of more modest means than residents on the county's northern end.

Manatee, which grew by 43 percent in the 1980s, has some residents who commute to work over the Sunshine Skyway Bridge to Tampa Bay. Leading employers in the county include Tropicana, which grows, picks and packs citrus, and Wellcraft Marine, which builds pleasure boats.

Bradenton, the county seat and retail center, has a somewhat diverse population both by income and ethnicity. It is also not quite as Midwestern-oriented as Sarasota.

The 13th also stretches south into Charlotte County to pick up parts of Port Charlotte and Murdock. Residents there are generally older, less affluent and more Democratic. It also extends north into Hillsborough County to pick up Sun City Center and Ruskin, where Republicans fare well.

1990 Population: 562,518. White 521,811 (93%), Black 30,631 (5%), Other 10,076 (2%). Hispanic origin 24,306 (4%). 18 and over 465,139 (83%), 62 and over 199,396 (35%). Median age: 47.

Committees

Budget (12th of 17 Republicans)

Education & Labor (15th of 15 Republicans)
Elementary, Secondary & Vocational Education; Human Resources; Postsecondary Education

Campaign Finance

1992	Receipts	Receipts from PACs		Expend-itures
Miller (R)	$453,193	$70,400	(16%)	$449,212
Snell (D)	$298,372	$38,300	(13%)	$298,309

Key Votes

1993

Require parental notification of minors' abortions	N
Require unpaid family and medical leave	N
Approve national "motor voter" registration bill	N
Approve budget increasing taxes and reducing deficit	N
Approve economic stimulus plan	N

Elections

1992 General		
Dan Miller (R)	158,836	(58%)
Rand Snell (D)	115,741	(42%)
1992 Primary Runoff		
Dan Miller (R)	33,965	(53%)
Brad Baker (R)	30,527	(47%)
1992 Primary		
Brad Baker (R)	22,055	(28%)
Dan Miller (R)	21,912	(28%)
Dave Thomas (R)	15,827	(20%)
Rick Louis (R)	13,828	(18%)
Jim Thorpe (R)	5,127	(7%)

District Vote for President

1992

D 100,950 (35%)
R 124,271 (43%)
I 65,297 (22%)

14 Porter J. Goss (R)

Of Sanibel — Elected 1988; 3rd Term

Born: Nov. 26, 1938, Waterbury, Conn.
Education: Yale U., B.A. 1960.
Military Service: Army, 1960-62.
Occupation: Businessman; newspaper founder; CIA agent.
Family: Wife, Mariel Robinson; four children.
Religion: Presbyterian.
Political Career: Sanibel City Council, 1974-80, 1981-82; mayor, 1975-77, 1982; Lee County Commission, 1983-88, chairman, 1985-86.
Capitol Office: 330 Cannon Bldg. 20515; 225-2536.

In Washington: At the start of the 102nd Congress, Goss — then beginning his second House term — asked to serve on the House ethics committee. He said he wanted the job in order to help improve Congress' standing with the public. But he insisted that he had no plans for a throw-the-rascals-out charge up Capitol Hill. "I'm not a crusader, and I'm not trying to change things," said Goss.

As it turned out, though, Goss had a lot more zeal in him than he had let on. As the controversy over members' no-penalty overdrafts at the House bank unfolded, Goss pushed for a thorough probe and full disclosure of the overdrafters' names.

An advocate of congressional term limits, Goss also produced a menu of legislation to reform Congress, including bills to limit payments for the expenses of former House speakers, roll back cost of living adjustments (COLAs) for House members and restrict members' mailing privileges.

At the start of the 103rd Congress, Goss obtained one of four Republican seats on the Rules Committee. Appointed to the Legislative Process Subcommittee, he intended to be in the forefront of Republican efforts to allow the introduction of more amendments during floor debate — a hot issue for GOP members who say the majority Democrats stack the deck by implementing restrictive rules on debate.

Minority Leader Robert H. Michel of Illinois also appointed Goss to the GOP Health Care Task Force, which had weekly meetings with key Clinton administration health advisers.

Goss has moved up within the House Republican Conference even though he is not one of his party's hard-line conservatives and certainly not an ideological drum-banger. His approach is usually well-modulated, and he veers from the party line on some environmental issues: the representative of a Florida Gulf Coast district with an economy that relies heavily on tourism, he strongly opposes oil drilling on the continental shelf off Florida.

Goss is to some extent a bridge between the more conciliatory veteran members, who take a pragmatic approach to achieving legislative results, and the more junior group of conservative activists, who favor confronting the long-dominant House Democratic leadership.

In February 1993, he blasted President Clinton's first federal budget proposal as typical Democratic "tax-and-spend" politics. But unlike some Republican activists in the House, Goss insisted that the GOP must produce concrete legislative alternatives of its own.

When Clinton released the outlines of his budget strategy, House Minority Whip Newt Gingrich of Georgia said Republicans should withhold their own budget proposals until the administration filled in its detailed plans for cutting programs and raising taxes. But Goss argued otherwise. "That's beautiful, wonderful politics," he said. "But this is not politics, this is our job."

He then submitted a proposal to cut 50 programs out of the federal budget for a savings of $190 billion. Although Goss said that some of his cuts would hit Florida's 14th District, most affected well-funded programs with benefits to parts of the country far from his home base: These included charging higher fees for Western ranchers who graze cattle on federal lands; reductions in farm subsidies, which would be most felt in the Midwestern grain-growing states; and elimination of the superconducting super collider, a super-expensive atom smasher being built in Texas.

However, these and other projects on Goss' list did have powerful Republican as well as Democratic sponsors.

While Goss, who supports a constitutional amendment to require a balanced budget, has been involved in money issues, his legislative efforts have been mainly on institutional reform.

One issue on which Goss took the lead during the 102nd Congress was the limitation of generous payments to the three surviving for-

Florida 14

Southwest — Lee and Collier counties; Cape Coral; Fort Myers; Naples

The 14th is an area of steadfast Republicanism and robust population growth. Fully 57 percent of district residents are registered Republicans, the highest percentage in the state. And the three counties that make up the district grew by more than 50 percent during the 1980s.

Lee County, which accounts for more than half the district's population, grew most slowly — at a 63 percent clip. The increase was pushed by Cape Coral, which grew by 134 percent and is now the district's largest city. Originally a retirement community, Cape Coral has been attracting young professionals, service industries and those involved in land development. Located near the gulf and along the Caloosahatchee River, the city features canals, easy access to the gulf and reasonable land costs.

To the west lie the barrier islands of Captiva and Sanibel, which have tried to restrict development to protect their natural beauty and preserve their images as upscale resort getaways. Across the river east of Cape Coral is Fort Myers, an older city once known for raising gladiolas. Acreage once devoted to gladiolas has since given way to land development. Health care is also an important employer here. Small pockets of blacks and blue-collar Democrats give Fort Myers a slightly less Republican cast than Cape Coral.

George Bush captured 68 percent of the Lee County vote in 1988, and his 44 percent in 1992 was still above his state average.

The region's growth spurred approval of a new state college, tentatively named Florida Gulf University, to be built in Lee County. The area also received boosts from the completion of Florida International Airport and the expansion of Interstate 75. The highway follows the gulf from Tampa, swinging east near Naples (Collier County) to cross the Everglades at Alligator Alley.

Naples, situated on the gulf, has some exclusive high-rise condominiums and large homes in its midst. The upper-income retirees, many from New England and the Midwest, support wide-ranging cultural activities, including the Naples Philharmonic center. Marco Island is a planned community noted for its wealthy residents and strong GOP inclination. Elsewhere in Collier County, citrus growers are increasingly attracted to the availability of open land and low risk of freezes. Immokalee, in the county's northern interior, has a large farm area and is home to many migrants and seasonal workers.

Collier, which grew 77 percent in the 1980s, is a solid Republican base; Bush captured 75 percent of the votes in 1988 and 53 percent in 1992.

Democrats often find their best chance in the district in Charlotte County, where Bush edged Democrat Bill Clinton in 1992, 39 percent to 37 percent.

Charlotte, known formerly as a retirement haven, has drawn a somewhat younger crowd recently, spurring a 90 percent population growth in the 1980s. Most of Charlotte County is in the 14th District except for some areas around Port Charlotte.

1990 Population: 562,518. White 517,105 (92%), Black 31,828 (6%), Other 13,585 (2%). Hispanic origin 37,384 (7%). 18 and over 455,977 (81%), 62 and over 170,636 (30%). Median age: 43.

mer House Speakers — Carl Albert, Thomas P. "Tip" O'Neill and Jim Wright — for office space and staff. "They are abusing the privileges afforded them," Goss said. "Anyone can see their official duties should wind down."

In late 1992, Goss was one of several Republican members of Congress who sued to block payment of a COLA for members; they argued that it violated the 27th Amendment, ratified in 1991, that bars members from raising their own pay. Although their suit failed, the House reacted to public anger over such pay raises by rolling back the COLA for 1993. Goss has proposed a bill to permanently limit House COLAs to no higher than those provided to recipients of Social Security benefits.

Social Security is a relevant issue to Goss, whose district has many retired elderly residents. As a member of a GOP task force on catastrophic health care, Goss promoted the repeal in 1989 of the 1988 Medicare Catastrophic Coverage Act after senior citizens angrily protested paying for the new benefits.

Goss reflects his home-base interests with his stand in favor of a permanent moratorium on offshore oil drilling in areas off Florida's coast. He has also sponsored legislation to allow a state to bar the capture of dolphins in its waters.

Goss pursued these issues on the Merchant Marine and Fisheries Committee, from which he took a leave when appointed to Rules. He also stepped down at least temporarily from the Foreign Affairs Committee.

There he showed an interest in Central America, serving on an Organization of American States delegation that observed the February 1990 elections in Nicaragua. Goss voices a typical Floridian's concern about communist Cuba, making a number of floor speeches about the continued perfidy of Fidel Castro.

At Home: After three elections, Goss appears to be well-suited for his district. He won his first bid for Congress with 71 percent of the vote in 1988, then ran unopposed for re-election. The district shed Sarasota County in redistricting, but it mattered little; Goss easily beat an independent challenger in 1992.

Local roots are not an obvious political selling point in fast-growing southwest Florida, where so many residents are new arrivals. But in 1988 Goss used his in local issues to convince voters that he would do the best job of protecting the environment that lured them there in the first place. A former employee of the CIA in Washington, D.C., and abroad, Goss moved to the district in 1971 and was drawn into politics by some of the same "quality-of-life" issues he stressed in the campaign. When picturesque Sanibel Island was hit by rapid development in the early 1970s, Goss played a major role in pushing for the town to incorporate and agree on growth-management laws. He became the small city's first mayor in 1975 and helped produce a development model that has been studied in public-policy schools and other localities.

Nearly a decade later, Goss was named to the Lee County Commission by then-Gov. Bob Graham, a Democrat. Goss, quickly tagged as the commission's environmentalist, got involved in controversial debates about managing growth countywide. But he easily won a full term, which positioned him to compete for the House seat when GOP Rep. Connie Mack decided to run for the Senate.

Goss had stiff competition for the GOP nomination: In particular, former Rep. L. A. "Skip" Bafalis, who had left the House for an unsuccessful gubernatorial bid in 1982, reappeared; among the three other GOP contenders was retired Army Brig. Gen. James Dozier, the victim of a well-publicized kidnapping by Italy's Red Brigades. Bafalis tried to label Goss a closet Democrat, saying Goss had contributed to Democratic candidates. But having moved back into the district shortly before launching his comeback bid, Bafalis' political strength had ebbed. His fundraising lagged (while Dozier's bid fizzled). Goss raised enough money to fund plenty of television and direct mail. He swept the October runoff and won the general election easily.

Committees

Rules (4th of 4 Republicans)
Legislative Process

Standards of Official Conduct (5th of 7 Republicans)

Elections

1992 General		
Porter J. Goss (R)	220,324	(82%)
James H. King (I)	48,156	(18%)
1990 General		
Porter J. Goss (R)	Unopposed	

Previous Winning Percentage: **1988** (71%)

District Vote for President

1992
D 87,856 (31%)
R 129,605 (46%)
I 63,149 (23%)

Campaign Finance

	Receipts	Receipts from PACs		Expend-itures
1992				
Goss (R)	$419,508	$41,900	(10%)	$414,185
King (I)	$17,382	0		$18,310
1990				
Goss (R)	$303,600	$122,125	(40%)	$244,740

Key Votes

1993	
Require parental notification of minors' abortions	Y
Require unpaid family and medical leave	N
Approve national "motor voter" registration bill	N
Approve budget increasing taxes and reducing deficit	N
Approve economic stimulus plan	N
1992	
Approve balanced-budget constitutional amendment	Y
Close down space station program	N
Approve U.S. aid for former Soviet Union	N
Allow shifting funds from defense to domestic programs	N
1991	
Extend unemployment benefits using deficit financing	N
Approve waiting period for handgun purchases	Y
Authorize use of force in Persian Gulf	Y

Voting Studies

	Presidential Support		Party Unity		Conservative Coalition	
Year	**S**	**O**	**S**	**O**	**S**	**O**
1992	75	25	91	9	85	15
1991	86	14	90	10	86	14
1990	72	28	88	11	85	15
1989	69	31	87	12	93	7

Interest Group Ratings

Year	ADA	AFL-CIO	CCUS	ACU
1992	5	17	75	88
1991	5	8	80	90
1990	33	8	86	79
1989	5	25	100	89

15 Jim Bacchus (D)

Of Merritt Island — Elected 1990; 2nd Term

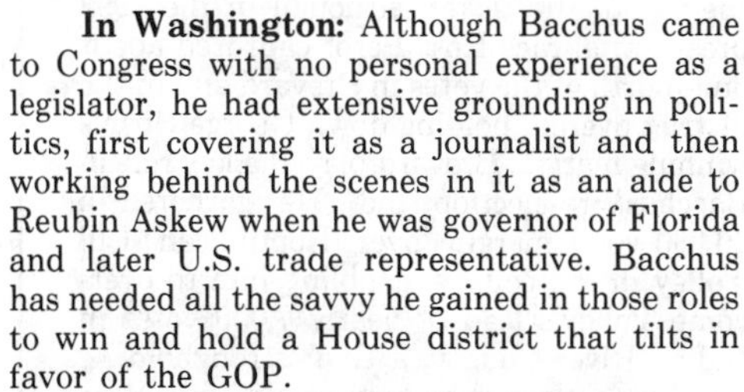

Born: June 21, 1949, Nashville, Tenn.
Education: Vanderbilt U., B.A. 1971; Yale U., M.A. 1973; Florida State U., J.D. 1978.
Military Service: Army Reserve, 1971-77.
Occupation: Lawyer; journalist.
Family: Wife, Rebecca McMillan; two children.
Religion: Presbyterian.
Political Career: No previous office.
Capitol Office: 432 Cannon Bldg. 20515; 225-3671.

In Washington: Although Bacchus came to Congress with no personal experience as a legislator, he had extensive grounding in politics, first covering it as a journalist and then working behind the scenes in it as an aide to Reubin Askew when he was governor of Florida and later U.S. trade representative. Bacchus has needed all the savvy he gained in those roles to win and hold a House district that tilts in favor of the GOP.

Bacchus' first legislative priority is clear: space. The 15th is home to the Kennedy Space Center at Cape Canaveral, and space and aeronautical matters are of paramount public concern here. Bacchus serves on the Science, Space and Technology Committee, where, not surprisingly, he supports ambitious plans for NASA, advocating establishment of a permanent moon base and exploring a possible mission to Mars. He is a big backer of NASA's controversial space station program.

"Space station *Freedom* is the next vital steppingstone for our space program," Bacchus has said. "Without *Freedom* we can forget about our dreams of building a base on the moon and landing a human being on Mars. We know of no other way to conduct the life sciences research that will tell us what long-term exposure to the harsh environment of space does to the human body."

In the 102nd Congress, Bacchus worked with Space Subcommittee Chairman Ralph M. Hall of Texas to get a provision he wanted into Hall's Commercial Space Competitiveness Act, which was later folded into the NASA authorization bill. Bacchus' section in the legislation authorized a new grant program to improve launch pads and other launch infrastructure for commercial purposes.

Bacchus' attention to space issues and his quietly intense personal demeanor help him deflect charges that he is too liberal for his district. In fact, Bacchus' overall voting record does look quite moderate for a Democrat in a marginal seat. For example, in 1991 he voted 83 percent of the time with labor, according to the AFL-CIO. In 1992, he voted for President Bush's stated position on legislation only 26 percent of the time. In the opening months of 1993, he was a down-the-line Bill Clinton supporter on several key votes, backing family leave, "motor voter" registration and the administration's budget and economic stimulus package while opposing parental notification of minors' abortions at federally funded clinics. He also has supported a waiting period for handgun purchases.

As a freshman, Bacchus drew favorable publicity at home for winning money for the Archie Carr Wildlife Refuge in Melbourne Beach and for successfully fighting to get a Veterans Administration hospital built in fast-growing Brevard County rather than Orlando.

In 1992, then-Department of Veterans Affairs Secretary Edward J. Derwinski picked a hospital site near Orlando International Airport, saying that location would best serve the area's more than 250,000 veterans. Bacchus disagreed with the recommendation and asked the General Accounting Office to study it.

GAO investigators criticized Derwinski's plan and supported Bacchus' position that it would be cheaper to build the hospital in Brevard. The VA has since agreed to build the hospital in Brevard.

Bacchus also serves on the Banking Committee, where he has been critical of the cost of the savings and loan bailout and has sought more accountability from the Resolution Trust Corporation.

At Home: Bacchus is a textbook case of how a Democrat can retain a House seat where Republicans outnumber Democrats. He has emphasized constituent service and issues important to the district, and worked hard to promote himself.

Growing conservatism in central Florida made the seat look ripe for a Republican pickup in 1990, when Democratic Rep. Bill Nelson ran for governor. Six Republican candidates feuded for the party nomination, while Bacchus was the unchallenged Democrat.

Though Bacchus had never held elective office, he knew the business. After working as a

Florida 15

Central — Brevard, Osceola and Indian River counties; Palm Bay; Melbourne

Brevard County is 72 miles long on the Atlantic Coast and only 20 miles wide. But it is less famous for its beaches than for what is launched from them. This is the self-proclaimed "Space Coast," home of NASA's Kennedy Space Center.

The county boomed during the era of Mercury, Gemini and Apollo space flights in the 1960s, then stalled when space exploration slipped as a national priority. The high-technology industries that had been lured to the area trimmed jobs, but a core of engineers and other skilled workers remained.

In the 1980s, the shuttle program and increased military spending brought new opportunities for aerospace and defense-related work, spurring another round of population growth. The 1986 explosion of the shuttle *Challenger* cast an economic and psychological pall over Brevard that began to lift when shuttle flights resumed in late 1988.

The space program still has an enormous economic impact on the county, and some of the companies it contracts with have taken on defense contracts as well. This reliance on government spending, either through space or defense funding, has forced several companies to adjust to a peacetime economy. Among the leading private employers are the Harris Corp., Collins General Aviation Division, Grumman and Lockheed.

Tourists are drawn to the space enterprises and to the beaches. The county still has some citrus, and cattle graze in southwest Brevard. Patrick Air Force Base provides support for the space program.

The county's population grew by 46 percent during the 1980s. Most residents live along the Indian River. Titusville, the county seat, is just north of the space center. Many of its residents are in working-class trades related to the space industry and are more prone to vote Democratic than the district as a whole. The Cocoa and Rockledge area, near the space center's entrance, tends to draw tourists. It is politically competitive. Farther south, Melbourne has more defense-related industries, and Palm Bay's largest employer is the Harris Corp., producing electronic systems and other high-tech equipment.

The 15th usually will vote Republican at the top of the ticket, although in the 1992 presidential race Ross Perot captured about one-fourth of the votes in Brevard and in the district overall, holding down George Bush's winning margin. Brevard played a key role in Bacchus' re-election bid. He garnered a 10,000-vote margin over Republican Bill Tolley in the county, enabling him to overcome Tolley's lead of nearly 7,000 votes in Indian River County, a GOP stronghold.

The retirees who have settled into Vero Beach and other coastal communities in Indian River County are fairly affluent and accustomed to voting Republican. Democrats have made few inroads there.

Bacchus also had a slight edge in the parts of Osceola County in the 15th. This area is largely agricultural. The small part of Polk County in the district is largely populated by cows, though Disney has plans to launch Celebration City, a mixed commercial and residential project there

---

1990 Population: 562,519. White 507,476 (90%), Black 42,761 (8%), Other 12,282 (2%). Hispanic origin 19,240 (3%). 18 and over 440,627 (78%), 62 and over 124,935 (22%). Median age: 37.

political reporter for The Orlando Sentinel and assisting Askew in Tallahassee and Washington, D.C., Bacchus had returned to Florida to practice law.

Bacchus kept a hand in Democratic politics and an array of civic groups, including a space-business roundtable and the Greater Orlando Chamber of Commerce, and commissions on the arts, the environment, the homeless and growth.

When Nelson left the House seat open, Bacchus launched what turned out to be an impeccably run campaign. He got organized quickly and challenged voters to get more involved in the community, creating "Citizen Saturdays." He devoted each Saturday to organizing volunteers to perform some community service, such as cleaning polluted beaches or building playgrounds.

Critics dismissed the Saturday programs as a campaign stunt, a knockoff of Lawton Chiles' walking tour of the state during his 1970 Senate campaign. But Bacchus insisted that the Citizen Saturdays were an end in themselves, an effort to get people mobilized within their own communities and the outgrowth of his "Jeffersonian" belief in participatory democracy.

GOP nominee Bill Tolley was strongly conservative and opposed to abortion. He blasted Bacchus for being too liberal for the district. Bacchus responded by spotlighting his business credentials and his support for a line-item veto and a balanced-budget constitutional amendment. He claimed Tolley was the extremist in the race, and he won with 52 percent of the vote.

Redistricting in 1992 removed Bacchus'

Orlando-area home from his district, prompting him to move to the Cape Canaveral area. A rematch was set when Tolley beat a moderate GOP legislator in the primary.

Tolley again portrayed Bacchus as too far left, and he said the incumbent used congressional franking privileges for self-promotion. But Bacchus' strong support for space programs and his high local profile on matters such as the VA hospital gave most voters no compelling reason to toss him from office. He emerged with a slim majority, and although Tolley contended that there were abnormalities in the count, Bacchus' victory stood up.

Committees

Banking, Finance & Urban Affairs (14th of 30 Democrats)
Financial Institutions Supervision, Regulation & Deposit Insurance; International Development, Finance, Trade & Monetary Policy

Science, Space & Technology (14th of 33 Democrats)
Space; Technology, Environment & Aviation

Elections

1992 General		
Jim Bacchus (D)	132,385	(51%)
Bill Tolley (R)	128,830	(49%)
1992 Primary		
Jim Bacchus (D)	31,216	(66%)
Larry Bessinger (D)	16,371	(34%)
1990 General		
Jim Bacchus (D)	120,991	(52%)
Bill Tolley (R)	111,970	(48%)

District Vote for President

1992

D 83,679 (31%)
R 117,685 (43%)
I 69,749 (26%)

Campaign Finance

	Receipts	Receipts from PACs		Expend-itures
1992				
Bacchus (D)	$841,298	$460,597	(55%)	$820,388
Tolley (R)	$216,346	$54,615	(25%)	$215,538
1990				
Bacchus (D)	$877,500	$412,573	(47%)	$875,386
Tolley (R)	$365,313	$106,100	(29%)	$364,926

Key Votes

1993	
Require parental notification of minors' abortions	N
Require unpaid family and medical leave	Y
Approve national "motor voter" registration bill	Y
Approve budget increasing taxes and reducing deficit	Y
Approve economic stimulus plan	Y
1992	
Approve balanced-budget constitutional amendment	Y
Close down space station program	N
Approve U.S. aid for former Soviet Union	Y
Allow shifting funds from defense to domestic programs	Y
1991	
Extend unemployment benefits using deficit financing	Y
Approve waiting period for handgun purchases	Y
Authorize use of force in Persian Gulf	Y

Voting Studies

	Presidential Support		Party Unity		Conservative Coalition	
Year	S	O	S	O	S	O
1992	26	71	77	18	58	42
1991	35	64	86	12	51	49

Interest Group Ratings

Year	ADA	AFL-CIO	CCUS	ACU
1992	70	55	13	29
1991	50	83	33	20

16 Tom Lewis (R)

Of North Palm Beach — Elected 1982; 6th Term

Born: Oct. 26, 1924, Philadelphia, Pa.

Education: Palm Beach Junior College, 1956-57; U. of Florida, 1958-59.

Military Service: Air Force, 1943-54.

Occupation: Real estate broker; aircraft testing specialist.

Family: Wife, Marian Vastine; three children.

Religion: Methodist.

Political Career: Councilman/Mayor of North Palm Beach, 1964-71; Fla. House, 1973-81, minority leader, 1979-81; Fla. Senate, 1981-83.

Capitol Office: 2351 Rayburn Bldg. 20515; 225-5792.

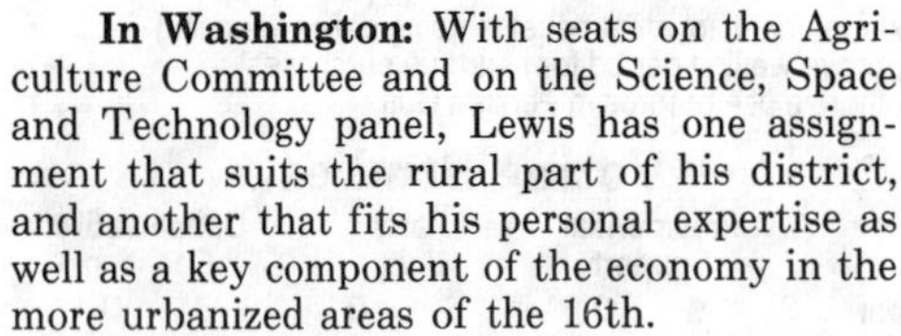

In Washington: With seats on the Agriculture Committee and on the Science, Space and Technology panel, Lewis has one assignment that suits the rural part of his district, and another that fits his personal expertise as well as a key component of the economy in the more urbanized areas of the 16th.

Though most of the turf in the 16th is south-central Florida farmland that produces vegetables, sugar, livestock and citrus, most of the district's people live in affluent communities along the Atlantic Coast, where aviation- and technology-oriented business is important. Hence, Lewis' two main interests in Congress are things that fly and things that grow (in that order).

Pratt & Whitney Aircraft — where Lewis once worked as a test engineer — employs thousands in the Palm Beach area. Lewis' personal expertise and his concerns for the district's economic health make him a natural proponent of programs promoting U.S. aerospace competitiveness, and a keen watcher of the Federal Aviation Administration (FAA).

In both the 102nd and 103rd Congresses, Lewis championed a bill providing a joint planning board from which NASA, the Defense Department and private companies would map out future research and development projects in the aerospace industry. Such a system would afford private companies the opportunity to advocate for defense-related projects that have commercial applications.

Although during the 102nd the bill stalled in committee, interest may increase given the Clinton administration's desire to spur research partnerships. Lewis is in a good position to weigh into the debate as ranking Republican on the Science Subcommittee on Technology, Environment and Aviation.

During the 102nd Lewis monitored the FAA's implementation of two measures for increasing aviation safety that he had passed in previous Congresses. His National Air Safety Act of 1988, which breezed through both houses of Congress, orders the FAA to spend a minimum of 15 percent of its annual research budget on a variety of safety issues. In the 101st Congress, Lewis wrote a law to require the FAA to perform additional research aimed at detecting problems that could lead to accidents involving aging airliners.

Lewis has long been a booster of the National Aerospace Plane, a proposed $5 billion-plus superfast orbital plane. However, in 1991 the plane fell victim to NASA budget traumas, and funding was nearly zeroed out. Pratt & Whitney was a contractor on the project.

Given the 16th's many miles of Atlantic Coast shoreline, it is not surprising that Lewis has fought to keep hurricane-hunting airplanes aloft until new radar tracking devices go into service. Preventing the Air Force from scrapping the hurricane plane program paid off in August 1992, when these planes flew into Hurricane Andrew to monitor its progress toward South Florida. During the 102nd, Lewis also shepherded through legislation that provides for a five-year study of hurricane behavior.

Lewis is now the No. 4 Republican on Agriculture, but he has not been one of the committee's more visible members, partly because of his low-key style and partly because most of the commodities grown in the 16th are not covered by federal programs. The 103rd Congress brought Lewis a new platform that may raise his profile: the ranking position on the Specialty Crops and Natural Resources Subcommittee.

One area in which Lewis has been passionate is agricultural trade. Farmers in the 16th are wary of the potential impact of the North American Free Trade Agreement, which would eliminate many restrictions on Mexican produce entering the United States. Lewis, working with the rest of the Florida delegation, wants to "harmonize" U.S. and Mexican environmental and worker-safety regulations before imple-

Florida 16

Central — Coastal Martin, Palm Beach and St. Lucie counties

The large 16th is something of a link between Central Florida and the southeast's Gold Coast. Although most of its land mass is in four lightly populated counties along the western edge of Lake Okeechobee, most of its population lives in three Atlantic coast counties.

Republicans hold a bare registration edge in the 16th, which means GOP candidates typically run better than their statewide average in top-of-the-ticket races.

The area has attracted newcomers from more congested areas farther south along the coast. Palm Beach County, which accounts for nearly half of the district's population, grew at an overall rate of 50 percent during the 1980s. St. Lucie County grew by 72 percent and Martin County grew by 58 percent. Growth management has become the most important local concern.

The 16th includes parts of north Palm Beach County. Controversies over the pace of development and its impact on the environment have been present in the community of Jupiter, which tripled in size in the 1970s and more than doubled in the 1980s. Many of the newcomers are young, middle-income families who commute south to work in an area from West Palm Beach to Boca Raton. Transportation is a concern here, deciding where to build access roads and how to move travelers through the county. Some bedroom communities are no longer interested in attracting more residents. Jupiter, a mix of conservative Democrats and Republicans, is enticing to boaters because of its access to the Atlantic as well as the Intracoastal Waterway.

Palm Beach Gardens is headquarters for the Professional Golfers Association and features a golf resort. Wellington is a GOP stronghold. Other areas attractive to retirees are Fountains of Lake Worth, where many residents live on a fixed income and lean Democratic, and Golden Lakes Village.

Farming is important in less-developed areas of the county, especially sugar, cattle, vegetables and citrus. Pratt & Whitney builds jet engines at a plant northwest of Palm Beach Gardens, while golf courses and beaches draw tourists to the coast.

Martin County faces some of the same issues of growth management. It has quite a few moderate- to high-income retirees and remains a GOP bastion.

Citrus is an important industry in St. Lucie County, where Indian River Citrus is known for its sweet grapefruit. Port St. Lucie quadrupled in population in the 1980s, with Republicans cutting into the county's traditional Democratic bent. Fort Pierce, which grew by a relatively modest 9 percent during the 1980s, has a wider spread of incomes than the rest of the coastal communities.

The other four counties in the district — Glades, Hendry, Highlands and Okeechobee — are largely agricultural, with some predominantly fixed-income retirees. Lake Okeechobee, which is adjacent, offers plenty of recreational opportunities for fishing and boating. In the 1992 presidential election, Ross Perot cut into George Bush's margin enough for Bill Clinton to carry Glades and Okeechobee counties.

1990 Population: 562,519. White 523,225 (93%), Black 22,616 (4%), Other 16,678 (3%). Hispanic origin 35,517 (6%). 18 and over 447,765 (80%), 62 and over 156,318 (28%). Median age: 40.

menting the agreement. Such a harmonization would slow down or prevent Mexican agricultural products from flooding U.S. markets.

Despite his dalliances in FAA regulations and with adding conditions to the free trade agreement, Lewis is normally an advocate of small-government, spend-less conservatism: In 1992, he got a 96 percent "correct" rating from the American Conservative Union. One of Lewis' more politically daring proposals — especially given Florida's large seniors population — is to freeze all government spending, including cost of living adjustments on entitlement programs such as Social Security.

But this does not mean that Lewis has not sought and won federal largess for his district — such as funding for a Veterans Administration hospital and for highway improvements.

Normally, however, Lewis functions as a voice of restraint on spending issues, advocating a balanced-budget constitutional amendment and a presidential line-item veto and opposing the costly superconducting super collider. He says his aerospace technology competitiveness proposals would cost nearly nothing to implement, and he occasionally grumbles about the price tag of other research and development projects passing through his subcommittee.

Lewis also voted in the 102nd against emergency appropriations for the Chicago flood and the Los Angeles riots (although he did vote to send money to South Florida after Hurricane Andrew hit).

He veers off the conservative line with his interest in the environment. Lewis opposes drilling for oil and gas off the Florida coast, and he has obtained federal funding to expand the Cypress National Preserve in South Florida. His priorities in the 103rd included authorizing research to study the diversity of plant and animal life in coastal wetlands.

At Home: Lewis did not enter politics until he was nearly 40, and he was 58 by the time he came to Congress. But if he was slow to start, he has played the game well, never losing an election.

Lewis' chance for a House seat came when the old 12th was created in 1981 redistricting. His state Senate district encompassed most of the House district, and many conservative Democrats were displeased with their party's nominee, Brad Culverhouse, a labor-backed lawyer and rancher.

At one point in the campaign, construction workers angered by economic downturn disrupted a Lewis rally featuring Vice President George Bush. Though Culverhouse disassociated himself from the protest, public reaction to the incident contributed to his defeat. Culverhouse's active campaigning did enable him to hold Lewis to 53 percent of the vote.

Lewis ran unopposed in the next four general elections, then beat Democrat John P. Comerford, an investment banker, in 1992. Comerford chipped away at the incumbent's popularity by criticizing his eight overdrafts at the House bank, his votes to cut Medicare and former acceptance of honoraria. Still, Lewis polled 61 percent.

Born in Philadelphia, Lewis was a gunner aboard a B-25 bomber in World War II, flying out of India and China. During the Korean War, he was on the ground directing American warplanes to their targets. After leaving the military in 1954, he settled in Florida.

He worked 16 years with Pratt & Whitney as chief of rocket and jet engine testing. During this time, he served on the North Palm Beach City Council, where he was chosen mayor, a post he held throughout his municipal career. When he assumed the more time-consuming duties of the Legislature, he quit Pratt & Whitney and entered the real estate business.

Committees

Agriculture (4th of 18 Republicans)
Specialty Crops & Natural Resources (ranking); Foreign Agriculture & Hunger; Livestock

Science, Space & Technology (4th of 22 Republicans)
Technology, Environment & Aviation (ranking)

Elections

1992 General		
Tom Lewis (R)	157,253	(61%)
John P. Comerford (D)	101,217	(39%)
1992 Primary		
Tom Lewis (R)	29,716	(64%)
John Anastasio (R)	16,621	(36%)
1990 General		
Tom Lewis (R)	Unopposed	

Previous Winning Percentages: **1988** (100%) **1986** (99%) **1984** (100%) **1982** (53%)

District Vote for President

1992
D 96,910 (36%)
R 107,257 (39%)
I 68,064 (25%)

Campaign Finance

	Receipts	Receipts from PACs	Expend-itures
1992			
Lewis (R)	$296,405	$129,015 (44%)	$363,795
Comerford (D)	$99,097	$40,200 (41%)	$97,871
1990			
Lewis (R)	$336,333	$80,425 (24%)	$401,225

Key Votes

1993	
Require parental notification of minors' abortions	Y
Require unpaid family and medical leave	N
Approve national "motor voter" registration bill	N
Approve budget increasing taxes and reducing deficit	N
Approve economic stimulus plan	N
1992	
Approve balanced-budget constitutional amendment	Y
Close down space station program	N
Approve U.S. aid for former Soviet Union	N
Allow shifting funds from defense to domestic programs	N
1991	
Extend unemployment benefits using deficit financing	Y
Approve waiting period for handgun purchases	N
Authorize use of force in Persian Gulf	Y

Voting Studies

	Presidential Support		Party Unity		Conservative Coalition	
Year	S	O	S	O	S	O
1992	70	27	90	6	94	2
1991	73	25	88	10	95	3
1990	68	31	86	8	93	2
1989	72	28	94	5	100	0
1988	69	28	93	5	95	0
1987	63	34	88	8	88	9
1986	71	26	82	14	86	8
1985	66	34	85	12	87	11
1984	58	40	81	16	93	7
1983	67	32	78	18	91	8

Interest Group Ratings

Year	ADA	AFL-CIO	CCUS	ACU
1992	10	27	83	96
1991	10	17	90	90
1990	6	0	79	90
1989	5	17	100	93
1988	5	14	93	100
1987	8	6	93	83
1986	15	21	76	70
1985	5	6	86	81
1984	20	23	88	79
1983	20	18	75	70

17 Carrie P. Meek (D)

Of Miami — Elected 1992; 1st Term

Born: April 29, 1926, Tallahassee, Fla.
Education: Florida A&M U., B.S. 1946; U. of Michigan, M.S. 1948; Florida Atlantic U., 1979.
Occupation: Educational administrator; teacher.
Family: Divorced; three children.
Religion: Baptist.
Political Career: Fla. House, 1979-83; Fla. Senate, 1983-93.
Capitol Office: 404 Cannon Bldg. 20515; 225-4506.

The Path to Washington: Meek arrives in Washington from an area still reeling from the ravages of Hurricane Andrew, and she says economic revitalization efforts for her Dade County district are a top priority.

She is well situated to deliver for her district: Of the 63 freshman Democrats elected in November, Meek was the only one to win a spot on the powerful Appropriations Committee.

Freshmen almost never make it onto Appropriations. It is considered an assignment that must be earned by voting with the leadership, working hard on other committees and making friends in high places. This year, however, Speaker Thomas S. Foley of Washington said he would make an exception because of the large bloc of new members.

(The leadership counts three freshmen among the new Democrats on Appropriations. The other two came to Congress in 1991 in special elections: Ed Pastor of Arizona and John W. Olver of Massachusetts.)

Meek's campaign for the committee seat was under way long before Foley agreed to break the no-freshmen rule.

During her career in Florida politics, Meek made a name for herself on social issues. She has been a longtime activist for blacks, the elderly and the poor. Her age — 66 — became an issue in the race. And one of her two primary opponents, Darryl Reaves, said he had challenged Meek so the new black-majority district would not "crown somebody queen."

After winning her primary in September with 83 percent of the vote, Meek faced no opponent in the general election. The 17th has the state's highest percentage of black residents, 58 percent, and is its most reliably Democratic constituency.

So while other candidates were still working to lock up their seats, Meek went to Washington and began campaigning anew — this time for a seat on the committee that decides how to spend the taxpayers' money.

She met the Democratic leadership — the Speaker, the majority leader, the whip, the deputy whips. She met the appropriators. She met the members of the Steering and Policy Committee, who make the committee assignments. She also talked to fellow members of the Congressional Black Caucus and spoke to influential women members. Even more important, Meek worked through the Florida delegation, which had lost two seats on Appropriations with the retirements of Democrats William Lehman and Lawrence J. Smith.

Meek also got a boost from the fact that the leadership was looking for diversity. Of the 12 new Democrats appointed to Appropriations, three are Hispanic and three are women, including Meek, who is black.

But while race and gender were factors in Meek's selection, a much bigger factor seemed to be the way she impressed the members she met.

She told them about herself and her background in politics. Meek is the child of sharecroppers and is one of three Florida blacks elected to Congress in 1992 — the first from the state since Reconstruction. She grew up in a poor Tallahassee neighborhood referred to as Black Bottom when segregation was the norm.

She served in the Florida House from 1979 to 1983 and then in the Florida Senate since 1983. In the Senate, she worked on the Appropriations Committee. She also worked as a college administrator and a teacher.

One point that she stressed was her experience as a veteran legislator who did not run against Congress. "I didn't run on coming up here and throwing the bozos out," Meek said.

Meek's assignment to the Military Construction Subcommittee may prove particularly useful as the fate of hurricane-damaged Homestead Air Force Base — targeted for closure — is weighed.

Besides helping to rebuild South Florida, Meek is concerned about how to deal with Haitian refugees seeking asylum in the United States. Early in the 103rd Congress, she delivered floor speeches calling for action on behalf of Haiti and its refugees in the United States and introduced a bill allowing certain Haitian refugees to be given permanent residency status.

Florida 17

Southeast — Parts of North Dade County; parts of Miami, Carol City

The 17th has the state's highest percentage of black residents and is Florida's most staunchly Democratic district. Democrats account for more than 75 percent of the registered voters, and they routinely deliver the highest percentage of votes for Democrats running statewide.

All three 1992 House aspirants were black Democrats. They were vying to represent a district that has seen widespread devastation. Starting at the Broward County line, the district runs through such northern Miami suburbs as Carol City and Opa-Locka, then picks up the impoverished Miami neighborhoods of Liberty City and Overtown. It follows U.S. 1 heading southwest to include predominantly black neighborhoods in Richmond Heights, Perrine, Homestead and Florida City. Some of these areas were leveled by Hurricane Andrew on Aug. 24, 1992.

Unincorporated Carol City is predominantly black and Hispanic. (Hispanics overall account for about one-quarter of the district's population.) Most residents are blue-collar workers who commute south to Miami. The area has a mix of single-family homes, apartments and housing projects. Opa-Locka, which suffers from high unemployment and high crime rates, is overwhelmingly black. As in the rest of the district, local political organizations usually center around churches. Opa-Locka is also noted for its Arabian theme and its large private airport.

Unincorporated Rolling Oaks is an affluent black neighborhood near Joe Robbie Stadium (home of football's Dolphins and baseball's Marlins). North Miami Beach contains some of the largest numbers of whites in the district, many of whom are Jewish retirees on fixed incomes. They are well-organized, Democratic and interested in health care and crime. The west side of North Miami, which is in the district, is a mix of blacks, whites and Hispanics, and somewhat less Democratic.

The Miami neighborhoods in the 17th include Little Haiti, which has a growing core of recent immigrants from the Caribbean. They tend to be Democrats but are not yet a political force. The black neighborhoods of Liberty City — where Rep. Meek lives — and Overtown have been plagued by economic despair and violence. A 1980 riot left 18 dead after an all-white jury acquitted four white Miami police officers in the beating death of a black insurance executive. Riots erupted again in 1989 after a Latino officer shot a black motorcyclist. Some improvements have been made — there are new apartment complexes and stores in Liberty City and the Miami Arena (home of pro basketball's Miami Heat) is reinvigorating part of Overtown — but progress is slow.

The district takes in the ethnically mixed areas of South Miami, then delves into the more rural communities near U.S. 1 that Andrew hit hard. Perrine, Richmond Heights and Florida City are heavily black; Homestead is mixed. Some residents were homeless or living in trailers for months after the hurricane struck, while others moved into northern Dade County. Homestead Air Force Base, which was hit hard by Andrew, was on the 1993 base-closure list.

1990 Population: 562,519. White 205,611 (37%), Black 328,316 (58%), Other 28,592 (5%). Hispanic origin 129,628 (23%). 18 and over 391,015 (70%), 62 and over 67,772 (12%). Median age: 30.

Committee

Appropriations (37th of 37 Democrats)
Energy & Water Development; Military Construction

Campaign Finance

1992	Receipts	Receipts from PACs	Expend-itures
Meek (D)	$574,719	$158,615 (28%)	$461,115

Key Votes

1993

Require parental notification of minors' abortions	N
Require unpaid family and medical leave	Y
Approve national "motor voter" registration bill	Y
Approve budget increasing taxes and reducing deficit	Y
Approve economic stimulus plan	Y

Elections

1992 General		
Carrie P. Meek (D)	102,732	(100%)
1992 Primary		
Carrie P. Meek (D)	31,262	(83%)
Darryl Reaves (D)	3,499	(9%)
Donald Jones (D)	3,122	(8%)

District Vote for President

1992	
D 101,901	(74%)
R 25,994	(19%)
I 9,820	(7%)

18 Ileana Ros-Lehtinen (R)

Of Miami — Elected 1989; 2nd Full Term

Born: July 15, 1952, Havana, Cuba.
Education: Miami-Dade Community College, A.A. 1972; Florida International U., B.A. 1975, M.S. 1986.
Occupation: Teacher; private school administrator.
Family: Husband, Dexter Lehtinen; two children, two stepchildren.
Religion: Roman Catholic.
Political Career: Fla. House, 1983-87; Fla. Senate, 1987-89.
Capitol Office: 127 Cannon Bldg. 20515; 225-3931.

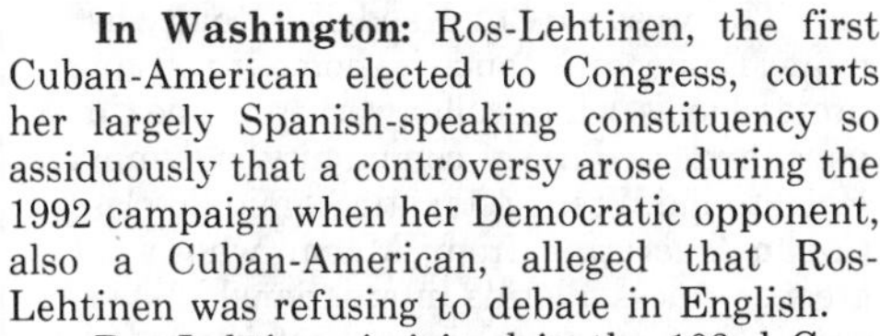

In Washington: Ros-Lehtinen, the first Cuban-American elected to Congress, courts her largely Spanish-speaking constituency so assiduously that a controversy arose during the 1992 campaign when her Democratic opponent, also a Cuban-American, alleged that Ros-Lehtinen was refusing to debate in English.

Ros-Lehtinen is joined in the 103rd Congress by another South Florida Cuban-American, fellow Republican Lincoln Diaz-Balart, but her emphasis on the interests of the Cuban-American constituency is unlikely to abate. Her redrawn district is still numbered the 18th, but it is now 67 percent Hispanic (up from 51 percent within the previous district lines).

During her time in the House, Ros-Lehtinen has focused on finding ways to isolate Cuban dictator Fidel Castro from the international community, with the hope of precipitating his downfall. After winning her special election to replace the late Democrat Claude Pepper in 1989, she got her dream assignment when the Democratic leadership agreed to give the GOP another slot on the Foreign Affairs panel.

In the 102nd Congress, Ros-Lehtinen forged a somewhat shaky alliance with Rep. Robert G. Torricelli, D-N.J., a fellow Foreign Affairs member and the principal author of a measure to address the Cuban situation through a variety of economic sanctions.

Torricelli's legislation, known as the Cuban Democracy Act, ultimately was incorporated into and adopted as part of the fiscal 1993 defense authorization. The measure prohibits foreign subsidiaries of U.S. corporations from conducting any new trade with Cuba.

While Torricelli and Ros-Lehtinen shared a determination to force a change in Cuba's leadership, they clashed more than once over the method. Ros-Lehtinen, a former Cuban refugee for whom the issue is personal, favored a hard-line approach, which would cut off the man that she has described as an "inhuman tyrant." Torricelli, though resolved to drive out Castro, was also mindful that the legislation needed the support of more liberal House members in order to win passage.

The tension between the two lawmakers became apparent to observers in the spring of 1992. One public exchange was reported in the Miami Herald. Torricelli, who was chairing a subcommittee hearing on the Cuban Democracy Act, interrupted Ros-Lehtinen during her questioning of a government witness. Infuriated by Torricelli's lapse of etiquette, Ros-Lehtinen stalked out of the hearing, announcing on her way out the door that she would be back. "Well, we won't be here," Torricelli replied.

During later consideration of the bill, Ros-Lehtinen objected to added provisions that would allow the donation and sale of medical supplies to the Cuban government. She argued that the allowances weakened the bill, telling her Foreign Affairs colleagues, "If Mr. Castro was a member of this committee, I'm sure he'd be a cosponsor of the bill with these amendments."

The language allowing the export of medicine and medical supplies remained in the final version of the Cuban Democracy Act. But it was eviscerated by a proviso requiring verification that the supplies would not be re-exported or used for purposes of torture.

While Ros-Lehtinen is not yet among the most prolific lawmakers, introducing only three bills in the 102nd Congress, she is a frequent contributor to the Extension of Remarks section of the Congressional Record. In the last Congress she submitted more than 600 such speeches. Many of them — with titles such as "Lixion A. Avila: First Cuban-American Hurricane Forecaster" and "Juan Morales: From Castro's Dungeons to Walt Disney World" — commemorate the achievements of Cuban-Americans and other immigrants in her district.

Ros-Lehtinen's pro-Israel stance appealed to the sizable Jewish population in the old 18th. When the United States supported a U.N. resolution criticizing Israel for the deaths of 19

Florida 18

Southeast — Parts of Dade County; part of Miami

This is one of two Hispanic-majority Florida districts. Although it includes much of downtown Miami, its spiritual heart is the inner-city neighborhood known as Little Havana.

Many of Miami's Cubans came to this country in the 1960s, fleeing Castro's takeover. Many were well-educated professionals and business people in Cuba, and they have achieved positions of status here. The Cubans, Puerto Ricans, Haitians, Nicaraguans and Colombians who have arrived more recently tend to be unskilled workers, and integrating them into society is more difficult.

The Cuban-American community for a time was consumed with discussing and plotting to overthrow Castro; U.S. elections were not a focus. They are now, and that is good news for the GOP. The party's hawkish anti-communist stance helped persuade most Cuban voters to register Republican. That makes this a safe GOP district.

The 18th is hardly homogenous, however. South Miami Beach, traditionally home to Jewish retirees, is attracting young professionals and some Hispanics. It features the Art Deco district of colorful hotels. Downtown Miami, hit by the bankruptcies of Eastern and Pan Am airlines, focuses on international trade. Brickell Avenue contains high-rise offices, and residences for Hispanics and the upper-middle class; it is a swing area politically.

Across a causeway is Key Biscayne, an upper-middle-class suburb and one of the city's first areas to turn Republican. Richard M. Nixon used to vacation here. Back on the mainland and heading south from downtown along the coast is Coconut Grove, a trendy neighborhood that attracts young liberals. Next comes Coral Gables, home of the University of Miami (14,000 students). The southern end of Coral Gables is more Anglo and has expensive houses and yacht clubs.

The 18th includes the east side of Kendall, an upper-middle class suburban area that leans Republican. The district extends farther south, to include small parts of Cutler Ridge and Perrine, then loops around endangered Homestead Air Force Base into South Miami Heights. This area includes blue-collar, conservative Democrats and Cubans and was hit by Hurricane Andrew in 1992.

The west side of Kendall is somewhat more Democratic and is home to young professionals, white-collar workers, some Cubans and a Jewish community. Olympia Heights and Westchester attract middle-class Cuban-Americans from Miami who want greener spaces. Florida International University (24,000 students) is in Westchester.

Most of Miami in the 18th is south of the Miami River except for Allapattah, an older section of the city that has become more Hispanic. While many of the Cubans who arrived in Little Havana have moved elsewhere, those who remain tend to be older and less affluent. Crime tends to be more of a problem with recent refugees. The west side of the city is also predominantly Hispanic but more middle class. The Orange Bowl is in the district, as is most of Miami International Airport.

1990 Population: 562,519. White 499,210 (89%), Black 23,351 (4%), Other 39,958 (7%). Hispanic origin 375,148 (67%). 18 and over 450,048 (80%), 62 and over 116,996 (21%). Median age: 38.

Palestinians during a September 1990 Sukkot holiday confrontation in Bethlehem, Ros-Lehtinen opposed the measure, saying the United States "should not support a resolution unless there has been a complete investigation of this tragic situation."

In 1991, she co-sponsored a bipartisan resolution calling on Arab states to recognize Israel and end the state of war in the Middle East. However, many of her Jewish constituents were ceded to other districts in the 1992 remap.

The new district extends as far south as Homestead and Florida City, areas that sustained significant damage from Hurricane Andrew in August 1992. In the wake of the hurricane, she demanded that greater attention be paid to minority contractors. "Priority for contracts and jobs should go to those affected areas, in this case, South Florida," she told her colleagues in a floor speech.

She also made an impassioned plea for the rebuilding of Homestead Air Force Base, which was devastated by Andrew, citing its strategic value because of its proximity to Cuba. The base has since shown up on the Pentagon's 1993 list of bases recommended for closure.

Ros-Lehtinen's overall conservative philosophy includes opposition to abortion and support for a constitutional amendment banning flag desecration. However, early in the 103rd Congress, she broke ranks with a majority of the GOP twice on key votes, casting hers in favor of family and medical leave and national "motor-voter" registration.

At Home: From the moment she announced for Pepper's seat, Ros-Lehtinen was the leading contender for the GOP nomination.

She has stood out politically since 1982, when she became, at age 30, the first Hispanic elected to the state Legislature. Although not a major power broker in Tallahassee, Ros-Lehtinen was an articulate campaigner and leading member of South Florida's Cuban-American community.

That community tends to vote Republican, and national GOP strategists were itching to rally that vote and snatch the 18th from Democratic hands. Ros-Lehtinen easily beat three other candidates for the GOP nomination.

Some Democratic insiders, building their own bridges to Cuban-Americans, backed Rosario Kennedy, also a Cuban-American. But Gerald Richman, a Miami Beach attorney with limited political experience, beat Kennedy in a runoff.

While Democrats struggled to unify, Ros-Lehtinen enjoyed generous GOP support, including visits from President George Bush and Vice President Dan Quayle. To reach the 18th's important bloc of Jewish voters, Ros-Lehtinen stressed her strong support for Israel, traveling there during the campaign. She also touted her crime-related work in the Legislature.

Richman, who is Jewish, reacted to GOP suggestions that Cuban-Americans deserved a voice in Congress by saying the 18th was "an American seat." Although Ros-Lehtinen and some media criticized Richman's comment as bigoted, he did strike a chord with some voters. Ros-Lehtinen won, but by a smaller margin than anticipated.

Richman's showing led some to believe Ros-Lehtinen's re-election was uncertain. But she prepared well, and several formidable Democrats skipped the race. The 1990 Democratic nominee was industrialist Bernard Anscher, who had won just 703 votes in the 1989 Democratic primary. He lost by 20 points to Ros-Lehtinen.

Two years later, Ros-Lehtinen lobbied the Legislature to draw as many Cuban-Americans as possible into her district. The plan that emerged from federal court created two districts with two-thirds Hispanic majorities and a firmly Republican character.

Her 1992 Democratic opponent, lawyer Magda Montiel Davis, criticized Ros-Lehtinen's anti-abortion stance and called for more travel and communication with Cuba. Ros-Lehtinen responded with a TV ad that tried to link Davis, through her husband's legal work, to Castro and former Panamanian leader Gen. Manuel Antonio Noriega. The incumbent won by 2-to-1.

Committees

Foreign Affairs (12th of 18 Republicans)
Western Hemisphere Affairs

Government Operations (9th of 16 Republicans)
Government Information, Justice, Transportation & Agriculture

Elections

1992 General		
Ileana Ros-Lehtinen (R)	104,715	(67%)
Magda Montiel Davis (D)	52,095	(33%)
1990 General		
Ileana Ros-Lehtinen (R)	56,364	(60%)
Bernard Anscher (D)	36,978	(40%)

Previous Winning Percentages: 1989* (53%)

** Special election.*

District Vote for President

	1992
D	52,615 (33%)
R	92,212 (57%)
I	16,761 (10%)

Campaign Finance

	Receipts	Receipts from PACs		Expend-itures
1992				
Ros-Lehtinen (R)	$662,297	$149,344	(23%)	$667,828
Davis (D)	$338,147	$38,150	(11%)	$335,408
1990				
Ros-Lehtinen (R)	$575,234	$168,784	(29%)	$560,847
Anscher (D)	$112,072	$750	(1%)	$112,071

Key Votes

1993	
Require parental notification of minors' abortions	Y
Require unpaid family and medical leave	Y
Approve national "motor voter" registration bill	Y
Approve budget increasing taxes and reducing deficit	N
Approve economic stimulus plan	N
1992	
Approve balanced-budget constitutional amendment	Y
Close down space station program	Y
Approve U.S. aid for former Soviet Union	N
Allow shifting funds from defense to domestic programs	N
1991	
Extend unemployment benefits using deficit financing	Y
Approve waiting period for handgun purchases	Y
Authorize use of force in Persian Gulf	Y

Voting Studies

	Presidential Support		Party Unity		Conservative Coalition	
Year	S	O	S	O	S	O
1992	61	36	73	24	79	19
1991	67	32	75	22	73	24
1990	50	45	70	26	70	24
1989	66 †	32 †	74 †	24 †	82 †	18 †

† Not eligible for all recorded votes.

Interest Group Ratings

Year	ADA	AFL-CIO	CCUS	ACU
1992	25	50	57	78
1991	40	42	50	70
1990	33	8	54	65
1989	--	40	100	100

19 Harry A. Johnston (D)

Of West Palm Beach — Elected 1988; 3rd Term

Born: Dec. 2, 1931, West Palm Beach, Fla.
Education: Virginia Military Institute, B.A. 1953; U. of Florida, LL.B. 1958.
Military Service: Army, 1953-55.
Occupation: Lawyer.
Family: Wife, Mary Otley; two children.
Religion: Presbyterian.
Political Career: Fla. Senate, 1975-87, president, 1985-87; sought Democratic nomination for governor, 1986.
Capitol Office: 204 Cannon Bldg. 20515; 225-3001.

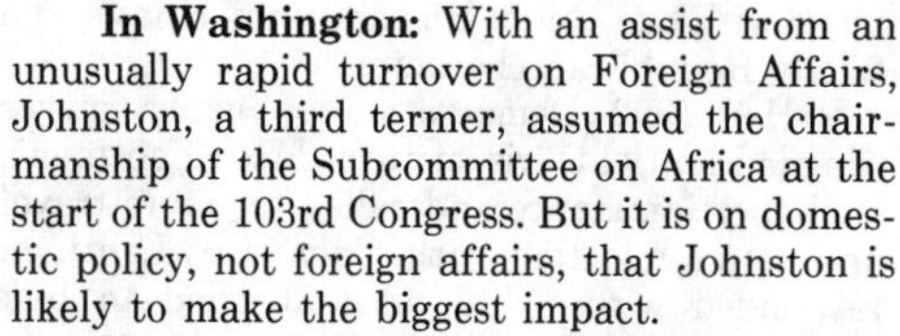

In Washington: With an assist from an unusually rapid turnover on Foreign Affairs, Johnston, a third termer, assumed the chairmanship of the Subcommittee on Africa at the start of the 103rd Congress. But it is on domestic policy, not foreign affairs, that Johnston is likely to make the biggest impact.

He has taken an especially active role in the debate on health-care reform. In 1991, Johnston introduced a bill that called for an overhaul of the nation's health-care system rather than the marginal changes favored by the Republican administration of George Bush.

"Supporters of incremental reform want to tinker with our current system under the guise of providing universal coverage; however, until we implement a system for managing costs, universal health insurance in the United States will remain an elusive dream," Johnston wrote in one of several op-ed pieces published in local and national newspapers during the course of the 102nd Congress.

The plan would have set up a national health insurance system funded by federal taxpayers but administered at the local level. Insurance companies would have bid to provide coverage to residents of localities; they would have been required to provide coverage to all people, regardless of income, employment status or pre-existing medical conditions.

Under Johnston's proposal, local and state governments would also have set up supervisory boards to set budgets for health-care providers and insurance companies and regulate the costs of physician services. It would also have sought to save money by streamlining the costs of health insurance administration.

The bill did not advance in Congress, but it gained the attention of then-presidential candidate Bill Clinton (Johnston was one of the earliest House endorsers of Clinton's candidacy). By the time he was elected president over Bush in November 1992, Clinton had come out in favor of a "managed competition" approach to health-care reform that contained elements similar to Johnston's provisions.

Although he lacked committee bona fides on the issue, Johnston was appointed to an 11-member task force advising House Majority Leader Richard A. Gephardt of Missouri on health-care reform. Johnston's legislative aide on the issue, Roger Berry, was chosen to serve on first lady Hillary Rodham Clinton's national task force that shaped the administration's health-care plan in 1993.

Johnston was expected to remain a key player in the effort to produce the reform legislation.

Johnston's main ongoing legislative role remains in the area of foreign policy. Although he had little background in African affairs — he did not even serve on the subcommittee before the 103rd Congress — and few African-Americans in his district to push him, Johnston pronounced an ambitious agenda shortly after taking over as subcommittee chairman.

After decades in which various African nations provided surrogate battlefields for the U.S.-Soviet rivalry, Johnston said he would fight the post-Cold War "marginalization" of African affairs. He told a March 1993 meeting of the Washington Office on Africa that he advocates a policy that recognizes "the critical interdependence between the U.S. and Africa." He promised to push for a strong U.S. role in conflict resolution and the promotion of democratic institutions in African nations.

To that end, Johnston called in early 1993 for a cutoff in aid to Zaire and the ouster of the corruption-plagued government of longtime totalitarian ruler Mobutu Sese Seko.

He also called for U.S. recognition of the elected government of Angola headed by President Jose Eduardo dos Santos, who had renounced the Soviet ties that spurred U.S. support for anti-communist Angolan guerrilla forces, headed by Jonas Savimbi, during the 1980s. Johnston condemned Savimbi, who, after losing to dos Santos in a September 1992 election, resorted to military action that reopened that nation's civil war. "It is high time

Florida 19

Southeast — Parts of Palm Beach and northern Broward counties; Boca Raton

The 19th is one of Florida'a most compact and most Democratic districts. It lies generally west of Interstate 95, running north-south from Lake Worth in Palm Beach County to Tamarac in Broward County. The district's population is nearly evenly split between the two counties.

The large registration edge that Democrats enjoy among voters in some other Florida districts is illusory in state and federal elections because conservative Democrats often vote Republican at the top of the ticket.

But the 19th is filled with devoted and lifelong Democrats who retired here from the Northeast. It routinely rolls up some of the state's most impressive margins for Democratic candidates. And it does so with the smallest percentage of black residents of any district in Florida. The 19th is the "whitest" of the four Florida districts that Michael S. Dukakis carried in the 1988 presidential race.

The district's retirees, many of whom are Jewish and from New York, give the area a Northeastern orientation. Delis and bagel bakeries are popular, and residents strongly support cultural offerings in nearby West Palm Beach and Fort Lauderdale. Health care and social security are vital concerns.

Although safely Democratic, the 19th has pockets of strong Republican support, and those areas are growing rapidly. Republicans are slightly more competitive in the district's Palm Beach County communities.

Lake Worth, Boynton Beach and Delray Beach are all less Democratic than the district as a whole. That is partly because they are somewhat less retirement-oriented and have a mix of young professionals and families living in single-family homes.

Boca Raton, which has some single-family homes as well as exclusive condominium subdivisions, is among the district's most Republican communities.

Also in the area are large private employers, including IBM and Siemens Stromberg Carlson (which produces telephone switching systems), both in Boca Raton, and Motorola in Boynton Beach.

Just south of the Palm Beach-Broward line lies Deerfield Beach. Many residents here are retired New Yorkers who live in middle-income condominium complexes; they vote Democratic in huge numbers.

To the west is fast-growing Coral Springs, the district's largest city, which grew by 113 percent in the 1980s.

Coral Springs is also friendly territory for the Republican Party. It features upper-middle-class houses that attract professionals, some of whom commute to Fort Lauderdale.

Continuing east and south, the district picks up more Democratic strongholds. They include Margate, which has some blue-collar workers, Tamarac and Coconut Creek, which grew by two-thirds in the 1980s.

Democrats can turn out impressive numbers in these areas because they are so well-organized.

1990 Population: 562,519. White 533,138 (95%), Black 15,447 (3%), Other 13,934 (2%). Hispanic origin 34,985 (6%). 18 and over 461,448 (82%), 62 and over 178,485 (32%). Median age: 42.

that we unequivocally tell Mr. Savimbi that enough is enough," Johnston said.

Johnston established himself early in his House career as an advocate of U.S. aid to promote democracy, demilitarization and market development in the former Soviet Union. He is co-chairman of the Congressional Roundtable on Post-Cold War Relations.

Like most Florida members, Johnston takes a strong interest in Latin American affairs. He supported aid to the Nicaraguan contras; in 1990, he helped monitor elections that ousted Nicaragua's leftist government. Although he expresses sympathy for the plight of potential refugees from Haiti — most of whom arrive in Florida — Johnston has called on the federal government to control such immigration until it relieves the state of the costs of dealing with the Haitian influx.

Though Johnston graduated from Virginia Military Institute, he is not hawkish: He favored sanctions in response to Iraq's invasion of Kuwait and opposed authorizing Bush to use force against Iraq in January 1991.

Endowed with one of Florida's most consistently Democratic-voting House districts, Johnston has an overall voting record that is one of the least conservative in the state's House delegation. In 1992, he supported Bush's position on just 18 percent of House votes on which Bush took a position.

During the 102nd Congress, Johnston held a seat on the Interior Committee, where he focused his efforts on an attempt to ban oil drilling in the waters off Florida's coast.

His 103rd Congress assignments include a

spot on the Budget Committee.

At Home: Although Johnston has the bearing of a Southern patrician, his politics are hardly Old Florida. As a state legislator who rose to Senate president, he took on the clique of rural legislators who had long ruled the state, helping replace them with a more urban coalition committed to open government. As a House candidate in 1988, he combined that experience with a sophisticated campaign to win easily over popular rivals.

Still, there were doubts about Johnston's campaigning ability when he announced for the 14th, which came open as Democrat Daniel A. Mica ran for the Senate. Johnston's 1986 bid for governor — highly touted at the outset — failed to reach the runoff. He is not a natural campaigner and once acknowledged worrying about invading voters' privacy.

In the Democratic House primary, he faced Dorothy Wilken, an outspoken Palm Beach County commissioner who presented herself as the grass-roots candidate. But Johnston, a wealthy fifth-generation Floridian, used his establishment contacts to gain a significant financial edge and dominate the TV ad battle.

Johnston's unexpectedly strong primary victory made him a slight favorite over GOP nominee Ken Adams, a popular county commissioner. Adams billed himself as a businessman with a conscience, noting his efforts to get funding for public housing and AIDS patients. He portrayed Johnston as "a liberal lawyer legislator," citing his votes for reducing penalties for criminals.

But Johnston forcefully dismissed Adams' charges as "a bucket of crap," and he played up some of his conservative stands, such as support for a presidential line-item veto. He won by 10 percentage points.

In 1990, Johnston faced even harsher GOP attacks from management consultant Scott Shore, who charged that Johnston faced too many conflicts of interest between his House duties and his partnership in a law firm. Johnston said his record was clean, but noted his plans to sever the law firm ties in compliance with new congressional ethics legislation, as he did in January 1991. Voters were deaf to Shore's pitch; Johnston romped.

The 1992 campaign was more civil. Republican Larry Metz, a lawyer and political newcomer, had little success tarring Johnston with Congress' shortcomings.

Committees

Budget (20th of 26 Democrats)

Foreign Affairs (7th of 27 Democrats)
Africa (Chairman); Economic Policy, Trade & the Environment; International Operations

Elections

1992 General		
Harry A. Johnston (D)	177,411	(63%)
Larry Metz (R)	103,848	(37%)
1990 General		
Harry A. Johnston (D)	156,055	(66%)
Scott Shore (R)	80,249	(34%)

Previous Winning Percentage: **1988** (55%)

District Vote for President

	1992
D	158,752 (54%)
R	88,829 (30%)
I	46,859 (16%)

Campaign Finance

	Receipts	Receipts from PACs	Expend-itures
1992			
Johnston (D)	$346,976	$179,800 (52%)	$231,449
Metz (R)	$62,630	0	$63,200
1990			
Johnston (D)	$508,525	$253,169 (50%)	$469,101
Shore (R)	$216,826	$9,800 (5%)	$213,139

Key Votes

1993	
Require unpaid family and medical leave	Y
Approve national "motor voter" registration bill	Y
Approve budget increasing taxes and reducing deficit	Y
1992	
Approve balanced-budget constitutional amendment	Y
Close down space station program	Y
Approve U.S. aid for former Soviet Union	Y
Allow shifting funds from defense to domestic programs	Y
1991	
Extend unemployment benefits using deficit financing	?
Approve waiting period for handgun purchases	Y
Authorize use of force in Persian Gulf	N

Voting Studies

	Presidential Support		Party Unity		Conservative Coalition	
Year	**S**	**O**	**S**	**O**	**S**	**O**
1992	18	76	86	10	33	65
1991	32	64	83	11	24	70
1990	23	72	81	11	30	69
1989	34	64	88	8	37	59

Interest Group Ratings

Year	ADA	AFL-CIO	CCUS	ACU
1992	90	67	38	12
1991	80	91	22	11
1990	83	83	38	25
1989	70	83	50	7

20 Peter Deutsch (D)

Of Lauderhill — Elected 1992; 1st Term

Born: April 1, 1957, Bronx, N.Y.
Education: Swarthmore College, B.A. 1979; Yale U., J.D. 1982.
Occupation: Lawyer; non-profit executive.
Family: Wife, Lori Ann Coffino; two children.
Religion: Jewish.
Political Career: Fla. House, 1983-93.
Capitol Office: 425 Cannon Bldg. 20515; 225-7931.

The Path to Washington: Deutsch's bruising campaign for the Democratic nomination in the 20th proved that when there is little philosophical difference between political combatants, there may be little left to do but sling mud.

A five-term Florida House member, Deutsch began gearing up for a run for the U.S. House in 1990 when he became chairman of the House congressional reapportionment subcommittee.

While Deutsch advanced his own interests in Tallahassee, he also actively represented those of his constituents, many of whom are retirees. He introduced bills prohibiting nursing home evictions, allowing the investment of state pension funds in Israeli bonds and extending grandparents' visitation rights. Cultivating the support of the area's seniors was shrewd politics on Deutsch's part because older voters typically turn out at the polls in higher numbers than their younger counterparts.

But during his tenure in the state House he also earned a reputation for arrogance. A Miami Herald columnist wrote that Deutsch was "viewed by colleagues as bright but abrasive, and an expert at using procedural rules to advance or torpedo legislation."

Deutsch's reputation cost him endorsements. When he learned that the final map placed him in the same district with Dante B. Fascell, a 38-year House veteran, Deutsch replied, "He's going to have to beat me." Fascell retired shortly thereafter, but not without a parting shot at Deutsch. Fascell, former Rep. Lawrence J. Smith and retiring Democratic Rep. William Lehman issued a formal letter of support for Deutsch's opponent, Broward County Commissioner Nicki Englander Grossman, saying she alone possessed the "knowledge and temperament" to represent the 20th.

Grossman, a commissioner since 1982, had the support of virtually all of the 20th's Democratic leaders and was considered the primary favorite by local pundits.

Because the two candidates differed little on substantive issues — both supporting abortion rights, Israel and universal health care — their campaigns turned personal.

Grossman hammered Deutsch for soliciting money from an out-of-town lobbyist, which a reporter witnessed. She also cited a magazine article that called Deutsch one of the least-effective legislators in Tallahassee.

Deutsch, who had a big financial edge over Grossman, fought back in an eleventh-hour blitz of mail and television ads. One flier depicted a bountiful table spread, with the caption "Nicki Grossman put this meal on our tab." The text charged that Grossman had entertained at Broward County taxpayers' expense.

Deutsch faced nominal competition in the general election from GOP nominee Beverly Kennedy. Kennedy tried to paint Deutsch as a political insider and emphasized her background as a businesswoman and political neophyte.

Voters in the 20th were unmoved by Kennedy's pitch; Deutsch won with 55 percent.

In Washington, Deutsch immediately created a minor stir when he hired a 19-year-old Harvard senior to be his chief aide.

Though he hoped for a spot on Energy and Commerce, from which he could help shape health-care reform, Deutsch instead wound up on Foreign Affairs, Banking and Merchant Marine.

Like his predecessors, Deutsch will need to be a strong voice in behalf of Israel because of the district's large Jewish constituency. Deutsch, Florida's only Jewish member, opposes arm sales to nations hostile to Israel.

Of the several Democratic freshmen on the Banking Committee's Financial Institutions Subcommittee, Deutsch seemed the most reluctant to cast a difficult vote to finance the final round of the thrift bailout early in the 103rd Congress. He said the GOP could more easily take the politically safe though "irresponsible" route and vote against funding the last round of the bailout.

On other issues, Deutsch opposes parental-consent requirements for abortions, favors an increase in federal funding for AIDS research, amending the Civil Rights Act of 1964 to include sexual orientation as a discriminatory classification and lifting the ban on gays in the military.

Florida 20

South — Southern and western Broward County; Hollywood; the Keys

While the two cultures that coexist in the 20th are as different as the music of Lawrence Welk and Jimmy Buffett, the retirees and suburbanites of Broward county hold the key to political success in the 20th.

The portion of Broward County in the 20th holds 75 percent of the district's residents. Though Republicans can be competitive here, voters typically support Democrats in statewide elections.

Democrats derive their pivotal backing in Broward from planned retirement villages with heavily Jewish populations, such as Sunrise Lakes. Many of the middle-income retirees who dwell in these sprawling developments hail from areas of New York where (generally speaking) everyone voted, and everyone voted Democratic. The city of Hollywood, part of which is in the district, also reflects that tradition.

But another important and growing voting bloc in the 20th are the young people who are moving into Broward bedroom communities such as Pembroke Pines (population 65,000), the largest city wholly within the district, and Cooper City (population 21,000). Pembroke Pines grew more than 80 percent in the 1980s, and Cooper City's population almost doubled.

With virtually no industry in the district, the mainly white professionals and midlevel managers commute to jobs in Miami and Fort Lauderdale. In the mid-1980s, I-595 was built largely to accommodate them.

The Dade County portion of the district is the least significant politically, with only 29,000 registered voters. Hurricane Andrew hammered the largely agricultural community of Homestead in 1992; community leaders hope that the planned closing of Homestead Air Force Base, part of which is in the 20th, will not cause a mass exodus of the active duty and retired military personnel who live in the area alongside a significant Hispanic population.

Much of the district's land area, particularly in western Dade and mainland Monroe counties, has practically no people, but it teems with life: The Florida Everglades is here; it is the largest subtropical wilderness in the United States.

Virtually all of Monroe County's 78,000 residents live on the Florida Keys, which stretch 135 miles from the mainland to Key West, the largest city on the Keys, in the Gulf of Mexico.

With its traditions of tolerance, independence and even lawlessness, Key West has a unique political culture. The significant homosexual community routinely forms alliances with Republican environmentalists who battle an entrenched Democratic power structure. Many of these Republicans will not hesitate to vote for a Democrat for statewide office, if he has strong environmentalist credentials.

The youth who came down in the 1980s to work in Key West's booming tourist-related businesses became a temporary political force: They helped elect their favorite bartender, a 70-year-old raconteur known as Captain Tony, mayor of Key West.

1990 Population: 562,518. White 518,114 (92%), Black 24,913 (4%), Other 19,491 (3%). Hispanic origin 69,459 (12%). 18 and over 440,467 (78%), 62 and over 107,945 (19%). Median age: 37.

Committees

Banking, Finance & Urban Affairs (17th of 30 Democrats)
Consumer Credit & Insurance; Financial Institutions Supervision, Regulation & Deposit Insurance; Housing & Community Development

Foreign Affairs (22nd of 27 Democrats)
Europe & the Middle East; Western Hemisphere Affairs

Merchant Marine & Fisheries (28th of 29 Democrats)

Campaign Finance

	Receipts	Receipts from PACs		Expend-itures
1992				
Deutsch (D)	$856,210	$162,599	(19%)	$849,785
Kennedy (R)	$90,009	$10,350	(11%)	$88,811

Key Votes

1993

Require parental notification of minors' abortions	N
Require unpaid family and medical leave	Y
Approve national "motor voter" registration bill	Y
Approve budget increasing taxes and reducing deficit	Y
Approve economic stimulus plan	Y

Elections

1992 General		
Peter Deutsch (D)	130,946	(55%)
Beverly Kennedy (R)	91,573	(38%)
James M. Blackburn (I)	15,340	(6%)
1992 Primary		
Peter Deutsch (D)	28,753	(63%)
Nicki Englander Grossman (D)	17,211	(37%)

District Vote for President

	1992	
D	115,902	(47%)
R	83,185	(34%)
I	48,672	(20%)

21 Lincoln Diaz-Balart (R)

Of Miami — Elected 1992; 1st Term

Born: Aug. 13, 1954, Havana, Cuba.

Education: U. of South Florida, B.A. 1976; Case Western Reserve U., J.D. 1979.

Occupation: Lawyer.

Family: Wife, Cristina Fernandez; two children.

Religion: Roman Catholic.

Political Career: Democratic nominee for Fla. House, 1982; Fla. House, 1987-89; Fla. Senate, 1989-92.

Capitol Office: 509 Cannon Bldg. 20515; 225-4211.

The Path to Washington: With the right name, the right money and the right district, Diaz-Balart is well-positioned to serve his Cuban-American constituents for as long as he wants.

That means he is free to pursue his principal — if not sole — goal as a member of Congress, keeping economic pressure on the regime that controls Cuba, his birthplace. Diaz-Balart is not exactly a single-issue candidate. But after making sure that sufficient federal aid has reached the sections of Miami ravaged by Hurricane Andrew last year, his first and last priority is the overthrow of Cuban President Fidel Castro.

He intends to use his seat on the Foreign Affairs Committee to enforce compliance with the 30-year-old U.S. embargo of Cuba, extended in 1992 to close a loophole through which foreign-based subsidiaries of U.S. businesses escaped the embargo's proscriptions. He calls for a U.N.-sanctioned international embargo.

In late January 1993, Diaz-Balart had his first opportunity to speak out on behalf of his Cuban-American constituents. When New York Democrat Charles B. Rangel accused certain exile groups of racism for successfully opposing the nomination of a black Cuban lawyer for a State Department post, Diaz-Balart took to the House floor to castigate Rangel for "impugning the honor of the Cuban-American community."

Diaz-Balart secured his election by first working overtime as a state senator to ensure that Miami would have a second Hispanic-majority district after redistricting. It ultimately took a court-drawn plan to accomplish what a deadlocked legislature and Diaz-Balart's efforts could not. The newly drawn 21st covers a compact section of northeast Dade County, and has a Hispanic population of 70 percent.

He then easily bested a fellow Cuban-American state senator in a two-way Republican primary that turned personal and nasty, and walked into office in November, drawing no general-election opposition.

Diaz-Balart's rise could be attributed as much to destiny as to ambition. He was born in Havana to a prosperous and politically active family. His grandfather, father and uncle all served in Cuba's House of Representatives before the family fled to the United States in 1960.

He was not always a Republican. As recently as 1982, he was head of the Florida Young Democrats and ran unsuccessfully under that banner for the state House.

But he is not like the many Cuban-Americans who abandoned the Democrats in the wake of the failed Bay of Pigs invasion in 1961. Instead, he traces his conversion to the early 1980s, when Democrats largely opposed Reagan administration policies in El Salvador and Nicaragua.

But Diaz-Balart will not be a wholly reliable GOP vote. In the state Legislature, he sided occasionally with Democrats on access to health care and other social welfare issues. In particular, he has been an advocate for farmworkers.

He opposes the North American Free Trade Agreement, principally because of the close ties that both Mexico and Canada maintain with Cuba. But he also is concerned that South Florida jobs will go to Mexico.

But when it comes to fiscal policy, he will be firmly in the mainstream of the Republican caucus: adamantly opposed to tax increases, in favor of spending cuts, and supportive of tax cuts on capital gains income and tax credits for new investment and first-time home buyers.

Diaz-Balart won against a less-polished fellow state senator, Javier D. Souto, whose anti-Castro credentials were more impeccable in the exile community than Diaz-Balart's. Souto also had fled Cuba in 1960 and trained in the United States for the invasion. He later infiltrated the country to set up organized resistance to Castro.

Souto ran a less visible, less-well-financed campaign, and despite his amiable style, he tried to make an issue over whose anti-Castro rhetoric was more believable. He subtly reminded voters that Diaz-Balart's aunt had once been married to Castro by noting in his campaign literature that the head of Cuba's nuclear energy program was Fidel Castro Diaz-Balart, the couple's son.

The negative campaigning appeared to backfire. Souto managed only 31 percent to Diaz-Balart's 69 percent, in a sparse, hurricane-delayed primary.

Florida 21

Southeast — Part of Dade County; Hialeah

Of South Florida's two Hispanic-majority districts, the 21st is the newest both politically and in its history as a Hispanic stronghold.

The 21st is immediately west of the black-majority 17th District and Hispanic-majority 18th. While the focus of the 18th is Little Havana, where 1960s Cuban exiles settled, the 21st centers on Hialeah, where many of those exiles later relocated.

Although Rep. Ileana Ros-Lehtinen hoped to amass as many Cuban-Americans as possible into her 18th District, the 21st actually has the state's highest percentage of Hispanics, 70 percent. Republicans make impressive showings here. George Bush captured 71 percent in 1988. Diaz-Balart, in his first congressional campaign, ran unopposed in the 1992 general election.

Much of the district's fierce Republicanism can be traced to Hialeah, which accounts for about one-third of district residents. Hialeah began growing rapidly after World War II, when many soldiers who trained in South Florida moved to the area.

In the 1960s and 1970s, it became increasing popular with middle- to low-income Cuban-Americans looking for more space than they could find in Miami. Its location near the airport made it accessible to jobs there, and it offered a mix of midsize single-family homes and apartment complexes.

Hialeah also has a large industrial area. Much of the apparel industry there has been struggling recently with competition from imports, especially from Caribbean Basin countries that have cheaper labor costs. UPS has its main South Florida facility near here. Also present is the Hialeah racetrack. State and national politicians make a point of stopping by Chico's to eat black beans and rice, drink Cuban coffee and shake hands.

Farther south is Miami Springs, a largely Republican and Anglo bedroom suburb of Miami. An unincorporated area west of the airport, known as Doral, is growing fast thanks to industry and corporate relocations. Ryder Systems, with its truck and airplane rentals, has its world headquarters here. Carnival Cruise Lines, a district office of the Federal Reserve and IVAX, a biotechnology company, also are in the area. There is also some light industry, primarily distribution centers with economic ties to the airport.

Sweetwater, another predominantly Hispanic municipality, attracts Cubans and Nicaraguans and has a high concentration of elderly residents.

The fast-growing area of Kendall in the district is generally Anglo; it also has some second-generation Cuban-Americans. It is considerably more Democratic than the district as a whole. Kendall Lakes is more compact, conservative and older, with smaller lots than Kendall and less rapid growth.

Tamiami is a generally Hispanic area, with young professionals in single-family homes. Its strong Republican orientation rivals that of Hialeah.

1990 Population: 562,519. White 492,513 (88%), Black 23,073 (4%), Other 46,933 (8%). Hispanic origin 391,534 (70%). 18 and over 424,355 (75%), 62 and over 70,384 (13%). Median age: 33.

Committees

Foreign Affairs (17th of 18 Republicans)
Africa; International Operations

Merchant Marine & Fisheries (15th of 18 Republicans)
Coast Guard & Navigation; Merchant Marine

Campaign Finance

	Receipts	Receipts from PACs	Expend-itures
1992			
Diaz-Balart (R)	$255,098	$71,800 (28%)	$251,177

Key Votes

1993

Require parental notification of minors' abortions	Y
Require unpaid family and medical leave	Y
Approve national "motor voter" registration bill	Y
Approve budget increasing taxes and reducing deficit	N
Approve economic stimulus plan	N

Elections

1992 General		
Lincoln Diaz-Balart (R)		Unopposed
1992 Primary		
Lincoln Diaz-Balart (R)	15,192	(69%)
Javier D. Souto (R)	6,941	(31%)

District Vote for President

	1992
D	45,561 (31%)
R	85,342 (58%)
I	15,501 (11%)

22 E. Clay Shaw Jr. (R)

Of Fort Lauderdale — Elected 1980; 7th Term

Born: April 19, 1939, Miami, Fla.

Education: Stetson U., B.S. 1961; U. of Alabama, M.B.A. 1963; Stetson U., J.D. 1966.

Occupation: Nurseryman; lawyer.

Family: Wife, Emilie Costar; four children.

Religion: Roman Catholic.

Political Career: Fort Lauderdale assistant city attorney, 1968; Fort Lauderdale chief city prosecutor, 1968-69; Fort Lauderdale associate municipal judge, 1969-71; Fort Lauderdale City Commission, 1971-73; vice mayor of Fort Lauderdale, 1973-75; mayor of Fort Lauderdale, 1975-81.

Capitol Office: 2267 Rayburn Bldg. 20515; 225-3026.

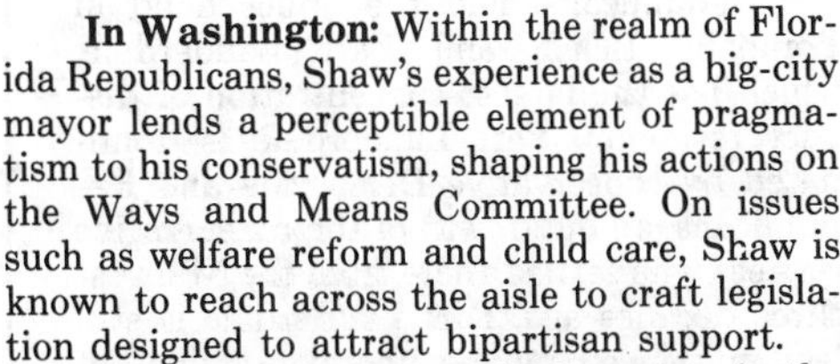

In Washington: Within the realm of Florida Republicans, Shaw's experience as a big-city mayor lends a perceptible element of pragmatism to his conservatism, shaping his actions on the Ways and Means Committee. On issues such as welfare reform and child care, Shaw is known to reach across the aisle to craft legislation designed to attract bipartisan support.

Appointed to Ways and Means late in the 100th Congress, Shaw found himself in the 101st the ranking Republican on the Subcommittee on Human Resources. In that role, which he relinquished in the 103rd, he successfully led resistance to increasing unemployment benefits (and raising employer taxes) proposed by Democrat Thomas J. Downey of New York, the panel's acting chairman.

He and Downey (who was defeated in 1992) could also find common ground. In 1992, they co-wrote an opinion piece in The Washington Post calling attention to the 1988 welfare reform law, which was aimed at helping welfare recipients find jobs while improving benefits for others.

Shaw continued to pursue welfare reform in the 103rd. He introduced a plan that included an enforceable two-year limit on those receiving Aid to Families with Dependent Children benefits, something Bill Clinton has supported. "If there's one issue where moderate Republicans and Democrats can work together in a bipartisan manner, this is it," he said in early 1993, as welfare reform plans were being devised.

Shaw drew notice during the 101st Congress by cosponsoring (with Texas Democrat Charles W. Stenholm) a comprehensive child-care package offered as an alternative to Downey's bill and a competing Democratic bill. Stenholm-Shaw, a somewhat leaner version of the main Democratic plans, won support from the Bush administration and the National Governors' Association. Although not enacted, it helped move Congress to resolve its child-care standoff.

Shaw seeks to repeal the luxury tax on yachts. He attracted 180 cosponsors to his bill in the 102nd Congress to lift the tax, which he says has devastated the boat-building industry. Two tax bills vetoed by President Bush in 1992 would have repealed the luxury tax. Shaw reintroduced it in the 103rd.

Shaw has also taken an interest in congressional reform. He introduced measures that would limit members' terms on committees. The concept has attracted bipartisan support.

Even as Shaw makes a name for himself on Ways and Means, most members still associate him with the drug issue. He chaired the Republican Research Committee's task force on drug abuse — an issue of pre-eminent concern to his South Florida coastal constituency. It was at least partly as a reward for his work on drugs that Shaw was given the coveted Ways and Means seat.

Before moving to Ways and Means, Shaw was a member of the Judiciary Committee and the Select Narcotics Abuse and Control panel. In both the 99th and 100th Congresses, he was appointed to GOP drug task forces set up by Minority Leader Robert H. Michel of Illinois, and a bill Shaw introduced became the basis of the 1988 Republican anti-drug legislative effort. His measure included several controversial provisions that were dropped two years earlier, but won approval in 1988: a death penalty for major drug traffickers, a drug "czar" to coordinate federal efforts and the use of the U.S. military for drug interdiction.

Shaw has met with considerably less success in his battle for widespread drug testing. In the 99th Congress, Shaw asked his staff to participate in a voluntary drug-testing program, but House rules barred him from paying for the tests with his official allowance.

While the House approved a Shaw amendment instructing conferees on an airline con-

Florida 22

Southeast — Coastal Broward, Dade and Palm Beach counties; Fort Lauderdale

The 22nd is a long shoestring of a district, hugging the south Atlantic coast from Juno Beach south to Miami Beach. It is roughly 90 miles long and in some places just a few blocks wide. Its width never extends beyond 3 miles.

The strange shape, which enables the 22nd to pick up fragments of about 50 different municipalities, was dictated largely by the desire to place minority-oriented neighborhoods in districts to the west, notably the 23rd. Four House incumbents lived within its borders when the 22nd was drawn in 1992.

Most residents of the coastal neighborhoods are white, and their economic status ranges from comfortable to wealthy. Corporate executives abound. There are also quite a few retirees on oceanfront condominiums.

The district is less Republican than the state overall, and thus competitive politically. Although George Bush captured 57 percent of the presidential vote here in 1988, he lost the district in 1992. The House race between Rep. Shaw and Democrat Gwen Margolis was one of the state's most fiercely fought in 1992.

Democrats start with a solid base in the Dade County portions of the district; Republicans have a clear edge in the Palm Beach part. Those two counties voted as expected in the Shaw-Margolis race, but Shaw swamped her in Broward County, which accounts for nearly half the district's population.

Within the borders of the 22nd are the ports of Palm Beach and Fort Lauderdale, as well as the mouth of the port of Miami. The district also contains the Miami Beach and Fort Lauderdale convention centers, the performing arts center in Miami Beach, the famous Breakers hotel in Palm Beach and Fountainbleau in Miami Beach, fashionable shopping areas such as Worth Avenue in Palm Beach and Las Olas Boulevard in Fort Lauderdale, and miles upon miles of beaches.

The city of Palm Beach is affluent and staunchly Republican. Democrats fare slightly better in the areas of West Palm Beach in the district.

Partisan orientations vary considerably among the municipalities within Broward County. Hallandale is strongly Democratic, while Hollywood is more competitive.

Republicans hold the upper hand in Pompano Beach and Fort Lauderdale, which has the largest concentration of district residents. Fort Lauderdale is dominated by conservative Democrats and Republicans, an outgrowth of the conservative retirees who settled there from the Midwest three decades ago. Fort Lauderdale is still less influenced by the liberal attitudes of Northeastern Jewish émigrés than are most other major South Florida cities. Even the Jewish voters who do live in the city tend not to vote as a bloc.

The Dade County portions of the district have more of the Northeastern influence. These southernmost stretches of the 22nd are heavily Jewish and Hispanic.

1990 Population: 562,519. White 529,651 (94%), Black 16,795 (3%), Other 16,073 (3%). Hispanic origin 72,140 (13%). 18 and over 490,832 (87%), 62 and over 196,619 (35%). Median age: 48.

sumer protection bill to include mandatory testing provisions, controversy over the issue contributed to the political stalemate that killed the bill in the 100th Congress. Shaw won passage of an amendment to a State Department authorization bill requiring drug tests for employees with access to secret information.

Also before his move to Ways and Means, Shaw served on the Public Works Committee, where he was often frustrated. His pet issue was restricting billboards on federal highways and limiting federal support for billboards. In 1986, Shaw won a modest victory with the adoption of a compromise amendment freezing the number of billboards allowed on federal highways while continuing to reimburse the billboard industry for taking down billboards.

At Home: Redistricting scrambled what had been a safe seat for Shaw, based in Fort Lauderdale. The new coastal district had a lot of unfamiliar territory.

Shaw was pitted against Democratic state Senate President Gwen Margolis in the most expensive and one of the most contentious House races in the state. She had an edge in the portions of Dade County in the 22nd, which she represented in the Legislature and which are strongly Democratic. Shaw's support began in the north, in coastal Palm Beach County, where Republicans predominate.

Margolis had a high-profile role in the state Senate, where she was occasionally criticized for being divisive. Her attempts to draw a favorable House seat for herself contributed to a remapping stalemate.

During the campaign, she characterized

Shaw as an extreme conservative who opposed abortion, handgun control and the family leave bill. Shaw attacked Margolis as a tax-and-spend liberal whose ineffective leadership created legislative chaos. He stressed that while he opposed federal funding for abortion, he supported a woman's right to an abortion in the first trimester of pregnancy.

Shaw's edge in Palm Beach County neatly canceled Margolis' advantage in Dade, and he swamped her by nearly 2-to-1 in the populous Broward County portions of the district.

It was Democratic squabbling that helped Shaw secure the old 15th District. In 1980, Democratic primary voters dumped 70-year-old Rep. Edward J. Stack for a younger candidate, former state Rep. Alan Becker. Shaw, who had been mayor of Fort Lauderdale since 1975, was unopposed for the GOP nomination.

Shaw denounced Becker as a liberal carpetbagger; the Democrat had moved into the 15th in 1979 after four terms in the Legislature representing North Miami. Shaw bragged that during his tenure in Fort Lauderdale, he had cut spending, broadened the economic base and burnished a more cosmopolitan image for the city. He won with 55 percent.

In 1982, another intraparty fight divided the Democrats. Stack was back, hoping to avenge his 1980 loss, and engaged in a bitter primary with a former ally. Stack eked out 51 percent to become the nominee, while Shaw again enjoyed an uncontested primary.

Stack had strong union support, but lingering Democratic disunity and his age dragged him down. Shaw, boosted by redrawn district lines that enhanced GOP strength in the 15th, won a second term with 57 percent.

Committee

Ways & Means (4th of 14 Republicans)
Human Resources; Trade

Elections

1992 General

E. Clay Shaw Jr. (R)	128,376	(52%)
Gwen Margolis (D)	91,605	(37%)
Richard "Even" Stephens (I)	15,467	(6%)
Michael F. Petrie (I)	6,311	(3%)
Bernard Anscher (I)	5,272	(2%)

1990 General

E. Clay Shaw Jr. (R)	104,295	(98%)
Charles Goodmon (write-in)	2,374	(2%)

Previous Winning Percentages: **1988** (66%) **1986** (100%) **1984** (66%) **1982** (57%) **1980** (55%)

District Vote for President

1992

D 114,847 (44%)
R 98,443 (38%)
I 45,259 (18%)

Campaign Finance

	Receipts	Receipts from PACs		Expend-itures
1992				
Shaw (R)	$948,514	$441,663	(47%)	$1,138,425
Margolis (D)	$939,410	$250,242	(27%)	$936,960
1990				
Shaw (R)	$413,387	$245,760	(59%)	$120,632

Key Votes

1993	
Require parental notification of minors' abortions	Y
Require unpaid family and medical leave	N
Approve national "motor voter" registration bill	N
Approve budget increasing taxes and reducing deficit	N
Approve economic stimulus plan	N
1992	
Approve balanced-budget constitutional amendment	Y
Close down space station program	N
Approve U.S. aid for former Soviet Union	Y
Allow shifting funds from defense to domestic programs	N
1991	
Extend unemployment benefits using deficit financing	N
Approve waiting period for handgun purchases	N
Authorize use of force in Persian Gulf	Y

Voting Studies

Year	Presidential Support S	Presidential Support O	Party Unity S	Party Unity O	Conservative Coalition S	Conservative Coalition O
1992	75	24	76	20	92	6
1991	80	17	78	16	97	0
1990	75	24	75	21	91	7
1989	77	22	65	32	95	5
1988	65	32	70	23	100	0
1987	70	29	76	20	95	5
1986	79	19	86	10	90	6
1985	70	25	88	8	89	9
1984	61	37	82	14	90	5
1983	78	16	87	8	93	4
1982	77	23	84	16	90	10
1981	78	22	94	6	95	5

Interest Group Ratings

Year	ADA	AFL-CIO	CCUS	ACU
1992	15	25	75	84
1991	0	17	100	90
1990	6	8	57	83
1989	5	17	90	89
1988	5	21	92	96
1987	4	13	93	78
1986	5	7	87	82
1985	5	18	81	81
1984	5	8	86	73
1983	5	0	80	96
1982	15	15	82	77
1981	10	0	89	100

23 Alcee L. Hastings (D)

Of Miramar — Elected 1992; 1st Term

Born: Sept. 5, 1936, Altamonte Springs, Fla.
Education: Fisk U., B.A. 1958; Howard U., 1958-60; Florida A&M U., J.D. 1963.
Occupation: Lawyer.
Family: Divorced; three children.
Religion: African Methodist Episcopal.
Political Career: Democratic nominee for Fla. secretary of state, 1990.
Capitol Office: 1039 Longworth Bldg. 20515; 225-1313.

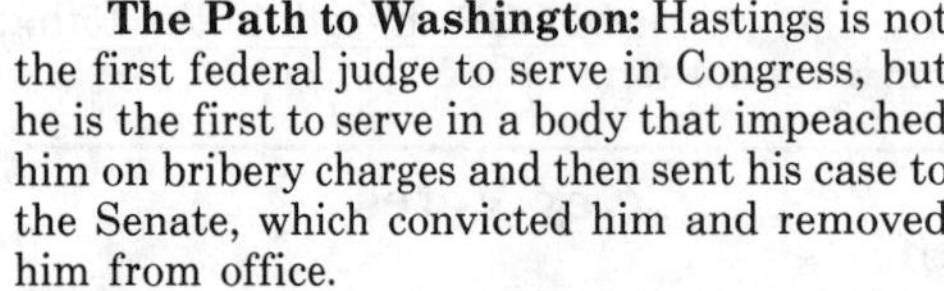

The Path to Washington: Hastings is not the first federal judge to serve in Congress, but he is the first to serve in a body that impeached him on bribery charges and then sent his case to the Senate, which convicted him and removed him from office.

On Sept. 17, 1992, a federal judge in Washington ruled that the Senate had improperly removed Hastings from office because a committee of senators, and not the full Senate, heard the case against him.

Hastings immediately referred to himself as an "unimpeached federal judge" but said he had no interest in returning to the bench. He had long since decided that he wanted to get involved in politics.

In January 1993, however, the Supreme Court ruled in a different case that federal courts have no constitutional authority to review the proceedings of Senate impeachment trials. Though the decision probably would have prevented Hastings from reassuming his judgeship, it had no effect on his new congressional career.

In an unsuccessful run for secretary of state in 1990, he had won a majority of the votes in what is now his district. When the 23rd was redrawn to be what Hastings calls a "minority access" district, he decided to seek the position, believing that a black with high name recognition could beat state Rep. Lois Frankel, a progressive white Democrat who would be able to run a well-financed campaign.

Hastings was correct about two things: Frankel did run (and it took a runoff for Hastings to win the party nomination); and he did have high name recognition — not only because of his impeachment but also because of his years as a judge and in private law practice.

During the campaign, Miami Herald Political Editor Tom Fiedler wondered in print: "Where do you start in attempting to characterize Alcee Hastings? Without question he is charming, inspirational, brilliant, gutsy and charismatic. He is also profane, audacious, proud, brazen, and pardon me for saying it, slick."

Hastings' campaign against Frankel helped prove the latter points. When she argued that her record demonstrated a commitment to issues important to white and black constituents, Hastings shot back that Frankel was a white opportunist who should not run in a district drawn to elect a minority candidate.

Calling her a wealthy outsider, Hastings said Frankel's claims that she understood the district were like trying "to convince B'nai B'rith that some sympathetic Arab millionaire ought to be prime minister of Israel." He told one reporter that "the bitch is a racist." He later said that although he made the comment, he had not intended it for publication.

After beating Frankel in the runoff by 15 percentage points, Hastings went on to defeat his GOP opponent, real estate developer Ed Fielding, 59 percent to 31 percent.

Hastings brings a liberal agenda to Congress. He campaigned for "the elimination of racism, ageism, anti-Semitism, and sexism"; for providing every American a decent job with job security; comparable pay for comparable work for women; and universal health care.

Where many other new members rush to embrace a balanced-budget amendment, Hastings calls it "a feel-good rhetorical statement" designed for campaigns.

Hastings assiduously avoided taking a seat on the House Judiciary Committee, the panel that drew up the articles of impeachment against him.

It was not because of disdain, he insists, but rather he felt reluctant to be a junior member on a panel that drafts laws for the federal judiciary when he would be the only one with firsthand knowledge of how those laws would work.

Despite his reputation for flamboyance, Hastings expects to make a smooth transition into the tradition-bound House. His aim, he says, is to get things done. "There are two methods as a legislator — to work through the committee process to gain stature or to be a maverick and scream. I don't intend to do the latter. It's not good for my constituents."

Hastings promised at the end of his campaign that he will "work my buns off to prove to everybody that I can be a good congressperson."

Florida 23

Southeast — Parts of St. Lucie, Martin, Broward and Palm Beach counties

One of the most unusual characteristics of Florida's congressional map for the 1990's is the kite-like 23rd.

The district extends over seven counties. Most of its land mass is in western St. Lucie, Martin and Palm Beach counties, near Lake Okeechobee. But most of the people in the 23rd live inland from the Atlantic, along a narrow strip that follows Interstate 95. Half the district residents live in Broward County; one-third live in Palm Beach County.

The district is heavily Democratic and designed to help black House candidates, but the election of a black is not assured. Blacks account for only a bare majority of the district's total population and about 44 percent of its voting-age population.

Agriculture dominates the western part of the district. Western St. Lucie and Martin counties as well as southeast Okeechobee County is citrus territory, with vegetable and lettuce crops also attracting some migrant workers. The sugar industry has a strong presence near Belle Glade in western Palm Beach County. Although Okeechobee is mostly white, the rest of this part of the district includes a high percentage of blacks and some Hispanics. The northeastern part of the district also extends into Fort Pierce to include most of its black neighborhoods.

The long strip of the district that runs adjacent to I-95 includes many public-sector workers, especially for county government and public schools. Public employee unions are strong political organizing forces, as are neighborhood associations.

The residents of Riviera Beach, an overwhelmingly black city, cast an extraordinarily high percentage of their votes for Democrats. Most residents are middle class, and some work at the nearby Pratt & Whitney plant. The portions of West Palm Beach in the district, which are also majority-black, include some neighborhoods that attract professionals. The portions that are in the 23rd from Delray Beach and Boynton Beach are about one-half black, Lake Worth is a little less so, and the part of Boca Raton included is overwhelmingly white and a GOP enclave.

Heading into Broward, the parts of Deerfield Beach and especially Pompano Beach in the 23rd are majority black. Deerfield Beach is mainly lower-middle class, with some farm workers commuting west, while Pompano is more middle-class oriented.

The district broadens somewhat in Broward County to include mainly black neighborhoods in Fort Lauderdale and, to the west, Lauderhill and Lauderdale Lakes. But it also includes predominantly white areas of Lauderdale Lakes that are middle class and, in some cases, retirement-oriented. This area was particularly supportive of state Rep. Bill Clark, a local resident and unsuccessful 1992 Democratic House candidate.

Norland, a predominantly black area, accounts for most of the district's residents in Dade County. Hastings' law office was located there, and though the area had relatively few votes, it did help him push past Clark into the Democratic runoff.

1990 Population: 562,519. White 251,923 (45%), Black 290,519 (52%), Other 20,077 (4%). Hispanic origin 52,706 (9%). 18 and over 407,318 (72%), 62 and over 86,056 (15%). Median age: 32.

Committees

Foreign Affairs (20th of 27 Democrats)
Africa; Europe & the Middle East

Merchant Marine & Fisheries (20th of 28 Democrats)
Coast Guard & Navigation; Merchant Marine

Post Office & Civil Service (15th of 15 Democrats)
Oversight & Investigations

Campaign Finance

	Receipts	Receipts from PACs	Expend-itures
1992			
Hastings (D)	$417,158	$98,200 (24%)	$427,931
Fielding (R)	$15,626	$2,250 (14%)	$15,622

Key Votes

1993

Require parental notification of minors' abortions	N
Require unpaid family and medical leave	Y
Approve national "motor voter" registration bill	Y
Approve budget increasing taxes and reducing deficit	Y
Approve economic stimulus plan	Y

Elections

1992 General		
Alcee L. Hastings (D)	84,232	(59%)
Ed Fielding (R)	44,800	(31%)
Al Woods (I)	14,873	(10%)
1992 Primary Runoff		
Alcee L. Hastings (D)	22,046	(58%)
Lois Frankel (D)	16,294	(43%)
1992 Primary		
Lois Frankel (D)	12,556	(35%)
Alcee L. Hastings (D)	10,237	(28%)
Bill Clark (D)	9,881	(28%)
Kenneth Donald Cooper (D)	1,872	(5%)
William Washington (D)	1,711	(5%)

District Vote for President

	1992	
D	96,926	(63%)
R	34,814	(23%)
I	22,026	(14%)

Georgia

STATE DATA

Governor: Zell Miller (D)
First elected: 1990
Length of term: 4 years
Term expires: 1/95
Salary: $92,088
Term limit: 2 terms
Phone: (404) 656-1776
Born: Feb. 24, 1932; Young Harris, Ga.
Education: Young Harris Junior College, 1951; U. of Georgia, A.B. 1957, M.A. 1958
Military Service: Marine Corps, 1953-56
Occupation: Professor
Family: Wife, Shirley Ann Carver; two children
Religion: Methodist
Political Career: Mayor of Young Harris, 1959-60; Ga. Senate, 1961-65; sought Democratic nomination for U.S. House, 1964, 1966; lieutenant governor, 1975-91; sought Democratic nomination for U.S. Senate, 1980

Lt. Gov.: Pierre Howard (D)
First elected: 1990
Length of term: 4 years
Term expires: 1/95
Salary: $60,141
Phone: (404) 656-5030

State election official: (404) 656-2871
Democratic headquarters: (404) 874-1994
Republican headquarters: (404) 365-7700

REDISTRICTING

Georgia gained one House seat in reapportionment, increasing from 10 seats to 11. Legislature passed map March 31, 1992; governor signed March 31. Justice Dept. approved April 2.

STATE LEGISLATURE

General Assembly. Meets January to mid-March.

Senate: 56 members, 2-year terms
1992 breakdown: 41D, 15R; 50 men, 6 women; 47 whites, 9 blacks
Salary: $10,641
Phone: (404) 656-0028

House of Representatives: 180 members, 2-year terms
1992 breakdown: 128D, 52R; 145 men, 35 women; 149 whites, 31 blacks
Salary: $10,641
Phone: (404) 656-5082

URBAN STATISTICS

City	Pop.
Atlanta	394,017
Mayor Maynard Jackson, D	
Columbus	178,681
Mayor Frank Martin, D	
Savannah	137,560
Mayor Susan S. Weiner, R	
Macon	106,612
Mayor Tommy Olmstead, D	
Albany	78,122
Mayor Paul Keenan, D	

U.S. CONGRESS

Senate: 1 D, 1 R
House: 7 D, 4 R

TERM LIMITS

For Congress: No
For state offices: No

ELECTIONS

1992 Presidential Vote

Bill Clinton	43.5%
George Bush	42.9%
Ross Perot	13.3%

1988 Presidential Vote

George Bush	60%
Michael S. Dukakis	40%

1984 Presidential Vote

Ronald Reagan	60%
Walter F. Mondale	40%

POPULATION

1990 population		6,478,216
1980 population		5,463,105
Percent change		+19%
Rank among states:		11
White		71%
Black		27%
Hispanic		2%
Asian or Pacific islander		1%
Urban		63%
Rural		37%
Born in state		65%
Foreign-born		3%
Under age 18	1,727,303	27%
Ages 18-64	4,096,643	63%
65 and older	654,270	10%
Median age		31.6

MISCELLANEOUS

Capital: Atlanta
Number of counties: 159
Per capita income: $17,364 (1991)
Rank among states: 29
Total area: 58,910 sq. miles
Rank among states: 21

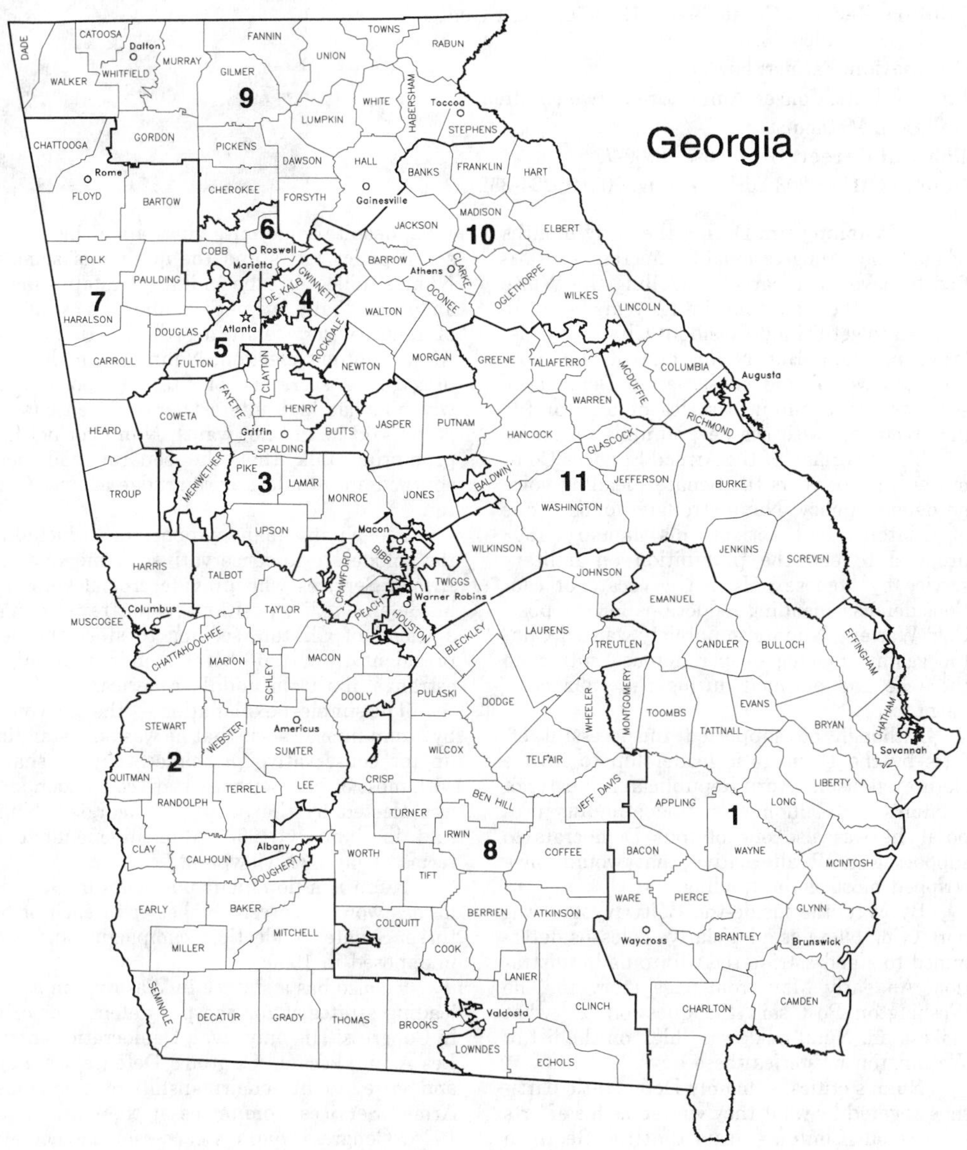
Georgia
1
2
3
4
5
6
7
8
9
10
11
DADE
CATOOSA
Dalton
MURRAY
WALKER
WHITFIELD
FANNIN
TOWNS
RABUN
UNION
GILMER
WHITE
HABERSHAM
Toccoa
STEPHENS
LUMPKIN
CHATTOOGA
GORDON
PICKENS
DAWSON
HALL
BANKS
FRANKLIN
HART
Rome
FLOYD
BARTOW
CHEROKEE
FORSYTH
Gainesville
MADISON
JACKSON
ELBERT
COBB
Roswell
Marietta
POLK
PAULDING
DE KALB
GWINNETT
BARROW
Athens
CLARKE
OCONEE
OGLETHORPE
WILKES
LINCOLN
HARALSON
DOUGLAS
Atlanta
ROCKDALE
WALTON
CARROLL
FULTON
CLAYTON
NEWTON
MORGAN
GREENE
TALIAFERRO
MCDUFFIE
COLUMBIA
Augusta
FAYETTE
HENRY
WARREN
COWETA
BUTTS
JASPER
PUTNAM
HANCOCK
RICHMOND
HEARD
Griffin
SPALDING
GLASCOCK
MERIWETHER
PIKE
LAMAR
BALDWIN
JEFFERSON
BURKE
TROUP
MONROE
JONES
WASHINGTON
UPSON
Macon
BIBB
HARRIS
TALBOT
CRAWFORD
WILKINSON
JENKINS
SCREVEN
TWIGGS
JOHNSON
Columbus
MUSCOGEE
TAYLOR
PEACH
Warner Robins
HOUSTON
EMANUEL
CHATTAHOOCHEE
BLECKLEY
LAURENS
EFFINGHAM
MARION
MACON
TREUTLEN
CANDLER
BULLOCH
SCHLEY
DOOLY
PULASKI
DODGE
WHEELER
MONTGOMERY
EVANS
STEWART
WEBSTER
Americus
TOOMBS
TATTNALL
BRYAN
CHATHAM
SUMTER
WILCOX
TELFAIR
Savannah
QUITMAN
TERRELL
LEE
CRISP
BEN HILL
JEFF DAVIS
LIBERTY
RANDOLPH
TURNER
APPLING
LONG
IRWIN
CLAY
Albany
CALHOUN
DOUGHERTY
WORTH
COFFEE
BACON
WAYNE
MCINTOSH
TIFT
WARE
PIERCE
EARLY
BAKER
BERRIEN
ATKINSON
GLYNN
COLQUITT
MITCHELL
Waycross
BRANTLEY
Brunswick
MILLER
COOK
LANIER
SEMINOLE
CLINCH
CHARLTON
CAMDEN
DECATUR
GRADY
THOMAS
BROOKS
Valdosta
LOWNDES
ECHOLS

Sam Nunn (D)

Of Perry — Elected 1972; 4th Term

Born: Sept. 8, 1938, Perry, Ga.
Education: Emory U., A.B. 1960, LL.B. 1962.
Military Service: Coast Guard, 1959-60; Coast Guard Reserve, 1960-66.
Occupation: Farmer; lawyer.
Family: Wife, Colleen Ann O'Brien; two children.
Religion: Methodist.
Political Career: Ga. House, 1969-72.
Capitol Office: 303 Dirksen Bldg. 20510; 224-3521.

In Washington: During the early months of 1993, most congressional Democrats — gratified to have their party controlling the White House for the first time in 12 years — were inclined to get behind President Clinton's legislative program. But Nunn, one of the most senior, powerful and conservative Democratic senators, stood out in a series of high-profile disagreements with the new administration.

The chairman of the Armed Services Committee and for years the Senate's leading voice on defense policy, Nunn strongly opposed one of Clinton's first actions: his January 1993 proposal to end the prohibition on military service by homosexuals. An advocate of cautious defense-spending reductions for the post-Cold War era, Nunn also publicly warned Clinton against making deeper defense cuts than those he had outlined during the 1992 campaign.

Although he supported unsuccessful efforts by the Democratic leadership to invoke cloture against an April Republican filibuster of Clinton's $16 billion economic stimulus proposal, he was also one of four Democrats to support a GOP alternative that would have stripped most of the funding.

By May, the inside-the-Beltway buzz was portraying Nunn as a legislative colossus determined to stand astride the Clinton administration. An early May front-page story in The Washington Post said the question of "what makes Sam Nunn tick" was "high on the list of Washington mysteries these days."

Nunn's critics — mainly Democratic partisans angered by what they viewed as his efforts to undercut Clinton — said that the Georgian was acting out his personal political frustrations. Long before Clinton's emergence as a centrist Democratic leader, Nunn was seen as a potential presidential candidate — some said the figure most likely to break the liberals' hold on the Democratic nominating process. Nunn was the founding chairman of the moderate-to-conservative Democratic Leadership Council (Clinton succeeded him).

Nunn supported Clinton's campaign in 1992, despite some misgivings about his liberal social policy views and the qualms of some of Nunn's allies in the military establishment about the "baby boomer" candidate's avoidance of military service during the Vietnam War. After Clinton's election, Nunn was in the running to be secretary of State (a position in which he had high interest) or of Defense (a job Nunn said he did not want). Nunn got neither, prompting talk that the senator had been spurned and would hold a grudge against Clinton.

But Nunn's many supporters — including the moderate-to-conservative Democrats on Armed Services who provide crucial votes for his defense policy positions — portrayed him as a friend of Clinton, seeking to steer the new president from too-liberal stands that might estrange him from middle America.

The simplest explanation — the one voiced by Nunn himself — is that he was only standing up for conservative principles that he shares with most of his Southern-state constituents. "I was elected by the people of Georgia," Nunn said in January 1993. "I'm independent in terms of my own viewpoint."

Nunn is a dominant politician in Georgia; he has won 80 percent or better in each of his three Senate re-election campaigns and was unopposed in 1990.

He also has a stature in Washington as the leading strategist for the pro-defense majority in Congress: His only rival, Democratic centrist Les Aspin, became Clinton's Defense secretary and gave up his chairmanship of the House Armed Services Committee at the start of the 103rd Congress. Aspin's successor, Democratic Rep. Ronald V. Dellums of California, is an eloquent liberal activist, but his support for deep cuts in the defense budget places him outside the current congressional mainstream.

Given Nunn's electoral security and his strong power base in the Senate, there are Democrats who say he could afford to bend a bit to help out the new Democratic president. But Nunn's stature and clout enable him to espouse right-of-Clinton views when he chooses without fearing that the administration will retaliate against programs that benefit his constituents.

The White House in early 1993 made an example of another conservative Southern Democrat — Alabama's Richard C. Shelby — when he publicly criticized aspects of Clinton's economic program: Some Alabama jobs in the space station program were shifted to Texas. But administration officials did little more than grumble about Nunn, a far more prominent and influential critic.

Nunn has denied throughout that he is out to get Clinton. "The news media's determined to put Clinton and me at odds," he said in March 1993. "It's not true, but that's the way the news media are going to report it."

In fact, Nunn throughout his career has stood on the right side of the Democratic spectrum. His strong-defense views made him the leading Democratic supporter of President Ronald Reagan's 1980s buildup of the military. As the era of defense spending retrenchment set in during the Bush administration, Nunn's support was crucial to saving such Pentagon priorities as the B-2 stealth bomber and other expensive, high-tech systems that more liberal Democrats wanted to eliminate.

Yet Nunn led the effort to defeat George Bush's 1989 nomination of former Texas Sen. John Tower as secretary of Defense. Also, Nunn opposed the January 1991 resolution that authorized Bush to use force to end Iraq's occupation of Kuwait, and he sponsored (with Senate Majority Leader George J. Mitchell, D-Maine) the defeated alternative to continue the existing policy of economic sanctions.

In those days, Republicans were the ones who accused Nunn of self-serving actions. After the brutal fight over the Tower nomination, many Republicans scoffed at Nunn's reputation for deaconlike probity: "Nunnpartisan" was what Senate Democrats had become, said Minority Leader Bob Dole, R-Kan.

Republicans charged that Nunn's efforts in the Tower and Iraq debates, as well as his 1990 switch to favor abortion rights, proved that he was positioning himself to run for president. Nunn's response: "When I agree with them, I'm a statesman," he said in November 1990. "When I don't . . . I'm running for president."

The image of Nunn as one of Clinton's main competitors in the Washington power game marks a comeback from his status just two years earlier. Nunn was then regarded — briefly — as a fading star because he had taken a politically inopportune stand on the Persian Gulf crisis.

Nunn's arguments against the use of military force were, as usual, pedagogic rather than demagogic. They were grounded in opinions — widely shared by military and geopolitical analysts — that the ongoing economic blockade against Iraq could break that nation's will, and that war would cause thousands of American casualties and become a political quagmire.

Nunn strongly backed Bush after the onset of war with Iraq. But the rapid victory of the U.S.-led coalition left Nunn looking politically vulnerable; then-Rep. Aspin had supported the war resolution and appeared to be eclipsing Nunn as Congress' defense guru.

Nunn's downturn was short-lived; he soon had an opportunity to show that he was still the man to beat on defense policy issues. In March 1991, he easily parried a Republican maneuver to advance a space-based Strategic Defense Initiative (SDI) system that Nunn strongly opposed.

Playing off the highly publicized use of Patriot missiles to shoot down Iraq's ballistic Scuds during the Persian Gulf War, ranking Armed Services Republican John W. Warner of Virginia proposed an amendment to a supplemental appropriations bill that would have accelerated development and deployment of a space-based anti-ballistic missile (ABM) system. However, Nunn countered with his own amendment, which would have steered SDI strongly toward his own favored concept of a limited ground-based ABM program. Warner withdrew his amendment.

However, later that year, Nunn lent his hand to a compromise plan, originally drafted by Warner and GOP Sen. William S. Cohen of Maine, that became the most major reorientation of the program since its inception.

Since President Reagan unveiled the SDI program in 1983, the White House had pushed a vision of a space-based system of Earth-orbiting weapons, which could shoot down at least some enemy ballistic missiles on launch. Nunn called such an approach technologically unrealistic; moreover, he insisted that it violated the 1972 U.S.-Soviet ABM treaty.

However, unlike many Democrats who tried to terminate the "star wars" program, Nunn did favor deployment of a ground-based ABM system to protect U.S. territory from more limited attacks. He also was amenable to renegotiation with Moscow of the ABM treaty to allow for a more expansive ground-based system.

Those were the salient features of the Warner-Cohen plan. It called for near-term deployment of a 100-missile ABM battery at Grand Forks, N.D., as allowed under the treaty, and recommended that the president reopen ABM talks with leaders of the then-Soviet Union. To maintain support of conservatives who favored the original SDI concept, the plan maintained "robust" funding for space-based weapons research. With Nunn on board, the SDI revisions passed easily as part of the defense authorization bill in 1991.

Nunn also joined with Aspin during the 102nd Congress to lay the groundwork for direct U.S. aid to the republics of the former

Soviet Union. Nunn framed the demilitarization of the formerly hostile communist superpower as a defense issue for the United States.

In 1991, Nunn and Aspin were leading advocates of a provision, attached to the defense authorization bill, to allow the president to spend up to $1 billion on aid to the then-collapsing Soviet Union. The money could be spent on humanitarian aid and on helping the Soviets disarm their nuclear arsenal.

However, by the time the bill's conference report came to the House floor, public dissatisfaction over an economic recession had made members wary about a new foreign aid program, and they dropped the Soviet aid plan from the bill. Nunn strongly criticized this isolationist approach. "I can't think of a better way to 'take care of your own' than by reducing the threat of [weapons] proliferation around the world," he told the Senate.

Nunn and Aspin quickly regrouped and pressed for a $500 million measure aimed strictly at aiding Soviet military dismantling. Less than a month after the original measure failed, a revised plan, providing $400 million, was enacted. In 1992, Nunn — working with Indiana Sen. Richard G. Lugar, the ranking Republican on the Foreign Relations Committee, and others — was again in the forefront of an effort to authorize greatly expanded aid to demilitarize and abet reforms in the now-former Soviet Union, enacted as the Freedom Support Act.

Nunn supported Bush in holding the line against forces in Congress that, with the fall of the Soviet Union, sought to divert large sums from the defense budget as a "peace dividend" to reduce the federal deficit or provide funds for domestic programs. "We should get rid of the notion floating around that by cutting defense we can get our national debt under control," Nunn said in February 1992.

A senator from a state with numerous military facilities and defense-related industries, Nunn is also a leading advocate of providing adjustment assistance to those financially affected by post-Cold War defense cuts.

Nunn's stature on defense issues continues traditions for both his family and his state. He is the grandnephew of Carl Vinson, a longtime chairman of the House Armed Services Committee, and he occupies the Senate seat once held by Georgia Democrat Richard Russell, who chaired Senate Armed Services.

Although the image of Nunn is justifiably that of a defense maven, he also has used his position as chairman of the Governmental Affairs Permanent Investigations Subcommittee to get involved in education policy, probing high default rates in student loan programs.

During the 101st Congress, Nunn held a yearlong investigation into outright fraud in such programs, particularly those that serve for-profit trade schools. Citing evidence of numerous trade-school scams, Nunn says the industry "attracted not just some bad apples, but bad orchards."

Nunn is also a member of the Small Business Committee and chairs its Government Contracting and Paperwork Reduction Subcommittee.

At Home: Nunn was a dark horse when he first decided to run for the Senate in 1972, but he turned out to be an ideal candidate against David H. Gambrell, the wealthy and urbane Atlanta lawyer whom Gov. Jimmy Carter named to the Senate after Russell's death.

Nunn also was a lawyer and state legislator, but his central Georgia roots and kinship with Carl Vinson allowed him to run as an old-fashioned rural Democrat. He called Gambrell a "fake conservative" who backed Democratic presidential nominee George McGovern, despite Gambrell's denials of any such link.

Though Gambrell finished first in the primary, he was forced into a runoff with Nunn, who intensified his attacks, all but saying Gambrell's wealthy family had bought the seat by contributing to Carter's gubernatorial campaign. It was enough to sink Gambrell.

The focus shifted in the general election, when Nunn encountered GOP Rep. Fletcher Thompson. This time, it was Thompson who used the McGovern issue. But Nunn countered by obtaining the blessing of Alabama Gov. George C. Wallace, then a conservative icon.

Despite his criticisms of busing and "welfare loafers," Nunn also got the support of black leaders, who claimed Thompson had not spoken to a black audience in four years, even though 40 percent of his Atlanta district was non-white. Further big-name help for Nunn came from Democratic Sen. Herman E. Talmadge, at the time an institution in state politics, whose critical support in rural areas helped Nunn offset his opponent's strength in the Atlanta suburbs. Nunn won with 54 percent.

Six years later, Nunn's fiscal conservatism and support for the military put him in such good position that no serious challenger emerged. The luckless Republican candidate, former U.S. Attorney John Stokes, had little money and ran a near-invisible campaign. Nunn's 83 percent was the highest vote any Senate candidate in the country received that fall against a major party opponent. In 1984, a banner year for Republican candidates in Georgia, Nunn took 80 percent of the vote.

Republicans paid Nunn the ultimate political compliment in 1990, opting not to challenge his bid for a fourth term. One Republican unknown did try to run, but when she could not come up with the filing fee, the state GOP, far from chipping in, asked that her name be removed from the ballot.

Though Nunn has established a reputation as electorally unassailable, he has had only mixed success using his popularity to elect other Democratic candidates. And in recent years, as GOP strength in Georgia has grown, he has at times seemed ambivalent about trying to do so.

In 1986, Nunn gave a crucial boost to Democratic Rep. Wyche Fowler Jr.'s successful campaign against GOP Sen. Mack Mattingly. Nunn's imprimatur helped Fowler mitigate a liberal reputation, developed during a decade representing Atlanta's majority-black 5th District, as he sought the votes of rural and suburban Georgians. Nunn campaigned vigorously and appeared in commercials that portrayed Fowler as an urban representative who looked out for rural voters.

In 1988, Nunn endorsed Michael S. Dukakis for president and made a well-publicized speech in his behalf at a rural Georgia rally in the last week of the campaign. But Dukakis lost Georgia badly to Bush, taking 40 percent of the vote.

In 1992, Clinton's chief campaigner in Georgia was not Nunn but Democratic Gov. Zell Miller. He embraced Clinton early on and helped him win the state's presidential primary, while Nunn held back. In November, Clinton did carry Georgia, but very narrowly. At the same time, the GOP picked up three House seats and ousted Fowler from the Senate, despite Nunn's efforts.

Committees

Armed Services (Chairman)

Governmental Affairs (2nd of 8 Democrats)
Permanent Subcommittee on Investigations (chairman); Oversight of Government Management; Regulation & Government Information

Small Business (2nd of 12 Democrats)
Government Contracting & Paperwork Reduction (chairman); Rural Economy & Family Farming; Urban & Minority-Owned Business Development

Elections

1990 General

Sam Nunn (D)	1,033,439	(100%)

Previous Winning Percentages: **1984** (80%) **1978** (83%) **1972** (54%) **1972** * (52%)

** Special election.*

Campaign Finance

	Receipts	Receipts from PACs	Expend-itures
1990			
Nunn (D)	$1,978,221	$627,010 (32%)	$882,336

Key Votes

1993	
Require unpaid family and medical leave	Y
Approve national "motor voter" registration bill	Y
Approve budget increasing taxes and reducing deficit	Y
Support president's right to lift military gay ban	Y
1992	
Approve school-choice pilot program	N
Allow shifting funds from defense to domestic programs	N
Oppose deeper cuts in spending for SDI	Y
1991	
Approve waiting period for handgun purchases	Y
Raise senators' pay and ban honoraria	Y
Authorize use of force in Persian Gulf	N
Confirm Clarence Thomas to Supreme Court	Y

Voting Studies

	Presidential Support		Party Unity		Conservative Coalition	
Year	**S**	**O**	**S**	**O**	**S**	**O**
1992	40	58	67	31	71	26
1991	57	38	69	29	83	15
1990	57	43	70	27	78	19
1989	72	28	68	30	87	11
1988	63	33	68	24	92	5
1987	46	53	77	22	91	6
1986	58	39	50	43	75	16
1985	58	42	57	41	88	10
1984	69	29	44	55	83	17
1983	64	33	49	48	84	11
1982	70	29	57	41	82	16
1981	59	31	59	39	84	15

Interest Group Ratings

Year	ADA	AFL-CIO	CCUS	ACU
1992	65	91	50	30
1991	50	58	40	48
1990	50	56	42	32
1989	35	80	63	37
1988	40	54	50	42
1987	55	100	28	23
1986	30	47	50	55
1985	30	43	59	57
1984	35	45	74	73
1983	40	35	42	28
1982	45	64	67	68
1981	35	32	72	47

Paul Coverdell (R)

Of Atlanta — Elected 1992; 1st Term

Born: Jan. 20, 1939, Des Moines, Iowa.
Education: U. of Missouri, B.A. 1961.
Military Service: Army, 1962-64.
Occupation: Financial executive; Peace Corps director.
Family: Wife, Nancy Nally.
Religion: Methodist.
Political Career: Ga. Senate, 1971-89, minority leader, 1975-89; candidate for U.S. House (special election), 1977; Ga. Republican Party chairman, 1985-87.
Capitol Office: 204 Russell Bldg. 20510; 224-3643.

The Path to Washington: Coverdell not only won a Senate seat in 1992, but also had the satisfaction of beating the man who denied him a seat in Congress 15 years earlier.

Coverdell lost to Democrat Wyche Fowler Jr. in a special House election in 1977 but returned the favor in 1992 by ousting Fowler from the Senate.

Victory, though, did not come easy for Coverdell. He had to survive an arduous, uphill campaign that saw him persevere through a tough July primary, an August primary runoff, a second-place finish on Nov. 3 and a late November general-election runoff. His margin of victory in both the primary and general-election runoffs was a scant 1 percentage point.

Fowler did not look that beatable at the beginning of the year, after the two Georgia Republicans with statewide visibility declined to run: former Sen. Mack Mattingly and former state House Minority Leader Johnny Isakson, who had waged a strong campaign for governor in 1990.

But Coverdell had decent credentials of his own. He was an Atlanta insurance marketing executive and former state GOP chairman with nearly two decades' experience in the state Senate (14 years as GOP minority leader) before serving a stint as Peace Corps director during the Bush administration.

Coverdell, though, did not win the Republican nomination by default. He slogged to a first-place finish in the multicandidate primary with less than 40 percent of the vote, then barely survived a runoff with U.S. Attorney Bob Barr.

Coverdell had a decided financial advantage in the GOP runoff and the endorsement of several big-name Republicans, including President Bush. But Barr used his anti-abortion stance to help woo conservatives and build a strong volunteer network.

Coverdell's narrow win over Barr provided little momentum for his fall campaign. Fowler enjoyed a hefty lead in early polls and led right up to Election Day. But Coverdell kept up a barrage of attacks and successfully cast Fowler as part of an entrenched network of self-serving Washington politicians.

He made a direct hit on the Fowler campaign with charges that linked the incumbent to the House bank scandal, despite Fowler's insistence that he never had any overdrafted checks during his House tenure from 1977 to 1987. Coverdell cited a deposition Fowler made in 1986 as part of child support proceedings, when he said he often ran short of cash, but "thankfully, we have a bank that doesn't zap me when I bounce a check because we have our own bank."

Coverdell also hammered Fowler for opposing the Persian Gulf War and for voting against the death penalty, which Coverdell said most Georgians favored. In short, Coverdell contended that the incumbent talked conservative in Georgia but voted liberal in Washington.

When Fowler tried to hit back, Coverdell proved a frustrating target. He was not vulnerable to the usual Democratic fire on the abortion issue because he favored abortion rights (while supporting parental notification for minors and opposing federal funding of abortion).

Still, Fowler would have won if not for Georgia election law, which required the winner to receive a majority of the vote. The final tally showed Fowler 35,000 votes ahead but short of the needed majority because of the 70,000 votes that went to the Libertarian candidate, Jim Hudson.

The unexpected result appeared to jostle Fowler into action. He worked hard to shore up votes within his liberal constituency, which some said he had taken for granted early in the race. But there was a widespread feeling that Fowler had missed his best chance for victory, as turnout among black and low-income voters for the runoff was expected to be light.

President-elect Bill Clinton and Vice President-elect Al Gore both campaigned during the runoff for Fowler, with Clinton arguing that Fowler's re-election was needed to help "break this gridlock in Washington."

But Coverdell had his share of visits from luminaries as well, including first lady Barbara Bush and Senate Minority Leader Bob Dole, who helped Coverdell argue that he was the candidate who best represented change.

Coverdell also drew support from Libertarian Hudson and an array of political organizations, such as the Christian Coalition, the National Rifle Association and leaders of Ross Perot's independent presidential campaign in Georgia.

In the end, Coverdell won the runoff by 16,237 votes out of 1.25 million cast, 1 million votes fewer than were cast Nov. 3.

Coverdell brought out his base in suburban Atlanta and made inroads in traditionally Democratic rural Georgia that offset Fowler's strong showing in Atlanta and neighboring DeKalb County. He became only the second Republican to win a Senate seat in Georgia since Reconstruction; Mattingly was the first in 1980 and lasted only one term before being defeated by Fowler in 1986.

Dole saw national implications in Coverdell's victory, saying it was a warning to Clinton: "Don't go too far or too fast."

For his part, Coverdell stressed the numerous areas of philosophical agreement he had with Georgia's Democratic senator, Sam Nunn. As the 103rd Congress opened, Coverdell joined Nunn on the Senate Small Business Committee. Coverdell also drew seats on Agriculture (a vital spot from which to defend Georgia's large agrarian sector) and Foreign Relations (a reflection of his Peace Corps experience).

Coverdell has plenty of experience operating in a Republican Senate minority, as that was his political lot in Georgia during the 1970s and 1980s. He tended then to be more bridge-builder than obstructionist, at one point chairing the Fulton County Senate delegation, a biracial, predominantly Democratic group.

Coverdell's legislative style was to pick an emerging issue such as pension law reform or consumer protection and become an expert on it. He has indicated that one of his early areas of focus in Congress will be the plight of small businesses.

Coverdell first made an effort to come to Congress in 1977, when he ran in the special election for the Atlanta House seat Andrew Young vacated to become Jimmy Carter's ambassador to the United Nations. The district, which included the poorest neighborhoods of the inner city as well as affluent communities to the north, was nearly one-half black.

While more than a half-dozen Democrats entered the race, Republicans rallied behind Coverdell. Still, that was not enough to get him into the runoff; he ran third in the initial round of voting behind Fowler, then president of the Atlanta City Council, and civil rights activist John Lewis. Fowler won the runoff, but Lewis ultimately won the seat nine years later when Fowler ran for the Senate.

Committees

Agriculture, Nutrition & Forestry (7th of 8 Republicans)
Rural Development & Rural Electrification (ranking); Agricultural Credit; Domestic & Foreign Marketing & Product Promotion

Foreign Relations (8th of 8 Republicans)
Western Hemisphere & Peace Corps Affairs (ranking); Near Eastern & South Asian Affairs; Terrorism, Narcotics & International Operations

Small Business (6th of 9 Republicans)
Export Expansion & Agricultural Development (ranking); Rural Economy & Family Farming

Campaign Finance

	Receipts	Receipts from PACs		Expend-itures
1992				
Coverdell (R)	$3,281,002	$585,557	(18%)	$3,193,774
Fowler (D)	$4,322,671	$1,592,996	(37%)	$4,894,620

Key Votes

1993	
Require unpaid family and medical leave	N
Approve national "motor voter" registration bill	N
Approve budget increasing taxes and reducing deficit	N
Support president's right to lift military gay ban	N

Elections

1992 General Runoff		
Paul Coverdell (R)	635,114	(51%)
Wyche Fowler Jr. (D)	618,877	(49%)
1992 General		
Wyche Fowler Jr. (D)	1,108,416	(49%)
Paul Coverdell (R)	1,073,282	(48%)
Jim Hudson (LIBERT)	69,878	(3%)
1992 Primary Runoff		
Paul Coverdell (R)	80,435	(50%)
Bob Barr (R)	78,887	(50%)
1992 Primary		
Paul Coverdell (R)	100,016	(37%)
Bob Barr (R)	65,471	(24%)
John Knox (R)	64,514	(24%)
Charles Tanksley (R)	32,590	(12%)
Dean Parkinson (R)	7,352	(3%)

1 Jack Kingston (R)

Of Savannah — Elected 1992; 1st Term

Born: April 24, 1955, Byron, Texas.
Education: U. of Georgia, A.B. 1978.
Occupation: Insurance broker.
Family: Wife, Libby Morris; four children.
Religion: Episcopalian.
Political Career: Ga. House, 1985-93.
Capitol Office: 1229 Longworth Bldg. 20515; 225-5831.

The Path to Washington: Although Kingston is the first Republican elected in this coastal district in more than a century, his victory was not a major upset. Republicans have had a solid base in the 1st District for years. Ronald Reagan won 59 percent of the vote in his 1984 re-election bid, and George Bush took 60 percent in 1988.

Kingston, an insurance agent who lives in Savannah, had represented Chatham County in the Georgia General Assembly since 1985. Joining the race to succeed retiring Democratic Rep. Lindsay Thomas, he vowed to overcome the "Chatham stigma": No Chatham County resident had been elected to Congress for 50 years in part because rural voters in the district felt alienated from them.

But Kingston's panel assignments may help him win over voters in rural and coastal areas. GOP leaders gave him posts on the Agriculture and Merchant Marine and Fisheries committees.

Those slots may also secure Kingston's Savannah base if he can succeed in using the posts to further his goal of making the city a world trade center. To accomplish that goal, Kingston wants to involve Georgia Southern University in developing agriculture-related businesses and increasing the export of Georgia farm products, particularly the Vidalia onion, a popular product of the district.

A conservative on fiscal and social issues, Kingston began his campaign by signing the "U.S. House Taxpayer Protection Pledge" — a promise to oppose all increases in personal or business income taxes — distributed by Americans for Tax Reform, a Washington-based group.

Kingston, who says the federal debt is the nation's most pressing problem, advocates a balanced-budget constitutional amendment and line-item veto for the president to force spending cuts.

Early in the 103rd Congress, Kingston emerged as a vocal critic of "motor voter" legislation that would require states to allow citizens to register to vote when they apply for or renew their driver's licenses. The bill also mandated that states expand the requirement to state agencies that provide public assistance.

Kingston charged that the purpose of the public assistance provision was not to expand voter participation, as Democratic supporters contended, but to register more Democrats.

Kingston easily secured the GOP nomination in a July 21 primary, while his eventual opponent, Barbara Christmas, a school principal in rural Camden County, had to fend off six other Democrats eager to succeed Thomas. Christmas won the Democratic nomination by defeating former Hinesville Mayor Buddy DeLoach in a runoff.

In Christmas, Democrats had two of the hottest commodities of the 1992 congressional campaign: a woman and an "outsider" who had been elected to only one other office — the Tattnall County Board of Education, where she served from 1976 to 1979.

Being an outsider worked to her advantage if only because it tempered the claim of Kingston, a four-term legislator, to that distinction.

Early in the campaign, Kingston positioned himself as an agent of change, emphasizing his support for term limits. But after the primary season, he adopted an argument reminiscent of past campaigns: Voters should choose him over Christmas because she lacked legislative experience.

Christmas also got some mileage out of her familiar last name. She chose "Christmas in November" as her campaign theme and dubbed her daylong visits to each of the district's 22 counties "Christmas Days."

But Christmas' gender made her vulnerable to attacks from Kingston. Christmas received a donation from the National Organization for Women, which regularly contributes to women running for office. Kingston's campaign pointed to the contribution as evidence of Christmas' liberal, feminist agenda, noting in a flier that NOW supports gay and lesbian rights.

Kingston's message prevailed and he defeated Christmas by more than 25,000 votes.

In February 1993, Kingston lost out to Howard P. "Buck" McKeon of California in his bid to lead the GOP freshmen.

Georgia 1

Southeast — Savannah suburbs; Brunswick; Statesboro

The 1st reaches from Georgia's Atlantic coast 100 miles inland to the state's timber and agricultural centers.

There is a solid Republican vote in the district's more-populous areas — around Savannah, Brunswick and Statesboro — while most of the rural areas are fairly reliably Democratic. All across the district, voters have a common preference for conservative candidates. In the 1992 House race, Kingston's success at portraying his Democratic opponent as a liberal helped him become the first Republican to represent the 1st since the Reconstruction era.

Farming provides a substantial part of the district's economic base — crops include Vidalia onions, corn, soybeans, wheat, peanuts and tobacco — but the tourism industry, federal government, frozen seafood companies and timber-related businesses are also large employers.

Chatham County (Savannah), where Kingston has a strong base of suburban support, casts more than one-fourth of the district vote. Coastal Southern cities typically have a richer ethnic mix than areas inland, and Savannah fits that mold, with Irish Catholics, French Huguenots, Greeks and a substantial Jewish community. The bulk of the city's black population is included in the black-majority 11th District.

Historic Savannah attracts thousands of tourists each year, and industry includes Union Camp (timber processing) and Gulfstream Aerospace (jet manufacturing), each employing more than 3,400 people. The largest government employers in this northern end of the district are Hunter Army Airfield in Savannah and Fort Stewart, in nearby Liberty County.

In Glynn County, the southern anchor of GOP strength in the district, the city of Brunswick is a large port for shipping agricultural products. Along the county's coast there are a number of upscale beach resort communities, such as St. Simon's Island and Jekyll Island. Wealthy retirees help give Glynn its GOP tilt, as do employees of the Federal Law Enforcement Training Center, which is located at a former naval air station that was converted in the 1970s.

During the 1980s, growth in the 1st was fastest in the district's southeastern corner, where population in coastal Camden County exploded by 126 percent. Much of the influx stemmed from the opening of the Kings Bay Nuclear Submarine Base, the East Coast homeport for Trident nuclear submarines. Also, the Cumberland Island National Seashore draws visitors. Camden County is more Democratic than neighboring Glynn; while George Bush carried both in 1992, Camden did not join Glynn in supporting Kingston for the House.

Inland, there are pockets of Republican strength in Bulloch County (Statesboro) and in Ware County (Waycross), but surrounding rural counties have provided a strong vote for most Democrats running statewide in recent years. In presidential elections, however, many rural voters side with the GOP. Bush carried the district comfortably over Bill Clinton in 1992.

1990 Population: 589,546. White 444,788 (75%), Black 133,616 (23%), Other 11,142 (2%). Hispanic origin 10,322 (2%). 18 and over 429,079 (73%), 62 and over 79,362 (13%). Median age: 31.

Committees

Agriculture (13th of 18 Republicans)
Department Operations; Specialty Crops & Natural Resources

Merchant Marine & Fisheries (11th of 18 Republicans)
Fisheries Management; Merchant Marine

Campaign Finance

	Receipts	Receipts from PACs		Expend-itures
1992				
Kingston (R)	$439,846	$113,985	(26%)	$418,883
Christmas (D)	$332,113	$106,050	(32%)	$332,319

Key Votes

1993

Require parental notification of minors' abortions	Y
Require unpaid family and medical leave	N
Approve national "motor voter" registration bill	N
Approve budget increasing taxes and reducing deficit	N
Approve economic stimulus plan	N

Elections

1992 General		
Jack Kingston (R)	103,932	(58%)
Barbara Christmas (D)	75,808	(42%)
1992 Primary		
Jack Kingston (R)	14,799	(81%)
W.B. "Bill" Jolley (R)	3,401	(19%)

District Vote for President

	1992
D	75,066 (39%)
R	89,692 (46%)
I	28,517 (15%)

2 Sanford D. Bishop Jr. (D)

Of Columbus — Elected 1992; 1st Term

Born: Feb. 4, 1947, Mobile, Ala.
Education: Morehouse College, B.A. 1968; Emory U., J.D. 1971.
Occupation: Lawyer.
Family: Divorced.
Religion: Baptist.
Political Career: Ga. House, 1977-91; Ga. Senate, 1991-93.
Capitol Office: 1632 Longworth Bldg. 20515; 225-3631.

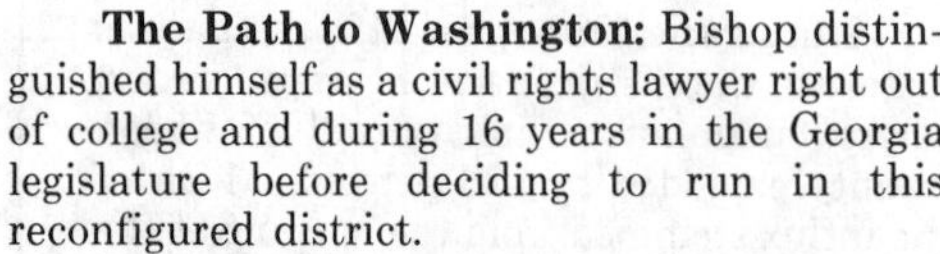

The Path to Washington: Bishop distinguished himself as a civil rights lawyer right out of college and during 16 years in the Georgia legislature before deciding to run in this reconfigured district.

But he owes his upset victory as much to his influential backers in Columbus, the troubles of his principal primary opponent — incumbent Democratic Rep. Charles Hatcher — and the Bush administration's Justice Department as he does to his own talents and background.

Bishop did not even want to make this race in 1992, preferring to wait a few years before trying to win election to Congress. But key Columbus business leaders talked him into running just days before the filing deadline, and then bankrolled his campaign against Hatcher's more significant resources.

Early in the year, Hatcher had been identified as one of the chief abusers of the House bank, with 819 overdrafts. Moreover, under pressure from some blacks in the legislature, the Justice Department had taken a tough line on the state's compliance with the Voting Rights Act. The department twice rejected redistricting plans that had left the 2nd with a majority of white residents. On the third try, the legislature produced a map for the 2nd that reached well beyond its rural base into Columbus, Macon and Warner Robins. That resulted in a 52 percent black voting-age population, and the third black-majority district in Georgia.

Bishop now has the difficult task of representing a more racially and economically diverse district. It is no longer possible to define the 2nd solely by its peanut farms and pine woods. It remains, however, one of the poorer regions of the state. And many of the problems facing residents cut across racial and urban-rural lines.

To help remedy some of those problems, he has argued strongly in the past for boosting federal aid to schools, especially through programs such as Head Start. He also favors tax incentives for small-city and rural enterprise zones, and he wants to diversify the 2nd's economy.

Farming is the district's economic cornerstone, and despite his urban orientation, Bishop sought and received a seat on the Agriculture Committee.

With Fort Benning in the northern corner of the 2nd, just east of Columbus, and Moody Air Force Base in Valdosta, Bishop also secured a seat on the Veterans' Affairs Committee.

Bishop eschews the liberal label to describe his views. He prefers the term "progressive" and even occasionally espouses mildly conservative positions, such as attacking government waste and cutting foreign aid to reduce the federal budget deficit. He is a strong supporter of family and medical leave and of abortion rights.

In March 1993, Bishop was one of only six House members to vote against a bill to give the FBI authority to obtain unlisted phone numbers without a warrant in cases of terrorism and espionage. Bishop said he believed the bill might have been unconstitutional.

While abortion was not an issue in the primary (the leading candidates all agreed with Bishop), his GOP opponent, Jim Dudley, an anti-abortion physician from Americus, raised the controversy in the general-election campaign.

Though the district has a nominal black majority, only 44 percent of its registered voters are black. That left Hatcher an outside chance in the six-way primary, in which three other blacks were vying with Bishop to unseat the incumbent.

Despite his check-writing problems, Hatcher finished first in the primary, garnering 40 percent of the vote. But Bishop forced Hatcher into a runoff, holding him below the absolute majority required under Georgia law. Bishop finished second with 21 percent, as the black vote split.

During the runoff campaign, Hatcher repeatedly apologized for his overdrafts. And he charged that Bishop's Columbus financial supporters were trying to buy a second seat. (Portions of Columbus also fall in the 3rd District.) But Bishop's call for a "new generation of leadership" resonated with rural voters and others disenchanted with Hatcher. Bishop won 53 percent to 47 percent. Bishop easily defeated Dudley in the general election, taking 64 percent of the vote.

Georgia 2

Southwest — Parts of Macon, Columbus, Albany and Valdosta

This is one of the three black-majority constituencies included in Georgia's redistricting plan for the 1990s, but it was by no means certain that the 2nd would elect a black to Congress in 1992. For while blacks make up 57 percent of the district's total population, they are only 52 percent of its voting-age population.

The district consists of parts of four urban areas — predominantly black sections of Macon (Bibb County), Columbus (Muscogee County), Albany (Dougherty County) and Valdosta (Lowndes County), connected by mostly rural counties that are dependent on agriculture for economic sustenance. Peanuts and tobacco are big here, but soybeans, pecans and cotton are also important.

In partisan terms, the 2nd is an open-and-shut case: solidly Democratic. Bill Clinton far outpaced George Bush here in 1992, and after Bishop got the Democratic nomination in hand, he glided to election in November.

Located on the Alabama border in the 2nd's northwestern corner is Columbus. It benefits from the Army's Fort Benning, the state's largest military base and its site for basic training. About 30,000 military and civilian personnel are employed at the base. Columbus also is home to several small colleges.

To the east is the old textile and railroad town of Macon, long a trading and processing center for the agricultural lands of middle Georgia that surround it. To the south, in the central part of the 2nd, is Albany, whose industrial activities include shelling and packing locally produced pecans and peanuts. Albany is also home to the Marine Corps Logistics Base, which is responsible for maintaining supplies for the Marines and employs about 7,300.

In the middle part of the district is Sumter County, where in the late 1970s the little town of Plains gained international fame as the home of President Jimmy Carter. Sumter backed Clinton in 1992, but it was one of just a handful of district counties that went against Bishop in the House race.

In the southeastern corner of the 2nd is Valdosta, which is surrounded by the vast reaches of southern Georgia's piney woods. Paper mills, sawmills and other wood-products manufacturers anchor the local economy, and Levi Strauss has a plant here. The Interstate 75 exits for Valdosta are a stopping-off point for many highway travelers heading to or just leaving Florida.

In winning the 2nd, Bishop carried the district's urbanized areas by huge margins: The combined November vote from Bibb, Muscogee, Dougherty and Lowndes counties was better than 3-to-1 Democratic in the House race.

The rural counties of the 2nd generally add to Democratic strength, particularly in state and local elections, but there are some GOP pockets, notably at the southern end of the district. Thomas County, which lies on the border with Florida, has a good share of Republican-minded retirees and supported Bush for president in 1992.

1990 Population: 591,699. White 248,315 (42%), Black 335,059 (57%), Other 8,325 (1%). Hispanic origin 9,880 (2%). 18 and over 415,777 (70%), 62 and over 85,102 (14%). Median age: 30.

Committees

Agriculture (25th of 28 Democrats)
Department Operations; General Farm Commodities; Specialty Crops & Natural Resources

Post Office & Civil Service (13th of 15 Democrats)
Postal Operations & Services

Veterans' Affairs (18th of 21 Democrats)
Hospitals & Health Care; Housing & Memorial Affairs

Campaign Finance

	Receipts	Receipts from PACs	Expend-itures
1992			
Bishop (D)	$353,162	$89,300 (25%)	$353,973
Dudley (R)	$223,736	$20,100 (9%)	$222,806

Key Votes

1993

Require parental notification of minors' abortions	N
Require unpaid family and medical leave	Y
Approve national "motor voter" registration bill	Y
Approve budget increasing taxes and reducing deficit	Y
Approve economic stimulus plan	Y

Elections

1992 General		
Sanford D. Bishop Jr. (D)	95,789	(64%)
Jim Dudley (R)	54,593	(36%)
1992 Primary Runoff		
Sanford D. Bishop Jr. (D)	41,593	(53%)
Charles Hatcher (D)	36,778	(47%)
1992 Primary		
Charles Hatcher (D)	40,833	(40%)
Sanford D. Bishop Jr. (D)	21,692	(21%)
Mary Young-Cummings (D)	19,363	(19%)
Lonzy Edwards (D)	11,819	(12%)
Phil Whigham (D)	4,762	(5%)
Stephanie A. Kaigler (D)	4,253	(4%)

District Vote for President

	1992
D	93,710 (60%)
R	46,229 (29%)
I	16,906 (11%)

3 Mac Collins (R)

Of Jackson — Elected 1992; 1st Term

Born: Oct. 15, 1944, Butts County, Ga.
Education: Graduated from Jackson H.S., 1962.
Military Service: National Guard, 1964-70.
Occupation: Trucking company owner.
Family: Wife, Julie Watkins; four children.
Religion: Methodist.
Political Career: Butts County Commission chairman, 1977-81; candidate for Ga. Senate, 1984, 1986; Ga. Senate, 1989-93.
Capitol Office: 1118 Longworth Bldg. 20515; 225-5901.

The Path to Washington: When Collins was a boy in Flowvilla, Ga., his introduction to politics came at the kitchen table. His mother, the first woman elected to the city council, and his father would regularly talk about politics while eating breakfast.

In 1992, his interest paid off. Taking advantage of redistricting and the strong anti-Washington mood in Georgia's 3rd District, Collins defeated 10-year incumbent — and a member of the powerful Armed Services Committee — Rep. Richard Ray by a margin of 55 percent to 45 percent.

From the beginning, both candidates ran as conservatives. Both opposed homosexuals in the military and supported anti-abortion policies, a capital gains tax cut and a balanced-budget amendment. Collins also favors a line-item veto, lower taxes and a moratorium on federal regulations. (In April 1993, Collins was one of only two Republicans to oppose GOP attempts to use a "vote-no" strategy on a key procedural vote on the line-item veto to get Democrats to bring a stronger measure to the floor. The Democrats' version passed with the support of about half the Republican caucus.)

But it was Collins — and his I'm-one-of-you campaign theme — with whom the voters in the largely working-class district identified. Collins, often dressed in blue jeans, a sweat shirt and cowboy boots, had a simple campaign slogan: "Send a Working Man to Congress."

He is a plain-speaking, down-home conservative who has shown a knack for campaigning and a disdain for the term "politician." He prefers the word "representative," saying "politician" implies making a career out of electoral politics. He supports a 12-year term limit.

Like many other freshmen, he has experience in local government. From 1977 to 1981, he served as a Butts County commissioner and, since 1989, as a state senator.

But the main factors that eventually helped Collins — and blocked Ray from a sixth term — were redistricting and an anti-incumbent mood.

Originally, House GOP Whip Newt Gingrich represented some areas that are now in the 3rd, but after redistricting, Gingrich opted to run in the new 6th, the most Republican district in the state.

The new lines robbed Ray of his political base in the old 3rd. The changes left the 3rd with a mixture of independent voters, Reagan Democrats and GOP suburbanites who did not know any of the candidates well.

All of this helped Collins. As a native of the southern part of the 3rd, he captured what remained of Ray's former district. Ray, in turn, lost many of the new northern suburban counties.

Throughout the campaign, Collins painted Ray as a corrupt politician who did not understand the people in the district. The strategy eventually took hold. Collins hit Ray hard with a commercial reviving a 1980s charge that Ray, who was a member of the Armed Services Committee, accepted an illegal contribution from Unisys, a defense contractor. Ray denied the charge.

But Ray struck back with an organized and visible campaign. And armed with an imposing $1 million (Collins spent $246,000), Ray unleashed some harsh advertisements of his own. In one commercial, Ray claimed that Collins charged the taxpayers excessively to tour the state. Collins called the allegation ludicrous and accused Ray of taking expensive congressional trips.

Collins promised an active, constituent-based agenda. His seat on the Public Works and Transportation Committee could help him keep an eye on the Hartsfield Atlanta International Airport and its concerns. He also got a slot on the Small Business Committee.

In May 1993, during debate of the competitiveness bill, Collins won approval of his first amendment, which specified that money from the bill should "benefit" U.S. citizens. That caught many Democrats by surprise, who switched their votes to support Collins.

Historically, his district win is noteworthy for another reason: It helped the Georgia send its largest GOP contingent to the House since Reconstruction — four, including Collins, Gingrich, Jack Kingston and John Linder.

Georgia 3

West Central — Griffin; Atlanta and Columbus suburbs

The 3rd is a mix of old-time Southern Democrats and Republican-leaning retirees and young professionals. Roughly (very roughly) triangular in shape, it starts at the peach orchards in aptly named Peach County, runs north to the Hartsfield Atlanta International Airport in Clayton County, then heads south and west to the suburbs of Columbus, in Muscogee County.

The booming population growth of the suburbs and exurbs to the south and west of Atlanta, along with increasing acceptance of the GOP among rural, traditionally Democratic conservatives, have made the 3rd fertile ground for Republican candidates.

The counties that contain these suburbs — Clayton (Jonesboro), Coweta (Newnan), Fayette (Fayetteville), Henry (McDonough) and Spalding (Griffin) — cast about 60 percent of the vote in the 3rd. All five went decisively for Republican Collins over Democratic Rep. Richard Ray in 1992. George Bush won all but Clayton on his way to victory over Bill Clinton.

The biggest growth occurred in the suburbs abutting Atlanta to the south. Clayton County grew 21 percent during the 1980s, and with more than 182,000 residents it is the biggest county in the 3rd, casting one-fifth of the district vote. The sprawling and ever-bustling international airport (which is split between the 3rd and 5th districts) is a prime driver of the district's economy. Ford also makes its hugely popular Taurus automobiles in Clayton and adjoining Fulton County.

Next door in Fayette County, population grew 115 percent in the past decade.

In Spalding County, textiles are still important to the Griffin economy. Dundee Mills, a towel manufacturer, is one of the largest employers here. The county is also home to the Atlanta Motor Speedway.

Moving into Coweta County, the atmosphere changes, although GOP voting habits do not. Newnan's wealth is tied less to Atlanta's recent growth than to the more distant past; spared during the Civil War, Newnan is known as the "the City of Homes" for its stately antebellum mansions.

In addition to the many district residents who depend on airport activity for their paychecks, thousands of others look to the military to put groceries on the table. Fort Gillem in Clayton County has the second largest payroll in the 3rd, after Delta Airlines. Others in the northern end of the district commute to the Army's Fort McPherson in the southern Atlanta suburbs in the neighboring 5th District. To the south (in the adjoining 2nd District) is Robins Air Force Base in Warner Robins. And a number who live in the Columbus area commute there to the Army's Fort Benning, the state's largest military base (also located in the 2nd District).

The most loyal support for Democratic candidates comes from a swath of mainly rural counties in the southern part of the 3rd — Peach, Monroe, Jones, Baldwin and Crawford. All went Democratic in the 1992 House race. Ray also managed just to nudge Collins in the Muscogee County (Columbus) part of the 3rd.

1990 Population: 591,328. White 474,999 (80%), Black 105,263 (18%), Other 11,066 (2%). Hispanic origin 8,057 (1%). 18 and over 429,343 (73%), 62 and over 71,465 (12%). Median age: 32.

Committees

Public Works & Transportation (15th of 24 Republicans)
Aviation; Economic Development; Surface Transportation

Small Business (9th of 18 Republicans)
Rural Enterprises, Exports & the Environment; SBA Legislation & the General Economy

Campaign Finance

	Receipts	Receipts from PACs		Expend-itures
1992				
Collins (R)	$255,683	$50,272	(20%)	$246,007
Ray (D)	$1,036,440	$353,971	(34%)	$1,128,552

Key Votes

1993

Require parental notification of minors' abortions	Y
Require unpaid family and medical leave	N
Approve national "motor voter" registration bill	N
Approve budget increasing taxes and reducing deficit	N
Approve economic stimulus plan	N

Elections

1992 General		
Mac Collins (R)	114,107	(55%)
Richard Ray (D)	94,271	(45%)
1992 Primary		
Mac Collins (R)	17,484	(55%)
Paul Broun (R)	14,546	(45%)

District Vote for President

1992

D 79,462 (37%)
R 103,640 (48%)
I 31,471 (15%)

4 John Linder (R)

Of Dunwoody — Elected 1992; 1st Term

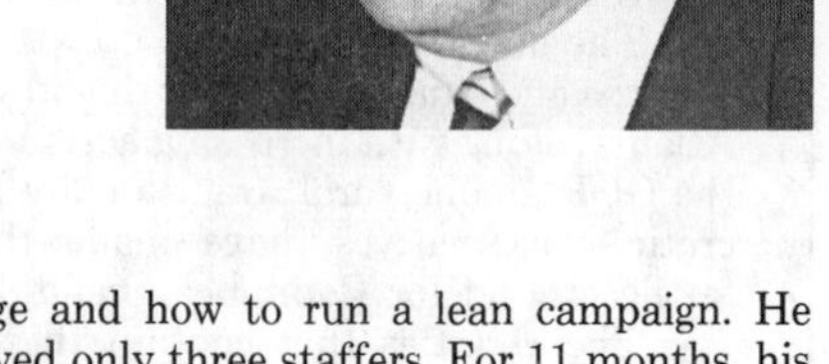

Born: Sept. 9, 1942, Deer River, Minn.
Education: U. of Minnesota, Duluth, B.S. 1963; U. of Minnesota, D.D.S. 1967.
Military Service: Air Force, 1967-69.
Occupation: Financial executive; dentist.
Family: Wife, Lynne Leslee Peterson; two children.
Religion: Presbyterian.
Political Career: Ga. House, 1975-81; GOP nominee for Ga. Senate, 1980; Ga. House, 1983-91; GOP nominee for U.S. House, 1990.
Capitol Office: 1605 Longworth Bldg. 20515; 225-4272.

The Path to Washington: When Linder arrived in Washington, one of his first acts at a House Republican caucus meeting was to introduce a proposal to limit anyone in their caucus holding a committee's top post to a six-year tenure.

That proposal won strong support from his fellow freshmen and marked an impressive start for the former Dunwoody state representative: The proposal passed on his ninth day in the nation's capital.

If his first proposal is any indication, Linder's style in Washington will be a marked departure from his liberal predecessor, Rep. Ben Jones, who opted to run in the 10th District this time (and lost).

With Linder, the House gains a soft-spoken, articulate businessman who is known for his intellect, his strong stand on political reform and his philosophical alignment with a fellow Georgian, GOP Whip Newt Gingrich.

A former dentist and former president of a financial lending company, Linder is no stranger to politics.

He served for 14 years in Georgia's House of Representatives and, with the backing of the late GOP National Chairman Lee Atwater, first ran for Congress in 1990 against Jones.

As a state representative, he introduced legislation to limit the Speaker of the House to three terms, reduce the number of state representatives and senators and cap state expenditures.

Those acts earned him the reputation — similar to Gingrich's — of a politician willing to battle the Democratic leadership.

His ascent to the House was the result of shrewd campaigning and a newly carved, more Republican district.

In his 1990 race against Jones, Linder captured 48 percent of the popular vote. But that loss gave him some valuable name recognition that served him well in 1992.

The loss also taught him some important lessons about congressional campaigning, including how to be comfortable with his political message and how to run a lean campaign. He employed only three staffers. For 11 months, his campaign manager worked from 4 a.m. to 10 p.m.

Linder campaigned on a platform of congressional reform. He called for term limits, an end to the franking privilege and staff reductions.

Linder voted in April 1993 against a Democratic bill giving the president limited line-item veto authority, in favor of an even stronger GOP substitute amendment. While most GOP freshmen chose to vote for both, Linder was one of only 12 GOP freshmen to only support the substitute amendment.

Early in the campaign, Linder showed a willingness to go for the political jugular: When he discovered that his GOP primary opponent, state Rep. Emory Morsberger (who was a former Democrat), had written a $103 check to the Gwinnett Democratic Party in 1990, Linder ran a television ad criticizing the contribution.

He led Morsberger in the primary, 34 percent to 28 percent, and then clinched a runoff, 62 percent to 38 percent.

During the general election, Linder's Democratic opponent, state Sen. Cathey Steinberg, labeled him an "extremist" and a "Pat Robertson with a Southern drawl" because of his conservative views.

Steinberg and Linder were ideological opposites. He is anti-abortion; she favored abortion rights. When Steinberg got money from EMILY's List, which raises funds for women candidates, Linder argued that this showed she was out of the Georgia political mainstream.

Linder, in turn, had strong backing from conservative religious activists, who campaigned heavily in the district.

Linder owed his 2,676-vote margin in part to support from conservative Democrats who did not feel comfortable with Steinberg.

Linder was given a seat on the Banking, Finance and Urban Affairs Committee because of his interest in small business. He also will sit on the Science, Space and Technology, and Veterans' Affairs committees.

Georgia 4

Atlanta suburbs — Parts of De Kalb and Gwinnett counties

As Atlanta blossomed into the South's financial capital during the 1960s and 1970s, De Kalb County (just east of the city) was the pacesetter of suburban growth. With more than a half-million people, De Kalb is now Georgia's second most populous county. But growth here has slowed as development has spread into outlying jurisdictions; lately, the hot spots have been farther east, in Gwinnett and Rockdale counties. Because of the expansion of suburbia there, the 4th tilts Republican. George Bush won the district in 1992, taking 46 percent of the vote.

Historically, this district has shifted between the parties. Two decades ago, the 4th was represented by a Republican, Ben Blackburn. He was ousted in 1974 by Democrat Elliott H. Levitas, who lost in 1984 to Republican Pat Swindall, who lost in 1988 to Democrat Ben Jones. After 1992 redistricting altered the 4th to Jones' disadvantage, he ran in the neighboring 10th District, but lost in the Democratic primary. Republican Linder captured the open 4th with 51 percent of the vote.

De Kalb and Gwinnett counties cast 47 percent and 41 percent of the district's vote in 1992. The 4th includes the north-central part of De Kalb and all but the northern section of Gwinnett. The two counties are quite different in their electoral behavior.

Democratic candidates get a warm reception in the central and western parts of De Kalb. Decatur, the county seat, was a 19th century commercial center until it lost out as a railroad center to Atlanta; it still has some industry and a Democratic complexion. As one of the district's largest employers, 9,500-student Emory University and the communities around it — many of them with substantial Jewish or black populations — give local politics a liberal slant. Chamblee, a blue-collar community in northern De Kalb, has a large immigrant community of both Asians and Hispanics, and they bolster the Democratic vote. Republicans' best showings in De Kalb generally come in the suburban neighborhoods around Stone Mountain. The mountain itself, with a gigantic carving of Robert E. Lee and other heroes of the Confederacy, is a big tourist draw.

Gwinnett County delivers a hefty Republican vote. In 1992, the margins that Bush and Linder piled up in Gwinnett offset their defeats in the De Kalb part of the 4th. Population in Gwinnett expanded nearly 50 percent during the 1980s; the county has newly established neighborhoods filled with recent arrivals who have no connection with the area's Democratic past.

To the south is Rockdale County. Long a rural and conservative Democratic area, Rockdale has been transformed by suburban growth. Dotted now with subdivisions, its vote has shifted dramatically to the GOP. In 1992, Bush won a majority in Rockdale, and Linder topped 60 percent. The county casts just under 10 percent of the vote in the 4th.

The district also has a small slice of Fulton County, on Atlanta's eastern edge, composed largely of white-collar suburbs.

1990 Population: 588,293. White 489,881 (83%), Black 67,968 (12%), Other 30,444 (5%). Hispanic origin 20,166 (3%). 18 and over 448,179 (76%), 62 and over 57,772 (10%). Median age: 32.

Committees

Banking, Finance & Urban Affairs (13th of 20 Republicans)
Consumer Credit & Insurance; Financial Institutions Supervision, Regulation & Deposit Insurance

Science, Space & Technology (18th of 22 Republicans)
Technology, Environment & Aviation

Veterans' Affairs (12th of 14 Republicans)
Hospitals & Health Care

Campaign Finance

	Receipts	Receipts from PACs		Expend-itures
1992				
Linder (R)	$543,357	$205,478	(38%)	$542,137
Steinberg (D)	$621,771	$151,832	(24%)	$603,399

Key Votes

1993

Require parental notification of minors' abortions	Y
Require unpaid family and medical leave	N
Approve national "motor voter" registration bill	N
Approve budget increasing taxes and reducing deficit	N
Approve economic stimulus plan	N

Elections

1992 General		
John Linder (R)	126,495	(51%)
Cathey Steinberg (D)	123,819	(49%)
1992 Primary Runoff		
John Linder (R)	21,807	(62%)
Emory L. Morsberger (R)	13,370	(38%)
1992 Primary		
John Linder (R)	17,628	(34%)
Emory L. Morsberger (R)	14,381	(28%)
Jimmy Fisher (R)	5,847	(11%)
Richard E. Robinson (R)	5,587	(11%)
Tom Phillips (R)	5,455	(11%)
Ray Miller (R)	2,480	(5%)

District Vote for President

	1992	
D	101,990	(41%)
R	116,418	(46%)
I	33,226	(13%)

5 John Lewis (D)

Of Atlanta — Elected 1986; 4th Term

Born: Feb. 21, 1940, Troy, Ala.
Education: American Baptist Theological Seminary, B.A. 1961; Fisk U., B.A. 1963.
Occupation: Civil rights activist.
Family: Wife, Lillian Miles; one child.
Religion: Baptist.
Political Career: Sought Democratic nomination for U.S. House (special election), 1977; Atlanta City Council, 1982-86.
Capitol Office: 329 Cannon Bldg. 20515; 225-3801.

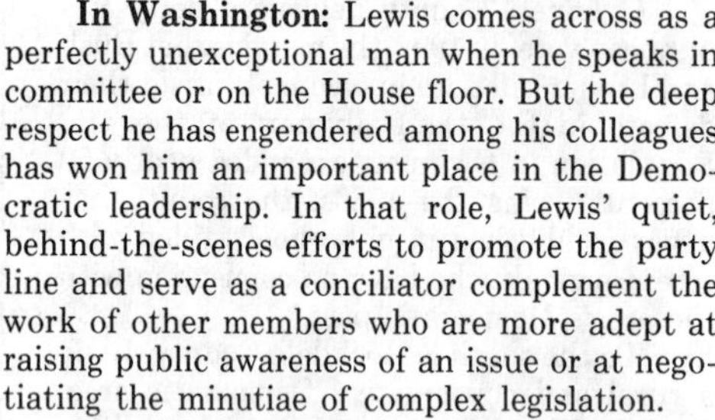

In Washington: Lewis comes across as a perfectly unexceptional man when he speaks in committee or on the House floor. But the deep respect he has engendered among his colleagues has won him an important place in the Democratic leadership. In that role, Lewis' quiet, behind-the-scenes efforts to promote the party line and serve as a conciliator complement the work of other members who are more adept at raising public awareness of an issue or at negotiating the minutiae of complex legislation.

From his first day in Congress in 1987, Lewis enjoyed a special status because of his exceptional role in the front lines of the civil rights movement. Many House members vividly recall the news photo of a young Lewis being beaten by state troopers as he and other civil rights leaders crossed the Edmund Pettus bridge in Selma, Ala., during a 1965 march. It was a seminal event in the civil rights movement. Yet the violence Lewis faced did not alter his strong commitment to nonviolent change. As a politician Lewis has sought biracial support and managed to win it. Lewis' early backing of Bill Clinton's 1992 presidential campaign undoubtedly helped the Democrat carry Georgia.

Lewis' appeal has won him two coveted assignments. In mid-1991, after William H. Gray III of Pennsylvania resigned from the House, the Democratic leadership decided it needed some diversity. Then an assembly of liberal, white males, the hierarchy sought to add a black, a woman and a conservative as chief deputy whips. Lewis campaigned for the job and got it.

Then, with the retirement of Georgian Ed Jenkins at the end of the 102nd Congress, a vacancy developed on the Ways and Means Committee. Lewis was the early and prohibitive favorite to succeed Jenkins on the panel.

Lewis opposed the use of force against Iraq in January 1991, and his deep commitment to peaceful change is well-known. But even about this Lewis is not ideological or rigid. His capacity to be flexible was evident at the end of 1992, when he led a House delegation to strife-torn Somalia. Lewis was so moved by the plight of starving Somali people and angered by the actions of heavily armed factions and street thugs who were keeping food from reaching the needy that he embraced sending U.S. troops to protect food shipments and, if necessary, disarm the warlords.

"It would seem somewhat out of the ordinary for me to support a military effort," he said in December. But the denial of "human decency," Lewis said, led him to conclude that "there are no other affirmative means to alleviate the situation except for the use of necessary military power to see that food and medical assistance be available to the people there."

A glimpse of the esteem Lewis commands came in the 1987 debate on imposing sanctions on the apartheid government of South Africa. All seven other Georgia House Democrats made a surprise last-minute decision to vote for the sanctions as a tribute to Lewis, who had let them know that passage of the bill was important to him.

A small gesture, perhaps, but those seven Democrats had strayed from the party line on several other key votes, leaving Lewis as the lone liberal vote in the traditionally conservative Georgia House delegation. Until 1991, Lewis consistently earned 100 percent ratings from the Americans for Democratic Action and AFL-CIO. (That his 1992 scores slipped to 85 percent and 92 percent, respectively, was offset by his perfect 0 rating from the American Conservative Union.)

Thanks to 1992 redistricting, Lewis now has more ideological company in his state delegation. The map for Georgia created two more black-majority districts, which elected black Democrats Sanford D. Bishop Jr. and Cynthia A. McKinney.

Lewis' liberalism — and his closeness to the leadership — caused him some difficult moments in the 102nd Congress. His record of support for environmentalists is about as strong as it is for labor. So when those two camps clashed over protecting "old growth" forests and their threatened animal inhabitants in the

Georgia 5

Parts of Atlanta

The obvious symbol of the 5th is Atlanta's alluring skyline, with the state Capitol, the steel-and-glass office skyscrapers and the towering hotels that make the city the commercial center of the Southeast and the symbolic capital of the New South.

However, in the shadows of those buildings is another Atlanta, a mostly black city struggling with typical urban social problems — unemployment, crime and drugs. While Atlanta's business boom spurred continued suburban sprawl through the 1980s, the city's population dropped slightly, to just over 394,000.

But as host city for the 1996 Summer Olympics, Atlanta is on the cusp of another building boom: Construction of Olympic venues could total $500 million. One of the largest Olympic construction projects is a new stadium that will be home to the Atlanta Falcons and the 1994 Super Bowl.

The 5th takes in most of Atlanta and surrounding Fulton County, as well as some suburban territory in neighboring counties, including the southern half of De Kalb County and fragments of northwest Clayton and southern Cobb counties. Blacks account for 62 percent of the district's population and 54 percent of its registered voters, and they help make the 5th a Democratic bastion. In the 1992 presidential contest, Bill Clinton took just over two-thirds of the vote in the 5th, his best showing in all of Georgia's 11 districts. Rep. Lewis topped 70 percent in winning re-election.

Fulton is reliable Democratic territory, though there are pockets of GOP strength in its northern suburbs. One of those communities is Sandy Springs, a booming area of white-collar, middle-level managers.

The heart of the district is Atlanta itself. Its downtown has enjoyed new attention with the recent opening of Underground Atlanta, a tourist shopping complex, and the nearby Coca-Cola museum. Tourists also can pay homage to late civil rights leader the Rev. Dr. Martin Luther King Jr. here; his birthplace, the church where he preached and his Center for Non-Violent Change are all in Atlanta.

South of Atlanta, the district takes in East Point, a lower-middle-class community. Many of its residents work at Hartsfield Atlanta International Airport, which is divided between the 5th and 3rd districts. The 1991 closure of Eastern Airlines took a bite out of aviation employment, costing 10,000 people their jobs. But TWA recently made Atlanta a mini-hub, and other job opportunities in the metropolitan area should mitigate the loss of Eastern.

Among the 5th's largest employers are Delta Airlines, the Fort McPherson Army Forces Command, Coca-Cola, Cable News Network, Bell South and timber giant Georgia Pacific.

More than 90 percent of the district's vote comes out of Fulton County. Of the rest, the biggest share (about 4 percent) comes from northwest Clayton County, home to many blue-collar, white middle-class airport workers and a growing Asian population.

1990 Population: 586,485. White 209,026 (36%), Black 365,206 (62%), Other 12,253 (2%). Hispanic origin 10,502 (2%). 18 and over 440,910 (75%), 62 and over 72,304 (12%). Median age: 31.

Pacific Northwest, or over saving timber jobs, Lewis found himself in the middle.

As a member of the Interior (now Natural Resources) Committee, Lewis was the swing vote when the National Parks and Public Lands Subcommittee voted to approve a controversial bill that would have placed millions of acres of forest off-limits to logging. When the subcommittee met to debate the bill in May 1992, Lewis first was opposed, and the measure was going to die on a 17-17 tie. During a half-hour break in the deliberations, full committee Chairman George Miller of California and subcommittee Chairman Bruce F. Vento of Minnesota leaned hard on Lewis. When the panel reconvened, Lewis asked for a new vote and supported the measure, sending it on to full committee, 18-16. "I want to see the process continue," he said after switching.

The full committee never acted on the bill, however. Heavy lobbying against it by Speaker Thomas S. Foley changed enough votes that Miller decided not to risk a defeat. Lewis did not commit to support it in full committee.

Lewis' interests are often close to home; he watches out for Atlanta's rapid transit system and airport. He has worked to designate as a National Historic Trail the route he marched from Selma to Montgomery, and he supports construction of a National African American Museum as part of the Smithsonian Institution on the Mall in Washington. He has also sought to clean up and limit construction of billboards on highways built with federal aid.

At Home: Lewis' 1986 victory in the 5th symbolized the rise of Southern blacks into the halls of political power. But to get to Congress, Lewis had to weather a bitter contest with a longtime ally, state Sen. Julian Bond.

The relationship between the civil rights leaders dated back to the early 1960s. Lewis, son of an Alabama sharecropper, was director of the Student Nonviolent Coordinating Committee (SNCC); Bond, from a middle-class Philadelphia background, was the group's spokesman.

Lewis spoke at the 1963 March on Washington. His fearlessness in the face of arrests and beatings was legendary. But when radical elements took over SNCC, Lewis moved on to head the Atlanta-based Voter Education Project.

Lewis lost his first political bid, a 1977 House primary, to Wyche Fowler Jr. In 1981, he won the first of two terms on the Atlanta City Council; he gained a following among blacks as well as whites in north Atlanta who appreciated his attention to neighborhood matters.

Bond, meanwhile, served 20 years in the Georgia legislature, where he pushed through a redistricting plan that transformed the 5th District from nearly half white to almost two-thirds black. When Fowler announced his 1986 challenge to Republican Sen. Mack Mattingly, Bond became the favorite to succeed him in the 5th.

Bond did finish ahead in the primary. But Lewis, whose biracial appeal brought him a sizable white vote, forced Bond into a runoff. The campaign became nasty. Bond belittled Lewis' command of issues. But Lewis delivered sharper blows, implying that Bond had held a desk job in the civil rights revolution and calling on Bond to join him in taking drug tests. Though he never accused Bond outright of using drugs, the implication was there for those who already saw Bond as a jet-setter.

Winning more than 80 percent of the vote in majority-white precincts and cutting into Bond's margin among blacks, Lewis won nomination with 52 percent. The Democratic rift had little effect on Lewis in the general election; he prevailed by a 3-to-1 margin. By his first reelection, Lewis was a settled incumbent, running without primary opposition and winning with ease in the general election. That pattern was repeated in 1990.

In 1992, redistricting deprived the 5th of some black voters, but the map kept the black majority in Lewis' turf well over 60 percent. Lewis drew both primary and general-election opponents, but neither offered a vigorous challenge, and he won both races with ease.

Committees

Chief Deputy Whip

District of Columbia (6th of 8 Democrats)
Government Operations & Metropolitan Affairs; Judiciary & Education

Ways & Means (16th of 24 Democrats)
Health; Oversight

Elections

1992 General		
John Lewis (D)	147,445	(72%)
Paul R. Stabler (R)	56,960	(28%)
1992 Primary		
John Lewis (D)	43,971	(76%)
"Able" Mable Thomas (D)	13,686	(24%)
1990 General		
John Lewis (D)	86,037	(76%)
J.W. Tibbs (R)	27,781	(24%)

Previous Winning Percentages: **1988** (78%) **1986** (75%)

District Vote for President

1992

D	140,270	(68%)
R	52,087	(25%)
I	15,214	(7%)

Campaign Finance

	Receipts	Receipts from PACs		Expenditures
1992				
Lewis (D)	$300,865	$225,195	(75%)	$246,913
Stabler (R)	$58,966	$8,000	(14%)	$58,612
1990				
Lewis (D)	$271,450	$175,510	(65%)	$108,118
Tibbs (R)	$1,992	0		$7,755

Key Votes

1993	
Require parental notification of minors' abortions	N
Require unpaid family and medical leave	Y
Approve national "motor voter" registration bill	Y
Approve budget increasing taxes and reducing deficit	Y
Approve economic stimulus plan	Y
1992	
Approve balanced-budget constitutional amendment	N
Close down space station program	N
Approve U.S. aid for former Soviet Union	N
Allow shifting funds from defense to domestic programs	Y
1991	
Extend unemployment benefits using deficit financing	Y
Approve waiting period for handgun purchases	Y
Authorize use of force in Persian Gulf	N

Voting Studies

	Presidential Support		Party Unity		Conservative Coalition	
Year	S	O	S	O	S	O
1992	11	81	95	1	6	83
1991	22	71	96	2	3	89
1990	16	84	95	5	6	94
1989	28	72	98	2	0	100
1988	13	82	93	3	5	92
1987	13	85	93	4	12	88

Interest Group Ratings

Year	ADA	AFL-CIO	CCUS	ACU
1992	95	92	13	0
1991	85	92	0	0
1990	100	100	21	4
1989	100	100	40	4
1988	100	100	17	0
1987	96	100	20	0

6 Newt Gingrich (R)

Of Marietta — Elected 1978; 8th Term

Born: June 17, 1943, Harrisburg, Pa.
Education: Emory U., B.A. 1965; Tulane U., M.A. 1968, Ph.D. 1971.
Occupation: Professor.
Family: Wife, Marianne Ginther; two children.
Religion: Baptist.
Political Career: GOP nominee for U.S. House, 1974, 1976.
Capitol Office: 2428 Rayburn Bldg. 20515; 225-4501.

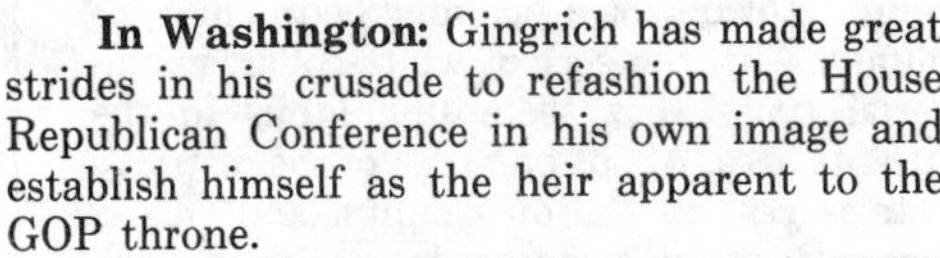

In Washington: Gingrich has made great strides in his crusade to refashion the House Republican Conference in his own image and establish himself as the heir apparent to the GOP throne.

In just a little over 14 years on Capitol Hill, Gingrich has played a big part in redefining what it is to be a Republican House member: On the wane is the pleasant-mannered, consensus-oriented Main Street conservatism exemplified by Minority Leader Robert H. Michel of Illinois. Coming to the fore is a harder-edged, avowedly confrontational style that markets the GOP as the low-tax party and bashes the Democrats as set in their wasteful-spending ways.

Gingrich was a surprise winner for minority whip in early 1989, yet in not quite four years, members sharing his conservative ideology and combative approach were occupying almost all the House GOP leadership positions except Michel's. The evolution has been so rapid that even Michel has adapted his formerly low-key style. "We're going to be a very militant, forceful force," he said as the 103rd Congress began.

Gingrich has made no secret of his desire to succeed Michel, who has been a subject of retirement speculation throughout the past four years. The conventional thinking has been that Gingrich's eventual move to be GOP leader would be opposed by a coalition of veteran "Old Bull" Republicans and party moderates. But in late 1992, when there were three contested elections for lower-level leadership spots, the confrontationalist wing identified with Gingrich prevailed each time. Most notably, Dick Armey of Texas unseated Republican Conference Chairman Jerry Lewis of California, who was criticized for forging cooperative relationships with Democrats; Lewis, the No. 3 man on the GOP ladder, had been seen as a potential challenger to Gingrich whenever the leader's job came open.

The rightward march provoked prominent moderates Steve Gunderson of Wisconsin and Fred Upton of Michigan to flee the leadership ranks; moderate Bill Gradison of Ohio left Congress altogether after losing his bid for a leadership spot. Indeed, the tenor of the Republican Conference is now such that Gingrich, when he makes his move to become party leader, may not be entirely immune from opposition on his right, from GOP elements even more confrontational than he is.

During the 12 years that Ronald Reagan and then George Bush held the presidency, Republicans in the House often were marginalized in policy-making. As a significantly outnumbered minority in Congress' lower chamber, they typically had less leverage with the White House than Senate Republicans (who controlled that chamber for six years and afterwards were a strong minority) and even the congressional Democratic leadership, which usually could muster enough votes to block presidential initiatives.

As whip, Gingrich was generally on the scene as the leaders of Congress tried to reach accord with the White House, but he never seemed very happy with a process that basically served to muddle the public's image of what the GOP stood for.

Now, unfettered from any obligation to support the White House line, Gingrich is freer to return to the role he loves best — Democrat-bashing, bill-slaying, fire-breathing antagonist.

On the first day of the 103rd Congress, Gingrich and fellow Republicans dispelled any notion that Bill Clinton's election would bring even a temporary "era of good feeling" between the parties in the House. The GOP fought with a vengeance a rules change engineered by the Democratic majority that abandoned precedent and allowed the chamber's four non-voting delegates and one resident commissioner (all of them Democrats) to vote in the Committee of the Whole, where the House does much of its serious legislative business.

Fuming that the new rule was unconstitutional and a partisan power grab, Republicans lost on the floor, but filed suit. A federal judge in 1993 declared the rule constitutional, but only because the delegates' votes had been rendered "meaningless" under the terms of the rule; in an attempt to quiet opposition, Democrats had crafted the rules change so that

Georgia 6

Atlanta suburbs — Roswell; part of Marietta

Anchored in Atlanta's burgeoning northern suburbs, the 6th covers parts of five counties that are laden with Republican voters who work in high-technology and other white-collar occupations. This area is commonly referred to as the Golden Crescent; it is sandwiched between three of the state's major interstate highways — I-75, I-85 and the I-285 perimeter highway.

Cobb County, which lies northwest of Atlanta, accounts for more than 50 percent of the district's vote. About three-fourths of Cobb's residents are in the 6th; most of the rest of the county is in the 7th. Voters in the 6th District part of Cobb gave George Bush a decisive 55 percent in the 1992 presidential contest. Republican Senate candidate Paul Coverdell also handily won Cobb.

Though it is well within Atlanta's orbit, Marietta (which is divided between the 6th and 7th districts) provides Cobb County with its own population and commercial center. A well-known Marietta landmark is the "big chicken," a 56-foot-tall, fowl-shaped sign with a Kentucky Fried Chicken outlet at its base. Marietta has a thriving base of service-oriented small businesses (the city won notice from The Wall Street Journal in 1989 as the nation's small-business development capital), and Cobb County is headquarters for a number of well-known larger concerns, including Sprint, Home Depot and The Weather Channel. Many workers in the district commute to jobs at the nearby Dobbins Air Reserve Base and an adjoining Lockheed facility (which are both located in the part of Marietta in the 7th District).

Marietta has three colleges — Kennesaw State College, Southern College of Technology and Life College (one of the largest chiropractic schools in the nation). An important local tourist attraction is the Kennesaw Mountain National Battlefield.

In the central part of the 6th are more GOP-leaning suburbs in northern Fulton County. Two major towns here are Alpharetta and Roswell. Alpharetta was once home to a number of large farms that have since been converted into suburban developments. Roswell used to be a cotton-milling center, but now is a booming bedroom community with the sort of white-collar, managerial types that seem ubiquitous in the Atlanta area. About one-fifth of the district's vote is cast in Fulton County, and this is where Bush ran strongest in the 6th in 1992, taking 58 percent of the vote.

The remaining share of the vote in the district — about 25 percent — comes from northern De Kalb County, northern Gwinnett County and southern Cherokee County. Again, all are solidly Republican.

In northern De Kalb County, affluent Dunwoody is a haven for the professional class, with well-manicured lawns and country clubs. Holiday Inn and United Parcel Service have their headquarters in Dunwoody.

Gwinnett and Cherokee counties were among the state's fastest-growing in the 1980s, also attracting newcomers with no connections to the region's traditional Democratic ties.

1990 Population: 587,118. White 535,627 (91%), Black 35,366 (6%), Other 16,125 (3%). Hispanic origin 12,092 (2%). 18 and over 438,847 (75%), 62 and over 40,467 (7%). Median age: 32.

anytime the delegates' votes spelled the difference between victory and defeat in the Committee of the Whole, there would be a re-vote in the full House.

Still, Republicans appealed the court ruling, and months later they were routinely demanding time-consuming re-votes on the House floor to protest the delegate-vote rule.

As Congress' Democratic majority moved early in the 103rd to pass the "motor voter" bill broadening voting registration opportunities, Gingrich let loose. "The bill would create a nationwide Chicago, where the dead can vote, illegal aliens can vote and the political machine can pressure people to vote for their candidate."

Also in the early months of 1993, in what some interpreted as an effort to burnish his credentials to be GOP leader, Gingrich broadened his legislative focus to include international affairs. He spoke skeptically of military intervention in Bosnia and had early meetings with President Clinton on possible Russian aid packages.

A brainy and extremely articulate former history professor, Gingrich began popularizing a more combative style for the House minority while he was still one of its backbenchers. Even as a freshman, he freely offered strategy advice to his party elders and drew scenarios for Republican dominance in crayon on a board in his office. He has made a career as a scourge on Democrats.

First elected in 1978, in the early 1980s he cofounded the Conservative Opportunity Society in the House and inaugurated the practice of giving late-afternoon floor speeches criticizing Democrats. The talks addressed an empty chamber but reached millions of homes via cable television, and he once so provoked the Democrats as to induce Speaker Thomas P. "Tip" O'Neill Jr. of Massachusetts to violate House rules in denouncing him.

Gingrich's 1988 complaint to the House ethics committee opened the inquiries that eventually toppled Speaker Jim Wright of Texas in 1989. It was also Gingrich who insisted the committee make a full disclosure of evidence gathered on Massachusetts Democrat Barney Frank's homosexuality.

Long dismissed by some as a personal fantast, Gingrich rode to institutional power on a wave of restlessness among House Republicans, frustrated by decades of minority status. His 1989 push for the the job of whip began within minutes of President Bush's announcement that he was nominating incumbent whip Dick Cheney of Wyoming to be secretary of Defense. At that moment, Gingrich had never held a leadership post and was regarded as a long-shot candidate.

His rival for the job, Edward Madigan of Illinois, had the consensus-building, bill-crafting skills traditionally associated with the whip's job. But Gingrich had what many House Republicans were looking for: something different.

His victory tapped into a growing feeling among Republicans that the Democratic majority was too heavy-handed in its use of power and that incumbent GOP leaders were too compliant. That disaffection ran so deep that some Republican moderates and even a few of the party's "Old Bulls" supported Gingrich, giving him a narrow, two-vote victory.

Gingrich owed his election as much to Wright as to anyone. Wright, in his drive to establish a reputation as a strong Speaker, galvanized all elements of the Republican Conference to a more confrontational style.

And Gingrich's ethics crusade against Wright, once it resulted in an investigation of unprecedented breadth, gave him legitimacy he would not otherwise have had.

Holding the party post has required Gingrich to channel his boundless intellectual and political energy more carefully, a challenge with which he constantly struggles.

"I've got to learn to make perfectly clear when I'm talking only about Newt Gingrich's view," he said in 1989.

When the GOP is riding high, Gingrich clearly relishes using his visibility as a leader to taunt the opposition. Throughout the Persian Gulf crisis, Gingrich goaded Democrats hesitant to support the use of military force. In the heady first days following the ouster of Iraqi troops from Kuwait, Gingrich crowed: "The last time they had a Democratic president they could not get eight helicopters across the desert" — an allusion to President Jimmy Carter's aborted effort to rescue U.S. hostages in Iran in 1980.

But in some high-profile situations, Gingrich has very clearly not been happy with the program set out by Republicans above him. Late in the 101st he rallied conservative House Republicans against the budget-summit agreement that incorporated Bush's capitulation on increasing taxes. Calling for aggressive tax cuts rather than compromise on the issue, Gingrich gave scores of House Republicans all the cover they needed to desert the president.

Times like those reinforce Gingrich's image as a partisan activist who cares primarily about cutting a sharper profile for his party, and only secondarily about passing legislation in the interim.

He earned a permanent place in the conservative pantheon in 1984, when he took on the apotheosis of liberalism: then-Speaker O'Neill.

Addressing a nearly empty chamber one night in May, Gingrich complained about a letter that 10 House Democrats had written to Nicaraguan leader Daniel Ortega, addressing him as "Dear Commandante" and calling for a settlement between political factions in that country. Gingrich said the letter was undermining U.S. foreign policy and possibly was illegal because it constituted negotiation by private citizens with a foreign power.

A few days later, O'Neill took the floor to charge that Gingrich had "challenged the Americanism of several Democratic members" at a time when they were not present to respond. O'Neill called that "the lowest thing that I have ever seen in my 32 years in Congress."

Republican whip Trent Lott of Mississippi moved that the Speaker's words be "taken down" — stricken from the record as inappropriate under House rules. Presiding officer Joe Moakley, a Massachusetts Democrat and close friend of O'Neill, had no choice but to accept Lott's motion — the first such embarrassment to a House Speaker since 1797.

Democrats have tried to draw attention to even the slightest whiff of impropriety on Gingrich's part, though with little success.

In 1989 he was accused of organizing various income streams that violated House rules, including a book deal some found comparable with the one that helped bring down Wright. But the ethics committee did not find enough merit in any of the allegations to justify any action.

And Gingrich was caught up in the House scandals of the 102nd, writing 22 overdrafts at the House bank and riding in a government-funded chauffeured car. He characterized the bank scandal and a subsequent controversy at the House Post Office as part of "a Democratic machine political scandal."

Gingrich's record of legislative accomplishment is as sparse as a backbencher's — as befits someone who cares more about big ideas and grand strategies than about passing bills.

But in his campaign as whip, Gingrich said

his ability to work with Democrats was abundantly evident in his work on two of the most bipartisan committees in Congress: Public Works and House Administration.

In a brief stint as ranking Republican on House Administration, Gingrich won a larger share of committee staff jobs for the GOP.

On Public Works, Gingrich could play the legislative game on the Aviation Subcommittee, where he became ranking minority member in 1987. That was a particularly useful spot for Gingrich, because Atlanta's huge Hartsfield International Airport was in his district.

At Home: After fighting hard to capture the 6th from Democratic hands in 1978, Gingrich appeared to have put his personal stamp on it. But complacence and a determined challenger dragged Gingrich to within 974 votes of a loss in 1990. His next election, thanks largely to redistricting and overdrafts at the House bank, was no easier.

The man who almost retired Gingrich in 1990 was Democrat David Worley, an aggressive young lawyer who was making his second bid for the 6th.

A party activist since his teens and a former aide to 4th District Democratic Rep. Elliott H. Levitas, Worley announced his first House campaign in mid-1987. His main thrust was a charge that Gingrich's proposed revamp of the nation's retirement system was actually a plot to destroy Social Security. He accused Gingrich of hypocrisy on ethics (pointing to, among other things, his efforts to have a political associate appointed a federal judge) and berated him for sympathizing with his scandal-plagued Georgia GOP colleague, Pat Swindall.

However, Gingrich proved again that he could give as good as he got. He portrayed Worley, a Harvard-educated district native, as a Boston liberal, and as a stooge of the ethically tarnished Speaker Wright. Gingrich ended up carrying all but one of the district's 12 counties.

Worley's 1988 showing left many Democrats unenthusiastic about 1990 — but not the candidate himself. Worley promptly announced he would try again and began an energetic campaign against Gingrich.

Worley's central argument in the rematch was that Gingrich had become enamored with national politics at the expense of district concerns. Worley slammed the incumbent for opposing federal mediation for the Eastern Airlines strike and stepping down from the Aviation Subcommittee during the airline's troubles. (Thousands of Eastern workers lived in the 6th.)

Worley also faulted Gingrich for supporting the 1989 congressional pay raise plan, although that stance appeared to cost him financial support from the Democratic Congressional Campaign Committee, due to a bipartisan agreement between party officials not to use the pay raise as a campaign issue.

Budget battles kept Gingrich in Washington most of the fall, bolstering Worley's portrait of the incumbent as out of touch. In the end, Gingrich prevailed by only 974 votes.

In 1992 redistricting, Gingrich saw his constituency completely carved up. His old district was south and west of Atlanta, but as redrawn, the 6th is anchored in Atlanta's northern suburbs. Even though it contains none of Gingrich's former constituents, it is laden with Republican voters, and Gingrich decided to move in and try for it.

That decision angered Republican Herman Clark, an Acworth attorney who had resigned his state House seat in the fall of 1991 to launch a House campaign in the redrawn 6th. Though Clark was not well-known in the district, he opted not to stand aside for the much higher-profile Gingrich and he dug in for a primary battle.

With a low-budget campaign, Clark hit Gingrich hard on the House bank scandal, congressional pay and members' perks. His most successful attack came in the form of a radio spot that had Georgians singing a ditty to the tune of "Old MacDonald Had a Farm" about Gingrich's 22 overdrafts, his support for a congressional pay raise and his use of a taxpayer-funded chauffeured Lincoln Town Car. Gingrich gave up the perk before the primary.

Gingrich did not fight back with the venom he had used in past campaigns, but his national visibility and superior financial resources helped him eke out a narrow victory over Clark.

Democrats, heartened by Gingrich's tepid victory in the primary, decided to take a second look at the winner of the Democratic primary, Tony Center, an Atlanta trial lawyer with a combative style. Center did not win the July primary outright but skated easily to victory in an August runoff.

Center, who also went after Gingrich on his overdrafts at the House bank and congressional perks, contended that Gingrich was vulnerable because he was in debt after spending $1.1 million for his bitter primary against Clark and because of the negative publicity from the primary race.

Both ran some of the campaign year's most personally nasty ads. Gingrich aired a spot claiming that Center had retained child-support payments owed to a single mother who had not paid Center's legal bill. Center retaliated with an ad saying Gingrich filed divorce papers the day after his first wife had cancer surgery, then left the family penniless.

But Center was not able to attract enough anti-Gingrich support, and Gingrich won a much more comfortable victory than in 1990.

Like many successful Republican politicians in the South, the Pennsylvania-born Gingrich is not a native. He spent his childhood in various military bases around the world before his family moved to Fort Benning, Ga. After receiving a graduate degree in European history, he taught history and geography at West Georgia College in Carrollton before launching his political career.

Gingrich set out after the 6th with his trademark intensity. Though Gingrich's 1974 campaign was his first political candidacy, he used professional polling and a hired staff, commodities rarely seen before in rural Georgia congressional contests. He surprised veteran Democratic Rep. John J. Flynt Jr., coming within 2,800 votes of victory. Two years later, Gingrich had to contend with a beefed-up Flynt campaign and Georgian Jimmy Carter heading the Democratic ticket. He lost again, but still drew more than 48 percent of the vote.

Flynt retired in 1978, leaving Gingrich as the best-known contender. In previous campaigns, Gingrich had been considered relatively liberal for a Georgia Republican, drawing much of his support from environmentalists. But in 1978 he relied on the tax-cut issue and stressed his opposition to U.S. transfer of the Panama Canal. He swept the northern portion of the district, defeating wealthy Democratic state Sen. Virginia Shapard by 7,600 votes.

After winning easily in 1980, Gingrich faced some difficulty in 1982 against Jim Wood, a Forest Park newspaper publisher and Democratic state representative who urged voters to pin the blame for harsh economic conditions on the GOP and Gingrich.

But the race was overshadowed by other contests around the state, and Wood had trouble getting his message out; Gingrich's ability to outspend him by better than 2-to-1 made the difference.

Gingrich had little trouble with the next two general election campaigns, taking 60 percent or better each time. His 1988 defeat of Worley had seemed to be another Democratic flub, but that race laid the groundwork for Worley's near-upset two years later.

Committees

Minority Whip

House Administration (2nd of 7 Republicans)
Accounts

Joint Printing

Elections

1992 General		
Newt Gingrich (R)	158,761	(58%)
Tony Center (D)	116,196	(42%)
1992 Primary		
Newt Gingrich (R)	35,699	(51%)
Herman Clark (R)	34,719	(49%)
1990 General		
Newt Gingrich (R)	78,768	(50%)
David Worley (D)	77,794	(50%)

Previous Winning Percentages: **1988** (59%) **1986** (60%) **1984** (69%) **1982** (55%) **1980** (59%) **1978** (54%)

District Vote for President

1992

D 82,355 (29%)
R 155,760 (56%)
I 41,876 (15%)

Campaign Finance

	Receipts	Receipts from PACs		Expend-itures
1992				
Gingrich (R)	$1,962,935	$653,712	(33%)	$1,963,810
Center (D)	$410,786	$129,650	(32%)	$410,807
1990				
Gingrich (R)	$1,538,827	$433,421	(28%)	$1,538,945
Worley (D)	$342,310	$163,190	(48%)	$333,873

Key Votes

1993	
Require parental notification of minors' abortions	Y
Require unpaid family and medical leave	N
Approve national "motor voter" registration bill	N
Approve budget increasing taxes and reducing deficit	N
Approve economic stimulus plan	N
1992	
Approve balanced-budget constitutional amendment	Y
Close down space station program	N
Approve U.S. aid for former Soviet Union	Y
Allow shifting funds from defense to domestic programs	N
1991	
Extend unemployment benefits using deficit financing	N
Approve waiting period for handgun purchases	N
Authorize use of force in Persian Gulf	Y

Voting Studies

	Presidential Support		Party Unity		Conservative Coalition	
Year	**S**	**O**	**S**	**O**	**S**	**O**
1992	76	10	82	5	85	2
1991	78	19	88	7	95	5
1990	66	29	83	8	94	4
1989	87	9	71	24	88	7
1988	62	32	80	6	92	3
1987	67	28	87	4	93	5
1986	72	23	85	8	80	14
1985	68	30	84	7	89	9
1984	60	29	83	9	86	8
1983	72	24	83	10	87	8
1982	70	26	78	18	75	12
1981	64	24	75	17	76	15

Interest Group Ratings

Year	ADA	AFL-CIO	CCUS	ACU
1992	10	22	88	100
1991	5	17	100	100
1990	17	25	92	86
1989	0	8	100	88
1988	5	15	100	100
1987	4	13	93	96
1986	0	14	94	81
1985	10	12	95	81
1984	5	8	60	78
1983	10	6	79	91
1982	5	10	75	86
1981	10	0	100	92

7 George "Buddy" Darden (D)

Of Marietta — Elected 1983; 5th Full Term

Born: Nov. 22, 1943, Hancock County, Ga.
Education: U. of Georgia, B.A. 1965, J.D. 1967.
Occupation: Lawyer.
Family: Wife, Lillian Budd; two children.
Religion: Methodist.
Political Career: Cobb County district attorney, 1973-77; Ga. House, 1981-83.
Capitol Office: 2303 Rayburn Bldg. 20515; 225-2931.

In Washington: Darden is a centrist Democrat who complained in 1989 that his party's House leadership was "a detriment to my electability" because it was shutting out Southerners. Times have changed. Now, two sons of the South are running the country and Darden himself does his House business from the lofty perch of the Appropriations Committee, where he won a place in 1993. A pretty fair legislative activist even in the 1980s, now Darden is positioned to be a real insider.

There had been signs before the 103rd Congress that the leadership and Darden were finding the same wavelength. He was named at-large whip, and in 1991 he was assigned to the House ethics committee, a position that usually goes to low-key and reliable party insiders.

Darden supported President Clinton on the two key economic votes of early 1993 — passage of the administration's budget plan and approval of its stimulus package — but Darden still can depart from the Democratic script on some high-profile issues. He opposed legislation mandating unpaid family and medical leave, for example, on the grounds that it could hurt business. "I think these situations ought to be worked out between employer and employee on an individual basis," Darden said.

And in January 1991, he voted for the resolution authorizing President Bush to use force to end Iraq's occupation of Kuwait.

In moving to Appropriations, Darden traded in his assignments on Armed Services and Interior, but he is in an excellent position to keep working in his (and his district's) major area of interest, defense. He sits on Appropriations' Defense Subcommittee, a good spot to look out for the interests of Lockheed, a major employer in his district.

When he was on Armed Services, Darden forged a close working relationship with then-Chairman Les Aspin, now the secretary of Defense. Darden backed Aspin during a 1987 challenge to his chairmanship waged by Marvin Leath of Texas. Aspin remembered Darden's loyalty, putting him on the Defense Policy Panel, which analyzed long-term defense policy issues.

From Armed Services, Darden in 1992 supported Lockheed's successful bid to secure a contract to build the F-22 Advanced Tactical Fighter; the contract is worth an estimated $80 billion over the next 10 to 15 years. Darden also played a role in seeing that the 1993 defense authorization bill contained $2.9 billion for aircraft built or modified at Lockheed.

Darden made his first big mark in the House with a determined, though unsuccessful, effort during the 100th Congress to save from extinction a Lockheed defense project, the C5-B cargo plane.

While on the Interior Committee and its National Parks and Public Lands Subcommittee in the 101st Congress, Darden worked on two controversial issues involving land use in the western United States.

Darden offered a proposal aimed at ending the regulations (in place since the 19th century) that allow ranchers to pay very low fees to graze their cattle on federally owned rangelands. His bill requiring ranchers to pay fair market value for grazing rights failed in the 101st and 102nd Congresses.

Darden also made his own bid to settle a long-running dispute over Nevada wilderness legislation. He put forward a bill that would have designated 1.4 million acres in 19 areas of Nevada for wilderness protection. A Senate bill, which covered 733,000 acres in 14 areas, was signed into law in 1989.

The ethics committee was quite busy during the 102nd Congress looking into the House bank and post office scandals. But Darden was one of several members who had to recuse themselves from participation in the bank inquiry; he had 35 overdrafts.

At Home: Darden's 1983 special-election victory over Rep. Larry McDonald's widow, Kathryn, was the first congressional victory in a decade for the 7th's mainstream Democrats. Larry McDonald, whose outspoken allegiance

Georgia 7

Northwest — Rome; part of Marietta

Starting in suburbs north and west of Atlanta, the 7th runs west to the Alabama border, taking in 10 full counties and part of another. But in terms of population concentration, it is bottom-heavy. Nearly half the district's voters live in just three counties that adjoin Atlanta's Fulton County — Cobb, Douglas and Carroll.

The 7th delivered a split verdict in the 1992 election. For president, the district preferred George Bush, who won 47 percent of the vote; Bill Clinton managed to carry only four largely rural counties on the Alabama border. But in voting for the House, Democratic Rep. Darden polled 57 percent, carrying all but one of the counties in the district.

The 7th takes in the southwestern part of Cobb County, including part of the city of Marietta. This is Darden's home base; he took 56 percent of the Cobb vote in 1992, even as those same voters backed Bush for president. The county is a collection of largely white-collar, middle-income suburbs.

The Marietta area has a diverse economic base, with numerous small businesses, several corporate headquarters and military- and aerospace-related employment at Lockheed and the Dobbins Air Reserve Base. The Lockheed facility laid off several thousand workers in the late 1980s, but a new contract to manufacture the F-22 advanced tactical fighter is expected to provide about 1,500 jobs in coming years.

Cobb's neighbor to the south is Douglas County, the only county in the 7th that gave a majority to Darden's Republican challenger in 1992. Bush carried Douglas with 50 percent. Thanks to the expansion of west-of-Atlanta bedroom communities, Douglas saw its population grow by 25 percent during the 1980s.

Moving beyond the metropolitan Atlanta orbit, the land is given over to agricultural pursuits, and there are a number of small towns traditionally reliant on textile trades. A number of the counties on the western edge of the 7th endured economic difficulties in the 1980s and are searching for new sources of income. Chattooga County now has a state prison; an Anheuser Busch brewery is coming into Bartow County. The biggest city in this part of 7th is Rome, the seat of Floyd County. Rome is a mill town that was once the district's largest city. Though eclipsed now by Marietta, it is a regional health-care center.

In 1992, Floyd County went narrowly for Bush but decisively for Darden; traditional Democratic voting patterns remain fairly strong in the district's more rural counties. Clinton carried Chattooga County, north of Floyd, and he also won three of the four counties directly to the south (Polk, Haralson and Heard). Jobs in these counties are found in the beef and timber industries and with a few manufacturers.

At the southwestern extreme of the district, Troup County may be poised for industrial expansion and population growth. It lies midway between Atlanta and Columbus, with I-85 slicing across its middle.

1990 Population: 588,071. White 505,415 (86%), Black 75,813 (13%), Other 6,843 (1%). Hispanic origin 6,576 (1%). 18 and over 431,939 (73%), 62 and over 77,830 (13%). Median age: 32.

to the New Right made him a Democrat in name only, had his own bipartisan conservative network. (McDonald died when the Korean jetliner on which he was a passenger was shot down over the Soviet Union.)

Darden was elected in 1972 as Cobb County district attorney after five years as an assistant D.A., and he developed a reputation as a firm law-and-order prosecutor. But his re-election effort in 1976 failed because he was dogged by charges that he had bungled a 1971 murder investigation.

Darden went into private law practice. But in 1980, when one of Cobb County's seats in the state House opened up, he got the support of local Democratic officials and won easily.

After McDonald's death, Darden entered the nonpartisan House special election. Calling himself a "responsible conservative," he promised to fight "big spenders in Congress." Though Darden earned a runoff position, he trailed Kathryn McDonald in first-round voting. However, McDonald's roughshod tactics — including an attempt to link Darden to gay rights through his ties to organized labor — alienated voters. Darden swept past her to win with 59 percent.

Again in 1984, Darden defended himself against charges of liberalism, this time from conservative airline pilot William Bronson. In the face of Ronald Reagan's 1984 landslide, Darden won re-election with 55 percent of the vote, and he was at 60 percent or above in the next three elections.

In 1992, Darden faced a rematch with Republican Al Beverly, a former Georgia Tech researcher who had gotten 40 percent of the vote in his 1990 challenge to Darden. Darden still won comfortably, but slipped a bit, largely due to the impact of redistricting.

The new district map for Georgia, approved in 1992, significantly altered Darden's constituency: It shifted the 7th southward into suburban Atlanta territory that Republican Newt Gingrich had represented, leaving Darden with only three full counties from the district he had served.

But Darden's centrist brand of politics, his moderate manner and his vigorous campaign made a good enough impression on voters new to Darden that he won with 57 percent.

Committees

Appropriations (28th of 37 Democrats)
Defense; Treasury, Postal Service & General Government

Standards of Official Conduct (2nd of 7 Democrats)

Elections

1992 General		
George "Buddy" Darden (D)	111,374	(57%)
Al Beverly (R)	82,915	(43%)
1990 General		
George "Buddy" Darden (D)	95,817	(60%)
Al Beverly (R)	63,588	(40%)

Previous Winning Percentages: **1988** (65%) **1986** (66%) **1984** (55%) **1983** * (59%)

** Special runoff election.*

District Vote for President

1992

D	77,103 (38%)
R	93,175 (47%)
I	30,097 (15%)

Campaign Finance

	Receipts	Receipts from PACs		Expend-itures
1992				
Darden (D)	$410,958	$226,940	(55%)	$510,547
Beverly (R)	$40,956	$4,200	(10%)	$40,778
1990				
Darden (D)	$463,055	$238,006	(51%)	$480,886
Beverly (R)	$19,028	0		$18,692

Key Votes

1993	
Require parental notification of minors' abortions	N
Require unpaid family and medical leave	N
Approve national "motor voter" registration bill	Y
Approve budget increasing taxes and reducing deficit	Y
Approve economic stimulus plan	Y
1992	
Approve balanced-budget constitutional amendment	Y
Close down space station program	N
Approve U.S. aid for former Soviet Union	N
Allow shifting funds from defense to domestic programs	N
1991	
Extend unemployment benefits using deficit financing	Y
Approve waiting period for handgun purchases	Y
Authorize use of force in Persian Gulf	Y

Voting Studies

	Presidential Support		Party Unity		Conservative Coalition	
Year	**S**	**O**	**S**	**O**	**S**	**O**
1992	30	68	81	17	79	21
1991	49	50	81	18	89	11
1990	43	57	75	24	87	13
1989	56	42	72	28	90	7
1988	41	58	75	25	92	5
1987	43	57	68	30	91	9
1986	49	48	60	37	80	8
1985	51	46	67	31	87	13
1984	48	51	58	39	86	12
1983	40 †	60 †	48 †	48 †	100 †	0 †

† Not eligible for all recorded votes.

Interest Group Ratings

Year	ADA	AFL-CIO	CCUS	ACU
1992	70	58	50	32
1991	40	58	60	35
1990	28	50	57	58
1989	35	50	90	43
1988	45	64	64	50
1987	48	56	53	39
1986	10	31	82	79
1985	15	44	64	71
1984	30	38	44	54
1983	--	50	--	50

8 J. Roy Rowland (D)

Of Dublin — Elected 1982; 6th Term

Born: Feb. 3, 1926, Wrightsville, Ga.
Education: Emory U., Oxford, 1943; South Georgia College, 1946-47; U. of Georgia, 1947-48; Medical College of Georgia, M.D. 1952.
Military Service: Army, 1944-46.
Occupation: Physician.
Family: Wife, Luella Price; three children.
Religion: Methodist.
Political Career: Ga. House, 1977-83.
Capitol Office: 2134 Rayburn Bldg. 20515; 225-6531.

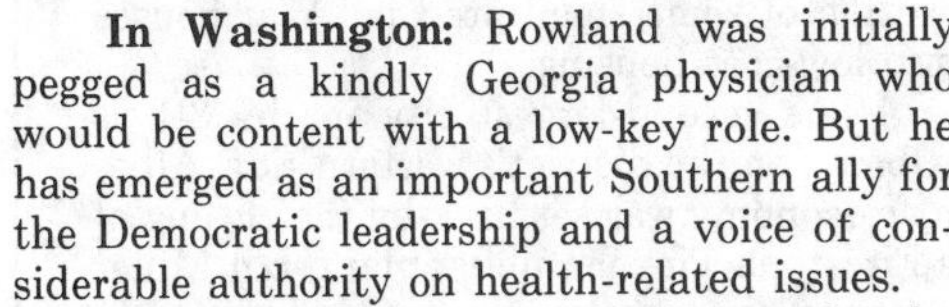

In Washington: Rowland was initially pegged as a kindly Georgia physician who would be content with a low-key role. But he has emerged as an important Southern ally for the Democratic leadership and a voice of considerable authority on health-related issues.

Rowland is not an automatic vote for the leadership. Like a number of other Southerners, he is more conservative than the majority of his party in the House, especially on fiscal matters. He voted for the balanced-budget constitutional amendment in 1992. And in 1993, he was one of just 22 House Democrats to vote against President Clinton's economic stimulus package, even though Clinton had telephoned him at home the night before the vote.

Rowland's background made him a key spokesman in the 102nd Congress on two abortion-related issues. Rowland spoke out against the "gag rule," which barred personnel at federally funded family planning clinics from mentioning abortion as an option for dealing with an unwanted pregnancy. He argued that the ban interfered with the doctor-patient relationship.

Rowland also joined those trying to overturn an executive branch ban on research using transplanted fetal tissue, saying that the Bush administration's plan to permit such research only with tissue from miscarriages "just won't work" because such tissue is often diseased. Although Congress failed to override President Bush's veto of bills lifting the gag rule and the fetal tissue ban, Clinton reversed the policies by executive action two days after taking office.

Early in the 103rd, Rowland voted to squelch a restrictive parental-notification rule on teenagers' abortions. He said he supported the concept of parental notice, but that the proposal pushed by Republican Thomas J. Bliley Jr. of Virginia went too far.

Rowland's manner does not mark him as an ambitious politician. He has always approached politics on Capitol Hill with the same soft voice and courteous manner that won him the nickname of "Marcus Welby, M.D." in the Georgia legislature. Even when addressing politically charged issues, he speaks in matter-of-fact, almost clinical language.

Still, Rowland put himself in the thick of two difficult issues in the 100th Congress, serving on leadership task forces dealing with controversial AIDS legislation and with contra aid. On both, his contribution proved valuable in terms both of substance and of symbolism. As a Southern conservative, Rowland is just the kind of Democrat the leadership needs to enhance its credibility across the political spectrum on sensitive issues. And on AIDS in particular, Rowland — one of only two physicians in the House — brings specific knowledge and even more authority.

Rowland's work won him a coveted slot on the Energy and Commerce Committee in the 101st Congress. Until then, Rowland had used his position on Veterans' Affairs to enter the AIDS debate. There in the 100th Congress, he introduced legislation, which ultimately became law, calling for an AIDS advisory commission, to succeed a much-criticized presidential panel.

Rowland was among those arguing that the Reagan administration had not done enough to address AIDS. "The AIDS virus does not stop at state boundary lines," he said. "It is a national problem and we need a national strategy."

At the end of 1988, Congress moved closer to mapping that strategy, authorizing $650 million for education, anonymous testing, and home and community-based health care.

During the 101st Congress, Rowland continued to speak out on AIDS issues from his new berth on the Health Subcommittee at Energy and Commerce. When some international scientists pledged to boycott an AIDS conference in San Francisco because of U.S. regulations forbidding entry to foreigners infected with the virus, Rowland introduced legislation to repeal the congressional mandate for the ban. His proposal passed as part of another bill, and the Bush administration subsequently lifted the restriction.

On another medical issue, Rowland won passage in the 101st Congress for his bill to streamline claim processing for Medicare.

Rowland's 1986 vote to give military aid to

Georgia 8

South Central — Warner Robins; parts of Albany, Valdosta and Macon

Covering a 32-county swath of south-central Georgia, the 8th is largely rural. In 1992, a majority of those 32 counties cast fewer than 5,000 votes apiece in the presidential contest.

But on the edges of the district, the 8th includes parts of four urbanized areas — Macon (Bibb County), Warner Robins (Houston County), Albany (Dougherty County) and Valdosta (Lowndes County).

Those four counties account for more than 40 percent of the total district vote. All four supported George Bush's re-election, and three of the four went against Rep. Rowland in his 1992 House election, which he won with 56 percent of the vote.

Redistricting in 1992 made the 8th more politically competitive. In his old district, Rowland had never gotten less than 69 percent of the vote. But remapping deprived him of many reliably Democratic black voters in the 8th's urban areas. Blacks now are 21 percent of the district's population, down from 35 percent in the 1980s.

Basically, what remains in those urban areas are whites — many of them conservative religious activists — who tend to vote Republican. On the strength of their support, Bush carried the 8th over Bill Clinton, even though Clinton won nearly all the 8th's less-populous counties.

Contributing to the 8th's conservative tenor are three large military bases — Robins Air Force Base (in Warner Robins), Moody Air Force Base (in Valdosta) and the Marine Corps Logistics Center (in Albany). The bases are the 8th's largest employers, but the district's economy also depends heavily on agriculture, particularly pecans and peanuts.

In the northwestern corner of the district is Macon, an old textile and railroad town that has long been a trading and processing center for the agricultural lands of middle Georgia that surround it. From here, Atlanta is just a little more than an hour up Interstate 75, but the boom in the capital region has not had a great impact in Macon. The city's population dropped almost 9 percent during the 1980s, to 107,000. Macon has a cherry blossom festival that draws thousands of visitors each spring, and there are redevelopment and preservation efforts, including renovation of some small pre-Civil War houses into low-cost housing.

The second-largest city in the 8th is Albany, on the district's western side. Albany's economy was set back by the closing of a Firestone Tire & Rubber plant, but Miller Brewing (beer), Procter & Gamble (paper products) and Coats and Clark (thread) remain as major employers.

Just a few miles short of Florida is Valdosta (Lowndes County). Surrounded by the vast reaches of south Georgia's Piney Woods, it makes much of its living from the forests, with planing and paper mills and sawmills providing many paychecks.

Although the 8th's more urbanized areas were a struggle for Rowland in 1992, he typically amassed sizable margins elsewhere in the district, where Democratic traditions are strong. He won Laurens County, his home base, with 72 percent.

1990 Population: 591,615. White 459,956 (78%), Black 124,257 (21%), Other 7,402 (1%). Hispanic origin 8,294 (1%). 18 and over 427,447 (72%), 62 and over 84,406 (14%). Median age: 32.

the Nicaraguan contras was no surprise, given Georgia's conservatism. But in 1988, Rowland stood apart from all but one of his state's House delegation — John Lewis of Atlanta — and voted against President Ronald Reagan's request for $36 million in military and non-military aid. Later, Rowland helped fashion a non-military aid package that became law, altering his image in the eyes of more liberal members.

Rowland predictably has directed most of his energy toward the health issues under Energy and Commerce's jurisdiction. But he also played a significant role in some non-health matters, including the laborious redrafting of the Clean Air Act. Rowland arrived on the committee just in time for the complex negotiations over that bill. Chairman John D. Dingell of Michigan and Health and Environment Subcommittee Chairman Henry A. Waxman of California had deadlocked over how much automakers should be required to do to limit auto emissions. Rowland worked behind the scenes to help fashion a compromise on that key provision, enabling the overall bill to move ahead.

Mostly, however, Rowland's legislative interests flow out of his medical career. Rowland takes a special interest in research to reduce infant-mortality rates and has served on a national and regional commission on the subject.

Rowland had been in the House less than a month in 1983 when he introduced legislation to make use of the drug methaqualone (Quaalude) illegal. It had been available as a prescription medicine for insomnia, but Rowland argued that it was being abused. A version of the bill became law in 1984.

Also during his first term, Rowland joined with Arkansas Republican John Paul Hammerschmidt to propose compensating veterans exposed to ionizing radiation during atomic-bomb tests; the measure was included in the Agent Orange bill passed by the House early in 1984.

At Home: Rowland grew up with politics as the common coin of dinner table conversations — his father was a district attorney and superior court judge, and his grandfather and uncle were members of the state legislature.

But Rowland himself opted for medicine. It was not until 1976, the year he turned 50, that he decided to run for office. He challenged his local Democratic state representative, with a coalition drawn largely from outside the area's political establishment, and won.

In 1982, he scored a similar victory for Congress. Democratic Rep. Billy Lee Evans had drawn embarrassing publicity when the Federal Election Commission fined his campaign for accepting illegal corporate contributions and illegal loans in 1980. The issue did its damage without much help from Rowland.

Rowland's reluctance to hit hard served him well. Evans became more acerbic as the campaign wore on, and this alienated voters. Evans accused his opponent of performing abortions. Rowland acknowledged that he had and said he had done two such operations to save the women's lives.

While Rowland was taking the high road, another challenger, lawyer Edd Wheeler, was attacking Evans directly. He attracted less than 10 percent of the primary vote, but he softened Evans up for Rowland. Still, Wheeler's presence deprived Rowland of an immediate victory in the primary and forced a runoff.

Evans sought the black vote during the runoff campaign. He did well in many black precincts, but it was not enough. Rowland increased his margin of victory the second time, carrying 20 of 30 counties, up from 13 in the primary. In his first two encounters with GOP opposition, in 1986 and 1990, he won both times.

Redistricting altered the geographic character of the 8th, depriving Rowland of much of the northern half of his old district for the 1992 election. It helped cut into Rowland's victory margin because his base of black voters was removed, but the changes were not enough to allow Republican Robert F. Cunningham to defeat Rowland in his second try. Cunningham took 44 percent to Rowland's 56 percent.

Committees

Energy & Commerce (16th of 27 Democrats)
Commerce, Consumer Protection & Competitiveness; Health & the Environment; Transportation & Hazardous Materials

Veterans' Affairs (6th of 21 Democrats)
Hospitals & Health Care (chairman); Education, Training & Employment

Elections

1992 General		
J. Roy Rowland (D)	108,472	(56%)
Bob Cunningham (R)	86,220	(44%)
1992 Primary		
J. Roy Rowland (D)	85,689	(68%)
Bill Lightle (D)	41,153	(32%)
1990 General		
J. Roy Rowland (D)	81,344	(69%)
Robert F. Cunningham (R)	36,980	(31%)

Previous Winning Percentages: **1988** (100%) **1986** (86%) **1984** (100%) **1982** (100%)

District Vote for President

	1992
D	80,093 (40%)
R	89,105 (45%)
I	30,399 (15%)

Campaign Finance

	Receipts	Receipts from PACs		Expend-itures
1992				
Rowland (D)	$454,319	$286,099	(63%)	$544,898
Cunningham (R)	$215,170	$5,000	(2%)	$210,233
1990				
Rowland (D)	$368,200	$228,050	(62%)	$365,513
Cunningham (R)	$106,278	$2,250	(2%)	$105,270

Key Votes

1993	
Require parental notification of minors' abortions	N
Require unpaid family and medical leave	N
Approve national "motor voter" registration bill	N
Approve budget increasing taxes and reducing deficit	Y
Approve economic stimulus plan	N
1992	
Approve balanced-budget constitutional amendment	Y
Close down space station program	Y
Approve U.S. aid for former Soviet Union	N
Allow shifting funds from defense to domestic programs	N
1991	
Extend unemployment benefits using deficit financing	#
Approve waiting period for handgun purchases	Y
Authorize use of force in Persian Gulf	Y

Voting Studies

	Presidential Support		Party Unity		Conservative Coalition	
Year	**S**	**O**	**S**	**O**	**S**	**O**
1992	44	52	70	29	85	10
1991	50	47	70	21	84	5
1990	42	58	73	22	91	9
1989	52	45	73	25	98	2
1988	36	62	79	18	82	8
1987	43	57	71	25	93	7
1986	44	56	73	27	88	12
1985	50	50	75	25	96	4
1984	50	48	71	27	78	19
1983	44	55	60	38	88	12

Interest Group Ratings

Year	ADA	AFL-CIO	CCUS	ACU
1992	50	58	63	48
1991	35	45	67	42
1990	33	42	57	42
1989	30	42	90	54
1988	55	57	69	46
1987	40	44	67	30
1986	40	50	56	55
1985	30	41	45	67
1984	45	62	44	42
1983	40	31	55	65

9 Nathan Deal (D)

Of Gainesville — Elected 1992; 1st Term

Born: Aug. 25, 1942, Millen, Ga.
Education: Mercer U., A.B. 1964, J.D. 1966.
Military Service: Army, 1966-68.
Occupation: Lawyer.
Family: Wife, Sandra Dunagan; four children.
Religion: Baptist.
Political Career: Ga. Senate, 1981-93, president pro tempore, 1991-93.
Capitol Office: 1406 Longworth Bldg. 20515; 225-5211.

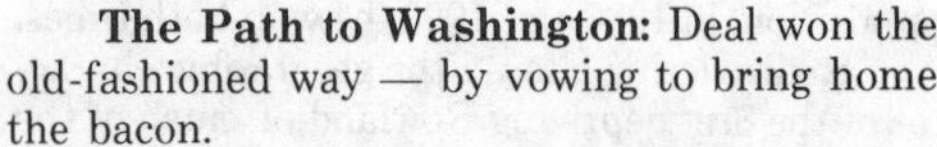

The Path to Washington: Deal won the old-fashioned way — by vowing to bring home the bacon.

Parochial interests took a back seat to national issues such as deficit reduction and congressional reform in most 1992 campaigns, but Deal overcame Daniel Becker in part because of his promise to seek federal funding for better roadways through the rugged mountains of the 9th District.

Deal will be in a good position to deliver on that promise. He won a seat on the Public Works and Transportation Committee, which authorizes funding for highway and bridge construction. Deal also won a slot on the Natural Resources Committee, which oversees the nation's parks and public lands, including the Chattahoochee National Forest and Chickamauga National Battlefield in the district.

Deal replaces retired Democratic Rep. Ed Jenkins, who was considered an expert in the quieter side of deal-making, often leaving few fingerprints on legislation. Jenkins had fended off challengers easily since 1976, but the affluent Atlanta suburbs, which tilt Republican, had begun to cut into his margins.

Deal, in his march to succeed Jenkins, voiced views in line with many voters in the conservative district, including support for a balanced-budget constitutional amendment, presidential line-item veto and capital gains tax cut. Deal also argued against a national single-payer health-care program, which he equated with "socialized medicine."

While ultimately voting for both President Clinton's budget and $16.3 billion stimulus package, he voted against a rule supported by the president and Democratic leadership that prevented opponents from amending the stimulus package, one of only 13 Democrats to do so.

An early ally of deficit hawk and Democratic Southern conservative Charles W. Stenholm of Texas, Deal supported a Stenholm amendment, blocked by the rule, that would have required that any money in the package spent after Sept. 30, 1993, be offset by spending cuts. Deal explained, "In my district 'change' means 'stop deficit spending.' "

Deal was also one of only 29 Democrats to vote against mandated family leave legislation that Clinton signed into law in February 1993.

After winning a seat in the state Senate in 1980, Deal had become accustomed to uneventful election victories during his tenure as a senator. He ran unopposed in his five re-election bids. But his road to Congress was not without obstacles.

He was forced into a runoff after winning 45 percent of the vote in the three-candidate primary; he won the runoff by 10 points. (Becker secured the GOP nomination with 53 percent of the vote in a runoff.)

The general-election campaign provided a challenge of a different sort. The 9th District contest was one of the few House races to attract national media coverage, but it was Becker who was the subject of that coverage.

Becker was one of more than a dozen congressional candidates to air anti-abortion television ads featuring graphic photos of allegedly aborted fetuses. He began airing the ads during the GOP primary and continued to air them until Election Day.

Although Deal supports abortion rights (with restrictions such as parental notification for minors), Becker's ads condemned abortion in general rather than criticizing Deal directly.

But while the ads did make voters aware of Becker's candidacy, the publicity may have done more harm than good.

Becker made abortion the focus of a "morality in government" campaign that sought to link the nation's social and economic ills to U.S. Supreme Court rulings outlawing prayer in public schools and legalizing abortion. Deal dismissed Becker's argument that the nation's problems would go away if the government did more to encourage morality.

Becker's conservative views appealed to a substantial bloc of voters but not enough to put the traditionally Democratic seat in the Republican column. Deal defeated Becker, winning 59 percent of the vote.

Georgia 9

North — Dalton; Gainesville; Toccoa

The 9th, anchored in north Georgia's mountains, runs across the state, from Alabama on the west to South Carolina on the east. At the local level, Democrats have long been dominant in most parts of the district, and when the 9th was open in 1992, Democrat Deal easily held it for his party.

The GOP, however, is gaining here.

The 9th has Republican pockets of long standing, particularly in the north-central counties of Union, Fannin, Gilmer and Towns counties; their allegiance to the GOP dates to the Civil War. And now, Republicans are becoming more prevalent in the southern part of the district, where Cherokee and Forsyth counties are filling up with Atlanta suburbanites.

Cherokee and Forsyth both gave a majority of their 1992 presidential votes to George Bush. In fact, despite his struggles nationally, Bush ran reasonably well all across the 9th, losing only two counties to Bill Clinton. The district also was strong for GOP Senate candidate Paul Coverdell.

In economic terms, the 9th is a blend of new and old. For many of those living in the metropolitan Atlanta orbit, white-collar and service-oriented occupations pay the bills. Elsewhere, apparel manufacturing, poultry processing and carpet-making are major providers, and tourism and recreation are increasingly important.

The raising and processing of chickens is big business in Hall County (Gainesville) and Whitfield County (Dalton), the district's two most populous. Gainesville calls itself the "poultry capital of the world," and in the center of town is the Georgia Poultry Federation's monument to the industry: an obelisk with a chicken statue on top. Hall went easily for Bush in 1992, but in the House race it voted by better than 2-to-1 for Deal, whose home is Gainesville.

Dalton, in the northwestern part of the district, is one of the country's top carpet-making centers. Despite its substantial blue-collar employment base, Whitfield County generally favors Republicans in competitive elections for state or federal office. Bush got 54 percent in Whitfield, and Coverdell also carried it. Deal ran below his districtwide average of 59 percent in the county, but he still won it comfortably.

In the district's extreme northwestern corner are Walker, Catoosa and Dade counties, conservative pillars whose economic fortunes are linked to Chattanooga, just over the border in Tennessee.

Millions who have never set foot in Georgia have seen its rugged northeastern corner on film. "Deliverance" was set in Rabun County, and "Smokey and the Bandit" was made in the area.

Tourist dollars play a crucial role in the district's economy. Dotting the mountains are an array of attractions, including Cloudland Canyon (Walker County), the manmade Lake Lanier (Hall County), the wineries of Habersham County, and, in White County, the hamlet of Helen, a Swiss village replica, and the Cabbage Patch Hospital, a shop decorated like a hospital where visitors can buy Cabbage Patch dolls.

1990 Population: 586,222. White 554,871 (95%), Black 21,516 (4%), Other 9,835 (2%). Hispanic origin 9,814 (2%). 18 and over 436,725 (74%), 62 and over 84,045 (14%). Median age: 33.

Committees

Natural Resources (21st of 28 Democrats)
Energy & Mineral Resources; Oversight & Investigations

Public Works & Transportation (34th of 39 Democrats)
Economic Development; Water Resources & the Environment

Science, Space & Technology (29th of 33 Democrats)
Technology, Environment & Aviation

Campaign Finance

	Receipts	Receipts from PACs	Expend-itures
1992			
Deal (D)	$420,897	$97,900 (23%)	$404,730
Becker (R)	$161,110	$3,174 (2%)	$161,060

Key Votes

1993

Require parental notification of minors' abortions	N
Require unpaid family and medical leave	N
Approve national "motor voter" registration bill	N
Approve budget increasing taxes and reducing deficit	Y
Approve economic stimulus plan	Y

Elections

1992 General		
Nathan Deal (D)	113,024	(59%)
Daniel Becker (R)	77,919	(41%)
1992 Primary Runoff		
Nathan Deal (D)	43,275	(55%)
Thomas P. Ramsey III (D)	35,213	(45%)
1992 Primary		
Nathan Deal (D)	40,634	(45%)
Thomas P. Ramsey III (D)	31,058	(35%)
Wyc Orr (D)	17,725	(20%)

District Vote for President

	1992
D	70,969 (35%)
R	98,184 (49%)
I	32,806 (16%)

10 Don Johnson (D)

Of Royston — Elected 1992; 1st Term

Born: Jan. 30, 1948, Royston, Ga.
Education: U. of Georgia, B.A. 1970, J.D. 1973; London School of Economics, LL.M. 1978.
Military Service: Air Force, 1973-77.
Occupation: Lawyer.
Family: Wife, Suzanne Spratlin; three children.
Religion: Baptist.
Political Career: Ga. Senate, 1987-93.
Capitol Office: 226 Cannon Bldg. 20515; 225-4101.

The Path to Washington: The retirement of 16-year incumbent Democrat Doug Barnard Jr. opened the door for newcomer Johnson to win this east Georgia district. But though he was a secure, inside player in the Georgia legislature, Johnson had to run hard against the Washington establishment to win.

A prominent member of the state Senate, Johnson helped draw the 10th to his liking. Its lines were moved north to incorporate Jackson, Banks, Franklin and Hart counties and take in Johnson's base. Johnson began the campaign as the best-known Democrat in a thinly Democratic district. Like Barnard, he is fairly conservative, especially on economic issues. He was one of 29 Democrats to vote against mandatory family leave legislation that Bill Clinton signed into law in February 1993, though he supported the president's budget and $16.3 billion economic stimulus package.

On social matters, Johnson has a more moderate record, which could prove troublesome if he is to hold on to this seat.

He made a name for himself as chairman of the state Senate Appropriations Committee, fighting against legislative pork barreling and helping to turn the appropriations process into one that targeted critical needs, not geographically balanced largess.

He prefers to try to eliminate the federal budget deficit without increasing taxes. But he says he would keep an open mind about tax increases to pay for programs that he thinks are underfinanced, such as education. (He sponsored a local-option sales tax for school construction that passed the state Senate in 1991.)

Johnson also claims credit for opening his committee's deliberations to women and minorities, and he would like to bring the same sort of reform to Congress by forcing more turnover in chairmanships and other leadership posts.

His seats on the Armed Services and Science committees will be of key interest to his constituents. Fort Gordon, home of the Army Signal Corps, lies at the bottom corner of the 10th. And the district is home to two significant research schools, the Medical College of Georgia in Augusta and the University of Georgia in Athens. Johnson favors federal aid to emerging technologies as a way to boost jobs, and he views biological science and health care as prime targets for such aid.

Two factors made winning this seat difficult for Johnson. The first was that he had to face an incumbent. Redistricting, which made a mess of Georgia's map in order to meet Justice Department requirements to create two new majority-black districts, forced several white incumbents to choose new districts. Among them was two-term Democrat Ben Jones, who abandoned his old 4th district, which had become marginally Republican, to run in the 10th.

Johnson was forced to run against Jones in the primary. In this Bible Belt district, however, Johnson found it easy to run to the right of Jones. Johnson tarred the incumbent with his votes for a pay raise and other congressional perks and against releasing to a special prosecutor documents involving bad checks drawn on the House bank.

Jones complained to no avail about the negative campaign. And Johnson deflected Jones' own charge that as Appropriations chairman he had known of abuse by legislators of a special state budget account. Johnson won 53 percent in a five-way primary.

Johnson's second obstacle proved to be the loss of Democratic areas becuause of redistricting. Although the 10th remained slightly Democratic, black precincts in Wilkes, Warren and Richmond (Augusta) counties were ceded to the new black-majority 11th. Although Augusta used to provide Barnard's victory margin, the portion left in the 10th was heavily Republican.

Nevertheless, Johnson won 54 percent in the general election to beat Republican Ralph Hudgens, state head of the Agricultural Stabilization and Conservation Service since 1989.

Hudgens, who ran unsuccessfully in 1988 against Democratic Rep. Charles Hatcher in the 2nd, tried but failed to paint Johnson as too liberal for the district, attacking his support for the Freedom of Choice Act and his local-option sales tax bill.

Georgia 10

Northeast — Athens; Augusta suburbs

This 19-county chunk of eastern Georgia has clumps of population at both ends and in the middle, and its voters are a mix of staunchly conservative Republicans, steadfast liberal Democrats and middle-of-the-roaders. In 1992, the contest for the open 10th District seat was one of Georgia's most competitive: Democrat Johnson won with 54 percent over GOP nominee Ralph Hudgens.

The district has two Republican bulwarks. The biggest is on the east, in the Augusta suburbs and exurbs of Richmond and Columbia counties. On the western edge of the 10th, the GOP is strong in Gwinnett County (which is split between the 10th, 4th and 6th districts).

Taken together, those two population concentrations cast almost 40 percent of the district vote, and they helped George Bush carry the 10th in 1992 presidential voting.

Between them is a stretch of counties that remains largely rural. Many of their voters are traditionally Democratic; Bill Clinton carried a half-dozen of the lightly settled counties in 1992.

But he found his strongest support at the center of the district, in Clarke County, home to the University of Georgia. Its 28,700 students and nearly 2,000 faculty members have moved Clarke well to the left of the district mainstream; Clinton carried the county with 53 percent of the vote. Tempering the liberal influence of the university community are military and civilian employees at the Navy Supply Corps School. It adds about $3 million yearly to the local economy.

In the Augusta area, conservative-minded white-collar suburbanites mingle with a substantial population of active-duty and retired military personnel associated with Fort Gordon, home of the Army Signal Corps. Though the city of Augusta itself is mostly in the 11th District, the 10th has the bulk of surrounding Richmond County. Bush won 52 percent here in 1992, and to the north in neighboring Columbia County, he soared to a 59 percent tally.

Other large employers in this part of the 10th are the Medical College of Georgia and the federal government's Savannah River nuclear facility, located just downriver in South Carolina's Aiken and Barnwell counties. The plant, which processed tritium for use in nuclear weapons, has been stymied by safety and environmental problems in recent years.

At the district's northeastern corner, bordering Hart County, is Hartwell Lake, one of the largest man-made lakes in the country. To the west, there is a Mitsubishi plant in Jackson County, and the little town of Braselton there made headlines recently when actress Kim Basinger purchased it for $20 million. Heading south, the 10th meanders through cotton, soybean, tobacco and corn-growing country.

At its western edge, the 10th's portion of Gwinnett County is less densely settled than the areas of the county in the 4th and 6th districts, but Republican preferences are almost as strong. Bush won 52 percent in the 10th District part of Gwinnett.

1990 Population: 591,644. White 475,141 (80%), Black 106,916 (18%), Other 9,587 (2%). Hispanic origin 6,964 (1%). 18 and over 439,254 (74%), 62 and over 75,138 (13%). Median age: 31.

Committees

Armed Services (23rd of 34 Democrats)
Military Installations & Facilities; Oversight & Investigations; Research & Technology

Science, Space & Technology (23rd of 33 Democrats)
Investigations & Oversight; Science; Technology, Environment & Aviation

Campaign Finance

	Receipts	Receipts from PACs		Expend-itures
1992				
Johnson (D)	$630,138	$161,235	(26%)	$623,406
Hudgens (R)	$189,780	$24,318	(13%)	$182,637

Key Votes

1993

Require parental notification of minors' abortions	N
Require unpaid family and medical leave	N
Approve national "motor voter" registration bill	Y
Approve budget increasing taxes and reducing deficit	Y
Approve economic stimulus plan	Y

Elections

1992 General		
Don Johnson (D)	108,426	(54%)
Ralph Hudgens (R)	93,059	(46%)
1992 Primary		
Don Johnson (D)	45,891	(53%)
Ben Jones (D)	25,924	(30%)
Marc Wetherhorn (D)	5,250	(6%)
Doug Bower (D)	5,018	(6%)
Chuck Pardue (D)	4,848	(6%)

District Vote for President

	1992	
D	81,014	(39%)
R	95,164	(46%)
I	29,452	(14%)

11 Cynthia A. McKinney (D)

Of Lithonia — Elected 1992; 1st Term

Born: March 17, 1955, Atlanta, Ga.
Education: U. of Southern California, B.A. 1978.
Occupation: Professor.
Family: Divorced; one child.
Religion: Roman Catholic.
Political Career: Democratic nominee for Ga. House, 1986; Ga. House, 1989-93.
Capitol Office: 124 Cannon Bldg. 20515; 225-1605.

The Path to Washington: A polite and helpful manner only partly masks McKinney's essentially tough nature. Her outspokenness and an unwillingness to compromise were hallmarks of McKinney's four years in the Georgia legislature. They were the keys to her electoral success, and they are likely to be her signature in the House.

McKinney has the distinction of being the first black woman ever elected to the House from Georgia, where she has a relatively meager record of legislative accomplishment.

She raised questions about the state government's willingness to contract with minority-owned businesses — scoring a modest success when Gov. Zell Miller issued an executive order requiring increased emphasis on minority contracting. But she failed in a bid to repeal the state's sodomy ban.

Rather, McKinney made her name by challenging the establishment at every turn. In January 1991, two-thirds of the state House walked out during her speech criticizing the Persian Gulf War. And McKinney gave herself a campaign issue by helping lead the charge for greater black representation in Congress and in state and local offices, challenging redistricting plans across the state.

Early in the 103rd Congress, McKinney forwarded to the White House health-care task force concerns from her constituents that proposals under consideration would harm minority health-care providers.

She won her seat by moving into a new black-majority district, running an aggressive, if low-budget, primary campaign and overwhelming two better-financed, better-connected black legislators.

McKinney went after longtime state Sen. Eugene Walker, a De Kalb resident and the presumptive favorite for the Democratic nomination when the campaign began, and state Rep. Michael Thurmond, chairman of the state House black caucus who won the endorsement of the Atlanta Constitution. McKinney branded both as being too closely connected to the state's dominant white Democratic power structure and unresponsive to Georgia's black voters.

Walker hit McKinney for abandoning the Fulton County constituency she had represented in the state House since 1989 to run for Congress. She officially moved to De Kalb County just after the General Assembly adjourned its 1992 session.

But McKinney may have done herself the most good with black voters in the 11th by helping lead the reapportionment fight in the legislature for a third black-majority district in the southwest part of the state.

Walker, an ally of Gov. Miller, chaired the Senate reapportionment committee and helped craft two different maps that would have left the new 2nd with a majority of white voters. Walker defended the plans and said McKinney was unwilling to compromise and thus was an ineffective legislator. But McKinney prevailed when the Justice Department rejected both maps for failing to protect minority interests under the Voting Rights Act. Eventually the legislature redrew the 2nd District to include a majority of blacks.

During the primary, McKinney won the endorsement of Andrew Young, for whom she campaigned during his failed 1990 gubernatorial bid against Miller. And a share of McKinney's victory was claimed by her father, J. E. "Billy" McKinney, who had served in the state House since 1973 and who in the 1980s ran three times unsuccessfully against then-Rep. Wyche Fowler Jr. The elder McKinney served as his daughter's campaign manager and treasurer.

Against all odds, McKinney led in the primary balloting and forced a runoff, which she won handily over George L. DeLoach, the only white candidate of five contenders. He finished a surprising second with the support of white voters from a core of rural counties in the otherwise largely suburban and urban district.

After that, McKinney won the general election in a walk, taking 73 percent of the vote over Woodrow Lovett, a farmer and political novice from the rural eastern edge of the 11th, who could not generate much of a spark in the heavily Democratic district.

Georgia 11

East Central — Atlanta suburbs; parts of Augusta and Savannah

The black-majority 11th begins in Atlanta's southeastern suburbs and then sweeps east and south across two-thirds of Georgia, ending 250 miles distant in the Atlantic coast city of Savannah. It includes all or part of 22 counties, but more than 60 percent of the vote comes out of just three urbanized counties — De Kalb (east of Atlanta), Richmond (Augusta) and Chatham (Savannah).

The 11th is one of two new majority-minority districts created by Georgia mapmakers in 1992 to comply with Voting Rights Act mandates to increase minority representation. (Atlanta's 5th District already was in the hands of black Democratic Rep. John Lewis.) Of the state's three minority districts, the 11th has the heaviest concentration of black residents: 64 percent. Blacks make up 60 percent of the district's registered voters.

Democrats dominate all across the district. With the exceptions of Henry and Glascock counties, Bill Clinton swept the 11th in 1992 presidential voting.

His victories were landslides in De Kalb (78 percent) and Chatham (79 percent). Richmond County gave him a more modest 60 percent. McKinney took even bigger margins in winning election to the House.

The southern part of De Kalb County is an unassuming area of modest residences, but economic activity here is likely to step up over the next few years as preparations are made for the 1996 Summer Olympics. With events scheduled for Atlanta as well as Savannah and Augusta, the 11th will have more sites of Olympic competition than any other district.

On the district's eastern edge, most of the conservative voters of Richmond County (Augusta) were placed by mapmakers in the 10th District, leaving a Democratic core in the 11th.

From Augusta, the district drops south along the South Carolina line and snakes into Savannah, taking in the city's heavily Democratic areas, including parts of historic Savannah, the port and its waterfront. The city's economy has gotten a boost from the success of River Street, a string of restaurants, nightclubs, shops and hotels along the waterfront that tourists frequent.

Between the urban pockets of the 11th are mile after mile of agricultural acreage. This area once was known as Georgia's cotton belt, but today many of the people here depend more on other crops, including corn, soybean and peanuts.

Also prominent in this part of the 11th is the kaolin mining industry, which provides the white clay for use in white paint, china and stationery.

The district is home to three of the four cities that have served as Georgia's capital. The first was Savannah, founded in 1736 by James Oglethorpe. Milledgeville (Baldwin County) was later designated the capital because of its central location, but during the Civil War, it was seen as vulnerable and Augusta became the capital. Later, Atlanta was given the honor.

1990 Population: 586,195. White 202,129 (34%), Black 375,585 (64%), Other 8,481 (1%). Hispanic origin 6,255 (1%). 18 and over 413,413 (71%), 62 and over 68,659 (12%). Median age: 30.

Committees

Agriculture (22nd of 28 Democrats)
Environment, Credit & Rural Development; Department Operations; Foreign Agriculture & Hunger

Foreign Affairs (18th of 27 Democrats)
Economic Policy, Trade & the Environment; Western Hemisphere Affairs

Campaign Finance

1992	Receipts	Receipts from PACs		Expend-itures
McKinney (D)	$311,365	$166,642	(54%)	$306,978
Lovett (R)	$27,801	$2,250	(8%)	$26,721

Key Votes

1993

Require parental notification of minors' abortions	N
Require unpaid family and medical leave	Y
Approve national "motor voter" registration bill	Y
Approve budget increasing taxes and reducing deficit	Y
Approve economic stimulus plan	Y

Elections

1992 General		
Cynthia A. McKinney (D)	120,168	(73%)
Woodrow Lovett (R)	44,221	(27%)
1992 Primary Runoff		
Cynthia A. McKinney (D)	39,301	(56%)
George L. DeLoach (D)	30,389	(44%)
1992 Primary		
Cynthia A. McKinney (D)	26,160	(31%)
George L. DeLoach (D)	21,122	(25%)
Eugene P. Walker (D)	18,805	(22%)
Michael Thurmond (D)	13,313	(16%)
Verdree Lockhart Sr. (D)	4,468	(5%)

District Vote for President

	1992	
D	118,708	(65%)
R	48,026	(26%)
I	16,883	(9%)

Hawaii

STATE DATA

Governor:
John Waihee III (D)
First elected: 1986
Length of term: 4 years
Term expires: 12/94
Salary: $94,780
Term limit: 2 consecutive terms
Phone: (808) 586-0034
Born: May 19, 1946; Honokaa, Hawaii
Education: Andrews U., B.A. 1968; Central Michigan U., M.A. 1973; U. of Hawaii, J.D. 1976
Occupation: Lawyer
Family: Wife, Lynne Kobashigawa; two children
Religion: Christian
Political Career: Hawaii House, 1981-83; lieutenant governor, 1983-87

Lt. Gov.: Benjamin J. Cayetano (D)
First elected: 1986
Length of term: 4 years
Term expires: 12/94
Salary: $90,041
Phone: (808) 586-0255

State election official: (808) 453-8683
Democratic headquarters: (808) 536-2258
Republican headquarters: (808) 526-1755

REDISTRICTING

Hawaii retained its two House seats in reapportionment. The map was adopted by a commission July 19, 1991; the governor's signature was not required.

STATE LEGISLATURE

Bicameral legislature. Meets January-April.

Senate: 25 members, 4-year terms.
1992 breakdown: 22D, 3R; 19 men, 6 women; 6 whites, 16 Asian-Americans, 3 others
Salary: $32,000
Phone: (808) 586-6720

House of Representatives: 51 members, 2-year terms.
1992 breakdown: 47D, 4R; 39 men, 12 women; 14 whites, 31 Asian-Americans; 6 others
Salary: $32,000
Phone: (808) 586-6400

URBAN STATISTICS

City	Pop.
Honolulu	365,272
Mayor Frank F. Fasi, R	
Hilo	37,808
Mayor Stephen Yamashiro, D	
Kailua	36,818
Mayor Frank F. Fasi, R	
Kaneohe	35,448
Mayor Frank F. Fasi, R	
Waipahu	31,435
Mayor Frank F. Fasi, R	

U.S. CONGRESS

Senate: 2 D, 0 R
House: 2 D, 0 R

TERM LIMITS

For Congress: No
For state offices: No

ELECTIONS

1992 Presidential Vote

Bill Clinton	48.1%
George Bush	36.7%
Ross Perot	14.2%

1988 Presidential Vote

Michael S. Dukakis	54%
George Bush	45%

1984 Presidential Vote

Ronald Reagan	55%
Walter F. Mondale	44%

POPULATION

1990 population		1,108,229
1980 population		964,691
Percent change		+15%
Rank among states:		40
White		33%
Black		2%
Hispanic		7%
Asian or Pacific islander		62%
Urban		89%
Rural		11%
Born in state		56%
Foreign-born		15%
Under age 18	280,126	25%
Ages 18-64	703,098	63%
65 and older	125,005	11%
Median age		32.6

MISCELLANEOUS

Capital: Honolulu
Number of counties: 4
Per capita income: $21,306 (1991)
Rank among states: 7
Total area: 6,471 sq. miles
Rank among states: 47

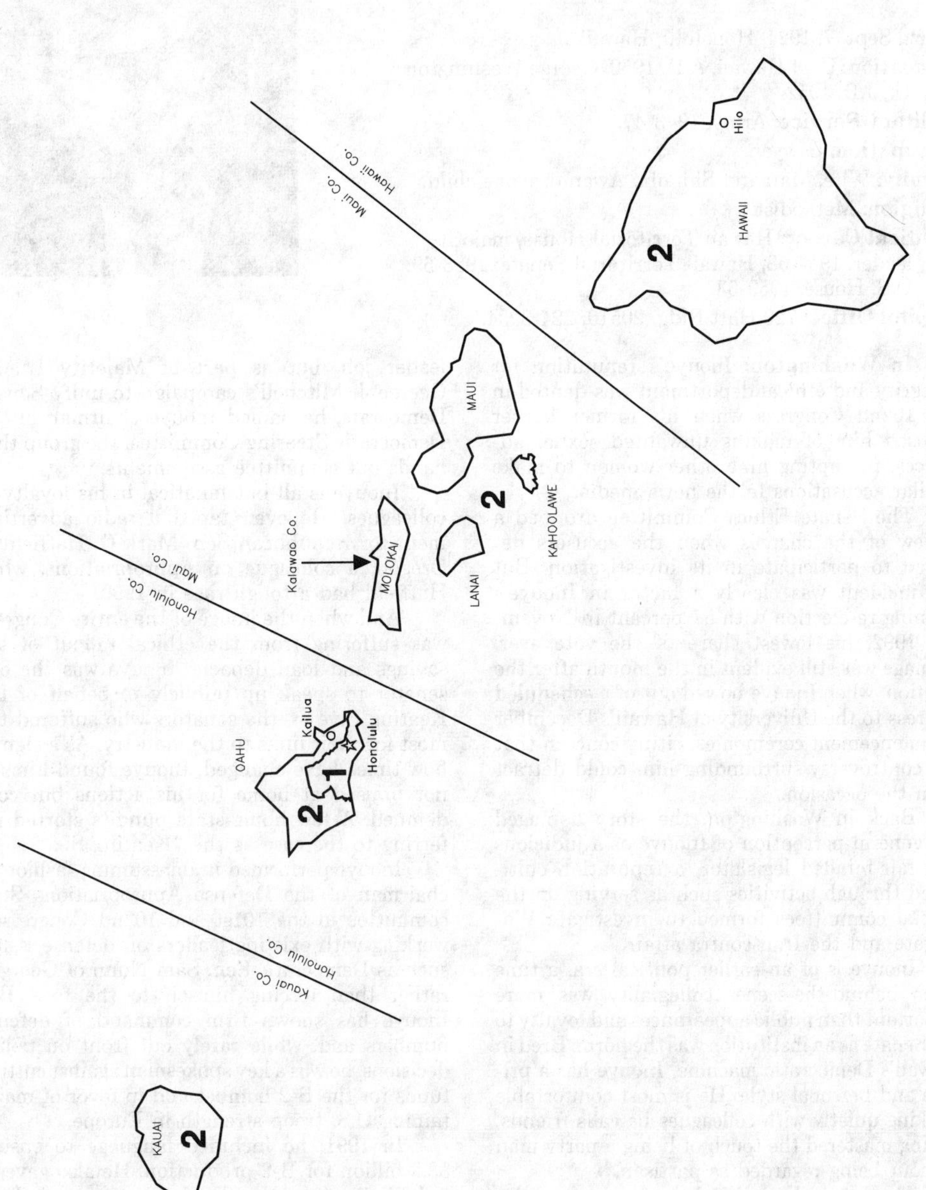
Hawaii Co.
Maui Co.
Hilo
HAWAII
2
MAUI
2
KAHOOLAWE
LANAI
MOLOKAI
Kalawao Co.
Maui Co.
Honolulu Co.
Kailua
Honolulu
OAHU
1
2
Honolulu Co.
Kauai Co.
KAUAI
2
NIIHAU

Daniel K. Inouye (D)

Of Honolulu — Elected 1962; 6th Term

Born: Sept. 7, 1924, Honolulu, Hawaii.
Education: U. of Hawaii, A.B. 1950; George Washington U., J.D. 1952.
Military Service: Army, 1943-47.
Occupation: Lawyer.
Family: Wife, Margaret Shinobu Awamura; one child.
Religion: Methodist.
Political Career: Hawaii Territorial House, majority leader, 1954-58; Hawaii Territorial Senate, 1958-59; U.S. House, 1959-63.
Capitol Office: 722 Hart Bldg. 20510; 224-3934.

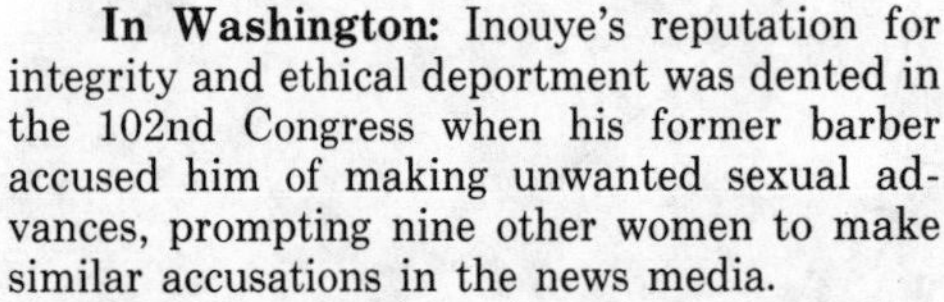

In Washington: Inouye's reputation for integrity and ethical deportment was dented in the 102nd Congress when his former barber accused him of making unwanted sexual advances, prompting nine other women to make similar accusations in the news media.

The Senate Ethics Committee dropped a review of the charges when the accusers declined to participate in its investigation. But the incident was clearly a factor in Inouye's winning re-election with 57 percent in November 1992, his lowest share of the vote ever. Damage was still evident in the month after the election, when Inouye bowed out of a scheduled address to the University of Hawaii's December commencement ceremonies, citing concern that the controversy surrounding him could detract from the occasion.

Back in Washington, the story damaged the general perception of Inouye as a judicious and fair-minded legislator, a reputation cultivated through activities such as serving on the special committees formed to investigate Watergate and the Iran-contra affair.

Inouye is of an earlier political era, a time when behind-the-scenes collegiality was more important than public appearances and loyalty to the Senate as an institution was the norm. Bred in Hawaii's Democratic machine, Inouye has a private and personal style. He is most comfortable working quietly with colleagues he calls friends, having mastered the touch of being a party man without being regarded as partisan.

The intensely political, impersonal tactics that now predominate, and the need to communicate the party's agenda outside the chamber, are all beyond Inouye. As a result, his 1989 bid for majority leader attracted only 14 of the Senate's 55 Democratic votes. Although he won some support by being the most senior member among those seeking the leadership, Inouye never expanded his base beyond old hands and colleagues on the Appropriations Committee.

Inouye gave up his post as secretary of the Democratic Conference to seek the majority leader job, but as part of Majority Leader George J. Mitchell's campaign to unify Senate Democrats, he named Inouye chairman of the Democratic Steering Committee, the group that hands out committee assignments.

Inouye is all but fanatical in his loyalty to colleagues. He even taped a radio advertisement for Republican Sen. Mark O. Hatfield of Oregon, a colleague on Appropriations, when Hatfield had a tough race in 1990.

And when the image of the entire Congress was suffering from the ethical fallout of the savings and loan debacle, Inouye was the one senator to speak up publicly in behalf of the Keating Five — the senators who suffered the most for their links to the industry. As a sign of how times have changed, Inouye found himself not praised at home for his actions but condemned. A few home-state pundits started referring to the case as the "Keating Six."

Inouye performed in unassuming fashion as chairman of the Defense Appropriations Subcommittee in the 101st and 102nd Congresses, working with existing leaders on defense issues such as Democratic Sen. Sam Nunn of Georgia, rather than forcing himself to the fore. But Inouye has shown firm command of defense numbers and, while rarely out front on policy decisions, he was a key spokesman against cutting funds for the B-2 bomber and in favor of maintaining U.S. troop strength in Europe.

In 1991, he included language to ensure $3.2 billion for B-2 production. He also gave in to lobbying from New England senators and got the panel to restore funding for the *Seawolf* submarine, which the Bush administration had sought to eliminate. During the 1992 Pentagon funding debate, Inouye was instrumental in preserving funding for the Strategic Defense Initiative, despite the opposition of many Democrats.

If Inouye has not been closely associated with national legislative achievements despite his many years in the Senate, his independence did help him take center stage during two congressional investigations of executive malfeasance.

His 1987 appointment to chair the select Senate committee investigating the Iran-contra affair stemmed not only from his evenhanded manner, but also from the esteem accorded him 14 years earlier during hearings on the illegal activities that led to the downfall of the Nixon administration. During the 1973 Watergate hearings, Inouye earned a reputation as a tough but judicious interrogator of President Richard M. Nixon's aides and associates.

Despite his low-key personality, polls during the Watergate hearings showed him with the highest nationwide "favorable" ratings of any committee member. Millions chortled when Inouye, unaware that his microphone was still live, muttered, "What a liar!" after hearing the testimony of White House aide John D. Ehrlichman. And support poured in when Ehrlichman's lawyer publicly called him "that little Jap."

Still, even when he finds himself in such highly public circumstances, Inouye shies from the limelight. After his appointment as the Iran committee chairman, he said, "You don't see me at press conferences. And I don't intend to be appearing before the mike . . . this often."

Inouye's work and rhetoric on the Iran panel, while competent, did not measure up to expectations. And so he missed a chance to shine at a time when he was still hoping to be the next majority leader.

His leadership campaign also suffered from the storm of protest that arose from a measure he put in a 1987 appropriations bill that would have spent $8 million to build schools for North African Jews in France. Unfortunately for Inouye, the project became a symbol of the kind of special interest projects members favor.

In early 1988, the Senate rescinded the money at Inouye's request, after news accounts that he had received a $1,000 contribution from a member of the board of a New York-based group that supports Jewish refugees and had lobbied Inouye for the project. In an emotional speech, Inouye conceded no impropriety, only an error in judgment, and he said he feared he had embarrassed his colleagues.

Before the 101st Congress, Inouye chaired Appropriations' Foreign Operations Subcommittee. He is a consistent advocate for increased aid to Israel. In 1991 he and then-Sen. Bob Kasten, a Wisconsin Republican, sponsored an amendment authorizing $10 billion in loan guarantees to Israel. In 1990, the two authored a successful amendment authorizing the president to provide the Israelis $700 million worth of equipment from Defense Department stockpiles.

Inouye also chairs the Commerce Subcommittee on Communications, where he shepherded the cable reregulation bill through the 102nd Congress. The bill passed with help from consumer groups and the broadcast industry after Inouye crafted a provision to allow broadcasters to seek compensation for cable use of over-the-air signals. The coalition supporting the bill was strong enough not only to win passage but to override a veto by Bush (the only such override of Bush's presidency).

In general, he has concentrated his Commerce work on helping his island home through shipping and tourism legislation. His work on the panel also prompted a rare reference to his service in the legendary Nisei regiment in World War II and the wound that took his right arm. In June 1986, as the committee was on its way to approving a $250,000 cap on certain court awards for pain and suffering, Inouye said, "I guess I can stand it, so I guess we can make [the cap] zilch. But I cannot speak for the rest of those who have lost their limbs." Support for the cap eroded, and the bill was doomed.

Inouye has also shown remarkable energy and passion to the Senate Indian Affairs Committee, where he became chairman in 1987. "This committee has been known as the scrap heap of the Senate," he said. "I'm going to do everything in my power to change that."

Inouye moved a score of tribal bills during the 102nd Congress, establishing standards for water use, fishing and agriculture rights, and wildlife protection on reservations.

At Home: A military hero, Inouye won his first election in 1954, helped guide Hawaii to statehood in 1959 and was a founder of the Democratic organization that has dominated state politics for three decades.

His stature in Hawaii's Japanese community approached reverence. During the war, he had fought in Europe as a member of the all Japanese-American 442nd Regiment. When his loss of an arm denied Inouye his ambition to be a surgeon, he went first into law and then eventually into politics.

He became one of Hawaii's first House members, then in 1962 became the first Japanese-American in the Senate. He went on to four more landslide wins over modest and mainly polite GOP opposition. But in 1992, Inouye's pedestal was rocked by a pair of maverick challengers: Democratic Maui County Commissioner Wayne K. Nishiki and Republican state Sen. Rick Reed.

Nishiki and Reed had been closely linked since the 1970s, when they published a local newspaper that showcased their strong environmentalist views. Nishiki and Reed then built careers out of challenging Hawaii's Democratic establishment, which they claimed had overly close ties with the state's business community, developers and even organized crime.

It was clear from the start that this would not be another deferential campaign. As Inouye prepared for the Dec. 7, 1991, ceremonies marking the 50th anniversary of Japan's attack on Pearl Harbor, Nishiki ran an ad in the Honolulu newspapers accusing the senator of being in league with Japanese real estate speculators who he said had contributed to high housing prices in Hawaii. The ad asked whether Inouye was "a traitor or simply incompetent." Inouye expressed outrage over the language and timing of the broadside.

Nishiki could not shake his image as a stalking horse for Reed and Inouye coasted to a better than 3-to-1 margin in the primary. But Reed, an easy winner in the GOP primary, did not wait until the general election to go after the Democrat. Reed tried to link Inouye with Hawaii businessman Larry Mehau, a Democratic Party insider whom Reed accused of being involved in organized crime. Reed referred to Inouye as "the kingpin" of Hawaii's political machine.

But sex, not crime, would be the main event in Reed's assault. A Reed ally — posing as a potential Inouye employee who had heard rumors of sexual misconduct by the senator — secretly recorded a conversation with Inouye's barber, Lenore Kwock. Although Reed denied authorizing the snooping, he ran a radio ad in October featuring Kwock's claims that Inouye had forced sex on her 17 years earlier and had made unwanted advances to her since.

Inouye called the accusation "unmitigated lies." And Kwock angrily rebuked Reed for publicizing her story without her permission. And Reed, faced with a strong backlash from the public and the media, withdrew the ad.

Yet the allegation did smudge Inouye's reputation and likely contributed to his diminished vote output: He won with under 60 percent, easily a career low. Much of the vote he lost did not go to Reed (who trailed by more than 100,000 votes) but to Linda B. Martin, the nominee of Hawaii's environmentalist Green Party.

Committees

Indian Affairs (Chairman)

Appropriations (2nd of 16 Democrats)
Defense (chairman); Commerce, Justice, State & Judiciary; Foreign Operations; Labor, Health & Human Services & Education; Military Construction

Commerce, Science & Transportation (2nd of 11 Democrats)
Communications (chairman); Aviation; Merchant Marine; National Ocean Policy Study; Surface Transportation

Rules & Administration (4th of 9 Democrats)

Elections

1992 General		
Daniel K. Inouye (D)	208,266	(57%)
Rick Reed (R)	97,928	(27%)
Linda B. Martin (GREEN)	49,921	(14%)
Richard O. Rowland (LIBERT)	7,547	(2%)
1992 Primary		
Daniel K. Inouye (D)	141,273	(76%)
Wayne K. Nishiki (D)	44,505	(24%)

Previous Winning Percentages: **1986** (74%) **1980** (78%) **1974** (83%) **1968** (83%) **1962** (69%) **1960 *** (74%) **1959 †** (68%)

* *House election.*

† *Special House election.*

Campaign Finance

	Receipts	Receipts from PACs		Expend-itures
1992				
Inouye (D)	$2,732,805	$805,465	(29%)	$2,971,128
Reed (R)	$440,852	$500	(0%)	$438,851

Key Votes

1993	
Require unpaid family and medical leave	Y
Approve national "motor voter" registration bill	Y
Approve budget increasing taxes and reducing deficit	?
Support president's right to lift military gay ban	Y
1992	
Approve school-choice pilot program	N
Allow shifting funds from defense to domestic programs	Y
Oppose deeper cuts in spending for SDI	Y
1991	
Approve waiting period for handgun purchases	Y
Raise senators' pay and ban honoraria	Y
Authorize use of force in Persian Gulf	N
Confirm Clarence Thomas to Supreme Court	N

Voting Studies

	Presidential Support		Party Unity		Conservative Coalition	
Year	**S**	**O**	**S**	**O**	**S**	**O**
1992	38	55	78	12	32	58
1991	51	47	77	19	50	43
1990	45	53	84	15	59	38
1989	60	37	83	17	47	53
1988	42	44	87	7	24	62
1987	33	63	91	5	41	53
1986	17	70	72	16	18	66
1985	20	72	80	7	20	58
1984	39	52	78	14	30	62
1983	33	42	70	9	9	66
1982	28	66	74	14	17	65
1981	47	44	74	13	20	69

Interest Group Ratings

Year	**ADA**	**AFL-CIO**	**CCUS**	**ACU**
1992	65	92	10	4
1991	80	92	20	14
1990	72	89	17	13
1989	70	90	50	11
1988	85	92	38	4
1987	95	90	29	0
1986	90	100	38	5
1985	95	95	24	5
1984	85	100	29	19
1983	75	93	27	9
1982	70	88	22	24
1981	70	89	44	0

Daniel K. Akaka (D)

Of Honolulu — Elected 1990; 1st Term

Appointed to the Senate April 1990.

Born: Sept. 11, 1924, Honolulu, Hawaii.
Education: U. of Hawaii, B.Ed. 1952, M.Ed. 1966.
Military Service: Army Corps of Engineers, 1945-47.
Occupation: Elementary school teacher and principal; state official.
Family: Wife, Mary Mildred Chong; five children.
Religion: Congregationalist.
Political Career: Sought Democratic nomination for lieutenant governor, 1974; U.S. House, 1977-90.
Capitol Office: 720 Hart Bldg. 20510; 224-6361.

In Washington: In a legislative body known for oversize personalities and powerful egos, the unassuming Akaka is virtually invisible. Among senators — members of what is sometimes called the world's most exclusive club — it's remarkable how unremarkable he is.

Akaka has continued the style he maintained during nearly 14 years in the House — a low profile and a very tight focus on Hawaiian interests. He delayed taking his Senate oath in order to ensure that funding for projects in Hawaii was advanced by House Appropriations.

Akaka sacrificed his seat on that committee when he moved to the Senate. However, he did get assignments to the Energy and Natural Resources, Governmental Affairs, Veterans' Affairs and Indian Affairs committees.

Akaka's votes are reliably liberal and Democratic, but on intraparty issues, his vote is seen as eminently "lobbyable." "He will always go with the last one to talk to him," says a colleague.

Few dispute his effectiveness in representing Hawaii's interests. In the 102nd Congress, he prodded the Federal Emergency Management Agency to establish a Hawaiian field office after Hurricane Iniki tore through the islands in September 1992. He got bills signed into law to aid Hawaii's tropical forests and to commend the civilians who played a role in Pearl Harbor.

Akaka also pushed for a joint resolution apologizing to Hawaiians for the 1893 U.S. overthrow of the islands' native government, a move that pleased constituents and adroitly skirted any endorsement of the popular movement that demands some measure of Hawaiian sovereignty.

In 1990, Akaka got an amendment to a crime bill increasing penalties for purveyors of a methamphetamine known as "ice," which had become a problem in Hawaii. A protector of Hawaii's sugar industry, he successfully fought an effort by Democratic Sen. Bill Bradley of New Jersey to cut the federal sugar subsidy by 2 cents a pound; Akaka's motion to table Bradley's amendment to the 1990 farm bill passed by a 54-44 vote.

Akaka is slight of stature, a fact he makes light of. Discussing his battle with Bradley, a towering former pro basketball star, Akaka told a Honolulu newspaper, "I'm only 5-feet-7, but I slam-dunked him."

That comment recalls an incident earlier in Akaka's career. In 1984, the House Democratic leadership was one vote short on a crucial roll call as it sought to block President Ronald Reagan's request for production of the MX missile. With time running out, Illinois Democrat Marty Russo located Akaka, who had been recorded as a pro-MX vote, lifted him out of a phone booth and escorted — carried, said some witnesses — him into the chamber. Akaka then changed his vote, giving the anti-MX forces a key victory.

At Home: When Democratic Sen. Spark M. Matsunaga died in April 1990, Akaka was a logical choice as his interim successor. Akaka had carried Hawaii's 2nd District by huge margins in seven House contests. A Native Hawaiian — the only one ever to serve in Congress — he was on good terms with Democratic Gov. John Waihee III, who made the appointment. Akaka was close to the leadership of the state Democratic Party and had received support throughout his career from Japanese-Americans, a crucial voting bloc.

However, with Akaka facing a special election in November 1990, there was a degree of trepidation about his ability to hold the seat. Akaka had been a rather sedate figure during his House career and was not readily identifiable to many Hawaiians. Some Democratic supporters feared that Akaka might be overwhelmed by his more aggressive opponent, 1st District Republican Rep. Patricia Saiki.

On paper, Akaka had major advantages over Saiki. He had won seven House elections to her two. He benefited from Hawaii's Democratic leanings and had solid backing from such towering state Democratic figures as senior Sen. Daniel K. Inouye. He also had demographics on his side: Population grew faster during the 1980s in his 2nd District than in Saiki's 1st.

Yet the image persisted that Saiki, a moderate with a more assertive personality and a base in Honolulu, was the favorite in the campaign. GOP strategists touted Hawaii as their best chance for a Senate "takeaway."

As it turned out, both Akaka and the state Democratic machine that backed him were underestimated. Akaka played to his strengths: his personality and his ability to deliver federal largess to Hawaii, proved as a member of the House Appropriations Committee. The organization got the party faithful to the polls: Akaka won by a surprisingly wide margin to fill out the final four years of Matsunaga's unexpired term.

Akaka rose through the Honolulu education bureaucracy before entering politics in 1971 as appointed head of the state Office of Economic Opportunity. In 1974, Democratic gubernatorial candidate George R. Ariyoshi tapped Akaka as his choice for lieutenant governor: Ariyoshi won, but Akaka lost in the Democratic primary. As governor, Ariyoshi appointed Akaka as his special assistant for human resources.

In 1976 the 2nd District opened up with the unsuccessful Senate candidacy of Democratic Rep. Patsy T. Mink. Akaka faced formidable primary opposition from state Sen. Joe Kuroda but won with a narrow plurality; he took the general election with 80 percent and won subsequent elections with similar ease.

Akaka's seat is up in 1994, and potential candidates began to position themselves even before the 1992 election.

But Akaka will have history on his side if he chooses to seek election to a full term in 1994: Hawaii voters have never turned out a Senate or House incumbent since statehood was achieved in 1959.

Committees

Energy & Natural Resources (6th of 11 Democrats)
Mineral Resources Development & Production (chairman); Public Lands, National Parks & Forests; Renewable Energy

Governmental Affairs (7th of 8 Democrats)
Federal Services, Post Office & Civil Service; General Services, Federalism & the District of Columbia; Oversight of Government Management

Indian Affairs (7th of 10 Democrats)

Veterans' Affairs (5th of 7 Democrats)

Elections

1990 Special Election		
Daniel K. Akaka (D)	188,901	(54%)
Patricia Saiki (R)	155,978	(45%)
Ken Schoolland (LIBERT)	4,787	(1%)
1990 Special Primary		
Daniel K. Akaka (D)	180,235	(91%)
Paul Snider (D)	18,427	(8%)

Previous Winning Percentages: **1988 *** (89%) **1986 *** (76%) **1984 *** (82%) **1982 *** (89%) **1980 *** (90%) **1978 *** (86%) **1976 *** (80%)

** House elections.*

Campaign Finance

	Receipts	Receipts from PACs	Expend-itures
1990			
Akaka (D)	$1,764,875	$854,107 (48%)	$1,760,839
Saiki (R)	$2,570,035	$902,829 (35%)	$2,398,961

Key Votes

1993	
Require unpaid family and medical leave	Y
Approve national "motor voter" registration bill	Y
Approve budget increasing taxes and reducing deficit	Y
Support president's right to lift military gay ban	Y
1992	
Approve school-choice pilot program	N
Allow shifting funds from defense to domestic programs	Y
Oppose deeper cuts in spending for SDI	N
1991	
Approve waiting period for handgun purchases	Y
Raise senators' pay and ban honoraria	Y
Authorize use of force in Persian Gulf	N
Confirm Clarence Thomas to Supreme Court	N

Voting Studies

	Presidential Support		Party Unity		Conservative Coalition	
Year	**S**	**O**	**S**	**O**	**S**	**O**
1992	30	70	92	8	26	74
1991	35	64	91	9	25	75
1990 *	23 †	75 †	88 †	10 †	23 †	73 †
House Service:						
1989	35	62	96	2	22	78
1988	22	74	88	2	13	82
1987	23	67	87	4	37	58
1986	18	79	89	6	28	68
1985	26	68	86	7	35	58
1984	31	63	85	8	22	75
1983	28	66	86	9	42	56
1982	40	53	81	8	32	58
1981	46	54	81	17	52	48

** Akaka was sworn in May 16, 1990. For 1990, his Senate scores are shown. In the House, his presidential support score in 1990 was 17 percent; his opposition score was 74 percent. His party-unity support score was 86 percent; his opposition score was 0 percent. His conservative coalition support score was 17 percent; his opposition score was 83 percent.*

† Not eligible for all recorded votes.

Interest Group Ratings

Year	ADA	AFL-CIO	CCUS	ACU
1992	90	92	20	0
1991	90	92	20	5
1990	100	88	10	11
House Service:				
1989	85	100	30	7
1988	85	93	23	0
1987	64	88	0	0
1986	90	86	18	9
1985	65	88	22	14
1984	85	92	38	10
1983	85	100	35	4
1982	65	90	21	15
1981	65	100	16	7

1 Neil Abercrombie (D)

Of Honolulu — Elected 1990; 2nd Full Term

Also served September 1986-January 1987.

Born: June 26, 1938, Buffalo, N.Y.
Education: Union College, B.A. 1959; U. of Hawaii, M.A. 1964, Ph.D. 1974.
Occupation: Educator.
Family: Wife, Nancie Caraway.
Religion: Unspecified.
Political Career: Sought Democratic nomination for U.S. Senate, 1970; Hawaii House, 1975-79; Hawaii Senate, 1979-86; sought Democratic nomination for U.S. House, 1986; Honolulu City Council, 1988-90.
Capitol Office: 1440 Longworth Bldg. 20515; 225-2726.

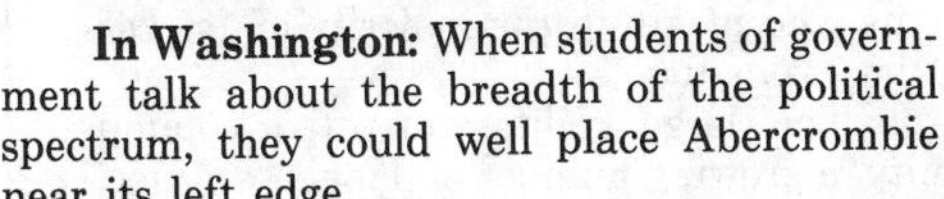

In Washington: When students of government talk about the breadth of the political spectrum, they could well place Abercrombie near its left edge.

With his full beard and flowing hair, Abercrombie looks as though he would be more comfortable on the road with the Grateful Dead — he was their guest at a June 1991 Washington concert — than in Congress. But this 1960s activist-turned-politician decided in the 1970s to run for the Hawaii Legislature and in the 1980s for the U.S. House.

During his tenure in the Legislature, Abercrombie was an avid, sometimes unyielding advocate of aid to the underprivileged. Naturally enough, he did not change his stripes when he came to Washington.

Abercrombie's voting record lists sharply to port: In the 102nd Congress he supported the Brady bill's seven-day waiting period for handgun purchases, a ban on permanent replacement of striking workers, the statutory guarantee of the right to abortion in the Freedom of Choice Act, a government-run system of national health insurance and imposition of human rights and other conditions on continued normalized trade with China.

Not surprisingly, the frequency with which Abercrombie voted on the House floor in 1992 in support of positions espoused by President Bush was exceedingly low; at 9 percent his was the third-lowest score in the House.

And Abercrombie still favors programs that aid the underprivileged. Early in the 103rd Congress, he was one of 85 Democrats to vote for a substitute budget blueprint crafted by the Congressional Black Caucus and the Progressive Caucus that would have cut more deeply into defense spending and raised taxes more sharply than the mainstream Democratic budget. The resulting savings would have been used to increase spending on education, job training, health and other domestic programs.

Typically a laid-back, friendly legislator, Abercrombie can nevertheless launch blistering attacks when his liberal instincts are riled. One such instance occurred in early 1993, when Republicans vigorously protested a change in the House rules to allow delegates from the District of Columbia, American Samoa, Guam, Puerto Rico and the Virgin Islands to vote on floor amendments in certain circumstances.

"If you are a member of the Danish Parliament and you live in Greenland, you can [vote]," Abercrombie said. "Greenland has the vote, but we do not give it to people in [territories of] the United States of America. And members sit here on the other side of the aisle and talk about democracy, and talk about freedom, and preach to me about the Constitution."

However enthusiastic Abercrombie may be about liberal causes, he has also proved that he will provide a needed partisan vote at an opportune time — even if it does not suit his ideological bent.

In April 1993, strong opposition from liberal Democrats and Republicans threatened to prevent the House from taking up a bill to grant the president a modified line-item veto. The necessary preliminary procedural vote seemed about to fail when Abercrombie and a few others were persuaded by House Speaker Thomas S. Foley to change their votes and allow the bill to go forward. The procedural measure was approved, 212-208; Abercrombie later voted against the bill itself.

Abercrombie's fleeting service as the winner of a special House election in 1986 gave him a leg up on committee assignments in the 102nd. During his few weeks in office at the end of the 99th Congress, he served on the Armed Services Committee, a position that enabled him to speak for defense budget cuts while promoting Hawaii's importance as a military center in the Pacific.

Upon his election in 1990, he rejoined the panel and picked up where he left off. Watching with satisfaction the nation's shift toward a smaller military, Abercrombie pushed for an even

Hawaii 1

Honolulu — Pearl City

The compact 1st takes in the narrow plain between the Koolau mountain range and the Leeward (western) coast of the island of Oahu. But this small area includes the city of Honolulu, the engine that drives all of Hawaii.

Honolulu is Hawaii's capital, home to most of its businesses and about one-third of its people. In its western end are the Pearl Harbor Naval Reservation and Hickam Air Force Base, major parts of a military sector that is vital to Hawaii's economy.

East of downtown Honolulu is Waikiki, heart of the tourist trade that is Hawaii's leading industry. Waikiki, with its numerous high-rise hotels, is one of the most densely populated places anywhere during tourist season. Those who come with dreams of "grass-shack" Hawaii are disappointed. But others who visit find it the perfect mix of stunning scenery, sandy beaches and urban amenities.

Farther east are Honolulu's most affluent neighborhoods, which include a large population of whites, known as *haoles* in the Hawaiian language.

The middle-class neighborhoods of central Honolulu are dominated by Americans of Japanese ancestry; for many in that ethnic group, employment in state government has been the route to economic security.

Kalihi, in northwest Honolulu, is a working-class community heavily populated by Filipinos and native Hawaiians. Scattered throughout are Chinese, Koreans, Vietnamese, Samoans, Portuguese, Puerto Ricans and other ethnic groups.

To the west are such towns as Pearl City, Aiea, Mililani Town and part of Kapolei, which is planned to become Oahu's "second city" by the 21st century.

Ewa Beach is connected to the district by a band rimming Pearl Harbor; Japan's attack on the naval base in December 1941 was the catalyst for the United States' entry into World War II. Inland is Camp H. M. Smith Marine Corps Base, the headquarters for the unified military command for the Pacific.

The 1st contributes to Hawaii's strong Democratic tilt. Japanese-Americans have long dominated the state Democratic Party; they are joined in their partisan tendencies by many other "minority group" constituents who make up the majority of 1st District residents.

The large military-oriented community, a growing number of Japanese-Americans gaining corporate advancement and the Republican leanings of many white residents occasionally allow a GOP candidate to carry the district. Republican Patricia Saiki made history by winning the House seat in 1986 and 1988.

But in 1990, Saiki lost a Senate bid to Democrat Daniel K. Akaka. Democrat Abercrombie easily won House contests that year and in 1992.

Bill Clinton carried the district by more than 8 percentage points, though his 48 percent plurality was below the Democratic norm.

1990 Population: 554,119. White 161,228 (29%), Black 13,807 (2%), Asian and Pacific Islander 368,904 (67%), Other 10,180 (2%). Hispanic origin 30,598 (6%). 18 and over 431,485 (78%), 62 and over 85,443 (15%). Median age: 34.

more scaled-back, less-expensive force than the one Armed Services Chairman Les Aspin preferred. At the same time, Abercrombie worked to secure money to build housing for more than 1,200 families on military bases in Hawaii.

He won assignment to Interior (now Natural Resources) in the middle of the 102nd Congress, a position from which he can concentrate on environmental issues. In his first year in the House, he had used a seat on Merchant Marine and Fisheries to publicize the danger of plutonium shipment by sea.

A legislator who is always willing to talk about his state, Abercrombie proved ready to legislate for his state, as well. By the end of the 102nd, he had helped defeat a proposed cut in cost of living adjustments for federal workers in Hawaii, secured authorization for the Hawaiian Islands Humpback Whale National Marine Sanctuary and exempted the state from an interstate milk inspection fee.

Lately, Abercrombie has been fighting to preserve a piece of Hawaii's history. He wants the federal government to buy an extrêmely rare collection of Hawaiian stamps for the Smithsonian Institution that includes envelopes with stamps affixed that were sent home by New England missionaries as long ago as 1851.

The collection is owned by the Persis Corp., which is not in a position to make use of the ordinary tax deduction permitted for charitable donations; some of the company's directors are agitating to auction off the stamps. So, prodded by Hawaii newspaper executive Thurston Twigg-Smith, who collected the stamps over a 30-year period, Abercrombie and Hawaii

Democratic Sen. Daniel K. Inouye introduced bills in 1992 to have the government buy the stamps for $8.25 million (which may be considerably less than their auction value).

The House Judiciary subcommittee to which such "private bills" are referred balked at the cost. Abercrombie reintroduced it in the 103rd.

At Home: With solid victories in 1990 and 1992, Abercrombie rebounded from his first House bid in 1986 and the political fluke that nearly relegated him to trivia question status: He had won and lost the 1st District seat on the same day.

Democratic Rep. Cecil Heftel had resigned the seat to run for governor, and a special election to fill out his term was scheduled to coincide with the September 1986 primary.

Abercrombie emerged as the favorite to succeed Heftel. A veteran of protest politics — he took 13 percent of the vote in the 1970 Democratic Senate primary as an antiwar candidate — Abercrombie had become a leading liberal activist in the state Legislature.

But Abercrombie's ideological cast and reputation for abrasiveness left him open to attacks from Republican activist Patricia Saiki, his main competitor in the open-ballot special election, and Democratic businessman Mufi Hannemann, an aggressive newcomer.

Hannemann scored the hardest hit: He unearthed a 17-year-old newspaper article in which Abercrombie suggested what seemed to be a favorable attitude about decriminalizing marijuana use. Although Abercrombie furiously denied that he countenanced drug use, the issue was damaging.

Abercrombie managed to win the special election with 30 percent to 29 percent for Saiki and 28 percent for Hannemann. But he narrowly lost the primary to Hannemann, making him ineligible to run for a full term that November. (GOP nominee Saiki went on to defeat Hannemann, making her the only Hawaii Republican ever to hold a House seat.)

Abercrombie restarted his political career in 1988 by winning a seat on the Honolulu City Council. When Saiki left the 1st District open in 1990 to challenge interim Democratic Sen. Daniel K. Akaka in the special election caused by the death of Democratic Sen. Spark M. Matsunaga, Abercrombie was primed for redemption.

Utilizing an engaging and less combative style, Abercrombie took 46 percent of the Democratic House primary vote to defeat state Sen. Norman Mizuguchi and lawyer Matt Matsunaga, the son of the late senator. He then had little trouble returning the seat to Democratic control, topping GOP state Rep. Mike Liu with 60 percent. The Republicans failed to recruit a well-known candidate in 1992, and Abercrombie coasted.

Committees

Armed Services (20th of 34 Democrats)
Military Acquisition; Military Installations & Facilities

Natural Resources (16th of 28 Democrats)
National Parks, Forests & Public Lands; Native American Affairs; Oversight & Investigations

Elections

1992 General		
Neil Abercrombie (D)	129,332	(73%)
Warner C. Kimo Sutton (R)	41,575	(23%)
Rockne Hart Johnson (LIBERT)	6,569	(4%)
1990 General		
Neil Abercrombie (D)	97,622	(60%)
Mike Liu (R)	62,982	(39%)

Previous Winning Percentage: 1986 * (30%)

** Special election.*

District Vote for President

1992
D 87,632 (48%)
R 72,156 (39%)
I 23,438 (13%)

Campaign Finance

	Receipts	Receipts from PACs		Expend-itures
1992				
Abercrombie (D)	$359,336	$176,568	(49%)	$359,681
Sutton (R)	$16,103	0		$16,103
1990				
Abercrombie (D)	$476,231	$143,600	(30%)	$442,211
Liu (R)	$271,319	$57,601	(21%)	$267,882

Key Votes

1993	
Require parental notification of minors' abortions	N
Require unpaid family and medical leave	Y
Approve national "motor voter" registration bill	Y
Approve budget increasing taxes and reducing deficit	Y
Approve economic stimulus plan	Y
1992	
Approve balanced-budget constitutional amendment	N
Close down space station program	Y
Approve U.S. aid for former Soviet Union	N
Allow shifting funds from defense to domestic programs	Y
1991	
Extend unemployment benefits using deficit financing	Y
Approve waiting period for handgun purchases	Y
Authorize use of force in Persian Gulf	N

Voting Studies

	Presidential Support		Party Unity		Conservative Coalition	
Year	**S**	**O**	**S**	**O**	**S**	**O**
1992	9	89	92	2	2	92
1991	21	78	95	2	8	92

Interest Group Ratings

Year	ADA	AFL-CIO	CCUS	ACU
1992	95	91	13	0
1991	100	100	10	0

2 Patsy T. Mink (D)

Of Honolulu — Elected 1990; 8th Full Term

Also served 1965-77.

Born: Dec. 6, 1927, Paia, Hawaii.
Education: U. of Hawaii, B.A. 1948; U. of Chicago, J.D. 1951.
Occupation: Lawyer.
Family: Husband, John Francis Mink; one child.
Religion: Protestant.
Political Career: Hawaii Territorial House, 1956-58; Hawaii Territorial Senate, 1958-60; Hawaii Senate, 1962-64; sought Democratic nomination for president, 1972; sought Democratic nomination for U.S. Senate, 1976; assistant U.S. secretary of State, 1977-78; Honolulu City Council, 1983-87; sought Democratic nomination for governor, 1986; sought Democratic nomination for mayor of Honolulu, 1988.
Capitol Office: 2135 Rayburn Bldg. 20515; 225-4906.

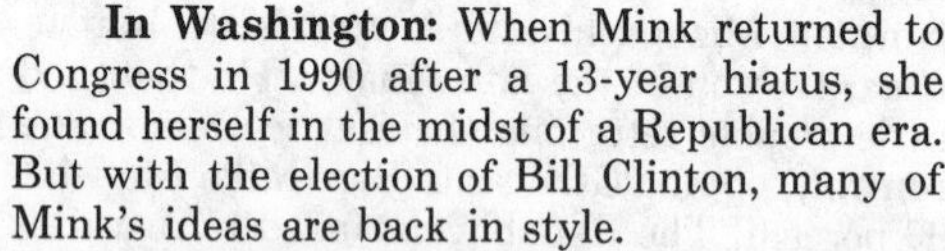

In Washington: When Mink returned to Congress in 1990 after a 13-year hiatus, she found herself in the midst of a Republican era. But with the election of Bill Clinton, many of Mink's ideas are back in style.

While the political fallout from the 1980s served to move some Republicans and Democrats closer to the middle, Mink, a New Deal Democrat, stayed decidedly to the left. On her return and appointment to the Education and Labor Committee, she quickly made it clear that her zeal for social programs had not changed substantially.

In the 103rd, Mink maintained that agenda as she was assigned to the Budget Committee, where her goal is to "redirect our budget priorities" toward such "human needs" as education, health care and job creation. A longtime proponent of social programs that confront issues facing the poor, women and American workers, Mink was an advocate of the family leave bill enacted early in 1993 and supports legislation that would bar permanent replacement of striking workers.

But despite more than 30 years in political life and some 15 years in Congress, Mink lacks the senior status that can mean political clout in Washington. She had to start over when she returned to Washington in 1990 despite her proven abilities as a legislator. And even though she helped create many of the programs that are the subject of debate today, such as Head Start and special education, her low ranking on the Education and Labor Committee places her years away from a subcommittee chairmanship.

While she is a contemporary of Chairman William D. Ford of Michigan (himself a product of the New Deal), Mink falls to the left of Ford on some issues. She epitomizes the subject of many a conservative Republican's bad dream — the "tax and spend" liberal.

In the 102nd, committee Democrats introduced a $700 million bill in response to America 2000, a Bush administration plan to reform the nation's schools. Mink criticized the Bush plan, but she was also frustrated by the committee's plan, which she thought came up short. During a subcommittee markup, Mink offered an amendment that would have authorized $5 billion for numerous programs, including an expansion of Head Start. Mink was the only Democrat to vote against the bill in committee.

However, Mink does not allow her policy differences to stymie her ability to make legislative contributions. In the 102nd, she crafted three provisions that were included in the higher education bill: providing Pell grants to students who are attending school less than half time; excluding the value of a family's home from the calculation of eligibility for financial aid; and providing loan forgiveness for students who become nurses and medical technicians.

A staunch advocate of women's civil rights in employment, she warned Democratic colleagues as long ago as 1970 that "women are still the victims of discrimination [in the workplace]. I think we as a party must recognize our moral responsibility for this injustice."

Disappointed by President Bush's veto of a 1990 civil rights bill, she was infuriated in 1991 when leadership proponents of the bill, in an effort to broaden its appeal, wrote in language that would limit damages for women and religious minorities who are the victims of job discrimination. Her efforts to persuade other House members to oppose the limit were unsuccessful, and after a civil rights measure without the cap failed on the House floor, she voted for the compromise. Mink has vowed to continue the fight in the 103rd.

Also in the 102nd, Mink pushed for increased federal funding for ovarian cancer research. The

Hawaii 2

Suburban and Outer Oahu — "Neighbor islands"

The heavily Democratic 2nd takes in seven major "neighbor islands," plus hundreds of reefs and atolls. But more than half the people in the 2nd live on Oahu.

Although it has a racial and ethnic patchwork similar to that in the 1st District, the 2nd has a somewhat higher proportion of white residents (more than one-third of the population is white). There are some predominantly white, conservative-leaning communities, mostly on Oahu and Maui, that regularly vote Republican.

But these areas barely dent Democrats' dominance of the 2nd. Rep. Mink won by better than 3-to-1 in 1992. Bill Clinton took 49 percent and bested George Bush by more than 14 percentage points.

Hilo, on the "Big Island" of Hawaii, is the district's largest city with nearly 38,000 people; but the Oahu cities of Kailua and Kaneohe are very close behind. Kailua, on Oahu's Windward (eastern) side, is one of the few majority-white cities in Hawaii. The Asian and Pacific Islander majority of neighboring Kaneohe is more typical of Hawaii's ethnic mix. Across the island at the edge of Pearl Harbor, working-class Waipahu is more than 80 percent Asian or Pacific Islander.

Oahu's numerous military installations are central to the life and economy of the 2nd. However, one facility, the Barber's Point Naval Air Station, showed up on the 1993 list of bases recommended for closing as the military continues to downsize.

Away from Honolulu, population on Oahu thins, and tourist outposts are more dispersed. Laie is a Mormon enclave that includes a campus of Brigham Young University. Oahu's north coast is famous for its surfing. The Leeward (western) side has many native Hawaiians.

The spacious island of Hawaii saw its population expand by nearly a third during the 1980s. Much of the growth was on the scenic Leeward, or Kona, coast. The city of Hilo is a commercial center on the rainy eastern part of the Big Island; its attraction to tourists is its proximity to the active Mauna Loa and Kilauea volcanoes and extinct Mauna Kea. Agricultural products — including sugar, macadamia nuts, flowers, cattle and coffee — make up a major segment of the island's economy.

After Oahu, the island of Maui has the state's most developed tourism industry. Maui County has three other islands, including Lanai, a longtime pineapple plantation, much of which is being converted into a tourist resort; relatively undeveloped Molokai; and deserted Kahoolawe, used from the late 1930s until 1990 as a military bombing range.

Although Kauai has a large sugar industry, the island makes much of its living from tourism. The coastal resorts and Kauai's populace were staggered in September 1992, when Hurricane Iniki scored a direct hit on the island. Kauai County includes the island of Niihau, set aside by its patrician owners as a place where native Hawaiians can maintain their traditional lifestyles; access by outsiders is limited.

1990 Population: 554,110. White 208,388 (38%), Black 13,388 (2%), Asian and Pacific Islander 316,332 (57%), Other 16,002 (3%). Hispanic origin 50,792 (9%). 18 and over 396,618 (72%), 62 and over 69,025 (12%). Median age: 31.

bill was not enacted, but the attention resulted in a boost in research dollars for the disease. And some women members pushed Mink as a candidate for chief deputy whip during the 102nd Congress.

She was selected in the 103rd to head a task force aimed at promoting equity for women and girls in job training and education programs. Mink wants to target gender bias in elementary and secondary education, and strengthen and update a bill she sponsored during her first House tenure — the Women's Educational Equity Act.

Mink is still as passionate about public health and environmental protection as she was in 1971, when she and 32 other members sued the Environmental Protection Agency and five other government agencies after they failed to disclose unclassified parts of a report on underground nuclear tests being conducted at the Alaskan Aleutian island of Amchitka.

In October 1990 she faced a similar incident closer to home. The Army had planned to assemble, test and launch missiles at the Pacific Missile Range facility on the Hawaiian island of Kauai. Mink and Sen. Daniel K. Akaka pushed for a bill mandating that the Army do an environmental impact statement before proceeding. The Army study, released in 1992, found that the program would have no significant effect on the island.

At Home: The congressional careers of Mink and Akaka are intertwined. Akaka succeeded Mink when she ended her first House stint with an unsuccessful 1976 Senate bid. Fourteen years later, Akaka's appointment to succeed the late Democratic Sen. Spark M. Matsunaga opened the way for Mink's return to the House.

Mink is one of the hardiest figures in Hawaii politics. In 1956, she won a seat in the territorial House, then moved to the Senate two years later. Mink was out of office during the early days of statehood but won a state Senate seat in 1962.

In 1964, Mink narrowly won a primary for a U.S. House seat and was elected along with incumbent Matsunaga. Quickly establishing herself as an outspoken activist, Mink easily won reelection in 1966 and 1968.

In her 1970 contest — her first in the new, 2nd District — Mink ran unopposed. With Richard M. Nixon scoring the first GOP presidential victory ever in Hawaii, Mink slipped to 57 percent of the vote in 1972. She rebounded to 63 percent in 1974.

However, Mink's rise was halted in 1976, when she bid for the seat of retiring Republican Sen. Hiram L. Fong. Her Democratic primary rival, House colleague Matsunaga, had backing from much of the state party leadership. Playing off his image as a conciliator against Mink's more ideological bearing, Matsunaga won with 51 percent to Mink's 41 percent and went on to serve in the Senate until his death in April 1990.

Mink then signed on with the liberal Americans for Democratic Action, serving as president from 1978 to 1981. She embarked on a bumpy return to politics, winning two terms on the Honolulu City Council, but losing primary bids for governor in 1986 and Honolulu mayor in 1988.

Thus, Mink's 1990 bid to succeed Akaka took the form of a comeback. In the September 1990 special election, her toughest foe was Mufi Hannemann, who had lost a 1986 House contest to Republican Patricia Saiki in the 1st District. A young, business-oriented candidate, Hannemann portrayed Mink as a candidate of a more liberal past. But touting her years of experience, Mink hung on, winning the special election by 2 percentage points and the primary for a full term by a slightly larger margin.

The November campaign was much easier. Republican Andy Poepoe, a businessman and longtime state officeholder, had run a distant fourth in the special election; Mink won easily. She breezed past her primary and general election opponents in 1992.

Committees

Budget (21st of 26 Democrats)

Education & Labor (12th of 28 Democrats)
Elementary, Secondary & Vocational Education; Labor-Management Relations; Postsecondary Education

Natural Resources (24th of 28 Democrats)
National Parks, Forests & Public Lands

Elections

1992 General		
Patsy T. Mink (D)	131,454	(73%)
Kamuela Price (R)	40,070	(22%)
Lloyd Jeffrey Mallan (LIBERT)	9,431	(5%)
1992 Primary		
Patsy T. Mink (D)	80,570	(83%)
David L. Bourgoin (D)	16,441	(17%)
1990 General		
Patsy T. Mink (D)	118,155	(66%)
Andy Poepoe (R)	54,625	(31%)
Lloyd Jeffrey Mallan (LIBERT)	5,508	(3%)

Previous Winning Percentages: **1990 *** (35%) **1974** (63%) **1972** (57%) **1970** (100%) **1964-68 †**

** Special election.*

† One of two Hawaii House members elected at large.

District Vote for President

	1992
D	91,630 (49%)
R	64,635 (35%)
I	29,558 (16%)

Campaign Finance

	Receipts	Receipts from PACs		Expend-itures
1992				
Mink (D)	$336,089	$113,425	(34%)	$287,017
Price (R)	$745	0		$772
1990				
Mink (D)	$641,324	$147,784	(23%)	$641,037
Poepoe (R)	$191,641	$42,460	(22%)	$204,153

Key Votes

1993	
Require parental notification of minors' abortions	N
Require unpaid family and medical leave	Y
Approve national "motor voter" registration bill	Y
Approve budget increasing taxes and reducing deficit	Y
Approve economic stimulus plan	Y
1992	
Approve balanced-budget constitutional amendment	N
Close down space station program	Y
Approve U.S. aid for former Soviet Union	Y
Allow shifting funds from defense to domestic programs	Y
1991	
Extend unemployment benefits using deficit financing	Y
Approve waiting period for handgun purchases	Y
Authorize use of force in Persian Gulf	N

Voting Studies

	Presidential Support		Party Unity		Conservative Coalition	
Year	S	O	S	O	S	O
1992	14	81	94	3	13	79
1991	19	77	96	3	3	97
1990	22 †	78 †	81 †	5 †	21 †	75 †

† Not eligible for all recorded votes.

Interest Group Ratings

Year	ADA	AFL-CIO	CCUS	ACU
1992	100	100	25	0
1991	100	100	20	0
1990	—	100	50	20

Idaho

STATE DATA

Governor:
Cecil D. Andrus (D)
First elected: 1986 (also served 1971-1977)
Length of term: 4 years
Term expires: 1/95
Salary: $75,000
Term limit: No
Phone: (208) 334-2100
Born: Aug. 25, 1931; Hood River, Ore.
Education: Oregon State U., 1948-49
Military Service: Navy, 1951-55
Occupation: Lumberjack; sawmill manager; insurance executive; management consultant
Family: Wife, Carol May; three children
Religion: Lutheran
Political Career: Idaho Senate, 1961-67; Democratic nominee for governor, 1966; Idaho Senate, 1969-71; governor, 1971-77; U.S. Interior secretary, 1977-81

Lt. Gov.: C. L. "Butch" Otter (R)
First elected: 1986
Length of term: 4 years
Term expires: 1/95
Salary: $20,000
Phone: (208) 334-2200

State election official: (208) 334-2300
Democratic headquarters: (208) 336-1815
Republican headquarters: (208) 343-6405

REDISTRICTING

Idaho retained its two House seats in reapportionment. Legislature passed the map Jan. 21, 1992; governor signed it Jan. 28.

STATE LEGISLATURE

Bicameral Legislature. Meets January-March.

Senate: 35 members, 2-year terms
1992 breakdown: 23R, 12D; 26 men, 9 women; 34 whites, 1 Hispanic
Salary: $12,000
Phone: (208) 334-2000

House of Representatives: 70 members, 2-year terms
1992 breakdown: 50R, 20D; 47 men, 23 women; 70 whites
Salary: $12,000
Phone: 208) 334-2000

URBAN STATISTICS

City	Pop.
Boise City	125,738
Mayor Dirk Kempthorne, R	
Pocatello	46,117
Mayor Peter Angstadt, I	
Idaho Falls	43,929
Mayor Thomas Campbell, I	
Nampa	28,365
Mayor Winston K. Goering, R	
Lewiston	28,082
Mayor Lovetta Eisele, I	

U.S. CONGRESS

Senate: 0 D, 2 R
House: 1 D, 1 R

TERM LIMITS

For Congress: No
For state offices: No

ELECTIONS

1992 Presidential Vote

George Bush	42.0%
Bill Clinton	28.4%
Ross Perot	27.0%

1988 Presidential Vote

George Bush	62%
Michael S. Dukakis	36%

1984 Presidential Vote

Ronald Reagan	72%
Walter F. Mondale	26%

POPULATION

1990 population		1,006,749
1980 population		943,935
Percent change		+7%
Rank among states:		42
White		94%
Black		<1%
Hispanic		5%
Asian or Pacific islander		1%
Urban		57%
Rural		43%
Born in state		51%
Foreign-born		3%
Under age 18	308,405	31%
Ages 18-64	577,079	57%
65 and older	121,265	12%
Median age		31.5

MISCELLANEOUS

Capital: Boise
Number of counties: 44
Per capital income: $15,401 (1991)
Rank among states: 44
Total area: 83,564 sq. miles
Rank among states: 13

Idaho - Congressional Districts

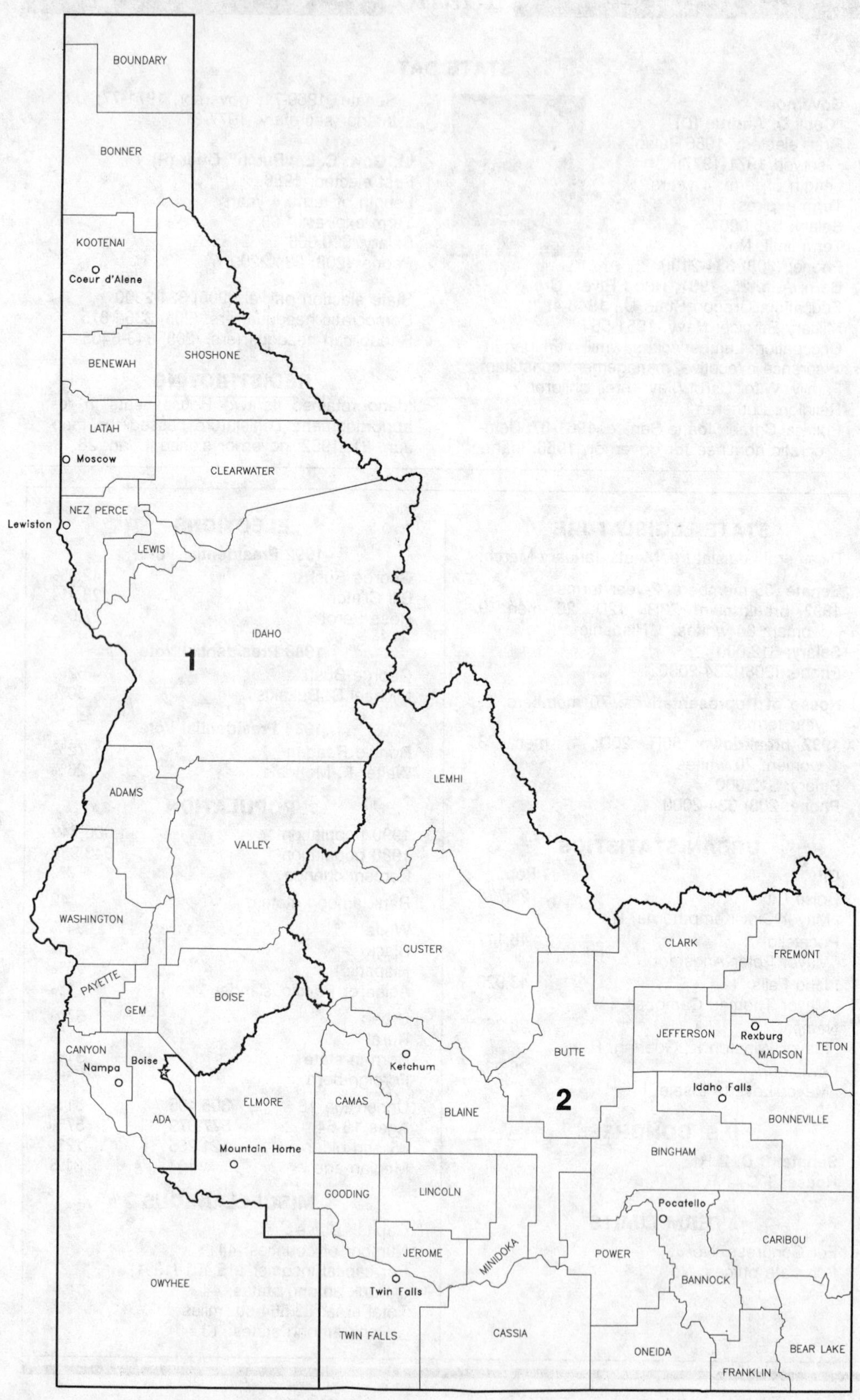

Larry E. Craig (R)

Of Payette — Elected 1990; 1st Term

Born: July 20, 1945, Council, Idaho.
Education: U. of Idaho, B.A. 1969; George Washington U., 1969-70.
Military Service: National Guard, 1970-71.
Occupation: Farmer; rancher.
Family: Wife, Suzanne Scott; three children.
Religion: Methodist.
Political Career: Idaho Senate, 1975-81; U.S. House, 1981-91.
Capitol Office: 313 Hart Bldg. 20510; 224-2752.

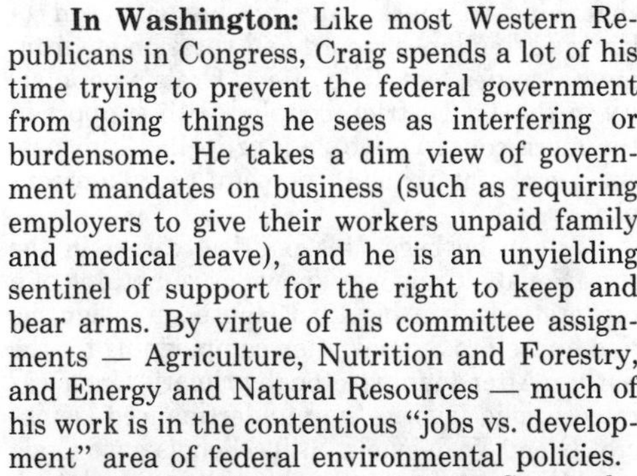

In Washington: Like most Western Republicans in Congress, Craig spends a lot of his time trying to prevent the federal government from doing things he sees as interfering or burdensome. He takes a dim view of government mandates on business (such as requiring employers to give their workers unpaid family and medical leave), and he is an unyielding sentinel of support for the right to keep and bear arms. By virtue of his committee assignments — Agriculture, Nutrition and Forestry, and Energy and Natural Resources — much of his work is in the contentious "jobs vs. development" area of federal environmental policies.

During his first two years in the Senate, he continued his efforts on several issues he pursued during his decade as the House member for western Idaho.

Craig has participated in the protracted debate over the designation of wilderness lands in Idaho. For years, environmental and commercial interests have been hung up on how much additional land to set aside.

In 1987, he opposed a 1.4 million-acre compromise plan unveiled by GOP Sen. James A. McClure (whom Craig succeeded in 1991) and Democratic Gov. Cecil D. Andrus. That plan dissolved. The state's congressional delegation met in January 1993 with Andrus to discuss the thorny issue, seeking a formula for balancing competing interests such as jobs, recreation and wilderness preservation.

In 1989, with many Northwesterners upset over proposed government intervention to protect the timberland habitat of the northern spotted owl, Craig introduced legislation aimed at weakening the Threatened and Endangered Species Act. His bill would have required public participation throughout the process of listing threatened and endangered species, rather than only after the Fish and Wildlife Service makes a proposed listing decision.

Early in the 103rd Congress, Craig sponsored legislation to counter Clinton administration proposals to impose steep royalty fees on minerals mined on public lands. Craig's bill, backed by the mining industry, called for 2 percent net royalty on hard-rock minerals extracted from federal lands. The bill easily passed the Senate by voice vote in late May.

The ease of passage, however, did not speak to the bill's chances of becoming law. The higher-royalty desires of the Clinton administration were much more closely reflected in a House bill sponsored by Democrat Nick J. Rahall II of West Virginia. Rahall's bill would impose an 8 percent royalty on the gross value of extracted minerals. Craig said Rahall's measure would cost his state thousands of jobs.

Craig portrayed his bill as "real" mining reform, but J. Bennett Johnston of Louisiana, chairman of the Senate Energy Committee, said it did not represent the Senate's substantive position and characterized the measure as merely a "ticket to conference committee." The assumption was that any compromise in conference would have to incorporate a royalty based on the gross value of the mineral as it is extracted, as Rahall's bill would require, rather than on the net value of the mineral after development costs are subtracted.

Craig's concerns about an overreaching federal government contributed to his strong opposition to legislation requiring businesses to provide employees with unpaid family and medical leave. In 1993, he wrote the GOP alternative that would have provided tax breaks for companies that offered leave programs. He accused his colleagues supporting mandatory leave of trying to "shove the costs off on the private sector." Craig lost 33-67, and the mandatory leave measure went on to become law with Clinton's signature.

Without exception, Craig finds that gun control proposals violate his concept that government's intrusion into citizens' lives should be limited. During a debate on anti-crime legislation in 1991, he contended that an amendment imposing a waiting period on the purchase of handguns would not take guns out of the hands of criminals: "We will never get the criminal element of this country marching in lockstep to the tune of the law."

Craig is a longtime crusader for a balanced-budget constitutional amendment, and he has carried that mission beyond the halls of Congress. Founder of CLUBB (Congressional Leaders United for a Balanced Budget), Craig urges state legislatures to demand that Congress enact a balanced-budget amendment or call a constitutional convention to draft one. Craig also supports giving the president enhanced rescission authority, a version of a line-item veto.

Craig's ardor for deficit reduction does not keep him from lobbying for home-state projects. But when he delivers, he seems to feel compelled to explain. In the 100th Congress, Craig helped secure the release of $300,000 to conduct a water-quality study in Idaho; he said it was "no pork barrel," but of "great importance" to several Western states. In a letter to constituents, Craig noted that a $1.35 million federal matching grant he helped secure for the Centennial Trail was "not one of the so-called budget-busting measures." The money was already set aside; he just earmarked it for Idaho.

One of 52 Republicans swept into the House in 1980, Craig proudly counted himself a front-ranks leader in the "Reagan Revolution." He shared with the new president roots in the West, a conservative ideology and a confrontational approach to government. But by the end of Ronald Reagan's tenure in the White House, Craig was among those Republicans who seemed more ideologically consistent than Reagan himself; at times he sounded dismayed that even after eight years under a president supposedly opposed to federal largess, the deficit had multiplied.

For the last four years of his House tenure, Craig served on the ethics committee, and early in the 103rd Congress, he was assigned to the Senate Ethics Committee, which was facing the task of looking into sexual harassment allegations against GOP Sen. Bob Packwood of Oregon.

At Home: Craig's ascent to the Senate was a fairly smooth affair, as he mobilized the renowned statewide organization of retiring Sen. McClure to roll over his Democratic opponent, Ron Twilegar, a former state legislator and Boise City Council member.

Idaho Democrats also cooperated to some extent by failing to field a well-known candidate. Rep. Richard Stallings, whose strong wins in the conservative 2nd District cast him as the party's best potential statewide candidate, opted against the race. After prolonged consideration, former Gov. John V. Evans, the 1986 nominee against GOP Sen. Steve Symms, also decided not to run.

Craig, by contrast, declared less than a week after McClure's January 1990 retirement announcement that he would vacate his 1st District seat and enter the race. Although State Attorney General Jim Jones also filed for the Republican nomination, he ran an underfunded campaign. He was no match for the well-funded, well-organized Craig, who won 59 percent of the primary vote. Twilegar, meanwhile, won his primary with 64 percent over an obscure Idaho Falls businessman.

Craig's reputation as a stalwart opponent of abortion produced one of the more awkward moments of his campaign. In a debate with Twilegar, Craig responded to a question by saying that if his wife were impregnated by rape, it would be up to her to decide if she should seek an abortion. Twilegar, who favored abortion rights, then archly asked whether Craig's wife should be the only woman in the country to have a choice.

But that was one of the few Twilegar shots that hit the mark. Mostly, his criticism of Craig's attendance record and votes on environmental issues had little effect. Craig's popularity in the 1st District, coupled with support in the more conservative 2nd, propelled him past the Democrat to a 61 percent to 39 percent victory.

When he began his political career in the state Senate, Craig was known as something of a moderate. But in his 1980 House campaign, he tied himself to Symms, then campaigning for the Senate. After winning a tough primary, Craig was rated a solid favorite over underfinanced Democrat Glenn W. Nichols. Still, Nichols gave Craig trouble, drawing attention by walking the length of the 1st, from Canada to Nevada, criticizing Craig's "Sagebrush Rebellion" sympathies.

Craig had one last tough House contest in 1982; his opponent that year was Democrat Larry LaRocco, who would win to succeed Craig in 1990.

LaRocco had worked in Idaho's Northern Panhandle as a field representative for former Democratic Sen. Frank Church. LaRocco said Craig favored wholesale privatization of federal lands. Craig complained he was the victim of "falsehoods, misrepresentations and misreporting." Despite strong support for LaRocco from the economically depressed northern part of the 1st, Craig again won with 54 percent.

After that, Craig developed a track record of success that was also marked by an eerie streak of bad fortune for his Democratic opponents. In 1984, the man who initially decided to challenge Craig was killed in a car crash. Craig soared to 69 percent against Bill Hellar, who was named the substitute Democratic nominee after the fatal car crash.

That tally was the highest vote by any 1st District candidate in nearly 50 years. Neither McClure nor Symms, both of whom held the 1st before moving to the Senate, had ever surpassed 60 percent.

In 1986, candidate Pete Busch, who two years before had mounted a spirited underdog campaign against McClure, died when the plane he was piloting crashed. Craig took 65 percent against Bill Currie, a former Boundary County commissioner who replaced Busch as the Democratic candidate.

The 1988 campaign was more conventional; the outcome was the same. Craig had no trouble turning back the challenge of two-term state legislator Jeanne Givens, a member of the Coeur d'Alene tribe.

Committees

Agriculture, Nutrition & Forestry (6th of 8 Republicans)
Agricultural Research, Conservation, Forestry & General Legislation (ranking); Agricultural Credit; Agricultural Production & Stabilization of Prices

Energy & Natural Resources (6th of 9 Republicans)
Energy Research & Development; Mineral Resources Development & Production (ranking); Public Lands, National Parks & Forests

Select Ethics (3rd of 3 Republicans)

Special Aging (8th of 10 Republicans)

Joint Economic

Elections

1990 General		
Larry E. Craig (R)	193,641	(61%)
Ron J. Twilegar (D)	122,295	(39%)
1990 Primary		
Larry E. Craig (R)	65,830	(59%)
Jim Jones (R)	45,733	(41%)

Previous Winning Percentages: **1988 *** (66%) **1986 *** (65%) **1984 *** (69%) **1982 *** (54%) **1980 *** (54%)

** House elections.*

Campaign Finance

	Receipts	Receipts from PACs		Expend-itures
1990				
Craig (R)	$1,734,617	$811,026	(47%)	$1,652,532
Twilegar (D)	$544,516	$212,049	(39%)	$544,419

Key Votes

1993	
Require unpaid family and medical leave	N
Approve national "motor voter" registration bill	N
Approve budget increasing taxes and reducing deficit	N
Support president's right to lift military gay ban	N
1992	
Approve school-choice pilot program	Y
Allow shifting funds from defense to domestic programs	N
Oppose deeper cuts in spending for SDI	Y
1991	
Approve waiting period for handgun purchases	N
Raise senators' pay and ban honoraria	Y
Authorize use of force in Persian Gulf	Y
Confirm Clarence Thomas to Supreme Court	Y

Voting Studies

	Presidential Support		Party Unity		Conservative Coalition	
Year	**S**	**O**	**S**	**O**	**S**	**O**
1992	83	15	99	1	97	3
1991	91	9	97	3	90	8
House Service:						
1990	59	25	75	8	89	2
1989	78	22	93	6	93	7
1988	66	23	87	5	76	5
1987	65 †	28 †	83 †	8 †	93 †	5 †
1986	79	21	85	9	92	6
1985	75	24	91	5	96	2
1984	73	22	86	4	93	5
1983	73	16	86	4	93	3
1982	75	23	85	7	86	8
1981	72	24	91	5	91	4

† Not eligible for all recorded votes.

Interest Group Ratings

Year	ADA	AFL-CIO	CCUS	ACU
1992	0	17	90	100
1991	5	25	100	86
House Service:				
1990	11	0	82	86
1989	0	0	100	96
1988	5	7	92	100
1987	8	13	93	86
1986	5	21	100	86
1985	0	0	91	90
1984	5	15	87	91
1983	0	0	84	100
1982	5	5	90	95
1981	0	13	95	100

Dirk Kempthorne (R)

Of Boise — Elected 1992; 1st Term

Born: Oct. 29, 1951, San Diego, Calif.

Education: U. of Idaho, B.A. 1975.

Occupation: Public affairs manager; securities representative; political consultant; building association executive.

Family: Wife, Patricia Merrill; two children.

Religion: Methodist.

Political Career: Mayor of Boise, 1986-92.

Capitol Office: 367 Dirksen Bldg. 20510; 224-6142.

The Path to Washington: Kempthorne's opponent in the 1992 Senate race was a four-term House Democrat, and the Republican got as much mileage as he could out of the line that he, unlike his foe, was not a Beltway-based officeholder.

But Kempthorne is hardly an outsider to politics. Before his Senate victory, he had spent six years as mayor of Boise, Idaho's largest city. His Senate candidacy was strongly backed by the Idaho Republican establishment, which was aiming to retain the hold the GOP has enjoyed since 1981 on both of Idaho's Senate seats. And at the top of Kempthorne's campaign structure was popular former GOP Sen. James A. McClure.

Kempthorne won the race to fill the seat vacated by retiring Republican Sen. Steve Symms by capitalizing on Idaho's sizable bedrock Republican vote as well as voter resentment toward Washington, which hampered Democratic Rep. Richard Stallings' bid.

Kempthorne calls himself a conservative Republican. He likes to say his role model is Arizona's Barry Goldwater, who rose from the Phoenix City Council to national prominence.

Yet he does not come on as strongly as his predecessor, the hard-charging, conservative Symms. In fact, after handling the relatively non-ideological post of mayor, Kempthorne seemed somewhat uneasy in his Senate campaign about signing on to a solidly conservative agenda.

For example, he says he is a free-trader, but his stance on the North American Free Trade Agreement is closer to President Clinton's qualified support than to George Bush's strong advocacy.

Kempthorne has said he is against foreign aid, but in a letter to the American Israel Public Affairs Committee during the campaign, he said he supported foreign aid to Israel. When that caused a flap, a campaign spokesman said "support" did not mean Kempthorne would vote for such aid.

On other issues his stance is less conditional. Kempthorne says he is a firm believer in limiting congressional terms. "I believe that is what the Founding Fathers intended," he said at one campaign debate. He suggested a limit of two terms for senators and six terms for members of the House.

In campaigning, Kempthorne took careful positions on natural resource issues, which are matters of wide debate in Idaho. He opposed giving federal wilderness lands a reserved water right, as happened in neighboring Nevada, although he endorsed negotiations among all interested state groups to devise a long-sought wilderness plan for Idaho.

He ran on a platform of balancing the federal budget. In one speech before a local Lions Club, he said the federal budget should be capped at its current level and that the federal budget could be balanced in five years if spending growth was limited to 3 percent or less each year.

Kempthorne opposes abortion except in cases of rape, incest and danger to the woman's life.

As a senator, Kempthorne plans to fight for Idaho's natural resources and infrastructure needs, balancing fellow Republican Sen. Larry E. Craig's spot on the Energy and Natural Resources Committee with his seat on the Environment and Public Works panel. Kempthorne also is a member of the Armed Services and Small Business committees.

During the campaign, Kempthorne early and often accused Stallings of being part of the gridlock paralyzing Capitol Hill. He also made an issue of Stallings' eight overdrawn checks at the House bank.

Stallings had secured eastern Idaho's formerly Republican House seat by compiling a moderate-to-conservative voting record, and he hoped to transfer that success statewide. Kempthorne's waffling on the foreign aid issue gave Democrats some cause for optimism that Stallings might close ground on the favored Republican. But in the end, Stallings could not break the voters' habit of sending Republicans to the Senate. Kempthorne won with 57 percent of the vote.

Kempthorne has moved easily between the worlds of business and government. From 1978 to 1981 he was executive director of the Idaho State Home Builders Association. His first direct involvement in statewide politics came in 1981, when he managed the unsuccessful gubernatorial campaign of Lt. Gov. Phil Batt. His successful run for mayor in 1985 was based on a platform of rebuilding the city's downtown. He was re-elected to a second term in 1989.

Committees

Armed Services (8th of 9 Republicans)
Coalition Defense & Reinforcing Forces; Defense Technology, Acquisition & Industrial Base; Nuclear Deterrence, Arms Control & Defense Intelligence

Environment & Public Works (7th of 7 Republicans)
Clean Air & Nuclear Regulation; Clean Water, Fisheries & Wildlife; Water Resources, Transportation, Public Buildings & Economic Development

Small Business (7th of 9 Republicans)
Innovation, Manufacturing & Technology; Rural Economy & Family Farming

Campaign Finance

	Receipts	Receipts from PACs		Expend-itures
1992				
Kempthorne (R)	$1,351,127	$599,151	(44%)	$1,305,338
Stallings (D)	$1,224,232	$605,068	(49%)	$1,222,222

Key Votes

1993	
Require unpaid family and medical leave	N
Approve national "motor voter" registration bill	N
Approve budget increasing taxes and reducing deficit	N
Support president's right to lift military gay ban	N

Elections

1992 General		
Dirk Kempthorne (R)	270,468	(57%)
Richard Stallings (D)	208,036	(43%)
1992 Primary		
Dirk Kempthorne (R)	67,001	(57%)
Rodney (Rod) W. Beck (R)	26,977	(23%)
Milt Erhart (R)	22,682	(19%)

1 Larry LaRocco (D)

Of McCall — Elected 1990; 2nd Term

Born: Aug. 25, 1946, Van Nuys, Calif.

Education: U. of Portland, B.A. 1967; Johns Hopkins U., 1968-69; Boston U., M.S. 1969.

Military Service: Army, 1969-72.

Occupation: Stockbroker.

Family: Wife, Chris Bideganeta; two children.

Religion: Roman Catholic.

Political Career: Democratic nominee for U.S. House, 1982; Democratic nominee for Idaho Senate, 1986.

Capitol Office: 1117 Longworth Bldg. 20515; 225-6611.

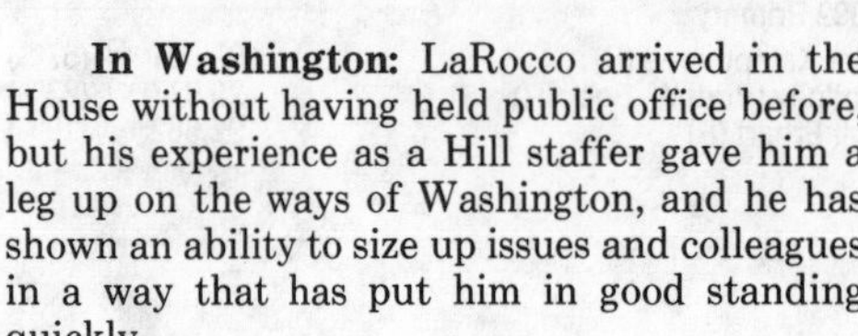

In Washington: LaRocco arrived in the House without having held public office before, but his experience as a Hill staffer gave him a leg up on the ways of Washington, and he has shown an ability to size up issues and colleagues in a way that has put him in good standing quickly.

LaRocco landed on the Banking and Interior (now Natural Resources) committees and got off to good starts there. Two LaRocco bills became law in the 102nd Congress: a measure to require consumer credit bureaus to include information on overdue child support payments, and a bill to issue silver medals from Congress to Persian Gulf War veterans.

The child-support bill, named after the late New York Democrat Ted Weiss, requires consumer credit agencies to include on credit reports any delinquency of $1,000 or more on court-ordered child-support payments. The bill was signed in October 1992 by President Bush.

The Defense Department initially opposed the Congressional Commemorative Medals, saying that enough honors had been bestowed upon the veterans, and that these latest were "not warranted or appropriate." LaRocco added an amendment to the bill directing the U.S. Mint to coin bronze replicas of the medals to be sold to the public to defray the costs of the silver versions.

LaRocco also worked during the 102nd Congress to allow the Forest Service to speed up harvests of "salvage timber" — dead and dying trees — that have otherwise been rotting and going to waste. The bill made it out of the Agriculture Committee but then stalled. LaRocco reintroduced it in the 103rd Congress.

In 1991, when Congress tried and failed to overhaul the nation's banking system, LaRocco succeeded in attaching an amendment to the bill that would have bucked the Bush administration and allowed healthy banks to continue to accept large certificates of deposit placed not by depositors but by brokers, who often search nationwide for the best interest rates.

"Anybody can call an '800' number and buy a CD. The fact that a broker is involved should not be a determining factor in whether deposit insurance applies," argued LaRocco, a former stockbroker.

LaRocco supports abortion rights, opposes gun control and favors a compromise in the longstanding debate over the use of 5 million acres of pristine Idaho "wilderness" land. He also worked toward providing federal protection of a natural area for birds of prey in southern Idaho.

LaRocco says that one of his major priorities in the 103rd Congress will be to win passage of an Idaho lands bill that would decide the status of lands frozen by the Wilderness Act of 1964. LaRocco wants to separate some lands out as wilderness and others as "special management areas" that can be used with some restrictions.

LaRocco introduced a wilderness bill early in the 103rd Congress dealing with national forests in his district and was negotiating with other members of Idaho's delegation and Gov. Cecil D. Andrus to craft a statewide bill. An attempt in 1988 to pass a similar Idaho lands bill failed.

At Home: LaRocco developed his political touch during the 1970s as an aide to Democratic Sen. Frank Church. Although his quest for public office was twice set back, LaRocco was able to win a close contest in 1990 for the 1st District seat that Republican Rep. Larry E. Craig left open to run for the Senate.

LaRocco settled in quickly. By 1992, district Republicans had trouble finding a candidate to contest LaRocco's re-election.

LaRocco was Church's north Idaho field representative from 1975 to 1981, when Church left office. Though he made friends and contacts while tending to Church's constituent matters, LaRocco had to overcome Idaho's conservative tendencies when he struck out on his own.

He did so in 1982 by challenging then-freshman Rep. Craig. LaRocco was able to carry the Northern Panhandle region, but not by a wide enough margin to offset the typically strong

Idaho 1

West — Boise; Nampa; Panhandle

Democratic Rep. LaRocco's sweeping win in 1992 (he carried every county) went against partisan form in the 1st. This mainly conservative district usually shows a strong Republican lean.

The 1st ranges nearly 500 miles from British Columbia to Nevada. Boise's white-collar constituency combines with voters in agricultural communities to provide Republicans with a solid base. George Bush finished first in all counties from Idaho County south, and victorious Republican Senate candidate (and then-Boise Mayor) Dirk Kempthorne defeated Democratic Rep. Richard Stallings by a whopping margin in the southern part of the 1st.

The most solid Democratic bloc is in blue-collar areas of the Northern Panhandle. Bill Clinton led the field in seven of the nine northernmost counties, and Stallings carried five.

The district also showed a strain of Sagebrush independence, giving Ross Perot more than a quarter of its presidential vote.

Ada County (Boise) has about 20 percent of Idaho's population. It is the only county split between the districts; the line bisects Boise, the state's capital and largest city. The 1st has most of Ada County's territory and about two-thirds of its population.

The 1st skips Boise's downtown and takes in its mainly residential western portion. Voters here and in the suburbs helped Bush win Ada County with 63 percent of the vote in 1988 and hang on with 45 percent in 1992.

The Republican grip is stronger in Canyon County (Nampa), on Ada's western border. Idaho's second-largest county gave Bush 51 percent in 1992, his best showing in the 1st; LaRocco's win in Canyon that year (also with 51 percent) broke sharply with partisan habit. The county is the state's top producer of cattle and corn and a leader in sugar beets.

To the north is a spread of mainly rural areas, including vast Idaho County. This Republican turf gives way to the Panhandle, where Democratic habits were implanted by a long period of labor activism in the timberlands, ore-mining areas and the industrial city of Lewiston.

Some Democratic-leaning areas have relatively stable economies. Lewiston, in Nez Perce County, has a grain-shipping port and the Potlatch pulp and paper factory; Latah County has the University of Idaho in Moscow (9,700 students). But the collapse of silver prices in the early 1980s crushed mining-dependent Shoshone County, which still has a jobless rate of more than 20 percent. Clinton took 49 percent in Shoshone, easily his best county showing in Idaho.

In some parts of this mountain and lake country, an expansion of the tourist industry and the arrival of many retirees have boosted the population and weakened the Democrats' position. Bush finished first in Kootenai County (Coeur d'Alene) — the Panhandle's most populous jurisdiction — and Kempthorne pulled down 57 percent.

1990 Population: 503,357. White 477,807 (95%), Black 1,112 (<1%), Other 24,438 (5%). Hispanic origin 23,070 (5%). 18 and over 358,537 (71%), 62 and over 77,332 (15%). Median age: 33.

Republican vote for Craig in the southern part of the 1st. Craig won with 54 percent overall.

In 1986, LaRocco set his sights on the state Senate and ran a tough challenge against a Republican incumbent, but again he fell short. But his ensuing strong House race showings in the south are attributed to his high visibility throughout the 1980s. As vice president of the Boise office of a large brokerage firm, LaRocco was tapped for commentaries by Boise TV and radio stations. In 1988, LaRocco led a successful statewide effort to amend the state constitution to allow a lottery.

LaRocco was thus a recognizable face in much the 1st when he bid to succeed Craig in 1990. He took 43 percent to beat two other candidates in the Democratic primary, and started out the general election campaign with an edge over Republican nominee C. A. "Skip" Smyser, a conservative state senator little-known outside his base in southern Idaho's Canyon County.

Smyser used LaRocco's backing for a wilderness compromise as well as his support from environmental groups such as the Sierra Club to try to pry away votes in the north, where loggers shared Smyser's opposition to setting aside additional land as wilderness.

Smyser's northern strategy had limited success. In the logging towns in Benewah County (St. Maries), the message took hold: Smyser won 52 percent in Benewah, which had backed LaRocco in his 1982 race. But elsewhere in the north, LaRocco ran much stronger than he had against Craig. In the nine northernmost counties (which cast about 40 percent of the

1st's vote), LaRocco received 60 percent against Smyser; those counties gave LaRocco 53 percent in 1982. In the swing county of Kootenai (Coeur d'Alene), LaRocco captured 55 percent, 11 points better than in 1982.

Although Smyser ran a game campaign, LaRocco lost the southern part of the 1st by a much smaller margin than in 1982. He took 53 percent districtwide.

Despite this fairly modest total, no leading Republican volunteered to take on LaRocco in 1992. The nomination went to former state Sen. Rachel S. Gilbert.

A hard-line conservative best known for her anti-tax stands, Gilbert had finished second in the 1990 GOP gubernatorial primary. Although she had a core of activist supporters, her strongly ideological profile and often-acerbic personality limited her electoral appeal. LaRocco won with nearly 60 percent.

Committees

Banking, Finance & Urban Affairs (12th of 30 Democrats)
Consumer Credit & Insurance; Financial Institutions Supervision, Regulation & Deposit Insurance; International Development, Finance, Trade & Monetary Policy

Natural Resources (15th of 28 Democrats)
Energy & Mineral Resources; National Parks, Forests & Public Lands

Elections

1992 General		
Larry LaRocco (D)	140,985	(58%)
Rachel S. Gilbert (R)	90,983	(37%)
John Abel (I)	6,255	(3%)
Henry "Sonny" Kinsey (I)	4,567	(2%)
1990 General		
Larry LaRocco (D)	85,054	(53%)
C.A. "Skip" Smyser (R)	75,406	(47%)

District Vote for President

1992	
D	75,499 (31%)
R	101,787 (42%)
I	67,677 (28%)

Campaign Finance

	Receipts	Receipts from PACs		Expend-itures
1992				
LaRocco (D)	$623,847	$408,955	(66%)	$623,327
Gilbert (R)	$222,858	$47,110	(21%)	$222,604
1990				
LaRocco (D)	$449,419	$238,753	(53%)	$447,895
Smyser (R)	$487,424	$198,459	(41%)	$480,994

Key Votes

1993	
Require parental notification of minors' abortions	N
Require unpaid family and medical leave	N
Approve national "motor voter" registration bill	Y
Approve budget increasing taxes and reducing deficit	Y
Approve economic stimulus plan	Y
1992	
Approve balanced-budget constitutional amendment	Y
Close down space station program	Y
Approve U.S. aid for former Soviet Union	Y
Allow shifting funds from defense to domestic programs	N
1991	
Extend unemployment benefits using deficit financing	Y
Approve waiting period for handgun purchases	N
Authorize use of force in Persian Gulf	N

Voting Studies

	Presidential Support		Party Unity		Conservative Coalition	
Year	S	O	S	O	S	O
1992	29	70	85	14	56	44
1991	41	55	81	18	59	35

Interest Group Ratings

Year	ADA	AFL-CIO	CCUS	ACU
1992	80	75	50	24
1991	45	64	60	16

2 Michael D. Crapo (R)

Of Idaho Falls — Elected 1992; 1st Term

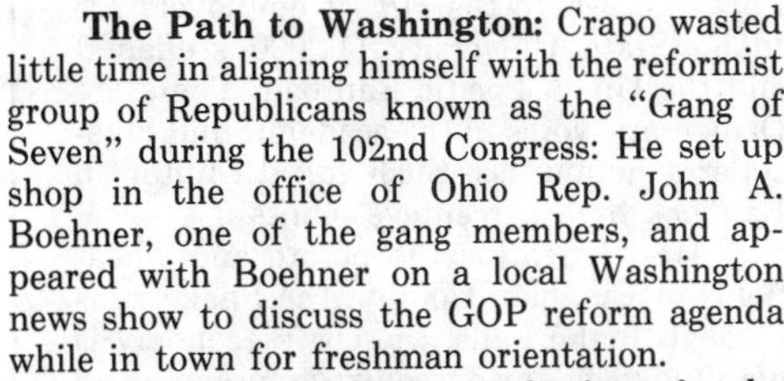

Born: May 20, 1951, Idaho Falls, Idaho.
Education: Brigham Young U., B.A. 1973; Harvard U., J.D. 1977.
Occupation: Lawyer.
Family: Wife, Susan Diane Hasleton; five children.
Religion: Mormon.
Political Career: Idaho Senate, 1985-93, president pro tempore, 1989-93.
Capitol Office: 437 Cannon Bldg. 20515; 225-5531.

The Path to Washington: Crapo wasted little time in aligning himself with the reformist group of Republicans known as the "Gang of Seven" during the 102nd Congress: He set up shop in the office of Ohio Rep. John A. Boehner, one of the gang members, and appeared with Boehner on a local Washington news show to discuss the GOP reform agenda while in town for freshman orientation.

To further signal their enthusiasm for the group, Crapo and about 30 other GOP freshmen also attended a GOP roundtable discussion on congressional reform during orientation.

Crapo's relationship with Boehner and other GOP incumbents paid off when GOP leaders doled out committee assignments.

Crapo landed a seat on the Energy and Commerce Committee, an assignment that will help him protect the interests of the 2nd District's farmers and guard the state's water rights, always an important issue in the water-thirsty West.

Crapo climbed aboard the congressional reform bandwagon long before he arrived in Washington. He chose reform as the centerpiece of his campaign to replace Democrat Richard Stallings, who passed up the chance for a fifth House term to run for the Senate.

A fiscal conservative, Crapo pledged to support a constitutional amendment to balance the budget with "no loopholes" and a line-item veto for the president. Along with about two-thirds of the GOP freshmen, Crapo voted in April 1993 for a Democratic version of the line-item veto, while also voting for a more potent GOP substitute.

Crapo also advocated a 12-year term limit for lawmakers; he later backed a proposal, approved by the Republican Conference during organizational meetings, prohibiting members of the GOP caucus from serving as any committee's ranking Republican for more than six consecutive years.

The general-election campaign was low-key compared with some other open-seat races across the country. Crapo and his Democratic opponent, state Auditor J. D. Williams, both of whom easily won their parties' nominations, had earned "nice guy" reputations during their political careers, and for the most part, both avoided mudslinging in the campaign.

First elected to the state Senate in 1984, Crapo became its president pro tempore, and thus the highest-ranking Republican policymaker in Idaho, in 1988. Crapo argued that he had helped stabilize Idaho's economy while serving in the state Senate, and he vowed to oppose any attempts to increase federal taxes or raise the federal debt limit.

Republicans had eagerly awaited Stallings' departure, believing that with the popular Democrat out of the picture they could regain control of the GOP-leaning 2nd. But the Democratic Party, with Williams as its candidate, had reason to hope that it could continue dominating the district as it had since Stallings first won in 1984.

Williams, who was appointed state auditor in 1989 and won election to that post in 1990, voiced views similar to those of Crapo, including opposition to abortion and gun control.

On economic issues, Crapo and Williams parted ways a bit. Crapo called for tax and spending cuts, and tax incentives for businesses to foster job growth. Williams argued that the government should invest more to stimulate growth industries and improve infrastructure.

Williams criticized Crapo for supporting tax hikes and a Senate pay raise while in the Legislature; Crapo tried to paint Williams as a liberal Democrat, citing contributions from numerous organized labor political action committees as evidence of Williams' ties to a liberal agenda.

Williams was hurt by charges late in the campaign that he had made improper campaign-related phone calls from his state auditor's office. He denied any wrongdoing, but he did stop making the calls.

Williams had hoped that running with Stallings on the ballot would increase his tally at the polls, but it was Crapo who benefited from his party's showing at the top of the ticket.

Idaho was one of 18 states that George Bush won, and Boise Mayor Dirk Kempthorne easily defeated Stallings in the Senate race. Crapo got more than 60 percent of the vote against Williams.

Idaho 2

East — Pocatello; Idaho Falls; Twin Falls

Republican Crapo's win ended the four-term Democratic hold, established by Richard Stallings, on the 2nd District seat. The Stallings era was a rare break in the Republicans' domination of this conservative region.

Although George Bush in 1992 ran far behind his 1988 vote in the 2nd, he carried all but one county. He won Madison County (Rexburg) with 59 percent; Bill Clinton hit bottom here with less than 10 percent. Ross Perot bested Clinton in all but six of the district's counties.

Stallings' failure to hold the 2nd in his 1992 Senate race sealed his fate against Republican Dirk Kempthorne.

By far, most district residents are of Northern European heritage. Members of the Church of Jesus Christ of Latter-day Saints make up the largest religious group; like Mormons everywhere, most have strongly conservative views.

Much of the district is farmland irrigated by the Snake River. At the district's western edge is the part of Boise that includes the state Capitol, major business offices and some affluent communities.

To the east, near Idaho Falls, is the Idaho National Engineering Laboratory (INEL), a federal research complex that is the state's largest single employment site (Westinghouse, the Department of Energy and Argonne all have workers here).

Boise is one of the nation's most economically vibrant small cities. Many of its businesses reflect the region's links to the land: The J. R. Simplot Co. raises potatoes and cattle, and Ore-Ida makes frozen french fries. Boise Cascade is a diversified forest products company. But some are industrial (the Morrison Knudsen heavy construction company) or cutting-edge (Micron Technology). Boise State University, with 14,200 students, is also in the district.

To the east is Elmore County, site of the Mountain Home Air Force Base. In the south-central part of the district is Twin Falls, hub of the Magic Valley region where potatoes, sugar beets, grain, livestock and trout are raised, and GOP votes are cast.

Farther east, in Bannock County, is Pocatello, where the largest employers are Idaho State University (11,000 students) and the Union Pacific Railroad. There are Democratic votes in the academic and blue-collar communities; Bush edged Clinton in Bannock by 3 percentage points.

After irrigating the potato and wheat fields of Bingham County, the Snake runs through Idaho Falls; the city's economy is highly dependent on contractors employed by the nearby INEL complex. In the Upper Snake River Valley is Rexburg, home of Mormon-run Ricks College (a two-year school with about 7,800 students).

In the mountainous center of the district is Blaine County and the bucolic Ketchum-Sun Valley area. Urban exiles, artists and outdoor enthusiasts boosted Blaine's population by 38 percent in the 1980s and gave it an un-Idaholike liberal tinge. It was the only county in the 2nd that Clinton carried (albeit with 36 percent).

1990 Population: 503,392. White 472,644 (94%), Black 2,258 (<1%), Other 28,490 (6%). Hispanic origin 29,857 (6%). 18 and over 339,807 (68%), 62 and over 67,196 (13%). Median age: 30.

Committee

Energy & Commerce (17th of 17 Republicans)
Energy & Power; Transportation & Hazardous Materials

Campaign Finance

	Receipts	Receipts from PACs		Expend-itures
1992				
Crapo (R)	$554,691	$234,599	(42%)	$572,532
Williams (D)	$253,051	$126,075	(50%)	$245,954

Key Votes

1993

Require parental notification of minors' abortions	Y
Require unpaid family and medical leave	N
Approve national "motor voter" registration bill	N
Approve budget increasing taxes and reducing deficit	N
Approve economic stimulus plan	N

Elections

1992 General		
Michael D. Crapo (R)	139,783	(61%)
J.D. Williams (D)	81,450	(35%)
Steven L. Kauer (I)	4,917	(2%)
David William Mansfield (I)	3,807	(2%)
1992 Primary		
Michael D. Crapo (R)	45,462	(68%)
Gary Glenn (R)	21,443	(32%)

District Vote for President

	1992	
D	61,514	(27%)
R	100,858	(45%)
I	62,718	(28%)

Illinois

STATE DATA

Governor: Jim Edgar (R)
First elected: 1990
Length of term: 4 years
Term expires: 1/95
Salary: $100,681
Term limit: No
Phone: (217) 782-6830
Born: July 22, 1946; Vinita, Okla.
Education: Eastern Illinois U., B.S. 1968; U. of Illinois, 1969-70
Occupation: Legislative aide
Family: Wife, Brenda Smith; two children.
Religion: American Baptist
Political Career: Candidate for Ill. House, 1974; Ill. House, 1977-79; Ill. secretary of state, 1981-91

Lt. Gov.: Bob Kustra (R)
First elected: 1990
Length of term: 4 years
Term expires: 1/95
Salary: $71,069
Phone: (217) 782-7884

State election official: (217) 782-4141
Democratic headquarters: (217) 528-3471
Republican headquarters: (217) 525-0011

REDISTRICTING

Illinois lost two seats in reapportionment, dropping from 22 districts to 20. The legislature failed to act on a new map by June 30, 1991, deadline. Federal court approved the map Nov. 6.

STATE LEGISLATURE

Bicameral General Assembly. Meets January-June.

Senate: 59 members, 4-year terms
1992 breakdown: 32R, 27D; 48 men, 11 women; 49 whites, 8 blacks, 2 Hispanics
Salary: $38,496
Phone: (217) 782-5715

House of Representatives: 118 members, 2-year terms
1992 breakdown: 67D, 51R; 88 men, 30 women; 102 whites, 12 blacks, 4 Hispanics
Salary: $38,496
Phone: (217) 782-8223

URBAN STATISTICS

City	Pop.
Chicago	2,783,726
Mayor Richard M. Daley, D	
Rockford	139,943
Mayor Charles E. Box, D	
Peoria	113,504
Mayor James A. Maloof, N-P	
Springfield	105,227
Mayor Ossie Langfelder, D	
Aurora	99,581
Mayor David L. Pierce, I	

U.S. CONGRESS

Senate: 2 D, 0 R
House: 12 D, 8 R

TERM LIMITS

For Congress: No
For state offices: No

ELECTIONS

1992 Presidential Vote

Bill Clinton	48.6%
George Bush	34.3%
Ross Perot	16.6%

1988 Presidential Vote

George Bush	51%
Michael S. Dukakis	49%

1984 Presidential Vote

Ronald Reagan	56%
Walter F. Mondale	43%

POPULATION

1990 population		11,430,602
1980 population		11,426,518
Percent change		+0%
Rank among states:		6
White		78%
Black		15%
Hispanic		8%
Asian or Pacific islander		2%
Urban		85%
Rural		15%
Born in state		69%
Foreign-born		8%
Under age 18	2,946,366	26%
Ages 18-64	7,047,691	62%
65 and older	1,436,545	13%
Median age		32.8

MISCELLANEOUS

Capital: Springfield
Number of counties: 102
Per capita income: $20,824 (1991)
Rank among states: 10
Total area: 56,345 sq. miles
Rank among states: 24

Illinois - Congressional Districts

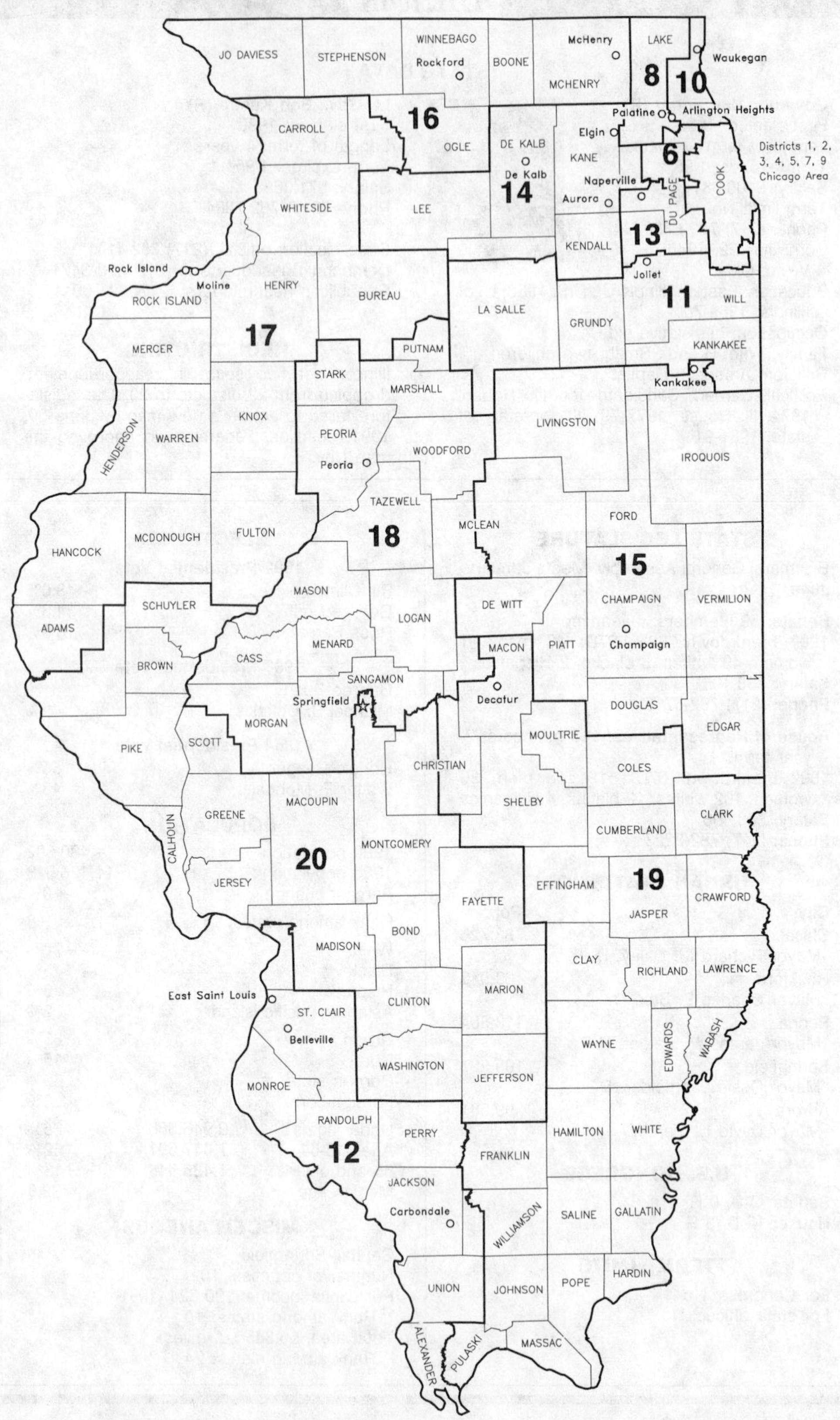

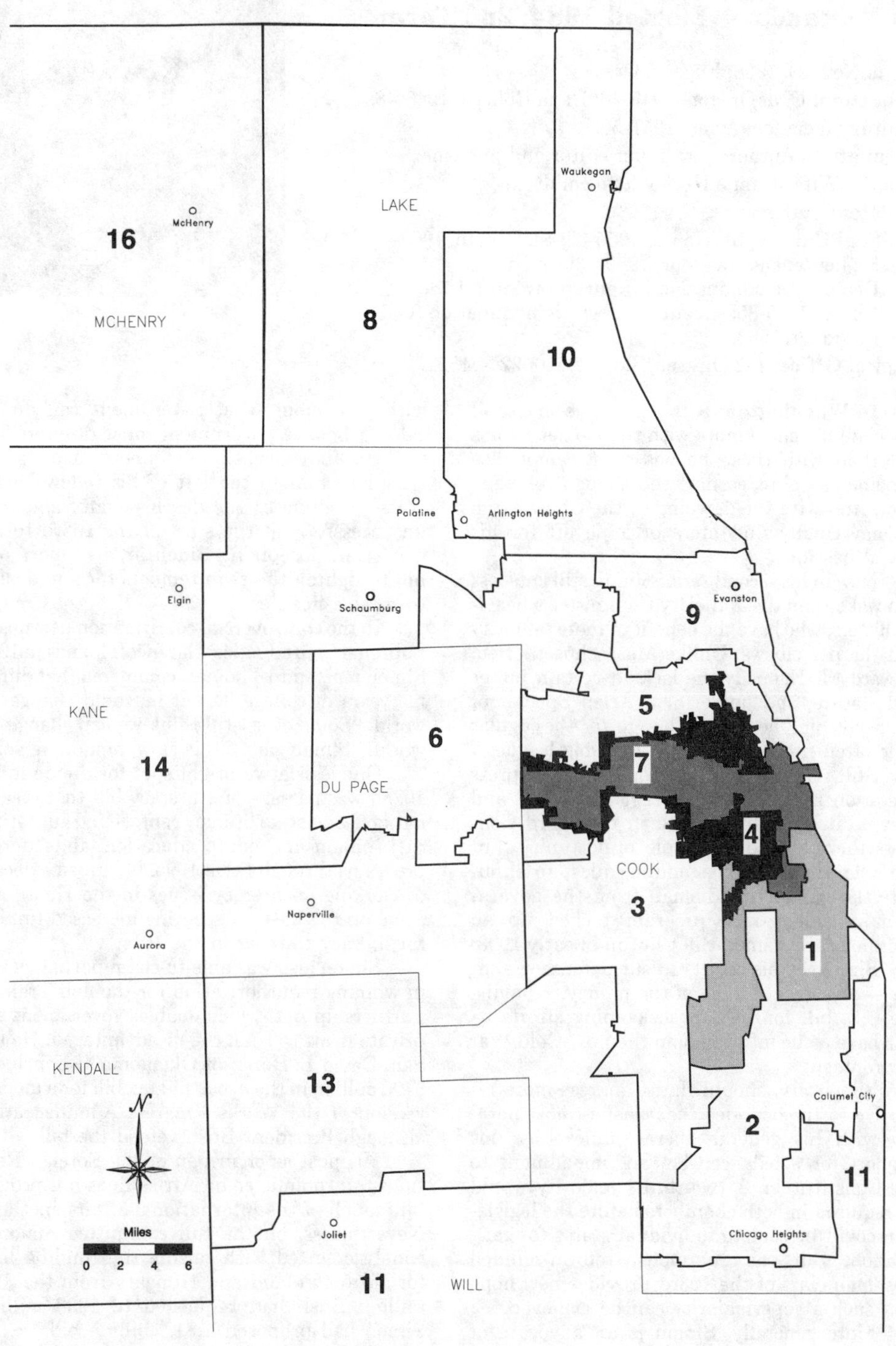

LAKE
Waukegan
16
McHenry
MCHENRY
8
10
Palatine
Arlington Heights
Elgin
Schaumburg
Evanston
9
5
KANE
14
6
7
DU PAGE
4
COOK
3
Naperville
Aurora
1
KENDALL
13
2
Calumet City
11
Miles
0 2 4 6
Joliet
Chicago Heights
11
WILL

Paul Simon (D)

Of Makanda — Elected 1984; 2nd Term

Born: Nov. 29, 1928, Eugene, Ore.
Education: U. of Oregon, 1945-46; Dana College, 1946-48.
Military Service: Army, 1951-53.
Occupation: Author; newspaper editor and publisher.
Family: Wife, Jeanne Hurley; two children.
Religion: Lutheran.
Political Career: Ill. House, 1955-63; Ill. Senate, 1963-69; lieutenant governor, 1969-73; sought Democratic nomination for governor, 1972; U.S. House, 1975-85; sought Democratic nomination for president, 1988.
Capitol Office: 462 Dirksen Bldg. 20510; 224-2152.

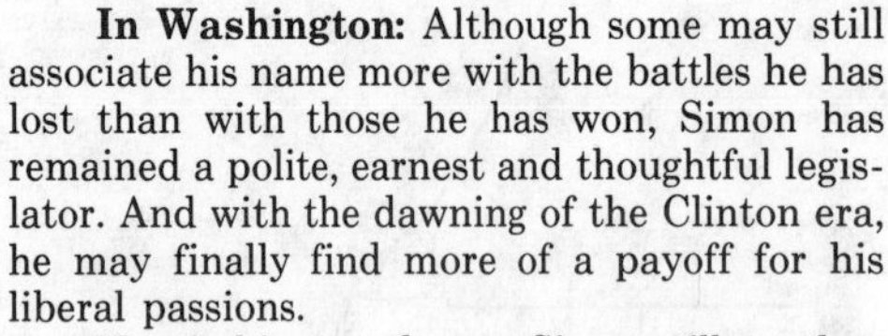

In Washington: Although some may still associate his name more with the battles he has lost than with those he has won, Simon has remained a polite, earnest and thoughtful legislator. And with the dawning of the Clinton era, he may finally find more of a payoff for his liberal passions.

Now in his second term, Simon still cuts less of a wake than the Judiciary Committee's heaviest hitters, who have the benefit of more seniority and sharper elbows. Unlike Massachusetts Sen. Edward M. Kennedy, he lacks a certain power and stature, and unlike Sen. Arlen Specter of Pennsylvania, he lacks the go-for-the-jugular style often needed in the political big leagues.

Still, Simon and his sophisticated press operation know how to market his issues, and they do it aggressively. And in the 103rd Congress there should be ample opportunity. For example, Simon's longstanding quest to eliminate the banker middleman from the government's student loan program picked up an enormous ally named Bill Clinton in early 1993.

Similarly, his efforts to cut defense spending — and devote some of the money to paying the U.S. bill for U.N. peacekeeping efforts — also have come into vogue in the post-Cold War environment.

Simon also should find Congress more receptive to the one idea that clashes most notably with his general liberal philosophy: his support for a balanced-budget amendment to the Constitution. A two-thirds majority would be required in both chambers before the legislation could be sent to individual states for ratification. But the enormous, reform-minded freshman class of the 103rd provides new hope that such a supermajority can be achieved.

More generally, Simon is an advocate of activist government who had to bide his time through a dozen years of Republican rule in the White House. So there was a certain vindication in hearing President Clinton declare in his first address to Congress: "Tonight, I want to talk with you about what government can do because I believe government must do more."

On Judiciary, Simon's liberal leanings often place him to the left of his fellow Democrats. He opposes the death penalty and tried unsuccessfully at the start of the 103rd to win Chairman Joseph R. Biden Jr.'s support of a bill to tighten the requirements for gun dealers to receive licenses.

In the controversial confirmation hearings of Supreme Court Justice Clarence Thomas in 1991, Simon reacted to Thomas' comments that during his years in college he felt he could change the world. "Some of us still think we can change the world," Simon said in his slow, monotone voice.

One legislative bright spot for Simon in the 102nd was passage of a literacy bill that created national and state literacy centers and authorized $1.1 billion for adult education and literacy programs through fiscal 1995. It capped a decade of working on literacy issues in the House and came on the heels of securing increased funding for literacy training in the 101st.

Simon also was able to claim partial victory in winning reauthorization for the Job Training Partnership Act, which enables government and private firms to train the disadvantaged. He and Sen. David L. Boren of Oklahoma also included $400 million in the urban aid tax bill for a modern version of the Works Progress Administration, although President Bush vetoed the bill.

His post as chairman of the Foreign Relations Subcommittee on Africa does not provide him much of the international affairs spotlight. Nevertheless, on the full committee Simon is widely credited with raising the funding level for aid for Poland and Hungary from the $146 million Bush had requested to $938 million. Simon had proposed a $1.2 billion bill.

Part of Simon's idiosyncratic vision is his support for a handful of conservative litmus test issues. The self-described liberal is also a former small-town newspaper publisher with an aversion to red ink. In the 101st Congress, he was also a lead sponsor of legislation to waive antitrust laws to allow the networks to develop guidelines on TV violence.

On most issues, Simon will eventually set aside his intransigent liberalism and compromise, once he is given a hearing. During the overhaul of legal immigration statutes in the 101st, Simon offered a proposal that would have expanded rather than capped immigration and kept the emphasis on family reunification, ensuring that the overwhelming majority of immigrants come from Mexico, Asia and Central America.

But on the Judiciary Immigration Subcommittee, Simon took a realistic approach and bargained to raise the immigration cap, successfully fought an English-language preference proposal and used his knowledge of the House to help the bill's lead Senate sponsors succeed.

His focus on Illinois sharpened after his 1988 presidential campaign failed. In that quest, Simon's anti-glamorous image as a big-eared, bow-tied egghead had a gleam of quixotic promise for a time. Simon was the candidate most willing to embrace his party and its history ("I am a not a neo-anything; I am a Democrat"), but his bid sputtered out after he got 5 percent in Wisconsin's primary. The highlight had been his home state's primary, which he won despite having to share favorite-son status with Jesse L. Jackson.

Simon's White House bid began auspiciously, with a close-second finish in the Iowa precinct caucuses. In the end, though, Simon garnered about 1 million votes and 170.5 delegates (by The Associated Press' count), but most of both came from Illinois. He never raised the money that the multistate Super Tuesday primaries required. And his "unreconstructed Democrat" approach, apparently pitched to lunch-bucket voters, ironically showed more appeal among liberals in affluent suburbs and academic communities.

At Home: Few will remember, after Simon's sweeping 1990 re-election victory, that he began his campaign near the top of the Republican target list. GOP optimism was based on the narrow margin by which Simon reached the Senate in 1984 (defeating three-term GOP Sen. Charles H. Percy) and on the failure of his 1988 presidential bid.

Simon was labeled "Senator No-Show" during his White House bid, as his Senate attendance record deteriorated. His liberal posture in 1988 also conflicted with the dour, moderate image he had crafted in his southern Illinois base.

The threat to Simon appeared fully deployed when GOP Rep. Lynn Martin announced against him. Martin was a fiscal conservative and liberal-basher, but her moderate record on social issues, including abortion and family leave, and her outgoing personality were expected to give her bipartisan appeal.

However, Simon proved he had not built a 35-year career in Illinois politics by being guileless. He lined up solid support from all elements of the Illinois Democratic Party and raised an enormous campaign fund.

Then Simon stood back as Martin's campaign imploded. Martin blew her chances in downstate Illinois early on; in an interview, she used the word "rednecks" to describe voters who might oppose her because of her gender. Later, she offended East European ethnics by referring to Simon's visit with Polish leader Lech Walesa as "crapola."

Simon ran into a couple of glitches. He angered some University of Illinois alumni and supporters when he signed a petition describing "Chief Illiniwek," the school's mascot, as insensitive to American Indians. Simon also faced reports that he had made a phone call to a savings and loan in behalf of an associate with foreclosure problems and had interceded with federal regulators in behalf of a pair of trade schools.

But Martin's furious effort to tie Simon's actions to the S&L scandal was a dud. Trailing badly in the polls, she ran short of money in late September. Then she had to apologize after her media consultant, Roger Ailes, called Simon "slimy" and "a weenie."

Simon ended up taking a whopping 65 percent of the vote. A few months later, he found himself in the ironic position of praising Martin's appointment as secretary of labor, a position she would hold through the last two years of the Bush administration.

Since Simon began his political career in the early 1950s, his anti-charismatic appearance has not changed much. But neither has the strong reputation for honesty and candor that first made him popular. Simon made a name for himself as editor of the Troy Tribune in southern Illinois in the early 1950s, crusading against local political corruption. In 1954, at age 25, he won a seat in the Illinois House. Eight years later, he moved to the state Senate, where he gained note as a political reformer.

Democratic leaders picked Simon for lieutenant governor in 1968, hoping his reform reputation would help a state ticket struggling against reported scandal and an expected Republican tide. The gubernatorial and Senate candidates lost, but Simon won.

That victory made Simon the front-runner in the Democratic gubernatorial primary in 1972. But Daniel Walker, a wealthy corporate lawyer, convinced voters that Simon was a tool of Mayor Richard J. Daley's Chicago Democrats — even though the Daley machine was clinging to Simon, rather than the other way around.

Simon lost, then retired briefly to teach political science at a Springfield college. In 1974, however, a retirement opened a southern Illinois House district. Although Simon had to move south from his old base, he was favored and won easily. He went on to four more terms, struggling only in 1980, when Ronald Reagan's popularity boosted Simon's opponent.

Simon's base in a traditionally Democratic

but conservative-leaning downstate area gave him a leg up when he jumped in against Percy in 1984. A business executive with a somewhat aristocratic manner, Percy had never achieved a large loyal following. Only his image as a moderate Republican had enabled him to outflank the more conservative Chicago Democrats who ran against him in 1972 and 1978.

By 1984, Percy was under fire from all sides. Conservatives thought him too liberal, while liberals disliked his support of the Reagan administration, especially as chairman of the Senate Foreign Relations Committee.

Simon was the best known of the Democrats' four Senate hopefuls. With support from organized labor and solid backing in Chicago's liberal lakefront wards and suburban areas, he took the nomination with 36 percent.

Percy had staved off a conservative primary challenge with an ad campaign stressing that he was "the Illinois advantage" in Washington. But he then took a rightward tack himself, portraying Simon as "ultraliberal."

The theme made it hard for Percy to hold his past coalition of blacks, suburbanites and conservative downstaters. Simon got a heavy vote in both the black and white ethnic wards of Chicago. Combining that strength with a more than respectable showing downstate, Simon won by 2 percentage points.

Illinois gave a temporary lift to Simon's 1988 presidential bid; under Illinois' modified winner-take-all system, Simon's 43 percent plurality earned him nearly 80 percent of the state's national convention delegates. But when it became obvious Simon would have to quit the race, Jackson backers urged him to withdraw before the state Democratic convention so primary runner-up Jackson could claim his delegates. Instead, Simon merely suspended his campaign, enabling his home-state loyalists to cinch their trips to Atlanta. Some blacks said the move would hurt Simon in future campaigns, but he won solid black support in 1990.

Committees

Budget (7th of 12 Democrats)

Foreign Relations (6th of 11 Democrats)
African Affairs (chairman); European Affairs; Terrorism, Narcotics & International Operations

Indian Affairs (6th of 10 Democrats)

Judiciary (7th of 10 Democrats)
Constitution (chairman); Antitrust, Monopolies & Business Rights; Immigration & Refugee Affairs

Labor & Human Resources (5th of 10 Democrats)
Employment & Productivity (chairman); Education, Arts & Humanities; Disability Policy

Elections

1990 General

Paul Simon (D)	2,115,377	(65%)
Lynn Martin (R)	1,135,628	(35%)

Previous Winning Percentages:	**1984**	(50%)	**1982 ***	(66%)

1980 *	(49%)	**1978 ***	(66%)	**1976 ***	(67%)	**1974 ***	(60%)

** House elections.*

Campaign Finance

	Receipts	Receipts from PACs		Expend-itures
1990				
Simon (D)	$8,462,209	$1,480,221	(17%)	$7,656,514
Martin (R)	$4,986,730	$1,193,942	(24%)	$4,921,613

Key Votes

1993	
Require unpaid family and medical leave	Y
Approve national "motor voter" registration bill	Y
Approve budget increasing taxes and reducing deficit	Y
Support president's right to lift military gay ban	Y
1992	
Approve school-choice pilot program	N
Allow shifting funds from defense to domestic programs	Y
Oppose deeper cuts in spending for SDI	N
1991	
Approve waiting period for handgun purchases	Y
Raise senators' pay and ban honoraria	Y
Authorize use of force in Persian Gulf	N
Confirm Clarence Thomas to Supreme Court	N

Voting Studies

	Presidential Support		Party Unity		Conservative Coalition	
Year	**S**	**O**	**S**	**O**	**S**	**O**
1992	27	73	88	10	16	84
1991	32	67	94	5	18	80
1990	20	80	90	8	8	92
1989	41	58	86	14	13	87
1988	31	42	70	1	0	54
1987	6	32	49	2	6	22
1986	19	78	89	11	13	86
1985	25	67	89	4	10	78
House Service:						
1984	12	31	42	3	7	44
1983	15	59	74	4	17	56
1982	31	56	81	4	16	73
1981	36	59	76	11	28	64

Interest Group Ratings

Year	**ADA**	**AFL-CIO**	**CCUS**	**ACU**
1992	95	92	10	7
1991	100	75	10	0
1990	94	78	25	13
1989	100	90	25	14
1988	85	91	42	0
1987	35	100	13	0
1986	85	80	32	9
1985	85	95	34	5
House Service:				
1984	45	100	67	13
1983	70	100	18	0
1982	75	95	15	6
1981	75	79	12	0

Carol Moseley-Braun (D)

Of Chicago — Elected 1992; 1st Term

Born: Aug. 16, 1947, Chicago, Ill.
Education: U. of Illinois, Chicago Circle, B.A. 1967; U. of Chicago, J.D. 1972.
Occupation: Lawyer.
Family: Divorced; one child.
Religion: Roman Catholic.
Political Career: Ill. House, 1979-88, assistant majority leader, 1983; Cook County recorder of deeds, 1988-92.
Capitol Office: 320 Hart Bldg. 20510; 224-2854.

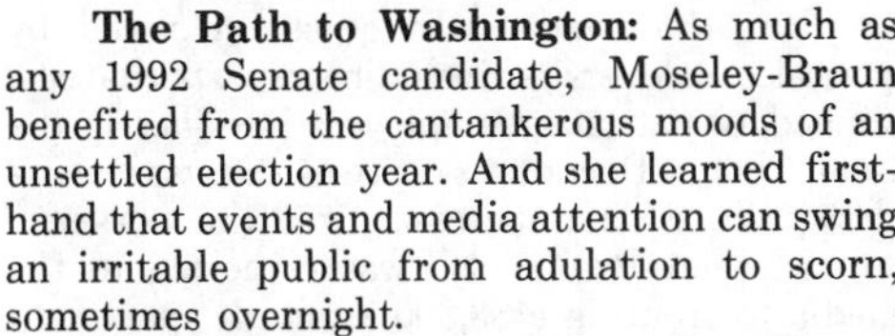

The Path to Washington: As much as any 1992 Senate candidate, Moseley-Braun benefited from the cantankerous moods of an unsettled election year. And she learned first-hand that events and media attention can swing an irritable public from adulation to scorn, sometimes overnight.

First, outrage over the Senate's handling of Anita F. Hill and her sexual harassment allegations against Supreme Court nominee Clarence Thomas propelled Moseley-Braun into the race and helped her upset two-term Democratic incumbent Alan J. Dixon in a three-way primary. Then voter disgust with the economy cinched a win over GOP challenger Richard S. Williamson, despite some serious flaws in her campaign that threatened to derail her election.

But in the weeks after she won, Moseley-Braun came under fire for questionable conduct and judgment. While her newly elected colleagues were traveling to Washington and otherwise preparing to assume their new jobs, Moseley-Braun left the country for a month-long vacation with her campaign manager, whom she later acknowledged to be her boyfriend.

Her absence merely attracted closer scrutiny, resulting in a spate of unfavorable news stories in Illinois and elsewhere that threw a damper over celebrations of her being sworn in as the first black woman elected to the Senate.

But after that rocky beginning, Moseley-Braun settled in, accepting her enhanced visibility but insisting that she should be judged on her performance in service to her constituents. In a January 1993 byline article in USA Today, Moseley-Braun wrote: "My presence in and of itself will change the U.S. Senate. But I cannot do the job that the people of Illinois have asked of me by being a symbol alone."

Moseley-Braun brought a strong liberal agenda to the Senate and displayed it right away. Soon after taking office, she beat most of her colleagues to the punch with an early maiden speech that eulogized retired Supreme Court Justice Thurgood Marshall. She was a visible presence on the floor in her first few months — appearing more frequently than most of the other freshmen, and speaking out on issues from family leave to voter registration to Republican efforts to block President Clinton's proposed economic stimulus bill.

One early speech that drew national attention was in defense of Clinton's call for an end to the ban on gays in military service. Moseley-Braun read from memoranda written in the 1940s objecting to racial integration of the military and the complaints of white soldiers at the time sounded very much like contemporary complaints about gays.

Winning a seat on Judiciary was initially not one of her top priorities, despite the outrage expressed by women nationwide that the panel was unresponsive to Anita Hill because it had no female members. Once she accepted the assignment, she was confronted with an uproar over attorney general nominee Zoë Baird, whose hiring of two undocumented aliens as domestic employees and whose failure to pay Social Security taxes for them eventually caused her to withdraw.

Moseley-Braun seemed unsure of herself at the Baird hearings, her first appearance as a member of the committee. She said that additional witnesses ought to be called to explore the details of the case. But later she expressed sympathy for Baird's plight.

Four months later, as the panel prepared to consider longtime Clinton friend Webster Hubbell for the post of associate attorney general, Moseley-Braun showed patience. An uproar arose over Hubbell's connections to an Arkansas country club whose membership had until recently been all-white, but Moseley-Braun did not publicly interject herself into the conflict. On the floor, she voted for Hubbell's confirmation, praising him for dropping his membership from the club.

On Banking, Moseley-Braun came to the defense of San Francisco Supervisor Roberta Achtenberg, who was confirmed as assistant secretary of Housing and Urban Development.

Achtenberg, apparently the first openly gay person ever nominated for a senior administration job, drew fire from conservatives.

Moseley-Braun told Achtenberg not to worry about the opposition: "I know from experience ... what it is like to break glass ceilings."

In the months that followed her stunning March 1992 primary win, Moseley-Braun metamorphosed from a little-known county official into a national emblem of a new politics. She was seen as part of a vanguard of women candidates at the national level, as well as of a broader movement of outsider politicians threatening white, male incumbents everywhere.

National money poured into her campaign, and Moseley-Braun found a perfect foil in GOP challenger Williamson, a wealthy, conservative lawyer who had held appointive jobs in the Reagan and Bush administrations. Summer polls placed her seemingly out of Williamson's reach, and there was confident talk of swearing in the Senate's first black woman.

But there were missteps along the way. Her campaign suffered from disorganization and infighting, while the candidate at times appeared ill-versed about certain national issues. Moseley-Braun's performance as recorder of deeds came under fire.

Then, in late September, Moseley-Braun was stung by strong criticism of her handling of her mother's finances. Moseley-Braun accepted, with her siblings, a $28,750 inheritance from her mother even though her mother was being supported by Medicaid and state law might have required that the income be applied to her mother's expenses. After a state investigation that concluded just before the election, Moseley-Braun paid the state roughly $15,000 in back medical expenses for her mother. There was no criminal investigation, and a state official described the payment as voluntary.

These problems were not enough to blunt her overall appeal as a personable and energetic politician.

The daughter of a police officer and a medical technician, Moseley-Braun grew up in Chicago's neighborhoods and had direct exposure to urban poverty. In 1978 voters elected her to the state Legislature where, for more than a decade, she worked as a legislative floor leader for the city and its first black mayor, the late Harold Washington. She rose to become the first woman assistant majority leader.

In her Senate race, Moseley-Braun ran strongly in Chicago and the southern part of the state, offsetting Williamson's strength in the Chicago suburbs. She won with 53 percent of the vote, spending nearly $6.6 million.

But the victory was quickly clouded by several controversies, including reports that she slipped 10 patronage employees into jobs in the Cook County Recorder's office as she was leaving that position. Her successor fired the workers.

Moseley-Braun also was criticized in the media for renting a $3,300 a month apartment at the same time some campaign workers went unpaid, and for her handling of anonymous accusations of sexual harassment raised against her campaign manager and boyfriend, Kgosie Matthews. She hired lawyers to investigate the accusations against Matthews, and several weeks later told the Chicago Sun-Times that the lawyers' report indicated that there had been no impropriety.

The issue continued to dog her in the weeks leading up to the swearing-in, compounded by reports that Matthews' salary as campaign manager was $15,000 per month. Moseley-Braun in late December acknowledged that she and Matthews were romantically involved, after they returned from a four-week trip to Africa and England.

Committees

Banking, Housing & Urban Affairs (10th of 11 Democrats)
Housing & Urban Affairs; Securities

Judiciary (10th of 10 Democrats)
Courts & Administrative Practice; Juvenile Justice

Small Business (12th of 12 Democrats)
Export Expansion & Agricultural Development; Urban & Minority-Owned Business Development

Campaign Finance

	Receipts	Receipts from PACs		Expenditures
1992				
Moseley-Braun (D)	$6,628,567	$646,746	(10%)	$6,594,570
Williamson (R)	$2,320,713	$472,839	(20%)	$2,300,924

Key Votes

1993

Require unpaid family and medical leave	Y
Approve national "motor voter" registration bill	Y
Approve budget increasing taxes and reducing deficit	Y
Support president's right to lift military gay ban	Y

Elections

1992 General		
Carol Moseley-Braun (D)	2,631,229	(53%)
Richard S. Williamson (R)	2,126,833	(43%)
Chad Koppie (CIL)	100,422	(2%)
1992 Primary		
Carol Moseley-Braun (D)	557,694	(38%)
Alan J. Dixon (D)	504,077	(35%)
Albert F. Hofeld (D)	394,497	(27%)

1 Bobby L. Rush (D)

Of Chicago — Elected 1992; 1st Term

Born: Nov. 23, 1946, Albany, Ga.
Education: Roosevelt U., B.A. 1973; U. of Illinois, Chicago Circle, 1977.
Military Service: Army, 1963-68.
Occupation: Insurance broker; political aide.
Family: Wife, Carolyn Thomas; five children.
Religion: Protestant.
Political Career: Candidate for Chicago Board of Aldermen, 1975; sought Democratic nomination for Ill. House, 1978; Chicago Board of Aldermen, 1983-93.
Capitol Office: 1725 Longworth Bldg. 20515; 225-4372.

The Path to Washington: Many politicians go through changes on their way to Congress. But Rush came about as far — geographically and philosophically — as is humanly possible.

He came first from rural, southern Georgia to a run-down neighborhood on the North Side of Chicago, not far from the rich, white Gold Coast. He was raised by a mother who worked as a Republican activist (because whites dominated the Democratic machine), yet he rose to become deputy chairman of the state Democratic Party.

He was a Boy Scout in an integrated troop and later volunteered for the Army. But, disillusioned by a racist commanding officer, Rush joined the Student Non-Violent Coordinating Committee and then went AWOL after the assassination of Martin Luther King Jr. (He was honorably discharged soon thereafter.)

He joined the Black Panthers, eventually heading the Illinois chapter, and spent six months in prison on a weapons charge. He quit the Panthers, went to college, and in the 1970s began running for the Chicago City Council and the state legislature, challenging the machine and losing. In 1983, riding the coattails of Harold Washington, who was elected in an upset as Chicago's first black mayor, Rush was elected as alderman.

After Washington's unexpected death in 1987, Rush allied himself with the regular Democrats. Many of Washington's — and Rush's — political allies, however, chose to form a more radical party named after the late mayor.

Rush's choice placed him at odds with some in the black community who charge that he has since been in league with the white establishment. But it allowed Rush a nearly 10-year stint on the council, where he became an activist on education, housing and community development issues. He also became a leader in efforts to curtail access to assault weapons and to curb drug use.

The soft-spoken Rush views his life as evolutionary and dismisses his critics for not understanding that he still holds to the Panther ideals of community-based leadership and service.

In the House, he expects to work aggressively within the system to boost the issues of greatest concern to his constituents.

The 1st reaches into some suburban neighborhoods in southwest Chicago, but it also contains the heart of the black South Side (more than two-thirds of the district's residents are black) and is among the most economically depressed districts in the country. Rush should be able to use his seat on the Banking, Finance and Urban Affairs Committee to advantage. He hopes to push more flexibility in urban banking policies, encouraging nonprofit, community-based credit unions — which he thinks better serve the needs of poorer neighborhoods — and community development banks.

Rush also took a seat on the Government Operations Committee.

To win the district, Rush first had to win a primary against four-term incumbent Charles A. Hayes, a Democrat elected in 1983. Hayes had won a special election to fill the seat vacated when Washington resigned to become mayor.

Hayes, at 74, was enjoying a second career after the decades as a labor leader he spent organizing the Chicago stockyards. But he was not known for legislative success. On the issues, little of substance separated the two candidates. So Rush offered his own energetic style in contrast, being careful not to say directly that Hayes was past his prime. Rush charged that Hayes had been ineffective and derided Hayes' periodic election-year gambit of introducing bills to create inner-city jobs with federal dollars — bills that never went anywhere.

The key to Rush's victory came just days before the March primary, when Hayes was named as one of the abusers in the House bank scandal. His 716 overdrafts focused the attention of the Chicago media on the race.

Rush managed 42 percent in the six-way primary and edged Hayes by 4,040 votes. In the general election, Rush easily defeated Republican Jay Walker, an administrative law judge.

Illinois 1

Chicago — South and southwest sides

As early as the 1920s, Chicago's near South Side was the center of a booming black population and the core of the nation's first urban black-majority House district, numbered the 1st. Even as the great migration from the South between 1940 and 1970 expanded the boundaries of Chicago's black neighborhoods, the 1st retained a rather compact form in the southeast section of Chicago.

In recent years, the territory covered by the 1st has grown, largely to compensate for the deterioration and depopulation of the 1st's low-income portions. During the 1980s, the district lost one-fifth of its population.

The 1st begins on the east side at 26th Street in the historic black hub, then moves south through mainly residential neighborhoods to 103rd Street, at the edge of a once-thriving industrial belt. At its midsection, the district swings west through inner-city communities. However, it also reaches an arm into Chicago's southwest side and close-in suburbs, home to most of the 1st's white residents and much of its sparse Republican vote.

The changing geography has had little impact on the district's demographics or politics. The 1st remains a majority-black Democratic stronghold. Although Rush's 1992 primary upset of Democratic Rep. Charles A. Hayes was a narrow one, his general-election victory was assured.

In some recent years, low voter turnout in the 1st undercut the chances of statewide Democratic candidates. But 1992 efforts by Rush — who headed Bill Clinton's national minority voter outreach program — and by Carol Moseley-Braun — who was bidding to become the first black woman senator — spurred a turnout that was above the average for Illinois' House districts.

The 1st has had just eight House members since 1929, all of them black. Rush, a 1960s Black Panther-leader-turned-liberal-pragmatist, has his base in the near South Side. Much of this area is fighting to stem urban blight.

Just east of the Dan Ryan Expressway is the crime-plagued Stateway Gardens housing project; the 1st crosses the highway to take in the new Comiskey Park, home of baseball's White Sox. To the southeast is Hyde Park, site of the University of Chicago (9,400 students) and its mainly white, largely liberal community. Then come Woodlawn and South Shore, black areas with alternating pockets of poverty and stability. In the southeast end of the 1st are solid middle-class black communities such as Chatham and Avalon Park.

The district crosses town through mainly low-income black areas such as Englewood, then banks south and crosses Western Avenue, the unofficial but widely recognized boundary between white and black Chicago. This area includes such communities as Lithuanian Village and Beverly, an enclave of affluent Irish-Americans, and suburban Evergreen Park. The 1st also takes in parts of Oak Lawn, Alsip and Blue Island.

1990 Population: 571,530. White 155,885 (27%), Black 398,318 (70%), Other 17,327 (3%). Hispanic origin 20,548 (4%). 18 and over 418,800 (73%), 62 and over 96,054 (17%). Median age: 33.

Committees

Banking, Finance & Urban Affairs (19th of 30 Democrats)
Consumer Credit & Insurance; Housing & Community Development; International Development, Finance, Trade & Monetary Policy

Government Operations (14th of 25 Democrats)
Commerce, Consumer & Monetary Affairs; Employment, Housing & Aviation

Campaign Finance

	Receipts	Receipts from PACs	Expend-itures
1992			
Rush (D)	$257,455	$132,300 (51%)	$260,389
Walker (R)	$14,050	$6,250 (44%)	$13,740

Key Votes

1993

Require parental notification of minors' abortions	N
Require unpaid family and medical leave	Y
Approve national "motor voter" registration bill	Y
Approve budget increasing taxes and reducing deficit	Y
Approve economic stimulus plan	Y

Elections

1992 General		
Bobby L. Rush (D)	209,258	(83%)
Jay Walker (R)	43,453	(17%)
1992 Primary		
Bobby L. Rush (D)	54,231	(42%)
Charles A. Hayes (D)	50,191	(39%)
Anna R. Langford (D)	14,094	(11%)
Roosevelt Thomas (D)	4,256	(3%)
Allen Smith (D)	3,486	(3%)
Smith Wiiams (D)	2,219	(2%)

District Vote for President

1992

D	214,045	(81%)
R	32,628	(12%)
I	17,195	(7%)

2 Mel Reynolds (D)

Of Chicago — Elected 1992; 1st Term

Born: Jan. 8, 1952, Mound Bayou, Miss.
Education: Chicago City College, A.A. 1972; U. of Illinois, B.A. 1974; Oxford U., LL.B. 1979, M.A. 1981.
Occupation: Professor.
Family: Wife, Marisol Concepcion; one child.
Religion: Baptist.
Political Career: Sought Democratic nomination for U.S. House, 1988, 1990.
Capitol Office: 514 Cannon Bldg. 20515; 225-0773.

The Path to Washington: Most people run for Congress because they want to serve. Reynolds had a second, equally compelling reason — to oust an incumbent whom he and others believed to be an embarrassment. Reynolds argued that Rep. Gus Savage was so ineffective as to be doing a disservice to his mostly black, poor, Democratic South Side Chicago constituents.

In an upset, the magnitude of which even stunned Reynolds, he ousted the 12-year incumbent with 63 percent of the vote in the Democratic primary. Savage had been tested in primaries before — even by Reynolds, who was making his third run at the seat — but never so proficiently.

Reynolds, like Savage, grew up poor in Chicago. But, with different opportunities in different times, the two took dramatically different paths. Reynolds won a Rhodes scholarship to Oxford University and became a community activist and mainstream political consultant; Savage stayed on the streets. He was a gang leader, then a civil rights leader and organizer of insurgent political campaigns against Chicago's white-run regular Democrats. That was how Savage earned the respect of his core constituency, who returned him to office despite his ethical scrapes and a flamboyant manner that offended many.

Reynolds is a coalition-builder, while Savage was divisive by choice. Reynolds has worked to improve race relations and is an unapologetic supporter of Israel. Savage filled his speeches with racial charges and blasted Reynolds in two campaigns for being a puppet of Jews who contributed to his candidacy. Reynolds says blacks have to take some responsibility for improving their condition — speaking out more forcefully against handgun violence, for example. Savage cited racism as the cause of all that he saw wrong with the world.

Early in the 103rd, Reynolds made gun control an immediate priority. He appeared on "Nightline" and wrote a Chicago Tribune opinion piece on the issue. He also introduced a bill to increase the excise tax on firearms and impose liability on gun manufacturers for injuries caused by their firearms.

His victory earned Reynolds a coveted assignment. He was the only freshman tapped for the Ways and Means Committee. Promoting government-private sector partnerships is a prime goal for Reynolds. And Ways and Means is a place where he can pursue tax policies to promote private investment in housing and other inner-city concerns.

For Reynolds, the third time was the charm. In 1988, he ran third in a four-way race, pulling only 14 percent to Savage's 52 percent. In 1990, he finished second with 43 percent to Savage's 51 percent (another candidate got 5 percent).

This time, Reynolds got the race that he wanted — and that he knew he could win. First, redistricting had stripped away some South Side voters who had been solidly in Savage's camp, substituting more middle-class voters — black and white — from the close-in suburbs. Second, it was a head-to-head clash. There was no third candidate to split the anti-Savage vote or to distract Reynolds.

Reynolds also took his message — and his attack on Savage's record — to the heart of the incumbent's own base of support. Reynolds never shut the campaign office he opened in 1989 for his last race. He used it for community outreach and to emphasize his contention that Savage never offered a helping hand to his constituents. And Reynolds poured $80,000 into radio spots during the last two weeks of the primary, to great effect.

In a strange twist, Reynolds was the victim of a drive-by shooting just days before the March primary. Riding in a rented car, with a huge campaign sign on top, Reynolds was cut slightly by flying glass when an unknown gunman in another car fired at him. Reynolds blamed the attack on a general climate of violence.

Reynolds won big in the suburbs, with the aid of some crossover Republican votes that he expected and a big turnout, and he edged Savage in the city portion of the 2nd.

Republicans, who ran no one in the primary, fielded a black candidate in the general election, business owner Ron Blackstone. And Savage's longtime chief of staff, Louanner Peters, ran an independent campaign. But neither made a dent in Reynolds' momentum.

Illinois 2

Chicago — Far South Side; south suburbs; Chicago Heights

More than two-thirds of the people in the 2nd are black, and Democrats dominate in contests from president right down the ballot. But redistricting for the 1990s, which added suburban turf to the 2nd, brought a major change in the district's House representation.

In the 1992 primary, Reynolds — an educator and community activist with a mainstream style — unseated Democratic Rep. Gus Savage, who had been a polarizing figure. Savage had appealed to a mainly urban constituency with hard-edged rhetoric that blamed white racism for the problems of his district's many low-income black residents; he had increasingly targeted Jews for criticism.

Under the new map, though, only slightly more than half the district's residents are within the Chicago city limits. Reynolds — who had lost two primary challenges to Savage — capitalized on this shift. Reynolds made a strong appeal to suburban voters, including Jews, conservative white ethnics and blacks with more moderate views. Reynolds steamrolled the incumbent in the suburbs, winning with 80 percent.

Even within the city, Savage had lost ground, particularly among middle-class blacks who found his attitude extreme and were drawn to Reynolds, a former Rhodes scholar. Reynolds edged Savage in the city part of the district. The district's huge Democratic advantage boosted Reynolds to an easy general election win.

Within the city, the 2nd is roughly U-shaped. Much of the western arm, which runs north to 63rd Street, is low-income. There are middle-class pockets, though, in such far South Side sections as Morgan Park and Pullman. The eastern arm begins at 71st Street in the South Shore area. In neighboring South Chicago, belching factories once employed thousands. The USX Corp.'s April 1992 closure of its already downsized South Works plant symbolized the decline of Chicago's industrial base.

For several years, Chicago Mayor Richard M. Daley pushed a pet project, a massive new airport in the Lake Calumet area, another former industrial hub. Backed by claims that the project would be a catalyst for cleaning up industrial pollution and would offer new employment opportunities, Daley in early 1992 gained Republican Gov. Jim Edgar's support for the airport. But the state legislature refused to go along, pleasing locals who complained about the displacement and noise a new airport would bring.

South of the city are working-class suburbs: Several, including Harvey, Markham and Robbins, are nearly all black. Some, including Ford Heights and parts of urbanized Chicago Heights, are poor, while others, such as Country Club Hills, are more affluent.

The district's southernmost reaches have most of its white population. Jewish residents are numerous in such well-to-do suburbs as Homewood, Flossmoor and Olympia Fields. Bloom Township has a longstanding Italian-American community; this is the most Republican area in the 2nd.

1990 Population: 571,530. White 154,902 (27%), Black 391,425 (68%), Other 25,203 (4%). Hispanic origin 37,860 (7%). 18 and over 402,216 (70%), 62 and over 69,334 (12%). Median age: 31.

Committee

Ways & Means (24th of 24 Democrats)
Human Resources; Social Security

Campaign Finance

1992	Receipts	Receipts from PACs		Expend-itures
Reynolds (D)	$532,031	$195,772	(37%)	$542,911
Blackstone (R)	$36,075	$1,000	(3%)	$35,848

Key Votes

1993

Require parental notification of minors' abortions	N
Require unpaid family and medical leave	Y
Approve national "motor voter" registration bill	Y
Approve budget increasing taxes and reducing deficit	Y
Approve economic stimulus plan	Y

Elections

1992 General		
Mel Reynolds (D)	182,614	(78%)
Ron Blackstone (R)	31,957	(14%)
Louanner Peters (LP)	19,293	(8%)
1992 Primary		
Mel Reynolds (D)	61,450	(63%)
Gus Savage (D)	36,865	(37%)

District Vote for President

	1992	
D	194,313	(80%)
R	31,710	(13%)
I	16,955	(7%)

3 William O. Lipinski (D)

Of Chicago — Elected 1982; 6th Term

Born: Dec. 22, 1937, Chicago, Ill.
Education: Loras College, 1957-58.
Military Service: Army Reserve, 1961-67.
Occupation: Parks supervisor.
Family: Wife, Rose Marie Lapinski; two children.
Religion: Roman Catholic.
Political Career: Chicago Board of Aldermen, 1975-83.
Capitol Office: 1501 Longworth Bldg. 20515; 225-5701.

In Washington: Representing southwest Chicago and some of its close-in suburbs, Lipinski is a member of a vanishing breed: a Democrat who symbolizes the kind of white ethnic, urban voters his party has had difficulty winning in recent presidential elections. But Lipinski is one hard-edged Chicago pol who has no intention of becoming extinct.

He survived a vicious election battle with fellow Democratic Rep. Marty Russo in 1992, and though both he and his wife went to the 1992 Democratic Convention as Clinton delegates, Lipinski quickly served notice that he is no Clinton Democrat.

To Lipinski and his constituents, national Democrats bear a heavy burden of proof on most social issue and tax matters, a burden Clinton isn't meeting by Lipinski's lights. In early 1993, Lipinkski was one of just 11 Democrats to oppose Clinton on the budget resolution, and he was a leader in the fight against the effort to lift the ban on gays in the military.

Of Polish descent, Lipinski is a friend of organized labor and many New Deal-type programs — allegiances that help make him a backroom traffic cop of competing Chicago delegation demands as well as the congressional liaison for the revitalized Democratic political machine of Chicago Mayor Richard M. Daley.

In the House, Lipinski operates in the shadow of a more prominent Polish-American, Ways and Means Committee Chairman Dan Rostenkowski — a position Lipinski bristles at.

As one of the members of the Public Works Committee who helped oust Chairman Glenn M. Anderson of California in 1991, he is well-positioned to look out for Chicago's needs on his own.

During consideration of the massive highway bill in 1991, Lipinski worked with state highway officials to guarantee local demonstration projects for his district and the districts of the four Illinois Democrats who serve with him on Public Works. "Who knows better where a certain amount of federal money should be spent locally than the congressman?" he said.

Lipinski was also instrumental in passing legislation to assess airline passenger fees that could give the city financial leverage in its quest for a new airport.

Lipinski honed his political savvy as a veteran leader of Chicago's 23rd Ward, which keeps its headquarters near his district offices.

Lipinski is a persistent and sometimes emotional spokesman for conservative ethnic values he thinks Democrats have discarded in recent years. The label "white ethnic," however, angers Lipinski. "These same political types who have made the term fashionable," he complains, "have at the same time tried to make it unfashionable to exhibit many of [the] beliefs real ethnics hold, implying that it's immoral to oppose all abortions, racist to support capital punishment."

Lipinski bitterly opposed the 1991 civil rights bill, denouncing its "quotas," and he introduced legislation that would provide remedies to those harmed by past "race-norming tests." In 1993, he bucked party leaders and voted against legislation to allow voters to register when they get driver's licenses.

Given this record, it is not surprising that Lipinski lost out to Illinois Rep. Richard J. Durbin in a 1993 bid to be regional representative on the Steering and Policy Committee, a Democratic panel that makes committee assignments. Lipinski intimated that his defeat came because Chicago freshman Mel Reynolds reneged on a promise and cast his secret ballot against Lipinski.

Lipinski does find some common ground with his party on family issues. He once criticized conservatives who, he says, base answers to current family problems on "an image of the family that no longer squares with the facts." He supported the Family and Medical Leave Act in 1993 and backs legislation to establish IRA-type accounts for postsecondary education and for first-time home buyers. He also supports a day-care tax credit.

At Home: Lipinski appeared to face long odds in 1992, when redistricting forced him into a primary matchup with fellow Democrat Russo. But Lipinski — who had already proved his mettle by unseating Democratic Rep. John G. Fary in the 1982 primary — survived one of the year's most bruising campaigns to win by a wide margin.

Illinois 3

Chicago — Southwest side; south and west suburbs

The working- and middle-class constituency on Chicago's southwest side provides a solid political base for Democratic Rep. Lipinski. This is part of the city's "Bungalow Belt," with block after block of small, neatly kept brick homes mainly occupied by people with ethnic roots in Poland and other Eastern European nations, Italy and Ireland.

During the 1980s, most of Lipinski's district was within the city limits. But in 1991 redistricting, his territory was shunted west, as a new Hispanic-majority district was created to go with the city's three black-majority districts.

The 3rd now roughly follows the pattern of white migration to the southwest suburbs. Only a quarter of its residents live within Chicago's borders.

Still, there is a strong similarity between the southwest side and the 3rd's close-in suburbs, including Berwyn, Burbank, Hometown and parts of Cicero and Oak Lawn. Residents in both areas tend to think of themselves as Democrats, but on social issues they are more conservative than the national Democratic Party's line.

There is a Republican vote in the more affluent suburbs in western Cook County and in some of the newer subdivisions at the southern end of the district. While Lipinski seems secure, the 3rd's conservative tilt makes it something of a swing district. George Bush in 1988 won 61 percent of the vote in the areas that make up the 3rd.

But in 1992, opposition to Bush's economic policies sent many of the district's "Reagan Democrats" back to their traditional party or to the populist campaign of Ross Perot. Bill Clinton carried the 3rd, though with his smallest plurality of any Chicago-based district.

Although the Chicago Democratic machine has atrophied in many parts of the city, Lipinski is one of the most successful remaining practitioners of ward-level organizing. His huge winning margin in the Chicago part of the 3rd gave Lipinski an unexpectedly easy win over Democratic Rep. Marty Russo in a 1992 primary forced by redistricting. Lipinski went on to trounce his Republican challenger in Chicago.

Midway Airport, located within the city and surrounded by southwest side residential communities, has been the district's largest employer. But the airport was dealt a blow in late 1991, when Midway Airlines shut down, and the facility could be threatened if a proposed new airport for the south Chicago area ever gets beyond the talking stage.

The 3rd is bisected by an industrial belt adjacent to Interstate 55 (the main route to the mostly residential suburban area) and the Chicago Sanitary and Ship Canal. Although close to downtown and surrounded by suburbia, this area has few residences among its factories and railroad yards. Bedford Park, home to a Corn Products Corp. factory and one of the district's largest communities in land area, had only 566 residents in 1990.

1990 Population: 571,531. White 533,458 (93%), Black 11,015 (2%), Other 27,058 (5%). Hispanic origin 42,101 (7%). 18 and over 442,224 (77%), 62 and over 110,981 (19%). Median age: 36.

The new 3rd's reach into the suburbs seemed to benefit Russo, whose former district was mainly suburban. Lipinski lost some of his Chicago base. But his edge within his remaining base was huge. Lipinski, a Democratic ward committeeman, had an army of precinct workers and the support of key members of the city's Democratic organization. In addition, many of the close-in suburbs also shared the ethnic characteristics and socially conservative views of his urban turf.

Russo placed his bets on his image as a rising figure in Congress. A member of Ways and Means, Russo touted his ties to Chairman Rostenkowski. His links with the leadership enabled him to run up a substantial fundraising advantage over Lipinski. Russo also played up his role as an advocate of a "Canadian-style" single-payer national health insurance plan.

But "anti-insider" sentiment was peaking at the time of Illinois' March 1992 primary. Lipinski guessed that his average-guy approach would play well against Russo's slick style.

In a campaign that became unceasingly negative on both sides, Lipinski portrayed Russo as a legislative front man for special interests. Russo cast Lipinski as a machine pol who hit up his employees for campaign contributions.

Lipinski compared his humble southwest side bungalow to Russo's large suburban home that, because of redistricting, was now outside the 3rd District. Russo revealed that Lipinski, who had called for strict limits on Japanese auto imports, owned an Italian sports car.

Organization ultimately won it for Lipinski. He swamped Russo by more than 25,000 votes in Chicago and ran within 3,500 votes of Russo in the suburbs.

GOP officials, whose redistricting map had been enacted by a federal court panel, initially had designs on the conservative-leaning 3rd. However, a popular state senator they hoped would run did not. Instead, Harry C. Lepinske, a businessman and local township official, won the nomination. A colorless campaigner, Lepinske was most notable for his sound-alike surname. Democrat Lipinski coasted to victory.

The predicted cliffhanger-turned-blowout was similar to Lipinski's first House bid in 1982, when he defeated Rep. Fary by a wide margin.

A lifelong Chicago resident, Lipinski developed his political contacts while working in city government. Beginning as a weekend athletic instructor, Lipinski spent 17 years in the Parks Department and rose to an administrative position.

In 1975 — the same year Fary first went to Congress — Lipinski was elected to the Board of Aldermen, where he lobbied for the establishment of the Southwest Rapid Transit Line; as chairman of the Education Committee, he opposed mandatory busing, a hot-button issue for his heavily ethnic constituency.

His 1982 challenge to Fary in the then-5th District was the result of an intraparty split. Fary had been a loyal supporter of Mayor Richard J. Daley. But after Daley's death, Fary aligned with Mayor Jane Byrne. By the early 1980s, Fary was being pressured to retire by allies of the mayor's son, Richard M. Daley, a prospective challenger to Byrne.

Fary resisted, and Lipinski ran as the candidate of the Daley forces. He won with 60 percent and went on to a series of easy general election victories in what was then a heavily Democratic, urban district.

Daley ran against Byrne in 1983, but both lost to Rep. Harold Washington, Chicago's first black mayor. Although much of the traditional Democratic machine withered during Washington's reform-minded tenure, Lipinski's organization remained mainly intact. He backed Daley's successful bids for mayor in 1989 and 1991.

Committees

Merchant Marine & Fisheries (5th of 29 Democrats)
Merchant Marine (chairman); Coast Guard & Navigation

Public Works & Transportation (8th of 39 Democrats)
Aviation; Economic Development; Surface Transportation

Elections

1992 General		
William O. Lipinski (D)	162,165	(64%)
Harry C. Lepinske (R)	93,128	(36%)
1992 Primary		
William O. Lipinski (D)	61,124	(58%)
Marty Russo (D)	38,802	(37%)
Aloysius A. Majerczyk (D)	3,551	(3%)
Paul J. Del Debbio (D)	1,773	(2%)
1990 General		
William O. Lipinski (D)	73,805	(66%)
David J. Shestokas (R)	34,440	(31%)
Ronald Bartos (ILSOL)	3,001	(3%)

Previous Winning Percentages: **1988** (61%) **1986** (70%) **1984** (64%) **1982** (75%)

District Vote for President

1992
D 108,211 (41%)
R 102,626 (39%)
I 52,892 (20%)

Campaign Finance

	Receipts	Receipts from PACs		Expend-itures
1992				
Lipinski (D)	$561,335	$316,350	(56%)	$556,847
Lepinske (R)	$67,070	$9,999	(15%)	$66,991
1990				
Lipinski (D)	$183,213	$137,317	(75%)	$171,746
Shestokas (R)	$43,950	0		$42,218

Key Votes

1993	
Require parental notification of minors' abortions	Y
Require unpaid family and medical leave	Y
Approve national "motor voter" registration bill	N
Approve budget increasing taxes and reducing deficit	N
Approve economic stimulus plan	Y
1992	
Approve balanced-budget constitutional amendment	Y
Close down space station program	N
Approve U.S. aid for former Soviet Union	N
Allow shifting funds from defense to domestic programs	Y
1991	
Extend unemployment benefits using deficit financing	Y
Approve waiting period for handgun purchases	Y
Authorize use of force in Persian Gulf	N

Voting Studies

	Presidential Support		Party Unity		Conservative Coalition	
Year	**S**	**O**	**S**	**O**	**S**	**O**
1992	34	52	67	20	63	29
1991	38	59	72	22	68	30
1990	41	57	76	20	56	43
1989	36	51	70	14	46	29
1988	33	56	68	20	47	42
1987	35	56	69	16	53	40
1986	42	54	74	18	52	42
1985	36	59	78	12	45	49
1984	45	46	71	14	46	41
1983	40	55	66	24	55	42

Interest Group Ratings

Year	ADA	AFL-CIO	CCUS	ACU
1992	50	67	29	48
1991	45	75	20	30
1990	44	75	54	54
1989	40	91	44	26
1988	55	100	45	35
1987	52	93	46	16
1986	45	92	27	45
1985	55	100	14	33
1984	60	92	33	35
1983	50	76	40	61

4 Luis V. Gutierrez (D)

Of Chicago — Elected 1992; 1st Term

Born: Dec. 10, 1954, Chicago, Ill.
Education: Northeastern Illinois U., B.A. 1975.
Occupation: Teacher; social worker.
Family: Wife, Soraida Arocho; two children.
Religion: Roman Catholic.
Political Career: Chicago Board of Aldermen, 1986-93.
Capitol Office: 1208 Longworth Bldg. 20515; 225-8203.

The Path to Washington: Whether on the job as a legislator or with the voters he had represented as alderman since 1986, Gutierrez speaks his mind. "Nobody doesn't have an opinion about me," he is proud to say.

Gutierrez swept to an easy victory as the first Hispanic elected to the House from Illinois. But fellow House members began to get a taste of Gutierrez's outspokenness even before they were sworn in. And he may have been denied a choice panel assignment as a result.

Along with others, Gutierrez tried to unite Democratic freshmen before many of them were certain of victory. On his own, he sent potential House freshmen copies of a disparaging little book about the federal budget called "Adventures in Porkland."

Like many new members, Gutierrez argued to open up membership on the Appropriations and Ways and Means committees. Unlike many, Gutierrez had a personal interest in Ways and Means. He had been lobbying for a seat on the panel since the primary defeat of Democrat Marty Russo, an 18-year member with close ties to Ways and Means Chairman Dan Rostenkowski, a fellow Chicagoan.

Gutierrez also has ties to Rostenkowski. They live perhaps a mile apart and the 4th includes a sizable slice of the Hispanic neighborhoods Rostenkowski represented for 20 years before 1992 redistricting. But their relationship had a rocky beginning.

They ended up on opposite sides of the Democratic fence in 1983, when Gutierrez backed Democrat Harold Washington for mayor and Rostenkowski supported Richard M. Daley, the son of Rostenkowski's political patron, the late Mayor Richard J. Daley.

Gutierrez later challenged Rostenkowski for his 32nd Ward Democratic Committee seat and got less than a fourth of the vote. After Washington's death in 1987, Gutierrez allied himself with Daley's camp. Rostenkowski has since supported Gutierrez in a council re-election bid in 1991 and in his race for Congress.

But although Gutierrez believed he was a shoo-in for Russo's seat on Ways and Means, that prize went to another Chicago freshman, Democrat Mel Reynolds. When it became clear that Gutierrez would not get the seat, he groused that Speaker Thomas S. Foley had applied a strict party loyalty test that he found unacceptable. Rostenkowski said Gutierrez might have opened his mouth too much.

The opening days of the 103rd Congress did not find Gutierrez any quieter. After President Clinton proposed a pay freeze for the executive branch, Gutierrez led a group of freshmen in moving to freeze Congress' own cost of living adjustment. The leadership later suspended the pay increase.

From the outset, Gutierrez was the prohibitive favorite to win the 4th District seat. He came into the race with several advantages, not least of which was Daley's endorsement the day after he announced. Hispanics make up 65 percent of the 4th's population but only 38 percent of its voters. Six percent of the voters are black. Daley's support almost guaranteed that the crucial non-Hispanic white vote would go to Gutierrez.

Gutierrez was left with one primary opponent, former alderman Juan M. Soliz, a Mexican-American, who was not as well financed as Gutierrez. Soliz lost a bid for re-election to his council seat in 1991, after a short-lived challenge to Daley for mayor. Gutierrez won the primary with nearly 60 percent, then jumped to 78 percent in the general election, where he bested Republican Hildegarde Rodriguez-Schieman.

Though he did not end up on Ways and Means, Gutierrez can be expected to use his Banking, Finance and Urban Affairs Committee assignment to advantage for a district plagued by poverty and gangs. To that end, he declined a seat on the Financial Institutions Subcommittee to settle onto the Housing and Community Development Subcommittee.

Gutierrez already has experience in housing policy. While on the City Council, he was instrumental in enacting an ordinance allowing the city to give away vacant lots to low-income housing developers. Gutierrez also won a seat on the Veterans' Affairs Committee.

Illinois 4

Chicago — Parts of North Side, southwest side

The 1990 census reported that Chicago had 545,852 Hispanic residents, more than twice as many as in 1970. A result of this boom has been a rise in political clout, as symbolized by the creation of the Hispanic-majority 4th.

Hispanics account for 65 percent of the district's population. But many of its Puerto Ricans are poor and have yet to establish community roots; many Mexicans are recent arrivals who are not citizens.

Because of these factors, the 4th lags in voter participation — its 1992 turnout was less than half the average for Illinois House districts — and provides opportunities for non-Hispanic whites, including many of Polish heritage, to influence local elections.

Two white Chicago aldermen filed to run in the 1992 Democratic House primary and could have threatened Hispanic control. But both dropped out, clearing the way for Gutierrez, then a Chicago alderman. Gutierrez, a native of Puerto Rico, defeated former Alderman Juan Soliz, a Mexican-American, with 60 percent of the vote.

Democratic primaries should be decisive in the 4th. The combination of minority-group and working-class ethnic voters makes the district a Democratic stronghold; Gutierrez won the 1992 general election by better than 3-to-1.

Drawing the 4th required a creative touch. Most Chicago Hispanics live in two blocs, one northwest of downtown and the other nearby to the southwest. However, a direct linkup would have cut through the black-majority 7th District. To avoid this, the 4th takes in a mostly Hispanic section of the North Side, follows a narrow, 10-mile band along the northern border of the 7th to the Cook County line, then moves south and east along the 7th to hook up with the other Hispanic concentration. Despite its reach, 92 percent of the 4th's population is within Chicago; 5 percent is in adjacent Cicero. Most of the suburban territory is composed of railroad tracks, forest preserves, cemeteries and interstates.

Puerto Ricans hold sway in much of the northern part of the 4th. The former "Polish downtown" along lower Milwaukee Avenue is now mainly Hispanic. Parts of the West Town community are "gentrifying," but nearby Humboldt Park is mainly low-income, and has one of the city's worst gang problems. To the north is Logan Square, which still has a substantial Polish community; there is industry there, in or adjacent to the narrow stretch to the west.

The southern part of the 4th is largely composed of two Mexican-American sections: Little Village, with a thriving business district and many single-family homes, and Pilsen, a poorer area that is upholding its heritage as a point of entry for immigrants.

In the 4th's southern reaches are ethnically mixed sections, including parts of Bridgeport and Back of the Yards. The latter area declined when the famed stockyards closed in the early 1970s, but community organizers have helped attract light industry and revive the retail trade.

1990 Population: 571,530. White 277,739 (49%), Black 36,193 (6%), Other 257,598 (45%). Hispanic origin 371,663 (65%). 18 and over 383,497 (67%), 62 and over 53,817 (9%). Median age: 27.

Committees

Banking, Finance & Urban Affairs (18th of 30 Democrats)
Consumer Credit & Insurance; Housing & Community Development

Veterans' Affairs (16th of 21 Democrats)
Hospitals & Health Care; Oversight & Investigations

Campaign Finance

	Receipts	Receipts from PACs		Expend-itures
1992				
Gutierrez (D)	$438,253	$187,945	(43%)	$420,227
Rodriguez-Schieman (R)	$3,857	$741	(19%)	$3,574

Key Votes

1993

Require parental notification of minors' abortions	N
Require unpaid family and medical leave	Y
Approve national "motor voter" registration bill	Y
Approve budget increasing taxes and reducing deficit	Y
Approve economic stimulus plan	Y

Elections

1992 General		
Luis V. Gutierrez (D)	90,452	(78%)
Hildegarde Rodriguez-Schieman (R)	26,154	(22%)
1992 Primary		
Luis V. Gutierrez (D)	36,377	(60%)
Juan M. Soliz (D)	24,609	(40%)

District Vote for President

1992

D	82,045 (65%)
R	28,890 (23%)
I	15,294 (12%)

5 Dan Rostenkowski (D)

Of Chicago — Elected 1958; 18th Term

Born: Jan. 2, 1928, Chicago.
Education: Loyola U., 1948-51.
Military Service: Army, 1946-48.
Occupation: Insurance executive; public official.
Family: Wife, LaVerne Pirkins; four children.
Religion: Roman Catholic.
Political Career: Ill. House, 1953-55; Ill. Senate, 1955-59.
Capitol Office: 2111 Rayburn Bldg. 20515; 225-4061.

In Washington: Rostenkowski found himself in a familiar position at the start of the 103rd Congress, with his Ways and Means Committee serving as the fulcrum upon which the success or failure of a president's agenda rested.

Comfortable in the spotlight, Rostenkowski has been known to brag that his committee *is* the House of Representatives. Indeed, the work that President Clinton promised to drop in the lap of the Ways and Means chairman was mountainous — deficit reduction, economic stimulus, tax-law changes, health care and welfare reform, not to mention several possible sweeping trade agreements.

It would have been burden enough to carry all that, but Rostenkowski also was operating under a storm cloud that threatened his congressional career. An investigation by the Justice Department into Rostenkowski's personal financial affairs began in mid-1992 and continued into 1993. What started as vague allegations of sham transactions involving fake stamp purchases at the House Post Office ballooned into what was apparently a full-bore investigation into Rostenkowski's financial dealings, going back more than a decade.

Among the allegations being pursued was that his office or campaign accounts were used to make bogus purchases of stamps to get cash from the post office. The Chicago Sun-Times said that questions had been raised about vehicle leasing arrangements and the payment of rent on an office owned by Rostenkowski and his sisters.

As spring turned to summer in 1993, Rostenkowski was faced with the possibility of an indictment that, if handed up, would require him to relinquish his chairmanship to the panel's No. 2 Democrat, Sam M. Gibbons of Florida. House Democratic rules forbid a member under indictment from acting as a chairman. Throughout, Rostenkowski professed his innocence.

He had passed two milestones as the 103rd began: His 65th birthday and the start of his 35th year in the House. Privately, he was said to be sleeping poorly, and observers noted that some of his closest friends on the committee had left Congress at the end of 1992. In 1991, there had been speculation that Rostenkowski, too, would retire. He was among those eligible to convert their campaign treasuries to personal use, had he left by the end of the 102nd Congress. That could have meant about $1 million to Rostenkowski, a man who repeatedly has complained that House members are not paid a salary commensurate with their managerial responsibilities.

But Rostenkowski has never been known as a quitter. "Suffice to say, I wouldn't have run for re-election if I didn't expect to be an active player," he said. "The leaks and vile rumors coming out of the House Post Office probe have been a sad distraction. But they will not keep me from the work at hand."

Notwithstanding his protests, Clinton strategists worried that an indictment might serve to stall progress on the administration's legislative agenda. Shortly after her confirmation in March 1993, Janet Reno, Clinton's attorney general, called for the resignations of all U.S. attorneys, including the one whose office was conducting the Rostenkowski probe. Republicans said it looked like an attempt to take the heat off the Ways and Means chairman; Reno made a public show of support for the interim U.S. attorney overseeing the Rostenkowski inquiry: "I told him if there was anything he needed, full steam ahead," Reno said.

There was one other uncommon feature to Rostenkowski's task for the 103rd: His designated role was as lieutenant to a Democrat in the White House, not as a leader of the loyal opposition. From the time he took over the committee in 1981 until Bill Clinton's inauguration, Rostenkowski had only served Republican presidents as chairman.

He freely acknowledged his changed status, however, and seemed not at all troubled by it; Clinton was "the boss," he told the House Democratic Caucus. "That's my man," Clinton said to Rostenkowski's wife, LaVerne, in a show of mutual respect.

Rostenkowski did make it clear to Clinton

Illinois 5

Chicago — North Side

The 5th, which spans the North Side of Chicago, can be thought of as two districts in one. On the city's east side is a mainly liberal, partly upscale area. Across town, the northwest side is part of Chicago's "Bungalow Belt," where middle- and working-class residents from a variety of Southern and Eastern European backgrounds hold more conservative views.

Both groups have Democratic traditions, but their voting behavior can vary widely. East Side liberals may balk at the local Democratic organization during primary campaigns, but they regularly vote Democratic in November. Democratic voters on the northwest side usually take cues from the party's organization in primaries, but the area can swing to GOP candidates in general elections for major office.

The result of this mix is a district that votes regularly though not certainly Democratic. After going strongly for Ronald Reagan in 1984 and narrowly for George Bush in 1988, the 5th went for Bill Clinton by a scant majority in 1992.

It is not inconceivable that Republicans could compete for this seat in a post-Rostenkowski future, but neither is it likely. Dealing in 1992 with a series of ethics allegations, Rostenkowski won an 18th House term by a margin that, while subpar for him, was still comfortable.

The district ranges to Lake Michigan just north of downtown, taking in some of the upscale high-rises along Lake Shore Drive's "Gold Coast." Nearby is the Lincoln Park community, home to numerous political activists, young professionals and DePaul University students.

Opponents of the city's Democratic Party machine had their heyday here in the 1970s, during the waning days of Richard J. Daley's reign as mayor. Somewhat dormant in recent years, the "lakefront liberals" emerged again when one of their number, activist Dick Simpson, challenged Rostenkowski in the 1992 primary.

The district follows Lincoln Avenue northwest past well-to-do Ravenswood and multi-ethnic Lincoln Square. To the west along Lawrence Avenue is a Korean-American community. The 5th then drops south to Jackowo, still a first stop for immigrants from Poland.

Much of the district's western end is a grid of small brick houses where families of city workers, commuters and O'Hare Airport employees live. Few blacks live here: In her 1992 bid to become the first black woman senator, Democrat Carol Moseley-Braun had trouble in parts of the northwest side. Harold Washington was anathema to many northwest voters during his tenure as Chicago's first black mayor in the mid-1980s.

The 5th also takes in two independent towns, Norridge and Harwood Heights, that are within Chicago's city limits, and such suburban Cook County communities as Franklin Park, Northlake and Melrose Park. Matsushita, the Japanese appliance maker, is expanding an existing Franklin Park facility into the world's largest microwave oven factory.

1990 Population: 571,530. White 496,212 (87%), Black 8,518 (1%), Other 66,800 (12%). Hispanic origin 75,841 (13%). 18 and over 467,584 (82%), 62 and over 103,218 (18%). Median age: 35.

that while he would carry the president's water, it would be up to Clinton to draw it from the well. Proposals to raise taxes would have to come from the White House, he said: "I do not plan to suggest revenue sources of my own."

And while Rostenkowski promised to be a good soldier, that did not stop him from objecting to Clinton administration proposals he found wanting. He complained that Clinton's plan to restore an investment tax credit to stimulate business purchases of equipment would be an unwelcome reversal of reform efforts in 1986 to streamline the tax code and make it broader and fairer. In an April speech, Rostenkowski weighed in on still-unfinished proposals to revamp the health-care system. "These plans are the domestic equivalent of Star Wars, where the plan was that a series of non-existent technologies would be developed and linked to one another so that they'd work flawlessly."

It was vintage Rostenkowski, sure of himself and undeterred by power in the hands of others.

The post office investigation may have been a huge burden for Rostenkowski in the latter months of 1992, but the 102nd Congress was otherwise an improvement for him over its predecessor. He managed to regain enough control of his committee to win passage of two big tax bills that were unmistakably Democratic in character. Both bills fell victim to vetoes by President Bush — as expected. But that had little or nothing to do with Rostenkowski's success at recovering some of the clout he appeared to have lost.

Life in the 101st Congress had been studded with setbacks for Rostenkowski. Legislative reversals, combined with the frustrations of the budget process and a cloudy political picture back home, had Capitol Hill guessing as to Rostenkowski's career plans.

Rostenkowski privately complained of the deterioration he saw in the quality of congressional life. Then, in rapid succession, he was slapped with defeats in committee on the capital gains tax and the extension of Medicare to catastrophic illness. He could not keep a limit on textile imports, which he opposed, from reaching the floor. In each case, Rostenkowski saw his coalition on the panel pulled apart by pressures greater than any he could bring to bear.

A close Rostenkowski associate, Ed Jenkins of Georgia, led five other Democrats and all 13 Ways and Means Republicans in backing a cut in the capital gains tax. At first, it was not clear whether Rostenkowski himself wanted to use such a cut as a bargaining chip with Bush, his old friend and former committee colleague. By the time the chairman had committed himself to fighting it, the die was cast. Jenkins prevailed in committee and again on the floor, even after the Democratic leadership had thrown in behind Rostenkowski.

The battle over catastrophic coverage, and the surtax passed in 1988 to pay for it, was even more disheartening. Rostenkowski was stunned by the vehemence of seniors' objection to the surtax, especially when he found his car pursued down a Chicago thoroughfare by an elderly throng shouting "Impeach Rotten-kowski!"

Rostenkowski has a reputation both in Chicago and Washington as a rather unsubtle ward politician. But it has become increasingly clear that Rostenkowski wants to be known by the end of his career for something beyond the hoarding of influence.

Such resolve to enlarge his legacy seemed evident in Rostenkowski's comprehensive March 1990 proposal for attacking the budget deficit. Few believed meaningful budget moves could be made in an election year, yet Rostenkowski proposed a deal of heroic proportions. It would raise taxes on gasoline and alcohol as well as on income. It carved deep into defense spending and froze domestic spending (including Social Security benefits) for a year to slow long-range spending growth. Widely praised by editorialists, Rostenkowski's plan received a surprisingly cordial nod from the White House, a precursor of later flexibility on taxes.

Whatever the future holds, it seems likely that Rostenkowski's chief legacy will be his remarkable achievement of the 99th Congress, when he maneuvered a new federal tax code through a reluctant House and into law. Many others played key roles in that drama, but none did quite what he did.

"I've had a reputation as a gut politician, a total political animal from the city of Chicago," he said early in 1985. "But I'm also trying ... to do the responsible thing."

The experience seemed to lead Rostenkowski to conclude that government could be just as much fun as politics. After nearly three decades in the House accumulating political power as if it were an end in itself, he began applying himself to larger legislative purposes, such as overhauling U.S. trade law and the welfare system.

Still, Rostenkowski has a pride in his raw political skills that is rare in an institution coming to be dominated by new-breed Democrats who are more inclined to distance themselves from their party and the institution. Both his pride and his irritation were on display in early 1989, when he chastised the House for lacking the self-respect to accept a pay raise.

"In my hometown of Chicago they call politics a blood sport," he said. "I have been pretty successful at it. I don't apologize for getting in the arena, and I'll be damned if I'll apologize for winning."

The key to Rostenkowski's legislative success has been the horse-trading skills he learned under Chicago Mayor Richard J. Daley. Indeed, Rostenkowski has turned Ways and Means into a well-oiled political machine of its own. He has treated his committee like a big-city ward, where personal loyalty counts far more than ideology. He has built members' allegiance the old-fashioned way, by doing favors, keeping his word and taking down the names of those who don't go along.

Despite his background in Democratic machine politics, Rostenkowski's preferred mode of legislating is bipartisan. He is willing to deal with Republicans as well as Democrats in his patented way of building coalitions within the committee: Give everyone an opportunity to participate in the decision-making process but exact a stiff price for participation.

His grip on the committee and its products is not always firm, as the capital gains defeat of 1989 showed. In 1981, his first year as chairman, Rostenkowski suffered an acutely embarrassing defeat when he laced a tax bill with special-interest provisions in an effort to beat President Ronald Reagan on the House floor. He ended up losing. "If we accept the president's substitute," he said on the floor, "we accept his dominance of the House in the months ahead." The House accepted the Reagan substitute by a vote of 238-195.

In the Congress after that, Rostenkowski won some notable legislative victories — his committee moved a bill restoring the solvency of the Social Security system — but he seemed most concerned with achieving control over the panel. He gradually restored the power of the Ways and Means chair, which had ebbed under the tenure of his predecessor, the well-informed but ineffectual Al Ullman of Oregon.

Rostenkowski's power-building efforts paid off handsomely when Reagan made overhauling the tax code the top domestic priority of his second term. In drafting the tax-overhaul bill, Rostenkowski asked members of both parties what it would take to win their support for the massive project. He agreed to consider meeting those demands only if the member, in return, would give an ironclad commitment to support the final product. If not, he saw no reason to deal. "You might as well kick a guy's brains out if he's not for you," he said at one point.

There is some irony in Rostenkowski's fame as a tax reformer: He never planned to be a tax specialist. For more than 20 years he played pure House politics, trading votes and committee assignments and angling for a top leadership position. His success in 1986 rekindled speculation that he might mount a campaign for Speaker in 1987. His opponent then would have been Jim Wright of Texas, whom he had helped make majority leader in 1976, but with whom he had since been at odds. Rostenkowski never made the move.

It was his last thought of getting a senior spot in the leadership. Before taking the committee chair, he had been in line to be whip, the third-ranking position in the leadership and steppingstone for the last two Speakers. Rostenkowski agonized and consulted friends for weeks before choosing the chairmanship.

Rostenkowski had once hoped the 1970s would see his career flower. But he was haunted by an event in 1968 that blocked what had seemed to be a steady rise in the party ranks. Rostenkowski stepped in at the command of President Lyndon B. Johnson to restore order at the tumultuous 1968 Democratic National Convention in Chicago. He physically took the gavel from House Majority Leader Carl Albert of Oklahoma, who had lost control of the situation. In 1971 Albert moved up from majority leader to Speaker. Rostenkowski threw his influence behind Hale Boggs of Louisiana for majority leader in exchange for a Boggs promise to appoint Rostenkowski as whip. Boggs won, but Albert, still angry over the convention squabble, vetoed Rostenkowski as whip. The man chosen instead was Thomas P. "Tip" O'Neill Jr. of Massachusetts. Six years later, after O'Neill was elected Speaker, a place was found for Rostenkowski as chief deputy whip.

At Home: Usually a winner of routine reelections, Rostenkowski in 1992 found himself the target of aggressive long-shot challengers who held him well below his typical victory margins in both the primary and general elections.

Rostenkowski's 1992 difficulties started with redistricting. Illinois lost two House seats in 1990 reapportionment, and when no House incumbents chose to step aside, the Democratic-controlled legislature stalemated on the remap. A federal court panel then enacted a Republican-drawn map. Under the plan, Rostenkowski picked up a big chunk of Chicago's Northwest Side that had been represented by veteran Democratic Rep. Frank Annunzio (who considered running against his colleague but instead retired) and a small piece on the city's east side that had been held by Democrat Sidney R. Yates.

The former Annunzio turf was similar to Rostenkowski's constituency — largely socially conservative working-class residents of a variety of European ethnic origins. But the former Yates territory was the haunt of the "Lakefront Liberals," a group of reform-minded activists who in the 1970s confronted the Democratic machine of then-Mayor Richard J. Daley (of which Rostenkowski was a member).

Although this group of reformers had faded from prominence, one of its leading figures, former Chicago Alderman Dick Simpson, challenged Rostenkowski in the March 1992 primary. Simpson portrayed Rostenkowski as the embodiment of the Old Guard and a servant of big-money special interests as Ways and Means chairman. He tried to make direct connections between Rostenkowski's legislative actions and political action committee contributions.

Rostenkowski largely ignored Simpson but showed a recognition of the danger he presented. After years of effortless campaigns, the longtime incumbent worked the streets, reminding voters of the federal dollars his position enabled him to bring to Chicago. Simpson managed to carry some of his lakefront base, but Rostenkowski won with relative ease elsewhere to take 57 percent overall.

Rostenkowski's GOP opponent pulled no punches about his "anti-insider" theme: He had himself listed on the ballot as Elias R. "Non-Incumbent" Zenkich. A Bosnian immigrant and owner of a medical products company, Zenkich tried to draw attention to the allegations linking Rostenkowski to the scandal-plagued House Post Office. While the little-known and underfunded challenger never was a real threat, he held the Democrat under 60 percent, a career low for a general election.

Until this slip, Rostenkowski's career was marked by a fast ascent and a long, near-level plateau. At 24, he became the youngest member of the Illinois House. At 26, he was the youngest in the Illinois Senate. And at 30, he was a member of Congress.

A talented baseball player who drew the attentions of pro scouts, Rostenkowski was instead steered into politics by his father, a city alderman and Democratic ward committeeman. The younger Rostenkowski developed an alliance with Daley, who became mayor in 1955. When Democratic Rep. Thomas Gordon of Chicago, chairman of the Foreign Affairs Committee, decided in 1958 to retire, Daley summoned Rostenkowski from the state legislature to succeed him.

Rostenkowski settled in for easy wins in a district dominated by the Democratic machine. His most uncomfortable moment came in 1966, a year of high racial tension in Chicago. His GOP opponent, cab driver John Leszynski, openly appealed to the white backlash against open-housing demonstrations. Still, Rostenkowski was re-elected with 60 percent.

Maintaining his position as Democratic ward committeeman for many years, Rostenkowski remained focused on Chicago politics and was seen as a likely successor to Daley. But by the time Daley died in office in 1976, Rostenkowski was a comfortable 18-year House veteran on track to become Ways and Means chairman.

Even after assuming that post in 1981, Rostenkowski stayed involved. In 1983, he strongly backed an initial bid by Richard M. Daley, his late ally's son, to unseat then-Mayor Jane Byrne; but a third candidate, Rep. Harold Washington, won to become Chicago's first black mayor.

Faced with a full plate of legislative responsibilities in the 1980s, Rostenkowski's focus increasingly turned to Washington and away from Chicago. When Daley made a successful run for mayor in 1989, Rostenkowski again supported him but did not play the strong personal role he would have in the past.

Committees

Joint Taxation (Chairman)

Ways & Means (Chairman)
Trade

Elections

1992 General		
Dan Rostenkowski (D)	132,889	(57%)
Elias R. "Non-Incumbent" Zenkich (R)	90,738	(39%)
Blaise C. Grenke (LIBERT)	8,456	(4%)
1992 Primary		
Dan Rostenkowski (D)	56,059	(57%)
Dick Simpson (D)	41,956	(43%)
1990 General		
Dan Rostenkowski (D)	70,151	(79%)
Robert Marshall (LIBERT)	18,529	(21%)

Previous Winning Percentages: **1988** (75%) **1986** (79%) **1984** (71%) **1982** (83%) **1980** (85%) **1978** (86%) **1976** (81%) **1974** (87%) **1972** (74%) **1970** (74%) **1968** (63%) **1966** (60%) **1964** (66%) **1962** (61%) **1960** (67%) **1958** (75%)

District Vote for President

1992

D 124,437 (51%)
R 80,139 (33%)
I 39,153 (16%)

Campaign Finance

	Receipts	Receipts from PACs		Expend-itures
1992				
Rostenkowski (D)	$1,587,108	$962,937	(61%)	$1,455,455
Zenkich (R)	$95,447	0		$83,293
1990				
Rostenkowski (D)	$378,282	$197,700	(52%)	$298,653

Key Votes

1993	
Require parental notification of minors' abortions	N
Require unpaid family and medical leave	Y
Approve national "motor voter" registration bill	Y
Approve budget increasing taxes and reducing deficit	Y
Approve economic stimulus plan	Y
1992	
Approve balanced-budget constitutional amendment	N
Close down space station program	Y
Approve U.S. aid for former Soviet Union	Y
Allow shifting funds from defense to domestic programs	Y
1991	
Extend unemployment benefits using deficit financing	Y
Approve waiting period for handgun purchases	Y
Authorize use of force in Persian Gulf	Y

Voting Studies

	Presidential Support		Party Unity		Conservative Coalition	
Year	S	O	S	O	S	O
1992	18	71	90	6	31	54
1991	36	52	80	10	51	43
1990	33	59	76	12	33	56
1989	36	59	85	10	39	54
1988	29	58	80	9	32	58
1987	20	66	73	5	37	47
1986	19	66	84	5	36	58
1985	28	61	82	6	18	73
1984	39	42	68	11	34	46
1983	41	52	77	12	33	64
1982	44	44	80	14	42	56
1981	50	49	77	18	44	52

Interest Group Ratings

Year	ADA	AFL-CIO	CCUS	ACU
1992	95	82	38	0
1991	45	73	30	16
1990	67	83	17	14
1989	70	100	10	19
1988	65	85	50	19
1987	68	77	22	18
1986	65	86	35	15
1985	75	81	36	20
1984	65	83	36	10
1983	65	81	39	9
1982	85	85	35	10
1981	55	73	26	14

6 Henry J. Hyde (R)

Of Bensenville — Elected 1974; 10th Term

Born: April 18, 1924, Chicago, Ill.
Education: Duke U., 1943-44; Georgetown U., B.S. 1947; Loyola U., J.D. 1949.
Military Service: Navy, 1942-46; Naval Reserve, 1946-68.
Occupation: Lawyer.
Family: Widowed; four children.
Religion: Roman Catholic.
Political Career: GOP nominee for U.S. House, 1962; Ill. House, 1967-75, majority leader, 1971-73.
Capitol Office: 2110 Rayburn Bldg. 20515; 225-4561.

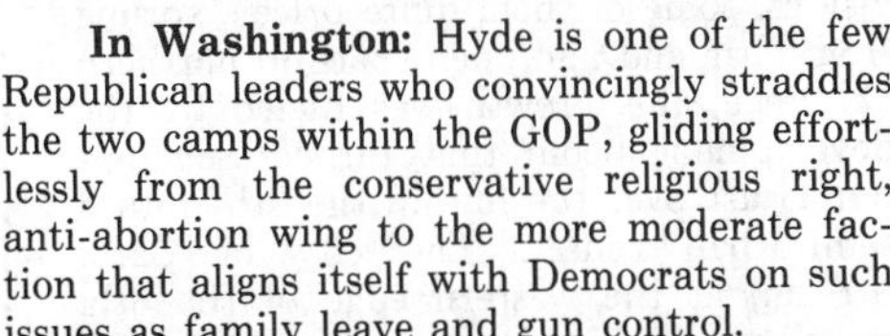

In Washington: Hyde is one of the few Republican leaders who convincingly straddles the two camps within the GOP, gliding effortlessly from the conservative religious right, anti-abortion wing to the more moderate faction that aligns itself with Democrats on such issues as family leave and gun control.

Articulate, smart and well-schooled in the art of making political friends, Hyde was unopposed in his campaign for chairman of the Republican Policy Committee at the start of the 103rd Congress. Confrontational enough to appeal to the brash, younger generation of House Republicans, yet practical enough to bargain occasionally with the opposition, Hyde remains a viable candidate for House GOP leader, should fellow Illinoisan Robert H. Michel retire.

But at age 69, with lingering questions about his health, the 103rd may be too late for Hyde to take advantage of generational opportunities.

He would be a prominent presence even if he were not a hulk of a man with a luminous white mane and enormous hands. No matter who is the sponsor of a conservative initiative, Hyde is likely to be its most impressive spokesman, waiting for flawed liberal arguments and then pouncing with all the wit and sarcasm he once used as a Chicago trial lawyer.

Though Hyde is criticized for having more zest for argument than for the less glamorous task of legislating, he says he is simply playing the proper role of a minority party member: "If you come to understand your role is to be a gadfly, a conscience factor, and try to work some influence in committee ... if that's enough, and you don't need to be chairman of a subcommittee or see your name on a bill, this can be very rewarding."

Hyde is savvy about polishing his image in the media, and he takes care not to overexpose himself. "You have to husband your pearls before you cast them profligately about the chamber," he says.

Despite his high profile on foreign policy matters in recent years and his increasing duties as the party's elder statesman, Hyde still is best known for the amendment bearing his name that prohibits federal funding of abortion. With the election of President Clinton, the issue returned to the fore in 1993 and promises to consume much of Hyde's time and energy in the 103rd.

Even before the legislative session was under way, Clinton, with the stroke of a pen, undid much of what Hyde and fellow abortion opponents had spent years working to achieve. Among the five federal abortion policies Clinton reversed were the 1988 "gag rule" prohibiting abortion counseling at federally funded clinics, the ban on fetal tissue research and the ban on performing abortions at overseas military medical clinics.

And anti-abortion activists know there is more to come. Clinton directed government researchers to study the use of the French abortion pill RU-486. And his proposed budget would reverse the Hyde amendment.

Passed when Hyde was a freshman in 1976, the amendment had become a routine part of annual appropriations legislation. Even when the Senate mustered enough votes to allow abortion funding for rape and incest victims in 1988, abortion opponents could rely on a presidential veto.

But without the veto leverage Hyde faces a difficult task in saving his amendment. And on the horizon looms the Freedom of Choice Act, a bill designed to prohibit most state restrictions on abortion.

Though he is most often recognized for his erudite conservatism, Hyde's words can sometimes put a biting edge on his rhetoric. In one abortion debate in the late 1980s, Hyde thundered: "This debate is not about forcing people to have children. It is [about] forcing taxpayers to pay for the extermination of unborn children."

One Hyde quip nearly resulted in fisticuffs

Illinois 6

Northwest and west Chicago suburbs

All the growth stages of Chicago's western suburbs are represented in the 6th. To the south are such long-established suburbs as Elmhurst, Villa Park, Lombard, Glen Ellyn and Wheaton, which grew up along an early commuter rail line. To the north are suburbs that boomed in the 1960s, as nearby O'Hare established itself as one of the world's busiest airports. In between are newer suburbs that have seen much of the area's recent population growth.

The 6th is mainly white-collar and overwhelmingly Republican. Two-thirds of its population is in Du Page County, often cited by political analysts as a symbol of GOP affluence; the remainder of the district is in equally Republican parts of suburban Cook County. Rep. Hyde has long been a politically dominant figure in the area.

Failure by a statewide Republican candidate to clean up in the 6th, and in Du Page County as a whole, means certain defeat. In 1992, George Bush carried Du Page with 48 percent. This was his best county total in Illinois, but his 63,707-vote victory margin over Bill Clinton here was barely half what Bush amassed in 1988 against Michael S. Dukakis. Ross Perot took 21 percent of the county vote.

O'Hare (an extension of the city of Chicago) is a major employer of district residents and the economic engine for much of the 6th. Rosemont, a Cook County suburb just east of the airport, has few residents, but it has business offices and thousands of hotel rooms. The Horizon arena is in Rosemont.

Des Plaines, the largest city wholly within the 6th, is pretty much built out, as is neighboring Park Ridge, a mainly Republican suburb whose best-known native is a Democrat: first lady Hillary Rodham Clinton. On the airport's west side are newer subdivisions in Elk Grove Village (where United Airlines has headquarters) and Bensenville (Hyde's hometown), which had double-digit growth rates during the 1980s.

The Du Page suburbs at the southern end of the 6th are mainly bedroom communities whose residents commute to downtown Chicago or to such burgeoning suburban employment centers as nearby Oak Brook and Naperville.

During the 1980s, residential subdivisions, some of them quite pricey, sprung from farmland and open space in northern Du Page; this growth was fueled by the development boom that turned Schaumburg (just over the line in the 8th) into a semi-urban center. The city of Carol Stream, at the western edge of the 6th, more than doubled in population during the 1980s. Such towns as Roselle, Bloomingdale and Glendale Heights also grew at healthy, albeit more modest, rates.

Years ago, Du Page's farms drew a number of migrant workers, including some Hispanics. Today, Hispanics make up 5 percent of the 6th's population, which is overwhelmingly white; blacks account for slightly more than 1 percent.

The 6th also butts back into western Cook County to take in LaGrange Park and parts of Westchester and Brookfield.

1990 Population: 571,530. White 524,739 (92%), Black 8,461 (1%), Other 38,330 (7%). Hispanic origin 30,126 (5%). 18 and over 437,195 (76%), 62 and over 84,164 (15%). Median age: 34.

at the end of the 101st, when nerves were frayed by endless budget talks. Angry over a sarcastic floor statement by liberal Barney Frank, Hyde suggested that the Massachusetts Democrat did not know what he was talking about because he had been in the "gymnasium doing whatever he does in the gymnasium." The comment referred to an unsubstantiated charge by a male prostitute that he had had sex with Frank in the gym. After Hyde and Democrat Craig Washington of Texas came near to a scrap over the comment, Hyde publicly apologized to Frank and asked that his remark be stricken from the record.

For all the intensity of his conservatism, Hyde is not always ideologically predictable. He often forms odd-couple alliances with liberal House Democrats, as he has done on an issue of importance to him: compelling parents to pay child support.

With help from Democrat Charles E. Schumer of New York, Hyde won passage in the 102nd Congress of a bill that establishes fines and jail time for failure to pay child support. The legislation makes interstate flight to avoid child support a federal crime.

In the 103rd, Hyde hopes to designate the Internal Revenue Service as the nation's principal child support collection agency. His proposal, which has received warm words from some Democratic leaders, including Clinton, would allow the IRS to garnishee wages and issue penalties for late payment.

In the past, Hyde has teamed up with liberal Henry A. Waxman, D-Calif., to expand Medicaid coverage to more poor women and children, and with Barbara Boxer, D-Calif., (who otherwise wrote proposals to undo the Hyde amendment in 1990 and 1992) to prohibit commercial surrogate mother contracts.

Some conservatives criticize the seeming contradictions in Hyde's voting record. In 1990, he voted to override President Bush's veto of the Family and Medical Leave Act.

But Hyde said the family leave bill that Clinton signed into law in 1993 would "reinforce the family by humanizing the relationship between employee and employer.... As one who shares a conservative vision for our society, I don't think my support for family leave is aberrational, but rather it's consistent with family values."

Reacting to speech codes on college campuses that penalize comments that might be controversial or offensive, Hyde formed an unusual partnership with the left-leaning American Civil Liberties Union. He drafted legislation that would prohibit schools receiving federal funds from disciplining students solely on the basis of speech. The bill would give students the right to seek an injunction against such speech codes on the basis that speech is protected under the First Amendment.

Although still the leader of the conservative forces on the Judiciary Committee, Hyde has devoted equal attention to the Foreign Affairs Committee, and, from 1985 through 1990, to the Intelligence panel.

Once brought together by the Cold War, Republicans on the Foreign Affairs panel now find themselves divided. Hyde, displaying a more internationalist stance, could become a key swing vote on the committee. Early in the Clinton administration, Hyde cautiously endorsed air strikes over Bosnia if carried out in concert with European allies, noting that he remained wary that the United States would get bogged down in an ensuing quagmire.

Hyde frequently is called upon to help investigate secretive foreign dealings by administration figures.

During the 102nd, Hyde and Democrat Lee H. Hamilton of Indiana led a special task force investigating allegations that operatives for the 1980 Reagan-Bush campaign conspired to delay the release of American hostages held in Iran. The panel announced in January 1993 that it had not found evidence to support the charges.

In the 100th, he was a member of the special Iran-contra investigating committee — where he emerged as President Ronald Reagan's leading defender. Hyde rarely questioned witnesses, instead favoring one-liners and long speeches. He once asked a question, then told the witness, "I'd rather answer it myself," and did.

One result of the hearings was a law to tighten controls on arms sales linked to terrorism. The author with California Democrat Howard L. Berman of a 1986 law requiring congressional notice of arms sales to terrorist nations, Hyde had criticized Reagan for not informing Congress about arms sales to Iran. In late 1989 Congress approved a new Berman-Hyde measure to close loopholes.

Release of Iran-contra figure Oliver L. North's notebooks in 1990 caused some discomfort for Hyde and three other House Republicans. The former White House aide, who was found guilty of three felony charges (later dismissed), said the four members were briefed in 1985 about third-country efforts to aid the contras.

Hyde is often noted for his appreciation of a worthy adversary. But at times, his intense feelings have made him less than charitable toward those who disagree with him. He even had harsh words for fellow Catholics who oppose U.S. policies in Central America, denouncing the "liberal clergy, the trendy vicars, the networking nuns."

Prominent in Hyde's office are both a bust and a portrait of St. Thomas More, the 16th-century English lord chancellor and Catholic martyr. Hyde notes that More is the patron saint of lawyers and a man who gave his life for his principles. More's career also reflected a mix of the secular and the religious that marks Hyde's own.

While Hyde believes it is appropriate to debate the morality of public-policy decisions, he tries to resist judging the morality of individuals.

In 1983 he opposed conservatives' motion to expel Illinois Republican Daniel B. Crane for sexual misconduct with a House page. "The Judeo-Christian tradition says, 'Hate the sin, love the sinner,'" Hyde said. "We are on record as hating the sin, some more ostentatiously than others. I think it is time to love the sinner."

In 1990, however, he joined a majority of Republicans to reject the recommendation of the ethics committee that Frank be reprimanded in connection with his involvement with the male prostitute. The GOP was unsuccessful in its effort to have Frank censured.

At Home: Though he has for years symbolized the stalwart Republican tendencies of Chicago's western suburbs, Hyde grew up in the city as an Irish Catholic Democrat. But he began having doubts about the Democratic Party in the late 1940s; by 1952, he had switched parties and backed Dwight D. Eisenhower for president.

In 1962, Hyde — a lawyer and Republican precinct committeeman — was the GOP choice to challenge Democratic Rep. Roman Pucinski in a northwest Chicago district. A Republican had represented the heavily ethnic district before Pucinski won it in 1958, and Hyde came within 10,000 votes of taking it back for the GOP.

Elected to the Illinois House in 1966, he was one of its most outspoken and articulate debaters. In 1971 Hyde became majority leader;

he unsuccessfully ran for Speaker in 1973.

In 1974, longtime GOP Rep. Harold Collier retired from the suburban 6th District just west of Chicago. Much of the 6th was unfamiliar to Hyde, but he dominated the six-man GOP primary anyway.

The general election was tougher. Hyde's Democratic opponent was Edward V. Hanrahan, a former Cook County state's attorney who had been indicted for attempting to obstruct a federal investigation into a 1969 incident in which Chicago police officers killed two Black Panther Party leaders. Hanrahan was acquitted but lost re-election as prosecutor in 1972.

Although Hanrahan's past exploits had made him a sort of folk hero among local blue-collar ethnics, he could not keep pace with Hyde in fundraising, organizing or personal campaigning.

Hyde's superior resources won out. Using phone banks and an army of precinct workers, his staff turned out enough voters to give him an 8,000-vote win over Hanrahan while GOP districts nationwide were falling to Democrats.

Hyde has since been invincible. The 1981 redistricting gave him an almost all-new constituency but one with a definite Republican lean; in each of his elections during the ensuing decade, Hyde carried two-thirds of the vote or better. The next remap, before the 1992 elections, was particularly kind, leaving Hyde's constituency largely intact. Hyde won re-election by his usual wide margin.

Committees

Foreign Affairs (6th of 18 Republicans)
International Operations

Judiciary (3rd of 14 Republicans)
Civil & Constitutional Rights (ranking)

Elections

1992 General		
Henry J. Hyde (R)	165,009	(66%)
Barry W. Watkins (D)	86,891	(34%)
1990 General		
Henry J. Hyde (R)	96,410	(67%)
Robert J. Cassidy (D)	48,155	(33%)

Previous Winning Percentages: **1988** (74%) **1986** (75%) **1984** (75%) **1982** (68%) **1980** (67%) **1978** (66%) **1976** (61%) **1974** (53%)

District Vote for President

1992
D 86,444 (33%)
R 121,863 (47%)
I 52,734 (20%)

Campaign Finance

	Receipts	Receipts from PACs	Expend-itures
1992			
Hyde (R)	$355,851	$170,882 (48%)	$408,987
Watkins (D)	$62,534	0	$62,423
1990			
Hyde (R)	$302,541	$130,648 (43%)	$270,435
Cassidy (D)	$1,520	0	$1,055

Key Votes

1993	
Require parental notification of minors' abortions	Y
Require unpaid family and medical leave	Y
Approve national "motor voter" registration bill	N
Approve budget increasing taxes and reducing deficit	N
Approve economic stimulus plan	N
1992	
Approve balanced-budget constitutional amendment	Y
Close down space station program	?
Approve U.S. aid for former Soviet Union	Y
Allow shifting funds from defense to domestic programs	N
1991	
Extend unemployment benefits using deficit financing	N
Approve waiting period for handgun purchases	Y
Authorize use of force in Persian Gulf	Y

Voting Studies

	Presidential Support		Party Unity		Conservative Coalition	
Year	**S**	**O**	**S**	**O**	**S**	**O**
1992	60	14	59	14	58	4
1991	85	14	83	13	92	8
1990	68	31	78	18	81	15
1989	66	16	58	12	61	10
1988	70	28	84	10	92	8
1987	65	32	76	18	86	9
1986	76	21	75	18	80	20
1985	71	19	75	17	85	9
1984	71	25	79	15	88	7
1983	89	10	83	15	88	12
1982	75	17	79 †	19 †	86	8
1981	79	20	77	19	81	16

† Not eligible for all recorded votes.

Interest Group Ratings

Year	ADA	AFL-CIO	CCUS	ACU
1992	15	44	75	94
1991	10	17	70	80
1990	11	17	64	88
1989	5	10	89	95
1988	15	14	100	92
1987	12	6	100	96
1986	5	7	75	90
1985	15	21	74	81
1984	10	8	87	88
1983	5	0	95	86
1982	15	11	81	85
1981	10	7	94	93

7 Cardiss Collins (D)

Of Chicago — Elected 1973; 10th Full Term

Born: Sept. 24, 1931, St. Louis, Mo.
Education: Northwestern U., 1949-50.
Occupation: Auditor.
Family: Widow of Rep. George W. Collins; one child.
Religion: National Baptist.
Political Career: No previous office.
Capitol Office: 2308 Rayburn Bldg. 20515; 225-5006.

In Washington: Collins is now into her third decade in Congress, and that long tenure has lifted her into a high-ranking position on the powerful Energy and Commerce Committee. She chairs its Subcommittee on Commerce, Consumer Protection and Competitiveness, and her range of interests includes equity in education, health problems of minorities, consumers' rights and environmental protection.

But on a committee stacked with overachievers, Collins has a tough time standing out. As a legislative operator, she does not rate with the others who chair Energy and Commerce subcommittees, a group that includes Henry A. Waxman of California, Edward J. Markey of Massachusetts and Philip R. Sharp of Indiana. And even some panel members junior to her are better-known as activist legislators, such as Mike Synar of Oklahoma, Ron Wyden of Oregon and Jim Cooper of Tennessee.

Though 1992 was widely proclaimed the "Year of the Woman" in politics, this did not serve to raise Collins' chronically low profile. Her status as Congress' senior black woman rarely got much notice, especially compared with the blaze of publicity surrounding another black female politician from Chicago, Carol Moseley-Braun, who became the first African-American Democrat elected to the Senate.

But the influx of new women into Congress could benefit Collins. After years as the lone woman on Energy, she has been joined by three freshman women, all Democrats. This could foster an environment more receptive to some of Collins' favorite issues, such as promoting business opportunities for women and minorities and bringing gender equity to college sports.

While she is generally considered a liberal, Collins tempers her liberalism in order to remain responsive to Chicago's financial and corporate interests as well as to her district's heavy industries.

In the 102nd Congress, her first term as chairman of the Energy subcommittee, Collins was credited with solid work on issues including international trade, banking regulations and solid waste disposal.

One longtime concern of Collins has been the small percentage of broadcasting licenses held by minorities and women. She has repeatedly introduced legislation to preserve preferences for minority and female applicants seeking such licenses from the Federal Communications Commission.

In the 103rd Congress, Collins proposed legislation to require college athletic departments to disclose how they divide their financial resources between men's and women's athletics. Collins says that colleges are ignoring Title IX of the Education Amendments of 1972, which mandates nondiscrimination in all programs, including sports, at colleges receiving federal aid.

Collins, who helped win Medicare coverage for two cancer-screening tests for women (Pap smears and mammograms), is now hoping to improve Medicaid coverage of services to low-income pregnant women and their infants.

Collins also is pushing for the addition of a 17th division to the National Institutes of Health; it would focus on minority health issues.

Her bill requiring safety warnings on toys with parts small enough to choke young children passed the House in the 102nd, though the Senate did not act on it. It passed the House again early in the 103rd.

Collins ranks even higher on a panel with less visibility than Energy and Commerce: She is the No. 2 Democrat on the Government Operations Committee, just behind Chairman John Conyers Jr. of Michigan.

Collins was a novice at politics in 1973, when the Chicago organization placed her in the House as successor to her husband, George W. Collins, who was killed in an airplane crash shortly after being elected to a second term. She soon became an active participant in the Congressional Black Caucus, and by 1979 was in line for the chairmanship. She took that post at a time of increasing black disillusionment with Jimmy Carter's administration, and she became a widely quoted voice of that discontent.

At Home: It was George Collins who seemed destined for a long tenure in a

Illinois 7

Chicago — Downtown; West Side

The black-majority 7th links Chicago's bustling downtown business district with the city's poorest minority neighborhoods. These economic extremes are symbolized by two stretches of apartment buildings. One lines Lake Shore Drive running north from downtown: These are the plush high-rises of the "Gold Coast." The other is in the 7th's southern end, on a barren stretch overlooking the Dan Ryan Expressway: a huge housing project, the Robert Taylor Homes. Abject poverty, crime, drugs, teenage pregnancy and other urban ills are rife here.

Poverty is also persistent on the city's West Side, home to most of the district's blacks. Parts of this area are moonscapes of abandoned factories and rubble-strewn lots.

Although the 7th fills up daily with white commuters, the permanent population is nearly two-thirds black. The district is reliably Democratic across the ballot.

Longtime Rep. Collins has been safe from general-election competition, but she faced tough primaries in 1984 and 1986. And there is cause for concern. In 1992, Democratic voters in the city's other majority-black districts (the 1st and 2nd) ousted veteran incumbents in favor of younger primary challengers.

At the eastern end of the district is downtown Chicago and the corporate headquarters, financial institutions and professional organizations that make it the Midwest's leading business center. Sears Tower, the world's tallest building, is here.

Across the Chicago River is the upscale "Magnificent Mile" shopping area, the skyscraping John Hancock Building and the Gold Coast. But even on the North Side there is anguish, in the troubled Cabrini-Green housing project. South of downtown, the 7th picks up Soldier Field (home of football's Bears), Chinatown and white, ethnic Bridgeport, the political base of the Daley family. The district then edges through black areas including the Robert Taylor Homes, whose buildings were once seen as exemplars of progressive social policy, but today are denounced as vertical ghettos.

The near West Side is bisected by the Eisenhower Expressway. To the north is a mainly black and poor area; Chicago Stadium, where basketball's Bulls and hockey's Black Hawks play, is here. To the south of the highway is the University of Illinois at Chicago (24,200 students) and the hospitals that make up the West Side Medical Center.

The West Side neighborhoods of Garfield Park and Lawndale define Chicago ghetto life. As late as the 1950s, Lawndale was a largely Jewish area. But an influx of blacks spurred a "white flight" exacerbated by block-busting real estate agents. Parts of Lawndale have never recovered from riots in the 1960s and a siege of "arson for profit" blazes in the 1970s.

Austin, at Chicago's western edge, has some better-off areas that border the largely prosperous suburbs of Oak Park and River Forest. Oak Park is the most settled of Chicago's western suburbs; 70 percent of its housing stock was built before 1940. Farther west are middle- and working-class suburbs, several of which are largely black.

1990 Population: 571,530. White 165,724 (29%), Black 375,170 (66%), Other 30,636 (5%). Hispanic origin 24,763 (4%). 18 and over 406,971 (71%), 62 and over 70,143 (12%). Median age: 30.

House district based in the low-income black communities of Chicago's West Side. The loyal lieutenant of longtime Mayor Richard J. Daley was awarded a City Council seat and then a seat in Congress in 1970.

But a month after his 1972 re-election, George Collins was killed in a plane crash near Chicago's Midway Airport. Although his widow had never before been involved directly in politics — she worked as an auditor in the Illinois Revenue Department — she obtained the Democratic organization's backing as his successor and won 93 percent in the ensuing special election.

In two decades as the member from an overwhelmingly Democratic black-majority district, she has never faced a serious general-election contest. But in the mid-1980s, she weathered a pair of competitive Democratic primaries.

Collins was caught in the cross-fire between the movement that elected Harold Washington as the first black mayor of Chicago in 1983 and the remnants of the Democratic political machine that had promoted her.

Collins had kept her distance from the city's black independent political movement, of which Washington was a leader. Although machine loyalties began unraveling in the West Side black community after Daley's 1976 death, Collins avoided the activists and even supported Mayor Jane M. Byrne in her unsuccessful 1983 bid for renomination against Washington.

Washington's supporters sought revenge in the 1984 House primary. Alderman Danny K.

Davis, a strong Washington supporter, took on Collins. By withholding her support from Washington, he said, she had "ignored the hue and cry of the people and turned her back on those who were looking to her and to her office for leadership." Davis tapped into the network of West Side ministers and grass-roots organizers who had supported Washington, and he tried to tie himself to the flood of "self-empowerment" sentiment that had powered Washington's campaign.

But the fervor of the mayoral campaign had died down, and Davis' cash-strapped bid had trouble stoking it. While several members of Washington's staff took prominent roles in Davis' effort, Washington did not endorse Davis until shortly before the election.

Collins, meanwhile, had help not only from old-line black machine Democrats, but also from labor unions and white liberals in Oak Park and lakefront Chicago who liked her environmentalist and feminist credentials. Collins took 49 percent to Davis' 38 percent.

Davis tried again in 1986, but the disgruntlement with Collins had peaked. Although Davis was somewhat better organized than in his first try, black turnout for the non-presidential year primary was low. Collins won 60 percent.

Collins then tamped the insurgents' anger by endorsing Washington's successful re-election effort in 1987. After Washington's death later that year, Davis turned his attentions back to local politics and Collins coasted to re-election in her next three campaigns.

But not all is quiet in the 7th. The 1992 primary upsets of Chicago's other veteran black House members, Charles A. Hayes and Gus Savage, by younger-generation candidates (Bobby L. Rush and Mel Reynolds) may serve to encourage Democrats in the 7th who feel it is time for a changing of the generational guard in this district, too.

Committees

Energy & Commerce (6th of 27 Democrats)
Commerce, Consumer Protection & Competitiveness (chairman); Oversight & Investigations

Government Operations (2nd of 25 Democrats)
Legislation & National Security

Elections

1992 General		
Cardiss Collins (D)	182,811	(81%)
Norman G. Boccio (R)	35,346	(16%)
Rose-Marie Love (ECR)	4,711	(2%)
Geri Knoll McLauchlan (NL)	2,413	(1%)
1992 Primary		
Cardiss Collins (D)	66,976	(88%)
Clarence D. Clemons (D)	8,980	(12%)
1990 General		
Cardiss Collins (D)	80,021	(80%)
Michael Dooley (R)	20,099	(20%)

Previous Winning Percentages: **1988** (100%) **1986** (80%) **1984** (78%) **1982** (86%) **1980** (85%) **1978** (86%) **1976** (85%) **1974** (88%) **1973 *** (93%)

* *Special election.*

District Vote for President

1992

D 184,383 (78%)
R 35,437 (15%)
I 15,952 (7%)

Campaign Finance

	Receipts	Receipts from PACs		Expend-itures
1992				
Collins (D)	$344,933	$285,067	(83%)	$390,942
Boccio (R)	$7,695	0		$6,978
1990				
Collins (D)	$278,392	$229,648	(82%)	$399,748

Key Votes

1993	
Require parental notification of minors' abortions	N
Require unpaid family and medical leave	Y
Approve national "motor voter" registration bill	Y
Approve budget increasing taxes and reducing deficit	Y
Approve economic stimulus plan	Y
1992	
Approve balanced-budget constitutional amendment	N
Close down space station program	Y
Approve U.S. aid for former Soviet Union	N
Allow shifting funds from defense to domestic programs	Y
1991	
Extend unemployment benefits using deficit financing	Y
Approve waiting period for handgun purchases	Y
Authorize use of force in Persian Gulf	N

Voting Studies

Year	Presidential Support S	Presidential Support O	Party Unity S	Party Unity O	Conservative Coalition S	Conservative Coalition O
1992	9	70	85	2	13	65
1991	23	73	88	2	5	89
1990	10	82	87	3	9	81
1989	14	38	51	0	2	51
1988	16	70	87	2	3	84
1987	8	85	85	2	0	86
1986	12	71	78	3	6	84
1985	16	76	87	1	2	89
1984	21	65	82	5	5	83
1983	5	80	85	3	7	88
1982	25	65	86	6	7	85
1981	28	70	83	7	4	85

Interest Group Ratings

Year	ADA	AFL-CIO	CCUS	ACU
1992	85	92	14	0
1991	90	100	20	0
1990	94	100	31	5
1989	40	100	57	0
1988	90	100	21	0
1987	92	100	0	0
1986	95	100	13	0
1985	95	100	10	5
1984	95	92	36	4
1983	90	100	15	0
1982	90	100	33	0
1981	85	87	6	0

8 Philip M. Crane (R)

Of Mount Prospect — Elected 1969; 12th Full Term

Born: Nov. 3, 1930, Chicago, Ill.
Education: DePauw U., 1948-50; Hillsdale College, B.A. 1952; U. of Michigan, 1952-54; U. of Vienna (Austria), 1953, 1956; Indiana U., M.A. 1961, Ph.D. 1963.
Military Service: Army, 1954-56.
Occupation: Professor; author; advertising executive.
Family: Wife, Arlene Catherine Johnson; eight children.
Religion: Protestant.
Political Career: Sought GOP nomination for president, 1980.
Capitol Office: 233 Cannon Bldg. 20515; 225-3711.

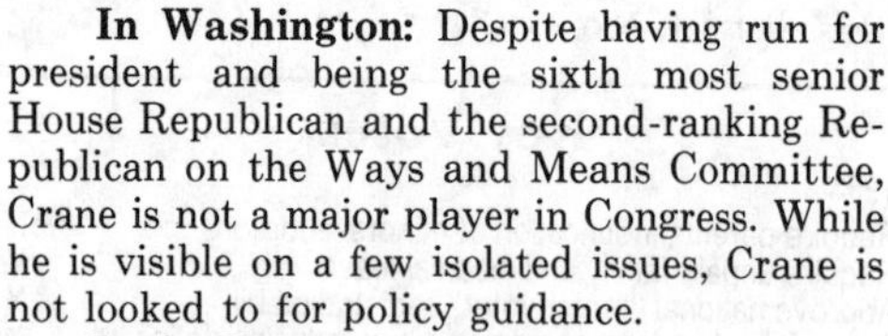

In Washington: Despite having run for president and being the sixth most senior House Republican and the second-ranking Republican on the Ways and Means Committee, Crane is not a major player in Congress. While he is visible on a few isolated issues, Crane is not looked to for policy guidance.

In the House, the torch has been seized by combative Republican conservatives who elected Newt Gingrich of Georgia as minority whip early in the 101st Congress and Dick Armey of Texas as conference chairman late in 1992. Both Gingrich and Armey are Crane's juniors in the House by a decade or more.

Recently, Crane has laid claim to a new cause in term limits. Though he is in his 12th full term, Crane sponsored a constitutional amendment limiting both House members and senators to six years in office. It was one of his few recent instances of national exposure. Another occurred when his daughters appeared as contestants on the syndicated television dating program "Studs," and yet another when ABC-TV's "Primetime Live" in April 1993 showed him and other members enjoying a Florida resort at lobbyists' expense.

Few question Crane's intellectual abilities or his oratorical skills. He received a perfect 100 percent rating from the American Conservative Union in all but one year from 1981 to 1992. But he has never displayed the mindset needed for the give-and-take of legislating. Even Crane describes some of his rigidly conservative legislative endeavors as "spitting in the wind."

Crane often acts to define the ideologically pure frontier. When funding for the National Endowment for the Arts became controversial in the 101st and 102nd Congresses, Crane called for the NEA's outright abolition, attracting the votes of less than one-third of his own party's colleagues. In June 1990, with Congress in high dudgeon over the savings and loan crisis, Crane stood alone against 420 members in a floor vote appropriating an extra $75 million for investigating and prosecuting S&L fraud cases.

In 1992, he was one of only seven House members — all Republicans — who voted against a 1992 bill to expand access to college loans. In the 101st Congress, Crane was part of the revolt against Democratic Ways and Means Chairman Dan Rostenkowski of Illinois that managed to repeal the funding mechanism for catastrophic health care and "Section 89" rules against discriminatory pension arrangements.

Crane was a fairly low-profile member of Ways and Means for a number of years, but in the 99th Congress, he assumed the ranking position on the Trade Subcommittee. He has emerged as a vocal proponent of free trade, battling other members' efforts to protect domestic industries from imports.

He has opposed attempts to link China's most-favored-nation trading status with changes in its human rights policies as "misguided." And he led the efforts to allow Taiwan to be part of the General Agreement on Tariffs and Trade. In the 102nd Congress he also supported legislation allowing duty-free exports from Bolivia, Colombia, Ecuador and Peru to allow the countries' economies to shift from illegal drug production.

Many other members share his concern about protectionist attempts to reduce the U.S. trade deficit, but few feel as strongly as Crane. Early in 1987, he was one of only two Ways and Means members to vote against reporting an omnibus trade bill to the floor. Although others complained about various parts of the legislation, Crane was virtually alone in questioning the need for any bill at all.

More than once in his career, Crane's opinions on tax policy have been ahead of the curve of debate on the subject. But when the ideas he was espousing began working their way through the legislative process, Crane was not known for fighting in the trenches for their passage.

He was one of the earliest congressional supporters of tax indexing, introducing legislation

Illinois 8

Northwest Cook County — Schaumburg; Palatine

There are House districts in the Chicago area where the major concerns are economic development and jobs. Then there are districts, such as the suburban and affluent 8th, where the main worries are overdevelopment and traffic.

The 8th is made up of the suburbs of northwest Cook County (which provide more than 60 percent of the district's votes); the developing exurbia of southwestern Lake County; and the more remote (but also growing) lake-country towns near Wisconsin. These areas combine to make the 8th the most Republican district in Illinois.

Although Democratic Sen. Paul Simon won every Illinois district in 1990, he took just 52 percent in the 8th. In 1992, the district returned to form, supporting Republican Senate candidate Rich Williamson over Democratic winner Carol Moseley-Braun.

Yet there are signs that recent suburban growth may have tempered the staunch conservatism that long made Rep. Crane virtually untouchable. In 1992, he struggled to fend off a more moderate GOP primary foe, then defeated his Democratic challenger with a subpar 56 percent. George Bush carried the 8th but with far less than the 71 percent he rang up in 1988.

The district has some well-established suburbs in its southeast corner, the nearest part to Chicago, including Mount Prospect and the southern part of Arlington Heights (the rest is in the 10th District). The biggest boom has been farther west; development has been abetted by access to Interstates 90 and 290 and proximity to O'Hare Airport (in the 6th District). Just 30 years ago, Schaumburg was still mainly rural. Today, it is a satellite city of 68,000 and the largest community totally within the 8th. The Motorola electronics company is in Schaumburg, as is Delta Air Lines' regional office. Hoffman Estates has expanded nearly as fast; Kmart Corp. is headquartered here, and retailer Sears has moved its merchandising group to the city.

Rolling Meadows, with some high-tech industry, and mainly residential Palatine lie to the north. At the west end of Cook County is a portion of Elgin that has experienced residential growth.

Some exclusive communities have sought to remain exclusive. Barrington Hills, which sprawls among Cook, Lake, McHenry and Kane counties, has slightly more than 4,000 residents. But growth is unbridled in other Lake County communities: Lake Zurich grew by 81 percent in the 1980s to 15,000 residents. The Kemper insurance company is based in nearby Long Grove.

The northern part of the district, with its "chain o' lakes," has a number of vacation homes but is far less densely populated. Residents who rely on seasonal employment are also less well-off than the district norm.

At the northeast edge of the 8th is Gurnee, across the 10th District line from Waukegan. Spurred by its location on Interstate 94, Gurnee nearly doubled in population in the 1980s, to just under 14,000.

1990 Population: 571,530. White 527,051 (92%), Black 9,442 (2%), Other 35,037 (6%). Hispanic origin 31,570 (6%). 18 and over 420,358 (74%), 62 and over 53,816 (9%). Median age: 32.

as far back as 1974. But while he could claim victory with its passage in 1981, he was not prominent in the key negotiations on the issue.

Well before tax-code revision became a major issue, Crane proposed a flat-rate tax of 10 percent on income, with no deductions or credits, and a $2,000 personal exemption. But in 1985, when Ways and Means produced a tax-revision bill incorporating some of his ideas, he described the bill — which had White House backing — as "poorly and thoughtlessly crafted" and burdensome on business. Unlike President Ronald Reagan and most House members, Crane did not want a revenue-neutral bill but one that would greatly lower the tax burden.

Crane launched his 1980 presidential campaign from his base as chairman of the American Conservative Union. After Crane spent a year trying to organize support for the New Hampshire primary, William Loeb, then the acerbic Manchester Union Leader publisher and political baron, ran articles accusing Crane of heavy drinking and womanizing. By the time New Hampshire voted, Crane was a minor candidate and received just 1.8 percent of the vote. He won five convention delegates but withdrew and endorsed Reagan.

At Home: For more than two decades, Crane thrived in the conservative environment of the affluent northwest Chicago suburbs and exurbs. It was thus a jarring change in 1992 when Crane faced threatening challenges in both the primary and general elections.

Crane's Republican opponent was Gary Skoien, a developer and former state official.

Skoien called himself a pragmatic conservative and portrayed Crane as an obstructionist. Bidding for suburban votes, Skoien contrasted his support for abortion rights to Crane's anti-abortion stance. He also said Crane had let his ties to the district attenuate.

But Crane responded with a vigorous campaign built around the slogan "the taxpayer's best friend." Skoien won several newspaper endorsements, but Crane maintained the loyalty of local Republican organizations and hung on to win with 55 percent.

In the fall, Crane faced Democrat Sheila A. Smith, owner of an appliance-light factory. While pursuing such Democratic Party issues as defense spending cuts and increased funding for public works, Smith told the usually Republican constituency that she was a different kind of Democrat. Crane promised to continue his practice of never voting for a tax increase. His share of the vote was lower than ever, but he still won by nearly 40,000 votes.

Prior to 1992, Crane had fallen below 60 percent only in his first two House contests. In 1969, he entered the Republican primary in a special election that followed then-Rep. Donald Rumsfeld's appointment by President Richard M. Nixon to head the Office of Economic Opportunity. With the aid of fellow conservative activists, Crane topped a seven-candidate field with 22 percent of the vote.

Crane's Democratic opponent in the special election tried to paint him as an ideological extremist. But Crane's soft-spoken and articulate manner helped him win with 58 percent. Crane matched that figure in his 1970 bid for a full term and increased his percentages thereafter.

Committee

Ways & Means (2nd of 14 Republicans)
Trade (ranking); Social Security

Joint Taxation

Elections

1992 General		
Philip M. Crane (R)	132,887	(56%)
Sheila A. Smith (D)	96,419	(40%)
Joe M. Dillier (ICONG)	9,327	(4%)
1992 Primary		
Philip M. Crane (R)	31,396	(55%)
Gary J. Skoien (R)	25,296	(45%)
1990 General		
Philip M. Crane (R)	113,081	(82%)
Steve Pedersen (ILSOL)	24,450	(18%)

Previous Winning Percentages: 1988 (75%) 1986 (78%) 1984 (78%) 1982 (66%) 1980 (74%) 1978 (80%) 1976 (73%) 1974 (61%) 1972 (74%) 1970 (58%) 1969 * (58%)

* *Special election.*

District Vote for President

1992
D 76,327 (31%)
R 118,714 (48%)
I 54,269 (22%)

Campaign Finance

	Receipts	Receipts from PACs		Expend-itures
1992				
Crane (R)	$477,110	0		$528,818
Smith (D)	$140,239	$71,557	(51%)	$138,921
1990				
Crane (R)	$163,442	0		$163,376

Key Votes

1993	
Require parental notification of minors' abortions	Y
Require unpaid family and medical leave	N
Approve national "motor voter" registration bill	N
Approve budget increasing taxes and reducing deficit	N
Approve economic stimulus plan	N
1992	
Approve balanced-budget constitutional amendment	Y
Close down space station program	Y
Approve U.S. aid for former Soviet Union	N
Allow shifting funds from defense to domestic programs	N
1991	
Extend unemployment benefits using deficit financing	N
Approve waiting period for handgun purchases	N
Authorize use of force in Persian Gulf	Y

Voting Studies

	Presidential Support		Party Unity		Conservative Coalition	
Year	S	O	S	O	S	O
1992	83	12	94	2	90	6
1991	71	20	87	5	89	5
1990	84	12	89	2	87	7
1989	63	30	86	5	90	5
1988	79	15	91	2	92	3
1987	71	16	83	2	72	9
1986	82	16	87	4	90	4
1985	80	11	79	5	76	9
1984	73	21	86	7	85	10
1983	76	16	92	4	92	6
1982	79	18	81	5	89	7
1981	64	28	81	9	80	13

Interest Group Ratings

Year	ADA	AFL-CIO	CCUS	ACU
1992	0	8	71	100
1991	0	0	89	100
1990	11	0	79	100
1989	5	0	90	100
1988	0	0	93	100
1987	4	0	92	100
1986	0	0	93	100
1985	5	6	82	95
1984	0	15	93	100
1983	5	6	85	100
1982	0	0	85	100
1981	10	0	89	100

9 Sidney R. Yates (D)

Of Chicago — Elected 1948; 22nd Term

Did not serve 1963-65.

Born: Aug. 27, 1909, Chicago, Ill.
Education: U. of Chicago, Ph.B. 1931, J.D. 1933.
Military Service: Navy, 1944-46.
Occupation: Lawyer.
Family: Wife, Adeline Holleb; one child.
Religion: Jewish.
Political Career: Democratic nominee for U.S. Senate, 1962.
Capitol Office: 2109 Rayburn Bldg. 20515; 225-2111.

In Washington: When Yates was first elected to Congress in 1948, Bill Clinton, the 10th president under which he has served, was still in diapers.

Yates is the oldest member of the House; he began his House career under President Harry S Truman. But he continues to fend off budget cuts with all the vigor he brought to past crusades for public housing in the 1950s and against the SST in the 1970s.

Though he has served four decades on the powerful Appropriations Committee, Yates is unlikely ever to be its chairman. If that bothers him, he characteristically does not show it. Instead, as a member of the panel's "college of cardinals," heading one of its 13 subcommittees, he contentedly has carved his own sphere of influence as a defender of the environment and the arts.

He has a reputation as one of Appropriations' toughest cardinals. His hearings are among the most detailed in the House; he does much of his own research on issues and always seems familiar with each budget item. He employs the probing style of a crafty lawyer to corner administration witnesses and to nudge his colleagues toward his position. But he is also personable and witty, and respected both for the grace of his argument and the quality of his work.

During debate over the fiscal 1992 energy and water bill, Yates engaged in a gentlemanly tussle with Energy and Water Development Subcommittee Chairman Tom Bevill of Alabama when he sought $43.5 million to upgrade a particle collider ring at a laboratory near Chicago. Bevill opposed the project, saying it would unravel the subcommittee's pact not to fund any new construction projects. During the dispute, Yates quoted Shakespeare, and Bevill responded with disarming though pointed wit. Yates' motion failed, 11-32; he later settled for $10 million.

Yates is fourth-ranking on Appropriations, but nowhere near as close to taking the chair as his proximity would suggest. He is older than all three men ahead of him, although one of them is Jamie L. Whitten, whom Democrats stripped of the chairmanship in 1992. (Yates was one of two subcommittee chairmen who did not sign a 1992 letter urging the ailing Whitten to step aside.)

So Yates' fiefdom probably will remain limited to his subcommittee, which itself holds broad sway over the budgets for the Interior Department, national parks, mines, Indian affairs, the national endowments for the arts and humanities, and the Smithsonian Institution.

Generally he works behind the scenes as chairman of the Interior Subcommittee, but he was often provoked into the spotlight during the Reagan years — from 1981, when he blocked a proposed 50 percent funding reduction for the National Endowment for the Arts (NEA), to 1988, when he engineered a far-reaching moratorium against administration plans to lease offshore lands for oil drilling. NEA funding cropped back up again during the Bush administration, although this time, the president was not leading the assault.

Yates stakes out the liberal ground, at times too liberal for some fellow Democrats. On the floor, however, he occasionally seems to lose his taste for a good fight. In 1985, he went more than halfway to accommodate conservative Republicans who proposed a 10 percent cut in an arts budget because they said the agency supported authors of sexually explicit poems. Rather than try to defeat the amendment outright, Yates agreed to a smaller reduction.

But his 1981 skirmish over arts spending was more typical. His subcommittee simply ignored Reagan's requested cuts. Reagan finally signed the measure and never again sought such major bites from arts funding.

The issue resurfaced, however, in 1989, when conservatives — upset by the works of two NEA grant recipients whose photographs were deemed pornographic or sacrilegious by many members — sought to cut the art agency's budget. Texas Republican Dick Armey proposed a 10 percent cut in the agency's appropriation. But Yates outmaneuvered Armey and

Illinois 9

Chicago — North Side Lakefront and suburbs; Evanston

The political core of the 9th is a wedge that takes in the northeast corner of Chicago and the near-in suburbs of Evanston and Skokie. This district, the most ethnically and racially diverse in the Chicago area, is also one of the most liberal-voting areas in Illinois. It provides a secure base for Democrats and offsets more conservative turf in the district's western end.

A bit more than two-thirds of the district's residents are non-Hispanic whites; the remaining constituency is divided nearly evenly among blacks, Hispanics and people of Asian heritage. Although the sizable minority population has an influence on its partisan direction, the 9th stands out as the most Democratic white-majority district in the state.

In 1992, Bill Clinton won comfortably here with 61 percent of the vote, and the 9th backed Democratic Senate nominee Carol Moseley-Braun, giving her 62 percent.

About two-thirds of the district's residents live within Chicago's boundaries. The 9th reaches a point at Diversey Street and Lake Michigan. A series of high-rises along Lake Shore Drive, many of them upscale, overlook Lincoln Park and the Lakeview community. This part of the 9th was home to some of the "lakefront liberals" who rose up to challenge the Democratic machine during the 1970s. The community of New Town is a center for the Chicago gay population.

To the north, at Addison and Clark, is venerable Wrigley Field, the Chicago Cubs' "friendly confines." The surrounding neighborhood had grown a bit seedy over the years, but an influx of young professionals has made "Wrigleyville" a hot real estate market.

The community of Uptown is mainly working-class, with some low-income areas. Much of the district's Hispanic population lives here; there is a settlement of Vietnamese immigrants as well. The largest black concentration in the Chicago part of the district is nearby.

Bordering the lake just to the north is the campus of Loyola University (15,800 students). Rogers Park, tucked in the city's northeast corner, is polyglot and mainly middle-class. Much of the district's Jewish population lives in the Chicago community of West Ridge and in Skokie, an adjacent suburb.

Evanston, with a population of more than 70,000, is the district's lakeside suburb. Blacks make up a fifth of the city's population and live mainly in the urbanized south part of the city. Northwestern University and its 14,200 students dominate northern Evanston; the surrounding residential areas anchor suburban Chicago's affluent North Shore region.

In the district's western reaches, its ethnicity and political attitudes change. Many of the residents are of Irish, Italian and Eastern European heritage and have moved from the city's "bungalow belt" to single-family homes in comfortable Norwood Park and Niles or upscale Forest Glen. Conservative attitudes prevail in much of this area.

1990 Population: 571,530. White 417,578 (73%), Black 69,034 (12%), Other 84,918 (15%). Hispanic origin 55,719 (10%). 18 and over 467,139 (82%), 62 and over 110,132 (19%). Median age: 35.

enlisted Texas Democrat Charles W. Stenholm, leader of the "Boll Weevils," to offer a substitute amendment cutting the NEA's appropriation by $45,000 — the amount of the two grants. The House adopted it overwhelmingly.

Yates' next task was to hold the line in the House-Senate conference. The Senate had adopted language by North Carolina Republican Jesse Helms prohibiting federal funding of obscene, indecent or anti-religious art.

But Yates trumped again: His procedural move enabled the House to avoid having to vote on Helms' language. The conferees watered down Helms' amendment; the bill barred the NEA and National Endowment for the Humanities from funding works that the endowments might find obscene or without merit.

That did not dispose of the issue, however. In the 102nd Congress, Yates' bill included a more than fourfold increase in grazing fees on public rangelands. The Senate bill contained no grazing fees. But both chambers approved another Helms amendment seeking to proscribe the NEA from funding certain projects.

For days, the conference was stymied. Even though the House had twice voted to include the Helms language, Yates ignored the votes. "The House did not instruct me to give up my better judgment," he said. Oregon Democratic Rep. Les AuCoin broke the logjam when he proposed a swap that called for no new restrictions on federal arts funding in exchange for no increase in grazing fees — a deal labeled "corn for porn."

Yates is a dedicated environmentalist, and his subcommittee is one of the few on Appropriations that regularly grapples with controversial policy, not just budget numbers. He played a key role in blocking some of the Reagan administration's resource-development policies, including leasing of federal lands for coal mining and offshore oil and gas drilling. Annually, over administration objections, Yates' panel would include more funding for energy conservation, park land acquisition and Indian health programs. In recent years, he has blocked oil and gas drilling in selective offshore areas and worked to obstruct efforts to open Alaska's Arctic National Wildlife Refuge for oil and gas exploration.

Yates' low-key style masks a stubbornness that allows him to stick with an issue for years, if necessary, to get what he wants. That was true in the long debate over the supersonic transport (SST) plane, which was first proposed in 1963 at an estimated cost of $1.5 billion but was sidelined until President Richard M. Nixon came into office in 1969.

Yates had opposed the idea from the beginning, complaining that it was an "incredible distortion of our national priorities" to spend that much public money for a private purpose. Throughout the 1960s, his amendments to eliminate SST funds had been defeated regularly, always on non-recorded votes. Millions of dollars already had been spent on preliminary planning when, in 1971, the House finally confronted the issue directly.

Newly adopted rules forced an on-the-record vote for the first time, and Yates was ready with stacks of facts and figures. Backing him was a well-organized environmental lobby and a carefully orchestrated publicity campaign. In the roll call vote, he won, 217-203.

Yates was just a freshman when he won a place on Appropriations in 1949. An energetic urban liberal in the 1950s, he became a leading advocate for the government's efforts to provide aid to older cities like Chicago.

When the GOP-controlled House sought to kill the public housing program in 1953, Yates fought back. "We need a program that will satisfy the housing needs of all Americans, of every economic level," he said, "not just those who can afford to buy their own houses." In the end, a compromise authorized 20,000 new housing units (compared with the 75,000 President Truman sought before leaving office). Yates also advocated legislation in those days to make mortgage credit money more easily available.

In his second term, he took up a different kind of campaign, to convince the Navy that it should promote Hyman G. Rickover to admiral. The renowned advocate of nuclear submarines had been bypassed and was about to leave the service. Yates thought that was wrong and said so, repeatedly. The resulting congressional hearings and public attention brought the desired result. Rickover was promoted and remained on active duty until 1982.

Yates was out of Congress for two years in the 1960s, after an unsuccessful Senate campaign. When he came back to the House in 1965, he returned to Appropriations. This time he was placed on the Transportation Subcommittee, where he was drawn into the SST fight. Later, Yates switched to the Interior Subcommittee; he became its chairman in 1975.

He also serves on Appropriations' Foreign Operations Subcommittee, where he is a strong supporter of aid to Israel. Otherwise, he does not invest much time or attention on the panel.

At Home: Only one member of the current House — Mississippi's Whitten — entered it before Yates did in January 1949. The two-year hiatus that followed Yates' gamble for the Senate in 1962, when he challenged then-Minority Leader Everett M. Dirksen, has prevented him from enjoying the full measure of that seniority. Yates nonetheless has been able to tout his influential Appropriations position to fend off the occasional younger challenger who insisted it was time for the long-tenured incumbent to go.

In 1982, Yates won two-thirds of the vote to swat aside Republican Catherine Bertini, an articulate moderate who later held appointed positions in the Reagan and Bush administrations. Since then, the local GOP has conceded to Yates. In the last five general elections, Yates has faced the same GOP candidate, Herbert Sohn, a lawyer-physician who has failed to top 33 percent. In fact, Yates has not had a close House race since 1956, when he won with 54 percent.

Yates' noisiest recent challenge came in the 1990 Democratic primary. His opponent, Chicago Alderman Edwin Eisendrath, was a proverbial young man in a hurry. A former schoolteacher from a wealthy family, Eisendrath spent $250,000 in his successful 1987 City Council race and said he intended to spend big in his effort to unseat Yates.

Eisendrath said Yates had focused on national issues, including his arts bailiwick, at the expense of local needs. He also accused Yates of campaign finance irregularities, citing a fundraising letter for Yates from an official of the American Association of Museums that the challenger described as a "shakedown."

Yates angrily rejected that charge, stating that he had no prior knowledge of the letter. Yates also burst any illusions Eisendrath might have had that he would be complacent. Yates made personal campaign appearances, ran newspaper ads signed by hundreds of well-known Chicagoans and engaged the support of most district Democratic officials. When the primary vote was tallied, Yates had flattened Eisendrath, winning with 70 percent.

Although redistricting changes gave him a number of new constituents in 1992, Yates effortlessly defeated two primary challengers with 68 percent.

Yates' long House career began with a long-shot candidacy. In 1948, recently returned to his Chicago law practice after World War II, Yates was drafted at the last minute by the Chicago Democratic organization to run against Republican Rep. Robert J. Twyman, who was expected to win re-election easily. But the Democratic ticket swept Illinois that year, and Yates came in with an 18,000-vote majority. He kept his seat with narrow wins in 1950 and 1952 before settling in comfortably.

After seven terms, Yates sacrificed his electoral security for a Senate challenge to Dirksen that had the backing of Chicago Mayor Richard J. Daley and the Democratic organization. But some Democrats thought Yates was undercut by his party's leadership: They contended that President John F. Kennedy secretly favored Dirksen, considering him the friendliest GOP Senate leader he was likely to get. The Cuban missile crisis took place in the final month of the campaign, and Dirksen was consulted often and openly by the White House.

But Yates, who received 47 percent of the vote, rejected rumors of a Kennedy-Dirksen compact. In 1963, Kennedy appointed him U.S. representative to the U.N. Trusteeship Council, a post he held for more than a year.

In the fall of 1964, the Chicago Democratic organization suddenly found a judgeship for Rep. Edward Finnegan, whom it had chosen to replace Yates in the House. Since Finnegan had already been renominated, the local party had the right to designate a candidate for the vacancy, and to no one's surprise, Yates was the choice. Spared the trouble of a primary, Yates easily won his way back to the House for the start of a second, much longer stay.

Committee

Appropriations (4th of 37 Democrats)
Interior (chairman); Foreign Operations, Export Financing & Related Programs

Elections

1992 General		
Sidney R. Yates (D)	162,942	(68%)
Herb Sohn (R)	64,760	(27%)
Sheila A. Jones (ECR)	12,001	(5%)
1992 Primary		
Sidney R. Yates (D)	63,211	(65%)
Glenn T. Sugiyama (D)	22,450	(23%)
William M. McTighe Jr. (D)	12,329	(13%)
1990 General		
Sidney R. Yates (D)	96,557	(71%)
Herb Sohn (R)	39,031	(29%)

Previous Winning Percentages: **1988** (66%) **1986** (72%) **1984** (68%) **1982** (67%) **1980** (73%) **1978** (75%) **1976** (72%) **1974** (100%) **1972** (68%) **1970** (76%) **1968** (64%) **1966** (60%) **1964** (64%) **1960** (60%) **1958** (67%) **1956** (54%) **1954** (60%) **1952** (52%) **1950** (52%) **1948** (55%)

District Vote for President

1992
D 155,124 (61%)
R 68,251 (27%)
I 29,236 (12%)

Campaign Finance

	Receipts	Receipts from PACs		Expend-itures
1992				
Yates (D)	$227,671	$34,350	(15%)	$228,812
Sohn (R)	$12,140	$1,000	(8%)	$12,599
1990				
Yates (D)	$779,125	$267,746	(34%)	$839,106
Sohn (R)	$11,545	$2,000	(17%)	$15,164

Key Votes

1993	
Require parental notification of minors' abortions	N
Require unpaid family and medical leave	Y
Approve national "motor voter" registration bill	Y
Approve budget increasing taxes and reducing deficit	Y
Approve economic stimulus plan	Y
1992	
Approve balanced-budget constitutional amendment	N
Close down space station program	Y
Approve U.S. aid for former Soviet Union	Y
Allow shifting funds from defense to domestic programs	Y
1991	
Extend unemployment benefits using deficit financing	Y
Approve waiting period for handgun purchases	Y
Authorize use of force in Persian Gulf	N

Voting Studies

	Presidential Support		Party Unity		Conservative Coalition	
Year	**S**	**O**	**S**	**O**	**S**	**O**
1992	14	77	88	2	4	90
1991	23	68	90	3	5	92
1990	17	79	88	4	6	89
1989	27	72	93	4	7	90
1988	17	66	81	5	8	71
1987	12	86	95	2	2	95
1986	18	77	88	3	2	86
1985	31	68	93	4	7	91
1984	28	71	91	8	5	93
1983	17	77	95	4	7	87
1982	19	53	75	4	4	70
1981	26	71	90	9	5	95

Interest Group Ratings

Year	ADA	AFL-CIO	CCUS	ACU
1992	95	100	29	0
1991	95	100	22	6
1990	100	92	17	5
1989	100	83	20	4
1988	80	100	36	5
1987	96	87	7	9
1986	90	85	12	0
1985	100	88	20	10
1984	95	92	31	0
1983	95	100	10	4
1982	75	100	13	0
1981	100	80	11	0

10 John Edward Porter (R)

Of Wilmette — Elected 1980; 7th Full Term

Born: June 1, 1935, Evanston, Ill.

Education: Massachusetts Institute of Technology, 1953-54; Northwestern U., B.A., B.S. 1957; U. of Michigan, J.D. 1961.

Military Service: Army Reserve, 1958-64.

Occupation: Lawyer.

Family: Wife, Kathryn Cameron; five children.

Religion: Presbyterian.

Political Career: GOP nominee for Cook County Circuit Court judge, 1970; Ill. House, 1973-79; GOP nominee for U.S. House, 1978.

Capitol Office: 1026 Longworth Bldg. 20515; 225-4835.

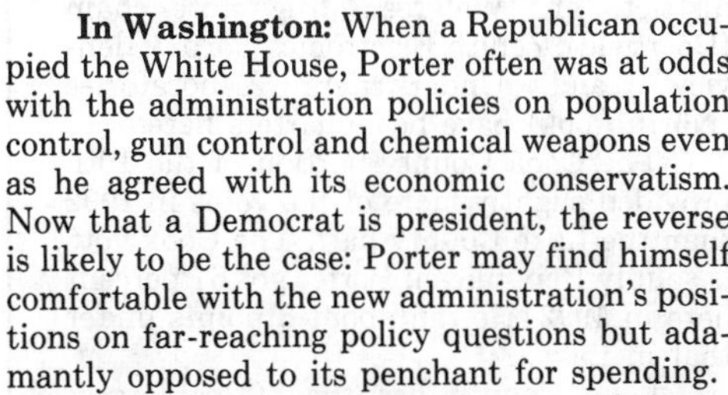

In Washington: When a Republican occupied the White House, Porter often was at odds with the administration policies on population control, gun control and chemical weapons even as he agreed with its economic conservatism. Now that a Democrat is president, the reverse is likely to be the case: Porter may find himself comfortable with the new administration's positions on far-reaching policy questions but adamantly opposed to its penchant for spending.

When he fights Republicans on such issues as abortion counseling, Porter lines up with the most liberal House members. But when he takes Democrats to task for wasting federal money, he sounds like a spokesman for the Chamber of Commerce.

Porter showed his liberal side in the 102nd Congress when he led the fight against a Bush administration ban on abortion counseling at federally funded family planning facilities. In both 1990 and 1991, Porter introduced legislation to overturn the counseling ban. During committee consideration of the fiscal 1992 Labor, Health and Human Services appropriations bill, he won approval of an amendment to block enforcement of the counseling ban, dubbed the "gag rule." "I think a lot of people on the Republican side who oppose abortion are real uncomfortable with this mind control the gag rule represents," he said. President George Bush vetoed the bill, and the override attempt failed.

Porter begins the 103rd Congress as the ranking member of the Labor-HHS Appropriations Subcommittee. Although he opposes federal funding for abortion, he thinks it should remain a legal option and supports family planning.

In his role as a member of the Appropriations Subcommittee on Foreign Operations, he is a leading advocate of restoring U.S. funding of the U.N. family planning agency. In the 102nd Congress, restoration of agency funding was added to, but ultimately dropped from, a foreign aid spending bill, as appropriators bowed to a standing veto threat.

Porter's conservative side emerged fully in early 1990, when a wide-ranging debate on Social Security arose from New York Sen. Daniel Patrick Moynihan's proposal to roll back the withholding tax for the program. Porter promoted his plan to gradually privatize Social Security. In an opinion piece in The Wall Street Journal, he suggested that the government refund Social Security taxes not needed to pay current benefits to mandatory Individual Social Security Retirement Accounts (ISSRA) for each wage earner. Porter proposed that when workers with ISSRAs retire the government adjust their federal Social Security benefit to reflect the income from their privately held ISSRA. The plan won editorial praise, but Porter's legislation, introduced in the 102nd Congress, did not get off the ground in Washington.

Porter has the freedom to pursue such provocative ideas in part because he is in an unusually comfortable political position. He represents a firmly Republican and relatively affluent district north of Chicago; most of his constituents do not have a pressing need for federal goods and services. Like Porter, they tend to be relatively liberal on many social issues but conservative on fiscal matters.

And true to his district, Porter's approach to the federal budget deficit is purely conservative. He voted for the 1990 budget summit plan that included a tax increase as an instrument to tame the deficit. The next year, during a House-Senate conference on the Labor-HHS appropriations bill, he expressed dismay at the use of an accounting device that allowed outlays to be pushed into the subsequent fiscal year in order to skirt deficit ceilings. Calling it "another phony attempt to live beyond our means," Porter said the effort to get around the 1990 budget agreement was "one of the most insane exercises I've ever seen."

Porter first made a name for himself in the 1980s as a critic of the Pentagon's contention

Illinois 10

North and Northwest Chicago suburbs — Wakegan

Drivers following lake-hugging Sheridan Road north from Evanston reach some of Chicago's oldest and wealthiest suburbs. Affluent North Shore communities here such as Wilmette, Kenilworth, Winnetka and Glencoe have long set a Republican tone in Illinois' northeastern section.

GOP candidates rarely sweat the outcome in the 10th, which includes northern Cook County suburbia and a swath of Lake County that reaches to Wisconsin. George Bush's struggles here in 1992 were not typical; he took 60 percent of the district vote in 1988. Sen. Paul Simon staged a rare Democratic win in 1990, but the 10th went against Democrat Carol Moseley-Braun in 1992.

When there is competition in district elections, it is almost always within the GOP. In the 1992 House primary, Rep. Porter — who combines a conservative stance on fiscal policy with more liberal positions on social issues — got 62 percent against an anti-abortion challenger. Porter won easily in November.

Most of the residences in the wealthy near-in suburbs were built before 1940; although these communities are hardly in decline, their growth days may be past. Highland Park, site of the summertime Ravinia music festival, won a national award for downtown revitalization.

Nearby is the Army's Fort Sheridan, which is being phased out under the 1989 base-closing law and Glenview Naval Air Station, which is on the 1993 base-closure list. However, the Great Lakes Naval Training Center a few miles north remains by far the 10th's largest single employer. In between are two affluent suburbs, Lake Forest and Lake Bluff, that have been gaining residents. The district's boom has been in newer subdivisions near its western border. Arlington Heights (partially in the 8th District) and surrounding communities expanded rapidly in the 1980s. Buffalo Grove's population grew by 64 percent; Wheeling and Prospect Heights were up by 29 percent. At the outer edge of the Chicago commuting zone, Lake County communities such as Mundelein, Vernon Hills and Libertyville also attracted numerous new residents.

Although most of the 10th's communities are known as bedroom suburbs, several major employers are scattered around the district. The Walgreen drug store chain (Deerfield), Zenith Electronics Corp. (Glenview) and Underwriters Laboratories (Northbrook) have headquarters here.

The Cook County portion of the 10th provided slightly more of the votes in 1992 than the Lake County part. The Cook vote is solidly Republican; Porter got 67 percent here in 1992. He ran about 6 points under that in Lake.

Lake County has the 10th's largest blocs of Democratic voters in the industrial cities of Waukegan and North Chicago. Just over half of Waukegan's residents are white, and the city has slightly more than half the entire district's minority-group residents. The Outboard Marine Corp., which makes boat motors, is based in Waukegan; Abbott Laboratories' home is in North Chicago.

1990 Population: 571,530. White 494,355 (86%), Black 35,228 (6%), Other 41,947 (7%). Hispanic origin 40,586 (7%). 18 and over 425,243 (74%), 62 and over 74,558 (13%). Median age: 34.

that chemical weapons could be quickly deployed in Europe in the event of armed confrontation with the Soviet Union. In 1989, he offered a successful amendment to the defense authorization bill expressing the sense of Congress that the president should intensify efforts to reach a non-proliferation treaty on chemical weapons with the Soviet Union.

As a result of Porter's conservative position on most budget questions, some of his colleagues bristle when he lobbies the Appropriations Committee to provide funds for projects in his district. But so far, little revenge seems to have been exacted. In October 1988, he was on hand for the dedication of a new air-traffic-control tower at Waukegan Regional Airport in his district.

At Home: The Republican leanings of the affluent North Shore suburbs in the 10th District would likely be enough to elect the fiscally conservative Porter. But his more liberal views on such social issues as abortion have earned Porter some support from independent and Democratic voters, enabling him to easily win his general-election contests.

However, those same positions unsettle the more conservative GOP factions. Porter's most vigorous challenge in recent years came from within the party in the 1992 primary.

His opponent was activist Kathleen M. Sullivan, founder of an organization that promotes sexual abstinence among teenagers. Trying to avoid the "single issue" label, Sullivan espoused an agenda of strong conservative positions on economic and social issues.

Still, abortion was the defining issue. Sullivan tried to portray Porter as an abortion advocate, citing his support for the 1992 Freedom of Choice bill. But Porter said his support for abortion rights was in keeping with his philosophy that government should stay out of individuals' lives. He also noted his opposition to federal funding of abortions in most cases.

Although Porter was never seriously threatened, Sullivan held him to 60 percent, his lowest percentage in 10 years. His 1992 general election was more routine: Porter defeated Democratic lawyer Michael J. Kennedy with 65 percent.

The son of a well-known judge in Evanston, Porter returned to the Chicago suburbs after a stint in Washington with the Justice Department in the early 1960s. Porter tried to follow his father into the judiciary in 1970 by running for Cook County circuit court judge. As a GOP candidate in the Democratic-dominated county, Porter's cause was hopeless. But the bid helped boost his credentials within GOP circles. He had no trouble winning a state House seat in 1972 and was re-elected twice.

Meanwhile, Democrat Abner J. Mikva, one of the most liberal House Democrats, had won the old 10th District by scanty margins in 1974 and 1976 and was looking ripe for a challenge. Porter won the 1978 primary over six other Republicans.

Although Porter waged a well-funded campaign, Mikva was not quite ready to be taken: He nudged Porter out by 650 votes. But Mikva was appointed to a federal judgeship a few months later, and Porter won the 1980 special election to fill out his term. Seeking a full term in November 1980, he was returned to office by a convincing margin.

When a 1981 redistricting plan placed Porter's Evanston home in the heavily Democratic 9th District, Porter announced that he would move to challenge 10-term GOP Rep. Robert McClory in the new solidly Republican 10th. McClory, then 74, decided to retire, clearing the way for Porter. Porter defeated an experienced Democratic state legislator, setting a pattern of easy November victories.

Committee

Appropriations (7th of 23 Republicans)
Labor, Health & Human Services, Education & Related Agencies (ranking); Foreign Operations, Export Financing & Related Programs

Elections

1992 General		
John Edward Porter (R)	155,230	(65%)
Michael J. Kennedy (D)	85,400	(35%)
1992 Primary		
John Edward Porter (R)	32,959	(60%)
Kathleen M. Sullivan (R)	21,895	(40%)
1990 General		
John Edward Porter (R)	104,070	(68%)
Peg McNamara (D)	47,286	(31%)
Herbert L. Gorrell (ILSOL)	2,243	(1%)

Previous Winning Percentages: **1988** (72%) **1986** (75%) **1984** (73%) **1982** (59%) **1980** (61%) **1980 *** (54%)

** Special election.*

District Vote for President

1992	
D	108,149 (41%)
R	112,401 (43%)
I	40,719 (16%)

Campaign Finance

	Receipts	Receipts from PACs	Expenditures
1992			
Porter (R)	$453,794	$160,649 (35%)	$485,778
Kennedy (D)	$37,334	0	$34,948
1990			
Porter (R)	$255,970	$110,025 (43%)	$313,498

Key Votes

1993	
Require parental notification of minors' abortions	N
Require unpaid family and medical leave	N
Approve national "motor voter" registration bill	N
Approve budget increasing taxes and reducing deficit	N
Approve economic stimulus plan	N
1992	
Approve balanced-budget constitutional amendment	Y
Close down space station program	Y
Approve U.S. aid for former Soviet Union	Y
Allow shifting funds from defense to domestic programs	N
1991	
Extend unemployment benefits using deficit financing	N
Approve waiting period for handgun purchases	Y
Authorize use of force in Persian Gulf	Y

Voting Studies

	Presidential Support		Party Unity		Conservative Coalition	
Year	S	O	S	O	S	O
1992	62	33	73	23	60	31
1991	67	30	69	27	78	22
1990	65	33	69	29	70	30
1989	65	35	54	41	71	24
1988	57	42	71	22	82	18
1987	54	41	69	25	81	19
1986	59	39	68	28	68	32
1985	68	30	71	25	73	25
1984	58	40	65	31	80	19
1983	73	22	69	29	67	30
1982	60	32	66	28	62	32
1981	68	32	65	33	61	36

Interest Group Ratings

Year	ADA	AFL-CIO	CCUS	ACU
1992	30	33	88	74
1991	30	17	80	80
1990	22	17	79	67
1989	30	8	100	63
1988	30	15	100	68
1987	20	6	100	62
1986	15	7	94	64
1985	20	24	82	71
1984	40	23	81	42
1983	25	6	95	52
1982	35	17	81	67
1981	30	7	89	67

11 George E. Sangmeister (D)

Of Mokena — Elected 1988; 3rd Term

Born: Feb. 16, 1931, Joliet, Ill.
Education: Elmhurst College, B.A. 1957; John Marshall Law School, J.D. 1960.
Military Service: Army, 1951-53.
Occupation: Lawyer.
Family: Wife, Doris M. Hinspeter; two children.
Religion: United Church of Christ.
Political Career: Will County justice of the peace/magistrate, 1961-64; Will County state's attorney, 1964-68; Ill. House, 1973-77; Ill. Senate, 1977-87; sought Democratic nomination for lieutenant governor, 1986.
Capitol Office: 1032 Longworth Bldg. 20515; 225-3635.

In Washington: Arriving in Washington as one of the older freshmen in the class of 1988, with a lengthy career in Illinois politics already behind him, Sangmeister suggested during his 1992 re-election campaign that he may not overstay his welcome: He signed the "lead or leave" pledge, signifying an intention not to seek re-election in 1996 if the federal budget deficit is not halved by then.

If Sangmeister was beginning to think about setting a personal limit on his congressional tenure, the outcome of Illinois redistricting in 1991 did nothing to dissuade him. Under the new map, Sangmeister's renumbered and reshaped district is considered more competitive for Republicans. Enduring biennial mud-wrestling matches to stay in the House may not look too enticing for Sangmeister, who as a 62-year-old House third-termer is still years away from gaining the kind of seniority and influence that he enjoyed in the Illinois legislature. There has been considerable district media speculation that Sangmeister, a lawyer and former chairman of the state Senate Judiciary Committee, would be interested in a seat on the federal bench.

Given his background and experience, Sangmeister was a natural candidate for a seat on the Judiciary Committee when he came to Congress. There, he has found a niche as a conservative-to-moderate voice on crime legislation.

He has quietly pursued issues such as limiting death sentence appeals, allowing victim-impact statements at sentencing, and modifying the exclusionary rule to allow the use of evidence obtained under faulty warrants in some cases. In the 102nd Congress, the Judiciary Committee voted to adopt a Sangmeister amendment on the exclusionary rule allowing evidence seized under such warrants to be used if the police were acting in the belief the warrant was valid. The Bush administration had sometimes wanted to allow the introduction of evidence seized without any warrant, provided police were acting in "good faith" that their actions were legal.

Sangmeister, an opponent of abortion, voted early in the 103rd Congress for a measure requiring parental notification of minors' abortions at federally funded clinics. In the 102nd, he was one of only two Democrats on the Judiciary Committee to vote against a bill codifying the Supreme Court's *Roe v. Wade* abortion rights decision, and he supported the Hyde amendment, which prohibits federal funding of abortions for those who cannot afford them.

Sangmeister also serves on the Veterans' Affairs Committee, where at the start of the 103rd Congress, he got the chairmanship of the Subcommittee on Housing and Memorial Affairs. He filed legislation to increase the loan limit on federally insured mortgages for veterans, to provide mortgage payment assistance to avoid foreclosures on such loans and to make more veterans' families eligible for payment of a cemetery plot allowance. However, Sangmeister's subcommittee is also likely to be considering legislation to increase mortgage fees charged to veterans, which the Clinton administration favors.

Sangmeister has said he hopes the chairmanship will help him win a Veterans Administration outpatient clinic for his district, as well as the creation of a national veterans' cemetery in the Chicago area.

A Korean War-era veteran, Sangmeister in 1991 successfully sponsored legislation declaring a Korean War Veterans' Remembrance Week that July, to mark the 38th anniversary

Illinois 11

South Chicago suburbs and exurbs — Joliet

The 11th may be contiguous, but it is not exactly coherent. It reaches from the working-class neighborhoods of far southeast Chicago past suburbs and exurbs to industrial Joliet, then through the farmland and small cities of Will, Kankakee, Grundy and La Salle counties.

With its mix of constituencies, the 11th shapes up as a classic swing district. George Bush carried the district in 1988 with 57 percent; in 1992, the 11th swung to Bill Clinton, even though he won Will, the district's largest county, by just 39 percent to 38 percent over Bush (Ross Perot pulled down 22 percent there).

Three of the district's counties, including Will, went against Democrat Carol Moseley-Braun in the 1992 Senate race. Rep. Sangmeister won thanks to big margins in his Will County base and in the areas of Cook County in the district; he narrowly lost the other three counties.

At the northeast corner of the 11th is a small chunk of Chicago that would have been largely depopulated had Chicago Mayor Richard M. Daley's plan for a third Chicago-area airport gone through. In 1992, he announced plans for an airport in the Lake Calumet area; he said the project would create jobs and clean up the polluted industrial site. But the thousands of residents who would be displaced — the blue-collar, ethnic community of Hegewisch would have been wiped out — protested; the state legislature, citing cost, blocked the plan; and Daley drew back. Airport proponents are now looking at other sites, including rural Will and Kankakee counties in the southern part of the 11th.

The district also rims the south suburban area of Cook County. There are mainly middle- and working-class communities in Calumet City, Lansing and South Holland, to the east; in the southern part is comfortable Park Forest. Just south of the Will County line is University Park, a mainly black, middle-class suburb that is the site of Governors State University.

The southern portion of Will County in the 11th has more than a third of the district's population. The loss of much of its industry sent Joliet into a downturn that hit bottom in the early 1980s; it has stabilized now, with regional malls and the Rialto Square performing arts center (an elaborate former movie theater) drawing people to town. There are still a number of factories, including a Caterpillar plant; the Statesville prison north of town is a major employer.

The towns of Mokena and Frankfort, Sangmeister's home base, are being absorbed into Chicago's south suburbia. Some rural communities to the east, along Interstate 57, are also growing. Farther south, the 11th takes in mainly rural northern Kankakee County, reaching to the edge but not into the city of Kankakee.

To the west, in Grundy County, is Morris, site of a nuclear power plant; Bush won this GOP-leaning county in 1992. However, Democrats compete in La Salle County, which has light industry in La Salle, Ottawa and Streator; Clinton beat Bush there by 14 percentage points.

1990 Population: 571,528. White 499,520 (87%), Black 48,897 (9%), Other 23,111 (4%). Hispanic origin 37,049 (6%). 18 and over 417,917 (73%), 62 and over 90,254 (16%). Median age: 33.

of the truce that ended the conflict and designated the 38th parallel as the border between North and South Korea.

In an emotional floor speech, the usually reserved Sangmeister described the conflict as a tragically forgotten war. "The recognition of those who served in the snowclad mountains of Korea is long overdue. Their pain and sacrifice must be recognized," Sangmeister said.

On the Public Works and Transportation Committee, Sangmeister has pushed for the development of high-speed rail in his district. A member of the Aviation Subcommittee, Sangmeister has had input into the controversial question of where to locate a new Chicago airport. One possible location is near Kankakee, which is part of Sangmeister's reshaped district.

At Home: Sangmeister's laconic style tempts Republican strategists to test him. But that moderate manner is ultimately his greatest strength, helping him offset GOP efforts to cast him as a liberal who is out of sync with a conservative-leaning constituency.

In 1992, Sangmeister faced an aggressive young GOP challenger, lawyer Robert T. Herbolsheimer, and a redistricting map that took away much of the suburban Cook County area he represented and replaced it with mainly rural territory. Yet Sangmeister won by a comfortable 12-percentage-point margin.

Sangmeister's success is based on strong support from Will County (Joliet), where his name is familiar. His father was mayor of the town of Frankfort for 32 years. The younger Sangmeister entered public life as a circuit court magistrate, then became Will County state's attorney. He won a state House seat in 1972, then ousted a Republican state senator in 1976.

Sangmeister had only one political slip-up, but it was hugely embarrassing. In the 1986 primary, he ran as the Democrats' slated candidate for lieutenant governor. However, the party failed to organize sufficiently for the primary, and Sangmeister lost to a disciple of fringe politician Lyndon H. LaRouche Jr.

However, Sangmeister rebounded smartly in 1988, unseating freshman Republican Rep. Jack Davis in the then-4th District. The campaign was heated: Sangmeister's operation portrayed Davis, a longtime GOP insider, as a shady politician. Davis played up the Democrat's ties to interest groups that Davis described as leftist. Sangmeister ended up on top by 1,039 votes.

Although Republicans touted their energetic 1990 nominee, suburban mayor Manny Hoffman, Sangmeister's dominance in his Will County base propelled him to a solid 59 percent victory.

In 1992, challenger Herbolsheimer tried to portray Sangmeister as a tax-and-spend liberal; he also cast the incumbent as a career politician. But Sangmeister countered that he had lived his entire life within the new 11th District, while Herbolsheimer — an administrator with the Environmental Protection Agency during the early 1980s — had left the area to go to college and had only recently returned after pursuing a career as a Washington insider.

Sangmeister won by carrying 59 percent of the vote in Will County and 56 percent in Cook. Herbolsheimer edged him in the three more rural counties, but by much smaller margins, and managed 44 percent districtwide.

Committees

Judiciary (14th of 21 Democrats)
Crime & Criminal Justice; International Law, Immigration & Refugees

Public Works & Transportation (18th of 39 Democrats)
Aviation; Water Resources & the Environment

Veterans' Affairs (9th of 21 Democrats)
Housing & Memorial Affairs (chairman); Compensation, Pension & Insurance

Elections

1992 General		
George E. Sangmeister (D)	135,387	(56%)
Robert T. Herbolsheimer (R)	107,860	(44%)
1990 General		
George E. Sangmeister (D)	77,290	(59%)
Manny Hoffman (R)	53,258	(41%)

Previous Winning Percentage: 1988 (50%)

District Vote for President

1992

D 108,447 (44%)
R 90,085 (36%)
I 50,200 (20%)

Campaign Finance

	Receipts	Receipts from PACs		Expend-itures
1992				
Sangmeister (D)	$339,478	$252,210	(74%)	$344,786
Herbolsheimer (R)	$283,199	$97,272	(34%)	$281,243
1990				
Sangmeister (D)	$477,551	$356,393	(75%)	$472,757
Hoffman (R)	$651,729	$87,725	(13%)	$642,391

Key Votes

1993	
Require parental notification of minors' abortions	Y
Require unpaid family and medical leave	Y
Approve national "motor voter" registration bill	Y
Approve budget increasing taxes and reducing deficit	Y
Approve economic stimulus plan	Y
1992	
Approve balanced-budget constitutional amendment	Y
Close down space station program	Y
Approve U.S. aid for former Soviet Union	N
Allow shifting funds from defense to domestic programs	Y
1991	
Extend unemployment benefits using deficit financing	Y
Approve waiting period for handgun purchases	Y
Authorize use of force in Persian Gulf	N

Voting Studies

	Presidential Support		Party Unity		Conservative Coalition	
Year	**S**	**O**	**S**	**O**	**S**	**O**
1992	29	70	85	14	48	52
1991	24	64	80	13	43	51
1990	32	67	77	19	50	46
1989	21	78	86	11	41	56

Interest Group Ratings

Year	ADA	AFL-CIO	CCUS	ACU
1992	70	83	25	24
1991	60	82	22	15
1990	56	75	38	33
1989	90	92	50	14

12 Jerry F. Costello (D)

Of Belleville — Elected 1988; 3rd Full Term

Born: Sept. 25, 1949, East St. Louis, Ill.
Education: Belleville Area College, A.A. 1970; Maryville College of the Sacred Heart, B.A. 1972.
Occupation: Law enforcement official.
Family: Wife, Georgia Cockrum; three children.
Religion: Roman Catholic.
Political Career: St. Clair County Board chairman, 1980-88.
Capitol Office: 119 Cannon Bldg. 20515; 225-5661.

In Washington: True to his roots in the back rooms of St. Clair County politics, Costello in Congress works mostly behind the scenes, and largely on local matters.

From his seat on the Public Works and Transportation Committee, Costello has been able to keep the folks at home happy with a stream of federal money for the 12th, including funding for bridge repairs, road and rail projects and the conversion of a military airport near Belleville to civilian use.

At the same time, he has made a favorable enough impression on House Democratic leaders to win a seat on the Budget Committee, all the while remaining firmly outside the spotlight — except for a personally wrenching moment in 1991. That was when Costello, with his son preparing for action with the 82nd Airborne Division near the Kuwait-Iraq border, voted against authorizing the use of military force against Iraq. Costello was one of only two members to have a son or daughter in the Persian Gulf.

At the time, he told The Washington Post that "if every member of Congress had a son or daughter in the Middle East, if the president had his son or his daughter in the Middle East in combat now, it might change their attitude to some extent."

Back on the meat-and-potatoes front, Costello worked on the 1991 highway bill, which included funds to rehabilitate two bridges across the Mississippi River; they link his economically distressed district in southwestern Illinois with the healthier job market of St. Louis.

In 1992, Costello also saw a project he had begun pushing as a county official move closer to realization, when the Federal Aviation Administration declared its intention to spend $140 million transforming Scott Air Force Base near Belleville into a joint civilian-military airport by the end of the century.

Also on Costello's watch, federal funds have been committed for a light-rail link from St. Louis' Lambert Airport to East St. Louis, Ill., and eventually to the projected joint-use airport, on the assumption that the site will someday be bustling with overflow from Lambert.

Costello also successfully shepherded legislation through Congress that extends the Jefferson National Expansion Memorial in St. Louis across the Mississippi River to include 100 acres in East St. Louis. The extension of the memorial (better known as the Gateway Arch) gives Illinois its first piece of national parkland. More important from the perspective of Costello's constituents, it gives East St. Louis, a grimly depressed area, a shot at some of the tourist business now confined to the other side of the river.

The extension had been opposed by the Reagan administration's Interior Department; the land in question was not part of President Thomas Jefferson's huge purchase of land for westward expansion. But after Congress passed Costello's bill designating the land, President George Bush signed it.

This is the record that has earned Costello the nickname of "Congressman Pork" at home. At the same time, Costello has stayed in step with the general public's sentiments about the profligate nature of the federal government by supporting a constitutional amendment requiring a balanced federal budget.

Also in step with local skepticism of federal spending with no obvious benefits for the 12th, Costello in the 102nd voted against aid to the former Soviet Union and in favor of deep cuts in the space program. His opposition to abortion and to gun control are counter to the national Democratic orthodoxy but in line with his district's socially conservative majority.

Early in the 103rd, Costello voted to support the Clinton administration's budget resolution and economic stimulus plan.

At Home: Costello's locally oriented legislative efforts solidified his position in his southwest Illinois district, the most Democratic seat outside Chicago. In 1992, Costello swamped his Republican opponent, Mike Starr, a Southern Illinois University professor, with 71 percent of the vote.

But political security was hard-won for Costello. His high-profile public career in populous St. Clair County had marked him as the

Illinois 12

Southwest — Carbondale; East St. Louis

The numbering system is one of the peculiarities of Illinois' House district map for the 1990s. Districts 1 through 13 are all in the Chicago metropolitan area — except the 12th, which is hundreds of miles away in the state's southwest corner.

The 12th also stands out for economic and demographic reasons. This is the most industrial district in southern Illinois, with a belt of factories and refineries on the Mississippi River near St. Louis and a coal-mining region south and east. Blacks are more numerous in the 12th than in any other district outside Chicago. The district contains some of the most economically depressed areas in Illinois.

Those factors combine to make this solidly Democratic turf. In 1992, Bill Clinton carried every county in the 12th, taking a majority in all but one. Senate candidate Carol Moseley-Braun won big even though she had upset a district native, then-Sen. Alan J. Dixon, in the primary.

St. Clair County, with more than two-fifths of the 12th's residents, is its hub. The district's most troubled community, East St. Louis, is here. As late as the 1960s, the city was an industrial center. But the closure of its stockyards set off an economic collapse. In the 1980s, East St. Louis lost a quarter of its population, and now has about 41,000 residents. Most who remain are black and poor; more than half of the city's children live below the poverty level.

Belleville, the St. Clair County seat and now its largest city with 43,000 people, is mainly white. It has a mix of poor, working-class and well-off residents, some of whom commute to St. Louis. Nearby is Scott Air Force Base, which is headquarters for the Air Mobility Command and is the district's largest employer. To the north, the district takes in the industrial western section of Madison County. Employers include the Laclede Steel plant in Alton and a Shell Oil refinery in Wood River. Alton was the first Illinois city to revive riverboat gambling. Although Alton is home to conservative activist Phyllis Schlafly, it is mainly Democratic.

South of St. Clair are Perry and Randolph counties, among Illinois' leading coal producers. Although demand for Illinois coal has remained steady, rapid mechanization during the past decade left thousands of miners looking for work. Coal is also mined in Jackson County; the county's economy is bolstered by Southern Illinois University in Carbondale, which has 25,000 students and more than 6,000 employees.

At the southern tip of the district is Alexander County and the weary Mississippi River town of Cairo. The scene of racial conflict in the 1960s, the city of about 4,800 residents is something of a microversion of East St. Louis. Alexander County gave nearly 60 percent to Clinton.

There is farm territory in the western part of the district; wheat is a major crop. This is one area where Democrats' hold is weak. Monroe was the only county in the 12th to go for GOP Senate nominee Rich Williamson over Moseley-Braun; Clinton won there by a narrow plurality.

1990 Population: 571,530. White 465,603 (81%), Black 97,185 (17%), Other 8,742 (2%). Hispanic origin 7,527 (1%). 18 and over 421,442 (74%), 62 and over 93,050 (16%). Median age: 32.

heir apparent to Democratic Rep. Melvin Price, an elderly House veteran.

The member of a prominent political family — his father served in the Illinois General Assembly and as sheriff and later treasurer of St. Clair County — Costello was elected chairman of the county commission in 1980. He emerged as a dominant figure in his heavily Democratic region, serving at one point as chairman of the metropolitan St. Louis Council of Governments.

However, Costello wielded clout, critics said, in the hardball tradition of an urban-based St. Clair County Democratic machine. In the March 1988 primary to succeed Price, Madison County Auditor Pete Fields tried to use Costello's image as a machine boss against him. A huge financial advantage (and the party structure) helped Costello survive, but with a 46 percent plurality, that turned out to be an omen for the August 1988 special election forced by Price's death that April.

Costello's Republican opponent in the special election was college official Robert H. Gaffner, who had run two futile challenges to Price before a close 1986 contest in which Price's failing health was an issue. Gaffner copied the line of attack used by Democrat Fields in the March primary: He ran ads suggesting that voters call Costello and quiz him about ethics questions.

The attacks stung Costello, who won the special election with a shockingly low 51.5 percent. The general election was a replay, with Gaffner belaboring the ethics issue to some effect. Costello again held on, winning just under 53 percent.

By 1990, Costello's clouds had lifted. Even the Belleville News Democrat, a longtime press adversary that Costello had once sued for libel, praised him for his efforts on behalf of district interests. Although Gaffner was once again drafted by the Republicans, he was burdened by a family illness and a lack of campaign funds and made a token effort; Costello coasted with 66 percent.

Committees

Budget (19th of 26 Democrats)

Public Works & Transportation (14th of 39 Democrats)
Aviation; Economic Development; Surface Transportation

Elections

1992 General		
Jerry F. Costello (D)	168,762	(71%)
Mike Starr (R)	68,115	(29%)
1990 General		
Jerry F. Costello (D)	95,208	(66%)
Robert H. Gaffner (R)	48,949	(34%)

Previous Winning Percentages: **1988** (53%) **1988 *** (51%)

** Special election.*

District Vote for President

	1992
D	132,556 (54%)
R	69,850 (29%)
I	42,191 (17%)

Campaign Finance

	Receipts	Receipts from PACs		Expend-itures
1992				
Costello (D)	$502,532	$145,175	(29%)	$580,559
Starr (R)	$21,177	0		$21,024
1990				
Costello (D)	$654,131	$231,550	(35%)	$380,559
Gaffner (R)	$24,670	0		$26,230

Key Votes

1993	
Require parental notification of minors' abortions	Y
Require unpaid family and medical leave	Y
Approve national "motor voter" registration bill	Y
Approve budget increasing taxes and reducing deficit	Y
Approve economic stimulus plan	Y
1992	
Approve balanced-budget constitutional amendment	Y
Close down space station program	Y
Approve U.S. aid for former Soviet Union	N
Allow shifting funds from defense to domestic programs	Y
1991	
Extend unemployment benefits using deficit financing	Y
Approve waiting period for handgun purchases	N
Authorize use of force in Persian Gulf	N

Voting Studies

	Presidential Support		Party Unity		Conservative Coalition	
Year	**S**	**O**	**S**	**O**	**S**	**O**
1992	32	65	78	18	50	50
1991	34	65	77	22	68	32
1990	26	73	86	14	48	52
1989	36	63	79	20	59	41
1988	24 †	76 †	86 †	11 †	67 †	33 †

† Not eligible for all recorded votes.

Interest Group Ratings

Year	ADA	AFL-CIO	CCUS	ACU
1992	60	83	14	43
1991	55	83	30	15
1990	67	92	36	29
1989	70	92	40	18
1988	--	100	--	57

13 Harris W. Fawell (R)

Of Naperville — Elected 1984; 5th Term

Born: March 25, 1929, West Chicago, Ill.
Education: North Central College, 1947-49; Chicago-Kent College of Law, J.D. 1952.
Occupation: Lawyer.
Family: Wife, Ruth Johnson; three children.
Religion: Methodist.
Political Career: Ill. Senate, 1963-77; candidate for Ill. Supreme Court, 1976.
Capitol Office: 2342 Rayburn Bldg. 20515; 225-3515.

In Washington: Rather than formulating major legislative strategies, Fawell prefers to preach the message of fiscal restraint and attempt to extract government waste from legislation. Wherever there is a bill that includes money for hometown projects and perks, Fawell will likely be found nearby shaking his head in disapproval.

His efforts have won him the informal title of co-chairman of the Porkbusters group, a largely Republican organization that jumps on large spending bills and targets hundreds of projects at a time in an attempt to show that lots of little programs add up to big dollars.

While the effort plays well back home, his critics in Congress find Fawell nitpicking, tiresome and limited in vision. Fawell knows that other members tend to take his efforts personally, but he does not seem to care.

"There is sort of a gathering of the clan to express their displeasure: 'This is not something you should be doing,'" Fawell says. "Even those without projects know: There but for the grace of God go I."

And Fawell does not make exceptions for projects in his home state. Early in the 103rd Congress, he and the 74 other porkbusters took aim at 747 projects approved by Congress in 1992 worth nearly $2 billion, including $1 million for tree planting in Chicago and a $1.7 million visitors center to be built in Springfield to honor Abraham Lincoln.

"It's not needed," Fawell said of the center.

Illinois Democrat Richard J. Durbin, who represents Springfield, argued that the center would help double the number of tourists who come to the area to visit Lincoln's hometown.

In 1992, however, Fawell found himself the target of other porkbusters. The House Appropriations Committee, in meeting President Bush's challenge to cut spending, unsuccessfully targeted a number of programs in districts held by Republicans, including a $3.4 million laboratory in the 13th. Fawell and others opposed the cut, and the money was left in.

As a member of the Education and Labor Committee, Fawell is part of a conservative bloc that consistently votes against labor issues and some education measures that Democrats favor. Conservative Dick Armey of Texas, chairman of the Republican Conference, is also a part of that bloc.

Fawell has shown an interest in internal Republican politics. He was recruited by Armey to help him win the conference chairmanship. Fawell made calls and worked the membership for Armey, whose positions he supports.

Fawell clearly reflects the attitudes and opinions of his affluent, suburban Republican district. On most issues, he quietly pursues the anti-tax, pro-business orientation of his constituents. It is not unusual for his voting record to earn a perfect score from the U.S. Chamber of Commerce.

Fawell supported most of Bush's economic and defense policies. But throughout Bush's administration, Fawell supported him on only about 70 percent of those votes on which Bush staked out a position.

Notably, Fawell parts company with Republican orthodoxy in his support of environmental legislation and his backing for funding of abortion in cases of rape and incest. In the 103rd, he voted for a bill that codified the Clinton administration's decision to overturn a ban on abortion counseling at federally funded family planning clinics.

Fawell achieved a measure of notoriety in 1988 during the controversy over "catastrophic" health insurance. When affluent senior citizens began grumbling about the costs of the bill, Fawell became their champion. A foe of the initial measure, he co-chaired the GOP task force pushing for its repeal and entered the discharge petition that helped shake the repeal out of the Ways and Means Committee, which was blocking action. In late 1989, Fawell claimed victory when Congress repealed the law.

By the time a measure comes before one of Fawell's committees, he not only has read it line by line, he is likely to have underlined and highlighted the document and scribbled notes

Illinois 13

Southwest Chicago suburbs — Naperville

As a leading critic of wasteful federal spending, Rep. Fawell receives little argument from his white-collar suburban constituency. The 13th, which covers southern Du Page County and parts of exurban Cook and Will counties, is a place of wide lawns and spacious houses where business executives live. It is one of the most inevitably Republican districts in the country.

George Bush's failure in 1992 to make the most of this advantage contributed to his crushing defeat by Bill Clinton in Illinois. In 1988, Bush took 69 percent of the 13th's vote; in 1992, he slipped all the way to 47 percent. Clinton did not get much more than the Democratic base vote, but even in this seat of suburban comfort, populist Ross Perot pulled down a fifth of the vote.

The major demographic changes in late 20th century America have included the emergence of suburban centers as satellite "downtowns" and population explosion in outlying exurbs. The 13th has prime examples of each, in the communities of Oak Brook and Naperville.

Oak Brook, just west of the Cook-Du Page County line, is not especially populous. But its location near the nexus of Interstates 88, 294 and 290 has abetted its development into a leading business center. Its corporate roster includes the headquarters of the McDonald's chain, the Ace Hardware Corp., Federal Signal Corp. and the Spiegel mail-order company.

South of Oak Brook along I-88 is a string of suburbs that grew up along the Burlington Northern commuter tracks and long served as the hub of southern Du Page County. (Overall, the county provides about three-fifths of the 13th's population.) With room to spread out, these cities — the largest of which is Downers Grove — gained population; the growth has given Lisle, one of the rare traditional working-class towns in the 13th, a more suburban veneer.

But the spectacular growth has been in Naperville. In 1970, Naperville was a small city amid Du Page and northern Will County farmland; by 1980, it caught up with Downers Grove in population. Then, over the next 10 years, Naperville doubled its population to more than 85,000, making it Illinois' sixth-largest city. It has also become an employment center: Allied Van Lines, Burlington Northern Railroad and Nalco Chemical have headquarters there.

Scientific research is a major source of jobs. Argonne National Laboratory is in southeast Du Page; district residents also work at the Fermi National Accelerator Laboratory, across the line in the 14th District.

Southern Du Page's fast growth has spilled over to the northern Will County city of Bolingbrook. The remainder of the 13th's section of Will County is mainly rural, dotted with towns — Lockport, Romeoville, Plainfield — whose links are mainly with the 11th District city of Joliet.

The 13th also takes in the mainly residential southwest corner of Cook County that includes the fast-growing exurbs of Orland Park and Tinley Park.

1990 Population: 571,531. White 523,801 (92%), Black 18,067 (3%), Other 29,663 (5%). Hispanic origin 16,929 (3%). 18 and over 412,733 (72%), 62 and over 55,223 (10%). Median age: 32.

in the margins about questions he wants to raise.

But for all his preparation, Fawell can come across as a rambling inquisitor of witnesses. At a 1991 hearing on striker protection legislation, he used his entire time allotment trying to articulate a question for AFL-CIO chief Lane Kirkland. When Fawell attempted to follow up on the answer, an exasperated chairman cut him off for exceeding the time limit.

At Home: Fawell reflects his constituency when he talks about issues "from a businessman's point of view" and pursues fiscal conservatism as his central theme. The political mainstream in the 13th ranges from the moderate to far right within the Republican Party.

Democrats have yet to put up a serious challenge to Fawell. He has won each of his five general elections with two-thirds of the vote or better.

Since winning a closely contested open seat primary in 1984, Fawell has had little opposition from within the GOP. In 1992, he easily brushed off a GOP primary challenge by Stuart A. Wesbury Jr., a well-financed health-care association executive who ran as an outsider candidate.

As the campaign treasurer for his longtime friend, veteran Rep. John N. Erlenborn, Fawell was well positioned in 1984 when Erlenborn announced his retirement after 20 years of service. Fawell picked up most of the veteran incumbent's political network; Erlenborn's chief aide became his campaign manager.

That help proved invaluable in winning

the GOP primary. Fawell, who as a state legislator had promoted measures to aid the disabled, faced two conservative opponents — state Sen. George Ray Hudson and former state Sen. Mark Rhoads — who tried to portray him as a liberal.

With backing from the formal Du Page and Cook County GOP organizations as well as conservative contacts, Hudson seemed at least an even bet to defeat Fawell. But he lost time and momentum after falling off a campaign stage and breaking a leg. Fawell took the nomination over Hudson by more than 3,000 votes, and has coasted since.

Committees

Education & Labor (6th of 15 Republicans)
Labor Standards, Occupational Health & Safety (ranking); Labor-Management Relations; Select Education

Science, Space & Technology (6th of 22 Republicans)
Energy (ranking)

Elections

1992 General		
Harris W. Fawell (R)	179,257	(68%)
Dennis Michael Temple (D)	82,985	(32%)
1992 Primary		
Harris W. Fawell (R)	46,417	(73%)
Stuart A. Wesbury Jr. (R)	17,202	(27%)
1990 General		
Harris W. Fawell (R)	116,048	(66%)
Steven K. Thomas (D)	60,305	(34%)

Previous Winning Percentages: **1988** (70%) **1986** (73%) **1984** (67%)

District Vote for President

1992
D 88,324 (32%)
R 128,627 (47%)
I 58,125 (21%)

Campaign Finance

	Receipts	Receipts from PACs		Expend-itures
1992				
Fawell (R)	$563,194	$215,917	(38%)	$657,908
Temple (D)	$4,327	0		$4,327
1990				
Fawell (R)	$336,789	$119,570	(36%)	$271,913

Key Votes

1993	
Require parental notification of minors' abortions	Y
Require unpaid family and medical leave	N
Approve national "motor voter" registration bill	N
Approve budget increasing taxes and reducing deficit	N
Approve economic stimulus plan	N
1992	
Approve balanced-budget constitutional amendment	Y
Close down space station program	Y
Approve U.S. aid for former Soviet Union	Y
Allow shifting funds from defense to domestic programs	N
1991	
Extend unemployment benefits using deficit financing	N
Approve waiting period for handgun purchases	Y
Authorize use of force in Persian Gulf	Y

Voting Studies

	Presidential Support		Party Unity		Conservative Coalition	
Year	S	O	S	O	S	O
1992	70	29	86	13	75	25
1991	75	22	80	16	84	11
1990	70	30	88	11	81	19
1989	60	40	73	25	88	10
1988	61	36	80	18	92	8
1987	64	34	74	23	84	16
1986	69	30	83	17	78	22
1985	85	15	79	18	78	22

Interest Group Ratings

Year	ADA	AFL-CIO	CCUS	ACU
1992	25	17	88	84
1991	15	8	100	84
1990	11	8	93	88
1989	10	0	100	93
1988	40	14	92	64
1987	24	0	100	70
1986	20	14	89	73
1985	15	6	95	81

14 Dennis Hastert (R)

Of Yorkville — Elected 1986; 4th Term

Born: Jan. 2, 1942, Aurora, Ill.
Education: Wheaton College, A.B. 1964; Northern Illinois U., M.A. 1967.
Occupation: Teacher; restaurateur.
Family: Wife, Jean Kahl; two children.
Religion: Protestant.
Political Career: Ill. House, 1981-87.
Capitol Office: 2453 Rayburn Bldg. 20515; 225-2976.

In Washington: As both a protégé and confidant of Minority Leader Robert H. Michel, Hastert's chief function in the House is to help protect his protector's turf.

During six years in the Illinois Legislature, Hastert honed the ability to work the inside. By applying those skills in the House, he has become a key behind-the-scenes operator for the Michel-Henry J. Hyde, traditional middle-America wing of the Republican Party. Increasingly he is called upon for a variety of tasks, from helping shape policy debates to strategic party decisions.

In 1993, he was chosen to be the Republican House member on Hillary Rodham Clinton's health-care task force, and he continues to serve on the GOP's Committee on Committees, which makes party committee assignments.

When Michigan Rep. Guy Vander Jagt was defeated in his August 1992 primary, Hastert emerged as a leading contender to replace the beleaguered Vander Jagt as the head of the National Republican Congressional Committee. Although the job ultimately went to Bill Paxon of New York, Hastert was elected a deputy whip at the start of the 103rd Congress. The NRCC mention and the whip post are two signs that suggest that Hastert has aspirations for a broader, more visible role.

A beefy former wrestling coach who once headed the National Wrestling Congress, Hastert is not a stereotypical jock. He is a serious legislator who came to Washington to serve as ombudsman for his constituents. And although he has been selected for tasks that extend beyond the concerns of the 14th, he manages to keep an eye on home-state issues.

At the start of the 102nd Congress, Hastert parlayed his contacts into a committee move of his own: He switched from Public Works to Energy and Commerce.

From that post, Hastert worked to ensure that ethanol, which is derived mainly from Midwestern corn, was included in the Clean Air Act as an acceptable alternative fuel.

He also secured money in the 102nd's comprehensive energy bill for the cleanup of low-level nuclear waste. West Chicago is home to many of Hastert's constituents in the 14th and also to a site where a now-defunct plant once buried low-level nuclear waste. The energy bill includes $40 million for the Illinois sites.

In his first term, Hastert tried to pass an amendment blocking the Nuclear Regulatory Commission (NRC) from designating a permanent waste site in the district until other alternatives had been studied.

"Certainly small communities should not be asked to gamble with the lives of their residents if better and safer solutions exist," Hastert said when he pushed for an amendment to the NRC authorization bill on the House floor. The amendment was accepted but did not become law.

Hastert also has repeatedly sought to remove penalties in the form of decreased Social Security benefits that are levied on senior citizens between 65 and 69 who continue to work after retirement. He made progress in the 102nd, winning approval for legislation to phase in increases in the amounts seniors may earn.

Hastert remains committed to outright repeal of the earnings limit, but he is pitted against powerful Ways and Means Committee Chairman Dan Rostenkowski of Illinois, who vehemently opposes repeal.

Hastert also serves as ranking member of the Environment, Energy and Natural Resources Subcommittee of the Government Operations Committee.

At Home: Hastert's ties to Michel have led to his rise within the Illinois Republican delegation. That was evident during the redistricting process that preceded the 1992 election: Hastert took the lead role in organizing the GOP House members behind a plan (favoring Republicans) that was eventually enacted by a three-judge federal court panel.

Not surprisingly, the remap left Hastert with an exurban-rural district similar to the one that had previously elected him to the House. Hastert breezed to victory, as he had in two previous re-election campaigns.

Only his first House general election con-

Illinois 14

North Central — Aurora; Elgin; De Kalb

A decade ago, the historically industrial cities of Aurora and Elgin in eastern Kane County were in a prolonged state of Rust Belt decline. However, the cities' location at the edge of metropolitan Chicago, their proximity to such booming satellite cities as Schaumburg and Naperville, and their reasonable land values gave them a new life and boosted their populations during the 1980s.

The growth here and in other Fox River Valley communities reinforced Kane County's dominance in the 14th; it contributes more than half the district's population. The rest of the people are distributed among a section of exurban Du Page County to the east and a mainly rural stretch south and west that includes Kendall, De Kalb, Lee and the northern part of La Salle counties. Exurban and rural Republican tendencies dominate the 14th's politics, offsetting the Democratic habits of some blue-collar whites and minority-group voters. After a tough 1986 contest against a Kane County Democratic official, Rep. Hastert has thrice won with better than two-thirds of the vote.

This GOP lean made the 14th one of George Bush's best Illinois districts in 1992, but that is faint praise. Although Bush won in five of the six full or partial counties in the 14th, he fell short of his 65 percent total in 1988. Ross Perot's populism struck a nerve here; he took 20 percent or better in every county.

Aurora, with nearly 100,000 residents, is the district's largest city. It maintains an industrial heritage, with Caterpillar Tractor Co. and the All-Steel office furniture company as major employers. But the growth sector is in white-collar operations, including Toyota's Midwest headquarters. The city's "Anywhere U.S.A." image has led to its current fame: It is the setting for "Wayne's World," first a TV skit and then a movie comedy about two middle-class teenage rock fans.

The economic mix is similar in Elgin, which has about 77,000 residents. Factory workers here still make a variety of products, including Elgin street sweepers. But the largest single private employer is First Chicago Corp.'s credit card processing center.

Much of the residential and retail growth has been in new subdivisions on the cities' east sides, leaving aging downtowns behind. Yet urban Kane County has attracted a growing number of Hispanic residents.

Between Elgin and Aurora are St. Charles, Geneva and Batavia, site of the Fermi National Accelerator Laboratory that extends into Du Page County. The 14th's section of Du Page includes West Chicago and part of Bartlett. To the south is lightly populated, conservative-voting Kendall County.

Just west of the Fox River Valley, the 14th leaves the metropolis and enters rural downstate Illinois. The only large break in the farmscape is De Kalb, site of Northern Illinois University (24,900 students): Clinton carried De Kalb County with 40 percent. In Lee County is Dixon, former President Ronald Reagan's boyhood hometown.

1990 Population: 571,530. White 507,488 (89%), Black 23,867 (4%), Other 40,175 (7%). Hispanic origin 56,145 (10%). 18 and over 407,741 (71%), 62 and over 63,855 (11%). Median age: 31.

test caused Hastert difficulty. He had already gone a long way in politics without breaking a sweat. Appointed to the Illinois House in 1981 to fill a vacancy, Hastert gained respect for his knowledge of state budget matters. An ally of then-GOP Gov. James R. Thompson, Hastert was selected in 1986 as the 14th District nominee by a Republican convention after GOP Rep. John E. Grotberg was forced to retire because of a terminal illness.

But in the general election, Hastert struggled to maintain the Republican hold on the district. His Democratic foe, Kane County coroner Mary Lou Kearns, enjoyed some advantages that made the election close.

Whereas Kearns was an official in the district's largest county, Hastert came from the southeast corner of the 14th, away from its population centers. And while Kearns had begun to campaign in summer 1985, Hastert was not nominated until June 1986, leaving him just a little more than four months to summon the district's normal GOP loyalties.

Hastert was hindered in that effort by the bruised feelings left over from the convention that nominated him. The backers of two other candidates — West Chicago lawyer Tom Johnson and Elgin Mayor Richard Verbic — complained that the convention was stacked in Hastert's favor.

While Hastert struggled to gain his footing, Kearns attaked him for supporting a utility measure in the Legislature that she claimed would result in rate increases. But in the final weeks, Hastert's sluggish effort finally came together. He promoted his experience in

Springfield, where he was GOP spokesman on the state House Appropriations Committee.

Hastert also went after Kearns, reminding district Republicans that she was a presidential convention delegate in 1984 for Walter F. Mondale. Hastert won with 52 percent. Kearns demurred on a rematch in 1988, and Hastert pinned a little-known Democratic opponent by a nearly 3-to-1 margin, establishing a solid hold on the seat.

Committees

Energy & Commerce (9th of 17 Republicans)
Energy & Power; Health & the Environment; Telecommunications & Finance

Government Operations (3rd of 16 Republicans)
Environment, Energy & Natural Resources (ranking)

Elections

1992 General		
Dennis Hastert (R)	155,271	(67%)
Jonathan Abram Reich (D)	75,294	(33%)
1990 General		
Dennis Hastert (R)	112,383	(67%)
Donald J. Westphal (D)	55,592	(33%)

Previous Winning Percentages: 1988 (74%) **1986** (52%)

District Vote for President

1992
D 83,107 (34%)
R 105,698 (44%)
I 52,914 (22%)

Campaign Finance

	Receipts	Receipts from PACs		Expend- itures
1992				
Hastert (R)	$601,812	$317,656	(53%)	$615,535
1990				
Hastert (R)	$461,002	$181,074	(39%)	$312,555

Key Votes

1993	
Require parental notification of minors' abortions	Y
Require unpaid family and medical leave	N
Approve national "motor voter" registration bill	N
Approve budget increasing taxes and reducing deficit	N
Approve economic stimulus plan	N
1992	
Approve balanced-budget constitutional amendment	Y
Close down space station program	Y
Approve U.S. aid for former Soviet Union	N
Allow shifting funds from defense to domestic programs	N
1991	
Extend unemployment benefits using deficit financing	N
Approve waiting period for handgun purchases	N
Authorize use of force in Persian Gulf	Y

Voting Studies

	Presidential Support		Party Unity		Conservative Coalition	
Year	S	O	S	O	S	O
1992	78	19	89	10	88	13
1991	84	14	90	6	95	3
1990	67	31	91	6	91	9
1989	76	23	90	9	90	10
1988	62	34	92	6	95	3
1987	66	33	90	7	91	9

Interest Group Ratings

Year	ADA	AFL-CIO	CCUS	ACU
1992	5	25	75	92
1991	0	8	100	95
1990	6	0	86	79
1989	10	17	100	85
1988	10	21	86	92
1987	8	13	87	87

15 Thomas W. Ewing (R)

Of Pontiac — Elected 1991; 1st Full Term

Born: Sept. 19, 1935, Atlanta, Ill.
Education: Millikin U., B.S. 1957; John Marshall Law School, J.D. 1968.
Military Service: Army, 1957; Army Reserve, 1957-63.
Occupation: Lawyer.
Family: Wife, Connie Lupo; three children, three stepchildren.
Religion: Methodist.
Political Career: Ill. House, 1975-91.
Capitol Office: 1317 Longworth Bldg. 20515; 225-2371.

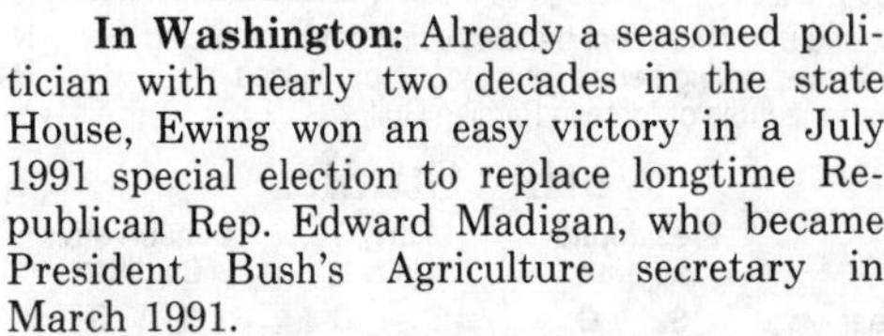

In Washington: Already a seasoned politician with nearly two decades in the state House, Ewing won an easy victory in a July 1991 special election to replace longtime Republican Rep. Edward Madigan, who became President Bush's Agriculture secretary in March 1991.

But anyone who thought Ewing would slip unnoticed into the well-worn seat of his predecessor was in for a surprise. Though both are conservative, Ewing is aggressive and confrontational, whereas Madigan was low-key and accommodating. Ewing's strong partisan streak brought him few Democratic allies in the state House, and he has made few in the U.S. House of Representatives; Madigan negotiated effectively with his many friends across the aisle.

Ironically, Ewing's hard-line approach aligns him with Georgia Republican Rep. Newt Gingrich, the leader of a more confrontational conservative faction who won the 1989 contest for House Republican whip over Madigan, the epitome of the Midwestern "Main Street" Republican.

Ewing targeted two highly polarized issues to kick off his congressional career. In November 1991 he introduced a House resolution to give the president a line-item veto and more authority to cut spending.

And as the White House Council on Competitiveness, chaired by Vice President Dan Quayle, came under bitter attack from Democrats who said it was circumventing the will of Congress in lifting federal safety and environmental regulations, Ewing put in a measure to sharpen the council's teeth.

In September 1992 Ewing and Republican Sen. Orrin G. Hatch of Utah introduced companion measures to ease government regulation on small business. "Let us work together, business and labor, to control excessive regulation so that we can protect jobs in America and improve our economy," Ewing said on the House floor.

He was also front and center in a related battle to freeze regulations. As an opening gambit to the 1992 election year, President Bush placed a 90-day moratorium on new regulations. Ewing was among the most vocal of the congressional conservatives calling on Bush to extend the moratorium.

While the moratorium and the competitiveness council went out with Bush, Ewing brought back his amendments to the Regulatory Flexibility Act in the 103rd Congress.

Like Madigan, Ewing has a seat on the Agriculture Committee, where he can look out for the interests of the soybean and corn growers in the 15th District.

Legislatively, however, little has been going on in Agriculture since the passage of the giant five-year farm bill in 1990, and perhaps as a result, Ewing has been slow to dig in. He introduced a bill geared at overhauling the Federal Crop Insurance Program and took note of the Midwest's drought conditions in 1991. Relief for farmers hit by the drought eventually came as part of a larger spending bill that fell outside the committee's purview.

The pace is much faster on the Public Works and Transportation Committee, where Ewing also has a seat. The $151 billion surface transportation bill that cleared Congress at the end of 1991 put big dollars in nearly every district — a whopping $437.8 million was earmarked for Illinois road projects and other big construction endeavors. By Ewing's own admission, the road projects in the 15th District all "are very small."

Ewing won both of his House elections by comfortable margins, but he deviates significantly from the Midwestern tradition of conservative pragmatism, and it is unclear how this will play over the long haul. Central Illinois was kind to Madigan, who ran unopposed in two of his last three House contests, and is home to a Republican of similar demeanor, House Minority Leader Robert H. Michel.

At Home: Although Ewing easily won the July 1991 special election to succeed Madigan, there was some question whether he had made

Illinois 15

East Central — Champaign; Kankakee

Most counties of downstate Illinois struggled with double-digit unemployment at the height of the recent recession. But two adjacent 15th District counties were islands of economic stability: McLean, which has an unusually thriving business sector, and Champaign, home of the University of Illinois.

This relative prosperity, combined with a traditional Republican base in surrounding farm country, makes the 15th a quintessential Midwestern Republican district. Though there are faded industrial areas and liberal academic communities that provide some Democratic votes, they are rarely enough to swing the partisan balance.

Thus, George Bush's weak 1992 district showing stands out. Bush — who in 1988 carried 10 of the 11 counties in the 15th — won just five in 1992, none with a majority.

Bloomington and Normal, in McLean County at the west end of the district, form its largest urban center. The cities have more than 90,000 residents between them. State Farm Insurance, the world's largest auto insurer, has its headquarters in Bloomington; Country Companies, another insurance firm, is based here. Normal has Illinois State University, with 22,000 students and nearly 4,000 employees; and Diamond-Star Motors, a joint venture of Mitsubishi and Chrysler, builds cars.

The rest of McLean County as well as De Witt County to the south and Livingston, Ford and Iroquois counties north and east contain some of the state's most prolific corn and soybean farms. These five counties, which Bush carried in 1992, make up the 15th's Republican core; the latter three gave Republican Senate candidate Rich Williamson 55 percent or better against Democrat Carol Moseley-Braun.

But a mix of academia, industry and farming makes Champaign County a swing-voting area.

Republican Ewing and Democrat Moseley-Braun won majorities in the county; Bill Clinton won a plurality. The University of Illinois dominates the economic landscape in the twin cities of Champaign and Urbana. Its payroll of 17,000 people supports a student enrollment of slightly more than 36,000. A Kraft food oils plant is the city's largest industrial facility.

Other urban areas of the district are not as economically healthy. Even in Champaign County, Rantoul is coping with the shutdown of Chanute Air Force Base under the 1989 base-closing law. Vermilion County has been hurt by factory layoffs in Danville and the demise of the tapped-out coal industry nearby. It was the only county to favor Ewing's Democratic challenger in 1992; Clinton beat Bush there by 17 percentage points.

Kankakee, at the district's northern edge, has been seeking an economic formula since the departure of two large industrial employers in the early 1980s. The city is one-third black, giving it the largest minority population in the 15th.

1990 Population: 571,532. White 512,928 (90%), Black 42,571 (7%), Other 16,033 (3%). Hispanic origin 9,300 (2%). 18 and over 433,424 (76%), 62 and over 87,262 (15%). Median age: 31.

the right career move. It seemed at the time that Ewing had given up a senior position in the state House — he was deputy Republican leader — for what might be a short stay in Washington.

Redistricting was around the corner; Illinois was slated to lose two House seats, and a third incumbent would be displaced to make room for a new Hispanic-majority district. Although the Democrats who controlled the state General Assembly conceded that two House Democrats would go, they also appeared ready to scrap a Republican seat by merging the districts of Ewing and Michel.

But the legislature stalemated over which Democratic incumbents would be hurt by redistricting. A federal court panel of three judges appointed by Republican presidents took over and enacted a plan drawn up by state GOP officials. Democratic members bore the entire burden of the seat shift; Ewing and Michel were given their own districts in which to run.

The new 15th District maintained most of Ewing's strongly Republican base. He did lose a bit of rural territory and picked up Democratic-leaning Vermilion County (Danville), with its struggling industrial economy. But even as his victory margin dropped a bit from 1991, Ewing still comfortably defeated Democrat Charles D. Mattis, a teacher from Danville.

Ewing entered the public arena in 1968 as an assistant state's attorney for Livingston County. His elective career began with his 1974 win for the state House. He rose through the leadership ranks, to assistant House minority leader and then to the deputy's position.

Ewing spent his first eight years in the state House on the Agriculture Committee. But he later focused on broader economic concerns as a member of the Labor and Commerce and Public Utilities committees and as co-chairman of the legislature's Economic and Fiscal Commission.

A Republican Party stalwart, Ewing drew no primary opposition for Madigan's vacated seat. He had no problems dealing with Democratic former state Rep. Gerald Bradley in the July special. Ewing won by nearly 2-to-1.

Committees

Agriculture (11th of 18 Republicans)
Department Operations; Environment, Credit & Rural Development; General Farm Commodities

Public Works & Transportation (10th of 24 Republicans)
Aviation; Economic Development; Water Resources & the Environment

Elections

1992 General		
Thomas W. Ewing (R)	142,167	(59%)
Charles D. Mattis (D)	97,190	(41%)
1991 Special		
Thomas W. Ewing (R)	25,675	(66%)
Gerald Bradley (D)	13,011	(34%)

District Vote for President

1992

D 107,962 (43%)
R 98,372 (39%)
I 47,259 (19%)

Campaign Finance

1992	Receipts	Receipts from PACs		Expend-itures
Ewing (R)	$381,502	$171,658	(45%)	$309,131
Mattis (D)	$6,338	$2,600	(41%)	$6,328

Key Votes

1993	
Require parental notification of minors' abortions	Y
Require unpaid family and medical leave	N
Approve national "motor voter" registration bill	N
Approve budget increasing taxes and reducing deficit	N
Approve economic stimulus plan	N
1992	
Approve balanced-budget constitutional amendment	Y
Close down space station program	Y
Approve U.S. aid for former Soviet Union	Y
Allow shifting funds from defense to domestic programs	N
1991	
Extend unemployment benefits using deficit financing	N

Voting Studies

	Presidential Support		Party Unity		Conservative Coalition	
Year	**S**	**O**	**S**	**O**	**S**	**O**
1992	74	25	80	17	71	27
1991	86 †	14 †	81 †	15 †	100 †	0 †

† Not eligible for all recorded votes.

Interest Group Ratings

Year	ADA	AFL-CIO	CCUS	ACU
1992	25	33	88	88
1991	0	13	100	100

16 Donald Manzullo (R)

Of Egan — Elected 1992; 1st Term

Born: March 24, 1944, Rockford, Ill.
Education: American U., B.A. 1967; Marquette U., J.D. 1970.
Occupation: Lawyer.
Family: Wife, Freda Tezlik; three children.
Religion: Baptist.
Political Career: Sought GOP nomination for U.S. House, 1990.
Capitol Office: 506 Cannon Bldg. 20515; 225-5676.

The Path to Washington: Perseverance — and tradition — won this seat for Manzullo, who pulled upsets against both a better-positioned primary opponent and one-term incumbent Democrat John W. Cox Jr.

A hard-line conservative with fundamentalist Christian leanings, Manzullo supports the death penalty and spending on a "star wars" defense system, and opposes gun control and government-run health care. In the 1980s, he crusaded against abortion, picketing clinics in Rockford. And he abhors allowing homosexuals to teach or serve in the military.

He has proposed that single mothers should clean houses to earn a living and defended the right of a woman to work by saying: "That's a decision she has to make with her husband."

Manzullo campaigned on a supply-side platform that echoed themes of former President Ronald Reagan. He called for a 10 percent income tax cut and elimination of the tax on capital gains, which he said would create millions of jobs. He argued that these measures, coupled with deep spending cuts, would help eliminate the deficit.

He can use his seat on the Small Business Committee to pursue his fight for a much lighter regulatory load on businesses, while his free-trade philosophy will dovetail with the export-promotion responsibilities of the Foreign Affairs Committee.

On the day after Manzullo was sworn in, he attacked the Democratic leadership over a rule that allows the five House delegates to vote on floor amendments, except when their votes would decide the question. He referred to the vote as "one of the most incredibly revolting spectacles that has ever taken place in the House of Representatives." He said that he "hung [his] head with shame over the fact that the Constitution, the very Constitution that Mr. Lincoln died for, was shredded at the hands of the Democrat majority."

Manzullo tried for this seat in 1990, losing in the GOP primary to John W. Hallock Jr., a more moderate state legislator. Hallock then lost the general election to Cox in an upset — the northwestern Illinois district along the Wisconsin border had sent a Republican to the House in every election since 1900.

Redistricting included McHenry County, whose rural character is being altered by development from the Chicago fringes. The county was Cox's biggest obstacle, but not just because his moderate leanings were unlikely to appeal to conservatives. McHenry was home to state Sen. Jack Schaffer, who had the backing of Lynn Martin — who left the 16th for a 1990 Senate bid — and GOP Gov. Jim Edgar in the primary.

It was taken for granted that Schaffer, with the party's backing and more money than Manzullo, would be Cox's challenger in the fall.

But Manzullo was undeterred. With a phalanx of traditional and evangelical volunteers still active after his failed bid two years earlier, Manzullo went after Schaffer, blasting him for supporting higher taxes. Schaffer had supported increased levies on gasoline, cigarettes and business purchases of computer software.

Manzullo also hit Schaffer for supporting a legislative pay raise and accepting contributions from liberal-leaning political action committees. Manzullo, who netted 46 percent in the 1990 primary, easily outran Schaffer, pulling 56 percent in his 1992 effort.

He then had to get by Cox, who had brought a low-key, forthright approach to the job that seemed to have plenty of appeal. Cox occasionally went against his district's conservative streak — opposing the use of force against Iraq, opposing capital punishment, and supporting abortion rights and the family leave bill that President Bush vetoed.

On the other hand, Cox embraced a balanced-budget amendment to the Constitution, middle-income tax relief, a modest capital gains tax cut and investment tax credits. In the middle of his re-election campaign, he presented a politically risky plan for a balanced budget that included program eliminations, entitlement cuts and tax increases. The new taxes were chiefly targeted at the wealthy, but included a 25-cents-per-gallon gasoline tax increase.

The voters were plainly unwilling to go against precedent anymore and gave Manzullo 56 percent of the vote.

Illinois 16

Northwest — Rockford; McHenry

After an uncharacteristic fling at Democratic voting, the 16th returned to its Republican form in 1992. GOP challenger Manzullo unseated one-term Democratic Rep. John W. Cox Jr., and George Bush carried the district, though by less than a Republican presidential candidate typically wins here.

The Yankees and Scandinavian farmers who settled the northern tier of Illinois gave it a lasting Republican tenor. Republicans held the region's House seat throughout the 20th century — until 1990.

The rare Republican setbacks that year in the 16th were in part the results of flawed candidacies. Cox's opponent, John W. Hallock Jr., faced questions about his personal ethics. And then-16th District GOP Rep. Lynn Martin's challenge to Democratic Sen. Paul Simon bombed; she got just 45 percent in her home base.

There is a core Democratic vote in the 16th, much of it centered in industrial Rockford (Winnebago County). But even within Winnebago County (which provides more than 40 percent of the 16th's votes), the Democratic edge is tempered by a Republican suburban and rural vote. And the overall Republican advantage in the 16th is cemented by McHenry County, a GOP bastion in exurban Chicago at the district's eastern end.

Rockford, with nearly 140,000 residents, is Illinois' second-largest city. Democrats rely on the city's blue-collar work force. Rockford has about 21,000 black residents, more than three-quarters of the district's black population.

A Chrysler plant and Sundstrand Corp. (a defense contractor based here) are the largest employers of Rockford's residents. Unemployment soared to 20 percent at one point during the early 1980s recession, but the city's extensive park system and other amenities made it harder to leave than some other industrial cities: Rockford had a net loss of fewer than 300 people between 1980 and 1990.

This relative stability pales, though, compared with McHenry County's boom during that period. Located at the northwest edge of Chicago's exurbia, McHenry increased its population by 24 percent during the 1980s.

This growth brought dramatic change to McHenry's larger towns: McHenry, Crystal Lake, Cary, Algonquin, Woodstock. But much of the county remains devoted to the traditional farming pursuits that emboldened the town of Harvard to call itself "the milk capital of the world." McHenry may be Illinois' most Republican county: Bush beat Bill Clinton here by 19 points, even though Ross Perot pulled down a quarter of the county's vote.

The other counties of this Wisconsin-border district are among Illinois' leading dairy producers. Jo Daviess County, in Illinois' northwest corner, leads the state in raising beef cattle. Galena, in rolling hills near the Mississippi River, has a tourist-based economy: It features the home of President Ulysses S. Grant and numerous bed-and-breakfast establishments.

1990 Population: 571,530. White 530,666 (93%), Black 26,845 (5%), Other 14,019 (2%). Hispanic origin 17,567 (3%). 18 and over 415,480 (73%), 62 and over 82,705 (14%). Median age: 33.

Committees

Foreign Affairs (16th of 18 Republicans)
Economic Policy, Trade & the Environment; International Operations

Small Business (16th of 18 Republicans)
Rural Enterprises, Exports & the Environment

Campaign Finance

	Receipts	Receipts from PACs		Expend-itures
1992				
Manzullo (R)	$440,379	$109,748	(25%)	$435,468
Cox (D)	$506,523	$338,389	(67%)	$491,002

Key Votes

1993

Require parental notification of minors' abortions	Y
Require unpaid family and medical leave	N
Approve national "motor voter" registration bill	N
Approve budget increasing taxes and reducing deficit	N
Approve economic stimulus plan	N

Elections

1992 General		
Donald Manzullo (R)	142,388	(56%)
John W. Cox Jr. (D)	113,555	(44%)
1992 Primary		
Donald Manzullo (R)	41,055	(56%)
Jack Schaffer (R)	31,705	(44%)

District Vote for President

1992

D	95,132 (37%)
R	108,949 (42%)
I	56,169 (22%)

17 Lane Evans (D)

Of Rock Island — Elected 1982; 6th Term

Born: Aug. 4, 1951, Rock Island, Ill.
Education: Augustana College (Rock Island, Ill.), B.A. 1974; Georgetown U., J.D. 1978.
Military Service: Marine Corps, 1969-71.
Occupation: Lawyer.
Family: Single.
Religion: Roman Catholic.
Political Career: No previous office.
Capitol Office: 2335 Rayburn Bldg. 20515; 225-5905.

In Washington: Evans entered the 103rd Congress having proved his political mettle and established himself as likely heir to the chairmanship of the Veterans' Affairs Committee.

He accomplished these ends by challenging Mississippi Democrat G. V. "Sonny" Montgomery, who had held the Veterans chairmanship for 12 years. Such a move would have seemed foolish just a few years before, but Evans has shown a knack for political timing. This bid was no exception, even if Evans did fall four votes shy of victory. Evans impressed many of his colleagues with his tough yet respectful campaign against Montgomery.

Evans and some veterans groups had been critical of Montgomery's handling of issues relating to Vietnam-era veterans. The conservative Montgomery also had put off his fellow Democrats by frequently allying himself with Republican Presidents Ronald Reagan and George Bush.

Evans was in the Marine Corps during the Vietnam War; and, although he was not assigned to Vietnam himself, he has become a leading advocate for programs benefiting veterans of that conflict. Evans distinguished himself as the premier House crusader to compensate victims of diseases linked to Agent Orange, a defoliant used during the Vietnam conflict. His four-year effort, which put him at loggerheads with Montgomery, paid off in his biggest legislative success: the enactment of Agent Orange legislation at the start of the 102nd Congress.

Vietnam veterans groups have claimed for years that several diseases contracted by some of their constituents were caused by exposure to Agent Orange. However, succeeding administrations had rejected the claims, saying science had yet to link the herbicide and the diseases. Montgomery also took this view, arguing that such benefits could be a dangerous precedent and drain the budget for veterans programs.

However, benefit supporters presented studies showing a link and portrayed Montgomery, a military officer in World War II and the Korean War, as an obstructionist intent on protecting his generation's programs at the expense of Vietnam veterans.

Strong opposition from the Reagan administration and Montgomery stymied Evans' early efforts. However, by the 101st Congress, the wave of public openness to Vietnam veterans and the growing political clout of that group gave momentum to the benefits cause.

Finally in early 1990, Bush administration Veterans Affairs Secretary Edward J. Derwinski announced that his department would provide benefits to victims of soft-tissue sarcomas and non-Hodgkins lymphoma who had been exposed to Agent Orange. But Evans pressed ahead, adapting his proposal to codify Derwinski's policy and to mandate a National Academy of Sciences review of Agent Orange-related studies.

Evans' amendment to the House cost of living adjustment (COLA) bill failed in the Veterans' Affairs Compensation Subcommittee, but the full committee passed the proposal by a 16-14 vote. The bill then passed the House by voice vote.

The victory for Evans' side would not be immediate. Senate opponents stalled the bill, while Montgomery tried and failed to win separate approval for the COLA alone. Montgomery tried to focus the veterans' anger over the failure of the COLA against those promoting the Agent Orange benefits. However, when the 102nd Congress opened, Montgomery's proposal of a "clean" bill was countered once again by Evans' COLA bill that included Agent Orange language. Montgomery then yielded to a compromise, under which his bill would pass first and be followed by Agent Orange legislation.

Given the 17th District's GOP history, Evans' record might seem to the left of much of his constituency. He was among the members with the highest percentages of floor votes in opposition to both Bush and Reagan administration positions. But his economic populism plays well at home, where the economy has been dependent on heavy industry that has declined in recent years.

Illinois 17

West — Rock Island; Moline

For western Illinois' 17th, the recession of the early 1990s was mild compared with the economic devastation that occurred in the previous decade. Then, the industrial regions centered on the neighboring cities of Rock Island and Moline (at the 17th's western end) and Peoria (across its eastern border in the 18th District) hit the skids.

Layoffs and factory closures in the district's essential industry — farm equipment manufacturing — caused severe hardship. Job-seekers left the area. Although economic stability has slowly and shakily returned, the earlier near-depression conditions had a lasting political impact: The 17th, a former GOP bastion, now leans to the Democrats.

Rep. Evans blazed the partisan trail by narrowly capturing this House seat in 1982. He has since dominated the 17th, winning two-thirds of the vote in 1990 before settling down to 60 percent in 1992 in a somewhat redrawn district.

The 17th remains more competitive in major-office contests; for example, Republican Jim Edgar took 53 percent for governor here in 1990. But in 1992, Bill Clinton carried the 17th, finishing first in 11 of the 14 counties that are all or part in the district. George Bush won just 29 percent in Fulton County, near Peoria.

Despite the district's economic problems and accompanying voter resentment, the 17th was not one of Ross Perot's strongest locales in Illinois.

Farm machinery is still king in the Quad Cities: Rock Island and Moline in Illinois, Davenport and Bettendorf in Iowa across the Mississippi River. Deere & Co., makers of John Deere tractors, has its headquarters in Moline as well as production and distribution facilities around the region. There is other farm-related industry, including meat packing; the federal arsenal at Rock Island is also a major employer.

Moline, with about 43,000 residents, is the district's largest city; Rock Island (Evans' base) is next with just over 40,000. Blacks and Hispanics make up more than 10 percent of Rock Island County, the largest minority-group concentration in the district. Clinton beat Bush by nearly 20 percentage points in the county.

Galesburg (Knox County) — the hometown of Illinois' late poet laureate, Carl Sandburg — is also broad-shouldered: Its largest employer is an Admiral refrigerator plant. At its southern end, the 17th takes in Quincy (Adams County), a river town that relies on agribusiness for jobs. Some coal is mined in McDonough and Fulton counties at the southeast end of the 17th.

The rest of the district is mainly rich farmland, with corn, hogs and soybeans abundant. Before the rise of Evans and the onset of economic difficulties, the large rural Republican vote usually offset the Democratic urban vote in the 17th.

At the district's north end, Carroll County and the part of Ogle County in the 17th were the only two to go against Evans in 1992. Bush also won these, though Clinton took most of the rural counties by pluralities.

1990 Population: 571,530. White 540,954 (95%), Black 18,609 (3%), Other 11,967 (2%). Hispanic origin 17,398 (3%). 18 and over 427,877 (75%), 62 and over 111,381 (19%). Median age: 35.

Evans has described himself as a "card-carrying capitalist," but argues that the economy should be organized with the interests of the average American in mind. "We're always consulted by corporations when they want something," he once complained. "When they want to leave town, they do it overnight."

While he holds strong views, Evans conducts himself in an engaging manner that makes it difficult for even conservative critics to dislike him. His high energy and hometown-boy style have been a hit with 17th District voters and generally with Hill colleagues as well.

On Armed Services, Evans has not yet found a major niche. His record on defense is generally as liberal as on economics. He opposed the 1991 resolution authorizing the use of force in the Persian Gulf.

At Home: Although Evans' capture of this traditionally Republican seat in 1982 was regarded at the time as stunning, his hard work soon established him as a fixture. In each of his re-election campaigns, district Republicans have tried to convince voters that Evans was an undesirable liberal extremist. Each time, Evans has won comfortably, hitting at least 60 percent in his last three contests.

Evans wins in part because he works tirelessly at home — conducting meetings to study the district's problems, popping up at every county and small-town celebration and making himself available to the local media.

In 1982, Evans emerged from his community legal clinic in Rock Island to make his first run for public office. It was an effort that seemed futile until the March primary that year, when former state Sen. Kenneth G. McMillan, a New Right stalwart, defeated Rep. Tom Railsback, a moderate eight-term Republican.

Railsback's defeat set up a clear ideological choice, one that benefited Evans in the recession year of 1982. Evans, who had worked in the presidential campaign of Massachusetts Sen. Edward M. Kennedy in 1980, urged voters in the economically troubled district to use his candidacy as a way to "send Reagan a message." McMillan defended President Reagan's economic program, and Evans managed to cast his opponent as a right-winger; the Democrat won with 53 percent of the vote.

The 1984 election brought a rematch. McMillan moderated his rhetoric, trying to appeal both to conservative voters in the rural counties of the district and to blue-collar voters in the industrial cities to the north. But Evans carried nine of the district's 14 counties.

In 1986, the GOP offered Rock Island lawyer Sam McHard, who came out of the party's moderate wing and had been an active supporter of Railsback in 1982. But Evans carried the same nine counties as in 1984.

Evans faced less serious Republican challenges in the next two cycles and won easily. In 1992, changes wrought by redistricting gave a boost to Republican nominee Ken Schloemer, a Moline restaurateur active in Rock Island County civic and economic development activities. Schloemer said the low ratings given Evans by some business and farm interest groups, and Evans' advocacy of gay rights in the military, proved the incumbent was out of step with the district.

Evans deflected the criticisms and kept his vote share at a still-comfortable 60 percent. He carried every county that had been in the old 17th and won the candidates' shared base (Rock Island County) with 63 percent. But he lost in Carroll and Ogle counties at the district's northern edge and took the part of Adams County that is on the district's southern fringe with a modest 53 percent.

Committees

Armed Services (15th of 34 Democrats)
Military Acquisition; Readiness

Natural Resources (26th of 28 Democrats)
Oversight & Investigations

Veterans' Affairs (4th of 21 Democrats)
Oversight & Investigations (chairman); Compensation, Pension & Insurance

Elections

1992 General		
Lane Evans (D)	156,233	(60%)
Ken Schloemer (R)	103,719	(40%)
1992 Primary		
Lane Evans (D)	47,351	(82%)
Richard E. Maynard (D)	10,545	(18%)
1990 General		
Lane Evans (D)	102,062	(67%)
Dan Lee (R)	51,380	(33%)

Previous Winning Percentages: **1988** (65%) **1986** (56%) **1984** (57%) **1982** (53%)

District Vote for President

1992

D 124,172 (47%)
R 95,180 (36%)
I 45,395 (17%)

Campaign Finance

	Receipts	Receipts from PACs		Expend-itures
1992				
Evans (D)	$370,096	$188,260	(51%)	$374,415
Schloemer (R)	$117,626	$34,994	(30%)	$117,624
1990				
Evans (D)	$417,626	$228,998	(55%)	$390,401
Lee (R)	$116,755	$26,830	(23%)	$115,495

Key Votes

1993	
Require parental notification of minors' abortions	N
Require unpaid family and medical leave	Y
Approve national "motor voter" registration bill	Y
Approve budget increasing taxes and reducing deficit	Y
Approve economic stimulus plan	Y
1992	
Approve balanced-budget constitutional amendment	N
Close down space station program	Y
Approve U.S. aid for former Soviet Union	N
Allow shifting funds from defense to domestic programs	Y
1991	
Extend unemployment benefits using deficit financing	Y
Approve waiting period for handgun purchases	Y
Authorize use of force in Persian Gulf	N

Voting Studies

Year	Presidential Support S	Presidential Support O	Party Unity S	Party Unity O	Conservative Coalition S	Conservative Coalition O
1992	11	88	95	5	6	94
1991	15	85	95	4	11	89
1990	16	84	97	3	9	91
1989	23	77	97	3	5	95
1988	17	83	97	2	8	92
1987	11	87	94	3	2	93
1986	13	86	95	4	6	92
1985	14	86	96	1	5	93
1984	24	73	94	6	7	92
1983	9	90	91	6	13	84

Interest Group Ratings

Year	ADA	AFL-CIO	CCUS	ACU
1992	95	100	13	4
1991	100	100	20	5
1990	100	100	21	4
1989	100	92	40	7
1988	100	100	14	0
1987	100	94	0	0
1986	100	93	11	0
1985	100	100	18	5
1984	90	85	38	0
1983	95	94	10	4

18 Robert H. Michel (R)

Of Peoria — Elected 1956; 19th Term

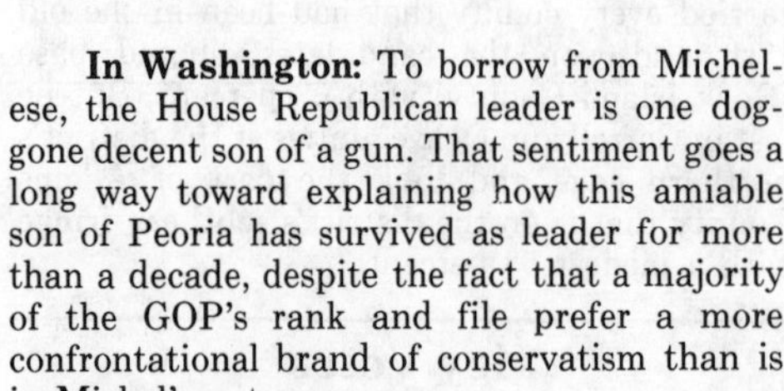

Born: March 2, 1923, Peoria, Ill.
Education: Bradley U., B.S. 1948.
Military Service: Army, 1942-46.
Occupation: Congressional aide.
Family: Wife, Corinne Woodruff; four children.
Religion: Apostolic Christian.
Political Career: No previous office.
Capitol Office: 2112 Rayburn Bldg. 20515; 225-6201.

In Washington: To borrow from Michelese, the House Republican leader is one doggone decent son of a gun. That sentiment goes a long way toward explaining how this amiable son of Peoria has survived as leader for more than a decade, despite the fact that a majority of the GOP's rank and file prefer a more confrontational brand of conservatism than is in Michel's nature.

The Young Turks took full control of the GOP leadership for the 103rd Congress, leaving Michel isolated among a group that sees making an ideological point as more important than getting something done. But accommodating himself to necessity is one of Michel's premier traits. To keep a firm grasp on his leadership post amid increasing restlessness from the far right, he has adopted a harsher, more assertive line.

That was evident in early 1993. With the Republicans now in full opposition mode, controlling neither the Congress nor the White House, it fell to Michel to deliver the GOP response to President Clinton's first address to Congress. In his nationally televised performance, Michel introduced himself to the American public in his own inimitable style.

"I have no props, no flip charts, no pointer, no electronic gimmicks. I don't even have a 1-800 number for you to call. I'd just like to talk with you as though we were having a cup of coffee back in my hometown of Peoria," he began.

But if his delivery was characteristically low-key and colloquial, the language of the speech was unusually harsh, given Michel's reputation and the newness of Clinton's presidency.

"After listening to the president tonight, I wonder if you know what the president's long-range economic strategy is. I don't — and I must say, I wonder if he does," Michel continued.

With tart references to "Clinton's spin doctors" and the "biggest propaganda campaign in recent political history," Michel mocked Clinton's calls for investment, change and "contribution."

"Contribution is now the new word for taxes.... [R]emember when you hear a Democrat call for taxes, do not ask for whom the tax rises — it will rise for you," he said.

The speech seemed yet another indication that Michel had fallen in step with the brasher group of Republicans who now occupy his leadership team.

Through retirements and competitive elections, conservatives won out over moderates in virtually every Republican leadership post for the 103rd. The theme was clearly stated by Dick Armey of Texas in his successful challenge to Conference Chairman Jerry Lewis of California: "The politics of confrontation works and the politics of appeasement fails."

The leadership turnover at the start of the 103rd Congress capped a trend that began with a bang in 1989 when firebrand Newt Gingrich of Georgia snatched the whip's job out from under Michel's old friend, Edward R. Madigan of Illinois.

Since then, Gingrich and his partisan acolytes have been steering Michel toward the door. With varying degrees of patience, the new crop of agitators seems to be marking time for what they expect will be their opportunity to rule the Republican roost.

Rumors have circulated on Capitol Hill for years that Michel was set to retire, particularly during rough points in the 101st, such as the several bitter budget fights and a loss of GOP House seats in 1990.

Michel chose to return for the 102nd and 103rd Congresses, and as for the future, he has coyly refused to tip his hand. But unburdened of the responsibilities of carrying a Republican administration's agenda on Capitol Hill, Michel has given indications early in the 103rd that he could lead the anti-Democratic charge.

In January, after the House changed rules to grant non-voting delegates some voting privileges on the floor, Michel filed a lawsuit in behalf of the GOP, calling the rules change a power grab by Democrats who in a sense picked up five more votes. Although a federal judge concluded the rules change was constitutional,

Illinois 18

Central — Peoria; part of Springfield

With its modest-sized industrial cities, small towns and farms, the 18th is in some ways a model of middle-class, Middle American conservatism.

In various permutations through a series of redistrictings, this central Illinois district has since 1956 elected Michel, the current House minority leader. Not for nothing did President Richard M. Nixon want to know how his policies would "play in Peoria."

Yet the 18th also has some concerns that make it less than a Republican bastion — including a Peoria-based industrial sector that has lost thousands of jobs in recent years and an economically worried working-class constituency.

Bill Clinton won by pluralities over George Bush in 1992 in Peoria and Tazewell, the 18th's most populous counties; he won four other counties in the Illinois River Valley and even won in the heavily Republican northern part of Sangamon County (Springfield) that is in the 18th. Bush finished first in just six mainly rural counties. Michel won comfortably, but even he was held to 55 percent in Peoria County and lost two other counties.

At some points during their House careers, several veteran House members have been forced by redistricting to move their residences in order to keep up with their constituencies. Michel is an opposite case; he has stayed in one place — his hometown of Peoria — while his district has been peripatetic.

In the 1960s, Peoria (Peoria County) anchored the southern end of the district held by Michel; in the 1970s, the city was at the district's center. In the 1980s, Peoria was near the northeast corner of a district that ran west to the Mississippi River; in the 1990s, it is in the northwest portion of a mainly north-south district.

The 18th's economic health is largely dependent on Caterpillar Inc. The manufacturer of earth-moving equipment and other heavy machinery is based in Peoria and employs nearly 18,000 people at its headquarters and plants, the largest of which is in East Peoria (Tazewell County, which also includes the cities of Pekin and Morton).

Caterpillar's slump in the early 1980s contributed to a migration from the region: Peoria, still Illinois' third-largest city with about 113,000 residents, lost about a tenth of its population during the 1980s. The company has rebounded somewhat in recent years, though a labor dispute closed Caterpillar's factories for six months beginning in November 1991 and caused regional hardship.

Any Democratic leanings in the industrial area are usually canceled out by the solid GOP rural vote: Michel in 1992 took 65 percent or better in three counties in the eastern part of the 18th. In the district's southern end, the 18th covers much of Sangamon County, reaching past soybean and corn farms to take in the northern, mainly white-collar portion of Springfield, the state capital.

1990 Population: 571,580. White 535,359 (94%), Black 29,414 (5%), Other 6,807 (1%). Hispanic origin 5,278 (1%). 18 and over 422,030 (74%), 62 and over 96,813 (17%). Median age: 35.

the Michel team won a moral and public relations victory: The judge explained his decision by calling the delegates' votes "meaningless." (If the delegates' votes are decisive, a re-vote is ordered.)

Michel also succeeded in persuading Speaker Thomas S. Foley to blunt a Democratic effort to curtail floor-speaking privileges known as special orders, which are treasured by conservative Republicans.

Michel became minority leader in 1981, and in the early years of the Reagan presidency, the White House had depended on him for a sense of strategy and timing in passing its budget and tax bills through the Democratic House.

But Michel's job got harder as the Republicans' numbers declined with succeeding elections and as Democrats reunited; he no longer had the working majority of Republicans and "Boll Weevil" Democrats he enjoyed in his first term as leader.

In the years from 1987 to 1993, with Democrats controlling both the House and the Senate and the GOP running the White House, Republicans in both chambers often felt like the odd men out of the agenda-setting process. But because GOP senators had larger individual platforms than did Republican House members, the anxiety was more acute among Michel's troops in the House.

As Clinton entered office, Michel and Senate Minority Leader Bob Dole announced the formation of Republican issue teams composed of conservative academics and former administration staff members to help plot the minority party's legislative strategy.

But all these efforts by Michel may not be

enough to satisfy the rabble-rousers on his right. At bottom, he remains a pragmatic legislator who sees the value of compromise and may not have the stomach for some of the go-for-the-jugular tactics promoted by his lieutenants.

In the opening week of the 103rd, Michel voiced the conflict in himself. First he engaged in a bitter partisan rules fight, then said: "But in every instance, ceremonial or political, mutual respect and good will should be at the heart of our endeavors."

Michel's adaptability, together with members' affection for him and his own instinct for House politics, have combined to carry him into a seventh term as leader. He holds the record for continuous House membership without ever being in the majority.

Just as he once had with Speaker Thomas P. O'Neill Jr., Michel has a competitive but relatively harmonious relationship with Speaker Foley.

The 1991 House bank scandal was a particularly difficult time for Michel. After a group of GOP freshman reformers and New York Times columnist William Safire sparked an uproar that prevented the leadership from dealing with the controversy quietly, Michel struck a deal with Foley to close the bank and order an ethics review. But that did little to quell the furor on the talk shows, fueled by strident calls for "full disclosure" from the freshmen.

Several months later, with several high-ranking Republicans tainted by overdrafts, Michel leaned toward adopting the ethics panel's recommendation to name only the 24 worst offenders. But the confrontational Gingrich faction of the GOP saw election-year help in full disclosure and balked at Michel's conciliatory approach. Their stance carried the day.

The tensions were still evident as Michel acknowledged rifts in GOP leadership in March 1993. "Newt's personality is Newt's, and mine is mine. We each do our own thing. I am not in a position to tell Newt what to say or do."

At the start of the 103rd, rank-and-file Republicans joined primarily Democratic freshmen in a surprising vote to kill the Select Committee on Narcotics. Emboldened by that victory, the group wanted to quickly abolish the remaining select committees, arguing they were redundant and costly. But Michel had instead been crafting a compromise with Foley to extend the panels one more year. (Ultimately, the leaders acquiesced to pressure and dissolved all four.)

Only a few years earlier, in 1989, Michel had been able to persuade his troops to keep sufficiently quiet to allow a pay raise and ethics reform package to pass. With Foley and Michel putting the full weight and prestige of their offices behind it, the proposal passed 252-174, with 84 Republicans voting to approve it.

The most drastic rent in the GOP quilt came in 1990, as Congress and the White House sought to craft an agreement on the fiscal 1991 budget. As pressure grew for high-level talks between congressional leaders and the White House, President Bush retracted his key 1988 campaign promise, saying he would consider a tax increase, though he also wanted a cut in the capital gains tax.

After 4½ months of struggle, Michel was one of five members of Congress who negotiated a final deal. A pivotal moment in the talks came when Michel backed away from including a capital gains proposal in the agreement, saying that Democrats were demanding too much in exchange for it. "The doggone price is too steep," he said. Since Michel was regarded as the president's most loyal soldier on the Hill, his comments were considered devastating for Bush.

But when the budget summit plan came to the floor, Gingrich defected along with most of the party's whip organization, leading a GOP revolt; the plan was rejected 179-254, and the federal government shut down. Congress stayed in session over the Columbus Day weekend to put together a fallback budget resolution.

Michel is hardly one of the House's best orators, and he has no special policy expertise. His parliamentary skills are good, but not unusual. He is neither charismatic nor intimidating. This is how he once described his method for rounding up votes from colleagues: "You can't treat two alike," he once explained. "I know what I can get and what I can't, when to back off and when to push harder. It's not a matter of twisting arms. It's bringing them along by gentle persuasion."

Yet one of his finest moments as Republican leader came in the U.S. military triumph in the Middle East in early 1991.

The World War II combat veteran had joined New York Democrat Stephen J. Solarz to lead the campaign for military force against Iraq. Michel made an emotional plea to members not to forget the lessons of the past: "Those of our generation know from bloody experience that unchecked aggression against a small nation is a prelude to international disaster.... Patience at any price is not a policy. It is a cop-out." The House passed the resolution 250-183, and Michel was the first member of Congress whom Bush notified when the U.S. bombing of Iraq started.

The success of the war resolution helped Michel counter criticism of his legislative style from junior GOP firebrands. In the mid-1980s they began winning national media attention under the banner of the Conservative Opportunity Society (COS).

Michel's initial advice to the militants was to calm down. "It's one thing to be out there on the stump, flapping your gums," he said, "and it is another thing to put something together. Some of the greatest talkers around here can't legislate their way out of a paper bag." In 1984, when Gingrich lambasted 10 Democrats for advocating talks with Nicaragua and O'Neill responded with a rare outburst that brought a rebuke from the presiding officer, many Republicans gave Gingrich a standing ovation. Michel kept his seat.

The current image of Michel as a moderate coming to terms with militant conservatism would surprise anyone familiar with the House in the 1960s, when he was clearly on the GOP right, an orthodox Midwestern Republican decrying wasteful government.

To carry out Reagan's economic program, he had to shelve his traditional conservative view that reducing deficits is a higher priority than reducing taxes. His ties to the moderate wing brought him their support when he ran for party leader in 1981, and they reluctantly backed Reagan's first budget partly as a favor to him.

Most Reaganites had backed Guy Vander Jagt of Michigan for House GOP leader in 1981. But Michel won the 103-87 decision on the same qualities that until recent years traditionally won GOP leadership races — cloakroom companionship, homespun Midwestern conservatism, aptitude for legislative detail and a grasp of the rules.

Like his immediate predecessors, John J. Rhodes and Gerald R. Ford, Michel is a product of the collegial Appropriations Committee. In a quarter-century there, he focused on details rather than broad policy but became an able negotiator in the process.

The Michel-Vander Jagt race began in December 1979, when Rhodes announced his impending retirement. Michel had an advantage among senior members and moderates, but Vander Jagt, as chairman of the campaign committee that donated money to GOP candidates, had the edge among those recently elected.

The 1980 election brought 52 new Republicans, more than even Vander Jagt had imagined. But by giving the GOP control of the White House and Senate, the election actually helped Michel; he argued that Reagan needed a legislative tactician in the House, not a fiery speaker. Vander Jagt got most of the newcomers, but Michel got the leadership job.

At Home: Michel's position at the top of the Republican leadership has earned him the respect, but not the awe, of his constituents. The member from a district centered on the economically challenged industrial city of Peoria, Michel has always had a large number of Democratic and independent-voting constituents. He has thus faced static for supporting Reagan and Bush administration policies that some voters believed were hurtful to the district's blue-collar workers and farmers.

Michel usually wins with votes to spare, but his margins are often unspectacular. His 1992 contest was typical: He defeated an underfunded Democratic challenger, surveyor Ronald C. Hawkins, with 58 percent of the vote (though he ran well ahead of Bush's failing re-election campaign).

The 1992 House campaign was placid compared with the one 10 years earlier, when Michel came as close as he ever has to being unseated. The local economy had hit bottom during the 1982 recession, and the aggressive Democratic nominee, labor lawyer G. Douglas Stephens, blamed it all on Reagan and Michel.

A 31-year-old, first-time candidate, Stephens caught Michel by surprise. Stephens told voters that Michel, in his role as chief mover of Reagan programs in the House, was neglecting the economic problems of the district's factory workers, farmers, small-business people, poor and elderly.

The Democrat criticized Michel particularly for failing to persuade Reagan to lift the United States' Cold War sanctions on selling natural gas pipeline equipment to the Soviet Union — a policy that cost Caterpillar Tractor Co. and other Illinois equipment companies lucrative contracts and exacerbated already high unemployment in Michel's district.

Initially slow to counterattack, Michel retaliated by casting Stephens as a puppet of organized labor. Reagan campaigned for Michel and hinted at the forthcoming removal of sanctions on the pipeline equipment sales. Held to slim majorities in the district's largest counties, Peoria and Tazewell, Michel hung on to win with 52 percent and a cushion of just 6,125 votes, both career lows.

By 1984, the worst of the recession was over and Reagan was more popular. Michel changed his political style, dropping his long-held aversion to trumpeting federal projects he had attained for the district. With Stephens bypassing the contest, Michel went over 60 percent and stayed there in 1986.

Yet Stephens decided to try again in 1988. His comeback bid was predicated on the hope that with the Reagan era ending, 1988 would be a year of Democratic revival. That turned out to be wishful thinking. En route to his presidential victory, George Bush carried the 18th District with 55 percent — a figure matched by Michel.

In 1990, district Democrats gave Michel a rare free pass. However, this was partially in anticipation that Michel might not seek re-election in 1992, either voluntarily or because of redistricting. Illinois was losing two House seats under the 1990 census, and it was rumored that the Democratic-controlled state Legislature would merge Michel's district with that of another member.

But legislators stalemated on the remap, and a federal court panel enacted a GOP-drawn plan that preserved for Michel a Peoria-based district. He ran and went on to his rather routine 1992 victory for a 19th term.

Born in Peoria, the son of a French immigrant factory worker, Michel got his start in politics working for Republican Harold Velde.

Velde became chairman of the old House Un-American Activities Committee during the Republican-dominated 83rd Congress (1953-55) and received much publicity for his hunt for communist subversives; Michel rose to become Velde's administrative assistant.

In 1956 Velde retired, and Michel ran for the seat. Backed by many county GOP organizations, for whom he had been a political contact in Washington, Michel won the primary with 48 percent against four opponents, then took 59 percent in the general election. Until 1982, his campaigns were mainly uneventful. He topped 60 percent several times, slipping as low as 54 percent only during President Lyndon B. Johnson's Democratic landslide in 1964.

Committee

Minority Leader

Joint Organization of Congress

Elections

1992 General

Robert H. Michel (R)	156,533	(58%)
Ronald C. Hawkins (D)	114,413	(42%)

1990 General

Robert H. Michel (R)	105,693	(98%)
Walter Gillin (write-in)	1,524	(1%)

Previous Winning Percentages: **1988** (55%) **1986** (63%) **1984** (61%) **1982** (52%) **1980** (62%) **1978** (66%) **1976** (58%) **1974** (55%) **1972** (65%) **1970** (66%) **1968** (61%) **1966** (58%) **1964** (54%) **1962** (61%) **1960** (59%) **1958** (60%) **1956** (59%)

District Vote for President

1992

D 116,533 (42%)
R 113,227 (41%)
I 46,810 (17%)

Campaign Finance

	Receipts	Receipts from PACs		Expend-itures
1992				
Michel (R)	$646,637	$404,027	(62%)	$636,430
1990				
Michel (R)	$705,878	$519,161	(74%)	$579,258

Key Votes

1993	
Require parental notification of minors' abortions	Y
Require unpaid family and medical leave	N
Approve national "motor voter" registration bill	N
Approve budget increasing taxes and reducing deficit	N
Approve economic stimulus plan	N
1992	
Approve balanced-budget constitutional amendment	Y
Close down space station program	N
Approve U.S. aid for former Soviet Union	Y
Allow shifting funds from defense to domestic programs	N
1991	
Extend unemployment benefits using deficit financing	N
Approve waiting period for handgun purchases	?
Authorize use of force in Persian Gulf	Y

Voting Studies

	Presidential Support		Party Unity		Conservative Coalition	
Year	**S**	**O**	**S**	**O**	**S**	**O**
1992	86	7	82	13	88	4
1991	81	9	78	10	95	0
1990	75	18	78	15	91	6
1989	88	9	75 †	17 †	90	7
1988	64	30	76	14	82	8
1987	77 †	17 †	85 †	9 †	93 †	2 †
1986	74	18	73	20	76	18
1985	85	11	78 †	15 †	91	7
1984	75	20	80	11	90	3
1983	84	7	71 †	20 †	81	15
1982	83	12	81	16	89	10
1981	80	17	82 †	11 †	83	13

† Not eligible for all recorded votes.

Interest Group Ratings

Year	ADA	AFL-CIO	CCUS	ACU
1992	10	25	88	87
1991	0	10	100	89
1990	11	0	71	76
1989	10	18	89	84
1988	10	31	85	92
1987	0	6	86	86
1986	5	8	88	86
1985	5	6	81	86
1984	5	8	81	82
1983	5	12	100	81
1982	5	10	80	82
1981	10	0	100	86

19 Glenn Poshard (D)

Of Carterville — Elected 1988; 3rd Term

Born: Oct. 30, 1945, Herald, Ill.
Education: Southern Illinois U., B.S. 1970, M.S. 1974, Ph.D. 1984.
Military Service: Army, 1962-65.
Occupation: Educator.
Family: Wife, Jo Roetzel; two children.
Religion: Baptist.
Political Career: Sought Democratic nomination for Ill. Senate, 1982; Ill. Senate, 1984-89.
Capitol Office: 107 Cannon Bldg. 20515; 225-5201.

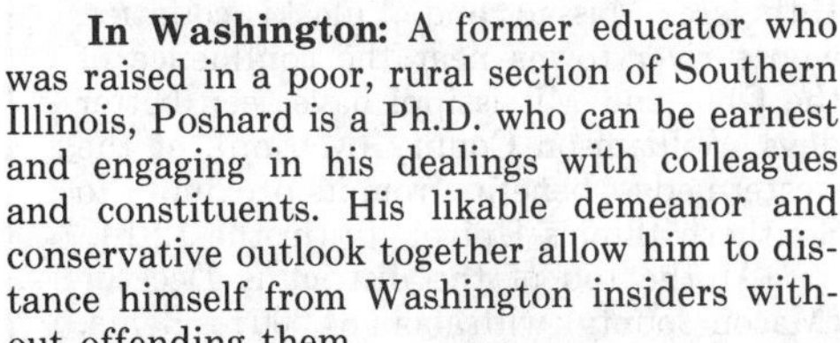

In Washington: A former educator who was raised in a poor, rural section of Southern Illinois, Poshard is a Ph.D. who can be earnest and engaging in his dealings with colleagues and constituents. His likable demeanor and conservative outlook together allow him to distance himself from Washington insiders without offending them.

That ability was vital to his return to Washington in 1993. Two terms into a career in the House, Poshard was pitted against fellow Democratic Rep. Terry L. Bruce in the district remapping that followed the 1990 census. Rejecting political action committee money and introducing legislation to ban such contributions and eliminate taxpayer-financed newsletters, Poshard successfully cast himself as an outsider and a populist who could still be an effective citizen-legislator.

While he votes like a traditional labor Democrat to meet the pressing economic needs of his rural district, Poshard can also be something of an outsider in his own party on certain social issues. He opposes abortion in most circumstances, and in early 1993, he opposed lifting the ban on gays serving in the military.

Poshard also endorses such conservative budgetary tools as the line-item veto and the balanced-budget amendment, yet he remains in the Democratic fold on most economic issues. In early 1993, he supported President Clinton on both the budget resolution and the stimulus package — and the year before he stood with House Democratic leaders for their tax bill and the effort to bring down the budget walls that prohibited defense dollars from being converted to domestic programs.

Overall, Poshard votes with a majority of Democrats roughly 80 percent of the time, a percentage close to the average for House Democrats. His opposition is generally quiet and closely tied to his district's conservative social posture or direct economic interests. One of his rare high-profile votes against the Democratic leadership was on the Clean Air Act in 1990. Stressing the devastating effect the legislation would have on his coal-mining district, he was one of 20 House members to oppose the bill.

On issues that fall outside the social or economic paradigm, Poshard often finds himself, after some deliberation, siding naturally with his Democratic colleagues. In early 1991 he voted against the use of force in the Persian Gulf, and in 1990 he opposed a constitutional amendment to ban flag desecration. The flag issue took some time to resolve itself in Poshard's mind. Having initially backed the amendment, Poshard later said that trips to Philadelphia and Gettysburg led him to conclude that First Amendment protection of freedom of speech extended to flag burning.

After serving his first term on the Education and Labor panel — a natural given his doctorate and years of practice in educational administration — Poshard switched to the Public Works Committee in 1991, where he is better able to help his mostly rural constituents. Congressional turnover quickly moved him to the middle tier on the panel, but a gavel likely remains years away from Poshard. He also serves on the Small Business panel.

Poshard drew national attention when he questioned the Navy's handling of the investigation of the April 1989 explosion aboard the USS *Iowa*. Unofficial news leaks from the Navy implicated Petty Officer Kendall Truitt, a constituent, in a murder-suicide pact with Clayton Hartwig, a sailor who died in the blast. Poshard questioned the source of the leaks and cited the need to protect Truitt's rights. After much publicity, the inquiry into Truitt's role was dropped and his name cleared.

At Home: When Democratic Rep. Kenneth J. Gray of the then-22nd District decided not to run in 1988, Poshard was the party's obvious pick. There were sharp contrasts between Gray and his successor. Gray, known for his flashy clothes and boisterous personality, never attended college and had worked as a car dealer and auctioneer.

But for all his academic and professional background, Poshard has working-class roots.

Illinois 19

Rural — Southern counties; Decatur

The northern part of the 19th is a familiar landscape of downstate Illinois. At the edge of the district is its only large city, Decatur, where heavy industry and grain processing plants employ a large blue-collar work force. For miles south, flat land produces corn and soybeans.

The southern part of the district, though, is different. The hilly territory produces coal and timber. Portions of this "border state" area are Appalachian-like. Of the 11 southernmost counties in the 19th, six have poverty rates above 20 percent.

This region was settled from the south and has a strong Southern Democratic tradition that tends to predominate in the 19th. Rep. Poshard, a native of rural White County, has staked his political success on an agenda that combines a populist economic message with conservative views on social issues.

Poshard, who had to defeat fellow Democratic Rep. Terry L. Bruce in a 1992 primary forced by redistricting, carried every district county in the general election. He is hugely popular in his base in the southern part of the district; he won four counties there with better than 80 percent of the vote.

Bill Clinton also carried the 11 southern counties in 1992. Although there is a Republican base in the heavily farmed northern part (which enabled George Bush to narrowly carry the 19th in 1988), Clinton won most counties there by pluralities.

Bush won just four of the district's 27 counties, three of them in a band across the 19th's midsection. One of these counties, Edwards, was one of two won by Republican Lynn Martin in her ill-fated 1990 challenge to Democratic Sen. Paul Simon. Although there are few blacks in the 19th, Democrat Carol Moseley-Braun carried 18 counties in her 1992 Senate bid.

Four of Illinois' 10 leading coal-producing counties are in the southern part of the 19th. Steady demand for coal has been offset in recent years by job losses caused by mechanization; unemployment is an endemic problem in much of the region.

Pope, Illinois' least populous county, is almost entirely within the Shawnee National Forest. At the southern tip of the 19th are Massac and Pulaski counties, whose river towns near the confluence of the Ohio and Mississippi have seen better days. Williamson County (Marion), at the western edge, benefits from its proximity to Southern Illinois University (in the 12th).

At the top of the district is Decatur (Macon County); with about 84,000 residents, the city is more populous than any of the 19th's other counties. Corn and soybean processors Archer Daniels Midland and A. E. Staley are economic mainstays, although a Caterpillar plant is the city's largest single employer. Industrial downsizing has taken a toll on Decatur. The city usually reinforces the southern Democratic vote.

In between is mainly farming country, dotted with such small cities as Mattoon and Effingham. Charleston, hometown of GOP Gov. Jim Edgar, is the site of Eastern Illinois University (10,500 students).

1990 Population: 571,530. White 546,051 (96%), Black 22,086 (4%), Other 3,393 (1%). Hispanic origin 2,727 (<1%). 18 and over 429,589 (75%), 62 and over 116,422 (20%). Median age: 36.

Like Gray, he favors a populist style that appeals to the district's coal-mining communities and Ohio River towns. Poshard had honed this appeal in five years in the state Senate, and it carried him to a series of easy general election victories.

Poshard's first run for office, in 1982, was a primary challenge to a veteran Democratic state senator. Though he fell short, Poshard's ability to address blue-collar concerns impressed party officials. When the senator died in mid-1984, district Democratic leaders picked Poshard for the vacancy.

Poshard went on to win two state Senate contests on his own. He specialized in education, labor, rural health care and coal-related issues in Springfield. Some colleagues complained that Poshard was too much a young man in a hurry. But he was named keynote speaker for the 1986 state party convention and chairman of the Senate Labor and Commerce Committee.

When Poshard decided he would try to succeed Gray in 1988, no Democrat stood in his way. His GOP foe, law professor Patrick Kelley, was articulate but little-known outside Carbondale, where he had served two terms on the City Council. Kelley's efforts to frame the election as an ideological contest were easily deflected by Poshard, who is opposed to abortion and supportive of school prayer. Poshard won with 65 percent of the vote. In 1990, he had no GOP opponent and collected 84 percent of the vote.

It appeared in early 1992 that a bad deal in redistricting would halt Poshard's rise. Instead, the ensuing campaign raised Poshard's reputation as a star campaigner higher than ever.

With Illinois losing two House seats following the 1990 census, Poshard was thrown into the new 19th District with fellow Democratic Rep. Terry L. Bruce. Poshard appeared disadvantaged: Bruce brought more of his former constituents into the district and, as a member of the Energy and Commerce Committee, had a much stronger fundraising base.

But Poshard was exceedingly strong on his turf and had ties beyond: His White County boyhood home gave him a beachhead in what had been Bruce's district. Even more essential was a campaign theme that was in tune with the electorate. Anti-insider sentiment in Illinois was peaking at the time of the March 1992 primary. Though an incumbent himself, Poshard ran as an outsider, declined PAC contributions and tied Bruce to special interests that had dealings with Energy and Commerce.

Poshard ran up 90 percent of the vote in the area he had represented. But he also edged Bruce on Bruce's own turf. Only in the northern end of the district, territory new to both, did Poshard run behind. Aided by the district's Democratic tilt, Poshard breezed by Republican lawyer Douglas E. Lee in the general election.

Committees

Public Works & Transportation (19th of 39 Democrats)
Surface Transportation; Water Resources & the Environment

Small Business (12th of 27 Democrats)
Rural Enterprises, Exports & the Environment; SBA Legislation & the General Economy

Elections

1992 General		
Glenn Poshard (D)	187,156	(69%)
Douglas E. Lee (R)	83,526	(31%)
1992 Primary		
Glenn Poshard (D)	57,566	(62%)
Terry L. Bruce (D)	35,574	(38%)
1990 General		
Glenn Poshard (D)	138,425	(84%)
Jim Wham (Jim Wham Party)	26,896	(16%)

Previous Winning Percentage: 1988 (65%)

District Vote for President

1992

D 131,631 (47%)
R 95,780 (34%)
I 50,705 (18%)

Campaign Finance

	Receipts	Receipts from PACs		Expend-itures
1992				
Poshard (D)	$317,043	0		$312,530
Lee (R)	$27,203	0		$25,303
1990				
Poshard (D)	$68,078	$5,150	(8%)	$103,396
Wham (Jim Wham Party)	$26,137	0		$16,737

Key Votes

1993	
Require parental notification of minors' abortions	Y
Require unpaid family and medical leave	Y
Approve national "motor voter" registration bill	Y
Approve budget increasing taxes and reducing deficit	Y
Approve economic stimulus plan	Y
1992	
Approve balanced-budget constitutional amendment	Y
Close down space station program	Y
Approve U.S. aid for former Soviet Union	N
Allow shifting funds from defense to domestic programs	Y
1991	
Extend unemployment benefits using deficit financing	Y
Approve waiting period for handgun purchases	N
Authorize use of force in Persian Gulf	N

Voting Studies

	Presidential Support		Party Unity		Conservative Coalition	
Year	**S**	**O**	**S**	**O**	**S**	**O**
1992	30	70	79	20	48	52
1991	30	70	79	19	57	43
1990	23	77	85	14	43	57
1989	35	65	79	20	41	59

Interest Group Ratings

Year	ADA	AFL-CIO	CCUS	ACU
1992	65	83	25	36
1991	65	75	30	25
1990	78	92	29	29
1989	80	92	40	21

20 Richard J. Durbin (D)

Of Springfield — Elected 1982; 6th Term

Born: Nov. 21, 1944, East St. Louis, Ill.
Education: Georgetown U., B.S.F.S. 1966, J.D. 1969.
Occupation: Lawyer; congressional and legislative aide.
Family: Wife, Loretta Schaefer; three children.
Religion: Roman Catholic.
Political Career: Democratic nominee for Ill. Senate, 1976; Democratic nominee for lieutenant governor, 1978.
Capitol Office: 2463 Rayburn Bldg. 20515; 225-5271.

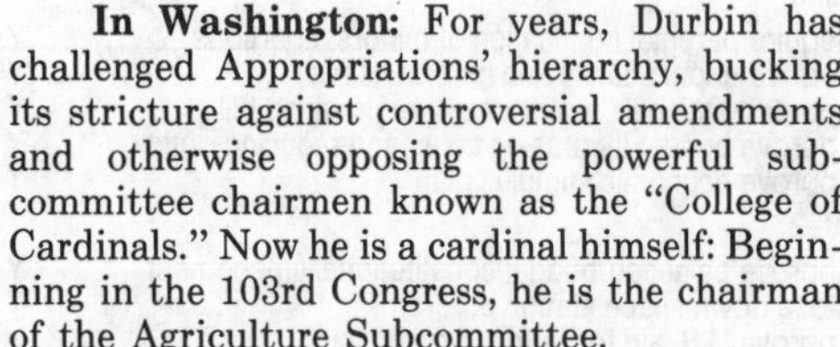

In Washington: For years, Durbin has challenged Appropriations' hierarchy, bucking its stricture against controversial amendments and otherwise opposing the powerful subcommittee chairmen known as the "College of Cardinals." Now he is a cardinal himself: Beginning in the 103rd Congress, he is the chairman of the Agriculture Subcommittee.

Durbin was lifted into the inner circle when the Democratic Caucus ousted the ailing Jamie L. Whitten of Mississippi from his chairmanship of the full committee; Appropriations Democrats then took away his Agriculture chair. Durbin's accession, and that of Bob Carr of Michigan (who took the helm of the Transportation Subcommittee), foreshadow a changing of the old guard of the Appropriations Committee. The movement may culminate in time with a bid for the full committee chairmanship by fifth-ranking David R. Obey of Wisconsin, a hard-charging reformer.

Durbin came to Congress with an understanding of its rules and a knack for playing its internal politics — a combination that has given him the savvy and self-assurance to act the parts of both insider and insurgent. He is well acquainted with legislative procedure, having been a parliamentarian of the Illinois Senate. Like a number of Democrats first elected in the 1982 recession, he is a budget-conscious liberal trying to rebuild his party's fiscal credibility. He quickly emerged as a popular figure among younger House members, while forging ties with current leaders that got him a prize seat on Appropriations in his second term.

Durbin is well placed on Appropriations to look after his district, which has both farmland and urban areas such as Springfield. Combining his roles on the Agriculture and Transportation subcommittees, Durbin is a spokesman for ethanol-based fuels, which are made from corn. He is co-chairman of the Alcohol Fuels Caucus.

By tradition, Appropriations operates on collegiality and stability. Durbin, however, set a perilous course in only his third year on the committee by taking on two of its most popular and influential members. The ensuing fight handed Durbin the victory of a lifetime when the 101st Congress approved a permanent ban on cigarette smoking on domestic airline flights.

The battle pitted the upstart against two Appropriations subcommittee chairmen, the tobacco lobby and conventional wisdom. But Durbin succeeded in putting Congress on record for the first time proscribing smoking for health reasons.

Durbin, whose chain-smoking father died of lung cancer when Durbin was 14, was roused to action in 1987 after taking a Phoenix-to-Chicago flight on which he had to sit between two smokers. He first tried to get the Appropriations Committee to approve an amendment to ban smoking on all flights. When that was defeated, he limited the ban and carried the battle to the House floor, a step akin to airing family laundry for an Appropriations member.

After an emotional debate, the House passed Durbin's measure, 198-193, surprising even him. With support from New Jersey Sen. Frank R. Lautenberg, chairman of the Transportation Appropriations Subcommittee, a similar measure passed in the Senate. The compromise that became law banned smoking on flights of two hours or less for a two-year trial period.

In the 101st Congress, Durbin bypassed the Appropriations Committee altogether, going instead to the Rules Committee with a request to offer a total ban as a floor amendment to the transportation spending bill. Rules rejected this, but with the acquiescence of the tobacco lobby — which was hoping to limit its losses — Durbin was allowed to offer an amendment making the existing ban permanent. It passed the House handily, and the Senate passed a total ban. Conferees agreed to the tougher language, excluding only a small number of flights, after Durbin threatened to bring his fight back to the floor on the conference report. The ban went into effect Feb. 25, 1991.

Two cardinals who will never forget this episode are Natcher and W. G. "Bill" Hefner, from the tobacco states of Kentucky and North Carolina, respectively. Natcher has since be-

Illinois 20

West Central — Part of Springfield; Collinsville

The 20th takes in a border-state portion of Illinois; its western edge lies along the Mississippi River, across from Missouri. Its Southern Democratic traditions are maintained by blue-collar voters near the Mississippi, many of the state employees in Springfield and coal industry workers in the southern part of the 20th.

This is a Democratic district, but the prevailing political tone is moderate-to-conservative, which means the 20th is not completely out of reach for the GOP; George Bush narrowly won here in 1988. The district has a portion of Springfield (the rest is in the 18th District), but otherwise there are no large cities, and there are few minority-group residents. Typically the farm-country constituency is Republican.

Still, in 1992, the 20th returned to Democratic form. Bill Clinton defeated Bush by a wide margin in 16 of the 19 counties, winning majorities in four. Senate winner Carol Moseley-Braun also ran well; Rep. Durbin, who became a politically dominant figure in the region during the 1980s, won by more than 35,000 votes, overcoming a tough challenger and a new, sharply changed district map.

Population is diffuse in the 20th. The section of Madison County in the district has about 20 percent of the total; the part of Sangamon County (Springfield) in the 20th is close behind. But the remaining residents are spread across 15 counties and parts of two others.

About half of Madison County's residents are in the 20th. Although most of the county's industry is located in the 12th District, the factories provide jobs for many residents in such 20th District communities as Edwardsville, Collinsville and Glen Carbon. Edwardsville is the site of a Southern Illinois University campus (11,800 students).

The southern part of Springfield, the state capital, is the 20th's largest single urban area; about two-thirds of the city's 105,000 residents are in the 20th. Nearly a fifth of these constituents are black, by far the largest minority concentration in the district.

The state government payroll provides economic stability, as do the city's academic institutions, Sangamon State University and Southern Illinois University's medical school. The county also has some industry.

The economy is not nearly as generous in some of the district's less populous areas, which have had bouts of double-digit unemployment in recent years. The jobless rate in sparsely populated Calhoun County, on the Mississippi, is among the highest in Illinois.

Farming is widespread through the district's more rural counties. Adams and Pike counties, in the northwest corner, are major livestock producers; nearby Scott County, also rural, stayed with Bush in 1992. Near the southern end is Illinois' wheat belt.

In Clinton and Washington counties, farms give way to coal mines. A rural Republican vote prevails in Washington. But neighboring Jefferson, a leading coal-producing county, is a Democratic stronghold.

1990 Population: 571,480. White 542,965 (95%), Black 23,928 (4%), Other 4,587 (1%). Hispanic origin 3,749 (1%). 18 and over 424,776 (74%), 62 and over 106,712 (19%). Median age: 35.

come the full Appropriations Committee chairman.

"It was clear to me from the start that there were political risks involved . . . because of the grudges that might result," Durbin said afterward. But so far, broad public support for his efforts has tempered any retribution.

Durbin continued his fight against cigarette smoking in the 102nd Congress, when he and Lautenberg sponsored legislation to require federally funded facilities that serve children to set up separately ventilated smoking areas to protect children from secondhand smoke.

He also joined with Minnesota Democrat Timothy J. Penny in attacking a proposal to permit smoking in Veterans Administration hospitals and to require VA health-care facilities to sell cigarettes. "How in God's name can we do this?" Durbin said. The House ultimately agreed to a compromise amendment by West Virginia Democrat Bob Wise that struck the provision requiring cigarette sales in VA facilities but kept the language mandating indoor smoking areas.

Durbin's geniality, articulate argument and sense of fair play have been enough to spare him the harsh judgment of colleagues, but they have not been enough to earn him a place on the party leadership ladder. He finished last in a four-way race for Democratic Caucus vice chairman in June 1989. He was mentioned in 1990 as a possible candidate for the chairmanship of the Democratic Congressional Campaign Committee but did not run.

Although Durbin is not a member of the Appropriations subcommittees that handle foreign aid or defense spending, he makes himself heard in foreign policy and defense debates. He chaired the Budget Committee Task Force on Defense, Foreign Policy and Space in the 102nd Congress, his last term on the committee.

Early in 1991, as the country headed toward war with Iraq, Durbin joined with Florida Democrat Charles E. Bennett to introduce a resolution asserting congressional war-making powers. "The decision to go to war should not be left to one man," the two wrote. With little controversy, the resolution passed 302-131. While Durbin argued passionately against the use of force, he said the subsequent congressional vote on that issue demonstrated that "the Constitution prevailed."

Early in 1991, Durbin called on the Bush administration to exert more pressure on the Soviet Union to withdraw from the Baltic States. A first-generation Lithuanian-American, Durbin a year earlier had led a congressional delegation to Lithuania; the delegation had hoped to observe the elections, but visa problems delayed their arrival until after the voting. He and Maryland Democrat Benjamin J. Cardin introduced legislation in early 1991 to withhold most-favored-nation trade status from the Soviets until they recognized the Baltic republics of Lithuania, Latvia and Estonia. The breakup of the Soviet Union saw the goals of congressional backers of Baltic independence finally realized.

In 1992, Durbin led an assault on the antimissile Strategic Defense Initiative. His proposal, which would have sliced nearly $1 billion from the $4.3 billion recommended by the Armed Services Committee for SDI, was rejected 161-211. But his effort to trim $700 million from the project failed by only 16 votes, 201-217.

He also opposed funding for two big-ticket science projects, the $8 billion-plus superconducting super collider and the $30 billion-plus space station, both of which have been plagued by massive cost overruns. Of the latter, he said, "If we fund this, it's clearly not for scientific projects, it's for the contractors who work on the project," adding that it had "become a WPA [Works Projects Administration] project for the aerospace industry."

Durbin made national headlines when he took to the floor, as colleagues debated a proposed constitutional amendment to ban flag desecration, to decry "the desecration of a great American symbol ... the baseball bat." His lampooning referred to baseball purists opposed to the shift away from wooden bats toward aluminum bats. "Are we ready to see the Louisville Slugger replaced by the aluminum ping dinger?" he asked. "Is nothing sacred?"

Humor aside, Durbin's vocal opposition to the flag amendment was consistent with his increasingly outspoken partisanship. During debate in 1992 on a constitutional amendment to mandate a balanced budget, Durbin offered a catastrophic view in opposition: "This amendment is the direct result of the mismanagement and misguided policies of Presidents Ronald Reagan and George Bush.... This amendment is Ronald Reagan's revenge.... He left a deficit behind him that is nothing short of a time bomb.... It's an act of political desperation that will haunt us for generations."

Early in the 103rd Congress, as Republican Dan Burton of Indiana was holding up floor proceedings on President Clinton's budget resolution by forcing a series of time-wasting roll-call votes, Durbin asked for a ruling on whether it "would be a violation of the House rules to characterize a member as petulant and puerile for continuing to call a series of unnecessary roll-call votes...."

Durbin opposes abortion, and he had opposed federal funding of abortion even in cases of rape and incest. But in 1989, with heightened attention on the issue, Durbin said his past votes had "haunted" him. After meeting with victims of incest in his district, he supported federal abortion funding for poor women who were victims of rape or incest or whose lives were in danger. In 1991, he reversed his opposition to permitting privately paid abortions in overseas military hospitals.

At Home: Durbin got to the House in 1982 by narrowly upsetting 11-term GOP Rep. Paul N. Findley, winning by 1,410 votes. As he rose rapidly to become a key player in the House, Durbin also became firmly ensconced in his district. He topped 60 percent in 1984 and hit two-thirds of the vote in his next three campaigns.

The 1992 election reintroduced Durbin to competitive politics. Redistricting had given him a district in which more than half the constituents were new to him, and he faced a tough young challenger in Madison County Treasurer John M. Shimkus. In the end, however, Durbin won a sixth term with room to spare.

By doing so, Durbin overcame the kind of circumstances to which Findley had fallen victim a decade earlier. The earlier remap had given Findley 175,000 new constituents and a district with a slight Democratic lean. Findley was also unfortunate in drawing so seasoned a challenger as Durbin, who had been an aide to Paul Simon (then the lieutenant governor) in 1969, and then top assistant to the state Senate leadership. Although he lost bids for state Senate in 1976 and lieutenant governor in 1978, those contests turned out to be training grounds.

The 20th District's farm and industrial sectors had been hit hard by the 1982 recession, and Durbin laid some blame at Findley's feet. Durbin also benefited from financing by pro-Israel groups offended by Findley's liaisons with the Palestine Liberation Organization. He sneaked through with barely 50 percent. Findley would later write a book excoriating the influence of the "Israel lobby," which he blamed in large part for his defeat.

After coasting through routine re-election contests, Durbin found himself the subject of an incumbent-bashing campaign in 1992. With polls showing voters unhappy with Congress, Shimkus called for congressional reform and chastised Durbin for having 12 overdrafts at the House bank. One Shimkus ad depicted members of Congress as pigs at a trough.

Durbin showed that his campaign reflexes had not slowed. A Durbin ad criticized Shimkus, who had won the county treasurer's post in 1990, for spending $31,000 on new office furnishings.

In August, President Bush set out on what he said would be a campaign to defeat Democratic House members and went to Springfield to make Durbin one of his first targets. The visit was supposed to be a boon to Shimkus. But Durbin shrugged off Bush's portrayal of him as too liberal and used the occasion to link Shimkus to Bush policies that were unpopular locally.

Durbin also worked hard to introduce himself to those voters who, because of redistricting, were unfamiliar with him. Although Shimkus, a 34-year-old West Point graduate, was an appealing candidate, he was far less known than Durbin outside his Madison County base.

Durbin ended up with nearly 57 percent. He won big in the holdover parts of the district and ran well overall, carrying 17 counties and losing the other two by close margins.

Committee

Appropriations (17th of 37 Democrats)
Agriculture, Rural Development, FDA & Related Agencies (chairman); District of Columbia; Transportation

Elections

1992 General		
Richard J. Durbin (D)	154,869	(57%)
John M. Shimkus (R)	119,219	(43%)
1990 General		
Richard J. Durbin (D)	130,114	(66%)
Paul E. Jurgens (R)	66,433	(34%)

Previous Winning Percentages: **1988** (69%) **1986** (68%) **1984** (61%) **1982** (50%)

District Vote for President

1992
D 130,673 (46%)
R 94,960 (34%)
I 56,004 (20%)

Campaign Finance

	Receipts	Receipts from PACs		Expend-itures
1992				
Durbin (D)	$666,110	$420,402	(63%)	$921,659
Shimkus (R)	$281,184	$44,271	(16%)	$278,357
1990				
Durbin (D)	$338,066	$207,978	(62%)	$209,360
Jurgens (R)	$44,565	$10,500	(24%)	$44,861

Key Votes

1993	
Require parental notification of minors' abortions	N
Require unpaid family and medical leave	Y
Approve national "motor voter" registration bill	Y
Approve budget increasing taxes and reducing deficit	Y
Approve economic stimulus plan	Y
1992	
Approve balanced-budget constitutional amendment	N
Close down space station program	Y
Approve U.S. aid for former Soviet Union	N
Allow shifting funds from defense to domestic programs	Y
1991	
Extend unemployment benefits using deficit financing	Y
Approve waiting period for handgun purchases	Y
Authorize use of force in Persian Gulf	N

Voting Studies

	Presidential Support		Party Unity		Conservative Coalition	
Year	S	O	S	O	S	O
1992	12	86	93	5	21	77
1991	25	73	92	6	30	70
1990	16	83	91	6	26	74
1989	24	76	95	4	12	88
1988	24	76	88	9	18	82
1987	13	84	91	5	19	77
1986	17	82	90	9	22	78
1985	28	73	79	19	20	78
1984	32	66	82	18	29	69
1983	13	85	77	17	31	69

Interest Group Ratings

Year	ADA	AFL-CIO	CCUS	ACU
1992	90	83	13	4
1991	95	92	30	5
1990	83	92	31	4
1989	95	83	30	4
1988	90	100	36	16
1987	92	94	0	4
1986	85	93	22	14
1985	65	82	36	19
1984	70	85	31	13
1983	85	76	20	13

Indiana

STATE DATA

Governor: Evan Bayh (D)
First elected: 1988
Length of term: 4 years
Term expires: 1/97
Salary: $77,200 — accepts $66,000
Term limit: 2 terms
Phone: (317) 232-4567
Born: Dec. 26, 1955; Terre Haute, Ind.
Education: Indiana U., B.S. 1978; U. of Virginia, J.D. 1981
Occupation: Lawyer
Family: Wife, Susan Breshears
Religion: Christian
Political Career: Ind. secretary of state, 1986-89

Lt. Gov.: Frank L. O'Bannon (D)
First elected: 1988
Length of term: 4 years
Term expires: 1/97
Salary: $64,000 + $11,600 for serving as head of Senate
Phone: (317) 232-4545

State election official: (317) 232-6531
Democratic headquarters: (317) 231-7100
Republican headquarters: (317) 635-7561

REDISTRICTING

Indiana retained its 10 House seats in reapportionment. The legislature passed the map June 13, 1991; the governor signed it June 14.

STATE LEGISLATURE

General Assembly. First session meets for 90 days between January and April; second session, 30 days between January and March.

Senate: 50 members, 4-year terms
1992 breakdown: 28R, 22D; 37 men, 13 women; 46 whites, 4 blacks
Salary: $11,600
Phone: (317) 232-9400

House of Representatives: 100 members, 2-year terms
1992 breakdown: 55D, 45R; 84 men, 16 women; 92 whites, 7 blacks, 1 Hispanic
Salary: $11,600
Phone: (317) 232-9700

URBAN STATISTICS

City	Pop.
Indianapolis	731,327
Mayor Stephen Goldsmith, R	
Fort Wayne	172,986
Mayor Paul Helmke, R	
Evansville	126,272
Mayor Frank F. McDonald II, D	
Gary	116,646
Mayor Thomas V. Barnes, D	
South Bend	105,511
Mayor Joseph Kernan, D	

U.S. CONGRESS

Senate: 0 D, 2 R
House: 7 D, 3 R

TERM LIMITS

For Congress: No
For state offices: No

ELECTIONS

1992 Presidential Vote

George Bush	42.9%
Bill Clinton	36.8%
Ross Perot	19.8%

1988 Presidential Vote

George Bush	60%
Michael S. Dukakis	40%

1984 Presidential Vote

Ronald Reagan	62%
Walter F. Mondale	38%

POPULATION

1990		5,544,159
1980		5,490,224
Percent change		+1%
Rank among states:		14
White		91%
Black		8%
Hispanic		2%
Asian or Pacific islander		1%
Urban		65%
Rural		35%
Born in state		71%
Foreign-born		2%
Under age 18	1,455,964	26%
Ages 18-64	3,391,999	61%
65 and older	696,196	13%
Median age		32.8

MISCELLANEOUS

Capital: Indianapolis
Number of counties: 92
Per capita income: $17,217 (1991)
Rank among states: 32
Total area: 36,185 sq. miles
Rank among states: 38

Indiana - Congressional Districts

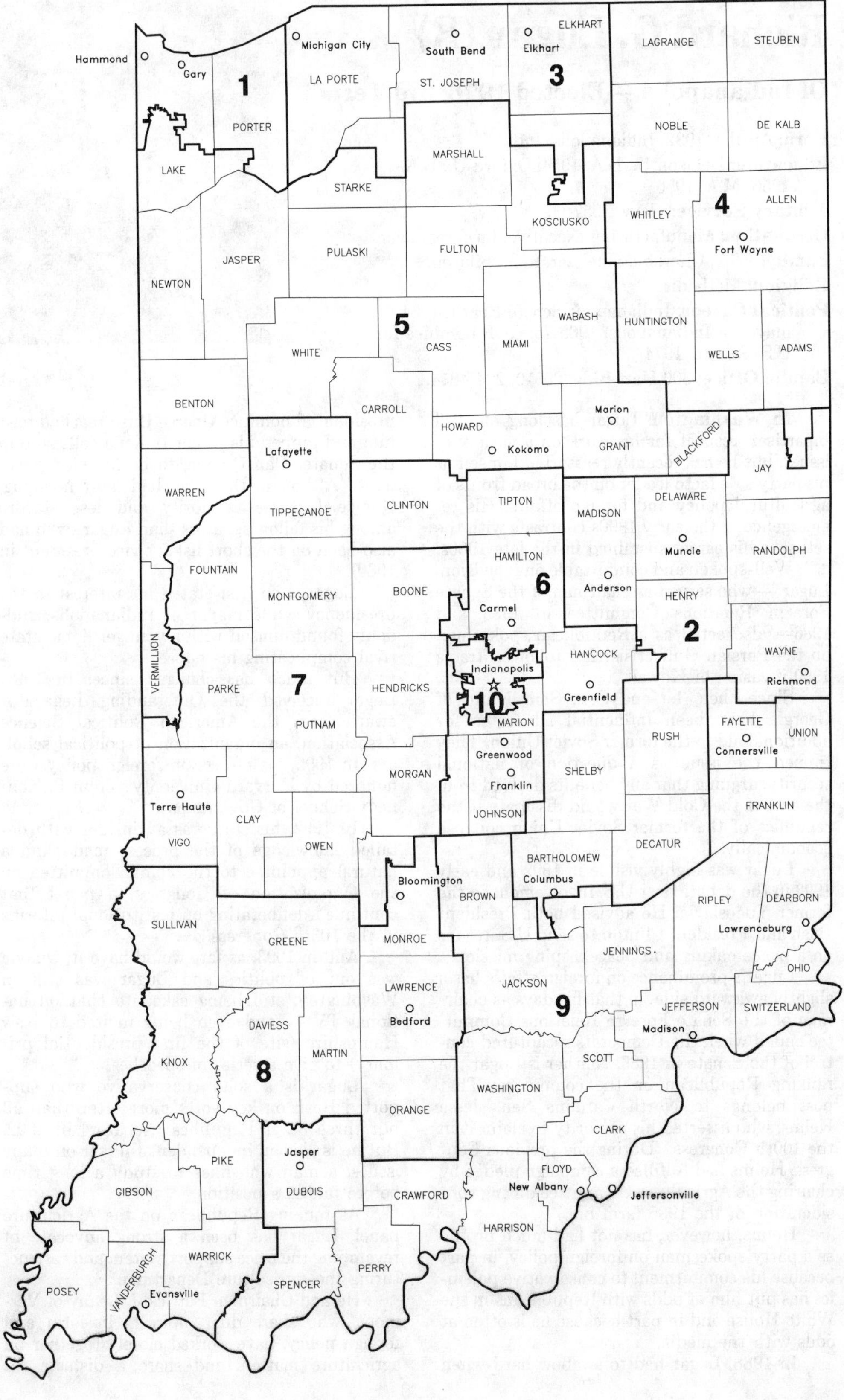

Indiana - Senior Senator

Richard G. Lugar (R)

Of Indianapolis — Elected 1976; 3rd Term

Born: April 4, 1932, Indianapolis, Ind.

Education: Denison U., B.A. 1954; Oxford U., B.A. 1956, M.A. 1956.

Military Service: Navy, 1957-60.

Occupation: Manufacturing executive; farm manager.

Family: Wife, Charlene Smeltzer; four children.

Religion: Methodist.

Political Career: Indianapolis School Board, 1964-67; mayor of Indianapolis, 1968-75; GOP nominee for U.S. Senate, 1974.

Capitol Office: 306 Hart Bldg. 20510; 224-4814.

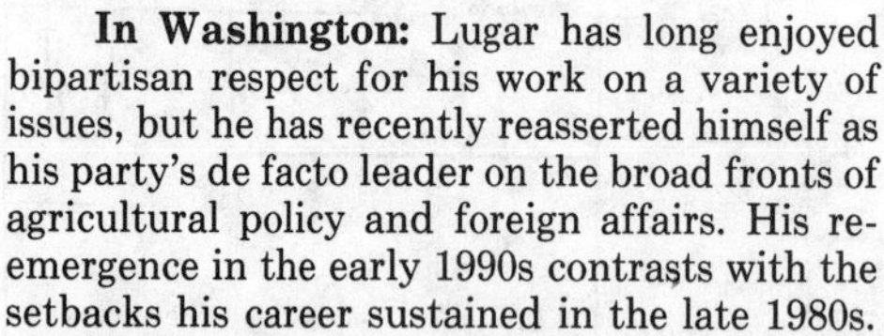

In Washington: Lugar has long enjoyed bipartisan respect for his work on a variety of issues, but he has recently reasserted himself as his party's de facto leader on the broad fronts of agricultural policy and foreign affairs. His re-emergence in the early 1990s contrasts with the setbacks his career sustained in the late 1980s.

Well-spoken and comfortable on television, Lugar — who served as chairman of the Senate Foreign Relations Committee in 1985 and 1986— also acted as a Republican spokesman on the Persian Gulf crisis that followed Iraq's 1990 invasion of Kuwait.

Since then, he and Sen. Sam Nunn of Georgia have been influential advocates for additional aid to the former Soviet Union. They framed the issue as a question of national security, arguing that any benefits derived from the end of the Cold War would dissipate if the republics of the former Soviet Union collapse economically.

Lugar was highly visible in 1992 and early 1993 in the debate over U.S. involvement in the former Yugoslavia. He advised both President Bush and President Clinton to send U.S. troops on a peacemaking and peacekeeping mission.

Lugar's prominence on foreign affairs has a slightly awkward side, in that his days as chairman of the Senate Foreign Relations Committee ended when the Democrats recaptured control of the Senate in 1986. Neither is Lugar the ranking Republican on the committee. That post belongs to North Carolina Sen. Jesse Helms, who asserted his seniority to claim it in the 100th Congress. (During the previous Congress, Helms had fulfilled a campaign pledge by chairing the Agriculture Committee during consideration of the 1985 farm bill.)

Helms, however, has not had much profile as a party spokesman on foreign policy, in part because his commitment to conservative polemics has put him at odds with Republicans in the White House and in part because he is often at odds with the media.

In 1988, Lugar had to swallow hard when presidential nominee George Bush reached past him and tapped his junior Indiana colleague in the Senate, Dan Quayle, to be his vice president. Although the two had gotten along, Quayle had less seniority and less stature among his fellow senators than Lugar (who had also been on the short list for vice president in 1980).

Lugar, who first stated his interest in the presidency while mayor of Indianapolis, suddenly found himself with a younger home-state rival complicating his hopes.

But much has changed since. In 1991, Lugar received the Outstanding Legislator award from the American Political Science Association, an organization of political scholars. In 1992, his efforts on foreign policy were honored by Harvard University's John F. Kennedy School of Government.

In 1992, his status as an insider with detailed knowledge of the process made him a natural appointee to the Joint Committee on the Organization of Congress, a panel that continued deliberating on institutional reforms in the 103rd Congress.

And in 1993, as fate would have it, Quayle was out of politics and Lugar was still in Washington, still being asked to chat on national TV — and even being invited to New Hampshire (site of the first presidential primary) to give a series of speeches.

Lugar is a solid conservative who supported Bush on key votes more often than all but three other Republican senators in 1992. But he is also an independent thinker on many issues, a man who likes to study a long time before taking a position.

As ranking Republican on the Agriculture panel, Lugar has been a strong advocate of revamping the price support system and restructuring the Agriculture Department.

He and Chairman Patrick J. Leahy of Vermont, who share dual interests in farm and foreign policy, have worked closely together on agriculture matters and share a distaste for farm subsidies.

The Bush administration was reluctant to dramatically alter policy and fought off efforts to close down some agricultural field offices (a Leahy-Lugar goal). And while Clinton administration Secretary of Agriculture Mike Espy has expressed support for Lugar and Leahy's ideas, no immediate action was taken in early 1993.

Lugar's chief assignment during the 101st Congress was the five-year reauthorization of the federal government's agriculture, soil-conservation and nutrition programs.

Lugar had already developed a close working relationship with Leahy. Before becoming Agriculture chairman in 1987, Leahy had devoted much of his time to other assignments and was happy to tap Lugar's detailed knowledge of agriculture policy. The bill passed in 1987 to bail out the nation's farm credit system bore Lugar's strong imprint.

Despite their differing partisan perspectives, Leahy and Lugar had the same basic goal: to produce a fiscally lean farm bill. Leahy looked to fashion agreements that could draw bipartisan support and avert the threat of a Bush veto; Lugar, who is philosophically opposed to farm-income subsidies, was determined to block efforts to boost spending on the programs.

Lugar's free-market approach is unusual on a committee whose members — Republicans and Democrats alike — tend to favor increased subsidies and trade favors for their constituents' programs. Given the integral role of the federal government in farm-income support, which was reinforced by the 1985 farm bill, Lugar recognized that his hope for a strictly market-based farm economy was a far-off goal. Still, he worked around the edges. He failed in committee in 1990 to end the controversial honey-subsidy program, which provides large payments to a small number of beekeepers. The amendment was adopted on the Senate floor. But, as in 1985, the program was preserved in conference with the House.

Those seeking increased subsidies were also kept off balance by Lugar's hints that he might stage a debate over the very nature of farm-subsidy programs, which he regards as akin to welfare. "At some point, maybe we should acknowledge that we are simply making transfer payments from one taxpayer to another," Lugar said.

Lugar's efforts benefited Leahy; the chairman had to fight off an insurgency from some liberal farm-state Democrats, who were not only determined to increase farm subsidies but viewed the issue as an effective one to use against Republicans back home. While Leahy gathered a group of moderate Democrats to freeze subsidy levels, Lugar maintained a solid bloc of GOP members on most votes.

Though overall a strong supporter of Bush's policies, Lugar expressed anger when administration officials, who had stayed on the sidelines during much of the deliberations, criticized the farm bill as not austere enough. "Without a great deal of assistance, I've managed to achieve a freeze of target prices and loan rates," Lugar said in July 1990. "And the failure of the administration to acknowledge this strikes me as curious."

Lugar's environmentalist tendencies are stronger than those of most Senate Republicans, and of many Agriculture Committee members of either party. He worked with Leahy to block changes sought by farm organizations in environmental restrictions in the 1985 farm bill, including the "swampbuster" provisions requiring cutoffs in federal payments to farmers who drain protected wetlands.

Despite their overriding attempts at cooperation, there were instances of partisan misunderstanding during the bill's birthing process. In the end, though, the fiscal crisis forced Leahy and Lugar to work together to make the unpalatable cuts that would be needed for the farm bill to meet budget guidelines and avoid a veto. The conference committee sliced nearly $14 billion out of the farm programs, though the cuts would be accounted for in a separate budget-reconciliation measure.

Lugar took the lead among Foreign Relations Republicans on the U.S. response to the August 1990 occupation of Kuwait by forces of Iraqi President Saddam Hussein. After the invasion, Lugar raced out ahead of Bush, whose stated goal was simply to get Iraq to give up Kuwait. "It seems to me important that Saddam Hussein must either leave or be removed," Lugar said.

Lugar also insisted that Congress needed to fulfill what he viewed as its constitutional responsibility to authorize the use of military force. Even before the 101st Congress adjourned in late October, Lugar said, "Congress ought to come back into session to entertain a declaration of war."

Still, Lugar emerged as a Senate point man for Bush's gulf policy. Lugar spoke frequently, in the Senate and during national television interviews, in favor of the January 1991 resolution authorizing military force.

Despite the U.S.-led military rout that liberated Kuwait, Lugar's hopes for Saddam's immediate downfall were not met; instead, the Iraqi strongman used what military might he had left to crush revolts among his nation's Kurdish and Shiite Muslim populations. Lugar nonetheless defended Bush against criticisms that he had stopped short of Saddam's removal and had reacted slowly to the plight of Iraq's minority groups.

Lugar was much more visible during the war than the laconic Foreign Relations chairman, Democrat Claiborne Pell of Rhode Island, or Helms, who uses the Foreign Relations post mainly to sustain his anti-communist crusades.

The conflicting approaches of the two Republicans had brought them to loggerheads even before Helms, by a 24-17 vote, pre-empted Lugar for the ranking position in 1987. They had clashed during deliberations on a 1986 bill mandating economic sanctions against South Africa, which Lugar had a key role in crafting. Lugar also made the difference when it came to overriding President Ronald Reagan's veto of that bill.

Although Lugar worked to engineer the veto override, he expressed regret over his disagreement with Reagan and chagrin that he had been unable to get the president to change his mind. However, Lugar did manage to convince a reluctant Reagan to accede to the ouster of a longtime U.S. ally, scandal-plagued President Ferdinand E. Marcos of the Philippines.

Early in 1986, Reagan asked Lugar to head a U.S. delegation monitoring the election between Marcos and challenger Corazon C. Aquino. Lugar quickly concluded that Marcos was stealing the election. Privately he implored Reagan to denounce Marcos, but Reagan argued instead that there had been fraud on both sides.

Lugar persisted. Eventually the administration pressured Marcos to leave office peacefully, in what came to be regarded as one of Reagan's chief foreign policy achievements. But in 1989, Aquino gave the credit to Lugar. "Without him," she said, "there would be no Philippine-U.S. relations to speak of by now." That year, Lugar was a chief sponsor of a measure that authorized U.S. participation in a multinational economic assistance program for the Philippines.

At Home: In 1994, Lugar is expected to stand for re-election and win. The one Hoosier Democrat in his electoral weight class, Gov. Evan Bayh, has shown no interest in a match. Any other Democrat nominated will need a reason for running other than an expectation of winning.

Lugar's long record of electoral success is remarkable given his modest gifts as a campaigner. He meets crowds woodenly and his style borders on lecturing. But he has always managed to impress the Indiana electorate as a man of substance.

Even in 1974, running for the Senate in a Watergate-dominated year with a reputation as "Richard Nixon's favorite mayor," he came within a respectable 75,000 votes against Democrat Birch Bayh. Two years later, against a much weaker Democrat, Sen. Vance Hartke, he won handily. In his 1982 re-election bid, Lugar's personal popularity — and massive campaign treasury — put him out of reach of his Democratic challenger, Rep. Floyd Fithian.

Lugar's record as mayor of Indianapolis still stands as the foundation of his political career. His conservative, efficiency-minded administration won him favorable notices all over Indiana, and he attracted national attention by defeating John V. Lindsay of New York City for vice president of the National League of Cities in 1970.

A Rhodes scholar, Lugar served in the Navy as a briefing officer at the Pentagon before returning home to run the family tool business. He won his first election in 1964, to the Indianapolis School Board.

Three years later, he saw an opportunity to take over the mayor's office. The Democrats were divided, and with the help of powerful Marion County GOP Chairman Keith Bulen, he beat incumbent Democrat John Barton.

Lugar's foremost accomplishment as Indianapolis mayor was creation of Uni-Gov, the consolidation of the city and its suburbs, which he lobbied through the state legislature.

Lugar's election over Lindsay was national news because he won it in an electorate of big-city mayors, most of whom were Democrats. He was a spokesman for Nixon administration policies, and from that time on the president began to take an interest in him.

He came to regret those ties in 1974, when he was saddled with the Nixon connection. In an attempt to deal with it, he declared that the Oval Office tape transcripts "revealed a moral tragedy" in the White House. But this alienated segments of the Republican right in Indiana and made his campaign against Birch Bayh even more difficult.

Still, he came close enough to be the logical contender in 1976 against Hartke. Hartke had nearly been beaten six years earlier and was severely damaged by a primary challenger who charged him with foreign junketing and slavish loyalty to the communications industry. Lugar coasted to an easy win.

Working to ensure the same result in 1982, Lugar began preparing two years in advance. By the time the election drew near, he had organizations in every county. By contrast, Democrat Fithian got off to a slow start. After his old 2nd District was dismembered in redistricting, Fithian initially announced plans to run for Indiana secretary of state, then switched to the Senate contest — angering other Democrats already in the race and prompting some observers to brand him "Flip-Flop Floyd."

Seeking to make up lost ground, Fithian attacked Lugar's record on Social Security, charging that the incumbent voted 16 times to reduce minimum benefits. He tied Lugar to Reagan policies Fithian claimed were responsible for Indiana's economic woes. Lugar acknowledged the troubled economic climate — billing himself as a "good man for tough times" — but put the blame on previous Democratic administrations. Lugar did not go to great lengths to identify himself with the White House, however. He criticized the president for vetoing the supplemental appropriation that included his own emergency housing legislation.

Fithian did manage to shore up support in

predominantly Democratic southern Indiana, taking 14 counties in this region. In most areas, though, Lugar was a comfortable winner, and he finished with 54 percent statewide.

In 1988, with Hoosier Democrats on the march (they captured the governorship and gained parity in the legislature), Lugar essentially drew a pass.

The only Democrat who filed to oppose him was Jack Wickes, an Indianapolis lawyer who had never run for office. Personable and energetic as Wickes was, his principal credential was that he had run Gary Hart's successful presidential primary campaign in Indiana in 1984. Wickes never raised enough money to make a serious race against Lugar. He was not even able to run television advertisements. Lugar got more votes (1.43 million) and a wider victory margin (761,747 votes) than any previous candidate in Indiana history. His vote share (68 percent) easily eclipsed the previous record for a Senate race in the state.

Committees

Agriculture, Nutrition & Forestry (Ranking)

Foreign Relations (2nd of 8 Republicans)
European Affairs (ranking); East Asian & Pacific Affairs; Western Hemisphere & Peace Corps Affairs

Select Intelligence (7th of 8 Republicans)

Joint Organization of Congress

Elections

1988 General

Richard G. Lugar (R)	1,430,525	(68%)
Jack Wickes (D)	668,778	(32%)

Previous Winning Percentages: 1982 (54%) 1976 (59%)

Campaign Finance

	Receipts	Receipts from PACs	Expend-itures
1988			
Lugar (R)	$3,029,708	$775,836 (26%)	$3,022,597
Wickes (D)	$338,465	$119,150 (35%)	$314,233

Key Votes

1993

Require unpaid family and medical leave	N
Approve national "motor voter" registration bill	N
Approve budget increasing taxes and reducing deficit	N
Support president's right to lift military gay ban	N
1992	
Approve school-choice pilot program	Y
Allow shifting funds from defense to domestic programs	N
Oppose deeper cuts in spending for SDI	Y
1991	
Approve waiting period for handgun purchases	Y
Raise senators' pay and ban honoraria	Y
Authorize use of force in Persian Gulf	Y
Confirm Clarence Thomas to Supreme Court	Y

Voting Studies

	Presidential Support		Party Unity		Conservative Coalition	
Year	S	O	S	O	S	O
1992	87	10	86	12	76	21
1991	93	7	88	11	83	10
1990	86	11	86	12	97	3
1989	93	2	83	15	89	11
1988	86	13	76	19	86	14
1987	76	21	77	20	78	13
1986	88	11	89	10	88	9
1985	89	10	92	8	88	12
1984	92	8	94	6	87	13
1983	95	5	92	8	95	5
1982	83	15	85	14	84	16
1981	90	9	93	7	90	10

Interest Group Ratings

Year	ADA	AFL-CIO	CCUS	ACU
1992	10	17	100	85
1991	10	17	90	76
1990	6	11	75	83
1989	10	0	100	75
1988	10	21	92	88
1987	5	20	88	72
1986	10	0	89	78
1985	5	10	90	74
1984	10	18	79	82
1983	15	12	68	44
1982	15	28	70	63
1981	5	0	94	100

Daniel R. Coats (R)

Of Fort Wayne — Elected 1990; 1st Full Term

Appointed to the Senate December 1988.

Born: May 16, 1943, Jackson, Mich.
Education: Wheaton College, B.A. 1965; Indiana U., J.D. 1971.
Military Service: Army Corps of Engineers, 1966-68.
Occupation: Lawyer.
Family: Wife, Marcia Anne Crawford; three children.
Religion: Presbyterian.
Political Career: U.S. House, 1981-88.
Capitol Office: 404 Russell Bldg. 20510; 224-5623.

In Washington: For years, Coats has labored in the shadow of a politician who did not cast a very long one. But events conspired at the start of the 103rd to enable Coats to leave behind the specter of his former boss and mentor, former Vice President Dan Quayle.

First of all, 1993 is the first year that Coats has held office when Quayle did not. But perhaps more important, Coats found himself the lightning rod for public antipathy toward one of the first acts of the new president, Bill Clinton.

When Republicans launched an offensive against Clinton's proposal to lift the ban on homosexuals serving in the military, they went looking for someone to take the point. Coats was their volunteer.

According to The Washington Post, the day before the confirmation hearing for Defense Secretary Les Aspin, Republican members of the Armed Services Committee met to discuss their questions. When Strom Thurmond of South Carolina wanted to know who would ask questions on the gay ban, no one spoke up.

"There was kind of a dead silence," Coats told The Post. "Assignments had been handed out and nobody said anything. I think my exact words were: 'Well, if no one else wants to take it, I'll ask the question.'"

It was a stroke of luck for the GOP. On morning network news shows and elsewhere, Coats expressed forcefully but without strident rhetoric the feelings of many Americans opposed to lifting the ban. He argued that Clinton was taking an "in your face" posture toward Congress and the military on the issue. Unlike some of his more uncompromising Republican colleagues — North Carolina's Jesse Helms, for instance — Coats, though a staunch conservative, brought a record of compromise and thus credibility to the debate.

In 1992, Coats had decided to break ranks with his party and president and become a supporter of a bill mandating that businesses allow their workers unpaid leave for family and medical emergencies.

Although he was still concerned about the costs it would impose on businesses, he said he had also felt uncomfortable opposing such a "pro-family" measure. Several compromises, including an exemption for key employees, satisfied Coats' concerns, but not those of the White House or most Republicans. The bill was vetoed by President Bush in 1992, but signed into law by Clinton early in 1993.

His willingness to compromise on family leave hardly makes Coats a moderate on most issues, much less a liberal. He was one of only five Republicans to oppose a compromise civil rights bill in 1991 that had Bush's support. Nonetheless, he is not viewed as one-dimensional, even by frequent adversaries. "I would not put him in the same class with Jesse Helms," one liberal Democrat, Paul Simon of Illinois, told The Post. "He is not totally predictable."

Coats sometimes seems to allow his emotions to overtake his reason, particularly on issues, such as abortion, that deeply divide the public and where he believes his position is morally correct.

During a 1993 debate in the Labor and Human Resources Committee on a bill that would provide a statutory guarantee of the right to abortion, Coats got into a heated exchange with Iowa Democrat Tom Harkin. "We wouldn't be here if women represented half the Supreme Court," Harkin said. "Abortions do not happen to men, they happen to women."

"And children," Coats said softly.

"Women," Harkin said a little louder.

"Children and fetuses," said Coats.

He then suggested amending the bill to allow states the option of regulating abortions performed in the ninth month of pregnancy, but dropped it, and the committee approved the bill, unchanged.

Coats is equally unbending on the issue of the military ban on gays. "You would think that someone who has not served a day in uniform would be particularly careful to consult his military chiefs," Coats said in a Senate floor speech, leveling a strategic jab at Clinton.

Coats argues that those seeking to lift the

ban have not fully confronted the implications of their position. To illustrate his point, he suggested that the armed forces would have to establish four sets of barracks — not only to segregate men and women, but also to separate those of each sex who are homosexual and heterosexual.

Though it is not unusual for one politician to be carried some distance by the career successes of another, few have come as far this way as has Coats.

Starting as Quayle's aide when Quayle represented northeast Indiana in the House, Coats has moved up behind his boss. When Quayle went to the Senate in 1980, Coats ran for and won his House seat. And after Quayle was elected vice president in 1988, Indiana's retiring GOP Gov. Robert D. Orr appointed Coats to succeed Quayle in the Senate.

Coats' appointment, lasting only through the 101st Congress, had to be ratified by the voters in November 1990, and he had to defend the seat in its regular re-election cycle in 1992.

During his tenure in the Senate, Coats has shown a particular zest for attacking trash — whether it be New Jersey tin cans or sexually explicit telephone messages. During the 101st Congress, Coats irritated New Jersey Democrats Frank R. Lautenberg and Bill Bradley when he won Senate approval of an amendment allowing state bans or limits on the importing of solid waste from other states. Coats, who ran campaign ads lampooning New Jerseyites dumping their garbage on a horrified Hoosier couple's lawn, denied political motivations for the provision, which was dropped in conference.

During the 102nd and into the 103rd, he has continued the fight, especially after the Supreme Court ruled in 1992 that states do not have the right to restrict out-of-state waste imports. The issue has developed into a crusade for Coats, whose state imports more than a million tons of waste a year, an amount that he argues is beginning to cause significant landfill problems for Indiana communities.

Coats tried in 1992 to have the garbage import ban included in a rewrite of the nation's broad main solid waste law. When that measure stalled, Coats said he would attempt to amend must-pass spending bills. That threat, in turn, precipitated action on a free-standing bill to give governors power to block some trash imports.

Later, on the floor of the Senate, Coats attempted to amend the bill to give the governors of four states — Indiana, Ohio, Pennsylvania and Virginia, which receive the most out-of-state trash — even greater authority to break existing contracts to meet waste-limit targets. But Lautenberg objected that allowing governors to break valid contracts would unfairly harm his home state, which has a severe landfill shortage.

After two days of negotiations, Coats and Lautenberg settled on a compromise that, starting in 1999, would have allowed the four governors to force limits on large landfill operators, despite the existence of contracts.

The Senate passed the bill, 89-2, but it was never considered by the House. Coats promises to pick up in 1993 where the Senate left off.

Known primarily as a serious social conservative given to pondering the implications of his Christian-based, pro-family politics, Coats also introduced legislation in 1990 to outlaw so-called "dial-a-porn" and to allow the sale of sexually explicit telephone messages only if adults specifically seek access through their telephone company.

He has urged the like-minded to move beyond such issues as school prayer and abortion to a concern for the material welfare of children and the poor. But his role is limited by his reluctance to depart from the conservative orthodoxy and suspicion of government he brought with him to Congress.

As a result, he often finds himself attempting the difficult balancing act of offering economic incentives without spawning government interference. He has called for doubling the personal tax exemption and creating tax credits for low-income families with children younger than 6. He also won adoption of several amendments in the 1989 child-care legislation to permit in-home care and to allow requirements that care-providers adhere to certain religious beliefs.

Coats is also a fiscal conservative, and he champions the cause of the line-item veto. Still, he was one of the House class of 1980 who not only survived electorally but built a detente with the government he opposed in getting elected. Many of his classmates who had ridden Ronald Reagan's 1980 coattails came a cropper in the recession of 1982; Coats actually ran stronger that year than in either of Reagan's landslides. He did it, in part, by watching out for his Fort Wayne-based district's economic interests.

At Home: When Orr named Coats to replace Quayle in the Senate a month after the 1988 presidential election, he was formalizing what many Indiana observers had considered a fait accompli. Coats was presumed to be Quayle's choice, just as he had been when Quayle left the House eight years earlier.

As Quayle's district representative from 1978 through 1980, Coats cultivated the role of surrogate congressman. He handled constituents' problems personally, and sometimes stepped in for Quayle to give a "government is too big" speech. When Quayle ran for the Senate in 1980, Coats had a spot on the ballot just below him and shared the highly effective organization both had helped build. Coats actually bested Quayle that November in the 4th.

Democrats in 1990 tried and failed to recruit a front-line candidate such as Rep. Lee Hamilton. Instead, they nominated little-known state Rep. Baron P. Hill, a former high school basketball star. Hill gained ground with clever television ads depicting the state as being flooded by Coats' franked mail. He also took a walking tour of the length of the state. Voters warmed to Hill's fiery stump style, which contrasted with Coats' stiff presence in crowds and reliance on television ads and mailings.

In the end, Hill did not have enough money and name recognition to overtake the incumbent, but he did do well enough to merit being mentioned as a possible repeat challenger in 1992.

But Hill decided not to try again. Instead Democrats offered up Indiana Secretary of State Joseph H. Hogsett, a close associate of Gov. Evan Bayh. Hogsett, who had helped run Bayh's gubernatorial campaign, was seen early as a strong threat to Coats. But the threat fizzled as Coats built up a large campaign treasury and a highly organized and effective campaign.

On Election Day, Coats pushed his tally to 57 percent.

When he first ran for the House in 1980, Coats was still a relative newcomer to the district. But he easily surmounted a bitter GOP primary against two candidates with much stronger local roots, winning the primary by carrying every county. In November, Coats smashed Democrat John D. Walda in Walda's second try. Four re-election campaigns produced no surprises.

Committees

Armed Services (6th of 9 Republicans)
Force Requirements & Personnel (ranking); Coalition Defense & Reinforcing Forces; Defense Technology, Acquisition & Industrial Base

Labor & Human Resources (3rd of 7 Republicans)
Children, Families, Drugs & Alcoholism (ranking); Aging; Education, Arts & Humanities; Employment & Productivity

Elections

1992 General		
Daniel R. Coats (R)	1,267,972	(57%)
Joseph H. Hogsett (D)	900,148	(41%)
Steve Dillon (LIBERT)	35,733	(2%)

Previous Winning Percentages: **1990** (54%) **1988** * (62%) **1986** * (70%) **1984** * (61%) **1982** * (64%) **1980** * (61%)

** House elections.*

Campaign Finance

	Receipts	Receipts from PACs		Expend-itures
1992				
Coats (R)	$3,642,012	$1,135,005	(31%)	$3,802,077
Hogsett (D)	$1,621,467	$436,042	(27%)	$1,584,173

Key Votes

1993	
Require unpaid family and medical leave	Y
Approve national "motor voter" registration bill	N
Approve budget increasing taxes and reducing deficit	N
Support president's right to lift military gay ban	N
1992	
Approve school-choice pilot program	Y
Allow shifting funds from defense to domestic programs	N
Oppose deeper cuts in spending for SDI	Y
1991	
Approve waiting period for handgun purchases	Y
Raise senators' pay and ban honoraria	N
Authorize use of force in Persian Gulf	Y
Confirm Clarence Thomas to Supreme Court	Y

Voting Studies

	Presidential Support		Party Unity		Conservative Coalition	
Year	**S**	**O**	**S**	**O**	**S**	**O**
1992	75	22	92	8	87	13
1991	85	15	91	9	85	15
1990	77	18	87	11	92	8
1989	81	19	92	8	92	8
House Service:						
1988	59	38	77	20	84	11
1987	64	36	83	16	86	12
1986	70	29	84	15	84	16
1985	74	26	81	17	80	20
1984	67	30	92	8	90	10
1983	78	21	88 †	12 †	84	16
1982	71	29	84	13	82	18
1981	74	26	86	14	91	9

† Not eligible for all recorded votes.

Interest Group Ratings

Year	ADA	AFL-CIO	CCUS	ACU
1992	10	33	90	93
1991	5	25	80	100
1990	0	22	83	96
1989	10	20	88	86
House Service:				
1988	10	29	93	92
1987	8	0	100	91
1986	10	14	94	82
1985	20	18	86	86
1984	5	0	69	92
1983	10	6	85	87
1982	30	15	73	73
1981	10	20	100	93

1 Peter J. Visclosky (D)

Of Merrillville — Elected 1984; 5th Term

Born: Aug. 13, 1949, Gary, Ind.
Education: Indiana U. Northwest, B.S. 1970; U. of Notre Dame, J.D. 1973; Georgetown U., LL.M. 1982.
Occupation: Lawyer.
Family: Wife, Anne Marie O'Keefe; two children.
Religion: Roman Catholic.
Political Career: No previous office.
Capitol Office: 2464 Rayburn Bldg. 20515; 225-2461.

In Washington: Visclosky came to Congress with a bold ambition: to accede to the influential role of numbers specialist held by his predecessor and mentor, Adam Benjamin Jr., on the Appropriations Committee. Finally, midway through his fourth term, Visclosky was awarded the assignment he had so long sought.

While he waited patiently for a position to open, Visclosky took care to avoid brash comments or a headline-grabbing style that would be inconsistent with that committee's method of doing business. When a slot opened up during the 102nd Congress, Visclosky — as House Speaker Thomas S. Foley of Washington promised him in 1990 — got it.

He has crafted a reputation as an intelligent and loyal Democrat and has been rewarded with four terms as an at-large whip. His floor statements honoring veterans, Lithuanians and the Rev. Dr. Martin Luther King Jr. reflect the roots and concerns of his solidly Democratic but diverse district. He also tends to the home front, working for funding of such projects as the Little Calumet River flood control project and a new airport in Gary.

Indiana's 1st District produces more steel than any other district, and it has suffered devastating economic losses in the past two decades. Visclosky rarely misses an opportunity to speak out for American steel. When the omnibus highway bill was debated on the floor, Visclosky reminded his colleagues how important highway projects are for the steel industry. When the House considered a foreign aid bill in early 1992, Visclosky extolled the merits of sending food aid to the former Soviet Union in steel cans.

As a member of the executive committee of the Congressional Steel Caucus, Visclosky advocated provisions in the 1988 trade bill to increase the U.S. trade representative's enforcement authority. The new law clarifies that foreign countries' voluntary steel import restrictions cannot be circumvented by processing the steel in a third country. In the 101st and 102nd Congresses, Visclosky worked to extend the voluntary restraint agreements on steel imports.

Visclosky has become well versed on pension issues and is an advocate for increasing employee input on investment decisions. He also successfully promoted legislation enlarging the Indiana Dunes National Lakeshore, a longtime *cause célèbre* for Midwest environmentalists and one of the few tourist attractions in northwest Indiana.

Even before winning his Appropriations assignment, Visclosky served the steel industry and its workers from his committee posts on Public Works and what was then called Interior and Insular Affairs. He also had a temporary assignment on Education and Labor.

When Public Works wrote a water resources bill in the 99th Congress, Visclosky was able to include about $100 million for flood and erosion control along the district's Lake Michigan shoreline.

At Home: After finishing law school in 1973, Visclosky linked his fortunes to Benjamin, then a state senator and rising star. Visclosky coordinated Benjamin's successful campaign for Congress in 1976 and worked with him in Washington for the next six years.

When Benjamin died in September 1982, Gary's longtime black mayor, Richard G. Hatcher, was the 1st District Democratic chairman, and thus had the legal right to choose the Democratic nominee. He picked Katie Hall, a black state senator and loyal ally. She survived the general election and sought renomination in 1984. Visclosky and Lake County prosecutor Jack Crawford, a well-known white politician, challenged her, and at first, Crawford seemed the more formidable of the two white candidates.

Everyone knew Hall would face renomination problems. Minorities made up less than one-third of the district's population, and Hall did not build much of a biracial constituency. But Visclosky's decision to run attracted little attention because Crawford was considered Hall's chief threat. Lake County accounted for 80 percent of the district vote, and Crawford had run two successful races there.

Indiana 1

Northwest — Gary; Hammond

With its large blue-collar work force and 21 percent black population, the 1st is a Democratic bastion. Industrial decline and urban decay in Gary and other cities along Lake Michigan cost the 1st nearly 10 percent of its population in the 1980s; Gary itself lost 23 percent, a steeper rate of decline than in any U.S. city during the 1980s. To compensate, 1991 redistricting added a substantial suburban swath in Lake and Porter counties.

Though Porter County, with its pockets of GOP voters, slightly dilutes the 1st's Democratic vote, it is still solidly Democratic. In 1992's three-way presidential race, Bill Clinton won a majority of the vote here, and Rep. Visclosky took 69 percent.

Gary and urban Lake County are Democratic pillars. Minorities have a major impact: Once packed with factory workers of Slavic extraction, Gary is now more than 80 percent black. The Hispanic presence has increased in Hammond and East Chicago.

Gary, named for turn-of-the-century steel baron Elbert H. Gary, has become the heart of U.S. steelmaking. While factories were abandoned in other Rust Belt regions, companies such as USX, Inland Steel and Bethlehem Steel modernized plants here. The 1st produces more steel than any other district in the country.

But the steelmakers' revival came after recessions and the effects of foreign competition had whittled payrolls. And the streamlined, automated factories require fewer workers. Socioeconomic problems are endemic.

Hammond, on the Illinois border and the 1st's other urban anchor, has a more varied economy, including a longstanding Lever Brothers bar soap plant. A marina has recently been built as part of an economic development effort. An Amoco oil refinery takes up most of the land area in neighboring Whiting.

As the 1st moves south of the Indiana Toll Road into such communities as Merrillville and Crown Point, the population becomes more white and the employment more white-collar.

Many residents of these suburbs are Eastern European ethnics who have maintained their Democratic loyalties. In recent decades, rivalry between white ethnics and blacks has been a feature of the 1st's Democratic politics. But of late, tension between the two camps has diminished, thanks in part to the governing style of Gary's black Mayor Thomas V. Barnes, who is a more consensus-oriented politician than his predecessor, Richard G. Hatcher.

Porter County's demographics and politics sharply contrast with Lake's. It is racially homogenous (less than 1 percent black) and growing. Chesterton, Valparaiso and other exurban communities are home to a number of former Lake Countians and to Chicago commuters, who came here seeking cheaper housing. Although there is a Democratic vote in Portage and Burns Harbor, Porter is friendly to GOP candidates. In 1992, George Bush won Porter County with 40 percent of the vote, edging past Clinton, who got 37 percent.

1990 Population: 554,416. White 411,190 (74%), Black 116,863 (21%), Other 26,363 (5%). Hispanic origin 47,320 (9%). 18 and over 400,197 (72%), 62 and over 81,439 (15%). Median age: 33.

In the end, though, Visclosky had greater appeal. To contrast his modestly funded bid with Crawford's high-budget operation, Visclosky put on dozens of "dog-and-bean" $2 dinners aimed at attracting the young, the elderly and the unemployed. His Eastern European background also helped him (he called himself "the Slovak Kid"), and older voters responded favorably because they remembered his father, John, who had served as Gary's comptroller in the 1950s and as the city's appointed mayor in 1962-63.

An added boost was the endorsement in late 1983 of Pat Benjamin, the congressman's widow, plus support from newspapers in Gary (Hall's home) and Hammond (Crawford's home).

Visclosky won over late-deciding white voters whose first priority was defeating Hall. She finished second, Crawford a close third. Visclosky swamped Republican Joseph B. Grenchik, the mayor of Whiting, in November.

In 1986, Hall tried a comeback. She retained her support in the black community, where Visclosky had alienated some voters by failing to close his congressional office on the Martin Luther King Jr. holiday in 1985. But with Hall as his only serious foe in this white-majority district, Visclosky's renomination was all but assured. Hall's 1990 primary bid fell flat.

In 1992, Visclosky reaffirmed his standing in the district, winning nearly 70 percent of the vote against a little-known Republican. Although the district picked up more of GOP-leaning Porter County in redistricting for the 1990s, it remains solidly Democratic.

Committee

Appropriations (25th of 37 Democrats)
Defense; Treasury, Postal Service & General Government

Elections

1992 General		
Peter J. Visclosky (D)	147,054	(69%)
David J. Vucich (R)	64,770	(31%)
1992 Primary		
Peter J. Visclosky (D)	53,383	(72%)
George T. Jancosek (D)	10,148	(14%)
Albert J. La Mere (D)	7,426	(10%)
Cyril B. Huerter (D)	3,389	(5%)
1990 General		
Peter J. Visclosky (D)	68,920	(66%)
William B. Costas (R)	35,450	(34%)

Previous Winning Percentages: **1988** (77%) **1986** (73%) **1984** (71%)

District Vote for President

1992
D 117,126 (53%)
R 68,403 (31%)
I 37,136 (17%)

Campaign Finance

	Receipts	Receipts from PACs		Expend-itures
1992				
Visclosky (D)	$275,278	$175,715	(64%)	$268,786
1990				
Visclosky (D)	$248,272	$168,020	(68%)	$299,280
Costas (R)	$21,358	0		$21,355

Key Votes

1993	
Require parental notification of minors' abortions	N
Require unpaid family and medical leave	Y
Approve national "motor voter" registration bill	N
Approve budget increasing taxes and reducing deficit	Y
Approve economic stimulus plan	Y
1992	
Approve balanced-budget constitutional amendment	N
Close down space station program	Y
Approve U.S. aid for former Soviet Union	Y
Allow shifting funds from defense to domestic programs	N
1991	
Extend unemployment benefits using deficit financing	Y
Approve waiting period for handgun purchases	Y
Authorize use of force in Persian Gulf	N

Voting Studies

	Presidential Support		Party Unity		Conservative Coalition	
Year	**S**	**O**	**S**	**O**	**S**	**O**
1992	22	78	91	9	38	63
1991	29	71	92	8	32	68
1990	22	76	90	8	30	69
1989	30	67	89	9	32	66
1988	22	78	91	9	18	82
1987	19	81	94	6	28	72
1986	19	81	93	7	20	80
1985	30	70	90	9	33	67

Interest Group Ratings

Year	ADA	AFL-CIO	CCUS	ACU
1992	85	100	50	16
1991	80	92	30	10
1990	72	92	14	13
1989	100	83	40	7
1988	100	100	36	0
1987	92	94	13	0
1986	90	93	33	0
1985	80	71	36	5

2 Philip R. Sharp (D)

Of Muncie — Elected 1974; 10th Term

Born: July 15, 1942, Baltimore, Md.
Education: Georgetown U., B.S.F.S. 1964; Oxford U., 1966; Georgetown U., Ph.D. 1974.
Occupation: Professor.
Family: Wife, Marilyn Augburn; two children.
Religion: Methodist.
Political Career: Democratic nominee for U.S. House, 1970, 1972.
Capitol Office: 2217 Rayburn Bldg. 20515; 225-3021.

In Washington: Sharp shifted his attention in the 103rd Congress to overseeing what he created in the 102nd: the Energy Policy Act of 1992, a sweeping piece of legislation that addresses oil conservation, nuclear power plant licensing and alternative fuels.

Nearly two years in the making, the Oct. 24, 1992, signing marked the pinnacle of Sharp's public career and a legislative high point in the otherwise rancorous and unproductive 102nd.

The Indiana Democrat was well-positioned and well-prepared to author the nation's first major energy policy in almost two decades.

Sharp began developing expertise in the field in the late 1970s when he helped usher President Jimmy Carter's package through Congress. Interest in energy policy waned during the 1980s, but when the issue re-emerged after the 1990 Iraqi invasion of Kuwait, Sharp was ready as chairman of the Energy and Power Subcommittee of Energy and Commerce. His influence was further enhanced by his seniority on two Interior subcommittees that oversee energy. (Interior is now the Natural Resources Committee.)

A former political science professor, Sharp was a quick standout in the large Democratic class of 1974: hard-working, sober and intellectually curious. Nevertheless, he took over what had been a Republican district and is one of the few House members who often has to fight hard to stay in office.

He is by nature careful, slow to step out front, and his politically competitive district further fuels that deliberative streak. Sharp's overall record is moderate to liberal, despite some concessions to his more conservative constituency.

As chairman of the Energy and Power Subcommittee, Sharp is committed to finding consensus but reluctant to pressure wavering Democrats, especially Chairman John D. Dingell of Michigan. Reflecting his academic bent, he conducts hearings like seminars and explores all sides of an issue. He is neither aligned with the environmental movement nor an industry advocate, a neutrality that served him well in the bill negotiations.

In late 1990 and early 1991, the Persian Gulf War sparked renewed interest in oil conservation, prompting Louisiana Sen. J. Bennett Johnston, chairman of the Energy and Natural Resources Committee, to jump out of the gate first with his version of an omnibus bill.

Sharp started out slower and smaller, filing five separate bills and stitching them together for markup in the summer of 1991. Some feared Sharp had squandered the gulf war momentum, but his judiciousness paid off. Unlike Johnston's draft, Sharp's met with near-unanimous committee support.

Johnston, an inside operator who bruised Democratic egos in the early going, failed to get his bill to the floor in 1991. When he returned in early 1992, he had sacrificed provisions allowing for drilling in the Arctic National Wildlife Refuge and higher gas mileage standards.

He got no complaints from Sharp, particularly on the gas mileage standards. Although Sharp had spoken in favor of mandating more fuel-efficient cars, he knew it would be a difficult battle against Detroit's leading protector, the powerful Chairman Dingell.

Early in the process, Dingell stayed in the shadows, allowing Sharp to lead the debate. But when turf battles broke out among some of the eight other House committees with jurisdiction over parts of the bill, Dingell gave his lieutenant a hand, employing some of the strong-arm tactics and parliamentary maneuvering for which he is best known.

On the House floor, however, Sharp suffered a major setback at the hands of Ways and Means Committee Chairman Dan Rostenkowski of Illinois, who successfully offered an amendment to remove language requiring oil importers and refiners to put 1 percent of their fuel into the nation's Strategic Petroleum Reserve. (During the 101st, Sharp had won passage of legislation requiring the administration to stockpile refined oil products as well as crude oil.)

In September 1992, 131 conferees began thrashing out major differences in the two bills. In the end, crafting a compromise came down to

Indiana 2

East Central — Muncie; Anderson; Columbus

Although manufacturing is a major factor in the medium-size cities across east-central Indiana, the 2nd's Democratic vote is outweighed by a GOP tradition in presidential elections. George Bush won easily here in 1988, and in 1992 he outdistanced Bill Clinton by almost 20,000 votes in the district.

Yet a series of industrial recessions and the financial uncertainties of family farmers have made the district's mainly conservative electorate more receptive to Democrats at other levels. Democratic Gov. Evan Bayh swept the district in his 1992 re-election victory. Rep. Sharp, first elected in 1974, had several competitive contests in the 1980s, but won comfortably in 1990 and 1992.

Unemployment throughout the 2nd is well below the near-depression levels of the early 1980s, when local auto-related industries laid off thousands. However, the long-term downscaling of the blue-collar work force has taken its toll: 1990 population in Delaware County (Muncie) was down more than 7 percent from 1980, and Madison County (Anderson) was down nearly that much. Rural areas such as Randolph and Henry counties also saw their economies and populations slip.

In the 1920s, Muncie was the model for "Middletown," a study of small-town American life. Today, with about 71,000 residents, it is the largest city in the 2nd. Muncie is Sharp's home base, and he typically carries Delaware County by overwhelming margins. Muncie's biggest private employer is Borg-Warner Automotive, which makes transmissions. The city's economy also benefits from Ball State University, which has 20,500 students and employs more than 2,700 people, and from the Ball Corp. It was founded and has its headquarters in Muncie, although most of its glass canning jars are made elsewhere.

Anderson's economy is heavily reliant on auto components manufacturing; the city is still trying to recover from layoffs and downsizing in that sector during the 1980s. Its largest employers are affiliates of General Motors: The Delco Remy division makes car ignition systems and electrical components; Inland Fisher Guide makes lighting equipment and bumpers. Officials in both Anderson and Muncie are working to use their locations on the White River for economic development and recreational purposes.

Although Columbus (Bartholomew County) has a strong industrial base — it is home to the Cummins Engine Co. and Arvin Industries — many of the voters are conservative: Bush took Bartholomew with 48 percent of the vote in 1992. Columbus boasts an array of modern buildings designed by leading architects; a local foundation helped fund the designs. Richmond (Wayne County), which Quakers founded in the 19th century, has an opera company.

The land outside the cities is rural and heavily farmed. Soybeans, oats and wheat are major crops in the northern part of the 2nd.

1990 Population: 554,416. White 526,723 (95%), Black 22,887 (4%), Other 4,806 (1%). Hispanic origin 3,322 (1%). 18 and over 416,400 (75%), 62 and over 91,595 (17%). Median age: 34.

Sharp and Johnston, and Sharp was forced to accept some compromises. In the House version, Sharp wanted power plants to contribute up to $500 million a year to clean up existing uranium enrichment facilities. He eventually agreed to cap payments at $150 million annually.

Sharp acknowledged the finished product had its limitations. "Neither the president, nor the Congress, nor the public is willing to support the massive energy tax increases, subsidies, regulations and changes in lifestyle that would be necessary to dramatically reduce our dependence on foreign oil," he said afterward.

But having to compromise did not mar the overall victory. "We have beaten gridlock," Sharp said.

While overseeing the new energy law will take up much of Sharp's attention in the 103rd Congress, he has also turned his attention to a key home-state concern: trash. He filed legislation early in the session allowing communities to restrict out-of-state garbage.

Sharp has long played a key role on energy and environmental issues.

During the 101st Congress, much of Sharp's energies were directed toward protecting Midwest interests in negotiations over the new clean air legislation.

The home-state pressures Sharp faces on the clean air issue are great: The auto industry is important in Indiana; the state ranks high in emissions of sulfur dioxide; and state utilities rely on high-sulfur coal. Sharp fought desperately to win help for Midwestern utilities expected to face demanding cleanup requirements. He stalled the acid rain provisions of the bill in his subcommittee, insisting that the "clean" states share in the costs of stopping pollution from the coal-fired Midwest plants.

Although he could not obtain direct financial aid for the utilities, he was instrumental in winning them some relief in the form of an emission "allowances" swap system. Under the trading scheme, utilities that exceeded cleanup requirements for sulfur dioxide emissions could sell the resulting credit to utilities in other areas that needed to expand.

During the 102nd, Congress approved a bill similar to Sharp's proposed Automobile Content Information Disclosure Act, which called on manufacturers to list on dealer stickers what portion of the car is made in America.

In the 100th Congress, Sharp's subcommittee successfully sponsored the repeal of a 1978 law aimed at encouraging industries and utilities to burn coal instead of oil or gas.

During his years as Fossil Fuels (now called Energy and Power) chairman, Sharp was at the center of debate over natural gas prices. When prices shot up in late 1982, liberal Democrats and some Midwestern Republicans began agitating for tighter regulation while President Ronald Reagan proposed eliminating all existing controls to boost supply.

Sharp steered through a bill that forced producers to lower their prices in some contracts in exchange for eased regulations. The bill stalled that year, but by 1989, after several years of low and stable gas prices, Sharp won congressional approval of price decontrol.

In the 100th, Sharp guided into law two conservation bills that reflected both his and Congress' more modest aims. A bill to set energy efficiency standards for large appliances, which Reagan had vetoed the Congress before, was enacted after a minor change. The second measure established pilot projects to promote alternative vehicle fuels, such as ethanol and methanol.

On Natural Resources, Sharp generally takes an environmentalist view, but his record and style are conciliatory enough that he sometimes serves as a bridge between differing factions.

His pragmatic drive for solutions was evident in the 100th Congress' effort to overhaul the 1957 Price-Anderson Act, which limited utilities' liability for nuclear reactor accidents. Sharp cosponsored a bill to raise utilities' joint liability tenfold, to $7 billion — still far below estimates of what a major accident would cost. The bill passed the House overwhelmingly and a House-Senate compromise version later became law.

Sharp had not been in the House long before he conceded that his experiences had deeply affected his attitude toward government. "In many cases we've gone toward excessive regulation," he said in late 1979. "I have a greater appreciation for the market than I did when I first ran."

At Home: Though never known as a stellar vote-getter, Sharp has shown that he can consistently win elections in adverse conditions. In the 1970s and 1980s he won election after election despite a redistricting map designed to work against him and despite a series of tough challenges. In 1992, redistricting may have enhanced the Democratic flavor of the district, but Sharp had a lot of explaining to do about his 120 overdrafts at the House bank. Still, he beat an old foe.

It took Sharp three tries before he even got to Congress. When Sharp began his campaign for Congress in 1970, he was a 28-year-old political science professor with little campaign experience and limited contacts in the district. He out-organized most of his six rivals to win the Democratic nomination with 22 percent of the vote. In November, with recession worrying people in the industrial cities of central Indiana, Sharp came within 2,500 votes against Republican David W. Dennis.

Sharp was better known and even better prepared in 1972, but President Richard M. Nixon won Indiana by 2-to-1, helping Dennis boost his share of the vote to 57 percent.

On his third try, Sharp had all the name recognition he needed, and it was the right year. Even in Indiana, Republicans were on the run in 1974; Sharp won with 54 percent.

In the next three elections, Sharp faced the same opponent — farmer William G. Frazier. A gregarious campaigner with a devoted core of rural followers, Frazier was unable to broaden his base for general elections. Sharp helped himself by assuming a high personal profile and by tending to the needs of constituents regardless of their partisan affiliation.

In the 1981 redistricting, Indiana's Republican legislature placed him in a redrawn district with clear Republican leanings. The GOP thought it had a good candidate in Ralph Van Natta, a former Shelbyville mayor who had gained further visibility as head of the state Bureau of Motor Vehicles. But Van Natta was encumbered by publicity about investigations of the state's patronage-controlled motor vehicle bureaus and Sharp, who had outspent him by nearly $100,000, won easily.

Kenneth MacKenzie, the 1984 GOP nominee, was different from Frazier and Van Natta. He was able to compete with Sharp in debating ability and fundraising. A former congressional aide on leave from his job as public affairs director for Muncie's Ball Corp., MacKenzie stressed his support for Reagan's efforts to give free enterprise a larger role in the economy. Once again, however, Sharp's attention to constituent service boosted him to victory.

The 1986 campaign provided an entirely new experience for Sharp, and a welcome one. In the aftermath of MacKenzie's costly failure, no prominent Republican wanted to bother challenging the incumbent. For the first time, Sharp broke 60 percent in a challenge by a

Republican with no political experience.

But the security was short-lived. In 1988, with neighbor Dan Quayle on the national GOP ticket, Sharp had to contend with another outpouring of Republican votes. His hope was that his underfinanced opponent, Mike Pence, would not be strong enough to ride the tide.

But Pence, a 29-year-old attorney from the Indianapolis area, turned his weakness to advantage. He not only ran his own campaign without any political action committee (PAC) money, he succeeded in making PACs the central issue of the local campaign by taking Sharp to task for his heavy PAC reliance.

For this Pence received favorable press both locally and nationally. He still came up short (47 percent).

Pence vowed to repeat his challenge, and in 1990 the national GOP had high hopes. But Pence, who again made campaign finance an issue, was hoist with his own petard when it was revealed that he was living on his campaign funds. The practice was not illegal, but even Republicans conceded that it was bad judgment.

Pence, who could not grasp presidential coattails this time around, stalled and never recovered. Sharp won 59 percent of the vote.

After a 12-year break, Frazier, riding the anti-incumbent, anti-Congress wave, returned to challenge Sharp in 1992. But Sharp, who was forced to spend campaign time explaining his overdrafts at the House bank, was helped by redistricting; Republican-leaning Johnson and Marion counties were transferred from the 2nd to the 6th District, a Republican stronghold, in exchange for Madison County — including blue-collar Anderson — and the balance of Delaware County, Sharp's home base which had been split between the 2nd and 6th. Sharp pushed up his tally to 57 percent, one of his best showings since he was first elected in 1974.

Committees

Energy & Commerce (3rd of 27 Democrats)
Energy & Power (chairman); Transportation & Hazardous Materials

Natural Resources (2nd of 28 Democrats)
Energy & Mineral Resources; Oversight & Investigations

Elections

1992 General		
Philip R. Sharp (D)	130,881	(57%)
William G. Frazier (R)	90,593	(40%)
Theodore Shaver (I)	7,821	(3%)
1990 General		
Philip R. Sharp (D)	93,495	(59%)
Mike Pence (R)	63,980	(41%)

Previous Winning Percentages: **1988** (53%) **1986** (62%) **1984** (53%) **1982** (56%) **1980** (53%) **1978** (56%) **1976** (60%) **1974** (54%)

District Vote for President

1992
D 81,915 (35%)
R 101,341 (43%)
I 50,424 (22%)

Campaign Finance

	Receipts	Receipts from PACs		Expend-itures
1992				
Sharp (D)	$624,265	$449,549	(72%)	$623,400
Frazier (R)	$176,488	$6,515	(4%)	$176,034
1990				
Sharp (D)	$714,491	$498,599	(70%)	$773,178
Pence (R)	$590,467	0		$595,457

Key Votes

1993	
Require parental notification of minors' abortions	?
Require unpaid family and medical leave	Y
Approve national "motor voter" registration bill	Y
Approve budget increasing taxes and reducing deficit	Y
Approve economic stimulus plan	Y
1992	
Approve balanced-budget constitutional amendment	Y
Close down space station program	Y
Approve U.S. aid for former Soviet Union	Y
Allow shifting funds from defense to domestic programs	N
1991	
Extend unemployment benefits using deficit financing	Y
Approve waiting period for handgun purchases	Y
Authorize use of force in Persian Gulf	N

Voting Studies

Year	Presidential Support S	Presidential Support O	Party Unity S	Party Unity O	Conservative Coalition S	Conservative Coalition O
1992	20 †	77 †	78	15	40 †	57 †
1991	28	67	81	12	38	57
1990	20	74	79	17	41	56
1989	28	66	76	17	39	51
1988	31	64	79	19	61	39
1987	25	73	81	14	47	51
1986	24	73	81	16	42	56
1985	43	56	76	21	36	62
1984	38	50	63	31	47	36
1983	22	77	79	20	35	64
1982	42	57	69	28	36	64
1981	43	57	70	27	52	47

† Not eligible for all recorded votes.

Interest Group Ratings

Year	ADA	AFL-CIO	CCUS	ACU
1992	85	75	38	25
1991	75	75	40	5
1990	67	83	46	22
1989	80	83	33	20
1988	75	100	50	20
1987	72	93	38	4
1986	65	86	41	10
1985	65	71	50	38
1984	50	54	14	43
1983	80	88	25	18
1982	80	95	41	14
1981	65	57	21	20

3 Tim Roemer (D)

Of South Bend — Elected 1990; 2nd Term

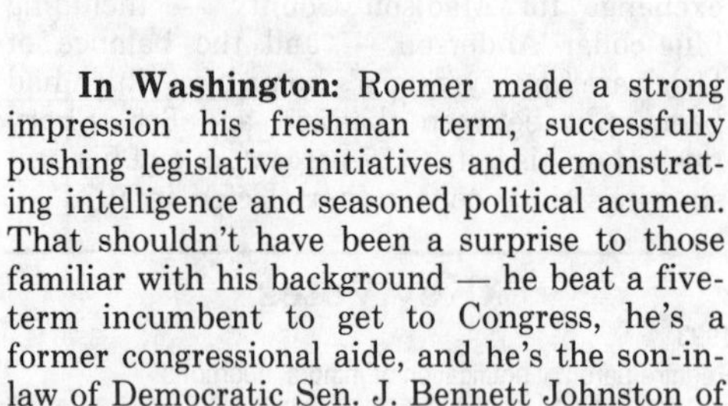

Born: Oct. 30, 1956, South Bend, Ind.
Education: U. of California, San Diego, B.A. 1979; U. of Notre Dame, M.A. 1982, Ph.D. 1986.
Occupation: Congressional aide.
Family: Wife, Sally Johnston; one child.
Religion: Roman Catholic.
Political Career: No previous office.
Capitol Office: 415 Cannon Bldg. 20515; 225-3915.

In Washington: Roemer made a strong impression his freshman term, successfully pushing legislative initiatives and demonstrating intelligence and seasoned political acumen. That shouldn't have been a surprise to those familiar with his background — he beat a five-term incumbent to get to Congress, he's a former congressional aide, and he's the son-in-law of Democratic Sen. J. Bennett Johnston of Louisiana.

A former college professor whose district includes Notre Dame University, Roemer is a strong supporter of higher education and upon arriving in Washington, he won a seat on the Education and Labor Committee. He sponsored legislation increasing the maximum amount of Pell grants to college students from $2,600 to $4,500. The language was incorporated in a bill passed by the House, but in conference the amount was reduced to $3,700.

Roemer also succeeded in getting the Education Department to stop using home equity as a means of determining loan eligibility.

Roemer also serves on the Science, Space and Technology Committee, and during the 102nd Congress he was an active opponent of the space station *Freedom*. He sponsored several amendments in 1992 that would have deleted its funding.

One Roemer amendment would have shifted $1.1 billion from the project to other NASA programs and $1.2 billion toward deficit reduction and veterans' health care and housing. The Science Committee rejected the amendment, 8-17, and the full House turned it back, 159-254.

Though Roemer was unsuccessful in the 102nd Congress, he has high hopes for the 103rd, in large because President Clinton has sought a scaled-back version of the space station.

In February 1993, Roemer wrote Clinton on the subject, saying, "This country may want to build a space station in the future. But it must have a clearly defined and advanced mission. We need to know in advance that it will serve as a way station to the moon and beyond, and not conjecture that we can modify it as time goes by."

During his freshman term, Roemer cosponsored Arkansas Democrat Ray Thornton's resolution calling for a "Marshall Plan for America" that would promote investment in infrastructure, education and business. It was overwhelmingly endorsed by the House.

In early 1993, Roemer introduced legislation to modify the portion of the Internal Revenue Code exempting companies from paying taxes on profits earned in offshore territories. "We're struggling hard enough as it is to keep our best jobs," he said. "We certainly don't need to spend U.S. tax dollars to help businesses move out of our communities."

During his freshman term, Roemer frequently defected from the party line. On partisan votes, he aligned himself with a majority of Democrats only about 70 percent of the time. On those issues on which President Bush staked out a position, he supported the president about 40 percent of the time.

Early in the 103rd Congress, Roemer was one of 22 House Democrats who opposed Clinton's economic stimulus package. He opposes abortion except in cases of rape, incest and when the women's life is in danger, and he supports a balanced budget amendment to the Constitution.

At Home: With a boost from redistricting, Roemer won re-election in 1992 with 57 percent of the vote over a strong Republican contender.

A swing district when he was first elected in 1990, the 3rd got a distinctly more Democratic flavor in 1992 when Michigan City was included in the new district lines.

That helped Roemer against Republican Carl H. Baxmeyer, a city planner. Baxmeyer initially seemed poised to give Roemer a vigorous challenge; in 1987, Baxmeyer ran for mayor of South Bend and took 48 percent of the vote. Fundraising problems made it difficult for Baxmeyer to maintain the momentum of his upset victory in the GOP House primary. That hurt him in getting solid name recognition outside of his South Bend base. He ended up with 43 percent of the vote.

Indiana 3

Northern Tier — South Bend; Elkhart

The 3rd, dominated by industrial cities that line the Indiana Toll Road near the state's northern border, has been something of a barometer of national political trends. At the peak of the Reagan Revolution, in 1980, Republicans took this district from the Democrats, as 27-year-old John Hiler ousted House Majority Whip John Brademas. Ten years later, the 3rd offered evidence that the Reagan-Bush era was drawing to a close, as Democrat Roemer ousted Hiler.

The 3rd has long been politically competitive. It has voters across the political spectrum, from staunchly conservative and Republican Elkhart (Elkhart County) to swing-voting La Porte city and more Democratic South Bend (St. Joseph County) and Michigan City (La Porte County).

La Porte County has two urban areas — La Porte and Michigan City. The latter is a blue-collar city with most of the county's minorities. Employers include Anco Inc., which makes automotive accessories, and the Jaymar-Ruby clothing company. Officials in Michigan City have oriented their economic growth efforts toward exploiting the tourist potential of its Lake Michigan location. Much of the development has been in shopping centers and vacation-home communities near the Indiana Dunes National Seashore.

To the southeast is the city of La Porte, which also has an industrial base. Employers include a Howmet Corp. plant that makes aerospace castings and a Whirlpool Corp. appliance distribution center.

With just over 105,000 residents, South Bend is the district's population nexus; neighboring Mishawaka adds 42,000 people. Although best known nationally for the University of Notre Dame, South Bend is also a center for tool-and-die manufacturing and the production of plastics. AM General Division, based in South Bend, makes military vehicles, including the "Humvee" transport. The manufacturing facility is in Mishawaka.

Like many industrial Midwestern locales, St. Joseph County has had its share of shocks. The collapse of the Studebaker Co. in the 1960s was a harbinger of the decline of the U.S. auto industry. The home-grown Bendix Corp. is now part of Allied-Signal Inc., which has headquarters elsewhere.

But the region has shown resilience. While foreign competition has hurt some local manufacturers, St. Joseph County has benefited from the location in New Carlisle of the supermodern I/N Tek steel plant, a joint venture of Inland Steel Co. and Japan's Nippon Steel Corp.

Elkhart is a center for manufactured housing and recreational vehicle construction, and it has long been known as the band instrument capital of the United States. One of the largest in that business is the Selmer Co., which gave Bill Clinton two saxophones just before his inauguration. Locally, the band instruments are far more likely to be played at GOP than Democratic rallies. Roemer lost Elkhart County in 1992.

Outside the cities, the landscape shifts to farmland. Elkhart County, with a large Amish population, is the state's largest milk-producer.

1990 Population: 554,416. White 502,899 (91%), Black 41,091 (7%), Other 10,426 (2%). Hispanic origin 10,717 (2%). 18 and over 407,768 (74%), 62 and over 86,726 (16%). Median age: 33.

Roemer's arrival in Washington in 1990 was a homecoming of sorts; he served as an aide to both former Democratic House Majority Whip John Brademas of Indiana and Democratic Sen. Dennis DeConcini of Arizona, and he taught at The American University in Washington.

Shaking off early primary criticism from some fellow Democrats that he was a carpetbagger from the East Coast, Roemer (who was born and raised in Indiana) took aim at Republican Rep. John Hiler, a veteran of four hard-fought re-elections in what had been a swing district.

As Johnston's son-in-law, Roemer was able to shake the Beltway money tree, and he set in place a sophisticated campaign with the help of Johnston's research and media consultants. Roemer raised his name recognition in the district with groups of volunteers called "Roemer's Roamers," who donned T-shirts and performed public services such as picking up trash and playing bingo with the elderly.

Roemer also benefited from the savings and loan scandal. The issue wounded Hiler, who sat on the House committee that oversees the thrift and banking industries.

Effectively steering a middle course during the campaign, Roemer sprinkled a traditional populism with occasional dashes of conservatism; one day he would hold a news conference at a plant rumored to be closing to lambaste the plight of the middle class; the next day he would out-Republican some Republicans by calling for a balanced budget and criticizing Bush for backing away from his no-taxes pledge.

Committees

Education & Labor (15th of 28 Democrats)
Elementary, Secondary & Vocational Education; Postsecondary Education

Science, Space & Technology (15th of 33 Democrats)
Energy; Space; Technology, Environment & Aviation

Elections

1992 General		
Tim Roemer (D)	121,269	(57%)
Carl H. Baxmeyer (R)	89,834	(43%)
1992 Primary		
Tim Roemer (D)	39,540	(88%)
Christopher Alan Mikulak (D)	3,110	(7%)
Anthony Vito Sims (D)	2,420	(5%)
1990 General		
Tim Roemer (D)	80,740	(51%)
John Hiler (R)	77,911	(49%)

District Vote for President

1992

D 82,483 (38%)
R 91,708 (43%)
I 41,358 (19%)

Campaign Finance

	Receipts	Receipts from PACs		Expend-itures
1992				
Roemer (D)	$467,094	$320,249	(69%)	$416,196
Baxmeyer (R)	$245,862	$16,706	(7%)	$245,500
1990				
Roemer (D)	$504,884	$269,313	(53%)	$473,055
Hiler (R)	$776,009	$257,112	(33%)	$745,145

Key Votes

1993	
Require parental notification of minors' abortions	Y
Require unpaid family and medical leave	Y
Approve national "motor voter" registration bill	Y
Approve budget increasing taxes and reducing deficit	Y
Approve economic stimulus plan	N
1992	
Approve balanced-budget constitutional amendment	Y
Close down space station program	Y
Approve U.S. aid for former Soviet Union	N
Allow shifting funds from defense to domestic programs	N
1991	
Extend unemployment benefits using deficit financing	Y
Approve waiting period for handgun purchases	Y
Authorize use of force in Persian Gulf	N

Voting Studies

	Presidential Support		Party Unity		Conservative Coalition	
Year	**S**	**O**	**S**	**O**	**S**	**O**
1992	40	58	70	29	71	29
1991	43	56	75	25	76	24

Interest Group Ratings

Year	ADA	AFL-CIO	CCUS	ACU
1992	55	58	63	40
1991	50	67	40	30

4 Jill L. Long (D)

Of Larwill — Elected 1989; 2nd Full Term

Born: July 15, 1952, Warsaw, Ind.
Education: Valparaiso U., B.S. 1974; Indiana U., M.B.A. 1978, Ph.D. 1984.
Occupation: Professor.
Family: Single.
Religion: Methodist.
Political Career: Valparaiso City Council, 1983-86; Democratic nominee for U.S. Senate, 1986; Democratic nominee for U.S. House, 1988.
Capitol Office: 1513 Longworth Bldg. 20515; 225-4436.

In Washington: Long has had a political tightrope to walk in Congress and back home, balancing the needs of her Democratic Party with her conservative, Republican-dominated district, which includes the hometown of former Vice President Dan Quayle.

Although Long is not known for significant legislative achievements, she is a friendly and agreeable legislator who has made her mark in her district through constituent service. She is also a skillful campaigner who has consistently won re-election despite the Republican bent of her district.

On social issues, Long has been loyal to her party, voting with the leadership on such key issues as family and medical leave, and abortion. In 1992, she supported the party nearly 90 percent of the time on issues that divided Democrats from Republicans.

In her first two years in Congress, she backed the Democratic position more than three-quarters of the time. She voted to allow federal funds for abortions in cases of rape and incest, and supported raising the minimum wage. In 1991, with a surprisingly comfortable re-election behind her, she voted against authorizing President Bush to use force in the Persian Gulf.

Long is more likely to desert the party on fiscal matters. Early in the 103rd Congress, she voted against adoption of President Clinton's budget resolution, which included tax increases. On the other hand, she voted for Clinton's economic stimulus plan, which would have boosted domestic spending and increased the deficit.

Democratic leaders clearly recognize her predicament and have repeatedly come to her aid. But the party has limits to how far it will go to accommodate someone who rode to Congress on an anti-tax vow and who opposed the leadership's 1990 budget package: A seat on the Budget Committee proved to be beyond Long's reach when she attempted to join for the 102nd Congress.

Until the 103rd, Long, who grew up on an Indiana wheat and dairy farm, was the only woman on the Agriculture Committee, where she has served since coming to Congress. Four other women joined the panel in 1993.

During debate on the 1990 farm bill, Long successfully sponsored a number of amendments, including two aimed at ensuring planting flexibility for farmers and providing incentives to farmers who practice effective conservation techniques.

In late 1992, when women's groups were pushing Clinton to appoint women to Cabinet-level posts, Long was widely mentioned as a candidate for the job of Agriculture secretary. After she was interviewed by Clinton, however, some key Democrats and some farm groups complained that Long lacked the necessary experience. Clinton instead chose Democratic Rep. Mike Espy of Mississippi, who had gained his colleagues' attention as an advocate of rural concerns.

Long is easygoing and low-key, and her personality has proved to be a political asset. In her first term, members helped Long fend off an attack on a provision in the 1990 defense authorization bill that had been added for her. Over strenuous GOP objections, the Armed Services Committee included $357,000 for North American Van Lines, headquartered in Fort Wayne, to reimburse the company for the destruction of a subsidiary's offices in the December 1989 U.S. invasion of Panama.

Kentucky Republican Larry J. Hopkins tried to delete the provision, blasting it as flagrant favoritism. But Democrats rallied around Long, and Hopkins' amendment was rejected 189-228. Some members said Long was the kind of friendly, agreeable colleague whom they routinely support on such matters.

Long has also been active on the Veterans' Affairs Committee. In the 102nd Congress, she successfully pushed for expanded hospice care services for terminally ill veterans.

She is also a strong advocate of comprehensive health-care services for women veterans, including counseling for those who have

Indiana 4

Northeast — Fort Wayne

Fort Wayne, which dominates the nine-county 4th, avoided the economic upheaval and population exodus that plagued many large Midwestern cities in the 1980s. The population of Indiana's second-largest city is nearly the same now as it was a decade ago, just under 173,000.

But if the 4th's economy has stayed fairly steady, its representation in the House has changed noticeably. In 1980, the 4th was held by a young conservative Republican named Dan Quayle, who successfully ran for the Senate that year. Today, a Democratic woman has the seat.

Quayle aide Daniel R. Coats succeeded his boss in the 4th in 1981, and Coats took Quayle's Senate seat when he became vice president in 1989. In the special House election to pick a replacement for Coats, Democrat Long prevailed, and she has since won two full terms, scoring an impressive 62 percent in 1992.

As the 4th evolved from a Republican stronghold to a district held by a Democrat, the GOP presidential vote here also slumped. In 1988, the Bush-Quayle ticket won two-thirds of the 4th District vote. In 1992, fewer than half the voters in the 4th cast a Republican ballot for president. At the same time, Democratic Gov. Evan Bayh carried every county in the district.

But Coats also swept the 4th in his 1992 Senate election, and this remains a conservative-minded area. Rep. Long's success is attributable more to her personal appeal and her agrarian background — she owns a farm in the Whitley County community of Larwill — than to her party label.

Although Fort Wayne is a GOP town, it has enough Democratic votes to help Long boost her margins. The city and its Allen County environs have several large industrial facilities: General Electric has a factory and General Motors builds trucks and buses at a plant just outside town.

But Fort Wayne's economy is buffered from industrial downturns by its large white-collar sector. The city's largest employer is the Lincoln National Life Insurance Co. Much of the area's manufacturing is technology-oriented: Magnavox's Government and Industrial Electronics Co. (which makes military radios) and ITT Corp.'s aerospace and communications division (producing meteorological instruments) are here.

German-Americans, a rather conservative constituency, remain Allen County's largest ethnic group: Fort Wayne's Germanfest is an annual social highlight.

Fort Wayne's cityscape gives way to some of Indiana's most fertile farms. Allen County leads the state in production of wheat, is No. 2 in oats, and is near the top in soybeans. Lagrange County trails only Elkhart County (in the 3rd) in milk production.

Small cities dot the 4th's fields: Huntington is Quayle's hometown. The town has a walking tour called The Quayle Trail, and in 1993, the Dan Quayle Commemorative Museum opened. Huntington County gave the GOP presidential ticket 57 percent in 1992.

1990 Population: 554,416. White 514,933 (93%), Black 30,635 (6%), Other 8,848 (2%). Hispanic origin 8,818 (2 %). 18 and over 396,224 (71%), 62 and over 79,975 (14%). Median age: 32.

been sexually harassed or assaulted during military service.

During the Persian Gulf War, Long proposed legislation that would restrict the stationing of single parents to locations where child-care facilities are available. But the Pentagon objected, saying it would create a special class of undeployable personnel "who don't pull their weight" and who would not be as likely to receive "training, assignments and promotions."

At Home: In winning the 4th District in a March 1989 special election, Long finally found a "Dan" she could beat. She had been routed by Dan Quayle in a 1986 Senate bid and by Dan Coats in a 1988 House race. But those campaigns gave her high name recognition and a volunteer network — crucial ingredients in her narrow victory over Fort Wayne lawyer and city administrator Dan Heath.

She did learn some valuable lessons from her earlier campaigns. In her 1986 Senate race, she laid out a liberal agenda. Since then, she has done her best to avoid ideological typecasting while calling on Democrats with more moderate reputations to campaign for her, such as then-Tennessee Sen. Al Gore and Indiana Gov. Evan Bayh.

Her 1989 House victory was an embarrassment to the state and national Republican Party. The seat had been held by both Quayle and Coats, whose appointment to Quayle's Senate seat in December 1988 created the need for the special election.

When Long sought her first full term in 1990, infighting among Republicans helped her.

GOP front-runner state Rep. Dan Stephan dropped out of the race just days before the primary after failing to energize the "Quayle-Coats" faction. Rick Hawks, a locally televised pastor, stepped in, delighting conservatives.

Hawks attempted to portray the race as a contest between ideologies, but Long dismissed him as a member of his party's "fringe element." Nor did revelations that Hawks was living on his campaign funds ease concerns of some residents about his religious fundraising background, despite the fact that he resigned his Baptist ministry to run for office. Long won easily with 61 percent.

While redistricting did not significantly alter the Republican bent of the 4th, Republicans once again helped Long in 1992 by nominating a candidate of limited appeal. Her GOP opponent, Charles W. Pierson, a conservative businessman, had a difficult time overcoming Long's personal appeal and tireless campaigning.

Until 1989, politics had been an avocation for her rather than a career. Most of her paychecks have come from college teaching. Long has a doctorate in business from Indiana University and had to balance her campaign schedule in 1989 with two business courses at Indiana University/Purdue University-Fort Wayne. Even on Election Day, she had to break away from greeting voters to teach a noontime class.

After teaching and politics, the third facet of Long's background is farming. Before her election to Congress, she lived on an 80-acre farm in Whitley County, and helped her parents run their farm nearby.

Committees

Agriculture (11th of 28 Democrats)
Environment, Credit & Rural Development; General Farm Commodities; Livestock

Veterans' Affairs (10th of 21 Democrats)
Hospitals & Health Care

Elections

1992 General		
Jill L. Long (D)	134,907	(62%)
Charles W. Pierson (R)	82,468	(38%)
1992 Primary		
Jill L. Long (D)	30,603	(87%)
J. Carolyn Williams (D)	4,724	(13%)
1990 General		
Jill L. Long (D)	99,347	(61%)
Richard W. Hawks (R)	64,415	(39%)

Previous Winning Percentage: 1989 * (51%)

** Special election.*

District Vote for President

1992
D 69,292 (31%)
R 102,779 (46%)
I 49,565 (22%)

Campaign Finance

	Receipts	Receipts from PACs		Expend-itures
1992				
Long (D)	$366,814	$263,182	(72%)	$346,011
Pierson (R)	$6,094	$500	(8%)	$6,489
1990				
Long (D)	$753,725	$448,381	(59%)	$752,362
Hawks (R)	$580,037	$79,448	(14%)	$575,363

Key Votes

1993	
Require parental notification of minors' abortions	N
Require unpaid family and medical leave	Y
Approve national "motor voter" registration bill	Y
Approve budget increasing taxes and reducing deficit	N
Approve economic stimulus plan	Y
1992	
Approve balanced-budget constitutional amendment	Y
Close down space station program	Y
Approve U.S. aid for former Soviet Union	Y
Allow shifting funds from defense to domestic programs	N
1991	
Extend unemployment benefits using deficit financing	Y
Approve waiting period for handgun purchases	N
Authorize use of force in Persian Gulf	N

Voting Studies

	Presidential Support		Party Unity		Conservative Coalition	
Year	**S**	**O**	**S**	**O**	**S**	**O**
1992	26	74	89	11	44	56
1991	32	68	85	15	59	41
1990	29	71	78	22	67	33
1989	33 †	67 †	89 †	11 †	35 †	65 †

† Not eligible for all recorded votes.

Interest Group Ratings

Year	ADA	AFL-CIO	CCUS	ACU
1992	80	75	63	24
1991	70	75	40	10
1990	50	67	43	38
1989	68	80	50	25

5 Steve Buyer (R)

Of Monticello — Elected 1992; 1st Term

Born: Nov. 26, 1958, Rensselaer, Ind.
Education: The Citadel, B.S. 1980; Valparaiso U., J.D. 1984.
Military Service: Army Reserve, 1980-84; Army, 1984-87; Army Reserve, 1987-present.
Occupation: Lawyer.
Family: Wife, Joni Geyer; two children.
Religion: Methodist.
Political Career: No previous office.
Capitol Office: 1419 Longworth Bldg. 20515; 225-5037.

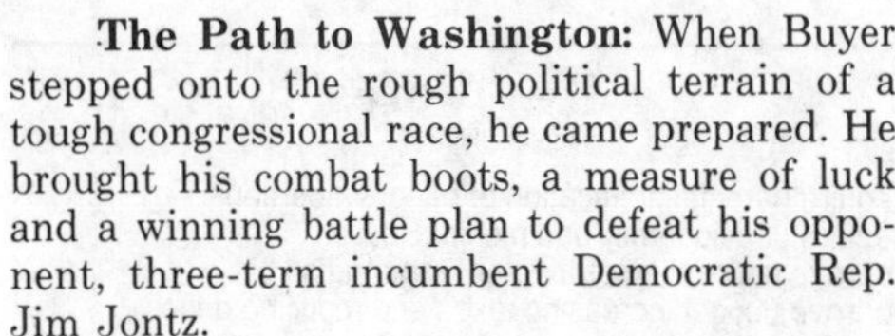

The Path to Washington: When Buyer stepped onto the rough political terrain of a tough congressional race, he came prepared. He brought his combat boots, a measure of luck and a winning battle plan to defeat his opponent, three-term incumbent Democratic Rep. Jim Jontz.

As a captain in the Army Reserve, Buyer served as lawyer for the troops in the Persian Gulf. Soon after he returned to U.S. soil, Buyer took to the stump. Brandishing his military service, he chided Jontz for voting against the use of force against Iraq. At some campaign stops, he brought his boots, placing them behind him in plain view of his audiences.

But when the war faded from the headlines and from the list of viable campaign issues, Buyer did not miss a beat. He immediately seized the theme of "change" that grew out of the House bank and Post Office scandals and successfully painted Jontz as part of a quagmire of corruption in Washington.

In the House bank matter, Jontz had only four overdrafts totaling less than $1,000 — not even placing him in the list of the top 200 offenders. Still, Buyer took him to task. Jontz's arguments that he was not trying to take advantage of the system — citing that one of the checks was for a scholarship fund that he supports with the congressional pay raise he refused — were no match for Buyer's onslaught.

Anti-incumbent fervor played just as big a role in Buyer's win.

During the campaign, Buyer stressed his "outsider" status, calling for term limits, an end to congressional perks including franked mail and a $600,000 cap on spending for House races. And he wrote to House Minority Leader Robert H. Michel of Illinois, calling for the resignation of House Speaker Thomas S. Foley of Washington.

Though social issues had not dominated his campaign, Buyer addressed school prayer early in the 103rd Congress. An Indiana high school rescinded its invitation for him to speak at graduation because of his previous promise to begin his speech with a prayer, in violation of a Supreme Court ban. On the House floor, Buyer criticized the court for its efforts "to sanitize religion from public conversation," ending his speech with the word "Amen."

Buyer broke a winning streak that began when Jontz was first elected to the Indiana House at age 22. Known as a tireless door-to-door campaigner who courted his constituents, Jontz stepped up his efforts during the campaign. However, Buyer tried to match Jontz's campaign fervor, knocking on 18,000 doors himself.

Buyer also had done his homework. In October 1991, Buyer said, he called a meeting, inviting every Republican whom Jontz had defeated since 1974. Having served as vice chairman of the White County Republican Party, he knew them all. And out of that meeting, he said, grew a united, strategic plan.

He also was able to take advantage of a small but growing level of voter discontent with Jontz. Some voters appeared ready to discount his hard work on agricultural concerns because of the time he spent working on environmental issues that affected the Pacific Northwest, not the 5th District.

Rather than scale back his environmental efforts in behalf of the northern spotted owl and the Northwest's old-growth forests, Jontz pressed ahead. In 1991, he relinquished his seat on the Veterans' Affairs Committee for a spot on the Interior and Insular Affairs Committee.

Buyer hit Jontz with pointed criticism of his efforts for environmental causes far from home. He even linked those efforts with higher lumber prices in Indiana and argued that Jontz could be costing the district jobs and hurting the economy. And just before the election, union members from the Northwest timber industry came to Indiana to campaign against Jontz.

By Election Day, Buyer and Jontz were in a dead heat. In one of the biggest surprise wins of the season, Buyer won with 51 percent of the vote.

In Washington, Buyer parlayed his military experience into seats on the Armed Services and Veterans' Affairs committees.

Indiana 5

Northern Rural — Kokomo

The 5th stretches across a mainly rural area that calls itself the "Hoosier Heartland." One would expect such a place to have a Republican tilt, and it does: George Bush carried 17 of the district's 20 counties in 1992. Redistricting in 1991 enhanced GOP strength in the 5th, and that helped Buyer narrowly defeat Democratic Rep. Jim Jontz, who had won the district three times with an energetic campaign style, assiduous constituent service and attention to agricultural concerns.

With economies heavily reliant on auto parts manufacturing, many of the district's small cities have struggled. Like many areas across the Midwest, several 5th District counties declined in population during the 1980s. Industrial Grant County (Marion) lost 8 percent of its population, while Howard County (Kokomo) fell by 7 percent. Warren, a farm county on Indiana's western border, was down by 9 percent.

Kokomo, with about 45,000 people, is the district's largest city. It was long a center for industrial innovation: Kokomo resident Elwood Haynes produced the first successful gasoline-powered car and later invented stainless steel (Haynes International Inc., a producer of metal alloys, is one of Kokomo's major employers). The biggest job-provider in the city is Delco Electronics Corp., known for its automobile sound systems. Much of Kokomo's hopes for economic growth are based on Delco's development of electronic pollution-control systems and safety devices such as air bags. Employment at Chrysler's transmission plant has been steady.

Economic recovery has been difficult in Marion and nearby Gas City. A General Motors auto body stamping plant is the largest employer in Marion.

To the north are a string of smaller working-class cities: Wabash, Peru and Logansport. Their distance from major highways is a hindrance to growth; locals are pushing for a "Hoosier Heartland Highway," which would modernize Routes 24 and 25 that connect these cities with Fort Wayne and Lafayette.

Peru has a colorful past — it was the hometown of songwriter Cole Porter and the base for a number of traveling circuses — but a tenuous present; nearby Grissom Air Force Base is on the Pentagon base-closing list and is set to close in 1994.

At its northwest corner, the 5th reaches into the smaller suburbs of central Lake County. In Porter County, only the town of Hebron is in the 5th.

Most of the remaining land in the 5th is farmed. In the district's northeast corner is part of Kosciusko County, which calls itself Indiana's leading agricultural county. This is strong Republican country: Bush beat Bill Clinton here by more than 2-to-1 in 1992, and Buyer took the county.

To the west, the 5th contains counties that are prolific producers of corn, soybeans and hogs. At its southwest extreme, the 5th's terrain and politics change quickly. Vermillion County, where Indiana's coal-mining territory begins, is heavily Democratic. Clinton won Vermillion in 1992, and Gov. Evan Bayh took three-fourths of its vote.

1990 Population: 554,415. White 536,008 (97%), Black 11,928 (2%), Other 6,479 (1%). Hispanic origin 7,463 (1%). 18 and over 403,843 (73%), 62 and over 89,590 (16%). Median age: 34.

Committees

Armed Services (16th of 22 Republicans)
Military Forces & Personnel; Research & Technology

Veterans' Affairs (9th of 14 Republicans)
Hospitals & Health Care; Housing & Memorial Affairs

Campaign Finance

	Receipts	Receipts from PACs		Expend-itures
1992				
Buyer (R)	$395,825	$135,834	(34%)	$392,922
Jontz (D)	$598,531	$352,065	(59%)	$583,029

Key Votes

1993

Require parental notification of minors' abortions	Y
Require unpaid family and medical leave	N
Approve national "motor voter" registration bill	N
Approve budget increasing taxes and reducing deficit	N
Approve economic stimulus plan	N

Elections

1992 General

Steve Buyer (R)	112,492	(51%)
Jim Jontz (D)	107,973	(49%)

District Vote for President

1992

D	70,893 (31%)
R	103,118 (46%)
I	52,354 (23%)

6 Dan Burton (R)

Of Indianapolis — Elected 1982; 6th Term

Born: June 21, 1938, Indianapolis, Ind.
Education: Indiana U., 1958-59; Cincinnati Bible College, 1959-60.
Military Service: Army, 1956-57; Army Reserve, 1957-62.
Occupation: Real estate and insurance agent.
Family: Wife, Barbara Logan; three children.
Religion: Protestant.
Political Career: Ind. House, 1967-69; Ind. Senate, 1969-71; GOP nominee for U.S. House, 1970; sought GOP nomination for U.S. House, 1972; Ind. House, 1977-81; Ind. Senate, 1981-83.
Capitol Office: 2411 Rayburn Bldg. 20515; 225-2276.

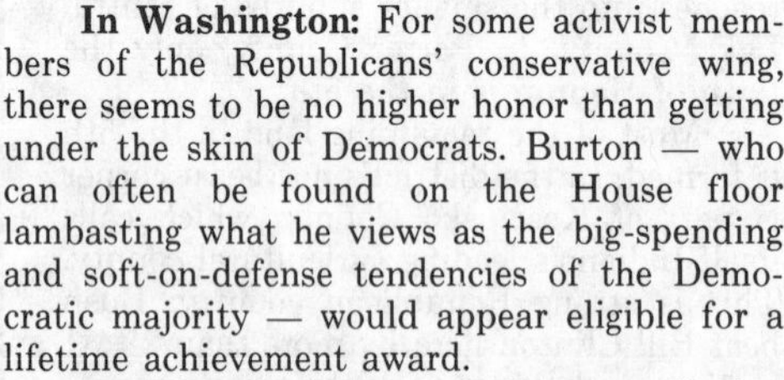

In Washington: For some activist members of the Republicans' conservative wing, there seems to be no higher honor than getting under the skin of Democrats. Burton — who can often be found on the House floor lambasting what he views as the big-spending and soft-on-defense tendencies of the Democratic majority — would appear eligible for a lifetime achievement award.

In early 1993, for example, Burton and other Republican members staged a campaign against the Democratic leadership's use of restrictive rules to limit debate on legislation. He warned during the early days of the 103rd Congress that he would resort to parliamentary tactics, including numerous roll call votes, until House Republicans receive a "modicum of fairness."

Burton did just that, and when he slowed action on President Clinton's first budget resolution in March by demanding a roll call on a sure-to-lose amendment, it was too much for Illinois Democratic Rep. Richard J. Durbin.

In an inquiry worded to avoid House rules against personal attacks, Durbin asked the chairman if "it would be a violation of the rules . . . to characterize a member as petulant and puerile for continuing to call a series of unnecessary roll call votes to interrupt the business of this House and orderly debate?"

Incidents such as these establish Burton as a competitor to Pennsylvania Republican Rep. Robert S. Walker as the leading antagonist of House Democrats. But it has earned him a following on his side of the aisle: Burton was elected at the start of the 103rd Congress as chairman of the House Republican Study Group.

This position could help Burton gain regard as a legislator and move away from his image as a bit of a loose cannon. It was just two years earlier, during the Persian Gulf War, that Burton raised eyebrows by promoting the use of tactical nuclear weapons against Iraqi military targets.

Foreign policy issues have been a major preoccupation of Burton's. The House Foreign Affairs Committee was an ideological battlefield during the Reagan and Bush administrations, and Burton was one of its leading Republican combatants.

Burton regarded communist governments and movements with unstinting hostility. He was not much kinder to fellow House members who did not see things his way. Burton unloosed one of his harshest attacks during a 1987 debate over U.S. aid to the contra rebels then fighting the leftist Sandinista government of Nicaragua. "My colleagues on the left," Burton said, "need to admit forthrightly that they support the communist government of Nicaragua and quit this charade that they try to put forth on the American people."

Although it had no obvious political benefit to a member from the Indiana heartland, Burton claimed the position as ranking Republican on the Foreign Affairs Africa Subcommittee in the 100th Congress, which he has held since.

This senior post was pivotal to his anticommunist crusade. He sponsored U.S. aid to anti-leftist insurgents — whom he described as "freedom fighters" — in such nations as Angola and Mozambique, but strongly opposed the use of sanctions to modify the behavior of African rulers known for anti-democratic practices but pro-Western sympathies.

The collapse of the Soviet Union ended the Cold War competition in the Third World and gave Burton some room for agreement with Democrats on Foreign Affairs. In early 1993, he joined Africa Subcommittee Chairman Harry A. Johnston of Florida in calling for the ouster of Zaire President Mobutu Sese Seko, a former ally of the United States who was accused of corruption and human rights violations. He supported the deployment of American troops to Somalia, started by President Bush and continued by President Clinton, to provide hu-

Indiana 6

Central — Suburban Indianapolis

Over the past couple of decades, the farms and undeveloped tracts of Hamilton, Johnson and outer Marion counties have been overtaken by Indianapolis subdivisions. Growth in some areas outside the city's widely looping beltway (Interstate 465) has been explosive. The population of once-pastoral Hamilton County has doubled since 1970, and it increased 33 percent in the 1980s, reaching about 110,000 in 1990.

The boom has changed the look, but not the politics, of the outlying areas that make up the core of the 6th. The wealthy and near-wealthy who have moved there are nearly as conservative as the farmers who live nearby. Republican vote totals are consistently high — George Bush won 62 percent of the Hamilton County vote in 1992. In neighboring Hancock County, Bush took 54 percent.

The Democrats in the state House who controlled redistricting in 1991 packed even more Republicans into the 6th than it contained in the 1980s: Increasingly suburban sections of Morgan and Boone counties, as well as mainly rural Clinton, Tipton, Hancock and a slice of Henry counties were transferred to the 6th. As a result, the district is not only the most Republican in Indiana, but also is one of the most GOP-oriented House districts in the nation. There is almost no minority-group constituency: Hamilton's black population in 1990 was 0.6 percent.

The 6th takes in the loyally Republican sections of northern and southern Marion County; the rest of Marion is in the Democratic-held 10th. Leaders in the GOP parade are the established suburbs of Washington Township, and the growth area to the northeast around Geist Reservoir. Castleton and part of the city of Lawrence are also in the district.

The northern sections of Marion County blend with the white-collar suburbs of Hamilton County. Although it is just 15 miles from downtown Indianapolis, Carmel in 1970 was a town of about 7,000 people; now, more than 25,000 live there. Noblesville and the nearby Morse Reservoir area also have grown significantly. Zionsville, in the southeast corner of Boone County, continues to advertise its quaint appearance even as it is further absorbed into the Indianapolis sphere.

There is suburban wealth in the district's southern reaches, but a number of residents of more modest means also live there. Some working-class Marion County suburbanites work at the Amtrak repair shops in Beech Grove and at Indianapolis Metropolitan Airport; the 6th takes in the city of Speedway, host of the Indianapolis 500 auto race. Johnson County, which grew by 14 percent in the 1980s, combines suburban sprawl with an industrial presence: Arvin Industries makes auto parts in Greenwood and Franklin.

The suburbs have encroached somewhat on Hancock County (Greenfield). However, the northernmost counties, Clinton and Tipton, are still primarily farmland.

1990 Population: 554,416. White 541,811 (98%), Black 5,888 (1%), Other 6,717 (1%). Hispanic origin 4,374 (1%). 18 and over 408,057 (74%), 62 and over 74,996 (14%). Median age: 34.

manitarian relief to its starving people. But in a role reversal that marked the change in party control of the White House, Burton bridles at giving Clinton open-ended authority to commit troops to peacekeeping forces there.

But if there has been a de-escalation of partisan conflict on foreign policy, it has only enabled Burton to step up his activism on his other hot-button issue: "pork barrel" spending in Congress, which he blames mainly on the Democratic majority.

Burton annually injects himself into debates on appropriations bills, seeking across-the-board cuts or deletions of specific items he sees as unnecessary.

Although most of his pork-busting efforts have gone for naught, he did score a coup in October 1991. Senate Appropriations Committee Chairman Robert C. Byrd was facing criticism for funneling programs to his home state of West Virginia, and Burton went after one of them: a $4.5 million grant for a hardwoods training and manufacturing center.

"Enough is enough," Burton said. "I do not mind giving a little bit of pork to West Virginia, but not the whole pig." The House voted to kill the spending provision.

Burton is not without his own parochial interests. The co-chairman of the Congressional Auto Caucus and a member of the Steel Caucus, he takes a more protectionist position than many Republicans, a reflection of the difficulties foreign competition has caused many of Indiana's blue-collar industries.

Burton's other committee assignments are Veterans' Affairs and Post Office and Civil

Service. He has found partisan battles to fight there as well. For example, in 1992, when the Post Office Subcommittee on Human Resources investigated the costs attributable to Bush's travels, Burton — the ranking Republican on the panel — accused Democrats of playing election-year politics and trying to deflect criticism of Congress' own perks.

"This is a political mission on the part of the Democratic leadership, and you guys are being used as pawns," he told subcommittee Democrats during a July 1992 hearing.

At Home: Redistricting, which made the 6th solid Republican terrain in 1982, helped put Burton in office and helped him win easily in his next four re-election bids. And redistricting should help him even more into the '90s: The Democrats who controlled redistricting in 1991 packed even more Republicans into the 6th than it contained in the 1980s.

Burton, a longtime state legislator, settled an old intraparty score by winning his 1982 primary.

A decade earlier he had lost to William Hudnut by 81 votes for the nomination in a nearby district; Hudnut served a term in the House and later became mayor of Indianapolis. When the new 6th was created in 1981, Mayor Hudnut hoped to secure the nomination for his GOP ally, state party Chairman Bruce Melchert. Against Melchert, however, Burton won.

Burton and Melchert agreed on most issues, and the competition was mostly amiable. But the Burton-Hudnut feud surfaced at one point, when Burton suggested that the mayor had engineered the last-minute candidacy of political unknown Ricky Bartl to deprive Burton of the first position on the alphabetical ballot.

Burton won the primary by 5,260 votes of over 72,000 cast, and in November took 65 percent, a winning margin that began a long streak of decisive general-election victories.

In 1992, he solidified his hold on the district by taking 72 percent of the vote.

Burton served 10 years in the state legislature, his tenure interrupted by two congressional campaigns — the losing 1972 primary against Hudnut and an unsuccessful 1970 bid against Democratic Rep. Andrew Jacobs Jr.

Committees

Foreign Affairs (9th of 18 Republicans)
Africa (ranking); International Security, International Organizations & Human Rights

Post Office & Civil Service (4th of 9 Republicans)
Civil Service (ranking)

Veterans' Affairs (3rd of 14 Republicans)
Housing & Memorial Affairs (ranking); Hospitals & Health Care

Elections

1992 General		
Dan Burton (R)	186,499	(72%)
Natalie M. Bruner (D)	71,952	(28%)
1992 Primary		
Dan Burton (R)	64,128	(80%)
George B. Tintera (R)	8,700	(11%)
William Russell Sparks II (R)	6,852	(9%)
1990 General		
Dan Burton (R)	116,470	(63%)
James P. Fadely (D)	67,024	(37%)

Previous Winning Percentages: **1988** (73%) **1986** (68%) **1984** (73%) **1982** (65%)

District Vote for President

1992

D 61,171 (23%)
R 153,280 (57%)
I 54,718 (20%)

Campaign Finance

	Receipts	Receipts from PACs		Expend-itures
1992				
Burton (R)	$591,300	$213,385	(36%)	$368,965
Bruner (D)	$32,156	0		$32,153
1990				
Burton (R)	$526,451	$203,426	(39%)	$311,727
Fadely (D)	$41,866	$9,000	(21%)	$41,180

Key Votes

1993	
Require parental notification of minors' abortions	Y
Require unpaid family and medical leave	N
Approve national "motor voter" registration bill	N
Approve budget increasing taxes and reducing deficit	N
Approve economic stimulus plan	N
1992	
Approve balanced-budget constitutional amendment	Y
Close down space station program	Y
Approve U.S. aid for former Soviet Union	N
Allow shifting funds from defense to domestic programs	N
1991	
Extend unemployment benefits using deficit financing	N
Approve waiting period for handgun purchases	N
Authorize use of force in Persian Gulf	Y

Voting Studies

	Presidential Support		Party Unity		Conservative Coalition	
Year	**S**	**O**	**S**	**O**	**S**	**O**
1992	75	23	94	4	85	10
1991	75	23	92	6	97	3
1990	77	22	95	2	94	2
1989	60	28	85	6	85	7
1988	84	16	96	2	95	0
1987	76	19	93	3	93	7
1986	81	18	94	4	96	4
1985	80	16	94	2	100	0
1984	73	20	93	3	90	5
1983	83	16	92	4	93	6

Interest Group Ratings

Year	ADA	AFL-CIO	CCUS	ACU
1992	10	25	86	100
1991	5	17	80	100
1990	11	17	85	96
1989	5	17	90	96
1988	0	0	93	100
1987	8	0	93	100
1986	5	21	89	100
1985	5	0	86	100
1984	0	23	86	83
1983	10	13	80	91

7 John T. Myers (R)

Of Covington — Elected 1966; 14th Term

Born: Feb. 8, 1927, Covington, Ind.
Education: Indiana State U., B.S. 1951.
Military Service: Army, 1945-46; Army Reserve, 1946-67.
Occupation: Banker; farmer.
Family: Wife, Carol Carruthers; two children.
Religion: Episcopalian.
Political Career: No previous office.
Capitol Office: 2372 Rayburn Bldg. 20515; 225-5805.

In Washington: Myers is the kind of old-fashioned, middle-American moderate Republican who was traditionally found within the inner circle of the House GOP leadership. His insider status has served him well over the years, earning him his seat on the Appropriations Committee, where he is now the No. 2 Republican in seniority.

A banker, a farmer, a Mason, an Elk and a Lion, Myers shares with other Appropriations members a pragmatic worldview in which deal-making skills are valued over ideology.

This philosophy, however, has spurred distrust among some of his party's House conservatives, who think Myers and other senior GOP appropriators are more loyal to their committee's products than to party principles of fiscal conservatism. Myers' sharpest critics may come from within the Republican Conference, whose upper echelons are now dominated by a newer, more confrontational breed.

With Appropriations' ranking Republican, Joseph M. McDade of Pennsylvania, facing criminal corruption charges, Myers could find himself in the ranking spot before long. When McDade was indicted in May 1992, Myers temporarily filled in for McDade. Beginning in the 103rd Congress, Myers is also the ranking Republican on the Post Office and Civil Service Committee.

Myers has never left any doubt about his affiliation with Appropriations politics. The ranking Republican on the Energy and Water Development Subcommittee, he likes to describe the panel's spending measure as "an all-American bill" that would "touch every congressional district in our country directly."

In 1990, as the fiscal 1991 energy and water appropriations bill breezed through the full committee, Myers took note of the lack of substantive amendments. "How can you improve upon perfection?" he joked.

He was particularly upset at Congress' 1992 vote to add a nuclear test moratorium to the energy appropriations bill.

Myers emerged in the 101st Congress as a supporter of the superconducting super collider, a multibillion-dollar atom smasher to be built in Texas by the Department of Energy. Defending the first-stage appropriation for the project, Myers pointed to the predicted technological spinoffs. "We don't know exactly where we're going," he said in July 1989. "But it's time to make an investment in our future." He opposed efforts in the 102nd Congress to kill the collider.

It is the subcommittee's control over the science research and water projects that many members covet for their districts — and conservatives deride as "pork" — that makes the panel an important power base for Myers. He also gets his share for his home turf: The fiscal 1992 bill included $10 million to build a cancer research center at Indiana University's medical school at Indianapolis, close to his district.

Myers can be a genial jokester in the Republican cloakroom, but he is noted for playing hardball on bills he has a hand in: He tracks closely those who vote with and against him. Once in a private meeting with Republicans, Myers pulled just such a list of names from his suit pocket and brandished it for all to see.

Myers can be sharp toward Republicans who try to demonstrate their fiscal conservatism by cutting the energy and water bill. In mid-1987, he told some members they would lose pet projects if they supported efforts to cut the bill on the House floor. Saying it would be hard in a House-Senate conference to defend projects of members who did not support the whole bill, Myers later explained, "It's not a threat. It's a fact of life."

The antagonism between old-school Republicans like Myers and the more confrontational activists led by Georgia Republican Newt Gingrich boiled up in 1989. At issue was whether Myers, then ranking Republican on the House ethics committee, and the other traditional Republican insiders on that panel would be tough enough in the investigation of Jim Wright of Texas, who was then Speaker.

Expressing concern that the ethics committee might "issue a whitewash," Gingrich asked a GOP leadership panel to call for the committee to release all of its testimony and documents. Myers headed off that suggestion, convincing his colleagues that the probe would be thorough. And he

Indiana 7

West — Terre Haute; Lafayette

The Wabash River recalls to Hoosier nostalgists the days when western Indiana was settled by newcomers who arrived on flatboats and steamers. The 7th, which ranges across this region, has long been identified with cities that sprang up along the river: Lafayette and Terre Haute.

However, rapid growth in the suburban counties west of Indianapolis has given the 7th a third population center. Adding to this new suburban clout is the northwest section of Monroe County, which contains expanding communities near Bloomington.

In the Indianapolis orbit is Hendricks County, the largest of the district's suburban counties; its population increased nearly 9 percent in the 1980s to 76,000. Growth was also flush to the south in Morgan County and to the north in Boone County, most of which are in the 7th.

Each of these counties is relatively affluent and has a minuscule minority population: just nine blacks were counted among Morgan County's 56,000 residents in 1990. The conservative tone of these counties has strongly reinforced the district's long-held Republican tendencies.

Lafayette and Terre Haute remain the 7th's major urban centers. The tale of these cities is a study in contrasts.

The Lafayette area (Tippecanoe County) has enjoyed economic growth. Some is attributed to Purdue University — which helps attract technology-oriented businesses — in West Lafayette. With nearly 36,000 students, Purdue employs more than 11,000 full-time workers, the most in the area.

Industry also has expanded around Lafayette: One of the most touted Japanese investments in Indiana, a Subaru-Isuzu plant that employs about 2,000 people, is here. Other facilities include an Eli Lilly chemical plant, an Alcoa aluminum plant and a Fairfield plant that makes gear shafts.

While its blue-collar sector provides some Democratic votes, Tippecanoe has held fast to its GOP traditions.

But Terre Haute (Vigo County) has a Democratic bent that economic hard times reinforced. Once a hotbed of radicalism — Terre Haute was the hometown of socialist Eugene V. Debs — Vigo supported Bill Clinton in 1992 with 43 percent of the vote. George Bush won here narrowly in 1988.

Terre Haute is coping with long-term industrial decline. At the northern end of Indiana's coal country, the city suffered from the national coal industry's ailments. Today, the largest area employer is Columbia House, the mail-order distributor of tapes and records. Several factories produce plastics and films; Pfizer has a pharmaceutical plant nearby. Local officials tout the city's colleges: Indiana State University (12,000 students) and the Rose-Hulman Institute.

The rest of the 7th is mainly GOP farmland, dotted with small cities such as Crawfordsville (Montgomery County), which has a large R. R. Donnelly printing plant. Greencastle (Putnam County) is home to Dan Quayle's alma mater, DePauw University (2,400 students).

1990 Population: 554,416. White 533,827 (96%), Black 10,899 (2%), Other 9,690 (2%). Hispanic origin 4,611 (1%). 18 and over 418,523 (75%), 62 and over 82,291 (15%). Median age: 32.

took umbrage at the interference. "If we don't hang somebody the first day of the trial, some people complain," he said in an interview.

The concerns of the GOP right proved unjustified. When the ethics committee voted to pursue charges against Wright in a trial-like proceeding, Myers voted "yes" on every count.

Myers also took a tough line on Democratic Rep. Barney Frank of Massachusetts, whose past relationship with a male prostitute was under investigation in 1990. When some committee Democrats suggested letting Frank off with the lightest punishment, a letter of reproval, Myers held out for a stricter sentence. The committee eventually compromised on a reprimand for Frank, which the House passed.

Myers' other assignment is Post Office and Civil Service, where he became ranking Republican at the start of the 103rd Congress. Early in the 103rd, Myers and Chairman William L. Clay of Missouri backed long-sought legislation overhauling the Hatch Act to ease restrictions on the political activities of federal workers.

At Home: Myers began his winning ways in 1966, when redistricting produced a 7th District without an incumbent. Myers had long been active in the party, mostly on the local level in Covington and in the Young Republicans. His 29 percent was enough for the GOP nomination over five opponents, one of whom, Daniel B. Crane, later served in the House from Illinois.

For years, Democrats helped Myers by nominating candidates of limited appeal. In 1966, Myers defeated Elden C. Tipton, a former naval officer and farmer who had been beaten twice before. Tipton tried two more campaigns against Myers but never came close. His son, J. Elden Tipton, ran a similarly weak campaign against Myers in 1976.

By 1978, many Democrats in the 7th were saying that Myers' only real strength was his ability to draw the Tiptons as his opposition. That year, Democrat Charlotte Zietlow, a former Bloomington City Council president, ran a spirited race against Myers. But Myers' rural support canceled out Democratic strength in Bloomington, and he won comfortably.

Democrats had a vigorous challenger in 1984 in Art Smith, a former congressional aide. But Smith's lopsided loss scared away significant opposition in 1986 and made Democratic leaders pessimistic about 1988. Their nominee, lawyer Mark R. Waterfill, wound up running the strongest Democratic campaign of the 1980s. Even so, he failed to reach 40 percent. In the anti-incumbent wave of 1990, Myers slipped to 58 percent against John W. Riley, a school bus driver and former carpenter.

And in 1992, even though the district was drawn to strengthen the Republicans' hold, Myers was held to 59 percent by Democrat Ellen E. Wedum, a chemist. Wedum, who had a difficult time raising campaign funds, was helped by voter backlash against Myers' 61 overdrafts at the House bank, a nationwide anti-incumbent atmosphere and the presence of Democratic Gov. Evan Bayh (who was easily re-elected) on the ballot.

Committees

Post Office & Civil Service (Ranking)

Appropriations (2nd of 23 Republicans)
Energy & Water Development (ranking); Agriculture, Rural Development, FDA & Related Agencies

Elections

1992 General		
John T. Myers (R)	129,189	(59%)
Ellen E. Wedum (D)	88,005	(41%)
1992 Primary		
John T. Myers (R)	32,238	(61%)
Charles J. Metzger (R)	20,382	(39%)
1990 General		
John T. Myers (R)	88,598	(58%)
John W. Riley Sr. (D)	65,248	(42%)

Previous Winning Percentages: **1988** (62%) **1986** (67%) **1984** (67%) **1982** (62%) **1980** (66%) **1978** (56%) **1976** (63%) **1974** (57%) **1972** (62%) **1970** (57%) **1968** (60%) **1966** (54%)

District Vote for President

1992
D 67,836 (32%)
R 97,908 (46%)
I 46,410 (22%)

Campaign Finance

	Receipts	Receipts from PACs		Expend-itures
1992				
Myers (R)	$329,387	$199,784	(61%)	$369,882
Wedum (D)	$51,495	$7,550	(15%)	$51,245
1990				
Myers (R)	$198,891	$98,870	(50%)	$228,556

Key Votes

1993	
Require parental notification of minors' abortions	Y
Require unpaid family and medical leave	N
Approve national "motor voter" registration bill	N
Approve budget increasing taxes and reducing deficit	?
Approve economic stimulus plan	?
1992	
Approve balanced-budget constitutional amendment	Y
Close down space station program	N
Approve U.S. aid for former Soviet Union	N
Allow shifting funds from defense to domestic programs	N
1991	
Extend unemployment benefits using deficit financing	N
Approve waiting period for handgun purchases	N
Authorize use of force in Persian Gulf	Y

Voting Studies

	Presidential Support		Party Unity		Conservative Coalition	
Year	**S**	**O**	**S**	**O**	**S**	**O**
1992	76	18	70	27	90	10
1991	75	22	66	29	100	0
1990	69	29	65	33	94	6
1989	73	27	56	40	88	10
1988	57	33	60	34	82	13
1987	65	29	59	36	88	7
1986	67	31	54	45	82	18
1985	69	28	58	39	91	9
1984	59	40	69	26	93	7
1983	68	27	72	25	88	8
1982	70	27	84	16	89	11
1981	75	25	77	21	91	9

Interest Group Ratings

Year	ADA	AFL-CIO	CCUS	ACU
1992	0	17	75	84
1991	0	17	90	70
1990	11	0	86	83
1989	20	25	100	74
1988	15	15	92	83
1987	8	19	60	87
1986	20	36	50	91
1985	20	18	73	71
1984	15	15	50	74
1983	10	0	90	83
1982	5	15	86	85
1981	0	29	83	93

8 Frank McCloskey (D)

Of Smithville — Elected 1982; 6th Term

Born: June 12, 1939, Philadelphia, Pa.
Education: Indiana U., A.B. 1968, J.D. 1971.
Military Service: Air Force, 1957-61.
Occupation: Lawyer; journalist.
Family: Wife, Roberta Ann Barker; two children.
Religion: Roman Catholic.
Political Career: Democratic nominee for Ind. House, 1970; mayor of Bloomington, 1972-82.
Capitol Office: 306 Cannon Bldg. 20515; 225-4636.

In Washington: Although McCloskey has three committee assignments — Armed Services, Foreign Affairs, and Post Office and Civil Service — he tends to throw his energy behind one issue at a time.

Some of his focus issues have been rather esoteric, as in his investigation during the 100th Congress into the efficacy of night-vision goggles used by military pilots, and his successful effort during the 101st Congress to crack down on deceptive mailings by fundraising or advocacy organizations.

But during the 102nd Congress, McCloskey stepped out front on an issue of historic moment: the violent disintegration of Yugoslavia. McCloskey became a fierce advocate of the Muslim population in Bosnia-Herzegovina, which found itself under siege by Bosnia's ethnic Serbs backed by the leaders of the former Yugoslav republic of Serbia.

McCloskey became engaged in the Bosnian issue in 1991 when the Serbian government — which already had engaged in a territorial battle with the republic of Croatia — was accused of genocide, under the name of "ethnic cleansing," against Bosnian Muslims.

McCloskey visited Croatia in 1991 and came back deeply moved. He had traveled to a town that only hours before had been devastated by an attack by Serb partisans. "There were between 40 and 50 people killed," McCloskey said. "I saw the bodies being brought in with half their faces gone."

Charging Serbia with Nazi-like fascism, McCloskey was one of the first House members to call on the United States and European nations to take strong action, including possible military intervention.

McCloskey was especially critical of President George Bush for taking a hands-off approach on negotiations between Yugoslavia's warring factions. In August 1992, he called for the lifting of an arms embargo affecting Bosnia. "If nothing else, we should let them defend themselves," McCloskey said.

Democratic presidential candidate Bill Clinton, during his 1992 campaign, also criticized Bush's handling of the issue. But after he became president, Clinton — faced with the lack of European support for intervention and concerns about sending U.S. troops into a military quagmire — also took a cautious approach.

In an impassioned speech on the House floor in March 1993, McCloskey, a member of the Foreign Affairs Subcommittee on International Security, International Organizations and Human Rights, placed primary blame for U.S. inaction on Bush. But McCloskey said both Bush and Clinton were guilty of "passivity in the face of Serb aggression in Croatia and Bosnia."

In a remarkably blunt letter to Clinton in March, McCloskey criticized the U.S. reliance on diplomatic pressure: "Your administration is saying that the U.S. will tolerate land grabs and the slaughter of a quarter of a million people in Europe.... This policy is an outrage."

McCloskey's stand on Bosnia surprised some because he had opposed U.S. military intervention elsewhere. An opponent of the Vietnam War when he entered politics in the 1970s, McCloskey in January 1991 voted against the resolution that authorized Bush to use force to end Iraq's occupation of Kuwait.

McCloskey is regarded as one of the more liberal members on Armed Services. He has supported several efforts to cut funding for the Strategic Defense Initiative. He is especially opposed to the concept of deploying weapons in space that could shoot down enemy missiles; McCloskey views that as a dangerous violation of the 1972 U.S.-Soviet ABM Treaty.

Most Armed Services members have favorite weapons programs, and McCloskey is no exception. He opposed the unsuccessful budget-based effort by the Bush administration to eliminate development of the V-22 Osprey, a hybrid airplane-helicopter. McCloskey's interest in the aircraft is based partially on the fact that its engines are built in Indiana.

McCloskey is still a couple of rungs down on the seniority ladder from an Armed Services subcommittee chairmanship, but he chairs the Post Office Subcommittee on Civil Service.

Overall, McCloskey's House voting record

Indiana 8

Southwest — Evansville; Bloomington

Heading toward the Ohio River, Indiana leaves the Corn Belt and enters the hilly border South. The political tradition in much of the 8th is of the Southern Democratic variety, and there is a significant GOP base vote.

Rep. McCloskey has won six consecutive elections but only once has topped 55 percent. His electoral troubles come in a handful of conservative, mostly rural counties — Knox, Daviess, Lawrence and Orange. They helped propel GOP House nominee Richard E. Mourdock to a districtwide tally of 45 percent in each of the past two elections.

But as McCloskey was struggling in 1992, Democrat Evan Bayh carried every county in the district in his gubernatorial re-election bid. And Bill Clinton won in the district's presidential voting, breaking a long dry spell: The 8th had not voted for a Democratic presidential candidate since 1964, when it contributed to Lyndon B. Johnson's landslide.

Three groupings provide much of the Democratic vote: industrial workers in Evansville and Bloomington; the university communities in those cities; and the miners who work the coal lodes in seven of the district's 12 counties.

Evansville (Vanderburgh County), an Ohio River port, is southern Indiana's industrial center. With just over 125,000 residents, it is Indiana's third-largest city. A Bristol-Myers pharmaceutical plant and a Whirlpool refrigerator factory are two of the leading employers; residents also commute east to an Alcoa aluminum plant in Newburgh (Warrick County) and west to a General Electric plastics plant in Mount Vernon (Posey County). Although Evansville has access to Interstate 64, it is the only large city in Indiana without a direct highway link to Indianapolis.

While the city hosts two small colleges, the University of Southern Indiana and the University of Evansville, it is Bloomington — home of Indiana University — that is the district's college town. "IU" has 35,000 students and employs 6,800 people.

Although the campus and blue-collar crowds rarely mix — tensions between students and working-class Bloomington youths were the background of the movie "Breaking Away" — they combine politically to give Democrats an edge. A General Electrics refrigerator factory, a French-owned Thomson electronics plant and an Otis Elevator factory are the city's largest industrial companies.

Past the limestone quarries of Monroe and Lawrence counties is the Naval Surface Warfare Center in Crane (Martin County), one of the district's largest employers, which develops naval systems and produces ammunition.

Then come the counties where coal is strip-mined. Indiana coal tonnage was 2.3 percent higher in 1991 than in 1982, but increasing mechanization came at the expense of jobs. Sullivan County was hit hard, losing 10 percent of its population in the 1980s. Most coal counties lean Democratic; in 1992, all but one of them backed Clinton for president.

1990 Population: 554,416. White 531,232 (96%), Black 17,093 (3%), Other 6,091 (1%). Hispanic origin 3,262 (1%). 18 and over 421,765 (76%), 62 and over 92,412 (17%). Median age: 33.

might appear somewhat liberal for southern Indiana. However, he has maintained his base by attending to 8th District issues, including those related to agriculture and coal mining.

McCloskey has succeeded in distancing himself from his reputation as "the four-vote wonder," a liability since his controversial 1984 re-election campaign.

McCloskey won an apparent narrow victory in 1984, but a recount gave the edge to Republican Richard D. McIntyre, who was certified the winner by Indiana's Republican secretary of state. The House Democratic leadership orchestrated a recount by the U.S. General Accounting Office, which declared McCloskey the winner by four votes. Some House Republicans still harbor a grudge over what they saw as a "railroad" job by the Democratic majority.

At Home: Of McCloskey's six House elections, only the 1988 election gave him a comfortable margin — 62 percent. His 1990 and 1992 victories were a different story, representing a slide back toward the narrow margins of his first three House elections.

After his four-vote win in 1984, Republican leaders in the House threatened retribution. Some members even proposed physically blocking McCloskey from taking the oath of office. Their ultimate response was symbolic: House Republicans staged a brief walkout.

Republicans also tried to get revenge at the polls. National GOP strategists thought voters were sufficiently convinced of Democratic misconduct to make McIntyre a winner in 1986. But McIntyre did not have the Reagan coattails that boosted him in 1984, and he had the disadvantage of coming from small Lawrence County.

McIntyre played hardball, reaching back into McCloskey's record as Bloomington mayor in the 1970s to argue that McCloskey had been irresponsible in his denunciations of the Vietnam War and soft in dealing with drug offenses. Once again, McCloskey won largely from support in populous Evansville, which had helped him significantly in 1984. He ended up with 53 percent of the vote.

McCloskey climbed above 60 percent against a weak foe in 1988 but ran into anti-incumbent sentiment in 1990, seeing his margin slip against Republican Richard E. Mourdock, an Evansville coal mining executive. Mourdock hit McCloskey on his votes for a congressional pay raise and for a federal deficit-reduction package that included tax increases.

McCloskey took 55 percent of the vote in 1990 and was expected to improve his margin in 1992 as the intended beneficiary of redistricting, which put the city of Bloomington, where he served as mayor for a decade, into the 8th.

However, McCloskey found himself in a rematch with Mourdock in a year when anti-incumbent sentiment was rampant nationwide. Mourdock was counting on the House bank scandal to influence the outcome in his favor; McCloskey had 65 overdrafts.

McCloskey campaigned tirelessly, reminding voters of his record, including how he preserved jobs at the Naval Surface Warfare Center at Crane. McCloskey won, but Mourdock's attacks on the House bank issue helped keep McCloskey to 52.5 percent of the vote.

Were it not for an auto accident, McCloskey might never have made it to the House. The Indiana General Assembly redrew the 8th in 1981 to make it secure for GOP Rep. Joel Deckard, and at the outset of his 1982 campaign, he was favored over challenger McCloskey. But Deckard drove his car into a tree in early October and admitted that he had been drinking. That incident, combined with Depression-level unemployment in parts of the 8th, boosted McCloskey to a 51 percent win.

A former newspaper reporter, McCloskey was first elected Bloomington's mayor in 1971, the year he finished law school. But after his 1975 re-election campaign, which he won by a narrower margin against a weaker opponent, he modified some of his more liberal positions and emphasized economic development and neighborhood restoration in Bloomington.

Committees

Armed Services (10th of 34 Democrats)
Military Acquisition; Military Installations & Facilities

Foreign Affairs (25th of 27 Democrats)
International Security, International Organizations & Human Rights

Post Office & Civil Service (3rd of 15 Democrats)
Civil Service (chairman); Census, Statistics & Postal Personnel

Elections

1992 General		
Frank McCloskey (D)	125,244	(53%)
Richard E. Mourdock (R)	108,054	(45%)
John W. Taylor (I)	3,098	(1%)
1990 General		
Frank McCloskey (D)	97,465	(55%)
Richard E. Mourdock (R)	80,645	(45%)

Previous Winning Percentages: **1988** (62%) **1986** (53%) **1984** (50%) **1982** (51%)

District Vote for President

	1992	
D	103,697	(43%)
R	97,070	(40%)
I	43,181	(18%)

Campaign Finance

	Receipts	Receipts from PACs		Expend-itures
1992				
McCloskey (D)	$498,192	$329,569	(66%)	$512,852
Mourdock (R)	$248,777	$100	(0%)	$248,152
1990				
McCloskey (D)	$467,981	$322,320	(69%)	$446,040
Mourdock (R)	$147,535	$13,125	(9%)	$146,961

Key Votes

1993	
Require parental notification of minors' abortions	N
Require unpaid family and medical leave	Y
Approve national "motor voter" registration bill	Y
Approve budget increasing taxes and reducing deficit	Y
Approve economic stimulus plan	Y
1992	
Approve balanced-budget constitutional amendment	Y
Close down space station program	Y
Approve U.S. aid for former Soviet Union	Y
Allow shifting funds from defense to domestic programs	Y
1991	
Extend unemployment benefits using deficit financing	Y
Approve waiting period for handgun purchases	Y
Authorize use of force in Persian Gulf	N

Voting Studies

	Presidential Support		Party Unity		Conservative Coalition	
Year	**S**	**O**	**S**	**O**	**S**	**O**
1992	17	80	93	5	27	71
1991	29	70	91	4	30	70
1990	20	78	93	6	26	72
1989	31	69	89	7	22	78
1988	20	78	91	7	29	71
1987	20	79	90	5	28	72
1986	24	76	84	13	52	48
1985	29 †	71 †	89 †	10 †	27 †	73 †
1984	37	59	84	9	25	69
1983	17	82	89	10	29	69

† Not eligible for all recorded votes.

Interest Group Ratings

Year	ADA	AFL-CIO	CCUS	ACU
1992	95	83	25	12
1991	90	83	20	0
1990	83	92	21	8
1989	85	92	30	7
1988	75	100	21	16
1987	80	94	14	4
1986	55	86	50	18
1985	68	76	30	28
1984	75	85	31	13
1983	85	94	20	22

9 Lee H. Hamilton (D)

Of Nashville — Elected 1964; 15th Term

Born: April 20, 1931, Daytona Beach, Fla.
Education: DePauw U., B.A. 1952; Goethe U. (Frankfurt, Germany), 1952-53; Indiana U., J.D. 1956.
Occupation: Lawyer.
Family: Wife, Nancy Nelson; three children.
Religion: Methodist.
Political Career: No previous office.
Capitol Office: 2187 Rayburn Bldg. 20515; 225-5315.

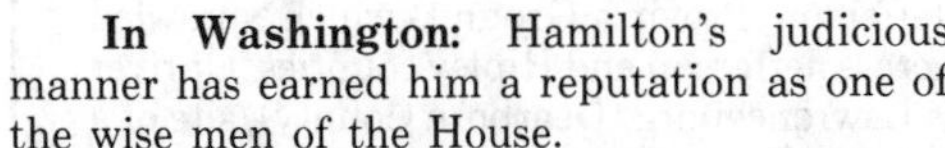

In Washington: Hamilton's judicious manner has earned him a reputation as one of the wise men of the House.

When probity is a requirement for a House assignment, Hamilton is likely to be called. He has served as chairman of the Intelligence Committee and of panels investigating such issues as the Iran-contra affair and the so-called October surprise allegations; during the 103rd Congress, he is co-chairman of the Joint Committee on the Organization of Congress, formed as a result of legislation introduced by Hamilton to examine institutional reform issues.

The latter role is fitting for Hamilton, who is known as a devotee of the legislative process. Although he disagreed with the substance of many Reagan and Bush administration policies, his statements were often colored by his annoyance at the Republican presidents for ignoring what he viewed as Congress' proper role in helping to shape foreign policy.

He should have ample opportunity to further define that role. At the start of the 103rd Congress, he became chairman of the Foreign Affairs Committee.

Hamilton shares many of the views of his predecessor, retired Rep. Dante B. Fascell of Florida, but the two did have their disagreements. Fascell supported the Republican administrations on such issues as aiding the anticommunist contra rebels in Nicaragua during the 1980s and giving President Bush the authority in 1991 to use military force against Iraq; Hamilton took the opposite views.

Yet when Hamilton became chairman, most of the comment had to do with process: that the rigorous Hamilton would run the committee with a firmer hand than Fascell, under whom Foreign Affairs functioned mostly as a debating society.

Hamilton is by no means devoid of opinions: He regularly spells out his views on foreign policy issues in the op-ed pages of newspapers, foreign policy journals and speeches to groups focused on international relations.

As chairman of the Europe and the Middle East Subcommittee (a position he retained after taking over as full committee chairman), Hamilton was in the forefront of efforts to provide U.S. aid to Eastern Europe following the thaw in U.S.-Soviet relations.

After communism fell in the Soviet Union, Hamilton advocated direct U.S. and multilateral aid to promote democracy and capitalism and to demilitarize the longtime U.S. adversary. In August 1992, he spoke for passage of the Freedom Support Act, which boosted such aid. "We cannot live safe and prosperous and free if there is turmoil and upheaval in a vast land that possesses some 30,000 nuclear warheads," Hamilton said. "If their reforms fail or are derailed, all of us are worse off."

Following the Persian Gulf War, Hamilton supported Bush administration efforts to organize negotiations to ease hostilities between Israel and its Arab neighbors. Hamilton tends to be a bit more critical of Israel than many Democrats, but he has not gone so far as to cause obvious unease among the large number of supporters of Israel in the ranks of Foreign Affairs.

With his rise to Foreign Affairs chairman coinciding with Democrat Bill Clinton's election as president, Hamilton is likely to have real influence: Seriously considered as a candidate for secretary of State, Hamilton is consulted frequently by Clinton's ultimate choice for that job, Warren M. Christopher.

Hamilton has on occasion been in the lead in voicing the Democratic leadership's position on foreign policy issues. As the Persian Gulf crisis reached its climax in January 1991, Hamilton and House Majority Leader Richard A. Gephardt of Missouri proposed a resolution that, while not foreclosing future military action to end Iraq's occupation of Kuwait, called for continued use of sanctions and diplomacy. Their measure was defeated by a vote of 183-250, a mirror image of the vote by which the House subsequently passed the resolution authorizing Bush to use force.

Voting with Hamilton and against Bush appeared to be a political liability as the U.S.-led military coalition stormed to a rapid victory.

Indiana 9

Southeast Hill Country — New Albany

Much of the 9th has more in common with Kentucky to the south than with the flatlands of Indiana to the north. The district's population centers — New Albany (Floyd County) and Jeffersonville (Clark County) — are just across the Ohio River from Louisville. The inland areas are scenic but remote and dependent on resource industries, such as timber and coal; rural poverty is present in the 9th.

The voting tendencies are those seen in many districts with Southern Democratic roots. Rep. Hamilton, with his mild, small-town manner, has been a good fit here since 1965; in 1992, he won comfortably in every county, and he took about three-quarters of vote in Floyd and Clark counties. In recent presidential balloting, though, Republicans have fared well in the 9th. The Bush-Quayle ticket carried the district in 1988, but lost it in 1992 by fewer than 1,000 votes.

The more Democratic part of the 9th is its hilly southern region: Bill Clinton won 10 southern counties in 1992. To the north, where the land levels out, patterns are similar to those in the rest of Indiana's farmland: Bush beat Clinton by a slight margin.

The towns in Louisville's sphere grew up as shipbuilding centers: The *Robert E. Lee* and other famed riverboats were built in New Albany. Although the largest area employer — a U.S. Census Bureau data preparation center — is white-collar, this remains an industrial region. New Albany's factories include a Pillsbury plant that makes refrigerated dough products. To the east, Clarksville has a Colgate-Palmolive plant topped by a clock 40 feet in diameter that is said to be the second largest in the world.

Jeffersonville still builds boats, including barges. Since 1974, it also has been home to the Hillerich and Bradsby sporting goods factory. Tourist interest in seeing its famous baseball bats has led the company to plan a new complex back across the river in the original home of the "Louisville Slugger."

Northeast along the Ohio is Madison; its industrial base includes producers of automotive equipment and women's shoes. The local economy is adjusting to the phaseout, under the 1989 base-closing law, of the Army's Jefferson Proving Ground, which sprawled across Jefferson and Ripley counties. Upriver is Lawrenceburg (Dearborn County), site of a Joseph E. Seagram whiskey distillery. Although Dearborn's economy has taken some blows — a Schenley distillery closed in 1988 — the county has grown, thanks to its proximity to Cincinnati: Population was up 13 percent in the 1980s.

At the district's extremes are two small industrial cities: In the northeast part of the 9th, Connersville is the site of a Ford auto air conditioning plant and a Frigidaire appliance factory. At the western end of the 9th is Jasper (Dubois County), a city dominated by German-Americans that bills itself as the nation's "wood office furniture capital." Some coal is mined in Dubois and in Spencer County to the south. In between are forests that attract recreationists to southern Indiana. But unemployment runs well above the state norm in most of the rural counties.

1990 Population: 554,416. White 541,899 (98%), Black 9,436 (2%), Other 3,081 (1%). Hispanic origin 2,458 (<1%). 18 and over 404,813 (73%), 62 and over 85,684 (15%). Median age: 34.

But even as many Democrats ran for cover, Hamilton stood by his position. "How do you calculate the cost" of U.S. and Iraqi casualties? Hamilton wrote in The Washington Post in March 1991. "Were we wrong to support a policy that might have spared these lives and that damage?"

This center-stage role, however, is not Hamilton's typical mode. Though he is sought out when hot foreign policy issues are before the public, the calm and measured Hamilton tends to be overshadowed by more activist members.

This was the case during the debate in early 1993 on whether the United States should intervene in the brutal civil war in the former Yugoslavian republic of Bosnia. Out in front on the issue were interventionists who described Serbian atrocities against Muslims and Croats as a "holocaust" and vocal opponents who said the situation could become another Vietnam-like quagmire for American troops.

Hamilton, meanwhile, was a well-modulated voice for cautious diplomacy, and as chairman of Foreign Affairs he is unlikely to change that. Early in the Clinton administration, he agreed to a strategy under which Bosnia's factions would agree to a partition of the republic, with U.S. forces joining in international peacekeeping efforts to enforce the pact. But when Bosnia's militarily dominant Serbs resisted, putting pressure on Clinton for U.S. military action during the spring of 1993, Hamilton suggested more time was needed to allow diplomacy and economic sanctions to work.

To Hamilton's many admirers, his caution

as a foreign policy-maker is an aid in deterring the nation from rushing into foreign policy mistakes. It also is a reflection of his consistent opposition to war; Hamilton in 1972 authored the first measure passed by Foreign Affairs to end the Vietnam War.

But Hamilton has his share of detractors who view his caution as indecisiveness. This was the theme of a broadside, titled "Nowhere Man," that was written by Jacob Weisberg in the New Republic in December 1992. "A reputation for integrity can disguise a hollowness within," Weisberg wrote in recommending that Clinton not choose Hamilton as secretary of State. "Hamilton is notably deficient in the forcefulness and vision that the chief American architect of the post-Cold War world ought to possess."

Hamilton fired back with a letter to the editor. "I would challenge Weisberg to find a member of Congress who has worked harder to spell out a Democratic foreign policy," Hamilton wrote.

Even within Democratic ranks, where he has widespread support, there has been dismay from some members that Hamilton lacks the sort of partisan edge needed in a leadership role.

In August 1991, House Speaker Thomas S. Foley named Hamilton to head a panel to investigate allegations that officials of Ronald Reagan's 1980 presidential campaign had collaborated with Iranian officials to prevent a release of U.S. hostages that might have boosted the flagging political prospects of President Jimmy Carter.

But Hamilton described himself as a "reluctant investigator," disappointing Democratic partisans who hoped an aggressive October surprise probe might reveal information that could damage the 1992 campaign of President George Bush (who in 1980 was Reagan's vice presidential running mate).

Hamilton led the task force in his usual low-key, bipartisan manner. In January 1993, the task force's final report said "there is wholly insufficient evidence" that the Reagan campaign had consorted with the Iranians.

Hamilton's earlier actions during the Iran-contra incident brought Hamilton his most serious bout of criticism.

Revelations that the Reagan administration had secretly sold arms to Iran and diverted the profits to the Nicaraguan contras burst into the news in November 1986. The facts might have emerged sooner if Hamilton, as Intelligence Committee chairman in 1985 and 1986, had not held back from probing early reports of illegal White House activity.

But Hamilton defended himself by pointing out that administration officials persistently lied about the Iran-contra events. In September 1985, he had called then-national security adviser Robert C. McFarlane before Intelligence; McFarlane assured Hamilton that National Security Council aide Oliver L. North had not "in any way been involved with funds for the contras."

"I for one am willing to take you at your word," Hamilton replied, and the matter was dropped.

Hamilton did a much-commended job as House chairman of the special committee that investigated the affair. In hindsight, however, some Democrats and outside legal experts have criticized Hamilton's support for providing witnesses with legal immunity for their testimony. They say this undercut efforts to pursue charges against such key operatives as North.

Hamilton's mild manner and willingness to work with Republicans were evident during the 101st Congress, when he chaired the Joint Economic Committee. In 1989 and 1990, the panel issued a bipartisan report — the first time that had been done since 1980. The price for consensus, however, was avoiding contentious issues.

The squeaky-clean, Middle American Hamilton was mentioned as a potential Democratic vice presidential candidate in 1988. Given his reserved manner, Hamilton surprised insiders in July 1992 when, in response to questions, he mentioned himself as a possible candidate for the second spot on the Democratic ticket with Clinton.

They were even more surprised a few days later when Hamilton, on NBC-TV's "Meet The Press," stated views on abortion that differed with those of abortion rights advocate Clinton. Saying he agreed with the Supreme Court decision that states could place some restrictions on abortion, Hamilton said, "I think it's perfectly appropriate to put some restraint on a woman seeking an abortion."

The issue may have played a role in his elimination from Clinton's list. Ironically, Hamilton faced a House challenge that fall by a hard-line anti-abortion Republican.

At Home: The son and brother of ministers, Hamilton has a devotion to work that comes out of his traditional Methodist family. From his days in Evansville High School in 1948, when he helped propel the basketball team to the state finals, to his race for Congress in 1964, he displayed a quiet, consistent determination.

When he graduated from DePauw University in 1952, he received an award as the outstanding senior. He accepted a scholarship to Goethe University in Germany for further study.

Hamilton practiced law for a while in Chicago, but soon decided to settle in Columbus, Ind., where his interest in politics led him into the local Democratic Party.

In 1960 he was chairman of the Bartholomew County (Columbus) Citizens for Kennedy. Two years later he managed Birch Bayh's Senate campaign in Columbus.

Lee H. Hamilton, D-Ind.

He was the consensus choice of the local Democratic organization for the 9th District House nomination in 1964, and won the primary with 46 percent of the vote in a field of five candidates. He went on to defeat longtime Republican Rep. Earl Wilson, a crusty fiscal watchdog who had represented the district for almost a quarter of a century.

Hamilton has been re-elected easily ever since. After a few years, Republicans gave up on defeating him and added Democrats to his district to give GOP candidates a better chance elsewhere in the state.

In 1992, Hamilton got a noisy yet fruitless challenge from Republican Michael E. Bailey. Much media attention was focused on Bailey, who ran anti-abortion television ads that showed what he said were dead fetuses in a pail. Despite all of the free publicity, Bailey got a negative response, capturing about 30 percent of the vote.

Hamilton's 1992 brush with a spot on the Clinton team was not the first time he had been mentioned as a candidate to leave the House.

In the early months of 1989, Indiana Democrats urged him to challenge junior GOP Sen. Daniel R. Coats in the 1990 special election to fill the remainder of Vice President Dan Quayle's Senate term.

Despite the limits of Hamilton's base in the state's rural southeast, Indiana political observers considered him the party's most promising candidate against Coats. So great was the respect for Hamilton in both the state and national party structures that the nomination was almost literally his to refuse.

But refuse it he did. Hamilton would have been forced to sacrifice his seat and House seniority to take on Coats. Even if he won, he would have faced another campaign just two years later, when the Quayle term expired. For a cautious man like Hamilton, that was a venture worth walking away from.

Committees

Foreign Affairs (Chairman)
Europe & the Middle East (chairman)

Joint Organization of Congress (Co-Chairman)

Joint Economic

Elections

1992 General		
Lee H. Hamilton (D)	160,980	(70%)
Michael E. Bailey (R)	70,057	(30%)
1990 General		
Lee H. Hamilton (D)	107,526	(69%)
Floyd Eugene Coates (R)	48,325	(31%)

Previous Winning Percentages: **1988** (71%) **1986** (72%) **1984** (65%) **1982** (67%) **1980** (64%) **1978** (66%) **1976** (100%) **1974** (71%) **1972** (63%) **1970** (63%) **1968** (54%) **1966** (54%) **1964** (54%)

District Vote for President

1992
D 98,063 (41%)
R 97,441 (41%)
I 44,873 (19%)

Campaign Finance

	Receipts	Receipts from PACs		Expend-itures
1992				
Hamilton (D)	$484,849	$199,150	(41%)	$477,591
Bailey (R)	$175,189	$6,400	(4%)	$175,013
1990				
Hamilton (D)	$399,758	$188,824	(47%)	$392,606

Key Votes

1993	
Require parental notification of minors' abortions	Y
Require unpaid family and medical leave	N
Approve national "motor voter" registration bill	Y
Approve budget increasing taxes and reducing deficit	Y
Approve economic stimulus plan	Y
1992	
Approve balanced-budget constitutional amendment	N
Close down space station program	Y
Approve U.S. aid for former Soviet Union	Y
Allow shifting funds from defense to domestic programs	N
1991	
Extend unemployment benefits using deficit financing	Y
Approve waiting period for handgun purchases	Y
Authorize use of force in Persian Gulf	N

Voting Studies

	Presidential Support		Party Unity		Conservative Coalition	
Year	**S**	**O**	**S**	**O**	**S**	**O**
1992	33	66	79	20	73	25
1991	43	57	80	20	57	43
1990	27	73	78	22	43	57
1989	42	58	77	23	54	46
1988	25	74	88	12	47	50
1987	26	74	84	16	51	49
1986	33	67	83	17	48	52
1985	38	63	82	18	42	56
1984	49	51	71	29	54	46
1983	35	65	82	17	42	58
1982	47	52	66	33	58	42
1981	47	51	71	27	56	44

Interest Group Ratings

Year	ADA	AFL-CIO	CCUS	ACU
1992	80	75	63	32
1991	65	58	50	15
1990	67	58	43	13
1989	60	67	60	21
1988	85	100	36	8
1987	72	69	47	9
1986	55	57	56	23
1985	60	69	57	33
1984	55	54	38	42
1983	75	71	45	17
1982	70	80	45	18
1981	65	67	28	20

10 Andrew Jacobs Jr. (D)

Of Indianapolis — Elected 1964; 14th Term

Did not serve 1973-75.

Born: Feb. 24, 1932, Indianapolis, Ind.
Education: Indiana U., B.S. 1955, LL.B. 1958.
Military Service: Marine Corps, 1950-52.
Occupation: Lawyer; police officer.
Family: Wife, Kimberly Hood; two children.
Religion: Roman Catholic.
Political Career: Ind. House, 1959-61; Democratic nominee for Ind. Senate, 1960; Democratic nominee for U.S. House, 1962; defeated for re-election to U.S. House, 1972.
Capitol Office: 2313 Rayburn Bldg. 20515; 225-4011.

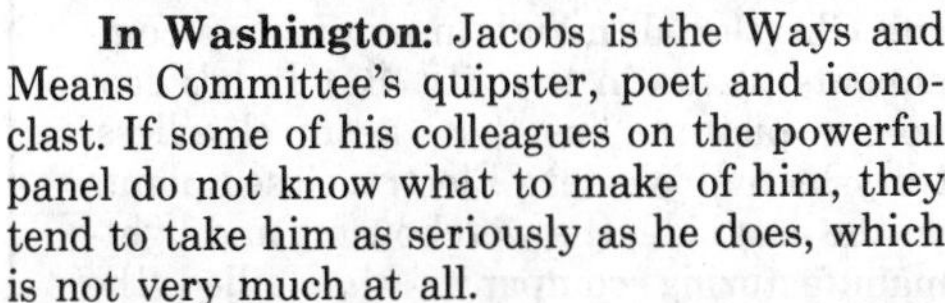

In Washington: Jacobs is the Ways and Means Committee's quipster, poet and iconoclast. If some of his colleagues on the powerful panel do not know what to make of him, they tend to take him as seriously as he does, which is not very much at all.

If that bothers Jacobs, he does not show it. The biography distributed by his office, like an ad for a hit movie, touts an Indianapolis newspaper's description of him as "refreshingly unpredictable." He chooses his legislative path irrespective of party, philosophy or other forms of political category — marching to drummers even Thoreau might not have heard. His voting record reflects allegiance neither to party nor president. "I am not the best go-alonger in the House," he once acknowledged. "Frankly, sometimes I do not get along very well."

His manner is perhaps least suited to Ways and Means' tight discipline. His colleagues may appreciate his offbeat sense of humor, but they do not look to him to provide vital input on the major legislation the committee handles. On a panel that operates on the slapped back and the cut deal, Jacobs' quirky personality excludes him — perhaps by choice — from its horse-trading culture. In early 1993, he skipped Ways and Means' annual retreat in Texas, which was being funded by public and private money. He told The Associated Press that he will not attend any congressional conference unless he can drive and pay his own way. "I can't afford it," he said. "Texas is too far away."

That is not to say that Jacobs is lazy or that he does not play a role in the committee's business. He is senior enough that he cannot be ignored; he chairs the Social Security Subcommittee. As a fiscal conservative on the House's tax-writing panel — he has described himself as a "parsimonious progressive" — he provides Chairman Dan Rostenkowski of Illinois with a point of view not widely held among committee Democrats — a perspective that can help get tax bills to the House floor.

But however eccentric he may seem to his colleagues in Washington, Jacobs remains keenly tuned into the wavelength of Indianapolis, where he continues to win re-election by healthy margins.

Though Jacobs was out of the House for two years after losing in 1972, the special relationship he maintains with his home folks frees him from the fear that tyrannizes some other incumbents whose tenure has been interrupted. Some who have known such setbacks hoard massive campaign treasuries to discourage challengers; Jacobs refuses political action committee (PAC) money and speaking fees and spends little on his campaigns.

Yet Indianans seem attracted by the same traits that have kept Jacobs an outsider in House politics. He is outspoken to the point of showmanship in his fiscal conservatism and attention to federal waste.

He has long opposed lawmakers' salary increases, and after the 101st Congress approved two rounds of raises, he launched a noisy crusade for their repeal that grated even on some colleagues who had opposed the raises in the first place.

Many members know Jacobs for his long-standing war on the perquisites of congressional office. Over the years he has returned tens of thousands of dollars to the Treasury from his salary, veterans' disability payments, mileage reimbursements and office allowances.

He issued dire pronouncements before the last round of House salary increases (to $125,100) although members cut off their speaking fees in exchange. Jacobs had long depicted such honoraria as barely legal bribery. "The only reason it is not bribery is because Congress gets to say what bribery is," he said. He has introduced legislation to repeal the pay raises and automatic increases contained in the 1989 pay raise and ethics package.

Being generally liberal on social questions and dovish on defense has not made Jacobs

Indiana 10

Central — Indianapolis

Geographically and figuratively, Indianapolis is at the center of Indiana life. With just over 730,000 residents in 1990, the state capital had more than four times the population of Fort Wayne, Indiana's second-largest city. Indianapolis is the state's banking and commercial hub, and it retains its traditional role as an industrial city.

Under a unitary city-county government instituted in 1970 (it collects all taxes and handles most services except schools and public safety), Indianapolis takes in all of Marion County except for the small cities of Lawrence, Beech Grove, Speedway and Southport. Consolidation brought large blocks of affluent suburbia into the city limits, reinforcing its standing as one of the most conservative large cities in the country. Its largely non-ethnic white population leans Republican. However, the 10th is crafted to take in the city's most Democratic areas, making it secure for Rep. Jacobs and others of his partisan persuasion. In 1992, Bill Clinton won the 10th, taking 47 percent of the vote. The district includes most of Indianapolis' black population, which makes up 23 percent of the city's total.

A downtown building boom in the 1980s and a relatively low unemployment rate have made Indianapolis a success story among Midwestern cities. Federal, state and city-county governments employ tens of thousands; the Indiana University-Purdue University campus, Butler University and numerous large health-care complexes are also major employers. Banks, insurance companies and the headquarters for the Eli Lilly pharmaceutical company add to the white-collar base.

Long known for its "500" auto race each Memorial Day weekend, Indianapolis has become a major-league sports city and convention site. Construction of the Hoosier Dome, just across the commons from the state Capitol, lured the National Football League Colts from Baltimore in 1984. The Indiana Pacers basketball team plays in nearby Market Square Arena. Indianapolis is also headquarters for the Amateur Athletic Union.

Heavy industry continues to play a role in the city's economy, with blue-collar workers turning out products such as turbine engines and transmissions. GM, Ford and Chrysler all maintain automotive components plants in the city. But Indy's economic picture has not been cloudless. Chrysler and Western Electric closed plants on the east side; the warehousing and light-manufacturing companies that filled the space are less labor-intensive. In general, the city's economic growth has been in white-collar and service industries that are inaccessible or unappealing to many former industrial workers. Indianapolis is also bracing for the phaseout of the Army's Fort Benjamin Harrison, scheduled to close by the summer of 1997. The base includes the Defense Finance and Accounting Center, which may be relocated before the base closes. Some of the district's workers commute to the Naval Air Warfare Center in the neighboring 6th.

1990 Population: 554,416. White 380,178 (69%), Black 165,372 (30%), Other 8,866 (2%). Hispanic origin 6,443 (1%). 18 and over 410,605 (74%), 62 and over 77,040 (14%). Median age: 31.

predictable. He usually votes against spending both for defense and public works projects. Like the most conservative Republicans, he supports a constitutional amendment to require a balanced budget. He has sponsored a constitutional amendment to limit terms of members of Congress and federal judges.

In 1989, Jacobs supplied the deciding vote on Ways and Means for a capital gains tax cut, contributing to his party leadership's biggest defeat in the 101st Congress.

Some observers were surprised by Jacobs' capital gains vote, given his usual rhetoric about taxes and the rich. But Jacobs said he liked the proposal because it allowed capital gains (profits on appreciated assets) to be adjusted for inflation.

In 1992, he backed a Democratic tax proposal, designed by Rostenkowski, that included indexing for capital gains as well as a 10 percent surtax on millionaires and a cut in taxes for the middle class. The support of Jacobs and other senior committee members hinged on Rostenkowski's inclusion of indexing in the bill, which was more an election-year manifesto for the Democratic Party than serious legislation.

Not that Jacobs has hesitated to defy party doctrine on other occasions. In 1981, he voted against the Democratic leadership's package of House rules at the beginning of the 97th Congress and was threatened with ouster from his seat on Ways and Means. Nothing was done, and Jacobs' reputation as a misfit was reinforced.

Jacobs looked like a target again in 1990 when the full Democratic Caucus decided it would henceforth choose the subcommittee chairmen on Ways and Means (as it does for Appropriations). But no challenge to Jacobs materialized. When the caucus voted in 1991, he easily won re-election, but he received more votes in opposition (21) than any Ways and Means or Appropriations subcommittee chairman.

Before becoming chairman of the Social Security Subcommittee, he had held the gavel on the Health Subcommittee. When the Social Security reform bill reached Ways and Means in 1983, Jacobs added a Medicare payment plan setting fixed costs for inpatient treatment of various diseases.

Jacobs also pushed to freeze Medicare payments to physicians and to prevent the charging of extra fees beyond those Medicare paid. "Vote for the canes, not for the stethoscopes," he said. That provoked the American Medical Association to mount a $300,000 independent effort to defeat him in 1986. (He won with 58 percent.)

But in the 100th Congress, Jacobs took another tack when a corporate constituent's interests were at stake. When Ways and Means drafted a bill expanding Medicare to cover catastrophic illness and outpatient prescription drugs, Jacobs succeeded in deleting a provision promoting generic drugs over more expensive name-brand versions.

The provision would have saved the government $400 million, it was estimated, but it would have cost drug manufacturers such as Indianapolis-based Eli Lilly. When another committee restored the generic drug requirement, Jacobs tried again to strike it. The House rejected his move, 161-265, despite drug companies' intense lobbying.

Ways and Means provides Jacobs with a platform to rail about the dangers of smoking. He was a sponsor of the laws that established separate smoking sections on commercial airliners and later banned smoking on virtually all domestic flights. He has also been a consistent advocate of doubling the cigarette tax and earmarking extra revenues for the Social Security hospital insurance trust fund.

When Ways and Means devoted most of its attention to overhauling the tax code in the 99th Congress, Jacobs dealt himself out of the major action by opposing the entire enterprise.

He is prolific in drafting bills and amendments. Some pass. In the 102nd Congress, the House approved a bill that Jacobs and Rostenkowski pushed to make the Social Security Administration an independent agency. The 101st Congress' welfare reform package included Jacobs' pilot program for college students to serve as "aunts and uncles" to welfare children. Another Jacobs effort made the Social Security system available to help blood banks find donors suspected of carrying the AIDS virus. He perennially sponsors legislation to slash expenditures for former presidents, meeting with mixed success.

Other endeavors, however, have proved less successful, such as his bill to make "America, the Beautiful" the national anthem. Or his measure to enclose the House galleries "with a transparent and substantial material." Or his proposal to repeal Article I, Section 8, Clause 11 of the Constitution — the one that gives Congress the power to declare war.

Jacobs' portfolio has also included animal-rights measures, a resolution aimed at providing meatless federal school lunches (he is a vegetarian) and a proposed anti-abortion constitutional amendment.

Early in his career, he was best known as a critic of the Vietnam War. Later, he vocally opposed military aid to the Nicaraguan contras, insisting that either side would rule as dictators, resulting in a flood of illegal immigrants to the United States.

At Home: In August 1989, 57-year-old Jacobs and his wife had their first child, an 11-pound boy named Andy. The name was no surprise: The congressman's father, Andrew Jacobs Sr., was elected to Congress from Indianapolis in 1948 but was turned out of office after one term. The younger Jacobs began moving early toward the congressional career his father never got to carry out.

In 1958, at the age of 26, Jacobs won a seat in the state House. Four years later he tried for Congress but was defeated by GOP Rep. Donald Bruce. In 1964 Bruce announced plans to retire, and Jacobs ran again. With the help of the national Democratic landslide, he edged into office by 3,000 votes out of 295,000 cast.

It would have been difficult for Jacobs to win re-election in 1966 within the same district boundaries. But under court mandate the lines were redrawn, and, with Democrats controlling that process, Jacobs got a more favorable district. He was re-elected regularly until 1972, when a Republican redistricting plan, combined with Richard M. Nixon's presidential landslide, temporarily cost him his seat. He lost that year to Republican William Hudnut, a Presbyterian minister. But he came back to beat Hudnut and reclaim his seat in the 1974 Democratic Watergate surge.

Redistricting after the 1980 census brought Jacobs new headaches. With Republicans again in control of the process, the remap eliminated Democrat David W. Evans' 6th District. Rather than run in one of several heavily Republican constituencies or launch a statewide campaign in 1982, Evans took the risk of a primary challenge to Jacobs, his fellow Democrat and friend.

Jacobs began with a geographic advantage: He had represented just over half the redrawn district. But Evans' tenuous political career — made up of four narrow House elections — had taught him how to fight. A near-fanatic on the campaign trail, Evans went after voters with everything from computerized direct mail to doorbell-ringing. Jacobs, however, had the party's endorsement and financial help. He outpolled Evans by as much as 4-to-1 in some black precincts, won the primary with 60 percent and had no trouble in November.

In 1986, Jacobs ran against the combined fundraising effort of his GOP opponent, Jim Eynon, a 40-year-old Indianapolis real estate manager, and the American Medical Association, which ran an independent barrage of ads. Jacobs, running with his usual low-budget ($40,000) nonchalance, took 58 percent.

In the last three elections, the GOP has been back to its less ambitious program against Jacobs, who skated to easy wins. And redistricting after the 1990 census did not change the fundamental character of the district.

Committee

Ways & Means (6th of 24 Democrats)
Social Security (chairman); Select Revenue Measures

Elections

1992 General		
Andrew Jacobs Jr. (D)	117,604	(64%)
Janos Horvath (R)	64,378	(35%)
Carolyn P. Sackett (NA)	1,849	(1%)
1992 Primary		
Andrew Jacobs Jr. (D)	31,710	(89%)
Joe L. Turner (D)	2,349	(7%)
Fred Ray (D)	1,551	(4%)
1990 General		
Andrew Jacobs Jr. (D)	69,362	(66%)
Janos Horvath (R)	35,049	(34%)

Previous Winning Percentages: **1988** (61%) **1986** (58%) **1984** (59%) **1982** (67%) **1980** (57%) **1978** (57%) **1976** (60%) **1974** (53%) **1970** (58%) **1968** (53%) **1966** (56%) **1964** (51%)

District Vote for President

1992
D 92,514 (47%)
R 70,458 (36%)
I 33,229 (17%)

Campaign Finance

	Receipts	Receipts from PACs		Expend-itures
1992				
Jacobs (D)	$15,690	0		$14,373
Horvath (R)	$67,192	$77	(0%)	$66,727
1990				
Jacobs (D)	$28,712	0		$14,816
Horvath (R)	$21,644	0		$13,201

Key Votes

1993	
Require parental notification of minors' abortions	N
Require unpaid family and medical leave	Y
Approve national "motor voter" registration bill	Y
Approve budget increasing taxes and reducing deficit	N
Approve economic stimulus plan	Y
1992	
Approve balanced-budget constitutional amendment	Y
Close down space station program	Y
Approve U.S. aid for former Soviet Union	N
Allow shifting funds from defense to domestic programs	N
1991	
Extend unemployment benefits using deficit financing	Y
Approve waiting period for handgun purchases	Y
Authorize use of force in Persian Gulf	N

Voting Studies

	Presidential Support		Party Unity		Conservative Coalition	
Year	S	O	S	O	S	O
1992	21	77	59	39	38	63
1991	27	68	61	34	32	65
1990	23	76	55	41	30	67
1989	27	67	48	47	37	61
1988	26 †	68 †	58 †	35 †	26 †	68 †
1987	18	82	61	36	19	81
1986	17	80	61	38	26	74
1985	35	65	53	44	27	71
1984	27	68	65	29	15	80
1983	23	68	61	31	31	64
1982	39	60	62	29	26	74
1981	34	64	73	24	25	75

† Not eligible for all recorded votes.

Interest Group Ratings

Year	ADA	AFL-CIO	CCUS	ACU
1992	85	83	25	20
1991	80	91	20	20
1990	78	83	43	25
1989	85	83	50	33
1988	95	100	42	12
1987	96	94	33	4
1986	85	79	50	0
1985	80	65	59	24
1984	80	69	44	25
1983	75	87	29	19
1982	85	90	41	32
1981	90	67	16	36

Iowa

STATE DATA

Governor:
Terry E. Branstad (R)
First elected: 1982
Length of term: 4 years
Term expires: 1/95
Salary: $76,700
Term limit: No
Phone: (515) 281-5211
Born: Nov. 17, 1946; Leland, Iowa
Education: U. of Iowa, B.A. 1969; Drake U., J.D. 1974
Military Service: Army, 1969-71
Occupation: Lawyer; farmer
Family: Wife, Christine Johnson; three children
Religion: Roman Catholic
Political Career: Iowa House, 1973-79; lieutenant governor, 1979-83

Lt. Gov.: Joy Corning (R)
First elected: 1990
Length of term: 4 years
Term expires: 1/95
Salary: $60,000
Phone: (515) 281-3421

State election official: (515) 281-5865
Democratic headquarters: (515) 244-7292
Republican headquarters: (515) 282-8105

REDISTRICTING

Iowa lost one seat in reapportionment, dropping from six districts to five. The legislature passed the map May 11, 1991; the governor signed it May 30.

STATE LEGISLATURE

Bicameral General Assembly. Meets January-May.

Senate: 50 members, 4-year terms
1992 breakdown: 27D, 23R; 44 men, 6 women; 50 whites
Salary: $18,100
Phone: (515) 281-3371

House of Representatives: 100 members, 2-year terms
1992 breakdown: 51R, 49D; 84 men, 16 women; 99 whites, 1 black
Salary: $18,100
Phone: (515) 281-3221

URBAN STATISTICS

City	Pop.
Des Moines	193,187
Mayor John P. Dorrian, D	
Cedar Rapids	108,780
Mayor Larry Serbousek, N-P	
Davenport	95,333
Mayor Patrick J. Gibbs, R	
Sioux City	80,505
Mayor Robert Scott, D	
Waterloo	66,467
Mayor Albert Manning Jr., R	

U.S. CONGRESS

Senate: 1 D, 1 R
House: 1 D, 4 R

TERM LIMITS

For Congress: No
For state offices: No

ELECTIONS

1992 Presidential Vote

Bill Clinton	43.3%
George Bush	37.3%
Ross Perot	18.7%

1988 Presidential Vote

Michael S. Dukakis	55%
George Bush	45%

1984 Presidential Vote

Ronald Reagan	53%
Walter F. Mondale	46%

POPULATION

1990 population		2,776,755
1980 population		2,913,808
Percent change		−5%
Rank among states:		30
White		97%
Black		2%
Hispanic		1%
Asian or Pacific islander		1%
Urban		61%
Rural		39%
Born in state		76%
Foreign-born		2%
Under age 18	718,880	26%
Ages 18-64	1,631,769	59%
65 and older	426,106	15%
Median age		34.0

MISCELLANEOUS

Capital: Des Moines
Number of counties: 99
Per capita income: $17,505 (1991)
Rank among states: 28
Total area: 56,275 sq. miles
Rank among states: 25

Iowa - Congressional Districts

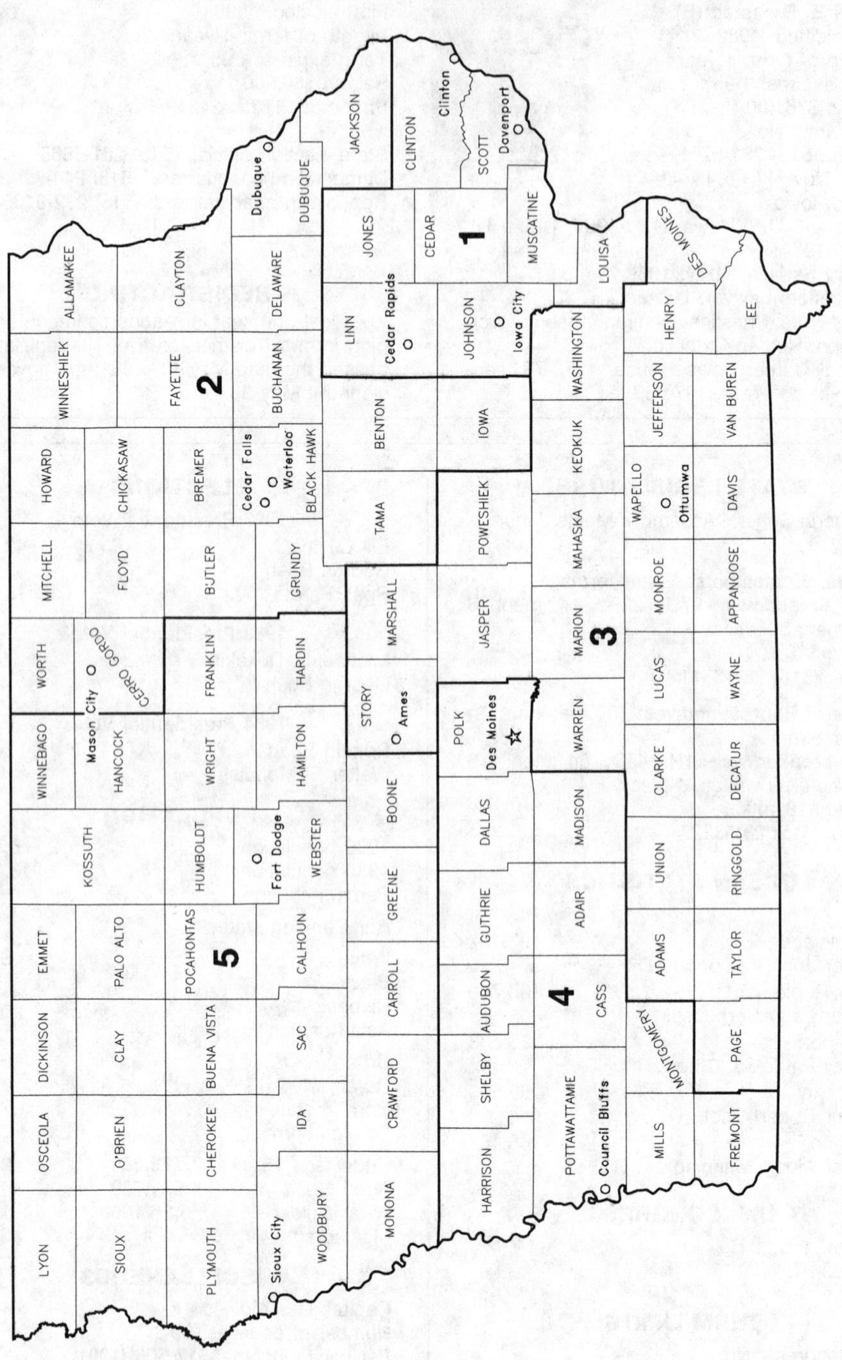

Charles E. Grassley (R)

Of New Hartford — Elected 1980; 3rd Term

Born: Sept. 17, 1933, New Hartford, Iowa.

Education: U. of Northern Iowa, B.A. 1955, M.A. 1956; U. of Iowa, 1957-58.

Occupation: Farmer.

Family: Wife, Barbara Ann Speicher; five children.

Religion: Baptist.

Political Career: GOP nominee for Iowa House, 1956; Iowa House, 1959-75; U.S. House, 1975-81.

Capitol Office: 135 Hart Bldg. 20510; 224-3744.

In Washington: Grassley has made a career out of playing the country bumpkin. "I'm just a farmer from Butler County," he once said. "What you see is what you get."

It is not entirely an act. Grassley's intellectual reach does have its limits. And aside from taking on obvious evils, his Senate accomplishments have been limited in scope even though he has a wide range of committee postings that includes Finance, Agriculture and Judiciary.

But if Grassley's slow-talking, farm-boy routine reinforces all the Eastern stereotypes of the rural Midwest, the liberals who once dismissed him as a right-wing rube now call him sly like a fox.

In 1992, as President Bush's fortunes were sagging, Grassley distanced himself from the losing party, complaining that the "Eastern snobs" running the GOP shunned him at their convention in Houston. They "don't want someone like Chuck Grassley with a Midwestern twang speaking on national television."

Knowing that Bush had lost Iowa in 1988 and was still unpopular there, Grassley could make the comment without risking much, but it did illustrate his knack for reading the political winds. He applies the same instincts to his legislative work.

After winning attention as the man who ferreted out expensive coffeepots and toilet seat covers purchased by the Pentagon, Grassley has turned his spotlight on broader Washington wrongdoings. By the opening of the 103rd Congress, he was zeroing in on issues that play to the Congress-bashing mood prevalent across America.

Grassley won an amendment to the Civil Rights Act of 1991 requiring the Senate to abide by the same civil rights and sexual harassment laws as everyone else. Aware he had hit a nerve with voters who see Washington's leaders as out of touch and unwilling to abide by the rules, Grassley promised to devote more of his time in the 103rd to efforts to apply other laws to Congress. And he began 1993 by criticizing the Clinton administration for holding its health-care task force meetings in secret.

Like his attempts to open up the health-care reform process, Grassley was part of an effort in the 102nd to declassify all government documents relating to Vietnam-era prisoners of war and servicemen missing in action. Taking a high-profile role in special Senate hearings, Grassley argued that the families of the servicemen deserved to finally resolve what happened nearly three decades earlier.

Swayed in particular by photographs of a rice paddy in Laos that appeared to show the letters "U-S-A," Grassley dissented from the special committee's conclusion that neither "live sighting" reports nor other sources of intelligence offered reason for optimism.

Grassley won a lot of publicity in the mid-1980s when he led the effort to trumpet Pentagon mismanagement.

No specialist in defense policy, Grassley strikes some professionals as simplistic with his criticisms of Defense Department procurement procedures. But he captured public attention by seizing the subject with the tenacity of a bulldog. In 1984, it was Grassley, as chairman of the Judiciary Subcommittee on Administrative Practices, who publicized the now-infamous $7,600 coffee maker bought by the Air Force.

In mid-1990, he drew attention with revelations of further procurement follies: Pentagon purchases of $999 pliers, $1,868 toilet seat covers and a mystifying $343 altar vase. No sweeping congressional investigation followed, but Grassley got his headlines.

In recent years, Grassley's concern with defense fraud has made him a major sponsor of legislation to protect workers who blow the whistle on abuse of tax dollars. After President Ronald Reagan issued a surprise veto, Grassley helped negotiate a compromise that Bush signed.

Grassley's first serious legislative attack on defense waste came in the 99th Congress, when he and Arkansas Democrat David Pryor unsuccessfully promoted Pentagon procurement reforms.

But Grassley succeeded in a 1986 attack on dishonest military contractors. He won passage of a bill updating the penalties and enforcement procedures of the federal False Claims Act, a law passed during the Civil War to crack down on suppliers who bilked the Union Army. In 1988, Grassley and Ohio Democrat Howard M. Metzenbaum succeeded in creating a new crime statute to impose tough prison penalties and fines to crack down on fraud in government contracts.

His endeavors have led to a few serious scrapes with those in his own party, but Grassley does not mind advertising that to Iowa's independent-minded electorate. After resisting Reagan's pleas to support the MX missile in 1985, Grassley revealed that a White House operative had summed up his feelings for the senator by saying, "I hope that son-of-a-bitchin' Grassley dies."

Grassley was far more circumspect in his decision to oppose President Bush with a vote against authorizing the use of force in the Persian Gulf in early 1991. He announced his decision in Iowa, where voters have always been wary of foreign conflict. But he did not make a statement before the Senate until after Bush had his victory in hand. He was one of two GOP senators to oppose the resolution.

Underlying all of Grassley's legislative work is a parochial view of his role in the Senate. Pigs and pork most often top his agenda.

He was commended by the National Pork Producers Council in late 1992 for helping win approval for the sale of pork to the former Soviet Union. Describing Grassley as a "fighter for the pork industry," the council said the export program would ensure the sale of at least 30,000 metric tons of pork.

During the 102nd, he pushed a resolution urging the Environmental Protection Agency to include corn-based ethanol as an acceptable clean-burning fuel. He is an advocate of subsidies for rural hospitals and helped win a substantial share of federal highway money for his state. Also in the 102nd, he won support for the federal "Farmers Market Program" that enables families receiving government assistance to purchase fresh produce from farmers, namely those in Iowa.

Even national debates take on a local feel with Grassley.

During 1991 deliberations over extending unemployment benefits, Grassley tenaciously fought a formula that would have denied retroactive payments to about 16,000 Iowans whose coverage had expired. The result was an extra 13 weeks of benefits for those people.

Looking out for Iowa interests was Grassley's chief role during the Finance Committee's 1986 debate on tax code revision. He won a tax break for farmers forced into bankruptcy and another benefiting a Des Moines trucking firm run by one of his campaign contributors. But Grassley, who characterizes himself as a "low-tax boy," has not been a significant player in broader debates over tax policy.

Grassley can be snappish sometimes, particularly with Democratic chairmen, a trait that rarely advances his legislative goals.

More than once, Grassley criticized Massachusetts Democrat John Kerry's management of the POW-MIA investigation. And on Judiciary, he and Chairman Joseph R. Biden Jr. of Delaware tussled over legislation that would have allowed rape victims to sue hard-core pornographers if the victims could prove the material influenced their attackers. Grassley, the leading committee proponent of the bill, sparred frequently with Biden over a series of amendments. The bill died in the 102nd, despite the renewed interest in so-called women's issues in the aftermath of Supreme Court nominee Clarence Thomas' hearings.

At Home: Grassley plays to the Iowa audience with understated artistry, blending shrewd political positioning with the homespun simplicity of the farm country he grew up in. This skill has earned him the moniker "the Kilimanjaro of Iowa politics" and enabled Grassley to crush an opponent who appeared to have all the right ingredients for a successful 1992 bid.

In a campaign season dubbed "The Year of the Woman," state Sen. Jean Lloyd-Jones looked strong on paper. Entering the race soon after the Thomas hearings, Lloyd-Jones was one of 10 female Senate nominees to appear on stage at the Democratic National Convention.

But her record in the General Assembly was spotty, and her candidacy never caught hold. It turned out to be one of the easiest Senate races in state history.

Grassley made his first congressional run from the enviable post of chairman of the state House Appropriations Committee. When veteran GOP Rep. H. R. Gross announced his retirement in 1974, Grassley organized the 3rd District's most conservative elements and won the GOP nomination with 42 percent. In November, he eked out 51 percent against an aggressive young Democrat in a Democratic year.

After conservative Republicans helped Roger W. Jepsen to victory over liberal Democratic Sen. Dick Clark in 1978, attention focused on Grassley as a 1980 challenger to Clark's liberal Senate colleague, John C. Culver.

Grassley's announcement of his Senate candidacy mobilized conservatives, who built a strong grass-roots organization across Iowa. Against a well-financed, moderate GOP primary opponent, Grassley won 90 of the state's 99 counties.

Then Grassley ran head-on into Culver, who conducted an insistent and impassioned defense of his liberal Senate voting record and characterized Grassley's legislative record as mediocre. Targeted for defeat by the Moral Majority and the National Conservative Political Action Committee, Culver lashed out at Grassley's New Right supporters, calling them a "poison in the political bloodstream."

But Grassley, an earnest, easygoing farmer, did not fit the part of a fanatic. He disassociated himself from New Right tactics without losing conservative support, and he turned voters' attention to pocketbook issues by charging that Democratic economic policies brought high inflation. Outpolling Reagan in Iowa, Grassley won 54 percent of the vote.

By 1986, Grassley's crusades against federal waste had built him a constituency that was unaffected by Iowa's massive farm discontent and anti-Reagan feelings. No prominent Democrat wanted to run against him, and the candidate who did, Des Moines lawyer John Roehrick, was never really in the contest.

In 1986 he cleared the 60 percent mark and six years later topped 70 percent.

Committees

Agriculture, Nutrition & Forestry (8th of 8 Republicans)
Agricultural Credit (ranking); Agricultural Production & Stabilization of Prices; Domestic & Foreign Marketing & Product Promotion

Budget (2nd of 9 Republicans)

Finance (7th of 9 Republicans)
Private Retirement Plans & Oversight of the Internal Revenue Service (ranking); International Trade; Medicare & Long Term Care

Judiciary (4th of 8 Republicans)
Courts & Administrative Practice (ranking); Patents, Copyrights & Trademarks

Special Aging (3rd of 10 Republicans)

Elections

1992 General		
Charles E. Grassley (R)	899,761	(70%)
Jean Lloyd-Jones (D)	351,561	(27%)
Stuart Zimmerman (NL)	16,403	(1%)

Previous Winning Percentages: **1986** (66%) **1980** (54%) **1978** * (75%) **1976** * (57%) **1974** * (51%)

* *House elections.*

Campaign Finance

	Receipts	Receipts from PACs		Expend-itures
1992				
Grassley (R)	$2,502,647	$1,002,585	(40%)	$2,322,262
Lloyd-Jones (D)	$415,829	0		$410,894

Key Votes

1993	
Require unpaid family and medical leave	N
Approve national "motor voter" registration bill	N
Approve budget increasing taxes and reducing deficit	N
Support president's right to lift military gay ban	N
1992	
Approve school-choice pilot program	Y
Allow shifting funds from defense to domestic programs	N
Oppose deeper cuts in spending for SDI	N
1991	
Approve waiting period for handgun purchases	N
Raise senators' pay and ban honoraria	N
Authorize use of force in Persian Gulf	N
Confirm Clarence Thomas to Supreme Court	Y

Voting Studies

	Presidential Support		Party Unity		Conservative Coalition	
Year	**S**	**O**	**S**	**O**	**S**	**O**
1992	70	30	81	19	68	32
1991	75	25	83	17	83	18
1990	70	30	85	15	70	30
1989	79	21	91	9	84	16
1988	78	20	87	13	86	14
1987	58	40	77	22	69	31
1986	67	31	72	28	82	18
1985	66	34	64	35	78	22
1984	74	25	79	18	89	11
1983	74	26	81	19	77	23
1982	84	16	82	17	86	12
1981	81	16	84	15	91	7

Interest Group Ratings

Year	ADA	AFL-CIO	CCUS	ACU
1992	30	17	90	74
1991	15	17	60	81
1990	17	33	83	87
1989	25	10	75	86
1988	5	21	93	88
1987	25	30	83	81
1986	30	27	74	70
1985	10	33	69	57
1984	15	9	79	73
1983	15	12	58	64
1982	30	19	62	60
1981	5	6	94	87

Tom Harkin (D)

Of Cumming — Elected 1984; 2nd Term

Born: Nov. 19, 1939, Cumming, Iowa.
Education: Iowa State U., B.S. 1962; Catholic U., J.D. 1972.
Military Service: Navy, 1962-67; Naval Reserve, 1968-74.
Occupation: Lawyer.
Family: Wife, Ruth Raduenz; two children.
Religion: Roman Catholic.
Political Career: Democratic nominee for U.S. House, 1972; U.S. House, 1975-85; sought Democratic nomination for president, 1992.
Capitol Office: 531 Hart Bldg. 20510; 224-3254.

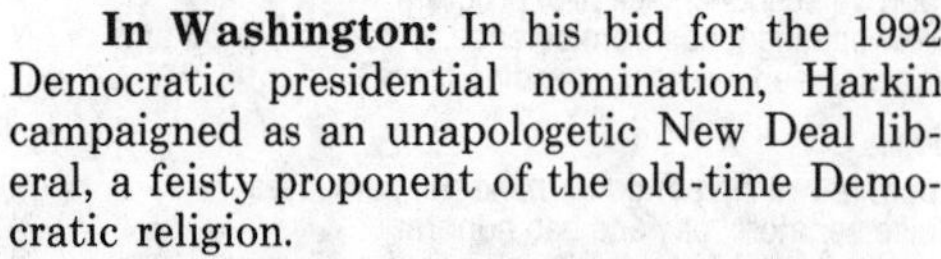

In Washington: In his bid for the 1992 Democratic presidential nomination, Harkin campaigned as an unapologetic New Deal liberal, a feisty proponent of the old-time Democratic religion.

"I've been called a [Hubert] Humphrey Democrat," he said. "And to that I say, amen."

The Iowa populist found few converts beyond his native state. He won the Iowa caucuses but then finished fourth in New Hampshire's primary. He pulled out of the race March 9, starved for cash.

But Harkin's impact was not inconsequential. In the summer of 1991, when President Bush was basking in the gulf war afterglow and Democrats such as Al Gore and Richard A. Gephardt were declaring their disinterest in carrying their party's 1992 presidential banner, Harkin was pounding away at the administration of "George Herbert Walker Bush and J. Danforth Quayle" (as he liked to call them), saying it was out of touch with the problems and concerns of ordinary Americans.

"I don't think the president is that popular," Harkin said. "He has feet of clay, and I intend to take a hammer to them."

For much of 1991, that sort of talk sounded like folly, and Harkin's advocacy of massive federal public works spending struck most as a political antiquity. But toward the end of 1991 and into 1992, as the gulf war faded from memory and the sputtering economy failed to find places for millions seeking jobs, Harkin turned out to be right: Bush *did* have clay feet. Democratic voters, however, wanted someone else to wield the hammer.

Harkin's hard-charging style ("Politics is a combat sport. Never defend. Always attack.") came across better at rallies than in debates on TV, where smooth Bill Clinton shined. Also, the glare of national media attention on Harkin's campaign served to clarify aspects of Harkin's personal and family background that had been indistinct.

The first concerned his military service during the early Vietnam War years. Harkin as a Navy pilot was stationed at an air base in Japan that repaired aircraft damaged in combat; he ferried planes into and out of the base. Some of Harkin's earlier statements and media accounts had created an incorrect impression that he was a combat pilot in Vietnam. Earlier, Harkin flew fighters at the U.S. base at Guantanamo Bay, Cuba, on patrols providing base defense and protection for ships and aircraft.

The second misimpression revolved around Harkin's brother, Frank. To illustrate one of his favorite themes — that greedy business interests in the 1980s and since repeatedly have stepped on the working man — Harkin relates that Frank (who is deaf) was a faithful worker for 23 years at a Des Moines factory but was thrown out of his job when new owners bought the plant and replaced its unionized work force.

Harkin's telling of Frank's story is quite affecting. When he spun the tale on the Senate floor in mid-1992 (during debate on a striker-replacement bill), he said that after Frank lost his job, he told him: "I feel like a piece of machinery. They used me up, and then they threw me out in the trash."

Some who hear this story are left with a picture of Frank as down on his luck; in fact, his firing happened years ago, and in the late 1970s Harkin helped Frank find a temporary job with the Postal Service, which he parlayed into full-time employment and a career that ended in retirement with full health and pension benefits. Harkin is not in the habit of mentioning that Frank lost his factory job well before the 1980s, or that he went on to another career.

But if Harkin's presidential campaign had a slashing tone and generated media comment about his truthfulness, the gracious way he departed the race left a favorable impression. He chose Gallaudet University in Washington, D.C., a school for the deaf, for his withdrawal speech. He called the school "a very real symbol of what my campaign has been all about" and delivered much of the speech in sign language.

The event called attention to the crown jewel of his Senate career: His sponsorship of legislation protecting the civil rights of the disabled, the 1990 Americans with Disabilities Act.

Harkin quickly endorsed Clinton and worked hard to win votes for him, especially among his labor union allies. His wife, Ruth, was named by Clinton in 1993 to head the Overseas Private Investment Corporation.

In Congress, Harkin sees himself as a defender of the interests of the common folk against the rich and powerful. He has two valuable posts from which to pursue his causes: the chairs of the Labor Subcommittee on Disability Policy and the Appropriations Subcommittee on Labor, Health and Human Services and Education.

In the 102nd Congress, he successfully pushed a measure to expand programs under the Individuals with Disabilities Education Act. He also won reauthorization of legislation aimed at protecting the rights of the mentally ill.

In addition, Harkin has been a successful activist for increased funding for breast cancer research; two of his sisters died of breast cancer. And he advocates cutting or eliminating funding for the superconducting super collider and the space station to free money for "human needs" programs.

Harkin has said that the proudest moment of his years in Congress came in 1990 when President Bush signed the Americans with Disabilities Act. The law, passed after years of effort and negotiations, extends broad civil rights protections to an estimated 43 million Americans with mental and physical disabilities. During final consideration, Harkin delivered a portion of his floor speech in sign language; it was addressed, he said, to Frank.

Harkin appeals most to those who feel they have little clout and distrust those who have. "In a free economic system," he once said, "there come times when too few people have too much wealth and too much power, and too many people have neither of both. It's the primary purpose of government to redress that imbalance."

Against the backdrop of a long and stressful 1990 re-election contest, Harkin reoriented his issue agenda in the 101st Congress, reflecting the changing focus of Iowa voters. In the mid-1980s, Harkin's extreme views on the importance of helping farmers were a centerpiece of his persona. But as Iowa's farm economy improved, Harkin assumed a higher profile on a number of social policy issues, and he continued as an outspoken liberal voice on foreign policy — always politically correct in dovish Iowa.

Harkin has had little success in advancing his theories on agriculture policy since the farm crisis began to ease in late 1987.

In 1985, he introduced the Save the Family Farm Act, a radically different approach to farm programs aimed at reducing supplies enough to cause much higher prices. Production controls would be implemented by the federal government if approved by referendum among farmers. Harkin lost, 36-56, when he offered the plan as an amendment to the 1985 farm bill. By 1990, Harkin was no longer loudly preaching the gospel of supply management and touting mandatory production controls. He was not an active player in shaping the 1990 farm bill.

Harkin has long been known for his outspokenness on U.S. foreign policy, especially involving Central America and the human rights records of other countries. When the 102nd Congress convened and turned its attention to the Persian Gulf crisis, Harkin led the liberals' charge. In November 1990, Harkin had joined 53 Democratic House members in a lawsuit seeking to prevent Bush from launching a military attack without Congress' approval.

Within minutes after the Senate went into session in 1991, Harkin sought to introduce a resolution demanding that Bush seek "explicit authorization" from Congress before acting militarily. The move surprised and visibly angered Majority Leader George J. Mitchell of Maine, who opposed immediate congressional action.

"Now is the time, and this is the place" for debate on the issue, he said. Mitchell coolly replied: "This may be the place. It is not the time."

At Home: Although Harkin was considered highly vulnerable in 1990, he pulled off a historic win, becoming the first Iowa Democrat ever to be re-elected to the Senate.

Harkin took nothing for granted en route to a second term. He opened his re-election battle early in 1989 by announcing his county-by-county campaign chairmen and stockpiled a sizable campaign fund.

That did not scare off Rep. Tom Tauke, perhaps the strongest candidate the Republicans could have nominated that year, other than Gov. Terry E. Branstad. Tauke also began early, raising money and seeking to build on his bipartisan base in the 2nd District.

Tauke pecked away at Harkin on a variety of issues, accusing him of franking abuses and of voting for excessive spending. But none of the attacks truly took hold, while Harkin stressed his work on legislation to help people with disabilities.

The two men also clashed over abortion — Harkin for abortion rights, Tauke opposed — although voters appeared divided on the issue, possibly making it a political wash. In the end Harkin won by a rather comfortable 9 points.

He may have a similar struggle on his hands in 1996 if popular 5th District GOP Rep. Fred Grandy decides to challenge him.

Harkin was no stranger to hard-fought campaigns; his 1984 race against GOP Sen. Roger W. Jepsen was one of that year's heavyweight bouts. Six years earlier, Jepsen had stunned Iowa Democrats by ousting Sen. Dick Clark. There never was much doubt Jepsen would be vulnerable in 1984, and Harkin, who had proved his campaign skills by securing a

GOP House district, was the logical opponent.

Jepsen's problem was that most of the events by which he had distinguished himself in office reflected badly on him. In 1983, for example, he had cited constitutional immunity to escape paying a traffic ticket while driving to work. Conservative organizations flocked to his defense, financing a barrage of TV and radio ads skewering Harkin for opposing a balanced-budget amendment and favoring higher taxes. Harkin came back with charges that Jepsen was freer with tax dollars than any other recent Iowa senator, dubbing him "Red Ink Roger."

The candidates traded charges, quarreling over who had a combat record and whose views on nuclear arms were more dangerous. Though polls showed a tight race, Harkin took 56 percent.

Republicans saw little cause for worry when Harkin first announced for Congress in 1972 against a well-entrenched GOP incumbent. But they soon found themselves up against one of the more resourceful Democrats in recent Iowa politics.

Harkin projected his concern for agriculture in rural western Iowa and drew publicity with his gimmick of "work days." (He revived the practice of spending a day at blue-collar jobs during his 1992 presidential bid.) Republican Rep. William Scherle defeated him, but by the lowest percentage of his House career.

Harkin launched his 1974 bid early, built a stronger organization and raised more money. Scherle made more appearances and tried to distance himself from the unpopular Republican administration. But Harkin won narrowly and quickly secured his hold on the seat.

Committees

Agriculture, Nutrition & Forestry (5th of 10 Democrats)
Nutrition & Investigations (chairman); Agricultural Production & Stabilization of Prices; Agricultural Research, Conservation, Forestry & General Legislation

Appropriations (10th of 16 Democrats)
Labor, Health & Human Services & Education (chairman); Agriculture, Rural Development & Related Agencies; Defense; Foreign Operations; Transportation

Labor & Human Resources (6th of 10 Democrats)
Disability Policy (chairman); Education, Arts & Humanities; Employment & Productivity; Labor

Small Business (4th of 12 Democrats)
Competitiveness, Capital Formation & Economic Opportunity; Export Expansion & Agricultural Development; Government Contracting & Paperwork Reduction

Elections

1990 General

Tom Harkin (D)	535,975	(54%)
Tom Tauke (R)	446,869	(45%)

Previous Winning Percentages: **1984** (56%) **1982 *** (59%) **1980 *** (60%) **1978 *** (59%) **1976 *** (65%) **1974 *** (51%)

** House elections.*

Campaign Finance

	Receipts	Receipts from PACs		Expend-itures
1990				
Harkin (D)	$4,983,819	$1,546,535	(31%)	$5,263,568
Tauke (R)	$4,941,809	$1,374,706	(28%)	$5,060,104

Key Votes

1993	
Require unpaid family and medical leave	Y
Approve national "motor voter" registration bill	Y
Approve budget increasing taxes and reducing deficit	Y
Support president's right to lift military gay ban	Y
1992	
Approve school-choice pilot program	?
Allow shifting funds from defense to domestic programs	+
Oppose deeper cuts in spending for SDI	N
1991	
Approve waiting period for handgun purchases	Y
Raise senators' pay and ban honoraria	Y
Authorize use of force in Persian Gulf	N
Confirm Clarence Thomas to Supreme Court	N

Voting Studies

	Presidential Support		Party Unity		Conservative Coalition	
Year	**S**	**O**	**S**	**O**	**S**	**O**
1992	18	62	66	3	5	66
1991	19	62	75	3	5	75
1990	22	78	85	15	8	92
1989	38	58	77	22	26	71
1988	42	57	89	6	8	86
1987	31	65	87	8	16	81
1986	19	78	91	5	5	91
1985	22	77	90	8	17	82
House Service:						
1984	29	66	79	14	17	80
1983	7	85	82	10	16	81
1982	26	69	83	12	12	86
1981	25	70	81	14	21	73

Interest Group Ratings

Year	ADA	AFL-CIO	CCUS	ACU
1992	85	91	17	0
1991	100	90	14	0
1990	94	78	17	22
1989	95	100	38	14
1988	95	92	36	0
1987	95	90	44	4
1986	90	93	28	14
1985	100	90	24	5
House Service:				
1984	75	46	33	21
1983	90	88	20	5
1982	95	95	24	0
1981	85	73	5	7

1 Jim Leach (R)

Of Davenport — Elected 1976; 9th Term

Born: Oct. 15, 1942, Davenport, Iowa.
Education: Princeton U., B.A. 1964; Johns Hopkins U., M.A. 1966; London School of Economics, 1966-68.
Occupation: Propane gas company executive; foreign service officer.
Family: Wife, Elisabeth Ann "Deba" Foxley; two children.
Religion: Episcopalian.
Political Career: GOP nominee for U.S. House, 1974.
Capitol Office: 2186 Rayburn Bldg. 20515; 225-6576.

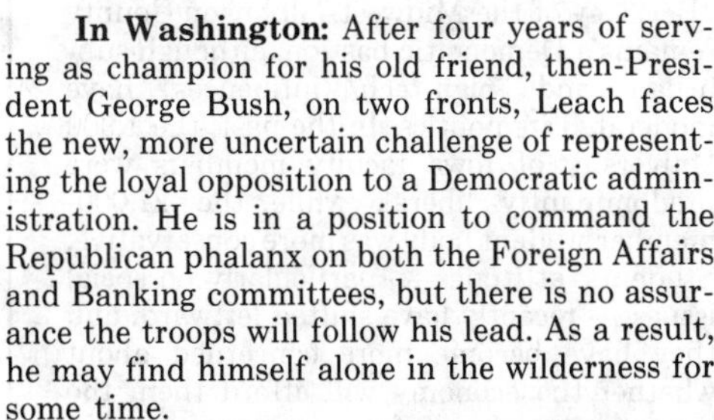

In Washington: After four years of serving as champion for his old friend, then-President George Bush, on two fronts, Leach faces the new, more uncertain challenge of representing the loyal opposition to a Democratic administration. He is in a position to command the Republican phalanx on both the Foreign Affairs and Banking committees, but there is no assurance the troops will follow his lead. As a result, he may find himself alone in the wilderness for some time.

Leach's outspoken foreign policy views have made him a pariah to his party's dominant right wing. It does not seem to bother Leach, who often relishes the chance to demonstrate his iconoclasm and prove that policy is more important to him than party. But he has risen to the No. 3 spot on Foreign Affairs, where his intellectual prowess could make him the alter ego to Henry J. Hyde of Illinois, leader of the panel's GOP conservatives.

Likewise, in the past on Banking, Leach had a tendency to free-lance and not consult his junior colleagues. He ascended to the ranking Republican seat in 1993, but he could have difficulty winning the allegiance of freshmen: Nine of the panel's 20 GOP members were elected in 1992.

Banking policy is set by shifting alliances on the committee that transcend seniority and party. Nonetheless, freshmen typically look for guidance to navigate between conflicting interests in debate. And Leach's views on banking issues usually clash with those of the panel's No. 2 GOP member, Bill McCollum of Florida, who is much more closely attuned to the confrontational strains of the Republican Conference.

Leach's grasp of the details — if not the politics — of banking issues greatly exceeds that of his uninventive predecessor as ranking Republican, Chalmers P. Wylie of Ohio (who retired). But Wylie had a close working relationship with the committee's mercurial chairman, Democrat Henry B. Gonzalez of Texas. Their cooperative venture enabled the panel to initiate a salvage plan for the savings and loan industry in the 101st Congress, and to enact a reauthorization of federal housing laws, and to revise the deposit-insurance system for banks and thrifts in the 102nd.

It is not just that Gonzalez and Leach have not worked closely in the past; relations between the two are strained. Gonzalez has openly criticized Leach's sometimes quixotic, if principled, stands. After Leach succeeded in stripping special-interest provisions from the thrift bailout bill in 1989, including one Gonzalez sponsored, the chairman called Leach a demagogue.

For his part, Leach took offense at Gonzalez's actions in the 102nd Congress that exposed the Bush administration's role in a scandal involving multibillion-dollar loans to Iraq from the Atlanta branch of an Italian government-run bank, the Banca Nazionale del Lavoro.

For years, Leach's cause has been to require financial institutions to keep more capital on hand and to make safer investments. He was among the first to warn of an impending crisis in the nation's thrift industry, and when it finally burst into public, he cast blame widely on Congress, the Reagan administration, the industry and state regulators.

Eventually, the House came around to Leach's views. In 1987, a Leach amendment to restrict speculative investments by thrifts was defeated on the floor 17-391. That did not deter him. In 1988, Leach tried a slightly different tack, suggesting that regulators use the same rules on risky investments for thrifts as for banks; that lost 20-29 in committee. But in the 1989 thrift bailout, he won as a leading proponent of the administration's plan to toughen up on the industry: The committee adopted 28-23 his amendment to apply federal restrictions on direct investments to all thrifts, even if they were state-chartered.

Leach cast one of two votes against the bailout bill in committee, saying it was not tough enough. And he opposed the final conference agreement — "not because the legislation

Iowa 1

East — Cedar Rapids; Davenport; Iowa City

The 1st is Iowa's most urbanized district, with three of the state's six most-populous cities. Cedar Rapids (Linn County) and Davenport (Scott County) grew up around heavy industry, and Iowa City (Johnson County) is home to the University of Iowa.

These urban centers give the 1st a Democratic tilt. In 1992 presidential voting, Bill Clinton prevailed by comfortable margins in all three counties. Rep. Leach has kept the 1st in GOP hands by mixing fiscal conservatism with more liberal social views.

Cedar Rapids emerged as Iowa's second-largest city in the late 1980s; nearly a third of the district's residents live in or around it. Long a prominent center for the grain-processing business, Cedar Rapids has weathered hard economic times of late with help from high-technology work, such as production of electronic and telecommunications equipment. Rockwell International, which makes avionics equipment, eclipsed Quaker Oats as the city's largest employer during the decade. In 1991, Eastman Kodak and Cultur Limited teamed up to build an $85 million biotechnology complex in Cedar Rapids.

Nearly 30 percent of the people in the 1st live in Scott County. Davenport and neighboring Bettendorf, along with the Illinois cities of Rock Island and Moline, make up the Quad Cities urban concentration. These are old, industrial Mississippi River cities whose economies suffered badly during the 1980s, as did the nearby manufacturing cities of Clinton and Muscatine.

Emblematic of the difficulties is a Caterpillar plant outside Davenport that once employed 4,000 people; briefly abandoned in the 1980s, it has recently found new life, but as a storage warehouse for several local businesses. Davenport and the other river cities are trying to rebound by capitalizing on tourist dollars drawn to riverboat gambling, permitted under a 1990 law. Scott voted Democratic for president in 1988 and 1992, but Leach has carried the county with more than 60 percent in the past four elections.

Iowa City, the next-largest population center, grew by nearly 18 percent in the 1980s. The city and Johnson County cast just under one-fifth of the district's vote. Once labeled "Berkeley of the Midwest," Johnson County remains a Democratic bastion, although suburban and high-tech influences have moderated its politics. In the past, the 1,900 University of Iowa faculty members were predominantly liberal, while the 27,000-member student body was more conservative. Students' attitudes — particularly on social issues — recently have shifted leftward, and they have become more concerned about whether the economy will afford them the opportunity of gainful employment after graduation.

Export sales by companies such as Stanley Engineering and Hon Industries give the district's economy an international dimension. But the traditional lifeblood, agriculture, is still important: By one estimate, there are four hogs to every person in the district, and its range of crops includes corn, tomatoes, soybean and watermelons.

1990 Population: 555,229. White 527,384 (95%), Black 14,624 (3%), Other 13,221 (2%). Hispanic origin 11,102 (2%). 18 and over 413,721 (75%), 62 and over 79,309 (14%). Median age: 32.

should necessarily be vetoed by the president," he said, "but because of my profound disappointment that Congress did not do better." He predicted that Congress would have to enact another bailout bill within 36 months; the next installment, a $30 billion measure to refinance the thrift salvage agency, was signed into law less than two years later.

Leach pursued his goal of imposing higher capital standards on banks in 1991 as part of an overhaul of banking law, but he failed to set them as high as he would have preferred. The same year, he failed on a vote of 119-298 to persuade the House to increase capital requirements on two federally sponsored corporations that finance a secondary market in mortgage loans.

Despite his allegiance to Bush, Leach was among the administration's chief antagonists in debate on the banking overhaul bill. He opposed permitting broad commercial ownership of banks and unfettered interstate branching. In committee, Leach's amendment to strike the commercial ownership provision failed 20-32, but the provision ultimately was dropped on the floor. He won a floor amendment to permit only the best-capitalized banks to affiliate with securities firms or to branch nationwide, but those grants of new powers also eventually disappeared from the bill.

Leach's background at the London School of Economics and his assignment on Foreign Affairs has made him one of the few members active on international debt issues, in contrast with the Main Street focus of most in Congress.

Leach was the author of a 1983 law that

was intended to require banks to maintain sizable cash reserves against Third World loans that were not likely to be repaid. In the 101st Congress, he pressed commercial banks to cooperate with the Bush administration's proposals for reducing Third World debt. But he resisted a measure that would have forced banks either to cooperate or set aside more cash reserves against potential losses on their loans.

The thrift crisis drew Leach from the cul-de-sac of Foreign Affairs, where the growing conservatism of the Republican contingent had left him isolated. Conservative Republicans resented the aura of bipartisanship he sometimes lent to Democrats by cosponsoring their bills or joining their initiatives, such as a trip to Cuba in 1984 with Rep. Bill Alexander of Arkansas (who was defeated in his 1992 primary).

In President Ronald Reagan's second term, Leach was often the leading GOP critic of administration policies on Central America, arms control and South Africa. In supporting sanctions against the apartheid regime in South Africa, he said, "All we ask of this Republican president is that he advance a foreign policy consistent with the views of the first Republican president, Abraham Lincoln."

Leach was a consistent opponent of U.S. aid to the Nicaraguan contras. When the Iran-contra affair began to unfold, Leach was harshly critical of the Reagan administration and Congress; he said that by watering down restrictions on covert involvement in 1985, Congress invited mischief. Democrats, he said, had buried their heads in the sand when reports of that mischief began to surface, out of fear that they would be blamed for "losing Central America" to communism. "The issue is backbone, not oversight," he said.

Occasionally Leach finds himself criticizing even the Democrats on Foreign Affairs as practicing too blatant an interventionism — as when he opposed the first proposals to give aid to rebels fighting the communist regime in Cambodia. But when Bush sought authority in 1991 to use military force in the Persian Gulf, Leach voted to give it to him. He praised Bush for working through the United Nations to line up international condemnation of Iraqi President Saddam Hussein's invasion of Kuwait.

It is not that Leach cannot be partisan; he simply wants the party to come to him. He has tried to use organizations such as the Ripon Society, which he chaired, and the Republican Mainstream Committee, which he founded, to raise a moderate voice in GOP politics.

But even with the White House in Bush's hands, Leach was still a party maverick. Fewer than 10 other Republicans opposed Bush's positions on roll call votes more often than Leach in each of the four years of the Bush presidency. He was one of 17 Republicans to vote against a constitutional amendment to ban desecration of the flag. He favors abortion rights and voted to allow the federal government to pay for abortions in cases of rape or incest. He earns roughly equal scores from both the liberal Americans for Democratic Action and the conservative Chamber of Commerce of the United States.

His restiveness with the domination of conservatives came to flower in 1981, when he was installed as president of the Ripon Society, a moderate GOP group that had fallen into quiescence during the 1970s. Leach all but declared war on the party's conservative social-issue activists. Leach said he had no intention of being "lashed to the guillotine of the New Right's social and security agenda." He declared a "moderate manifesto" touting the need for arms control and the Equal Rights Amendment. In 1984, Leach formed the Republican Mainstream Committee, a loose coalition of moderates, to fight on the GOP platform.

At Home: Redistricting made the 1st slightly more Democratic, but for moderate Leach the new district posed no problems. Pitted against a little-known actuary who had trouble getting support from his own party, Leach took every county in the new 1st.

As his party's leadership clung to conservative themes at the 1992 national convention in Houston, Leach led the charge for a middle course. It not only won him national exposure but assuaged his Democratic constituents.

Leach brought a varied background to his first campaign, in 1974, against first-term Democrat Edward Mezvinsky. Leach had studied at Princeton and at the London School of Economics, worked in the Office of Economic Opportunity and in the Foreign Service, was assigned to the Arms Control and Disarmament Agency, then returned to Iowa to run the propane gas manufacturing firm that his family owned.

He lost to Mezvinsky in 1974 by 12,147 votes, but that was a good showing for a Republican newcomer in a Democratic year. During the next two years, he spoke regularly in the district, held his organization together and built a $200,000 campaign fund.

In 1976 Leach stressed his ties to Robert Ray, Iowa's moderate Republican governor. He described himself as a "Bob Ray Republican" and called Mezvinsky a "Bella Abzug Democrat." Leach won by carrying his home base of Scott County (Davenport), which Mezvinsky had taken in 1974. (Leach now serves with Mezvinsky's wife: Democrat Marjorie Margolies-Mezvinsky won an open Pennsylvania seat in 1992.)

In 1978 Leach's courting of the voters in the areas where he had run poorly two years earlier paid off.

He drew 64 percent, the first time in 16 years that a House candidate in the 1st had won more than 55 percent. He carried every county that year and again in 1980.

The only Democrat who has given Leach any trouble since he won the seat was the 1982 nominee, former Scott County Supervisor William E. Gluba, a forceful campaigner with a populist flair and more than 10 years of political involvement in the 1st's most populous county.

But Gluba was so little known outside his home county that he gave up 37 percent of the Democratic primary vote to a candidate who had spent several years in prison for a variety of offenses, including burglary and armed robbery.

That embarrassment made it difficult for Gluba to convince potential contributors he could win, and he never obtained the resources necessary to match Leach's organization. Also, Gluba was unsuccessful at tying Leach to Reaganomics. Leach could point to his role as a leading Republican critic of Reagan's priorities for defense, education and social services. Gluba ended up with two counties.

Gluba was back in 1988, winning the nomination after former gubernatorial nominee Lowell Junkins had passed on it. But Gluba was even more woefully underfunded than in 1982. He again carried just two counties, and his share of the districtwide vote slipped below 40 percent.

In 1990 Democrats did not bother to challenge Leach at all. In 1992, they tried again with Jan J. Zonneveld: Leach took 68 percent of the vote.

Committees

Banking, Finance & Urban Affairs (Ranking)
Financial Institutions Supervision, Regulation & Deposit Insurance

Foreign Affairs (3rd of 18 Republicans)
Asia & the Pacific (ranking); Europe & the Middle East

Elections

1992 General		
Jim Leach (R)	178,042	(68%)
Jan J. Zonneveld (D)	81,600	(31%)
1990 General		
Jim Leach (R)	90,042	(100%)

Previous Winning Percentages: **1988** (61%) **1986** (66%) **1984** (67%) **1982** (59%) **1980** (64%) **1978** (64%) **1976** (52%)

District Vote for President

1992
D 128,655 (46%)
R 95,660 (34%)
I 52,983 (19%)

Campaign Finance

	Receipts	Receipts from PACs	Expenditures
1992			
Leach (R)	$213,649	0	$259,804
1990			
Leach (R)	$115,051	0	$87,489

Key Votes

1993	
Require parental notification of minors' abortions	N
Require unpaid family and medical leave	Y
Approve national "motor voter" registration bill	Y
Approve budget increasing taxes and reducing deficit	N
Approve economic stimulus plan	N
1992	
Approve balanced-budget constitutional amendment	Y
Close down space station program	Y
Approve U.S. aid for former Soviet Union	Y
Allow shifting funds from defense to domestic programs	N
1991	
Extend unemployment benefits using deficit financing	Y
Approve waiting period for handgun purchases	Y
Authorize use of force in Persian Gulf	Y

Voting Studies

	Presidential Support		Party Unity		Conservative Coalition	
Year	S	O	S	O	S	O
1992	52	47	65	33	54	40
1991	59	41	61	35	59	41
1990	38	59	62	37	52	48
1989	45	52	59	34	51	44
1988	35	65	62	35	61	39
1987	38	59	58	32	42	58
1986	47	52	58	39	37 †	63 †
1985	34	64	53	40	22	78
1984	42	53	51	42	36	58
1983	39	55	40	51	28	71
1982	45	52	43	54	36	62
1981	58	42	54	45	48	51

† Not eligible for all recorded votes.

Interest Group Ratings

Year	ADA	AFL-CIO	CCUS	ACU
1992	60	33	63	40
1991	60	42	70	35
1990	61	42	57	21
1989	65	25	67	46
1988	75	79	64	32
1987	52	31	79	38
1986	55	21	61	32
1985	60	53	50	33
1984	50	8	67	30
1983	50	33	65	18
1982	65	45	45	23
1981	55	20	79	73

2 Jim Nussle (R)

Of Manchester — Elected 1990; 2nd Term

Born: June 27, 1960, Des Moines, Iowa.
Education: Luther College, B.A. 1983; Drake U., J.D. 1985.
Occupation: Lawyer.
Family: Wife, Leslie Harbison; two children.
Religion: Lutheran.
Political Career: Delaware County attorney, 1986-90.
Capitol Office: 308 Cannon Bldg. 20515; 225-2911.

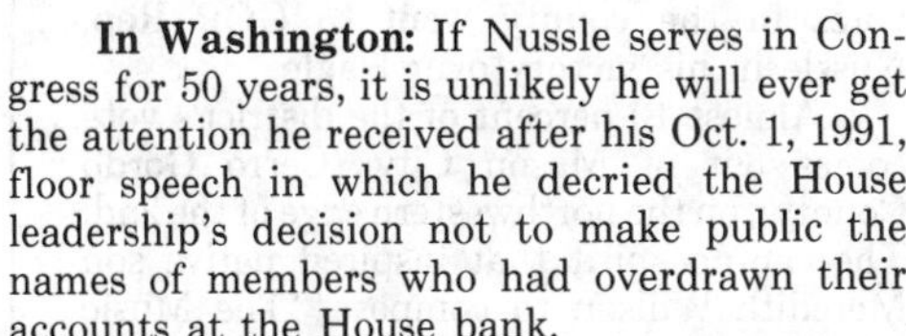

In Washington: If Nussle serves in Congress for 50 years, it is unlikely he will ever get the attention he received after his Oct. 1, 1991, floor speech in which he decried the House leadership's decision not to make public the names of members who had overdrawn their accounts at the House bank.

It wasn't what he said but that he delivered it with a brown paper bag over his head. The moment — captured by C-SPAN and reproduced by the national media — seemed to symbolize the public image problems of the 102nd Congress and Nussle's outspoken reform efforts.

"Mr. Speaker," Nussle said on floor, "it is time to take the mask off this institution. It is time to expose the check-writing scandal that I like to call Rubbergate. It is time to bring some honor back to this institution."

Nussle was chastised by Democratic Rep. G. V. "Sonny" Montgomery of Mississippi, the acting Speaker, for "inappropriate use of an exhibit" and roundly criticized by editorial writers at home.

But voters did not seem to mind, and, for some, the incident served to break the House into two groups: those members who had overdrafts and those who were damned mad at the first group. Nussle was clearly among the angry ones.

Nussle was one of the "Gang of Seven" in the 102nd Congress — a group of House Republican first-termers who aggressively agitated for changes in the ways Congress operated.

Most of Nussle's legislative efforts focused on institutional changes.

Bills he introduced in the 102nd Congress would have cut members' pay when the country ran a fiscal deficit; eliminated the frank for mailings to constituents; adjourned Congress by Sept. 30 each year to get members home to hear from their constituents; and called for ratification of a constitutional amendment limiting congressional terms.

These measures went nowhere in the 102nd Congress; Nussle reintroduced them in the 103rd.

Nussle sits on the Agriculture and Banking committees. He showed interest in family issues; he was adopted, and his daughter has Down's syndrome.

Nussle touts his Danish heritage and stresses conservative themes such as individualism and family values, criticizing what he says is over-reliance on government to cure social ills. He campaigned against strict government controls mandating soil conservation and drew criticism from environmentalists after he admitted that, until a few years ago, he was unaware of where his garbage went.

At Home: Two squeaker elections would seem to signify tough times ahead for Nussle. But having defeated a powerful three-term Democrat after a not-so-favorable redistricting, he should enjoy better numbers in the future.

Nussle's re-election campaign serves as a textbook case for the congressional upheaval of 1992. From redistricting to House bank overdrafts, the freshman's razor-thin victory over Democratic Rep. Dave Nagle illustrates why the 103rd Congress is populated by dozens of newcomers who pledged to eradicate perks, limit terms and balance the federal budget.

When Iowa lost a seat in reapportionment, Nagle and Nussle were thrown into battle in the new 2nd. Redistricting took something from each incumbent, setting the stage for a vicious, expensive campaign — by Iowa standards.

Initially ridiculed for his brown-bag stunt, Nussle continued his reform theme into the campaign, hammering Nagle for four overdrafts at the House bank. He also took a "Lead or Leave" pledge, promising not to run again if the federal deficit is not halved by 1996.

Nagle, often praised for helping Democratic leaders corral crucial floor votes, did not shy away from the insider label. But he did object to a stream of attack ads by Nussle, some distorting the overdraft controversy. Nagle characterized the matchup as a choice between anger and hope.

On the issues, the two were polar opposites. And in the end, Nussle was the beneficiary when it came to the subject of abortion. His anti-abortion position kept Nussle within a 22-vote margin in the heavily Catholic — often Democratic — Dubuque County. The remain-

Iowa 2

Northeast — Waterloo; Dubuque

The 2nd is dominated by two midsize industrial cities, Waterloo and Dubuque, and a university town, Cedar Falls. But nearly two-thirds of the vote comes from their rural surroundings.

Black Hawk County, with Waterloo and Cedar Falls, is Iowa's fourth-largest metropolitan area and traditionally a strong Democratic base. The county casts more than one-fifth of the 2nd's vote. Waterloo had the first gasoline-tractor manufacturer, and it now has a large John Deere facility. The city grew up around the farm-implement and meatpacking industries. Hogs are still slaughtered here at the world's largest pork plant. (Neighboring Delaware County leads the nation in hog production.)

Until 1986, the GOP prevailed in House voting in Black Hawk County, despite the industrial and union influences in Waterloo and an academic community at the University of Northern Iowa in Cedar Falls. The majority in Black Hawk seemed politically more akin to those in the surrounding Republican-voting farmlands.

In the mid- to late 1980s, Black Hawk County voters occasionally split their tickets. But in 1988 with Michael S. Dukakis and Dave Nagle and in 1992 with Bill Clinton and Nagle, Democrats easily carried the county.

Dubuque is the district's other population center. Together with Dubuque County, the area contributes more than 15 percent of the 2nd's vote.

Built on and against the bluffs facing the Mississippi River, Dubuque is Iowa's oldest city. Its economic base shifted from lead mines and lumbering to manufacturing and meatpacking, which suffered in the 1980s. The city is now seeking to lure tourists with a new industry, riverboat gambling. Dubuque also has gotten a lift from people trekking to nearby Dyersville to see the site featured in the movie "Field of Dreams."

Dubuque is predominantly Democratic by registration, but elections reveal the conservative outlook of this ethnic and heavily Catholic city. Republican Rep. Tom Tauke carried the county throughout the 1980s and in his unsuccessful 1990 Senate bid. Clinton won in Dubuque, although half the votes in the county went to GOP Rep. Nussle in his victory over Nagle.

Almost 10 percent of the district's vote comes out of Mason City (Cerro Gordo County), on the northwestern edge of the 2nd. The can-do spirit that inspired native son Meredith Willson to compose "The Music Man" helped the city weather the farm crisis; the city has emerged as a health-care hub. Residents here demonstrate their independence at the polls; in 1990 Democrat Tom Harkin narrowly carried Cerro Gordo County in his Senate contest, but in 1992 Republican Sen. Charles E. Grassley and Democrat Nagle both won Cerro Gordo County.

While pork, grain and dairy remain integral industries in the 2nd, much of the district is rural, with dairying and a bucolic Northern European flavor. The German-influenced Amana Colonies are in Iowa County and Decorah in Winneshiek County has a fine Norwegian museum.

1990 Population: 555,494. White 540,713 (97%), Black 9,511 (2%), Other 5,270 (1%). Hispanic origin 3,673 (1%). 18 and over 408,469 (74%), 62 and over 107,097 (19%). Median age: 35.

der of his slim margin came from the more rural counties of the 2nd.

Nussle also engaged in some fierce campaigning in his first bid for Congress. In 1990 Democrat Eric Tabor charged Nussle had exaggerated his work experience on his résumé. Nussle claimed he had served as a "staff assistant, legal counsel" for Gov. Terry E. Branstad in 1985 and was an "attorney at law" the same year.

In fact, Nussle did not receive his law degree from Drake University until 1985, and he was an unpaid intern in Branstad's office.

Nussle entered the 1990 homestretch as an underdog against Tabor, who had gained a degree of name recognition from two prior unsuccessful efforts to unseat GOP Rep. Tom Tauke.

But Tabor's campaign blew up in his face just days before the election when it was revealed that an aide had registered his father, mother and sister as Democrats to vote absentee ballots in the district even though they lived in what was then the 4th District.

Tabor moved quickly to staunch the damage by firing the aide, but local GOP officials questioned whether there might be other such examples yet uncovered.

In the end, voters — by a 1,642-vote margin — chose a man whose confrontational conservatism is a marked departure from the moderate Republicanism of Tauke, who like Nussle came to Congress at the tender age of 28.

Nussle, a lawyer and former Delaware County attorney, was an assistant in Washington for Tauke, whose strong grass-roots organization helped Nussle carry six of the 11 counties in the old 2nd District.

Committees

Agriculture (9th of 18 Republicans)
Environment, Credit & Rural Development; General Farm Commodities

Banking, Finance & Urban Affairs (9th of 20 Republicans)
Economic Growth; Financial Institutions Supervision, Regulation & Deposit Insurance; International Development, Finance, Trade & Monetary Policy

Elections

1992 General		
Jim Nussle (R)	134,536	(50%)
Dave Nagle (D)	131,570	(49%)
1990 General		
Jim Nussle (R)	82,650	(50%)
Eric Tabor (D)	81,008	(49%)
Jan J. Zonneveld (I)	2,325	(1%)

District Vote for President

1992

D 120,228 (44%)
R 95,005 (35%)
I 55,279 (20%)

Campaign Finance

	Receipts	Receipts from PACs		Expend-itures
1992				
Nussle (R)	$867,359	$350,565	(40%)	$865,838
Nagle (D)	$835,449	$486,347	(58%)	$853,637
1990				
Nussle (R)	$469,933	$146,558	(31%)	$466,259
Tabor (D)	$567,456	$389,847	(69%)	$568,659

Key Votes

1993	
Require parental notification of minors' abortions	Y
Require unpaid family and medical leave	N
Approve national "motor voter" registration bill	N
Approve budget increasing taxes and reducing deficit	N
Approve economic stimulus plan	N
1992	
Approve balanced-budget constitutional amendment	Y
Close down space station program	Y
Approve U.S. aid for former Soviet Union	Y
Allow shifting funds from defense to domestic programs	N
1991	
Extend unemployment benefits using deficit financing	N
Approve waiting period for handgun purchases	N
Authorize use of force in Persian Gulf	Y

Voting Studies

	Presidential Support		Party Unity		Conservative Coalition	
Year	**S**	**O**	**S**	**O**	**S**	**O**
1992	71	29	89	10	65	35
1991	80	20	85	14	81	19

Interest Group Ratings

Year	ADA	AFL-CIO	CCUS	ACU
1992	25	25	88	76
1991	20	8	90	85

3 Jim Ross Lightfoot (R)

Of Shenandoah — Elected 1984; 5th Term

Born: Sept. 27, 1938, Sioux City, Iowa.
Education: U. of Iowa; U. of Tulsa.
Military Service: Army, 1955-56; Army Reserve, 1956-63.
Occupation: Radio broadcaster; store owner; police officer; flight instructor; charter pilot; farmer.
Family: Wife, Nancy Harrison; four children.
Religion: Roman Catholic.
Political Career: Corsicana (Texas) City Commission, 1974-76.
Capitol Office: 2444 Rayburn Bldg. 20515; 225-3806.

In Washington: As the 102nd Congress drew to a close, Lightfoot could look back with satisfaction and relief. He had secured a seat on the coveted Appropriations Committee and weathered a flurry of negative media coverage to score a stunning, come-from-way-behind re-election victory in November 1992.

For much of the election year, Lightfoot was distracted from business in Washington by a redistricting map for Iowa that was harmful to him, by publicity and criticism over his 105 overdrafts at the House bank, and by a forceful female opponent. Having survived all that, he has an opportunity in the 103rd to focus more on Capitol Hill matters.

As the House bank scandal unfolded in 1992, a number of the House members involved retired, and some lost in primaries. Others raced home offering mea culpas for abusing congressional privileges.

Not Lightfoot. He blamed his overdrafts on Democratic mismanagement of the House bank, including tardy deposits of his paychecks. "[The bank] was run by the House Democrats, and I should have known better," he said in one campaign swing home.

This head-on approach — as well as countless hours of retail politicking — worked just well enough for Lightfoot. He won with 49 percent of the vote.

Lightfoot is still getting settled on Appropriations, where his efforts to bring federal dollars to Iowa will likely be aided by home-state colleague Neal Smith, the committee's third-ranking Democrat. In June 1992, Lightfoot was able to take partial credit for securing $1.45 billion over six years to build the so-called Avenue of the Saints highway, which runs through Iowa.

The seat on Appropriations also may give Lightfoot more leverage to persuade airlines to require child-restraint seats. A pilot and certified flight instructor, Lightfoot took up that cause after five infants died in the 1989 crash of a United jet in Sioux City. When the Federal Aviation Administration ruled in October 1992 that it would not require the safety seats, Lightfoot said he "would not rule out using the power of the purse as a last resort."

Usually this former radio broadcaster is an easygoing man with a homespun wit, but he can turn quite serious. During wrangling over the budget in 1990, Lightfoot took to the floor for a rare emotional display, calling Congress "the only insane asylum run by its own inmates."

And during debate in the 101st Congress over increasing federal funding for abortion, Lightfoot spoke for "a bunch of people whose natural mothers decided to let us live." Lightfoot, who was adopted as an infant and who has a daughter born with spina bifida, debated the issue with California Democratic Rep. Barbara Boxer on TV's "Donahue" show. "So they'll never call him a wimp, this guy Lightfoot," said Donahue after the show. "Nobody's going to accuse him of waffling."

Lightfoot has usually followed a conservative line, not only on agricultural issues but also on many of the defense and foreign policy questions that excite Iowa's dovish, quasi-isolationist instincts.

During the 102nd, he voted against reductions in the Strategic Defense Initiative and supported a balanced-budget constitutional amendment. At the start of the 103rd, Lightfoot opposed the Family and Medical Leave Act and supported elimination of the House's select committees.

"Of course, it's true that $45 million will not retire the national debt," he said of the committees' cost. "But our government is rife with this nonsense."

In June 1992, Lightfoot won approval of an amendment to reduce the House's budget for franked mailings by 10 percent. His proposal came the same week that he appeared on a list as the 17th-highest spender on franked mailing in the House.

After being turned away from the Agriculture Committee upon arriving in Washington — with two Iowans on the panel, the state was

Iowa 3

South Central — Ames; Burlington

Taking in 27 counties, nearly 14,000 square miles and six media markets, the 3rd gives a fair picture of Iowa. Within its borders are relatively well-off urban and suburban areas, depressed rural counties and industrial cities, and scattered towns with high hopes for economic development. Although this area trended Democratic during the 1980s, district voters frequently split their tickets.

The largest city is Ames (Story County), home to Iowa State University (25,000 students). Coupled with the state Department of Transportation office, the university ensures stability for Ames in hard times. The city, just 25 miles north of Des Moines, is positioned for future growth.

Story County makes up nearly 15 percent of the 3rd's population and is essentially Democratic. Story did vote narrowly for Republican Gov. Terry E. Branstad in 1990, but it went Democratic in the 1992 presidential and House elections.

Roughly one-quarter of the district's people live in the other four counties near Des Moines. Many of the voters here are independents; they backed all but one statewide Democratic candidate in 1990 but were divided in the 1992 presidential race.

Some of Iowa's most productive farms are in this area, but the number of Des Moines bedroom communities is growing, and some towns have developed independent economic bases. Newton, in Jasper County, is Maytag Corp.'s headquarters — where F. L. Maytag built the first mechanized washer in 1909. Pella, in Marion County, is home to the windowmaker Pella Corp. Tourists visit the Dutch-influenced town's restored Victorian center, known for its tulips and glockenspiel.

The 3rd's other population concentration is to the southeast, along the Mississippi River in Des Moines County (Burlington) and Lee County (Fort Madison). They account for 15 percent of the district's residents. These two old manufacturing cities, set in rolling hills and forests, have turned to tourism and riverboat gambling to spur the economy. Des Moines, Lee and Wapello counties all voted Democratic for president in 1992, though by narrower margins than in 1988.

The rest of the district's population is spread across Iowa's southern tier, bordering Missouri. Once forest and rough grazing land, much of this area was put into production during the 1970s.

Although hard times helped Democratic candidates here in the 1980s, voters moved back toward their traditional Republican roots in 1992. On the western side of the 3rd, several smaller, rural counties — including Page, Taylor, Union, Adams and Ringgold — helped GOP Rep. Lightfoot stave off a tough re-election challenge. Only two southern counties show much potential for growth: Jefferson (Fairfield) and Henry (Mount Pleasant). Maharishi International University, which moved to Fairfield in 1972, helped lure several small software companies. Mount Pleasant got a boost when Wal-Mart Stores Inc. opened a regional distribution center there.

1990 Population: 555,299. White 541,358 (97%), Black 5,219 (1%), Other 8,722 (2%). Hispanic origin 4,481 (1%). 18 and over 417,743 (75%), 62 and over 107,335 (19%). Median age: 35.

thought to have its share of seats — Lightfoot took a seat on Public Works. When a seat on Agriculture opened up in his second term, he decided to keep Public Works, and there he lobbied for a flood-control project and a federal buyout of farmers' land flooded by a lake in the district.

Lightfoot underwent double-bypass heart surgery in 1988, and judging from his performance on the campaign trail in 1992, his health is not a problem.

At Home: If anyone in Congress has a right to appropriate Mark Twain's famous line, it is Lightfoot. To put it mildly, reports of his political demise were greatly exaggerated.

As the pundits were dotting the i's and crossing the t's on Lightfoot's electoral obituary, he sneaked back into Congress by a mere 5,000 votes.

Lightfoot entered the 1992 campaign for the 3rd as only something of an incumbent. Redistricting put him in a substantially reshaped constituency that included just 10 of the 27 counties he had represented in his old 5th District.

Democrats avoided an expensive and potentially divisive primary by quickly rallying around Secretary of State Elaine Baxter, who had won two statewide campaigns. She benefited from media and contributors' interest in the "Year of the Woman" phenomenon, receiving national attention and money. Baxter targeted the larger Democratic counties new to Lightfoot, but her margins there were too slim to overcome Lightfoot's advantage in the more Republican southern counties, where GOP Sen.

Charles E. Grassley's big re-election win boosted Lightfoot.

And Baxter's emphasis on criticizing Lightfoot told voters little about herself. When he began firing back, accusing her of voting as a state legislator for tax increases and taking junkets on taxpayers' money, there was not much of a reservoir of good will for her to tap.

In virtually every county Baxter ran just off the pace set by Bill Clinton, while Lightfoot ran significantly ahead of George Bush. Backers of Ross Perot's White House bid evidently were more prone to back Lightfoot for the House.

Affable and unassuming, Lightfoot fit his old district like a comfortable pair of dungarees. In 1984, he brought the GOP its first victory in the 5th in a decade.

When Democrat Tom Harkin left the 5th to run for the Senate, Lightfoot was an obvious contender. For 16 years, off and on, he had been a farm editor and announcer for KMA, the major farm station in southwest Iowa. With his highly personal reports on weather, farm news and the markets, he had developed a following.

He also had ready access to networks of pork producers and cattlemen, and to GOP regulars. Urged to run for Congress after returning from a well-publicized trip to the Far East with President Ronald Reagan in 1983, Lightfoot agreed, proving his potency in a four-way primary.

The general election proved much tougher. Southern Iowa's farm economy was in wretched shape, and voters were in no mood to accept generic GOP assurances. Moreover, Democrat Jerry Fitzgerald, a former state House majority leader who had run twice for governor, was well-known in the northern counties and had extensive ties to Democratic activists.

Lightfoot's campaign cultivated a neighborly image — on the back of the campaign cards he handed out was a recipe for "Florence Falk's sour cream apple pie."

Fitzgerald, more cerebral and reserved, could not compete on the level of personality but came across as the more substantive. As has often been the case, Lightfoot was attacked as being ill-informed about federal policy.

Lightfoot built up huge support in his home territory, and he won by just over 3,000 votes.

Democrats were optimistic they could unseat Lightfoot in 1986 amid the deepening farm discontent, but they never quite came together. As depressed as conditions were in southwest Iowa, voters seemed unwilling to blame Lightfoot. He won every county and took the next two elections by an even larger margin.

Committee

Appropriations (15th of 23 Republicans)
Treasury, Postal Service & General Government (ranking); Foreign Operations, Export Financing & Related Programs

Elections

1992 General		
Jim Ross Lightfoot (R)	125,931	(49%)
Elaine Baxter (D)	121,063	(47%)
Larry Chroman (NL)	10,181	(4%)
1992 Primary		
Jim Ross Lightfoot (R)	15,757	(58%)
Ronald J. Long (R)	11,251	(42%)
1990 General		
Jim Ross Lightfoot (R)	99,978	(68%)
Rod Powell (D)	47,022	(32%)

Previous Winning Percentages: **1988** (64%) **1986** (59%) **1984** (51%)

District Vote for President

	1992	
D	120,495	(46%)
R	96,515	(37%)
I	47,028	(18%)

Campaign Finance

	Receipts	Receipts from PACs		Expend-itures
1992				
Lightfoot (R)	$623,098	$260,302	(42%)	$755,552
Baxter (D)	$657,055	$287,902	(44%)	$645,342
1990				
Lightfoot (R)	$497,363	$146,243	(29%)	$418,134
Powell (D)	$67,655	$34,920	(52%)	$63,591

Key Votes

1993	
Require parental notification of minors' abortions	Y
Require unpaid family and medical leave	N
Approve national "motor voter" registration bill	N
Approve budget increasing taxes and reducing deficit	N
Approve economic stimulus plan	N
1992	
Approve balanced-budget constitutional amendment	Y
Close down space station program	N
Approve U.S. aid for former Soviet Union	Y
Allow shifting funds from defense to domestic programs	N
1991	
Extend unemployment benefits using deficit financing	N
Approve waiting period for handgun purchases	N
Authorize use of force in Persian Gulf	Y

Voting Studies

	Presidential Support		Party Unity		Conservative Coalition	
Year	**S**	**O**	**S**	**O**	**S**	**O**
1992	78	15	81	13	88	8
1991	81	19	86	12	95	5
1990	68	30	90	7	98	2
1989	72	27	91	7	98	2
1988	63	26	76	8	92	3
1987	65	34	89	10	88	12
1986	70	30	83	16	84	16
1985	63	38	85	14	84	16

Interest Group Ratings

Year	ADA	AFL-CIO	CCUS	ACU
1992	15	25	88	87
1991	0	8	100	100
1990	6	0	93	92
1989	5	0	90	79
1988	10	15	85	90
1987	8	6	87	74
1986	10	14	94	64
1985	10	24	82	81

4 Neal Smith (D)

Of Altoona — Elected 1958; 18th Term

Born: March 23, 1920, Martinsburg, Iowa.
Education: U. of Missouri, 1945-46; Syracuse U., 1946-47; Drake U., LL.B. 1950.
Military Service: Army Air Corps, 1941-45.
Occupation: Lawyer; farmer.
Family: Wife, Beatrix Havens; two children.
Religion: Methodist.
Political Career: Sought Democratic nomination for U.S. House, 1956.
Capitol Office: 2373 Rayburn Bldg. 20515; 225-4426.

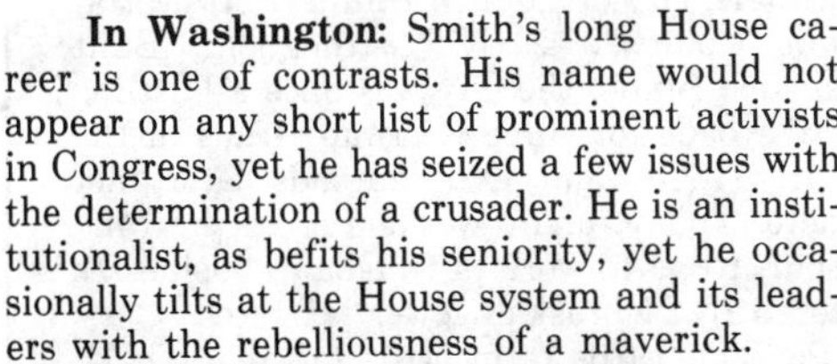

In Washington: Smith's long House career is one of contrasts. His name would not appear on any short list of prominent activists in Congress, yet he has seized a few issues with the determination of a crusader. He is an institutionalist, as befits his seniority, yet he occasionally tilts at the House system and its leaders with the rebelliousness of a maverick.

Like most effective appropriators, Smith spends the bulk of his time outside the spotlight, tending to his chairmanship of the Appropriations Subcommittee on Commerce, Justice, State and Judiciary. He tenaciously defends programs under his jurisdiction against budget assaults and tinkers with crop subsidies, dam construction and other appropriations business that affects his district.

Smith always has in mind the possibility that he eventually could chair the powerful Appropriations Committee. Smith acknowledged as far back as 1986 that he thinks about running the show someday. "I can't help it," he said. "Everyone keeps telling me I'll be chairman." With the removal of Chairman Jamie L. Whitten in the 102nd Congress, Smith is unofficially next in line to chair the committee.

Though he is a fair and honest broker as subcommittee chairman — he is known to keep debate going until agreement can be reached without voting — Smith has the political strength and personal willpower to fight for ideas dear to him. A man of liberal instincts rooted in Depression-era Iowa, he cannot fathom how other members, particularly Democrats, can put deficit reduction ahead of addressing society's needs.

The spending bill under his jurisdiction is diverse enough to give Smith entree to a host of areas, and he is intimately familiar with the details of the bill, which funds three Cabinet departments, the federal courts and 23 agencies, including the Federal Trade, Communications, and Securities and Exchange commissions, and the Small Business Administration.

Perhaps more than any other subcommittee chairman in Appropriations' "college of cardinals," Smith resists the strictures imposed on appropriations bills by 1980s budget laws and by free-lance attacks from junior budget-cutters on the House floor.

During 1989 consideration of the legislative spending bill, he went as far as offering an amendment to cut off funding for the House Budget Committee staff if the budget process was not revamped by January 1990. While that idea was not treated seriously, the Budget Committee did, ironically, lose some influence as a result of the 1990 budget summit. The summit fixed overall spending limits through fiscal 1995, but appropriators have leeway to operate within those limits. Smith clamored to tear down the budget "walls" erected in 1990 that prevented money for defense programs from being shifted into domestic accounts.

Typically quiet and understated — "bland and boring," a GOP foe once said — Smith can turn fierce when his priorities are challenged. He angrily protests what he sees as some colleagues' politically opportunistic attempts to have it both ways — voting to authorize new initiatives but later opposing appropriations for them in the name of deficit reduction. "Some members that talk big about wanting to control deficits, they also want all these things — drug abuse, homeless money," he once groused.

Like all the cardinals, Smith ardently defends his panel's spending prerogatives — sometimes even to their recipients. In his July 1991 newsletter to constituents, he blasted officials at Iowa State University and in the state government for their failure to support the research and development projects he had steered back to the university. "I have recently been surprised, if not shocked, to find that some of the major players do not even understand, let alone appreciate, the game plan," he wrote in his newsletter, which was reprinted in The Des Moines Register. "... Congress has provided the funds, [and two university presidents] ... followed through over the objections of the old lethargic establishment at Iowa State — who apparently view the new nationally recognized mission as a threat to their

Iowa 4

Southwest — Des Moines; Council Bluffs

Though the new 4th sprawls from central Iowa all the way west to the Missouri River, its anchor is Des Moines (Polk County), the region's commercial, financial and governmental center and home to Iowa's influential statewide newspaper, the Des Moines Register. Nearly 60 percent of the 4th's voters live in Polk County, a dominance that is apt to increase if current population trends continue through the 1990s. Polk grew nearly 8 percent in the 1980s, though the state lost residents.

Des Moines emerged fairly unscathed from the farm and manufacturing recessions that racked Iowa in the 1980s. The relative prosperity helped spawn the phrase "Golden Circle" to describe the towns and suburbs within a 50-mile radius of the city. The web of skywalks in downtown Des Moines, built during a $1 billion development spree during the 1980s, gives it a gleam of success.

Des Moines managed to flourish in part because of its white-collar employment base and its independence from agriculture. It is home to the state government and also is the nation's second-largest insurance center. About 60 insurance companies have headquarters or major offices in the city, led by Principal Financial Group. And Des Moines' role in the state's commerce grew as economies crumbled in the small towns that once offered medical care and other basic services.

Des Moines always has been more like Minneapolis than Chicago or Milwaukee: It is predominantly white, Protestant and middle class. Polk County's Democratic tradition has strengthened in recent years. Des Moines' prosperity has created a comfortable middle class that is largely missing disaffected white ethnics and go-go entrepreneurs — two groups that voted Republican in other parts of the country during the 1980s.

Polk has been more reliably Democratic than most parts of the country, supporting Walter F. Mondale, Michael S. Dukakis and Bill Clinton in recent presidential elections. In 1992, Democratic Rep. Smith as usual trounced his opponent here. Even popular GOP Gov. Terry E. Branstad fell 7 points behind his statewide tally in 1990.

This voting pattern and the city's size minimize the influence in the 4th of the western city of Council Bluffs (Pottawattamie County), a GOP stronghold. Built against bluffs, the city was once a bustling crossroads for three westward trails in the early 1800s and five railroads later met here. Today, many workers cross the Missouri River to work in Omaha in businesses lured by Nebraska's lower tax rates.

The 1980s farm crisis failed to shake the GOP grip on Pottawattamie and the rural counties surrounding it. In 1992, the liberal Smith managed to capture just a slight edge in Pottawattamie and it was also one of the few Iowa counties to give George Bush a solid victory in the 1992 presidential voting.

The farmers in Harrison and Shelby counties have been relatively prosperous, thanks to fertile soil. To the south and east, the land is rough and relatively dry, more suitable for grazing than farming.

1990 Population: 555,276. White 529,118 (95%), Black 15,395 (3%), Other 10,763 (2%). Hispanic origin 8,329 (1%). 18 and over 412,171 (74%), 62 and over 91,013 (16%). Median age: 34.

peaceful process of merely assigning pages in books and grading papers. . . ."

Traditionally, Smith has refused to fund unauthorized programs, preferring to leave such accounts unfunded until the bill goes to conference. It is a stance that has spared him from House fights but strengthened the hand of Senate appropriators, as it leaves him with little leverage to ask for more money.

In 1991, however, he relented, and his panel funded all the programs under its jurisdiction. He changed, he said, because a conference with the Senate was difficult without a full appropriation and because of a fear that other subcommittees might sop up unappropriated money.

One consequence of his stance has been that the Senate has dictated terms on the funding of controversial programs such as the Legal Services Corporation (LSC), a program that provides legal services to the poor and a target for elimination in the Reagan and Bush years. At Smith's request, Judiciary Committee Democrat Barney Frank of Massachusetts, a prime LSC supporter, introduced an LSC authorization bill in 1992. The House passed it, giving Smith added clout in the appropriations conference.

For several years, Smith has used his position on Appropriations to block the government almost single-handedly from tearing down the unfinished, bug-riddled U.S. Embassy in Moscow. During construction, the building was seeded with listening devices by Soviet operatives, and the State Department and many members of Congress — including Smith's counterpart on the Senate Appropriations Committee, Ernest F. Hollings of South Carolina — favored razing the building and starting over.

Smith adamantly opposed that idea, estimated to cost $300 million, and year after year foiled attempts to fund demolition. The State Department gave in; in 1991, the Bush administration threw its support to a less costly plan, under which secure floors would be built on top of the bugged building. But critics of the "top hat" plan vowed to resist it.

Congress and the White House agreed in 1991 to allow the State Department to decide whether to replace it, and in 1992, President Bush and Russian President Boris N. Yeltsin agreed to allow a new facility to be built nearby. But in 1993, under close questioning from Smith, Secretary of State Warren M. Christopher said it might no longer be necessary to build the $240 million chancery building.

Outside Appropriations, Smith was active in the late 1980s in fighting for tougher poultry inspection laws, a drive that recalls a crusade early in his House career that resulted in perhaps his single most-notable achievement.

That effort began in 1961, and it ended with passage of the 1967 Wholesome Meat Act and the 1968 Wholesome Poultry Products Act. The legislation was the first major overhaul of the law regulating the meatpacking industry since its passage during the Theodore Roosevelt administration, in the wake of the exposé "The Jungle." Similarly, Smith's long-sought success in the 1960s followed reports of scandalous conditions in meatpacking houses, this time by The Des Moines Register, which won a Pulitzer Prize.

Though his quiet persistence had been largely responsible for forcing the issue, the 1967 law did not go nearly as far as Smith wanted. He tried to amend it to impose federal standards on the industry but failed. Congress eventually cleared a bill simply providing funds for states to upgrade their facilities.

Smith's reformist approach to agriculture has been a consistent theme in his career. He was instrumental in creating the Commodity Futures Trading Commission to guard against grain trading abuses and in setting up strict federal procedures for grain inspection.

One of his landmark reforms, however, had nothing to do with agriculture. It was a rule against nepotism on congressional payrolls. As of the late 1960s, more than 50 members had hired relatives as aides. Smith's measure prevented that, although it "grandfathered" those already employed.

To get his rule past the House, Smith had to offer it as an amendment to a related bill, and he found a vehicle in legislation increasing federal salaries. Before most members knew what had happened, the House had passed it.

That bit of parliamentary gamesmanship demonstrated the fascination Smith has with House procedure. He has proposed a variety of rules changes over the years, including the one in 1973 that reduced the dominance of the seniority system by making committee chairmen subject to a Democratic Caucus vote at the start of each Congress.

Despite his parliamentary skill and the wide respect he enjoys, Smith never has excelled at internal politics. In 1975, he tried to become Budget Committee chairman, but lost to Brock Adams of Washington, 148-119. In the 99th Congress, he mounted a quixotic challenge to a member of the Democratic Steering and Policy Committee, though no incumbent on that leadership panel had ever been defeated that way. Eventually Smith gave up.

At Home: Smith always has won votes beyond the normal Democratic constituency in Iowa, and 1992 was no different. Even in the revamped 4th, Smith won Pottawattamie County, a solid Republican base added in redistricting. He then racked up a huge margin in Democratic Polk County (Des Moines), proving his broad-based appeal.

His long run of easy re-elections was interrupted by a poor showing in 1980, but he rebounded convincingly two years later and has had no problems since.

Until 1980, Smith had not seen tough elections since the early years of his political career. He first ran for Congress in 1956, losing the Democratic primary to state Rep. William Denman.

In 1958 Smith finished first in a five-man Democratic primary. But he fell short of winning the 35 percent plurality required by state party rules, so the party's district convention was left to choose the nominee. Overcoming opposition from Des Moines labor unions, he won the nomination easily.

Cunningham's narrow 1956 victory marked him as vulnerable in 1958, but Democratic unity had been damaged by the bitter nomination fight. Smith had to struggle to win with 52 percent, aided by a national Democratic tide that took three Iowa congressional seats from the GOP.

In 1960 Smith was the sole survivor among the state's three first-term Democrats. His Republican opponent, Des Moines physician Floyd Burgeson, was a forceful speaker but an inexperienced politician. Smith took 53 percent and won easily during the next decade.

Redistricting after the 1970 census threw Smith into the same district with Republican Rep. John Kyl. The national Democratic Party and labor groups gave Smith extra support, and he easily overcame Kyl (whose son Jon now serves in the House from Arizona). Smith coasted through subsequent elections until he met Republican Don Young in 1980.

Smith's close call against Young capped a year of unusual activity among 4th District Republicans. A Des Moines physician, Young used financial and organizational help from the national GOP to build a respectable campaign organization and raise about $250,000. He called Smith an entrenched fixture of a Democratic Congress that had weakened the nation's economy and defense.

Disquieted by polls showing a sharp drop in his popularity, Smith fought back with radio, TV and billboard advertisements in the closing weeks of the campaign. He won just over 55 percent in Polk County and Wapello County (Ottumwa), but lost two rural, small-town counties and was held to a bare majority in six others. For the first time in 20 years, Smith was held below 60 percent.

The strong showing by Young generated considerable optimism among Republicans that Smith could be toppled in 1982. The optimism faded, however, when Young announced in late 1981 that he would forgo a rematch and concentrate on running his medical clinic.

Des Moines state Sen. Dave Readinger stepped in to take the GOP nomination. He blanketed the district with billboards to increase his name recognition and tried to portray Smith as having spent too much time in Washington to be attuned to Iowa concerns.

But the conservative mood that aided Young in 1980 had passed. Smith won two-thirds of the vote, and since then, Republicans have invested little in the 4th.

Committees

Appropriations (3rd of 37 Democrats)
Commerce, Justice, State & Judiciary (chairman); Agriculture, Rural Development & Related Agencies; Labor, Health & Human Services, Education & Related Agencies

Small Business (2nd of 27 Democrats)
SBA Legislation & the General Economy

Elections

1992 General		
Neal Smith (D)	158,610	(62%)
Paul Lunde (R)	94,045	(37%)
1990 General		
Neal Smith (D)	127,812	(98%)

Previous Winning Percentages:				**1988**	(72%)	**1986**	(68%)
1984	(61%)	**1982**	(66%)	**1980**	(54%)	**1978**	(65%)
1976	(69%)	**1974**	(64%)	**1972**	(60%)	**1970**	(65%)
1968	(62%)	**1966**	(60%)	**1964**	(70%)	**1962**	(63%)
1960	(53%)	**1958**	(52%)				

District Vote for President

1992
D 117,863 (43%)
R 107,745 (39%)
I 47,835 (17%)

Campaign Finance

	Receipts	Receipts from PACs		Expend-itures
1992				
Smith (D)	$324,231	$210,300	(65%)	$197,159
Lunde (R)	$11,178	$381	(3%)	$11,178
1990				
Smith (D)	$167,829	$116,970	(70%)	$56,903

Key Votes

1993	
Require parental notification of minors' abortions	N
Require unpaid family and medical leave	Y
Approve national "motor voter" registration bill	Y
Approve budget increasing taxes and reducing deficit	Y
Approve economic stimulus plan	Y
1992	
Approve balanced-budget constitutional amendment	N
Close down space station program	Y
Approve U.S. aid for former Soviet Union	Y
Allow shifting funds from defense to domestic programs	Y
1991	
Extend unemployment benefits using deficit financing	Y
Approve waiting period for handgun purchases	N
Authorize use of force in Persian Gulf	N

Voting Studies

	Presidential Support		Party Unity		Conservative Coalition	
Year	S	O	S	O	S	O
1992	36	60	83	11	48	50
1991	37	54	81	12	41	54
1990	27	72	88	10	41	59
1989	31	56	82	8	22	59
1988	30	63	79	12	37	53
1987	27	69	87	8	47	49
1986	22	70	80	13	44	52
1985	30	66	85	11	35	62
1984	38	55	71	17	42	47
1983	30	68	84	13	29	66
1982	40	56	83	17	30	67
1981	42	55	76	20	40	55

Interest Group Ratings

Year	ADA	AFL-CIO	CCUS	ACU
1992	75	75	57	17
1991	55	82	40	11
1990	83	83	29	8
1989	70	75	40	11
1988	80	86	46	16
1987	76	81	14	9
1986	70	83	22	14
1985	75	75	24	10
1984	70	62	53	21
1983	70	76	61	17
1982	80	70	45	19
1981	55	64	18	20

5 Fred Grandy (R)

Of Sioux City — Elected 1986; 4th Term

Born: June 29, 1948, Sioux City, Iowa.
Education: Harvard U., B.A. 1970.
Occupation: Actor; congressional aide.
Family: Wife, Catherine Mann; three children.
Religion: Episcopalian.
Political Career: No previous office.
Capitol Office: 418 Cannon Bldg. 20515; 225-5476.

In Washington: Singled out early in his House career as someone to watch, Grandy holds a secure seat and a plum assignment on the Ways and Means Committee. These days, however, he operates with the freedom of someone who knows he is not long for the institution.

Partly, Grandy seems increasingly impatient with the pace of legislative life. Harvard-educated, he often gets to the point quickly, and he does not like to wait for the slowpokes to catch up. Perhaps more significantly, he has departed just enough from the orthodoxy of the Republican right to make him an occasional Democratic ally and thus suspect in the eyes of the new crop of GOP leaders.

If the opportunity seems right, he will almost certainly make a bid for statewide office in the next few years.

There should be little reason to doubt Grandy's bona fides as a member of the party in good standing. He is a staunch fiscal conservative and willing antagonist of profligate Democrats. He opposes abortion and votes with his party more often than the average Republican.

But he has earned a few black marks. Early in 1993, Grandy joined with another potential rising star from the party's moderate wing — Steve Gunderson of Wisconsin — to offer a package of insider reforms that would have increased the minority leader's power within the Republican Conference.

He traveled to a freshman get-together in Omaha shortly after the 1992 elections to try to sell the package. But it fell flat in mid-December during a party caucus that also saw the election of a phalanx of more conservative members to leadership posts. Not long after, Gunderson resigned his appointive job as chief deputy whip.

More than once Grandy has taken on the right wing on the floor. In 1990, when conservatives tried to gut the National Endowment for the Arts after an uproar over government-supported art projects that some members considered obscene or sacrilegious, Grandy defended the NEA. "I defy anyone in this chamber to find me a federal agency that has a better record of success," he said. Conservatives lobbying for restrictions, he said, "do not necessarily speak for all of the families of America."

He was also one of only 17 House Republicans to oppose a constitutional amendment to ban flag desecration in 1990. Less than a week after that vote, he chastised delegates at his state's GOP convention after they backed a flag-burning amendment. "You can't trash the First Amendment to protect our flag," he said.

A one-time congressional aide, Grandy already had a working knowledge of the House when he arrived in 1987. In his first two terms, he primarily focused on the Agriculture Committee, where he earned a reputation for intelligence, incisiveness and homework. He was named to the House-Senate conference committee on the 1987 farm-credit bill, the most important agriculture legislation of the 100th Congress. He was also a co-author of the Drought Assistance Act of 1988.

In his two terms on Education and Labor, Grandy was usually allied with the committee's more combative conservative Republicans and for years led the charge against a mandatory parental leave bill that was finally enacted in early 1993.

In the middle of 1989, Grandy was appointed to the House ethics committee, where he had to judge abusers of the House bank in 1992. In the 103rd Congress, he became ranking Republican.

As a new member of the Ways and Means Committee in the 102nd Congress, he chose to move slowly, learn the issues and pick his fights carefully. But he was willing to spar with Democrats over the need for a permanent extension of unemployment benefits and to insist that any benefit increase be paid for.

Early on he joined in the health-care debate, introducing his own "managed care" plan and relying on changes in the existing health insurance system to lower costs and expand coverage.

He joined with Democrats Tony Hall of Ohio and Mike Espy of Mississippi to promote a change in welfare policy that would allow

Iowa 5

Northwest — Sioux City; Fort Dodge

The 5th takes in nearly 18,000 square miles of fertile soil and gently undulating hills. The farms here are some of the nation's most productive, turning out impressive yields of corn, soybeans and hogs.

The bountiful land has allowed the region to remain more like the Iowa of old than any other part of the state. Virtually every town has a working grain elevator, and nearly every adult is involved in the farm-to-market agricultural network. Politically, Iowa's GOP tradition holds sway. The 5th is the only district in which registered Republicans outnumber Democrats; to win statewide, GOP candidates need lopsided margins here.

Yet even here, demographic and political change is evident. The area suffered dramatic population losses during the 1980s as many small-scale farmers sold their land to agribusiness operations. Each of the district's 30 counties lost population, and 18 lost more than 10 percent. In 1992, George Bush took 42 percent of the vote while Bill Clinton took 38 percent.

The smallest population loss was in Woodbury County (Sioux City), which is the district's largest, accounting for about 20 percent of the 5th's population. Once a meat-packing town, Sioux City has evolved into a more service-oriented center for a region that includes part of South Dakota and Nebraska. Some Sioux City businesses have moved across the river to take advantage of more favorable tax laws in South Dakota and Nebraska, but Woodbury County has sprouted numerous bedroom communities to house their employees — who prefer Iowa's schools and government services.

Politically, Sioux City has long leaned Republican. This pattern held during the 1980s, as the shift of voters to the Democrats on economic and peace issues was offset by the declining influence of labor. In 1992, Bush and GOP Sen. Charles E. Grassley both won Woodbury County, although Grassley's 3-to-1 margin was considerably larger than Bush's.

The district's only other significant population center is Fort Dodge (Webster County). The county is home to less than 10 percent of the 5th's voters — a figure that underscores the region's rural character. An industrial center near large gypsum mines, Fort Dodge emerged as a leader in veterinary pharmaceuticals in the 1980s. The city is in the heart of a region first settled by Irish Catholics. Webster and its heavily Catholic neighbor, Greene County, typically vote Democratic. Clinton carried both counties, although Grassley had no trouble here.

If Iowa has a playground, it is Dickinson County on the Minnesota border. With Spirit Lake and East and West Okoboji lakes, the county attracts tourists, making it the rare Iowa community debating how fast and how much it should grow.

Elsewhere, county fairs are the annual highlight: Clay County's is the nation's second-largest. The September Tulipfest in conservative, Dutch-settled Orange City (Sioux County) is a must-attend event for GOP candidates, and performers attend the annual Donna Reed Festival in her hometown of Denison (Crawford County).

1990 Population: 555,457. White 544,517 (98%), Black 3,341 (1%), Other 7,599 (1%). Hispanic origin 5,062 (1%). 18 and over 405,771 (73%), 62 and over 118,656 (21%). Median age: 36.

beneficiaries to start a small business and not immediately lose their state and federal assistance. The proposal was incorporated into a sweeping urban aid tax bill in late 1992 that President Bush vetoed the day after he was defeated for re-election. Grandy was one of 39 Republicans to vote for the tax bill.

A former actor, Grandy is known to TV trivia buffs as "Gopher Smith," the bumbling and likable ship's purser on the "Love Boat" series, which made Grandy famous. He came to the Hill with the desire to put the sitcom behind him. And as he has gained acceptance as a serious player, he has largely succeeded. But he is a bit touchy about the subject and does not take kindly to even innocent jokes at his expense.

At Home: Redistricting gave Grandy a solid partisan base. His popularity at home scared off any competition in 1992. It also makes him well-positioned to run for governor in 1994, if Terry E. Branstad steps down, or for Senate in 1996, when Democrat Tom Harkin will be up for re-election.

Grandy has traveled back and forth between the two worlds he loves: politics and theater. He first chose the former, becoming a legislative aide and speechwriter to Wiley Mayne, then the GOP representative for northwest Iowa. But show business beckoned. Grandy was soon appearing in off-Broadway productions and films, and in 1975 he began work on the "Love Boat" series.

As that commercial success wound down, Grandy looked again to Washington. The road to Congress lay through Sioux City, where luck gave him a shot at an open seat in 1986.

When Grandy first started running for Congress in 1985, his bid was viewed as just a curiosity. An actor from California who had left Iowa as a young teenager, he returned to an area where he had never even voted to take on popular six-term Rep. Berkley Bedell (who had defeated Mayne in 1974). But early in 1986, Bedell decided not to run.

Democrats nominated Bedell's agricultural aide, Clayton Hodgson. Despite his late start and low name recognition, Hodgson had strengths Grandy lacked: a solid agricultural background, lifelong residency in the state and strong support from Bedell.

But Grandy proved successful at deflecting carpetbagger charges and jokes about his show business career. Grandy set out early to, as he put it, "make people understand that there is a long-pants version of Fred Grandy, not just Gopher Smith in short pants." He worked hard to master the issues and built a large campaign treasury.

Grandy noted that his father's name still graced an insurance company in Sioux City, the 6th's largest city. He criticized his former home state of California as a "superficial environment" and praised Iowa's sense of community.

Ideological differences between the candidates were largely overshadowed by questions of background and style, but they did exist. Grandy tried to have the best of both worlds, appearing with President Reagan at the signing of the 1985 farm bill, but taking care not to defend the administration's agricultural policies. To troubled farmers he stressed the need to expand exports, with federal subsidies if necessary. Hodgson called Grandy's farm proposals "a welfare check for farmers."

Grandy's first victory was far from overwhelming. He carried only 11 of 23 counties in the district. But those who expected him to fall in his first re-election bid were soon surprised by both the job he did in Washington and his high-profile presence back home.

Democrats had thought Grandy vulnerable for his vote on contra aid and for the time he had spent campaigning for other GOP candidates or visiting in California. But the party was unable to field a strong candidate.

Their nominee was 30-year-old lawyer David O'Brien of Sioux Falls. Although he had excellent political contacts in the district, O'Brien was far outspent and made no headway with his attacks on Grandy for being less attuned to the district than Bedell. Grandy easily carried every county and won by an even larger margin two years later.

Committees

Standards of Official Conduct (Ranking)

Ways & Means (8th of 14 Republicans)
Health; Human Resources

Elections

1992 General		
Fred Grandy (R)	196,942	(99%)
1990 General		
Fred Grandy (R)	112,333	(72%)
Mike D. Earll (D)	44,063	(28%)

Previous Winning Percentages: **1988** (64%) **1986** (51%)

District Vote for President

1992
D 99,112 (38%)
R 109,966 (42%)
I 50,343 (19%)

Campaign Finance

	Receipts	Receipts from PACs		Expend-itures
1992				
Grandy (R)	$382,626	$296,149	(77%)	$292,752
1990				
Grandy (R)	$409,067	$251,675	(62%)	$322,563
Earll (D)	$44,250	$17,350	(39%)	$42,597

Key Votes

1993	
Require parental notification of minors' abortions	Y
Require unpaid family and medical leave	N
Approve national "motor voter" registration bill	N
Approve budget increasing taxes and reducing deficit	N
Approve economic stimulus plan	N
1992	
Approve balanced-budget constitutional amendment	Y
Close down space station program	Y
Approve U.S. aid for former Soviet Union	Y
Allow shifting funds from defense to domestic programs	N
1991	
Extend unemployment benefits using deficit financing	N
Approve waiting period for handgun purchases	N
Authorize use of force in Persian Gulf	Y

Voting Studies

	Presidential Support		Party Unity		Conservative Coalition	
Year	**S**	**O**	**S**	**O**	**S**	**O**
1992	78	19	81	16	77	19
1991	83	17	81	19	76	24
1990	63	37	81	17	76	22
1989	74	26	86	13	90	10
1988	52	43	70	27	87	11
1987	63	37	77	20	86	14

Interest Group Ratings

Year	ADA	AFL-CIO	CCUS	ACU
1992	15	25	88	88
1991	25	17	100	85
1990	28	0	86	42
1989	25	8	100	64
1988	40	57	86	64
1987	20	19	80	57

Kansas

STATE DATA

Governor: Joan Finney (D)
First elected: 1990
Length of term: 4 years
Term expires: 1/95
Salary: $76,091
Term limit: 2 terms
Phone: (913) 296-3232
Born: Feb. 12, 1925; Topeka, Kan.
Education: Kansas City Conservatory of Music, 1946; College of St. Teresa, 1950; Washburn U., B.A. 1981
Occupation: Congressional aide; public official
Family: Husband, Spencer Finney Jr.; three children
Religion: Roman Catholic
Political Career: Republican candidate for U.S. House, 1972; Kan. treasurer, 1975-91

Lt. Gov.: James L. Francisco (D)
First elected: 1990
Length of term: 4 years
Term expires: 1/95
Salary: $20,998
Phone: (913) 296-2213

State election official: (913) 296-4561
Democratic headquarters: (913) 234-0425
Republican headquarters: (913) 234-3416

REDISTRICTING

Kansas lost one seat in reapportionment, dropping from five districts to four. The legislature passed the map May 7, 1992; the governor signed it May 11. Federal court finalized that map with minor changes June 3.

STATE LEGISLATURE

Bicameral Legislature. Meets January-June.

Senate: 40 members, 4-year terms
1992 breakdown: 14D, 26R; 26 men, 14 women; 36 whites, 2 blacks, 2 Hispanics
Salary: $61.50/day salary, $73/day expenses while in session
Phone: (913) 296-7344

House of Representatives: 125 members, 2-year terms
1992 breakdown: 59D, 66R; 92 men, 33 women; 119 whites, 4 blacks, 2 Hispanics
Salary: $61.50/day salary, $73/day expenses while in session
Phone: (913) 296-7500

URBAN STATISTICS

City	Pop.
Wichita	304,011
Mayor Elma Broadfoot, N-P	
Kansas City	149,800
Mayor Joseph E. Steineger, N-P	
Topeka	119,883
Mayor Harry "Butch" Felker, N-P	
Overland Park	111,790
Mayor Ed Eilert, R	

U.S. CONGRESS

Senate: 0 D, 2 R
House: 2 D, 2 R

TERM LIMITS

For Congress: No
For state offices: No

ELECTIONS

1992 Presidential Vote

George Bush	38.9%
Bill Clinton	33.7%
Ross Perot	27.0%

1988 Presidential Vote

George Bush	56%
Michael S. Dukakis	43%

1984 Presidential Vote

Ronald Reagan	66%
Walter F. Mondale	33%

POPULATION

1990 population		2,477,574
1980 population		2,363,679
Percent change		+5%
Rank among states:		32
White		90%
Black		6%
Hispanic		4%
Asian or Pacific islander		1%
Urban		69%
Rural		31%
Born in state		61%
Foreign-born		3%
Under age 18	662,002	27%
Ages 18-64	1,473,001	59%
65 and older	342,571	14%
Median age		32.9

MISCELLANEOUS

Capital: Topeka
Number of counties: 105
Per capita income: $18,511 (1991)
Rank among states: 21
Total area: 82,277 sq. miles
Rank among states: 14

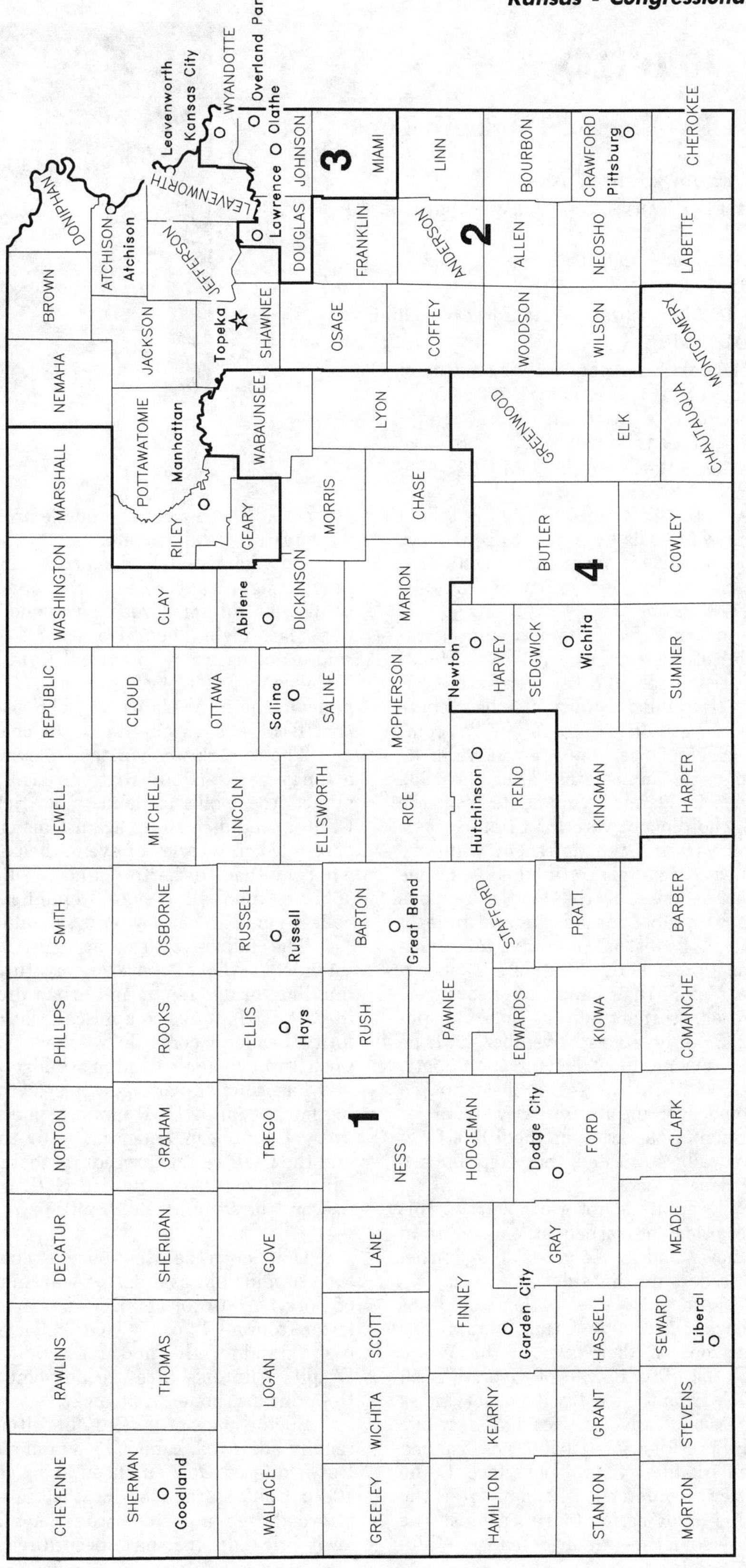
1
2
3
4
CHEYENNE
RAWLINS
DECATUR
NORTON
PHILLIPS
SMITH
JEWELL
REPUBLIC
WASHINGTON
MARSHALL
NEMAHA
BROWN
DONIPHAN
SHERMAN
Goodland
THOMAS
SHERIDAN
GRAHAM
ROOKS
OSBORNE
MITCHELL
CLOUD
CLAY
RILEY
POTTAWATOMIE
Manhattan
JACKSON
ATCHISON
Atchison
JEFFERSON
LEAVENWORTH
Leavenworth
Kansas City
WYANDOTTE
WALLACE
LOGAN
GOVE
TREGO
ELLIS
Hays
RUSSELL
Russell
LINCOLN
OTTAWA
Abilene
DICKINSON
GEARY
WABAUNSEE
Topeka
SHAWNEE
DOUGLAS
Lawrence
JOHNSON
Olathe
Overland Park
GREELEY
WICHITA
SCOTT
LANE
NESS
RUSH
BARTON
Great Bend
ELLSWORTH
SALINE
Salina
MORRIS
OSAGE
FRANKLIN
MIAMI
HAMILTON
KEARNY
FINNEY
Garden City
HODGEMAN
PAWNEE
STAFFORD
RICE
MCPHERSON
MARION
CHASE
LYON
COFFEY
ANDERSON
LINN
GRAY
Dodge City
EDWARDS
Hutchinson
RENO
Newton
HARVEY
SEDGWICK
Wichita
BUTLER
GREENWOOD
WOODSON
ALLEN
BOURBON
STANTON
GRANT
HASKELL
FORD
KIOWA
PRATT
KINGMAN
ELK
WILSON
NEOSHO
CRAWFORD
Pittsburg
MORTON
STEVENS
SEWARD
Liberal
MEADE
CLARK
COMANCHE
BARBER
HARPER
SUMNER
COWLEY
CHAUTAUQUA
MONTGOMERY
LABETTE
CHEROKEE

Bob Dole (R)

Of Russell — Elected 1968; 5th Term

Born: July 22, 1923, Russell, Kan.
Education: U. of Kansas, 1941-43; Washburn U., A.B. 1952, LL.B. 1952.
Military Service: Army, 1943-48.
Occupation: Lawyer.
Family: Wife, Mary Elizabeth Hanford; one child.
Religion: Methodist.
Political Career: Kan. House, 1951-53; Russell County attorney, 1953-61; U.S. House, 1961-69; GOP nominee for vice president, 1976; sought GOP nomination for president, 1980, 1988.
Capitol Office: 141 Hart Bldg. 20510; 224-6521.

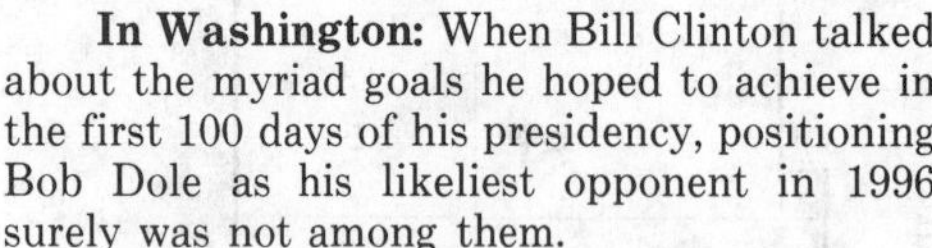

In Washington: When Bill Clinton talked about the myriad goals he hoped to achieve in the first 100 days of his presidency, positioning Bob Dole as his likeliest opponent in 1996 surely was not among them.

In the first months of the new administration, a series of missteps by the White House and Senate Democrats and the unexpected appearance of Republican unity in the Senate gave Dole a battlefield promotion to commander in chief of the opposition, a rank he assumed in name immediately after the 1992 election when he claimed a mandate from the 57 percent who did not vote for Clinton.

By orchestrating the defeat of Clinton's $16.3 billion economic stimulus package through the exercise of the GOP's tenuous filibuster power, Dole earned the gratitude of his fellow Republicans and promoted talk of his prospects as a presidential candidate — speculation he was more than happy to encourage.

The recent turnaround in Dole's disposition is striking. As late as November 1991, he was publicly musing about leaving the Senate, disconsolate with the prospect of leading a dwindling and ever unruly minority. In anger and frustration, Dole twice in the 101st Congress sardonically suggested that Republicans find a new Senate leader.

"Party discipline is not a problem on this side of the aisle," he carped at one point in 1990. "We never had it. We are all free spirits. We are all leaders on this side."

On the surface, Dole's situation would not appear to have improved now that Republicans do not have one of their own in the White House. But the 1992 defeat of George Bush liberated Dole from the frustration of serving as chief congressional advocate for his erstwhile rival for the presidency — a job Dole carried out with remarkable loyalty. "Let's face it," he said at a news conference the day after the election, "it's a lot easier to run against the White House sometimes than defend a White House.... I won't have to hustle around to get 34 votes to sustain a veto."

Dole immediately signaled his intention to play a significant role in the opposition. "I think you got some good news and some bad news last night about Governor Clinton," he said, drawing on his preferred formula for political comedy. "The good news is, he's getting a honeymoon in Washington. The bad news is that Bob Dole is going to be his chaperone."

The remark was vintage Dole: humor with a tangy partisan bite that can also accurately depict the political landscape. Before long, Clinton would come up against his chaperone's curfew when a series of events helped Dole do what he had hitherto found so difficult to achieve: bind all Senate Republicans into a cohesive unit to bat down the stimulus package.

The failure of the package, which was intended to boost the economy through road building, bridge repair and urban projects, was in part attributable to a miscalculation by Majority Leader George J. Mitchell of Maine to push through both Clinton's budget blueprint and his stimulus package while neither soliciting nor accepting GOP input. Democrats killed every Republican amendment to the budget, and the GOP had no procedural tool to block it. But a filibuster by a unified GOP was able to prevent the stimulus bill from coming to a final vote.

Dole and the Republicans characterized the stimulus bill as a deficit-leavening package of pork barrel projects. Dole was armed with a letter from all 42 of his GOP colleagues pledging to stand together and stop action on the bill. Despite Clinton's pressure on some moderate Republicans, none broke away.

Such a show of unified opposition, as Dole readily admitted, cannot be summoned at will. But it offered Dole an encouraging start to the 103rd Congress and — for the time being — afforded him a respite from having to swat away brickbats that have been directed at him in recent years from some of the younger, more ideological members of the Republican Conference. Dole is a true conservative and a man skilled at bare-knuckles politics. But foremost he is a legislative pragmatist, a deal-maker, and that trait has caused him problems with some of the GOP troops he tries to lead.

Dole always has seen himself as the personification of the American ideal, proof certain that hard work and determination can lift a man from humble roots and carry him through adversity to great success. Dole's belief in that ethic drove him with unbroken success from the Kansas House to the top job in the U.S. Senate.

He thought that his message would find a sympathetic national audience, but in 1980 and again in 1988, he was defeated as he tried to move up to the presidency. Dole has never been a visionary or an idealist, and by revealing his occasionally caustic side in 1988 he lost voters seeking inspiration, intimacy and a sense of what his election would mean for them.

None of those challenges will be absent should he try again in 1996. And Dole, now 70, would be 73 by the time of the 1996 GOP national convention (Ronald Reagan, by contrast, was 69 when he was nominated in 1980). But even though he earned stripes throughout the Reagan-Bush era as a most loyal soldier, Dole — alone among Republicans most frequently named as potential 1996 candidates — emerged from those 12 years with his credibility as a fiscal conservative intact, having balked at the policies of cutting taxes and increasing spending that ballooned the budget deficit and quadrupled the national debt.

The question will be whether, after four years of opposing Clinton's agenda, his image will be so indelibly negative that he will be unable to inspire the kind of following that politicians with sunnier perspectives have been able to attract.

Dole laid out his message in his post-election news conference: "I'd like to get back to traditional Republican philosophy, where you deal with the deficit, and you couple that with tax cuts. You don't just have tax cuts with no deficit reduction." He immediately began cultivating independent Ross Perot, whose anti-deficit, anti-Washington campaign attracted 19 percent of the vote in the 1992 presidential race. Perot and his devoted followers hold the key to a successful challenge to Clinton in 1996, and Dole may argue that he deserves their consideration, given his long-standing wariness of GOP economic policies.

Early in 1982, Dole began telling a joke he repeats to this day: "The good news," he said, "is that a bus full of supply-siders went off a cliff. The bad news is that two seats were empty." That joke symbolized Dole's doubts about the philosophy behind President Ronald Reagan's 1981 tax cut. Dole wanted targeted tax incentives aimed at boosting savings, investment and productivity, rather than across-the-board reductions. But as Finance Committee chairman he dutifully shepherded the Reagan plan through the Senate, though he did persuade Reagan to scale back the cut from 30 percent to 25 percent over three years.

That would be merely one of the earliest examples of Dole's loyalty to a White House policy that may have conflicted with his own beliefs. However deep Dole's reservations, he is also a staunch Republican partisan, and a fighter who fights to win.

Any questions Republicans might have had about Dole's willingness to wage Bush's wars on Capitol Hill after their bitter presidential feud were put to rest early on, when Dole clawed in an attempt to win confirmation of Bush's nomination of John Tower as Defense secretary, the first test of Bush's presidency. Throughout Bush's tenure, Dole was steadfast in his support for the administration. As he had done with Reagan, Dole sometimes took up the White House cause reluctantly, only to become totally committed once engaged.

Given his immediate past with Bush, Dole's performance on the Tower nomination was remarkable. In 1988, Bush and Dole were the main combatants in a six-man GOP presidential field, fighting what came to resemble class conflict more than any political or ideological battle. In Dole's eyes, it was Dole the self-made son of the heartland against Bush the son of Eastern privilege. Both men competed for Reagan's mantle, but Dole cast himself as the man who helped shape it legislatively while Bush merely stood by for ceremonial occasions.

Just before the Iowa caucuses, when Bush happened to be presiding over the Senate, Dole confronted him audibly for his "lowdown, nasty, mean politics." Dole won that pivotal first contest, proving his farm-state appeal. But then he went on to New Hampshire, where he set up such high expectations of his victory and eventual nomination that he looked all the more foolish when he lost. Worse, he looked like a sore loser; that night on network television, he snapped at Bush, "Stop lying about my record."

Weeks later, on Super Tuesday, his campaign was effectively over when he failed to win a single one of the 17 GOP events held that day, most in the South. Still, he persisted for three embarrassing weeks before conceding at the end of March. Through the November election, the only time he and Bush would speak to each other was at the time of the Republican National Convention, when Bush called to say that Dole was not his choice for vice president. Despite their feuding, Dole had plainly wanted the job.

Finally, weeks after the election, they met and pledged cooperation. "We've both been in politics for quite a while," Dole said. "We understand that when the election is over, it's over." Later, Bush named Dole's wife, Elizabeth, to be Labor secretary.

Much has been made of the impact on Dole of his handicap — a nearly useless right arm and an impaired left one resulting from combat in Italy late in World War II — and of the years the once-athletic farm boy spent recovering. Clearly his character was indelibly marked. "I do try harder," he once said. "If I didn't, I'd be sitting in a rest home, in a rocker, drawing disability."

Elected in 1968, after eight years in the House, Dole is the Senate's fourth most senior Republican, and he is coping with a Congress far different from the one he entered a generation ago. As Senate GOP leader, Dole has shown a will and a capacity to exercise power and exert control, but he now finds around him a greater number of younger conservatives, impatient with their elders' more pragmatic approach. In the Senate, this internal GOP rift is not as wide or as public as it has been in the House, but in organizing for the 102nd and 103rd Congresses, several conservatives won leadership positions over more moderate competition.

The political crosscurrents Dole fights to tame roiled during the protracted budget debate of 1990. Recession had forced legislators to make a more concerted effort to cut the deficit, and with Democrats scoring political points with demands for "tax fairness," Bush dropped his 1988 campaign pledge not to raise taxes.

Dole quickly defended Bush's new line, saying he was merely trying to get Democrats to bargain seriously. But politically and personally, it was a tough sell for the minority leader because Bush's anti-tax rhetoric had been echoed by countless Republicans after it blistered Dole in the 1988 New Hampshire presidential primary.

Still, Dole could not resist a gibe at Bush, whose 1988 convention speech made "read my lips, no new taxes" his rallying cry. Asked how GOP candidates should react to Bush's changed signals, he cracked, "Tell them to get some lip balm; it's good for cracked lips."

But from there, Dole went on to be perhaps Bush's most relentless ally in the budget-summit process. During weeks of congressional-White House negotiations, Dole propelled the talks forward at several tense junctures. When the final agreement failed to gain congressional approval, it was not for a lack of a fight by Dole — liberals had balked at its program cuts and conservatives at its tax increases.

Dole then joined with Mitchell to put up a united front for a budget much like the summit agreement. Arguing that any amendment would unravel the deal, Mitchell and Dole managed to keep reluctant troops in line.

The budget-summit episode illustrated Dole's frustration with the White House and some of his Republican colleagues, as well as his relatively cordial relationship with Mitchell. After becoming majority leader in 1989, Mitchell made a point of keeping Dole informed of scheduling plans, easing Republican fears of procedural sneak attacks. The two worked as a team during the Senate's long debate on a major overhaul of the Clean Air Act in 1990, sharing strategy and vote counts to defeat amendments that might have crippled a compromise they had negotiated with the White House. The honeymoon lasted until mid-1990, when Democrats forced a partisan showdown on civil rights that Dole had hoped to avoid.

Throughout the 1980s, Dole was a key broker on civil rights legislation. He overrode Reagan administration objections and formulated a compromise that allowed the 1982 Voting Rights Act extension to emerge from a divided Judiciary Committee with provisions making it easier to prove violations. In 1990, he had expressed reservations about whether a new law was needed to address employment discrimination, but civil rights activists appeared to believe that Dole would come around.

When Democrats fast-tracked the employment discrimination bill, however, Dole unleashed a tirade that was unusually biting even for a man renowned for his caustic wit. Voice trembling, he complained that the vote to end debate was a partisan ploy designed to cast Republicans as opposing civil rights even as negotiations with the White House were close to an agreement. "This senator's never voted against a civil rights bill," he said. "But he has never had one shoved down his throat before."

Dole's outburst, however, was also directed at some wayward Republicans — this time not conservatives, but moderates — who helped Mitchell win the pivotal 62-38 cloture vote. In a closed meeting just before the vote, Republican senators had been urged to oppose cloture. No head count was taken, but none of the eight who would defect spoke up. "If we are going to let Democrats run the Senate and throw away eight or nine Republican votes to help them, then I don't want any part of it," Dole said afterward. "Maybe we should get together and elect another leader."

He made a similar threat during the budget debate. As conservatives balked at the package he had labored to produce, Dole challenged Malcolm Wallop of Wyoming to run against him for leader. "If you feel that way, fine," one senator quoted Dole saying in a private meeting. "Let's have a ballot right here."

All of this was a far cry from the days when Dole led the Senate with his unique blend of go-it-alone determination and deal-cutting savvy. Though his two-year stint as majority leader was brief, it proved a point that badly needed proving at the time: The Senate could be led.

"You have to produce, and you have to prove leadership," he said shortly after Republicans elected him over four contenders in late 1984. Dole did both, even if he failed to achieve a number of his most important goals.

Beyond the major bills that passed with his help — tax revision, a new immigration law, a five-year farm bill and aid to the Nicaraguan contras, among others — Dole's chief accomplishment was to undermine the ability of small groups of senators to bring the chamber regularly to a standstill. His success rested on the palpable sense of his will to use power. "I did not become majority leader to lose," he once said.

Dole's style contrasted with that of his predecessor, the amiable Howard H. Baker Jr. of Tennessee, who allowed his colleagues to fight it out in hopes that eventually, exhausted, they would agree to something. "I don't wait for the consensus," Dole said. "I try to help build it."

His aggressive use of power occasionally embittered colleagues, mostly Democrats. During consideration of South Africa sanctions in 1985, Dole had the official copy of the bill locked in a safe, preventing further action on it. In 1986, Dole averted defeat on a vote to confirm a bitterly contested judicial nominee, Daniel A. Manion, by persuading two opponents to withhold their votes as a traditional courtesy to two Republican supporters who were absent. When it was learned that the absent Republicans had not made up their minds, Democrats and some Republicans complained they had been misled.

As a member of Agriculture, and of Judiciary until 1985, Dole has built a supportive record on two issues — civil rights and food stamps — that stands out from his otherwise consistent conservatism. He has also been a crusader for federal aid to the handicapped. He routinely has broken conservative ranks to protect and enlarge the food stamp program, popular among Kansas farmers as well as the poor.

A member of a special national commission on Social Security, Dole played a key role in the compromise that led to the commission's recommendations on saving the system, which Congress used as the basis for its 1983 rescue bill. In 1985, this gave him credibility to cajole GOP colleagues to support a freeze in Social Security benefits in order to pass a budget.

Dole still hails that budget, with its estimated $50 billion in deficit reduction, as one of his proudest achievements. It reflected his old-line Republican fealty to balanced budgets, a goal for which Dole was willing to raise taxes until his 1988 presidential campaign made him a subscriber to anti-tax rhetoric. To his lasting chagrin, Reagan later disowned the budget, and it was said to have contributed to the Republicans' 1986 loss of the Senate.

Dole's partisanship, and his loyal support for Republican presidents, is consistent with the man who first arrived in the Senate more than a quarter century ago. If anything, leadership has tempered him. He was President Richard M. Nixon's staunchest Senate backer, defending in often abrasive terms Nixon's Vietnam policies, his Supreme Court nominations, his ABM program and almost every other move the president made.

Dole's performance did not sit well with some Senate colleagues; in 1971, Ohio Republican William B. Saxbe said Dole was a "hatchet man" who "couldn't sell beer on a troopship." But Nixon rewarded Dole in 1971 by naming him national party chairman. Dole never got along with the White House staff, however, and was pushed from the party leadership in January 1973 — a stroke of good fortune because he escaped the subsequent Watergate scandal. Although he had been GOP chairman when the June 1972 burglary occurred, Dole never knew what was going on at the Nixon re-election committee. "Watergate happened on my night off," he later said.

He re-emerged as Gerald R. Ford's vice presidential running mate in 1976, but his subsequent denunciation of the 20th century's "Democrat wars" gave national circulation to the hatchet-man label that haunts Dole still. Only after days of controversy did Dole grudgingly back away from the remark.

That campaign may have been a turning point. While Dole never accepted the notion that his negative style cost Ford the presidency, he has rarely sounded so strident since. Some attribute this to the influence of his wife, whom he married in 1975 when she was a federal trade commissioner.

When she appeared before a Senate committee before her confirmation as Reagan's Transportation secretary in 1983, Dole said, "I regret that I have but one wife to give for my country's infrastructure."

At Home: While his presidential ambitions have been twice thwarted, Dole has built and maintained his status as the foremost political figure from Kansas.

Dole's strong partisanship and rough edges will never make him universally loved even in Kansas: His recent re-election totals have fallen short of those run up by his moderate and mild-mannered Republican Senate colleague, Nancy Landon Kassebaum. Still, he beat Democratic activist Gloria O'Dell in 1992, only a fair Republican year in Kansas, with 63 percent of the vote, the same figure he won with during the 1980 Reagan landslide.

Although his ride has been smooth in his last three elections, Dole's road to political security was rough. He faced a series of contests early in his career in which the swing of not many votes would have sent him home to Russell.

Dole emerged from his World War II ordeal with ambition and an ample share of discipline. Before completing his law degree, he won a term in the Kansas House. Two years later, he became Russell County prosecutor.

In 1960, Dole ran in the Republican primary for an open House seat against Keith G. Sebelius. Dole defeated him by 982 votes, forcing Sebelius to wait eight years for a House vacancy. In the fall, Dole was an easy winner, keeping the old 6th District in its traditionally Republican hands.

In 1962, the state's two western districts were combined, and Dole had to run against a Democratic incumbent, J. Floyd Breeding. He beat him by more than 20,000 votes. Dole had a more difficult time coping with the 1964 national Democratic landslide and with Bill Bork, a farmers' co-op official, but still managed to win by just over 5,000 votes.

In 1968, Republican Frank Carlson announced his retirement from the Senate, and Dole competed for the GOP nomination with former Gov. William H. Avery, who had been ousted from the governorship just two years earlier. Dole scored an easy victory.

That fall, Dole also had an easy time against Democrat William I. Robinson, a Wichita attorney who criticized him for opposing federal aid to schools. Dole talked about the social unrest of that year and blamed much of it on the Johnson administration.

The 1974 campaign was different. Dole was burdened by his earlier Nixon connections, which were played up, probably to an unwise degree, by Democratic challenger William Roy, a two-term House member. Roy continued to refer to Nixon and Watergate even though he had built a comfortable lead against Dole. This enabled Dole to strike back with an ad in which a mud-splattered poster of himself was gradually wiped clean as he insisted on his honesty. Dole came from behind to win.

Since then, he has had nothing to worry about. He met only weak opposition for a third term in 1980. In 1986, as the defeats of several Senate GOP colleagues cost him the job of majority leader, Dole coasted.

Committees

Minority Leader

Agriculture, Nutrition & Forestry (2nd of 8 Republicans)
Agricultural Production & Stabilization of Prices; Nutrition & Investigations; Rural Development & Rural Electrification

Finance (2nd of 9 Republicans)
Social Security & Family Policy (ranking); Energy & Agricultural Taxation; Medicare & Long Term Care

Rules & Administration (5th of 7 Republicans)

Joint Organization of Congress

Joint Taxation

Elections

1992 General

Bob Dole (R)	706,246	(63%)
Gloria O'Dell (D)	349,525	(31%)
Christina Campbell-Cline (I)	45,423	(4%)
Mark B. Kirk (LIBERT)	25,253	(2%)

1992 Primary

Bob Dole (R)	244,480	(80%)
Richard Warren Rodewald (R)	59,589	(20%)

Previous Winning Percentages: **1986** (70%) **1980** (64%) **1974** (51%) **1968** (60%) **1966 *** (69%) **1964 *** (51%) **1962 *** (56%) **1960 *** (59%)

** House elections.*

Campaign Finance

	Receipts	Receipts from PACs		Expend-itures
1992				
Dole (R)	$2,362,936	$1,237,318	(52%)	$1,990,098
O'Dell (D)	$246,056	$40,150	(16%)	$249,359

Key Votes

1993

Require unpaid family and medical leave	N
Approve national "motor voter" registration bill	N
Approve budget increasing taxes and reducing deficit	N
Support president's right to lift military gay ban	N

1992

Approve school-choice pilot program	Y
Allow shifting funds from defense to domestic programs	N
Oppose deeper cuts in spending for SDI	Y

1991

Approve waiting period for handgun purchases	Y
Raise senators' pay and ban honoraria	Y
Authorize use of force in Persian Gulf	Y
Confirm Clarence Thomas to Supreme Court	Y

Voting Studies

	Presidential Support		Party Unity		Conservative Coalition	
Year	**S**	**O**	**S**	**O**	**S**	**O**
1992	88	12	94	6	92	8
1991	96	4	93	7	98	3
1990	80	20	86	14	95	5
1989	94	4	89	11	87	13
1988	68	19	70	12	86	5
1987	71	24	85	10	81	6
1986	92	8	92	7	95	4
1985	92	7	92	6	92	5
1984	90	9	90	8	96	2
1983	78	21	88	8	89	7
1982	86	13	91	8	85	10
1981	85	7	94	5	92	5

Interest Group Ratings

Year	ADA	AFL-CIO	CCUS	ACU
1992	5	17	90	93
1991	5	17	80	86
1990	0	33	75	83
1989	5	0	88	86
1988	15	33	91	91
1987	5	20	83	77
1986	0	0	89	91
1985	0	10	90	91
1984	10	0	83	86
1983	5	19	56	64
1982	15	20	62	80
1981	5	11	100	76

Nancy Landon Kassebaum (R)

Of Burdick — Elected 1978; 3rd Term

Born: July 29, 1932, Topeka, Kan.
Education: U. of Kansas, B.A. 1954; U. of Michigan, M.A. 1956.
Occupation: Broadcasting executive.
Family: Divorced; four children.
Religion: Episcopalian.
Political Career: Maize School Board, 1973-75.
Capitol Office: 302 Russell Bldg. 20510; 224-4774.

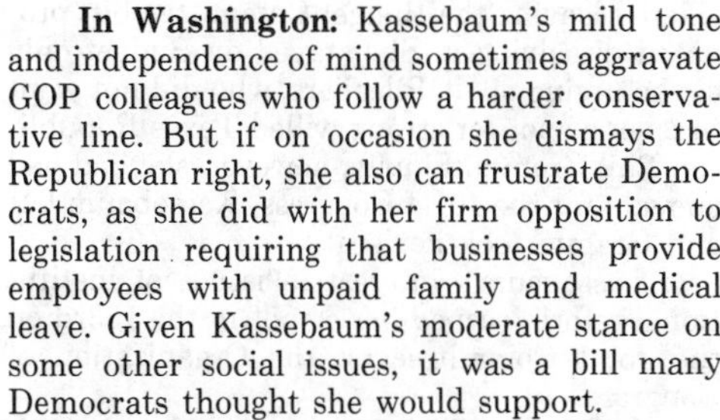

In Washington: Kassebaum's mild tone and independence of mind sometimes aggravate GOP colleagues who follow a harder conservative line. But if on occasion she dismays the Republican right, she also can frustrate Democrats, as she did with her firm opposition to legislation requiring that businesses provide employees with unpaid family and medical leave. Given Kassebaum's moderate stance on some other social issues, it was a bill many Democrats thought she would support.

But Kassebaum, who came to Congress before the Reagan era and now has outlasted it, charts her own course. And during her years in the Senate she has quietly established an image as a positive force in the institution.

In the 103rd Congress, Kassebaum became the ranking Republican on the Labor and Human Resources Committee, replacing Orrin G. Hatch of Utah, who left that spot to take the ranking seat on Judiciary. Although Hatch did develop a working relationship with committee Chairman Edward M. Kennedy of Massachusetts, having Kassebaum at the top of the GOP side probably broadens the possibilities for bipartisan cooperation. Kassebaum, for instance, supports abortion rights — although she also endorses giving states the right to impose restrictions such as parental notification and waiting periods.

However, Kassebaum's first major action as ranking member in the 103rd was to oppose the family leave bill. She held firm despite the wide appeal of the legislation; three of her six Republican colleagues on Labor supported it.

"I always feel like the skunk at the picnic on this issue," she said. "But I feel it is wrong for us to mandate benefits."

Her opposition put her at odds with her daughter, Linda K. Johnson, a pathologist with two children. "We discussed it until we realized we had discussed it to death," Kassebaum said.

The Senate passed the bill 71-27. The House followed suit, and President Clinton's signature made it law.

Many who reach Congress promising to be short-term "citizen legislators" soon become just as concerned about partisan advantage as the professional politicians they once reviled. But her years in the Senate have not worked that change on Kassebaum. She still conveys the plain-spoken honesty and common sense she had when she arrived in 1979 as an almost complete political neophyte.

Kassebaum still appears on occasion to be shy and uneasy in a public role. "Someday I'm going to hit someone over the head for calling me diminutive and soft-spoken," she once said. "But I am." She chafes at comparisons to Dorothy in "The Wizard of Oz," yet has enough humor about her image that her staff felt free to include representations of the film in a patchwork quilt they made for her.

Kassebaum eschews harsh partisan rhetoric and tries to act as a mediator on some of the Senate's more contentious issues. As a member of the Foreign Relations and Labor and Human Resources committees, she finds no shortage of opportunities to employ her conciliatory nature.

In 1990, members sharply divided over a bill to provide legal remedies for certain instances of job discrimination: Democratic leaders defined the bill as a civil rights act, while President Bush described it as a "jobs-quota bill" and threatened to veto it.

Kassebaum sought middle ground. Her alternative would have established an easier test than in the Democratic bill for employers to prove they had not discriminated, and lowered the maximum monetary payments that courts could order employers to pay to victims of intentional discrimination.

Her efforts went for naught, though. With the 1990 elections looming, the civil rights debate had taken on a partisan dimension that dwarfed the details of the legislation; Kassebaum's proposal died without a vote in the Senate. When the plan was picked up by Minority Leader Robert H. Michel as a GOP alternative in the House, it was defeated 188-238.

On Foreign Relations, Kassebaum's moderate approach clashes with that of the ranking Republican, conservative confrontationalist

Jesse Helms of North Carolina. The contrast was sharply cast during the presidency of Ronald Reagan. While Helms drew an ideological line in the sand on such issues as U.S. aid to the Nicaraguan contras, Kassebaum sought to steer an independent course between Reagan and his mainly Democratic critics.

While Kassebaum supported military aid for the contras, she grew increasingly critical of both the rebels and the president as Nicaragua's civil war dragged on. In 1986, she was a principal architect of a $100 million military aid package that included Reagan's promises to push contra leaders to curb human rights abuses and to end their internal disunity. She lambasted aid supporters for portraying the issue as "a disagreement between Republicans in white hats and Democrats in red banners."

From the Africa Subcommittee, which she chaired when Republicans controlled the Senate, Kassebaum has influenced the debate on policy toward South Africa. She was initially skeptical about the value of sanctions, warning they could harm oppressed blacks. But in 1986, a campaign of repression by South Africa's government allayed Kassebaum's doubts. She prodded Reagan to take action. When he did not, she backed sanctions and opposed his veto in order to "send a decisive message" of U.S. condemnation.

At the start of the 103rd Congress, Kassebaum gave up the ranking spot on the Africa subcommittee to take the top GOP seat on the International Economic Policy, Trade, Oceans and Environment panel.

During the 1991 congressional debate on the U.S. military response to Iraq's August 1990 invasion of Kuwait, Kassebaum stood solidly behind Bush. She praised the international coalition mobilized by Bush against Iraq as a "landmark achievement."

However, Kassebaum had not been satisfied with U.S. policy toward Iraq before its invasion of Kuwait. Viewing Iraq as a bulwark against Iran, the Reagan and Bush administrations sought better relations with Iraqi President Saddam Hussein and blocked congressional efforts to mandate economic sanctions in response to reports of Saddam's human rights violations. Kassebaum favored sanctions, even though they would have affected Kansas farmers who had found an export market in Iraq.

When a sanctions bill reached Foreign Relations in July 1990, administration officials said ending farm credit guarantees to Iraq would hurt American farmers more than Iraq. "I cannot believe that any farmer in this nation would want to send his products ... to a country that has used chemical weapons and to a country that has tortured and injured their children," Kassebaum responded.

Despite her status as one of only two Republican women in the Senate, Kassebaum has refused to be used by her party as a symbol. When officials of the 1984 GOP convention sought to have her appear on the podium with other prominent Republican women, she pointedly declined. "I'd be happy to speak on substantive issues," she said, "but to be treated as a bauble on a tree is not particularly constructive."

Kassebaum likewise has charted her own course on economic issues. As a member of the Budget Committee, Kassebaum opposed the 1985 Gramm-Rudman-Hollings budget-balancing law after sponsors exempted Social Security and other programs from its strictures. It could not work, she said, if Congress singled out sacred cows for special protection.

Kassebaum became so frustrated by the ongoing deficit impasse that she not only considered leaving the Budget Committee but proposed dissolving it. She stayed on Budget only at the urging of GOP leaders, who did not want to open a spot for strong-willed Texas Republican Phil Gramm. Finally, however, she had had enough; for the 101st Congress, Kassebaum left and Gramm took her seat.

Kassebaum's interest in issues of institutional reform earned her a spot in the 103rd on the Joint Committee on the Organization of Congress.

At Home: The Landon in Kassebaum's name marks her deep roots in Kansas politics. Her father, Alfred M. Landon, was a governor of Kansas and the 1936 GOP presidential nominee. (He died in 1987, just after his 100th birthday.)

But by the end of her second term, Kassebaum had established a more lasting political legacy than her father. Her modesty and moderate philosophy made her an overwhelming favorite for a third term in 1990.

In fact, her biggest obstacle was a pledge she made in 1978 to serve just two terms. Republican officials lobbied Kassebaum to run again and she assented, noting that she had tried without success to get Congress to consider term limits.

Any uncertainty about her re-election ended when she ended up being opposed in November by the *loser* of the Democratic Senate primary.

Prominent Democrats had backed off, and it seemed that Kassebaum would face Dick Williams, a little-known college instructor and an opponent of U.S. policies in Central America. But on the last day for candidate filing, former Democratic Rep. Bill Roy Sr. walked into the race. One week later, the 64-year-old Roy, who had lost to Kassebaum in 1978, walked back out, saying he lacked the stamina for campaigning. However, his name remained on the ballot, and was so much better known than Williams' that Roy won the primary.

A physician who said he wanted to emphasize health care issues, Roy reconsidered his withdrawal, but finally renounced the nomination. Williams was then chosen by a state party committee. He never made a dent in Kassebaum's support; she won with 74 percent.

Before 1978, Kassebaum's political activity had been confined to the School Board in a town of 785 people and one year as an aide to GOP Sen. James B. Pearson. But when Pearson announced plans to retire, she joined eight other contestants in the Republican primary. Kassebaum's middle name helped her stand out in the crowded field. She built upon that advantage with a series of TV ads featuring her father. The result was a clear victory.

That fall, she faced Roy, who had nearly ousted GOP Sen. Bob Dole in 1974. However, the Watergate backlash that helped Roy against Dole had faded. Kassebaum had no record for Roy to aim at, and her gentle style made attacks on her inexperience seem unmannerly. She beat Roy more comfortably than had Dole.

By 1984, Kassebaum was entrenched. The Democratic line went to investment executive Jim Maher, loser in two earlier Senate bids. Kassebaum won 76 percent.

Committees

Labor & Human Resources (Ranking)
Children, Families, Drugs & Alcoholism; Education, Arts & Humanities; Labor

Foreign Relations (3rd of 8 Republicans)
International Economic Policy, Trade, Oceans & Environment (ranking); African Affairs; European Affairs

Indian Affairs (6th of 8 Republicans)

Joint Organization of Congress

Elections

1990 General		
Nancy Landon Kassebaum (R)	578,605	(74%)
Dick Williams (D)	207,491	(26%)
1990 Primary		
Nancy Landon Kassebaum (R)	267,946	(87%)
R. Gregory Walstrom (R)	39,379	(13%)

Previous Winning Percentages: **1984** (76%) **1978** (54%)

Campaign Finance

	Receipts	Receipts from PACs		Expend- itures
1990				
Kassebaum (R)	$481,852	$187,858	(39%)	$407,387
Williams (D)	$16,827	$500	(3%)	$16,627

Key Votes

1993	
Require unpaid family and medical leave	N
Approve national "motor voter" registration bill	N
Approve budget increasing taxes and reducing deficit	N
Support president's right to lift military gay ban	N
1992	
Approve school-choice pilot program	Y
Allow shifting funds from defense to domestic programs	N
Oppose deeper cuts in spending for SDI	N
1991	
Approve waiting period for handgun purchases	Y
Raise senators' pay and ban honoraria	Y
Authorize use of force in Persian Gulf	Y
Confirm Clarence Thomas to Supreme Court	Y

Voting Studies

	Presidential Support		Party Unity		Conservative Coalition	
Year	**S**	**O**	**S**	**O**	**S**	**O**
1992	72	28	76	22	74	26
1991	79	20	69	30	75	23
1990	68	29	67	31	76	16
1989	85	14	71	27	84	16
1988	69	28	61	32	81	8
1987	59	28	65	22	72	22
1986	70	24	77	21	80	13
1985	76	19	79	17	75	22
1984	79	19	75	24	81	17
1983	78	20	71	25	59	36
1982	78	19	74	24	77	21
1981	82	17	77	20	80	18

Interest Group Ratings

Year	ADA	AFL-CIO	CCUS	ACU
1992	25	25	100	67
1991	35	17	80	62
1990	44	22	67	64
1989	20	0	63	57
1988	30	23	71	61
1987	30	20	71	60
1986	45	21	58	41
1985	35	10	69	48
1984	45	45	61	55
1983	35	24	42	36
1982	50	29	53	42
1981	35	5	88	60

1 Pat Roberts (R)

Of Dodge City — Elected 1980; 7th Term

Born: April 20, 1936, Topeka, Kan.
Education: Kansas State U., B.A. 1958.
Military Service: Marine Corps, 1958-62.
Occupation: Journalist; congressional aide.
Family: Wife, Franki Fann; three children.
Religion: Methodist.
Political Career: No previous office.
Capitol Office: 1126 Longworth Bldg. 20515; 225-2715.

In Washington: Roberts' enormous district requires him to pay attention to the concerns of constituents in the western two-thirds of Kansas, a territory larger than a good many states. But in 1993, Roberts has come to represent an even broader constituency as the ranking Republican on the Agriculture Committee. The defeat of two senior Republicans and the retirement of a third enabled him to vault from fourth-ranking in the 102nd Congress to ranking in the 103rd.

Roberts has long been an active player on Agriculture, where he is viewed not only as an advocate for Kansas wheat farmers but also as the resident wit. Pleasantly irascible, Roberts has a sarcastic sense of humor similar to that of Kansas' senior senator, Republican Bob Dole, who represented the 1st in the 1960s. Sometimes, deliberately or not, he even projects inflections and mannerisms similar to Dole's.

Colleagues also compare Roberts to Dole in another way. He is widely viewed as a man with both the interest and ability to serve in the other chamber of Congress in the event Dole or GOP Sen. Nancy Landon Kassebaum moves on.

Committee members consider Roberts' working knowledge of farm programs to be voluminous. His instincts may be conservative, but he is an unwavering defender of government spending programs that help his state's farmers. His outlook is nearly always a reflection of his rural district first and of his partisan label second. During the debate over the 1985 farm bill in the 99th Congress, he freely attacked the unpopular Reagan farm policy, and he once warned that Air Force One would get a "pitchfork in the belly" if it flew too low over Kansas. This farmer-first mentality is one reason he is expected to work well with Agriculture Committee Chairman E. "Kika" de la Garza of Texas.

Roberts' partisan colors can blaze more distinctly on his other committee assignment, House Administration, which oversees the day-to-day operations of the House.

In the 102nd Congress, Roberts was the lead Republican on a six-member task force investigating allegations of embezzlement and drug dealing at the House Post Office. Although the panel was evenly divided between Democrats and Republicans, bipartisan unity crumbled when Republicans proposed naming members in the panel's report. "A report without names is not a credible report," Roberts said. In the end, the panel issued a report with separate sections for each party.

Earlier in the 102nd, Roberts had helped publicize another unflattering aspect of members' business. As ranking Republican on the Personnel and Police Subcommittee, Roberts had joined Democratic chairman Mary Rose Oakar in announcing that members owed hundreds of thousands of dollars to the House restaurants in overdue bills.

The episode brought Roberts some unaccustomed personal criticism from colleagues. "Gee whiz, I just got excoriated," he told the Kansas City Times.

During consideration of the fiscal 1993 legislative appropriations bill, Roberts won approval for his amendment to end the 20-cents-per-mile payments to members for one round-trip visit to the district each session (a payment first authorized in 1866). He was rebuffed, however, in his attempt to bar spending on so-called legislative service organizations, issue-oriented confederations of like-minded members such as the Congressional Black Caucus.

Roberts spent much of his time in the 101st Congress working on the 1990 farm bill. The centerpiece of the bill was a plan, long backed by Roberts and Texas Democrat Charles W. Stenholm, to reduce the amount of cropland eligible for government income-support payments.

Construction of the 1990 farm bill took place amid palpable pressure to cut spending. When the farm economy was in a near depression during the 1985 farm bill debate, Roberts was uncomfortable about killing a plan that would have imposed production controls on farmers — and forced prices up. But with the mood on the farm comparatively tranquil in the 101st Congress, Roberts was willing to argue for

Kansas 1

Rural West — Salina; Hutchinson; Dodge City

Sprawling across 66 counties and more than two-thirds of Kansas' land area, the "Big First" is larger than many Eastern states. This is wheat-growing and cattle-raising country, dotted with small cities (none with more than 42,500 residents) and otherwise sparsely populated.

While much of the nation was enjoying an economic boom during the 1980s, western Kansas endured a period of "farm crisis" along with the typical vagaries of drought and freeze. These factors, along with continuing farm mechanization and concentration of land ownership, exacerbated population decline: Most counties in the 1st lost people in the 1980s.

But those who want to work in western Kansas can. Unemployment is extraordinarily low: In December 1992, several western counties had jobless rates below 2 percent.

1992, a year of GOP trial nationwide, proved the strength of the 1st's rural Republican voting traditions. George Bush finished first in all but one 1st District county. Bill Clinton finished third behind Bush and Ross Perot in 47 of the 66 counties. (Perot carried Wabaunsee and Morris counties in the eastern end of the 1st.) Republican Sen. Bob Dole, a native of the 1st, and Rep. Roberts swept the district.

The two largest population centers are in the 1st's eastern reaches. Salina (Saline County) is a traditional farm-market town, but it has an industrial element. Beech Aircraft has a factory here; food products, car batteries and light bulbs are also produced. Not far east is Abilene (Dickinson County), site of Dwight D. Eisenhower's burial place and his presidential library.

Industry in Hutchinson (Reno County) is largely farm- and food-related. Located 54 miles northwest of Wichita, Hutchinson is the site of the annual Kansas State Fair. The city of McPherson is nearby to the north; Emporia is at the district's eastern edge.

In recent years, the nation's meatpacking industry has dispersed from big-city stockyards to smaller towns closer to the Midwest's cattle ranches. Such southwest Kansas locales as Garden City and Dodge City have benefited from the trend and bucked Kansas' population slump. Finney County (Garden City) had the state's largest population increase (32 percent) during the 1980s, a boost fueled by Mexican and Asian immigrants who came to work in the huge IBP and Monfort beef-processing plants.

An Excel beef plant is the heart of Dodge City's economy. But the town also relies on a tourist trade based on its "Wild West" history. At the district's western edge is a sparsely populated rural region that was one of the strongest areas in the nation for Bush in 1992; he pulled down 64 percent in Wallace County, along the Colorado border.

At the district's center is Russell, Dole's hometown. But just west is Ellis County: Populated largely by farmers of German and Russian extraction, Ellis developed a Democratic habit that is abetted by Fort Hays State University's academic community. It was the only 1st District county that Clinton carried — with just 37 percent.

1990 Population: 619,370. White 583,625 (94%), Black 8,155 (1%), Other 27,590 (4%). Hispanic origin 31,962 (5%). 18 and over 452,729 (73%), 62 and over 124,511 (20%). Median age:35

some fiscal restraint in farm programs.

Roberts was less concerned about budget stringencies when Kansas farmers were hit by drought in 1988 and 1989. His district bore the brunt of the drought, and he sought disaster relief for his constituents.

In 1991, he and other farm-state members chafed under the fiscal constraints imposed by the 1990 budget agreement as they sought to revamp subsidy programs for dairy and grain farmers hit by low prices. When the Bush administration issued a veto threat, an exasperated Roberts said, "What can we tell farmers? Are our hands tied? Have we lost control of agriculture policy?"

As ranking member on the Agriculture Subcommittee on Department Operations, Research and Foreign Agriculture, Roberts was involved in efforts to write pesticide laws. He fought efforts during deliberations over the 1990 farm bill to reduce farmers' use of chemicals, and he opposed provisions designed to break the "circle of poison" by greatly restricting the export of pesticides banned in the United States.

Roberts has other rural interests outside the Agriculture Committee. In the 100th Congress he was a member of the bipartisan Rural Health Care Coalition, a group that worked to make changes in the Medicare system, which many legislators consider unfair and harmful to rural health services. Just before the 102nd Congress began, he and Stenholm were named co-chairmen of the coalition.

At Home: As the long-tenured member from the sprawling 1st District, Roberts is often mentioned as a potential statewide contender. But the Senate route has been blocked by the ongoing careers of fellow Republicans Dole and Kassebaum.

Roberts understudied his House role for 12 years as top aide to GOP Rep. Keith G. Sebelius. When Sebelius retired in 1980, Roberts was ready. Most GOP county chairmen backed Roberts in the primary, and he won with 56 percent.

Roberts' victory in November was scarcely in doubt. Capitalizing on the popularity of Sebelius, Roberts referred to "our record" so frequently that he sounded like an incumbent. He defeated Democratic state Rep. Phil Martin with 62 percent of the vote.

In 1984, Roberts faced some loud opposition: Democrat Darrell Ringer, who declared that the government would neglect the nation's agricultural problems unless more farmers went to Congress. But most voters concluded that Ringer, an activist in the American Agricultural Movement, would be more strident than successful; Roberts won by 3-to-1.

After a similar Roberts performance in 1986, Democrats left him unopposed in 1988.

In 1990, district Democrats challenged Roberts with lawyer Duane West, the prosecutor in the 1958 murder case that inspired Truman Capote's book "In Cold Blood." Although Roberts won easily with 63 percent, West did better than past 1st District Democratic challengers and sought a rematch. But West barely won a three-way Democratic primary in 1992 and was no match for Roberts, who again approached 70 percent of the vote in November.

Roberts' father, C. Wesley Roberts, was the state GOP chairman in the late 1940s. In 1953, he was chosen chairman of the Republican National Committee. But the Kansas City Star accused him of having improperly used his influence as a state party leader to affect an appropriation by the state Legislature. Nine weeks after taking his national GOP post, he resigned.

Committees

Agriculture (Ranking)

Joint Printing (Ranking)

House Administration (3rd of 7 Republicans)
Accounts (ranking); Elections; Libraries & Memorials

Joint Library

Elections

1992 General		
Pat Roberts (R)	194,912	(68%)
Duane West (D)	83,620	(29%)
Steven A. Rosile (LIBERT)	6,765	(2%)
1990 General		
Pat Roberts (R)	102,974	(63%)
Duane West (D)	61,396	(37%)

Previous Winning Percentages: **1988** (100%) **1986** (77%) **1984** (76%) **1982** (68%) **1980** (62%)

District Vote for President

1992

D 81,526 (28%)
R 123,019 (42%)
I 85,550 (29%)

Campaign Finance

	Receipts	Receipts from PACs		Expend-itures
1992				
Roberts (R)	$313,020	$185,085	(59%)	$601,655
West (D)	$64,899	0		$64,850
1990				
Roberts (R)	$222,760	$132,250	(59%)	$152,249
West (D)	$16,965	$250	(1%)	$16,701

Key Votes

1993	
Require parental notification of minors' abortions	Y
Require unpaid family and medical leave	N
Approve national "motor voter" registration bill	N
Approve budget increasing taxes and reducing deficit	N
Approve economic stimulus plan	N
1992	
Approve balanced-budget constitutional amendment	Y
Close down space station program	N
Approve U.S. aid for former Soviet Union	Y
Allow shifting funds from defense to domestic programs	N
1991	
Extend unemployment benefits using deficit financing	N
Approve waiting period for handgun purchases	N
Authorize use of force in Persian Gulf	Y

Voting Studies

	Presidential Support		Party Unity		Conservative Coalition	
Year	**S**	**O**	**S**	**O**	**S**	**O**
1992	87	11	93	4	96	4
1991	82	17	90	6	97	3
1990	71	27	87	11	87	9
1989	79	21	86	12	93	5
1988	62	33	86	10	95	3
1987	63	31	83	10	81	9
1986	69	31	87	11	90	8
1985	63	38	83	10	80	16
1984	63	35	84	8	85	10
1983	73	27	87	11	85	13
1982	62	36	86	11	84	14
1981	67	30	86	11	91	5

Interest Group Ratings

Year	ADA	AFL-CIO	CCUS	ACU
1992	10	17	88	88
1991	5	0	90	83
1990	6	0	79	75
1989	5	0	100	79
1988	10	25	100	79
1987	4	0	100	86
1986	0	7	94	82
1985	15	12	95	71
1984	5	8	80	96
1983	10	6	90	91
1982	15	0	90	82
1981	10	0	84	100

2 Jim Slattery (D)

Of Topeka — Elected 1982; 6th Term

Born: Aug. 4, 1948, Good Intent, Kan.
Education: Netherlands School of International Economics and Business, 1969-70; Washburn U., B.S. 1970, J.D. 1974.
Military Service: National Guard, 1970-75.
Occupation: Real estate broker.
Family: Wife, Linda Smith; two children.
Religion: Roman Catholic.
Political Career: Kan. House, 1973-79; Kan. acting secretary of revenue, 1979.
Capitol Office: 2243 Rayburn Bldg. 20515; 225-6601.

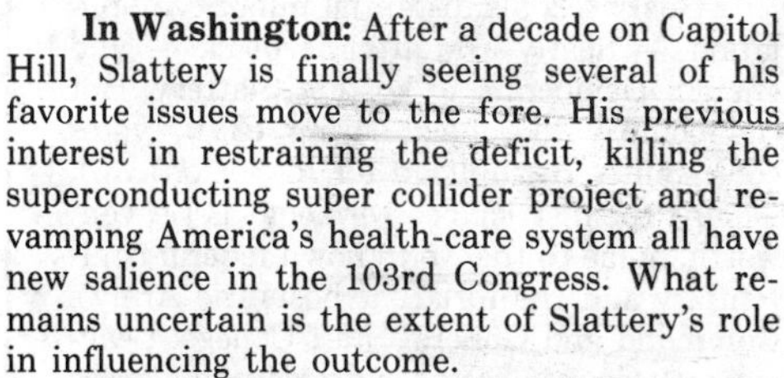

In Washington: After a decade on Capitol Hill, Slattery is finally seeing several of his favorite issues move to the fore. His previous interest in restraining the deficit, killing the superconducting super collider project and revamping America's health-care system all have new salience in the 103rd Congress. What remains uncertain is the extent of Slattery's role in influencing the outcome.

Now in his sixth term, Slattery is no longer the youthful rising star. His full head of dark hair has streaks of gray, and a great political opportunity was bypassed in 1990 when Slattery decided to forgo the gubernatorial race (and watched a lesser-known Democrat oust the sitting Republican governor).

It could take years for another statewide opportunity that good, and with a mid-level slot on the Energy and Commerce Committee, Slattery might wait another decade before controlling his own turf in the House.

Nevertheless, Slattery is a reliable yeoman, willing to work hard for a single amendment. His doggedness has produced results, particularly for his constituents. In the 102nd, Slattery helped win millions of federal dollars for two new highways and a veterans medical center in Kansas. He also persuaded the U.S. trade representative to impose an import duty on Mexican cellophane, a move that helps protect a major employer in Tecumseh, Kan.

Another example of Slattery's attentiveness to district concerns was his bill pertaining to greyhound racing. The National Greyhound Association is based in Kansas, and Slattery's bill sought to give dog owners a share of the profits when races are simulcast across state lines. Slattery got the bill through Energy and Commerce, but it died at the end of the 101st Congress. It was reintroduced in the 102nd and again in the 103rd.

When he arrived in the House in 1983, Slattery quickly became part of a group trying to form a new center of gravity within the Democratic Party on budget issues — even if it meant bucking the Democratic leadership.

Slattery was one of three moderate-to-conservative Democrats appointed to the Budget Committee in 1985 when Speaker Thomas P. O'Neill Jr. was under pressure to change its liberal tilt. In 1985 the group proposed a budget that called for a freeze on most federal programs, domestic as well as military, and included Social Security among those eligible to be frozen. It lost on the floor 56-372.

Slattery pressed on, and during the 101st Congress his fiscal concerns inspired a battle against the B-2 stealth bomber. Slattery had earlier supported the bomber, but changed his mind after its cost overruns mounted. In early 1990, he joined with 13 Armed Services Committee members seeking to stop production of the B-2. The House voted to cap the fleet at 20 bombers, instead of the 132 requested by President Bush.

Slattery also has shown a willingness to go after smaller expenditures, even at the expense of embarrassing colleagues. Near the end of the 101st Congress, he set his sights on a $500,000 appropriation for a German-Russian interpretive center at the North Dakota birthplace of band leader Lawrence Welk. Slattery's move to rescind the funding prevailed in the House, but the well-publicized crusade angered then-Rep. Byron L. Dorgan, a North Dakota Democrat and advocate for the project.

Slattery's self-described role as a pork-buster and his accessibility have won him a generous share of media coverage. Colleagues joke about which Kansan will tally more floor speeches: Slattery or Rep. Dan Glickman.

But Slattery's frequent appearances on the front page belie his internal role in the House. His distaste for public criticism of the institution, coupled with his Midwestern sensibilities, make him a valued sounding board for Majority Leader Richard A. Gephardt and other high-ranking Democrats.

In his freshman year, Slattery won a spot on the coveted Energy Committee, where he is

Kansas 2

East — Topeka; Leavenworth; Pittsburg

The 25-county 2nd sweeps from Kansas' eastern corners, touching Nebraska to the north and Oklahoma to the south and making up most of Kansas' border with Missouri in between.

Two-thirds of the residents live in or north of Shawnee County. Topeka (the state capital and the third-biggest city in Kansas, with nearly 120,000 residents), Leavenworth and Manhattan are here. The small city of Pittsburg, with 17,800 residents, is the biggest town in the 2nd's southern reaches.

The 2nd has a conservative bent, but Rep. Slattery has thrived, winning solidly in 1992 even though redistricting gave him much new turf in the district's southern end.

George Bush finished first in 1992, but just barely. He did best in 1992 in the district's more rural northern and south-central regions; even there, he topped 40 percent in just four counties. Bill Clinton ran first in the urbanized north-central area influenced by Topeka and Kansas City, Mo., and in the blue-collar, southeast corner of Kansas. The 2nd showed an independent streak: Ross Perot topped 30 percent in 13 district counties and won two.

The 11 northern counties that make up Slattery's longtime base include numerous state employees and a scattering of minority-group concentrations. The coal mines and oil fields of southeastern Kansas long ago drew Southern Democrats and Eastern European immigrants (because of whom this hilly area was nicknamed "the Balkans"). Although these resource industries faded, there is enough remaining manufacturing to sustain a blue-collar Democratic vote.

State government is Topeka's largest employer. Medical centers, including the Menninger Foundation's psychiatric facilities, employ thousands. The economy includes an industrial component. A Goodyear tire factory and the Atchison, Topeka & Santa Fe Railway are leading employers.

To the west is Manhattan with Kansas State University (20,700 students); this agriculture-oriented school gives Riley County a conservative tone that is reinforced by the military community at Fort Riley, which sprawls into Geary County and is home to the Army's 1st Infantry Division.

Geary has a substantial minority population — nearly a quarter is black — and enough Democrats to sustain Slattery. But the county, like neighboring Riley, votes consistently Republican for higher offices.

At the district's eastern edge is Leavenworth, home to the well-known federal penitentiary and the fort that hosts the Army's Command and General Staff College. Leavenworth County has been drawn into Kansas City, Mo.'s, suburban sphere; its population grew 17 percent in the 1980s.

To the north and south of Topeka is mainly farmland where soybeans are grown, hogs are raised and mostly Republican votes are cast. The two counties Slattery lost in 1992 — Coffey and Linn — are in the south-central region. Most of the rural counties have suffered the kind of population slump seen in the western 1st District.

1990 Population: 619,391. White 558,318 (90%), Black 38,940 (6%), Other 22,133 (4%). Hispanic origin 18,390 (3%). 18 and over 458,157 (74%), 62 and over 104,237 (17%). Median age: 33.

considered close to business but often supports measures pushed by environmental groups. In the 102nd, he authored a provision of the cable reregulation bill that bans negative options, a procedure in which cable companies provide new channels without approval from the customer. The provision was included in the final bill, which was enacted when both chambers overrode Bush's veto.

He also joined the push to let the regional Bell companies manufacture telecommunications equipment. The debate revived in the 103rd.

Although Slattery failed to kill the $8.5 billion atom-smashing superconducting super collider project in the 102nd, his proposal picked up votes. Slattery resumed the fight amid talk of belt tightening in the 103rd.

On health care, Slattery focuses on small business and rural issues. Among his goals: guaranteed health coverage — or tax deductions — for farmers.

After a single term on Banking and the maximum three-term stint on the Budget Committee, Slattery limited his committee work in the 103rd to Energy and Veterans' Affairs.

At Home: After winning a formerly Republican seat by a comfortable margin in 1982, Slattery settled in for a series of no-sweat victories over modest GOP competition. His 1992 contest fit the mold: It was a rematch against Republican Jim Van Slyke, whom Slattery had defeated with 60 percent of the vote in 1984.

But in 1992, Slattery's 50 overdrafts at the House bank gave Van Slyke an issue. Slattery also faced a 2nd District constituency that had been greatly changed by redistricting. Because the state lost a House seat following the 1990 census, the 2nd District annexed a 13-county swath of largely rural, conservative-leaning southeast Kansas.

Slattery received at least 57 percent in all 12 northeast Kansas counties where he had run before. But he topped that mark in only three of his new counties, and lost two of them outright. Still, Slattery defeated Van Slyke with more than 40,000 votes to spare.

Slattery has never made a secret of his political ambitions. He was 24 and still in law school in 1972 when he defeated a Republican state representative.

After six years in the state House, Slattery took a break to develop his Topeka real-estate business and prepare a run for Congress. His chance soon came: Republican Jim Jeffries had won the 2nd in 1978, but decided not to run in 1982 after redistricting made some unfavorable changes to the district.

Slattery bid for the open seat and fended off efforts by his Republican opponent, former state legislator Morris Kay, to brand him a liberal. Appealing for bipartisan support by stressing his farm background and his ties to the Topeka business community, Slattery carried all but two of the district's 13 counties. Slattery defeated Van Slyke in 1984 and went on to easy wins in 1986 and 1988.

Slattery initially seemed likely in 1990 to challenge Republican Gov. Mike Hayden, whose popularity had declined. But Slattery deferred to former Democratic Gov. John Carlin, who had entered the gubernatorial primary.

Although Slattery would breeze by Republican Scott Morgan, a former Hayden aide, for House re-election, he had to be somewhat frustrated as state Treasurer Joan Finney upset Carlin for the Democratic nomination and went on to unseat the beleaguered Hayden.

Committees

Energy & Commerce (12th of 27 Democrats)
Commerce, Consumer Protection & Competitiveness; Health & the Environment; Telecommunications & Finance

Veterans' Affairs (7th of 21 Democrats)
Compensation, Pension & Insurance (chairman); Education, Training & Employment

Elections

1992 General		
Jim Slattery (D)	151,019	(56%)
Jim Van Slyke (R)	109,801	(41%)
Arthur L. Clack (LIBERT)	7,986	(3%)
1990 General		
Jim Slattery (D)	99,093	(63%)
Scott Morgan (R)	58,643	(37%)

Previous Winning Percentages: 1988 (73%) **1986** (71%) **1984** (60%) **1982** (57%)

District Vote for President

1992
D 98,527 (36%)
R 98,999 (36%)
I 75,600 (28%)

Campaign Finance

	Receipts	Receipts from PACs		Expend-itures
1992				
Slattery (D)	$702,306	$439,255	(63%)	$742,215
Van Slyke (R)	$36,704	$4,870	(13%)	$36,704
1990				
Slattery (D)	$467,018	$327,550	(70%)	$504,861
Morgan (R)	$87,021	$8,054	(9%)	$84,568

Key Votes

1993	
Require parental notification of minors' abortions	N
Require unpaid family and medical leave	N
Approve national "motor voter" registration bill	Y
Approve budget increasing taxes and reducing deficit	Y
Approve economic stimulus plan	Y
1992	
Approve balanced-budget constitutional amendment	N
Close down space station program	N
Approve U.S. aid for former Soviet Union	Y
Allow shifting funds from defense to domestic programs	N
1991	
Extend unemployment benefits using deficit financing	Y
Approve waiting period for handgun purchases	N
Authorize use of force in Persian Gulf	Y

Voting Studies

	Presidential Support		Party Unity		Conservative Coalition	
Year	**S**	**O**	**S**	**O**	**S**	**O**
1992	30	69	73	23	56	44
1991	38	62	71	26	76	24
1990	32	67	73	25	48	48
1989	45	55	74	24	59	41
1988	32	61	78	19	61	29
1987	38	60	73	24	63	33
1986	34	66	68	30	62	38
1985	43	58	71	27	65	35
1984	39	61	60	39	49	51
1983	39	61	57	38	58	38

Interest Group Ratings

Year	ADA	AFL-CIO	CCUS	ACU
1992	75	83	50	28
1991	40	67	50	40
1990	61	67	43	22
1989	55	75	60	21
1988	55	85	38	33
1987	68	69	47	4
1986	45	57	56	27
1985	55	53	36	33
1984	50	38	44	38
1983	55	71	55	36

3 Jan Meyers (R)

Of Overland Park — Elected 1984; 5th Term

Born: July 20, 1928, Lincoln, Neb.
Education: William Woods College, A.F.A. 1948; U. of Nebraska, B.A. 1951.
Occupation: Homemaker; community volunteer.
Family: Husband, Louis "Dutch" Meyers; two children.
Religion: Methodist.
Political Career: Overland Park City Council, 1967-72, president, 1970-72; Kan. Senate, 1973-85; sought GOP nomination for U.S. Senate, 1978.
Capitol Office: 2338 Rayburn Bldg. 20515; 225-2865.

In Washington: When she came to the House from a position of some influence in the Kansas Legislature, Meyers had high hopes for a prestige committee post. Almost a decade later — at the start of the 103rd Congress — she had advanced only to the top GOP slot on a secondary panel, the Small Business Committee. Still, it was clearly a move up the Republican hierarchy, and it gave her the distinction of being the first woman to assume a ranking minority committee post in 20 years.

Since her election in 1984, Meyers has steadily carved a niche for herself at Small Business through persistent efforts to protect entrepreneurs. She repeatedly has won high ratings from the U.S. Chamber of Commerce and the National Federation of Independent Business, the latter group awarding her a 100 percent score in the 102nd Congress. She has worked especially hard at extending the health insurance deduction for the self-employed, while maintaining the GOP line against federal mandates on employers. She sided against the high-profile Family and Medical Leave Act, even on the pivotal vote in 1993 when the bill finally became law.

Early in the 103rd Congress, Meyers introduced legislation calling for 12 steps to help small-business entrepreneurs. They included elevating the Small Business Administration to Cabinet rank, making permanent several tax credits for small business, increasing the health-care deduction for the self-employed to 100 percent and restoring the small-business exemption to minimum wage laws.

Meyers has long tried to climb the party ladder but with limited success. She started by taking on low-visibility party housekeeping tasks for GOP leader Robert H. Michel of Illinois, with whom she shares a proclivity for legislative compromise. But by the time Meyers ran for conference secretary, a more confrontational style was ascendant among House Republicans, embodied by Newt Gingrich and his Conservative Opportunity Society (COS). The genteel Meyers was swept aside by COS member Vin Weber of Minnesota. However, after his 1989 election as GOP whip, Gingrich appointed her deputy whip for theme development.

Meyers has made a semi-career of serving on various task forces and policy bodies, such as the Republican Task Force on Health Care Policy. Besides her post in that 1992 group, she was elected in 1989 as vice chairman of the Environmental and Energy Study Conference. In 1993 she was appointed to Michel's Economic and Health Task Force. She was also reappointed as an at-large member of the Republican Policy Committee.

Meyers has not played a particularly visible role on her other committee — Foreign Affairs — although she was outspoken on one issue. During the 102nd Congress she opposed the administration's so-called Mexico City policy, named for the 1984 conference at which restrictions were unveiled on U.S. aid to family planning organizations abroad.

Meyers took on fellow Republican Christopher H. Smith of New Jersey at Foreign Affairs and offered an amendment to a foreign aid authorization bill to eliminate the restriction, which she said would bar U.S. aid to several African nations with high rates of population growth.

Usually a staunch Bush administration loyalist, Meyers readily accepted that her actions might have triggered a possible veto. "The president has to do what he has to do," she said, "and I have to do what I have to do."

The Foreign Affairs Committee adopted Meyers' language, but it ultimately was dropped in conference.

Meyers' other efforts typically have a home-base angle. In 1990, her bill to study improvements in firefighter safety became law; she came to the issue after a 1988 incident in Kansas City, Mo., in which a trailer containing volatile materials exploded, killing six firefighters. Meyers also successfully lobbied for funding of a federal building and courthouse in Kansas City, Kan. Drug-abuse prevention is another Meyers priority. She proposed increas-

Kansas 3

Kansas City region — Overland Park; Lawrence

The 3rd, hard by Missouri in eastern Kansas, is not like the state's other districts. Geographically compact, it is almost entirely within the metropolitan sphere of Kansas City, Mo. Its population is mainly in the graceful suburbs of Johnson County, in the grittier urban environs of Kansas City, Kan., and in Lawrence (home to the University of Kansas and its 29,200 students).

There are sharp contrasts within the 3rd. Non-Hispanic whites make up more than 90 percent of Johnson County's population. But more than a third of the residents in Kansas City (in neighboring Wyandotte County) are black or Hispanic. The 1990 census reported a poverty rate in Johnson County of 3.6 percent; Wyandotte's rate was nearly five times higher.

Johnson County, with more than 350,000 people, dominates the 3rd; its strong Republican lean usually tips the district to GOP candidates, including Rep. Meyers, a county native. But Wyandotte County sometimes provides a counterbalance that gives Democrats a fighting chance. The 1992 campaign, in which Bill Clinton scored a rare Democratic win over George Bush in the 3rd, was illustrative. Bush won Johnson (though with 44 percent, nearly 20 percentage points below his 1988 figure). Clinton took Wyandotte with 55 percent, by far his best showing in Kansas; Bush's 20 percent put him in third, behind Ross Perot, who won nearly a quarter of the 3rd's vote overall.

Johnson County has been booming since the 1960s. The growth has turned Overland Park into a satellite city with more than 110,000 residents. Numerous companies are based in Johnson, which bills itself as "Executive Country." Westwood is home to U.S. Sprint. Residential growth has spread to exurban areas west of Overland Park: Olathe, the county seat, has more than 63,000 residents.

Bordering to the north is Wyandotte County and Kansas City. Overshadowed by its namesake across the Missouri River, Kansas City, Kan., is an industrial town that has had its share of Rust Belt blues due to factory closures and the long-term decline of urban stockyards. But Kansas City maintains a large industrial base and has attracted some growth in its biotechnology sector. Successful efforts by Kansans in Congress to place a new federal courthouse here and to transfer a regional Housing and Urban Development office from Kansas City, Mo., have provided a boost.

To the west, the 3rd takes in Lawrence and most of Douglas County. The county's eastern portions along state Route 10 are becoming increasingly suburban. University-centered Lawrence has some liberal activists, but the outlying farm areas lean Republican. Bush in 1988 carried Douglas, but with just 50 percent; the county swung to Clinton in 1992 by 46 percent to 31 percent. Meyers carried Douglas narrowly.

At the district's southern end is Miami County, which is lightly populated and has a Republican tilt, though that has been tempered by some recent economic troubles. Clinton narrowly won it in 1992.

1990 Population: 619,439. White 540,210 (87%), Black 55,263 (9%), Other 23,966 (4%). Hispanic origin 20,395 (3%). 18 and over 455,833 (74%), 62 and over 77,999 (13%). Median age: 32.

ing criminal penalties for operators of common carriers, who, while under the influence of drugs or alcohol, are involved in accidents that cause death and injury; provisions of her bill were attached to the 1988 omnibus drug act.

Similarly, she proposed a comprehensive energy conservation program in March 1991 with an eye toward expanding business opportunities for her more entrepreneurial constituents. The provisions geared toward home and commercial energy efficiency were folded into the 1992 omnibus energy bill signed by the president.

At Home: The consensus-oriented Meyers said she is representative of the "moderate majority" in the 3rd District, which is dominated by the Johnson County suburbs of Kansas City, Mo. In 1984, Meyers, then a 12-year state senator, outdistanced four GOP opponents in the primary to succeed retiring Republican Rep. Larry Winn Jr. She then went to defeat a prominent Democrat, Mayor Jack Reardon of Kansas City, with 55 percent of the vote.

For the next several elections, Meyers scored easy victories over mild Democratic opposition and faced no trouble within the district Republican Party. That changed in 1992, when state Rep. Kerry Patrick, a conservative activist, staged an aggressive primary challenge to Meyers.

Patrick had a reputation as a maverick who spoke out whenever the Legislature's Republican leadership showed a willingness to compromise with Democrats on state fiscal issues. Also known for his conservative views on social issues, Patrick sought to brand Meyers as a liberal. The main thrust of his campaign, though, was to tarnish Meyers' ethical image. He played up the findings of a House task force, which reported just before the August primary that Meyers was one of seven members for whom House Post Office employees had delivered campaign-related mail.

While Meyers conceded that her staff had arranged such deliveries early in her tenure, she said she stopped the practice as soon as she learned of it. She also dropped her mild manner long enough to castigate Patrick as a gadfly and an ineffective legislator.

Although Meyers slipped to 56 percent, she finished with a comfortable lead over Patrick (33 percent) and two other candidates. In November, she breezed past Democratic state Rep. Tom Love, winning 66 percent in Johnson County to offset Love's much slighter advantage in his Wyandotte County (Kansas City, Kan.) base.

Meyers began her political career in 1967 when she was elected to the Overland Park City Council. After five terms, she moved to the state Senate, making a mark on such issues as care for the elderly, and prevention of child abuse and drunken driving. In 1978, Meyers ran in the GOP primary for an open U.S. Senate seat. She finished fourth with 10 percent in a contest won by Nancy Landon Kassebaum.

Committees

Small Business (Ranking)
SBA Legislation & the General Economy (ranking)

Foreign Affairs (10th of 18 Republicans)
Europe & the Middle East; Economic Policy, Trade & the Environment

Elections

1992 General		
Jan Meyers (R)	169,929	(58%)
Tom Love (D)	110,071	(38%)
Frank Kaul (LIBERT)	12,791	(4%)
1992 Primary		
Jan Meyers (R)	35,911	(56%)
Kerry Patrick (R)	20,953	(33%)
Jim Hall (R)	3,947	(6%)
Gary Adams (R)	3,014	(5%)
1990 General		
Jan Meyers (R)	88,725	(60%)
Leroy Jones (D)	58,923	(40%)

Previous Winning Percentages: **1988** (74%) **1986** (100%) **1984** (55%)

District Vote for President

1992
D 116,729 (38%)
R 114,220 (37%)
I 75,608 (25%)

Campaign Finance

	Receipts	Receipts from PACs		Expend-itures
1992				
Meyers (R)	$431,501	$209,895	(49%)	$430,833
1990				
Meyers (R)	$211,505	$110,641	(52%)	$209,986
Jones (D)	$78,289	$51,299	(66%)	$76,007

Key Votes

1993	
Require parental notification of minors' abortions	N
Require unpaid family and medical leave	N
Approve national "motor voter" registration bill	Y
Approve budget increasing taxes and reducing deficit	N
Approve economic stimulus plan	N
1992	
Approve balanced-budget constitutional amendment	Y
Close down space station program	N
Approve U.S. aid for former Soviet Union	Y
Allow shifting funds from defense to domestic programs	N
1991	
Extend unemployment benefits using deficit financing	N
Approve waiting period for handgun purchases	Y
Authorize use of force in Persian Gulf	Y

Voting Studies

	Presidential Support		Party Unity		Conservative Coalition	
Year	**S**	**O**	**S**	**O**	**S**	**O**
1992	63	37	76	20	73	25
1991	68	32	73	27	76	22
1990	65	35	70	29	78	22
1989	69	31	53	46	88	12
1988	52	45	71	24	87	13
1987	59	41	71	26	77	21
1986	59	39	73	27	70	30
1985	68	31	68	26	78	18

Interest Group Ratings

Year	ADA	AFL-CIO	CCUS	ACU
1992	30	36	88	72
1991	25	33	70	75
1990	22	0	57	67
1989	15	17	100	64
1988	35	23	85	58
1987	12	6	93	61
1986	25	14	78	55
1985	15	19	86	71

4 Dan Glickman (D)

Of Wichita — Elected 1976; 9th Term

Born: Nov. 24, 1944, Wichita, Kan.
Education: U. of Michigan, B.A. 1966; George Washington U., J.D. 1969.
Occupation: Lawyer.
Family: Wife, Rhoda Yura; two children.
Religion: Jewish.
Political Career: Wichita Board of Education, 1973-76, president, 1975-76.
Capitol Office: 2371 Rayburn Bldg. 20515; 225-6216.

In Washington: Glickman has eschewed the customary path to influence in the House — specializing in one legislative area — but he cannot be accused of being a scattershot. Rather, his approach is more like saturation bombing: Health-care reform, farm policy, television violence, campaign finance reform, eliminating members' parking perks — all this is part of Glickman's legislative arsenal.

As the chairman of the House Intelligence Committee (a job he got at the start of the 103rd Congress), Glickman has launched a campaign to "demystify" the nation's intelligence operations, promising to hold more frequent open sessions of the panel in addition to the usual closed-door meetings. He is also emerging as an advocate of using CIA resources to deter economic espionage by foreign corporations and of sharing intelligence with U.S. companies to help them compete internationally.

The intelligence budget, now an estimated $29 billion per year, is expected to face especially close scrutiny in the 103rd, with the increasing strain on federal resources. Glickman signaled that his committee will be taking a hard look at intelligence spending, telling CIA Director James Woolsey in March 1993 that "times have changed." The nation's intelligence agencies tripled in size during the 1980s.

House Speaker Thomas S. Foley picked Glickman for the top spot on Intelligence, replacing Dave McCurdy of Oklahoma. Foley's move was seen as an attempt to give the House leadership more control over the committee.

In addition to chairing Intelligence, Glickman serves on the Judiciary and Science committees. If the past is any indication, Glickman will continue to be a serious player on both. He has been described by one colleague as "a legislative factory." Such industry has helped Glickman move past his early reputation as something of a media-seeking maverick — though he is still regarded as having a yen for publicity.

In accepting the chairmanship of Intelligence, Glickman stepped down from chairing the Agriculture Subcommittee on Wheat, Soybeans and Feed Grains, a position that gave him considerable clout on matters of interest to Kansas farmers. However, Glickman's term on Intelligence will expire at the end of the 103rd — in time for him to return to the subcommittee, now expanded and called General Farm Commodities, for work on the 1995 farm bill.

A central player on the 1985 farm bill, Glickman was one of a group of younger House Democrats who wanted Congress to try new approaches for the federal price-support program. At the start of the 100th Congress, he inherited the subcommittee chair and again played a pivotal role in the 1990 farm bill. Glickman's work on Agriculture has been characterized by an understanding that a line must be drawn in accommodating farm-state interests to produce farm legislation that can pass on the floor.

Glickman has been a sharp critic of unnecessary bureaucracy at the U.S. Department of Agriculture; he filed a bill in the 102nd to consolidate hundreds of USDA field offices while reducing the paperwork that farmers must complete to receive federal subsidy payments.

In the 102nd, Glickman moved one step closer to realizing a controversial goal: establishing a national park in the tall grass plains of Kansas' Flint Hills. His bill creating an 11,000-acre park was passed by the House but not acted on by the Senate. The idea has been around since the 1970s, but many Kansas ranchers and farmers oppose it.

In the 103rd, Glickman has tied together home-state interests and global concerns with a bill that would provide additional grain shipments to the republics of the former Soviet Union in exchange for actions by those countries to dismantle their nuclear arsenals.

Glickman, whose 1992 re-election bid was complicated by his 105 overdrafts at the House bank, criticized House Democratic leaders for moving too slowly to clean up the mess. "The leadership has a special responsibility to protect the institution and to protect the members," he said. "And by 'protect' I don't mean cover up — I mean clean up." Glickman filed

Kansas 4

South central — Wichita

The 4th takes in an 11-county stretch in south-central Kansas. But the district is dominated by Kansas' largest city, Wichita (Sedgwick County). Sedgwick provides more than two-thirds of the district's population; Wichita alone, with more than 300,000 residents, makes up nearly half.

A center for military, commercial and general aviation aircraft production, Wichita has a large number of blue-collar whites with roots in Oklahoma, Texas and elsewhere in the South. Blacks and Hispanics make up about 16 percent of Wichita's population, a modest proportion by big-city standards but huge compared with the rest of the 4th.

The Democratic traditions of the district's Southern whites and the strong partisan affiliation of minority voters has boosted Rep. Glickman and some centrist Democratic candidates for statewide office. But with its overall conservative tone, the 4th is not a "Democratic" district.

George Bush took 40 percent of the 4th's vote in 1992, yet easily defeated Bill Clinton, carrying all 11 counties. Clinton was second in Sedgwick, but ran third behind Ross Perot in all but three other counties.

Glickman's close 1992 election exposed a divide in the 4th. He carried the seven western counties (including Sedgwick), most of which he had long represented. But he lost the four easternmost counties in a mainly rural region that was added to the 4th in 1992 redistricting.

While many industrial cities struggled during the 1980s, Wichita rode the wings of its aviation industry. The decade's big growth in defense spending boosted Boeing's military aircraft lines in Wichita; the national business boom aided Learjet, Cessna and Beech, civilian plane-builders affiliated with larger companies but based in Wichita.

The decline in defense spending is creating local concerns not only about the aviation industry but also the future of McConnell Air Force Base, site of a B-1 bomber fleet. The early 1990s recession and the downward spiral of the nation's passenger airlines have already rocked aviation's commercial side. Once rock-solid, Boeing announced in February 1993 that it planned to cut its Wichita work force by about 30 percent.

The city is hardly a one-industry town. The Coleman recreation equipment company and the Pizza Hut restaurant chain are headquartered here, as is Koch Industries, a leader in development of southern Kansas' oil and gas resources. Wichita State University (15,800 students) is also a major employer.

Wichita has developed a growing suburbia. Derby, a few miles south on Kansas 15, has nearly 15,000 residents, almost double its population 20 years ago. There has been some spillover into Butler County (El Dorado).

Much of the rest of the 4th (including rural parts of Sedgwick) is farmland. Sumner County, on the Oklahoma border, is Kansas' leading wheat-growing county; that crop is also important to Harper and Kingman counties to the west. Cattle graze in sparsely populated Greenwood, Elk and Chautauqua counties to the east.

1990 Population: 619,374. White 549,833 (89%), Black 40,718 (7%), Other 28,823 (5%). Hispanic origin 22,923 (4%). 18 and over 449,241 (73%), 62 and over 99,483 (16%). Median age: 33.

legislation to prevent such problems in the future by hiring a professional administrator and auditor for the House.

House Speaker Thomas S. Foley apparently took Glickman's comments as constructive, not personal, criticism. He backed the House administrator bill and was not dissuaded from picking Glickman to replace McCurdy, who had rankled Foley and other leaders, at Intelligence.

Another Glickman interest is campaign finance reform. Together with Democrat Mike Synar of Oklahoma, he has pushed legislation to institute public financing of campaigns.

At Home: After narrowly unseating a GOP incumbent in 1976, Glickman quickly settled in to become the most successful vote-getter among major Democratic officeholders in Kansas. He got at least 64 percent of the vote in each of his next seven elections.

A tough 1992 campaign proved his prowess. For the first time in years, Republicans put up a well-known foe, state Senate Vice President Eric R. Yost. Yet Glickman overcame Yost and other obstacles to win by 10 percentage points.

At first, it was uncertain Glickman would seek a ninth House term: He was seen as a likely challenger to GOP Sen. Bob Dole of Kansas, and a certain candidate if Dole chose not to go for a fifth term. But Dole decided to run, and Glickman stuck with the 4th.

The campaign was anything but routine. Glickman had to answer questions about his overdrafts at the House bank. That provided an issue for Yost, who ran on a congressional reform theme. And Yost showed strength during the GOP primary, defeating one-term Rep.

Dick Nichols, whose then-5th District had been carved up in redistricting.

But Glickman touted his record on district issues and attacked Yost as too conservative for the 4th. A supporter of abortion rights, Glickman implied (despite Yost's objections) that Yost was in league with anti-abortion activists who caused turmoil in Wichita during 1991.

Yost also was overshadowed in the campaign's closing weeks by an overreaching effort to help him. The owners of Wichita's cable television system, angered by Glickman's support of the cable reregulation bill, ran ads attacking the incumbent and urging support for Yost. But Glickman portrayed himself as a victim of a vengeful special interest and obtained time on the cable system to respond.

Glickman's only other tough House contest was his first one, in 1976. A member of a wealthy and prominent local family, Glickman was the youthful president of the Wichita school board when he decided to challenge veteran GOP Rep. Garner E. Shriver, who had been re-elected by a surprisingly small margin in 1974.

Campaigning in the usually Republican district as a fiscal conservative and a moderate on other issues, Glickman painted Shriver as a tired, inactive House member; he called for a six-term limit on House tenure and won narrowly.

Glickman quickly became a popular figure and an overwhelming winner. By 1980, he was being mentioned as a potential statewide candidate. But he has several times bypassed chances to challenge Dole or popular GOP junior Sen. Nancy Landon Kassebaum.

Glickman's six-term limit proposal from 1976 provided fodder for his 1988 opponent, attorney Lee Thompson, a GOP moderate and Kassebaum ally. But Glickman easily deflected this thrust, noting that he had tried with no success as a freshman to push his term-limit plan.

Committees

Select Intelligence (Chairman)
Program & Budget Authorization (chairman)

Agriculture (5th of 28 Democrats)
Department Operations; General Farm Commodities

Judiciary (8th of 21 Democrats)
Administrative Law & Governmental Relations; Crime & Criminal Justice; Economic & Commercial Law

Science, Space & Technology (3rd of 33 Democrats)
Technology, Environment & Aviation

Elections

1992 General		
Dan Glickman (D)	143,671	(52%)
Eric R. Yost (R)	117,070	(42%)
Seth L. Warren (LIBERT)	17,275	(6%)
1990 General		
Dan Glickman (D)	112,015	(71%)
Roger M. Grund (R)	46,283	(29%)

Previous Winning Percentages: **1988** (64%) **1986** (65%) **1984** (74%) **1982** (74%) **1980** (69%) **1978** (70%) **1976** (50%)

District Vote for President

1992

D 93,652 (33%)
R 113,713 (40%)
I 75,600 (27%)

Campaign Finance

	Receipts	Receipts from PACs		Expend-itures
1992				
Glickman (D)	$873,194	$421,726	(48%)	$1,046,769
Yost (R)	$397,565	$76,011	(19%)	$396,254
1990				
Glickman (D)	$520,945	$294,865	(57%)	$355,581
Grund (R)	$4,227	$300	(7%)	$4,317

Key Votes

1993	
Require parental notification of minors' abortions	N
Require unpaid family and medical leave	N
Approve national "motor voter" registration bill	Y
Approve budget increasing taxes and reducing deficit	Y
Approve economic stimulus plan	Y
1992	
Approve balanced-budget constitutional amendment	Y
Close down space station program	N
Approve U.S. aid for former Soviet Union	Y
Allow shifting funds from defense to domestic programs	N
1991	
Extend unemployment benefits using deficit financing	Y
Approve waiting period for handgun purchases	Y
Authorize use of force in Persian Gulf	Y

Voting Studies

	Presidential Support		Party Unity		Conservative Coalition	
Year	**S**	**O**	**S**	**O**	**S**	**O**
1992	27	71	78	21	60	40
1991	35	61	70	22	62	30
1990	27	72	81	17	37	61
1989	37	60	80	18	59	34
1988	32	65	75	20	61	39
1987	26	74	80	17	58	42
1986	28	70	76	21	60	40
1985	36	63	76	22	53	45
1984	40	59	69	29	44	53
1983	43	57	73	23	46	53
1982	47	53	74	26	45	53
1981	47	53	70	30	48	51

Interest Group Ratings

Year	ADA	AFL-CIO	CCUS	ACU
1992	75	64	63	32
1991	50	67	33	32
1990	72	67	31	17
1989	80	67	50	18
1988	80	86	43	16
1987	80	75	47	9
1986	55	64	50	32
1985	55	59	41	35
1984	60	62	38	29
1983	70	63	55	22
1982	70	80	24	18
1981	75	60	26	27

Kentucky

STATE DATA

Governor:
Brereton C. Jones (D)
First elected: 1991
Length of term: 4 years
Term expires: 12/95
Salary: $81,647
Term limit: 1 term*
Phone: (502) 564-2611
Born: June 27, 1939; Gallipolis, Ohio
Education: U. of Virginia, B.S. 1961
Occupation: Rancher
Family: Wife, Elizabeth Lloyd; two children
Religion: Presbyterian
Political Career: W.Va. House, 1965-69; Ky. lieutenant governor, 1987-91

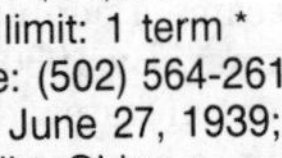

** Jones is limited to one term; when he leaves office in 1995, a new 2-term limit takes effect.*

Lt. Gov.: Paul E. Patton (D)
First elected: 1991
Length of term: 4 years
Term expires: 12/95
Salary: $69,412
Phone: (502) 564-7562

State election official: (502) 564-7100
Democratic headquarters: (502) 695-4828
Republican headquarters: (502) 875-5130

REDISTRICTING

Kentucky lost one seat in reapportionment, dropping from seven districts to six. The legislature passed the map Dec. 18, 1991; the governor signed it Dec. 20.

STATE LEGISLATURE

General Assembly. Meets January through mid-April.

Senate: 38 members, 4-year terms
1992 breakdown: 25D, 13R; 37 men, 1 woman; 37 whites, 1 black
Salary: $100/day and $75/day expenses
Phone: (502) 564-8100

House of Representatives: 100 members, 2-year terms
1992 breakdown: 72D, 28R; 95 men, 5 women; 97 whites, 3 blacks
Salary: $100/day and $75/day expenses
Phone: (502) 564-8100

URBAN STATISTICS

City	Pop.
Louisville Mayor Jerry Abramson, D	269,063
Lexington Mayor Pam Miller, I	225,366
Owensboro Mayor David Adkisson, D	53,549
Covington Mayor J. Dennis Bowman, D	43,264
Bowling Green Mayor Johnny Webb, R	40,641

U.S. CONGRESS

Senate: 1 D, 1 R
House: 4 D, 2 R

TERM LIMITS

For Congress: No
For state offices: No

ELECTIONS

1992 Presidential Vote

Bill Clinton	44.6%
George Bush	41.3%
Ross Perot	13.7%

1988 Presidential Vote

George Bush	56%
Michael S. Dukakis	44%

1984 Presidential Vote

Ronald Reagan	60%
Walter F. Mondale	39%

POPULATION

1990 population		3,685,296
1980 population		3,660,777
Percent change		+1%
Rank among states:		23
White		92%
Black		7%
Hispanic		1%
Asian or Pacific islander		<1%
Urban		52%
Rural		48%
Born in state		77%
Foreign-born		1%
Under age 18	954,094	26%
Ages 18-64	2,264,357	61%
65 and older	466,845	13%
Median age		33

MISCELLANEOUS

Capital: Frankfort
Number of counties: 120
Per capita income: $15,539 (1991)
Rank among states: 42
Total area: 40,410 sq. miles
Rank among states: 37

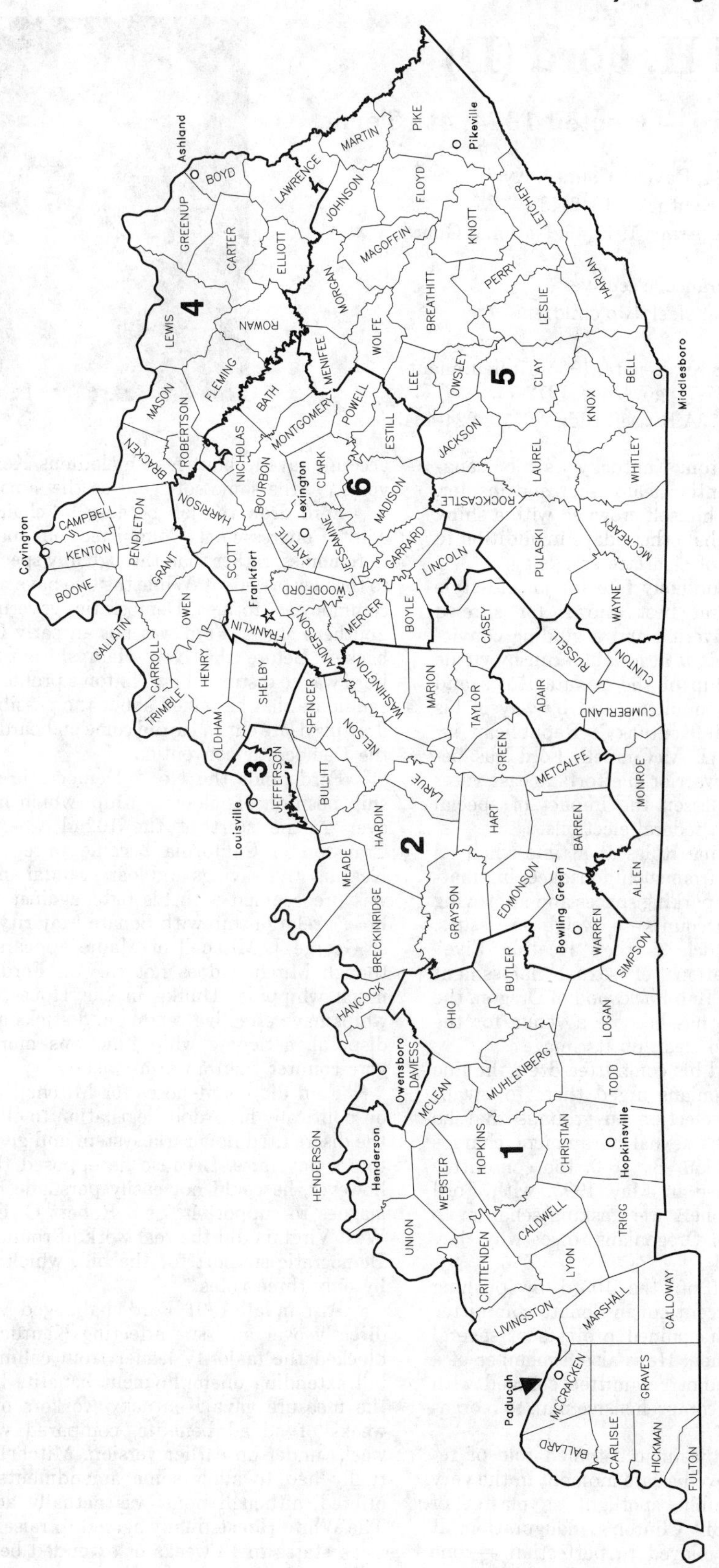
1
2
3
4
5
6
Ashland
Covington
Louisville
Frankfort
Lexington
Pikeville
Middlesboro
Owensboro
Henderson
Hopkinsville
Bowling Green
Paducah
BOYD
GREENUP
LAWRENCE
MARTIN
PIKE
CARTER
ELLIOTT
JOHNSON
FLOYD
LEWIS
ROWAN
MORGAN
MAGOFFIN
KNOTT
LETCHER
MASON
FLEMING
BATH
MENIFEE
WOLFE
BREATHITT
PERRY
HARLAN
LESLIE
BRACKEN
ROBERTSON
NICHOLAS
MONTGOMERY
POWELL
LEE
OWSLEY
CLAY
BELL
KNOX
CAMPBELL
KENTON
BOONE
PENDLETON
HARRISON
BOURBON
CLARK
ESTILL
JACKSON
LAUREL
WHITLEY
GRANT
SCOTT
FAYETTE
MADISON
ROCKCASTLE
GALLATIN
OWEN
WOODFORD
JESSAMINE
GARRARD
MCCREARY
PULASKI
CARROLL
HENRY
FRANKLIN
ANDERSON
MERCER
BOYLE
LINCOLN
TRIMBLE
SHELBY
SPENCER
WASHINGTON
CASEY
WAYNE
OLDHAM
JEFFERSON
BULLITT
NELSON
MARION
TAYLOR
RUSSELL
CLINTON
ADAIR
CUMBERLAND
MEADE
HARDIN
LARUE
GREEN
METCALFE
MONROE
BRECKINRIDGE
HART
BARREN
GRAYSON
EDMONSON
ALLEN
HANCOCK
OHIO
BUTLER
WARREN
SIMPSON
DAVIESS
MCLEAN
MUHLENBERG
LOGAN
TODD
HENDERSON
WEBSTER
HOPKINS
CHRISTIAN
UNION
CRITTENDEN
CALDWELL
TRIGG
LYON
LIVINGSTON
MARSHALL
CALLOWAY
MCCRACKEN
GRAVES
BALLARD
CARLISLE
HICKMAN
FULTON

Wendell H. Ford (D)

Of Owensboro — Elected 1974; 4th Term

Born: Sept. 8, 1924, Daviess County, Ky.
Education: U. of Kentucky, 1942-43.
Military Service: Army, 1945-46; National Guard, 1949-62.
Occupation: Insurance executive.
Family: Wife, Jean Neel; two children.
Religion: Baptist.
Political Career: Ky. Senate, 1965-67; lieutenant governor, 1967-71; governor, 1972-74.
Capitol Office: 173A Russell Bldg. 20510; 224-4343.

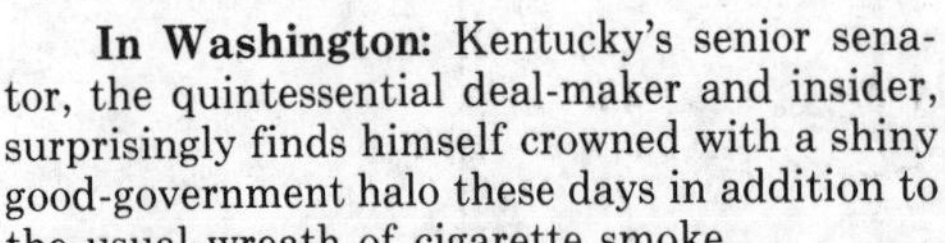

In Washington: Kentucky's senior senator, the quintessential deal-maker and insider, surprisingly finds himself crowned with a shiny good-government halo these days in addition to the usual wreath of cigarette smoke.

It seems an unlikely fate for an old-style Southern Democrat best known for shrewd back-room maneuvering and a guiding conviction that everything is negotiable. But by virtue of his chairmanship of the Senate Rules and Administration Committee, and by way of his fierce rivalry with Kentucky's Republican junior senator, Mitch McConnell, Ford has become a front-line warrior in efforts to ease voter registration and lessen the impact of special interest money on federal elections.

Ford is heading Rules at a time when its focus is changing from such housekeeping matters as dispensing parking spaces and approving postage stamp accounts to weightier issues. Amid scandals such as the "Keating Five" affair and allegations of sexual harassment against GOP Sen. Bob Packwood of Oregon, the Rules Committee has become a venue for the Senate's efforts to clean up its image.

But Ford and his committee drew the line when some Oregonians urged them to invalidate Packwood's election on grounds that he had lied about the sexual harassment charges prior to the election. By 16-0, the committee dismissed the case in May 1993, with Ford saying the petitioners were asking senators to read the minds of Oregonians to see why they voted as they did.

Ford started off the 103rd by pushing through a 7.5 percent cut in Senate committee spending, over the pained protests of several committee chairmen. He is also a member of a new, temporary joint committee charged with coming up with a comprehensive plan to reorganize Congress.

Along with the unaccustomed role of reformer, Ford enjoyed a rare moment in the very center of the public spotlight as master of ceremonies for Bill Clinton's inauguration. It was a role Ford played to perfection — one account raved about his "melodious Kentucky voice . . . the same soft gold as the sunshine."

Ford drew the job because he chaired the Joint Congressional Committee on Inaugural Ceremonies, rather than through any special link to the new president. While the two have much in common as former Democratic governors of Southern states, Ford was not an early Clinton backer. Before the New Hampshire primary, Ford was so disturbed by Clinton's problems as a candidate that he talked about the possibility of drafting a late entry. He did come on board before the Democratic convention.

Ford holds the No. 2 Democratic leadership position of majority whip, which he took over at the start of the 102nd when Alan Cranston of California became mired in the Keating Five savings and loan scandal and then was preoccupied with his fight against cancer. Ford's relationship with Senate Majority Leader George J. Mitchell of Maine appears solid, though Mitchell does not call on Ford to do much whipping: Unlike in the House, where whips have effective carrots and sticks at their disposal, a Senate whip functions more as a vote-counter than an arm-twister.

Ford did count noses for Mitchell in 1991 on politically hazardous legislation to eliminate the discredited honoraria system and give senators a pay raise. Because he opposed the bill, however, he could not easily persuade his colleagues to support it. Sen. Robert C. Byrd of West Virginia did the real work of rounding up Democratic support for the bill, which passed by only three votes.

Also in late 1991, Ford challenged Mitchell directly over an issue affecting Kentucky. He blocked the majority leader from calling up a bill extending unemployment benefits because the measure gave Kentucky workers only six weeks of added benefits, compared with 13 weeks under an earlier version. Mitchell eventually had to allow some amendments to be offered, although none was actually adopted. The White House finally agreed to raise all six-week states to 13 weeks of extended benefits.

For three years, Ford was a frequent supporter of Bush administration positions, voting with President Bush 57 percent of the time in 1991 on issues where Bush took a position.

In a striking example of Ford's ability to cut deals with a Republican administration, Bush Transportation Secretary Samuel K. Skinner traveled to Louisville in 1991 to deliver a federal pledge of $144 million to expand the city's airport. The pledge was one of the largest federal commitments to any airport. As chairman of the Senate Commerce Aviation Subcommittee, Ford initially had opposed Skinner's plan to allow airports to charge a new passenger fee to fund capital improvements. But Skinner persuaded Ford to go along with the fee, in exchange for adoption of a federal airport noise policy and more spending from the federal airport trust fund.

The deal did not stop Ford from blasting Skinner on other issues, including an administration decision to allow foreign investors to own up to 49 percent of an airline's equity and to increase foreign carriers' access to domestic airports.

While Ford is happy to do business with Republicans, he is also happy to do battle with them. In 1990, he traveled to South Dakota to campaign for Sen. Larry Pressler's Democratic opponent, Ted Muenster. As Rules chairman, he is said to dole out parking places, office space and other perks on a Democratic rather than democratic basis.

Ford typically pursues his legislative aims through private negotiations in committee, at the conference table or in the cloakroom. He is a loyal friend to business interests, particularly those important to his state — tobacco, liquor and coal — and the one he knows best, insurance.

Ford owned two Kentucky insurance companies during most of his first decade in the Senate, and recused himself when insurance-related issues came before the Commerce Committee. But after selling his business interests to family members in 1985, he began to work actively on the industry's behalf. In 1986, he fought to weaken a provision requiring insurance companies to report certain information to the federal government, and opposed a bill making it easier for other businesses to form their own liability insurance pools.

In 1991, Ford worked to change a family and medical leave bill in ways responsive to business concerns. Ford won amendments exempting small companies from the bill, and limiting the right of part-time and temporary workers to take such leave.

Ford is a critic of much federal business regulation and opposes efforts to control billboards, a key advertising medium for liquor and tobacco companies.

His ever-present cigarette is not the only measure of his loyalty to tobacco interests. In 1991, he filed the portentously named Veterans' Dignity in Health Care Act, which would have required the Veterans Administration to make sure patients in VA hospital have access to tobacco products and places to consume them.

In 1984, Ford blocked a bill mandating new health warnings on cigarettes until winning an agreement to soften the language. In 1985, Ford and North Carolina Republican Sen. Jesse Helms engineered a complex deal establishing a new tobacco price-support program in return for tobacco interests' agreeing to a permanent extension of the 16-cents-a-pack cigarette tax. The deal became law in 1986.

Having long helped bury legislation requiring warning labels on liquor, Ford joined in Commerce's unanimous approval of a labeling bill in 1988. The industry publicly objected, but privately favored the federal warning as a potential defense against liability lawsuits and as a uniform standard to prevent a proliferation of state-passed requirements.

All of this seems to contrast oddly with Ford's suddenly high profile on election reform issues. But those are the focus of his increasingly intense rivalry with McConnell, a leader of GOP efforts to block Democratic proposals such as campaign spending limits and the "motor voter" bill. McConnell, a member of the Rules Committee, is a constant thorn in Ford's side. The irritation seems to have led Ford to unusual efforts on behalf of issues in which he would appear to have little vested interest.

In addition to Rules and Commerce, Ford is a member of the Energy Committee, where he looks out for Kentucky's coal providers. He has repeatedly sought repeal of tough federal strip-mining regulations. In 1987, he agreed to a repeal of a 1978 law requiring utilities to use coal rather than oil and gas, but he did add language that new power plants must be adaptable to coal use. Ford opposes Western coal producers' push for a coal-slurry pipeline to transport their coal more cheaply and make it competitive with Appalachian coal in Eastern and Southern markets.

In the 102nd, he won Senate approval of a bill to revamp the Energy Department's uranium enrichment enterprise. The government-owned plant in Paducah, Ky., sells fuel to nuclear power producers and is the second largest employer in Western Kentucky.

At Home: Ford plays Kentucky politics to win, and he plays it just about full time. Faced with the likelihood of weak opposition in his first Senate re-election (in 1980), Ford still amassed a huge campaign treasury. No serious challenger emerged, but he conducted an exhausting campaign anyway and crushed long-shot Republican Mary Louise Foust.

In 1986, he actually had a reason to be cautious. Two years before, his Democratic colleague, Walter D. Huddleston, had been ousted by McConnell in an upset, and Republicans hoped for a repeat performance. But in the wake of Huddleston's defeat, Ford commissioned a series of polls to test where in the state he might be in danger. He again began raising money early, and by the end of 1985 had more than enough to scare off any top-drawer opposition. He won 74 percent of the vote in 1986.

Armed with an overflowing campaign kitty again in 1992, Ford parried charges by underfunded state Sen. David Williams that Ford was a Washington insider whose ascent to the Democratic leadership was accompanied by a leftward veer in his voting record. Outside the rock-ribbed GOP mountain counties, not many voters believed Williams; Ford won without blinking.

While building his insurance business, Ford started in politics as a protégé of Democratic Gov. Bert Combs, for whom he worked as an aide from 1959-63. But that relationship turned sour. By 1971, after a term in the state Senate and one as lieutenant governor, Ford was ready for the governorship. Combs, however, decided on a comeback the same year.

Their contest for the Democratic nomination was rough. Ford said Combs was the candidate of the "fat cats and the courthouse crowd." Combs said Ford was a "punchless promiser with both hands tied behind him by special interests." Combs had his traditional base in eastern Kentucky, but Ford did better in Louisville and the counties to the west and defeated his old mentor soundly. He had little trouble beating Republican Tom Emberton that fall.

As governor, Ford earned popularity by cutting taxes imposed under his Republican predecessor, Louie B. Nunn. This left him in good stead when he ran for the Senate in 1974 against one-term GOP incumbent Marlow W. Cook. The Ford-Cook race was no more pleasant than the earlier gubernatorial contest. Cook accused Ford of using state contracts as governor to reward his political allies. Ford labeled Cook "marvelous Marlow, the wonderful wobbler." Cook was hurt by his earlier defense of Richard M. Nixon. In a Democratic year, Ford won comfortably.

After deciding not to run for governor in 1983, Ford conducted the race vicariously by helping an ally, Lt. Gov. Martha Layne Collins, win. In 1984, he was notably less successful. He volunteered to chair the state campaign for Democratic presidential nominee Walter F. Mondale, hoping to hold down Reagan's margin and thereby protect Huddleston. Mondale lost badly, and Huddleston fell with him.

Committees

Majority Whip

Rules & Administration (Chairman)

Joint Printing (Chairman)

Commerce, Science & Transportation (3rd of 11 Democrats)
Aviation (chairman); Communications; Consumer; National Ocean Policy Study

Energy & Natural Resources (3rd of 11 Democrats)
Energy Research & Development (chairman); Mineral Resources Development & Production; Water & Power

Joint Organization of Congress

Elections

1992 General

Wendell H. Ford (D)	836,888	(63%)
David L. Williams (R)	476,604	(36%)
James A. Ridenour (LIBERT)	17,366	(1%)

Previous Winning Percentages: **1986** (74%) **1980** (65%) **1974** (54%)

Campaign Finance

	Receipts	Receipts from PACs	Expend-itures
1992			
Ford (D)	$2,317,149	$1,312,902 (57%)	$2,076,069
Williams (R)	$345,291	$19,940 (6%)	$335,304

Key Votes

1993

Require unpaid family and medical leave	Y
Approve national "motor voter" registration bill	Y
Approve budget increasing taxes and reducing deficit	Y
Support president's right to lift military gay ban	Y

1992

Approve school-choice pilot program	N
Allow shifting funds from defense to domestic programs	Y
Oppose deeper cuts in spending for SDI	N

1991

Approve waiting period for handgun purchases	Y
Raise senators' pay and ban honoraria	X
Authorize use of force in Persian Gulf	N
Confirm Clarence Thomas to Supreme Court	N

Voting Studies

	Presidential Support		Party Unity		Conservative Coalition	
Year	**S**	**O**	**S**	**O**	**S**	**O**
1992	35	65	70	29	82	16
1991	57	43	67	33	95	5
1990	55	45	69	30	86	14
1989	60	39	64	35	71	29
1988	64	33	70	29	78	22
1987	35	64	85	13	66	34
1986	34	66	74	25	47	53
1985	39	60	76	23	68	28
1984	45	51	76 †	22 †	55	38
1983	40	56	81	17	52	43
1982	32	60	75	24	66	33
1981	56	44	84	14	58	41

† Not eligible for all recorded votes.

Interest Group Ratings

Year	ADA	AFL-CIO	CCUS	ACU
1992	75	92	10	15
1991	50	75	10	47
1990	39	89	33	35
1989	45	100	25	25
1988	65	93	21	24
1987	75	100	22	19
1986	55	67	53	35
1985	50	81	48	43
1984	80	82	39	23
1983	70	88	32	20
1982	70	81	55	55
1981	70	63	50	13

Mitch McConnell (R)

Of Louisville — Elected 1984; 2nd Term

Born: Feb. 20, 1942, Sheffield, Ala.
Education: U. of Louisville, B.A. 1964; U. of Kentucky, J.D. 1967.
Occupation: Lawyer.
Family: Wife, Elaine Chao; three children.
Religion: Baptist.
Political Career: Jefferson County judge/executive, 1978-85.
Capitol Office: 120 Russell Bldg. 20510; 224-2541.

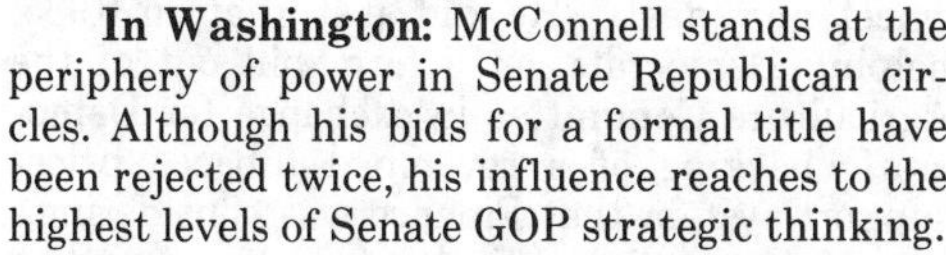

In Washington: McConnell stands at the periphery of power in Senate Republican circles. Although his bids for a formal title have been rejected twice, his influence reaches to the highest levels of Senate GOP strategic thinking.

Most important is the close relationship that has developed between McConnell and Senate Minority Leader Bob Dole of Kansas. Even though McConnell was one of the few senators who supported George Bush over Dole during the 1988 presidential primary, his political savvy earned him a recommendation by Dole to be general chairman of the Republican National Committee (RNC).

McConnell has taken on jobs for the party that seem thankless, but he has accomplished them in ways that have earned him acclaim. He led the charge against the popular "motor voter" bill and has staked out the GOP position on the prickly issue of campaign finance reform.

On the Foreign Relations Committee, he took a leading role in the 102nd Congress in crafting legislation authorizing foreign aid, working with Democrats and the Bush administration on a perennially unpopular cause.

He will retain a central role in foreign aid in the 103rd as the ranking Republican on Appropriations' Foreign Operations Subcommittee. He also took the vice chairmanship of the Ethics Committee, one of the least desirable assignments in the Senate and thus one that demonstrates fealty to the leadership.

In early 1993, as Republicans battled over who would lead the RNC, Dole proposed McConnell as the man for the job. But McConnell was never a declared candidate.

The cerebral, methodical McConnell clashes sharply in style and personality with his Kentucky colleague, backslapping, down-home Democrat Wendell H. Ford, the majority whip. But if McConnell lacks Ford's old-boys-club cachet, he has honed a superb constituent-service operation and is one of the better practitioners of finding and pushing the hot buttons back home with TV ads and franked mail.

Neither has any love lost for the other, particularly after Ford actively campaigned for McConnell's Democratic opponent in 1990. And Ford must put up with his upstart junior colleague in his own back yard — the Rules and Administration Committee — where McConnell has developed the reputation as an expert on campaign finance and the leading GOP obstructionist of Democratic proposals to pay for congressional campaigns with public funds.

A former political science professor, McConnell compensates for what he lacks in charm by studying an issue to the point where he knows more about it than most of his colleagues.

In the 100th Congress, he found a chance to move down the learning curve with one of the most divisive issues to come before the Senate by helping to lead the Republican filibuster against Democratic campaign finance legislation. The Democrats tried, and failed, to shut off debate a record eight times.

McConnell's stance has become the GOP line in the Senate. He has proposed banning political action committee (PAC) contributions and decreasing out-of-state individual contributions, and he seeks to enhance the role of party committees by letting them spend more on campaigns. In essence, the system he envisions plays to the strengths of the GOP, which has a large individual donor base and a sophisticated party operation, but a worsening record of collecting PAC money. McConnell's opposition to Democratic plans stems from the Democrats' attempt to limit campaign spending and from their reliance on various public financing schemes to induce adherence to the spending limit. (He calls them "food stamps for politicians.")

In the 101st and 102nd Congresses, McConnell was the Republican floor leader on the bill. But he could not prevent passage of a Democratic measure that offered incentives such as reduced television and mail costs, as well as public funds in some instances, to candidates who limited their spending. The measure died in conference in the 101st; President Bush vetoed the bill in the 102nd. When President Clinton in 1993 proposed a campaign-finance reform bill that included public financing, McConnell quickly denounced it. In 1990, McConnell tried to parlay his success in protecting GOP fundraising into the chairmanship of the National Republican Senatorial Committee. But he suffered the first electoral defeat of his career when colleagues chose Phil Gramm of Texas by 26-17. He tried again in 1992, losing 20-19.

The motor-voter debate early in the 103rd Congress presented a test of GOP ability to influence policy in the Clinton era. It also matched up the two Kentucky senators. Ford led the efforts in the 102nd and 103rd to pass the bill, which would direct states to register voters at driver's license and welfare bureaus.

Republicans charged that the bill would invite voter fraud and was aimed primarily at increasing Democratic registration. McConnell warned that it would not increase turnout at the polls and could cheapen the electoral process by including more people in the electorate who do not care enough to learn about candidates or the issues. "If we wanted to make elections really easy for voters, we could eliminate both voter registration and voting at the polls, and just have everyone vote with their remote control units while watching interactive TV. They wouldn't even have to think," he said.

Congress passed the bill in the 102nd Congress, but Bush vetoed it; the Senate failed to override the veto. With Clinton's endorsement, the bill appeared set to pass in 1993. But McConnell and other opponents successfully used parliamentary tactics and extensive floor debate to slow the bill and to win key concessions. The Senate-passed bill encouraged — but no longer required — states to provide registration forms at public assistance offices.

The GOP's successful filibuster provided an early sign that Senate Republicans could stop a fast-moving legislative vehicle and wring concessions from the Democratic majority, proving at least that they cannot be ignored.

While McConnell waves the GOP banner on election-related issues, his partisanship fades on the question of foreign aid. In 1985, he broke with the party line on U.S. policy toward South Africa. The middle-ground proposal he and Delaware Republican William V. Roth Jr. offered served as a starting point for the Foreign Relations Committee as it went on to write the sanctions bill that eventually became law over President Ronald Reagan's veto.

The venture seemed to whet McConnell's appetite for the foreign policy realm; at the beginning of the 100th Congress, he left his seats on the Judiciary and Intelligence committees and took a spot on Foreign Relations.

In the 102nd Congress, committee members, hoping to get a foreign aid authorization bill enacted for the first time since 1985, ceded much of the responsibility for crafting that legislation to the International Economic Policy Subcommittee. Committee Chairman Claiborne Pell and ranking Republican Jesse Helms stepped aside in favor of subcommittee Chairman Paul S. Sarbanes of Maryland and McConnell, the ranking Republican. The system functioned well; Sarbanes and McConnell proved far more adept at moving the bill to the floor than Pell and Helms.

The Senate passed the authorization 74-18. But an intense backlash against foreign aid and a Bush veto threat doomed the bill, which died in the House. Also in the 102nd, Bush signed McConnell's bill reaffirming U.S. relations with Hong Kong after the British colony becomes part of China in 1997.

On Agriculture, McConnell's interest is tobacco. His philosophy has been, in his words: "When it comes to tobacco, I'm prepared to wheel and deal." He did just that in 1985, helping Democrats get a farm bill out of the Agriculture Committee in exchange for Democratic backing of a revamped tobacco price-support system that Finance was considering.

McConnell's political antennae, as good as they are, have occasionally malfunctioned. In 1989, McConnell proposed allowing federal law enforcement agents to shoot down planes suspected of drug trafficking. But the proposal, after being initially adopted, ultimately was rejected after Democrat John Glenn of Ohio took to the floor: "If I have ever seen anything that I thought was posturing on behalf of the U.S. Senate, this is it."

At Home: Three things brought McConnell to Congress: bloodhounds, Reagan and dogged persistence in the face of daunting odds.

And three things have kept him there: bloodhounds, infighting between state Democrats and a record of looking out for Kentucky's interests that spurred even some Democrats to move into his camp in 1990.

For much of 1984, few people believed McConnell had much chance of defeating two-term Democratic Sen. Walter D. Huddleston. Even some GOP leaders complained that McConnell had a "citified" image that would not play well in most parts of Kentucky; his base was metropolitan Louisville, where he had twice been elected Jefferson County judge, the county's top administrative post.

McConnell's campaign struggled for quite a while; he even lost the endorsement of Marlow Cook, the last Republican to win a Senate election in Kentucky and McConnell's boss when he was a Senate aide in the 1960s. At times, it seemed that McConnell's bid was surviving on little more than his fierce ambition to be a senator, a goal he admitted having harbored for two decades.

Then McConnell hit upon a clever, homey gimmick to get across his claim that Huddleston had limited influence and was often absent from committee meetings. McConnell aired TV ads showing bloodhounds sniffing frantically around Washington in search of the incumbent.

The hound dog gimmick got people talking about a race they had ignored, and many concluded that McConnell had a point — they were not exactly sure what Huddleston had been doing since he went to Congress in 1973. The incumbent, an easygoing mainstream Democrat, had worked behind the scenes on Kentucky issues, such as tobacco and coal, never causing much controversy and never earning much publicity. With Reagan crushing Walter F. Mondale by more than 280,000 votes statewide, McConnell had long coattails to latch on to. He won by four-tenths of a percentage point.

In 1990, McConnell was tabbed as one of the most vulnerable Republicans up for reelection. But, unlike his predecessor, McConnell came out early and tough. He brought back the TV bloodhounds, this time to bark up the fact that he had made 99 percent of the votes cast during his first term.

Former Louisville Mayor Harvey I. Sloane emerged from a bloody Democratic primary as one of the best-heeled Senate challengers in the country. But McConnell, a polished debater with a flair for cutting, sometimes snide repartee, kept Sloane on the defensive from the start. Sloane, a non-practicing physician, was also plagued throughout the campaign by revelations that he had prescribed himself sleeping pills during a 20-month period, contrary to accepted medical practice and without renewing his permit for prescribing drugs.

McConnell effectively portrayed himself as the defender of the common man against what he said was Sloane's East Coast liberalism. Although several local Democratic officials endorsed McConnell, Sloane belatedly managed to rally top Democrats into his fold, including Ford and Louisville Mayor Jerry Abramson, who agreed to appear in TV spots. In the final days of the campaign, Sloane appeared to ride the wave of anti-incumbent sentiment to close the gap, but he came up short with 48 percent.

A lifelong political overachiever, McConnell was student body president in high school and college and president of the student bar association at law school. After earning his law degree in 1967, he worked for Cook and then served as deputy assistant U.S. attorney general in the Ford administration. In his 1977 campaign for Jefferson County judge, McConnell defeated a Democratic incumbent; four years later, he won reelection by a narrow margin and started laying the groundwork for a statewide campaign.

Committees

Select Ethics (Vice Chairman)

Agriculture, Nutrition & Forestry (5th of 8 Republicans)
Nutrition & Investigations (ranking); Agricultural Production & Stabilization of Prices; Domestic & Foreign Marketing & Product Promotion

Appropriations (11th of 13 Republicans)
Foreign Operations (ranking); Commerce, Justice, State & Judiciary; Energy & Water Development; Military Construction

Rules & Administration (6th of 7 Republicans)

Elections

1990 General		
Mitch McConnell (R)	478,034	(52%)
Harvey I. Sloane (D)	437,976	(48%)
1990 Primary		
Mitch McConnell (R)	64,063	(89%)
Tommy Klein (R)	8,310	(11%)

Previous Winning Percentage: **1984** (50%)

Campaign Finance

	Receipts	Receipts from PACs		Expend-itures
1990				
McConnell (R)	$4,073,583	$1,076,029	(26%)	$5,074,187
Sloane (D)	$2,571,559	$518,688	(20%)	$2,927,624

Key Votes

1993	
Require unpaid family and medical leave	N
Approve national "motor voter" registration bill	N
Approve budget increasing taxes and reducing deficit	N
Support president's right to lift military gay ban	N
1992	
Approve school-choice pilot program	Y
Allow shifting funds from defense to domestic programs	N
Oppose deeper cuts in spending for SDI	Y
1991	
Approve waiting period for handgun purchases	N
Raise senators' pay and ban honoraria	N
Authorize use of force in Persian Gulf	Y
Confirm Clarence Thomas to Supreme Court	Y

Voting Studies

	Presidential Support		Party Unity		Conservative Coalition	
Year	**S**	**O**	**S**	**O**	**S**	**O**
1992	77	23	91	8	92	8
1991	93	7	95	5	98	3
1990	78	22	84	15	92	5
1989	82	18	94	6	97	3
1988	85	15	80	18	92	8
1987	65	32	85	13	91	6
1986	87	13	90	10	92	8
1985	85	14	82	16	90	8

Interest Group Ratings

Year	ADA	AFL-CIO	CCUS	ACU
1992	15	18	100	89
1991	0	17	90	90
1990	0	33	92	87
1989	10	20	75	89
1988	5	29	93	92
1987	10	33	89	80
1986	0	7	89	83
1985	5	10	79	78

Kentucky - 1st District

1 Tom Barlow (D)

Of Paducah — Elected 1992; 1st Term

Born: Aug. 7, 1940, Washington, D.C.
Education: Haverford College, B.A. 1962.
Occupation: Sales director; conservation consultant.
Family: Wife, Shirley Pippin; two children, three stepchildren.
Religion: Methodist.

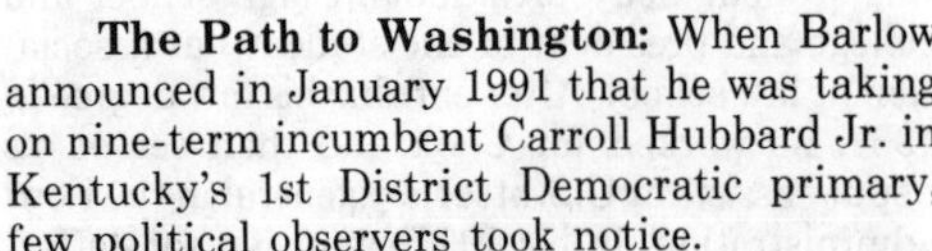

Political Career: Candidate for Barlow City Council, 1987; sought Democratic nomination for U.S. House, 1986.
Capitol Office: 1533 Longworth Bldg. 20515; 225-3115.

The Path to Washington: When Barlow announced in January 1991 that he was taking on nine-term incumbent Carroll Hubbard Jr. in Kentucky's 1st District Democratic primary, few political observers took notice.

After all, Hubbard had defeated the little-known Barlow in the 1986 Democratic primary by better than a 4-to-1 margin. Bolstered by broad name recognition and a well-financed campaign treasury, Hubbard had scared off more formidable challengers.

But Barlow's long-shot bid paid off when, in April, Hubbard was implicated in the House bank scandal. After Hubbard denied that he had overdrafts at the infamous bank, the House ethics committee released a list showing that he had 152.

Making matters worse, the first acknowledgment of Hubbard's involvement with the bank came not from the congressman, but from his wife. Carol Brown Hubbard, a Democratic candidate in Kentucky's 5th District, broke the news at a press conference for her campaign.

Barlow also hammered away at Hubbard — chair of the House Banking Subcommittee on General Oversight — for failing to foresee the massive financial problems of the nation's savings and loan industry.

"People in Western Kentucky thought it was time for a change," Barlow said. "And they were given enough reasons to make a switch."

Taking advantage of being a political outsider, Barlow scored a narrow primary victory over Hubbard, who had represented the 1st District since 1975.

Redistricting did not hurt Barlow, either. Even though mapmakers added several Republican counties to the edge of the district, it is one of the state's most Democratic districts. In the general election, Barlow outpolled Republican Steve Hamrick 60 percent to 39 percent.

Barlow's rise was all the more remarkable when one considers that, in 1987, he finished last in a five-person field in the election for four city council seats in Barlow, Ky. He says he dropped out of that race.

Barlow is determined to avoid the mistakes of Hubbard, whom some voters had accused of losing touch with the district. He plans on maintaining his home in Paducah and returning to the district each week.

Barlow hopes that his assignments on the Agriculture, Merchant Marine and Fisheries, and Natural Resources committees will enable him to assist his constituents. Agriculture-related business brings in an estimated $500 million each year to the 1st. Paducah, on the shores of the Ohio River, is a center for the nation's barge industry.

Barlow was one of a group of Democratic freshmen who successfully insisted that any vote on the president's $16.3 billion economic stimulus package be preceded by a vote on the budget resolution and its deficit-reduction targets. He ultimately voted for both the resolution and the package.

Barlow has an unlikely background for a candidate who benefited from popular discontent with government and Washington. He was born in the nation's capital and graduated from a private high school there.

Barlow also is no stranger to the Agriculture Committee, having lobbied the panel during the 1970s on behalf of the Natural Resources Defense Council (NRDC).

During the campaign, Hubbard seized on Barlow's 11-year tenure with the NRDC — an influential environmental lobbying group — to portray him as anti-business. He also criticized Barlow for his support of the Clean Air Act, which is controversial in coal-rich Kentucky.

Barlow says his work for the NRDC was largely related to agricultural issues, and that he lobbied the Agriculture Committee on soil conservation and forestry matters.

With Barlow viewed as vulnerable by many in Kentucky, several candidates are already said to be weighing challenges to him in 1994.

But having just overcome long odds to win his seat, Barlow says he is not concerned: "There are going to be people out there, but I'm not looking over my shoulder."

Kentucky 1

West — Paducah

Western Kentucky's 1st District is the state's version of the Deep South. In the Civil War era, regional sentiment here strongly favored the Confederacy — Jefferson Davis was born here in 1808 — and slaves helped cultivate the tobacco and cotton crops. Kentucky's eight westernmost counties even plotted to secede and form their own state along with some renegade Tennessee counties.

The Confederate legacy translates into Democratic votes. When the birth of quintuplets caused a sensation in Mayfield (Graves County) in 1896, the local paper ran a picture with the caption "Five New Democrats." Today, politics is much the same: 95 percent of registered voters in Graves County are Democrats.

That is the story in the rest of Western Kentucky as well. Most counties are, at the very least, 80 percent Democratic. In the 1980s, the region began drifting toward supporting Republican candidates for president, but Bill Clinton brought them home in 1992.

Four television markets reach Western Kentucky, but no city in the 1st has more than 30,000 people. Many of the district's people are employed in agriculture, from soybeans and tobacco to chicken processing in Mayfield.

Hopkins, Muhlenberg, Ohio and Union counties have a coal-country tradition, but jobs in the mining industry have waned in recent years. In 1980, mining jobs accounted for about a quarter of all jobs in Muhlenberg and Ohio counties, but by 1990 that share had dropped to under 10 percent. Hopkins County has better weathered the post-World War II coal industry decline by evolving into a regional industrial and medical center.

Tourism and recreation also play a role in the regional economy, especially in the area around the Land Between the Lakes Recreation Area. Nearby Murray has become a preferred retirement destination.

The Ohio River port of Paducah (McCracken County) has traditionally been the political and population center of Western Kentucky, but its population has been surpassed by Hopkinsville (Christian County), an agricultural market center with a dependence on nearby Fort Campbell military base.

The Atomic Energy Commission plant steered to Paducah by native son Alben W. Barkley — the longtime Democratic senator and then vice president under Harry S Truman — is a major employer, though new uranium-generation technology has cast doubts on its future.

The main source of Republican votes in the 1st comes from the economically disadvantaged mountain counties on the far eastern edge of the district. Bordering Tennessee to the south and the 5th District to the east, counties such as Adair, Clinton, Cumberland, Monroe and Russell have been turning in GOP majorities since the Civil War.

This cluster even stayed true to GOP Rep. Larry J. Hopkins in his ill-fated 1991 gubernatorial run, when he won only 13 of Kentucky's 120 counties.

1990 Population: 614,226. White 561,481 (91%), Black 47,932 (8%), Other 4,813 (1%). Hispanic origin 4,458 (1%). 18 and over 460,899 (75%), 62 and over 110,855 (18%). Median age: 34.

Committees

Agriculture (19th of 28 Democrats)
Environment, Credit & Rural Development; Foreign Agriculture & Hunger; General Farm Commodities

Merchant Marine & Fisheries (24th of 29 Democrats)
Coast Guard & Navigation

Natural Resources (27th of 28 Democrats)
Energy & Mineral Resources

Campaign Finance

1992	Receipts	Receipts from PACs		Expenditures
Barlow (D)	$204,295	$104,825	(51%)	$197,396
Hamrick (R)	$67,051	$13,500	(20%)	$66,705

Key Votes

1993

Require parental notification of minors' abortions	N
Require unpaid family and medical leave	Y
Approve national "motor voter" registration bill	Y
Approve budget increasing taxes and reducing deficit	Y
Approve economic stimulus plan	Y

Elections

1992 General		
Tom Barlow (D)	128,524	(60%)
Steve Hamrick (R)	83,088	(39%)
1992 Primary		
Tom Barlow (D)	40,014	(48%)
Carroll Hubbard Jr. (D)	37,188	(45%)
Charles T. Banken Jr. (D)	6,019	(7%)

District Vote for President

	1992	
D	116,637	(48%)
R	96,602	(40%)
I	30,869	(13%)

2 William H. Natcher (D)

Of Bowling Green — Elected 1953; 20th Full Term

Born: Sept. 11, 1909, Bowling Green, Ky.
Education: Western Kentucky U., B.A. 1930; Ohio State U., LL.B. 1933.
Military Service: Navy, 1942-45.
Occupation: Lawyer.
Family: Widowed; two children.
Religion: Baptist.
Political Career: Warren County attorney, 1937-49; 8th Judicial District commonwealth attorney, 1951-53.
Capitol Office: 2333 Rayburn Bldg. 20515; 225-3501.

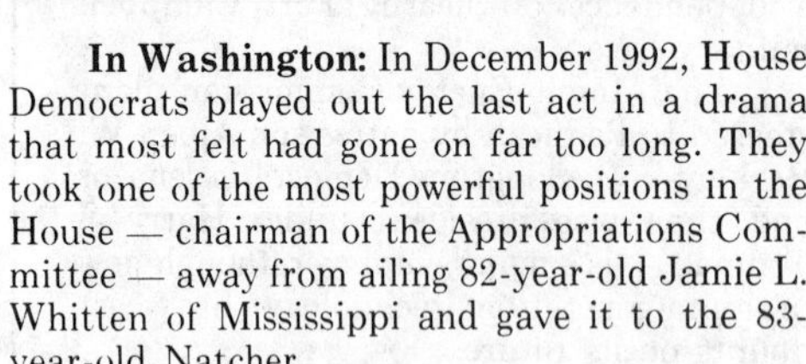

In Washington: In December 1992, House Democrats played out the last act in a drama that most felt had gone on far too long. They took one of the most powerful positions in the House — chairman of the Appropriations Committee — away from ailing 82-year-old Jamie L. Whitten of Mississippi and gave it to the 83-year-old Natcher.

Under pressure from colleagues since suffering a stroke in early 1992, Whitten had already turned over his day-to-day responsibilities to his friend Natcher, who also runs the subcommittee that funds health, education and social service programs.

While there were some rumors of a challenge from a younger member, David R. Obey of Wisconsin, Natcher proved too strong a candidate. "Who can argue against Bill Natcher just because he's 83 years old? He's exquisitely fair and responsive," said Minnesota Democrat James L. Oberstar.

Natcher's victory was also due in large part to his stewardship of the panel in Whitten's absence. When Natcher took over, committee insiders said one test of his leadership would be whether he managed to get all 13 regular fiscal 1993 spending bills done on time or reasonably close to it. He did — and he also delivered every bill under President Bush's budget request.

While unquestionably a vestige of another era, Natcher is more in tune than Whitten with those clamoring for congressional reform and railing against members' perquisites and privileges. He eschews publicity, maintains a tiny personal staff and never misses a vote on the House floor, and has long opposed efforts to add pork projects to appropriations bills. Ever since he won his first House race in 1953, he has been running for re-election the old-fashioned way — with no campaign contributions, no television advertising — just roaming his district without entourage.

Natcher's gentlemanly manner and commitment to the House as an institution has earned him respect even from the most partisan Republicans. "He reminds you of the world that once was, in which politics happens in your district and governing happens in Washington," Republican firebrand Newt Gingrich of Georgia once said.

When contentious floor debates are imminent, Natcher is often called to the Speaker's chair. Respected for his evenhanded, controlled judgment, Natcher keeps partisan members in order with legendary parliamentary precision. He memorized Roberts Rules of Order while in law school in 1933 and first presided over the House in 1954, shortly after arriving in Congress.

Natcher's exacting nature carries over to many aspects of his life. He dresses carefully, votes carefully and keeps a detailed diary of his everyday life.

A member of the Appropriations Committee since his second year in the House, Natcher helped set the standard of collegiality that for decades has defined the panel. But members of both parties are loath to cross him because he is reputed to forget no slight, no matter how minor.

While his refusal to fund unauthorized projects and his great reluctance to earmark funds for specific projects may have seemed out of step, he is not a man to bend with the times. Rather, with the increased saliency of the anti-pork theme in 1992's political contests, it is the times that appear to be bending with Natcher.

One man who is not likely to bend, however, is Robert C. Byrd, the mighty chairman of the Senate Appropriations Committee and a man as intimate with the wiles of Senate procedure as Natcher is schooled in the House rules. Both chairmen are fastidious traditionalists, but their concepts of tradition with respect to the appropriations process are diametrically different. Unlike Natcher, Byrd has no qualms about earmarks or added projects, as he has shown by funneling millions of dollars to his home state of West Virginia. How Natcher performs matched up against such a master of the appropriations process may affect whether House Democrats elect to retain him as chairman in the future.

Natcher began the 103rd Congress in strong form as well. Although President Clinton's $16.3 billion economic stimulus package

Kentucky 2

West central — Owensboro

The wide Democratic registration advantage in the 2nd is misleading. This is a competitive district in state and national elections. The 2nd includes three distinct areas of the state: the outer Bluegrass region in the east, suburban Louisville to the north and the rolling hill country of the Pennyrile in the southwest.

More than two-thirds of the district's voters are registered as Democrats. But they have an independent streak and a penchant for backing Republicans at the federal level. In good GOP years, statewide candidates have a shot at the 2nd's three major population centers: Daviess County (Owensboro), Hardin County (the Fort Knox area) and Warren County (Bowling Green).

GOP Sen. Mitch McConnell won Hardin and Warren counties in his 1990 reelection effort; George Bush won the district in 1992, but failed to prevail in Daviess County.

There are some smaller counties that Republicans can always count on. Casey County gave Bush a better than 2-to-1 margin in 1992. Grayson and Edmonson, centers of Union support during the Civil War, also voted for Bush in 1992. And Edmonson was one of just 13 counties — out of 120 — that GOP Rep. Larry J. Hopkins carried in his failed 1991 gubernatorial bid.

Owensboro, along the Ohio River in the far northwestern edge of the district, is the largest city in the 2nd. Tobacco, oil and coal are mainstays of the local economy, making it Western Kentucky's leading trade center.

At the other end of the Green River Parkway lies Bowling Green (Warren County), the district's second-largest city. Metals and machinery are some of Bowling Green's industrial output, but the GM Corvette assembly plant there draws more attention. Western Kentucky University, the largest college in the state west of Louisville, overlooks the city.

Hardin County, home to Fort Knox, is between Owensboro and Louisville. Adjacent to the military reservation is the Treasury Department's Gold Depository, where bars of almost pure gold are locked in a vault behind a door weighing more than 20 tons. Active-duty military families and retired military help fuel the economies of nearby Radcliff and Elizabethtown.

Closer to Louisville, the 2nd includes some Republican-leaning Jefferson County suburbs and Bullitt County, an extension of Louisville's suburbs. White flight from Louisville fueled a 66 percent population increase in Bullitt in the 1970s, though growth tapered off considerably in the 1980s. The county's sizable blue-collar element frequently bolts the Democratic ticket, but Bullitt went narrowly for Bill Clinton in 1992.

Bardstown (Nelson County) claims to be the "The Bourbon Capital of the World," and several distilleries are in the vicinity, including Maker's Mark in Loretto. As if to balance the worldly pleasure that bourbon brings, the names of several area towns connote ethereality, including Holy Cross, Calvary, St. Mary, St. Francis, Saint Catharine and Gethsemane.

1990 Population: 614,833. White 574,373 (93%), Black 33,700 (5%), Other 6,760 (1%). Hispanic origin 5,103 (1%). 18 and over 448,234 (73%), 62 and over 84,999 (14%). Median age: 32.

ultimately failed in the Senate, it sailed through the House under Natcher's stewardship. To fend off attempts to cut the bill on the House floor, Natcher asked the Rules Committee for a rule barring amendments. It was the first time in his 39 years in the House, Natcher said, that he had sought to bar amendments.

Another element of Natcher's leadership that members will watch is how his longstanding opposition to abortion affects efforts to overturn laws restricting abortion funding. Natcher's Subcommittee on Labor, Health and Human Services, and Education produces the bill that funds Medicaid. Since 1981, the Labor-HHS bill has carried the so-called Hyde amendment, which bans the use of federal funds for abortions except when the life of the woman is in danger. Abortion rights supporters seek to end the ban.

In the past, Natcher has supported the ban, but he also puts paramount priority on getting his bill signed into law. Asked in early 1993 if he would support a bill without the ban, he said, "I've come to no conclusion, no conclusion. I've come to no conclusion."

Sometimes it seems that Natcher cares more about getting his bill signed into law than about what it contains. After assertive abortion rights members amended the Hyde language to allow funding for abortions in cases of rape and incest in 1989, Natcher was caught between his desire to pass his appropriations bill and his opposition to abortion. He wound up voting for the bill on passage, despite the abortion amendment he opposed, and then voted to override Bush's veto. When the override failed, Natcher introduced a bill that was identical except it lacked the abortion language, and the House passed it.

In 1992, Natcher warned members that he would object if they attached language to his bill blocking implementation of the so-called gag rule, which prohibited abortion counseling in federally funded family planning clinics. In deference to his new status as acting chairman of the full committee, members held off. But Natcher's concern was to prevent his bill from being vetoed. Indeed, he voted earlier in the year in favor of a bill that included language overturning the ban.

The Labor-HHS panel has more expansive jurisdiction than any other subcommittee except Defense. The panel's share of the budget pie has grown to almost $250 billion, even after more than a decade of budget cuts. But the percentage left to discretionary funds has fallen to just a little more than a quarter of that budget, as demands on the untouchable entitlements have grown. Even so, Natcher proudly points out that funding for the National Institutes of Health has grown from $73 million when he was first elected to more than $10 billion today. On his 83rd birthday, groundbreaking began on a new office building complex at the National Institutes of Health to be named after Natcher.

"I have always believed that if you take care of the health of your people and educate your children, you continue living in the strongest country in the world," he says time and again.

All the while he is overseeing a huge slice of the federal budget, Natcher makes sure his predominantly rural Kentucky district gets its share. He has secured local funding for programs from flood control to education of the disadvantaged.

Despite a tooth-and-nail fight, though, he could not prevent a major defeat for his district's powerful tobacco interests in 1987, when Congress passed an amendment banning smoking on airplane flights of at least two hours' duration. After Natcher blocked the ban in committee, it passed on the House floor and in 1989 was made permanent.

Natcher inherited the Labor-HHS Subcommittee chair in 1979. He soon attracted attention by announcing that he wanted to close the subcommittee's markup session and then presiding over an 8-4 vote that closed it for the first time in many years. Lobbyists swarmed outside the committee room, and Natcher said it would be difficult to produce a fiscally responsible bill had they been allowed to record how the members voted. Natcher has kept his subcommittee markups closed ever since.

Before that, he spent 18 years as chairman of one of the least politically appealing Appropriations subcommittees, on the District of Columbia. Natcher clashed often with Washington city officials — particularly over the subway system then on the drawing boards. Three years in a row he delayed the D.C. budget for months while he pressured local officials to finish their highway projects before demanding subway money. Natcher got much of what he wanted.

Natcher's response to media criticism is to ignore it. He seldom grants interviews. He refuses to allow reporters to accompany him on campaign trips. Natcher does issue one news release a year. It announces the new record he has set for attendance at roll calls on the floor — 17,756 by the end of the 102nd Congress.

Natcher says he did not notice his perfect record until five years into his term, when a House clerk pointed it out. While he made up his mind to keep the record, Natcher has sacrificed personally and professionally to sustain it, and he advises junior members to miss a vote early on. For two weeks some years ago, he flew between Kentucky and Washington daily to be with his ill wife, and in 1979 he missed a trip to his district by President Jimmy Carter — all to keep his streak unbroken.

At Home: Nearly as important to Natcher as his perfect voting record is his persistent refusal to accept campaign contributions. The small political expenses he incurs, seldom more than $7,000 per election, he pays himself. "Some people are spending $1 million on House races," Natcher once lamented. "That's wrong. It's morally wrong. I don't believe they can really represent their people if they are taking money from these groups [political action committees]."

It was no great burden for Natcher to pay his campaign expenses; he usually escaped serious opposition. But in 1982 and 1984, Natcher faced primary fights that would have induced most other incumbents to collect and spend bundles of cash. Natcher stuck to his old ways; he spent only about $21,000 in both years combined, all from his own pocket.

In 1982, three major challengers thought Natcher might be ripe for an upset. They contended that he was too eccentric and too liberal for the rural 2nd. His personal frugality, they said, masked a liberal big spender who voted for all major appropriations bills. Altogether, Natcher's foes spent more than $400,000, not including thousands of dollars that the National Conservative Political Action Committee pumped into an independent anti-Natcher ad campaign.

To Natcher's advantage, his primary rivals came from the three corners of the far-flung district; none was well-known outside his home area. With a low turnout and a regional split in the anti-Natcher vote, the incumbent carried all but one of the district's 18 counties, winning renomination with 60 percent.

In 1984, Natcher was challenged by Democratic state Sen. Frank Miller, who as chairman of the Senate Banking and Insurance Committee had access to ample funding. Miller, copying the 1982 attempt to portray Natcher as penny-wise but pound-foolish, complained that he had not used his leadership position on Appropriations to curb the federal deficit. But Natcher won with 70 percent of the vote.

No matter who challenges him, Natcher campaigns in his same old-fashioned manner. He shuns "media events," reporters and other campaign entourage, preferring to drive through the district unaccompanied and stop to chat with people in courthouses and Main Street stores, delivering a simple message: "I'm Bill Natcher, up there in Washington trying to do a good job for you."

Though Natcher does not command a formidable political machine — many of those who helped him secure the district in the 1950s are no longer politically active — he still keeps in touch with a few influential people in most towns. And most average voters know about his refusal to accept campaign contributions, about his attendance record and about the millions of dollars in federal money he has brought the district. Also, the accumulated weight of nearly four decades of constituent service means that Natcher's work has touched just about every family in the 2nd.

Natcher had congressional ambitions even as a teenager. After serving in several local political offices in Warren County (Bowling Green) and as president of the Kentucky Young Democrats, he got his chance in 1953, when Democratic Rep. Garrett L. Withers died. Party leaders united behind him, and he won without opposition in a special election.

Since then, the success of GOP presidential and statewide candidates in the 2nd has occasionally encouraged the party to make bids to unseat Natcher. But Republicans came close to beating him only once, in 1956, when Dwight D. Eisenhower's coattails pulled the GOP candidate to within 3,000 votes of victory.

Committee

Appropriations (Chairman)
Labor, Health & Human Services, Education & Related Agencies (chairman)

Elections

1992 General		
William H. Natcher (D)	126,894	(61%)
Bruce R. Bartley (R)	79,684	(39%)
1992 Primary		
William H. Natcher (D)	35,351	(71%)
Bob Evans (D)	10,072	(20%)
Paul D. Hamm (D)	4,428	(9%)
1990 General		
William H. Natcher (D)	77,057	(66%)
Martin A. Tori (R)	39,624	(34%)

Previous Winning Percentages: **1988** (61%) **1986** (100%) **1984** (62%) **1982** (74%) **1980** (66%) **1978** (100%) **1976** (60%) **1974** (73%) **1972** (62%) **1970** (100%) **1968** (56%) **1966** (59%) **1964** (68%) **1962** (100%) **1960** (100%) **1958** (76%) **1956** (51%) **1954** (100%) **1953** *(100%)

** Special election.*

District Vote for President

1992
D 98,955 (41%)
R 107,339 (45%)
I 33,192 (14%)

Campaign Finance

	Receipts	Receipts from PACs		Expend-itures
1992				
Natcher (D)	$6,623	0		$6,624
Bartley (R)	$1,125	0		$1,125
1990				
Natcher (D)	$6,768	0		$6,766
Tori (R)	$144,166	$1,600	(1%)	$144,315

Key Votes

1993	
Require parental notification of minors' abortions	N
Require unpaid family and medical leave	Y
Approve national "motor voter" registration bill	Y
Approve budget increasing taxes and reducing deficit	Y
Approve economic stimulus plan	Y
1992	
Approve balanced-budget constitutional amendment	Y
Close down space station program	N
Approve U.S. aid for former Soviet Union	Y
Allow shifting funds from defense to domestic programs	Y
1991	
Extend unemployment benefits using deficit financing	Y
Approve waiting period for handgun purchases	N
Authorize use of force in Persian Gulf	N

Voting Studies

	Presidential Support		Party Unity		Conservative Coalition	
Year	**S**	**O**	**S**	**O**	**S**	**O**
1992	38	62	89	11	60	40
1991	35	65	88	12	57	43
1990	29	71	86	14	67	33
1989	49	51	83	17	61	39
1988	26	74	94	6	42	58
1987	34	66	91	9	65	35
1986	29	71	89	11	58	42
1985	30	70	87	13	56	44
1984	34	66	85	15	46	54
1983	32	68	83	17	53	47
1982	48	52	74	26	63	37
1981	54	46	69	31	75	25

Interest Group Ratings

Year	ADA	AFL-CIO	CCUS	ACU
1992	85	83	50	16
1991	50	100	30	20
1990	61	75	36	25
1989	65	83	50	25
1988	75	100	21	16
1987	76	94	13	13
1986	65	93	28	23
1985	60	76	23	24
1984	60	69	44	29
1983	65	82	25	26
1982	55	80	55	41
1981	35	80	26	20

3 Romano L. Mazzoli (D)

Of Louisville — Elected 1970; 12th Term

Born: Nov. 2, 1932, Louisville, Ky.

Education: U. of Notre Dame, B.S. 1954; U. of Louisville, J.D. 1960.

Military Service: Army, 1954-56.

Occupation: Lawyer; professor.

Family: Wife, Helen Dillon; two children.

Religion: Roman Catholic.

Political Career: Ky. Senate, 1968-70; sought Democratic nomination for mayor of Louisville, 1969.

Capitol Office: 2246 Rayburn Bldg. 20515; 225-5401.

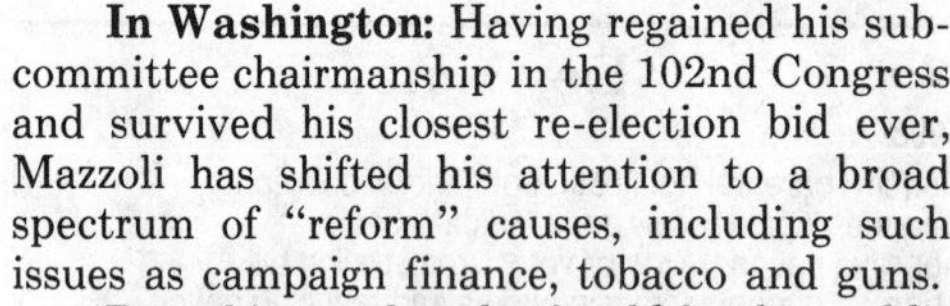

In Washington: Having regained his subcommittee chairmanship in the 102nd Congress and survived his closest re-election bid ever, Mazzoli has shifted his attention to a broad spectrum of "reform" causes, including such issues as campaign finance, tobacco and guns.

But taking on the role of scold for the world's excesses is a risky chore for the upright Louisville Democrat. The challenge for Mazzoli as he begins something of a second career on Capitol Hill is to not sound sanctimonious as he fights for the issues about which he cares deeply.

Mazzoli has been on an emotional and political roller coaster ride for several years. The up side: 1986, when the landmark immigration bill bearing his name was passed; the downside: 1989, when he was stripped of his chairmanship of the Judiciary Committee's Immigration Subcommittee.

The seeds of rejection were sown during the long, stormy legislative battle over the Simpson-Mazzoli bill, when he was alternately contentious and withdrawn. He became even more isolated and stolid in the two years after final passage. But at bottom, Mazzoli lost his chairmanship for being a Republican sympathizer on a committee dominated by activist liberal Democrats.

A last-minute lobbying blitz of Judiciary Democrats brought Mazzoli just five of 21 votes. "The subcommittee did kind of get a little bit sloppy, a little directionless," he conceded, citing his preoccupation with a tough 1988 primary race. "I was a bit of an absentee landlord," he said after having held the post for eight years.

Despite his bitterness, Mazzoli set out to refurbish his image with his Democratic colleagues by highlighting their common interests.

In the 101st Congress, he sharply criticized President Bush for his reluctance to ban assault rifles, he joined the Democratic chorus for a surtax on millionaires, and he shied away from close, public association with Republicans, especially on abortion policy.

All those efforts help explain why Judiciary's liberal bloc was willing to let Mazzoli retake the subcommittee chair in 1991 when his replacement gave up his House seat to run for governor. But perhaps the overriding reason for their generosity was the fact that little action was slated for the Immigration panel in the 102nd Congress.

In the 102nd, he was on the panel that makes Democratic committee assignments; in the 103rd he became a regional whip — two more signs that his rehabilitation effort has paid off.

The unresolved question of how to deal with Haitian refugees provides an opportunity for the Immigration panel to raise its profile again in the 103rd. (Mazzoli won House passage in the 102nd of legislation that would have granted temporary protections and asylum hearings for Haitian refugees.)

But after devoting himself to immigration issues for two decades, Mazzoli is looking in other directions. He saves his most passionate rhetoric for gun control, anti-smoking legislation and campaign finance revision.

In the fall of 1992, in a speech on the House floor, Mazzoli urged party leaders to pass the Brady bill before adjourning. At the start of the 103rd he refiled the legislation to require a seven-day waiting period for handgun purchases.

In June 1992 Mazzoli wrote to RJR Nabisco asking it to curtail its Camel cigarettes' "Old Joe" advertising campaign that appealed to youngsters. In the 102nd and 103rd Congresses, he was an original cosponsor of a bill prohibiting smoking in certain federal offices.

Mazzoli has made allies on those efforts, but he found few companions to join him in his quest to revise the nation's campaign finance laws.

At a House Democratic whip meeting in February 1993, Mazzoli urged President Clinton to push for legislation to eliminate donations by political action committees (PACs) and to set campaign spending limits. He said reform was needed to restore the public's faith in the political process.

Mazzoli, who stopped accepting PAC money

Kentucky 3

Louisville and suburbs

Rural and small-town Kentuckians have always considered themselves different from Louisville, the state's largest city. In a state where blacks make up just 7 percent of the population, Louisville is 30 percent black. The city also has an exceptionally large Catholic population, a legacy of a massive German immigration in the mid-19th century. And Louisville's Courier-Journal newspaper is a leading liberal voice in a state that generally prefers moderate-to-conservative politicians.

That suspicion of Louisville is usually reflected at the ballot box in statewide elections, when the rest of the state bands together to vote against the Louisville-based candidate. GOP Sen. Mitch McConnell, serving in his second term, has been an exception.

Every first Saturday in May, though, the rest of the state turns to Louisville, to be serenaded with the state's official song "My Old Kentucky Home" and to witness one of horse-racing's biggest spectacles, the Kentucky Derby.

In a state known for its contentious politics, Louisville is no exception. Court-ordered busing of students in the 1970s inflamed passions throughout Jefferson County, leading to riots and violent demonstrations. And in the 1980s, Louisville became known as "Strike City" for its fractious labor-management relations.

Despite some job losses from industrial decline, labor strength runs deep among the blue-collar, white residents of the South End; it translates into Democratic votes. Blacks who live near downtown in the West End turn in even larger Democratic majorities. Republicans live in the affluent East End by the Ohio River.

Louisville's newer jobs are more service-oriented, with employers such as United Parcel Service, which operates a hub out of Standiford Airport, and Galen (formerly Humana), which runs for-profit hospitals.

In the 1970s, the city of Louisville — with the addition of a few suburbs — held enough population for its own congressional district. But massive white flight to the suburbs forced mapmakers in the two subsequent rounds of redistricting to expand the 3rd District's lines even farther into the Jefferson County suburbs. Louisville now accounts for less than half the district vote.

That has meant a shift in the 3rd District balance of power. Before the black Democratic vote became a force in the mid-to late 1960s, Jefferson County was fertile ground for Republicans. And in the 3rd, the pendulum is swinging back in that direction, as the suburbs increasingly flex their muscles.

This version of the 3rd is considerably more receptive to Republicans, particularly in the higher-income areas (such as the Brownsboro Road-Interchange 71 corridor) outside the city and in areas closer to the Oldham County border. The turf between St. Matthews and Middletown — on the 2nd District border — is Republican, well-educated and affluent. The new suburban majority made the 1992 congressional election the closest in more than 20 years.

1990 Population: 613,603. White 494,625 (81%), Black 112,290 (18%), Other 6,688 (1%). Hispanic origin 4,075 (1%). 18 and over 465,371 (76%), 62 and over 103,277 (17%). Median age: 34.

and contributions of more than $100 despite two tough re-election campaigns, was met with "deafening silence," The Washington Post reported.

Mazzoli's views and votes span the political spectrum, which is perhaps not surprising for a member from an urban district in the border South. He first won election in 1970 as an anti-war candidate; he is a strong opponent of abortion, supports handgun controls and often votes with conservatives on budget issues. In the eyes of many Democrats, his most offensive departure from the party script came on the party-line 1985 vote to seat Democratic incumbent Frank McCloskey rather than his GOP rival in a disputed Indiana election. Mazzoli sided with the GOP.

The highlight of his career came Oct. 17, 1986, when Congress cleared the Simpson-Mazzoli immigration bill. The law penalizes employers who knowingly hire illegal aliens and offered amnesty to illegal aliens who could prove that they had been in the United States before 1982.

By the time of final passage, however, Mazzoli had relinquished the leadership role he had played for most of the process. Emotionally spent from polarizing fights in the two past Congresses, he was content to work behind the scenes, lending technical expertise to the debate while others stepped into the spotlight. "The fight's gone out of the dog," one House Democrat said of Mazzoli.

If Mazzoli sometimes seemed like the forgotten man in the final stages of the immigration bill, GOP Sen. Alan K. Simpson of Wyoming and others who conducted the concluding negotiations left no doubt that Mazzoli had helped make it all possible. Moreover, the Kentucky Democrat had emerged in the end to deal with one of the bill's most controversial aspects: the proposal to establish a permanent "guest worker" program for growers who rely on foreign labor. He helped draft a compromise between growers, who said they needed the help, and organized labor, which insisted the program was exploitative, just when the dispute threatened to sink the entire bill for the third consecutive time.

In the 97th and 98th Congresses, the Senate passed the immigration bill only to see it withdrawn from the House floor — by Mazzoli the first time and by then-Speaker Thomas P. "Tip" O'Neill Jr. of Massachusetts the next session.

Stung by criticism that he was stifling a needed reform for political purposes, O'Neill relented later in the 98th. But it was impossible for the House to agree with the Senate on a bill that drew opposition from Hispanics and Democratic presidential nominee Walter F. Mondale. The bill became law in the 99th Congress.

Once the bill was in place, immigration experts monitored implementation. By its first anniversary in late 1987, Mazzoli would proudly say, "Even the most implacable foes of the bill have had to eat some crow."

Meanwhile, his Judiciary colleagues were restless to do more than savor past successes. In 1987, Mazzoli was the only Democrat on his subcommittee and the full committee to join Republicans in opposing a bill to allow extended stays in the United States for refugees of El Salvador and Nicaragua until conditions in those countries improved. Then Mazzoli proposed an alternative safe-haven bill for refugees of armed conflict or environmental disaster, but it died in the Senate.

His fellow subcommittee Democrats also wanted to extend the 1986 immigration law's amnesty period for another year, to ensure that all eligible aliens took advantage of the opening. And having successfully tackled illegal immigration, they wanted to begin work on revising the legal-immigration system, with its country-by-country quotas and eligibility standards that were widely considered outdated. Mazzoli wanted to undertake neither effort.

Pressed by a majority of his panel, however, Mazzoli finally agreed to a vote on the proposed amnesty extension just weeks before the law's May 1988 deadline. He proposed a six-month extension as a compromise; the full committee, acting within an hour of the subcommittee, settled on seven months. The measure narrowly was passed by the House, but died in a Senate filibuster. The amnesty deadline passed, leaving committee Democrats resentful that Mazzoli had waited until it was too late for action.

At Home: Mazzoli's most serious opposition usually comes from those in his own party. On four occasions since 1976, he has faced competitive primary opponents. But in 1992, it was his Republican foe, state Rep. Susan B. Stokes, who gave him his closest general-election scare since 1970.

At the outset of the race, redistricting was a concern. The new map added a chunk of Republican-leaning suburbs in Jefferson County, though the district retained a significant Democratic voter registration advantage.

The biggest hurdle for Mazzoli turned out to be a lack of money. Because he eschewed PAC money — a practice he started in 1990 — and limited donations to less than $100, he was unable to match Stokes' spending. As one of the nation's most competitive female GOP challengers — and an abortion rights supporter — Stokes had little trouble outpacing Mazzoli's fundraising.

Stokes hammered Mazzoli in television commercials, without any response from the incumbent. Lacking deep pockets, Mazzoli was limited to newspaper ads touting his inability to purchase TV time.

But on the heels of Kentucky's 1991 gubernatorial race, where a record $19 million was spent, voters found Mazzoli's stance appealing. He won with 53 percent.

A furor over school busing had provided the ammunition for the 1976 challenge. Mazzoli at first accepted busing as a means of desegregating the Louisville schools, then switched to an anti-busing position after the city's turmoil began. But the shift in positions came too late and was too mild for vocal busing foes. He was held to 56 percent of the primary vote.

The second primary challenge came in 1982, fueled by lingering resentment over the busing crisis and an unfavorable 1982 remap that extended his district deep into Louisville's GOP suburbs. His opponent, state Rep. Mark O'Brien, sought to tie the busing issue to a school-tax referendum, saying that if there were no busing, the proposed county surtax on the state income tax would be unnecessary. But because O'Brien's campaign was underfinanced and starting late, it turned out to be more smoke than fire; Mazzoli comfortably surpassed the 60 percent mark.

The third primary challenge came in 1988, from Jeffrey Hutter, administrative director of the Humana Heart Institute and a former Louisville TV reporter. He was not especially well-financed either, but he made up for it with brashness. He accused Mazzoli of ignoring Louisville and voting against its interests. Hutter had support from the 80,000-member Greater Louisville Central Labor Council, which was upset with Mazzoli for his support of a smoking ban on domestic airplane flights of two hours or less (a vote labor saw as a threat to jobs in the state's lucrative tobacco industry) and his opposition to the Gephardt "fair trade" amendment.

Yet while Hutter carried blue-collar precincts, he could not crack the base that Mazzoli had constructed among the district's many Catholic and elderly voters. Mazzoli got 61 percent of the vote.

Hutter tried again in 1990, this time with the backing of several district and city officials. But Mazzoli had a surprisingly easy time in turning back both Hutter and city alderman Paul Bather in the primary.

In the general election, Mazzoli faced Al Brown, a black labor-relations consultant and a member of the Kentucky Lottery Commission. Brown gained the attention and blessing of the national GOP, always eager to promote its black candidates.

Brown, like Hutter, argued that Mazzoli was ineffective in bringing federal projects home. Although he described himself as moderate to conservative, Brown supported abortion rights, contrasting himself with Mazzoli and his staunch anti-abortion position. Yet Brown, plagued by a lack of funds, could manage only 39 percent of the vote.

Mazzoli's base has shifted a bit since he first ran for the House in 1970. Then, he was an opponent of the Vietnam War, with a strong base among blacks, young liberals and blue-collar Catholics. But the decisive factor in his House victory that year was the bitter intraparty feud between GOP incumbent William O. Cowger and Republican Gov. Louie B. Nunn over local patronage. The breach never healed, and Mazzoli took advantage of it to win a 211-vote victory.

Committees

Judiciary (4th of 21 Democrats)
International Law, Immigration & Refugees (chairman); Crime & Criminal Justice; Intellectual Property & Judicial Administration

Small Business (4th of 27 Democrats)
SBA Legislation & the General Economy

Elections

1992 General		
Romano L. Mazzoli (D)	148,066	(53%)
Susan B. Stokes (R)	132,689	(47%)
1992 Primary		
Romano L. Mazzoli (D)	52,748	(76%)
Ron Greene (D)	16,758	(24%)
1990 General		
Romano L. Mazzoli (D)	84,750	(61%)
Al Brown (R)	55,188	(39%)

Previous Winning Percentages: **1988** (70%) **1986** (73%) **1984** (68%) **1982** (65%) **1980** (64%) **1978** (66%) **1976** (57%) **1974** (70%) **1972** (62%) **1970** (49%)

District Vote for President

1992
D 143,824 (50%)
R 105,520 (37%)
I 35,902 (13%)

Campaign Finance

	Receipts	Receipts from PACs		Expend-itures
1992				
Mazzoli (D)	$223,091	0		$216,638
Stokes (R)	$446,807	$170,123	(38%)	$364,659
1990				
Mazzoli (D)	$301,713	0		$333,885
Brown (R)	$329,060	$33,675	(10%)	$327,390

Key Votes

1993	
Require parental notification of minors' abortions	Y
Require unpaid family and medical leave	Y
Approve national "motor voter" registration bill	Y
Approve budget increasing taxes and reducing deficit	Y
Approve economic stimulus plan	Y
1992	
Approve balanced-budget constitutional amendment	Y
Close down space station program	Y
Approve U.S. aid for former Soviet Union	N
Allow shifting funds from defense to domestic programs	N
1991	
Extend unemployment benefits using deficit financing	Y
Approve waiting period for handgun purchases	Y
Authorize use of force in Persian Gulf	N

Voting Studies

	Presidential Support		Party Unity		Conservative Coalition	
Year	**S**	**O**	**S**	**O**	**S**	**O**
1992	28	72	90	10	38	63
1991	38	62	88	11	35	65
1990	31	68	87	12	44	52
1989	50	50	80	19	59	41
1988	33	62	84	14	42	50
1987	42	57	84	15	74	26
1986	40	58	78	20	62	38
1985	48	52	74	25	62	36
1984	40	57	79	20	47	53
1983	40	59	78	20	51	48
1982	44	53	75	22	49	49
1981	47	43	62	29	49	36

Interest Group Ratings

Year	ADA	AFL-CIO	CCUS	ACU
1992	70	75	38	28
1991	65	67	20	10
1990	78	83	29	13
1989	40	25	80	32
1988	75	77	54	21
1987	52	56	33	30
1986	50	64	24	32
1985	55	47	50	33
1984	65	38	38	38
1983	65	53	55	35
1982	70	90	41	27
1981	60	64	44	36

4 Jim Bunning (R)

Of Southgate — Elected 1986; 4th Term

Born: Oct. 23, 1931, Campbell County, Ky.
Education: Xavier U., B.S. 1953.
Occupation: Investment broker; sports agent; professional baseball player.
Family: Wife, Mary Catherine Theis; nine children.
Religion: Roman Catholic.
Political Career: Fort Thomas City Council, 1977-79; Ky. Senate, 1979-83; Republican nominee for governor, 1983.
Capitol Office: 2437 Rayburn Bldg. 20515; 225-3465.

In Washington: People who watched Bunning as an athlete generally described him as a tough, stubborn competitor who hated to lose and never liked to yield an inch to an opposing batter. Those who have watched him in politics have found exactly the same characteristics. Democrats sometimes describe him as obstinate and unyielding in the legislative process. Republicans prefer to stress his diligence at mastering the details of the job.

Bunning does not apologize for throwing partisan hardballs in the House. "Sometimes when you believe very deeply in an issue — very deeply — people take that for being arrogant and aggressive. I think it's being honest," he told The (Louisville) Courier-Journal in 1992.

As a freshman, Bunning was elected by his classmates to be their representative on the GOP Committee on Committees, which determines committee assignments. His contacts there with more senior Republicans enabled Bunning to secure a seat on the highly coveted Ways and Means Committee for the 102nd Congress after falling short in a previous bid.

Perhaps to balance that choice assignment, Bunning was also placed on the ethics committee, arguably one of the least desirable posts in the House. He remained on the ethics panel in the 103rd, but his first term came during two of the committee's most tumultuous years — 1991-92 — when it was inundated by scandals involving the House bank and post office.

Throughout the painful bank scandal, Bunning insisted on full disclosure of members' names and all aspects of their overdrafts. He was one of four committee Republicans who branded as a "whitewash" early proposals to name only the most egregious abusers of the bank. Their refusal to go along with the other 10 ethics committee members was central to the House's later decision to release the list of all bank overdrafts. (Bunning had none.)

Bunning was the sole dissenter on a 12-1 vote not to require members to report overdrafts as loans or gifts on their financial disclosure statements. Most ethics committee members apparently thought that most representatives did not have enough information to accurately state the size of their overdrafts. Bunning said he considered any overdraft a loan that ought to be reported.

Despite a reputation early in his House career as having only one pitch in his arsenal, Bunning has impressed some more junior conservatives with his effort to develop a more practical approach to some issues. That is especially true on Ways and Means, where Bunning managed in his first term to play a few bit parts, while remaining an ideological beacon among the younger Republicans. Because of his turn toward a slightly more accommodating legislative posture, Bunning occasionally found himself lined up against the Bush administration.

He was one of only 39 House Republicans to vote for the last-ditch urban aid tax bill that President Bush vetoed the day after losing his re-election bid. The bill's increased taxes on the wealthy had a decidedly Democratic air, but Bunning had worked on several issues the bill covered, including urban enterprise zones, a "taxpayers' bill of rights" and fraud protections for senior citizens. He also had worked hard on a provision to protect a private foundation in Louisville. The James Graham Brown Foundation was paying to clean up a toxic-waste site, a cost that cut into its charitable giving and in turn subjected the foundation to excise taxes. Bunning (along with Kentucky Sens. Wendell H. Ford and Mitch McConnell) won passage of a provision to count the cleanup costs toward the foundation's contribution requirement.

Bunning also went against the president to support a bill requiring China to improve its human rights record before it would qualify for renewal of normalized trade status with the United States. He worked with liberal New York Democrat Thomas J. Downey to add an amendment insisting that China not aid other countries in developing nuclear weapons. And he voted to override Bush's veto of the bill. (The veto stood when the Senate failed to

Kentucky 4

North and East — Covington; Ashland

Of the state's six congressional districts, the 4th is the least distinctly Kentuckian. Almost half the district's population is located in the Cincinnati suburbs; Ashland, the 4th's second-largest city, is on the far eastern fringe, near where the Ohio River forms a border with Ohio and West Virginia.

Boone, Campbell (Newport) and Kenton (Covington) counties are associated much more closely with Cincinnati — where much of the area's population commutes to work — than with Lexington or Louisville. The Greater Cincinnati International Airport is actually in Kentucky, a few miles west of Covington.

Newport has battled its reputation as a "sin city" — for its go-go bars and nightclubs — where some of Cincinnati's residents go to blow off steam. Ohioans also escape their state-run liquor stores by buying less expensive alcohol in Covington.

A frequently voiced complaint in Covington is that the state ignores them because of their close ties to Ohio. But the federal government certainly has not: A regional center of the Internal Revenue Service is the city's largest employer. The peak of tax season adds even more jobs to the district's largest city.

Boone County attracted population spillover from Campbell and Kenton counties in the 1970s and 1980s, growing more than 75 percent over the past two decades.

The politics of these three counties is nominally Democratic, but increasingly Republican-friendly. George Bush won all three easily in 1992; Rep. Bunning won by more than 2-to-1 in each.

For a Democrat to win the 4th, the candidate must remain competitive in these counties and then run up sizable margins in the eight rural-suburban counties closer to Louisville.

Most of these rural counties are Democratic, but suburban Oldham County (at the 4th's western edge, closest to Louisville) is leaning Republican. In the 1970s, Oldham's population swelled by 91 percent, thanks to white-collar out-migration from Louisville and an influx of out-of-state business executives. Population growth tapered off considerably in the 1980s, but Oldham has an unmistakable GOP stamp.

Any Democratic strategy for the 4th also has to factor in the industrial city of Ashland (Boyd County), home to Ashland Oil and Armco Steel. Strong unions kept the oil refinery workers and steelworkers of Boyd and neighboring Greenup counties in the Democratic column for decades, but their grip has weakened. Still, Bill Clinton and 1992 Democratic House challenger Floyd Poore carried Boyd and Greenup.

Before redistricting, these counties clustered by the West Virginia border were part of Eastern Kentucky's heavily Democratic, coal-producing Appalachian district. That voting tradition lives on in sparsely populated and 98 percent Democratic Elliott County. Lewis County marches to its own GOP beat, dating to the time when it was a stop on the Underground Railroad.

1990 Population: 614,245. White 597,696 (97%), Black 13,180 (2%), Other 3,369 (1%). Hispanic origin 2,666 (<1%). 18 and over 449,764 (73%), 62 and over 90,033 (15%). Median age: 33.

muster a two-thirds majority to override.)

In committee, Bunning joined with liberal Democrat Pete Stark to amend a broad trade bill to bar imports from companies that helped foreign countries build nuclear weapons. But on the floor he opposed the bill, which was viewed as protectionist. It died when the Senate did not act on it.

If Bunning has found reason to cooperate on occasion, he is still capable of rising vigorously to defend the minority's rights in the House or to rail against some liberal ideology that he finds wanting. Bunning's legislative style is entirely in keeping with the confrontational conservatives who are gaining prominence in the House GOP. Conservatives evidently liked his approach: They elected him chairman of the Conservative Opportunity Society for the 102nd Congress.

His combative nature carries over into electoral politics. In a 1989 fundraising letter that discussed impending redistricting, he exhorted supporters not to "cave in to the plots and schemes of the Frankfort Democrats who want to change our district."

Bunning's presence offers House Republicans a chance for guaranteed supremacy in one of the few areas of partisan competition they have dominated in recent years — the congressional baseball game. Not since 1975 has there been a major league player in the House, and there has never been one like Bunning, who pitched two no-hitters and won 224 games over a 15-year big-league career.

At Home: After winning re-election easily in his first two tries, in 1992 Bunning found himself imperiled by the changes wrought by redistricting. Sensing an opportunity, Democrats recruited Dr. Floyd G. Poore, a prolific fundraiser coming off an unsuccessful 1991 gubernatorial bid.

Given the more than 2-to-1 Democratic registration edge in the refigured district, Poore was considered a serious threat to capture the seat. But Bunning was able to resurrect enough of the character questions raised during Poore's gubernatorial run to keep the Democrat off balance. Just in case Poore did get close, Bunning raised more than $900,000.

After retiring as an active player in 1971, Bunning tried minor league managing for a while, then returned to his native Kentucky, where he set up as an investment broker and agent to professional athletes.

He also got involved in civic activities that led him to a seat on the Fort Thomas City Council, where in 1977 he began his rapid political rise. After just two years, Bunning unseated a longtime Democratic state senator. He quickly became the minority leader for the small group of Senate Republicans.

In 1983, Kentucky Republicans, searching for a viable gubernatorial candidate, recruited Bunning. In his uphill campaign against Democrat Martha Layne Collins, he contended that the state's economy had stagnated during a long period of Democratic rule. He also took a "tough man" approach that seemed designed for voters uncomfortable with the idea of a female governor. Bunning got a respectable 44 percent.

He initially had planned on another try for the governorship in 1987. But GOP Rep. Gene Snyder announced his retirement in 1986, and GOP officials were worried about holding the 4th. They needed a strong candidate, and they enlisted Bunning.

His opponent was Democratic state Rep. Terry Mann, who had lost to Snyder by only 12,000 votes in 1982 and had considerable strength in Bunning's Campbell County political base, just across the Ohio River from Cincinnati. Mann contrasted his 14 years in the legislature to Bunning's four. But Mann drew negative press in March, when it was reported that he had rigged his state House voting lever with a rubber band so he would be recorded as present while he was absent from a session.

That episode, coupled with Bunning's image as a conservative in Snyder's mold and a big GOP financial edge, helped Bunning build a winning margin in the Cincinnati-area counties of Kenton and Boone and in the populous Louisville suburbs of Jefferson County.

Committees

Budget (7th of 17 Republicans)

Standards of Official Conduct (3rd of 7 Republicans)

Ways & Means (7th of 14 Republicans)
Social Security (ranking)

Elections

1992 General		
Jim Bunning (R)	139,634	(62%)
Dr. Floyd G. Poore (D)	86,890	(38%)
1990 General		
Jim Bunning (R)	101,680	(69%)
Galen Martin (D)	44,979	(31%)

Previous Winning Percentages: **1988** (74%) **1986** (55%)

District Vote for President

1992
D 94,240 (39%)
R 106,605 (44%)
I 40,425 (17%)

Campaign Finance

	Receipts	Receipts from PACs		Expend-itures
1992				
Bunning (R)	$946,781	$439,491	(46%)	$984,180
Poore (D)	$311,111	$106,573	(34%)	$311,121
1990				
Bunning (R)	$532,775	$225,900	(42%)	$563,409
Martin (D)	$76,407	$32,900	(43%)	$76,580

Key Votes

1993	
Require parental notification of minors' abortions	Y
Require unpaid family and medical leave	N
Approve national "motor voter" registration bill	N
Approve budget increasing taxes and reducing deficit	N
Approve economic stimulus plan	N
1992	
Approve balanced-budget constitutional amendment	Y
Close down space station program	N
Approve U.S. aid for former Soviet Union	N
Allow shifting funds from defense to domestic programs	?
1991	
Extend unemployment benefits using deficit financing	N
Approve waiting period for handgun purchases	N
Authorize use of force in Persian Gulf	Y

Voting Studies

	Presidential Support		Party Unity		Conservative Coalition	
Year	**S**	**O**	**S**	**O**	**S**	**O**
1992	77	21	89	6	85	8
1991	76	23	94	4	97	3
1990	71	28	94	2	96	2
1989	78	17	95	3	88	10
1988	65	29	92	3	97	0
1987	74	24	95	4	95	5

Interest Group Ratings

Year	ADA	AFL-CIO	CCUS	ACU
1992	10	27	71	90
1991	10	8	90	100
1990	6	8	79	87
1989	5	17	100	96
1988	0	8	100	100
1987	4	6	93	87

5 Harold Rogers (R)

Of Somerset — Elected 1980; 7th Term

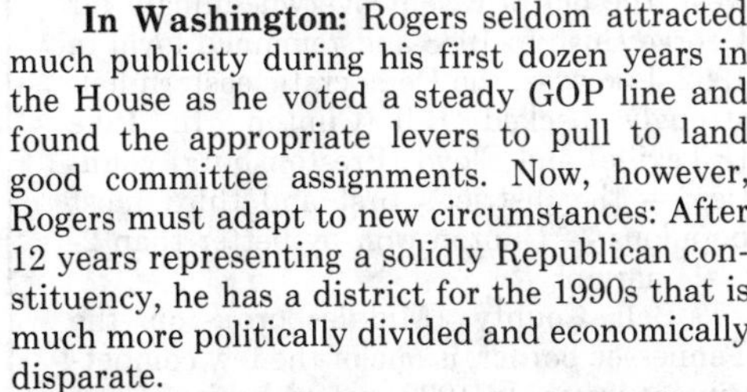

Born: Dec. 31, 1937, Barrier, Ky.
Education: Western Kentucky U., 1956-57; U. of Kentucky, B.A. 1962, LL.B. 1964.
Military Service: National Guard, 1956-63.
Occupation: Lawyer.
Family: Wife, Shirley McDowell; three children.
Religion: Baptist.
Political Career: Pulaski and Rockcastle counties commonwealth attorney, 1969-79; GOP nominee for lieutenant governor, 1979.
Capitol Office: 2468 Rayburn Bldg. 20515; 225-4601.

In Washington: Rogers seldom attracted much publicity during his first dozen years in the House as he voted a steady GOP line and found the appropriate levers to pull to land good committee assignments. Now, however, Rogers must adapt to new circumstances: After 12 years representing a solidly Republican constituency, he has a district for the 1990s that is much more politically divided and economically disparate.

Redistricting grafted onto the unfailingly Republican mountain counties of Rogers' old 5th the coal counties that border West Virginia and Virginia, which have turned out mighty Democratic majorities since the New Deal. Rogers won re-election with a career-low 55 percent, and there are signs that representing a more Democratic-friendly district will have some impact on his voting behavior.

In March 1993, Rogers was one of only three Republicans to vote for President Clinton's $16.3 billion economic stimulus package. He explained that his district still had high unemployment and had not shown signs of economic recovery. For the 103rd Congress, he dropped his slot on Appropriations' Treasury-Postal Service Subcommittee in favor of a position on the Energy and Water Development panel; it funds the flood-control projects that Rogers has steered into his district as well as the Tennessee Valley Authority and the Appalachian Regional Commission.

Rogers' behind-the-scenes skills are well-suited to Appropriations, where Democrats and Republicans usually work together closely to draft money bills that all panel members can support; Rogers follows the panel's ethic of bipartisan cooperation and picks up plums for his district. He is ranking Republican on the Commerce, Justice and State Subcommittee.

Rogers' personality and legislative pursuits set him apart from the more visible and confrontational Republicans who have come to the House in recent years. His day-to-day frame of reference more mirrors that of the Democratic chairmen of his two subcommittees, Neal Smith on Commerce-Justice-State and Tom Bevill on Energy and Water, two old-style politicians with an institutional perspective.

The top spot on the Commerce Subcommittee puts Rogers in a position to influence that and other spending bills, particularly those that might benefit Kentucky in general and his economically struggling district in particular. The fiscal 1992 bill from his subcommittee included a $4.5 million Small Business Administration special project for the University of Kentucky at Lexington, to go toward the construction of its Advanced Science and Technology Commercialization Center. A major flood control project on the Upper Cumberland River, a tunnel at the Cumberland Gap and the Southern Kentucky Rural Development project also attest to Rogers' skill as an appropriator.

But Rogers' news releases announcing new federal funds pair with those proclaiming his staunch opposition to tax increases, and that has drawn some critical press at home. One 1990 headline read, "Rep. Rogers' dilemma: Pet Projects vs. Tax Hikes."

Rogers says he is just trying to make up for years of neglect his area suffered from the federal government.

"Just because [my constituents] have been ignored all these years, it's no reason to say, 'Sorry, you're out of the picture. We don't have the money,' " he says.

Tobacco is a subject that can get the easy-going Rogers excited: He is a smoker, and he views the "right to smoke" as an issue of personal liberty. That is good politics because tobacco-growing puts a lot of groceries on the table in the 5th. There are 40,000 allotments in the district, most of them held by small-scale farmers.

In 1985, perturbed by Reagan administration proposals to phase out parts of the tobacco price-support system, Rogers "took a walk" during a high-profile Appropriations Committee vote on the MX missile. His refusal to vote

Kentucky 5

Southeast — Middlesboro; Pikeville

Appalachian Eastern Kentucky has long been one of the state's most downtrodden areas. Lexington and Louisville are culturally, economically and geographically distant from the 5th District, the state's poorest, sickest and least-educated.

With no city that has more than 15,000 residents, the 5th spans 26 counties and part of Lawrence County. Most of Democratic Eastern Kentucky is within its confines, along with the Republican southeastern region along the Tennessee border.

One tie that binds the district is the staggering poverty that differentiates it from the rest of the state. About one in five households lacks a telephone or makes less than $5,000 per year.

The 1970s coal boom brought many former residents from the urban Midwest back to the hills and hollows of Appalachia. But the revival died out as coal production began to shift from the East to the West, where, typically, it is cheaper and easier to mine coal.

The decline of the once-mighty coal industry — the state lost 20,000 mining jobs in the 1980s — has brought even harder times to the region's mountain people, who never had it easy to begin with.

Besides the abandoned mines and scarred hillsides, King Coal is leaving behind a legion of crippled miners, whether they suffer from black lung disease or are disabled by some other mine-related injury. Fourteen percent of the people in the district have a work-related disability that prevents them from working.

The United Mine Workers union (UMW) speaks loudly for these residents and carries a big stick in the coal counties in the eastern half of the district. These counties bordering Virginia and West Virginia have turned in huge Democratic majorities since the New Deal.

Pitted against the coal counties is a firewall of mountain counties that have been voting Republican since the 1860s; they used to form the backbone of the old GOP 5th District before it was merged with the Democratic 7th in 1992 redistricting. Taken as a whole, the district has a slight Democratic voter registration advantage.

Counting Leslie County and moving west, the old 5th went overwhelmingly for George Bush in 1988 and remained loyal in 1992. Likewise, the Democratic eastern half strongly backed Bill Clinton. In Pike (Pikeville) and Floyd (Prestonsburg) counties — the district's first and third most populous — Clinton won by better than 2-to-1 margins.

Bell County (Middlesboro), on the Tennessee border, is one of the few competitive counties. In 1992, voters backed Clinton while crossing over for Rep. Rogers.

Population in the western section is concentrated in Pulaski (Somerset) and Laurel (London) counties. Like the rest of the west, Somerset — the 5th's second-largest city after Middlesboro — relies heavily on tourism and recreation. Lake Cumberland is nearby, as is the Big South Fork National River and Recreation area.

1990 Population: 614,119. White 606,222 (99%), Black 5,884 (1%), Other 2,013 (<1%). Hispanic origin 1,635 (<1%). 18 and over 441,744 (72%), 62 and over 88,669 (14%). Median age: 32.

on the issue had the intended effect — it attracted attention at the White House. Quickly, a meeting was arranged for Rogers with Chief of Staff Donald T. Regan. The Kentucky Republican fully vented his tobacco concerns before agreeing to back the president on the MX.

Fighting to protect tobacco, however, has increasingly been a rear-guard action. In 1987, Rogers helped snuff out in subcommittee a plan by Illinois Democrat Richard J. Durbin to ban smoking on airplane flights — only to have Durbin win on the House floor and in conference. The trend is not lost on Rogers, who has been seeking funds for aquaculture and crop diversification to broaden his district's economic base. He also sponsored a task force to entice vacationers to southeastern Kentucky's parks and lakes.

During three terms on the Budget Committee, Rogers put enough zing into his anti-deficit rhetoric to win friends among the brasher Republicans, who chafe at the way Democrats control the budget debate in Congress. At the start of the 102nd Congress, Rogers made a bid for the ranking spot on Budget. Though his effort was solid, he ended up losing to Bill Gradison of Ohio, a supreme legislative pragmatist and the preferred choice of Minority Leader Robert H. Michel of Illinois. Rogers cycled off the panel at the end of the 102nd Congress.

At Home: Rogers had not even faced a Democratic opponent since 1984, but he was well-prepared in 1992 when redistricting threw him into a distinctly Democratic district. The new 5th merged Rogers' old rock-ribbed Republican 5th and retiring Democratic Rep. Carl C. Perkins' 7th, in Democratic-voting coal country.

Rogers started early laying groundwork for a strenuous campaign, amassing a hefty campaign treasury and making contacts in counties new to him as a crowded field of Democratic primary aspirants bickered among themselves. Rogers was unopposed for his party's nomination.

By the fall, Rogers' greatest concern was the unpopularity of the Bush-Quayle ticket, which ended up losing the 5th by 6 percentage points. The Democratic nominee, former state Sen. John Doug Hays, wrapped himself in the Clinton-Gore banner, but his bid was sidetracked in late October when it was revealed that his second wife hid a court file on their brief divorce. The file indicated that Hays divorced his first wife in 1991 and remarried three weeks later. Six weeks into that marriage, his second wife filed for divorce. But they reconciled, and she said she hid the file to protect Hays. Rogers carried 16 of the district's 27 counties en route to a 10-point victory.

Rogers made his name locally in the 1960s as a civic activist promoting industrial development in Somerset (Pulaski County). He took over as the commonwealth's attorney in 1969 and continued to play a conspicuous role in politics as the prosecutor for Pulaski and Rockcastle counties. He was unsuccessful as the GOP nominee for lieutenant governor in 1979, but the race helped him build name recognition, and that paid off in his first House campaign in 1980.

GOP Rep. Tim Lee Carter's retirement touched off a scramble, but Rogers quickly moved to the front of the 11-candidate GOP field. The primary revolved around personalities, geography and political alliances, not issues. Rogers drew barely one-fifth of the vote, but carried 11 of the district's 28 counties, most of them around his home base in the center of the old 5th.

Committees

Appropriations (8th of 23 Republicans)
Commerce, Justice, State & Judiciary (ranking); Energy & Water Development

Elections

1992 General		
Harold Rogers (R)	115,255	(55%)
John Doug Hays (D)	95,760	(45%)
1990 General		
Harold Rogers (R)	64,660	(100%)

Previous Winning Percentages: **1988** (100%) **1986** (100%) **1984** (76%) **1982** (65%) **1980** (68%)

District Vote for President

1992
D 109,581 (48%)
R 95,818 (42%)
I 23,886 (10%)

Campaign Finance

	Receipts	Receipts from PACs		Expend-itures
1992				
Rogers (R)	$651,821	$233,890	(36%)	$885,966
Hays (D)	$280,313	$58,150	(21%)	$274,753
1990				
Rogers (R)	$180,606	$71,025	(39%)	$103,286

Key Votes

1993	
Require parental notification of minors' abortions	Y
Require unpaid family and medical leave	N
Approve national "motor voter" registration bill	N
Approve budget increasing taxes and reducing deficit	N
Approve economic stimulus plan	Y
1992	
Approve balanced-budget constitutional amendment	Y
Close down space station program	Y
Approve U.S. aid for former Soviet Union	N
Allow shifting funds from defense to domestic programs	N
1991	
Extend unemployment benefits using deficit financing	Y
Approve waiting period for handgun purchases	N
Authorize use of force in Persian Gulf	Y

Voting Studies

	Presidential Support		Party Unity		Conservative Coalition	
Year	**S**	**O**	**S**	**O**	**S**	**O**
1992	67	30	80	19	88	13
1991	70	25	76	21	86	5
1990	69	31	85	14	94	2
1989	80	20	83	16	95	5
1988	62	38	85	11	87	11
1987	62	34	77	18	91	5
1986	70	29	76	23	92	8
1985	64	34	75	21	89	9
1984	54	41	66	28	92	7
1983	70	29	80	19	89	10
1982	70	29	73	20	86	12
1981	72	28	81	18	88	9

Interest Group Ratings

Year	ADA	AFL-CIO	CCUS	ACU
1992	25	50	88	80
1991	10	25	90	79
1990	6	17	86	83
1989	10	25	80	71
1988	5	21	100	96
1987	4	13	80	78
1986	10	43	67	86
1985	10	18	76	76
1984	25	38	73	71
1983	5	12	74	87
1982	15	30	77	76
1981	10	40	84	93

6 Scotty Baesler (D)

Of Lexington — Elected 1992; 1st Term

Born: July 9, 1941, Lexington, Ky.
Education: U. of Kentucky, B.A. 1963, J.D. 1966.
Military Service: Army Reserve, 1967-73.
Occupation: Lawyer; farmer.
Family: Wife, Alice Woods; two children.
Religion: Independent Christian.
Political Career: Vice mayor of Lexington, 1974-78; candidate for mayor of Lexington, 1977; Fayette County district judge, 1979-81; mayor of Lexington, 1982-92; sought Democratic nomination for governor, 1991.
Capitol Office: 508 Cannon Bldg. 20515; 225-4706.

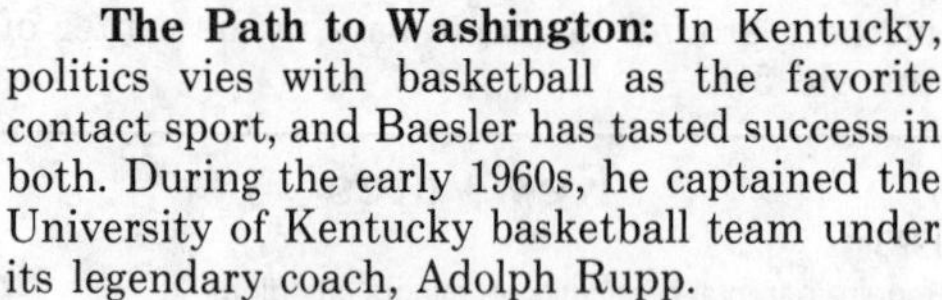

The Path to Washington: In Kentucky, politics vies with basketball as the favorite contact sport, and Baesler has tasted success in both. During the early 1960s, he captained the University of Kentucky basketball team under its legendary coach, Adolph Rupp.

After a decade as mayor of Lexington, hometown of his alma mater, Baesler now represents the city and its environs on the Hill. He handily defeated Republican Charles W. Ellinger in winning the open 6th District seat in November and replaces GOP Rep. Larry J. Hopkins.

Hopkins' gubernatorial race was derailed in 1991 after his admission that he had 32 overdrafts at the House bank — making him one of the scandal's first victims. (The ethics committee later reported that he had 83 overdrafts.)

Hopkins could have run for re-election in 1992, but with the popular Baesler gearing up for a challenge, Hopkins elected to retire.

Hopkins might have had trouble with Baesler even without the bad checks and a losing gubernatorial bid. The 6th has GOP leanings, but Baesler has built a formidable political operation as mayor of its most-populous city. His career had gone so smoothly that he tried to make the big leap from the Bluegrass region of central Kentucky to the governorship in 1991, losing in the primary by about 7 percentage points.

But Baesler immediately regrouped and went after Hopkins' seat, tuning up for the fall 1992 race by routing four opponents in the Democratic primary. In November, he outpolled Ellinger, a member of the Urban County Council, by more than 20 percentage points.

Unlike many successful candidates in 1992, Baesler did not run against Congress or against the perceived problems of the federal government. "I don't think my race had a thing to do with what was going on in Washington," he said.

He has pledged to maintain his focus on local education and employment issues even as he acclimates himself to Congress. "My heavy concentration for the first few months will be down there," he said.

Baesler already has discovered that Capitol Hill can be an inhospitable place for newcomers. He was rebuffed in a determined attempt to win a seat on the Energy and Commerce Committee or on the Public Works Committee, the latter of which accepted 15 other freshman Democrats as members.

Shortly after that rejection, Baesler told his hometown newspaper, the Lexington Herald-Leader, that his first experience in Congress had been "very educational — like sticking your hand in a fire is educational."

The blow was softened a bit when he subsequently won a seat on the Agriculture Committee and on its Subcommittee on Specialty Crops and Natural Resources, a perch from which he can look out for the district's important tobacco interests. He also will serve on Education and Labor and Veterans' Affairs.

Early in the 103rd, Baesler voted for both President's Clinton's budget and $16.3 billion stimulus package, but he was one of only 13 Democrats to vote against a rule supported by the president and Democratic leadership that prevented opponents from amending the package.

Baesler is viewed as well-positioned to hold the 6th for the Democrats if he pursues a career in Congress. But after his election, rumors began to circulate that the former mayor was only biding his time before making another run for statewide office.

The speculation was fueled in part by the new rules regarding gubernatorial succession, which Kentucky voters approved in a constitutional amendment in November 1992. While the current Democratic governor, Brereton Jones, can serve only one term, the next governor — to be elected in 1995 — will be able to succeed himself.

Baesler insists that he is content in Congress and has no plans for another run for the statehouse. "I think I might like it here for a while," he said.

Kentucky 6

North Central — Lexington; Frankfort

The 6th embodies the culture and the economic pursuits that most outsiders associate with the state of Kentucky. This district is the heart of the Bluegrass region, which regularly spawns Kentucky Derby champions and is host to considerable tobacco and liquor interests.

Lexington, the district's largest city, is known best as the hub of the country's horse-breeding industry. Hundreds of horse farms — ranging in size from just a few acres to more than 6,000 — cover the rich bluegrass pastureland within a 35-mile radius of the city.

Consolidated with Fayette County in 1974, Lexington experienced moderate growth in the 1970s and 1980s, spurred by the arrival of some clean, high-tech industry. By the early 1990s, the growth flattened out, in part because of some job losses associated with IBM's sale of its printer division to Lexmark.

But, as the market center of the state's burley tobacco industry and home to the University of Kentucky, the city has been able to avoid an economic free fall.

The areas outside Fayette County experienced more rapid population growth and industrial development in the 1980s, raising concerns about overdevelopment. Bourbon distilleries, tobacco and horse farms used to dominate the landscape, but they are being joined by new residential divisions and light industrial sprawl.

In Georgetown (Scott County), a Toyota Camry assembly plant that opened in 1988 is already expanding. Neighboring Woodford County is reaping some of the economic rewards of the plant; it ranks as the state's second-highest in per capita income.

Within commuting distance of Lexington, the northern portion of Madison County — the district's second-most populous — includes bedroom communities for Lexington workers. Eastern Kentucky University (16,500 students) is in the southern portion of the district in the tobacco market town of Richmond.

The influx of white-collar executives and engineers to Lexington, and the changing landscape in the farming counties to the south and west, have increased Republican competitiveness across the district.

The region's partisan roots are reflected in voter registration figures that favor the Democratic Party, but Republicans now regularly carry Fayette County. In 1992, George Bush carried almost all the counties south and west of Fayette. At the congressional level, though, every county in the 6th voted for longtime Lexington Mayor Baesler in the open-seat House race.

Bill Clinton was able to carry Franklin County on the strength of state government workers in Frankfort. Chosen as the state capital in a compromise between Lexington and Louisville, this Kentucky River Valley city has always stayed modest-sized and content to do the business of government.

East of Lexington, Democratic strength is found in the farming counties that remain largely untouched by Lexington sprawl.

1990 Population: 614,270. White 557,435 (91%), Black 49,921 (8%), Other 6,914 (1%). Hispanic origin 4,047 (1%). 18 and over 465,190 (76%), 62 and over 85,226 (14%). Median age: 32.

Committees

Agriculture (23rd of 28 Democrats)
Environment, Credit & Rural Development; Foreign Agriculture & Hunger; Specialty Crops & Natural Resources

Education & Labor (27th of 28 Democrats)
Human Resources

Veterans' Affairs (17th of 21 Democrats)
Hospitals & Health Care

Campaign Finance

	Receipts	Receipts from PACs	Expend-itures
1992			
Baesler (D)	$301,557	0	$273,727
Ellinger (R)	$70,095	$9,291 (13%)	$65,643

Key Votes

1993

Require parental notification of minors' abortions	N
Require unpaid family and medical leave	Y
Approve national "motor voter" registration bill	Y
Approve budget increasing taxes and reducing deficit	Y
Approve economic stimulus plan	Y

Elections

1992 General		
Scotty Baesler (D)	135,613	(61%)
Charles W. Ellinger (R)	87,816	(39%)
1992 Primary		
Scotty Baesler (D)	49,954	(82%)
Roy Tudor (D)	4,701	(8%)
J.T. Underwood (D)	2,627	(4%)
Harvey Carroll Jr. (D)	2,425	(4%)
Christopher Bush (D)	1,438	(2%)

District Vote for President

	1992	
D	101,762	(41%)
R	105,191	(43%)
I	39,655	(16%)

Louisiana

STATE DATA

Governor:
Edwin W. Edwards (D)
First elected: 1991 *
Length of term: 4 years
Term expires: 1/96
Salary: $73,440
Term limit: 2 terms
Phone: (504) 342-7015
Born: Aug. 7, 1927; Marksville, La.
Education: Louisiana State U., LL.B. 1949, J.D. 1974
Military Service: Navy Air Corps, 1945-46
Occupation: Lawyer
Family: Divorced; four children
Religion: Roman Catholic
Political Career: Crowley City Council, 1954-62; La. Senate, 1964-65; U.S. House, 1965-72; * governor, 1972-80; La. Supreme Court, 1980; * governor, 1984-88

Lt. Gov.: Melinda Schwegmann (D)
First elected: 1991
Length of term: 4 years
Term expires: 1/96
Salary: $63,372
Phone: (504) 342-7009

State election official: (504) 342-4971
Democratic headquarters: (504) 336-4155
Republican headquarters: (504) 383-7234

REDISTRICTING

Louisiana lost one seat in reapportionment, dropping from eight districts to seven. The legislature passed the map May 29, 1992; the governor signed it June 1. The Justice Department approved the map July 6.

STATE LEGISLATURE

Bicameral Legislature. Meets March-June yearly.

Senate: 39 members, 4-year terms
1992 breakdown: 33D, 6R; 38 men, 1 woman; 31 whites, 8 blacks
Salary: $16,800
Phone: (504) 342-2040

House of Representatives: 105 members, 4-year terms
1992 breakdown: 88D, 16R, 1I; 96 men, 9 women; 81 whites, 24 blacks
Salary: $16,800
Phone: (504) 342-7263

URBAN STATISTICS

City	Pop.
New Orleans Mayor Sidney Barthelemy, D	496,938
Baton Rouge Mayor Tom Edward McHugh, D	219,531
Shreveport Mayor Hazel Beard, R	198,525
Metairie Parish President Michael Yenni, D	149,428
Lafayette Mayor Kenneth Bowen, D	94,440

U.S. CONGRESS

Senate: 2 D, 0 R
House: 4 D, 3 R

TERM LIMITS

For Congress: No
For state offices: No

ELECTIONS

1992 Presidential Vote

Bill Clinton	45.6%
George Bush	41.0%
Ross Perot	11.8%

1988 Presidential Vote

George Bush	54%
Michael S. Dukakis	44%

1984 Presidential Vote

Ronald Reagan	61%
Walter F. Mondale	38%

POPULATION

1990 population		4,219,973
1980 population		4,205,900
Percent change		+<1%
Rank among states:		21
White		67%
Black		31%
Hispanic		2%
Asian or Pacific islander		1%
Urban		68%
Rural		32%
Born in state		79%
Foreign-born		2%
Under age 18	1,227,269	29%
Ages 18-64	2,523,713	60%
65 and older	468,991	11%
Median age		31

MISCELLANEOUS

Capital: Baton Rouge
Number of parishes: 64
Per capita income: $15,143 (1991)
Rank among states: 45
Total area: 47,752 sq. miles
Rank among states: 31

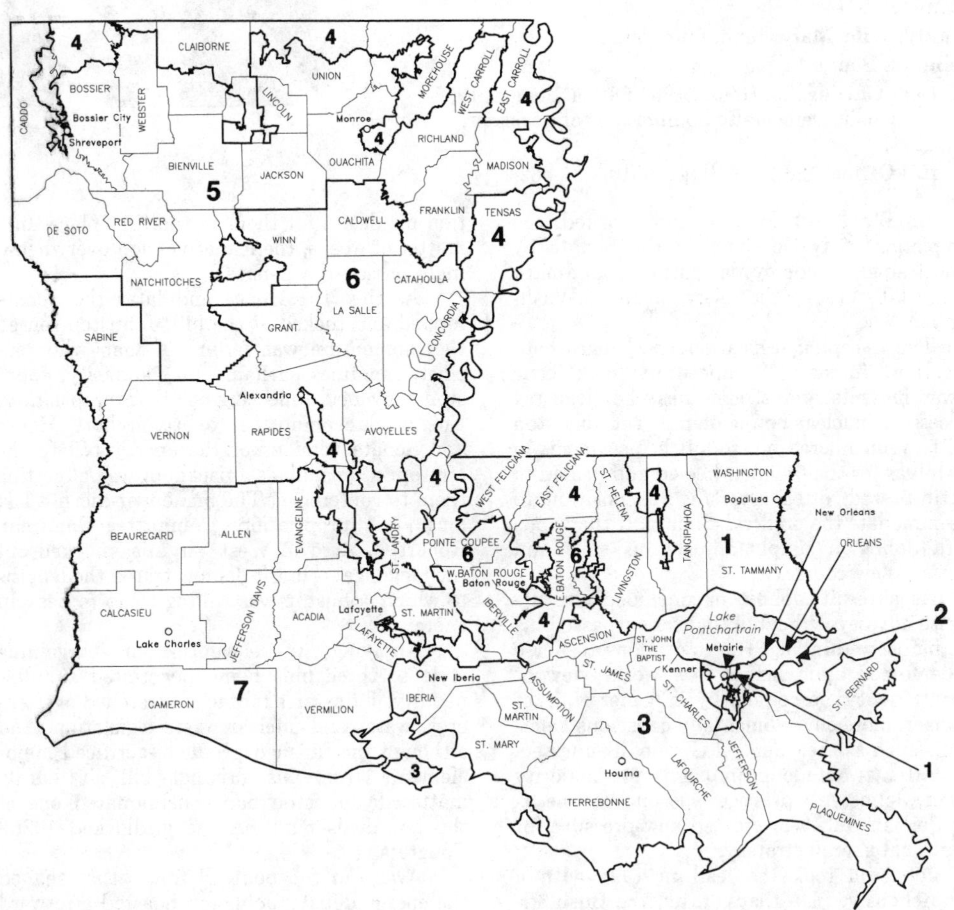
CADDO
BOSSIER
Bossier City
Shreveport
CLAIBORNE
WEBSTER
LINCOLN
UNION
MOREHOUSE
WEST CARROLL
EAST CARROLL
Monroe
RICHLAND
OUACHITA
MADISON
BIENVILLE
JACKSON
CALDWELL
FRANKLIN
TENSAS
DE SOTO
RED RIVER
WINN
NATCHITOCHES
CATAHOULA
LA SALLE
GRANT
SABINE
CONCORDIA
Alexandria
VERNON
RAPIDES
AVOYELLES
WEST FELICIANA
EAST FELICIANA
ST. HELENA
WASHINGTON
Bogalusa
BEAUREGARD
ALLEN
EVANGELINE
ST. LANDRY
POINTE COUPEE
W. BATON ROUGE
Baton Rouge
E. BATON ROUGE
LIVINGSTON
TANGIPAHOA
ST. TAMMANY
New Orleans
ORLEANS
CALCASIEU
Lake Charles
JEFFERSON DAVIS
ACADIA
Lafayette
ST. MARTIN
LAFAYETTE
IBERVILLE
ASCENSION
Lake Pontchartrain
Metairie
Kenner
ST. JOHN THE BAPTIST
ST. JAMES
ST. CHARLES
ST. BERNARD
CAMERON
VERMILION
New Iberia
IBERIA
ASSUMPTION
ST. MARTIN
ST. MARY
Houma
TERREBONNE
LAFOURCHE
JEFFERSON
PLAQUEMINES
1
2
3
4
5
6
7

J. Bennett Johnston (D)

Of Shreveport — Elected 1972; 4th Term

Born: June 10, 1932, Shreveport, La.
Education: Washington and Lee U., 1950-51; U.S. Military Academy, 1951-52; Washington and Lee U., 1952-53; Louisiana State U., LL.B. 1956.
Military Service: Army, 1956-59.
Occupation: Lawyer.
Family: Wife, Mary Gunn; four children.
Religion: Baptist.
Political Career: La. House, 1964-68; La. Senate, 1968-72; sought Democratic nomination for governor, 1971.
Capitol Office: 136 Hart Bldg. 20510; 224-5824.

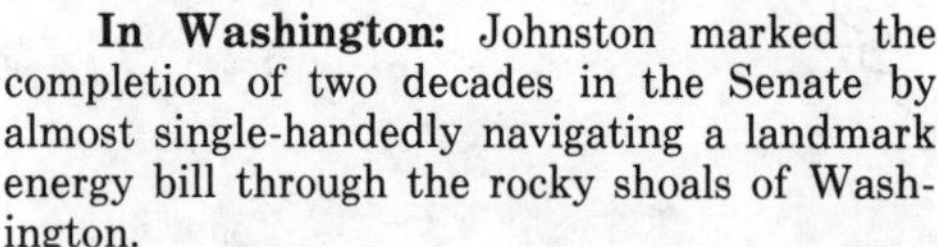

In Washington: Johnston marked the completion of two decades in the Senate by almost single-handedly navigating a landmark energy bill through the rocky shoals of Washington.

The sweeping legislation encourages conservation, increases competition in electric power markets and streamlines the licensing process for nuclear power plants. Yet Johnston will be remembered not so much for what is in the bill as for the way he wheeled and dealed to get it passed, often reversing his position to accommodate the political climate. If the winds shift, Johnston simply adjusts his sails and charts a new course.

As a result, Johnston concluded the 21-month odyssey with a bill that far surpassed his pro-industry thinking. His invitations to horse trade forced upon him a new world view of energy policy embodied by a generation of younger, more environmentally conscious Democrats such as then-Sen. Al Gore of Tennessee.

After two failed campaigns for majority leader, Johnston's prestige was on the line as the Persian Gulf War created new pressure for a national energy strategy.

Johnston took the lead in 1991 with a comprehensive plan that courted the Bush administration and Republican senators on his Energy and Natural Resources Committee.

But that approach, which included allowances to drill for oil in the Arctic National Wildlife Refuge, cost key Democratic votes. On substance, the environmentalist senators objected to the drilling proposal; on pure politics, others were miffed that Johnston steamrolled the bill through without consulting them. Forty-four senators — including nine fellow committee chairmen — blocked the bill from coming to the floor.

Enter Johnston the deal-maker.

Just as quickly as they were written, Johnston dropped the drilling provisions and higher gas mileage standards, prompting some to question his desire for them in the first place. In a matter of weeks, the leaner version overwhelmingly passed the Senate.

As first the House and later the Senate nipped and tucked at the bill, Johnston sensed the momentum was fading. A man who routinely redefines parliamentary audacity, Johnston convened a meeting of his Appropriations Energy Subcommittee to attach both House and Senate versions of the energy bill to the appropriations bill as a backdoor way of getting them to conference. The maneuver did not last long — Appropriations Committee Chairman Robert C. Byrd of West Virginia knocked out the language — but it demonstrated the lengths to which Johnston was willing to go to pass an energy bill.

Applying his eleventh-hour bargaining style to three bills being negotiated simultaneously, Johnston's tentacles stretched over energy, water and nuclear waste legislation. And although the finished product sacrificed major elements from his original bill, it hardly mattered; Johnston had consummated one of the few deals made in the gridlocked 102nd Congress.

Aware of the political forces that shaped the energy debate, Johnston boasted afterward about key provisions that initially were not top priorities of his. In a letter summarizing his achievements, he underscored "the very extensive environmental agenda" in the bill.

Some find Johnston's horse-trading unsavory, but he gladly acts the part. Waiting for other senators to bring amendments to the floor, he will open his arms and flash a big grin as he says: "We're open for business here."

For those unwilling to do business, Johnston has sharp elbows and no qualms about bruising his way past a foe. This method gets things done, but it does not facilitate formation of the kind of personal relationships that are paramount in leadership races.

In mid-1986, Johnston announced his challenge to then-Minority Leader Byrd, hoping to transform inchoate dissatisfaction with his leadership into an insurgency. But when the Democrats regained the Senate majority that November, Byrd was widely interviewed in post-election analysis as the presumed new majority leader, with nary a mention of his challenger. Days later, Johnston quit the race, saying he could not dissolve Byrd's "aura of electability."

Johnston's second try began late in 1987 when rumors flourished that Byrd would step down as majority leader to take over Appropriations.

A master of the poker-faced political bluff, Johnston brought that game to the intraparty election, working hard to create a perception that his success was assured. The job, however, went easily to George J. Mitchell of Maine, whose campaign for the post was as low-key as Johnston's was brash.

As those two failed efforts suggest, Johnston's wheeler-dealer style is increasingly out of step with the emerging political trends of the 1990s. With the environmental and energy agendas being set by a Democratic White House, Johnston faces an entirely different challenge from the days when he used his bargaining skills to craft pragmatic coalitions with the GOP.

Before the omnibus energy bill, one of Johnston's biggest legislative victories came in 1989 when Congress lifted price controls from natural gas. In contrast to previous years, when it was one of the most contentious issues on Capitol Hill, gas decontrol moved easily through the 101st Congress, as members from gas-producing and gas-consuming states alike agreed that controls kept very little gas below market prices and had thus become largely irrelevant to consumers.

Johnston introduced his bill in April, encountering opposition from a longtime gas-decontrol foe, Ohio Democrat Howard M. Metzenbaum. The committee, however, shrugged off amendments in May and voted overwhelmingly to approve Johnston's bill for floor action.

Metzenbaum continued to oppose the bill on the floor, issuing attacks on the Energy Committee and oil-and-gas state senators supporting the bill that drew an angry response from Johnston. "I would be severely and personally resentful of the remarks of my distinguished colleague from Ohio had I not heard this story before. It is the same old tired rhetoric," Johnston said. The Senate passed the measure easily in June.

Emboldened by Iraq's invasion of Kuwait in August 1990 — and the resulting worldwide embargo against Iraq that crimped oil supplies, raised gas prices and renewed concerns over the country's dependence on foreign fuel — Johnston was a prime mover behind a bill that expanded the nation's rainy-day supply of crude oil. The bill forced the administration to expand its plan to fill the Strategic Petroleum Reserve to 1 billion barrels, up from the existing goal of 750 million.

Arguing that the nation needed a bigger fuel cushion in case of another embargo, Johnston had pushed for a billion-barrel reserve for some time. The Louisiana Land and Exploration Co., a large oil and gas producer, wanted Congress to increase the 750 million-barrel cap so it could lease the government some of its extra salt domes for storage, a deal that could be worth millions of dollars a year.

Johnston also crafted compromise legislation in 1990 that withheld from timber-cutting more than 1 million additional acres of Alaska's Tongass National Forest.

Johnston's panel also has jurisdiction over the status of Puerto Rico, an issue the chairman has personally adopted. Legislation to give Puerto Ricans the right to determine their future relationship with the United States stalled at the end of the 101st Congress and was killed in committee during the 102nd.

Energy Appropriations is another important legislative showcase for Johnston, one where he boldly flexes his muscle. As usual, the panel's fiscal 1992 money bill was full of home-state projects for well-placed senators such as Johnston. The bill included $10 million for the Institute of Micromanufacturing at Louisiana Tech University and $6 million for the Biomedical Research Institute of Louisiana State University in Shreveport.

Johnston also snatched $1 million from wetlands study accounts to renovate a stadium in New Orleans.

If there is a Louisiana angle on a piece of legislation, Johnston will find it. Although he once seemed skeptical of the Texas-based superconducting super collider (SSC), Johnston is now a leading proponent of the expensive atom-smasher; two companies bidding to build the massive magnets for the SSC promised to set up factories in Louisiana. (In early 1991, General Dynamics was awarded a $240 million contract to build the magnets.)

From his Appropriations subcommittee chair, Johnston in July 1990 pushed through President George Bush's full 1991 request of $318 million for the SSC; a highly favorable committee report contained no mention of the projected $2 billion cost increase for the project. After the House voted to kill the project in 1992, Johnston restored its funding when the energy and water spending bill reached his subcommittee.

With President Clinton and others scouring for big-ticket budget savings, Johnston is likely to remain a crucial defender of the collider.

Divide and conquer is another well-known Johnston legislative device. He employed this tactic in 1987, when he almost single-handedly rammed a nuclear-waste plan through Congress. Johnston's initial plan was to abandon a search for an Eastern disposal site and put all waste in one of three Western states. He assembled a Senate majority by uniting states with one thing in common: None wanted to host the nation's permanent radioactive-waste dump.

In tense negotiations on a variety of details, Johnston engineered a plan to put all the waste in Nevada. Angry Nevadans cried foul, but the plan passed, and Johnston calmly noted, "If I were a Nevadan living in the real world, I would be happy with this bill. I would bet that in a very few years, Nevada will deem this one of their most treasured industries."

In crafting the 1992 energy bill, Johnston went one step further. Under threats of a filibuster by Nevada's senators, he brazenly added language that would make it easier for the government to open the dump. "We can't let one man stop the whole energy bill," he declared.

If Johnston is easy to read on energy matters — protecting oil and gas industries at all costs — he is far from predictable on the myriad of other issues facing the Senate. And for Johnston, virtually every vote is up for grabs.

One of just 10 Senate Democrats to authorize the use of force in the Persian Gulf, Johnston nevertheless passed on entreaties from Mitchell to take a tough stance on free trade with China after the Tiananmen Square protests.

He has switched votes on funding the space station *Freedom* and on proposals to revamp campaign finance laws. In 1992, only one Senate Democrat — Alabama's Richard C. Shelby — voted more frequently with Bush.

Johnston dropped out of active participation on the Budget Committee in 1988 when it recommended less spending for energy programs than he wanted. He even publicly questioned the relevance of the committee in 1991 during the panel's consideration of the budget resolution, saying it made "absolutely no difference" what the committee did.

Johnston's role in 1987 in leading the opposition to archconservative Supreme Court nominee Robert H. Bork surprised those who remembered him as a young lawyer defending segregation. As late as 1981, when a controversy raged over busing to achieve integration in Baton Rouge schools, he took the lead on a Senate proposal to bar the courts from ordering busing except in limited cases. After a protracted floor struggle, he got the measure through the Senate, though the House balked.

At Home: Another 5,000 votes would have made Johnston governor of Louisiana in 1972. Rather than slowing him down, however, Johnston's near-miss in the Democratic runoff against Edwin W. Edwards brought him the public attention he needed for a successful Senate campaign a few months later.

Still, it took an unexpected turn of events to bring Johnston to Washington. After losing the governor's race, he decided on a primary challenge to veteran Sen. Allen J. Ellender, who despite his age (81) was a man of remarkable vigor; he also was chairman of the Appropriations Committee and a master at providing federal money for Louisiana. But three weeks before the primary, Ellender died of a heart attack. Johnston had a clear path to election.

Before his 1971 campaign for governor, Johnston had been just a moderately visible conservative state legislator from northern Louisiana and a lawyer practicing with his father in Shreveport. In the Legislature, his major issue was completion of an interstate highway linking his home city with New Orleans.

Campaigning against each other in the Democratic runoff, Johnston and Edwards differed politically, regionally and personally. Edwards, a Catholic from Cajun southern Louisiana, had moderate social views and a flamboyant manner. Johnston called for racial moderation, but was more aloof in style, and, as a Baptist from the Protestant north, was universally perceived as being to Edwards' right.

There was little anyone could do to stop Johnston in 1972 once Ellender died. Former Gov. John J. McKeithen tried a last-minute move to reopen filing for the August primary, but the state Democratic committee turned him down. Johnston easily won nomination.

In the fall, McKeithen ran as an independent, bidding for the votes of blacks and low-income whites by characterizing Johnston as the candidate of the wealthy. The former governor had a problem, however, in the well-publicized indictments of key members of his administration. McKeithen himself was never accused of wrongdoing, but Johnston campaigned on the need for a return to honest government.

The GOP nominee was Ben C. Toledano, who had run unsuccessfully for mayor of New Orleans in 1970. He sought to link Johnston to Democratic presidential nominee George McGovern, but Johnston sloughed off that charge and won 55 percent of the vote.

By 1978, Johnston had some problems at home. He had a reputation among some local Democrats as being aloof and Washington-oriented, and among others as insufficiently conservative. He drew a serious challenge from Democratic state Rep. Louis "Woody" Jenkins, who had worked for George C. Wallace in national politics.

Jenkins labeled the senator a devotee of high taxes and spending, and seemed to be making inroads. But after a slow start, Johnston put on an aggressive drive for renomination. He had taken away Jenkins' best issue earlier in the year by voting against ratification of the Panama Canal treaties. Johnston won 59 percent of the primary vote, assuring him reelection under Louisiana law.

Johnston had clear sailing in 1984, yet in

1990 there were renewed complaints that Johnston had "Potomac fever." But Republicans, after failing to draft a top-drawer candidate, ended up scrambling just to avoid national embarrassment. The sanctioned GOP candidate, little-known state Sen. Ben Bagert, could not raise the money needed to run a credible campaign. Pressured by some Republicans, Bagert dropped out of the race just days before the state's open primary, a move aimed at averting a November runoff between Johnston and rogue GOP candidate David Duke.

Duke, a state representative, former Ku Klux Klan leader and former Nazi sympathizer, ran stronger than expected in a heavy primary turnout, gaining 44 percent against Johnston. Many Republicans — including eight GOP senators — campaigned for Johnston, fearing a Duke upset.

Before Bagert withdrew, Johnston had stayed above the fray, allowing former boxer Bagert to bloody Duke on the hustings. But as the primary approached, Johnston reversed his strategy, stumping the parishes in the populist tradition of the state while running ads showing Duke at cross-burnings and giving white power salutes.

Despite Johnston's win, Democrats and traditional Republicans were clearly shaken by Duke's strong showing, which presaged his 1991 gubernatorial bid (in which he made the runoff) and his brief 1992 run for the Republican presidential nomination.

Committees

Energy & Natural Resources (Chairman)

Appropriations (4th of 16 Democrats)
Energy & Water Development (chairman); Agriculture, Rural Development & Related Agencies; Defense; Interior; VA, HUD & Independent Agencies

Budget (3rd of 12 Democrats)

Select Intelligence (9th of 9 Democrats)

Special Aging (4th of 11 Democrats)

Elections

1990 Primary †

J. Bennett Johnston (D)	752,902	(54%)
David Duke (R)	607,391	(44%)
Nick Joseph Accardo (D)	21,485	(2%)
Larry Crowe (D)	14,335	(1%)

† In Louisiana the primary is open to candidates of all parties. If a candidate wins 50 percent or more of the vote in the primary, no general election is held.

Previous Winning Percentages: **1984** (86%) **1978** (59%) **1972** (55%)

Campaign Finance

	Receipts	Receipts from PACs		Expend-itures
1990				
Johnston (D)	$4,167,111	$1,416,331	(34%)	$4,989,521
Duke (R)	$2,670,311	0		$2,615,267

Key Votes

1993	
Require unpaid family and medical leave	Y
Approve national "motor voter" registration bill	Y
Approve budget increasing taxes and reducing deficit	Y
Support president's right to lift military gay ban	Y
1992	
Approve school-choice pilot program	N
Allow shifting funds from defense to domestic programs	Y
Oppose deeper cuts in spending for SDI	N
1991	
Approve waiting period for handgun purchases	N
Raise senators' pay and ban honoraria	Y
Authorize use of force in Persian Gulf	Y
Confirm Clarence Thomas to Supreme Court	Y

Voting Studies

	Presidential Support		Party Unity		Conservative Coalition	
Year	S	O	S	O	S	O
1992	52	45	66	33	79	21
1991	56	43	65	34	80	18
1990	53	41	65	29	84	11
1989	70	30	71	29	63	37
1988	63	35	77	20	86	11
1987	44	54	82	17	88	13
1986	58	42	61	37	67	30
1985	45	53	63	33	68	27
1984	61	30	51	44	83	11
1983	55	44	54	40	82	5
1982	61	37	47	48	93	6
1981	68	26	49	45	93	3

Interest Group Ratings

Year	ADA	AFL-CIO	CCUS	ACU
1992	70	75	20	23
1991	40	75	40	52
1990	39	86	33	38
1989	30	70	63	32
1988	55	86	50	36
1987	70	90	33	20
1986	50	67	44	35
1985	60	80	28	45
1984	55	56	47	59
1983	20	43	67	56
1982	35	50	67	63
1981	25	35	82	27

John B. Breaux (D)

Of Crowley — Elected 1986; 2nd Term

Born: March 1, 1944, Crowley, La.
Education: U. of Southwestern Louisiana, B.A. 1964; Louisiana State U., J.D. 1967.
Occupation: Lawyer.
Family: Wife, Lois Daigle; four children.
Religion: Roman Catholic.
Political Career: U.S. House, 1972-87.
Capitol Office: 516 Hart Bldg. 20510; 224-4623.

In Washington: Breaux, whose cloakroom reputation is that of a serious politician with a hawk's eyes for trouble as well as opportunity, found himself early in the 103rd Congress trying with limited success to show President Clinton where his economic plan had run off the track.

He was not the only right-leaning Southern Democrat to warn the new president that his program lacked the necessary finesse to survive the rigors of Senate scrutiny. But Breaux did not throw his objections right in Clinton's face — unlike Alabama's Richard C. Shelby, who strayed so far off the reservation that he drew heavy fire from the White House, or even Oklahoma's David L. Boren, who seemed to dance right up to the edge of the cliff.

Like both Boren and Shelby, Breaux criticized Clinton's proposed $16.3 billion stimulus bill and his proposed energy tax; both needed refinements, he said.

But unlike Shelby, Breaux cast no early votes against Clinton, ultimately supporting Clinton's failed effort to bring the stimulus package to a vote.

And unlike Boren, Breaux did not place himself squarely in the path of the energy tax. Instead, Breaux — who along with Boren is a member of the Finance Committee — tried to suggest ways by which Clinton could steer the energy tax through the Senate with a few changes that he said would make it more palatable.

"We have a mission as a result of this election, and that is to show that we are different from past Democratic administrations," Breaux said, in explaining why he — a longtime friend and ally of Clinton's — was making waves for the president.

Breaux is the sort who simply cannot get enough of politics, whether fundraising, strategizing or legislating. True to the Cajun tradition — *"laissez les bons temps roulez"* — he makes it look like great fun.

He has as much talent as any of his colleagues with loftier ambitions, and a record that puts him just inside the Democratic Party mainstream. But his and his state's political image would be a tough sell to Democrats nationally: Breaux is a backer of the oil industry, an unapologetic protégé of controversial Gov. Edwin W. Edwards, and a roguish charmer in his own right.

So, Breaux has set his sights on gaining power within the chamber, and has climbed the ladder rapidly in his brief time as a senator.

Because of the accrued seniority from his lengthy House experience, Breaux had a privilege in his first term: immediately chairing two subcommittees. Then late in 1988, newly elected Majority Leader George J. Mitchell of Maine picked Breaux for the position that Mitchell himself had parlayed into his leadership victory: chairman of the fundraising Democratic Senatorial Campaign Committee (DSCC).

During the 101st Congress, Breaux was awarded his coveted seat on the Finance Committee, the same panel where former Louisiana Democrat Russell B. Long wielded great institutional power as chairman for 14 years. In the 103rd, Breaux became chairman of the Finance Subcommittee on Social Security and Family Policy, a position of some import in the expected debate over reforming welfare policy that Clinton has promised to initiate.

Also in the 103rd, Breaux was given a spot on the leadership team as chief deputy whip.

Breaux was chosen to head the DSCC even though he managed the majority leader campaign for Mitchell's rival, home-state colleague J. Bennett Johnston. The choice appeared to be an olive branch from Mitchell, but the fact was, no one was better for the job than Breaux.

He could look back with satisfaction when he completed his DSCC term after the 1990 elections. While Republicans had spoken of using 1990 as a springboard for retaking Senate control in 1992 — Breaux said in 1989 "my goal is to hold the line" — the Democrats actually increased their majority by one seat, with Breaux raising record amounts of money for his party's candidates.

As one who simply loves the legislative game for its own sake, Breaux does not bring ideology or great policy objectives to the table. However, like other moderate-to-conservative Southerners, he has called for the Democratic

Party to move rightward. Breaux followed Clinton as chairman of the Democratic Leadership Council, a group founded with a reorientation of the party as its chief aim.

In 1989, Breaux opposed the selection of a black, Ronald H. Brown, as national party chairman, frankly arguing that Democrats needed to court white males who had left the party. Breaux's objections sparked some controversy, given his status as a party campaign spokesman and the fact that he owed his 1986 election in part to overwhelming black support.

Later, in 1993, when Clinton picked Brown to be secretary of Commerce, Breaux welcomed the nomination: "I happen to think that he is the right person for the right job at the right time. There's a little history in that, but I think the president-elect has made a great choice."

Breaux is unabashed about courting business. His shrewd pragmatism is almost shameless, although endearingly so, as illustrated by his now-legendary remark in 1981 explaining that he would support President Ronald Reagan's proposed social spending cuts in return for concessions on natural gas policy and sugar subsidies. Breaux quipped that while his vote could not be bought, "it can be rented."

Above all, Breaux is an advocate for Louisiana's interests, especially energy and commercial fishing. On Commerce, Science and Transportation, he chairs the Merchant Marine panel. On Environment and Public Works, he headed the Nuclear Regulation Subcommittee before leaving the committee to join Finance.

In 1990, he used his position to secure funding to help Louisiana address its coastal erosion problems, a concern not only of environmentalists, but also of business. Late in the 101st Congress, during consideration of the deficit-reduction package, Breaux persuaded his colleagues on Finance to include in the measure a $50 million "wetlands preservation" trust fund, with about $35 million going to Louisiana.

Earlier, he had proposed a bill to restore eroding wetlands — like his state's shrimp-rich coast — by using a share of federal oil-leasing revenues. To protect Louisiana shrimpers further, Breaux joined with Johnston in 1989 to gain approval of a measure to bar shrimp imports from any country that does not take actions to protect endangered sea turtles. With American shrimpers subject to turtle-protection regulations, Breaux and Johnston said, foreign imports had an unfair advantage. The senators successfully attached the provision to a spending measure approved by Congress in October.

Despite a dedication to nuclear power and the petrochemical industry, Breaux also has to balance the safety and environmental concerns of Louisianans. When Environment Committee members offered their first rewrite of the Clean Air Act in April 1989, Breaux was considered a pivotal backer. "Those of us in Louisiana want not only jobs, we want to be able to breathe the air and breathe it safely," he said. While his state is home to many oil refineries and chemical manufacturers affected by the bill, it is also hard-hit by air-toxics emissions and has a high incidence of health problems suspected to be caused by those emissions.

During committee debate on strengthening the act, Breaux generally represented industry viewpoints, but early in 1989 he cosponsored legislation against toxic emissions. When administration and congressional representatives bogged down in early 1990 over a number of the bill's provisions, Breaux participated in three weeks of back-room negotiations that produced a compromise aimed at satisfying environmentalists without forfeiting administration support. Breaux fought on the floor to prevent any amendments designed to tighten controls on toxic air pollution even further, fearing such regulations would unduly burden industry and would lead the administration to oppose the measure.

In 1991, he persuaded his Commerce Committee colleagues to amend a pipeline safety bill to require that abandoned underwater pipelines be subject to federal safety regulations.

Breaux also played a role in oil-spill liability legislation during the 101st Congress. When the Senate considered an amendment to raise significantly the liability limits approved by the Environment Committee, an angry Breaux argued that the higher insurance costs mandated by higher liability limits would bring higher oil prices. In part to accommodate him, the limits were scaled back and the legislation was enacted in 1990.

At Home: Breaux learned his trade from one of Louisiana's masters — Edwards, the state's four-term governor and a former U.S. representative. Breaux was Edwards' junior law partner and served for four years as one of his top congressional aides.

When Edwards first won the governorship in February 1972, he pushed for Breaux to be his successor in the House. With Edwards' organization, Breaux easily paced the field of six Democratic primary candidates, then won the September runoff with 55 percent of the vote over TV newscaster Gary Tyler, the same man Edwards had defeated to win his first congressional term seven years earlier.

Breaux does not, however, owe his ascent to the Senate to Edwards' influence. If anything, his one-time mentor made his 1986 bid to replace retiring Democrat Long more difficult. During Edwards' third term, Louisiana's oil industry had foundered, and by the time of the 1986 Senate contest the state's economy was reeling. Many voters were in a mood to blame the Democrats. Moreover, Edwards' image had suffered during two trials on corruption charges, even though he was eventually acquitted.

Those circumstances gave the GOP one of its best openings in years. Early in 1986, GOP Rep. W. Henson Moore began airing ads designed to exploit voters' restlessness. Democrats, Moore charged, had squandered the state's resources and prostituted the political system to their own advantage. Republicans, Moore argued, were the party of reform. He quickly took the lead.

If Moore had continued on the same tack, he might have won. But as the nonpartisan September primary approached, he pushed to win more than 50 percent of the vote and avoid a runoff. He shifted his emphasis, beginning a wave of ads and mailings that attacked Breaux directly. "The politician's politician, always putting himself first," one mailer called the Democrat. At the same time, the national GOP mounted a program to purge ineligible voters in black precincts.

None of those tactics sat well with Louisiana's basically Democratic electorate. Moore seemed mean-spirited, especially in contrast with Breaux's Cajun charm. And the "ballot security" program infuriated black voters — a boost for Breaux, since many blacks had considered him too conservative.

The primary was a turning point. Moore came in first, but he did not run as strongly as many had expected. Over the next month, Breaux worked to take the high ground Moore had abandoned, arguing that the state's problems stemmed not from the state government, but from a GOP administration that had followed misguided trade and farm policies. Moore's first allegiance, he charged, was to his party and to President Reagan, not to Louisiana. Moore tried to recoup, but Breaux carried 42 of 64 parishes.

Six years later, the state GOP was in disarray, coming off a disastrous election year in 1991 that was marked by the defeat of both its endorsed gubernatorial candidate (Rep. Clyde C. Holloway) and the incumbent governor, Democrat-turned-Republican Buddy Roemer, and the embarrassment of having Republican David Duke, a former Ku Klux Klan leader and former Nazi sympathizer, make the gubernatorial runoff against Edwards.

With Breaux's popularity at seemingly unassailable heights, no prominent Republican stepped forward. Breaux won re-election in the five-way primary with 73 percent.

Committees

Chief Deputy Whip

Commerce, Science & Transportation (7th of 11 Democrats)
Merchant Marine (chairman); Communications; National Ocean Policy Study; Surface Transportation

Finance (10th of 11 Democrats)
Social Security & Family Policy (chairman); Energy & Agricultural Taxation; International Trade

Special Aging (5th of 11 Democrats)

Elections

1992 Primary †		
John B. Breaux (D)	616,021	(73%)
Jon Khachaturian (I)	74,785	(9%)
Lyle Stockstill (R)	69,986	(8%)
Nick Joseph Accardo (D)	45,839	(5%)
Fred Clegg Strong (R)	36,406	(4%)

† In Louisiana the primary is open to candidates of all parties. If a candidate wins 50 percent or more of the vote in the primary, no general election is held.

Previous Winning Percentages: **1986** (53%) **1984 *** (86%) **1982 *** (79%) **1980 *** (100%) **1978 *** (60%) **1976 *** (83%) **1974 *** (89%) **1972 †** (100%)

** House elections.*

† Special House election.

Campaign Finance

	Receipts	Receipts from PACs	Expenditures
1992			
Breaux (D)	$2,449,803	$1,318,635 (54%)	$1,446,199

Key Votes

1993	
Require unpaid family and medical leave	Y
Approve national "motor voter" registration bill	Y
Approve budget increasing taxes and reducing deficit	Y
Support president's right to lift military gay ban	Y
1992	
Approve school-choice pilot program	Y
Allow shifting funds from defense to domestic programs	Y
Oppose deeper cuts in spending for SDI	N
1991	
Approve waiting period for handgun purchases	N
Raise senators' pay and ban honoraria	Y
Authorize use of force in Persian Gulf	Y
Confirm Clarence Thomas to Supreme Court	Y

Voting Studies

	Presidential Support		Party Unity		Conservative Coalition	
Year	**S**	**O**	**S**	**O**	**S**	**O**
1992	42	58	68	29	76	21
1991	65	33	59	37	83	13
1990	57	41	68	31	95	5
1989	71	28	62	38	87	13
1988	61	36	73	25	92	5
1987	42	58	84	15	81	19
House Service:						
1986	21	28	24	11	32	0
1985	49	44	53	36	89	5
1984	50	38	49	36	80	8
1983	52	40	41	50	85	9
1982	58	27	44	42	64	14
1981	61	24	35	42	63	7

Interest Group Ratings

Year	**ADA**	**AFL-CIO**	**CCUS**	**ACU**
1992	60	67	10	30
1991	30	67	40	57
1990	33	78	33	39
1989	40	100	50	30
1988	50	85	43	44
1987	70	90	28	19
House Service:				
1986	30	100	25	63
1985	35	53	62	62
1984	15	25	40	52
1983	20	31	65	70
1982	15	22	67	71
1981	0	20	84	69

1 Robert L. Livingston (R)

Of Metairie — Elected 1977; 8th Full Term

Born: April 30, 1943, Colorado Springs, Colo.
Education: Tulane U., B.A. 1967, J.D. 1968.
Military Service: Navy, 1961-63; Naval Reserve, 1963-67.
Occupation: Lawyer.
Family: Wife, Bonnie Robichaux; four children.
Religion: Episcopalian.
Political Career: GOP nominee for U.S. House, 1976; GOP candidate for governor, 1987.
Capitol Office: 2368 Rayburn Bldg. 20515; 225-3015.

In Washington: Life as a senior member of the Appropriations Committee is an existence fraught with dilemmas for a conservative Republican like Livingston. But he has achieved a certain peace with himself on the question of what constitutes justified spending.

In general, "I do all in my power to see to it and vote to see to it that the bills stay within . . . the budget requirements set forth by the president," he said in a 1991 interview with Congressional Quarterly. ". . . But once you get to the point that money is going to be spent, then it seems to me that I have the discretion and the responsibility to see to it that it is spent properly. And I have to tell you that sometimes that means that it might be more properly spent in my district than in somebody else's, but I don't think I take that to excess."

Livingston's ideology and legislative temperament give him much in common with the younger generation of House GOP confrontationalists, led by party Whip Newt Gingrich of Georgia. But Livingston came to Congress in 1977, a bit before the New Wave-conservative Republicans hit Washington in 1979, and, in greater numbers, in 1981. Livingston at times seems to have a foot in the "Old Bull" camp of veteran Republicans, who are more accommodating in their legislative dealings with Democrats benefiting them, and were more loyal to the Bush White House line.

When President Bush and Minority Leader Robert H. Michel pleaded with conservatives to stick with the 1990 budget summit agreement despite its tax increases, Livingston was with them. After a White House meeting, he said, "For us Republicans, we owe it to our president to listen to his fears." He supported the agreement on the House floor, where Gingrich was busily — and successfully — mobilizing his GOP allies to defeat it.

When National Republican Congressional Committee Chairman Guy Vander Jagt lost in his 1992 primary, Livingston initially expressed interest in running for the NRCC chair as a compromise candidate, but he chose not to.

On Appropriations in the 1980s, Livingston was a leading supporter of the Strategic Defense Initiative and of military aid to Central America. During the Reagan-era battles over contra aid, Livingston seemed to view each vote on the issue as a test of patriotism. Democrats usually failed the test by advancing what he saw as a policy of appeasement. Beginning in the 103rd Congress, Livingston takes over as ranking Republican on the Foreign Operations Subcommittee, chaired by an equally combative Democrat, David R. Obey of Wisconsin.

When not battling liberals on matters of foreign policy, Livingston spends his time looking for ways to bring defense dollars home. He also works to protect the state's offshore oil drilling industry.

Being on Appropriations sometimes means confronting pork busters with whom a conservative such as Livingston would normally ally. In October 1991, he was the target of Dan Burton, a conservative Indiana Republican who was trying to strip from the Interior appropriations conference report an amendment earmarking $1 million to refurbish a sports stadium in New Orleans. Livingston defended the money, saying the stadium would be used for upcoming Olympic trials. With the help of his fellow appropriators and the House's Democratic majority, Livingston prevailed on a 243-164 vote.

"Everybody's got his vision of pork, but very, very rarely does pork even remotely exist in one's own district," Livingston said. "It's always in the 434 other districts. So, Burton did focus on [the stadium], and I didn't think that he was right on that one . . . and the floor vote ruled in my favor."

On the House Administration Committee, which Livingston joined in the 102nd Congress, he waves the GOP flag on issues such as public financing of campaigns, which he stoutly opposes. He was a vocal opponent in the 102nd and 103rd Congresses of the so-called motor-voter bill, which would require states to allow citizens to register to vote when they apply for or renew a driver's license.

Louisiana 1

Southeast — Metairie; Kenner

The 1st is conservative territory dominated by the mostly white suburban communities that ring New Orleans. The district starts in New Orleans' upper-class northwest corner, takes in the city's southwestern suburbs in east Jefferson Parish and then runs north to include the northeastern corner of southern Louisiana.

The east bank of Jefferson Parish anchors the district. The area is made up of affluent New Orleans suburbs such as Metairie, the base of the state legislative seat held until 1992 by David Duke, the former Ku Klux Klansman-turned-GOP-conservative who waged high-profile Senate and gubernatorial campaigns. Nearly half the district resides in east Jefferson; the area is packed with white-collar conservatives, many of whom sleep in the affluent suburbs dotting the shore of Lake Pontchartrain and work in New Orleans.

Historically, conservative candidates have done well in the 1st. District voters gave Duke 56 percent of the vote in his 1990 Senate primary and George Bush received 56 percent in 1992. Redistricting for the 1990s pushed the 1st further to the right, as cartographers struggled to carve a second black-majority district. The mapmakers' effort left the 1st with the smallest black population in any district in the state, 10 percent. Blacks constitute 31 percent of the statewide populace.

From east Jefferson the 1st skips across Lake Pontchartrain to take in most or all of four parishes north of New Orleans: St. Tammany, Washington, Tangipahoa and Livingston. The richest parish in the state, St. Tammany is home to nearly a quarter of the 1st's voters. Once an isolated vacation area for residents escaping the heat and humidity of New Orleans, St. Tammany has been the fastest-growing parish in the state in the last two decades. In the 1970s its population grew nearly 70 percent; in the 1980s it grew more than 30 percent. Many of the newcomers are transplants from the East and Midwest who have maintained GOP voting habits.

To the west of St. Tammany lies the former strawberry capital of the world, Tangipahoa Parish. It is now home to many New Orleans and Baton Rouge commuters, but Tangipahoa farms still produce great amounts of strawberries and bell peppers. The parish economy has diversified and is sustained by Southeastern Louisiana University (11,400 students) and distribution centers for Winn-Dixie and Superfine supermarkets. A General Dynamics plant chosen to build magnets for the federal superconducting super collider project is expected to bring more than 1,000 new jobs to the parish.

Redistricting bolstered the conservative nature of the 1st by adding rural Washington Parish to the district's northeastern corner. Voters there in 1968 gave George Wallace more than 70 percent of the presidential vote, and they supported Duke in his 1990 campaign for senator and 1991 run for governor. Predominantly a farming community that grows watermelons and breeds chickens, Washington Parish bears a striking resemblance to the Mississippi counties it borders.

1990 Population: 602,859. White 528,079 (88%), Black 60,895 (10%), Other 13,885 (2%). Hispanic origin 24,562 (4%). 18 and over 444,144 (74%), 62 and over 87,961 (15%). Median age: 33.

At Home: The 1st District did not come close to electing a Republican to the House for a century after Reconstruction, but now that it has one, it seems quite satisfied. Livingston has had no difficulty holding the seat he won in a 1977 special election.

But Livingston has shown some restlessness in Congress. Late in 1986 he told the Baton Rouge tabloid Gris Gris, "I've been here 10 years and I'm 43 years old. In all likelihood, in 10 years I'll be 53 years old and still broke and the only thing I can say then is that I've been here 20 years."

That led in part to his decision to run for governor in 1987. Livingston's visibility among Republicans in the New Orleans area put him in a strong position to finish near the top of a field of five major candidates, which included colorful and scandal-tainted Democratic Gov. Edwin W. Edwards, and Democratic Reps. W. J. "Billy" Tauzin and Buddy Roemer.

But Roemer, the eventual winner, was a dynamic candidate who successfully appealed to many conservatives who might have voted Republican. Meanwhile, Livingston proved to be a somewhat plodding candidate; during one televised debate he lost his train of thought and fell silent during a statement on education. Livingston finished third, behind Roemer and Edwards. Roemer won the governorship, and in 1991 switched to the GOP.

A prosperous New Orleans lawyer, former assistant U.S. attorney and veteran party worker, Livingston made his first bid for Congress in 1976, when Democrat F. Edward Hebert retired. He lost narrowly to a labor-backed

Democrat, state Rep. Richard A. Tonry.

Livingston did not have to wait long, however, for a second try. Tonry's 1976 primary opponent succeeded in pressing a vote-fraud case against him, and Tonry resigned from the House in May 1977. He sought vindication in a second Democratic primary that June, but lost to state Rep. Ron Faucheux. Tonry later pleaded guilty to violations of federal campaign finance law and went to prison.

Livingston was ready to run as soon as Tonry resigned. He mounted a well-financed campaign against Faucheux that drew significant blue-collar support as well as backing from more traditional GOP voters in white-collar areas. Spending more than $500,000, Livingston launched an ad blitz that showed him in his earlier job as a welder and as a devoted family man (in contrast to Faucheux, a young bachelor). With organized labor refusing to support Faucheux, Livingston won easily, and he has met no formidable Democratic challenger since.

The only threat to his House career was posed in 1981 by the Democratic Legislature, which passed a redistricting bill that would have forced Livingston to run in a new district heavily weighted with blue-collar sections of Jefferson Parish. When GOP Gov. David C. Treen threatened a veto, the Legislature backed off.

Court-ordered redistricting in 1983 further strengthened Livingston's position, when the Legislature shifted most of New Orleans out of the 1st in exchange for the "east bank" of Jefferson Parish, including its upscale neighborhoods.

Redistricting in 1992 did not harm Livingston, even though his nemesis, Edwards, was now back in office, and some Democrats were urging mapmakers to combine the districts of Livingston and GOP Rep. Richard H. Baker. But Livingston warned that if that happened, he would run against Tauzin in the 3rd District. Edwards did not warm to the proposal, either. The 1st District emerged largely undisturbed.

Committees

Appropriations (5th of 23 Republicans)
Foreign Operations, Export Financing & Related Programs (ranking); Defense

House Administration (4th of 7 Republicans)
Elections (ranking); Personnel & Police

Elections

1992 Primary †		
Robert L. Livingston (R)	83,685	(73%)
Anne Thompson (R)	11,620	(10%)
Vincent J. Bruno (R)	7,847	(7%)
Richie Martin (R)	4,789	(4%)
Jules W. Hillery (I)	4,442	(4%)
Greg V. Reinhard (I)	2,641	(2%)
1990 Primary †		
Robert L. Livingston (R)	132,855	(84%)
Vincent J. Bruno (R)	25,494	(16%)

† In Louisiana the primary is open to candidates of all parties. If a candidate wins 50 percent or more of the vote in the primary, no general election is held.

Previous Winning Percentages: **1988** (78%) **1986** (100%) **1984** (88%) **1982** (86%) **1980** (88%) **1978** (86%) **1977 *** (51%)

** Special election.*

District Vote for President

1992
D 86,886 (31%)
R 155,411 (56%)
I 34,613 (12%)

Campaign Finance

	Receipts	Receipts from PACs	Expend-itures
1992			
Livingston (R)	$337,316	$133,247 (40%)	$321,487
1990			
Livingston (R)	$279,603	$140,878 (50%)	$108,207

Key Votes

1993	
Require parental notification of minors' abortions	Y
Require unpaid family and medical leave	N
Approve national "motor voter" registration bill	N
Approve budget increasing taxes and reducing deficit	N
Approve economic stimulus plan	N
1992	
Approve balanced-budget constitutional amendment	Y
Close down space station program	N
Approve U.S. aid for former Soviet Union	Y
Allow shifting funds from defense to domestic programs	N
1991	
Extend unemployment benefits using deficit financing	N
Approve waiting period for handgun purchases	N
Authorize use of force in Persian Gulf	Y

Voting Studies

	Presidential Support		Party Unity		Conservative Coalition	
Year	**S**	**O**	**S**	**O**	**S**	**O**
1992	72	11	66	17	73	6
1991	86	14	77	20	100	0
1990	75	23	71	23	87	7
1989	79	21	68	29	98	2
1988	63	26	78	11	95	3
1987	43	22	41	16	70	2
1986	76	19	71	21	92	6
1985	74	24	81	15	96	4
1984	75	24	86	12	95	5
1983	77	18	76	17	85	12
1982	79	14	76	20	84	11
1981	76	21	71	20	76	17

Interest Group Ratings

Year	ADA	AFL-CIO	CCUS	ACU
1992	10	30	83	95
1991	0	8	100	90
1990	6	8	79	83
1989	5	17	90	93
1988	5	8	100	100
1987	0	7	78	73
1986	0	21	78	82
1985	0	12	86	86
1984	5	15	81	96
1983	5	6	95	90
1982	5	5	82	80
1981	20	27	94	71

2 William J. Jefferson (D)

Of New Orleans — Elected 1990; 2nd Term

Born: March 14, 1947, Lake Providence, La.
Education: Southern U. and A&M College, B.A. 1969; Harvard U., J.D. 1972.
Military Service: Army, 1969-75.
Occupation: Lawyer.
Family: Wife, Andrea Green; five children.
Religion: Baptist.
Political Career: La. Senate, 1980-91; candidate for mayor of New Orleans, 1982, 1986.
Capitol Office: 428 Cannon Bldg. 20515; 225-6636.

In Washington: In one term, Jefferson quietly impressed enough colleagues to land a coveted seat on the Ways and Means Committee, a powerful slot that will give him a chance to use his expertise on economic issues.

Although understated in style, Jefferson has more than a decade of legislative experience to draw upon. During his 11 years in the Louisiana Legislature, Jefferson was a major player, especially on economic development and budget matters. He served on the Senate Finance Committee for much of the 1980s and headed the special Budget Stabilization Committee created to cut state spending and find more accurate ways of projecting state revenue. And it didn't hurt his overall political influence that he was chairman of the Governmental Affairs Committee, which had jurisdiction over reapportionment.

Jefferson belongs to the new generation of black leaders, who flow with ease from black communities to halls of power filled with white establishment tradition.

He is generally a quiet party loyalist, rarely breaking ranks to vote against Democratic-backed legislation. He voted for gun control legislation supported by Democrats that would have required a seven-day waiting period for handgun purchases to allow local law enforcement authorities to check the background of prospective buyers. He also joined with most Democrats in voting against the resolution authorizing the use of military force in the Persian Gulf.

In 1992, Jefferson became a soldier in the Democratic leadership apparatus when he was elected whip for first-term Democrats; he quickly secured a reputation as an accurate vote-counter.

In the 1992 presidential election, he was one of a number of members who became key supporters of Bill Clinton. Jefferson arrived in Washington as the first African American elected to Congress from Louisiana since Reconstruction. After the 1992 election, he was joined by Cleo Fields from the 4th District.

In the 102nd Congress, Jefferson served on the Education and Labor Committee, where he took an active role in trying to push small legislative initiatives of his own, including measures to boost education opportunities for minorities and provide temporary care for disabled children to provide a respite for families of children who require constant care.

But he gained the most attention when he entered the national debate over school choice. Under a plan put forth by President Bush, states could have used their federal funds to implement programs that allowed poor parents to choose whether to send their children to public or private schools with public funds. Jefferson opposed the plan, arguing that choice would result in flight from financially strapped inner-city schools.

A deal hammered out among Education Committee Chairman William D. Ford of Michigan, ranking Republican Bill Goodling of Pennsylvania and the Bush administration included a watered-down version of Bush's plan. It allowed local school districts to decide what approach they favored, and if they wanted to adopt a choice plan, federal funding would be provided.

Although committee leaders on both sides agreed to the compromise, Jefferson led a two-day battle for an amendment to eliminate the choice plan altogether.

When the full committee began marking up the bill, it held off debate on Jefferson's amendment while members negotiated further with administration officials. The next day, the White House signaled in a letter that it would support the committee bill only if its choice provisions were left in.

Jefferson pressed ahead with his amendment, arguing that states would still have the option to institute choice programs, as some have done. "It leaves states and local districts as free as they are to implement choice plans," he said. "My amendment takes away the carrot of federal dollars."

Ford and a number of other members said

Louisiana 2

East — New Orleans

New Orleans' melange of temptations, sensations and attractions gives it a unique mystique in America and lures a steady stream of visitors. But the city of just under a half-million residents has more on its mind than granting hedonists their fancies.

In recent years the city has endured population decline, budget crunches, teacher strikes, drug problems and racial hostility. Mardi Gras itself — a $500 million golden goose for the local economy every year — has been caught up in controversy.

Since the 1992 passage of a city ordinance outlawing many social clubs' exclusive practices, there has been considerable debate over whether the krewes (carnival organizations) that are the backbone of the Mardi Gras parade should be punished for discriminatory practices.

New Orleans' economy is rooted in service industries. A few energy, mining and construction firms have headquarters here, including McDermott International Inc., but retail and hospitality services such as hotels, restaurants and bars employ a majority of the city's workers. The French Quarter is famous for its art galleries and fine dining. Nearby, sports fans descend on the 75,000 seat Louisiana Superdome — site of the 1988 Republican National Convention — to root for pro football's Saints. The dome also has hosted the Super Bowl and the NCAA's basketball Final Four.

New Orleans is an ethnic potpourri, with blacks, Italians, Irish, Cubans and the largest Honduran population outside Central America. The city also has more than 50,000 college students; schools include the University of New Orleans, Tulane University, Loyola University and Xavier University, the nation's only Catholic college with a predominantly black student population.

The Algiers section, which sits on the west bank of the Mississippi River, is a blend of high- and low-income residents, new condominiums and well-tended historic buildings. On the east bank between the Mississippi and Lake Pontchartrain is a fascinating variety of neighborhoods: comfortable Carrolton, an area of middle-class whites on the west side of the city; the wealthy Uptown section, with its professionals and academics; the predominantly black Lower 9th Ward; and fast-growing New Orleans East, reaching into the city's marshland and home to middle-class black and white families.

Created by court order in 1983, the 2nd was Louisiana's first black-majority House district. Despite its demographics, the 2nd continued to elect white Democrat Lindy (Mrs. Hale) Boggs. But when she retired in 1990, Jefferson moved in. As it emerged from 1992 redistricting, the 2nd includes 85 percent of New Orleans and has a black population of 61 percent. It takes in southern parts of Kenner, a growing suburb west of New Orleans that includes the international airport. A quarter of the district's people live in northern Jefferson Parish.

The electorate is overwhelmingly Democratic. Bill Clinton won nearly 70 percent here in 1992.

1990 Population: 602,689. White 213,832 (35%), Black 367,460 (61%), Other 21,397 (4%). Hispanic origin 22,107 (4%). 18 and over 426,275 (71%), 62 and over 80,928 (13%). Median age: 30.

they believed in Jefferson's amendment but, in the interest of holding onto the deal with the administration, could not support it.

The committee defeated Jefferson's amendment 17-23.

At Home: Jefferson's election to succeed Democrat Lindy (Mrs. Hale) Boggs was notable on several counts. He became Louisiana's first black congressman since Reconstruction, and his constituency was the last black-majority House district of the 1980s to gain black representation.

In Jefferson, it has a representative whose life has almost literally been a rags-to-riches story. Raised in poverty in rural northeast Louisiana as one of 10 children, he quickly showed brains and ambition. He was student body president at Southern University in Baton Rouge, winner of a scholarship to Harvard Law School, a law clerk in New Orleans for veteran federal appellate court Judge Alvin Rubin and then a legislative assistant to Louisiana Democratic Sen. J. Bennett Johnston.

Like Boggs, he is regarded as a liberal Democrat; and like the politically well-connected widow of a one-time House majority leader, Jefferson boasts of being a coalition-builder who can steer federal largess to economically slumping New Orleans.

In 1979, Jefferson launched his political career by winning a seat in the Louisiana Senate, ousting a white incumbent in a racially mixed New Orleans district that included much of the affluent Uptown area.

When Boggs announced her retirement in 1990, Jefferson was well-positioned to succeed her. With the backing of Mayor Sidney Barthelemy, many of the city's white officials and the Interdenominational Ministerial Alliance (the city's largest organization of black clergy), he ran first in the crowded Oct. 6 voting, then beat attorney Marc H. Morial, the 32-year-old son of the city's first black mayor, Ernest N. "Dutch" Morial, in the bitter November runoff, winning by roughly 5,000 votes.

Morial mocked Jefferson's experience in the Legislature ("We don't want to take Baton Rouge shenanigans to Washington," he said) and hit hard at questions surrounding Jefferson's personal finances. The two candidates ran virtually neck and neck in the city's black precincts. Jefferson won on the strength of his showing on the largely white, working-class West Bank.

Committees

District of Columbia (7th of 8 Democrats)
Fiscal Affairs & Health; Government Operations & Metropolitan Affairs

Ways & Means (22nd of 24 Democrats)
Oversight; Social Security

Elections

1992 Primary †		
William J. Jefferson (D)	67,030	(73%)
Wilma Knox Irvin (D)	14,121	(15%)
Roger C. Johnson (I)	10,090	(11%)
1990 General		
William J. Jefferson (D)	55,621	(53%)
Marc H. Morial (D)	50,232	(47%)

† In Louisiana the primary is open to candidates of all parties. If a candidate wins 50 percent or more of the vote in the primary, no general election is held.

District Vote for President

1992

D	153,342 (69%)
R	54,555 (25%)
I	13,813 (6%)

Campaign Finance

	Receipts	Receipts from PACs	Expend-itures
1992			
Jefferson (D)	$376,227	$223,735 (59%)	$352,058
1990			
Jefferson (D)	$448,100	$104,950 (23%)	$446,743
Morial (D)	$492,323	$26,500 (5%)	$487,171

Key Votes

1993	
Require parental notification of minors' abortions	N
Require unpaid family and medical leave	Y
Approve national "motor voter" registration bill	Y
Approve budget increasing taxes and reducing deficit	Y
Approve economic stimulus plan	Y
1992	
Approve balanced-budget constitutional amendment	N
Close down space station program	?
Approve U.S. aid for former Soviet Union	N
Allow shifting funds from defense to domestic programs	Y
1991	
Extend unemployment benefits using deficit financing	Y
Approve waiting period for handgun purchases	Y
Authorize use of force in Persian Gulf	N

Voting Studies

	Presidential Support		Party Unity		Conservative Coalition	
Year	S	O	S	O	S	O
1992	14	74	81	5	25	65
1991	26	63	82	5	19	68

Interest Group Ratings

Year	ADA	AFL-CIO	CCUS	ACU
1992	85	92	29	0
1991	85	92	20	0

3 W.J. "Billy" Tauzin (D)

Of Thibodaux — Elected 1980; 7th Full Term

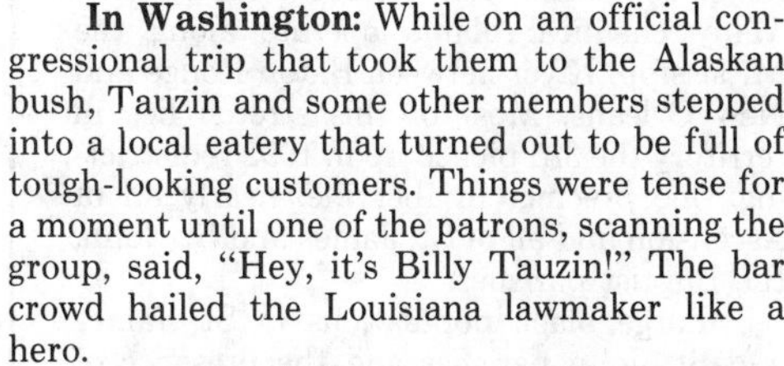

Born: June 14, 1943, Chackbay, La.
Education: Nicholls State U., B.A. 1964; Louisiana State U., J.D. 1967.
Occupation: Lawyer.
Family: Divorced; five children.
Religion: Roman Catholic.
Political Career: La. House, 1971-80; candidate for governor, 1987.
Capitol Office: 2330 Rayburn Bldg. 20515; 225-4031.

In Washington: While on an official congressional trip that took them to the Alaskan bush, Tauzin and some other members stepped into a local eatery that turned out to be full of tough-looking customers. Things were tense for a moment until one of the patrons, scanning the group, said, "Hey, it's Billy Tauzin!" The bar crowd hailed the Louisiana lawmaker like a hero.

In Alaska, where people rely heavily on satellite dishes to pick up television programming, Tauzin is a hero indeed. Dubbed by one Hill colleague the "king of the satellite dish guys," Tauzin cemented his claim to that title in 1992 with his amendment to the cable television reregulation bill. It forbade cable program vendors from discriminating against such cable TV competitors as satellite broadcasters.

The reregulation bill hit the House floor in July 1992 with all its major components settled except for Tauzin's amendment, which was vehemently opposed by the cable industry and by Energy and Commerce Committee Chairman John D. Dingell of Michigan. The vote on the amendment was a blowout: 338-68 — much more support than had been predicted. In addition to winning votes from members who agreed with him on the merits, Tauzin also apparently benefited from a widespread view that voting for the amendment was a painless way to "stick it" to Dingell, who has a reputation as one of the Hill's biggest bullies.

Notwithstanding that run-in with the chairman, Energy and Commerce has proven to be a good spot for Tauzin, a truck driver's son who made his way to Washington with unusual purpose. By the age of 10, his grandfather was referring to him as "the lawyer," but he had to overcome a rustic naiveté and a lisp before becoming student body president in high school. Tauzin went to law school at Louisiana State, where he was a classmate of John B. Breaux, now the state's junior senator. At ease in the recondite world of Louisiana politics, Tauzin is able to think on several planes at once — a valuable asset when operating in the shadow of the vulpine Dingell.

Tauzin's penchant for Cajun storytelling masks a shrewd legislative mind and a knowledge of energy policy that helps him bargain skillfully on the fiercely competitive Energy and Commerce panel.

And Tauzin is more than just a player on the committee. He is a legislative play-maker, building coalitions to win support for his point of view. His involvement is usually a signal that a given proposal must be taken seriously.

Tauzin's hopes to move beyond the House were dashed in 1987 when his gubernatorial bid flopped. But he quickly rebounded and plunged back into the familiar bayous of his committee.

Energy and Commerce is a key committee for Louisiana's oil and gas industry, and Tauzin is one of the industry's most knowledgeable allies.

Tauzin's expertise kept him in the thick of clean-air negotiations in the 101st Congress, but he was unable to stop two House members from Texas from diluting an alternative fuels requirement for automobiles. Louisiana's natural gas is one of the alternative fuels that would have been promoted more forcefully under the original provision.

Tauzin took over the Coast Guard and Navigation Subcommittee of the Merchant Marine Committee in early 1989, just in time for the *Exxon Valdez* oil spill in Alaska.

Tauzin held the first congressional hearing on the spill and began prodding his colleagues to pass federal oil spill prevention and compensation legislation. They did, but not the version he had hoped for; Tauzin, whose pro-industry views sometimes leave him outside the more environmentally tilted mainstream in the House, complained that the bill did not limit liability for shippers and would make it impossible for some to get liability insurance.

In the 102nd Congress, Tauzin used his subcommittee post to lobby for more money for the Coast Guard than was favored by the Appropriations Subcommittee on Transportation.

On non-industry issues that come before Energy and Commerce, Tauzin is often a crucial

Louisiana 3

South Central — Houma; New Iberia

The 3rd begins below Lafayette, in the Cajun heartland of Louisiana, and sweeps east. New Iberia, whose nearby Avery Island produces Tabasco hot sauce, marks a western boundary. The Gulf of Mexico lies to the east and south.

Bayous, grassy marshes and hardwood swamps finger into the gulf for hundreds of miles here, making this a major wetlands area where ecosystems and the economy often intertwine. Alligators, game fish and water birds abound, but so do offshore oil and gas rigs and shrimp boats.

Intertwining is not always easy. Commercial fishermen required to attach turtle-excluder devices to their nets complain that the trapdoor releases free not only turtles but also their catch. Environmentalists contend that channels dredged so that rigs can be hauled offshore accelerate coastal erosion. Local residents have begun recycling Christmas trees as reef-builders in the gulf.

Economically, though, the 3rd has not been a Christmasy kind of place for a long time. The lushness of the land has belied a Dust Bowl economy during much of the last decade. And Hurricane Andrew added to the malaise late in August 1992.

After devastating Homestead, Fla., the storm tore through the district, causing more than $500 million in damage. Everyone feared the worst for the sugar cane, the agricultural mainstay here, but farmers turned in a record crop, up 10 percent in harvested acres from a year earlier.

In the oil and gas industry, no such storybook recovery has been forthcoming. The district, a dominant player in the oil extraction business, has been retrenching ever since Louisiana crude oil prices fell from a 1981 high of $37 a barrel to $10.50 a barrel in 1986. Prices have climbed back to about $20 a barrel, but after a modest rally, drilling activity in the 3rd has gone sluggish.

Louisiana produces nearly 30 percent of the nation's natural gas, which is abundant in the 3rd. Drilling for gas took up some economic slack here, but lower demand led to a glut and tumbling prices in the early 1990s, and the district economy wobbled again.

Chemical manufacturing has made a major comeback from its 1980s hard times. Many chemical plants operate along the Mississippi River between Baton Rouge and New Orleans. Most of this stretch lies in territory the 3rd picked up in 1992 redistricting: one precinct in Iberville, nearly all of Ascension and all of St. James and St. John, the Baptist parishes.

Large black populations in St. James and St. John parishes and the presence of labor unions in the chemical plants produce a more liberal tilt here than in the rest of the 3rd. St. James, which is 50 percent black, cast 60 percent of its 1992 presidential vote for Bill Clinton.

Redistricting otherwise left the 3rd largely unchanged. White-dominated, Catholic and strongly Democratic at the local levels, the district remains inclined to vote Republican (or at least not Democratic) for president. The combined George Bush-Ross Perot tally in 1992 was 55 percent.

1990 Population: 602,950. White 454,235 (75%), Black 131,735 (22%), Other 16,980 (3%). Hispanic origin 14,719 (2%). 18 and over 414,995 (69%), 62 and over 68,464 (11%). Median age: 30.

swing vote, reluctant to take sides in advance and eager to negotiate.

When he does take a stand, it often has a populist flavor, as with his championing the cause of satellite-dish owners. Tauzin was a strong proponent of cable reregulation from the start; he boils his thinking on the issue down to: "Who controls the clicker?" — that is, should the cable industry or the consumer be in charge of the TV remote control? During the effort to construct the cable bill, Tauzin turned a blind eye to the $5,000 campaign contribution he got from the Home Shopping Network and opposed requiring cable systems to carry locally broadcast home-shopping channels.

At Home: Tauzin won his House seat in 1980 with the help of an influential ally, Edwin W. Edwards, who was then between terms as governor. Seven years later the two ended up as rivals in a hot gubernatorial contest.

Tauzin's decision to run for governor in 1987 came as no great surprise; many had expected him to be a strong contender for statewide office someday. But his bid was greatly complicated by Edwards, a colorful figure whose political stock had plummeted as a result of well-publicized indictments (he was eventually acquitted). Even when Edwards insisted he would seek another term, many suspected he would eventually drop out of the race.

He did not. And in a field of five major candidates, that spelled trouble for Tauzin. Both Edwards and Tauzin were popular among southern Louisiana Cajuns and blacks. And while Tauzin was critical of Edwards' candidacy, he also had difficulty distancing himself from his one-time mentor. In the end, there was a surge for Democratic Rep. Buddy Roemer, and Tauzin ran a poor fourth. Edwards finished second, while GOP Rep. Robert L. Livingston, who competed on the same ballot, was third.

Most of Tauzin's political outings have been more successful. His victory in a 1980 special election restored control of the 3rd District to French-speaking, Democratic south Louisiana, after nearly a decade under a Republican from suburban New Orleans, David C. Treen.

When Treen vacated the seat after winning the governorship, he tried to pick a successor, James J. Donelon, a Democrat-turned-Republican. Edwards campaigned ardently for Tauzin.

Like Edwards, Tauzin is as comfortable speaking French as English. After practicing law in the bayou towns of Houma and Thibodaux, he won a state legislative seat in 1971. In eight years in the Legislature he emerged as Edwards' protégé, serving as his floor leader in the lower chamber.

Again with Edwards' help, Tauzin finished a strong second in the first round of the special election to fill Treen's House vacancy. Donelon led the four-man field, but not by enough to avoid a runoff. The second round was bitter and expensive. Tauzin won by more than 7,000 votes, building a big lead in the Cajun parishes to offset Donelon's home-base advantage in New Orleans' suburbs. The margin discouraged GOP leaders, who have not fielded a serious candidate against Tauzin since.

Committees

Energy & Commerce (8th of 27 Democrats)
Energy & Power; Telecommunications & Finance; Transportation & Hazardous Materials

Merchant Marine & Fisheries (4th of 29 Democrats)
Coast Guard & Navigation (chairman); Environment & Natural Resources

Elections

1992 Primary †		
W.J. "Billy" Tauzin (D)	82,047	(82%)
Paul I. Boynton (R)	18,402	(18%)
1990 Primary †		
W.J. "Billy" Tauzin (D)	155,351	(88%)
Ronald P. Duplantis (I)	14,909	(8%)
Millard F. Clement (I)	6,562	(4%)

†In Louisiana the primary is open to candidates of all parties. If a candidate wins 50 percent or more of the vote in the primary, no general election is held.

Previous Winning Percentages: **1988** (89%) **1986** (100%) **1984** (100%) **1982** (100%) **1980** (85%) **1980** * (53%)

** Special election.*

District Vote for President

1992
D 115,406 (45%)
R 105,989 (41%)
I 36,200 (14%)

Campaign Finance

	Receipts	Receipts from PACs		Expend-itures
1992				
Tauzin (D)	$590,179	$442,559	(75%)	$311,112
1990				
Tauzin (D)	$460,418	$243,922	(53%)	$474,224

Key Votes

1993	
Require parental notification of minors' abortions	Y
Require unpaid family and medical leave	N
Approve national "motor voter" registration bill	Y
Approve budget increasing taxes and reducing deficit	Y
Approve economic stimulus plan	N
1992	
Approve balanced-budget constitutional amendment	Y
Close down space station program	?
Approve U.S. aid for former Soviet Union	N
Allow shifting funds from defense to domestic programs	N
1991	
Extend unemployment benefits using deficit financing	Y
Approve waiting period for handgun purchases	N
Authorize use of force in Persian Gulf	Y

Voting Studies

	Presidential Support		Party Unity		Conservative Coalition	
Year	**S**	**O**	**S**	**O**	**S**	**O**
1992	55	42	55	37	85	10
1991	53	44	50	45	95	5
1990	46	49	56	40	100	0
1989	69	29	48	48	93	5
1988	45	54	61	37	97	3
1987	19	24	36	20	37	5
1986	49	51	56	44	98	2
1985	54	43	55	37	91	5
1984	44	53	46	47	83	17
1983	54	45	35	60	90	10
1982	57	36	35	63	82	15
1981	67	28	36	60	91	7

† Not eligible for all recorded votes.

Interest Group Ratings

Year	ADA	AFL-CIO	CCUS	ACU
1992	40	55	75	71
1991	10	50	80	70
1990	22	25	85	58
1989	20	25	80	74
1988	45	86	62	64
1987	20	75	56	53
1986	20	50	72	64
1985	25	53	65	65
1984	15	31	53	67
1983	25	35	70	74
1982	5	20	73	73
1981	0	21	79	71

4 Cleo Fields (D)

Of Baton Rouge — Elected 1992; 1st Term

Born: Nov. 22, 1962, Baton Rouge, La.

Education: Southern U. and A&M College, B.A. 1984, J.D. 1987.

Occupation: Public official.

Family: Wife, Debra Horton.

Religion: Baptist.

Political Career: La. Senate, 1987-93; Democratic candidate for U.S. House, 1990.

Capitol Office: 513 Cannon Bldg. 20515; 225-8490.

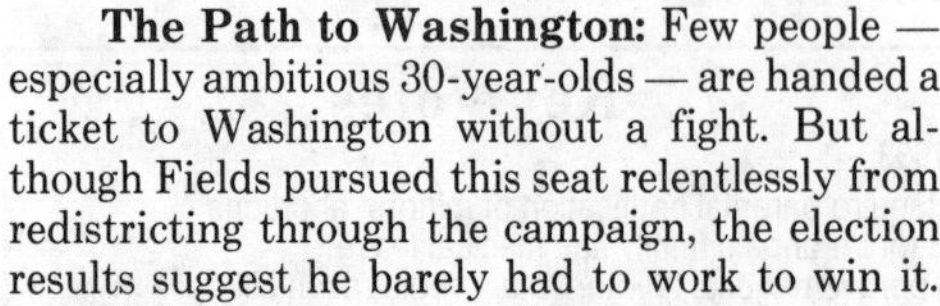

The Path to Washington: Few people — especially ambitious 30-year-olds — are handed a ticket to Washington without a fight. But although Fields pursued this seat relentlessly from redistricting through the campaign, the election results suggest he barely had to work to win it.

Fields nearly captured an out-and-out victory in the state's unique, all-party primary, winning 48 percent of the vote in an eight-candidate field. His closest competitor, fellow Democratic state Sen. Charles "C. D." Jones, netted only 14 percent. Thrown into a November runoff with Jones, Fields continued his student-led, grass-roots campaign and walked away with 74 percent, virtually assuring himself of similar electoral successes for years to come.

Fields campaigned on the same three issues as virtually every other congressional candidate in 1992 — creating jobs, improving the availability and reducing the cost of health care, and reducing the federal budget deficit. But he took few specific positions — chiefly because he was not forced to — preferring to wait for initiatives from the White House or his future congressional colleagues.

In April 1993, Fields had to resolve an early conflict of loyalties over the issue of granting the president modified line-item veto authority. Though apparently opposed to the concept and in opposition to the position of the Congressional Black Caucus, Fields supported the Democratic leadership on a close procedural vote that allowed the bill to come to the floor. He ultimately voted with most of the black caucus against final passage, though the bill passed easily.

He hopes to parlay his assignments on the Banking, Finance and Urban Affairs, and Small Business committees into benefits for his relatively impoverished district. To Fields, that mostly means trying to find ways of leveraging capital into small businesses that will locate in rural or inner-city areas.

Unlike many members of the Class of '92, Fields is not concerned with congressional reform. In the state Senate, he opposed the imposition of term limits on constitutional grounds, arguing that such restraints on voters are undemocratic. And he is opposed to the idea in Congress. Likewise, he has no beefs about Capitol Hill's seniority system, knowing that one day it could work in his favor.

Fields became the youngest state senator in Louisiana history, having entered office at age 24. He has been a leader against illicit drug use and is regarded favorably by environmentalists, but not so much that he is perceived as an enemy of the state's powerful natural gas industry.

Mostly Fields knows how to position himself to win elections. And he has the drive and energy to see that he does.

In the Senate, he chaired the reapportionment committee and worked to craft a second majority-black district for the state in compliance with the Voting Rights Act. He competed with Senate rival Jones, a 13-year incumbent from Monroe, over the shape of the district, and eventually Jones prevailed.

The Legislature moved the 4th's boundaries north to Monroe and beyond, but Fields also managed to hold onto his Baton Rouge base — and the crucial student population at Southern University in particular. From his early years in the Senate, Fields cultivated younger voters. He won enactment of bills to get high school students registered at age 17, before they graduated, and to register college students on campus as they signed up for classes.

The bizarrely drawn, Z-shaped 4th stretches east and west from Baton Rouge, where a fourth of its voters reside, then north from the Delta along the Mississippi River to the Arkansas border, then west all the way to Shreveport. Its 66 percent black population is found in both rural parishes and in corners of the half-dozen cities that it touches.

The 4th also includes a fair number of white Baton Rouge voters, and Fields campaigned hard to win their support. Fields has always played down racial issues and done as much as possible to raise the comfort level of his white constituents. At one point in the campaign, he distanced himself from Jones, who attacked a white newspaper editor as "some racist cracker."

Louisiana 4

North and east — Parts of Monroe, Shreveport and Baton Rouge

A Z-shaped creature, the far-flung 4th zigzags through all or part of 28 parishes and five of Louisiana's largest cities, digesting black communities to create the state's second black-majority district.

From industrial Shreveport, the district snakes east along the Arkansas border, then follows the Mississippi River southward. At Pointe Coupee Parish it splits: One finger plunges west, deep into central Louisiana, and the other continues east and south to the Cajun city of Lafayette. The bizarre shape of the 4th represents what the Louisiana Legislature had to do to make a new district winnable by a black candidate. Until 1992 redistricting, Louisiana had only one black-majority district (New Orleans' 2nd), although blacks make up 31 percent of the state's population. With a 66 percent black population, it is a safe bet that the 4th will continue to elect a black representative.

Poverty permeates many of the nooks and crannies of this overwhelmingly Democratic district. Registered Democrats outnumber registered Republicans by more than 8-to-1. In 1988, when Michael S. Dukakis lost Louisiana decisively, he still got 64 percent of votes cast in areas that now make up the 4th.

While the 4th includes rural farming areas, it is dominated by the black communities of five Louisiana cities. As chairman of the 1992 state redistricting committee, then-state Sen. Fields made sure Baton Rouge, his home base, anchored the 4th. The Baton Rouge metropolitan area is home to 28 percent of the district's people. The district's part of the city also includes Louisiana State University (26,100 students) and predominantly black Southern University, both of which were key Fields support bases in 1992.

Splitting the city with the 6th District, the 4th captures all of northern and parts of southern Baton Rouge, which includes lower- and middle-income black and racially mixed neighborhoods. Many residents work in nearby chemical plants, including the Exxon Court Manufacturing Complex, the city's largest private employer.

The 4th winds through the rich cotton and soybean farmlands of northern Louisiana, taking in much of the city of Monroe, longtime trading hub of northeast Louisiana. The district ends in Shreveport in the northwest corner of the state. The 4th gobbles up almost every black resident in the city, including populous Cooper Road, among Louisiana's oldest black communities. Once a booming oil and gas town, Shreveport now counts AT&T Consumer Products and a General Motors plant in its economic mix.

Outside Baton Rouge in central and northeastern Louisiana the amoeba-like district is anchored by the black sections in blue-collar Alexandria and Lafayette, the center of the state's Cajun culture. Along the Mississippi border, the 4th picks up most or all of the timber and potato producing parishes of St. Helena and West and East Feliciana.

1990 Population: 602,884. White 198,389 (33%), Black 400,493 (66%), Other 4,002 (1%). Hispanic origin 5,366 (1%). 18 and over 413,500 (69%), 62 and over 82,836 (14%). Median age: 29.

Committees

Banking, Finance & Urban Affairs (25th of 30 Democrats)
Consumer Credit & Insurance; Housing & Community Development; International Development, Finance, Trade & Monetary Policy

Small Business (18th of 27 Democrats)
Minority Enterprise, Finance & Urban Development; SBA Legislation & the General Economy

Campaign Finance

1992	Receipts	Receipts from PACs		Expend-itures
Fields (D)	$304,719	$49,020	(16%)	$305,336
Jones (D)	$85,552	$4,400	(5%)	$129,003

Key Votes

1993

Require parental notification of minors' abortions	N
Require unpaid family and medical leave	Y
Approve national "motor voter" registration bill	Y
Approve budget increasing taxes and reducing deficit	Y
Approve economic stimulus plan	Y

Elections

1992 General		
Cleo Fields (D)	143,980	(74%)
Charles Jones (D)	50,851	(26%)
1992 Primary †		
Cleo Fields (D)	62,697	(48%)
Charles Jones (D)	18,305	(14%)
Joe Shyne (D)	14,157	(11%)
Faye Williams (D)	11,264	(9%)
Steve Myers (R)	10,275	(8%)
Emile K. Ventre (R)	8,982	(7%)
James Ross (D)	2,791	(2%)
Ralph Hall (D)	2,675	(2%)

†In Louisiana the primary is open to candidates of all parties. If a candidate wins 50 percent or more of the vote in the primary, no general election is held.

District Vote for President

	1992	
D	149,733	(67%)
R	54,587	(25%)
I	17,697	(8%)

5 Jim McCrery (R)

Of Shreveport — Elected 1988; 3rd Full Term

Born: Sept. 18, 1949, Shreveport, La.
Education: Louisiana Tech U., B.A. 1971; Louisiana State U., J.D. 1975.
Occupation: Lawyer; congressional aide; government relations executive.
Family: Wife, Johnette Hawkins.
Religion: Methodist.
Political Career: Candidate for Leesville City Council, 1978.
Capitol Office: 225 Cannon Bldg. 20515; 225-2777.

In Washington: The 102nd Congress was a tumultuous one for McCrery: He had to defend himself against accusations about his personal life made in a national gay and lesbian magazine, and then to stay in office he had to endure a redistricting-forced matchup with a more senior Democratic incumbent.

But McCrery cleared the hurdles and at the beginning of the 103rd Congress settled in to a plum assignment on the Ways and Means Committee.

On that panel, there is little doubt what kind of record this former business lobbyist will compile. Since coming to the House in April 1988 after a special election victory, McCrery has won high ratings from the Chamber of Commerce, hitting 100 his first year. His ratings from the AFL-CIO, on the other hand, are often in the single digits.

In his House floor votes during the Bush administration, McCrery almost without exception followed the line laid down by the White House on economic, social policy and foreign policy questions. And in the early months of 1993, he found little to like in the Clinton administration program. He opposed the new president's budget and tax priorities and his economic stimulus package, voted against family leave legislation and the "motor voter" registration bill and supported parental notification of minors' abortions at federally funded clinics.

In fact, McCrery's only high-profile departure from his top party leadership's wishes came in October 1990, when he joined with the GOP wing most hostile to tax increases and voted against a budget compromise crafted by President Bush and House and Senate leaders, which included tax increases.

McCrery voted for the final budget plan that year, but unhappily. Blaming Democratic "tax and spend" policies for the budget morass, McCrery said that voters "... cannot continue to elect a Republican to the White House to keep their taxes low and to do the right thing for the country, and then send Democrats to Congress to fatten all of the federal programs they think are important, and even to create new ones."

Before moving up to Ways and Means in 1993, McCrery had served on the Budget Committee, where he strongly supported a balanced-budget constitutional amendment, and on the Armed Services Committee, where he looked out for the interests of Barksdale Air Force Base and Fort Polk.

The normally quiet McCrery made an unusual splash when he first came to Congress. A 1989 article in the Capitol Hill newspaper Roll Call described McCrery's visit to a topless club in South Carolina, where he wore a dancer's bra on his head. "I'm not going to live like a monk while I'm in Congress," he said.

At Home: McCrery was one of four Louisiana incumbents paired against another incumbent due to 1992 redistricting. He was matched with eight-term Democrat Jerry Huckaby.

Huckaby chaired the Agriculture Subcommittee on Cotton, Rice and Sugar — commodities of great concern to Louisiana — and represented some of the state's most conservative areas. Before remapping, he had relied on the 31 percent black population in his 5th District to help keep serious conservative challenges at bay. But he had his back to the wall in the new 5th, with its smaller (22 percent) black population and the conservative GOP incumbent from the former 4th district on the ballot.

To win re-election, McCrery had to withstand some unflattering personal publicity: The Advocate, a national gay and lesbian magazine, published an article that said McCrery had had several homosexual affairs. McCrery, recently married, said the story was not true. Voters in the conservative district did not appear to be troubled by the publicity. They gave McCrery a 44 percent to 29 percent lead over Huckaby in the five-candidate primary.

Huckaby appeared to suffer more lasting damage from his own troubles: He had 88 overdrafts at the House bank; McCrery had none. Huckaby nearly lost his spot in the runoff

Louisiana 5

North — Bossier City; parts of Shreveport and Monroe

While the 5th is anchored in the northwestern Louisiana city of Shreveport, it runs for miles to the east, taking in expanses of both hilly and flat agricultural land and reaching nearly to the Mississippi River along the state's eastern border.

Shreveport (Caddo Parish), Louisiana's third-largest city, has been a bastion of conservatism since the 1930s when it voted against Gov. Huey P. Long. Redistricting in 1992 reinforced Republican dominance of the district by carving all of Shreveport's black communities out of the district and placing them in the new majority-minority 4th District. In the part of Caddo Parish that falls within the 5th, 82 percent of the population is white. Overall, almost 30 percent of people in the 5th live in Caddo Parrish.

In the beginning of the 20th century, oil was discovered near Shreveport, providing the region with prominence and wealth. The city has never fully recovered from the fading of the oil boom; in the 1980s, its population growth was quite slow. Today the city's largest employers include AT&T Consumer Products, General Motors and Southcentral Bell. Shreveport is also the home of the Frymaster Corp. and the site of the annual Poulan Weedeater Independence Bowl.

Just across the Red River from Shreveport is the district's third-largest city, Bossier City (population 52,700). The largest single employer for both cities is Barksdale Air Force Base, headquarters for a unit of the Air Combat Command and home to most of the Air Force's fleet of B-52s. The base employs 1,200 civilians and 5,900 military personnel.

The central part of the district, made up of Union, Lincoln, Jackson and a portion of Winn parishes, is the hilly timber region where Louisiana's softwood pine is harvested. These parishes are dotted with small lumber and paper mills. The rural voters here have leaned Republican in presidential voting; in 1988, George Bush carried all four of these parishes. Bush did not fare as well in 1992, though, carrying only Lincoln and Union.

Monroe (Ouachita Parish) is the district's second-largest city (population 54,900) and an agricultural trading hub, and falls squarely between the forest section and the fertile Delta region. International Paper Co. is the city's largest single employer. Ouachita gave Bush 69 percent of the vote in 1988; in 1992, he got 67 percent.

West Carroll, Madison, Franklin and Morehouse parishes are part of Louisiana's Northern Delta Region. The alluvial soil and the flat land of the Delta lend it naturally to the cultivation of such row crops as cotton, rice and soybeans. These crops take up nearly 900,000 acres in the eastern reach of the 5th.

Despite Bush's recent falling fortunes in the 5th, it appears that the district has not developed any special affection for Democratic presidential candidates. In 1992, George Bush took 49 percent to Bill Clinton's 37 percent and Ross Perot's 14 percent.

1990 Population: 602,816. White 463,168 (77%), Black 133,329 (22%), Other 6,319 (1%). Hispanic origin 6,809 (1%). 18 and over 437,021 (72%), 62 and over 94,240 (16%). Median age: 32.

to Robert Thompson, a political neophyte who blared an anti-incumbent message. In the runoff, McCrery breezed past Huckaby, outpolling him by 26 percentage points as Bush carried the district by 12 percentage points over Clinton.

McCrery, a former Democrat and once an aide to 4th District Rep. Buddy Roemer, was well-positioned to make a bid for the House when Roemer left Congress after his 1987 election as Louisiana governor.

McCrery's GOP label, acquired in late 1987 before his House bid began, helped his victory. Originally from Leesville, in the southern end of the 4th, he served at one time as assistant city attorney in Shreveport. In recent years he had worked in Baton Rouge, the state capital, as a lobbyist for Georgia-Pacific Corp.

This background, and his work for Roemer, did not make him well-known in the 4th; he stood out in the 10-person March primary field largely because he was the only Republican, and he impressed many with his knowledge of legislative issues.

And while linking himself to Roemer, he also associated himself with Republican figures, running ads featuring President Ronald Reagan. In a district that tends to favor Republicans in national and state elections, McCrery's conservative ties helped him outdistance the large field; Democratic state Sen. Foster L. Campbell Jr. ran second, earning a place in the April runoff.

Campbell was a flamboyant, populist-style campaigner, and his base was in the 4th's northern rural parishes. But a month before the election, Campbell was seriously injured in a car crash while driving on a closed highway.

After the special election, McCrery had little time to prepare for November. Fortunately for him, the Democratic effort in the 4th fizzled. Potential challengers stopped in their tracks when Roemer's mother, Adeline, entered the race. She lost badly.

Campbell, having just paid off debts from his previous campaign, came back unexpectedly strong in 1990, buoyed by polls late in the race suggesting that he could beat McCrery. McCrery lost valuable campaign time because he was shuttling back and forth from Washington while the House was debating the budget. He also took heat for his opposition to plant-closing notification and family leave bills, and his support for a constitutional amendment permitting abortion only for rape or incest.

But McCrery got his campaign back on track in the final days of the race and won re-election with 55 percent.

Committee

Ways & Means (11th of 14 Republicans)
Health; Select Revenue Measures

Elections

1992 General		
Jim McCrery (R)	153,501	(63%)
Jerry Huckaby (D)	90,079	(37%)
1992 Primary †		
Jim McCrery (R)	69,511	(44%)
Jerry Huckaby (D)	46,386	(29%)
Robert Thompson (D)	35,306	(22%)
L.D. "Nota" Knox (I)	3,369	(2%)
Donal A. Milton (R)	2,971	(2%)
1990 Primary †		
Jim McCrery (R)	89,859	(55%)
Foster L. Campbell Jr. (D)	74,388	(45%)

†In Louisiana the primary is open to candidates of all parties. If a candidate wins 50 percent or more of the vote in the primary, no general election is held.

Previous Winning Percentages: 1988 (69%) 1988 * (51%)

** Special election.*

District Vote for President

	1992
D	95,048 (37%)
R	127,436 (49%)
I	36,584 (14%)

Campaign Finance

	Receipts	Receipts from PACs		Expend-itures
1992				
McCrery (R)	$768,933	$225,593	(29%)	$743,254
Huckaby (D)	$519,141	$232,241	(45%)	$792,318
1990				
McCrery (R)	$469,766	$190,623	(41%)	$481,504
Campbell (D)	$316,703	$139,450	(44%)	$305,348

Key Votes

1993	
Require parental notification of minors' abortions	Y
Require unpaid family and medical leave	N
Approve national "motor voter" registration bill	N
Approve budget increasing taxes and reducing deficit	N
Approve economic stimulus plan	N
1992	
Approve balanced-budget constitutional amendment	Y
Close down space station program	N
Approve U.S. aid for former Soviet Union	Y
Allow shifting funds from defense to domestic programs	N
1991	
Extend unemployment benefits using deficit financing	N
Approve waiting period for handgun purchases	N
Authorize use of force in Persian Gulf	Y

Voting Studies

	Presidential Support		Party Unity		Conservative Coalition	
Year	S	O	S	O	S	O
1992	77	6	74	6	83	2
1991	84	12	78	15	95	3
1990	68	25	62	23	87	7
1989	85	15	71	21	95	2
1988	61 †	35 †	80 †	18 †	94 †	0 †

† Not eligible for all recorded votes.

Interest Group Ratings

Year	ADA	AFL-CIO	CCUS	ACU
1992	5	10	83	91
1991	0	8	90	85
1990	17	8	86	88
1989	0	8	90	86
1988	12	20	100	94

6 Richard H. Baker (R)

Of Baton Rouge — Elected 1986; 4th Term

Born: May 22, 1948, New Orleans, La.
Education: Louisiana State U., B.A. 1971.
Occupation: Real estate broker.
Family: Wife, Kay Carpenter; two children.
Religion: Methodist.
Political Career: La. House, 1972-86; Democratic candidate for La. Senate, 1981.
Capitol Office: 434 Cannon Bldg. 20515; 225-3901.

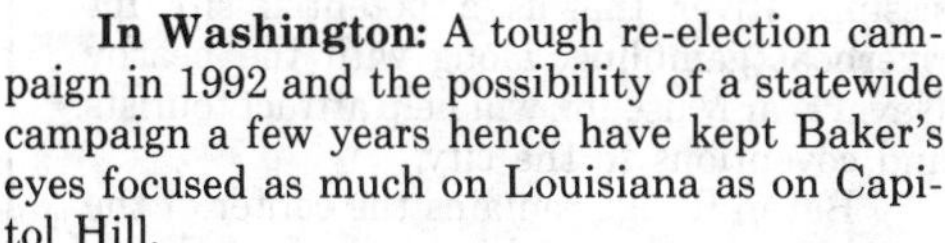

In Washington: A tough re-election campaign in 1992 and the possibility of a statewide campaign a few years hence have kept Baker's eyes focused as much on Louisiana as on Capitol Hill.

Despite his relative youth, Baker is a seasoned veteran of Bayou politics. By the time he was 24, he had already made it to the state House, where he spent most of his 14 years as a labor-oriented Democrat. But when he switched parties and made his way to Congress, he showed an ability to maneuver with calculated care. Baker's voting record in Washington is decidedly pro-business and anti-labor. And his name is now routinely included when talk turns to possible statewide candidates. It is no secret that Baker is considering a 1995 gubernatorial bid.

Baker has proved to be one of the most low-key members of his class in the House. He spent his first two years on the Interior Committee, but in the 101st Congress he moved onto the Banking Committee, where he could better pursue business-oriented interests. Through attrition, he has risen to rank eighth of 20 Republicans on the panel, but his role is often at the margins of legislative action. During a yearlong debate over restructuring the deposit insurance system in 1991, his major contribution was a provision that relaxed rules limiting the amount of non-housing loans that savings and loan associations could make.

In the middle of the 102nd Congress, Baker reclaimed a seat on Interior (renamed Natural Resources for the 103rd). But because of his absence he ranks just above freshmen elected in 1992. He also serves on the Small Business Committee.

A conservative party loyalist, he sided with the leadership on two especially contentious votes in the 101st Congress, backing the 1989 pay raise and ethics reform package and the 1990 budget summit agreement. During the 102nd, he was among the most reliable votes in support of President George Bush. In 1991 he was among the few Republicans to consistently support administration requests to pump additional taxpayer money into the thrift bailout. And he bolted only on issues of conservative principle, such as his opposition to a 1992 package of aid for Russia and other former republics of the Soviet Union.

Even before 1992 brought Baker his first re-election challenge, he was more visible at home than in Washington. In addition to regular political and constituent work, he chaired Bush's 1988 Louisiana campaign and led the state's delegation at the Republican National Convention in New Orleans.

In the 101st Congress, Baker fueled speculation that he was moderating his voting record to appeal to a statewide audience. After voting in 1988 to bar federal funds for abortions in cases of rape and incest, Baker voted in 1989 to permit the use of funds in those cases — three months after the Supreme Court's landmark *Webster* ruling.

Baker said that earlier votes on the issue "were reflections of my own personal judgment. Now I have a better feel" for the opinions of his constituents through "heightened public awareness of the issue. . . . My vote is a reflection of public sentiment that abortion in cases of rape and incest is very different from abortion for the convenience of the woman."

He opposed a 1990 amendment that would have allowed privately paid abortions at military hospitals for overseas military personnel. And he supported Bush's veto of a 1992 bill that would have reversed the administration's ban on abortion counseling at federally supported family planning clinics.

At Home: After GOP Rep. W. Henson Moore announced plans to run for the Senate in 1986, Baker put together an unusual coalition of country-club Republicans and blue-collar Democrats to defeat a better-financed Democratic opponent, state Senate President Pro Tempore Thomas Hudson.

It was an odd election. Baker had spent 12 years in the Legislature as a Democrat, switching parties in 1985 at the urging of GOP leaders who saw him as the only candidate who could stop Hudson. Representing a blue-collar Baton

Louisiana 6

Central — Parts of Alexandria, Baton Rouge and Lafayette

The kite-shaped 6th is an economic microcosm of Louisiana, taking in both an urban center and rural agricultural country. But politically speaking, the 6th is lopsidedly conservative; it is the only Louisiana district where a majority of voters supported former Ku Klux Klan leader David Duke in his 1990 Senate race and 1991 gubernatorial bid.

Thanks to 1992 redistricting, the 6th is no longer compact. It now sprawls across 17 parishes. It begins in Sabine Parish along the Texas border, cuts a wide swath across the state nearly to the Mississippi River, and then meanders south to the state capital, Baton Rouge. The district includes former Gov. Huey P. Long's birthplace in rural Winn Parish as well as his grave on the grounds of the state Capitol.

Within its boundaries, the 6th contains a variety of business pursuits linked to the land. In Caldwell Parish in the northeastern reach of the district, 72 percent of the acreage is devoted to commercial forestry. Farther south, in Avoyelles Parish, rice is the primary cash crop. Sugar cane fields dot Point Coupee Parish and soybeans are grown in southernmost Iberville Parish.

In electoral terms, Baton Rouge is the single biggest influence in the 6th. Remappers splintered the capital city, ceding all of the predominantly black neighborhoods to the majority-minority 4th District. However, East Baton Rouge Parish is still home to more than one-third of the 6th's population.

Downtown Baton Rouge, like so many other center cities, has been strapped economically by suburban flight; there has been relatively little major construction here in the past 20 years. Many state agencies, requiring more space than is available near the Capitol, lease space in other parts of the city. Recently, though, in an attempt to lure businesses and agencies back to the capital area, the state began buying up downtown parcels in the hope of building more than 500,000 square feet of office space. (A budget shortfall could cause some problems, however.) City officials also are hopeful that Catfish Town, a city-assisted retail development on the Mississippi River that is a potential site for riverboat gambling, along with the nearby Naval War Museum, will help attract tourists and coventions to the city.

Baton Rouge remains the center of the South's petrochemical industry. The Exxon Corp. Manufacturing Complex in Baton Rouge has the nation's second-largest chemical manufacturing facility. The petrochemical industry employs more than 14,000 in the Baton Rouge area.

Voter registration in the 6th belies its decidedly GOP tilt, with registered Democrats outnumbering Republicans nearly 3-to-1. In the 1988 presidential election, 60 percent of the vote in the old 6th went to George Bush. LaSalle Parish in the northern part of the 6th gave him nearly 75 percent of the vote. But in 1992, Bush's tally in LaSalle fell off precipitously, to 48 percent, and districtwide he took just 52 percent to Bill Clinton's 35 percent.

1990 Population: 602,854. White 502,982 (83%), Black 87,718 (15%), Other 12,154 (2%). Hispanic origin 11,941 (2%). 18 and over 434,678 (72%), 62 and over 78,365 (13%). Median age: 31.

Rouge district, he had been identified for most of his career as a labor-oriented lawmaker. Hudson, on the other hand, represented a white-collar constituency.

Baker could not compete with Hudson when it came to endorsements from organized political forces. Baker's 1976 stand against right-to-work legislation cost him important business backing, and his party switch cost him backing from the previously supportive AFL-CIO. Only in the rural parishes, where he had Farm Bureau support, did Baker receive help from a significant pressure group.

But Baker had a core of committed GOP volunteers, many of them affluent suburbanites who had supported Moore. TV ads linked Baker to the popular Republican incumbent, and he benefited from his reputation as a "clean government" reformer.

Baker also developed an effective appeal to diverse religious groups. He had been a Methodist lay preacher, and he expanded his support among fundamentalists with an endorsement from Baton Rouge-based TV evangelist Jimmy Swaggart, who at the time was an influential figure. Many Catholics appreciated Baker's opposition to abortion and his support for state aid to parochial schools.

TV advertisements showing him with his wife and children contrasted Baker with his twice-divorced foe. And Baker made many personal appearances, especially in blue-collar areas where he needed to reinforce his popularity. On Election Day, Baker nearly carried Hudson's Senate district, and he did carry Hudson's home precinct.

In 1992, Baker was paired with Republican Rep. Clyde C. Holloway, a conservative who had won three terms in a district that was roughly 85 percent Democratic. But redistricting reduced Holloway's 8th District to splinters.

Baker raised nearly twice as much money as Holloway. But Holloway, a nurseryman who earned praise for his attention to his district, had a profile closer to that of voters in the 6th's rural parishes.

Holloway came in first in the primary. Democrat Ned Randolph, the popular conservative mayor of Alexandria, finished a close third behind Baker, outpolling him in all but four of the 17 parishes in the district. But one of those was Baker's home parish, East Baton Rouge, source of the 6th's largest chunk of votes.

In the runoff, Baker carried only two parishes — East Baton Rouge and Livingston — but his nearly 44,000-vote margin in East Baton Rouge enabled him to withstand losses across the rest of the 6th. Holloway won 64 percent of the vote in the 6th, minus East Baton Rouge. But Baker's home parish cast 41 percent of the vote. Baker squeaked past Holloway to a 2,728-vote victory.

Committees

Banking, Finance & Urban Affairs (8th of 20 Republicans)
Consumer Credit & Insurance; Financial Institutions Supervision, Regulation & Deposit Insurance; Housing & Community Development; International Development, Finance, Trade & Monetary Policy

Natural Resources (11th of 15 Republicans)
National Parks, Forests & Public Lands; Native American Affairs

Small Business (3rd of 18 Republicans)
Procurement, Taxation & Tourism (ranking)

Elections

1992 General		
Richard H. Baker (R)	123,953	(51%)
Clyde C. Holloway (R)	121,225	(49%)
1992 Primary ‡		
Richard H. Baker (R)	46,990	(33%)
Clyde C. Holloway (R)	52,012	(37%)
Ned Randolph (D)	42,819	(30%)
1990 Primary ‡		
Richard H. Baker (R)	Unopposed	

‡ In Louisiana the primary is open to candidates of all parties. If a candidate wins 50 percent or more of the vote in the primary, no general election is held. A candidate unopposed in the primary and general election is declared elected and the candidate's name does not appear on the ballot.

Previous Winning Percentages: **1988** (100%) **1986** (51%)

District Vote for President

1992

D 92,042 (35%)
R 135,915 (52%)
I 35,656 (14%)

Campaign Finance

	Receipts	Receipts from PACs		Expend-itures
1992				
Baker (R)	$711,147	$268,350	(38%)	$770,203
Holloway (R)	$374,471	$193,475	(52%)	$424,870
1990				
Baker (R)	$382,622	$153,761	(40%)	$332,905

Key Votes

1993	
Require parental notification of minors' abortions	Y
Require unpaid family and medical leave	N
Approve national "motor voter" registration bill	N
Approve budget increasing taxes and reducing deficit	N
Approve economic stimulus plan	N
1992	
Approve balanced-budget constitutional amendment	Y
Close down space station program	N
Approve U.S. aid for former Soviet Union	N
Allow shifting funds from defense to domestic programs	N
1991	
Extend unemployment benefits using deficit financing	N
Approve waiting period for handgun purchases	N
Authorize use of force in Persian Gulf	Y

Voting Studies

	Presidential Support		Party Unity		Conservative Coalition	
Year	S	O	S	O	S	O
1992	81	9	88	5	94	2
1991	79	14	88	6	92	0
1990	69	27	81	7	85	7
1989	70	27	87	11	98	2
1988	63	32	80	10	97	3
1987	66	30	76	16	84	5

Interest Group Ratings

Year	ADA	AFL-CIO	CCUS	ACU
1992	0	20	86	100
1991	0	8	100	95
1990	0	18	83	86
1989	5	17	90	79
1988	5	15	100	100
1987	4	6	100	81

7 Jimmy Hayes (D)

Of Lafayette — Elected 1986; 4th Term

Born: Dec. 21, 1946, Lafayette, La.

Education: U. of Southwestern Louisiana, B.S. 1967; Tulane U., J.D. 1970.

Military Service: Air National Guard, 1968-74.

Occupation: Lawyer; real estate developer.

Family: Wife, Leslie Owen; three children.

Religion: Methodist.

Political Career: La. commissioner of financial institutions, 1983-85.

Capitol Office: 2432 Rayburn Bldg. 20515; 225-2031.

In Washington: Hayes showed a few signs early in his House career that he might become a key moderate Southern ally of the liberal House Democratic leadership, but since then he has settled into a mode that more often looks like defiance. Even with Southerners Bill Clinton and Al Gore calling the shots, early in the 103rd Congress Hayes was at best an iffy vote for administration priorities.

He was one of just 22 Democrats voting against Clinton's economic stimulus package, he opposed requiring businesses to provide employees unpaid family and medical leave, and he supported a requirement that parents be notified when minors seek abortions at clinics that receive federal funding.

Hayes did vote for Clinton's budget blueprint and for the "motor voter" registration bill, but overall he seems to be going down a path not unlike the one he followed in the Reagan and Bush administrations, when conservative organizations such as the U.S. Chamber of Commerce found much more to like in his voting record than did liberal interest groups. He supports a balanced-budget constitutional amendment, is an opponent of gun control and voted in 1991 to authorize the use of force against Iraq.

While House leaders will often cut a Southerner some slack, to them Hayes' district looks like one that might tolerate a Democrat more in step with the party program. In 1988 presidential voting, Michael S. Dukakis came within a eyelash of carrying Hayes' old 7th District, and his redrawn constituency in 1992 gave Clinton a 47 percent to 38 percent victory over George Bush.

This helps explain why the Democratic leadership has bypassed the Louisianan when filling openings on key committees. Hayes has snapped about being snubbed. In a 1992 interview with the Atlanta Journal-Constitution, he complained that the leadership "would not tolerate anything but blind obedience ... as a measurement for committee assignments on either Ways and Means or the Appropriations committees."

So Hayes instead keeps occupied with his duties on the Public Works and Transportation Committee, where he is vice chairman of the Subcommittee on Water Resources and Environment, and on the Science, Space and Technology Committee, where he chairs the Investigations and Oversight Subcommittee.

The Water Resources Subcommittee will be in the spotlight as Congress moves to reauthorize the controversial clean water act. The panel also wrestles with other divisive environmental matters, such as striking a balance between protecting wetlands and permitting economic development. For some time, Hayes has worked on the issue of how to preserve coastal wetlands without resorting to what he sees as overregulation.

In the 102nd Congress, he introduced legislation to tighten the definition of what constitutes a wetland, to prioritize wetlands according to their ecological and economic value, and to compensate owners of lands designated for preservation. He complained about federal enforcement of a regulation that broadened the definition of wetlands, saying it was "so overreaching that it has in effect denied property rights, which is unconstitutional."

Committee hearings were held on the legislation, but no action was taken. Hayes reintroduced it at the start of the 103rd Congress.

Soon after he entered the House in 1987, there were high hopes for Hayes among the Democratic leadership. As a freshman, he made a name for himself by emerging as the party point man in a battle over controversial drug-related amendments. He impressed colleagues with his acumen and amused them with his wit. When it came time to orient new freshmen in 1988, Hayes was asked to help them learn the ropes, and he was tapped as a whip for four Southern states (a post he no longer holds).

Hayes in 1988 gained notice for deftly dealing with Rep. Robert S. Walker, a Pennsylvania Republican, in the "drug-free work place" controversy. Walker, like Hayes a member of

Louisiana 7

Southwest — Lake Charles; part of Lafayette

Literally, the Cajun expression "Lache pas la patate" means "Don't drop the potato." Figuratively, it comes closer to "Hang in there," and that is what the 7th has been doing with increasing success since the oil bust of the mid-1980s.

The district, which begins in the Cajun core of south-central Louisiana, runs to Texas on the west and borders the Gulf of Mexico on the south.

Dotted with waterfowl and wildlife refuges, the 7th's gulf edge also serves sports and commercial fishermen. Menhaden, which is ground into feed and industrial oil, accounts for a large share of the commercial catch. Back on land, some of the farms north and west of Crowley that grow rice now alternately raise crawfish in fallow rice fields.

Lake Charles, a refining and chemical-producing hub in the southwest corner of the district, offers a sharp industrial contrast to the 7th's rural areas. A union and Democratic stronghold, the city has seen a rebound in chemical sales abroad, and many refineries have been able to offer hundreds of construction jobs because of environmentally oriented projects undertaken to meet looming deadlines set in the 1990 Clean Air Act.

The closing of a Boeing repair facility cost Lake Charles 2,000 jobs early in the decade. But Grumman, which builds JSTARS radar planes, moved in and expects to employ 1,500 by 1997.

Defense downsizing worries De Ridder, the largest town in the 7th's northwest corner, which depends on Fort Polk as an economic mainstay. The army base, about 20 miles to the north in the 6th District, was due for realignments and cutbacks.

Oakdale, east of De Ridder, hosts a federal detention center and a federal correctional institution, which together employ about 575 people.

The timber industry is also an important employer in this area. Boise Cascade Corp. employs almost 1,200 in Beauregard and Allen parishes.

Southwest of Oakdale on U.S. Highway 165 lies the little town of Kinder, which hopes to gain a big name for itself with a gambling casino run by the Coushatta Indians. The tribe is planning a 100,000-square-foot gaming facility, to open early in 1994, employing as many as 1,200 — Indians and non-Indians alike. If they tire of the tables, visitors might head east to sample Cajun fare and the Acadian lifestyle in nearby communities.

The largest city in the 7th, the economically diversified Lafayette is as close to a political opposite of Lake Charles as the district offers. George Bush, who lost the 7th by 9 percentage points in 1992, made his strongest showing in Lafayette Parish. He took 51 percent of the vote, compared with Bill Clinton's 35 percent and Ross Perot's 14 percent.

Redistricting in 1992 only slightly realigned the 7th. The main loss was of sections of Lafayette Parish, moved into the black-majority 4th District. The 7th remains overwhelmingly Democratic, with 75 percent of registered voters aligning themselves with the party.

1990 Population: 602,921. White 478,453 (79%), Black 117,651 (20%), Other 6,817 (1%). Hispanic origin 7,540 (1%). 18 and over 422,091 (70%), 62 and over 79,446 (13%). Median age: 31.

the Science Committee, began pushing amendments to bills barring spending for any grant or contract "until the recipient shall certify to the government that they will provide a drug-free work place."

Democrats cried that the amendment could wreak havoc on contracts and create a police-state mentality, but they were clearly in a political pinch. Hayes volunteered to try to forge a compromise. Working with Walker, Hayes helped hammer out a softer version that prevented the government from withholding payments for a single violation.

At Home: Hayes had never run for office when he began his 1986 House campaign, and he was not the clear choice of Democratic regulars. But thanks to his loyalty to traditional Democratic issues, he benefited from the same coalition of unions, blacks and courthouse politicians that lifted his predecessor, John B. Breaux, to victory in the 1986 Senate contest.

Hayes, an investor and developer, had the money to court any audience. The son of a prominent independent oilman, he launched his campaign with a flurry of ads stressing his concerns about two issues crucial to troubled south Louisiana: jobs and agriculture.

But Hayes, who resigned his appointed job as state commissioner of financial institutions to campaign, was challenged from the right and left: On the right was state Rep. Margaret Lowenthal, a wealthy pro-business Democrat; on the left was state Rep. James David Cain, a labor-oriented legislator backed by many blacks and blue-collar workers.

Hayes' strong personality initially put off

some, but he improved steadily as a campaigner, and built support in his hometown of Lafayette. That, added to his media effort, put him in a runoff with Lowenthal.

Despite the blue-collar tilt of her legislative district, Lowenthal was regarded as anti-labor by many Cain supporters. Hayes seized the center, won Cain's backing and made a special effort to woo his labor and rural allies. Lowenthal, known as a maverick in the Legislature, stressed her independence and reformist image: Noting Hayes' state job, she tried to tie him to scandal-tainted Democratic Gov. Edwin W. Edwards. Hayes won with 57 percent.

In 1990, Hayes turned back David Thibodaux, who ran third in the 1986 open primary. A professor at the University of Southwestern Louisiana and a conservative GOP activist, Thibodaux got campaign help from former Marine Lt. Col. Oliver L. North.

For a time, Hayes appeared to face a difficult and unusual challenge in 1992. It ended up being only unusual.

Former Republican Lt. Gov. Paul J. Hardy met the candidate filing deadline to run against Hayes, as did Hayes' older brother, Fredric Hayes, also a Republican. Fredric had served as a Democrat in the state House from 1968 to 1972.

But Hardy withdrew from the race. The incumbent younger Hayes dismissed his brother's challenge as little more than a family feud, and he won easily over Fredric and Republican Robert J. Nain.

Committees

Government Operations (19th of 25 Democrats)
Environment, Energy & Natural Resources

Public Works & Transportation (12th of 39 Democrats)
Water Resources & the Environment (vice chairman); Aviation

Science, Space & Technology (11th of 33 Democrats)
Investigations & Oversight (chairman); Space

Elections

1992 Primary †		
Jimmy Hayes (D)	84,149	(73%)
Fredric Hayes (R)	23,870	(21%)
Robert J. Nain (R)	7,184	(6%)
1990 Primary †		
Jimmy Hayes (D)	103,308	(58%)
David Thibodaux (R)	68,530	(38%)
Johnny Myers (D)	7,369	(4%)

† In Louisiana the primary is open to candidates of all parties. If a candidate wins 50 percent or more of the vote in the primary, no general election is held.

Previous Winning Percentages: **1988** (100%) **1986** (57%)

District Vote for President

1992
D 123,250 (47%)
R 100,140 (38%)
I 38,283 (15%)

Campaign Finance

	Receipts	Receipts from PACs		Expend-itures
1992				
Hayes (D)	$429,546	$240,552	(56%)	$436,331
1990				
Hayes (D)	$317,295	$164,850	(52%)	$309,229
Thibodaux (R)	$158,918	$7,957	(5%)	$157,656

Key Votes

1993	
Require parental notification of minors' abortions	Y
Require unpaid family and medical leave	N
Approve national "motor voter" registration bill	Y
Approve budget increasing taxes and reducing deficit	Y
Approve economic stimulus plan	N
1992	
Approve balanced-budget constitutional amendment	Y
Close down space station program	?
Approve U.S. aid for former Soviet Union	N
Allow shifting funds from defense to domestic programs	N
1991	
Extend unemployment benefits using deficit financing	N
Approve waiting period for handgun purchases	N
Authorize use of force in Persian Gulf	Y

Voting Studies

	Presidential Support		Party Unity		Conservative Coalition	
Year	**S**	**O**	**S**	**O**	**S**	**O**
1992	43	40	49	28	67	8
1991	54	40	55	37	86	11
1990	38	49	63	24	85	6
1989	59 †	38 †	64 †	33 †	88 †	10 †
1988	35	57	70	23	87	13
1987	36	57	72	19	79	19

† Not eligible for all recorded votes.

Interest Group Ratings

Year	ADA	AFL-CIO	CCUS	ACU
1992	30	55	100	65
1991	20	50	67	80
1990	22	45	75	55
1989	30	67	60	56
1988	55	92	62	52
1987	48	69	53	22

Maine

STATE DATA

Governor:
John R. McKernan Jr. (R)
First elected: 1/86
Length of term: 4 years
Term expires: 1/95
Salary: $70,000 (Actual salary is $65,819.40 after furlough days are taken into account.)
Term limit: 2 consecutive terms
Phone number: (207) 289-3531
Born: May 20, 1948; Bangor, Maine
Education: Dartmouth College, A.B., 1970; U. of Southern Maine, J.D. 1974.
Occupation: Lawyer
Family: Wife, Olympia J. Snowe
Religion: Protestant
Political Career: Maine House, 1973-77, assistant GOP floor leader, 1975-77; U.S. House, 1983-87

No Lieutenant Governor

State election official: (207) 287-4186
Democratic headquarters: (207) 622-6233
Republican headquarters: (207) 622-6247

REDISTRICTING

Maine retained its two House seats in reapportionment. The legislature will consider redistricting in its 1993 session; the 1992 House elections were run under the current map.

STATE LEGISLATURE

Legislature. In even years meets December-June; odd years, January-April.

Senate: 35 members, 2-year terms
1992 breakdown: 20D, 15R; 24 men, 11 women; 35 whites
Salary: $18,000 over 2 years
1st year: $10,500; 2nd year: $7,500
Phone: (207) 289-1500

House of Representatives: 151 members, 2-year terms
1992 breakdown: 90R, 61D; 104 men, 47 women; 151 whites
Salary: $18,000 over 2 years
1st year: $10,500; 2nd year: $7,500
Phone: (207) 289-1300

URBAN STATISTICS

City	Pop.
Portland	64,358
Mayor Charles Harlow, D	
Lewiston	39,757
Mayor James Howaniec, D	
Bangor	31,181
Mayor John W. Bragg, R	
Auburn	24,309
Mayor Richard Trafton, N-P	

U.S. CONGRESS

Senate: 1 D, 1 R
House: 1 D, 1 R

TERM LIMITS

For Congress: No
For state offices: No

ELECTIONS

1992 Presidential Vote

Bill Clinton	38.8%
George Bush	30.4%
Ross Perot	30.4%

1988 Presidential Vote

George Bush	55%
Michael S. Dukakis	44%

1984 Presidential Vote

Ronald Reagan	61%
Walter F. Mondale	39%

POPULATION

1990 population		1,227,928
1980 population		1,124,660
Percent change		+9%
Rank among states:		38
White		98%
Black		<1%
Hispanic		1%
Asian or Pacific islander		1%
Urban		45%
Rural		55%
Born in state		68%
Foreign-born		3%
Under age 18	309,002	25%
Ages 18-64	755,553	62%
65 and older	163,373	1.3%
Median age		33.9

MISCELLANEOUS

Capital: Augusta
Number of counties: 16
Per capita income: $17,306 (1991)
Rank among states: 30
Total area: 30,265 sq. miles
Rank among states: 39

Maine - Congressional Districts

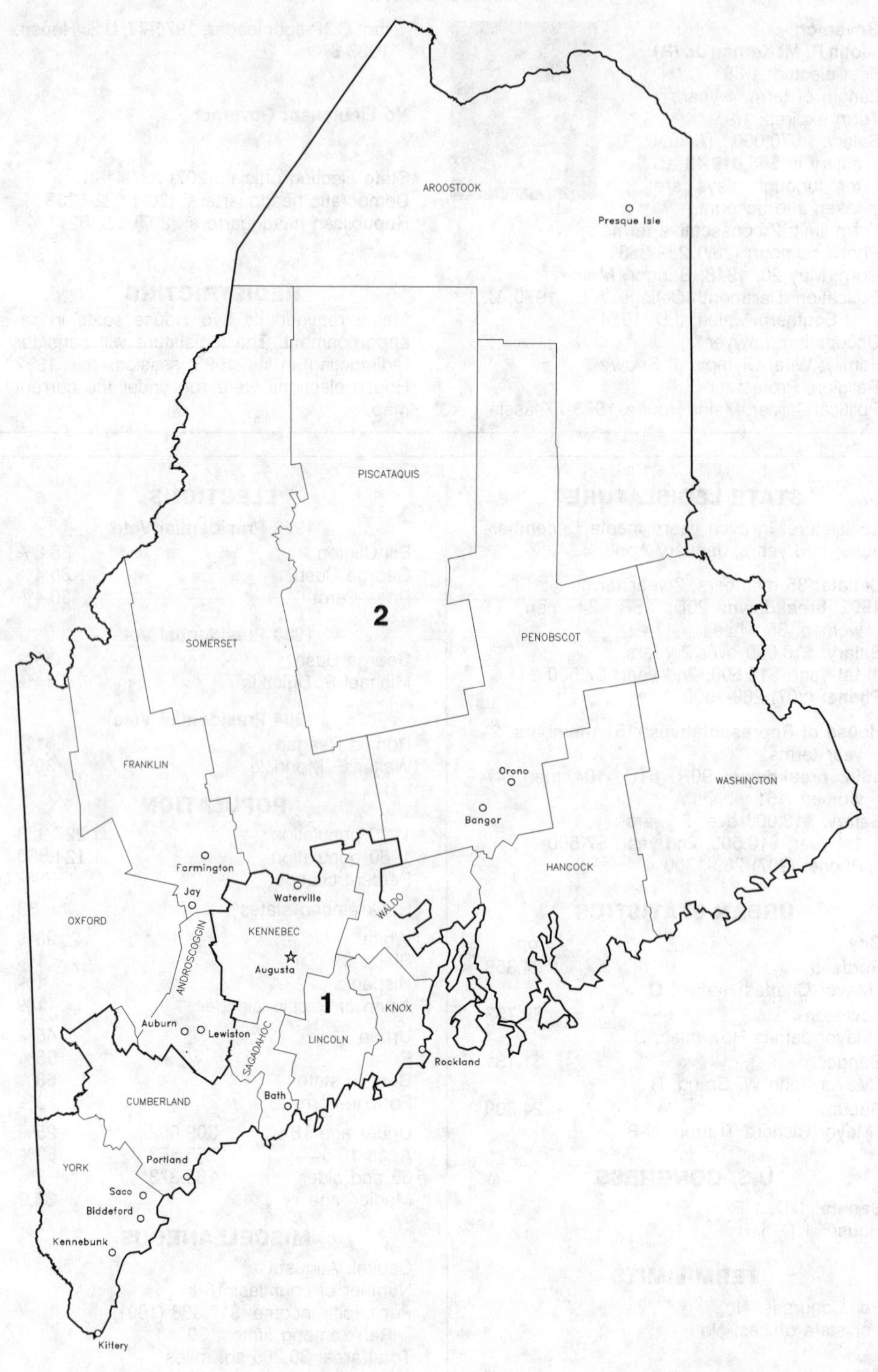

William S. Cohen (R)

Of Bangor — Elected 1978; 3rd Term

Born: Aug. 28, 1940, Bangor, Maine.
Education: Bowdoin College, B.A. 1962; Boston U., LL.B. 1965.
Occupation: Lawyer.
Family: Divorced; two children.
Religion: Unitarian.
Political Career: Bangor City Council, 1969-72, mayor, 1971-72; U.S. House, 1973-79.
Capitol Office: 322 Hart Bldg. 20510; 224-2523.

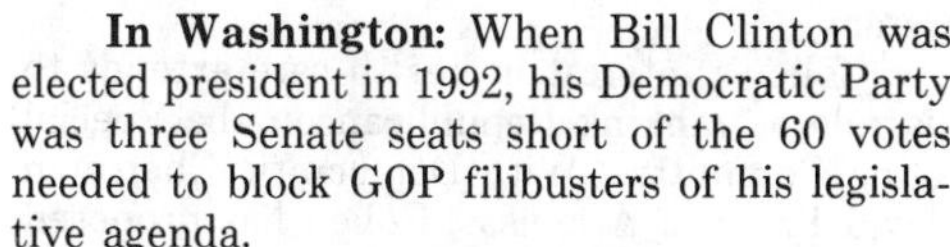

In Washington: When Bill Clinton was elected president in 1992, his Democratic Party was three Senate seats short of the 60 votes needed to block GOP filibusters of his legislative agenda.

It seemed certain Clinton would have to court votes from moderate Republican senators, of which Cohen is one. Although Cohen generally voted more often with than against GOP Presidents Ronald Reagan and George Bush on policy issues, he was outspoken when he disagreed. This, after all, is a Republican whose first bask in the national spotlight came when he voted, as a House member, to impeach President Richard M. Nixon.

Yet Cohen remains a loyal Republican. And when Clinton — buoyed by his success in early 1993 at rolling over Republican opposition to his budget and "economic stimulus" plans in the House — decided to rely on the Senate's Democratic majority to enact his program, Cohen stuck with his own kind.

Joining in a unanimous Republican effort organized by Minority Leader Bob Dole, Cohen voted against Clinton's budget plan (which passed) and supported the GOP filibuster that ultimately killed Clinton's $16.3 billion stimulus package. Cohen was unshaken by the influence of Majority Leader George J. Mitchell, Maine's junior senator.

Cohen's moderate image is something of a median of his views on individual issues. On social policy matters, he is left of his party's leadership. In 1992, Cohen became a founder of the Republican Majority Coalition, formed to counter the influence of conservative religious activists in the GOP.

But Cohen is generally conservative on national security issues (representing a state with numerous military facilities and defense industries, Cohen is the third-ranking Republican on the Armed Services Committee). Citing widespread instability in the post-Cold War world, he warns against cutting deeply into the budgets for defense and intelligence.

Cohen also takes a more standard Republican line on fiscal policy. But he is willing to work with Democrats — especially those of moderate and conservative leanings. In May 1993, he was part of a bipartisan Senate coalition headed by Oklahoma Democrat David L. Boren that sought to scrap Clinton's proposed energy tax and place more emphasis on budget cuts to reduce the federal deficit.

There are also times when Cohen clearly disagrees with his party on defense and fiscal policies. With Maine burdened in 1991 by a recession that predated the national downturn, Cohen was one of only eight GOP senators voting to override Bush's October 1991 veto of an extension of unemployment benefits. On Armed Services, Cohen was the lead Republican during the 101st and 102nd Congresses in efforts to terminate production of the costly B-2 stealth bomber.

There are two aspects of Cohen's actions that flesh out his moderate image: his interest in executive-branch ethics and his reflective, non-ideological approach to policy debates.

The former trait was set in place by Cohen's pursuit of the Watergate allegations as a freshman member of the House Judiciary Committee in 1974. In 1987, Cohen served on the special committee that investigated the "Iran-contra" affair. Cohen was the most outspoken Republican detractor of Reagan's actions relating to Iran-contra. He was one of only three Republicans to join Democrats in signing the majority report that held Reagan responsible for his "cabal of zealots."

Then a member of the Senate Intelligence Committee (he later would serve as ranking Republican, or vice chairman, during the 101st Congress), Cohen also introduced a bill to require the president to notify Congress within 48 hours of the start of any covert military or intelligence operation.

With Republicans holding the White House for 16 of his first 20 years in Congress, Cohen's dogged interest in presidential ethics was unusual within his party. This was borne out in 1992, when Cohen's push to reauthorize the expiring "independent counsel" law — which he helped author in the 1970s — was blocked by other Republican members.

The law, which presumed potential conflicts of interest in Justice Department investigations of executive branch wrongdoing, mandated appointment of an independent counsel to probe allegations against certain top-level officials. Because of the GOP's dominance of the White House, the law had been invoked most often against Republican officials. As the law came up for renewal in 1992, many Republicans had grown enraged by the drawn-out investigation of the Iran-contra affair by independent counsel Lawrence E. Walsh.

With support from the Bush administration, a group of GOP senators blocked the renewal by threatening an end-of-session filibuster. But Cohen — the ranking Republican on the Governmental Affairs Subcommittee on Oversight of Government Management — argued that their attitude seemed predicated on a continued Republican hold on the White House. Cohen said that should Clinton be elected, Republicans "might rue the day they presided over the final rites of this legislation."

Clinton, however, favored renewing the independent counsel law. One committee that would have a say on the resubmitted legislation was Senate Judiciary, where Cohen took a seat at the start of the 103rd Congress.

Cohen also has shown an interest in congressional reform: He was appointed to the Joint Committee on the Organization of Congress, which began its examination of institutional procedures in January 1993.

A poet and author of eight books (including three mystery novels), Cohen often laces his speeches with literary references. During the January 1991 Senate debate on authorizing Bush to employ force to end Iraq's occupation of Kuwait, Cohen noted that members had come to different conclusions based on the United States' experience in previous conflicts. "So we are left to make judgments while doubt sits like a raven on our shoulders and taunts us," Cohen said.

But no one mistakes Cohen for some dreamy dilettante. He is widely respected as an artful legislator. In 1991, Cohen joined with Virginia Sen. John W. Warner, then the ranking Republican on Armed Services, in crafting a compromise on the Strategic Defense Initiative (SDI) anti-ballistic missile program.

Warner and Cohen sought to bridge the rift between conservatives who supported the original Reagan-Bush vision of a "shield" of space-based defensive weapons, and others (mainly Democrats) who derided SDI as a "star wars" fantasy and a potentially destabilizing violation of the 1972 U.S.-Soviet ABM treaty.

The Warner-Cohen plan appealed to Armed Services Chairman Sam Nunn of Georgia by emphasizing the sort of ground-based ABM system he favored. It drew in conservatives by continuing funding for research on space-based weapons and calling for negotiations with Moscow on amending the ABM Treaty to allow for a more expansive system. A program along these lines was incorporated into that year's defense authorization bill.

Cohen is involved in complex issues outside his main committee assignments. His activism on health-care reform was piqued in 1990, when his Democratic challenger spent freely on a campaign that focused on his support for a Canadian-style government-run health-care system. Cohen countered with a free-market-oriented approach to providing health insurance; it emphasized tax incentives for the self-employed and small businesses, a refundable tax credit for low- and moderate-income people, and an overhaul of the medical malpractice system.

Cohen's interest in health care extends to his role as ranking Republican on the Special Aging Committee. With Democratic Chairman David Pryor of Arkansas, Cohen has proposed tax penalties against drug manufacturers whose price increases exceed the rate of inflation.

Cohen's moonlighting career as an author sparked a jocular — and perhaps prescient — exchange between Clinton and Dole. In March 1993, the president visited Senate Republicans to discuss his agenda. The GOP members presented him with a copy of Cohen's latest book, "Murder in the Senate." When Clinton noted that the book's murder victim was a Democrat, Dole — famous for his razor-sharp wit — quipped, "So it had a happy ending."

At Home: Cohen's image as a moderate, independent Republican and his attentions to defense-industry concerns and other issues affecting Maine have made him a political force. Despite an unexpectedly game challenge from Democratic state Rep. Neil Rolde in 1990, Cohen easily won a third Senate term.

Cohen entered the campaign with huge advantages, including a statewide base built in his two previous Senate campaigns. He also had the benefits of incumbency: He received front-page coverage for his late summer visit to U.S. forces deployed to Saudi Arabia after Iraq's August 1990 invasion of Kuwait.

But Rolde spent more than $1 million, much of it his own money, on TV ads that focused on his proposal for a universal health-care plan based on the system in Canada. Cohen criticized the concept, citing reports that Canada's system was plagued by debt and service delays; he countered with his own plan, which included incentives to insurers to supply inexpensive "no frills" coverage. The issue gained Rolde a share of media attention, but Cohen won with 61 percent of the vote.

Cohen had an easier time of it in 1984. After then-Gov. Joseph E. Brennan declined to challenge him, the Democratic nomination went to state House Majority Leader Elizabeth H. Mitchell. Although Mitchell was well-grounded on state-level issues, she took a strident approach that centered on her support for a nuclear weapons freeze. Her rejection of political action committee money led much of the Democratic establishment to write off her campaign as quixotic. Cohen got 73 percent.

Cohen has been a political star in Maine since the day he spoke out for Nixon's impeachment, carving an image as a Republican of conscience. His good looks, easygoing manner and careful questioning were perfect for television.

Cohen had risen quickly from local to national politics. After three years as a Bangor City Council member and one as mayor, Cohen in 1972 won easily for the 2nd District House seat that Democratic Rep. William D. Hathaway vacated for a successful Senate bid.

After the 1974 period of Watergate celebrity, Cohen spent nearly a year considering a 1976 campaign against Maine's senior Democratic senator, Edmund S. Muskie. Private polls showed it might be a close contest, but prudence dictated a two-year wait and a campaign against Hathaway, more liberal and less of an institution than Muskie.

Hathaway worked hard to save himself in 1978, but Cohen had almost no weaknesses. The personal glamour of 1974 lingered, and state and national media refurbished it for the campaign. Cohen shifted slightly to the right, arguing that Hathaway was too liberal for most of Maine. At the same time, he worked for Democratic votes, concentrating his efforts in such places as Portland's Irish-Catholic Munjoy Hill section. Although the incumbent had done nothing in particular to offend the voters, Cohen won 57 percent to 34 percent.

Committees

Special Aging (Ranking Member)

Armed Services (3rd of 9 Republicans)
Regional Defense & Contingency Forces (ranking); Coalition Defense & Reinforcing Forces; Defense Technology, Acquisition & Industrial Base

Governmental Affairs (3rd of 5 Republicans)
Oversight of Government Management (ranking); Permanent Subcommittee on Investigations; Regulation & Government Information

Judiciary (7th of 8 Republicans)
Juvenile Justice (ranking); Courts & Administrative Practice

Joint Organization of Congress

Elections

1990 General

William S. Cohen (R)	319,167	(61%)
Neil Rolde (D)	201,053	(39%)

Previous Winning Percentages: **1984** (73%) **1978** (57%) **1976 *** (77%) **1974 *** (71%) **1972 *** (54%)

** House elections.*

Campaign Finance

	Receipts	Receipts from PACs	Expend-itures
1990			
Cohen (R)	$1,452,273	$549,194 (38%)	$1,572,195
Rolde (D)	$1,635,717	$29,647 (2%)	$1,630,894

Key Votes

1993	
Require unpaid family and medical leave	Y
Approve national "motor voter" registration bill	N
Approve budget increasing taxes and reducing deficit	N
Support president's right to lift military gay ban	N
1992	
Approve school-choice pilot program	N
Allow shifting funds from defense to domestic programs	N
Oppose deeper cuts in spending for SDI	Y
1991	
Approve waiting period for handgun purchases	Y
Raise senators' pay and ban honoraria	N
Authorize use of force in Persian Gulf	Y
Confirm Clarence Thomas to Supreme Court	Y

Voting Studies

	Presidential Support		Party Unity		Conservative Coalition	
Year	**S**	**O**	**S**	**O**	**S**	**O**
1992	63	37	59	38	45	55
1991	67	33	59	41	58	43
1990	44	56	47	53	30	70
1989	74	26	52	48	71	29
1988	52	43	39	59	41	54
1987	55	42	57	42	63	38
1986	78	22	63	33	74	25
1985	63	27	55	38	55	32
1984	62	30	42	53	53	47
1983	66	29	60	36	73	23
1982	67	31	62	36	47	52
1981	76	19	69	25	59	36

Interest Group Ratings

Year	ADA	AFL-CIO	CCUS	ACU
1992	40	33	70	48
1991	65	42	40	43
1990	61	33	42	48
1989	45	30	75	50
1988	35	57	57	46
1987	55	40	67	58
1986	50	20	63	52
1985	35	45	68	55
1984	80	73	28	45
1983	45	47	33	30
1982	55	27	42	50
1981	35	33	76	47

George J. Mitchell (D)

Of Portland — Elected 1982; 2nd Full Term

Appointed to the Senate 1980.

Born: Aug. 20, 1933, Waterville, Maine.
Education: Bowdoin College, B.A. 1954; Georgetown U., LL.B. 1960.
Military Service: Army, 1954-56.
Occupation: Judge; lawyer.
Family: Divorced; one child.
Religion: Roman Catholic.
Political Career: Maine Democratic Party chairman, 1966-68; Democratic National Committee, 1969-77; assistant county attorney, 1971-77; Democratic nominee for governor, 1974; U.S. attorney for Maine, 1977-79; U.S. District Court judge, 1979-80.
Capitol Office: 176 Russell Bldg. 20510; 224-5344.

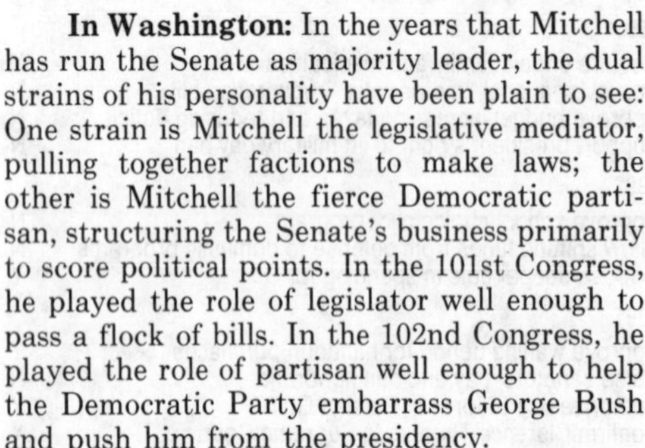

In Washington: In the years that Mitchell has run the Senate as majority leader, the dual strains of his personality have been plain to see: One strain is Mitchell the legislative mediator, pulling together factions to make laws; the other is Mitchell the fierce Democratic partisan, structuring the Senate's business primarily to score political points. In the 101st Congress, he played the role of legislator well enough to pass a flock of bills. In the 102nd Congress, he played the role of partisan well enough to help the Democratic Party embarrass George Bush and push him from the presidency.

Soon after taking over as majority leader in 1989, Mitchell began using his new power to push to enactment legislation in a range of areas, including health, human services and the environment. His crowning achievement of the 101st Congress was passage of a revitalized Clean Air Act. When Mitchell arrived in the Senate in 1980, he declared clean air to be his No. 1 legislative priority. It took a decade, but he got it done, not coincidentally in his first term as leader.

In the process, Mitchell revealed that he believes in making accommodations when necessary to achieve his broad aims, even if that means disappointing the faithful. "We've had 13 years of speeches on the subject," Mitchell said during the clean air debate. "The question is: Do we want to continue to make statements or do we want to make law?"

Watching Mitchell in this mode — judicious and conciliating — it is sometimes possible to forget that, at core, Mitchell is a devout Democrat. The son of a janitor, he is a strong believer in the Democratic Party's working-class roots, and he seemed at times to take personal offense at the whole style and philosophy of the Reagan and Bush administrations. He is not shy about using the tools at his disposal as leader to differentiate Republicans from Democrats for political advantage. There were some notable legislative achievements in the 102nd Congress — including enactment of energy, transportation and civil rights bills — all of which required a degree of compromise. But in the lead-up to the 1992 presidential election Mitchell regularly used the Senate floor to draw a bright line between his party's priorities and those of the party of President Bush.

Time and again after being defeated on bills he pushed, he claimed a moral victory for the Democratic Party. A family leave bill, a bill intended to increase voter registration, one reversing an administration ban on abortion counseling in federally supported clinics, another overhauling campaign finance laws, another imposing conditions on the continued favorable trade status enjoyed by China in the wake of the Tiananmen Square massacre, and two tax bills intended to help boost a stagnant economy — all died under Bush's veto.

But if Bush won the battles with his veto pen, Mitchell won the rhetorical war with his claim that Bush was ignoring the nation's growing domestic problems.

After Bush vetoed the first of the tax bills, Mitchell accused him of playing politics: "The president wants to cut taxes on the very wealthy. We Democrats want to cut taxes on the middle class. The president says that's class warfare. Why is it class warfare when Democrats want to cut taxes to help the middle class, but not class warfare when Republicans want to cut taxes to help the very wealthy?"

With Bill Clinton in the White House, the pressure is on Democrats to produce policy, and that may put a burden on Mitchell to submerge his partisan soul. In the early going of the 103rd Congress, however, Mitchell found himself still campaigning against Senate Republicans, who found an uncommon ability to unite against the new president's economic proposals. As Mitchell complained that they were wrongly thwarting the majority's will, Republicans gibed that Clinton had not commanded a majority of the presidential vote in 1992.

Mitchell three times stepped to the plate to press for Senate action on a $16.3 billion economic "stimulus" bill that Clinton said was urgently needed. Each time a united bloc of Republicans denied him the 60 votes needed to shut off debate and move to a vote. Mitchell then proposed scaling back the spending package, but by then the GOP position was hardened. The Republicans offered a version that was significantly more slimmed down than his own, but Mitchell rejected that as not even half a loaf: "It wasn't even a slice of bread. It was not a credible proposal." Four strikes and Mitchell, Clinton and their stimulus package were out.

The beginnings of the 103rd Congress were not all bad for Mitchell. The voter registration and family leave bills left over from 1992 were easily enacted with bipartisan support, even if the number of GOP votes for the bills was small. And Clinton's fiscal 1994 budget blueprint was passed in March, despite unanimous Republican opposition.

But in looking to increase his number of marks in the win column, Mitchell faced some tough issues in the spring and summer of 1993: campaign finance reform, overhauling the nation's health-care system and a budget reconciliation bill with a new broad-based energy tax that was a centerpiece of Clinton's plan to cut the federal deficit by nearly $500 billion over five years.

All in all, Mitchell's achievements have impressed colleagues on both sides of the aisle and surprised skeptics who had thought him too cerebral for the job, and too inexperienced, since he had held only an honorific leadership post before the 101st Congress.

So successful has Mitchell been as leader that unfriendly editorialists compare him with Lyndon B. Johnson, the legendary cloakroom bully. But unlike Johnson, Mitchell has a quiet bearing, one of almost exaggerated dignity. After hours of floor maneuvering and off-the-floor negotiating, he still strives for an even temper and a moderate tone. Even his anger is well-rehearsed, and one admiring GOP colleague marveled at Mitchell's steely patience that enables him to endure Republicans' maneuvers, when he has the votes.

But if Mitchell's appearance and demeanor suggest the federal judge that he used to be, and not the political beast he is, that is just further proof of his studied and controlled disposition.

In his leadership tour to date, Mitchell has caused many an ally and adversary to perhaps recall his years as a wiry point guard for the Bowdoin College basketball team. Mitchell is reputed to have personified the terrier-like tenacity demanded by his position, and he continues to do so in the Senate.

As a lawyer, a judge and a politician, Mitchell relates to interviews as debates and treats questions as three-dimensional traps. He often responds to questions not by answering them but by questioning their premises — usually with a few words of courteous preface such as "with all due respect."

For example, asked why some Democrats oppose a fast-track procedure for approving trade agreements, Mitchell will cite the names of several prominent Democratic leaders who do not oppose such procedures. But if asked why Democrats are not doing more to assert the rights of the Congress over trade, he can argue that he and others like him are doing everything they can to protect the livelihoods of American workers.

Mitchell can, as the old joke goes, "preach it both ways." But he is at his most effective on issues about which he feels most deeply. In January 1991 he delivered one of the most riveting of all the solemn speeches preceding the vote on military force in the Persian Gulf.

"Just this morning I heard it said that there may be only a few thousand American casualties. For the families of those few thousand — the fathers and mothers, husbands and wives, daughters and sons — the word 'only' will have no meaning," said Mitchell. With the chamber hushed, Mitchell went on to state the case for sanctions: "If we go to war now, no one will ever know if sanctions would have worked if given a full and fair chance."

Once the Senate had voted 52-47 to authorize the use of force, Mitchell swiftly switched modes. He made sure that a resolution supporting the troops was so written that all Democrats could support it. And when a package of benefits for returning Persian Gulf veterans was put together in March, Mitchell made sure every Democratic senator would be on board for the vote. He also reintroduced what had been controversial legislation to compensate Vietnam veterans who had been exposed to Agent Orange. Previous efforts to compose House and Senate bills on the issue had failed. In the January 1991 atmosphere, an agreement was reached with remarkable ease.

It was, in a sense, a victory for Mitchell and other congressional leaders just to have a meaningful vote on the use of military force in the gulf crisis. Through much of the period between Iraq's invasion of Kuwait and the onset of hostilities, the Bush administration intimated that it did not need congressional authority to act under the authority of a U.N. mandate.

As he showed in 1992, Mitchell can also become exercised on the subject of taxes. In 1989, when the House had passed a substantial cut in capital gains taxes and the Senate was thought likely to follow suit, Mitchell seemed almost alone in resisting the tide.

But when Finance Chairman Lloyd Bentsen of Texas kept the tax cut out of his committee's version of the relevant legislation, Mitchell had the parliamentary tool he needed. Senate Republicans needed 60 votes to insert the provision on the floor, and Mitchell kept enough Democrats behind him to deny the president the up-or-down vote that would have favored the cut.

Indeed, Mitchell seems to be involved in the substance and strategy of nearly every piece of important legislation brought to the floor since he was elected leader. In 1991, he was in the thick of negotiations to craft a civil rights bill that could either avoid or survive a veto. Similarly, he sought to amend the seven-day waiting period for handguns (the Brady bill) so it, too, could become law as part of a broad crime bill in 1992. The civil rights bill was enacted; the crime bill died when Mitchell could not break a GOP filibuster.

Mitchell's election as leader on Nov. 29, 1988, was declared unanimous after he had dominated two rivals on the first ballot. The victory capped a remarkable seven-month campaign in which Mitchell overcame seniority, regional rivalry, and reservations about his liberal views and low-key style.

In the end, he won with a certain flair, not just because he got more votes but because he had held his coalition together under intense pressures — both internal and external. His competitors, J. Bennett Johnston of Louisiana and Daniel K. Inouye of Hawaii, both attempted to declare themselves the winners in advance and create momentum — with Inouye making his pitch in the cloakroom and Johnston making his in the media.

But Mitchell, who probably led the race wire to wire, was cautious in public statements while pursuing his votes systematically in private. Not until a few days before the secret ballot did he discuss his own vote tally — which, in the end, proved accurate.

Mitchell's coalition was based on liberals, Easterners, senators elected in the 1980s and senators with strong interest in the environment. But he supplemented these categories with votes from all levels of seniority, every region and most of the Senate Democrats' ideological range. Mitchell divided the spoils of his triumph, both the real positions of power and the more honorific posts, with generosity to the defeated and their supporters.

In the early months of 1989, Mitchell assumed his new power with what might be called due deliberate speed. He ceded often to others, as he had promised to do. He had Bentsen deliver the Senate Democrats' TV response to President Bush's first address to Congress. He stepped aside while Armed Services Chairman Sam Nunn of Georgia led the first battle with Bush, the rejection of former Sen. John G. Tower, Bush's nominee for secretary of Defense. He did the same later when Nunn led the Democratic opposition to Bush's use-of-force resolution in the gulf in 1991.

He seemed intent on rationalizing the Senate floor routine, as he had promised. This particular effort has met with mixed success. For four years he generally hewed to a schedule in which every fourth week was either a recess or a light-work session without recorded votes. He has also tried to encourage senators not to put formal "holds" on bills, a traditional practice that contributes to the logjam of legislative business at the end of a session.

But he has found, as all other reformers have before him, that much of the Senate's obfuscation endures because it serves the purposes of too many senators too well. In May 1993, after abandoning the "three-on, one-off" policy, he warned senators that they would have to be available for votes whenever the Senate is in session, including Mondays and Fridays. And in May 1993, after senators blocked confirmation of a long list of Clinton administration appointees through the use of anonymous holds, he said he would no longer tolerate such delays. "No senator has ever had, to my knowledge, the right to kill outright legislation or a nomination through this process," he said.

When Mitchell came to town as an appointed senator in 1980, he struck colleagues as a fellow with a judicial temperament who generally kept partisan rhetoric out of his speeches. Few could have imagined then that he would soon chair the Democratic Senatorial Campaign Committee and lead his party's 1986 charge to retake control of the Senate.

But Mitchell's long public career has been as much politics as it has law — he was a Democratic state chairman years before he was a judge — and it did not take him much time in the Senate to show that there was a vocal and aggressive politician lurking behind the soft-spoken intellectual facade.

During the 1986 campaign, Mitchell's combative side was often in evidence. Responding to President Ronald Reagan's 1986 State of the Union speech, Mitchell portrayed Reagan as a man who relied on "rhetoric that refuses to face the real world." After the Iran-contra arms revelations convinced many Americans that Reagan was, at best, absent-minded, Mitchell all but gloated. "Never again will there be the period of the dominant Reagan presidency of the first six years," he said.

Mitchell took the campaign committee job for 1986 knowing that history clearly favored Democratic chances of toppling the GOP's 53-47 Senate majority. Ever since popular Senate elections began in 1914, an administration's sixth-year election had cost the president's party an average of seven Senate seats.

But with the GOP enjoying its typically large financial advantage and Reagan campaigning all-out to protect vulnerable GOP incumbents, no one expected the Democrats to retake the chamber so decisively, with 55 seats.

To reward Mitchell when they organized the 100th Congress, Senate Democrats gave him the position of deputy president pro tempore, a job that was created for Hubert H. Humphrey in 1977 and had not been occupied since Humphrey's death. Winning such a prestigious post clearly marked Mitchell as a man on the move, but another role lay ahead — one that would add a critical dimension to his drive for majority leader: He became one of six Democrats on the special Senate committee investigating the Iran-contra affair.

In July 1987, Mitchell took over the public questioning of Oliver North and walked the former Marine through a series of lawyerly questions. He cut off the show-stealing answers North had given other interrogators on the panel, and delivered one of the most memorable lines of the hearings. " . . . Recognize that it is possible for an American to disagree with you on aid to the contras and still love God and still love this country just as much as you do," he told North.

Later, when Reagan delivered his national address on the subject in August, Mitchell was chosen to give the Democrats' response. It was a measured, serious performance that made little effort to charm. But it was a hit. Mitchell blends his partisanship with a keen memory for detail and an ability to pursue several complicated tasks at once.

On the Finance Committee, Mitchell did not play a prominent role in shaping tax bills in the 97th and 98th Congresses, but he was active in the tax-code overhaul enacted by the 99th Congress. Mitchell argued that middle-income taxpayers should benefit as much from revision as those in high- and low-income groups, and he sought to ensure that new restrictions on real-estate tax shelters would not eliminate the incentive to build and maintain low-income housing.

The tax bill that came out of Finance also called for a two-tiered rate structure for individuals. On the Senate floor, Mitchell tried to add a third tier, an effort to get more tax revenue from the highest-income taxpayers. In the end, Mitchell's plan lost by 71-29; the decisive margin sent a signal that the Senate would resist all major changes in the tax rates and basic reform elements of the Finance Committee's bill.

Later, Mitchell did get the Senate to approve a tax credit that preserved incentives for investing in low-income housing.

At Home: Mitchell's feats on the national stage were matched by his political accomplishments in Maine in the 1980s. He started the decade as an appointed senator scrapping to win election on his own; by 1988, he was the holder of the state record for the most lopsided Senate victory.

Mitchell was assured an easy re-election campaign in 1988 when GOP Rep. Olympia J. Snowe, his most threatening potential adversary, decided not to challenge him. Instead, he faced Jasper Wyman, a leader in the 1986 anti-pornography state referendum campaign and head of the state's Christian Civic League.

For the Senate contest, Wyman stepped back from his conservative social agenda and focused on taxes and national defense. But he was no match for Mitchell, who won 81 percent of the vote, the highest percentage for any 1988 Senate candidate.

As resounding a victory as that was, the thrill was much greater for Mitchell when he won in 1982. A year before that election, appointee Mitchell had looked like a sitting duck: He had failed in his only previous attempt to win statewide office, and he trailed by 36 points in a poll released by Republican David F. Emery, a four-term House member with designs on Mitchell's seat.

Yet on Election Day, Mitchell crushed Emery with 61 percent of the vote, a stronger showing than even the invincible Democrat Edmund S. Muskie had posted when winning his fourth Senate election in 1976.

Emery's campaign was guilty of some well-publicized blunders. One of the worst was a letter Emery sent to veterans in which he boasted that the Veterans of Foreign Wars (VFW) had rated his voting record at 92, while giving a zero to Mitchell. The VFW statistics were compiled in June 1980, just a month after Mitchell took office. They contained no votes in which the senator could have participated. That incident prompted newspaper editorials criticizing Emery for practicing the "politics of distortion," an especially unkind cut in Maine, where voters disdain negative campaigning.

Mitchell, meanwhile, came home often and impressed many. Running at the height of the 1982 recession, he promised that Democrats would not accept high unemployment. Working-class voters who had been laid off or feared for their jobs favored Mitchell over Emery, who had the then-unenviable task of defending Reagan's economic policies.

In the end, Mitchell won all but one county and dealt a blow to Emery's political career from which the Republican never recovered (Emery attempted a House comeback in 1990 but was trounced by Democrat Thomas H. Andrews in Maine's 1st District).

Mitchell got into the Senate thanks to the last of a series of boosts he received from Muskie, his mentor and longtime political ally. In the early 1960s, Mitchell worked as Muskie's administrative assistant. On Muskie's recommendation, President Jimmy Carter named Mitchell U.S. attorney for Maine in 1977; two years later the same connection won Mitchell a federal judgeship.

Mitchell held that lifetime appointment

for just a few months. When Carter chose Muskie as secretary of State in 1980, Muskie suggested that Mitchell be named to succeed him in the Senate. Democratic Gov. Joseph E. Brennan agreed.

Mitchell had defeated Brennan in the 1974 gubernatorial primary, but that contest had left no ill feelings. Mitchell had few enemies and seemed the perfect compromise, allowing Brennan to bypass the more prominent but more controversial contenders.

The campaign for governor in 1974 had been Mitchell's one statewide effort, and it had been an embarrassing defeat. Widely considered the favorite that fall, he underestimated the independent candidacy of James Longley, a Lewiston businessman running on a platform of reduced state spending. Longley drew thousands of blue-collar votes that Mitchell took for granted, and he won by 15,000 votes.

From working-class roots, Mitchell worked his way through law school as an insurance adjuster and spent two years in the Justice Department's antitrust division before joining Muskie's staff. He returned to Maine to practice law in 1965, later serving as Democratic state chairman and national committeeman. In the wake of the 1972 defeat of George S. McGovern, he staged an unsuccessful drive to become chairman of the Democratic National Committee. As the choice of the party's liberal faction, he lost to Robert S. Strauss of Texas.

Committees

Majority Leader

Conference Chairman

Environment & Public Works (3rd of 10 Democrats)
Clean Water, Fisheries & Wildlife; Water Resources, Transportation, Public Buildings & Economic Development

Finance (5th of 11 Democrats)
Health for Families & the Uninsured; International Trade; Medicare & Long Term Care

Veterans' Affairs (3rd of 7 Democrats)

Joint Organization of Congress

Elections

1988 General

George J. Mitchell (D)	452,590	(81%)
Jasper S. Wyman (R)	104,758	(19%)

Previous Winning Percentage: 1982 (61%)

Campaign Finance

1988	Receipts	Receipts from PACs		Expend-itures
Mitchell (D)	$1,810,602	$724,547	(40%)	$1,340,157
Wyman (R)	$147,981	$2,599	(2%)	$147,760

Key Votes

1993

Require unpaid family and medical leave	Y
Approve national "motor voter" registration bill	Y
Approve budget increasing taxes and reducing deficit	Y
Support president's right to lift military gay ban	Y
1992	
Approve school-choice pilot program	N
Allow shifting funds from defense to domestic programs	Y
Oppose deeper cuts in spending for SDI	N
1991	
Approve waiting period for handgun purchases	Y
Raise senators' pay and ban honoraria	Y
Authorize use of force in Persian Gulf	N
Confirm Clarence Thomas to Supreme Court	N

Voting Studies

	Presidential Support		Party Unity		Conservative Coalition	
Year	S	O	S	O	S	O
1992	25	75	93	7	21	79
1991	35	65	92	8	20	80
1990	34	66	89	11	22	78
1989	57	43	86	14	37	63
1988	43	57	95	4	5	95
1987	36	64	90	10	31	69
1986	31	66	84	14	25	74
1985	33	67	87	13	30	70
1984	36	61	84	15	15	85
1983	40	60	84	15	30	70
1982	35	63	89	11	16	84
1981	45	51	88	10	24	75

Interest Group Ratings

Year	ADA	AFL-CIO	CCUS	ACU
1992	95	83	20	0
1991	90	83	30	5
1990	83	56	17	9
1989	80	100	50	11
1988	95	100	21	0
1987	95	90	28	8
1986	85	87	32	14
1985	65	86	31	17
1984	90	73	37	9
1983	80	76	42	12
1982	95	88	30	40
1981	90	95	35	7

1 Thomas H. Andrews (D)

Of Portland — Elected 1990; 2nd Term

Born: March 22, 1953, North Easton, Mass.
Education: Bowdoin College, B.A. 1976.
Occupation: Association director; political activist.
Family: Wife, Debra Johnson.
Religion: Unitarian.
Political Career: Maine House, 1983-85; Maine Senate, 1985-91.
Capitol Office: 1530 Longworth Bldg. 20515; 225-6116.

In Washington: Andrews wasted no time in making his mark in Congress. He was elected president of the 1991 freshman class and very visibly staked out his consistently liberal views on a wide variety of issues throughout the 102nd Congress.

The waters look good for a repeat performance. In the 103rd, Andrews has a new committee, Merchant Marine and Fisheries, which will take up several issues close to the heart of Maine's 1st District, and he will be working under a new Armed Services chairman, Democrat Ronald V. Dellums of California, who is seen as more in sync with Andrews than was the former chairman, Defense Secretary Les Aspin.

Andrews went against his home-state GOP colleagues, Rep. Olympia J. Snowe and Sen. William S. Cohen, by voting in 1991 to support the closing of Loring Air Force Base in Snowe's 2nd District. His Armed Services Committee vote hardly determined the 46-8 outcome, but it showed his determination to draw down defense costs regardless of where the pain was felt.

In May 1993, Andrews remained true to his principle when the Portsmouth Naval Shipyard with more than 8,000 civilian and military jobs was put on a new list of bases being considered for closure by an independent commission. "The commission's decision is not surprising and it is not unreasonable.... The bottom line for the commission in making its final decision is the national defense needs of the country and providing the best value to the American taxpayer," Andrews said in a statement.

Andrews' cost-cutting approach showed itself again in June 1992 when he offered an amendment to the defense authorization bill that would have barred the procurement of additional B-2 bombers.

Aspin and Democratic Rep. John P. Murtha of Pennsylvania managed to get most Republicans and a group of conservative Democrats together to spike the amendment, but Andrews refused to go down quietly. "Democrats can either rise above the pack or try in vain to rationalize yet another bum decision — buying weapons we don't need with money we don't have to confront an enemy we no longer face," he said.

Later in June, the Defense Appropriations Subcommittee (under its chairman, Murtha) voted to fund fewer Navy destroyers than the Navy requested — ships that would have been built at Bath Iron Works in Andrews' district. The maneuver — which didn't stick — was seen by some as Murtha's slap at Andrews for his B-2 amendment.

Andrews is expected to have an easier time in the 103rd serving on Dellums' Armed Service Committee. He agrees with Dellums' minimalist approach to defense and may be able to fill Dellums' old shoes in staking out the liberal argument when Dellums as chairman cannot.

Andrews is also focusing on themes expected to be emphasized in his new committee, Merchant Marine, under its new chairman, Democrat Gerry E. Studds of Massachusetts. Early in the 103rd, he sponsored bills that would boost the nation's commercial shipbuilding industry and that would exempt certain ferries from water excise taxes.

Andrews played a very visible, if unsuccessful, role in 1992 presidential politics. With Bill Clinton faltering in the public opinion polls early in the year, Andrews led the movement to draft New York Gov. Mario M. Cuomo for the Democratic nomination. Andrews' effort gained steam until Cuomo's write-in votes failed to materialize in the New Hampshire primary and Cuomo disavowed Andrews' efforts.

At Home: Andrews says he has been involved in social causes since high school. A personal trauma reinforced Andrews' activist tendencies.

When he was 15, Andrews learned he had cancer on one knee; seven years later, that leg had to be amputated. After several years of working on causes related to the poor, Andrews — who is fitted with a prosthesis — signed on in 1981 as executive director of the Maine Association of Handicapped Persons.

Andrews was also involved in a variety of environmentalist campaigns in the early 1980s and developed a group of activist supporters

Maine 1

South — Portland; Augusta

Maine's Democratic core follows Interstate 95 through the heart of the 1st, from industrial Biddeford and Saco in the south through urban Portland and on to blue-collar Waterville in the north. This base has enabled liberal populist Rep. Andrews to dominate his two House campaigns.

But the 1st is hardly a sure thing for Democratic candidates; Maine's Yankee Republican heritage is still respected in many suburbs of Portland, inland rural areas and small coastal towns (including Kennebunkport, the vacation hometown of George Bush).

In 1988, Bush carried the 1st by more than 38,000 votes. But his fortunes faded here, and he lost to Bill Clinton in 1992 by nearly 30,000 votes. The 1st's status as a swing district is cemented by a large bloc of independent voters; Ross Perot carried more than a quarter of the 1st's votes in 1992.

Powered by the waters of Maine's rivers, industries here have made shoes, textiles, lumber, paper and ships throughout the 20th century.

Portland is Maine's largest city with about 63,000 people, including large numbers of Irish- and Franco-Americans. Working-class communities combine with an environmentalist white-collar vote to provide Democrats with a base that often enables them to carry Cumberland County.

The spread of high-tech industry from Boston brought a modest boom to Portland in the 1980s; high-rise office buildings sprouted, and downtown streets welcomed trendy boutiques and restaurants. But recent hard times have heightened some urban problems, including an upswing in homelessness.

Impending post-Cold War defense cuts cause concerns in communities that depend on the 1st's military-related employers, such as Brunswick Naval Air Station in Cumberland County and Bath Iron Works, a Navy shipbuilder in Sagadohoc County. In 1993, the Portsmouth Naval Shipyard was targeted for possible closure, and the district was nicked in the 1991 round by the closing of Pease Air Force Base (just across the New Hampshire border) and by cutbacks in the naval shipyard at Kittery.

Kittery is at the tip of York, Maine's southernmost county; Biddeford and Saco, with their large Franco-American populations and Democratic leanings, are in northern York. While Bush managed to win with 48 percent in Kennebunkport, he narrowly lost the county to Clinton.

In the northern part of the 1st is Augusta, the state capital, which is split rather evenly between white-collar government workers and factory workers. Augusta and the textile city of Waterville usually give Democrats an edge in Kennebec County.

The GOP heartland lies along the northern coast. Lincoln, Knox and Waldo counties consist mainly of coastal towns that help make Maine the No. 1 lobster state.

In 1992, Maine used congressional district lines that had been in place since 1983. Redistricting for the remainder of the 1990s is under way.

1990 Population: 636,486. White 627,035 (99%), Black 2,816 (<1%), Other 6,635 (1%). Hispanic origin 3,742 (<1%). 18 and over 478,547 (75%), 62 and over 101,137 (16%). Median age: 34.

who helped him win a state House seat in 1982. After just one term, he moved on to the state Senate, where during a six-year tenure he would chair the Legislature's Taxation Committee and the Economic Development Committee.

In 1990, 1st District Democratic Rep. Joseph E. Brennan decided to give up the House seat in an attempt to reclaim his former position as Maine's governor. Andrews bid for the open seat in a crowded Democratic primary field and outorganized his opponents, winning with a 36 percent plurality.

With Maine in a recession, Andrews' populist themes and activist base gave him an advantage over former Rep. David F. Emery, the Republican nominee. Emery played up his past House tenure (1975-83) and tried to brand Andrews as an extreme liberal who supported defense cuts that would hurt 1st District workers. But Emery, who had been out of politics since a failed 1982 challenge to Democratic Sen. George J. Mitchell of Maine, ran a lackluster campaign, and Andrews won easily with 60 percent.

Andrews appeared to face a threat in his first re-election campaign. Unlike the moderate Emery, 1992 GOP candidate Linda Bean was a staunch conservative who provided a sharp contrast with Andrews. Bean, the wealthy granddaughter of the late Maine retailer L. L. Bean, spent more than $1 million combined in the Republican primary and general election.

However, Bean's aggressive, expensive campaign backfired. She received media criticism for negative TV advertising. One Bean ad featured a disgruntled constituent who said

Andrews failed to help him resolve a veterans' issue. Andrews responded with a folder of papers documenting his office's efforts on the man's behalf.

Andrews again emphasized economic issues and tied Bean to the sinking fortunes of 1st District vacationer George Bush. He won in a walk.

Committees

Armed Services (21st of 34 Democrats)
Military Acquisition

Merchant Marine & Fisheries (16th of 29 Democrats)
Merchant Marine

Small Business (25th of 27 Democrats)
Regulation, Business Opportunities & Technology

Elections

1992 General

Thomas H. Andrews (D)	232,696	(65%)
Linda Bean (R)	125,236	(35%)

1990 General

Thomas H. Andrews (D)	167,623	(60%)
David F. Emery (R)	110,836	(40%)

District Vote for President

1992

D 145,191 (40%)
R 115,697 (32%)
I 102,828 (28%)

Campaign Finance

	Receipts	Receipts from PACs		Expend-itures
1992				
Andrews (D)	$861,564	$392,357	(46%)	$850,122
Bean (R)	$1,469,959	$57,176	(4%)	$1,464,720
1990				
Andrews (D)	$696,604	$244,473	(35%)	$693,165
Emery (R)	$465,551	$162,121	(35%)	$463,873

Key Votes

1993	
Require parental notification of minors' abortions	N
Require unpaid family and medical leave	Y
Approve national "motor voter" registration bill	Y
Approve budget increasing taxes and reducing deficit	Y
Approve economic stimulus plan	Y
1992	
Approve balanced-budget constitutional amendment	N
Close down space station program	Y
Approve U.S. aid for former Soviet Union	Y
Allow shifting funds from defense to domestic programs	Y
1991	
Extend unemployment benefits using deficit financing	Y
Approve waiting period for handgun purchases	Y
Authorize use of force in Persian Gulf	N

Voting Studies

	Presidential Support		Party Unity		Conservative Coalition	
Year	S	O	S	O	S	O
1992	14	86	90	8	13	85
1991	23	76	93	6	8	92

Interest Group Ratings

Year	ADA	AFL-CIO	CCUS	ACU
1992	100	92	25	4
1991	100	92	20	0

2 Olympia J. Snowe (R)

Of Auburn — Elected 1978; 8th Term

Born: Feb. 21, 1947, Augusta, Maine.
Education: U. of Maine, B.A. 1969.
Occupation: Public official.
Family: Husband, John R. McKernan Jr.
Religion: Greek Orthodox.
Political Career: Maine House, 1973-77; Maine Senate, 1977-79.
Capitol Office: 2268 Rayburn Bldg. 20515; 225-6306.

In Washington: After enjoying more than a decade of sure footing in House politics, Snowe struggled through a difficult balancing act in the early 1990s.

Although she had not previously taken flak for pursuing international issues on the Foreign Affairs Committee, Snowe had to fend off criticism that she had not focused on the problems of Maine's recession-plagued 2nd District. One of the more moderate House Republicans, she also had to justify her continued alliance with President Bush, even as she held more liberal positions on such issues as abortion rights and aid to the unemployed.

Snowe also found herself linked to the flagging political popularity of her husband, Maine Republican Gov. John R. McKernan Jr., who presided over a series of painful state budget cuts and tax increases.

A hairbreadth win in 1990 over Democrat Patrick K. McGowan appeared to reorder Snowe's priorities. While continuing in her role as ranking Republican on the Foreign Affairs International Operations Subcommittee, she redoubled her efforts for her district. Her most publicized stand during the 102nd Congress was an unsuccessful effort to block the closure of Loring Air Force Base, located in the 2nd.

Though she backed Bush for re-election in 1992, she sharply criticized him for his reluctance to extend unemployment benefits and his vetoes of abortion-related bills. A longtime advocate of issues relating to women's equality and health, Snowe sought a higher profile for her work as co-chair of the Congressional Caucus for Women's Issues.

Although these efforts helped Snowe survive McGowan's 1992 comeback attempt, her plurality victory in a three-way race will probably leave her cautious for some time.

But Snowe is hardly abandoning her post at Foreign Affairs, where she made a mark on a long-lived issue: the fate of the "bugged" U.S. Embassy building in Moscow.

Since 1987, when U.S. officials revealed that the Soviets had seeded the new, unfinished embassy with listening devices, Snowe demanded that it be torn down and rebuilt. But fiscal concerns led to a search for a cheaper option.

In 1991, the Bush administration first turned to the "Top Hat" plan to build new secured floors on top of the bugged portion of the building. Later that year, the House overrode Snowe's objections and ceded the decision to the administration; the State Department subsequently announced that it would build a new embassy. (But in March 1993, Secretary of State Warren M. Christopher suggested that the issue might still be open.)

While Snowe's counterpart on International Operations, Chairman Howard L. Berman, D-Calif., differed with her on the embassy, they work compatibly in shaping the bill that authorizes State Department operations.

As an advocate of U.S. assistance to Greece — the homeland of her ethnic forebears — Snowe is averse to calls for deep cuts in foreign aid. But she has made numerous sallies against what she calls wasteful spending in the foreign policy bureaucracy. A supporter of a constitutional amendment mandating a balanced federal budget, Snowe took a seat on the Budget Committee in the 103rd Congress.

There are areas, though, in which Snowe favors increased spending. Along with Rep. Patricia Schroeder of Colorado, the Democratic co-chairman of the women's caucus, Snowe has called for more research into health problems that mainly affect women. She also backed more research into diseases affecting the elderly as a member of the Select Aging Committee.

When Snowe makes a commitment on an issue, her rhetoric can take on a rough edge. When then-Foreign Affairs Chairman Dante B. Fascell of Florida favored the "Top Hat" plan for the Moscow embassy, Snowe lectured him, "You should be ashamed of yourself."

At Home: After a tussle for an open House seat in 1978, Snowe settled in for a series of easy victories. Democrat McGowan ended her comfort in 1990.

A young political veteran and state House member, McGowan used populist themes to his

Maine 2

North — Lewiston; Auburn; Bangor

America's largest congressional district east of the Mississippi, the 2nd accounts for the vast bulk of Maine's territory. Its northern reaches are heavily forested; its people are clustered at the southern end, closer to the state's industrial core.

Heavily dependent on factories, farms and fishing, the 2nd is the less affluent of Maine's House districts.

Pockets of poverty are found in coastal Washington County, which is less accessible to tourists than the seaside regions in the 1st District, and in remote Aroostook County, where economic problems are being deepened by the 1991 decision to close Loring Air Force Base.

Until recently, rural Republican traditions remained sturdy in the 2nd. Rep. Snowe coasted through the 1980s; in 1988, George Bush carried the district by 10 percentage points.

But the recession of the early 1990s soured many voters on Republicans and created opportunities for Democrats and independent candidates. Snowe has struggled to hold the seat in her last two campaigns.

In 1992 presidential voting, Bill Clinton won the 2nd with a plurality, while Ross Perot captured fully a third of the vote; Bush collapsed to third place with 29 percent.

The 2nd's Democratic base is in Androscoggin County, a part of Maine's industrial belt. The Democratic vote is anchored in blue-collar Lewiston (Maine's second-largest city with nearly 40,000 people); Snowe's Democratic challenger Patrick K. McGowan took 58 percent here in 1992. But she held on narrowly in her hometown of Auburn, which claims to be the birthplace of Maine's shoe industry.

The only other city of significant size in the 2nd is Bangor, which has slightly more than 33,000 people. Bangor's heyday as a shipmaking center is over. But its wood-products industry and modest port remain in operation, and its international airport is a refueling station for many transoceanic flights.

Democrats are competitive in local elections, but GOP Sen. William S. Cohen's hometown is usually more dependable for Republicans seeking higher office. The University of Maine (12,800 students) is nearby in Orono.

The rest of the district is rural, much of it covered with the forests that supply trees to Maine's lumber and paper mills. The district also produces potatoes (mainly in Aroostook County), apples, corn and chickens.

In making a case against pork barrel spending in 1992, Bush nicked not only Democratic Sen. George J. Mitchell but also Republican Snowe by proposing to eliminate a federally funded research program on low-bush wild blueberries, one of Washington County's few economic mainstays.

In 1992, Maine used congressional district lines that had been in place since 1983. Redistricting for the remainder of the 1990s is under way.

1990 Population: 591,442. White 581,325 (98%), Black 2,322 (<1%), Other 7,795 (1%). Hispanic origin 3,087 (1%). 18 and over 440,379 (74%), 62 and over 94,848 (16%). Median age: 34.

advantage. The 2nd — the less affluent of Maine's districts — was being hit by the effects of a recession; McGowan's major thrust was that Snowe spent too much time on foreign policy and not enough addressing local economic problems.

When Snowe debated McGowan, she engaged in a series of heated exchanges, surprising pundits who expected Snowe to ignore the rookie challenger. As it turned out, Snowe had reason for concern. She won with 51 percent and a plurality of 4,900 votes.

The outcome encouraged McGowan to try again in 1992. But it also shook up the incumbent, and she geared up early for the rematch.

McGowan again tried to tie Snowe to the unpopular economic policies of Bush and McKernan. But Snowe took the offense herself, branding McGowan as a longtime loyalist of a state House Democratic leadership that was also facing the public's wrath. She highlighted her efforts on such domestic issues as the budget and women's health.

A big difference in this campaign was a strong bid by Green Party candidate Jonathan K. Carter. He ran as an outsider, reinforcing the "change" theme McGowan used against Snowe. He also siphoned off liberal voters, especially environmentalists, from McGowan. Carter, who pulled down 9 percent, appeared to hurt McGowan more. Snowe was held to a plurality, but increased her margin over McGowan to more than 22,000 votes.

Even with her close recent brushes, Snowe has experienced a storybook rise. Orphaned at 9 and raised by an aunt and uncle in blue-collar surroundings, she worked as an intern for Democratic Gov. Kenneth M. Curtis. In 1969, she married Peter Snowe, an Auburn businessman involved in Republican politics.

The next year, Peter Snowe won a state House seat. But in 1973, he was killed in an automobile accident. Olympia Snowe — who was working in the district office of then-Republican Rep. William S. Cohen — was elected to fill his seat. She won one full term, then was elected in 1976 to the state Senate.

Two years later, Cohen ran for the Senate, and Snowe was nominated to succeed him. She faced a scrap with Democrat Markham L. Gartley, Maine's secretary of state and a Vietnam veteran who had been the first prisoner of war released by the North Vietnamese. Though she won with a bare majority, she held a 10 percentage point edge over Gartley.

Over her next five campaigns, Snowe never received less than two-thirds of the vote.

In 1989, Snowe married McKernan, Maine's governor since 1987 and a former House colleague.

Committees

Budget (5th of 17 Republicans)

Foreign Affairs (5th of 18 Republicans)
International Operations (ranking); International Security, International Organizations & Human Rights

Elections

1992 General		
Olympia J. Snowe (R)	153,022	(49%)
Patrick K. McGowan (D)	130,824	(42%)
Jonathan K. Carter (GREEN)	27,526	(9%)
1990 General		
Olympia J. Snowe (R)	121,704	(51%)
Patrick K. McGowan (D)	116,798	(49%)

Previous Winning Percentages: **1988** (66%) **1986** (77%) **1984** (76%) **1982** (67%) **1980** (79%) **1978** (51%)

District Vote for President

1992
D 118,229 (38%)
R 90,807 (29%)
I 103,992 (33%)

Campaign Finance

	Receipts	Receipts from PACs		Expend-itures
1992				
Snowe (R)	$746,628	$246,095	(33%)	$746,611
McGowan (D)	$382,445	$134,462	(35%)	$382,410
Carter (GREEN)	$16,849	0		$16,793
1990				
Snowe (R)	$278,223	$97,655	(35%)	$306,289
McGowan (D)	$229,478	$65,903	(29%)	$228,344

Key Votes

1993	
Require parental notification of minors' abortions	N
Require unpaid family and medical leave	Y
Approve national "motor voter" registration bill	N
Approve budget increasing taxes and reducing deficit	N
Approve economic stimulus plan	N
1992	
Approve balanced-budget constitutional amendment	Y
Close down space station program	Y
Approve U.S. aid for former Soviet Union	N
Allow shifting funds from defense to domestic programs	N
1991	
Extend unemployment benefits using deficit financing	Y
Approve waiting period for handgun purchases	N
Authorize use of force in Persian Gulf	Y

Voting Studies

	Presidential Support		Party Unity		Conservative Coalition	
Year	S	O	S	O	S	O
1992	41	59	58	41	69	31
1991	47	47	52	47	89	11
1990	48	51	57	43	67	33
1989	51	48	47	52	76	22
1988	37	63	54	46	82	18
1987	38	58	48	50	65	35
1986	44	54	53	47	64	36
1985	48	52	56	43	69	31
1984	49	51	47	53	64	36
1983	50	50	46	53	49	49
1982	47	52	53	46	58	40
1981	67	33	68	32	69	31

Interest Group Ratings

Year	ADA	AFL-CIO	CCUS	ACU
1992	50	58	50	60
1991	35	67	40	55
1990	28	33	43	54
1989	35	25	90	54
1988	60	86	50	40
1987	56	44	73	22
1986	50	64	61	48
1985	35	53	59	48
1984	55	38	38	25
1983	35	29	75	43
1982	50	35	57	36
1981	45	40	89	87

Maryland

STATE DATA

Governor:
William Donald Schaefer (D)
First elected: 1986
Length of term: 4 years
Term expires: 1/95
Salary: $120,000
Term limit: 2 terms
Phone: (410) 974-3901
Born: Nov. 2, 1921; Baltimore, Md.
Education: U. of Baltimore, LL.B. 1942, LL.M. 1951
Military Service: Army, 1942-45; Army Reserve, 1945-79
Occupation: Lawyer
Family: Single
Religion: Episcopalian
Political Career: Baltimore City Council, 1955-71 (president, 1967-71); mayor of Baltimore, 1971-87

Lt. Gov.: Melvin A. Steinberg (D)
First elected: 1986
Length of term: 4 years
Term expires: 1/95
Salary: $100,000
Phone: (410) 974-2804

State election official: (410) 974-3711
Democratic headquarters: (410) 280-2300
Republican headquarters: (301) 269-0113

REDISTRICTING

Maryland retained its eight House seats in reapportionment. The legislature passed the map Oct. 22, 1991; the governor signed it Oct. 23.

STATE LEGISLATURE

General Assembly. Meets January-April.

Senate: 47 members, 4-year terms
1992 breakdown: 38D, 9R; 37 men, 10 women; 40 whites, 7 blacks
Salary: $28,000
Phone: (410) 841-3700

House of Representatives: 141 members, 4-year terms
1992 breakdown: 116D, 25R; 107 men, 34 women; 117 whites, 24 blacks
Salary: $28,000
Phone: (410) 841-3100

URBAN STATISTICS

City	Pop.
Baltimore	736,014
Mayor Kurt Schmoke, D	
Silver Spring	76,046
County Executive Neil Potter, D	
Columbia	75,885
County Executive Charles I. Ecker, R	
Dundalk	65,800
County Councilman Donald C. Mason, D	
Bethesda	62,936
County Executive Neil Potter, D	

U.S. CONGRESS

Senate: 2 D, 0 R
House: 4 D, 4 R

TERM LIMITS

For Congress: No
For state offices: No

ELECTIONS

1992 Presidential Vote

Bill Clinton	49.8%
George Bush	35.6%
Ross Perot	14.2%

1988 Presidential Vote

George Bush	51%
Michael S. Dukakis	48%

1984 Presidential Vote

Ronald Reagan	53%
Walter F. Mondale	47%

POPULATION

1990 population		4,781,468
1980 population		4,216,975
Percent change		+13%
Rank among states:		19
White		71%
Black		25%
Hispanic		3%
Asian or Pacific islander		3%
Urban		81%
Rural		19%
Born in state		50%
Foreign-born		7%
Under age 18	1,162,241	24%
Ages 18-64	3,101,745	65%
65 and older	517,482	11%
Median age		33.6

MISCELLANEOUS

Capital: Annapolis
Number of counties: 23
Per capita income: $22,080 (1991)
Rank among states: 5
Total area: 10,460 sq. miles
Rank among states: 42

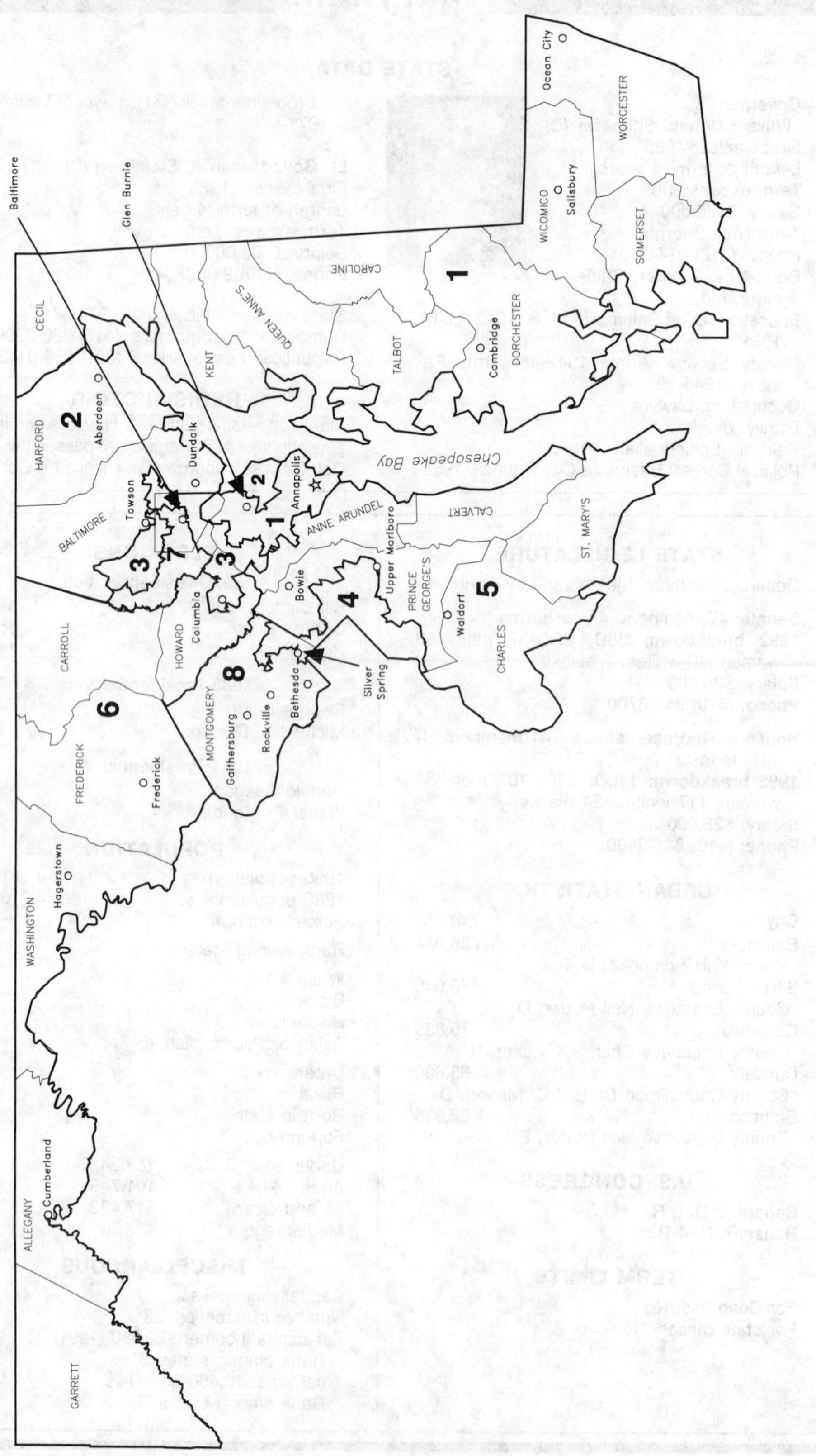
Baltimore
Glen Burnie
CECIL
HARFORD
Aberdeen
2
Dundalk
Towson
BALTIMORE
3
7
CARROLL
6
FREDERICK
Frederick
Hagerstown
WASHINGTON
Cumberland
ALLEGANY
GARRETT
HOWARD
Columbia
MONTGOMERY
Gaithersburg
Rockville
Bethesda
Silver Spring
8
3
Bowie
4
Upper Marlboro
PRINCE GEORGE'S
Waldorf
CHARLES
5
ST. MARY'S
CALVERT
ANNE ARUNDEL
1
Annapolis
2
Chesapeake Bay
KENT
QUEEN ANNE'S
CAROLINE
TALBOT
Cambridge
DORCHESTER
1
WICOMICO
Salisbury
SOMERSET
WORCESTER
Ocean City

Paul S. Sarbanes (D)

Of Baltimore — Elected 1976; 3rd Term

Born: Feb. 3, 1933, Salisbury, Md.
Education: Princeton U., A.B. 1954; Oxford U., B.A. 1957; Harvard U., LL.B. 1960.
Occupation: Lawyer.
Family: Wife, Christine Dunbar; three children.
Religion: Greek Orthodox.
Political Career: Md. House, 1967-71; U.S. House, 1971-77.
Capitol Office: 309 Hart Bldg. 20510; 224-4524.

In Washington: When asked a question, Sarbanes is apt to fold his arms, furrow his brow and slip into quiet reflection, sometimes for a very long while. When deliberating thusly, he is rarely deciding where to stand — Sarbanes almost always comes out on the liberal side of debate. Instead, the meditation reflects his methodical and reserved personality.

"It is quite true I don't make decisions off the top of my head," he once explained. "I don't think important decisions ought to be made that way."

Legislatively, Sarbanes' agenda meshes with his style: He concentrates on important, if obscure, details, whether it be the global consequences of Third World debt, or the intricacies of deliberations by the Federal Reserve's policy-making committee. Politically, Democratic leaders turn to Sarbanes when they need a spokesman resistant to partisan fire: In 1987, he was selected to serve on the panel investigating the Iran-contra scandal.

In the past, Sarbanes' painstaking approach and penchant for a narrow legislative focus have frustrated his admirers, who feel he should be more of a leader. One of the Senate's most penetrating intellects, he has the skills to leave opponents sputtering, but he is not a provocateur.

On occasion, Sarbanes does stand in the forefront. In 1991, at the behest of Foreign Relations Chairman Claiborne Pell of Rhode Island, he took the lead on a foreign aid authorization bill and managed to steer a conference report through the Senate for the first time since 1985. It was no fault of Sarbanes' that the bill was killed in the House.

Still, Sarbanes often vexes colleagues by targeting minor issues, leading some to conclude that his judgment on the importance of subjects does not always equal his thoroughness in examining them. When he spars at length with witnesses over technicalities, he sometimes seems to miss the big picture by nit-picking minutiae.

For a man who has made politics his life's work, Sarbanes has a curious, if refreshing, distaste for publicity. When he does make headlines, it is generally because he has unearthed a detail offensive to his good-government sensibilities. This was the case in 1989, when Sarbanes held up the consideration of ambassadorial nominees who were major contributors to the GOP. Acknowledging that the practice of rewarding political supporters with ambassadorships has a long bipartisan history, Sarbanes argued that the Bush administration had pursued the practice to excess. (He would later warn President Clinton that his concerns about ambassadorships were bipartisan.)

The nomination of Florida real estate magnate Joseph Zappala to be ambassador to Spain was Sarbanes' test case. "We propose to send as ambassador to Spain [a man] with no particular interest [in] or knowledge of Spain," he said, adding that Mr. Zappala's $145,000 in contributions "appear to be the sole reason" for his selection. While many senators concurred that Zappala's résumé was thin, Foreign Relations narrowly approved his nomination, as did the full Senate.

When Donald P. Gregg was nominated to be ambassador to South Korea, Sarbanes dwelt not on political connections, but on the Iran-contra affair. Sarbanes grilled Gregg, the former national security adviser to then-Vice President Bush, about his knowledge of the diversion of funds to the contras. But after a heated debate, the Senate approved his nomination 66-33.

On the select committee investigating the Iran-contra affair in 1987, Sarbanes' performance drew mixed reviews in part because expectations for him were high. His cool, legalistic approach seemed perfect to untangle the complex web of evidence. Many recalled his critical role in the 1974 hearings to impeach President Richard M. Nixon; then a member of the House Judiciary Committee, Sarbanes drafted the most important article of impeachment, charging the president with obstruction of justice.

But what was overlooked about Sarbanes' role in the Watergate hearings was that he had taken center stage for a time precisely because of his cautious nature. The case he built against Nixon was tightly constructed and cogently argued, but he was selected for the job in part because he had avoided the spotlight and withheld an opinion until the committee's work was well under way.

On Foreign Relations and as former chairman of the Banking Subcommittee on International Finance, Sarbanes developed a reputation as an expert on the problem of Third World debt and its relationship to U.S. banking and trade. In the 102nd Congress, he managed measures to reauthorize the Export-Import Bank and the Overseas Private Investment Corporation.

In the 103rd Congress, he joined the Budget Committee and assumed the chairmanship of the Banking Subcommittee on Housing, where he can more directly attempt to increase federal spending on urban needs. He and Budget Chairman Jim Sasser of Tennessee were the first to propose an urban aid-fiscal stimulus bill in early 1992, at a time when the economy appeared permanently mired in recession. But their idea for adding $55 billion to the federal deficit found few supporters.

In each of the last three Congresses, Sarbanes also served a year as chairman of the Joint Economic Committee, which he treated as an almost pedagogical post from which to criticize Republican economic policies and pursue his view that there should be a more activist fiscal and monetary response to the business cycle.

Although Sarbanes may never match Maryland's junior senator, Barbara A. Mikulski, when it comes to bringing home the bacon — she chairs an Appropriations subcommittee — he nonetheless makes an effort to tout his role as leader of the state delegation. In the 102nd Congress, he won enactment of a bill enlarging the Assateague Island National Seashore. In the 101st, he was the chief Senate sponsor of legislation to clean up the Chesapeake Bay. In 1986, he launched the first filibuster of his career over legislation that would have transferred control over two major Washington, D.C.-area airports from the federal government to a regional authority. Marylanders saw the bill as an economic threat to their state's major airport. Sarbanes talked for five days, with an uncharacteristic enthusiasm that won concessions aimed at providing some protection for Maryland's interests.

At Home: The son of Greek immigrant parents, Sarbanes grew up on Maryland's Eastern Shore, attended Princeton, won a Rhodes scholarship and graduated from Harvard Law School magna cum laude.

After settling in Baltimore to practice law, Sarbanes entered politics and won a state House seat in 1966. Having developed the quiet, meticulous approach to problem-solving that would mark his Washington career, Sarbanes left the legislature in 1970 to challenge veteran Democratic Rep. George H. Fallon. Running as an anti-war, anti-machine insurgent, Sarbanes defeated the aging chairman of the House Public Works Committee for the Democratic nomination in Baltimore's multi-ethnic then-4th District. With Democrats enjoying nearly a 4-to-1 registration advantage in the 4th, he had no general-election trouble.

Two years later, redistricting threw him together with another old-time Democrat, Rep. Edward Garmatz, but Garmatz retired.

By 1976 Sarbanes was ready to move to the Senate, and he did so by unseating one-term Republican J. Glenn Beall Jr. Sarbanes first parried a primary comeback attempt by former Democratic Sen. Joseph D. Tydings, deflecting Tydings' charges that Sarbanes was too liberal. In the fall, Beall called him an inactive legislator, and Sarbanes responded with TV ads playing up his Judiciary Committee role during Watergate. Sarbanes won with 57 percent of the vote.

There were early signs that his 1982 reelection campaign might be more difficult. Emboldened by their 1980 successes, Republicans put Sarbanes on their target list. The National Conservative Political Action Committee (NCPAC) launched a half-million-dollar advertising attack in 1981.

But by early 1982, Sarbanes' opponents had lost their confidence. Many felt the NCPAC campaign had backfired: The Democrat had stepped up his schedule of personal appearances, lashed out at NCPAC as "an alien force" and raised money aggressively.

When state GOP leaders failed to enlist a big-name challenger, the nomination went to Prince George's County Executive Lawrence J. Hogan — a former House member who had a chilly relationship with many Maryland Republican activists, stemming from his Watergate-era criticisms of President Nixon.

Hogan called Sarbanes "the phantom," a do-nothing senator who complained about Reaganomics but offered no alternatives. Sarbanes was unfazed. Sweeping all but three counties, he won 64 percent of the vote.

Approaching 1988, state Republicans again talked a good game, describing Sarbanes' liberal politics as out of step in a state that had voted for Ronald Reagan in 1984. But the talk failed to produce a single top-drawer entrant in a nine-candidate March primary. Wealthy businessman Thomas L. Blair spent freely and easily won nomination. But he withdrew in May, citing business obligations.

At a state party convention to replace Blair on the ballot, conservatives lobbied for Alan L. Keyes, a former State Department official who had served as a top assistant to U.N. Representative Jeane J. Kirkpatrick. Though Keyes had not previously been active in the state party, he gained the nomination.

Keyes drew attention as one of two black Senate contenders in 1988, and he campaigned aggressively. In a basically liberal-voting state with a large urban black population, he denounced "welfare state" policies that he said promoted dependency, and he opposed anti-apartheid sanctions against South Africa.

But Keyes also exhibited an independent streak that alienated some Republicans. Invited to speak at the Republican National Convention, he rejected as tokenistic a draft of a convention speech that was suggested by the Bush campaign. And he called on the state GOP chairman to resign after the mailing of a party fundraising letter linking Democratic presidential nominee Michael S. Dukakis with furloughed rapist Willie Horton.

Meanwhile, Sarbanes raised a large treasury, kept a big lead in the polls and spent nearly as much time plugging for Dukakis as for himself. Bush carried Maryland, but Sarbanes won with 62 percent.

Keyes argued that his 38 percent was a strong showing — given his late start and low name recognition — that would lay a base for future success. But instead of waiting for another shot at Sarbanes in 1994, Keyes went after popular Democratic Sen. Barbara A. Mikulski in 1992 and was flattened, taking less than 30 percent.

Committees

Banking, Housing & Urban Affairs (2nd of 11 Democrats)
Housing & Urban Affairs (chairman); International Finance & Monetary Policy

Budget (10th of 12 Democrats)

Foreign Relations (3rd of 11 Democrats)
International Economic Policy, Trade, Oceans & Environment (chairman); European Affairs; Near Eastern & South Asian Affairs

Joint Economic

Joint Organization of Congress

Elections

1988 General		
Paul S. Sarbanes (D)	999,166	(62%)
Alan L. Keyes (R)	617,537	(38%)
1988 Primary		
Paul S. Sarbanes (D)	309,919	(86%)
B. Emerson Sweatt (D)	25,932	(7%)
A. Robert Kaufman (D)	25,450	(7%)

Previous Winning Percentages: **1982** (64%) **1976** (57%) **1974** * (84%) **1972** * (70%) **1970** * (70%)

* *House elections.*

Campaign Finance

	Receipts	Receipts from PACs		Expend-itures
1988				
Sarbanes (D)	$1,477,516	$604,799	(41%)	$1,466,477
Keyes (R)	$684,383	$63,352	(9%)	$662,651

Key Votes

1993	
Require unpaid family and medical leave	Y
Approve national "motor voter" registration bill	Y
Approve budget increasing taxes and reducing deficit	Y
Support president's right to lift military gay ban	Y
1992	
Approve school-choice pilot program	N
Allow shifting funds from defense to domestic programs	Y
Oppose deeper cuts in spending for SDI	N
1991	
Approve waiting period for handgun purchases	Y
Raise senators' pay and ban honoraria	Y
Authorize use of force in Persian Gulf	N
Confirm Clarence Thomas to Supreme Court	N

Voting Studies

	Presidential Support		Party Unity		Conservative Coalition	
Year	S	O	S	O	S	O
1992	27	73	96	4	11	89
1991	30	70	96	4	13	88
1990	31	69	93	7	11	89
1989	45	53	95	4	11	87
1988	40	59	96	4	8	92
1987	31	67	95	4	6	94
1986	18	81	96	3	3	95
1985	22	74	90	5	8	87
1984	30	64	94	2	0	98
1983	41	58	88	9	11	84
1982	25	65	91	3	2	78
1981	38	61	93	6	7	93

Interest Group Ratings

Year	ADA	AFL-CIO	CCUS	ACU
1992	100	92	10	0
1991	100	92	10	0
1990	83	67	8	4
1989	85	100	25	7
1988	90	100	29	4
1987	100	90	28	0
1986	100	100	16	0
1985	100	100	25	0
1984	100	100	21	0
1983	95	100	16	0
1982	85	92	15	28
1981	95	95	11	0

Barbara A. Mikulski (D)

Of Baltimore — Elected 1986; 2nd Term

Born: July 20, 1936, Baltimore, Md.
Education: Mount Saint Agnes College, B.A. 1958; U. of Maryland, M.S.W. 1965.
Occupation: Social worker.
Family: Single.
Religion: Roman Catholic.
Political Career: Baltimore City Council, 1971-77; Democratic nominee for U.S. Senate, 1974; U.S. House, 1977-87.
Capitol Office: 709 Hart Bldg. 20510; 224-4654.

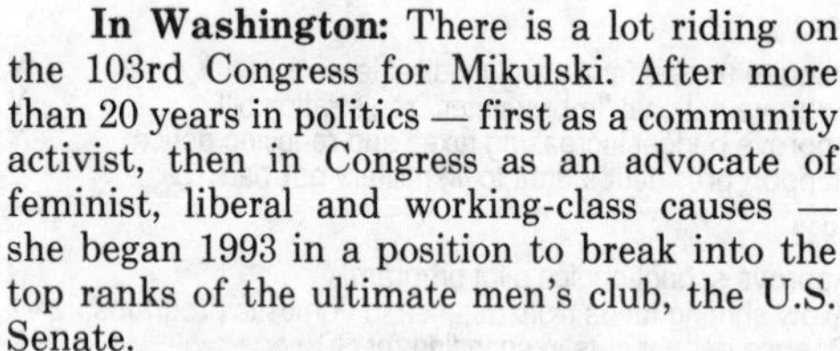

In Washington: There is a lot riding on the 103rd Congress for Mikulski. After more than 20 years in politics — first as a community activist, then in Congress as an advocate of feminist, liberal and working-class causes — she began 1993 in a position to break into the top ranks of the ultimate men's club, the U.S. Senate.

After her 1992 election for a second Senate term, Mikulski was named to the post of assistant floor leader. Top Senate Democrats, sensitive about the lack of diversity in their leadership ranks, turned to Mikulski, the dean of the chamber's five Democratic women — all newcomers except for her. Along with her junior leadership post (the first held by a woman in the Senate), Mikulski got another new responsibility: a seat on the Ethics Committee. She retained her chairmanship of a powerful Appropriations subcommittee and picked up the gavel on the Labor and Human Resources Aging subcommittee.

It's a full agenda, even for the hard-driving, streetwise Mikulski.

Mikulski's work on the Ethics Committee is likely to receive special scrutiny in 1993, as the panel examines charges of sexual harassment against Republican Sen. Bob Packwood of Oregon. She is the only woman on Ethics, and her place there is an outgrowth of negative public reaction to the all-male Judiciary Committee's handling of sexual harassment allegations that arose in the process of confirming Clarence Thomas to the Supreme Court in 1991. After the allegations against Packwood were published in The Washington Post in November 1992, Senate leaders made a priority of finding a woman to serve on Ethics.

In a statement issued just after the Post article appeared, Mikulski said: "The allegations made against Sen. Packwood are serious. They should be and must be dealt with seriously and responsibly through the Ethics Committee's procedures."

Two months later, Mikulski was put on Ethics, and as the panel looks into the Packwood matter, Mikulski's sex gives her a special role in making the committee's work come across to the public as thorough and sensitive. Yet she also must take care not to appear overzealous; that could damage her relationships and legislative effectiveness in what is still an overwhelmingly male Senate.

If the past is any indication, Mikulski probably will devote much of her considerable energy to her role as chair of the Appropriations Subcommittee on VA, HUD and Independent Agencies.

Despite the belt-tightening environment of the 102nd Congress, Mikulski showed an uncanny ability to unearth more money for the diverse federal programs under her jurisdiction, and to distribute that money in a way that quelled infighting. As a result, she was able to head off what many predicted would be a collision between competing interests such as veterans, environmentalists, housing advocates and NASA for shares of a smaller budget pie.

She and her counterpart on the House Appropriations Committee, then-Rep. Bob Traxler of Michigan, more than doubled the money available for earmarked projects in the HUD budget between fiscal 1991 and fiscal 1992 — from \$73 million to \$150 million. "They went too far," grumbled HUD Secretary Jack F. Kemp. In fiscal 1993, they went further, funding \$260 million worth of VA/HUD earmarks. Mikulski and Traxler also defended their right to distribute such largesse, going up against Mississippi Rep. G. V. "Sonny" Montgomery, chairman of the Veterans' Affairs Committee, who argued that appropriators should not fund VA projects that had not been approved by an authorizing committee.

So far, Mikulski has been able to avoid making tough choices between her support for traditional Democratic social programs such as housing and veterans' programs, and NASA, which provides thousands of high-paying jobs in her state. But with the Clinton administration eagerly searching for ways to cut the deficit while also increasing funding for "human needs" priorities, pressure has intensified to target big-ticket items such as the space station.

In the 102nd, Mikulski successfully defended NASA's space station *Freedom* from repeated efforts to pull the funding plug. In 1991, she squeezed enough money out of the fiscal 1992 VA/HUD total to continue funding the station. She nibbled at numerous programs, but approved key projects for all the major VA/HUD constituencies and thereby kept them from lashing out against the station.

In 1992, Mikulski successfully employed a similar strategy in committee, but she had to defend the space station against attack on the floor. She made it clear that her support is grounded in earthly realities. "I truly believe that in space station *Freedom*, we are going to generate jobs today and jobs tomorrow," said Mikulski. "Jobs today in terms of the actual manufacturing of space station *Freedom*, but jobs tomorrow because of what we will learn."

Mikulski also has been an ardent defender of another "big science" program at NASA — the Mission to Planet Earth, a long-term project with a multibillion-dollar price tag that involves using unmanned satellites to collect environmental data about Earth.

Mikulski at times has been hard on NASA. When it was revealed in June 1990 that the Hubble Space Telescope had been deployed with a faulty lens, she fumed. However, NASA repaired some of the trouble using earmarked funds that Mikulski had put in the budget.

Mikulski has been a harsh critic of another agency that comes under her funding purview, the Federal Emergency Management Agency. After Hurricane Andrew, which devastated portions of Florida in August 1992, Mikulski characterized FEMA officials' disaster relief efforts as "pathetically sluggish" and "dysfunctional." In early 1993, she introduced legislation that would completely overhaul FEMA in order to improve the effectiveness of federal disaster response.

Mikulski has successfully used her power as an appropriator to benefit Maryland. In 1991, she lobbied for $200 million in funding for new buildings for the Food and Drug Administration. Both Montgomery and Prince George's counties wanted a piece of the action, so the FDA decided to consolidate its operations in two new facilities, one in each county.

Also in 1991, Mikulski used the appropriations process to compel the VA to award a prestigious geriatric research grant to a Baltimore VA facility, even though it had not won the grant in an earlier peer-review process.

The fiscal 1992 budget for the Environmental Protection Agency, also part of Mikulski's turf, included more than $47 million for Maryland projects, including a $40 million wastewater treatment plant in Baltimore.

In addition to the varied subjects she has pursued as chairman, Mikulski has continued to seek legislative expression for her liberal and feminist concerns. In the 102nd, she successfully amended the transportation spending bill to require automakers to label new cars to detail the city and country in which the car was made, and the percentage of U.S. labor and parts that went into the car.

She played a key role in negotiating a compromise child-care assistance bill that President Bush signed into law in 1989. She is a staunch supporter of abortion rights, and repeatedly challenged the Bush administration's ban on U.S. contributions to the U.N. population fund. In 1990, Mikulski successfully pushed legislation that created a women's health research office within the National Institutes of Health.

In March 1993, Mikulski called for a General Accounting Office investigation into sexual harassment at the 171 VA hospitals. She cited a January report by the VA inspector general that documented numerous charges of sexual harassment at the Atlanta VA medical center.

At Home: When she ran to succeed retiring GOP Sen. Charles McC. Mathias Jr. in 1986, many questioned whether the pudgy, 4-foot-11 Mikulski would strike voters as "senatorial." But then-Rep. Mikulski proved her skills, easily outrunning Rep. Michael D. Barnes and outgoing Gov. Harry R. Hughes in the Democratic primary, then drubbing Republican Linda Chavez with 61 percent of the vote.

In her 1992 re-election campaign, Mikulski became a political giant. She took 71 percent to trounce Alan L. Keyes, a black conservative activist who had run against Democratic Sen. Paul S. Sarbanes in 1988.

The granddaughter of Polish immigrants, Mikulski first gained a following by discussing the plight of the "forgotten" ethnic residents of America's cities. Mikulski also organized a fight against a highway that would have leveled several Baltimore neighborhoods. She won a City Council seat in 1971 and became prominent in the feminist movement.

In 1974, Mikulski challenged the heavily favored GOP Sen. Mathias and drew 43 percent of the vote. She was well positioned in 1976, when then-Rep. Sarbanes vacated his Baltimore House seat for his first Senate campaign. Mikulski had no trouble winning the Democratic House primary, and she breezed through five general elections.

With Mathias retiring in 1986, Mikulski's vibrant style was a big asset in the Senate primary against two well-known but colorless Democratic rivals. She won by more than 112,000 votes over Barnes; Hughes was a distant third.

Mikulski then had to overcome conservative Linda Chavez, a staff director of the U.S. Commission on Civil Rights under President Ronald Reagan. Though never more than a long shot, Chavez did not go quietly, describing

Mikulski as a "San Francisco style" liberal. Mikulski resisted the bait to brawl with an opponent who was no electoral threat and coasted to victory.

Maintaining high approval ratings and compiling a large campaign treasury, Mikulski deterred the most prominent Maryland Republicans in 1992. The GOP nomination went to Keyes, a State Department official during the Reagan presidency who had gained attention for his eloquent opposition to the liberal orthodoxy of most black leaders. When Keyes took 38 percent against Sarbanes, he called it a springboard for a future contest.

But his challenge to Mikulski got off on the wrong foot when it was revealed that Keyes was paying himself $8,500 a month from his campaign treasury. The practice was legal, but politically dubious in a recession year.

Mikulski played a featured role at the Democratic National Convention, conducting a program featuring female candidates and nominating Tennessee Sen. Al Gore for vice president. Keyes, meanwhile, clashed with the organizers of the Republican National Convention; when they were slow to offer him a speaking slot during TV's prime time, Keyes accused the party of racism. In October, the National Republican Senatorial Committee, citing Keyes' poor showing in opinion polls, cut off funding to his campaign; Keyes declared himself an "independent Republican."

Mikulski ended up carrying all but one of Maryland's counties. Although Maryland was Clinton's best state after Arkansas, Mikulski outran him there by 21 percentage points.

Committees

Appropriations (11th of 16 Democrats)
VA, HUD & Independent Agencies (chairman); Foreign Operations; Legislative Branch; Transportation; Treasury, Postal Service & General Government

Labor & Human Resources (7th of 10 Democrats)
Aging (chairman); Children, Families, Drugs & Alcoholism; Education, Arts & Humanities; Employment & Productivity

Select Ethics (2nd of 3 Democrats)

Elections

1992 General

Barbara A. Mikulski (D)	1,307,610	(71%)
Alan L. Keyes (R)	533,688	(29%)

1992 Primary

Barbara A. Mikulski (D)	376,444	(77%)
Thomas M. Wheatley (D)	31,214	(6%)
Walter Boyd (D)	26,467	(5%)
Don Allensworth (D)	19,731	(4%)
Scott David Britt (D)	13,001	(3%)
James Leonard White (D)	12,470	(3%)
B. Emerson Sweatt (D)	11,150	(2%)

Previous Winning Percentages: **1986** (61%) **1984*** (68%) **1982*** (74%) **1980*** (76%) **1978*** (100%) **1976*** (75%)

** House elections.*

Campaign Finance

	Receipts	Receipts from PACs		Expend-itures
1992				
Mikulski (D)	$2,940,047	$876,062	(30%)	$3,161,104
Keyes (R)	$1,185,385	$31,150	(3%)	$1,175,682

Key Votes

1993

Require unpaid family and medical leave	Y
Approve national "motor voter" registration bill	Y
Approve budget increasing taxes and reducing deficit	Y
Support president's right to lift military gay ban	Y

1992

Approve school-choice pilot program	N
Allow shifting funds from defense to domestic programs	Y
Oppose deeper cuts in spending for SDI	N

1991

Approve waiting period for handgun purchases	Y
Raise senators' pay and ban honoraria	N
Authorize use of force in Persian Gulf	N
Confirm Clarence Thomas to Supreme Court	N

Voting Studies

	Presidential Support		Party Unity		Conservative Coalition	
Year	**S**	**O**	**S**	**O**	**S**	**O**
1992	23	77	87	10	24	74
1991	33	67	91	8	33	65
1990	26	73	89	6	16	81
1989	41	56	94	5	11	89
1988	40	58	93	3	5	92
1987	28	64	93	4	13	84
House Service:						
1986	11	80	75	4	10	64
1985	18	83	89	4	18	82
1984	24	65	84	6	12	75
1983	15	84	90	6	18	76
1982	31	68	90	7	18	79
1981	32	68	84	9	11	87

Interest Group Ratings

Year	ADA	AFL-CIO	CCUS	ACU
1992	100	92	0	0
1991	90	83	20	10
1990	94	75	10	5
1989	90	100	38	8
1988	95	100	29	0
1987	100	100	28	4
House Service:				
1986	90	93	20	5
1985	80	100	32	10
1984	85	83	21	0
1983	90	94	11	9
1982	90	100	19	23
1981	100	87	16	7

1 Wayne T. Gilchrest (R)

Of Kennedyville — Elected 1990; 2nd Term

Born: April 15, 1946, Rahway, N.J.
Education: Wesley College, A.A. 1971; Delaware State U., B.A. 1973; Loyola College (Baltimore), 1990.
Military Service: Marine Corps, 1964-68.
Occupation: High school teacher.
Family: Wife, Barbara Rawley; three children.
Religion: Methodist.
Political Career: GOP nominee for U.S. House, 1988.
Capitol Office: 412 Cannon Bldg. 20515; 225-5311.

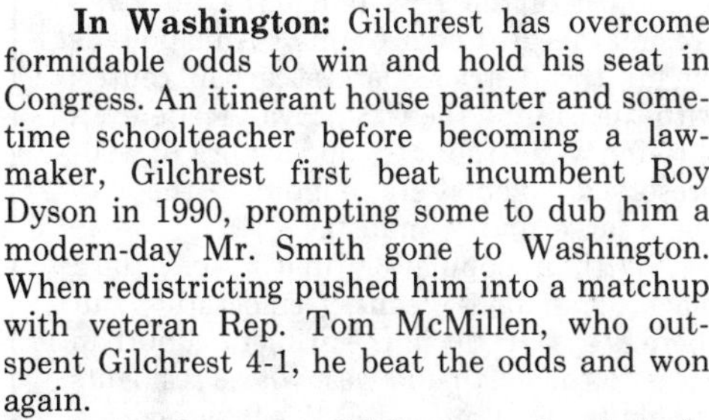

In Washington: Gilchrest has overcome formidable odds to win and hold his seat in Congress. An itinerant house painter and sometime schoolteacher before becoming a lawmaker, Gilchrest first beat incumbent Roy Dyson in 1990, prompting some to dub him a modern-day Mr. Smith gone to Washington. When redistricting pushed him into a matchup with veteran Rep. Tom McMillen, who outspent Gilchrest 4-1, he beat the odds and won again.

In his first term, Gilchrest stuck relatively close to the "Mr. Smith" image. He commuted daily to his home in Kennedyville and eschewed the usual Capitol Hill power uniform (he owned two suits when he was elected, and the family cars had 25 years between them). His genuine, approachable, and at times wide-eyed, demeanor gives the impression of an idealist at heart, and he has earned a reputation as a legislator who grapples with issues rather than just voting on them.

His Republican peers probably wish he grappled less. In the biggest splash of his first term, Gilchrest balked at his party's attempt to ease restrictions on wetlands. Conservatives, complaining that the 1989 definition of wetlands classified too much land as protected, attempted to gut Army Corps of Engineers guidelines of much of their restrictive language. Attempting to forestall this move, Gilchrest proposed an amendment to an emergency supplemental appropriations bill requiring a one-year study to scientifically define the word "wetland" before making any changes in the standing law. The Eastern Shore part of Gilchrest's district has many miles of such protected wetlands.

"We need a policy based on fact, not a policy based on politics," Gilchrest told his colleagues. Despite this plea, the amendment fell to defeat, 181-241, and eventually Congress did ease the definition to allow more land to stay in private hands. In 1992, however, Gilchrest saw a similar study provided as part of an appropriation for the Environmental Protection Agency.

Beyond wetlands, Gilchrest counts other environmental issues among his concerns. Assiduously guarding district interests, he sponsored a bill allowing the National Park Service to acquire more land at Assateague Island National Seashore, and brought in the EPA to clean up a wood treatment plant on the Eastern Shore.

Dipping into national issues, Gilchrest called for a moratorium on the construction of chemical munitions incinerators until the Department of Defense certified this process as the safest of all options. Gilchrest's bill died in committee, although then-Rep. Larry J. Hopkins, R-Ky., managed to include similar provisions in the 1992 defense authorization bill.

While Gilchrest distances himself from the GOP on environmental issues, his fiscal conservatism guarantees him a spot on the team. According to a local interest group, he is Maryland's staunchest pro-business legislator. Opposition to unpaid family leave, national health insurance and higher taxes complements his support for cuts in the capital gains tax and decreasing government spending.

On social and military issues, however, Gilchrest again parts ways with mainstream Republicans. He favored a seven-day waiting period for the purchase of a handgun (although he voted against a proposed assault weapons ban) and supported overturning the Bush administration's restrictions on abortion counseling at federally funded clinics. In 1991, he was one of 37 Republicans voting to pare back U.S. troop strength in Europe to less than 100,000 by 1995, a position partly driven by his hawkish views on the deficit.

As a former Marine who served in Vietnam, Gilchrest takes an interest in prisoner-of-war issues. In 1991, he traveled to countries involved in the Southeast Asian war to talk with government officials about POWs/MIAs. While he once insisted that all questions about missing military personnel should be resolved before normalizing relations with Vietnam, he later decided that normalization was an important step toward answering those questions.

Maryland 1

Cross Bay — Eastern Shore; Annapolis; Glen Burnie

The 4.3-mile-long Chesapeake Bay Bridge links the mainly rural counties of the Bay's Eastern Shore and the fast-growing suburbia of Anne Arundel County. These regions are different in many ways, but they share a conservative tilt that often benefits Republican candidates. George Bush swept the 1st in 1988 and bettered Bill Clinton here by 7 percentage points in 1992.

Yet the 1st is no lock for a Republican House candidate, as illustrated by Rep. Gilchrest's close 1992 contest against Democrat McMillen. Much of the Eastern Shore has a Democratic tradition (albeit of the conservative Southern brand). Annapolis, the state capital, has many government employees. Blacks make up 15 percent of the 1st's population; Annapolis, as well as Salisbury and Cambridge on the Eastern Shore, have large minority communities.

About three-fifths of the district's population is spread across the nine counties of the Eastern Shore. Isolated until the Bay Bridge was completed in the 1950s, most of the region remains rural. The Perdue poultry company has a large work force at its Salisbury headquarters and plants.

But the shore's rusticity is disrupted on summer weekends by vacationers from the Washington and Baltimore areas heading for Ocean City on the Atlantic or such villages as St. Michael's and Crisfield on the bay. The shore's larger communities have some manufacturing. An upswing in cross-bay commuting has boosted the populations of such central areas as Queen Anne's and Talbot counties.

Gilchrest in 1992 benefited from the regionalism of Eastern Shore residents (McMillen was from across the bay) and their Republican tilt in federal contests. The small town and farm country in the central part of the district is the GOP heartland: Gilchrest ran up better than 70 percent in Talbot and Kent counties. But he slipped below 55 percent in the southernmost part, with its larger working-class and black constituencies. He won narrowly in Cecil County, at the edges of the Baltimore and Philadelphia metropolitan areas in Maryland's northeast corner.

Most of the 1st's remaining residents are in Anne Arundel County. Annapolis is by far the district's largest urban center; with the capitol, the U.S. Naval Academy, a thriving waterfront area and a stock of well-preserved colonial-era buildings, the city has a large tourist industry.

With a population that is one-third black, Annapolis leans Democratic. But there is a GOP tilt in the affluent suburban areas to the north and west whose residents commute to Baltimore, Washington and Annapolis. At the county's north end are Glen Burnie and other working-class suburbs that lean Democratic but are rather conservative. McMillen carried his home base with 58 percent, but Bush edged Clinton, 43 percent to 38 percent, in the Anne Arundel part of the 1st.

The 1st also covers a small, blue-collar part of Baltimore city that is heavily Democratic but has few voters.

1990 Population: 597,684. White 498,523 (83%), Black 89,773 (15%), Other 9,388 (2%). Hispanic origin 6,580 (1%). 18 and over 454,906 (76%), 62 and over 91,037 (15%). Median age: 34.

Gilchrest ran on a "Clean up Congress" ticket even before it recently became fashionable, but has not joined all phases of the reform movement. By 1992, he had abandoned campaign promises to seek congressional term limits and had garnered criticism in the local media for abandoning a pledge not to have districtwide mailings.

He has embraced strict limits on contributions that will severely limit his fundraising options. In April 1992 he announced he would no longer accept money from political action committees or from individuals outside his district. He also introduced legislation to impose the same limits on all members of Congress.

Moderate social views, a penchant for independent thought and a focus on working for his district have led Gilchrest to take a low-profile seat on the GOP team, so far. He seems content to remain on Merchant Marine and Fisheries, where he can worry about wetlands and influence decisions about the fishing industry so important to his district. In the 103rd, Gilchrest joined Public Works, a spot that may force him to balance his interest in promoting district projects with his habit of trying to pare back transportation spending.

At Home: Gilchrest's easygoing manner and prosaic background may have led the House incumbents he has beaten to underestimate him. Among other occupations, he has labored as a barn builder, forest ranger and chicken slaughterhouse employee. When he first ran for the House in 1988, he was a high school teacher moonlighting as a house painter.

Gilchrest spent just $300 that year to win the little-sought nomination to oppose Dyson — a conservative Democrat who previously had won easily in the Eastern Shore-based 1st District. However, Dyson subsequently saw his popularity sink in 1988 after the suicide of his top House aide and reports of Dyson's ties to contractors involved in a Pentagon procurement scandal. Although long-shot Gilchrest got wan support from GOP officials, he came within 1,540 votes of winning.

Facing a rematch in 1990, a chastened Dyson came in with a well-funded campaign. But he was shadowed by the ethics cloud, and the hawkish Democrat faced more bad publicity when it was revealed that he was a conscientious objector during the Vietnam War.

Gilchrest was still laid back but more seasoned. Playing off Dyson's military flap, Gilchrest ran an ad late in the campaign that emphasized his service as a decorated Vietnam veteran. He won with surprising ease, taking 57 percent of the vote.

That did not spare him in 1992. The state legislature, in creating a new black-majority district near Washington, D.C., carved up Democratic Rep. McMillen's Annapolis-based district and threw him into a cross-bay contest with Gilchrest in the redrawn 1st.

Gilchrest first had to fend off Republican businesswoman Lisa G. Renshaw, a conservative who said Gilchrest's positions on abortion and wetlands made him a liberal; Gilchrest won the primary with a plurality.

Although Gilchrest had more constituents than McMillen in the new district — about three-fifths of the residents came from his Eastern Shore base — the Democrat had more flash and cash. A towering former basketball star for the University of Maryland and the Washington Bullets, McMillen had celebrity glamour. A prodigious fundraiser, he far outspent Gilchrest.

But Gilchrest's average-guy appeal again won out. Targeting his base in the largely rural and politically parochial Eastern Shore region, Gilchrest portrayed McMillen as a rich Washington insider and junketeer.

The strategy worked, but not by much. Gilchrest outran McMillen on the Eastern Shore by more than 25,000 votes, offsetting McMillen's 17,000-vote advantage in his base on the western side of the Chesapeake Bay.

Committees

Merchant Marine & Fisheries (9th of 18 Republicans)
Coast Guard & Navigation; Environment & Natural Resources

Public Works & Transportation (11th of 24 Republicans)
Aviation; Investigations & Oversight; Water Resources & the Environment

Elections

1992 General		
Wayne T. Gilchrest (R)	120,084	(52%)
Tom McMillen (D)	112,771	(48%)
1992 Primary		
Wayne T. Gilchrest (R)	17,469	(47%)
Lisa G. Renshaw (R)	10,933	(30%)
Robert P. Duckworth (R)	6,915	(19%)
Edward F. Taylor (R)	1,261	(3%)
Michael P. Jackson (R)	482	(1%)
1990 General		
Wayne T. Gilchrest (R)	88,920	(57%)
Roy Dyson (D)	67,518	(43%)

District Vote for President

1992
D 93,165 (37%)
R 109,039 (44%)
I 47,188 (19%)

Campaign Finance

	Receipts	Receipts from PACs		Expend-itures
1992				
Gilchrest (R)	$394,794	$94,529	(24%)	$395,104
McMillen (D)	$1,256,666	$699,296	(56%)	$1,553,849
1990				
Gilchrest (R)	$266,930	$60,074	(23%)	$264,932
Dyson (D)	$759,213	$497,700	(66%)	$771,809

Key Votes

1993	
Require parental notification of minors' abortions	Y
Require unpaid family and medical leave	N
Approve national "motor voter" registration bill	Y
Approve budget increasing taxes and reducing deficit	N
Approve economic stimulus plan	N
1992	
Approve balanced-budget constitutional amendment	Y
Close down space station program	N
Approve U.S. aid for former Soviet Union	N
Allow shifting funds from defense to domestic programs	N
1991	
Extend unemployment benefits using deficit financing	Y
Approve waiting period for handgun purchases	Y
Authorize use of force in Persian Gulf	Y

Voting Studies

	Presidential Support		Party Unity		Conservative Coalition	
Year	S	O	S	O	S	O
1992	56	42	68	29	71	27
1991	70	30	78	21	86	14

Interest Group Ratings

Year	ADA	AFL-CIO	CCUS	ACU
1992	30	36	75	64
1991	20	17	90	70

2 Helen Delich Bentley (R)

Of Lutherville — Elected 1984; 5th Term

Born: Nov. 28, 1923, Ruth, Nev.
Education: U. of Nevada, 1941-42; George Washington U., 1943; U. of Missouri, B.A. 1944.
Occupation: International trade consultant; journalist.
Family: Husband, William Roy Bentley.
Religion: Eastern Orthodox.
Political Career: Chairman, Federal Maritime Commission, 1969-75; GOP nominee for U.S. House, 1980, 1982.
Capitol Office: 1610 Longworth Bldg. 20515; 225-3061.

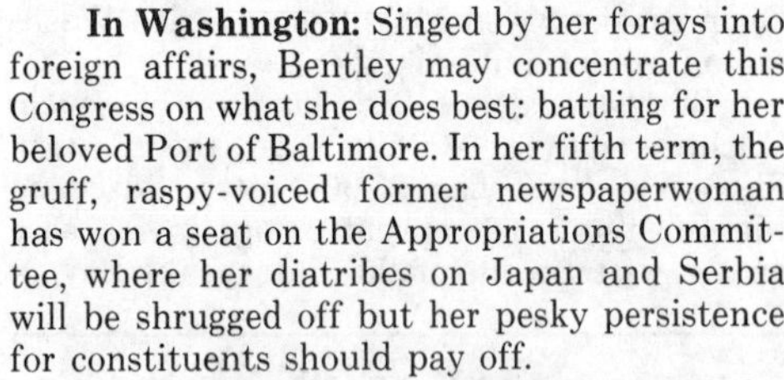

In Washington: Singed by her forays into foreign affairs, Bentley may concentrate this Congress on what she does best: battling for her beloved Port of Baltimore. In her fifth term, the gruff, raspy-voiced former newspaperwoman has won a seat on the Appropriations Committee, where her diatribes on Japan and Serbia will be shrugged off but her pesky persistence for constituents should pay off.

In the 102nd Congress, Bentley provided a lonely voice in support of Serbia, even attending meetings of committees to which she did not belong to remind colleagues that the Bosnian Serbs were not the only ones at fault in the complex ethnic struggle. But her position grew so unpopular that she quit talking about it in public.

That was a rare instance of Bentley holding her tongue. Before that, she had been best known for her frequent denunciations of Japan, whose trading practices she blamed for the disappearance of factory and harbor jobs among her blue-collar constituents.

In the summer of 1987, Bentley gained attention by organizing a media event on the steps of the Capitol in which she and several other GOP members used sledgehammers to destroy a Toshiba radio. It was a symbolic protest against the Japanese company's sale of sensitive technology to the Soviet Union.

Bentley wrote late in 1989 that Japanese foreign investment in the United States "is the modern Pearl Harbor" — the 50th anniversary of which she greeted in 1991 with a bill demanding that Japan apologize. She frequently takes to the House floor to lament Japanese inroads into bastions of American culture and life, such as the 1989 purchase of Columbia Pictures by Sony Corp. and the 1991 purchase of California's Pebble Beach golf course by Japanese investors. "Instead of crying 'fore,' golfers can cry 'banzai,' " she complained.

Bentley's interest in foreign affairs stems from hearthside concerns even when it comes to Serbia. Her parents were born there, and she saw a duty to speak up for a long-suffering people cast as villains on the world stage. In 1991, Bentley helped form SerbNet, a pro-Serb lobbying group, and served until mid-1992 as its president. She used congressional stationery for a pro-Serb mailing, which she later said was a mistake, although she insisted that she was "not walking away from the Serbian people." Bentley said she was not defending misbehavior by the Bosnian Serbs, but that other sides were equally to blame for a "horrible tragedy."

Shortly before the 1992 election, her press secretary resigned, calling on her to change her stand. Bentley said the aide's resignation resulted from his personal problems. However, she quit talking to the media about Serbia.

Bentley has demonstrated she can work with Democrats, steering to enactment in 1992 a bill to combat overweight shipments that were causing road damage and safety problems when hauled by trucks. She won approval of the measure not only from her own committees, but also from Energy and Commerce.

Bentley was first elected on a promise to pry loose funds for dredging the Port of Baltimore. She used her seat on the Public Works and Transportation Committee to lobby for inclusion of the project in a water resources bill, and then fought to get the funds into a 1986 supplemental appropriation.

Before joining Appropriations, an "exclusive" committee, Bentley served on the Public Works, Merchant Marine and Fisheries, Budget and Select Aging committees. As a former chairman of the Federal Maritime Commission, she had valuable contacts in the Republican administrations and the maritime agency.

Bentley drew some unusual attention in June 1990 when a process server accused her of assaulting him as he was handing her a subpoena as a potential witness in a murder trial. Although the assault charges were dropped within a month, those who know Bentley well did not think it ridiculous that at 66, the feisty 5-foot-2 woman could have wrangled with a 230-pound former police officer.

But the same woman won respect from

Maryland 2

Baltimore and Harford counties

The 2nd has more than enough Republican territory to provide a base for GOP Rep. Bentley. In Baltimore County — home to slightly more than 60 percent of the 2nd's residents — the district takes in middle-class areas of Towson and such upper-income communities as Lutherville, Cockeysville and Hunt Valley, then sweeps north into horse country. The district also includes conservative-minded Harford County, which has experienced a burst of exurban growth.

Yet it is the support Bentley derives from blue-collar workers in the grimy southeastern part of Baltimore County that has made her so successful. To the traditionally Democratic voters there, Bentley's party label is less important than her support for the port of Baltimore and her strong views that unfair foreign competition has cost thousands of jobs at Bethlehem Steel and other local industrial mainstays.

Bethlehem Steel's complex at Sparrows Point is still Baltimore County's largest employer, but its 7,000 jobs are a fraction of the number during the steel industry's heyday. Many of the workers live across the Baltimore Beltway in Dundalk, at the Baltimore city line. Essex and nearby Middle River are largely blue-collar.

To the north, the 2nd moves into more suburban environs, including the county's most affluent communities and its burgeoning employment centers. Diversification has helped keep Baltimore County moving forward even as its heavy-industry sector has declined. The McCormick food company's headquarters are in Hunt Valley; tool manufacturer Black & Decker is based in Towson.

However, several county employers (Martin Marietta, AAI, Allied-Signal and Westinghouse, for example) rely on defense contracts, a cause for concern in an era of Pentagon cuts. Westinghouse has laid off about 4,500 workers in the past two years. But AAI is trying to diversify and recently won a contract to build weather monitoring systems for airports.

Job and other economic concerns dampened the GOP advantage here in 1992. Although Bentley again dominated in her home base, George Bush carried the part of Baltimore County that is in the 2nd by just 44 percent to 38 percent over Bill Clinton. His subpar performance here — combined with the typically strong Democratic vote in the parts of the county that are in the 3rd and 7th districts — allowed Clinton to become the first Democratic presidential candidate to win Baltimore County since 1964.

Republican loyalties are stronger to the east in Harford County. Bush beat Clinton by 11 percentage points. Harford grew by 25 percent in the 1980s, as commuters poured into subdivisions in such towns as Bel Air and Joppa. Much of Harford's economic base is defense-related: With more than 14,000 employees, the Aberdeen weapons proving ground is by far the region's largest employer.

At its southern end, the 2nd leaps across the Patapsco River into an upscale, strongly Republican corner of Anne Arundel County, including parts of suburban Pasadena and Severna Park.

1990 Population: 597,683. White 547,999 (92%), Black 35,295 (6%), Other 14,389 (2%). Hispanic origin 7,242 (1%). 18 and over 457,201 (76%), 62 and over 88,673 (15%). Median age: 34.

both sides as a conciliator after she stepped forward to mediate a heated 1989-90 strike at the Baltimore port.

At Home: Persistence paid big dividends for Bentley. It took her three tries to convince suburban Baltimore voters that veteran Democrat Clarence D. Long had overstayed his welcome. But just two years after her 1984 victory, Bentley beat back a $1 million challenge by Democrat Kathleen Kennedy Townsend, the eldest child of the late Sen. Robert F. Kennedy.

Bentley, who dubbed herself "the fighting lady," lost to Long in 1980 and 1982, but she improved with each campaign. Her theme was that Long had mishandled Baltimore's harbor economy.

Bentley had expertise on harbor issues, having worked for 25 years as a maritime reporter and editor for The Sun of Baltimore. She also produced a weekly TV program on the harbor that ran for 15 years. In 1969, Bentley was appointed chairman of the Federal Maritime Commission by President Richard M. Nixon, becoming the highest-ranking woman in the federal government at that time.

In 1984, Bentley was aided by a redistricting change that bolstered the GOP presence in the 2nd and by Ronald Reagan's strong showing there. She won with 51 percent.

Bentley's first-term emphasis on harbor dredging and trade issues helped secure her base, but they did not earn her any respite from a vigorous challenge in 1986. The Democratic candidate was a relative newcomer to the district but had no name identification problem. As a member of the Kennedy family, Townsend, a 35-year-old attorney, drew considerable media attention, both locally and from national and foreign journalists.

While Bentley was slowed by a kidney ailment, Townsend campaigned vigorously. Many observers speculated that Townsend's broad smile and cheerleader-like enthusiasm would contrast well with Bentley's gruff persona.

Yet Bentley trumped Townsend by touting her constituent service and focusing heavily on the largess she had brought to the 2nd. Her incumbency also helped her raise even more money than the heavily financed Democrat. Bentley won an impressive 59 percent victory.

Bentley coasted in the next two elections, taking more than 70 percent each time. Despite her differences with the Republican White House on trade, Bentley emerged as a dominant force in the Maryland GOP and chaired George Bush's 1988 and 1992 campaigns in the state.

Redistricting gave Bentley some nervous moments prior to the 1992 election. The overwhelmingly Democratic state legislature appeared likely at one point to pass a plan that would have placed Bentley and fellow Republican Rep. Wayne T. Gilchrest in a single district.

But Bentley turned up with an unexpected political bodyguard: Democratic Gov. William Donald Schaefer. Another thorny political personality, Schaefer had a longtime alliance with Bentley based on their shared passion for the Port of Baltimore. Never a strong partisan — he would later raise Democratic hackles by endorsing Bush's 1992 re-election bid — Schaefer made it clear he would veto any redistricting plan that jeopardized Bentley.

Bentley retained a safely Republican district in the Baltimore suburbs and exurbs. Instead, Democratic Rep. Tom McMillen was thrown in with Gilchrest (in the new 1st District) and lost.

The 1992 campaign was not effortless for Bentley. Democrat Michael C. Hickey Jr., a lawyer, ran aggressively, criticizing Bentley's stand on Serbia and arguing that, for all her rhetoric on trade, she had failed to stem the loss of local blue-collar jobs. But Bentley still managed to roll up 65 percent in a year when Democrat Bill Clinton was carrying Maryland handily.

With a district drawn to fit her, about the only threat to her longevity in Congress appears to be a likely appeal from officials of the flaccid Maryland GOP who wish she would bear the party standard for governor or senator in 1994.

Committee

Appropriations (18th of 23 Republicans)
Labor, Health & Human Services, Education & Related Agencies; Military Construction

Elections

1992 General		
Helen Delich Bentley (R)	165,443	(65%)
Michael C. Hickey Jr. (D)	88,658	(35%)
1992 Primary		
Helen Delich Bentley (R)	29,814	(87%)
Robert T. Petr (R)	4,435	(13%)
1990 General		
Helen Delich Bentley (R)	115,398	(74%)
Ronald P. Bowers (D)	39,785	(26%)

Previous Winning Percentages: **1988** (71%) **1986** (59%) **1984** (51%)

District Vote for President

1992

D	98,267 (36%)
R	121,087 (45%)
I	52,668 (19%)

Campaign Finance

	Receipts	Receipts from PACs		Expend-itures
1992				
Bentley (R)	$959,100	$240,620	(25%)	$956,821
Hickey (D)	$49,031	$4,000	(8%)	$48,841
1990				
Bentley (R)	$781,008	$214,305	(27%)	$730,852

Key Votes

1993	
Require parental notification of minors' abortions	Y
Require unpaid family and medical leave	N
Approve national "motor voter" registration bill	N
Approve budget increasing taxes and reducing deficit	N
Approve economic stimulus plan	N
1992	
Approve balanced-budget constitutional amendment	Y
Close down space station program	N
Approve U.S. aid for former Soviet Union	Y
Allow shifting funds from defense to domestic programs	N
1991	
Extend unemployment benefits using deficit financing	Y
Approve waiting period for handgun purchases	Y
Authorize use of force in Persian Gulf	Y

Voting Studies

	Presidential Support		Party Unity		Conservative Coalition	
Year	**S**	**O**	**S**	**O**	**S**	**O**
1992	62	32	77	19	85	8
1991	60	36	72	25	84	14
1990	61	36	76	17	87	11
1989	51	40	74	17	80	5
1988	46	45	74	16	87	11
1987	49	48	68	25	84	16
1986	57	38	60	30	80	14
1985	64	34	74	19	85	13

Interest Group Ratings

Year	ADA	AFL-CIO	CCUS	ACU
1992	25	50	100	80
1991	25	50	40	60
1990	11	25	77	83
1989	20	50	90	86
1988	10	69	79	86
1987	32	63	73	57
1986	15	67	63	62
1985	20	24	73	76

3 Benjamin L. Cardin (D)

Of Baltimore — Elected 1986; 4th Term

Born: Oct. 5, 1943, Baltimore, Md.
Education: U. of Pittsburgh, B.A. 1964; U. of Maryland, LL.B. 1967.
Occupation: Lawyer.
Family: Wife, Myrna Edelman; two children.
Religion: Jewish.
Political Career: Md. House, 1967-87, speaker, 1979-87.
Capitol Office: 227 Cannon Bldg. 20515; 225-4016.

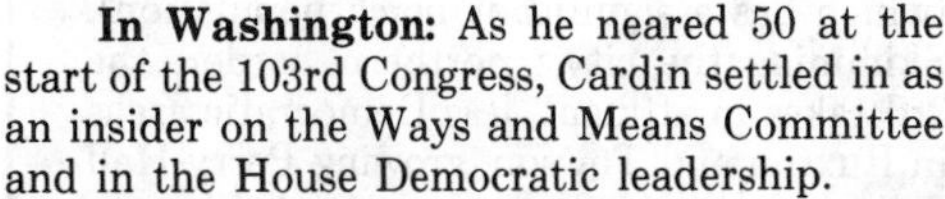

In Washington: As he neared 50 at the start of the 103rd Congress, Cardin settled in as an insider on the Ways and Means Committee and in the House Democratic leadership.

He was well-positioned on the panel's Health Subcommittee to play an important role in what was expected to be the biggest legislative challenge in years — the overhaul of the nation's health-care delivery and financing systems. In his first two years on the committee, he proved to colleagues his ability to grasp and manipulate the complex issues involved in such technical and legalistic subjects as living wills and pre-authorized treatment.

And as 13th of 24 Democrats on the full committee, Cardin was no longer relegated to sitting next to equally junior Republicans on the lower tier of the dais, where he previously would wait to get a shot at questioning a witness.

Cardin was once a young man in a hurry: A state legislator before he had finished law school, a committee chairman at 32 and Speaker of the Maryland House at 35, he arrived in Washington with uncommon momentum. But the erstwhile boy wonder appears to have tempered the impatient streak that led him to protest outside a closed session of the budget summit in September 1990. He was there on behalf of members left out of the deal-making. "Even if we weren't happy with what was going on," he complained, "we'd be a lot more comfortable if we knew *what* was going on."

With his rising stature on one of the premier House committees, Cardin found a reason to curb his appetite and to shelve for now his idea to run for the Maryland statehouse. The fact that a Democrat would occupy the White House for at least four years also made Washington more desirable than Annapolis.

At the same time that he found a channel for his energy on Ways and Means in the 102nd Congress, Cardin also was named to the Committee on Standards of Official Conduct, the panel that passes judgment on colleagues' ethics. The assignment is hardly sought after and often results from having won some coveted seat, such as Ways and Means. But it generally indicates that a member has won the leadership's confidence.

Cardin accepted the task with uncommon vigor, serving on high-profile task forces that investigated scandals involving the House bank and Post Office. His involvement was not likely to win him favor with colleagues, but that did not deter him from playing a visible role.

Before joining Ways and Means, Cardin already had a vote of confidence from its chairman, Dan Rostenkowski of Illinois. As an at-large whip in 1988, Cardin was part of the task force apparatus organized to help pass Rostenkowski's catastrophic health insurance plan (since repealed). Cardin also had a key ally in fellow Marylander Steny H. Hoyer, who became Democratic Caucus chairman in 1989.

Cardin enhanced his standing with Rostenkowski in 1993 by claiming a seat on the insider's panel of House Administration, which manages internal affairs, including committee budgets. And his value to the leadership was further signaled with his selection before the 103rd as a member of the Caucus Steering and Policy Committee, which makes committee assignments.

On Ways and Means, Cardin has generally joined with the panel's bloc of younger, more liberal members who think the federal tax structure became unacceptably regressive during the 1980s. He has supported changes in that structure that would roll back Reagan-era tax cuts for the highest income groups and opposed tax cuts (such as the partial exclusion of capital gains income) that would principally benefit the wealthy.

In one way, Cardin has veered from that stance. He joined in early 1993 with Florida Republican E. Clay Shaw Jr. to press for repeal of a tax enacted in 1990 on luxury items, including boats. Though the tax was aimed at the wealthy, it was widely viewed as contributing to a decline in the boat industry, which is critical to Maryland's Chesapeake Bay economy.

Cardin arrived in Congress brimming with confidence that his reputation as a legislative deal-maker and budgetary expert would win him a coveted seat on Budget, if not Ways and Means. When those seats proved unreachable, Cardin did not waste time sulking. He spent considerable time on the floor, listening to the

Maryland 3

Downtown and ethnic Baltimore; Columbia

The city of Baltimore has long had an ethnically diverse, Democrat-dominated district. But today that district ranges far and wide to take in thousands of city natives who moved to the suburbs.

The 3rd, a reverse-C shape, wends in and out of Baltimore to pick up the Democratic voters who enable Rep. Cardin to dominate his House contests. Democratic Sen. Barbara A. Mikulski, a former 3rd District House member, has also run very well here. With its large suburban constituency, the 3rd can be somewhat more competitive in presidential contests; but Bill Clinton easily bested George Bush in 1992, with Ross Perot lagging a weak third.

The city still has the largest share (about two-fifths) of the 3rd's residents. At the heart of the district is Baltimore's rejuvenated downtown. Spurred by the success of Harborplace, a retail-and-entertainment complex along the once-forsaken waterfront, Baltimore's downtown has sprouted hotels and office buildings: The USF&G insurance company, Maryland National Bank and Crown Central Petroleum have headquarters here.

In 1992, baseball's Orioles moved into a new stadium just west of downtown. To the south, the 3rd moves through gentrifying Federal Hill, takes in a blue-collar stretch around the harbor leading to Fort McHenry, then jumps across the Patapsco River's Middle Branch to mainly black Cherry Hill.

East of downtown is the city's ethnic heartland: Little Italy and Highlandtown (whose Polish and German voters gave Mikulski her political start). There is a working-class accent here: The city is "Bawlamer" and its ball team is the "Eryals." General Motors has a factory in East Baltimore. The 3rd moves north through working-class sections on the city's east edge, then west to pick up some of Baltimore's wealthier communities. The mainly Jewish areas of northwest Baltimore make up Cardin's base.

In its part of Baltimore County (about a third of the total population), the 3rd follows the path of Jewish migration north from wealthy Pikesville to middle-class Reisterstown and west to Randallstown (which has a significant black population). Skimming the city's northern border, the 3rd takes in affluent, less Democratic areas in Ruxton and Towson, growing Perry Hall and modest suburbs such as Parkville.

On the other side of the city, the 3rd includes middle-class suburbs in south Baltimore County and northwest Anne Arundel County near Baltimore-Washington International Airport: Linthicum — site of a Westinghouse facility pinched by defense cuts — and the part of Fort Meade that houses the National Security Agency are here.

The 3rd also includes the eastern portion of Howard County and Columbia, with its planned racial mix and liberal-leaning electorate. The city has become an economic engine in the middle of the newly combined Washington-Baltimore metropolitan area. The Rouse development company, which built Columbia and Harborplace, and several high-tech companies are here.

1990 Population: 597,680. White 475,260 (80%), Black 104,380 (17%), Other 18,040 (3%). Hispanic origin 10,264 (2%). 18 and over 459,113 (77%), 62 and over 94,865 (16%). Median age: 34.

proceedings and talking with members one-on-one. Despite his evident ambitions, he stayed on friendly personal terms with most colleagues. When he did rise to speak during the 100th Congress, it was often about the plight of individual Soviet Jewish "refuseniks," an important concern in his district.

He dug into the work of his two committees and served his party's interests when needed. On Judiciary, he offered an amendment to the 1988 drug bill to strike "user accountability" language. Like many liberals, Cardin maintained that convicted drug users who had gone to jail had paid their debt to society and should not be disqualified from federal benefits, such as education and job training. His amendment was rejected in favor of one requiring drug offenders to complete rehabilitation programs.

For all his ambition, Cardin has not been one to forget the home folk. In his time on Capitol Hill, he has compiled a creditable record of service — including not just the usual constituent errands but chief sponsorship of the Chesapeake Bay Restoration Act and active defense of Maryland's unusual system for reimbursing hospitals under Medicare.

He has also brought home such projects as the preservation of the Coast Guard base at Curtis Bay, the restoration of Fort McHenry in Baltimore, and development assistance for a light rail system in Baltimore and a prototype magnetic levitation train between Baltimore and Washington.

At Home: Like most state legislators, Cardin was perceived as having taken a step up when he moved to Congress from the Maryland House. But Cardin gave up considerable power in doing so. He had served as House Speaker in Annapolis for almost a decade, growing accustomed to calling the legislative shots.

Cardin's legislative talents helped him acquire a leadership role in the Maryland House at an extraordinarily young age. He was 23 when first elected to the legislature, and in 1975 he was chairman of the House Ways and Means Committee. Four years later, Cardin became the youngest Speaker in the history of the Maryland House.

Cardin was generally popular among his Annapolis colleagues. Those who viewed him as tough but fair outnumbered critics who complained that he planted pliable allies in chairmanships and rushed favored bills through without debate. On such difficult issues as pension laws and bank deregulation, Cardin adopted a conciliatory and bipartisan approach. Though he opposed extreme tax-limitation measures, Cardin established a Spending Affordability Committee to restrain the growth in state spending.

Cardin initially hoped that his strong legislative record would earn him his party's nomination in 1986 to succeed outgoing Democratic Gov. Harry R. Hughes. But William Donald Schaefer, the popular Democratic mayor of Baltimore, also decided to run for governor. Cardin recognized that Schaefer would overshadow him, so he opted to seek the 3rd District seat that Democrat Barbara A. Mikulski was leaving to run for the Senate.

Cardin's reserved demeanor is in sharp contrast to Mikulski's pugnacity. But the strength of his credentials easily offsets the relative mildness of his personality. His House elections have been non-events: He drew no significant primary opposition for the open seat in 1986, and has won at least 70 percent in his four general-election contests.

Cardin's growing clout in the House and longstanding ties to the state legislature benefited him during the redistricting that preceded the 1992 elections. Although the state map faced major changes to accommodate a second black-majority district, Cardin's interests were protected: He retained a Democratic-leaning district with his base in the heavily Jewish neighborhoods of northwest Baltimore and nearby suburbs.

Committees

House Administration (12th of 12 Democrats)
Accounts; Elections

Standards of Official Conduct (3rd of 7 Democrats)

Ways & Means (13th of 24 Democrats)
Health; Human Resources

Elections

1992 General		
Benjamin L. Cardin (D)	163,354	(74%)
William T.S. Bricker (R)	58,869	(26%)
1992 Primary		
Benjamin L. Cardin (D)	63,793	(84%)
Carl A. Mueller (D)	11,707	(16%)
1990 General		
Benjamin L. Cardin (D)	82,545	(70%)
Harwood Nichols (R)	35,841	(30%)

Previous Winning Percentages: **1988** (73%) **1986** (79%)

District Vote for President

1992
D 136,829 (54%)
R 82,494 (32%)
I 34,973 (14%)

Campaign Finance

	Receipts	Receipts from PACs		Expend-itures
1992				
Cardin (D)	$591,234	$292,553	(49%)	$646,863
Bricker (R)	$6,635	$521	(8%)	$8,832
1990				
Cardin (D)	$532,752	$200,790	(38%)	$363,847
Nichols (R)	$4,325	0		$4,234

Key Votes

1993	
Require parental notification of minors' abortions	N
Require unpaid family and medical leave	Y
Approve national "motor voter" registration bill	Y
Approve budget increasing taxes and reducing deficit	Y
Approve economic stimulus plan	Y
1992	
Approve balanced-budget constitutional amendment	N
Close down space station program	N
Approve U.S. aid for former Soviet Union	Y
Allow shifting funds from defense to domestic programs	Y
1991	
Extend unemployment benefits using deficit financing	Y
Approve waiting period for handgun purchases	Y
Authorize use of force in Persian Gulf	N

Voting Studies

	Presidential Support		Party Unity		Conservative Coalition	
Year	**S**	**O**	**S**	**O**	**S**	**O**
1992	17	82	93	5	27	71
1991	32	67	91	8	22	78
1990	21	79	95	4	13	87
1989	36	63	94	5	22	76
1988	22	76	93	4	18	79
1987	22	75	90	3	19	81

Interest Group Ratings

Year	ADA	AFL-CIO	CCUS	ACU
1992	95	83	38	4
1991	75	92	30	0
1990	83	92	14	4
1989	90	100	30	7
1988	90	93	36	4
1987	88	94	13	0

4 Albert R. Wynn (D)

Of Largo — Elected 1992; 1st Term

Born: Sept. 10, 1951, Philadelphia, Pa.
Education: U. of Pittsburgh, B.S. 1973; Howard U., 1973-74; Georgetown U., J.D. 1977.
Occupation: Lawyer.
Family: Separated.
Religion: Baptist.
Political Career: Md. House, 1983-87; Md. Senate, 1987-93.
Capitol Office: 423 Cannon Bldg. 20515; 225-8699.

The Path to Washington: Wynn appealed across both racial and county lines — which were in this case equally broad divides — to win the Democratic primary, the race that mattered in this overwhelmingly Democratic district. From there it was a relatively easy walk to a win in November.

A solid Democrat in the state legislature for 10 years, Wynn is a supporter of abortion rights and an ally of organized labor. His close friendship with Rep. Steny H. Hoyer, chairman of the House Democratic Caucus and a fellow resident of Maryland's Prince George's County, should be an asset to both.

Wynn advocates gun control and tough approaches to criminal sentencing, key concerns for his middle-class district, parts of which have seen the murder rate skyrocket in recent years. In the legislature, Wynn fought to ban concealable handguns and to send convicted murderers to prison with no chance for parole.

Like many in 1992 contests, Wynn made the economy a central tenet of his campaign, focusing his attacks on President Bush.

Wynn hopes to use his seat on the Banking, Finance and Urban Affairs Committee to boost the availability of capital to small and minority-owned businesses. He is especially concerned that existing rules for collateral and owner's equity are blocking many loans.

In April 1993, he voted to give the president limited line-item veto authority in opposition to the stated position of the Congressional Black Caucus.

This newly drawn, black-majority district in the close-in Washington suburbs posed multiple challenges for aspiring candidates. First, there was an early March primary that left little time for fundraising or campaigning. Second, the race drew 20 candidates — 13 Democrats and seven Republicans — several with significant name recognition, making it all the more difficult to escape from the pack.

Third, the district straddles the Montgomery-Prince George's line, with about three-fourths of its voters in black-majority Prince George's and the rest in mostly white Montgomery.

Wynn took his high-energy, personal campaign across the border into Montgomery, hoping that a win there, coupled with sufficient support from his Prince George's base, would be enough. It proved to be the right strategy, but the outcome was very close.

Wynn's principal opponent was popular Prince George's State's Attorney Alexander Williams Jr., who had proved his ability to win white votes in past countywide elections but who concentrated his efforts at home. Williams edged Wynn by 400 votes in Prince George's, but Wynn out-polled Williams in Montgomery by 1,700 votes.

State Rep. Dana Lee Dembrow of Montgomery, the leading white candidate in the race, ran well ahead in his home county and finished third overall. But black leaders' fears that a large number of black candidates might split the black vote and allow a white to sneak in proved unfounded.

Endorsements from key county elected officials aided Wynn's strong showing in Montgomery. Many Montgomery Democrats saw the chance to win another voice on Capitol Hill by supporting Wynn, who showed a desire to bridge the gap that usually separates the counties.

Redistricting had left the balance of Montgomery in the 8th, which was in the firm grip of GOP Rep. Constance A. Morella.

It also helped Wynn's cause that turnout in Montgomery was significantly higher than in Prince George's.

Though the general election appeared a foregone conclusion even before the primary, Republican Michele Dyson, a black business owner from Montgomery County, tried to make it a race. The two differed little on substance, but her business credentials and support for tax cuts on capital gains income earned her the endorsement of the U.S. Chamber of Commerce.

The overwhelming Democratic registration and Wynn's name recognition in Prince George's left Dyson in the dust. Wynn won 75 percent of the vote and seems secure in the seat for as long as he wants it.

Maryland 4

Inner Prince George's County; Silver Spring

The emergence of Prince George's as one of the nation's few suburban counties with a black majority sparked the creation of the 4th. Blacks are about three-fifths of the district's population; most of them live in Prince George's, which makes up the major part of the 4th. Adding Hispanics, whose numbers have steadily grown in recent years, more than two-thirds of the 4th's residents are of minority groups.

Still, there is a substantial white population, particularly in the southeast section of Montgomery County that contributes slightly more than a quarter of the district's residents. When the first House primary was held in the new black-majority 4th in 1992, black Democratic activists worried that a white candidate might maneuver through a large crowd of black contenders. But Wynn used a biracial appeal in both counties to take the nomination.

The primary was the hard part in this sure Democratic district. In the general election, Wynn piled up 84 percent of the vote in Prince George's County and took 59 percent in Montgomery. Bill Clinton ran just slightly behind Wynn in Prince George's but ahead of him in the Montgomery section.

Prince George's is in many ways a success story of black upward mobility. For blacks, it is among the nation's leading jurisdictions in business formation, home ownership and education. Many residents work in Washington, D.C., and at a complex in Suitland (which includes the Census Bureau and the National Weather Service) and at Andrews Air Force Base. There are large private employers in Landover (such as the Giant supermarket chain that dominates the area) and in the New Carrollton business center. The Capital Centre arena is in Largo.

For some residents, however, there has been no escape from the drugs and guns that many hoped to leave behind when they moved from the District of Columbia. Drug trafficking and attendant violence plague a number of the 4th's low-income communities, which are mostly inside the Capital Beltway that rings Washington.

The largest concentrations of Hispanics are in working-class and low-income communities in western Prince George's County and in the Silver Spring area of eastern Montgomery County. Takoma Park, which straddles the county line, has a bohemian image: Liberal activists declared it a "nuclear free zone" in the 1980s.

Silver Spring, one of Washington's first suburbs, saw its once-bustling downtown grow seedy as the retail trade moved to regional malls. Local officials have finally resolved a years-long battle between developers and residents over how to rejuvenate the city; developers now plan a new mall and office buildings, while residents will enjoy a civic plaza and the restoration of the downtown's Art Deco elements.

North of Silver Spring the 4th follows the Route 29 business corridor. The middle- and upper-middle-income communities in this area are whiter and more conservative than communities in the rest of the district.

1990 Population: 597,690. White 200,081 (33%), Black 349,499 (58%), Other 48,110 (8%). Hispanic origin 37,962 (6%). 18 and over 447,123 (75%), 62 and over 54,791 (9%). Median age: 31.

Committees

Banking, Finance & Urban Affairs (24th of 30 Democrats)
Consumer Credit & Insurance; Housing & Community Development

Foreign Affairs (23rd of 27 Democrats)
Economic Policy, Trade & the Environment; Western Hemisphere Affairs

Post Office & Civil Service (11th of 15 Democrats)
Census, Statistics & Postal Personnel

Campaign Finance

	Receipts	Receipts from PACs		Expend-itures
1992				
Wynn (D)	$571,408	$238,477	(42%)	$386,186
Dyson (R)	$137,717	$18,192	(13%)	$135,945

Key Votes

1993

Require parental notification of minors' abortions	N
Require unpaid family and medical leave	Y
Approve national "motor voter" registration bill	Y
Approve budget increasing taxes and reducing deficit	Y
Approve economic stimulus plan	Y

Elections

1992 General		
Albert R. Wynn (D)	136,902	(75%)
Michele Dyson (R)	45,166	(25%)
1992 Primary		
Albert R. Wynn (D)	18,353	(28%)
Alexander Williams Jr. (D)	17,067	(26%)
Dana Lee Dembrow (D)	9,928	(15%)
Hilda R. Pemberton (D)	8,480	(13%)
Francis J. Aluisi (D)	3,774	(6%)
Tommie L. Broadwater (D)	2,564	(4%)
Linda A. Kelly (D)	1,448	(2%)
Maria Turner (D)	1,325	(2%)
Robert Bates (D)	908	(1%)
Michael B. DuPuy (D)	686	(1%)

District Vote for President

	1992	
D	149,262	(74%)
R	37,716	(19%)
I	14,160	(7%)

5 Steny H. Hoyer (D)

Of Berkshire — Elected 1981; 6th Full Term

Born: June 14, 1939, New York.
Education: U. of Maryland, B.S. 1963; Georgetown U., J.D. 1966.
Occupation: Lawyer.
Family: Wife, Judith Pickett; three children.
Religion: Baptist.
Political Career: Md. Senate, 1967-79, president, 1975-79; sought Democratic nomination for lieutenant governor, 1978; Md. Board of Higher Education, 1978-81.
Capitol Office: 1705 Longworth Bldg. 20515; 225-4131.

In Washington: Hoyer's defeat in his July 1991 bid for majority whip raised a critical question as to his future in the House: With his leadership tenure apparently about to expire, will the portfolio of an Appropriations "cardinal" be enough for a man who is identified as one of the people most ambitious for a high-level leadership position in the House?

After losing the whip's race, Hoyer returned to his lower-profile position as chairman of the Democratic Caucus, a post he must relinquish at the end of the 103rd Congress. But at the start of the 103rd, Hoyer was elevated to the "College of Cardinals," taking the chairmanship of the Appropriations Subcommittee on Treasury, Postal Service and General Government.

For now, there are no openings in the leadership available to Hoyer, who was a wheeler-dealer in the Maryland Senate before bringing his political skills to Washington in 1981. He has thought of himself as an important national player, but for one reason or another, many of his House colleagues have not quite taken to him.

That was demonstrated in his race for whip against Michigan Democrat David E. Bonior, who prevailed despite his opposition to abortion, which put him at odds with most of the Democratic Caucus, including Hoyer, who is a leading abortion rights advocate. Overall, though, Bonior was considered slightly more liberal than Hoyer, who has been more hawkish on some defense issues.

Hoyer and Bonior began feverishly contacting colleagues for support even before the sitting whip, Pennsylvania Democrat William H. Gray III, officially confirmed that he would leave the House to become president of the United Negro College Fund. Bonior gained early momentum by campaigning more aggressively than Hoyer, which is ironic because Hoyer has been labeled too ambitious.

Some members said they were backing Hoyer because of his abortion rights stance. But in the end, Bonior prevailed by a decisive 160-109 vote. Members attributed Bonior's victory to his work in the lower echelons, his more easygoing personality and his quick-off-the-mark bid. And he also seemed to benefit from the perception that Hoyer, who is four years behind Bonior in House seniority, was trying to move too far too fast in the Democratic hierarchy.

Hoyer has never been shy about getting ahead. Defeated in a statewide race at age 39, he got back on track when an incumbent's illness left a House seat open. After just a year in the House, he scratched his way to a seat on Appropriations, succeeding despite the opposition of a senior Maryland colleague already on the panel.

Hoyer's most consistent issue concerns have related to the federal employees who populate his district in the Washington suburbs. His base of operations has been the Treasury-Postal Service Subcommittee — a secondary assignment that many members ignore, but for Hoyer, a gold mine of constituent service.

Hoyer and another Washington-area appropriator in the House, Virginia Republican Frank R. Wolf, have often teamed up to push area projects such as funding for the Metro public transportation system. They also try to stem the stream of federal jobs and agencies that are drained from the Washington metropolitan area and diverted to West Virginia, the home state of Senate Appropriations Chairman Robert C. Byrd.

One of the latest to make the move to the Mountain State is the Bureau of the Public Debt, which plans to have relocated 700 of its 824 Washington employees to West Virginia by 1995. Hoyer and Wolf countered in the fiscal 1992 Treasury-Postal Service bill with a provision ensuring that any employee who does not want to move will be given another metropolitan-area job within the Treasury Department.

The fiscal 1992 bill also contained Hoyer's $11 million request for an additional courtroom in a new U.S. courthouse in Prince George's

Maryland 5

Outer Prince George's; Southern Maryland

The 5th has a different makeup and outlook from the primarily suburban district that Hoyer represented during his first decade in the House. The creation of the black-majority 4th in 1991 redistricting siphoned off many black Democrats, while pushing Hoyer into less urbanized areas of Prince George's County, southern Anne Arundel County and Southern Maryland (Charles, St. Mary's and Calvert counties).

The southern counties have a rural heritage, with tobacco as a major crop. The political tradition is Democratic but conservative, a tendency augmented by an influx of commuters and exurbanites. Winning candidates for major office here are usually conservatives and are often Republicans.

The reshaping of the 5th to include this territory was expected to cause Hoyer trouble in 1992, and it did. After years of easy victories, Hoyer had to campaign vigorously to defeat Republican Lawrence J. Hogan Jr. by 9 percentage points. Hoyer was saved by a solid Democratic vote in his remaining portion of Prince George's County, where he took 60 percent; he trailed Hogan elsewhere in the 5th. Similarly, Bill Clinton failed to crack 38 percent in any of the Southern Maryland counties, but won a plurality in the 5th thanks to his 53 percent in Prince George's.

P.G. County (as some locals call it) accounts for nearly half the 5th's population. In the northern part of the county, the 5th ducks inside the Capital Beltway to pick up such heavily black communities as Hyattsville. Also in Prince George's County is the University of Maryland's flagship campus at College Park, with 40,000 students.

The university is among the public employers that bolster the district's job base. Up the I-95/Baltimore-Washington Parkway corridor toward Greenbelt and Laurel are NASA's Goddard Space Flight Center and the National Agricultural Research Center. Fort Meade, despite downsizing as part of the 1989 military base-closing plan, still assists numerous government organizations.

The 5th sweeps east through Bowie, whose location between Washington and Annapolis brought a growth spurt in the 1980s, then around Andrews Air Force Base into southern Prince George's. The 5th also takes in a portion of southern Anne Arundel County that contributes about 15 percent of the district's residents; upscale communities such as Crofton and Davidsonville are here, but much of the area retains a rural feel.

The southern counties all grew rapidly in the 1980s. Charles County's population grew 39 percent to more than 100,000, as commuters poured into subdivisions along Route 301 and Indian Head Highway. Population in St. Mary's County increased 27 percent. There is much defense-related work in the southern counties: Charles County has the Naval Ordnance Station at Indian Head, and St. Mary's has the Patuxent River Naval Air Test Center and the Naval Electronics Systems center, which appeared on the 1993 base-closure list. Calvert County's population grew 48 percent, but it remains the state's second-least-populous county west of the Chesapeake Bay.

1990 Population: 597,681. White 461,610 (77%), Black 110,953 (19%), Other 25,118 (4%). Hispanic origin 14,520 (2%). 18 and over 450,198 (75%), 62 and over 56,900 (10%). Median age: 31.

County, Md. He also won $2.7 million to plan and design a computer center for the Census Bureau to be built in Bowie, Md.

Hoyer and Wolf, then the ranking Republican on the panel, worked together on the fiscal 1993 bill to obtain a $5 million earmark from the General Services Administration's new construction funds. The money would go toward establishing three "flexi-place" telecommuting centers — two in Maryland and one in Virginia — allowing federal employees who commute as much as four hours each day to report to the same job much closer to home.

In the 100th Congress, he bucked the tide on drug testing for federal employees, fighting random testing as unconstitutional. Early in 1989, Hoyer was an outspoken supporter of the 51 percent pay increase for Congress set in motion by a presidential commission; many federal employees expected the raise to ripple through the rank and file. And early in the 103rd Congress, Hoyer was a vocal critic of President Clinton's proposal to freeze the pay of federal workers.

Hoyer, who has long taken an interest in the Baltic States of Latvia, Lithuania and Estonia, chairs the Commission on Security and Cooperation in Europe, known as the Helsinki commission, an international human rights organization. In February 1991, he led a congressional delegation to those states, visiting their new, democratically elected presidents. After the new government in Moscow granted independence to the three former Soviet republics, he sponsored legislation with Illinois Democrat Richard J. Durbin to grant most-favored-nation trade status to the Baltics.

Hoyer's leadership track began as early as the 100th Congress, when he was tapped to direct leadership task forces on AIDS and on welfare reform. He endured a setback at the outset of that Congress when the deputy whip job he had hoped for went instead to Bonior. Hoyer reset his clock, waiting for his next chance to move up and busying himself with the Helsinki commission.

Hoyer got back in the leadership scramble sooner than expected. He became vice chairman of the caucus in the 101st Congress and moved up in June 1989 after Gray succeeded Tony Coelho of California as majority whip. Coelho, who had resigned facing ethics charges, had also been the prime sponsor of the Americans with Disabilities Act. Hoyer soon became that bill's designated shepherd.

It was an unfamiliar assignment for Hoyer, steeped as he was in the different customs and politics of the Appropriations Committee. But his work on the disabilities bill got good marks. The legislation was submitted to seven subcommittee and full committee markups, and Hoyer was present and pacing like an expectant father at each.

One apparent sign of Hoyer's ever-deepening loyalty to the leadership was his vote in January 1991 favoring sanctions over military force in the Persian Gulf crisis. Hoyer previously had warned his party about its national security posture. Early in 1985, when the House debated the MX missile program, Hoyer urged Democrats to change their soft-on-defense image. He voted for the MX, angering liberals and breaking with party leadership.

But in 1992, Hoyer also displayed sensitivity to his new, more politically marginal constituency when he reversed his opposition and voted for a constitutional amendment to balance the federal budget. Hoyer stood out as one of the few senior members to vote for it who was neither from the South nor especially conservative (though his redrawn district picked up areas in Southern Maryland that look and vote like the South).

At Home: Hoyer's rise to prominence on Capitol Hill has coincided with an increased political challenge in his district just a few miles to the east. Consistently a huge winner during his first decade in the House, Hoyer was held to a modest victory margin of 9 percentage points in 1992.

This slip was largely the result of a redistricting plan enacted before the 1992 election. The 5th District that previously had elected Hoyer was mainly in the close-in Washington suburbs of Prince George's County, and it had a large and growing black constituency whose liberal Democratic leanings provided Hoyer with a solid political base. But the black migration to the suburbs also spurred demands for creation of a new black-majority district.

Hoyer, who faced a primary challenge from a black opponent in 1990, supported the creation of the black-majority district. The Democratic-dominated state legislature in turn tried hard to protect Hoyer (a former state Senate president) by giving him the traditionally Democratic area of Southern Maryland to replace the inner-suburban area he had to give up.

Still, the changes left Hoyer at risk. Southern Maryland was until recently a mainly rural area that has started to give way to suburbs and exurbs. Its Democratic tradition is of the Southern, conservative variety.

Republicans sensed that the generally liberal Hoyer might have trouble in the newly drawn 5th. So they recruited an aggressive candidate with a well-known name: Lawrence J. Hogan Jr., the son of a former House member and former Prince George's County executive.

Hogan ran on conservative themes such as deficit reduction and crime control. But the main thrust of his campaign was to hammer at Hoyer's status as a congressional insider. The challenger insisted that Hoyer, as a member of the leadership, bore a good deal of responsibility for what he called the House's legislative and institutional failures, including the House bank and Post Office scandals.

However, Hoyer adroitly pointed out the advantage of his senior status. He took a spot on the Appropriations Military Construction Subcommittee, which could benefit military facilities in Southern Maryland. Enjoying a big fundraising edge, Hoyer flooded the airwaves in the campaign's closing days with ads highlighting his efforts on local issues.

The results showed both Hoyer's strengths and weaknesses in the new 5th. He cinched his win by carrying 60 percent in the Prince George's base he shared with Hogan. But Hogan edged Hoyer by smaller margins in each of the district's other four counties.

Hoyer was just out of law school when he was elected to the Maryland Senate in 1966. An ally of Democratic Gov. Marvin Mandel, Hoyer was chosen Senate president after two terms, becoming the youngest person to take that post.

A 1978 setback briefly slowed Hoyer's rise. After first declaring for governor, he agreed to run for lieutenant governor on a Democratic ticket headed by acting Gov. Blair Lee III. But the ticket was defeated in the primary.

Hoyer rebounded by winning a 1981 special House election. The seat had been declared vacant when it became clear that Democratic Rep. Gladys Noon Spellman — who was reelected in 1980 despite a heart attack that left her in a coma — was unable to serve. A stampede of 31 candidates, including her husband, entered the contest to succeed Spellman. But Hoyer was able to call on his past coalition of liberal, labor and black supporters to win the primary.

He then defeated Republican Audrey

Scott, the mayor of Bowie, with 55 percent and went on to a string of easy general election wins. Over the course of the 1980s, though, Hoyer faced growing restiveness among black Democrats, who called for empowerment of the suburbs' growing minority population.

In 1990, that sentiment spurred a primary challenge from Abdul Alim Muhammad, a spokesman for Nation of Islam leader Louis Farrakhan. Hoyer swamped Muhammad with nearly 80 percent of the vote. But the contest was a harbinger of the redistricting changes that thrust Hoyer into a competitive district in 1992.

Committees

Caucus Chairman

Appropriations (15th of 37 Democrats)
Treasury, Postal Service & General Government (chairman); Labor, Health & Human Services, Education & Related Agencies; Military Construction

House Administration (7th of 12 Democrats)
Accounts; Elections

Elections

1992 General		
Steny H. Hoyer (D)	118,312	(53%)
Lawrence J. Hogan Jr. (R)	97,982	(44%)
William D. Johnston III (I)	6,990	(3%)
1992 Primary		
Steny H. Hoyer (D)	46,400	(84%)
Ricardo V. Johnson (D)	8,802	(16%)
1990 General		
Steny H. Hoyer (D)	84,747	(81%)
Lee F. Breuer (R)	20,314	(19%)

Previous Winning Percentages: **1988** (79%) **1986** (82%) **1984** (72%) **1982** (80%) **1981** * (55%)

** Special election.*

District Vote for President

1992

D 107,618 (45%)
R 95,356 (40%)
I 37,441 (16%)

Campaign Finance

	Receipts	Receipts from PACs		Expenditures
1992				
Hoyer (D)	$1,304,867	$711,367	(55%)	$1,584,271
Hogan (R)	$267,271	$51,409	(19%)	$265,065
1990				
Hoyer (D)	$725,418	$417,235	(58%)	$716,469
Breuer (R)	$9,084	0		$8,709

Key Votes

1993	
Require parental notification of minors' abortions	N
Require unpaid family and medical leave	Y
Approve national "motor voter" registration bill	Y
Approve budget increasing taxes and reducing deficit	Y
Approve economic stimulus plan	Y
1992	
Approve balanced-budget constitutional amendment	Y
Close down space station program	Y
Approve U.S. aid for former Soviet Union	Y
Allow shifting funds from defense to domestic programs	Y
1991	
Extend unemployment benefits using deficit financing	Y
Approve waiting period for handgun purchases	Y
Authorize use of force in Persian Gulf	N

Voting Studies

	Presidential Support		Party Unity		Conservative Coalition	
Year	**S**	**O**	**S**	**O**	**S**	**O**
1992	27	72	89	8	52	48
1991	33	67	90	7	19	81
1990	19	79	96	2	22	76
1989	35	63	93	3	29	68
1988	23	77	98	1	18	82
1987	25	75	93	3	28	72
1986	21	79	95	3	26	72
1985	29	71	93	5	29	71
1984	42	57	89	9	32	63
1983	32	67	91	6	29	70
1982	38	57	92	5	25	71
1981	40 †	55 †	86 †	11 †	32 †	67 †

† Not eligible for all recorded votes.

Interest Group Ratings

Year	ADA	AFL-CIO	CCUS	ACU
1992	90	75	38	17
1991	80	92	30	0
1990	89	100	14	0
1989	80	100	20	0
1988	95	100	21	0
1987	84	100	7	0
1986	95	93	22	5
1985	75	94	32	14
1984	75	92	33	8
1983	80	100	25	9
1982	75	85	32	18
1981	72	92	12	0

6 Roscoe G. Bartlett (R)

Of Frederick — Elected 1992; 1st Term

Born: June 3, 1926, Moreland, Ky.
Education: Columbia Union College, B.S. 1947; U. of Maryland, M.S. 1948, Ph.D. 1952.
Occupation: Teacher; engineer.
Family: Wife, Ellen Louise Baldwin; 10 children.
Religion: Seventh-day Adventist.
Political Career: GOP nominee for U.S. House, 1982.
Capitol Office: 312 Cannon Bldg. 20515; 225-2721.

The Path to Washington: Few 1992 races gave voters a clearer, more ideological choice than the one in Maryland's 6th District. But by the tone of the campaign few observers could have guessed that there were substantive issues of government policy at stake.

Bartlett's 54 percent to 46 percent win over Thomas H. Hattery was perhaps a mild upset. Bartlett would have had a much tougher race against incumbent Democrat Beverly B. Byron, who held the seat for seven terms and lost to Hattery in a bitter primary. Bartlett's victory margin was much narrower than those typically run up by the conservative Byron, suggesting that suburban growth in the 6th's eastern end may be compensating for the district's conservative lean and that Bartlett may be more conservative than is the district as a whole.

Bartlett's views are rooted in his strongly held religious beliefs and his Depression-era upbringing. He believes that the federal government is far too large and intrusive in people's business and personal lives. He opposes taxes and gun control, and he favors a presidential line-item veto. He was one of only four House newcomers who signed a pledge to cut the federal budget deficit in half by 1996 or not seek re-election.

He opposes congressional term limits, favoring instead a ceiling on campaign spending as a means to induce turnover. His only departure from an anti-government line is his firm opposition to abortion.

Once in office, Bartlett did not disappoint those who expected him to be controversial. He offended many in the Asian community when in discussing the high percentage of Asian scholarship winners, he made a reference to Asians not having "normal" names. Bartlett later contended that his remarks were taken out of context.

The Baltimore Sun later reported that Bartlett refused to sign a letter requesting federal emergency snow removal aid after a March 1993 blizzard, saying it would fly in the face of his promises to reduce the deficit. Though the paper reported that he angered several members of the Maryland delegation, such stands could play well in the conservative-leaning 6th.

He claimed a seat on the Armed Services Committee and on the Science, Space and Technology Committee, which is of interest to the high-technology companies that have located along the I-270 corridor in Frederick County. That assignment also dovetails with Bartlett's background as a research scientist and patent holder.

Bartlett, who ran in 1982 against Byron and pulled only 26 percent of the vote, won his own, relatively quiet, three-way primary by 646 votes over Thurmont businessman and political newcomer Michael Downey. Former Cumberland Mayor Frank K. Nethken finished a distant third.

Bartlett won the general election by besting Hattery at his own game of negative campaigning. Hattery had capitalized on an anti-incumbent year by sharply criticizing Byron's vote in favor of a $35,000 congressional pay raise at a time when the district was suffering high unemployment. And he hit her for extensive overseas travel at taxpayer expense. Hattery won 56 percent of the vote, out-polling Byron in all six of the district's counties.

Hattery had barely won the primary, however, when Bartlett struck, setting up Hattery as the nominal incumbent and charging him with padding his legislative expense account. That started a mudfest that left most voters angrier at Hattery because he started it with Byron.

Bartlett accused Hattery of failing to buy workers' compensation insurance for the employees at his family-owned printing company. Hattery accused Bartlett of failing to remedy a tainted water supply that served tenants at his Frederick County farm.

Redistricting altered the 6th only modestly, taking away its wealthy western Montgomery County suburbs, and adding more of suburban Howard County. The district is slightly more Republican than Democratic in registration, but it is substantially Republican in its voting habits. It had, however, previously elected conservative Democrats for 22 consecutive years: Byron for 14 and her husband, Goodloe E. Byron, from 1970 until his death in 1978.

Maryland 6

Central and West — Frederick; Hagerstown

During the 14 years (1978-1992) that Democrat Beverly B. Byron dominated the 6th, local Republicans insisted that it was only her record as one of the most conservative House Democrats that kept the GOP-leaning district from falling into their hands.

The events of 1992 justified their contention. Byron was upset by a more liberal Democrat, Thomas H. Hattery, in the March primary. But in November, the 6th stuck to its conservative form, electing Republican Bartlett by a margin of nearly 20,000 votes.

The 6th takes in the five westernmost counties along Maryland's northern border — Garrett, Allegany, Washington, Frederick and Carroll — and more than half the population of Howard County. These places include some of the state's most reliably Republican territory. George Bush swept all the counties in 1992; his 48 percent here was by far his best in any state district. Garrett — one of Maryland's least populous counties and one with a "mountain Republican" tradition — was the only county to go against Democratic Sen. Barbara A. Mikulski's landslide, giving 59 percent of its vote to Republican Alan L. Keyes.

Most of the 6th's people live in the rapidly growing exurban areas of central Maryland. At its southern end, the 6th takes in the recently built subdivisions of western Howard County, then skirts south past the city of Columbia. The growth in the southern part of the 6th drew in a less conservative sort of Democrat who turned against Byron in 1992. But the district's conservative majority, including a number of traditional Democratic voters, rebelled against that result, and the GOP captured the district.

Frederick County's population also blossomed over the past decade; many residents commute on I-270 to Washington or on I-70 to Baltimore, or to high-tech businesses along those highways. The National Cancer Institute and the Defense Department's Medical Research Center are in the city of Frederick. The Camp David retreat is in Thurmont, in northern Frederick County.

To the east is Carroll County, parts of which have turned into bedroom suburbs of Baltimore. Both Frederick and Carroll counties still have a good deal of farmland and are Republican strongholds.

While development is an issue in central Maryland, slow growth is the problem in the hilly Western Panhandle. Though the largest private employer in Hagerstown (Washington County) is a Mack Truck factory, the manufacturing sector has diminished; a Citicorp credit card service center has taken up some of the employment slack.

In Cumberland (Allegany County), officials are laboring to replace jobs lost in the late 1980s, when Kelly-Springfield (which has headquarters here) closed its tire plant. Hard times give Democrats a chance — Hattery narrowly edged Bartlett in the county — but conservatism usually prevails.

With few economic options, Garrett County is trying to make the most of its remote location. Its tourism industry draws visitors to man-made Deep Creek Lake and winter-sport players to its mountain towns.

1990 Population: 597,688. White 560,853 (94%), Black 26,838 (4%), Other 9,997 (2%). Hispanic origin 5,495 (1%). 18 and over 447,788 (75%), 62 and over 83,167 (14%). Median age: 34.

Committees

Armed Services (22nd of 22 Republicans)
Military Forces & Personnel; Research & Technology

Science, Space & Technology (22nd of 22 Republicans)
Energy; Technology, Environment & Aviation

Campaign Finance

	Receipts	Receipts from PACs		Expend-itures
1992				
Bartlett (R)	$293,736	$82,050	(28%)	$252,227
Hattery (D)	$598,213	$279,492	(47%)	$596,051

Key Votes

1993

Require parental notification of minors' abortions	Y
Require unpaid family and medical leave	N
Approve national "motor voter" registration bill	N
Approve budget increasing taxes and reducing deficit	N
Approve economic stimulus plan	N

Elections

1992 General		
Roscoe G. Bartlett (R)	125,564	(54%)
Thomas H. Hattery (D)	106,224	(46%)
1992 Primary		
Roscoe G. Bartlett (R)	15,374	(42%)
Michael Downey (R)	14,728	(41%)
Frank K. Nethken (R)	6,201	(17%)

District Vote for President

	1992	
D	88,196	(34%)
R	125,494	(48%)
I	46,376	(18%)

7 Kweisi Mfume (D)

Of Baltimore — Elected 1986; 4th Term

Born: Oct. 24, 1948, Baltimore, Md.
Education: Morgan State U., B.S. 1976; Johns Hopkins U., M.A. 1984.
Occupation: Professor; radio station program director; talk show host.
Family: Divorced; five children.
Religion: Baptist.
Political Career: Baltimore City Council, 1979-87.
Capitol Office: 2419 Rayburn Bldg. 20515; 225-4741.

In Washington: Mfume, whose adopted Swahili name means "conquering son of kings," blends the collegial style typical of younger-generation black House members with a bit of the provocative rhetoric of their elders.

He spent his first years in the House presiding over floor proceedings, where his radio-trained voice and impeccable clothes, not to disregard his mastery of the rules, earned him notice. Having quietly built bridges to the House Democratic leadership and between the newer and older members of the Congressional Black Caucus, Mfume was ready in the 103rd Congress to assert his own brand of leadership from two new positions of responsibility.

As chairman of an enlarged and thus empowered black caucus, Mfume was expected to elevate its status to pressure the Democratic hierarchy, while working within the system to achieve the legislative goals of its minority constituents. And as chairman of the newly reconfigured Minority Enterprise, Finance and Urban Development Subcommittee of the Small Business Committee, Mfume could pursue the economic agenda he adopted when first elected.

Representing some of Baltimore's poorest black neighborhoods, Mfume could have succeeded politically by simply voicing anger and frustration with "the system." Instead, he has become known as a thoughtful lawmaker who tries to help the disadvantaged by making legislative allies. Mfume learned the importance of coalitions on the Baltimore City Council, where his confrontations with Mayor William Donald Schaefer were legend. Upon Mfume's election to the House and Schaefer's to the governorship in 1986, Mfume made peace, knowing that they would one day need to work together.

Mfume's willingness to accommodate earned him a challenge for the black caucus chair from Texas Democrat Craig Washington, who promised a more aggressive style. Mfume was elected by acclamation after winning a first ballot, 27-9.

Lest anyone think Mfume would shirk from confronting the leadership or the White House, he moved quickly to declare the caucus' concerns. In March 1993, he blasted the Clinton administration for continuing its predecessor's policy of intercepting Haitians seeking to escape their strife-torn nation, and returning them to Haiti. Mfume, like other black leaders, had given President Clinton time to alter the policy, but when the administration asked the Supreme Court to uphold it, he said, "The time has passed for this kind of grace period."

A few weeks later, the black caucus supplied a key bloc of Democratic votes to join with Republicans in thwarting for a time the leadership's effort to pass a version of the line-item veto that Clinton sought. In what Mfume described on the floor as "a pure position of principle," most black caucus members opposed the measure, saying it would cede too much power to the president.

The combination of Republicans, who thought the measure too weak, and the black caucus caused House leaders to pull the measure from the floor even before it came to a vote. A few weeks later the leadership used its muscle to pare away enough black members from the caucus position to pass the bill.

Mfume is outspoken in his support for civil rights and other traditional minority concerns, but he has always seen his role as one of fostering "economic development and economic empowerment" for his minority constituents. In his first term on the Banking Committee, he worked to learn the issues. Later, in the 102nd Congress, he relinquished a seat on the Education and Labor Committee to move to the Joint Economic Committee, where he could advance his ideas.

At the start of the 103rd Congress, Mfume unveiled a seven-point plan to revitalize the nation's cities, incorporating existing ideas, such as enterprise zones and a plan for national service for young people, with enough fine-tuning that he could call it his own.

And he worked with Republican Christopher Shays of Connecticut to introduce a bill creating tax credits for long-term investments in small businesses started by minorities.

Maryland 7

Inner-city Baltimore; Western Baltimore County

Downtown Baltimore's resurgence looks like a mirage to residents of the low-income black neighborhoods of west Baltimore and to those living north and east of the city center. The areas' ills — crime, drugs, teen pregnancies, school dropouts, lack of job opportunities — starkly contrast the vitality of the Inner Harbor.

Baltimore's population reached 939,000 in the 1960s, but the subsequent spread of urban problems sparked an exodus. By 1990, the city's population was 736,000, and an increasing number of middle-class blacks were joining whites in the suburbs.

As a result, the 7th — once wholly within the city — now swings out across western Baltimore County. But by following the black migration west on Liberty Heights toward Randallstown and down the Baltimore National Pike to Catonsville, the 7th maintains a 71 percent black population.

During his tenure as Baltimore mayor, Democratic Gov. William Donald Schaefer was berated by black activists for funneling development money into downtown. Since becoming mayor in 1987, Democrat Kurt L. Schmoke has channeled some resources to low-income communities in the flats east of downtown to row houses along Broadway and to tenements in west Baltimore. But major improvements have been slow.

The picture within the city (which contributes nearly 80 percent of the 7th's population) is not all bleak. Just north of the downtown business district is the gentrified Mount Vernon area, home of the Walters Art Gallery and the Peabody music academy. Farther north are Johns Hopkins University and the Baltimore Museum of Art.

To the west is Druid Hill Park and the Baltimore Zoo. To the east is integrated Waverly and Memorial Stadium, home of the baseball Orioles for 37 years; the team left for a new downtown park in 1992. To the northeast is Morgan State University.

Though overshadowed by Harborplace, the old retail section west of the downtown hub survives; the Lexington food market and Baltimore Arena are here. There are middle-class black communities along Liberty Heights Road in west Baltimore. The national headquarters of the NAACP is near the city's western border. Over the line in Baltimore County are mainly black suburban settlements in Woodlawn and Lochearn. The Social Security Administration complex and Security Square Mall in Woodlawn are important sources of jobs.

To the south is Catonsville, site of the University of Maryland at Baltimore County. To the north, the 7th reaches to Randallstown, then leaps through a mostly undeveloped area to Reisterstown (both suburbs are shared with the 3rd). Although black residents have a strong presence in many of the 7th's suburban areas, the Baltimore County portion of the 7th is three-fifths white.

Democrats are assured of victories in the 7th. But getting the vote out can be a problem for Democrats; only 67 percent of the registered voters in the city part of the 7th turned out in November 1992, well below the 81 percent rate for the state.

1990 Population: 597,680. White 162,648 (27%), Black 424,132 (71%), Other 10,900 (2%). Hispanic origin 5,268 (1%). 18 and over 448,177 (75%), 62 and over 87,650 (15%). Median age: 32.

On Banking, Mfume gives voice to the concerns of public housing residents. In 1990, the Housing Subcommittee approved a Mfume amendment to change the way tenants calculate their rents, allowing them to pay according to their actual income, not their estimated income, which could include alimony or child support payments that do not come through.

He has been a participant in debate on bills to keep the savings and loan bailout operating. He won adoption of an amendment to increase business for minority contractors with the Resolution Trust Corporation, the bailout agency. And he engineered another to allow minority investors to operate branches of failed thrifts in minority neighborhoods rent-free for at least five years. But he largely has opposed providing more money to finance the bailout.

In 1992 he and other black caucus members opposed a Russian aid bill, which included a $12 billion increase in the U.S. contribution to the International Monetary Fund, on the ground that more money should be devoted to domestic needs first.

Amid the chorus of voices expressing concern over drug abuse and proposing grand plans to combat it, Mfume has tried to make a dent in the problem by focusing on a small corner of the issue. In 1989, he began pushing to curb sales of electronic beepers to minors, who, he said, use them to arrange drug deals. He reintroduced his bill in the 102nd Congress.

In mid-1992, Mfume was named to the House ethics committee to fill a vacancy when Gary L. Ackerman of New York resigned. Mfume had served temporarily on the panel when it was investigating the House bank scandal because Chairman Louis Stokes, who had overdrafts, recused himself. Mfume did not know it at the time, but he had 12 overdrafts.

At Home: Before his 1986 House election, Mfume was well-known in Baltimore for his broadcasting and City Council careers. But his background was anything but typical for a congressional candidate.

Mfume was born Frizzell Gray in the slums of West Baltimore. After his mother died when he was 16, he quit high school, drifted through a series of jobs and, between the ages of 17 and 22, fathered five sons by four different women. But in his early 20s, he adopted a new name and way of life, climbing the career ladder at Morgan State University's radio station. Mfume finished high school, graduated from Morgan State at 27 and earned an advanced degree from Johns Hopkins University.

After achieving popularity as a radio talk show host, Mfume won a seat on the City Council, where he promoted the causes of his inner-city constituents. Criticized early by some colleagues for his confrontational style, Mfume developed a more temperate approach that helped win some victories, including a law ordering the city to divest itself of investments in companies doing business with South Africa.

Although Mfume entered the 1986 Democratic House race as an underdog, he was well-positioned when the front-runners slipped. State Sen. Clarence M. Mitchell, the nephew of retiring Rep. Parren J. Mitchell, was damaged by reports on his personal finances and his alleged relationship with a jailed drug dealer. Another prominent contender, the Rev. Wendell H. Phillips, a civil rights activist, was hurt by accusations that he was cozy with the city's white power structure.

Mfume quietly promoted himself as the compromise candidate. Assisted by a group of black clergy, Mfume swept to an easy primary victory.

Though Mfume was unbeatable in the heavily Democratic 7th, his GOP opponent, Saint George I. B. Crosse III, harassed him by making an issue of his children. Mfume stated that he supported his sons financially and emotionally, and the local media portrayed his rise from poverty in a positive light.

Mfume won with 87 percent of the vote, an outcome that would become typical. In both 1990 and 1992, he defeated Republican Kenneth Kondner, a dental technician, with 85 percent.

Committees

Banking, Finance & Urban Affairs (10th of 30 Democrats)
Financial Institutions Supervision, Regulation & Deposit Insurance; Housing & Community Development

Small Business (9th of 27 Democrats)
Minority Enterprise, Finance & Urban Development (chairman); Procurement, Taxation & Tourism

Standards of Official Conduct (5th of 7 Democrats)

Joint Economic

Elections

1992 General		
Kweisi Mfume (D)	152,689	(85%)
Kenneth Kondner (R)	26,304	(15%)
1992 Primary		
Kweisi Mfume (D)	55,842	(84%)
Michael Vernon Dobson (D)	10,310	(16%)
1990 General		
Kweisi Mfume (D)	59,628	(85%)
Kenneth Kondner (R)	10,529	(15%)

Previous Winning Percentages: 1988 (100%) **1986** (87%)

District Vote for President

1992
D 159,191 (78%)
R 32,431 (16%)
I 13,009 (6%)

Campaign Finance

	Receipts	Receipts from PACs		Expend-itures
1992				
Mfume (D)	$255,269	$131,687	(52%)	$216,518
1990				
Mfume (D)	$224,826	$128,000	(57%)	$205,671

Key Votes

1993	
Require parental notification of minors' abortions	N
Require unpaid family and medical leave	Y
Approve national "motor voter" registration bill	Y
Approve budget increasing taxes and reducing deficit	Y
Approve economic stimulus plan	Y
1992	
Approve balanced-budget constitutional amendment	N
Close down space station program	Y
Approve U.S. aid for former Soviet Union	N
Allow shifting funds from defense to domestic programs	Y
1991	
Extend unemployment benefits using deficit financing	Y
Approve waiting period for handgun purchases	Y
Authorize use of force in Persian Gulf	N

Voting Studies

	Presidential Support		Party Unity		Conservative Coalition	
Year	S	O	S	O	S	O
1992	12	87	90	6	13	88
1991	23	76	89	6	5	95
1990	15	81	86	7	9	91
1989	31	66	86	5	15	83
1988	23	76	93	4	21	79
1987	13	86	93	3	9	88

Interest Group Ratings

Year	ADA	AFL-CIO	CCUS	ACU
1992	95	92	13	0
1991	100	100	20	5
1990	94	92	29	13
1989	90	100	30	8
1988	95	100	21	4
1987	100	100	7	0

8 Constance A. Morella (R)

Of Bethesda — Elected 1986; 4th Term

Born: Feb. 12, 1931, Somerville, Mass.

Education: Boston U., B.A. 1954; American U., M.A. 1967.

Occupation: Professor.

Family: Husband, Anthony C. Morella; nine children.

Religion: Roman Catholic.

Political Career: Candidate for Md. House, 1974; Md. House, 1979-87; sought Republican nomination for U.S. House, 1980.

Capitol Office: 223 Cannon Bldg. 20515; 225-5341.

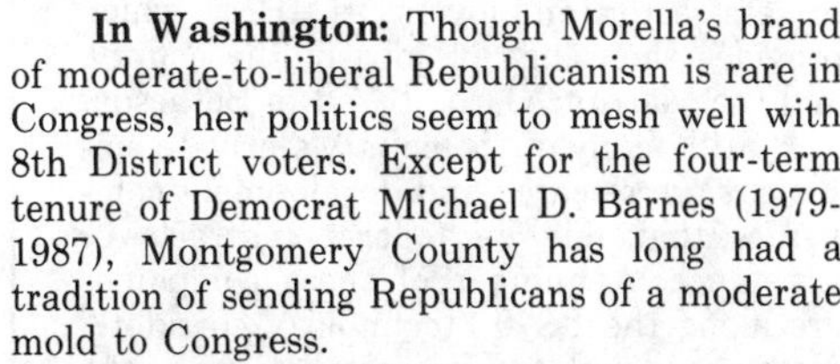

In Washington: Though Morella's brand of moderate-to-liberal Republicanism is rare in Congress, her politics seem to mesh well with 8th District voters. Except for the four-term tenure of Democrat Michael D. Barnes (1979-1987), Montgomery County has long had a tradition of sending Republicans of a moderate mold to Congress.

But while Morella's moderation plays well at home, it is not looked upon so kindly by some of her GOP colleagues. She was consistently among the the Republicans least likely to support Presidents Ronald Reagan and George Bush.

Early in the 102nd Congress, Morella was one of only three Republicans opposing the resolution authorizing Bush to use force in the Persian Gulf.

And in 1992, she supported Bush on House votes only 39 percent of the time when he took a position, and she voted with her party only 46 percent of the time when a majority of Democrats opposed a majority of Republicans.

Morella has taken other steps to separate herself from the national GOP. It wasn't until 1992, after 30 years as a Republican, that she attended her first national Republican convention. And then it was only as a staunch abortion rights supporter who wanted to oppose a GOP platform plank that described abortion as murder.

But if Republicans are unlikely to take Morella into their inner circle, neither do they give her the cold shoulder. She is too personally pleasant to get brusque treatment, and many Republicans recognize that a more conservative member would have trouble holding the 8th, which is packed with federal bureaucrats and liberal political activists.

Inside the GOP, it helps Morella that she has largely focused her liberalism on local concerns. While many members curry favor with party bigwigs to get on "prestige" committees, Morella's lower-profile assignments suit her fine.

The Post Office and Civil Service Committee handles issues of interest to the working and retired federal employees in her district; the Science, Space and Technology Committee is important to the many research laboratories in Montgomery County.

In 1989, Morella joined most members in voting against a proposed 51 percent congressional pay raise. But she then submitted a bill to give up to 20 percent pay increases to judges and senior officials of federal agencies, whose raises also were killed by the House vote.

She has backed repeal of the Hatch Act, which restricts political activity by federal employees; Bush vetoed a repeal measure in June 1990.

Early in the 102nd Congress, Morella submitted legislation that would allow higher pay for federal workers in the high-cost Baltimore-Washington, D.C., metropolitan area. In the 103rd Congress, one of her priorities is to oppose President Clinton's efforts to hold down pay for federal workers.

Morella also has become a voice on women's issues. In the 102nd Congress she sponsored and managed passage of three pieces of legislation relating to women.

The Women in Apprenticeship and Nontraditional Occupations Act was to provide grants to community-based organizations that give technical assistance to private employers who wish to recruit, train and retain women in apprenticeships or jobs traditionally held by men; the Battered Women's Testimony Act increased the use of expert testimony in trials of battered women accused of killing their abusers; and the Judicial Training Act provided training for judges and other court personnel on dealing with child custody cases in families affected by domestic violence.

In the 103rd Congress, she planned to work to win passage of legislation she introduced to focus more federal medical research on women with AIDS, to strengthen laws on violence against women and to make it a federal crime to obstruct the entrance to an abortion clinic.

At Home: Even more than Morella's earlier election victories, the 1992 contest proved the appeal of her personal style and liberal

Maryland 8

Montgomery County

A huge federal government presence and a burgeoning private sector spurred a boom in Montgomery County during the 1980s, increasing population by nearly a third to more than 750,000. That put Montgomery ahead of the city of Baltimore as Maryland's largest jurisdiction.

With its steady employment base and large population of educated professionals, Montgomery County is one of the nation's most affluent places. In Potomac, million-dollar homes are interspersed with horse farms. Upscale stores in Chevy Chase and Bethesda anchor a bustling retail trade along Route 355.

Still, the recession of the early 1990s slowed the real estate development and retail sales that keyed Montgomery County's growth. And the county is not entirely dominated by upper-income residents. Most of the county's recent growth has been in middle-income communities in outer suburbs such as Gaithersburg, Germantown and Olney.

Older parts of Rockville, Gaithersburg and the Kensington-Wheaton area have working-class and some low-income areas, home to many of the county's black residents. There are also growing numbers of Hispanic and Asian immigrants.

Public employment — there are about 60,000 federal employees and more than 20,000 county workers — underpins Montgomery's economy and sets its political tone. Democrats have long dominated local politics here.

Yet GOP Rep. Morella has thrived, largely because of her reputation as one of the most liberal House Republicans. And the county is suburban enough to make it a challenge for Democratic presidential candidates. Bill Clinton mastered Montgomery, beating George Bush in the 8th by 53 percent to 35 percent (and taking the whole county, part of which is in the 4th District, with 55 percent). But the 1984 and 1988 Democratic tickets won Montgomery narrowly.

Despite Clinton's 1992 surge, there are Republicans who view Montgomery County as a potential partisan growth area. They point to the increased importance of such private-sector employers as IBM, which provides thousands of jobs in the county, and the Marriott Corp., based in Bethesda.

Still, many of the county's private employers are research and development companies that rely on federal contracts or assistance. A number of these companies are along the I-270 "technology corridor." Nearby are such federal installations as the National Institutes of Health (Bethesda), the National Institute of Standards and Technology (Gaithersburg) and Department of Energy labs (Germantown). Montgomery County is a national center for biotechnology research.

County officials have tried to preserve the remnants of Montgomery's farming heritage in the northern and western areas of the county. Attitudes in these areas are more conservative and Republican habits stronger than elsewhere in the county.

1990 Population: 597,682. White 486,990 (81%), Black 49,029 (8%), Other 61,663 (10%). Hispanic origin 37,771 (6%). 18 and over 454,721 (76%), 62 and over 76,602 (13%). Median age: 34.

Republican politics in suburban Montgomery County.

The Montgomery County Democratic Party, which has dominated the affluent but liberal-leaning county for years, worked hard to energize voters on behalf of the Clinton-Gore ticket and Democratic Sen. Barbara A. Mikulski's re-election bid. But the party made a tepid effort for Morella's challenger, Edward J. Heffernan, a former House aide making his first try for elective office. Although Clinton and Mikulski easily carried the 8th District, Morella kept the House seat Republican with 73 percent of the vote.

Although Democrat Michael D. Barnes held the 8th for four terms prior to his 1986 retirement for a Senate bid, the district previously had favored such moderate-to-liberal Republicans as Charles McC. Mathias Jr., Gilbert Gude and Newton I. Steers Jr. (Steers had thwarted Morella's first House bid in a 1980 primary.) Morella successfully tied herself to that tradition.

Although Morella, a community college English professor, was involved in environmental and social issues during her eight years in the Maryland House, the biggest factor in her 1986 House victory was her vivacious personality. She played up her family's immigrant heritage and her working-class upbringing and noted that she and her husband had raised nine children (including her late sister's six).

Her Democratic foe, state Sen. Stewart Bainum, was a millionaire businessman with liberal views. But his wooden campaign style contrasted poorly with Morella's manner.

Morella won with 53 percent.

Morella's high visibility as a Washington-area member and her voting record enabled her to brush aside state Delegate Peter Franchot in 1988 with 63 percent. She won 74 percent in 1990 against a little-known opponent.

Committees

Post Office & Civil Service (5th of 9 Republicans)
Compensation & Employee Benefits (ranking); Civil Service

Science, Space & Technology (7th of 22 Republicans)
Investigations & Oversight; Technology, Environment & Aviation

Elections

1992 General		
Constance A. Morella (R)	203,377	(73%)
Edward J. Heffernan (D)	77,042	(27%)
1990 General		
Constance A. Morella (R)	130,059	(74%)
James Walker Jr. (D)	39,343	(22%)
Sidney Altman (I)	7,485	(4%)

Previous Winning Percentages: 1988 (63%) **1986** (53%)

District Vote for President

1992
D 156,043 (53%)
R 103,477 (35%)
I 35,599 (12%)

Campaign Finance

	Receipts	Receipts from PACs		Expend-itures
1992				
Morella (R)	$430,301	$184,373	(43%)	$328,516
Heffernan (D)	$75,483	$10,606	(14%)	$74,454
1990				
Morella (R)	$542,961	$239,709	(44%)	$353,959

Key Votes

1993	
Require parental notification of minors' abortions	N
Require unpaid family and medical leave	Y
Approve national "motor voter" registration bill	Y
Approve budget increasing taxes and reducing deficit	N
Approve economic stimulus plan	N
1992	
Approve balanced-budget constitutional amendment	Y
Close down space station program	N
Approve U.S. aid for former Soviet Union	Y
Allow shifting funds from defense to domestic programs	N
1991	
Extend unemployment benefits using deficit financing	Y
Approve waiting period for handgun purchases	Y
Authorize use of force in Persian Gulf	N

Voting Studies

	Presidential Support		Party Unity		Conservative Coalition	
Year	**S**	**O**	**S**	**O**	**S**	**O**
1992	39	56	46	48	44	44
1991	43	54	39	58	41	57
1990	26	70	32	65	24	72
1989	41	58	18	76	34	63
1988	28	68	30	67	32	66
1987	34	65	29	66	40	60

Interest Group Ratings

Year	ADA	AFL-CIO	CCUS	ACU
1992	70	50	38	35
1991	65	67	60	15
1990	67	58	29	17
1989	80	67	80	21
1988	90	79	46	8
1987	60	50	40	22

Massachusetts

STATE DATA

Governor:
William F. Weld (R)
First elected: 1990
Length of term: 4 years
Term expires: 1/95
Salary: $75,000
Term limit: No
Phone: (617) 727-3600
Born: July 31, 1945; Smithtown, N.Y.
Education: Harvard U., B.A. 1966; Oxford U., 1966-67; Harvard U., J.D. 1970
Occupation: Lawyer
Family: Wife, Susan Roosevelt; five children
Religion: Episcopalian
Political Career: Republican nominee for Mass. attorney general, 1978; U.S. attorney for Mass., 1981-86; assistant U.S. attorney general, 1986-88

Lt. Gov.: Argeo Paul Cellucci (R)
First elected: 1990
Length of term: 4 years
Term expires: 1/95
Salary: $60,000
Phone: (617) 727-7200

State election official: (617) 727-2830
Democratic headquarters: (617) 426-4760
Republican headquarters: (617) 725-1994

REDISTRICTING

Massachusetts lost one House seat in reapportionment, dropping from 11 districts to 10. The legislature passed the map July 8, 1992; the governor signed it July 9.

STATE LEGISLATURE

General Court. Meeting time varies; usually year-round.

Senate: 40 members, 2-year terms
1992 breakdown: 24D, 15R, 1 vacancy; 31 men, 9 women; 28 whites, 1 black, 1 Hispanic
Salary: $30,000
Phone: (617) 722-1455

House of Representatives: 160 members, 2-year terms
1992 breakdown: 124D, 35R, 1I; 123 men, 37 women; 150 whites, 7 blacks, 3 Hispanics
Salary: $30,000
Phone: (617) 722-2000

URBAN STATISTICS

City	Pop.
Boston	574,283
Special mayoral election set for 11/93	
Worcester	169,759
Mayor Jordan Levy, D	
Springfield	156,983
Mayor Robert T. Markel, N-P	
Lowell	103,439
Mayor Tarsy T. Poulios, D	
New Bedford	99,922
Mayor Rosemary Tierney, D	

U.S. CONGRESS

Senate: 2 D, 0 R
House: 8 D, 2 R

TERM LIMITS

For Congress: No
For state offices: No

ELECTIONS

1992 Presidential Vote

Bill Clinton	47.5%
George Bush	29.0%
Ross Perot	22.7%

1988 Presidential Vote

Michael S. Dukakis	53%
George Bush	45%

1984 Presidential Vote

Ronald Reagan	51%
Walter F. Mondale	48%

POPULATION

1990 population		6,016,425
1980 population		5,737,037
Percent change		+5%
Rank among states:		13
White		90%
Black		5%
Hispanic		5%
Asian or Pacific islander		2%
Urban		84%
Rural		16%
Born in state		69%
Foreign-born		10%
Under age 18	1,353,075	22%
Ages 18-64	3,844,066	64%
65 and older	819,284	14%
Median age		33.6

MISCELLANEOUS

Capital: Boston
Number of counties: 14
Per capita income: $22,897 (1991)
Rank among states: 3
Total area: 8,284 sq. miles
Rank among states: 45

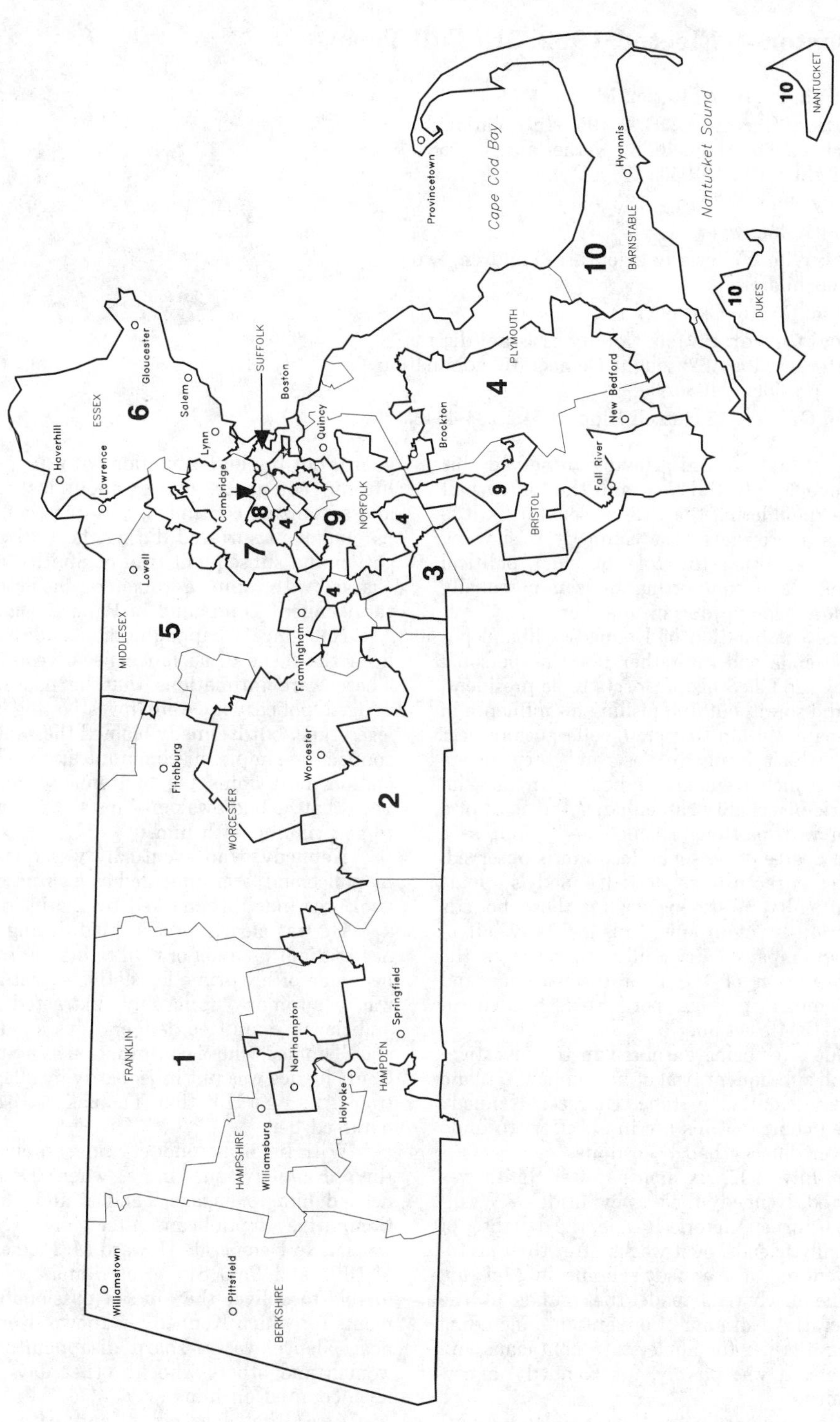
Haverhill
Lawrence
ESSEX
6
Gloucester
Salem
Lynn
SUFFOLK
Boston
Cambridge
Quincy
8
7
4
9
NORFOLK
Lowell
MIDDLESEX
5
3
Framingham
Fitchburg
Worcester
WORCESTER
2
Springfield
HAMPDEN
Holyoke
Northampton
Williamsburg
HAMPSHIRE
FRANKLIN
1
Williamstown
Pittsfield
BERKSHIRE
Brockton
PLYMOUTH
4
New Bedford
Fall River
9
BRISTOL
10
BARNSTABLE
Hyannis
Provincetown
Cape Cod Bay
Nantucket Sound
10
DUKES
10
NANTUCKET

Edward M. Kennedy (D)

Of Boston — Elected 1962; 5th Full Term

Born: Feb. 22, 1932, Boston, Mass.

Education: Harvard U., B.A. 1956; International Law School, The Hague (The Netherlands), 1958; U. of Virginia, LL.B. 1959.

Military Service: Army, 1951-53.

Occupation: Lawyer.

Family: Wife, Victoria Reggie; three children, two stepchildren.

Religion: Roman Catholic.

Political Career: Suffolk County assistant district attorney, 1961-62; sought Democratic nomination for president, 1980.

Capitol Office: 315 Russell Bldg. 20510; 224-4543.

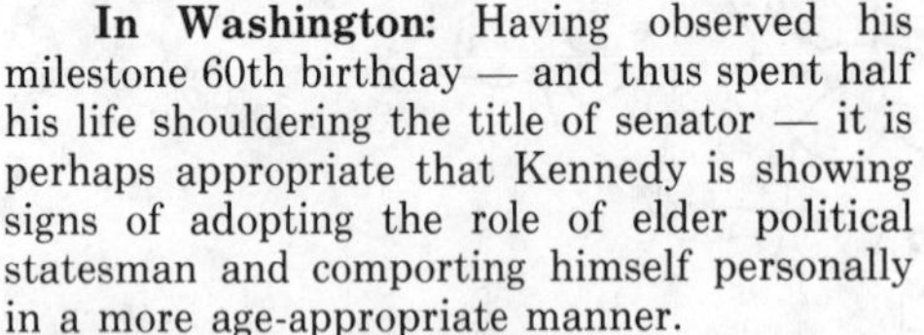

In Washington: Having observed his milestone 60th birthday — and thus spent half his life shouldering the title of senator — it is perhaps appropriate that Kennedy is showing signs of adopting the role of elder political statesman and comporting himself personally in a more age-appropriate manner.

The combination of Kennedy's liberal political agenda and his rather libertine personal life long ago killed his prospects to be president, but it did so without diminishing his influence in the Senate. Within that club, colleagues respect power, which Kennedy has, and they revere history, which Kennedy embodies. In fact, an eccentric personality can enhance the clout of a senator with passionate beliefs — as long as a certain degree of personal decorum is observed.

Yet as recently as 1991, Kennedy's apparent difficulty in staying within those bounds had seriously compromised his legislative effectiveness, impaired his ability to serve as the personification of the liberal conscience and placed him in political peril as he headed toward a 1994 election.

But after being ensnared in the investigation and subsequent trial of his nephew William Kennedy Smith on rape charges, Kennedy grabbed control of his life in an effort to undo whatever damage had been done.

In July 1992, six months after Smith was acquitted, Kennedy took a new bride — Washington attorney Victoria Reggie, the daughter of old family friends. Just weeks after their secretive wedding at Kennedy's home in McLean, Va., the newlyweds made the rounds at the Democratic National Convention, including hosting a cruise for home-state politicians and reporters. It was plainly, for Kennedy, a new beginning.

The legendary name that is so large a part of Kennedy's influence also shines a glaring light on his personal life. After relinquishing his national ambition, Kennedy seemed to drop his guard, but public fascination with his personal life did not abate. Stories about his drinking and socializing continued, and questions about his judgment surfaced during the 1991 investigation and subsequent trial of Smith, who was charged with raping a woman on the grounds of the Kennedy compound in Palm Beach, Fla.

Not since Chappaquiddick had Kennedy been the focus of so much negative publicity. There were intimations that he had initially dodged police who were investigating the alleged rape, but Kennedy blamed their failure to connect on simple miscommunication. The revelation most damaging to Kennedy may have been that he had awakened his son and nephew to go drinking with him.

Kennedy, who eventually was questioned by police and later appeared as a witness at the trial, was indelibly marked by the incident.

He was clearly preoccupied during crucial negotiations on a major civil rights bill that had been one of his prime legislative objectives. He was even more noticeably distracted during Judiciary Committee deliberations about Clarence Thomas, whose confirmation as a Supreme Court justice was put in jeopardy by allegations from Anita F. Hill that Thomas had sexually harassed her.

With his own conduct under intense scrutiny, Kennedy sat mute when Democrats needed him to engage Thomas and Judiciary Committee Republicans effectively. The task was left to Democrats Howard M. Metzenbaum of Ohio and Paul Simon of Illinois, who were unable to deliver the kind of passionate arguments for which Kennedy is known. Kennedy's near silence was a sharp disappointment to women and others who, in other days, would have counted on him.

After that low point, and with an eye toward his upcoming election, Kennedy heeded the warning signs.

He went on yet another diet, steered clear of

the social circuit and delivered a personal mea culpa of sorts in October 1991 at Harvard University's John F. Kennedy School of Government. "I recognize my own shortcomings — the faults in the conduct of my private life. I realize that I alone am responsible for them, and I am the one who must confront them," he said.

At the start of the 103rd Congress, he appeared to be moving beyond the recent controversial incidents that have clouded his tenure. Having risen to the No. 3 Democrat in the chamber, armed with a new public persona and backed by a Democratic president, he stands to be a legislative force on both health care and welfare reform as the chairman of the Labor and Human Resources Committee.

If indeed he has weathered this latest period of personal controversy, he will have no difficulty enduring Republican efforts to sink Democratic initiatives by labeling them as "Kennedy-style liberalism."

The label dates to the early 1980s, when the Reagan revolution had Democrats running scared. Kennedy stood almost alone articulating an opposing view of social justice and equality. Admirers praise Kennedy's steadfast liberalism during this period; it reinforced his singular stature among civil rights activists, advocates for the poor and other liberals.

Kennedy's opposition to President Ronald Reagan encouraged GOP image-makers and fundraisers to make him out as the caricature of a big-government, bleeding-heart liberal. While the label stuck, those who work with Kennedy in the Senate, especially in recent years, do not see him that way. There, his commitment to social programs is increasingly tempered by concern about the federal deficit, and an appreciation of what taxpayers will bear.

Kennedy signaled an important shift in his attitudes when he proclaimed in 1985 that "those of us who care about domestic progress must do more with less." In early 1991, as Congress began debate on reducing the federal student loan default rate, Kennedy warned, "The American taxpayer is not going to support that program unless we get a grip on it."

On the Judiciary Subcommittee on Immigration, which he chairs, Kennedy works closely with Wyoming Republican Alan K. Simpson, one of the more caustic Senate conservatives. After years of work, the two crafted successful compromise legislation in 1990 to limit the flow of legal immigration into the United States. Both Kennedy and Simpson were committed to providing more visas to European immigrants who may not have immediate family here.

Kennedy has achieved some of his recent successes by joining with a Republican ally, then keeping in the background so as not to spark controversy — even as he and his staff work to broker compromises to woo conservative Democrats. This was the case during debate on the 1990 civil rights bill, when he worked with Republican John C. Danforth of Missouri to fashion a bill that won the votes of all the Southern Democrats and 10 Republicans. But President Bush vetoed the bill, labeling it a "quota bill," and an an override attempt fell one vote short. In the process, Bush engendered a store of bad will among Democrats. The bill was finally enacted in 1991 after a deal was cut that both sides could live with. The compromise limited money damages for victims of harassment and other intentional discrimination based on sex, religion or disability; no such cap exists for racial discrimination. Kennedy was the only Democrat to attend the bill's signing, but he remained dissatisfied with the deal.

"That particular limitation [caps on damages] I found obnoxious and extremely offensive," Kennedy said in 1992. "It was necessary to accept because of the legislative realities."

Women's groups in particular were incensed. Kennedy vowed to revisit the issue in 1992, but his attempts to remove the limit were met with charges that he was trying to go back on the deal struck only months before.

Kennedy is expected to employ this same strategy of laying low and negotiating behind the scenes when health care comes to the fore in the 103rd. For at least 25 years, Kennedy has proposed a national system of health care, and for most of that time, no one listened. He long ago gave up the idea of a plan completely financed by the government and instead proposed a hybrid system requiring private employers to insure workers while government covers the poor and unemployed. The idea is similar to those being heard from the Clinton administration in early 1993.

Kennedy was more successful in the 101st Congress ushering to enactment legislation to protect the disabled from discrimination. During debate, he spoke movingly of his mentally retarded sister, Rosemary, and his son Teddy, who lost a leg to cancer.

On the Judiciary Committee, Kennedy has been the most consistent vote against conservative Supreme Court nominations. He was the lone panelist to oppose Bush's appointment of David H. Souter in 1990. But Kennedy did not seek to make Souter a cause célèbre, as he did nominee Robert H. Bork in 1987.

While other Senate Democrats withheld their fire after Reagan nominated the controversial conservative, Kennedy delivered a salvo against Bork within an hour of the announcement. On the Senate floor, he blasted Bork, saying that he "stands for an extremist view of the Constitution and the role of the Supreme Court." In 1991, Kennedy just as firmly opposed Thomas, although much of the fiery rhetoric was missing.

He uses his celebrity to champion the anti-apartheid movement in South Africa. His heavily publicized trip there in early 1985 helped harden public opinion against the white-minority government, setting in motion the events that led to passage of tough economic sanctions in 1986.

Though his Oval Office prospects are gone, Kennedy is still able to assemble a staff that is regarded as the most powerful on Capitol Hill. It is also far larger than most — Kennedy's seniority has brought him a major committee chairmanship and two subcommittee chairs.

This combination gives him a conglomerate of experienced, creative professionals who are fiercely loyal. They screen his contacts, prepare him thoroughly, and churn out countless program initiatives. With their backing, Kennedy can march into a markup with a fistful of amendments, and even if most are dropped, he still ends up with more than his share of successes.

Kennedy started his career without any of the leadership pressures that descended on him later. He was 30 years old, his brothers were running the country, and he voted with them while looking out for his state's interests.

In time, he became an innovative and often successful legislator, particularly during the early 1970s, after not only the 1969 Chappaquiddick tragedy but also his most embarrassing Senate defeat, his ouster as majority whip in 1971.

Kennedy had been elected whip in 1969, beating Finance Chairman Russell B. Long, who had performed erratically in the post. The vote was taken only months after New York Sen. Robert F. Kennedy's assassination, which made the youngest Kennedy the rising star.

But he was bored with the odd parliamentary jobs that make effective leaders. Then that summer, his image was shattered for all time when he drove his car off a bridge at Chappaquiddick and his companion in the car, Mary Jo Kopechne, drowned. When Senate Democrats elected their leaders in 1971, they chose Robert C. Byrd of West Virginia for whip, 31-24.

As he would do more than a decade later upon shelving his national ambitions, Kennedy returned to legislating. As chairman of Labor's Health Subcommittee, he formed a productive partnership with his House counterpart, Florida Democrat Paul G. Rogers. Together they wrote legislation financing research into cancer and heart and lung diseases, family planning and doctor training. Every year brought a greater federal role in health.

He became chairman of Judiciary in 1979, but his tenure did not last long. By fall, he was running for president, and the next year's elections brought a Republican Senate takeover.

Since 1968, people had looked to Kennedy to run for president. In the fall of 1979, apparently tempted by early polls showing him far ahead of President Jimmy Carter, Kennedy launched his campaign without offering any clear idea of why he wanted to be president. He talked of the need for stronger leadership, but so clumsily as to raise the question of whether he could provide it.

Only in the campaign's second half — by which time Kennedy was essentially beaten — did he present the clear liberal argument he took to the convention. The changes did not bring him any closer to nomination, but they kept him alive as a liberal leader. His stirring Democratic convention speech, with its liberal affirmation that "the work goes on, the cause endures, the hope still lives, and the dream shall never die," helped restore some lost luster. Kennedy was considered a potential candidate for 1988, but late in 1985 he announced he would not seek the nomination. He acknowledged that his decision meant he probably would never occupy the White House. "The pursuit of the presidency is not my life," he said. "Public service is."

At Home: Like Chappaquiddick 22 years earlier, the Palm Beach incident renewed doubts about Kennedy's judgment and revived Republican hopes of defeating him in 1994. However, his marriage and more staid personal persona have netted him a popularity surge.

The new Mrs. Kennedy has been a hit. Shortly after the 1992 Democratic convention, one prominent columnist predicted the best of Kennedy may be yet to come. A January 1993 poll published in the Boston Globe showed "a political recovery for the recently married Kennedy," and observed that "any time you see Ted these days you see his wife with him." As if to underscore their inseparability and her modifying influence on him, they appeared at his annual and well-attended Capitol Hill Christmas party in 1992 as Beauty and the Beast.

Despite Kennedy's near-hero status with many Massachusetts voters, a smaller — but equally vocal — number seem to despise him. Almost always, regardless of his opponent, Kennedy hovers around the 60 percent mark.

Kennedy's challenge has been to live up to the standard he set in 1964, when he ran for his first full term less than a year after his brother John's assassination. Bedridden after an airplane crash, he beat Republican Howard Whitmore Jr. by the widest margin in state history: 1,129,244 votes.

That number, rather than GOP candidate Josiah Spaulding, was the real test in 1970. There was no way Kennedy could pass it. The Chappaquiddick accident had occurred the year before and even loyal Bay Staters had doubts. His 62 percent showing that year established the love-hate yardstick that still holds.

In 1976, he brushed aside three anti-busing and anti-abortion challengers in the primary, then crushed GOP businessman Michael Robertson by 1 million votes.

In 1982, Kennedy met his first Republican foe able to draw attention on his own. Raymond Shamie, a wealthy inventor, spent more than $1 million in a quixotic but imaginative campaign. In an effort to force Kennedy to debate him, Shamie had airplanes circle baseball games, county fairs and freeways, towing banners offering $10,000 to whoever could "GET TED KENNEDY TO DEBATE RAY SHAMIE."

Kennedy fought back with his own attention-getting ploy. A month before the election, Kennedy accepted Shamie's offer, asking that the reward go to a Catholic school in Hanover, Mass. The debate had little impact on the race; Kennedy won with 61 percent of the vote.

In 1988, Kennedy had a trouble-free reelection. Joseph D. Malone, a 33-year-old former state GOP executive director, saw his bid more as a party-building endeavor than a contest with Kennedy. He made scant progress against Kennedy but established a base and positive image to run successfully for state treasurer in 1990.

Kennedy burst into politics in 1962 by winning the election to fill the remaining two years of his brother's Senate term. John F. Kennedy had arranged for family friend Benjamin A. Smith to get the seat when he became president in 1961, and Smith then stepped aside for the younger Kennedy in 1962.

Edward J. McCormack, nephew of House Speaker John W. McCormack, was not as obliging. He derided Kennedy's qualifications, noting his meager experience as an assistant district attorney in Boston and said in a Democratic primary debate: "If your name were Edward Moore [instead of Edward Moore Kennedy], your candidacy would be a joke." Kennedy did not lose his temper and the attacks created a backlash against McCormack.

Kennedy easily won the primary, carrying every ward in Boston and winning outstate as well. In November, he took 55 percent of the vote against Republican George Cabot Lodge.

Committees

Labor & Human Resources (Chairman)
Children, Families, Drugs & Alcoholism; Education, Arts & Humanities; Labor

Armed Services (4th of 11 Democrats)
Regional Defense & Contingency Forces (chairman); Defense Technology, Acquisition & Industrial Base; Force Requirements & Personnel

Judiciary (2nd of 10 Democrats)
Immigration & Refugee Affairs (chairman); Constitution; Patents, Copyrights & Trademarks

Joint Economic

Elections

1988 General

Edward M. Kennedy (D)	1,693,344	(65%)
Joseph D. Malone (R)	884,267	(34%)

Previous Winning Percentages: **1982** (61%) **1976** (69%) **1970** (62%) **1964** (74%) **1962** * (55%)

** Special election.*

Campaign Finance

	Receipts	Receipts from PACs		Expend-itures
1988				
Kennedy (D)	$3,304,580	$322,972	(10%)	$2,702,865
Malone (R)	$617,806	0		$587,323

Key Votes

1993	
Require unpaid family and medical leave	Y
Approve national "motor voter" registration bill	Y
Approve budget increasing taxes and reducing deficit	Y
Support president's right to lift military gay ban	Y
1992	
Approve school-choice pilot program	N
Allow shifting funds from defense to domestic programs	Y
Oppose deeper cuts in spending for SDI	N
1991	
Approve waiting period for handgun purchases	Y
Raise senators' pay and ban honoraria	Y
Authorize use of force in Persian Gulf	N
Confirm Clarence Thomas to Supreme Court	N

Voting Studies

	Presidential Support		Party Unity		Conservative Coalition	
Year	**S**	**O**	**S**	**O**	**S**	**O**
1992	25	73	95	3	5	92
1991	31	67	92	7	13	88
1990	25	70	89	7	14	81
1989	48	49	90	7	18	79
1988	36	55	84	4	3	89
1987	29	62	85	5	6	81
1986	28	69	79	16	24	70
1985	27	69	81	7	17	73
1984	30	58	84	7	6	91
1983	36	54	70	17	11	82
1982	29	64	83	5	2	88
1981	31	60	80	9	4	87

Interest Group Ratings

Year	ADA	AFL-CIO	CCUS	ACU
1992	100	92	20	0
1991	95	83	20	0
1990	100	89	0	0
1989	85	90	29	7
1988	95	100	27	0
1987	90	100	24	0
1986	80	77	47	10
1985	85	90	39	9
1984	85	100	24	5
1983	85	100	22	0
1982	75	96	0	6
1981	100	94	6	0

John Kerry (D)

Of Boston — Elected 1984; 2nd Term

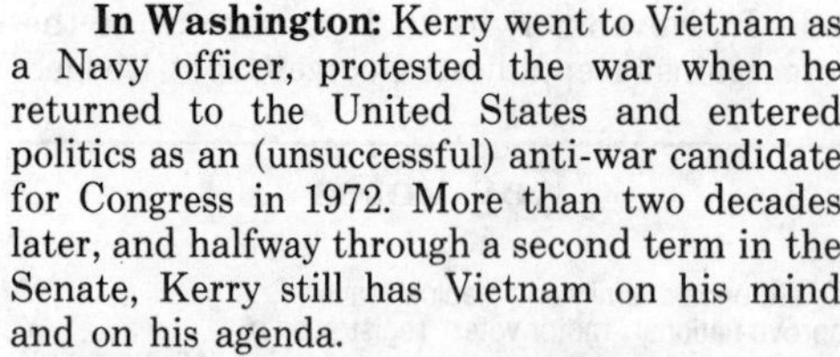

Born: Dec. 11, 1943, Denver, Colo.
Education: Yale U., B.A. 1966; Boston College, J.D. 1976.
Military Service: Navy, 1968-69.
Occupation: Lawyer.
Family: Divorced; two children.
Religion: Roman Catholic.
Political Career: Democratic nominee for U.S. House, 1972; lieutenant governor, 1983-85.
Capitol Office: 421 Russell Bldg. 20510; 224-2742.

In Washington: Kerry went to Vietnam as a Navy officer, protested the war when he returned to the United States and entered politics as an (unsuccessful) anti-war candidate for Congress in 1972. More than two decades later, and halfway through a second term in the Senate, Kerry still has Vietnam on his mind and on his agenda.

In March 1993, a document that had been languishing in Soviet files since 1972 became public, purporting to show that Hanoi had held far more prisoners of war than it ever acknowledged. At the time, Hanoi had pegged the number at 368, but the document indicated there were actually more than 1,200 American POWs.

"This document clearly smacks of authenticity," Kerry said on ABC's "Nightline" in April. "But there's a distinction between authenticity and accuracy."

Kerry had reason to dispute the allegation. In the 102nd Congress, he had been chairman of the Senate Select Committee on POW/MIA Affairs, investigating the possibility that there were still U.S. prisoners Americans alive in Vietnam. But after a 15-month inquiry, including 22 days of public hearings and several trips to Vietnam, Laos and Cambodia, the committee concluded: "There is, at this time, no compelling evidence that proves that any American remains alive in captivity in Southeast Asia."

The 1,000-page final report was signed by all 12 members of the committee, six from each party. It said some evidence had suggested that at least some POWs may have languished in Vietnam years after the war ended.

"This report does not close the issue," Kerry said at the time. "It is not meant to. This report provides a reality base from which we can now make real judgments about probabilities and possibilities."

Indeed, Vietnam never seems to be closed. And for those who, like Kerry, showed empathy for both sides of the national division, the conflict is especially persistent. During one hearing of the select committee, Kerry had a testy exchange with former Secretary of State Henry Kissinger, who bristled at Kerry's suggestion that the Nixon administration had failed to pressure Vietnam to return POWs after the Paris peace accords were signed in 1973. Kissinger said he found it a "bizarre situation" that people "who were parading and arguing that we shouldn't be doing what we were doing now say we should have been more aggressive."

"Look, I didn't ask for this job," Kerry shot back. "I'm here because 20 years later the questions still confound America."

Kerry's history also influenced his thinking in 1993 on the crisis in Bosnia, as he warned Secretary of State Warren M. Christopher, during an appearance before the Senate Foreign Relations Committee in May, that the Senate might lose patience with the administration's apparent drift.

Kerry was one of those who seemed best-prepared to handle the political dilemma posed by the January 1991 vote authorizing the use of military force in the Persian Gulf. Kerry voted against the resolution authorizing President Bush to use force. "There is no consensus in America for war," he said. Yet he took pains to note his overall support for confrontation with Iraq and warned the world "not to draw too sharp a line" between the parties or the branches of government on the question of Kuwait's sovereignty.

Kerry also chairs the Foreign Relations Subcommittee on Terrorism, Narcotics and International Operations, and he used his panel to dig into the domestic and international activities of the Bank of Credit and Commerce International (BCCI). He had started investigating in 1987, and for almost three years, Kerry was alone in his effort to pursue a probe of questionable dealings by BCCI. By the fall of 1991, the Senate and House Banking committees had started their own investigations. Kerry serves on the Senate Banking Committee and had urged the panel to look into BCCI.

In his subcommittee chair, Kerry had gained

some note in the 100th Congress by taking on Panamanian strongman Manuel Antonio Noriega. Kerry's subcommittee investigators looked for ties between drug smuggling and illegal shipments of weapons to the Nicaraguan contras. Kerry suggested that Noriega was being protected by the United States because of what he knew about the connection. Bush, then vice president and the 1988 GOP presidential nominee, attacked Kerry by name.

Later, however, when Bush decided to invade Panama and root out Noriega, Kerry voiced his support. By then, Kerry had moved away from gaudy hearings on drug-running and money laundering. In the later stages of his first term, he immersed himself in work that, while often smaller-scale, was generally more productive.

Typical was his amendment to the 1990 crime bill that doubled the funding available to help local police cope with drug-related crime. Many of his more successful moments related to the business of Massachusetts — including his support of a third tunnel for Boston Harbor and a proposed high-speed rail link between Boston and New York.

Kerry also was active in such wider arenas as the Clean Air Act and campaign finance reform. Some of the amendments he offered to the former legislation were adopted, and he also submitted at least one toughening amendment on smog that lost only narrowly (when Majority Leader George J. Mitchell of Maine decided its adoption would endanger the deal with the White House).

He also pressed for restructuring federal campaign financing to rely on voluntary public funding for 90 percent of campaign costs. Kerry continued to push for such a formula when the issue was rejoined in the 102nd Congress.

Moreover, in the later years of his first Senate term, Kerry found himself compelled to do some heavy political lifting. He chaired his party's Senate campaign committee through a successful electoral round in 1988, even as his former boss in the Massachusetts state government, Gov. Michael S. Dukakis, faltered in his bid for the presidency.

Kerry then turned in a strong performance in his own behalf, winning a solid re-election victory in 1990. He turned back a self-financing GOP citizen-candidate despite the worst anti-incumbent sentiment to hit Massachusetts Democrats in years.

Kerry no longer appears on everyone's list of senators running for president, and for his Senate career, at least, that is good news. The White House may well be his ultimate goal, but he has benefited in his colleagues' estimation by restraining his ambition.

Early in his Senate years, Kerry's reputation suffered somewhat from his apparent preoccupation with image. He got a reputation for caring about how things looked, and when he had corrective jaw surgery it was regarded by some as an effort to improve his appearance.

Kerry has also been seen as overly aware of the characteristics he shares with a legendary Massachusetts politician with the same initials. Like John F. Kennedy, Kerry is a product of social privilege (his middle name, Forbes, salutes his mother's blue-blood family). Like Kennedy, Kerry was decorated for his daring as a small-craft commander in the Navy and went quickly into politics in the party of the lower-income classes. But Kerry's career has been more anti-establishment than Kennedy's, especially at critical junctures.

He first came to prominence protesting the Vietnam War, and at times in his first years in the Senate he still seemed to be carrying a protester's banner. The dutiful study he devoted to complex issues such as anti-satellite weapons testing was appreciated, but his effort to address the issue with amendments on other senators' unrelated bills was not.

At Home: In 1971, Kerry, a leader of Vietnam Veterans Against the War, joined with other demonstrators as they threw their medals over the White House fence. When the incident is recounted, Kerry takes pains to explain that he opposed the returning of medals as a tactic and returned none of his own (three Purple Hearts, a Silver Star and a Bronze Star). He did throw the medals of a veteran from Worcester, Mass., who could not come to Washington, and he also threw several of the ribbons he had received with his own medals.

He gained front-page coverage in 1971 by asking the Senate Foreign Relations Committee, "How do you ask a man to be the last man to die for a mistake?" He tried to exploit the publicity by moving to Lowell and running in the open 5th District in 1972. Kerry won his 10-way primary but lost in the fall to Republican Paul Cronin.

After that defeat, Kerry went to law school and then worked as assistant district attorney in Middlesex County. In 1980, he bowed out of a House campaign in a second suburban district in favor of fellow liberal Barney Frank.

In 1982, he challenged the regular Democratic establishment by running for lieutenant governor. With help from Ray Flynn, a member of the Boston City Council who later became mayor, he carried Suffolk County and edged out Evelyn Murphy in the primary.

The anti-establishment theme surfaced again in 1984, in his fight with U.S. Rep. James M. Shannon for the nomination to replace retiring Sen. Paul E. Tsongas. Kerry contrasted his image as an independent liberal to Shannon's reputation as a House insider.

Shannon argued that his knowledge of Capitol Hill was an asset Kerry could not match. But Kerry called Shannon a "back-room" politician, and cast himself as an outsider who could stand up to the Reagan administration. He won 41 percent of the vote, to

Shannon's 38 percent.

In the general election, Kerry faced conservative businessman Raymond Shamie, who had won the GOP nomination in a stunning upset over longtime national figure Elliot Richardson. Indications that Shamie had picked up primary votes from working-class Democrats, along with Reagan's popularity in lunch-bucket territory, forced Kerry to moderate his image. He played down foreign policy, talked about economics, and muted his anti-war background.

It turned out there was little to worry about. The Boston Globe ran articles tying Shamie to the ultra-conservative John Birch Society, and Shamie was not helped when some of his supporters questioned Kerry's loyalty as a U.S. citizen. Kerry took Boston by better than 2-to-1 and defeated Shamie in most other cities, winning with 55 percent overall.

In 1990, Kerry sought a second term amid a maelstrom of statewide anti-incumbent fervor. Departing Gov. Dukakis' popularity had fallen to subterranean levels and the commonwealth's economy was sinking. Voters' enmity toward Dukakis spilled over onto the overwhelmingly Democratic state Legislature and to others on the public payroll.

Millionaire real estate developer and lawyer Jim Rappaport tried to handcuff Kerry to the Democratic structure under siege. The son of a prominent real estate magnate, Rappaport tapped the family fount to siphon a reported $4.2 million of personal money into his campaign, his first political bid.

Able to battle Kerry on an equal financial footing, Rappaport invested heavily in TV advertisements lashing Kerry to Dukakis and accusing Kerry of being a tax-and-spend liberal. His most memorable ad showed a photograph of Dukakis' face slowly metamorphosing into one of Kerry's. His strategy was simple: Persuade voters to think of Dukakis' 1982 running mate as a "Dukakis clone."

But Kerry parried Rappaport's negative ads with ones of his own. His radio and TV ads ridiculed Rappaport for his business affairs in Hawaii and Vermont and accused him of earning business profits at taxpayers' expense. Kerry also ran effective ads highlighting his career. By the end, a race that polls had shown as extremely close in September widened to a 57 percent to 43 percent victory for Kerry.

Committees

Banking, Housing & Urban Affairs (6th of 11 Democrats)
Economic Stabilization & Rural Development; Housing & Urban Affairs; International Finance & Monetary Policy

Commerce, Science & Transportation (6th of 11 Democrats)
Foreign Commerce & Tourism (chairman); National Ocean Policy Study (vice chairman); Aviation; Communications; Science

Foreign Relations (5th of 11 Democrats)
Terrorism, Narcotics & International Operations (chairman); East Asian & Pacific Affairs; International Economic Policy, Trade, Oceans & Environment

Select Intelligence (7th of 9 Democrats)

Small Business (5th of 12 Democrats)
Urban & Minority-Owned Business Development (chairman); Innovation, Manufacturing & Technology

Elections

1990 General

John Kerry (D)	1,321,712	(57%)
Jim Rappaport (R)	992,917	(43%)

Previous Winning Percentage: **1984** (55%)

Campaign Finance

	Receipts	Receipts from PACs		Expend-itures
1990				
Kerry (D)	$6,215,076	0		$6,234,887
Rappaport (R)	$5,185,061	$177,205	(3%)	$5,177,801

Key Votes

1993	
Require unpaid family and medical leave	Y
Approve national "motor voter" registration bill	Y
Approve budget increasing taxes and reducing deficit	Y
Support president's right to lift military gay ban	Y
1992	
Approve school-choice pilot program	N
Allow shifting funds from defense to domestic programs	Y
Oppose deeper cuts in spending for SDI	N
1991	
Approve waiting period for handgun purchases	Y
Raise senators' pay and ban honoraria	N
Authorize use of force in Persian Gulf	N
Confirm Clarence Thomas to Supreme Court	N

Voting Studies

	Presidential Support		Party Unity		Conservative Coalition	
Year	**S**	**O**	**S**	**O**	**S**	**O**
1992	23	77	92	8	8	89
1991	28	72	92	8	10	90
1990	25	70	85	11	5	86
1989	47	53	86	14	18	82
1988	40	55	88	4	0	92
1987	38	59	89	8	9	84
1986	22	75	85	12	16	79
1985	26	73	91	7	13	87

Interest Group Ratings

Year	ADA	AFL-CIO	CCUS	ACU
1992	100	83	10	0
1991	95	83	20	5
1990	94	89	18	5
1989	95	100	50	11
1988	90	93	36	0
1987	85	100	25	4
1986	90	93	32	9
1985	85	95	38	5

1 John W. Olver (D)

Of Amherst — Elected 1991; 1st Full Term

Born: Sept. 3, 1936, Honesdale, Pa.
Education: Rensselaer Polytechnic Institute, B.S. 1955; Tufts U., M.S. 1956; Massachusetts Institute of Technology, Ph.D. 1961.
Occupation: Professor.
Family: Wife, Rose Richardson; one child.
Religion: Unspecified.
Political Career: Mass. House, 1969-73; Mass. Senate, 1973-91.
Capitol Office: 1323 Longworth Bldg. 20515; 225-5335.

In Washington: Olver replaced Silvio O. Conte in the 1st District and, in the 103rd Congress, took his seat on the Appropriations Committee. Olver also shares much of his predecessor's worldview. But it will take some time before he can match the power and popularity Conte enjoyed.

Conte was beginning his 17th term and was the ranking Republican on Appropriations when he died in February 1991. Olver was elected in a special election the following June.

At a glance, the two men could not be more different. Olver, originally from Pennsylvania, is a lanky, shy and thoughtful academic. He received his college degree at 18 and his master's at 19, and he earned his doctorate from the Massachusetts Institute of Technology at 24. He first came into the district as a member of the faculty of the University of Massachusetts at Amherst.

Conte, a graduate of Boston College, was a gruff but ebullient product of the Italian wards in blue-collar Pittsfield. He was a stocky man who loved cigars and good talk and could entertain a single colleague or the entire House with great ease.

Yet the two men's approaches to government are not dissimilar. On Appropriations, Olver undoubtedly will reprise Conte's dedication to funding biomedical research, maternal and child health programs, and student aid. Much of this funding will benefit the numerous colleges and universities in the district — including the state university where Olver once taught chemistry.

Olver has seats on the subcommittees dealing with Foreign Operations and the Treasury. He adds to the geographic diversity of the Treasury panel as the only member from the Northeast.

Though Conte was the top Republican on Appropriations, he often voted with the Democrats. He felt government funds should be spent generously to improve people's lives. But he also objected to what he felt were efforts by colleagues to promote wasteful pork barrel projects. To dramatize his protest, he occasionally would don a pig mask on the House floor.

The Appropriations position was in part a reward for Olver's party loyalty and to New England. Despite the closeness of his election margin and the probability of future challenges, Olver was willing to vote with his party majority 96 percent of the time in 1991 and 93 percent of the time in 1992 on votes that divided along party lines.

He has genuine faith in the ability of government to solve society's programs, telling his cheering supporters on the night he was first elected that "compassion still has a place in government.... It isn't all number-crunching and policy papers. People do count."

At Home: Olver has yet to establish himself in his district, where a liberal tradition of long standing was carried on by a breed of Republicans now largely vanished from the U.S. House. Conte, one of the House's most liberal Republicans, exemplified the tradition by which Republicans had represented the western counties of Massachusetts since the 1800s.

But Democrats have grown more numerous in the 1st in recent years due to growth around the campuses of several colleges and the arrival of younger refugees from the Boston area. Democratic presidential nominee Walter F. Mondale had come close to winning the district in 1984, and the national Democratic ticket carried it easily in 1988 and 1992.

Democrats also have become more common in local and state office. When Conte died, no fewer than 10 Democrats lined up to vie for the nomination to succeed him. Among them was Olver, who had been serving quietly in the state legislature since the 1960s.

He was first elected to the state House in the highly charged political atmosphere of 1968. Four years later, backed by a small army of volunteers, he bucked the national GOP trend by unseating an incumbent Republican state senator in a district once represented by Calvin Coolidge.

As a state senator, Olver voted for gay rights,

Massachusetts 1

West — Berkshire Hills; Fitchburg; Amherst

The enormous 1st, which is framed by Connecticut on the south, New York on the west and Vermont and New Hampshire on the north, seems more like three districts than one.

Residents of the bucolic Berkshire Hills identify most naturally with New Yorkers; they get their news from Albany and many of their visitors from Manhattan. In the central part of the 1st lies the Connecticut River Valley, a rural region known for its maple syrup and a scenic 63-mile stretch of state Route 2 (the Mohawk Trail), which runs from Greenfield to Williamstown. On the eastern side of the 1st are a handful of medium-sized industrial cities more closely linked to Worcester in the 3rd District than to the rest of the 1st.

A theme repeats itself across the district: Major textile industries have died, workers have left, and a handful of educational institutions and small businesses are struggling to revive the region. Shoe factories have closed, Gardner is no longer a furniture capital, and in Pittsfield, General Electric's work force has plummeted from 15,000 in the 1950s to 3,000 in the 1990s. (Martin Marietta purchased GE's aerospace division in 1992, creating even more uncertainty for the Pittsfield workers.) Paper mills still thrive in the district and plastic production is lively in Pittsfield and Leominster.

The residents of Western Massachusetts see themselves as a hardy, self-reliant lot. For years this was the only state district sending a Republican to Congress, although ironically, a major contributor to the long tenure of GOP Rep. Silvio O. Conte (1959-91) in the 1st was his success at using his Appropriations Committee seat to produce federal dollars and jobs. After Conte's death, the GOP lost the 1st in a 1991 special election, and it stayed Democratic in 1992.

Rep. Olver carved out a second win with the help of liberal enclaves such as Amherst, Belchertown, Williamstown and Pelham. Heavily Catholic communities such as Holyoke, Westfield and Pittsfield have many people who like to vote an anti-abortion line, but they will often support Democrats if both parties nominate abortion-rights supporters (as was the case in the 1992 House race).

Bill Clinton trailed Olver in most of the district's communities in 1992, but he still carried the 1st.

The district's schools provide an injection of youth and growth potential to the otherwise aging region. In addition to Williams College, eight of the 30 state college campuses are in the 1st; the largest is the University of Massachusetts at Amherst, with 22,000 students. Its world-class Polymer Research Center has spawned several small businesses in the area.

By the standards of overwhelmingly white Western Massachusetts, a few towns in the 1st have minority populations of some significance. One-third of Holyoke is Hispanic, and there are small black and Asian communities in Fitchburg and Leominster. But the district's predominant non-Yankee groups are Poles, French-Canadians and Italians.

1990 Population: 601,643. White 566,587 (94%), Black 10,183 (2%), Other 24,873 (4%). Hispanic origin 28,927 (5%). 18 and over 457,863 (76%), 62 and over 99,882 (17%). Median age: 33.

for allowing minors access to abortion, for universal health care and for an override of the famed ballot proposition that limited taxes and spending in Massachusetts state government.

As much as he lacks charisma, Olver excels in preparation and organization. In the 1991 primary and general election campaigns, he carefully targeted his vote. After winning the primary, he collected endorsements from his rivals to go with those of labor unions, teachers, environmentalists, women's groups and supporters of abortion rights.

Uncomfortable at times in the media glare, Olver has never been thought a barn-burner in campaigning. But he has steadily built a following in the liberal precincts around Amherst, where his habits of handball, cross-country skiing and rock-climbing in a Grateful Dead T-shirt seem as fitting as Conte's cigar and Red Sox cap did in blue-collar Pittsfield.

Olver emerged from the big primary field in 1991 with surprising ease, outdistancing his nearest competitor, state Sen. Linda J. Melconian, by more than 10 percentage points.

But the Massachusetts Republican Party, flush from its recent success in electing William Weld governor the previous November, was not about to let Conte's seat go without a fight (it was the only seat in the delegation held by a Republican at the time).

The Republican champion was Steven D. Pierce, a former state House Minority Leader who had lost the GOP primary for governor to Weld the previous year. Weld had since appointed him to a cabinet job and backed him enthusiastically for Congress.

Pierce tried to depict Olver as too liberal for the district by echoing some of the same charges on economic and cultural issues that George Bush had used against Michael S. Dukakis in 1988. He also criticized Olver as an architect of the state's high taxes in view of Olver's position as chairman of the state Senate Taxation Committee.

Olver fought back by reminding voters that Weld had called Pierce a "right-wing ideologue" during their 1990 GOP gubernatorial primary. Olver also benefited from the National Abortion Rights Action League's independent campaign against Pierce, who supported abortion only in cases of rape, incest or a threat to the mother's life.

In the end, the abortion issue may have been pivotal. Olver eked out a 50 percent share and won by fewer than 2,000 votes.

In 1992, Olver was unopposed in the primary. But he was not able to expand much on the share of the vote he had drawn the previous year.

His GOP opponent was Patrick Larkin, once the top staff aide to Conte, who had many personal contacts in the district but whose TV ads left swing voters unmoved. Larkin did reach 45 percent, but three minor-party candidates divided another 5 percent of the vote. Olver, whose own campaign was hobbled by uncharacteristic misfires, barely managed to record a majority.

Committee

Appropriations (35th of 37 Democrats)
Foreign Operations, Export Financing & Related Programs; Treasury, Postal Service & General Government

Elections

1992 General		
John W. Olver (D)	135,049	(52%)
Patrick Larkin (R)	113,828	(43%)
Louis R. Godena (PJJ)	7,162	(3%)
Dennis M. Kelly (PDR)	4,355	(2%)
1991 Special		
John W. Olver (D)	70,022	(50%)
Steven D. Pierce (R)	68,052	(48%)
Patrick Joseph Armstrong (I)	1,859	(1%)

District Vote for President

1992
D 130,311 (48%)
R 72,246 (27%)
I 68,541 (25%)

Campaign Finance

	Receipts	Receipts from PACs		Expend-itures
1992				
Olver (D)	$705,906	$296,780	(42%)	$704,238
Larkin (R)	$398,618	$96,685	(24%)	$384,625

Key Votes

1993	
Require parental notification of minors' abortions	N
Require unpaid family and medical leave	Y
Approve national "motor voter" registration bill	Y
Approve budget increasing taxes and reducing deficit	Y
Approve economic stimulus plan	Y
1992	
Approve balanced-budget constitutional amendment	N
Close down space station program	Y
Approve U.S. aid for former Soviet Union	Y
Allow shifting funds from defense to domestic programs	Y
1991	
Extend unemployment benefits using deficit financing	Y
Approve waiting period for handgun purchases	I

Voting Studies

	Presidential Support		Party Unity		Conservative Coalition	
Year	S	O	S	O	S	O
1992	11	87	93	5	10	90
1991	20 †	80 †	96 †	1 †	5 †	95 †

† Not eligible for all recorded votes.

Interest Group Ratings

Year	ADA	AFL-CIO	CCUS	ACU
1992	100	92	25	0
1991	100	100	33	0

Massachusetts - 2nd District

2 Richard E. Neal (D)

Of Springfield — Elected 1988; 3rd Term

Born: Feb. 14, 1949, Worcester, Mass.
Education: American International College, B.A. 1972; U. of Hartford, M.P.A. 1976.
Occupation: Public official; college lecturer.
Family: Wife, Maureen Conway; four children.
Religion: Roman Catholic.
Political Career: Springfield City Council, 1978-84; mayor of Springfield, 1984-89.
Capitol Office: 131 Cannon Bldg. 20515; 225-5601.

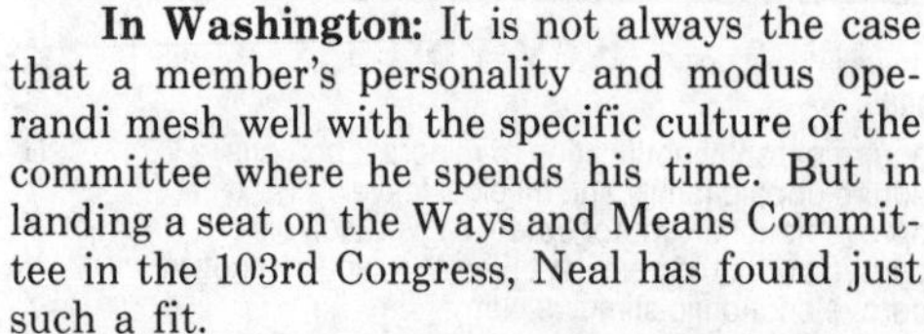

In Washington: It is not always the case that a member's personality and modus operandi mesh well with the specific culture of the committee where he spends his time. But in landing a seat on the Ways and Means Committee in the 103rd Congress, Neal has found just such a fit.

Ways and Means is very different from the Banking Committee, in whose uneasy venue Neal spent two relatively quiet terms. Where Banking can be a quicksand of shifting alliances and uncertain politics, the relative terra firma of Ways and Means is the perfect platform from which a member from a secure district can confidently build a career.

It is also a serious place, where Neal's academic and lengthy professional background in public administration will be seen as an asset. And Neal's reluctance to seek the spotlight puts him in the mold of typical Ways and Means members, who do much of their work in private conversations with Chairman Dan Rostenkowski of Illinois or in head-knocking markups behind closed doors.

While learning the ropes on Banking, Neal tried to impress colleagues with a sober approach to legislating. He took a seat on the Financial Institutions Subcommittee, which was charged with, among other things, drafting legislation to bail out the deposit insurance fund for savings and loan institutions and restructure the industry's deposit insurance system.

In 1989, Neal voted to stiffen capital standards for savings and loans and supported the original thrift bailout bill. But since then he has voted consistently against putting additional taxpayer funds into the bailout.

In 1991, as the committee prepared to embark on an overhaul of banking law, Neal expressed doubts about some proposals in the Bush administration's package of reforms, which many feared would lead to even more concentration of financial markets.

"I've watched decision-making move from Springfield to Boston; I'm concerned about it moving on to New York, then to London and Tokyo," he told one administration witness.

Neal was particularly troubled about the seeming lack of available credit in New England during the early 1990s recession and the possibility that lenders were discriminating in their allocation of loans. His amendment to the big banking bill to require reports on lending practices regarding small businesses, small farms and minority-owned companies was adopted 28-23. Critics said it would add costly paperwork to banks that were struggling. But Neal convinced his colleagues that that sort of public information would give Congress insight into whether further action was needed. It was one of the few consumer-oriented measures enacted as part of the 1991 bill.

Neal generally has voted the Democratic line, but on several high-profile votes, he strayed from the leadership's position.

As an abortion opponent from a heavily Catholic district, he voted against federal funding for abortions in cases of rape or incest, though he twice voted to overturn an administration ban on abortion counseling in federally financed family planning clinics. He also opposed the 1989 pay raise and ethics reform package, the 1990 budget summit agreement and the 1992 aid bill to former Soviet Union.

In 1990, Neal backed constitutional amendments to ban flag desecration and to require a balanced federal budget. But in 1992 he switched at the last minute to oppose the balanced-budget amendment in the face of the Democratic leadership's stiff lobbying against the measure. Neal had even told President Bush, who telephoned from Air Force One the morning of the vote, that he was planning to vote yes.

Neal has been a unwavering supporter of Democratic tax proposals. In 1989, for instance, he opposed Bush's proposed cut in the capital gains tax, preferring a Democratic alternative to restore the tax deductibility of contributions to Individual Retirement Accounts. Neal introduced bills in the 102nd and 103rd Congresses to restore IRA deductibility.

Neal also advocated reregulating the cable

Massachusetts 2

West Central — Northampton; Springfield; Sturbridge

The city of Springfield dwarfs all other communities in the 2nd in size, population and economic importance. Located on the banks of the Connecticut River, Springfield was named in 1636 by fur trader William Pynchon after his hometown in England.

Since then, Springfield has laid claim to a string of "firsts," including the first federal armory (approved by Congress in 1794), the first gasoline-powered car, the first Pullman rail car and the first basketball game.

Many of the city's successes of the 1990s are tied to that rich history. Companies such as Spalding Sports Worldwide and Smith & Wesson guns have kept the economy going as heavy manufacturing has fallen off. And attractions such as the Basketball Hall of Fame and the Springfield Armory National Historic Site have helped lure tourists.

Ultimately, the region's future rests with the insurance and financial services industries. Despite staff reductions in late 1992, Massachusetts Mutual Life Insurance Co. remains a major employer. Some small manufacturers remain, although others (such as the R. E. Phelon machine parts company) are moving to Southern locales where the cost of doing business is lower.

Residents in the district also worry about defense spending cutbacks, specifically those affecting United Technologies, the largest private employer in neighboring Connecticut and an important source of jobs for the 2nd as well.

A sizable Hispanic population moved into the 2nd in the 1950s to work in tobacco fields. Although the business has dwindled, West Springfield and Hadley still have many laborers picking leaves that form cigar wrappers. The minority population in the 2nd now tops 10 percent.

Springfield and Chicopee, the second-largest city in the district, together offer a reliable base of votes for any Democratic candidate. Democratic voter registration in the 2nd is four times that of the GOP. Bill Clinton surpassed 60 percent here in 1992 presidential voting. Neal's anti-abortion stance sits well with this heavily Catholic city.

A drive through the rest of the 2nd is a glimpse of New England at its quaintest. In towns such as Longmeadow, Hadley, Palmer and Ware, village life is still focused on a town green. Two of the "Seven Sisters" schools — Mount Holyoke College and Smith College — add to the traditional New England look. Northampton has a more modern claim to fame: A couple of artists there created an icon of child culture: the Teenage Mutant Ninja Turtles.

Although not as well-known as the nearby Berkshire Hills or Cape Cod along the coast, the 2nd is a popular recreational area. Boating and cross-country skiing are popular, and the brilliant fall foliage always draws a crowd. Virtually every town capitalizes on the scenery with a variety of special events, from Chicopee's World Kielbasa Festival to cider-making at Sturbridge Village.

1990 Population: 601,642. White 539,107 (90%), Black 33,960 (6%), Other 28,575 (5%). Hispanic origin 36,181 (6%). 18 and over 454,404 (76%), 62 and over 101,193 (17%). Median age: 33.

TV industry, sponsoring a sense of Congress resolution in 1989 and backing reregulation bills in the 101st and 102nd Congresses. In 1990, he introduced a bill aimed at creating jobs for federal prison inmates to try to quell disciplinary problems stemming from idleness.

At Home: Redistricting, anti-incumbent fever, 87 overdrafts at the House bank and a close shave in the primary contributed to Neal's lowest congressional margin ever in 1992. His appointment to Ways and Means should enable him to fortify his wobbly base before the 1994 election when he won't have Bill Clinton at the top of the ticket.

For Neal, part of the challenge always has been smoothing over tensions created when former Rep. Edward P. Boland all but handed him the seat. As the only Democrat told about Boland's pending retirement after 36 years representing the 2nd, Neal had plenty of time to cull signatures and dollars for his first congressional bid.

For more than a year, he had been touring the district's 38 towns and cities and had amassed a $200,000 campaign treasury before Boland stepped down in April. Neal won the Democratic nomination unopposed and crushed a weak GOP foe. Although he won, Neal is still deflecting resentment from fellow Democrats and some voters who believe that he inherited the seat rather than earned it.

Neal began his political career in 1972, as co-chairman of George McGovern's presidential campaign in western Massachusetts. After a five-year stint working as an aide to Springfield Mayor William C. Sullivan, Neal in 1977 was elected to the first of the three terms on the City Council.

In 1983, his preparations to challenge Springfield's Democratic mayor helped persuade the incumbent, Theodore E. Dimauro, to retire. Neal then won the office with a landslide margin that he matched in 1985 and 1987. With about 40 percent of the 2nd District's voters living in Springfield and its suburbs, these electoral successes gave Neal a solid base from which to run for the House. During his tenure as mayor, public criticism of Neal was rare, and usually mild; Springfield's newspaper is very supportive of Neal.

Heading into 1990, one local politician was grumbling that Neal had an unfair advantage in 1988 — former Mayor Dimauro. He challenged Neal in the Democratic primary, running an angry, bitter campaign that criticized Neal's tenure as mayor and battered the freshman as a Washington insider. But any progress Dimauro made evaporated at the end of August when he admitted spreading a false rumor about one of the region's largest banks. Dimauro said federal regulators had recommended liquidating the troubled Bank of New England, causing the institution's stock to plunge.

Threatened with lawsuits and criminal prosecution and unable to verify his claim, Dimauro retracted his statement, apologized, and blamed and fired his campaign manager. But his credibility was shot. Neal pulverized Dimauro in the primary, winning all but one community. In January 1991, federal regulators took over the Bank of New England.

In 1992 Neal was painted with the same brush as other Massachusetts Democratic incumbents. Relatively speaking though, he was not nearly as threatened as Rep. Nicholas Mavroules, who was under indictment on 17 criminal counts, or Rep. Joseph D. Early, who lost much of his former district in redistricting and was humiliated during the bank scandal. Both men lost.

Nevertheless, Neal's problems at the House bank prompted two local Democrats to challenge him in the primary, and he finished with a mediocre 48 percent. The Democratic leanings of the 2nd and the power of incumbency enabled Neal to hang on in 1992 and should continue to bolster his electoral position.

Committee

Ways & Means (18th of 24 Democrats)
Select Revenue Measures; Trade

Elections

1992 General		
Richard E. Neal (D)	131,215	(53%)
Anthony W. Ravosa Jr. (R)	76,795	(31%)
Thomas R. Sheehan (FTP)	38,963	(16%)
1992 Primary		
Richard E. Neal (D)	30,370	(48%)
Kateri Walsh (D)	21,709	(34%)
Charles Platten (D)	11,513	(18%)
1990 General		
Richard E. Neal (D)	134,152	(100%)

Previous Winning Percentage: 1988 (80%)

District Vote for President

1992
D 121,750 (46%)
R 76,244 (29%)
I 65,924 (25%)

Campaign Finance

	Receipts	Receipts from PACs		Expend- itures
1992				
Neal (D)	$384,741	$208,395	(54%)	$355,367
Ravosa (R)	$108,758	$7,550	(7%)	$102,179
1990				
Neal (D)	$462,672	$248,878	(54%)	$534,345

Key Votes

1993	
Require parental notification of minors' abortions	N
Require unpaid family and medical leave	Y
Approve national "motor voter" registration bill	Y
Approve budget increasing taxes and reducing deficit	Y
Approve economic stimulus plan	Y
1992	
Approve balanced-budget constitutional amendment	N
Close down space station program	N
Approve U.S. aid for former Soviet Union	N
Allow shifting funds from defense to domestic programs	Y
1991	
Extend unemployment benefits using deficit financing	Y
Approve waiting period for handgun purchases	Y
Authorize use of force in Persian Gulf	N

Voting Studies

	Presidential Support		Party Unity		Conservative Coalition	
Year	S	O	S	O	S	O
1992	14	85	90	5	15	83
1991	26	71	89	6	19	81
1990	19	72	85	6	19	72
1989	30	64	88	6	15	83

Interest Group Ratings

Year	ADA	AFL-CIO	CCUS	ACU
1992	90	92	13	0
1991	90	100	20	5
1990	83	92	29	18
1989	85	100	30	11

3 Peter I. Blute (R)

Of Shrewsbury — Elected 1992; 1st Term

Born: Jan. 28, 1956, Worcester, Mass.
Education: Boston College, B.A. 1978.
Occupation: Public relations director.
Family: Wife, Roberta Crudale.
Religion: Roman Catholic.
Political Career: Mass. House, 1987-93.
Capitol Office: 1029 Longworth Bldg. 20515; 225-6101.

The Path to Washington: In the 3rd District of Massachusetts, the voters seemed to be more interested in voting out their congressman than in voting in his replacement.

Rep. Joseph D. Early was known for shouting on the House floor, "They ran like rats!" at members of the ethics committee during their investigation of members who overdrew their House bank accounts. Early was one of those tainted. He had 140 overdrafts. And despite testimonials by other politicians and by members of the Massachusetts medical establishment, the combination of the scandal and a newly drawn district did Early in.

But now that Blute is in, he plans on doing everything it takes to stay there.

Upon arriving in Washington, he met with quick success, getting appointments to both committees he sought — Public Works and Transportation, and Science, Space and Technology. Blute believes that the two committees are an ideal match for his newly drawn district.

No Massachusetts representative has sat on Public Works in recent years. Within the district, the interchange between the Massachusetts Turnpike and Route 146 (which connects Worcester, Mass. and Providence, R.I.) needs upgrading. In Fall River, the sewers are old and routinely overflow during heavy rains. Blute hopes to use Public Works to help fund those projects.

In Worcester, there are numerous biotechnology companies. Blute views the Science Committee as a perch from which to aid those and other emerging high-tech businesses and to preserve and create jobs in the area.

Blute, however, is following on the heels of an expert at funneling projects to his state. Early's pet projects included the University of Massachusetts Medical School, the Tufts Veterinary School and a biotechnology park.

Before taking on Early, Blute beat out two primary opponents, David Lionett and Michelle Flaherty. For the most part, the race was between Blute and Lionett and centered on their differences on abortion — Lionett supports abortion rights; Blute opposes abortion, except in cases of rape, incest or danger to the woman's life.

Blute served since 1987 as a representative in the Massachusetts House. There he was known for attacking a variety of taxes and for his attempts to privatize Boston's convention center, thus taking it out of the grasp of the patronage system.

Blute said that one of the things he learned as a Republican in a liberal, Democratic state, is that "if Republicans don't work together, including those who call themselves conservatives and those who call themselves moderates and liberals, then we don't win."

Nevertheless, he says he is willing to work with the new Democratic administration, particularly on issues that they agree on: reducing the deficit, putting in place the line-item veto and tracking down "deadbeat dads" who fail to pay child support.

He also was one of only 40 Republicans to vote for mandatory unpaid family leave legislation that President Clinton signed into law in February 1993.

On a host of other issues, however, Blute could be termed a traditional conservative. He is against "political" gun control measures but says he would support reasonable background checks.

He also is opposed to tax increases. As evidence of this, he points to his sponsorship in the state House of legislation that repealed Massachusetts' tax on service. He also has pushed to privatize state services, which led to turning over management of Boston Common's garage to a private company and privatizing laundry services within the Mental Health Department.

During the campaign, the secretary of state's office accidentally left Blute's state representative title off the ballots. To reprint the ballots would have cost $75,000. Blute said he was upset that voters would not be reminded about his public service position, but he declined to insist that taxpayers foot the bill.

Health-care reform is a priority. He favors a system using tax credits and government vouchers to make health care more affordable. He wants to increase funding for child immunization and has suggested diverting the money used for franking privileges to pay for the shots.

Massachusetts 3

Central and Southeast — Worcester; coastal towns

Political wags dubbed the snakelike 3rd the "Ivy League" district because it stretches from the town of Princeton in central Massachusetts to Dartmouth on the southeastern coast. (The schools by those names are located elsewhere.)

The nickname is ironic because the 3rd is anchored by two of the state's grittier cities, Fall River and Worcester. In 1992 House voting, Republican Blute lost in those two cities, but he compensated for the deficit by taking solid margins in the suburban areas of the 3rd.

Fall River, at the southern end of the 3rd, is a fishing community that routinely has the highest unemployment of any city in Massachusetts. Split between the 3rd and 4th districts, Fall River long has been a bastion of blue-collar, white ethnic Democrats.

To the north of Fall River is another working-class city and the population hub of the 3rd: Worcester, with 170,000 people. It was once a thriving industrial center but did not benefit much from the "Massachusetts Miracle" of the 1980s that saw a boom in high-technology employment elsewhere in the state. Missing out on the "miracle," however, spared Worcester severe pain when the statewide economy nosedived in the late 1980s. As other communities were reeling, Worcester was plotting for the future.

Building on a foundation of respected hospitals in the region, Worcester is working to expand its role in the medical services field. New laboratories, research institutes and drug-manufacturing plants dot the city; the Biotechnology Research Park is growing. On the drawing board are plans for Medical City, a downtown complex that would include a hospital, medical labs, offices, restaurants and shops. Several banks, insurance companies and colleges are also located in Worcester.

Federal, state and city officials have committed money to a $27 million expansion of the Worcester Centrum, a popular arena that draws sporting events and big concerts. And by the mid- to late 1990s, the city may have commuter rail stations on a line to Boston.

Suburban communities to the north and south of Worcester already have as many votes as the urban areas of the district, and they are likely to have increasing influence on elections in the 3rd. A number of these suburbanites commute to jobs outside the district in Boston or Providence, R.I.

Democratic candidates traditionally have had an overall edge in the areas that make up the 3rd, but "unenrolled voters" are more numerous than Republicans or Democrats, and a number of them are conservative-leaning. Anti-abortion sentiment is widespread in the 3rd, and the National Rifle Association claims that the largest share of its Massachusetts members live here. Blute won in 1992 thanks to Democratic Rep. Joseph Early's ethics problems and to strong support from Republicans in communities such as Westboro, Attleboro and Shrewsbury, Blute's hometown.

1990 Population: 601,642. White 567,923 (94%), Black 11,024 (2%), Other 22,695 (4%). Hispanic origin 22,454 (4%). 18 and over 458,187 (76%), 62 and over 97,996 (16%). Median age: 34.

Committees

Public Works & Transportation (20th of 24 Republicans)
Economic Development; Surface Transportation

Science, Space & Technology (19th of 22 Republicans)
Science; Technology, Environment & Aviation

Campaign Finance

1992	Receipts	Receipts from PACs	Expend-itures
Blute (R)	$438,994	$43,900 (10%)	$435,911
Early (D)	$829,258	$220,725 (27%)	$924,384

Key Votes

1993

Require parental notification of minors' abortions	Y
Require unpaid family and medical leave	Y
Approve national "motor voter" registration bill	N
Approve budget increasing taxes and reducing deficit	N
Approve economic stimulus plan	N

Elections

1992 General		
Peter I. Blute (R)	131,473	(50%)
Joseph D. Early (D)	115,587	(44%)
Leonard J. Umina (IV)	9,691	(4%)
Michael T. Moore (NL)	4,130	(2%)
1992 Primary		
Peter I. Blute (R)	11,989	(49%)
David Lionett (R)	8,984	(37%)
Michelle Flaherty (R)	3,558	(14%)

District Vote for President

1992

D 122,900 (45%)
R 84,711 (31%)
I 63,596 (23%)

4 Barney Frank (D)

Of Newton — Elected 1980; 7th Term

Born: March 31, 1940, Bayonne, N.J.
Education: Harvard U., B.A. 1962, J.D. 1977.
Occupation: Lawyer.
Family: Lives with Herb Moses.
Religion: Jewish.
Political Career: Mass. House, 1973-81.
Capitol Office: 2404 Rayburn Bldg. 20515; 225-5931.

In Washington: Frank continues to evolve as a trusted emissary between the leadership and House liberals, and as one of the preeminent deal-makers in the chamber. With a quick mind and agile debating style, Frank has always grasped the substance and process of legislation as well as anyone. And his rapid-fire repartee is legend for both its wit and its sting.

If some of his closest allies carp about his attention span or his occasionally gratuitous ripostes, they pardon him because of his talent. Even his adversaries concede his skill at matching liberalism with hard-nosed pragmatism in order to move the legislative ball. In his 1992 book, "Speaking Frankly," Frank addressed the need for Democrats to reconcile their liberal agenda with mainstream values, writing: "Mainstream liberal Democrats have been intimidated by the left politically to some degree, but morally to an even greater extent."

Neither Frank's increasingly visible role as a key Democratic strategist on defense nor his longstanding pursuit of housing and social concerns were significantly impaired by his 1989 entanglement in a sex scandal and the resulting House reprimand a year later. Frank's comeback is a testament to his perseverance, intelligence and hard work, qualities admired across the political spectrum, even by those who disagree with his views and lifestyle.

As the first member of Congress to acknowledge that he is gay, Frank is quick to rise to the defense of homosexual rights. But the pragmatic Frank riled some members of the gay community when he offered a compromise to President Clinton's controversial call for an end to the military's ban on gays: Frank proposed allowing military personnel to lead openly gay lives, but only off-base and off-duty.

In June 1989, when a GOP memo called new Speaker Thomas S. Foley an "out of the liberal closet" Democrat, and compared him to Frank and no one else, Frank vowed that he would name prominent gay Republicans if the GOP didn't "cut the crap." He said later he believed "that if we did not threaten retaliation, they would continue unilateral shelling."

Frank prefers the direct approach in discussing his lifestyle, explaining simply that he "lives with Herb Moses," and eschewing common euphemisms such as "companion." "I answer every other question I'm asked," he said in disclosing his homosexuality in 1987. "I have nothing to hide, nothing to advertise."

In 1984, Frank embarked on a wholesale makeover of his image with a diet and exercise regime that helped him shed 70 pounds. Now, Frank appears to be wearying a bit of keeping up appearances.

But the passage of time has not cost him a step as a legislator; Frank continues to be found everywhere. He well understands that winning is a long-term proposition, requiring a constant effort of probing for cracks, finding leverage and slowly wearing away the stone. If his constant motion and shifting of gears annoys and confounds his colleagues, it is Frank's way of staying vital and avoiding burnout.

Though Frank has for several years been a liberal spark plug on defense issues, until his 1991 assignment to Budget he had no formal post from which to agitate for reducing defense spending in favor of domestic programs.

With the collapse of the Soviet Union at the end of 1991, he pressed anew for deep defense cuts, taking the lead in calling for a repudiation of the 1990 budget agreement, which barred transferring anticipated defense outlays to domestic uses. Budget hawks, fearful that such a change would drive up the federal deficit, prevailed in that fight.

But in 1992, Frank took advantage of his legislative loss the year before to win a key House floor vote to cut $3.5 billion from funds allocated to station U.S. forces in Europe, Japan and South Korea. He credited the help of Connecticut Republican Christopher Shays, a cosponsor of the amendment, and the fact that deficit-conscious members could vote to cut defense without a worry that the money would flow into other uses.

Les Aspin, then the House Armed Services chairman, opposed Frank's effort at imposing defense burden-sharing on U.S. allies, so most

Massachusetts 4

Boston suburbs — Newton; New Bedford; part of Fall River

The contorted shape of the 4th is proof positive that the state where the term gerrymander was coined remains true to its tradition of politically motivated mapmaking.

The district begins just over the Boston line in Brookline, juts out west to Sherborn, descends to Fall River and New Bedford on the southern coast and then runs back north to Pembroke. At least there is some political timeliness to the curving lines: They roughly trace the shape of a saxophone, Democrat Bill Clinton's instrument of choice.

Clinton and Rep. Frank both won the 4th easily in 1992, in part a reflection of the hard economic times plaguing many people here. Fall River, a fishing port where the median income is less than $15,000, struggles with a declining business base that has resulted in double-digit unemployment. Anderson Little shut down its Fall River clothing plant in 1992; soon thereafter, shoemaker Stride Rite moved out of New Bedford to Louisville, Ky.

New Bedford boasts the largest dollar-volume catch in the nation, thanks primarily to its lucrative scallop industry. But with the American waters being fished out of other seafood, local fishermen are traveling over the line to fish in Canadian waters, which is illegal. The city lost at least 1,300 jobs in the early 1990s, and no new companies were expressing a desire to move in.

The early textile mills drew large groups of Portuguese and Cape Verdeans to the coastal communities. Today, Portuguese own most of New Bedford's fleet.

To the northeast, in an area known as the South Shore, cranberry bogs in Carver and Lakeville compete with bogs in Wisconsin.

Even some of the wealthiest communities in the 4th suffered tough economic times in the late 1980s and early 1990s, as computer companies such as Wang Laboratories laid off thousands and the credit crunch crippled smaller entrepreneurial firms.

A sign of the times in 1992: lines down the block to get into the food pantry at the Unitarian Church in West Newton. Waiting their turn in this well-to-do suburb were teachers, computer programmers and other professionals trying to feed their families and hang on to their expensive homes.

Brookline, another comfortable suburb just over the line from Boston, became famous in 1988 when native Michael S. Dukakis ran for president. As governor, he commuted to work on the trolley line that connects Brookline to downtown. There are now more students and other transient types mixed in with Brookline's homeowners, but the town still boasts one of the best public school systems in the state.

Despite the dramatic socioeconomic differences between the district's southern cities and its Boston suburbs, the communities share a strong loyalty to the Democratic Party.

Republicans are numerous only in a handful of upper-crust towns such as Dover, Sherborn and Wellesley.

1990 Population: 601,642. White 562,771 (94%), Black 13,165 (2%), Other 25,706 (4%). Hispanic origin 15,011 (2%). 18 and over 461,073 (77%), 62 and over 97,324 (16%). Median age: 34.

of the amendment was dropped in conference with the Senate. But the episode was widely seen as an incremental victory for Frank.

Frank has long been active on the Judiciary Committee, and as chairman of Administrative Law Subcommittee, was a stalwart for the Legal Services Corporation. Often, Legal Services battles have been fought on appropriations bills because it has been impossible to enact an authorization bill since 1977. But in 1992, Frank managed to win House passage of an authorization bill, turning back most amendments aimed at restricting the agency's activities. Though the authorization bill never made it to the Senate floor, House passage had the effect of changing the tone of the debate for the House appropriations fight.

Frank achieved a significant long-term goal in the 101st Congress with the rewrite of the McCarthy-era McCarran-Walter Act, which established grounds for denying visas to foreigners, including some based on political ideology or expression. Late in 1987, he won a one-year change in the law, mandating that aliens be judged by their actions rather than their beliefs. In 1990, the change was made permanent. Congress also repealed language that barred people with AIDS from entering the country.

At the start of the 103rd Congress, Frank abruptly decided to abandon his Judiciary subcommittee chairmanship and increase his focus on the Banking Committee, where he claimed the chairmanship of the International Development Subcommittee. From that seat, he will have a close view of U.S. efforts to aid the emerging economies of Russia and other former Soviet Republics, as well as Third World concerns generally. Before the 1991 Soviet collapse, Frank was a vocal opponent of aid unless the Soviets made significant moves toward installing a free market and cutting their own defense spending.

Although he was a major supporter of the failed effort to overhaul banking laws in 1991 to permit banks to open branch offices across state lines and affiliate with securities firms, Frank has mostly been a marginal player on banking matters, choosing to confine his efforts to defending the special circumstances that benefit a class of New England savings banks, and to concentrate instead on housing issues.

Frank considers his advocacy for poor people one of his primary missions in Congress. During consideration of the 1989 savings and loan bailout, he forcefully pushed language to give low-income housing groups first pick at property seized from failed thrifts. In 1991, he took advantage of a sweeping bill to overhaul the federal deposit insurance system to expand that idea to cover real estate seized from failed banks.

Frank has also played instrumental roles in pushing a reform bill for the Department of Housing and Urban Development and two housing reauthorization bills through Congress since 1989, gaining credit for devising strategies both to win passage and to avoid presidential vetoes.

Frank has also served as the chief go-between in the leadership's dealings with Banking Chairman Henry B. Gonzalez of Texas, whose eccentricities can drive others to distraction. Frank is among Gonzalez's most prominent defenders in the House.

Frank's steady march to a prominent role was almost derailed in 1989. In August of that year, The Washington Times published a story alleging that Frank had hired a male prostitute, Steve Gobie, a felon on probation, as a sexual companion in 1985 and later made the man a household employee. At a Boston news conference the day the story broke, Frank confirmed many of its details, but he denied that he knew Gobie was running a prostitution business out of Frank's Capitol Hill apartment.

Frank, the cocky, brainy reformer, found himself before the nation humbly admitting that he had done something "incredibly stupid." Attributing his misconduct to the strain of concealing his homosexuality, he called for an ethics committee investigation of the matter and then went into a self-imposed exile. After 11 months of investigation, the ethics panel unanimously recommended Frank be reprimanded for improperly using his office, a decision upheld by the House in a July 1990 vote of 408-18.

Frank did not contest the finding that his actions had brought "discredit" on the House, and ethics committee Chairman Julian C. Dixon made a passionate appeal for the House to sustain the panel's decision, casting the matter as a vote of confidence in the panel itself. A GOP effort to censure Frank was turned back 141-287, and a move to expel him lost 38-390.

At Home: Massachusetts mapmakers twice have taken aim at Frank's district and two times he has easily survived. His sharp political mind — matched only by his sharp tongue — has made Frank one of the most formidable politicians in the state.

Frank left his pursuit of studying government to experience it firsthand in 1967. Studying for a Ph.D. in political science at the time, he left Harvard to help Democrat Kevin H. White win his first term as Boston's mayor. Frank became White's executive assistant, establishing ties to local leaders and learning the ways of Boston politics.

Relying on political contacts he developed at city hall and a large presidential-election turnout in his district, Frank won a ticket to the Statehouse in 1972. "I'm one of the few people in the country who can say he benefited from George McGovern's coattails," he later commented. Frank compiled an unabashedly liberal record in the Legislature, scrapping frequently with its entrenched Democratic leadership.

When Democratic Rep. Robert F. Drinan decided to leave Congress in 1980, bowing to the papal prohibition against priests holding public office, Frank went for his seat. He had to move into the district to run, but his record in the Legislature and high profile in national liberal Democratic circles won him endorsements from Drinan and many liberal organizations.

Frank won the primary by 5 percentage points. But instead of coasting through the general election, he nearly lost under a last-minute flurry of ads by his little-known GOP opponent attacking his liberal stands in the Legislature.

Two years later, Massachusetts had to lose one House seat in redistricting; hostile former colleagues in the Legislature paired him with GOP Rep. Margaret M. Heckler in a district that drew 70 percent of its vote from Heckler's old territory. "If you asked legislators to draw a map in which Barney Frank would never be a congressman again," he said, "this would be it."

But Frank overcame his initial hesitation. From the beginning of 1982 until Election Day, he pursued Heckler relentlessly, raising money and building steam while she largely rested on her record over eight terms in the House.

Heckler's 1981 votes for President Reagan's economic program gave Frank his issue in the 4th. Hammering at her support for Reagan, appealing to the district's elderly, blue-collar and poor residents, Frank gradually drew former Heckler backers to his side.

Taken aback by his criticism, Heckler appeared defensive during her rare public appearances. Her campaign consisted largely of attacks on Frank's stands in the Legislature on behalf of homosexuals and the creation of an "adult entertainment" zone in Boston.

But while Frank's 1980 Republican opponent had used that theme with some success, it made little difference in 1982. He won by nearly 40,000 votes, surprising even his own managers.

Heckler's departure for Reagan administration appointments as secretary of Health and Human Services and as ambassador to Ireland left the GOP without a serious threat to Frank. After winning easily in 1984, he ran without Republican opposition in 1986.

If there was any lingering doubt about Frank's popularity in the 4th, his 1988 reelection eliminated it. After he acknowledged publicly in mid-1987 that he is homosexual, Frank prepared for the possibility that his candor about his personal life would generate a political challenge. While his Republican opponent Debra Tucker — a little-known supporter of religious broadcaster Pat Robertson's presidential campaign — tried to make an issue of it, she failed. Frank won with 70 percent.

In 1990, the GOP nominee, Attleboro accountant and lawyer John R. Soto, had almost no money, no name recognition and entered the race without the backing of the state Republican party. Soto had no qualms about raising questions over Frank's actions in the Gobie scandal. He said Frank had "failed miserably" to exhibit good judgment and challenged him to undergo a test for AIDS and release the results, as he had. Frank won two-thirds of the vote.

Two years later, redistricting took half of the city of Fall River from Frank's 4th and added the Portuguese fishing community of New Bedford and all or portions of more than 20 smaller towns. The remap had no real impact on Frank: he finished with 68 percent of the vote.

Committees

Banking, Finance & Urban Affairs (6th of 30 Democrats)
International Development, Finance, Trade & Monetary Policy (chairman); Financial Institutions Supervision, Regulation & Deposit Insurance

Budget (9th of 26 Democrats)

Judiciary (9th of 21 Democrats)
Administrative Law & Governmental Relations; Civil & Constitutional Rights; Intellectual Property & Judicial Administration

Elections

1992 General		
Barney Frank (D)	182,633	(68%)
Edward J. McCormick III (R)	70,665	(25%)
Luke Lumina (IV)	13,670	(5%)
Dennis J. Ingalls (FFL)	2,797	(1%)
1990 General		
Barney Frank (D)	143,473	(66%)
John R. Soto (R)	75,454	(34%)

Previous Winning Percentages: **1988** (70%) **1986** (89%) **1984** (74%) **1982** (60%) **1980** (52%)

District Vote for President

1992
D 144,352 (51%)
R 75,080 (27%)
I 63,040 (22%)

Campaign Finance

	Receipts	Receipts from PACs		Expend-itures
1992				
Frank (D)	$498,997	$185,360	(37%)	$376,829
McCormick (R)	$51,540	0		$51,350
1990				
Frank (D)	$643,920	$220,517	(34%)	$718,160
Soto (R)	$32,078	$2,250	(7%)	$31,903

Key Votes

1993	
Require parental notification of minors' abortions	N
Require unpaid family and medical leave	Y
Approve national "motor voter" registration bill	Y
Approve budget increasing taxes and reducing deficit	Y
Approve economic stimulus plan	Y
1992	
Approve balanced-budget constitutional amendment	N
Close down space station program	Y
Approve U.S. aid for former Soviet Union	Y
Allow shifting funds from defense to domestic programs	Y
1991	
Extend unemployment benefits using deficit financing	Y
Approve waiting period for handgun purchases	Y
Authorize use of force in Persian Gulf	N

Voting Studies

	Presidential Support		Party Unity		Conservative Coalition	
Year	**S**	**O**	**S**	**O**	**S**	**O**
1992	16	80	93	5	4	96
1991	29	68	90	7	16	84
1990	19	76	90 †	5 †	11	85
1989	27	72	92	5	10	88
1988	17	79	87	8	0	97
1987	14	79	92	3	12	88
1986	18	81	91	8	12	88
1985	25	74	91	4	5	91
1984	30	66	87	7	8	88
1983	17	82	88	8	9	89
1982	34	62	81	10	15	78
1981	29	64	85	11	9	87

† Not eligible for all recorded votes.

Interest Group Ratings

Year	ADA	AFL-CIO	CCUS	ACU
1992	100	83	25	0
1991	100	83	20	5
1990	94	100	23	4
1989	95	92	30	7
1988	100	93	21	0
1987	100	94	7	0
1986	100	86	17	0
1985	100	94	23	10
1984	95	69	25	0
1983	95	100	20	0
1982	90	100	30	15
1981	100	87	11	7

5 Martin T. Meehan (D)

Of Lowell — Elected 1992; 1st Term

Born: Dec. 30, 1956, Lowell, Mass.
Education: U. of Massachusetts, Lowell, B.A. 1978; Suffolk U., M.A. 1981, J.D. 1983.
Occupation: Lawyer.
Family: Single.
Religion: Roman Catholic.
Political Career: No previous office.
Capitol Office: 1223 Longworth Bldg. 20515; 225-3411.

The Path to Washington: A brash newcomer, Meehan has quickly adapted to the ways of Capitol Hill. Cultivating a newborn friendship with Rep. Joe Moakley, dean of the Massachusetts delegation and chairman of the powerful Rules Committee, Meehan maneuvered for several coveted committee assignments.

His stroking of Moakley and intense lobbying of leadership was reminiscent of the assertive style that helped him oust Rep. Chester G. Atkins in the Democratic primary.

Although his efforts to secure a slot on the Appropriations Committee failed, he was ultimately awarded spots on the Armed Services Committee, as well as on the Small Business Committee.

From his position on Small Business, Meehan has promised to work for a capital gains tax cut and programs to encourage new companies specializing in emerging technologies. He describes himself as a pro-business Democrat in the mold of 1992 presidential aspirant Paul E. Tsongas, who once held this seat.

Meehan arrived in Congress armed with his own 1,000-page plan to erase the federal deficit. The proposal includes a mix of spending cuts, new taxes and a 50 percent reduction in defense spending.

Meehan also will give an amount equal to his cost of living increase — $2,500 — to charity in protest of the perk. He supported a ban on lobbyists' gifts and voted to kill four House select committees in early 1993.

Meehan has also attempted to deal with problems in his district. The city of Lawrence suffered a 250 percent increase in fires from 1991 to 1992, more than 25 percent of which were arson cases. Meehan has since co-sponsored the Arson Prevention Act of 1993, which would provide up to $10.5 million over the next two years for the training of arson investigators.

A career bureaucrat, Meehan has been positioning himself for a congressional run since he graduated from college. Still, he was not supposed to win.

In 1992 Massachusetts carved up its congressional districts after it lost one seat to reapportionment. Republican Gov. William F. Weld negotiated a 5th District he was betting would elect Republican Paul W. Cronin in a November matchup with incumbent Atkins. But when Meehan trounced Atkins in the September Democratic primary, all bets were off.

If incumbents were feeling the heat from disgruntled voters in 1992, Atkins inadvertently was stoking the fire. The working-class voters who dominate Lawrence and Lowell, the two largest cities in the district, never had been totally comfortable with the Swiss-born Atkins. He further alienated those constituents when he hinted he would like to drop the cities from the district. Atkins looked even more vulnerable when his base, Framingham, was sliced from the 5th.

During the campaign, Meehan branded Atkins as an unsavory political insider. When he assailed Atkins for supporting a House pay raise and for having 127 overdrafts at the House bank, Meehan struck a responsive chord with voters.

Meehan came on strong to overwhelm Atkins in the primary, taking nearly two-thirds of the vote. After dispatching Atkins, Meehan was favored over his GOP opponent, businessman and former one-term Rep. Cronin.

Going into the general election, Meehan, a former prosecutor, portrayed himself as a Democratic moderate who was tough on crime. On the other hand, Cronin argued that as the owner of a fiberglass company he was better suited to represent the business-oriented 5th.

The two men lambasted each other's professional qualifications in criticisms often peppered with personal attacks. Cronin accused Meehan of being nothing more than a political gofer, paid to do no more than hold the coats of the politicians he served. Meehan countered that Cronin was "a career politician" who had made eight previous runs for office and lost four of them.

Boosted in part by a large turnout in his hometown of Lowell, Meehan won by more than 37,000 votes.

Massachusetts 5

North Central — Lawrence; Lowell

Although located on the northeastern edges of the 5th, the gritty cities of Lawrence and Lowell dominate this otherwise suburban district.

An intense rivalry between the two mill cities dates back to the 1900s: Lowell, the model "company town," was watched over by paternalistic Yankee Protestants, while immigrant workers in Lawrence labored in unsafe factories and lived in substandard quarters. Ever since, it seems Lawrence has trailed the city to the south.

With the help of some federal dollars and arm-twisting in Congress, downtown Lowell was designated a national historic park in 1978. Earning that status was a boost to tourism, and it helped draw business.

But Lowell and its 103,400 people have not been able to escape the recessionary times of the 1990s. Wang Laboratories, the lifeblood of the city's resurgence and a onetime employer of 10,000, filed for bankruptcy protection and announced massive layoffs.

There are similar troubles elsewhere in the district. Digital Equipment moved a plant from Maynard to New Hampshire. The Fort Devens Army Base in Ayer is to close by 1995, taking with it about 3,800 military and civilian jobs. By one estimate, the 5th lost 30,000 jobs from 1988 through 1991.

Lawrence, a city of 70,000, has problems on a scale normally reserved for only the largest of metropolitan areas: arson, drug trafficking, car thefts, teen pregnancy and double-digit unemployment. Police set up barricades in one neighborhood and checked the license of every person entering to try to curtail the drug trade. Minorities are about 45 percent of the city's population: The largest single group, Hispanics, have begun to flex political muscle, electing the first Hispanic to the school board.

Despite the tough times, some of the district's smaller non-traditional businesses are finding profitable niches. Marlboro, situated on Interstate 495, is home to snack maker Smartfoods and Stratus Computer.

Businesses in the northern tier of the 5th are competing more successfully with no-sales-tax New Hampshire, thanks to a relaxation of state blue laws that allows merchants within 10 miles of the border to open on Sundays.

Sprinkled through the Merrimack Valley are some of the country's most well-known preparatory schools, including Phillips Academy in Andover and the Groton School and Lawrence Academy, both in Groton. The 5th is also home to Walden Pond in Concord, where authors Henry David Thoreau and Ralph Waldo Emerson derived inspiration in the 19th century.

Lawrence and Lowell continue to give Democrats a strong anchor in the 5th. In 1992, they were the key to the district going for Bill Clinton and Meehan. But independents, or "unenrolled" voters, outnumber those registered in either major party, which makes the district competitive. Republican William F. Weld won here in his successful 1990 gubernatorial bid against Democrat John Silber.

1990 Population: 601,643. White 537,800 (89%), Black 13,762 (2%), Other 50,081 (8%). Hispanic origin 49,014 (8%). 18 and over 446,756 (74%), 62 and over 76,460 (13%). Median age: 32.

Committees

Armed Services (27th of 34 Democrats)
Military Forces & Personnel; Readiness; Research & Technology

Small Business (14th of 27 Democrats)
Regulation, Business Opportunities & Technology; SBA Legislation & the General Economy

Campaign Finance

1992	Receipts	Receipts from PACs		Expend-itures
Meehan (D)	$832,266	0		$831,544
Cronin (R)	$565,565	$240	(0%)	$551,896

Key Votes

1993

Require parental notification of minors' abortions	N
Require unpaid family and medical leave	Y
Approve national "motor voter" registration bill	Y
Approve budget increasing taxes and reducing deficit	Y
Approve economic stimulus plan	Y

Elections

1992 General

Martin T. Meehan (D)	133,844	(52%)
Paul W. Cronin (R)	96,206	(37%)
Mary J. Farinelli (I)	19,077	(7%)
David E. Coleman (I)	7,214	(3%)

1992 Primary

Martin T. Meehan (D)	50,300	(65%)
Chester G. Atkins (D)	26,855	(35%)

District Vote for President

	1992	
D	112,959	(42%)
R	85,260	(32%)
I	70,391	(26%)

6 Peter G. Torkildsen (R)

Of Danvers — Elected 1992; 1st Term

Born: Jan. 28, 1958, Milwaukee, Wis.
Education: U. of Massachusetts, B.A. 1980; Harvard U., M.P.A. 1990.
Occupation: Public official.
Family: Single.
Religion: Roman Catholic.
Political Career: Mass. House, 1985-91; Mass. commissioner of labor and industries, 1991-92.
Capitol Office: 120 Cannon Bldg. 20515; 225-8020.

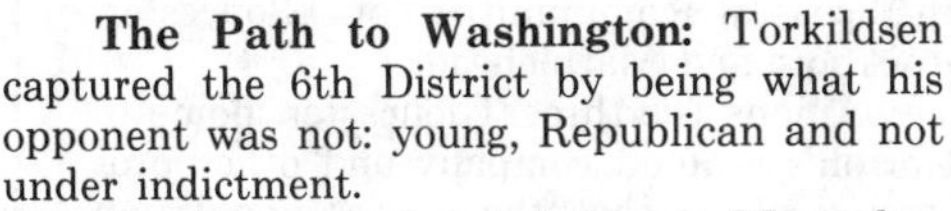

The Path to Washington: Torkildsen captured the 6th District by being what his opponent was not: young, Republican and not under indictment.

The Harvard-educated former Massachusetts labor commissioner portrayed himself as a youthful reformer, dedicated to creating jobs for his constituents. His squeaky-clean image stood in contrast to that of Democratic Rep. Nicholas Mavroules, who was indicted in August 1992 on bribery, extortion and tax evasion charges.

Torkildsen is no stranger to the world of government. By the age of 34, he already had served six years as a state representative and two years as the Massachusetts commissioner of labor and industries.

Torkildsen displayed his political savvy in his campaign for a spot on the Armed Services Committee, the panel on which Mavroules had served to great benefit for the district.

While some freshmen wasted time trying to land on the powerful Ways and Means or Appropriations committees, Torkildsen shot just a bit lower. He secured his top two choices, Armed Services and Small Business.

While supporting some cuts in defense spending, Torkildsen is committed to fighting the deeper five-year reductions of 40 percent to 50 percent discussed by some. The 6th is home to two defense facilities and Hanscom Air Force Base and a host of defense contractors.

Like his former boss, Republican Gov. William F. Weld, Torkildsen has a fiscally conservative, pro-business legislative agenda while supporting abortion rights. Torkildsen expects to work with the Clinton administration on restoring the investment tax credit and passing a targeted capital gains tax cut.

Two of Torkildsen's top priorities are reforming the nation's health-care system and passing an economic stimulus package.

Fulfilling a campaign promise, Torkildsen launched an unsuccessful effort early in the 103rd to persuade the GOP caucus to adopt a rule to force ranking members of committees and subcommittees to step down if indicted. His efforts put him at odds with the powerful ranking Republican on the Appropriations Committee, Joseph M. McDade of Pennsylvania, who had been indicted in May 1992 on criminal charges.

Known as affable and polite, Torkildsen ran few negative ads during the campaign. He relied on the media to spotlight his opponent's legal difficulties and his own record to carry him to victory in November. He highlighted his role in repealing an unpopular state surtax and cleaning up hazardous waste around the state. He did slam Mavroules for accepting contributions from defense-oriented political action committees — money he refused during the campaign.

Torkildsen first made a name for himself by bouncing an entrenched incumbent from office. In 1984, he captured his first elected office by upsetting then-Democratic state House Majority Leader John E. Murphy Jr.

Ultimately, though, it was Mavroules' legal problems that were key to Torkildsen's victory.

In 1992 Mavroules faced an uphill fight for re-election. In the September primary he squeaked by little-known state Rep. Barbara Hildt by fewer than 600 votes. Backed into a political corner, Mavroules launched an aggressive general campaign in the blue-collar 6th.

Despite the 17-count federal indictment, Mavroules tried to rely on a strong base of political support built up over 40 years in local politics. He sought an eighth term in a Democratic district that had changed little since he was elected mayor of Peabody in the late 1960s.

As his supporters rallied around him hoisting signs of the tireless "Energizer Bunny," Mavroules criticized Torkildsen for reversing his position as a state legislator on such issues as abortion rights and education funding. After opposing abortion for several years, Torkildsen came out in favor of abortion rights in April 1992, the same month he launched his campaign.

But Mavroules ran out of steam in the campaign's closing weeks, and it became obvious he was in serious trouble. He reported having only $3,000 on hand on Oct. 14, and shortly thereafter, he fired his campaign manager.

In the end, by fewer than 29,000 votes, the district preferred the clean-cut Republican.

Massachusetts 6

North Shore — Lynn; Peabody

The North Shore area is more open to Republican entreaties than most communities in Massachusetts, a state with a strong affinity for Democrats. Republican William F. Weld won his 1990 campaign for governor, and in 1992 Torkildsen followed suit, capturing the House seat with the aid of then-Rep. Nicholas Mavroules' pending criminal indictment.

Registered Democrats outnumber Republicans in much of Massachusetts, but the 6th is dominated by independent voters. GOP candidates can succeed by targeting them, holding the votes of wealthy Republican suburbanites who support abortion rights, and picking off some conservative lunch-bucket Democrats who are angry about high taxes and expensive social programs.

The 35½ cities and towns that constitute the 6th are a melange of scruffy fishing ports, aristocratic suburbs, unspoiled coastland and well-worn factory towns.

Lynn, with 81,000 people, is by far the largest community in the 6th. Lynn's major employer is the General Electric Co., which makes aircraft engines for the F/A-18 Hornet, helicopters and some commercial planes. Employment at the GE plant has dropped from 13,000 workers in 1981 to 6,500 as of early 1993. Torkildsen will be under pressure to duplicate the success Mavroules had at funneling federal contracts into the district; he was a senior member of the Armed Services Committee. In 1992, Mavroules helped the GE plant secure a $754 million contract for work on engines for the next generation of F-18 fighter planes.

Despite the relative proximity of Lynn to Boston, the city's officials often feel isolated from the state capital. In early 1993 state leaders began debating the prospects of extending one of Boston's subway lines to Lynn. If approved, the project would create jobs and provide a smoother trip from Lynn to Boston's airport, financial district and tourist attractions.

The coast north of Lynn includes some of the most beautiful landscapes in the state. Each town has its own personality and attitudes. Tourists and fishermen share the coastal communities of Gloucester, Rockport and Marblehead.

Among the three, Gloucester, home to Gorton's seafood company and other processing plants, has the largest population and fishing catch and the most visitors.

Most of the beaches on the North Shore are pristine, protected and open to the public. Manchester-by-the-Sea is something of an exception; a tony town of 5,000 that voted to change its name from just plain Manchester, it discourages outsiders from using its beaches by enforcing a residents-only parking rule. The area has a number of antique shops that draw visitors.

In 1992, Salem marked the tricentennial of the city's 1692 witch trials with a series of re-enactments, lectures and museum exhibits.

Redistricting in 1992 added Bedford, home of the Hanscom Air Force Base, to the 6th.

1990 Population: 601,643. White 573,352 (95%), Black 11,405 (2%), Other 16,886 (3%). Hispanic origin 17,373 (3%). 18 and over 480,390 (80%), 62 and over 99,624 (17%). Median age: 35.

Committees

Armed Services (17th of 22 Republicans)
Military Installations & Facilities; Research & Technology

Small Business (17th of 18 Republicans)
Regulation, Business Opportunities & Technology

Campaign Finance

1992	Receipts	Receipts from PACs		Expend-itures
Torkildsen (R)	$464,007	0		$461,934
Mavroules (D)	$612,064	$240,125	(39%)	$671,110

Key Votes

1993

Require parental notification of minors' abortions	N
Require unpaid family and medical leave	N
Approve national "motor voter" registration bill	N
Approve budget increasing taxes and reducing deficit	N
Approve economic stimulus plan	N

Elections

1992 General		
Peter G. Torkildsen (R)	159,165	(55%)
Nicholas Mavroules (D)	130,248	(45%)
1992 Primary		
Peter Torkildsen (R)	16,556	(56%)
Alexander T. Tennant (R)	13,043	(44%)

District Vote for President

1992

D 134,424 (44%)
R 96,857 (32%)
I 75,893 (25%)

7 Edward J. Markey (D)

Of Malden — Elected 1976; 9th Full Term

Born: July 11, 1946, Malden, Mass.
Education: Boston College, B.A. 1968, J.D. 1972.
Military Service: Army Reserve, 1968-73.
Occupation: Lawyer.
Family: Wife, Susan Blumenthal.
Religion: Roman Catholic.
Political Career: Mass. House, 1973-77.
Capitol Office: 2133 Rayburn Bldg. 20515; 225-2836.

In Washington: If proof was still needed in 1992 that Markey had graduated into the ranks of serious legislators, he provided it with the enactment of a sweeping measure to regulate the services and prices of cable television companies. It was the only bill in four years to be enacted into law over President Bush's otherwise impregnable veto.

The measure combined Markey's continuing focus on consumers with a growing interest in cutting-edge information services. Its enactment was seen as a tribute to Markey's evolution as a deal-maker: As principal House sponsor, he adjusted his strategy as needed to steer the measure past jurisdictional shoals to reach the floor with key provisions intact.

Markey showed his ability to maneuver by working with Energy and Commerce Chairman John D. Dingell of Michigan on the jurisdictional fight by excluding from the House bill language giving local broadcasters the right to charge cable companies for retransmitting their signals. The provision was restored in conference with the Senate. But Markey also opposed Dingell and beat him on the floor over another controversial provision, guaranteeing home satellite and other "wireless" cable systems access to programs now produced by and for the cable industry.

During his early years in Congress, Markey was the toast of liberal activists, a fierce opponent of the nuclear-power industry and a champion of consumer rights. In the face of pecuniary scandals in the 1980s and technological advances to come in the 1990s, he has steeped himself in telecommunications and financial issues, where he has found it necessary to be more pragmatic.

Markey's activist approach attracts critics who believe he has never seen a problem that he couldn't regulate. But consumer advocates still find a lot to like about Markey. The cable bill is one reason; his 1990 bill to limit advertising on children's television shows and encourage quality programming by making stations' performance a factor in their license renewal is another.

When consumer activist Ralph Nader was offering himself as a "none of the above" candidate for president in early 1992, he described Markey as one of the two best members of the House. At the same time, Markey's increasing influence and his willingness to negotiate have given his consumerist friends some ambivalent moments. It was also Nader who told The Boston Globe that Markey was "getting on a first-name basis with too many people in the industries he oversees, having too many dinners with them."

His great success as a campaign fundraiser — despite essentially free rides to re-election since 1984 — reveals a similar paradox: Markey eschews political action committee contributions in an effort to avoid the taint of special interest money, but most of his huge campaign fund has come from people affiliated with businesses that his subcommittee oversees. In 1990, his biggest cadre of contributors were Washington-based lawyer-lobbyists. For a February 1993 fundraiser, held at a restaurant in Washington's upscale Georgetown neighborhood, Markey sent invitations at $1,000 a head to lobbyists around town, reminding them that he is chairman of a "powerful" subcommittee "at the center of telecommunications policy."

About that, he is right. Now in his fourth term as chairman of the Energy and Commerce Subcommittee on Telecommunications and Finance, Markey oversees those industries at a time of rapidly evolving changes on Wall Street and in the banking, telephone, broadcast and entertainment industries. Away from the subcommittee, he remains personally committed to the two issues for which he previously was best known, arms control and nuclear power.

A witty sort, Markey is sometimes almost too quick with an apt one-liner or sound bite. But he is also conversant in the mind-numbing details of today's most complex issues, which come before his subcommittee. His tendency to actually read about subjects in depth leads him to move methodically. And it has given him a vision of the future of electronic information-sharing that does not hew to the desires or needs of any one industry.

Trying to develop that vision into reality will occupy him for much of the 103rd Congress,

Massachusetts 7

Northwest suburbs — Woburn; Framingham; Revere

Although the 7th lies outside Boston, the city is the occupational and cultural focal point for most residents of this district. It is a collection of medium-sized cities and towns that almost completely rings Boston, giving the 7th a strong commuter orientation.

The well-educated, liberal-minded suburbanites are reliably Democratic. In his competitive 1990 re-election bid, Democratic Sen. John Kerry took the 7th with 62 percent of the vote. Bill Clinton ran 21 points ahead of George Bush here in 1992 (although Ross Perot got a solid 21 percent), and Rep. Markey carried every community except Weston. Malden, Framingham and Woburn provide a solid start for building large Democratic margins.

Redistricting in 1992 added Framingham and Natick to the western end of the district, boosting the presence of high technology in the 7th. Route 128, often compared with California's Silicon Valley, has a variety of large and small computer, telecommunications and engineering companies. The 7th's largest employer is Lexington-based Raytheon, maker of the Patriot missile system. The company has weathered defense cuts in part by diversifying into commercial products such as refrigerators and stoves.

Waltham, a working-class city once known for its watch factories, has experienced a technological surge in recent years. Smaller new companies — such as Kendall Square Research, a supercomputer manufacturer, and IDG, a computer magazine publishing house — are off Route 128 in Waltham. The Charles River Museum of Industry pays tribute to the city's grand industrial past.

Nearby universities, such as Harvard and the Massachusetts Institute of Technology, have helped fuel the local electronics industry. Boston Technologies in Wakefield began in 1986 with just five people. By 1993 the "voice mail" firm employed 200 and had signed a contract to provide voice mail services to a Japanese phone company.

The cities of Medford and Malden are often seen as one metropolitan area, with some shared city services and a rivalry in football. Although many of the residents commute to blue-collar jobs in Boston, the New England processing center for Fleet Bank is a major employer in Malden. Houses in Medford, Malden, Everett and Melrose have been passed on through several generations of Irish and Italian families.

Irish immigrants originally settled in Revere, too, but Southeast Asian immigrants began moving into that coastal city in the 1980s. Revere offers the growing Asian community affordable housing and easy access to service-sector jobs in downtown Boston.

Weston, Lincoln and Lexington are the most affluent communities in the 7th, home to professional athletes and media celebrities such as Boston Globe columnist Mike Barnacle. Lexington, site of the first Revolutionary War conflict, is popular with out-of-state visitors and Massachusetts students. Re-enactments of the Battle of Lexington are held every April.

1990 Population: 601,642. White 564,252 (94%), Black 13,639 (2%), Other 17,816 (3%). Hispanic origin 17,980 (3%). 18 and over 498,567 (83%), 62 and over 109,360 (18%). Median age: 35.

and perhaps afterward. And it will begin with his effort to ease the entry of the seven Baby Bell regional telephone companies into new service markets while protecting consumers and competitiveness from potential Bell abuses. The Baby Bells want to be allowed into long-distance manufacturing and video delivery to give them financial incentives to upgrade the nation's information networks.

Before 1985, Markey's critics considered him less a legislator than a mouthpiece for the outside groups dedicated to his liberal causes; more conservative House colleagues in particular complained that he preferred the moral high ground to the lowly work of political compromise. But returning to the House that year after an abortive Senate campaign, Markey immediately impressed his skeptics with his willingness and ability to make deals.

First as chairman of the Energy Conservation and Power Subcommittee in the 99th Congress, and then as the Telecommunications and Finance head since the 100th, he has proved adept at building consensus. With his affability, evenhanded attention to substance and, most important, his habit of consulting with members individually on pending matters, Markey has coopted Democrats and Republicans alike.

The best evidence of his having learned the art of compromise is the frequency with which his bills are brought to the House floor under expedited procedures that prohibit amendments and require two-thirds majorities for passage; most of the time, the procedure is reserved for the least controversial bills. Markey also has learned to pick off his opponents with rifle shots. In the 100th and 101st Congresses, he pushed to enactment a raft of bills overhauling securities regulation in the wake of the stock market crashes of 1987 and 1989, the Ivan Boesky insider trading scandal and general concerns about the integrity of the markets. But rather than combine them into an omnibus measure that might face an assembly of opposition that could kill it, Markey moved them carefully, one by one, limiting the obstacles and winning enactment of each one.

When Markey has veered from this strategy, the results have not been good. In the 102nd Congress, following revelations of a bid-rigging scandal in the federal government securities market by the prestigious Wall Street firm of Salomon Brothers, Markey decided that it was time to overhaul completely the regulation of trading in government bonds. Markey's vehicle of choice was the reauthorization of the 1986 Government Securities Act, which had itself imposed new statutory controls on the market.

The Senate Banking Committee reacted delicately to the scandal, and crafted a relatively narrow measure, essentially imposing specific penalties for the activities uncovered in the Salomon case. Markey, who was working with Dingell on the issue, went farther afield, and sought to impose a new layer of regulation on banks, who were the largest dealers in government bonds, subjecting them for the first time to regulation by the Securities and Exchange Commission.

The House Banking Committee hollered, viewing Markey's action as poaching of the worst kind. Banking Chairman Henry B. Gonzalez of Texas complained, but House leaders turned a deaf ear. When Markey and Dingell brought up their version of the bill under the procedure that barred amendments, Gonzalez went to the floor and succeeded in killing the bill.

In the 99th Congress, as both the Energy Conservation and Power chairman and a member of the Interior Committee's Energy Subcommittee, Markey led the effort to set national energy efficiency standards for major appliances. Though Ronald Reagan vetoed it on free-market grounds, the bill was revived early in the 100th Congress with a minor change, and the president signed it into law.

Markey also successfully resolved a long-running battle between private and public utilities over the relicensing of hydropower plants. And the Energy Conservation and Power chair gave him an official platform for his crusade against the nuclear power industry.

The climate for Markey's criticisms had improved, particularly in the wake of the Chernobyl nuclear accident in the Soviet Union, and Markey regularly attacked the Nuclear Regulatory Commission, the Energy Department and private companies. He blocked legislation to streamline nuclear plant licensing and reduce public participation in licensing decisions, pointing to Chernobyl as "a glaring example of the dangers of nuclear power if public pressure for safety is stifled."

His most visible anti-nuclear effort in the 100th Congress was a locally oriented one. He repeatedly tried and failed to pass an amendment that would bar operating licenses for the Seabrook power plant in New Hampshire and the Shoreham plant on Long Island, which were opposed, respectively, by officials in Massachusetts and New York.

In the arms control realm, Markey and a small cadre of liberal arms controllers exploited widespread unease with Reagan's arms policies. They succeeded for three years running, 1986 through 1988, in winning House approval of a ban on nuclear testing, contingent on Soviet restraint. But in all three years, the test ban was dropped under pressure from the Senate, reflecting members' desire to close ranks behind Reagan once he finally had begun arms control talks with Soviet leader Mikhail S. Gorbachev.

In 1988, however, conferees accepted an alternative Markey amendment requiring the Energy Department to devise a non-explosive method of testing the nuclear arsenal's reliability. He had lost in the House, 201-220, but at his prodding Armed Services Committee Chairman Les Aspin of Wisconsin pressed for Markey's provision in the conference.

At Home: The 1992 redistricting took aim at almost every Massachusetts incumbent. The fact that Markey's 7th District was barely knicked by the district-carvers is evidence he has finally solidified his electoral position after a close call in 1984.

When Democratic Sen. Paul E. Tsongas quit the Senate, Markey was the first Democrat to announce for his seat. His prominence on the nuclear weapons freeze and on nuclear energy issues had earned him a following of anti-nuclear enthusiasts, and they became the core of his campaign.

But Markey's candidacy did not keep several other prominent contenders from entering the Senate contest, including then-Rep. James M. Shannon and John Kerry, who was lieutenant governor. As the campaign heated up, it became clear that Markey was at best an even bet against his chief competitors; he dropped out of the Senate race and filed again for reelection to his House seat.

Markey said he wanted to return to the House to continue working on nuclear arms issues. He told reporters it no longer made sense to him to "go out and scrap for another nine months in the campaign, when I had a chance to advance the freeze in the House."

Markey had to struggle just to win renomination in his district against former state Sen. Samuel Rotondi, a combative campaigner who chose to stay in the House contest, hoping the reaction to Markey's indecision would help his campaign.

"First he was going to be a senator," a Rotondi ad noted, "now he wants to be a congressman some more. It kind of makes you dizzy, doesn't it, seeing Ed Markey twirling around like that?" But Markey struck back with charges that Rotondi had received campaign contributions from executives of utility companies and nuclear industries. Rotondi, he said at a debate, "has so much radioactive money in his Federal Election Commission report it glows in the dark."

Markey ended up winning the primary with 54 percent, and a routine victory in the general election. He has not had a primary opponent since and Republicans did not even put up a sacrificial lamb for the 7th until 1992.

Then, a doctor rented a house in the district to challenge Markey. Polar opposites, Markey and Stephen A. Sohn engaged in a bitter contest. Sohn's criticism of Markey's 92 overdrafts at the House bank put a dent in Markey's armor, but he still won with 62 percent of the vote.

Before 1984, Markey's only difficult congressional campaign was his first, in 1976. When the critically ill Torbert H. MacDonald announced his retirement that year after serving 21 years in the House, virtually every prominent Democrat thought about trying to replace him.

It was clear that a primary with a dozen aspirants would be decided mostly by simple name identification. Markey had received a fair amount of attention for his battles in the legislature with the Democratic leadership, which had once closed his office and banished him to a desk in the hall. "They can tell me where to sit," Markey boasted, "but they can't tell me where to stand."

Endorsed by then-Rep. Michael J. Harrington, Markey won his own hometown, Malden, and six of the remaining 11. That gave him 21 percent of the vote, enough for a comfortable win.

Committees

Energy & Commerce (4th of 27 Democrats)
Telecommunications & Finance (chairman); Energy & Power; Transportation & Hazardous Materials

Natural Resources (3rd of 28 Democrats)
Energy & Mineral Resources; National Parks, Forests & Public Lands

Elections

1992 General		
Edward J. Markey (D)	174,837	(62%)
Stephen A. Sohn (R)	78,262	(28%)
Robert B. Antonelli (I)	28,421	(10%)
1990 General		
Edward J. Markey (D)	155,380	(100%)

Previous Winning Percentages: **1988** (100%) **1986** (100%) **1984** (71%) **1982** (78%) **1980** (100%) **1978** (85%) **1976** (77%)

District Vote for President

1992
D 150,102 (50%)
R 87,432 (29%)
I 61,965 (21%)

Campaign Finance

	Receipts	Receipts from PACs	Expend-itures
1992			
Markey (D)	$444,628	0	$892,994
Sohn (R)	$289,756	0	$290,304
1990			
Markey (D)	$336,209	0	$207,273

Key Votes

1993	
Require parental notification of minors' abortions	N
Require unpaid family and medical leave	Y
Approve national "motor voter" registration bill	Y
Approve budget increasing taxes and reducing deficit	Y
Approve economic stimulus plan	Y
1992	
Approve balanced-budget constitutional amendment	N
Close down space station program	Y
Approve U.S. aid for former Soviet Union	Y
Allow shifting funds from defense to domestic programs	Y
1991	
Extend unemployment benefits using deficit financing	Y
Approve waiting period for handgun purchases	Y
Authorize use of force in Persian Gulf	N

Voting Studies

	Presidential Support		Party Unity		Conservative Coalition	
Year	**S**	**O**	**S**	**O**	**S**	**O**
1992	11	82	91	3	8	88
1991	23	76	94	3	11	89
1990	15	82	92	2	7	89
1989	28	71	94	1	2	93
1988	17	78	93	3	3	97
1987	13	86	94	1	5	95
1986	11	80	86	5	8	84
1985	23	76	90	4	2	98
1984	17	58	76	3	0	85
1983	21	77	91	6	8	90
1982	32	62	90	3	8	92
1981	34	66	91	8	8	88

Interest Group Ratings

Year	ADA	AFL-CIO	CCUS	ACU
1992	100	83	25	0
1991	100	100	20	0
1990	94	100	21	4
1989	100	100	40	0
1988	90	100	23	0
1987	96	100	0	0
1986	95	85	13	0
1985	100	100	29	10
1984	90	85	23	5
1983	90	94	20	0
1982	100	100	9	0
1981	90	80	5	0

8 Joseph P. Kennedy II (D)

Of Boston — Elected 1986; 4th Term

Born: Sept. 24, 1952, Boston, Mass.
Education: U. of Massachusetts, B.A. 1976.
Occupation: Energy company executive.
Family: Divorced; two children.
Religion: Roman Catholic.
Political Career: No previous office.
Capitol Office: 1210 Longworth Bldg. 20515; 225-5111.

In Washington: Since his arrival on Capitol Hill, Kennedy has labored under the assumption that the House is merely a stopover on his way to a bid for statewide office.

But in turning 40, the eldest son of the late Robert F. Kennedy underwent a passage of sorts, making choices that would indicate a desire to settle into the House for at least the next four years, if not longer, and to engage seriously in the business of legislating in behalf of the disadvantaged.

Kennedy passed up an opportunity to move to the high-profile Ways and Means Committee before the 103rd Congress. At the time, he was encouraging speculation that he would run for governor in 1994 against Republican William F. Weld; in opinion polls, Kennedy was the only Democrat to evidence a chance of unseating Weld. His decision to stay on the Banking Committee, where he could chair the Consumer Credit and Insurance Subcommittee, was viewed as a way for Kennedy to get more headlines — and more favorable ones — during his gubernatorial race.

But he stunned observers in February 1993, announcing that he would not run for governor. In saying that he did not want to limit further the time he had to spend with his twin sons, he added that he felt comfortable in the House: "I feel I can make a difference," he said. "There's a tremendous opportunity for me."

Kennedy made his reputation as grasping and headstrong at the start of his first term, when he disregarded the advice of his elders to be patient and asked House leaders for a seat on the Energy and Commerce Committee. He lost.

Two years later, he chose to challenge a more senior Massachusetts colleague — Chester G. Atkins — for a vacant seat on the Appropriations Committee. Kennedy called on his uncle, Sen. Edward M. Kennedy, to lobby on his behalf. Kennedy was expected to win by a single vote, but he lost 8-9; a round of finger-pointing for the unknown defector added a final note of bitterness to the whole affair.

But Kennedy has demonstrated that he can channel his limitless energy into the work of the Banking Committee, where he shares with Chairman Henry B. Gonzalez of Texas an instinct for helping the poor and minorities. When Gonzalez was abruptly challenged for the chairmanship in late 1990, Kennedy drew on his inbred political skills to help organize a war room and line up key commitments to preserve Gonzalez's job.

Kennedy's accomplishments include amending a 1987 housing bill to include incentives for units affordable to low-income families. Earlier, he joined about a dozen members for a cold night on a steam grate to draw attention to the homeless. (Kennedy has used his seat on the Veterans' Affairs Committee to agitate for aid to homeless vets.)

In the 101st Congress, the Banking Committee worked on the most sweeping overhaul of federal housing programs since 1974. The bill included Kennedy's Community Housing Partnership program, providing $300 million in grants to cities, states and nonprofit groups to rehabilitate, acquire and build low-income housing — and to help low-income families buy homes.

Kennedy's most significant accomplishment is his success in strengthening laws against bank "redlining," the practice of refusing to lend in low-income or minority neighborhoods.

His amendment to require public disclosure of bank and thrift evaluations under the 1977 law that prohibits redlining and to require mortgage lenders to report data on applications by race, sex and income level was rejected by the Banking Committee. But the House narrowly adopted it 214-200, and most of its provisions remained in the bill as enacted. The result was a round of reports in 1992 disclosing continued widespread discrimination by lenders.

A further effort by Kennedy to buttress anti-redlining rules failed in 1991 as part of a sweeping bank overhaul bill. In battling forces on the committee who wanted to roll back existing laws, Kennedy and his allies agreed to hold off pursuing any change at all.

Kennedy has also engaged in a quixotic quest to pay for the savings and loan bailout either through a tax increase or spending cuts, not more borrowing. And his growing aversion

Massachusetts 8

Parts of Boston and suburbs — Cambridge; Somerville

The 8th, with a population almost 40 percent minority, is an outgrowth of mapmakers' attempt in 1992 to create a district where minorities would have substantial political influence. It links Hispanics in Chelsea, Haitians in Somerville and blacks in the Boston neighborhoods of Dorchester, Roxbury and Mattapan. Blacks are 23 percent of the district's population, Hispanics 11 percent and Asians 6 percent.

The large minority population helps fuel the service economy that dominates the 8th. Many work as custodians, clerical staff, orderlies and cooks at the local hospitals, universities, hotels and government offices. There is a degree of tension in the 8th between these laborers and white-collar professionals who work at the same institutions, but they coexist in reasonable peace partly because of their shared liberalism.

Two of the world's most renowned universities — Harvard and the Massachusetts Institute of Technology — lie along the banks of the Charles River in Cambridge. Jokingly known as the Kremlin on the Charles, the exceedingly liberal city of 96,000 votes staunchly Democratic. It helped Bill Clinton carry the 8th with 68 percent in 1992, by far his best showing in any Massachusetts district.

The two universities employ about 24,000 and educate nearly 28,000. Their research activities helped spawn a bevy of highly specialized computer and biotechnology firms in the area.

One of the few cities that still enforces rent-control laws, Cambridge has grown increasingly crowded, and that has sent students and young workers looking for quarters in neighboring Somerville.

Despite the influx of yuppies and a handful of upscale restaurants and boutiques in the 1980s, Somerville remains a working-class, tight-knit community of triple-decker houses, neighborhood pubs and home-style eateries.

More than half the district's residents live in Boston, a city with a metropolitan air but small-town charm, thanks to its many and varied neighborhoods. At least 10 distinct Boston sections are within the 8th. They include: Fenway, home to the Red Sox baseball stadium (Fenway Park) and a large gay population; Mattapan, where black professionals have refurbished single family homes; Jamaica Plain, a thriving liberal enclave with popular ethnic restaurants and retail shops; Beacon Hill, the historic district of stately brick townhouses behind the Massachusetts Statehouse; and Roxbury, an overwhelmingly poor black neighborhood rife with vacant lots.

The 8th also has Chelsea, a destitute city polluted by toxic waste discharged by oil ships traveling up Chelsea Creek. Things got so dire here in the early 1990s that the city government was put into state receivership and the schools were handed over to Boston University to manage.

Belmont, with its bankers, lawyers and other professionals, is the 8th's only suburban turf. One of the nation's largest concentrations of Armenians lives in neighboring Watertown.

1990 Population: 601,643. White 394,209 (66%), Black 140,276 (23%), Other 67,158 (11%). Hispanic origin 64,055 (11%). 18 and over 505,856 (84%), 62 and over 76,956 (13%). Median age: 30.

to the federal debt placed him in an elite group of liberal Democrats who switched in 1992 to support a constitutional amendment requiring a balanced federal budget.

Given his pedigree and personality, it was inevitable that Kennedy would earn an international reputation. In late 1992, after repeated instances of assaults on foreigners in Germany, Kennedy traveled to Berlin to meet with German officials and for several public appearances. To a crowd at the same spot where his uncle, President John F. Kennedy, expressed solidarity in 1963 with West Berliners besieged by Soviet troops, Joe Kennedy declared: "Ich bin ein auslander" ("I am a foreigner"). The incident upset some officials, who mistakenly thought he had come as an emissary of President-elect Bill Clinton.

Kennedy's activities in behalf of Catholics in Protestant Northern Ireland have gained notice. In a 1988 visit to Northern Ireland, the Irish Catholic Kennedy traded insults with a British soldier after his car was stopped at gunpoint. In March 1990, he co-chaired a hearing of the Congressional Human Rights Caucus on the case of the so-called "Birmingham Six," six Irish men who said they were unjustly jailed in 1975 after being convicted of bombing British pubs. The Birmingham Six were released in March 1991 after their convictions were overturned.

At Home: Reapportionment gave Kennedy the state's first minority-dominated district in 1992. But leaders of the black community said they have found a friend in the liberal Kennedy scion and did not field a serious challenge.

From the earliest days of his political career, Kennedy has been a powerhouse at the polls. The only remaining question is where does he go next? In a December 1987 interview with The Boston Globe, Kennedy mused about his political future: "I mean, I know I love the job, but I don't know that it is right for me or my family ... and I am just trying to figure it out." Throughout his first term, he bristled at suggestions he might run for governor in 1990. In early 1989, Kennedy rejected a run; he also announced he was separating from his wife. With Weld's election, liberals again whispered Kennedy's name until he squelched speculation in early 1993.

Being the front-runner in his 1986 House race to replace the retiring incumbent, Speaker Thomas P. O'Neill Jr., did not spare Kennedy a tough campaign. In addition to his familial advantages, Kennedy had attained favorable press on his own as founder of the nonprofit Citizens Energy Corporation, which buys oil wholesale and provides discounts on heating oil to low-income residents of New England.

But in the primary, he became the target for a large field of opponents — and some journalists, who questioned his qualifications. Voters were reminded that Kennedy struggled through high school and graduated from college through the aid of correspondence courses. Stories rehashed the 1973 accident that crippled a passenger in the Jeep Kennedy was driving.

Kennedy's opponents also derided him as an inexperienced newcomer. He was labeled as inarticulate after some stumbling campaign performances; one Boston columnist said Kennedy had "vapor lock on the brain."

But Kennedy grew more sure of himself and the issues. He espoused liberal positions on such matters as health care and education but positioned himself as the moderate in a field of liberals. This centrist move provoked a liberal backlash that fueled the campaign of state Sen. George Bachrach, who became Kennedy's closest rival. But Kennedy's moderate posture appealed to blue-collar voters, including many elderly and longtime Kennedy loyalists. Carrying working-class wards by huge margins while running even on Bachrach's home turf of Somerville, Kennedy easily won the 11-candidate primary.

Although not the most articulate politician, Kennedy draws crowds, particularly in the ethnic neighborhoods around Boston where his family always has been revered. At home, his big grin and blue eyes seem to be all he needs to charm constituents. Since 1988, Kennedy has coasted to re-election every two years, racking up his largest margin to date in 1992.

Committees

Banking, Finance & Urban Affairs (8th of 30 Democrats)
Consumer Credit & Insurance (chairman); Financial Institutions Supervision, Regulation & Deposit Insurance; International Development, Finance, Trade & Monetary Policy

Veterans' Affairs (8th of 21 Democrats)
Hospitals & Health Care

Elections

1992 General		
Joseph P. Kennedy II (D)	149,903	(83%)
Alice Harriett Nakash (I)	30,402	(17%)
1992 Primary		
Joseph P. Kennedy II (D)	45,993	(81%)
Charles Calvin Yancey (D)	11,005	(19%)
1990 General		
Joseph P. Kennedy II (D)	125,479	(72%)
Glenn W. Fiscus (R)	39,310	(23%)
Susan C. Davies (NA)	8,806	(5%)

Previous Winning Percentages: 1988 (80%) **1986** (72%)

District Vote for President

1992
D 136,582 (68%)
R 39,284 (20%)
I 25,503 (13%)

Campaign Finance

	Receipts	Receipts from PACs		Expend-itures
1992				
Kennedy (D)	$769,635	$146,030	(19%)	$767,161
1990				
Kennedy (D)	$805,013	$108,550	(13%)	$832,815

Key Votes

1993	
Require parental notification of minors' abortions	N
Require unpaid family and medical leave	Y
Approve national "motor voter" registration bill	Y
Approve budget increasing taxes and reducing deficit	Y
Approve economic stimulus plan	Y
1992	
Approve balanced-budget constitutional amendment	Y
Close down space station program	Y
Approve U.S. aid for former Soviet Union	Y
Allow shifting funds from defense to domestic programs	Y
1991	
Extend unemployment benefits using deficit financing	Y
Approve waiting period for handgun purchases	Y
Authorize use of force in Persian Gulf	N

Voting Studies

	Presidential Support		Party Unity		Conservative Coalition	
Year	**S**	**O**	**S**	**O**	**S**	**O**
1992	15	79	85	7	17	81
1991	24	74	94	3	14	86
1990	21	73	90	4	13	80
1989	23	73	95	4	10	90
1988	18	80	95	3	3	89
1987	14	86	90	5	12	88

Interest Group Ratings

Year	ADA	AFL-CIO	CCUS	ACU
1992	95	83	25	8
1991	95	100	20	0
1990	89	92	21	4
1989	95	100	40	4
1988	95	100	21	4
1987	96	88	13	9

9 Joe Moakley (D)

Of Boston — Elected 1972; 11th Term

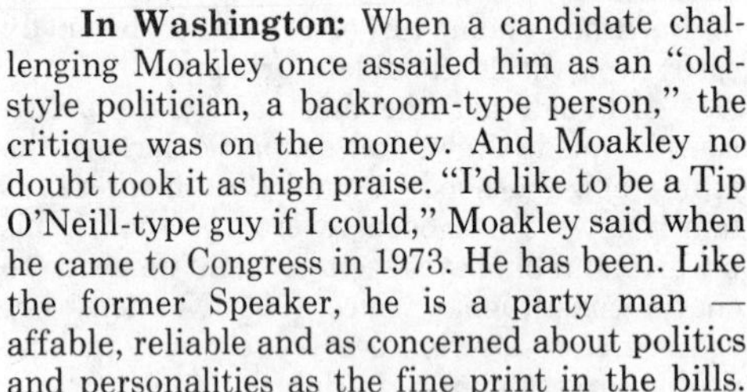

Born: April 27, 1927, Boston, Mass.
Education: U. of Miami; Suffolk U., J.D. 1956.
Military Service: Navy, 1943-46.
Occupation: Lawyer.
Family: Wife, Evelyn Duffy.
Religion: Roman Catholic.
Political Career: Mass. House, 1953-65; Mass. Senate, 1965-69; sought Democratic nomination for U.S. House, 1970; Boston City Council, 1971-73.
Capitol Office: 235 Cannon Bldg. 20515; 225-8273.

In Washington: When a candidate challenging Moakley once assailed him as an "old-style politician, a backroom-type person," the critique was on the money. And Moakley no doubt took it as high praise. "I'd like to be a Tip O'Neill-type guy if I could," Moakley said when he came to Congress in 1973. He has been. Like the former Speaker, he is a party man — affable, reliable and as concerned about politics and personalities as the fine print in the bills.

These traits have served Moakley well as chairman of the Rules Committee, where process is sometimes more important than policy. The committee is often described as the gatekeeper of the House, because it works in concert with the leadership to control the flow of legislation and set the terms of floor debate. This makes the chairman one of Congress' premier horse-traders.

Moakley became chairman after the May 1989 death of Florida Democrat Claude Pepper. As principal traffic cop, Moakley has brought a distinctly congenial spirit to the necessarily partisan deliberations of the Rules panel, where Democrats wield a lopsided majority, almost always to their own benefit.

Moakley has shown a willingness, uncommon among chairmen, to listen to all sides. And his personable style — his humor helps defuse tense situations and make bitter political pills easier to swallow — has helped tame some of the more outspoken Rules Republicans, in particular ranking member Gerald B. H. Solomon of New York. "The days of snarling chairmen who look through junior members are long gone," said Moakley at the end of 1990. "To survive, you have to be gracious even when you say no."

Under the leadership of Speaker Thomas S. Foley of Washington, whose own style keeps him above the fray as much as possible, the Rules Committee is freer than under previous Speakers to resolve disputes among committees with competing jurisdictions and to grant members' requests for special floor procedures that give them an advantage in debate. At the same time, Foley has shown an inclination to exert tighter control over floor deliberations. That translates into closely crafted rules and more power for the committee — and by extension, Moakley.

Foley and Moakley described their relationship at the end of 1991 as one of consultation not mandate. "I don't direct chairmen of committees," Foley protested when asked if he had demanded a specific outcome. "I don't even direct the Rules Committee. I consult with it." Moakley concurred, to a point: "He tells you what the bottom line is he'd like to see, and lets you get there the way you want."

That approach was in evidence during a tense period before a broad energy bill was brought to the floor in May 1992. Foley ordered the chairmen of nine committees with jurisdiction over the bill to work out differences of jurisdiction and policy. All managed to do so, except Energy and Commerce Chairman John D. Dingell of Michigan and Interior Chairman George Miller of California.

Miller, who was seeking both to reclaim jurisdiction lost to Energy and Commerce over the years and to take a more aggressive posture on nuclear generating plant licensing and disposal of radioactive waste, wanted a floor fight. Dingell was more disposed to backroom logrolling. Moakley mediated the problem by putting some of Miller's proposals into the bill, leaving some out entirely, and subjecting some to the will of the membership.

That is not to say that Moakley doesn't have an ear that is finely tuned for instructions from the leadership. In May 1991, when the Brady bill, mandating a seven-day waiting period for handgun purchases, headed to the floor, Foley was in an awkward spot.

As a longtime opponent of gun control, Foley could have ordered Rules to structure the debate to give maximum advantage to a competing proposal to establish an instantaneous computer check for buyers. Brady bill supporters doubted that the computer check would work and viewed the proposal as an end-run by gun owners. They preferred the cooling-off period their approach provided. Foley's tact was

Massachusetts 9

Part of Boston, southern suburbs — Taunton; Braintree; part of Brockton

In coming years, Boston and the 9th will be an interesting venue to watch in assessing the Clinton administration's ability to use federal public works dollars to fuel economic revitalization.

Three major projects will be under way in Boston through the 1990s: construction of a third tunnel under Boston Harbor connecting downtown to Logan International Airport; the depression and reconstruction of a north-south highway called the Central Artery; and cleanup of the polluted Boston Harbor. Some estimates say that the three projects will employ 20,000 once they are in full swing. And with construction under way for a new arena to house basketball's Celtics and hockey's Bruins, even more jobs will be created.

The projects are especially important to the 9th, where many working-class residents have not had a steady paycheck since the bottom fell out of the commercial real estate market in the late 1980s, halting new construction work. These blue-collar Democrats live primarily in Boston's ethnic neighborhoods. Italians reside in the North End, a compact section near the waterfront where suburbanites trek for some of the region's best food. South Boston, still overwhelmingly white and Irish, was the center of bitter opposition to school busing in the 1970s. Most of the residents of middle-class West Roxbury and Roslindale work downtown at banks, insurance companies, law offices and government agencies.

The 9th takes in nearly all the white sections of Boston. Redistricting in 1992 put most of the city's black, Hispanic and Asian neighborhoods into the 8th to create a minority-influence district.

South of Boston, the 9th includes half the city of Brockton. This former shoemaking capital has struggled since those factories departed in the 1960s. Brockton's population slipped slightly in the 1980s to just under 93,000. Brockton went Republican in the three presidential elections of the 1980s, but Bill Clinton carried it in 1992.

Despite the presence of Boston, Brockton and (farther south) the city of Taunton, the 9th is evenly divided between urban and suburban communities. Many Boston executives live in and give a conservative flavor to the towns of Milton, Randolph, Medfield and Braintree. These communities (south and west of Boston) are known for their neatly manicured lawns, good schools and predominantly white populations. The state's burgeoning anti-abortion movement is centered in Braintree.

In a state where many areas saw significant population decline in the 1980s, Milton held steady and Randolph grew. Adding to Milton's appeal is the nearby Blue Hills Reservation, a 6,500-acre preserve with hiking trails, tennis courts, a golf course and small ski slope. Although Milton is George Bush's birthplace, it went narrowly for Clinton; Bush won Medfield.

Many of the 9th's suburban residents work outside the district, traveling the Route 128 beltway to companies such as Raytheon and Digital Equipment Corp.

1990 Population: 601,643. White 526,931 (88%), Black 40,197 (7%), Other 34,515 (6%). Hispanic origin 27,953 (5%). 18 and over 486,597 (81%), 62 and over 105,018 (17%). Median age: 34.

to claim he had his hands off the process, and he merely instructed that the floor fight be "fair." Moakley and his Rules colleagues permitted a slight advantage in the floor debate to the Brady bill's foes, by allowing the computer check as an amendment that if adopted would wipe out the waiting period. But the computer check was rejected by a wide margin; not a single Rules Democrat voted for it.

On more than one occasion, Moakley has defused potentially ugly situations when the two parties were at each other's throats. In 1990, when partisan rancor threatened debate over child-care legislation, Moakley agreed that Republicans had not been given a fair chance to view the latest version of the measure, so he delayed committee votes by a day. The limits to his bipartisanship were soon clear, though; the committee rejected five GOP amendments on party-line votes the next day.

Often, Moakley's work has a local angle; he has used his post to block legislation offensive to Boston's Logan Airport, and he has also looked after New England's financial institutions.

Moakley managed to win a special $10 million grant for Bridgewater State College in his district to build a high-tech center to train students for jobs in the region's advanced industries. "There are other schools besides Harvard, Yale and MIT," he said without apology. And Moakley was quick to call the White House and object when President Clinton proposed in his first budget request to Congress that earmarked appropriations be eliminated — especially one to clean up Boston Harbor, whose pollution was made famous by President Bush in the 1988 presidential campaign.

Even Moakley's forays into foreign relations hew to the dictum that all politics are local. Making the district rounds in 1983, he met some constituents working through their church with Salvadoran refugees. Since then, he has been a proponent of granting special immigration status to people immigrating illegally to the United States from the civil wars in El Salvador and Nicaragua. Such a bill passed the House in 1989 but never made it to the Senate.

When Congress passed an immigration overhaul measure in 1990, Moakley fought again for an 18-month stay-of-deportation provision for Salvadorans. The issue pitted Moakley against lead Senate negotiators, who argued against singling out one country for special treatment. But Moakley noted that he had been willing in other years to back off in the interest of whatever immigration bill was on the table. This time, he said, he was not going to budge.

For Moakley, tolerance for rights abuses perpetrated by the Salvadoran military reached a breaking point in 1990. Lawmakers from both parties agreed that the character of the issue changed substantially in November 1989, when six Jesuit priests and their two housekeepers were murdered. Eight soldiers were arrested after the execution-style slayings, and there were suspicions that high-ranking officers had prior knowledge of the murders.

Shortly after the slayings, Foley appointed Moakley to chair a 19-member task force, with a mandate to monitor the Salvadoran government's response to the killings. While focusing on the Jesuits' case, the Moakley task force used its report to denounce what it said were the failures of the Salvadoran judicial and military systems — both of which had been heavily subsidized by U.S. aid. In general, the task force said, El Salvador's judicial system did not work. Even Republicans, while challenging some parts of the Moakley report, said most of it was fair.

After the March 1993 release of a U.N. commission's report on Salvadoran violence that mirrored the Moakley task force's findings, he called for declassifying government records to show just how much the Reagan and Bush administrations knew about the case.

During debate on a foreign aid authorization measure, lawmakers in 1990 first tackled the El Salvador aid issue. In May, the House approved a Moakley amendment calling for a 50 percent cut in military aid. "Enough is enough," Moakley said in an impassioned speech. "The time to act has come. They killed six priests in cold blood. I stood on the ground where my friends were blown away by men to whom the sanctity of human life bears no meaning — and men who will probably never be brought to justice."

Moakley's attention to the Salvadoran cause earned him a special salute in 1993 on his 66th birthday, with a charity dinner dedicated to establishing an endowment for the University of Central America in El Salvador. The week before, the John W. McCormack Institute of Public Affairs at the University of Massachusetts gave its first John Joseph Moakley Award for Distinguished Public Service.

For most of his years on Rules, Moakley's priorities were O'Neill's. But he also showed streaks of independence. Perhaps the most publicized — and personally painful — demonstration of Moakley's independence came early in 1984 during an ugly exchange between the Speaker and conservative "Young Turk" Republicans. O'Neill and Georgia Republican Newt Gingrich engaged in a shouting match, with the Speaker denouncing Gingrich's tactics as "the lowest thing that I have ever seen in my 32 years in Congress."

Recognizing a breach of the prohibition against personal insults on the floor, Republicans demanded that O'Neill be declared out of order. The parliamentarian concurred, and Moakley had no choice but to rule against his friend and mentor, telling O'Neill "that type of characterization should not be used in debate." It was the first time since 1797 that a Speaker had been officially rebuked for his language.

At Home: Surgery to remove a benign lesion from his kidney and a slow recovery afterward made Moakley keenly aware of his own mortality as the 1992 election loomed.

Moreover, Moakley had been caught up in the House bank scandal, having written 90 overdrawn checks. He was worried that his "human error," as he described it, might hasten an end to his public career. So he quickly confronted the check problem and moved to defuse it: "It seems I should have majored in accounting rather than sheet metal when I was at Southie High," he quipped in April 1992.

Redistricting called for Massachusetts to lose one of its 11 congressional seats. And although Rep. Brian Donnelly's retirement helped ease the way, Moakley made it clear he was in no mood for a tough campaign in unfamiliar territory.

As the dean of the delegation and chairman of Rules, Moakley was a valuable asset to Massachusetts officials, Democrats and Republicans alike. And after four decades in politics he had a long list of allies willing to protect his turf in reapportionment. Nicknamed the "cloutmeister" by one columnist, Moakley ran in a 9th whose partisan makeup was barely changed by map-carvers. He won with 69 percent, spending more than $1 million along the way.

Moakley is from the same school of party politics as is O'Neill, but it took a striking display of independence to elect him to Congress.

He was a state representative by age 25 and knew early on he would like to succeed John W. McCormack in the House. He spent 16 years in the state Legislature and waited for McCormack to retire. But when the Democratic Speaker finally stepped down in 1970, Moakley found himself overmatched in the primary against the more visible Louise Day Hicks. She took the nomination and won in November.

Then things began to turn Moakley's way. Hicks lost her second mayoral try in 1971, straining her reputation as a political force, and the next year the district was substantially rearranged. Moakley, meanwhile, won a seat on Boston's City Council.

By 1972, Hicks was highly vulnerable. In the primary, she was held to 37 percent; she won renomination only because five other candidates split the opposition.

Moakley was not one of the primary challengers. In the smartest political gamble of his life, he had decided to run as an independent. Insisting he was a lifelong Democrat, he staked out a position well to Hicks' left. Hicks carried the part of Boston remaining in the district, but by only 192 votes, as Moakley cut into her vote in Irish neighborhoods and swept the black areas. He won the seat with 5,000 votes to spare.

Since then, only twice has Moakley's re-election tally fallen below 70 percent. In 1982, Republicans drafted state Rep. Deborah R. Cochran, promising to produce her ads. Though she carried several small towns in Bristol and Plymouth counties, Moakley's urban constituents gave him 74 percent of their vote. His 64 percent total was convincing enough to ward off GOP opposition in the next four elections.

Committee

Rules (Chairman)
Legislative Process; Rules of the House

Elections

1992 General		
Joe Moakley (D)	175,550	(69%)
Martin D. Conboy (R)	54,291	(21%)
Lawrence C. Mackin (I)	15,637	(6%)
Robert W. Horan (I)	8,084	(3%)
1990 General		
Joe Moakley (D)	124,534	(70%)
Robert W. Horan (I)	52,660	(30%)

Previous Winning Percentages: **1988** (100%) **1986** (84%) **1984** (100%) **1982** (64%) **1980** (100%) **1978** (92%) **1976** (70%) **1974** (89%) **1972** (43%)

District Vote for President

1992
D 131,539 (48%)
R 85,981 (31%)
I 56,609 (21%)

Campaign Finance

	Receipts	Receipts from PACs		Expend-itures
1992				
Moakley (D)	$855,533	$430,075	(50%)	$1,056,446
Conboy (R)	$15,105	$2,159	(14%)	$12,616
1990				
Moakley (D)	$512,858	$279,274	(54%)	$318,847

Key Votes

1993	
Require parental notification of minors' abortions	N
Require unpaid family and medical leave	Y
Approve national "motor voter" registration bill	Y
Approve budget increasing taxes and reducing deficit	Y
Approve economic stimulus plan	Y
1992	
Approve balanced-budget constitutional amendment	N
Close down space station program	Y
Approve U.S. aid for former Soviet Union	Y
Allow shifting funds from defense to domestic programs	Y
1991	
Extend unemployment benefits using deficit financing	Y
Approve waiting period for handgun purchases	Y
Authorize use of force in Persian Gulf	N

Voting Studies

	Presidential Support		Party Unity		Conservative Coalition	
Year	**S**	**O**	**S**	**O**	**S**	**O**
1992	15	71	89	2	13	85
1991	32	66	90	7	22	73
1990	24	75	95	4	28	69
1989	31	65	89	4	10	83
1988	21	77	95	3	5	92
1987	19	78	91	1	12	84
1986	16	79	87	3	16	84
1985	23	65	80	4	11	85
1984	29	63	86	5	12	76
1983	22	74	89	5	11	82
1982	39	52	89	5	25	70
1981	36	47	81	8	23	63

Interest Group Ratings

Year	ADA	AFL-CIO	CCUS	ACU
1992	85	92	25	4
1991	90	100	20	5
1990	78	100	14	4
1989	95	100	44	4
1988	90	100	21	8
1987	84	100	7	5
1986	85	100	18	5
1985	90	100	23	5
1984	85	92	33	4
1983	80	94	21	5
1982	75	100	18	9
1981	55	86	6	7

10 Gerry E. Studds (D)

Of Cohasset — Elected 1972; 11th Term

Born: May 12, 1937, Mineola, N.Y.
Education: Yale U., B.A. 1959, M.A.T. 1961.
Occupation: High school teacher.
Family: Single.
Religion: Episcopalian.
Political Career: Democratic nominee for U.S. House, 1970.
Capitol Office: 237 Cannon Bldg. 20515; 225-3111.

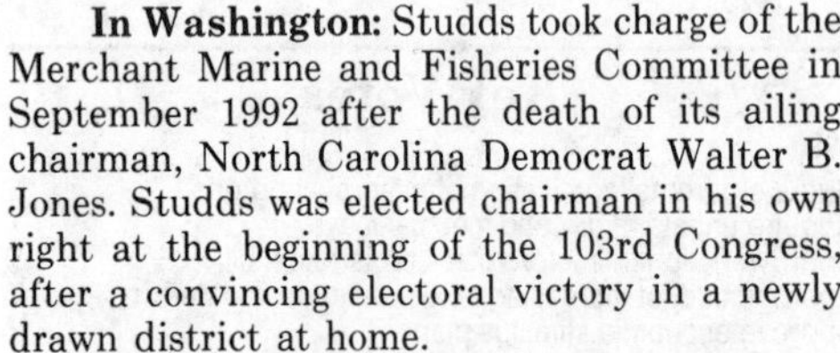

In Washington: Studds took charge of the Merchant Marine and Fisheries Committee in September 1992 after the death of its ailing chairman, North Carolina Democrat Walter B. Jones. Studds was elected chairman in his own right at the beginning of the 103rd Congress, after a convincing electoral victory in a newly drawn district at home.

The two elections resolved any lingering doubts that Studds' House career is fully back on course after going seriously off-track in the early 1980s, when the House censured him for sexual misconduct with a young male page.

An experience that would have reshaped the personality of a different member left Studds the same self-confident, argumentative and articulate liberal, just as tough on his opposition as before. "My sexual preference has nothing to do with my ability to do this job well or to do it badly," he said at the height of the controversy. "I'm a good or bad congressman quite apart from my sexual preference." He is still known as one of the funniest members of the House, with a piercing wit that rivals any in the chamber.

The censure briefly cost Studds his base of legislative power as chairman of Merchant Marine's Coast Guard and Navigation Subcommittee. But he got that back after he was re-elected in 1984, and, in 1987, he inherited what he called "the premier subcommittee," the Fisheries and Wildlife panel.

Studds broadened his legislative territory at the start of the 102nd Congress by joining one of the most active committees in Congress, Energy and Commerce. In doing so, he passed up a chance to take the chairmanship of a Foreign Affairs subcommittee that oversees Central America, a significant area of interest to Studds. He gave up his seat on Foreign Affairs at the beginning of the 103rd.

The Energy and Commerce post gives Studds an opportunity to keep an eye on the panel's chairman, John D. Dingell, D-Mich., whose always-stretching jurisdiction often overlaps with that of Merchant Marine.

But Studds will have to find another way to keep an eye on another jurisdictional rival, Democrat George Miller of California, the chairman of the Natural Resources Committee, which also tends to overlap Merchant Marine's territory.

Like Miller, Studds is showing every sign of charting a far more aggressive course for his committee than his predecessor. These paths will almost certainly collide in the 103rd Congress on such issues as the reauthorization of the Endangered Species Act and the clean water act.

Studds has reason to be nervous about turf encroachment; with efforts to streamline Congress under way over at the Joint Committee on the Organization of Congress, Merchant Marine is likely to come under particularly hard scrutiny; the panel is a possible candidate for elimination.

In bypassing Foreign Affairs' Western Hemisphere chair in favor of Energy and Commerce and the Merchant Marine chair, Studds has put himself in a position to pursue closer-to-home issues.

As a rookie congressman in the mid-1970s, he decried the tendency of senior members to grow so accustomed to Washington that they lost touch with their districts. Over time, Studds has seemed to become even more oriented toward the parochial concerns of his coastal district — fishing, shipping and boating, ocean and coastal pollution and the Coast Guard — perhaps more than he ever imagined when he arrived in the House as a veteran of the civil rights and anti-war movements.

In the past, Studds trod gingerly between environmentalists and Jones, his committee chairman, on the issue of whether to open Alaska's vast Arctic National Wildlife Refuge (ANWR) to oil exploration. In 1988, in deference to Jones, he moved Jones' bill to permit limited oil leasing through his subcommittee, though he himself voted against it.

But the 1989 oil spill of the *Exxon Valdez* clouded the prospects for any expansion of oil exploration, and in the debate in the 102nd Congress over President Bush's energy bill proposals, Studds voiced his doubts on the pros-

Massachusetts 10

South Shore — Cape Cod; islands

A researcher at Woods Hole Oceanographic Institution starts his own business to produce a new medicine he developed from squid blood.

The Maritime Administration moors the Southern Cross, a 450-foot ship, at the all but abandoned Fore River Shipyard in Quincy. The boat becomes the first floating classroom in the nation.

These are the kind of small but notable developments that are helping the coastal communities of the 10th shift gears into the 1990s. Just as whaling gave way to textiles after the Civil War, and textiles were replaced with fishing and shipbuilding in the 1920s, now newly emerging technologies offer economic promise for the residents of Cape Cod, the Islands and Massachusetts' South Shore.

Since the 10th has never relied on the defense industry and did not partake in the high-tech boom of the 1980s, its economy has stayed more constant than much of the state's.

The coastal towns, particularly on Cape Cod, rely on tourists to help them survive the long, arduous winters. Though the Cape is referred to as a single locale, it is an eclectic mix of communities, some of them ritzy summer vacation spots, some of them middle-class communities with year-round residents; one — Provincetown, at the tip of the cape — is a liberal, predominantly gay artists' colony. Martha's Vineyard and Nantucket are summer retreats for the rich (and often, famous).

The mainland coastal towns of the 10th are commonly referred to as the South Shore communities. With the exception of a handful of thriving cranberry bogs, most of the South Shore towns consist of bedroom developments for Boston's professionals or Quincy's blue-collar workers. Commuter boats shuttle lawyers and doctors from Hingham and Hull across Boston Harbor to downtown.

Cape Cod, Hingham, Duxbury and Cohasset can offer a trove of votes to the right Republican. Although Rep. Studds handily defeated his two opponents in those communities in 1992, the presidential contest was closer; George Bush won several towns in the south, including Duxbury, Chatham, Hingham and Hanover.

Quincy, popularized in the mid-1970s by white Bostonians fleeing the city's forced busing policies to integrate the schools, continues its tradition as an ethnic melting pot. Irish and Italian immigrants led the way south; now Asian-Americans are becoming a visible presence in Quincy.

The city of Brockton dominates the inland communities of the 10th. Split between the 9th and 10th districts, it has been suffering ever since the decline of its shoemaking industry in the 1960s.

The 10th overall is one of the Democrats' weaker districts in Massachusetts. Bush did better here than in any other district (though he still got only 32 percent), and the 10th was independent candidate Ross Perot's second-best district, giving him almost 26 percent.

1990 Population: 601,642. White 572,442 (95%), Black 12,519 (2%), Other 16,681 (3%). Hispanic origin 8,601 (1%). 18 and over 480,850 (80%), 62 and over 113,463 (19%). Median age: 36.

pects of ANWR drilling. "It is absurd for this administration to base its entire national energy strategy on potential oil development in ANWR," he said.

Studds supports the argument that whatever oil could be gained in Alaska would be unnecessary if Congress would restore auto fuel-efficiency standards to their pre-Reagan administration level.

The *Valdez* spill helped break a 15-year deadlock over increasing oil spillers' federal liability limits. Studds first introduced oil-spill liability legislation in 1975; in August 1990, Bush signed a liability bill into law. The bill also would compensate those economically injured by accidents, enhance cleanup efforts and attempt to prevent spills. It contained another longtime Studds goal, mandating double hulls, bottoms or sides on oil vessels, though the shipping industry persuaded members to stretch out the phase-in over 25 years.

Studds successfully sponsored a mound of legislation in the 102nd Congress that addressed such issues as a dolphin protection treaty, enforcement of the driftnet fishing ban, striped bass and wild bird conservation and an international fisheries agreement.

Another bill Studds managed to get signed into law requires the federal government to ensure that Pacific yew trees in federal forests are harvested, not discarded. The yew is the source of the cancer-fighting drug Taxol.

In his first term, Studds enjoyed perhaps his single most important success when he pushed a bill extending U.S. territorial waters to a 200-mile limit, a change the fishing industry felt was essential to fight foreign competition. Later, when President Carter proposed a new U.S.-Canadian fishing treaty, Studds opposed it because his state's fishermen thought it favored Canada. One of Studds' priorities in the 103rd Congress is getting the 200-mile limit reauthorized.

In a move in the 102nd Congress that directly benefited his district, Studds managed to ease pending Commerce Department rules aimed at replenishing New England's fish populations. The rules would have meant deep cuts in the number of fish allowed to be caught; Studds' bill stretched the recovery out over a longer period. The bill also called on the government to find new markets for America's fish: "There's no reason that the new McDonald's in Moscow should not be serving McMackerels," Studds said.

Early in the 103rd Congress, Studds focused attention on the problem that came up during the Persian Gulf War of merchant marines losing their jobs after going to war. Military reservists who are called up are guaranteed their jobs back when they return from active duty, but merchant marines who volunteer for the Ready Reserve Force are not. Studds' remedy would give civilian sailors essentially the same re-employment rights as military reservists.

The assiduous attention Studds pays his constituents' interests is a matter of political survival; it has allowed him to survive a round of redistricting that ripped the heart out of his old territory, and a scandal that would have toppled many members.

Though Studds has worked hard to move beyond the incident, he probably will always be best remembered outside Congress as the member censured in 1983 for having had sex with a 17-year-old male page. He publicly acknowledged his homosexuality and admitted an "error in judgment," but he never apologized. "I do not believe," he said in a prepared statement, "that a relationship which was mutual and voluntary; without coercion; [and] without any preferential treatment express or implied ... constitutes 'improper sexual conduct.'"

In contrast, GOP Rep. Daniel B. Crane of Illinois, who was cited at the same time for having sex with a teenage female page, appeared at a press conference in tears to ask for forgiveness. When the two cases came to the floor, the House voted for censure — a more severe penalty than the reprimand recommended by the ethics committee, but milder than expulsion, which several members demanded.

Censure requires that a member appear before the House to hear the reading of punishment. Crane faced his colleagues as Speaker Thomas P. O'Neill Jr. read the resolution against him, Studds stood stoically facing O'Neill, his back to his colleagues. Crane left the chamber after the reading; Studds remained. He later issued a statement thanking his constituents for their support, adding, "All members of Congress are in need of humbling experiences from time to time."

At Home: Studds' biography reads like a how-to book on political survival. No matter what is thrown his way, he endures.

In 1984, in the midst of the scandal surrounding his censure, Studds proved his popularity and political acumen by winning with 56 percent of the vote.

If the sex scandal did not serve to oust him, Republicans thought a new district might. Led by GOP Gov. William F. Weld, the mapmakers carved out a new 10th that eliminated Studds' base of support: New Bedford. He inherited more blue-collar conservative communities just outside Boston, including the city of Quincy.

So abysmal was the remap that a Democratic state senator challenged Studds in the primary. But when Studds easily disposed of Quincy's Paul Harold, talk of his likely demise abated.

The 1992 brawl was a repeat of 1990 — only worse. After two tries against Studds in 1988 and 1990 (when he got 47 percent), airline pilot Jon L. Bryan decided to try a third time. But this time he entered the fray without the blessing of the GOP. Angered by the Republican power-brokers, Bryan ran as an independent, serving to play the role of spoiler and finishing with only 13 percent.

Bryan's vendetta against Studds manifested itself in the form of nasty personal attacks, terming the incumbent a "rapist" and a "child molester." GOP nominee Dan Daly, handpicked by Weld, floundered to make a convincing argument either against Studds or on behalf of himself. Even earlier theories that the only way for Studds to win would be to eke out a slim margin in the three-way fight proved foolish. He finished by taking more votes than any other congressional winner in the state.

The son of a Long Island architect, Studds went through a flurry of Washington jobs in the early 1960s before "retiring" to teach in an exclusive boarding school in New Hampshire.

In 1967, motivated by his opposition to the war in Vietnam, he enlisted in Eugene J. McCarthy's presidential campaign and ended up as one of the coordinators of the senator's New Hampshire primary effort. Then he moved to Massachusetts' old 12th District, sensing that incumbent Republican Hastings Keith was potentially vulnerable for 1970.

Studds won a four-way Democratic primary with a clear majority of the vote, while Keith had an ominously hard time winning renomination over moderate state Sen. William D. Weeks. In the general election, Studds' labor support in New Bedford and anti-war loyalists on Cape Cod brought him tantalizingly close. Keith won by just 1,522 votes.

Over the next two years, redistricting made the 10th slightly more Democratic and Studds never stopped campaigning. He learned Portuguese to communicate better with New Bedford's Portuguese fishing community. He began talking less about Vietnam, although he remained a "peace" candidate, and more about unemployment and President Richard M. Nixon's economic programs. The outcome was even closer than in 1970 — 1,118 votes — but Studds won.

When Studds returned home after his censure, he embarked on a round of town meeting-style gatherings that have since become legendary. He waited until early 1984, after the furor subsided, to announce he would run again.

The censure brought out two primary opponents, but only one posed a threat: Plymouth County Sheriff Peter Y. Flynn, a law-and-order Democrat with close ties to the conservative wing of the party. When it became clear he was making no headway, Flynn started denouncing Studds for the incident, accusing him of "seducing a young child." The attacks backfired; Studds carried all but four of the towns in the district on primary day.

In the general election, Studds' opponent was Lewis Crampton, a former official of the Environmental Protection Agency. Crampton scrupulously stayed away from the censure issue except to argue that it had diminished Studds' effectiveness in the House. He cast himself as a fiscal conservative who was moderate on environmental and some foreign policy issues.

Democrats feared that Crampton's moderate approach and freedom from scandal might be enough to overcome Studds' superior organization and past popularity. But Studds was tireless in reassuring voters that his effectiveness was unimpaired, pointing to recent accomplishments on fishing and foreign policy issues. Boosted by his usual massive margins in New Bedford and the coastal communities at the southern end of the district, Studds prevailed.

Committees

Merchant Marine & Fisheries (Chairman)
Environment & Natural Resources (chairman)

Energy & Commerce (19th of 27 Democrats)
Health & the Environment; Transportation & Hazardous Materials

Elections

1992 General		
Gerry E. Studds (D)	189,342	(61%)
Daniel W. Daly (R)	75,887	(24%)
Jon L. Bryan (I)	39,265	(13%)
Michael P. Umina (IV)	6,020	(2%)
1992 Primary		
Gerry E. Studds (D)	57,640	(61%)
Paul Harold (D)	34,280	(36%)
William G. Zissulis (D)	3,175	(3%)
1990 General		
Gerry E. Studds (D)	137,805	(53%)
Jon L. Bryan (R)	120,217	(47%)

Previous Winning Percentages: **1988** (67%) **1986** (65%) **1984** (56%) **1982** (69%) **1980** (73%) **1978** (100%) **1976** (100%) **1974** (75%) **1972** (50%)

District Vote for President

1992
D 133,776 (42%)
R 101,936 (32%)
I 80,791 (26%)

Campaign Finance

	Receipts	Receipts from PACs		Expend-itures
1992				
Studds (D)	$1,438,264	$413,068	(29%)	$1,440,376
Daly (R)	$241,250	$8,160	(3%)	$238,739
Bryan (I)	$224,792	0		$230,617
1990				
Studds (D)	$600,325	$221,581	(37%)	$620,387
Bryan (R)	$281,651	0		$41,129

Key Votes

1993	
Require parental notification of minors' abortions	N
Require unpaid family and medical leave	Y
Approve national "motor voter" registration bill	#
Approve budget increasing taxes and reducing deficit	Y
Approve economic stimulus plan	Y
1992	
Approve balanced-budget constitutional amendment	N
Close down space station program	Y
Approve U.S. aid for former Soviet Union	Y
Allow shifting funds from defense to domestic programs	Y
1991	
Extend unemployment benefits using deficit financing	Y
Approve waiting period for handgun purchases	Y
Authorize use of force in Persian Gulf	N

Voting Studies

	Presidential Support		Party Unity		Conservative Coalition	
Year	**S**	**O**	**S**	**O**	**S**	**O**
1992	13	83	93	4	8	92
1991	20	76	96	2	5	92
1990	18	82	95	4	4	96
1989	27	73	97	2	2	98
1988	16	77	94	4	0	97
1987	12	86	93	2	2	95
1986	16	84	93	3	6	88
1985	21	78	93	3	5	95
1984	23	66	85	5	5	83
1983	18	77	91	5	6	88
1982	32	66	92	8	10	90
1981	33	67	91	9	7	93

Interest Group Ratings

Year	ADA	AFL-CIO	CCUS	ACU
1992	100	83	25	0
1991	90	100	20	0
1990	100	100	21	4
1989	100	100	40	0
1988	100	100	21	0
1987	100	100	0	0
1986	95	86	19	0
1985	100	100	27	10
1984	90	75	29	0
1983	85	88	32	0
1982	95	95	23	14
1981	100	80	11	7

Michigan

STATE DATA

Governor: John Engler (R)
First elected: 1990
Length of term: 4 years
Term expires: 1/95
Salary: $106,690
Term limit: 2 terms
Phone: (517) 373-3400
Born: Oct. 12, 1948; Mount Pleasant, Mich.
Education: Michigan State U., B.S. 1971; Thomas M. Cooley Law School, J.D. 1981
Occupation: Lawyer
Family: Wife, Michelle Dumunbrun
Religion: Roman Catholic
Political Career: Mich. House, 1971-79; Mich. Senate, 1979-91

Lt. Gov.: Connie Binsfeld (R)
First elected: 1990
Length of term: 4 years
Term expires: 1/95
Salary: $80,300
Phone: (517) 373-6800

State election official: (517) 373-2540
Democratic headquarters: (517) 371-5410
Republican headquarters: (517) 487-5413

REDISTRICTING

Michigan lost two House seats in reapportionment, dropping from 18 districts to 16. Federal court issued the map March 23, 1992.

STATE LEGISLATURE

Legislature. Meets January-June, September-December.

Senate: 38 members, 4-year terms
1992 breakdown: 22R, 16D; 35 men, 3 women; 35 whites, 3 blacks
Salary: $45,450 + $8,500 expenses
Phone: (517) 373-2400

House of Representatives: 110 members, 2-year terms
1992 breakdown: 55D, 54R, 1 vacancy; 84 men, 26 women; 99 whites, 11 blacks
Salary: $45,450 + $8,500 expenses
Phone: (517) 373-0135

URBAN STATISTICS

City	Pop.
Detroit	1,027,974
Mayor Coleman A. Young, N-P	
Grand Rapids	189,126
Mayor John H. Logie, N-P	
Warren	144,864
Mayor Ronald L. Bonkowski, N-P	
Flint	140,761
Mayor Woodrow Stanley, N-P	
Lansing	127,321
Mayor Terry J. McKane, N-P	

U.S. CONGRESS

Senate: 2 D, 0 R
House: 10 D, 6 R

TERM LIMITS

For Congress: Yes
Senate: 2 terms in 24-year period
House: 3 terms in 12-year period
For state offices:
Senate: 2 terms
House: 3 terms

ELECTIONS

1992 Presidential Vote

Bill Clinton	43.8%
George Bush	36.4%
Ross Perot	19.3%

1988 Presidential Vote

George Bush	54%
Michael S. Dukakis	46%

1984 Presidential Vote

Ronald Reagan	59%
Walter F. Mondale	40%

POPULATION

1990 population		9,295,297
1980 population		9,262,078
Percent change		+<1%
Rank among states:		8
White		83%
Black		14%
Hispanic		2%
Asian or Pacific islander		1%
Urban		71%
Rural		29%
Born in state		75%
Foreign-born		4%
Under age 18	2,458,765	26%
Ages 18-64	4,675,687	50%
65 and older	1,108,461	12%
Median age		32.6

MISCELLANEOUS

Capital: Lansing
Number of counties: 83
Per capita income: $18,697 (1991)
Rank among states: 20
Total area: 58,527 sq. miles
Rank among states: 23

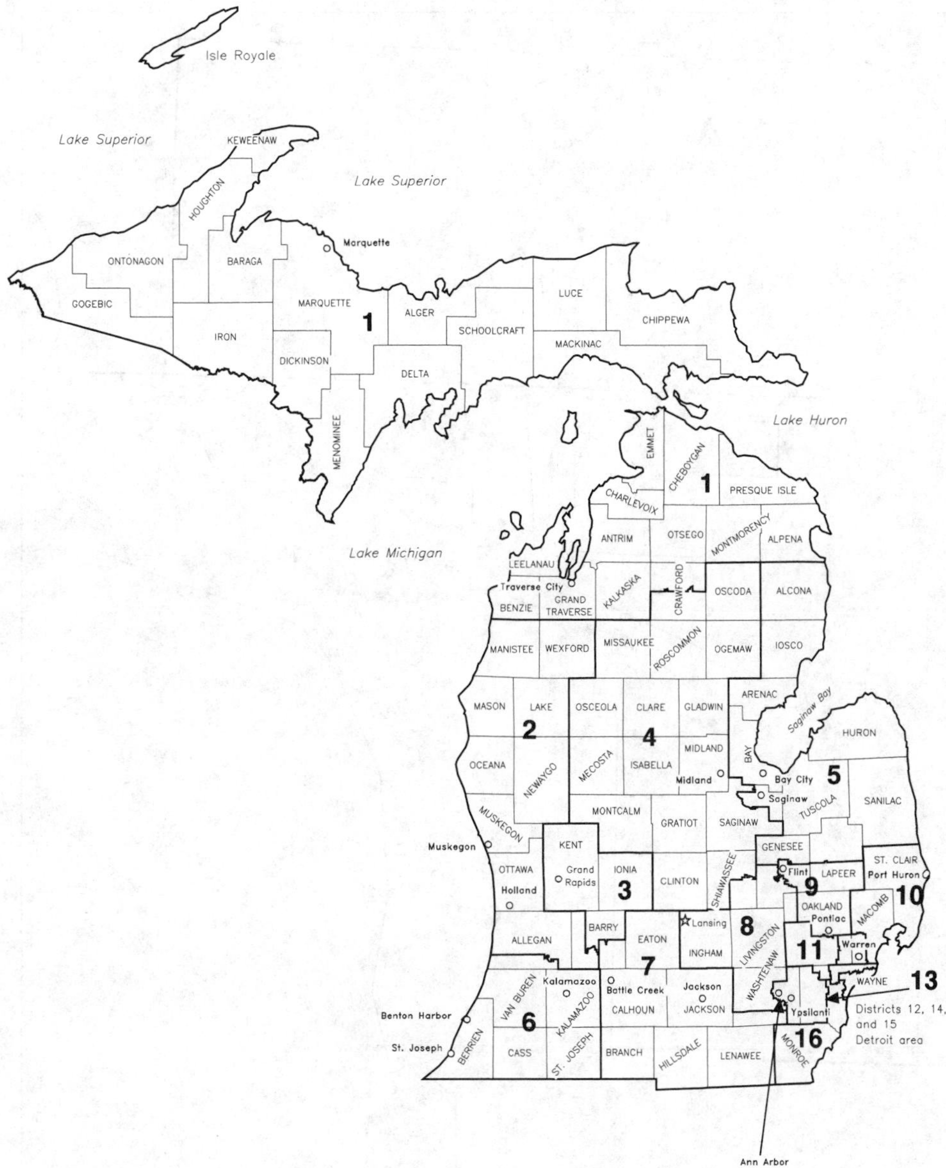
Isle Royale
Lake Superior
Lake Superior
KEWEENAW
HOUGHTON
ONTONAGON
BARAGA
GOGEBIC
IRON
MARQUETTE
Marquette
DICKINSON
MENOMINEE
DELTA
ALGER
SCHOOLCRAFT
LUCE
MACKINAC
CHIPPEWA
1
Lake Michigan
Lake Huron
EMMET
CHEBOYGAN
PRESQUE ISLE
CHARLEVOIX
ANTRIM
OTSEGO
MONTMORENCY
ALPENA
LEELANAU
Traverse City
GRAND TRAVERSE
BENZIE
KALKASKA
CRAWFORD
OSCODA
ALCONA
MANISTEE
WEXFORD
MISSAUKEE
ROSCOMMON
OGEMAW
IOSCO
MASON
LAKE
OSCEOLA
CLARE
GLADWIN
ARENAC
Saginaw Bay
HURON
2
4
5
OCEANA
NEWAYGO
MECOSTA
ISABELLA
MIDLAND
Midland
BAY
Bay City
Saginaw
TUSCOLA
SANILAC
MUSKEGON
Muskegon
MONTCALM
GRATIOT
SAGINAW
KENT
Grand Rapids
IONIA
CLINTON
SHIAWASSEE
GENESEE
Flint
LAPEER
ST. CLAIR
Port Huron
OTTAWA
Holland
3
9
10
OAKLAND
Pontiac
MACOMB
BARRY
EATON
Lansing
INGHAM
LIVINGSTON
8
11
Warren
ALLEGAN
7
WASHTENAW
WAYNE
13
Kalamazoo
Battle Creek
Jackson
VAN BUREN
KALAMAZOO
CALHOUN
JACKSON
Ypsilanti
Districts 12, 14, and 15 Detroit area
Benton Harbor
6
16
St. Joseph
BERRIEN
CASS
ST. JOSEPH
BRANCH
HILLSDALE
LENAWEE
MONROE
Ann Arbor

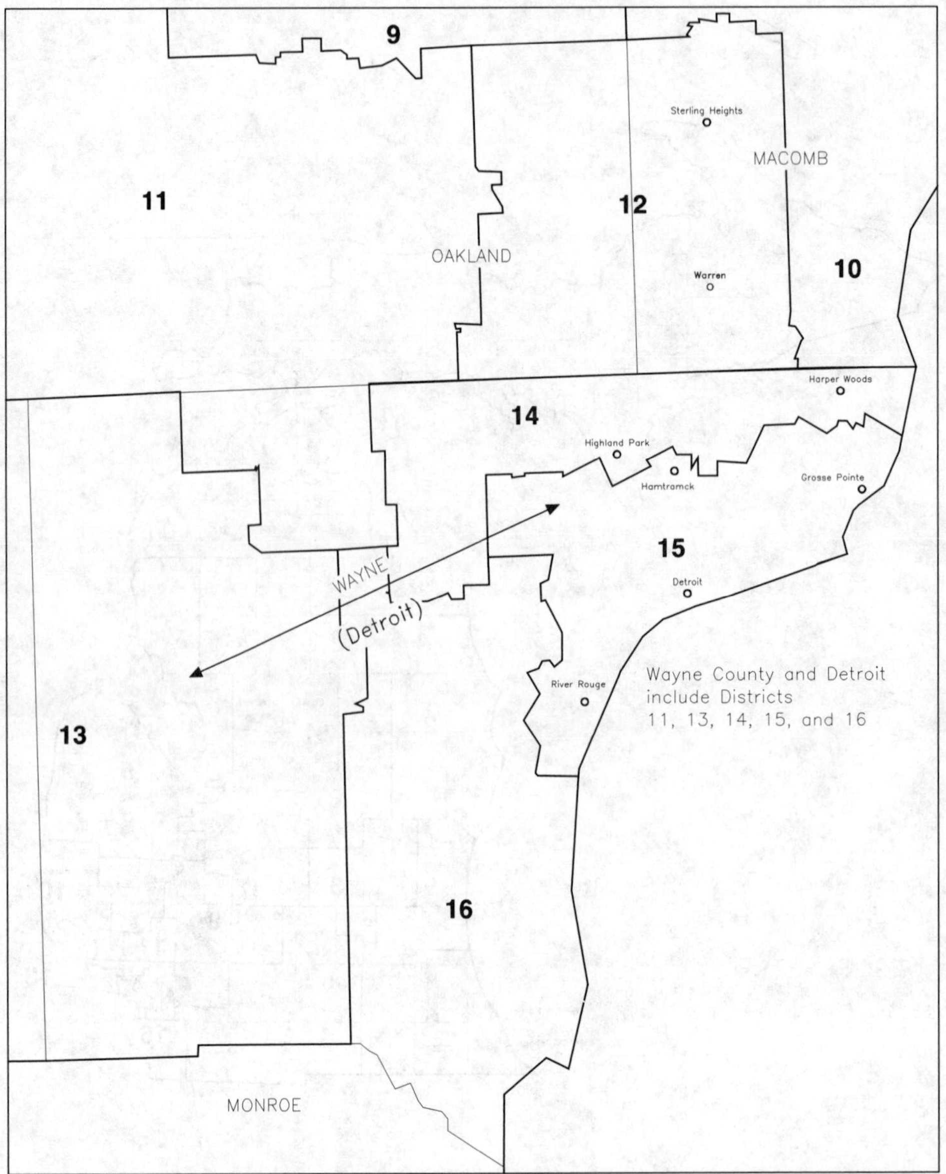
9
11
12
10
OAKLAND
MACOMB
Sterling Heights
Warren
14
Harper Woods
Highland Park
Hamtramck
Grosse Pointe
15
WAYNE
(Detroit)
Detroit
River Rouge
Wayne County and Detroit
include Districts
11, 13, 14, 15, and 16
13
16
MONROE

Donald W. Riegle Jr. (D)

Of Flint — Elected 1976; 3rd Term

Born: Feb. 4, 1938, Flint, Mich.
Education: Flint Junior College, 1956-57; Western Michigan U., 1957-58; U. of Michigan, B.A. 1960; Michigan State U., M.B.A. 1961; Harvard U. Business School, 1964-66.
Occupation: Business executive; professor.
Family: Wife, Lori Hansen; five children.
Religion: Methodist.
Political Career: U.S. House, 1967-76.
Capitol Office: 105 Dirksen Bldg. 20510; 224-4822.

In Washington: Known at home as a fierce political competitor, Riegle lately has behaved on Capitol Hill like a man trying to outrun his troubles and ward off a premature electoral demise.

He set an ambitious agenda for the 102nd Congress and achieved an impressive share of it. In his second term as Banking Committee chairman, he finally was able to complete the transformation he began years earlier from *enfant terrible* to inside player. In doing so, he did not entirely abandon the intense partisanship that described his transitional persona.

In 1990, during his first term as chairman, Riegle saw his course hijacked by the Senate Ethics Committee's investigation into his relationship with Arizona thrift operator Charles H. Keating Jr. Ultimately rebuked for his "poor judgment" in intervening with federal regulators on Keating's behalf, Riegle was contrite with his colleagues.

The scrape seemed to focus Riegle's attention. He turned his committee into a veritable legislative machine, overhauling the banking industry, imposing a tough new regulatory regime on some of the nation's largest financial entities and reauthorizing federal housing programs — all the while tending to a long list of more mundane senatorial chores.

Though much of the work was of a caliber to achieve note inside the Capital Beltway, it was perhaps of only marginal interest to the voters whom Riegle will face in 1994, as he seeks a fourth Senate term. But in addition to Banking, Riegle sits on the Budget and Finance committees, and he chairs the Finance Subcommittee on Health for Families and the Uninsured.

Those diverse assignments will permit him in the 103rd Congress to play a central role in three arenas that his home state's declining industrial base cares about deeply — jobs, health care and trade.

Late in the 102nd Congress, he took center stage during debate over a proposal by President Bush to aid Russia's transformation to a market economy. Describing the president as "drunk on foreign policy," Riegle offered an amendment to the bill that would have matched about $1 billion in aid to the former Soviet Union with a similar amount of domestic assistance for those struggling to cope with the aftermath of the 1990-91 recession. Riegle's amendment was killed on a 64-32 vote.

Then, at the start of the 103rd, Riegle used the setting of a confirmation hearing for one of President Clinton's top economic advisers to lambaste the pending North American Free Trade Agreement. Asserting that the trade pact "provides a brand-new incentive to take jobs to Mexico" — in conflict with Clinton's promise to create jobs — he signaled that he might wind up voting against it.

The Keating scandal could have turned out much worse for Riegle. Of the Keating Five senators (Riegle, Democrats Alan Cranston of California, Dennis DeConcini of Arizona and John Glenn of Ohio, and Arizona Republican John McCain), Riegle had the shortest relationship with Keating.

Keating was chairman of American Continental Corp. of Phoenix, which owned Lincoln Savings and Loan Association of California: He met Riegle in 1986 at the grand opening of an old downtown Detroit hotel that Keating had bought and renovated.

In early 1987, Keating, seeing that Riegle would soon become Banking chairman, sought a closer association with him. In 1987, Keating hosted a fundraiser for Riegle, who was seeking re-election. He raised $78,250.

At about the same time, Keating and his assistants were attempting to persuade Riegle that regulators from the Federal Home Loan Bank Board were unjustly pressuring Lincoln over some of its investments. Riegle spoke to bank board Chairman Edwin J. Gray, and told him to expect to hear from senators concerned with Lincoln's treatment. Later he suggested to DeConcini that senators meet with Gray; that meeting occurred April 2, 1987, but Riegle was the only one of the five not to attend.

Donald W. Riegle Jr., D-Mich.

Riegle did attend an April 9 meeting between all five senators and several bank board regulators. There, the senators were informed that Lincoln's mismanagement was so serious that the thrift faced criminal investigation by the Justice Department. After the meeting, Riegle, Glenn and McCain stopped their inquiries into Lincoln. In March 1988, Riegle returned the money Keating and his associates had raised for his re-election.

The Ethics Committee's special counsel, Robert S. Bennett, focused on the proximity of Keating's fundraising and Riegle's efforts in his behalf. Riegle said he did nothing improper in his contacts with regulators.

In the end, the committee concluded that Riegle's conduct "gave the appearance of being improper and was certainly attended with insensitivity and poor judgment ... [but] did not reach a level requiring institutional action" — the same verdict given DeConcini.

Apologetic, Riegle called the findings "fair and constructive.... I certainly regret and accept responsibility for this [conflict of interest] appearance problem, even though no conflict or wrongful conduct" occurred. He added that "every senator is vulnerable" to a problem of apparent conflict of interest given the existing campaign finance system.

In 1990, Common Cause issued a study that showed Riegle having received more campaign contributions in the 1980s from the thrift industry than all but one member of Congress. He later announced that he would turn over to the Treasury all thrift-related campaign contributions he had received since 1983; he estimated that it would total about $120,000. He also vowed not to accept contributions from companies whose principal business falls under the panels he chairs, the Banking Committee or his Finance subcommittee.

By 1992, Riegle's pledge was causing him some difficulty in raising the $7 million or so that he anticipated needing for his 1994 re-election campaign. The Wall Street Journal reported that Riegle was "trying to work around" his pledge by soliciting contributions from individuals and political action committees tied to the insurance industry (other than health insurers) and from lawyer-lobbyists with long and diverse client lists, even those that regularly lobbied on banking and health issues.

Riegle explained what some saw as a shift in his promise by saying the insurance industry was principally overseen by the Commerce Committee, though it often petitions the Banking panel to protect its turf from encroaching banks. And he told The Detroit News he would apply "a rule of reason" to lawyer-lobbyists' contributions, based on how much they appeared to be tied to a single industry.

Even in the 101st Congress, Riegle maintained a weighty agenda, having to cope with both a major housing authorization bill and the Bush administration's plan to salvage the ailing savings and loan industry.

Riegle concentrated his early attention on the Bush proposal to finance the initial $50 billion cost to bail out the bankrupt Federal Savings and Loan Insurance Corporation. He failed in committee and on the floor to replace the administration's call for off-budget borrowing with a complicated alternative that would have been recorded on the government's books and thus added to the deficit. But, he argued, it would have saved as much as $4.5 billion in interest costs over several decades.

Despite losing that fight, the new Banking chairman won high marks from committee members for steering a bill quickly through the rough waters of industry infighting, with bipartisan courtesy and without being swamped.

In his second term as chairman, Riegle took the lead in trying to overhaul the deposit insurance system, but was skeptical about Bush administration calls for major changes in banking law to allow banks broad authority to affiliate with securities and insurance companies or to open branch offices across state lines. Before the administration forwarded its sweeping bill to Congress, Riegle argued for taking on the task in two stages: first, shoring up deposit insurance, then finding ways to modernize the banking system.

By default — not Riegle's design — that is effectively what happened. Riegle walked his committee through a minefield of closed-door negotiations on the bill as well as a vigorous, three-day drafting session. The committee's bill permitted some new securities affiliations and interstate branching. It passed on a 12-9 vote. Opponents included some who thought the measure too restrictive and some who thought it too lax.

On the floor, the measure was pared even further by a Riegle amendment that knocked out the securities provisions. Though he was not an early advocate of interstate branching, he was, in the end, almost the only voice calling for keeping it in the final bill. The measure that was enacted did not include interstate branching, but it did impose stiff new rules on bank capital and requirements for closing banks before they were completely insolvent — provisions Riegle had a central role in crafting.

Also in the 102nd, Riegle managed to push three separate bills through the Senate to keep the savings and loan bailout operating. The House was not as successful and only two were enacted, requiring the bailout effectively to shut down in April 1992.

After long struggles, he also managed to win enactment of bills reauthorizing the Defense Production Act (which incorporated new language geared to stimulate U.S. manufacturers) and imposing a regulatory regime on several "government-sponsored enterprises" that helped create secondary markets for home mortgages, but whose financial stability was in part dependent upon implicit federal backing of their securities.

Riegle, however, failed in repeated attempts to persuade the House to support a "Fair Trade in Financial Services" measure that was intended to force foreign governments to open their markets wider to U.S. banks and securities firms.

On the Budget Committee, Riegle has been a relentless opponent of cuts in domestic spending programs. In 1985, he strongly resisted efforts to freeze Social Security cost of living adjustments (COLAs). When the committee endorsed that step as part of a spending plan it approved in March 1985, Riegle denounced the Republicans who drafted it. "You didn't have the courage to run on that basis," he said, noting President Ronald Reagan's 1984 campaign pledge not to touch Social Security. Reagan himself eventually derailed the COLA freeze.

And Riegle's long record of devotion to the automobile industry and the United Auto Workers is well-known.

Some years ago, when he was grand marshal of a parade in Traverse City, Mich., he refused to ride in the foreign car assigned to him; flustered organizers of the event hastily located a Chevrolet for the senator.

In 1977, when the Clean Air Act was up for renewal, Riegle offered the industry's principal amendment to relax standards for carbon monoxide emissions from automobiles. And in 1990, Riegle led the floor fight against a bill to raise automobile fuel-efficiency standards.

Riegle was crucial in the 1979 passage of a bailout for the Chrysler Corp., arranging a compromise that averted a filibuster and moving the plan through the Senate just before the year's recess. The compromise involved more than $500 million in wage concessions by Chrysler employees, in addition to federal protection for the company's future loans.

At Home: Riegle's first plunge into politics was enough to give anyone visions of grandeur. He was working toward a business degree at Harvard in 1966 when his hometown Republican Party, scrounging for candidates, recruited him to run against Democratic Rep. John C. Mackie. Riegle's name had some advantage; his father was active as a GOP officeholder in Flint and surrounding Genesee County.

Ignoring the odds in his heavily Democratic district, Riegle campaigned furiously, winding up his handshaking only after the polls closed on Election Day. Mackie, ignoring the warnings of friends, felt he would have no trouble winning and lapsed into a somnolent campaign. He woke up with an 11,000-vote deficit. Riegle quickly concluded that if he could win a Democratic House seat that easily, there was no reason to restrain his ambitions.

A House freshman in 1967 at age 28, he was seen as a brash and transparently ambitious young man who overstepped the bounds of protocol by announcing the timetable for his presidential aspirations — 15 years.

Although he quickly developed a maverick reputation in the House, Riegle managed to stay on good terms with his party leader, Gerald R. Ford. Even after Riegle tried to take the 1970 Michigan Senate nomination away from Lenore Romney, the choice of GOP leaders, Ford seemed to remain an ally.

The Vietnam War, however, turned Riegle from maverick to full-time rebel. He was one of a small group of anti-war Republicans backing Rep. Paul N. McCloskey Jr. of California against President Richard M. Nixon during the 1972 GOP primaries. Also that year, he further ruffled feathers with the publication of "O Congress," his legislate-and-tell look at life in the Capitol.

By then he had burned his Republican bridges and was winning re-election by comfortable margins mainly because he was popular among Flint's blue-collar Democratic majority. He became a Democrat in 1973, won a fifth term the next year and began a well-financed effort to win the Senate seat vacated in 1976 by Democrat Philip A. Hart.

In the 1976 Democratic primary, he upset the favorite, black Secretary of State Richard H. Austin. Austin was hurt by criticism of alleged irregularities in the collection of his campaign funds and by his refusal to debate. Riegle, campaigning with his usual vigor, contrasted his age (38) and Austin's (63).

Sparking a crossover primary vote by liberal Republicans and independents, Riegle won stunning victories in all the state's Democratic strongholds except Wayne County (Detroit), which he lost by just 2,000 votes.

Riegle's primary win put him on a clear path toward a Senate victory that fall against moderate GOP Rep. Marvin Esch. Despite Esch's attempt to woo suburban Detroit Democrats by attacking busing and abortion, Riegle maintained a comfortable lead.

Then The Detroit News published transcripts of taped conversations between Riegle and a staff member with whom he had had an affair in 1969. Riegle acknowledged the affair, calling it a "foolish mistake." He also sought to create a sympathetic backlash in his favor, charging that Esch's campaign had been misrepresenting his policy positions. "I hold Marvin Esch personally responsible for the gutter-level tone of this campaign," Riegle declared. The defense worked, and Riegle withstood a last-minute media flurry by Esch.

In 1982, although few vestiges were left of the earlier "young man in a hurry," Riegle again had to fight off attacks on his character. His opponent, former GOP Rep. Philip E. Ruppe, latched onto a Washington Post article in which GOP senators were quoted to the effect that Riegle's confrontational approach cost him legitimacy.

That was Ruppe's best weapon against Riegle. With Michigan in the throes of a depression that many voters blamed on GOP policies, the time was anything but auspicious for a Republican. Moreover, Riegle's work in behalf of the auto industry had already pre-empted some traditional sources of GOP funding in Michigan, including Henry Ford II. Riegle had little trouble, winning even the Upper Peninsula, Ruppe's base.

Six years later, Michigan's Republican Party was fractured by feuding caused by their complex presidential delegate-selection process. With party regulars — loyalists of Bush — openly battling supporters of religious broadcaster Pat Robertson, the GOP scarcely had time to think about challenging Riegle. The GOP nomination fell to former Rep. Jim Dunn, an East Lansing developer who had been on the outs with the party hierarchy after a bitter and unsuccessful Senate primary bid in 1984.

While Dunn was never considered a serious threat, Riegle took no chances. His campaign produced more than 20 TV commercials, including an environmental spot featuring the senator fishing with his 4-year-old daughter, and a testimonial by New Jersey Sen. Bill Bradley likening Riegle's work on the 1988 omnibus trade bill to that of an athletic star leading his team to a championship. Pumping well over $3 million into his campaign, Riegle outspent Dunn nearly 8-to-1 and won 60 percent of the vote.

Committees

Banking, Housing & Urban Affairs (Chairman)

Budget (4th of 12 Democrats)

Finance (7th of 11 Democrats)
Health for Families & the Uninsured (chairman); Deficits, Debt Management & Long-Term Economic Growth; International Trade

Elections

1988 General

Donald W. Riegle Jr. (D)	2,116,865	(60%)
Jim Dunn (R)	1,348,219	(38%)

Previous Winning Percentages: **1982** (58%) **1976** (53%) **1974 *** (65%) **1972 *†** (71%) **1970 *†** (69%) **1968 *†** (61%) **1966 *†** (54%)

** House elections.*
† Riegle was elected as a Republican in 1966-72.

Campaign Finance

	Receipts	Receipts from PACs		Expend-itures
1988				
Riegle (D)	$3,289,327	$1,281,641	(39%)	$3,383,849
Dunn (R)	$470,976	$8,055	(2%)	$442,693

Key Votes

1993

Require unpaid family and medical leave	Y
Approve national "motor voter" registration bill	Y
Approve budget increasing taxes and reducing deficit	Y
Support president's right to lift military gay ban	Y

1992

Approve school-choice pilot program	N
Allow shifting funds from defense to domestic programs	Y
Oppose deeper cuts in spending for SDI	N

1991

Approve waiting period for handgun purchases	Y
Raise senators' pay and ban honoraria	N
Authorize use of force in Persian Gulf	N
Confirm Clarence Thomas to Supreme Court	N

Voting Studies

	Presidential Support		Party Unity		Conservative Coalition	
Year	**S**	**O**	**S**	**O**	**S**	**O**
1992	28	68	83	8	24	68
1991	33	67	93	7	28	73
1990	30	63	85	12	27	70
1989	45	54	93	5	13	84
1988	41	57	94	3	24	73
1987	35	64	92	6	19	78
1986	18	82	96	4	5	95
1985	24	74	87	10	22	75
1984	31	68	92	6	2	98
1983	34	64	93	4	14 †	86 †
1982	24	66	89	3	4	86
1981	34	60	88	4	7	87

† Not eligible for all recorded votes.

Interest Group Ratings

Year	ADA	AFL-CIO	CCUS	ACU
1992	95	92	38	4
1991	90	83	10	14
1990	83	78	25	9
1989	85	100	38	12
1988	90	93	36	4
1987	100	100	17	4
1986	95	93	26	9
1985	95	90	24	4
1984	100	100	28	5
1983	85	94	28	4
1982	80	92	16	24
1981	90	89	22	14

Carl Levin (D)

Of Detroit — Elected 1978; 3rd Term

Born: June 28, 1934, Detroit, Mich.
Education: Swarthmore College, B.A. 1956; Harvard U., LL.B. 1959.
Occupation: Lawyer.
Family: Wife, Barbara Halpern; three children.
Religion: Jewish.
Political Career: Detroit City Council, 1970-77, president, 1974-77.
Capitol Office: 459 Russell Bldg. 20510; 224-6221.

In Washington: Levin, who is midway through his third Senate term, is intelligent, reasonable, aware of Michigan interests and liberal. He has prospered in the not-so-liberal world of Michigan politics by emphasizing the first three traits — and playing down the fourth.

Levin votes much like the majority of his Democratic colleagues on social policy issues. He favors abortion rights and was one of only three Democrats on the Senate Armed Services Committee to announce support quickly for President Clinton's January 1993 proposal to end the ban on homosexuals serving in the military.

Levin also backs most federal programs that benefit the poor, but he acknowledges the need to rethink some old-fashioned liberal assumptions. "We messed up those social programs," he likes to say. "Those of us who believe in them have an obligation to make them work."

Levin is very cautious about throwing money at social problems. The theme of fiscal responsibility is a popular one in Michigan, where a large constituency of voters is dissatisfied with government economic policy and especially angry about taxes. In keeping with that, Levin has established himself as a "hawk" on reducing the federal deficit. In June 1992, he was one of six senators who appeared on ABC-TV's "Nightline" to propose a series of one-hour televised sessions in which the presidential candidates would be grilled on their plans for deficit reduction.

Levin cheered in January 1993 when Leon E. Panetta, Clinton's nominee to direct the Office of Management and Budget, told the Governmental Affairs Committee that deficit reduction was a top administration priority and that all items — including entitlement cuts and unpopular tax increases — would be on the table for discussion. "Stick to your guns," said Levin, a senior member of the committee. "Without all of them, we're not going to get any of them."

Levin showed no inclination to stray from the new administration's position when Republicans and some conservative Democrats criticized Clinton's initial budget proposals as leaning too heavily on raising taxes and not enough on cutting spending. Levin voted in March 1993 for the budget resolution that upheld Clinton's economic outline.

Although the Michigan Democrat expressed concern about the budgetary impact of Clinton's proposed $16 billion "economic stimulus" package, he voted in April 1993 in favor of the unsuccessful efforts by the Democratic leadership to end a Republican filibuster.

As a member of Armed Services, Levin has taken a high-profile role in arguing to preserve funding for conventional weapons systems, especially the M-1 tank built in Michigan. But he was sharply critical of much of the Reagan and Bush administrations' defense policy.

Levin, now a well-tenured chairman of an Armed Services subcommittee (known as Coalition Defense and Reinforcing Forces in the 103rd Congress), complained that the Republican administrations put too much emphasis on buying complicated new weapons systems, especially nuclear ones, while skimping on maintenance and production of conventional weaponry.

Though he was once one of the few liberal members to support the radar-evading, ultra-expensive B-2 "stealth" bomber, he changed his mind during the 102nd Congress. He proposed an unsuccessful amendment in 1992 that would have blocked funding of an additional four B-2s for a total fleet of 20. Citing their cost, Levin said they "don't add $2.5 billion worth of military capability."

Levin also bases his defense arguments on strategic grounds. He opposed the Reagan-Bush vision of the Strategic Defense Initiative — a network of space-based weapons armed to shoot down enemy missiles — as a destabilizing violation of the Anti-Ballistic Missile (ABM) treaty with the Soviet Union.

In 1991, Armed Services Committee Chairman Sam Nunn, who favored a ground-based ABM system, reached an agreement with conservative Republicans who wanted a more expansive system: SDI funding would emphasize research into a ground-based system, but a renegotiation to liberalize the ABM treaty would be urged. Levin opposed this pact as opening the door to removal of all ABM restrictions. Although other measures proposed by Democratic SDI opponents to rein in the deal failed, Levin attached a provision stating that the legislation did not authorize any violation of the ABM Treaty.

In January 1991, Levin voted against giving President Bush authorization to use force against Iraq. But he took a more hawkish stand against Serb forces accused of committing atrocities against Muslims and Croats in the former Yugoslav republic of Bosnia.

The Senate in June 1992 passed Levin's resolution calling on President Bush to urge the United Nations' leadership to draw up plans for "such intervention as may be necessary" to enforce its demand to Serbian forces for a cease-fire. The next month, Levin made a floor speech urging military force if necessary to stop atrocities in Serb-run internment camps.

Outside of defense issues, much of Levin's legislative effort is devoted to issues that could fall into the broad category sometimes known as "good government." The chairman of the Governmental Affairs Subcommittee on Oversight of Government Management, he is the author of a bill, first proposed in the 102nd Congress and passed by the Senate early in the 103rd, to require stricter reporting requirements for Washington lobbyists.

In December 1992, Levin praised the ethics guidelines that Clinton instituted for top government officials. "No one has a God-given right to 'cash in' on his or her public service," Levin said.

Levin is also co-author with Republican Sen. William S. Cohen of Maine of a bill to reauthorize the independent counsel law for five years. The law, which required the attorney general to appoint an independent prosecutor to investigate criminal allegations against certain top executive branch officials, expired in December 1992.

The law lapsed after Levin's efforts to pass an extension fell short in the 102nd Congress. He was blocked by Republicans who argued that the Justice Department was capable of investigating executive branch wrongdoing without an independent council and who objected that the law was not mandatory for members of Congress. But their main complaint was that Democrats had wielded the law against Republican administrations, pointing to the lengthy, expensive probe by independent counsel Lawrence E. Walsh into the Iran-contra affair.

Levin said that Republicans were "killing the most important single Watergate reform on the books." He also reacted angrily in December 1992 when Bush pardoned former Defense Secretary Caspar W. Weinberger and five other Reagan administration officials who had been indicted or convicted on charges relating to the Iran-contra scandal.

Governmental Affairs was also the forum for Levin's most conspicuous crusade to reform the federal bureaucracy: He favored a legislative veto that would allow Congress to revoke federal regulations of all sorts. Levin had some success here early in his Senate career, but it was largely overturned by the Supreme Court in 1983.

At Home: Levin has made it through two re-election campaigns waged in years not entirely favorable to his party. In 1984, Levin survived a big Reagan presidential victory in Michigan; six years later, Levin won comfortably even as the state's Democratic governor was being ousted from office.

Levin had been anticipating a tough race in 1984 and pumped up his fundraising with dire warnings that the national GOP planned to spend millions against him. The warnings worked so well that Levin outspent his Republican opponent, former astronaut Jack Lousma, who went heavily into debt in the primary and was strapped for funds in the fall campaign.

But Levin needed more than a monetary advantage as Walter F. Mondale's presidential campaign faded and it became apparent that Ronald Reagan's coattails could cause Levin real problems. So he unveiled an "October surprise." He aired a film clip of Lousma warming up a Japanese audience in 1983 by telling them about the Toyota he owned. In Michigan, where Japanese cars mean joblessness for auto workers, Lousma's statement was a major embarrassment. Few were soothed by his plea that the Toyota belonged not to him, but to his son.

The Toyota film clip meshed well with Levin's overall campaign theme; he had billed himself as "A Proven Fighter for Michigan" and stressed his work to limit auto imports, extend unemployment benefits and help relieve the state unemployment compensation debt.

Lousma, who had flown on Skylab and space shuttle missions in the 1970s and early 1980s, was strongly supported by anti-abortion forces, anti-tax advocates and other conservative Republicans, who helped him win nomination. But he suffered from his own unfamiliarity with politics and Michigan issues. He had retired from NASA in Houston and moved to his boyhood home of Grand Rapids just before launching his campaign.

In spite of those handicaps, Lousma might have been able to ride Reagan's coattails to victory had Levin's fundraising been less vigorous and his strategy less well devised. Reagan carried Michigan with 59 percent, but Levin held on to win with 52 percent.

In 1990, Levin's political skills were again on view. With national GOP leaders sharpening their knives for him, Levin amassed a daunting campaign treasury and early on aired television ads touting his accomplishments. Only after his opponent, GOP Rep. Bill Schuette, began attacking did Levin fire back, thereby preserving his "nice guy" image.

Schuette tried to link Levin to senior Sen. Donald W. Riegle Jr. — then under scrutiny for his ties to the S&L crisis — by charging that both men were party to "cozy deals" in Washington. He also tried to paint Levin as soft on defense.

But Levin's past support for conventional weaponry protected him from Schuette's assault. And the Republican, who had battled perceptions of superficiality, never developed the stature he needed to get into Levin's weight class. As Democratic Gov. James J. Blanchard lost his bid for a third term, Levin won a decisive 57 percent of the vote.

Levin's older brother, Sander, now in the House, first spread the family name statewide with gubernatorial campaigns in 1970 and 1974. Carl Levin made his name in politics in the mid-1970s as president of the Detroit City Council, where he teamed with black Mayor Coleman A. Young to provide for demolition of thousands of abandoned buildings. The two strayed apart at times in the late 1970s, but this probably helped Levin in later statewide races by showing suburban voters that he was not inextricably tied to Detroit's black majority.

The big break in Levin's successful 1978 Senate challenge was a major misstep by the GOP incumbent, Robert P. Griffin. Disappointed at losing the contest for Senate Republican leader in 1977, Griffin announced that he would retire the next year and began skipping votes on the floor. He eventually changed his mind about running, but by that time had missed a third of the Senate votes over an entire year. Levin said Griffin was obviously tired of the job, and the voters agreed that the incumbent deserved a rest.

Committees

Armed Services (3rd of 11 Democrats)
Coalition Defense & Reinforcing Forces (chairman); Defense Technology, Acquisition & Industrial Base; Nuclear Deterrence, Arms Control & Defense Intelligence

Governmental Affairs (3rd of 8 Democrats)
Oversight of Government Management (chairman); Permanent Subcommittee on Investigations; Regulation & Government Information

Small Business (3rd of 12 Democrats)
Innovation, Manufacturing & Technology (chairman); Rural Economy & Family Farming

Elections

1990 General

Carl Levin (D)	1,471,753	(57%)
Bill Schuette (R)	1,055,695	(41%)
Susan Farquhar (WW)	32,796	(1%)

Previous Winning Percentages: 1984 (52%) **1978** (52%)

Campaign Finance

	Receipts	Receipts from PACs		Expend-itures
1990				
Levin (D)	$6,948,096	$1,392,502	(20%)	$6,930,262
Schuette (R)	$2,488,958	$735,932	(30%)	$2,417,705

Key Votes

1993	
Require unpaid family and medical leave	Y
Approve national "motor voter" registration bill	Y
Approve budget increasing taxes and reducing deficit	Y
Support president's right to lift military gay ban	Y
1992	
Approve school-choice pilot program	N
Allow shifting funds from defense to domestic programs	Y
Oppose deeper cuts in spending for SDI	N
1991	
Approve waiting period for handgun purchases	Y
Raise senators' pay and ban honoraria	N
Authorize use of force in Persian Gulf	N
Confirm Clarence Thomas to Supreme Court	N

Voting Studies

	Presidential Support		Party Unity		Conservative Coalition	
Year	**S**	**O**	**S**	**O**	**S**	**O**
1992	32	67	91	8	21	76
1991	37	63	90	10	30	70
1990	33	66	82	18	35	65
1989	50	50	80	16	39	61
1988	42	52	91	6	14	84
1987	32	67	89	8	28	69
1986	23	77	91	9	11	88
1985	25	73	89	6	25	72
1984	34	61	89	8	9	85
1983	33	66	86	12	14	82
1982	34	63	92	6	5	94
1981	35	63	92	5	6	93

Interest Group Ratings

Year	ADA	AFL-CIO	CCUS	ACU
1992	100	92	20	0
1991	90	75	0	5
1990	78	78	33	22
1989	80	100	25	14
1988	80	92	21	0
1987	90	90	17	4
1986	90	87	26	9
1985	85	90	31	4
1984	100	82	35	14
1983	95	94	16	8
1982	95	96	14	20
1981	100	100	0	7

1 Bart Stupak (D)

Of Menominee — Elected 1992; 1st Term

Born: Feb. 29, 1952, Milwaukee, Wis.
Education: Northwestern Michigan College, A.A. 1972; Saginaw Valley State College, B.S. 1977; Thomas M. Cooley Law School, J.D. 1981.
Occupation: Lawyer; state trooper; patrolman.
Family: Wife, Laurie Ann Olsen; two children.
Religion: Roman Catholic.
Political Career: Mich. House, 1989-91; sought Democratic nomination for Mich. Senate, 1990.
Capitol Office: 317 Cannon Bldg. 20515; 225-4735.

The Path to Washington: Stupak's brand of moderate-to-liberal economics and conservative social values proved to be the perfect combination to win in this vast, rural northern Michigan district. Democrats have won here only twice before in the past 60 years. But Stupak may have put together a strong enough résumé to hold on to the 1st for as long as he wants.

In a general-election campaign where the two major-party candidates agreed on almost everything except the scope of reform of the nation's health-care system, Stupak, the home-grown outsider, easily beat his better-financed, more experienced opponent, Philip E. Ruppe. Stupak stung him with a 54 percent to 44 percent margin, even though late summer polls had indicated a Ruppe victory.

A lawyer previously in private practice in Menominee, far out on the UP — the Upper Peninsula on the Wisconsin border — Stupak prides himself on his "Yooper" background. He was once a state trooper and served one term in the state House before quitting to run unsuccessfully for the state Senate.

Stupak, like most of the Roman Catholics on the UP, opposes abortion. And he opposes gun control. But he is far more concerned about jobs in the district, where the copper and iron mines have largely played out and the military is about the biggest employer.

Like his predecessor, Stupak will serve on two committees essential to the district's livelihood — Armed Services and Merchant Marine and Fisheries. The continued operation of the K. I. Sawyer Air Force Base south of Marquette is crucial to the UP economy, and Stupak had hoped that his Armed Services seat would bring him the opportunity to send defense contracts north. Instead, he found himself fighting for the base's very existence when Sawyer appeared on the 1993 Base Closure Commission's list.

Merchant Marine will be important if Stupak is to achieve his goal of stopping all waste discharges into the Great Lakes.

To win the seat, Stupak had to survive both a three-way primary and a general-election fight that Republicans worked hard to win.

Ruppe had represented the district from 1967 until 1979, when he was caught in the political equivalent of musical chairs. Ruppe yielded his secure seat to run for the Senate, when it appeared that Republican incumbent Robert P. Griffin would not run again. But Griffin changed his mind, leaving Ruppe with no place to go.

Republican Robert W. Davis inherited the district, and almost certainly would have retained it in 1992, except for the House bank scandal. Tagged as the third leading abuser with 878 overdrafts, Davis made an appeal to the 1st's voters. But when it became clear they would neither forgive nor forget, he quit his reelection bid.

Two Republicans and three Democrats (including Stupak) were soon in the race. And state and national GOP leaders were concerned that their candidates were not strong enough to hold the seat. They recruited Ruppe to return from Washington, where he worked as a lobbyist for a Michigan mining company.

Ruppe easily won his primary; Stupak had more trouble.

He carried the UP, where most Democrats are concentrated, and restaurateur Mike McElroy took most of the votes from Lower Michigan, where he lives. That gave Stupak a 49 percent to 43 percent plurality, with the balance going to a third LP candidate, respiratory therapist Daniel F. Herringa, who ran a no-budget campaign.

Stupak then turned his fire on Ruppe, branding him a carpetbagger and the choice of insiders.

Stupak and Ruppe agreed on the need to eliminate the federal government's red ink. However, Stupak favors a balanced-budget constitutional amendment only if other efforts fail. Their biggest disagreement was over health care. Ruppe insisted that fine-tuning the existing private insurance-based system was sufficient. Stupak called for a national health insurance system.

Michigan 1

Upper Peninsula; northern Lower Michigan

Built in 1957, the Mackinac Bridge connects the 1st's two regions — Michigan's Upper Peninsula (UP) and northern Lower Michigan.

Above the Straits of Mackinac, the UP covers 315 miles of woodland, bordering Wisconsin and Canada. Three of the Great Lakes form its boundaries — Huron to the southeast, Michigan to the south and Superior to the north.

The UP's rugged terrain breeds a special brand of independence, qualities ascribed to the "Yoopers" that live here. They must contend with prevailing northwesterly winds that dump several hundred inches of snow every year in the northern reaches of the area. And economic opportunity has been in short supply since the mining industries began to fade at the turn of the century.

The western UP has been hit the hardest. The extraction of copper, iron and timber long supported the area, but mining is almost non-existent and timber jobs have dwindled. Tourism and recreation are the only growth industries.

Known as "Copper Country," these western counties once produced about 90 percent of the copper mined in the United States. But by 1890, most of the purest copper had been mined and prices began to fall.

Calumet, located in the northwestern arm of the UP, was once a booming copper-mining town of 50,000. Now it is a village of 4,000. On Lake Superior, Marquette tells the same story. Some shipping still departs from the city, but many of the ore docks are abandoned. Still, Marquette County is the UP's most populous.

Marquette's economy was hit hard again when K. I. Sawyer Air Force Base showed up on the 1993 base-closure list. The base's payroll for 3,000 military and civilian employees is responsible for about 20 percent of the local economy.

The descendants of the miners, loggers, mill workers and longshoremen retain a union-oriented tradition, thus making the western UP a Democratic stronghold. In the open 1992 House race, Stupak won every county north of the Straits of Mackinac — the dividing line between the UP and Lower Michigan.

The UP's eastern section votes more like the counties south of the bridge. Chippewa and Mackinac counties lean Republican and are more dependent on tourism and farming. The only major city in this area is Sault Ste. Marie (Chippewa), a port city on the Canadian border. In 1992, Chippewa was the only UP county to vote for George Bush.

About half the district vote is cast on the Republican turf south of the bridge. The population center of northern Lower Michigan is Traverse City (Grand Traverse County), a GOP stronghold. Tourists and vacationers come for the resorts, golf courses and sandy beaches of Grand Traverse Bay.

Outside the Traverse City area, the communities are a conservative lot, though newly arrived retired autoworkers have boosted the Democratic vote in Cheboygan, Emmet, and Presque Isle counties.

1990 Population: 580,956. White 558,614 (96%), Black 4,909 (1%), Other 17,433 (3%). Hispanic origin 3,308 (1%). 18 and over 431,643 (74%), 62 and over 108,423 (19%). Median age: 35.

Committees

Armed Services (26th of 34 Democrats)
Military Acquisition; Military Forces & Personnel

Merchant Marine & Fisheries (25th of 29 Democrats)
Coast Guard & Navigation; Merchant Marine

Campaign Finance

	Receipts	Receipts from PACs		Expend-itures
1992				
Stupak (D)	$225,699	$104,950	(46%)	$225,572
Ruppe (R)	$458,270	$131,250	(29%)	$449,464

Key Votes

1993

Require parental notification of minors' abortions	N
Require unpaid family and medical leave	Y
Approve national "motor voter" registration bill	Y
Approve budget increasing taxes and reducing deficit	Y
Approve economic stimulus plan	Y

Elections

1992 General		
Bart Stupak (D)	144,857	(54%)
Philip E. Ruppe (R)	117,056	(44%)
Gerald Aydlott (LIBERT)	4,094	(2%)
1992 Primary		
Bart Stupak (D)	24,034	(49%)
Mike McElroy (D)	21,304	(43%)
Daniel F. Herringa (D)	4,085	(8%)

District Vote for President

1992

D 118,879 (42%)
R 100,997 (35%)
I 65,339 (23%)

2 Peter Hoekstra (R)

Of Holland — Elected 1992; 1st Term

Born: Oct. 30, 1953, Groningen, Netherlands.
Education: Hope College, B.A. 1975; U. of Michigan, M.B.A. 1977.
Occupation: Furniture company executive.
Family: Wife, Diane M. Johnson; three children.
Religion: Christian Reformed.
Political Career: No previous office.
Capitol Office: 1319 Longworth Bldg. 20515; 225-4401.

The Path to Washington: A furniture executive who never before held or aspired to political office, Hoekstra, who unseated veteran Rep. Guy Vander Jagt in the GOP primary, is one of the few true outsiders in the freshman class.

He brings to Washington few notions about what government should or should not do. Instead, he talked as much in his campaign about his family, his religious upbringing and his job as product manager for one of the country's largest furniture manufacturers as he did about issues facing Congress.

He cast himself as a coalition builder, and said restoring the public's confidence in government was his chief goal as a freshman.

He is nevertheless quite conservative, and lists reducing the deficit, curtailing government intrusion on business and elimination of waste and pork-barreling as priorities. He claims a bias against increasing taxes, but said he will support policies that result in a fair sharing of the burden of deficit reduction.

He refused to embrace quick fixes for the deficit, saying that the unwavering anti-deficit pledges issued by many candidates were but hollow campaign gimmicks that failed to account for the complexity of issues that bedevil Congress.

Hoekstra worries that the pending North American Free Trade Agreement represents a threat to his district's sizable asparagus industry. But his solution is not to reject reduced tariffs on Mexican growers, but rather to ease the regulatory and paperwork burden on domestic producers to make it easier and less costly for them to compete.

Like many freshmen, Hoekstra supports term limits for House members, pledging to depart after 12 years in office. Unlike many freshmen, Hoekstra accepted no political action committee funds in the latest election cycle — he was one of only 11 to decline the money.

The Netherlands-born Hoekstra provided a textbook case of how money and other advantages of incumbency can be overcome by good old-fashioned politicking. He upset Vander Jagt, attacking the 26-year veteran for being too concerned with national party fundraising — he was chairman of the National Republican Congressional Committee — and out of touch with the voters at home.

Lacking name recognition, Hoekstra embarked on an intense grass-roots campaign. He saved his vacation to take a county-by-county bicycle tour of the 2nd, which runs 140 miles along Lake Michigan, the state's western border.

Unable to afford television ads, Hoekstra advertised on radio and campaigned door to door. The latter proved an especially useful way to show that if Vander Jagt was no longer close to the people, at least Hoekstra would be.

The incumbent had barely survived the 1990 general election, winning 55 percent against a relatively unknown Democrat in an overwhelmingly Republican district. His chief liability was an ABC News exposé that October of House Ways and Means Committee members cavorting on a Barbados beach with lobbyists, while ostensibly on a trade study mission. Vander Jagt ranked No. 2 on the GOP side of the committee aisle, and his gamboling in the Caribbean, which was nearly fatal in 1990, was a killer when Hoekstra gave voters a conservative alternative.

Vander Jagt also wounded himself by coming to the defense of GOP Rep. Robert W. Davis, who represented the northern part of Michigan and was named as one of the abusers in the 1992 House bank overdraft scandal. (Davis eventually decided to retire.)

But Vander Jagt did not go down without a fight. He was well-financed during the 1992 campaign and embarked on a last-minute media blitz touting his effectiveness in Washington. The message did not sell, however, and Hoekstra won with 46 percent to Vander Jagt's 40 percent in a three-way race.

It was perhaps to Hoekstra's advantage that the redrawn district included most of one large county, and part of a second, that were new territory for Vander Jagt. Though the incumbent carried the other eight counties in the 2nd, these two — Allegan and Ottawa, the district's most populous — went for Hoekstra.

The general election was largely an afterthought. Hoekstra took 63 percent.

Michigan 2

West — Holland; Muskegon

In terms of GOP hegemony, the 2nd is rivaled only by the 3rd District as the state's staunchest Republican district. From the fruit and vegetable farmers to the conservative Dutch communities on the 2nd's southern border, Democrats find little sympathy.

The district covers nearly 100 miles of Lake Michigan shoreline, from Manistee County south to Allegan County, but population is concentrated in three counties — Allegan, Muskegon and Ottawa.

The city of Holland, on the border between Allegan and Ottawa counties, is a GOP bastion with a strong Dutch influence. The westernmost point of the "Dutch Triangle" (formed by Holland, Grand Rapids and Kalamazoo), Holland and its environs were settled by immigrants from the Netherlands in the mid-19th century.

That heritage is highlighted at an entertainment complex — Dutch Village — where life in the Old Country is replicated, or at the city's two wooden shoe factories. In May, the city hosts a Tulip Festival.

Ottawa County has voted Republican in every presidential election since 1928. In 1988, it voted for George Bush by better than 3-to-1, and gave 68 percent to the GOP's ill-fated Senate nominee, Jim Dunn. Four years later, Bush took 59 percent, 22 points higher than his statewide average. Even Hoekstra, the relatively unknown Republican who upset longtime incumbent GOP Rep. Guy Vander Jagt in the 1992 primary, won 63 percent in November.

Hoekstra's career as an executive with office furniture maker Herman Miller Inc. was a mark in his favor. Three of the nation's four top office furniture makers are based in western Michigan, and the fourth has a major plant in the region. Two of the companies — Herman Miller and Haworth Inc. — have headquarters here.

The 2nd's limited Democratic strength is found north of Ottawa and Allegan counties in and around the industrial city of Muskegon. The city has one of western Michigan's heaviest manufacturing bases, including a number of primary metal industries (such as foundries), fabricated metal producers, and machinery operations, all of which have been struggling.

The black inland precincts and the city's ethnic neighborhoods turn out a strong Democratic vote, though the surrounding suburbs often offset their votes. Heavily forested Lake and Manistee counties are also sources of Democratic votes, as is the small industrial city of Cadillac (Wexford County).

Tourism, farming and food-processing are the economic mainstays for the rest of the district. Towns along the Lake Michigan shoreline, such as Manistee, are heavily reliant on retirees, Chicago tourists and boaters who sail across the lake into their municipal marinas.

Cherries and asparagus are among the products grown by local farms and processed within the district. Fremont, in Newaygo County, is home to the international headquarters of Gerber baby foods.

1990 Population: 580,956. White 539,604 (93%), Black 25,324 (4%), Other 16,028 (3%). Hispanic origin 17,586 (3%). 18 and over 414,968 (71%), 62 and over 86,799 (15%). Median age: 32.

Committees

Education & Labor (13th of 15 Republicans)
Labor-Management Relations; Labor Standards, Occupational Health & Safety; Postsecondary Education

Public Works & Transportation (23rd of 24 Republicans)
Economic Development; Water Resources & the Environment

Campaign Finance

	Receipts	Receipts from PACs		Expend-itures
1992				
Hoekstra (R)	$104,861	0		$100,278
Miltner (D)	$21,447	$6,000	(28%)	$20,518
Jacobs (LIBERT)	$1,757	0		$981

Key Votes

1993

Require parental notification of minors' abortions	Y
Require unpaid family and medical leave	N
Approve national "motor voter" registration bill	N
Approve budget increasing taxes and reducing deficit	N
Approve economic stimulus plan	N

Elections

1992 General		
Peter Hoekstra (R)	155,577	(63%)
John H. Miltner (D)	86,265	(35%)
Dick Jacobs (LIBERT)	4,840	(2%)
1992 Primary		
Peter Hoekstra (R)	34,572	(46%)
Guy Vander Jagt (R)	30,203	(40%)
Melvin J. DeStigter (R)	10,141	(14%)

District Vote for President

	1992	
D	95,342	(34%)
R	127,008	(45%)
I	58,258	(21%)

3 Paul B. Henry (R)

Of Grand Rapids — Elected 1984; 5th Term

Born: July 9, 1942, Chicago, Ill.
Education: Wheaton College, B.A. 1963; Duke U., M.A. 1968, Ph.D. 1970.
Occupation: Professor.
Family: Wife, Karen Anne Borthistle; three children.
Religion: Christian Reformed.
Political Career: Mich. House, 1979-83; Mich. Senate, 1983-85.
Capitol Office: 1526 Longworth Bldg. 20515; 225-3831.

In Washington: In the spring of 1993, Henry took out an ad in Roll Call, a Capitol Hill newspaper, addressed to his colleagues. In the ad he talked about his struggle with cancer, his abiding religious faith and his gratitude for his colleagues' emotional support during his ordeal.

"I count as one of God's great blessings the opportunity I have to serve with so many fine people. Caring and thoughtfulness know no political party," Henry said in the ad. "Please know that despite the frustration of continuing my recovery at home, I remain determined to return to the fray on Capitol Hill."

Coming from Henry, the ad, filled with passionate feeling and candor about God and Henry's fondness for his friends in Congress, was not surprising. Long before he was diagnosed with a malignant brain tumor, Henry had not been one to hide his evangelical Christian beliefs.

Henry was diagnosed as having a lethal form of cancer in the fall of 1992 and underwent surgery just two weeks before being elected to his fifth term. Doctors removed a 3-inch tumor from his brain. At the start of the 103rd Congress, he was continuing periodic chemotherapy. He returned to the House chamber in the 103rd for his swearing-in Jan. 5 to a tearful reception from colleagues.

During his first four terms in Congress, Henry had the ability to sound eminently reasonable and somewhat self-righteous at the same time. He strikes this curious balance by combining the conservative instincts of an evangelical Christian, the open mind of a former Peace Corps volunteer and the intellectual approach of a political scientist.

This combination of traits has made Henry a much talked-about politician. As far back as 1984, when he was seeking his first House term, syndicated columnist David S. Broder foresaw a career in the Senate for the gifted Republican.

But for all the respect his integrity earns him personally, his independence has tended to isolate rather than ingratiate him politically.

Over the years Henry has developed a reputation as one who defies labels — neither a rigid conservative, nor a moderate. He generally votes with his party (70 to 80 percent of the time) and he most often takes the party line in Education and Labor Committee sessions. Despite all this, Henry has remained independent-minded, and he has broken ranks on some key issues when his principles dictated.

Although Henry is a longtime opponent of abortion, in the 102nd Congress he voted for legislation that would have lifted the government ban on fetal tissue research. Henry said he thought it "destructive to the cause" for abortion foes to oppose research aimed at "restoring the wholeness and fullness of life, not destroying it." The bill was vetoed, however, and the House could not muster the necessary two-thirds vote to override.

In the 101st Congress, Henry parted ways with his party to vote for civil rights legislation that the Bush administration had labeled a "quota bill." In the 102nd, when the bill came up again, he voted for the compromise that finally became law. The bill reversed the conservative Rehnquist Court, which in 1989 had restricted the reach and remedies of federal anti-discrimination laws. Henry also voted for an anti-crime package that included a waiting period for handgun purchases. (Michigan already has such a law.) Most Republicans opposed the bill.

But it is not possible to categorize Henry as a liberal Republican, either. In the 102nd Congress, as ranking Republican of the Subcommittee on Health and Safety, Henry opposed stricter federal safety guidelines under legislation aimed at protecting construction workers, who face among the highest rates of death and injury of any workers.

Henry argued that the proposed new reporting requirement for companies would overburden the Occupational Safety and Health Administration, impeding its ability to inspect construction sites and investigate accidents.

In the 103rd, Henry moved to ranking on the Subcommittee on Human Resources. He also became ranking member on the Investiga-

Michigan 3

West Central — Grand Rapids

Politically, the Grand Rapids-based 3rd looks a lot like it did when Gerald R. Ford represented the area. Both the middle-class residents of the city and the farmers and small-town denizens of the surrounding counties make it a GOP stronghold.

Kent County is home to more than 85 percent of the population, most of whom live in Grand Rapids, Michigan's second-largest city. With its diversified economic base, the city was one of the few outside the Sunbelt to emerge relatively unscathed from the recession.

Part of the reason can be attributed to the variety of products made in Kent County. The 10 largest employers count nine different industries, including footwear and leather products, fabricated metal products, office furniture, avionics systems, automotive stampings, and children's apparel.

The furniture-making industry is one of Kent County's largest employers. Unlike the furniture industry of North Carolina, western Michigan's furniture makers mostly produce office furniture, much of it the metal variety.

Beginning with the 1970s invention of systems furniture, local companies prospered and experienced record growth. That slowed, however, by the the early 1990s as growth in office space stagnated and companies nationwide began to cut their white-collar work forces.

General Motors has a significant presence in Grand Rapids, but the city has not felt the same pain that southeastern Michigan has. Another major employer is the Amway Corp., a home- and personal-care products company whose Amway Grand Hotel dominates the newly emerging skyline. The DeVos family, which runs the company, is a leading financial supporter of the state Republican Party.

Grand Rapids has a sizable blue-collar work force — and a high number of black and Hispanic residents for western Michigan — many of whom have moved to townships north and south of the city. Still, it is not nearly enough to offset the GOP wave from the rest of the city and county.

The local GOP has two wings. The "Dutch Wing" is more conservative, made up of white-collar executives and the small Christian college communities. The "Ford Wing" is a more moderate brand of Republicanism, found mostly in the northeast, East Grand Rapids and Kentwood.

George Bush breezed in Kent County in 1992, and Rep. Henry did even better, despite the disclosure of his life-threatening illness. Across the district, Bush won easily, carrying the 3rd with 47 percent.

Outside Kent, in Ionia County and part of Barry County, the 3rd is Republican and agriculture-oriented, though not fruit-producing like coastal western Michigan. Ionia County has no town or village even close to having 10,000 residents.

Flat, rural and Republican Barry County is home to Hastings, which boasts the distinction of being listed in a 1993 book as one of America's 100 best small towns.

1990 Population: 580,956. White 520,262 (90%), Black 43,356 (7%), Other 17,338 (3%). Hispanic origin 16,069 (3%). 18 and over 416,628 (72%), 62 and over 75,777 (13%). Median age: 31.

tions and Oversight Subcommittee of Science, Space and Technology.

Henry also has pushed for funds for his district. In the 102nd, $2.4 million Henry requested was included in the highway bill to construct a bypass in Grand Rapids.

During debate in the 101st Congress over the National Endowment for the Arts' funding of controversial works, Henry was committed to saving the NEA and convincing Congress that restrictions on obscenity were only fair to taxpayers. "I am your friend, I support the arts personally," he said. "But please do not blind yourself to political reality. . . . In order to save [the NEA] we are going to have to reform it."

His proposal would have restricted funding of projects that "deliberately denigrate" the United States or religious, racial or ethnic groups, and he called for the NEA to uphold "general standards of decency." As the debate wore on, however, Henry's attempt to find a middle ground placed him well to the right of those in the thick of the legislative fight. In a nod to his efforts, his language on "standards of decency" was included in the final measure.

In the 102nd, Henry continued to work to advance his national bottle bill, which has been bottled up in committee for years. Modeled on Michigan's legislation, Henry's plan would require a 5-cent deposit on beverage containers — glass, aluminum and plastic.

In the 100th Congress, when the Education and Labor Subcommittee on Health and Safety debated legislation to require notification of workers who might be exposed to hazardous substances, Henry commended the bill's "very laudable goals" but took a lead in warning of "an avalanche" of new liability problems. A substitute he offered to mandate stricter enforcement of existing laws was rejected on a largely party-line vote.

At Home: Though the national GOP was touting Reagan-style conservatism when Henry won his seat in 1984, he built his political credentials in the party's moderate wing. A political scientist by profession, his introduction to the practical side of politics came when he worked as an aide to Illinois Rep. John B. Anderson in the late 1960s. Elected to the state House in 1978, Henry backed Anderson in Michigan's 1980 GOP presidential primary.

Henry's centrist outlook was the norm for the state GOP in the 1970s, when moderate William G. Milliken was governor. But after the GOP lost the governorship in 1982, the state party shifted right. In his initial House campaign, Henry tried to keep step while retaining his moderate image. "I'm a fiscal conservative," he said, "but not a Scrooge." In the GOP primary, Henry was challenged from the right by Keary W. Sawyer, the son of retiring GOP Rep. Harold S. Sawyer.

But Henry contrasted his record in the state House, where he was assistant floor leader, and in the state Senate, where he chaired the Education and Health Committee, with his foe's lack of experience.

Sawyer had never sought public office and was not plugged into the local party network because his father lacked close ties with the GOP establishment. Henry won the nomination decisively. That fall, he faced Democrat Gary J. McInerney, a lawyer and businessman who seemed to have appeal beyond his party's normal base. But the political neophyte was no match for Henry, who as a state legislator had served about half the people in the old 5th.

Henry won that first fall race with 62 percent and went on to win three more terms with vote shares in excess of 70 percent. With that trajectory, he was often mentioned as potential statewide candidate, and his base has remained solid. Even after redistricting and after the disclosure of his medical condition late in the 1992 campaign, Henry managed to win with more than 60 percent of the vote.

Committees

Education & Labor (7th of 15 Republicans)
Human Resources (ranking); Postsecondary Education

Science, Space & Technology (5th of 22 Republicans)
Investigations & Oversight (ranking)

Elections

1992 General		
Paul B. Henry (R)	162,451	(61%)
Carol S. Kooistra (D)	95,927	(36%)
Richard Whitelock (LIBERT)	3,232	(1%)
Susan Normandin (NL)	3,228	(1%)
1990 General		
Paul B. Henry (R)	126,308	(75%)
Thomas Trzybinski (D)	41,170	(25%)

Previous Winning Percentages: **1988** (73%) **1986** (71%) **1984** (62%)

District Vote for President

	1992
D	94,721 (34%)
R	128,677 (47%)
I	52,779 (19%)

Campaign Finance

	Receipts	Receipts from PACs		Expend-itures
1992				
Henry (R)	$349,444	$72,650	(21%)	$282,472
Kooistra (D)	$43,258	$20,600	(48%)	$44,866
1990				
Henry (R)	$398,627	$92,880	(23%)	$241,151

Key Votes

1993	
Require parental notification of minors' abortions	?
Require unpaid family and medical leave	?
Approve national "motor voter" registration bill	?
Approve budget increasing taxes and reducing deficit	?
Approve economic stimulus plan	?
1992	
Approve balanced-budget constitutional amendment	Y
Close down space station program	Y
Approve U.S. aid for former Soviet Union	Y
Allow shifting funds from defense to domestic programs	N
1991	
Extend unemployment benefits using deficit financing	Y
Approve waiting period for handgun purchases	Y
Authorize use of force in Persian Gulf	Y

Voting Studies

	Presidential Support		Party Unity		Conservative Coalition	
Year	**S**	**O**	**S**	**O**	**S**	**O**
1992	59	39	78	19	73	27
1991	64	35	74	24	78	22
1990	58	40	75	21	70	30
1989	66	33	69	29	80	20
1988	49	48	81	17	84	11
1987	56	42	75	22	77	23
1986	43	57	67	31	66	34
1985	60	40	69	29	65	35

Interest Group Ratings

Year	ADA	AFL-CIO	CCUS	ACU
1992	35	58	88	80
1991	30	25	80	65
1990	33	9	86	63
1989	30	8	90	68
1988	50	57	93	52
1987	36	40	87	45
1986	40	43	89	45
1985	25	24	68	67

4 Dave Camp (R)

Of Midland — Elected 1990; 2nd Term

Born: July 9, 1953, Midland, Mich.
Education: Albion College, B.A. 1975; U. of California, San Diego, J.D. 1978.
Occupation: Lawyer.
Family: Single.
Religion: Roman Catholic.
Political Career: Mich. House, 1989-91.
Capitol Office: 137 Cannon Bldg. 20515; 225-3561.

In Washington: Camp has made an unusually rapid rise to prominence, moving in just six years from serving as a congressional staffer to sitting as a junior GOP House member on the influential Ways and Means Committee.

At a time when the House Republican Conference is taking on a more aggressively confrontational tone, Camp has described himself in language that sets him a bit apart from some conservative GOP colleagues whose top priority is challenging the Democratic majority.

"You can be committed to principle and yet understand that you're working within a process that requires compromise," Camp told the Detroit News in May 1991.

Notwithstanding such intimations of pragmatism, Camp's opening bid is almost always a firmly conservative one. In his initial House campaign, he pledged he would never vote to raise taxes. On the major early priorities of the Clinton administration, Camp went down the line with his party: opposing the new president's budget blueprint and economic stimulus package, opposing unpaid family and medical leave and opposing the "motor voter" bill to broaden registration opportunities.

Camp supports a presidential line-item veto and a balanced-budget constitutional amendment, has opposed a waiting period for handgun purchases and would permit abortion only in cases of rape or incest or threat to the pregnant woman's life. When minors seek abortions at clinics that receive federal funds, he would mandate parental notification.

In a few high-profile instances as a freshman, Camp did part ways with the majority of Republicans and go against positions taken by President Bush.

In 1991, Camp voted to extend unemployment benefits to the long-term unemployed; in 1992, he voted in favor of closing down the space station program and against providing aid to the former republics of the Soviet Union. All three of those issues were sensitive ones in a district that has seen its share of economic troubles. Voters' pocketbook concerns in 1992 were sufficient to give Clinton a razor-thin victory over Bush in the 4th District's presidential voting.

But overall, Camp's party loyalty was sufficient to earn him the Ways and Means promotion, as well as an appointment as an assistant regional whip and the chairmanship of a party task force on agriculture — the latter a reflection of the important role that farming plays in his district's economy.

In his first term, Camp was the only Michigander of either party on the 45-member Agriculture Committee; he had to give up that post to move to Ways and Means, where he is expected to speak out in behalf of farmers, automobile manufacturers and other Michigan business interests.

Amid the whirl of activity on Capitol Hill aimed at changing campaign finance laws to limit the role of political action committees (PACs), Camp joins with those taking exception to the view that PACs are nefarious special-interest influences. "PACs are organizations of people who think similarly on an issue who are involved in the political process," he told the Midland Daily News. "I think we need more people involved in the political process."

In 1991, Camp took strong exception to a media account that drew a connection between his personal finances and a piece of legislation he cosponsored with 138 other members. An article in the Detroit News reported his support for a bill to provide uniform state and federal regulation of pesticides, and noted that Camp owns between $100,000 to $250,000 of stock in Midland-based Dow Chemical Co., which has a subsidiary that produces pesticides.

In a lengthy written response to the paper, Camp led off by saying, "I vehemently deny any conflict of interest...." He went on to explain that farmers and farm organizations in his district (not Dow) had urged him to support the bill; he said he favors uniform standards in order to spare farmers and other pesticide users from facing a maze of potentially conflicting local regulations.

At Home: When GOP Rep. Bill Schuette announced his campaign for the Senate in 1990,

Michigan 4

North Central — Midland

While the 4th is Michigan's second-largest district in terms of land mass (after the massive 1st), most of the district's residents live in the southern half. North of Midland, much of the terrain is forested and sparsely populated.

With few cities of size, most of the vote is cast in the small towns and farming communities that traditionally favor the GOP. Bill Clinton ran competitively in the 4th in 1992, but he is an exception to recent Democratic presidential nominees. In 1992, Rep. Camp won every county.

Midland, the site of one of the largest single chemical complexes in the United States, is the 4th's population and industrial center. There, on 1,900 acres, the Dow Chemical Co. keeps its international headquarters and produces more than 500 products. Between Dow Chemical and the Dow Corning Corp., there are more than 10,000 employees in the Midland area. Dow Corning is the world's largest producer of silicone.

Accordingly, the Dow name is firmly stamped on Midland. Residents can browse at the Grace A. Dow Memorial Library or learn about the man who started it all at the Herbert H. Dow Historical Museum. Their son, Alden, designed many of the city's churches, homes, schools and business complexes. For botanists, there is Dow Gardens.

The company also sets the tone for Midland County's Republican politics. In 1990, GOP then-Rep. Bill Schuette — a Midland native — carried the county against Democratic Sen. Carl Levin, while Republican challenger John Engler did the same in his successful gubernatorial bid against Democratic Gov. James J. Blanchard. Two years later, George Bush carried Midland County rather easily.

South of Midland, the district is primarily agricultural. The second-leading source of votes in the 4th is Saginaw County, although the city of Saginaw belongs to the 5th. The city is heavily Democratic and unionized, but the farmers to the south and west generally favor Republicans.

Clinton County sports a fair number of Lansing commuters, but they, along with farmers and small-town voters, favor Republican candidates.

Owosso (Shiawassee County) and Alma (Gratiot County) are more traditional, small manufacturing cities. Gratiot tilts Republican, but both produce some Democratic votes.

Tourism and recreation fuel the economy north of these areas. Local residents are more likely to travel farther north toward the Upper Peninsula for vacations, but many autoworkers from Michigan's industrial southeast favor the lakes and woodland of Montcalm and Mecosta counties.

Retirees from the southeastern cities have also made their mark in the far northern portion of the 4th. Counties such as Clare, Gladwin, Ogemaw and Roscommon are no longer routinely Republican; Blanchard carried three of the four in 1990 and Clinton carried all four in 1992.

1990 Population: 580,956. White 564,340 (97%), Black 6,182 (1%), Other 10,434 (2%). Hispanic origin 10,175 (2%). 18 and over 425,655 (73%), 62 and over 87,007 (15%). Median age: 32.

he endorsed Camp, a friend of his since childhood days in Midland and a former administrative assistant in his Capitol Hill office.

After a two-year stint with Schuette in Washington, Camp returned to Michigan in 1986 to manage Schuette's re-election campaign and resume his law career. But in 1988, a state representative from the district including Midland and neighboring communities announced his retirement, and Camp decided to run for the job. He won, and had barely found his chair in the Legislature when GOP strategists began talking up Schuette to run against Democratic Sen. Carl Levin; almost in the same breath, they suggested Camp as a replacement for Schuette in the House.

But several ambitious Republicans decided to try for the GOP nomination. The result was a heated four-way primary that included Camp, former U.S. Rep. Jim Dunn, and former state Sens. Al Cropsey and Richard J. Allen.

Camp, who ran an unexciting but polished campaign, faced a strong challenge from Cropsey, a hard-line conservative backed by many abortion foes and religious fundamentalists. But like Schuette, Camp enjoyed strong support from GOP establishment figures and from executives at Dow Chemical. He won nomination on the strength of a strong margin in his Midland base.

From there, the campaign was an extended prelude to Camp's inaugural party. The GOP would have been strongly favored in any case, but Camp lucked out when dairy farmer Joan L. Dennison pulled an upset in the sparsely attended Democratic primary. Dennison espoused support for some ideas of political extremist Lyndon H. LaRouche Jr., and she advocated discarding much of the public school curriculum because she felt that the schools were being run by atheists. Camp won with nearly two-thirds of the vote.

Though Michigan lost two House seats in reapportionment, the redistricting map preserved a district for Camp (renumbered from the 10th to the 4th), and his second general election turned out to be nearly as lopsided as his first. He prepared for the worst, however, raising more than $500,000 (40 percent of it from PACs) and outspending his Democratic opponent, homemaker Lisa Donaldson, by more than 30-to-1. Camp tallied 63 percent, down a bit from 1990, but vastly better than Bush's showing in the 4th.

Committee

Ways & Means (14th of 14 Republicans)
Human Resources; Select Revenue Measures

Elections

1992 General		
Dave Camp (R)	157,337	(63%)
Lisa A. Donaldson (D)	87,573	(35%)
Joan L. Dennison (TIC)	3,344	(1%)
1990 General		
Dave Camp (R)	99,952	(65%)
Joan L. Dennison (D)	50,923	(33%)
Charles Congdon (LIBERT)	2,496	(2%)

District Vote for President

1992

D 104,709 (38%)
R 103,464 (37%)
I 67,873 (25%)

Campaign Finance

	Receipts	Receipts from PACs		Expend-itures
1992				
Camp (R)	$507,855	$204,537	(40%)	$518,118
Donaldson (D)	$15,650	$2,500	(16%)	$15,650
1990				
Camp (R)	$667,713	$175,075	(26%)	$657,229

Key Votes

1993	
Require parental notification of minors' abortions	Y
Require unpaid family and medical leave	N
Approve national "motor voter" registration bill	N
Approve budget increasing taxes and reducing deficit	N
Approve economic stimulus plan	N
1992	
Approve balanced-budget constitutional amendment	Y
Close down space station program	Y
Approve U.S. aid for former Soviet Union	N
Allow shifting funds from defense to domestic programs	N
1991	
Extend unemployment benefits using deficit financing	Y
Approve waiting period for handgun purchases	N
Authorize use of force in Persian Gulf	Y

Voting Studies

	Presidential Support		Party Unity		Conservative Coalition	
Year	**S**	**O**	**S**	**O**	**S**	**O**
1992	70	30	85	14	73	27
1991	71	29	88	12	95	5

Interest Group Ratings

Year	ADA	AFL-CIO	CCUS	ACU
1992	5	25	75	84
1991	15	8	100	80

5 James A. Barcia (D)

Of Bay City — Elected 1992; 1st Term

Born: Feb. 25, 1952, Bay City, Mich.
Education: Saginaw Valley State College, B.A. 1974.
Occupation: Congressional aide.
Family: Wife, Vicki Bartlett.
Religion: Roman Catholic.
Political Career: Mich. House, 1977-83, majority whip, 1979-83; Mich. Senate, 1983-93.
Capitol Office: 1717 Longworth Bldg. 20515; 225-8171.

The Path to Washington: For Barcia, the magic number is three. Elected to the Michigan House of Representatives at the tender age of 24, he served three terms before jumping over to the state Senate. He won three terms there, then ran for Congress.

He finished first in a three-way race with about 60 percent of the vote. Now Barcia is looking forward to a maximum of three terms in the U.S. House, if Michigan's new term-limits law is upheld. He questioned the wisdom of those limits during the campaign but is not likely to challenge them.

Barcia inherits most of his district from Democratic Rep. Bob Traxler, a nine-term veteran who announced in 1991 that he felt too frustrated and helpless in Congress to run for re-election.

Traxler had used his post as chairman of the VA-HUD Appropriations Subcommittee to steer two major federal projects to his district. Now it will be Barcia's job to keep the money flowing to those projects — a NASA earth sciences center and an Environmental Protection Agency Great Lakes research and conference facility.

That job will be complicated by the fact that Barcia will not follow Traxler onto the Appropriations Committee. Instead, he will serve on the Public Works and the Science, Space and Technology committees, which handle the authorizing legislation for those projects.

Barcia gained a reputation in the Legislature as a middle-of-the-road Democrat, one who did not toe the line for unions or management. Barcia won the business community's support by often being a voice for compromise on environmental issues. He also sided with the business community on a measure to cut the cost of workers' compensation, breaking a deadlock in the state Senate.

As a reflection of the business community's support, the local, state and national chambers of commerce endorsed Barcia over Republican Keith Muxlow, a real estate developer and former dairy farmer from Brown City. The labor unions backed Barcia, too, but not until two liberal Democrats lost in the primary.

The general-election campaign was relatively friendly, with the candidates taking similar positions. Unlike Barcia's opponents in the Democratic primary, Muxlow could hardly criticize Barcia for being a career politician. Muxlow had spent the previous 12 years in the state Legislature and was mayor of Brown City for eight years before that.

The issue for Barcia and Muxlow, as it was for candidates throughout Michigan, was jobs. To spur employment, Barcia supported an investment tax credit, reduced regulation and a milder capital-gains tax, while opposing the North American Free Trade Agreement. He also pledged to be an advocate for the faltering domestic automobile industry.

Barcia started the campaign with an advantage over Muxlow, having represented a far larger portion of the district as a state senator than Muxlow had as a state representative. Muxlow did not have the money to close the gap — he ran no TV ads and did only a limited amount of radio advertising and direct mail. In the final tally, Barcia collected almost 150,000 votes, Muxlow a little more than 93,000, and Lloyd Clarke of the Workers World Party had about 4,300.

On several fronts, Barcia has carved out positions closer to the GOP leadership in Congress than to the Democratic leadership. He opposes abortion rights, calls for less burdensome environmental regulation and favors health-care reform based on the current system of private insurers.

Barcia also established himself early in the 103rd Congress as a supporter of a strong line-item veto. In addition to supporting a Democratic version the House passed in April 1993, Barcia was one of only 33 Democrats to support the more potent GOP substitute.

In addition, he was one of only 28 Democrats in the House to oppose legislation codifying President Clinton's overturning of the so-called gag rule, which prohibited staff at federally funded family planning clinics from discussing abortion.

Michigan 5

East — Saginaw; Bay City

The 5th covers more than 200 miles of Lake Huron shoreline, but population is centered along the Bay City-Saginaw corridor. There, the heavy Democratic vote is usually enough to offset the Republican-voting areas that outline the district.

Saginaw, the largest city in the 5th, has a manufacturing sector that includes a heavy General Motors presence. Accordingly, the United Auto Workers (UAW) union carries a big stick.

Outside the city, Saginaw County's rich agricultural land produces sugar beets, dry beans, corn and soybeans. The importance of such commodities — along with the auto industry's presence — make the North American Free Trade Agreement of great interest. Many sugar beet growers, for example, fear cheap sugar imports from Mexico.

UAW strength and a significant blue-collar base make the city a Democratic stronghold. Democrat Michael S. Dukakis carried Saginaw County by 3,215 votes in 1988, and Bill Clinton had a much easier time winning it in 1992.

The second-largest city in the 5th is Bay City (Bay County). Once situated in the midst of a vast pine forest, Bay City was weaned on the lumber industry. Inhabitants used to refer to their home as the "Lumber Capital of the World," in deference to the more than 50 mills that once operated here.

The economy now, like Saginaw's, is more reliant on heavy manufacturing. Its blue-collar workers make boats, auto parts, jet engine components and tubing. The city is also one of the Great Lakes' top-ranked ports in terms of waterborne tonnage.

Bay County voters are even more reliably Democratic than their neighbors in Saginaw County. In the 1992 open seat House race, Barcia won 75 percent of the county vote.

Forested Arenac County, north of Bay County, is a popular vacation spot and home to retired autoworkers. Their UAW loyalties are reflected at the ballot box, where Democrats usually prevail. In 1990, all four Democrats running for statewide office won in Arenac. Clinton and Barcia captured the county in 1992.

North of Arenac, Alcona and Iosco counties are preferred weekend destinations for Detroit suburbanites. Military retirees from Wurtsmith Air Force Base help keep Iosco County competitive for the GOP, but in 1992, voters expressed their dissatisfaction over the scheduled shutdown of Wurtsmith by voting for Bill Clinton. Alcona County backed George Bush in 1992, along with Republican Keith Muxlow in the House race.

The other source of GOP votes is in Michigan's Thumb. Once heavily forested, the vast flat reaches of the region produce sugar beets, dry beans, corn, wheat and dairy products; Sanilac and Huron are top dairy counties. Just as Saginaw and Bay City experienced population losses in the 1980s, the counties of the Thumb declined also, though not as dramatically. Along the Lake Huron coastline, small fishing villages and lakeside resorts dot the landscape.

1990 Population: 580,956. White 516,255 (89%), Black 48,758 (8%), Other 15,943 (3%). Hispanic origin 19,611 (3%). 18 and over 418,962 (72%), 62 and over 91,368 (16%). Median age: 33.

Committees

Public Works & Transportation (35th of 39 Democrats)
Economic Development; Investigations & Oversight; Water Resources & the Environment

Science, Space & Technology (18th of 33 Democrats)
Science; Space

Campaign Finance

1992	Receipts	Receipts from PACs		Expenditures
Barcia (D)	$289,443	$138,251	(48%)	$288,755
Muxlow (R)	$93,876	$14,906	(16%)	$93,557

Key Votes

1993

Require parental notification of minors' abortions	Y
Require unpaid family and medical leave	Y
Approve national "motor voter" registration bill	Y
Approve budget increasing taxes and reducing deficit	Y
Approve economic stimulus plan	Y

Elections

1992 General		
James A. Barcia (D)	147,618	(60%)
Keith Muxlow (R)	93,098	(38%)
Lloyd Clarke (WW)	4,270	(2%)
1992 Primary		
James A. Barcia (D)	27,138	(46%)
John D. Cherry Jr. (D)	16,890	(29%)
Don Hare (D)	14,761	(25%)

District Vote for President

1992

D 118,699 (45%)
R 84,525 (32%)
I 60,990 (23%)

6 Fred Upton (R)

Of St. Joseph — Elected 1986; 4th Term

Born: April 23, 1953, St. Joseph, Mich.
Education: U. of Michigan, B.A. 1975.
Occupation: Congressional aide; budget analyst.
Family: Wife, Amey Rulon-Miller; two children.
Religion: Protestant.
Political Career: No previous office.
Capitol Office: 2439 Rayburn Bldg. 20515; 225-3761.

In Washington: Upton made headlines at the start of the 103rd Congress when he resigned his post as a minority deputy whip, citing ideological differences with more strident conservative GOP leaders, such as Newt Gingrich of Georgia and Dick Armey of Texas.

Whether he was forced out or stepped down, there is no doubt that Upton increasingly found himself bucking the leadership structure he was a part of. His descent inevitably closes some doors with the Republican Party, but it may open others with the Democrats, particularly fellow Energy and Commerce Committee members.

Upton has already proved that he can get along with members of the opposition party, teaming up with a handful of Democrats on issues he cares about. Joint ventures with Energy and Commerce Chairman John D. Dingell, D-Mich., and subcommittee chairs Henry A. Waxman of California and Edward J. Markey of Massachusetts may present the greatest opportunities for Upton to leave his mark in the House.

In his early tenure in Congress, Upton used his background at the Office of Budget and Management (OMB) to carve a niche as a budget-cutter.

As a freshman, he joined an effort, led by Republican Tom Tauke of Iowa and Democrat Timothy J. Penny of Minnesota, to shrink the deficit with small cuts in appropriations bills.

His most noticed first-term victory involved blocking an effort to declare a one-time federal holiday on Sept. 17, 1987, honoring the bicentennial of the U.S. Constitution. "We all realize that the Constitution is a working document," Upton said. "If this is true, does it really make sense to celebrate a working document by taking a day off work?"

Citing OMB estimates of a potential $330 million in savings, Upton gained passage of an amendment that struck out the federal holiday provisions and instead proposed a "National Day of Recognition."

Upton remained conservative on economic issues and in 1990 came out sharply against the bipartisan budget deal that called for higher taxes. His opposition endeared him to die-hard conservatives but prompted White House Chief of Staff John H. Sununu to explode: "What are you smoking?"

Upton continued shifting away from the administration in the 102nd Congress, defying President Bush and party leaders on several high-profile issues. In 1992 House floor votes, Upton opposed Bush on issues on which the president had a declared position 43 percent of the time — about double the Republican average.

Upton has consistently voted against the space station *Freedom* and the $8.5 billion superconducting super collider, two projects that Bush favored. Upton also favored reductions in expensive weapons systems such as the B-2 bomber and the Strategic Defense Initiative, in keeping with his longstanding attempts to control federal spending and reduce the deficit.

Upton also opposed Bush when he voted in 1992 to extend unemployment benefits, a reflection of the tough economic times in Michigan. Nearly the entire state delegation supported the extension.

Upton's high-profile support of fetal tissue research and the so-called Brady Bill, which would establish a waiting period before the purchase of a handgun, placed him foursquare against his party's hierarchy in the 102nd Congress.

Democrat Waxman chose Upton to close the debate on the House floor on the National Institutes of Health reauthorization, legislation which codified Clinton's repeal of the ban on fetal tissue research.

"As a Republican it is never easy for me to oppose the administration," Upton said in opening his impassioned plea in favor of the research that supporters believe is vital to curing such diseases as Parkinson's, Alzheimer's and diabetes.

Upton's resignation from the leadership only seemed to free him further. Early in the 103rd, he and eight other Republicans crafted their own alternative budget plan that included raising taxes on the wealthy, eliminating the atom-smashing super collider and reducing the

Michigan 6

Southwest — Kalamazoo; Benton Harbor; St. Joseph

Nestled in the southwestern corner of Michigan, bordered to the west by Lake Michigan and to the south by Indiana, the 6th is prime agricultural and Republican turf.

With 80,000 residents, Kalamazoo is the largest city in the 6th by far. A significant manufacturing sector provides the base for a strong union presence and blue-collar vote, despite the scheduled closure of Kalamazoo County's second-largest employer, a General Motors body-stamping plant. Other employers make printing and packaging paper, aircraft components, automotive parts and medical equipment.

The Upjohn Co., maker of pharmaceuticals, medical equipment and chemicals, has its worldwide headquarters in Portage, just outside the city of Kalamazoo.

Education and health-care services also have emerged as major employers. The city has a large academic community that includes the students of Western Michigan University — where former Democratic Rep. Howard Wolpe once taught — and Kalamazoo College (29,200 combined).

The area's Dutch heritage, when combined with corporate managers and the agriculture-oriented townships on the outskirts of Kalamazoo County, helps turn out a moderate-to-conservative vote. GOP Rep. Upton easily carried the county in 1992, but Bill Clinton also won here. Split tickets were also the rule in 1990, when Kalamazoo County voted for successful Republican challenger John Engler over Democratic Gov. James J. Blanchard while sticking with Democratic Sen. Carl Levin against GOP then-Rep. Bill Schuette.

The twin cities of Benton Harbor and St. Joseph make Berrien County the second-most populous in the district. Outside these cities, fruits and berries are grown; there is some food-processing industry. The area along the wooded Lake Michigan shoreline, where many affluent Chicagoans maintain second homes and vacation cottages, is known as "Harbor Country."

The cities are more geared toward industry. Separated by the St. Joseph River, more populous Benton Harbor and St. Joseph eye each other warily. Benton Harbor — once a stop along the Underground Railroad — is more than 90 percent black; St. Joseph is more than 90 percent white.

St. Joseph used to be a bedroom community for Benton Harbor, but a migration of Southern blacks to nearby fruit farms sparked a wave of white flight to St. Joseph. Today, St. Joseph is noticeably more prosperous and less gripped by urban decline.

Democrats run well in this area, but votes for them usually are negated by the rural voters and retirees of the outlying Republican towns. Both Engler and Schuette won Berrien County in 1990; in 1992, the county stuck with George Bush.

The flat croplands of Republican Cass and St. Joseph counties form the northeastern edge of the Corn Belt. Dowagiac (Cass) and Three Rivers (St. Joseph) have some industry, but the workers are conservative Democrats at best.

1990 Population: 580,956. White 512,029 (88%), Black 55,474 (10%), Other 13,453 (2%). Hispanic origin 10,506 (2%). 18 and over 426,902 (73%), 62 and over 85,915 (15%). Median age: 33.

deficit by $171.5 billion more than President Clinton proposed. Included in the group were Steve Gunderson, the Wisconsin member who left the GOP leadership at the same time as Upton, and Nancy L. Johnson of Connecticut, who joined Upton at the White House to lobby Bush in favor of the fetal tissue bill.

"The first task at hand is for Congress and the White House to drop their usual partisan agenda and solve the budget deficit," Upton said when introducing the alternative budget.

And there were clear signs he himself will seek out allies in both parties. He and fellow Michigander Dingell are promoting a high-speed rail line from Detroit to Chicago, which would make three stops in Upton's district. He joined forces with Markey and Republican Paul B. Henry of Michigan in the 103rd Congress to revive their national bottle bill.

At Home: In 1986, Upton was the only House Republican to unseat an incumbent in a primary. But his victory over GOP Rep. Mark D. Siljander was not a total shock.

Much of the local GOP establishment had long disliked Siljander, an activist in the religious right whose efforts to link religion and politics had often fed controversy. And Upton was unusually well-positioned to challenge the vulnerable incumbent.

Upton is a member of one of the district's most prominent families — his grandfather was a founder of the Whirlpool appliance company. And although he had never sought office before, Upton had a strong résumé. He spent 10 years as an aide to David A. Stockman during Stockman's tenures as 4th District House member and as

President Ronald Reagan's OMB director.

Siljander had emerged on the scene in 1981, winning a special election after Stockman's move to OMB. He beat a longtime Stockman ally by mobilizing his fundamentalist backers, and he went on to establish a reputation as a conservative firebrand known to denounce the "perverted" philosophy of "secular humanists." Although his voting record was in line with the majority philosophy of the then-4th, Siljander's style alienated GOP regulars. Upton decided to run when he returned to the district in 1985 after Stockman resigned his OMB post.

Upton generally avoided challenging Siljander's issue positions; instead, he hoped to convince voters that he was simply a more appealing, less confrontational conservative. He got a break late in the campaign, when Siljander committed an astounding gaffe. He taped an appeal to fundamentalist ministers, implying that the challenge to him was linked to evil forces, and calling on voters to "break the back of Satan." Upton aides claim that Upton would have won anyway, but the tape clinched his victory.

Religious activists mounted a 1990 primary challenge to Upton, in the form of conservative state Sen. Ed Fredricks. But Upton won the nomination and since then has continued his string of solid general-election victories.

Committee

Energy & Commerce (10th of 17 Republicans)
Health & the Environment; Oversight & Investigations; Transportation & Hazardous Materials

Elections

1992 General		
Fred Upton (R)	144,083	(62%)
Andy Davis (D)	89,020	(38%)
1990 General		
Fred Upton (R)	75,850	(58%)
JoAnne McFarland (D)	55,449	(42%)

Previous Winning Percentages: 1988 (71%) **1986** (62%)

District Vote for President

1992

D 100,461 (39%)
R 97,057 (38%)
I 61,008 (24%)

Campaign Finance

	Receipts	Receipts from PACs		Expend-itures
1992				
Upton (R)	$432,851	$149,585	(35%)	$367,596
Davis (D)	$42,048	$19,600	(47%)	$42,769
1990				
Upton (R)	$445,881	$152,654	(34%)	$503,164
McFarland (D)	$82,095	$48,100	(59%)	$78,392

Key Votes

1993	
Require parental notification of minors' abortions	N
Require unpaid family and medical leave	N
Approve national "motor voter" registration bill	Y
Approve budget increasing taxes and reducing deficit	N
Approve economic stimulus plan	N
1992	
Approve balanced-budget constitutional amendment	Y
Close down space station program	Y
Approve U.S. aid for former Soviet Union	Y
Allow shifting funds from defense to domestic programs	N
1991	
Extend unemployment benefits using deficit financing	Y
Approve waiting period for handgun purchases	Y
Authorize use of force in Persian Gulf	Y

Voting Studies

	Presidential Support		Party Unity		Conservative Coalition	
Year	**S**	**O**	**S**	**O**	**S**	**O**
1992	57	43	78	22	73	27
1991	60	40	78	21	86	14
1990	61	39	89	11	85	15
1989	74	26	85	15	88	12
1988	60	40	86	14	87	13
1987	60	40	90	10	91	9

Interest Group Ratings

Year	ADA	AFL-CIO	CCUS	ACU
1992	30	50	88	72
1991	25	25	100	80
1990	17	17	93	71
1989	20	8	100	75
1988	30	50	100	64
1987	16	13	87	70

7 Nick Smith (R)

Of Addison — Elected 1992; 1st Term

Born: Nov. 5, 1934, Addison, Mich.
Education: Michigan State U., B.A. 1957; U. of Delaware, M.S. 1959.
Military Service: Air Force, 1959-61.
Occupation: Dairy farmer.
Family: Wife, Bonnalyn Atwood; four children.
Religion: Congregationalist.
Political Career: Somerset Township Board of Trustees, 1962-66; Hillsdale County Board of Supervisors, 1966-68; Mich. House, 1979-83; Mich. Senate, 1983-93.
Capitol Office: 1708 Longworth Bldg. 20515; 225-6276.

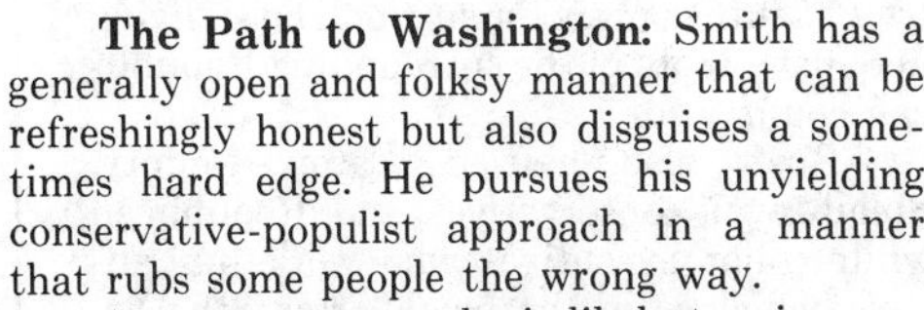

The Path to Washington: Smith has a generally open and folksy manner that can be refreshingly honest but also disguises a sometimes hard edge. He pursues his unyielding conservative-populist approach in a manner that rubs some people the wrong way.

As a consequence, he is likely to win some friends among GOP House freshmen, but he may not influence very many people in a chamber where compromise is still the name of the game.

Smith is a decided fan of lower taxes — he claims more tax-cutting success during his tenure in the Michigan Senate than any of his colleagues there — and he brought that philosophy to Washington. He has promised not to vote for any tax increase that is not balanced by an offsetting tax cut elsewhere. He was a persistent advocate of cuts in the state's inheritance tax and supported GOP Gov. John Engler's proposal to cut property taxes and cap assessments.

In addition, tax policy changes to boost saving and investment are at the top of his list, chiefly because he believes the nation faces the threat of a shortage of capital. He favors trying to eliminate the federal budget deficit with deep spending cuts — since higher taxes do not fit into his scheme — and he is willing to spread the pain.

In April 1993, he voted to give the president a modified line-item veto, voting for a Democratic version and a stronger GOP substitute.

Though he often sounds fixated on taxes and the economy, Smith's conservative credentials extend to his law-and-order record and his vigorous opposition to abortion. He took on the rising cost of health care — and the state's trial lawyers (a popular GOP target) — during the 1991 legislative session. He proposed that health insurance plans include mandatory arbitration clauses that would prevent malpractice lawsuits — and theoretically hold down the cost of malpractice insurance. Consumer advocates argued that there was no direct connection between malpractice suits and the overall cost of health care, and they worried that Smith's approach would close off an avenue of relief for injured patients.

Smith will have an opportunity to put some of these ideas into play — he won a seat on the Budget Committee and on the Science, Space and Technology Committee.

Smith kept his head down and his hands relatively clean during a bitter Republican primary. He won with almost 44 percent in a four-way race and thereby essentially won the general election. The newly drawn district was so heavily tilted to the GOP that no Democrat filed: Smith won 88 percent of the vote in November against Libertarian Kenneth L. Proctor.

Smith's chief adversary was fellow GOP state Sen. John Schwartz, whose name recognition rivaled that of Smith and who raised about twice as much money. There is little doubt that Smith was the most conservative candidate in the primary. Though Schwartz also opposes abortion, Smith won the endorsement of Michigan Right to Life. The two lesser-known candidates, Thomas Dooley Wilson and Brad Haskins, advocated abortion rights.

Smith was an indirect beneficiary of Haskins' repeated attacks on Schwartz. Haskins ran 15-second television ads saying Schwartz assaulted a veterans hospital security officer with his car after the guard gave him a ticket. Schwartz denied the charge and gave a different version. But a Battle Creek physician later said that Schwartz had once beaten him.

The mud stuck to both Schwartz and Haskins and left Smith untainted.

Smith went on the offensive against Schwartz, using his longstanding opposition to political action committees (PACs) to raise questions about Schwartz's fundraising and his loyalties. Smith pledged to carry his anti-PAC crusade to Congress. He was one of 14 Republican freshmen who attended the post-election "Omaha summit." There he advocated putting a $1,000-per-election limit on PAC contributions to congressional candidates, the same level that applies to individual donations.

Michigan 7

South Central — Battle Creek; Jackson

When Bill Clinton carried the Republican 7th by 600 votes in 1992, it was less an indication of his popularity than a protest vote against George Bush.

This is a district of conservative small towns and agricultural communities, with a few midsize cities thrown in for good measure. In 1990, GOP challenger John Engler won every county in the 7th against Democratic incumbent Gov. James J. Blanchard. In 1992's open-seat House race, Democrats did not even bother to put up a candidate.

Battle Creek, or "Cereal City," is the largest city in the 7th. It is the home of "Tony the Tiger" of Frosted Flakes fame and to the breakfast cereal plants that employ many of the city's residents.

The Kellogg Co., headquartered in Battle Creek, is the top individual employer and a prominent force in the city. The federal government also has a heavy local presence; almost half the federal employees work at a Veterans Administration medical center.

Besides the money that Kellogg has poured into civic improvements, the company also left its imprint on local government. In the early 1980s, Kellogg told Battle Creek in no uncertain terms to merge the city and Battle Creek Township governments. Fearful that the company would move its headquarters, the city annexed the township, adding 21,000 residents to its population.

With a fair amount of blue-collar Democrats, Battle Creek often makes Calhoun County competitive for Democrats. Outside the city, the vote of corporate executives and outlying small towns tilts Republican. In 1992, Clinton posted 44 percent in Calhoun County, his best showing in the district.

About an hour's drive away on I-94, the industrial city of Jackson is another source of Democratic votes. The city is smaller in population than Battle Creek, but as a whole, Jackson is the most populous county wholly within the 7th.

Layoffs at the tool-and-die and auto parts shops have caused some pain in the city, but Bush was able to carry Jackson County in 1992 on the strength of the outlying towns and farming areas.

Bush drew some support from city-based Democrats — a socially conservative lot, with a tendency to pull the lever for the GOP at the presidential level. Unlike Detroit's autoworkers, many of those living here have roots in the surrounding Republican countryside.

Bush also carried Eaton County. Small-town conservatives and Republican white-collar executives who work in Lansing (which is in the neighboring 8th District) boosted Bush to 39 percent.

Next door to Eaton County, Barry County is divided among the 2nd, 3rd and 7th districts. The southwestern 7th portion provides fewer than 5,000 votes.

The agricultural flatland of Branch, Hillsdale, Jackson and Lenawee counties long has been fertile ground for the GOP. Until Bush lost in Lenawee County in 1992, all four counties on the northern edge of the Corn Belt had voted Republican in presidential contests since 1964.

1990 Population: 580,957. White 535,970 (92%), Black 32,742 (6%), Other 12,245 (2%). Hispanic origin 14,170 (2%). 18 and over 424,301 (73%), 62 and over 86,007 (15%). Median age: 33.

Committees

Budget (15th of 17 Republicans)

Science, Space & Technology (15th of 22 Republicans)
Science; Technology, Environment & Aviation

Campaign Finance

	Receipts	Receipts from PACs	Expend-itures
1992			
Smith (R)	$242,908	0	$231,043

Key Votes

1993

Require parental notification of minors' abortions	Y
Require unpaid family and medical leave	N
Approve national "motor voter" registration bill	N
Approve budget increasing taxes and reducing deficit	N
Approve economic stimulus plan	N

Elections

1992 General		
Nick Smith (R)	133,972	(88%)
Kenneth L. Proctor (LIBERT)	18,751	(12%)
1992 Primary		
Nick Smith (R)	26,174	(43%)
John Schwarz (R)	21,823	(36%)
Thomas Dooley Wilson (R)	7,067	(12%)
Brad Haskins (R)	5,598	(9%)

District Vote for President

1992

D 96,940 (38%)
R 96,336 (38%)
I 62,673 (24%)

8 Bob Carr (D)

Of East Lansing — Elected 1974; 9th Term

Did not serve 1981-83.

Born: March 27, 1943, Janesville, Wis.
Education: U. of Wisconsin, B.S. 1965, J.D. 1968.
Occupation: Lawyer.
Family: Wife, Kate Smith; two stepchildren.
Religion: Baptist.
Political Career: Democratic nominee for U.S. House, 1972; defeated for re-election to U.S. House, 1980.
Capitol Office: 2347 Rayburn Bldg. 20515; 225-4872.

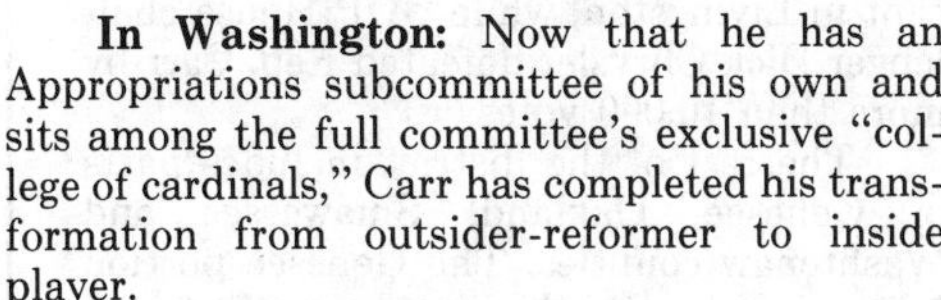

In Washington: Now that he has an Appropriations subcommittee of his own and sits among the full committee's exclusive "college of cardinals," Carr has completed his transformation from outsider-reformer to inside player.

With the retirement of Democratic Rep. William Lehman of Florida and the resignation of Democratic Rep. William H. Gray III of Pennsylvania, Carr became chairman of the Appropriations Subcommittee on Transportation. This should enable him to channel federal money to his state while keeping an eye on issues related to the automobile industry — still a mainstay for much of his district.

Like many of his fellow "Watergate babies" who were first elected in 1974, Carr came to Congress with considerable interest in, and a relatively radical perspective on, national issues. He even looked like the University of Wisconsin campus activist he had recently been. He also made an instant reputation as a hothead by calling for the resignation of House Speaker Carl Albert of Oklahoma. Years later, he referred to this particular gambit as "sheer, naive stupidity."

What made the difference for Carr was his defeat at the polls in 1980, the year his class and party were purged in Ronald Reagan's first electoral landslide. That defeat did more than keep him out of office for two years — it transformed his legislative profile. Since returning to office in 1983, he has rarely expended political capital except on matters of local concern.

At times Carr seems highly sensitive to prevailing political winds. During the 101st Congress, he recommended stripping flag burners of their citizenship and then expediting deportation procedures for them. "Putting them in jail or giving them a fine like a common purse snatcher is not appropriate," he explained. "Raising questions about their citizenship is."

On Appropriations, Carr's favorite transporation issues have to do with automobile travel and aviation, the latter interest stemming from his own background as a pilot. He has a keen interest in the Federal Aviation Administration (FAA), and when aviation is discussed, he can speak eloquently on technically complex matters with no notes to guide him.

Although most of his attention is geared to bringing federal funds home, Carr is not above criticizing others for doing the same. Carr's zealous support for $11.5 million for three demonstration highway projects in Michigan caused one of his colleagues to criticize him for supporting pork. An impassioned Carr replied, "The people who die on our highways, the people who sit in congestion on our highways ... should resent your calling them pigs and hogs. They're not pigs and they do not regard this as pork."

At the same conference, he also got the National Highway Traffic Safety Administration to study the usefulness of crash test data and standardize the types of crash dummies used in tests. Older-model dummies can skew results and make cars appear less safe.

But Carr is not loath to criticize other members' funding: He advocated cuts in several urban rail projects during an October 1991 conference committee. "This is not an entitlement program," he said, defending his opposition to a $30 million appropriation for a monorail in Houston.

He also showed his concern for the automobile industry by sponsoring a bill to amend the tax code to allow people to deduct interest payments on car loans from their federal taxes.

At Home: After running unopposed in 1990, Carr had all the opposition he could handle from Republican Dick Chrysler in 1992. Having lost a 1986 gubernatorial bid in the primary, Chrysler did not scrimp in his challenge to Carr. He spent more than $1.7 million and owed more than $1.5 million when it was all over.

Carr was able to keep pace with Chrysler financially, but he had lost some valuable ground in redistricting. The new 1992 map put the Democratic city of Pontiac out of the district, making a once-marginal district more Republican-leaning.

The race remained tight until, near the

Michigan 8

Central — Part of Lansing

The 8th reaches from the state capital of Lansing to the outskirts of Flint and Ann Arbor, but the majority of voters live in just two counties, Ingham (Lansing) and Livingston. Between them, they hold almost 70 percent of the district population.

While Bill Clinton won here and a Democrat represents the 8th, the district has a Republican character.

Residents of Lansing, the largest city in the 8th, live by the area's three Cs: cars, campus and the Capitol. General Motors is the city's largest employer, employing more than 20,000 workers who build Pontiacs, Buicks and Oldsmobiles. Ransom Eli Olds founded his Olds Motor Vehicle Co. here in 1897, at first turning out horseless carriages.

The state Capitol complex is the next largest employer, followed by Michigan State University in East Lansing. The 42,100 students are a source of Democratic votes, which, when combined with autoworkers, state employees and the university faculty who live in places such as Okemos Township, tilts Ingham County toward Democrats.

Livingston County retains much of its agricultural character, despite a population influx over the past two decades. In the 1970s, Livingston was the state's second-fastest-growing county, though growth slowed in the 1980s. Many of these new residents were whites fleeing Detroit, Flint, Lansing and Pontiac.

Much of the vote comes from small towns and farming communities such as Fowlerville and Howell, which celebrates the muskmelon harvest with its annual Melon Festival.

The county's traditional conservatism has not been affected by the newcomers. Settled by German Protestant farmers, it was a center of German-American Bund activism in the 1930s. In 1990, GOP challenger John Engler won 62 percent against Democratic Gov. James J. Blanchard; Republican Rep. Bill Schuette also carried the county against Democratic Sen. Carl Levin that year, though he won just 41 percent statewide.

In 1992, Clinton garnered just 29 percent in Livingston, while GOP House challenger Dick Chrysler defeated Rep. Carr by more than 10,000 votes.

The rest of the district includes parts of Genesee, Oakland, Shiawassee and Washtenaw counties. The Genesee portion takes in the southwestern part of the county, reaching to the Flint city limits. The strongly Democratic heritage of Flint spills over into these areas, and they turn out a Democratic vote.

The northwestern Washtenaw County portion, starting from the edge of Ann Arbor, is mostly small townships and part of the city of Saline. Unlike the Democratic university community in Ann Arbor, these areas prefer Republican candidates. Bush and Chrysler carried the county in 1992.

The small segment of Oakland County in the district adds a small number of voters, most of whom vote the same way the rest of the county does — Republican.

1990 Population: 580,956. White 525,215 (90%), Black 33,900 (6%), Other 21,841 (4%). Hispanic origin 16,947 (3%). 18 and over 431,535 (74%), 62 and over 64,226 (11%). Median age: 31.

end, Chrysler was forced to respond to questions about his business practices that were first raised in his 1986 gubernatorial run.

Carr was a political newcomer when he first ran for the House in 1972, but he did better than expected against veteran GOP Rep. Charles E. Chamberlain, taking advantage of the new 18-year-old vote in the college town of East Lansing to come within 2,500 votes. When Chamberlain retired in 1974, Carr won the election to replace him.

Carr's liberalism seemed out of place in his traditionally GOP district, but his strong constituent service helped him defeat his next two challengers. After pulling in 57 percent in 1978, Carr looked secure.

But in 1980, conservative building contractor Jim Dunn poured money into a hard-hitting campaign. A complacent Carr failed at first to see the threat; when he did, it was too late.

After losing narrowly, there was little question Carr would try again in 1982. He was helped by a Democratic-led redistricting and a recession-ravaged local economy. Carr tied Dunn to Reaganomics and won back his seat.

Dunn bypassed the 1984 House race for an unsuccessful GOP Senate primary bid. Carr prepared carefully anyway. He emphasized his work on district concerns and collected over a half-million dollars.

His efforts paid off against Republican Tom Ritter, though not as richly as expected. Carr carried Oakland County with 57 percent and Ingham County with 53 percent. But Ritter, whose family produce business was a fixture in what was then the 6th's eastern end, did well in

Livingston County. Carr's slim 52 percent victory emboldened Republicans.

Dunn's negative tone during his 1984 Senate primary against eventual nominee Jack Lousma angered many GOP insiders, but his image as Carr's strongest challenger forced them to shelve their reservations when Dunn decided to tackle Carr again in 1986.

From the outset, there was a bitter edge to Dunn's effort. Republican officials claimed Carr owned an airplane, a horse and a Florida condo, but did not have a district residence because he said he could not afford homes in both Washington and Michigan.

Carr denied each charge. He claimed he did have a district residence — a rented room in a friend's East Lansing home. He also said he had sold his airplane and the Florida home, which was built for his mother; the horse, Carr said, belonged to his estranged wife.

Dunn resurrected a 14-year-old newspaper article in which Carr supported marijuana decriminalization. Carr said he had changed his opinions on many issues and noted that Dunn campaigned as a foe of abortion, but had voted for federal abortion funding in the House. Despite Dunn's attacks, or perhaps in part because of them, Carr won with surprising ease.

Committee

Appropriations (16th of 37 Democrats)
Transportation (chairman); Commerce, Justice, State & Judiciary; Legislative Branch

Elections

1992 General		
Bob Carr (D)	135,517	(48%)
Dick Chrysler (R)	131,906	(46%)
Frank D. McAlpine (I)	12,155	(4%)
Michael E. Marotta (LIBERT)	5,115	(2%)
1990 General		
Bob Carr (D)	97,547	(100%)

Previous Winning Percentages: **1988** (59%) **1986** (57%) **1984** (52%) **1982** (51%) **1978** (57%) **1976** (53%) **1974** (49%)

District Vote for President

1992
D 117,654 (41%)
R 103,725 (36%)
I 67,983 (23%)

Campaign Finance

	Receipts	Receipts from PACs		Expenditures
1992				
Carr (D)	$1,107,973	$568,003	(51%)	$1,355,199
Chrysler (R)	$1,763,305	0		$1,762,766
1990				
Carr (D)	$397,155	$208,550	(53%)	$223,595

Key Votes

1993	
Require parental notification of minors' abortions	N
Require unpaid family and medical leave	N
Approve national "motor voter" registration bill	Y
Approve budget increasing taxes and reducing deficit	Y
Approve economic stimulus plan	Y
1992	
Approve balanced-budget constitutional amendment	Y
Close down space station program	N
Approve U.S. aid for former Soviet Union	N
Allow shifting funds from defense to domestic programs	Y
1991	
Extend unemployment benefits using deficit financing	Y
Approve waiting period for handgun purchases	N
Authorize use of force in Persian Gulf	N

Voting Studies

	Presidential Support		Party Unity		Conservative Coalition	
Year	**S**	**O**	**S**	**O**	**S**	**O**
1992	30	67	78	18	58	40
1991	34 †	61 †	79 †	14 †	43	41
1990	29	69	81	15	46	52
1989	30	67	80	13	37	63
1988	31	65	80	10	50	47
1987	21	74	82	11	40	56
1986	21	74	75	21	56	44
1985	29	68	81	14	38	56
1984	26	72	87	11	34	66
1983	12	83	86	10	25	72

† Not eligible for all recorded votes.

Interest Group Ratings

Year	ADA	AFL-CIO	CCUS	ACU
1992	70	75	57	22
1991	75	58	40	21
1990	72	67	57	25
1989	85	67	50	25
1988	80	93	46	21
1987	88	100	31	9
1986	70	86	33	24
1985	65	76	50	15
1984	80	85	38	22
1983	85	88	10	17

9 Dale E. Kildee (D)

Of Flint — Elected 1976; 9th Term

Born: Sept. 16, 1929, Flint, Mich.
Education: Sacred Heart Seminary, B.A. 1952; U. of Detroit, 1954; U. of Peshawar (Pakistan), 1958-59; U. of Michigan, M.A. 1961.
Occupation: Teacher.
Family: Wife, Gayle Heyn; three children.
Religion: Roman Catholic.
Political Career: Mich. House, 1965-75; Mich. Senate, 1975-77.
Capitol Office: 2239 Rayburn Bldg. 20515; 225-3611.

In Washington: A former divinity student who switched to political science, Kildee takes a liberal, do-gooder outlook on social problems but approaches potential remedies with the deft maneuvering of a seasoned politician. He says the roots of his liberalism come from his "deep respect for human life."

The concern Kildee voices about social programs, which put him out of sync during the Reagan-Bush years, should blend more smoothly into President Clinton's game plan for overhauling the health and welfare systems. However, an off note may be sounded during the abortion debate when he sides against the president.

Seldom one to break rank with the Democrats, Kildee's anti-abortion conviction put him in the opposing camp on Nov. 19, 1991, when the House answered the biggest abortion-related question of the year. The chamber failed by a dozen votes to override President George Bush's veto of a spending bill that had included language to stop the government from enforcing controversial rules barring abortion counseling in federally funded family planning clinics.

The vote was particularly difficult for Kildee because he had worked so hard for many of the funding increases in the bill. He said his ultimate decision to vote with the president was because blocking the regulations "still could and would lead to the death of unborn babies."

In the House, Kildee champions most all social programs to aid the poor, the elderly and the very young. In Michigan, he has filled out tax forms for senior citizens and helped fix their leaky roofs. A local headline in 1989 proclaimed, "Kildee to the Rescue" for his efforts to improve the food at a senior citizen center.

At the start of the 101st Congress, Kildee won a seat on the Budget Committee, where he is a consistent voice for increasing funds for social programs at the expense of the defense budget. But Kildee is no militant liberal. Though he debates with a degree of philosophical purity, he is more comfortable in coalitions than crusades.

Kildee is low-key but persistent in his efforts to increase funds for Head Start, child care and education. While he occasionally meets with success — in 1989, the committee approved his language to allow as much as $1.8 billion for a new child-care package — his is a frustrating role in an era of limited resources. After a particularly tense, closed-door meeting in 1989, Kildee said, "Everyone wanted a little more for their own programs. We did a lot of shouting. I did some shouting myself."

He came back fighting in the 102nd Congress, proposing an increase in Head Start funding that was double President Bush's request.

Kildee devotes most of his energy to his work on the Education and Labor Committee, where he chaired the Human Resources Subcommittee for several years. In the 102nd Congress, he took over the Elementary, Secondary and Vocational Education Subcommittee, which attempted to reauthorize education programs. Although the House in the 102nd Congress passed legislation to provide block grants to states to improve education, Senate Republicans kept the bill from reaching the White House.

Kildee's more ambitious plans for social welfare rarely go far, but his Act for Better Child Care Services — the ABC bill sponsored by Connecticut Democrat Christopher J. Dodd in the Senate — became a touchstone for many Democratic candidates in 1988. That helped create a political climate to pass child care legislation in the 101st Congress. Though the final bill included key portions of Kildee's original proposal, the legislation's passage was tangled in a bitter turf battle he shunned.

In the 100th Congress, the bill snagged on the issue of whether church-sponsored day care centers should receive federal funds. While the issue was again controversial in the 101st, it was eventually resolved by allowing government vouchers to be used at church-sponsored centers.

In the 100th Congress, Kildee was a key

Michigan 9

East Central — Flint; Pontiac

Nearly any conversation about the city of Flint nowadays invariably includes mention of the 1989 documentary "Roger and Me." Produced by a local filmmaker, it painted a scathing portrait of General Motors (GM) and the effects of its massive layoffs on this company town.

This was the birthplace of GM in 1908, and later, the United Auto Workers (UAW). Thirty years after the first plant opening, the modern labor movement sprouted forth from UAW sit-down strikes that paralyzed two GM factories.

At its employment peak, 80,000 people worked at Flint's GM plants. Today, that number is close to 40,000, with little hope of recovery. No longer do residents enjoy the benefits of what used to be GM's "womb to tomb" paternalism.

Abandoned neighborhoods and shuttered businesses reflect the city's population decline. The city has tried valiantly to retain its residents and draw in visitors through numerous civic projects, but unemployment remains high and tourism revenues low.

The UAW is still potent, although it has suffered as members have moved in search of jobs. The city continues to be a Democratic bastion, but the outlying Genesee County vote is less partisan.

In 1984, Ronald Reagan managed to win Genesee, but in 1988 and 1992, the county voted for a Democrat for president. Flint's high unemployment rates spurred a backlash against George Bush in 1992, when he won 24 percent in Genesee, barely enough to squeak by Ross Perot.

Michigan's 1992 redistricting radically redrew the district, so that Genesee is divided among the 5th, 8th and 9th districts. Only Flint, Grand Blanc and the southeastern portion of the county remain in the 9th. Flint is still the largest city in the district, but the bulk of the vote now comes from Republican Oakland County.

Pontiac, Oakland's largest city in the 9th, is made up of low-income blacks, Hispanics and socially conservative whites, whose families migrated from the South to work in the auto industry. They lean Democratic but are more independent than their counterparts in Flint.

Outside Pontiac, the townships in the northeastern corner of the county are less developed and more Republican. The GOP vote from areas such as Auburn Hills and Rochester, along with Addison, Orion and Oakland townships, counters the Flint vote and keeps the district competitive for Republicans. In 1992, Democratic Rep. Kildee faced the closest race of his career, in part because his GOP opponent racked up 57 percent in Oakland County.

Lapeer County, whose southern half is in the district, is also less-than-receptive to Democratic candidates. Eastern Lapeer has a more Democratic cast, a vestige of Flint-UAW spillover, but the county as a whole is more rural than the rest of the district. The rural Republican vote is often enough to tilt the county toward the GOP side as it did in 1992, when Bush and GOP House challenger Megan O'Neill won.

1990 Population: 580,956. White 461,400 (79%), Black 103,133 (18%), Other 16,423 (3%). Hispanic origin 16,436 (3%). 18 and over 420,886 (72%), 62 and over 65,534 (11%). Median age: 31.

negotiator on the bilingual education provision of the omnibus education bill. But the deal he helped strike to ensure passage was as much capitulation as compromise. The massive reauthorization was threatened by Republican demands to increase funding for programs using English-only methods instead of native-language instruction. Kildee and then-GOP Rep. Steve Bartlett of Texas sought a middle ground, but when none was found, GOP demands largely prevailed. Hispanic House members were furious. "It was not a happy compromise," Kildee said. "There would be wounds no matter what we would do. This preserved bilingual education and minimized bloodletting."

Kildee is also a strong labor loyalist. His AFL-CIO rating has averaged more than 90 percent; it was a perfect 100 from 1982 to 1990. His near-perfect liberal record on social issues is marred only by his opposition to federal funding of abortion.

Kildee has taken an increasingly strong role on trade issues, especially as they affect the American auto industry, the major financial base of his district. Claiming that Japanese motor vehicle manufacturers were exploiting the U.S. open market, he took a lead role in the 102nd Congress on a bill that sought to raise the import tariffs on four-door minivans. The measure passed the House as part of a wide-ranging tariff bill, but the Senate failed to endorse it.

In the 103rd Congress, Kildee is co-chairman of the Congressional Automotive Caucus.

At Home: Having to answer for 100 overdrafts at the House bank was hard enough in 1992, but Kildee had that problem compounded by redistricting. Not only did he have to answer to the constituents that knew him, but he also had to explain himself to the 49 percent of the district that was new to him.

His opponent, Republican Megan O'Neill, ran a spirited campaign and gained on Kildee in the final weeks. But the district still retained a Democratic edge, and O'Neill was unable to match Kildee in spending in the home stretch. Kildee won with 54 percent.

As a Democrat from the General Motors town of Flint, Kildee draws his political strength from the labor movement he supports in Washington.

The United Auto Workers and the AFL-CIO have deserted him only once — when he first ran for Congress in 1976. Trying to succeed five-term Rep. Donald W. Riegle Jr., who was running for the Senate, Kildee left a state Senate seat he had won only two years before. Labor, which had worked exceptionally hard to help Kildee oust a 26-year state Senate veteran in 1974, felt he should have served out his four-year term. But Kildee insisted on making his move.

Winning was relatively easy, even with division in the ranks of labor. Kildee beat a local union official with 76 percent in the Democratic primary and went on to trounce his general-election opponent. Before 1992, he had never won less than two-thirds of the vote, and often he would take considerably more.

Committees

Budget (3rd of 26 Democrats)

Education & Labor (5th of 28 Democrats)
Elementary, Secondary & Vocational Education (chairman); Human Resources; Labor-Management Relations; Postsecondary Education

House Administration (9th of 12 Democrats)
Accounts

Elections

1992 General		
Dale E. Kildee (D)	133,956	(54%)
Megan O'Neill (R)	111,798	(45%)
1990 General		
Dale E. Kildee (D)	90,307	(68%)
David J. Morrill (R)	41,759	(32%)

Previous Winning Percentages: **1988** (76%) **1986** (80%) **1984** (93%) **1982** (75%) **1980** (93%) **1978** (77%) **1976** (70%)

District Vote for President

1992
D 117,872 (44%)
R 92,262 (35%)
I 55,077 (21%)

Campaign Finance

	Receipts	Receipts from PACs		Expend-itures
1992				
Kildee (D)	$762,758	$464,970	(61%)	$795,484
O'Neill (R)	$135,192	$13,751	(10%)	$129,840
1990				
Kildee (D)	$259,480	$187,746	(72%)	$222,531
Morrill (R)	$6,382	0		$6,382

Key Votes

1993	
Require parental notification of minors' abortions	Y
Require unpaid family and medical leave	Y
Approve national "motor voter" registration bill	Y
Approve budget increasing taxes and reducing deficit	Y
Approve economic stimulus plan	Y
1992	
Approve balanced-budget constitutional amendment	N
Close down space station program	Y
Approve U.S. aid for former Soviet Union	Y
Allow shifting funds from defense to domestic programs	Y
1991	
Extend unemployment benefits using deficit financing	Y
Approve waiting period for handgun purchases	Y
Authorize use of force in Persian Gulf	N

Voting Studies

	Presidential Support		Party Unity		Conservative Coalition	
Year	**S**	**O**	**S**	**O**	**S**	**O**
1992	16	84	96	4	8	92
1991	29	71	95	5	14	86
1990	19	81	95	5	9	91
1989	35	65	94	6	10	90
1988	17	83	95	5	11	89
1987	16	84	98	2	0	100
1986	13	87	97	2	6	94
1985	18	78	94	3	4	96
1984	26	74	94	6	7	93
1983	11	89	92	8	9	91
1982	36	64	92	8	10	90
1981	26	74	90	10	15	85

Interest Group Ratings

Year	ADA	AFL-CIO	CCUS	ACU
1992	90	92	25	4
1991	95	92	10	5
1990	94	100	21	4
1989	95	100	20	11
1988	95	100	14	4
1987	96	100	7	4
1986	95	100	17	0
1985	85	100	25	5
1984	95	100	38	8
1983	90	100	5	13
1982	95	100	23	9
1981	90	80	5	0

10 David E. Bonior (D)

Of Mount Clemens — Elected 1976; 9th Term

Born: June 6, 1945, Detroit, Mich.
Education: U. of Iowa, B.A. 1967; Chapman College, M.A. 1972.
Military Service: Air Force, 1968-72.
Occupation: Probation officer; adoption caseworker.
Family: Wife, Judy; three children.
Religion: Roman Catholic.
Political Career: Mich. House, 1973-77.
Capitol Office: 2207 Rayburn Bldg. 20515; 225-2106.

In Washington: Bonior's first 18 months in the No. 3 Democratic leadership post coincided with public dissatisfaction over gridlock, the House bank scandal and a president who seemed out of touch with working-class Americans. He fit into the role nicely, thumping President Bush on issues such as family leave while drawing attention to proposed Democratic solutions.

With a Democrat in the White House and gridlock allegedly over, Bonior is point man in a whole new game. The team captain has changed, as has the playbook. And the challenge for Bonior in the 103rd Congress is to deliver votes for the new president's agenda, a job that requires lots of arm twisting, horse trading and sweet talking.

The job will not be easy, given the competing interests on Capitol Hill, the lack of federal dollars and a leadership structure that has sometimes hesitated to apply enough pressure to command unwavering loyalty.

The difficulties became quickly apparent when, at the start of the 103rd, Speaker Thomas S. Foley's leadership team was caught off guard on attempts to eliminate four select committees and give non-voting delegates partial floor voting privileges. Both efforts were successful.

Still, Bonior's colleagues saw in him an ability to pull together the disparate groups in the House, and on three more substantive matters early in the 103rd, House leaders had more to brag about than did their counterparts in the Senate. The Foley team won House passage of President Clinton's 1994 budget and his $16 billion economic stimulus package, which died in the Senate, and of Clinton's reconciliation bill, including a controversial energy tax.

Bonior exhibits traits from his two long-held passions: marathon running and basketball. He has retained the qualities of the solitary marathoner — patience, endurance and a disdain for flashiness — while evolving into a team player with a knack for parliamentary tactics.

While some members grumble he lacks a certain focus, he is more often praised for his low-key diligence and a keen appreciation of the value of teamwork. His rise through the Democratic ranks, to chief deputy whip in 1987 and whip in 1991, certified the progress Bonior had made since his early House years, when he was a restless Vietnam-era veteran searching for a role.

Having first run for whip in 1989, Bonior was well-prepared when William H. Gray III of Pennsylvania announced in June 1991 that he was leaving Congress. Using skills he learned the hard way when Gray beat him out for the job in 1989, Bonior was campaigning even before Gray's decision. In fact, Bonior first approached colleagues in April when speculation surfaced that Gray might run for the Senate seat vacated by the death of John Heinz.

Many of the House members who supported Gray over Bonior in 1989 pledged to back Bonior at the next opportunity. When it happened two years later, in Bonior's race against Maryland Rep. Steny H. Hoyer, many were good to their word. Others said they supported Bonior because he had helped them move a key piece of legislation or simply because they liked him.

He received early support from several senior powerhouses: Rules Committee Chairman Joe Moakley of Massachusetts and fellow Michiganders John D. Dingell, chairman of the Energy and Commerce Committee, and William D. Ford, chairman of the Education and Labor Committee. But Bonior also appealed to members of his own generation by arguing Democrats needed to be more aggressive in promoting their legislative agenda. He also told colleagues he favored expanding the leadership to make room for more women, minorities and Southerners.

Some liberals were reluctant to elevate a leader who opposed abortion rights, but Bonior disposed of those concerns by promising not to be "an impediment in letting the caucus [members] express their views."

Perhaps foreshadowing his ability to count votes, Bonior predicted his winning margin precisely, 160-109.

Michigan 10

Southeast — Macomb County; Port Huron

This is the home of the famed voters of Macomb County. Every four years, national reporters lug their laptops and cameras to the county to get an earful of what working-class America has to say. Political consultants probe their sentiments in focus groups. For presidential candidates, it is a must-stop.

Some of its renown stems from its reputation as an electoral bellwether. In 15 of the past 17 elections for president, governor or U.S. senator, the winner in Macomb has also been the statewide winner. But in 1992, George Bush became one of the exceptions.

Back in 1960, Macomb was solidly Democratic, suburban territory and proved it by delivering an almost 2-to-1 margin for John F. Kennedy. Voters stayed true to the party through most of the decade, backing Lyndon B. Johnson in 1964 and Hubert H. Humphrey in 1968.

But the late 1960s were a time of political transition for local residents, as they became increasingly disenchanted with the counterculture movement and frightened by the Detroit riots. By 1972, Richard M. Nixon had claimed the county.

As busing and civil rights emerged as prominent local issues, voters associated the national Democratic Party with the policies of the far left; by 1984, Ronald Reagan won by a 2-to-1 margin.

Strong union loyalties have not been enough to override the social conservatism of the Catholic Italians and Eastern European working-class voters. Democrats are still stigmatized as the party of permissiveness, one that is soft on crime and intent on raising taxes.

Bush won here on those issues in 1988 and in 1992 despite deep discontent among local voters. Japanese trade practices and layoffs weighed heavily on residents' minds, so in one visit, Bush spoke at a machine tooling plant in Fraser about his plan for a federal jobs training program.

In statewide and local races, Democrats are more competitive. In 1990, Macomb showed its ticket-splitting tendency by backing GOP challenger John Engler against Democratic Gov. James J. Blanchard, while choosing Democratic Sen. Carl Levin. In 1992, Democratic Rep. Bonior captured the county while Bill Clinton lost it.

Not all of Macomb County is in the 10th: The district includes the newer subdivisions north of Mount Clemens and Clinton Township, and extends to the grittier neighborhoods, such as East Pointe (formerly called East Detroit), which is shared with the 12th. Fraser and Roseville are in the 10th, but Warren and Sterling Heights are on the 12th District side.

The rest of the vote comes from St. Clair County. More rural in composition, it leans Republican. Port Huron, a source of blue-collar voters, is beginning to feel the effects of residential and commercial spillover from the Detroit metro area. Retailers and developers are moving into the city because it is less developed than areas closer to Detroit and for the potential market of Canadian consumers from nearby Ontario.

1990 Population: 580,956. White 560,595 (96%), Black 11,755 (2%), Other 8,606 (1%). Hispanic origin 7,430 (1%). 18 and over 434,093 (75%), 62 and over 86,557 (15%). Median age: 33.

When he was chosen chief deputy whip by then-Speaker Jim Wright of Texas in 1987, Bonior served as a bridge to liberals and Midwesterners. He has been playing on the team for some time, having been named to the Rules Committee in 1981 and appointed one of seven deputy Democratic whips in 1985. On the Rules Committee, he remains a voice for House liberals, often floor-managing high-profile legislation, such as the major oil-spill bill Congress passed in 1990.

He took the lead in the fight against proposals to amend the Constitution to ban flag desecration and he backed the controversial pay raise package enacted in late 1989.

Bonior also typified the group of liberals who were the nucleus of opposition to authorizing use of force in the Persian Gulf. Earlier, in the politically charged atmosphere created by Iraq's occupation of Kuwait, Bonior won approval of a burden-sharing amendment that became a lightning rod for festering congressional anger at Japan's modest defense efforts and its aggressive commercial policies.

Bonior's measure required Japan to pay the costs for U.S. military troops stationed in the country. An overwhelming number of members wanted to signal their unhappiness with Japan's foot-dragging in supporting the multinational effort against Iraq, and Bonior's amendment was adopted 370-53. Two days later, Japan quadrupled to $4 billion the amount it pledged to support the multilateral campaign against Iraq.

On foreign policy, Bonior was passionate in his opposition to military aid to the Nicaraguan contras. And after traveling to Central America in 1990 to investigate human rights violations by the Salvadoran military, he became part of a vocal group of House liberals urging a significant cut in aid to El Salvador.

But as the economy worsened at home, and Bonior's own electoral grip weakened, he found a new passion: the United States.

Although best known nationally as a leading critic of the Reagan administration's policies in Central America, in Michigan Bonior talked about the environment and the economy. (He is known for the pine tree seedlings he has planted all over the district.)

Around the time he became whip, Bonior hit on three new priorities: middle-class tax relief, health care and extended unemployment benefits.

The pitch, he discovered, not only had resonance in Michigan, but with the Democratic Caucus in Washington as well.

In the fall of 1991, when Bush killed an extension of unemployment benefits by refusing to declare a budget emergency, Bonior was there with one of the most-quoted soundbites: "The fact is the administration is ignoring people with mouths to feed and is serving them a bunch of baloney."

That same month, he wrote a column for The Washington Post arguing restraint on foreign aid during "our domestic crisis."

"Now, until we have addressed our more pressing domestic problems, aid to other nations simply has to take second place," he wrote.

In October, Bonior helped organize a marathon, all-night vigil at the Capitol to heighten public awareness on domestic problems such as homelessness and unemployment.

Bonior threatened to hold up a foreign aid package in 1992 unless more money was dedicated to domestic spending. In August, he endorsed the $12.3 billion increase in the U.S. commitment to the International Monetary Fund after receiving assurances from the Bush administration it would accelerate about $370 million in public works projects.

He has not abandoned entirely his interest in foreign affairs. In April 1993, Bonior joined Majority Leader Richard A. Gephardt of Missouri and other House members on a trip to Russia and Ukraine.

Bonior breaks with party leaders on occasion; besides opposing abortion, he voted against the 1990 budget summit agreement, and he opposes the free-trade pact with Mexico.

Estimating that Michigan stands to lose between 500,000 and 1 million jobs, Bonior has led the fight in Congress either to reject or revise the pact, known as the North American Free Trade Agreement. He has supported the free trade pact with Canada because he says the economies, wage scales and environmental laws of the two nations are similar.

Some staunch supporters of Israel have objected to Bonior's record on issues important to that country, such as his vote against authorizing the president to withhold funds from the United Nations if the World Health Organization admitted the Palestine Liberation Organization. He also voted against an amendment adopted overwhelmingly in April 1990 stating that Jerusalem "is and should remain" the capital of Israel.

Bonior was instrumental in forming the Vietnam-era Veterans Congressional Caucus in 1977. He has long sought to make the Vietnam War and its veterans a topic of discussion. "No one even wants to talk about the war," he once complained. "It was a disaster."

If Bonior is able to keep both his conservative constituents and the divergent Democratic Caucus appeased, history suggests he may be on his way to even greater things. Three of the past four House Speakers (Foley, Thomas P. O'Neill Jr. and Carl Albert) began their climb on the leadership ladder as majority whip.

At Home: Bonior's liberal politics have kept him under 60 percent in five of his eight re-election bids in his blue-collar district. And, as long as he is a member of House leadership, he will have difficulty matching the 66 percent he won in 1982 and 1986.

One Republican, state Sen. Douglas Carl, has kept Bonior under 55 percent twice. In 1986, Carl upset an incumbent GOP legislator with the help of activists associated with Pat Robertson's presidential campaign. He immediately began building bridges to party establishment figures and, midway through 1988, won their unanimous backing to challenge Bonior.

Aided by two visits to the Macomb County district by President Ronald Reagan and one by Vice President George Bush, Carl won 46 percent. Bush carried the district by 21 points.

Bonior's 1988 endorsement from Michigan's Right to Life organization helped him undercut Carl's base, but Bonior owed his victory to his hefty financial advantage and his campaign apparatus, which persuaded many voters going Republican for president to swing back and return a Democrat to the House.

Four years later, in 1992, Carl decided on a rematch after redistricting added 90,000 new residents to the district. Bonior's 76 overdrafts at the House bank looked to be a potent issue. And this time, Carl carried the banner of the Michigan Right to Life organization.

But Bonior was ready for the fight. He raised well over $1 million, and outspent Carl by a ratio of more than 5-to-1. On top of the financial disadvantage, Carl was hampered by a split in the local GOP between moderates and evangelical Christians. Bush's weak 42 percent performance sealed Carl's fate. Bonior notched 53 percent.

In 1990, Republicans came at Bonior with businessman and developer Jim Dingeman. He tossed the too-liberal charge at Bonior again, citing the incumbent's opposition to the death penalty and his support for a congressional pay raise.

But Bonior responded with another aggressive and well-financed effort. He faulted Dingeman's business record and charged him with carpetbagging; Dingeman had lived in Colorado, and even held elective office there, as recently as 1988. By late fall, national Republican officials had stopped talking up the race, and Bonior went on to win handily.

All of Bonior's re-election campaigns have been supported by organized labor and the Macomb County Democratic organization, but he has not been on the closest of terms with either. In the crowded 1976 contest to find a successor to Democratic Rep. James G. O'Hara, the unions were split and the Macomb Democratic Party favored Bonior's major primary opponent. Bonior narrowly won the primary and general election with an aggressive personal campaign; he went door to door handing out pine tree seedlings.

At the time, Bonior was a two-term state representative, having been elected to the Legislature only months after completing military duty; he served stateside as an Air Force cook.

Committee

Majority Whip

Rules (5th of 9 Democrats)
Rules of the House

Elections

1992 General		
David E. Bonior (D)	138,193	(53%)
Douglas Carl (R)	114,918	(44%)
David A. Weidner (LIBERT)	7,098	(3%)
1990 General		
David E. Bonior (D)	98,232	(65%)
Jim Dingeman (R)	51,119	(34%)
Robert W. Roddis (LIBERT)	2,472	(2%)

Previous Winning Percentages: **1988** (54%) **1986** (66%) **1984** (58%) **1982** (66%) **1980** (55%) **1978** (55%) **1976** (52%)

District Vote for President

1992
D 100,587 (36%)
R 115,849 (42%)
I 60,927 (22%)

Campaign Finance

	Receipts	Receipts from PACs		Expend-itures
1992				
Bonior (D)	$1,295,553	$934,613	(72%)	$1,345,011
Carl (R)	$253,607	$19,562	(8%)	$258,057
1990				
Bonior (D)	$1,189,127	$728,055	(61%)	$1,188,905
Dingeman (R)	$296,051	$31,156	(11%)	$295,184

Key Votes

1993	
Require parental notification of minors' abortions	N
Require unpaid family and medical leave	Y
Approve national "motor voter" registration bill	Y
Approve budget increasing taxes and reducing deficit	Y
Approve economic stimulus plan	Y
1992	
Approve balanced-budget constitutional amendment	N
Close down space station program	N
Approve U.S. aid for former Soviet Union	Y
Allow shifting funds from defense to domestic programs	Y
1991	
Extend unemployment benefits using deficit financing	Y
Approve waiting period for handgun purchases	Y
Authorize use of force in Persian Gulf	N

Voting Studies

	Presidential Support		Party Unity		Conservative Coalition	
Year	S	O	S	O	S	O
1992	12	72	79	3	10	71
1991	30	68	94	5	8	89
1990	18	81	95	4	6	94
1989	36	63	92	4	15	83
1988	19	80	93	2	3	92
1987	11	73	79	1	5	88
1986	16	79	90	1	6	84
1985	19	76	90	3	5	84
1984	25	69	84	4	10	83
1983	21	78	87	6	13	81
1982	26	58	85	5	12	71
1981	25	74	86	8	9	85

Interest Group Ratings

Year	ADA	AFL-CIO	CCUS	ACU
1992	80	91	29	0
1991	95	100	20	0
1990	94	100	31	8
1989	95	100	30	4
1988	95	100	21	4
1987	88	100	8	0
1986	95	100	6	0
1985	90	94	25	5
1984	75	92	33	5
1983	80	94	25	4
1982	70	100	5	11
1981	90	79	5	0

11 Joe Knollenberg (R)

Of Bloomfield Hills — Elected 1992; 1st Term

Born: Nov. 28, 1933, Mattoon, Ill.
Education: Eastern Illinois U., B.S. 1955.
Military Service: Army, 1955-57.
Occupation: Insurance broker.
Family: Wife, Sandra; two children.
Religion: Roman Catholic.
Political Career: Oakland County Republican Party chairman, 1978-86.
Capitol Office: 1218 Longworth Bldg. 20515; 225-5802.

The Path to Washington: If there was a place in the country in 1992 where abortion was supposed to be the defining issue in a House race, it was in Michigan's 11th District. Knollenberg's victory, however, indicates that voters were not swayed by the single-issue campaign.

The 11th is an upscale Republican district in suburban Detroit that abortion rights advocates thought they could win. Knollenberg supports abortion only to save the life of a pregnant woman, not in cases of rape or incest.

By electing Knollenberg, voters got an abortion foe and an otherwise traditional conservative Republican. He does not bring a long list of original ideas for congressional action and seems more concerned about holding the line against the perceived excesses of the Democratic majority than advancing an agenda.

Knollenberg campaigned as an outsider but won his seat with an insider's skill, capitalizing on experience gained in his years as local Republican chairman and campaign chairman for the district's 36-year incumbent, William S. Broomfield, who retired.

Like most candidates who ran hard against the established order, Knollenberg called for a constitutional amendment to require a balanced budget and for granting a presidential line-item veto. He also favors congressional reform and term limits for members.

Knollenberg voted early in the 103rd Congress against a Democratic bill giving the president limited line-item veto authority, backing only an even stronger GOP substitute amendment. While most of the 47 GOP freshmen chose to vote for both, Knollenberg was one of 12 to support only the substitute amendment.

He pledged to assault the deficit, especially entitlements, but he said he would exclude Social Security. He cited the Grace commission and Heritage Foundation as sources of ideas for spending cuts and promised to oppose tax increases. In line with his other views, he favors a reduction in the tax on capital gains income.

As do most Michigan members, Knollenberg opposes any increase in automobile fleet gasoline mileage standards.

But, atypically, he favors the North American Free Trade Agreement, saying the number of jobs gained from increased exports would more than compensate for any lost.

Knollenberg got into the race when Broomfield — who had been nearly untouchable because of his reputation for looking out for the district's needs — decided in April not to seek re-election.

Abortion rights advocates quickly persuaded longtime Oakland County Circuit Judge Alice L. Gilbert to give up her seat on the bench to run in the primary. State Sen. Dave Honigman also was in the race, and Gilbert's supporters were discomfited by Honigman's ambiguous — but presumed negative — stand on abortion.

All three candidates ran vigorous negative ads. Millionaires Gilbert and Honigman used television extensively. Gilbert attacked her opponents' positions on abortion and singled out Honigman as being overly ambitious. Honigman zeroed in on Gilbert, charging that she was the laziest judge in Detroit.

Knollenberg, whose abortion views were well-known, otherwise seemed to escape the name-calling. And though he could not afford television advertising, he attacked both Gilbert and Honigman on radio for trying to buy the election.

Knollenberg won more than 43 percent in the primary. Despite expectations that abortion rights supporters would rally for Gilbert, she finished third.

In the general election, Democrat Walter Briggs made his second run at the seat, hoping that redistricting — which had loosened slightly the GOP's hold — would give him a chance. Briggs, grandson of the man who built Tiger Stadium and nephew of respected former Sen. Philip A. Hart, had taken on Broomfield in 1990. Then, Briggs won only 34 percent of the vote. Casting himself as a moderate, hoping to capitalize on a Michigan victory by Democrat Bill Clinton and focusing on Knollenberg's abortion views, this time Briggs managed 40 percent. Knollenberg's 58 percent was right around the district's GOP registration.

Michigan 11

Southeast — Part of Oakland County

The 11th is the lone Republican stronghold in metropolitan Detroit. Unlike the other suburban districts, which sometimes flirt with local GOP candidates and flock to Republican presidential candidates, the 11th is GOP turf in good times and bad. In 1992, George Bush won quite easily here, as did Knollenberg in the open seat House race.

A mixture of white, upper- and middle-class residents, the 11th covers the southwestern portion of Oakland County and the city of Livonia in Wayne County. Much of the vote is cast in the populous eastern section, which is better-educated and more affluent than the western half of the county.

Birmingham and Bloomfield hold the mansions and homes of auto executives and professionals. Birmingham's tony downtown shopping district used to be considered Michigan's version of Rodeo Drive while Bloomfield Hills was George Romney's hometown in his days as an auto executive (before he was governor and a presidential candidate). More than half the housing units in Bloomfield and Bloomfield Hills have four bedrooms or more.

Farmington Hills, Southfield and West Bloomfield are population centers whose recent growth has qualified them for "edge city" status. Located north of 8 Mile Road — Detroit's northern boundary — these municipalities sit in the corridor between Grand River Avenue and the Northwestern Freeway that has served as one of the primary routes for white flight from the city.

While the rest of Oakland County is hostile to Detroit and unreceptive to blacks moving out of the city, Southfield has a relatively large and growing black population. Nearly 30 percent of the city's residents are black; many are middle-class families trying to escape Detroit's high crime rates. As Detroit has declined, businesses have flocked to surrounding suburbs such as Southfield. Southfield now has more multipurpose office space than Detroit.

The rest of the 11th is overwhelmingly white. Lathrup Village is slightly more than 20 percent black, but outside of it and Southfield, there is little racial diversity.

The northwestern part of the 11th is covered with lakes and recreation areas. Places such as Novi, South Lyon and Wixom in the southwest have newer subdivisions and are populated with a fair number of socially conservative blue-collar workers.

Wayne County's portion of the 11th consists of Redford Township and part of Livonia. Professionals and middle-level managers from the area's auto plants give a GOP tilt to Livonia, which is shared with the 13th District. Those sentiments may change, however, once General Motors completes the scheduled closure of its Livonia plant.

Of the five districts that delve into Wayne County, the portion of the 11th there was the only one to back Bush in 1992. Accounting for about one-fifth of the district vote, these voters also backed Knollenberg.

1990 Population: 580,956. White 540,408 (93%), Black 23,967 (4%), Other 16,581 (3%). Hispanic origin 7,404 (1%). 18 and over 444,245 (76%), 62 and over 89,326 (15%). Median age: 35.

Committees

Banking, Finance & Urban Affairs (14th of 20 Republicans)
Consumer Credit & Insurance; Housing & Community Development

Small Business (13th of 18 Republicans)
Minority Enterprise, Finance & Urban Development; Procurement, Taxation & Tourism

Campaign Finance

	Receipts	Receipts from PACs		Expend-itures
1992				
Knollenberg (R)	$496,036	$116,436	(23%)	$490,926
Briggs (D)	$272,984	$78,350	(29%)	$272,422

Key Votes

1993

Require parental notification of minors' abortions	Y
Require unpaid family and medical leave	N
Approve national "motor voter" registration bill	N
Approve budget increasing taxes and reducing deficit	N
Approve economic stimulus plan	N

Elections

1992 General		
Joe Knollenberg (R)	168,940	(58%)
Walter Briggs (D)	117,725	(40%)
Brian Richard Wright (LIBERT)	4,144	(1%)
1992 Primary		
Joe Knollenberg (R)	30,022	(43%)
Dave Honigman (R)	20,641	(30%)
Alice L. Gilbert (R)	18,954	(27%)

District Vote for President

	1992	
D	117,274	(37%)
R	149,109	(47%)
I	50,675	(16%)

12 Sander M. Levin (D)

Of Southfield — Elected 1982; 6th Term

Born: Sept. 6, 1931, Detroit, Mich.
Education: U. of Chicago, B.A. 1952; Columbia U., M.A. 1954; Harvard U., LL.B. 1957.
Occupation: Lawyer.
Family: Wife, Victoria Schlafer; four children.
Religion: Jewish.
Political Career: Mich. Senate, 1965-71; Democratic nominee for governor, 1970, 1974.
Capitol Office: 106 Cannon Bldg. 20515; 225-4961.

In Washington: Levin will have ample opportunity in the 103rd Congress to apply his studious, issue-oriented approach to two areas in which he has been increasingly active on the Ways and Means Committee in recent years: trade and health care.

A believer in international cooperation and a liberal on many foreign policy questions, Levin has nonetheless been confrontational on trade matters when they affect his hard-pressed working-class constituents. Some think his views on automobile imports, in particular, have become increasingly inflexible.

In other ways, as well, Levin has been something of a political hybrid. He shares the fiscal concerns of the younger Democrats elected with him in 1982, a year of recession and concern about the federal deficit. At the start of the 103rd Congress, he became co-chairman with Pete Peterson of Florida of the Democratic Budget Study Group, a loose organization of mostly fiscally conservative members who meet weekly to keep abreast of budgetary issues. Yet he retains the orthodox liberalism of his first days in politics in the mid-1960s, and thus a zeal to address today's social needs on the scale of the Great Society.

Now in his sixth House term, he has won considerable respect as a judicious legislator determined to find right answers even if they are not simple answers.

He has applied that approach to health-care matters, focusing his attention on solving narrow, finite problems, rather than embracing big-picture solutions.

In the 101st Congress he was given high marks for shepherding into law a carefully crafted provision requiring Medicare and Medicaid providers to inform patients of their rights under state law to execute "living wills" or give advance directives about their care should they later be unable to communicate.

In the 102nd Congress, he pushed for revisions to the Medicare program to permit cancer treatments using cutting-edge drugs, for which reimbursement is generally prohibited.

Levin's standing would be even higher were it not for his penchant for discussing complex issues in all their details and abstractions, a trait that contributed to his losses in two elections for the Michigan governorship in the 1970s.

It might also have cost him a coveted seat on Ways and Means, but his dogged pursuit of that prize and his support of the panel's 1986 tax-overhaul bill overcame whatever qualms Chairman Dan Rostenkowski, an Illinois Democrat, may have had that Levin would make himself too obtrusive on the tightly controlled panel. Also, Michigan had a geographic claim on the seat.

Joining the committee in the 100th Congress, Levin used the assignment largely to pursue his interest in trade. Along with his close ally, Majority Leader Richard A. Gephardt of Missouri, Levin has promoted the renewal of the "Super 301" retaliation provisions of a 1987 trade act, which expired in 1990.

The House passed a Gephardt-Levin bill in 1992 that would have restored Super 301 language requiring negotiations with and possible sanctions against countries that discriminate against U.S.-made goods. The measure included a Levin amendment added on the floor that would have specifically required negotiations with Japan over both the number of cars that country exports to the United States and the quantity of U.S.-made parts included in cars produced in the United States by Japanese-owned companies.

Lest Levin be seen as a blunt Japan-basher, however, he proved his willingness to step into his adversaries' shoes in 1990. At the time, the hottest book in Washington was "The Japan That Can Say No," Shintaro Ishihara's tough-talking defense of Japan's economic nationalism. While trade hawks critical of Japanese trade policies were incensed by the book, Levin invited its author to accompany him to a Michigan factory town crippled by competition from Japanese imports. And he went a long step further, going to visit some of the people

Michigan 12

Suburban Detroit — Warren; Sterling Heights

Think of the suburban 12th as a square. The top half contains fast-growing Troy and Sterling Heights. The southwest corner includes some older, racially mixed areas, while the city of Warren anchors the southeastern corner.

The auto industry is the thread that binds the 12th and with the industry comes the United Auto Workers (UAW) as a force. But unlike in the other heavily unionized districts of southeastern Michigan, that does not automatically translate into Democratic votes.

In Troy, a burgeoning high-tech sector revolves around auto industry consulting work that has been farmed out to smaller companies. EDS — one of the largest of these firms — is a major employer; it does computer consulting for General Motors. Another economic presence is Kmart, which keeps its world headquarters in Troy.

On the western side of the district, along what is known as the Golden Corridor, more traditional methods of car-making are evident. From 8 Mile Road — the northern border of Detroit — to Utica in the northern extreme of the 12th, this stretch includes a number of auto plants that make virtually every aspect of the car.

Close by the industrial corridor, in Warren, stands the GM Tech Center, a design and engineering center. Not far from there is a General Dynamics tank assembly plant, where in 1988 Democratic presidential nominee Michael S. Dukakis took his ill-advised tank ride.

Across the district, Democrats have an edge, but at the presidential level, a large contingent of Reagan Democrats boost the GOP. In 1992, George Bush lost the 12th by fewer than 4,000 votes.

With a large number of blue-collar workers, the 12th is fertile ground for Democratic candidates.

Warren, the district's largest city, is a traditional Democratic stronghold, yet socially conservative. Within the city, Republicans have run well in the north, where voters are better off.

A solid Democratic vote is also cast in majority-black Royal Oak Township and in Oak Park, where more than a third of the population is black. A sizable Jewish population in affluent Huntington Woods, Oak Park and Southfield, which is shared with the 11th District, favors Democratic candidates.

Voters in Troy are more likely to be transplants to the area and less likely to be strongly affiliated with a political party than those in the southern half of the 12th. They lean toward the GOP. Sterling Heights is less transient; a large number of its residents are upwardly mobile, former Warren residents.

Republican strength in Troy — supplemented by the white-collar influx — and the swing voters of Sterling Heights kept Bush and Rep. Levin's GOP challenger competitive in 1992. Bush managed to carry the Macomb County portion of the 12th, which includes Warren and Sterling Heights.

1990 Population: 580,956. White 541,953 (93%), Black 21,717 (4%), Other 17,286 (3%). Hispanic origin 6,796 (1%). 18 and over 442,863 (76%), 62 and over 89,874 (15%). Median age: 34.

Ishihara represents in the Japanese Diet.

In the mid-1980s, Levin supported the controversial Gephardt "fair trade" amendment, defending it against those who called it protectionist. Responding to a negative editorial, Levin described himself as a non-isolationist and "a committed internationalist." But, he added, that "doesn't mean allowing others to run roughshod over our home market or lock us out of theirs."

Levin again expressed the auto industry's concerns when Ways and Means turned to legislation implementing a U.S.-Canada trade agreement phasing out tariffs between the two nations over 10 years, though he ultimately supported the pact. And as the 103rd Congress anticipated action on the North American Free Trade Agreement, incorporating tariff cuts and other trade concessions among the United States, Mexico and Canada, Levin warned that it was "doomed" unless supplemental agreements were reached addressing concerns about wages, worker safety and environmental protections.

Levin has had something substantive to say on just about every major issue the panel considered. He was among the core group of Democrats most opposed to cutting taxes on capital gains in the 101st Congress. And, scoring points with Rostenkowski, he was also among the last defenders of the 1988 Medicare insurance for catastrophic illness. Levin continued to support the program after most of Congress had bowed to senior citizens enraged by the associated surtax.

Like his brother Carl in the Senate, Levin was a leader in the House minority opposing a new federal death penalty included in the 1988 antidrug package. Unable to block pre-election support for the provision, opponents could merely pick at it; Levin won adoption of his amendment barring execution of the mentally retarded. Unlike 30 fellow liberals, he voted for the drug bill on final passage despite the capital punishment provision.

At Home: Levin's 1982 election capped his unexpected return to politics after an eight-year absence from the public eye. Levin first won office in 1964, taking a state Senate seat in the heavily Jewish Oakland County suburbs north of Detroit. He served as state Democratic Party chairman in the late 1960s and was viewed as one of the party's rising stars in 1970, when he challenged incumbent Republican William G. Milliken for the governorship.

But the low-key, even-tempered manner that had made Levin a successful legislator and party leader was less useful against Milliken. Levin won almost 49 percent of the vote in 1970, but four years later, he slipped under 47 percent.

After that, Levin's name left the front pages. But when Democratic Rep. William M. Brodhead decided not to seek re-election 12 weeks before the 1982 primary, Levin returned to the area he represented in the state Senate and announced his candidacy. Levin's name and his support from the party establishment helped him overcome five primary opponents.

Critics accused Levin of trying to regain public office on the popularity of his younger brother, Sen. Carl Levin, although Sander Levin's statewide races had in fact helped pave the way for Carl Levin's 1978 victory. Sander Levin won the old 17th easily, and since then has been seriously challenged only once.

It came in 1992, as a result of redistricting. After a federal panel merged Levin's district with Democratic colleague and friend Dennis M. Hertel's 14th, Hertel decided to retire.

Still, Levin had some convincing to do. Besides Hertel's constituents, there were voters from other districts who were added when the map was radically redrawn. Even though Levin spent about more than $1 million to woo them, he could manage only 53 percent against Oakland County commissioner John Pappageorge.

Committee

Ways & Means (12th of 24 Democrats)
Health; Human Resources

Elections

1992 General

Sander M. Levin (D)	137,514	(53%)
John Pappageorge (R)	119,357	(46%)
Charles Hahn (LIBERT)	2,751	(1%)

1990 General

Sander M. Levin (D)	92,205	(70%)
Blaine L. Lankford (R)	40,100	(30%)

Previous Winning Percentages: **1988** (70%) **1986** (76%) **1984** (100%) **1982** (67%)

District Vote for President

1992

D	119,055	(42%)
R	115,065	(41%)
I	49,519	(17%)

Campaign Finance

	Receipts	Receipts from PACs		Expend-itures
1992				
Levin (D)	$1,028,481	$504,521	(49%)	$1,185,400
Pappageorge (R)	$192,095	$16,800	(9%)	$190,203
1990				
Levin (D)	$356,280	$241,525	(68%)	$271,072

Key Votes

1993	
Require parental notification of minors' abortions	N
Require unpaid family and medical leave	Y
Approve national "motor voter" registration bill	Y
Approve budget increasing taxes and reducing deficit	Y
Approve economic stimulus plan	Y
1992	
Approve balanced-budget constitutional amendment	N
Close down space station program	Y
Approve U.S. aid for former Soviet Union	Y
Allow shifting funds from defense to domestic programs	Y
1991	
Extend unemployment benefits using deficit financing	Y
Approve waiting period for handgun purchases	Y
Authorize use of force in Persian Gulf	N

Voting Studies

	Presidential Support		Party Unity		Conservative Coalition	
Year	**S**	**O**	**S**	**O**	**S**	**O**
1992	18	82	96 †	4 †	30 †	70 †
1991	28	72	95	5	8	92
1990	19	81	97	3	19	81
1989	31	69	98	2	20	80
1988	24	73	94	2	11	89
1987	19	80	97	2	19	81
1986	19	81	97	2	12	86
1985	23	78	97	3	13	87
1984	30	70	93 †	7 †	15	85
1983	28	72	94	6	19	81

† Not eligible for all recorded votes.

Interest Group Ratings

Year	ADA	AFL-CIO	CCUS	ACU
1992	95	83	38	4
1991	100	100	30	0
1990	89	100	21	4
1989	95	100	20	0
1988	100	100	31	0
1987	84	100	13	0
1986	85	100	33	0
1985	85	88	32	10
1984	90	85	25	5
1983	95	94	25	0

13 William D. Ford (D)

Of Taylor — Elected 1964; 15th Term

Born: Aug. 6, 1927, Detroit, Mich.

Education: Nebraska State Teachers College, 1946; Wayne State U., 1947-48; U. of Denver, B.S. 1949, J.D. 1951.

Military Service: Navy, 1944-46; Air Force Reserve, 1950-58.

Occupation: Lawyer.

Family: Wife, Mary Whalen; three children.

Religion: United Church of Christ.

Political Career: Taylor Township justice of the peace, 1955-57; Melvindale city attorney, 1957-59; Taylor Township attorney, 1957-63; Mich. Senate, 1963-65.

Capitol Office: 2107 Rayburn Bldg. 20515; 225-6261.

In Washington: Raised by working-class parents — New Deal disciples who told him, "The Democratic Party cared and the Republican Party didn't" — Ford came to the House in time to champion Lyndon B. Johnson's Great Society.

For a man so steeped in party dogma, the 1980s were trying times, as Ford faced a Republican administration hostile to the idea of government as social engineer.

With the arrival of the 1990s, everything began to fall into place again. The country's mood shifted, just as Ford's political clout began a steady climb upward. In 1991, at the start of the 102nd Congress, he was elevated to the chairmanship of the Education and Labor Committee. Then in 1992, Bill Clinton was elected president, giving Ford a Democratic mandate and an even higher profile.

However, Clinton's election also brought the outspoken Ford a new mission and responsibility. After battling administrations with practical impunity for more than a decade, he is charged with being a good soldier for Clinton. He must now take orders from a higher authority.

Early in the 103rd, with his handling of Family and Medical Leave Act, he showed a willingness to be a team player, accepting Clinton's version of the bill rather than pushing for the stronger provisions he favored.

A former labor lawyer, Ford is a union stalwart. As with other pieces of his legislative agenda, life experience contributed to Ford's personal commitment to organized labor. His father worked at Kaiser-Frazer, and when he collapsed at the auto plant, at age 42, officials claimed he died of a heart attack. Suspicious, Ford, then 20, began a personal investigation and learned that his father had been killed by toxic smoke inhalation. When confronted with the facts, the company offered the family $5,000.

Ford is known as a tenacious legislator, with one of the best institutional memories in Congress. He spent 14 years working to pass legislation to give workers 60 days' notice before a plant closed, and he is said to remember the name of every member who voted against the successful 1987 bill. Ford's keen memory, however, can be a double-edged sword, as it occasionally leads him to hold forth long after those listening are ready to move on.

Passage of the 1987 plant-closing bill was the end of a long struggle for Ford. Some 14 years and many compromises after he first introduced the legislation, it became the Democrats' *cause célèbre* in the 100th Congress, the issue they hoped would prove GOP callousness to workers and win back the Reagan Democrats in the 1988 election.

The proposal was attached to a major trade bill in the House. With typical bluntness, Ford repeatedly warned his party's waverers, many from the oil states, that if his provision were challenged, he would go after the section in the trade bill repealing the windfall profits tax on oil.

After Reagan vetoed the trade bill, citing the plant-closing language, Congress passed the bill separately by a margin that indicated a veto could not hold. Ultimately, the president allowed the plant-closing bill to become law without his signature.

For years, many considered Ford the de facto chairman of Education and Labor. The previous chairman, Augustus F. Hawkins of California, who retired at the end of the 101st Congress at the age of 83, shared Ford's New Deal ideology. But Ford is more involved in legislative details and more aggressive in pushing the Democratic line as well as his own. Upon his election to the chairmanship, Ford quickly imposed a new ban on foreign cars parking in committee spaces at the Capitol.

Temperamentally, Ford is a crusty old-school pol — blunt, aggressive and partisan.

Michigan 13

Southeast — Ann Arbor; Westland; Ypsilanti

One of the first things Rep. Ford did upon his election as House Education and Labor chairman in 1990 was to inform staff members that all staff parking spaces would be reserved for American cars only.

There was good reason behind his edict: Back then, as now, his district had about two dozen auto plants scattered across eastern Washtenaw and western Wayne counties. That number may soon diminish, as General Motors continues its employment cutbacks and completes the scheduled closing of the Willow Run assembly plant in Ypsilanti Township.

Western Wayne County provides more than 60 percent of the vote, much of it coming from the cities east of I-275, on the eastern edge of the 13th. Many of these cities, such as Garden City, Inkster, Romulus and Westland, are primarily blue collar, with a heavy dependence on auto industry jobs. These residents turn out a reliably Democratic vote, as do the mostly black voters of Inkster.

In recent presidential elections, many have crossed over to vote for GOP nominees, but auto industry cutbacks and the recession brought them back to Bill Clinton in 1992.

Farther west, closer to Washtenaw County, the townships are less industrialized and more Republican. Canton, Northville and Plymouth generally have higher incomes than their county neighbors who live closer to Detroit; they are receptive to GOP candidates. Recognizing the area as one of the few sources of GOP votes in southeastern Michigan, George Bush made several campaign stops here in 1992.

Democratic Ann Arbor, the state's seventh-largest city, casts the bulk of Washtenaw County's ballots. Before 1992 redistricting, back when the city was part of the old 2nd District, the liberal community of the University of Michigan was a surefire source of Democratic votes against then-GOP Rep. Carl D. Pursell. A large number of blacks in Ypsilanti and Ypsilanti Township also boosts local and statewide Democrats.

Traditionally, Washtenaw County as a whole has swung back and forth at the presidential level, as a result of the GOP small towns and farmers who populate the rest of the county. It was the only county in the nation to support George McGovern in 1972, then back Gerald R. Ford in 1976.

Fortunately for 13th District Democrats, most of the Republicans in Washtenaw County now live in the 7th and 8th districts. While the auto industry remains a vital source of jobs, an emerging high-tech corridor has taken shape in the Ann Arbor-Detroit corridor, between I-94 and I-96. Known as "automation alley," this stretch draws on the engineering skills and brainpower of the University of Michigan, and to a lesser extent, Eastern Michigan University in Ypsilanti. Robotics companies have clustered in the area, making factory automation equipment that, eventually, will lead to even more job losses in the auto industry.

1990 Population: 580,956. White 494,938 (85%), Black 64,052 (11%), Other 21,966 (4%). Hispanic origin 10,131 (2%). 18 and over 442,445 (76%), 62 and over 62,132 (11%). Median age: 31.

Ford counts fellow Michigan Democrat John D. Dingell, powerful chairman of the House Energy and Commerce Committee, as a close friend. Now hunting buddies, the two first met when Ford was a justice of the peace outside Detroit and Dingell a young prosecutor there. Institutional observers are watching to see if Ford, like Dingell, will strive to expand his committee's jurisdiction.

Over the years, the committee has had something of a split personality. The panel tends to function in a cooperative, bipartisan manner on education issues, while resorting to partisan fisticuffs on labor issues.

This still holds true for the most part, but under Ford's chairmanship, battles also have erupted over education.

Twice during Ford's first session as chairman, he reneged on deals he had cut with Republicans on education bills. The first incident, said moderate Wisconsin Republican Steve Gunderson, "was the committee's darkest hour of this session."

On private school choice, the centerpiece of President Bush's education plan, Ford worked out a deal with ranking Republican Bill Goodling of Pennsylvania, who was negotiating on behalf of then-White House Chief of Staff John H. Sununu, to allow a limited amount of private school choice with federal dollars. After the Senate voted down a school choice plan, however, Ford angered Republicans by scuttling his bill and introducing a new one with no mention of choice. Ford said his deal was with Sununu, and, by then, Sununu no longer worked at the White House.

Relations between Ford and Republicans also grew more tense during the reauthorization of the Higher Education Act.

Tom Coleman of Missouri, then the ranking Republican of the subcommittee responsible for the bill, thought he had a commitment from Ford to put a cap on spending on one provision. But when the bill was printed, the cap was gone. Ford denied that an agreement ever existed. Coleman took his name off the bill.

If Ford ever forgets for a moment the conservative Republican presence on the committee, he has a GOP stalwart just as brash and pedantic as himself to remind him.

Dick Armey of Texas, chairman of the House Republican Conference and a keeper of the GOP flame in that chamber, is Ford's sworn enemy. Armey, who has only warm thoughts of former Chairman Hawkins, has not adjusted well to Ford's style, which is much like his own.

"If Bill Ford were not chairman of Ed and Labor, I'd probably get off. Somebody's got to talk back to him," Armey says.

Ford describes Armey as "just kind of a pain in the ass."

Ford still has the advantage of a moderate ranking member in Goodling as well as another moderate committee player in Gunderson.

Armey is not Ford's only concern on the committee. As chairman, he must soothe the interests of those in his own party who are more prone to federal spending and less to compromise than he is. Patsy T. Mink of Hawaii and some other more liberal committee Democrats sometimes have preferred that Ford be less accommodating.

In education, college aid has been Ford's specialty over the years, and his priority for the 102nd was the reauthorization of the Higher Education Act. He had a hand in its 1965 creation as well as numerous reauthorizations since. Ford's interest is in helping not just the poor but also the middle class, whose support he believes is politically crucial to the programs' survival.

The Higher Education Act, signed by Bush, opened aid programs to more middle-class students by removing a family's home or farm equity from calculations of how much aid a student needs to attend school. Under the law, about 300 schools would participate in a direct loan project, with 35 percent of the institutions allowing students to repay their loans according to how much money they earned after graduation. Other students would pay a fixed amount each month, regardless of how much money they earned.

Ford succeeded in getting the Higher Education Act reauthorized in 1985 by brokering a complex bipartisan bill, packed with enough pork barrel projects for each panel member to have a vested interest in its fate. He also had to accommodate Congressional Black Caucus members who were protective of aid for historically black colleges. "I have real difficulty," Ford said, with the idea "that a school that was created to keep blacks separate from other people in college should have money on a continuing basis." A compromise funneled funds to black colleges and to institutions with minority enrollments.

As chairman of the Post Office and Civil Service Committee, Ford was best known for his role as the undertaker eager to bury any proposals that would block pay raises for lawmakers and federal employees, indulging his love for legislative sleight of hand. Back then, Ford could afford to lead the pro-pay-raise side because he had never had serious political problems at home. "I know for a fact that the vast majority of the people I represent think I'm vastly underpaid," he once boasted.

In 1978, Ford was labor's negotiator on President Jimmy Carter's civil service revision bill, expressing the unions' fears that merit incentives written into the bill would weaken job protection. Ultimately, he reached a compromise on behalf of the unions with the administration and with the bill's chief sponsor, Arizona Democrat Morris K. Udall.

One issue that Ford has been politically cautious about over the years is busing to achieve racial balance in schools. He signed congressional petitions, held hearings and voted for measures aimed against busing. But when he balked in 1972 at signing a petition to pry an anti-busing constitutional amendment out of the Judiciary Committee, demonstrators marched around his Michigan office, chanting, "Sign or Resign." Ford insisted he simply did not like stripping a committee of its jurisdiction, but the groups were not appeased. In 1979 he voted for an anti-busing amendment on the floor.

At Home: Ford's third round of redistricting in 1992 was perhaps his most difficult. A significant number of unfamiliar voters were added, though the district retained its Democratic edge.

Almost as difficult as reaching these new voters was cranking up Ford's political apparatus, which had not faced a tough challenge in decades. Since 1964, Ford's lowest re-election score was 60 percent.

His 1992 opponent, GOP state Sen. R. Robert Geake, had several advantages. A proven vote-getter serving his fourth full term in the state Senate, Geake had ties to the University of Michigan in Ann Arbor. The liberal college town, which had been added to the district, was supposed to be a key wellspring of Democratic votes for Ford.

If Ford was worried, he did not let on. News stories detailing Ford's penchant for flying first class and dining well failed to spark much reaction from Ford.

Republican strategists touted the race as an upset special in the waning weeks of the campaign, but Bush's anemic showing in populous Washtenaw County doomed Geake's effort. Ford won 52 percent.

Winning his seat in 1964 was much easier. The newly created 15th District had no incumbent, and most local party leaders favored Ford for the opening. His only significant primary opposition came from township politician William Faust, who later became majority leader of the state Senate. Ford defeated Faust 45 percent to 36 percent, with the rest of the vote split among three others.

Ford drew more publicity than most secure incumbents in the early 1980s when he had to contend with Gerald Carlson, a "white rights" advocate who once had ties to the Ku Klux Klan and the American Nazi Party. Carlson ran against Ford as a Republican in 1980 and 1984, and as a Democrat in 1982.

Carlson's 1982 candidacy went nowhere, but in November 1984 he polled 40 percent, a result that shocked and embarrassed local Republican officials, who had disavowed him.

Committee

Education & Labor (Chairman)
Postsecondary Education (chairman)

Elections

1992 General		
William D. Ford (D)	127,642	(52%)
R. Robert Geake (R)	105,169	(43%)
Randall F. Roe (I)	8,626	(4%)
Paul Steven Jensen (TIC)	3,314	(1%)
1990 General		
William D. Ford (D)	68,742	(61%)
Burl C. Adkins (R)	41,092	(37%)
David R. Hunt (LIBERT)	2,497	(2%)

Previous Winning Percentages: **1988** (64%) **1986** (75%) **1984** (60%) **1982** (73%) **1980** (68%) **1978** (80%) **1976** (74%) **1974** (78%) **1972** (66%) **1970** (80%) **1968** (71%) **1966** (68%) **1964** (71%)

District Vote for President

1992
D 125,913 (49%)
R 86,769 (34%)
I 42,875 (17%)

Campaign Finance

	Receipts	Receipts from PACs		Expend-itures
1992				
Ford (D)	$681,981	$520,850	(76%)	$872,349
Geake (R)	$188,860	$35,031	(19%)	$188,138
1990				
Ford (D)	$384,737	$280,598	(73%)	$354,964
Adkins (R)	$42,511	$5,200	(12%)	$42,834

Key Votes

1993	
Require parental notification of minors' abortions	N
Require unpaid family and medical leave	Y
Approve national "motor voter" registration bill	Y
Approve budget increasing taxes and reducing deficit	Y
Approve economic stimulus plan	Y
1992	
Approve balanced-budget constitutional amendment	N
Close down space station program	Y
Approve U.S. aid for former Soviet Union	Y
Allow shifting funds from defense to domestic programs	Y
1991	
Extend unemployment benefits using deficit financing	Y
Approve waiting period for handgun purchases	Y
Authorize use of force in Persian Gulf	N

Voting Studies

	Presidential Support		Party Unity		Conservative Coalition	
Year	**S**	**O**	**S**	**O**	**S**	**O**
1992	13	81	88	2	17	69
1991	22	73	84	3	16	73
1990	12	65	67	3	9	65
1989	24	73	90	2	7	90
1988	13	80	83	2	5	89
1987	11	84	88	3	9	88
1986	18	79	84	4	12	78
1985	16	76	71	2	7	87
1984	23	65	82	5	17	75
1983	12	78	87	2	8	82
1982	30	62	90	1	8	77
1981	26	58	84	3	12	68

Interest Group Ratings

Year	ADA	AFL-CIO	CCUS	ACU
1992	95	100	25	0
1991	95	100	13	0
1990	78	100	33	5
1989	95	91	40	0
1988	100	100	23	0
1987	92	100	0	0
1986	80	93	6	5
1985	80	100	20	5
1984	85	100	38	0
1983	90	100	10	0
1982	85	100	14	5
1981	70	100	6	0

14 John Conyers Jr. (D)

Of Detroit — Elected 1964; 15th Term

Born: May 16, 1929, Detroit, Mich.
Education: Wayne State U., B.A. 1957, LL.B. 1958.
Military Service: National Guard, 1948-52; Army 1952-53; Army Reserve, 1953-57.
Occupation: Lawyer.
Family: Wife, Monica Ann Esters; one child.
Religion: Baptist.
Political Career: Candidate for mayor of Detroit, 1989.
Capitol Office: 2426 Rayburn Bldg. 20515; 225-5126.

In Washington: While many of his African-American peers have toned down their rhetoric over the years, Conyers has not. He is seen as a more accomplished legislator after two terms chairing the Government Operations Committee, but he is still prone to preach — even when it does not boost his stature in the House.

As the senior member and co-founder of the Congressional Black Caucus, Conyers has long viewed his role as more than that of lawmaker. When an issue affects minorities, Conyers often takes it on and seems to relish the spotlight.

In 1992, he led an unsuccessful last-ditch effort to defeat the nomination of Edward Earl Carnes Jr. for the 11th Circuit Court of Appeals. Conyers joined the NAACP in opposing Carnes because, as an assistant attorney general in Alabama, Carnes had defended death sentences imposed on blacks in cases where prosecutors had intentionally excluded black jurors.

In 1983, he won creation of a federal holiday to commemorate the Rev. Dr. Martin Luther King Jr. He has seen far less success, however, with his plan to authorize a study of the impact of slavery on living African Americans. The study would include recommendations to Congress on possible remedies including reparations.

Though Conyers represents an overwhelmingly black urban district, his actions are rooted in the soil of the civil rights movement, of which he is a veteran. He has spent considerable time outside Washington and his district campaigning for other black politicians. In 1988, he claimed to have spent more days campaigning for Jesse Jackson than any other black member of the House. In early 1993, he spent more than a week in Mississippi, helping to elect Democrat Bennie Thompson, who won a special House election.

Conyers shows no signs of relaxing his activist role. While other committee chairmen are primed to be good soldiers for President Clinton, Conyers got off to a tense start.

When Clinton seemed bent on nominating a white woman for attorney general, Conyers urged the White House to expand the field, arguing that appointment of a black would send a strong signal to a black community that has historically felt ill-served by the criminal justice system. But Conyers told The Detroit News that communication between the black caucus and the president on the issue was "a one-way street."

Conyers faces other political challenges in the 103rd Congress. While other chairmen look forward to pushing a Democratic mandate, the Government Operations Committee is charged with overseeing and ferreting out problems in the federal government on a broad scale.

During recent Republican administrations, the committee has leveled blasts at agencies and presidents on any number of issues that drew national attention. Conyers' challenge as chairman under a Democratic president will be to work with Clinton to push measures that could improve government functions.

Conyers succeeded in 1990 with one attempt to boost government efficiency, winning enactment of a bill to install chief financial officers in federal departments and agencies. The aim was to centralize financial reporting and shore up the management arm of the Office of Management and Budget. The bill had bipartisan support, though the Bush administration wanted it to go further.

He may finally prevail in the 103rd Congress with a measure he has pushed since the 101st to elevate the Environmental Protection Agency to Cabinet status. President Bush's opposition to specifics of the bill helped stall the effort in the past, but Clinton favors the idea.

Conyers remains the No. 3 Democrat on the Judiciary Committee, where he is known best for the bills he opposes — in recent years, attempts to roll back the federal anti-racketeering law.

During most of his three decades in Congress, Conyers has seemed more interested in being a rebel than in becoming a power broker. Some colleagues found his style sarcastic and abrasive, making it difficult for him to coordi-

Michigan 14

Parts of Detroit; Harper Woods; Highland Park

Henry Ford built his first large factory in Highland Park in 1909, followed by Buick, R. E. Olds and the Fisher brothers. Soon afterward the nascent automobile industry attracted rural Michiganders, residents of Appalachia, Southern blacks and Eastern Europeans, many of whom sought housing in the sea of single and two-family homes on Detroit's north side.

The industry kept Detroit working and prosperous for much of the century, but over the past few decades, the city has been losing jobs and people rapidly. The auto industry jobs have moved to Mexico and other non-unionized areas. The residents have moved to the mainly white suburbs that ring the city.

In 1960, the city contained about 1.7 million inhabitants, two-thirds of whom were white. By 1990, the city barely exceeded 1 million residents, three-quarters of whom were black. Highland Park exemplifies this demographic change.

Completely enveloped by Detroit, Highland Park was once a white-ethnic bastion and home to the Chrysler Corp. headquarters. Now it is primarily black, with a significant contingent of retired autoworkers. Rising unemployment and tough economic times have gradually chipped away at the city's middle-class character. Conditions may worsen now that Chrysler has decided to move to suburban Auburn Hills.

The rest of the district is centered on the north side of Detroit, taking in Harper Woods, Grosse Pointe Woods and Grosse Pointe Shores on the eastern edge and a handful of precincts from Dearborn Heights (the rest are in the 16th District) on the southwestern fringe. It is generally more residential and better off than the city's other congressional district, the 15th.

Rosedale is home to larger residences that were built for General Motors executives in the 1930s. North of 7 Mile Road, there are racially mixed communities with a relatively high percentage of professionals and white-collar city employees. Toward the west side are some of the city's largest and most politically active black churches.

Politically, this is a Democratic stronghold where Republicans have virtually no presence.

In presidential elections, Democratic nominees regularly rack up the state's highest percentages here and in the 15th District. In statewide politics, Democratic candidates must run up huge margins in Detroit to offset their losses outside of southeastern Michigan. Democratic then-Gov. James J. Blanchard's 1990 upset loss to Republican John Engler was partly attributed to his inability to win big in the Motor City.

The only places where Republicans find quarter are outside the city. The blue-collar and middle-class denizens of Harper Woods lean Republican at the statewide and national levels, but they are swing voters who often split tickets. The doctors, lawyers and auto executives of affluent Grosse Pointe Woods and Grosse Pointe Shores are even more receptive to GOP candidates.

1990 Population: 580,956. White 169,875 (29%), Black 401,444 (69%), Other 9,637 (2%). Hispanic origin 6,127 (1%). 18 and over 408,963 (70%), 62 and over 80,771 (14%). Median age: 31.

nate the alliances needed to legislate. But Conyers managed to alter that image in the 100th Congress, with his leadership on the impeachment of former U.S. District Judge Alcee L. Hastings.

As chairman of the Judiciary Subcommittee on Criminal Justice, Conyers was obliged to investigate Hastings, who had been accused of conspiring to solicit a bribe and leaking wiretap information. For Conyers, investigating a black judge who claimed the allegations against him were racially motivated presented a particularly sticky political problem. Complicating matters, Hastings had been acquitted by a jury.

When Conyers began the proceedings in 1987, he indicated that he, too, saw the possibility of racial bias in the charges. But as the investigation progressed, Conyers reached what he later called the most difficult decision of his House career: that Hastings was guilty and had fabricated his court defense.

"We did not fight the civil rights struggle to replace one sort of judicial corruption with another," Conyers said, recalling the difficulties blacks had faced with white judges.

The impeachment resolution was easily approved by the subcommittee and full committee, and Conyers gave a floor speech on the case that brought him a standing ovation and helped to deliver a vote of 413-3.

In an ironic twist for Conyers, Hastings joined the black caucus in 1993, having been elected to the House from South Florida.

At Home: The son of an autoworker, Conyers became interested in politics while in law school and worked loyally in the party apparatus. The creation in 1964 of a second black-majority district in Detroit gave him his first opportunity. He ran for Congress on a platform of "Equality, Jobs and Peace," pledging to strengthen the United Nations and to exempt low-income families from paying federal income tax.

Among the qualifications Conyers cited for holding office were three years as a district aide to Democratic Rep. John D. Dingell of Michigan and service on a panel of lawyers picked by President John F. Kennedy to look for ways of easing racial tensions in the South. Conyers won the primary by just 108 votes over Richard H. Austin, a Detroit accountant who has remained a political rival ever since.

Racial troubles in Conyers' district exploded in 1967, when rioting destroyed many blocks in the heart of the district. Conyers was booed when he stood atop a car telling rioters to return to their homes. Later his office was gutted by fire. But those episodes had no lasting political impact, nor did his initial reluctance to support Hubert H. Humphrey for the presidency in 1968.

Conyers' primary challenges have been infrequent and minor, though he has not always been on the best of terms with Mayor Coleman A. Young and the United Auto Workers, the major political powers in the city. In 1989, Conyers challenged Young's re-election and finished third in the September primary, ceding a runoff berth against Young to accountant Tom Barrow. The next year, however, Conyers was unchallenged for the Democratic nomination for his House seat and breezed to a November win.

In 1992, Conyers faced re-election after disclosure of his 273 overdrafts at the House bank. And he had to run in a significantly changed district. Though heavily Democratic, much of the territory was new and accustomed to representation from two white Democrats, Sander M. Levin and Dennis M. Hertel. Blacks retained the balance of power, however, and in a primary against a white state senator, Conyers won easily.

Committees

Government Operations (Chairman)
Legislation & National Security (chairman)

Judiciary (3rd of 21 Democrats)
Crime & Criminal Justice; Intellectual Property & Judicial Administration; Economic & Commercial Law

Small Business (7th of 27 Democrats)
Minority Enterprise, Finance & Urban Development

Elections

1992 General		
John Conyers Jr. (D)	165,496	(82%)
John W. Gordon (R)	32,036	(16%)
Richard R. Miller (NL)	2,043	(1%)
1992 Primary		
John Conyers Jr. (D)	39,324	(64%)
John Kelly (D)	15,780	(26%)
Martha G. Scott (D)	5,281	(9%)
Frederick H. Strickland (D)	1,041	(2%)
1990 General		
John Conyers Jr. (D)	76,556	(89%)
Ray Shoulders (R)	7,298	(9%)
Robert Mays (I)	1,134	(1%)
Jonathan Paul Flint (LIBERT)	764	(1%)

Previous Winning Percentages: **1988** (91%) **1986** (89%) **1984** (89%) **1982** (97%) **1980** (95%) **1978** (93%) **1976** (92%) **1974** (91%) **1972** (88%) **1970** (88%) **1968** (100%) **1966** (84%) **1964** (84%)

District Vote for President

1992

D	180,007	(81%)
R	28,937	(13%)
I	12,600	(6%)

Campaign Finance

	Receipts	Receipts from PACs		Expend-itures
1992				
Conyers (D)	$309,396	$215,008	(69%)	$332,818
1990				
Conyers (D)	$300,877	$178,360	(59%)	$288,906
Shoulders (R)	$545	0		$545

Key Votes

1993	
Require parental notification of minors' abortions	N
Require unpaid family and medical leave	Y
Approve national "motor voter" registration bill	Y
Approve budget increasing taxes and reducing deficit	Y
Approve economic stimulus plan	Y
1992	
Approve balanced-budget constitutional amendment	N
Close down space station program	?
Approve U.S. aid for former Soviet Union	N
Allow shifting funds from defense to domestic programs	Y
1991	
Extend unemployment benefits using deficit financing	Y
Approve waiting period for handgun purchases	Y
Authorize use of force in Persian Gulf	N

Voting Studies

	Presidential Support		Party Unity		Conservative Coalition	
Year	S	O	S	O	S	O
1992	10	72	69	4	4	79
1991	23	75	91	2	3	89
1990	16	81	86	3	7	85
1989	14	57	72	2	2	85
1988	13	74	83	1	3	89
1987	8	81	82	2	5	81
1986	11	73	71	4	4	78
1985	13	68	69	6	7	67
1984	21	73	88	6	5	92
1983	6	73	73	6	4	73
1982	22	60	68	8	8	75
1981	32	59	78	9	9	85

Interest Group Ratings

Year	ADA	AFL-CIO	CCUS	ACU
1992	90	89	13	0
1991	95	100	20	0
1990	78	100	15	0
1989	90	88	30	5
1988	90	100	21	0
1987	92	100	0	0
1986	85	92	9	0
1985	75	92	28	12
1984	95	85	21	4
1983	100	100	11	0
1982	80	88	6	6
1981	90	93	0	9

15 Barbara-Rose Collins (D)

Of Detroit — Elected 1990; 2nd Term

Born: April 13, 1939, Detroit, Mich.
Education: Wayne State U.
Occupation: Public official.
Family: Widowed; two children.
Religion: Shrine of the Black Madonna (Pan-African Orthodox Christian).
Political Career: Detroit Public School Board, 1971-73; Mich. House, 1975-81; Detroit City Council, 1982-91; sought Democratic nomination for U.S. House, 1988.
Capitol Office: 1108 Longworth Bldg. 20515; 225-2261.

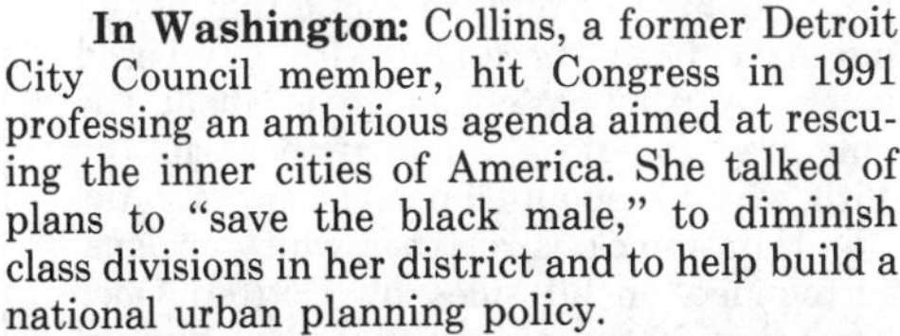

In Washington: Collins, a former Detroit City Council member, hit Congress in 1991 professing an ambitious agenda aimed at rescuing the inner cities of America. She talked of plans to "save the black male," to diminish class divisions in her district and to help build a national urban planning policy.

That's a tall order for any member, especially a freshman holding low-ranking seats on committees of second-tier influence, as Collins did in the 102nd Congress.

But if her portfolio of first-term legislative endeavors was skinny, Collins did raise her voice from time to time in advocacy for the poor and the disenfranchised. And at the start of the 103rd Congress, she got a couple of posts that hold the promise of giving her a modicum of visibility. She took the chairmanship of the Post Office and Civil Service Subcommittee on Postal Operations and Services, and she was given vice-chair responsibilities at the Public Works and Transportation Subcommittee on Investigations and Oversight, under panel chairman Robert A. Borski of Pennsylvania.

Also in 1993, the Democratic leadership made Collins one the party's at-large whips, and she picked up a seat on the Government Operations Committee.

Detroit is among the U.S. cities most associated with the violence, poverty and decline plaguing many urban centers. So it is not surprising that Collins sees urban decay and the underclass as major concerns. In these areas she can speak from personal experience: She was a teenage mother who had a baby die at two months, and in 1990, her son Christopher was jailed for armed robbery.

In the spring of 1991, as the nation focused on the beating of black motorist Rodney King by Los Angeles police officers after a high-speed chase, Collins added her voice to the chorus expressing outrage over police brutality, which she called "an old enemy of the black community." Throughout U.S. history, she said, lynchings and other violence against blacks "happened with the knowledge of and/or the participation of local police officers." Collins said that black males are such frequent targets of abuse that they live in "constant terror and fear of the police."

One of Collins' ideas for addressing the problem of hunger in America's inner cities is to have the Agriculture Department encourage growers and producers to donate to homeless shelters and soup kitchens food that is edible but unmarketable and would otherwise go to waste.

Collins' seat on Public Works could help give her a role in seeing that Detroit and other cities get more federal dollars for infrastructure projects. In her first term, she said she had a hand in the approval of funding for Detroit road improvements and a light rail study.

At Home: A Detroit native, Collins already was a well-known figure in city politics when she waged a strong but unsuccessful 1988 challenge to veteran Democratic Rep. George W. Crockett Jr.

After many years as a community activist, Collins in 1970 was elected to the Detroit school board, where she served until 1973. In 1975, she moved on to the state House. During her six years in the Legislature, Collins focused on consumer and civil rights, economic development and women's issues. She sponsored bills on sex education, sexual harassment and urban enterprise zones.

In 1982, she took a seat on the Detroit City Council, where she became known as an ally of Mayor Coleman A. Young. Collins carried over into her council work some of the issues she had pursued in the Legislature, including support for urban enterprise zones and other economic development initiatives. She sponsored legislation calling for the city to divest its South Africa-linked investments. But Collins also drew criticism from some quarters for not putting in the careful work needed to translate her rhetoric into legislative action.

Collins' 1988 run against Crockett was characteristic of her outspoken, ambitious style.

Michigan 15

Parts of Detroit; Grosse Pointe; Hamtramck; River Rouge

The depopulation of Detroit has been under way for decades, leading the city to be called the Beirut of America, a desolate, burned-out hulk showing few signs of life. By 1992, a local editorial columnist asked "Has the city of Detroit ceased to exist?"

If it has, a variety of factors contributed over the past four decades. In 1960, Detroit was a metropolis of 1.7 million people. Thirty years later, local officials fretted when a preliminary census count showed fewer than 1 million residents. The final census numbers confirmed that Detroit had just over 1 million inhabitants.

The domestic automobile industry's woes economically devastated southeastern Michigan and Detroit, but some of the population decline can be linked to the 1967 riots, the worst in terms of property damage and deaths this century.

Particularly hard hit was the area that now makes up the 15th. Taking in the older parts of the city, the 15th contains the skeletal remains of an era when Detroit was a manufacturing powerhouse. Even though the 15th contains the city's downtown and waterfront areas, it also houses many of the city's most downtrodden residents, who live in bombed-out, boarded-up neighborhoods largely clustered south of the Ford Freeway.

The city's downtown and riverfront areas have been the focus of numerous redevelopment projects over the years, aimed at luring residents back. The 73-story Renaissance Center was opened in 1977 to try to revitalize the city's commercial core. Those efforts have met with some success, but the emergence of the outlying suburban cities as commercial centers has made the task even more daunting.

In sharp contrast to the city's mostly poor and working-class blacks are the wealthy white communities of Grosse Pointe Park, Grosse Pointe and Grosse Pointe Farms, nestled in the northeast corner of the district.

Like the rest of the white suburban communities that surround Detroit, residents here are usually hostile toward the city, with a particular disdain for black Mayor Coleman Young. In 1992, Democratic House primary challenger Tom Barrow appealed to their vote by trying to link Rep. Collins to Young, a tactic that would not have been successful with city-based voters. A primary challenge is about the only way to knock an incumbent in the 15th, which is about 80 percent Democratic.

Hamtramck is another white enclave, surrounded on all sides by Detroit. Once home to 50,000 people, many of whom worked at the huge and now closed Dodge plant at the southern end of town, the city's population has dwindled to below 20,000. Still, a tight-knit Polish community exists, leavened by newly arrived Yugoslavs, Albanians and some Middle Eastern immigrants. Other Arab communities of Syrians, Palestinians and Chaldeans exist in southeast Detroit.

River Rouge and Ecorse are grafted on to the 15th's southern extreme; they are populated with autoworkers and steelworkers, many of whom are black.

1990 Population: 580,956. White 153,464 (26%), Black 406,905 (70%), Other 20,587 (4%). Hispanic origin 24,808 (4%). 18 and over 418,224 (72%), 62 and over 97,630 (17%). Median age: 32.

Most black leaders were reluctant to challenge Crockett, a pioneer in the civil rights movement, but Collins said she was "tired of waiting" for him to retire. In the Democratic primary, she finished just 8 points behind the incumbent, which helped persuade him to retire in 1990. Collins was the immediate front-runner to succeed him, and Young's endorsement helped her stand out in a crowded Democratic primary field. Once she was nominated, the general election was a formality.

While Collins may not have been very visible in Washington during her first term, she aggressively used the congressional franking privilege to boost herself at home. One newsletter she sent to constituents in 1991 featured six photos of her and mentioned her name more than 30 times.

Collins' legislative low profile and negative publicity about irregularities in her campaign finances helped generate a return challenge from Tom Barrow in the 1992 Democratic primary. Barrow had finished second to Collins in the 1990 primary.

Barrow had name recognition from two unsuccessful mayoral bids and from his 1990 House effort. Criticizing Collins' House record, he talked about the "urgent need for responsible representation in Washington." Barrow also tried to turn Young's support for Collins into a negative, sending targeted mailings highlighting their alliance into white communities that had been added to the district in remapping.

But Barrow, who is also black, could not crack Collins' black urban base, and she won renomination with ease. In November, GOP physician Charles Vincent also flopped. A dean at the Wayne State University School of Medicine, Vincent had finished third behind Collins and Barrow in the 1990 primary. He switched parties to run as a Republican in 1992, but managed just 17 percent in this Democratic stronghold.

Committees

Government Operations (21st of 25 Democrats)
Commerce, Consumer & Monetary Affairs; Employment, Housing & Aviation

Post Office & Civil Service (8th of 15 Democrats)
Postal Operations & Services (chairman)

Public Works & Transportation (22nd of 39 Democrats)
Investigations & Oversight (vice chairman); Aviation

Elections

1992 General		
Barbara-Rose Collins (D)	148,908	(81%)
Charles C. Vincent (R)	31,849	(17%)
James E. Harris Jr. (I)	2,704	(1%)
1992 Primary		
Barbara-Rose Collins (D)	37,272	(68%)
Tom Barrow (D)	17,728	(32%)
1990 General		
Barbara-Rose Collins (D)	54,345	(80%)
Carl R. Edwards Sr. (R)	11,203	(17%)
Joyce Ann Griffin (WW)	1,090	(2%)
Jeff J. Hampton (LIBERT)	649	(1%)
Cleve Andrew Pulley (I)	530	(1%)

District Vote for President

1992

D 144,092 (81%)
R 26,421 (15%)
I 8,278 (5%)

Campaign Finance

	Receipts	Receipts from PACs		Expend-itures
1992				
Collins (D)	$278,723	$121,721	(44%)	$284,049
Vincent (R)	$98,434	$10,020	(10%)	$94,260
1990				
Collins (D)	$335,736	$68,620	(20%)	$274,688

Key Votes

1993	
Require parental notification of minors' abortions	N
Require unpaid family and medical leave	Y
Approve national "motor voter" registration bill	Y
Approve budget increasing taxes and reducing deficit	Y
Approve economic stimulus plan	Y
1992	
Approve balanced-budget constitutional amendment	N
Close down space station program	?
Approve U.S. aid for former Soviet Union	N
Allow shifting funds from defense to domestic programs	Y
1991	
Extend unemployment benefits using deficit financing	Y
Approve waiting period for handgun purchases	Y
Authorize use of force in Persian Gulf	N

Voting Studies

	Presidential Support		Party Unity		Conservative Coalition	
Year	S	O	S	O	S	O
1992	12	79	84	3	10	73
1991	23	77	93	3	5	95

Interest Group Ratings

Year	ADA	AFL-CIO	CCUS	ACU
1992	95	90	13	0
1991	100	100	20	0

16 John D. Dingell (D)

Of Trenton — Elected 1955; 19th Full Term

Born: July 8, 1926, Colorado Springs, Colo.
Education: Georgetown U., B.S. 1949, J.D. 1952.
Military Service: Army, 1944-46.
Occupation: Lawyer.
Family: Wife, Deborah Insley; four children.
Religion: Roman Catholic.
Political Career: Wayne County assistant prosecutor, 1953-55.
Capitol Office: 2328 Rayburn Bldg. 20515; 225-4071.

In Washington: In more than a decade as chairman of the Energy and Commerce Committee, Dingell has turned the panel into a powerhouse. With a combination of ruthless expansionism and crafty deal-cutting, he has built a remarkable fiefdom, attracting some of the brightest young talents on Capitol Hill.

Today, many of those rising stars are subcommittee chairmen; Dingell's protégés have become his lieutenants, entrusted with crafting major policy changes in communications, energy, transportation, solid waste disposal and health care.

The 1992 election brought turnover that dramatically altered the dynamics of the committee. The retirement of New Yorker James H. Scheuer, the panel's No. 2 Democrat, put an end to his decadelong feud with Dingell. And while the chairman lost a friend when ranking Republican Norman F. Lent retired, he gained a considerably less formidable opponent in Carlos J. Moorhead of California, who moved up to ranking minority member.

While the gruff chairman still rules his empire with an iron gavel — punishing those who dare cross him and bestowing favors on a select few — he is increasingly concerned with people and events outside the committee. Having amassed the broadest jurisdiction in the House, Dingell now spends much of his time defending his committee's turf against other strong-minded chairmen.

With the Clean Air Act and National Energy Policy Act behind him, Dingell is less preoccupied with protecting the interests of the Detroit auto industry and free to focus on health care in the 103rd Congress. That could produce the most potent one-two punch in Congress on the issue. Henry A. Waxman, D-Calif., chairman of Energy and Commerce's Subcommittee on Health and the Environment, is perhaps the most influential House voice on health policy, and even though Dingell and Waxman have often feuded on environmental issues, they are allies on health care.

President Clinton has courted Dingell, and the man known as "Big John" has returned the attention with enthusiastic support for the administration. Dingell is also close to Clinton's legislative point man, Howard Paster, guaranteeing him a central role in the debate.

Health care is not just another policy battle for Dingell; it is a personal crusade, begun by his father when the latter served in the House. After surviving a bout with tuberculosis, John Dingell Sr. wrote the first national health insurance bill, legislation his son has introduced every Congress since. While it is unlikely that Congress will approve the tax-subsidized, health-care-for-all plan Dingell prefers, the Michigan Democrat sees an opportunity to move in that direction in the 103rd.

If he succeeds, it will be Dingell's legacy; if not, he is likely to pass the cause — along with his House seat — to his son, Christopher.

Dingell is considered one of the House's most skillful legislators and hard-nosed negotiators. His mastery of House rules and procedural minutiae is renowned, as is his maxim about the power such knowledge gives him: "If you let me write procedure and I let you write substance," he told the Rules Committee in 1982, "I'll screw you every time."

Several significant pieces of legislation came out of Energy and Commerce in the 102nd Congress, including a sweeping energy policy act, a cable reregulation bill and tightened regulation of generic drugs. Dingell's Oversight and Investigations Subcommittee also spotlighted illegal billing practices by major universities such as Stanford and the Massachusetts Institute of Technology.

The energy overhaul was one of the few major bills to win enactment in the 102nd. For much of the debate, Dingell remained behind the scenes, relying on Philip R. Sharp, D-Ind., chairman of his Energy and Power Subcommittee, to oversee the process. The pair often operate as a good-cop, bad-cop team.

On gas mileage standards, for instance, Sharp said at the outset he planned to include language requiring more energy-efficient vehicles, anathema to Dingell's Detroit automakers. But the Senate knocked the provision out of its

Michigan 16

Southeast Wayne County; Monroe County

A gray stretch of gritty communities along the Detroit River, the 16th is one of the most industrialized districts in the country.

In a previous incarnation, two rounds of redistricting ago, the Detroit News called it "the most polluted congressional district in the nation." The borders are somewhat different now, but the character is quite similar.

Dearborn, its largest city, is home to the Ford Motor Co. and the factory that was once the largest on Earth. Known simply as "the Rouge," spread over 1,200 acres, its assembly line employed nearly 100,000 workers during its heyday. Now the automotive facilities employ fewer than one-tenth of that number.

The tool-and-die shops, foundries, assembly lines and chemical plants of the 16th served as a powerful magnet for U.S. and international job-seekers in the early and mid-20th century. Residents of Appalachia, Germans, Poles, Czechs, Italians, and Southern blacks all migrated here in search of jobs, filling communities such as Melvindale, Wyandotte and Allen Park.

Another wave of migration brought large numbers of Arabs to the Dearborn area. Some Shiite Moslems came during World War I, after Henry Ford opened the massive plant in the southern end of the city. For decades afterwards, Egyptians, Iraqis, Lebanese, Syrians, Palestinians, Jordanians, Saudis and Yemenis would come into the city in spurts. Today, the Arab business district along Warren Avenue supports the nation's largest Arab-American community.

The migration to the state's ninth largest city has not included blacks. Whites make up 98 percent of Dearborn; relations with majority-black Detroit are strained.

Nearby Dearborn Heights is shared with the Detroit-based 14th District; most of the city is in the 16th. Farther south, just inside the Wayne County limits on the southern edge, is the Flat Rock automotive plant, a joint U.S.-Japanese venture and one of the district's larger employers. The plant produces the Mazda MX-6 and Ford Probe.

The Wayne County portion of the district is the most populous. Thoroughly unionized and mostly blue-collar, this area regularly turns in Democratic margins. There are some pockets of Republican affluence, mainly in Riverview and Grosse Ile.

Monroe County, south of Wayne, is more politically competitive. Local factories have a union presence, but farther west, the turf is less industrialized and more conservative. Some retirees from the Detroit and Toledo areas have moved to communities on the county's Lake Erie shoreline.

Bill Clinton won Monroe in 1992, but two years before, voters displayed their independence by splitting their tickets in statewide races.

Democratic Sen. Carl Levin carried the county in his 1990 re-election bid, but successful GOP gubernatorial challenger John Engler captured 53 percent against Democratic Gov. James J. Blanchard.

1990 Population: 580,956. White 561,164 (97%), Black 8,088 (1%), Other 11,704 (2%). Hispanic origin 14,092 (2%). 18 and over 434,219 (75%), 62 and over 93,030 (16%). Median age: 34.

draft and Sharp never fought to put it back in, a decision many saw as Dingell's handiwork.

Whereas Sharp, the consensus-builder, crafted a bill that received near-unanimous support in committee, Dingell, the power-grabber, was left to fight turf battles with eight other chairmen. Through his special blend of strong-arm tactics and creative horse-trading, Dingell resolved conflicts with all but one: Interior Chairman George Miller of California.

When the bill reached a mammoth, 131-person conference, the negotiations were dominated by some of Congress' most adept bargainers. Ultimately, Dingell, Miller, Sharp and Senate Energy Chairman J. Bennett Johnston of Louisiana orchestrated a complicated agreement involving three separate pieces of legislation that were conferenced simultaneously. The Byzantine solution affected not only energy policy but also laws on California water rights and nuclear waste dumping.

Dingell often slips behind a closed door and emerges with unpredictable results. Such was the case when House Judiciary Committee Chairman Jack Brooks of Texas and Dingell did battle in 1992 over cable reregulation and new rules for the so-called Baby Bells.

Dingell, this time working with Telecommunications Subcommittee Chairman Edward J. Markey of Massachusetts, stripped a retransmission provision from the proposed cable bill to keep the legislation away from the Judiciary Committee, which was claiming jurisdiction over that question.

Brooks used a similar strategy to snatch the Baby Bells issue from Energy, writing his version completely in the lexicon of antitrust law, not regulatory law.

The two men, among Congress' closest friends and fiercest competitors, jostled for months with no apparent resolution in sight. Yet, in the end, Dingell won sole jurisdiction over cable legislation and Brooks nabbed the Baby Bells bill. Was it a deal? The two wouldn't say. (The cable bill passed in the 102nd; Baby Bells legislation did not.)

Dingell provided some insight into his modus operandi early in the 103rd when he testified on possible committee restructuring. He said lawmakers should hash out their differences in private. "Sunlight is the best disinfectant, but too much disinfectant can be toxic."

Because of the array of issues that pass through his committee, Dingell is a force to reckon with at some point for nearly every member of the House. But his legislative imperialism has met with increasing resistance in recent years.

When the cable bill reached the floor in July 1992, Louisiana Democrat W. J. "Billy" Tauzin offered an amendment to force cable-affiliated programmers to sell their shows at fair prices to competitors, such as the backyard satellite dish industry. Lobbyists speculated that Tauzin was 100 votes shy of winning, especially since he was pitted against Dingell and the cable industry. His surprising win was read as a show of force by underling House members who relished the opportunity to hand Dingell a rare defeat.

In previous Congresses, Public Works Chairman James J. Howard of New Jersey and Agriculture Chairman E. "Kika" de la Garza of Texas tapped into resentment against Dingell to score similar victories.

As renowned as Dingell is for his territorial prowess, he does not win legislative battles as often as his bravado suggests. But he has shown that one need not always score a clear victory to be perceived as powerful.

In the 101st Congress, Dingell's most significant legislative accomplishment was a bill he fought through much of the 1980s: reauthorization of the Clean Air Act. Passage of the measure was not seen as a defeat for Dingell. Instead, he was credited with holding off action far longer than most lawmakers could have and then driving a decent bargain for automakers.

The years of debate, which required hand-to-hand combat with Waxman, proved Dingell's power to obstruct is not to be underestimated.

Initially, Dingell felt that environmentalists were seeking to impose drastic restrictions on industry with little regard to the costs. In 1982, Waxman blocked Dingell's effort to loosen auto emissions standards. Afterward, Dingell spent years thwarting Waxman's attempts to strengthen those standards.

The scales began to tip against Dingell late in 1987, when he lost a floor fight over how long to extend the deadline for cities to comply with air-quality standards. When, in June 1989, President Bush submitted a new clean air bill, Dingell decided to sponsor the working document.

Dingell's committee work showcased all the tools he can bring to bear on an issue. Well-versed in the technical issues underlying many of the bill's provisions, Dingell often could outargue less informed opponents. He let committee meetings run on, even into the small hours, seemingly hoping to wear down his foes.

But Dingell kept the bill moving through committee, forging several compromises with Waxman, the most significant on auto emissions. The result was a bill strong enough for environmentalists to support, but more favorable toward the auto industry than many would have anticipated.

After the bill passed, Dingell told the Detroit Free Press that he made no apology for looking out for the auto industry in his district: "That's what I'm sent here to do."

Much of Dingell's reputation for ruthlessness comes from his role as the House's most aggressive and merciless investigator. At his Oversight Subcommittee, Dingell zealously probes the propriety and performance of federal agencies. He can force some sluggish federal regulators into action merely by threatening to call them before his subcommittee.

For many who elude testifying before the subcommittee, there are "Dingell-grams," the tart rebukes and testy inquiries penned by the chairman at a rate of hundreds per year.

His admirers say his exposés of such problems as pesticides in food and improperly tested prescription drugs are a service to the public. His detractors say his oversight of executive agencies is meddlesome, intrusive and an example of congressional government run amok.

The panel's reputation was clouded in March 1989, when Dingell aired allegations that a private investigator had impersonated a member of his subcommittee staff. But in 1991, the subcommittee won favorable headlines for its scrutiny of university misuse of government research grants. The investigation helped lead to the resignation of Stanford University's president and resulted in more money for monitoring the colleges.

Dingell is known for bullying witnesses and badgering members. Even as he drapes an arm over a colleague's shoulder "asking" for support, there is an air of intimidation. Personally, he is a complex man, stubborn and vindictive on occasion, self-confident to the point of arrogance. Yet one must wonder whether Dingell's "meanness" is a device for building a public reputation he believes will serve his causes. And while other committee chairmen are routinely criticized for dominating their own hearings, Dingell is usually content to sit back and let the more junior members speak first.

At Home: The Dingell family has represented the Detroit area in Congress since 1932. For 23 years, John D. Dingell Sr., a New Deal champion of national health insurance, served from the city's west side. When the elder Dingell died unexpectedly in 1955 while undergoing a routine physical examination, his 29-year-old son stepped in.

John Dingell Jr. grew up on Capitol Hill — not in Detroit. It was only when he received his law degree and went to work as an assistant prosecutor that he learned the intricacies of Detroit politics. But after three years as "my father's ears and eyes," he was ready for the 1955 special election. With backing from organized labor, he trounced a dozen Democratic candidates in the primary and went on to overwhelm his 26-year-old GOP opponent.

Since then, Dingell has had to worry about re-election only once, in 1964, when part of his constituency was combined with a larger part of the district held by Democratic Rep. John Lesinski Jr., who also had succeeded his father in the House. The Dingell-Lesinski primary got national attention because it was thought to be a measure of "white backlash" over recent civil rights legislation. Dingell, whose old district was about one-third black, had voted for the 1964 Civil Rights Act. Lesinski, whose district was nearly all white, was one of four Northern Democrats who had voted against it.

The issue was not brought up in the campaign, but both sides knew it was the main reason Dingell received such strong help from labor, civil rights groups and the state Democratic Party. Dingell won with 55 percent of the vote and has not had any problems since.

Committee

Energy & Commerce (Chairman)
Oversight & Investigations (chairman)

Elections

1992 General		
John D. Dingell (D)	156,964	(65%)
Frank Beaumont (R)	75,694	(31%)
Max J. Siegle (TIC)	4,048	(2%)
1990 General		
John D. Dingell (D)	88,962	(67%)
Frank Beaumont (R)	42,629	(32%)
Roger Conant Pope (LIBERT)	2,019	(2%)

Previous Winning Percentages:				**1988**	(97%)	**1986**	(78%)
1984	(64%)	**1982**	(74%)	**1980**	(70%)	**1978**	(77%)
1976	(76%)	**1974**	(78%)	**1972**	(68%)	**1970**	(79%)
1968	(74%)	**1966**	(63%)	**1964**	(73%)	**1962**	(83%)
1960	(79%)	**1958**	(79%)	**1956**	(74%)	**1955** *	(76%)

** Special election.*

District Vote for President

1992

D	118,079	(44%)
R	97,968	(36%)
I	52,963	(20%)

Campaign Finance

	Receipts	Receipts from PACs		Expend-itures
1992				
Dingell (D)	$1,112,141	$767,931	(69%)	$1,086,152
Beaumont (R)	$5,402	0		$5,401
1990				
Dingell (D)	$843,579	$625,727	(74%)	$602,952
Beaumont (R)	$3,775	0		$3,774

Key Votes

1993	
Require parental notification of minors' abortions	N
Require unpaid family and medical leave	Y
Approve national "motor voter" registration bill	Y
Approve budget increasing taxes and reducing deficit	Y
Approve economic stimulus plan	Y
1992	
Approve balanced-budget constitutional amendment	N
Close down space station program	Y
Approve U.S. aid for former Soviet Union	Y
Allow shifting funds from defense to domestic programs	Y
1991	
Extend unemployment benefits using deficit financing	Y
Approve waiting period for handgun purchases	N
Authorize use of force in Persian Gulf	Y

Voting Studies

	Presidential Support		Party Unity		Conservative Coalition	
Year	**S**	**O**	**S**	**O**	**S**	**O**
1992	19	74	87	6	31	56
1991	28	67	81	11	51	49
1990	20	78	87	5	37	61
1989	35	62	81	7	34	61
1988	22	75	88	3	29	61
1987	16	78	88	1	16	74
1986	24	70	80	5	32	58
1985	23	71	76	5	27	64
1984	30	59	84	7	31	63
1983	23	67	84	6	16	78
1982	44	55	90	7	25	74
1981	36	55	73	11	27	55

Interest Group Ratings

Year	ADA	AFL-CIO	CCUS	ACU
1992	90	83	25	0
1991	65	92	22	22
1990	67	100	15	4
1989	75	82	20	8
1988	80	100	29	13
1987	92	100	7	0
1986	75	92	6	19
1985	85	88	25	14
1984	75	92	33	9
1983	90	100	28	0
1982	80	100	18	14
1981	70	86	21	15

Minnesota

STATE DATA

Governor: Arne Carlson (R)
First elected: 1990
Length of term: 4 years
Term expires: 1/95
Salary: $109,053
Term limit: No
Phone: (612) 296-3391
Born: Sept. 24, 1934; New York, N.Y.
Education: Williams College, B.A. 1957; U. of Minnesota, 1957-58
Military Service: Army, 1959-60
Occupation: Computer executive
Family: Wife, Susan Shepard; three children
Religion: Protestant
Political Career: Minneapolis City Council, 1965-67; Minn. House, 1971-79; Minn. auditor, 1979-91

Lt. Gov.: Joanell Drystad (R)
First elected: 1990
Length of term: 4 years
Term expires: 1/95
Salary: $59,981
Phone: (612) 296-3391

State election official: (612) 296-2805
Democratic headquarters: (612) 293-1200
Republican headquarters: (612) 854-1446

REDISTRICTING

A 1993 Supreme Court decision upheld a state-drawn redistricting map and invalidated a plan crafted by the federal courts. The Minnesota delegation was elected under the federal plan and will use the new state map for the 1994 elections.

STATE LEGISLATURE

Legislature. Meets odd years, January-May; even years, January-March.

Senate: 67 members, 4-year terms
1992 breakdown: 45D, 22R; 47 men, 20 women; 66 whites, 1 other
Salary: $27,979
Phone: (612) 296-0504

House of Representatives: 134 members, 2-year terms
1992 breakdown: 86D, 48R; 99 men, 35 women; 131 whites, 1 black, 2 Hispanics
Salary: $27,979
Phone: (612) 296-2146

URBAN STATISTICS

City	Pop.
Minneapolis Mayor Donald Fraser, D	368,383
St. Paul Mayor Jim Scheibel, N-P	272,235
Bloomington Mayor Neil W. Peterson, R	86,335
Duluth Mayor John Fedo, N-P	85,493
Rochester Mayor Chuck Hazama, N-P	70,745

U.S. CONGRESS

Senate: 1 D, 1 R
House: 6 D, 2 R

TERM LIMITS

For Congress: No
For state offices: No

ELECTIONS

1992 Presidential Vote

Bill Clinton	43.5%
George Bush	31.9%
Ross Perot	24.0%

1988 Presidential Vote

Michael S. Dukakis	53%
George Bush	46%

1984 Presidential Vote

Walter F. Mondale	50%
Ronald Reagan	50%

POPULATION

1990 population		4,375,099
1980 population		4,075,970
Percent change		+7%
Rank among states:		20
White		94%
Black		2%
Hispanic		1%
Asian or Pacific islander		2%
Urban		70%
Rural		30%
Born in state		74%
Foreign-born		3%
Under age 18	1,166,783	27%
Ages 18-64	2,661,382	61%
65 and older	546,934	13%
Median age		32.5

MISCELLANEOUS

Capital: St. Paul
Number of counties: 87
Per capita income: $19,107 (1991)
Rank among states: 17
Total area: 84,402 sq. miles
Rank among states: 12

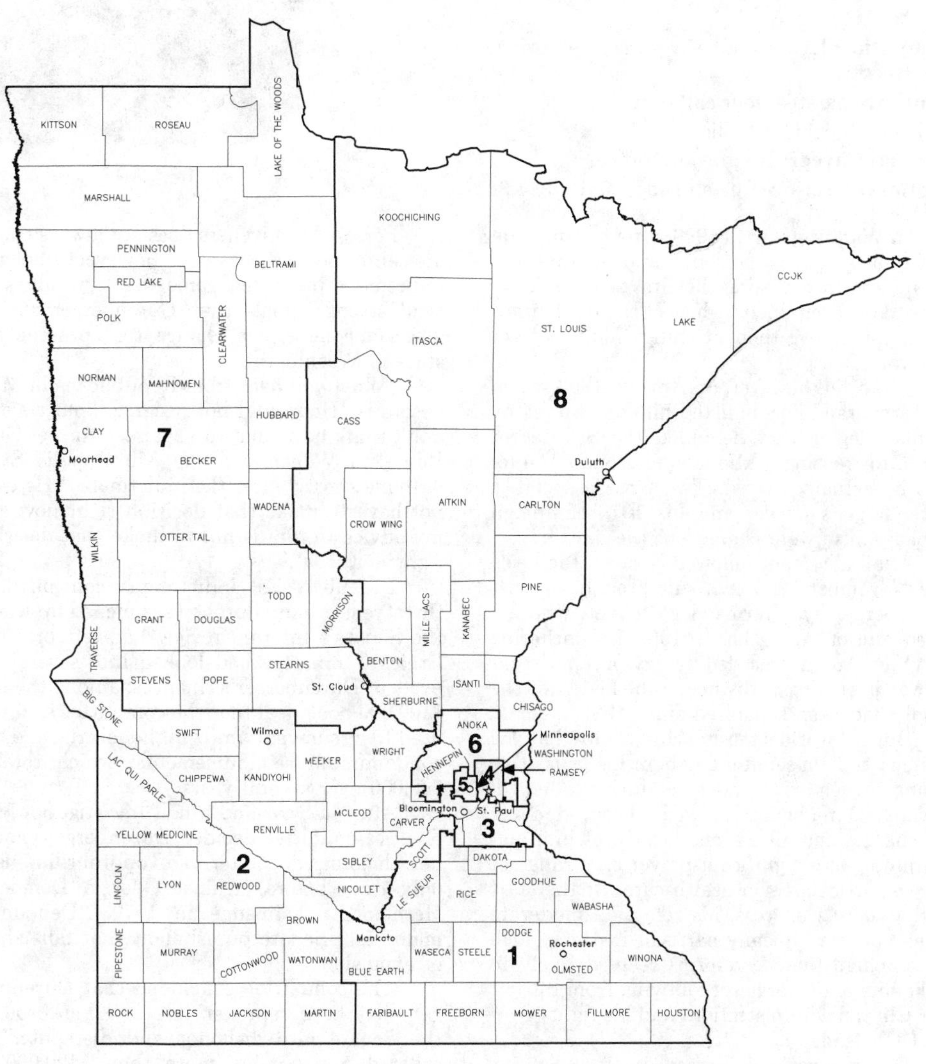
KITTSON
ROSEAU
LAKE OF THE WOODS
MARSHALL
KOOCHICHING
PENNINGTON
BELTRAMI
RED LAKE
COOK
POLK
CLEARWATER
ST. LOUIS
LAKE
ITASCA
NORMAN
MAHNOMEN
8
HUBBARD
CASS
CLAY
7
Moorhead
BECKER
Duluth
AITKIN
CARLTON
WADENA
CROW WING
WILKIN
OTTER TAIL
PINE
TODD
MORRISON
MILLE LACS
KANABEC
GRANT
DOUGLAS
TRAVERSE
BENTON
STEARNS
ISANTI
STEVENS
POPE
St. Cloud
SHERBURNE
CHISAGO
BIG STONE
ANOKA
SWIFT
Wilmar
6
Minneapolis
WASHINGTON
MEEKER
WRIGHT
HENNEPIN
LAC QUI PARLE
CHIPPEWA
KANDIYOHI
4
RAMSEY
5
MCLEOD
Bloomington
St. Paul
CARVER
YELLOW MEDICINE
RENVILLE
3
SCOTT
DAKOTA
2
SIBLEY
LINCOLN
LYON
REDWOOD
GOODHUE
NICOLLET
LE SUEUR
RICE
WABASHA
BROWN
DODGE
Mankato
Rochester
PIPESTONE
MURRAY
COTTONWOOD
WATONWAN
WASECA
STEELE
1
WINONA
BLUE EARTH
OLMSTED
ROCK
NOBLES
JACKSON
MARTIN
FARIBAULT
FREEBORN
MOWER
FILLMORE
HOUSTON

Dave Durenberger (R)

Of Minneapolis — Elected 1978; 2nd Full Term

Born: Aug. 19, 1934, Collegeville, Minn.
Education: St. John's U., B.A. 1955; U. of Minnesota, J.D. 1959.
Military Service: Army, 1955-56; Army Reserve, 1956-63.
Occupation: Lawyer; adhesives manufacturing executive.
Family: Separated; four children.
Religion: Roman Catholic.
Political Career: No previous office.
Capitol Office: 154 Russell Bldg. 20510; 224-3244.

In Washington: In 1990, after a multitude of troubles in his personal and official life culminated in his being the first senator in 11 years to be disciplined by his colleagues, Durenberger must have thought things could not get any worse.

They did, however, on April 2, 1993, when a federal grand jury indicted him on two felony counts alleging that he billed the Senate for $3,825 for renting a Minneapolis condominium that he actually owned. Two close associates, Durenberger's lawyer and his 1978 campaign manager, also were charged in the matter.

The indictment followed close on the heels of a November 1992 civil suit brought against Durenberger by a former legal client, who accused him of raping her in 1963 and fathering her child. And it preceded by days a report that he was a seeking a divorce from his wife; the couple had been separated since 1985.

But the world's most exclusive club has the capacity to let a senator go about his legislative business even when he is enduring personal travails. Durenberger plowed ahead, denying the charges and allegations leveled at him and continuing as a significant player on a range of issues, particularly on health care. At the start of the 103rd Congress, his role as a moderate swing vote on typically partisan matters (such as campaign finance reform) seemed likely to make him a key target of lobbying from his left (the Clinton administration) and his right (Senate GOP leaders).

Durenberger's resilience in the Senate, however, may not carry home to Minnesota, where his chances for re-election in 1994 appeared rapidly to fade after the indictment.

There had been some home-state calls for his resignation in 1990, after the Senate disciplinary action, but Durenberger returned to Minnesota to apologize for his actions and to attend the state Republican convention. Despite their past coolness toward Durenberger, delegates embraced the embattled senator at the time.

Personal forgiveness does not always translate into political loyalty, however, and the indictment prompted some one-time allies to send strong signals that Durenberger should give someone else a chance to represent the state in Washington.

"What you hear from Republicans in Minnesota is, 'He should not resign ... but we also don't think he should run again,' " former GOP Rep. Vin Weber told the Minneapolis Star-Tribune shortly after the indictment. "He does not have to make that decision right now and my advice to him is not to make that decision right now."

Durenberger's indictment concluded a three-year criminal probe that picked up where the Senate's internal review had left off. The Ethics Committee had looked into several aspects of Durenberger's finances, among them: a $100,000 book deal that the committee said was used to circumvent limits on honoraria, and the condominium reimbursements, which totaled $40,000 over several years.

After its year-and-a-half investigation, the Ethics Committee decided Durenberger should be "denounced," a term of opprobrium used only once before, against Georgia Democrat Herman E. Talmadge in 1979. "Denouncement" is a Senate punishment that falls short of expulsion.

The committee concluded that Durenberger "has been reprehensible and has brought the Senate into dishonor and disrepute." It ordered him to pay more than $120,000 in restitution for the housing reimbursements and speaking fees. Durenberger called denouncement too harsh a penalty, but he did not challenge the verdict or the version of events presented on the Senate floor by committee Chairman Howell Heflin, an Alabama Democrat. After the Senate voted 96-0 to denounce him, Durenberger rose to seek his colleagues' forgiveness.

He was rewarded by a return to legislative normalcy in the 102nd Congress, during which he tried in his typical bipartisan fashion to accelerate debate on overhauling the nation's health-care system, and on addressing the teetering system of government-backed student loans.

Durenberger joined with Finance Committee Chairman Lloyd Bentsen of Texas to promote a plan to make health insurance both more readily available and less expensive for small businesses. The plan was included in two separate tax bills that passed the Senate in 1992, but conference committee members from the House objected to such an "incremental" approach to health care reform and insisted that the language be dropped.

Durenberger also worked with Illinois Democrat Paul Simon on a proposal to replace the government's guaranteed student loan program, which was chiefly financed by banks and plagued by rising costs and inefficiencies. Their idea was to substitute a direct government loan program that would eliminate the bank middlemen. All students would be eligible and the IRS would collect repayments. The General Accounting Office said such a change could save the government billions of dollars.

Banks objected to government intrusion into the business of making student loans, and against stiff Bush administration objections, Congress included a demonstration of the plan, involving 500 schools, in a broad bill reauthorizing higher education programs. Though President Bush at one point had threatened to veto the bill because of the provision, he signed it.

Even before the Senate's disciplinary action, Durenberger had been working to reassert his influence. With seats on the Finance and Environment committees, Durenberger has been able to exercise his legislative skills on an impressive variety of domestic policies over the years. In the 101st Congress, he joined the Labor and Human Resources Committee, which with Finance writes most health and human services laws.

He was aiming to rebuild the reputation for thoughtful legislating that had marked his career before he entered, as he once said, his "so-called flake period." Compounding his ethics problems in the late 1980s were personal difficulties; he went through a particularly trying "midlife crisis," about which he spoke frankly to newspapers in interviews that detailed his separation from his family and search for happiness.

Durenberger has always been one of the least ideological Republicans in the Senate, frequently abandoning the party or GOP White House line to vote his own way. In early 1993, he negotiated a deal with Democrats to enable enactment of a "motor voter" bill designed to increase voter registration by requiring states to allow citizens to register as they apply for a driver's license or public assistance. Strong GOP opposition had blocked the bill with a filibuster, but Durenberger satisfied himself with language intended to cut down opportunities for coercion; his became the 60th vote Democrats needed to break the filibuster.

A backer of the Democrats' campaign finance bill in the 102nd Congress, Durenberger decries the importance in modern campaigning of contributions from political action committees, lobbyists and large out-of-state donors. He was courted again early in the 103rd Congress as the Clinton administration renewed efforts to enact campaign finance reform.

On Environment, Durenberger has been one of a small group of Republicans who often ally with environmental groups in pushing for tighter safeguards. In the 101st Congress, he was the chief Senate sponsor of the Clean Air Act's air toxics proposal, which imposed tough new controls to reduce industrial emissions of 189 toxic substances, most of which had never been regulated by the federal government.

Durenberger was chairman of the Finance Subcommittee on Health during Republican control of the Senate; he kept the ranking slot with the change in party control in 1987. At the start of the 101st Congress, the committee split the Health Subcommittee in two; Durenberger became ranking Republican on the new Medicare and Long-Term Care panel.

He was a leading sponsor of provisions in the 1983 Social Security bill that established the "prospective payment" system for Medicare, perhaps the most significant measure enacted in the 1980s to cut health-care costs. The plan, originally proposed by the Reagan administration, established the principle that Medicare would pay hospitals fixed amounts for treatment of various types of diseases — replacing the old system under which Medicare paid hospitals their costs to treat patients. In a similar vein, Durenberger helped craft a key compromise in 1989 when Congress overhauled the way Medicare pays doctors.

Durenberger was a strong supporter of the 1988 law that expanded Medicare to cover catastrophic health expenses for the elderly. But senior citizens' groups were angry at having to pay the entire cost of their new benefits, and in 1989, Congress repealed virtually the entire law. Durenberger joined former backers in opposing efforts to change the law, but the momentum for repeal was irresistible.

Durenberger's rise to the chairmanship of the Senate Intelligence Committee in 1985 brought repeated confrontations with the Reagan administration and criticism from his colleagues. He had to cope with a series of disturbing revelations about Soviet and Israeli espionage activity in the United States, a public break with the GOP administration over Nicaragua and a nasty feud with William J. Casey, the CIA director.

Then, just as Durenberger was about to leave the chairmanship at the end of 1986, news of the Iran-contra affair broke. Within days, he was caught up in an extremely sensitive political inquiry, topped off by a heated dispute with some of his committee colleagues over whether to release the results of their investigation.

He incurred the wrath of many of his colleagues after deciding to brief President Reagan on the contents of the committee's report in December 1986. It was the second time in a year Durenberger was criticized for talking to outsiders about Intelligence Committee business. After a U.S. citizen was caught spying for Israel, Durenberger told a group of American Jews that the United States had once tried to recruit a spy in Israel; he was criticized, but not punished, by the Ethics Committee.

At Home: Several Minnesota newspapers had issued calls for Durenberger's resignation after the Senate denunciation; immediately after he was indicted, those cries were heard again.

But Durenberger ignored their counsel, professed his innocence and stressed that his effectiveness as a legislator had not been diminished. Nevertheless, there was widespread feeling among Republicans that Durenberger's standing with the public — already low because of his Senate troubles — could not recover enough to make him a viable candidate for reelection.

Durenberger's ethics case and his subsequent denunciation by the Senate dominated the first half of 1990 and was but the first in a series of incidents that soured Minnesota voters on the party establishment and on politicians in general that year.

The mood of antipathy helped elect three anti-establishment candidates running against entrenched incumbents: Democrat Paul Wellstone, who defeated GOP Sen. Rudy Boschwitz; Republican Arne Carlson, who dethroned 10-year Democratic Gov. Rudy Perpich; and Democrat Collin C. Peterson, who ousted scandal-tainted GOP Rep. Arlan Stangeland.

News of Durenberger's erratic personal behavior in the 99th Congress seemed to make him a prime target as the 1988 election cycle began. Democrats, frustrated by Durenberger's ability to present himself as a quiet and independent problem-solver in two impressive Senate campaigns, saw an opportunity to present him as an unpredictable "flake." And they had a very well-known candidate to do the job: Hubert H. "Skip" Humphrey III, son of former Vice President Hubert H. Humphrey, the revered Democrat who once held this Senate seat.

But Humphrey's campaign against Durenberger proved to be one of the most disappointing challenger efforts in the country. Throughout his Senate bid, Humphrey, who had built his own popularity as state attorney general, struggled to meet high expectations that came with his famous name. Instead of keeping the focus on Durenberger, Humphrey was fending off unflattering comparisons between himself and his father. Often it was Humphrey's fellow Democrats who were the most critical.

Durenberger, meanwhile, carefully reinforced his old image as a thoughtful legislator. Always a personable campaigner, he spent considerable time traveling the state, holding hearings and forums on health care, rural development and the environment. And Durenberger ignored Humphrey for much of the campaign, much to the frustration of the challenger, who was consistently trailing in the polls and searching for an effective theme.

Humphrey's slow start and inability to meet high fund-raising expectations made it difficult for him to run the sort of media effort many had expected. In the fall, he started throwing some populistic punches. Humphrey accused Durenberger of having misguided priorities, that, among other things, led him to cast votes for the Nicaraguan contras and against Medicare. Humphrey also accused Durenberger of voting for a tax break for corporations that paid for a vacation he took in Puerto Rico.

But by October there was not much evidence he had done himself any good, and there was some sense Minnesota voters were tiring of negative media assaults. Durenberger, who had run ads accusing Humphrey of being soft on crime, halted his negative advertising and challenged the Democrat to do the same. After trying to get Durenberger to drop all ads for the last 10 days of the campaign, Humphrey switched to positive spots. On Election Day, he was swamped, losing 56-41 percent.

Durenberger waged his first two Senate campaigns in a period of four years. In 1978, he rode a Minnesota Republican tide to a comfortable victory. Four years later, he had to buck the economic failures of national and state GOP administrations and the unlimited financial resources of his Democratic rival. Although he won by a narrower margin, his second victory was a more striking personal triumph.

Durenberger's presence in the Senate is the result of an unusual set of events. When the 1978 political year began, he was preparing a gubernatorial challenge that seemed to be going nowhere. When the year ended, he was the state's senior senator.

Durenberger had hovered on the periphery of public office for years, as chief aide to GOP Gov. Harold Levander during the late 1960s and as a well-connected Minneapolis lawyer after that. But he was politically untested, and, in spite of a yearlong campaign, he was given little chance to wrest the nomination for governor from popular U.S. Rep. Albert H. Quie.

When interim Sen. Muriel Humphrey announced that she would not run for the remaining four years of her late husband's term, Republican leaders asked Durenberger to switch contests. He was easy to persuade.

Democratic disunity aided Durenberger

immensely. The party's endorsed candidate, U.S. Rep. Donald M. Fraser, was defeated in a primary by Bob Short, a blustery conservative whose campaign against environmentalists alienated much of the Democratic left. Some Democrats chose not to vote in the general election, but even more deserted to Durenberger, who had the endorsement of Americans for Democratic Action. He won a solid victory.

Durenberger's moderate views antagonized some in the GOP's conservative wing. At the 1980 state party convention, a group of conservative activists, mainly from southern Minnesota, warned him to move right if he wanted their backing for re-election in 1982. Durenberger publicly dismissed the Republicans' warning, calling it "minority party mentality."

Durenberger cleared a major hurdle in early 1981 when former Vice President Walter F. Mondale, a Minnesota senator from 1964 to 1976, announced he would not seek the office again. That made Durenberger a heavy favorite, while opening the Democratic side for Mark Dayton, liberal young heir to a department store empire. Although politically inexperienced, Dayton sank about $7 million of his fortune into a two-year Senate campaign.

Dayton made no apologies for his spending; he said that unlike Durenberger, he was not dependent on special-interest contributions, and that lavish spending was the only way he could offset the incumbent's perquisites and hefty campaign treasury.

For months, Dayton saturated the media with ads that sought to tie Durenberger to Reaganomics. This expensive blitz pulled Dayton up in the polls, but Durenberger was well positioned for re-election. He contended that while he was an independent voice in Washington, he had the president's respect and could help moderate the administration's course. Dayton swept the economically depressed Iron Range and the Democratic Twin Cities, but little else. Durenberger's wide lead in the suburbs of Minneapolis-St. Paul and most of rural Minnesota carried him to a 53 percent victory statewide.

Committees

Environment & Public Works (3rd of 7 Republicans)
Superfund, Recycling & Solid Waste Management (ranking); Clean Water, Fisheries & Wildlife; Water Resources, Transportation, Public Buildings & Economic Development

Finance (6th of 9 Republicans)
Medicare & Long Term Care (ranking); Health for Families & the Uninsured; Social Security & Family Policy

Labor & Human Resources (7th of 7 Republicans)
Disability Policy (ranking); Aging; Children, Families, Drugs & Alcoholism; Education, Arts & Humanities

Special Aging (7th of 10 Republicans)

Elections

1988 General		
Dave Durenberger (R)	1,176,210	(56%)
Hubert H. "Skip" Humphrey III (D)	856,694	(41%)
1988 Primary		
Dave Durenberger (R)	112,413	(93%)
Sharon Anderson (R)	5,464	(5%)
John Zeleniak (R)	2,379	(2%)

Previous Winning Percentages: **1982** (53%) **1978 *** (61%)

** Special election.*

Campaign Finance

	Receipts	Receipts from PACs		Expend-itures
1988				
Durenberger (R)	$4,969,448	$1,499,382	(30%)	$5,410,783
Humphrey (D)	$2,483,491	$557,234	(22%)	$2,477,068

Key Votes

1993	
Require unpaid family and medical leave	Y
Approve national "motor voter" registration bill	Y
Approve budget increasing taxes and reducing deficit	N
Support president's right to lift military gay ban	Y
1992	
Approve school-choice pilot program	Y
Allow shifting funds from defense to domestic programs	N
Oppose deeper cuts in spending for SDI	Y
1991	
Approve waiting period for handgun purchases	Y
Raise senators' pay and ban honoraria	Y
Authorize use of force in Persian Gulf	Y
Confirm Clarence Thomas to Supreme Court	Y

Voting Studies

	Presidential Support		Party Unity		Conservative Coalition	
Year	**S**	**O**	**S**	**O**	**S**	**O**
1992	63	33	56	41	63	37
1991	83	17	68	30	65	35
1990	62	35	55	40	76	19
1989	77	18	56	42	63	37
1988	57	38	43	48	32	59
1987	51	44	54	43	47	50
1986	64	33	65	32	66	34
1985	70	21	59	34	62	25
1984	71	23	68	25	70	21
1983	75	19	60	28	57	36
1982	60	28	45	41	39	48
1981	73	24	68	25	59	33

Interest Group Ratings

Year	ADA	AFL-CIO	CCUS	ACU
1992	25	50	60	42
1991	40	33	50	48
1990	44	56	25	45
1989	40	30	50	41
1988	60	77	43	26
1987	55	90	56	28
1986	40	40	58	43
1985	30	47	54	48
1984	50	25	65	55
1983	40	19	61	38
1982	70	59	28	25
1981	40	26	72	47

Paul Wellstone (D)

Of Northfield — Elected 1990; 1st Term

Born: July 21, 1944, Washington, D.C.
Education: U. of North Carolina, B.A. 1965, Ph.D. 1969.
Occupation: Professor.
Family: Wife, Sheila Ison; three children.
Religion: Jewish.
Political Career: Democratic nominee for Minn. auditor, 1982; Democratic National Committee, 1984-91.
Capitol Office: 717 Hart Bldg. 20510; 224-5641.

In Washington: Early returns declared the quirky, ultraliberal Wellstone a gadfly, and a shabbily dressed, impertinent one at that. Now in his third year on Capitol Hill, he has retooled his image, boned up on Senate etiquette and made a few friends.

In short, the evolution of Paul Wellstone has begun. But it has been a bumpy trip and it's far from over.

His 1990 upset of GOP Sen. Rudy Boschwitz had scarcely been certified before Wellstone had offended at least two of his colleagues and violated several unwritten canons of senatorial manner.

First he told reporters that ever since the age of 19 he had "despised" and "detested" North Carolina Republican Sen. Jesse Helms. Then Wellstone asked former Minnesota Sen. (and Vice President) Walter F. Mondale to escort him to be sworn in, bypassing the tradition of having the other home-state sitting senator — Republican Dave Durenberger in this case — do the honors.

Then Wellstone's relentless, highly publicized attempts to lobby the Bush administration to change its policy in the Persian Gulf prompted President Bush to ask members of the Minnesota delegation, "Who is this chickenshit?"

Top aides quit, complaining publicly that Wellstone's frenetic unfocused pace was too much to endure.

His style was not an instant hit with the chairman of the Energy and Natural Resources Committee, Democrat J. Bennett Johnston of Louisiana. As Johnston sought to speed his comprehensive energy bill through the committee, Wellstone persevered in reading his opening statement despite Johnston's admonition.

Nevertheless, Wellstone had some serious legislative goals and with the prodding of some of his colleagues and the assistance of a few top-notch staffers he began to realize that some relatively minor cosmetic changes could help him accomplish those goals.

After decades of flannel shirts and do-it-yourself haircuts, Wellstone now sports a professional hairdo and almost looks comfortable in a suit and tie. More valuable are the bonds he has built with other senators — sponsoring a bill with Helms, stumping in Pennsylvania for Democrat Harris Wofford. He has developed relationships with Majority Leader George J. Mitchell of Maine and Rules Committee Chairman Wendell H. Ford of Kentucky.

Wellstone's most notable achievement in the 102nd was something he helped prevent rather than anything he won passage of.

He and some of the Senate's most ardent environmentalists successfully knocked language out of a sweeping energy bill that would have permitted drilling in the Arctic National Wildlife Refuge. (In 1992, Mitchell appointed Wellstone a member of the Senate delegation to the "Earth Summit" in Rio de Janeiro.)

Wellstone was also one of the Senate's most passionate opponents of the Persian Gulf War. "I could not accept the loss of life of any of our children in the Persian Gulf right now, and that tells me in my gut I do not believe it is time to go to war," he said during debate on authorizing Bush to use military force against Iraq. "I do not believe the administration has made the case to go to war. And if I apply this standard to my children, then I have to apply this standard to everyone's children. I have to apply this standard to all of God's children."

In the post-Cold War, post-Gulf War era, Wellstone is a vocal advocate of shifting military dollars to diversification projects.

A former college professor, Wellstone devotes much of his time to educational issues. In the 102nd, his amendments to the Pell Grant program gave block grant money to some colleges and expanded eligibility of the grant program.

With a new Democratic administration and the addition of several liberal-leaning senators, Wellstone finds himself in less hostile territory. He was an early supporter of President Clinton's national service proposal and was expected to play a major role in the school funding debate.

Early in the 103rd, he filed bills to create a national health-care system, eliminate the congressional cost of living increase and study the prospects of the French abortion pill RU 486.

After making little progress in the 102nd to revamp the nation's campaign finance laws, Wellstone has promised to take another crack at the system. He wants to eliminate all political action committee donations and reduce the spending and contribution limits.

At Home: In a state with a reputation for clean government and politics to match, 1990 set a new standard for Minnesota. Voters' disillusionment with their elected officials began with Durenberger's hearings before the Senate Ethics Committee and his subsequent denunciation (he was indicted in early 1993). Some state legislators also had well-publicized scandals. Questions about Republican Rep. Arlan Stangeland's office phone bill further contributed to Minnesotans' gloom, as did the October surprise of Republican gubernatorial nominee Jon Grunseth, who was edged off the ballot after he was accused of sexual indiscretions.

Touting a fresh, anti-establishment message, Wellstone found himself perfectly positioned to exploit voters' antipathy and topple a senator who as late as mid-October had been considered a safe bet for re-election.

It was an upset unrivaled since 1980, when several surprise Republican victories propelled the GOP to a 12-seat pickup and a Senate majority. In ideological terms, the switch from Rudy Boschwitz to Wellstone is as stark as any in 1980. A political science professor at Carleton College, Wellstone co-chaired Jesse Jackson's 1988 presidential campaign in Minnesota.

Wellstone's humorous television campaign caught the imagination of voters. In some of the most original advertisements of the year, Wellstone starred in a Minnesota version of Michael Moore's sardonic documentary "Roger and Me," in which Wellstone, instead of stalking General Motors Corp. Chairman Roger Smith, seeks out Boschwitz. In another ad, Wellstone raced across the state speaking increasingly rapidly, explaining that he must talk fast because he did not have Boschwitz's $6 million treasury.

On Election Day, Minnesotans revolted against establishment candidates. They threw out 10-year Democratic Gov. Rudy Perpich, voting in maverick Republican Arne Carlson, who had replaced Grunseth as the party's nominee only a week earlier. (Carlson beat Wellstone in the 1982 auditor's race.) Stangeland lost his re-election bid. And Wellstone beat Boschwitz by less than 50,000 votes, 50 percent to 48 percent.

Boschwitz said early on that he would seek a rematch in 1996. But with Durenberger's indictment, Boschwitz may find an opening before then.

Wellstone meanwhile, realizing many dismissed his 1990 upset win as a fluke, has paid close attention to strengthening his base in Minnesota and reaching out to new voters. Early in 1993, the Minneapolis Star Tribune declared him arguably the most powerful, most popular politician in the state.

Committees

Energy & Natural Resources (8th of 11 Democrats)
Renewable Energy (vice chairman); Energy Research & Development; Public Lands, National Parks & Forests

Indian Affairs (8th of 10 Democrats)

Labor & Human Resources (9th of 10 Democrats)
Children, Families, Drugs & Alcoholism; Education, Arts & Humanities; Labor

Small Business (7th of 12 Democrats)
Rural Economy & Family Farming (chairman); Urban & Minority-Owned Business Development

Elections

1990 General		
Paul Wellstone (D)	911,999	(50%)
Rudy Boschwitz (R)	864,375	(48%)
Russell B. Bentley (GR)	29,820	(2%)
1990 Primary		
Paul Wellstone (D)	226,306	(60%)
Jim Nichols (D)	129,302	(35%)
Gene Schenk (D)	19,379	(5%)

Campaign Finance

	Receipts	Receipts from PACs		Expend-itures
1990				
Wellstone (D)	$1,403,208	$294,520	(21%)	$1,340,708
Boschwitz (R)	$6,086,588	$1,211,209	(20%)	$6,221,333

Key Votes

1993	
Require unpaid family and medical leave	Y
Approve national "motor voter" registration bill	Y
Approve budget increasing taxes and reducing deficit	Y
Support president's right to lift military gay ban	Y
1992	
Approve school-choice pilot program	N
Allow shifting funds from defense to domestic programs	Y
Oppose deeper cuts in spending for SDI	—
1991	
Approve waiting period for handgun purchases	Y
Raise senators' pay and ban honoraria	N
Authorize use of force in Persian Gulf	N
Confirm Clarence Thomas to Supreme Court	N

Voting Studies

	Presidential Support		Party Unity		Conservative Coalition	
Year	**S**	**O**	**S**	**O**	**S**	**O**
1992	23	75	92	5	8	92
1991	22	75	91	5	8	88

Interest Group Ratings

Year	ADA	AFL-CIO	CCUS	ACU
1992	100	92	10	0
1991	95	83	20	5

1 Timothy J. Penny (D)

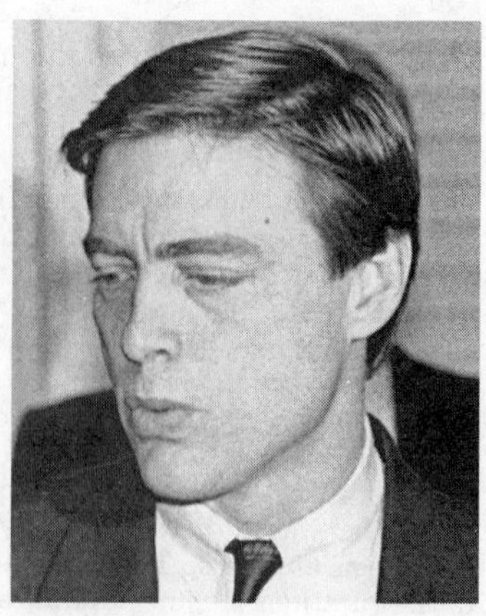

Of New Richland — Elected 1982; 6th Term

Born: Nov. 19, 1951, Albert Lea, Minn.
Education: Winona State U., B.A. 1974; U. of Minnesota, 1975.
Military Service: Naval Reserve, 1986-present.
Occupation: Sales representative.
Family: Wife, Barbara Christianson; four children.
Religion: Lutheran.
Political Career: Minn. Senate, 1977-83.
Capitol Office: 436 Cannon Bldg. 20515; 225-2472.

In Washington: Throughout his career, Penny has been preoccupied by the intractability of federal fiscal problems and the unwillingness of senior members of Congress to strike out in new directions. As a budget watchdog trying to restrain the Democratic Party's inclinations toward generosity in spending, he often jousts with party leaders. He sealed his commitment to the cause in 1992 with his promise to leave Congress if the budget deficit is not cut in half by 1996.

When Penny and other like-minded budget deficit "hawks" began their assaults on spending bills in the 1980s, it was easy for Democratic leaders to dismiss those efforts as quixotic adventures with no chance of affecting policy. But as the economy and the size of the deficit took greater prominence in the public debate in the 102nd and 103rd Congresses, a larger segment of the Democratic Caucus has joined the campaign for fiscal restraint.

Penny, who considers himself a strong Democrat, tries to balance his readiness to challenge his party's leaders and their prerogatives against his own party loyalties. Although he joined conservative Democrats seeking to change President Clinton's economic stimulus package early in the 103rd Congress, in the end he voted for the bill.

Still, senior Democrats do not always take to Penny's maverick conduct. He failed in his bid to join the Ways and Means Committee in the 103rd Congress. He was, however, named by Speaker Thomas S. Foley of Washington, to his Working Group on Policy Development created at the start of the 103rd, which is designed to help set the legislative agenda.

Deficit hawks registered several high-profile victories in the 102nd Congress, including House adoption of a budget resolution that devoted defense savings to deficit reduction. Penny and Texas Democrat Charles W. Stenholm, who heads the Conservative Democratic Forum, led a conservative Democratic revolt that blocked a proposed shift of funds from the defense budget to a variety of social programs. They argued, successfully, that any money cut from defense should be used to reduce the deficit, as required by the 1990 budget agreement. Republicans joined with Democratic deficit hawks to reject the plan, giving Democratic leaders an embarrassing defeat.

Less than a year later, Penny and Stenholm led the clamor to alter President Clinton's $16.3 billion economic stimulus package. But the White House, fueled by what one Democrat called "good will and momentum," rebuffed their efforts to trim the package, banking on the large Democratic majority in the House. United Republican opposition in the Senate ultimately killed the bill.

Unlike Stenholm, Penny decided to vote for the stimulus package. He said he informed the White House that "some noses would be out of joint" if the Senate received the deal that House conservatives craved. Good will and momentum, Penny said, are finite commodities. "You can only bank on that a couple of times." At a White House reception the morning after the vote, according to The Washington Post, he told Clinton: "I hope you understand I voted with you because I was trying to be helpful." Penny told the Post that Clinton noted that it was a tough vote and added, "I'll never forget it."

Penny established an early beachhead from which to wage his war on deficits. In 1983 he became chairman of the Freshman Budget Task Force, a group of Democratic first-termers touting an across-the-board budget freeze. This effort begat the Budget Study Group, an organization that discusses deficit-reduction options and that has grown in both size and acceptance.

In 1987, Penny and Iowa Republican Tom Tauke formed the Truth-in-Budgeting Task Force, of which Penny is still a co-chairman. "The only way we can meet our deficit reduction is to cut a little more as each opportunity arises," Penny said. Since then, Penny and other allies have offered numerous amendments to appropriations bills making across-the-board cuts in funding levels. They meet with limited success; most — but not all — of the amendments lose, many by sizable margins.

Minnesota 1

Southeast — Rochester; part of Mankato

When he talks to audiences unfamiliar with the 1st, Rep. Penny describes it this way: "It's Redwing Shoes, the Mayo Clinic, Hormel and the valley of the Jolly Green Giant."

The "valley" is still mostly rural, and agriculture — corn, grains, dairy and hog farming — is the major focus. The rolling hills that extend from the Mississippi River to the great bend in the Minnesota River offer farmers some of the state's most productive land.

Except for Rochester and some Mississippi River towns, the population centers in the 1st are devoted to serving the surrounding farms, or in the case of Austin, processing the main local product — hogs.

Austin's economy is fed by the meat- and food-processing plants in the area, and the name Hormel says it all. George A. Hormel founded the company in 1891. At the Mower County Historical Center, visitors can see the original Hormel building, along with steam locomotives and horse-drawn carriages.

And while there are pockets of Democratic strength (Mower County is the most consistently Democratic in the 1st), the district as a whole is overwhelmingly Republican with a keen independent streak.

The state's redistricting odyssey has not changed that configuration. A 1993 Supreme Court decision upheld a state-drawn redistricting map and invalidated a plan crafted by the federal courts. The federally drawn plan was used in the 1992 election. However, the new state-drafted districts will be in effect for the 1994 congressional election. Although the 1st will change little, it gained North Mankato. Now the whole metropolitan area of Mankato, the district's second largest city, will be in the same congressional district.

In 1992, the district gave Ross Perot about 27 percent of the vote — more than in any state district except the 2nd. The state overall was one of Perot's biggest successes. In 1988, George Bush won the old 1st with only 51 percent of the vote; Bill Clinton narrowly carried the 1st in 1992.

Still a fixture in the 1st is Redwing Shoes. Located in Red Wing, the company employs more than 1,000 people. The district is also known for the world-famous Mayo Clinic, located in Rochester. The facility now employs about 1,000 physicians in the 19-story facility. And IBM's largest domestic facility, which employs about 7,600 people, is in Rochester.

Rochester (Olmsted County) has a more white-collar orientation than the rest of the district. Its voters are more reliably Republican than many of the 1st's farmers, who often stray from GOP traditions.

Another of the 1st's claims to fame is as the scene of one of the last chapters of Old West history. It was in Northfield (Rice County) that Jesse James and his gang were finally stopped in 1876 when they attempted to rob the Northfield Bank and were ambushed by townfolk. Each Labor Day weekend, thousands attend the "Defeat of Jesse James Days" celebration.

1990 Population: 546,887. White 535,088 (98%), Black 1,752 (<1%), Other 10,047 (2%). Hispanic origin 5,347 (1%). 18 and over 399,063 (73%), 62 and over 90,709 (17%). Median age: 33.

Penny also has been willing to take his budget philosophy personally. In 1991, he founded the Porkbusters group. He continues to co-chair Porkbusters as well as the Democratic Budget Group. In August 1992, he joined the anti-deficit "Lead ... or Leave" drive, signing a pledge committing himself to quitting in 1996 if the deficit is not reduced to half of the $333 billion figure used by the group.

On the Agriculture Committee, the assignment most crucial to Penny politically, he is a defender of his home-state dairy farmers, though he can work with others seeking a middle ground on dairy provisions. Penny joined other Midwestern and Northeastern lawmakers in 1991 when they tried unsuccessfully to revise dairy programs in response to plummeting milk prices.

At the start of the 103rd Congress, Penny took the helm of Agriculture's Foreign Agriculture and Hunger Subcommittee. With the demise of the House Select Committee on Hunger, Penny instantly became a leading legislative player on programs addressing world hunger.

On the issue of using military force in the Persian Gulf in early 1991, Penny, a member of the Veterans' Affairs Committee, agonized about his vote. He met with peace marchers and military families, with the confused and the passionate. In the end, Penny voted to rely on sanctions and delay the use of force. He later professed to being comfortable with his choice but added, "I'll probably have fewer doubts the next time around."

At Home: The first Democrat to hold this

district in nearly a century, Penny defied GOP predictions that he would be a one-term fluke.

Penny has been running for office virtually his entire adult life. In 1976, barely a year out of graduate school, he ran for the state Senate in south-central Minnesota. Treading in staunchly GOP territory, Penny visited each household in the district three times and drew 52 percent to oust a Republican incumbent.

Redistricting carved up his state Senate district and left him without a familiar place to seek re-election. So he decided to run for Congress in 1982. His chances of making it seemed minimal until a vicious quarrel developed between two GOP incumbents, Tom Hagedorn and Arlen Erdahl, who ended up running against each other after redistricting.

When Hagedorn won the GOP district convention, Penny worked to exploit lingering bitterness, calling himself a moderate in the Erdahl tradition. As the race tightened, Hagedorn unleashed a barrage of charges, including criticism that Penny had never worked in the private sector. Penny responded with ads that showed him with his young family, a contrast with the divorced Hagedorn. Penny prevailed with 51 percent of the vote.

In 1984, Penny defeated Republican Keith Spicer, a Rochester sales manager with close ties to southern Minnesota's fundamentalist Christian community. Although President Ronald Reagan swept the 1st District, Spicer had little appeal to the district's large contingent of moderate Republicans, whom Penny had cultivated.

GOP leaders hoped Erdahl would run in 1986, but he bowed out in late 1985, choosing a position in the national office of the Peace Corps. Republicans fielded a weak challenger then, and again in 1988.

In early 1990, Republican state Rep. Dave Bishop, a popular moderate from Rochester, said he was considering challenging Penny because the Democrat was too conservative. But Bishop opted against running, and once again the GOP settled for insignificant opposition. Penny racked up his biggest House election mark: 78 percent. In 1992, Penny won with 74 percent of the vote.

Committees

Agriculture (8th of 28 Democrats)
Foreign Agriculture & Hunger (chairman); Environment, Credit & Rural Development

Veterans' Affairs (5th of 21 Democrats)
Education, Training & Employment

Elections

1992 General		
Timothy J. Penny (D)	206,369	(74%)
Timothy R. Droogsma (R)	72,367	(26%)
1992 Primary		
Timothy J. Penny (D)	29,816	(92%)
E. Douglas Andersen (D)	1,618	(5%)
Joseph B. Campbell (D)	1,131	(3%)
1990 General		
Timothy J. Penny (D)	156,749	(78%)
Doug Andersen (R)	43,856	(22%)

Previous Winning Percentages: **1988** (70%) **1986** (72%) **1984** (57%) **1982** (51%)

District Vote for President

1992
D 109,829 (39%)
R 98,384 (35%)
I 75,227 (27%)

Campaign Finance

	Receipts	Receipts from PACs	Expend-itures
1992			
Penny (D)	$244,518	$92,743 (38%)	$292,920
Droogsma (R)	$96,568	$10,981 (11%)	$93,620
1990			
Penny (D)	$230,040	$113,050 (49%)	$197,442

Key Votes

1993	
Require parental notification of minors' abortions	Y
Require unpaid family and medical leave	N
Approve national "motor voter" registration bill	Y
Approve budget increasing taxes and reducing deficit	Y
Approve economic stimulus plan	Y
1992	
Approve balanced-budget constitutional amendment	Y
Close down space station program	Y
Approve U.S. aid for former Soviet Union	Y
Allow shifting funds from defense to domestic programs	N
1991	
Extend unemployment benefits using deficit financing	N
Approve waiting period for handgun purchases	N
Authorize use of force in Persian Gulf	N

Voting Studies

	Presidential Support		Party Unity		Conservative Coalition	
Year	**S**	**O**	**S**	**O**	**S**	**O**
1992	41	59	60	37	48	52
1991	50	50	66	32	57	41
1990	34	66	66	33	56	44
1989	57	43	67	33	68	32
1988	37	63	59	41	66	34
1987	35	65	59	41	49	51
1986	34	66	61	39	48	52
1985	25	75	53	47	35	65
1984	35	65	69	31	36	64
1983	13	87	84	16	29	69

Interest Group Ratings

Year	ADA	AFL-CIO	CCUS	ACU
1992	45	50	50	52
1991	50	42	60	30
1990	67	50	43	25
1989	55	50	80	46
1988	60	71	64	36
1987	64	50	53	30
1986	75	64	50	18
1985	60	47	50	24
1984	75	38	50	33
1983	75	76	40	17

2 David Minge (D)

Of Montevideo — Elected 1992; 1st Term

Born: March 19, 1942, Clarkfield, Minn.
Education: St. Olaf College, B.A. 1964; U. of Chicago, J.D. 1967.
Occupation: Lawyer.
Family: Wife, Karen Aaker; two children.
Religion: Lutheran.
Political Career: Montevideo School Board, 1989-92.
Capitol Office: 1508 Longworth Bldg. 20515; 225-2331.

The Path to Washington: In early 1992, Republican Rep. Vin Weber, who was preparing to retire after six terms in the House, disparagingly predicted that the huge freshman class of the 103rd Congress would arrive with its only mandate to be fat and not to bounce checks — a tongue-in-cheek reference to the House bank scandal and controversy over congressional perks, such as the House gymnasium.

But Minge, who succeeds Weber in the 2nd District, has higher aspirations.

"I kept on seeing all the problems we faced as a nation, and I didn't feel they were being addressed," said Minge, a self-described "country lawyer" whose only previous political experience was a four-year stint on the local Montevideo Board of Education. "So instead of going fishing, I decided to do something about it."

Minge's first major achievement was getting elected at all. The mostly rural 2nd was little changed by redistricting; it is a heavily Republican area where the popular Weber had enjoyed ever-increasing margins in his last three races.

Weber bowed out after he was caught up in the House bank scandal himself. Still, Minge was expected to play sacrificial lamb to his better-known GOP opponent, Cal R. Ludeman, a former state representative who was the party's nominee for governor in 1986.

Indeed, Minge looked anything but strong heading into the general election. Despite winning the party endorsement at the district's convention (an event that often makes primaries in the state anticlimactic), Minge received an anemic 53 percent in the primary, barely beating one challenger who was a supporter of jailed political extremist Lyndon H. LaRouche and another who spent less than $100 on the race.

But Minge successfully painted Ludeman — seen as the logical successor to conservative media darling Weber — as too radical for the district's voters.

One campaign brochure noted that Ludeman, during his tenure in the state Legislature, was one of only three members who voted against a bill to require that employers pay workers the minimum wage, and the only dissenter on legislation urging that areas of the state hit by storms be declared federal disaster areas.

"Ludeman has a record of voting based on ideology, not on what is in the best interest of the district," Minge's brochure said.

Minge also took one-on-one campaigning seriously, including a nine-day, 478-mile bicycle trek through the 2nd's 27 counties.

In the end, Minge managed to squeak past Ludeman, winning by 569 votes out of more than 275,000 cast.

In the House, agriculture will obviously be a priority, given the district's rural bent, and Minge met one of his first-term goals early when he was appointed to the Agriculture Committee. His other committee assignment is to Science, Space and Technology.

While Minge supports such mainstream Democratic positions as abortion rights, family leave and full funding for Head Start, he is not an automatic liberal vote.

He also supports what has become the GOP freshman mantra — congressional term limits, a balanced-budget amendment to the Constitution and a presidential line-item veto.

In addition to supporting a Democratic version of a line-item veto that the House passed in April 1993, Minge was one of only 33 Democrats to vote for a more potent GOP substitute.

Minge's national policy priorities are also in line with the majority of the freshman class: lowering the federal deficit and improving the economy, reforming the nation's health-care system and overhauling the campaign finance system.

But his personal policy interests are diverse. When asked, he quickly rattles off a virtual laundry list, including banking, small-business issues and export policy.

"I've been a generalist in my community in terms of being a country lawyer," Minge says, noting that he taught six or seven different courses during his years as a law professor at the University of Wyoming. "I've always been curious about a lot of things, so there are a lot of things I can see doing that would be exciting."

Minnesota 2

Southwest — Willmar

Much of the landscape of the 2nd District is dotted for mile upon mile with silos and grain elevators, broken up occasionally by small crossroads market centers. The 2nd's largest town, Willmar, has only about 18,000 people.

The 2nd supports a small industrial economy, which includes three 3M facilities — one in New Ulm and two in Hutchinson. (Hutchinson is the site of the company's largest facility, which employs about 2,000 people.) Turkey growing and processing is big business in Worthington (Nobles County).

But the economy is still driven by farming. Bisected by the broad Minnesota River, the sprawling 27-county district includes some of the best farmland in the state. The well-to-do farmers in the south along the Iowa border enjoy bountiful harvests of corn and soybeans. Moving north along the Minnesota River, dairy farms become more common.

The political flavor of the 2nd tends to be Republican with an independent streak. In 1992, Democrat Bill Clinton carried the 2nd with 37 percent of the vote; George Bush took 35 percent, Ross Perot 28 percent.

In the prairie counties north of the Minnesota River, the land is sandy and rocky and the politics more unpredictable. Farmers here have to work harder to scratch out a living, and they display a frequent dissatisfaction with any party that is in power.

Many voters in the southern tier of counties are of German ethnic stock. Like those in the adjoining 1st District, they share a strong Republican tradition and an allegiance to the Farm Bureau, the most conservative of the state's major farm organizations.

At the turn of the century, the Scandinavian settlers here battled constantly with railroads, bankers and grain merchants. Disillusioned by Republicans and Democrats, they were ripe for third-party alternatives.

The Farmer-Labor Party found early support in this region, as did presidential candidate Robert LaFollette in 1924, when his Progressive Party carried many of the counties in this area.

Today, with strong support from the National Farmers Union, Democrats often run well in this part of the district.

The economies of some small towns — Morton, Redwood Falls and Granite Falls in the southern part of the district — have benefited from casinos that are owned and operated by the Sioux Indians. The casinos have produced an influx of visitors and jobs to the towns; Redwood Falls has been building new lodging facilities to accommodate the added traffic.

In 1993, the Supreme Court rejected the federally drawn redistricting map that had been used in the 1992 election. Candidates will run under a state-drawn plan in 1994.

Changes for the 2nd were minimal: North Mankato moved to the 1st.

1990 Population: 546,887. White 538,611 (98%), Black 836 (<1%), Other 7,440 (1%). Hispanic origin 5,279 (1%). 18 and over 390,480 (71%), 62 and over 98,947 (18%). Median age: 34.

Committees

Agriculture (16th of 28 Democrats)
Environment, Credit & Rural Development; General Farm Commodities; Specialty Crops & Natural Resources

Science, Space & Technology (28th of 33 Democrats)
Science; Technology, Environment & Aviation

Campaign Finance

1992	Receipts	Receipts from PACs		Expend-itures
Minge (D)	$365,394	$159,958	(44%)	$355,400
Ludeman (R)	$432,038	$14,415	(3%)	$429,100

Key Votes

1993

Require parental notification of minors' abortions	N
Require unpaid family and medical leave	Y
Approve national "motor voter" registration bill	Y
Approve budget increasing taxes and reducing deficit	Y
Approve economic stimulus plan	Y

Elections

1992 General		
David Minge (D)	132,156	(48%)
Cal R. Ludeman (R)	131,587	(48%)
Stan Bentz (I)	12,146	(4%)
1992 Primary		
David Minge (D)	13,468	(53%)
Pat O'Reilly (D)	7,465	(30%)
Andrew Olson (D)	4,282	(17%)

District Vote for President

1992

D 103,447 (37%)
R 98,015 (35%)
I 79,610 (28%)

3 Jim Ramstad (R)

Of Minnetonka — Elected 1990; 2nd Term

Born: May 6, 1946, Jamestown, N.D.
Education: U. of Minnesota, B.A. 1968; George Washington U., J.D. 1973.
Military Service: Army Reserve, 1968-74.
Occupation: Lawyer; legislative aide.
Family: Single.
Religion: Protestant.
Political Career: Minn. Senate, 1981-91.
Capitol Office: 322 Cannon Bldg. 20515; 225-2871.

In Washington: As a junior member of the minority wing of the minority party, one might expect Ramstad to be fairly invisible. However, he has been active and successful in several policy areas and seems to be following in the path of his activist predecessor, Bill Frenzel. Despite the inevitable setbacks Ramstad has had, it is likely that the leadership will be keeping an eye on his actions.

A member of the Judiciary, Small Business and the Joint Economic committees, he has not limited his activities to the jurisdictions of those panels. He managed to get included in the higher education reauthorization bill an amendment to order universities to establish sexual assault policies.

He also pushed legislation that would have forced convicted child offenders and kidnappers to register their addresses with local law enforcement officials for 10 years after leaving prison. He also sponsored a bill that would have provided felony punishment for assaults against children under 16 that result in substantial bodily harm. Ramstad's law-and-order policy approach carried over from his days in the Minnesota state Senate, where he backed mandatory prison sentences for dealing drugs and committing violent crimes, and "boot camps" for felony drug offenders.

Ramstad, a recovering alcoholic who has devoted much energy to ensure that alcohol and drug education is available to young people, speaks often to schools and community groups on the subject. He also frequently addresses other groups of recovering alcoholics to discuss his experiences.

"I'm a grateful recovering alcoholic who is committed to alcohol and drug education for our young people. I'm also committed to providing treatment opportunities for chemically dependent people who meet and want help. I really believe that, more than anything else, the chemical abuse problem threatens to undermine the social fiber of our country," he said in a 1992 interview.

Ramstad also received attention during the 102nd Congress for not always adhering to the Republican leadership's position. He voted to override President Bush's vetoes on family leave and abortion counseling at federally funded clinics. Such votes did little to endear him to his more conservative colleagues and probably were a factor in his failure at the start of the 103rd Congress to get on the House Ways and Means Committee, where his mentor and former boss, Frenzel, made his mark.

Ramstad had gotten an earlier taste of Washington power politics in 1991, when he voted to cut funding for the office of then-Transportation Secretary Samuel K. Skinner: $2 million that was to have funded the upgrade of a 3rd District highway instead went to a project in Democrat Martin Olav Sabo's neighboring 5th District.

Ramstad's abortion rights stance has put him at odds with many in his party and has caused him some political problems at home because of the heavy influence of the anti-abortion forces within the Independent-Republican Party. But Ramstad has gotten some help smoothing the waters with abortion opponents from former Republican Sen. Rudy Boschwitz.

The onset of the Clinton era may make Ramstad more of a GOP team player — especially on economic issues, where Ramstad is a more traditional, conservative Republican. He criticized Clinton's economic proposal in early 1993 as being too short on spending cuts.

"History shows that higher taxes always lead to more government spending and higher deficits," he said. "We're repeating history's mistakes."

At Home: As Frenzel's heir apparent, Ramstad fairly cruised into office in 1990.

During the campaign, Ramstad sought to paint his election as a continuation of the Frenzel legacy. His most daunting obstacle was the district Independent-Republican convention, where his abortion rights stance placed him at odds with the anti-abortion delegates who dominate the state's Republican conventions.

In the affluent suburban Twin Cities district, voters prefer Republicans of a moderate stripe, such as Frenzel (who represented the

Minnesota 3

Southern Twin Cities suburbs — Bloomington; Minnetonka

With its abundance of high-tech industries, white-collar workers, golf courses and middle-class homes, the 3rd is for the most part the very picture of suburban living.

The last round of the state's redistricting pingpong was good news for Rep. Ramstad. The 3rd, already a Republican safe haven, became slightly more so when the Supreme Court rejected the federally drawn map that had been used in the 1992 elections. In 1993, the high court ruled that federal courts must stand aside until challenges to redistricting plans run their course in state courts. In 1994, candidates will run in districts drawn by the state court in 1992.

In 1992, the district included parts of Dakota, Hennepin, Scott and Washington counties. Under the state plan upheld by the Supreme Court, the 3rd will include more Wright County than Washington County, will pick up Republican Plymouth and western Hennepin County communities, and gain the largely Democratic cities of Brooklyn Park and Brooklyn Center.

The 3rd extends beyond the western and southern extremities of the metropolitan area. Surburbanization has touched most of the 3rd except the very farthest reaches, which remain rural.

The district is a popular home for Fortune 500 companies. Several, including Cargill Inc., the world's largest privately owned corporation, are here. Cargill, which is based in Minnetonka and employs about 2,000 people there, is a diversified company that handles everything from wheat and corn processing to financial trading. Other Fortune companies with headquarters in the 3rd include lawnmower maker Toro; food giant General Mills; Medtronic, which produces heart pacemakers; high-tech Control Data; Cray Research, which makes supercomputers; and grocery chain Super-value. Honeywell has three factories here.

But perhaps most crucial to many local businesses is the fate of the district's largest employer, the financially troubled Northwest Airlines, which employs about 18,000 people.

The 3rd also has another claim to fame — the nation's largest shopping mall. The Mall of America in Bloomington (Hennepin County) measures 4.2 million square feet. Nearly a third of the 30 million people who visited the mall during the first two months after it opened in 1992 were tourists, some coming from as far as Japan, England and Germany.

A few Democrats can be found in Dakota County, but its comparatively small number of voters will not be enough to loosen the hold the GOP typically enjoys in the 3rd. Ramstad has won the 3rd twice with about two-thirds of the vote. Republican influence is so strong here that in 1984, home-state Democratic presidential nominee Walter F. Mondale drew less than one-third of the vote in a number of precincts.

In 1988, George Bush won the old 3rd with 54 percent of the vote. However, voters were not as enthusiastic in 1992, giving Bush 36 percent to Bill Clinton's 40 percent and Ross Perot's 24 percent.

1990 Population: 546,888. White 524,804 (96%), Black 7,291 (1%), Other 14,793 (3%). Hispanic origin 5,880 (1%). 18 and over 398,813 (73%), 62 and over 55,647 (10%). Median age: 32.

area from 1971 to 1991). Although Democrats had not held the seat since Dwight D. Eisenhower was president, they saw a chance to compete if Republicans chose an anti-abortion candidate at the convention. Such a choice likely would have mired the Republican Party in an abortion rights debate through the primary in mid-September.

But Boschwitz, an abortion opponent, put pragmatism over personal preference and wrote to convention delegates urging them to unify and support Ramstad. Another anti-abortion Republican, 2nd District then-Rep. Vin Weber, also endorsed Ramstad before the convention.

Anti-abortion delegates greeted Boschwitz coolly as he worked the floor in Ramstad's behalf, but ultimately they acceded to his lobbying. After seven ballots, Ramstad defeated four other candidates to win the convention endorsement. He easily defeated a minor foe in the primary and then began a push against his Democratic rival, investment executive Lewis DeMars.

With the most serious impediment behind him, Ramstad lost little time demonstrating how formidable he could be. Known for his fundraising skills, Ramstad vaulted to the top ranks of congressional candidates in contributions raised. With three weeks to go before voting, Ramstad had raised a half-million dollars more than DeMars and went on to crush him 2-to-1 in the general election.

In 1992, Ramstad held on to his base in a year when the Republican Party was struggling at the top of the ticket, winning 64 percent of the vote against an opponent making his first run at elective political office.

Committees

Judiciary (10th of 14 Republicans)
Administrative Law & Governmental Relations; Crime & Criminal Justice

Small Business (6th of 18 Republicans)
Rural Enterprises, Exports and the Environment; Minority Enterprise, Finance & Urban Development; SBA Legislation & the General Economy

Joint Economic

Elections

1992 General		
Jim Ramstad (R)	200,240	(64%)
Paul Mandell (D)	104,606	(33%)
Dwight Fellman (GR)	9,164	(3%)
1990 General		
Jim Ramstad (R)	195,833	(67%)
Lewis DeMars (D)	96,395	(33%)

District Vote for President

1992
D 130,810 (40%)
R 118,458 (36%)
I 80,412 (24%)

Campaign Finance

	Receipts	Receipts from PACs		Expend-itures
1992				
Ramstad (R)	$1,010,791	$260,016	(26%)	$695,521
Mandell (D)	$18,609	$8,670	(47%)	$18,164
1990				
Ramstad (R)	$936,208	$237,745	(25%)	$935,454
DeMars (D)	$338,261	$107,925	(32%)	$337,321

Key Votes

1993	
Require parental notification of minors' abortions	N
Require unpaid family and medical leave	Y
Approve national "motor voter" registration bill	Y
Approve budget increasing taxes and reducing deficit	N
Approve economic stimulus plan	N
1992	
Approve balanced-budget constitutional amendment	Y
Close down space station program	Y
Approve U.S. aid for former Soviet Union	N
Allow shifting funds from defense to domestic programs	N
1991	
Extend unemployment benefits using deficit financing	N
Approve waiting period for handgun purchases	N
Authorize use of force in Persian Gulf	Y

Voting Studies

	Presidential Support		Party Unity		Conservative Coalition	
Year	S	O	S	O	S	O
1992	53	47	78	22	56	44
1991	65	34	81	18	86	14

Interest Group Ratings

Year	ADA	AFL-CIO	CCUS	ACU
1992	30	42	75	68
1991	25	33	80	85

Minnesota - 4th District

4 Bruce F. Vento (D)

Of St. Paul — Elected 1976; 9th Term

Born: Oct. 7, 1940, St. Paul, Minn.
Education: U. of Minnesota, A.A. 1961; Wisconsin State U., B.S. 1965; U. of Minnesota, 1965-70.
Occupation: Science teacher.
Family: Divorced; three children.
Religion: Roman Catholic.
Political Career: Minn. House, 1971-77.
Capitol Office: 2304 Rayburn Bldg. 20515; 225-6631.

In Washington: Vento made his reputation as a legislative workhorse under the less-than-ideal conditions of divided government, and he should have greater opportunities for accomplishment with a Democrat in the White House.

He chairs the Natural Resources (formerly Interior) Subcommittee on National Parks and Public Lands, a panel with a huge mandate and a workload to match. He should be a central player — and a potential ally for President Clinton — in the turbulent debate over protecting the threatened northern spotted owl and the ancient, old-growth forests that are its habitat. At the same time, Vento remains active on the Banking Committee, on issues as diverse as aiding the homeless and addressing the savings and loan crisis.

But even those who admire Vento's diligence acknowledge that he has one problem: He talks and talks and talks. Even his closest associates acknowledge that he will often go to great lengths to explain an issue, a trait that springs from his genuine interest in educating people. Were he any less conscientious a lawmaker, his unpunctuated verbosity might make it hard for him to build the delicate coalitions needed to pass legislation.

Vento shares the philosophy of the conservationist majority on the Natural Resources Committee, where his productivity helps them tolerate his garrulous style. In the 101st Congress, by his count, he shepherded 109 bills through the House and saw 92 of them enacted.

Vento's subcommittee mandate allows him to offer colleagues tangible benefits to attract them to his side. His panel can approve historical sites and designate trails and rivers, national parks and wilderness land. In the 99th Congress, Vento helped guide the creation of Nevada's Great Basin National Park, the first full-scale national park added to the system outside Alaska since 1971.

In the 1990s, Vento's biggest effort has been devoted to protecting ancient forests in Oregon, Washington and Northern California and their wildlife habitats — without making loggers an endangered species.

In the 101st and 102nd Congresses, Vento pushed bills that would have placed millions of acres of forest off-limits to logging. Both times, he steered the measures through his subcommittee on close votes only to see them blocked in full committee by disgruntled lawmakers who appealed to Speaker Thomas S. Foley of Washington to reopen negotiations.

In the 103rd, Clinton and Vice President Al Gore took a personal interest in the issue by convening a "timber summit" (later rechristened a "forest conference") in April 1993 in Portland, Ore. But Vento and his colleagues will have to decide whether the ideas emerging from that meeting become law.

Vento remains influential on the Banking Committee, having escaped any major repercussions after his coup attempt against Chairman Henry B. Gonzalez before the start of the 102nd Congress. Much of the Democratic Caucus had been frustrated with Gonzalez's first two years as Banking chairman, and Vento offered himself as the vessel for this dissatisfaction. More than one-third of the caucus rallied to him; but the competing personalities within the Banking Committee failed to coalesce behind his effort, which was not launched until the very day of balloting. Gonzalez held on by a vote of 163-89.

Vento has been involved in a range of issues on Banking. He was a principal in the 1991 fight to overhaul banking regulations and reform the federal system of deposit insurance. His Midwestern populist views placed him in the path of administration officials and big-bank interests that wanted to open branch offices across state lines. He sponsored a successful floor amendment to the banking bill that would have given states the opportunity to "opt out" of a federally mandated regime of interstate branching. Ultimately, other pressures forced the entire branching issue to be dropped.

In the 101st Congress, he devoted considerable time to succoring the nation's ailing savings and loan industry. In 1989, as the Banking Committee was considering a bill to provide $50

Minnesota 4

St. Paul and suburbs

The 4th, with its deep roots in the labor movement and its liberal academic communities, is in many ways a Democratic candidate's dream.

The economy of the 4th is fueled by the government, education and industry. St. Paul, the capital, is the hub of state government, whose agencies employ thousands of unionized workers. The headquarters for the Minnesota Mining and Manufacturing Co., better known as 3M Co., is in a suburb of St. Paul and employs about 20,000 people, many of whom also are union members.

The district, which includes Ramsey County and parts of Dakota and Washington counties, also has numerous college campuses, including parts of the University of Minnesota and its 39,300 students.

St. Paul (population 272,000), located in Ramsey County, is a traditionally Democratic city with a large German and Irish-Catholic population. The city developed as a major port and railroading center and still has a strong labor tradition. Many portions of the district are middle- or high-income areas.

The city became more diverse during the 1970s and 1980s, when there was an influx of Hmong refugees from Southeast Asia. In some neighborhoods in mostly northern and eastern sections of the city, some business signs are written in Hmong. The first Hmong elected to public office in the nation was elected to St. Paul's school board in 1991.

The city's Hispanic population has also increased. On the west side of the city (and in the city of West St. Paul) is a well-organized, solidly Democratic Hispanic community.

The working-class neighborhoods on St. Paul's East Side are drab and solidly Democratic. The precincts here have routinely supported virtually every major statewide Democratic candidate of recent years.

More than 30 years ago, when Eugene J. McCarthy represented St. Paul in the House, nearly 90 percent of the district vote came from the city. But with the growth of the suburbs and a decline in St. Paul's population (from its 1960 peak of 313,000), St. Paul now accounts for just half the district vote.

Most of the suburban vote lies north of the city in Ramsey County. While Rep. Vento never has difficulty carrying any section of St. Paul, he has sometimes struggled in several areas in suburban Ramsey. Farther north are the more-affluent suburbs of Shoreview, North Oak and White Bear Lake, which vote Republican more often.

A 1993 Supreme Court decision upheld a state-drawn redistricting map, rejecting a plan crafted by the federal courts and used in the 1992 election. The state plan will be used in the 1994 election.

Under the state plan approved by the high court, Mendota Heights, which votes Republican, was returned to the 4th. Redistricting also added Sunfish Lake, a small conservative suburb.

1990 Population: 546,887. White 486,403 (89%), Black 23,229 (4%), Other 37,255 (7%). Hispanic origin 15,600 (3%). 18 and over 410,455 (75%), 62 and over 78,838 (14%). Median age: 32.

billion to salvage the industry, Vento brokered a compromise that gave thrifts more time to meet stricter capital standards, while at the same time stiffening those standards.

Later, Vento served as the vocal and critical chairman of a task force on the Resolution Trust Corporation, the government's thrift salvage agency, to oversee the implementation of the bailout. In the 102nd, he was instrumental in enacting changes to the RTC's operations.

In the 101st Congress, the Banking Committee also worked on the most sweeping overhaul of federal housing programs since 1974. Vento teamed with Pennsylvania Republican Tom Ridge to remedy the Federal Housing Administration's troubled mortgage insurance program, proposing a plan that would curtail losses without shutting out families from home ownership. (Ridge eventually backed out of the partnership.)

Vento was one of the first members to urge congressional action on the homeless, pushing for money to finance temporary shelters in 1982. In the 100th Congress, he was the prime sponsor of the $1.3 billion McKinney homeless-aid reauthorization bill, which won widespread support and was reauthorized in 1990. At the start of the 103rd, Foley named Vento to chair a special task force on the homeless whose formation was requested by Clinton.

At Home: Vento has the right personal and political background to represent his labor-dominated district.

The son of a Machinists' union official, he was a union steward at a plastics plant, then worked in a brewery and on a refrigerator assembly line before becoming a junior high school teacher and state representative.

During his three terms in the Legislature he echoed the interests of the working-class residents of St. Paul's Phalen Park. A loyal team player, he won the assistant majority leader post under Speaker Martin Olav Sabo, now his Minnesota congressional colleague.

When nine-term House veteran Joseph E. Karth decided to retire in 1976, he endorsed Vento for the seat. Karth's backing and labor support gave Vento the party endorsement.

Still, Vento faced four foes in the Democratic primary. Two were significant: St. Paul attorney John S. Connolly, running as an even more liberal alternative to Vento, and 27-year-old state Auditor Robert W. Mattson, who twice defeated party-endorsed candidates. But Vento had too many factors working in his favor. He won a convincing primary victory with 52 percent. The November election was just as easy for Vento as it usually had been for Karth.

In 1978, Vento met an aggressive, conservative GOP challenger who held the incumbent under 60 percent. But with the same candidate and a much better-financed campaign in 1980, Republicans got no closer. Since then they have offered only token opposition. In 1986 Vento easily turned back a challenge from one of the nation's foremost perennial candidates, Harold E. Stassen, making his first bid for the House after numerous tries for other offices. In 1988, 1990 and 1992, he easily repelled challenges by Republican Ian Maitland, a professor at the University of Minnesota.

Committees

Banking, Finance & Urban Affairs (4th of 30 Democrats)
Financial Institutions Supervision, Regulation & Deposit Insurance; Housing & Community Development

Natural Resources (6th of 28 Democrats)
National Parks, Forests & Public Lands (chairman); Oversight & Investigations

Elections

1992 General		
Bruce F. Vento (D)	159,796	(57%)
Ian Maitland (R)	101,744	(37%)
James L. Willess (I)	6,732	(2%)
Dan R. Vacek (GR)	4,418	(2%)
Lynn Marvin Johnson (NL)	3,602	(1%)
1990 General		
Bruce F. Vento (D)	143,353	(65%)
Ian Maitland (R)	77,639	(35%)

Previous Winning Percentages: **1988** (72%) **1986** (73%) **1984** (74%) **1982** (73%) **1980** (59%) **1978** (58%) **1976** (66%)

District Vote for President

1992

D	148,046 (52%)
R	79,690 (28%)
I	59,361 (21%)

Campaign Finance

	Receipts	Receipts from PACs		Expend-itures
1992				
Vento (D)	$280,123	$207,495	(74%)	$348,920
Maitland (R)	$83,114	0		$82,563
1990				
Vento (D)	$259,456	$187,095	(72%)	$265,699
Maitland (R)	$57,086	0		$57,415

Key Votes

1993	
Require parental notification of minors' abortions	N
Require unpaid family and medical leave	Y
Approve national "motor voter" registration bill	Y
Approve budget increasing taxes and reducing deficit	Y
Approve economic stimulus plan	Y
1992	
Approve balanced-budget constitutional amendment	N
Close down space station program	Y
Approve U.S. aid for former Soviet Union	Y
Allow shifting funds from defense to domestic programs	Y
1991	
Extend unemployment benefits using deficit financing	Y
Approve waiting period for handgun purchases	Y
Authorize use of force in Persian Gulf	N

Voting Studies

	Presidential Support		Party Unity		Conservative Coalition	
Year	S	O	S	O	S	O
1992	13	86	95	4	6	92
1991	26	70	94	4	5	86
1990	13	86	95	4	7	91
1989	30	69	92	7	12	85
1988	21	77	94	4	11	89
1987	12	85	95	2	5	88
1986	19	81	94	5	6	94
1985	21	78	95	3	4	91
1984	28	67	90	6	3	95
1983	17	82	94	4	4	96
1982	34	65	94	5	5	92
1981	29	61	86	9	9	84

Interest Group Ratings

Year	ADA	AFL-CIO	CCUS	ACU
1992	100	92	25	0
1991	90	92	10	0
1990	100	100	21	4
1989	100	83	30	4
1988	90	100	36	4
1987	100	94	8	0
1986	90	93	28	0
1985	95	100	18	5
1984	95	92	43	0
1983	90	94	20	0
1982	100	100	14	9
1981	90	80	13	0

5 Martin Olav Sabo (D)

Of Minneapolis — Elected 1978; 8th Term

Born: Feb. 28, 1938, Crosby, N.D.
Education: Augsburg College, B.A. 1959; U. of Minnesota, 1960.
Occupation: Public official.
Family: Wife, Sylvia Ann Lee; two children.
Religion: Lutheran.
Political Career: Minn. House, 1961-79, minority leader, 1969-73, Speaker, 1973-79.
Capitol Office: 2336 Rayburn Bldg. 20515; 225-4755.

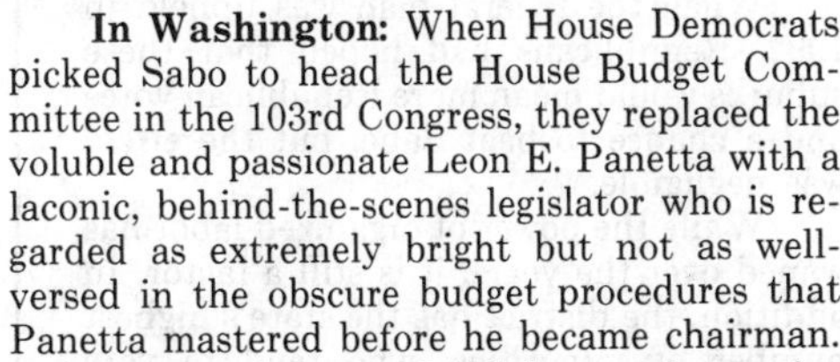

In Washington: When House Democrats picked Sabo to head the House Budget Committee in the 103rd Congress, they replaced the voluble and passionate Leon E. Panetta with a laconic, behind-the-scenes legislator who is regarded as extremely bright but not as well-versed in the obscure budget procedures that Panetta mastered before he became chairman.

Quiet and thoughtful, Sabo matches an innate liberalism with an attention to detail and political strategy that earns him respect from many quarters. Sabo's victory over centrist John M. Spratt Jr., D-S.C., in the chairmanship fight, appeared to be more the result of the well-liked congressman's networking and preemptive campaigning than a measure of House Democrats' political temperature.

Sabo began rounding up commitments well before President-elect Bill Clinton in December 1992 named Panetta to be the new director of the White House Office of Management and Budget (OMB). By the time others tried to get into the race, Sabo had established what turned out to be an insurmountable lead.

Suddenly subjected to intense scrutiny by the media and under great pressure to articulate House Democrats' views on the budget, Sabo occasionally looked as if he would rather be almost anywhere but in the TV lights, and he answered many questions with a mantralike assertion that he would wait to hear what Clinton wanted. Democrats insisted they had no doubt the smart and able Sabo was the right man for the job, despite any initial awkwardness.

Sabo takes over a committee whose role will be sharply altered by a Democratic administration bristling with budget ideas of its own. A key outpost for congressional Democrats in their budget wars with successive GOP administrations over the past 12 years, the committee is expected to shift from aggressive policy formulator to team-playing policy implementer.

Sabo's patient negotiating and the Democrats' own desire to stay united behind Clinton gave the president's first budget blueprint a smooth path through the House. By the time it was adopted on a mostly party-line vote in March 1993, Democrats had voted down every substantive GOP effort to change it, including an alternative plan from John R. Kasich of Ohio, ranking Republican on the Budget panel.

Sabo's low-key approach is well-suited to the Appropriations Committee, where he has added a liberal's perspective to defense and transportation debates for more than a decade. In the 101st Congress, he began to play a broader role when he took a seat on Budget and assumed the chairmanship of the Democratic Study Group (DSG). In the 102nd, he notched upward again with an appointment to the Intelligence Committee. He gave up both Intelligence and the DSG job at the start of the 103rd.

As DSG chairman, Sabo was credited with helping restore the liberal-leaning policy group as a source of agitation. The group had been a key agent for change during the late 1970s but was less visible in the 1980s. During the protracted budget debate in late 1990, the DSG issued meaty and highly partisan reports on "tax fairness," dubbing Bush's capital gains tax cut as a sop to the rich.

At the start of the 102nd Congress, the DSG went on record for a more legislatively assertive Democratic Caucus when it helped orchestrate the ouster of two old-school Democratic chairmen. Sabo contributed to the episode with a letter to Foley raising questions about whether Banking Chairman Henry B. Gonzalez of Texas had violated caucus rules by taping a political ad for a Republican. While Gonzalez survived the flap, he was served notice that the caucus took seriously complaints about his coziness with committee Republicans.

Sabo's new responsibilities on Budget, more than his job at the helm of the DSG, may help satisfy his desire for the kind of leadership role he played in the state Legislature, where he was House Speaker. Sabo once tried for a top leadership job in the U.S. House, seeking the Democratic whip post for the 100th Congress (he was already a deputy whip). But he ran an oddly taciturn campaign and gave it up in mid-1986 for a seat on the Appropriations Subcommittee on Defense. "I think I know how to

Minnesota 5

Minneapolis and suburbs

In 1992, when many a voter was rediscovering his more liberal roots, most residents of the 5th could honestly say they never left the Democratic fold.

Minneapolis residents account for nearly three-fourths of the 5th's voters, and except for those on the city's southwest side, they predictably choose liberal candidates over conservatives.

The district is also home to former Vice President Walter F. Mondale. Voters here gave him 63 percent of the vote against Ronald Reagan in 1984. Michael S. Dukakis and Bill Clinton also won the 5th in 1988 and 1992 with about 60 percent of the vote.

Scandinavians remain the most conspicuous ethnic group; it is no coincidence that Sabo includes his middle name, Olav, on all his official papers to eliminate any doubt that he is of Norwegian heritage.

Although many of the flour mills that once lined the Mississippi River at St. Anthony's Falls have moved, the major companies that settled in Minneapolis — Pillsbury and General Mills — have remained and diversified. They are among the major employers in the Twin Cities, along with the new "brain power" companies that find Minneapolis ideally suited for their needs. Honeywell has its worldwide headquarters here. The white-collar professionals who have been attracted by these "clean" industries help to give the city an image that is reflected in the glistening towers of its downtown area.

However, even the presence of Fortune 500 companies could not halt a late 1980s downturn in the regional economy.

In 1993, the Supreme Court rejected the federally drawn redistricting map that had been used in the 1992 elections. Candidates will now run under a state-drawn plan. The state redistricting barely changed the boundaries of the 5th, and made little change in the political landscape.

Past redistricting efforts have added considerable suburban territory to the 5th. A number of suburban areas — including Golden Valley and New Hope — were added under the federal plan and will remain here in 1994.

When the federal plan was upheld in 1992, Republicans had hoped that these suburbs would mean more Republican votes and a chance to beat Sabo, but the effect was negligible.

While the power of organized labor has waned over the years, it is still a factor. In addition, the district has the state's highest number of minorities, who tend to vote Democratic. Hennepin County has the state's largest number of Hispanic and black voters at 60,114 and 13,978, respectively.

Minneapolis is not only parks, lakes, glass and chrome. Northwest of the downtown office towers are some poor neighborhoods, home to blacks and some of the city's Chippewa Indian population. East of the Mississippi are older, more traditional blue-collar areas adjoining the main campus of the University of Minnesota (39,300 students).

1990 Population: 546,887. White 457,891 (84%), Black 52,345 (10%), Other 36,651 (7%). Hispanic origin 9,756 (2%). 18 and over 434,263 (79%), 62 and over 87,690 (16%) Median age: 33.

count," he said. "My chances of winning are remote."

The Defense Subcommittee seat was a reasonable consolation prize. Sabo had long had an interest in arms control issues, and anti-Pentagon Democrats wanted him on the panel. Until the Minnesotan's arrival, Oregon's Les AuCoin had been the only subcommittee member with a critical attitude toward the Reagan administration's defense buildup and controversial new weapons systems.

Sabo has surprised and offended liberals with his opposition to across-the-board defense cuts. He says he is opposed to such untargeted cuts on principle and will not vote for one, regardless of the subject matter.

On Appropriations, Sabo mixes parochial interests and national policy on spending bills through his interest in scientific research. He looks out for the major high-technology firms in his district as well as for the University of Minnesota, while advocating development of a federal policy on supercomputers. He supported amendments to the 1988 and 1989 defense appropriations bills to require the Pentagon to buy only American-made supercomputers.

In 1990, he offered legislation to fund a national bicycle coordinator within the Department of Transportation and to require a study of ways to promote bicycles as an alternative mode of transportation. The concept squared with his energy-efficiency policy goals and his personal reputation for physical fitness. Though a few years older than others in the Democratic "basketball caucus" — an informal and influential group that regularly competes at the House gym — he is one of its stalwarts.

At Home: Sabo has never been a flashy campaigner, but he has been a significant presence in Minnesota politics virtually all his adult life.

When Democrat Donald Fraser left the House for his unsuccessful Senate try in 1978, nearly a dozen candidates began maneuvering to succeed him. But when Sabo announced that he wanted the job, nearly all bowed out of the contest. Those who remained either lost at the endorsing convention or badly trailed Sabo's 81 percent primary victory.

One of the reasons for Sabo's strength has been his amazing combination of youth and longevity. Elected to the state Legislature at 22, he had been in the public spotlight for 18 years and served as Speaker for six years before running for Congress. He was seen by most voters as the logical liberal successor to Fraser.

Sabo's first Republican opponent, dentist Mike Till, conducted a much more visible campaign than Republicans usually wage in this heavily Democratic district. When businessman Bob Short defeated Fraser in a bitter Senate primary, Till hoped some of the animosity liberals felt toward Short would rub off on Sabo for the general election. But Sabo carefully avoided making any connection between his campaign and Short's, which was a wise move. Short received less than 24 percent in the 5th.

Sabo's winning percentage in 1978 was not quite up to what Fraser had been receiving. But by his second election, he had achieved solid support throughout the area, even in the communities of the district where he was weakest against Till.

Committees

Budget (Chairman)

Appropriations (11th of 37 Democrats)
Defense; Transportation; Treasury, Postal Service & General Government

Elections

1992 General		
Martin Olav Sabo (D)	174,139	(63%)
Stephen A. Moriarty (R)	77,093	(28%)
Russell B. Bentley (GR)	6,786	(2%)
Sandra Coleman (NA)	5,927	(2%)
Mary Mellen (NL)	5,499	(2%)
Glenn Mesaros (I)	4,809	(2%)
1992 Primary		
Martin Olav Sabo (D)	35,168	(67%)
Lisa Niebauer-Stall (D)	14,519	(28%)
James W. Therkelsen (D)	2,456	(5%)
1990 General		
Martin Olav Sabo (D)	144,682	(73%)
Raymond C. "Buzz" Gilbertson (R)	53,720	(27%)

Previous Winning Percentages: **1988** (72%) **1986** (73%) **1984** (70%) **1982** (66%) **1980** (70%) **1978** (62%)

District Vote for President

1992
D 167,941 (58%)
R 68,072 (24%)
I 52,374 (18%)

Campaign Finance

	Receipts	Receipts from PACs		Expend-itures
1992				
Sabo (D)	$408,981	$247,703	(61%)	$585,831
Moriarty (R)	$16,870	$1,742	(10%)	$16,781
1990				
Sabo (D)	$355,684	$226,950	(64%)	$321,644
Gilbertson (R)	$7,950	0		$9,497

Key Votes

1993	
Require parental notification of minors' abortions	N
Require unpaid family and medical leave	Y
Approve national "motor voter" registration bill	Y
Approve budget increasing taxes and reducing deficit	Y
Approve economic stimulus plan	Y
1992	
Approve balanced-budget constitutional amendment	N
Close down space station program	Y
Approve U.S. aid for former Soviet Union	Y
Allow shifting funds from defense to domestic programs	Y
1991	
Extend unemployment benefits using deficit financing	Y
Approve waiting period for handgun purchases	Y
Authorize use of force in Persian Gulf	N

Voting Studies

	Presidential Support		Party Unity		Conservative Coalition	
Year	S	O	S	O	S	O
1992	15	83	96	2	8	92
1991	30	68	91	5	8	89
1990	19	81	95	3	15	83
1989	30	69	97	2	12	88
1988	20	80	96	2	8	92
1987	17	80	91	2	12	84
1986	20	80	95	3	12	88
1985	16	84	98	1	5	95
1984	26	70	92	4	12	80
1983	18	80	93	3	9	90
1982	35	64	92	5	10	89
1981	29	70	89	8	7	92

Interest Group Ratings

Year	ADA	AFL-CIO	CCUS	ACU
1992	100	92	25	0
1991	90	92	10	0
1990	94	100	14	0
1989	95	92	20	0
1988	100	100	21	0
1987	100	94	7	0
1986	95	93	11	0
1985	95	94	18	5
1984	95	85	31	4
1983	100	94	30	0
1982	100	95	29	0
1981	90	93	5	0

6 Rod Grams (R)

Of Anoka — Elected 1992; 1st Term

Born: Feb. 4, 1948, Princeton, Minn.

Education: Anoka-Ramsey Community College, 1970-72; Carroll College, 1974-75.

Occupation: Contractor; television journalist.

Family: Wife, Laurel Servaty; four children.

Religion: Lutheran.

Political Career: No previous office.

Capitol Office: 1713 Longworth Bldg. 20515; 225-2271.

The Path to Washington: Grams made it to Congress by being in the right place at the right time. The right place was Minnesota's 6th District, and the right time was just as five-term incumbent Democrat Gerry Sikorski was reaching his political nadir.

A leading environmental voice in the House, Sikorski managed to dodge one scandal in 1988, when The Washington Post published a story detailing how he required his staff to perform personal errands. The House ethics committee investigated, but closed the case in 1990 without taking action.

Sikorski was not so lucky in 1992, when the ethics committee put him on its list of House bank abusers because he had written 697 overdrafts.

The already-weakened Sikorski then outraged a significant portion of his electorate by switching from a strong anti-abortion position to one supporting abortion rights. Sikorski was originally elected in 1982 with the strong backing of the powerful anti-abortion Minnesota Citizens Concerned for Life. The group responded in 1992 by throwing its weight behind Hennepin County Commissioner Tad Jude in a September primary that quickly grew ugly. Sikorski ultimately won the primary, but just barely, garnering 49 percent of the vote to Jude's 46 percent. Two minor candidates split the rest.

Sikorski's brutal primary softened the incumbent up enough for Grams, a builder and real estate developer with no political experience but whose face and name were well-known to voters from his 10 years as a Minneapolis TV news anchorman. Grams easily won his primary.

Like Jude, Grams opposes abortion. With the two major candidates on opposite sides, that issue promised to influence the outcome. Mostly, however, the race was about Sikorski's checks. Until the ethics committee disclosed that he was one of the House bank's abusers, Sikorski was considered a safe bet for re-election.

The ballot presence of independent Dean Barkley was a wild card. Barkley, an abortion rights proponent, adopted some of independent presidential candidate Ross Perot's economic rhetoric. He won the endorsement of the Minneapolis Star-Tribune. Barkley captured 16 percent of the vote, much of his support likely coming at Sikorski's expense. Sikorski ended up with 33 percent of the vote, as Grams won the election with 44 percent, the third-lowest winning percentage of any 1992 House candidate.

Only four months after his improbable win, however, the Supreme Court may have dealt a blow to Grams' future electoral prospects by abolishing the current Minnesota congressional map. Under the likely 1994 replacement plan, Grams would be disadvantaged in his already swing district, though Grams' office notes that the new plan also adversely affects a potential Democratic challenger, state Sen. Bill Luther.

Grams' campaign from the outset focused on voters' outrage at what he called the "air of royalty" Congress had adopted. "I don't think we need free haircuts or prescriptions or shoe polishing or separate and privileged dining areas," he told a news conference in May 1992.

Among Grams' proposed solutions were eliminating all congressional perks except parking places, cutting the legislative branch's budget and staff by 30 percent and requiring rotation of committee chairmanships every six years.

During organizational meetings in December, Republicans actually adopted that last proposal for its ranking members on full committees, with the six-year clock to begin running with the start of the 103rd Congress. The proposal was offered by another GOP freshman, John Linder of Georgia.

On other issues, Grams voices concern about the budget deficit. He also supports lowering taxes and decreasing government regulation.

From his position on the Banking Committee, Grams said he wants to make loans more readily available to small businesses by eliminating some regulation on banks and other lenders.

Grams' other committee assignment is Science, Space and Technology, a perch from which he will be able to monitor the interests of the major high-tech firms at home, including Honeywell, 3M and Control Data.

Minnesota 6

Northern Twin Cities suburbs

The horseshoe-shaped 6th District wraps around the Twin Cities, taking in surrounding suburbs, plus a bit of farmland farther out. The district includes marginally Democratic areas, some Democratic strongholds and GOP-leaning suburbs. Redistricting made the area slightly more Democratic.

In the latest round of the state's redistricting pingpong, the Supreme Court in 1993 rejected the federally drawn map that had been used in the 1992 election. The high court ruled that federal courts must stand aside until challenges to redistricting plans run their course in state courts. In 1994, candidates will run under a state-drawn plan.

Most of the areas lost by the 6th under the state plan, including the northern and western Hennepin County suburbs, were represented by Republicans in the state Legislature.

The district gained east and central Dakota County and southern Washington County. These areas are developed or emerging suburbs with white-collar voters. However, these voters tend to favor abortion rights and increased funding of education; the Republican Party cannot count on them for reliable support.

The state court also added Farmington, Hastings and Inver Grove Heights, which tend to be more Democratic than their neighbors. (Apple Valley, Eagan and Rosemount in Dakota County were also added for the 1994 elections.)

Anoka County, which casts nearly 45 percent of the vote, is the strongest Democratic area in the 6th. It was the cornerstone of former Rep. Gerry Sikorski's congressional victories, and it remained loyal to Walter F. Mondale in 1984, Michael S. Dukakis in 1988 and Bill Clinton in 1992. But in 1992, the county chose Grams over Sikorski at least in part because of Sikorski's 697 overdrafts at the House bank.

Anoka is a mix of new suburbs, farms and small towns. Lake Wobegon, the mythical town in Garrison Keillor's one-time weekly radio program "A Prairie Home Companion," is modeled after Keillor's boyhood home in Anoka County.

But the Lake Wobegons of this part of Minnesota are quickly disappearing as the Twin Cities metropolitan area continues to expand farther into the surrounding counties.

The major employer is Northwest Airlines, which is in Eagan. The airline's headquarters employs about 18,000 people, and its survival is crucial to the economy. Cray Research, which makes supercomputers, and West Publishing Co., the nation's largest publisher of legal books, are also in Eagan.

One of the district's largest employers is FMC Corp., a defense contractor in Fridley, a Minneapolis suburb.

The Fridley operation is home to the company's Naval Systems Division, and employs about 2,300 people. The division makes gun and missile launching systems for Navy ships.

1990 Population: 546,888. White 528,078 (97%), Black 6,291 (1%), Other 12,519 (2%). Hispanic origin 4,936 (1%). 18 and over 382,305 (70%), 62 and over 39,295 (7%). Median age: 31.

Committees

Banking, Finance & Urban Affairs (16th of 20 Republicans)
Consumer Credit & Insurance; Financial Institutions Supervision, Regulation & Deposit Insurance; Housing & Community Development

Science, Space & Technology (17th of 22 Republicans)
Energy; Technology, Environment & Aviation

Campaign Finance

1992	Receipts	Receipts from PACs		Expend-itures
Grams (R)	$464,693	$138,784	(30%)	$439,718
Sikorski (D)	$905,875	$607,683	(67%)	$1,217,832
Barkley (I)	$64,269	$25	(0%)	$64,170

Key Votes

1993

Require parental notification of minors' abortions	Y
Require unpaid family and medical leave	N
Approve national "motor voter" registration bill	N
Approve budget increasing taxes and reducing deficit	N
Approve economic stimulus plan	N

Elections

1992 General		
Rod Grams (R)	133,564	(44%)
Gerry Sikorski (D)	100,016	(33%)
Dean Barkley (I)	48,329	(16%)
James H. Peterson (IFP)	16,411	(5%)
1992 Primary		
Rod Grams (R)	11,818	(69%)
James C. Hillegass (R)	5,404	(31%)

District Vote for President

	1992	
D	120,226	(40%)
R	101,314	(33%)
I	82,064	(27%)

7 Collin C. Peterson (D)

Of Detroit Lakes — Elected 1990; 2nd Term

Born: June 29, 1944, Fargo, N.D.
Education: Moorhead State U., B.A. 1966.
Military Service: National Guard, 1963-69.
Occupation: Accountant.
Family: Divorced; three children.
Religion: Lutheran.
Political Career: Minn. Senate, 1977-87; sought Democratic nomination for U.S. House, 1982; Democratic nominee for U.S. House, 1984, 1986; sought Democratic nomination for U.S. House, 1988.
Capitol Office: 1133 Longworth Bldg. 20515; 225-2165.

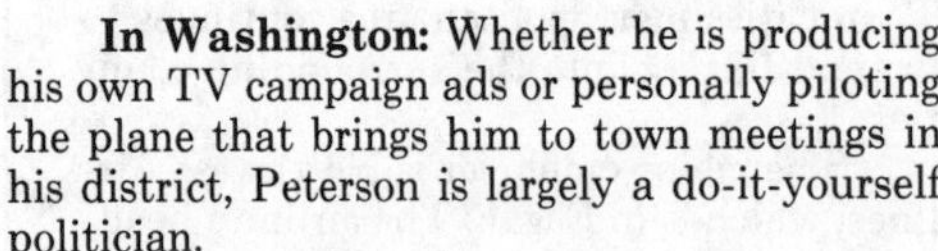

In Washington: Whether he is producing his own TV campaign ads or personally piloting the plane that brings him to town meetings in his district, Peterson is largely a do-it-yourself politician.

Although they are 35 year apart in age, Peterson has been likened to Democratic Appropriations Chairman William H. Natcher of Kentucky, a House mentor. In comparing the two, the Minneapolis Star-Tribune observed that both were doggedly self-sufficient and intentionally low profile — getting by with small, multifunctional staffs. At first glance, Peterson's occupation does not seem a natural fit for the 7th. In a sprawling, rural district where many people make their living in agriculture, he is a certified public accountant.

But Peterson was raised on a farm near Moorhead and boasted that as an accountant he had a detailed understanding of the farm economy. During a decade in the state Senate, he was a key player on taxation and natural resource matters, helping to draft Minnesota's original "superfund" toxic waste law.

But he also got his name around in his younger days as a musician. As a guitar player and singer-songwriter he once toured the state with a band called Collin and the Establishment. And when he traveled to Washington to lobby for the Democratic alternative to the 1985 farm bill, he recorded a song called "Don't Do Nothin.' "

A thorough-going "prairie populist" on farm issues, Peterson's views on fiscal matters and such social issues as abortion are decidedly conservative. The mix has produced a balance reflective of the attitudes common in his rural district (which sent a Republican to House in seven straight elections before choosing Peterson). In his first Congress, he sided with the GOP on about one-fifth of the votes that split along party lines.

He resisted an attempt by fellow Democrats to repeal the "gag rule," a measure barring abortion counseling in federally funded family planning clinics, voting to keep the measure in place. He also voted for continued funding for both the B-2 bomber and the Strategic Defense Initiative (SDI). He also supported a balanced-budget constitutional amendment and opposed a disaster relief package after Chicago's downtown floods and the Los Angeles riots.

Peterson chose a seat on the Agriculture Committee, where he devotes himself to representing the interests of dairy, wheat and sugar beet farmers. In one of two floor speeches he gave in his first term, he delivered a vehement defense of dairy farmers. The matter at hand was a joint resolution offered by Sen. Patrick J. Leahy of Vermont calling for higher farm supports to offset falling milk prices.

Peterson lashed out at The Washington Post for calling the amendment "a joke" in a 1991 editorial and for concluding that higher milk prices would be "regressive." He also attacked critics for their "vendetta" against America's farmers.

"The family farmer who cares for his cows and never sees the inside of a corporate boardroom is the loser here today," he said.

Peterson likes to apply his accountant's background to the issues he tackles on the Government Operations Committee. Turnover before the 103rd Congress propelled him to the chairmanship of the subcommittee on Employment, Housing and Aviation. The subcommittee oversees the Department of Housing and Urban Development (HUD), an agency rocked by fraud and mismanagement in the 1980s.

Wasting little time in investigating the agency's practices, Peterson sought explanations from HUD officials regarding the agency's failure in 1992 to distribute billions of dollars in federal housing funds earmaked for low-income housing projects in urban communities.

At Home: Peterson did not take office until 1991, but he showed up for freshman orientation way back in December 1986. Peter-

Minnesota 7

Northwest — Moorhead; part of St. Cloud

From the prairie wheat fields along the Red River to the hills, forests and lakes in the middle of the state, this vast district is Minnesota's most marginal — economically as well as politically.

While some district counties, including Kittson, Mahnomen and Beltrami, continue to struggle economically, many of the lake regions are either stable or growing. The area's economy is fueled by farming — dairy, grains and row crops — light manufacturing, tourism and education (the 7th has 17 community colleges). Many farmers struggle each year to meet high operating costs on land that does not match the quality of the soil farther south. The region's lumber business, once in decline, has revived. And the snowmobile industry has recovered from a spell of dry winters and the 1980s recession.

Politically, the district has been in the marginal category since popular Democrat Bob Bergland left it in 1977 to become Jimmy Carter's secretary of Agriculture. Republican Arlan Stangeland, who represented the 7th from 1977 until 1991, won five of six re-elections with less than 55 percent of the vote, including a 121-vote win over Peterson in 1986.

The district's map changed little under recent redistricting, and neither did the political landscape. In 1993, the Supreme Court rejected the federally drawn map that had been used in the 1992 election. The decision upheld a state redistricting plan.

St. Cloud, which was placed in the 8th District in the federal plan, is included in the 7th under the state map. The seat of Stearns County, St. Cloud, with 49,000 residents, is the district's largest city and one of the fastest growing in the state. For years, it was a major center for granite quarrying. Today the descendants of the old stonecutters share their ancestors' support of the Democratic Party on economic issues, but they often stray to the GOP when social issues, especially abortion, become paramount.

The state plan also returned a major employer. St. Cloud is home to Fingerhut, a mail-order house that sells gadgets and novelty items. Employing more than 4,000 people, Fingerhut is the district's largest employer.

Apart from St. Cloud and Moorhead, a sister city to Fargo, N.D., there are few population centers. But many of the district's towns are vintage Americana. Sauk Centre — about 40 miles northwest of St. Cloud — was the birthplace of novelist Sinclair Lewis, who used his hometown as the model for his novel "Main Street." Signs along the prime thoroughfare, in fact, call it the "Original Main Street."

The wheat-growing central sections of the district are slightly more populous than the rest and also more Republican.

Sugar beets are grown around Moorhead in the Red River Valley, which possesses some of the 7th's most fertile farmland. In the rolling countryside just to the east, hunters, fishermen and summer tourists are drawn to hundreds of lakes.

1990 Population: 546,888. White 529,380 (97%), Black 1,008 (<1%), Other 16,500 (3%). Hispanic origin 4,302 (1%). 18 and over 394,926 (72%), 62 and over 98,640 (18%). Median age: 33.

son came to Washington that month thinking he had defeated incumbent Republican Arlan Stangeland the previous month (a recount showed him the loser of that race by 121 votes). Peterson needed two more election cycles to finally subdue 13-year incumbent Stangeland and reclaim the 7th District — a vast farming district on the Canadian border — for the Democrats.

Peterson is, in fact, one of Capitol Hill's monuments to persistence, having run for Congress four times before his winning campaign. His victory in 1990 owed much to Stangeland's personal baggage. Having been re-elected with more than 55 percent of the vote only once, the Republican had been living on the political edge; in 1990, he went over it.

The end began in January, when The St. Cloud Daily Times reported that Stangeland had used his House credit card to charge several phone calls to or from the phone of a female Virginia lobbyist. A subsequent story revealed that he allowed a lobbyist to use his House parking space. Stangeland denied any wrongdoing, but he was never able to dispel the impression of impropriety.

Peterson might not have run again in 1990 had it not been for Stangeland's problems. After four defeats, his own political image was in disrepair. Some Democrats had resented him since his first congressional bid in 1982, when, as a state senator, he challenged Gene Wenstrom for the Democratic nomination. Wenstrom had held Stangeland to 52 percent in two previous elections, and many Democrats felt Wenstrom deserved a third shot without having to hurdle intraparty competition.

In 1984, Wenstrom did not run, and Peterson won the nomination. But lacking money and name identification, he was trampled by Stangeland.

The farm crisis helped pull Peterson close in 1986. But he was less than graceful in defeat; he lashed out at the Democratic Congressional Campaign Committee for failing to provide adequate support, and he refused to concede his loss without a recount. Two years later, he was beaten in the Democratic primary.

When Peterson decided to try once more in 1990 he was careful to present himself as a "new Collin Peterson," more mellow than in his past campaigns and ready to mend fences with Democratic activists he had previously offended. At the district convention, he won the party endorsement over a field that included a female abortion rights supporter (Peterson is anti-abortion).

That fall, he ran a virtually error-free campaign, uniting the district's often-divided Democratic Party and creating a more sophisticated voter targeting effort than ever before. Peterson harnessed the anti-incumbent tide that ran strongly across Minnesota — the only state in 1990 to turn out both an incumbent governor and senator — carrying all but three of the 23 counties that were entirely or partially within the 7th.

In 1992, like other incumbents, Peterson was battered by the call for change. In addition, his GOP opponent, state Rep. Bernie Omann, said Peterson had not been assertive enough in aiding the state's dairy industry. Omann also accused Peterson of overusing the congressional franking privilege. (He was No. 11 in use of the frank for the first nine months of his first year; thereafter he was not in the top 50.)

Peterson received the endorsement of the Star-Tribune, which praised him as a hard worker for the district's interests.

In the end, Peterson had just enough going for him to win. But his 3,490-vote margin emphasized how hard it is for an incumbent to feel secure in the 7th.

Committees

Agriculture (13th of 28 Democrats)
Environment, Credit & Rural Development; General Farm Commodities; Livestock; Specialty Crops & Natural Resources

Government Operations (12th of 25 Democrats)
Employment, Housing & Aviation (chairman)

Elections

1992 General		
Collin C. Peterson (D)	133,886	(50%)
Bernie Omann (R)	130,396	(49%)
1992 Primary		
Collin C. Peterson (D)	30,917	(71%)
Lorelei Kraft (D)	12,464	(29%)
1990 General		
Collin C. Peterson (D)	107,126	(54%)
Arlan Stangeland (R)	92,876	(46%)

District Vote for President

1992

D 104,359 (38%)
R 103,624 (38%)
I 63,610 (23%)

Campaign Finance

	Receipts	Receipts from PACs		Expenditures
1992				
Peterson (D)	$488,844	$321,507	(66%)	$495,882
Omann (R)	$218,216	$35,300	(16%)	$218,951
1990				
Peterson (D)	$266,773	$185,598	(70%)	$242,864
Stangeland (R)	$489,490	$298,670	(61%)	$487,224

Key Votes

1993	
Require parental notification of minors' abortions	Y
Require unpaid family and medical leave	Y
Approve national "motor voter" registration bill	Y
Approve budget increasing taxes and reducing deficit	Y
Approve economic stimulus plan	Y
1992	
Approve balanced-budget constitutional amendment	Y
Close down space station program	Y
Approve U.S. aid for former Soviet Union	Y
Allow shifting funds from defense to domestic programs	Y
1991	
Extend unemployment benefits using deficit financing	Y
Approve waiting period for handgun purchases	N
Authorize use of force in Persian Gulf	N

Voting Studies

	Presidential Support		Party Unity		Conservative Coalition	
Year	S	O	S	O	S	O
1992	35	64	82	17	44	54
1991	39	60	76	20	57	43

Interest Group Ratings

Year	ADA	AFL-CIO	CCUS	ACU
1992	65	75	63	24
1991	65	67	40	15

8 James L. Oberstar (D)

Of Chisholm — Elected 1974; 10th Term

Born: Sept. 10, 1934, Chisholm, Minn.
Education: College of St. Thomas, B.A. 1956; College of Europe (Bruges, Belgium), M.A. 1957.
Occupation: Language teacher; congressional aide.
Family: Widowed; four children.
Religion: Roman Catholic.
Political Career: Sought Democratic nomination for U.S. Senate, 1984.
Capitol Office: 2366 Rayburn Bldg. 20515; 225-6211.

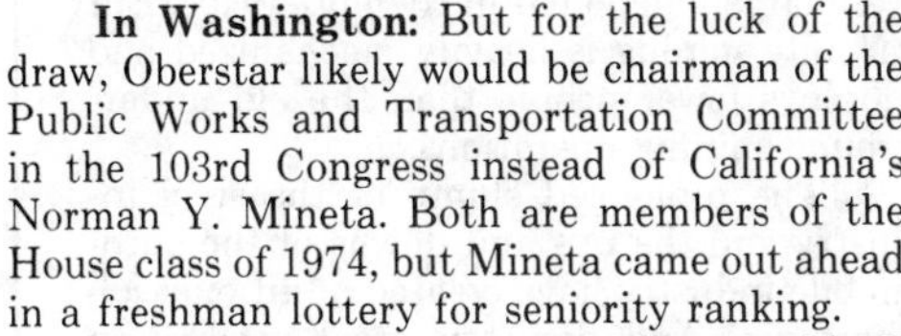

In Washington: But for the luck of the draw, Oberstar likely would be chairman of the Public Works and Transportation Committee in the 103rd Congress instead of California's Norman Y. Mineta. Both are members of the House class of 1974, but Mineta came out ahead in a freshman lottery for seniority ranking.

That little-noticed act of long ago paid off for Mineta in 1993, when he assumed the chairmanship upon the retirement of Robert A. Roe of New Jersey. Oberstar was content to remain head of the Aviation Subcommittee and did not challenge Mineta for the chairmanship of the full committee.

In some ways Oberstar seems miscast for the Public Works Committee at all, despite his quarter-century there as staff member and congressman. He has the instincts of a scholar and reformer, but Public Works is a place where members like to dig first and ask questions later; policy analysts take a back seat to pork-barrelers.

At the same time, Oberstar is only part scholar. The rest of him is Minnesota Iron Range street fighter, a self-described bohunk. He is the son of a miner and a shirt-factory worker, and is an unrepentant New Deal-style Democrat with deep faith in the job-creating potential of public works and deeper faith yet in his party.

Oberstar has made his career and built seniority at Public Works. Even so, not long ago he was restless enough to want to surrender it for something more. He unsuccessfully sought the Democratic Senate nomination in 1984 and returned to the House in 1985. Then he lost his bid for a seat on the Ways and Means Committee and went back to Public Works.

Oberstar's restlessness came to the fore again at the start of the 102nd Congress, when he joined a group of younger Public Works members in engineering the ouster of politically weak Chairman Glenn M. Anderson of California. As fourth-ranking Democrat then, Oberstar was willing to run for the post, but he instead lent his support to Mineta, then the panel's No. 3 Democrat. The coup, however, was not completed; Roe, then the second-ranking Democrat, gained the chair.

Even before the late 1990 coup, Public Works had been in some turmoil. Oberstar unsuccessfully proposed at the start of the 101st Congress that subcommittee chairmen get more power over staff and budgeting decisions. He was opposed by Roe, who as chairman-in-waiting did not want to inherit a weakened position, and by other subcommittee heads who felt that under the passive Anderson they already enjoyed greater power without changing committee rules.

With the 101st Congress, Oberstar assumed his third subcommittee chairmanship on the panel. Having headed the Economic Development and the Investigations and Oversight subcommittees, he took charge of the one covering aviation.

As a subcommittee chairman, Oberstar generally is considered fair and bipartisan by Republicans, despite his occasional partisan flashes in House debates. More conservative Democrats consider him someone they can deal with.

Oberstar in 1990 reached a compromise with House appropriators to spend some of the Airport and Airway Trust Fund on improving the nation's airports. Public Works members and the aviation industry had long contended that the White House hoarded the trust fund surplus to disguise the size of the general budget deficit. Oberstar also shed his previous opposition to President Bush's proposal of assessing airline travelers a user fee as another way to fund increased airport capacity and air traffic control improvements.

As chair of the Aviation Subcommittee, Oberstar has operated from the view that airline deregulation prompted concentration in the industry, which in turn has brought higher prices and fewer choices for passengers.

Oberstar's attempts to craft comprehensive legislation to meet the problem ran afoul of the Bush administration's laissez faire approach to the airline industry. Oberstar subsequently promoted incremental changes to en-

Minnesota 8

Northeast — Iron Range; Duluth

If the 8th were dropped onto a map of the East Coast, it would reach from Washington to Connecticut. The district measures about 26,000 square miles and is generally Democratic territory. The mostly rural area encompasses a vast stretch of land that includes flat farmland, steep bluffs and lakes. The district's largest city, Duluth (population 85,500), is also the state's fourth largest. From here much of the grain from the Plains states is shipped east.

Singer Bob Dylan grew up in Hibbing, which calls itself the "Iron Ore Capital of the World." Hibbing also produced Boston Celtics great Kevin McHale, who is a hero in his hometown. A local bus line that started in Hibbing in 1914 with one open touring car became the Greyhound Bus Lines. And the nation's only gas station designed by Frank Lloyd Wright is in Cloquet.

Based in the barren and remote northern reaches of Minnesota, the district has a long Democratic tradition.

Immigrants from Sweden, Finland and Eastern Europe settled here after the turn of the century to work in the iron mines scattered throughout the Mesabi and Vermillion iron ranges. Strongly allied with unions, the workers on the Iron Range today are unswerving in their allegiance to the Democrats.

The economy is fueled by a variety of industries.

Tourism is crucial and the timber industry is also a major employer, both in timber harvesting and in the production of paper and wood products.

In the southern counties farmers grow corn and small grain. Dairy farming slowed in the south during the mid-1980s when many farmers here sold their herds. The federal government paid milk producers to send their herds to slaughter in order to cut milk production and reduce the government's purchases of dairy surpluses.

The economy has taken its share of knocks. The discovery of new taconite mining technology helped boost the local economy after the high-quality iron ore mines were largely depleted in the mid-1940s. But taconite mining is heavily mechanized and employs fewer people than the old underground mining operations.

The prolonged slump of the steel industry and the ups and downs of the automobile industry have created additional job shortages. And domestic steel production has faced intense foreign competition.

Casinos on Indian reservations have been one economic bright spot. The gambling enterprises have brought jobs and spurred sales and construction in many nearby towns.

The district changed only slightly in the last act of the state's redistricting odyssey. In 1993, the Supreme Court rejected the federally drawn map that had been used in the 1992 election.

In 1994, candidates will run under a state-drawn plan. The 8th lost portions of Benton and Sherburne counties to the 7th.

1990 Population: 546,887. White 530,140 (97%), Black 2,192 (<1%), Other 14,555 (3%). Hispanic origin 2,784 (1%). 18 and over 398,011 (73%), 62 and over 100,080 (18%). Median age: 35.

courage greater competition, from alterations in the computerized reservation system to making the Federal Aviation Administration independent of the Transportation Department.

With the blessing of the Clinton administration, Oberstar pushed early in the 103rd Congress for legislation to expand and accelerate the work of the National Commission to Ensure a Strong Competitive Airline Industry, a body created by Congress in 1992 to study the financial woes of the airline and airplane manufacturing industries.

A political scientist and amateur linguist, Oberstar can theorize at length about the proper balance for public works policy. In fact, he talks a lot, whether intensively questioning witnesses or explaining a bill. He opened one hearing in early 1989 with a long reading from the prize-winning Thornton Wilder novel "The Bridge of San Luis Rey." He occasionally beseeches the committee to "rise above" pork barrel thinking and seek innovative ways to address problems.

On the other hand, Oberstar has not been known to turn down a new project for northern Minnesota. He spent years learning how to use Public Works to bring Duluth and the Iron Range a share of the pie, as an aide and protégé to John A. Blatnik, the Minnesota Democrat who chaired Public Works until 1975, when he retired and Oberstar won his seat.

As chairman of Public Works' Economic Development Subcommittee before 1985, Oberstar was in a key position to help bring federal money to depressed areas like the Iron Range. With ranking Republican William F. Clinger of Pennsylvania, he worked to preserve the Economic Development Administration against President Reagan's repeated efforts to abolish it.

Oberstar's partisan instincts tend to flash when the issue is jobs. In 1982 he helped write a jobs bill that, with changes, became law the next year. "I just never cease to be amazed," he said in 1982, "by our colleagues on the other side of the aisle who refuse to do anything to help the unemployed but complain about those who try."

He was even more critical of fellow Democrats in 1985 when the House agreed to end a supplemental compensation program for the long-term unemployed. "We cannot let our party be Reaganized," he declared, adding that Democrats must make clear "we're not backing away" from employment issues.

In 1989, Oberstar, the pro-labor partisan, quickly jumped into the controversy surrounding a strike against Eastern Airlines that was aimed at its chairman, Frank Lorenzo, a hated symbol of union-busting to organized labor nationwide. When President Bush refused to intervene, Oberstar became the Democratic leadership's point man in a strategy designed to paint the president as anti-labor. He sponsored a bill requiring Bush to set up an emergency panel to forge a settlement.

The Aviation Subcommittee approved it 21-12, and a week later it passed the House 252-167, both tallies roughly along party lines. "A vote for this legislation is a vote for the continued survival of competition in the airline industry," Oberstar told the House. But the bill died in the Senate, where Democratic leaders lacked the votes to choke a threatened GOP filibuster.

Oberstar has defended protectionist efforts to promote domestic employment by limiting imports. He cites his experience as a graduate student during the formation of Europe's Common Market, which, as Oberstar recalls, promoted economic development by protecting domestic markets.

Oberstar took a seat on the House Foreign Affairs Committee in 1993 following a six-year stint on the Budget Committee. He owed his Budget assignment to a Public Works connection, former committee member Jim Wright.

When Wright became Speaker in 1987, he appointed Oberstar to the Democratic Steering and Policy Committee, the leadership panel that makes committee assignments. Oberstar was among those who spoke up for Wright during the long ethics probe that eventually forced the Speaker to resign in June 1989.

Oberstar earlier had a voice in budget and tax debates as chairman of the liberal Democratic Study Group (DSG) in the 99th Congress. He was among those urging, unsuccessfully, that the budget include a tougher minimum tax on corporations. And when Ways and Means was drafting its landmark rewrite of the tax code, Oberstar and the DSG argued that revenues raised by closing loopholes should be used for deficit reduction, not more tax cuts.

A couple of issues provide the only exceptions to Oberstar's traditional liberalism. He opposes gun control bills and abortion. "Democrats have made it uncomfortable for other Democrats to be pro-life," he said in late 1991.

Oberstar is also against the death penalty. When the House debated a capital punishment provision that became law as part of Congress' 1988 drug bill, Oberstar supported instead an unsuccessful substitute that would have required mandatory life imprisonment for drug-related killers.

At Home: Republicans have not cost Oberstar much sleep since he inherited the 8th in 1974 from Blatnik, his employer and predecessor. But fighting within the Democratic Party has made his life far from tranquil.

For years there was a feud between the Blatnik wing of the Democratic Party and the faction headed by the three Perpich brothers, whose leader, Rudy, would become governor of Minnesota.

The battle between the two sides broke into the open in 1974 and flared up again in 1980. In 1974 Blatnik tried to anoint Oberstar as his successor, but the result was an acrimonious party-endorsing convention lasting 30 ballots. Eventually Blatnik and Oberstar lost, and the party's endorsement went to state Sen. A. J. "Tony" Perpich. Blatnik then threw all his prestige and political power behind Oberstar in the Democratic primary, and Oberstar won by more than 20,000 votes.

Six years later, Oberstar faced a second Perpich. This time it was Tony's younger brother, George. When Rudy was elected lieutenant governor in 1970, George took his seat in the state Senate and carried on the populist Perpich crusade against the mining companies.

At the 1980 nominating convention, George tried to keep the party endorsement out of the incumbent's hands, arguing for a neutral party stand. But Oberstar won the endorsement with just one-third of a vote more than the 60 percent needed.

Perpich decided not to force a primary, but Duluth City Councilman Thomas E. Dougherty did. Concentrating his campaign in the northern part of the district where unemployment was high, Dougherty picked up votes from Perpich supporters bent on protest. Oberstar was saved by his backing at the southern end of the district, in the Twin Cities media area.

The two faced each other again in 1984 after Oberstar's bid for the Democratic Senate nomination fell short. As in 1980, Dougherty pounded away at Oberstar as inattentive to his Iron Range constituents and their declining economic status, using as his slogan: "Our District Is His First Choice."

But Oberstar was well-prepared for the

1984 rematch. He emphasized his work to promote the local iron industry through support of temporary quotas on steel and iron ore imports. And he launched one of the most extensive voter identification programs ever seen in northeast Minnesota.

Dougherty, who netted 44 percent of the primary vote in 1980, was beaten by a margin of nearly 2-to-1 in 1984.

Oberstar's Senate candidacy earlier that year had enjoyed the support of much of the state's labor movement. But he could not match the strength of his major rival, Secretary of State Joan Growe, who was the favorite of the liberal activists who dominated the Democratic endorsement process.

Growe got the party endorsement on the 19th ballot at the state convention in June. Oberstar could have continued the fight into a September primary, but he decided instead to switch races and run again for his House seat.

Oberstar has had no trouble at the ballot box since 1984. He easily won the Democratic primary in 1992 over a convicted murderer who was still in prison for killing his attorney.

In the fall, Oberstar faced a Perot supporter, a terms-limit candidate and a Republican. He was held to 59 percent of the vote, his lowest share ever in a general election, but still won easily in the crowded field.

Committees

Foreign Affairs (10th of 27 Democrats)
Economic Policy, Trade & the Environment; Western Hemisphere Affairs

Public Works & Transportation (2nd of 39 Democrats)
Aviation (chairman); Economic Development; Water Resources & the Environment

Elections

1992 General		
James L. Oberstar (D)	167,104	(59%)
Phil Herwig (R)	83,823	(30%)
Harry Robb Welty (PCP)	22,619	(8%)
Floyd A. Henspeter (TLC)	8,602	(3%)
1992 Primary		
James L. Oberstar (D)	52,392	(78%)
Leonard J. Richards (D)	14,535	(22%)
1990 General		
James L. Oberstar (D)	151,145	(73%)
Jerry Shuster (R)	56,068	(27%)

Previous Winning Percentages: **1988** (75%) **1986** (73%) **1984** (67%) **1982** (77%) **1980** (70%) **1978** (87%) **1976** (100%) **1974** (62%)

District Vote for President

1992
D 138,357 (48%)
R 80,586 (28%)
I 70,539 (24%)

Campaign Finance

	Receipts	Receipts from PACs		Expend-itures
1992				
Oberstar (D)	$340,642	$202,005	(59%)	$386,646
Herwig (R)	$41,039	$500	(1%)	$32,416
1990				
Oberstar (D)	$364,577	$248,780	(68%)	$229,262
Shuster (R)	$16,696	0		$16,681

Key Votes

1993	
Require parental notification of minors' abortions	Y
Require unpaid family and medical leave	Y
Approve national "motor voter" registration bill	Y
Approve budget increasing taxes and reducing deficit	Y
Approve economic stimulus plan	Y
1992	
Approve balanced-budget constitutional amendment	N
Close down space station program	Y
Approve U.S. aid for former Soviet Union	Y
Allow shifting funds from defense to domestic programs	Y
1991	
Extend unemployment benefits using deficit financing	Y
Approve waiting period for handgun purchases	N
Authorize use of force in Persian Gulf	N

Voting Studies

	Presidential Support		Party Unity		Conservative Coalition	
Year	**S**	**O**	**S**	**O**	**S**	**O**
1992	17	82	94	5	15	85
1991	30	59	83	8	16	76
1990	17	82	92	4	13	83
1989	35	64	88	10	10	90
1988	21	77	93	6	8	92
1987	12	87	93	3	5	95
1986	18	79	92	4	18	82
1985	16	84	91	3	7	93
1984	19	71	88	4	5	83
1983	12	84	90	6	9	89
1982	34	65	95	4	10	89
1981	33	67	89	8	16	81

Interest Group Ratings

Year	ADA	AFL-CIO	CCUS	ACU
1992	90	92	25	4
1991	85	83	20	11
1990	78	100	15	0
1989	95	83	30	4
1988	90	100	21	12
1987	96	94	7	4
1986	85	93	6	5
1985	95	100	18	5
1984	80	89	33	4
1983	90	94	15	9
1982	100	100	14	9
1981	85	87	5	7

Mississippi

STATE DATA

Governor:
Kirk Fordice (R)
First elected: 1991
Length of term: 4 years
Term expires: 1/96
Salary: $75,600
Term limit: No
Phone: (601) 359-3150
Born: Feb. 10, 1934; Memphis, Tenn.
Education: Purdue U., B.S. 1956, M.S. 1957
Military Service: Army, 1957-59; Army Reserve, 1959-77
Occupation: Construction executive
Family: Wife, Patricia Owen; four children
Religion: Methodist
Political Career: No previous office

Lt. Gov.: Eddie Briggs (R)
First elected: 1991
Length of term: 4 years
Term expires: 1/96
Salary: $40,800
Phone: (601) 359-3200

State election official: (601) 359-6357
Democratic headquarters: (601) 969-2913
Republican headquarters: (601) 948-5191

REDISTRICTING

Mississippi retained its five House seats in reapportionment. The legislature passed the map Dec. 20, 1991; the governor signed it Dec. 20. Justice Department approved the map Feb. 21, 1992.

STATE LEGISLATURE

Legislature. Meets January-April.

Senate: 52 members, 4-year terms
1992 breakdown: 39D, 13R; 48 men, 4 women; 42 whites, 10 blacks
Salary: $10,000
Phone: (601) 359-3202

House of Representatives: 122 members, 4-year terms
1992 breakdown: 93D, 27R; 107 men, 15 women; 90 whites, 32 blacks
Salary: $10,000
Phone: (601) 359-3360

URBAN STATISTICS

City	Pop.
Jackson Mayor Kane Ditto, D	196,637
Biloxi Mayor Pete Halat, D	46,319
Greenville Mayor C.C. Franks Self, D	45,226
Hattiesburg Mayor J. Ed Morgan, D	41,882
Meridian Mayor Jimmy Kemp, R	41,036

U.S. CONGRESS

Senate: 0 D, 2 R
House: 5 D, 0 R

TERM LIMITS

For Congress: No
For state offices: No

ELECTIONS

1992 Presidential Vote

George Bush	49.7%
Bill Clinton	40.8%
Ross Perot	8.7%

1988 Presidential Vote

George Bush	52%
Michael S. Dukakis	48%

1984 Presidential Vote

Ronald Reagan	60%
Walter F. Mondale	40%

POPULATION

1990 population		2,573,216
1980 population		2,520,638
Percent change		+2%
Rank among states:		31
White		63%
Black		36%
Hispanic		1%
Asian or Pacific islander		1%
Urban		47%
Rural		53%
Born in state		77%
Foreign-born		10%
Under age 18	746,761	29%
Ages 18-64	1,505,181	58%
65 and older	321,284	12%
Median age		31.2

MISCELLANEOUS

Capital: Jackson
Number of counties: 82
Per capital income: $13,343 (1991)
Rank among states: 50
Total area: 47,689 sq. miles
Rank among states: 32

Mississippi - Congressional Districts

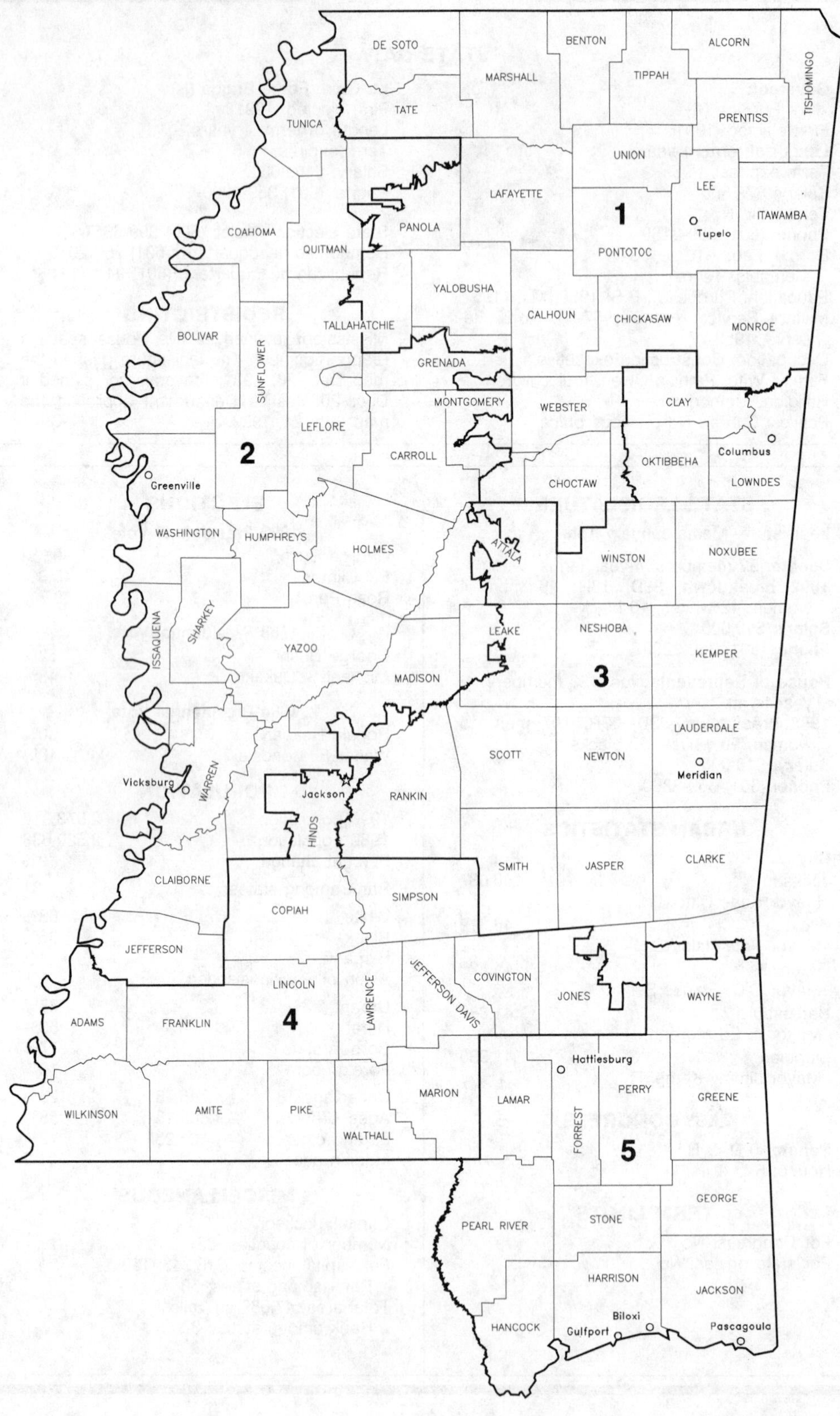

Thad Cochran (R)

Of Jackson — Elected 1978; 3rd Term

Born: Dec. 7, 1937, Pontotoc, Miss.
Education: U. of Mississippi, B.A. 1959; Trinity College (U. of Dublin, Ireland), 1963-64; U. of Mississippi, J.D. 1965.
Military Service: Navy, 1959-61.
Occupation: Lawyer.
Family: Wife, Rose Clayton; two children.
Religion: Baptist.
Political Career: U.S. House, 1973-78.
Capitol Office: 326 Russell Bldg. 20510; 224-5054.

In Washington: Mississippi will have significant influence in Republican Party politics in the 1990s. With both Cochran and junior Sen. Trent Lott now in the Republican leadership and the 1993 election of Mississippian Haley Barbour to chair the Republican National Committee, the Mississippi GOP has matured into a national force.

Just when Mississippi Democrats have relinquished their grip on congressional power, Mississippi Republicans have reached a new zenith. The 1989 retirement of Senate Appropriations Committee Chairman John C. Stennis and ailing Jamie L. Whitten's 1992 removal from the House Appropriations chair ended an era for Mississippi Democrats.

Cochran, the chairman of the Republican Conference (the No. 3 post in the leadership hierarchy), and Lott, the new Republican Conference secretary (fourth-ranking), differ in style and to some degree in substance. Lott has honed a sharper, more confrontational edge to his conservatism.

By contrast, Cochran comes close to defining the modern paradigm of a statewide political success.

Although a relative moderate in a state GOP dominated by conservatives, he has established himself or made peace with every important state constituency. That kind of home base security usually leads to power and influence in the Senate — and beyond — even if it takes a few terms for it to happen.

Unlike Lott, Cochran has managed to succeed in state politics without alienating the state's large black population. His decision in 1988 not to work to defeat then-freshman Rep. Mike Espy, the state's first black congressman in a century, may pay dividends in the 1990s, given Espy's position as President Clinton's Agriculture secretary.

Cochran is a leading voice for Southern interests on farm issues, and he is a vital bridge between GOP conservatives and moderates.

He is not immune to the partisan impulse. When U.S.-led military forces drove Iraqi invaders out of Kuwait, Cochran noted that "most of the Democrats in Congress voted to the left of the United Nations — that's something the voters are going to have to consider and will consider."

And he has tried to make good on his promise of a sharper profile for his party in the Senate since gaining the conference chair in November 1990. He has pressed for blocks of floor time for Republicans to present coordinated policy speeches — rather like the "special orders" of rebellious junior Republicans on the House side.

But he has avoided strong identification with the conservatives — "I vote on the social issues because I have to," he once said — and he has been a supporter of funding for food stamps, rural housing and traditionally black colleges. In 1989, he supported continued federal funding for the Martin Luther King Jr. Federal Holiday Commission.

While Cochran stalwartly defends the party line, his Senate work demonstrates that his interests lie in legislative accomplishment rather than partisan stonewalling. "We ought not be here just throwing rocks at the Democrats," he said after the 1992 election. In 1992, The Washington Times quoted him defending President Bush from conservative critics, saying, "You get the impression they're Republicans. They're professional complainers."

Still, Cochran is no liberal. His conservative inclinations came out most clearly on issues before the Judiciary Committee, where he served during his first two years in the Senate. He becomes livid at the mention of language in the Voting Rights Act requiring Southern states to get Justice Department approval before changing their election procedures.

"Local officials have to go to Washington, get on their knees, kiss the ring and tug their forelock to all these third-rate bureaucrats," Cochran once complained. But his effort to make all states comply with the same requirements was rejected by the Senate, 16-74.

Perhaps because he has made his mark in

agriculture, a policy area that invites bipartisan cooperation, he has been able for much of his career to escape the roiling partisanship for which he seems temperamentally unsuited.

As ranking Republican on the Appropriations Subcommittee on Agriculture, the panel he chaired in the early 1980s, Cochran was given wide latitude by the panel's languid chairman, Quentin N. Burdick. When amendments were made during 1991 floor action, it was Cochran who supported and explained the committee position, managed the floor time and made most of the requisite motions to move the bill forward. The fiscal 1993 agriculture appropriations bill came out of the Senate studded with $1.6 billion for Mississippi projects.

During the 102nd Congress, Cochran, an abortion opponent, worked with Rhode Island Republican John H. Chafee, an abortion rights supporter, to overturn Bush administration rules that banned family planning clinics from giving abortion advice. After Cochran hinted that he opposed the regulations but was concerned about how Chafee's amendment was drafted, Chafee rewrote his amendment. Cochran chose to draw up his own amendment. His plan pleased neither opponents nor supporters of abortion rights and was rejected 14-85.

He had more success in the 102nd on the reauthorization of the Older Americans Act. Then the ranking Republican on the Labor and Human Resources Subcommittee on Aging, he won approval of an amendment to authorize $15 million for in-home services for older, infirm people.

Cochran also worked with the Bush administration on school reform. He worked out a compromise to give more money to states that want to try to create model public schools. His proposal to increase the amount of its block grant a state could set aside for "break the mold" public schools was adopted 96-0.

Cochran has played an important behind-the-scenes role in mediating splits within the Agriculture Committee, which is torn by conflicts among commodity interests. He works well with ranking Republican Richard G. Lugar of Indiana, and is acknowledged as the GOP leader on Southern agricultural interests. His reasoned, gentlemanly style (he has been called "the Southern Lugar") is well-suited to settling disagreements. Cochran generally enjoys high credibility among committee Democrats, in part because he is more supportive of the programs being authorized than many of his GOP brethren, including Lugar. He is the ranking Republican on its Domestic and Foreign Marketing Subcommittee.

Precocious in authority, Cochran was already writing key sections of major farm bills in the early 1980s. His influence was even more significant during work on the 1985 farm bill. Allied with then-Majority Leader Bob Dole of Kansas, he worked to develop an overall GOP stance on farm issues out of competing regional interests.

Cochran hardly overlooked the interests of Mississippi and other Southern farmers, though, especially those raising cotton or rice. Making full use of the key tactical position they had during action on the farm bill, Cochran and a few other Southerners pushed through a radically new and potentially expensive form of price support for growers of the two crops.

Cochran's seniority and leadership rank invite some intriguing speculation about his future. If Republicans regain control of the Senate in the 1990s, Cochran could reach the chairmanship of the Appropriations Committee before he is 60. The two Republicans ahead of him on Appropriations are both reasonable candidates for retirement after their current term.

Alternatively, Cochran could find himself chairman of the Agriculture Committee (where he ranks fourth), a candidate for party leader or part of a national ticket.

At Home: Each time Cochran has run for the Senate, he has made history. In 1978, he became the first Republican to win a Mississippi Senate seat in a century. Six years later, he became the first GOP candidate for any major statewide office to capture a majority of the vote since Reconstruction. In 1990, he became the first statewide Republican to go without Democratic opposition this century.

The lack of Democratic enthusiasm for challenging Cochran was understandable, considering his 1984 outing. Facing Democrat William F. Winter, the state's popular governor from 1980 to 1984, Cochran won by a decisive 61 percent to 39 percent.

Little had happened in the interim to encourage Democrats to believe they could beat Cochran in 1990. And by the beginning of the year he had more than $865,000 on hand.

He has shown a talent for making friends across the political spectrum. Despite his conservative House voting record, Cochran drew significant support in most of his House campaigns from blacks, who made up more than 40 percent of his 4th District. After a close first election in 1972, when the presence of a black independent allowed him a narrow victory, he drew more than 70 percent in his 1974 and 1976 campaigns.

In 1976 the Mississippi GOP was beset by an internal struggle between supporters of Gerald R. Ford and Ronald Reagan for the presidential nomination. Cochran sided with Ford at the national convention in Kansas City, and the delegation voted 30-0 for Ford's position in the critical rules fight that played a large role in ending Reagan's chances. Although there was considerable anger within the delegation at the time, Cochran suffered no lasting damage.

His election to the Senate in 1978 was made possible in part by another independent black campaign siphoning off votes from the Democratic nominee, ex-Columbia Mayor Maurice Dantin. Democrat James O. Eastland retired in 1978 after 36 years in the Senate and endorsed Dantin to succeed him. But a flamboyant campaign by Fayette Mayor Charles Evers, a veteran black activist, drew more attention than Cochran and Dantin combined.

In a state where Democrats must have the black vote, Evers virtually guaranteed GOP success. Drawing 45 percent statewide, Cochran finished nearly 80,000 votes ahead of Dantin.

Many Democrats regarded Cochran's election as a fluke, but he proved his vote-getting ability in 1984 against Winter. Winter's administration was highlighted by passage of a landmark education bill designed to improve the quality of public schools and make Mississippi attractive to new industry.

But Winter dissipated much of the good will when he accepted, then rejected, the University of Mississippi chancellorship in late 1983. By taking more than six weeks after that to decide whether to challenge Cochran, he reinforced an image of indecisiveness. Winter sought to make up ground with an increasingly aggressive campaign. He criticized Cochran as a likable but ineffective "backbencher" whose Senate approach was to "go along to get along."

But with a smooth-running, well-financed operation, Cochran gave Winter few openings. He dominated the airwaves, dismissing Winter's candidacy as Washington-inspired and stressing his own seniority and growing stature in the Senate. Cochran swept all but a handful of Mississippi's 82 counties, including nearly half those with majority-black populations. In 1990, he won a unanimous victory.

Committees

Conference Chairman

Agriculture, Nutrition & Forestry (4th of 8 Republicans)
Domestic & Foreign Marketing & Product Promotion (ranking); Agricultural Production & Stabilization of Prices; Agricultural Research, Conservation, Forestry & General Legislation

Appropriations (3rd of 13 Republicans)
Agriculture, Rural Development & Related Agencies (ranking); Defense; Energy & Water Development; Interior; Labor, Health & Human Services & Education

Governmental Affairs (4th of 5 Republicans)
Regulation & Government Information (ranking); Federal Services, Post Office & Civil Service; Oversight of Government Management; Permanent Subcommittee on Investigations

Indian Affairs (3rd of 8 Republicans)

Rules & Administration (7th of 7 Republicans)

Elections

1990 General

Thad Cochran (R)	274,244	(100%)

Previous Winning Percentages: **1984** (61%) **1978** (45%) **1976** * (76%) **1974** * (70%) **1972** * (48%)

** House elections.*

Campaign Finance

	Receipts	Receipts from PACs	Expend-itures
1990			
Cochran (R)	$1,316,810	$534,450 (41%)	$567,446

Key Votes

1993

Require unpaid family and medical leave	N
Approve national "motor voter" registration bill	N
Approve budget increasing taxes and reducing deficit	N
Support president's right to lift military gay ban	N

1992

Approve school-choice pilot program	Y
Allow shifting funds from defense to domestic programs	N
Oppose deeper cuts in spending for SDI	Y

1991

Approve waiting period for handgun purchases	N
Raise senators' pay and ban honoraria	Y
Authorize use of force in Persian Gulf	Y
Confirm Clarence Thomas to Supreme Court	Y

Voting Studies

	Presidential Support		Party Unity		Conservative Coalition	
Year	**S**	**O**	**S**	**O**	**S**	**O**
1992	82	15	92	6	89	8
1991	90	9	89	9	95	5
1990	85	15	83	15	100	0
1989	94	6	85	14	97	0
1988	70	22	66	22	97	0
1987	68	26	78	19	97	3
1986	88	10	88	10	91	4
1985	80	14	81	14	87	5
1984	87	8	93	5	96	2
1983	71	22	69	28	77	16
1982	77	20	88	9	85	3
1981	82	9	87	11	88	7

Interest Group Ratings

Year	ADA	AFL-CIO	CCUS	ACU
1992	10	17	100	85
1991	5	25	80	76
1990	0	33	83	87
1989	0	10	75	78
1988	5	15	100	96
1987	20	40	78	68
1986	5	0	89	78
1985	5	15	81	74
1984	10	9	74	82
1983	20	18	74	48
1982	10	16	63	72
1981	10	16	94	53

Trent Lott (R)

Of Pascagoula — Elected 1988; 1st Term

Born: Oct. 9, 1941, Grenada County, Miss.
Education: U. of Mississippi, B.P.A. 1963, J.D. 1967.
Occupation: Lawyer.
Family: Wife, Patricia Elizabeth Thompson; two children.
Religion: Baptist.
Political Career: U.S. House, 1973-89.
Capitol Office: 487 Russell Bldg. 20510; 224-6253.

In Washington: Lott's ascent in the 103rd Congress to the position of Republican Conference secretary — the No. 4 GOP leadership slot — formally confirmed what had been clear in the Senate for some time: A new generation of aggressively conservative Republicans is exercising more and more influence on their party's posture in the chamber.

In personal terms, Lott's election was another sign that as a senator he is reprising a role he perfected as House minority whip: afflicting the Democratic majority.

These days when there is a partisan Republican duty to be done, likely as not Lott is involved — whether the job is putting a little heat on President Clinton's Cabinet appointees, or rallying his colleagues to oppose administration budget plans, or tearing into Clinton's desire to lift the ban on homosexuals serving in the military.

To these tasks and others like them, Lott brings a blend of qualities: conservative indignation, public relations savvy and strategic smarts.

Early in the 103rd, after Clinton's proposed $16 billion economic stimulus package passed the House and headed to the Senate, Lott worked to plant the notion in members' minds that the American people wanted any new federal spending to be paired with budget cuts. Playing off Clinton's campaign mantra, "It's the economy, stupid," Lott distributed buttons with the phrase "It's spending, stupid." Clinton failed to counter the GOP attack effectively, and with Republican senators across the ideological spectrum holding firm to a filibuster strategy, Democrats had to shelve the stimulus plan.

Lott also quickly snatched center stage on the issue of the military gay ban, joining with Texas Sen. Phil Gramm in forcing a vote on Clinton's proposed ban during the February 1993 debate on family leave.

Some who support the gay ban tread cautiously, regarding it as risky to appear to be denying civil rights to any group. But Lott has no qualms about opposing what he sees as special rights for practitioners of an aberrant lifestyle. Invoking the biblical story of Sodom and Gomorrah, he worked successfully in the summer of 1992 to prohibit the District of Columbia from implementing a new "domestic partnership" ordinance, which extends health and other benefits to unmarried couples.

Minority Leader Bob Dole of Kansas turned to Lott in early 1993 to act as the GOP's point man on reviewing the backgrounds of Clinton's Cabinet nominees and passing on pertinent information to the committees reviewing their nominations. In this instance, Lott ended up with little to show for his efforts. Virtually all the nominees sailed through without difficulty, and in the case of the one who didn't — attorney general designee Zoë Baird — Lott and the GOP failed to anticipate and capitalize on the public's outrage at the revelation that Baird had hired illegal aliens as domestic help. Baird withdrew her nomination.

Busy with his many party duties — another in 1993 is sitting on the Joint Committee on the Organization of Congress — Lott has not made a name for himself as an initiator of legislation. But he is vigilant in protecting Mississippi interests, particularly the state's military-related businesses.

Long an ardent defense hawk, Lott is casting a more critical eye on some military expenditures as the Pentagon's share of the budget decreases. In the 102nd Congress, Lott announced that he was speaking against a weapons system for the first time in his 19 years in Congress; he faulted the *Seawolf* nuclear submarine as "a Cold War weapon ... overdeveloped for a post-Cold War [defense] posture."

But even as he was criticizing the submarine and raising doubts about the B-2 bomber, Lott argued that the defense budget should see a "planned, controlled, steady decline we can cope with." Referring to Mississippi's Ingalls Shipbuilding, a major defense contractor, he added: "The best thing I can do for my constituents is to keep those ships coming."

During his House years and then into his Senate tenure as well, Lott's ideological firmness has from time to time placed him at odds even with the party line espoused by leaders above him. In 1985, he abandoned President

Ronald Reagan on his top priority, tax overhaul, and when George Bush was president, he did not shy from criticizing the administration when he thought it insufficiently conservative.

While congressional leaders (including Dole) and the Bush White House labored to produce a budget-summit agreement in 1990, Lott warned, "I am not going to vote for just any package that comes out of these negotiations, especially if 50 percent of it comes out of tax increases and where the priorities are clearly not in the proper order."

Before the budget summit deal went down to defeat in the House, Lott said that if the White House expected easy approval of spending cuts and tax increases, "They're smoking something."

Lott's sharp rhetoric, however, is most often aimed at liberals. In late 1990, he used the legal definition of treason to warn Democrats to stick with the president in the Persian Gulf crisis. "If we start allowing this to be a backing away from [administration] policy," he said, "it could be giving aid and comfort to [Iraqi President] Saddam Hussein." Discussing the suit filed by some Democrats to block offensive military action unless Congress had given prior approval, Lott said, "It's typical that would come from the loony left."

He makes plain his delight in sparring with the opposition. After losing a vote in the 102nd on a tax bill with a new 36 percent top tax bracket and a surtax for millionaires, Lott said he was not upset. "We almost killed a real bad tax-raising bill, and besides that, I just love to watch [Majority Leader George] Mitchell squirm," he said.

Dole put Lott on the Ethics Committee in 1989, and many Democrats feared that he would use the panel as a partisan grandstand during the investigation of five senators — four of them Democrats — associated with savings and loan tycoon Charles H. Keating Jr. Lott was said to be most closely allied with North Carolina Republican Jesse Helms, an Ethics panelist who backed tough sanctions on three of the senators involved (all Democrats).

But if Lott had any notion that the Keating affair could besmirch the Democratic Party, the slow pace of the investigation instead caused him to worry that the affair was damaging the reputation of the entire Senate.

As the panel labored over the minutiae of the report language, Lott reportedly attempted to detonate the committee into action by stalking out or threatening to do so. In the end, the Ethics panel unanimously decided to scold four of the senators and further investigate the fifth. Lott said he opposed further action against the four because it would have amounted to "setting the standards after the fact."

Lott came out of the proceedings concerned about the "appearance standard" the case seemed to set. "You've got to be prepared to tell a constituent, 'If you contribute, you've got to understand, I might not be able to help you,' " he said. (Lott left the Ethics Committee at the start of the 103rd.)

In the House, Lott was a key GOP strategist both on the Rules Committee and as minority whip. In 1981, he became the first Deep South Republican to take the No. 2 GOP position.

At the beginning of his House career, on Judiciary, he took part in the historic impeachment proceedings of President Richard M. Nixon in 1973 and 1974. Lott was a staunch defender of Nixon, which was not a liability for him back home, as Nixon remained popular with many Gulf Coast conservatives.

At Home: The 1988 presidential election created a favorable atmosphere for Lott to wage a Senate campaign, but he also rose to the occasion. Mississippi, though conservative, was then still traditional Democratic territory that had regularly elected Lott's predecessor, Democratic Sen. John C. Stennis, beginning in 1947. It took a strong campaign for Lott to overcome a skilled opponent, Rep. Wayne Dowdy, with a solid 54 percent of the vote.

While Dowdy depleted his financial resources to win a tough primary, Lott was free to focus on the fall election. He took the offensive with an early media blitz Dowdy could not afford to answer for much of the summer. Lott, long identified as a strong supporter of Reagan's policies, used the airwaves to stress issues that often had been turned against Republicans in the 1980s. To Democrats' dismay, he positioned himself as a champion of Social Security, student loans and public works.

To appeal to rural and blue-collar conservatives often sympathetic to Democrats, Lott stressed his background. Though he has the polished appearance of a blue-suit conservative, Lott reminded voters that his father farmed cotton and drove a school bus. He said Dowdy, whose rumpled appearance and folksy manner belied his family's wealth, was a "millionaire, country-club type."

Dowdy faulted Lott for election-year conversions on issues, and insisted that the Republican was out of step with Mississippi. His late-starting ad campaign included a spot criticizing Lott for having a $50,000 per-year "chauffeur," George Awkward. But Lott blasted the ad, which featured a limousine cruising through the countryside, saying that Awkward was a member of the Capitol security force, funded by a bill Dowdy supported. He added that Awkward showed up for work more often than Dowdy, whose House attendance dropped dramatically during the campaign year.

By summer's end, the sophistication of Lott's effort was apparent, and Democrats were complaining that Dowdy, though a good stump candidate, had an inadequate organization. Michael S. Dukakis' almost non-existent campaign in the state did not boost party spirits.

But Democrats held out hope that Dowdy's strength might not be apparent until Election

Day. Part of that optimism stemmed from his apparent appeal in the black community, which accounts for more than a third of Mississippi's population. While Dowdy was first elected as a champion of the Voting Rights Act, Lott had cast several votes that alienated black leaders, including those against renewal of that act and against the Martin Luther King Jr. holiday.

But Lott came through on Election Day. In addition to his strong showing among whites, he got a surprising 13 percent of the black vote, according to CBS News-New York Times exit polls.

Lott suffered a public relations black eye in 1989 when he helped steer the GOP nomination in a special House election to a longtime aide rather than the widow of GOP Rep. Larkin Smith, whose death in a plane crash necessitated the new election. The treatment of Smith's widow was considered by many as brusque and heavy-handed; Republicans lost the seat Lott had won and held since 1973, and they have failed to regain it.

Lott did not become a Republican until the eve of his first House campaign, in 1972. As Democratic Rep. William M. Colmer's administrative assistant, he had remained a nominal Democrat. But when the venerable Rules chairman decided to retire in 1972 at age 82, Lott filed in the GOP primary, saying he was "tired of the Muskies and the Kennedys and the Humphreys and the whole lot.... I will fight against the ever-increasing efforts of the so-called liberals to concentrate more power in the government in Washington."

The wisdom of Lott's switch was soon confirmed. Running that fall against Democrat Ben Stone, chairman of the state Senate Banking Committee, Lott stayed on the offensive by linking Stone with the national Democratic Party. Aided by the Nixon landslide and an endorsement from Colmer, Lott carried all but two of the district's 12 counties.

Committees

Conference Secretary

Armed Services (5th of 9 Republicans)
Nuclear Deterrence, Arms Control & Defense Intelligence (ranking); Defense Technology, Acquisition & Industrial Base; Regional Defense & Contingency Forces

Budget (6th of 9 Republicans)

Commerce, Science & Transportation (8th of 9 Republicans)
Merchant Marine (ranking); National Ocean Policy Study; Science; Surface Transportation

Energy & Natural Resources (9th of 9 Republicans)
Energy Research & Development; Public Lands, National Parks & Forests; Renewable Energy

Joint Organization of Congress

Elections

1988 General

Trent Lott (R)	510,380	(54%)
Wayne Dowdy (D)	436,339	(46%)

Previous Winning Percentages: **1986 *** (82%) **1984 *** (85%) **1982 *** (79%) **1980 *** (74%) **1978 *** (100%) **1976 *** (68%) **1974 *** (73%) **1972 *** (55%)

** House elections.*

Campaign Finance

	Receipts	Receipts from PACs		Expend-itures
1988				
Lott (R)	$3,602,481	$1,118,111	(31%)	$3,405,242
Dowdy (D)	$2,195,960	$962,719	(44%)	$2,355,957

Key Votes

1993	
Require unpaid family and medical leave	N
Approve national "motor voter" registration bill	N
Approve budget increasing taxes and reducing deficit	N
Support president's right to lift military gay ban	N
1992	
Approve school-choice pilot program	Y
Allow shifting funds from defense to domestic programs	N
Oppose deeper cuts in spending for SDI	Y
1991	
Approve waiting period for handgun purchases	N
Raise senators' pay and ban honoraria	Y
Authorize use of force in Persian Gulf	Y
Confirm Clarence Thomas to Supreme Court	Y

Voting Studies

	Presidential Support		Party Unity		Conservative Coalition	
Year	**S**	**O**	**S**	**O**	**S**	**O**
1992	83	17	93	3	97	3
1991	88	10	91	7	93	5
1990	76	24	82	16	97	0
1989	82	16	92	6	95	3
House Service:						
1988	51	33	59	13	84	0
1987	63	24	83	8	88	5
1986	78	18	79	14	84	4
1985	73	24	82	9	89	5
1984	73	25	86	8	97	2
1983	73	22	86	7	97	1
1982	75	17	78	19	88	11
1981	84	16	90	6	95	3

Interest Group Ratings

Year	ADA	AFL-CIO	CCUS	ACU
1992	10	17	90	100
1991	5	27	78	86
1990	0	22	100	91
1989	5	20	88	96
House Service:				
1988	5	33	82	95
1987	4	19	77	91
1986	5	23	86	95
1985	0	12	95	90
1984	0	8	80	96
1983	0	6	85	100
1982	5	5	70	85
1981	0	7	95	93

1 Jamie L. Whitten (D)

Of Charleston — Elected 1941; 26th Full Term

Born: April 18, 1910, Cascilla, Miss.
Education: U. of Mississippi, 1927-32.
Occupation: Elementary school teacher and principal; lawyer; author.
Family: Wife, Rebecca Thompson; two children.
Religion: Presbyterian.
Political Career: Miss. House, 1931-33; Miss. 17th Judicial District attorney, 1933-41.
Capitol Office: 2314 Rayburn Bldg. 20515; 225-4306.

In Washington: As the 103rd Congress unfolded, Whitten, always a solitary figure, could be seen in the House, seated alone, activity swirling about him. For the first time in decades, no one felt compelled to consult, cajole or ingratiate himself with the legendary Mississippi Democrat. Stripped of his two chairmanships — on the full Appropriations Committee, over which he had presided since 1979, and the Agriculture Appropriations Subcommittee, his source of power since 1949 — Whitten remains a repository of institutional knowledge, a relic of historical significance, a last link to the New Deal — but no longer a force in Congress.

Only a year earlier it had been very different. Whitten, if not at the height of his powers, still had immense influence. By the midpoint of the 102nd Congress, he had managed to produce "dire emergency" supplemental spending bills to steer money to distressed farmers while evading the caps set by the 1990 budget agreement. He was promoting his bill that would provide $8 billion in spending and loans to create jobs. And he was using his subcommittee to maintain his unofficial position as a chief administrator of U.S. agriculture policy, a post that had long ago earned him the sobriquet "permanent secretary of Agriculture." On Jan. 6, 1992, he broke the record for longest service in the House: 50 years, two months and two days, surpassing Georgia Democrat Carl Vinson.

Soon after he set the record, however, his health deteriorated and he was hospitalized. Close associates said he had a stroke. After he returned to the House in March, he often seemed disoriented and unable to manage without considerable assistance. In June, during a conference on a supplemental appropriations bill, he tried to lead the House delegation, but his voice was so weak that he had trouble being understood; he eventually allowed William H. Natcher of Kentucky, the No. 2 Appropriations Democrat, to take over.

Pressure for Whitten to relinquish his authority had been building for weeks because appropriators were entering their busiest season. A letter urging him to do so was signed by all of the panel's subcommittee chairmen except Natcher and Sidney R. Yates of Illinois, the Interior Subcommittee chairman.

Speaker Thomas S. Foley met with Whitten, but he refused to budge. It was only when a resolution was pending with the Democratic Caucus that would have forced him to step aside that Whitten gave Natcher a letter asking him to stand in while he recovered from his illness. Stubborn to the end, however, he refused to give up the chairmanship itself, yielding only day-to-day public duties, such as presiding over committee meetings, House-Senate conferences and floor debate.

In December, as Democrats organized for the 103rd Congress, Whitten again refused to cede his chairmanships. But the Steering and Policy Committee stripped him of his full committee title and his fellow appropriators took away his subcommittee chair. Natcher, seven months Whitten's elder, was elected full committee chairman. Whitten was replaced on Agriculture by Richard J. Durbin of Illinois, who was born three years after Whitten took office.

Throughout his long career in Congress Whitten has kept alive the spirit of the New Deal. A Depression survivor, he is a true believer in government's pump-priming potential. A shrewd trader in appropriations pork, Whitten always presented his role in grander terms than that, in keeping with his theme that the nation's wealth is measured not in money but in its physical assets. He has given that lecture often, stupefying committee colleagues and exasperating senators and administration officials who may have provoked it by challenging him on some spending item.

During an interview in January 1992 with Congressional Quarterly, Whitten was asked if, in his view, there was any such thing as "pork barrel spending." He replied: "In the minds of newspapers. Pork barrel is something that the press stirred up back yonder — anything that you get in your district.

"It only started way back yonder when Congress didn't have public works, and you did not meet local problems with federal programs.

Mississippi 1

North — Tupelo

Change has slowly crept into this overwhelmingly rural area, awakening the sluggish economy and bringing some jobs and industries that might have been unthinkable to residents 20 years ago. While much of the district remains loyally Democratic, the economic evolution has brought an increase in Republican white-collar voters.

One recent sign of the shift came with groundbreaking for a Lockheed Corp. manufacturing plant that will produce Advanced Solid Rocket Motors for NASA. A Whitten-backed enterprise, the plant is under construction in Iuka in Tishomingo County and currently employs about 1,000 people. The project has spurred construction of a hospital and a high school in the county.

In addition, northeastern Mississippi has become a hub for furniture manufacturing, particularly lower-priced pieces such as recliners. A national furniture market is held twice a year in the Lee County city of Tupelo, which is the district's biggest, with 31,000 people. However, Tupelo is still best known as the birthplace of Elvis Presley. The shotgun house where Presley was born is now a tourist attraction.

Another boost to local economic development came with the 1985 opening of the Tennessee-Tombigbee Waterway, a project that Whitten and other area legislators strongly advocated. The Tenn-Tom cuts through a handful of counties in the northeastern corner of the 1st, connecting the Tennessee and Tombigbee rivers to create an unbroken link to the Gulf of Mexico.

On the western side of the district in Lafayette County is Oxford, site of the University of Mississippi (11,000 students). Popularly known as "Ole Miss," the university is the home of the Center for the Study of Southern Culture. Square Books, on the town square, attracts area literati, including local authors such as Willie Morris and John Grisham. Oxford was the home base for William Faulkner, whose stately home, Rowan Oak, is host to thousands of Faulkner enthusiasts each year.

Beyond a handful of built-up areas, the district remains largely rural. It takes in the flat, rich farmland on the edge of the Delta region in northwestern Mississippi and the less fertile plots of the northeastern Hill Country. Although cotton was once the dominant crop in this region, 1st District farmers now also produce soybeans, rice, corn, wheat, livestock and poultry.

Over the past two decades, the steadiest population growth in the 1st has come in the Memphis, Tenn., suburbs of De Soto County. Population has nearly doubled there since 1970, and De Soto now casts more votes than any other county in the 1st — about 13 percent of the total. In a district where many retain their traditional allegiance to the Democratic Party, white-collar De Soto is unmistakably Republican. Since 1976, the county has supported GOP presidential candidates (George Bush won 59 percent here in 1992), and it also voted against Whitten in the past two elections, giving his 1992 challenger 61 percent.

1990 Population: 514,548. White 395,070 (77%), Black 117,126 (23%), Other 2,352 (<1%). Hispanic origin 2,386 (<1%). 18 and over 373,928 (73%), 62 and over 81,130 (16%). Median age: 32.

Anything special that you did for your district was unusual. But since I've been here, more and more we've met local problems with federal programs. And I'm proud of that...."

From deciding where to build roads, dams and inland waterways to telling the White House how to run its internal affairs, Whitten called the shots from his seemingly invisible perch on the Agriculture Subcommittee. Better than anyone else, he understood arcane and labyrinthine farm programs — some of which he helped to create.

"Agriculture affects 84 percent of the geography of this country," he would say repeatedly. "I'm proud to have my name on rural electricity, water systems, telephones and highway service roads in 84 percent of the country."

For decades, the Agriculture Subcommittee was Whitten's virtual fiefdom. From it, as late as the 1960s, he was railing against integration and social programs and dictating crop subsidies without much challenge. But it was his views on the environment (he called environmentalists a "small, vocal group of extremists") that so angered liberals that they plotted to oust him in 1975. Armed with a new rule requiring Appropriations subcommittee chairmen to be elected by the Democratic Caucus, they were finally assuaged by Appropriations Chairman George Mahon of Texas, who arranged for Whitten to give up environmental and consumer issues in return for keeping the chair.

Through the years, various bills have allowed Whitten to pour money into Mississippi. Often, he would slip in provisions unnoticed or explain them in his famous Mississippi mumble that leaves listeners more perplexed than enlightened. He is not apologetic: "Somebody told me, 'Jamie, you're the biggest pork barreler in Congress.' I said, 'I guess I am, because pork barrel is what you do in the other fella's district, and I've helped more districts than anybody.' "

One program that Whitten has managed to retain against vigorous opposition is the Advanced Solid Rocket Motor project, a controversial and expensive new launch system estimated to cost about $3 billion and being built in Yellow Creek, Miss., in Whitten's district. In 1992, the House voted to cut all but $100 million of the $480 million allotted for fiscal 1993, but House-Senate conferees restored the funding level to $360 million.

Perhaps the largest monument to Whitten's power is the Tennessee-Tombigbee waterway that cuts through his district. Completed in 1985, the project was his pet cause for two decades. To Whitten it is one of his proudest contributions; to critics, a symbol of pork barrel excess.

Whitten inherited the full committee chairmanship that let him build that waterway and scores of other projects over the objections of House liberals when Mahon retired in 1979. Liberals favored Edward P. Boland of Massachusetts, longtime roommate of Speaker Thomas P. O'Neill Jr. of Massachusetts, for the job. But O'Neill was on good terms with Whitten and would not breach seniority.

In turn, O'Neill and every Speaker since has had a loyal chairman. Whitten, who once voted against civil rights bills, Medicare and anti-poverty programs, now backs party goals even at the risk of political controversy back home. Once an avowed segregationist, Whitten signed the 1956 Southern Manifesto and said the Supreme Court's 1954 school desegregation decision had started the nation "on the downhill road to integration and amalgamation and ruin." Today, he represents a district that is 23 percent black, a smaller population than in the past but one that votes in significant numbers now. He is as free of racial rhetoric as the younger Southern Democrats who have joined him since the 1970s.

A one-time grammar school principal and county prosecutor, Whitten claims, "I came to Congress by accident; my ambition was to practice law." But after winning a special election the month before Pearl Harbor, he has stayed to become the dean of the House. In that role, Whitten takes pride in having sworn in the Speaker in the last nine Congresses, including the 103rd.

Whitten is the last of a breed — the conservative Southern Democrats who once ruled Capitol Hill — and like the others who survived, he had to adjust.

In the House, Whitten became a vassal to Democratic leaders and answerable to junior activists who have been willing to take on and even topple chairmen they deem unsuitable for the job.

Though never a back slapper, Whitten nevertheless reveled in retail legislative politics. He dealt with members one on one, in private, but with an abiding sense of where each one came from.

"We have tried to deal fairly with members and their problems," he said in 1991 when unveiling the last spending bill that he personally oversaw. "And when I say members I mean sections of the United States."

But even as Whitten's ability to get pet projects into the enacted agriculture appropriations bill made him invaluable to members, it also may have contributed to his demise. With Whitten severely weakened, members apparently sought assurance that their needs, so long cultivated by Whitten, would be addressed.

"The majority didn't think he was strong enough to do it," said Iowa Democrat Neal Smith, a longtime Appropriations colleague. That was the only reason, Smith said, that Whitten lost the position that really mattered to him.

At Home: Whitten accrued his seniority with barely a scent of opposition in his northern Mississippi district. Only in 1992, with his health and control on Capitol Hill in question, was Whitten challenged by a solid and well-financed Republican opponent, former Tupelo Mayor Clyde Whitaker. While Whitten bested Whitaker easily with 59 percent of the vote, for the first time his armor was battered.

Whitten, who has never debated his opponents, did not accept Whitaker's offer to debate. Nor did he campaign extensively in the 1st, relying instead on lengthy ads in local newspapers to spur voter loyalty. That he won despite only modest personal campaigning is a testament to voters' affection and respect for Whitten. In addition, despite his ill health, many voters still believed that Whitten could continue to deliver badly needed federal dollars to the state.

Although Whitaker did not make an issue of Whitten's health and waning power in Washington, The (Memphis) Commercial Appeal did so gently in its endorsement of Whitaker and tried to prepare voters for the eventuality of Whitten's departure from politics.

The editorial's writer cautioned voters that not only were the days of the titan pork barreler fading in Washington, but that Whitten's days as chairman of the Appropriations Committee might be numbered as well. Because of his health problems, "it's highly questionable whether Whitten would continue to be chairman of the full Appropriations Committee." Between 1941, when he first won his House seat, and 1978, the year he inherited the Appropriations chairmanship, Whitten had faced GOP opposition only once. Nor had he seen much opposition inside the Democratic Party; the only real threat was in 1962, when redistricting forced him to battle Rep. Frank Smith for the nomination.

The son of a Tallahatchie County farmer, Whitten has spent his entire adult life in politics. He was elected to the Mississippi House at 21, and two years later was chosen district attorney. At 31, he was elected to Congress to succeed Wall Doxey, who had moved to the Senate. For the next two decades, Whitten ran virtually unopposed. But in 1962, Mississippi lost one House seat in reapportionment. The state Legislature combined the northern Delta region's two districts, forcing a bitter showdown between Whitten and Smith. The two had been on opposite sides during the 1960 presidential election, when Smith backed John F. Kennedy while Whitten supported an unpledged slate of segregationist electors.

The new district's population was more than half black, but virtually none of the blacks voted. Each congressman tried to outdo the other in support of segregation. Smith was a populist, and Whitten claimed that he worked with Northern liberals and the Kennedy administration rather than trying to "preserve the Southern way of life." Smith said Whitten was more of a "prima donna" than an effective champion of Southern rights.

Building a huge lead in the counties of his old constituency, Whitten won easily with 60 percent of the vote. Smith was appointed by President Kennedy to the board of the Tennessee Valley Authority.

Mississippi's resurgent Republicans have been challenging Whitten in most recent election years, but until 1992, the closest anyone came was in 1980, when GOP challenger T. K. Moffett picked up 37 percent.

Committee

Appropriations (2nd of 37 Democrats)
Agriculture, Rural Development, FDA & Related Agencies

Elections

1992 General		
Jamie L. Whitten (D)	121,664	(59%)
Clyde E. Whitaker (R)	82,952	(41%)
1992 Primary		
Jamie L. Whitten (D)	36,817	(82%)
Rex N. Weathers (D)	8,114	(18%)
1990 General		
Jamie L. Whitten (D)	43,668	(65%)
Bill Bowlin (R)	23,650	(35%)

Previous Winning Percentages: **1988** (78%) **1986** (66%) **1984** (88%) **1982** (71%) **1980** (63%) **1978** (67%) **1976** (100%) **1974** (88%) **1972** (100%) **1970** (87%) **1968** (100%) **1966** (84%) **1964** (100%) **1962** (100%) **1960** (100%) **1958** (100%) **1956** (100%) **1954** (100%) **1952** (100%) **1950** (100%) **1948** (100%) **1946** (100%) **1944** (99%) **1942** (100%) **1941** * (69%)

** Special election.*

District Vote for President

1992
D 83,581 (42%)
R 99,264 (49%)
I 17,713 (9%)

Campaign Finance

	Receipts	Receipts from PACs	Expend-itures
1992			
Whitten (D)	$82,667	$30,700 (37%)	$267,223
Whitaker (R)	$229,172	$6,400 (3%)	$229,004
1990			
Whitten (D)	$183,612	$129,450 (71%)	$96,254
Bowlin (R)	$14,780	$250 (2%)	$14,750

Key Votes

1993	
Require parental notification of minors' abortions	N
Require unpaid family and medical leave	Y
Approve national "motor voter" registration bill	Y
Approve budget increasing taxes and reducing deficit	Y
Approve economic stimulus plan	Y
1992	
Approve balanced-budget constitutional amendment	Y
Close down space station program	N
Approve U.S. aid for former Soviet Union	Y
Allow shifting funds from defense to domestic programs	Y
1991	
Extend unemployment benefits using deficit financing	Y
Approve waiting period for handgun purchases	?
Authorize use of force in Persian Gulf	Y

Voting Studies

	Presidential Support		Party Unity		Conservative Coalition	
Year	S	O	S	O	S	O
1992	27	36	60	10	52	19
1991	39	55	78	15	57	27
1990	34	62	79	16	69	30
1989	52	47	79	19	66	34
1988	28	68	90	8	45	53
1987	33	61	82	10	70	21
1986	30	64	76	16	60	34
1985	33	68	79	13	55	35
1984	39	58	76	18	56	39
1983	30	66	71	22	63	31
1982	40	53	66	27	49	34
1981	50	49	63	36	67	31

Interest Group Ratings

Year	ADA	AFL-CIO	CCUS	ACU
1992	50	78	50	29
1991	25	75	60	33
1990	44	75	38	43
1989	50	67	70	42
1988	65	100	15	20
1987	68	88	13	13
1986	55	69	31	16
1985	55	75	20	26
1984	50	69	60	33
1983	60	88	33	18
1982	45	70	38	52
1981	30	67	22	20

2 Bennie Thompson (D)

Of Bolton — Elected 1993; 1st Term

Born: Jan. 28, 1948, Bolton, Miss.
Education: Tougaloo College, B.A. 1968; Jackson State U., M.S. 1972.
Occupation: Teacher.
Family: Wife, London Johnson; one child.
Religion: Methodist.
Political Career: Bolton Board of Aldermen, 1969-73; mayor of Bolton, 1973-79; Hinds County Board of Supervisors, 1980-93.
Capitol Office: 1408 Longworth Bldg. 20515; 225-5876.

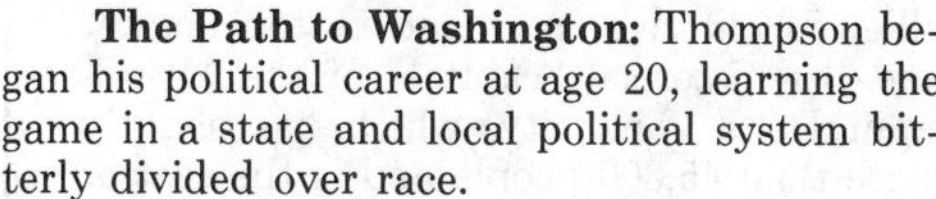

The Path to Washington: Thompson began his political career at age 20, learning the game in a state and local political system bitterly divided over race.

In the late 1960s, when Thompson began challenging that system, the black officeholders were few and the discouragements many. If a black candidate got elected, white officials sometimes refused to seat him.

"In each instance that I ran for office I had to go to court," Thompson said.

When he was sworn in as a member of Congress in the spring of 1993, Thompson was solidifying some of the gains made by African-Americans in their ongoing struggle for power in Mississippi. The seat he won had previously been held by Mike Espy, who in 1986 had become the state's first black representative in Congress since Reconstruction. Espy resigned in January to become secretary of Agriculture.

Thompson won his seat with 55 percent of the vote over Republican Hayes Dent, an adviser to Republican Gov. Kirk Fordice who briefly entertained hopes of breaking the Democrats 5-0 shutout in the state's House delegation.

Unlike Espy, Thompson has not been viewed as a candidate who could appeal both to blacks and to moderate and conservative whites in the district. His participation in the state's civil rights battles over the past generation made him less attractive to some whites, and he did not go out of his way to court white voters as Espy had.

Thompson was also thought to have suffered somewhat in the free-for-all Democratic field of contenders in the initial voting March 30. Dent had finished first in that test with 34 percent. Thompson finished second with 28 percent to 20 percent for the third-place finisher: Espy's brother, Henry, the mayor of Clarksdale.

With just two weeks to the runoff, the campaign was intense. Both candidates were plagued by unfavorable publicity. Dent had to answer for a simple assault conviction from 1983. And stories were revived from the 1980s questioning whether Thompson's friendship with a state official had helped to prevent an investigation into Thompson's practices as a Hinds County supervisor.

But the latter stories did not gain much momentum in the retelling in 1993, nor did they prevent Thompson from uniting and galvanizing blacks, who constitute 58 percent of the voting-age population in the 2nd. Turnout was considered high for a special election (more than 130,000 votes were cast).

With the election behind him, Thompson said he planned to emphasize the concerns of the majority in the district. He also vowed to work to unify the district.

"I hope to bridge that gap, but right now it's still very much divided," he said after his election April 13.

Thompson met with House Speaker Thomas S. Foley of Washington to push for a seat on the Agriculture Committee, hoping to safeguard the state's farm interests. Foley accommodated him.

Although Thompson should have the ear of his predecessor Espy on farm issues, he may find the going tougher in the House and in its Agriculture Committee. He will not have the political assistance all Mississippians once enjoyed from the presence of their Democratic colleague Jamie L. Whitten at the pinnacle of the House Appropriations Committee (and its Agriculture Subcommittee). Whitten, who turned 83 in 1993, was relieved of his chairmanship late in 1992 due to persistent ill health.

Thompson was educated in segregated elementary and secondary schools in the state. As a student at Tougaloo College, he met civil rights activist Fannie Lou Hamer, who inspired him to pursue a career in politics.

At 20, he ran for alderman in his native Bolton. He won but was denied a seat by white officials until a court order forced the town to relent. Four years later, Thompson was elected mayor of Bolton. And at 32, he took a seat on the Board of Supervisors for Hinds County, which includes the state's capital city of Jackson.

Mississippi 2

West central — Mississippi Delta

The 2nd is known both for the rich culture and extreme poverty of its people. The latter has produced an atmosphere that is kinder to Democratic candidates than elsewhere in the state. Bill Clinton took 58 percent here in 1992.

"The Birthplace of the Blues," the Delta was home to many musicians. Muddy Waters was born in Rolling Fork, near Greenville, and grew up on a Clarksdale plantation in Coahoma County. Ike Turner and John Lee Hooker are also from Clarksdale, which boasts a blues museum.

Ever since swamp-draining technology and cheap black labor transformed the Delta into an agricultural gold mine in the years after the Civil War, the region has had a far larger population of poor rural blacks than affluent white cotton growers.

In the past generation, thousands of Delta blacks, pushed out of work by farm mechanization, moved to Chicago, St. Louis and closer Sun Belt cities such as Little Rock and Memphis.

While a black middle class has always existed in the 2nd, many blacks here live in abject poverty. With 50 percent of majority-black Tunica County living below the poverty line, the county is the poorest in the state and one of the poorest in the nation. However, those figures are expected to change with the advent of casino gambling. Long lines of patrons from across the region wait for a chance to play at the Splash Casino, which has generated nearly $200,000 a month since it opened in October 1992. The state gaming commission says the casino has cut the county's unemployment figures in half.

Some residents of the 2nd still make a living off the land. While soybeans have replaced cotton as the largest cash crop, more acreage is devoted to cotton.

More recently the Delta has become synonymous with "aquaculture" because it produces about 75 percent of the nation's catfish. While the catfish processing industry has provided jobs, it has been criticized for the low wages it pays. Striking workers have gained some concessions from the plant owners. The Catfish Institute, an industry trade group, is based in Belzoni.

The largest city in the 2nd is Greenville, an old river port and cotton market and the historical "capital" of the Mississippi Delta. The city, which has slightly more than 45,000 people and is the seat of Washington County, is one of the few areas that has grown in recent years.

In the southern part of the district, in Warren County, is the city of Vicksburg. It is still best known for the Battle of Vicksburg, a 47-day siege in 1863 that resulted in the city's surrender to Union Gen. Ulysses S. Grant. Two regional medical centers are here. And the U.S. Army Corps of Engineers employs about 4,000 people in environmental and water resources projects.

Redistricting added 13 precincts in Jackson, the state capital, to the 2nd. (One more was added just outside the city.) Many of those residents added were poor blacks, leaving more affluent blacks in the more conservative 4th.

1990 Population: 514,845. White 188,309 (37%), Black 324,199 (63%), Other 2,337 (<1%). Hispanic origin 2,731 (1%). 18 and over 345,943 (67%), 62 and over 78,756 (15%). Median age: 29.

Committees

Agriculture (26th of 28 Democrats)

Merchant Marine & Fisheries (30th of 30 Democrats)
Environment & Natural Resources; Merchant Marine

Campaign Finance

	Receipts	Receipts from PACs		Expenditures
1993				
Thompson (D)	$502,559	$193,688	(39%)	$498,397
Dent (R)	$469,511	$103,313	(22%)	$465,485

Elections

1993 Special Runoff		
Bennie Thompson (D)	72,561	(55%)
Hayes Dent (R)	58,995	(45%)
1993 Special		
Hayes Dent (R)	34,766	(34%)
Bennie Thompson (D)	29,041	(28%)
Henry Espy (D)	20,800	(20%)
Unita Blackwell (D)	7,412	(7%)
David M. Halbrook (D)	6,027	(6%)
Steve Richardson (D)	3,036	(3%)

District Vote for President

1992

D	105,052	(58%)
R	66,350	(37%)
I	9,805	(5%)

3 G.V. "Sonny" Montgomery (D)

Of Meridian — Elected 1966; 14th Term

Born: Aug. 5, 1920, Meridian, Miss.
Education: Mississippi State U., B.S. 1943.
Military Service: Army, 1943-46; National Guard, 1946-80 (Active duty, 1951-52).
Occupation: Insurance executive.
Family: Single.
Religion: Episcopalian.
Political Career: Miss. Senate, 1956-66.
Capitol Office: 2184 Rayburn Bldg. 20515; 225-5031.

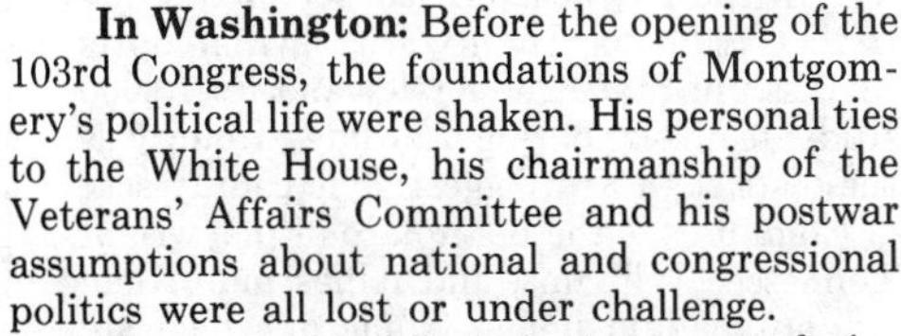

In Washington: Before the opening of the 103rd Congress, the foundations of Montgomery's political life were shaken. His personal ties to the White House, his chairmanship of the Veterans' Affairs Committee and his postwar assumptions about national and congressional politics were all lost or under challenge.

The venerable Mississippian was truly incredulous at finding that senior, pro-military, conservative Southern Democrats, so powerful in the 1980s, had gone out of style overnight.

The most startling of these events was the challenge to his chairmanship. Although change was in the air (the House Democratic Caucus underwent its biggest turnover in 18 years), Montgomery was the only chairman challenged. He prevailed, but by just four votes, 127-123.

The instigator of the challenge was the boyish, liberal Lane Evans of Illinois. Evans had respectfully but steadily criticized Montgomery's handling of Vietnam veterans issues over the years. Montgomery, the polite Southern gentleman, can be intransigent when it comes to liberal ideas, and he has made some Democrats feel left out. The committee had also been undergoing a gradual infusion of new blood, and Montgomery was caught off guard.

In the 102nd Congress, for example, California Democrat Maxine Waters swept aboard and took issue with a Montgomery proposal on her first day on the committee. Tension between the two brought into the open some philosophical differences between liberals and conservatives that had been papered over in the past. Waters accused Montgomery of having difficulty dealing with an assertive black woman who "had the audacity to challenge him." She criticized the scarcity of minority committee aides and suggested he hire some. And when the folksy Montgomery tried to break the ice and call her "Maxine," she told him not to do it again.

Montgomery sought advice from political friends in the Congressional Black Caucus on getting along with Waters. An additional black committee staffer was hired. But Montgomery was not about to change his style or his politics, both of which had stood him in good stead with his constituents and not a few presidential administrations. Montgomery had been good friends with President Bush, for example, since they were House freshmen together in 1967.

But even friendships come with a price. And Montgomery has been called to pay for his ties to Bush. When forced to battle for his chair, Montgomery found out how many Democrats had chafed at his frequent alliance with Republican presidents. During the Reagan presidency, Montgomery's leadership role among the "Boll Weevils," a coalition of conservative Democrats who backed the president's policies, caused consternation in the Democratic Caucus: At the start of the 98th Congress, he received a less-than-resounding 179-53 vote for re-election as chairman.

Montgomery then adopted a lower profile in the conservative coalition. However, his voting record did not change much. The only year in which he voted against Ronald Reagan's positions more than half the time was in 1988.

In 1989, Montgomery supported Bush's position on 78 percent of House floor votes before cooling off to 66 percent in 1992.

With such a political résumé, Montgomery will not likely be an insider in this Democratic era. It partly explains why he did not try for the chairmanship of the Armed Services Committee, where he was second in line to replace Chairman Les Aspin, now the Defense secretary. In an era of defense conversion, Montgomery still wants to protect defense expenditures. Realistic about his standing with the caucus in general, Montgomery backed the nomination of Californian Ronald V. Dellums for the chair.

The other explanation for Montgomery staying put is that veterans issues have been his trademark. He spent more than half his life in the military. He was decorated for his Army service in World War II and Korea and retired as a major general from the Mississippi Na-

Mississippi 3

East central — Meridian

The 3rd combines east Mississippi Hill Country with suburbs of the city of Jackson in Rankin County. Although Rep. Montgomery wins re-election with ease, all the building blocks of this district — the rural areas, the small cities and especially the Jackson suburbs — are fertile ground for Republican candidates.

In the 1992 presidential contest, Bill Clinton managed only about one-third of the vote in the 3rd. Texas billionaire Ross Perot also fared poorly here, finishing in single digits, well below his national average of 19 percent. By contrast, George Bush soared toward 60 percent in the district.

Nearly one-fifth of the total district vote is cast in Rankin County, one of the fastest-growing areas of the state during the 1980s. The white-collar professionals here, most of whom have jobs in and around the state capital of Jackson, are among the most faithful GOP voters in the South.

Rankin went solidly Republican in the 1987 gubernatorial contest, helping the GOP nominee to an unexpectedly strong statewide showing, and in 1991 Rankin was instrumental in making Kirk Fordice the first Republican governor of Mississippi since Reconstruction. Rankin gave Bush nearly 80 percent of its presidential vote in 1988. Four years later, as Bush was falling below 40 percent nationally, he still took 68 percent of the vote in Rankin.

Due east of Rankin on the Alabama border is Lauderdale County (Meridian), the district's second most populous. Meridian is an industrial city with Lockheed and General Motors facilities, and the Meridian Naval Air Station trains naval pilots. An Air National Guard facility in the area appeared on the 1993 base-closure list. Lauderdale County was just a step behind Rankin in loyalty to Bush in 1992, giving him 63 percent of the vote.

In the center of the 3rd is one of Mississippi's most infamous locales: the Neshoba County seat of Philadelphia. Near here in 1964, three civil rights workers were murdered. The annual Neshoba County fair is a must stop for any Mississippi politician. In presidential election years, even White House aspirants have been known to include the fair on their itinerary.

In the northeastern corner of the district, Oktibbeha County (Starkville) hosts Mississippi State University and its 13,000 students. Neighboring Lowndes County is the district's third biggest. The county seat of Columbus is the birthplace of playwright Tennessee Williams, and it has more than 100 antebellum homes, some of which are open for viewing each April.

Columbus also has a major Air Force base that provides basic training for prospective pilots, and the military-related population helps boost the GOP in Lowndes County. In 1992, Bush won 56 percent of the county's presidential vote.

The rest of the district is mostly rural and agricultural territory. There are a significant number of poultry and poultry-processing businesses, as well as employers in the timber and oil and gas industries.

1990 Population: 515,314. White 345,115 (67%), Black 161,458 (31%), Other 8,741 (2%). Hispanic origin 2,901 (1%). 18 and over 370,290 (72%), 62 and over 75,457 (15%). Median age: 31.

tional Guard. Even though he hung up his uniform in 1980 — his House and military careers overlapped for 14 years — Montgomery never really left the service.

A bachelor, Montgomery regards the men and women of the armed forces almost as family members, whose interests he oversees from his strategic committee positions. Yet as a lawmaking guardian, Montgomery is caring but stern. He will invest all his energies to protect and expand benefits he believes veterans have coming to them; but he fights tooth and nail against program initiatives — even those with strong constituencies — that he sees as unwarranted or fears may divert funds from established programs that he favors.

So strong is Montgomery's devotion to educational and training benefits for veterans that when Congress passed a major revision of these programs during the 100th Congress, it was named the Montgomery GI Bill. On the other hand, for four years, he blocked legislation providing compensation to cancer sufferers exposed to Agent Orange, yielding only after being outmaneuvered by Evans and other benefits supporters at the start of the 102nd Congress.

Montgomery's assertive leadership on veterans issues gives him a command over the committee he chairs. However, some members, particularly those of the Vietnam generation, bridle at Montgomery's efforts to set priorities for all veterans programs.

Evans led the fight to set up benefits for victims of Agent Orange-related diseases. A Vietnam War-era Marine veteran (he was not assigned to fight in that conflict), Evans first proposed in 1987 to provide compensation to veterans who had contracted five types of cancer linked to the dioxin-based defoliant. Montgomery opposed the measure — citing studies by the Defense Department and the Centers for Disease Control that showed no definitive evidence that the diseases were caused by Agent Orange — and supported efforts by Presidents Reagan and Bush to block the new benefits.

Montgomery insisted that his opposition was no sign of bias against Vietnam veterans. However, some veterans groups argued that Montgomery was trying to protect programs for World War II and Korean War veterans at the expense of their younger counterparts.

In early 1990, then-Veterans Affairs Secretary Edward J. Derwinski announced that compensation would be provided to Agent Orange-exposed veterans suffering from non-Hodgkin's lymphoma or soft-tissue sarcoma. Evans adopted a new approach after Montgomery blocked his more sweeping measure at the subcommittee level. His amendment to codify Derwinski's rules and to mandate a National Academy of Sciences review of Agent Orange studies was attached to a bill providing a cost of living adjustment (COLA) for recipients of veterans' retirement and disability payments. The amendment passed the Veterans' Affairs Committee in October 1990 by a 16-14 vote, a rare defeat for Montgomery.

Montgomery then tried to get the provisions stripped out. He failed, and a Senate deadlock ensued that scuttled both the COLA and Agent Orange measures for the 101st Congress. Montgomery tried to lay blame for the COLA's failure on supporters of Agent Orange benefits and proposed a clean bill in January 1991. After Evans persisted, proposing a combined COLA and Agent Orange bill, Montgomery agreed to compromise. The COLA and Agent Orange benefits passed separately.

Montgomery is far more often the advocate of veterans programs than an opponent. One of his pet projects, the enactment of a 60-year-old proposal to convert the Veterans Administration into a Cabinet-level Department of Veterans Affairs, reached fruition during the 100th Congress.

After the U.S.-led military campaign to end Iraq's occupation of Kuwait in early 1991, Montgomery constructed a $1 billion House measure to provide benefits for veterans of that conflict. The provisions of this bill were not controversial, but its funding mechanism was. Under the 1990 federal budget agreement, new entitlement spending was to be offset by an across-the-board cut or a revenue-raising change in other programs. But Montgomery promoted the benefits bill as an "emergency" measure resulting from the war, which would have permitted a waiver of the pay-as-you-go rule.

The Bush administration, backed by the leadership of the House Budget Committee, argued that the bill mainly funded expansions of existing programs, and they opposed Montgomery's funding language as a loophole that could slacken the new regimen of fiscal discipline. However, when then-Budget Committee Chairman Leon E. Panetta, D-Calif., tried to get the House to dedicate funding for the program, Montgomery cast the debate as a matter of patriotism and fairness. "All we're trying to do here is be fair to these Persian Gulf veterans, do the same thing we did for others who fought in different wars," Montgomery said.

Panetta's amendment to remove the bill's emergency spending designation was defeated by a 175-248 vote.

Although Panetta was himself highly regarded during his House tenure, he learned early in his Budget chairmanship the risks of tangling with Montgomery on veterans issues. During committee debate in early 1989 on a budget resolution for fiscal 1990, Panetta parried attempts to raise veterans' medical benefits by $600 million over the previous year's levels. Montgomery mobilized veterans to lobby for more funds.

"I sent a brigade of wheelchair people to see Panetta," Montgomery said. "He saw that we weren't just whistling 'Dixie' — that there are needs out there." Eager to avoid a floor fight, Panetta and other Budget leaders agreed to add back $525 million for the veterans programs, to be financed by a small across-the-board cut in other discretionary spending.

Prominent as he has been on Veterans' Affairs, Montgomery's star on Armed Services was eclipsed long ago. In 1985, Wisconsin Democrat Les Aspin jumped the seniority line as leader of the coup that deposed the aged and infirm Armed Services chairman, Melvin Price of Illinois. Montgomery was one of the conservative "Old Guard" that had long dominated the committee. He rarely criticizes weapons programs and has not been a dominant force in debate over spending priorities. He concentrates now on issues involving the National Guard and reserve forces.

Montgomery first ran for Congress in 1966 as a supporter of the war in Vietnam. "The time is past when we can discuss whether this is the wrong war," he said in 1967. "Our flag is committed." He visited South Vietnam several times; his exposure to Agent Orange without ill effect shaped his views on the benefits issue.

At Home: For years, Montgomery has had the best of both worlds — personal popularity in Congress and bipartisan support back home. In 1992, he won the general election with 81 percent of the vote. Before that, he had not won a primary or general election with less than 89 percent of the vote since 1968.

Montgomery's 1988 GOP opponent, Columbia contractor Jimmie Ray Bourland, was so frustrated by the lack of attention to his effort that he climbed a TV tower to protest. He soon descended back into obscurity, eventually winning 11 percent of the vote.

Montgomery was a state senator and prominent National Guard officer when he first ran for the House in 1966. The 3rd District had gone Republican on a fluke in 1964, electing little-known chicken farmer Prentiss Walker, the only Republican who had filed for Congress anywhere in the state that year. Barry Goldwater carried Mississippi easily in his 1964 presidential campaign, and he propelled Walker into office. Two years later, Walker ran for the Senate — he would have been beaten for reelection to the House anyway — leaving the 3rd open.

There were three other candidates for the Democratic House nomination in 1966, but Montgomery won with little difficulty. He drew 50.1 percent of the primary vote, avoiding a runoff.

His general-election campaign was easier. Describing himself as "a conservative Mississippi Democrat," Montgomery said he opposed the new, big-spending Great Society programs but favored older ones such as Social Security and rural electrification. He claimed that his Republican opponent, state Rep. L. L. McAllister Jr., was against all federal programs, and he linked McAllister with the national GOP, which he called the "party of Reconstruction, Depression and 'me-too' liberalism." Montgomery won every county.

Committees

Veterans' Affairs (Chairman)
Education, Training & Employment (chairman)

Armed Services (2nd of 34 Democrats)
Military Forces & Personnel; Military Installations & Facilities

Elections

1992 General		
G.V. "Sonny" Montgomery (D)	162,864	(81%)
Michael E. Williams (R)	37,710	(19%)
1992 Primary		
G.V. "Sonny" Montgomery (D)	26,468	(85%)
Henry P. Clanton (D)	4,563	(15%)
1990 General		
G.V. "Sonny" Montgomery (D)	49,162	(100%)

Previous Winning Percentages: **1988** (89%) **1986** (100%) **1984** (100%) **1982** (93%) **1980** (100%) **1978** (92%) **1976** (94%) **1974** (100%) **1972** (100%) **1970** (100%) **1968** (70%) **1966** (65%)

District Vote for President

1992
D 61,645 (33%)
R 111,222 (59%)
I 15,122 (8%)

Campaign Finance

	Receipts	Receipts from PACs	Expend-itures
1992			
Montgomery (D)	$172,603	$97,600 (57%)	$174,165
1990			
Montgomery (D)	$112,779	$55,250 (49%)	$71,181

Key Votes

1993	
Require parental notification of minors' abortions	Y
Require unpaid family and medical leave	N
Approve national "motor voter" registration bill	Y
Approve budget increasing taxes and reducing deficit	Y
Approve economic stimulus plan	N
1992	
Approve balanced-budget constitutional amendment	Y
Close down space station program	Y
Approve U.S. aid for former Soviet Union	Y
Allow shifting funds from defense to domestic programs	N
1991	
Extend unemployment benefits using deficit financing	N
Approve waiting period for handgun purchases	N
Authorize use of force in Persian Gulf	Y

Voting Studies

	Presidential Support		Party Unity		Conservative Coalition	
Year	**S**	**O**	**S**	**O**	**S**	**O**
1992	66	34	65	35	88	13
1991	66	33	53	44	97	3
1990	56	44	60	37	94	6
1989	78	22	57	41	98	2
1988	45	53	64	34	89	8
1987	53	43	56	38	93	5
1986	58	42	53	45	92	8
1985	66	34	53	44	98	0
1984	59	41	34	59	97	3
1983	68	30	28	67	94	3
1982	74	23	29	66	90	5
1981	78	21	26	68	97	3

Interest Group Ratings

Year	ADA	AFL-CIO	CCUS	ACU
1992	30	25	88	64
1991	5	17	90	70
1990	22	25	71	63
1989	10	25	90	59
1988	25	57	71	71
1987	16	19	71	65
1986	5	29	76	86
1985	15	18	82	76
1984	0	31	50	70
1983	10	13	80	96
1982	5	5	73	91
1981	0	13	83	93

4 Mike Parker (D)

Of Brookhaven — Elected 1988; 3rd Term

Born: Oct. 31, 1949, Laurel, Miss.
Education: William Carey College, B.A. 1970.
Occupation: Funeral director.
Family: Wife, Rosemary Prather; three children.
Religion: Presbyterian.
Political Career: No previous office.
Capitol Office: 1410 Longworth Bldg. 20515; 225-5865.

In Washington: While Parker is not known for high-profile legislative achievements in Congress, neither does he attempt to lay claim to any. Instead, he proudly acknowledges that his first priority is constituent service.

"As a congressman, my focus has been on economic development efforts within my district along with an unequaled devotion to constituent casework rather than legislative initiatives," Parker said.

More than most, Parker makes it a point to keep in close touch with his mostly conservative district — through six district offices and a mobile office.

Keeping his ear to the ground has helped him look out for constituents and to reflect their political bent.

In the 102nd Congress, Parker came to the aid of a county school system in the 4th. He pushed through a bill to provide relief for the Wilkinson County School District, one of the nation's poorest, after it was discovered the school system had paid too much in taxes. The statute of limitations for correcting the overpayment had run out, and the only way to secure a refund was through an act of Congress.

Parker, a member of both the Budget and the Public Works and Transportation committees, planned to push hard in the 103rd Congress for the not necessarily consistent goals of deficit reduction and full funding for the $151 billion highway law enacted in the 102nd.

Then a member of the Public Works Subcommittee on Surface Transportation (he is now on the Aviation, Economic Development and Water Resources subcommittees), Parker pushed for provisions that would rebuild the nation's roads, including those at home. In Parker's district, where most of the roads are still two lanes wide, funding would provide jobs and modernize an outdated highway system.

Parker also reflects the clear conservative bent of his constituents — a fact that frequently puts him at odds with House Democratic leaders.

He was a strong supporter of many of President Bush's positions, and he has voted with Republicans about half the time on issues that split the two major parties.

"Maybe that's why I'm not on the leadership track," Parker said.

Parker was one of only 10 Southern Democrats voting against the 1990 civil rights bill, although more than 40 percent of Parker's constituency is African-American.

Since 1991, Parker has been pushing for the establishment of the Margaret Walker Alexander National African-American Research Center at Jackson State University. The center would be named for the acclaimed black Mississippi author of "Jubilee." Parker reintroduced the bill in the 103rd.

On another vote important to Democratic leaders — approval of the tax-raising 1990 bipartisan budget compromise — Parker voted "yea"; not coincidentally, he got a seat on the Budget Committee at the start of the 102nd Congress.

Some Republicans who knew businessman Parker before his 1988 House bid had hoped he would seek the GOP nomination. He did not, but did give himself the rather laborious label of "Mike Parker, mainstream Mississippi Democrat." Still, in the campaign, he tried to reassure the party faithful. "I support the broad principles of the Democratic Party," he said. "The party that gave us Social Security, Medicaid, Medicare, veterans' benefits ... gave us [Rep. G. V.] 'Sonny' Montgomery and [Sen.] John [C.] Stennis."

As a freshman, Parker took seats on Public Works and Veterans' Affairs, where partisan distinctions are less obvious and ideological sparring less prevalent than in the House as a whole. There, he worked to secure funds for several highway and airport development projects. He also pushed for continued funding of the Natchez National Historical Park.

At Home: Parker was a political novice when he began his 1988 campaign, but as a funeral home director and one-time drama student, he was no neophyte at presenting himself to the public. Parker's 55 percent showing — which came in the face of a solid Bush victory in

Mississippi 4

Southwest — Jackson

The 4th holds a mixture of old Southern charm and New South savvy.

Natchez, with a population of just over 19,000, sits on the banks of the Mississippi River in Adams County and is the embodiment of the old South. Dripping with Spanish moss, it is home to 500 antebellum mansions ever-popular with tourists.

In the recession of the late 1980s and early 1990s, the southwestern counties of the 4th were hit hard. While its oil and gas industry suffered, Natchez's economy stayed afloat with other enterprises, with tourism topping the list. The small river city and its antebellum homes attract 150,000 people a year. Other residents find work in the timber industry in such businesses as wood processing and paper production. One such facility in Brookhaven in Lincoln County converts logs into wood chips.

North of Natchez is Jackson, the state capital, in Hinds County. Burned during the Civil War, Jackson has refashioned itself into an urban center and the state's largest city, with a population of nearly 200,000. About 56 percent of the city's population is black, up from 47 percent in 1980.

Jackson and surrounding Hinds County gives Republicans a strong political base to build on. Jackson is home to many of the state GOP's financial kingpins, and Hinds County has not voted Democratic in a presidential election since 1956. But the part of Hinds County that is in the neighboring 2nd is Democratic territory, which helped keep George Bush's 1992 margin to about 2,000 votes over Democrat Bill Clinton.

Redistricting may have made that GOP base even more formidable. The 4th picked up most of Republican-leaning Jones County, including the industrial city of Laurel, population 19,000, and its timber-related industry fueled by its proximity to Mississippi's Piney Woods. Redistricting also moved less-affluent black sections of Jackson into the 2nd District, leaving the more well-to-do black sections of the city in the much more conservative 4th.

Black voters, however, have shown political strength in the 4th, making it winnable for any Democrats who could link black voters with rural white voters. In the 1970s, independent black candidates were a force. In 1972, 1978 and 1980, independent black challengers siphoned enough votes from Democratic House nominees to elect Republican Sen. Thad Cochran and Jon C. Hinson. But the GOP lost the 4th after a sex scandal drove Hinson from office in April 1981.

Along with the Gulf Coast 5th, the Jackson-based 4th is the backbone of the GOP resurgence in Mississippi. These are the only two districts in the state in modern times to elect two Republican representatives in a row, and the 4th is the base of Cochran, who in 1979 became the state's first GOP senator in more than a century. Yet Rep. Parker — and Wayne Dowdy before him — have built a winning coalition of rural white and black votes and have kept the 4th in the Democratic column since 1981.

1990 Population: 513,853. White 301,976 (59%), Black 209,352 (41%), Other 2,225 (<1%). Hispanic origin 2,135 (<1%). 18 and over 367,753 (72%), 62 and over 81,456 (16%). Median age: 32.

the 4th — was proof he possesses campaign skills beyond his political years.

An early wave of TV ads helped Parker distinguish himself from more than a dozen contenders, Democrats and Republicans, after Democratic Rep. Wayne Dowdy launched a Senate bid. Drawing on sizable personal loans, Parker touted his business background and dedication to "family" values.

In the primary, Parker ran second to Jackson attorney Brad Pigott, who had better party connections. In the runoff, Parker won endorsements from the third- and fourth-place primary finishers and stormed past Pigott.

Parker's strong runoff showing made him the November favorite against GOP nominee Thomas Collins, but in the conservative-minded 4th (which has elected GOP House members in the recent past), Parker had to run a careful general-election campaign.

Collins, who spent nearly eight years as a POW during the Vietnam War, had significant patriotic appeal — a real plus against the backdrop of a presidential campaign that focused on flag-waving issues such as the Pledge of Allegiance. And Collins' appeal to veterans was enhanced by his recent service as director of the Mississippi Veterans Farm and Home Board.

Collins tried to tie Parker to Democratic presidential nominee Michael S. Dukakis, but Parker disconnected himself with an ad that said he was not endorsing Dukakis. Parker's blunt denial of his party's national nominee temporarily infuriated some local party activists. But if it struck some as disloyal, Parker's move was not a dramatic shift in his campaign, which never had embraced the national Democratic agenda.

Parker, who comes from a Republican-leaning county in the southern half of the 4th, was actually very close to Collins on a number of national issues. Both supported the Strategic Defense Initiative and military aid for the Nicaraguan contras. And Parker, son of a Baptist preacher, also spoke in favor of organized prayer in schools.

Stressing the need for "business principles" in Washington, Parker was successful at adding to his rural base the votes of many business-oriented Republicans in Hinds County (Jackson), home to roughly half of the district's voters. Parker won by 11 percentage points and was virtually unopposed in 1990. In 1992, he swept the district with 67 percent of the vote.

Committees

Budget (12th of 26 Democrats)

Public Works & Transportation (15th of 39 Democrats)
Aviation; Economic Development; Water Resources & the Environment

Elections

1992 General		
Mike Parker (D)	130,927	(67%)
Jack L. McMillan (R)	43,705	(22%)
Liz Gilchrist (I)	10,523	(5%)
James H. Meredith (I)	9,389	(5%)
1990 General		
Mike Parker (D)	57,137	(81%)
Jerry Parks (R)	13,754	(19%)

Previous Winning Percentage: 1988 (55%)

District Vote for President

1992	
D	84,089 (41%)
R	102,666 (50%)
I	16,744 (8%)

Campaign Finance

	Receipts	Receipts from PACs	Expend-itures
1992			
Parker (D)	$416,677	$240,200 (58%)	$156,969
1990			
Parker (D)	$526,415	$286,473 (54%)	$479,651

Key Votes

1993	
Require parental notification of minors' abortions	Y
Require unpaid family and medical leave	N
Approve national "motor voter" registration bill	Y
Approve budget increasing taxes and reducing deficit	Y
Approve economic stimulus plan	N
1992	
Approve balanced-budget constitutional amendment	Y
Close down space station program	Y
Approve U.S. aid for former Soviet Union	Y
Allow shifting funds from defense to domestic programs	N
1991	
Extend unemployment benefits using deficit financing	N
Approve waiting period for handgun purchases	N
Authorize use of force in Persian Gulf	Y

Voting Studies

	Presidential Support		Party Unity		Conservative Coalition	
Year	S	O	S	O	S	O
1992	63	36	62	37	88	13
1991	58	41	50	47	95	3
1990	56	44	52	46	96	4
1989	71	23	47	45	93	5

Interest Group Ratings

Year	ADA	AFL-CIO	CCUS	ACU
1992	30	25	88	68
1991	20	33	80	75
1990	22	25	79	63
1989	20	27	100	68

5 Gene Taylor (D)

Of Bay St. Louis — Elected 1989; 2nd Full Term

Born: Sept. 17, 1953, New Orleans, La.
Education: Tulane U., B.A. 1976; U. of Southern Mississippi, Gulf Park, 1978-80.
Military Service: Coast Guard Reserve, 1971-84.
Occupation: Sales representative.
Family: Wife, Margaret Gordon; three children.
Religion: Roman Catholic.
Political Career: Bay St. Louis City Council, 1981-83; Miss. Senate, 1983-89; Democratic nominee for U.S. House, 1988.
Capitol Office: 215 Cannon Bldg. 20515; 225-5772.

In Washington: Before Taylor won an October 1989 special election to succeed the late Rep. Larkin Smith, the GOP held the 5th for more than 16 years; George Bush took 69 percent in the old 5th District in 1988 and 54 percent in 1992, making it one of the strongest Bush districts in the country that still elected a Democrat to the House.

As a result, Taylor would be expected to have an independent, conservative voting record, and for the most part, he has.

Early in the 103rd Congress, Taylor was one of only a few Democrats who opposed President Clinton on both his budget resolution and his economic stimulus package.

During the Bush administration, Taylor sided almost as often with Republicans as with Democrats. A member of the Armed Services Committee, Taylor in 1990 rejected cutting funds for the Strategic Defense Initiative. On the proposed Civil Rights Act of 1990 and the effort to override Bush's veto of family leave legislation, Taylor voted "no."

He supported Bush on those votes on which Bush took a position 49 percent of the time in 1990, 55 percent in 1991 and 58 percent in 1992 — the last being one of the top scores among House Democrats.

Yet in January 1991, Taylor voted against the resolution authorizing Bush to commit U.S. troops to war against Iraq. He said government often finds "the most costly way to accomplish our goals," adding, "Must that apply to the waste of young men and women as well? True conservatives know the value of conserving all of our resources, not just our money."

Taylor had sought a seat on Armed Services — and was promised one by the Democratic leadership during his 1989 campaign — in order to oversee the interests of such 5th District military facilities as Camp Shelby near Hattiesburg and the proposed Navy homeport in Pascagoula.

On the committee, Taylor has aligned himself with the bloc of centrist Democrats that had been headed by its chairman, Les Aspin of Wisconsin, who is now the defense secretary. But while he has generally shown himself to be a supporter of military programs, he has also been critical of weapons systems that fall behind and run over budget.

During one hearing on the troubled C-17 military transport plane in March 1993, after Air Force officers described the program as "on track" and having turned the corner on its problems, Taylor demanded, "How many corners are there in this program?"

During his first term, Taylor cannily tapped the support of a powerful Mississippian, Appropriations Committee Chairman Jamie L. Whitten, to delay the closure of an ammunition plant in his district. "I'm a little bitty fish, but I've got some big fish helping me," he said.

Another big fish Taylor knows is Michigan Democrat John D. Dingell, chairman of the Energy and Commerce Committee. Taylor has a special connection to the chairman: His father served as an Army sergeant under then-Lt. Dingell in World War II.

While Taylor knows he often has to vote with Republicans to keep his seat, he is also able on occasion to show that he is a full member of his own party.

He introduced a bill to deny a government car and chauffeur to House political party whips — a bipartisan move on its face, but since Majority Whip David E. Bonior of Michigan had already given up the privileges, the bill affected only Minority Whip Newt Gingrich of Georgia. The bill went nowhere, but the pressure it generated forced Gingrich to grudgingly give up both driver and car.

On the Merchant Marine and Fisheries Committee, Taylor looks out for the interests of the shipbuilders, shrimpers and fishermen of his Gulf Coast district.

Taylor sponsored a bill in the 102nd Congress that reversed a law prohibiting U.S.-flagged oceangoing cruise ships to offer gambling. Foreign-flagged ships already had

Mississippi 5

Southeast — Gulf Coast; Hattiesburg

At the core of the 5th's economy is defense-related industry, so much so that it would be hard to imagine the district without it.

Some observers estimate that at least half the district's residents have some connection to one of these enterprises. The 5th is home to the state's biggest private employer, Ingalls Shipbuilding, a division of Litton Industries, located in Pascagoula (Jackson County). It employs about 15,000 people.

In 1992, the city of 26,000 saw the opening of Naval Station Pascagoula at Singing River Island. The facility employs about 1,100 military personnel and will eventually employ about 150 civilians.

The Gulf Coast counties, with their white sand beaches and resort cities, bear little resemblance to the rest of the state. The Harrison County cities of Gulfport and Biloxi attract thousands of tourists each year. The area is also home to gulf shrimpers and seafood-processing plants. Gulfport is the site of the annual four-day Mississippi Deep Sea Fishing Rodeo held during the week of July 4.

Biloxi is also home of Keesler Air Force Base, the premier training center for the Air Force and one of the four largest bases in the country. Keesler employs about 7,100 military personnel and nearly 5,000 civilians, and specializes in communications, electronics and medical training. Beauvoir, the last home of Jefferson Davis, the president of the Confederacy, is also in Biloxi.

In neighboring Hancock County is the Stennis Space Center, named for the late Sen. John C. Stennis, who represented the state from 1947 to 1989. A division of NASA, the center tests rocket engines.

Hattiesburg, the seat of Forrest County, is the sole population center in the northern part of the 5th. The leading employer in the predominantly white-collar town is the University of Southern Mississippi, with 12,300 students. The tier of counties above the coast — George, Stone, Pearl River, Greene, Perry, Forrest and Lamar — are part of the poorer Piney Woods region, where the economy is driven by the production of wood products, poultry and dairy farming.

In addition, the textile industry has also been a significant employer in the district with several manufacturing plants.

Mississippi's long-dormant Republican Party made its initial inroads in the 5th, a solidly conservative region where Democrats are no longer competitive in national elections. Ronald Reagan carried Mississippi in 1980 only because of a 30,000-vote edge in the 5th. As George Bush carried the state easily in 1988, the 5th was his strongest district. In 1992, Bush carried every county in the district.

Yet while the district has been a GOP beachhead, it is not impregnable, evidenced by Democratic Rep. Taylor's special election victory in 1989, his smashing re-election win in 1990 (81 percent of the vote) and his comfortable victory in 1992 with 63 percent of the vote.

1990 Population: 514,656. White 402,991 (78%), Black 102,922 (20%), Other 8,743 (2%). Hispanic origin 5,778 (1%). 18 and over 368,541 (72%), 62 and over 69,164 (13%). Median age: 31.

gambling on board, which he said put American ships at a serious competitive disadvantage. The bill was signed by Bush in March 1992; U.S.-flagged ships operating outside the three-mile state limit are now allowed to offer gambling if it is not the main purpose of the trip.

At Home: The Democratic Party was cool to Taylor in his first two campaigns for the 5th — in 1988 and the special election the following year to succeed Smith, who died in an August 1989 plane crash. But he drew a respectable 45 percent against Smith in 1988, when both were competing for the seat vacated by Senate aspirant Trent Lott. He captured 65 percent of the vote in dispatching Lott's longtime Hill aide, Tom Anderson Jr., in a 1989 special election. And he drew 81 percent against Smith's widow, Sheila, to win re-election in 1990.

A sales representative for a company that manufactured cardboard boxes, Taylor entered politics in 1981 to run for the Bay St. Louis City Council. In 1983, he won election to the state Senate. He focused on education issues, such as raises and merit pay for teachers.

In 1988, Taylor was considered the strongest candidate in the Democratic field for the open 5th, and he easily dispatched Hattiesburg District Attorney Glenn White in a runoff. But he seemed slow to organize for the fall; national party sources concluded that they could better spend their money elsewhere.

Taylor tried to make political capital out of the absence of national Democratic support. He told voters he was being snubbed by party officials for his refusal to moderate his conservative posture on issues such as aid to the

Nicaraguan contras (which he backed) and federal funding for abortion (which he opposed). But Taylor had trouble raising money and was outspent by Smith by more than 3-to-1.

Taylor was heavily outspent in 1989 as well, but Anderson had an unflattering image as Lott's "anointed" successor and Democratic state Attorney General Mike Moore, who had the backing of organized labor, Mississippi's main association of educators and Democratic Gov. Ray Mabus, struck many voters as politically overambitious; he had just been elected attorney general in 1987. In the primary, Taylor took 42 percent to Anderson's 37 percent and Moore's 21 percent. The one-on-one match-up with Anderson was a Taylor runaway.

The size of Taylor's victory was due in part to a feeling among many voters that Smith's widow should have been given the GOP nomination. She was in 1990, but it quickly became apparent her chance came a year too late.

In 1992, it was assumed that Taylor's vote against the use of military force in the Persian Gulf would hurt in the 5th, a district economically dependent on military facilities and the shipbuilding industry. Republicans nominated retired Air Force Gen. Paul Harvey, former commander of Keesler Air Force Base in the district, to challenge him. However, Taylor's conservative record continued to hold him in good stead with voters, who returned him to Washington with 63 percent of the vote.

Committees

Armed Services (19th of 34 Democrats)
Military Acquisition; Military Installations & Facilities

Merchant Marine & Fisheries (13th of 29 Democrats)
Coast Guard & Navigation; Fisheries Management; Merchant Marine

Elections

1992 General		
Gene Taylor (D)	120,766	(63%)
Paul Harvey (R)	67,619	(35%)
Shawn O'Hara (I)	2,673	(1%)
1990 General		
Gene Taylor (D)	89,926	(81%)
Sheila Smith (R)	20,588	(19%)

Previous Winning Percentage: 1989 * (65%)

** Special election.*

District Vote for President

	1992
D	56,411 (32%)
R	96,589 (54%)
I	24,248 (14%)

Campaign Finance

	Receipts	Receipts from PACs		Expend-itures
1992				
Taylor (D)	$340,357	$158,535	(47%)	$340,311
Harvey (R)	$237,123	$20,310	(9%)	$236,140
O'Hara (I)	$7,114	0		$100
1990				
Taylor (D)	$316,052	$143,426	(45%)	$322,048
Smith (R)	$205,068	$10,400	(5%)	$205,067

Key Votes

1993	
Require parental notification of minors' abortions	Y
Require unpaid family and medical leave	Y
Approve national "motor voter" registration bill	Y
Approve budget increasing taxes and reducing deficit	N
Approve economic stimulus plan	N
1992	
Approve balanced-budget constitutional amendment	Y
Close down space station program	N
Approve U.S. aid for former Soviet Union	N
Allow shifting funds from defense to domestic programs	N
1991	
Extend unemployment benefits using deficit financing	N
Approve waiting period for handgun purchases	N
Authorize use of force in Persian Gulf	N

Voting Studies

	Presidential Support		Party Unity		Conservative Coalition	
Year	S	O	S	O	S	O
1992	58	42	57	42	83	17
1991	55	42	50	49	86	14
1990	49	51	57	43	93	7
1989	68 †	32 †	67 †	33 †	71 †	29 †

† Not eligible for all recorded votes.

Interest Group Ratings

Year	ADA	AFL-CIO	CCUS	ACU
1992	30	50	50	76
1991	15	33	80	84
1990	28	50	64	63
1989	--	100	--	100

Missouri

STATE DATA

Governor: Mel Carnahan (D)
First elected: 1992
Length of term: 4 years
Term expires: 1/97
Salary: $88,541
Term limit: 2 terms
Phone: (314) 751-3222
Born: Feb. 11, 1934; Birch Tree, Mo.
Education: George Washington U., B.A. 1954; U. of Missouri, J.D. 1959
Military Service: Air Force, 1954-56
Occupation: Lawyer
Family: Wife, Jean Carpenter; four children
Religion: Baptist
Political Career: Municipal judge, 1961-62; Mo. House, 1963-67; Rolla School Board, 1976-80; Mo. treasurer, 1981-85; lieutenant governor, 1989-93; sought Democratic nomination for Mo. Senate, 1968; sought Democratic nomination for governor, 1984

Lt. Gov.: Roger Wilson (D)
First elected: 1992
Length of term: 4 years
Term expires: 1/97
Salary: $54,343
Phone: (314) 751-4727

State election official: (314) 751-4875
Democratic headquarters: (314) 636-5241
Republican headquarters: (314) 636-3146

REDISTRICTING

Missouri retained its nine House seats in reapportionment. The legislature passed the map May 16, 1991; the governor signed it July 8.

STATE LEGISLATURE

General Assembly. Meets January-May.

Senate: 34 members, 4-year terms
1992 breakdown: 19D, 15R; 33 men, 1 woman; 31 whites, 3 blacks
Salary: $22,863
Phone: (314) 751-3766

House of Representatives: 163 members, 2-year terms
1992 breakdown: 100D, 62R, 1 vacancy; 126 men, 37 women; 150 whites, 13 blacks
Salary: $22,863
Phone: (314) 751-3659

URBAN STATISTICS

City	Pop.
Kansas City	435,146
Mayor Emanuel Cleaver II, N-P	
St. Louis	396,685
Mayor Freeman Bosley Jr., D	
Springfield	140,494
Mayor N. L. McCartney, N-P	
Independence	112,301
Mayor Bill Carpenter, N-P	

U.S. CONGRESS

Senate: 0 D, 2 R
House: 6 D, 3 R

TERM LIMITS

For Congress: Yes *
Senate: 2 terms
House: 4 terms
For state offices: Yes *
Senate: 2 consecutive terms
House: 2 consecutive terms

** Take effect when 50% of states have adopted term limits*

ELECTIONS

1992 Presidential Vote

Bill Clinton	44.1%
George Bush	33.9%
Ross Perot	21.7%

1988 Presidential Vote

George Bush	52%
Michael S. Dukakis	48%

1984 Presidential Vote

Ronald Reagan	60%
Walter F. Mondale	40%

POPULATION

1990 population		5,117,073
1980 population		4,916,686
Percent change		+4.1%
Rank among states:		15
White		88%
Black		11%
Hispanic		1%
Asian or Pacific islander		1%
Urban		69%
Rural		31%
Born in state		70%
Foreign-born		2%
Under age 18	1,314,826	26%
Ages 18-64	3,084,566	60%
65 and older	717,681	14%
Median age		33.5

MISCELLANEOUS

Capital: Jefferson City
Number of counties: 114
Per capita income: $17,842 (1991)
Rank among states: 25
Total area: 69,697 sq. miles
Rank among states: 19

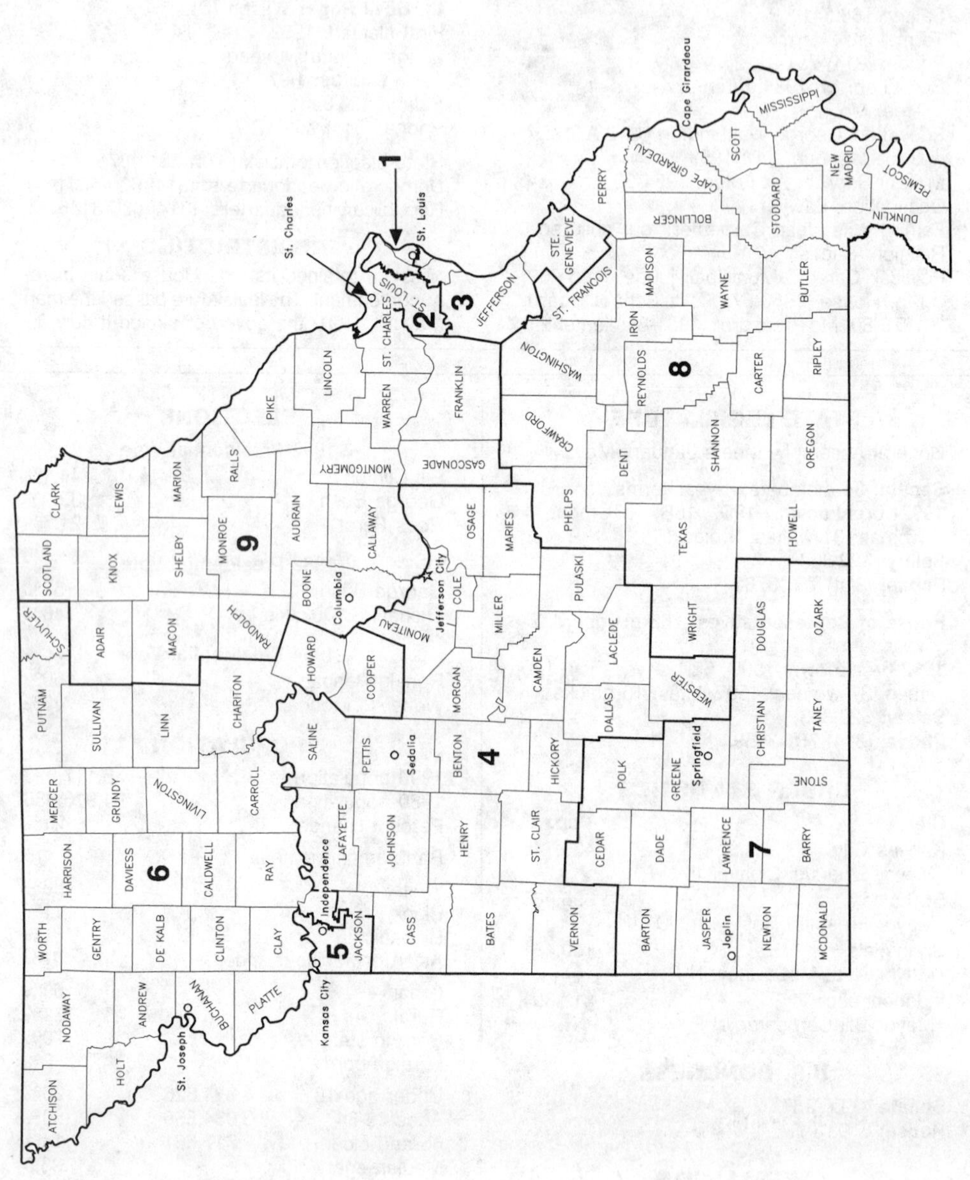

1
2
3
4
5
6
7
8
9
St. Charles
St. Louis
Cape Girardeau
Columbia
Jefferson City
Sedalia
Springfield
Independence
Kansas City
St. Joseph
Joplin
MISSISSIPPI
SCOTT
CAPE GIRARDEAU
PERRY
NEW MADRID
PEMISCOT
DUNKLIN
STODDARD
BOLLINGER
STE. GENEVIEVE
ST. LOUIS
JEFFERSON
ST. FRANCOIS
MADISON
WAYNE
BUTLER
IRON
ST. CHARLES
WASHINGTON
REYNOLDS
CARTER
RIPLEY
LINCOLN
PIKE
WARREN
FRANKLIN
CRAWFORD
SHANNON
OREGON
RALLS
MONTGOMERY
GASCONADE
DENT
MARION
AUDRAIN
CALLAWAY
OSAGE
MARIES
PHELPS
TEXAS
HOWELL
CLARK
LEWIS
SCOTLAND
KNOX
SHELBY
MONROE
BOONE
COLE
PULASKI
SCHUYLER
ADAIR
MACON
RANDOLPH
MONITEAU
MILLER
WRIGHT
DOUGLAS
OZARK
HOWARD
COOPER
MORGAN
CAMDEN
LACLEDE
WEBSTER
PUTNAM
SULLIVAN
LINN
CHARITON
SALINE
PETTIS
BENTON
HICKORY
DALLAS
CHRISTIAN
TANEY
MERCER
GRUNDY
LIVINGSTON
CARROLL
LAFAYETTE
JOHNSON
HENRY
ST. CLAIR
POLK
GREENE
STONE
HARRISON
DAVIESS
CALDWELL
RAY
CEDAR
DADE
LAWRENCE
BARRY
WORTH
GENTRY
DE KALB
CLINTON
CLAY
JACKSON
CASS
BATES
VERNON
BARTON
JASPER
NEWTON
MCDONALD
NODAWAY
ANDREW
BUCHANAN
PLATTE
HOLT
ATCHISON

John C. Danforth (R)

Of Newburg — Elected 1976; 3rd Term

Born: Sept. 5, 1936, St. Louis, Mo.
Education: Princeton U., A.B. 1958; Yale U., B.D., LL.B. 1963.
Occupation: Lawyer; clergyman.
Family: Wife, Sally Dobson; five children.
Religion: Episcopalian.
Political Career: Mo. attorney general, 1969-77; GOP nominee for U.S. Senate, 1970.
Capitol Office: 249 Russell Bldg. 20510; 224-6154.

In Washington: In a chamber that glorifies individualism, Danforth will always stand out.

Heir to the Ralston Purina fortune and a former Wall Street lawyer, he is among the wealthiest members of the Senate. He is also the only ordained minister in the chamber.

Danforth's ideology is distinct. Obvious in his battle for civil rights, famine relief and even cable reregulation is a compassion for those less fortunate that sometimes puts him in positions at odds with his conservative Republican colleagues.

But Danforth came through in a big way for the party in 1991. He shepherded Supreme Court Justice Clarence Thomas through one of the most heated confirmation battles in congressional history. Although Danforth was motivated as much by personal fealty — Thomas was a longtime friend and former employee — as by party loyalty, the result was the same: a face-saving victory for Republican President George Bush.

Danforth demonstrated his individuality again early in 1993 when he announced that he would not seek a fourth term. Danforth said he plans to return to St. Louis and become more active in the Episcopalian ministry; he may also resume his legal career. "I would rather start a new phase in my life when I am 58 than when I am 64," he said in February.

It is rare for an incumbent to announce so early in an election cycle his decision to retire. But Danforth's announcement was even more unusual in that he had no apparent political problem heading into 1994. After narrowly winning a second term in 1982, Danforth rebounded with a solid victory in 1988; he would have been a heavy favorite had he sought a fourth term.

The decision and its early announcement are typical of Danforth's character: Though he can be as calculating as any politician when pursuing a cause, he is driven by more than political concerns. He has survived unblemished through more than two decades of public service precisely because he operates on his own wavelength.

Danforth's ability to remain above the fray even when enmeshed in it was apparent in the controversy surrounding Thomas' nomination. Danforth was Thomas' most visible defender from the start, accompanying him on visits to senators' offices and taking to the floor to respond to any attacks leveled against him. He sat behind Thomas during Senate Judiciary Committee confirmation hearings, occasionally signaling members when he thought their questions or comments were unfair.

When Anita F. Hill, a law professor and former employee of Thomas' at the Department of Education and Equal Employment Opportunity Commission, accused Thomas of sexual harassment two days before the scheduled Senate confirmation vote, Danforth initially downplayed the development. But he angrily defended Thomas — and decried Hill's charges — when the controversy snowballed and Republicans reluctantly delayed the Senate vote on Thomas' nomination so the Judiciary Committee could conduct hearings on the charges.

Danforth maintained that Hill's story was not credible: "This is a very weak but sensational case." During the Thomas-Hill hearings, he released an affidavit from a former coworker of Hill's that raised questions about some of her testimony and her veracity.

Throughout the ordeal, few people challenged his role in defending Thomas. Although some Democratic senators chastised Danforth for releasing the affidavit, it was other Republican senators — namely Judiciary members Arlen Specter of Pennsylvania and Orrin G. Hatch of Utah — who bore the brunt of the criticism for bitter attacks on Hill's character.

Danforth emerged from the battle, resolved Oct. 15 on a 52-48 vote confirming Thomas, unscathed. He was seen not as a part of the Senate's "good-old-boy" network decried once Hill's allegations were made public, but as a loyal friend.

Danforth's championing of Thomas paved the way for another high-profile legislative victory for the Missouri Republican in 1991: a compromise with the Bush administration on civil rights legislation. Having saved Bush from an embarrassing setback, Danforth found himself in a position to broker a deal with the Republican president who had vetoed civil rights legislation a year earlier.

Bush and Senate Republicans were reluctant at first to compromise on a bill aimed at reversing several Supreme Court job-bias rulings. Their argument in 1990 that the proposal would encourage hiring quotas had given Republicans an explosive campaign issue. Danforth pursued a deal with the White House early in 1991, but he halted negotiations in June. Compromise seemed out of reach even when negotiations resumed after Thomas' confirmation. Danforth pressed on, however, and in late October the Bush administration found what it considered an acceptable middle ground.

Some said that political circumstances of the day prompted the deal. One section of the bill allowed women to collect damages for sexual harassment on the job, a tough measure to vote against in light of the Thomas-Hill hearings. And Bush, proud of his unbroken string of sustained vetoes, was not assured victory in a second civil rights veto fight. Danforth was reluctant to take any credit for the agreement, but Senate leaders on both sides of the aisle said Danforth laid the groundwork that led to the deal.

Danforth also played a major role in the battle to reregulate the cable industry. He pushed hard for the bill despite opposition from Bush and his GOP colleagues, who saw the measure as unnecessary government interference in business.

Danforth tried to persuade Republicans to his side. "This is not wild-eyed regulation," he said after the Senate overwhelmingly approved the final version of the bill in September 1992. But Bush could not be convinced that cable reregulation was necessary. He vetoed the bill, and Danforth was among the Senate Republicans who voted with the majority in the first and only successful override of a Bush veto.

Danforth's successes stand in contrast to the acutely personal disappointment he suffered in the final act of the tax-reform drama in 1986. The problem then was not that Danforth, a member of the Finance Committee, opposed the conference version of the tax-revision bill, or that he switched from supporter to critic because tax-accounting changes in the final version of the bill adversely affected McDonnell Douglas Corp. and other major defense contractors in Missouri.

It was the manner in which Danforth both supported and opposed the bill that proved disturbing to colleagues. In both cases, he took a strongly moralistic approach in criticizing those who disagreed with his views. Some of his colleagues suspected that Danforth was using a tone of righteous indignation to cover his pique at losing out on his home-state concerns.

Important as he has been on Finance, Danforth's first committee responsibility has been on Commerce, Science and Transportation. In addition to his efforts to reregulate the cable industry, Danforth has been active in the areas of airline regulation and auto safety, two more issues that put him at odds with Republican administrations.

Danforth's reluctance to abandon regulation was most apparent on the issue of auto safety. During the 101st and 102nd Congresses, Danforth stepped up congressional efforts to encourage the installation of air bags in passenger cars and light trucks. He sponsored a bill in 1991 to require air bags in all such vehicles by 1995; in 1990, he had pushed an amendment on fuel efficiency legislation to give credit to automakers that installed air bags in their vehicles.

Danforth has similarly involved himself in the airline industry and efforts to reregulate it. Concerned about the continued industry shakeout — more and more carriers filing for bankruptcy — he has started to promote legislation to ensure competition. In 1990, Danforth strongly backed successful efforts to impose new airline ticket fees of up to $3 per flight to pay for facility improvements.

Early in the 103rd Congress, Danforth played a role in the debate over a bill to create a long-delayed congressional commission to study the airline and aerospace industries. Danforth insisted the bill was unnecessary, given the more than 50 federal studies that had already been conducted on the industry, but when passage became inevitable he successfully amended the measure to increase the number of non-voting members on the committee from nine to 11.

Danforth has encouraged the Senate to act before the commission completes its study on two bills he has sponsored. One calls for a probe of European subsidies of Airbus, which competes with the commercial aviation division of McDonnell Douglas headquartered in Missouri; the second would create a government-subsidized aerospace research consortium modeled after Sematech, the semiconductor research consortium.

Some of Danforth's legislative efforts reflect the humanitarian and moral ideals that led him into the ministry. Deeply concerned about world hunger, he helped win $150 million in emergency food aid for Africa after touring the drought-ravaged continent early in 1984. He also was active in pushing the Reagan administration to step up the pace of nuclear arms reduction talks with the Soviet Union. In 1990, he offered "living-will" legislation to allow people in advance of a medical crisis to dictate what kind of treatment they would want.

Danforth has also been disturbed by the growing negativity of political campaigns and has pushed for revisions in their financing and conduct. In an attempt to raise the level of political dialogue, Danforth has pushed legislation to require federal candidates to appear personally in ads that refer to their opponents and to require television stations to offer free air time for candidates to respond to direct attacks. In 1992, Danforth won approval of a non-binding measure urging candidates for office to suggest ways to cut the deficit and debate the issue during their campaigns. The measure also urged that the three presidential candidates agree to a formal discussion dedicated entirely to the deficit.

At Home: A former Wall Street lawyer and Ralston Purina heir hardly seems the type to represent a state whose political hero is Harry S Truman, champion of the common folk. Moreover, Danforth's air of detachment struck some as a sign of political vulnerability. Before his re-election in 1988, there was talk of his spot being ripe for the taking. But Danforth showed he had learned the lessons of his first re-election (which he won with just 51 percent). He raised millions of dollars early and made manifest to all his intent to fight for his job.

Partly because of Danforth's early effort, the Democrats failed to field a challenger in his weight class. Prominent Democratic Rep. Richard A. Gephardt decided to run for president and popular six-term Democratic Rep. Ike Skelton chose to stay in the House. The party's top state official, Lt. Gov. Harriett Woods, was retiring and opted to skip the race. She had given Danforth his scare in 1982, but had also lost a bruising Senate race in 1986 to former Gov. Christopher S. Bond.

So the party turned to youthful state Sen. Jay Nixon, a 32-year-old in his first legislative term. Nixon struggled to raise a quarter of the money Danforth had at his disposal. He also struggled to find an effective theme. Danforth never had to run hard. He won all 114 counties, losing only in the city of St. Louis. His share was 68 percent, and he drew over a third of a million votes more than George Bush.

Danforth's patrician pedigree was no hindrance in his early political career; he won his first election in 1968 as an outsider, a young insurgent vowing to rid the state attorney general's office of deadwood that had collected during a succession of Democratic administrations.

But in 1982, after eight years in state office and six more in Washington, Danforth struck many Missouri voters not as a reformer but as a wealthy man distant from their economic concerns. That was why he was nearly ambushed by Woods, a clever liberal Democrat who sold herself as a populist under the slogan "Give 'em hell, Harriett."

Woods' entry had initially brought little cheer to party leaders. She had gained valuable media exposure representing a liberal St. Louis County constituency, but offered a record of questionable appeal to rural and conservative voters and to business interests the Democrats needed to compete with Danforth's fundraising. Woods also supported legalized abortion and the use of busing as a tool to desegregate schools.

But Woods managed to portray herself as an average working person and hit Danforth as an aristocrat who supported cuts in health care, social services and education. As the only female Democratic candidate for the Senate in 1982, her candidacy became a priority for women's groups.

Danforth's fundraising advantage over Woods was more than 2-to-1. But his money and excellent organization were offset by Woods' most important asset: desire. Voters were impressed with her enthusiastic dawn-to-midnight campaigning, while Danforth gave the impression he was not really hungry to be re-elected. More than once, he lamented that the campaign was making it difficult for him to watch the baseball playoffs (the St. Louis Cardinals were on their way to a World Series championship).

But Danforth's strategy changed abruptly Oct. 15, when the St. Louis Globe-Democrat's poll showed his comfortable lead of a month earlier had vanished. The incumbent went on the attack. He called Woods a liberal and a throwback to an era of discredited Democratic tax-and-spend practices. He accused her of demagoguery for portraying the Republican Party as a menace to Social Security without offering any constructive suggestions of her own. He brought up abortion and busing, topics he had avoided earlier in the campaign.

The shift to a negative campaign had the desired effect. Some conservative Democrats took a second look at Woods and lost their enthusiasm, and complacent Republicans were jolted into realizing that a high GOP turnout would be necessary to keep the seat.

Woods won where Democrats usually do in Missouri — St. Louis, Kansas City and the majority of rural counties — but in each of those areas, her liberalism cost her just enough votes to enable Danforth to escape.

His 1982 struggle, however, did not sully his reputation as the founder of the modern-day Missouri GOP. Elected state attorney general in 1968 in his political debut, Danforth became the first Republican in 22 years to win statewide office. Republicans point to his victory as the seminal event in the party's revival.

He lured bright young lawyers to the attorney general's office — among them Bond, who served two non-consecutive terms as governor before his 1986 election to the Senate, and John Ashcroft, who followed Bond, serving two terms as governor from 1985 to 1993. Danforth also developed a reputation as a protector of consumers and the environment.

John C. Danforth, R-Mo.

In 1970, Danforth was the GOP's only hope to dislodge Democratic Sen. Stuart Symington, who was seeking a fourth term. In an expensive campaign that introduced Missouri to modern media-oriented politics, Danforth won 48 percent of the vote. Two years later, he was returned as attorney general by more than 450,000 votes and awaited his next Senate chance.

It came, as expected, when Symington retired in 1976. Democrats appeared to seize the momentum by nominating U.S. Rep. Jerry Litton, described by a state political expert as "one of the most exciting political personalities to come along in years." But Democratic enthusiasm was tragically brief. Litton died in a primary-night plane crash, and Danforth was suddenly the favorite.

The state Democratic committee chose as its replacement former Gov. Warren Hearnes, whose courthouse-style administration had been the focus of Danforth's campaign attacks in 1968. Hearnes had finished a poor second to Litton in the primary. Against Litton, Danforth would have had a difficult contest; against Hearnes, he won easily.

Committees

Commerce, Science & Transportation (Ranking)
National Ocean Policy Study

Finance (4th of 9 Republicans)
International Trade (ranking); Health for Families & the Uninsured; Taxation

Select Intelligence (3rd of 8 Republicans)

Elections

1988 General

John C. Danforth (R)	1,407,416	(68%)
Jay Nixon (D)	660,045	(32%)

Previous Winning Percentages: **1982** (51%) **1976** (57%)

Campaign Finance

1988	Receipts	Receipts from PACs		Expenditures
Danforth (R)	$4,077,855	$1,149,207	(28%)	$3,992,995
Nixon (D)	$884,513	$241,231	(27%)	$880,160

Key Votes

1993

Require unpaid family and medical leave	Y
Approve national "motor voter" registration bill	N
Approve budget increasing taxes and reducing deficit	N
Support president's right to lift military gay ban	N
1992	
Approve school-choice pilot program	Y
Allow shifting funds from defense to domestic programs	N
Oppose deeper cuts in spending for SDI	Y
1991	
Approve waiting period for handgun purchases	N
Raise senators' pay and ban honoraria	Y
Authorize use of force in Persian Gulf	Y
Confirm Clarence Thomas to Supreme Court	Y

Voting Studies

	Presidential Support		Party Unity		Conservative Coalition	
Year	**S**	**O**	**S**	**O**	**S**	**O**
1992	78	22	77	20	79	21
1991	77	16	72	24	68	28
1990	74	25	71	29	81	19
1989	90	10	75	24	76	21
1988	75	23	65	28	76	22
1987	60	37	68	30	75	19
1986	80	20	77	21	82	17
1985	81	17	77	20	70	20
1984	86	13	85	15	83	17
1983	80	16	72	27	64	32
1982	71	19	72	21	76	18
1981	85	13	84	15	83	16

Interest Group Ratings

Year	ADA	AFL-CIO	CCUS	ACU
1992	25	25	90	74
1991	20	25	70	60
1990	39	44	67	43
1989	15	20	63	71
1988	20	42	71	72
1987	35	80	61	54
1986	30	33	61	57
1985	15	19	75	65
1984	35	27	63	68
1983	40	13	53	32
1982	40	23	52	50
1981	25	17	89	73

Christopher S. Bond (R)

Of Mexico — Elected 1986; 2nd Term

Born: March 6, 1939, St. Louis, Mo.
Education: Princeton U., A.B. 1960; U. of Virginia, LL.B. 1963.
Occupation: Lawyer.
Family: Wife, Carolyn Reid; one child.
Religion: Presbyterian.
Political Career: GOP nominee for U.S. House, 1968; Mo. assistant attorney general, 1969-70; Mo. auditor, 1971-73; governor, 1973-77; GOP nominee for governor, 1976; governor, 1981-85.
Capitol Office: 293 Russell Bldg. 20510; 224-5721.

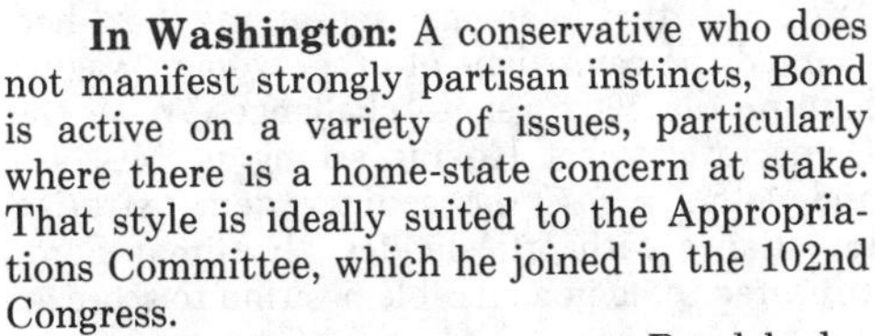

In Washington: A conservative who does not manifest strongly partisan instincts, Bond is active on a variety of issues, particularly where there is a home-state concern at stake. That style is ideally suited to the Appropriations Committee, which he joined in the 102nd Congress.

Like other former governors, Bond had a little trouble adjusting to the Senate's competing egos. But unlike some others, he took a low-key approach to the adjustment. He willingly cut a modest figure in his first Congress, finding his way gradually, choosing his shots with care.

By the 101st Congress, he appeared to have become more accustomed to the ways of the Senate. He ran for a party leadership position before the start of the 102nd Congress, losing 26-17 to Bob Kasten of Wisconsin in a bid for Republican Conference secretary. After the 1992 defeat, he tried again, this time losing to Mississippi Republican Trent Lott, 20-14; Alaska Republican Frank H. Murkowski received five votes.

Although Bond is generally a Chamber of Commerce conservative, his vote is not always easy to predict. Most would place him to the right of Republican John C. Danforth, the state's senior senator, but an ideologue he is not. Usually if he is involved in an issue, he is attempting to craft a compromise that will win broad support in Congress, even if that means crossing a Republican president.

During the 102nd Congress, Bond worked on legislation to mandate that most businesses offer unpaid family leave to their employees. He and Connecticut Democrat Christopher J. Dodd, the bill's original sponsor, forged a bipartisan compromise. But President George Bush opposed forcing businesses to offer family leave, and he vetoed the bill when it reached his desk in 1992. The election of Bill Clinton, however, ended White House opposition to family leave. Early in 1993, Clinton signed into law a bill nearly identical to the 1992 version.

Bond took a leading role in the 102nd Congress in a fight over highway funding. Bond and other senators from so-called donor states (which pay more in gasoline taxes than they get back in transportation projects) threatened to filibuster the 1991 highway authorization bill unless the formulas divvying up money for projects were changed. The final bill tossed aside longstanding formulas and also authorized lump sum payments to donor states.

In 1992, Bond had to work to ensure that the Appropriations Committee did not undo the agreement reached on the highway bill. On a 39-57 vote, he lost his bid to get the Senate to adhere to the agreement, as contained in the House fiscal 1993 transportation appropriations bill. But he rounded up the signatures of a number of other donor-state senators and sent a "Dear Colleague" letter to Senate Transportation Appropriations panel Chairman Frank R. Lautenberg of New Jersey, urging him to support the House version. In the House-Senate conference, the Senate conferees relented.

Having tweaked the Reagan administration in his 1986 campaign for being "too slow to respond" to the farm crisis, Bond found himself on the spot as one of four freshmen — and the only first-term Republican — on the Agriculture Committee.

Bond's early bills on Agriculture tended toward the dull but doable — improving meat and fowl inspection, providing flood relief, reducing farmers' paperwork.

In the 101st Congress, the committee assembled the 1990 farm bill. Bond's most active parochial interest was soybeans. Although Bond was considered a potential Republican vote for Democratic proposals to secure a generous new marketing loan for soybean growers, he was unwilling to buck the GOP leadership to do so. The 1990 farm bill included a marketing loan plan for soybeans, though the loan rate was far lower than that sought by members from soybean-producing states.

The pet proposal of committee Chairman Patrick J. Leahy of Vermont would have curtailed the so-called "circle of poison," in which domestically banned pesticides re-enter the United States on imported fruit and vegetables. Bond opposed Leahy's plan, arguing that the plan would export some pesticide production, costing U.S. jobs. "If these pesticides can be manufactured offshore," he said, "we will then be in a position to have no control over them." Monsanto Co., one of the world's largest chemical companies, has headquarters in St. Louis.

On the Banking Committee in the 101st Congress, Bond took a keen interest in an overhaul of housing programs, even though he did not sit on the Housing Subcommittee. He helped broker a compromise by California Democrat Alan Cranston, the panel's chairman, enabling it to attract GOP votes in winning committee approval. He was later appointed to the House-Senate conference. The bill contained $5.9 million to authorize the sale of more than 200 public housing units to residents at the Carr Square Village project in St. Louis. Bond worked hard trying to craft a bipartisan compromise on the 102nd Congress' housing reauthorization bill. Beginning in the 103rd Congress, Bond is the subcommittee's ranking Republican.

Bond has delved into defense policy to help workers at the St. Louis-based McDonnell Douglas Corp., which announced in July 1990 that it would lay off 17,000 workers. In 1991, the Defense Appropriations Subcommittee approved his amendment making the purchase of more F-15 Air Force fighter planes a legal requirement. It included $722 million for F-15 spare parts and maintenance gear. The F-15 is made by McDonnell Douglas.

In 1992, Bond pushed the Bush administration to approve the sale of 72 advanced F-15s to Saudi Arabia. Without the sale, company officials warned, 40,000 aerospace jobs would be lost at McDonnell Douglas. At a September campaign appearance in St. Louis, Bush announced the F-15 sales.

One consistent motivation for Bond is his deference to the states. That often aligns him with other former governors, including Democrats such as David L. Boren of Oklahoma and Bob Graham of Florida, who favor letting states make regulatory decisions. When the Banking Committee mulled banks' right to sell insurance, and when the Agriculture Committee debated who would distribute rural development grants, Bond spoke up for letting each state decide.

During Senate consideration in the 101st Congress of a bill creating child-care grant programs, Bond offered an amendment to permit states to make grants to school districts for before- and after-school programs for so-called latchkey children. The Senate adopted his proposal by voice vote. It became law as part of the year-end deficit-reduction bill.

At Home: In his six statewide races, Bond has not proved himself to be an overwhelming favorite with Missouri voters. He has won by more than 10 percentage points only once — his first contest, the 1970 state auditor race. In five subsequent statewide runs, he has reached 55 percent only once (his 1972 election as governor) and lost once (in his 1976 gubernatorial re-election bid).

But in 1992, despite Bond's apparent inability to inspire enthusiasm at the polls and the prospects for a good Democratic year, Missouri Democrats did not field a prominent candidate to oppose him. With most of the state's attention focused on the race for the open governor's office, 14 little-known Democrats competed in the Senate primary.

The winner was St. Louis County Council member Geri Rothman-Serot, the ex-wife of former Democratic Lt. Gov. Kenneth J. Rothman. Rothman-Serot sought to capitalize on the "Year of the Woman" sensation that had charged the campaigns of other women waging high-profile 1992 Senate challenges. With the Democratic ticket looking strong in Missouri and voters across the country demonstrating impatience with officeholders, Rothman-Serot appeared to be in a credible position to score an upset.

But Bond had prepared well. His campaign treasury was four times larger than Rothman-Serot's. His approval ratings remained healthy, bolstered by campaign ads touting him as an effective problem solver. His image as a pragmatic conservative did not engender strong partisan antipathy among Democrats.

Rothman-Serot was criticized for taking issue stands that were long on personal anecdote but short on policy specifics. And she was not very visible in conservative Democratic areas such as rural southeast Missouri. Her liberal stands and her reluctance to court rural conservatives reminded some Democrats of Bond's 1986 challenger, then-Lt. Gov. Harriett Woods.

On Election Day, Clinton carried Missouri, and Democrats won all but one statewide race on the ballot: Bond was the GOP's only victorious statewide candidate. As he had in 1986, Bond lost in Kansas City and St. Louis but performed strongly in most rural areas. While he received only 52 percent of the vote, his nearly 164,000-vote margin over Rothman-Serot was his best showing against an opponent in 20 years.

Missouri is unique in having two senators who not only attended the same private out-of-state university but studied there at the same time. Like Danforth, Bond is a product of a wealthy family who attended Princeton in the 1950s and then earned a law degree from an exclusive law school. In Bond's case, the family money came from making bricks. At law school, he was class valedictorian.

(The extent and condition of Bond's fortune, however, was called into doubt in the spring of 1993, when he sued his investment adviser, whom he accused of squandering his $1.3 million blind trust. Bond was forced to sell his million-dollar home in Washington.)

Bond broke into politics in 1968, seeking a seat in the U.S. House from northeastern Missouri. Although he lost, it was the year the modern GOP in Missouri was born. Richard M. Nixon carried the state, and Danforth was elected attorney general. Bond took a job with Danforth and in 1970 won the office of state auditor. Two years later, he was elected the state's first GOP governor since World War II.

He had a troubled first term. Democrats in the Legislature found him aloof; Republicans chafed at his efforts to abolish patronage jobs. In 1976, he lost to Democrat Joseph P. Teasdale. But he avenged this loss in 1980, riding Ronald Reagan's popularity atop the ticket and exploiting Teasdale's image as an incompetent administrator. In his second term, Bond warmed up to the Legislature and generally won points for being more accessible.

In 1986, Bond was one of the few Republican success stories in a Senate election year fraught with disaster for the GOP. He overcame an aggressive, well-known challenger and the rumblings of farm protest to win the seat vacated by retiring Democrat Thomas F. Eagleton. As a result, he was the only Republican to capture an open Democratic seat in 1986.

His contest with Woods was a bitter one. Bond offered himself as a budget-conscious conservative, citing his two-term gubernatorial record of avoiding major tax increases. He painted Woods as a liberal with values out of sync with most Missourians.

Woods portrayed herself as a scrappy Truman-style populist, a strategy she had used in nearly upsetting Danforth in 1982. She called Bond a passive governor, an aloof aristocrat and a likely rubber stamp for Reagan.

Woods' campaign foundered, however, when she ran a TV ad depicting a weeping farmer describing how he was foreclosed by a company on whose board Bond served. The ad provoked a firestorm of controversy, as Republicans and editorialists branded it a crass attempt to put farm troubles to political use. The ad damaged Woods' attempts to win conservative rural Democrats.

Bond, too, had past problems with members of his party. Many conservatives remembered his support of Gerald R. Ford over Reagan at the 1976 national GOP convention and never really considered him one of their own. But any doubts they might have had about Bond were drowned out by their antipathy toward Woods; he won with 53 percent.

Committees

Appropriations (9th of 13 Republicans)
Treasury, Postal Service & General Government (ranking); Agriculture, Rural Development & Related Agencies; Defense; VA, HUD & Independent Agencies; Labor, Health & Human Services & Education

Banking, Housing & Urban Affairs (3rd of 8 Republicans)
Housing & Urban Affairs (ranking); International Finance & Monetary Policy; Securities

Budget (5th of 9 Republicans)

Small Business (3rd of 9 Republicans)
Government Contracting & Paperwork Reduction (ranking); Competitiveness, Capital Formation & Economic Opportunity

Elections

1992 General		
Christopher S. Bond (R)	1,221,901	(52%)
Geri Rothman-Serot (D)	1,057,967	(45%)
Jeanne F. Bojarski (LIBERT)	75,048	(3%)
1992 Primary		
Christopher S. Bond (R)	337,795	(83%)
Wes Hummel (R)	70,626	(17%)

Previous Winning Percentage: **1986** (53%)

Campaign Finance

	Receipts	Receipts from PACs		Expend-itures
1992				
Bond (R)	$4,069,717	$1,420,459	(35%)	$4,577,895
Rothman-Serot (D)	$1,113,647	$306,860	(28%)	$1,112,187

Key Votes

1993	
Require unpaid family and medical leave	Y
Approve national "motor voter" registration bill	N
Approve budget increasing taxes and reducing deficit	N
Support president's right to lift military gay ban	N
1992	
Approve school-choice pilot program	?
Allow shifting funds from defense to domestic programs	N
Oppose deeper cuts in spending for SDI	Y
1991	
Approve waiting period for handgun purchases	N
Raise senators' pay and ban honoraria	N
Authorize use of force in Persian Gulf	Y
Confirm Clarence Thomas to Supreme Court	Y

Voting Studies

	Presidential Support		Party Unity		Conservative Coalition	
Year	**S**	**O**	**S**	**O**	**S**	**O**
1992	70	23	76	14	66	24
1991	85	11	86	12	85	15
1990	82	16	86	12	100	0
1989	86	12	85	12	89	3
1988	75	20	73	19	89	8
1987	64	23	86	11	94	0

Interest Group Ratings

Year	ADA	AFL-CIO	CCUS	ACU
1992	25	33	100	76
1991	20	27	70	81
1990	11	44	67	77
1989	5	10	100	85
1988	0	23	86	88
1987	10	25	82	81

1 William L. Clay (D)

Of St. Louis — Elected 1968; 13th Term

Born: April 30, 1931, St. Louis, Mo.
Education: St. Louis U., B.S. 1953.
Military Service: Army, 1953-55.
Occupation: Real estate and insurance broker.
Family: Wife, Carol Ann Johnson; three children.
Religion: Roman Catholic.
Political Career: St. Louis Board of Aldermen, 1959-64; St. Louis Democratic Committee, 1964-67.
Capitol Office: 2306 Rayburn Bldg. 20515; 225-2406.

In Washington: When he came to Congress a quarter-century ago, Clay was labeled a black militant. Over the years, he gradually has adjusted his political focus and rhetoric to match his slightly more white and more conservative district, but he remains a strident liberal on the issues he cares deeply about — especially civil rights and labor.

Clay remains popular back home, and he pays close attention to the needs of his district. Although he was tossed about during the 102nd Congress, he always seemed to land on firm ground. Despite having overdrawn 328 checks at the House bank, he was returned to Congress by a vote of 2-to-1.

In Congress, Clay is known for a sharp tongue and biting attacks. When riled, he can be belligerent and prone to verbal fisticuffs.

Some examples: During the 101st Congress, Clay called then-Rep. Mike Espy, a black Democrat from Mississippi, a "gigolo" at a Congressional Black Caucus hearing on the complaints of striking workers about sub-poverty wages at catfish farms in Espy's Mississippi Delta district.

During the 102nd Congress, Clay took a swipe at President Bush over the administration's rejection of affirmative action in debate over civil rights legislation. "As far as I'm concerned," Clay said, "there is about as much difference between David Duke and George Bush as there is between Tweedledee and Tweedledum."

At the start of the 102nd Congress, Clay became chairman of the Post Office and Civil Service Committee, a political backwater that generates few pieces of major legislation. But Clay has used the position to champion unions and to make life miserable for the Postal Service.

In 1992, after a committee investigation, Clay issued a report highly critical of Postal Service management. The committee questioned the Post Office's purchase of a building from a St. Louis real estate investment group for $12.5 million. The company had bought the building only five hours earlier for $5 million. He demanded a response from the Post Office within 30 days, insisting that Postal Service officials "should be held fully accountable for its amateur performance," Clay said.

He also raised questions about Postal Service streamlining, under which some employees were given an option of taking a bonus to retire or a possible downgrade to stay on.

Clay also has been an influential voice on the Education and Labor Committee, where he served as chairman of the Labor-Management Relations Subcommittee until 1991. Most of his efforts fizzled in the early 1980s, as labor-backed initiatives met with strong opposition from the newly installed Reagan administration. But Clay slowly chipped away at his agenda, enacting several major pieces of legislation and coming close on others.

He was the author and lead Education and Labor Committee conferee on a bill to ban so-called pension reversions. The provisions, stripped at the last minute from legislation in 1989, sought to protect employees' pension assets from employer raids of overfunded pension plans. Congress in 1990 did pass, as part of its omnibus deficit-reduction bill, provisions expected to slow the practice by sharply increasing taxation of any excess pension plan funds retained by an employer.

In the 101st and 102nd Congresses, Clay was a leading advocate of legislation that made other sweeping changes in the nation's pension protection law, the Employee Retirement Income Security Act (ERISA). His efforts were spurred on by the plight of workers in troubled industries that were sidestepping promised pension benefits, and by the soaring deficits of the Pension Benefit Guaranty Corporation.

As the original sponsor and floor manager of compromise legislation in 1990 reversing a Supreme Court ruling that allowed age-based discrimination in employee benefits, Clay helped steer the measure through Congress late in the session. Despite opposition from GOP lawmakers and business groups, Bush ultimately signed the measure.

Clay was also a primary House sponsor of committee Chairman William D. Ford of Michi-

Missouri 1

North St. Louis; Northeast St. Louis County

Almost everything that outsiders identify with the city of St. Louis is in the 1st. The Gateway Arch, Laclede's Landing, Busch Stadium and Forest Park all lie north of the line that divides the two city-dominated districts.

The other, equally familiar St. Louis is also here: the crime-ridden streets, the run-down neighborhoods, the closed factories and businesses. Parts of the downtown area have declined so far that they shock even visitors accustomed to inner-city blight.

Blacks and whites have fled the city. The well-off have gone to distant suburbia and the less affluent to neighborhoods just outside the city limits. Blacks have also begun to move to the predominantly white neighborhoods of south St. Louis, and, as a consequence, many south St. Louis whites have headed for the suburbs. Once the nation's third-largest city, St. Louis' population has shrunk to less than half its 1950 total. It fell by 12 percent during the 1980s; with about 400,000 residents in the 1990 census, St. Louis has fallen behind Kansas City as Missouri's most-populous city. Politically, the 1st is Missouri's most reliably Democratic district.

The St. Louis area has been rocked in recent years by plant closings and layoffs. In 1991, Chrysler closed one of its two St. Louis County assembly plants. McDonnell Douglas has cut thousands of workers through attrition and layoffs; cancellation of McDonnell Douglas' A-12 attack plane in January 1991 prompted another wave of layoffs. Trans World Airlines, whose domestic hub is at St. Louis' Lambert International Airport, filed for bankruptcy in July 1991. General Dynamics Corp. moved its corporate headquarters to Northern Virginia in January 1992.

North St. Louis is not uniformly dilapidated. There remain pockets of stable older residential areas, such as the Central West End and adjacent neighborhoods north and east of Forest Park, as well as the Mark Twain and Walnut Park neighborhoods near the northern city limits.

But most of north St. Louis is in decay. Some of the worst areas lie just north and west of downtown. Much of the central city has become a battle zone of drive-by shootings and drug deals.

The city has waged an ambitious program to renovate its historic buildings. Monumental Union Station, for example, has been rehabilitated into an upscale marketplace with shops, restaurants, nightclubs and a hotel. But these efforts offer scant solace to the poor residents of crime-ravaged north St. Louis.

The 1st also takes in many of the blacks who have left the city for nearby St. Louis County suburbs. Affluent black professionals live in University City, Clayton and Florissant. Clayton was once the prototypical prosperous suburb, but its profile has been changing of late, as tony shops relocate west to more-affluent locales.

The rest of the 1st is composed largely of white working-class conservatives who work in the auto assembly and aerospace manufacturing facilities ringing the city.

1990 Population: 568,285. White 262,955 (46%), Black 297,331 (52%), Other 7,999 (1%). Hispanic origin 5,090 (<1%). 18 and over 418,731 (74%), 62 and over 94,234 (17%). Median age: 32.

gan's plant-closing notification bill that finally won approval in 1988.

Clay has been a consistent primary sponsor of family and medical leave legislation, and was again during the 103rd, when the bill was finally enacted. In addition, he lent his support to legislation that would prevent businesses from permanently replacing striking workers.

Clay also has been active on education issues. In the 102nd Congress, he cosponsored a bill with fellow Missouri Democrat Alan Wheat aimed at helping black colleges and universities finance the rebuilding of their physical plants. The bill authorizes the secretary of Education to provide insurance on the bonds to be issued by some schools for the purpose of improvements to libraries, dormitories and other buildings. The measure was included in the Higher Education Act of 1992.

Clay is also a dependable liberal voice on such issues as abortion and the death penalty.

A long and frustrating battle for Clay has been his effort to revise the Hatch Act, which restricts political activity by government workers. He came close to obtaining the modifications sought by federal employee unions in 1975, when Congress passed his Hatch Act bill but failed to override President Gerald R. Ford's veto. Clay has introduced legislation to reform the act in each Congress since. Early in the 103rd, the House passed the Hatch Act revisions 333-86. However, they faced an uncertain future in the Senate.

Over the years, Clay has had a number of confrontations with the House ethics committee. The most contentious was in 1992 when the panel found that he had overdrawn his account at the House bank 328 times. Clay blasted the committee for the way it handled the issues; he was livid over the panel's piecemeal release of the names of the overdraft offenders. At one point, Clay charged that some of the six subcommittee members lied to him. He said four members told him they had voted to take his name off the list.

In 1980, when the committee recommended censure of his close friend and Postal Operations Subcommittee ally, Charles H. Wilson of California, he called the panel a "kangaroo court" that was "perverted" and "devoid of fairness, justice and equity."

In the 101st Congress, Clay was one of just 18 members to vote against reprimanding Democrat Barney Frank of Massachusetts for misusing his official position to help a male prostitute.

In the mid-1970s, Clay was accused of billing the House for trips home that he did not take. His administrative assistant went to jail in 1976 for fraudulently placing a sister-in-law on the federal payroll. The Justice Department spent months scrutinizing Clay's tax returns and campaign finances. But no charges were ever filed against him. He settled the House travel account by repaying some of the money, saying there had been a bookkeeping error. When the Justice Department dropped its probe, Clay charged that it had been politically motivated.

At Home: Clay had to survive redistricting and overcome the House bank fallout to win a 13th term in 1992. As it turned out, neither hazard proved particularly difficult to overcome.

After her 54-vote upset of 2nd District GOP Rep. Jack Buechner in 1990, Democrat Joan Kelly Horn sought a more Democratic composition for her district. But she was up against an informal arrangement made before the 1990 elections among Clay, Buechner and 3rd District Democrat Richard A. Gephardt to enhance the partisan makeup in each member's seat.

Neither Clay nor Gephardt would concede Horn a part of St. Louis, which they share. Clay did return one-third of Democratic Florissant (which had been entirely in the 2nd) to Horn, but that was not enough to stave off her defeat. Clay and Gephardt won by wider margins than in 1990, but Horn lost to Republican state Rep. James M. Talent. The bank scandal hardly slowed Clay, who dispatched his primary and general-election opponents by more than 2-to-1.

For someone who has spent more than 20 years in Washington, Clay remains unusually active in local politics and repeatedly has clashed with St. Louis' longtime mayor, Vincent C. Schoemehl Jr.

In 1987, he used a franked letter to constituents to criticize two Schoemehl-backed tax proposals. (Both measures passed.)

Clay won a 1986 round against Schoemehl when he opposed the mayor's decision to turn control of a city-run health-care facility over to a private, nonprofit corporation. The dispute prompted Schoemehl to field a slate of candidates to challenge Clay-backed contenders for city offices in the Democratic primary, but Clay's slate swept Schoemehl's. In 1992, Clay worked energetically for Schoemehl's opponent in the Democratic gubernatorial primary, then-Lt. Gov. Mel Carnahan. Not only did Schoemehl lose the nomination to Carnahan, he lost his home city by 10,000 votes.

Clay's career has thrived on confrontation. His own campaign literature once noted that he had been "arrested, convicted of contempt of court [and] served 110 days in jail" for demonstrating at a St. Louis bank.

That incident took place years before his election to the House in 1968. But it was one of a string of such confrontations that gave him a reputation as a civil rights activist. In 1954, while going through military training at Fort McClellan in Alabama, Clay found the post swimming pool and barber shop closed to blacks, and the non-commissioned officers' club off-limits when there were white women present. He led blacks to swim en masse in the pool, boycott haircuts and picket the club.

After returning to St. Louis, Clay became active in the NAACP and CORE, the Congress on Racial Equality. He was elected to the city's Board of Aldermen in 1959 and became an official in the politically active Pipefitters Union in 1966. While keeping his identification as a civil rights militant, he moved closer over the years to the patronage politics of the local Democratic Party.

Redistricting by the Missouri legislature in 1967 placed most of St. Louis' 257,000 blacks in the 1st District, ending years of fragmentation of the black vote. Democrat Frank M. Karsten, the 1st District representative for 22 years, decided to retire rather than seek re-election in 1968.

With the backing of most local black leaders, Clay emerged from a racially divided four-way primary with a 48 percent plurality. In the general election, he ran on a platform geared to the district's 55 percent black majority. He called for more federal money for jobs, housing, health and education, and for changes in police agencies and the court system to eliminate bias against blacks. Clay won 64 percent against black Republican Curtis C. Crawford to become Missouri's first black congressman.

As Clay extended his tenure in the House, the population in his district dwindled steadily. The 1st lost one-quarter of its people during the 1970s, and redistricting in 1981 gave Clay nearly 200,000 new constituents, many of them blue-collar workers in largely white sections of St. Louis County. In Clay's old district, two-thirds of the population was black; in the redrawn 1st, blacks barely formed a majority, and more whites than blacks were registered to vote.

A sizable number of Clay's new constituents fiercely objected to his support for abortion and for busing of students to integrate schools. Anti-Clay Democrats coalesced behind a white candidate, state Sen. Al Mueller, an opponent of abortion and busing.

Clay maintained that his stands on abortion and busing were consonant with current laws and court rulings.

He also criticized his opponent for ignoring important national problems, such as unemployment and cutbacks in federal aid to the disadvantaged.

Mueller carried the St. Louis County portion of the 1st, but Clay, strongly backed by organized labor, crushed him in the city en route to a 61 percent victory districtwide.

Committees

Post Office & Civil Service (Chairman)
Oversight & Investigations (chairman)

Education & Labor (2nd of 28 Democrats)
Labor-Management Relations; Labor Standards, Occupational Health & Safety

House Administration (3rd of 12 Democrats)
Libraries & Memorials (chairman); Administrative Oversight; Personnel & Police

Elections

1992 General		
William L. Clay (D)	158,693	(68%)
Arthur S. Montgomery (R)	74,482	(32%)
1992 Primary		
William L. Clay (D)	57,242	(68%)
Donald Cross (D)	26,677	(32%)
1990 General		
William L. Clay (D)	62,550	(61%)
Wayne G. Piotrowski (R)	40,160	(39%)

Previous Winning Percentages: **1988** (72%) **1986** (66%) **1984** (68%) **1982** (66%) **1980** (70%) **1978** (67%) **1976** (66%) **1974** (68%) **1972** (64%) **1970** (91%) **1968** (64%)

District Vote for President

1992
D 161,794 (68%)
R 44,980 (19%)
I 29,586 (13%)

Campaign Finance

	Receipts	Receipts from PACs		Expend-itures
1992				
Clay (D)	$300,187	$251,680	(84%)	$297,635
Montgomery (R)	$20,587	$550	(3%)	$21,862
1990				
Clay (D)	$213,965	$182,550	(85%)	$196,909
Piotrowski (R)	$12,767	0		$12,666

Key Votes

1993	
Require parental notification of minors' abortions	N
Require unpaid family and medical leave	Y
Approve national "motor voter" registration bill	Y
Approve budget increasing taxes and reducing deficit	Y
Approve economic stimulus plan	Y
1992	
Approve balanced-budget constitutional amendment	N
Close down space station program	Y
Approve U.S. aid for former Soviet Union	N
Allow shifting funds from defense to domestic programs	Y
1991	
Extend unemployment benefits using deficit financing	Y
Approve waiting period for handgun purchases	Y
Authorize use of force in Persian Gulf	N

Voting Studies

	Presidential Support		Party Unity		Conservative Coalition	
Year	**S**	**O**	**S**	**O**	**S**	**O**
1992	9	86	80	9	10	77
1991	24	69	80	10	3	86
1990	16	80	75	12	7	89
1989	28	62	71	21	7	88
1988	12	67	68	12	0	82
1987	11	74	72	12	2	91
1986	8	78	71	11	2	74
1985	15	80	73	18	4	91
1984	19	65	83	3	2	92
1983	9	80	83	2	2	85
1982	19	43	74	5	3	67
1981	22	68	86	2	4	89

Interest Group Ratings

Year	ADA	AFL-CIO	CCUS	ACU
1992	95	91	13	0
1991	90	100	20	0
1990	94	100	31	4
1989	95	92	33	0
1988	90	100	18	0
1987	92	100	0	0
1986	75	100	15	0
1985	100	100	24	5
1984	95	100	33	5
1983	90	100	17	0
1982	65	100	29	13
1981	95	87	0	0

2 James M. Talent (R)

Of Chesterfield — Elected 1992; 1st Term

Born: Oct. 18, 1956, St. Louis, Mo.
Education: Washington U., B.A. 1978; U. of Chicago, J.D. 1981.
Occupation: Lawyer.
Family: Wife, Brenda Lyons; two children.
Religion: Presbyterian.
Political Career: Mo. House, 1985-93, minority leader, 1989-93.
Capitol Office: 1022 Longworth Bldg. 20515; 225-2561.

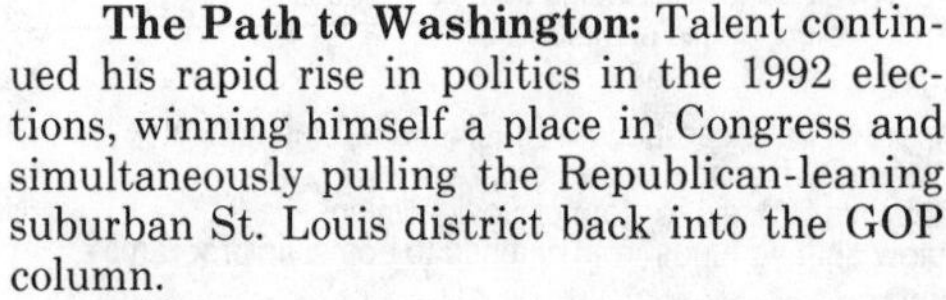

The Path to Washington: Talent continued his rapid rise in politics in the 1992 elections, winning himself a place in Congress and simultaneously pulling the Republican-leaning suburban St. Louis district back into the GOP column.

Talent captured the seat after winning a challenging primary battle and then toppling one-term Democratic incumbent Joan Kelly Horn.

He arrives in Washington with substantial legislative experience, a strong conservative agenda and a taste for political combat. Particularly on social issues such as abortion rights, he is likely to offer a sharp contrast with his liberal predecessor.

Talent's interest in politics, always with a strong conservative tilt, dates back to his late teens.

After finishing law school and clerking for a Chicago judge, Talent returned to the St. Louis area and quickly ran for a seat in the Missouri House of Representatives. Talent won that 1984 race, capturing a vacant seat in safe Republican territory, and had little trouble holding on to it.

In 1988, he was elected minority floor leader in the Democratic-controlled House chamber.

In the state legislature, Talent was known as a strong fiscal and social conservative — even bucking Republican Gov. John Ashcroft on a proposed package of education reforms that included a tax increase.

Republican ambitions naturally focused on Horn after her 54-vote, hairsbreadth victory in 1990. And Horn saw her position further weakened by redistricting, which removed several Democratic neighborhoods from a district where Republican presidential and statewide candidates tend to run strongly.

But Talent did not have an easy path to a November victory.

In the GOP primary, he faced Bert Walker or, more precisely, George Herbert Walker III — a cousin of President Bush. Walker deployed two Cabinet members and roughly $600,000 in his campaign for the nomination, but Talent beat him soundly with far less money but far more grass-roots support. His impressive districtwide network boosted him to a 16,000-vote win.

That victory drained Talent's campaign treasury as he headed into the general-election battle with Horn. Horn, a former political consultant, was a relatively strong candidate despite the redrawn district's Republican slant.

She had ample money against Talent and had assiduously tended to district concerns during her term. And Horn tried to galvanize support on the basis of her abortion rights stand, in sharp contrast to Talent's position that abortion should be allowed only in cases of rape, incest or to protect the woman's life.

But Talent allied himself with the popular yen for change, advocating term limits and attacking Horn for allegedly flip-flopping to vote against a proposed constitutional amendment to balance the budget she had helped sponsor.

Talent ultimately eked out a narrow win, even as St. Louis County, which anchors the district, went for Bill Clinton over Bush at the presidential level.

Talent cites his experience within the Democrat-led Missouri House as proof that he can have an impact even as part of the minority party.

He sees room for cooperation with Democrats on issues such as an investment tax credit and a line-item veto for the president, and is willing to consider health-care reform based on "managed competition."

Talent, however, voted early in the 103rd Congress against a Democratic bill giving the president limited line-item veto authority, in favor of an even stronger GOP substitute amendment. While most of the 47 GOP freshmen chose to vote for both, Talent was one of 12 to support only the substitute amendment.

At the same time, Talent sounds a more belligerent tone when it comes to fending off some potential liberal drives — such as universal health care or unduly large defense cuts.

"We have got to be prepared to fight those to the last ditch," Talent said. "If those things are going to happen, I want them to happen over a lot of Republican dead bodies."

Missouri 2

Western St. Louis County; Eastern St. Charles County

The suburban 2nd has some of Missouri's most affluent suburbs and some of the fastest-growing communities in the country. Republicans dominate much of the terrain, but enough independent voters and blue-collar households remain for a Democratic candidate to compete.

Separate from the city of St. Louis since 1876, St. Louis County, the largest in Missouri, makes up about 80 percent of the 2nd's population. The county has steadily filled with St. Louisans fleeing the declining urban center.

The heaviest concentration of Republicans is along the U.S. 40 corridor, across the heart of the 2nd. Communities such as Ladue and Frontenac have some of the area's wealthiest residents; the GOP vote is unshakable.

The affluent suburban vote has been spreading as the St. Louis suburbs have expanded west and northwest. Municipalities such as Chesterfield, Town and Country, and Ballwin are attracting the suburbanites who used to settle in Webster Groves, Kirkwood and other suburbs closer to the city. In the western part of the county, where subdivisions give way to unincorporated areas and farmland, affluent new arrivals mix with longtime residents of less lofty incomes and less predictable voting habits.

The southwestern part of the 2nd is home to the ghost town of Times Beach, site of one of the worst U.S. environmental disasters. Residents were threatened by health problems associated with dioxin-tainted soil.

The auto industry is a major employer in the district. At the southeastern corner, the district takes in the Chrysler assembly plant at Fenton. Two plants operated at the Fenton site until mid-1991, when Chrysler closed one, laying off about 4,000 workers. The second plant continues to turn out minivans. Ford's Hazelwood plant is here. General Motors' Wentzville facility, in the 9th District, provides jobs for many residents of the 2nd.

McDonnell Douglas Corp. has its headquarters in the 2nd and a plant adjacent to St. Louis' Lambert International Airport, which is one of the largest employers here. These workers lend a blue-collar tinge to the "North County." Traditional working-class communities such as St. Ann, Overland, Bridgeton and Olivette are Democratic strongholds. A proposed airport expansion, which would eliminate almost 1,000 homes in predominantly white Bridgeton, has added a volatile element to local politics. The 2nd also takes in two-thirds of reliably Democratic Florissant.

About 20 percent of the district lies over the Missouri River in St. Charles County, which in each of the past two decades has grown about 50 percent.

Settled by a French Canadian fur trader in 1769, the city of St. Charles served as Missouri's first capital from 1821 to 1826. The historic buildings on South Main Street have been restored, including the original Capitol. McDonnell Douglas manufactures the Harpoon missile at its St. Charles plant.

The rest of the 2nd in St. Charles County is rural. Soybeans and corn grow in the rich soil of the northern flood plain.

1990 Population: 568,306. White 535,626 (94%), Black 21,149 (4%), Other 11,531 (2%). Hispanic origin 5,803 (1%). 18 and over 420,651 (74%), 62 and over 72,790 (13%). Median age: 34.

Committees

Armed Services (20th of 22 Republicans)
Military Forces & Personnel; Research & Technology

Small Business (12th of 18 Republicans)
Minority Enterprise, Finance & Urban Development; SBA Legislation & the General Economy

Campaign Finance

	Receipts	Receipts from PACs		Expend-itures
1992				
Talent (R)	$920,895	$213,472	(23%)	$910,893
Horn (D)	$827,576	$372,427	(45%)	$832,813

Key Votes

1993

Require parental notification of minors' abortions	Y
Require unpaid family and medical leave	N
Approve national "motor voter" registration bill	N
Approve budget increasing taxes and reducing deficit	N
Approve economic stimulus plan	N

Elections

1992 General		
James M. Talent (R)	157,594	(50%)
Joan Kelly Horn (D)	148,729	(48%)
Jim Higgins (LIBERT)	6,119	(2%)
1992 Primary		
James M. Talent (R)	35,791	(58%)
Bert Walker (R)	19,555	(32%)
Tom McCoy (R)	4,322	(7%)
Hugh V. Murray (R)	1,915	(3%)

District Vote for President

1992

D 114,792 (36%)
R 126,788 (40%)
I 73,048 (23%)

3 Richard A. Gephardt (D)

Of St. Louis — Elected 1976; 9th Term

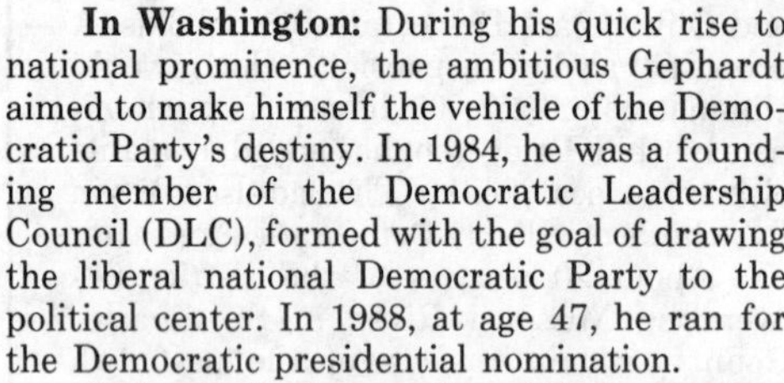

Born: Jan. 31, 1941, St. Louis, Mo.
Education: Northwestern U., B.S. 1962; U. of Michigan, J.D. 1965.
Military Service: Air National Guard, 1965-71.
Occupation: Lawyer.
Family: Wife, Jane Ann Byrnes; three children.
Religion: Baptist.
Political Career: St. Louis Board of Aldermen, 1971-76; sought Democratic nomination for president, 1988.
Capitol Office: 1432 Longworth Bldg. 20515; 225-2671.

In Washington: During his quick rise to national prominence, the ambitious Gephardt aimed to make himself the vehicle of the Democratic Party's destiny. In 1984, he was a founding member of the Democratic Leadership Council (DLC), formed with the goal of drawing the liberal national Democratic Party to the political center. In 1988, at age 47, he ran for the Democratic presidential nomination.

Although that campaign failed, a leadership shake-up in 1989 boosted Gephardt to the second-highest spot in the House hierarchy, majority leader. But the move up was widely seen as another step toward the White House rather than toward the Speaker's chair. The Missourian was seen as likely to run again for president, perhaps as early as 1992.

Gephardt, however, decided in July 1991 that he would not make a second consecutive bid. He stayed out despite intermittent coaxing from House allies who had doubts about Democratic front-runner Bill Clinton's electability.

Clinton, for whom Gephardt campaigned hard, surged to become the first "baby boomer" president, likely foreclosing the options of other Democrats for the rest of the 1990s. With the even-younger Vice President Al Gore in the national wings — and no apparent Gephardt interest in a bid for Senate or other statewide office — Gephardt's foreseeable future appears to be as a member of the House leadership.

Not that there aren't a few hundred denizens of Capitol Hill who would love to be in Gephardt's shoes. He is on track someday to succeed House Speaker Thomas S. Foley, who already relies on the boyish-looking and rhetorically able Gephardt as the partisan spokesman for the House Democratic viewpoint.

Also, after spending his first years in the House leadership as point man in a often-frustrating partisan standoff with the Republican Reagan and Bush administrations, Gephardt now gets to rally his House troops behind the activist legislative agenda of Democratic President Clinton.

Gephardt's influence in the Clinton White House is enhanced by the placement in high positions of several former members of his impressive House staff — including Clinton policy adviser George Stephanopoulos and political consultant Paul Begala.

But Gephardt also must accommodate himself to a midcareer adjustment. His drive for power, once a hot-rod sprint, is now part of a motorcade. His success is tied to that of others: Foley as top leader of the House Democrats and now Clinton as president.

There is a risk to that situation, as Gephardt learned during the scandal concerning members' check overdrafts at the House bank. Following the September 1991 release of a critical report about the bank by the General Accounting Office, Gephardt joined Foley in his initial effort to keep a lid on the scandal: As Foley closed down the bank that October, Gephardt made lawyerly arguments to exonerate his colleagues. "No taxpayer funds were used to cover insufficiencies," Gephardt argued.

However, the issue stirred an angry reaction from an American electorate that in the midst of an economic recession, was already dissatisfied with Congress. Voter ire was fueled by Republican activists, who viewed this as a damaging issue for the majority Democratic leadership. While Foley and Gephardt backed a House ethics committee recommendation in March 1992 that only the worst bank abusers be identified, a panicky House overwhelmingly voted for "full disclosure," even of the names of members with few overdrafts.

The result was fierce criticism — from members angry at the leadership for failing to protect their troops and letting the issue get so out of control, and from reform-minded members who blamed the leaders for failing to recognize the seriousness of the scandal. While most of the anger was targeted at Foley, it seemed possible for a time that Gephardt too might be vulnerable to a leadership challenge.

However, the storm passed. Foley moved

Missouri 3

South St. Louis; southeast St. Louis County; Jefferson and Ste. Genevieve counties

For years, south St. Louis has been a collection of white working-class neighborhoods that reflect the European heritage of their residents. While the city's high-crime and low-income areas are primarily associated with north St. Louis (the 1st District), the south has not been immune. Crime has risen in south St. Louis and spilled over the city limits into St. Louis County.

With its declining population, the city accounts for less than a third of the vote in the new 3rd. Much of that vestige still has a heavily ethnic cast. Italians are clustered in The Hill, where family-owned businesses have survived for generations. Bevo Mill and Carondelet are old-line German communities. Mounting threats of crime have energized the growth of powerful neighborhood associations to arrest the decline of housing values in south St. Louis. In some neighborhoods, these groups rival the Democratic ward machines for power and organization.

McDonnell Douglas Corp., Anheuser-Busch, Monsanto, Barnes Hospital and the area automobile assembly plants are major employers of the blue-collar workers in the 3rd. Many have been affected by recent shutdowns and layoffs. In 1991, Chrysler closed one of its two assembly plants in Fenton in south St. Louis County, just across the line in the 2nd District. McDonnell Douglas has reduced its work force by thousands through attrition and layoffs.

The wards along the Mississippi, near the Anheuser-Busch brewery, are home to the poorest whites. Affluent whites live in the St. Louis Hills neighborhood, in the southwest part of the city. It is the only Republican area in the city. For the most part, south St. Louis is residential and middle class.

Monsanto and Mallinckrodt chemical facilities and barge operations along the Mississippi are important to the 3rd's economy. But the most prominent enterprise in this part of the city is Anheuser-Busch, which employs 6,000 people.

Looking to escape from typical urban ills in many north St. Louis neighborhoods, blacks have been moving into the south wards. Whites, in turn, have sought the St. Louis County suburbs, in communities such as Lemay, Afton and Concord. Some kept on going until they reached Jefferson County, where the population ballooned from about 146,000 to more than 171,000 during the 1980s. The southern part of Jefferson remains predominantly rural. Farmers in the Hillsboro area regularly truck their produce to markets in downtown St. Louis. Jefferson, which cast nearly as many 3rd District votes in 1992 as the city of St. Louis, is a swing area. George Bush carried Jefferson in 1988, but in 1992, Bill Clinton won it by 16 percentage points.

Ste. Genevieve County has escaped the rapid residential expansion of its neighbors. Founded by French lead miners in the 1720s, the city of Ste. Genevieve was the first permanent settlement in Missouri. Its roots are evident in restored French homes downtown. The Mississippi Lime Co. tops the list of city employers, but much of the county's land is devoted to corn, soybeans and hogs.

1990 Population: 568,326. White 547,496 (96%), Black 13,342 (2%), Other 7,488 (1%). Hispanic origin 6,513 (1%). 18 and over 428,779 (75%), 62 and over 100,122 (18%). Median age: 34.

quickly to eliminate some controversial perks for House members, hired a professional administrator for the House and set in motion task forces to produce suggested reforms of management and legislative procedures. And as the presidential election campaign and the voters' overriding concern with the economy refocused the House on legislative issues, House Democrats were reminded why they favored the two as their top leaders in the first place.

Gephardt has long been well-regarded by his Democratic colleagues. On a personal level, Gephardt projects a clean-cut image with his pressed shirts and polite Midwestern manner. He is a good listener and an able negotiator.

Thus, Gephardt, like the low-key Foley, was seen as an antidote to the heavy-handed leadership of House Speaker Jim Wright, whose ethics problems forced him to resign from the House in 1989. Wright's leadership style relied heavily on arm-twisting, and his habit of setting his own policy course without first achieving a consensus within the House Democratic Caucus irritated many members.

Gephardt, on the other hand, takes a strongly consensus-oriented approach to leadership of the ideologically diverse and often-fractious Democratic forces. To define party themes, Gephardt institutionalized morning "message" meetings with House Democratic colleagues. He organizes and often heads task forces that try to shape consensus on divisive issues.

Discussing his efforts as organizer of a House Democratic task force on health-care reform in 1992, Gephardt described his leadership philosophy. "We do not operate here by the leadership bringing tablets of stone to the members and telling them what they will do," Gephardt said. "We build a consensus from the bottom up, not the top down."

Gephardt has also shown an inclination to subsume his own agenda to the common good of the conference. This was the case on the trade issue during the 102nd Congress.

Gephardt had made trade the centerpiece of his 1988 presidential campaign. Appealing to factory workers and farmers, he argued for a retaliatory economic policy against nations such as Japan that had large export surpluses with the United States.

The issue has remained at the top of Gephardt's personal agenda; he has offered various legislative proposals to toughen the U.S. trade stance. But his actions as a Democratic leader have indicated a recognition that the party has both free-trade and protectionist elements. Thus it was, in May 1991, that Gephardt, who opposed the proposed North American Free Trade Agreement with Mexico, endorsed a procedural measure that allowed President Bush to go forward with negotiations.

While this flexibility keeps Gephardt from alienating wings of his party, it recalls a criticism of him during his 1988 presidential bid: that he has no fixed political philosophy. Gephardt's critics pointed out that he had switched within four years from DLC centrist to angry populist. Over the years, Gephardt also had switched from an anti-abortion position to mainly supporting abortion rights.

Now, there are those, particularly in the liberal Democratic bloc, who wish that Gephardt would take a more consistent and less conciliatory line, cracking the whip if needed to draw the party's centrifugal parts together.

Yet it would take some convincing to make Republicans think that Gephardt is not partisan enough. Gephardt is regarded by GOP members as Foley's co-conspirator in depriving the minority party of its rights by pushing for closed rules that limit floor debate on issues.

Even more aggravating to Republicans is Gephardt's barbed rhetoric in the political arena. He was one of Bush's leading antagonists and played a role in framing the image of the president as an elitist who did not understand the economic worries of average Americans.

The turning point in Bush's one-term presidency came in late 1991, when he insisted in the face of public concern that the economy was doing fine. When Bush told a Republican gathering that a bill to extend unemployment benefits was "a bunch of garbage," Gephardt was ready with a sharp retort. "Unemployment compensation isn't garbage," Gephardt said, "and neither are the people who need it."

In his end-of-session statement at the close of the 102nd Congress in October 1992, Gephardt took a parting shot at Bush, who had made a strategic re-election campaign decision to run against the unpopular Congress. "The president's repeated, gratuitous use of the veto and meaningless deadlines were the major sources of gridlock," Gephardt said.

Gephardt shaped his partisan approach as a member of the Ways and Means Committee, on which he took a seat during his freshman term and remained through the Reagan presidency. Gephardt left the panel in 1989, taking an ex officio seat on the Budget Committee, where he had served from 1979 through 1984.

Gephardt's hard work on the presidential hustings in 1988 enabled him to score a victory in the campaign-opening Iowa caucuses. But his protectionist theme and "It's your fight, too" slogan played less well in conservative, free-trade-oriented New Hampshire. He lost there, and his effort quickly faded.

Gephardt returned to an uncertain future in the House. But that changed as ethics controversies undermined the careers of Wright and Democratic whip Tony Coelho of California. When Coelho abandoned an expected race for majority leader in May 1989 and resigned from Congress, Gephardt ran and defeated Georgia Democrat Ed Jenkins by 181-76.

In the 99th Congress, he had had even less trouble winning the chairmanship of the Democratic Caucus; his main opponent, David R. Obey of Wisconsin, dropped out nearly a year before the vote.

At Home: Redistricting in 1991 helped Gephardt halt a trend that saw his vote share fall from 69 percent in 1986 to 63 percent in 1988 to 57 percent in 1990 — by far his lowest tally since he first won the seat in 1976. In 1992, Gephardt pushed his vote share back up to 64 percent.

As a leader in Congress, Gephardt has been tied by recent GOP challengers to Congress' negative image. And in 1990, Gephardt was also victimized by the nationwide anti-incumbent mood that struck particularly hard in Missouri; six of the state's nine House members fell below the 60 percent mark.

Gephardt might really have had to sweat in 1990 if state and national Republicans had been able to run their preferred candidate, St. Louis County Election Board member Stephen Doss. He was lured into the race with broad hints that he would be assured a hefty campaign treasury.

But at the same time, a number of St. Louis County Republicans were lining up behind Malcolm L. "Mack" Holekamp, a former Webster Groves City Council member. Both filed for the GOP primary and, after several weeks of finger-pointing, Doss quit the race.

At that point, the national GOP lost interest in the contest and Holekamp had trouble raising money. But he proved to be a feisty challenger, lambasting Gephardt as "a PAC rat" and the Democrats' "No. 1 Bush-whacker." At one point he reportedly dressed up as a "dark horse" to draw attention to his campaign.

Gephardt was no less unlikely to encounter anti-incumbent sentiment in 1992, and he again faced Holekamp. In addition, Gephardt was the target of GOP radio ads mocking him for misstating the number of overdrafts he thought he had incurred at the House bank.

But by retaining its stake in St. Louis and adding Democratic Ste. Genevieve County, Gephardt's district became more comfortably Democratic, thanks to an informal arrangement made before the 1990 elections between Gephardt, 1st District Democrat William L. Clay and then-2nd District Republican Jack Buechner to enhance the partisan makeup in each member's seat. (Buechner lost in 1990, but Clay and Gephardt retained their monopoly on the city of St. Louis.)

Gephardt paid close attention to his race. As a result, he led all other incumbents in fundraising in the 1991-92 election cycle. Holekamp's vote share dropped to 33 percent, as Gephardt outpolled him by nearly 84,000 votes.

Gephardt was first elected to Congress in 1976 on the strength of his reputation as a young activist on the machine-dominated St. Louis Board of Aldermen. While on the board, he had sponsored zoning laws to preserve ethnic neighborhoods, building a constituency among German-American working-class communities on the city's South Side, the core of the 3rd District electorate. He also supported a constitutional amendment to restrict abortions, a position that he abandoned later in his career.

In the 1976 Democratic primary, Gephardt defeated state Sen. Donald J. Gralike, head of an electrical workers local. Gephardt's November opponent was Republican Joseph L. Badaracco, who had served eight years as a St. Louis alderman, six of those as board president.

Badaracco stressed his reputation for honesty in city politics and tried to convince voters that Gephardt was really a rich downtown lawyer groomed for Congress by the pin-striped establishment. Gephardt promised to emulate the moderate approach of Democratic Rep. Leonor K. Sullivan, who was retiring. He won with ease, rolling up a 2-to-1 advantage in St. Louis and taking nearly 60 percent of the vote in St. Louis County.

Committees

Majority Leader

Budget (2nd of 26 Democrats)

Joint Organization of Congress

Elections

1992 General		
Richard A. Gephardt (D)	174,000	(64%)
Mack Holekamp (R)	90,006	(33%)
Robert Stockhausen (LIBERT)	7,828	(3%)
1992 Primary		
Richard A. Gephardt (D)	71,773	(76%)
Leif Johnson (D)	13,433	(14%)
Ned L. Abernathy (D)	8,957	(10%)
1990 General		
Richard A. Gephardt (D)	88,950	(57%)
Malcolm L. Holekamp (R)	67,659	(43%)

Previous Winning Percentages: **1988** (63%) **1986** (69%) **1984** (100%) **1982** (78%) **1980** (78%) **1978** (82%) **1976** (64%)

District Vote for President

1992

D 120,866 (44%)
R 87,406 (32%)
I 64,511 (24%)

Campaign Finance

	Receipts	Receipts from PACs		Expend-itures
1992				
Gephardt (D)	$3,237,531	$1,240,597	(38%)	$3,316,784
Holekamp (R)	$426,168	$18,529	(4%)	$425,966
1990				
Gephardt (D)	$1,647,415	$762,687	(46%)	$1,455,794
Holekamp (R)	$82,784	$4,966	(6%)	$82,077

Key Votes

1993	
Require parental notification of minors' abortions	N
Require unpaid family and medical leave	Y
Approve national "motor voter" registration bill	Y
Approve budget increasing taxes and reducing deficit	Y
Approve economic stimulus plan	Y
1992	
Approve balanced-budget constitutional amendment	N
Close down space station program	N
Approve U.S. aid for former Soviet Union	Y
Allow shifting funds from defense to domestic programs	Y
1991	
Extend unemployment benefits using deficit financing	Y
Approve waiting period for handgun purchases	Y
Authorize use of force in Persian Gulf	N

Voting Studies

	Presidential Support		Party Unity		Conservative Coalition	
Year	**S**	**O**	**S**	**O**	**S**	**O**
1992	16	76	88	4	33	58
1991	30	68	90	5	22	70
1990	14	74	89	2	17	74
1989	33	63	95	3	22	78
1988	18	58	73	4	16	76
1987	5	22	18	0	5	21
1986	16	53	69	1	18	54
1985	26	71	84	6	31	65
1984	33	60	87	7	27	69
1983	26	70	90	6	25	69
1982	44	53	71	24	56	40
1981	54	43	64	33	69	27

Interest Group Ratings

Year	**ADA**	**AFL-CIO**	**CCUS**	**ACU**
1992	85	78	25	0
1991	75	92	30	0
1990	83	100	14	4
1989	90	100	30	4
1988	75	92	20	10
1987	20	100	0	0
1986	70	100	18	0
1985	60	88	19	19
1984	75	92	38	14
1983	85	94	25	9
1982	55	80	35	33
1981	45	73	11	27

4 Ike Skelton (D)

Of Lexington — Elected 1976; 9th Term

Born: Dec. 20, 1931, Lexington, Mo.
Education: Wentworth Military Academy, A.A. 1951; U. of Edinburgh (Scotland), 1953; U. of Missouri, A.B. 1953, LL.B. 1956.
Occupation: Lawyer.
Family: Wife, Susan Anding; three children.
Religion: Christian Church.
Political Career: Lafayette County prosecuting attorney, 1957-60; Mo. special assistant attorney general, 1961-63; Mo. Senate, 1971-77.
Capitol Office: 2227 Rayburn Bldg. 20515; 225-2876.

In Washington: A senior member of the Armed Services Committee, Skelton is a pro-defense Democrat. He was a key member of the centrist Democratic coalition headed by then-Wisconsin Rep. Les Aspin during his tenure as Armed Services chairman.

Now, Aspin is President Clinton's defense secretary. Skelton, chairman of Armed Services' Military Forces and Personnel Subcommittee since the start of the 103rd Congress, finds himself with an ally at the Pentagon.

Skelton urges caution in reducing the nation's post-Cold War defense commitment and will find room to disagree with Clinton's pledge to cut military spending. But Clinton and Aspin appear to favor a phased-in approach to the cutbacks, which should enable Skelton to stay in line with the administration.

Skelton and his fellow Democratic centrists on the panel may prove useful to Aspin as a counterweight to liberals — including Aspin's successor as chairman, Ronald V. Dellums of California — who want much deeper cuts than the administration will bear.

Despite his support for maintaining defense spending, Skelton shows an interest in the structure of the U.S. services that makes some of the military leadership uncomfortable. He is not a reflexive supporter of the Defense Department bureaucracy.

Skelton plans to closely monitor the armed services' examination of their traditional mission in light of the collapse of the Soviet bloc and growing concern about the deficit. "You have to come up with an end-strength number," he said, referring to the total number of people the military will need in the future. "To get to that number, you have to determine the force structure. To get force structure, you have to look at roles and missions."

Skelton's chairmanship of the Military Forces and Personnel subcommittee put him in the middle of a debate on homosexuals in the military. When Clinton set off a firestorm in January 1993 by proposing to revoke the military's "gay ban," Skelton quietly expressed qualms. But he withheld judgment pending hearings before his subcommittee projected for mid-1993.

Skelton has a track record on military reform. He has made a cause of upgrading and streamlining the Defense Department's institutions for midcareer officer training; he was appointed by Aspin as chairman of a special panel on military education. In the mid-1980s, Skelton was active in efforts to reform the command structure, providing more authority to the chairman of the Joint Chiefs of Staff and strengthening coordination among the branches. Advocates say the changes reduced interservice rivalries and provided the foundation for the near-flawless U.S. military operation against Iraq in early 1991.

On defense policy issues, the laconic Skelton made his strongest stand as a supporter of the B-2 bomber, an expensive "stealth" plane designed to evade enemy radar. Skelton's position was influenced by the fact that his district includes Whiteman Air Force Base, home to a B-2 bomber force. But his arguments were weighted to the aircraft's strategic importance.

Since the late 1980s, Skelton had labored to stop opponents from killing the program; he held out for the Air Force's plan to build 75 planes. But by 1992, the tightening fiscal situation made that figure unsustainable. Skelton went along with a compromise to set a production cap of 20 B-2s.

A childhood polio victim who later attended a military academy, Skelton took to the House floor several times in 1991 during the Persian Gulf War to praise the U.S. troops — never mentioning that his son James, an Army lieutenant, was stationed in the war zone.

Along with his strong support for defense spending, Skelton divides with the liberal majority of House Democrats on many social issues. An opponent of abortion in most cases, Skelton supported the Bush administration's "gag rule" on abortion counseling at federally

Missouri 4

West Central — Kansas City suburbs; Jefferson City

The 4th is splayed two-thirds of the way across the state, stretching south and east from suburban bedroom communities in Jackson County (Kansas City) to encompass rural farmland, resort areas and small cities — including the state capital of Jefferson City. The easternmost point of the 4th in Osage County is just 75 miles from St. Louis.

Voters in the 4th are conservative, and outside Jackson County the GOP presidential nominee usually fares well: George Bush in 1988 carried every county wholly within the 4th except Saline. But the district is more conservative Democratic than rock-ribbed Republican, and the right kind of Democrat can do quite well, as Rep. Skelton's comfortable re-elections regularly demonstrate. In 1992, Bill Clinton carried 13 whole counties plus the 4th's share of Jackson; he came within 1,801 votes of winning the 4th.

Democrats running for statewide office can find support in the western portion of the 4th. In 1992, successful Democratic gubernatorial nominee Mel Carnahan won every county west of Laclede. Toward the east, however, voter tendencies take a Republican turn. Democrats in competitive contests rarely top one-third of the vote in Cole, Miller and Osage counties.

Much of the 4th is devoted to small farming. While the farm economy has brightened considerably since the mid-1980s, it remains unsettled. Here, as elsewhere in the state, young people are leaving the farms to find steadier employment.

Corn, wheat and soybeans are grown in the rich soil along the Missouri River, on the 4th's northern frontier, as well as in the west. Livestock and dairy production dominate the southern part of the district, where the terrain turns hilly and rocky.

The greatest growth in the 1980s within the 4th was registered in the Lake of the Ozarks resort area and in the suburbs outside Kansas City (especially the burgeoning Cass County suburbs to the south). Retirees have been drawn to the Lake of the Ozarks area, in the center of the district.

State government has been a fairly reliable source of jobs in Cole County, just slightly less populous than Cass. But budget constraints have introduced some uncertainty in the area's economy, threatening state workers with layoffs. Jefferson City also has some light industry. Chesebrough Ponds makes Q-Tips at its Jefferson City plant.

Military installations have been a major factor in the economy. Whiteman Air Force Base in Johnson County is to house the first wing of B-2 stealth bombers, which are expected to begin arriving late in 1993. The Pentagon's 1991 base-closing plan ordered the closure of Richards-Gebaur Air Force Base in Cass County, but the Army's Fort Leonard Wood in Pulaski County has escaped shutdown in 1991 and 1993 rounds.

Sedalia (Pettis County) once was a railhead of the Missouri Pacific Railroad and an entertainment mecca for railworkers. Ragtime composer Scott Joplin got his start in a Sedalia club. Every June, Sedalia holds the Scott Joplin Ragtime Festival, attracting artists from across the country.

1990 Population: 569,146. White 542,723 (95%), Black 18,271 (3%), Other 6,214 (1%). Hispanic origin 8,152 (1%). 18 and over 420,347 (74%), 62 and over 98,757 (17%). Median age: 34.

funded family planning clinics.

But Skelton is more like his party colleagues on domestic spending, especially on programs for rural areas like those in his district. Skelton is a strong supporter of efforts to improve rural health care, law enforcement and economic development. He is a member of the Small Business Committee and formerly chaired a subcommittee that dealt with programs to increase tourism in rural areas.

At Home: Although Skelton won easy reelection in 1990, he was brushed by the anti-incumbent sentiment that swept Missouri. His vote fell to 62 percent, the lowest since redistricting threw him together with freshman Republican Rep. Wendell Bailey in 1982. But by 1992, he was back to form, winning with 70 percent of the vote.

Mapmakers gave Skelton a head start in the 1982 race. When Bailey's old 8th District was dismembered, the largest single block of his constituents was added to Skelton's 4th. So Bailey decided that was the place to seek a second term. But for every one of his old constituents in the new district, there were nearly two of Skelton's.

The Skelton-Bailey match was billed as a referendum on Reaganomics in the rural heartland. The candidates responded appropriately: Skelton called Bailey a "rubber stamp" because he supported nearly all of Reagan's budget and tax proposals, and Bailey countered that Skelton's mixed record of support for Reaganomics showed him to be a liberal who occasionally waffled to appease conservatives.

Bailey, known as one of Missouri's most

effective campaigners, was relying on the gregarious, hard-charging style he developed as a car salesman to help him pull Democrats away from the less dynamic Skelton.

But Skelton, a small-town lawyer with a sincere, low-key style, benefited from greater familiarity with the new district's voters. Of the seven counties that had been part of Bailey's old 8th District, Bailey carried six. But Skelton had represented 13 counties and managed to carry 12 of them. That brought him in nearly 18,000 votes ahead.

Skelton's only other tough election was in 1976, when he won the seat of retiring Democratic Rep. William Randall. As a rural state legislator with a narrow political base, Skelton did not look particularly well-positioned when the campaign began. Only two counties in his state Senate district were within the borders of the 4th District as it was then drawn. His major rivals for the Democratic nomination were state senators from the Kansas City suburbs, which cast about 40 percent of the district vote.

Skelton emphasized his rural roots and campaigned successfully for farm and small-town support. He ran third in the suburbs, but with the rural vote he won with 40 percent.

Independence Mayor Richard A. King was the GOP nominee. A protégé of Gov. (and now Sen.) Christopher S. Bond, King tied his campaign to the GOP ticket of Bond and Senate candidate John C. Danforth. Skelton cited his farm background and fiscal conservatism. And the top of the GOP ticket did not give King much coattail pull. Danforth carried the 4th, but Bond lost it. Skelton won by 24,350 votes.

Committees

Armed Services (5th of 34 Democrats)
Military Forces & Personnel (chairman)

Small Business (3rd of 27 Democrats)
Regulation, Business Opportunities & Technology

Elections

1992 General		
Ike Skelton (D)	176,977	(70%)
John Carley (R)	74,475	(30%)
1992 Primary		
Ike Skelton (D)	60,347	(79%)
Ron Beller (D)	11,540	(15%)
Lewis E. Seay (D)	4,638	(6%)
1990 General		
Ike Skelton (D)	105,527	(62%)
David Eyerly (R)	65,095	(38%)

Previous Winning Percentages: **1988** (72%) **1986** (100%) **1984** (67%) **1982** (55%) **1980** (68%) **1978** (73%) **1976** (56%)

District Vote for President

1992
D 94,951 (37%)
R 96,752 (38%)
I 65,231 (25%)

Campaign Finance

	Receipts	Receipts from PACs		Expend-itures
1992				
Skelton (D)	$310,017	$211,391	(68%)	$426,867
Carley (R)	$4,706	0		$4,628
1990				
Skelton (D)	$390,115	$242,050	(62%)	$306,485
Eyerly (R)	$7,115	0		$7,137

Key Votes

1993	
Require parental notification of minors' abortions	Y
Require unpaid family and medical leave	N
Approve national "motor voter" registration bill	Y
Approve budget increasing taxes and reducing deficit	Y
Approve economic stimulus plan	Y
1992	
Approve balanced-budget constitutional amendment	Y
Close down space station program	Y
Approve U.S. aid for former Soviet Union	Y
Allow shifting funds from defense to domestic programs	X
1991	
Extend unemployment benefits using deficit financing	Y
Approve waiting period for handgun purchases	N
Authorize use of force in Persian Gulf	Y

Voting Studies

	Presidential Support		Party Unity		Conservative Coalition	
Year	**S**	**O**	**S**	**O**	**S**	**O**
1992	57	38	66	31	83	15
1991	52	47	65	32	92	5
1990	50	48	68	29	94	4
1989	59	34	62	25	85	12
1988	43	52	63	30	92	8
1987	45	48	66	24	81	19
1986	48	47	66	26	76	20
1985	44	46	66	25	85	15
1984	54	38	63	27	76	15
1983	45	50	56	37	74	22
1982	48	34	40	41	73	14
1981	58	39	45	45	91	5

Interest Group Ratings

Year	ADA	AFL-CIO	CCUS	ACU
1992	45	67	86	65
1991	30	67	60	47
1990	33	50	62	50
1989	35	58	70	56
1988	40	83	62	58
1987	48	86	40	38
1986	35	86	47	55
1985	40	63	33	50
1984	35	77	33	36
1983	50	82	30	57
1982	10	50	63	65
1981	25	67	37	43

5 Alan Wheat (D)

Of Kansas City — Elected 1982; 6th Term

Born: Oct. 16, 1951, San Antonio, Texas.
Education: Grinnell College, B.A. 1972.
Occupation: Legislative aide; federal economist.
Family: Wife, Yolanda Townsend; one child.
Religion: Church of Christ.
Political Career: Mo. House, 1977-83.
Capitol Office: 2334 Rayburn Bldg. 20515; 225-4535.

In Washington: Although political observers have made much in recent years of the new generation of young black politicians, Wheat gained notice long ago as a skilled political communicator — effective at reaching out both to whites and African-Americans.

Wheat has the largest white constituency of any Democratic black member, with 73 percent. He appeals to a broad and moderate, but loyally Democratic, base. Since he was elected in 1982, he has succeeded in cultivating white voters and building coalitions across racial and ethnic lines.

Throughout his career in Congress, Wheat has paid close attention to his district, winning points from all corners for his efforts to secure federal funding for hometown projects. He has used his seat on the Rules Committee to win concessions for his urban district, including a number of multimillion-dollar flood-control projects. Other committee leaders are eager to accommodate members of Rules, given its role as traffic cop for nearly all legislation.

In the 102nd, he won federal money for the South Riverfront Expressway and for federal studies on a proposed light-rail system for the Kansas City metropolitan area. In addition, Wheat successfully pushed for funding for a new federal courthouse in Kansas City.

Even as he has concentrated on local concerns and his work on Rules, Wheat has shown strong ambition as well in a number of attempts to move up in the Democratic hierarchy.

In 1992 at the Democratic National Convention, he secured a co-chairmanship of the Credentials Committee.

He considered a race for Democratic Caucus vice chairman in the 101st Congress, and then unsuccessfully sought a seat on the Budget Committee.

He assumed a more prominent role in the Black Caucus Foundation, serving as its president since 1990. In 1991, the caucus voted to urge Speaker Thomas S. Foley of Washington to name Wheat chief deputy majority whip. However, the venerable Democrat John Lewis of Georgia launched his own campaign and won, according to a columnist for Gannett News Service.

Wheat has consistently spoken out on issues that have an impact on African-Americans. In the 102nd, he cosponsored a bill with fellow Missouri Democrat William L. Clay aimed at helping financially strapped historically black colleges and universities make needed but costly building and other improvements. The measure was included in the Higher Education Act enacted in 1992.

In January 1990, he traveled to South Africa and later met with African National Congress leader Nelson Mandela. During debate over U.S. relations with South Africa, Wheat echoed a suggestion by Mandela, urging that sanctions continue until the United States determines that the nation's movement toward democracy is "irreversible."

Wheat was a reserved, deferential apprentice when he first arrived in the House, heeding the advice of his respected predecessor and mentor, Richard Bolling. Wheat got a ringside seat in his first term, landing on the prestigious Rules Committee, which Bolling had chaired. Bolling died in 1991.

Wheat rarely introduces legislation of his own but instead sponsors Rules' resolutions for floor debate on issues of interest to him, such as the Civil Rights Act of 1990 and the leadership's high priority homeless-aid bill in 1987. That helped him win a 1990 appointment to the now-defunct House Select Committee on Hunger.

Wheat's success in Congress has some suggesting he has a shot at the Senate seat coming open in 1994. Republican John C. Danforth announced at the beginning of the 103rd Congress that he would not seek another term.

At Home: Wheat's election in 1982 breached the custom that candidates of his race win only those districts dominated by liberals and minority voters. Just one-fourth of his district's residents are black and, though the white majority usually votes Democratic, most of the electorate stands to his right.

After attending Grinnell, a prestigious lib-

Missouri 5

Kansas City and eastern suburbs; Independence

From its fountains and skyscrapers to its barbecue joints and sports complex, one-time cowtown Kansas City is now a modern, front-line U.S. city. In the 1990 census, it passed St. Louis as Missouri's most populous city.

While it remains a nationally prominent feeder cattle and hard winter wheat market, the city's economy is far more diverse than its longtime image implies. The stockyards' heyday ended decades ago. Diversity enabled Kansas City to weather economic doldrums better than many urban areas.

The district is solidly Democratic: Presidential nominees Michael S. Dukakis and Bill Clinton both carried the 5th by wide margins in 1988 and 1992. That has helped Rep. Wheat, who has always attracted biracial support, maintain a steady hold on his white-majority district.

Long a center for automobile production, metropolitan Kansas City is the nation's sixth-largest auto producer. Ford has a plant north of the city in Claycomo (in the 6th District); General Motors' Fairfax assembly plant is just across the Missouri River in Kansas. Many autoworkers live in blue-collar neighborhoods in Kansas City and in the nearby city of Independence.

Other blue-collar workers who live in the district work at Kansas City International Airport (KCI), north of the city. Trans World Airlines, which filed for bankruptcy in July 1991, has a large base where it overhauls its aircraft. KCI is a contender in the bidding war for the production facility for McDonnell Douglas' new passenger airplane.

With many regional offices in the city and across the Kansas border, the federal government is one of the area's largest employers. Hallmark Cards is a hometown corporation and has spent millions on commercial redevelopment within the city. It built Crown Center, which includes an array of restaurants, shops, pricey apartments and a luxury hotel. Hallmark and other major corporations received some unflattering attention in 1991 with their "screening committee" to dub an acceptable mayoral candidate. Ultimately, City Council member Emanuel Cleaver, who had been snubbed by the corporate elite, won the election, becoming Kansas City's first black mayor.

Though Kansas City has not suffered the flight of people and businesses that has drained St. Louis, its population has declined to about 435,000 — fewer people than were living in the city 30 years ago. For a generation there has been steady out-migration to Jackson County suburbs and into Johnson County, Kan.

But Kansas City has not capitulated. Yuppies have been lured back to the central city by projects such as the restoration of the Quality Hill section, one of Kansas City's oldest areas, and of City Market, an outdoor market in use since the 1800s. And the city boasts an outstanding housing stock around the University of Missouri-Kansas City.

To the east, the 5th includes Independence (population 112,300), the fourth most populous city in Missouri and hometown of Harry S Truman.

1990 Population: 569,130. White 416,843 (73%), Black 134,608 (24%), Other 17,679 (3%). Hispanic origin 18,032 (3%). 18 and over 428,226 (75%), 62 and over 93,429 (16%). Median age: 33.

eral-arts school in Iowa, Wheat worked in Kansas City for the Department of Housing and Urban Development, and was an aide to the Jackson County executive. Elected at age 25 to the state House, he served three terms and chaired its Urban Affairs Committee.

In 1982, Wheat was one of eight Democrats to enter the congressional primary following Bolling's retirement announcement. The only black candidate in the field, Wheat won nomination with 31 percent of the vote.

The bulk of Wheat's support in the primary came from 10 Kansas City wards where the black political organization, Freedom Inc., is an influential force. But he refuted those who said he was the candidate only of blacks by amassing about one-third of his primary vote in mostly white and relatively prosperous neighborhoods in southwest Kansas City.

Republicans nominated state Rep. John A. Sharp, who sought to woo moderate and conservative Democrats who found Wheat too liberal. Though Sharp did not portray the contest in racial terms, he often warned that Wheat would be a tool of Freedom Inc.

But Wheat found a unifying theme, holding up Reaganomics as a threat to working-class voters of all races. Armed with Bolling's endorsement, Wheat found support among local business people and union members alike, and he took an impressive 58 percent.

Wheat's liberal leanings and narrow margin of victory in the 1982 primary prompted some conservative white Democrats to seek an alternative candidate for 1984. But no prominent challenger came forward. Wheat had no trouble winning re-election in 1986, 1988 and 1990.

In 1990 Wheat did face opposition but won with 62 percent of the vote.

But 1992 proved tougher. When it was disclosed that Wheat had overdrawn his House bank account 86 times, four Democratic challengers filed against him.

The one with the greatest potential was Fred Arbanas, who was a star with the Kansas City Chiefs before beginning his 20-year career as a Jackson County (Kansas City) legislator. Arbanas fit the profile of the candidate most threatening to Wheat: a white, moderate-to-conservative Democrat with a base in the blue-collar eastern area of the district.

But Arbanas ran a curiously restrained campaign, choosing not to attack Wheat aggressively for his check problems. And Arbanas' fundraising was lackluster.

In addition, Wheat's well-established record of returning home and tending to constituent services served him well. His door-to-door campaigning, while perhaps more aggressive in 1992 than in most years, was no aberration.

Unlike some of his less-fortunate colleagues, Wheat also benefited from a late-summer primary. By August, the bank stories had virtually disappeared. Wheat topped Arbanas by more than 20 percentage points.

In November, Wheat faced former mayoral candidate Edward "Gomer" Moody, a prominent businessman who ran unsuccessfully for mayor in 1991. In the strongly Democratic 5th, Moody was far from an ideal fit. Wheat beat Moody by 22 percentage points, but the presence of two third-party candidates held him to 59 percent, the first time he came in below 60 percent in 10 years.

Committees

District of Columbia (3rd of 8 Democrats)
Government Operations & Metropolitan Affairs (chairman); Fiscal Affairs & Health

Rules (7th of 9 Democrats)
Legislative Process

Elections

1992 General		
Alan Wheat (D)	151,014	(59%)
Edward "Gomer" Moody (R)	93,562	(37%)
Tom Danaher (NL)	6,107	(2%)
Grant Stauffer (LIBERT)	4,629	(2%)
1992 Primary		
Alan Wheat (D)	50,873	(58%)
Fred Arbanas (D)	32,773	(38%)
Michael Boatright (D)	1,972	(2%)
Lou Ferro Jr. (D)	1,682	(2%)
1990 General		
Alan Wheat (D)	71,890	(62%)
Robert H. Gardner (R)	43,897	(38%)

Previous Winning Percentages: **1988** (70%) **1986** (71%) **1984** (66%) **1982** (58%)

District Vote for President

1992
D 134,932 (52%)
R 67,503 (26%)
I 55,763 (22%)

Campaign Finance

	Receipts	Receipts from PACs		Expend-itures
1992				
Wheat (D)	$488,439	$344,588	(71%)	$652,137
Moody (R)	$55,395	$2,000	(4%)	$57,400
1990				
Wheat (D)	$311,266	$224,435	(72%)	$245,132

Key Votes

1993	
Require parental notification of minors' abortions	N
Require unpaid family and medical leave	Y
Approve national "motor voter" registration bill	Y
Approve budget increasing taxes and reducing deficit	Y
Approve economic stimulus plan	Y
1992	
Approve balanced-budget constitutional amendment	N
Close down space station program	Y
Approve U.S. aid for former Soviet Union	N
Allow shifting funds from defense to domestic programs	Y
1991	
Extend unemployment benefits using deficit financing	Y
Approve waiting period for handgun purchases	Y
Authorize use of force in Persian Gulf	N

Voting Studies

	Presidential Support		Party Unity		Conservative Coalition	
Year	**S**	**O**	**S**	**O**	**S**	**O**
1992	12	88	93	3	10	85
1991	23	77	97	3	5	95
1990	13	86	95	3	11	87
1989	27	71	80	17	7	90
1988	15	83	79	18	5	92
1987	9	91	97	2	5	95
1986	14	86	96	3	12	88
1985	15	84	97	1	5	95
1984	23	77	96	4	3	97
1983	12	87	97	3	10	90

Interest Group Ratings

Year	ADA	AFL-CIO	CCUS	ACU
1992	95	91	13	0
1991	100	100	10	0
1990	100	100	21	4
1989	95	100	40	0
1988	100	93	21	0
1987	100	100	0	0
1986	95	86	22	0
1985	100	100	14	0
1984	100	92	38	0
1983	95	100	15	0

6 Pat Danner (D)

Of Smithville — Elected 1992; 1st Term

Born: Jan. 13, 1934, Louisville, Ky.
Education: Northeast Missouri State U., B.A. 1972.
Occupation: Congressional aide; federal official.
Family: Husband, Markt Meyer; four children.
Religion: Roman Catholic.
Political Career: Sought Democratic nomination for U.S. House, 1976; Mo. Senate, 1983-93.
Capitol Office: 1217 Longworth Bldg. 20515; 225-7041.

The Path to Washington: Danner's strategy for winning the 6th was a two-fisted one: With one hand, hammer the sitting incumbent; with the other, cloak herself in the image of a beloved and departed local political figure.

During the campaign, Danner, a state senator since 1983, frequently invoked the memory of former Democratic Rep. Jerry Litton of Missouri, for whom she had been chief district aide.

Litton, who represented the district from 1973 to 1976, died in a plane crash after winning the 1976 Democratic Senate nomination. He is a folk hero among northwest Missouri natives who believe that, had he lived, he eventually would have become president.

The first signs of trouble for Republican incumbent Tom Coleman arose as early as 1990, when a little-known and underfinanced Democratic opponent held him to 52 percent.

The poor showing prompted eight Democrats to file for the 6th in 1992, with Danner and state Rep. Sandra Reeves leading the field.

Reeves, who favored abortion rights, went on the offensive before the primary, accusing Danner of misleading voters by suggesting that Danner, too, supported abortion rights. Reeves cited news stories from 1991 in which Danner referred to herself as "pro-life."

Danner countered that she would not seek to outlaw abortion and would vote for a version of the Freedom of Choice Act, as long as it included a parental notification provision and barred use of taxpayers' money for abortions.

Danner's campaign stance on abortion conflicted with her state Senate record. She voted for a 1986 bill that banned the use of public facilities for abortion and declared that life begins at conception. That statute was upheld in the Supreme Court's landmark 1989 *Webster v. Reproductive Health Services* decision.

In 1988, Danner introduced a bill by the chairman of Missouri Citizens for Life to ban use of fetal tissue and organs obtained from abortions for medical transplants and to prohibit abortions that are performed for the purpose of obtaining fetal tissue or organs. (In the 103rd Congress, however, she voted for a bill codifying the Clinton administration's lifting of the ban on fetal tissue research.)

Reeves' charges failed to stick, though, and Danner won the nomination with 52 percent of the vote. Reeves trailed with 25 percent.

Danner benefited from a perception of Coleman, both at home and in Washington, as aloof and inaccessible. The farm economy in northwest Missouri has yet to rebound from the decline of the 1980s. While Coleman, the ranking Republican on the Agriculture Committee, often touted his disagreements with White House farm policies, farmers in the largely agricultural 6th District complained that he was unresponsive to the crisis.

Unlike Coleman's 1990 opponent, Danner was both amply funded and well-known. Between Danner and her son, state Sen. Steve Danner, 20 of the 26 counties wholly within the 6th were represented by a Danner in the state Senate.

Danner capitalized on swelling voter resentment toward Congress, attacking the incumbent for his travel, his vote for a congressional pay raise and his use of the frank. Coleman blasted back with a heavy TV ad campaign assailing her voting record in the legislature and questioning her ethics.

Danner was slow to respond to Coleman's attacks. But voters apparently were not swayed by the incumbent's charges. As Bill Clinton amassed a 21,000-plus victory in the 6th, she outran Coleman by nearly 30,000 votes.

Despite her campaign litany on the evils of Congress, it is not clear that Danner will be one to buck the system once in Washington. During the race, she spoke with House Speaker Thomas S. Foley of Washington and met with House Majority Leader Richard A. Gephardt of Missouri. "Those are the kind of friends you want in Congress," she said.

Farmers formed a key block of support for Danner, and to reward them she had hoped to win a spot on the Agriculture Committee or the Appropriations Committee and its Agriculture Subcommittee. Instead she was awarded positions on the Public Works and Transportation and the Small Business committees.

Missouri 6

Northwest — St. Joseph

The 6th encompasses prosperous suburbs east and north of Kansas City and struggling farms along the Iowa border. The economic disparities are mirrored in its political diversity: It is the state's most marginal district. George Bush carried what was then the 6th in 1988, but just barely. In 1992, Democrat Bill Clinton carried all but two of the 28 counties wholly or partly within the 6th. That year, Democratic gubernatorial nominee Mel Carnahan carried all but four counties, while GOP Sen. Christopher S. Bond won all but three district counties.

The substantial population losses in the 1980s in the district's northern tier reflect the devastation of the farm economy. Northwest Missouri is still recovering from the mid-1980s farm crisis; erosion, drought and flooding have taken their toll. Some soybean and corn farmers and their families have turned up on welfare rolls. In towns such as Princeton (Mercer County), businesses that sold farm equipment are boarding up. Being far from the state's four-lane highways perpetuates the sense of isolation.

Farther west in the district, farming is becoming more of a part-time occupation, as many farmers take second jobs. Small to medium-size companies dot the region. Agricultural research critical to the local economy is conducted at Northwest Missouri State University (5,900 students) in Maryville (Nodaway County).

The river city of St. Joseph (Buchanan County) gained a place in history as the eastern end of the Pony Express. A booming supply depot for gold prospectors heading to California in the 1800s, St. Joseph had more than 100,000 people in 1900. But the city shrank steadily thereafter as the stockyards declined, and people looked to jobs and metropolitan life in Kansas City, 35 miles to the south. Things seemed to hit bottom in the 1960s with the exodus of meatpacking companies, and St. Joseph's 1990 population (about 71,900) was its lowest in 100 years.

Attempting to right itself, the city's business sector has diversified. Recent location decisions by new and existing businesses have offered some hope of improvement.

Times have not been as hard in the southwestern part of the 6th, where Kansas City-area workers opting for a more bucolic exurb moved into surrounding counties. Platte and Clay counties registered double-digit percentage gains in population in the 1980s. The portion of Jackson County in the 6th contains affluent, Republican-leaning suburban voters; it was one of only three counties that Danner lost to GOP Rep. Tom Coleman in her 1992 election.

Kansas City International Airport (KCI) is another vital organ of the regional economy. Cutbacks at KCI, particularly by Trans World Airlines, have upset the economy. The airport is now considered a focus of agricultural exports. An export facility there ships cattle by air to the Far East.

Other areas have turned to some innovative economic development ideas. Cameron (Clinton County), for example, has a private minimum-security prison and is eager to host another.

1990 Population: 569,131. White 549,059 (96%), Black 11,997 (2%), Other 8,075 (1%). Hispanic origin 8,478 (2%). 18 and over 421,046 (74%), 62 and over 96,559 (17%). Median age: 34.

Committees

Public Works & Transportation (29th of 39 Democrats)
Aviation; Economic Development; Surface Transportation

Small Business (15th of 27 Democrats)
Rural Enterprises, Exports & the Environment

Campaign Finance

1992	Receipts	Receipts from PACs		Expend-itures
Danner (D)	$490,277	$188,992	(39%)	$482,984
Coleman (R)	$501,200	$343,299	(68%)	$533,305

Key Votes

1993

Require parental notification of minors' abortions	N
Require unpaid family and medical leave	Y
Approve national "motor voter" registration bill	Y
Approve budget increasing taxes and reducing deficit	Y
Approve economic stimulus plan	Y

Elections

1992 General		
Pat Danner (D)	148,887	(55%)
Tom Coleman (R)	119,637	(45%)
1992 Primary		
Pat Danner (D)	43,821	(52%)
Sandra Lee Reeves (D)	20,842	(25%)
John J. Kauffman (D)	6,795	(8%)
John Gallagher (D)	4,671	(6%)
Jeff Bailey (D)	3,327	(4%)
Gene Simmons (D)	2,045	(2%)
Don Pine (D)	1,245	(1%)
Ed O'Herin (D)	1,099	(1%)

District Vote for President

1992

D 110,064 (40%)
R 89,005 (32%)
I 75,185 (27%)

7 Mel Hancock (R)

Of Springfield — Elected 1988; 3rd Term

Born: Sept. 14, 1929, Cape Fair, Mo.
Education: Southwest Missouri State U., B.S. 1951.
Military Service: Air Force, 1951-53; Air Force Reserve, 1953-65.
Occupation: Security company executive.
Family: Wife, Alma "Sug" McDaniel; three children.
Religion: Church of Christ.
Political Career: Sought GOP nomination for U.S. Senate, 1982; GOP nominee for lieutenant governor, 1984.
Capitol Office: 129 Cannon Bldg. 20515; 225-6536.

In Washington: After spending much of his first two terms in Congress proclaiming his distaste for the institution and musing about retirement, Hancock begins his third term with a seat on the traditional preserve of House insiders, the Ways and Means Committee.

It is not a case of Hancock changing, but of his blunt, outspoken, anti-tax fervor becoming the coin of the realm among House Republicans.

Long before many younger members of the House GOP had even entered politics, the chain-smoking Hancock was honing his anti-tax rhetoric. He authored an anti-tax measure that revolutionized — some say hamstrung — Missouri government beginning in 1980.

Hancock, though, has not had long to hone his skills as a legislator. He had not held elective office before winning a seat in Congress in 1988, and at age 59, he was the oldest freshman in his class.

Still, Hancock is less likely to be noticed for his age than for his energy, his size (he is almost a head taller than Ronald Reagan in a 1976 photo of the two) and the big, bass-baritone voice that he says "tends to carry."

Hancock is in top form expressing his visceral antipathy to government. He opposes government involvement in economic affairs and has endorsed the privatizing of even such basic governmental activities as air traffic control.

Long after the Cold War had lost its chill, his speeches at times recalled the heartland anti-government rhetoric of a generation ago, sprinkled with references to "the road to socialism" and "the kind of system they have in Russia."

Even with a friendly regime in Moscow, Hancock has found it difficult to support aid to Russia. During the 102nd Congress he teamed with fellow Banking, Finance and Urban Affairs Committee member John J. "Jimmy" Duncan Jr., R-Tenn., in an unsuccessful effort to strike the funding authorization for the International Monetary Fund, a prime source of aid to Russia and other former republics of the Soviet Union.

In August 1992, Hancock made one of his rare breaks from party ranks on the House floor to oppose a broader Russian aid package. President George Bush and a majority of House Republicans supported its passage.

Hancock came under fire from primary opponents in 1992 who complained that his fight to hold down government spending was costing the district badly needed federal funds. In particular, they criticized Hancock for opposing the 1991 highway bill, which contained funding for road projects in the southwest Missouri district.

Hancock made amends of sorts in 1992 by using his perch on the Public Works and Transportation Committee to push for $7.6 million to build a highway loop around the burgeoning country-and-western resort town of Branson, Mo. The money was added as a "technical correction" to the 1991 highway bill.

During his first two terms in Congress, Hancock spent much of his time on parochial interests as well as issues that affected his aging Ozark constituency. He promoted the creation of tax-free savings accounts for parents and grandparents saving for college for their children and grandchildren.

And he pursued the legislative repeal of the Supreme Court ruling in *Missouri v. Jenkins.* The case arose when a federal judge in Kansas City ordered the school district to raise taxes to finance court-ordered integration. Hancock's ban on "judicial taxation" had 147 cosponsors in the 101st Congress, but no hearings were held on it.

From his new position on the Ways and Means Committee, Hancock could become a visible player in national affairs, although it is doubtful that he will ever be heavily lobbied by President Clinton, who has little chance of winning over Hancock.

Hancock indicated in early 1993 that he supported a freeze in government spending.

Missouri 7

Southwest — Springfield; Joplin

Two decades of rapid growth have helped lift southwestern Missouri from poor hillbilly hideaway to burgeoning resort region with a growing industrial base. Since the 1970s, this part of Missouri has outpaced the rest of the state in population growth. It is solidly Republican territory.

The 7th boomed during the 1980s as a stream of retirees and other newcomers settled in the resort area around Table Rock Lake. Branson (Taney County) has become a magnet for country music fans, attracting 4 million visitors a year to its many theaters and studios.

The recreational trade nourishes local services and industries. Bass Pro Shops, which manufactures and sells fishing boats and other sporting goods, is based in Springfield (Greene County), the district's industrial and commercial center. Nationwide customers of Bass Pro's mail-order catalog are lured to the Springfield store much as devotees of L. L. Bean descend on its site in Maine.

Springfield also counts Kraft, Litton, 3M and Rockwell among its major employers, and it is home to Southwest Missouri State University (19,500 students). More than 40 percent of the 7th's residents live in Greene and neighboring Christian County.

Joplin is the district's other population center. An old lead- and zinc-mining town, Joplin is now a manufacturing and trucking center. Nearby Carthage, the Jasper County seat, competes for attention with its larger neighbor.

Wheat, soybeans and corn are grown in the 7th's western counties. The hillier Ozark counties raise beef and dairy cattle. Poultry farming and production also contribute to the district's economy.

The rural and agricultural character of the Ozarks has not entirely yielded to development and modernization. There remain many small, isolated communities, legacies of the region's settlers — Scots-Irish mountaineers from eastern Tennessee, western Virginia and Kentucky. Many of these rural counties struggle economically.

Southwestern Missouri is a breeding ground for statewide GOP politicians. The last Republican governor, secretary of state, attorney general and state treasurer all had roots in the southwest. George Bush carried every county in the 7th in 1992 even as he lost by 10 points statewide. Losing 1992 GOP gubernatorial nominee William L. Webster won every county but Greene.

The area's Republican lineage dates from the Civil War. Though there was some slave trading on Springfield's town square, most of the Ozark settlers had no use for slavery on their small, hilly farms; pro-Union sentiment was strong. The GOP preference in the Joplin area was cemented when President Woodrow Wilson lowered tariffs on lead and zinc and crippled the mining industry.

The 7th's conservatism is also reflected in its politically active religious organizations. The national headquarters of the Assemblies of God, the nation's largest Pentecostal church, is in Springfield, and the Pentecostal Church of God's international headquarters is in Joplin.

1990 Population: 568,017. White 552,934 (97%), Black 5,295 (1%), Other 9,788 (2%). Hispanic origin 4,443 (1%). 18 and over 428,827 (75%), 62 and over 105,271 (19%). Median age: 35.

"There's a lot of spending they could cut — foreign aid, welfare, get rid of the bureaucracy," he said. "You can streamline government just like you can a business."

That kind of talk may have helped him win a GOP slot on Ways and Means. Certainly his partisanship did. Although Hancock has cultivated a reputation as a maverick, his party unity scores have been among the highest in Congress. On votes that divided mostly along party lines in 1992, he voted with the GOP House majority 98 percent of the time, a mark exceeded by only two other Republican members.

At Home: When veteran GOP Rep. Gene Taylor announced that he was stepping down in 1988, competitive races ensued in both parties. Hancock won his primary by dominating the rural counties and holding off Gary Nodler, Taylor's district aide, whose base was in Joplin.

The Democrats nominated former Greene County (Springfield) Circuit Judge Max E. Bacon, a tough judge whose nickname was "Maximum Max" and who was best known for singing gospel duets with GOP Gov. John Ashcroft (also from Springfield). Bacon came within 500 votes in Greene County. But Hancock ran up a 6,000-vote margin in the three counties bordering Kansas and swept the 13 outlying counties.

Most House freshmen enjoy a "sophomore surge" when they first run for re-election, but not Hancock. He saw his vote share decline from 53 percent in 1988 to 52 percent in 1990, even though his Democratic opponent was neither as well-known nor as well-financed as the one Hancock faced in 1988.

Hancock was apparently hurt by his "Congressman No" image, especially in Greene County, the most cosmopolitan part of the district. He lost that county in 1990 by more than 3,000 votes to Democrat Thomas Patrick Deaton, a Springfield lawyer. Of the other 16 counties in the historically Republican district, Hancock carried 15, but his share outside Greene County was still a modest 55 percent.

Hardly anyone expected the election to be so close. Before the campaign began, Hancock told the St. Louis Post-Dispatch that he would "rather be back home, hunting," and might not run for re-election. He quickly changed his mind, though, and seemed to clear his only real hurdle for re-election early in the year when Bacon announced that he would not run.

Hancock took his 1992 opposition seriously, campaigning aggressively in both the primary and general elections. He faced two primary challengers: Taney County Commission Clerk Ronald Houseman and schoolteacher Stephen Pennington. Both accused Hancock of being excessively doctrinaire in his anti-government conservatism, but neither was well-known or well-funded. Hancock crushed them, winning with 77 percent of the vote.

Deaton had returned for a rematch in the general election, but Democratic disunity helped scuttle his effort. Deaton won an acrimonious primary over state Rep. Doug Harpool of Springfield, who had switched from the state attorney general race to run for Congress. But the caustic primary cleaved a rift in Democratic ranks that never closed. Hancock prevailed with 62 percent of the vote and carried every county in the 7th.

Committee

Ways & Means (12th of 14 Republicans)
Select Revenue Measures (ranking); Oversight

Elections

1992 General		
Mel Hancock (R)	160,303	(62%)
Thomas Patrick Deaton (D)	99,762	(38%)
1992 Primary		
Mel Hancock (R)	66,667	(77%)
Ronald Houseman (R)	13,469	(16%)
Stephen Keith Pennington (R)	6,304	(7%)
1990 General		
Mel Hancock (R)	83,609	(52%)
Thomas Patrick Deaton (D)	76,725	(48%)

Previous Winning Percentage: **1988** (53%)

District Vote for President

1992
D 96,621 (37%)
R 118,817 (45%)
I 48,824 (18%)

Campaign Finance

	Receipts	Receipts from PACs		Expend-itures
1992				
Hancock (R)	$393,638	$164,430	(42%)	$426,525
Deaton (D)	$309,432	$183,268	(59%)	$310,658
1990				
Hancock (R)	$280,787	$122,782	(44%)	$182,474
Deaton (D)	$103,759	$47,445	(46%)	$103,265

Key Votes

1993	
Require parental notification of minors' abortions	Y
Require unpaid family and medical leave	N
Approve national "motor voter" registration bill	N
Approve budget increasing taxes and reducing deficit	N
Approve economic stimulus plan	N
1992	
Approve balanced-budget constitutional amendment	Y
Close down space station program	N
Approve U.S. aid for former Soviet Union	N
Allow shifting funds from defense to domestic programs	N
1991	
Extend unemployment benefits using deficit financing	N
Approve waiting period for handgun purchases	N
Authorize use of force in Persian Gulf	Y

Voting Studies

	Presidential Support		Party Unity		Conservative Coalition	
Year	**S**	**O**	**S**	**O**	**S**	**O**
1992	81	19	98	2	96	4
1991	79	19	95	3	100	0
1990	80	20	98	2	94	6
1989	78	22	98	1	95	5

Interest Group Ratings

Year	ADA	AFL-CIO	CCUS	ACU
1992	10	25	75	96
1991	5	8	90	100
1990	11	0	79	100
1989	0	8	90	96

8 Bill Emerson (R)

Of Cape Girardeau — Elected 1980; 7th Term

Born: Jan. 1, 1938, Hillsboro, Mo.
Education: Westminster College, B.A. 1959; U. of Baltimore, LL.B. 1964.
Military Service: Air Force Reserve, 1964-92.
Occupation: Government relations executive; congressional aide.
Family: Wife, Jo Ann Hermann; four children.
Religion: Presbyterian.
Political Career: No previous office.
Capitol Office: 2454 Rayburn Bldg. 20515; 225-4404.

In Washington: Emerson has a streak of ideological conservatism that reveals itself on certain issues through his votes and rhetoric. But the hallmark of his legislative identity is pragmatism. That often showed up on the Select Committee on Hunger, where he was vice chairman, as well as on Agriculture, where, beginning in the 103rd Congress, he was the ranking Republican on the General Farm Commodities Subcommittee.

Emerson first came to the House as a high school student in the 1950s, when he served as a page. Later, he worked as both a House and Senate staffer and as a lobbyist. He cultivates an image as a man who knows how the game is played. And his history on the Hill made him a logical choice for the Joint Committee on the Organization of Congress, a 28-member bipartisan panel formed at the end of the 102nd Congress.

Early in the 103rd, Emerson gave indications that his sights may not be set permanently on the House. When Missouri Republican Sen. John C. Danforth announced that he would not seek a fourth term in 1994, Emerson considered making the statewide run.

Emerson fought the creation of a new House Select Committee on Hunger. Still, he accepted appointment to it. By the 101st Congress, he was the committee's vice chairman.

As a member of the Hunger Committee, Emerson was a sort of conservative watchdog, willing to challenge the assumptions of the Democratic majority. Like other conservative Republicans, he is concerned about Democrats using hunger in America as a political issue. But he has taken an interest in the world famine problem. He went to Somalia in November 1992, focusing attention on the mass starvation there before President Bush ordered U.S. military intervention to aid that nation.

When House Republicans proposed rule changes to abolish the four select (non-legislative) panels, Emerson defended the Hunger panel. "Some years ago, I would have agreed with this goal," he said in September 1992. ". . . However . . . my experience has changed my mind. . . . The Hunger Committee plays a valid role in addressing . . . problems that otherwise would not have been dealt with." He was one of 15 Republicans voting to reauthorize the Select Narcotics Committee in 1993. The four House Select panels were killed.

Emerson's major crop interest is soybeans. He has long advocated legislation to require the Agriculture secretary to start a new marketing loan program. It would allow soybean farmers to repay their price-support loans at the market price, which could be significantly lower than the loan rate. The 1990 farm bill included a marketing loan plan for soybeans, though the loan rate was far lower than that sought by members from soybean-producing states.

The more partisan and combative Emerson emerges in areas such as federal spending. Emerson, who supports a constitutional amendment to require a balanced budget, avers, "We've had enough of the budget chicanery from the liberals in Congress."

An abortion foe, he introduces a bill each Congress to prohibit using federal funds for abortion except when the woman's life is in danger. He opposed efforts in the 102nd Congress to overturn a 1988 ban on federally funded research using tissue from aborted fetuses, rejecting arguments that the research could help those stricken with Parkinson's disease and diabetes. "This is an issue of abortion and an issue of abortion only. The simple truth is we already have enough fetal tissue," he said.

Emerson joined the Public Works Committee in the 101st Congress, leaving his post on the Interior Committee. Just as he had on Interior, he uses his Public Works seat as a vehicle for tending to local concerns. He secured funding for the Ste. Genevieve and Cape La Croix flood control projects in his district.

In March 1988, Emerson voluntarily began a 30-day treatment program for alcohol dependency. Remarkably, his adversities seemed to strengthen him. Reaction was almost uniformly sympathetic. By openly seeking help, he seemed to win respect and even admiration from colleagues and constituents alike.

At Home: In North Carolina, there are

Missouri 8

Southeast — Cape Girardeau

Within the borders of the 8th is some of the state's most bountiful farmland, and the district's agricultural diversity is matched by its political breadth. The 8th spans the spectrum from solidly Republican counties in the west and northeast along the Mississippi River to "yellow dog" Democratic territory in the southeastern Bootheel.

The 8th's growth during the 1980s came primarily in its northernmost counties, not far from metropolitan St. Louis. Washington and St. Francois counties both had double-digit growth as commuters settled into bedroom communities. Both counties solidly backed Bill Clinton in 1992.

In the southeastern corner is the Bootheel, a cluster of counties that look and vote like the Old South. Predominantly a wheat-growing region until the mid-1920s, the Bootheel was transformed when cotton growers and black sharecroppers from Mississippi, Alabama and Tennessee, driven north by the boll weevil, discovered the area's rich delta land and settled. The seven counties in the southeastern corner — Mississippi, New Madrid, Pemiscot, Dunklin, Butler, Stoddard and Scott — grow 35 percent of the state's cash crops. Clinton carried all seven in 1992.

The Bootheel is the northernmost area in the country where cotton and rice grow. The port at New Madrid has Missouri's only rice mill; it opened in 1988. Dunklin is the nation's No. 3 watermelon-harvesting county and is in the top 50 for peach production.

Soybeans and corn have supplanted cotton as the Bootheel's leading crops, but the Southern Democratic habits forged during cotton's heyday have persisted. A search of the Bootheel counties' courthouses would reveal only the occasional Republican. But in statewide contests, these Democratic strongholds are largely offset by Republican votes from Cape Girardeau and Perry counties. The cluster of Cape Girardeau, Perry and Bollinger counties makes up three of the four district counties George Bush won in 1992.

Above the Bootheel, along the Mississippi River, dairy production and beef cattle fuel the economy. Livestock, timber and fruit production flourish in other parts of the 8th. Wright is Missouri's foremost dairy county. Oregon County breeds feeder pigs for Iowa slaughterhouses. Apples are grown in the Mark Twain National Forest.

Even the ground beneath the 8th yields riches. The vast majority of the nation's lead — and most of the world's — is mined in southeast Missouri. The discovery of a "New Lead Belt" called the Viburnum Trend during the late 1950s revitalized an industry that dates back to the early 1700s, when French explorers mined in Mine La Motte (Madison County). Most of today's lead mining is centered in the New Lead Belt of western Iron County and Reynolds County.

The forests of the Ozarks once provided the timber that built St. Louis. Small lumber mills in the area still produce pallets and other wood products. The Ozarks also attract recreation-seekers who fish and canoe in the Eleven Point and Current rivers and in the Ozark National Scenic Riverways.

1990 Population: 568,385. White 538,611 (95%), Black 25,155 (4%), Other 4,619 (1%). Hispanic origin 2,907 (1%). 18 and over 418,339 (74%), 62 and over 109,113 (19%). Median age: 35.

"Jessecrats"; in southeast Missouri, there are "Emercrats": conservative Democrats who support members of their own party for local office but Republican Emerson for the House.

Emerson ousted an ethically tainted Democrat in 1980 and has relied on Emercrat votes to win re-election ever since, though Democrats control virtually all the area's county courthouses and state legislative seats. Democratic challengers ran best against Emerson in 1982 and 1986, holding him to 53 percent of the vote each time.

He had to overcome the effects of recession and redistricting in 1982. Remapping moved Emerson's Jefferson County base from the district, and he relocated 80 miles to the southeast in Cape Girardeau, the 8th's largest city.

That gave Democrats an opening to label Emerson a "carpetbagger." But Emerson, stressing support from several prominent Democrats and the state Farm Bureau, held on to win against Democratic state Rep. Jerry Ford.

After winning easily in 1984, Emerson faced a serious 1986 challenge from Democrat Wayne Cryts, who burst into national prominence in 1981 by leading a band of frustrated cohorts to a bankrupt grain elevator and seizing more than 30,000 bushels of soybeans.

But Cryts did not command unanimous support in the farm community; the Missouri Farm Bureau and the heads of many state and local farm commodity groups backed Emerson. Even some farmers sympathetic to Cryts recalled that the incumbent had worked to help spring Cryts from jail following the 1981 soybean raid. Cryts carried 15 counties, but that was not enough to overcome Emerson's nearly

5,000-vote margin in Cape Girardeau County.

In 1988, Cryts was back. He compiled a sizable campaign treasury, raising twice as much as he had in 1986. Emerson's admission of alcohol dependency in early 1988 suggested vulnerability. But there was a lessened sense of economic crisis among Bootheel farmers in 1988. In the end, Emerson won 22 counties, including Cryts' one-time base, Stoddard.

In 1990, he defeated Russ Carnahan, the son of then-Lt. Gov. (now Gov.) Mel Carnahan and a grandson of the late Democratic Rep. A. S. J. Carnahan, who represented the 8th for seven terms (1945-47, 1949-61). In 1992, Democrats gave Emerson a virtual free ride. He got 63 percent against Thad Bullock, a 75-year-old piano store owner and perennial candidate.

The Washington bug bit Emerson early — when he was a teenage page in the 83rd and 84th Congresses. After finishing college in Missouri, he returned to Capitol Hill and worked as a lobbyist in the 1960s and 1970s.

In 1979 he returned to Missouri to challenge 10th District Democratic Rep. Bill D. Burlison. The incumbent was hurt by charges that he had an affair, then interceded improperly in the woman's behalf in a dispute involving her performance in a federal job. Burlison denied all charges, but many conservative Democrats deserted him. Aided also by Ronald Reagan's coattails, Emerson became the first Republican in 50 years to take the 10th.

Committees

Agriculture (2nd of 18 Republicans)
General Farm Commodities (ranking); Department Operations; Specialty Crops & Natural Resources

Public Works & Transportation (6th of 24 Republicans)
Public Buildings & Grounds; Surface Transportation; Water Resources & the Environment

Joint Organization of Congress

Elections

1992 General		
Bill Emerson (R)	147,398	(63%)
Thad Bullock (D)	86,730	(37%)
1992 Primary		
Bill Emerson (R)	28,973	(69%)
E. Earl Durnell (R)	12,807	(31%)
1990 General		
Bill Emerson (R)	81,452	(57%)
Russ Carnahan (D)	60,751	(43%)

Previous Winning Percentages: **1988** (58%) **1986** (53%) **1984** (65%) **1982** (53%) **1980** (55%)

District Vote for President

1992
D 109,858 (46%)
R 89,238 (37%)
I 41,558 (17%)

Campaign Finance

	Receipts	Receipts from PACs		Expend-itures
1992				
Emerson (R)	$518,998	$299,188	(58%)	$488,949
Bullock (D)	$12,650	$6,000	(47%)	$11,974
1990				
Emerson (R)	$625,060	$326,541	(52%)	$704,447
Carnahan (D)	$250,002	$120,950	(48%)	$246,595

Key Votes

1993	
Require parental notification of minors' abortions	Y
Require unpaid family and medical leave	N
Approve national "motor voter" registration bill	N
Approve budget increasing taxes and reducing deficit	N
Approve economic stimulus plan	N
1992	
Approve balanced-budget constitutional amendment	Y
Close down space station program	N
Approve U.S. aid for former Soviet Union	Y
Allow shifting funds from defense to domestic programs	N
1991	
Extend unemployment benefits using deficit financing	Y
Approve waiting period for handgun purchases	N
Authorize use of force in Persian Gulf	Y

Voting Studies

	Presidential Support		Party Unity		Conservative Coalition	
Year	**S**	**O**	**S**	**O**	**S**	**O**
1992	76	24	84	15	92	8
1991	71	29	71	28	97	3
1990	57	41	65	31	96	2
1989	78	21	75	22	95	2
1988	47	38	75	14	84	3
1987	60	38	86	13	95	2
1986	69	31	82	18	92	8
1985	60	36	78	17	95	2
1984	57	42	78	19	93	5
1983	70	27	85	13	90	9
1982	58	34	88	9	85	10
1981	78	22	90	10	99	1

Interest Group Ratings

Year	ADA	AFL-CIO	CCUS	ACU
1992	20	42	88	92
1991	15	25	90	85
1990	11	17	85	78
1989	10	17	100	93
1988	10	50	83	90
1987	4	25	87	78
1986	10	29	72	77
1985	10	25	81	80
1984	15	31	75	83
1983	5	12	85	87
1982	10	15	86	91
1981	0	20	89	100

9 Harold L. Volkmer (D)

Of Hannibal — Elected 1976; 9th Term

Born: April 4, 1931, Jefferson City, Mo.
Education: U. of Missouri, LL.B. 1955.
Military Service: Army, 1955-57.
Occupation: Lawyer.
Family: Wife, Shirley Ruth Braskett; three children.
Religion: Roman Catholic.
Political Career: Mo. assistant attorney general, 1955; Marion County prosecuting attorney, 1960-66; Mo. House, 1967-77.
Capitol Office: 2409 Rayburn Bldg. 20515; 225-2956.

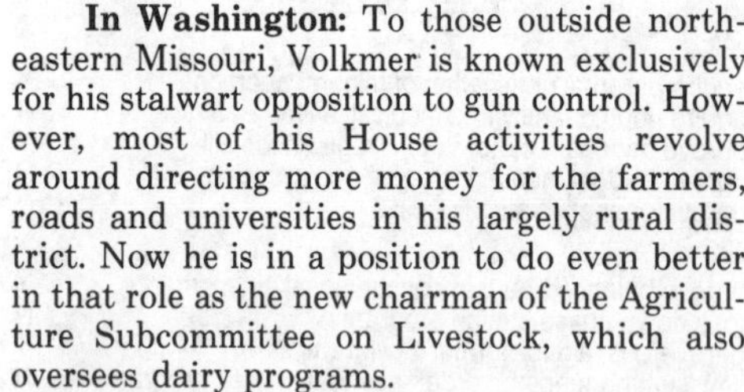

In Washington: To those outside northeastern Missouri, Volkmer is known exclusively for his stalwart opposition to gun control. However, most of his House activities revolve around directing more money for the farmers, roads and universities in his largely rural district. Now he is in a position to do even better in that role as the new chairman of the Agriculture Subcommittee on Livestock, which also oversees dairy programs.

Winning friends has never been Volkmer's strong suit in the House. He can be surly when he disagrees with someone, which is not infrequently. And his recent elections demonstrate that his particular combination of social conservatism and pork barrel politics is showing signs of wear with a significant segment of his constituency. But if his social skills fail to charm some colleagues, that has not kept him from having an influence on legislation.

Volkmer is the National Rifle Association's leading House ally. The NRA's lobbying has buoyed Volkmer's efforts against gun control; but lobbyists don't kill bills, legislators do, and Volkmer has shown he can be effective.

Volkmer's most notable achievement in this area came in 1986, when he won passage of a bill rolling back gun control laws that had been on the books nearly 20 years.

Opponents of Volkmer's proposal, which lifted a ban on the interstate sale of rifles, shotguns and handguns and eased other restrictions, called it "cop killer" legislation. But Volkmer said he was simply protecting the right to bear arms. The House adopted his package by a 286-136 vote, though opponents managed to retain a ban on interstate sale of handguns.

In the 100th Congress, he helped scuttle a portion of a drug bill requiring a seven-day waiting period for the purchase of handguns. The proposal, known as the "Brady bill," gained steam in the 102nd Congress when former President Ronald Reagan endorsed it. The House passed a seven-day waiting period in early 1991; but a five-day waiting period died at the end of the 102nd as part of the omnibus crime bill.

During House consideration of the crime bill, Volkmer succeeded in removing a provision that would have banned 13 semiautomatic weapons and limited gun magazines to seven rounds of ammunition. The debate was sparked by an incident in which a man with an automatic pistol shot and killed 22 people at a Texas cafeteria. But Volkmer and others complained that the language could lead to banning many sporting weapons. A day after the Texas shooting spree, members voted 247-177 to strip out the ban.

Volkmer has shown a particular aptitude for legislating on the Agriculture Committee. He is an active participant in committee debates and can be a team player who will work to whip up support for the panel's legislation. But his willingness to play ball wanes when the subject turns to price supports for feed grains and dairy; he will scrap to the last for those.

The 1990 farm bill was assembled amid budget-cutting pressures, but Volkmer had little sympathy for the cost-cutters. He championed the proposal of a national group of dairy farmer cooperatives; it called for a 50-cent increase in the existing dairy price-support level. But when the full committee considered the bill, a plan backed by the chairman and ranking Republican of the dairy subpanel, Charles W. Stenholm of Texas and Steve Gunderson of Wisconsin, prevailed.

Volkmer joined the 1991 effort by dairy-state members to increase the dairy price support and limit the amount of milk that farmers could produce. A Stenholm bill would have raised the support price by $1.50, but the subcommittee, by a 10-9 vote, backed Volkmer's amendment to increase it by $2.50. The bill proved politically unacceptable because it would have increased the consumer price of milk; it never reached the floor.

Volkmer's strength as a legislator, and his weakness in personal relations, stem from his stubbornness. He is a familiar figure in the chamber as he hunches down over a micro-

Missouri 9

Northeast — Columbia

Stark contrasts of prosperity and penury define the 9th. Population in the southeastern part of the district skyrocketed in the 1980s as the St. Louis suburbs expanded into adjacent counties: St. Charles County grew by 48 percent; the populations of Lincoln and Warren counties increased by about 30 percent.

Many of the new arrivals commute to St. Louis; others work at the General Motors assembly plant in Wentzville or at McDonnell Douglas Corp. in St. Charles and St. Louis counties. Local concerns revolve around bridges and roads to support the population crunch.

But the blossoming at this end of the district is countered by bleak conditions in the northern counties, where farm families find it increasingly difficult to survive. The agricultural depression of the 1980s has abated elsewhere but lingers in many parts of the 9th. Young people, leaving their hometowns for more reliable employment, often cross the border to work in Iowa or Illinois.

Agriculture remains the mainstay of the 9th's economy. Winter wheat, corn and soybeans are grown throughout the district. St. Charles County still has some wheat and corn fields. Cattle and hogs are raised across the district. Vineyards in Gasconade and Warren counties grow grapes for area wineries that date back more than 150 years. Among Missouri's first settlers were Virginians and Kentuckians who found the rich soil to their liking. Those settlers had pro-Southern sympathies during the Civil War, but they could not pull Missouri into the Confederacy; their descendants still vote Democratic.

Their allegiance toward the national party faded in the early 1980s. Of the core Little Dixie counties in the 9th — Ralls, Pike, Monroe, Audrain, Callaway, Randolph and Boone — Ronald Reagan won four in 1980. Four years later, he carried them all. But by 1988, farmers hurt by the farm crisis returned to the Democratic Party. Michael S. Dukakis carried all but Callaway. In 1992, Bill Clinton won everywhere but Gasconade and St. Charles.

The economy in Boone County is steadied by the University of Missouri in Columbia (24,700 students), the oldest state university west of the Mississippi River, and by the Ellis Fischel State Cancer Center in Columbia. The moderate-to-liberal university community lends uncertainty to Boone elections. In 1988, Boone County voted Democratic for president and Republican for governor. In 1992, Boone went Democratic for president and governor but Republican for Senate.

East of Boone is Callaway County, whose residents declared it a kingdom unto itself in defiance of the Union during the Civil War. Many state government employees who work in Jefferson City live here.

On the banks of the Mississippi lies Hannibal, where a once-thriving cement industry provided jobs for Italians, Hungarians, Czechs and other European immigrants in the 19th century. Hannibal is best known as Mark Twain's birthplace, and it attracts more than 250,000 visitors a year to view his boyhood home and "Tom Sawyer's fence."

1990 Population: 568,347. White 539,981 (95%), Black 21,060 (4%), Other 7,306 (1%). Hispanic origin 4,222 (1%). 18 and over 417,301 (73%), 62 and over 85,744 (15%). Median age: 32.

phone, waiting as long as necessary for a chance to jump into the debate. One day many years ago, Volkmer asked California Democrat John Burton how long he planned to keep talking. If Burton talked much longer, Volkmer said, he would go back to his office. "I think I could probably get unanimous consent," Burton responded, "for the gentleman to go back to his office for the rest of the evening."

But Volkmer is not swayed by criticism of his personality. "I'm not short-tempered," he said in 1986. "Someone's got an erroneous impression. Gruff, possibly. Short shrift sometimes. Sometimes I can cut people off short."

At Home: Though it can irk colleagues in the House, Volkmer's tireless, hard-charging style has brought him political success in Missouri. When told that his 1982 opponent called him "abrupt and abrasive," Volkmer replied, "Could be." He took 61 percent of the vote.

A lawyer from the Mississippi River town of Hannibal, Volkmer has always been popular among rural northeast Missouri voters. But his popularity has shown signs of eroding. His vote percentages have declined in his last three races; in 1992, he was held below 50 percent.

Redistricting and general anti-incumbent sentiment combined in 1992 to present Volkmer with his biggest test. Although the 9th was redrawn to become more Democratic by shedding solidly Republican Osage County, the new demographics were not necessarily an improvement for Volkmer, as suburban voters in booming St. Charles were substituted for rural ones in Osage. In the Democratic primary, he got 57 percent against five unheralded challengers.

Those signs encouraged GOP nominee Rick Hardy, a popular political science professor at the University of Missouri in Columbia.

Hardy began with the Boone County base any Volkmer foe can expect and sought to employ his grass-roots organization of former students to gain support in rural areas. He carried Boone by nearly 2-to-1 over Volkmer, and remained close in many of the rural counties. But Volkmer carried St. Charles by a wide margin and scored big in Franklin County, enabling him to edge past Hardy by 5,883 votes.

Volkmer may have benefited from two third-party candidates on the ballot who helped siphon away some of the anti-Volkmer vote; they received 17,830 votes.

With the announcement by Democratic Rep. William L. Hungate that he would retire in 1976, Volkmer and 10 other Democrats sought to succeed him. Drawing on his reputation as a five-term member of the Missouri House, Volkmer sewed up a comfortable 17,000-vote margin over his closest primary competitor. Although his November opponent, GOP state Sen. J. H. Frappier, was well-known near St. Louis, Volkmer held his own there and mustered enough rural support to capture 56 percent of the vote.

Volkmer faced a tougher test in 1984, squaring off with Republican Carrie Francke, a former assistant state attorney general with close ties to Sen. John C. Danforth and a Boone County base. Danforth lent his support, and the national GOP helped her establish a healthy treasury. Francke, however, had trouble making inroads into the 9th's rural territory. Volkmer's strength in St. Charles County and the rural reaches again pulled him through.

Francke sought a rematch in 1986 but was defeated in the primary by state Sen. Ralph Uthlaut, a conservative farmer whose constituency gave him a base at the 9th's southern end.

Uthlaut supported a gradual withdrawal of government price supports, while Volkmer called for higher price supports, and argued that he was positioned to try to help farmers from his post on the Agriculture Committee. Bolstered further in rural Missouri by media reports of his influence in scaling back federal gun controls, Volkmer racked up a comfortable 57 percent victory.

Committees

Agriculture (7th of 28 Democrats)
Livestock (chairman); Department Operations; General Farm Commodities

Science, Space & Technology (4th of 33 Democrats)
Space

Elections

1992 General		
Harold L. Volkmer (D)	124,694	(48%)
Rick Hardy (R)	118,811	(45%)
Jeff Barrow (GREEN)	10,565	(4%)
Duane Neil Burghard (I)	7,265	(3%)
1992 Primary		
Harold L. Volkmer (D)	45,899	(57%)
Justus D. Griffin (D)	16,785	(21%)
Joseph P. Caulfield (D)	9,124	(11%)
Anthony DeFranco (D)	3,567	(4%)
Duane Messick (D)	2,630	(3%)
Rob Shiverdecker (D)	2,340	(3%)
1990 General		
Harold L. Volkmer (D)	94,156	(58%)
Don Curtis (R)	69,514	(42%)

Previous Winning Percentages: **1988** (68%) **1986** (57%) **1984** (53%) **1982** (61%) **1980** (57%) **1978** (75%) **1976** (56%)

District Vote for President

	1992	
D	109,995	(41%)
R	90,669	(34%)
I	65,032	(24%)

Campaign Finance

	Receipts	Receipts from PACs		Expend-itures
1992				
Volkmer (D)	$354,612	$247,010	(70%)	$511,550
Hardy (R)	$144,157	0		$139,860
1990				
Volkmer (D)	$308,533	$218,715	(71%)	$238,679
Curtis (R)	$36,020	$1,000	(3%)	$36,045

Key Votes

1993	
Require parental notification of minors' abortions	Y
Require unpaid family and medical leave	Y
Approve national "motor voter" registration bill	Y
Approve budget increasing taxes and reducing deficit	Y
Approve economic stimulus plan	Y
1992	
Approve balanced-budget constitutional amendment	Y
Close down space station program	N
Approve U.S. aid for former Soviet Union	N
Allow shifting funds from defense to domestic programs	N
1991	
Extend unemployment benefits using deficit financing	Y
Approve waiting period for handgun purchases	N
Authorize use of force in Persian Gulf	Y

Voting Studies

	Presidential Support		Party Unity		Conservative Coalition	
Year	**S**	**O**	**S**	**O**	**S**	**O**
1992	42	57	70	26	81	15
1991	49	50	71	28	89	11
1990	35	65	73	25	81	19
1989	53	47	72	28	80	20
1988	35	60	72	23	79	13
1987	34	66	77	20	74	26
1986	33	67	79	20	60	40
1985	30	70	77	21	55	44
1984	42	56	72	27	56	44
1983	26	74	71	29	46	54
1982	35	60	66	34	55	41
1981	43	51	65	31	67	29

Interest Group Ratings

Year	ADA	AFL-CIO	CCUS	ACU
1992	50	91	50	40
1991	35	75	40	42
1990	39	75	36	38
1989	60	83	40	25
1988	60	93	50	35
1987	64	88	27	9
1986	45	79	33	32
1985	40	59	36	33
1984	55	69	44	25
1983	80	88	20	17
1982	45	65	52	55
1981	30	67	26	29

Montana

STATE DATA

Governor:
Marc Racicot (R)
First elected: 1992
Length of term: 4 years
Term expires: 1/97
Salary: $55,288
Term limit: 8 years in a 16-year period
Phone: (406) 444-3111
Born: July 24, 1948; Thompson Falls, Mont.
Education: Carroll College, B.A. 1970; U. of Montana, J.D. 1973
Military Service: Army, 1973-76
Occupation: Lawyer
Family: Wife, Theresa Barber; five children

Religion: Roman Catholic
Political Career: Candidate for Mont. Supreme Court, 1980; for Mont. District Court, 1982, 1984; Mont. attorney general, 1989-93

Lt. Gov.: Dennis Rehberg (R)
First elected: 1992
Length of term: 4 years
Term expires: 1/97
Salary: $40,310
Phone: (406) 444-5551

State election official: (406) 444-4732
Democratic headquarters: (406) 442-9520
Republican headquarters: (406) 442-6469

STATE LEGISLATURE

Legislature. Meets January-April.

Senate: 50 members, 4-year terms
1992 breakdown: 30D, 20R; 42 men, 8 women; 49 whites, 1 other
Salary: $57 per day in session
Phone: (406) 444-4880

House of Representatives: 100 members, 2-year terms
1992 breakdown: 53R, 47D; 79 men, 21 women; 98 whites, 2 others
Salary: $57 per day in session
Phone: (406) 444-4819

URBAN STATISTICS

City	Pop.
Billings Mayor Richard L. Larsen, N-P	81,151
Great Falls Mayor Gayle Morris, N-P	55,097
Missoula Mayor Daniel Kemmis, D	42,918
Butte-Silver Bull Mayor Jack Lynch, D	33,336
Helena Mayor Kay McKenna, N-P	24,569

U.S. CONGRESS

Senate: 1 D, 1 R
House: 1 D, 0 R

TERM LIMITS

For Congress: Yes
Senate: 12 years in a 24-year period
House: 6 years in a 12-year period
For state offices: Yes
Senate: 8 years in a 16-year period
House: 8 years in a 16-year period

ELECTIONS

1992 Presidential Vote

Bill Clinton	37.6%
George Bush	35.1%
Ross Perot	26.1%

1988 Presidential Vote

George Bush	52%
Michael S. Dukakis	46%

1984 Presidential Vote

Ronald Reagan	60%
Walter F. Mondale	38%

POPULATION

1990 population		799,065
1980 population		786,690
Percent change		+2%
Rank among states:		44
White		93%
Black		<1%
Hispanic		2%
Asian or Pacific islander		1%
Urban		53%
Rural		47%
Born in state		59%
Foreign-born		2%
Under age 18	222,104	28%
Ages 18-64	470,464	59%
65 and older	106,497	13%
Median age		33.1

MISCELLANEOUS

Capital: Helena
Number of counties: 56
Per capita income: $16,043 (1991)
Rank among states: 39
Total area: 147,046 sq. miles
Rank among states: 4

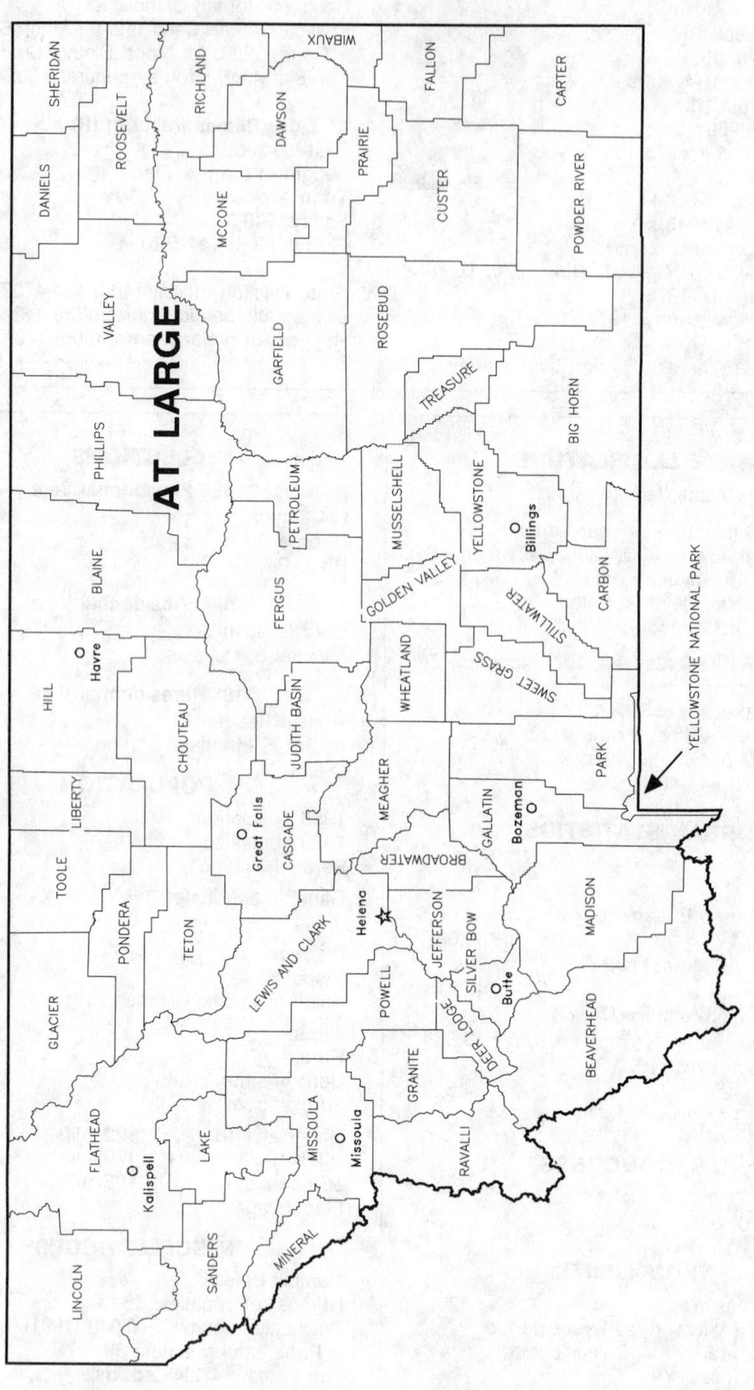
AT LARGE
SHERIDAN
ROOSEVELT
DANIELS
VALLEY
PHILLIPS
BLAINE
HILL
Havre
LIBERTY
TOOLE
CHOUTEAU
PONDERA
TETON
GLACIER
FLATHEAD
Kalispell
LAKE
LINCOLN
SANDERS
MINERAL
MISSOULA
Missoula
RICHLAND
WIBAUX
DAWSON
MCCONE
PRAIRIE
FALLON
CARTER
CUSTER
POWDER RIVER
GARFIELD
ROSEBUD
TREASURE
BIG HORN
PETROLEUM
FERGUS
MUSSELSHELL
YELLOWSTONE
Billings
GOLDEN VALLEY
STILLWATER
CARBON
JUDITH BASIN
WHEATLAND
SWEET GRASS
CASCADE
Great Falls
MEAGHER
PARK
GALLATIN
Bozeman
BROADWATER
Helena
LEWIS AND CLARK
JEFFERSON
SILVER BOW
Butte
MADISON
POWELL
DEER LODGE
GRANITE
RAVALLI
BEAVERHEAD
YELLOWSTONE NATIONAL PARK

Max Baucus (D)

Of Missoula — Elected 1978; 3rd Term

Born: Dec. 11, 1941, Helena, Mont.
Education: Stanford U., B.A. 1964, LL.B. 1967.
Occupation: Lawyer.
Family: Wife, Wanda Minge; one child.
Religion: United Church of Christ.
Political Career: Mont. House, 1973-75; U.S. House, 1975-78.
Capitol Office: 511 Hart Bldg. 20510; 224-2651.

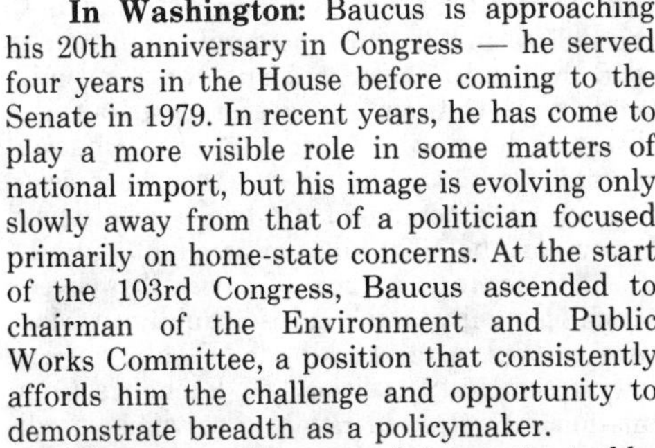

In Washington: Baucus is approaching his 20th anniversary in Congress — he served four years in the House before coming to the Senate in 1979. In recent years, he has come to play a more visible role in some matters of national import, but his image is evolving only slowly away from that of a politician focused primarily on home-state concerns. At the start of the 103rd Congress, Baucus ascended to chairman of the Environment and Public Works Committee, a position that consistently affords him the challenge and opportunity to demonstrate breadth as a policymaker.

There's no shortage of issues to tackle: Among the items facing the committee are reauthorizations of the clean water act, the Endangered Species Act, the "superfund" law and the solid-waste law (the Resource Conservation and Recovery Act, or RCRA).

Also on his to-do list is a Montana wilderness bill, under consideration in the Energy and Natural Resources Committee.

RCRA and the wilderness bill are initiatives Baucus pressed for in the 102nd, only to see them fall short of passage. Baucus' new position — and a White House more disposed to such legislation — may help give these bills extra momentum.

The Environment chair came open in the 102nd Congress when North Dakota Democrat Quentin N. Burdick died in September 1992. Taking over from Burdick was Democrat Daniel Patrick Moynihan of New York, but in 1993, when Finance Committee Chairman Lloyd Bentsen, D-Texas, left the Senate to become Treasury secretary, Moynihan moved into the Finance chair and passed the Environment gavel to Baucus.

Baucus got a taste during the 101st Congress of the legislative skills and expertise the job will require. Then, in his role as chairman of the Environmental Protection Subcommittee, he had authority within the Senate over the Clean Air Act reauthorization. (The ailing Burdick had essentially turned over the work of the committee to the subcommittee chairs.) Successfully moving the legislation was a weightier role than most Baucus had played over the course of his career in Congress, but one he handled to critical acclaim.

In other ways, though, the demands of being chairman will require an adjustment from Baucus. As generally a second-line participant in Congress' past doings, he was able to show sympathy for farmers in his Agriculture Committee work, and for environmentalists in his Environment Committee work. Both groups are important constituencies in Montana. But the Environment chair is a more visible front-line post with responsibility for actually striking a balance between competing interests.

In earlier years, Baucus spent considerably more time tending to home-state interests than to staking out positions on the controversies of the day. His "Montana First" politics and low profile on most national issues cushioned him against the effects of a voting record that sometimes strays to the left of majority opinion in Montana. His approach is evidently a hit back home: In 1990, Montana voters re-elected him by better than a 2-to-1 margin over his Republican opponent, Montana's lieutenant governor.

In the 101st Congress, the Clean Air Act gave Baucus a chance to redress the assessment of him as a senator whose interests seldom strayed beyond his state's borders. As the new chairman of the Environmental Protection subcommittee, he had a choice position at an opportune time. With the guidance of Senate Majority Leader George J. Mitchell of Maine (Baucus' predecessor in the Environmental Protection chair), Baucus steered the clean-air bill through committee, managed it on the floor and chaired the House-Senate conference.

By 1989, the combination of a sympathetic majority leader, a president who actively sought a bill, and the resolution of major House-side disputes had dislodged some of the most stubborn impediments to enacting legislation to deal with the problems of acid rain and auto pollution.

Baucus sponsored urban smog provisions that would set new tailpipe emission standards and require auto manufacturers to implement by 1993 strict vehicle emission standards similar to California's. Baucus and Democrats on his subcommittee supported a controversial second round of reductions to go into effect in 2003 that would require a 50 percent reduction beyond first-round emission levels.

The second-round question produced a rare partisan split on the subcommittee. Automakers and their allies argued that it would cost about $500 a car to develop new technology to meet the requirement; Democrats countered with estimates of $100 per car. "It's about the cost of a new hubcap — a nice, new hubcap — to meet [the second round]," Baucus said. The subcommittee approved it on a 7-6 vote.

Armed with Mitchell's request that the Environment Committee report a clean-air package before Thanksgiving, Baucus had a mandate to barrel the bill through. The committee met Nov. 16, 1989, to mark up the massive package. "Keep going, keep going," Baucus implored members, as the session stretched into the evening. "We have got to get done." In a single day, the committee approved the bill, on a 15-1 vote.

Baucus was a key player in the closed-door Senate-White House negotiations that produced a compromise. As Democratic floor manager of the bill, he joined the Senate leadership in fending off assaults on the bill from senators seeking to make the bill more environmentally stringent. Arguing against one amendment by a liberal Democrat, he said, "I'm much less ideological about this. I'm much more practical. I want a bill that works."

The House-Senate conference pitted Baucus against formidable House Energy and Commerce Chairman John D. Dingell, D-Mich. After three months of agonizing negotiations, the gridlock broke and an agreement was reached, producing the first clean-air rewrite in 13 years.

An issue that came in over Baucus' transom in the 102nd Congress was trade with China. With an eye firmly on his state's wheat exports, Baucus supported President Bush and opposed efforts to rescind China's most-favored-nation trade status as a way of expressing U.S. displeasure with the human rights situation in that country. In March 1992, Baucus was one of only four Democrats voting to sustain Bush's veto of a bill to rescind the trading status.

Before the 101st Congress, Baucus had been cultivating a higher profile on a politically potent issue, and the most fashionable trade concept of the day: America's economic "competitiveness" in the world economy. In the 101st Congress, he acquired a forum to vent his views on unfair foreign trading practices — particularly by U.S. trading partners in the Pacific Rim — as chairman of the Finance Subcommittee on International Trade. In the 103rd Congress, he expects to use this perch to exert influence in the debate on the proposed North American Free Trade Agreement.

On the Agriculture Committee, Baucus has aligned himself with the group of partisan Midwestern "prairie populist" Democrats. They battled to make the 1990 farm bill a more distinctly Democratic product. He lacks their profound knowledge of farm programs, however. Baucus did participate when the committee worked on the farm bill, working on its trade provisions, but he ended up voting against the bill in committee and on the floor.

Baucus offered an amendment that would have increased so-called target prices — the guaranteed minimum prices farmers receive for their crops — by whatever percentage inflation exceeds 4.3 percent. It was rejected in committee and on the floor.

He also opposed Chairman Patrick J. Leahy's "whole-herd buyout" program, added to the 1985 farm bill, which paid milk producers to send their entire herds to slaughter to cut milk production. Cattlemen viewed the buyout as a threat to depress beef prices. Baucus, who represents the sixth-leading state for beef cows, offered an amendment to bar a whole-herd buyout on the 1990 bill; it was adopted 16-2.

At Home: The son of a wealthy Helena ranching family, Baucus rose rapidly in Montana politics. After working in Washington as a lawyer for the Securities and Exchange Commission, he returned home to serve as coordinator of the state constitutional convention in 1972. The same year, he won his state legislative seat.

In 1974, Baucus moved up to the U.S. House, dislodging Republican Richard G. Shoup, who was trying for a third term. To gain publicity for the race, Baucus walked 631 miles across his congressional district. He managed to impress the labor-oriented Democrats who dominate the party in western Montana, and he did little to antagonize Republicans. He was a comfortable winner over Shoup in 1974 and an easy re-election winner in 1976.

Meanwhile, he was focusing on the Senate. His hopes were temporarily frustrated in early 1978 by Democratic Gov. Thomas L. Judge, a political rival. After the death of veteran Democrat Lee Metcalf, the governor bypassed Baucus and appointed Paul Hatfield, chief justice of the Montana Supreme Court, to succeed Metcalf in the Senate.

But Baucus already had begun his 1978 Senate campaign, and he did not step aside for Hatfield. The newly appointed senator could not match Baucus' head start in organizing, and he hurt himself by voting for the Panama Canal treaties. Baucus did not oppose the treaties, but as a member of the House, he did not have to vote on the issue. He easily won the primary.

That fall, he had a hard-nosed Republican competitor in financier Larry Williams, who castigated him as too liberal. But just as Williams seemed on the verge of overtaking him, Baucus' Democratic allies released their "bombshell" — a picture of the "conservative" Williams in shaggy hair and love beads, taken before he moved from California to Montana. Baucus kept his distance from the issue, but the AFL-CIO made sure the picture was all over Montana in the weeks before the election. Baucus won a comfortable victory.

Heading into 1984, Baucus organized and raised money at a feverish pace. His preparations daunted Republican recruiting efforts: No well-known GOP figure stepped forward to take on the incumbent. Former state Rep. Chuck Cozzens won the GOP primary.

Cozzens had trouble attracting the attention he needed to be viewed as a credible challenger to Baucus. He tried to solve that problem by airing a series of radio advertisements calling Baucus a "wimp" who "talks out of both sides of his mouth." But the "wimp" portrayal backfired; many editorial writers and even some Republicans criticized Cozzens for running a mudslinging campaign. In spite of President Reagan's 60 percent showing in Montana, Baucus took 57 percent of the vote.

In 1990, national Republicans, fresh from their 1988 upset in Montana of Democratic Sen. John Melcher, hungrily eyed Baucus' slot. But things went right for Baucus from the start. Lt. Gov. Allen C. Kolstad, the putative GOP front-runner, was held under 44 percent in the June primary, while Baucus breezed to renomination.

In the general election, Baucus' polished, energetic campaign style complemented his superior campaign operation. In contrast, Kolstad's effort was lackluster and ineffective. Baucus won 68 percent, the best showing of any Montana Senate candidate since Mike Mansfield won a second term in 1958.

Committees

Environment & Public Works (Chairman)

Agriculture, Nutrition & Forestry (8th of 10 Democrats)
Agricultural Credit; Agricultural Production & Stabilization of Prices; Domestic & Foreign Marketing & Product Promotion

Finance (2nd of 11 Democrats)
International Trade (chairman); Medicare & Long Term Care; Taxation

Select Intelligence (8th of 9 Democrats)

Joint Taxation

Elections

1990 General		
Max Baucus (D)	217,563	(68%)
Allen C. Kolstad (R)	93,836	(29%)
Westley F. Deitchler (LIBERT)	7,937	(2%)
1990 Primary		
Max Baucus (D)	81,687	(83%)
John B. Driscoll (D)	12,622	(13%)
"Curly" Thornton (D)	4,367	(4%)

Previous Winning Percentages: 1984 (57%) **1978** (56%) **1976 *** (66%) **1974 *** (55%)

** House elections.*

Campaign Finance

	Receipts	Receipts from PACs		Expend-itures
1990				
Baucus (D)	$2,667,328	$1,377,663	(52%)	$2,409,262
Kolstad (R)	$748,100	$74,898	(10%)	$747,661

Key Votes

1993	
Require unpaid family and medical leave	Y
Approve national "motor voter" registration bill	Y
Approve budget increasing taxes and reducing deficit	Y
Support president's right to lift military gay ban	Y
1992	
Approve school-choice pilot program	N
Allow shifting funds from defense to domestic programs	Y
Oppose deeper cuts in spending for SDI	N
1991	
Approve waiting period for handgun purchases	N
Raise senators' pay and ban honoraria	Y
Authorize use of force in Persian Gulf	N
Confirm Clarence Thomas to Supreme Court	N

Voting Studies

	Presidential Support		Party Unity		Conservative Coalition	
Year	**S**	**O**	**S**	**O**	**S**	**O**
1992	35	65	83	17	45	55
1991	40	58	83	17	45	55
1990	51	49	70	28	51	46
1989	48	48	69	27	50	47
1988	47	51	86	12	51	49
1987	33	65	86	13	44	56
1986	30	66	74	22	37	54
1985	30	68	83	15	47	52
1984	40	58	76	21	34	66
1983	38	60	77	21	45	55
1982	44	53	80	18	31	67
1981	45	50	84	14	29	66

Interest Group Ratings

Year	ADA	AFL-CIO	CCUS	ACU
1992	95	75	20	4
1991	70	58	20	24
1990	56	44	45	41
1989	80	100	43	19
1988	80	86	29	8
1987	75	80	28	8
1986	80	60	37	13
1985	65	75	37	9
1984	75	50	50	14
1983	75	71	32	25
1982	85	85	40	16
1981	85	67	39	13

Conrad Burns (R)

Of Billings — Elected 1988; 1st Term

Born: Jan. 25, 1935, Gallatin, Mo.
Education: U. of Missouri, 1952-54.
Military Service: Marine Corps, 1955-57.
Occupation: Radio and television broadcaster.
Family: Wife, Phyllis Kuhlmann; two children.
Religion: Lutheran.
Political Career: Yellowstone County Commission, 1987-89.
Capitol Office: 183 Dirksen Bldg. 20510; 224-2644.

In Washington: Burns could find Washington a lonely place in the 103rd Congress. With the 1992 loss of Rep. Ron Marlenee, he is now the only Republican in Montana's congressional delegation, and he can no longer look to a Republican president or administration to check the anti-development, pro-wilderness tendencies of many members of Congress: The Clinton administration is tilted toward environmentalists.

However, Burns has tried in his first four years to achieve results by bridging differences, an approach that contrasts with Marlenee's blunt and confrontational style. While he shares Marlenee's rugged and rambunctious conservative populism, his personality is folksier and his manner is more appealing than Marlenee's. He was rewarded in the 103rd Congress when he won a seat on the Appropriations Committee.

In both philosophy and style, Burns has little in common with Democratic Senate colleague Max Baucus, a liberal with an intellectual approach.

Burns' willingness to compromise to achieve results was evident in the 102nd Congress on one of the most contentious and longest-running issues in the state: wilderness preservation, a topic he addressed from his seat on the Energy and Natural Resources Committee.

Burns, like many Western conservatives, is wary of extensive wilderness protections and is sympathetic to the arguments of developers and recreationists who want access to the lands. Baucus proposed a solution to a Montana wilderness stalemate in the 101st Congress, but Burns offered his own plan, which covered less acreage.

Burns stepped on some toes when he criticized a land-management agreement for Montana's Lolo and Kootenai national forests worked out by an ad hoc council of millworkers, environmentalists and others. Baucus had incorporated the agreement into his bill. Supporters of the plan accused Burns of undercutting a hard-won agreement. By year's end, Burns had softened his tone. "I think the way they've approached that problem up there has been very good," he said. "I still want to involve more people."

In November 1991, Burns and Baucus finally agreed on a compromise. Their painfully crafted plan would have set aside about 1.2 million acres as wilderness land. Energy and Natural Resources approved it on a 20-0 vote; the Senate passed it, 75-22, in March 1992.

But environmentalists and Hollywood stars such as Harrison Ford, Goldie Hawn and Glenn Close argued that the bill would not protect enough land and would allow undue mining and logging. Minnesota Democrat Bruce F. Vento, chairman of the House subcommittee that oversees public lands, agreed. He introduced a substitute that would set aside nearly 1.5 million acres and pushed it through his subcommittee and the full Interior Committee. The House passed the Vento bill on a 282-123 vote. It died at adjournment.

When he arrived in the Senate, Burns was faced with a difficult political balancing act. A former rancher and farm broadcaster with little political experience, Burns sought credibility as a legislator while maintaining the crowd-pleasing cowboy image that helped him overcome Democratic Sen. John Melcher in the biggest Senate upset of 1988.

Burns plunged into his Senate work, engaging in issues as detailed as telephone industry regulation. Yet the countrified image Burns projected at a freshman orientation session — to which he wore aged cowboy boots and a leather belt with a "C" on the buckle — remains his persona to most Senate-watchers.

Burns' back-roads image was reinforced by incidents during his first few years in Congress. After a tree-planting ceremony near the Lincoln Memorial, Burns walked over to a police horse and examined its mouth to see how old the animal was; a syndicated story on the incident was carried by Burns' hometown newspaper, The Billings Gazette. In November 1990, Burns suffered minor wounds when a young member of his pheasant-hunting party accidentally winged him with shotgun pellets. A year later, after a vote on civil rights legislation, some civil rights lobbyists heard Burns say that he was going home to a "slave auction." A Burns aide later clarified that he was referring to a charity event in which students are "bought" to do chores, and Burns subsequently apologized.

Burns' style, which has made him a popular dinner speaker, has caught the eyes of the Eastern media. USA Today, one of several media outlets to run friendly profiles of Burns, reported that the tobacco-chomping newcomer had promised, "I'll never take a chew under the Capitol dome."

To his acolytes back home, Burns is an expression of themselves: natural, independent and not bound by elitist (read: Eastern) pretensions. To his critics, Burns is feeding damaging stereotypes of Montana as a remote and unsophisticated backwater. "Thanks, Conrad, thanks for telling the world what hicks we are," the Gazette has written. The harshest criticism came over Burns' glib remark that "there are awful good folks" in Montana, including some who "can read and write."

But the comment, far from being an attack on his constituents, was typical of the joshing and often self-deprecating humor that made Burns popular on the campaign stump in 1988. Burns denied that his cowboy characterization would make him an ineffective spokesman for Montana interests. "I don't take myself seriously. I take my job damn serious," Burns told The Washington Post.

Burns sought to prove that in his work on his committee assignments. A member of the Senate Commerce Committee, Burns used his experience as a broadcaster to make a mark on telecommunications issues.

During the 1992 debate on a bill to reinstitute rate and programming regulations on the cable television industry, Burns became a leading advocate of allowing local telephone companies to offer cable television services under certain conditions. The phone companies are barred from such services under provisions of federal law.

Burns and other advocates argued that allowing telephone companies to provide TV programming over their lines would create competition for cable companies, most of which have local monopolies. They also said the phone companies need to expand in order to provide the financial base to build a nationwide fiber-optics network; fiber optics, in turn, are hailed as opening American households to an array of communications services. Burns and then-Sen. Al Gore of Tennessee introduced legislation in the 102nd Congress that would have allowed independent phone companies — and potentially the Bell companies — to offer cable television in exchange for a commitment from phone companies to develop a nationwide fiber-optics network by 2015.

Also in the 102nd Congress, Burns fought to block legislation to reregulate the cable industry, which was accused of gouging its customers with unchecked rate increases. He said that Congress was punishing the cable industry for its successes and blasted the regulatory costs of the bill. But the bill had widespread appeal, and Congress overrode President Bush's veto, its only successful override attempt in Bush's four years in office.

Although he is not on the Agriculture Committee, Burns' background enabled him to speak freely on the 1990 farm bill. Discussing the bill's cattle provisions, Burns was every bit the independent Westerner. He noted in May 1990 that there was a dairy title in the bill but none for beef cattle. "That is precisely the way that those of us involved in the beef cattle industry want it . . . ," Burns said. "To them, the stability comes from keeping the government out of the cattle business."

At Home: When he entered the 1988 Senate contest, Burns had served less than two years in his only elective office, Yellowstone County (Billings) commissioner. He had no broad expertise on national or international issues. And he seemed to be a fallback candidate, recruited by the National Republican Senatorial Committee (NRSC) for a state party that failed to find a well-known elected official to challenge the two-term Melcher.

However, Burns actually had a much stronger political base than most observers, including Melcher, recognized. His broadcasts on the Northern Agricultural Network, which he cofounded, had given him a statewide following and far greater name recognition than any of the state legislators the GOP had tried to recruit. He also had a lifetime of experience in agriculture, a crucial economic sector in Montana.

Melcher, for his part, was a far less formidable incumbent than widely presumed. A veterinarian widely known as "Doc," Melcher had built his popularity with his own folksy charm. But he was a stumbling campaigner, and his Senate voting record, which often earned him 100 percent ratings from the Americans for Democratic Action, left him vulnerable to charges that he was to the left of the state mainstream.

The NRSC spotted this vulnerability early on and promoted Burns, to a disbelieving political and media establishment, as their "upset special." The campaign committee poured in nearly $200,000, enough to buy plenty of TV ad time in a state where airtime is inexpensive. Many of the ads blasted Melcher as too liberal and as ineffective in promoting Montana's agenda.

Burns' campaign planted doubt in voters' minds, and Melcher's double-digit lead in the polls slowly began to evaporate. Melcher tried to strike back by portraying Burns as a packaged candidate, bought and controlled by the national Republican political machine. He even reprised a previously successful TV ad concept, "talking" cows who derided the "greenhorn" Republican.

But not even talking cows could save Melcher from an onslaught of untimely news headlines in the last weeks of the campaign. Burns benefited from an article in the Great Falls Tribune detailing Melcher's interest in Philippine issues; Burns had labored to draw attention to the fact that the incumbent had visited the Philippines three times in five years. Burns also gained from the publicity attending a Billings campaign visit by Republican presidential nominee Bush in late October.

But the event that may have clinched the win for Burns was President Ronald Reagan's veto of a wilderness bill, authored by Melcher, just days before the election. The bill, which had long been stalled in Congress, had been an albatross for Melcher, endearing him neither to development interests, who opposed wilderness legislation in general, nor environmentalists, who wanted more land protected than the bill provided. Then, when Reagan vetoed the bill, it appeared to reinforce Burns' claim that Melcher lacked the clout to get his proposals enacted.

Burns won by a fairly narrow 52 percent-48 percent margin, but his support was well distributed across the state. In fact, he ran slightly better in the usually Democratic 1st District than in the Republican 2nd, a home base he shared with Melcher.

The NRSC intervention in the campaign remained controversial, however. In 1989, a former Montana Republican Party official filed a federal lawsuit against the state and national GOP organizations, alleging he was fired for raising questions about financial transactions on behalf of Burns' campaign.

In 1990, a Democratic state representative from Montana and the public interest group Common Cause filed complaints with the Federal Election Commission, alleging that the NRSC transferred funds to the Montana Republican Party for Burns' use that were in excess of legal limits. The FEC investigation is continuing.

Committees

Appropriations (13th of 13 Republicans)
District of Columbia (ranking); Interior; Legislative Branch; VA, HUD & Independent Agencies

Commerce, Science & Transportation (6th of 9 Republicans)
Science (ranking); Communications; Consumer; Surface Transportation

Small Business (4th of 9 Republicans)
Innovation, Manufacturing & Technology (ranking); Rural Economy & Family Farming

Special Aging (9th of 10 Republicans)

Elections

1988 General		
Conrad Burns (R)	189,445	(52%)
John Melcher (D)	175,809	(48%)
1988 Primary		
Conrad Burns (R)	63,330	(85%)
Tom Faranda (R)	11,427	(15%)

Campaign Finance

	Receipts	Receipts from PACs		Expend-itures
1988				
Burns (R)	$1,099,488	$315,387	(29%)	$1,076,010
Melcher (D)	$1,237,661	$812,560	(66%)	$1,338,622

Key Votes

1993	
Require unpaid family and medical leave	Y
Approve national "motor voter" registration bill	N
Approve budget increasing taxes and reducing deficit	N
Support president's right to lift military gay ban	N
1992	
Approve school-choice pilot program	N
Allow shifting funds from defense to domestic programs	N
Oppose deeper cuts in spending for SDI	Y
1991	
Approve waiting period for handgun purchases	N
Raise senators' pay and ban honoraria	Y
Authorize use of force in Persian Gulf	Y
Confirm Clarence Thomas to Supreme Court	Y

Voting Studies

	Presidential Support		Party Unity		Conservative Coalition	
Year	**S**	**O**	**S**	**O**	**S**	**O**
1992	85	15	94	6	95	5
1991	89	11	93	7	95	5
1990	81	19	92	7	95	5
1989	86	12	92	7	92	5

Interest Group Ratings

Year	ADA	AFL-CIO	CCUS	ACU
1992	5	25	100	89
1991	5	17	90	86
1990	6	11	83	91
1989	0	0	88	85

AL Pat Williams (D)

Of Helena — Elected 1978; 8th Term

Born: Oct. 30, 1937, Helena, Mont.

Education: U. of Montana, 1956-57; William Jewell College, 1958; U. of Denver, B.A. 1961; Western Montana College, 1962.

Military Service: Army, 1960-61; National Guard, 1962-69.

Occupation: Elementary and secondary school teacher.

Family: Wife, Carol Griffith; three children.

Religion: Roman Catholic.

Political Career: Mont. House, 1967-71; sought Democratic nomination for U.S. House, 1974.

Capitol Office: 2457 Rayburn Bldg. 20515; 225-3211.

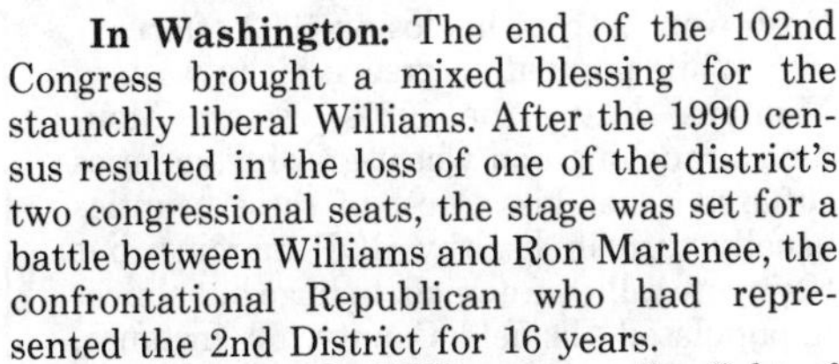

In Washington: The end of the 102nd Congress brought a mixed blessing for the staunchly liberal Williams. After the 1990 census resulted in the loss of one of the district's two congressional seats, the stage was set for a battle between Williams and Ron Marlenee, the confrontational Republican who had represented the 2nd District for 16 years.

On the up side, Williams won the fight of his political career and became the state's lone representative in Congress. Working in his favor were a personal style and a political wisdom that proved more effective in Congress and with voters than did his opponent's. Throughout his congressional career, Williams has shown an ability to match his partisanship with healthy doses of pragmatism, and that has earned him some significant legislative accomplishments.

But in the end, only half of Montana's voters supported him. Now he has the daunting job of single-handedly representing a geographically large state where nearly half the voters are much more conservative than he is. Wooing the eastern half of the politically divided state may not be easy.

The eastern half, besides being more conservative, is deeply concerned about the impact of environmental initiatives on jobs in the timber and mining industries. Williams, a traditional New Deal liberal who is willing to champion new government programs when most politicians are talking about cutbacks, has become known as a champion of the environment.

In the 102nd Congress, he tried to push through a bill to protect the state's vast wild federal lands for wildlife and fish habitat and for recreational use. Marlenee sided with Montanans in the timber and mining industry. At times, the two turned the Interior Committee into a battleground over the issue.

Williams, who has an above-average rating from the League of Conservation Voters, argued that "one cannot hunt if there is nothing to shoot at, and we can't fish if streams are polluted and the spawning grounds ruined."

Montana's senators, Democrat Max Baucus and Republican Conrad Burns, had compromised on a bill that would have protected 2.2 million acres. The House bill, crafted by Williams and Democrat Bruce F. Vento of Minnesota, would have protected an additional 300,000. A House-Senate compromise died in the final days of the 102nd, a victim of an unrelated filibuster and senators' objections to the bill.

Williams' ties to organized labor first helped bring him to Congress, and he has been faithful to the union movement. He is a deputy whip designated to watch labor issues in the House, and he serves the same function from his post on the Education and Labor Committee. At the start of the 102nd Congress, he became chairman of the Labor-Management Relations Subcommittee. Williams was a prime cosponsor of family and medical leave legislation enacted under President Clinton at the start of the 103rd.

As subcommittee chairman, Williams will take on striker replacement legislation, pension reform and changes in the Employee Retirement Income Security Act. His panel is also one of three in the House with jurisdiction over health-care reform.

Williams has long argued for legislation barring striker replacement, saying that without the ban on permanent replacements, "workers have not so much a right to strike as a right to quit."

In the 100th Congress, Williams was the prime mover behind successful labor-backed legislation to bar most private employers from requiring workers and job applicants to take lie-detector tests. "Thumbscrews and the rack, even if they are now electronic, should be outlawed," he said.

A former schoolteacher, Williams took a middle course on the problem of student-loan defaults. He echoed the conservative demand to crack down on "charlatans" but said the default

Montana

At large

Only the invisible hand of the U.S. Census would have dared join the rugged west of Montana's old 1st District and the eastern plains of the 2nd. But because the state's population grew little during the 1980s (up 2 percent, to 799,065), reapportionment cost Montana a House seat, bringing western labor Democrats and eastern Republican ranchers into an at-large constituency. A match made in heaven this is not.

In economic and political terms, eastern and western Montana seem more like separate states than two halves of the same. The west is mountains, mines and lumber mills; the east is flat country, largely given over to wheat and cattle. Throughout the 1980s, the west was represented in the House by Democrat Pat Williams, a labor liberal. The east elected Republican Ron Marlenee, a crusty conservative.

When Williams and Marlenee faced off in 1992, the result was predictably close: Williams 50.5 percent, Marlenee 47 percent.

In fact, close elections were the rule in Montana in 1992. Republican Marc Racicot won the governorship over Democrat Dorothy Bradley by 2 percentage points. And Bill Clinton had a 2-point advantage over George Bush in presidential voting, which made him the first national Democrat to win the state since 1964.

But Clinton's tally was a lukewarm 38 percent and Bush's an even more tepid 35 percent. The only candidate who truly showed a surge in Montana was independent Ross Perot, who took 26 percent — his seventh-best showing in the country.

The current political behavior of eastern and western Montana is rooted in their historic economic underpinnings.

The mountains of western Montana begat lumber mills and mines early in this century. While the prodigious lodes of copper, zinc and lead in Butte's "richest hill on Earth" produced some of the nation's richest mine owners, they also spawned strong unions to represent the miners.

Though forestry and mining have not always provided a steady living, union-inspired Democratic voting habits have been quite regular in most western counties.

Nowhere is this clearer than in heavily unionized Silver Bow County (Butte) and its neighbor Deer Lodge County (Anaconda). In 1992, Clinton won 55 percent in Silver Bow and 61 percent in Deer Lodge; Bush ran in the teens in both counties, trailing Perot.

Clinton also carried the two western counties with sizable urban centers — Missoula County (Missoula) and Lewis and Clark County (Helena).

Missoula, lying at the hub of several agricultural valleys, is a lumber-processing center and home to the University of Montana. Helena, the capital, got its start when gold was discovered in Last Chance Gulch during the Civil War.

There are pockets of GOP strength in the west, most notably Flathead County in the north (where visitors to Glacier National Park help sustain Kalispell and Whitefish), and Gallatin County in the south (site of Bozeman and Montana State University). Bush won both in his losing 1992 effort.

While population grew a bit in western Montana during the 1980s, eastern Montana's ranching and wheat-growing counties suffered a net loss. Most of these counties usually turn in healthy GOP margins, but their vote tallies are small. In huge but almost unpopulated Garfield County, for instance, Bush won 50 percent; 809 people voted.

In the east are Montana's two largest cities, Billings (Yellowstone County) and Great Falls (Cascade County). Billings has generally been the more dependable of the two for Republicans, but while Bush carried Yellowstone County in 1992, Democrat Williams won it narrowly. Cascade County voted for both Clinton and Williams.

From its beginnings as a market center for sugar beets and other farm products, Billings grew in the 1970s to become headquarters for many energy ventures. In Great Falls, cheap hydroelectric power drawn from nearby falls on the Missouri River spurred industrial development early in the century, as well as a surviving tradition of union activism.

A new phenomenon drawing attention to Montana — and giving a boost to Democrats — is the state's status as a getaway for the rich and famous. Celebrities including Tom Brokaw, Jeff Bridges, Ted Turner and Jane Fonda have property in the state. Glenn Close has a coffee shop in Bozeman.

And an increasing number of new-age professionals are relocating from the rat race to Montana, where they continue to take care of business by using fax machines and other such telecommuting technology.

1990 Population: 799,065. White 741,111 (93%), Black 2,381 (<1%), Other 55,573 (7%). Hispanic origin 12,174 (2%). 18 and over 576,961 (72%), 62 and over 126,919 (16%). Median age: 34.

rate had skyrocketed in part because the loan program, intended as a supplement for middle-income students, instead had become the principal path to college for low-income students, who often are ill-equipped to repay their loans. In the 101st Congress, he backed legislation to crack down on trade schools with exceptionally high default rates.

In the 102nd, two of Williams' proposals were included in the reauthorization of higher education legislation enacted in 1992. The first authorized grants to states to improve teacher training programs at colleges and scholarships for students who want to become teachers.

The other, the Middle Income Student Assistance Act, expanded loans and grants for middle-income families. Also under the act, equity in family farms and ranches is no longer counted as annual income for eligibility purposes.

In the 101st Congress, Williams stepped outside his primary interests in labor and education to become a front-line player in the debate on decency standards for the National Endowment for the Arts. The issue placed him in rare alliance with Bush, who supported Williams' five-year NEA reauthorization without the restrictions sought by those who complained that the organization was funding obscene art. "A little bit of censorship is like being a little bit pregnant," Williams said.

Williams was thrust into the debate as chairman of the Postsecondary Education Subcommittee, which had jurisdiction over the NEA's authorization bill. When the subcommittee could not agree on whether or how to write language restricting the agency from funding certain types of work, it sent along Williams' bill to the full committee. When it, too, failed to come up with a solution and sent the bill to the full House, a major floor fight was slated.

But Williams spent weeks negotiating with key Republican activists. They eventually reached an agreement that would ban funding of obscene art but leave it to the courts to determine whether a project has crossed that line. The amendment eventually passed the House 382-42 and formed the basis of the legislation that was ultimately signed into law.

In the 103rd, Williams will again be in charge of moving NEA legislation though the House.

For three terms (through 1988), Williams served on the Budget Committee, where he reveled in the fierce partisan rivalry that prevailed early in his tenure, but in later years joined the move toward bipartisanship.

At Home: Until 1992, Williams had won at least 60 percent of the vote in every congressional re-election race, but in that year he was locked in a true Western showdown between two veteran incumbents. It was anti-abortion versus abortion rights; Marlenee, the so-called "Earth's enemy," against Williams, the environmentalist. After a bruising campaign fight in which both men spent more than $1 million, Williams won with 50.5 percent to Marlenee's 47 percent.

It was a race in which a long list of small factors came together to spell "win" for Williams. To begin with, his district, the western part of the state, had a higher population than Marlenee's east. According to the 1990 census, western Montana grew by 6 percent, while eastern Montana's population fell by 3 percent. In addition, Williams did slightly better in his old district than Marlenee did in his.

Williams was also a winner in urban areas of the state and on Indian reservations, while Marlenee did better in rural areas and picked up some votes in western counties with large timber interests. Women favored Williams because of his stance on such issues as abortion rights and parental leave.

Finally, with the certainty of having only one legislator representing the whole state, personal styles became an issue as well. Newspaper endorsements of Williams compared his effectiveness as a consensus builder to Marlenee's more confrontational methods.

Williams was also buoyed by Clinton's popularity. Clinton won the state's three electoral votes, becoming the first Democratic presidential candidate to win the state since President Lyndon B. Johnson defeated Sen. Barry Goldwater in 1964.

Williams scored his first congressional victory in 1978, a year in which districts all over the mountain West were voting Republican.

Williams entered a multicandidate primary and was blessed with strong labor backing. He campaigned on the need for more jobs in the western part of Montana, but also on the need to keep the district's industry clean. He won nomination with 41 percent of the vote.

Williams' Republican opponent was 29-year-old Jim Waltermire, then a Missoula County commissioner. At the time, Waltermire was not well-known outside his home county, and his pro-development views were a liability against Williams, an environmental moderate who stressed the need for protection as well as job development. Williams comfortably defeated Waltermire (who went on to become Montana's secretary of state and a 1988 candidate for governor, but died in a plane crash).

Before 1978, Williams had filled a variety of positions besides serving two terms in the state Legislature. He was Montana director of Hubert H. Humphrey's presidential campaign in 1968 and chairman of the Jimmy Carter campaign in western Montana in 1976. He spent two years on Capitol Hill as an aide to Democrat John Melcher, who was then representing Montana's other district in the House and later served two Senate terms.

His political career was temporarily derailed in 1974, when he lost the Democratic House nomination to Max Baucus. But when

Baucus ran for the Senate in 1978, Williams had another shot.

In 1990 — his final election in the 1st District before reapportionment reduced Montana's House representation to one seat — Williams took 61 percent against first-time Republican candidate Brad Johnson.

In early 1991, there was speculation that Williams would run for governor in 1992 rather than face a House contest against Marlenee for the state's new at-large seat. But Williams announced he would not go for governor.

Committees

Agriculture (27th of 28 Democrats)
General Farm Commodities

Education & Labor (6th of 28 Democrats)
Labor-Management Relations (chairman); Postsecondary Education; Select Education

Natural Resources (7th of 28 Democrats)
National Parks, Forests & Public Lands; Native American Affairs

Elections

1992 General

Pat Williams (D)	203,711	(50%)
Ron Marlenee (R)	189,570	(47%)
Jerome J. Wilverding (LIBERT)	10,454	(3%)

1990 General

Pat Williams (D)	100,409	(61%)
Brad Johnson (R)	63,837	(39%)

Previous Winning Percentages: **1988** (61%) **1986** (62%) **1984** (66%) **1982** (60%) **1980** (61%) **1978** (57%)

District Vote for President

1992

D 154,507 (38%)
R 144,207 (36%)
I 107,225 (26%)

Campaign Finance

	Receipts	Receipts from PACs		Expend-itures
1992				
Williams (D)	$1,190,716	$501,505	(42%)	$1,336,673
Marlenee (R)	$1,220,494	$384,885	(32%)	$1,292,583
1990				
Williams (D)	$458,293	$296,640	(65%)	$345,258
Johnson (R)	$86,542	$4,300	(5%)	$90,238

Key Votes

1993

Require parental notification of minors' abortions	N
Require unpaid family and medical leave	Y
Approve national "motor voter" registration bill	Y
Approve budget increasing taxes and reducing deficit	Y
Approve economic stimulus plan	Y

1992

Approve balanced-budget constitutional amendment	N
Close down space station program	Y
Approve U.S. aid for former Soviet Union	N
Allow shifting funds from defense to domestic programs	Y

1991

Extend unemployment benefits using deficit financing	Y
Approve waiting period for handgun purchases	N
Authorize use of force in Persian Gulf	N

Voting Studies

	Presidential Support		Party Unity		Conservative Coalition	
Year	**S**	**O**	**S**	**O**	**S**	**O**
1992	17	75	77	14	33	56
1991	31	61	75	14	32	51
1990	24	72	77	12	20	72
1989	31	60	72	12	22	71
1988	14	77	70	5	13	79
1987	18	79	81	5	21	74
1986	12	82	76	8	18	74
1985	18	80	76	4	7	87
1984	30	65	72	14	17	75
1983	18	72	77	9	18	74
1982	35	61	81	11	16	79
1981	34	62	86	10	21	73

Interest Group Ratings

Year	ADA	AFL-CIO	CCUS	ACU
1992	85	92	50	8
1991	65	73	44	20
1990	89	82	33	9
1989	80	91	40	7
1988	85	100	15	0
1987	96	94	7	0
1986	85	92	20	5
1985	95	94	23	10
1984	90	82	33	13
1983	90	94	37	9
1982	85	100	23	9
1981	95	93	6	20

Nebraska

STATE DATA

Governor:
Ben Nelson (D)
First elected: 1990
Length of term: 4 years
Term expires: 1/95
Salary: $65,000
Term limit: 2 terms
Phone: (402) 471-2244
Born: May 17, 1941; McCook, Neb.
Education: U. of Nebraska, B.A. 1963, M.A. 1965, J.D. 1970
Occupation: Lawyer
Family: Wife, Diane Lyle; four children
Religion: Methodist
Political Career: Neb. director of insurance, 1975-76

Lt. Gov.: Maxine B. Moul (D)
First elected: 1990
Length of term: 4 years
Term expires: 1/95
Salary: $47,000
Phone: (402) 471-2256

State election official: (402) 471-2554
Democratic headquarters: (402) 475-4584
Republican headquarters: (402) 475-2122

REDISTRICTING

Nebraska retained its three House seats in reapportionment. The legislature passed the map June 5, 1991; the governor signed it June 10.

STATE LEGISLATURE

Unicameral Legislature. Meets January-May in odd years, January-April in even years.

Legislature: 49 nonpartisan members, 4-year terms
1992 breakdown: 39 men, 10 women; 48 whites, 1 black
Salary: $12,000
Phone: (402) 471-2271

URBAN STATISTICS

City	Pop.
Omaha Mayor P. J. Morgan, R	335,795
Lincoln Mayor Mike Johanns, R	191,972
Grand Island Mayor Ernest L. Dobesch, I	39,457
Belleview Mayor Inez Boyd, I	30,982
Kearney Mayor Ron Larsen, I	24,396

U.S. CONGRESS

Senate: 2 D, 0 R
House: 1 D, 2 R

TERM LIMITS

For Congress: Yes
Senate: 2 terms
House: 4 consecutive terms
For state offices: Yes
Unicameral legislature: 2 terms

ELECTIONS

1992 Presidential Vote

George Bush	46.6%
Bill Clinton	29.4%
Ross Perot	23.6%

1988 Presidential Vote

George Bush	60%
Michael S. Dukakis	39%

1984 Presidential Vote

Ronald Reagan	71%
Walter F. Mondale	29%

POPULATION

1990 population		1,578,385
1980 population		1,569,825
Percent change		+.01%
Rank among states:		36
White		94%
Black		4%
Hispanic		2%
Asian or Pacific islander		1%
Urban		66%
Rural		34%
Born in state		70%
Foreign-born		2%
Under age 18	429,012	27%
Ages 18-64	926,305	59%
65 and older	223,068	14%
Median age		33

MISCELLANEOUS

Capital: Lincoln
Number of counties: 93
Per capita income: $17,852 (1991)
Rank among states: 24
Total area: 77,355 sq. miles
Rank among states: 15

Nebraska - Congressional Districts

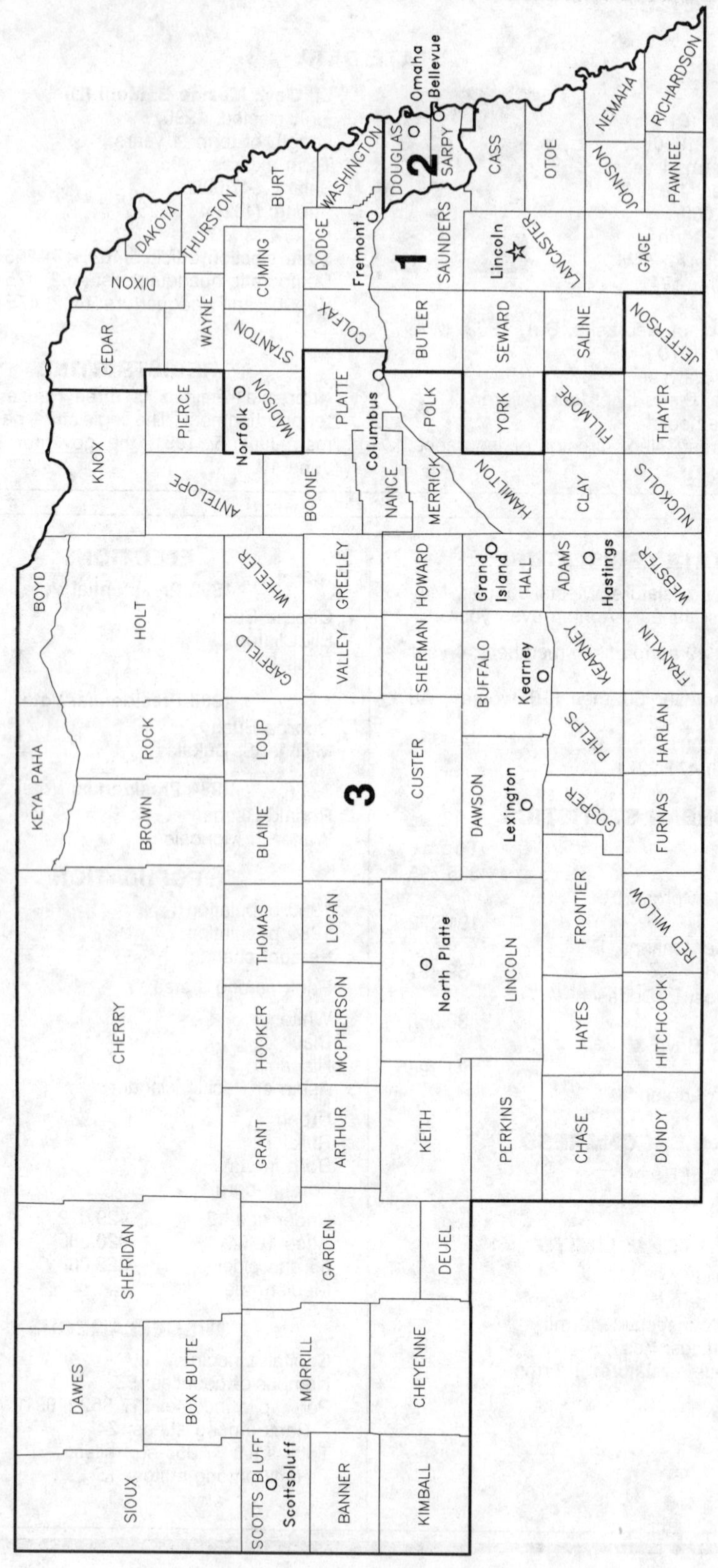

Jim Exon (D)

Of Lincoln — Elected 1978; 3rd Term

Born: Aug. 9, 1921, Geddes, S.D.
Education: U. of Omaha, 1939-41.
Military Service: Army, 1941-45; Army Reserve, 1945-49.
Occupation: Office equipment dealer.
Family: Wife, Patricia Ann Pros; three children.
Religion: Episcopalian.
Political Career: Democratic National Committee, 1968-70; governor, 1971-79.
Capitol Office: 528 Hart Bldg. 20510; 224-4224.

In Washington: Despite his 14 years in the Senate, Exon has not been a major player on most legislative issues. But he wields considerable influence on selected policy areas involving defense, budget policy, business and transportation. Well-liked by his colleagues, he is a middle-of-the-road Democrat with an independent streak. His vote cannot be taken for granted by the party leadership.

When the new Clinton administration submitted a budget resolution to Congress for approval without allowing members to review a budget document, Exon balked: "By placing the budget resolution cart before the budget horse, the Senate is forced to respond like a horse with blinders. Don't look around — just charge ahead. The president has asked us to make a leap of faith." Exon eventually voted for the budget resolution, although, iconoclastic to the end, he was the sole Senate Democrat to vote against one floor amendment calling for full funding of President Clinton's education reform proposals by 1998.

He also opposed Clinton's initial economic stimulus package as too costly and said it would add to the deficit. Although he stuck with his party on unsuccessful votes to invoke cloture and cut off a Republican filibuster against the package, Exon and Nebraska's junior senator, Bob Kerrey, were among the handful of Democrats who supported a GOP amendment to cut back the bill.

From his spot on the Budget Committee, Exon has often preached fiscal conservatism. He introduced a balanced-budget constitutional amendment in 1991 and 1993. And to do his share for deficit reduction, Exon regularly returns a substantial portion of his office allowance to the Treasury.

Exon came to Clinton's defense during the 1992 campaign when he participated in a news conference saying that Clinton's lack of military service should not be used as a campaign issue against him. As a World War II veteran and the second-ranking Democrat on the Armed Services Committee, Exon's support for the embattled candidate was highly valued.

On Armed Services, Exon fits in well with the panel's pro-Pentagon leanings. He generally works smoothly with Chairman Sam Nunn of Georgia and has agreed with him on such volatile issues as the Persian Gulf War and lifting the ban on homosexuals in the military. Before the start of 1993 committee hearings on gays in the military, Exon stated his views with his usual bluntness: "Am I open-minded on the proposition that homosexuality be open and approved in the service? No way."

Exon's backing for Nunn on one controversial issue — opposing the nomination of former GOP Sen. John Tower of Texas as secretary of Defense in 1989 — was especially vocal. Although Tower had served as chairman of the Armed Services Committee for four years in the 1980s, Exon said Tower was not up to the top Pentagon job. And he differed with Republicans who said Tower's colleagues would have known if he were alcohol dependent: "Just because we did not see anything ... does not necessarily mean that it did not happen."

In 1990, a still-angry Tower went to Nebraska to campaign against Exon and made the unsubstantiated charge that the Nebraskan had a reputation as "one of the two or three biggest boozers in the Senate."

Exon, though usually a supporter of the military, sponsored an amendment during the 1992 budget debate that would have roughly doubled the defense cuts proposed by the Bush administration. Instead of slashing big-ticket items such as the B-2 bomber, which Exon supported, he proposed cutting scores of smaller procurement and research and development expenditures. His amendment drew considerable support, but it was finally defeated, 45-50.

Later in 1992, Exon was one of three sponsors of a measure to restrict and eventually end U.S. testing of nuclear weapons. The ban was ultimately approved. Exon has long been involved in testing issues as chairman of the Nuclear Deterrence, Arms Control and Defense Intelligence Subcommittee.

At the outset of the 101st Congress, the panel faced a different sort of nuclear challenge:

the waste-cleanup crisis at the nation's nuclear-weapons plants. Exon joined in the promotion of an oversight board to ensure the cleanup and modernization of the facilities and worked to establish a council in 1990 to apply the resources of the Energy and Defense departments to such environmental problems.

A longtime supporter of the B-2 bomber, Exon worked for years to save the weapon. He and Nunn, along with other backers of the bomber, succeeded in keeping the program alive, although Congress allocated less money than they wanted.

Threats to the bomber's production grew with the gradual end of the Cold War. An amendment in 1989 to curb production of the B-2 was rejected by 42 votes; in 1990, an amendment to kill the program was rejected by just 13 votes. By late 1990, even Exon conceded the B-2 was "in big, big trouble." In 1992, Congress approved President Bush's request for $2.7 billion to build the last four B-2s (for a total of 20), but specified that the funds could be released only by a follow-up vote after Congress received a report from the Pentagon on the bomber's cost and ability to evade radar detection.

On another weapons issue, Exon in the 101st Congress decided to support Bush's request for $100 million for the Midgetman missile, even though he previously had backed the rail-based MX missile as a cheaper alternative. Exon's move came as part of a political compromise to secure congressional funding for both weapons. Congress ultimately apportioned $680 million between the two projects but also said the country would not be able to afford both missiles as U.S. defense budgets continued to decline.

Exon's interests in defense and business issues came together when he sponsored legislation to strengthen and make permanent the Exon-Florio law giving the president the right to stop a foreign takeover of U.S. companies if the takeover threatened national security.

In the 101st Congress, he sponsored a bill aimed at improving federal agencies' collection and analysis of data from foreign-owned businesses. "It matters a great deal who owns businesses, assets and technologies," said Exon, a leading critic of foreign control of American enterprise. "American economic policy must be concerned about the creation of American wealth and international economic leadership, as well as the creation of American jobs."

On the Commerce Committee, Exon chairs the Surface Transportation Subcommittee, where he has been quite active, particularly on safety issues. In 1993, he joined the full committee's ranking Republican, John C. Danforth of Missouri, in sponsoring legislation to provide incentive grants to states that agree to grant only provisional licenses to teenage drivers and take other steps to get high-risk drivers off the highways. During the 102nd Congress, he sponsored legislation that froze the length of multiple-trailer trucks at their current size and also froze the number of highways these trucks may use. He also successfully sponsored legislation that required high-tech braking devices to be installed in trains and authorized more funding for safety and research programs and increased penalties for safety violations. And he sponsored another law that stiffened Department of Transportation regulation of pipeline safety and required more attention to the environmental impact concerns.

Exon was also the original sponsor of two earlier safety-related laws, though his fingerprints on each grew faint as it moved through Congress. One, designed to prevent the release of chemicals and other hazardous materials in transit across the country, beefed up laws governing the transportation of hazardous materials. The other was aimed at prohibiting "backhauling" (transporting food in the same trucks used to ship garbage or chemicals). Both bills were passed by Congress and signed by Bush in 1990.

At Home: After his narrow, 52 percent win over a little-known challenger in 1984, Exon ranked near the top of the Republican target list for 1990. GOP Senate strategists — who recruited heavily from the House that year — failed to coax 1st District Rep. Doug Bereuter into the contest. But they did get former four-term 2nd District Rep. Hal Daub, who had been seen as promising prior to his defeat by interim Sen. David K. Karnes in the 1988 Republican Senate primary.

Daub had angered many Republicans by challenging Karnes (who eventually lost to Democrat Kerrey), but his 1990 entry received strong backing from the party leadership. He drew quick attention with a January 1990 salvo in which he renounced political action committee contributions and challenged Exon to do the same. Exon refused.

Exon said rejecting PAC money would imply that he might be corrupted by it. He also recalled Daub dismissing a similar "no PACs" campaign by a 1984 Democratic House challenger as "a gimmick."

Exon aired an early flight of TV ads, playing on his biggest strengths: his grandfatherly image and his long career of public service to Nebraska.

Daub, by contrast, had been known for his gratingly intense manner. He tried to soften his image, campaigning in a more relaxed style as "the new Hal Daub." But these efforts were undercut, and the challenge doomed, by the controversy over Tower's allegations concerning Exon's drinking.

When Daub declined to apologize for the incident, Exon said Daub's "pit bull" image had been revived. The incumbent maintained wide leads in the polls and won with 59 percent.

With his strong campaign effort, Exon lent credence to his argument that his weaker 1984 showing was attributable to his own complacency and to the coattails of President Reagan, who took 71 percent of the Nebraska vote that year. Exon's 1984 opponent, University of Nebraska Regent Nancy Hoch, surprised even her GOP supporters with her performance.

The 1984 aberration was the only close contest of Exon's political career. The owner of an office supply business in Lincoln, he broke into politics in the 1950s as a local Democratic Party coordinator. In 1964, he ran Lyndon B. Johnson's 1964 presidential campaign in Nebraska, and in 1968 he became a Democratic National Committee member.

Although Exon had never run for office himself before 1970, he did not start small: He challenged incumbent Republican Gov. Norbert T. Tiemann. Exon benefited in that campaign from public disenchantment over newly enacted state income and sales taxes. The anti-tax backlash spurred a strong primary challenge to Tiemann, who was then swept aside by Exon.

His 1974 re-election campaign caused Exon no problems. Running on a fiscal austerity program that had produced a state government surplus that year, Exon turned back GOP state Sen. Richard D. Marvel.

His 1978 bid to move up to the Senate was nearly as easy. Republican Carl T. Curtis chose to retire after four terms, and his former aide, Donald E. Shasteen, was overmatched against Exon from the start. The ease with which Exon collected 68 percent of the vote may have set him up for the tumble his winning percentage would take in 1984.

Committees

Armed Services (2nd of 11 Democrats)
Nuclear Deterrence, Arms Control & Defense Intelligence (chairman); Coalition Defense & Reinforcing Forces; Regional Defense & Contingency Forces

Budget (5th of 12 Democrats)

Commerce, Science & Transportation (4th of 11 Democrats)
Surface Transportation (chairman); Aviation; Communications

Elections

1990 General

Jim Exon (D)	349,779	(59%)
Hal Daub (R)	243,013	(41%)

Previous Winning Percentages: 1984 (52%) **1978** (68%)

Campaign Finance

	Receipts	Receipts from PACs		Expend-itures
1990				
Exon (D)	$2,598,356	$1,503,897	(58%)	$2,349,739
Daub (R)	$1,461,846	0		$1,452,681

Key Votes

1993	
Require unpaid family and medical leave	Y
Approve national "motor voter" registration bill	Y
Approve budget increasing taxes and reducing deficit	Y
Support president's right to lift military gay ban	Y
1992	
Approve school-choice pilot program	N
Allow shifting funds from defense to domestic programs	N
Oppose deeper cuts in spending for SDI	Y
1991	
Approve waiting period for handgun purchases	Y
Raise senators' pay and ban honoraria	Y
Authorize use of force in Persian Gulf	N
Confirm Clarence Thomas to Supreme Court	Y

Voting Studies

	Presidential Support		Party Unity		Conservative Coalition	
Year	**S**	**O**	**S**	**O**	**S**	**O**
1992	43	57	74	26	55	45
1991	52	48	68	32	75	23
1990	54	42	63	34	68	30
1989	65	35	53	46	79	21
1988	65	31	66	30	86	11
1987	44	56	74	23	72	28
1986	34	64	66	31	45	53
1985	43	45	54	30	65	28
1984	58	36	51	45	68	28
1983	54	46	56	43	70	25
1982	55	40	64	33	70	26
1981	56	41	69	27	67	31

Interest Group Ratings

Year	ADA	AFL-CIO	CCUS	ACU
1992	75	83	30	26
1991	50	67	20	38
1990	33	67	55	61
1989	35	100	25	36
1988	35	71	50	48
1987	65	80	50	38
1986	35	53	32	48
1985	25	43	46	59
1984	55	36	65	48
1983	40	44	61	60
1982	40	48	55	74
1981	45	33	50	47

Bob Kerrey (D)

Of Lincoln — Elected 1988; 1st Term

Born: Aug. 27, 1943, Lincoln, Neb.
Education: U. of Nebraska, B.S. 1966.
Military Service: Navy, 1966-69.
Occupation: Restaurateur.
Family: Divorced; two children.
Religion: Congregationalist.
Political Career: Governor, 1983-87; sought Democratic nomination for president, 1992.
Capitol Office: 303 Hart Bldg. 20510; 224-6551.

In Washington: In the spring of 1993, Kerrey raised some eyebrows around Washington when he joined three other Democrats and a unified GOP in supporting a Republican amendment to cut President Clinton's $16.3 billion economic stimulus package.

Kerrey had said — after sticking with the administration on some tough votes on the fiscal 1994 budget resolution — that he would not be swayed by a "Win one for the Gipper" argument. "I'm doing a lot for the Gipper," he said. "I'm doing essentially the budget resolution."

But the inevitable question arose: Was Kerrey, who had lashed Clinton with one of the sharpest remarks of the 1992 primary campaign, still harboring hard feelings toward his vanquisher for the Democratic presidential nomination? No answer was easily discernible.

Kerrey is one of the most enigmatic Democrats to have risen recently in national party circles. A glamorous former governor with a streak of quirkiness, he was tagged upon his arrival in the Senate as someone who would eventually run for president. His story had mesmerized Nebraska voters for years: a telegenic wounded war hero who returned from Vietnam, built a successful business career and became a popular vote-getter in a Republican state. He defeated an incumbent Republican for the governorship, had a romance with a Hollywood actress (Debra Winger), renounced a virtually guaranteed re-election and then beat a Republican appointee for a Senate seat. He has a mischievous relish for the provocative quip. (Asked in April 1993 by Washington radio personalities if he is still seeing Winger, he replied, "Not as a stimulus package.")

Kerrey had shown little interest in a 1992 campaign until the late summer of 1991. When he did enter on Sept. 30, he seemed to do so more on impulse than by contemplative strategy. His message was diffuse, and those unfamiliar with his penchant for impulsive discourse regarded him as an oddity. As late as November, when The Miami Herald asked him why he wanted to be president, he said, "I don't know why; I just believe I can do it."

Kerrey began honing his message, accenting his pay-as-you-go national health-care plan and a proposal to streamline the federal executive branch within the visionary framework of "building for greatness again."

Then in mid-November, an open TV microphone at a New Hampshire political roast caught Kerrey telling Clinton an off-color joke involving both lesbianism and former California Gov. Edmund G. "Jerry" Brown Jr. Kerrey responded to his gaffe with a stream of mea culpas. "It was an insensitive, stupid joke told by, hopefully, a temporarily stupid politician," he said.

That stumble behind him, Kerrey righted himself with a strong performance in the first candidates' debate in December. He earned praise for challenging Brown's attacks on corrupt politicians. "I've got to tell you I resent all this ... special-interest stuff that you are putting out," Kerrey said, "because you seem to be saying that I'm somehow bought and paid for. Is that what you're saying?"

After finishing fifth in Iowa, which was won overwhelmingly by Iowa Sen. Tom Harkin, Kerrey came in third in New Hampshire, winning 11 percent of the vote but no delegates. His sole occasion for celebration came in South Dakota, where, against a full field, he collected 40 percent of the primary vote.

The South Dakota win briefly resuscitated his candidacy. Kerrey went to Georgia, where he played up the contrast between his Vietnam service and Clinton's draft avoidance. Kerrey did not attack Clinton's anti-war stance or nonservice, but he suggested that the Republicans would do precisely that in the fall if Clinton won the nomination. Clinton, he said in his most memorable line of the campaign, "is going to be opened up like a soft peanut." But after failing to win any of the seven contests on March 3, Kerrey ended his campaign.

He proved gallant in his departure, saying that he could be "very" enthusiastic about Clinton if he were nominated. He dismissed his prior remarks as "political hyperbole" and added, "If he's the nominee of the party, I will campaign feverishly to make certain that he wins." He also said that he expected to try for the White House again.

Kerrey appeared on some "short lists" for vice president; he flew to Little Rock for an interview with Clinton. But according to Newsweek magazine, Kerrey "crashed the list, telling all of Washington he was on it."

He proved to be a stalwart Clinton supporter during the general-election campaign. In September, he rose on the Senate floor to castigate President Bush for attacking Clinton's Vietnam War draft record. "When you began your presidency, you said you wanted to put the Vietnam memory behind us.... Now, when the hunger for re-election has gotten the better of you and the smell of political blood is in the air, you abandon your earlier, and correct, intention....

"While my first concern and sympathy goes to those men and women who fought in the war, I am also sympathetic with those like Bill Clinton who made other decisions. I am also here to argue that whatever memory difficulties faced by Bill Clinton they are of a much smaller order than the memory loss and lack of shame shown by you."

In his first two years in the Senate, Kerrey impressed his colleagues with his swift acclimation in matters legislative and political. His quick mastery of the arcana of agriculture policy propelled him into a central role in negotiations on the 1990 farm bill. And by the end of the 101st Congress, he had become an articulate moral compass for the left wing of the Democratic Party on volatile partisan issues such as the Persian Gulf War and flag burning.

Kerrey has a belief in activist government that stems in part from his personal experience. He credits assistance from federal programs in helping him make the transformation from an embittered Vietnam veteran to a wealthy businessman.

Kerrey was the only member of his class to win a seat on the Appropriations Committee for the 101st Congress. His other committee assignment, Agriculture, was promised to him by Chairman Patrick J. Leahy during his election campaign.

Although Kerrey did not enter the Senate with a detailed grounding in the intricacies of agriculture, he hired respected staff and immersed himself in government farm programs. By the time the committee turned to the 1990 farm bill, he was prepared to spearhead the activist, prairie populist wing on the panel.

Early in the 103rd Congress, Kerrey and five other farm-state Democrats, concerned that Leahy would not forcefully protect grain-state interests, formed an unofficial Midwestern caucus. They sent a list of their ideas to Agriculture Secretary Mike Espy.

Kerrey's record as a war hero in Vietnam — he lost part of his right leg in combat and earned a Medal of Honor — gave him credibility, and other anti-war Democrats cover, when he launched his early opposition to the U.S. buildup of forces in the Persian Gulf in 1990. After supporting the initial dispatch of troops to Saudi Arabia, saying it was justifiable to prevent an Iraqi invasion, he became one of the most conspicuous opponents of Bush's gulf policy as it escalated toward creating an offensive force.

"I question the response that says we're going to go there and have our young people die so we can have cheap oil and cheap gasoline here at home," he said in August 1990. He chastised the administration for its record of passivity while Iraqi President Saddam Hussein amassed weapons and oppressed his citizens.

Earlier, Kerrey had lent his patriotic prestige to liberals' debate when he denounced vehemently Bush's initiative to amend the Constitution to ban physical desecration of the flag. He accused Bush of trying "to divide the nation" by pushing the amendment. "I am ashamed of what he did," he said in a passionate floor speech in 1990. He concluded, "I grieve for us. I weep for America today."

At Home: "Charismatic" and "enigmatic" are the two descriptors commonly applied to Kerrey during his rise in Nebraska public life. An unconventional style and disregard for the accepted rules of political behavior vaulted Kerrey into the governorship in 1982, and sent him to the Senate six years later.

Although Kerrey was known locally as a war hero and a successful restaurateur, he was a political novice when he bid against Republican Gov. Charles Thone in 1982. However, Thone had a reputation for being bland and indecisive. Employing an aggressive campaign style and a wry, self-deprecating sense of humor, Kerrey attracted publicity and scored a narrow upset.

Kerrey soon showed he was unafraid to buck political trends: He became a critic of President Ronald Reagan, who in 1984 would carry 71 percent of the Nebraska vote. Kerrey attacked Reagan's economic and farm policies and accused the president of taking an approach to foreign affairs that "drapes euphemism and simplistic slogans over the realities of war." His views on war were well-known: After accepting the Medal of Honor, he had protested the Vietnam War as immoral.

But it was Kerrey's relationship with Winger, not his political agenda, that left the most enduring impression from his gubernatorial tenure. Kerrey, who was divorced, met Winger in 1983 while she was making a movie in Lincoln.

While Kerrey's public romance made him something of a dashing figure, it also led to criticisms that he was long on style and short on substance. Although he cut an activist image early in his term, pushing deficit reduction and banking-law-reform measures to passage, his relationship with the unicameral Legislature soured somewhat.

Still, Kerrey was heavily favored to win a second term; his job-approval rating hung at about 70 percent. He thus sealed his reputation for unpredictability when he announced he would not run for re-election in 1986. Although some observers tied the decision to distress over the breakup of his romance with Winger, Kerrey cited business obligations and a desire to spend more time with his two children.

With both Senate seats held by Democrats, it appeared that Kerrey might have plenty of quality time before seeking higher office. However, Democratic Sen. Edward Zorinsky died unexpectedly in March 1987; Republican Gov. Kay A. Orr picked an obscure businessman, David K. Karnes, as a replacement. Knowing his political base was much stronger than Karnes', Kerrey needed no arm-twisting before entering the 1988 contest for a full Senate term.

As it turned out, Kerrey received an unexpected assist from a would-be Republican rival. Four-term 2nd District GOP Rep. Hal Daub, angered that Orr had passed him over in favor of Karnes, jumped into the Republican Senate primary. Bolstered by his brief incumbency and the support of the state Republican leadership, Karnes held on to win with 55 percent of the vote. But he was bloodied, and entered the fall campaign against Kerrey as a distinct underdog.

Kerrey, who had token opposition for the Democratic nomination, had already filled the airwaves with image-building biographical ads. He was able to stick to his own script for the general election, touting his support for catastrophic health insurance, parental leave legislation and an overhaul of the welfare system. He called for a mix of spending cuts and tax increases to reduce the deficit.

Karnes, meanwhile, had spent much of his money on the primary, and was $200,000 in debt by the end of June. He also made a disastrous gaffe: In discussing improved agricultural technology, Karnes said, "We need fewer farmers at this point in time," a remark that provoked jeers from a state-fair audience. Karnes immediately retreated, saying he had misspoken, but the damage was done.

Even a flawless campaign might have fallen short of upending the popular Kerrey; one as fraught with errors as Karnes' was doomed. Kerrey won by 15 percentage points, running nearly 20 points ahead of Democratic presidential nominee Michael S. Dukakis.

Committees

Agriculture, Nutrition & Forestry (9th of 10 Democrats)
Agricultural Production & Stabilization of Prices; Agricultural Research, Conservation, Forestry & General Legislation; Nutrition & Investigations

Appropriations (13th of 16 Democrats)
Agriculture, Rural Development & Related Agencies; Commerce, Justice, State & Judiciary; Energy & Water Development; Treasury, Postal Service & General Government; VA, HUD & Independent Agencies

Select Intelligence (4th of 9 Democrats)

Elections

1988 General		
Bob Kerrey (D)	378,717	(57%)
David K. Karnes (R)	278,250	(42%)
1988 Primary		
Bob Kerrey (D)	156,498	(91%)
Ken L. Michaelis (D)	14,248	(8%)

Campaign Finance

	Receipts	Receipts from PACs		Expend-itures
1988				
Kerrey (D)	$3,485,728	$799,279	(23%)	$3,461,148
Karnes (R)	$3,423,237	$883,895	(26%)	$3,411,361

Key Votes

1993	
Require unpaid family and medical leave	Y
Approve national "motor voter" registration bill	Y
Approve budget increasing taxes and reducing deficit	Y
Support president's right to lift military gay ban	Y
1992	
Approve school-choice pilot program	?
Allow shifting funds from defense to domestic programs	Y
Oppose deeper cuts in spending for SDI	N
1991	
Approve waiting period for handgun purchases	Y
Raise senators' pay and ban honoraria	Y
Authorize use of force in Persian Gulf	N
Confirm Clarence Thomas to Supreme Court	N

Voting Studies

	Presidential Support		Party Unity		Conservative Coalition	
Year	S	O	S	O	S	O
1992	25	58	74	9	18	58
1991	32	52	70	13	45	35
1990	40	60	84	16	49	51
1989	51	49	88	12	26	74

Interest Group Ratings

Year	ADA	AFL-CIO	CCUS	ACU
1992	90	91	25	0
1991	75	78	29	5
1990	83	67	25	13
1989	80	100	50	11

1 Doug Bereuter (R)

Of Lincoln — Elected 1978; 8th Term

Born: Oct. 6, 1939, York, Neb.
Education: U. of Nebraska, B.A. 1961; Harvard U., M.C.P. 1963, M.P.A. 1973.
Military Service: Army, 1963-65.
Occupation: Urban planner; professor; state official.
Family: Wife, Louise Anna Meyer; two children.
Religion: Lutheran.
Political Career: Neb. Legislature, 1975-79.
Capitol Office: 2348 Rayburn Bldg. 20515; 225-4806.

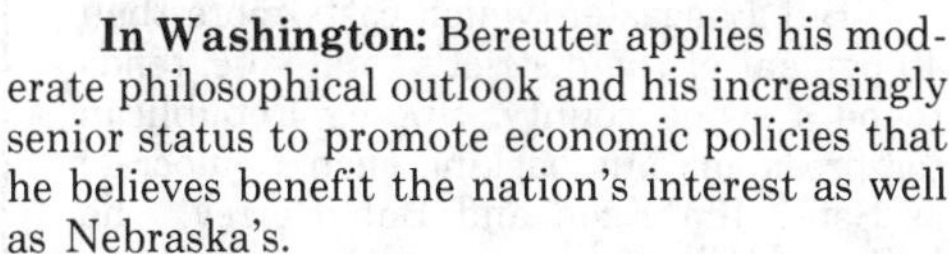

In Washington: Bereuter applies his moderate philosophical outlook and his increasingly senior status to promote economic policies that he believes benefit the nation's interest as well as Nebraska's.

On the domestic front, he has been instrumental in devising rural housing programs, and in pressing a populist concern for small borrowers and small lenders alike. But he is perhaps best known on Capitol Hill for his work on international economic issues. He combines the overlapping jurisdictions of the Banking and Foreign Affairs committees to focus on multinational lending activities and export promotion, an area where his activities have often redounded to the benefit of his state's agricultural producers.

In the 103rd Congress, he took over as ranking Republican on the Banking Subcommittee on International Development, Finance, Trade and Monetary Policy, where he is an ally of the Democratic chairman, Barney Frank of Massachusetts. He also retained his ranking spot on the Foreign Affairs Subcommittee on International Security, International Organizations and Human Rights.

Bereuter has taken a leadership role in the Nebraska GOP and is viewed as a potential Senate candidate. So, his earnest efforts as a committed internationalist might be seen to entail some political risk. Some in central Nebraska still regard foreign entanglements, especially foreign aid programs, with suspicion. But Bereuter's attention to Farm Belt concerns mitigates any problem that his less parochial activities might provoke.

A free-trader, he has been a leading opponent of cargo-preference laws (which require that a share of U.S.-financed exports be carried on U.S.-flag vessels). Bereuter says such laws hurt American farmers whose foreign competitors can export goods anyway they choose. But he is not often successful at blocking their passage, or at replacing them with language more hortatory than mandatory.

At the same time, Bereuter is not averse to criticizing barriers other countries erect to U.S. trade. A Bereuter-sponsored resolution that passed the House in 1992 noted Japan's resistance to some U.S. agricultural goods. The resolution urged the administration to solicit more Japanese aid to poor nations in the form of purchased U.S. food.

Bereuter is a rare moderate Republican on the ideologically divided Foreign Affairs Committee. During debates over such issues as aid to the Nicaraguan contras in the 1980s, Bereuter was often one of the committee's few voices urging compromise. His background as an Army intelligence officer and his continuing service on the House Select Intelligence Committee give him a broad view of complex international events.

Bereuter took umbrage in early 1990 at the State Department's efforts to develop a closer relationship with Iraq. Citing the "abysmal" record of Saddam Hussein's Iraqi regime — which included the use of poison gas in 1988 against the nation's Kurdish minority — Bereuter cosponsored a non-binding resolution with Democratic subcommittee Chairman Gus Yatron of Pennsylvania condemning Iraq for a "consistent pattern" of human rights violations.

Though the resolution easily passed the subcommittee, the Bush administration blocked its advance. After Iraq's invasion of Kuwait, Bereuter supported the president's request to use force against Iraq, and said economic sanctions that had been instituted against Iraq had proved insufficient.

Concern about the ability of foreign countries to buy U.S. goods has led Bereuter to take an interest in efforts to reduce debts developing nations owe to U.S. banks — an issue that overlaps his Foreign Affairs and Banking beats. He generally supported a 1989 plan by Treasury Secretary Nicholas F. Brady to reduce total loan obligations or to spread out payments in a way that would ensure that a portion of the loans would be repaid. But he was wary of proposals to force banks to grant relief, fearing that if banks were mandated to take a loss they would be reluctant to lend to Third World countries in the future.

Nebraska 1

East — Lincoln; Norfolk

Not long ago, Lincoln was a sleepy town that came to life only during the Legislature's sessions and on autumn Saturdays when the University of Nebraska played football. Back then, Cornhusker crowds nearly matched the city's population. Today, however, Lincoln is thriving: Its population has nearly doubled over the past 40 years to 192,000. A diversified employment base makes Lincoln (Lancaster County) a picture of economic health.

The city's boom has been led by the expanding state and city governments and by the university, which has 24,600 students. Lincoln has three major hospital complexes, and the white-collar base features banks and insurance companies. In addition, Lincoln (like Omaha) is fast becoming a telecommunications hub. Gallup Organization Inc., the polling company, is in Lincoln. Lincoln does have industrial employers, including a Goodyear factory that makes rubber belts and hoses. There are also a number of food-processing companies.

The 1st has pockets of population growth elsewhere. Norfolk (Madison County) is known for pursuing industry; beef products, electronic components and steel products are made here. The district includes Omaha exurbs to the north (Washington County) and south (most of Cass County), as well as Dakota County suburbs of Sioux City, Iowa (where IBP, the nation's largest beef processor, is headquartered), and Dodge County.

In the more sparsely populated rural sections of the 1st is some of the nation's most productive farmland. Counties in the northern part of the 1st are among Nebraska's leaders in hog and milk production; York County, to the west, is a leading corn producer. Farming in the rural parts of Lancaster County outside Lincoln makes the county the biggest sorghum producer.

The rural Republican vote gives the GOP an advantage in the 1st. In 1992, Madison County gave 57 percent to George Bush, although that was well below his 1988 tally of 76 percent. Rep. Bereuter won re-election in 1992 with 60 percent of the vote, carrying all but one county in the 1st.

But Lancaster, which casts more than 40 percent of the district's total vote, tends to be a swing county, tipping Republican for president but backing such Democrats as Sens. Jim Exon and Bob Kerrey, who hail from Lincoln.

In 1992, Bush won Lancaster over Bill Clinton by just 193 votes, out of more than 104,000 cast. Four years earlier, Bush won the county by 345 votes. Bereuter in 1992 took 53 percent in Lancaster, below his district average.

The strongest Democratic counties are at opposite corners of the district. In the northeast are Dakota County, with a large blue-collar contingent and some Hispanic and Asian residents, and Thurston County, made up almost entirely of Winnebago and Omaha Indian reservations. In the southwest is rural Saline County, dominated by people of Czech heritage with a longstanding Democratic tradition.

1990 Population: 526,297. White 507,343 (96%), Black 5,544 (1%), Other 13,410 (3%). Hispanic origin 7,106 (1%). 18 and over 389,852 (74%), 62 and over 91,091(17%). Median age: 33.

A city planner by profession, Bereuter has been active on the Banking Committee on housing and development issues. In 1990, he helped shepherd to enactment a pilot program of mortgage loan guarantees for lower income residents of small communities in rural areas. In 1992, the program was extended to all 50 states and broadened to include middle-income households.

He has also been active promoting an overhaul of federal flood insurance. The measure would require property owners in threatened areas to buy insurance and deny insurance in 10-year flood zones. Supported by some conservationists and opposed by coastal resort developers, the bill passed the House in the 102nd Congress, but died in the Senate. Bereuter reintroduced it at the start of the 103rd.

Bereuter has been less involved in banking matters, but he has been supportive of the savings and loan bailout. He called a House decision in 1992 not to continue financing the bailout "irresponsible." During debate on a major banking overhaul bill in 1991, Bereuter sided with smaller banks to oppose Bush administration proposals to roll back deposit insurance coverage and to permit banks to open branch offices across state lines without limit.

At Home: In September 1989, Bereuter was the only House Republican to vote against President Bush's proposed capital gains tax cut. But he rejected the media theory that he had done so to get even for a personal slight. The theory had it that Bush was displeased that Bereuter, without consulting him, decided not to run against Democratic Sen. Jim Exon.

When Bush visited Lincoln shortly thereafter, Bereuter was not invited to sit on the stage.

The flap, such as it was, caused no problems for Bereuter at the polls. He won a seventh term in 1990 with 65 percent of the vote, even as the GOP lost both the governorship and the Senate race. He continues to be mentioned as a possible Senate candidate, should the right opportunity arise.

Bereuter's background is unusual for a Nebraska politician. He held the state's top city planning post under moderate GOP Gov. Norbert Tiemann from 1969 to 1971. Then he served one four-year term in the Legislature, winning a reputation as one of the more liberal members by sponsoring a land-use planning bill. Farming and ranching interests regarded the bill as an intrusion into private-property decisions.

Bereuter used conservative rhetoric during his 1978 House campaign, but he was still seen as a moderate in Lincoln. His big margin in Lancaster (Lincoln) County pushed him past a conservative state senator.

In November he drew united GOP support and a large independent vote to collect 58 percent against Hess Dyas, the former Democratic state chairman. Thereafter he won every two years with 64 percent or better, until 1992, when redistricting added some of the Omaha metropolitan area to his Lincoln-based district. He won again in 1992, but his share slipped to 60 percent.

Committees

Banking, Finance & Urban Affairs (4th of 20 Republicans)
International Development, Finance, Trade & Monetary Policy (ranking); Consumer Credit & Insurance; Housing & Community Development

Foreign Affairs (7th of 18 Republicans)
International Security, International Organizations & Human Rights (ranking); Economic Policy, Trade & the Environment

Select Intelligence (2nd of 7 Republicans)
Oversight & Evaluation; Program & Budget Authorization

Elections

1992 General		
Doug Bereuter (R)	142,713	(60%)
Gerry Finnegan (D)	96,309	(40%)
1990 General		
Doug Bereuter (R)	129,654	(65%)
Larry Hall (D)	70,587	(35%)

Previous Winning Percentages: **1988** (67%) **1986** (64%) **1984** (74%) **1982** (75%) **1980** (79%) **1978** (58%)

District Vote for President

1992
D 80,700 (33%)
R 107,092 (43%)
I 59,979 (24%)

Campaign Finance

	Receipts	Receipts from PACs		Expend-itures
1992				
Bereuter (R)	$315,824	$194,482	(62%)	$365,386
Finnegan (D)	$86,028	$27,521	(32%)	$84,533
1990				
Bereuter (R)	$254,654	$147,250	(58%)	$223,898
Hall (D)	$65,064	$43,400	(67%)	$65,064

Key Votes

1993	
Require parental notification of minors' abortions	Y
Require unpaid family and medical leave	N
Approve national "motor voter" registration bill	N
Approve budget increasing taxes and reducing deficit	N
Approve economic stimulus plan	N
1992	
Approve balanced-budget constitutional amendment	Y
Close down space station program	Y
Approve U.S. aid for former Soviet Union	Y
Allow shifting funds from defense to domestic programs	N
1991	
Extend unemployment benefits using deficit financing	N
Approve waiting period for handgun purchases	N
Authorize use of force in Persian Gulf	Y

Voting Studies

	Presidential Support		Party Unity		Conservative Coalition	
Year	S	O	S	O	S	O
1992	68	30	77	21	73	25
1991	79	21	77	22	78	22
1990	62	38	73	25	87	13
1989	69	29	58	41	80	17
1988	56 †	42 †	79 †	20 †	87 †	13 †
1987	59	41	63	35	81	19
1986	58	42	73	26	78	22
1985	58	43	74	22	78	18
1984	54	43	64	35	71	29
1983	61	37	69	26	70	29
1982	75	25	77	23	79	21
1981	68	30	75	23	79	19

† Not eligible for all recorded votes.

Interest Group Ratings

Year	ADA	AFL-CIO	CCUS	ACU
1992	20	33	88	79
1991	10	17	100	85
1990	17	0	100	67
1989	15	33	80	61
1988	20	57	93	76
1987	24	19	80	57
1986	15	21	72	59
1985	15	12	82	67
1984	35	23	63	54
1983	25	6	95	70
1982	26	20	86	68
1981	20	0	89	87

2 Peter Hoagland (D)

Of Omaha — Elected 1988; 3rd Term

Born: Nov. 17, 1941, Omaha, Neb.
Education: Stanford U., A.B. 1963; Yale U., LL.B. 1968.
Military Service: Army, 1963-65.
Occupation: Lawyer.
Family: Wife, Barbara Erickson; five children.
Religion: Episcopalian.
Political Career: Neb. Legislature, 1979-87.
Capitol Office: 1113 Longworth Bldg. 20515; 225-4155.

In Washington: Hoagland's intelligence is not questioned, and his work ethic was rewarded at the start of his third term with a seat on the Ways and Means Committee. But Hoagland's political acumen is quixotic; at times he pursues legislative goals that plainly cannot be achieved.

His image at home and on Capitol Hill as a sincere, diligent member helped his first reelection campaign and made him a plausible, though unsuccessful, candidate for a spot on the Appropriations Committee in late 1990. In partial recompense for not landing on Appropriations, he acquired seats on Interior and Judiciary for the 102nd Congress, while retaining his assignment to the Banking Committee. And his perseverance paid off in the 103rd with the move to Ways and Means.

Hoagland has a reputation for being principled — some say too much so. As a freshman, he worked hard on the bill that initiated the savings and loan bailout, even winning inclusion in the final bill of an amendment important to some Omaha constituents. But at the last minute, Hoagland joined with some senior House Democrats to oppose a compromise method of paying the bailout's first installment. His speech on the floor against the compromise and subsequent "no" vote on final passage earned him a year's worth of silent treatment from Banking Chairman Henry B. Gonzalez of Texas.

Hoagland thought the deal, which the Bush administration had demanded and which Gonzalez had accepted, was bad policy. Gonzalez was particularly miffed because — except for Hoagland's provision that protected a pair of Omaha-based partnerships that owned thrifts — the bailout bill had been stripped of most special-interest language. Gonzalez thought that Hoagland should have supported the bill, since his amendment was included.

The amendment later became a key element in a book about Hoagland, "House Rules" by Robert Cwiklik, who had access to Hoagland in 1989. The bill broadly required related thrifts to guarantee each other's balance sheets. But Hoagland argued that the two Omaha partnerships were effectively unrelated. Rather than giving them a special benefit, he convinced his colleagues that an exemption from the bill's general rule would, in fact, be good policy.

Some of Hoagland's colleagues think that he worries too much about political consequences. Before a high-profile vote in 1992 on a constitutional amendment requiring a balanced federal budget, Democratic leaders lobbied Hoagland intensively to drop his support for the measure. He agonized but eventually voted for it. His refusal to bend did not appear to affect his request for a more desirable committee assignment.

As his vote on the balanced-budget amendment suggests, Hoagland gives a moderate tint to his representation of the politically marginal 2nd. Though he votes with his party more often than the average Democrat, he can regularly be found casting a conservative vote, particularly on fiscal issues.

As a freshman, Hoagland backed abortion rights and a higher minimum wage and opposed a constitutional amendment banning flag desecration. In his second term, he supported a Democratic tax bill and aid to Russia, but he opposed shifting additional money from defense to domestic spending or further cutting the Strategic Defense Initiative.

In his first two terms, Hoagland was an active member of the Banking Committee. In the 102nd Congress, he was a key Democratic ally of administration efforts to overhaul banking law. He supported proposals to permit banks to open branch offices across state lines and to enter prohibited lines of business, such as mutual funds underwriting. He became so deeply connected to banking reform that he refused to give up after an overhaul bill failed at the end of 1991. With the tide clearly against him, he continued pressing the issue in 1992 and at the start of the 103rd Congress.

In 1989, during committee action on the thrift bailout bill, Hoagland took a tough stand on stiffening capital standards for the industry, despite heavy lobbying by a large Omaha-based savings and loan.

Nebraska 2

East — Omaha; Sarpy County suburbs

Omaha grew up as a blue-collar city: a railroad center, a Missouri River port and a place where cattle became steaks. To outsiders, this broad-shouldered, gritty image remains. But Omaha (Douglas County) has become mainly a place of white-collar jobs and new downtown office buildings. The county is also reliably Republican, voting for the GOP White House candidate every time but once in the post-Roosevelt era. In 1992, George Bush won the county with 50 percent of the vote.

Omaha's economic health is reflected in its continued growth: Its 1990 population topped 335,000, up by 7 percent since 1980. Once-rural Sarpy County, which borders Douglas County to the south, continued to blossom: Now with more than 102,000 people, it is the state's third most-populous.

As its core has filled with people through the years, the Omaha-based 2nd has become more compact. It now covers just Douglas and Sarpy counties and a tiny slice of Cass County including the city of Plattsmouth.

Metropolitan Omaha's economy is a mix of new and old. The largest employer is the Strategic Air Command at Offutt Air Force Base in Sarpy County, another Republican stronghold. A large telemarketing and credit-processing industry has been established in Omaha. Yet the Mutual of Omaha insurance company, long a community pillar, remains its largest private employer. Downtown includes the corporate headquarters for ConAgra — the agricultural products giant that ranks 25th among the Fortune 500 — and the Union Pacific Railroad. While most of Omaha's stockyards are now obsolete, more than 20 food processing companies are here.

Blue-collar jobs historically drew an ethnic population — including large numbers of Irish, Italians, Germans and Eastern Europeans — to Omaha's south side. Mainly Roman Catholics, they set the political tone for the 2nd. It has a Democratic tradition, and victory here is essential for Democrats who hope to win statewide.

However, the longtime partisan leanings are tempered by a strong conservative streak, especially on social issues. Many working-class residents vote with more affluent residents, which has enabled recent GOP presidential candidates to carry the 2nd. Bush won the county by 13 points over Bill Clinton in 1992. The city is 13 percent black, a large proportion by Nebraska standards; more than three-fourths of the state's entire black population lives in Omaha.

Long known mainly for the Boys Town orphanage, western Omaha is now heavily residential, with some new, affluent subdivisions. Nearby, onetime crossroads communities are now burgeoning cities. Bellevue, with nearly 31,000 people, is Nebraska's fourth-largest city.

The area benefits from Omaha's status as Nebraska's cultural and sports capital. It is home to the Ak-Sar-Ben (Nebraska spelled backward) racetrack and hosts the World Series of college baseball each spring.

1990 Population: 526,567. White 460,519 (87%), Black 50,907 (10%), Other 15,141 (3%). Hispanic origin 14,865 (3%). 18 and over 379,331 (72%), 62 and over 64,581 (12%). Median age: 31.

And as a member of the Housing Subcommittee in the 101st Congress, he participated in the first major rewrite of federal housing programs since 1974. Hoagland joined a bloc of moderate and conservative Democrats who forged compromise language to provide incentives for landlords to continue renting to low-income families.

On Interior (renamed Natural Resources in the 103rd), Hoagland successfully pushed along with Nebraska's two Democratic senators for enactment of a bill designating parts of the Niobrara River in Nebraska and a segment of the Missouri River in Nebraska and South Dakota as part of the national wild and scenic rivers system.

At Home: Largely because of the blue-collar population in Omaha, the 2nd is regarded as Nebraska's most Democratic turf. However, the district votes Republican for president and was won four times by Republican Hal Daub, who served from 1981 to 1989. Hoagland had tough campaigns in 1988, 1990 and 1992.

Hoagland's opportunity came when Daub sought the GOP Senate nomination in 1988. With eight years' experience in Nebraska's Legislature, Hoagland entered the contest with a large political base. A fifth-generation Omahan, he had spent his young adulthood away from home: in college, in the Army, in law school and in Washington, D.C., where he was a law clerk and trial lawyer. Hoagland returned to Omaha in 1973 to practice law, and he got involved in public affairs.

Hoagland began his own political career in 1978, winning a seat in the Legislature, where he backed initiatives on water conservation, hospital cost containment and education. He did not seek a third term in 1986, but he ran in the 1988 Democratic House primary and defeated Cece Zorinsky, the widow of Democratic Sen. Edward Zorinsky, 51 percent to 43 percent.

His Republican foe, pathologist Jerry Schenken, was little known but had a war chest that bought instant credibility. However, Hoagland linked up with the Senate campaign of former Gov. Bob Kerrey, who was headed for a resounding victory over appointed GOP Sen. David K. Karnes. Hoagland won by 2,981 votes.

In 1990, Hoagland's GOP foe was lawyer Ally Milder, a conservative former aide to Iowa Sen. Charles E. Grassley. Milder stressed her opposition to abortion and called Hoagland a liberal. Hoagland styled himself as an independent voice for the 2nd and emphasized his efforts to reform the savings and loan system and fight drug-related crime. He also gained when Secretary of Veterans Affairs Edward J. Derwinski visited Omaha for Milder and created a huge flap by calling Hispanics "wetbacks." Hoagland won with 58 percent.

Killer anti-incumbent sentiment and a surprisingly strong challenger made Hoagland more vulnerable in 1992. In June, he carried nearly a 30-point lead over former Douglas County Attorney Ron Staskiewicz. A week before Election Day, the margin had dwindled significantly after a bitter campaign.

Staskiewicz, a restaurant owner, got into the race early and immediately went on the attack, leveling charges at the front-runner, forcing him into a defensive posture. Hoagland returned fire, and the two traded charges in radio ads for weeks. Although he was not a veteran politician, Staskiewicz had run a successful campaign in the district, winning election as Douglas County attorney. Douglas County still casts four-fifths of the district's vote.

Known as an unorthodox campaigner and candidate, the flamboyant Staskiewicz called his style "Stas-o-mania." He ran on a congressional reform theme, using Cwiklik's unflattering book as evidence that Hoagland was an opportunist. Hoagland said the book, which received mixed reviews both at home and in The New York Times, was "unfair."

Staskiewicz also accused Hoagland of accepting too many donations from political action committees and using his Washington office staff to work on his campaign. Hoagland struck back, criticizing his opponent for renting office space and a school bus from two of his own corporations for his campaign. In addition, Hoagland said Staskiewicz had ignored judgments against him and his corporation for unpaid debts.

Both men said the charges against them were either false or misleading and seemed to bounce back from the onslaught. When the smoke cleared, Hoagland had held on to enough of the support he had cornered in his two terms to capture about 51 percent of the vote.

Committee

Ways & Means (19th of 24 Democrats)
Select Revenue Measures; Trade

Elections

1992 General		
Peter Hoagland (D)	119,512	(51%)
Ronald L. Staskiewicz (R)	113,828	(49%)
1992 Primary		
Peter Hoagland (D)	42,825	(85%)
Jess M. Pritchett (D)	7,501	(15%)
1990 General		
Peter Hoagland (D)	111,903	(58%)
Ally Milder (R)	80,845	(42%)

Previous Winning Percentage: **1988** (50%)

District Vote for President

1992
D 78,697 (32%)
R 115,244 (48%)
I 48,652 (20%)

Campaign Finance

	Receipts	Receipts from PACs		Expend-itures
1992				
Hoagland (D)	$701,282	$457,190	(65%)	$699,387
Staskiewicz (R)	$379,153	$83,110	(22%)	$378,721
1990				
Hoagland (D)	$935,652	$615,587	(66%)	$929,247
Milder (R)	$632,229	$152,769	(24%)	$625,716

Key Votes

1993	
Require parental notification of minors' abortions	N
Require unpaid family and medical leave	Y
Approve national "motor voter" registration bill	Y
Approve budget increasing taxes and reducing deficit	Y
Approve economic stimulus plan	Y
1992	
Approve balanced-budget constitutional amendment	Y
Close down space station program	Y
Approve U.S. aid for former Soviet Union	Y
Allow shifting funds from defense to domestic programs	N
1991	
Extend unemployment benefits using deficit financing	Y
Approve waiting period for handgun purchases	Y
Authorize use of force in Persian Gulf	Y

Voting Studies

	Presidential Support		Party Unity		Conservative Coalition	
Year	**S**	**O**	**S**	**O**	**S**	**O**
1992	30	67	88	10	58	38
1991	42	58	83	17	54	46
1990	27	73	84	16	50	50
1989	35	65	86	14	49	51

Interest Group Ratings

Year	ADA	AFL-CIO	CCUS	ACU
1992	85	75	50	24
1991	50	83	10	15
1990	72	83	50	29
1989	70	92	40	25

3 Bill Barrett (R)

Of Lexington — Elected 1990; 2nd Term

Born: Feb. 9, 1929, Lexington, Neb.
Education: Hastings College, B.A. 1951.
Military Service: Navy, 1951-52.
Occupation: Real estate and insurance broker.
Family: Wife, Elsie Carlson; four children.
Religion: Presbyterian.
Political Career: Neb. Legislature, 1979-91, Speaker, 1987-91.
Capitol Office: 1213 Longworth Bldg. 20515; 225-6435.

In Washington: Barrett spent his first term pushing to expand his role in Congress and attempting to nail down support in the district he struggled to win in 1990. He succeeded on both counts.

From the day he arrived in Washington, Barrett pursued his goals on several fronts. He was quickly elected — and later re-elected — as president of his Republican freshman class.

He won a seat on the Agriculture Committee, where he could represent the farmers in his rural district.

He accepted a position on the House Administration Committee, where he could use his experience as Speaker of Nebraska's unicameral Legislature and get noticed by the Republican leadership. (He was one of three Republicans named to the six-member panel created to investigate mismanagement of the House Post Office.)

And he made frequent trips home to his district, making sure his constituents knew who he was and what he was doing for them. They seemed to appreciate it: They re-elected him with 72 percent of the vote.

From his seat on the Agriculture Committee, Barrett pushed successfully for provisions, including one in the 1991 modification of the 1990 farm bill, to give farmers increased planting flexibility. Another successful Barrett proposal provided assistance to help beginning farmers and ranchers get started.

In 1992, with corn farmers in the 3rd in mind, Barrett asked then-candidate Bill Clinton to endorse ethanol use and waive restrictions imposed under the Clean Air Act. He suggested that Clinton should announce his support for President Bush's Oct. 1 decision to grant ethanol a waiver from the act's restrictions.

"I hope the Clinton administration will uphold this decision, one that is so important to Nebraska's farmers, the ethanol industry and the overall economy," Barrett said in the Omaha World-Herald.

Barrett also sits on the Education and Labor Committee. He was one of a number of committee members who sponsored legislation that would preclude government consideration of equity in a family's home or farm as an asset when determining student loan eligibility.

A Barrett amendment authorizing $1 million a year for four years for states to provide grants for recovery programs for homeless and runaway youth was included in juvenile justice legislation signed into law in 1992.

Barrett suffered one big disappointment in the 102nd Congress when a longstanding feud over land and water finally ended.

Barrett fought against members of his own delegation who wanted to designate a scenic stretch along the Niobrara River as protected federal land.

He knew when he arrived in Washington that he faced an uphill battle to stop Congress from including a portion of the river under federal land protection laws.

A 76-mile stretch of the Niobrara targeted under the bill that became law runs through the 3rd. Barrett argued to no avail that the legislation, which designates that stretch as part of the Wild and Scenic Rivers System, was unfair to land owners near the waterway because some would have their land taken and others would see their property values fall.

When the bill was approved by the House Interior Committee, Barrett, because he is not a member of the panel, sat helpless in the room, watching as a spectator.

When the bill moved to the House floor, Barrett attempted to amend it to require further study but the amendment failed 109-293.

Early in the 103rd Congress Barrett opposed President Clinton's economic stimulus package and a budget resolution backed by the president. He also opposed family planning legislation that overturned the "gag rule," the Bush administration's ban on abortion counseling at federally funded family planning clinics.

At Home: Barrett's first run for the House looked a lot like his predecessor's first House campaign. Like retiring Rep. Virginia Smith, he struggled to hold the traditional GOP bastion.

When Smith first ran for the open 3rd, she

Nebraska 3

Rural West — Grand Island; North Platte

As ever, agriculture is king in the 3rd. To the east are the state's most productive corn-growing regions and several leading hog-raising counties; the west has the biggest wheat farms. Western Nebraska is also a national leader in production of sugar beets and dry beans.

On the plains in the northern and central parts of the 3rd, the old saw that there are more cows than people is a gross understatement. Vast Cherry County, with fewer than 7,000 people, had more than 300,000 head of cattle in 1992.

In this part of Nebraska, one can drive for hours along straight, flat roads without passing any community larger than a village. Between 1980 and 1990, 63 of the 66 counties in the 3rd lost population.

The 3rd is traditionally the most Republican district in the state — its '80s incarnation gave more than 70 percent of its vote to Ronald Reagan in 1980 and 1984, and 67 percent to George Bush in 1988. In 1992, Bush carried the district with 50 percent. Bush's decline was no help to Bill Clinton, though; he finished third in the district with 24 percent, behind Ross Perot's 27 percent.

The only city in the 3rd with more than 30,000 people is Grand Island (Hall County), a retail center for the surrounding farmlands. Grand Island's major industries are farm implements and meatpacking. The Principal Financial Group also has offices here.

North of Grand Island are the only counties in the district with a significant Democratic registration lead (Sherman, Greeley and Howard). Another, Nance, has a slimmer Democratic registration edge. Their residents tend to vote almost as Democratic as their Polish and Irish ancestors did generations ago.

The smaller population centers of Kearney, North Platte and Scottsbluff are strung along the Platte River west of Grand Island. Much of Kearney's growth has come from its campus of the University of Nebraska.

West of Kearney along the Platte is Lexington, a town of 6,600. It struggled in the mid-1980s farm crisis, but was revitalized in 1990 with the opening of a huge IBP meatpacking plant.

North Platte, located in the valley where the North and South Platte rivers meet, was the home of William F. "Buffalo Bill" Cody; it tries to coax Omaha-to-Denver travelers into staying awhile by putting on Buffalo Bill shows and rodeos. The Union Pacific runs through North Platte and is its biggest employer. Corn and livestock are raised in the valley, with wheat fields to the west and huge cattle ranches to the north.

The Oregon and Mormon trails run through Scottsbluff, which has the only sizable Hispanic population in western Nebraska, a legacy of the migrant labor used to harvest sugar beets over a period of several decades. Great northern beans are a major crop in the farm areas surrounding Scottsbluff. The major employer is the Regional West Medical Center, a health-management organization.

1990 Population: 525,521. White 512,696 (98%), Black 953 (<1%), Other 11,872 (2%). Hispanic origin 14,998 (3%). 18 and over 380,190 (72%), 62 and over 108,148 (21%). Median age: 35.

won by 737 votes in the Watergate election of 1974. Barrett's 51 percent win over Democratic state Sen. Sandra K. Scofield in 1990 was unexpectedly narrow in a district in which two-thirds of the 1988 presidential vote went to George Bush.

His House bid received no help from the top of the ticket. Embattled Republican Gov. Kay A. Orr's mediocre performance in western Nebraska sealed her defeat at the hands of Democrat Ben Nelson. In addition, Democratic Sen. Jim Exon scored a big win over his GOP challenger, former 2nd District Rep. Hal Daub.

Barrett found that his greatest strength — his position as Speaker of Nebraska's Legislature — was also his greatest weakness in a year of anti-incumbent sentiment. While Barrett's position gave him a boost in stature over Scofield, it also let Scofield link him to some of the more unpopular Orr policies.

Scofield's popularity and her aggressive campaign made her a contender, but it was not enough to put her over the top. Barrett carried 41 of the district's 62 counties, generally dominating the eastern two-thirds (although he carried populous Hall County with barely 50 percent). His margins there enabled him to overcome the strength of his opponent in the west — where she won her home base, Dawes County, with 62 percent of the vote.

By 1992, Barrett had solidified support in the 3rd by tirelessly courting the district's voters and by maintaining his conservative stance in the Republican-leaning district. He returned to Nebraska most weekends for informal meetings with constituents.

And it did not hurt that he faced a political novice in Lowell Fisher, a Spencer rancher who entered the race at the eleventh hour. Barrett did not hesitate to remind voters of Fisher's inexperience, but often ignored him otherwise. Barrett won easily with 72 percent of the vote.

Committees

Agriculture (8th of 18 Republicans)
Department Operations; Environment, Credit & Rural Development; General Farm Commodities

Education & Labor (10th of 15 Republicans)
Human Resources; Labor-Management Relations; Select Education

House Administration (5th of 7 Republicans)
Libraries & Memorials (ranking); Administrative Oversight; Office Systems

Joint Library (Ranking)

Elections

1992 General		
Bill Barrett (R)	170,857	(72%)
Lowell Fisher (D)	67,457	(28%)
1990 General		
Bill Barrett (R)	98,607	(51%)
Sandra K. Scofield (D)	94,234	(49%)

District Vote for President

1992

D 57,467 (24%)
R 121,342 (50%)
I 65,473 (27%)

Campaign Finance

	Receipts	Receipts from PACs		Expend-itures
1992				
Barrett (R)	$485,326	$197,875	(41%)	$487,992
Fisher (D)	$92,706	$19,400	(21%)	$91,170
1990				
Barrett (R)	$644,559	$193,583	(30%)	$624,575
Scofield (D)	$457,931	$239,816	(52%)	$457,655

Key Votes

1993	
Require parental notification of minors' abortions	Y
Require unpaid family and medical leave	N
Approve national "motor voter" registration bill	N
Approve budget increasing taxes and reducing deficit	N
Approve economic stimulus plan	N
1992	
Approve balanced-budget constitutional amendment	Y
Close down space station program	N
Approve U.S. aid for former Soviet Union	Y
Allow shifting funds from defense to domestic programs	N
1991	
Extend unemployment benefits using deficit financing	N
Approve waiting period for handgun purchases	N
Authorize use of force in Persian Gulf	Y

Voting Studies

	Presidential Support		Party Unity		Conservative Coalition	
Year	S	O	S	O	S	O
1992	85	15	91	8	85	13
1991	84	14	92	6	97	0

Interest Group Ratings

Year	ADA	AFL-CIO	CCUS	ACU
1992	10	25	88	84
1991	0	8	90	89

Nevada

STATE DATA

Governor: Bob Miller (D)
First elected: 1990
Length of term: 4 years
Term expires: 1/95
Salary: $90,000
Term limit: 2 terms
Phone: (702) 687-5670
Born: March 30, 1945; Chicago, Ill.
Education: U. of Santa Clara, B.A. 1967; Loyola U. (Los Angeles), J.D. 1971
Military Service: Air Force Reserve, 1967-73
Occupation: Lawyer
Family: Wife, Sandy Searles; three children
Religion: Roman Catholic
Political Career: Clark County deputy district attorney, 1971-73; Las Vegas Township justice of the peace, 1975-78; Clark County district attorney, 1979-86; lieutenant governor, 1987-89; acting governor, 1989-90

Lt. Gov.: Sue Wagner (R)
First elected: 1990
Length of term: 4 years
Term expires: 1/95
Salary: $83,700 (Wagner did not accept last pay raise. She reports a salary of $83,700.)
Phone: (702) 687-3037

State election official: (702) 687-3176
Democratic Party Chairman: (702) 388-7788
Republican headquarters: (702) 258-9182

REDISTRICTING

Nevada retained its two House seats in reapportionment. Legislature passed the map June 11, 1991; governor signed it June 20.

STATE LEGISLATURE

Legislature. Meets January-June.

Senate: 21 members, 4-year terms.
1992 breakdown: 11R, 10D; 16 men, 5 women; 18 whites, 1 black, 2 Hispanics
Salary: $130 per day for 60 days plus salary for official meetings during interim
Phone: (702) 687-5742

Assembly: 42 members, 2-year terms.
1992 breakdown: 29D, 13R; 30 men, 12 women; 40 whites, 2 blacks
Salary: $130 per day for 60 days plus salary for official meetings during interim
Phone: (702) 687-5739

URBAN STATISTICS

City	Pop.
Las Vegas	258,204
Mayor Jan Laverty Jones, N-P	
Reno	133,850
Mayor Peter J. Sferrazza, N-P	
Paradise	124,682
County Commissioner Karen Hayes, D	
Sunrise Manor	95,362
County Commissioner Jay Bingham, D,	

U.S. CONGRESS

Senate: 2 D, 0 R
House: 1 D, 1 R

TERM LIMITS

For Congress: No
For state offices: No

ELECTIONS

1992 Presidential Vote

Bill Clinton	37.4%
George Bush	34.7%
Ross Perot	26.2%

1988 Presidential Vote

George Bush	59%
Michael S. Dukakis	38%

1984 Presidential Vote

Ronald Reagan	66%
Walter F. Mondale	32%

POPULATION

1990 population		1,201,833
1980 population		800,493
Percent change		+50%
Rank among states:		39
White		84%
Black		7%
Hispanic		10%
Asian or Pacific islander		3%
Urban		88%
Rural		12%
Born in state		22%
Foreign-born		9%
Under age 18	296,948	25%
Ages 18-64	777,254	65%
65 and older	127,631	11%
Median age		33.3

MISCELLANEOUS

Capital: Carson City
Number of counties: 16
Per capita income: $19,175 (1991)
Rank among states: 15
Total area: 110,561 sq. miles
Rank among states: 7

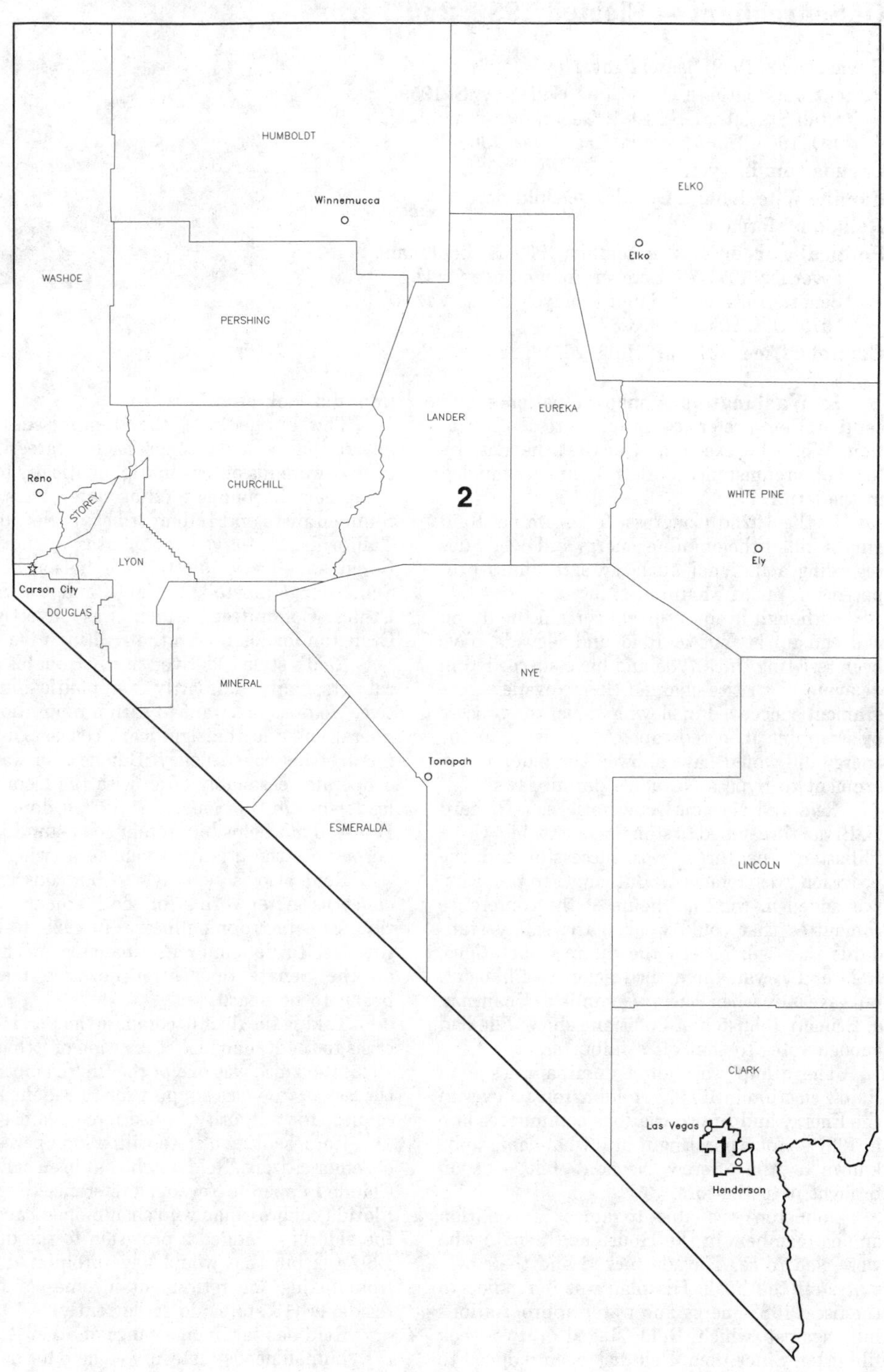
HUMBOLDT
ELKO
Winnemucca
Elko
WASHOE
PERSHING
LANDER
EUREKA
Reno
CHURCHILL
STOREY
2
WHITE PINE
Ely
LYON
Carson City
DOUGLAS
NYE
MINERAL
Tonopah
ESMERALDA
LINCOLN
CLARK
Las Vegas
1
Henderson

Harry Reid (D)

Of Searchlight — Elected 1986; 2nd Term

Born: Dec. 2, 1939, Searchlight, Nev.
Education: Southern Utah State College, A.S. 1959; Utah State U., B.A. 1961; George Washington U., J.D. 1964; U. of Nevada, Las Vegas, 1969-70.
Occupation: Lawyer.
Family: Wife, Landra Gould; five children.
Religion: Mormon.
Political Career: Nev. Assembly, 1969-71; lieutenant governor, 1971-75; Democratic nominee for U.S. Senate, 1974; candidate for mayor of Las Vegas, 1975; U.S. House, 1983-87.
Capitol Office: 324 Hart Bldg. 20510; 224-3542.

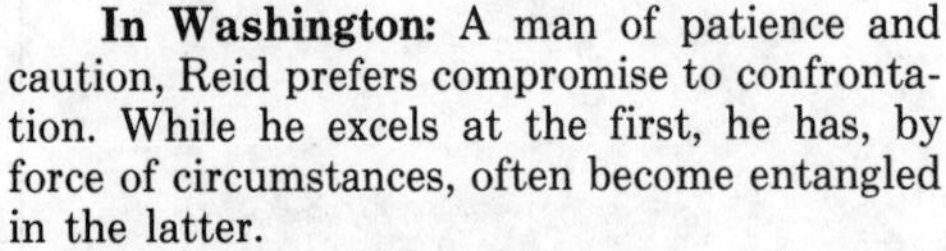

In Washington: A man of patience and caution, Reid prefers compromise to confrontation. While he excels at the first, he has, by force of circumstances, often become entangled in the latter.

In the 102nd Congress, for example, Reid almost killed the omnibus energy bill over rules regarding a national nuclear-waste dump proposed for Yucca Mountain, Nev.

Although it now appears certain the dump will end up at Yucca, Reid and Nevada have been resisting since 1985 and have succeeded in delaying it. Critics charged that Nevada's government succeeded in slowing down the process by wrapping it in red tape. A provision in the energy bill would have allowed the federal government to bypass Nevada's permit laws.

Reid and Nevada Democratic Sen. Richard H. Bryan threatened to stop the energy bill with a filibuster. The threat was successful and the provision was removed. But another provision was added in the final hours of the conference committee that could weaken the safety standards that will govern the dump's operations. Reid and Bryan threatened again to filibuster, but gave it up when Energy Committee Chairman J. Bennett Johnston of Louisiana showed he had enough votes to shut off a filibuster.

The dump was not a dominant issue in Reid's election in 1986, but Johnston's moves in the Energy and Appropriations committees late in 1987 — incorporating it into what came to be known as the "Screw Nevada" bill — soon brought it to the fore.

Johnston was able to amass a coalition among members in the House and Senate who were glad to see Nevada picked and their own states off the hook. His plan was embodied in the fiscal 1988 energy and water appropriations bill, against which Reid staged a two-week filibuster. Since then, Reid has been reduced to a rear-guard action as the site-selection process grinds on. One lingering hope is that scientists will find something wrong with Yucca Mountain and look elsewhere.

The intensity of the dump issue is an aberration in Reid's congressional career. More typical were his efforts in diplomatically forging an agreement among feuding water users, environmentalists and Indian tribes in Nevada and California. He served for months in the 102nd Congress — very quietly — as liaison between Sen. Alan Cranston, D-Calif., and the Senate Ethics Committee, which was investigating Cranston for his role in the Keating Five affair.

Reid's style is derived partly from his political personality and partly from political imperative. He does not want to earn a reputation as a liberal and rile the significant conservative element of his constituency. But he also wants to cooperate reasonably often with the Democratic leadership in the Senate, as he had done in the House. That helps him retain good standing and perpetuate the attention paid to a swing voter.

Reid also is sensitive to his constituents' concerns. After voting for the Medicare expansion for catastrophic illnesses in 1988, Reid was the first to denounce its financing mechanism on the Senate floor after negative reactions began to be heard.

Taking the floor to compare the Persian Gulf crisis to the Italian fascist invasion of Ethiopia in 1935, Reid also was one of the first Democrats in the Senate to voice support for President Bush's request for authority to use force against Iraq.

Representing a state with a high percentage of senior citizens, Reid — who has been called the Claude Pepper of Nevada, a reference to the late Florida congressman who championed causes for the elderly — added a provision to the doomed 1992 tax bill that would have prohibited states from taxing the retirement incomes of former residents (13 states do so currently).

Reid has taken on a range of other issues in the "human needs" category — help for battered women; a children's bill of rights that would aid prosecution of sexual abuse; and limiting the use of certain chemicals used on test animals to measure toxicity. Reid began pushing for additional funds to research women's diseases when three women who suffered from interstitial cystitis showed up at his office asking for help.

During the 101st Congress, Reid and Bryan overcame years of debate and opposition from the state's lone GOP member of Congress, Barbara F. Vucanovich, to carve out more than 700,000 acres of protected Nevada wilderness. The law gave the state its first wilderness area in 25 years.

But Reid opposed the changes to the 1872 Mining Act that came up in 1991, citing the importance of mining to Nevada: "A hole in the ground can look pretty good to some people," he said.

In the House, Reid staked out a conservative position on a few highly publicized issues, then voted with the majority of Democrats much of the rest of the time. Reflecting the cultural values of his state and his own Mormonism, he shared Ronald Reagan's opposition to the Equal Rights Amendment and legalized abortion. He has also supported the MX missile program. But on a range of other issues — the nuclear-weapons freeze, aid to the Nicaraguan contras, anti-satellite missile testing and funding for several social programs — Reid has sided with the more liberal Democratic leadership.

Reid took on a new, more visible role at the start of the 103rd Congress when he was named to the Joint Committee on the Organization of Congress, which was charged with making recommendations to reform congressional procedures.

Reid got a lot of publicity in March 1993 when he locked horns publicly with Ross Perot. While most of the rest of the panel seemed star-struck when the former presidential candidate testified, Reid took Perot to task for his tone and his lack of specifics. "You've now given us 45 minutes of sound bites and five minutes of material," he told the Texas billionaire. He went on to advise Perot to "start checking your facts a little more and stop listening to the applause as much."

Reid is also chairman of the Legislative Branch Appropriations Subcommittee. With one eye on Congress' organization and the other on Congress' budget, he tried and failed in early 1993 to abolish yet another of his panel assignments, Special Aging.

At Home: While Reid has fashioned a long career in Nevada politics, he is hardly a premier vote-getter. His early fundraising success scared off big-name challengers in 1992, yet he still struggled to win both the primary and the general election with bare majorities.

Wealthy broadcast executive Charles Woods proved an unexpectedly strong foe in the primary. An Alabama native, Woods had run early in the year in the Democratic presidential primaries, then shifted to the Senate race even though he admitted a limited knowledge of Nevada's problems.

Reid failed to make this an issue. Instead he largely ignored Wood's candidacy, allowing the challenger to saturate the airwaves with advertising that stressed the need to elect a businessman like himself to the Senate.

Woods appeared in his own ads, making no effort to hide the vivid scars from a World War II plane crash that disfigured his face and hands. Some in the Nevada political community believe he drew a sizable sympathy vote. He was also able to tap support from voters upset with Reid's anti-abortion stance as well as those who just wanted to protest the federal government in Washington.

Woods swept most of Nevada's rural "Cow counties." Reid rolled up his winning margin in the state's major population centers, Clark (Las Vegas) and Washoe (Reno) counties.

A similar voting pattern recurred in the general election. Rancher Demar Dahl, the Republican nominee, tried to harness the same anti-Washington sentiment that Woods did. But Reid retaliated this time. He had saved his money for the fall campaign and outspent Dahl by a margin of more than 5-to-1.

The 1992 campaign was not out of character for Reid. His self-made career has been part skyrocket and part slow, hard climb. He was born into modest circumstances in remote Searchlight. He worked his way through school, including a stint as a policeman in the U.S. Capitol while attending law school in Washington. Within five years he was a successful lawyer in booming Las Vegas, well on his way toward becoming a millionaire, and a freshly elected member of the state Legislature — all before he was 30.

In 1970, he ran successfully for lieutenant governor on a ticket with his former high school boxing coach, Mike O'Callaghan, who was elected governor. After one term in the No. 2 job, at age 34, Reid came within 625 votes of election to the U.S. Senate. It was 1974, and the Watergate scandal almost lifted Reid past the state's Republican former governor, Paul Laxalt.

But Reid's youth and even more boyish appearance did not wear well over the course of the campaign; the firm, articulate and mature Laxalt seemed to fit the part of a senator better.

Seeking a quick rebound a year later, Reid lost a bid to be mayor of Las Vegas. Some thought he was through in politics.

Then, in 1977, O'Callaghan appointed him chairman of the Nevada Gaming Commission. While Reid held that job, the FBI uncovered evidence of organized-crime influence in the Nevada gaming industry, and one reputed mobster accused Reid of being on the take.

Reid was cleared of charges that he intervened in behalf of organized-crime figures before the Gaming Commission. When he left the commission in 1981, Reid was praised for helping to eliminate criminal elements from the gaming industry. Politically, he was alive again.

Redistricting in 1981 created a House seat for Las Vegas separate from the rest of Nevada; it would have been held by the state's popular

Democratic congressman at-large, Jim Santini, but he decided to run in 1982 against Democratic Sen. Howard W. Cannon. Reid announced his House campaign early, seeking support from friends and from business leaders he dealt with as Gaming Commission chairman.

Reid faced an attractive, articulate Republican, former state Rep. Peggy Cavnar. But her House bid was strapped for funds because she had embarrassed the Las Vegas GOP establishment by defeating its handpicked candidate in the primary. Reid's superior financial resources and organization resulted in a 58 percent win.

In a 1984 rematch, both Reid and Cavnar were in a stronger position to compete. Reid had the advantages of incumbency, while Cavnar had gained the backing of the GOP establishment. The new advantages offset each other, and Reid won convincingly, with just a slightly lower percentage than he took in 1982.

In 1986, Reid squared off against Santini in one of the year's most closely watched Senate races. Retiring Sen. Laxalt had helped woo Santini to the GOP in 1985 and helped clear the way for him to have the GOP nomination.

But Santini's campaign had headaches from the start. Supporters of GOP Rep. Vucanovich only slowly warmed to Santini because his entry derailed her Senate ambitions. And his candidacy outraged many Nevada Democrats.

There was heated byplay between the candidates that obscured the fact that they held similar positions on many issues. Reid clearly had been more sympathetic to organized labor, but both he and Santini were opposed to abortion, the ERA and gun control. Both supported the death penalty and said they were generally supportive of Reagan's foreign policy.

Reagan helped raise money for Santini, and Laxalt campaigned extensively for him. But Reid minimized their impact by tapping the state's distrust of Washington with an "us vs. them" campaign.

When all the votes were counted, Reid had carried only two of the state's 16 counties. But one of them was Clark County, Reid's political base and home for a majority of Nevada voters. Reid amassed a 32,000-vote lead in the county, enough to offset Santini's 18,000-vote advantage in the rest of the state.

Committees

Appropriations (12th of 16 Democrats)
Legislative Branch (chairman); Energy & Water Development; Interior; Labor, Health & Human Services & Education; Military Construction

Environment & Public Works (5th of 10 Democrats)
Toxic Substances, Environmental Oversight, Research & Development (chairman); Clean Water, Fisheries & Wildlife; Water Resources, Transportation, Public Buildings & Economic Development

Indian Affairs (5th of 10 Democrats)

Special Aging (7th of 11 Democrats)

Joint Organization of Congress

Elections

1992 General		
Harry Reid (D)	253,150	(51%)
Demar Dahl (R)	199,413	(40%)
None of these candidates	13,154	(3%)
Joe S. Garcia Jr. (IA)	11,240	(2%)
Lois Avery (NL)	7,279	(1%)
H. Kent Cromwell (LIBERT)	7,222	(1%)
1992 Primary		
Harry Reid (D)	64,828	(53%)
Charles Woods (D)	48,364	(39%)
None of these candidates	4,429	(4%)
Norman Hollingsworth (D)	3,253	(3%)
God Almighty (D)	1,869	(2%)

Previous Winning Percentages: **1986** (50%) **1984 *** (56%)

1982 * (58%)

** House elections.*

Campaign Finance

	Receipts	Receipts from PACs	Expend-itures
1992			
Reid (D)	$2,142,152	$871,102 (41%)	$2,725,713
Dahl (R)	$481,653	0	$471,371

Key Votes

1993	
Require unpaid family and medical leave	Y
Approve national "motor voter" registration bill	Y
Approve budget increasing taxes and reducing deficit	Y
Support president's right to lift military gay ban	Y
1992	
Approve school-choice pilot program	N
Allow shifting funds from defense to domestic programs	Y
Oppose deeper cuts in spending for SDI	N
1991	
Approve waiting period for handgun purchases	Y
Raise senators' pay and ban honoraria	N
Authorize use of force in Persian Gulf	Y
Confirm Clarence Thomas to Supreme Court	N

Voting Studies

	Presidential Support		Party Unity		Conservative Coalition	
Year	**S**	**O**	**S**	**O**	**S**	**O**
1992	37	62	75	22	45	55
1991	51	49	75	25	60	38
1990	44	55	79	20	32	68
1989	63	37	71	28	61	39
1988	56	40	76	20	54	46
1987	40	58	88	11	44	56
House Service:						
1986	26	74	84	16	48	52
1985	44	55	87	13	40	60
1984	42	58	84	16	42	58
1983	29	67	86	13	35	65

Interest Group Ratings

Year	ADA	AFL-CIO	CCUS	ACU
1992	80	73	10	23
1991	65	92	10	33
1990	61	67	17	30
1989	65	100	38	21
1988	55	92	29	28
1987	80	90	22	19
House Service:				
1986	60	93	44	32
1985	55	82	32	29
1984	75	100	38	17
1983	70	82	25	35

Richard H. Bryan (D)

Of Las Vegas — Elected 1988; 1st Term

Born: July 16, 1937, Washington, D.C.
Education: U. of Nevada, B.A. 1959; U. of California, Hastings Law School, LL.B. 1963.
Military Service: Army, 1959-60.
Occupation: Lawyer.
Family: Wife, Bonnie Fairchild; three children.
Religion: Episcopalian.
Political Career: Nev. Assembly, 1969-73; Nev. Senate, 1973-79; Nev. attorney general, 1979-83; governor, 1983-89; Democratic nominee for Nev. attorney general, 1974.
Capitol Office: 364 Russell Bldg. 20510; 224-6244.

In Washington: Since arriving in the Senate in 1989, former Gov. Bryan has compiled a businesslike record as a middle-of-the-road Democrat who votes a moderate line and often performs thankless duties for his party and its leadership.

Bryan became chairman of the Ethics Committee in the 103rd Congress, the only member of the panel who also served on it in the previous Congress. He had initially turned down the chair offered him by Majority Leader George J. Mitchell of Maine, but in time he relented. The committee's immediate agenda included allegations of sexual harassment against Oregon Republican Bob Packwood and an investigation into Texas Republican Phil Gramm's dealings with the owner of a savings and loan association.

Bryan's most visible exertions have been expended on issues having to do with energy, even though he was still waiting in the 103rd Congress for a seat on the Energy and Natural Resources Committee. Undaunted by the fact that four members more junior have been given seats while he waited, Bryan has continued his work on automobile fuel efficiency, nuclear waste and other issues.

His quest to raise federal automobile fuel-efficiency standards dominated his first term. The issue remains in play, and Bryan is by no means assured of success; but the effort has helped establish him as a serious legislator.

Heavy lobbying by the auto industry and the administration of President George Bush stalled Bryan's attempt at the end of the 101st Congress. The Senate fell three votes short of the 60 votes needed to limit debate on a bill that would have required automakers to increase 1988 Corporate Average Fuel Economy (CAFE) levels by 20 percent by 1995 and by 40 percent by 2001. The existing standard is 27.5 miles per gallon.

The legislation got a boost after the August 1990 Iraqi invasion of Kuwait set off renewed debate over U.S. energy policy. Bryan said his bill would save 2.8 million barrels of oil per day and lead automakers to produce fleets with an average rating of 40 mpg.

Bryan redoubled his efforts at the start of the 102nd Congress, when prospects for moving new CAFE legislation improved amid efforts by Congress and the White House to come up with a new national energy policy.

But despite maneuvering for several months, including threats of filibusters and Senate floor amendments, the fuel efficiency mandates were left out of the energy bill that finally cleared Congress. It was part of a deal worked out by Energy and Natural Resources Chairman J. Bennett Johnston of Louisiana, and Bryan agreed to drop his proposal, noting the financial problems of the auto industry. "Pretty clearly the economic climate makes for some additional obstacles," he said. But the compromise on the energy bill afforded Bryan and five other like-minded senators a victory on another issue — opening Alaska's Arctic National Wildlife Refuge to oil and gas drilling. The Bush administration had argued vigorously for opening up the Alaska refuge, but Bryan countered that this option was "fatally flawed."

"It is worshiping at the shrine of production," Bryan said. "We cannot drill our way out of our dependence on oil."

Closer to home for Bryan is the disposing of high-level radioactive waste from the nation's commercial nuclear plants. Johnston and much of the rest of the government settled in the late 1980s on Yucca Mountain in Nevada as the site for the nation's nuclear repository. But Bryan arrived in the Senate with a mandate to defend his state aggressively against that plan.

The dump site had been a salient issue for Bryan in unseating one-term GOP Sen. Chic Hecht in 1988. Hecht's failure to block the siting decision, or even to oppose it in its formative stage, lent weight to criticism that he was out of his league in the Senate.

When Bryan got to Washington, while he did not get a seat on Johnston's Energy Committee, he did join with his fellow Nevada Democrat in the Senate, Harry Reid, to battle the proposed Yucca Mountain site whenever they could. The most obvious opportunity was presented by the omnibus energy legislation that moved in the 102nd Congress. Bryan began a filibuster against the legislation, but it was quickly shut down, prompting him to complain that "every time there is an opportunity to screw Nevada there is an appetite to do so."

Though the energy bill was enacted with the dump site proposal in it, Bryan was unbowed and promised to continue his opposition in the 103rd Congress.

Bryan also serves on the Commerce and Banking committees, somewhat unusual assignments for a Western senator, but ones that suit the businesslike Bryan well. On Commerce, Bryan has the chairmanship of the Consumer Subcommittee, where in the 101st Congress he oversaw the reauthorization of the Consumer Product Safety Commission, the first standalone reauthorization of the watchdog agency since 1981.

The bill, a long-sought victory for consumer activists, was aimed at jump-starting the commission, which for a decade had seen its budget and staff cut and its role as a consumer watchdog diminished by Reagan administration appointees. After some effort, Bryan succeeded in keeping the reauthorization measure free of product-specific provisions that had stopped earlier bills.

Bryan also sponsored legislation before the Commerce panel to strengthen the authority of the Federal Trade Commission in dealing with fraud committed in connection with telephone sales. Bryan said the legislation was needed to combat the "bad actors who are out to defraud and harass the consumer," adding that he supported legislation "carefully crafted to avoid unduly burdening the many legitimate telemarketers." The bill passed the Senate but died at the end of the 101st Congress.

Bryan so far has compiled a generally moderate record in the Senate. On a number of high-profile issues — abortion, civil rights, the nomination of former Sen. John Tower as secretary of Defense and the nomination of Clarence Thomas to the Supreme Court — he has voted in step with most Democrats. Bryan was one of 13 Democrats who had announced that they would vote to confirm Thomas before Anita F. Hill leveled her allegations of sexual harassment. After the hearings into the matter, Bryan changed his mind and opposed the nominee.

Bryan is also a fiscal conservative and has gone his own way on some defense and foreign policy issues.

He has backed a cut in the capital gains tax and opposed banning certain semiautomatic weapons and halting production of the B-2 stealth bomber, and he supported a constitutional amendment to ban flag desecration. He was also one of the 10 Democratic senators to support the January 1991 resolution authorizing the president to use force in the Persian Gulf.

A lawyer and former state attorney general, Bryan was chosen to serve on the 12-member ad hoc committee that took testimony in the impeachment trial of U.S. District Judge Alcee L. Hastings in 1989. And in the aftermath of the Keating Five scandal — five senators accused of unduly assisting a wealthy contributor to their campaigns — Senate leaders in April 1991 named Bryan to a new six-member task force to decide where to draw the line of propriety in such situations.

Bryan was also a freshman member of the Senate Democratic Policy Committee and took an interest in strategy sessions for the party's campaign committee in 1990. After the 1990 elections, however, Majority Leader Mitchell selected the more nationally known Charles S. Robb of Virginia over Bryan to head the Democratic Senatorial Campaign Committee for the 1992 election cycle.

At Home: Bryan first ran for the Senate in the middle of his second term as governor. He had first been elected governor in 1982, and in 1986 he was re-elected with 72 percent of the vote. As he rode to that easy re-election, it was widely assumed he would challenge Hecht in 1988.

Bryan won his reputation as a fiscal conservative when he cut hundreds of state government jobs in a budget-balancing drive in his first term. He was helped by growth in the state's revenues from gambling, which made higher burdens on the state's taxpayers largely unnecessary. In his second term, a health-cost-containment bill, successfully steered through the Legislature, was one of his major projects.

Bryan began his political career as a public defender and prosecutor in Clark County (Las Vegas), which includes slightly more than half the state's population. He had also served a decade in the state Assembly and Senate before winning his first statewide office, state attorney general, in 1978.

By the time Bryan sought the Senate, Hecht offered an irresistible target. He had been elected in 1982 in large part because the Democratic incumbent, Howard W. Cannon, was rendered vulnerable by a tough primary and by the trial of Teamsters union officials charged with trying to bribe him. Despite these circumstances, Hecht won with just 50 percent.

In the interim, Hecht had enjoyed some sunny moments, including passage of his amendment restoring the 65 mph speed limit. But he had also been battered by the nuclear waste controversy. When Hecht finally turned against siting the dump in Nevada, the momentum in Congress for choosing the state was unstoppable. For years before, Hecht had viewed the dump as a patriotic duty and as a potential source of federal money and jobs.

Hecht also had to compensate for an unimposing personal presence and a tendency to utter malapropisms (he once said the state should not become a "a nuclear suppository"). After Bryan announced his candidacy early in 1988, he emphasized these perceptions of Hecht. At one point he referred to the state's senior senator as being "unable to find the men's room."

These tactics played into the hands of Hecht's campaign managers, who used some of their $2 million treasury for a TV blitz that defined the early stage of the campaign. The ads portrayed a humble, hard-working Hecht, devoted to helping the little guy. Bryan, by contrast, came off seeming harsh and a touch arrogant.

But Bryan righted his campaign in the summer, moving belatedly to counter Hecht's efforts on the airwaves and shifting his aim to issues. He kept up the heat on the nuclear waste dump, an issue that had helped Reid move up from the House in 1986.

Bryan's other attacks on Hecht also helped contrast the two on domestic issues: He targeted Hecht's votes to eliminate cost-of-living adjustments to Social Security recipients and against restoration of certain Medicare benefits. Bryan found support from labor groups; he backed the bill Congress passed in 1988 to give workers 60 days' notice of plant closings. Hecht opposed it. Bryan's support for contra aid, however, placed him apart from the mainstream of Democrats nationally.

With all his ammunition, and despite a resurgent lead in the summer polls, Bryan could not knock Hecht flat. The plucky incumbent had to deal with a state GOP rife with internal disputes involving new leaders associated with the presidential campaign of Pat Robertson. He was distracted when the Clark County GOP chairman impugned Bryan's marital fidelity on a radio program. Still, Hecht pressed his case, raking Bryan for leaving the governorship in midterm and for being too close to the power elements of the national Democratic Party.

The race was close to the end. At one point on election night, at least one TV network projected Hecht the winner. Bryan ran nearly 43,000 votes ahead of his party's presidential ticket but still got just over 50 percent.

Committees

Select Ethics (Chairman)

Banking, Housing & Urban Affairs (7th of 11 Democrats)
Economic Stabilization & Rural Development; Housing & Urban Affairs; Securities

Commerce, Science & Transportation (8th of 11 Democrats)
Consumer (chairman); Aviation; Foreign Commerce & Tourism; Science

Select Intelligence (5th of 9 Democrats)

Elections

1988 General		
Richard H. Bryan (D)	175,548	(50%)
Chic Hecht (R)	161,336	(46%)
1988 Primary		
Richard H. Bryan (D)	62,278	(79%)
None of these candidates	7,035	(9%)
Pat M. Fitzpatrick (D)	4,721	(6%)
Manny Beals (D)	2,656	(3%)
Larry Kepler (D)	1,655	(2%)

Campaign Finance

1988	Receipts	Receipts from PACs		Expend- itures
Bryan (D)	$2,986,727	$802,792	(27%)	$2,957,789
Hecht (R)	$2,907,927	$977,024	(34%)	$3,007,864

Key Votes

1993	
Require unpaid family and medical leave	Y
Approve national "motor voter" registration bill	Y
Approve budget increasing taxes and reducing deficit	Y
Support president's right to lift military gay ban	Y
1992	
Approve school-choice pilot program	N
Allow shifting funds from defense to domestic programs	Y
Oppose deeper cuts in spending for SDI	N
1991	
Approve waiting period for handgun purchases	Y
Raise senators' pay and ban honoraria	N
Authorize use of force in Persian Gulf	Y
Confirm Clarence Thomas to Supreme Court	N

Voting Studies

	Presidential Support		Party Unity		Conservative Coalition	
Year	S	O	S	O	S	O
1992	32	68	78	22	47	50
1991	47	53	78	22	73	28
1990	44	55	81	19	51	49
1989	59	40	75	24	58	39

Interest Group Ratings

Year	ADA	AFL-CIO	CCUS	ACU
1992	80	67	10	19
1991	70	83	20	38
1990	56	78	25	30
1989	55	100	25	30

1 James Bilbray (D)

Of Las Vegas — Elected 1986; 4th Term

Born: May 19, 1938, Las Vegas, Nev.

Education: American U., B.A. 1962; Washington College of Law, J.D. 1964.

Military Service: National Guard, 1955-63.

Occupation: Lawyer.

Family: Wife, Michaelene Mercer; three children.

Religion: Roman Catholic.

Political Career: Clark County deputy district attorney, 1964-68; Democratic nominee for U.S. House, 1972; Nev. Senate, 1981-87.

Capitol Office: 2431 Rayburn Bldg. 20515; 225-5965.

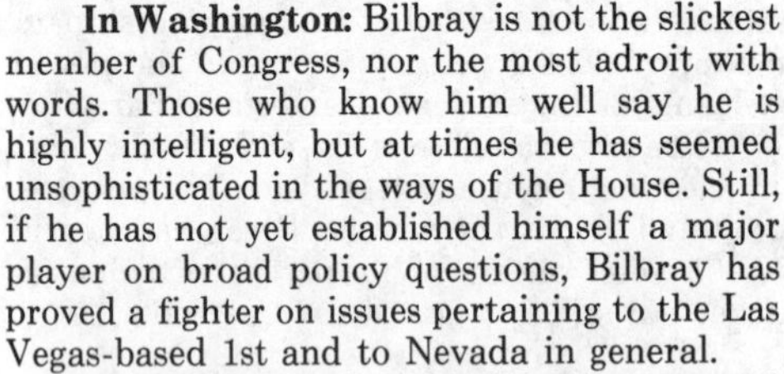

In Washington: Bilbray is not the slickest member of Congress, nor the most adroit with words. Those who know him well say he is highly intelligent, but at times he has seemed unsophisticated in the ways of the House. Still, if he has not yet established himself a major player on broad policy questions, Bilbray has proved a fighter on issues pertaining to the Las Vegas-based 1st and to Nevada in general.

In 1993 he introduced legislation to extend a duty suspension on behalf of the Nishika Corp., an employer of 135 people in Henderson, Nev., which produces 3-D cameras. A few years before Bilbray defended the honor of his hometown's pride and joy, the University of Nevada at Las Vegas basketball team. Although UNLV won the National Collegiate Athletic Association championship in 1990, its program faced NCAA penalties over its recruiting and academic practices. In the 101st Congress, Bilbray proposed a bill to guarantee due process to schools that face NCAA sanctions. But the legislation did not get past its public hearing.

For as long as he has been in Congress, Bilbray has been plagued by the specter of radioactive remnants of nuclear facilities in his district.

In 1990, Congress enacted legislation Bilbray had supported authorizing compensation of $50,000 per person to cancer victims in Nevada, Utah and Arizona who had been exposed to radiation from open-air nuclear weapons testing during the 1950s. Bilbray described these "downwinders" as "no different from the veterans of World War II, Korea and Vietnam — they are veterans of the Cold War."

In 1987, Bilbray's first year in the House, Congress enacted legislation which Nevadans refer to as the "Screw Nevada" bill, designating Yucca Mountain in southern Nevada as the sole site to be considered for the nation's high-level nuclear waste dump. The provisions were part of that year's budget-reconciliation bill, which Bilbray and other members of the delegation voted against in vain.

In 1992, Bilbray irritated the rest of the Nevada delegation and drew criticism from some hometown papers when he supported House passage of the big national energy policy bill, even though it contained language that pre-empted the state's ability to regulate federal activities at the Yucca Mountain site. Bilbray did not apologize. "I had to make a policy decision of my own," he told the Las Vegas Review Journal. "My decision was that we need an energy policy."

By fall, however, Bilbray had rearranged his priorities. In a House floor tirade, he lambasted Senate Energy Committee Chairman J. Bennett Johnston, a Louisiana Democrat, for skewering Nevada twice — in the energy legislation and in a bill focusing on the Waste Isolation Pilot Plant (WIPP) in New Mexico. Nevadans were angry that the latter bill, which paved the way for opening a storage facility for defense-related nuclear waste, contained provisions that could indirectly allow the Energy Department to use weaker safety standards at the Yucca Mountain site than those required at the WIPP facility. Agreeing with the three other Nevadans in Congress, Bilbray voted against the final energy policy conference report.

The fall of 1992 was an active season for Bilbray. He also secured $17.5 million from the Highway Trust Fund for improving two Las Vegas-based interchanges on Interstate 15.

Early in the 103rd Congress, Bilbray was supportive of the new administration's efforts to stimulate the economy, reduce the deficit and liberalize some social policies. He also continued to express interest in international affairs and has proposed a couple of bills to protect Nevada resources.

However, Bilbray's earlier days of politicking brought fewer rewards.

In his first House term, bucking for a seat on the Science Committee, he took the unusual step of standing outside the room where the Democratic Steering and Policy Committee was

Nevada 1

South — Las Vegas

For the second time this century, Las Vegas is undergoing a transformation. Once a dusty railroad stop on the Union Pacific Line, the town evolved after World War II into Sin City, a garish neon pleasure palace where gambling flourished and visiting businessmen could hop a private plane to a rural bordello.

The gaming industry is still king — it's the building block of the local economy — but albino tigers, flaming man-made volcanoes and Wayne Newton are no longer the only stories in Vegas.

Economic diversification is the city's new buzzword, and it's coming none too soon. Some of the older casinos, such as The Dunes, have gone under. Meanwhile, high-tech companies have joined such well-known gambling establishments as Bally's, Caesar's Palace, the Golden Nugget and the Mirage on the local business roster.

Attracted by low taxes and a pro-business environment, nearly 100 companies relocated to the Las Vegas area during the past decade. The jobs they offered were a magnet for newcomers: 275,000 people moved to the Las Vegas valley in the 1980s. Local authorities claim that the population influx is continuing at the rate of about 3,500 per month.

While Chamber of Commerce officials drool, many longtime residents are clamoring for a development slowdown. The valley is experiencing air quality problems, traffic congestion worsens daily, and schools are bursting at the seams. Water resources are severely strained.

Mormon conservatism flavors Clark County politics, but within the city limits of Las Vegas, Democrats have the edge. The 1st encompasses the downtown areas and the city of Henderson, to the southeast, which despite recent development maintains its blue-collar image.

Unionized service workers, many of whom work in the glittery resort hotels along "The Strip" just south of Las Vegas, include a number of blacks who live on the city's west side. Democrats also can tap the city of North Las Vegas (which is 37 percent black) for votes. Under the 1980s map, North Las Vegas was divided between the 1st and 2nd districts. Now, virtually all of it is in the 1st.

During World War II, Henderson produced magnesium; it still supports itself with chemical manufacturing. Green Valley, home to professionals, young families and California transplants, is a GOP oasis. Workers at Nellis Air Force Base (just northeast of Las Vegas), and at the Energy Department's Nevada Test Site also tend to favor GOP candidates.

Rural portions of Clark County were pared from the 1st in 1991 redistricting, creating a constituency that is almost exclusively urban.

Overall, Clark County casts more than half the vote in Nevada, so winning it has become crucial to statewide victory. In 1992, Bill Clinton carried only two of Nevada's 17 counties; Democratic Sen. Harry Reid carried just six. But each won statewide with the help of a substantial lead in Clark County.

1990 Population: 600,957. White 477,946 (80%), Black 62,809 (10%), Other 60,202 (10%). Hispanic origin 73,184 (12%). 18 and over 456,137 (76%), 62 and over 82,602 (14%). Median age: 34.

meeting, and lobbying the members as they arrived. Bilbray told them that shaking hands door-to-door worked for him in his House campaign and that he hoped it would get him his desired committee assignment. It did not.

Bilbray then tried twice during the 100th Congress to get on the Armed Services Committee and failed. He finally got on during the 101st Congress, but only after two more junior members were chosen. Now he also sits on the Select Intelligence and Small Business committees.

At Home: When Democrat Harry Reid vacated this House seat to run for the Senate in 1986, Bilbray was a logical replacement. Son of the longtime Clark County assessor, he had close personal ties to the Las Vegas hotel and casino establishments. He had chaired the Taxation Committee in the state Senate. And he was running in a district with a 3-to-2 Democratic advantage. But by Election Day, Bilbray's campaign had run into so many problems that his victory over Republican state Sen. Bob Ryan turned out to be a surprise.

For example, at a meeting of the state AFL-CIO in September, Bilbray warned of the dangers of a sympathy vote for Ryan because the Republican was blind. "Voters feel sorry for a man who knocks on their door with a white cane," he said. Bilbray personally apologized to Ryan the next day.

Meanwhile, Bilbray had to fend off questions about his personal ethics. Both in the primary and general election, Bilbray was questioned as to why he acted as legal counsel to companies that stood to benefit from legislation he promoted in the state Senate.

Bilbray survived with some hardball of his own. On election eve, he sent out an anti-Ryan mailer that pictured Sirhan Sirhan and Charles Manson on the cover and suggested that Ryan supported measures that would let killers such as Sirhan and Manson out of jail. Ryan protested, but the mailer, coupled with Bilbray's superior grass-roots organization and fundraising, brought him a 10 percentage-point victory. In 1988 and 1990, Bilbray surpassed 60 percent.

In June of 1992, a redistricting "handshake" between Bilbray and 2nd District Republican Barbara F. Vucanovich greased passage of the new Nevada map. With little debate, the Legislature passed and Democratic Gov. Bob Miller signed a redistricting bill.

Nevada's population had increased by 50 percent over the decade, from 800,493 in 1980 to 1,201,833 in 1990. But the state, which just gained its second House seat in the 1980 reapportionment, fell short of adding a third in 1990.

The booming growth was distributed evenly between the Las Vegas-based 1st and the more rural sprawling 2nd, which takes in the remainder of the state.

Bilbray got more of the Democratic-leaning city as well as nearly all of North Las Vegas, which has a significant black population. At the same time, the 1st donated some surrounding Republican turf in the Las Vegas suburbs (Clark County) to Vucanovich's 2nd.

In the fall election, Bilbray garnered only 58 percent. But with a third-party candidate taking 4 percent, he still defeated GOP state Rep. J. Coy Pettyjohn by 20 percentage points. Pettyjohn was a retired U.S. Air Force brigadier general, but, like Bilbray's earlier GOP challengers, had little money with which to promote himself.

Bilbray's recent successes have softened the memories of a 1972 House effort. Then, as a youthful and more liberal Democrat, he upset 10-term House veteran Walter S. Baring in the Democratic primary. But Baring and many of his supporters remained cool to Bilbray, and a virtually unknown Republican defeated him in the general election.

Committees

Armed Services (16th of 34 Democrats)
Military Forces & Personnel; Military Installations & Facilities; Research & Technology

Select Intelligence (8th of 12 Democrats)
Legislation; Program & Budget Authorization

Small Business (8th of 27 Democrats)
Procurement, Taxation & Tourism (chairman); Regulation, Business Opportunities & Technology

Elections

1992 General		
James Bilbray (D)	128,278	(58%)
J. Coy Pettyjohn (R)	84,217	(38%)
Scott A. Kjar (LIBERT)	8,993	(4%)
1990 General		
James Bilbray (D)	84,650	(61%)
Bob Dickinson (R)	47,377	(34%)
William "Bill" Moore (LIBERT)	5,825	(4%)

Previous Winning Percentages: 1988 (64%) 1986 (54%)

District Vote for President

1992
D 98,801 (43%)
R 70,586 (31%)
I 56,058 (25%)

Campaign Finance

	Receipts	Receipts from PACs		Expend-itures
1992				
Bilbray (D)	$698,431	$228,534	(33%)	$667,018
Pettyjohn (R)	$114,362	$9,613	(8%)	$113,776
1990				
Bilbray (D)	$686,010	$218,056	(32%)	$705,037
Dickinson (R)	$149,863	$9,775	(7%)	$149,778

Key Votes

1993	
Require parental notification of minors' abortions	N
Require unpaid family and medical leave	Y
Approve national "motor voter" registration bill	Y
Approve budget increasing taxes and reducing deficit	Y
Approve economic stimulus plan	Y
1992	
Approve balanced-budget constitutional amendment	Y
Close down space station program	Y
Approve U.S. aid for former Soviet Union	Y
Allow shifting funds from defense to domestic programs	N
1991	
Extend unemployment benefits using deficit financing	Y
Approve waiting period for handgun purchases	N
Authorize use of force in Persian Gulf	Y

Voting Studies

	Presidential Support		Party Unity		Conservative Coalition	
Year	S	O	S	O	S	O
1992	31	68	81	19	67	33
1991	41	57	81	16	78	19
1990	33	67	83	15	63	37
1989	45	53	83	17	78	22
1988	30	67	79	16	68	29
1987	34	66	79	17	67	30

Interest Group Ratings

Year	ADA	AFL-CIO	CCUS	ACU
1992	70	75	63	33
1991	35	100	20	40
1990	50	75	29	25
1989	55	75	50	25
1988	60	93	43	44
1987	68	94	33	26

2 Barbara F. Vucanovich (R)

Of Reno — Elected 1982; 6th Term

Born: June 22, 1921, Camp Dix, N.J.
Education: Manhattanville College, 1938-39.
Occupation: Congressional aide; travel agency owner.
Family: Husband, George F. Vucanovich; five children.
Religion: Roman Catholic.
Political Career: No previous office.
Capitol Office: 2202 Rayburn Bldg. 20515; 225-6155.

In Washington: In her 10 years in Washington, Vucanovich has seen the political environment change in ways that any conservative Westerner would find disquieting. When she arrived, Ronald Reagan was in the White House and Republicans Paul Laxalt and Chic Hecht held Nevada's seats in the Senate. But both Reagan and his close friend Laxalt (who was also Vucanovich's mentor) have long since left office. The White House is occupied by a Democrat, and Vucanovich is the only Republican left in Nevada's congressional delegation.

Things have not been particularly comforting back home lately, either. Vucanovich's share of the vote in her district has been below 60 percent since 1986, and in 1992 a field of four opponents held her below 50 percent.

Still, Vucanovich has persevered in a body dominated by members far more liberal than she. And as the most-senior Republican woman from anywhere west of New Jersey, she enjoys two committee assignments important to Nevada. One is Appropriations, which she joined in the 102nd Congress and where she is the top Republican on the Military Construction Subcommittee. Although Appropriations is usually an exclusive committee, Vucanovich won permission to remain on Natural Resources (formerly Interior), where she is now the No. 3 Republican overall and the ranking member on the Energy and Mineral Resources Subcommittee.

There, she battles governmental efforts to dictate policy in Nevada, 85 percent of which is federally owned land. The 100th Congress, for example, enacted a law to put all of the nation's high-level nuclear waste in Yucca Mountain. And the omnibus energy bill signed by President George Bush during the 102nd Congress included new language to help the government open the proposed dump.

Vucanovich was a bit slow to join opponents of the waste site, but once she did, she did so ardently. She contributed to a bill that would have established a special commission to study placement of a waste site. But the issue was largely decided in the Senate, where Louisiana Democrat J. Bennett Johnston, chairman of the Senate Energy and Natural Resources Committee, was able to speed up the site-selection process. With no Nevadans on the House-Senate conference committee considering the bill, Johnston struck a deal to name Nevada as the dump site. Vucanovich condemned this but could not stop it. The bill became law in 1987.

In the 102nd Congress, the Nevada delegation fought to block Johnston's energy bill. This time, some environmentalists sided with the Nevadans, fearing that the bill's provision for federal pre-emption of state permit requirements would weaken safety standards. The Interior Committee stripped the pre-emption provision from the bill. Johnston then finessed the showdown in the House-Senate conference (and a threatened filibuster by Nevada's senators, Richard H. Bryan and Harry Reid) by removing his original provision.

This done, Johnston proceeded to strike a deal with House negotiators on a different provision regarding the dump. It again drew complaints about weakening safety standards, but this time Vucanovich had to take her case not to her own committee but to House conferees. They voted to accept the Senate provision, and on the Senate floor, Johnston had the votes to quell Bryan and Reid's filibuster.

In the mid-1980s, Vucanovich became embroiled in the controversy over designating wilderness lands off-limits to development. Reid (who was then the state's other House member) and Bryan (who was then governor) wanted wilderness areas totaling 592,000 acres; Vucanovich was willing to go for 137,000 acres.

As long as she had two GOP senators as a backstop, Vucanovich held off House Interior's wilderness bills. But when both Reid and Bryan had reached the Senate, the stalemate ended. Bush signed a Nevada wilderness bill into law in 1989 over Vucanovich's objections.

Vucanovich has also been a last-bastion defender of the 1892 mining law, arguing that proposed retooling would devastate the Western mining industry and cost jobs. But an overhaul bill reached the House floor in 1992, and the Clinton administration backed mining

Nevada 2

Reno, the Cow Counties and part of Clark County

Campaigning in the 2nd is an awesome undertaking. It contains 99.8 percent of the land area (nearly 110,000 square miles) of the nation's seventh-largest state.

While redistricting enlarged the 2nd so it now encompasses all but the heart of Las Vegas and its immediate environs, the district's population nexus is in the north, in the Reno (Washoe County) area. Reno is older, more conservative and less reliant on the gaming industry than Las Vegas. Proximity to California and the Pacific Northwest make warehousing an important part of the local economy.

Formerly a GOP stronghold, Reno's politics have been moderated by an influx of environmentally conscious newcomers (its population grew 33 percent in the 1980s). Catholics make up a significant portion of the electorate, but they tend not to be as politically active as their Mormon brethren in Clark County.

The state capital of Carson City is in the 2nd, as is Lake Tahoe, a year-round resort area astride the California-Nevada line that attracts visitors to its golf courses, casinos and chalets.

The rural Cow Counties cover most of the state but hold few of its residents: Several of these enormous counties are home to fewer than 10,000 people. Agriculture and ranching are the main pursuits, and huge expanses of uninhabited mountain and desert land are used as military test ranges.

Yucca Mountain looms ominously over Nye County as the site Congress has proposed for a federal nuclear waste dump. Nevadans share a bipartisan resentment of what they call the "Screw Nevada" dump bill, which Congress passed in 1987.

Resentment of the federal government — which owns nearly 90 percent of the district's land — is most adamant in the conservative-voting "Cows." Federal water and grazing regulations generate animosity, as do airspace restrictions that local pilots face near the bombing ranges.

Retired military personnel are numerous in Hawthorne (Mineral County), site of the Hawthorne Army Ammunition Plant. State politicians rarely miss the small town's annual armed forces parade.

A modern-day mining boom has spurred growth in a number of rural communities to the north, particularly in Elko (Elko County), Lovelock (Pershing County) and Battle Mountain (Lander County).

The location of Ely (White Pine County) on the eastern end of U.S. 50 makes it a regional center for commerce and business. The highway, snaking across central Nevada past Carson City, became known as "the loneliest road in America" after a Life magazine article claimed travelers needed survival skills to cross this stretch of empty and desolate desert.

In 1992, all but two of the counties in the 2nd voted for George Bush. Storey County, which includes the famous 19th century mining center of Virginia City, backed Ross Perot. White Pine County, where a unionized work force once mined copper and other minerals from huge pits, voted for Bill Clinton.

1990 Population: 600,876. White 534,749 (89%), Black 15,962 (3%), Other 50,165 (8%). Hispanic origin 51,235 (9%). 18 and over 448,748 (75%), 62 and over 76,899 (13%). Median age: 33.

reform in the 103rd Congress.

Beyond her committee work, Vucanovich is a member of the GOP whip organization and a consistent conservative, even on social issues such as abortion and family and medical leave, where she finds herself voting against most of the other women in Congress. But she has been a champion of other women's causes. She testified before the Energy and Commerce Committee and the Select Committee on Aging in the 101st Congress on mammogram screening. She introduced legislation to provide annual coverage under the Social Security Act of mammography screening for women 65 or older.

At Home: Vucanovich fell for the first time into the ranks of "embattled incumbents" in 1992. Reno Mayor Pete Sferrazza ran a feisty campaign that held Vucanovich without a majority for the first time ever. It was a rematch for the two. Vucanovich had beaten Sferrazza by 24,000 votes in 1986. But this time the challenger had more money and a better campaign environment, as he pounded away at the theme that he was "the candidate of change."

Sferrazza criticized Vucanovich for opposing abortion rights, supporting a congressional pay raise and accepting out-of-state political action committee money. Vucanovich fired back, charging Sferrazza with backing a pay increase of his own as a member of the Reno city government and chiding him for spending much of his career at the public trough.

The race was at times ugly — Sferrazza at one point called Vucanovich "an old bag." And at the end, it was close. Sferrazza ran virtually even with the incumbent in the Reno area and the suburbs of Las Vegas. Vucanovich built up nearly all of her 12,000-vote victory margin in the conservative "Cow Counties."

Their first contest in 1986 was also spirited. Sferrazza sought to make an issue of the proposed placement of a nuclear-waste dump in the vast desert reaches of the district, saying he had been against it while Vucanovich was trying to make up her mind.

Yet, before 1992 her most serious challenge had come from Sparks Mayor James Spoo in 1988. Presidential-year voting trends helped ensure Vucanovich's victory. George Bush won 61 percent in the 2nd, and Vucanovich was close behind with 57 percent.

In 1990, state Assemblywoman Jane Wisdom moved to the district to challenge Vucanovich. But Wisdom's abortion rights, pro-labor message did not suit the conservative 2nd. Vucanovich took 59 percent, her second-highest re-election tally.

Vucanovich's first election to the House rewarded her long involvement in Republican politics. She had worked in presidential campaigns since the Eisenhower era and had been president of several GOP women's groups. In 1962 she signed on with Laxalt, whom she served for two decades as grass-roots organizer and constituent-service specialist. Laxalt returned the favor in 1982 by actively helping her win the newly created 2nd District.

His backing all but guaranteed her the GOP nomination against five others.

In the 1982 general-election campaign, Democrat Mary Gojack urged voters not to elect a Laxalt clone. A former state senator and unsuccessful challenger to Laxalt in 1980, Gojack was a stronger personal campaigner than Vucanovich. But she suffered in much of the district from her reputation as a feminist liberal closer to the politics of the East than to those of Nevada. Vucanovich stressed her ties to Laxalt less, played up her own devout conservatism more and won with 56 percent.

Committees

Appropriations (14th of 23 Republicans)
Military Construction (ranking); Agriculture, Rural Development, FDA & Related Agencies

Natural Resources (3rd of 15 Republicans)
Energy & Mineral Resources (ranking); Insular & International Affairs; Oversight & Investigations

Elections

1992 General		
Barbara F. Vucanovich (R)	129,575	(48%)
Pete Sferrazza (D)	117,199	(43%)
Daniel M. Hansen (IA)	13,285	(5%)
Dan Becan (LIBERT)	7,552	(3%)
Don Golden (POP)	2,850	(1%)
1992 Primary		
Barbara F. Vucanovich (R)	45,792	(69%)
Don Hensley (R)	9,843	(15%)
Dick Baker (R)	5,697	(9%)
Terry L. Flower (R)	4,583	(7%)
1990 General		
Barbara F. Vucanovich (R)	103,508	(59%)
Jane Wisdom (D)	59,581	(34%)
Dan Becan (LIBERT)	12,120	(7%)

Previous Winning Percentages: **1988** (57%) **1986** (58%)
1984 (71%) **1982** (56%)

District Vote for President

1992
D 90,347 (33%)
R 105,242 (39%)
I 76,522 (9%)

Campaign Finance

	Receipts	Receipts from PACs		Expend-itures
1992				
Vucanovich (R)	$686,022	$256,119	(37%)	$688,379
Sferrazza (D)	$207,252	$19,100	(9%)	$202,888
Hansen (IA)	$17,350	0		$17,015
1990				
Vucanovich (R)	$445,465	$166,275	(37%)	$441,075
Wisdom (D)	$41,771	$22,500	(54%)	$41,287

Key Votes

1993	
Require parental notification of minors' abortions	Y
Require unpaid family and medical leave	N
Approve national "motor voter" registration bill	N
Approve budget increasing taxes and reducing deficit	N
Approve economic stimulus plan	N
1992	
Approve balanced-budget constitutional amendment	Y
Close down space station program	N
Approve U.S. aid for former Soviet Union	Y
Allow shifting funds from defense to domestic programs	N
1991	
Extend unemployment benefits using deficit financing	N
Approve waiting period for handgun purchases	N
Authorize use of force in Persian Gulf	Y

Voting Studies

	Presidential Support		Party Unity		Conservative Coalition	
Year	S	O	S	O	S	O
1992	84	12	84	13	81	10
1991	84	14	87	9	95	5
1990	72	23	84	8	89	2
1989	79	19	91	5	98	2
1988	68	32	92	4	92	3
1987	63	31	89	7	91	9
1986	69	24	84	12	90	10
1985	70	29	87	9	91	7
1984	64	31	83	11	90	5
1983	78	16	87	6	90	7

Interest Group Ratings

Year	ADA	AFL-CIO	CCUS	ACU
1992	5	17	75	96
1991	0	9	78	100
1990	6	8	79	88
1989	5	8	100	89
1988	10	14	77	92
1987	20	19	86	74
1986	0	7	89	86
1985	10	13	95	86
1984	10	8	75	96
1983	0	0	90	96

New Hampshire

STATE DATA

Governor:
Stephen Merrill (R)
First elected: 1992
Length of term: 2 years
Term expires: 1/95
Salary: $79,541 (voluntary 10% pay cut)
Term limit: No
Phone: (603) 271-2121
Born: June 21, 1946; Norwich, Conn.
Education: U. of New Hampshire, B.A. 1969; Georgetown U., J.D. 1972
Military Service: Air Force, years not reported
Occupation: Lawyer; federal official; gubernatorial aide
Family: Wife, Heather MacLean
Religion: Episcopalian
Political Career: Chief of staff to Gov. John H. Sununu, 1983-85; N.H. attorney general, 1985-89

No lieutenant governor

State election official: (603) 271-3242
Democratic headquarters: (603) 225-6899
Republican headquarters: (603) 225-9341

REDISTRICTING

New Hampshire retained its two House seats in reapportionment. The legislature passed the map March 24, 1992; the governor signed it March 27. Justice Department approved the map June 12.

STATE LEGISLATURE

General Court. Meets January-July.

Senate: 24 members, 2-year terms.
1992 breakdown: 13R, 11D; 15 men, 9 women; 24 whites
Salary: $100/year + mileage
Phone: (603) 271-2111

House of Representatives: 400 members, 2-year terms
1992 breakdown: 258R, 136D, 1 I, 4 others; 268 men, 132 women; 398 whites, 2 blacks
Salary: $100/year + mileage
Phone: (603) 271-3661

URBAN STATISTICS

City	Pop.
Manchester	98,332
Mayor Raymond J. Wieczorek, R	
Nashua	79,662
Mayor Rob Wagner, D	
Concord	36,006
Mayor William Veroneau, N-P	
Derry	29,603
Mayor May Casten, R	
Rochester	26,630
Mayor Roland Roberge, D	

U.S. CONGRESS

Senate: 0 D, 2 R
House: 1 D, 1 R

TERM LIMITS

For Congress: No
For state offices: No

ELECTIONS

1992 Presidential Vote

Bill Clinton	38.9%
George Bush	37.6%
Ross Perot	22.6%

1988 Presidential Vote

George Bush	62%
Michael S. Dukakis	36%

1984 Presidential Vote

Ronald Reagan	69%
Walter F. Mondale	31%

POPULATION

1990 population		1,109,252
1980 population		920,610
Percent change		+20%
Rank among states:		40
White		98%
Black		1%
Hispanic		1%
Asian or Pacific islander		1%
Urban		51%
Rural		49%
Born in state		44%
Foreign-born		4%
Under age 18	278,755	25%
Ages 18-64	705,468	64%
65 and older	125,029	11%
Median age		32.8

MISCELLANEOUS

Capital: Concord
Number of counties: 10
Per capita income: $20,951 (1991)
Rank among states: 9
Total area: 9,279 sq. miles
Rank among states: 44

New Hampshire - Congressional Districts

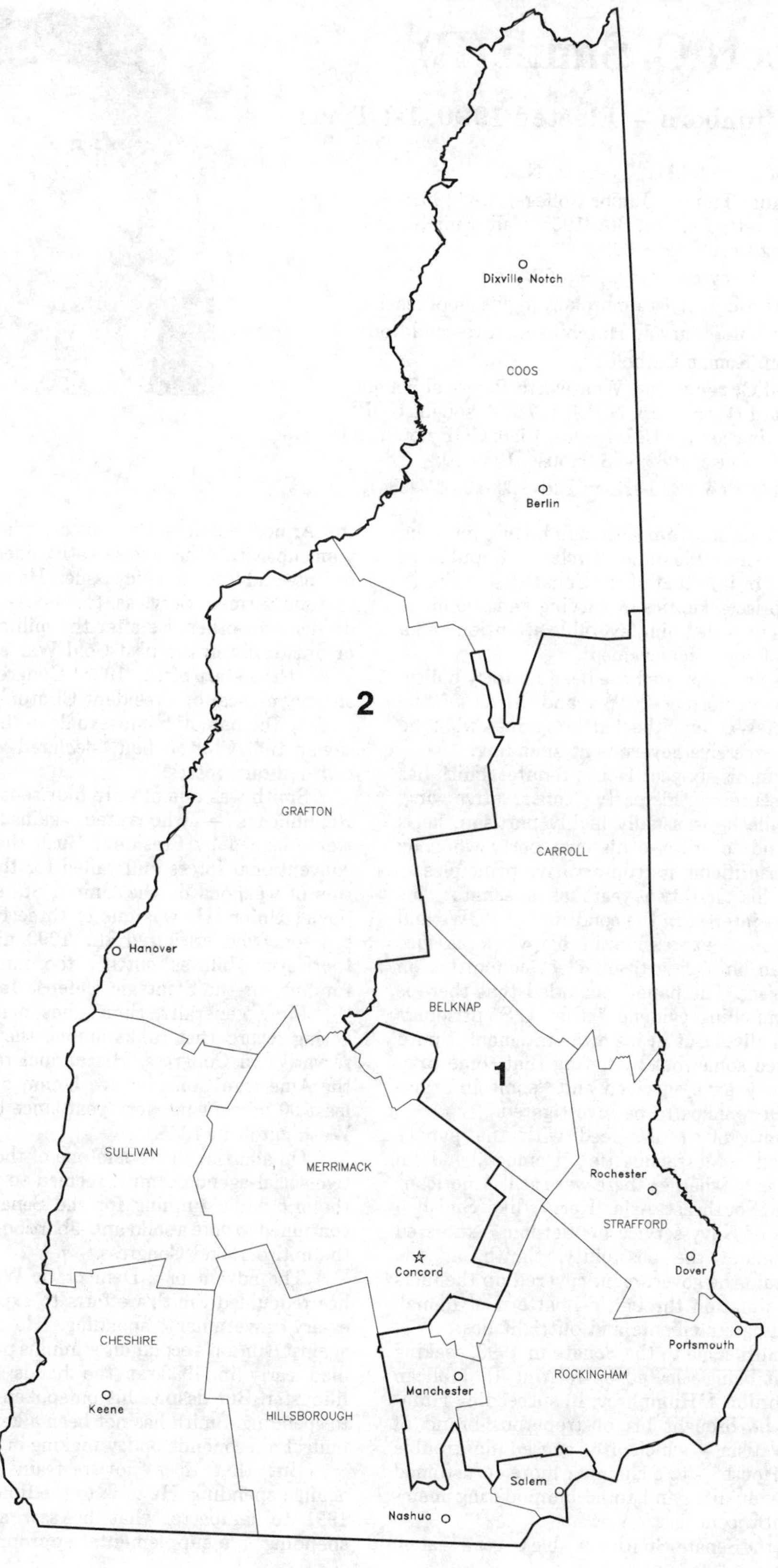

Robert C. Smith (R)

Of Tuftonboro — Elected 1990; 1st Term

Born: March 30, 1941, Trenton, N.J.

Education: Trenton Junior College, A.A. 1963; Lafayette College, B.A. 1965; California State U., Long Beach, 1968-69.

Military Service: Navy, 1965-67.

Occupation: Real estate broker; high school teacher.

Family: Wife, Mary Jo Hutchinson; three children.

Religion: Roman Catholic.

Political Career: Gov. Wentworth Regional School Board (Wolfeboro, N.H.), 1978-84; sought GOP nomination for U.S. House, 1980; GOP nominee for U.S. House, 1982; U.S. House, 1985-90.

Capitol Office: 332 Dirksen Bldg. 20510; 224-2841.

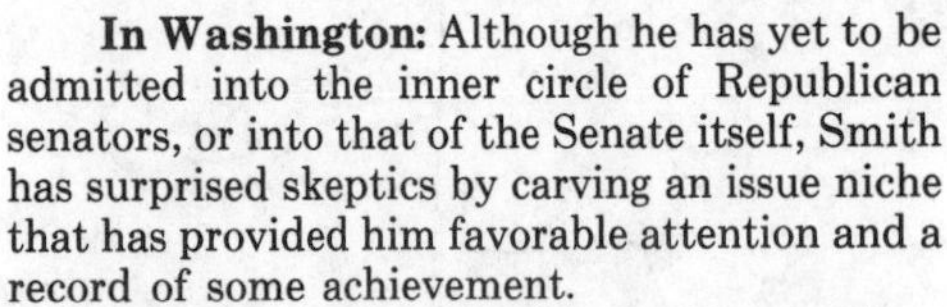

In Washington: Although he has yet to be admitted into the inner circle of Republican senators, or into that of the Senate itself, Smith has surprised skeptics by carving an issue niche that has provided him favorable attention and a record of some achievement.

His key interests have been military policy, the fate of former POWs and MIAs of the Vietnam War and the battle against what he sees as excessive government spending.

As in his six-year House tenure, Smith has dwelt securely in his party's conservative wing. And while he is usually highly partisan, he is not afraid to criticize his own party when he sees it sacrificing its conservative principles.

In his first two years as a senator, his longtime interest in the condition of POWs and MIAs found expression in his work as vice chairman on a bipartisan select committee on the subject. The panel concluded that there is no "compelling evidence" that U.S. prisoners are still alive. But in his own statement, Smith demurred somewhat by noting that some prisoners may have survived and "some information still remains to be investigated."

Smith often disagreed with the panel's chairman, Massachusetts Democrat John Kerry, as to whether there were still Americans alive in Southeast Asia. Kerry, like Smith a veteran of Navy service in Vietnam, expressed doubt about the possibility. Smith, at one point, said the government covered up the facts of the situation through a "pattern of denial, misleading statements and outright lies."

Smith came to the Senate in 1990, seeking the seat being vacated by retiring Republican Sen. Gordon J. Humphrey. In succeeding Humphrey, he brought his obstreperous brand of conservatism — which often caused him trouble in the House — to a chamber more accustomed to individualism and to accommodating members with iconoclastic views.

In the Senate, Smith was able to get a seat on the Armed Services Committee, where he can team up with other conservative ideologues on defense and foreign policy issues. He has used his seat on Armed Services to oppose efforts to downsize or otherwise alter the military quickly or drastically in the post-Cold War era.

At the start of the 103rd Congress, he was sharply critical of President Clinton's proposal to drop the ban on homosexuals in the military, saying that Clinton had "declared war on his own military forces."

Smith was one of only four senators — all Republicans — who voted against the 1991 treaty signed by President Bush that reduced conventional forces and called for the destruction of weapons by the United States and the Soviet Union. He was one of three Republican senators who criticized the 1992 defense authorization bill as cutting too much of the funding for the Strategic Defense Initiative.

More generally, Smith has maintained a voting record that ranks among the most conservative in Congress. His annual rating from the American Conservative Union has been at least 90 percent in every year since he came to Washington in 1985.

On abortion, a cornerstone of the conservative social agenda, Smith seemed to temper his rhetoric while running for the Senate. But he continued to vote a solid anti-abortion line during the entire 102nd Congress.

The advent of a Democratic White House has redoubled Smith's efforts to expose unnecessary government spending. He spoke out against Clinton's economic stimulus package that died early in 1993 at the hands of a GOP filibuster. But despite his outspoken opposition to spending, Smith has not been a key player on budget or economic policy-making in the Senate.

But that does not restrain his railing against spending. He took to the floor in March 1991 to lambaste what he saw as wasteful spending in a supplemental appropriations bill that had just passed the Senate. He proudly points to his consistently high ratings from groups such as the National Taxpayers Union; he was among the first members of Congress to urge President Bush in mid-1990 to reject any budget deal that included any tax increase; and he is a strong proponent of a constitutional amendment requiring a balanced budget.

In the House, Smith was a vocal opponent of congressional pay raises. When the House voted in February 1989 to block a proposed 51 percent salary hike for members of Congress, Smith was both a big winner and a big loser.

He was a winner because he helped lead the fight against a procedure that would have allowed the raise to be enacted without a House vote.

"Would I like to have a $45,000 raise? You're damned right I would," Smith said. "But that's not the way to get it. If we can't convince the American people we should have a raise, then we shouldn't have it."

Smith lost, though, in that he had to wait longer for the seat he wanted on the House Armed Services Committee — a wait he attributed to his activism on the pay issue. He gained a seat on Armed Services in November 1989 when a slot opened up in midterm.

However, Smith's positions have served him very well in fiscally conservative New Hampshire, which has neither an income nor sales tax, and prides itself on its bare-bones state and local governments.

At the start of the 103rd Congress, he was named to the Senate Ethics Committee. During his House service, he wrote a chapter on ethics in a 1987 book by conservative Republicans entitled "House of Ill Repute." In it, Smith said, "I happen to believe that being ethical is like being pregnant — you either are or you are not!"

Smith parts company with his conservative stalwarts and joins with environmentalists on acid rain, an issue that cuts across party and ideological lines in New Hampshire, whose lakes and streams show signs of damage from the pollution problem. In the 101st Congress, Smith was elected co-chairman of the House Republican Task Force on Acid Rain, and when he joined the Senate in the 102nd Congress, he got a seat on the Environment and Public Works Committee.

At Home: A small-town real estate agent and one-time junior high school teacher, New Hampshire's senior senator has cultivated the image of a real-life "Mr. Smith Goes to Washington." But he also exhibited a good bit of political savvy in 1990 in navigating his crossing from one side of Capitol Hill to the other.

In three terms of representing New Hampshire's 1st District, Smith had forged a reputation as an ardent Congress-basher and hard-right conservative immersed in few issues other than accounting for Vietnam MIAs.

But when Sen. Humphrey announced in early 1989 that he would not seek re-election, Smith moved quickly to assume the mantle. He announced his candidacy for the open seat, wrapped up the support of key Republican leaders (including John H. Sununu, then-White House chief of staff and former New Hampshire governor) and began to project a more moderate position on several key issues.

In the GOP primary, Smith's well-heeled campaign rolled up nearly two-thirds of the vote against Tom Christo, a wealthy lawyer specializing in computer law who was backed by the National Abortion Rights Action League. Smith ran just as well in the general election, crushing the comeback bid of former Democratic Sen. John A. Durkin (1975-80).

Smith was favored to win the seat, but the ease of his victory was a surprise. On paper, Durkin looked like the best candidate the Democrats could nominate. He was a proven vote-getter with a tart-tongued manner that seemed capable of skewering the affable Smith. Durkin certainly tried, mocking Smith as "Bumbling Bob" and the "abominable no-man" and portraying him as a simplistic ideologue who would be intellectually over his head in the Senate.

But Smith was able to give as good as he got, keeping Durkin on the defensive in part by attacking aspects of Durkin's own Senate record in the late 1970s. Smith accused Durkin of being a tax-and-spend liberal who supported the federal bailout of New York City but opposed the Kemp-Roth tax cut.

And he charged that Durkin was a flip-flopper to boot. During his Senate years, Durkin was strongly against abortion and readily accepted political action committee (PAC) money. In 1990, Durkin backed abortion rights and refused PAC donations. Heavily outspent, Durkin was in no position to compete effectively in the final days of the campaign. In Republican New Hampshire, the result was a rout.

Smith's early campaigns were far more modest: short on money, long on Rotary Club luncheons. But they gave him a chance to demonstrate his persistence. On his first House try in 1980, Smith lost in the GOP primary. On his second try, in 1982, he won the primary but lost the general election to Democratic Rep. Norman E. D'Amours (1975-85). On his third try in, 1984, when D'Amours ran for the Senate, Smith finally won the seat. In beating the highest-ranking Democrat in state government, Executive Councilor Dudley Dudley, he returned the eastern New Hampshire House seat to the GOP for the first time in a decade.

Unlike D'Amours, whose roots were in ethnic Manchester, Smith reflected small-town Yankee New Hampshire. It was there that he wrote his brief political résumé as a member and chairman of the Wolfeboro School Board. In private life, he was a civics and gym teacher at the local junior high school.

Rather than embellish his modest credentials when he ran for the House, Smith presented himself as a citizen-politician who understood New Hampshire's common-sense values. Each campaign played up the down-home manner of the big, burly baseball coach and emphasized his fervent conservatism.

Smith began the 1984 campaign with a lingering debt from his earlier efforts. But with wide name identification and staunch support from the state's largest newspaper, the conservative Manchester Union Leader, he easily outdistanced a crowded GOP primary field.

Dudley, by contrast, struggled through an unexpectedly close primary race, burdened by a reputation as a liberal Democrat that Smith reinforced with references to her as "Dudley Dudley, Liberal Liberal." Smith won by about a 3-to-2 margin, sweeping not only rural portions of the 1st but also blue-collar cities such as Manchester and Rochester.

In 1986, Smith had to put down a Republican primary challenge from Executive Councilor Louis J. Georgopoulos, a Manchester haberdasher whose political post and gregarious nature gave him high name identity. He called Smith, who grew up in New Jersey and boasted close ties to national conservative groups, an "outsider." He also criticized Smith's preoccupation with tracing the whereabouts of missing Vietnam-era servicemen, contrasting it with his own work to keep nuclear waste out of the state. But Smith had perfected his "man of the people" style of campaigning and again enjoyed strong support from the Union Leader. He won by more than 3-to-1.

In the fall, he faced an aggressive challenger in former state Rep. James M. Demers, who won the Democratic primary easily after falling 1,100 votes short of nomination two years earlier. Demers offered himself as a centrist Democrat, not saddled with the liberal reputation that hurt Dudley in 1984.

Demers had legislative experience as assistant minority whip in the Democratic state House leadership; he had a French name that sounded similar to that of the district's previous Democratic incumbent; and he had been campaigning virtually non-stop since 1984.

Demers carried Democratic coastal cities such as Portsmouth, Rochester and his home town of Dover, but won little else. In spite of his French name, he lost heavily ethnic Manchester by about 2,000 votes.

In 1988, Democratic nominee Joseph F. Keefe, a Manchester lawyer, began and ended his campaign with less of a following than Demers had enjoyed. Smith reached 60 percent of the vote for the first time.

Committees

Armed Services (7th of 9 Republicans)
Defense Technology, Acquisition & Industrial Base (ranking); Coalition Defense & Reinforcing Forces; Military Readiness & Defense Infrastructure

Environment & Public Works (5th of 7 Republicans)
Toxic Substances, Environmental Oversight, Research & Development (ranking); Superfund, Recycling & Solid Waste Management; Water Resources, Transportation, Public Buildings & Economic Development

Select Ethics (3rd of 3 Republicans)

Elections

1990 General		
Robert C. Smith (R)	189,630	(65%)
John A. Durkin (D)	91,262	(31%)
John Elsnau (LIBERT)	9,717	(3%)
1990 Primary		
Robert C. Smith (R)	56,215	(65%)
Tom Christo (R)	25,286	(29%)
Theo De Winter (R)	2,768	(3%)
Ewing E.J. Smith (R)	2,009	(2%)

Previous Winning Percentages: **1988 *** (60%) **1986 *** (56%) **1984 *** (59%)

** House elections.*

Campaign Finance

	Receipts	Receipts from PACs	Expend-itures
1990			
Smith (R)	$1,509,288	$663,400 (44%)	$1,420,172
Durkin (D)	$334,025	0	$319,879

Key Votes

1993	
Require unpaid family and medical leave	N
Approve national "motor voter" registration bill	N
Approve budget increasing taxes and reducing deficit	N
Support president's right to lift military gay ban	N
1992	
Approve school-choice pilot program	Y
Allow shifting funds from defense to domestic programs	N
Oppose deeper cuts in spending for SDI	Y
1991	
Approve waiting period for handgun purchases	N
Raise senators' pay and ban honoraria	Y
Authorize use of force in Persian Gulf	Y
Confirm Clarence Thomas to Supreme Court	Y

Voting Studies

	Presidential Support		Party Unity		Conservative Coalition	
Year	**S**	**O**	**S**	**O**	**S**	**O**
1992	73	27	92	8	89	11
1991	85	14	93	6	85	15
House Service:						
1990	73	27	91	8	87	13
1989	62	37	91	9	88	12
1988	73	26	97	2	95	5
1987	80	20	95	5	81	19
1986	82	18	96	4	94	6
1985	84	16	91	8	82	18

Interest Group Ratings

Year	**ADA**	**AFL-CIO**	**CCUS**	**ACU**
1992	5	25	90	96
1991	10	17	70	90
House Service:				
1990	6	17	71	91
1989	10	8	100	96
1988	5	14	93	100
1987	4	13	100	96
1986	0	14	100	91
1985	5	18	95	90

Judd Gregg (R)

Of Greenfield — Elected 1992; 1st Term

Born: Feb. 14, 1947, Nashua, N.H.
Education: Columbia U., A.B. 1969; Boston U., J.D. 1972, LL.M. 1975.
Occupation: Lawyer.
Family: Wife, Kathleen MacLellan; three children.
Religion: Congregationalist.
Political Career: N.H. Governor's Executive Council, 1979-81; U.S. House, 1981-89; governor, 1989-93.
Capitol Office: 393 Russell Bldg. 20510; 224-3324.

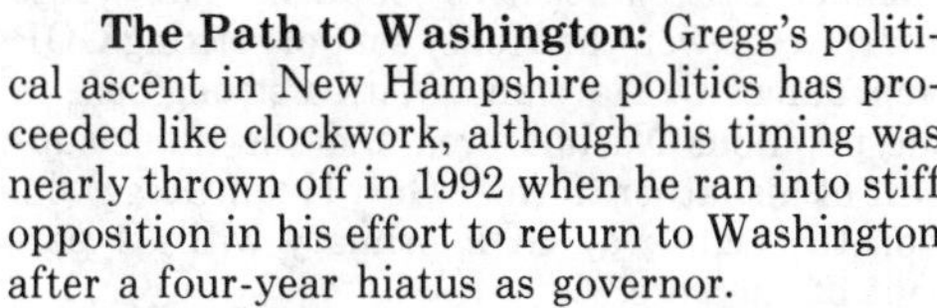

The Path to Washington: Gregg's political ascent in New Hampshire politics has proceeded like clockwork, although his timing was nearly thrown off in 1992 when he ran into stiff opposition in his effort to return to Washington after a four-year hiatus as governor.

A tenacious campaigner and scion of one of New Hampshire's most famous political families, Gregg had won convincingly in four House races and two gubernatorial contests since the fall of 1980.

But in 1992, New Hampshire's economic woes fired up an angry electorate, helping Bill Clinton win the state and putting pro-business Democrat John Rauh in a position to give Gregg his toughest electoral fight ever in his bid to replace retiring GOP Sen. Warren B. Rudman.

As governor and Senate candidate, Gregg took the heat for the state's economic troubles. In the Republican primary, wealthy developer Harold "Hal" Eckman pounded away at Gregg with a lavishly financed media campaign that held Gregg to a bare majority of the vote.

Rauh, a millionaire businessman who moved to Sunapee, N.H., from Ohio in 1986, continued the attack in the fall. He repeatedly reminded voters that Gregg had presided over some of the worst fiscal times in New Hampshire's history, including a tripling of the unemployment rate and the loss of 70,000 jobs over the previous four years. With hard times on their minds, New Hampshire voters appeared ready to send a Democrat to the Senate for the first time since 1975.

The voters had displayed their distaste for incumbents earlier in the year by handing President Bush a surprisingly lackluster victory in the state's presidential primary, giving 37 percent of the vote to his GOP primary challenger, Patrick J. Buchanan. It was an embarrassment for Gregg, who had led Bush's state campaign.

And Rauh's business credentials were appealing. Rauh, who personally financed much of his campaign, stressed his experience as former chief executive officer of a Cincinnati-based plastics company. Though strongly liberal, Rauh tailored his campaign to fit New Hampshire sensibilities by backing such Republican notions as the line-item veto and the balanced-budget amendment.

In a state whose motto is "Live Free or Die," Rauh also made an issue of Gregg's lack of a military record, noting that Gregg had eluded the Vietnam draft on a medical exemption (he suffered acne, bad knees and sleep-walking). Rauh was an Army veteran.

Gregg responded with an aggressive, often negative campaign of his own that was in sync with the Granite State's values of low taxes and minimalist government. He focused on traditional Republican themes, calling Rauh a "tax-and-spend liberal," ridiculing Rauh's proposal to cut defense spending by 50 percent and likening him to Massachusetts Democratic Sen. Edward M. Kennedy.

While acknowledging the state's economic hardships, Gregg frequently added that he had kept a tight lid on spending and remained staunchly opposed to state income and sales taxes. He sloughed off criticism that he was only able to keep the state government solvent during his governorship by raiding federal Medicaid funds.

The race went down to the wire. Gregg lost most of the counties on the rural western side of New Hampshire that were in his old congressional district. But he won the populous southeast corner of the state and the Republican "North Country" by enough votes to take Rudman's Senate seat.

Gregg, who served in the House from 1981 to 1989, brings to the Senate the same fiscal conservatism of his predecessor and outdoes Rudman as a social conservative. He signed a pledge to cut the budget deficit in half within four years or not seek re-election, said he opposes large defense cuts and supported the nomination of Clarence Thomas to the Supreme Court.

But unlike Rudman, Gregg opposes abortion rights and one of the first votes he cast as a member of the 103rd Congress was against passage of the bill providing workers in large businesses with 12 weeks of unpaid family and medical leave. Gregg and his New Hampshire

GOP colleague, Robert C. Smith, were the only New England senators to oppose the measure.

Gregg's return to Congress may evoke a sense of déjà vu. As one of the 52 Republicans elected to the House in 1980 — a group known as the "Reagan robots" — Gregg played the backbench antagonist. He joined Newt Gingrich's Conservative Opportunity Society in 1983 and fought to force floor votes on the issues of school prayer, abortion, a balanced budget and a line-item veto. It is a role he likely will resume under the Clinton administration — particularly on the issues that were the source of Rudman's frustration: congressional reform and eliminating the budget deficit.

"Yes, I am cheap. We need some skinflints in the U.S. Senate," Gregg told The Boston Globe in the final days of the campaign. "I am going to stand up and be counted on the basis of fiscal conservatism."

The lone issue on which Gregg often parted company with conservatives during his House career was the environment. He bucked the Reagan administration during his first term by leading an effort, along with two other freshmen on the Science Committee, to block funding for the Clinch River nuclear breeder reactor in Tennessee.

He also criticized Reagan for inaction on acid rain, which has harmed lakes and forests in northern New England and Canada. In 1987, he introduced legislation to impose financial penalties for emissions that cause acid rain.

Gregg's personal style is more subdued than Rudman's. Gregg is articulate but reserved, and can seem uncomfortable with the flesh-pressing aspects of politics. However, he has devoted almost his entire adult life to public service.

He practiced law only a short time before launching his political career in 1978 by unseating a GOP incumbent for a seat on the five-member state Executive Council. Two years later, Gregg won the House seat of retiring GOP Rep. James C. Cleveland. With a strong base in the populous Nashua area and the quiet support of his father (former Gov. Hugh Gregg), he won the eight-way GOP primary with 34 percent of the vote.

From then until 1992, Gregg coasted at the polls, winning every primary and general election with at least 60 percent of the vote.

Committees

Budget (9th of 9 Republicans)

Commerce, Science & Transportation (9th of 9 Republicans)
Foreign Commerce & Tourism (ranking); National Ocean Policy Study; Science; Surface Transportation

Labor & Human Resources (4th of 7 Republicans)
Aging (ranking); Children, Families, Drugs & Alcoholism; Education, Arts & Humanities; Employment & Productivity

Elections

1992 General		
Judd Gregg (R)	249,591	(48%)
John Rauh (D)	234,982	(45%)
Katherine M. Alexander (LIBERT)	18,214	(4%)
Larry Brady (I)	9,340	(2%)
1992 Primary		
Judd Gregg (R)	57,141	(50%)
Harold Eckman (R)	43,264	(38%)
Jean T. White (R)	10,642	(9%)
Mark W. Farnham (R)	2,295	(2%)

Previous Winning Percentages: **1986** * (74%) **1984** * (76%) **1982** * (71%) **1980** * (64%)

** House elections.*

Campaign Finance

	Receipts	Receipts from PACs		Expend-itures
1992				
Gregg (R)	$990,836	$367,605	(37%)	$875,675
Rauh (D)	$834,000	0		$833,967

Key Votes

1993

Require unpaid family and medical leave	N
Approve national "motor voter" registration bill	N
Approve budget increasing taxes and reducing deficit	N
Support president's right to lift military gay ban	N

Voting Studies

	Presidential Support		Party Unity		Conservative Coalition	
Year	**S**	**O**	**S**	**O**	**S**	**O**
House Service:						
1988	56	25	71	8	79	8
1987	69	26	83	8	84	16
1986	74	24	85	9	84	10
1985	70	25	78	13	73	25
1984	67	28	82	15	83	15
1983	78	20	85	10	73	20
1982	68	30	84	15	77	19
1981	68	29	80	17	72	25

Interest Group Ratings

Year	ADA	AFL-CIO	CCUS	ACU
House Service:				
1988	16	13	93	82
1987	20	21	88	80
1986	20	21	88	80
1985	10	29	86	76
1984	15	23	69	71
1983	10	6	89	74
1982	35	5	81	76
1981	25	7	89	93

1 Bill Zeliff (R)

Of Jackson — Elected 1990; 2nd Term

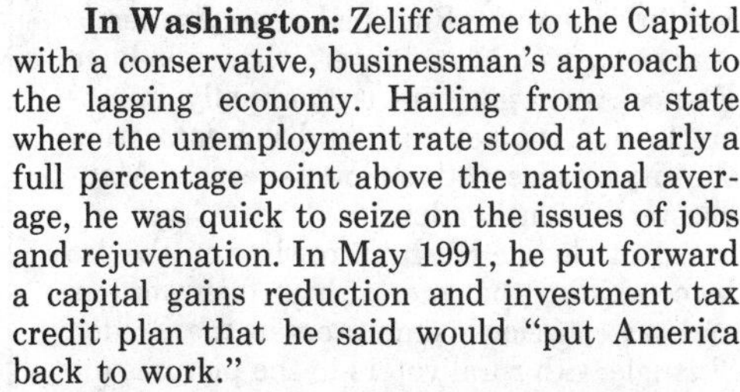

Born: June 12, 1936, East Orange, N.J.
Education: U. of Connecticut, B.S. 1959.
Military Service: National Guard, 1959-64.
Occupation: Hotel owner.
Family: Wife, Sydna Taylor; three children.
Religion: Protestant.
Political Career: Sought GOP nomination for N.H. Senate, 1984.
Capitol Office: 224 Cannon Bldg. 20515; 225-5456.

In Washington: Zeliff came to the Capitol with a conservative, businessman's approach to the lagging economy. Hailing from a state where the unemployment rate stood at nearly a full percentage point above the national average, he was quick to seize on the issues of jobs and rejuvenation. In May 1991, he put forward a capital gains reduction and investment tax credit plan that he said would "put America back to work."

Zeliff told colleagues in a House speech that "investment in our companies will expand operations, make businesses more profitable, allow us to hire more workers and, ultimately, pay more taxes." His economic proposal drew 74 cosponsors, including three Democrats, but not the requisite support of the Ways and Means Committee.

Undeterred, Zeliff brought his plan back to the 103rd Congress.

Despite the jobless rate at home, Zeliff opposed two separate Democratic efforts in 1991 to extend emergency unemployment benefits, denouncing them as "budget busters." President Bush vetoed one bill and signed the second.

While he sided with the White House on most issues, he broke with Bush and conservative Republicans over abortion rights. In November 1991, he voted to block enforcement of an administration "gag rule" that barred abortion counseling in federally funded family planning clinics. He cast a similar vote against the administration position in 1992.

Although he sits on the Public Works and Transportation, Government Operations and Small Business committees, his legislative interests take him outside those committee jurisdictions to more high-profile issues. Besides the economy and jobs, Zeliff's interest gravitates toward environmental problems, military base closures and health care.

He played a role in forming a superfund task force responsible for making recommendations to Congress on cleanup of sites, including 17 in New Hampshire. The reauthorization of "superfund" hazardous waste cleanup legislation is high on the legislative priority list for the 103rd Congress.

As a freshman, Zeliff succeeded in winning passage of his bill to designate a nine-mile stretch of New Hampshire's Lamprey River for study under the National Wild and Scenic Rivers System. The genesis of that legislation was a proposed hydroelectric facility that threatened to diminish the water quality of the river. Energy output from the facility was estimated to reach 30 homes, which Zeliff argued is a lower priority than the hundreds of people who enjoy the river each year.

On nuclear energy, Zeliff has been heavily influenced by the controversy over the Seabrook nuclear power plant in his district. The plant's original owner fell into bankruptcy before startup, in large part because of repeated public intervention over safety that delayed its operations. (Northeast Utilities bought Seabrook; operations began in August 1990.)

During debate on the 1992 energy bill, Zeliff argued for "an improved, rational nuclear licensing process," and he supported provisions in the bill that streamlined nuclear power licensing.

Zeliff split with the Bush administration in both 1991 and 1992 when he voted to eliminate funding for the multibillion-dollar atom smasher in Texas. The superconducting super collider holds great opportunities for physicists and Texans, but offers little to a fiscally conservative New Englander.

The proposed orbiting space station *Freedom* would spread federal dollars more widely but would not help New Hampshire's 1st District much. Yet Zeliff voted with Bush in 1991 and 1992 to continue funding for the beleaguered project. He said his support for the space project was rooted in the jobs, scientific gains and economic boost it promises.

Despite his breaks with Bush over abortion and the super collider, Zeliff remained loyal until the end. He voted with Bush more than 80 percent of the time on those issues on which the president staked out a position.

At Home: Zeliff may have the public demeanor of a genial innkeeper, but he is not

New Hampshire 1

East — Manchester

The 1st qualifies as New Hampshire's urban district. It covers barely one-quarter of the state's land area yet contains seven of the 11 largest communities in New Hampshire, including the largest, Manchester, which has nearly 100,000 people.

As in the neighboring 2nd, most of the district's population lives in the southern tier within 30 miles of the Massachusetts border, with the largest concentration of voters in the "Golden Triangle." It is an area extending roughly from Nashua and Salem on the south to Manchester on the north that straddles the line between the two most populous counties in the state, Hillsborough and Rockingham.

Within the Triangle are many of the high-tech companies and bedroom communities (all within easy commuting range of Boston) that have helped New Hampshire nearly double its population since 1960.

The southern half of the Triangle along the Massachusetts line is in the 2nd District. But the 1st includes many of the faster-growing towns that stretch to the north along Interstate 93 and Route 3. During the 1980s, Derry grew by 57 percent, Londonderry by 45 percent, Merrimack by 44 percent. Each town currently boasts a population in excess of 19,000.

The growth has been stymied in the 1990s by the slump in New Hampshire's economy. But the biggest hit in the 1st was suffered along the Atlantic seacoast with the 1991 closure of Pease Air Force Base in Newington. Commuter airlines have begun to use the facility, but that has not offset the thousands of jobs that were lost. The region avoided a double whammy when the government decided in early 1993 to keep open the Portsmouth Naval Shipyard in nearby Kittery, Maine.

The economic uncertainties helped the Democrats in 1992 carry more than their usual beachheads in Durham (Strafford County), the home of the University of New Hampshire, and the gentrified seaport of Portsmouth (Rockingham County).

Bill Clinton not only swept old mill towns such as Rochester and Somersworth, but also carried the historic Yankee town of Exeter, site of the Phillips Exeter Academy. And he carried Manchester, where the huge Franco-American vote is nominally Democratic but subject to blandishments from the city's conservative newspaper, the Manchester Union Leader.

But George Bush narrowly won the 1st by combining the votes of high-tech workers and tax-conscious commuters in the Golden Triangle with rural voters in the picturesque land of lakes and mountains to the north. Carroll County, which anchors the northern end of the district, has voted for a Democratic presidential candidate in only one election this century, 1912. Still, independent Ross Perot carved deeply enough into the GOP vote, especially in the Golden Triangle, to enable Clinton to carry the state.

In 1992 redistricting, the 1st shed a half-dozen towns on its western fringe near Concord, from Sanborntown on the north to Chichester on the south.

1990 Population: 554,360. White 543,105 (98%), Black 4,052 (1%), Other 7,203 (1%). Hispanic origin 5,771 (1%). 18 and over 415,884 (75%), 62 and over 73,828 (13%). Median age: 32.

averse to playing political hardball. Both sides of his personality have been on display during his first two congressional campaigns.

Zeliff's friendship with former White House Chief of Staff John H. Sununu was crucial in launching his political career. During Sununu's tenure as governor (1983-89), he encouraged Zeliff to run for office.

Zeliff lost a bid for the state Senate in 1984, but Sununu appointed him to Vice President Bush's campaign steering committee for the 1988 New Hampshire presidential primary. When Rep. Robert C. Smith decided in 1990 to run for the Senate, Zeliff ran with Sununu's support for the vacated seat.

Among Zeliff's strengths was his image as a successful businessman. In 1976, he gave up his job as a corporate executive in Pennsylvania and purchased the Christmas Farm Inn in New Hampshire's North Country. With his wife, Zeliff converted the aging inn into a year-round resort with whirlpool baths and other upscale comforts.

Zeliff referred to his business success often during the 1990 campaign, linking it to the Yankee traditions of entrepreneurialism and frugality. To make the point, he carried a jar of pennies, stating, "Watch the pennies and the dollars will take care of themselves."

With his ties to Sununu and friends in the hotel industry, Zeliff proved to be a lucrative fundraiser. He collected more than $1.5 million for his first two congressional races, nearly a half-million dollars of that from political action committees.

Still, both campaigns were hard-edged. In

1990, Zeliff branded one primary opponent, state House Speaker Douglas Scamman Jr., as a "taxer" and another, international trade consultant Larry Brady, as a "foreign agent." They, in turn, accused Zeliff of trying to buy the election. After Zeliff edged Brady by 314 votes, the runner-up refused to endorse him.

But the Manchester Union Leader, the staunchly conservative newspaper that dominates the district's media, lined up behind Zeliff. Its editorials lauded his fiscal conservatism, particularly his adherence to the "no new taxes" principle that is political gospel in New Hampshire. The paper also assailed Democratic nominee Joseph F. Keefe — who challenged Smith in 1988 — as an arch-liberal.

Zeliff's image as a party regular helped him secure the support of GOP loyalists, while his antitax stance appealed to angry conservatives. Despite polls indicating that the contest was a tossup, Zeliff won by 10 percentage points.

His second House campaign mirrored the first. The residue of the 1990 GOP infighting brought Zeliff a pair of primary challengers in 1992, including Scamman's finance chairman, Ovide Lamontagne.

Zeliff escaped the primary with just 50 percent of the vote, although he had an easier time in the general election against former Democratic Senate Minority Leader Bob Preston.

The incumbent had to fend off charges that he and his staff spent lavishly on travel around the district. But Zeliff had the money to press his own theme — that he was a frugal-minded congressional reformer who kept in frequent contact with his constituents.

In neither the primary nor general election, though, did Zeliff have the backing of the Union Leader. Bothered by Zeliff's pro-abortion rights stance, the paper endorsed Lamontagne in the primary and Preston in the fall. It was the Union Leader's first general election endorsement of a Democrat in more than 20 years.

Committees

Government Operations (12th of 16 Republicans)
Commerce, Consumer & Monetary Affairs

Public Works & Transportation (9th of 24 Republicans)
Investigations & Oversight; Surface Transportation; Water Resources & the Environment

Small Business (8th of 18 Republicans)
SBA Legislation and the General Economy

Elections

1992 General		
Bill Zeliff (R)	135,936	(53%)
Bob Preston (D)	108,578	(42%)
Knox Bickford (LIBERT)	5,633	(2%)
Richard P. Bosa (I)	3,537	(1%)
1992 Primary		
Bill Zeliff (R)	28,877	(50%)
Ovide Lamontagne (R)	20,493	(35%)
Maureen E. Barrows (R)	8,447	(15%)
1990 General		
Bill Zeliff (R)	81,684	(55%)
Joseph F. Keefe (D)	66,176	(45%)

District Vote for President

1992
D 101,415 (38%)
R 104,653 (39%)
I 61,571 (23%)

Campaign Finance

	Receipts	Receipts from PACs		Expend-itures
1992				
Zeliff (R)	$776,283	$325,915	(42%)	$778,358
Preston (D)	$174,566	$62,287	(36%)	$174,565
1990				
Zeliff (R)	$807,514	$130,601	(16%)	$802,680
Keefe (D)	$378,930	$175,279	(46%)	$377,993

Key Votes

1993	
Require parental notification of minors' abortions	N
Require unpaid family and medical leave	N
Approve national "motor voter" registration bill	N
Approve budget increasing taxes and reducing deficit	N
Approve economic stimulus plan	N
1992	
Approve balanced-budget constitutional amendment	Y
Close down space station program	N
Approve U.S. aid for former Soviet Union	Y
Allow shifting funds from defense to domestic programs	N
1991	
Extend unemployment benefits using deficit financing	N
Approve waiting period for handgun purchases	N
Authorize use of force in Persian Gulf	Y

Voting Studies

	Presidential Support		Party Unity		Conservative Coalition	
Year	**S**	**O**	**S**	**O**	**S**	**O**
1992	79	17	88	6	92	8
1991	80	20	86	11	97	3

Interest Group Ratings

Year	ADA	AFL-CIO	CCUS	ACU
1992	20	25	88	92
1991	10	8	100	80

2 Dick Swett (D)

Of Bow — Elected 1990; 2nd Term

Born: May 1, 1957, Bryn Mawr, Pa.
Education: Yale U., B.A. 1979.
Occupation: Architect.
Family: Wife, Katrina Lantos; six children.
Religion: Mormon.
Political Career: No previous office.
Capitol Office: 230 Cannon Bldg. 20515; 225-5206.

In Washington: Swett surprised Washington insiders when he won a House seat in 1990 as a Mormon and Democrat in a district dominated by Protestant Republican Yankees. He further confounded them in 1992 when he managed to win re-election by a wide margin.

There are two ready explanations for his success: As the son-in-law of Democratic Rep. Tom Lantos of California, Swett has been able to shake the Beltway money tree to help solidify his position in the 2nd District. But his ability to steer a middle course — voting conservatively on several high profile issues yet remaining loyal to the Democratic Party on other issues — helped him easily win re-election with 62 percent of the vote.

Among those high-profile conservative votes were his support for the use of force against Iraq in the Persian Gulf War in 1991, his support for the balanced-budget amendment in 1992 and his opposition to ending the Strategic Defense Initiative program in 1991. Swett also appealed to his independent-thinking constituents by knowing when to part company with President Bush; Swett supported the former president's position only 28 percent of the time in 1992 on issues on which he had a stated position, down from 46 percent in 1991.

Swett is on the Science, Space and Technology and Public Works and Transportation committees, where he has expressed an interest in alternative energy sources and alternative modes of transportation.

As the only professional architect to be elected to Congress this century, Swett is inclined to design logical solutions to problems, but his junior status limits his legislative influence.

Among his successes: On the Public Works Committee, Swett authored provisions of the 1991 surface transportation reauthorization measure calling for earmarking funds for alternative transportation uses and for enhancing statewide transportation planning requirements.

On the Science Committee, he has become known for taking stands opposite those of committee Chairman George E. Brown Jr., a California Democrat. For example, in 1992, Swett voted for legislation that would have killed the NASA space station *Freedom*, legislation that Brown strongly opposed.

On issues closer to home, he lobbied for funding for the expansion of the White Mountain National Forest and for continued funding of the Northern Forest Lands Council in fiscal 1993.

At Home: If the Republicans are to win control of the House anytime soon, they will probably need to regain a seat like the one held by Swett. Historically, the New Hampshire 2nd has been one of the most Republican districts in the country. Before Swett won it in 1990, it had not elected a Democrat since 1912.

But the GOP's initial efforts to regain the seat in 1992 failed miserably, as Swett rolled up more than 60 percent of the vote.

Part of Swett's success has been due to his assiduous courtship of district voters, extensive fundraising and middle-of-the-road political posture. But his success has also been due to a pair of Republican rivals who were anathema to a sizable segment of the district's large GOP base.

Swett is not a natural politician. Though he was raised in New Hampshire, he lived in California for many years before returning in 1987 with the idea of developing alternative energy projects with his father. He had never held political office and had a limited background in community service when he ran in 1990.

But Swett was able to tap atypical political expertise and connections through his wife, Katrina Lantos-Swett. That backing helped him to exploit Republican incumbent Chuck Douglas' weaknesses, including overconfidence about his first re-election campaign.

The contest centered more on the candidates' personal qualities than on their issue papers. Douglas' conservative views were palatable to many voters in the 2nd, but his demeanor was not. Douglas' combative style had led to run-ins with advocates for the mentally ill and with the Presbyterian Synod of the

New Hampshire 2

West — Concord; Nashua

Through most of the century, the 1st has been regarded as one of the most rock-ribbed Republican districts in the country. Only once before 1990 did the district elect a Democrat to Congress — that in 1912 during the GOP-Bull Moose bloodletting and then for only two years.

But in 1990, western New Hampshire voters elected Democrat Swett to the House, and two years later they not only re-elected him overwhelmingly but also gave Bill Clinton a 10,000-vote plurality. That helped Clinton become the first Democratic presidential candidate since Lyndon B. Johnson in 1964 to carry the Granite State.

It is too early to tell whether the Democratic inroads are an aberration or an indicator of a basic overhaul in the district's politics. But New Hampshire's sharp economic downturn in the early 1990s has affected normal voting patterns — shaking loose a number of Republican-oriented rural voters while bringing back to the Democratic fold blue-collar voters in old mill towns such as Berlin (Coos County) and Claremont (Sullivan County).

The only reliable source of Democratic votes in the 2nd had been the liberal college town of Hanover (Grafton County), home of Dartmouth College. It is arguably the only recession-proof community in the district.

The economy of the heavily forested "North Country" is closely tied to paper manufacturing and wood products. The populous southern tier along the Massachusetts border has gone boom and bust with high-tech industries deeply involved in computers and defense electronics. In between, many of western New Hampshire's picturesque small towns depend on tourist dollars — from summer vacationers at the myriad lakes to wintertime skiers in the White Mountains. Each area has suffered during New Hampshire's downturn.

Loaded with well-educated, upwardly mobile refugees from "Taxachusetts," many of the towns along the southern tier have remained reliably Republican despite the recession. The largest city in the 2nd, Nashua (with almost 80,000 residents) voted for Clinton. But the nearby bedroom communities of Hudson, Milford and Salem all backed George Bush.

That was not the case in major communities of the 2nd outside the southern tier. Newcomers there are apt to be more attuned to environmental concerns than taxes. The state capital of Concord (Merrimack County) and the college town of Keene (Cheshire County) both backed Clinton.

Altogether, five of the six New Hampshire counties that Clinton won were totally or primarily within the 2nd. So were four of the five counties that went Democratic for Senate in 1992, and both of the counties that voted Democratic for governor. (Statewide, Republicans won both contests.)

Yet it is hard to see the 2nd becoming a nest of Yankee bolshevism. Conservative commentator Patrick J. Buchanan made his best showing in the 1992 New Hampshire GOP primary in Sullivan and Coos, cracking 40 percent of the vote in both.

1990 Population: 554,892. White 544,328 (98%), Black 3,146 (<1%), Other 7,418 (1%). Hispanic origin 5,562 (1%). 18 and over 414,613 (75%), 62 and over 77,176 (14%). Median age: 33.

Northeast, among others.

Douglas' three divorces also made some voters uneasy. In the closing campaign push, Swett sent out mailings featuring quoted remarks by Nancy Sununu — wife of former New Hampshire governor and then-White House Chief of Staff John H. Sununu — questioning Douglas' morals and values.

Douglas countered with his own attacks, casting Swett as the puppet of his liberal father-in-law and of out-of-state political action committees. But Douglas, as a freshman House member with a sharp tongue, had not stockpiled the credibility he needed to make his charges stick.

Republican strategists placed Swett near the top of their target list in 1992, but he gave them few openings.

Swett was not easy to tag as a liberal, with his support of a balanced-budget constitutional amendment, a presidential line-item veto, the use of force in the Persian Gulf and restrictions on abortions after the first trimester.

The abortion issue brought a primary challenge from Keene State College economics professor Emily Northrop, who favored the Freedom of Choice Act. She won more than one-third of the primary vote and carried the city of Keene and a number of communities nearby.

But Swett was well-positioned for the fall campaign against former GOP state Rep. Bill Hatch. With the support of the Manchester Union Leader, Hatch established himself during the GOP primary as the most conservative candidate in the field.

But the Republican primary was bitter and

closely contested. Hatch and his main rival, former state Rep. Stephen M. Duprey, each tried to depict the other as a closet big spender. And Hatch got his fall campaign off to a stumbling start by holding up a photograph of Swett with the cross hairs of a gun sight superimposed on it. He was never able to pull together the Republican base.

Committees

Public Works & Transportation (20th of 39 Democrats)
Aviation; Economic Development; Surface Transportation

Science, Space & Technology (17th of 33 Democrats)
Energy; Technology, Environment & Aviation

Elections

1992 General		
Dick Swett (D)	157,328	(62%)
Bill Hatch (R)	91,126	(36%)
John A. Lewicke (LIBERT)	5,977	(2%)
1992 Primary		
Dick Swett (D)	27,552	(65%)
Emily Northrop (D)	14,543	(35%)
1990 General		
Dick Swett (D)	74,829	(53%)
Chuck Douglas (R)	67,063	(47%)

District Vote for President

	1992
D	107,625 (41%)
R	97,831 (37%)
I	59,766 (23%)

Campaign Finance

	Receipts	Receipts from PACs		Expend-itures
1992				
Swett (D)	$872,187	$403,900	(46%)	$785,452
Hatch (R)	$231,226	$35,118	(15%)	$232,617
1990				
Swett (D)	$470,252	$186,000	(40%)	$465,160
Douglas (R)	$575,748	$223,050	(39%)	$540,605

Key Votes

1993	
Require parental notification of minors' abortions	N
Require unpaid family and medical leave	Y
Approve national "motor voter" registration bill	Y
Approve budget increasing taxes and reducing deficit	Y
Approve economic stimulus plan	Y
1992	
Approve balanced-budget constitutional amendment	Y
Close down space station program	Y
Approve U.S. aid for former Soviet Union	Y
Allow shifting funds from defense to domestic programs	Y
1991	
Extend unemployment benefits using deficit financing	Y
Approve waiting period for handgun purchases	Y
Authorize use of force in Persian Gulf	Y

Voting Studies

	Presidential Support		Party Unity		Conservative Coalition	
Year	S	O	S	O	S	O
1992	28	71	75	24	50	50
1991	46	53	72	25	78	22

Interest Group Ratings

Year	ADA	AFL-CIO	CCUS	ACU
1992	85	83	38	32
1991	45	92	30	40

New Jersey

STATE DATA

Governor:
James J. Florio (D)

First elected: 11/89
Length of term: 4 years
Term expires: 1/94
Salary: $85,000 (By law, governor's salary is $130,000; Florio receives only $85,000.)
Term limit: 2 consecutive terms
Phone: (609) 292-6000
Born: Aug. 29, 1937; Brooklyn, N.Y.
Education: Trenton State College, B.A. 1962; Columbia U., 1962-63; Rutgers U., J.D. 1967.
Military Service: Navy, 1955-58; Naval Reserve, 1958-74
Occupation: Lawyer
Family: Wife, Lucinda Coleman; three children
Religion: Roman Catholic
Political Career: N.J. Assembly, 1970-74; Democratic nominee for U.S. House, 1972; U.S. House, 1975-90; sought Democratic nomination for governor, 1977; Democratic nominee for governor, 1981

No lieutenant governor

State election official: (609) 292-3760
Democratic headquarters: (609) 392-3367
Republican headquarters: (609) 989-7300

REDISTRICTING

New Jersey lost one House seat in reapportionment, dropping from 14 districts to 13. Legislature established bipartisan commission Jan. 13, 1992; commission issued map March 20.

STATE LEGISLATURE

Legislature. Meets year-round.

Senate: 40 members, 4-year terms
1992 breakdown: 27R, 13D; 38 men, 2 women; 38 whites, 2 blacks
Salary: $35,000
Phone: (609) 292-5199

General Assembly: 80 members, 2-year terms
1992 breakdown: 58R, 22D; 67 men, 13 women; 70 whites, 10 blacks
Salary: $35,000
Phone: (609) 292-5339

URBAN STATISTICS

City	Pop.
Newark Mayor Sharpe James, D	275,221
Jersey City Mayor Bret Schundler, R	228,537
Paterson Mayor William J. Pascrell Jr., D	140,891
Elizabeth Mayor J.C. Bollwage, D	110,002
Woodbridge Mayor James McGreevey, D	93,086

U.S. CONGRESS

Senate: 2 D, 0 R
House: 7 D, 6 R

TERM LIMITS

For Congress: No
For state offices: No

ELECTIONS

1992 Presidential Vote

Bill Clinton	43.0%
George Bush	40.6%
Ross Perot	15.6%

1988 Presidential Vote

George Bush	56%
Michael S. Dukakis	43%

1984 Presidential Vote

Ronald Reagan	60%
Walter F. Mondale	39%

POPULATION

1990 population		7,730,188
1980 population		7,364,823
Percent change		+5%
Rank among states:		9
White		79%
Black		13%
Hispanic		10%
Asian or Pacific islander		4%
Urban		89%
Rural		11%
Born in state		87%
Foreign-born		13%
Under age 18	1,799,462	23%
Ages 18-64	4,898,701	63%
65 and older	1,032,025	13%
Median age		34.5

MISCELLANEOUS

Capital: Trenton
Number of counties: 21
Per capita income: $25,372 (1991)
Rank among states: 2
Total area: 7,787 sq. miles
Rank among states: 46

New Jersey - Congressional Districts

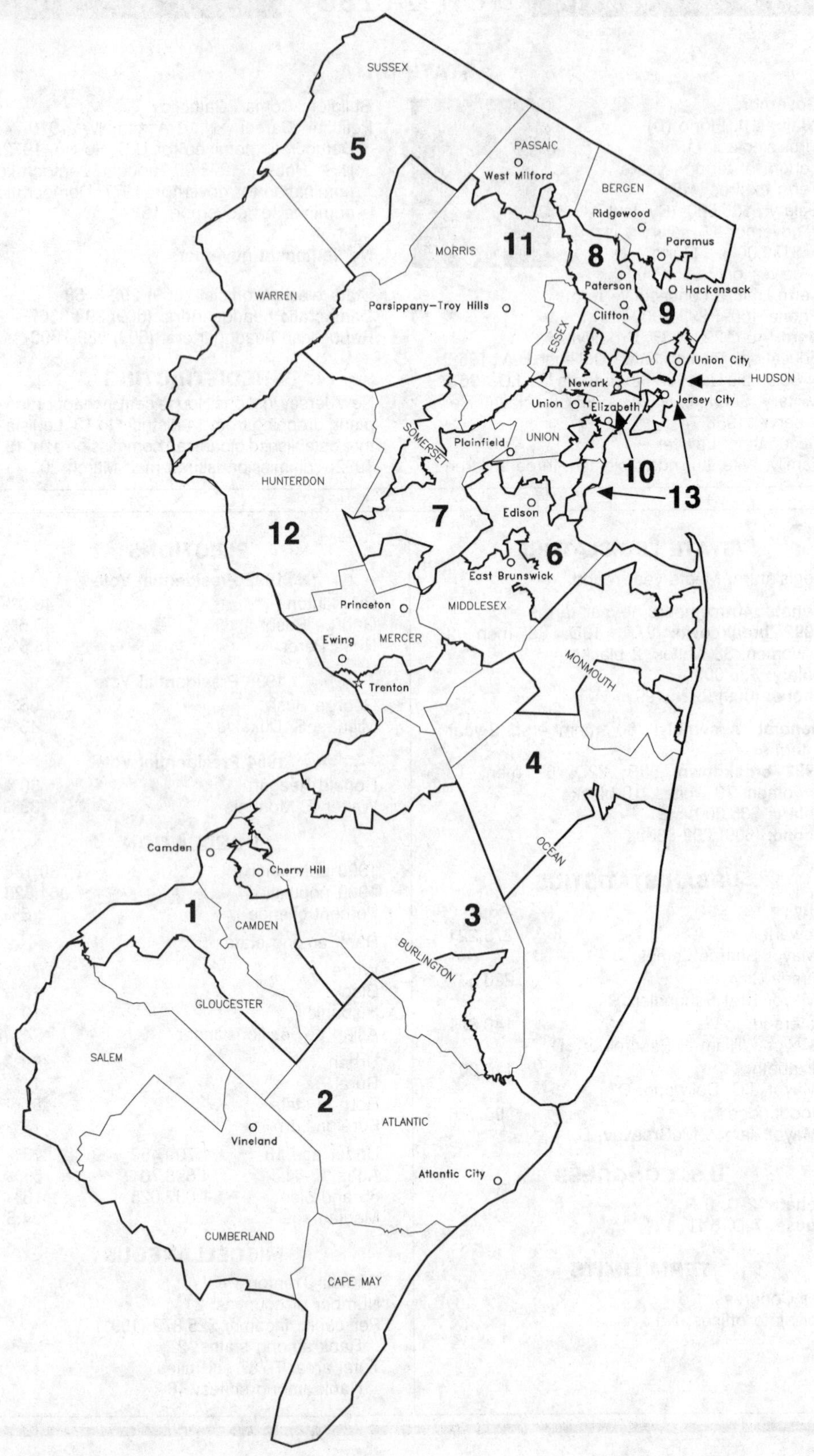

Bill Bradley (D)

Of Denville — Elected 1978; 3rd Term

Born: July 28, 1943, Crystal City, Mo.
Education: Princeton U., B.A. 1965; Oxford U., M.A. 1968.
Military Service: Air Force Reserve, 1967-78.
Occupation: Professional basketball player; author.
Family: Wife, Ernestine Schlant; one child, one stepchild.
Religion: Protestant.
Political Career: No previous office.
Capitol Office: 731 Hart Bldg. 20510; 224-3224.

In Washington: Bradley continues to confound both his allies and adversaries, proving lately perhaps that he retains some of the skill for which he earned fame as a New York Knick, notably his ability to get into position to score, even before he has the ball.

If not for his height and giraffe-like lope, it might be easy to forget that a basketball court rather than the Senate floor provided Bradley's first professional arena. Well into his third term in office, he has shown a zest for the tedious substance of policy-making, and little of the backslapping collegiality and street-smart style expected of sports figures — or successful national political figures.

After years of viewing Bradley as a potential savior of the Democratic Party — if not the country — Congress-watchers and Democratic operatives alike have seen their hopes give way to a realization that they may have set their expectations too high. Bradley's 1990 election-night squeaker showed that New Jersey voters also no longer view him with unyielding awe.

While hard legislative work earned Bradley a place on Democrats' short list of potential presidential candidates throughout the 1980s, he has yet to emerge as an institutional leader. Though he played a major and well-documented role in the enactment of the landmark 1986 tax revision law, with each passing Congress his greatest achievement fades further in memory.

In the 102nd Congress, however, he countered a common notion that he does not like to dirty his hands with the nitty-gritty of legislating. From his position as chairman of the Energy Committee's Water and Power Subcommittee, Bradley did yeoman work on a sweeping water bill. He succeeded in restructuring California's massive Central Valley Project, specifying for the first time that environmental and wildlife preservation were official purposes of the project and breaking the stranglehold that agricultural interests had on the state's water.

When the full Energy and Natural Resources Committee dumped Bradley's version of the water bill in favor of one crafted by growers and backed by Republican John Seymour of California, Bradley went to work negotiating with House sponsor George Miller, D-Calif., and Senate Energy Chairman J. Bennett Johnston, D-La. The bill that emerged from a House-Senate conference committee, and was finally enacted, achieved many of Bradley's initial aims.

A strong supporter of traditional Democratic causes — middle-class tax relief and the special financial needs of women and children, in particular — Bradley has been a maverick within his party on other issues. He touts free trade, and on one occasion backed aid to the Nicaraguan contras. In early 1993, he attracted attention with a change of heart that led to his support for a line-item presidential veto not only for appropriations, but also for tax code provisions that reduce revenue collections.

His support for the line-item veto coincided with his conversion to deficit hawk. A growing concern about the crushing burden of the nation's debt fits the charter of his newly reconfigured Finance subcommittee: Deficits, Debt Management and Long-Term Economic Growth.

For Bradley, the 101st Congress, which ended with his near defeat at the polls, had an inauspicious start. In a move seen as a sign of his ambition, Bradley considered trying to seize the chairmanship of the Intelligence Committee from Oklahoma Democrat David L. Boren. But precedent was not on Bradley's side, and as chairman in the 100th Congress, Boren had generated no antagonism. Bradley's plan was quickly aborted for lack of support.

When he seemed adrift, even Bradley's supporters and admirers questioned the absence of a clear theme in his agenda. At the start of the 102nd Congress, Democratic Rep. Robert E. Andrews of New Jersey told a New Jersey magazine that Bradley needed to rethink and sharpen his message. "It was almost like the ghost of Dan Quayle got inside Bill Bradley," said Andrews. "I think he needs to start saying something again."

He did. Bradley seized upon civil rights, first blasting President Bush on the Senate floor in

July 1991 for allowing race to be invoked in the 1988 campaign with Willie Horton. A week later at the National Press Club, Bradley spoke from personal experience and implored blacks and whites to "begin an honest dialogue about race in America by clearing away the phony issues that can never bring us together."

Then, in the spring of 1992, Bradley again went to the Senate floor. In March, he lamented the plight of America's cities and called for new solutions to their problems that departed from both the liberal and conservative bromides of the past. A month later he returned, decrying the acquittal of Los Angeles police officers accused of using unnecessary force in the beating of Rodney L. King. "Just as we saw the missiles over Baghdad, or the murders in Tiananmen Square, so we saw the four police officers beating Rodney King. It was clear cut. Fifty-six times in 81 seconds.... Pow. Pow. Pow. Pow....," Bradley recited slowly.

That Bradley has failed to reach the level of influence that his boosters have wished should not detract from his contributions in the Senate. A hard-liner on dealing with the Soviet Union, Bradley stood out from many in his party in his wariness toward Mikhail S. Gorbachev's regime — and events in that nation during the early 1990s seemed to vindicate his opinions. He warned of a crackdown in the Baltic States and scolded Bush for his muted criticism of the situation there. Later, he opposed Bush's move to grant the Soviet Union normalized trade relations, without special protections for the Baltics. But, after the country's disintegration, Bradley urged wholehearted support for Russia.

Bradley also used the 101st Congress to reaffirm free trade policies. He was one of just nine Democrats to vote against a protectionist textile quota bill and one of the few Finance Committee members to praise the administration's April 1990 decision not to cite Japan for unfair trade practices. In 1992, he was an early supporter of the North American Free Trade Agreement to unite the economies of Mexico, Canada and the United States.

In many ways, though, Bradley's role in the remarkable legislative history of the tax law illustrates and defines this paradoxical man. On the tax bill, as throughout his public life, he went about his business without taking much notice of the customary rules of politics. His sheer determination and intellectual persistence kept the idea alive for years and, in the end, his seeming indifference to political advantage and to tactical maneuvering was crucial in pushing the bill through Congress. He succeeded where a craftier political operator — one whose suits were less rumpled, and whose demeanor was less professorial — might well have failed.

Long before President Ronald Reagan and others had adopted his tax ideas, Bradley was urging that the accumulated layers of deductions and special-interest provisions be replaced by a simpler system based on lower tax rates. Though the prospects for tax restructuring did not look particularly bright when Bradley presented his "Fair Tax" proposal in 1982, gradually his perseverance began to pay off.

A crucial player throughout, Bradley's most significant contribution came when the Senate Finance Committee drafted its bill in the spring of 1986. Patiently but to little avail, Bradley reminded his colleagues that they were reducing the bill's benefits for the middle class every time they approved a costly tax advantage for corporations and the wealthy.

When committee members realized they had a package that would cut federal revenues by about $30 billion, the bill seemed doomed. In desperation, Chairman Bob Packwood, R-Ore., huddled with Bradley and a few others to produce a radically new proposal that looked a lot like Bradley's original plan. With Bradley as intermediary between Packwood and House Ways and Means Chairman Dan Rostenkowski, D-Ill., conferees soon produced the compromise that led to the most profound change in the tax code in a generation.

With the passage of the tax bill, Bradley turned his attention to another idea of limited appeal and great complexity — relief from the huge debt burden carried by Third World nations, particularly those in Latin America.

As chairman at the time of Finance's International Debt Subcommittee, Bradley opposed Reagan administration policies to increase loans to developing nations, charging that debt was being piled on debt. In 1986, he proposed his own debt relief plan, calling for interest-rate reductions and selective forgiveness of loans, combined with new policies aimed at promoting economic growth within debtor nations.

Although allied with the Reagan administration on tax revision, Bradley was a forceful critic of Reagan's overall economic policies. He was the only member of Finance to vote against the 1981 tax cut, which he opposed as excessive and too generous to the wealthy. Since enactment of the 1986 tax law, Bradley has spent years fending off attempts to revise it. He has been an outspoken opponent of a cut in the capital gains tax, arguing that it would disproportionately benefit the rich. "If capital gains gets put back in the code," said Bradley, "it's a knife in the back of tax reform." In early 1993, Bradley did not hesitate to criticize his friend President Clinton's tax proposals in those places where he thought they went against the gospel of reform as written in 1986.

Bradley also has taken advantage of Finance's responsibility for taxes and federal health policies to become one of the leading and most innovative proponents of aid to the poor. A son of privilege who came of age in the civil rights and Great Society years, and a man grown rich thanks to his physical and intellectual gifts, Bradley exhibits a sense of social obligation to those lacking his advantages.

He has focused extensive time and energy toward children's issues; in the 101st Congress, he pushed a measure aimed at cutting infant mortality, helped pass legislation that reauthorized a program that helps pay for childhood vaccines, and got the Senate in 1990 to back an international effort to establish basic standards of protection for children.

It is not unusual for Bradley to act as a sort of Senate conscience or to scold, even if it is not a role that endears him to colleagues.

During action on the 1988 welfare-overhaul bill, Bradley embarrassed lawmakers into preserving a tax credit for child care. "We are paying for welfare reform with a tax on child care," Bradley objected. "I am against punishing women for their success." He proposed instead to end the business entertainment deduction for those making more than $360,000 a year. The Senate agreed, although another financing measure was substituted in conference.

He wages other fights that, taken alone, might not cost much. But collectively, they aggravate a good many senators. Bradley espouses higher cigarette taxes and other anti-smoking measures, provoking tobacco-state members. In the interests of his oil-consuming state, Bradley battles the oil industry and its allies. He unsuccessfully opposed elements of a 1992 energy bill that granted tax advantages to independent oil drillers.

On Intelligence, Bradley received special insight into Reagan administration policies against Nicaragua. Bradley stunned colleagues in 1986 by voting for a $100 million military aid package; he said he did so to keep pressure on Nicaragua's rulers to democratize. But by 1988, Bradley again opposed contra aid, citing Reagan's failure to pursue diplomatic moves. In 1989, he was one of just nine senators who voted against the compromise contra aid package, arguing that the Bush administration had failed to adequately define its policy toward the country.

In 1991, Bradley led Senate opposition to Bush's nomination of Robert M. Gates to head the CIA. Gates, a longtime CIA employee with close connections to former director William Casey, had been tarnished by the Iran-contra scandal. "Why do we want someone as director who has to carry the burden of the Casey years?" Bradley asked. Gates was confirmed, 64-31.

At Home: Under normal circumstances, the retirement of two-term GOP Gov. Thomas H. Kean after the 1989 election would have given Bradley an undisputed position as New Jersey's most popular officeholder. Republicans were not expected to put up much of a struggle as Bradley sought re-election in 1990.

But 1990 proved to be anything but normal circumstances, and Bradley came within a whisker of seeing his political career come to a halt. His 50 percent to 47 percent victory against an unheralded opponent was one of the more startling results of election night.

Democratic Gov. James J. Florio's $2.8 billion tax increase, enacted in response to a state budget deficit, enraged New Jersey voters and touched off waves of anti-tax protests. Democrats across the state scurried for cover as voters hunted for targets against whom to vent their fury.

With no state legislative seats on the ballot, the tallest target was the well-known two-term senator. Bradley had not voiced an opinion on the tax plan, but his Republican opponent, former state Public Utilities Commissioner Christine Todd Whitman, did everything in her power to equate a vote for her with a vote against Florio. One of her radio advertisements attacked Florio and exhorted voters to "send a message that higher taxes are just not acceptable . . . by supporting someone who's not just another politician." Her campaign also ordered bumper stickers that proclaimed: "Get Florio, Dump Bradley."

Bradley, who had been a force for tax reform in the mid-1980s, campaigned as if oblivious to the ferocious disapproval thousands of voters were expressing toward the tax package. He avoided commenting on the plan; armed with a massive fundraising advantage, he strove to avoid specifics altogether. Bradley's television ads were "warm and fuzzy," depicting the senator walking on a beach or playing basketball. In post-election interviews by The New York Times, voters said they were insulted by the ads, considering the economic problems confronting the state and federal governments.

Late in the campaign, when polls showed the race tightening, Bradley ran ads criticizing Whitman for backing tax increases when she was a freeholder in Somerset County.

Many voters said they did not intend to defeat Bradley, merely to send him and his fellow state Democrats a message. "I got the message! I got the message!" Bradley insisted after the election.

Bradley was already well-known in New Jersey from his basketball success with Princeton and the New York Knicks before he began his first campaign. During his 10-year pro career, Bradley was looking ahead to politics. In the off-season, he spoke at Democratic Party gatherings, worked as a reading teacher in Harlem and spent a summer doing administrative work in the federal Office of Economic Opportunity in Washington.

His interest in politics came early, nurtured by his father, a Republican banker in Crystal City, Mo., and by his days at Princeton, where he wrote his senior thesis on Harry S Truman's 1940 Senate campaign. Bradley considered returning to Missouri to seek office, but marriage to a New Jersey college professor and years of television exposure in the New York metropolitan area persuaded him to run in the

Garden State. To finance his 1978 Senate bid, he relied on some of his own wealth, then valued at nearly $1.6 million, and on fundraising events by such prominent friends as singer Paul Simon and actor Robert Redford.

With superior name recognition, Princeton and Oxford degrees and a clean-cut reputation, he scored an easy Democratic primary victory over Gov. Brendan T. Byrne's candidate, former state Treasurer Richard C. Leone.

Bradley drew as his general-election opponent Jeffrey Bell, a former campaign aide to Ronald Reagan. Bell had ousted four-term Sen. Clifford P. Case in the Republican primary, and his campaign had split the GOP badly. Without the liberal Case on the November ballot, labor and minorities felt free to go with Bradley. Bell spoke enthusiastically of the Kemp-Roth tax-cut plan, but his campaign lacked substance outside the issue of taxes. Though not much as a campaigner, Bradley made the most of his fresh face in a state dominated by organization politicians. He won with 55 percent.

His first term coincided with efforts, particularly by Kean, to improve the image of a state that had been derided for years as a chemical junkyard and a playground for organized crime. Bradley, with his intellectual bearing and distance from grimy organization politics, was a model for how New Jerseyans preferred their state to be viewed.

By 1984, Bradley was poised for a landslide re-election. Once clearly uncomfortable on the stump, he worked crowds now with more ease. He had learned the nuts and bolts of politics, assembling a talented political organization and showing an impressive ability to raise funds. He had $2 million salted away before the Republicans even came up with an opponent.

The candidate they finally settled on was Mary Mochary, the mayor of Montclair, who hitched her wagon to Reagan's re-election campaign, trying to convince Reagan supporters that the Democrat would stand in the way of the president's goals. It made no difference. Bradley won close to two-thirds of the vote.

Committees

Energy & Natural Resources (4th of 11 Democrats)
Water & Power (chairman); Public Lands, National Parks & Forests; Renewable Energy

Finance (4th of 11 Democrats)
Deficits, Debt Management & Long-Term Economic Growth (chairman); Health for Families & the Uninsured; International Trade

Special Aging (3rd of 11 Democrats)

Elections

1990 General		
Bill Bradley (D)	977,810	(50%)
Christine Todd Whitman (R)	918,874	(47%)
John L. Kucek (POP)	19,978	(1%)
Louis M. Stefanelli (LIBERT)	13,988	(1%)
1990 Primary		
Bill Bradley (D)	197,454	(92%)
Daniel Z. Seyler (D)	16,287	(8%)

Previous Winning Percentages: **1984** (64%) **1978** (55%)

Campaign Finance

	Receipts	Receipts from PACs		Expend-itures
1990				
Bradley (D)	$8,134,268	$1,062,309	(13%)	$9,563,942
Whitman (R)	$827,006	$10,782	(1%)	$801,660

Key Votes

1993	
Require unpaid family and medical leave	Y
Approve national "motor voter" registration bill	Y
Approve budget increasing taxes and reducing deficit	Y
Support president's right to lift military gay ban	Y
1992	
Approve school-choice pilot program	Y
Allow shifting funds from defense to domestic programs	Y
Oppose deeper cuts in spending for SDI	N
1991	
Approve waiting period for handgun purchases	Y
Raise senators' pay and ban honoraria	N
Authorize use of force in Persian Gulf	N
Confirm Clarence Thomas to Supreme Court	N

Voting Studies

	Presidential Support		Party Unity		Conservative Coalition	
Year	S	O	S	O	S	O
1992	23	68	80	10	18	74
1991	32	64	84	11	15	83
1990	32	66	80	19	14	86
1989	46	51	82	14	16	74
1988	48	45	81	9	22	70
1987	32	55	81	12	38	56
1986	51	48	66	24	36	61
1985	33	59	69	23	17	73
1984	42	45	66	25	28	60
1983	42	58	82	18	23	75
1982	37	63	87	13	14	85
1981	44	48	80	10	11	77

Interest Group Ratings

Year	ADA	AFL-CIO	CCUS	ACU
1992	85	91	22	4
1991	90	75	10	10
1990	94	67	8	13
1989	85	80	25	15
1988	75	75	25	9
1987	80	100	28	21
1986	85	87	31	23
1985	85	81	28	9
1984	85	64	29	35
1983	85	82	32	16
1982	100	85	29	15
1981	90	82	13	7

Frank R. Lautenberg (D)

Of Secaucus — Elected 1982; 2nd Term

Born: Jan. 23, 1924, Paterson, N.J.
Education: Columbia U., B.S. 1949.
Military Service: Army, 1942-46.
Occupation: Computer firm executive.
Family: Separated; four children.
Religion: Jewish.
Political Career: No previous office.
Capitol Office: 506 Hart Bldg. 20510; 224-4744.

In Washington: Lautenberg may never be counted among the lions of the Senate, but he has amassed a fair share of achievements and approaches his second re-election year in 1994 as a solid member of the chamber's middle rank.

In the 102nd Congress, Lautenberg was a major mover of the 1991 highway bill, owing to his pivotal position as chairman of the Transportation Subcommittee on Senate Appropriations. That legislation not only demonstrated his readiness to handle large tasks, it also funded a list of improvements Lautenberg can point to when he goes home.

When it came to the "demonstration projects" that measure legislators' individual clout, New Jersey got $35.7 million — more than New York or California.

Lautenberg's attention to the state has been his hallmark. First elected in 1982 pledging to put "New Jersey first," he won a second term in 1988 in part by demonstrating that he had. And throughout both terms he has concentrated on the responsibilities he has assumed in transportation and pollution policy.

Lautenberg's interests range well beyond the Jersey shores, however, and he is fortunate that his state provides a base to delve into issues of national and international scope as well. As a result, he has set up his Senate office much like a diversified business venture that explores all types of legislative activity.

But learning to make the system work should not be confused with liking it. Lautenberg came to politics from a business career, and, like many self-made men, he has trouble dealing with the slow grind of legislation. The tough, hard-driving entrepreneur has elbowed his way into issues where his presence was not always welcome. While he generally has done so without alienating colleagues, there have been exceptions.

In 1989, Lautenberg showed he had learned to play hardball when he steered a smoking ban on domestic airline flights through the Senate. A former two-pack-a-day smoker himself, he counseled tobacco farmers to "grow soybeans or something." This brought down the wrath of Republican Jesse Helms of North Carolina and other tobacco senators, who howled that Lautenberg had bypassed their committees by attaching the ban to an appropriations bill, Lautenberg snapped: "The committee system is safe. The flying public is not."

Lautenberg is among those who would confer Cabinet status on the Environmental Protection Agency (EPA), and in 1987 he became chairman of the Environment and Public Works subcommittee that has jurisdiction over EPA's "superfund" toxic waste cleanup program — an issue important to New Jersey, home to dozens of toxic waste sites bad enough to make the superfund list.

New Jersey has long resented New York City's sludge washing up on its shores, and Lautenberg has helped enact legislation to prevent recurrences. He has also pressed for laws against ocean dumping of plastics that do not degrade like organic materials. Allied with environmentalists, he was deeply involved in the ultimately successful effort to reauthorize the superfund program.

Lautenberg's subcommittee broadened its scope in the 101st Congress, enhancing its reach on New Jersey matters. Ocean dumping, drinking water, groundwater and indoor pollution were added to its jurisdiction.

In 1990, Lautenberg ran afoul of Republican Daniel R. Coats of Indiana, who sought to block New Jersey's export of garbage, some of which ends up in landfills. Regarding the issue as a campaign effort by Coats, Lautenberg managed in conference to remove the provision from the appropriations bill it was riding. Lautenberg was not as successful on 1990 clean air legislation. He broke with Majority Leader George J. Mitchell of Maine and led a floor fight for tighter controls on toxic air pollution caused in large part by auto emissions. The Senate rejected his amendment.

In the 102nd Congress Lautenberg was able to earmark funding in fiscal 1992 and 1993 spending bills for several New Jersey-related projects, including money to study the effects of sewer overflows off the New Jersey coast, to preserve an undersea research project based at Rutgers University and for continuing EPA research of sediment decontamination in New York Harbor.

Also in the 102nd Congress, Lautenberg pushed a bill through the Senate to expand the EPA's authority to monitor and help improve indoor air quality, but the House did not act on it. He also steered passage of a bill to reauthorize programs aimed at reducing levels of radon, a colorless, odorless gas that can cause lung damage, but the House failed to act on this as well.

Lautenberg's other subcommittee chairmanship, the Transportation Subcommittee on Appropriations, allows him to plunge even deeper into issues of rail, air and highway safety. He has pushed for more transportation funds for densely populated East Coast states and has fought attempts to eliminate federal funding for Amtrak.

In the 98th Congress, Lautenberg won legislation aimed at curbing drunken driving by forcing states to raise their minimum drinking age to 21. To get the bill through the Senate, Lautenberg worked out a "stick and carrot" compromise — threatening states that refused to raise their drinking age with the loss of up to $500 million a year in federal highway money, while also offering them incentives to try other measures to reduce drunken driving.

Lautenberg hounded the Reagan administration to rehire air-traffic controllers who were fired after they went on strike in 1981. Contending that the current controllers are so overworked that the Federal Aviation Administration is hard-pressed to keep the skies safe, Lautenberg tried to get the rehiring ban lifted. The Senate endorsed his proposal in 1986 but backed down when Reagan threatened to veto the transportation funding bill to which it was attached.

With his leverage increased in the 100th Congress, he continued to harass the FAA, saying it could make the system even safer with additional measures. He sought more money for air safety, including air-traffic control.

In the 102nd Congress Lautenberg clashed with the Bush administration over provisions in the fiscal 1993 transportation bill that would have helped flight attendants and other displaced airline employees. One provision would have limited flight attendants' working hours, and the other would have required a carrier picking up routes from a failed airline to give hiring priority to employees from that failed line. The Bush administration insisted that the provisions were unwise and unworkable and threatened a veto, so Senate sponsors backed down.

During the 101st Congress, Lautenberg got a seat on the Defense Appropriations subcommittee largely to try to save Fort Dix, a New Jersey army base slated for closing.

At Home: For the New York and Philadelphia TV stations that provide most of New Jersey's news coverage, Lautenberg's workmanlike performance on state issues has been pretty dull stuff, especially compared with the activities of senior Democratic Sen. Bill Bradley and former GOP Gov. Thomas H. Kean, both of whom have been players on the national stage in their parties. So when Lautenberg began his 1988 re-election campaign, he had a fairly low public profile.

But by the end of the contest, Lautenberg's name and deeds were widely known, and he had beaten back an aggressive challenge from Republican Pete Dawkins by 250,000 votes.

Dawkins was the national GOP's premier "résumé" candidate for the Senate in 1988. His life had been an unbroken string of accomplishments — winner of the Heisman Trophy (while playing for Army in 1958), a Rhodes scholar, the Army's youngest brigadier general, a high-ranking Pentagon official, a Wall Street financial executive. He tried to mold his golden image to political advantage, describing himself as a potential national leader in the Bradley-Kean mold. He denigrated Lautenberg as "the junior senator."

But Dawkins soon found his superstar image challenged. An article in a Manhattan business magazine described him as a failure in a variety of military and business positions, who still was promoted because of the public relations value of his all-American image. It was said that he had shopped for a state in which to seek public office and settled on New Jersey, moving in just before announcing his Senate candidacy.

While Dawkins denied that assertion and dismissed the magazine story, he and his campaign were caught in several instances of résumé-padding that had to be retracted. These included statements that Dawkins had played a major combat role in Vietnam and that he had been an innovator in international finance as an executive for a Wall Street brokerage firm.

Dawkins spent $1 million-plus in the spring to get his name in front of voters, but he entered the fall trailing Lautenberg in the polls. At that point, Lautenberg went on the attack, beginning with an unusual ad showing Dawkins himself making a flowery statement about the glories of New Jersey. "Be Real, Pete" was superimposed on the film clip, conveying Lautenberg's theme that Dawkins was a carpetbagger and a phony. Another ad accused Dawkins of viewing New Jersey as a pit stop on his route to national office.

Dawkins bemoaned Lautenberg's mudslinging but then got into a tit-for-tat war of negativism that sank to its lowest when Dawkins charged multimillionaire Lautenberg with using his Senate seat for personal profit.

Lautenberg's lead weathered the fierce exchanges, Dawkins' money dried up and the incumbent at the end switched to positive ads extolling his work for the state. In spite of George Bush's solid victory in New Jersey,

Lautenberg won 54 percent of the vote.

While Lautenberg had been involved for years as a Democratic activist and fundraiser — his $90,000 contribution to George McGovern's campaign in 1972 earned him a place on President Richard M. Nixon's "enemies list" — he had never sought office prior to his 1982 bid for the seat vacated by appointed Republican Sen. Nicholas F. Brady.

After winning with a plurality in a Democratic primary, he came from behind to defeat Republican Rep. Millicent Fenwick.

Both candidates were wealthy. But while Fenwick inherited her fortune, Lautenberg, the son of an immigrant silk mill worker, was a self-made man. The Democrat spent some $4 million of his own money to drive home that contrast. At one campaign stop, he pointed to the gap between his front teeth and said, "If my parents had money I wouldn't have this. I keep it as a badge of my roots."

Irreverent, witty and eccentric, Fenwick was frequently profiled and quoted in the national media and was a heroine to numerous good-government causes. She started out with a sizable lead over Lautenberg.

But Lautenberg overcame Fenwick's reformist credentials and personal popularity by painting her and the GOP as insensitive to working-class people. He touted himself as an expert on creating jobs, talking about how he had turned his company, Automatic Data Processing, from a three-man business into one of the world leaders in computer services.

To erase organized labor's doubts about him, Lautenberg advocated a minimum tax on corporations and elimination of the third year of Reagan's tax cut for those earning more than $40,000 per year. Labor finally went along with him against Fenwick, overlooking the absence of unions at ADP. Lautenberg said no one had tried to organize the firm.

With the endorsements of several major newspapers, the unions and such liberal forces as the National Organization for Women, Lautenberg showed that Fenwick's lead was soft. He hammered on her votes for the 1981 Reagan economic package. She could not equal his media effort, as she would not dip as heavily into her wealth and refused donations from political action committees. Lautenberg rejected her request that each side limit spending to $1.6 million. He won with 51 percent of the vote.

Committees

Appropriations (9th of 16 Democrats)
Transportation (chairman); Commerce, Justice, State & Judiciary; Defense; Foreign Operations; VA, HUD & Independent Agencies

Budget (6th of 12 Democrats)

Environment & Public Works (4th of 10 Democrats)
Superfund, Recycling & Solid Waste Management (chairman); Clean Water, Fisheries & Wildlife; Toxic Substances, Environmental Oversight, Research & Development

Small Business (10th of 12 Democrats)
Competitiveness, Capital Formation & Economic Opportunity; Export Expansion & Agricultural Development

Elections

1988 General		
Frank R. Lautenberg (D)	1,599,905	(54%)
Peter M. Dawkins (R)	1,349,937	(45%)
1988 Primary		
Frank R. Lautenberg (D)	362,072	(78%)
Elnardo J. Webster (D)	51,938	(12%)
Harold J. Young (D)	41,303	(10%)

Previous Winning Percentage: 1982 (51%)

Campaign Finance

	Receipts	Receipts from PACs		Expenditures
1988				
Lautenberg (D)	$7,087,476	$1,410,360	(20%)	$7,289,663
Dawkins (R)	$7,766,535	$855,144	(11%)	$7,616,249

Key Votes

1993	
Require unpaid family and medical leave	Y
Approve national "motor voter" registration bill	Y
Approve budget increasing taxes and reducing deficit	Y
Support president's right to lift military gay ban	Y
1992	
Approve school-choice pilot program	N
Allow shifting funds from defense to domestic programs	Y
Oppose deeper cuts in spending for SDI	N
1991	
Approve waiting period for handgun purchases	Y
Raise senators' pay and ban honoraria	N
Authorize use of force in Persian Gulf	N
Confirm Clarence Thomas to Supreme Court	N

Voting Studies

	Presidential Support		Party Unity		Conservative Coalition	
Year	S	O	S	O	S	O
1992	22	78	92	8	5	95
1991	31	69	89	11	10	90
1990	25	75	88	12	8	92
1989	49	50	87	12	24	76
1988	42	53	92	4	0	92
1987	33	63	87	6	19	72
1986	30	69	79	15	12	86
1985	28	69	85	14	7	92
1984	35	61	85	12	6	91
1983	40	56	77	20	14	80

Interest Group Ratings

Year	ADA	AFL-CIO	CCUS	ACU
1992	100	92	30	4
1991	95	67	10	5
1990	100	78	17	4
1989	80	90	29	7
1988	90	100	17	0
1987	85	89	33	8
1986	85	100	22	17
1985	90	95	32	4
1984	100	91	24	0
1983	85	94	26	16

1 Robert E. Andrews (D)

Of Bellmawr — Elected 1990; 2nd Term

Born: Aug. 4, 1957, Camden, N.J.
Education: Bucknell U., B.A. 1979; Cornell U., J.D. 1982.
Occupation: Professor.
Family: Single.
Religion: Episcopalian.
Political Career: Camden County Board of Chosen Freeholders, 1987-90, director, 1988-90.
Capitol Office: 1005 Longworth Bldg. 20515; 225-6501.

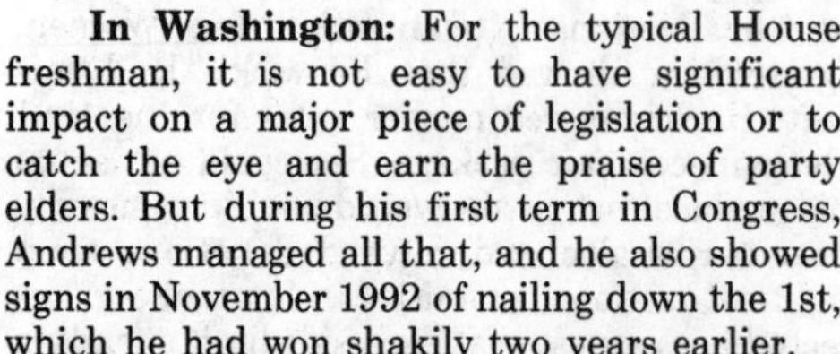

In Washington: For the typical House freshman, it is not easy to have significant impact on a major piece of legislation or to catch the eye and earn the praise of party elders. But during his first term in Congress, Andrews managed all that, and he also showed signs in November 1992 of nailing down the 1st, which he had won shakily two years earlier.

Andrews successfully pushed through the legislative maze a plan that would have the federal government provide direct loans to college students, a shift from the established practice of having the government guarantee loans that students obtain from private banks. Initially, the plan drew fire from Republicans, who questioned whether direct loans would truly be a cost-saver. Andrews argued strenuously that the new approach would save the government money and thus free up resources to provide more help for students. "This will be a true test of who supports corporate welfare and who doesn't," he said.

Andrews' detailed knowledge of the proposal and his tenacity in pushing it on the Education and Labor Committee impressed the panel's chairman, Michigan Democrat William D. Ford, who over the course of the 102nd came to regard Andrews as something of a protégé.

White House displeasure with the direct-loan plan prompted President Bush to threaten to veto the reauthorization of the Higher Education Act, of which it was a part. A House-Senate conference ultimately included in the reauthorization bill a limited version of the idea Andrews was pushing.

Under the Higher Eduction Act passed in 1992, 300 schools would participate in a direct loan project, and an income-contingent repayment approach would be tested. Thirty-five percent of the participating institutions would allow students to repay their loans according to how much money they earned after graduation. Other students would repay a fixed amount each month, regardless of how much money they earned.

In the opening months of the 103rd Congress, the direct loan plan stayed in the political spotlight. President Clinton included the proposal in his budget plan for fiscal 1994. (Clinton also advocated direct loans in his book "Putting People First.") Clinton's budget projected that the government would reap substantial savings by gradually replacing the existing guaranteed student loan system with a direct loan program.

Another of Andrews' first-term endeavors was sponsorship of legislation to require the Occupational Safety and Health Administration (OSHA) to target its inspections of work sites at companies with a high potential for serious, and perhaps fatal, injuries or exposure to toxic chemicals. The Education and Labor Committee incorporated Andrews' amendment into a bill that would have overhauled the OSHA Act of 1970. But the bill died at the end of 1992 when Democrats could not reach a compromise with Republicans who were concerned about an increased regulatory burden on businesses.

Andrews also boosted his political profile by joining with Pennsylvania Republican Curt Weldon (whose suburban Philadelphia district is across the Delaware River from Andrews') to form the Congressional Empowerment Caucus. The group aims to look for and promote innovative proposals to deal with the problems of the nation's poor. Caucus members hope to advance initiatives such as enterprise zones and tenant management of public housing, ideas advanced by the likes of former Housing and Urban Development Secretary Jack F. Kemp.

The bipartisan group, which includes more than a dozen members, held an early 1993 conference in Washington attended by about 250 community activists.

In March 1993, Andrews stood out as a Democratic defector — and showed his acute sensitivity to the issue of tax increases — by being one of only 11 in his party to vote against the Clinton administration's fiscal 1994 budget plan that included higher taxes. Andrews' 1990 House campaign was a strain because of fervent public opposition to a state tax increase that New Jersey Gov. James J. Florio had imposed. Florio served the 1st before Andrews. In the 1990

New Jersey 1

Southwest — Camden

More than two-thirds of the 1st District hails from Camden County, an amalgam of older suburbs, developing countryside and the city of Camden.

Once a major industrial center and Delaware River port, Camden now is one of the nation's most distressed cities. More than 70 percent of its children live below the poverty line. Businesses and middle-class residents have fled in droves to the suburbs, decimating the tax base.

City officials have pinned their hopes for economic revival on a new $52 million aquarium, the anchor for an ambitious waterfront redevelopment that is designed to draw suburban residents back into the city and provide a tourism lure for the neighbors across the river in Philadelphia.

Camden was once the hub of Camden County's powerful Democratic machine. Democratic Gov. James J. Florio was a product of the their farm system. But as population decreased precipitously over the past three decades, suburban GOP strength has made the county more competitive.

The city now holds less than 20 percent of county residents. Most of the county is in the 1st, with the exception of Cherry Hill and several smaller municipalities that are in the 3rd District.

Along the Delaware River, the cities are gritty and industry-oriented. The factories and oil storage yards of mostly working-class and poor Pennsauken, on the northern tip of the 1st, give it a Democratic character. Democrats can also find refuge in the older blue-collar towns farther south along the Black Horse Pike. East of Camden, the district becomes more suburban and Republican. Florio won 62 percent in the 1st in his gubernatorial bid in 1989, but after passing a $2.8 billion tax package in his first year in office, some of the most virulent opposition in the state came from the county's suburban voters. During the 1990 elections, Democrats lost control of the freeholder board for the first time in nearly two decades.

Republicans have experienced gains in the growing southern portion of Camden County and in suburban Gloucester County, which is shared with the 2nd. Roughly a quarter of the district's population hails from Gloucester County.

Commercial growth in and around Cherry Hill has spurred runaway population growth in Camden County locales such as Washington, middle-class Gloucester and white-collar Voorhees townships, though the growth is beginning to stabilize. Many residents moved to escape the older suburbs closer to Camden, but others sought the relatively easy access to Center City Philadelphia or Cherry Hill.

Not so long ago, Voorhees was a farming hamlet. But between 1970 and 1980, population more than doubled. From 1980 to 1990, it doubled again.

While Republican strength is more pronounced in the suburbs, the suburban vote also has an independent streak, with a tendency to split tickets. In 1992, Rep. Andrews breezed past a GOP assemblyman who represented many of these areas.

1990 Population: 594,630. White 465,929 (78%), Black 94,014 (16%), Other 34,687 (6%). Hispanic origin 37,350 (6%). 18 and over 435,857 (73%), 62 and over 84,651 (14%). Median age: 32.

race, Andrews promised to oppose all tax increases during his first term. He also has declined to take his congressional pay raise, instead using the money to establish a scholarship fund for high school students in his district.

At the start of his second term, Andrews signaled an interest in issues beyond the domestic front by taking a seat on the Foreign Affairs Committee. (He left the Small Business panel.)

At Home: In 1990, anger toward Florio among those he used to represent in Congress gave a scare to Andrews, his heir apparent.

Florio, who left the 1st in January 1990 to become governor, ignited a statewide voter revolt when he raised taxes early in his tenure as chief executive. Running to keep the vacant 1st in Democratic hands in November, Andrews had to sweat out a victory in a contest that originally figured to be a cakewalk for him. Also on Nov. 6, Andrews won the special election to fill Florio's vacant seat for the balance of the 101st Congress.

After Florio moved to Trenton, Andrews, director of the Camden County Board of Chosen Freeholders, looked like a good bet to succeed him in the 1st. A political ally of the governor, Andrews was known as a young reformer in the Florio mold. He lined up the backing of the Camden County Democratic Party organization and brushed off faint primary opposition.

His GOP opponent, businessman Daniel J. Mangini, backed into the nomination after a better-known candidate could not be found. While Mangini, a Gloucester County freeholder, directed his understaffed, underfunded effort from the back of an appliance store, Andrews was headquartered in the spacious end unit of a Somerdale shopping center. Andrews outraised Mangini by more than 6 to 1.

But the $2.8 billion increase in sales and income taxes Florio pushed through the Legislature in June leveled the playing field. Democrats at every level, alarmed at bumper stickers and signs across the state with exhortations such as "Flush Florio," attempted to distance themselves from the governor.

Mangini repeatedly referred to Andrews as "Florio's handpicked protégé," but Andrews held steady and refrained from directly repudiating Florio.

The "Florio factor" did not prove powerful enough to offset Andrews' money and organization. The Democrat carried all three counties in the 1st, winning with 54 percent.

Andrews' first foray into electoral politics came in 1986, after he had practiced law at several area firms and taught at Rutgers University College of Law. He was elected to the Camden County Board of Chosen Freeholders and two years later was chosen freeholder director by the board.

Although Andrews' experience was in county government, during his initial House campaign he spoke smoothly on local as well as federal issues, and he moved easily among both inner-city and suburban voters.

In 1992, having employed the advantages of incumbency to establish a stronger position in the 1st, Andrews piled up 67 percent of the vote against a credible opponent.

Committees

Education & Labor (13th of 28 Democrats)
Human Resources; Labor Standards, Occupational Health & Safety; Postsecondary Education

Foreign Affairs (15th of 27 Democrats)
Europe & the Middle East; International Operations

Elections

1992 General		
Robert E. Andrews (D)	153,525	(67%)
Lee A. Solomon (R)	65,123	(29%)
James E. Smith (PLPFVET)	3,761	(2%)
Jerry Zeldin (LIBERT)	2,641	(1%)
1990 General †		
Robert E. Andrews (D)	73,522	(54%)
Daniel J. Mangini (R)	57,801	(43%)
Jerry Zeldin (LIBERT)	1,599	(1%)
Walter E. Konstanty (PH)	1,431	(1%)
William Henry Harris (POP)	1,078	(1%)

† Elected to a full term and to fill a vacancy at the same time.

District Vote for President

1992

D 118,060 (48%)
R 78,095 (32%)
I 48,157 (20%)

Campaign Finance

	Receipts	Receipts from PACs		Expend-itures
1992				
Andrews (D)	$758,301	$345,800	(46%)	$762,588
Solomon (R)	$176,601	$22,631	(13%)	$176,586
1990				
Andrews (D)	$542,535	$236,190	(44%)	$541,960
Mangini (R)	$83,705	$23,850	(28%)	$79,662

Key Votes

1993	
Require parental notification of minors' abortions	N
Require unpaid family and medical leave	Y
Approve national "motor voter" registration bill	Y
Approve budget increasing taxes and reducing deficit	N
Approve economic stimulus plan	Y
1992	
Approve balanced-budget constitutional amendment	Y
Close down space station program	N
Approve U.S. aid for former Soviet Union	N
Allow shifting funds from defense to domestic programs	Y
1991	
Extend unemployment benefits using deficit financing	Y
Approve waiting period for handgun purchases	Y
Authorize use of force in Persian Gulf	N

Voting Studies

	Presidential Support		Party Unity		Conservative Coalition	
Year	S	O	S	O	S	O
1992	38	58	78	18	50	48
1991	35	64	78	18	41	59

Interest Group Ratings

Year	ADA	AFL-CIO	CCUS	ACU
1992	70	83	38	32
1991	70	92	10	15

2 William J. Hughes (D)

Of Ocean City — Elected 1974; 10th Term

Born: Oct. 17, 1932, Salem, N.J.
Education: Rutgers U., A.B. 1955, J.D. 1958.
Occupation: Lawyer.
Family: Wife, Nancy L. Gibson; four children.
Religion: Episcopalian.
Political Career: Cape May County assistant prosecutor, 1960-70; Democratic nominee for U.S. House, 1970; Ocean City solicitor, 1970-74.
Capitol Office: 241 Cannon Bldg. 20515; 225-6572.

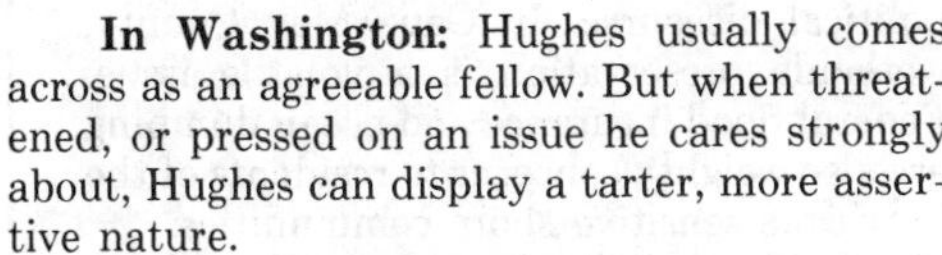

In Washington: Hughes usually comes across as an agreeable fellow. But when threatened, or pressed on an issue he cares strongly about, Hughes can display a tarter, more assertive nature.

The trials of the 102nd Congress — on Capitol Hill and back home in New Jersey — pushed the limits of his patience.

After a string of easy re-election campaigns, Hughes struggled for survival in 1992, targeted by a feisty state legislator and the National Rifle Association. Hughes battled his way to a 56 percent win, his lowest election tally ever. In Washington, however, where Hughes sits on the Judiciary Committee, the NRA generally has held the upper hand.

Stubborn and something of a loner, Hughes is a diligent member who pursues complicated matters.

After dedicating more than a decade on Capitol Hill to crime-related policy — he was chairman of the Crime Subcommittee from 1981-91 — Hughes shifted emphasis in the 102nd as he took over Judiciary's Subcommittee on Intellectual Property and Judicial Administration.

As chairman, he ushered into law new copyright protections for music, written materials and information contained on computer software. The recording fee bill adds royalty fees to digital tapes and recording equipment to help cover financial losses from illegal copying.

At the start of the 103rd, Hughes and his Senate counterpart, Dennis DeConcini of Arizona, announced they would push legislation to end the Copyright Royalty Tribunal, a three-member commission that sets copyright fees for jukebox records and television programs rebroadcast on cable stations.

The subcommittee also has jurisdiction over federal courts and prisons. In 1992, he ran a series of hearings on prison conditions and promised to continue the effort in 1993. His bill providing money for alternatives to incarceration, such as "boot camps," was signed into law in the 101st.

During his chairmanship of the Crime Subcommittee, Hughes left his mark on the law enforcement provisions of the 1986, 1988 and 1990 drug bills, the 1984 overhaul of the federal criminal code, a stronger law against child pornography and a measure to ban "plastic" guns.

When he sets his mind to it, Hughes can use his place between Judiciary liberals and the more conservative House to moderate dissent. A supporter of the death penalty in certain instances, Hughes offered the "racial justice" language adopted by the House in 1990. Although his amendment diluted language sought by liberals on Judiciary, it maintained the basic premise that there should be more precautions against racism in sentencing. The measure was dropped, however, in conference.

Hughes' frustrations on crime legislation have been matched by those on gun control. Though he owns hunting rifles, his sympathies lie with law enforcement officials who favor certain restrictions on gun ownership.

Once Hughes did find common ground with the NRA, and it helped bring about a rare victory. In the 100th Congress, the NRA reluctantly joined a coalition of police groups in opposing the sale of firearms made mostly of plastic, which could not be picked up by conventional metal detectors. Hughes was instrumental in obtaining congressional passage of the bill.

After fighting for years to pass a mandatory waiting period for handgun purchases, Hughes finally has a president more sympathetic to the issue. "If you pass the Brady bill, I'll sure sign it," President Clinton told Congress in February 1993.

During the 101st and 102nd, Hughes sponsored legislation to limit private damage suits under the federal anti-racketeering law known as RICO. Hughes' proposal required federal judges to throw out civil RICO suits unless they meet strict criteria, including that the triple-damages remedy in the RICO law be "appropriate because of the magnitude or significance of the injury." The Judiciary Committee has supported the legislation, but it has gotten no further in the past.

When not preoccupied with Judiciary,

New Jersey 2

South — Atlantic City; Vineland

The Mason-Dixon Line does not cross the Delaware River, but if it did, the 2nd would fit right in with the South. Like the rest of South Jersey (Burlington and all counties south of it), the 2nd is generally less affluent than the northern half of the state, median home values are lower and the area is less densely populated.

Though New Jersey is known better as an urban and suburban state, agriculture is a leading industry in the 2nd. The district is also known for its dislike of gun control measures.

Taking in all of Atlantic, Cape May, Cumberland and Salem counties — along with part of Gloucester County and one township from Burlington — the 2nd covers the bottom portion of New Jersey.

The towns along the Delaware River are more industrialized, and many residents work in the chemical plants across the river from Wilmington and in refineries on the Jersey side, just south of Philadelphia.

Farther inland, in Salem and Cumberland counties, there are pockets of rural poverty in an agricultural area that is one of the nation's leading egg producers. There is glass-making in Vineland and Millville.

The 2nd's best-known city is Atlantic City (Atlantic County). Once known as "Sodom by the Sea" for its seedy nightlife, this resort town fell on hard times before gambling was legalized in the mid-1970s.

But while glitzy casinos and hotels have sprouted up on the Boardwalk and property values have soared, the prosperity has been slow to trickle down to the mainly black and poor residents of the city.

The shore communities south of Atlantic City, in Cape May County, have fared much better. From north to south, the county takes in family-oriented Ocean City, wealthy Avalon and Stone Harbor, then rowdier Wildwood.

On the southern tip, the city of Cape May has prospered as GOP-voting retirees have flocked to this old seaside resort of Victorian homes and small cottages.

The coastal character — and vast pinelands west of the shoreline — places environmental issues at the forefront of political discourse. In Cape May County, wetlands preservation is a volatile issue. Federal flood insurance and ocean dumping are also weighty concerns to residents of the hurricane-sensitive shore communities.

Politically, the 2nd has a Republican tilt. Ronald Reagan and George Bush easily carried it in 1984 and 1988, but in statewide elections, Democrats have fared well.

Sen. Bill Bradley won every county in the district in his tight 1990 victory; then-Democratic Rep. James J. Florio also carried all the counties in his successful 1989 gubernatorial bid. In 1992, Bush managed to hold only two counties that are wholly within the district — agricultural Salem and Cape May.

In the more industrial towns such as Bridgeton, Millville and Vineland — which has a significant number of Hispanic and black voters — and in Atlantic City, Democrats have an advantage.

1990 Population: 594,630. White 480,000 (81%), Black 83,902 (14%), Other 30,728 (5%). Hispanic origin 39,494 (7%). 18 and over 450,384 (76%), 62 and over 105,491 (18%). Median age: 34.

Hughes usually can be found defending the interests of his coastal district as the second-ranking Democrat on the Merchant Marine and Fisheries Committee.

On June 30, 1992, the final shipment of sewage sludge left New York City on a barge headed for the ocean, marking the end of a 17-year effort by Hughes to stop the dumping. (The anti-sewage dumping legislation, passed in the 100th Congress, also included Hughes' provisions making it a crime to dispose of medical waste in U.S. coastal or navigable waters.)

In 1992, President Bush signed into law Hughes' bill designating 129 miles of the Great Egg Harbor River as "wild and scenic."

Blueberries thrive in the sandy soil of Hughes' coastal district, and when a series of record harvests caused a glut in the frozen blueberry market in 1990, Hughes successfully lobbied the Department of Agriculture to buy 6 million pounds of the berries for school menus and other nutrition programs.

Hughes was poised to assume the chairmanship of the Select Aging Committee at the start of the 103rd. As pressure mounted to eliminate the panels, which cost about $3.5 million annually, Hughes proposed reducing the committee staff from 37 to 18. The offer was not enough to spare the committee.

At Home: Though Hughes votes a standard Democratic line on most issues, he occasionally goes against the grain. In the 100th, for instance, he was the only New Jersey Democrat to oppose the retaliatory Gephardt "fair trade" amendment. Such actions, combined with his tough-on-crime image, have made him a popular figure in the Republican-leaning 2nd District.

His closest scare came in 1992, when state Rep. Frank A. LoBiondo staged a noisy and well-publicized challenge. Hughes had not faced a tough opponent in years; only once was he re-elected with less than 60 percent of the vote. But with the NRA in his corner, LoBiondo spooked Hughes with his aggressive tactics aimed at convincing voters Hughes had become "part of the problem."

If Hughes was startled at first by the intensity of the assault, he soon shook it off. He accelerated his fundraising efforts and fought back as aggressively as LoBiondo; Hughes won with 56 percent.

Now the dean of the delegation, Hughes was Ocean City solicitor in 1974 when he challenged four-term GOP Rep. Charles W. Sandman Jr. He had run against Sandman once before, in 1970, coming within 6,000 votes. The second time he began in a stronger position, because Sandman had hurt himself badly with slashing attacks on President Nixon's detractors during the 1974 impeachment debate. The result was as much a judgment of Sandman as it was a triumph for Hughes; the incumbent drew only 41 percent.

Committees

Judiciary (5th of 21 Democrats)
Intellectual Property & Judicial Administration (chairman)

Merchant Marine & Fisheries (2nd of 29 Democrats)
Coast Guard & Navigation; Fisheries Management

Elections

1992 General

William J. Hughes (D)	132,465	(56%)
Frank A. LoBiondo (R)	98,315	(41%)
Roger W. Bacon (LIBERT)	2,575	(1%)

1990 General

William J. Hughes (D)	98,734	(88%)
William A. Kanengiser (POP)	13,246	(12%)

Previous Winning Percentages: **1988** (66%) **1986** (68%) **1984** (63%) **1982** (68%) **1980** (57%) **1978** (66%) **1976** (62%) **1974** (57%)

District Vote for President

1992

D 101,718 (41%)
R 97,696 (39%)
I 50,870 (20%)

Campaign Finance

	Receipts	Receipts from PACs		Expend-itures
1992				
Hughes (D)	$500,308	$219,025	(44%)	$579,771
LoBiondo (R)	$324,027	$39,862	(12%)	$284,773
1990				
Hughes (D)	$282,731	$91,270	(32%)	$211,686

Key Votes

1993	
Require parental notification of minors' abortions	N
Require unpaid family and medical leave	Y
Approve national "motor voter" registration bill	Y
Approve budget increasing taxes and reducing deficit	Y
Approve economic stimulus plan	Y
1992	
Approve balanced-budget constitutional amendment	N
Close down space station program	Y
Approve U.S. aid for former Soviet Union	N
Allow shifting funds from defense to domestic programs	Y
1991	
Extend unemployment benefits using deficit financing	Y
Approve waiting period for handgun purchases	Y
Authorize use of force in Persian Gulf	Y

Voting Studies

	Presidential Support		Party Unity		Conservative Coalition	
Year	**S**	**O**	**S**	**O**	**S**	**O**
1992	23	77	83	17	27	71
1991	29	68	79	18	41	59
1990	26	73	79	19	39	59
1989	30	69	84	14	51	49
1988	30	68	85	15	47	50
1987	24	75	79	17	49	51
1986	28	72	78	20	32	68
1985	30	70	76	23	40	60
1984	41	58	71	24	46	47
1983	34	66	74	26	38	62
1982	43	57	80	19	40	59
1981	41	58	64	31	41	59

Interest Group Ratings

Year	ADA	AFL-CIO	CCUS	ACU
1992	80	83	25	20
1991	70	92	33	26
1990	78	91	38	13
1989	70	75	50	14
1988	70	100	43	16
1987	80	81	27	9
1986	75	79	22	9
1985	75	82	41	19
1984	60	46	40	25
1983	70	82	25	17
1982	80	90	27	18
1981	65	71	24	13

3 H. James Saxton (R)

Of Vincentown — Elected 1984; 5th Term

Born: Jan. 22, 1943, Nicholson, Pa.

Education: East Stroudsburg State College, B.A. 1965; Temple U., 1967-68.

Occupation: Real estate broker; elementary school teacher.

Family: Separated; two children.

Religion: Methodist.

Political Career: N.J. Assembly, 1976-82; N.J. Senate, 1982-84.

Capitol Office: 438 Cannon Bldg. 20515; 225-4765.

In Washington: Saxton is steadily emerging from the shadows, especially on the Armed Services Committee.

While still no mover-and-shaker, his questions on a wide range of issues are frank and intelligent and far more frequent than in his earlier years. And he has begun to attract the notice of others.

One of the major battles of Saxton's tenure has been over the closing of Fort Dix, a move first proposed in late 1988 by the Defense secretary's commission charged with drawing up recommendations for closing military bases.

Fort Dix and its 4,600 base-related jobs lie partly in the 3rd District. Saxton and Republican Rep. Christopher H. Smith, whose 4th District contains the other part of Fort Dix, objected to the commission's findings. On the House floor in early 1989, Saxton said the commission used incomplete information on Fort Dix; he called the base-closing plan "flawed, seriously flawed." But an effort to kill the plan failed, 43-381.

Saxton continued to press for relief, but to no avail. When he was named to Armed Services, Saxton made no promises about Fort Dix, only that he would make sure "New Jersey gets its fair share" of military money and projects.

The 1991 base-closing plan recommended shutting down Fort Dix, and all subsequent attempts by Saxton and the rest of the New Jersey delegation to save the base have been for naught. The base retained its military hospital and a reserve presence and the base is now being used by agencies such as the FBI and the Bureau of Prisons. But the site no longer employs anything close to the number that it used to.

Another issue Saxton has spoken up on is the C-17 transport plane, which he has supported throughout its myriad development troubles. "As we bring our forces back from overseas, there's going to be a time when we want to get them back there," he said.

He also introduced a bill in March 1991 that would urge the establishment of an international military tribunal that would prosecute war crimes arising out of the Persian Gulf War.

"We continue to hear of sadistic atrocities Iraqi soldiers committed against Kuwaiti citizens," he said as he introduced the bill. "And we are incensed by the fact that Kuwait's oilfields are being burned and that its people were being executed even as Iraq was preparing to surrender.

"We all believe Saddam should be held accountable. We should bring him to justice with the same international cooperation we displayed in expelling him from Kuwait."

When Saxton moved to the Armed Services Committee, he gave up a slot on the Banking panel. But he still sits on the Merchant Marine Committee.

There he carefully tends to the ample environmental concerns of his district, with its high concentration of hazardous waste sites.

He began the 102nd Congress as ranking Republican on the Oversight and Investigations Subcommittee. In 1988, after a summer of continued reports of medical waste washing up on New Jersey beaches, Saxton and New Jersey Democrat William J. Hughes, a fellow Merchant Marine member, sponsored a bill to ban the dumping of medical waste in oceans and the Great Lakes.

In the 102nd, Saxton introduced a bill that would require each state to mirror New Jersey's current practice of monitoring waste levels along the coast and notifying beachgoers when levels are unhealthy. It was a weaker version of a bill he wrote in 1990 that would have also required states to shut down beaches that do not meet Environmental Protection Agency standards.

Despite Saxton's efforts, the 1990 bill failed in the waning weeks of the 101st, and the second effort stalled in the Senate after passing in the House by voice vote.

Saxton advocates creating the National Institutes for the Environment to fund environmental research. He and New Jersey Democratic Sen. Bill Bradley, sponsor of a companion bill, testified before the House Science Commit-

New Jersey 3

South central— Cherry Hill

On the surface, the Camden and Burlington County suburbs would seem to have little in common with the shore communities of Ocean County. But both share an affinity for Republican candidates and concerns about the spiraling growth that is affecting their quality of life.

Only four Camden County municipalities are included in the 3rd, but they include Cherry Hill, a city that has experienced uninterrupted growth over the past three decades as a result of out-migration from Philadelphia and Camden.

The new housing developments, office parks and shopping malls have changed the complexion of this once-rural hamlet, but at a price: traffic congestion.

The young, mostly white suburbanites who live here lean Republican, but they are an independent lot.

During the political tax revolt spurred by Democratic Gov. James J. Florio's 1990 tax increase — while Democrats across the state were being swept out of the Legislature — Republicans actually lost a local state Senate seat. In 1992, voters split their tickets for Bill Clinton and GOP Rep. Saxton.

A much larger share of the 3rd District vote is cast in the suburbs of Burlington County. Democrats run well in the industrial towns along the Delaware River, and in Willingboro, a Levittown-style community which is more than 50 percent black. Cinnaminson and Delran are more affluent, though not as upscale as Moorestown.

West of these towns, suburban sprawl takes over. Population has exploded in places such as Mount Laurel and Evesham, which are situated by highways that facilitate white-collar employees who commute to Trenton, Philadelphia and corporate facilities in north Jersey.

Away from the riverfront, the vote is more Republican. Though Clinton carried the county by more than 5,000 votes, Saxton won in a breeze in 1992.

After Burlington County, the second-largest population cluster is in rapidly growing Ocean County (which is split between the 3rd and 4th districts). Many live in the Toms River area, and the rest are scattered in smaller, seaside communities. Retirees are an important constituency; there are age-restricted housing developments in Berkeley Township.

Retirees have not been the only ones moving to Ocean County. The 1950s extension of the Garden State Parkway to the shore area made the area attractive for commuters and spawned Parkway bedroom communities. Closer to the fragile Atlantic coastline, barrier beach development has pitted builders against environmentalists.

The newcomers have helped keep Ocean County in the GOP column. Florio carried the county in his successful 1989 gubernatorial bid, but a year later, GOP Senate challenger Christine Todd Whitman bested Democratic Sen. Bill Bradley. Of the three counties that make up the 3rd, Ocean was the only one to back George Bush in 1992.

1990 Population: 594,630. White 528,533 (89%), Black 47,565 (8%), Other 18,532 (3%). Hispanic origin 15,477 (3%). 18 and over 451,821 (76%), 62 and over 108,169 (18%). Median age: 36.

tee in the 101st Congress in behalf of legislation to have the National Academy of Sciences study the feasibility of such an institute.

As Saxton has gained more attention in Congress, he has begun to play a role in party politics. He is now a vice chairman of the House GOP campaign committee.

At Home: Saxton struggled to win the nomination for the seat left open by the 1984 death of GOP Rep. Edwin B. Forsythe. But after surviving a tough primary, he has had little trouble in this heavily Republican district.

A state legislator for eight years, Saxton came in with the backing of the strong GOP organization in Burlington County, the most populous in the district. But the district also includes Camden and Ocean counties, and each supplied a candidate.

M. Dean Haines and his Ocean County organization gave Saxton his stiffest challenge. Assemblyman John A. Rocco of Camden County entered the primary, but his differences with his county organization resulted in the GOP endorsement of Saxton.

The lesser-known Haines concentrated his efforts on Ocean County, where turnout was traditionally high. Saxton, with his large state Senate constituency, ran ads on Philadelphia TV stations to reach voters in Camden and Burlington counties.

The strategy paid off. With Saxton and Haines winning on their home turf, the contest was decided in Camden County. Saxton's second-place showing behind Rocco there allowed him to win the primary by about 1,400 votes.

In 1990, Saxton faced aggressive young

Democrat John H. Adler, a former Cherry Hill City Council member. With voters furious over Democratic Gov. James J. Florio's $2.8 billion tax package and looking for victims at the polls, the House race attracted a decade-high turnout. While 1990 may have been a dicey year for Democrats elsewhere, Adler managed to hold Saxton under 60 percent for the first time.

In 1992, Saxton beat Timothy Ryan, 59 percent to 37 percent.

Committees

Armed Services (13th of 22 Republicans)
Military Acquisition; Military Installations & Facilities

District of Columbia (3rd of 4 Republicans)
Government Operations & Metropolitan Affairs (ranking); Fiscal Affairs & Health

Merchant Marine & Fisheries (4th of 18 Republicans)
Environment & Natural Resources (ranking); Oceanography, Gulf of Mexico & the Outer Continental Shelf

Post Office & Civil Service (9th of 9 Republicans)
Oversight & Investigations

Joint Economic

Elections

1992 General		
H. James Saxton (R)	151,368	(59%)
Timothy E. Ryan (D)	94,012	(37%)
Helen L. Radder (LIBERT)	2,711	(1%)
1992 Primary		
H. James Saxton (R)	25,388	(89%)
Frank W. Drake (R)	3,044	(11%)
1990 General		
H. James Saxton (R)	100,537	(58%)
John H. Adler (D)	68,286	(39%)
Howard Scott Pearlman (WWW)	4,178	(2%)

Previous Winning Percentages: 1988 (69%) **1986** (65%) **1984 *** (61%)

** Elected to a full term and to fill a vacancy at the same time.*

District Vote for President

1992

D 114,503 (40%)
R 113,583 (40%)
I 54,989 (19%)

Campaign Finance

	Receipts	Receipts from PACs		Expend-itures
1992				
Saxton (R)	$647,329	$278,875	(43%)	$416,807
Ryan (D)	$30,561	$6,950	(23%)	$30,015
1990				
Saxton (R)	$628,142	$250,149	(40%)	$730,989
Adler (D)	$210,993	$56,599	(27%)	$203,147

Key Votes

1993	
Require parental notification of minors' abortions	Y
Require unpaid family and medical leave	Y
Approve national "motor voter" registration bill	N
Approve budget increasing taxes and reducing deficit	N
Approve economic stimulus plan	N
1992	
Approve balanced-budget constitutional amendment	Y
Close down space station program	N
Approve U.S. aid for former Soviet Union	Y
Allow shifting funds from defense to domestic programs	N
1991	
Extend unemployment benefits using deficit financing	?
Approve waiting period for handgun purchases	Y
Authorize use of force in Persian Gulf	Y

Voting Studies

	Presidential Support		Party Unity		Conservative Coalition	
Year	**S**	**O**	**S**	**O**	**S**	**O**
1992	73	25	79	18	88	10
1991	69	29	76	19	86	11
1990	57	42	68	29	78	22
1989	65	33	50	48	83	15
1988	57	42	80	19	82	16
1987	58	42	73	27	91	9
1986	64	34	67	33	78	22
1985	61	39	81	19	76	24

Interest Group Ratings

Year	ADA	AFL-CIO	CCUS	ACU
1992	15	50	75	80
1991	10	27	67	74
1990	33	17	92	63
1989	20	42	100	64
1988	30	50	79	72
1987	24	38	73	52
1986	30	57	56	64
1985	15	12	82	81

4 Christopher H. Smith (R)

Of Robbinsville — Elected 1980; 7th Term

Born: March 4, 1953, Rahway, N.J.
Education: Trenton State College, B.A. 1975.
Occupation: Sporting goods executive.
Family: Wife, Marie Hahn; four children.
Religion: Roman Catholic.
Political Career: GOP nominee for U.S. House, 1978.
Capitol Office: 2353 Rayburn Bldg. 20515; 225-3765.

In Washington: Smith represents a largely urban and industrial district, and his pro-labor sentiments have contributed to him compiling one of the more centrist records among House Republicans. On average over the 12-year course of the Reagan and Bush administrations, he opposed the stated White House position on House floor votes 49 percent of the time.

But if voters in Smith's district know that he takes positions such as supporting family and medical leave and backing a waiting period for handgun purchases, the name Smith has made for himself nationally is as a staunch opponent of abortion.

Smith sees his work against abortion and his international interests on the Foreign Affairs Committee as springing from the same concern for human rights.

"In this society, the least and the throw-aways are the unborn. In many of these other societies, it's the person who's different in another way.... But to me it's anyone who's weak and vulnerable," he told the Asbury Park Press.

Vulnerable was how Democrats regarded Smith after anti-abortion activists helped him upset scandal-plagued Democratic Rep. Frank Thompson Jr. in 1980. But Smith survived the counterattack in 1982 and since then has topped 60 percent in each of five re-elections.

Smith's fight agaist abortion has long been at the top of his legislative agenda. When the Supreme Court in early 1989 took up *Webster v. Reproductive Health Services* — involving a Missouri law that restricted abortion and declared life as beginning at conception — Smith led a group of House signatories to a legal brief urging the Supreme Court to use the case to overturn the 1973 *Roe v. Wade* decision that legalized abortion.

The court did not overturn *Roe* but did uphold the Missouri law, thus giving tacit permission for other states to pass restrictive abortion laws. Smith applauded the decision, but said he would continue to pursue federal legislation limiting abortion.

But the upswing in abortion rights activism after the *Webster* decision emboldened abortion-rights members of Congress, and during the 102nd Smith had to fight to stop efforts to lift the federal bans against abortion counseling at federally funded facilities, against fetal tissue research and against allowing abortions at overseas military hospitals.

During debates on abortion, Smith's arguments typically cut to the quick: He said the controversy about abortion counseling "isn't about free speech. It is about taxpayer subsidized abortion advocacy." He warned that the military hospitals would become "abortion mills." In 1990, he said, "The 'choice' rhetoric is hollow and shallow. A choice to do what? To dismember a child?"

Smith usually was fighting an uphill battle in the House during the 102nd, but he had President Bush's veto pen to back him up. However, Bill Clinton's inauguration as president in 1993 put the federal government on an abortion rights track, as Clinton had promised during his 1992 campaign.

Smith has taken his anti-abortion crusade international through his work on the Foreign Affairs Committee. Since 1985, he has led successful efforts to block U.S. funding for population control programs run by the International Planned Parenthood Foundation and the U.N. population fund. Smith accuses the latter organization of supporting China's "one-child-per-couple" policy, which he says relies on forced abortions and sterilizations.

Smith is an active member of the Foreign Affairs Subcommittee on Human Rights, and a member of the Commission on Security and Cooperation in Europe (the Helsinki commission); Bush appointed Smith in 1989 as a congressional delegate to the United Nations, where he served on the Human Rights Committee.

Smith's "pro-life" politics include supporting additional funding for child health care in the Third World. In 1989, he attached an amendment to a foreign aid bill authorizing $245 million for "child survival" programs, such as immunization; in doing so, he defied Bush's express request that Congress limit its "earmarks" for specific foreign aid programs. He

New Jersey 4

Central — Trenton

Stretching from Trenton to the Atlantic Ocean, the 4th covers the state's midsection, an area where the Garden State begins to make the transition from South Jersey to North Jersey.

The motto of the state capital — and the district's largest city — is "Trenton Makes, the World Takes." That catchy phrase refers to the city's industrial heritage, but nowadays, the city makes less and takes a lot more federal aid.

Minorities make up more than half the city's population, though there are a few remaining white ethnic enclaves such as the Italian section of Chambersburg.

Hispanics and blacks, when combined with the contingent of state employees, help Trenton turn out a fairly sizable Democratic vote. It is usually enough to put Mercer County into the Democratic column in statewide elections. In 1988, Michael S. Dukakis edged out George Bush there, and Democratic Sen. Frank R. Lautenberg carried the county by more than 30,000 votes in his competitive reelection bid. In 1992, Mercer backed Bill Clinton, though he lost the district. At the same time, Mercer gave GOP Rep. Smith a relatively easy victory.

Countering Trenton is a burgeoning suburban voice, made up mostly of Trenton expatriates. These white suburbanites are more independent voters who, at the federal level, tend to prefer GOP candidates.

Many blue-collar Irish and Italians settled in Hamilton Township after leaving Trenton. Its population has boomed as Trenton's declined; now it is only slightly smaller.

Ocean County is the site of the top concentration of voters in the district. If a Democratic candidate comes out ahead in Mercer, that lead is likely to be blunted by the Republican advantage in Ocean County. Retirement communities have sprouted up in Lakewood, and in Brick and Manchester townships, sparking creation of new service industries geared to the elderly. Ocean County — which the 4th shares with the 3rd District — houses one of the largest concentrations of retirees in the Northeast.

These retirees come out in large numbers on Election Day, enough so that in 1992, Ocean County easily bested Mercer County in voter turnout percentage in the 4th.

Parts of Monmouth and Burlington counties round out the district. The Monmouth County portion includes some fast-growing inland communities such as Howell, where white-collar employees commute to Trenton or New York City. Monmouth voters backed Smith by a better than 2-1 margin; Bush outdistanced Clinton by more than 7,000 ballots.

The Burlington County portion is slightly smaller than Monmouth's but more Democratic. The industrial areas closer to the Delaware River favor Democrats, but farther east, Republicans fare better because of places such as Mansfield, a community where posh housing developments are growing in number, facilitated by access to Princeton, Philadelphia and Trenton.

1990 Population: 594,630. White 497,624 (84%), Black 74,309 (12%), Other 22,697 (4%). Hispanic origin 31,141 (5%). 18 and over 451,927 (76%), 62 and over 115,364 (19%). Median age: 35.

also went against the Bush administration in demanding human rights improvements in China as a condition for renewing the country's most-favored-nation trading status.

Smith does not need to worry much about ideology in his other major field of legislative endeavor: He joins in the bipartisan consensus in favor of veterans programs as a member of the Veterans' Affairs Committee, where he is the second-ranking Republican.

At Home: Smith became ensconced in the 4th with surprising ease, demolishing Democratic hopes of recapturing a district that was long theirs.

Smith's diligent constituent work and well-run campaigns were important, but the secret of his success was his unexpectedly moderate voting record. Though steadfast in the anti-abortion activism that drew him into politics, his attention to the interests of blue-collar workers and organized labor has given Smith considerable crossover appeal.

Even redistricting, which gave him a constituency about one-third new in 1992, failed to faze Smith. Democrat Brian M. Hughes, son of former Democratic Gov. Richard J. Hughes, tried to convince voters in the reconfigured 4th that Smith's high-profile House opposition to abortion came at the expense of local interests.

But that is a charge Democrats throw at Smith every two years, so far to no avail. Without a fresh issue to keep voters' attention, Hughes struggled to stay in the public eye. When local media finally got interested in the contest, it was mostly to detail charges of résumé padding that were leveled against

Hughes. Smith breezed with 63 percent.

In 1980, Smith ousted 13-term Democrat Thompson solely because of Thompson's involvement in Abscam. In 1978, as a political novice running almost exclusively on his contacts in the anti-abortion movement, Smith had failed to draw even 40 percent against Thompson. On the second try, after Thompson's bribery indictment, Smith won with 57 percent.

Despite that solid showing, Smith was viewed as nearly certain to fall in 1982 to Democrat Joseph P. Merlino, the former president of the New Jersey Senate. As it turned out, Merlino came across in areas outside Trenton as a gruff, horse-trading pol. After one debate, when Smith approached him to exchange pleasantries, Merlino growled, "Beat it, kid." Smith won with 53 percent.

In 1984, Democrats tried again with a protégé of Merlino, former Mercer County Freeholder James C. Hedden. Hedden took Smith seriously, accusing his opponent of being obsessed with abortion. But Smith soared to 61 percent and hasn't won less than that since.

Committees

Foreign Affairs (8th of 18 Republicans)
Western Hemisphere Affairs (ranking); International Security, International Organizations & Human Rights

Veterans' Affairs (2nd of 14 Republicans)
Hospitals & Health Care (ranking)

Elections

1992 General		
Christopher H. Smith (R)	149,095	(62%)
Brian M. Hughes (D)	84,514	(35%)
Benjamin Grindlinger (LIBERT)	2,984	(1%)
1990 General		
Christopher H. Smith (R)	101,508	(63%)
Mark Setaro (D)	55,454	(34%)
Carl Peters (LIBERT)	2,168	(1%)
Joseph J. Notarangelo (POP)	1,219	(1%)
J.M. Carter (God We Trust)	1,029	(1%)

Previous Winning Percentages: **1988** (66%) **1986** (61%) **1984** (61%) **1982** (53%) **1980** (57%)

District Vote for President

1992

D 105,335 (40%)
R 109,907 (41%)
I 50,768 (19%)

Campaign Finance

	Receipts	Receipts from PACs		Expend-itures
1992				
Smith (R)	$369,949	$110,958	(30%)	$413,493
Hughes (D)	$176,898	$23,761	(13%)	$164,038
1990				
Smith (R)	$280,579	$113,126	(40%)	$292,826
Setaro (D)	$55,701	$4,000	(7%)	$55,772

Key Votes

1993	
Require parental notification of minors' abortions	Y
Require unpaid family and medical leave	Y
Approve national "motor voter" registration bill	Y
Approve budget increasing taxes and reducing deficit	N
Approve economic stimulus plan	N
1992	
Approve balanced-budget constitutional amendment	Y
Close down space station program	N
Approve U.S. aid for former Soviet Union	Y
Allow shifting funds from defense to domestic programs	N
1991	
Extend unemployment benefits using deficit financing	Y
Approve waiting period for handgun purchases	Y
Authorize use of force in Persian Gulf	Y

Voting Studies

	Presidential Support		Party Unity		Conservative Coalition	
Year	S	O	S	O	S	O
1992	61	38	61	37	83	17
1991	62	37	58	40	73	24
1990	43	56	44	54	56	44
1989	55	44	36	61	66	34
1988	40	59	44	53	68	32
1987	38	62	39	59	77	23
1986	46	54	32	66	60	40
1985	45	55	43	53	55	44
1984	56	44	45	48	63	37
1983	50	50	44	56	60	39
1982	49	51	41	57	52	47
1981	64	36	65	35	67	33

Interest Group Ratings

Year	ADA	AFL-CIO	CCUS	ACU
1992	40	67	75	68
1991	45	75	40	60
1990	56	50	64	63
1989	45	75	70	43
1988	60	100	43	48
1987	52	81	53	39
1986	45	93	33	45
1985	65	88	41	52
1984	45	69	50	43
1983	40	53	40	48
1982	50	75	57	41
1981	40	40	79	87

5 Marge Roukema (R)

Of Ridgewood — Elected 1980; 7th Term

Born: Sept. 19, 1929, West Orange, N.J.
Education: Montclair State College, B.A. 1951.
Occupation: High school government and history teacher.
Family: Husband, Richard Roukema; two children.
Religion: Protestant.
Political Career: Ridgewood Board of Education, 1970-73; GOP nominee for U.S. House, 1978.
Capitol Office: 2244 Rayburn Bldg. 20515; 225-4465.

In Washington: After 12 years in the House, Roukema has acquired the seniority that could propel her into a leading role; yet she finds herself in an increasingly awkward position within the Republican Conference. She is the second most senior Republican woman in the House and the third-ranking Republican on both her major committees, where she can influence most bills. But her philosophy, her views and even her votes diverge from those of the conference majority with striking frequency.

Her role in the early 1993 enactment of the Family and Medical Leave Act is a case in point. Roukema would have received even more credit for this legislation had it been signed when first passed, under the Republican rule of President Bush. But Roukema's efforts over eight years on what she called "a bedrock family issue" failed to convince enough of her GOP colleagues to support it. Bush vetoed it twice, and solid GOP voting in Congress sustained both vetoes. Passed again in 1993, the bill became the first legislative trophy of the Clinton administration.

Roukema had been the lead Republican sponsor of the bill, which requires large and medium-sized businesses to provide unpaid leave to new parents, disabled workers and those caring for a seriously ill family member. Her work led to moderating revisions that allowed the bill to win passage for the first time in 1990, only to be vetoed by Bush — as it was again in 1992. In neither year were there enough GOP votes to override.

Roukema opposes the majority of House Republicans on about one floor vote in three. That is more than enough to cause the party's most conservative wing to view her with suspicion — particularly because her apostasy often crops up on high-profile issues. In 1992, she opposed Bush on nearly half the votes on which his administration expressed a specific opinion. But it mattered far more to party insiders that the half on which Roukema went her own way included such emotionally charged issues as family leave and abortion.

In 1989, she took pains to distance herself from Bush's veto of federal financing of abortions in limited cases. "How could such a leader make such a harsh choice and throw the gauntlet down to Congress on an indefensible position," she asked, "namely, that we vote, yet again, to deny the poor victims of rape and incest a legal right to an abortion, a right open to all other women in our society?"

Roukema's standing with the conference's leaders has not been helped by her votes on intraparty matters. In 1989, Roukema backed moderate Edward Madigan of Illinois for GOP whip against conservative Georgian Newt Gingrich — who won.

Roukema has some conservative credentials of her own. She is tough on fiscal discipline — not only supporting a balanced-budget amendment to the Constitution but putting her money where her mouth is on floor votes to reduce spending, especially on big-ticket items that do not have universal appeal. That principled stance, in fact, put her at odds with Bush at times — as when she backed cuts in the strategic defense initiative and the termination of funding for the space station and the superconducting super collider.

Alongside her highly visible defections from the business line over the years, Roukema has cast scores of pro-business votes on more mundane matters. In the 101st Congress, for instance, she offered a successful amendment to strike a proposal to give workers equal representation with management on trustee boards that run single-employer pension plans. Similarly, she argued that "fairness and common sense" dictated that business be given extra time to comply with the legislation to prevent age discrimination.

On the Banking Committee, during a 1991 debate on a complex bill overhauling the federal deposit insurance system, she fought — with partial success — to preserve the rights of pension plans to deposit huge sums in banks and have the deposits fully insured. Her theory was that $100,000 in deposit insurance should pass through to a pension fund for each of its future beneficiaries.

New Jersey 5

North and West — Ridgewood

The 5th has little in common with the stereotype of New Jersey as a state within a turnpike. In fact, the New Jersey Turnpike actually stops short of entering the district in Bergen County.

This is one of the state's least densely packed districts, stretching from Warren County north to the New York border, then all the way across the northern tier to the Hudson River. No municipality has more than 30,000 residents. It includes some of the state's most scenic, wealthiest and Republican areas.

Ronald Reagan captured 70 percent here in 1984; four years later, George Bush racked up 67 percent. Bush had a tougher time in 1992 but managed to win with 50 percent.

Northern Bergen County provides the bulk of the vote. These affluent voters are so heavily Republican that Democrats often have a hard time finding sacrificial candidates to run in legislative races.

Property values and income levels are among the highest in the state. Alpine is home to sports stars and celebrities; Saddle River is where Richard M. Nixon resides. Less famous denizens include the corporate executives and white-collar New York commuters who live in places such as Ridgewood and Oradell. It is only fitting that the company that makes the car of choice for many upscale buyers — BMW — keeps its U.S. headquarters in Woodcliff Lake. Park Ridge also serves as a corporate headquarters site.

In his too close-for-comfort 1990 reelection bid, Democratic Sen. Bill Bradley ran poorly in these areas. He lost Bergen County — as well as the rest of the district. Voters were equally hostile to Bill Clinton in 1992: George Bush won 50 percent in the 5th District portion of Bergen.

The rest of the population lives in Warren County and in parts of Passaic and Sussex counties.

The mountains of Warren and affluent Sussex counties are dotted with sparsely populated small towns. Phillipsburg, situated across the Delaware River from Easton, Pennsylvania, has some industry and is Warren County's only town with as many as 15,000 residents.

The scenic backcountry of western Sussex attracts some tourists, especially around the Delaware Water Gap region. Much of the county remains rural, despite experiencing a 13 percent jump in population in the 1980s as affluent, young professionals stretched the New York metropolitan orbit even farther west.

The small towns and boroughs of Sussex are much like those in Warren, but even more Republican. In 1992, Rep. Roukema won 72 percent in Sussex County. Bush won here by more than 2-1.

The less-populous portion of upper Passaic County contributes four municipalities to the 5th. It is more Republican and less industrialized than its southern section, which is mostly in the 8th District. It includes West Milford Township, which, at about 25,000 in population, barely beats out suburban Paramus (Bergen County) as the 5th's most populous.

1990 Population: 594,630. White 556,154 (94%), Black 7,906 (1%), Other 30,570 (5%). Hispanic origin 16,567 (3%). 18 and over 452,587 (76%), 62 and over 91,998 (15%). Median age: 36.

Roukema does not always reject her party's position on social issues. In 1991, after having supported an earlier Democratic effort to overturn Supreme Court rulings on a variety of anti-discrimination laws, she switched at Bush's request and voted no. She has also vociferously opposed legislation to lift a ban on permitting people with AIDS to immigrate to the United States.

Roukema's more liberal social views are sometimes influenced by personal experience. After years of fighting for the family leave bill, Roukema in mid-1990 revealed a personal facet to her commitment. In 1976, when she was a graduate student, Roukema had dropped out of her academic program to care for her 17-year-old son, who was dying of leukemia. "What would I have done if not only did I have the tragedy and trauma of caring for my child," she asks, "but also had to worry about losing a job and the roof over my head?"

Roukema is often the Democrats' most ready ally on the Housing subcommittee, where she is the ranking Republican and is considered a housing advocate. During consideration of the 1990 housing bill, she was the lone Republican to back an amendment prohibiting those buying homes through a new federal program from reaping a profit on a later sale.

At the same time, Roukema watches out for her largely affluent district. She opposed a housing bill provision that would have targeted more Community Development Block Grant money to anti-poverty programs, a move some thought would make those funds hard to use in rural and well-heeled communities. She has also carried the banner for the real estate industry as a preserver of the home-mortgage interest deduction (including for second homes).

At Home: Roukema struggled to wrest a seat from a Democratic incumbent in 1980. But redistricting has since given her a constituency content with moderate GOP representation.

The Democratic Legislature's 1981 remap paired her with fellow Republican Jim Courter, but Courter moved to the 12th. Roukema then coasted in 1982 against Democratic lawyer Fritz Cammerzell. In 1984, a second redistricting plan gave her a more compact but equally Republican district. Roukema won 71 percent.

Two years later, Roukema had to dismiss a challenge from conservative businessman Bill Grant before going on to defeat a little-known Democrat with three-fourths of the vote, a feat she repeated in 1988 and 1990. Unfazed by redistricting, she did it again in 1992.

Elections were much more difficult for Roukema in her original district. The old 7th was less Republican, and she had to run twice there to unseat liberal Democrat Andrew Maguire. In her first challenge, in 1978, she was a former teacher returning to politics five years after leaving the Ridgewood Board of Education. She attacked Maguire for being "anti-defense" and lost by 8,815 votes. In 1980, she focused on complaints that Maguire, a critic of big oil companies during the 1979 gasoline shortage, was anti-business. With a strong showing by Ronald Reagan in northern New Jersey, she won by nearly 10,000 votes.

Committees

Banking, Finance & Urban Affairs (3rd of 20 Republicans)
Housing & Community Development (ranking); Economic Growth; International Development, Finance, Trade & Monetary Policy

Education & Labor (3rd of 15 Republicans)
Labor-Management Relations (ranking); Elementary, Secondary & Vocational Education; Postsecondary Education

Elections

1992 General		
Marge Roukema (R)	196,198	(72%)
Frank R. Lucas (D)	67,579	(25%)
William J. Leonard (I)	6,182	(2%)
1992 Primary		
Marge Roukema (R)	27,030	(62%)
Lou Sette (R)	10,243	(24%)
Ira M. Marlowe (R)	4,839	(11%)
C. "Larry" Fischer (R)	1,372	(3%)
1990 General		
Marge Roukema (R)	118,101	(76%)
Lawrence Wayne Olsen (D)	35,010	(22%)
Mark Richards (POP)	2,998	(2%)

Previous Winning Percentages: **1988** (76%) **1986** (75%) **1984** (71%) **1982** (65%) **1980** (51%)

District Vote for President

1992
D 99,733 (34%)
R 146,004 (50%)
I 48,666 (17%)

Campaign Finance

	Receipts	Receipts from PACs		Expend-itures
1992				
Roukema (R)	$439,150	$224,598	(51%)	$504,596
Lucas (D)	$2,080	0		$2,117
1990				
Roukema (R)	$446,589	$219,068	(49%)	$443,540

Key Votes

1993	
Require parental notification of minors' abortions	Y
Require unpaid family and medical leave	Y
Approve national "motor voter" registration bill	N
Approve budget increasing taxes and reducing deficit	N
Approve economic stimulus plan	N
1992	
Approve balanced-budget constitutional amendment	Y
Close down space station program	Y
Approve U.S. aid for former Soviet Union	Y
Allow shifting funds from defense to domestic programs	N
1991	
Extend unemployment benefits using deficit financing	Y
Approve waiting period for handgun purchases	Y
Authorize use of force in Persian Gulf	Y

Voting Studies

	Presidential Support		Party Unity		Conservative Coalition	
Year	S	O	S	O	S	O
1992	48	45	66	30	56	35
1991	54	41	56	37	62	35
1990	45	45	58	32	63	24
1989	53	42	60	37	68	29
1988	42	55	68	28	79	21
1987	45	51	61	36	70	28
1986	56	43	62	26	64	36
1985	49	50	56	41	60	40
1984	51	45	57	38	56	42
1983	61	35	49	47	47	51
1982	62	34	57	39	60	37
1981	66	32	70	29	56	41

Interest Group Ratings

Year	ADA	AFL-CIO	CCUS	ACU
1992	50	42	71	68
1991	35	55	67	50
1990	28	42	58	59
1989	30	33	90	57
1988	40	79	69	50
1987	36	38	87	52
1986	30	43	78	36
1985	45	29	68	40
1984	45	15	63	36
1983	40	18	80	30
1982	50	30	68	41
1981	35	27	89	80

6 Frank Pallone Jr. (D)

Of Long Branch — Elected 1988; 3rd Term

Born: Oct. 30, 1951, Long Branch, N.J.
Education: Middlebury College, B.A. 1973; Tufts U., M.A. 1974; Rutgers U., J.D. 1978.
Occupation: Lawyer.
Family: Wife, Sarah Hospodor.
Religion: Roman Catholic.
Political Career: Long Branch City Council, 1982-88; N.J. Senate, 1984-88.
Capitol Office: 420 Cannon Bldg. 20515; 225-4671.

In Washington: Pallone may not be the most popular member in Congress, as witnessed by the New Jersey delegation's attempts to leave him without a district in 1992 redistricting. But he survived that and challenges from both parties.

At the start of the 103rd Congress, he traded up for a seat on the influential Energy and Commerce Committee, a testament to his persistent ambition and a sign perhaps that he has larger goals in mind.

Both in New Jersey and Washington, Pallone encourages his lone wolf image. His 1992 campaign was marked by his "Declaration of Independence," emphasizing his opposition to Democratic Gov. James J. Florio's huge tax increase and other differences with party leaders. He voted with President Bush's agenda 29 percent of the time in 1992.

Yet with the redistricting behind him and the retirement of a powerful detractor, Rep. Robert A. Roe, Pallone may have an opportunity to put some of those tensions behind him.

From his posts on the Merchant Marine and Public Works committees, Pallone as a freshman looked for ways to please the voters of his coastal district. Three of his ideas made it into the 101st Congress' Water Resources Development Act, including a provision to reduce disposal of floatable and dredge material on ocean waters. He also joined in the successful fight to repeal Coast Guard fees for pleasure boats.

Shortly after winning his third term Pallone promised his constituents that he would use his seat on Public Works to secure federal money for New Jersey's roads and bridges. He gave up that seat, but his Merchant Marine slot will keep him in a position to work in behalf of the waterways. At the start of the 103rd, he filed legislation that would extend a moratorium on striped bass fishing off the coasts of states that do not follow federal conservation guidelines.

Pallone and the delegation also managed to keep the Army's Fort Monmouth open, but the 1993 base-closure list recommended severe cutbacks there.

On money matters, Pallone votes a politically careful line, opposing congressional pay raises and rejecting the budget summit agreement of October 1990 and a later Democratic spending plan, both of which included higher taxes. He advocates cutting agriculture subsidies and the budgets of the space station and the superconducting super collider.

He also was an early supporter of lifting the ban on homosexuals in the military.

Pallone takes a minimalist approach to drafting legislation; the short list in the 102nd included a resolution to commend the maritime community for its commitment during Operation Desert Shield, a bill repealing the luxury tax on passenger vehicles, a resolution designating "Animal Awareness Week," and a bill to designate "The Most Beautiful Lady in the World" as the official anthem of the Statue of Liberty.

Pallone took one high-profile risk in the 101st, shifting from his longtime anti-abortion stance. After the Supreme Court's *Webster* decision giving states more authority to regulate abortion, Pallone said, "I have come to the conclusion that it is inappropriate for me to impose my religious beliefs on those who do not share those beliefs or whose circumstances demand that other choices be available."

At Home: When some members of New Jersey's House delegation got together to draw up their version of the new congressional map, Pallone was conspicuously absent. So, too, was Pallone's district when a final plan was handed down in March 1992.

It was partly a reflection of Pallone's status as a loner, earned when he criticized the congressional pay raise of 1989. It was also rooted in the political reality of reapportionment. (New Jersey lost one seat.)

Pallone's 3rd District was merged with Democratic Rep. Bernard J. Dwyer's 6th. Instead of his old Monmouth County-based "shore" district, Pallone had to run in a district rooted in unfamiliar Middlesex County. He dodged a bullet when Dwyer retired, but state

New Jersey 6

Central — New Brunswick; Long Branch; Asbury Park

From industrial Middlesex County to the shore communities of Monmouth County, the 6th is one of the most competitive districts in the state.

This mostly middle-class and independent-voting slice of New Jersey is a crucial component of any successful statewide effort.

The 1992 presidential campaign emphasized the district's competitive nature. Both Bill Clinton and George Bush made concerted efforts here, but in the Monmouth County portion, neither could gain a decisive advantage: Bush won by about 1,100 votes.

In 1984 and 1988, Ronald Reagan and George Bush won the 6th, respectively, but in 1989, Democrat James J. Florio carried the district with 56 percent.

Jobs and the economy are pressing issues in Middlesex County, where almost 60 percent of the district population comes from 13 towns. Democrats traditionally run well in the county, though more recently, residents have shown few qualms about splitting tickets.

Edison — a part of which is in the 7th District — is the largest city in the district, and home to some manufacturing concerns and corporate headquarters. Some of Edison's white-collar employees live nearby in Metuchen.

Black voters and the Rutgers University community boost Democrats in New Brunswick. Across the Raritan River, Republicans are competitive in more affluent Piscataway and Highland Park. Suburban ticket-splitting and independent voting is more prevalent in populous Old Bridge and Sayreville.

The inland portion of Monmouth County is suburban, and less affluent and Republican than the rest of the county, which is divided into the 4th, 6th and 12th districts. In the 4th and 12th districts, Republicans carried the House and presidential races relatively easily. But in the 6th, Bush barely squeaked by, while Democratic Rep. Pallone won by more than 7,000 votes.

Most of the suburban, Republican turf of Middletown — the largest town in Monmouth County — is in the 6th, but a part of it is in the 12th District. Working-class Red Bank is fertile ground for Democrats.

In coastal Monmouth County, the environment weighs heavily in political debates. Ocean dumping, beach erosion and hurricane protection are matters of import to locals. The coastal region begins with the Sandy Hook part of the Gateway National Recreation Area, which extends like a thin finger from the top of Monmouth County.

Farther south, the shore communities used to attract the 19th century elite. President James A. Garfield was brought to his summer cottage in Long Branch in 1881 after he was shot; he died there a few weeks later. The aging seaside resort of Asbury Park — glorified by singer and local hero Bruce Springsteen — has faded in prominence. The black community in Asbury Park helps keep it in the Democratic column. Deal is a wealthier, residential community.

1990 Population: 594,630. White 486,512 (82%), Black 66,850 (11%), Other 41,268 (7%). Hispanic origin 36,492 (6%). 18 and over 465,699 (78%), 62 and over 88,181 (15%). Median age: 33.

Rep. Bob Smith stepped up to take Dwyer's place in the primary.

Endorsed by Dwyer, Smith ran a high-spending, hard-hitting campaign, portraying Pallone as ineffective. But Pallone sidestepped the charges by positioning himself as an outsider. Pallone's campaign slogan described him as "Our best hope — their worst nightmare." He painted Smith, a former county party chairman in Middlesex County, as an insider.

In the general election, both Pallone and the Republican nominee, state Sen. Joseph M. Kyrillos, wooed the district's mostly moderate, independent, middle-of-the-road voters. Kyrillos distanced himself from the national party line on social issues such as abortion, while Pallone stressed his outsider credentials.

But as George Bush's prospects faded in New Jersey, so did Kyrillos'. And Pallone's 2-1 fundraising edge proved too much to overcome in the end.

Pallone was a protégé of Democratic Rep. James J. Howard, who was chairman of the Public Works Committee until he died in 1988 during his 12th term and left the 3rd District open. Many Democratic insiders, including Howard's widow, lined up behind Pallone, who had won re-election to the state Senate in 1987 with 60 percent of the vote. He won the Democratic House nomination without a contest and faced Republican Joseph Azzolina, a former state legislator, in the general election.

Though both candidates had name-recognition problems outside their home areas, Pallone enjoyed an advantage because of his work on environmental issues in the pollution-conscious 3rd. Pallone won with 52 percent of the vote.

In 1990, Democrats across the state fretted over what voters, angered by Gov. Florio's $2.8 billion tax increase, might do to them.

Pallone's little-known Republican challenger, lawyer Paul A. Kapalko, successfully attacked the incumbent with an anti-Florio message. Pallone barely held off the anti-tax fury, beating Kapalko by 4,258 votes.

Committees

Energy & Commerce (21st of 27 Democrats)
Commerce, Consumer Protection & Competitiveness; Health & the Environment; Transportation & Hazardous Materials

Merchant Marine & Fisheries (10th of 29 Democrats)
Coast Guard & Navigation; Environment & Natural Resources

Elections

1992 General		
Frank Pallone Jr. (D)	118,266	(52%)
Joseph M. Kyrillos (R)	100,949	(45%)
1992 Primary		
Frank Pallone Jr. (D)	19,087	(55%)
Bob Smith (D)	12,769	(37%)
Barbara Jensen (D)	1,784	(5%)
Jeffrey R. Gorman (D)	1,286	(4%)
1990 General		
Frank Pallone Jr. (D)	77,709	(49%)
Paul A. Kapalko (R)	73,451	(46%)
Richard D. McKean (I)	4,390	(3%)
William Stewart (LIBERT)	1,875	(1%)
Joseph A. Plonski (POP)	867	(1%)

Previous Winning Percentages: 1988 * (52%)

** Elected to a full term and to fill a vacancy at the same time.*

District Vote for President

	1992
D	110,821 (44%)
R	98,397 (39%)
I	41,646 (17%)

Campaign Finance

	Receipts	Receipts from PACs		Expend-itures
1992				
Pallone (D)	$932,079	$531,079	(57%)	$929,541
Kyrillos (R)	$408,460	$97,881	(24%)	$403,153
1990				
Pallone (D)	$632,450	$394,464	(62%)	$634,109
Kapalko (R)	$118,692	$11,050	(9%)	$115,202

Key Votes

1993	
Require parental notification of minors' abortions	N
Require unpaid family and medical leave	Y
Approve national "motor voter" registration bill	Y
Approve budget increasing taxes and reducing deficit	Y
Approve economic stimulus plan	Y
1992	
Approve balanced-budget constitutional amendment	Y
Close down space station program	Y
Approve U.S. aid for former Soviet Union	Y
Allow shifting funds from defense to domestic programs	Y
1991	
Extend unemployment benefits using deficit financing	Y
Approve waiting period for handgun purchases	Y
Authorize use of force in Persian Gulf	Y

Voting Studies

	Presidential Support		Party Unity		Conservative Coalition	
Year	S	O	S	O	S	O
1992	29	71	82	18	33	67
1991	33	66	75	24	54	46
1990	29	71	79	20	54	46
1989	34	65	82	16	59	39

Interest Group Ratings

Year	ADA	AFL-CIO	CCUS	ACU
1992	90	83	38	28
1991	60	92	10	30
1990	61	83	43	29
1989	75	92	40	25

7 Bob Franks (R)

Of New Providence — Elected 1992; 1st Term

Born: Sept. 21, 1951, Hackensack, N.J.
Education: DePauw U., B.A. 1973; Southern Methodist U., J.D. 1976.
Occupation: Newspaper owner.
Family: Single.
Religion: Methodist.
Political Career: N.J. Assembly, 1980-92; N.J. Republican Party chairman, 1988-92.
Capitol Office: 429 Cannon Bldg. 20515; 225-5361.

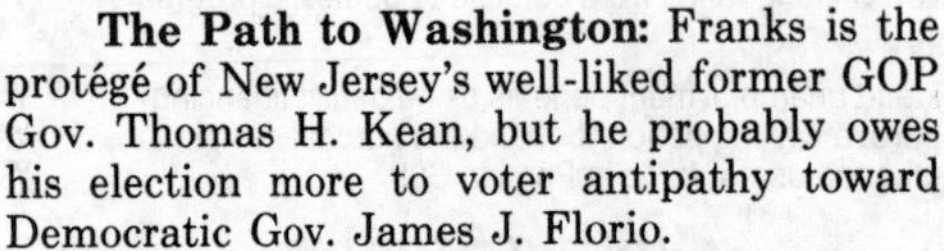

The Path to Washington: Franks is the protégé of New Jersey's well-liked former GOP Gov. Thomas H. Kean, but he probably owes his election more to voter antipathy toward Democratic Gov. James J. Florio.

Franks caught voters' attention in 1991 by spearheading the anti-tax, anti-Florio campaign that resulted in an ouster of the Democratic majorities in both chambers of the state Legislature and their replacement with Republican majorities capable of overriding any Florio veto.

Franks had not anticipated that 1992 would find him a candidate for the House. Many believed that he was preparing to run for governor in 1993. However, the GOP nomination for the 7th District virtually fell into his lap when 10-term House veteran Matthew J. Rinaldo unexpectedly announced his retirement after the primary.

A member of the state Assembly for 13 years and a former GOP state chairman, Franks was well-positioned to succeed Rinaldo in the 7th, a district that eluded Democrats' grasp for 20 years even though it included blue-collar Elizabeth and predominantly black Plainfield.

Redistricting gave the GOP an edge in the district, carving Elizabeth from the 7th and replacing it with more affluent, GOP-leaning towns that Franks represented in the state Legislature.

The Democratic nominee, real estate developer Leonard R. Sendelsky, had an advantage bringing in money as one of the state's top Democratic fundraisers, but he did not have Franks' name recognition.

Franks' rather extensive political résumé had the potential to be a handicap, though, in 1992. Sendelsky fit the popular outsider image, having held no previous political office.

"Three words sum up Franks' adult life," Sendelsky charged during the campaign: "Politics, politics, politics."

Franks countered by pointing to his support of initiatives and referendums for New Jersey voters as evidence of his desire to change the status quo. He also touted his successful efforts to roll back sales taxes in the wake of Florio's much-loathed $2.8 billion 1990 tax increase.

Fortunately for Franks, the anti-insider spark never quite caught fire in the 7th, and he won 53 percent to Sendelsky's 43 percent.

Franks' involvement in the GOP goes back to his junior high school days in Chicago, when he volunteered on Charles H. Percy's unsuccessful 1964 bid for governor of Illinois.

His introduction to New Jersey politics came in 1967 when he worked on Kean's campaign for the Legislature. He later played a leading role in Kean's successful 1981 gubernatorial bid, and in 1987, Kean reciprocated by naming Franks state GOP chairman.

Throughout the campaign Franks called for reining in federal spending, saying the deficit could be cut without raising taxes — a position popular with New Jersey voters, many of whom still felt the sting of the Florio tax increase.

He supported a balanced-budget constitutional amendment, a line-item veto for the president and an annual 15 percent reduction in the congressional operating budget.

Like most GOP freshmen, Franks voted in April 1993 both for a Democratic bill giving the president modified line-item veto authority as well as for an even more potent GOP substitute.

To revitalize the manufacturing sector, he promised to try to eliminate conflicting regulations and to promote public-private sector partnerships to provide specialized job training.

Franks will have an opportunity to work directly for these goals: He won assignments to the Budget Committee and the Public Works and Transportation Committee.

Franks promised voters that his first priority would be to push through Congress a package of bills promoting economic growth and job creation.

While Franks favors conservative fiscal policy, he is a social moderate, supporting abortion rights and a lifting of the ban on homosexuals in the military. He was one of 51 Republicans to vote for a bill codifying President Clinton's lifting of the "gag rule" that prohibited staff at federally funded family planning clinics from discussing abortion.

New Jersey 7

North and Central — Parts of Woodbridge and Union

Before GOP Rep. Matthew J. Rinaldo unexpectedly announced his post-primary retirement in 1992, it was assumed that he would easily win re-election to the Republican 7th. Redistricting removed urban, industrial and Democratic Elizabeth, though it had hardly been a problem for Rinaldo in the past since the Republican suburbs usually drowned out Elizabeth's vote.

After Rinaldo dropped out, Democrats harbored illusions that they might pull an upset here in the open race, only to be doused with a splash of reality: Democratic nominee Leonard R. Sendelsky managed only 43 percent. Republican Franks carried all the parts of four counties that make up the 7th — Essex, Middlesex, Somerset and Union.

Franks' open-seat victory was presaged by previous election results in the 7th: In 1984, Ronald Reagan won 64 percent and four years later, George Bush captured 60 percent. In the open 1989 gubernatorial race, Republican Rep. Jim Courter carried the district with 51 percent, though he won just 37 percent statewide.

Roughly half the vote is cast in Union County. Predominantly black and Democratic Plainfield is the most-populous place in the Union County portion, followed closely by Union Township (a small part of Union Township is in the 10th District). Plainfield was one of the first of New Jersey's cities to explode in the riots of 1967.

North of Plainfield, the towns are mostly suburban, white and Republican. Summit, Westfield and Cranford are bedroom communities for New York City and Newark.

About a quarter of the population comes from each of Middlesex and Somerset counties. Middlesex only contributes two whole municipalities and parts of two others, but they constitute a significant voting bloc. It includes most of New Jersey's largest suburb, middle-class Woodbridge, along with part of Edison. (Most of Edison is in the neighboring 6th District.) Woodbridge experienced explosive growth between 1950 and 1970; it is now larger than Camden.

Farther west, in southern Somerset County, corporate and industrial growth along Interstate 287 and U.S. 22 has led to growth in Bridgewater and Hillsborough.

Somerset generally backs Republican candidates. In 1990, GOP Senate challenger Christine Todd Whitman carried the county over Democratic Sen. Bill Bradley. But Democratic votes can be found in the industrial boroughs, such as Manville and Bound Brook, to the south.

The Johns-Manville plant that gave Manville its name attracted large numbers of Poles and other Slavic immigrants in the 1930s and '40s. By 1982, though, the company was forced to file for bankruptcy after being slapped with tens of thousands of asbestos-related lawsuits. In 1985, the factory shut down.

A small section of western Essex County is also grafted onto the 7th. It adds parts of two towns, Maplewood and affluent Millburn.

1990 Population: 594,629. White 497,273 (84%), Black 60,532 (10%), Other 36,824 (6%). Hispanic origin 29,712 (5%). 18 and over 467,393 (79%), 62 and over 101,000 (17%). Median age: 36.

Committees

Budget (14th of 17 Republicans)

Public Works & Transportation (19th of 24 Republicans)
Economic Development; Surface Transportation

Campaign Finance

1992	Receipts	Receipts from PACs		Expend-itures
Franks (R)	$460,998	$131,032	(28%)	$453,991
Sendelsky (D)	$224,844	$36,965	(16%)	$223,704

Key Votes

1993

Require parental notification of minors' abortions	Y
Require unpaid family and medical leave	Y
Approve national "motor voter" registration bill	Y
Approve budget increasing taxes and reducing deficit	N
Approve economic stimulus plan	N

Elections

1992 General

Bob Franks (R)	132,174	(53%)
Leonard R. Sendelsky (D)	105,761	(43%)
Eugene J. Gillespie Jr. (I)	4,043	(2%)
Bill Campbell (NNG)	2,612	(1%)

District Vote for President

1992

D 115,846 (41%)
R 125,592 (45%)
I 40,708 (14%)

8 Herb Klein (D)

Of Clifton — Elected 1992; 1st Term

Born: June 24, 1930, Newark, N.J.
Education: Rutgers U., B.A. 1950; Harvard U., J.D. 1953; New York U., LL.M. 1958.
Military Service: Air Force, 1954-56.
Occupation: Lawyer.
Family: Wife, Jacqueline; one child.
Religion: Jewish.
Political Career: N.J. Assembly, 1972-76, assistant majority leader, 1973-76; Passaic County Democratic Committee executive director, 1977-81.
Capitol Office: 1728 Longworth Bldg. 20515; 225-5751.

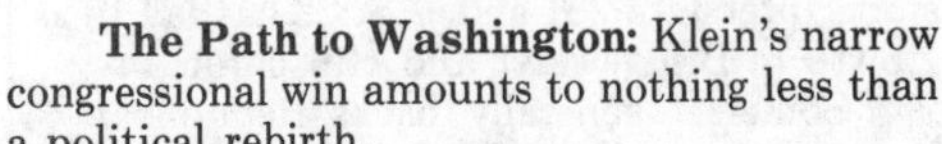

The Path to Washington: Klein's narrow congressional win amounts to nothing less than a political rebirth.

Ousted from the state Assembly after he supported a controversial state income tax in 1974, Klein had been relegated to the political back rooms for the past decade. As his wife took center stage as a national committeewoman, Klein developed a reputation as a prodigious fundraiser. He also gave willingly to fellow Democrats, donating $25,000 to James J. Florio's 1989 gubernatorial campaign.

When Rep. Robert A. Roe made his surprise announcement in March 1992 that he was retiring after serving 23 years, Klein was a relatively new face in the 8th.

Although not the first choice of party activists, Klein eventually won Roe's endorsement. The notion of Roe passing the congressional mantle to Klein was a powerful symbol, particularly with elderly residents in the district.

Klein's campaign was reminiscent of his school days, when he put himself through college and law school selling Fuller brushes door to door. Throughout the contest there was nary a senior center, local fair or coffee klatch that Klein would pass up.

Klein and his Republican opponent, state Sen. Joseph L. Bubba, ran old-style campaigns in the northern New Jersey district. Bubba appealed to Italian voters in Totowa, Nutley, Belleville and his hometown of Wayne, while Klein campaigned hard in Jewish communities such as Passaic, Montclair and his hometown of Clifton.

Sensing that Klein's weakness was his 1974 tax vote and knowing that voters were still seething over Florio's massive 1990 tax increase, Bubba stumped on a no-tax pledge.

Klein retaliated with promises that he would work to create jobs in the desperately depressed region. He trolled for votes at unemployment offices and job fairs. He blamed GOP presidents for the nation's financial woes, mocking "trickle down" theories and the savings and loan crisis.

Despite his mild demeanor, Klein proved he could get tough when the election got tense in the final month. He ran tart-tongued radio spots accusing Bubba of accepting $46,000 from a contractor convicted of bribery. (The contractor was convicted after Bubba received the money.)

Klein does not shy away from his liberal Democratic leanings. He supports universal health care, abortion rights and stringent gun control laws.

The Democrat handily won both counties in the densely populated district, but he sacrificed more than 16,000 votes to independent candidate Gloria J. Kolodziej.

Although the Science, Space and Technology Committee was not Klein's first choice, it should put him in a better position to deliver on a campaign pledge to convert military and foreign aid dollars into domestic job programs.

As one of 11 freshmen on the Banking Committee's Financial Institutions Subcommittee, Klein impressed members and staff during April 1993 drafting of the unpopular thrift bailout funding bill. He was rewarded with the opportunity to offer an amendment, which carried easily in subcommittee, to cut almost $7 billion from the money the bill would have provided for the Resolution Trust Corporation.

Klein was drawn to politics after studying the career of Harry S Truman at Rutgers University. After volunteering with local Democratic groups, Klein won his first term to the New Jersey Assembly in 1971. He served a second term before the tax flap cost him the seat.

The loss dissuaded Klein from seeking office until Roe's retirement. In the interim years, he built up a lucrative law firm in Clifton and served on a number of civic boards.

Klein's seat did not come cheap. He lent his campaign more than $575,000 and finished the cycle with a large debt. To begin to pay it back, he took the second-highest amount of PAC donations of any House freshman in the two months after the election.

New Jersey 8

North — Paterson

After surveying the Great Falls of the Passaic River in the late 18th century, Treasury Secretary Alexander Hamilton figured it would be an ideal place to develop some homegrown industry, independent of England. So he created the Society for Establishing Useful Manufactures to build facilities to harness the water power in Paterson.

The industrial complex was slow to develop, but by the mid-19th century, Paterson had attracted a wave of English, Irish and Dutch immigrants to staff its silk mills. A second wave would bring Italians, Poles and Slavs to work the looms.

Hamilton's vision thrived, and "Silk City" (as Paterson became known) developed into one of the world's leading textile producers. But the introduction of rayon and other 20th century synthetic fabrics triggered an economic freefall from which the city has never fully recovered. Today, Paterson suffers from chronic unemployment and the side effects of industrial decline.

Though the jobs left, Paterson's (Passaic County) minority population increased: Blacks and Hispanics currently make up 74 percent. Combined with the city's strong labor tradition, Paterson turns out a reliable Democratic vote.

The city of Passaic is a smaller but equally troubled version of Paterson. For a Democrat to win the district, the candidate must carry both cities handily. That is no small task, especially in Paterson, where voter turnout and registration is low.

The white ethnics who left these cities moved to Passaic County suburbs such as Wayne and Clifton, one of New Jersey's largest and oldest suburban communities.

Along with suburban Essex County voters, these suburbanites keep GOP candidates competitive. The Essex County portion — about a third of the 8th's population — is mainly suburban turf, from the more affluent areas such as Montclair and South Orange to the blue-collar and middle-class towns of Nutley and Belleville. Italian Catholics make up a notable segment; there are also pockets of Jewish voters.

Democrats hold the edge in districtwide registration, but they usually run best at the local and statewide levels. In 1989, Democrat James J. Florio won the district in his successful gubernatorial bid. At the presidential level, the GOP often flexes its muscle: In 1984, Ronald Reagan racked up 59 percent and in 1988, George Bush won 54 percent.

Essex is one of New Jersey's traditional Democratic strongholds, and its party politics are rife with the usual internecine battles. The 8th District portion does not include the Democratic stronghold of Newark, but the county's Democratic machine still casts a long shadow.

Bloomfield, Essex County's largest city in the 8th, even managed to play a role in the 1988 presidential election. It was at a local flag factory that Bush met with the local makers of Old Glory, in order to publicize the controversy surrounding Democratic nominee Michael S. Dukakis and the Pledge of Allegiance.

1990 Population: 594,629. White 444,372 (75%), Black 77,145 (13%), Other 73,112 (12%). Hispanic origin 105,764 (18%). 18 and over 461,457 (78%), 62 and over 104,868 (18%). Median age: 35.

Committees

Banking, Finance & Urban Affairs (15th of 30 Democrats)
Economic Growth; Financial Institutions Supervision, Regulation & Deposit Insurance; Housing & Community Development

Science, Space & Technology (19th of 33 Democrats)
Energy; Technology, Environment & Aviation

Campaign Finance

	Receipts	Receipts from PACs		Expend-itures
1992				
Klein (D)	$1,295,113	$178,920	(14%)	$1,249,023
Bubba (R)	$435,590	$115,849	(27%)	$432,784
Kolodziej (IFC)	$12,643	0		$3,850

Key Votes

1993

Require parental notification of minors' abortions	N
Require unpaid family and medical leave	Y
Approve national "motor voter" registration bill	Y
Approve budget increasing taxes and reducing deficit	Y
Approve economic stimulus plan	Y

Elections

1992 General		
Herb C. Klein (D)	96,742	(47%)
Joseph L. Bubba (R)	84,674	(41%)
Gloria J. Kolodziej (IFC)	16,170	(8%)
Thomas Caslander (IFC)	2,916	(1%)
Carmine O. Pellosie (IPPN)	2,135	(1%)
1992 Primary		
Herb C. Klein (D)	9,456	(39%)
Harry A. McEnroe (D)	6,786	(28%)
Clare I. Lagermasini (D)	6,510	(27%)
Joseph C. Iozia (D)	1,127	(5%)
Roger P. Ham (D)	502	(2%)

District Vote for President

	1992	
D	107,304	(46%)
R	99,974	(43%)
I	27,797	(12%)

9 Robert G. Torricelli (D)

Of Englewood — Elected 1982; 6th Term

Born: Aug. 26, 1951, Paterson, N.J.
Education: Rutgers U., A.B. 1974, J.D. 1977; Harvard U., M.P.A. 1980.
Occupation: Lawyer.
Family: Divorced.
Religion: Methodist.
Political Career: No previous office.
Capitol Office: 2159 Rayburn Bldg. 20515; 225-5061.

In Washington: When Torricelli was elected to the House at age 31, he was regarded as a young man in a hurry. He was forced to defer his hopes for a quick jump to higher office in 1989, when more senior Democratic House colleague Jim Florio claimed the New Jersey governorship that Torricelli coveted.

But Torricelli, still just in his early 40s, keeps himself plenty busy in the House as he awaits another opportunity to move up. Exuding intelligence and a brash self-assurance, he has muscled his way into several major policy debates. Along the way he has attracted allies — mainly Democrats who admire his intensity and partisan zeal — and detractors, including Republicans nettled by his rhetoric and some "good government" reformers who see his aggressive fundraising as emblematic of a campaign system in which politicians are too preoccupied with the money chase.

The chairman of the Foreign Affairs Subcommittee on Western Hemisphere Affairs, Torricelli in the 102nd Congress authored legislation that tightened economic sanctions against communist-run Cuba. When the Cuba Democracy Act came up in 1992, Cuba's economy was reeling from the loss of aid from its fallen communist sponsor, the Soviet Union. Torricelli promoted his sanctions bill as a means of hastening the fall of Cuban dictator Fidel Castro. The bill extended the existing embargo on U.S. trade with Cuba to foreign subsidiaries of companies based in the United States and barred from U.S. ports any ships that had stopped in Cuba.

The measure's passage in October 1992 earned Torricelli a denunciation from Havana. The official Cuban news agency described him as "the equivocal, opportunistic politico from New Jersey who has tried to build a career by cultivating the most reactionary and fascist elements of the counter-revolutionary Cuban exile community."

The bill also earned Torricelli some negative publicity from another quarter. A Wall Street Journal article in August 1992 implied a connection between Torricelli's anti-Castro activism and campaign contributions he received from Cuban exiles. Torricelli strongly denied a link.

Helping prompt media interest in Torricelli's efforts to weaken Castro — a goal promoted by the Reagan and Bush administrations — was the fact that in his work on other Latin American issues, Torricelli had been a sharp critic of GOP policies.

Torricelli was one of the staunchest opponents of U.S. military assistance to the government of El Salvador in its battle with leftist guerrillas, and he also opposed U.S. backing of the Nicaragua contras who sought to overthrow that nation's communist Sandinista government.

Political settlements in both countries led to democratic elections, which Republicans declared as vindication of the Reagan-Bush policies. But Torricelli seems unwilling to let the matter rest at that.

In March 1993, a United Nations-sponsored commission issued a report on El Salvador's civil war; among its findings was that Reagan administration officials had reason to know that Salvadoran armed forces murdered non-combatants and committed other human rights abuses; allegations of such actions had fueled Torricelli's opposition to military aid.

From his Foreign Affairs perch, Torricelli reacted viscerally to the report. "It is now clear that while the Reagan administration was certifying human rights progress in El Salvador they knew the terrible truth that the Salvadoran military was engaged in a widespread campaign of terror and torture," he said. "This committee," he warned, "will review every word uttered by every Reagan administration official" for evidence of perjury.

Republicans accused him of using "McCarthyite" tactics to justify his own opposition to 1980s Republican policies.

There is no doubting Torricelli's sense of partisanship: In 1989, he was the House lawyer for Speaker Jim Wright, D-Texas, then facing ethics charges that would end his career.

Yet despite his partisan edge, he occasionally will take a high-profile step away from the party line. Torricelli said in early 1993 that he

New Jersey 9

North — Fort Lee; Hackensack

Sports fans and concertgoers are familiar with the Meadowlands stadium complex in East Rutherford, but otherwise, there is little to distinguish the 9th from other suburban New Jersey districts.

By one measure — money — the 9th stands out. With more than half the population of Bergen County, one of the country's wealthiest counties, the district is more affluent than its suburban and urbanized north Jersey counterparts.

It covers southeastern Bergen County and part of Hudson County, with prestigious Bergen addresses clustered in Englewood and the northern reaches of the 9th. The blue-collar areas are in the south.

The George Washington Bridge, connecting Manhattan's 181st Street and the New Jersey Palisades, is a fitting symbol for the 9th. Opened in 1931, the span spurred the growth of Bergen County.

South of posh Englewood, Fort Lee is home to affluent Asian-Americans, including a thriving Japanese community. Farther west from the Hudson River, the Jewish voters of Teaneck and Fair Lawn — part of which is in the 5th District — help turn out a Democratic vote, despite the towns' relative affluence. Hackensack has some affluent sections, but is more blue-collar, with a large black population.

Beginning south of the city of Hackensack, the Hackensack Meadowlands area is a 30-mile commercial and residential engine, experiencing increasing development amid the swamps of the region.

The southern reaches of the 9th contain working-class towns with large numbers of white ethnics, in places such as North Arlington, Lyndhurst and Kearny (Hudson County). Most of Kearny is in the 9th, with the exception of about 300 residents who live in the 13th.

Hudson County contributes about a fifth of the district population and contains a mix of Hispanics and white ethnics, drawn from parts of Jersey City, Kearny, North Bergen and all of Secaucus.

The Jersey City segment is carved from the northern part of the city; it includes many Hispanics. The 9th is one of three districts that splice into Jersey City, the other two being the majority-minority 10th and 13th districts.

The 9th has no single dominant industry. Englewood Cliffs houses some corporate headquarters; Secaucus has attracted new restaurants, offices, hotels and shopping outlets. It is also a warehousing and distribution center.

The politics of the 9th are firmly Democratic. Bergen, as a whole, backed GOP Senate challenger Christine Todd Whitman over incumbent Democrat Bill Bradley in 1990 — and George Bush in 1992 — but the 9th District portion does not include the rock-ribbed Republican communities on the northern tier.

In 1992, Bill Clinton won 48 percent in this part of Bergen. Rep. Torricelli carried Bergen by almost 42,000 votes at the same time, against a highly touted GOP challenger.

1990 Population: 594,630. White 497,644 (84%), Black 38,517 (6%), Other 58,469 (10%). Hispanic origin 67,913 (11%). 18 and over 480,677 (81%), 62 and over 115,521 (19%). Median age: 37.

would "reserve judgment" on some controversial elements of the Clinton administration's agenda, such as lifting the ban on homosexuals serving in the military and raising taxes on upper-income individuals.

On occasion, Torricelli also has pushed House Speaker Thomas S. Foley, D-Wash., about as far as he could dare. In 1990, Torricelli forcefully disagreed with Foley's priority of passing a campaign-finance reform bill. Foley may have been sending Torricelli a message when he persuaded Rep. Vic Fazio of California to take the chairmanship of the Democratic Congressional Campaign Committee, a position Torricelli wanted.

In the wake of the House bank scandal in the 102nd Congress, Torricelli was one of a handful of Democrats who openly criticized Foley for lax management of the institution. But Foley ultimately reasserted firm control, and Torricelli pronounced himself satisfied. "I wanted to see him fight and he fought," Torricelli said in August 1992.

A sign that Torricelli apparently had made amends came at the start of the 103rd Congress, when Foley appointed him to the Select Intelligence Committee. He is also a member of the Science Committee. His interests range beyond his formal assignments: He is a leading House advocate of controlling sales of handguns and assault weapons.

At Home: At the outset of the 1992 redistricting process, Torricelli looked like a prime prospect to get squeezed. But when the election was done, he was unscathed.

New Jersey lost a House seat in 1990

reapportionment, and as the least-senior white Democrat in north Jersey — an area where population had declined — Torricelli was at risk of seeing his district eliminated.

But he armed himself with a $1 million-plus campaign treasury and plotted a steady course through the year. When a map merging his district with another Democrat's was considered, talk surfaced that Torricelli might challenge Gov. Florio in the 1993 primary unless he got a better deal in redistricting. A better deal did come his way: The final map left Torricelli's district intact and put two other Democratic incumbents together.

Still, Torricelli faced an aggressive GOP challenger. State Rep. Patrick J. Roma relentlessly hammered Torricelli for his 27 overdrafts at the House bank and his use of the franking privilege. But Roma knocked himself offstride by waffling on gun control, and that was enough to doom him in a district with a Democratic edge as Clinton carried the state for president. Torricelli beat Roma by 21 points.

In 1982, after redistricting had made the 9th District attractive to Democrats, Torricelli moved there from his home in northern Bergen County and launched a campaign against GOP Rep. Harold Hollenbeck. A moderate Republican with labor support, Hollenbeck had survived three terms in his blue-collar constituency, but had never before faced strong opposition.

Hollenbeck played down his partisan affiliation, but he had backed President Reagan's economic plan in 1981, something Torricelli used against him. The incumbent also suffered from his lackadaisical manner, staying in Washington while Torricelli campaigned door-to-door. Hollenbeck returned home during the October recess, but even his staff sometimes did not know where to find him. Torricelli won 53 percent of the overall vote.

Torricelli's big winning margins in 1986 and 1988 sparked speculation about his potential as a future statewide candidate, speculation he fueled by testing the waters for a 1989 gubernatorial campaign. But by early 1989, Florio had established himself as the front-runner and Torricelli took himself out of contention.

Committees

Foreign Affairs (4th of 27 Democrats)
Western Hemisphere Affairs (chairman); Africa; Asia & the Pacific

Science, Space & Technology (8th of 33 Democrats)
Space; Technology, Environment & Aviation

Select Intelligence (5th of 12 Democrats)
Oversight & Evaluation; Program & Budget Authorization

Elections

1992 General		
Robert G. Torricelli (D)	139,188	(58%)
Patrick J. Roma (R)	88,179	(37%)
Peter J. Russo (CUC)	4,491	(2%)
1992 Primary		
Robert G. Torricelli (D)	24,010	(80%)
Nancy Harrigan (D)	4,733	(16%)
Matthew C. Guice (D)	1,429	(5%)
1990 General		
Robert G. Torricelli (D)	82,736	(57%)
Peter J. Russo (R)	59,759	(41%)
Chester Grabowski (POP)	2,573	(2%)

Previous Winning Percentages: 1988 (67%) **1986** (69%) **1984** (63%) **1982** (53%)

District Vote for President

1992
D 122,676 (48%)
R 102,578 (40%)
I 31,527 (12%)

Campaign Finance

	Receipts	Receipts from PACs		Expend-itures
1992				
Torricelli (D)	$1,190,045	$350,495	(29%)	$1,001,343
Roma (R)	$176,768	$29,550	(17%)	$172,946
1990				
Torricelli (D)	$818,917	$236,389	(29%)	$495,219
Russo (R)	$34,591	$1,600	(5%)	$34,513

Key Votes

1993	
Require parental notification of minors' abortions	N
Require unpaid family and medical leave	Y
Approve national "motor voter" registration bill	Y
Approve budget increasing taxes and reducing deficit	Y
Approve economic stimulus plan	Y
1992	
Approve balanced-budget constitutional amendment	Y
Close down space station program	N
Approve U.S. aid for former Soviet Union	Y
Allow shifting funds from defense to domestic programs	Y
1991	
Extend unemployment benefits using deficit financing	Y
Approve waiting period for handgun purchases	Y
Authorize use of force in Persian Gulf	Y

Voting Studies

	Presidential Support		Party Unity		Conservative Coalition	
Year	**S**	**O**	**S**	**O**	**S**	**O**
1992	25	66	82	10	48	40
1991	33	60	81	10	38	54
1990	20	65	83	8	35	57
1989	34	56	86	5	29	66
1988	23	71	88	6	39	58
1987	18	78	81	5	33	63
1986	19	74	85	7	20	68
1985	24	71	87	4	18	78
1984	31	61	76	17	31	66
1983	17	78	82	6	16	80

Interest Group Ratings

Year	ADA	AFL-CIO	CCUS	ACU
1992	85	83	33	16
1991	60	92	30	20
1990	83	100	31	10
1989	75	100	30	0
1988	85	100	25	4
1987	84	93	15	5
1986	70	100	13	9
1985	80	100	19	5
1984	70	69	31	13
1983	85	100	15	4

10 Donald M. Payne (D)

Of Newark — Elected 1988; 3rd Term

Born: July 16, 1934, Newark, N.J.
Education: Seton Hall U., B.A. 1957.
Occupation: Community development executive.
Family: Widowed; two children.
Religion: Baptist.
Political Career: Essex County Board of Chosen Freeholders, 1972-78; sought Democratic nomination for Essex County executive, 1978; sought Democratic nomination for U.S. House, 1980; Newark Municipal Council, 1982-88; sought Democratic nomination for U.S. House, 1986.
Capitol Office: 417 Cannon Bldg. 20515; 225-3436.

In Washington: Payne has established a reputation among his colleagues and in his district as a hard worker whose effectiveness comes from quiet perseverance and a pleasant, low-key style.

"I would not call myself electrifying," Payne once related. "But I think there is a lot of dignity in being able to achieve things without having to create rupture."

Payne, usually a reliable vote for the Democratic leadership line, is primarily interested in trying to address the problems of urban areas — not surprising for a member who represents a district plagued with a list of social ills. The 10th includes Newark, which, like many cities, is struggling with high rates of poverty and unemployment. Newark also is coping with an unusually high percentage of residents with AIDS; their medical problems severely strain the health-care system.

An African-American member from a district with a 60 percent black-majority population, Payne also devotes attention to U.S. policies affecting Africa. He has a seat on the Foreign Affairs Committee.

Payne generally has been skeptical of U.S. military intervention abroad. He opposed authorizing the use of force against Iraq in 1991, and after the air war began, he was one of several members to vote "present" on a resolution supporting President Bush and the military. Later, he was one of 42 members to sign a letter urging Bush not to launch a ground offensive.

But in late 1992, Payne supported the president's decision to send U.S. troops to Somalia. Payne traveled to the country to get a firsthand look at the widespread suffering caused there by the collapse of order and factional violence.

During organizing for the 103rd Congress, Payne was a leader in a successful effort to preserve the Foreign Affairs Subcommittee on Africa. A leadership mandate to trim subcommittees gave rise to a proposal that the panel be combined with another subcommittee. But Payne and his allies argued that the affairs of the continent were too important not to retain a separate subcommittee. The panel survived, as Foreign Affairs was allowed to keep seven subcommittees, one over its limit.

Payne also backed retention of another of his committees that got caught in the House's cost-trimming efforts — the Select Committee on Narcotics. Early in 1993 he voted to preserve the panel, where he served under chairman Charles B. Rangel, N.Y., another black Democrat from an urban district. But Select Narcotics was killed, falling prey to critics who said its work was being duplicated by other permanent committees.

Although Payne introduces some legislation, most often in Washington he spends his time helping promote the Democratic leadership's legislative initiatives. Indeed, Payne is more likely to call a news conference back home in Newark than to opt for a stately Capitol Hill backdrop. In the 102nd, when Payne wanted to bring attention to the family and medical leave bill he favored, he and fellow New Jersey Democrat Robert G. Torricelli held a news conference at the headquarters of the Newark Teachers Union to drum up support.

"No 'kinder, gentler nation' would inflict additional hardships on working Americans during times of crisis," Payne said.

After New York Democrat Ted Weiss died in 1992, Payne ran his Government Operations Subcommittee on Human Resources and Intergovernmental Affairs for the remainder of the 102nd. Shortly after becoming chairman, Payne held a subcommittee hearing in Newark to call attention to a sharp upturn in cases of AIDS-related tuberculosis in Newark and other cities where AIDS is a big problem.

Also in the 102nd, Payne worked with his state's two senators to secure $1.5 million in funding for a safe house for children suffering from lead poisoning.

New Jersey 10

Parts of Newark and Jersey City

At midcentury, Newark was a city of nearly a half-million people. Nine percent of the state's population lived here; it was a commercial center that held about 15 percent of all jobs in New Jersey.

Now, as the century winds down, Newark tells a different story. Population has declined to about 275,000. The city is still the most populous in the state — and the largest employment center — but its share of New Jersey's jobs is only about 4 percent.

The decade after the riots of the late 1960s saw a steep decline in the number of jobs and an increase in the number of whites moving out of the city. As the Irish and Italians who used to vie for political power fled to the suburbs, blacks became a majority, and accordingly, grabbed the reins of power at City Hall; an African-American has held the mayoralty since 1970. Districtwide, blacks make up about 60 percent of the population.

Blacks and whites have lived an uneasy coexistence in Newark, but both communities are as one in their inurement to the political intrigue and ethical improprieties of local politics.

In political circles, Essex County Democrats have been stabbing each other in the back since the late 1970s, when the county switched to a county executive form of government, thus diminishing the influence of local party bosses.

Redistricting split the city between the 10th and 13th districts, but more than half the residents of Newark live in the 10th. The 10th District portion is made up of the primarily black central and south wards, with some Hispanics and Portuguese from the east ward.

The central ward was decimated in the riots of 1967 and has never fully recovered. There have been efforts to revitalize the area, but the desperate living conditions and deep poverty have changed little.

From Newark, the district extends into the Essex County suburbs that combine with the city to make up almost two-thirds of the district's population.

Outside the city are some racially mixed, working-class suburbs such as Irvington and Montclair (which is shared with the 8th District).

Orange and populous East Orange are majority-black. More affluent are South and liberal West Orange, although most of both places are in the 8th.

Union County adds a little more than a quarter of the vote. Democratic and blue-collar Elizabeth is a hefty chunk of this portion, even though it is divided between the 13th and the 10th. Republicans can find votes in Rahway and Roselle.

Parts of two Democratic Hudson County municipalities — Jersey City and Bayonne — round out the 10th. This section of Jersey City includes about one-fourth of New Jersey's second-largest city; the Bayonne segment consists of about 5,000 residents. Like virtually everywhere else in the district — which is far and away the most Democratic in the state — they churn out healthy Democratic margins.

1990 Population: 594,630. White 194,097 (33%), Black 357,671 (60%), Other 42,862 (7%). Hispanic origin 72,877 (12%). 18 and over 444,087 (75%), 62 and over 83,709 (14%). Median age: 32.

In addition to keeping a high profile in the 10th, Payne works hard at being a role model there. He visits schools to encourage young people to stay in school and stay straight. While some members are bashful about the pay they receive because it looks lavish to the average American, Payne touts his six-figure salary as part of his pitch to youth that hard work pays off: He says he earns a lot more than any drug peddler.

At Home: Perseverance enabled Payne to pull himself from poverty and become a successful businessman and community and political leader in his hometown of Newark.

It took the same kind of perseverance — three campaigns — to win election in the black-majority 10th: His path was blocked by the legendary Democratic Rep. Peter W. Rodino Jr., who held the seat for 40 years. Rodino, chairman of the Judiciary Committee, achieved national fame during the 1974 Watergate hearings, but it was Rodino's steadfast advocacy of civil rights legislation that earned him the loyalty — and votes — of many black residents in the 10th.

Insisting that the time had come for Newark-area blacks to be represented by one of their own, Payne challenged Rodino in the 1980 Democratic primary, and again in the 1986 primary. However, black good will toward Rodino, combined with his base in Newark's mainly Italian North Ward, enabled the incumbent to win easily. Payne got 23 percent of the vote in 1980 and 36 percent in 1986.

But when Rodino said the 1986 contest would be his last, local Democrats got behind Payne, a longtime party insider who had served on the Essex County Board and was in his second term on the Newark Municipal Council.

Payne's only opposition came in the Democratic primary from City Council colleague Ralph T. Grant Jr. But Payne's advantages — party support, a sizable campaign treasury and recognition earned in his earlier campaigns — brought him the nomination in a landslide. Payne's November victory was a formality in the overwhelmingly Democratic district.

For a man so determined to become a black political pioneer, the soft-spoken Payne does not cut a dynamic figure. A high school teacher and football coach after college, he moved into business in 1963 as community affairs director for the Newark-based Prudential Insurance Co. More recently, he was vice president of a computer forms company founded by his brother.

The head of a "storefront YMCA" in inner-city Newark in the late 1950s, Payne became the first black president of the National Council of YMCAs in 1970, and later served two four-year terms as chairman of the YMCA's international committee on refugees. While participating in all these activities, the widowed Payne was raising two children and building his political career.

Committees

Education & Labor (10th of 28 Democrats)
Elementary, Secondary & Vocational Education; Labor-Management Relations; Select Education

Foreign Affairs (14th of 27 Democrats)
Africa

Government Operations (17th of 25 Democrats)
Human Resources & Intergovernmental Relations

Elections

1992 General		
Donald M. Payne (D)	117,287	(78%)
Alfred D. Palermo (R)	30,160	(20%)
1992 Primary		
Donald M. Payne (D)	31,846	(74%)
Willie L. Flood (D)	4,167	(10%)
Brian Connors (D)	3,601	(8%)
Stanley J. Moskal (D)	3,502	(8%)
1990 General		
Donald M. Payne (D)	42,616	(81%)
Howard E. Berkeley (R)	9,072	(17%)
George Mehrabian (SW)	617	(1%)

Previous Winning Percentage: **1988** (77%)

District Vote for President

1992

D 125,922 (71%)
R 35,930 (20%)
I 14,854 (8%)

Campaign Finance

	Receipts	Receipts from PACs		Expend-itures
1992				
Payne (D)	$358,688	$183,606	(51%)	$285,455
Palermo (R)	$26,277	$1,305	(5%)	$26,276
1990				
Payne (D)	$282,420	$185,642	(66%)	$162,612

Key Votes

1993	
Require parental notification of minors' abortions	N
Require unpaid family and medical leave	Y
Approve national "motor voter" registration bill	Y
Approve budget increasing taxes and reducing deficit	Y
Approve economic stimulus plan	Y
1992	
Approve balanced-budget constitutional amendment	N
Close down space station program	Y
Approve U.S. aid for former Soviet Union	N
Allow shifting funds from defense to domestic programs	Y
1991	
Extend unemployment benefits using deficit financing	Y
Approve waiting period for handgun purchases	Y
Authorize use of force in Persian Gulf	N

Voting Studies

	Presidential Support		Party Unity		Conservative Coalition	
Year	**S**	**O**	**S**	**O**	**S**	**O**
1992	10	85	92	3	4	92
1991	24	72	95	2	0	97
1990	16	81	92	5	9	89
1989	24	62	86	2	2	90

Interest Group Ratings

Year	ADA	AFL-CIO	CCUS	ACU
1992	95	91	13	0
1991	95	100	20	0
1990	89	100	29	4
1989	90	100	30	4

11 Dean A. Gallo (R)

Of Parsippany — Elected 1984; 5th Term

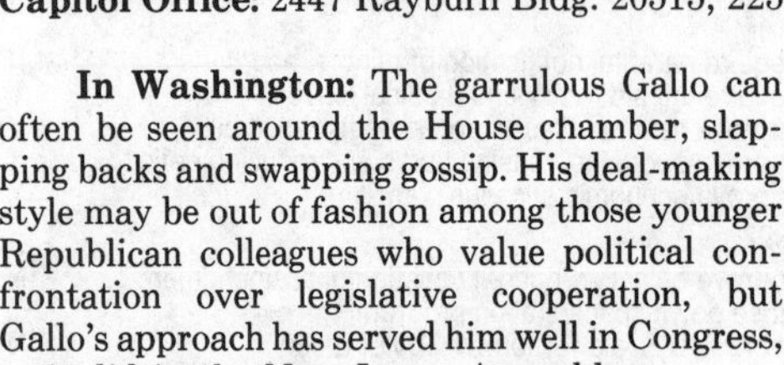

Born: Nov. 23, 1935, Hackensack, N.J.
Education: Graduated from Boonton H.S., 1954.
Occupation: Real estate broker.
Family: Divorced; two children.
Religion: Methodist.
Political Career: Parsippany-Troy Hills Township Council, 1968-71; Morris County Board of Chosen Freeholders, 1971-75; N.J. Assembly, 1976-84, minority leader, 1982-84.
Capitol Office: 2447 Rayburn Bldg. 20515; 225-5034.

In Washington: The garrulous Gallo can often be seen around the House chamber, slapping backs and swapping gossip. His deal-making style may be out of fashion among those younger Republican colleagues who value political confrontation over legislative cooperation, but Gallo's approach has served him well in Congress, as it did in the New Jersey Assembly.

With the retirement of several senior New Jersey members in 1992, Gallo at the start of the 103rd Congress moved to the front rank of the delegation. With a seat on the Appropriations Committee, he is the only member from New Jersey on either of the "money committees" (Appropriations and Ways and Means) that control federal spending and taxing. The rest of the delegation will need to go to him for help funding projects in their districts. And he can also pile up chits from members across the country.

On the home front, the focus of Gallo's attention will be the massive — and controversial — Passaic River flood control project that is partly in his district. Gallo in 1991 gave up a position on the Foreign Operations Subcommittee to get on the Energy and Water Development Subcommittee, which controls funding for such projects, and he has helped get federal monies flowing. The complex tunnel and levee system has been demanded by labor unions and property owners in a 935-square-mile area prone to periodic flooding, but environmentalists oppose the project.

In early 1993, Gallo put the squeeze on Democratic Gov. James J. Florio, who was seeking minor funding to keep the $2 billion project alive but refusing to make a commitment to it in an election year. Gallo demanded Florio's full support if the project was to get more money.

A Northeastern Republican with a sizable urban constituency, Gallo votes with his party less often than the average Republican, but he is more loyal to the conservative GOP majority than are most of his regional neighbors. In 1993, for instance, Gallo was the only member of the New Jersey delegation to follow the GOP leadership line and vote against a family leave bill, even though New Jersey Republican Marge Roukema was a leading advocate of the measure. Such loyalty to party and his convivial style make him useful to the leadership as a vote-counter, a role he serves as regional whip. He is co-chair of the Northeast-Midwest Congressional Coalition, a caucus of Rust Belt members.

The Northeasterner in Gallo shows most clearly on environmental issues. In the 101st Congress, he won House approval for an amendment to the oil-spill liability bill that required tankers to have double hulls. Gallo's amendment was weakened in conference to impose the requirement only on newly built tankers, but it was one of the few specific congressional actions taken in response to the *Exxon Valdez* oil spill in Alaska.

In the 102nd Congress, he was among those who worked to help commuters nationwide by supporting a provision in a big energy bill that nearly tripled the tax break employers could get from subsidizing mass transit for their workers.

In the 99th Congress, Gallo staked out a portion of the "superfund" legislation as his specialty by proposing a "community right to know" amendment, joining with Bob Wise, a West Virginia Democrat. The final bill included their language to provide federal money for local committees to gather information about dangerous substances and develop plans for dealing with any emergency that might occur.

Gallo got in a tough spot in 1989, when Democrats used the District of Columbia funding bill to force the first House vote on abortion since the Supreme Court's *Webster* decision. As the ranking Republican on the D.C. Appropriations Subcommittee, he took part in meetings to discuss strategy for repealing a ban on using D.C. funds to pay for abortion in cases of rape or incest. Gallo supported repealing the ban, a position at odds with the majority GOP view, and he apparently neglected to tip off his party about the strategy of the abortion-rights activists. An amendment repealing the ban won

New Jersey 11

North — Morris County

The 11th covers all of Morris County and parts of four others, but it can be described best by one word: Republican.

By all standards, this is the most rock-ribbed Republican district in the state. In 1984, Ronald Reagan captured 71 percent of the vote, when its boundaries were similarly drawn. Four years later, his vice president, George Bush, racked up 68 percent.

If that is not enough evidence of the 11th's voting habits, witness the 1989 gubernatorial election results: Democrat James J. Florio, who won 61 percent statewide, posted an anemic 35 percent here, his worst showing of all the state's 13 congressional districts.

The Republican dominance continued in the 1992 campaign, despite tough times for north Jersey white-collar employees. Bush won 52 percent, his best showing in New Jersey. Rep. Gallo won by about 120,000 votes.

More than two-thirds of the vote comes from Morris County. The middle-class Parsippany-Troy Hills community is the largest in the district; it is occasionally receptive to Democratic candidates. After years of rapid growth, population stabilized by the late 1980s.

Central and northern Morris County is mostly white and affluent, populated by well-educated white-collar professionals, bankers, lawyers and stockbrokers who live in upscale places such as Chatham, Kinnelon and Mendham. Harding is especially well-off, even by Morris County standards.

Minorities make up a tiny portion of the 11th's population. Morristown has a relatively large black community; Hispanics live in blue-collar Dover and Victory Gardens.

Toward the west, the county has lost some of its pastoral landscape to newer tract developments which are rapidly altering the character of the area.

Eastern Morris is home to a number of Fortune 500 companies that keep headquarters in local corporate office complexes.

During the 1980s, a number of corporate complexes sprouted up across the county, but the recession and white-collar downsizing have left the area with a glut of vacant office space.

After Morris County, Essex County is the most-populous portion with about 66,000 residents. This handful of western municipalities is wealthier than the county as a whole. Livingston, hometown of former GOP Gov. Thomas H. Kean, is Republican but contains a large Jewish community that leans Democratic.

A grab bag of towns from Somerset and Sussex counties are also grafted onto the 11th, along with Bloomingdale, the lone town from Passaic County. Somerset adds Bernards township, Raritan borough, Somerville and Bridgewater — which is shared with the 7th District. Hopatcong and Sparta are the largest towns from Sussex County.

Their voting tendencies fit right in with Morris County Republicans; Gallo carried them all effortlessly in 1992.

1990 Population: 594,630. White 548,691 (92%), Black 15,995 (3%), Other 29,944 (5%). Hispanic origin 24,567 (4%). 18 and over 458,657 (77%), 62 and over 79,766 (13%). Median age: 35.

congressional approval but prompted a presidential veto.

Despite such occasional discomfort, the insider's role suits Gallo's experience and his instincts. In a 1992 article, he bemoaned the recent ascendancy in Congress of strident ideological advocacy over problem-solving. "Talking about problems gets more attention than solving them," he complained.

At Home: Gallo is well-connected in state GOP circles and popular among moderates and conservatives alike. In 1981, Gallo, then the state Assembly Republican leader, joined U.S. Rep. Jim Courter as a co-chairman of Thomas H. Kean's successful gubernatorial campaign. With Kean retiring in 1989, Gallo signed on as chairman of Courter's campaign for the GOP nomination.

In 1983, the U.S. Supreme Court struck down the Democratic-drawn district map used for the 1982 elections; a new court-drawn plan gave the 11th a GOP hue, placing veteran Democratic Rep. Joseph G. Minish at a disadvantage. Gallo was seen as Minish's greatest threat. A business-oriented moderate, he had been elected minority leader of the Assembly in 1981, and represented the eastern half of heavily Republican Morris County, added to the 11th by the remap. Gallo, unopposed in the primary, got an early start against Minish.

In letters to GOP and independent voters, Gallo hammered at the incumbent, a former union official, calling him anti-business and criticizing his opposition to Ronald Reagan's tax and budget policies. An old-school personal campaigner, Minish reacted slowly but eventually went on the offensive, criticizing Gallo for supporting tax increases in the Legislature. But Gallo, helped by Reagan's strong showing, won easily.

He has had no trouble since then. In 1992, Democrat Ona Spiridellis, a state consumer affairs official, attacked Gallo as "a career politician and a foot soldier of the Reagan/Bush administration who has been taking a biennial cakewalk to re-election." But when the music stopped, she was left with only 26 percent of the vote in a field crowded with minor candidates.

Committees

Appropriations (13th of 23 Republicans)
Energy & Water Development; Veterans Affairs, Housing & Urban Development & Independent Agencies

Elections

1992 General		
Dean A. Gallo (R)	188,165	(70%)
Ona Spiridellis (D)	68,871	(26%)
Richard S. Roth (LIBERT)	3,538	(1%)
Barry J. Fitzpatrick (TFC)	3,127	(1%)
1990 General		
Dean A. Gallo (R)	95,198	(65%)
Michael Gordon (D)	47,782	(33%)
Jasper Gould (POP)	3,610	(2%)

Previous Winning Percentages: **1988** (70%) **1986** (68%) **1984** (56%)

District Vote for President

1992

D 97,697 (33%)
R 153,731 (52%)
I 46,418 (16%)

Campaign Finance

	Receipts	Receipts from PACs		Expend-itures
1992				
Gallo (R)	$567,280	$187,284	(33%)	$618,448
Spiridellis (D)	$123,342	$21,150	(17%)	$132,520
1990				
Gallo (R)	$652,386	$189,245	(29%)	$694,735
Gordon (D)	$106,599	$5,850	(5%)	$105,031

Key Votes

1993	
Require parental notification of minors' abortions	Y
Require unpaid family and medical leave	N
Approve national "motor voter" registration bill	N
Approve budget increasing taxes and reducing deficit	N
Approve economic stimulus plan	N
1992	
Approve balanced-budget constitutional amendment	Y
Close down space station program	N
Approve U.S. aid for former Soviet Union	Y
Allow shifting funds from defense to domestic programs	N
1991	
Extend unemployment benefits using deficit financing	Y
Approve waiting period for handgun purchases	Y
Authorize use of force in Persian Gulf	Y

Voting Studies

	Presidential Support		Party Unity		Conservative Coalition	
Year	**S**	**O**	**S**	**O**	**S**	**O**
1992	71	26	73	24	88	10
1991	67	31	67	30	84	14
1990	60	37	65	29	85	13
1989	64	34	48	50	73	27
1988	59	40	84	14	87	13
1987	55	44	71	27	88	12
1986	70	29	71	27	86	14
1985	63	38	80	19	82	18

Interest Group Ratings

Year	ADA	AFL-CIO	CCUS	ACU
1992	25	33	75	76
1991	20	42	90	60
1990	17	8	77	65
1989	25	25	100	61
1988	30	31	79	72
1987	32	44	67	57
1986	35	57	61	68
1985	20	29	68	81

12 Dick Zimmer (R)

Of Flemington — Elected 1990; 2nd Term

Born: Aug. 16, 1944, Newark, N.J.
Education: Yale U., B.A. 1966, LL.B. 1969.
Occupation: Lawyer.
Family: Wife, Marfy Goodspeed; two children.
Religion: Jewish.
Political Career: GOP nominee for N.J. Assembly, 1979; N.J. Assembly, 1982-87; N.J. Senate, 1987-91.
Capitol Office: 228 Cannon Bldg. 20515; 225-5801.

In Washington: A strong fiscal conservative and a veteran advocate of tax cuts, Zimmer has nonetheless emerged as a moderate voice within the House Republican Conference of the early 1990s.

In his first term he introduced legislation that would require a two-thirds vote in both houses to raise taxes. And he used his spot on the Science Committee to become a leading opponent of the space station project, an undertaking he derides as wasteful pork barrel spending. The station is still alive, but Zimmer believes his efforts have found a sympathetic audience within the Clinton administration.

At the same time, Zimmer has attracted environmentalists' approval with bills that would mandate a 10-year moratorium on oil and gas leasing off the New Jersey coast and make it easier for individuals to sell or donate land to the government or private organizations for conservation purposes.

In New Jersey, he chairs the Coalition Against Higher Taxes, a grass-roots organization that lobbies at the federal and state level against what it perceives as excessive spending.

His identification with these efforts helped his star rise in the early 1990s, when Gov. James J. Florio's tax increases proved decidedly unpopular.

Zimmer sees the Clinton administration as an opportunity for the GOP to reshape its image as "giving voice to the concerns of the average taxpayer." Zimmer has been an equal opportunity skeptic, however. While in the New Jersey Legislature in 1989, Zimmer opposed Republican Gov. Thomas H. Kean's budget, arguing that it was based on false economic projections. He also predicted the Kean budget would produce big deficits, which proved to be true.

Zimmer's criticism was especially noteworthy in view of the fact that he had held important roles in all of Kean's gubernatorial campaigns.

The Clinton administration's activities in health care will also be of interest to Zimmer, a former attorney for Johnson & Johnson. Clinton has made the pharmaceutical industry, which employs more than 50,000 people in New Jersey, a favorite target of criticism.

Zimmer also will be fighting efforts by the Base Closure Commission to transfer 589 personnel from New Jersey's Fort Monmouth to Georgia. There is some irony in this, as Zimmer came to Congress as the successor to former GOP Rep. Jim Courter, who has since served as chairman of the base-closing panel.

At Home: Despite Clinton's victory in New Jersey, Zimmer's electoral strength remained unchanged in 1992. He received 64 percent of the vote, just as he had in winning his first term in 1990, but getting there was far quieter the second time. Zimmer's first race was the most expensive race in the country in 1990, largely because the Democrats nominated millionaire businesswoman Marguerite Chandler. Democrats had expected to pose Chandler against incumbent Courter, but after his devastating defeat in the 1989 gubernatorial race, Courter chose to retire rather than seek another House term. Chandler proceeded to spend $1.7 million, but she was unable to flank Zimmer and wound up with just 52,000 votes.

Zimmer co-chaired Courter's 1989 campaign and was campaign counsel in all of Kean's gubernatorial bids — his two successful ones (in 1981 and 1985) and his failed primary run (in 1977).

He chaired New Jersey Common Cause from 1974 to 1977. In 1979, he narrowly lost a campaign for the state Assembly, but two years later he prevailed; he was re-elected in 1983 and 1985. In the spring of 1987, he won a special election for the state Senate.

In the Legislature, he complemented a "good government" agenda with a resolutely conservative approach to fiscal matters. He was in the forefront of efforts to give New Jersey voters the right of initiative and referendum, and he backed campaign finance reform. He also sponsored environmental bills dealing with radon gas testing and farmland preservation.

One of three Republicans on the Senate Appropriations Committee, Zimmer was an unswerving opponent of new taxes. But his fiscal conservatism was not bound by partisan bonds.

New Jersey 12

North and central — Flemington; Princeton

Reaching from the Delaware River, on its western border, almost to the Atlantic Ocean, the 12th meanders across New Jersey's midsection.

Parts of four counties — and all of Hunterdon County — make up the district, all with one common trait: an affinity for Republican candidates.

More than a third of the population lives in Republican-leaning Monmouth County. Mostly middle-class or affluent, this portion includes rapidly growing towns such as Manalaplan and Marlboro. Voters favor Republican candidates down to the local level, particularly so in wealthy Rumson and Shrewsbury. The district border stops just short of the fragile strip of Atlantic coastline, which belongs to the neighboring 6th District.

Hunterdon, Mercer and Middlesex counties each contribute about one-fifth of the district's population. The Mercer portion includes the affluent, white-collar Trenton suburbs and middle-class, blue-collar Ewing. Colonial Princeton — home to the Ivy League institution of the same name and its 6,400 students — is a source of Democratic votes cast by the liberal academic community.

Commercial and residential spillover from the Princeton and Route 1 corridor has translated into new growth in southern Middlesex County, especially in Plainsboro and South Brunswick.

Upscale East Brunswick — the district's largest city — is as far north as the 12th's border stretches in Middlesex.

Hunterdon is the lone county wholly contained in the 12th. Here the green pastureland and riverside hamlets breed a brand of Republicanism that permeates every level of governance.

The river towns, such as Frenchtown and Lambertville, are filled with quaint antique shops and bed-and-breakfasts. Flemington, the county seat, is a shopping outlet center. The 1980s rousted this sleepy county to the reality of soaring land values and development as it became a popular East Coast weekend getaway destination and second-home community.

These changes did little to alter the county's traditional Republican character. In 1992, George Bush easily carried Hunterdon. Rep. Zimmer ran even better, winning here by a more than 4-to-1 margin.

Northern Somerset County adds a handful of lightly populated, wealthy communities, including Far Hills and Peapack, from the hunt country.

Taken as a whole, the old-money towns and affluent suburbs of the 12th give Republicans a near lock. Ronald Reagan won 64 percent in 1984, followed by Bush's 61 percent in 1988. Even in the 1989 gubernatorial election, when Democrat James J. Florio carried the state with 61 percent, the GOP nominee, then-Rep. Jim Courter, took 53 percent here.

1992 was another breezy year for Republicans, as Bush defeated Democrat Bill Clinton and Rep. Zimmer cruised in his first re-election bid.

1990 Population: 594,630. White 532,833 (90%), Black 31,114 (5%), Other 30,683 (5%). Hispanic origin 15,792 (3%). 18 and over 455,824 (77%), 62 and over 83,469 (14%). Median age: 35.

He attracted attention during 1989 budget action when he opposed Kean's budget as relying on erroneous revenue projections and thus being out of balance. Zimmer's pronouncements were later verified: Kean left the state with an estimated $600 million deficit.

In the Legislature, Zimmer took his commitment to ethics in government quite far: To avoid conflicts of interest with his work for Johnson & Johnson, he abstained from voting on legislation that would affect the company. (Chandler ridiculed the practice in a radio ad, chiding Zimmer for "ducking" issues.)

Courter had performed miserably in his 1989 statewide race, collecting a meager 37 percent of the vote and frittering away his political credibility by running a stumbling campaign and equivocating on his opposition to abortion. Still, his March 1990 announcement that he would not seek re-election stunned many in the 12th. Courter had been considered potentially vulnerable to a challenge from a candidate with Chandler's profile — a woman advocating abortion rights, with good funding and ties to the area business community.

But Chandler, a political neophyte, was unproven and largely unknown in the heavily Republican 12th.

Zimmer was a co-chairman of Courter's ill-starred bid for governor in 1989. When Courter lost and retired, Zimmer stepped up to run for Courter's seat. Among others running were Assemblyman Rodney P. Frelinghuysen and former New York Giants football star Phil McConkey. Frelinghuysen had the most famous political name in the race: His family's tradition of public service dated back to the Revolutionary War. Four Frelinghuysens had served in the U.S. Senate, and Frelinghuysen's father had served in the House from New Jersey from 1953 to 1975.

During the GOP primary, Zimmer unveiled a plan that would, among other things, reduce a political action committee's (PAC) maximum allowable contribution to a congressional candidate from $5,000 to $2,000, raise maximum allowable individual contributions from $1,000 to $2,000, remove limits on the amount political parties may contribute to campaigns and eliminate members' franking privileges as well as PACs controlled by members.

Zimmer criticized Frelinghuysen for supporting Kean's budget and had an edge among environmental activists.

He also was helped by McConkey's anti-establishment campaign, which hurt the blue-blooded Frelinghuysen more than it did Zimmer.

Committees

Government Operations (11th of 16 Republicans)
Legislation & National Security

Science, Space & Technology (11th of 22 Republicans)
Space; Technology, Environment & Aviation

Elections

1992 General		
Dick Zimmer (R)	174,216	(64%)
Frank Abate (D)	83,035	(30%)
Carl J. Mayer (I)	11,051	(4%)
1990 General		
Dick Zimmer (R)	108,173	(64%)
Marguerite Chandler (D)	52,498	(31%)
Joan I. Bottcher (Back to Basics)	4,443	(3%)
C. Max Kortepeter (Independent Reform)	2,442	(1%)
Michael A. Notarangelo (POP)	1,408	(1%)

District Vote for President

1992
D 121,447 (40%)
R 130,651 (43%)
I 50,477 (17%)

Campaign Finance

	Receipts	Receipts from PACs		Expend-itures
1992				
Zimmer (R)	$943,548	$214,214	(23%)	$911,638
Abate (D)	$63,184	$19,970	(32%)	$62,937
1990				
Zimmer (R)	$1,227,742	$204,983	(17%)	$1,224,626
Chandler (D)	$1,716,554	$51,864	(3%)	$1,707,539

Key Votes

1993	
Require parental notification of minors' abortions	Y
Require unpaid family and medical leave	Y
Approve national "motor voter" registration bill	Y
Approve budget increasing taxes and reducing deficit	N
Approve economic stimulus plan	N
1992	
Approve balanced-budget constitutional amendment	Y
Close down space station program	Y
Approve U.S. aid for former Soviet Union	N
Allow shifting funds from defense to domestic programs	N
1991	
Extend unemployment benefits using deficit financing	Y
Approve waiting period for handgun purchases	N
Authorize use of force in Persian Gulf	Y

Voting Studies

	Presidential Support		Party Unity		Conservative Coalition	
Year	S	O	S	O	S	O
1992	58	42	83	17	67	33
1991	60	39	79	19	89	11

Interest Group Ratings

Year	ADA	AFL-CIO	CCUS	ACU
1992	40	42	63	76
1991	20	42	70	70

13 Robert Menendez (D)

Of Union City — Elected 1992; 1st Term

Born: Jan. 1, 1954, New York, N.Y.
Education: St. Peter's College, B.A. 1976; Rutgers U., J.D. 1979.
Occupation: Lawyer.
Family: Wife, Jane Jacobsen; two children.
Religion: Roman Catholic.
Political Career: Union City Board of Education, 1974-78; mayor of Union City, 1986-92; N.J. Assembly, 1987-91; N.J. Senate, 1991-92.
Capitol Office: 1531 Longworth Bldg. 20515; 225-7919.

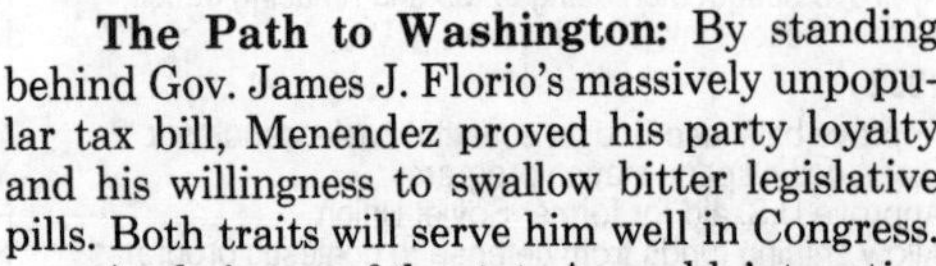

The Path to Washington: By standing behind Gov. James J. Florio's massively unpopular tax bill, Menendez proved his party loyalty and his willingness to swallow bitter legislative pills. Both traits will serve him well in Congress.

As chairman of the state Assembly's taxation subcommittee in 1990, Menendez carried Florio's $2.8 billion income tax bill, despite the risk of political consequences. He argued that the measure benefited his Hudson County constituency by easing a disproportionate property tax burden, increasing aid for municipalities — especially for schools — and stabilizing the tax base.

For his troubles, Menendez suffered no electoral consequences — which could not be said of many of the state's other prominent Democratic political figures. He was appointed to fill a state Senate vacancy in early 1991 and the following November was elected to that seat.

Menendez, the son of Cuban immigrants, has been a fixture in Hudson County politics and a central figure in the Cuban-American community. He is a lifelong Democrat — unusual for a Cuban-American politician — a position that he says best reflects his belief in an activist government. He won his first election to the school board in 1974 while still in college. He became mayor of Union City in May 1986 and simultaneously served in the Legislature beginning in January 1987.

Besides his Assembly work on the tax bill, creases. He was singled out by the National Conference of Mayors in 1987 for an antipoverty program in which the city helped finance private, nonprofit day-care centers.

Redistricting nearly doubled the district's Hispanic population, but that may not have been the most important factor in Democratic Rep. Frank J. Guarini's decision to retire after 14 years in the House. It did provide Menendez with a strong incentive to consider the race. And once Guarini made up his mind to step down, Menendez found himself with a virtually clear field for the primary and general election.

He faced Jersey City lawyer Robert P. Haney Jr. in the Democratic primary and a host of candidates in the general election, including Republican Fred J. Theemling Jr., who had lost twice to Guarini.

Menendez won the primary with 68 percent of the vote and the general with 64 percent. In both cases turnout was light, which could be attributable to typically low voter participation among Hispanics.

Menendez is proud of the fact that he is the first Hispanic to represent New Jersey in the House, but he sees himself first as an urban voice for all the constituents in this dense, ethnically diverse district. (Union City is the most densely populated municipality in the nation's most densely populated state.)

Menendez favors taxing and spending policies that promote economic growth in declining areas. He supports tax incentives for businesses to locate in designated enterprise zones, but he wants to target rewards at small companies and to require employers to try to hire first from within their zones.

He also takes a page out of Bill Clinton's economic plan, calling for tax and other incentives for high-technology infrastructure development, and from his seat on the Public Works and Transportation Committee, he may have a chance to put his ideas to work.

His seat on the Foreign Affairs Committee is of prime interest to his Cuban-American constituents. Menendez has also shown an interest in Northern Ireland. Early in the 103rd Congress, he cosponsored and delivered a short speech in support of a resolution by Democrat Joseph P. Kennedy II of Massachusetts calling for the establishment of a bill of rights for the people of the beleaguered province.

Given his background, Menendez had hoped to land a seat on the Ways and Means Committee. He was aided by New Jersey's senior senator, Democrat Bill Bradley, and the fact that Guarini, whom he was replacing in the House, had been put on the committee as a freshman. But the competition was fierce — only one freshman got a seat.

New Jersey 13

Parts of Jersey City and Newark

Not far from the place that welcomed the tired, the poor and the huddled masses yearning to be free rests Jersey City, a modern-day melting pot. Ellis Island, the onetime processing point for countless numbers of immigrants, and the Statue of Liberty are appropriately situated a short ferry ride away from the city's Liberty State Park. Although the subject is of some dispute, city boosters say the statue is within city limits.

Legendary political boss Frank "I Am the Law" Hague's machine controlled Hudson County politics from 1917 to the late 1940s, oiled by the votes of those white, working-class European immigrants. But now more than half the votes in Jersey City come from minorities, many of whom came in a second wave of immigration, primarily from Spanish-speaking countries.

About half of Jersey City — the state's second-largest city — is in the 13th, with the rest shared between the 9th and 10th districts. This portion consists mainly of the eastern parts of the city, including the downtown area, which has experienced some gentrification as young professionals have been forced across the Hudson River by New York City's housing prices.

There are Russian immigrants living downtown, and scattered pockets of Indian, Korean and Filipino immigrants, but blacks and Hispanics together make up more than half the city's population.

The local Hispanic community is far from monolithic; it consists of immigrants from more than 20 countries. The 13th as a whole has a Hispanic population of 41 percent, so it was not surprising that the district sent the state's first Hispanic representative to Washington.

The Hispanic communities are scattered across the district, as far south as Elizabeth (Union County) and Perth Amboy (Middlesex County). Union City, North Bergen, Guttenberg, and especially West New York have politically active Cuban communities that tend to vote Republican at the presidential level and Democratic in local elections.

Outside of those Republican votes, the GOP presence is muted. The various Hispanic communities and large numbers of blue-collar whites favor Democratic candidates.

Another Hudson County locale that has been gentrified is Hoboken, where yuppies have taken over the city's eastern section. The city may be better known, though, as Frank Sinatra's birthplace and the setting for the 1954 film "On the Waterfront."

From Hudson County, the 13th extends to Newark (Essex County) to siphon Puerto Rican and Italian voters from the city's north and east wards.

Middlesex and Union counties also contribute voters, but on a smaller scale. All of Perth Amboy and Carteret along with a small portion of suburban Woodbridge together make up about 10 percent of the district. Parts of Elizabeth and Linden round out the Union County contingent.

1990 Population: 594,630. White 400,803 (67%), Black 81,305 (14%), Other 112,522 (19%). Hispanic origin 246,715 (41%). 18 and over 454,356 (76%), 62 and over 87,646 (15%). Median age: 32.

Committees

Foreign Affairs (16th of 27 Democrats)
International Operations; Western Hemisphere Affairs

Public Works & Transportation (31st of 39 Democrats)
Economic Development; Surface Transportation; Water Resources & the Environment

Campaign Finance

1992	Receipts	Receipts from PACs	Expend-itures
Menendez (D)	$668,659	$226,497 (34%)	$645,640
Theemling (R)	$7,500	$1,500 (20%)	$7,499

Key Votes

1993

Require parental notification of minors' abortions	N
Require unpaid family and medical leave	Y
Approve national "motor voter" registration bill	Y
Approve budget increasing taxes and reducing deficit	Y
Approve economic stimulus plan	Y

Elections

1992 General

Robert Menendez (D)	93,670	(64%)
Fred J. Theemling Jr. (R)	44,529	(31%)
Joseph D. Bonacci (STI)	2,363	(2%)
Len Flynn (LIBERT)	1,539	(1%)
John E. Rummel (COM)	1,525	(1%)

1992 Primary

Robert Menendez (D)	24,245	(68%)
Robert P. Haney Jr. (D)	11,409	(32%)

District Vote for President

	1992
D	95,144 (54%)
R	64,727 (37%)
I	14,911 (9%)

New Mexico

STATE DATA

Governor: Bruce King (D)
First elected: 1990 *
Length of term: 4 years
Term expires: 1/95
Salary: $90,692
Term limit: 2 consecutive terms
Phone: (505) 827-3000
Born: April 6, 1924; Stanley, N.M.
Education: U. of New Mexico, 1943-44
Military Service: Army, 1944-46
Occupation: Farmer; rancher; businessman
Family: Wife, Alice Martin; two children
Religion: Baptist
Political Career: Santa Fe County Commission, 1954-59; N.M. House, 1959-69; sought Democratic nomination for governor, 1968; N.M. Democratic Party chairman, 1968-69; * governor, 1971-75, 1979-83

Lt. Gov.: Casey E. Luna (D)
First elected: 1990
Length of term: 4 years
Term expires: 1/95
Salary: $65,500
Phone: (505) 827-3050

State election official: (505) 827-3621
Democratic headquarters: (505) 842-8208
Republican headquarters: (505) 298-3662

REDISTRICTING

New Mexico retained its three House seats in reapportionment. Legislature passed the map Sept. 18, 1991; governor signed it Oct. 4.

STATE LEGISLATURE

Legislature. Meets January-March in odd years; January-February in even years.

Senate: 42 members, 4-year terms
1992 breakdown: 27D, 15R; 34 men, 8 women; 23 whites, 17 Hispanics, 2 others
Salary: $75/day
Phone: (505) 986-4714

House of Representatives: 70 members, 2-year terms
1992 breakdown: 52D, 18R; 56 men, 14 women; 37 whites, 28 Hispanics, 5 others
Salary: $75/day
Phone: (505) 247-4321

URBAN STATISTICS

City	Pop.
Albuquerque	384,736
Mayor Louis E. Saavedra, N-P	
Las Cruces	62,126
Mayor Ruben Smith, N-P	
Santa Fe	56,551
Mayor Sam Pick, D	
Roswell	44,654
Mayor William F. Brainerd, N-P	

U.S. CONGRESS

Senate: 1 D, 1 R
House: 1 D, 2 R

TERM LIMITS

For Congress: No
For state offices: No

ELECTIONS

1992 Presidential Vote

Bill Clinton	45.9%
George Bush	37.3%
Ross Perot	16.1%

1988 Presidential Vote

George Bush	52%
Michael S. Dukakis	47%

1984 Presidential Vote

Ronald Reagan	60%
Walter F. Mondale	39%

POPULATION

1990 population		1,515,069
1980 population		1,302,894
Percent change		+16%
Rank among states:		37
White		76%
Black		2%
Hispanic		38%
Asian or Pacific islander		1%
Urban		73%
Rural		27%
Born in state		52%
Foreign-born		5%
Under age 18	446,741	29%
Ages 18-64	905,266	60%
65 and older	163,062	11%
Median age		31.3

MISCELLANEOUS

Capital: Santa Fe
Number of counties: 33
Per capita income: $14,844 (1991)
Rank among states: 46
Total area: 121,593 sq. miles
Rank among states: 5

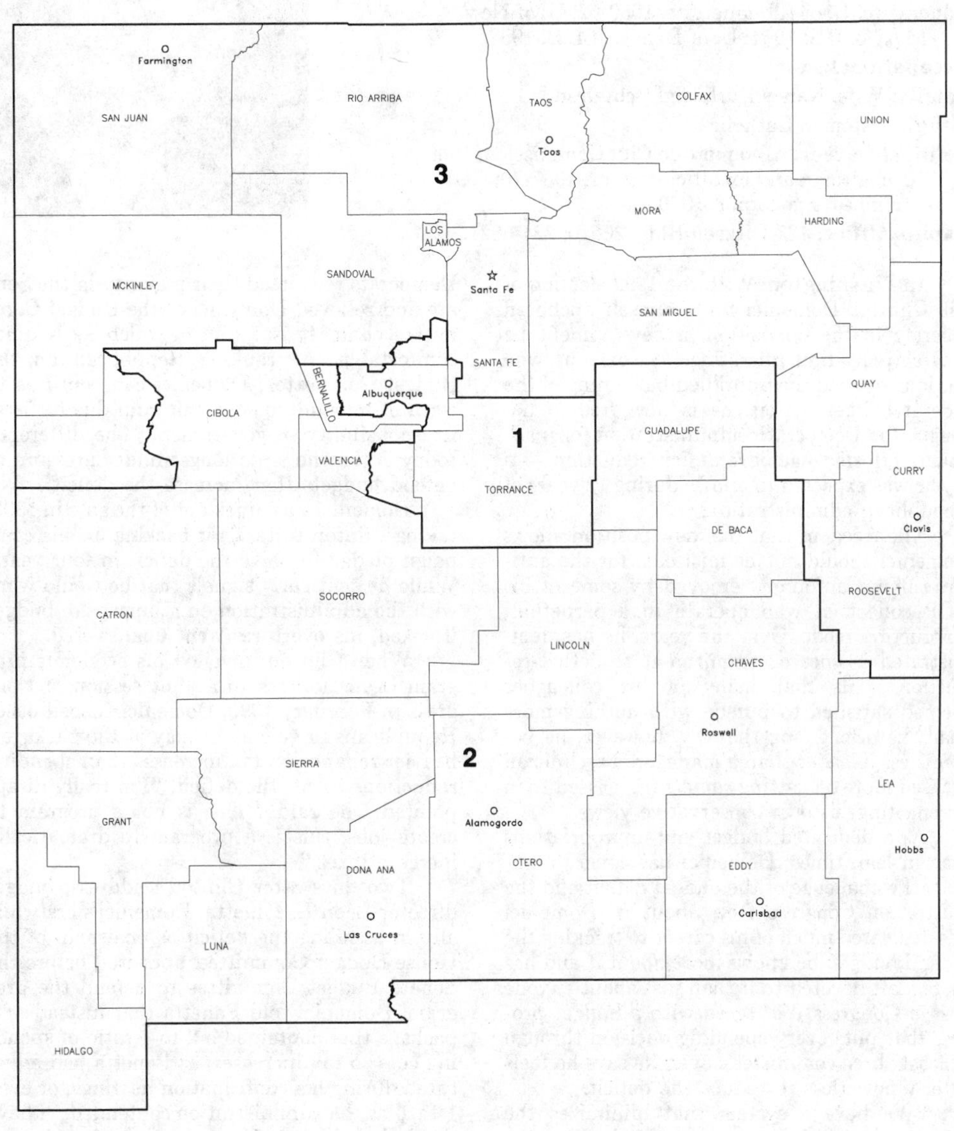
Farmington
SAN JUAN
RIO ARRIBA
TAOS
Taos
COLFAX
UNION
3
MORA
HARDING
LOS ALAMOS
MCKINLEY
SANDOVAL
Santa Fe
SAN MIGUEL
SANTA FE
BERNALILLO
Albuquerque
CIBOLA
QUAY
GUADALUPE
1
VALENCIA
CURRY
TORRANCE
Clovis
DE BACA
ROOSEVELT
CATRON
SOCORRO
LINCOLN
CHAVES
Roswell
SIERRA
2
LEA
GRANT
Alamogordo
Hobbs
OTERO
DONA ANA
EDDY
Carlsbad
LUNA
Las Cruces
HIDALGO

Pete V. Domenici (R)

Of Albuquerque — Elected 1972; 4th Term

Born: May 7, 1932, Albuquerque, N.M.

Education: U. of Albuquerque, 1950-52; U. of New Mexico, B.S. 1954; U. of Denver, LL.B. 1958.

Occupation: Lawyer.

Family: Wife, Nancy Burk; eight children.

Religion: Roman Catholic.

Political Career: Albuquerque City Commission, 1966-70, chairman and ex-officio mayor, 1967-70; GOP nominee for governor, 1970.

Capitol Office: 427 Dirksen Bldg. 20510; 224-6621.

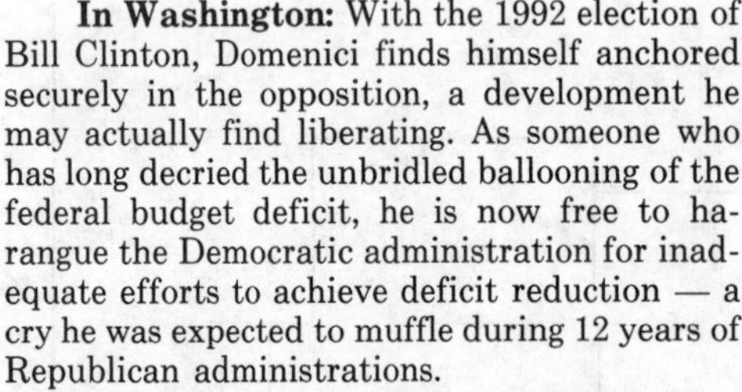

In Washington: With the 1992 election of Bill Clinton, Domenici finds himself anchored securely in the opposition, a development he may actually find liberating. As someone who has long decried the unbridled ballooning of the federal budget deficit, he is now free to harangue the Democratic administration for inadequate efforts to achieve deficit reduction — a cry he was expected to muffle during 12 years of Republican administrations.

The freedom that this new position allows Domenici should not be mistaken for the anti-government autonomy enjoyed by some of his GOP colleagues who operate in a perpetual-obstruction mode. Over the years, he has demonstrated a sincere commitment to deficit-reduction goals that many of his colleagues seemed satisfied to pursue with nothing more than rhetoric. Along the way, however, he became less a leader than a manager, a technician focused more on getting *something* passed than on enacting his own conservative views.

As a dedicated budget-and-appropriations man in lean times, Domenici has come to embody the challenge of the budget deficit and the frustration Congress feels about it. Domenici has dedicated much of his career to tracking the federal budget; he knows more about it and has more staff devoted to it than just about anyone else in Congress. Yet faced with a budget process that puts every spending decision through at least three committees, even he says he feels utterly powerless to reduce the deficit.

"We have a system that minimizes the opportunity to be courageous and wilts the willpower to address tough issues," he has said. "It befuddles the minds of our citizens. We have made our work unintelligible." Domenici joined Democratic Sen. David L. Boren of Oklahoma, Democratic Rep. Lee H. Hamilton of Indiana and GOP Rep. Bill Gradison of Ohio in successfully pressing for a bipartisan joint committee in the 103rd Congress to look into improving how Congress works.

Domenici's return to full-opposition mode completes a transition begun in 1986 when Democrats reclaimed their majority in the Senate and relieved Domenici of the Budget Committee chair. It is a role in which he is quite comfortable. As ranking Republican on the Budget Committee, Domenici can continue to warn of impending economic ruin due to fiscal irresponsibility in government. The difference today is that he is no longer under pressure to defend budgets that increase the deficit.

Domenici was quick out of the gate in 1993, taking Clinton to task for backing off his campaign pledge to halve the deficit in four years. While he sent early signals that he would work with the administration on a bipartisan budget if asked, his overtures went unanswered.

When Clinton unveiled his economic program in an address to a joint session of Congress in February 1993, Domenici echoed other Republicans in voicing dismay at the package's heavier reliance on tax increases than spending reductions to cut the deficit. "I'm really disappointed," he said. "This is not a program to create jobs; this is a program to dramatically increase taxes."

Two days after Clinton's address, budget director Leon E. Panetta, Domenici's erstwhile ally in assailing the deficit as chairman of the House Budget Committee, appeared before the Senate Budget Committee to defend the program. Domenici told Panetta that instead of a package that contained a 2-to-1 ratio of spending cuts to tax increases, as Panetta had advocated during his confirmation hearings, or even 1-to-1, as the administration contended, "I have concluded that it's $1 in new taxes for 44 cents in expenditures reductions."

In an op-ed article in The Washington Post the following weekend, Domenici chided: "More than anything else, [Clinton] campaigned on a theme of putting people first by increasing job growth, generating higher-paying jobs and reducing taxes on the middle class. Thus far, his plan puts government first, not people."

After Clinton's budget blueprint won Senate approval, Domenici charged that the plan "will not create jobs, will not grow the economy

[and] will not reduce the deficit."

Domenici is conservative, but not nearly enough so to suit some of his colleagues. As a result, he suffered when the Senate GOP moved rightward in choosing its leaders for the 102nd Congress. Oklahoman Don Nickles, a product of the Reagan revolution of 1980, was chosen over him to be chairman of the Republican Policy Committee.

That rebuff, Domenici's second in a bid for leadership, demonstrated the thanklessness of the fiscal issues on which he has spent his Senate career. When the leadership election was held in November 1990, the party had just lost ground in the midterm elections and was generally perceived to be losing the momentum of the previous decade. Some of the blame descended on the drawn-out budget process of that summer and fall, which left President Bush's no-new-taxes pledge broken and embarrassed both him and the Congress. Outright rebellion had flared in the House, where the first version of the budget agreement was roundly rejected. But frustration festered in the Senate, too, and Domenici got a taste of it when Nickles got 23 votes to his 20.

In his six years as Budget chairman, Domenici worked hard to build unity on his committee, heeding colleagues' wishes on everything from meeting times to spending priorities. He avoided using high-pressure tactics to persuade senators to do things they did not want to do.

But Domenici's earnest temperament sometimes produced irritated outbursts that worked against his consensus-building efforts. He is an intense presence, a sensitive man who appears genuinely distressed when a colleague is angry at him. He does not suffer criticism lightly, and frequently bristles at reporters and others who question his actions.

Domenici's record as chairman loomed over his bid to become majority leader at the start of the 99th Congress. His fellow Republicans saw him as hard-working and intelligent, but without the flair for firm direction that an eventual majority saw in Dole. Domenici was eliminated on the second ballot.

At times during the 1980s, the budget struggle seemed to push Domenici to the brink of despair. "I think we're getting very close to abandoning the notion of ever truly balancing the budget," he said in 1986.

The 1992 presidential campaigns of Democrat Paul E. Tsongas and independent Ross Perot focused national scrutiny on the deficit and elected officials' inability to rein it in. Their appeal among voters — suggesting that a serious attempt to curb the deficit could also be a vote-winner — spawned efforts in Congress to craft long-term deficit-reduction plans.

Domenici was intrigued by Bush budget director Richard G. Darman's proposal to cap mandatory spending for programs like Medicaid and Medicare. During consideration of the fiscal 1993 budget resolution, Domenici and three cosponsors (including two Democrats) offered the highly controversial proposal. Their plan would have imposed a cap on all mandatory spending, except for Social Security and interest on the debt, beginning in 1994; only increases to accommodate population growth, inflation and an additional sliding factor would be allowed. Domenici said the plan was the only way to constrain out-of-control entitlement spending that threatens the nation with bankruptcy. But he withdrew his amendment after the Senate approved, 66-28, what promised to be the first of a series of amendments exempting veterans and other groups from the cap.

In September, a bipartisan commission headed by Domenici and Georgia Democrat Sam Nunn presented a $2 trillion package of spending cuts and tax increases designed to balance the budget by 2002. It, too, included a cap on all mandatory spending except Social Security. It also called for scrapping the current income tax system and replacing it with a consumption-based tax that would exempt new savings and investment.

Domenici serves on Appropriations as well as Budget — he has been an active member of as many as four committees, even in his days as Budget chairman — and so he knows firsthand how evanescent Budget's influence can be. But he believes the committee has a role to play, even under the post-1990 "pay as you go" system. He still thinks Budget leaders should function as "good enforcers."

Domenici chaired the Budget Committee in all six of the years (from 1981 through 1986) Republicans controlled the Senate. In the historic session of 1981, he led the committee and the full Senate in approving the spending cuts President Ronald Reagan wanted. But he was more interested in balancing the federal budget than in providing the fiscal stimulus sought by "supply side" conservatives (Reagan budget director David A. Stockman called him "a Hooverite"). He feared the full tax-cut program of the Reagan administration would deepen the deficit, and he later worked with Finance Chairman Bob Dole and Majority Leader Howard H. Baker Jr. to pass the $98 billion tax bill of 1982.

Domenici's budget odyssey proved equally difficult in 1985, and even more dramatic. He had to cope not only with a deadlock over spending priorities, but with a dominant new ally in Dole, who had succeeded Baker as leader and threatened to overshadow the Budget chairman. The two worked for months to forge a consensus GOP plan and then to force a compromise budget to passage by a single vote.

By his last year in the chair, Domenici was openly critical of the Reagan administration and worked closely with ranking Democrat Lawton Chiles of Florida to achieve a bipartisan budget resolution. Chiles responded in kind after the Democrats recaptured the Senate majority in 1986.

The budget summit was born in 1987 and soon became a regular feature of the budget process. In its first few outings, the summit concept proved useful for the GOP. It enabled the minority Republicans on the Hill to bring their big gun, the president, to bear at the outset of congressional budget deliberations.

By 1990, however, a summit was no longer a last resort so much as a prior assumption of the process (beginning this time in May and lasting 4½ months). Members in both parties who were not part of the summit felt excluded and therefore not bound by its result. The summit deal collapsed and was replaced by an unlovely, hurried compromise built around the pay-as-you-go concept.

Before the Republican takeover of the Senate in 1981 thrust the Budget chair on Domenici, he had been a legislative dabbler, stubborn and intense about promoting a variety of issues but not widely identified with any. Much of his hardest work was oriented to New Mexico.

Since he joined the Appropriations Committee in the 98th Congress, Domenici has been a voice for spending restraint — as one would expect — and for the traditional Western concerns of water, power and rangeland agriculture. But he has also been a strong, often impassioned advocate of spending on science and research. Some of his concern stems from the role of the Los Alamos and Sandia national weapons laboratories in New Mexico. But he has also warned that a diminished commitment to pure science, including the National Science Foundation's programs, will diminish the nation's future.

In 1991, Domenici pulled off a legislative coup by persuading appropriators to shift an additional $200 million in overall defense spending into the energy and water bill. He earmarked most of the money for research and development at the national defense labs, including Los Alamos and Sandia.

Domenici brings a Westerner's perspective to issues before Appropriations' Interior Subcommittee, where fault lines split along regional, not partisan boundaries. Since the bulk of the nation's public lands are in the West, it is there that the battles are fought. "It appears every year that somebody wants to scalp someone in the West," Domenici has said. "I'm not only frustrated by it, but it is the worst way to affect people and their lives."

Domenici and Wyoming Republican Malcolm Wallop bitterly opposed a provision to the fiscal 1992 Interior spending bill that would have raised states' share of the costs of collecting royalties from oil and gas wells on public land. The change could have cost New Mexico nearly $21 million a year. Since mineral-rich states such as New Mexico and Wyoming get a higher percentage of the royalties, they would have suffered a disproportionate cut. Domenici warned of a floor fight; Wallop sent word that he was considering a filibuster. The provision was later dropped to avert a Wallop filibuster.

Domenici is also a member of Energy and Natural Resources. During committee consideration of the massive energy bill in the 102nd Congress, Domenici and Colorado Democrat Tim Wirth complained that Canadian natural gas producers have been exploiting a regulatory peculiarity to undercut American gas producers. At their urging, the committee tentatively adopted an amendment they said would correct the alleged regulatory loophole. But three wary committee members registered objections, and Energy Department officials worried that the amendment could violate the free-trade agreement. The committee rejected a move to delete the language, but it was left off the final bill.

Domenici was an active member of the Environment Committee for several years. In the 99th Congress, he helped hammer out the compromise in the toxic-waste "superfund" cleanup bill regarding settlement terms for private entities responsible for cleanup costs. He was a vocal proponent of the industry point of view on reauthorization of the Clean Air Act, urging relaxation of some pollution standards.

At Home: Seeking a first term in 1972, Domenici had the advantage of speaking Spanish in a state that was 37 percent Hispanic. He also had a Hispanic-sounding surname, even though he was born Pietro Vichi Domenici, the son of an immigrant Italian grocer. He drew more votes in Hispanic northern New Mexico than Republicans normally do.

Domenici's background was in municipal government. After law school, he had made his first political foray by winning a seat on the Albuquerque City Commission, and later became chairman, the equivalent of mayor. As a city official, he prided himself on neighborhood meetings he held to hear residents' complaints.

Counting on his Bernalillo County (Albuquerque) base, which cast a third of the vote in the state, Domenici ran for governor in 1970. He captured the GOP nomination in a six-way race with slightly less than 50 percent of the vote. Domenici was seen as a moderate. His closest primary rival was Stephen C. Helbing, the GOP floor leader in the state House, who advocated a crackdown on student demonstrators.

In the fall, Bernalillo County did not come through for Domenici the way he had hoped. He carried it by only 8,909 votes, not enough for him to win statewide against Democrat Bruce King, the state House Speaker (and now the governor once again). King had the party registration advantage and was better known statewide. Domenici tried to raise doubts about King by criticizing his lack of administrative experience, but with little success.

Undeterred, Domenici came back in 1972, this time running for the Senate seat being vacated by Democrat Clinton P. Anderson. His Democratic opponent was former state Rep. Jack

Daniels, who had also run for governor in 1970 but lost to King in the Democratic primary.

Daniels, a wealthy banker, differed little from Domenici on the issues. But Domenici pointed out that Daniels had stood on the same platform as Sen. George McGovern that year and pledged to back him as the Democratic presidential nominee. While Daniels had repudiated McGovern's call for reduced defense spending, the association hurt him. Domenici won with 54 percent.

Domenici's percentage dropped slightly in 1978. The Democratic candidate, state Attorney General (and later one-term governor) Toney Anaya, was Hispanic. Domenici had taken most of the heavily Hispanic counties in 1972, but six years later he lost most of them. In addition, his 1972 plurality of 31,240 votes in Bernalillo shrank to 6,766 in 1978.

Fortunately for Domenici, Anaya did not have a united Democratic Party behind him. As chief state prosecutor, he had secured indictments against several important party figures, arousing resentment among regulars and prompting many of them not to vote.

With a massive campaign treasury and his new national role as chairman of the Budget Committee, Domenici's re-election in 1984 was never much in doubt. He all but locked up the victory when no prominent Democrats chose to challenge him. He defeated liberal state Rep. Judith A. Pratt with more than 70 percent.

In 1990, Domenici's continued popularity with voters was reaffirmed when he trounced Democratic state Sen. Tom R. Benavides, a legislative maverick who once introduced a bill to legalize ostrich and camel racing in the state and tried to create a new county near Albuquerque to be named "Benavides County."

Committees

Budget (Ranking)

Appropriations (6th of 13 Republicans)
Commerce, Justice, State & Judiciary (ranking); Defense; Energy & Water Development; Interior; Transportation

Banking, Housing & Urban Affairs (8th of 8 Republicans)
Housing & Urban Affairs; Securities

Energy & Natural Resources (3rd of 9 Republicans)
Energy Research & Development (ranking); Public Lands, National Parks & Forests; Renewable Energy

Indian Affairs (5th of 8 Republicans)

Joint Organization of Congress (Vice Chairman)

Elections

1990 General

Pete V. Domenici (R)	296,712	(73%)
Tom R. Benavides (D)	110,033	(27%)

Previous Winning Percentages: **1984** (72%) **1978** (53%) **1972** (54%)

Campaign Finance

	Receipts	Receipts from PACs		Expend-itures
1990				
Domenici (R)	$2,110,973	$773,374	(37%)	$1,925,057
Benavides (D)	$38,643	$13,250	(34%)	$38,510

Key Votes

1993

Require unpaid family and medical leave	N
Approve national "motor voter" registration bill	N
Approve budget increasing taxes and reducing deficit	N
Support president's right to lift military gay ban	N

1992

Approve school-choice pilot program	Y
Allow shifting funds from defense to domestic programs	N
Oppose deeper cuts in spending for SDI	Y

1991

Approve waiting period for handgun purchases	Y
Raise senators' pay and ban honoraria	Y
Authorize use of force in Persian Gulf	Y
Confirm Clarence Thomas to Supreme Court	Y

Voting Studies

	Presidential Support		Party Unity		Conservative Coalition	
Year	S	O	S	O	S	O
1992	82	18	88	11	89	11
1991	93	6	88	11	88	10
1990	67	29	69	24	84	8
1989	90	7	74	23	76	24
1988	76	19	77	19	97	0
1987	69	31	78	20	88	13
1986	88	12	89	10	95	5
1985	82	15	90	6	88	8
1984	88	8	86	14	91	9
1983	74	18	72	14	75	9
1982	85	15	90	9	97	3
1981	84	13	86	8	94	4

Interest Group Ratings

Year	ADA	AFL-CIO	CCUS	ACU
1992	15	17	78	78
1991	10	17	90	76
1990	22	56	67	50
1989	10	11	88	88
1988	15	46	79	72
1987	20	30	78	65
1986	5	13	79	83
1985	5	10	83	82
1984	25	36	63	77
1983	15	19	35	44
1982	15	19	80	55
1981	15	11	94	64

Jeff Bingaman (D)

Of Santa Fe — Elected 1982; 2nd Term

Born: Oct. 3, 1943, El Paso, Texas.
Education: Harvard U., A.B. 1965; Stanford U., J.D. 1968.
Military Service: Army Reserve, 1968-74.
Occupation: Lawyer.
Family: Wife, Anne Kovacovich; one child.
Religion: Methodist.
Political Career: N.M. attorney general, 1979-83.
Capitol Office: 110 Hart Bldg. 20510; 224-5521.

In Washington: Bingaman is a detail man, a relative rarity in a body whose members are often more comfortable expounding on the state of the world than examining esoteric issues. Nearing the end of his second term, he has fully emerged from the shadow of New Mexico's GOP senior senator, Pete V. Domenici. Although rarely seen on the network news shows or even on C-SPAN, Bingaman in his own quiet way has established himself as a major player on a range of issues, from defense and foreign affairs to energy and education.

The serious-minded Bingaman is not one for the colorful quip. Once or twice a week, he abandons his Senate office for a quiet corner of the Supreme Court library down the street. He had a similarly secluded cubbyhole in Santa Fe when he was New Mexico attorney general — a place where he could retreat to think.

This studious style has served him well on the Armed Services Committee, where his mastery of military research and management issues impresses defense specialists. He chairs the Defense Technology, Acquisition and Industrial Base Subcommittee — formerly the Defense Industry and Technology Subcommittee. The change in emphasis is important; it reflects the priority Bingaman puts on retaining the nation's military-industrial base in an era of draconian military spending cuts.

Liberal by instinct, Bingaman is nonetheless a frequent ally of the conservative committee chairman, Sam Nunn of Georgia, whose leadership of Senate defense policy he acknowledges.

Bingaman is a leader in the push toward dual-use technologies, those that have applications for commercial development as well as defense. The concept was shunned by President Bush, but it is embraced wholeheartedly by the Clinton administration.

Bingaman was a major architect of the section of the 1993 defense authorization bill that provided $1.6 billion for defense conversion.

The technology initiatives Bingaman introduced in the 102nd Congress would require the Defense Department to work more closely with private industry and to map out the research and development of each of 22 technologies the administration has designated as crucial for U.S. security. The technologies include high-definition television, superstrong ceramics, sensors and signal processing.

"Nobody has ever suggested we could go to the moon without a plan of action," Bingaman says. "To suggest that we can be a world leader without a plan of action is just not the real world. This sorts out the priorities."

Bingaman has been close to Nunn on two of the salient defense debates of the 1990s: the Persian Gulf War and the development of an anti-ballistic missile defense system. Early in 1991, he rejected the argument that Congress was micromanaging the Persian Gulf policy by debating the resolutions just before the Jan. 15 deadline for Iraq's withdrawal from Kuwait, which had been set by the United Nations at Bush's request.

At the end of Bingaman's speech, Pennsylvania Republican Arlen Specter implied that the debate was a forum for Democrats "second-guessing the president." Bingaman responded that "the Congress is doing what it is required under our Constitution to do today, and that is meeting to debate whether we should go to war. . . ."

During the 101st and 102nd Congresses, Bingaman made his mark in the debate over the Strategic Defense Initiative (SDI). Like Nunn, Bingaman opposed the Reagan/Bush vision of a space-based "shield" of anti-ballistic missile (ABM) weapons as infeasible under current technology and as violative of the 1972 ABM treaty between the United States and the Soviet Union. But Bingaman was not opposed to SDI research: He wanted to see priorities reordered in favor of ground-based anti-missile systems with near-term possibilities.

In August 1990, Bingaman joined with Alabama Democrat Richard C. Shelby on an amendment to the fiscal 1991 defense authorization bill diverting money from Brilliant Pebbles, a system of small interceptor missiles that was the current favorite of those advocating rapid deployment of a space-based SDI. The funds would be applied to research on ground-based systems and on exotic space-based technologies that could not be deployed for years. The Senate adopted the measure by a 54-44 vote.

Hoping for a comeback, SDI advocates tried in early 1991 to ride the success of Patriot anti-ballistic missiles at shooting down Iraq's Scuds during the Persian Gulf War. However, Bingaman warned against what he viewed as pro-SDI hype: "The public should not be mesmerized by the [Patriots'] great success against Iraqi missiles . . . into believing that the SDI program should receive blanket support."

In his second term, Bingaman has turned more often to policy areas beyond the U.S. borders. A report he wrote with Nunn and Republican Sens. Richard G. Lugar of Indiana and John W. Warner of Virginia after a March 1992 trip to Russia and Ukraine was credited with galvanizing support for more aid to those countries.

He was active in the controversy over China's trade status, arguing that rescinding most-favored-nation status would cut into the $1 billion in wheat that the U.S. exports to China annually.

Bingaman follows national energy policy as a member of the Energy and Natural Resources Committee and chairman of the Renewable Energy, Energy Efficiency and Competitiveness Subcommittee. Like Domenici, he guards the interests of New Mexico's coal, natural gas and uranium industries.

Bingaman, whose state is home to the Los Alamos National Laboratory, is a proponent of efforts to reduce such facilities' dependence on weapons research. As the 101st Congress worked to shape a plan to clean up toxic waste sites and other hazards at the nation's defense installations, Bingaman fell in behind a proposal by Nunn that was heavy on environmental research, some of which would be performed by the Department of Energy labs.

In October 1992, Congress cleared legislation allowing the Energy Department to open the Waste Isolation Pilot Plant (WIPP) in Carlsbad, N.M., a facility designed to hold defense-related nuclear waste. Bingaman pushed hard — but failed — to reduce the amount of waste to be allowed at the site during the roughly six-year test phase.

After a long effort, Bingaman in 1990 pushed through a measure that would allow the Defense and Energy departments to raise the pay of certain engineers and scientists nearer to private-sector levels. To accomplish this goal, he had to overcome the opposition of Democrat John Glenn of Ohio, the chairman of the Senate Governmental Affairs Committee (of which Bingaman was then a member).

In May 1990, Bingaman left Governmental Affairs to fill a vacancy on the Labor and Human Resources Committee. But he did not lose interest in governmental issues. In April 1991, Bingaman was named to a Senate task force formed in the aftermath of the Keating Five controversy to develop standards for "constituent service."

Bingaman was chairman of the special trial committee that heard evidence in the 1989 impeachment case against federal Judge Alcee L. Hastings. The committee convicted and removed Hastings from the bench, although Bingaman voted against the conviction. (Hastings' impeachment was overturned in 1992 by a federal judge; he is now a freshman representative from Florida's 23rd District.)

Bingaman joined the Ethics Committee in May 1991 in the midst of its deadlocked misconduct proceedings against Sen. Alan Cranston, D-Calif. Bingaman was filling in for Arkansas Democrat David Pryor, who had suffered a heart attack the month before. Fortunately, Pryor's heart attack was mild — he was called back into service when Bingaman announced in July that potential conflicts with his wife's legal work had forced him to disqualify himself from the case.

Bingaman shed the onerous Ethics assignment at the end of the 102nd Congress. If he hadn't, he would likely be chairing the committee: Richard H. Bryan, who now wields that gavel, wasn't even on the committee at the beginning of the 102nd Congress. Not a single senator who began the 102nd Congress on Ethics continues in that assignment in the 103rd.

At Home: When he launched his 1982 Senate campaign, Bingaman was in his third year as New Mexico's attorney general, little-known outside the legal and political communities but politically unscarred. Whether by luck or shrewdness, he remained relatively fresh through the primary (against former Democratic Gov. Jerry Apodaca) and then against incumbent GOP Sen. Harrison Schmitt.

In the primary, the ex-governor was hamstrung by reports that he had ties to underworld figures. Bingaman did not directly mention Apodaca's problems, but he gave voters a not-so-subtle reminder with his slogan — "a senator we can proudly call our own."

Bingaman was endorsed by the state AFL-CIO, then narrowly won the support of the party convention. In the primary, he swept to nomination by a ratio of nearly 3-to-2.

Incumbent Schmitt, a former Apollo astronaut, lacked Apodaca's political baggage. But he appeared more interested in pet subjects such as 21st-century technology than in the state's struggling economy. Bingaman lambasted Schmitt for supporting supply-side economics, sharp increases in defense spending and cuts in Social Security payments. With statewide unemployment at 10 percent, Schmitt's ties to President Ronald Reagan were a campaign liability.

Schmitt also ran poorly researched advertisements that accused Attorney General Bingaman of condoning the release of a convicted murderer and failing to prosecute the instigators of a deadly prison riot. The charges backfired when the head of the state Supreme Court and an archbishop of the Catholic Church in New Mexico defended Bingaman. Labor backing, a voter-targeting program by the Democratic National Committee and a heavy Hispanic turnout for gubernatorial candidate Toney Anaya all helped Bingaman.

Bingaman also owed a literal debt of thanks to his wife, a successful Santa Fe lawyer. She and Bingaman lent his campaign more than $600,000, making it possible to compete with Schmitt's well-funded effort. Bingaman took 54 percent of the vote.

Long before 1988, national GOP operatives were portraying Bingaman as one of their top targets. His low-profile manner had left him with a fairly fuzzy image after one term in the Senate, and the GOP wanted to define it, claiming that Bingaman lacked stature and had achieved little in Congress.

But the GOP line lost credibility when the party chose a nominee with his own stature problems who was no more compelling on the stump than Bingaman.

GOP state Sen. Bill Valentine had trouble whipping up enthusiasm or money for his campaign. Bingaman had made few enemies, and he had the cash to run waves of advertising that began early in the year. Valentine managed less than 40 percent of the vote.

Bingaman grew up in the isolated New Mexico mining town of Silver City, the son of a professor and nephew of John Bingaman, a confidant of Democratic Sen. Clinton Anderson. At Stanford Law School, Bingaman worked for Robert F. Kennedy's 1968 presidential campaign. Returning to New Mexico, he served as counsel to the 1969 state constitutional convention, joined a politically connected law firm and ran for attorney general six years later.

Committees

Armed Services (5th of 11 Democrats)
Defense Technology, Acquisition & Industrial Base (chairman); Military Readiness & Defense Infrastructure; Nuclear Deterrence, Arms Control & Defense Intelligence

Energy & Natural Resources (5th of 11 Democrats)
Renewable Energy (chairman); Energy Research & Development; Public Lands, National Parks & Forests

Labor & Human Resources (8th of 10 Democrats)
Children, Families, Drugs & Alcoholism; Education, Arts & Humanities; Employment & Productivity; Disability Policy

Joint Economic

Elections

1988 General

Jeff Bingaman (D)	321,983	(63%)
Bill Valentine (R)	186,579	(37%)

Previous Winning Percentage: **1982** (54%)

Campaign Finance

	Receipts	Receipts from PACs		Expend- itures
1988				
Bingaman (D)	$3,176,793	$1,100,451	(35%)	$3,164,973
Valentine (R)	$661,825	$91,363	(14%)	$659,624

Key Votes

1993	
Require unpaid family and medical leave	Y
Approve national "motor voter" registration bill	Y
Approve budget increasing taxes and reducing deficit	Y
Support president's right to lift military gay ban	Y
1992	
Approve school-choice pilot program	N
Allow shifting funds from defense to domestic programs	Y
Oppose deeper cuts in spending for SDI	Y
1991	
Approve waiting period for handgun purchases	Y
Raise senators' pay and ban honoraria	Y
Authorize use of force in Persian Gulf	N
Confirm Clarence Thomas to Supreme Court	N

Voting Studies

	Presidential Support		Party Unity		Conservative Coalition	
Year	S	O	S	O	S	O
1992	40	50	70	23	39	55
1991	51	48	78	20	65	35
1990	35	54	76	18	32	57
1989	54	46	84	16	34	66
1988	52	47	71	22	68	30
1987	32	60	74	21	53	38
1986	41	58	70	29	41	59
1985	33	66	75	24	37	60
1984	40	56	79	19	28	72
1983	45	54	81	15	25	73

Interest Group Ratings

Year	ADA	AFL-CIO	CCUS	ACU
1992	75	92	20	4
1991	65	67	20	19
1990	67	56	17	19
1989	65	90	38	15
1988	70	77	43	20
1987	65	90	40	13
1986	65	73	26	35
1985	70	81	34	13
1984	100	91	42	9
1983	90	94	42	4

1 Steven H. Schiff (R)

Of Albuquerque — Elected 1988; 3rd Term

Born: March 18, 1947, Chicago, Ill.
Education: U. of Illinois, Chicago Circle, B.A. 1968; U. of New Mexico, J.D. 1972.
Military Service: Air National Guard, 1969-91; Air Force Reserve, 1991-present.
Occupation: Lawyer.
Family: Wife, Marcia Lewis; two children.
Religion: Jewish.
Political Career: Candidate for district judge, 1978; Bernalillo County district attorney, 1981-89.
Capitol Office: 1009 Longworth Bldg. 20515; 225-6316.

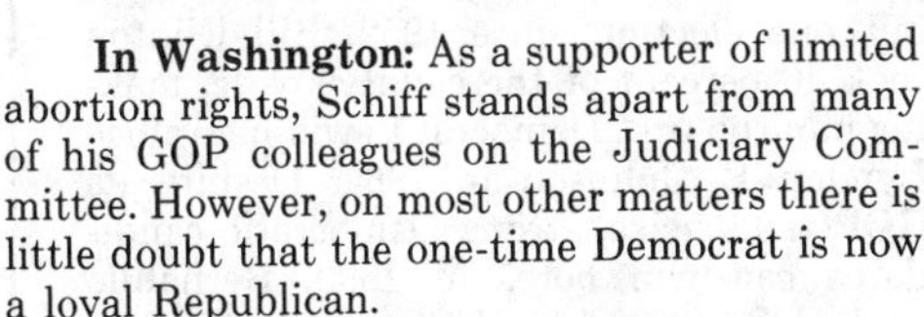

In Washington: As a supporter of limited abortion rights, Schiff stands apart from many of his GOP colleagues on the Judiciary Committee. However, on most other matters there is little doubt that the one-time Democrat is now a loyal Republican.

After parting with President Bush on nearly half the 1990 House floor votes, the thoughtful Schiff found himself able to support the president's agenda 67 percent of the time in the following two years. He also improved his party stock by joining a handful of high-profile Republican attacks on the Democratic leadership.

In the summer of 1991, Schiff and other Republicans sported "100 days" buttons, accusing House leaders of failing to respond to Bush's request to pass crime and transportation legislation within 100 days. They blamed Judiciary Chairman Jack Brooks of Texas in particular for slowing the crime bill.

At the start of the 103rd Congress, Republican leaders appointed Schiff to the ethics committee, a recognition of both his prosecutorial background and his methodical — some might say bland — personality. He is expected to bring an evenhanded, lawyerly approach to the panel that handles sensitive internal investigations.

His easygoing personality and moderate social views often make Schiff a sought-after swing vote on Judiciary. He was one of three Republican committee members to support the civil rights bill in 1991 and 1990. He has also lobbied for legislation to require Congress to comply with laws in the areas of civil rights, age discrimination, health and safety.

Although operating in the minority party, Schiff had significant input into the crime bill, thanks in part to a good working relationship with New York Democrat Charles E. Schumer, chairman of Judiciary's Crime and Criminal Justice Subcommittee.

The bill that passed included four amendments drafted by Schiff: giving grant money to prosecutors to bind over to adult court 16- and 17-year-olds who commit violent crimes; making possession of a stolen firearm a federal crime; increasing the penalties for interstate gun trafficking; and setting a 10-year minimum sentence for a violent career criminal with prior felony convictions who is caught with a firearm.

While tough on criminals who use guns, Schiff is not eager to restrict access to handguns and consistently has opposed the so-called Brady bill, which would require a seven-day waiting period before the purchase of a handgun.

He has called for regulation of private jails housing federal prisoners and has encouraged state legislatures to adopt uniform treatment of juveniles, including the right to prosecute as adults people 15 or older who commit certain violent crimes. He successfully included in the 1990 crime bill a provision barring convicted criminals from escaping court-ordered restitution by declaring bankruptcy.

Schiff, who is chairman of the House Republican Research Committee's Task Force on Crime, filed two bills in March 1993 aimed at assisting states in the prosecution of drunken driving offenses. And he is working to reduce prisoners' credits for good behavior to a maximum of 25 percent of their sentence.

A lieutenant colonel in the New Mexico Air National Guard, Schiff was called for active service during the Persian Gulf crisis; he did not go overseas but volunteered to serve three days drafting wills and performing other legal aid for reservists. Schiff, whose wife is in the Army Reserve, opposed bills introduced during the war that would have exempted some military parents with dependent children from combat service. Schiff argued that such risks are accepted when one joins a volunteer army.

In June 1992 he introduced an amendment to the fiscal 1993 defense authorization bill that guarantees veterans' benefits to remarried widows who later lose their second husbands.

Arguing from a constitutional perspective, Schiff voted against a bill to ban physical

New Mexico 1

Central — Albuquerque

Albuquerque's postwar emergence as New Mexico's commercial hub and a GOP stronghold was fueled by the development of a prosperous military-aerospace industry. Despite a Democratic edge in registration (55 percent to 38 percent), the GOP has maintained its hold on the seat by offering fiscally conservative, defense-oriented moderate candidates.

However, the existence of a large state and local government work force and a big minority population gives Democrats a foothold in Bernalillo County, alongside Republican-voting white-collar professionals employed in the area's defense and aerospace industries. About 38 percent of the 1st District's population is Hispanic. The city and the county together cast about one-third of the state vote.

Before World War II, Albuquerque was a lightly populated regional trade center, better known as a health resort where tubercular patients could alleviate their suffering by taking advantage of the dry climate.

Since the A-bomb was developed in 1945 (less than 100 miles north at Los Alamos), Albuquerque has seen its population multiply from 35,000 people in 1940 to about 385,000 today. The district has a high concentration of scientists and engineers who work in the military-aerospace industry. A large employer is Sandia National Laboratories, which specializes in nuclear and solar research and testing. Kirtland Air Force Base is also in the district. Defense and aviation technology companies such as Honeywell and General Electric are here as are scores of newer electronics, computer and communications companies. (Honeywell and GE have suffered a few layoffs in the post-Cold War era.)

Teachers also form an important bloc; the University of New Mexico and Albuquerque public school system account for 23,000 jobs.

Much of the GOP vote is cast in the city's heavily white, upper-middle-class and residential Northeast Heights section. The Hispanic-majority South Valley, on the south and west sides of the Rio Grande, boosts Democratic totals.

Until 1992, Bernalillo County had supported the GOP presidential nominee in all but one election since 1952. Bill Clinton took 46 percent of the county's vote, making him the first Democrat to win here since Lyndon B. Johnson in 1964. Despite its GOP tendencies, strong Democratic candidates can win here. In 1990, Bernalillo backed Democrats Jeff Bingaman for Senate and Bruce King for governor.

Bernalillo serves as the population center of the district, but rural Torrance County has most of the land area with 3,300 square miles. Torrance accounts for only about 1 percent of the district vote.

Portions of three other counties make up the balance of the 1st. About 13,000 voters — mainly professionals — live in Albuquerque bedroom communities in eastern Valencia County, and about 11,000 voters hail from a primarily rural section of Sandoval County, just north of Bernalillo County.

1990 Population: 505,491. White 392,124 (78%), Black 13,434 (3%), Other 99,933 (20%). Hispanic origin 192,384 (38%). 18 and over 371,875 (74%), 62 and over 64,551 (13%). Median age: 32.

desecration of the flag. He was one of only 43 House members voting against the legislation.

Schiff maintains his Republican Party credentials by supporting a host of traditional conservative proposals, including a balanced-budget amendment and the presidential line-item veto.

At Home: Schiff won his 1988 House election on a pledge to deliver constituent service, a rather modest agenda for a Republican who toppled two family dynasties to win in a politically competitive district. But constituent service had been the hallmark of his GOP predecessor, Manuel Lujan Jr.

When Lujan announced his plans to leave the House after 20 years (he later served as George Bush's Interior secretary), a dozen candidates jockeyed to succeed him, including his brother, former state GOP Chairman Edward Lujan, and Democrat Tom Udall, the son of former Interior Secretary Stewart Udall and nephew of former Arizona Rep. Morris K. Udall.

Schiff had been contemplating a Senate bid but quickly shifted his sights to the open House seat. In eight years as popular district attorney in Bernalillo County, Schiff had become a familiar face in the media; he directed the prosecution of numerous high-profile criminal cases. Outspent in the House primary by nearly 2-to-1, Schiff came under fire for his willingness to plea-bargain. But the charge did not stick because Schiff's image as a law-and-order figure was well-known to voters.

In Democrat Udall, a lawyer and environmental activist, Schiff faced a well-funded and well-organized foe whose name had helped him win a 10-way primary. While Schiff boasted that his office had won the most death-penalty cases in state history, he was again accused of letting criminals off easy. He also was accused of lacking legislative experience.

In 1990, Democrat nominee Secretary of State Rebecca Vigil-Giron was sent reeling by revelations that she had exaggerated her academic record, had once defaulted on a student loan and had witnessed her roommate forge a signature on her 1986 ballot petition. Schiff coasted to a 70 percent victory.

In 1992, Schiff captured more than 60 percent of the vote in his win against Robert Aragon.

Committees

Government Operations (6th of 16 Republicans)
Human Resources & Intergovernmental Relations (ranking)

Judiciary (9th of 14 Republicans)
Crime & Criminal Justice; Intellectual Property & Judicial Administration

Science, Space & Technology (9th of 22 Republicans)
Energy; Space

Standards of Official Conduct (7th of 7 Republicans)

Elections

1992 General		
Steven H. Schiff (R)	128,426	(63%)
Robert J. Aragon (D)	76,600	(37%)
1990 General		
Steven H. Schiff (R)	97,375	(70%)
Rebecca Vigil-Giron (D)	41,306	(30%)

Previous Winning Percentage: **1988** (51%)

District Vote for President

1992
D 95,677 (46%)
R 81,046 (39%)
I 33,032 (16%)

Campaign Finance

	Receipts	Receipts from PACs		Expend-itures
1992				
Schiff (R)	$573,884	$186,910	(33%)	$589,743
Aragon (D)	$81,585	0		$81,541
1990				
Schiff (R)	$554,465	$223,203	(40%)	$538,273
Vigil-Giron (D)	$127,218	$34,732	(27%)	$123,215

Key Votes

1993	
Require parental notification of minors' abortions	N
Require unpaid family and medical leave	N
Approve national "motor voter" registration bill	N
Approve budget increasing taxes and reducing deficit	N
Approve economic stimulus plan	N
1992	
Approve balanced-budget constitutional amendment	Y
Close down space station program	N
Approve U.S. aid for former Soviet Union	Y
Allow shifting funds from defense to domestic programs	N
1991	
Extend unemployment benefits using deficit financing	N
Approve waiting period for handgun purchases	N
Authorize use of force in Persian Gulf	Y

Voting Studies

	Presidential Support		Party Unity		Conservative Coalition	
Year	**S**	**O**	**S**	**O**	**S**	**O**
1992	67	31	72	26	85	15
1991	67	33	64	33	86	14
1990	55	44	56	41	78	22
1989	69	30	63	37	78	22

Interest Group Ratings

Year	ADA	AFL-CIO	CCUS	ACU
1992	25	58	88	72
1991	20	33	80	65
1990	22	17	71	58
1989	15	25	90	86

2 Joe Skeen (R)

Of Picacho — Elected 1980; 7th Term

Born: June 30, 1927, Roswell, N.M.
Education: Texas A&M U., B.S. 1950.
Military Service: Navy, 1945-46; Air Force Reserve, 1949-52.
Occupation: Sheep rancher; soil and water engineer; flying service operator.
Family: Wife, Mary Jones; two children.
Religion: Roman Catholic.
Political Career: N.M. Senate, 1961-71, minority leader, 1965-71; N.M. GOP chairman, 1962-65; GOP nominee for lieutenant governor, 1970; GOP nominee for governor, 1974, 1978.
Capitol Office: 2367 Rayburn Bldg. 20515; 225-2365.

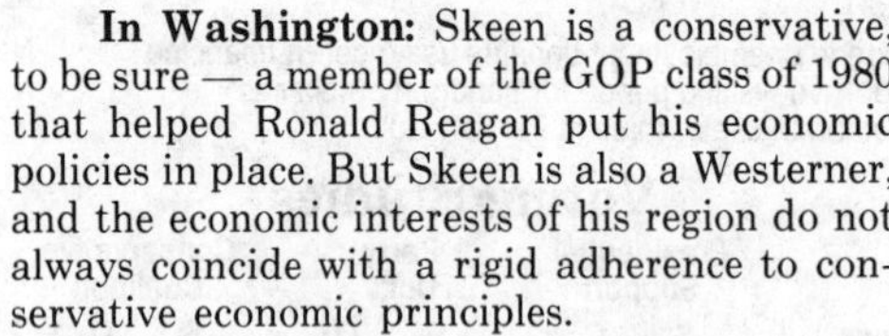

In Washington: Skeen is a conservative, to be sure — a member of the GOP class of 1980 that helped Ronald Reagan put his economic policies in place. But Skeen is also a Westerner, and the economic interests of his region do not always coincide with a rigid adherence to conservative economic principles.

Skeen, a member of the Appropriations Committee, has observed that issues in Congress increasingly seem to break not along party lines, but along Western vs. Eastern and rural vs. urban fissures. Nowhere has that been more apparent than in the battle over increasing grazing fees on public rangeland.

At the start of the 102nd Congress, Skeen became the ranking Republican on Appropriations' Agriculture Subcommittee, which puts him in a choice position to watch out for his district's cattle and sheep ranchers. Through the 102nd, he also had a seat on the Interior Subcommittee, site of the grazing-fee fight.

A former rancher, Skeen is a staunch opponent of proposals to increase fees charged for use of federal grazing land. Advocates of higher fees say the current charges amount to a government giveaway that adds to the deficit.

Over the objections of Skeen and other Western members, the Interior Subcommittee voted in the 102nd to raise grazing fees on public land by 33 percent. "This is something that Eastern folks simply don't understand," Skeen said, after trying unsuccessfully to stop the increase. He said the move would cost ranchers $10 million annually. "They don't have that kind of money." But his plaints went for naught as the subcommittee voted 4-3 to raise the fee.

Realizing he did not have enough support to reverse that vote in the full committee, Skeen received the assurance of Democratic subcommittee Chairman Sidney R. Yates of Illinois that committee members would not object if he attempted during floor debate to strip the provision.

Skeen lost the initial skirmish on the floor when the House voted for an amendment by Oklahoma Democrat Mike Synar to raise fees. Earlier, lawmakers had removed from the bill language containing a more moderate fee hike after Skeen raised a technical objection. Skeen argued that the grazing fees were not too low, but actually too high, given the amount of work ranchers must do to keep up federal rangelands as part of their grazing permit.

Opposition in the Senate to raising the grazing fees thwarted Synar in the 102nd, but all sides in the dispute geared up for another go-round in 1993, when the Clinton administration reopened the issue of raising the fees.

Skeen is one of the few House members willing to entertain the idea of locating a nuclear-waste site in his district. The Waste Isolation Pilot Plant, to be located in underground salt caverns near the 2nd District city of Carlsbad, would make the site the first permanent facility to store defense-generated low-level waste. It is designed to store plutonium-tainted waste from the nation's nuclear weapons factories.

After years of deadlock, the House in 1992 voted to begin limited trial storage at the $1 billion facility. The legislation, which would transfer the repository to the Energy Department and set certain conditions — including Environmental Protection Agency oversight — before site-testing could begin, became law at the end of the 102nd Congress.

Like his Appropriations Committee colleagues, Skeen looks for ways to bring home federal dollars. As part of the fiscal 1992 agriculture appropriations bill, he was able to secure $230,000 for the Agriculture Department's Extension Service to promote tourism in New Mexico. The fiscal 1993 bill contained $200,000 for research into eradicating the broom snakeweed, a menace in New Mexico and the South-

New Mexico 2

South — Little Texas; Las Cruces; Roswell

Southern New Mexico was once firmly Democratic, but traditional party ties have eroded here. During the 1970s, the area developed a strong habit of voting Republican in statewide contests, as ranchers and other Southern-style Democrats came to resent their party's national program.

In 1991, redistricting wrought more changes. To try to make the district more competitive for Democrats, the state's Democratic Legislature drew district lines to include more liberal voters. The population of Hispanics jumped from 34 percent to 42 percent.

In addition, the 2nd District lost Curry, Quay and Roosevelt counties, all Democratic but conservative. The district picked up De Baca and Guadalupe, where ranching is the mainstay.

In what was once resolutely GOP country, George Bush in 1992 lost the district to Bill Clinton by 1 percentage point.

Other Democratic strongholds are in the Mexican Highlands, along the Arizona border, where copper and lead mines have attracted union labor. But they have provided less than 10 percent of the vote.

"Little Texas," the southeastern corner of New Mexico, remains an important focus, making up about 50 percent of the 2nd. This region, settled by Texans early in the 20th century, is more culturally and economically attuned to conservative, Baptist West Texas than to the more liberal capital city of Santa Fe. Most of the land here is devoted to grazing cattle or sheep. But oil and military projects have reshaped voting habits in a Republican direction.

The oil- and gas-producing centers of Chaves and Lea counties are bastions of conservatism.

Near Carlsbad in Eddy County are the nation's most productive salt mines. Democratic miners occasionally influence county elections. The subterranean salt beds will be the site of the nation's first nuclear waste dump, the controversial Waste Isolation Pilot Plant, which is scheduled to begin operations in late 1993 or early 1994. Many in the Carlsbad area support the project, expected to inject millions of dollars into the stagnant local economy; meanwhile, the safety of the Carlsbad nuclear repository has ignited a firestorm of criticism statewide.

To the west are Otero and Doña Ana counties, which account for more than one-third of the 2nd's population. Otero County favors the GOP. Doña Ana, which includes Las Cruces, has a Hispanic majority, giving the Democrats a substantial base, but Republicans generally carry it. Parts of Doña Ana, Otero and Sierra counties hold the sprawling White Sands Missile Range.

Holloman Air Force Base in Otero County also provides GOP strength. Just north of Otero, in the southeastern corner of Socorro County, the world's first atomic bomb was exploded in 1945.

Billy the Kid stood trial in the tiny village of Mesilla, in Las Cruces, but escaped. The village also served briefly as the Confederate capital of the Arizona Territory.

1990 Population: 504,659. White 423,661 (84%), Black 10,662 (2%), Other 70,336 (14%). Hispanic origin 212,355 (42%). 18 and over 350,557 (69%), 62 and over 72,656 (14%). Median age: 31.

west.

In the 101st Congress, he helped win $36 million to bring a stealth fighter wing to Holloman Air Force Base in the 2nd. In his first term on Appropriations, he attached an amendment to the omnibus drug bill providing $350,000 for the Los Alamos National Laboratory's research on a low-level radar detection system that could aid in catching drug smugglers.

One of Skeen's best-known legislative causes is a perennial effort with Indiana Democrat Andrew Jacobs Jr. to reduce the allowances and pensions for former presidents. The usual routine is for Jacobs to propose a draconian cut, and then for Skeen to offer a more modest reduction that is often adopted by the House.

Skeen left the Interior Subcommittee in the 103rd Congress in favor of a seat on the Defense Subcommittee.

At Home: After narrowly losing two carefully planned bids for governor, Skeen won a House seat in 1980 without even being on the ballot. He is one of the few write-in candidates ever elected to the House.

Skeen's unusual victory came after Democratic Rep. Harold E. Runnels, who was unopposed for re-election, died on Aug. 5, 1980. Runnels' death set off three months of complex maneuvering, with Skeen and Runnels' widow, Dorothy, mounting unsuccessful court challenges to win a spot on the ballot against the substitute Democratic nominee, David King.

Skeen and Mrs. Runnels pursued separate write-in campaigns, aided by negative publicity that hit King. A former state finance commissioner, King moved to the district only after Harold Runnels' death, and there were complaints that his choice was arranged by his uncle, Democratic Gov. Bruce King.

Skeen based his campaign on the contention that no one should be appointed to Congress. His write-ins totaled 38 percent of the vote, enough to win the three-way contest.

Skeen then went on a streak of comfortable re-elections, drawing no Democratic foe at all in 1988 and 1990. But in 1992, he got a serious opponent with officeholding credentials and name recognition: Dan Sosa Jr. Sosa had served 17 years on the state's Supreme Court, including five as chief justice, before retiring in 1991. And Sosa, a Hispanic, hoped to benefit from the fact that 1992 redistricting added more than 65,000 Hispanics to the 2nd, making its population 42 percent Hispanic.

Sosa ran a campaign against the status quo and longtime incumbency. He also faulted Skeen for his opposition to family leave legislation and for voting no on civil rights and extended unemployment compensation legislation.

But Skeen has remained well-liked in his district, and he was able to draw on a deep reservoir of support that he had built with years of steady attention to constituents. He won with 56 percent of the vote, running 15 points ahead of George Bush in the district.

Committee

Appropriations (9th of 23 Republicans)
Agriculture, Rural Development, FDA & Related Agencies (ranking); Defense

Elections

1992 General		
Joe Skeen (R)	94,838	(56%)
Dan Sosa Jr. (D)	73,157	(44%)
1990 General		
Joe Skeen (R)	80,677	(100%)

Previous Winning Percentages: **1988** (100%) **1986** (63%) **1984** (74%) **1982** (58%) **1980*** (38%)

* *Write-in candidate.*

District Vote for President

1992	
D	70,646 (41%)
R	68,754 (40%)
I	31,782 (19%)

Campaign Finance

	Receipts	Receipts from PACs		Expend-itures
1992				
Skeen (R)	$387,893	$160,125	(41%)	$493,406
Sosa (D)	$39,561	$1,750	(4%)	$40,973
1990				
Skeen (R)	$197,830	$109,210	(55%)	$80,737

Key Votes

1993	
Require parental notification of minors' abortions	N
Require unpaid family and medical leave	N
Approve national "motor voter" registration bill	N
Approve budget increasing taxes and reducing deficit	N
Approve economic stimulus plan	N
1992	
Approve balanced-budget constitutional amendment	Y
Close down space station program	N
Approve U.S. aid for former Soviet Union	Y
Allow shifting funds from defense to domestic programs	N
1991	
Extend unemployment benefits using deficit financing	N
Approve waiting period for handgun purchases	N
Authorize use of force in Persian Gulf	Y

Voting Studies

	Presidential Support		Party Unity		Conservative Coalition	
Year	**S**	**O**	**S**	**O**	**S**	**O**
1992	76	24	67	32	92	8
1991	75	25	69	30	89	11
1990	68	32	63	35	91	9
1989	86	14	70	29	100	0
1988	56	43	80	19	89	11
1987	63	34	76	24	93	7
1986	68	30	79	20	94	6
1985	68	31	81	17	93	4
1984	62	38	84	15	93	7
1983	82	17	89	8	94	4
1982	82	16	90	10	100	0
1981	75	24	83	15	96	4

Interest Group Ratings

Year	ADA	AFL-CIO	CCUS	ACU
1992	20	42	88	76
1991	0	17	90	85
1990	6	8	79	71
1989	0	0	90	96
1988	5	29	93	100
1987	12	25	80	83
1986	10	7	67	82
1985	0	6	86	76
1984	15	15	69	75
1983	5	0	90	91
1982	5	5	82	82
1981	0	20	89	100

3 Bill Richardson (D)

Of Santa Fe — Elected 1982; 6th Term

Born: Nov. 15, 1947, Pasadena, Calif.
Education: Tufts U., B.A. 1970, M.A. 1971.
Occupation: Business consultant.
Family: Wife, Barbara Flavin.
Religion: Roman Catholic.
Political Career: N.M. Democratic Party executive director, 1978-80; Democratic nominee for U.S. House, 1980.
Capitol Office: 2349 Rayburn Bldg. 20515; 225-6190.

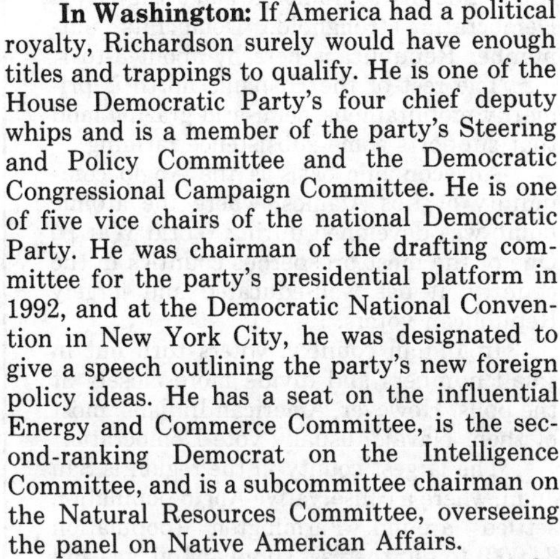

In Washington: If America had a political royalty, Richardson surely would have enough titles and trappings to qualify. He is one of the House Democratic Party's four chief deputy whips and is a member of the party's Steering and Policy Committee and the Democratic Congressional Campaign Committee. He is one of five vice chairs of the national Democratic Party. He was chairman of the drafting committee for the party's presidential platform in 1992, and at the Democratic National Convention in New York City, he was designated to give a speech outlining the party's new foreign policy ideas. He has a seat on the influential Energy and Commerce Committee, is the second-ranking Democrat on the Intelligence Committee, and is a subcommittee chairman on the Natural Resources Committee, overseeing the panel on Native American Affairs.

In recognition of his position as one of the nation's top Hispanic politicians, Richardson made the long list of Bill Clinton's possible vice presidential picks. After Clinton's election, Richardson was touted for Interior Secretary by groups wanting another Hispanic in the Cabinet (to join Housing and Urban Development's Henry G. Cisneros). But national environmental groups objected, and Transportation Secretary Federico F. Peña filled the bill instead.

A more realistic goal for Richardson — and one his House colleagues widely see him as actively pursuing — is statewide office in New Mexico. Richardson came close to entering the 1990 Democratic gubernatorial primary but demurred. A media kit his office prepared in early 1993 included an article from the Santa Fe New Mexican reporting on a poll that showed Richardson leading Democratic Gov. Bruce King if the two met in a primary. King is up for re-election in 1994.

If Richardson chooses instead to stay in the House, he faces the challenge of demonstrating to his colleagues that he can juggle all the responsibilities he has taken on. Even those who work amicably with Richardson wonder if he has too many irons in the fire. Less charitable observers of Richardson's work say he wrongly equates activity and media publicity with genuine legislative influence.

Richardson has heard the criticisms that he can get overcommitted and is a hog for personal credit. "The rap is that I'm spread too thin," Richardson told a reporter from the Albuquerque Journal in 1990. "And there's another rap. That I seek publicity." But Richardson believes many are unaware of how much he has achieved. "For all the criticism I might get, I have done more than most," he told the paper. "That's not because of ambition, that's because I want to do things. I mean, look at my schedule compared to most members of Congress.'

Richardson's overall voting record is solidly liberal, but on a number of issues he has tried to take into account the desires of business interests, such as the oil, gas and uranium industries, and liberal activist groups, such as environmentalists. Both are important players in New Mexico politics, but their priorities often conflict.

For a number of years, Richardson was a vocal critic of plans to open and operate the Waste Isolation Pilot Project, a nuclear waste repository in underground salt beds near Carlsbad, N.M. That stance pleased environmentalists, but some of them soured on him during the 102nd Congress, when it appeared WIPP would become reality: Richardson shifted his focus to passing legislation addressing safety concerns about the project.

During negotiations on the Clean Air Act reauthorization during the 101st Congress, Richardson drew fierce attacks from oil lobbyists when he pushed a plan to promote non-gasoline car fuels. Richardson's proposal required the use of special, cleaner burning gasolines in the most polluted cities.

Opposed by Energy and Commerce Chairman John D. Dingell of Michigan, the proposal was narrowly defeated in subcommittee and again in full committee. But the Senate had approved similar provisions in its clean air bill, and the committee later agreed to a compromise that included parts of Richardson's amendment.

Other of Richardson's legislative endeavors have been less auspicious. Colleagues still cite the incident in the 100th Congress when Richardson

New Mexico 3

North and East Central — Farmington; Santa Fe

With more than half its voters either Hispanic or Indian, the 3rd is more liberal and more Democratic than either of the state's other districts. It contains eight of the 10 New Mexico counties that Michael S. Dukakis carried in 1988. In 1992, Bill Clinton took 51 percent of the 3rd's vote.

However, 1991 redistricting made the district a bit less Democratic, trading a chunk of Hispanic territory for a piece of conservative GOP turf.

Richardson now represents a constituency that is about 35 percent Hispanic, down from 39 percent in the 1980s. Anglos make up about 40 percent; the remainder is American Indian. The population is divided between the Hispanic counties of northern New Mexico and some energy-rich Indian lands along the Arizona border.

Areas of the 3rd, particularly Cibola, McKinley and Mora counties, are plagued with high unemployment and poverty. In most of the counties that ring the Santa Fe-Taos area, between one-third and one-half of the residents, many of whom are unskilled minorities, live in poverty. Unemployment levels here routinely run about 10 percent for most of these counties; the Mora County jobless rate hovered above 30 percent for much of the 1980s. And although programs have targeted alcoholism, it remains a problem in poorer pockets of the 3rd.

The scenery in parts of the 3rd is breathtaking, making it a trendy tourist spot. Taos, home of Taos Ski Valley and many art galleries and specialty shops, attracts thousands of tourists.

The 3rd gained some conservative farming and ranching territory when it picked up Curry, Quay and Roosevelt counties in 1991 redistricting. Curry is home to Cannon Air Force base and a considerable number of military retirees who make this area a conservative bastion.

The centerpiece of the region is Santa Fe, the third-largest city in the state. The city has evolved into a regional arts center, supporting more than 150 art galleries and hundreds of shops that peddle distinctive southwestern and Indian art styles. Artists, state employees, Hispanics, Indians and Anglo liberals combine to make the city a Democratic stronghold; Democrats outnumber Republicans here by about 3-to-1.

The rest of the Hispanic north is primarily mountainous, semi-arid grazing land that supports some subsistence farming.

An economic oasis is the Anglo community of Los Alamos, where the atomic bomb was developed during World War II. One of the most prosperous counties in the country, it has well-educated and largely Republican voters.

In Indian country, voters turn out in small numbers and divide more closely at the polls. However, American Indians, most of them Navajo, usually vote Democratic.

The largest county in the region is San Juan, where a conservative Anglo population settled around Farmington (population 34,000) to tap the vast supply of oil, gas and coal in the Four Corners area. San Juan went solidly for George Bush in 1988 and 1992.

1990 Population: 504,919. White 330,243 (65%), Black 6,114 (1%), Other 168,562 (33%). Hispanic origin 174,485 (35%). 18 and over 345,896 (69%), 62 and over 61,140 (12%). Median age: 31.

did not show for the first day of Energy and Commerce's work on a product-liability bill for which he was chief sponsor. Richardson has said a family illness kept him away, but he was missing at other times throughout the deliberations on the measure, and colleagues came to identify the bill with its other, more active proponents.

Richardson's work over the years on issues of concern to American Indians — a significant constituency in New Mexico — made him an obvious choice to chair the Native American Affairs subcommittee, newly created for the 103rd.

Addressing a joint session of the New Mexico legislature shortly after he took the subcommittee gavel, he called the federal Bureau of Indian Affairs "the worst agency in the United States." A variety of Richardson proposals addressing alcohol and drug abuse among Indians, as well as their health, education and job training needs, have become law.

Richardson has been a high-profile advocate of the North American Free Trade Agreement, writing columns favoring NAFTA that appeared in The Wall Street Journal, The Los Angeles Times and The Washington Post.

During the 102nd, Richardson supported granting the Bush administration "fast track" authority to negotiate NAFTA. He praised candidate Clinton for endorsing NAFTA in 1992, and in 1993, with worries growing in the United States about NAFTA's environmental and economic impact, Richardson called on President Clinton to work with Mexico to negotiate side agreements to the pact that would ease U.S.

concerns.

At Home: A former staff member of the Senate Foreign Relations Committee, Richardson made his entry into politics in 1978, when he moved to New Mexico to become executive director of the Democratic State Committee. Within months he was planning a 1980 congressional campaign against GOP Rep. Manuel Lujan Jr. He was criticized as a carpetbagger, but he responded that his ethnic heritage — he was raised in Mexico City by a Mexican mother and an American father — made heavily Hispanic New Mexico a logical home.

By coming within 5,200 votes of the seemingly entrenched Lujan, Richardson became a star in his state party overnight. When the northern New Mexico 3rd District was created the next year, he was the early favorite to win.

His campaign survived some serious problems. He had to retract a statement in his literature that he had been a "top" foreign policy adviser to Sen. Hubert H. Humphrey. Questions about a $100,000 campaign loan produced a probe by the Federal Election Commission. Although he was eventually cleared of any wrongdoing, the probe did bring him negative publicity.

Richardson countered the bad press by campaigning dawn to dusk through the small towns and pueblos, reaching the Hispanic and Indian voters who together cast a majority of the ballots. With his 1980 organization still in place and a substantial campaign treasury, Richardson won the four-way primary with 36 percent of the vote. In the most loyally Democratic House constituency in the state, his nomination was tantamount to election.

Richardson has not had any problems since then, although one of his campaigns attracted some attention. In 1986, he was challenged for re-election by former GOP Gov. David F. Cargo, who was seeking a political comeback 15 years after leaving office, following a long absence from the state. But Richardson topped 70 percent.

Richardson almost passed up politics for a career in baseball. After his boyhood in Mexico City, he moved to the United States to attend school. At age 18, he was drafted by the Kansas City (now Oakland) Athletics. But an elbow injury ended his sports career.

Committees

Chief Deputy Whip

Energy & Commerce (11th of 27 Democrats)
Health & the Environment; Telecommunications & Finance; Transportation & Hazardous Materials

Natural Resources (11th of 28 Democrats)
Native American Affairs (chairman); National Parks, Forests & Public Lands

Select Intelligence (2nd of 12 Democrats)
Program & Budget Authorization

Elections

1992 General		
Bill Richardson (D)	122,850	(67%)
F. Gregg Bemis Jr. (R)	54,569	(30%)
Ed Nagel (LIBERT)	4,798	(3%)
1990 General		
Bill Richardson (D)	104,225	(74%)
Phil T. Archuletta (R)	35,751	(26%)

Previous Winning Percentages: **1988** (73%) **1986** (71%) **1984** (61%) **1982** (65%)

District Vote for President

1992

D	95,294 (51%)
R	63,024 (34%)
I	27,081 (15%)

Campaign Finance

	Receipts	Receipts from PACs		Expend-itures
1992				
Richardson (D)	$680,154	$387,551	(57%)	$600,683
Bemis (R)	$49,879	$1,000	(2%)	$48,064
1990				
Richardson (D)	$531,096	$346,707	(65%)	$420,907
Archuletta (R)	$19,557	$5,500	(28%)	$20,902

Key Votes

1993	
Require parental notification of minors' abortions	N
Require unpaid family and medical leave	Y
Approve national "motor voter" registration bill	Y
Approve budget increasing taxes and reducing deficit	Y
Approve economic stimulus plan	Y
1992	
Approve balanced-budget constitutional amendment	Y
Close down space station program	N
Approve U.S. aid for former Soviet Union	Y
Allow shifting funds from defense to domestic programs	N
1991	
Extend unemployment benefits using deficit financing	Y
Approve waiting period for handgun purchases	N
Authorize use of force in Persian Gulf	N

Voting Studies

	Presidential Support		Party Unity		Conservative Coalition	
Year	**S**	**O**	**S**	**O**	**S**	**O**
1992	29	65	83	10	44	46
1991	33	67	91	8	54	46
1990	29	69	84	10	54	44
1989	37	58	86	11	54	46
1988	28	66	83	12	55	34
1987	26	71	88	9	58	42
1986	24	76	90	9	52	44
1985	25	71	89	6	33	65
1984	31	66	89	9	19	80
1983	16	82	87	9	29	71

Interest Group Ratings

Year	ADA	AFL-CIO	CCUS	ACU
1992	75	73	57	33
1991	50	92	30	20
1990	61	92	21	26
1989	70	92	44	21
1988	75	93	42	21
1987	80	88	29	9
1986	75	100	41	18
1985	70	76	32	14
1984	85	100	43	17
1983	95	88	20	13

New York

STATE DATA

Governor:
Mario M. Cuomo (D)
First elected: 1982
Length of term: 4 years
Term expires: 1/95
Salary: $130,000
Term limit: No
Phone: (518) 474-8390
Born: June 15, 1932; Queens, N.Y.
Education: St. John's U., B.A. 1953, LL.B. 1956
Occupation: Lawyer
Family: Wife, Matilda Raffa; five children
Religion: Roman Catholic
Political Career: Sought Democratic nomination for lieutenant governor, 1974; N.Y. secretary of state, 1975-79; sought Democratic nomination for New York City mayor, 1977; Liberal Party nominee for mayor of New York City, 1977; lieutenant governor, 1979-83

Lt. Gov.: Stan Lundine (D)
First elected: 1986
Length of term: 4 years
Term expires: 1/95
Salary: $110,000
Phone: (518) 474-4623

State election official: (518) 474-6220
Democratic headquarters: (518) 462-7407
Republican headquarters: (518) 462-2601

REDISTRICTING

New York lost three House seats in reapportionment, dropping from 34 districts to 31. Legislature passed map June 9, 1992; governor signed June 11. Justice Department approved July 2.

STATE LEGISLATURE

Legislature. Officially meets year-round; usually meets January-June.

Senate: 61 members, 2-year terms
1992 breakdown: 35R, 26D; 54 men, 7 women; 52 whites, 5 blacks, 4 Hispanics
Salary: $57,500
Phone: (518) 455-3216

Assembly: 150 members, 2-year terms
1992 breakdown: 101D, 49R; 124 men, 26 women; 122 whites, 21 blacks, 7 Hispanics
Salary: $57,500
Phone: (518) 455-4218

URBAN STATISTICS

City	Pop.
New York City	7,322,564
Mayor David Dinkins, D	
Buffalo	328,175
Mayor James D. Griffin, D	
Rochester	231,636
Mayor Thomas P. Ryan Jr., D	
Yonkers	188,082
Mayor Terrance Zaleski, D	
Syracuse	163,860
Mayor Thomas G. Young, D	

U.S. CONGRESS

Senate: 1 D, 1 R
House: 18 D, 13 R

TERM LIMITS

For Congress: No
For state offices: No

ELECTIONS

1992 Presidential Vote

Bill Clinton	49.7%
George Bush	33.9%
Ross Perot	15.7%

1988 Presidential Vote

Michael S. Dukakis	52%
George Bush	48%

1984 Presidential Vote

Ronald Reagan	54%
Walter F. Mondale	46%

POPULATION

1990 population		17,990,455
1980 population		17,558,072
Percent change		+2%
Rank among states:		2
White		74%
Black		16%
Hispanic		12%
Asian or Pacific islander		4%
Urban		84%
Rural		16%
Born in state		68%
Foreign-born		16%
Under age 18	4,259,549	24%
Ages 18-64	11,367,184	63%
65 and older	2,363,722	13%
Median age		33.9

MISCELLANEOUS

Capital: Albany
Number of counties: 62
Per capita income: $22,456 (1991)
Rank among states: 4
Total area: 49,108 sq. miles
Rank among states: 30

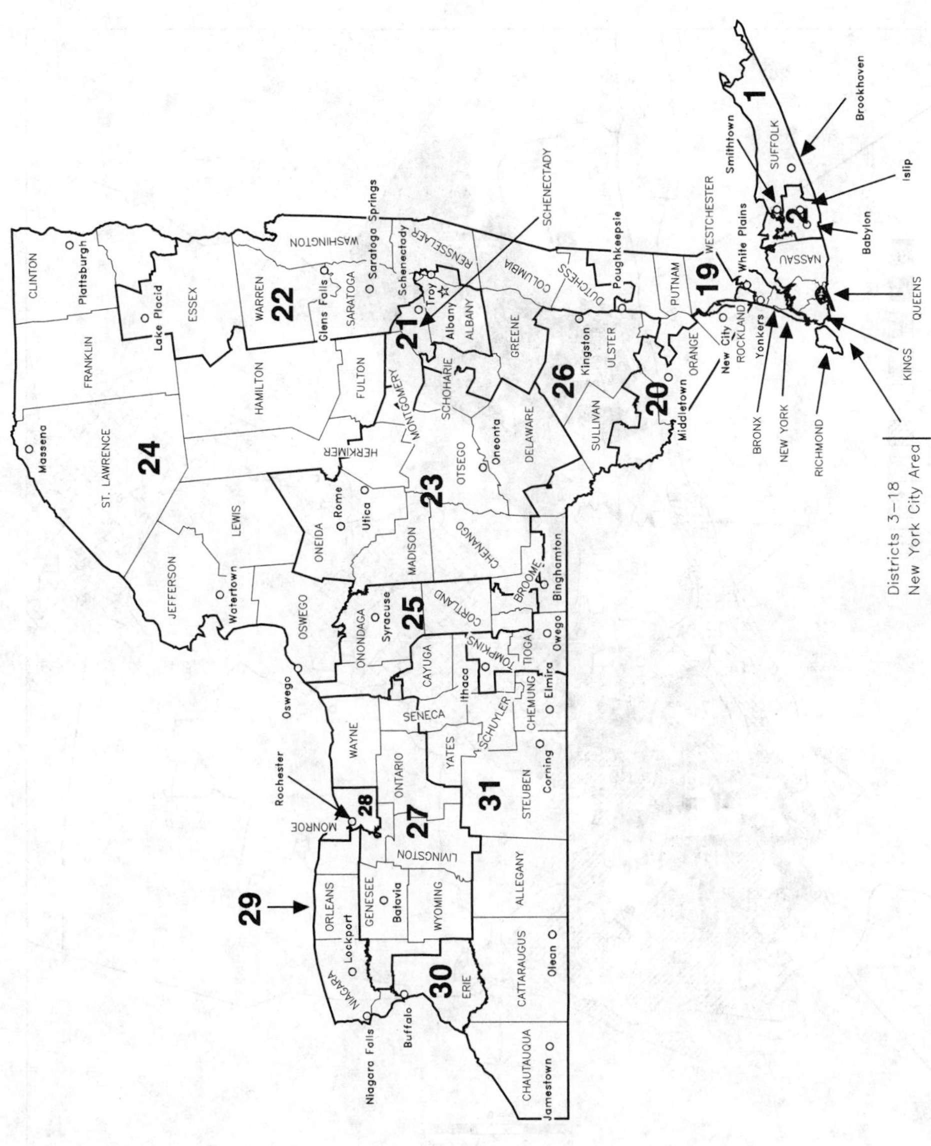

CLINTON
Plattsburgh
ESSEX
Lake Placid
FRANKLIN
Massena
ST. LAWRENCE
24
HAMILTON
WARREN
22
WASHINGTON
Saratoga Springs
Glens Falls
SARATOGA
Schenectady
SCHENECTADY
RENSSELAER
Troy
Albany
ALBANY
21
FULTON
MONTGOMERY
SCHOHARIE
GREENE
COLUMBIA
DUTCHESS
Poughkeepsie
Kingston
ULSTER
26
SULLIVAN
DELAWARE
Oneonta
OTSEGO
HERKIMER
23
Utica
Rome
ONEIDA
LEWIS
JEFFERSON
Watertown
OSWEGO
Oswego
MADISON
CHENANGO
ONONDAGA
Syracuse
25
CORTLAND
BROOME
Binghamton
Owego
TIOGA
TOMPKINS
Ithaca
CAYUGA
SENECA
WAYNE
ONTARIO
YATES
SCHUYLER
CHEMUNG
Elmira
Corning
STEUBEN
31
Rochester
MONROE
28
27
LIVINGSTON
ALLEGANY
29
ORLEANS
GENESEE
Batavia
WYOMING
NIAGARA
Lockport
Niagara Falls
Buffalo
30
ERIE
CATTARAUGUS
Olean
CHAUTAUQUA
Jamestown
PUTNAM
19
WESTCHESTER
White Plains
ORANGE
20
Middletown
New City
ROCKLAND
Yonkers
BRONX
NEW YORK
RICHMOND
KINGS
QUEENS
NASSAU
2
Babylon
Islip
Smithtown
SUFFOLK
Brookhaven
1
Districts 3–18
New York City Area

New York City Area Districts

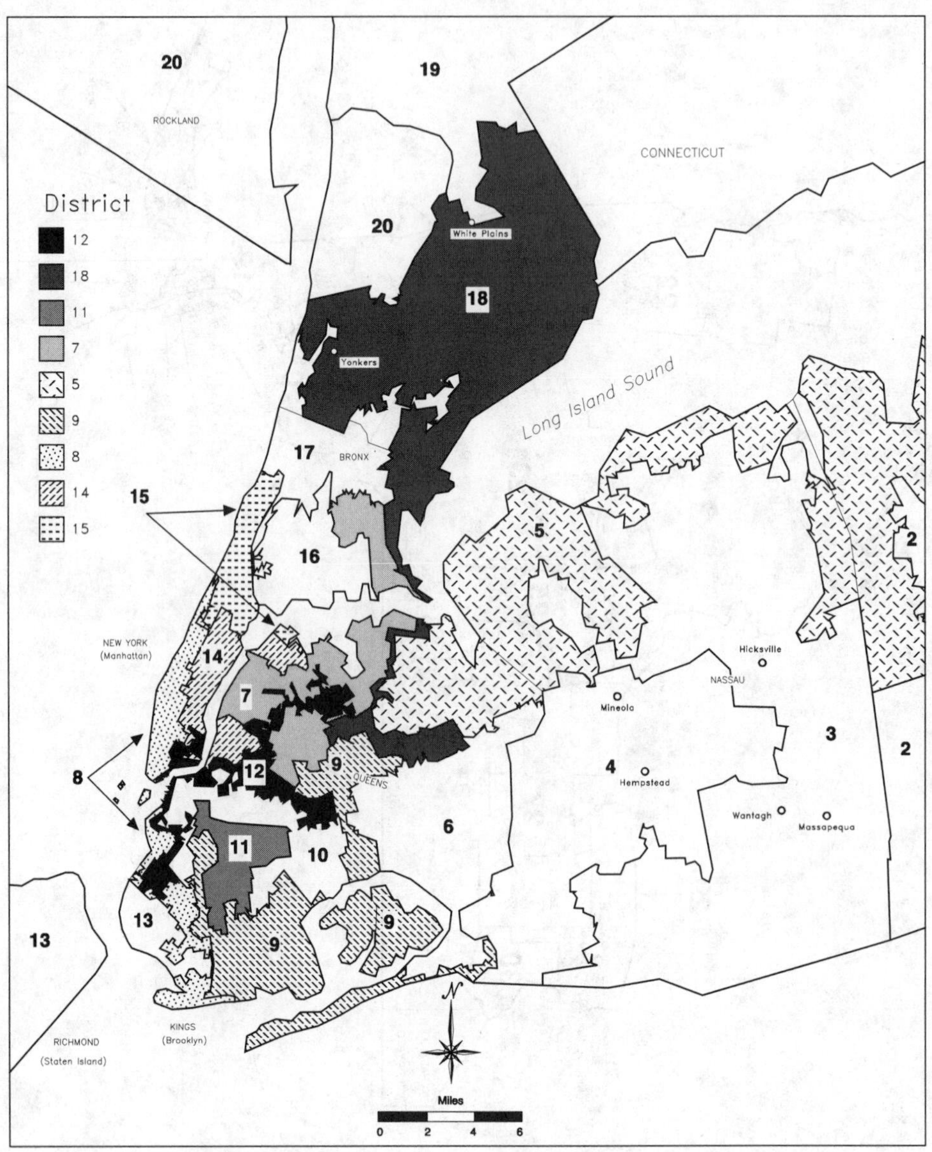

Daniel Patrick Moynihan (D)

Of Pindars Corners — Elected 1976; 3rd Term

Born: March 16, 1927, Tulsa, Okla.
Education: City U. of New York, City College, 1943; Tufts U., B.N.S. 1946, B.A. 1948; Fletcher School of Law and Diplomacy, M.A. 1949, Ph.D. 1961.
Military Service: Naval Reserve, 1944-66.
Occupation: Professor; writer.
Family: Wife, Elizabeth Brennan; three children.
Religion: Roman Catholic.
Political Career: Sought Democratic nomination for N.Y. City Council president, 1965.
Capitol Office: 464 Russell Bldg. 20510; 224-4451.

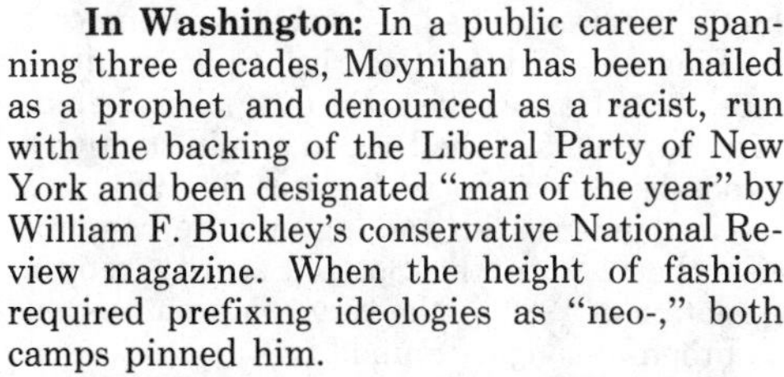

In Washington: In a public career spanning three decades, Moynihan has been hailed as a prophet and denounced as a racist, run with the backing of the Liberal Party of New York and been designated "man of the year" by William F. Buckley's conservative National Review magazine. When the height of fashion required prefixing ideologies as "neo-," both camps pinned him.

Now he has a new title: committee chairman. Directing the work of the Finance Committee is a demanding job that does not quite fit with Moynihan's popular image as a genuine intellectual of considerable scholarly accomplishment, a senator who loves to debate but does not often summon the patience or interest to engage in legislating.

But Moynihan is *sui generis* in today's Senate, and he will no doubt find a way to accommodate both the responsibilities of his new position and his inclination to ruminate and theorize. He is also a good Democrat, and one who professed early support for President Clinton. "The party has to show it can run a campaign, then get a program through," he told The New York Times shortly after the election.

At the same time, Moynihan was quick to chastise a leaked administration proposal to reduce the deficit by trimming cost-of-living adjustments for Social Security pensioners. Nothing is more sacred to Moynihan than Social Security, and he dismissed the notion, branding it a "death wish" on Clinton's part.

Few seem happier than Moynihan with life as a senator. The body appreciates high oratory but forgives the merely partisan. Moynihan can deliver both.

At certain moments, listening to him is both an education and a treat, as when he interrupts routine debate with a personal discourse on the impossibility of free trade with a country like Mexico that lacks an independent judiciary, or discusses an algebraic formula for determining national income and explains in comprehensible terms how it works. When he focuses his attention on an issue, his pronouncements are invariably provocative.

Impressed colleagues do not always appreciate his manner, though; his digressions can cross the border to pomposity and appear as self-aggrandizement wrapped in disheveled, professorial tweed.

Moynihan has been a player on the world stage, and he prefers to act much as he speaks, on the grand scale. That has led critics to sometimes overlook his refined capacity both for legislative and purely political maneuvering.

It might seem as if Moynihan is ill-suited to take over the reins of the Finance Committee from Lloyd Bentsen, who resigned his Senate seat to become Treasury secretary. Moynihan's long devotion to Social Security and welfare issues is understood; his general lack of interest in the intricacies of trade and tax law is likewise a hallmark of his tenure in the Senate.

But Moynihan has proved his ability twice in recent years as an adept operator of the legislative mill.

He was key to Senate passage of a comprehensive surface transportation bill in 1991. And he saw much of his effort to rethink the purpose of federal transportation spending survive in the conference committee, where he led Senate negotiators as chairman of the Environment and Public Works Subcommittee on Water Resources and Transportation. As enacted, the measure moves far from the highway construction emphasis of the past, and establishes a new emphasis on alternatives to single-passenger vehicles and to maintenance of existing roadways.

The central tenet of the measure was challenged by an amendment from Republican Trent Lott of Mississippi, who wanted to have the federal government pay 90 percent of the cost of interstate highway maintenance and bridge construction. With state highway administrators lobbying hard for the amendment, Moynihan argued against "the notion that this is all free money"; it was defeated 53-44.

Moynihan can frustrate by refusing to engage in the mundane that others must attend to. On the transportation bill, he was caught short when he insisted on an unrelated provision to pay to renovate a Brooklyn, N.Y., courthouse. His lack of attention to budget scorekeeping details threatened to lop $1.2 billion in spending from the bill, when a little creative bill-drafting could have averted the problem. Eventually, Congress had to repeal the courthouse provision to save the highway money.

Previously, in the 100th Congress, Moynihan rose to the occasion as the chief Senate sponsor of welfare legislation. Long one of the nation's foremost authorities on work and family in the welfare state, he was challenged as never before to make social policy of social science, as momentum built to try for the third time in 20 years to overhaul the nation's welfare system.

Moynihan did homework and legwork along with brain work writing an entitlement program designed to move welfare recipients into the work force. It was in many ways vindication, but one he would have preferred not to have collected, for experience had come to support his theory that black families in urban ghettos would break up even if the nation as a whole prospered.

The restructured welfare program aims first to hold families together, and then, if they break apart, to move welfare recipients, mostly mothers, from the dole into the work force. Moynihan's ideas about poverty and the black family structure, which caused him to be denounced as a racist a generation ago, came to be seen by many as farsighted and the key to the restructuring of the welfare system.

Moynihan's interest in defending Social Security is legend. So, it was somewhat of a shock when he disrupted economic politics in both parties in the 101st Congress, proposing to cut Social Security taxes and stop building surpluses in the Social Security trust funds.

He said the 1990 rate increase in the payroll tax should be repealed and refunded. He sought to restore the initial pay-as-you-go approach to funding Social Security, under which it operated before 1983, and to make the tax plan progressive by giving a cut to lower- and middle-class workers and placing higher taxes on upper-income workers. He said surpluses in the trust funds allowed the administration to disguise the true size of the federal deficit.

In a city where the promise of new ideas is extolled but infrequently fulfilled, officials in Washington were confronted with a concept that upended traditional alignments. Prominent conservatives endorsed it. President Bush called it a "charade," warning against "messing around" with Social Security. Democratic congressional leaders approached it warily. It dominated fiscal debate for the first several weeks of 1990 and loomed over budget discussions throughout the year.

Few Democrats joined Moynihan initially. House Ways and Means Committee Chairman Dan Rostenkowski, Ill., called the idea irresponsible; Bentsen expressed deep misgivings as well. But the Democratic National Committee endorsed it, as did New York Gov. Mario M. Cuomo. The proposal became a political club Democrats could wield during budget talks: If the president pressed for a cut in the capital gains tax, Democrats could counter with the Moynihan plan. Republican congressional leaders lined up their members behind Bush.

For two days in October, the Senate debated Moynihan's plan but decided to kill it. The vote, however, was on a parliamentary motion and did not require senators to go on record on the merits of the plan. The Senate voted it down again in 1991.

Moynihan's plan caught many by surprise, chiefly because he had been the top Democrat on Finance's Social Security Subcommittee since 1981. He was the most outspoken Democratic opponent of the Reagan administration's proposals to trim Social Security in 1981, and was instrumental in working out the compromise that led to the Social Security reform legislation of 1983 — the very compromise that his proposal sought to undo.

On many other domestic issues, Moynihan has been less intent on rethinking fundamental questions than on lining up emotionally with liberal Democrats in support of preserving the New Deal and Great Society. His ringing declarations of support for traditional Democratic Party ideas strike some colleagues as cynical political rhetoric, since they remember him as a critic of those ideas.

And foreign policy questions no longer preoccupy Moynihan the way they did when, as U.N. ambassador, he was a staunch anti-communist and the scourge of radical Third World regimes. In the Senate, Moynihan has figured prominently as an arms-control supporter and backer-turned-critic of aid for the Nicaraguan contras. His was a lonely voice on Finance arguing to deny normal trading status to China in the 101st Congress after the Chinese government's massacre of pro-democracy demonstrators and subsequent repression.

Known at the United Nations for his outspoken defense of Israel, Moynihan has been equally militant in the Senate. He sponsored a resolution, unanimously adopted by the Senate, threatening to pull the United States out of the United Nations if Israel was expelled.

He opposed authorizing Bush to use force to oust Iraq from Kuwait when the Senate debated the question in January 1991, denouncing Kuwait's prior behavior. "I remember Kuwait at the United Nations as a particularly poisonous enemy of the United States," he said. "One can be an antagonist of the United States in a way that leaves room for further discussions afterwards. But the Kuwaitis were singularly nasty. Their anti-Semitism was at the level of the personally loathsome."

At Home: The professorial Moynihan may not have the populist appeal of his earthier colleague, Republican Sen. Alfonse M. D'Amato. But Moynihan's image of *gravitas* and avoidance of scandal has protected him from the sort of electoral scrape that D'Amato barely survived in 1992.

Moynihan's election results powerfully attest to his political popularity. After unseating Republican Sen. James Buckley in 1976, Moynihan won his first re-election in 1982 with 65 percent of the vote. In 1988, he defeated Republican attorney Robert R. McMillan with 67 percent — breaking his own state record for Senate vote percentage.

At the outset of the 1988 campaign, a Moynihan landslide was no given: Possible Republican opponents included U.S. Attorney Rudolph W. Giuliani, the high-profile prosecutor of organized crime figures and corrupt Wall Street financiers, and Rep. Jack F. Kemp, then a candidate for the GOP presidential nomination. Moynihan prepared as if for the fight of his life, raising money early and running TV ads in January. He even took the unusual step of denying a persistent but unsubstantiated rumor that he had a problem with alcohol.

His concerns turned out to be unfounded. Giuliani decided to stay on as prosecutor (he went on to lose narrowly for New York City mayor in 1989, and is expected to again bid for that office in 1993). Kemp was courted after ending his 1988 White House bid, but also declined.

New York Republicans then resorted to McMillan. The longtime GOP activist had many friends inside the state party, but was virtually unknown to the voting public. He had run one previous race, a losing campaign for New York City Council in 1964.

McMillan campaigned hard, caustically criticizing Moynihan. Running as a "compassionate conservative," McMillan described Moynihan's support for a federal grant for a homosexual "safe sex" program as a vote for "safe sodomy." He portrayed Moynihan as aloof and lazy, with poor management skills that resulted in high turnover on his Senate staff.

But few New Yorkers heard McMillan's attacks. Republican financial backers wrote off the race as a loss; McMillan raised a meager half-million dollars, enough to buy one week of one ad in the expensive New York TV market. Meanwhile, Moynihan was flooding the airwaves with ads lauding his accomplishments, including his September 1988 victory on welfare reform. He swept the state, losing just a single rural county in upstate New York.

The landslide was a crowning moment in Moynihan's rise from Manhattan's ethnic, blue-collar precincts to the heights of academia and government. Moynihan's father, a hard-drinking journalist, walked out on the family when the senator was age 6; his mother ran a saloon near Times Square. Moynihan walked into the entrance exam for City College with a longshoreman's loading hook in his back pocket.

After establishing himself as an academic — he taught his personal combination of economics, sociology and urban studies at Harvard and at the Joint Center for Urban Studies — Moynihan turned to government service in the 1960s. He worked in the Labor Department in the Kennedy and Johnson administrations, and as an urban affairs expert for Nixon.

In the latter role, Moynihan was the architect of the ill-fated Nixon "family assistance" welfare proposal, whose history he detailed in a book. He also caused himself great trouble when he counseled "benign neglect" toward minorities. The dispute caused by this advice revived accusations that Moynihan's scholarship was highbrow racism, an issue that first surfaced in 1965, when his book "Beyond the Melting Pot" attributed social problems among blacks to unstable family structure. Though Moynihan insisted he had been misunderstood, his social views created a gulf between him and some minority-group leaders that had to be bridged after he entered elective politics.

But the positive press Moynihan earned in his other roles in GOP administrations — as ambassador to India and to the United Nations under Presidents Nixon and Ford — set him on the road to political success. In his last year in New Delhi, Moynihan drew attention for his articles criticizing a lack of firmness in U.S. foreign policy, especially toward the Third World. His reputation made him a logical choice in 1975 for the U.N. post, whose most recent appointees, including future President George Bush, had been inconspicuous.

Moynihan's service at the United Nations clearly helped his political prospects in New York, although he denied any connection. His staunch defense of Israel earned him support among New York's sizable Jewish constituency, and his televised militance at the United Nations in 1975 allowed him to begin the 1976 campaign as a celebrity, rather than just an articulate Harvard professor. "He spoke up for America," one campaign advertisement said. "He'd speak up for New York."

Given his previous work for GOP presidents and his neo-conservative profile, Moynihan would have had difficulty running in a Democratic primary against a single liberal candidate in 1976. But he found himself challenged not only by Rep. Bella Abzug, the flamboyant feminist leader, but also by two other well-known figures of the Democratic left: former U.S. Attorney General Ramsey Clark and New York City Council President Paul O'Dwyer. Moynihan's chief political sponsor, Erie County Democratic Chairman Joseph Crangle, kept the liberal vote split by pushing the state Democratic convention to guarantee ballot spots for all three liberal candidates.

Abzug depicted Moynihan as a Buckley in Democratic clothing and emerged as his main rival. But Clark and O'Dwyer took a combined 19 percent, enough to sink her. Moynihan came in first with 36 percent, 10,000 votes up on Abzug.

Buckley had won the seat six years earlier as the Conservative Party candidate, taking advantage of a three-way contest involving liberal Republican incumbent Charles Goodell and liberal Democratic challenger Richard L. Ottinger. He had no such advantage in 1976.

Moynihan started with a strong lead over Buckley in the polls, and he neither said nor did anything in the fall to fracture his tenuous party harmony. He spent much of his time in Massachusetts, teaching at Harvard to protect his tenure. When he did speak out, he called Buckley a right-wing extremist out of step with the state's politics — citing Buckley's initial opposition in 1975 to federal loan guarantees for New York City. He sailed to victory over Buckley by a half-million votes.

For the first few years of his Senate career, it seemed likely he would be challenged from the left in seeking renomination in 1982. But by the time of the primary, his belligerent and unexpected defense of traditional Democratic policies had had its effect. New York's Democratic left was pacified, and the National Conservative Political Action Committee unwittingly helped Moynihan by airing TV ads calling him "the most liberal United States senator." Even the Liberal Party, which had been upset by his support of tuition tax credits for non-public schools, backed Moynihan in 1982.

Former U.S. Rep. Bruce F. Caputo wanted the GOP nomination, and he might have made an attractive candidate. But he was forced to withdraw after disclosure that he had exaggerated his military record. Conservative state Assemblywoman Florence Sullivan won the nomination; she carried only 16 rural counties in November.

Committees

Finance (Chairman)
International Trade; Private Retirement Plans & Oversight of the Internal Revenue Service; Social Security & Family Policy

Environment & Public Works (2nd of 10 Democrats)
Water Resources, Transportation, Public Buildings & Economic Development (chairman); Clean Air & Nuclear Regulation; Superfund, Recycling & Solid Waste Management

Foreign Relations (7th of 11 Democrats)
Near Eastern & South Asian Affairs (chairman); African Affairs; Terrorism, Narcotics & International Operations

Rules & Administration (6th of 9 Democrats)

Joint Library

Joint Taxation

Elections

1988 General

Daniel Patrick Moynihan (D)	4,048,649	(67%)
Robert R. McMillan (R)	1,875,784	(31%)

Previous Winning Percentages: 1982 (65%) 1976 (54%)

Campaign Finance

	Receipts	Receipts from PACs		Expenditures
1988				
Moynihan (D)	$4,350,271	$892,773	(21%)	$4,809,810
McMillan (R)	$536,445	$33,495	(6%)	$528,989

Key Votes

1993	
Require unpaid family and medical leave	Y
Approve national "motor voter" registration bill	Y
Approve budget increasing taxes and reducing deficit	Y
Support president's right to lift military gay ban	Y
1992	
Approve school-choice pilot program	N
Allow shifting funds from defense to domestic programs	Y
Oppose deeper cuts in spending for SDI	N
1991	
Approve waiting period for handgun purchases	Y
Raise senators' pay and ban honoraria	Y
Authorize use of force in Persian Gulf	N
Confirm Clarence Thomas to Supreme Court	N

Voting Studies

	Presidential Support		Party Unity		Conservative Coalition	
Year	**S**	**O**	**S**	**O**	**S**	**O**
1992	35	65	90	10	34	66
1991	35	65	92	7	25	75
1990	31	69	89	9	11	89
1989	52	45	90	7	24	71
1988	48	47	91	6	27	70
1987	37	60	93	5	19	78
1986	40	59	72	25	36	63
1985	33	65	81	13	27	67
1984	36	53	68	25	21	66
1983	46	51	74	21	16	80
1982	28	71	86	11	14	84
1981	41	47	71	14	8	87

Interest Group Ratings

Year	ADA	AFL-CIO	CCUS	ACU
1992	100	83	10	0
1991	95	92	10	0
1990	94	78	17	4
1989	75	100	38	4
1988	90	93	31	8
1987	95	100	31	0
1986	85	67	39	13
1985	90	100	33	4
1984	85	80	39	18
1983	80	82	26	8
1982	95	96	22	22
1981	75	94	33	13

Alfonse M. D'Amato (R)

Of Island Park — Elected 1980; 3rd Term

Born: Aug. 1, 1937, Brooklyn, N.Y.
Education: Syracuse U., B.S. 1959, J.D. 1961.
Occupation: Lawyer.
Family: Wife, Penny Collenburg; four children.
Religion: Roman Catholic.
Political Career: Nassau County public administrator, 1965-68; Town of Hempstead tax receiver, 1969-71; Hempstead town supervisor, 1971-77; Nassau County Board of Supervisors, 1971-81, presiding supervisor, 1977-81.
Capitol Office: 520 Hart Bldg. 20510; 224-6542.

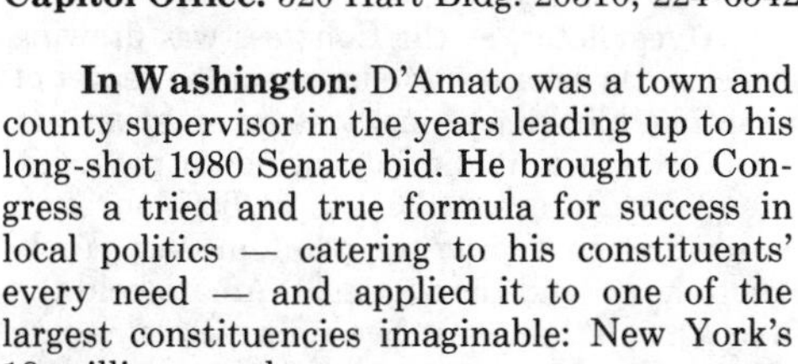

In Washington: D'Amato was a town and county supervisor in the years leading up to his long-shot 1980 Senate bid. He brought to Congress a tried and true formula for success in local politics — catering to his constituents' every need — and applied it to one of the largest constituencies imaginable: New York's 18 million people.

He has two more attributes that he uses to good effect in the Senate and on the stump — chutzpah and luck. When an ethical cloud descended on D'Amato before the 1992 elections, he brushed it away in typical, D'Amato fashion, despite a rebuke from the Ethics Committee for negligence in the way he conducted his office's affairs. At the polls, he narrowly won a third term — garnering the same 81,000-vote plurality by which he was first elected — after sitting by while his potential Democratic opponents carved up one another in the primary.

D'Amato ran on the right in his 1980 Senate campaign and voiced strong support for Ronald Reagan. But he quickly established himself as an independent-minded legislator who would fight for every dime he could get for New York, especially for the transportation and housing programs crucial to his heavily urbanized state. On the Appropriations Committee, he has pursued federal aid in a brazen and persistent manner, earning the nickname "Senator Pothole."

With the retirement of Jake Garn of Utah at the end of the 102nd Congress, D'Amato captured a new seat from which to play to the galleries for his beloved New York: the ranking Republican slot on the Banking Committee.

The Ethics Committee's investigation of D'Amato concluded in August 1991, more than two years after the first news reports linked a scandal involving influence-peddling in the Department of Housing and Urban Development to D'Amato. In July 1989, The New York Times published allegations that D'Amato had developed a too-cozy relationship with HUD's New York regional office (which included New Jersey and Puerto Rico as well); the article said he used his contacts there to steer federal housing money to his campaign contributors and other associates, including members of his family.

That December, the Ethics panel, acting on a complaint from D'Amato's 1986 Democratic Senate foe, Mark Green, decided to begin a formal, preliminary investigation of the accusations, which by then had broadened considerably into other areas. Eventually, the committee probed 16 specific allegations. It found "no evidence" of rules violations in two cases, "no credible evidence" in 12, and "insufficient credible evidence" in two more.

The committee decided to rebuke D'Amato, finding him "negligent in failing to establish appropriate standards for the operation of his office." But it said no further action was warranted by the full Senate.

The case involved D'Amato's brother, Armand, who claimed to be representing Unisys Corp., which was seeking contracts from the Defense Department. D'Amato's office twice sent letters to Defense over the senator's signature, but D'Amato said the staff acted without telling him, and he denied knowing that his brother worked for Unisys. The committee found the letters to be "ordinary and routine," and said there was no evidence that any actions were taken as a result of campaign contributions.

In a footnote to the case, Armand D'Amato was convicted in May 1993 of defrauding Unisys, having engaged in a sham consulting scheme to hide the fact that he was being paid to provide access to the senator. He was not charged with exerting improper influence and prosecutors said there was no evidence that the senator knew what was going on.

In another case, involving help from D'Amato for campaign contributors in Puerto Rico who were seeking HUD grants, the committee said the evidence was insufficient because "essential witnesses" had invoked the Fifth Amendment to avoid testifying. The committee said granting them immunity would have placed related criminal investigations at risk.

After the committee concluded its probe, D'Amato claimed vindication: "I'm pleased and delighted ... that the committee has found that I did nothing wrong. It's ironic that I've been attacked for what I'm proudest of. That's being a fighter for the people of New York."

The long-running investigation produced its share of attendant publicity — not always to D'Amato's liking. In April 1991, the CBS News program "60 Minutes" broadcast a scathing recitation of D'Amato's problems, dating back to his ties to Nassau County Republican boss Joseph Margiotta. Reporter Mike Wallace said that during a phone conversation, D'Amato agreed to appear only in an unedited interview, then unleashed a stream of obscenities and hung up.

The incident highlighted D'Amato's hot-and-cold relationship with the media. The same D'Amato who avoids the cameras when his ethics are questioned has used them to his political advantage throughout his career.

Many New Yorkers have the enduring image of D'Amato — a crusader in the federal war against illegal drugs and advocate of the death penalty for drug "kingpins" — dressed in battle fatigues and participating in a filmed undercover cocaine sting in 1986. In 1990, D'Amato showed his support for independence in the Soviet Baltic states by trying to enter Lithuania without a Soviet visa.

There is more to D'Amato than his ethics problems, his parochial pursuits and his knack for publicity. He may not have the biggest legislative portfolio in the Senate, but he has made his mark.

For more than three years leading up to its enactment in November 1990, D'Amato worked with Housing Subcommittee Chairman Alan Cranston, D-Calif., to craft an omnibus housing bill. As the administration's point man during the conference on the bill, D'Amato secured many priorities sought by President Bush and HUD Secretary Jack F. Kemp. These included a new program to help residents of low-income housing purchase their homes.

D'Amato also took the lead in shoring up the Federal Housing Administration's troubled mortgage insurance program. Warning of a potential disaster on the scale of the savings and loan crisis, D'Amato pushed through provisions raising the down payment required of home buyers with FHA-backed mortgages and adding an annual premium to buyers' mortgages.

In the 102nd Congress, D'Amato's principal legislative endeavors were more typical of his grandstanding style. As Congress was considering a sweeping bill to overhaul the banking industry in 1991, D'Amato was not much in evidence, despite his senior position on the Banking Committee. But when the bill reached the Senate floor, D'Amato was there with an amendment calculated to win him maximum attention — a proposal to cap credit card interest rates.

The amendment caught bill sponsors and Senate leaders by surprise, and its populist appeal was hard to counter — even though bankers said the result would be that many consumers with marginal credit histories would lose their cards as a result. The Senate voted 74-19 for the amendment and for a time the House appeared poised to go along. But Treasury Secretary Nicholas F. Brady called D'Amato's ploy "wacky, senseless legislation," and the conference committee meeting on the banking bill quietly dropped the amendment. D'Amato barely mentioned it after the brief flurry on the floor.

A year later, as the Congress was drawing to a close, D'Amato was once again the center of attention, blocking a final vote on an urban aid tax bill because it did not include a provision intended to prevent the loss of 850 jobs at a Smith-Corona typewriter plant in New York. For 15 hours and 15 minutes, D'Amato held the floor, the sixth-longest live filibuster in Senate history. But his protest went for naught, when the House adjourned while he was still talking and without acting on his call for passage of a free-standing bill incorporating the typewriter provision.

The show was reminiscent of another election-year filibuster by D'Amato, that one in October 1986. Then, D'Amato held up consideration of a must-pass omnibus appropriations bill in an attempt to block an amendment to halt production of the T-46 trainer airplane, built by the Fairchild Republic Co. on Long Island. "To this product, to this company, this is life or death.... I'm not going to sit by and allow that company to be closed," he said. At noon that Oct. 17, there was still no compromise and no catchall spending bill, so nonessential federal functions were shut down. Later that day, D'Amato won a temporary reprieve for his plane. In the end, the program was canceled.

As ranking Republican on the Appropriations Subcommittee on Transportation, D'Amato is a leading proponent of mass transit. This issue caused some of D'Amato's strongest conflicts with the Reagan administration. When Reagan proposed huge cuts in transit spending in 1982, D'Amato said, "There's no way I'm going to be a good ol' boy and roll along with the team."

D'Amato is also on the Appropriations Subcommittee on Foreign Operations, where he voices the international interests of the dozens of ethnic communities residing in New York. His strong support of Israel reflects that of his large Jewish constituency.

A hard-line anti-communist and a human rights supporter, D'Amato generally backed

Reagan and Bush foreign policies. When he disagreed, it was usually because he favored a tougher line than the White House had taken. For example, D'Amato responded in April 1990 to Iraqi dictator Saddam Hussein's threats toward Israel by proposing trade sanctions against Iraq. His efforts were stalled by the Bush administration, which viewed Saddam as a key player in Middle East politics, and by farm-state senators, who feared a cutoff of agricultural exports. With Iraqi troops massing on the border of Kuwait that July, however, D'Amato's sanctions were approved, 83-12, as an amendment to the 1990 farm bill.

At Home: D'Amato's many critics may never stop declaiming his ethical standards or his parochial agenda. But after his come-from-behind victory in 1992, no one can doubt D'Amato's survival skills.

The 1992 campaign was just another loop in D'Amato's roller-coaster career. A local official little-known outside his Nassau County base when he entered the 1980 Senate race, D'Amato upset four-term Republican Sen. Jacob K. Javits in the primary and then won by a very narrow plurality over Democratic Rep. Elizabeth Holtzman. But D'Amato's home-state orientation and his straight talk — delivered with his distinctive "LongIsland" accent — quickly made him a popular figure; in 1986, he swept aside Democrat Mark Green, a consumer activist, with 57 percent of the vote.

D'Amato then appeared to fall fast: During his second term, he was battered by the allegations of ethical misconduct. D'Amato's low approval ratings early in 1992 marked him as the most vulnerable GOP incumbent that year. Yet D'Amato — dogged, controversial and colorful as ever — never lost his fighting edge in his bid for a third term.

There is another adjective that may apply as well: lucky. Most of D'Amato's good fortune stemmed from New York's mid-September primary. D'Amato had no GOP opponent, thanks to arcane New York election laws that barred a prospective challenger, environmental lawyer Laurence Rockefeller, from the ballot.

But the eventual Democratic nominee, state Attorney General Robert Abrams, was stuck in a primary brawl with 1984 vice presidential nominee Geraldine A. Ferraro, black activist Al Sharpton and New York City Comptroller Holtzman, seeking a rematch with D'Amato.

Abrams had a strong ethical reputation that made some Democrats see him as an ideal contrast to D'Amato. But his lackluster manner left him trailing the more charismatic Ferraro through much of the primary campaign.

In the closing weeks, though, Ferraro was attacked — by Abrams and more so by Holtzman — over rumors that she had ties to organized crime (similar allegations had hurt her vice presidential campaign). Ferraro, an Italian-American, argued that she was the victim of an ethnic smear. But the issue damaged her and helped Abrams win by 1 percentage point.

Abrams then entered the six-week general-election campaign bruised and broke. D'Amato had used the primary respite to remind voters of his legislative efforts on behalf of New York interests. Though well behind in the polls after the Democratic primary, D'Amato had a bulging campaign treasury that he quickly put to use. He ended up spending nearly $9.2 million on the campaign, second only to California Democrat Barbara Boxer.

Seeking to bolster his Republican base, D'Amato ran a barrage of TV ads branding Abrams as "hopelessly liberal." He also tried to turn the tables by accusing Abrams of accepting campaign money from interests that had official dealings with the state attorney general's office.

After losing precious days to raise funds, Abrams returned fire, hanging the scandal cloud over D'Amato and scoffing at him for raising the ethics issue. He engaged D'Amato in debates notable for their harsh tone.

But Abrams also made a major gaffe. At a rally, he responded to heckling by D'Amato supporters by calling the senator a "fascist." D'Amato, near tears, demanded an apology, called the epithet an ethnic slur and ran ads with images of Benito Mussolini to underline the point.

Although New York's presidential vote went heavily to Clinton, D'Amato held on, winning by just under 81,000 votes. The outcome may have had less to do with loyalty to the incumbent than voter disgust with both candidates for a campaign widely described as a vicious gutter fight.

D'Amato's narrow win recalled his first Senate bid in 1980. His decision to run that year was a surprise. Then a township presiding supervisor and product of the Nassau County Republican machine led by Margiotta, D'Amato was headed for a modest step — such as county executive — up the ladder.

But D'Amato gambled that the conservative wave spurred by Ronald Reagan's presidential campaign would enable him to unseat Javits, one of the Senate's most liberal Republicans. D'Amato also made an issue of Javits' age (76) and infirmity (he suffered from a progressive motor neuron disease), drawing a scathing rebuke from some Javits loyalists. But D'Amato won with votes to spare.

Javits' insistence on a last hurrah may have ensured D'Amato's election. Running as the nominee of New York's Liberal Party, Javits pulled off more than 10 percent of the vote, and likely drew more from the liberal Holtzman than D'Amato. Although Holtzman tried to link D'Amato to alleged corruption in the Nassau GOP, he won by 45 percent to 44 percent.

D'Amato then faced a brush with scandal

within his first year in office. Margiotta, his mentor, was convicted of fraud and extortion. D'Amato himself would be the subject of three separate investigations, all of which absolved him of any wrongdoing.

Meanwhile, D'Amato's aggressive attention to New York interests won him widespread praise. Better-known Democrats took a pass at challenging him in 1986, so the nomination went to Green, a former associate of consumer crusader Ralph Nader.

Green again made D'Amato's ethics the issue, particularly his activities as then-chairman of the Banking Subcommittee on Securities (a news report said D'Amato had received generous campaign contributions from Wall Street firms he had aided legislatively). But the accusations rolled off his back, and he won easily.

Even as he struggled to maintain his public standing, D'Amato stumbled a bit in his efforts to assume a power-broker role in New York Republican politics. In 1988, he gave his presidential endorsement to Senate colleague Bob Dole of Kansas, who would be swamped by George Bush in the New York primary. A political feud with former federal prosecutor and New York City mayoral contender Rudolph W. Giuliani led D'Amato to endorse another candidate for mayor in 1989; but Giuliani won in a landslide.

D'Amato did score one intraparty victory in early 1991. His longtime aide William Powers was elected chairman of the state GOP. During the 1992 campaign, he mended fences with Giuliani, who lost narrowly to Democrat David Dinkins for mayor of New York City in 1989 and is seeking another shot in 1993.

Committees

Banking, Housing & Urban Affairs (Ranking)

Appropriations (4th of 13 Republicans)
Transportation (ranking); Defense; Foreign Operations; VA, HUD & Independent Agencies; Treasury, Postal Service & General Government

Select Intelligence (2nd of 8 Republicans)

Elections

1992 General

Alfonse M. D'Amato (R, C, RTL)	3,166,994	(49%)
Robert Abrams (D, L)	3,086,200	(48%)
Norma Segal (LIBERT)	108,530	(2%)

Previous Winning Percentages: **1986** (57%) **1980** (45%)

Campaign Finance

1992	Receipts	Receipts from PACs		Expend-itures
D'Amato (R)	$6,533,230	$922,922	(14%)	$9,175,533
Abrams (D)	$6,764,365	$590,769	(9%)	$6,408,981

Key Votes

1993

Require unpaid family and medical leave	Y
Approve national "motor voter" registration bill	N
Approve budget increasing taxes and reducing deficit	N
Support president's right to lift military gay ban	Y

1992

Approve school-choice pilot program	+
Allow shifting funds from defense to domestic programs	N
Oppose deeper cuts in spending for SDI	Y

1991

Approve waiting period for handgun purchases	Y
Raise senators' pay and ban honoraria	N
Authorize use of force in Persian Gulf	Y
Confirm Clarence Thomas to Supreme Court	Y

Voting Studies

	Presidential Support		Party Unity		Conservative Coalition	
Year	S	O	S	O	S	O
1992	58	38	59	36	42	45
1991	79	21	75	25	80	20
1990	68	31	68	32	65	32
1989	67	32	52	46	66	32
1988	68	30	70	28	84	16
1987	58	38	65	33	69	28
1986	77	23	66	32	66	30
1985	71	28	69	28	88	8
1984	68	25	67	25	72	19
1983	67	28	67	30	70	27
1982	71	26	76	22	78	17
1981	82	14	81	13	78	17

Interest Group Ratings

Year	ADA	AFL-CIO	CCUS	ACU
1992	30	70	60	52
1991	15	67	50	86
1990	28	44	67	70
1989	35	70	63	48
1988	15	57	64	80
1987	30	70	44	56
1986	35	53	56	70
1985	20	62	62	70
1984	25	36	78	85
1983	20	33	63	44
1982	15	46	47	50
1981	10	22	94	64

1 George J. Hochbrueckner (D)

Of Coram — Elected 1986; 4th Term

Born: Sept. 20, 1938, Queens, N.Y.

Education: State U. of New York, 1959-60; Hofstra U., 1960-61; Pierce College, 1961-62; California State U., Northridge, 1962-63.

Military Service: Navy, 1956-59.

Occupation: Aerospace engineer.

Family: Wife, Carol Ann Joan Seifert; four children.

Religion: Roman Catholic.

Political Career: N.Y. Assembly, 1975-85; Democratic nominee for U.S. House, 1984.

Capitol Office: 229 Cannon Bldg. 20515; 225-3826.

In Washington: A member of the Armed Services Committee, Hochbrueckner is best-known in the House for his unceasing promotion of the F-14 fighter jet — produced by Grumman Corp. in his Long Island district. A Navy veteran and one of the designers of the F-14, he has long insisted that it is better suited to the Navy's needs than planes built by contractors in other parts of the United States.

Although largely unsuccessful in his efforts, Hochbrueckner has received local accolades for his efforts, which have helped him hold onto his seat in the Republican-leaning 1st District. Hochbrueckner's avid support for Grumman and other local defense contractors has also helped him fend off Republican challengers who tried to cast him as a liberal.

The F-14 was targeted for budget savings soon after George Bush became president, even before the Cold War was declared over.

When the F-14 debate began in 1989, Hochbrueckner brought a special edge to his lobbying efforts on Armed Services. Before entering politics, he worked on electronic systems for the F-14 and other Navy planes built by Grumman. Although he lacked academic certification as an engineer, Hochbrueckner — who learned technical skills while serving in the Navy — held the equivalent of an engineering position. His House office is decorated with scale models of Grumman-built planes.

During the 101st Congress, Hochbrueckner lavished his colleagues with explanations of the plane's technical specifications. He noted that the fighter had performed well since its introduction in 1970.

But Navy policy-makers opted for the F/A-18, built by McDonnell Douglas, which had a shorter flight range but lower operating costs than the F-14.

Warning that a cancellation would ruin the F-14's manufacturer and damage the nation's "defense-industrial base," Hochbrueckner and others in the bipartisan Long Island delegation won House passage of an amendment to the fiscal 1990 defense authorization bill to include funding for 12 advanced F-14Ds.

But the Senate went along with the Navy, and Hochbrueckner's side was forced to accept an amendment closing out production of the Grumman plane, although funding was provided for a final 18 F-14D's. He subsequently was part of a successful effort to obtain funding for a one-year program to upgrade existing F-14s with up-to-date equipment.

During the 102nd Congress, Defense Secretary Dick Cheney canceled the program to develop the A-12 attack plane, which had been plagued by cost overruns. Hochbrueckner saw an opening and argued that the Navy should use a slightly modified version of the F-14D for air-to-ground combat until the next-generation plane was available.

He fumed when the Navy instead chose a version of the F/A-18 with major modifications. He said that the Navy was ordering "essentially a new airplane" that would take four to five years to develop, while a modified F-14D would be more readily deployable.

Although Hochbrueckner's doggedness earned him reams of positive publicity back home, it antagonized some colleagues, including some Republicans who noted that he often votes against defense spending. In recent years, he has favored deep funding cutbacks for the Strategic Defense Initiative anti-missile program.

Hochbrueckner supported Bush on just 18 percent of the 1992 House votes on which Bush staked out a position.

Hochbrueckner, who wants to be known as the "compost man of Congress," has proposed measures to require federal agencies to turn more of their disposable waste into compost; he is a strong advocate of this and other recycling mea-

New York 1

Eastern Suffolk County — Brookhaven; Smithtown

Located more than 100 miles from downtown Manhattan, Long Island's lightly populated East End presents a tableau of the Suffolk County of 40 years ago. Farms, fishing villages and the vacation homes of the wealthy (in such enclaves as the Hamptons and Shelter Island) remain this region's most prominent features.

Nonetheless, suburban sprawl has thoroughly overtaken the closer-in areas on the western side of the 1st. Brookhaven Town, the 1st's core jurisdiction, increased in population more than ninefold between 1950 and 1990, from 44,500 to 408,000.

Suburbanization has not greatly changed the Republican tilt that dates to the 1st District's rural days. George Bush took 60 percent of the 1st's vote in 1988; although he fell off sharply in 1992, he still managed to eke out a win over Democrat Bill Clinton here.

Yet fourth-term Rep. Hochbrueckner has proved that a Democrat can win here. There is a small minority population on which to build a Democratic base, and the district has large numbers of Irish- and Italian-Americans, many with blue-collar, urban roots. The 1st has some industrial employment, including a defense-production base that has become tenuous in the post-Cold War era. A reliance on seasonal employment in many of the 1st's exurban and rural areas provides modest incomes for many district residents.

Constituents' environmental concerns have also benefited Hochbrueckner. He was a leader in the successful effort to decommission a nuclear power plant in Shoreham and has pushed to clean up the ocean waters that are vital to the 1st's fishing and tourism industries.

The bulk of the 1st's residents live in a part of Smithtown, at the district's western end, and in Brookhaven, which covers a large swath spanning the width of Suffolk County. The North Shore area along Long Island Sound has several well-off subdivisions, but most of the 1st's suburbs are middle class.

Coram, with just over 30,000 residents, is the largest of Brookhaven's many sizable suburban communities. The mainly residential area includes the state university at Stony Brook (11,000 students), a center for scientific research. In the exurbs to the east is Brookhaven National Laboratory. Nearby, in Riverhead, is Calverton and a Grumman Inc. factory that has been hit hard by cutbacks in Navy aviation programs.

Five less-populous towns — Riverhead, East Hampton, Shelter Island, Southampton and Southold — make up the East End. There are still many potato and duck farms here; a number of small vineyards also have been established on Long Island's North Fork, which has a climate and soil similar to the Burgundy region of France.

The beaches along the 1st's southern edge are summer playgrounds; parts of Fire Island are long-established retreats for New York's gay community. But these coastal areas are vulnerable to damage by storms, such as the fierce nor'easters that hit during the winter of 1992-93.

1990 Population: 580,338. White 539,824 (93%), Black 23,691 (4%), Other 16,823 (3%). Hispanic origin 27,210 (5%). 18 and over 433,173 (75%), 62 and over 81,669 (14%). Median age: 33.

sures. Reflecting the environmental concerns of residents of his ecologically fragile coastal district, Hochbrueckner supported legislation in the 100th Congress to phase out sludge dumping off New York and other coastal areas.

A member of the Merchant Marine and Fisheries Committee, Hochbrueckner obtained funding to dredge Shinnecock Inlet, a Long Island waterway that had become treacherous for mariners.

Hochbrueckner's advocacy of federally funded research into Lyme disease also has a local angle: Eastern Long Island has an unusually high incidence of the debilitating nerve illness, caused by the bite of the deer tick.

Hochbrueckner also supports funding for research on X-ray lithography, a process that may produce smaller, faster computer chips; much of the research is being performed at Long Island's Brookhaven National Laboratory.

At Home: Far from entrenched, Hochbrueckner has shown a knack for surviving hard-fought campaigns by very modest margins. Hochbrueckner won his first two House contests, in 1986 and 1988, with 51 percent of the vote. In 1992, he won a rematch against his 1988 opponent, local Republican official Edward P. Romaine, with 52 percent.

Hochbrueckner's activism in the 1970s against the Shoreham nuclear power plant project gave him a foothold in Suffolk County politics. From his seat in the state Assembly, which he held from 1975 to 1985, Hochbrueckner became a leader among those who viewed Shoreham as dangerous because of its location in a densely populated area. (The plant ultimately was completed but later scrapped in the face of public opposition.)

In 1984, Hochbrueckner sought a House seat by challenging Republican Rep. William Carney, a Shoreham supporter, and came within about 12,000 votes of winning. In 1986, Carney chose to not seek re-election.

Republicans replaced him with county legislator Gregory J. Blass. Like Hochbrueckner, Blass was also a Shoreham opponent, but Hochbrueckner stood out as the candidate who had opposed Shoreham earlier and louder. Hochbrueckner got 51 percent, allowing him to beat Blass by a comfortable margin; a Conservative Party candidate drained off 9 percent.

In 1988, Republican Romaine made his first try. Then a county legislator, he appealed to his GOP base by calling the incumbent a liberal, but profiled himself as a moderate on environmental, education and other domestic issues. He got a boost from Bush's winning 1988 campaign in the 1st. But Hochbrueckner was well-financed, with a big chunk of defense PAC money. He won again with 51 percent, though his margin over the GOP candidate shrunk to 2 percentage points.

Hochbrueckner enjoyed a relative breather in 1990, when Republicans bollixed their candidate recruitment. In succession GOP officials tapped three separate individuals — state Rep. John Behan, former New York Stock Exchange Chairman James J. Needham and Suffolk County Supervisor Fred Thiele — to run against Hochbrueckner, only to have each of them drop out of the race.

Finally, in July, the Republicans settled on a novice candidate, retired Army Col. Francis W. Creighton. A 27-year military veteran, Creighton tried to show how his background melded with interests of the district's defense industry. But Hochbrueckner had already geared up for a more formidable foe. His ads stressed his efforts to save the F-14, increase spending on Lyme disease research and protect the regional coastline. He won with 56 percent.

The elements of Hochbrueckner's 1992 rematch with Romaine, by then the Suffolk County clerk, were familiar. The incumbent touted his efforts on the district's behalf; the challenger called him too liberal by half.

With Grumman's troubles adding to the harsh effects of recession, Bush's popularity sagged in the 1st; Hochbrueckner tried to tie Romaine to Bush's policies. Romaine distanced himself from the 1990 tax increase and other unpopular Bush policies and sounded the theme of "change" that was prevalent among 1992 House challengers. He called for reform of Congress and criticized Hochbrueckner for having 49 overdrafts at the House bank.

Despite the new wrinkles, the outcome was close to that in their 1988 bout: Hochbrueckner won by just under 4 percentage points.

Committees

Armed Services (12th of 34 Democrats)
Military Installations & Facilities; Research & Technology

Merchant Marine & Fisheries (9th of 29 Democrats)
Coast Guard & Navigation; Environment & Natural Resources

Elections

1992 General		
George J. Hochbrueckner (D, LIF)	117,940	(52%)
Edward P. Romaine (R, C, RTL, TCP-LI)	110,043	(48%)
1990 General		
George J. Hochbrueckner (D)	75,211	(56%)
Francis W. Creighton (R)	46,380	(35%)
Clayton Baldwin Jr. (C)	6,883	(5%)
Peter J. O'Hara (RTL)	5,111	(4%)

Previous Winning Percentages: 1988 (51%) **1986** (51%)

District Vote for President

1992

D	96,890 (38%)
R	101,160 (40%)
I	54,128 (21%)

Campaign Finance

	Receipts	Receipts from PACs		Expend-itures
1992				
Hochbrueckner (D)	$628,248	$296,600	(47%)	$606,190
Romaine (R)	$235,259	$26,761	(11%)	$226,283
1990				
Hochbrueckner (D)	$655,297	$398,062	(61%)	$638,635
Creighton (R)	$45,545	$550	(1%)	$45,544

Key Votes

1993	
Require parental notification of minors' abortions	N
Require unpaid family and medical leave	Y
Approve national "motor voter" registration bill	Y
Approve budget increasing taxes and reducing deficit	Y
Approve economic stimulus plan	Y
1992	
Approve balanced-budget constitutional amendment	N
Close down space station program	N
Approve U.S. aid for former Soviet Union	Y
Allow shifting funds from defense to domestic programs	Y
1991	
Extend unemployment benefits using deficit financing	Y
Approve waiting period for handgun purchases	Y
Authorize use of force in Persian Gulf	N

Voting Studies

Year	Presidential Support S	Presidential Support O	Party Unity S	Party Unity O	Conservative Coalition S	Conservative Coalition O
1992	18	81	94	5	23	77
1991	29	68	91	6	32	68
1990	23	77	94	6	22	78
1989	33	64	92	5	32	68
1988	22	78	89	10	37	63
1987	18	81	87	5	19	81

Interest Group Ratings

Year	ADA	AFL-CIO	CCUS	ACU
1992	95	92	25	4
1991	75	100	20	0
1990	89	100	21	13
1989	85	100	30	7
1988	80	93	36	12
1987	92	93	27	4

2 Rick A. Lazio (R)

Of Brightwaters — Elected 1992; 1st Term

Born: March 13, 1958, West Islip, N.Y.
Education: Vassar College, B.A. 1980; American U., J.D. 1983.
Occupation: Lawyer.
Family: Wife, Patricia; one child.
Religion: Roman Catholic.
Political Career: Suffolk County Legislature, 1990-93.
Capitol Office: 314 Cannon Bldg. 20515; 225-3335.

The Path to Washington: Lazio may regret once referring to himself as a "bad boy Republican," but the label may remain apt if GOP leaders insist on challenging the new administration at every turn in the 103rd Congress. Lazio is no Democrat. But he is a confirmed moderate who expects to wind up among the Democrats' most consistent GOP allies.

Even Lazio's aversion to taxes — his principal Republican credential — is anything but categorical. He is resolute in his disdain for tax increases that would penalize his middle-class constituency, a position that extends to higher taxes on gasoline. But in some circumstances, he would consider an income tax rate increase or surtax on the wealthy.

And Lazio sided with Democrats on two issues that had generated showdowns between President Bush and Democrats in the 102nd Congress — family leave and abortion counseling. He was one of 40 Republicans to vote for a family leave bill that President Clinton signed in February and one of 51 to vote for a bill codifying Clinton's overturning of the "gag rule" that prohibited staff at federally funded family planning clinics from discussing abortion.

Lazio has also staked out ground firmly in the middle on health care. He does not support a federally run national health-care program, but neither did he support the Bush administration's plan for an all-private effort at cutting costs and extending care.

On the Budget and Banking committees, Lazio could provide a receptive ear for the administration whenever Clinton makes an effort to lure moderate Republicans.

Lazio likes the idea of a short-term economic stimulus. And he can be expected to oppose any tax increase that is not coupled with deficit reduction. He also wants to improve the availability of affordable housing and promote the growth of community-based financial institutions, both of which dovetail with Clinton's ideas.

In winning this seat, Lazio pulled an upset over 18-year incumbent Democrat Thomas J. Downey that on some levels resembled Downey's 1974 win over the 2nd's last GOP representative, James R. Grover.

Grover was an entrenched, senior member, and Downey won by waging an aggressive campaign that painted the incumbent as being out of touch. It did not hurt that Downey — then a brash 25-year-old member of the Suffolk County Legislature — was running in the Watergate year of 1974. The district was and is dominated by Republicans, but Downey managed a 5,000-vote victory.

In 1992, Downey was the entrenched incumbent and Lazio the upstart from the Suffolk Legislature (representing Downey's old district, in fact). This year, too, there was a scandal, involving the House bank. Downey was doubly vulnerable: He had 151 overdrafts and his wife, Chris, was an employee of the House sergeant at arms (who ran the bank) with the unfortunate, if imprecise, title of auditor.

Neither candidate had a primary opponent, which left Lazio free to concentrate his significantly smaller campaign treasury on Downey. Concentrate he did, attacking Downey about the bank and reminding voters that Downey took a junket to Barbados in 1990 that received embarrassing national publicity.

Though Downey was well-known in Washington for his attention to national issues — welfare reform, unemployment and arms control, for example — Lazio turned the incumbent's high profile against him.

Unlike Grover in 1974, Downey took the challenge from Lazio seriously. He countered Lazio's criticism that he had abandoned Long Island for Washington by noting that he had held 300 meetings in the district in the past two years and spent virtually every weekend there.

In September, Downey launched his own negative attack, blasting Lazio for supporting a plan to borrow money to cover a county revenue shortfall. Downey said Lazio's refusal to support a sales tax increase to raise the money was just a political move for the election campaign.

Downey's spending, defense and counterattacks did not prove enough, however, and he lost by 13,000 votes.

New York 2

Western Suffolk County — Islip; Babylon

During an 18-year House career, Democrat Thomas J. Downey withstood the Republican tendencies of western Suffolk County's well-established, middle-class suburbs. But the 2nd's partisan tilt meant that any error would leave Downey vulnerable.

That slip came in 1992, when Downey got entangled in the House bank controversy. The timing was fortuitous for Republican Lazio, his party's strongest House challenger in years. A moderate with some appeal to independents and even Democrats disappointed in Downey, Lazio reinstated the GOP claim on the 2nd District.

The 1992 presidential contest provided an odd counterpoint to the House race: The middle-class dissatisfaction with Washington that toppled Downey also hindered George Bush in the 2nd. He got only 41 percent of the district's vote in 1992 (well below his 1988 tally); Bill Clinton took 40 percent.

Despite the district's overall tendencies, Democratic candidates do have a base that is sizable by suburban Long Island standards. While the district's mainly white-collar work force includes many who commute to New York City, there is a blue-collar constituency, including a number of workers dependent on Long Island's defense-related industries that have been hit hard by funding cutbacks.

The 2nd has more than 56,000 Hispanics — the largest Hispanic population among the Long Island districts — and as many blacks. More than a third of the 45,000 residents of Brentwood (the largest community in Islip town) are Hispanics; blacks make up three-quarters of the nearly 14,000 residents of North Amityville in Babylon town.

Islip and Babylon — the two townships that make of the southwest corner of Suffolk County — took full part in the post-World War II suburban boom, but they hit a plateau in the 1970s. Islip, where population jumped from about 71,500 in 1950 to 279,000 in 1970, gained a net of just 20,000 people over the next 20 years. Babylon (which had 45,000 residents in 1950) topped 200,000 in 1970 but stuck there.

Islip town — which takes in such communities as Brentwood, West Islip, Central Islip and Bay Shore — contains much of the district's employment base. The Estee Lauder cosmetics company and an Entenmann's Bakery are leading employers. Hauppauge, the seat of Suffolk County's government, is shared with the 1st District; the 2nd has the county office complex and much of the community's commercial real estate.

While Babylon town is made up mainly of residential communities — the largest of which, with just over 42,000 residents, is West Babylon — there is some industry: AIL Systems makes defense electronics in Deer Park. But defense-industry employment has been faltering since a Fairchild Republic aircraft plant in Farmingdale closed in the late 1980s.

The northern part of the 2nd also takes in parts of Huntington town and Smithtown. These areas have large Jewish populations and Democratic leanings.

1990 Population: 580,337. White 496,052 (85%), Black 56,722 (10%), Other 27,563 (5%). Hispanic origin 56,302 (10%). 18 and over 437,435 (75%), 62 and over 70,884 (12%). Median age: 33.

Committees

Banking, Finance & Urban Affairs (15th of 20 Republicans)
Consumer Credit & Insurance; Financial Institutions Supervision, Regulation & Deposit Insurance; Housing & Community Development

Budget (13th of 17 Republicans)

Campaign Finance

	Receipts	Receipts from PACs		Expend-itures
1992				
Lazio (R)	$276,487	$43,663	(16%)	$276,191
Downey (D)	$1,085,414	$457,222	(42%)	$1,446,911

Key Votes

1993

Require parental notification of minors' abortions	Y
Require unpaid family and medical leave	Y
Approve national "motor voter" registration bill	N
Approve budget increasing taxes and reducing deficit	N
Approve economic stimulus plan	N

Elections

1992 General

Rick A. Lazio (R, C, TCP-LI)	109,386	(53%)
Thomas J. Downey (D, LIF)	96,328	(47%)

District Vote for President

1992

D	91,430 (40%)
R	92,762 (41%)
I	44,603 (19%)

3 Peter T. King (R)

Of Seaford — Elected 1992; 1st Term

Born: April 5, 1944, Manhattan, N.Y.
Education: St. Francis College, B.A. 1965; U. of Notre Dame, J.D. 1968.
Military Service: National Guard, 1968-73.
Occupation: Lawyer.
Family: Wife, Rosemary; two children.
Religion: Roman Catholic.
Political Career: Hempstead Town Council, 1978-81; Nassau County comptroller, 1981-93.
Capitol Office: 118 Cannon Bldg. 20515; 225-7896.

The Path to Washington: It is not surprising that King's favorite movie is "High Noon."

A veteran of 17 years in the rough-and-tumble of local politics on Long Island, he relishes political showdowns. He believes confrontation and partisanship are the best ways to do legislative and political business. He describes politics as a contact sport, "somewhere between roller derby and a 25-round fight."

King has been criticized for championing causes critics say have little relevance to his constituents. He is an avid and outspoken supporter of the Irish Republican Army. A November editorial by Newsday blasted him for his alleged preoccupation with the IRA effort to oust the British from Northern Ireland.

But if King is a sometime crusader, he also can be a pragmatic politician. Like his predecessor, 22-year veteran Norman F. Lent, King is a product of the Nassau County Republican machine. He joined the GOP's executive committee in 1975 and served as comptroller of Nassau County throughout the 1980s.

Tax and budget issues are primary interests for King, who plans to work for passage of a 5 percent across-the-board cut in personal income taxes and a reduction of capital gains tax rates, arguing that both would stimulate the nation's economy. He also has called for a balanced-budget amendment to the Constitution.

King, who was elected vice president of the GOP freshmen, voted in the 103rd Congress against a Democratic bill giving the president limited line-item veto authority, in favor of an even stronger GOP substitute amendment. Most of the 47 GOP freshmen chose to vote for both, but King was one of 12 to support only the GOP substitute.

To expand health-care coverage, he advocates a tax credit for small businesses that provide health insurance for their employees.

Having won a seat on the Banking, Finance and Urban Affairs Committee, King will push for the creation of enterprise zones, an idea he has supported for years. Also, King succeeds Lent on the Merchant Marine and Fisheries Committee. There he is well placed to defend the district's waterways, beaches and fishing industry. Long Island Sound lies along one side of the 3rd; the Atlantic Ocean lies along the other.

Lent announced in June 1992 that he was not seeking re-election, and King moved with characteristic dispatch to establish himself as his successor. Defying the vogue enjoyed by political outsiders in 1992, King touted his governmental experience as proof that he could get things done in Washington.

He coasted through the primary. The general election proved more difficult, as King drew a strong and well-financed opponent in Democrat Steve A. Orlins, a senior consultant to American Express.

Although the district is normally Republican turf, Orlins held a potent trump card. During the campaign he raised more than four times as much money as King, including $775,000 from his own resources. This allowed him to bombard the district with mass mailings and radio advertisements.

True to form, however, King came out firing. He accused Orlins of being "a carpetbagging millionaire" who was "trying to buy the election." Orlins, who grew up on Long Island, had lived in Manhattan until he rented a house in the district in July.

Orlins countered that as part of the long-dominant Nassau Republican machine, King had to take his share of responsibility for the county's $130 million deficit and high tax rates.

Throughout the campaign, Orlins trumpeted his support of abortion rights. King, strongly opposed to abortion in most cases, stressed his support for parental notification laws restricting minors' access to abortion. Orlins also called for increased federal spending to stimulate the economy and defense cuts to finance deficit reduction and job retraining. King relied on his tax-cut plans to serve the same ends.

In the end, King's history of local involvement helped him hold the district's GOP votes. Although he fell short of a majority, he turned back Orlins' challenge by 4 percentage points.

New York 3

Eastern Nassau County — Oyster Bay

During 22 years (1971-93) of representing much of eastern Nassau County, Republican Rep. Norman F. Lent faced few serious election challenges. The elements of this successful GOP track record in the 3rd — made up mainly of Lent's former turf — remain firmly in place. The 3rd's suburban population is more than 90 percent non-Hispanic white; it has more pockets of affluence than of poverty.

In addition, a Republican machine has controlled Nassau County politics for decades. Its most prominent alumnus, third-term GOP Sen. Alfonse M. D'Amato, hails from Island Park in the southwest part of the 3rd.

Yet the economic problems of the early 1990s hit home in the 3rd and loosened the GOP grip in 1992. The impact of the national recession on the 3rd's mainly white-collar work force was amplified by the district's dependence on a declining defense industrial base; Grumman, a contractor that has lost several large Navy aircraft projects, has its headquarters and a production facility in Bethpage.

The resulting dissatisfaction with George Bush's economic program in the 3rd was matched by anger toward local GOP officials held largely responsible for a county budget gap and burdensome property tax rates. As a result, Bush — who in 1988 defeated Democrat Michael S. Dukakis by more than 40,000 votes in the 3rd — lost to Bill Clinton in 1992. Republican King defeated Democrat Steve Orlins by a narrow plurality to succeed Lent. However, D'Amato won easily in the 3rd, a more typical GOP outcome.

The 3rd reaches a finger into northwest Nassau County, taking in such well-off communities as Plandome Manor, Manhasset and North Hills. The district then broadens to cover much of eastern Nassau County.

The Long Island Expressway (LIE) roughly bisects this area. To the north is estate country in such communities as Brookville and Old Westbury. The Sagamore Hill estate of President Theodore Roosevelt is near Long Island Sound. The district's campuses of the State University of New York, C.W. Post College and the New York Institute of Technology are in the north part of the 3rd.

The bulk of the 3rd's people are in the portions of Hempstead Town and Oyster Bay south of the LIE. This is mainly white-collar suburbia, with many commuters to the financial and corporate offices of Manhattan. Despite cutbacks, Grumman is the largest employer in the 3rd, which also has the headquarters of the Long Island Lighting Co. in Hicksville and National Westminster Bank USA in Jericho.

The 3rd has just over half the residents of Levittown, the development that sparked Long Island's suburban boom in the 1940s. The district has a large number of Italian-American and Jewish residents: Massapequa, in the southeast corner, was once nicknamed "Matzo-Pizza" for its ethnic mix, though it is now mainly Italian.

1990 Population: 580,337. White 547,567 (94%), Black 11,702 (2%), Other 21,068 (4%). Hispanic origin 25,545 (4%). 18 and over 455,840 (79%), 62 and over 99,657 (17%). Median age: 37.

Committees

Banking, Finance & Urban Affairs (20th of 20 Republicans)
Consumer Credit & Insurance; Economic Growth; International Development, Finance, Trade & Monetary Policy

Merchant Marine & Fisheries (14th of 18 Republicans)
Coast Guard & Navigation; Merchant Marine

Campaign Finance

1992	Receipts	Receipts from PACs		Expend-itures
King (R)	$244,526	$117,550	(48%)	$263,345
Orlins (D)	$1,142,476	0		$1,127,239

Key Votes

1993

Require parental notification of minors' abortions	Y
Require unpaid family and medical leave	N
Approve national "motor voter" registration bill	N
Approve budget increasing taxes and reducing deficit	N
Approve economic stimulus plan	N

Elections

1992 General		
Peter T. King (R, C)	124,727	(50%)
Steve A. Orlins (D)	116,915	(46%)
Louis P. Roccanova (RTL)	6,888	(3%)
Ben-Zion J. Heyman (L)	3,092	(1%)
1992 Primary		
Peter T. King (R)	8,346	(68%)
Robert Previdi (R)	3,955	(32%)

District Vote for President

1992

D 126,112 (44%)
R 121,176 (42%)
I 40,450 (14%)

4 David A. Levy (R)

Of Baldwin — Elected 1992; 1st Term

Born: Dec. 18, 1953, Johnson County, Ind.
Education: Hofstra U., B.A. 1974, J.D. 1979.
Occupation: Lawyer; radio journalist; legislative aide; utility company executive.
Family: Wife, Tracy Burgess; two children.
Religion: Jewish.
Political Career: Hempstead Town Council, 1989-93.
Capitol Office: 116 Cannon Bldg. 20515; 225-5516.

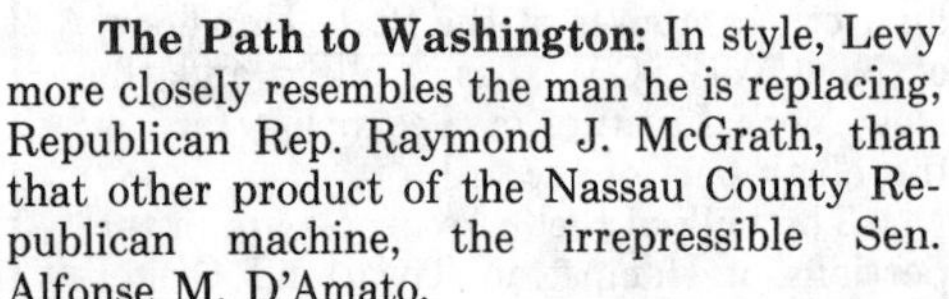

The Path to Washington: In style, Levy more closely resembles the man he is replacing, Republican Rep. Raymond J. McGrath, than that other product of the Nassau County Republican machine, the irrepressible Sen. Alfonse M. D'Amato.

Though he campaigned as an outsider, Levy brings to Congress an insider's appreciation for the institution. He recalls first visiting Washington at age 8. He was impressed with the city's aura of power and resolved to return one day as one of the decision-makers.

He learned about politics as the top aide to Nassau GOP Chairman Joseph Mondello (with whom Levy also served on the Hempstead Town Board, where Mondello is presiding supervisor). And like McGrath, he is more likely to become an inside player on Capitol Hill than to mimic D'Amato's high-visibility style.

But like D'Amato, Levy is a conservative. He opposes tax increases — he ran on his record in Hempstead, where the board has consistently held down property taxes.

During the campaign, he opposed the Bush administration's ban on abortion counseling at federally funded clinics, the so-called "gag rule." But in 1993, when the House considered legislation supported by President Clinton that included language lifting the counseling ban, Levy voted "no," in line with a majority of House Republicans. He said he objected to the level of funding for family planning programs that was included in the bill. Levy opposes Medicaid funding of abortions, and he opposes the Freedom of Choice Act, believing that regulation of abortions should be left to the states.

Like most Nassau politicians, Levy has a very parochial perspective. Defense cuts — which could wreck major Long Island employers — must be careful and deliberate, he believes. And he plans to use his seat on the Public Works and Transportation Committee to improve the movement of people and goods through his district's maze of roads.

Levy's views on the Middle East — and his opposition to the Bush administration policy placing restrictions on loan guarantees for Israel — suits the Jewish neighborhoods that occupy a corner of the 4th. His seat on the Foreign Affairs Committee will give him a platform to speak out on their concerns.

Redistricting prompted a nasty intraparty squabble that grew out of a 1980s split between Mondello and Joseph Margiotta. The latter lost his job as party boss when he went to prison on extortion charges arising from a municipal insurance scheme. State Rep. Daniel Frisa got into the primary, running to the right of Levy and attacking him for being Mondello's puppet. Levy shot back that Margiotta was running Frisa's campaign, a charge that Frisa denied.

In the end, Levy prevailed handily, winning 53 percent to Frisa's 41 percent.

The general election was by comparison a relatively aboveboard, issue-dominated affair. And Levy survived a close contest that exposed the weakened state of the Nassau GOP. Despite a huge registration advantage for the Republicans, he won with 50 percent. Democrat Philip Schiliro pulled 45 percent.

The result was partly due to the appeal in the district of Democratic presidential candidate Bill Clinton. It also stemmed from a stronger-than-typical Democratic challenge for an open seat. And partly it was because recession-racked voters were unhappy with the Nassau GOP's hold on local offices and its failure to get the local government's books balanced.

Schiliro, the top aide to California Democratic Rep. Henry A. Waxman, took a leave of absence to make the race. Though born in the district, he had not lived there for more than a dozen years. That left Schiliro open to carpetbagger charges, but he still secured the local party leadership's endorsement. He edged wealthy consultant Joan F. Axinn by 528 votes in the primary.

Differences in the general election reflected partisan splits — Schiliro, for example, made an issue of Levy's support for some restrictions on abortion. And each tried to tie the other to failures of their respective parties — Levy to the Nassau GOP, Schiliro to the Democratic-controlled Congress.

New York 4

Southwest Nassau County — Hempstead; Mineola

The 4th shares many Republican traits with the neighboring 3rd District. The 4th has some of New York City's longest established suburbs: its middle-to-upper-income residents head to work on the Long Island Railroad and such congested routes as the Southern State Parkway and Long Island Expressway. The 4th, which includes the Nassau County seat of Mineola, is a stronghold for the county's GOP organization.

Yet the 4th does have some elements that can make it potentially competitive for a Democratic candidate. Nearly a quarter of the district's residents are black or Hispanic, the largest minority-group constituency of any Long Island House district.

There are a number of working-class residents who work at John F. Kennedy International Airport (across the district line in Queens), the Belmont Park horse track in Floral Park and such large shopping centers as Roosevelt Field and Green Acres. Even some of the district's wealthiest communities, in its southwestern corner, are mainly Jewish and lean Democratic.

These constituencies provide Democrats with a foothold in the 4th. This base — combined with the national recession, cutbacks in the region's defense and banking industries and fiscal problems in the Republican-controlled county government — enabled Bill Clinton to defeat George Bush here in 1992. That year, House candidate Levy, a Republican organization stalwart and a moderate, won with barely half the vote.

More than 80 percent of the district's population is in the sprawling township of Hempstead; the remainder is in North Hempstead. The foundation of GOP success is such middle- and upper-middle income suburbs as Valley Stream, New Hyde Park, Garden City and Franklin Square; these communities are nearly all white.

The ethnic mix of the district includes many Italian- and Irish-Americans. Rockville Centre is the seat of suburban Long Island's Roman Catholic diocese.

The district's black population, and much of its Democratic vote, is mainly in such east side communities as Roosevelt, Uniondale, Hempstead and New Cassel. While these are largely middle-class areas, their poverty rates are well above the district's average.

The other Democratic bloc is at the other end of the district and income scale, in the largely Jewish "Five Towns" of Inwood, Lawrence, Cedarhurst, Woodmere and Hewlett. Nearby Atlantic Beach makes up the 4th's coastline, the shortest of any suburban Long Island district.

At the district's eastern end is about half of the historic suburban development of Levittown. The largest employment hub is between Garden City and Uniondale. It includes the Roosevelt Field shopping complex and the former site of the Mitchell Field airport, which now supports the Nassau County Veterans' Memorial Coliseum and the campuses of Hofstra University and Nassau Community College. Adelphi University is also in the district.

1990 Population: 580,338. White 454,297 (78%), Black 94,141 (16%), Other 31,900 (5%). Hispanic origin 43,751 (8%). 18 and over 450,745 (78%), 62 and over 104,547 (18%). Median age: 36.

Committees

Foreign Affairs (15th of 18 Republicans)
Europe & the Middle East; International Operations

Public Works & Transportation (17th of 24 Republicans)
Aviation; Surface Transportation

Campaign Finance

	Receipts	Receipts from PACs		Expend- itures
1992				
Levy (R)	$217,319	$60,880	(28%)	$209,225
Schiliro (D)	$506,217	$258,530	(51%)	$502,513

Key Votes

1993

Require parental notification of minors' abortions	Y
Require unpaid family and medical leave	N
Approve national "motor voter" registration bill	N
Approve budget increasing taxes and reducing deficit	N
Approve economic stimulus plan	N

Elections

1992 General		
David A. Levy (R, C)	110,710	(50%)
Philip M. Schiliro (D, L)	100,386	(45%)
Vincent P. Garbitelli (RTL)	9,548	(4%)
1992 Primary		
David A. Levy (R)	12,646	(53%)
Daniel Frisa (R)	9,890	(41%)
Francis A. Lees (R)	1,410	(6%)

District Vote for President

1992

D 119,947 (47%)
R 106,016 (41%)
I 30,476 (12%)

5 Gary L. Ackerman (D)

Of Queens — Elected 1983; 5th Full Term

Born: Nov. 19, 1942, Brooklyn, N.Y.
Education: Queens College, B.A. 1965.
Occupation: Teacher; publisher and editor; advertising executive.
Family: Wife, Rita Gail Tewel; three children.
Religion: Jewish.
Political Career: Sought Democratic nomination for N.Y. City Council at large, 1977; N.Y. Senate, 1979-83.
Capitol Office: 238 Cannon Bldg. 20515; 225-2601.

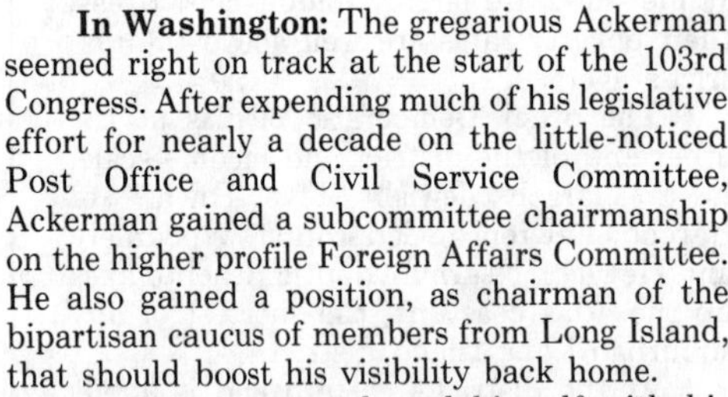

In Washington: The gregarious Ackerman seemed right on track at the start of the 103rd Congress. After expending much of his legislative effort for nearly a decade on the little-noticed Post Office and Civil Service Committee, Ackerman gained a subcommittee chairmanship on the higher profile Foreign Affairs Committee. He also gained a position, as chairman of the bipartisan caucus of members from Long Island, that should boost his visibility back home.

As Ackerman conducted himself with his trademark joviality, it was hard to tell that he had just survived a near-fatal political year in 1992. Ackerman suffered a double blow from the House bank investigation. He had 111 overdrafts of his own. And he was accused of leaking a preliminary list of the worst bank offenders, presumably because the list included his political rival. Ackerman strongly denied being the source of the leak, but the accusation forced him to step down from the House ethics committee.

His political situation was complicated further by redistricting. An urban liberal, Ackerman was placed in a district that removed much of his base in the New York City borough of Queens and gave him new voters in suburban (and more conservative) Long Island. To return for the 103rd Congress, Ackerman fended off a primary challenger, then edged a Republican candidate with just 52 percent of the vote.

The House bank scandal was interwoven with the redistricting issue. In July 1992, the ethics committee received a letter requesting a probe into whether Ackerman leaked the House bank list. The letter was signed by Democratic Reps. Edward F. Feighan of Ohio and Charles A. Hayes of Illinois, whose House bank overdrafts contributed to the ending of their House careers.

But published reports indicated that the letter was actually produced by retiring New York Democrats Robert J. Mrazek and James H. Scheuer, who contributed many constituents to the new 5th District. Scheuer considered running in a primary against Ackerman but opted to retire after the bank scandal.

Ackerman "absolutely and unequivocally" denied being the source of the leak, but quit the ethics committee anyway, declaring it a "thankless task." The ethics committee then decided not to pursue an investigation into the leak allegation.

Ackerman's troubles slowed what had been his increasingly successful campaign to be regarded as a serious legislator.

During his early years in the House, Ackerman was identified mainly with his idiosyncrasies: His glib wit, considerable girth, goatee, boutonniere and unusual residence (a houseboat docked in a Potomac River marina).

But by the late 1980s, a diet, a shave and a diligent effort on mundane issues as chairman of various Post Office and Civil Service subcommittees had helped Ackerman craft a more solonic image.

As chairman of the Subcommittee on Compensation and Employee Benefits, Ackerman helped win passage in the 101st Congress of a federal pay raise plan to help close the gap between public- and private-sector salaries. During the 102nd Congress, he proposed a plan to reform the health-care benefits system for federal employees; although the proposal never got off the ground, it included elements, such as hospital cost containment, that were similar to those later presented in President Clinton's health-care reform package in 1993.

Earlier on the full committee, Ackerman gained note for opposing proposals for widespread drug testing of federal workers.

At the start of the 103rd Congress, Ackerman gave up his Post Office subcommittee gavel for the chairmanship of the Foreign Affairs Subcommittee on Asia and the Pacific. This move broadens Ackerman's foreign policy agenda, which previously focused on Israel, world hunger and human rights issues.

Ackerman, who like many of his constituents is Jewish, is a strong supporter of U.S. aid to Israel. He was an early supporter of U.S. military involvement in the Persian Gulf.

Ackerman's interest in human rights often has centered on oppression faced by Jews, including the emigration rights of Soviet Jewish

New York 5

Northeast Queens; northern Nassau and Suffolk counties

One of the noted wits in the House, Democratic Rep. Ackerman used humor to express his displeasure with the 1992 redistricting plan that created the elongated, politically competitive 5th.

Congressional districts are supposed to be compact and contiguous. When state legislators showed the proposed remap to Ackerman, he asked how the shore-hugging district — which is connected in three places only by the waters of Long Island Sound — could be contiguous. By that reasoning, Ackerman said, Maine, New Jersey and Florida, connected only by the Atlantic Ocean, are contiguous.

But the 5th remained as drawn, one of several irregularly shaped districts on the new New York map. And its difficult navigability turned out to be just one of Ackerman's problems in 1992. Almost exactly half the district's population lives in suburban Long Island; even the portion of the New York City borough of Queens (Ackerman's base) that is in the 5th is more suburban than urban. As such, Democrats have no lock on the district.

The 1992 election results indicated that the 5th, while Democratic-leaning, has potential to be a political swing district. Ackerman edged a local Republican official by just 7 percentage points; Bill Clinton's majority win here was strong by suburban Long Island standards but weak compared with his performance in other New York City-based districts.

The portion of Queens that makes up the western end of the 5th is the Democratic base: Ackerman won 61 percent here in 1992. It has many Jewish residents and a large number of Asians (including a Chinese-American constituency centered on the community of Flushing). Flushing, one of Queens' "downtown" centers, is the most urbanized area of the district and has some low-income population.

Among the major employers in the Queens part of the 5th are Queens College of the City University of New York in South Flushing and the Long Island Jewish Medical Center in New Hyde Park.

Just across the Nassau County border are two peninsulas that contain some of the nation's wealthiest communities, including Sands Point, Kings Point and Great Neck. Despite its affluence, this area, which has a large Jewish population, is usually strong for Democrats. Ackerman pulled down nearly 60 percent here.

The U.S. Merchant Marine Academy is in Kings Point. Unisys, a maker of high-tech defense systems, is in Great Neck; Canon USA is based in Lake Success.

The exurban part of the district on Suffolk County's North Shore provides a sharp political contrast. Taking in most of the town of Huntington before terminating in the western part of Smithtown, the Suffolk County portion of the 5th votes steadily Republican.

Melville, at Suffolk's western border, is a commercial center. The newspaper Newsday and the Long Island offices of Chase Manhattan and Chemical Bank are there.

1990 Population: 580,337. White 487,569 (84%), Black 20,140 (3%), Other 72,628 (13%). Hispanic origin 42,440 (7%). 18 and over 462,505 (80%), 62 and over 109,899 (19%). Median age: 38.

"refuseniks" and Ethiopian Jews. He also was one of the early House members trying to draw attention to hunger in Africa.

Whatever Ackerman does on broader issues, it is his position at the head of the Long Island caucus that may be key to improving his re-election prospects in a difficult district.

It is a role he could not have imagined playing before 1992: Ackerman's constituency was completely within Queens. But after redistricting, half of Ackerman's constituency was in suburban Nassau and Suffolk counties. And all of Long Island's more senior members either retired or were defeated.

Ackerman adjusted to the leadership role quickly, organizing the group — which includes fourth-term Democratic Rep. George J. Hochbrueckner and three GOP freshmen: Peter T. King, Rick A. Lazio and David A. Levy — on such issues as flood-damage relief for coastal areas ravaged by winter storms and help for the region's economically crucial defense industry, which has been hit hard by post-Cold War cutbacks.

If Ackerman has worked hard for respect, he is still capable of burlesque. After U.S. forces began the bombing campaign against Iraq in January 1991, Ackerman read a poem on the House floor that began, "Slam, bam, thanks Saddam," and concluded, "Now take the loss, reverse the course, because it ain't going to get no better."

On the House floor in 1990, Ackerman displayed swimming trunks, pantyhose and other paraphernalia emblazoned with a flag motif to convey the impracticality of a constitutional ban on flag desecration.

At Home: Although he faced a contest in

his initial House race, a 1983 special election, Ackerman cruised through his first four re-election campaigns in the then-7th District. His mainly urban constituency included many loyally Democratic Jewish and Hispanic voters. He ran without opposition in 1988 and 1990.

But in 1992, the outlook changed. His House bank-related problems and redistricting spurred the first real threat to Ackerman's career.

New York lost three seats in reapportionment, and the House map had to squeeze a new Hispanic-majority district into New York City. Ackerman was one of the odd members out; his district was carved into several pieces.

Ackerman opted to run in the mainly suburban 5th. He avoided a showdown when Scheuer decided to retire. Still, a Democratic primary challenge revealed Ackerman's vulnerability.

Opponent Rita Morris was a grandmotherly college librarian who had never run for office (though her son was a political consultant). Her emphasis on Ackerman's check problems and his insider status hurt him. Ackerman pulled through, but with just 62 percent of the Democratic vote, and he lost Suffolk County to Morris.

Suffolk was the base of Ackerman's Republican opponent, County Legislator Allan E. Binder. A former aide to Texas Republican Rep. Tom DeLay, Binder ran on a theme of congressional reform and pounded Ackerman on ethics issues.

However, the much better-financed Ackerman touted his record on such issues as hunger and support for abortion rights. He hung on by 7 percentage points, his big margin in Queens offsetting Binder's advantage in Suffolk.

Ackerman came to the House to succeed Democratic Rep. Benjamin S. Rosenthal, who died in early 1983. A former social studies teacher, Ackerman had run-ins with the Queens Democratic machine as a publisher of a weekly newspaper and had run as an independent in an unsuccessful 1977 challenge to a City Council incumbent. But he won a state Senate seat in 1978, and convinced Democratic leaders in 1983 that he was the party's best hope in a House race against a wealthy independent candidate, pollster Douglas Schoen, and a less competitive GOP candidate. Ackerman won the special election with 50 percent of the vote.

Committees

Foreign Affairs (6th of 27 Democrats)
Asia & the Pacific (chairman); International Security, International Organizations & Human Rights

Merchant Marine & Fisheries (29th of 29 Democrats)
Merchant Marine

Post Office & Civil Service (4th of 15 Democrats)
Compensation & Employee Benefits

Elections

1992 General		
Gary L. Ackerman (D, L)	110,476	(52%)
Allan E. Binder (R, C)	94,907	(45%)
Andrew J. Duff (RTL)	5,448	(3%)
1992 Primary		
Gary L. Ackerman (D)	25,328	(62%)
Rita-Louise A. Morris (D)	15,656	(38%)
1990 General		
Gary L. Ackerman (D, L)	51,091	(100%)

Previous Winning Percentages: **1988** (100%) **1986** (77%) **1984** (69%) **1983** * (50%)

* *Special House election.*

District Vote for President

	1992	
D	131,095	(52%)
R	88,586	(34%)
I	30,475	(12%)

Campaign Finance

	Receipts	Receipts from PACs		Expend-itures
1992				
Ackerman (D)	$674,901	$342,775	(51%)	$917,483
Binder (R)	$125,965	$9,250	(7%)	$123,206
1990				
Ackerman (D)	$305,414	$186,537	(61%)	$272,549

Key Votes

1993	
Require parental notification of minors' abortions	N
Require unpaid family and medical leave	Y
Approve national "motor voter" registration bill	Y
Approve budget increasing taxes and reducing deficit	Y
Approve economic stimulus plan	Y
1992	
Approve balanced-budget constitutional amendment	N
Close down space station program	Y
Approve U.S. aid for former Soviet Union	Y
Allow shifting funds from defense to domestic programs	Y
1991	
Extend unemployment benefits using deficit financing	Y
Approve waiting period for handgun purchases	Y
Authorize use of force in Persian Gulf	Y

Voting Studies

	Presidential Support		Party Unity		Conservative Coalition	
Year	S	O	S	O	S	O
1992	13	57	76	1	6	52
1991	25	64	86	3	8	78
1990	14	79	92	2	7	85
1989	27	66	92	1	10	83
1988	15	74	93	0	3	87
1987	19	74	93	2	7	86
1986	12	79	91	0	4	82
1985	20	74	87	3	4	95
1984	22	66	85	5	5	86
1983	20 †	79 †	91 †	4 †	12 †	87 †

† *Not eligible for all recorded votes.*

Interest Group Ratings

Year	ADA	AFL-CIO	CCUS	ACU
1992	70	91	33	0
1991	85	100	20	10
1990	94	100	15	0
1989	90	100	40	0
1988	95	100	23	0
1987	96	100	14	0
1986	85	100	13	0
1985	100	100	20	10
1984	95	92	36	9
1983	85	100	22	0

6 Floyd H. Flake (D)

Of Queens — Elected 1986; 4th Term

Born: Jan. 30, 1945, Los Angeles, Calif.
Education: Wilberforce U., B.A. 1967; Payne Theological Seminary, 1968-70; Northeastern U., 1974-75; St. John's U., 1982-85.
Occupation: Minister.
Family: Wife, M. Elaine McCollins; four children.
Religion: African Methodist Episcopal.
Political Career: No previous office.
Capitol Office: 1035 Longworth Bldg. 20515; 225-3461.

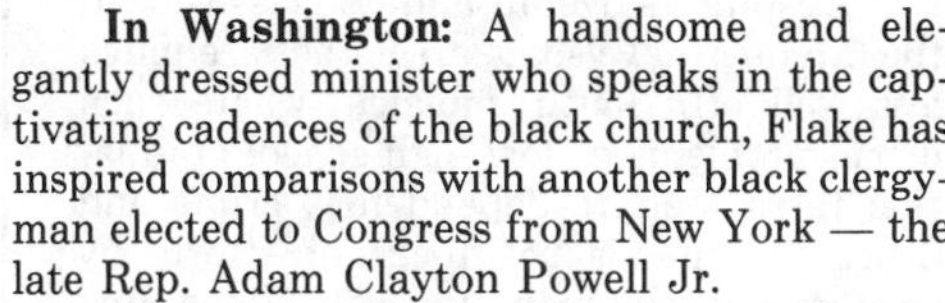

In Washington: A handsome and elegantly dressed minister who speaks in the captivating cadences of the black church, Flake has inspired comparisons with another black clergyman elected to Congress from New York — the late Rep. Adam Clayton Powell Jr.

For a time, the parallel with Powell, who faced legal and ethical problems during much of his House career, seemed to be getting uncomfortably close.

Flake is a contemporary of the new generation of black House members who view their role less in racial terms than do some more senior Congressional Black Caucus members. Democrats Kweisi Mfume of Maryland and Alan Wheat of Missouri exemplify this new generation; they try to effect change by working through the power structure, rather than by agitating primarily from the outside.

But in style and ideology, Flake does not fit quite so readily with the new generation, as he can be more vociferous and controversial.

Almost since arriving in the House, Flake has endured legal and political trials that have distracted him from legislative pursuits and given members pause about lining up with him on projects. Twice he was passed over for choice committee assignments. He had been the Black Caucus candidate for the Budget Committee in the 101st Congress. And when two New York Democrats left the Appropriations Committee prior to the 103rd, Flake made a bid. Two more junior New Yorkers — Nita M. Lowey and Jose E. Serrano — were tapped for the vacancies.

Flake's most difficult time came after he was indicted in August 1990 on 17 counts of evading taxes and diverting $141,000, including federal housing funds, from his church.

The Allen African Methodist Episcopal Church in Queens, of which Flake has been pastor for 17 years, is one of the city's oldest churches, with one of its largest black congregations. Prosecutors accused Flake and his wife, M. Elaine, of embezzling funds from a senior citizens housing project run by the church and failing to report the income on their tax returns.

In April 1991, the government's case was dismissed after a federal judge barred prosecutors from presenting what one called "the heart" of the case to the jury.

With that behind him — and a subsequent re-election tempest calmed — Flake is hoping to settle into a player's role in House affairs. He could be aided by a silver lining to his failure to move off the Banking Committee. Thanks to attrition, Flake rose to ninth of 30 Democrats on the panel at the start of the 103rd Congress and was thus eligible to claim the chairmanship of the General Oversight Subcommittee. Though the panel has no legislative responsibilities and in the past has been largely overlooked, Flake may try to use it to enhance his influence, in part by watching over the continuing savings and loan bailout.

In previous years, Flake sat on the Housing Subcommittee, which gave him a role in shaping housing programs for lower-income people. In the 101st Congress, he battled to ensure that more low-income families benefited from a $300 million rental-housing production program. The program, devised by New York Democrat Charles E. Schumer, was included in a bill overhauling the nation's federal housing programs. It established a revolving loan fund to provide advances to developers, nonprofit groups and public housing agencies to construct or rehabilitate affordable rental housing.

Republicans called it "a scandal waiting to happen" and tried to kill it. Flake, too, was troubled, and his reservations threatened to spark additional Democratic opposition to the program. Flake met with Schumer and agreed to return to the fold in exchange for a promise to modify the program so that either 40 percent of a building's tenants would be low-income or 20 percent would be lower-income. That proposal, offered by Flake, was adopted by the committee.

When the Banking Committee worked on legislation in 1989 to bail out and restructure the savings and loan industry, Flake stood with some in the industry in offering an amendment to allow thrifts that carried on their books "supervisory good will" — a form of phantom capital — to count it toward their required amount of capital.

New York 6

Southeast Queens — Jamaica; St. Albans

The southeast portion of Queens has sent an African-American to the House only since 1986; its black majority (about 56 percent of the population) is one of the most narrow of any district served by a black member. But a challenge to black representation here appears unlikely: Hispanics (about 17 percent) contribute to a minority-group voting bloc, while non-Hispanic whites (less than a quarter of the population) provide little counterweight.

The 6th provides a dependable partisan base for Rep. Flake and other Democrats. In his first election under the current district lines in 1992, Flake took 81 percent of the general-election vote; Bill Clinton dominated the 6th, winning 76 percent. Any political action here is going to be in the Democratic primaries: Flake proved his sure footing with his easy 1992 primary win over a black primary challenger supported by the Queens Democratic organization (with which Flake has had a long-running feud).

With an eastern border that follows the line between the New York City borough of Queens and suburban Nassau County, the 6th is one of the most economically sound minority-majority districts. Its poverty rate is less than the rate for New York state as a whole; the poverty rates for blacks and Hispanics are about half the figures for those groups statewide.

More than a generation ago, such communities as Springfield Gardens and St. Alban's were settled by a burgeoning Roman Catholic middle class. Today, the economic profile of these areas is not much different: Its brick homes house many civil servants, teachers and small-business owners. But the demographics are completely different. Instead of Irish- and Italian-Americans, most of the residents now are blacks.

John F. Kennedy International Airport, by far the district's largest employer, provides a steady job base. It is also the district's most prominent geographical feature: Originally named Idlewild for the marshlands on which it was built, "JFK" occupies a huge swath of the 6th along the north shore of Jamaica Bay.

Despite its overall middle-class veneer, the 6th does have some areas that are much less well off. South Jamaica, where such urban problems as low high school graduation rates, welfare dependency, crime and drugs are rife, is the focus of efforts by economic development advocates (including Flake). The 6th's portion of the Rockaway peninsula — across Jamaica Bay from the airport with no direct land link to the rest of the district — has several public housing projects.

Much of the district's mainly middle-class white population is in its northeast end, in such communities as Bellerose and Queens Village, and near its western border, in Ozone Park. These areas are mainly Irish and Italian, with a scattering of Jewish residents. They lean Democratic, though the Republican vote is heavier than in the rest of the 6th. The Aqueduct horse track is in South Ozone Park.

1990 Population: 580,337. White 170,071 (29%), Black 326,335 (56%), Other 83,931 (14%). Hispanic origin 98,209 (17%). 18 and over 432,187 (74%), 62 and over 79,944 (14%). Median age: 32.

Even though the proposal had previously been debated and withdrawn, Flake offered it again. When debate clearly showed it would fail, he withdrew it. On the floor, Flake voted for the unsuccessful good will amendment sponsored by Illinois Republican Henry J. Hyde.

From his spot on the Small Business panel, Flake has worked on legislation overhauling the minority set-aside program for federal contracts.

At Home: Flake's wide victory margins give him the appearance of an entrenched incumbent. Yet he has actually had a stormier career than most tenured members.

Running as an insurgent House candidate in 1986, he wrestled with the Queens Democratic machine: He first lost to party-endorsed state Rep. Alton R. Waldon Jr. in a special election, then unseated Waldon in the primary that followed. Though never seriously threatened in his ensuing re-election bids, Flake was shadowed by the allegations of improprieties.

Even after surviving legal battles, Flake had other problems in 1992. First, he continued a feud with the Queens Democrats by organizing a slate of primary candidates to challenge party regulars for elective and party positions, after they endorsed his opponent in the Democratic primary. The party organization retaliated by challenging the ballot status of Flake and the slated challengers. An out-of-court compromise was reached under which most of the challengers withdrew and Flake stayed on the ballot.

The incumbent then had to fend off black businessman Simeon Golar, a former New York City housing official who had earlier staged four failed House bids.

In a primary campaign notable for its strong rhetoric, Golar reminded voters constantly of Flake's previous legal problems. While Flake touted the federal funds he had obtained for the district, Golar argued that most benefits had gone to members of the church Flake heads.

Golar, however, was not able to establish himself as a credible alternative. He had run two strong primary challenges, in 1982 and 1984, against white Democratic Rep. Joseph P. Addabbo after the 6th District gained a black majority in redistricting. But he was a late entry into the 1986 Democratic primary that followed Addabbo's death and was drubbed.

Then, in 1990, Bronx Republicans wanted to test the depths of black antipathy to Hispanic control of the seat of resigned Democratic Rep. Robert Garcia, and Golar agreed to be their candidate against Democrat Jose E. Serrano. Golar went on to tally 7 percent of the vote in the overwhelmingly Democratic district.

Flake breezed past Golar by a 3-1 margin and won easily in November.

Flake has a diverse background in corporate marketing and in education. But it was his long tenure as pastor of the Allen African Methodist Episcopal Church — and the economic and social programs that he sponsored in that role — that gave Flake a base for a political career.

Flake made his political debut in the June 1986 special election. The party's backing gave Waldon an organizational advantage, and he was aided by a filing technicality that prevented Flake from appearing on absentee ballots. Yet Waldon won only a narrow victory over Flake, whose followers, angered by the absentee ballot flap, believed the election was stolen by a corrupt Queens machine.

That sentiment gave Flake momentum going into the September primary to choose a nominee for a full term in the 100th Congress. Fusing his support in the black church with elements of black organized labor, Flake defeated Waldon and went on to an easy general election win.

By 1988, Flake drew no significant opposition. His only difficulty was of a personal nature. In May, a woman who had worked for Flake at his Queens church accused Flake of harassing her to quit after she broke off a sexual affair with him. Flake denied the accusations.

In 1990, Flake carried the burden of his tax-evasion indictment into his campaign. But many of his supporters rallied to his side. Flake defeated a strong Republican with 73 percent of the vote.

Committees

Banking, Finance & Urban Affairs (9th of 30 Democrats)
General Oversight, Investigations & the Resolution of Failed Financial Institutions (chairman); Consumer Credit & Insurance; Financial Institutions Supervision, Regulation & Deposit Insurance

Government Operations (18th of 25 Democrats)
Employment, Housing & Aviation

Small Business (10th of 27 Democrats)
Minority Enterprise, Finance & Urban Development

Elections

1992 General		
Floyd H. Flake (D)	96,972	(81%)
Dianand D. Bhagwandin (R, C)	22,687	(19%)
1992 Primary		
Floyd H. Flake (D)	34,914	(75%)
Simeon Golar (D)	11,462	(25%)
1990 General		
Floyd H. Flake (D, L)	44,306	(73%)
William Sampol (R)	13,224	(22%)
John Cronin (RTL)	3,111	(5%)

Previous Winning Percentages: **1988** (86%) **1986** (68%)

District Vote for President

1992
D 115,253 (76%)
R 27,855 (18%)
I 9,335 (6%)

Campaign Finance

	Receipts	Receipts from PACs		Expend-itures
1992				
Flake (D)	$272,263	$142,490	(52%)	$281,172
Bhagwandin (R)	$50,090	$1,379	(3%)	$45,015
1990				
Flake (D)	$240,869	$122,440	(51%)	$205,031

Key Votes

1993	
Require parental notification of minors' abortions	Y
Require unpaid family and medical leave	Y
Approve national "motor voter" registration bill	Y
Approve budget increasing taxes and reducing deficit	Y
Approve economic stimulus plan	Y
1992	
Approve balanced-budget constitutional amendment	N
Close down space station program	Y
Approve U.S. aid for former Soviet Union	N
Allow shifting funds from defense to domestic programs	Y
1991	
Extend unemployment benefits using deficit financing	Y
Approve waiting period for handgun purchases	Y
Authorize use of force in Persian Gulf	N

Voting Studies

	Presidential Support		Party Unity		Conservative Coalition	
Year	**S**	**O**	**S**	**O**	**S**	**O**
1992	10	76	87	3	10	83
1991	23	65	87	4	0	95
1990	14	81	85	5	9	80
1989	27	67	85	4	7	93
1988	14	74	82	3	5	82
1987	13	75	79	2	12	70

Interest Group Ratings

Year	ADA	AFL-CIO	CCUS	ACU
1992	90	92	13	0
1991	100	100	20	0
1990	89	91	38	4
1989	95	100	30	4
1988	95	100	30	0
1987	92	100	0	0

7 Thomas J. Manton (D)

Of Queens — Elected 1984; 5th Term

Born: Nov. 3, 1932, New York, N.Y.
Education: St. John's U., B.B.A. 1958, LL.B. 1962.
Military Service: Marine Corps, 1951-53.
Occupation: Lawyer.
Family: Wife, Diane Mason Schley; four children.
Religion: Roman Catholic.
Political Career: N.Y. City Council, 1970-84; sought Democratic nomination for U.S. House, 1972, 1978.
Capitol Office: 203 Cannon Bldg. 20515; 225-3965.

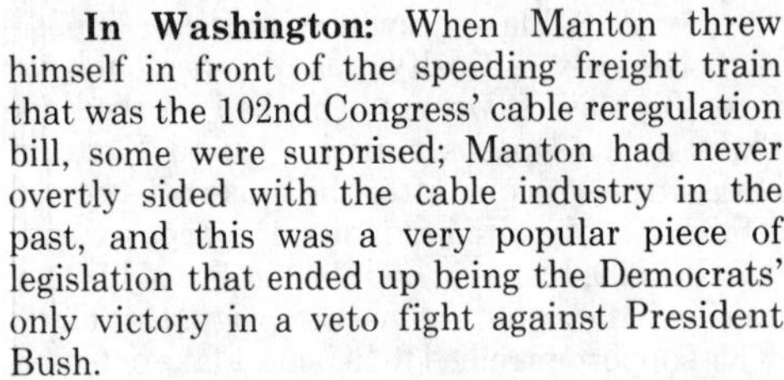

In Washington: When Manton threw himself in front of the speeding freight train that was the 102nd Congress' cable reregulation bill, some were surprised; Manton had never overtly sided with the cable industry in the past, and this was a very popular piece of legislation that ended up being the Democrats' only victory in a veto fight against President Bush.

But media giant Time Warner Inc. sits right in Manton's district, employing more than 2,000 of his constituents. The company is the nation's second-largest cable operator and a major cable program producer.

Manton could not stop the reregulation bill, but the cable industry still was grateful for his help. "You gave it your best shot," said James P. Mooney, president of the National Cable Television Association, after a key markup session.

It was a rare kind of foray for Manton, who is less known for getting into the details of legislating than for playing institutional inside baseball on House Administration, which oversees internal House matters such as committee budgets, and on Steering and Policy, a Democratic Party panel that determines committee assignments.

Behind-the-scenes politics is Manton's natural orientation; as chairman of the Democratic organization in Queens, he is deeply involved in complex parochial politics. In Washington, Manton has worked to find the centers of power and has gravitated toward them.

In the 101st Congress, he won a place on Energy and Commerce, a committee with considerable legislative reach whose members thus have entree to a wide range of political action committees (PACs) that closely follow congressional action. Manton typically draws about two-thirds of his campaign money from PACs, and he spent more than $1 million on his 1992 re-election.

Manton had tried to get onto Energy and Commerce in the 100th Congress, but failed to win the backing of the New York delegation. He then laid careful groundwork, playing an active role on the Democratic Congressional Campaign Committee, serving as a regional co-chairman and raising money for party candidates.

He was also careful to court committee Chairman John D. Dingell of Michigan, who worked hard to add members to his panel who would not undermine his efforts to block tough clean air legislation.

During consideration of such legislation in 1990, Manton returned the favor. Despite the urgings of lobbyists for New York, Manton joined Dingell in successfully opposing an amendment to require cleaner car fuels. "We're here in a political climate of give-and-take, with amendments we may need some help on," Manton said. "People don't need to fracture my arm to get my attention."

A former policeman, Manton touts his sponsorship of federal disability pay to law enforcement officials injured in the line of duty, passed as part of omnibus anti-crime legislation in 1990. He also has supported levying the federal death penalty against those who commit gun murders.

At Home: Although Manton served for 14 years on the New York City Council, he had some initial trouble gaining political stature. He twice lost House nomination races during the 1970s. During his first successful House campaign, in 1984, Manton was overshadowed by his predecessor, Democrat Geraldine A. Ferraro, who was then on the national Democratic ticket as Walter F. Mondale's vice presidential running mate.

Soon thereafter, Manton obtained prominence in his own right, taking over as Queens Democratic chairman and stabilizing a party organization that had been wracked by scandal. Manton's party position provided him with a ready-made organization for a series of easy re-election campaigns.

However, 1992 was a year marked by voter skepticism about politicians, and Manton's image as a political insider provided fodder for his Republican opponent, aggressive first-time candidate Dennis C. Shea.

New York 7

Parts of Queens and the Bronx — Long Island City

Democrats have a strong registration advantage in the 7th, a multi-ethnic, mainly middle-class, urban district that connects northern Queens with the southern Bronx. There is a substantial minority presence: Over a fifth of the residents are Hispanic, with blacks and Asians (including a Chinese-American concentration in Flushing) each making up about a tenth of the population.

Yet the Democratic vote here is somewhat less dependable than in most of New York City. Non-Hispanic whites make up just under 60 percent of the 7th's population but vote in greater numbers than its minority-group residents, and many of these whites are of working-class backgrounds and of ethnic groups that have conservative tendencies on social issues.

The creators of the 1970s TV show "All in the Family" placed the home of its conservative blue-collar protagonist, Archie Bunker, in the Queens community of Astoria, located mainly in the 7th.

The 7th supported Ronald Reagan in the 1980s, even in 1984 when Geraldine A. Ferraro — who then represented much of the 7th District in the House — was the Democratic vice presidential nominee. The 7th narrowly returned to the Democratic side in the 1988 presidential contest, but Bill Clinton won it by a wide margin.

That year, Democratic Rep. Manton easily defeated his GOP opponent. But nearly all of his 17,000-vote margin came from Queens, where he is county Democratic chairman. Manton won barely more than half the vote in the Bronx portion of the 7th.

The 7th owes its irregular shape in Queens (which has about three-quarters of the district's population) to the Hispanic-majority 12th District, which winds around northern Queens to pick up pockets of Hispanic residents.

At the 7th's western end is Long Island City, which faces Manhattan across the East River. This longtime industrial center still has blue-collar employers, including the Swingline stapler company, but has lost many of its factories in recent years.

A Citicorp skyscraper, the tallest building in Queens, is in Long Island City. The Astoria Film Center, a studio used since the silent-movie days, is nearby, as is much of Astoria's Greek community. Sunnyside has Amtrak and Long Island Rail Road yards.

The 7th picks up a largely Irish section in Jackson Heights, then wraps around the 12th to take in much of its own Hispanic population in such areas as East Elmhurst and Corona. Bordering Flushing Bay are LaGuardia Airport and Flushing Meadow Park, site of Shea Stadium, the National Tennis Center (site of the U.S. Open) and the 1939 and 1964-65 world's fairs.

To the east, the district covers residential College Point and Whitestone, then moves across the Bronx-Whitestone Bridge. The 7th's portion of the Bronx is shaped roughly like the number seven. Italian-Americans make up the predominant ethnic group. The Bronx section has a large hospital complex that includes Yeshiva University's Albert Einstein College of Medicine.

1990 Population: 580,337. White 406,394 (70%), Black 58,788 (10%), Other 115,155 (20%). Hispanic origin 123,495 (21%). 18 and over 472,528 (81%), 62 and over 116,640 (20%). Median age: 37.

Manton touted his efforts on behalf of his constituents as a member of Energy and Commerce and other committees. But Shea — a 31-year-old lawyer who once served as legal counsel to Republican Sen. Bob Dole of Kansas — portrayed the incumbent as a local party boss who went to Congress to take overseas junkets, enjoy perks and vote for House pay raises. He also played up Manton's 17 overdrafts at the House bank.

Manton's precinct organization in the Queens part of the redrawn 7th District assured his victory; he took 59 percent of the vote there. But it was no help in the part of the Bronx added to Manton's base in redistricting: He edged Shea there with 52 percent. Overall, Manton's 57 percent was his lowest election tally since his 1984 race.

That contest marked a turnaround for Manton. In 1972, as a junior member of the New York City Council, Manton unsuccessfully challenged longtime Democratic Rep. James J. Delaney in the House primary. He tried again for the seat when Delaney retired in 1978; Ferraro defeated him decisively.

But when Mondale tapped Ferraro in 1984, Manton, by then a veteran councilman, became a front-runner to replace her. He eked out a narrow primary win over a field that included a state assemblyman, a prominent lawyer and a Queens election official. He then defeated conservative Republican Serphin R. Maltese, whose vigorous campaign held the heavily favored Manton to 53 percent.

By 1986, Manton had a firm grip on his district (then numbered the 9th), racking up 69 percent against Queens attorney Salvatore Calise. He ran unopposed in 1988, and took 64 percent — 40 points better than his GOP rival — in 1990.

Meanwhile, Manton devoted much of his political effort to his position as Queens Democratic chairman. Manton won the post in October 1986, after pledging to improve the image of the party organization. He succeeded an interim replacement to Donald Manes, the Queens borough president and longtime party chairman who committed suicide earlier that year following his implication in a city corruption scandal.

Committees

Energy & Commerce (17th of 27 Democrats)
Commerce, Consumer Protection & Competitiveness; Telecommunications & Finance; Transportation & Hazardous Materials

House Administration (6th of 12 Democrats)
Personnel & Police (chairman)

Merchant Marine & Fisheries (7th of 29 Democrats)
Fisheries Management (chairman); Merchant Marine

Joint Library

Elections

1992 General		
Thomas J. Manton (D)	72,280	(57%)
Dennis C. Shea (R, C)	54,639	(43%)
1990 General		
Thomas J. Manton (D)	35,177	(64%)
Ann Pfoser Darby (R)	13,330	(24%)
Thomas V. Ognibene (C)	6,137	(11%)

Previous Winning Percentages: **1988** (100%) **1986** (69%) **1984** (53%)

District Vote for President

1992

D 91,803 (56%)
R 57,783 (35%)
I 15,118 (9%)

Campaign Finance

	Receipts	Receipts from PACs		Expend-itures
1992				
Manton (D)	$643,780	$427,492	(66%)	$1,013,635
Shea (R)	$216,128	$25,832	(12%)	$182,737
1990				
Manton (D)	$620,609	$452,323	(73%)	$316,301

Key Votes

1993	
Require parental notification of minors' abortions	Y
Require unpaid family and medical leave	Y
Approve national "motor voter" registration bill	Y
Approve budget increasing taxes and reducing deficit	Y
Approve economic stimulus plan	Y
1992	
Approve balanced-budget constitutional amendment	N
Close down space station program	N
Approve U.S. aid for former Soviet Union	Y
Allow shifting funds from defense to domestic programs	Y
1991	
Extend unemployment benefits using deficit financing	Y
Approve waiting period for handgun purchases	Y
Authorize use of force in Persian Gulf	N

Voting Studies

	Presidential Support		Party Unity		Conservative Coalition	
Year	**S**	**O**	**S**	**O**	**S**	**O**
1992	30	63	84	9	40	52
1991	35	58	86	6	22	76
1990	26	72	89	6	35	61
1989	38	53	82	12	41	56
1988	24	67	89	6	32	63
1987	19	78	92	2	23	77
1986	18	77	88	3	30	60
1985	23	71	88	5	24	69

Interest Group Ratings

Year	ADA	AFL-CIO	CCUS	ACU
1992	85	83	29	8
1991	80	92	20	10
1990	67	100	21	9
1989	70	100	40	4
1988	60	100	23	18
1987	80	100	7	4
1986	75	100	29	9
1985	70	81	27	10

8 Jerrold Nadler (D)

Of Manhattan — Elected 1992; 1st Term

Born: June 13, 1947, Brooklyn, N.Y.

Education: Columbia U., A.B. 1969; Fordham U., J.D. 1978.

Occupation: City official; lawyer.

Family: Wife, Joyce L. Miller; one child.

Religion: Jewish.

Political Career: N.Y. Assembly, 1977-92; candidate for Manhattan Borough President, 1985; candidate for New York City Comptroller, 1989.

Capitol Office: 424 Cannon Bldg. 20515; 225-5635.

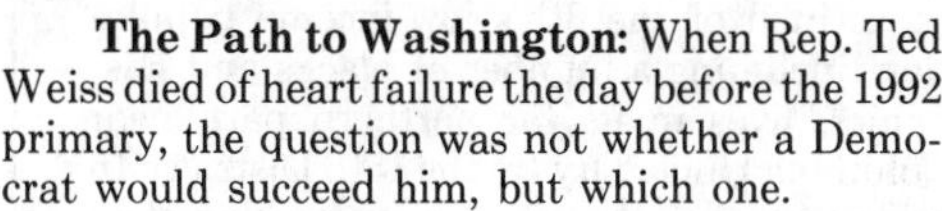

The Path to Washington: When Rep. Ted Weiss died of heart failure the day before the 1992 primary, the question was not whether a Democrat would succeed him, but which one.

Nadler quickly emerged as the front-runner for the Democratic nomination and, with that in hand, had little trouble sweeping the general election for the district that includes Manhattan's liberal West Side.

Voters can expect little ideological change from Nadler, who shares Weiss' liberal inclinations on issues such as gay rights and women's rights and limited defense spending.

But the hard-charging Nadler will present a stylistic departure from his predecessor's usually calm demeanor. Intelligent and hard-working, Nadler's political trademark is also a persistence that some say can occasionally border on obsession.

Weiss had become a fixture in the Manhattan-based seat and appeared on his way to easy re-election when he died on the eve of the September Democratic primary. Primary voters endorsed him nonetheless, giving party officials the right to pick a successor.

Weiss' death set off a scramble among the district's ample cadre of Democratic activists, with six candidates jumping into the frenetic nine-day race for the nomination.

Nadler quickly became the presumptive leader: While other potential nominees such as former Rep. Bella S. Abzug were better-known to the public, Nadler had longstanding ties to the insiders who would cast the vote.

Nadler served the remainder of Weiss' term immediately after the November election.

Brooklyn-born, Nadler spent his early years on a poultry farm in New Jersey. But his family moved back to New York City after the farm failed, and Nadler attended a yeshiva before graduating from Stuyvesant High School.

He kept close to city limits thereafter, earning a bachelor's degree in government at Columbia University. Later, while working as assistant branch manager of an Off-Track Betting office, he attended Fordham Law School in the Bronx at night.

Nadler's political involvement dates to his college days in the 1960s, when he was a community activist and an organizer against the Vietnam War. Nadler himself was disqualified from military service for medical reasons.

His early political ventures found him organizing anti-war students to campaign for Eugene J. McCarthy in the 1968 New Hampshire presidential primary, warning tenants about lead paint and campaigning for Weiss in one of his early unsuccessful bids for Congress.

In 1976, he narrowly won an open seat in the state Legislature and served there for 16 years.

In the Legislature, Nadler was a solid liberal vote but not always a predictable one. For example, in 1987 he was among only a handful of legislators to oppose a popular tax cut, arguing that it would lead to large deficits.

He was best-known for work on women's issues, including legislation to fight domestic violence and enforce child-support payments.

Nadler also crusaded in behalf of mass transit and rail freight. Nadler advocates rail freight both as a means to reduce truck traffic and pollution and to preserve manufacturing jobs.

He will be able to pursue some of those concerns as a member of the Public Works and Transportation Committee. Nadler also won a seat on the Judiciary panel.

Nadler played a role in the deliberations over the Freedom of Choice Act early in the 103rd Congress. In a subcommittee markup on the bill, he succeeded in stripping language that gave states permission to enact parental notification and consent laws. Though Nadler's actions did nothing to preclude states from enacting such restrictions, he said that the language would encourage states to pass such laws.

Known as something of a maverick in the state Legislature, Nadler said he is likely to be a more loyal vote in Congress, where he believes the Democrats must show they can enact party goals.

During the December organizational meetings, Nadler was elected second vice president for the freshman class.

New York 8

West Side Manhattan; parts of southwest Brooklyn

A strong strain of liberalism prevails on the West Side of Manhattan. Containing nearly three-fifths of the 8th's population, this area gives Democrats a lock on the district. This part of the island is Democratic Rep. Nadler's base, as it was for his predecessor, the late Ted Weiss. The West Side has many liberal-voting Jewish residents and one of the nation's largest concentrations of homosexuals.

The portion of Brooklyn that has the remainder of the 8th's population does not look very different. Like the Manhattan side, this is a thoroughly urban area of apartment dwellers; Jews are a large constituency.

But while most of Manhattan's Jewish residents lead mainly secular lifestyles, the Brooklyn part of the 8th has large communities of Hasidic Jews, whose religion-centered lives and orthodox reading of the Old Testament set a more conservative political tone. Though Democrats have a huge registration advantage, these communities are not averse to supporting socially conservative Republicans who meet a major condition: strong support for Israel. One such figure, Sen. Alfonse M. D'Amato, was backed by key Hasidic leaders during his 1992 campaign against a liberal Jewish Democrat.

Although Democrats still typically dominate the Brooklyn part, their numbers are slightly lower than in Manhattan. Nadler won 84 percent of the vote in the Manhattan part of the 8th and 73 percent in Brooklyn. Bill Clinton easily carried both sections.

The district's liberal lean belies its status as a world center of finance and commerce. The Wall Street financial district is at the southern tip of Manhattan in the 8th, as are the twin towers of the World Trade Center, second in height only to Chicago's Sears Tower and the site of a terrorist bomb attack in February 1993. The Empire State Building, in midtown, long reigned as the world's tallest skyscraper.

The 8th is also a world-famous cultural center. On the Upper West Side is Lincoln Center; the Broadway theater district and Madison Square Garden are farther downtown. Greenwich Village, a longtime magnet for artists, is also the hub for the gay community. New York University is also here.

Much of the 8th's low-income population, including a number of blacks and Hispanics, lives in its far northern part, near Columbia University (in the 15th District). In midtown near the river is a working-class area, initially populated by Irish-Americans, that was long known as one of the city's roughest areas: Officially named Clinton, it was better known as "Hell's Kitchen."

After crossing the Brooklyn-Battery Tunnel and skimming along the Brooklyn waterfront, the 8th takes in mainly residential areas, including the orthodox Jewish center of Borough Park and part of ethnically mixed, racially tense Bensonhurst. At its southern end, the district meets the Atlantic Ocean at Brighton Beach, the setting for Neil Simon's autobiographical plays; Coney Island, whose century-old amusement park is a place of faded glory, has a population mix of minorities and Jews, many of them elderly.

1990 Population: 580,337. White 466,355 (80%), Black 49,725 (9%), Other 64,257 (11%). Hispanic origin 73,580 (13%). 18 and over 486,296 (84%), 62 and over 103,793 (18%). Median age: 37.

Committees

Judiciary (17th of 21 Democrats)
Civil & Constitutional Rights; International Law, Immigration & Refugees

Public Works & Transportation (25th of 39 Democrats)
Economic Development; Surface Transportation; Water Resources & the Environment

Campaign Finance

	Receipts	Receipts from PACs		Expend-itures
1992				
Nadler (D)	$49,685	$37,750	(76%)	$45,505
Askren (R)	$2,150	0		$2,150

Key Votes

1993

Require parental notification of minors' abortions	N
Require unpaid family and medical leave	Y
Approve national "motor voter" registration bill	Y
Approve budget increasing taxes and reducing deficit	Y
Approve economic stimulus plan	Y

Elections

1992 General		
Jerrold Nadler (D, L)	138,296	(81%)
David L. Askren (R)	25,548	(15%)
Margaret V. Byrnes (C)	5,180	(3%)
1992 Special †		
Jerrold Nadler (D,L)	151,122	(100%)

† On Election Day, Nadler was elected to a full term and to fill out the remainder of the term of Ted Weiss, D-N.Y., who died Sept. 14, 1992.

District Vote for President

1992

D	169,005	(77%)
R	37,614	(17%)
I	12,216	(6%)

9 Charles E. Schumer (D)

Of Brooklyn — Elected 1980; 7th Term

Born: Nov. 23, 1950, Brooklyn, N.Y.
Education: Harvard U., B.A. 1971, J.D. 1974.
Occupation: Lawyer.
Family: Wife, Iris Weinshall; two children.
Religion: Jewish.
Political Career: N.Y. Assembly, 1975-81.
Capitol Office: 2412 Rayburn Bldg. 20515; 225-6616.

In Washington: If any member of the House — an immense and impossibly broad institution — can be called ubiquitous, it is Schumer. Indeed, everything about him is outsized: his agenda, his ego and his legislative trophies.

Were he not as effective as any three less ambitious members, his colleagues would scorn him; instead they are merely envious. They covet his success and they are jealous of his ability to find the spotlight, almost as if without looking. It is a wonder that Schumer can do so much and get so much attention, and still be unhappy that some of his good works go unnoticed.

Schumer thrives not only in the public eye, but also in the back rooms that are the incubators of legislative accomplishment. He is shrewd and tough, sees the big picture but attends to detail, and can make necessary compromises. A keen mind and an abundance of energy enabled him, in six terms all under Republican presidents, to put his imprint on housing, trade, immigration, crime, farm and banking policy.

Though the Judiciary Subcommittee on Crime is where he hangs his hat most often these days, Schumer still is exceedingly active just around the corner in the Rayburn Building on the Banking Committee, where he became chairman of the panel's Democratic caucus in the 103rd Congress. Schumer ranks fifth below Chairman Henry B. Gonzalez and three somewhat more senior Democrats. But whenever Gonzalez decides it is time to move on (and he shows no signs of fatigue), Schumer will be ready to make a bid to leapfrog into the chair.

Most New York City liberals tend to be suspect in Democratic leadership circles, but Schumer has made his way in the House as a leadership insider. He has benefited from sharing a house on Capitol Hill that has more political wattage than any residence in the city, except a famous address on Pennsylvania Avenue. Currently Democrats Richard J. Durbin of Illinois, Sam Gejdenson of Connecticut and George Miller of California are Schumer's housemates; Californian Leon E. Panetta moved out when he was tapped by President Clinton to run the Office of Management and Budget.

When he needs to build support for a key legislative proposal, he can also call on allies in the Wall Street business community or on the editorial board of The New York Times. He makes skillful use of the media, publishing countless opinion pieces in national newspapers and appearing so often on TV news talk shows that it is sometimes hard to tell whether he is a guest or a host.

At the start the 102nd Congress, Schumer became chairman of the Crime Subcommittee, after it was merged with his old subcommittee on Criminal Justice. He is proud of having used the position to move his party toward the center on crime issues, defusing the partisanship that kept Democrats on the defensive.

He poked and prodded Democrats into accepting a broad anti-crime bill that had something for all sides to hate and love. It included a compromise version of the Brady bill, imposing a five-day waiting period for handgun purchases. And it would have extended the federal death penalty to more than 50 crimes and limited the ability of death row inmates to challenge their sentences in federal court. The death penalty was too much for some liberals, and conservatives, particularly Republicans, objected to the handgun language and thought the death row appeal limits too weak. But the House adopted a conference report on the bill by a 205-203 vote in November 1991. Senate supporters, however, could not muster enough votes to break a Republican filibuster, and the bill died.

In the 103rd Congress, he renewed the fight for the handgun bill and began pushing another measure to make blockading an abortion clinic a federal crime.

In 1992, Schumer had success with a bill to make a federal crime of "carjacking" — defined as armed theft of an automobile when the driver is present. Introduced in March, the measure languished until several grisly deaths in carjacking

New York 9

Parts of Brooklyn and Queens — Sheepshead Bay; Forest Hills

Contiguity, a supposed criterion for congressional districts, may be in the eye of the beholder. But it would be hard to find a more geographically disparate district anywhere than the 9th, which takes in widely separated parts of Brooklyn and Queens.

One of the most interesting of the many abstract designs on the current map, the 9th reaches a point in the Park Slope section of central Brooklyn, then follows a narrow corridor south before broadening out along that borough's waterfront. It jumps across an inlet to the Rockaways, running the length of the narrow peninsula that forms the southern part of Queens. It also heads back across Jamaica Bay (touching several islands that make up a wildlife refuge) to the mainland and follows another narrow band north, before broadening out across a swath of west-central Queens.

The only connections between the three regions are the two auto causeways to and from the Rockaways and the broad waters of Jamaica Bay. At the south side of the mainland, the district's pieces are separated by about a mile across the 10th District. But at the northern extremes, the Queens and Brooklyn branches of the 9th are more than four miles apart, with parts of the 10th, 11th and 12th districts in between.

It is only when the demographics of the 9th are considered that its design begins to make sense. Under the mandates of the Voting Rights Act, remappers drew the 9th around the minority-group concentrations in the intervening districts, two of which are majority-black, the other majority-Hispanic. As a result, the population is about 82 percent non-Hispanic white.

The lack of a large minority base does not keep the 9th from being a regularly Democratic district that is tailor-made for Rep. Schumer. Like the all-Brooklyn district Schumer represented during the 1980s, the mostly middle-class and residential 9th has large Jewish and ethnic populations (mainly Italian- and Irish-Americans) that give it a strong Democratic flavor. Schumer had no GOP opponent in 1992; Bill Clinton won the 9th by 26 percentage points.

There are pockets of social conservatism, however, and racial tension is not unknown. The Howard Beach community in Queens is still living down a 1986 incident in which a gang of whites chased a black man onto a highway, where he was struck by a car and killed.

From its Brooklyn tip in Park Slope, an upscale community hard by sprawling Prospect Park, the 9th takes in the Brooklyn College campus and such middle-class areas as Sheepshead Bay and Canarsie. It then crosses the Marine Parkway Bridge to Queens, running the length of the peninsula from Breezy Point to Far Rockaway (where it abuts the 6th District).

Cross Bay Boulevard carries the district back to the mainland at Howard Beach, then north to Woodhaven. At the northeast corner of the 9th are two of its wealthiest communities, Forest Hills (site of the West Side Tennis Center, the former home of the U.S. Open) and Kew Gardens.

1990 Population: 580,338. White 508,396 (88%), Black 19,156 (3%), Other 52,786 (9%). Hispanic origin 49,220 (8%). 18 and over 469,579 (81%), 62 and over 134,443 (23%). Median age: 39.

cases received national attention. The bill roared through both the House and Senate in October, passing by voice votes in both chambers. It had taken some doing on Schumer's part, however, to get it to the floor.

He wanted automakers to label all major car parts with identification numbers that the FBI would keep on file. Energy and Commerce Chairman John D. Dingell of Michigan said such a proposal would not help and would be exceedingly costly to his home state's biggest industry. Schumer persevered and cut a deal with Dingell in which major car parts would be marked on most car lines, but the system would be phased in, and the attorney general was told to determine if the program was effective in deterring crime.

Schumer was a key negotiator on the 1990 legal immigration reform bill, supporting an increase in the number of job-related visas and creation of a category of "diversity" visas for individuals from countries that under the current system are all but shut out. He entered that debate with considerable credibility from the 99th Congress, when his work helped lead to passage of landmark new U.S. immigration laws.

Schumer's visibility on the Banking Committee tends to wax and wane, depending on the issue and how deeply he is involved in non-Banking affairs.

He attempted to play a dominant role in 1991 on a major overhaul of banking laws, and was instrumental in several key sections. In a somewhat dramatic shift, Schumer had decided prior to the 1991 debate that the time had come to change Depression-era laws banning bank affiliations with securities firms. The last time the House considered the issue, in 1988, he was staunchly opposed to such affiliations.

Concerned about the threat to the deposit insurance system (and the competitive advantage that such affiliations might give to banks), Schumer in 1991 offered a proposal to bifurcate the industry into "core banks" that would continue to have insurance, and "wholesale banks" that would not have insurance but also would be exempted from many regulatory barriers.

The idea was hailed by many as original and possibly meritorious. But the proposal's novelty was its downfall. After failing to persuade his committee colleagues to embrace it, Schumer lost a floor vote on the proposal, 106-312. Soon thereafter, any hope of permitting banks broader latitude in which to operate vanished for the year.

Schumer's involvement in the banking bill was almost marginal, however, when seen alongside his skillful navigation of the savings and loan bailout bill in 1989. He managed to be at once the Bush administration's biggest helper and hindrance, and if his willingness to cut deals frustrated allies and adversaries alike, it also enabled the House to pass the legislation by a wide bipartisan margin.

Then a senior Democrat on the Budget Committee and a member of Banking and Judiciary, Schumer was uniquely well-placed to seize control of the debate. Then when the bill was drafted, he became a pivotal expert witness as the Rules Committee deliberated how to send it to the floor.

Schumer's fingerprints are on virtually every one of the 732 pages of the House thrift bill. Both in committee and the floor, he championed the tough capital standards sought by the administration and ultimately adopted by Congress. He succeeded in his own efforts to increase civil and criminal penalties for banking law violations. And he made the rhetorical case for adding the cost of the bailout directly to the budget, in direct opposition to the administration.

Schumer was also in top form during the widely publicized 1989 Banking Committee investigation of influence peddling at the Department of Housing and Urban Development. When former Interior Secretary James Watt testified about his $420,000 consulting fee, a disgusted Schumer asked, "Was it moral, what you did? ... Were you lured by the crumbs of subsidies? Were you? Everyone else in this room sees the hypocrisy of what you've done."

Before Schumer rotated off the Budget Committee at the start of the 102nd Congress, he helped establish an aggressive faction of liberals that became a force to be reckoned with, particularly in keeping social programs from bearing the brunt of spending cuts. For a city slicker, Schumer has earned a reputation as a knowledgeable and articulate critic of arcane farm law. During consideration of the 1990 farm bill, Schumer and conservative Texas Republican Dick Armey led a coalition of urban liberals and free-market conservatives who waged war on waste and inequity in federal farm programs. While their more ambitious cutback legislation failed, 159-263, their efforts did lead the Agriculture Committee to exercise spending restraint in drafting the farm bill.

After leaving Budget, Schumer took a temporary seat on Interior, where he was not much in evidence. He left that spot in the 103rd to join the Foreign Affairs Committee, where he will be one of the most visible defenders of Israel in the House.

At Home: Schumer began his political career as a state Assembly aide to Brooklyn Democrat Stephen J. Solarz, who moved to the House in 1974. After winning three Assembly terms on his own, Schumer also won a House seat in 1980 and renewed his alliance with Solarz.

However, by the end of the 1980s, Schumer and Solarz were rivals for local and national political stature. Their relationship was further undercut by speculation that the two might be thrown together in the redistricting that would follow the 1990 reapportionment, in which New York ultimately would lose three seats. Untested at the polls over the decade in their heavily Democratic districts, both Schumer and Solarz piled up more than $2 million in campaign funds in case they were matched up in 1992.

But the face-off never came to pass. The state Legislature did enact a plan that dismembered Solarz' former 13th District, and part of his constituency was placed in the new 9th, where Schumer planned to run. But Schumer had a substantial territorial advantage there, and Solarz opted instead for a major gamble: He ran in the newly created Hispanic-majority 12th.

It was an ill-fated decision. Despite his huge financial advantage, Solarz could not overcome the sentiment among Hispanic voters that he was an interloper: He lost a six-way primary to Puerto Rican activist Nydia M. Velázquez.

Schumer made out much better. The new 9th maintained his largely Jewish turf in southeast Brooklyn. The strangely shaped district also annexed a swatch of central Queens, but it was a Democratic-leaning area not unlike his base.

Schumer's large campaign bankroll and track record of political success further helped ward off opposition. He faced no major-party challenger in either the primary or general elections, winning a seventh term with nearly 90 percent over a Conservative Party candidate.

The 1992 campaign marked the second time Schumer had dodged a redistricting-related matchup with Solarz. The first came in 1982, when freshman Schumer first faced reelection. Even then, the more senior Solarz got the short end, but that time he survived. Schumer was given a comfortable district; Solarz's district was merged with that of scandal-plagued Democratic Rep. Fred Richmond, who then retired.

Schumer came to the House as the successor to Democratic Rep. Elizabeth Holtzman, who was engaged in what would be an unsuccessful Senate campaign. A liberal who had a voter base in his Assembly district, front-runner Schumer had Holtzman's endorsement.

To win his House seat, Schumer had to beat two more conservative candidates in the Democratic primary. Theodore Silverman attracted Orthodox Jewish support with his stand in favor of the death penalty; Susan Alter criticized Schumer for not fighting hard enough against pornography. But Schumer had the best organization, and he won centrist support and an endorsement from Mayor Edward I. Koch. He took almost 60 percent of the vote, and sailed through the general election.

After clearing the redistricting hurdle in 1982, Schumer won 72 percent in 1984. Even that landslide figure would turn out to be his career low.

His strength at home and rising prominence in Washington have led some to speculate on Schumer's potential as a statewide candidate. Should Schumer entertain an opportunity to run for higher office at a future date, though, he may find himself handicapped by the lack of coverage that local television stations give to individual House members in the crowded New York City media market. Comparing New York members with those from broader geographical areas who dominate their media markets, Schumer has said, "Local television is a far less important part of our lives."

Schumer added that most New York-area members are lucky to get on local TV twice a year. But unlike most of his metropolitan colleagues, Schumer has made up some of the media deficit by availing himself of frequent opportunities to appear on national television.

Committees

Banking, Finance & Urban Affairs (5th of 30 Democrats)
Financial Institutions Supervision, Regulation & Deposit Insurance; Housing & Community Development

Foreign Affairs (11th of 27 Democrats)
Economic Policy, Trade & the Environment; Europe & the Middle East

Judiciary (10th of 21 Democrats)
Crime & Criminal Justice (chairman); International Law, Immigration & Refugees

Elections

1992 General		
Charles E. Schumer (D, L)	116,545	(89%)
Alice E. Gaffney (C)	14,985	(11%)
1990 General		
Charles E. Schumer (D, L)	61,468	(80%)
Patrick J. Kinsella (R, C)	14,963	(20%)

Previous Winning Percentages: **1988** (78%) **1986** (93%) **1984** (72%) **1982** (79%) **1980** (77%)

District Vote for President

	1992	
D	121,110	(59%)
R	66,917	(33%)
I	17,574	(9%)

Campaign Finance

	Receipts	Receipts from PACs		Expend-itures
1992				
Schumer (D)	$923,272	$187,114	(20%)	$387,059
1990				
Schumer (D)	$819,952	$163,612	(20%)	$93,863

Key Votes

1993	
Require parental notification of minors' abortions	N
Require unpaid family and medical leave	Y
Approve national "motor voter" registration bill	Y
Approve budget increasing taxes and reducing deficit	Y
Approve economic stimulus plan	Y
1992	
Approve balanced-budget constitutional amendment	N
Close down space station program	Y
Approve U.S. aid for former Soviet Union	Y
Allow shifting funds from defense to domestic programs	Y
1991	
Extend unemployment benefits using deficit financing	Y
Approve waiting period for handgun purchases	Y
Authorize use of force in Persian Gulf	N

Voting Studies

	Presidential Support		Party Unity		Conservative Coalition	
Year	**S**	**O**	**S**	**O**	**S**	**O**
1992	18	76	90	5	13	81
1991	28	70	89	6	19	78
1990	19	78	89	6	6	89
1989	26	70	91	2	10	88
1988	20	77	90	5	5	92
1987	18	76	88	4	9	86
1986	17	78	88	5	14	82
1985	28	64	84	7	7	84
1984	29	68	87	6	3	93
1983	23	73	89	5	13	84
1982	29	64	91	4	7	92
1981	30	67	83	11	12	83

Interest Group Ratings

Year	ADA	AFL-CIO	CCUS	ACU
1992	95	82	25	0
1991	85	92	20	0
1990	94	92	21	4
1989	95	100	30	0
1988	100	86	36	4
1987	88	81	21	9
1986	85	86	29	5
1985	90	93	32	14
1984	90	83	33	4
1983	85	100	25	0
1982	95	100	16	0
1981	100	93	6	0

10 Edolphus Towns (D)

Of Brooklyn — Elected 1982; 6th Term

Born: July 21, 1934, Chadbourn, N.C.
Education: North Carolina A&T State U., B.S. 1956; Adelphi U., M.S.W. 1973.
Military Service: Army, 1956-58.
Occupation: Professor; hospital administrator.
Family: Wife, Gwendolyn Forbes; two children.
Religion: Independent Baptist.
Political Career: Brooklyn Borough deputy president, 1976-82.
Capitol Office: 2232 Rayburn Bldg. 20515; 225-5936.

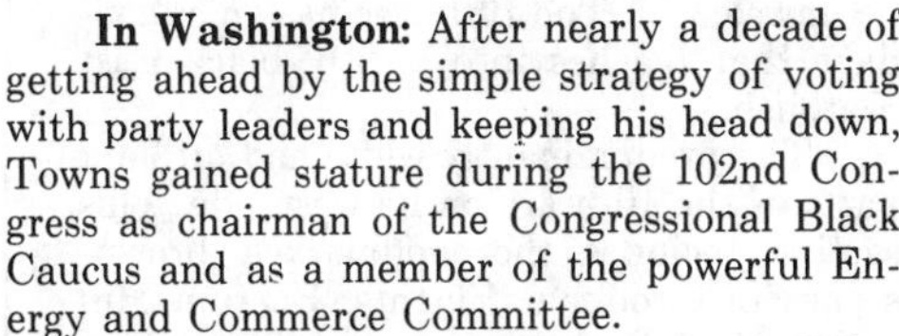

In Washington: After nearly a decade of getting ahead by the simple strategy of voting with party leaders and keeping his head down, Towns gained stature during the 102nd Congress as chairman of the Congressional Black Caucus and as a member of the powerful Energy and Commerce Committee.

But if his career was seen in a new light, the House bank scandal added an unwelcome glare: With 408 overdrafts on his record, Towns was cited by the House ethics panel as having abused banking privileges. But in 1993, Towns received a letter from federal authorities informing him the investigation into his accounts had been closed.

As caucus chairman, Towns worked to help Bill Clinton mend fences with congressional blacks before the Democratic National Convention. Towns hosted a meeting in June 1992 between the apparent Democratic nominee and caucus members. Although the meeting covered many topics, it took place amid tension engendered by Clinton's criticism of black rapper Sister Souljah for her racially inflammatory views and his implicit criticism of Jesse Jackson for giving her a public platform. After the meeting, however, many caucus members declared their support.

The overdraft issue did not appear to hurt Towns at home. He said that a receptionist in his office embezzled $28,000 from his account to support a drug habit and hid his accounts. "I was the victim," Towns argued. Publicity from the incident, however, combined with 1991 news reports that the Congressional Black Caucus had used funds from the office account of a retiring member to pay delinquent taxes, contributed to a perception that Towns and the caucus should have been paying closer attention to their financial affairs.

While the chairmanship increased Towns' visibility, critics say Towns failed to do the same for the caucus, at least in any positive way. Now that the membership has grown from 26 to 40, some expect Towns to fade into the background again while his successor, Kweisi Mfume, D-Md., works to make the most of the increased black presence on Capitol Hill.

Despite his junior status on the Energy and Commerce panel, Towns was appointed to the conference committee on the national energy bill in the 102nd Congress, an apparent reward for loyalty to Chairman John D. Dingell of Michigan.

Towns' legislative agenda reflects his liberal background and the interests of his urban district. He has pushed for Medicaid coverage for drug and alcohol treatment for pregnant women, and for higher reimbursement rates for non-physicians, such as nurse midwives and physician's assistants, as a way to improve access to health care in poor communities.

During debate over the 1991 civil rights bill, Towns teamed up with Patricia Schroeder, D-Colo., in an unsuccessful effort to eliminate caps on punitive damages for cases dealing with sex discrimination and certain cases of religious bias. Early in the 103rd, Towns sponsored a measure to bar discrimination on the basis of "affectional or sexual orientation."

But some of Towns' votes belie his liberal label and confound those who support his work to improve the health of poor and minority citizens. He is considered a reliable vote for the tobacco industry (he was born and raised in North Carolina). Critics also saw him working within the Energy panel's Health and Environment Subcommittee to weaken proposed regulations aimed at reducing the levels of toxic lead in drinking water, homes and schools.

Towns maintained that the strong regulations lacked the votes to prevail as written and that he had been working with subcommittee Chairman Henry A. Waxman, D-Calif., to work out a compromise between those who supported the regulations and those who believed they would unduly burden large cities. Towns has also opposed stricter auto emissions standards, despite their popularity in some quarters of New York, endearing himself to Chairman Dingell of Detroit.

Votes such as these prompted one col-

New York 10

Parts of Brooklyn — Bedford-Stuyvesant; Brooklyn Heights

During the 1980s, Democrat Towns represented a Brooklyn district in which blacks made up just a plurality of the population; a large Hispanic constituency composed a competing power bloc. But in the 1992 redistricting, many of these Hispanic constituents were drawn off into the new Hispanic-majority 12th District, which forms the western and northern borders of the 10th.

Now blacks make up more than three-fifths of the 10th's population; non-Hispanic whites and Hispanics are roughly one-fifth each. This breakdown appears enough to ensure the election of a black representative. In 1992, Towns faced a primary challenge from Susan Alter, a white city councilwoman with a largely black constituency. Towns won with 62 percent of the vote.

If there is political action here, it is almost certain to be in the Democratic primary. More than 80 percent of the 10th's registered voters are Democrats. Towns had no GOP opponent in the general election; Bill Clinton cleaned up, winning 83 percent.

The district is roughly the shape of an upside-down U. It runs from just inside Brooklyn's industrial waterfront along New York Bay to the Queens border and the shores of Jamaica Bay. Connecting the east and west parts of the district is Atlantic Avenue, one of Brooklyn's main east-west thoroughfares and commercial corridors.

In the central part of the district is Bedford-Stuyvesant, a mainly low-income black area. Once a well-off white area, "Bed-Stuy" has long since been a minority ghetto. Though troubles still abound, the community has been a target for economic revival efforts since the 1960s, when Sen. Robert F. Kennedy promoted an urban industrial park regarded as a forerunner of the "enterprise zone" concept.

To the east is the even more devastated part of East New York, which has one of New York City's highest murder rates. The 10th then follows Pennsylvania Avenue south to the Belt Parkway and Jamaica Bay. Nearby is Starrett City, a high-rise apartment complex that is racially integrated. But there are parts of working-class Canarsie, which has a large Italian-American population, where blacks are known to be unwelcome. The 10th also has an appendage that reaches into mostly black East Flatbush.

The predominantly white and affluent parts of the 10th are on its west side. This section includes the landmarked brownstones of Brooklyn Heights, Boerum Hill and part of Park Slope, and middle-class, Italian-American Carroll Gardens. Much of Brooklyn's civic life — including Borough Hall, its court houses, St. Francis College and the Brooklyn campus of Long Island University — is here.

The biggest problem here is the district's aging infrastructure. One of the oldest areas of the city, its water and sewer lines are prone to collapse. Heavy truck traffic is eroding the Brooklyn-Queens Expressway and residential streets leading up to the Brooklyn and Manhattan bridges (located in the 12th District, which hugs the waterfront).

1990 Population: 580,335. White 155,496 (27%), Black 352,521 (61%), Other 72,318 (12%). Hispanic origin 114,153 (20%). 18 and over 414,607 (71%), 62 and over 69,073 (12%). Median age: 30.

league to say of Towns, "He's the special interests' best friend."

Towns has shown continued interest in college athletics and the rights of student athletes, the scene of his one high-profile legislative success, passage of the Student Athlete Right to Know Act. Towns worked with two former professional basketball players, then-Rep. Tom McMillen, D-Md., and Senate cosponsor Bill Bradley, D-N.J., in helping to enact the law requiring colleges to provide information about the graduation rates of their scholarship athletes. In the 102nd Congress, Towns filed a bill to require the National Collegiate Athletic Association to afford due process to coaches and players affected by the association's regulatory activities.

At Home: After winning a 1982 primary in a newly drawn, majority-minority district (then the 11th), Towns settled in for a decade of political quiet. Towns' calm was disrupted in 1992, when Democratic City Council member Susan D. Alter staged a primary challenge in the redrawn and renumbered 10th District.

A 12-year city council incumbent, Alter — who in 1980 lost a primary for an open House seat — touted her record on community level issues. She argued that Towns was too busy cultivating special interest contacts as an Energy and Commerce member, and assailed Towns for being high on the House bank overdraft list.

Before the 1992 election, redistricting had boosted the district's black population share to 61 percent. Alter, who is white, dealt with the demographics by emphasizing that she represented a black-majority council district.

But most of the 10th's black leaders stuck with Towns; some challenged Alter's decision to run in a district drawn to preserve black representation. Towns won with 62 percent of the vote, more than doubling Alter's total. The November result was, as usual, a foregone conclusion.

If the remap of 1992 caused him some discomfort, Towns had the remap of 1982 to thank for paving his way into the House. New York's Legislature wanted to make the 11th a largely Hispanic district, but black Democrats in Brooklyn objected to the plan and the Justice Department ultimately threw it out. The final version, creating a constituency almost evenly split between blacks and Hispanics, was much more congenial to Towns.

The new district included some Brooklyn territory that had been represented by white Democratic Rep. Frederick W. Richmond. But Richmond, who had been indicted (and later was convicted) of income-tax evasion and marijuana possession, resigned from the House in 1982.

A social worker who served as deputy Brooklyn borough president, Towns bid for the open 11th and attracted support from both party regulars and a rival faction calling for reform. Towns fended off two Hispanic primary contenders to win with 50 percent. He easily won in November, setting a pattern of general election landslides in the Democratic stronghold. After his comfortable 1984 victory over another Hispanic Democrat, Towns got a pass in the primary in every re-election cycle until 1992.

Committees

Energy & Commerce (18th of 27 Democrats)
Commerce, Consumer Protection & Competitiveness; Health & the Environment

Government Operations (9th of 25 Democrats)
Human Resources & Intergovernmental Relations (chairman); Environment, Energy & Natural Resources

Elections

1992 General		
Edolphus Towns (D, L)	97,509	(96%)
Owen Augustin (C)	4,315	(4%)
1992 Primary		
Edolphus Towns (D)	33,490	(62%)
Susan D. Alter (D)	15,207	(28%)
Frank R. Seddio (D)	5,078	(9%)
1990 General		
Edolphus Towns (D, L)	36,286	(93%)
Ernest Johnson (C)	1,676	(4%)
Lorraine Stevens (NA)	1,094	(3%)

Previous Winning Percentages: **1988** (89%) **1986** (89%) **1984** (85%) **1982** (84%)

District Vote for President

1992

D 125,206 (83%)
R 19,177 (13%)
I 5,711 (4%)

Campaign Finance

	Receipts	Receipts from PACs	Expend-itures
1992			
Towns (D)	$560,977	$241,165 (43%)	$699,589
1990			
Towns (D)	$335,807	$186,250 (55%)	$282,933

Key Votes

1993	
Require parental notification of minors' abortions	N
Require unpaid family and medical leave	Y
Approve national "motor voter" registration bill	Y
Approve budget increasing taxes and reducing deficit	Y
Approve economic stimulus plan	Y
1992	
Approve balanced-budget constitutional amendment	N
Close down space station program	?
Approve U.S. aid for former Soviet Union	N
Allow shifting funds from defense to domestic programs	Y
1991	
Extend unemployment benefits using deficit financing	Y
Approve waiting period for handgun purchases	Y
Authorize use of force in Persian Gulf	N

Voting Studies

	Presidential Support		Party Unity		Conservative Coalition	
Year	**S**	**O**	**S**	**O**	**S**	**O**
1992	11	64	70	4	10	60
1991	21	69	83	3	3	86
1990	11	82	88	4	6	93
1989	19	67	83	1	0	95
1988	13	71	76	2	0	76
1987	14	77	80	1	2	86
1986	14	77	81	4	8	86
1985	11	75	81	3	2	87
1984	18	69	78	4	3	86
1983	12	87	90	2	7	89

Interest Group Ratings

Year	ADA	AFL-CIO	CCUS	ACU
1992	80	82	14	0
1991	90	100	13	0
1990	94	100	31	4
1989	90	100	33	0
1988	90	100	33	0
1987	92	100	0	0
1986	95	100	15	0
1985	95	93	15	5
1984	85	100	36	5
1983	95	100	25	0

New York - 11th District

11 Major R. Owens (D)

Of Brooklyn — Elected 1982; 6th Term

Born: June 28, 1936, Memphis, Tenn.
Education: Morehouse College, B.A. 1956; Atlanta U., M.L.S. 1957.
Occupation: Librarian.
Family: Wife, Maria Cuprill; five children.
Religion: Baptist.
Political Career: N.Y. Senate, 1975-83.
Capitol Office: 2305 Rayburn Bldg. 20515; 225-6231.

In Washington: If Owens ran the country, it would look something like this: Every American would be guaranteed a job, and spanking children would be outlawed. There would be few guns, because the Second Amendment — the right to bear arms — would be repealed. The government would spend hundreds of billions of dollars more on social programs, and the nation's borders would be open to Haitian refugees, among others.

Owens' responsibilities in Congress are considerably more limited than his objectives and ideals. But this does not dampen his liberal convictions or his efforts. Owens, a dependable Democratic vote, is passionate, and sometimes even belligerent, about issues affecting people he believes are oppressed or discriminated against.

According to a survey by the the National Taxpayers Union Foundation, which tracks the cost of bills in Congress, Owens ranked first on a list of the institution's biggest potential spenders. By this group's calculations, Owens' bills call for spending a total of $425 billion.

Although many of his pricier or more revolutionary initiatives are quickly stalled, the Education and Labor Subcommittee on Select Education and Civil Rights, which he chairs, has successfully taken on relatively minor proposals on the rights of children and those with disabilities. There, he works alongside his wife Maria Cuprill, who is the subcommittee's staff director.

In the 102nd Congress, Owens sponsored legislation to authorize early education for children with disabilities. He also pushed a bill that would expand grants to states for programs serving victims of domestic violence and their children. Both measures stalled at the end of the session as time ran out.

Owens did push through legislation that would reauthorize grants to states to maximize job opportunities for the disabled. It would authorize funding for independent living centers, rehabilitative training centers, and employment, transportation and technical assistance programs. Another successful Owens initiative reauthorized funding for education of the deaf.

Owens is reserved and sometimes gruff, but he is a diligent legislator capable of impassioned oratory in defense of causes important to his poor, mostly black, district. He has even brought the rhythm of the streets to Congress, expressing his frustration through rap music. During the 1990 budget-summit talks between the White House and congressional leaders, the Congressional Record reported his lyrics: "At the big white D.C. mansion/There's a meeting of the mob/And the question on the table/Is which beggars will they rob."

Owens says he likes rap for the same reasons it has mass appeal. "Rap is a way that angry young men are getting things off their chest," he says. "So it seemed a good way to get some things off my chest."

Owens had been angry on the floor before. When the House approved the 1989 minimum wage bill with a subminimum wage, Owens said that the latter would create a class of "peons or serfs or simply slave workers."

In 1992, he blasted President Bush's policy of repatriating Haitian boat people intercepted at sea without first giving them a chance to apply for political asylum, calling it a "David Duke immigration policy."

At the beginning of the 103rd Congress, he was also critical of President Clinton's decision to continue Bush's Haiti policy, although he was not as vitriolic about it.

While many of Owens' ambitious goals have stalled in recent years, he has made a name on Education and Labor as an advocate for the disabled. After he failed to win support for a 5 percent set-aside in the Vocational Education Act for disabled students, the 1990 enactment of the Americans with Disabilities Act achieved many of his goals. The bill authorized programs to help preschoolers, train teachers and develop technologies to help the disabled.

Owens guided the bill to passage as chairman of the Select Education Subcommittee, making productive use of the panel's somewhat narrow scope. In the 101st Congress, he cleared the way for the federal volunteer agency AC-

New York 11

Central Brooklyn — Flatbush; Crown Heights; Brownsville

The concentration of black residents in the central core of Brooklyn allowed House mapmakers to construct the 11th as a rather compact district; its minority majority is one of the largest of any of the House districts. More than two-thirds of the 11th's residents are non-Hispanic blacks, with Hispanics topping 10 percent; non-Hispanic whites make up less than a fifth of the population.

The 11th follows the overwhelmingly Democratic pattern of minority-dominated districts nationwide. More than 80 percent of the registered voters are Democrats. In 1992, Democratic Rep. Owens ran without Republican opposition (as he had in the 1990 general election). Bill Clinton ran up 87 percent of the vote here; George Bush got 10 percent.

The heart of the 11th is Flatbush. Through the years immediately after World War II, this was a mainly white, working-class area whose residents identified with such early TV characters as the Kramdens (of "The Honeymooners" fame) and the Goldbergs.

Today, Flatbush has a sizable black plurality and a number of Hispanics; much of the white population (about a third of Flatbush's total) is elderly. Though there is some poverty, this remains a working-class area, as does much of adjacent, predominantly black East Flatbush. A large medical complex that includes Kings County Hospital, Kingsbrook Jewish Medical Center and the State University of New York Health Sciences Center is in Flatbush.

To the north, across Eastern Parkway, is Crown Heights, where a black majority and a Hasidic Jewish community have a tense relationship. When the car of an assistant to an orthodox rabbi struck and killed a black child in 1991, rioting broke out, and a Jewish theological student was killed.

Ebbets Field, the home of baseball's Brooklyn Dodgers, was in Crown Heights. The team's departure for Los Angeles after the 1957 season deprived the borough of much of its national identity. The stadium site is now a housing project.

At the eastern extreme of the 11th is Brownsville, its most economically troubled community. More than 40 percent of its residents are on some kind of government income support, nearly a third on public assistance.

However, the rapid depopulation that occurred during the 1970s was reversed in the last decade, in part because of an influx of immigrants from the Caribbean, including many Jamaicans, Haitians and Guyanans. (West Indians have also located in many other black communities in the 11th.)

Much of the district's white population lives on its west side, in heavily Jewish, middle-class Kensington and Midwood and in well-to-do Park Slope.

Such attractions as the Brooklyn Museum, Botanical Garden and Academy of Music are in this west section, which rims sprawling Prospect Park (mostly in the 9th District).

1990 Population: 580,337. White 108,289 (19%), Black 429,728 (74%), Other 42,320 (7%). Hispanic origin 67,014 (12%). 18 and over 414,564 (71%), 62 and over 60,151 (10%). Median age: 31.

TION to be reauthorized and for wide-ranging reforms in the VISTA program. Congress also approved Owens' relatively modest proposals for programs assisting abused and disabled children.

The only trained librarian in Congress, Owens regularly emphasizes the importance of libraries. He also works to protect funding for historically black colleges and aid for poor students. Sometimes Owens draws on his library background for non-book issues. During one committee session, he suggested that a variation of the Dewey Decimal System be used on child-welfare program information.

In the 102nd Congress, Owens' name appeared on a list of members with overdrafts at the House bank. However, his 48 overdrafts were never an issue back home, where he won re-election with 94 percent of the vote.

At Home: Owens cofounded the black "reform" faction of the Brooklyn Democratic Party, and his 1982 primary victory over an organization stalwart testified to the movement's progress.

A community organizer in Brooklyn's economically depressed Brownsville section in the mid-1960s, Owens was tapped by Mayor John V. Lindsay to head New York City's Community Development Agency.

In 1974, Owens made his first bid for elective office. Leading a slate of candidates opposing incumbents backed by the Brooklyn Democratic machine, he won a state Senate seat that he held for eight years.

When Owens set his sights on the House in 1982, he faced a tough opponent, state Sen.

Vander Beatty, who as deputy Democratic leader in the state Senate had built a patronage empire in the Brooklyn black community. But Owens capitalized on Beatty's unsavory connections: A longtime Beatty ally, former City Councilman Samuel Wright, was convicted of extortion and conspiracy in 1978. Owens emphasized his own reputation for honesty and his scandal-free tenure as community development chief. He won by a narrow margin.

Beatty challenged the result, accusing Owens' forces of forging signatures on voter registration cards. Although an acting state Supreme Court judge in Brooklyn ordered a second vote, Owens ultimately triumphed in the New York Court of Appeals, which canceled the rerun and cleared his path to Congress.

Since then, Owens has faced only one foe of note. In the 1986 primary, he met Congress of Racial Equality Chairman Roy Innis, who had drawn attention with his brashly conservative stands against crime. Owens romped to victory.

Republicans have never posed a threat to Owens, whose solidly Democratic district has more African-Americans than any other in New York. In the last two elections, Owens has had no GOP opponent.

Owens' actor son Geoffrey is also in the public eye. He had a recurring role on TV's long-running "The Cosby Show."

Committees

Education & Labor (8th of 28 Democrats)
Select Education and Civil Rights (chairman); Elementary, Secondary & Vocational Education; Human Resources; Labor-Management Relations

Government Operations (8th of 25 Democrats)
Government Information, Justice, Transportation & Agriculture

Elections

1992 General		
Major R. Owens (D, L)	80,028	(94%)
Michael Gaffney (C)	4,287	(5%)
Ernest N. Foster (NA)	1,179	(1%)
1990 General		
Major R. Owens (D, L)	40,570	(95%)
Joseph Caesar (C)	1,159	(3%)
Mamie Moore (NA)	1,021	(2%)

Previous Winning Percentages: **1988** (93%) **1986** (91%) **1984** (91%) **1982** (91%)

District Vote for President

1992
D 104,678 (87%)
R 11,709 (10%)
I 3,916 (3%)

Campaign Finance

	Receipts	Receipts from PACs	Expend-itures
1992			
Owens (D)	$173,365	$89,972 (52%)	$177,235
1990			
Owens (D)	$161,086	$111,525 (69%)	$172,498

Key Votes

1993	
Require parental notification of minors' abortions	N
Require unpaid family and medical leave	Y
Approve national "motor voter" registration bill	Y
Approve budget increasing taxes and reducing deficit	Y
Approve economic stimulus plan	Y
1992	
Approve balanced-budget constitutional amendment	N
Close down space station program	Y
Approve U.S. aid for former Soviet Union	N
Allow shifting funds from defense to domestic programs	Y
1991	
Extend unemployment benefits using deficit financing	Y
Approve waiting period for handgun purchases	Y
Authorize use of force in Persian Gulf	N

Voting Studies

	Presidential Support		Party Unity		Conservative Coalition	
Year	**S**	**O**	**S**	**O**	**S**	**O**
1992	11	85	89	4	6	92
1991	21	77	87	3	0	97
1990	12	80	86	3	2	93
1989	21	70	91	1	2	93
1988	13	73	79	3	3	79
1987	9	85	88	3	7	88
1986	11	83	89	2	6	90
1985	16	76	86	1	4	82
1984	18	78	90	4	3	93
1983	12	77	79	2	6	78

Interest Group Ratings

Year	ADA	AFL-CIO	CCUS	ACU
1992	85	92	13	0
1991	100	100	11	0
1990	94	100	29	4
1989	100	100	20	4
1988	95	100	15	0
1987	100	100	0	0
1986	95	93	20	0
1985	95	100	14	0
1984	90	100	44	5
1983	85	100	26	0

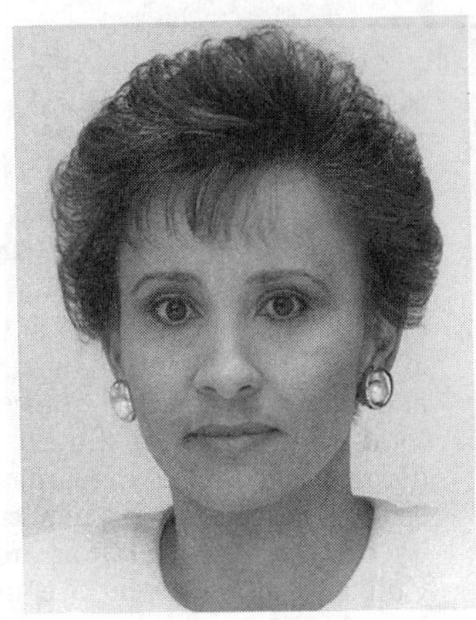

12 Nydia M. Velázquez (D)

Of Brooklyn — Elected 1992; 1st Term

Born: March 22, 1953, Yabucoa, Puerto Rico.
Education: U. of Puerto Rico, B.A. 1974; New York U., M.A. 1976.
Occupation: Professor.
Family: Divorced.
Religion: Roman Catholic.
Political Career: Appointed to N.Y. City Council, 1984; defeated for election to N.Y. City Council, 1984.
Capitol Office: 132 Cannon Bldg. 20515; 225-2361.

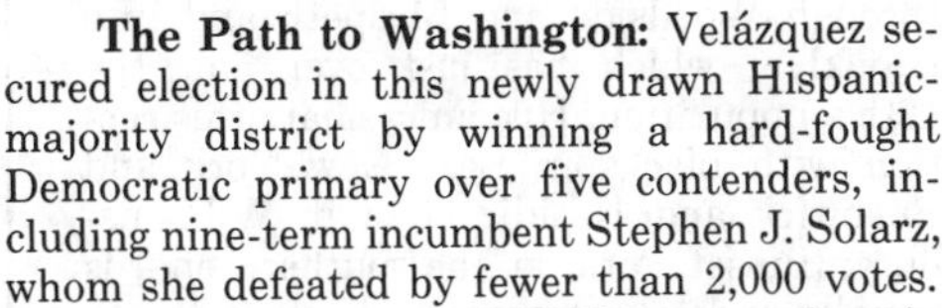

The Path to Washington: Velázquez secured election in this newly drawn Hispanic-majority district by winning a hard-fought Democratic primary over five contenders, including nine-term incumbent Stephen J. Solarz, whom she defeated by fewer than 2,000 votes.

The victory assured Velázquez a place in history as the first Puerto Rican woman in Congress. A liaison between the Puerto Rican government and Latino communities in the United States from 1986 until her election, she plans to continue to work for the constituencies she has focused on during her public career — Hispanics, women and the poor.

Velázquez serves on the Banking, Finance and Urban Affairs, and Small Business committees. She planned to focus on educational issues, including reducing the school dropout rate and developing measures to ensure safety in public schools.

Born in the sugar cane farming region of Puerto Rico, Velázquez was the first member of her family to earn a high school diploma. She became the first Hispanic woman to serve on the New York City Council.

But her local name recognition grew dramatically shortly before her 1992 race, when she ran a Hispanic voter registration effort financed by the Puerto Rican government. She contended that the effort registered 200,000 voters nationwide, but critics said she targeted the Brooklyn sections that later became part of her congressional district.

Her biggest obstacle was Solarz, whose district had been dismantled in redistricting. Solarz decided to run for re-election in the redrawn 12th District, and many in the Hispanic community complained that it was unfair for a powerful, well-financed white candidate to run in a district specifically carved to expand Hispanic representation in Congress. Solarz's former district had encompassed predominantly Jewish sections of Brooklyn.

Solarz targeted his advertising to the Hispanic media, hired Hispanic advisers and learned a few Spanish phrases. But as an unknown to many of his would-be constituents, he was branded as a carpetbagger and wealthy outsider.

Velázquez, if the local favorite, was not the only Latino candidate. With four other Hispanics in the primary, many predicted that Solarz would benefit from a fractious community that could not unite behind any one candidate.

But Velázquez won the primary, all but ensuring election in a district that is 58 percent Hispanic and nearly three-quarters Democratic.

She then found herself on the defensive again after an anonymous source faxed to news organizations hospital records showing that she had attempted suicide in 1991. The records also revealed that she had been battling depression with alcohol and pills.

"It was a sad and painful experience for me — and one I thought was now in the past," she said at a news conference in Brooklyn at the time. Friends said her depression stemmed from being torn between duty to her ailing parents in Puerto Rico and her work with the New York Hispanic community. She said counseling had helped her overcome her depression.

Velázquez also faced attacks from some in New York's Puerto Rican community, who branded her as an outsider who did not understand the problems of Puerto Ricans born in the United States. She also faced accusations by others in the community that she was merely a puppet of the Puerto Rican government.

She spent most of her general-election campaign answering her critics. "There are people who just cannot accept that I have won," she told The New York Times.

In the end, she defeated Republican Angel Diaz with 77 percent of vote. Two minor candidates were not factors.

With almost $300,000 in campaign debt, the fourth-highest of any freshman House member, however, Velázquez has been unable to leave the difficult campaign season behind her. To help offset the debt, she took in more than $63,000 in political action committee money, more than all but two other House freshmen, in the two months after the election.

New York 12

Lower East Side of Manhattan; parts of Brooklyn and Queens

One certainty of New York's most recent redistricting was that a second Hispanic-majority district would be created. As a result of an ongoing influx that began just after World War II, Hispanic population had grown to nearly a quarter of the city's total. Yet only the South Bronx House district had sent a Hispanic to Congress.

The execution of a new Hispanic-majority district, however, was no easy matter. Unlike blacks — who are mainly in large concentrations — Hispanic immigrants had located in disparate low- and middle-income communities scattered across the city's five boroughs. The mapmakers had to go block-by-block to build a district that could reasonably assure a Hispanic's election. The result was the 12th, one of the most unusually shaped House districts in the nation's history. It follows a wildly meandering path through parts of three New York City boroughs: Queens, Brooklyn and Manhattan.

Along with its geographic sampling, the 12th also has an ethnic variety that the generic term Hispanic — which applies to nearly three-fifths of the district's residents — fails to capture. Puerto Ricans, by far the largest single group, make up nearly half the Hispanic population. The other groups came from Mexico, the Caribbean, Central America and South America.

The district's design had its desired effect in 1992: Democrat Velázquez, a Puerto Rican activist, won out over a crowded Democratic primary field that included non-Hispanic Democratic Rep. Stephen J. Solarz. She then easily won the general election in this overwhelmingly Democratic district. But voter participation in the 12th is greatly dampened by such factors as recent immigration status and poverty. While most New York House districts had turnouts of more than 200,000 voters, fewer than 75,000 cast ballots for the 12th District seat.

The district's northeastern terminus is well into Queens (the borough has slightly more than a quarter of the population). The district's parts of Jackson Heights, Corona and Elmhurst are largely Hispanic (many residents are of South American origin).

The district then moves southwest through Woodside and Maspeth and into Brooklyn, which has just over half the 12th's population. Hispanics share this section with blacks in East New York and Bushwick and Hasidic Jews in Williamsburg; Sunset Park, at the southern end, is racially and ethnically mixed.

From there, the 12th crosses the East River — on the Brooklyn and Manhattan bridges and the Brooklyn-Battery Tunnel — to Manhattan's Lower East Side. There is a mainly low-income Hispanic concentration in "Alphabet City," where the streets have letter names — Avenue A, Avenue B. But the Manhattan portion (about a fifth of the district), is the only one where Hispanics are in the minority. Asians are the largest racial group; the district takes in most of Chinatown. There are also remnants of the Lower East Side's once-teeming Jewish population.

1990 Population: 580,340. White 196,368 (34%), Black 79,265 (14%), Other 304,707 (53%). Hispanic origin 335,817 (58%). 18 and over 417,933 (72%), 62 and over 60,819 (10%). Median age: 30.

Committees

Banking, Finance & Urban Affairs (23rd of 30 Democrats)
Consumer Credit & Insurance; Economic Growth; General Oversight, Investigations & the Resolution of Failed Financial Institutions; Housing & Community Development

Small Business (17th of 27 Democrats)
Minority Enterprise, Finance & Urban Development

Campaign Finance

1992	Receipts	Receipts from PACs		Expenditures
Velázquez (D)	$480,174	$155,000	(32%)	$461,749
Franco (L)	$88,971	0		$85,840
Diaz (R)	$5,300	0		$5,390

Key Votes

1993

Require parental notification of minors' abortions	N
Require unpaid family and medical leave	Y
Approve national "motor voter" registration bill	Y
Approve budget increasing taxes and reducing deficit	Y
Approve economic stimulus plan	Y

Elections

1992 General

Nydia M. Velázquez (D)	55,926	(77%)
Angel Diaz (R, C, RTL)	14,976	(20%)
Ruben Franco (L)	1,556	(2%)

1992 Primary

Nydia M. Velázquez (D)	11,007	(33%)
Stephen J. Solarz (D)	9,138	(28%)
Elizabeth Colon (D)	8,529	(26%)
Ruben Franco (D)	2,568	(8%)
Rafael Mendez (D)	1,141	(3%)
Eric Ruano Melendez (D)	847	(3%)

District Vote for President

	1992	
D	67,114	(69%)
R	25,622	(26%)
I	5,121	(5%)

13 Susan Molinari (R)

Of Staten Island — Elected 1990; 2nd Full Term

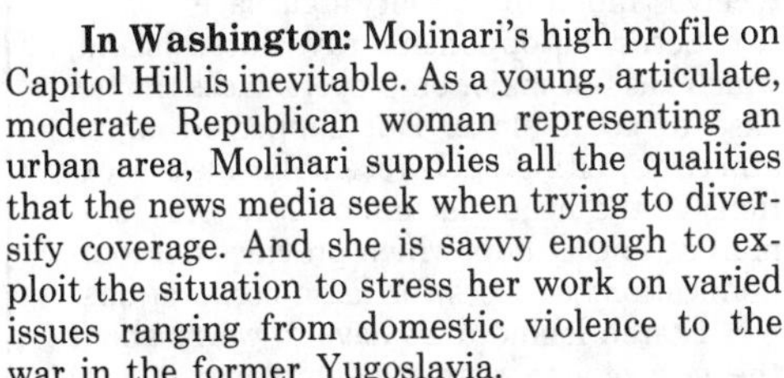

Born: March 27, 1958, Staten Island, N.Y.
Education: State U. of New York, Albany, B.A. 1980, M.A. 1982.
Occupation: Political aide.
Family: Divorced.
Religion: Roman Catholic.
Political Career: N.Y. City Council, 1985-90.
Capitol Office: 123 Cannon Bldg. 20515; 225-3371.

In Washington: Molinari's high profile on Capitol Hill is inevitable. As a young, articulate, moderate Republican woman representing an urban area, Molinari supplies all the qualities that the news media seek when trying to diversify coverage. And she is savvy enough to exploit the situation to stress her work on varied issues ranging from domestic violence to the war in the former Yugoslavia.

To many, it may seem surprising to find Molinari in the Republican fold, but to Molinari, it is home. She comes from a long line of Republican politicians: Her grandfather was a fixture in Staten Island politics, and she succeeded her father in the House. And though she espouses liberal social issues, she is conservative on many others. In the 102nd Congress, she voted against the civil rights bill and voted to oppose a ban on semi-automatic weapons (though she backed the Brady bill and its waiting period for handgun purchases).

Her rising star status in the party and on the Hill is evident in her committee assignments. On the Public Works and Transportation Committee, she is the ranking member of the Economic Development Subcommittee. And she has a seat on the Education and Labor Committee.

On Public Works, she has been a leader in the effort to close or regulate her district's Fresh Kills landfill because of past environmental problems. On the Education and Labor Committee, she has been active on issues affecting women, including strengthening laws to punish sexual and domestic violence, and helping women break through the so-called "glass ceiling" into the upper ranks of management. She introduced legislation to encourage businesses to further diversify their work forces and to create a commission to investigate sex discrimination.

Besides her committee work, Molinari has been very involved in issues concerning the war in the former Yugoslavia. Her district is made up largely of middle- and upper-middle-class "ethnics," some of whom have family ties to the war-torn region. Molinari traveled to Croatia in early 1992 and again in April 1993 and has worked to win U.S. government recognition of the republic and to facilitate aid efforts.

While Molinari was a week short of turning 32 when she won a House special election, she quickly proved herself as a legislator in 1990 when she succeeded in striking an amendment to the defense authorization bill that would have closed down the Navy homeport being built in her Staten Island district. Arguing that the facility had been unfairly singled out, Molinari lined up fellow Republicans and trumped the opposition of most of New York City's delegation, noting that Democratic Gov. Mario M. Cuomo backed the homeport. But her energy and efforts have not been enough in the face of persistent pressures to trim defense spending: The homeport showed up on the Pentagon's 1993 base-closing list.

One local movement has captured her attention: Staten Island's effort to secede from New York to become a separate city. Molinari has advocated secession, if it is economically feasible. The issue was scheduled for a Nov. 2, 1993, referendum.

Molinari's father, Guy V. Molinari, gave up the then-14th District in January 1990 after he was elected Staten Island borough president. His daughter quickly emerged as the front-runner to succeed him, in part because her political profile as a council member was much like her father's in the House. She balances her anti-crime, anti-tax conservatism with an environmentalist streak. The biggest issue difference between the two is on abortion; the younger Molinari supports abortion rights.

Although many sons have succeeded their fathers in the House, Molinari is one of few daughters to do so. Illinois Republican Winnifred Mason Huck was elected in 1922 to replace her father, William Mason, who died in midterm, but she served only that partial term. In 1992, Democrat Lucille Roybal-Allard of California joined the list; she succeeded long-time Rep. Edward R. Roybal.

Like many of the women House members, Molinari has her share of stories to tell about

New York 13

Staten Island; part of southwest Brooklyn

With Staten Island — the most suburban of the five boroughs — making up nearly two-thirds of its population, the 13th stands out among New York City's House districts. It is the only consistently Republican district in the otherwise Democratic-dominated city.

The 13th, with a working population of mainly middle- to upper-middle-class commuters, has the lowest poverty rate of any district wholly in New York City. Italian-Americans, many of them social conservatives, make up the largest ethnic group in the 13th (which also includes part of Brooklyn across the New York Bay Narrows); Irish-Americans are also a large constituency. The non-Hispanic white population is more than 85 percent; there are few minority voters to provide a Democratic base.

Although there are some Democratic pockets in the more working-class ethnic parts of Brooklyn, the district seems tailor-made for Republican Rep. Molinari. George Bush carried Staten Island (officially Richmond County) by 9 percentage points over Bill Clinton in 1992; his 48 percent there was exactly double his percentage for New York City as a whole.

If some community activists have their way, the 13th will no longer be the most Republican district in New York City — because Staten Island would no longer be part of New York City. A once-belittled movement to secede from the city has become serious: If a November 1993 referendum is approved by borough voters, a secession measure would be presented to the state Legislature.

Staten Island has always been distant, both physically and psychologically, from the rest of the city. It is the least populous of the boroughs, with about 380,000 residents, and the most remote (its only land link is the Verrazano-Narrows Bridge, opened in 1964, that connects it with Brooklyn; the Staten Island Ferry is still the only direct route to Manhattan).

Residents have become increasingly angry over the use of Staten Island as a literal dumping ground: Its Fresh Kills landfill, one of the world's largest facilities, receives much of the city's garbage.

Secession opponents say Staten Island, which has few major employers, lacks the tax base to go it alone. But supporters argue otherwise, citing such recent business locations as the headquarters of Teleport Communications Group, which provides telecommunications services for large corporations.

Staten Island does have to worry about the fate of one potential employer: a new Navy homeport. Molinari fought to preserve funding for the project, a result of the Reagan-era plan to greatly expand the U.S. naval force. But that plan has been scrapped, and the Staten Island base was placed on the preliminary 1993 base-closing list.

The Brooklyn portion of the 13th includes Bay Ridge — setting for the 1977 disco movie "Saturday Night Fever" — and part of Bensonhurst, a mainly Italian community and the site of unrest after the murder of a black youth in 1989.

1990 Population: 580,337. White 502,925 (87%), Black 32,474 (6%), Other 44,938 (8%). Hispanic origin 43,336 (7%). 18 and over 449,571 (77%), 62 and over 97,316 (17%). Median age:35.

working in a male-dominated organization. After her first speech on the House floor, addressing military base closures, the freshman Molinari heard some criticism because she wore tailored slacks instead of a skirt. And when the 103rd Congress opened, she toured the halls of Congress for a segment of "CBS This Morning" and made a point of showing how the women representatives have to use tourist bathrooms three stair flights below the House chamber.

At Home: Guy Molinari's victory for Staten Island borough president forced a special election in a House district where Democrats once were competitive. But there was little doubt that the major effect of the 14th District transition would be a change in the House nameplates to read "Ms. Molinari" rather than "Mr. Molinari."

Susan Molinari entered the House contest with huge advantages over any potential Democratic candidate. Her father blazed a path for her in the 14th, winning strongly both in his Staten Island base and in the Brooklyn part of the district. In winning two terms on the New York City Council, Molinari had established herself as a popular officeholder.

After stints with the Republican Governors' Association and the Republican National Committee, Molinari ran for the council in 1985 and won. Her status on the council was singular: She was the only Republican in the city's legislative body. Although she earned the title of minority leader by default, Molinari gained entree to the council's decision-making process and ex officio status on major committees.

Several well-known Democrats nonetheless

expressed interest in the March 1990 special election, but Democratic leaders put their muscle behind lawyer and party insider Robert Gigante. While he secured the nomination, Gigante's campaign never got off the ground. From the outset, he trailed far behind Molinari in name identification, and he lacked the financial resources to build recognition.

Hoping to make up the difference with a splash in the media, Gigante wound up splattering himself. In an early campaign forum, Gigante described himself as more typical of the district voter by noting that he and his wife had four children while Molinari, who was recently married, had none. A reporter for the Staten Island Advance then criticized the Democrat for trying to make family size a qualification for office.

Molinari won easily, taking 58 percent to Gigante's 34 percent. She won a first full term in 1990 over Democratic lawyer Anthony J. Pocchia by a similar margin. In 1992, she took 56 percent of the vote.

Committees

Education & Labor (9th of 15 Republicans)
Elementary, Secondary & Vocational Education; Human Resources

Public Works & Transportation (8th of 24 Republicans)
Economic Development (ranking); Investigations & Oversight; Water Resources & the Environment

Elections

1992 General		
Susan Molinari (R, C)	107,903	(56%)
Sal F. Albanese (D, L)	73,520	(38%)
Kathleen M. Murphy (RTL)	10,825	(6%)
1992 Primary		
Susan Molinari (R)	9,110	(71%)
Kathleen M. Murphy (R)	3,731	(29%)
1990 General		
Susan Molinari (R, C)	58,616	(60%)
Anthony J. Pocchia (D, L)	34,625	(35%)
Christine Sacchi (RTL)	4,370	(4%)

Previous Winning Percentage: 1990 * (58%)
** Special election.*

District Vote for President

1992
D 82,796 (39%)
R 100,761 (48%)
I 26,317 (13%)

Campaign Finance

	Receipts	Receipts from PACs	Expend-itures
1992			
Molinari (R)	$523,755	$195,775 (37%)	$507,962
Albanese (D)	$251,248	$94,500 (38%)	$247,739
Murphy (RTL)	$29,435	$350 (1%)	$24,514
1990			
Molinari (R)	$157,229	$71,788 (46%)	$141,216
Pocchia (D)	$35,054	$1,080 (3%)	$35,052

Key Votes

1993	
Require parental notification of minors' abortions	N
Require unpaid family and medical leave	Y
Approve national "motor voter" registration bill	N
Approve budget increasing taxes and reducing deficit	N
Approve economic stimulus plan	N
1992	
Approve balanced-budget constitutional amendment	Y
Close down space station program	Y
Approve U.S. aid for former Soviet Union	Y
Allow shifting funds from defense to domestic programs	N
1991	
Extend unemployment benefits using deficit financing	Y
Approve waiting period for handgun purchases	Y
Authorize use of force in Persian Gulf	Y

Voting Studies

	Presidential Support		Party Unity		Conservative Coalition	
Year	S	O	S	O	S	O
1992	65	33	77	21	81	19
1991	62	33	72	26	76	24
1990	56 †	44 †	70 †	28 †	79 †	19 †

† Not eligible for all recorded votes.

Interest Group Ratings

Year	ADA	AFL-CIO	CCUS	ACU
1992	35	58	88	64
1991	30	58	70	70
1990	31	40	57	57

14 Carolyn B. Maloney (D)

Of Manhattan — Elected 1992; 1st Term

Born: Feb. 19, 1948, Greensboro, N.C.
Education: Greensboro College, A.B. 1968.
Occupation: Legislative aide; teacher.
Family: Husband, Clifton H.W. Maloney; two children.
Religion: Presbyterian.
Political Career: N.Y. City Council, 1982-93.
Capitol Office: 1504 Longworth Bldg. 20515; 225-7944.

The Path to Washington: Former New York City Council member Maloney comes to Congress with commitments to help urban areas — particularly New York City — and to combat government waste, fraud and abuse.

Maloney's victory over seven-term incumbent Republican Bill Green contained many of the elements that energized voters in 1992: a female Democrat who upset a powerful, entrenched incumbent, thanks in large part to a newly drawn congressional district.

Green, an affable, liberal Republican with a liberal-leaning constituency, had defeated in the past such visible names as former Rep. Bella S. Abzug and then-Manhattan Borough President Andrew Stein. Running in the so-called Silk Stocking district, long dominated by landed Republican gentry, Green is heir to a family supermarket fortune.

Nor is Maloney a pauper, though she was vastly outspent by Green. A former teacher, Maloney's early campaign slogan "there are too many millionaires and not enough women" in the House of Representatives referred to Green and her primary challenger, real estate tycoon Abraham J. Hirschfeld. But she and her husband, a successful businessman, also are worth $3 million to $5 million, with most assets in real estate holdings, according to her financial disclosure form.

Maloney also benefited from a redrawn district that brought in Democratic Upper West Side neighborhoods in Manhattan and middle-class areas of Queens and Brooklyn.

In fact, Green edged out Maloney in Manhattan precincts, but voters in the newly added areas — which make up 20 percent of the congressional district's residents — favored Maloney by a nearly 2-to-1 margin.

Maloney also profited from a high level of name recognition as a 10-year veteran of the City Council.

In Congress, Maloney wants to revise what she sees as inequitable formulas for distributing federal funds to urban and rural areas. She points to recent reports indicating that New York pays out $33 billion more to the federal government than it takes back in aid.

She and other freshmen with urban constituencies will try to form regional coalitions that include lawmakers from cities and outlying areas.

Maloney won a seat on the Banking, Finance and Urban Affairs Committee. She also got a slot on Banking's Housing and Community Development Subcommittee, where she seeks to help increase community development and housing funds to cities, while working to facilitate lending to urban communities.

She was one of several freshmen on the Financial Institutions Subcommittee to make their mark on the drafting of the 1993 thrift bailout bill. She pressed for bill language to bar bulk sales of Resolution Trust Corporation-held real estate until smaller investors were given the opportunity to purchase individual properties.

Her other committee post, Government Operations, also is tailor-made for Maloney. She was New York City's top watchdog against government waste, having chaired the City Council's Committee on Contracts. Among her achievements was setting up a computerized tracking system that could more easily uncover wrongdoing in government contracting.

Other priorities Maloney points to include campaign finance reform and women's and children's issues. She is part of a group of freshman women who vowed to push for full funding for the Head Start children's program, protections for Capitol Hill employees from sexual harassment and abortion rights legislation.

Maloney also supports a constitutional amendment to balance the budget, deeper cuts in defense spending, and new taxes on gasoline and the wealthy as the means to bring down the federal deficit. In addition, she hopes to cut by 3 percent annually the amount spent on the administration of the federal government.

Despite this campaign theme, Maloney raised eyebrows in May 1993 by voting against President Clinton's deficit-reduction bill. She was the only New York Democrat to side with Republicans on the close, party-line vote. She said the bill relied too much on tax increases rather than spending cuts.

New York 14

East Side Manhattan; Parts of Queens and Brooklyn

A bastion of urban liberalism, the House district centered on Manhattan's East Side presented a paradox during the 1980s. Voters strongly supported all Democratic presidential candidates, including landslide losers such as Walter F. Mondale in 1984. Yet during this same period, the district sent a liberal Republican, Bill Green, to the House.

Yet even Green, who had won eight House contests, could not buck the Democratic surge in 1992. The 14th District, which backed Bill Clinton by a wide margin, also chose Democrat Maloney over Green for the House seat.

Green, in fact, was able to narrowly carry his Manhattan base (shared with then-City Council member Maloney). But he was undone by a redistricting plan that added two working-class areas, in Queens and Brooklyn, where voters had more regularly Democratic habits in House contests. Maloney's wide margins in these areas carried her to victory.

The east side of Manhattan has a Republican heritage. Known as the "Silk Stocking" district, its avenues were once lined with the mansions of Republican industrialists. (Most have long since been replaced by apartment buildings; others, such as the Frick mansion owned by a steel magnate, have been preserved as museums).

But by the 1960s, young urban liberals, Jewish voters and other Democratic support groups had gained dominance. The social and cultural liberalism of even some wealthy residents gave rise to the term "limousine liberal." Today, the only Republicans who have a shot in the 14th are liberals like Green. Democrats have a 3-1 voter registration advantage here.

The East Side district has many of the office towers that make up the skyline, including the Citicorp and AT&T buildings. The U.N. building, the Chrysler Building, Grand Central Station and the main New York Public Library touch on 42nd Street. Such landmarks as Rockefeller Center and the Metropolitan Museum of Art are in the 14th, as is all of Central Park (which the 14th crosses to take in a small piece of the West Side).

The district's population is 80 percent non-Hispanic white. The largest minority-group concentrations are at the north end, near Harlem, and south in the Lower East Side, which has a large Hispanic population. The 14th also takes in part of Chinatown, as well as the East Village, a nexus for artists and counterculturalists.

The rest of the 14th is one of those marvels of New York redistricting. It crosses the East River to parts of Astoria in Queens and Greenpoint in Brooklyn, which are three miles apart on either side of the 7th District.

Despite being more conservative than the Manhattan side, these parts were decisive in a Democrat's winning the 1992 House race. The mainly ethnic residents (Greeks and Italians in Astoria, Poles and Italians in Greenpoint) generally stick with their Democratic traditions, but there is a strain of social conservatism.

1990 Population: 580,337. White 498,371 (86%), Black 26,844 (5%), Other 55,122 (9%). Hispanic origin 63,398 (11%). 18 and over 515,981 (89%), 62 and over 107,359 (18%). Median age: 39.

Committees

Banking, Finance & Urban Affairs (16th of 30 Democrats)
Consumer Credit & Insurance; Financial Institutions Supervision, Regulation & Deposit Insurance; Housing & Community Development

Government Operations (15th of 25 Democrats)
Environment, Energy & Natural Resources; Legislation & National Security

Campaign Finance

	Receipts	Receipts from PACs		Expend-itures
1992				
Maloney (D)	$283,909	$73,935	(26%)	$277,223
Green (R)	$850,661	$211,300	(25%)	$1,141,470

Key Votes

1993

Require parental notification of minors' abortions	N
Require unpaid family and medical leave	Y
Approve national "motor voter" registration bill	Y
Approve budget increasing taxes and reducing deficit	Y
Approve economic stimulus plan	Y

Elections

1992 General		
Carolyn B. Maloney (D, L)	101,652	(50%)
Bill Green (R, INN)	97,215	(48%)
Abraham J. Hirschfeld (BES)	2,970	(1%)
1992 Primary		
Carolyn B. Maloney (D)	34,935	(65%)
Abraham J. Hirschfeld (D)	12,360	(23%)
Charles W. Juntikka (D)	3,476	(7%)
Frederick D. Newman (D)	2,697	(5%)

District Vote for President

	1992	
D	159,750	(70%)
R	53,675	(23%)
I	16,419	(7%)

15 Charles B. Rangel (D)

Of Manhattan — Elected 1970; 12th Term

Born: June 11, 1930, New York, N.Y.
Education: New York U., B.S. 1957; St. John's U., LL.B. 1960.
Military Service: Army, 1948-52.
Occupation: Lawyer.
Family: Wife, Alma Carter; two children.
Religion: Roman Catholic.
Political Career: N.Y. Assembly, 1967-71; sought Democratic nomination for N.Y. City Council president, 1969.
Capitol Office: 2252 Rayburn Bldg. 20515; 225-4365.

In Washington: After more than two decades of proving himself as a member of the club, Rangel should be savoring his accomplishments and his elevation in the House, making the most of his pragmatic skill at back-room negotiation. Instead, Rangel is confronting frustration from all sides.

Defeated in his bid for the majority whip's job in 1987, Rangel has watched as a new generation of Democrats moved up. Chastened by a dozen years served under Republican presidents, these Democrats do not share Rangel's unalloyed liberalism or his brand of intense partisanship.

And, though it did not slow him, at the start of the 103rd Congress, Rangel was among the few House members still under investigation because of kited checks at the House bank; Rangel had 64 overdrafts before the bank was shut down in 1992. Rangel finally got his letter saying the investigation had ended in May 1993.

In another affront, Rangel was denied the committee platform from which he has battled vigorously against illegal drugs. Chosen as chairman of the Select Committee on Narcotics in 1983, he was among the first members of Congress to focus on the impact of drugs on society — a problem he has seen up close at home.

At the start of the 103rd Congress, cost-conscious House members decided that Select Narcotics, and three similar non-legislative committees, were too costly and duplicative to retain. In a surprise 180-237 vote, the House voted against reauthorizing Rangel's panel, and all four passed into oblivion without another vote.

The action was not aimed at Rangel or the three other chairmen whose panels were abolished. But Rangel took it hard, pleading with members to keep his panel alive until a joint committee studying the organization of Congress had a chance to review their merits. It did not work.

Drugs are not the only subject that can stir his passions. In the 102nd Congress, he thought he might finally succeed in winning creation of a series of urban enterprise zones where tax incentives and federal job training and education assistance might induce real economic advancement in inner-city districts such as his in Harlem.

To hold on to his dream, Rangel forged deals with former colleague Jack F. Kemp, the best-known Republican champion of enterprise zones, who was President Bush's secretary of Housing and Urban Development. He also negotiated with Democratic liberals and with Ways and Means Chairman Dan Rostenkowski of Illinois. Enterprise zones on Rangel's model became a central element in a broader urban aid tax bill. Finally, after Rangel thought he had everyone lined up, Bush vetoed the bill (citing unrelated provisions, but complaining as well about the terms of the enterprise zone proposal).

While his politics have not changed, Rangel's words have taken on a sharp confrontational tone. Once regarded as the least ideological of the senior black members of Congress — the one most likely to choose modest but tangible help for his constituents over the opportunity to express outrage — Rangel has warmed to the idea of positioning the Congressional Black Caucus as a counterbalance to those who would pull the Democratic Party to the right. "We are the conscience of the Congress," Rangel says. "We protect the truest traditions of the Democratic Party."

Shortly after President Clinton took office, anti-Castro Cuban-Americans and others managed to block the nomination of a black, Cuban-American lawyer for a key State Department post concerned with Latin America. In raising doubts about the potential nominee's qualifications and his willingness to maintain a hard line against the Cuban government, the opponents raised Rangel's ire.

In a January 1993 column for the Miami Herald, Rangel lashed out at "the bullying tactics of a pressure group motivated by racism." Freshman Republican Lincoln Diaz-Balart of Florida then took to the House floor to denounce Rangel for "impugning the honor

New York 15

Northern Manhattan — Harlem; Washington Heights

One of the original seats of black political power, the Upper Manhattan area centered on Harlem has been transformed in recent decades: There has been a major influx of Hispanics, mainly from Puerto Rico and the Dominican Republic, with a large sampling of other Latin American ethnicities.

Hispanics now make up a large plurality (46 percent) of the population in the 15th, which blankets Upper Manhattan from 96th Street to its northern tip. But in part because of low Hispanic voter participation rates, the non-Hispanic blacks who make up about 37 percent of the population continue to have the political upper hand.

Since first sending an African-American to Congress, the Harlem-based district has had just two House members, both Democrats: the flamboyant Adam Clayton Powell Jr., who won a landmark election in 1944, and the low-key Rangel, who unseated the ailing and scandal-plagued Powell in 1970 and has held the seat since.

Democrats have a lock on the constituency covered by the 15th. Throughout his career, Rangel has received the endorsement not only of the local Democrats, but of the minuscule GOP organization as well.

At the turn of the 20th century, Harlem, located about 10 miles north of New York City's original hub, was an upscale suburb with a nearly all-white population. But in 1904, blacks — steered by a black real estate agent named Philip A. Payton Jr. — began to move in. By the 1920s, the height of its cultural "renaissance," Harlem was mainly black and upscale. By the 1940s, the trickle of low-income blacks arriving there became a flood, turning much of Harlem into the economically troubled area it remains.

The largest concentration of blacks in the 15th is in west-central Harlem. Puerto Ricans dominate in East Harlem; West Harlem and Washington Heights farther north have large Dominican communities. Most of the 15th's non-Hispanic whites live in three areas: its south end in the Upper East and West sides; the Inwood section at the north end; and a longtime Italian-American community in East Harlem.

Large parts of the 15th have the array of social problems plaguing low-income minority communities. A third of its residents live in poverty; less than 60 percent of persons 25 and older graduated high school. Harlem has some relatively affluent areas, such as Strivers' Row and Lenox Terrace. There has been some reversal of the outflow of upwardly mobile blacks in such areas as Mount Morris Park, where once-grand brownstones are being restored.

On the west side of the 15th are the campuses of Columbia University and the City College of New York. The district contains such historic sites as the massive Cathedral of St. John the Divine and the tomb of Ulysses S. Grant. The George Washington Bridge crosses the Hudson River to connect Upper Manhattan with New Jersey.

An incongruous appendage to the 15th is Rikers Island, located two miles off Manhattan in the East River. A New York City prison complex occupies the island.

1990 Population: 580,337. White 160,127 (28%), Black 272,063 (47%), Other 148,147 (26%). Hispanic origin 269,051 (46%). 18 and over 437,484 (75%), 62 and over 81,239 (14%). Median age: 32.

of the Cuban-American community." Rangel subsequently introduced legislation to lift the U.S. trade embargo on Cuba.

Now the fourth most senior Democrat on Ways and Means, Rangel has enjoyed close rapport with Chairman Rostenkowski. But he has griped from time to time — as he did during budget talks in 1990 — about being shut out.

Rangel doesn't like sitting on the sidelines. After criticizing the new House leadership in the 101st Congress for its hesitancy in challenging Bush's proposed capital gains tax head-on, Rangel was elated when the new Democratic leadership took up the cause. After Speaker Thomas S. Foley of Washington spoke to Ways and Means Democrats, Rangel said, "Foley was eloquent. He was good.... Goddamn, we're going to the mat. I'm ready."

Rangel also has played an active role in House debates on South Africa. A strong advocate of tougher sanctions against the apartheid regime, Rangel authored a far-reaching provision enacted as part of the 1987 budget reconciliation to end foreign tax credits for income derived from South African holdings.

And of late, he has been a prominent supporter of restoring the elected Haitian government of Jean-Bertrand Aristide and has been critical of the policy, carried over from Bush to Clinton, of returning refugee boats to Haiti.

At Home: Rangel's 1970 primary victory over flamboyant Democratic Rep. Adam Clayton Powell was big news; his contests since have been routine. Rangel has never faced a Republican opponent or a serious primary challenger during his long House tenure.

A high school dropout, Rangel joined the Army and fought in the Korean War. He then returned to Manhattan and entered college in his mid-20s. He got his law degree in 1960 and the next year was appointed assistant U.S. attorney for the Southern District of New York.

In 1966 Rangel won a seat in the New York Assembly. Three years later, he made a quixotic bid for citywide office by running for City Council president in the Democratic primary on a ticket headed by U.S. Rep. James H. Scheuer. Rangel ran last in a field of six but received publicity in black areas as the only citywide black candidate.

Rangel bounced back the next year, applying the *coup de grâce* to Powell's fading political career. The veteran Democrat had been "excluded" from the 90th Congress on charges that he had misused committee funds for parties and travel to the Caribbean. The Supreme Court ruled the exclusion unconstitutional, and Powell was seen as a martyr by constituents. But when he took a seat in the 91st Congress and then spent most of the following year out of the country, that view changed.

Rangel had the backing of a coalition of younger black politicians who were tired of Powell's behavior and wanted someone who would work harder for blacks and for New York: He portrayed Powell as an absentee representative and promised to work full-time for his constituents. Although the anti-Powell vote was split four ways, Rangel's coalition of younger blacks and liberal whites prevailed.

The primary win established Rangel as the dominant political figure in his district and gave him influence in New York City politics. He was a frequent critic of longtime Mayor Edward I. Koch, who had an often-adversarial relationship with the city's minorities.

Rangel was mentioned as a possible challenger to Koch in 1989. He, however, eventually endorsed Manhattan Borough President David Dinkins, who became the city's first black mayor.

Rangel has maintained his electoral lock despite the changing demographics of his constituency, brought on by a continuing influx of Hispanics. The Harlem-based district that first elected Rangel was mainly black. In the current 15th District, Hispanics outnumber non-Hispanic blacks by more than 50,000.

Committee

Ways & Means (4th of 24 Democrats)
Select Revenue Measures (chairman); Oversight

Elections

1992 General		
Charles B. Rangel (D)	105,011	(95%)
Jose A. Suero (C, INF)	4,345	(4%)
Jessie Fields (NA)	1,337	(1%)
1992 Primary		
Charles B. Rangel (D)	38,076	(81%)
Jessie Fields (D)	4,725	(10%)
Harry C. Fotopoulos (D)	4,355	(9%)
1990 General		
Charles B. Rangel (D, R, L)	55,882	(97%)
Alvaader Frazier (NA)	1,592	(3%)

Previous Winning Percentages: **1988** (97%) **1986** (96%) **1984** (97%) **1982** (97%) **1980** (96%) **1978** (96%) **1976** (97%) **1974** (97%) **1972** (96%) **1970** (87%)

District Vote for President

1992

D	124,594	(86%)
R	15,589	(11%)
I	4,726	(3%)

Campaign Finance

	Receipts	Receipts from PACs		Expend-itures
1992				
Rangel (D)	$539,183	$325,850	(60%)	$669,095
1990				
Rangel (D)	$541,762	$353,900	(65%)	$601,550

Key Votes

1993	
Require parental notification of minors' abortions	N
Require unpaid family and medical leave	Y
Approve national "motor voter" registration bill	Y
Approve budget increasing taxes and reducing deficit	Y
Approve economic stimulus plan	Y
1992	
Approve balanced-budget constitutional amendment	N
Close down space station program	Y
Approve U.S. aid for former Soviet Union	N
Allow shifting funds from defense to domestic programs	Y
1991	
Extend unemployment benefits using deficit financing	Y
Approve waiting period for handgun purchases	Y
Authorize use of force in Persian Gulf	N

Voting Studies

	Presidential Support		Party Unity		Conservative Coalition	
Year	**S**	**O**	**S**	**O**	**S**	**O**
1992	12	84	90	4	15	81
1991	25	71	92	2	0	97
1990	13	81	85	3	6	87
1989	27	59	86	2	0	93
1988	14	71	80	2	5	87
1987	9	76	85	2	2	79
1986	17	73	89	2	4	92
1985	16	75	89	1	7	91
1984	23	67	84	4	8	85
1983	20	71	88	4	9	87
1982	31	69	87	5	10	88
1981	33	63	83	6	4	92

Interest Group Ratings

Year	ADA	AFL-CIO	CCUS	ACU
1992	95	92	25	0
1991	95	100	20	0
1990	89	100	29	4
1989	85	100	11	0
1988	85	100	31	0
1987	88	100	0	0
1986	100	93	11	0
1985	90	100	10	0
1984	90	92	27	0
1983	100	94	20	0
1982	100	95	19	0
1981	95	93	6	0

16 Jose E. Serrano (D)

Of the Bronx — Elected 1990; 2nd Full Term

Born: Oct. 24, 1943, Mayaguez, Puerto Rico.
Education: Graduated from Dodge Vocational H.S., 1961.
Military Service: Army Medical Corps, 1964-66.
Occupation: Public official.
Family: Wife, Mary Staucet; three children, two stepchildren.
Religion: Roman Catholic.
Political Career: N.Y. Assembly, 1975-90; sought Democratic nomination for Bronx borough president, 1985.
Capitol Office: 336 Cannon Bldg. 20515; 225-4361.

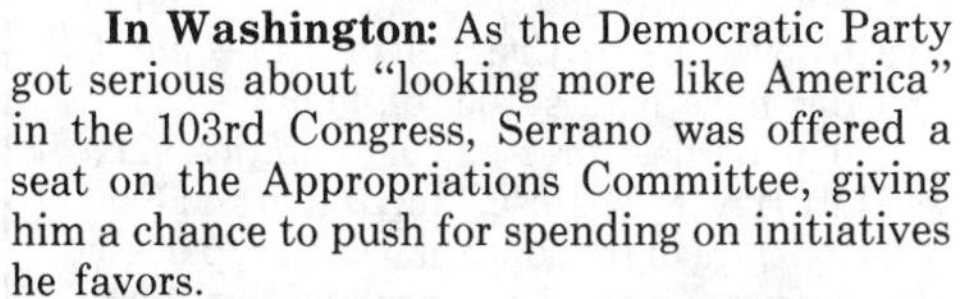

In Washington: As the Democratic Party got serious about "looking more like America" in the 103rd Congress, Serrano was offered a seat on the Appropriations Committee, giving him a chance to push for spending on initiatives he favors.

Serrano gained notice as an active Democratic soldier on a list of issues that affect minorities. He has a reputation as a serious legislator who never leaves behind his own sense of identity or his sense of the economic plight of his Hispanic-majority district, which is among the most poverty-ridden in the nation.

His colleagues still remember a moving speech Serrano delivered on the House floor shortly after he was sworn in. In the speech he recalled how his parents, now deceased, immigrated to the United States from Puerto Rico when he was 7.

Serrano will likely have a higher profile in the 103rd. In 1992, he was unanimously elected chairman of the Congressional Hispanic Caucus. Serrano was elected to the post just as the number of Hispanic members reached a new high at 19 (including delegates from the U.S. Virgin Islands and Puerto Rico, whose voting privileges are limited).

Serrano was elected despite some members' concern that he would give the organization too much of a liberal bent. Serrano has worked closely with the more liberal Congressional Black Caucus to boost his own group's leverage in Congress.

"I am personally liberal, but I will lead the caucus by consensus," Serrano said.

He will have to work to heal divisions within his caucus on issues involving Cuba and abortion rights, as well as differences arising from the group's increasing political and cultural diversity. Unlike its black counterpart, the Hispanic caucus has a substantial nucleus of Republicans.

In the 102nd, Serrano successfully led the fight for the Voting Rights Language Assistance Act. The legislation reauthorized and expanded sections of the Voting Rights Act of 1965 to guarantee bilingual balloting and other assistance in areas with high concentrations of non-English-speaking citizens.

Before the bill was enacted, a language-minority group had to constitute 5 percent of a county's population to qualify for language assistance. Under the new law, assistance is available to counties in which any one such minority group exceeds 10,000 people. This serves to make localities such as Philadelphia or Queens, N.Y., eligible.

In addition, when the 102nd Congress considered a new civil rights bill, Serrano took up the Hispanic cause. Amid reports that the Equal Employment Opportunity Commission was not responding adequately to the needs of Hispanic workers, Serrano successfully pushed the Education and Labor Committee to adopt an amendment authorizing a new public information and outreach program at the commission.

Representing a district that is 60 percent Hispanic, Serrano demonstrates a great deal of interest in his native Puerto Rico. During consideration of a measure to set up a plebiscite for the island's residents to let them decide their status, Serrano sought to attach a provision allowing mainland Puerto Ricans to vote in the referendum, which lost out when both political parties in Puerto Rico objected. After passing the House, the plebiscite measure died in the Senate during the 101st Congress. Likewise, efforts to move the issue forward went nowhere in the 102nd. Serrano plans to push for a referendum again in the 103rd.

Building on his experience in the state Legislature, in his first term Serrano got a seat on the Education and Labor Committee. Through his position there he saw one of his bills enacted during his first year in the House. Congress passed a measure designed to prevent students from dropping out of school by requir-

New York 16

South Bronx

One of the most economically devastated areas in the United States, the mostly Hispanic South Bronx had by the 1970s become a metaphor for the nation's urban ills. Its stretches of refuse-strewn lots and burned-out buildings provide backdrops for visiting politicians of both parties, who prescribed varying solutions to revive the inner cities. Residents have complained bitterly that these photo sessions have resulted in no improvements for the low-income communities of the South Bronx.

But the fragile seedlings of an economic turnaround have begun to take root in parts of the area that forms the 16th. Like frontier settlements, several developments of single-family homes and low-rise apartments have been built on vacated lots by subsidized economic development organizations and occupied by working-class, minority families. These areas, together with more settled, middle-class Hispanic communities in the eastern part of the 16th, provide hope for improvement.

The South Bronx, overtaken by the post-World War II influx of Hispanics to New York City, has since 1970 elected Democrats of Puerto Rican origin to the House. That year, Herman Badillo became the first Puerto Rican to serve in Congress. In 1978, he was succeeded by Robert Garcia. In 1989, Serrano stepped in and has easily held the seat since.

Once largely the province of working-class white ethnics, Jews and blacks, the 16th's territory is now 60 percent Hispanic. About a third of the residents are non-Hispanic blacks; fewer than 5 percent are non-Hispanic whites, one of the lowest proportions in any district. Overwhelming Democratic strength here is consistent with other mainly minority districts. Another consistent pattern is low voter turnout, a result of such factors as recent immigration status, political alienation and poverty. A turnout effort in 1992 boosted the number of votes cast in the House contest to more than 90,000 (91 percent went to Serrano). But that was still less than half the average for New York House districts.

A range of inner-city problems affects the residents of the 16th. It has the lowest median family income of the 435 House districts. More than 40 percent of all residents (and nearly half the Hispanic residents) live in poverty. Less than half of the people 25 or older have high school diplomas.

The hardest-pressed communities, such as Mott Haven, Melrose, Morrisania and East Tremont, are in the south and central parts of the district. Some of the new developments are scattered here among the ruins of urban decay. Across the Bronx River, in Soundview and Clason Point, are communities of middle-class Hispanic homeowners.

Once a major factory area, the South Bronx still has a handful of industrial employers, as well as two large wholesale food centers, the Hunts Point and the Bronx terminal markets; Yankee Stadium is near the latter. The 16th comes to a northern point in Bronx Park, site of the Bronx Zoo and the New York Botanical Garden.

1990 Population: 580,338. White 116,116 (20%), Black 244,636 (42%), Other 219,586 (38%). Hispanic origin 349,190 (60%). 18 and over 385,188 (66%), 62 and over 51,111 (9%). Median age: 27.

ing school districts to create plans to reduce dropout rates.

At Home: Although Serrano's state Assembly career had made him a fixture in New York Hispanic politics, his avenues for advancement had looked narrow before 1989. Democratic Rep. Robert Garcia, first elected in 1978, was still in his 50s and seemed unlikely to leave his House seat soon.

But Garcia's career was shattered by his October 1989 conviction on charges of extortion. The case involved Wedtech Corp., a Bronx defense contractor that had aggressively pursued business under minority set-aside programs in the 1980s. Wedtech's lobbying techniques included bribes to several politicians.

Garcia resigned his seat in what was then numbered the 18th District in January 1990, and a March election was set to fill his unexpired term. Serrano moved quickly to stake his claim.

Serrano breezed to the Democratic House nomination in 1990 despite some dissent from African-American activists incensed at allusions to the 18th, then nearly half-black, as a "Puerto Rican" seat. Bronx Republican officials, who seldom contest Democratic dominance in the South Bronx, probed that rift by running black businessman Simeon Golar. But Serrano ran away with 92 percent of the vote in the special election. He won a full term with 93 percent in November of that year.

As a politician in a place plagued by unemployment and crime, Serrano has touted his own up-from-poverty story. An immigrant who had been brought up in a housing project,

Serrano graduated from a vocational high school and served in the Army. Thereafter, he worked for a New York City bank and took a position on a community school board in the Bronx that helped him develop a core group of political allies.

In 1974, those contacts helped him win a state Assembly seat. By 1983, he was chairman of the Assembly Education Committee, a post from which he could look out for schools in New York City in general and for his minority constituents in particular.

Serrano twice sought the office of Bronx borough president. In 1985, he nearly upset incumbent Democrat Stanley Simon in a primary. Two years later, Serrano tried to become the party's appointed interim replacement for Simon, who also had been convicted in the Wedtech case and forced from office. Party officials rejected him after he referred to Bronx politics as "a fetid sinkhole of corruption." But he retained his electoral clout in the Assembly and then the House.

In 1992, the already well-entrenched Serrano gained insurance from House redistricting plan that made his Democratic district more Hispanic and lowered the chances of a primary challenge.

Committee

Appropriations (31st of 37 Democrats)
Foreign Operations, Export Financing & Related Programs; Labor, Health & Human Services, Education & Related Agencies

Elections

1992 General

Jose E. Serrano (D, L)	85,222	(91%)
Michael Walters (R, C)	7,975	(9%)

1990 General

Jose E. Serrano (D, L)	38,024	(93%)
Joseph Chiavaro (R)	1,189	(3%)
Mary Rivera (NA)	866	(2%)
Anna Johnson (C)	717	(2%)

Previous Winning Percentage: **1990 *** (92%)

** Special election.*

District Vote for President

1992

D	100,602	(81%)
R	18,834	(15%)
I	4,042	(3%)

Campaign Finance

	Receipts	Receipts from PACs	Expend-itures
1992			
Serrano (D)	$112,982	$93,350 (83%)	$96,339
1990			
Serrano (D)	$111,390	$74,550 (67%)	$132,359

Key Votes

1993

Require parental notification of minors' abortions	N
Require unpaid family and medical leave	Y
Approve national "motor voter" registration bill	Y
Approve budget increasing taxes and reducing deficit	Y
Approve economic stimulus plan	Y

1992

Approve balanced-budget constitutional amendment	N
Close down space station program	Y
Approve U.S. aid for former Soviet Union	N
Allow shifting funds from defense to domestic programs	Y

1991

Extend unemployment benefits using deficit financing	Y
Approve waiting period for handgun purchases	Y
Authorize use of force in Persian Gulf	N

Voting Studies

	Presidential Support		Party Unity		Conservative Coalition	
Year	**S**	**O**	**S**	**O**	**S**	**O**
1992	9	89	90	3	4	92
1991	19	71	86	3	5	89
1990	17†	77†	93†	2†	6†	90†

† Not eligible for all recorded votes.

Interest Group Ratings

Year	ADA	AFL-CIO	CCUS	ACU
1992	95	91	13	0
1991	100	100	10	0
1990	88	100	14	0

17 Eliot L. Engel (D)

Of the Bronx — Elected 1988; 3rd Term

Born: Feb. 18, 1947, Bronx, N.Y.
Education: Hunter-Lehman College, B.A. 1969; Lehman College, M.A. 1973; New York Law School, J.D. 1987.
Occupation: Teacher; guidance counselor.
Family: Wife, Patricia Ennis; two children.
Religion: Jewish.
Political Career: Bronx Democratic district leader, 1974-77; N.Y. Assembly, 1977-88.
Capitol Office: 1433 Longworth Bldg. 20515; 225-2464.

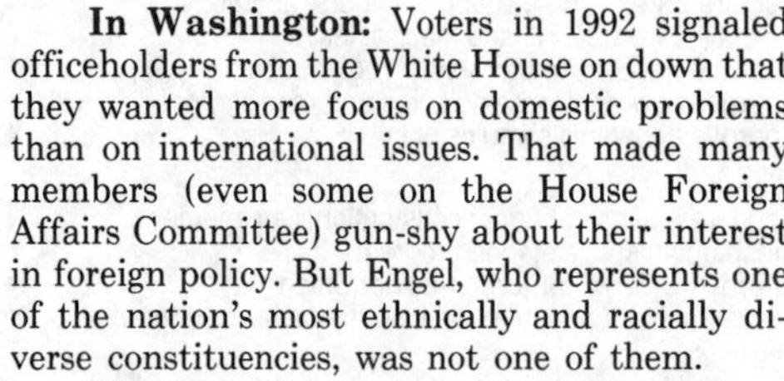

In Washington: Voters in 1992 signaled officeholders from the White House on down that they wanted more focus on domestic problems than on international issues. That made many members (even some on the House Foreign Affairs Committee) gun-shy about their interest in foreign policy. But Engel, who represents one of the nation's most ethnically and racially diverse constituencies, was not one of them.

The 17th District, based in the borough of the Bronx, is split about evenly among whites, blacks and Hispanics. It includes dozens of ethnic groups, including many people with roots in Ireland, Italy and Eastern Europe. Like Engel, many of the district's residents are Jewish.

Engel accordingly is unafraid to talk about his interest in international issues. In fact, he takes on foreign policy issues almost as a type of constituent service.

Engel's strong support for the Jewish state of Israel is a given. In early 1990, President Bush appeared to question Israel's hold on all of Jerusalem when he opposed new Jewish settlements in East Jerusalem. Engel led a House protest, sponsoring a resolution stating that Jerusalem "is and should remain" the capital of Israel.

Although Engel has generally supported a smaller defense budget through the years, he was among those backing strong U.S. action to end the Iraqi occupation of Kuwait that began in August 1990. Israel's adversarial relationship with Iraq was a factor in Engel's position.

Engel condemned efforts by Iraqi leader Saddam Hussein to link his country's occupation of Kuwait to the Palestinian issue. "Saddam Hussein did not invade Kuwait to help the Palestinians," he said. "He invaded Kuwait because he is a ruthless, evil dictator and aggressor."

Engel voted for the resolution authorizing the use of force against Iraq in January 1991. But after the defeat of Iraq by U.S.-led forces, Engel broke sharply with Bush over the president's subsequent actions toward Israel.

Bush had resumed his policy of pressuring the Israeli government headed by Yitzhak Shamir to stop building Jewish settlements in the disputed West Bank territory taken by Israel from Jordan in the 1967 war. Bush's effort in September 1991 to delay legislation providing $10 billion in U.S. loan guarantees to Israel — and his public criticism of pro-Israel lobbyists — drew a strong response from Engel.

Accusing the secretary of state and other administration officials of an "anti-Israel bias," Engel said that a showdown between Bush and American Jewish organizations was inevitable. "This is as good a place to draw the line as any," Engel said. But Congress drew no such line. It went along with Bush and allowed the loan guarantees to be delayed until after the 1992 election defeat of Shamir by Shimon Peres, who promised to restrict the settlements.

Engel's involvement in the problems of Northern Ireland also has a constituent link: His district's many Irish-Americans include a number of activists who favor expanded rights for the Catholic minority and an eventual end to British rule of Northern Ireland. Engel has proposed a resolution urging the British to eliminate employer discrimination against Roman Catholics; during the 102nd Congress he joined Rep. Joseph P. Kennedy II, D-Mass., in proposing a resolution calling on the president to urge Great Britain to open peace talks on Northern Ireland including all parties to the conflict.

Picking up where his House predecessor, Democrat Mario Biaggi, left off, Engel is the annual sponsor of a resolution declaring October Italian-American Heritage and Culture Month.

In February 1993, Engel joined in a bipartisan coalition that urged President Clinton to lift a U.N. arms embargo against the besieged former Yugoslav republic of Bosnia. The coalition supported an increased arms flow to allow Bosnia to defend itself against its well-armed neighbor, Serbia.

Engel does pursue some broader issues as a member of the Foreign Affairs Subcommittee on Economic Policy, Trade and the Environment. During the prolonged debate on authorizing the Export Administration Act (which has spanned several Congresses), Engel has sup-

New York 17

North Bronx; parts of southern Westchester

Reflective of the demographic changes the borough of The Bronx has undergone in recent years, the 17th is one of the most ethnically and racially diverse congressional districts. Blacks, with a more than two-fifths plurality, make up the largest racial group in the 17th (which takes in nearly all of the northern part of The Bronx as well as urbanized parts of Yonkers, Mount Vernon and New Rochelle in Westchester County). But Hispanics and non-Hispanic whites are just behind, almost tied with about a third of the population each.

The non-Hispanic white constituency subdivides among dozens of ethnic groups, with longstanding communities of Italian- and Irish-Americans, Eastern Europeans and Jews.

Many ethnics are traditionally Democratic but hold conservative views on social issues: They provided the political base for such figures as former Rep. Mario Biaggi, who held the North Bronx district for nearly two decades before running afoul of the law in 1988.

But the 17th, as configured by redistricting in 1992, is a majority-minority district where the liberal views of current Rep. Engel may be more in keeping. Like Biaggi, Engel has signed onto the various foreign policy causes of his district's European ethnics. But he must maintain a liberal voting record and build multiracial coalitions to forestall future primary challenges by minority-group candidates.

Any serious House contest in the 17th will almost have to be in the primary: Nearly three-quarters of the registered voters are Democrats. Bill Clinton triumphed with 76 percent in the 17th.

There are some low-income pockets in the 17th, including some housing projects located in an odd arm that follows the Major Deegan Expressway into an area of the South Bronx adjacent to (but not including) Yankee Stadium. The poverty rate for Hispanic residents, about 30 percent, is on par with New York state's rate.

But by and large, this is a middle- to working-class district where the city meets the suburbs. The poverty rate for blacks in the 17th is well below that for the state. A composite of the district can be found in middle-income Co-Op City, a massive complex of high-rise apartments in the eastern part of the 17th. It has a large Jewish population that is Engel's political base, but also many black and Hispanic residents.

At the western border of the Bronx is its most affluent and suburbanlike community, heavily Jewish Riverdale. Just to the north, though, is much of the western part of the city of Yonkers, which is two-thirds minority and mainly low-income. The concentration of minorities in this section has led to a drawn-out federal court battle over housing discrimination in Yonkers.

On its east side, the 17th takes in a part of Mount Vernon that is three-quarters black, a small and racially mixed part of Pelham, and a part of New Rochelle (including its downtown) that is two-thirds black.

1990 Population: 580,337. White 233,703 (40%), Black 243,182 (42%), Other 103,452 (18%). Hispanic origin 168,791 (29%). 18 and over 438,290 (76%), 62 and over 97,471 (17%). Median age: 33.

ported loosening restrictions on exports of goods that are no longer of national security importance. But he has proposed even stronger restrictions on exports of "dual use" items, which could have military as well as civilian applications, to nations that support terrorism.

Of course, as the representative of a mainly middle-class district that has many low-income residents, not even Engel can afford to seem entirely focused on foreign issues. This became particularly true after the 1992 redistricting, which made the 17th a "majority-minority" district. Although Engel has a strongly liberal House voting record, he could find himself vulnerable in the future if the district's black and Hispanic voters were to coalesce behind a single primary challenger.

In the 103rd Congress, Engel has secured a new committee assignment, Education and Labor, which should help him forestall such a challenge. The former public school guidance counselor says his priorities include education programs, such as Head Start, that are targeted to low-income families.

Engel's district is also home to many unionized public employees, and at the start of the 102nd Congress he tried to get on another domestic-oriented committee, Post Office and Civil Service. But Chairman William L. Clay of Missouri, angry about Engel's 1989 vote against a controversial federal pay raise proposal, blocked that bid.

At Home: Engel earned a House seat in 1988 by defeating former 10-term Democratic Rep. Biaggi, who had been convicted earlier that year on federal charges of bribery and extortion. Engel had a relatively routine re-election campaign in 1990, then solidified his position in 1992 by stifling Biaggi's unlikely last hurrah.

A low-key figure during more than a decade in the New York Assembly, Engel held positions that served him well in his initial House race. He had chaired a committee on drug and alcohol abuse and a subcommittee that handled moderate-income housing issues.

Nevertheless, it was the gamble of his career when Engel gave up the Assembly to mount a primary challenge to Biaggi in what was then numbered the 19th District. Biaggi was about to be tried in a federal case involving alleged bribes by Wedtech Corp. (a defunct Bronx defense contractor), and he had been convicted of accepting illegal gratuities in a separate 1987 case. But he remained highly popular in the 19th, where he was known as a decorated former police officer and neighborhood hero. So most Democrats stood aside when he defiantly announced he would seek re-election in 1988.

In August, Biaggi was convicted and resigned his seat. His name remained on the ballot, however, for both the primary and the general election (the latter because he regularly received the endorsement of district Republicans who had long before ceded the seat to him). Engel won both contests, taking 50 percent of the primary vote (Biaggi split the rest with a third candidate) and then winning the general election with 56 percent to Biaggi's 27 percent.

In 1991, Biaggi was given early release from his jail sentence because of heart and neurological problems. But a year later, he pronounced himself hale and determined to reclaim his seat. Renowned for his constituent service efforts during his House tenure, Biaggi insisted he understood the problems of district residents better than Engel.

Biaggi retained a loyal core of supporters and even obtained the endorsement of a former New York City police commissioner. But his comeback try, likely doomed in any election year, was especially ill-timed in a year that voters were attuned to corruption in Congress. Engel, while touting his own record of delivering for the district, blasted Biaggi for having "weaseled his way out of prison" with health complaints.

Engel won the primary by a nearly 3-1 margin. Running in a district (now the 17th) that had been made even more Democratic by the addition of minority group residents, Engel coasted to an easy win in November.

Committees

Education & Labor (16th of 28 Democrats)
Elementary, Secondary & Vocational Education; Labor-Management Relations

Foreign Affairs (8th of 27 Democrats)
Africa; Economic Policy, Trade & the Environment; Europe & the Middle East

Elections

1992 General		
Eliot L. Engel (D, L)	98,068	(80%)
Martin Richman (R)	16,511	(13%)
Kevin Brawley (C)	3,143	(3%)
Martin J. O'Grady (RTL)	3,067	(3%)
Nana LaLuz (NL)	1,592	(1%)
1992 Primary		
Eliot L. Engel (D)	35,859	(74%)
Mario Biaggi (D)	12,680	(26%)
1990 General		
Eliot L. Engel (D, L)	45,758	(61%)
William J. Gouldman (R)	17,135	(23%)
Kevin Brawley (C, RTL)	11,868	(16%)

Previous Winning Percentage: **1988** (56%)

District Vote for President

1992	
D	120,286 (76%)
R	30,133 (19%)
I	7,945 (5%)

Campaign Finance

	Receipts	Receipts from PACs		Expend-itures
1992				
Engel (D)	$465,735	$285,450	(61%)	$469,220
1990				
Engel (D)	$399,619	$324,173	(81%)	$389,698

Key Votes

1993	
Require parental notification of minors' abortions	N
Require unpaid family and medical leave	Y
Approve national "motor voter" registration bill	Y
Approve budget increasing taxes and reducing deficit	Y
Approve economic stimulus plan	Y
1992	
Approve balanced-budget constitutional amendment	N
Close down space station program	N
Approve U.S. aid for former Soviet Union	Y
Allow shifting funds from defense to domestic programs	Y
1991	
Extend unemployment benefits using deficit financing	Y
Approve waiting period for handgun purchases	Y
Authorize use of force in Persian Gulf	Y

Voting Studies

	Presidential Support		Party Unity		Conservative Coalition	
Year	**S**	**O**	**S**	**O**	**S**	**O**
1992	16	75	85	5	25	73
1991	27	71	93	4	14	86
1990	18	75	83	2	13	80
1989	30	65	92	1	10	80

Interest Group Ratings

Year	ADA	AFL-CIO	CCUS	ACU
1992	95	91	25	4
1991	90	100	30	15
1990	100	100	21	9
1989	95	100	33	4

18 Nita M. Lowey (D)

Of Harrison — Elected 1988; 3rd Term

Born: July 5, 1937, Bronx, N.Y.
Education: Mount Holyoke College, B.A. 1959.
Occupation: Public official.
Family: Husband, Stephen Lowey; three children.
Religion: Jewish.
Political Career: N.Y. assistant secretary of state, 1985-87.
Capitol Office: 1424 Longworth Bldg. 20515; 225-6506.

In Washington: When the House Democratic leadership was looking to fill seats on the Appropriations Committee in a way that would give it more diversity, Lowey lobbied hard for a spot and got it.

She is one of two Jewish members serving on the 60-member committee in the 103rd Congress and one of seven women. But Lowey had a lot more to offer than gender or religion. She has a gregarious personality, keen political instincts and a lot of party loyalty. On votes that split Democrats and Republicans in the 102nd Congress, she voted with her party at least 95 percent of the time. And Lowey has been one of the few members of her class to make personal contributions to her colleagues' campaigns.

Lowey was assigned to the Appropriations Subcommittee for Labor, Health and Human Services, and Education, which will allow her to influence programs she feels strongly about.

A leading advocate of abortion rights, Lowey sponsored legislation in the 102nd Congress that would bar the government from awarding Community Development Block Grant funding to communities that do not enforce laws to protect those involved in the abortion process, from doctors to patients. She reintroduced the bill in the 103rd.

The bill is aimed at protecting women, their families and health-care professionals from harassment and violence from anti-abortion forces.

She was one of the most vocal critics of the so-called "gag rule" that barred abortion counseling and referral in federally funded family planning clinics. It was lifted in 1993.

Lowey also supports the use of Medicaid to pay for abortions for poor women.

"My position is that funding should be available through Medicaid because poor women shouldn't be denied the right to have an abortion," she said.

In addition, Lowey has introduced legislation that reflects strong feeling about her religious background. In the 102nd, she pushed a resolution that would have Congress weigh in on the ongoing Middle East conflict between Israel and the Arab states. The resolution would urge the Arab states to recognize and make peace with Israel. Although dozens of members cosponsored the resolution, it never came to a vote on the House floor. Another measure passed by the House in 1992 would commend those who rescued Jews from concentration camps during World War II as well as the Jewish Foundation for Christian Rescuers.

Despite the general affluence of her Westchester district, Lowey has pushed for a list of measures aimed at helping the poor. She has introduced legislation to increase educational opportunites for low-income students as well as for women and minorities.

In the 102nd, her legislation expanding the preventive health services and disease prevention programs for the elderly was included in the Older Americans Act reauthorization bill.

When Lowey entered the 101st Congress as a freshman, she got a seat on the Education and Labor Committee, a good fit for her interests, and she was a reliable liberal vote there. Looking out for the interests of working mothers and poor families, Lowey pushed an amendment to encourage public-private partnerships in developing new child-care facilities. She also sponsored an amendment to double the authorized funding to $10 million for the Nutrition Education and Training program, which provides nutritional information to students, teachers and other school personnel.

Lowey shepherded an anti-drug bill through the legislative mill in 1990. The bill authorized funding for drug education and counseling services for students, and after it won committee approval, the leadership gave her a go-ahead to bring it to the House floor under an expedited rule. But the rule allowed a slim one-third vote of those present to derail the measure, and shortly before her bill was up, Lowey learned that the GOP intended to block its passage because of an unrelated amendment tacked on by another member. With floor time scarce as Congress wound down, Lowey pragmatically severed the amendment and won unanimous approval for her bill.

On the Merchant Marine and Fisheries

New York 18

Parts of Westchester, Bronx and Queens counties

The 18th is one of many jigsaw-puzzle pieces in New York's district map. It stretches from the southern part of Westchester County (which has two-thirds of the district's population), down a ribbon of the East Bronx bordering Long Island Sound, across the mouth of the East River and down a narrow corridor into central Queens.

Before 1992 redistricting, Democrat Lowey's constituency was wholly within Westchester. But the drastic reshaping left the political makeup pretty much intact: The 18th is one of New York's most competitive districts, with a slight Democratic lean in recent elections.

The remap removed mainly black, Democratic-voting communities on the urban southern edge of Westchester. But it replaced them with heavily Jewish parts of Queens, where Lowey took 71 percent of the vote in 1992, cinching her victory over the Republican she unseated four years earlier, former Rep. Joseph J. DioGuardi.

The Westchester portion of the district is a tossup: Lowey won 53 percent there in 1992. This section has some of the most affluent communities in New York state. Most — including such places as Bronxville and Harrison — lean Republican, though Scarsdale, with its large Jewish population, often goes Democratic. The 18th's coastal location along the Long Island Sound also breeds an environmental consciousness that has benefited Lowey.

The most Democratic sections are in the low- to middle-income areas of the large cities, including parts of New Rochelle and White Plains, the county's seat and commercial center. The 18th has the largest portion of Yonkers, Westchester's most populous city (which is split among three districts).

While Yonkers provides some Democratic votes from its ethnic white, working-class population, it is not a liberal place; it has been tied up for years in a federal court battle over whether there is intentional housing discrimination. The part of the city in the 18th (mainly on the east side) is nearly 90 percent non-Hispanic white, while the southwest part in the 17th District is two-thirds minority.

While there is much commuting to New York City, the portion of Westchester in the 18th has several large employers, including the headquarters of Texaco (White Plains) and Pepsico (Purchase). There is a significant retail trade, much of it in White Plains. Educational institutions include Iona College in New Rochelle and exclusive Sarah Lawrence College in Yonkers.

On its east side, the district takes in an edge of The Bronx, including Pelham Bay Park and City Island. This area's small population, mainly working-class Italian-Americans, is heavily Republican.

The 18th then enters Queens via the Throgs Neck Bridge and follows a winding path through urban Flushing, which gives it much of its Asian population. After enveloping the southern part of Flushing Meadow Park, the district spreads west to take in the community of Rego Park and east to Utopia, site of St. John's University.

1990 Population: 580,337. White 470,717 (81%), Black 43,506 (7%), Other 66,114 (11%). Hispanic origin 60,202 (10%). 18 and over 467,381 (81%), 62 and over 117,660 (20%). Median age: 38.

Committee, Lowey advocated measures to clean up Long Island Sound. She backed legislation to create the Long Island Sound Conservancy office within the Environmental Protection Agency.

She gave up her seats on Education and Labor and Merchant Marine in the 103rd Congress to move to Appropriations.

At Home: Lowey made a stunning political debut in 1988 when she unseated two-term Rep. Joseph J. DioGuardi in the then-20th District. Her outgoing personality and district-oriented legislative efforts enabled her to quickly settle in, defeating a poorly funded Republican candidate in 1990, then brushing aside a comeback attempt by DioGuardi in 1992.

By the time she entered the political arena, Lowey had spent years as a Democratic activist. In 1974, Lowey, then a homemaker in Queens, worked in an early campaign of a neighbor, Mario M. Cuomo. When Cuomo was later appointed by then-Democratic Gov. Hugh Carey as New York secretary of state, he hired Lowey to work in his department's anti-poverty division.

By the mid-1980s, Cuomo was governor; Lowey was the top aide to Secretary of State Gail Schaffer and a resident of the Westchester suburb of Harrison. Meanwhile, DioGuardi in 1984 had captured a swing Westchester House district that had long been held by Democrats.

In 1988, Lowey aimed for DioGuardi. She survived a primary against Hamilton Fish III, publisher of The Nation magazine and son of a House member, and businessman Dennis Mehiel. Lowey also raised $1.3 million, a huge treasury for a challenger.

DioGuardi outspent her, but his fundraising prowess also turned into his downfall. A newspaper reported in October that a New Rochelle auto dealer had funneled $57,000 in corporate contributions to DioGuardi's campaign through his employees. DioGuardi denied knowledge of the pass-through scheme, but the revelations damaged him. Despite DioGuardi's effort to brand her as an extreme liberal, Lowey won — though by fewer than 6,000 votes.

Although GOP officials had trouble recruiting a candidate in 1990, allowing Lowey to coast, they found DioGuardi eager for another shot in 1992. The ousted Republican again argued that Lowey, who profiled herself as a moderate, was too far to the left. He continued to deny prior knowledge of the 1988 funding scheme, and noted that Lowey had been fined for late reporting of personal funds that she had put into the 1988 campaign.

But Lowey denied wrongdoing, saying the fine was the result of an innocent oversight, and she tied DioGuardi to the Reagan-Bush policies she blamed for the nation's economic problems. This time she won with a cushion of more than 20,000 votes.

Committee

Appropriations (29th of 37 Democrats)
Foreign Operations, Export Financing & Related Programs; Labor, Health & Human Services, Education & Related Agencies

Elections

1992 General		
Nita M. Lowey (D)	115,841	(56%)
Joseph J. DioGuardi (R, C, RTL)	92,687	(44%)
1990 General		
Nita M. Lowey (D)	82,203	(63%)
Glenn D. Bellitto (R)	35,575	(27%)
John M. Schafer (C, RTL)	13,030	(10%)

Previous Winning Percentage: **1988** (50%)

District Vote for President

1992
D 117,937 (50%)
R 94,754 (40%)
I 22,019 (9%)

Campaign Finance

	Receipts	Receipts from PACs		Expend-itures
1992				
Lowey (D)	$1,153,696	$307,977	(27%)	$1,277,433
DioGuardi (R)	$583,458	$79,357	(14%)	$583,905
1990				
Lowey (D)	$1,223,045	$448,797	(37%)	$911,766
Bellitto (R)	$15,505	0		$15,356

Key Votes

1993	
Require parental notification of minors' abortions	N
Require unpaid family and medical leave	Y
Approve national "motor voter" registration bill	Y
Approve budget increasing taxes and reducing deficit	Y
Approve economic stimulus plan	Y
1992	
Approve balanced-budget constitutional amendment	N
Close down space station program	Y
Approve U.S. aid for former Soviet Union	Y
Allow shifting funds from defense to domestic programs	Y
1991	
Extend unemployment benefits using deficit financing	Y
Approve waiting period for handgun purchases	Y
Authorize use of force in Persian Gulf	N

Voting Studies

	Presidential Support		Party Unity		Conservative Coalition	
Year	**S**	**O**	**S**	**O**	**S**	**O**
1992	13	87	96	3	15	85
1991	24	74	95	3	8	92
1990	14	83	94	4	15	81
1989	28	70	94	3	15	85

Interest Group Ratings

Year	ADA	AFL-CIO	CCUS	ACU
1992	100	92	25	0
1991	100	100	20	0
1990	100	100	21	4
1989	95	100	40	7

19 Hamilton Fish Jr. (R)

Of Millbrook — Elected 1968; 13th Term

Born: June 3, 1926, Washington, D.C.
Education: Harvard U., A.B. 1949; New York U., LL.B. 1957.
Military Service: Naval Reserve, 1944-46.
Occupation: Lawyer.
Family: Wife, Mary Ann Tinklepaugh; four children.
Religion: Episcopalian.
Political Career: GOP nominee for U.S. House, 1966.
Capitol Office: 2354 Rayburn Bldg. 20515; 225-5441.

In Washington: When Fish joined the Judiciary Committee as a House freshman in 1969, he aligned with the numerous moderate Republicans who supported liberal social causes. Today, Fish is alone at the top, the committee's senior Republican and one of its few liberal GOP voices on behalf of such issues as civil rights, gun control and abortion counseling.

As party leaders reorganized for the 103rd Congress, Fish was among a group of senior, old-style Republicans mentioned as potential coup targets by the more combative conservatives rising through the GOP ranks. The purging began with the defeat of California moderate Jerry Lewis in his re-election bid for GOP conference chairman. Next, Steve Gunderson of Wisconsin and Fred Upton of Michigan resigned their deputy whip posts — some say under pressure — citing philosophical differences with the more strident Republicans.

But Fish has avoided ouster attempts, largely on the strength of his good word and decency. And he is appreciated for his willingness to free the committee staff to pursue the party line on key issues, rather than his own view.

Fish manages each session to find a handful of key votes that allow him to side with Republican leaders. In the 102nd, the issue was allowing the so-called Baby Bells to enter new markets.

Fish, who generally finds common ground with Judiciary Chairman Jack Brooks of Texas handed Brooks a major setback when he won an amendment in committee to eliminate the waiting period for an expansion of regional phone companies. The bill never reached the House floor, providing both sides with the opportunity to rejoin the battle in the 103rd.

In past years, Fish developed a reputation for rolling up his sleeves and forging compromises with the majority party. But as the tensions between the confrontational "Young Turk" Republicans and the mainstream Democrats who now control both Congress and the White House have become more emotionally charged, Fish's influence as a bridge-builder has lost some of its capital.

Few were surprised when Brooks and Fish teamed up in the 102nd to push for legislation protecting victims of job discrimination. But the ranking Republican's role as negotiator had waned from previous civil rights fights.

In mid-1990, Fish helped craft a compromise package that cleared the way for approval of legislation to extend civil rights protections to the disabled. He brought together the chairman and ranking member of the subcommittee working on the bill — California Democrat Don Edwards and Wisconsin Republican F. James Sensenbrenner Jr. — as well as representatives of small businesses and the disabled to craft a deal on the Americans with Disabilities Act.

Fish's pivotal role was plainly evident in the 100th Congress' debate on amending the Fair Housing Act as well. He initiated negotiations between civil rights advocates and Democrats on the left, and Realtors and the Reagan administration on the right. After more than six weeks of talks, the two sides agreed to allow either the Department of Housing and Urban Development or the alleged discriminator to opt for a full jury trial. This breakthrough ensured House passage; the bill was signed into law soon afterward.

Before taking over the senior Republican position on the full committee in 1983, Fish held the ranking post on the Immigration Subcommittee. His expertise in immigration dates to the 1950s, when he was a foreign service officer stationed in Dublin, Ireland. During the major immigration debates of the 1980s and early 1990s, he was not a primary GOP strategist, but he lent assistance without upstaging the lead sponsors.

Fish finds commonality with his conservative colleagues on issues involving the Justice Department, as well as on matters of copyright and antitrust law. He is ranking Republican on Judiciary's Economic and Commercial Law Subcommittee; in the 101st Congress, he was among the critics of "vertical" price-fixing legislation, which consumer groups said was needed to prohibit manufacturers from setting a minimum retail price.

In the ongoing debate over reauthorization

New York 19

Hudson Valley — Poughkeepsie

From its southern edge in Westchester County, the 19th links the densely packed New York City constituencies to the spacious districts of upstate New York. Though it takes in part of White Plains and Poughkeepsie, the 19th is largely exurban and even partially rural.

The 19th provides a comfortable base for veteran GOP Rep. Fish, though it is not the state's most Republican district. The New York City-oriented Westchester part of the 19th, which provides just under half the population, can be competitive: Fish took 54 percent of the 1992 vote. The rest of the district is solidly Republican: Fish took nearly two-thirds in Putnam and parts of Dutchess and Orange counties in the 19th.

Still, George Bush could not avoid a sharp dropoff in 1992. He lost to Bill Clinton by a plurality in the Westchester County portion of the 19th. He carried the northern part of the district, but he fell from 66 percent in 1988 to 46 percent in Putnam County in 1992.

Much of the 19th's Democratic vote comes from White Plains and working-class communities along the Hudson River. A General Motors plant in North Tarrytown is closing under a corporate restructuring plan. Ossining is the site of the Sing Sing correctional facility; its location on the Hudson gave rise to the warning about being "sent up the river." In Buchanan, near Peekskill, is the Indian Point nuclear power plant. Minority groups make up a higher proportion of the population in these areas than in the rest of the Westchester part of the 19th.

That portion is otherwise made up mainly of white-collar and middle- to upper-middle-class homeowners. During its boom years, International Business Machines — which has its corporate headquarters in Armonk and an international marketing office in White Plains — spurred rapid residential growth in exurban northern Westchester. IBM's recent financial downturn has brought on unprecedented job cuts and economic worries for the 19th.

Among other employers based here is the Reader's Digest Co. in Pleasantville. The Rockefeller family estate, much of it now a state park, is in Pocantico Hills.

Putnam County has experienced some exurban growth, but much of it remains relatively rural. The same can be said about eastern Dutchess County, estate country that has a number of horse farms. Across the Hudson, the 19th takes in a piece of Orange County that includes the U.S. Military Academy at West Point.

The population in the Dutchess County portion is concentrated near its western border with the Hudson. IBM's fallout has also shaken this area. Vassar and Marist colleges are in Poughkeepsie.

The Dutchess County town of Hyde Park is just north of the 19th, but it remains a historic touchstone for the Fish political dynasty. The late Rep. Hamilton Fish Sr. was one of the most fervent opponents of the New Deal policies of President Franklin D. Roosevelt, whose Hyde Park estate was in Fish's House district.

1990 Population: 580,337. White 516,568 (89%), Black 42,260 (7%), Other 21,509 (4%). Hispanic origin 30,293 (5%). 18 and over 444,315 (77%), 62 and over 78,595 (14%). Median age: 34.

of the independent counsel statute, Fish has said he supports the concept of an outside investigator but wants the law to include tougher controls on the prosecutor's discretion and budget.

In the 103rd Congress, Fish is cosponsoring a bill to allow voluntary prayer in schools, and he supports a presidential line-item veto and a balanced-budget amendment.

At Home: Although Fish's re-election was never really in doubt in 1992, his victory over Democratic lawyer Neil McCarthy fell short of the landslides to which the veteran Republican had become accustomed.

Redistricting played a role in Fish's shrinking margin. The remap that created the new 19th District took away a big chunk of Fish's strongly Republican Hudson Valley base in Orange County and expanded his constituency in the New York City suburbs of Westchester County, which have larger numbers of Democratic and independent voters.

The result was telling: Fish, who held a typically large lead in the 19th's more rural counties, carried the Westchester part with 54 percent. This pulled Fish down to 60 percent overall, his lowest re-election tally ever and the first time since 1974 that he fell below 70 percent.

Fish came to the House with one of the most impressive pedigrees in politics. His great-grandfather Hamilton Fish was governor of New York, U.S. senator and secretary of State. His grandfather Hamilton Fish was a U.S. representative. And his father, also Hamilton Fish, spent 24 years in the House arguing for American business and against President Franklin D.

Roosevelt's New Deal.

The current Rep. Fish had long been engaged in civic activities on his ancestral turf of Dutchess County when an opportunity came to run for the House in 1966. Historically Republican, the district had gone Democratic in 1964, and the GOP was eager to retake it.

Fish engaged in a highly publicized "patrician primary" against Alexander Aldrich, cousin of Gov. Nelson A. Rockefeller. Fish won, but was beaten in November by the Democratic incumbent, Joseph Y. Resnick.

In 1968 Resnick ran for the Senate. Fish won his primary against a then-little-known lawyer, G. Gordon Liddy. Fish won the general election with a 48 percent plurality; by 1970, he was winning with 71 percent en route to a long string of easy re-elections.

In 1988, Fish's son, Hamilton Fish III, tried to extend the family's political reach by running for the then-20th District in southern Westchester County. However, the youngest Fish was of a far more liberal bent — he had been publisher of The Nation, a liberal opinion journal — and entered the Democratic primary, aiming for GOP Rep. Joseph J. DioGuardi. He finished second to Nita M. Lowey, who went on to upset DioGuardi.

Committee

Judiciary (Ranking)
Economic & Commercial Law (ranking); Intellectual Property & Judicial Administration

Elections

1992 General		
Hamilton Fish Jr. (R, C)	139,610	(60%)
Neil McCarthy (D)	92,854	(40%)
1990 General		
Hamilton Fish Jr. (R, C)	99,866	(71%)
Richard L. Barbuto (D)	34,128	(24%)
Richard S. Curtin II (RTL)	5,925	(4%)

Previous Winning Percentages: **1988** (75%) **1986** (77%) **1984** (78%) **1982** (75%) **1980** (81%) **1978** (78%) **1976** (71%) **1974** (65%) **1972** (72%) **1970** (71%) **1968** (48%)

District Vote for President

1992
D 104,950 (40%)
R 109,965 (42%)
I 45,088 (17%)

Campaign Finance

	Receipts	Receipts from PACs		Expend-itures
1992				
Fish (R)	$489,831	$229,000	(47%)	$617,832
McCarthy (D)	$131,097	$14,100	(11%)	$132,279
1990				
Fish (R)	$348,209	$204,990	(59%)	$411,614
Barbuto (D)	$935	0		$729

Key Votes

1993	
Require parental notification of minors' abortions	Y
Require unpaid family and medical leave	Y
Approve national "motor voter" registration bill	Y
Approve budget increasing taxes and reducing deficit	N
Approve economic stimulus plan	N
1992	
Approve balanced-budget constitutional amendment	Y
Close down space station program	Y
Approve U.S. aid for former Soviet Union	Y
Allow shifting funds from defense to domestic programs	N
1991	
Extend unemployment benefits using deficit financing	Y
Approve waiting period for handgun purchases	Y
Authorize use of force in Persian Gulf	Y

Voting Studies

	Presidential Support		Party Unity		Conservative Coalition	
Year	**S**	**O**	**S**	**O**	**S**	**O**
1992	54	43	56	40	65	31
1991	52	43	40	53	57	43
1990	42	51	44	47	56	41
1989	65	33	37	57	63	34
1988	37	59	37	59	58	42
1987	45	54	40	56	72	28
1986	40	56	33	60	56	38
1985	45	46	42	45	44	44
1984	50	43	38	51	53	37
1983	54	37	45	47	55	40
1982	45	44	41	51	49	44
1981	57	38	48	46	40	56

Interest Group Ratings

Year	ADA	AFL-CIO	CCUS	ACU
1992	40	58	43	48
1991	45	75	40	35
1990	56	50	43	32
1989	45	42	70	41
1988	60	86	71	32
1987	44	44	53	35
1986	45	57	44	32
1985	35	80	55	40
1984	40	42	69	23
1983	20	29	74	43
1982	45	55	33	43
1981	50	27	78	57

20 Benjamin A. Gilman (R)

Of Middletown — Elected 1972; 11th Term

Born: Dec. 6, 1922, Poughkeepsie, N.Y.
Education: U. of Pennsylvania, B.S. 1946; New York Law School, LL.B. 1950.
Military Service: Army, 1943-45; New York Guard, 1981-present.
Occupation: Lawyer.
Family: Wife, Rita Gail Kelhoffer; two children, two stepchildren.
Religion: Jewish.
Political Career: Assistant N.Y. attorney general, 1953-55; N.Y. Assembly, 1967-73.
Capitol Office: 2185 Rayburn Bldg. 20515; 225-3776.

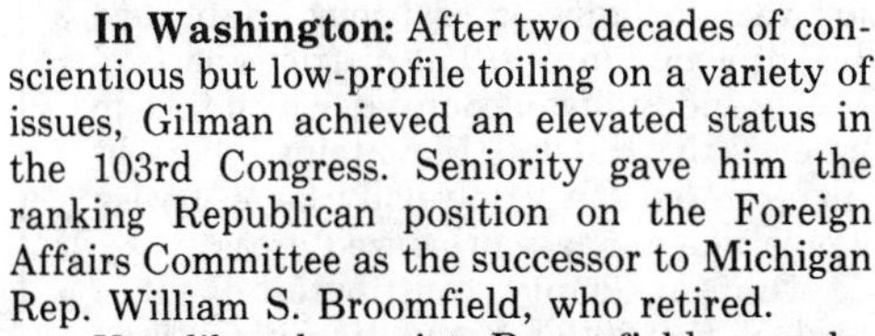

In Washington: After two decades of conscientious but low-profile toiling on a variety of issues, Gilman achieved an elevated status in the 103rd Congress. Seniority gave him the ranking Republican position on the Foreign Affairs Committee as the successor to Michigan Rep. William S. Broomfield, who retired.

Yet like the quiet Broomfield — who ended a 36-year House career virtually unknown outside his district — Gilman is likely to remain overshadowed by the committee's more loquacious or combative Republican members.

With a Democrat in the White House for the first time in 12 years, congressional Republicans will shape their alternatives to President Clinton's foreign policy.

But barring a sharp change in Gilman's approach, GOP members will look to such spokesmen as Illinois Rep. Henry J. Hyde to shape the foreign policy agenda. Gilman has shown little inclination in the past for global strategizing. Instead, he has focused his energy on issues of particular interest to him, such as U.S. aid to Israel, human rights and combating drug trafficking.

As the House Republican Conference organized for the 103rd Congress, some activist conservative elements wanted a more assertive figure for the ranking position.

Some also had qualms about Gilman's voting record: As one of the few remaining "Rockefeller Republicans" in the New York delegation, Gilman has liberal views on social issues, which consistently ranked him as one of the leading House Republicans in voting against Reagan and Bush policies. During the 102nd Congress, Gilman voted against President Bush's positions on a contentious civil rights bill, family leave legislation and a Democratic-sponsored anti-crime bill; he was one of two House Republicans who voted against a constitutional amendment requiring a balanced budget, which Bush strongly advocated in his 1992 campaign.

But there was no desire from within Foreign Affairs to deny Gilman the spot. While he parted ways with his party on many domestic issues, his was a loyal GOP vote on most foreign policy matters. And members simply like the mild-mannered Gilman.

That sentiment is not restricted to the Republican side. Gilman is expected to work well with Foreign Affairs Chairman Lee H. Hamilton of Indiana (who also moved up in 1993, succeeding retired Democrat Dante B. Fascell of Florida). They have teamed up before without rancor, as chairman and ranking Republican on the Europe and Middle East Subcommittee; they also headed a task force that issued a report in 1989 calling for reform of the much-criticized foreign aid bureaucracy.

Gilman agreed with most of the report's conclusions, but expressed reservations about a proposal to end completely the congressional practice of earmarking aid to nations of strategic importance. Though he said the practice — which is criticized for limiting presidential flexibility in targeting foreign aid — should be restricted, he stressed the need to maintain earmarks for such critical U.S. allies as Israel and Egypt.

Gilman's support for Israel, as much as party loyalty, informed his January 1991 vote in favor of using force to end the occupation of Kuwait by Iraq, an adversary of Israel. At a hearing held after combat had broken out, Gilman drew out a testy affirmation from Secretary of State James A. Baker III that Iraq's withdrawal from Kuwait would not be linked to settlement of the Israeli-Palestinian conflict.

During the 1980s, Gilman was a leading advocate of the rights of Soviet Jews to emigrate to Israel. His human rights agenda led him in April 1992 to propose a House resolution calling for a greater U.S. role in ending the Somalian civil war, in which thousands have died.

Gilman pursues his interest in drug interdiction as a member of the Foreign Affairs task

New York 20

Rockland and parts of Westchester, Orange and Sullivan counties

The 20th, near the outer edge of New York City's sphere, has a Republican lean but not a full tilt. Its Rockland and Orange county subdivisions have been populated since World War II largely by relocated New York City residents, many of them Irish- and Italian-Americans and Jews; a number brought Democratic voting traditions that were tempered by their new exurban lifestyles. A moderate, such as Rep. Gilman, can draw out a solid GOP vote. But in races featuring more conservative GOP candidates, the 20th is somewhat more competitive.

In 1992, Gilman took 66 percent of the vote in the 20th, a typical figure for him; Republican Sen. Alfonse M. D'Amato carried the district by a somewhat lower margin. But Democrat Bill Clinton defeated George Bush here. In Rockland County — which has just less than half the district's population — Clinton got 47 percent and defeated Bush by 6 percentage points.

The 20th actually starts fairly close in to New York City, in the Westchester County suburbs. It takes in the northeast corner of Yonkers (including its affluent Beech Hill section), Greenburgh (a mainly middle-class town that includes part of the Central Avenue retail corridor) and such mainly comfortable riverside communities as Hastings-on-Hudson, Dobbs Ferry and Tarrytown. A 17 percent combined black and Hispanic population contributes to making this the most Democratic part of the 20th; Gilman took just 52 percent of the vote there in 1992.

But Gilman dominated in his home base of Rockland County, winning two-thirds of the vote. Though Rockland does not have a single urban center — its population is spread among such communities as Spring Valley, Pearl River, Nyack, Congers, New City and Suffern — it is rather thoroughly developed: More than 90 percent of the population is classified by the Census Bureau as urban.

Rockland has a number of employers, the largest of which is a facility of the Lederle Laboratories pharmaceutical company in Pearl River. But many residents drive across the Tappan Zee Bridge to offices in Westchester or make the long commute into New York City.

The county has a large Jewish population that includes several long-established Hasidic communities. The district's parts of Orange and Sullivan counties, which take in some of the Catskill Mountains' "borscht belt" resorts, have unusually large Jewish populations for less urbanized areas.

Orange County contributes about a third of the 20th's population; its largest towns are Warwick and Middletown. On the county's north side, near the 26th District city of Newburgh, is Stewart Airport, a former Air Force base that is now a major cargo terminal. Much of the county is rural, with dairy, stud horse and onion farms.

Sullivan County has less than 5 percent of the 20th's population, but has its most famous latter-day cultural site. The Woodstock music festival was held in a farm field near the town of Bethel in 1969.

1990 Population: 580,338. White 502,759 (87%), Black 47,504 (8%), Other 30,075 (5%). Hispanic origin 35,263 (6%). 18 and over 429,329 (74%), 62 and over 79,090 (14%). Median age: 34.

force on international narcotics control. He was also a longtime member of the select committees on Narcotics Abuse and Control and Hunger, which were eliminated in 1993 as part of the effort to reduce federal spending.

In order to claim the ranking position on Foreign Affairs, Gilman gave up the senior Republican spot on Post Office and Civil Service (though he remains on the committee). On one of the few contentious issues handled by that committee in the 102nd Congress, Gilman opposed efforts to adjust the 1990 population census to account for an alleged undercount said to mainly affect localities with large minority-group constituencies.

At Home: Although many House incumbents from New York saw their districts drastically reshaped in redistricting that preceded the 1992 elections, Gilman got off light. Retaining his political base in exurban Rockland and Orange counties, Gilman easily defeated Democratic lawyer Jonathan L. Levine, running to five his streak of House elections in which he has taken two-thirds of the vote or better.

The 1992 contest was a far cry from the one in 1972, in which Gilman unseated a Democratic incumbent, and 1982, when he prevailed over House colleague Democrat Peter A. Peyser.

Gilman earned his initial House nomination by quietly working his way through the ranks of appointive and elective office. A former New York state assistant attorney general, Gilman in 1966 won an Assembly seat from Orange County. After three terms in the Assembly, Gilman challenged Democratic Rep. John G. Dow for the House. Viewed as a moderate,

Gilman defeated conservative builder Yale Rapkin for the Republican nomination.

Dow had carried a traditional Republican district in the 1964 Johnson presidential landslide and held it for six of the next eight years. But redistricting in 1972 had made the district even more Republican. Gilman won with a comfortable plurality, even though Rapkin siphoned off 13 percent as the Conservative Party candidate.

After deflecting a 1974 comeback attempt by Dow, Gilman's re-elections went smoothly until his district was combined with that of Peyser in 1982. A result of New York's loss of five House seats in reapportionment, their contest was described as a fair fight: Peyser had the party-registration advantage and Gilman the edge in familiar territory.

It was an angrier campaign than Gilman had been used to. Peyser criticized him for opposing a nuclear-weapons freeze and for backing military aid to El Salvador. The usually soft-spoken Gilman fired back, calling Peyser — who once had been a Republican House colleague of Gilman's before switching parties — as an "ultra-liberal Democratic congressman."

Gilman's close ties to his geographically dominant Rockland-Orange base paid off: He carried those two counties solidly. Gilman was almost able to carry a usually Democratic, heavily Jewish portion of Sullivan County that had been placed in the district for the first time. Peyser took the Westchester County portion, his home base, but it was not enough.

Since then, Gilman has easily fended off all challenges, including the most unusual comeback attempt of 1990. His Democratic opponent was 85-year-old former Rep. Dow. But the contest was a mild attempt at a "last hurrah" for Dow. Gilman won with 69 percent.

Committees

Foreign Affairs (Ranking)
Europe & the Middle East (ranking)

Post Office & Civil Service (2nd of 9 Republicans)
Postal Operations & Services

Elections

1992 General		
Benjamin A. Gilman (R)	150,301	(66%)
Jonathan L. Levine (D)	66,826	(29%)
Robert F. Garrison (RTL)	10,204	(4%)
1990 General		
Benjamin A. Gilman (R)	95,495	(69%)
John G. Dow (D)	37,034	(27%)
Margaret M. Beirne (RTL)	6,656	(5%)

Previous Winning Percentages: **1988** (71%) **1986** (69%) **1984** (69%) **1982** (53%) **1980** (74%) **1978** (62%) **1976** (65%) **1974** (54%) **1972** (48%)

District Vote for President

1992
D 116,294 (45%)
R 107,107 (41%)
I 37,011 (14%)

Campaign Finance

	Receipts	Receipts from PACs		Expend-itures
1992				
Gilman (R)	$566,773	$212,397	(37%)	$576,538
Levine (D)	$30,135	0		$27,833
1990				
Gilman (R)	$445,481	$195,968	(44%)	$497,635
Dow (D)	$4,038	0		$3,473

Key Votes

1993	
Require parental notification of minors' abortions	N
Require unpaid family and medical leave	Y
Approve national "motor voter" registration bill	Y
Approve budget increasing taxes and reducing deficit	N
Approve economic stimulus plan	N
1992	
Approve balanced-budget constitutional amendment	N
Close down space station program	N
Approve U.S. aid for former Soviet Union	Y
Allow shifting funds from defense to domestic programs	N
1991	
Extend unemployment benefits using deficit financing	Y
Approve waiting period for handgun purchases	Y
Authorize use of force in Persian Gulf	Y

Voting Studies

	Presidential Support		Party Unity		Conservative Coalition	
Year	**S**	**O**	**S**	**O**	**S**	**O**
1992	41	58	42	57	56	44
1991	50	50	39	61	57	43
1990	33	66	35	63	52	48
1989	44	55	29	69	44	56
1988	41	54	39	58	55	42
1987	38	61	33	60	58	42
1986	43	53	31	67	66	30
1985	44	55	43	53	60	38
1984	45	55	43	57	58	42
1983	57	43	42	56	61	38
1982	53	42	41	56	45	52
1981	51	29	42	48	48	51

Interest Group Ratings

Year	**ADA**	**AFL-CIO**	**CCUS**	**ACU**
1992	75	92	50	32
1991	60	92	20	30
1990	61	83	14	29
1989	55	92	60	43
1988	55	93	50	42
1987	68	88	21	26
1986	40	92	28	55
1985	45	82	27	43
1984	40	62	44	33
1983	45	65	45	57
1982	50	75	36	38
1981	45	43	72	66

21 Michael R. McNulty (D)

Of Green Island — Elected 1988; 3rd Term

Born: Sept. 16, 1947, Troy, N.Y.
Education: College of the Holy Cross, A.B. 1969.
Occupation: Public official.
Family: Wife, Nancy Ann Lazzaro; four children.
Religion: Roman Catholic.
Political Career: Green Island supervisor, 1970-77; Democratic nominee for N.Y. Assembly, 1976; mayor of Green Island, 1977-83; N.Y. Assembly, 1983-89.
Capitol Office: 217 Cannon Bldg. 20515; 225-5076.

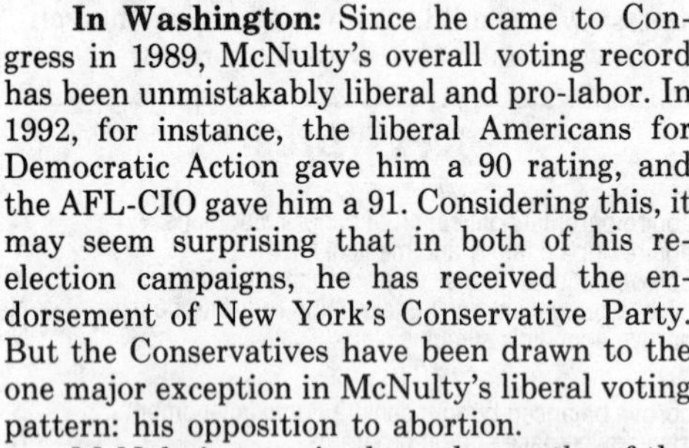

In Washington: Since he came to Congress in 1989, McNulty's overall voting record has been unmistakably liberal and pro-labor. In 1992, for instance, the liberal Americans for Democratic Action gave him a 90 rating, and the AFL-CIO gave him a 91. Considering this, it may seem surprising that in both of his re-election campaigns, he has received the endorsement of New York's Conservative Party. But the Conservatives have been drawn to the one major exception in McNulty's liberal voting pattern: his opposition to abortion.

McNulty's votes in the early months of the 103rd Congress were typical of his usual posture: He voted almost down the line with the Democratic leadership, supporting President Clinton's budget, tax and economic stimulus bills, voting to require businesses to provide unpaid family and medical leave and backing the "motor voter" bill broadening registration opportunities.

But McNulty and 40 other Democrats went against Clinton — a supporter of abortion rights — in voting to require parental notification when minors seek abortions at federally funded clinics. McNulty says he does not support an outright ban of abortion, but he opposes public funding of the procedure except in cases of rape or incest or danger to the woman's life. McNulty did, however, support lifting the ban on abortion counseling in federally funded clinics.

If McNulty takes exception to his national party's line on abortion issues, it has not prevented him from rising fairly quickly to an influential post in the House — a seat on the Ways and Means Committee. He got the assignment at the start of the 103rd Congress, partly as a reward for toiling away quietly as a vote-counter for the party. In his first term, McNulty served as one of two whips for his freshman class. In his second, he was an at-large party whip.

After all the 1992 election turnover in the House, a number of seats on plum committees opened up, and initially McNulty had his eyes on Appropriations. But New York was not going to get more than two Democratic seats there, and the leading contenders were a woman, Nita M. Lowey, and a Hispanic, Jose E. Serrano. McNulty was persuaded to shift his ambitions to Ways and Means, which had only one other New York Democrat, Charles B. Rangel. After winning the seat, McNulty joined the Select Revenue Measures Subcommittee, which Rangel chairs.

McNulty's move to Ways and Means and its broad legislative portfolio marks his definitive emergence from the shadow cast by his predecessor in the House, longtime Rep. Samuel S. Stratton. A hawkish Democrat and defense specialist who rose to a high-ranking seat on the Armed Services Committee, Stratton looked out for his district's defense-related industries. When McNulty first ran in 1988 to succeed Stratton, he said that if elected he would try to get on Armed Services.

The Democratic leadership did put McNulty on Armed Services, and there he generally took a more pro-defense line than many of his Democratic colleagues. He voted in 1989 against capping production of the B-2 stealth bomber and in 1990 against a deep slash in funding for the Strategic Defense Initiative. In January 1991, he voted to give President Bush authority to use military force against Iraq.

But in keeping with his basic impulse to be loyal to his party leadership, McNulty first voted for the unsuccessful Democratic-sponsored resolution calling for continued economic sanctions against Iraq rather than war. He was one of only three Democrats who voted for both sanctions and force. McNulty said he felt that defeat of both measures would have sent a signal of weakness to Iraqi President Saddam Hussein.

At Home: Running in a district dominated by Albany, a Democratic stronghold, McNulty has won three times with more than 60 percent of the vote.

His easy 1992 win over GOP challenger Nancy Norman was most notable for the paradox of his getting the Conservative Party endorsement, while Norman, an abortion rights supporter, was backed by New York's Liberal Party.

McNulty said in 1988 that serving in Congress had been a lifelong goal. But he did not

New York 21

Capital District — Albany; Schenectady; Troy

With government employment and manufacturing as its economic mainstays, New York's Capital District has long provided Democrats — including Rep. McNulty and his predecessor, the late Samuel S. Stratton — with a solid political base.

Yet the 21st is no liberal stronghold; its minority population is not large, and its major ethnic groups are Irish- and Italian-Americans, many of whom are conservative on social issues. McNulty is one of the few New York Democrats who seeks and receives the endorsement of the state's Conservative Party.

Bill Clinton carried the 21st in 1992, but won a majority of the vote only in Albany County (which has just over half the district's residents). Ross Perot took more than 20 percent of the vote in Schenectady, Rensselaer and Montgomery counties.

The 21st covers most of the Albany-Schenectady-Troy metropolitan area. Albany, the capital, is the district's largest city with just over 100,000 residents. It has the 21st's largest minority concentration; more than half the district's blacks live there.

Albany provides the foundations for Democratic wins in the 21st; despite pockets of Republican votes in the suburbs (the largest of which is adjacent Colonie), Albany County usually goes Democratic. It was one of only three upstate counties to favor Democrat Robert Abrams over Republican Sen. Alfonse M. D'Amato in 1992.

The state bureaucracy and regional federal offices in Albany provide economic stability (even though fiscal problems have forced some public agencies to trim their payrolls). Nearly half of all employment in Albany is in the public sector.

Albany County, on the west bank of the Hudson River, has a longstanding industrial sector that includes the arsenal in Watervliet. But its private-sector growth has been in such fields as health care and insurance. The state university campus in Albany (15,300 students) is the largest higher educational institution in the 21st; others include Rensselaer Polytechnic Institute (6,800 students) in Troy and Union College (2,300 students) in Schenectady.

Industrial employment remains more integral in Troy, across the Hudson in Rensselaer County, and west along the Mohawk River in Schenectady and Amsterdam (Montgomery County). General Electric makes power-generating equipment and has its research and development center in Schenectady.

Even though it remains the 21st's largest employer, GE cut its work force deeply over the past decade; overall industrial employment in Schenectady County declined by more than a third during the 1980s. The blow was cushioned by an aggressive economic development effort that attracted smaller manufacturers and service providers.

But Montgomery County has been struggling since its major employer, a Mohawk Carpet plant, moved south in the 1960s. It has the lowest median household income among the district's counties.

1990 Population: 580,337. White 529,568 (91%), Black 36,352 (6%), Other 14,417 (2%). Hispanic origin 11,963 (2%). 18 and over 451,775 (78%), 62 and over 106,092 (18%). Median age: 34.

expect to have the chance that year, since Stratton had filed for re-election in the then-23rd District.

When New York's candidate filing deadline passed, McNulty had already re-upped to run for a fourth term in the New York Assembly. However, Stratton, a 30-year House member who had been in ill health, suddenly announced his retirement. Democratic leaders in the 23rd met within hours of the announcement and selected McNulty to replace Stratton on the ballot.

While taking typically Democratic positions on domestic issues, McNulty said he had no major differences with Stratton's conservative stance on defense. With endorsements from Stratton and environmentalist groups, McNulty defeated local Republican official Peter Bakal with 62 percent. Two years later, he won the Conservative Party endorsement and topped GOP public relations consultant Margaret Buhrmaster with 64 percent.

Deeply rooted in Albany County politics, McNulty's family is virtually dynastic in its home base of Green Island. His grandfather was elected town tax collector in 1914, and went on to serve as town supervisor, county board chairman and county sheriff. McNulty's father was supervisor for eight years, mayor for 16 years and county sheriff for six.

McNulty joined his elders in 1969, winning a seat on the town board at age 22. While in this post, he waged his only unsuccessful campaign, a 1976 challenge to a Republican assemblyman. He recouped the next year by winning a contest for Green Island mayor, then won the first of three state Assembly terms in 1982.

Committee

Ways & Means (20th of 24 Democrats)
Select Revenue Measures; Trade

Elections

1992 General		
Michael R. McNulty (D, C)	166,371	(63%)
Nancy Norman (R, L)	91,184	(34%)
William J. Donnelly (RTL)	7,723	(3%)
1990 General		
Michael R. McNulty (D, C)	117,239	(64%)
Margaret B. Buhrmaster (R)	65,760	(36%)

Previous Winning Percentage: 1988 (62%)

District Vote for President

1992
D 140,251 (48%)
R 99,094 (34%)
I 51,086 (18%)

Campaign Finance

	Receipts	Receipts from PACs		Expend-itures
1992				
McNulty (D)	$220,997	$126,386	(57%)	$252,821
1990				
McNulty (D)	$240,736	$149,179	(62%)	$149,204
Buhrmaster (R)	$23,300	$250	(1%)	$23,299

Key Votes

1993	
Require parental notification of minors' abortions	Y
Require unpaid family and medical leave	Y
Approve national "motor voter" registration bill	Y
Approve budget increasing taxes and reducing deficit	Y
Approve economic stimulus plan	Y
1992	
Approve balanced-budget constitutional amendment	N
Close down space station program	N
Approve U.S. aid for former Soviet Union	Y
Allow shifting funds from defense to domestic programs	Y
1991	
Extend unemployment benefits using deficit financing	Y
Approve waiting period for handgun purchases	Y
Authorize use of force in Persian Gulf	Y

Voting Studies

	Presidential Support		Party Unity		Conservative Coalition	
Year	S	O	S	O	S	O
1992	27	72	87	10	54	46
1991	31	68	93	6	35	65
1990	27	72	92	7	35	65
1989	42	57	83	14	56	44

Interest Group Ratings

Year	ADA	AFL-CIO	CCUS	ACU
1992	90	91	38	13
1991	80	100	10	10
1990	78	92	21	21
1989	75	100	40	25

22 Gerald B.H. Solomon (R)

Of Glens Falls — Elected 1978; 8th Term

Born: Aug. 14, 1930, Okeechobee, Fla.
Education: Siena College, 1949-50; St. Lawrence U., 1952-53.
Military Service: Marine Corps, 1951-52.
Occupation: Insurance executive.
Family: Wife, Freda Parker; five children.
Religion: Presbyterian.
Political Career: Queensbury town supervisor, 1968-72; Warren County Legislature, 1968-72; N.Y. Assembly, 1973-79.
Capitol Office: 2265 Rayburn Bldg. 20515; 225-5614.

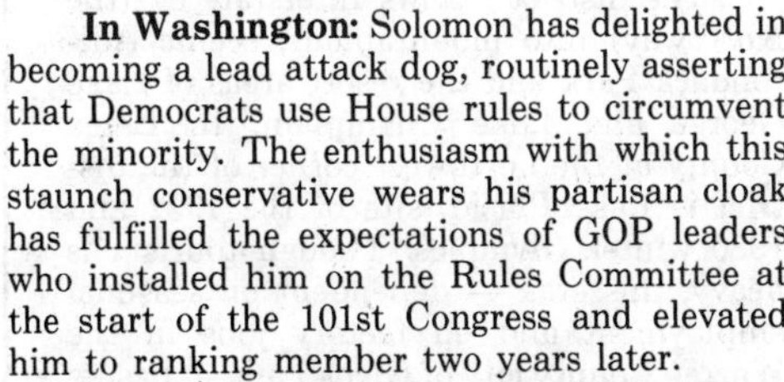

In Washington: Solomon has delighted in becoming a lead attack dog, routinely asserting that Democrats use House rules to circumvent the minority. The enthusiasm with which this staunch conservative wears his partisan cloak has fulfilled the expectations of GOP leaders who installed him on the Rules Committee at the start of the 101st Congress and elevated him to ranking member two years later.

In some quarters, it was thought that Democrat Thomas S. Foley of Washington would be a more conciliatory Speaker than his predecessor, Democrat Jim Wright of Texas. And the elevation of Joe Moakley of Massachusetts to Rules chairman was likewise expected to signal more genial interparty dealings. But that has proved to be only partly the case, as Foley has adopted a particular fondness for restrictive rules that greatly limit floor debate.

"I will say that we have a much more cordial working relationship with the new Speaker and Rules Committee chairman," Solomon said in 1990. "But that has not yet translated into greater procedural fairness." Rules, he said on another occasion, "can literally break the law legally, and we do it all the time."

With the Democrats capturing the White House and ascendant in the 103rd Congress, Solomon was presented with more opportunities to protest majoritarianism. The Democrats pushed through a series of rules changes, most of which were intended to make the House more efficient. But in several instances, Republicans perceived the changes as grossly unfair.

Most egregious to Republicans was allowing the delegates from the District of Columbia, American Samoa, Guam, Puerto Rico and the Virgin Islands — all Democrats — to vote on floor amendments in certain circumstances. Amendments to bills are voted on in a parliamentary setting called the Committee of the Whole House; delegates were still not permitted to vote as regular House members. Solomon persisted at the start of the 103rd in demanding — as House rules permit — repeat votes by the full House on amendments on which delegates cast ballots in the Committee of the Whole.

Solomon plainly revels in allowing his temper to flare on occasion. When Democrat Louise M. Slaughter of New York, a fellow Rules member, tried to cut off a typical Solomon outburst in March 1993, Solomon erupted: "You had better not do that, ma'am. You will regret that as long as you live. Who do you think you are?" Solomon's words in the Congressional Record were edited to a more polite objection.

His move onto Rules did not come without a cost: He had to give up his seats on the Foreign Affairs Committee, a forum for his anti-communist rhetoric, and Veterans' Affairs, where the ex-Marine was one of the most stalwart defenders of veterans benefit programs and where he showed he could work with the equally pro-veteran committee Democrats.

Solomon remains a vocal participant in foreign policy debates. In January 1991, the day after President Bush launched the ground offensive against Iraq, Solomon took to the House floor to issue a ringing endorsement of the actions and to call once again for a constitutional amendment to ban flag burning. "What we cannot be proud of," Solomon said, "is the unshaven, shaggy-haired, drug culture, poor excuses for Americans, wearing their tiny round wire-rim glasses, a protester's symbol of the blame-America-first crowd, out in front of the White House burning the American flag."

Solomon has also been in the forefront of congressional efforts to deny normal trade relations to China as punishment for its crackdown on pro-democracy demonstrators in June 1989. In the 101st and 102nd Congresses, Solomon's measure to revoke China's most-favored-nation status passed the House but died in the Senate.

Early in the 103rd, he renewed his call for a ban on the export of satellites for launch by China. That stance, intended to hamstring China's development of advanced rockets, reflects

New York 22

Rural East — Glens Falls; Saratoga Springs

The 22nd runs nearly 200 miles south to north, from the Dutchess County estate country at the edge of the New York City metropolis, around Albany and on to the Adirondack mountain region not far from Canada. It takes in most of New York's eastern border with the New England states.

This largely rural and conservative district has held more strongly to its Yankee Republican voting traditions than its New England neighbors. The 22nd is carried overwhelmingly by Republican Rep. Solomon, one of the most outspoken conservatives in the House.

In 1992, Solomon carried the four full and five partial counties in the 22nd with no less than 62 percent of the vote (and as much as 69 percent). Republican Sen. Alfonse M. D'Amato topped 55 percent in all 22nd District counties as he narrowly won re-election in 1992.

George Bush, who won nearly 60 percent of the district's vote in 1988, fell off sharply in 1992, but still managed a plurality win over Bill Clinton, who failed to reach 40 percent in any of the district's county portions. Ross Perot topped a fifth of the vote in every county.

The 22nd is 97 percent non-Hispanic white; it has the smallest minority population among New York districts.

The population hub of the 22nd is in its center, in the Albany-Schenectady-Troy metropolitan area. This district has none of those cities, but much of their GOP suburbia.

Saratoga County, just north of Albany at the confluence of the Hudson and Mohawk rivers, has by far the district's largest population share (with about 30 percent of the district's residents). The ongoing suburbanization of the southern part of the county, in such communities as Half Moon and Clifton Park, was reflected in Saratoga County's 18 percent population increase during the 1980s.

Across the Hudson, the 22nd takes in much of Rensselaer County. But its largest bloc of Democratic votes, in industrial Troy, is snatched away by the 21st District, leaving the 22nd with its suburbs and dairy lands.

In northern Saratoga County is the resort town of Saratoga Springs. Nearby is a Revolutionary War battlefield, one of many 18th century historical sites in the 22nd.

The district follows Interstate 87 (the Northway) into mountainous, scenic Adirondack Park and the resort areas of Lake George and Lake Champlain. In Essex County at the northwest corner of the district is Lake Placid, site of the 1932 and 1980 winter Olympics. Though tourism is heavy, this area — dependent on seasonal employment and on factory jobs in the Warren County city of Glens Falls — has its share of economic problems.

The southern end of the 22nd is made up of mainly rural territory in Schoharie, Greene, Columbia and northern Dutchess County. Near the south edge of the district is Hyde Park and the estate of President Franklin D. Roosevelt, the patrician Democrat who in his time was regarded by much of the area's landed gentry as a "traitor to his class."

1990 Population: 580,337. White 560,652 (97%), Black 12,548 (2%), Other 7,137 (1%). Hispanic origin 8,807 (2%). 18 and over 434,538 (75%), 62 and over 89,550 (15%). Median age: 34.

his longstanding opposition to allowing U.S. technology to get into the hands of certain foreign governments. In 1989, Solomon opposed the joint development with Japan of the new FS-X fighter plane, and in 1991 he warned against selling Patriot missile and other technology to the Soviet Union.

Because he is somewhat of a trade hawk — a position anathema to the basic free-trade GOP philosophy — he defers to Californian David Dreier to handle most trade matters on Rules.

During his tenure on the Foreign Affairs Committee, Solomon regularly excoriated panel Democrats for being too hard on U.S. allies and too soft on anti-American regimes and insurgent movements. One of the staunchest supporters of the Nicaraguan contras, Solomon charged during one of the debates to cut off U.S. aid to the contras that the panel was "about to sell the United States down the drain and is aiding and abetting the spread of communism in Central America."

Solomon's legislative achievements in recent years have been focused on penalizing drug abusers and those who shirk military duty.

He has sponsored successful amendments requiring random drug testing of employees in the CIA, the Coast Guard, at NASA and within the Washington Metro transit system. And he has persuaded Congress to reduce federal highway aid to states that do not suspend the driver's licenses of those convicted of drug offenses and to make students convicted of drug possession ineligible for financial aid.

Since 1982, Solomon has also successfully

sponsored amendments barring men who avoid their draft-registration requirements from receiving federal student aid, job training assistance and contracted defense work.

At Home: Solomon's stalwart conservatism is his armor in a mainly rural eastern New York district, where Yankee Republican traditions have proved sturdier than in the neighboring New England states. Running in one of the few New York House districts that Bush carried in 1992, Solomon won with two-thirds of the vote.

Solomon has never been seriously threatened since his easy win to unseat Democratic Rep. Ned Pattison in 1978. Pattison had been one of the upset Democratic winners in the Watergate year of 1974, becoming the first Democrat to represent the then-29th District in the 20th century. He managed to hold his seat in 1976, when a Republican and a Conservative Party candidate split the vote against him.

But in Solomon, Pattison faced a popular state legislator who had support from both the GOP and the Conservatives. Solomon's Assembly constituency lay entirely within the 29th, so he had a solid base from which to run.

Pattison also created his own problems with an interview in Playboy magazine, in which he admitted that he had smoked marijuana: Conservatives referred to him derisively as "Pot-tison." Solomon went on to win with 54 percent and has tallied much larger margins in his seven re-election campaigns.

Co-founder of an insurance and investment firm, Solomon got his start in politics in 1968, winning election as Queensbury town supervisor. He held that post and served simultaneously as a member of the Warren County Legislature. In 1972, he won the Assembly seat that he held until his election to the House.

Committees

Rules (Ranking)
Rules of the House

Joint Organization of Congress

Elections

1992 General		
Gerald B.H. Solomon (R, C, RTL)	164,436	(65%)
David Roberts (D)	86,896	(35%)
1990 General		
Gerald B.H. Solomon (R, C, RTL)	121,206	(68%)
Bob Lawrence (D)	56,671	(32%)

Previous Winning Percentages: **1988** (72%) **1986** (70%) **1984** (73%) **1982** (74%) **1980** (67%) **1978** (54%)

District Vote for President

1992

D 99,988 (36%)
R 116,238 (42%)
I 62,533 (22%)

Campaign Finance

	Receipts	Receipts from PACs		Expend-itures
1992				
Solomon (R)	$382,251	$283,180	(74%)	$286,286
Roberts (D)	$33,625	0		$32,189
1990				
Solomon (R)	$255,758	$147,715	(58%)	$240,615
Lawrence (D)	$98,649	$32,340	(33%)	$95,100

Key Votes

1993	
Require parental notification of minors' abortions	Y
Require unpaid family and medical leave	Y
Approve national "motor voter" registration bill	N
Approve budget increasing taxes and reducing deficit	N
Approve economic stimulus plan	N
1992	
Approve balanced-budget constitutional amendment	Y
Close down space station program	Y
Approve U.S. aid for former Soviet Union	N
Allow shifting funds from defense to domestic programs	N
1991	
Extend unemployment benefits using deficit financing	N
Approve waiting period for handgun purchases	N
Authorize use of force in Persian Gulf	Y

Voting Studies

	Presidential Support		Party Unity		Conservative Coalition	
Year	**S**	**O**	**S**	**O**	**S**	**O**
1992	70	26	88	9	83	13
1991	71	25	89	8	95	3
1990	67	32	84	13	87	13
1989	67	33	86	13	90	10
1988	65	32	90	9	95	5
1987	69	29	92	5	88	7
1986	79	16	84	10	92	4
1985	70	20	86	5	82	13
1984	64	34	85	10	83	14
1983	76	21	92	5	94	4
1982	60	26	85	9	78	10
1981	70	24	92	5	93	4

Interest Group Ratings

Year	ADA	AFL-CIO	CCUS	ACU
1992	15	58	63	96
1991	15	45	56	90
1990	22	36	64	83
1989	15	33	80	79
1988	15	57	86	88
1987	4	20	86	91
1986	0	21	83	81
1985	15	25	86	84
1984	5	31	81	79
1983	5	6	80	96
1982	5	22	76	90
1981	5	7	89	100

23 Sherwood Boehlert (R)

Of New Hartford — Elected 1982; 6th Term

Born: Sept. 28, 1936, Utica, N.Y.
Education: Utica College, A.B. 1961.
Military Service: Army, 1956-58.
Occupation: Congressional aide; public relations executive.
Family: Wife, Marianne Willey; four children.
Religion: Roman Catholic.
Political Career: Sought GOP nomination for U.S. House, 1972; Oneida County executive, 1979-82.
Capitol Office: 1127 Longworth Bldg. 20515; 225-3665.

In Washington: Like others in the small band of moderate-to-liberal House Republicans, Boehlert can pinch pennies with the most frugal members of his party. But on social issues and campaign reform questions, he often makes common cause with Democrats.

In the early days of the 103rd Congress, as confrontational conservatives in the House GOP were butting heads with the newly installed Clinton administration, Boehlert sided with the Democratic president in several key legislative battles. The New Yorker was one of just 40 House Republicans to vote for passage of a bill requiring businesses to provide family and medical leave. He was one of only 34 Republicans opposing an effort to require parental notification when minors seek abortions at federally funded clinics. He was one of 21 Republicans to back House passage of the "motor voter" registration bill. And he was one of just three GOP members to join the Democratic majority in supporting Clinton's ill-starred $16 billion economic stimulus package.

At first glance, Boehlert's vote for the stimulus plan appeared odd for a man who often has decried what he sees as excessive federal spending. But Boehlert found the plan appealing on several counts. As a former county executive, he applauded its community development block grant money for local governments. And since his district formerly included the Schoharie Creek bridge (a span on the New York State Thruway that collapsed several years ago with loss of life), he welcomed the funds earmarked for infrastructure repair.

Boehlert's willingness to stray from the more conservative GOP House majority is nothing new. He was weaned on politics when New York Gov. Nelson A. Rockefeller was at his apogee.

Despite a personal friendship with President Bush that dated to the 1960s (when Bush was a young congressman and Boehlert a congressional aide), Boehlert's presidential support score during the Bush years never exceeded 58 percent; he consistently voted less than half the time with the majority of House Republicans.

To those who call him a GOP apostate, Boehlert says that he actually is a defender of true Republican values. "Unless we realize that the overwhelming majority of Republicans are moderate," he said in late 1992, "we're destined to be the minority party forever more."

From time to time, Boehlert was helpful to the Bush White House. He stood with Bush in support of the controversial October 1990 budget agreement, which the GOP right denounced for its tax increases. He backed the use of force in the Persian Gulf in 1991. And in 1992 he sided with his fellow House Republicans on a number of key economic votes, including support for a balanced-budget constitutional amendment. In 1993, he was part of the unanimous House GOP vote against Clinton's budget plan. And to the surprise of many, Boehlert in early 1989 backed conservative champion Newt Gingrich in his successful bid for House GOP whip. Boehlert sees Gingrich as a creative thinker and a more pragmatic politician than his reputation would suggest.

Still, Boehlert is viewed warily by some in his party, and he has yet to gain a seat on a prestige House committee. During the Reagan years, he tried to win appointment to Ways and Means or Appropriations but was passed over for members more loyal to the party line. As a representative from solid GOP territory, Boehlert is cut little slack from party leaders in Washington, who see no political necessity behind his independent voting habits.

He is a member of two second-line panels, Public Works and Science. Both committees operate in the kind of bipartisan fashion that suits Boehlert's affable manner and preference for seeking consensus.

Boehlert has found other forums in which he can stake out his views. In April 1993, he was re-elected chairman of the Ripon Society, a nationwide organization of moderate Republicans.

Also beyond his committee work, he was a leader in the 1980s fight against acid rain,

New York 23

Central — Utica; Rome

The 23rd, which takes in four full counties and parts of five others in central New York, is a demographic sampler. It has a few cities, including Utica and Rome in Oneida County, many more small towns and rural stretches that make up most of this large district's land area.

A Republican heritage in this upstate region allows most GOP candidates to carry the 23rd. Rep. Boehlert's record as a moderate has appealed to the mix of farm, Main Street and urban voters; he has never been seriously challenged. Against three opponents in 1992 — a liberal Democrat and two conservatives — Boehlert won at least 58 percent of the vote in every county; he topped 60 percent in all but three.

However, many of the 23rd's voters showed their disaffection with George Bush in 1992. He carried the district, but won more than 40 percent in just four counties. Economic problems in some blue-collar and rural areas gave Ross Perot an audience; he topped a fifth of the vote in all district counties.

Oneida County, Boehlert's home base, has more than 40 percent of the district's population. The biggest concentration is in the short stretch of the Mohawk River Valley that connects Utica and Rome.

Blue-collar jobs continue to be important in these aging industrial cities: The largest private-sector employer is the Oneida silverware company. But the manufacturing sector has declined over the years. Utica's poverty rate is above 20 percent. Local officials look to service industry jobs and such high-tech fields as fiber optics and photonics for growth. Rome's economy has been cushioned by nearby Griffiss Air Force Base. But that good fortune may soon run out: A military-base downsizing proposal submitted in March 1993 by a federal commission targeted Griffiss for a major realignment.

The remainder of Oneida County is mainly rural. Although there is some Democratic vote in the cities, the county usually sets a Republican tone for the district. Boehlert took two-thirds of the vote and GOP Sen. Alfonse M. D'Amato took 61 percent here in 1992.

Other areas of the 23rd have concerns about the post-Cold War defense budget. A Simmonds plant in Chenango County makes military jet engines. The area of Broome County in the southern end of the 23rd is affected by cutbacks in nearby Binghamton's defense-related industries.

There are other industrial facilities, including Remington Arms and Chicago Pneumatic Tool plants in Herkimer County. The district's educational institutions include Colgate University in Hamilton (Madison County; 2,700 students), Hartwick College in Oneonta (Otsego County; 1,400 students) and the state university in Oneonta (4,200 students).

At the south end of Otsego Lake (the source of the Susquehanna River) is Cooperstown, a small village that hosts the Baseball Hall of Fame. It was here that James Fenimore Cooper wrote the stories of frontier days that gave central New York its nickname — the "Leatherstocking Region."

1990 Population: 580,337. White 556,069 (96%), Black 16,565 (3%), Other 7,703 (1%). Hispanic origin 8,922 (2%). 18 and over 436,162 (75%), 62 and over 103,010 (18%). Median age: 34.

reflecting not only his parochial concern for the acidic Adirondack lakes, but also his general worry about his party's image. "A lot of people have the traditional belief that Republicans don't give a damn about the environment," he said in 1989. "Well, a lot of people are wrong."

Boehlert cited 1990 passage of clean air legislation as the major accomplishment of the 101st Congress. And for years he has supported legislation to elevate the Environmental Protection Agency to Cabinet status in a new Department of the Environment.

On Public Works' Aviation Subcommittee, he has been a voice for airline consumer and safety bills. On Science, he has joined critics who say NASA's budget is too big.

But Boehlert's primary fire has been aimed at the superconducting super collider (SSC) — an atom-smasher under construction in Texas that could be the largest public works project in U.S. history.

Boehlert spoke out loudly during the 101st Congress against excessive spending on the super collider. Imploring the project's staunchest backers to practice moderation, Boehlert said, "The SSC will not cure cancer, will not solve the problem of male pattern baldness and will not guarantee a World Series victory for the Chicago Cubs."

Boehlert has continued his attacks on the SSC. He signed a letter with five other members in February 1993 asking President Clinton to scrap the project altogether.

At Home: Having proved the appeal of his left-of-center Republican philosophy by winning big early in his House career, Boehlert earned a free pass in the 1988 and 1990 elections. He faced no major-party opposition.

In 1992, he faced a surfeit of challengers but still won with 64 percent, a solid showing in a poor Republican year. One of his opponents was quite well known: Randall Terry, leader of the controversial anti-abortion group Operation Rescue, who ran as the Right to Life Party candidate. But Terry was distracted by his organization's national efforts — he was arrested during the summer for violating court orders restricting his protest activities at the Democratic and Republican national conventions — and did not actively campaign against Boehlert.

This present electoral security was hard-won for Boehlert, a longtime congressional aide whose House ambitions were deferred for a decade after an initial defeat in 1972. That year, Boehlert had hoped to succeed his boss, retiring GOP Rep. Alexander Pirnie, but he lost to Donald J. Mitchell in a Republican primary.

Boehlert swallowed his disappointment and went to work for Mitchell. In 1977, he left Washington to run Mitchell's Utica office, then in 1979 restarted his own political career by winning the Oneida County executive post.

By 1982, Mitchell was ready to retire. Boehlert was driving along an interstate highway in Oneida County when he heard the news. He pulled into a rest stop, called a radio station and announced his candidacy.

As county executive he had earned high marks from labor unions, and he was one of only two New York state Republicans to get the state AFL-CIO's endorsement in the 1982 elections. After winning the Republican primary comfortably, Boehlert capitalized on a huge organizational and financial advantage over Democrat Anita Maxwell, a dairy farmer who had lost badly to Mitchell in 1976. He won with 56 percent.

Boehlert's moderate voting record vexed some of the more conservative Republican elements in his district (then the 25th). In 1986, they put forward music professor Robert S. Barstow to challenge Boehlert in the GOP primary. But Boehlert won renomination by 2-to-1, and he nailed down the seat that November by taking nearly 70 percent of the vote.

Committees

Post Office & Civil Service (8th of 9 Republicans)
Oversight & Investigations (ranking)

Public Works & Transportation (4th of 24 Republicans)
Water Resources & the Environment (ranking); Aviation; Economic Development

Science, Space & Technology (3rd of 22 Republicans)
Science (ranking)

Elections

1992 General		
Sherwood Boehlert (R)	139,774	(64%)
Paula DiPerna (D)	61,835	(28%)
Randall A. Terry (RTL)	8,688	(4%)
Geoffrey P. Grace (C)	8,011	(4%)
1990 General		
Sherwood Boehlert (R)	91,348	(84%)
William L. Griffen (L)	17,481	(16%)

Previous Winning Percentages: **1988** (100%) **1986** (69%) **1984** (73%) **1982** (56%)

District Vote for President

1992

D 92,549 (37%)
R 99,497 (40%)
I 55,902 (23%)

Campaign Finance

	Receipts	Receipts from PACs		Expend-itures
1992				
Boehlert (R)	$368,179	$197,496	(54%)	$372,109
DiPerna (D)	$64,018	$5,500	(9%)	$63,220
1990				
Boehlert (R)	$303,746	$130,950	(43%)	$272,533
Griffen (L)	$12,882	0		$10,577

Key Votes

1993	
Require parental notification of minors' abortions	N
Require unpaid family and medical leave	Y
Approve national "motor voter" registration bill	Y
Approve budget increasing taxes and reducing deficit	N
Approve economic stimulus plan	Y
1992	
Approve balanced-budget constitutional amendment	Y
Close down space station program	N
Approve U.S. aid for former Soviet Union	Y
Allow shifting funds from defense to domestic programs	N
1991	
Extend unemployment benefits using deficit financing	Y
Approve waiting period for handgun purchases	Y
Authorize use of force in Persian Gulf	Y

Voting Studies

	Presidential Support		Party Unity		Conservative Coalition	
Year	**S**	**O**	**S**	**O**	**S**	**O**
1992	42	58	50	49	58	40
1991	58	41	46	54	62	38
1990	40	60	47	52	61	39
1989	51	47	46	51	44	56
1988	37	59	58	40	58	37
1987	37	60	46	49	65	35
1986	46	54	53	45	66	32
1985	41	59	54	44	56	44
1984	58	39	38	59	61	37
1983	52	43	34	61	49	47

Interest Group Ratings

Year	ADA	AFL-CIO	CCUS	ACU
1992	75	75	50	40
1991	45	75	40	40
1990	61	50	50	33
1989	65	75	70	43
1988	65	86	64	24
1987	60	69	67	9
1986	50	93	56	41
1985	45	65	57	52
1984	65	62	47	25
1983	45	47	55	30

24 John M. McHugh (R)

Of Pierrepont Manor — Elected 1992; 1st Term

Born: Sept. 29, 1948, Watertown, N.Y.
Education: Syracuse U., B.A. 1970; State U. of New York, Albany, M.P.A. 1977.
Occupation: City official; legislative aide; insurance broker.
Family: Wife, Katharine Sullivan.
Religion: Roman Catholic.
Political Career: N.Y. Senate, 1985-93.
Capitol Office: 416 Cannon Bldg. 20515; 225-4611.

The Path to Washington: Whoever represents the sprawling 24th in New York's North Country has one job above virtually all others: Find a way to keep the largely rural, economically struggling district's two big military bases open and healthy. Six-term GOP Rep. David O'B. Martin managed to help do that from his seat on the Armed Services Committee. Now McHugh is poised to do the same.

McHugh made a name for himself in New York's state Senate in part through his aggressive advocacy for dairy farmers, a major presence in his district. But when he had to focus on the committee he most wanted, it was not Agriculture but Armed Services, where he snagged the seat left open by Martin's retirement.

From there, he will help guide the fortunes of the Army's Fort Drum and Plattsburgh Air Force Base (and Griffiss Air Force Base just outside his district), which must struggle to survive in an era of defense cuts and base shutdowns. In January 1993, McHugh hired Martin as a special aide to help him monitor any action on the bases by the commission studying the closure list.

A socially moderate but fiscally conservative Republican, McHugh appears to be a good match for his heavily Republican district, where he has a reputation for diligent constituent service and has never had a close election since he won his state Senate seat in 1984.

A supporter of abortion rights and an opponent of increased taxes, McHugh warded off challenges from more conservative, anti-abortion Republicans in a district where Democrats generally failed to field strong candidates. He has a reputation as a smart bargainer, but his willingness to deal with Democrats in Albany helped put him on conservative hit lists.

He showed evidence of this flexibility early in the 103rd Congress as one of only 40 Republicans to vote for the family leave bill. He also voted for a bill codifying the Clinton administration's lifting of the so-called "gag rule" that prohibited staff at federally funded family planning clinics from discussing abortion.

But McHugh voted in April 1993 against a Democratic bill giving the president limited line-item veto authority, in favor of a stronger GOP substitute amendment. While most of the GOP freshmen voted for both, McHugh was one of 12, including fellow New Yorker Peter T. King, to support only the GOP substitute.

McHugh is a career politician who got his start as a confidential assistant to the city manager of his hometown of Watertown, the congressional district's largest city. From there he moved to the staff of state Sen. H. Douglas Barclay, where his duties included acting as a liaison to local governments in the district — a job that helped McHugh prepare for a successful run for the Senate when Barclay retired.

In Albany, McHugh worked in the Republican-majority Senate to pass legislation designed to help farmers and pushed to develop a compact of Northeastern states that would have enabled dairy farmers to get higher milk prices.

When Martin decided to retire, McHugh jumped into the race.

He beat his more conservative, anti-abortion primary opponent, local business owner and Hamilton town supervisor Morrison J. Hosley Jr., with 70 percent of the vote. In the general election, the two strongest candidates he faced were Hosley, who ran on the Conservative and Right to Life tickets, and Democrat Margaret M. Ravenscroft, a retired math teacher.

The two combined to hold McHugh to the lowest winning percentage of his career — a nonetheless comfortable 61 percent.

McHugh's congressional district, which borders Canada in extreme northern New York, is the state's largest — larger than nine states — and one of its poorest, with a double-digit unemployment rate that McHugh notes is consistently higher than the state and national averages.

He campaigned on the need to cut the unemployment rate and to revitalize New York's sagging economy, outlining a 12-point plan to help the district's farmers and small-business owners. Among his proposals were tax credits for businesses that invest in research and development and a targeted capital gains tax cut for small businesses.

New York 24

North Country — Plattsburgh; Watertown; Oswego

The 24th, which forms the northern border of New York state, is one of the East's most sprawling congressional districts. It covers all of eight counties and parts of two others. Beginning in the east along Lake Champlain, the 24th tracks north to the Canadian border, west along the St. Lawrence River, then south along Lake Ontario as far as Oswego. Its southern edge reaches east to the outskirts of metropolitan Albany. The Adirondack Mountains make up much of the district's middle.

Although there is blue-collar industry along its waterways, the 24th is a mainly rural district that holds strongly to a Yankee Republican tradition. The importance of defense-related facilities — including the Army's Fort Drum and Plattsburgh Air Force Base — and the lack of a significant minority population reinforce the GOP strength.

Republican McHugh easily won the open House seat in 1992; GOP Sen. Alfonse M. D'Amato swept the 24th's counties, winning most with 60 percent or more.

The district's GOP tendencies have remained solid despite its rather stagnant economy, a result of its reliance on heavy industry and its remote location. But economic concerns took a toll on George Bush in 1992. Though he carried all but two counties in the 24th, his margins were mainly meager pluralities. He did, however, manage 53 percent in sparsely populated Hamilton, the only county in New York in which he won a majority.

The counties that form the 24th's western border, Oswego, Jefferson and St. Lawrence, are its most populous. Oswego has a number of industrial employers, including a Miller Brewing plant and three nuclear power stations. There is a State University of New York campus in the city of Oswego.

Industry in Jefferson County is centered in Watertown, the 24th's largest city. A Champion pulp and paper mill and the New York Air Brake Co. are major employers. But Fort Drum, home of the Army's 10th Mountain Division, is the driving economic force: It has more than 13,000 military and civilian employees.

Massena, in St. Lawrence County, depends on the factories of the Aluminum Company of America, Reynolds Metals and General Motors. An organized labor presence makes St. Lawrence and Franklin counties the most Democratic areas in the 24th. Bill Clinton won both in 1992.

Although Fort Drum, which received a heavy investment in new facilities during the 1980s, has not yet felt the post-Cold War fiscal squeeze, Plattsburgh Air Force Base (near the 24th's eastern edge) came close to the brink in 1991; it was on an initial list of the military base-closing commission that year. But it escaped with most of its jobs intact when the commission decided to close Maine's Loring Air Force Base instead.

The interior of the 24th includes some of New York's leading dairy farming areas (including parts of Jefferson and St. Lawrence counties) and the mountain-and-lake country of the Adirondacks, where much of the economy is recreation- and tourist-oriented.

1990 Population: 580,338. White 553,432 (95%), Black 15,043 (3%), Other 11,863 (2%). Hispanic origin 9,424 (2%). 18 and over 426,525 (73%), 62 and over 82,732 (14%). Median age: 31.

Committees

Armed Services (19th of 22 Republicans)
Military Installations & Facilities; Oversight & Investigations

Government Operations (13th of 16 Republicans)
Employment, Housing & Aviation; Environment, Energy & Natural Resources

Campaign Finance

1992	Receipts	Receipts from PACs	Expend-itures
McHugh (R)	$177,033	$96,351 (54%)	$170,749
Hosley (C)	$112,240	$1,573 (1%)	$149,493

Key Votes

1993

Require parental notification of minors' abortions	Y
Require unpaid family and medical leave	Y
Approve national "motor voter" registration bill	N
Approve budget increasing taxes and reducing deficit	N
Approve economic stimulus plan	N

Elections

1992 General		
John M. McHugh (R, VR)	122,257	(61%)
Margaret M. Ravenscroft (D)	47,675	(24%)
Morrison J. Hosley Jr. (C, RTL)	26,763	(13%)
Stephen Burke (L)	4,374	(2%)
1992 Primary		
John M. McHugh (R)	21,452	(70%)
Morrison J. Hosley Jr. (R)	9,320	(30%)

District Vote for President

	1992
D	85,078 (38%)
R	86,357 (38%)
I	54,537 (24%)

25 James T. Walsh (R)

Of Syracuse — Elected 1988; 3rd Term

Born: June 19, 1947, Syracuse, N.Y.
Education: St. Bonaventure U., B.A. 1970.
Occupation: Marketing executive; social worker.
Family: Wife, DeDe Ryan; three children.
Religion: Roman Catholic.
Political Career: Syracuse Common Council, 1978-88, president, 1986-88; sought GOP nomination for Onondaga County executive, 1987.
Capitol Office: 1330 Longworth Bldg. 20515; 225-3701.

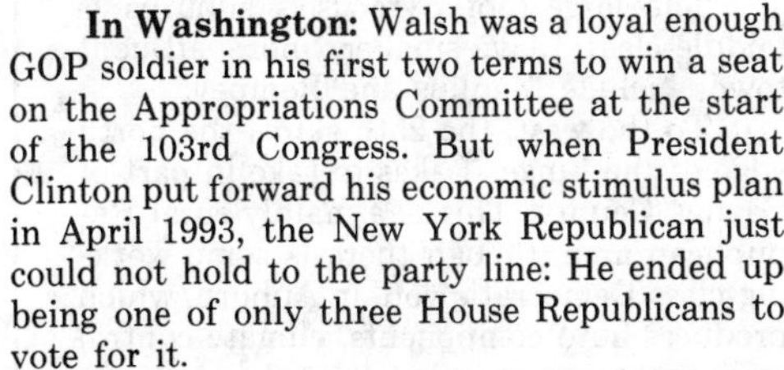

In Washington: Walsh was a loyal enough GOP soldier in his first two terms to win a seat on the Appropriations Committee at the start of the 103rd Congress. But when President Clinton put forward his economic stimulus plan in April 1993, the New York Republican just could not hold to the party line: He ended up being one of only three House Republicans to vote for it.

Walsh takes his share of conservative stands — he opposes abortion, supports a balanced-budget constitutional amendment and opposed Clinton's budget blueprint with its higher taxes, for instance — but he will diverge from the party script from time to time, especially on issues affecting Syracuse's large blue-collar population.

Walsh's urbanized district was slammed hard by the recession; in explaining his support for Clinton's stimulus plan, he said its extension of unemployment benefits and educational and community development grants were "badly needed" in the 25th.

That vote called to mind an earlier Walsh defection on a blue-collar "pocketbook" issue: In 1989, he voted to override President Bush's veto of a Democratic-backed bill increasing the minimum wage.

In 1993, Walsh also was in a minority of Republicans who supported the family and medical leave bill and the "motor voter" registration measure, both primarily pushed by Democrats. He voted in 1992 to force cable programmers to provide their product to satellite and other potential cable competitors at rates comparable to what they charge cable companies — a stand that was seen as pro-consumer.

When Walsh first came to Washington and began lobbying for his place in the committee system, he calculated that a good way to broaden his appeal beyond his urban base and protect his district's dairy, apple-growing and other farming interests would be to get on the Agriculture Committee.

Capitalizing on contacts with senior Republicans who had served with his father (GOP Rep. William F. Walsh, 1973-79), Walsh became the only Republican freshman to win assignment to Agriculture in 1989.

As the panel deliberated on the 1990 farm bill, Walsh showed a knack for gauging when his input would be helpful and when he would be best-served by listening to his elders. On the House floor, he offered an amendment that combined his dairy interests with his concern for a balanced budget. The aim of Walsh's proposal was to reduce federal payouts to dairy farmers while providing them with the income security derived from operating in a tighter market, one without surpluses. Walsh's amendment was adopted by the House, but was dropped in a House-Senate conference.

However, Walsh was successful in his proposal to establish a clearinghouse for national data on farm safety, which he said would facilitate lower insurance rates for farmers.

When Walsh moved onto Appropriations in 1993, he took subcommittee assignments that reflect both his agricultural interests and his familiarity with big-city problems. He is on the Agriculture subcommittee, and he is the ranking Republican on the District of Columbia subcommittee.

In joining Appropriations, Walsh gave up his Agriculture Committee seat as well as his post on the House Administration Committee. There he had drawn on his background as a Nynex telephone executive in pushing for implementation of a new telephone system that established dedicated lines for members to transfer information electronically between Washington and their districts.

From House Administration in the 102nd Congress, Walsh got involved in campaign finance reform.

An opponent of public financing of campaigns, he was among many Republicans criticizing a Democratic-backed overhaul proposal for not adequately addressing where the government would get the money to fund campaigns.

At Home: Walsh had a rather easy time against Democrats in his first two House contests — winning 57 percent against a seasoned oppo-

New York 25

Central — Syracuse

Syracuse, the dominant city in the 25th, is in the center of Onondaga County. That county has more than 80 percent of the district's population, and the traditional Republican advantage there gives GOP candidates a jump on carrying the district.

The economic evolution of Syracuse was similar to that of many northern industrial towns, but its politics were all upstate New York. While the ethnic populations of other blue-collar cities were drafted into Democratic machines, it was a Republican organization that for years held the loyalties of the various Syracuse constituencies, including large Irish, Italian, Polish and Jewish populations. The electorate's GOP leanings were reinforced by the typical upstate antipathy toward Democratic New York City.

The Republican hold on the city itself has weakened; the GOP machine has faded, and the decline of the city's once-thriving industrial sector has helped the Democratic Party gain ground. Aided by minority-group residents who make up more than a quarter of the city's population, Democrats have dominated the mayor's office in recent years.

But the sizable Republican base that remains in the city is coupled with a strong GOP lean in suburban and outlying areas, and that tips the partisan balance in Onondaga County. Facing a grumpy electorate in 1992, Rep. Walsh (a Syracuse native) held the county with 54 percent of the vote; GOP Sen. Alfonse M. D'Amato took 57 percent. Yet not even Republican tradition could salvage George Bush, who narrowly lost the 25th.

Once the nation's leading producer of salt, Syracuse grew into a thriving but grimy center for such industries as glass, steel and chemicals. But the manufacturing sector faded, with service industries picking up some slack.

The city's clearer skies make Syracuse somewhat more livable, though it is harder for some blue-collar workers to make a living. Today, Syracuse University (16,000 students) competes with General Electric to be the area's top employer, and has surpassed the Carrier Corp. (a division of United Technologies), which not long ago financed the university's domed stadium.

The largest of Syracuse's suburbs is middle-class Clay; smaller, more affluent towns include Manlius and Pompey.

To the west, the 25th skims the north edge of the Finger Lakes to take in part of Cayuga County. This is a mainly rural Republican area, though there is some working-class Democratic vote in Auburn, which produces auto components, climate-control equipment and recycled steel.

South of Syracuse, the district follows I-81 into Cortland County, a hilly dairy farming area that has some industry. The county will take a big job hit if Smith-Corona carries out plans to move its Cortland factory operations to Mexico; it is the last large-scale producer of typewriters and word processors in the United States.

At the southern end of the 25th are a chunk of Broome County northwest of Binghamton and a lightly populated piece of Tioga County.

1990 Population: 580,337. White 528,110 (91%), Black 38,527 (7%), Other 13,700 (2%). Hispanic origin 7,950 (1%). 18 and over 435,923 (75%), 62 and over 90,166 (16%). Median age:33.

nent in 1988 and defeating a newcomer in 1990 with 63 percent. But in 1992, a prevalent anti-incumbent mood and a rare Democratic presidential victory in the 25th cost Walsh a few points.

Walsh first campaigned for the House in 1988 after four-term Republican Rep. George C. Wortley — with a nudge from GOP officials — decided to retire. Although the then-27th District had a Republican lean, its tone was centrist: Staunch conservative Wortley had barely survived a 1986 challenge by Democrat Rosemary S. Pooler.

Walsh, an advocate of urban programs and a former Peace Corps volunteer, had the desired centrist profile. But his background as a Nynex executive reassured Syracuse's mainly Republican business community.

Walsh also had a politically potent name. His father had served in the House and also as mayor. James Walsh served 10 years on the Syracuse City Council, the last two as its president. In 1987, he lost a GOP primary for Onondaga County executive by a razor-thin margin.

Pooler, set for a rematch with Wortley, instead faced the stronger Walsh. A consumer advocate and former state public service commissioner, Pooler blamed the Reagan-Bush administration for the loss of local blue-collar jobs. But Walsh portrayed Pooler as an extreme liberal and turned an expected close race into a runaway.

In 1990, Walsh defeated 30-year-old political consultant Peggy L. Murray with little trouble. He appeared en route to another easy victory in 1992. Although the newly drawn 25th

District altered Walsh's territory, it maintained a Syracuse base and Republican lean. His opponent, teacher Rhea Jezer, trailed Walsh by 3-to-1 in campaign funds.

However, Jezer worked hard, tying Walsh to the public's unhappiness with Congress. She assailed him for his 30 recorded overdrafts at the House bank and for backing fast-track authority for negotiating the U.S.-Mexico trade pact while a district employer was shifting jobs to Mexico. She also compared her support for abortion rights with Walsh's opposite position; exit polls showed she did well among women voters. Walsh was never seriously threatened with defeat, but his victory margin did slip to a career-low 12 percentage points.

Committee

Appropriations (19th of 23 Republicans)
District of Columbia (ranking); Agriculture, Rural Development, FDA & Related Agencies

Elections

1992 General		
James T. Walsh (R, C)	135,076	(56%)
Rhea Jezer (D, CSP)	107,310	(44%)
1990 General		
James T. Walsh (R, C)	95,220	(63%)
Peggy L. Murray (D, L)	52,438	(35%)
Stephen K. Hoff (RTL)	3,097	(2%)

Previous Winning Percentage: 1988 (57%)

District Vote for President

1992
D 108,334 (41%)
R 95,476 (36%)
I 58,239 (22%)

Campaign Finance

	Receipts	Receipts from PACs		Expend-itures
1992				
Walsh (R)	$284,162	$82,495	(29%)	$294,850
Jezer (D)	$99,340	$22,345	(22%)	$96,083
1990				
Walsh (R)	$365,536	$140,186	(38%)	$340,553
Murray (D)	$11,934	$2,200	(18%)	$11,779

Key Votes

1993	
Require parental notification of minors' abortions	Y
Require unpaid family and medical leave	Y
Approve national "motor voter" registration bill	Y
Approve budget increasing taxes and reducing deficit	N
Approve economic stimulus plan	Y
1992	
Approve balanced-budget constitutional amendment	Y
Close down space station program	N
Approve U.S. aid for former Soviet Union	N
Allow shifting funds from defense to domestic programs	N
1991	
Extend unemployment benefits using deficit financing	Y
Approve waiting period for handgun purchases	Y
Authorize use of force in Persian Gulf	Y

Voting Studies

	Presidential Support		Party Unity		Conservative Coalition	
Year	**S**	**O**	**S**	**O**	**S**	**O**
1992	64	35	65	33	83	13
1991	70	28	67	32	76	22
1990	44	54	54	41	74	24
1989	69	30	57	42	85	12

Interest Group Ratings

Year	ADA	AFL-CIO	CCUS	ACU
1992	25	75	75	72
1991	25	50	70	63
1990	44	33	62	58
1989	35	33	80	64

26 Maurice D. Hinchey (D)

Of Saugerties — Elected 1992; 1st Term

Born: Oct. 27, 1938, New York, N.Y.

Education: State U. of New York, New Paltz, B.S. 1968, M.A. 1970.

Military Service: Navy, 1956-59.

Occupation: State employee.

Family: Wife, Ilene Marder; three children.

Religion: Roman Catholic.

Political Career: Democratic nominee for N.Y. Assembly, 1972; N.Y. Assembly, 1975-93.

Capitol Office: 1313 Longworth Bldg. 20515; 225-6335.

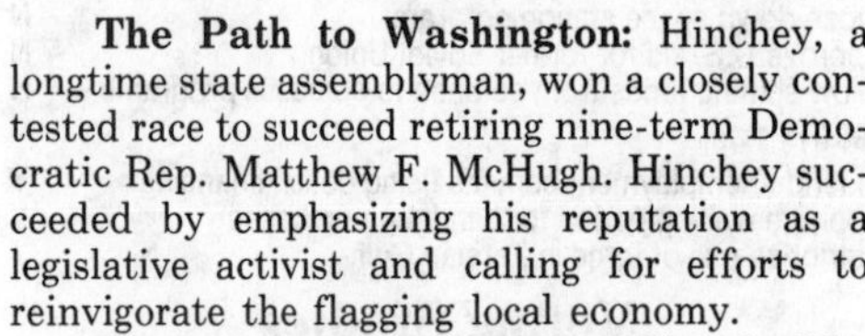

The Path to Washington: Hinchey, a longtime state assemblyman, won a closely contested race to succeed retiring nine-term Democratic Rep. Matthew F. McHugh. Hinchey succeeded by emphasizing his reputation as a legislative activist and calling for efforts to reinvigorate the flagging local economy.

Hinchey has a tough act to follow in McHugh, with his modest demeanor, reputation for integrity and strong constituent service.

One of the most well-regarded and influential House members, McHugh stunned colleagues with his announcement in May 1992 that he would retire because of a general dissatisfaction with Congress. McHugh headed the ethics task force that investigated the House bank scandal. The job was an unrewarding one that brought McHugh personal abuse from colleagues and left him dispirited at the way the scandal was perceived by the news media and the public.

McHugh's retirement touched off a scramble to succeed him. Hinchey decided to give up his 18-year state Assembly tenure and gamble on the race.

He started as the underdog in the Democratic primary, facing Binghamton Mayor Juanita M. Crabb, a well-known politician who had once been talked about as a potential running mate for Gov. Mario M. Cuomo.

But Hinchey prevailed by pushing a New Deal-like plan to revitalize the economy of the recession-hit region — and by holding on to his base.

Hinchey drew 80 percent of the Ulster vote in the primary and took away enough votes on Crabb's home turf in Broome County at the district's western end to win nearly 55 percent.

The general election again pitted Hinchey against a foe from the western end of the district, and the contest became a microcosm of the presidential race, matching populist Democrat Hinchey against a conservative Republican, six-year Broome County legislator Bob Moppert, owner of a Binghamton moving company.

Hinchey and Moppert echoed the tops of their respective tickets in prescribing cures for their economically ailing district, where defense cutbacks and the recession have badly hurt high-tech employers such as IBM Corp. and General Electric Co.

While Moppert preached a get-the-government-off-our-backs brand of business-led economic fundamentalism, Hinchey countered with Clinton-style calls for an activist federal government and investment in infrastructure. Like Clinton, Hinchey called for an end to the "trickle-down" economics of the past two Republican administrations and a scaling back of tax breaks for the wealthiest taxpayers.

Moppert attacked Hinchey as a "professional politician," but Hinchey's nine terms in the state Legislature had made him enormously popular in his heavily Republican Assembly district, where he won re-election by strong margins. An activist on consumer and environmental issues, Hinchey chaired the Assembly's Environmental Conservation Committee and also built a record of support for issues affecting women, including abortion rights.

During his campaign, Hinchey echoed Clinton's call for national health-care reform. He noted that he had sponsored a bill in the Assembly to bring more family practice physicians to the area, a program he said has resulted in a reduction in Ulster County's prenatal and infant mortality rates.

Hinchey took seats on the House's Banking and Natural Resources committees and likely will focus his legislative efforts in part on programs that could help revive his district's economy. He favors federal assistance for defense-oriented businesses seeking to convert to production of civilian goods.

Early in the 103rd Congress, Hinchey impressed members and staff during the April 1993 drafting of the unpopular thrift bailout funding bill. He received the opportunity to offer an amendment, which passed easily in subcommittee, to cut $5 billion from a new taxpayer-financed thrift insurance fund.

New York 26

South — Kingston; Binghamton; Ithaca

The elongated 26th reaches from high above Cayuga Lake's waters to the banks of the Hudson River. Most of the population is found in pockets at the district's extremes: the Ithaca and Binghamton areas to the west, and the Hudson Valley region — which includes the cities of Kingston, Newburgh and Beacon — on the eastern edge.

Although the 26th, like most upstate districts, has a Republican heritage, its demographics have made it a political swing district. A Democratic hold on the region's House seat was established by longtime Rep. Matthew F. McHugh in 1974 and continued by Hinchey in 1992, but the 26th can still go Republican in contests for major office.

With Cornell University (18,600 students) and Ithaca College (6,400 students) fostering a liberal academic community, Tompkins County is one of the Democrats' strongholds in New York. The part of Broome County in the 26th takes in the "Triple Cities" of Binghamton, Johnson City and Endicott; its mix of high-tech employees and a traditional blue-collar constituency make Broome politically competitive. Ulster County (Kingston) has industry, but much rural territory; Republicans usually win it.

However, the 26th showed its unpredictability in 1992. Hinchey, whose populist style earned him a long career in the state Assembly, carried Ulster (his home county) with 58 percent of the vote; his 64 percent in Tompkins cinched his victory. But Broome County, usually essential to Democratic victory, gave 56 percent to the locally based GOP candidate, Bob Moppert. Bill Clinton carried the 26th with a plurality; Republican Sen. Alfonse M. D'Amato won every county but Tompkins.

One thing that binds this diverse district is its reliance on a major employer: International Business Machines (IBM), which was founded in Endicott. IBM's preeminence in mainframe computer technology made it a corporate giant; it also led the transition of Broome County's traditional smokestack economy to a high-tech base. But IBM's failure to keep up with rapid changes in the industry has caused huge financial losses and unprecedented job cutbacks.

Layoffs in IBM facilities have stung such cities as Kingston and Owego (Tioga County). And the Binghamton area, whose defense contractors produce such products as aircraft components and flight simulators, has been further battered by post-Cold War budget cuts.

But economic development officials base hopes for future high-tech growth on the region's skilled work force and the presence of such academic institutions as Cornell and the state university campus in Binghamton (11,900 students).

The economy in less-populous areas relies largely on farming (Ulster County's crops include apples and wine grapes) and recreation. The portion of Sullivan County in the district includes much of the Catskill Mountain resort area, a longtime magnet for middle-class Jews and Italians from the New York City area.

1990 Population: 580,338. White 525,498 (91%), Black 33,076 (6%), Other 21,764 (4%). Hispanic origin 24,829 (4%). 18 and over 446,405 (77%), 62 and over 91,776 (16%). Median age: 33.

Committees

Banking, Finance & Urban Affairs (27th of 30 Democrats)
Consumer Credit & Insurance; Financial Institutions Supervision, Regulation & Deposit Insurance; General Oversight, Investigations & the Resolution of Failed Financial Institutions

Natural Resources (22nd of 28 Democrats)
National Parks, Forests & Public Lands; Oversight & Investigations

Campaign Finance

	Receipts	Receipts from PACs	Expend-itures
1992			
Hinchey (D)	$374,264	$145,258 (39%)	$368,777
Moppert (R)	$209,386	$32,750 (16%)	$203,274

Key Votes

1993	
Require parental notification of minors' abortions	N
Require unpaid family and medical leave	Y
Approve national "motor voter" registration bill	Y
Approve budget increasing taxes and reducing deficit	Y
Approve economic stimulus plan	Y

Elections

1992 General		
Maurice D. Hinchey (D, L)	119,557	(50%)
Bob Moppert (R, C)	110,738	(47%)
Mary C. Dixon (RTL)	6,821	(3%)
1992 Primary		
Maurice D. Hinchey (D)	19,426	(54%)
Juanita M. Crabb (D)	14,226	(40%)
Barbara A. Wolfson (D)	2,002	(6%)

District Vote for President

1992

D	116,525	(45%)
R	91,625	(35%)
I	52,886	(20%)

27 Bill Paxon (R)

Of Amherst — Elected 1988; 3rd Term

Born: April 29, 1954, Buffalo, N.Y.
Education: Canisius College, B.A. 1977.
Occupation: Public official.
Family: Single.
Religion: Roman Catholic.
Political Career: Erie County Legislature, 1978-82; N.Y. Assembly, 1983-89.
Capitol Office: 1314 Longworth Bldg. 20515; 225-5265.

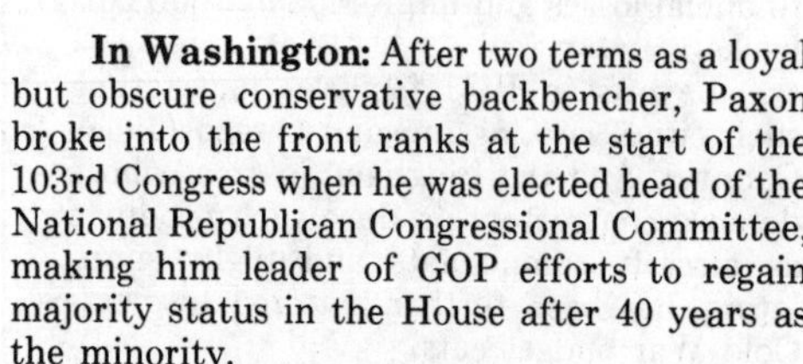

In Washington: After two terms as a loyal but obscure conservative backbencher, Paxon broke into the front ranks at the start of the 103rd Congress when he was elected head of the National Republican Congressional Committee, making him leader of GOP efforts to regain majority status in the House after 40 years as the minority.

He succeeds Rep. Guy Vander Jagt of Michigan, who chaired the NRCC for 18 years but was defeated in his 1992 primary.

Paxon faces a decidedly uphill battle because Democrats have the power of incumbency and all the advantages attached to it. In addition, Democrats used their majorities at the state level in 1992 to draw new district lines that will help secure their House majority.

In his first few months in office Paxon took several steps to improve the NRCC's effectiveness. In the 1992 cycle it raised twice as much as its Democratic counterpart, although the GOP panel gave out less money directly to candidates because of higher overhead costs, and as of April 1993 still had a debt of about $4 million.

To help eliminate the debt, Paxon reduced the number of full-time employees from 89 to 37, a move that prompted questions and criticism. Paxon also proposed creation of an Incumbent Support Program that would ask relatively safe members to contribute up to $7,500 to provide funding for members who face close races.

The House successor to Jack F. Kemp, President Bush's Housing and Urban Development secretary, Paxon was named to the Energy and Commerce Committee at the start of the 103rd Congress. He had gone after a slot on the committee in the 102nd Congress, but failed to make it.

Previously, Paxon had served on the Banking, Finance and Urban Affairs Committee. Though a fan of Kemp's enterprise zone initiative to encourage investment and create jobs in economically depressed areas, chiefly through tax incentives, Paxon was not a visible force on the panel, nor does it have a say in tax matters.

Paxon has maintained a consistently conservative voting record. On partisan issues in 1992, he voted with Republicans 94 percent of the time. He supported President Bush 80 percent of the time on votes on which Bush staked out a position.

At Home: Paxon went to work early to assure his 1992 re-election, taking the battle not so much to his opponent but to the state legislature, which had the daunting task of redrawing district boundaries to take into account the loss of three New York House seats.

Concerned about rumors that he would be thrown into the same district as veteran western New York Democratic Rep. John J. LaFalce, Paxon contributed or raised more than $50,000 in campaign funds to help New York Republicans defend their majority in the state Senate and promised to do whatever he could in the future to help the Republican State Senate Campaign Committee.

Although Republican officials came up with a plan that gave Paxon a safe district, their effort became moot when the Senate and Democratic-controlled state Assembly stalemated. But Paxon did all right in the end, even though the new district map was ultimately drawn by a state Supreme Court panel with a Democratic majority.

Paxon lost part of his Erie County base, but the new 27th District retained a big chunk of the Republican-leaning Buffalo suburbs. He picked up a substantial number of new voters to the east, but most were from rural areas with Republican tendencies.

Paxon was thus able to easily handle Democrat W. Douglas Call, a lawyer and former Genesee County sheriff who in 1984 had run an unsuccessful House race in a Rochester-based district.

Call, while profiling himself as a Democratic moderate, tried to portray Paxon as an ineffective conservative ideologue. One of many "outsider" challengers in 1992, Call also pointed to Paxon's 96 recorded overdrafts at the House bank.

Paxon ably deflected Call's efforts, high-

New York 27

Suburban Buffalo and rural west — Amherst

During 1992 redistricting, Rep. Paxon lobbied former colleagues in the state Legislature for a comfortably Republican constituency. His efforts appeared endangered when a Democratic-dominated state court panel took control of the process from the deadlocked legislators. Yet the jurists produced a map that created the suburban-and-rural 27th, which is as solidly a Republican district as Paxon could have designed himself.

The 27th takes in the northeastern suburbs of Buffalo, some suburbia to the south and west of Rochester and a largely farming region stretching 100 miles across northwestern New York. In 1992, Paxon carried the five full and four partial counties in the 27th, most by wide margins. George Bush won the 27th with a solid plurality, topping 45 percent of the vote (a strong showing for him in New York) in four counties.

There was voter dissatisfaction, but it did not do much to help Bill Clinton, who received less than a third of the vote in most jurisdictions and finished third in rural Wyoming County with 25 percent. Ross Perot ran strongly, especially in Wyoming County, where he took 30 percent.

Amherst, a Buffalo suburb at the western end of the 27th, is the district's anchor; with more than 111,000 residents, it has nearly a fifth of the people in the 27th. The main campus of the State University of New York at Buffalo (23,600 students) is here. Greater Buffalo International Airport, just across the Buffalo city line (in the 30th District), is another jobs producer.

Unlike Buffalo, the Erie County suburbs in the 27th have little blue-collar industry and a small minority population. Republicans usually run well in Amherst (Paxon's hometown) and even better in the towns east and south, where the landscape quickly shifts from suburban to exurban to rural.

The New York Thruway links Erie County to the Rochester suburbs of Monroe County. The largest of these communities in the 27th is Chili, with about 25,000 residents. Republicans usually carry these mainly middle-class suburbs.

Between and to the east are the dairy, vegetable and grain farms of rural western New York. In Genesee County is Batavia, a small city that lost a Sylvania television plant in the mid-1980s and has been fighting further industrial decline since. Batavia's leading employers include companies that make electrical insulation and canned food.

Wyoming County is heavily agricultural, but it has a facility that is distinctly unbucolic: the state penitentiary at Attica, the site in 1971 of one of the worst prison riots in U.S. history.

In Ontario and Seneca counties, the 27th moves into the part of the Finger Lakes region, including some of its grape vineyards and the cities of Geneva and Seneca Falls (the site of a convention in 1848 that is regarded as the origin of the women's rights movement). The western end of Wayne County (which borders Lake Ontario) is within Rochester's sphere; in its southern reaches are several towns that grew up along the Erie Canal.

1990 Population: 580,337. White 554,426 (96%), Black 14,748 (3%), Other 11,163 (2%). Hispanic origin 7,391 (1%). 18 and over 433,948 (75%), 62 and over 90,096 (16%). Median age: 34.

lighting conservative stands that played well in the Republican-leaning district. Paxon pulled down a House career-high vote percentage and carried every county in the 27th, running close only in Call's Genesee County base.

When Kemp stepped aside to run for president in 1988, Paxon was touted as his heir apparent in the then-31st District. Though only 34 years old, he was already a political veteran. The son of an Erie County family court judge, Paxon was elected at age 23 as the youngest-ever member of the Erie County Legislature. Twice reelected to county office by huge margins, he then easily won an open Assembly seat in 1982.

Paxon established his conservative credentials in Albany, promoting efforts to cut state welfare costs and often opposing efforts to expand state regulation. He also gained the ranking position on the Assembly corrections committee.

But Paxon's move to the House in 1988 did not go as smoothly as expected. He weathered a vigorous challenge from Democratic Erie County Clerk David Swarts.

Swarts — who had honed his campaign skills in a futile 1983 challenge to a Republican Erie County executive and in a successful 1986 county clerk bid — denounced Paxon as an ideologue with a reflexive opposition to business regulation. The well-known Democrat's aggressive effort made the contest close in Erie County. But Paxon had breathing room in the district's more rural precincts, enabling him to win with 53 percent overall.

Paxon's 1990 Democratic opponent, lawyer Kevin P. Gaughan, tried to tie the Banking

Committee member to the savings and loan scandal, noting his receipt of campaign contributions from banking industry sources just before voting on the 1989 S&L bailout bill. But Paxon denied any impropriety, and national Democratic officials, who targeted the 31st in 1988, paid it little notice in 1990. Paxon won 57 percent.

Committee

Energy & Commerce (12th of 17 Republicans)
Commerce, Consumer Protection & Competitiveness; Health & the Environment; Transportation & Hazardous Materials

Elections

1992 General		
Bill Paxon (R, C, RTL)	156,596	(64%)
W. Douglas Call (D)	89,906	(36%)
1990 General		
Bill Paxon (R, C, RTL)	90,237	(57%)
Kevin P. Gaughan (D, L)	69,328	(43%)

Previous Winning Percentage: **1988** (53%)

District Vote for President

	1992
D	90,194 (33%)
R	115,432 (42%)
I	67,721 (25%)

Campaign Finance

	Receipts	Receipts from PACs		Expend-itures
1992				
Paxon (R)	$845,163	$329,412	(39%)	$1,017,327
Call (D)	$72,481	$11,900	(16%)	$71,370
1990				
Paxon (R)	$692,799	$239,020	(35%)	$506,934
Gaughan (D)	$101,182	$51,492	(51%)	$100,353

Key Votes

1993	
Require parental notification of minors' abortions	Y
Require unpaid family and medical leave	N
Approve national "motor voter" registration bill	N
Approve budget increasing taxes and reducing deficit	N
Approve economic stimulus plan	N
1992	
Approve balanced-budget constitutional amendment	Y
Close down space station program	N
Approve U.S. aid for former Soviet Union	N
Allow shifting funds from defense to domestic programs	N
1991	
Extend unemployment benefits using deficit financing	Y
Approve waiting period for handgun purchases	N
Authorize use of force in Persian Gulf	Y

Voting Studies

	Presidential Support		Party Unity		Conservative Coalition	
Year	**S**	**O**	**S**	**O**	**S**	**O**
1992	80	20	94	5	96	4
1991	75	23	90	7	97	3
1990	69	30	93	5	94	6
1989	73	26	89	9	90	10

Interest Group Ratings

Year	ADA	AFL-CIO	CCUS	ACU
1992	10	33	75	92
1991	10	17	80	85
1990	6	8	86	88
1989	0	8	100	93

28 Louise M. Slaughter (D)

Of Fairport — Elected 1986; 4th Term

Born: Aug. 14, 1929, Harlan County, Ky.
Education: U. of Kentucky, B.S. 1951, M.P.H. 1953.
Occupation: Market researcher.
Family: Husband, Robert Slaughter; three children.
Religion: Episcopalian.
Political Career: Monroe County Legislature, 1975-79; N.Y. Assembly, 1983-87.
Capitol Office: 2421 Rayburn Bldg. 20515; 225-3615.

In Washington: Now in her fourth term, Slaughter not only has solidified her position as an important inside player but has begun to spread her legislative wings as well.

From her earliest days, she has proved to be a favorite of the Democratic hierarchy. When House Democrats caucused to organize for the 101st Congress, Slaughter was asked to make nominating speeches for four members of the leadership, including Speaker Thomas S. Foley, then majority leader. Having friends in such high places benefited Slaughter, who was awarded a high-profile Rules Committee seat early in her second term.

Her position as the only woman on Rules was magnified when she was assigned as well to the Budget Committee in 1991, where she is the only New York Democrat.

In 1991, she was named to chair the Committee on Organization, Study and Review of the Democratic Caucus, which proposed a package of rules changes for the 103rd Congress intended to make the House more efficient. Most of the committee's recommendations were adopted, including trims in the number of subcommittees and a method for removing recalcitrant committee chairmen.

There were moments when Caucus Chairman Steny H. Hoyer of Maryland seemed to upstage Slaughter on the rules changes, such as when the package was presented to incoming freshmen. But Slaughter gamely carried the leadership's water, even though some of the panel's proposals angered Republicans.

One, which was adopted over strong GOP protests, permitted delegates from the District of Columbia, American Samoa, Guam, Puerto Rico and the Virgin Islands — all Democrats — to vote on floor amendments in certain circumstances. Another, which was dropped, would have curtailed after-hours House floor speeches, known as special orders. Republicans charged that since the Democrats control the floor schedule, special orders are often their only opportunity to speak at length on some issues. Slaughter defended the change as a money saver, noting the cost of keeping the chamber open and of printing the proceedings.

Slaughter does not disguise her Kentucky accent, which emphasizes her self-contained regional balance — a Northerner from the South. And her Harlan County upbringing instilled in her a nature that is gracious when appropriate and tough when necessary, as when she bears in on an administration witness from her seat on Budget. She has proved she could go far in the House on the force of her personality. But her ability to win and hold what was until 1992 a nominally Republican district and her record as a liberal Democratic loyalist further ingratiated Slaughter with the party leadership.

She could probably write the book on achieving quick popularity and success in a marginal district and within the ranks of Congress — if such a book hadn't already been written about her. Two local political science professors chose the district as a case study for a book on congressional campaigns. The book, "Political Ambition: Who Decides to Run for Congress," published in June 1989, analyzed Slaughter's election and the reasons for her success.

Despite her visibility in Washington as a liberal activist — she was one of seven House women who marched on the Senate in October 1991 to urge a delay in the vote on the nomination of Clarence Thomas to the Supreme Court — Slaughter takes care to consider the views of her constituents. She voted against the controversial 1990 budget summit agreement — and in a rare case against the Democratic leadership — in a bow to her district's conservative nature. And she has supported bills that died repeatedly under presidential veto to impose quotas on imported textiles and shoes, reflecting threats to her industrial region.

The Rules Committee, though a prestigious spot that offers a venue for scoring points with the leadership and making friends — and enemies — among the rank and file, provides its members few opportunities to enmesh themselves in the business of legislation. Budget, too, has no nitty-gritty legislative responsibilities, but she has used the seat to advantage, agitating for increased spending on women and chil-

New York 28

Rochester and most of suburban Monroe County

Rochester's location on Lake Ontario and the Erie Canal made it an industrial center by the early 19th century. Yet unlike many northern cities with blue-collar bases, Rochester long held to a Republican tradition typical of upstate New York. Only in recent years has the city — which dominates the 28th — developed a lean toward Democratic candidates.

Known early on as the "Flour City" (for its grain mills) and then the "Flower City" (for its commercial nurseries), Rochester grew to be New York's third-largest city with a push from a pair of giant corporations: Eastman Kodak (founded in the 1880s) and the Xerox Corp. (which began producing copying machines in the 1940s).

These companies spawned a large white-collar managerial class that leaned Republican. They also pursued a rather paternalistic management style that rubbed off on Rochester's civic life. The Republicans who long dominated Rochester politics were generally moderates: Barber B. Conable, who served a Rochester-based district from 1965 to 1985, was typical.

But Fred J. Eckert, his staunchly conservative GOP successor, lasted one term before his 1986 loss to Democrat Slaughter. And the city's tilt away from conservatism benefited Democratic presidential candidates in 1988 and 1992.

Still, to carry the 28th, Democrats must do exceedingly well within the city (which has about two-fifths of the 28th's population). More than half the registered voters in the city are Democrats, but Republicans hold a wide plurality among registrants in suburban Monroe County. While the city has a large blue-collar population, the suburbs are mainly white-collar. Rochester's population is nearly one-third black and nearly a tenth Hispanic, but less than 5 percent of the suburban population is black or Hispanic.

Kodak remains the district's largest employer, but has undergone a serious downsizing in recent years, from 60,000 local jobs in 1981 to less than 40,000 today. Employment has remained rather constant at Xerox, the Bausch and Lomb optical company, and a pair of General Motors parts plants; among the region's smaller companies are a number of high-tech startups that benefit from their proximity to the major corporations and the area's major academic institutions, Rochester Institute of Technology (13,000 students) and the University of Rochester (8,800 students).

While the jobless rate has remained relatively moderate in recent years, much of the job slack has been picked up by service industries, which generally provide lower salaries than the manufacturing sector. This transition has exacerbated the problems of Rochester's low-income residents: the city's poverty rate tops 20 percent.

The recent recession took an unusually hard toll on white-collar workers, but the Monroe County suburbs in the 28th are relatively affluent compared with the city. The most populous suburbs, Greece and Irondequoit, are north of the city; Pittsford, the wealthiest suburb, is southeast.

1990 Population: 580,337. White 472,733 (81%), Black 81,107 (14%), Other 26,497 (5%). Hispanic origin 24,703 (4%). 18 and over 439,156 (76%), 62 and over 90,688 (16%). Median age: 33.

dren's health and high-speed rail development.

But Slaughter, a bacteriologist with a master's degree in public health, has scored some legislative successes. Her bill to increase education about health risks of exposure to the drug DES was enacted in 1992. And she successfully attached an amendment to a 1990 homeless-aid bill to reduce barriers preventing homeless children from attending school by providing incentive grants to states. In the Budget Committee in 1992, she took on Bush administration budget director Richard G. Darman over the proposed elimination of $7 million that had previously been appropriated for the education program for the homeless. Ultimately the money was not only restored but increased.

Slaughter is also the prime mover in the House for a special tax break that allows small manufacturers and farmers to issue tax-exempt bonds through local governments. The continued existence of these small-issue bonds is dependent on a periodic reauthorization, which Slaughter routinely sponsors.

At Home: Slaughter's charm, grass-roots organization and fundraising skill weighed heavily in her narrow 1986 upset of conservative GOP Rep. Fred J. Eckert. The same factors, plus her rapid rise to a prestige committee position, enabled Slaughter to breeze past her next two Republican opponents, pushing close to 60 percent of the vote in 1990.

Redistricting before the 1992 election appeared to further solidify her position. The old 30th District where she ran her first three races took in only the more Republican part of Rochester and stretched into some heavily Republican rural areas outside Monroe County. The newly drawn 28th District, by contrast, takes in all of Rochester, is contained wholly within Monroe County and shows a Democratic tilt.

Yet Slaughter saw her 1992 vote drop a bit, though not dangerously. Her problem was a locally well-known Republican opponent, Monroe County Legislator William P. Polito.

Given the district's centrist profile, the strongly conservative Polito was assumed to pose little threat to Slaughter. But Polito worked to take advantage of a widespread anti-Congress mood. His TV ads, which accused Slaughter of supporting spending on wasteful programs and congressional perks, drew attention with the catch phrase, "Jeez, Louise." Although he played down ideology in his campaign statements, he had strong backing from some Christian right and other conservative activists who opposed Slaughter's liberal positions on social issues.

Given the district's moderate tendencies, Polito's rightward lean might have provided Slaughter with some ammunition. But she eschewed negative advertising and emphasized actions she had taken in behalf of local constituents. Polito's criticisms had some effect, as Slaughter slipped to an 11 percentage point victory margin.

With her liberal views and Southern accent (she moved north from Kentucky in the 1950s), Slaughter has been a rather singular figure in western New York politics since the mid-1970s. She entered public life as a Monroe County legislator and as an assistant to Mario M. Cuomo, then New York's secretary of state.

In 1982, Slaughter upset a GOP state assemblyman. Slaughter's arguments with the state's private power companies earned her support from liberals and labor activists and gave her a base for her 1986 challenge to Eckert.

Although Eckert had won the seat in 1984, he was far more conservative than his predecessor, veteran GOP Rep. Barber B. Conable Jr. Democratic PACs that had targeted Eckert for defeat helped Slaughter raise nearly $600,000. Depicting Eckert as a right-wing obstructionist and parrying Eckert's efforts to portray her as an ultraliberal, Slaughter won with 51 percent of the vote.

Slaughter's continued fundraising success made her a strong front-runner in 1988. Her Republican opponent, Monroe County legislator John D. Bouchard, ran a two-pronged campaign, patterning himself after Conable while portraying Slaughter as a puppet of organized labor. But his campaign never jelled; Slaughter won with 57 percent. She bumped that up two more points in 1990, easily defeating Republican lawyer John M. Regan Jr.

Committees

Budget (11th of 26 Democrats)

Rules (9th of 9 Democrats)
Rules of the House

Elections

1992 General		
Louise M. Slaughter (D)	140,908	(55%)
William P. Polito (R, C)	112,273	(44%)
1990 General		
Louise M. Slaughter (D)	97,280	(59%)
John M. Regan Jr. (R, C, RTL)	67,534	(41%)

Previous Winning Percentages: **1988** (57%) **1986** (51%)

District Vote for President

1992
D 119,055 (44%)
R 103,544 (38%)
I 48,467 (18%)

Campaign Finance

	Receipts	Receipts from PACs		Expend-itures
1992				
Slaughter (D)	$473,871	$297,050	(63%)	$526,345
Polito (R)	$245,768	0		$245,526
1990				
Slaughter (D)	$446,664	$282,817	(63%)	$322,216
Regan (R)	$24,863	0		$24,712

Key Votes

1993	
Require parental notification of minors' abortions	N
Require unpaid family and medical leave	Y
Approve national "motor voter" registration bill	Y
Approve budget increasing taxes and reducing deficit	Y
Approve economic stimulus plan	Y
1992	
Approve balanced-budget constitutional amendment	N
Close down space station program	Y
Approve U.S. aid for former Soviet Union	Y
Allow shifting funds from defense to domestic programs	Y
1991	
Extend unemployment benefits using deficit financing	Y
Approve waiting period for handgun purchases	Y
Authorize use of force in Persian Gulf	N

Voting Studies

	Presidential Support		Party Unity		Conservative Coalition	
Year	**S**	**O**	**S**	**O**	**S**	**O**
1992	16	84	96	3	17	83
1991	25	73	93	3	24	73
1990	16	84	94	5	11	89
1989	27	71	93	4	20	80
1988	23	73	92	8	37	61
1987	17	78	83	9	35	60

Interest Group Ratings

Year	ADA	AFL-CIO	CCUS	ACU
1992	95	92	25	4
1991	95	100	20	5
1990	94	92	29	17
1989	95	100	40	4
1988	85	100	43	8
1987	76	87	29	10

29 John J. LaFalce (D)

Of Tonawanda — Elected 1974; 10th Term

Born: Oct. 6, 1939, Buffalo, N.Y.
Education: Canisius College, B.S. 1961; Villanova U., J.D. 1964.
Military Service: Army, 1965-67.
Occupation: Lawyer.
Family: Wife, Patricia Fisher; one child.
Religion: Roman Catholic.
Political Career: N.Y. Senate, 1971-73; N.Y. Assembly, 1973-75.
Capitol Office: 2310 Rayburn Bldg. 20515; 225-3231.

In Washington: Those who work with LaFalce regard him as one of the smartest members of the House. The chairman of the Small Business Committee, LaFalce has labored to change the panel's backwater image and give it a role in the setting of tax and regulatory policy. And as the No. 3 Democrat on the Banking Committee, LaFalce stays closely involved in regulatory issues and the savings and loan bailout.

However, even endorsements of LaFalce's acumen tend to be qualified: His intense public manner and his intellectual certitude can be off-putting. An observer once said that LaFalce "has an innate ability to rub people the wrong way." And in his zeal for pursuing a broad range of legislative interests, LaFalce has run over some big feet, both in and out of Congress.

There is no doubt that LaFalce has expanded the reach of the Small Business Committee. The committee remains something less than a powerhouse, but LaFalce has managed to weigh in frequently from his corner, in particular concentrating on ways to improve the availability of capital and credit to small businesses.

In the 102nd Congress he succeeded in pushing to enactment bills to authorize more Small Business Administration loans to companies that could not get bank credit and to increase the share of federal research expenditures earmarked for small firms.

And LaFalce continues to press for creation of a government-sponsored secondary market to buy and sell small-business loans. His hope is that a secondary market similar to that for home mortgages will further stimulate small business lending. To oversee this market, LaFalce would create the Venture Enhancement and Loan Development Administration for Smaller Undercapitalized Enterprises, a title crafted to yield Velda Sue as its nickname, in imitation of Fannie Mae, Farmer Mac and other government-created financial entities.

Early in 1989, LaFalce conceded that "99 out of 100" issues in which he gets involved are outside the committee's jurisdiction, adding, "I can either say we'll tend to our knitting or we can become the aggressive ombudsman of the small-business community."

To do this, he has had to encroach on the turf of some of the most powerful House members. His biggest victory came in 1989 at the expense of Democratic Ways and Means Committee Chairman Dan Rostenkowski of Illinois.

At issue was the repeal of Section 89 of the 1986 Tax Reform Act. The goal of this provision was widely accepted: eliminate disparities in employee health programs that provided greater benefits to higher-paid workers. But the measure required a complicated series of tests to prove non-discrimination that business groups decried as burdensome to employers.

With the provision due to take effect a year later, LaFalce proposed in January 1989 to repeal Section 89. Rostenkowski, who helped craft the section, resisted at first. But members were getting their ears singed by small-business constituents, and LaFalce lined up a cosponsors' list that included more than half the House.

"I didn't sit down and talk until I had 218 cosponsors," he said. Rostenkowski backed down, introducing a bill easing the testing requirements and making it easier for employers to meet anti-discrimination guidelines.

LaFalce pledged to work with Rostenkowski. However, he discovered that the issue had taken on a life of its own. House members of both parties pressed for outright repeal. Some Republicans jumped on the issue to reinforce the GOP's image as the party of business and deregulation.

LaFalce appeared somewhat melancholy in September 1989 when the House passed a Section 89 repeal bill by a 390-36 vote. Referring to his belated outreach to the rolled-over Rostenkowski, LaFalce told a colleague, "I wanted a Ways and Means victory."

This would not be the only time during the 101st Congress that LaFalce, as a small-business advocate, would break some china in the

New York 29

Northwest — Part of Buffalo; Niagara Falls

The many industrial workers in the Buffalo-Niagara Falls region provide a political base for Rep. LaFalce and other Democratic candidates in the 29th. However, the district also has a piece of GOP-leaning Buffalo suburbia and Rochester suburbs at its eastern extreme; in between is some solidly Republican rural turf. Many traditional Democratic voters in the Buffalo area are socially conservative white "ethnics" with roots in Italy, Eastern Europe and Ireland.

These factors make the 29th potentially competitive. LaFalce (a leading Democratic opponent of abortion) has maintained his party's grasp on the seat, but his once-dominant hold has slipped: He took 55 percent in 1990 and 54 percent in 1992.

In 1992, Bill Clinton beat George Bush in the 29th, but his plurality was one of the smallest of any district that he carried in the state. Working-class unhappiness with the two major parties led to an exceptional turnout for independent Ross Perot: In Niagara County, Clinton won 37 percent to 32 percent for Bush and 31 percent for Perot.

Most of the district's residents live in northwest Erie County and all of Niagara County (each of these jurisdictions provides about 40 percent of the 29th's population).

The 29th takes in the northwest corner of the city of Buffalo. Though it has a small part of downtown and the Peace Bridge that connects the city with Fort Erie, Ontario, this is a mainly residential area, where Italian-Americans make up the predominant constituent group.

To the north are such mixed blue- and white-collar suburbs as Tonawanda and Grand Island. Like the rest of Buffalo, this area is adjusting from an economy dependent on heavy industry to one based on service providers and lighter manufacturers. Unemployment is down but so are wages for formerly unionized blue-collar workers.

The natural grandeur of Niagara Falls makes its namesake city one of the world's leading tourist stops. But the Niagara River also made the region a major industrial center. Its chemical industry provides thousands of jobs but has given the area a somewhat sinister ecological reputation. A community had to be abandoned in 1978 because of toxic dumping in the city's Love Canal; part of the area has been cleaned up and reoccupied.

Though there has been some retrenchment, blue-collar industry is still central: Occidental Chemical, Du Pont and Carborundum factories are in Niagara Falls, as is a Nabisco shredded-wheat factory. General Motors' components plant in Lockport has thus far avoided the financially struggling company's downsizing: GM committed $50 million to the Lockport facility in 1992 for air-conditioning equipment that will not use ozone-depleting refrigerants.

The remainder of Niagara and Orleans County to the east are largely rural, with many dairy and produce farms. Orleans is by far the most Republican part of the 29th: Bush beat Clinton there by 45 percent to 30 percent.

1990 Population: 580,337 . White 537,547 (93%), Black 26,118 (5%), Other 16,672 (3%). Hispanic origin 16,241 (3%). 18 and over 441,716 (76%), 62 and over 102,578 (18%). Median age: 34.

Democratic pantry. Well into deliberations on the proposed Civil Rights Act of 1990, LaFalce intervened with a substitute proposal that became a rallying point for House Republicans and provoked the wrath of some on his own side of the aisle.

The Democratic leadership had made an election-year priority of the bill, which aimed at reversing court decisions limiting the right to sue and recover compensatory damages for claims of job discrimination. However, LaFalce took seriously President Bush's threat to veto the measure as a "quotas" bill, and he produced a plan that addressed some of the small-business community's objections. LaFalce's measure would have established an easier test for employers to prove they had not discriminated and set a lower cap on damages that could be claimed.

However, LaFalce did not pick up on two political realities: House Democrats had adopted a hard-line strategy to put Bush on the spot on civil rights issues, and House Republicans were floundering for a counter to the main bill. When LaFalce was blocked from offering his measure as a Democratic alternative, Minority Leader Robert H. Michel of Illinois put his name on it and promoted it as a GOP plan. With the Democratic leadership whipping against it, the alternative failed by a 188-238 vote. LaFalce voted for the Michel substitute, but he also voted for the Democrats' bill. And he voted for the final House-Senate compromise version, which died under Bush's promised veto.

In another effort to avoid a Bush veto and

to accommodate his small-business constituency, LaFalce in late 1991 tried to devise a compromise to grant workers guaranteed unpaid leave for family needs. LaFalce's alternative, crafted with Minnesota Democrat Timothy J. Penny, appeared unlikely to win the two-thirds margin on the House floor, however, that it would have needed to overcome a veto. Since LaFalce's alternative was less palatable to family leave supporters, and would have met the same fate as the leadership's version, it was never offered.

LaFalce gained the Small Business helm in 1987, after the retirement of the previous chairman, Parren Mitchell of Maryland. With his hard-charging style, LaFalce presented a sharp contrast to the low-key Mitchell, a black Democrat who expended much of his effort on minority contracting set-aside programs.

When he took the Small Business position, LaFalce gave up his chairmanship of the Banking Subcommittee on Economic Stabilization. LaFalce had tried to use that position to shape the diverse proposals for a "national industrial policy" into legislation, but had limited practical success. Republicans, led by President Ronald Reagan, opposed industrial policy as "micromanagement" of the economy and an attempt by the federal government to pick the economy's "winners and losers."

Although he no longer chairs a Banking panel, LaFalce remains one of the committee's more active members, though he does not always find himself on the prevailing side among the committee's shifting coalitions.

A sometime critic of Congress' efforts to impose stiffer capital standards on financial institutions, LaFalce tried to minimize the effects that a 1991 regulatory overhaul bill would have had on weakly capitalized banks. His amendment to give regulators more discretion to close banks that could not meet tough, new minimum standards being set in the bill was rejected on a 21-28 vote.

LaFalce likewise disapproved of many provisions in the thrift bailout bill in 1989, and typically tried to blaze his own path. During debate in the Subcommittee on Financial Institutions, a LaFalce amendment, requiring states with large numbers of failed thrifts to pick up part of the tab, was defeated by voice vote. He objected to the off-budget financing mechanism in the bill; his amendment to place the bailout "on-budget" was ruled non-germane by Democratic Banking Chairman Henry B. Gonzalez of Texas, who said it was a tax-writing issue under Ways and Means' jurisdiction.

Gonzalez and LaFalce, both headstrong and prickly House veterans, have a cat-and-dog relationship on Banking.

LaFalce's aggressiveness extends to issues outside his committee assignments. He is among the House Democrats most opposed to abortion, and warned in 1989 that the Democratic leadership's advocacy of abortion rights could create a lasting rift between the party and working-class voters. "We're just inviting people to vote against us," LaFalce said. "It's suicide within our party. We're alienating the ethnics and the Catholics that have built the party."

Yet LaFalce risked the wrath of his large Roman Catholic constituency in June 1990 when he criticized the head of the archdiocese of New York. Cardinal John J. O'Connor had said that Catholic politicians might face excommunication if they supported abortion rights. Remarking that such comments might energize the abortion rights cause, LaFalce said, "He has no political smarts.... The cardinal and his cause would be better off if he kept his mouth shut."

LaFalce's pro-small business attitude and his anti-abortion position might indicate that he is a conservative Democrat. However, on most issues, he votes with his Democratic colleagues. LaFalce voted against Bush's position on House legislation more than two-thirds of the time during the 102nd Congress.

At Home: His aggressive manner, an ethnic link to many of his constituents and the Democratic lean in his Niagara region district enabled LaFalce to dominate his first eight House contests. However, in each of his past two bids, LaFalce has tallied no more than 55 percent of the vote.

Though he slipped from the 73 percent he obtained in 1988 in what was then the 32nd District, LaFalce was never threatened with defeat in 1990. His Republican opponent, communications executive Michael T. Waring, received only 31 percent, while Conservative Party candidate Kenneth J. Kowalski drew off 14 percent.

LaFalce blamed his slippage on complacency and his absence from the district during the 101st's long session. However, there also was evidence of dissatisfaction in LaFalce's blue-collar base, which likely stemmed from a general unhappiness with Congress.

LaFalce dodged a bullet in the redistricting that preceded the 1992 election. An early remap proposal would have placed LaFalce in the same district as rising GOP Rep. Bill Paxon. But the final plan gave each incumbent his own district.

However, voters' dissent continued to simmer, and Republicans recruited a higher-profile candidate to challenge LaFalce in the new 29th District. Lawyer William E. Miller Jr. was young, aggressive and had a well-known name: His late father, a longtime House member from the area, was the vice presidential candidate on the 1964 Republican ticket with Barry Goldwater.

Miller ran hard on an anti-incumbent theme, pointing to LaFalce's votes for a House pay raise and the 1990 tax increase and against a balanced-budget amendment. He tried to tar LaFalce, as a senior Banking Committee member, with some responsibility for the savings and loan scandal. He also contrasted his support for abortion rights with LaFalce's anti-abortion position.

But LaFalce fought back vigorously. He said he was an early advocate of banking law reform and blamed the thrift crisis on regulatory failures by Republican administrations. Despite the "anti-insider" sentiment so widely expressed, he benefited from his seniority: The western New York region was already faced with the retirement of longtime Democratic Rep. Henry J. Nowak of Buffalo. Although Miller gained a higher percentage than the 1990 GOP candidate, LaFalce prevailed by more than 30,000 votes.

LaFalce, a lawyer in his hometown of Buffalo, burst into politics in 1970 with an upset victory for the state Senate. When a redistricting plan gave him an impossible district to run in two years later, he moved down to the state Assembly, where he served one term.

In 1974, when GOP Rep. Henry P. Smith retired, LaFalce campaigned in a semi-suburban district that had not been won by a Democrat in 62 years. He carried 60 percent of the vote, then proceeded to win with even greater margins until his 1990 dropoff.

Committees

Small Business (Chairman)
SBA Legislation & the General Economy (chairman)

Banking, Finance & Urban Affairs (3rd of 30 Democrats)
Economic Growth; Financial Institutions Supervision, Regulation & Deposit Insurance; Housing & Community Development; International Development, Finance, Trade & Monetary Policy

Elections

1992 General		
John J. LaFalce (D, L)	128,230	(54%)
William E. Miller Jr. (R, C)	98,031	(42%)
Kenneth J. Kowalski (RTL)	7,367	(3%)
1990 General		
John J. LaFalce (D, L)	68,367	(55%)
Michael T. Waring (R)	39,053	(31%)
Kenneth J. Kowalski (C, RTL)	16,853	(14%)

Previous Winning Percentages: **1988** (73%) **1986** (91%) **1984** (69%) **1982** (91%) **1980** (72%) **1978** (74%) **1976** (67%) **1974** (60%)

District Vote for President

1992
D 103,528 (40%)
R 86,732 (33%)
I 70,231 (27%)

Campaign Finance

	Receipts	Receipts from PACs		Expend-itures
1992				
LaFalce (D)	$588,616	$312,570	(53%)	$467,841
Miller (R)	$83,924	$1,000	(1%)	$83,110
Kowalski (RTL)	$50	0		$51
1990				
LaFalce (D)	$339,919	$196,675	(58%)	$145,079
Kowalski (C)	$273	0		$231

Key Votes

1993	
Require parental notification of minors' abortions	Y
Require unpaid family and medical leave	Y
Approve national "motor voter" registration bill	Y
Approve budget increasing taxes and reducing deficit	Y
Approve economic stimulus plan	Y
1992	
Approve balanced-budget constitutional amendment	N
Close down space station program	Y
Approve U.S. aid for former Soviet Union	Y
Allow shifting funds from defense to domestic programs	Y
1991	
Extend unemployment benefits using deficit financing	Y
Approve waiting period for handgun purchases	Y
Authorize use of force in Persian Gulf	N

Voting Studies

	Presidential Support		Party Unity		Conservative Coalition	
Year	S	O	S	O	S	O
1992	27	70	86	9	29	65
1991	32	67	89	8	22	78
1990	30	67	80	14	35	61
1989	34	59	81	15	41	51
1988	24	70	85	11	32	61
1987	20	77	83	9	26	74
1986	19	76	80	11	20	64
1985	30	66	77	15	22	73
1984	35	56	78	13	25	68
1983	30	67	84	12	19	75
1982	38	57	80	10	21	73
1981	36	61	78†	15†	27	68

† Not eligible for all recorded votes.

Interest Group Ratings

Year	ADA	AFL-CIO	CCUS	ACU
1992	85	100	25	12
1991	90	83	30	10
1990	72	67	46	21
1989	90	83	50	12
1988	80	93	38	8
1987	88	87	14	5
1986	85	83	25	10
1985	70	94	38	14
1984	80	83	43	24
1983	80	94	35	9
1982	85	94	24	5
1981	70	87	17	7

30 Jack Quinn (R)

Of Hamburg — Elected 1992; 1st Term

Born: April 13, 1951, Buffalo, N.Y.
Education: Siena College, B.A. 1973; State U. of New York, Buffalo, M.A. 1983.
Occupation: Teacher.
Family: Wife, Mary Beth McAndrews; two children.
Religion: Roman Catholic.
Political Career: Town of Hamburg Council, 1982-84; Hamburg town supervisor, 1985-93.
Capitol Office: 331 Cannon Bldg. 20515; 225-3306.

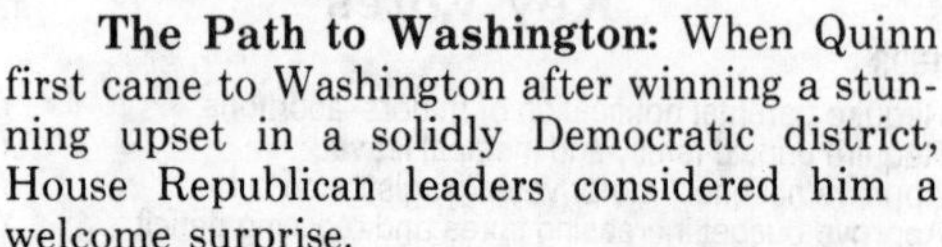

The Path to Washington: When Quinn first came to Washington after winning a stunning upset in a solidly Democratic district, House Republican leaders considered him a welcome surprise.

Quinn then gave his elders the bad news — to keep the seat, he would have to stray from the party line on many issues that face Congress. "I said I need to vote for what's best for my district, and that may not always be where the party is," said Quinn, a former English teacher and school athletic coach.

Translation: Quinn, the first Republican in decades to represent downtown Buffalo in the House, likely will be one of the chamber's more moderate GOP members.

Quinn did not waste any time proving his willingness to stray. He was one of only 40 Republicans to vote for mandatory unpaid family leave legislation that President Clinton signed in February 1993.

Quinn says he became a Republican almost by chance — his uncle, a local GOP elections official, happened to be the one who sent him his voter registration papers. Though now one of the party faithful — he was the Erie County campaign coordinator for George Bush's 1988 presidential race — Quinn repeatedly has been re-elected chief executive (supervisor) of the Democratic suburb of Hamburg. In his congressional race, the Erie County Conservative Party endorsed his Democratic opponent, County Executive Dennis Gorski.

Unlike most Republicans in Congress, Quinn is leery of the proposed North American Free Trade Agreement, thinks Clinton's $20 billion-a-year infrastructure program is $30 billion too modest and considers himself anti-abortion but hedges on whether he'll oppose federal funding for the procedure.

In March 1993, he voted against a bill codifying the Clinton administration's lifting of the "gag rule" that prohibited staff at federally funded family planning clinics from discussing abortion.

Quinn successfully pushed hard for a seat on the Public Works Committee, from which his predecessor, Democrat Henry J. Nowak, reportedly brought home $1 billion in federal aid during his 18 years in Congress.

During the campaign, Quinn distanced himself from George Bush and made congressional reform his issue. He had two spots on the ballot, one for the Republican Party and one for his own "Change Congress Party."

The main pitch of his campaign was an 11-point reform platform, calling for limits on franking, members' travel, Congress' budget, closed debating rules and political action committee contributions.

Quinn promised not to accept Congress' latest pay raise, a $4,100 increase, though even at the 1992 level of $129,500 a year his salary will more than double what he was paid as Hamburg supervisor.

Though Quinn also supported 12-year term limits for members of Congress, he did not pledge to limit his own service. "I'm thrilled to come to the United States Congress for however long I can be productive to the district," he said.

After securing the GOP's nomination with little fuss, Quinn said the Democrats considered him little more than a nuisance. But he quickly went on the attack, dovetailing his gibes against the status quo with sharp criticisms of his opponent, telling voters that Gorski was a typical politician who represented "more of the same."

Quinn battered Gorski for not releasing the 1993 county budget before the election, implying that Gorski was hiding bad fiscal news. Quinn also made the most of reports that much of Gorski's campaign fund came from contributions from county employees.

Quinn ended up taking 52 percent of the vote, but he is aware of how vulnerable he remains. To secure his seat, Quinn plans a congressional office operation tilted heavily toward constituent service.

Most of his staff, including the top aide and press secretary, likely will be based in his district office. His wife and two children will live in Hamburg, and he will commute home each weekend.

New York 30

West — Buffalo

The 30th, dominated by its part of Buffalo, provided a paradoxical result in the 1992 election. The district, with its large, economically worried working-class population, went to Democrat Bill Clinton by a wide margin; George Bush finished behind independent candidate Ross Perot.

Yet even as the district was resoundingly rejecting Bush, it elected Republican Quinn in the House. His win was a major upset: Over the previous 18 years, the territory covered by much of the 30th had elected retiring Democratic Rep. Henry J. Nowak without a serious GOP challenge.

Quinn's win was based much less on his partisan status than on his theme of political reform. However, this dissatisfaction with the political status quo affected the presidential contest in the 30th, fueling Perot's campaign there and hurting both major-party candidates. Although he carried the district by 46,000 votes, Clinton won with a 46 percent plurality, well below the 66 percent won by Democrat Michael S. Dukakis in 1988.

Political alienation is one lingering effect of the decline of the region's traditional heavy industry base. Decades of Rust Belt decline had a corrosive effect on Buffalo's morale and national image. Though still one of the nation's 50 largest cities with just over 328,000 people, Buffalo lost 29 percent of its population in the 1970s, and 9 percent in the 1980s.

The city is slowly resurrecting its economic prospects. The U.S.-Canada free-trade agreement enacted in 1989 is paying business dividends for Buffalo; there was a major upswing in its financial industry. The unemployment rate, as high as 15 percent in the early 1980s, was just over 6 percent at the end of 1992. Pilot Field, a 19,000-seat ballpark widely praised by baseball fans, has drawn record-breaking crowds to AAA-level minor league games.

Still, the city's transition has hardly been painless for blue-collar whites or the large low- to middle-income black constituency. The manufacturing jobs in the Buffalo area declined by 45,000 between 1980 and 1991. The once-dominant steel industry is now a fragment: Much of the steel-making center in Lackawanna is a wasteland. Though service industry jobs grew by even more than manufacturing jobs fell, many of them provide a fraction of the wages to which unionized factory workers were accustomed.

About two-thirds of the city of Buffalo, including most of its downtown, is in the 30th. Black residents make up about 43 percent of the Buffalo section. Polish-Americans are the largest ethnic group in both Buffalo and Cheektowaga. South Buffalo has a large Irish population.

South of the city along the lake are the industrial parts of Lackawanna and Hamburg that provide a usually dependable Democratic vote. But the southern and eastern reaches of the 30th are suburban and exurban areas, some of which provide a Republican counterweight. Orchard Park is the site of Rich Stadium, home of football's Buffalo Bills.

1990 Population: 580,337. White 472,761 (81%), Black 97,103 (17%), Other 10,473 (2%). Hispanic origin 8,922 (2%). 18 and over 441,308 (76%), 62 and over 104,483 (18%). Median age: 34.

Committees

Public Works & Transportation (24th of 24 Republicans)
Economic Development; Water Resources & the Environment

Veterans' Affairs (10th of 14 Republicans)
Education, Training & Employment; Oversight & Investigations

Campaign Finance

	Receipts	Receipts from PACs		Expend-itures
1992				
Quinn (R)	$205,843	$10,665	(5%)	$199,257
Gorski (D)	$456,099	$119,525	(26%)	$459,349

Key Votes

1993	
Require parental notification of minors' abortions	Y
Require unpaid family and medical leave	Y
Approve national "motor voter" registration bill	N
Approve budget increasing taxes and reducing deficit	N
Approve economic stimulus plan	N

Elections

1992 General		
Jack Quinn (R, CHGC)	125,734	(52%)
Dennis Gorski (D, C)	111,445	(46%)
Mary F. Refermat (RTL)	6,025	(2%)

District Vote for President

	1992
D	119,115 (46%)
R	68,172 (26%)
I	73,333 (28%)

31 Amo Houghton (R)

Of Corning — Elected 1986; 4th Term

Born: Aug. 7, 1926, Corning, N.Y.
Education: Harvard U., A.B. 1950, M.B.A. 1952.
Military Service: Marine Corps, 1945-46.
Occupation: Glassworks company executive.
Family: Wife, Priscilla Dewey; four children, three stepchildren.
Religion: Episcopalian.
Political Career: No previous office.
Capitol Office: 1110 Longworth Bldg. 20515; 225-3161.

In Washington: Not many corporate chief executive officers cap their careers by becoming members of the minority party in a legislative chamber of 435. But Houghton, former CEO for Corning Glass Works and scion of one of the nation's wealthiest families, has done just that.

Houghton abandoned plans to work as a missionary in Africa and headed to Capitol Hill instead. At age 66, he does not plan a long stay in Washington, but while here, he has a missionary's enthusiasm for making a contribution.

Congress, however, has shown a resistance to being converted to Houghton's view that government's fiscal affairs should be run like those of a corporation. Houghton's business acumen helped him get a seat on the Budget Committee as a freshman, which he was able to parlay into a seat on the Ways and Means Committee at the beginning of the 103rd Congress.

While he participated actively in the budget panel's business, he gained no special influence on the committee, where Republicans often are shut out by Democrats who view the budget as a partisan statement more than as an economic blueprint.

His skills and inclinations may serve him better on Ways and Means, a less partisan committee where a solution-oriented House Republican can influence policy and process.

The switch to Ways and Means comes at a good time for Houghton; many of the issues he has pursued over his career are now key parts of the Clinton agenda. He introduced his own health-care package in 1992 and 1993, along with an alternative family leave bill.

During debate on the family leave bill in February 1993, Houghton argued in favor of the concept but against the bill that passed. "I probably am one of the only people around here that has ever put in a family leave program," he told the House. "We did it with a paid family leave ... but I did it in a company that had about 30,000 employees. I have worked in smaller companies and I have advised smaller companies. If a company does not have the money, it is not a good idea."

Houghton has been able to do some things for his district. Late in the 101st Congress, he worked to resolve a conflict between the Seneca Indian Nation and the U.S. government over the renegotiation of federal leases of Indian lands.

The dispute centered on the 1991 expiration of 99-year leases of Seneca lands — negotiated on terms very unfavorable to the Senecas — upon which the town of Salamanca was built. With the leases due to expire, Houghton helped craft a deal under which the federal and state governments paid the Indian nation $60 million, and the Senecas renewed the land leases on terms acceptable to the governments.

Not surprisingly for a Northeastern Republican, Houghton stands to the left of the House GOP line on a number of issues. He was one of only 17 Republicans opposing a constitutional amendment to ban flag desecration. He now opposes a balanced-budget amendment, saying that it is "legal fancy footwork" and that it is Congress' responsibility to control spending.

As a member of the Foreign Affairs Committee for two terms — he gave up both Budget and Foreign Affairs in the 103rd — Houghton made trips to the Soviet Union and Nicaragua. But unlike colleagues who travel abroad on military aircraft, Houghton paid for all such travel himself.

Houghton opposed military aid for the Nicaraguan contras, preferring another way to make an impact in Central America: In the 100th Congress, he worked to put together private funding for a scholarship program to bring Nicaraguan students to colleges and universities in western New York. "Many times when congressmen go down there ... they come back and have a press conference and that's all. Here is a way of saying 'we want to help' in a human way," Houghton said of his plan.

In November 1992, Houghton also urged a strong international response to the crisis in Somalia.

The Republican end of the House chamber is a long way from the Corning boardroom, but for a man used to giving orders, Houghton has shown little frustration. He is affable, with a

New York 31

Southern Tier — Jamestown; Corning; Elmira

The 31st stretches across the bottom of New York state — the Southern Tier — for more than 100 miles, from Lake Erie on the west to Elmira in the east. This hilly, mainly rural country strongly favors Republicans.

Although the landscape is dotted with small industrial cities, Democrats have never been able to make many inroads here. GOP Rep. Houghton's 71 percent in 1992 was typical of his strong showings since his election in 1986. His predecessor, Democrat Stan Lundine (now New York's lieutenant governor), did hold the Southern Tier's House seat for a decade, but he was an exception.

The nation's economic problems have been felt in parts of the 31st (most counties in the district had small net population losses during the 1980s), and residents' concerns were reflected in the 1992 presidential results: George Bush, who took about three-fifths of the 31st's vote in 1988, fell to 40 percent.

Still, Bush won a solid plurality here. The district was no friendlier to Bill Clinton than to previous Democratic candidates; he received less than 30 percent in three 31st District counties, including Cattaraugus, where his 29 percent placed him third behind Ross Perot. (The independent Perot took 31 percent there and won more than a quarter of the vote in most other counties.)

Chautauqua County, at the district's western end, is the 31st's most populous; it has about a quarter of the district's residents. Jamestown, which with its population of nearly 35,000 is the 31st's largest city, is a furniture-making center.

The county (Lundine's home base) is the only one in the district where Democrats are often competitive. Clinton carried the county, albeit with just 36 percent (to 34 percent for Bush and 30 percent for Perot). GOP Sen. Alfonse M. D'Amato's Chautauqua tally of 53 percent in 1992 was by far his weakest showing in the 31st.

But Republicans dominate in the counties to the east, including Cattaraugus; its big town is industrial Olean, also home to St. Bonaventure University (2,800 students). Agribusiness plays an important role in neighboring Allegany County. Welch's, a grape-growing cooperative best known for its juice products, is based in Wellsville.

Steuben County contains Corning, one of America's better-known company towns. Houghton's family has long controlled Corning Inc., which produces utilitarian dishes, cookware and medical glass products; its Steuben Glass Works makes more costly decorative crystal pieces.

The Elmira area (Chemung County) is also industrial. Its largest employers are Hardinge Brothers, which makes precision machines, and a Toshiba Display Devices facility.

To the north, the 31st moves into the vineyards and vacation lands of the Finger Lakes region. The large Taylor and Great Western wineries are here, along with numerous small family-run operations. The district also takes in part of Auburn, the commercial center of Cayuga County.

1990 Population: 580,337. White 556,495 (96%), Black 13,485 (2%), Other 10,357 (2%). Hispanic origin 8,614 (1%). 18 and over 428,519 (74%), 62 and over 100,899 (17%). Median age: 34.

sense of humor he can turn on himself.

At Home: Houghton's easy manner and non-ideological approach seem to suit his constituents in upstate New York's Southern Tier. Since taking 60 percent of the vote in 1986 to win an open House seat previously held by a Democrat, Houghton has dominated.

He is carrying on the traditions of a patrician family that for years has run Steuben County's Corning Inc. Houghton served 19 years as chief executive officer of Corning Glass. Then, at age 60, he entered the public sector, as had his father and grandfather.

Houghton's political opportunity appeared suddenly in 1986, when Democratic incumbent Stan Lundine of the Southern Tier's then-34th District was tapped by New York Gov. Mario M. Cuomo to run for lieutenant governor.

Before Lundine's departure, Houghton had been spending much of his time on efforts to provide economic relief for Zimbabwe. When the congressional vacancy appeared, he switched his sights closer to home.

Houghton was popular in his hometown, where Corning Glass is the major employer. The company helped finance restoration after a flood devastated the city in 1972. While he had never been particularly active in local Republican affairs, he had little trouble securing the GOP nomination.

Seeking across-the-board appeal, Houghton pointed to his experience at creating jobs — a key issue in a district where unemployment remains well above the national average. He pointed to his service as co-chairman of the Labor-Industry Coalition on International

Trade, a group that had lobbied heavily for the Democratic trade bill in the 99th Congress.

The Democratic nominee, Cattaraugus County District Attorney Larry Himelein, portrayed Houghton as an elitist, and his case was boosted by a satirical profile of Houghton in The Wall Street Journal. It focused on Houghton's posh campaign style: He traveled either in a plush motor home stocked with liquor, cigars and homemade cookies or in his private plane.

With Houghton spending more than any candidate had ever spent in the district, Himelein hoped to pick up support from voters who considered the Republican too much of a Brahmin. "Running for Congress isn't going to finishing school, it's not going to the country club," Himelein told a reporter during the campaign.

But Houghton ably deflected criticism. A 3-1 margin in his Steuben County base propelled him to victory.

Committee

Ways & Means (9th of 14 Republicans)
Oversight (ranking); Social Security

Elections

1992 General		
Amo Houghton (R, C)	150,696	(71%)
Joseph P. Leahey (D)	52,010	(24%)
Gretchen S. McManus (RTL)	10,848	(5%)
1990 General		
Amo Houghton (R, C)	89,831	(70%)
Joseph P. Leahey (D)	37,421	(29%)
Nevin K. Eklund (L)	1,807	(1%)

Previous Winning Percentages: 1988 (96%) 1986 (60%)

District Vote for President

	1992
D	82,959 (34%)
R	97,447 (40%)
I	62,325 (26%)

Campaign Finance

	Receipts	Receipts from PACs		Expend-itures
1992				
Houghton (R)	$359,995	$117,060	(33%)	$444,296
Leahey (D)	$5,849	$500	(9%)	$5,850
1990				
Houghton (R)	$333,962	$102,000	(31%)	$178,401
Leahey (D)	$6,483	0		$6,462

Key Votes

1993	
Require parental notification of minors' abortions	N
Require unpaid family and medical leave	N
Approve national "motor voter" registration bill	N
Approve budget increasing taxes and reducing deficit	N
Approve economic stimulus plan	N
1992	
Approve balanced-budget constitutional amendment	Y
Close down space station program	N
Approve U.S. aid for former Soviet Union	Y
Allow shifting funds from defense to domestic programs	N
1991	
Extend unemployment benefits using deficit financing	Y
Approve waiting period for handgun purchases	N
Authorize use of force in Persian Gulf	Y

Voting Studies

	Presidential Support		Party Unity		Conservative Coalition	
Year	S	O	S	O	S	O
1992	66	32	64	33	79	19
1991	71	27	58	37	65	30
1990	57	39	58	36	72	22
1989	65	26	45	46	71	20
1988	52	45	61	32	92	8
1987	63	35	62	33	84	14

Interest Group Ratings

Year	ADA	AFL-CIO	CCUS	ACU
1992	30	50	88	68
1991	20	50	70	70
1990	33	25	54	43
1989	20	10	90	65
1988	45	57	100	56
1987	28	38	80	39

North Carolina

STATE DATA

Governor:
James B. Hunt Jr. (D)
First elected: 1992 *
Length of term: 4 years
Term expires: 1/97
Salary: $91,938
Term limit: 2 consecutive terms
Phone: (919) 733-7350
Born: May 16, 1937; Greensboro, N.C.
Education: North Carolina State U., B.S. 1959, M.S. 1962; U. of North Carolina, J.D. 1964
Occupation: Lawyer; cattle rancher
Family: Wife, Carolyn Leonard; four children
Religion: Presbyterian
Political Career: Lieutenant governor, 1973-77; * governor, 1977-85; Democratic nominee for U.S. Senate, 1984

Lt. Gov.: Dennis Wicker (D)
First elected: 1992
Length of term: 4 years
Term expires: 1/97
Salary: $75,774
Phone: (919) 733-7350

State election official: (919) 733-7173
Democratic headquarters: (919) 821-2777
Republican headquarters: (919) 828-6423

REDISTRICTING

North Carolina gained one House seat in reapportionment, increasing from 11 districts to 12. The legislature passed the map Jan. 24, 1992; the Justice Department approved it Feb. 6.

STATE LEGISLATURE

Bicameral General Assembly. Meets January-July.

Senate: 50 members, 2-year terms
1992 breakdown: 39D, 11R; 43 men, 7 women; 43 whites, 7 blacks
Salary: $13,026
Phone: (919) 733-7350

House of Representatives: 120 members, 2-year terms
1992 breakdown: 78D, 42R; 96 men, 24 women; 101 whites, 18 blacks, 1 other
Salary: $13,026
Phone: (919) 733-3451

URBAN STATISTICS

City	Pop.
Charlotte	395,934
Mayor Richard Vinroot, R	
Raleigh	207,951
Mayor Avery C. Upchurch, N-P	
Greensboro	183,894
Mayor V. M. Nussbaum Jr., D	
Winston-Salem	143,485
Mayor Martha S. Wood, D	
Durham	136,611
Mayor Harry E. Rodenhizer Jr., R	

U.S. CONGRESS

Senate: 0 D, 2 R
House: 8 D, 4 R

TERM LIMITS

For Congress: No
For state offices: No

ELECTIONS

1992 Presidential Vote

George Bush	43.4%
Bill Clinton	42.7%
Ross Perot	13.7%

1988 Presidential Vote

George Bush	58%
Michael S. Dukakis	42%

1984 Presidential Vote

Ronald Reagan	62%
Walter F. Mondale	38%

POPULATION

1990 population		6,628,637
1980 population		5,881,766
Percent change		+13%
Rank among states:		10
White		76%
Black		22%
Hispanic		1%
Asian or Pacific islander		1%
Urban		50%
Rural		50%
Born in state		70%
Foreign-born		2%
Under age 18	1,606,149	24%
Ages 18-64	4,218,147	64%
65 and older	804,341	12%
Median age		33.1

MISCELLANEOUS

Capital: Raleigh
Number of counties: 100
Per capita income: $16,642 (1991)
Rank among states: 34
Total area: 52,669 sq. miles
Rank among states: 28

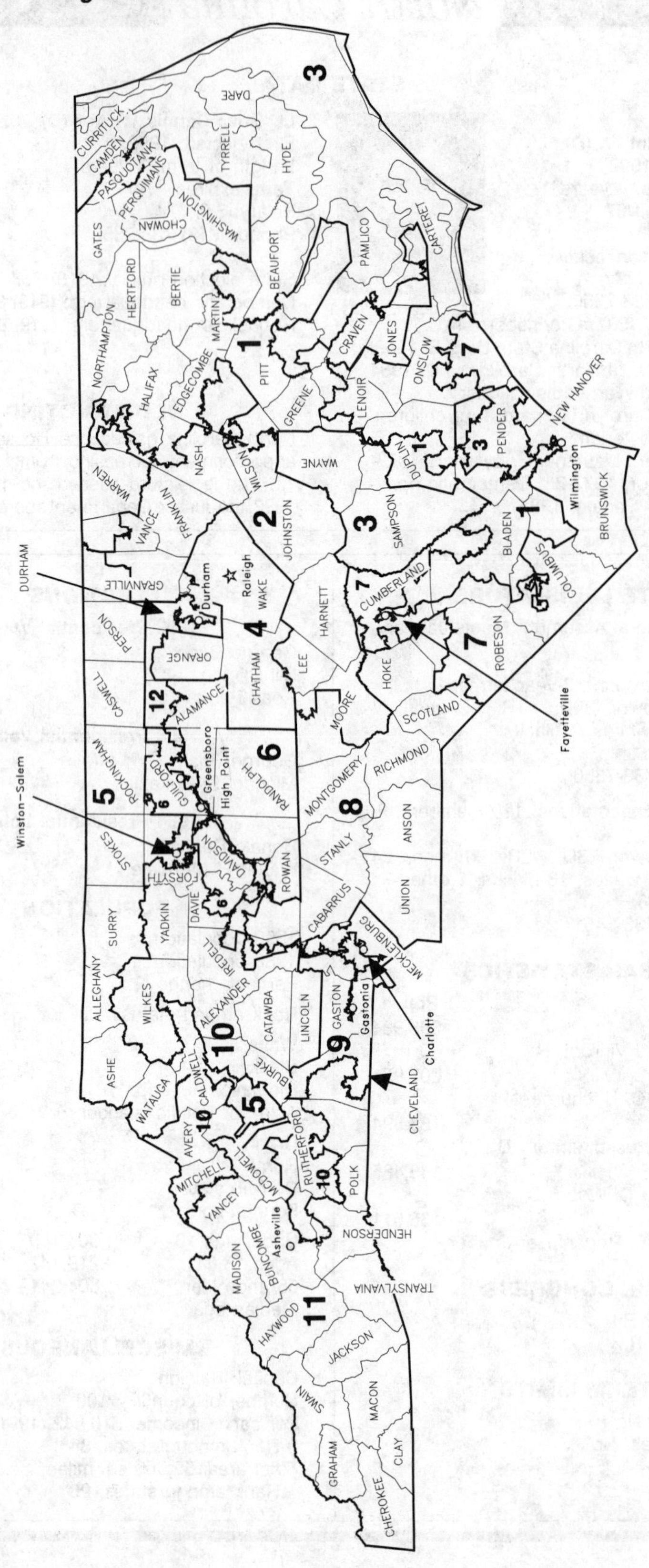

CURRITUCK
CAMDEN
PASQUOTANK
PERQUIMANS
GATES
CHOWAN
HERTFORD
BERTIE
NORTHAMPTON
HALIFAX
WARREN
VANCE
GRANVILLE
PERSON
CASWELL
ROCKINGHAM
STOKES
SURRY
ALLEGHANY
ASHE
WATAUGA
WILKES
YADKIN
FORSYTH
GUILFORD
ALAMANCE
ORANGE
DURHAM
Durham
WAKE
Raleigh
FRANKLIN
NASH
EDGECOMBE
MARTIN
WASHINGTON
TYRRELL
DARE
HYDE
BEAUFORT
PITT
WILSON
JOHNSTON
WAYNE
GREENE
LENOIR
CRAVEN
PAMLICO
CARTERET
JONES
ONSLOW
DUPLIN
PENDER
NEW HANOVER
Wilmington
BRUNSWICK
COLUMBUS
BLADEN
SAMPSON
CUMBERLAND
Fayetteville
HARNETT
LEE
CHATHAM
RANDOLPH
Greensboro
High Point
Winston-Salem
MOORE
HOKE
ROBESON
SCOTLAND
RICHMOND
MONTGOMERY
ANSON
STANLY
UNION
ROWAN
DAVIDSON
DAVIE
IREDELL
CABARRUS
MECKLENBURG
Charlotte
GASTON
Gastonia
LINCOLN
CATAWBA
ALEXANDER
CALDWELL
BURKE
CLEVELAND
RUTHERFORD
POLK
HENDERSON
McDOWELL
AVERY
MITCHELL
YANCEY
MADISON
BUNCOMBE
Asheville
HAYWOOD
TRANSYLVANIA
JACKSON
SWAIN
MACON
GRAHAM
CHEROKEE
CLAY

Jesse Helms (R)

Of Raleigh — Elected 1972; 4th Term

Born: Oct. 18, 1921, Monroe, N.C.
Education: Wingate College, 1938-39; Wake Forest U., 1939-40.
Military Service: Navy, 1942-45.
Occupation: Journalist; broadcasting executive; banking executive; congressional aide.
Family: Wife, Dorothy Jane Coble; three children.
Religion: Baptist.
Political Career: Raleigh City Council, 1957-61.
Capitol Office: 403 Dirksen Bldg. 20510; 224-6342.

In Washington: Two decades of tirades against communism, liberalism, big government, abortion and homosexuality have made Helms the paragon of hard-line conservatism in the Senate. While conservative activists lionize him, liberal Democrats vilify him as an extremist; even in his own Republican Party, more moderate members sometimes shrink from his stark rhetoric on social and national security issues.

Yet Helms has proved time and again that he knows the issues that energize the Middle American, overwhelmingly white constituency that has carried him through a series of fierce Senate campaigns. In the process, he often sets a tone that the national party eventually adopts.

Now in his 70s, Helms is undiminished in his battles despite health problems that probably would have quieted any other senator. In 1991, he was diagnosed with a rare bone disease, and he revealed that he was undergoing treatment for prostate cancer. In June 1992, he underwent quadruple-bypass heart surgery.

Although he missed some time for treatment and recuperation, he still was a force to be dealt with in debates throughout the 102nd Congress. And the Clinton administration — which early on proposed lifting the military's ban on homosexuals — promised to provide him with plenty of targets for his social-issue crusades.

Even before coming to the Senate, Helms worked as a craftsman of the GOP's "Southern strategy." By contrasting conservative stands on defense, crime, civil rights and traditional morality with the liberalism of national Democrats, Helms helped transform politics in the once solidly Democratic South. Winning a Senate seat in the process, Helms by the early 1970s was a "Reaganite" — well before Ronald Reagan became a dominant national figure.

During the 1970s and 1980s, Helms helped set the New Right's social agenda. He remains one of the Senate's fiercest opponents of abortion and one of its strongest supporters of school prayer. He has made a crusade of limiting access to telephone "dial-a-porn" services.

Homosexuality has also become a defining issue in Helms' social agenda. In 1993, he told The Washington Times that he would try to block President Clinton's openly homosexual nominee for an assistant secretary job at the Department of Housing and Urban Development "[b]ecause she's a damn lesbian. I'm not going to put a lesbian in a position like that. If you want to call me a bigot, fine."

Helms, who has said that the crisis caused by AIDS is overstated, has tried without success to shift money for AIDS research to efforts against other diseases. He has also used the anxiety surrounding the disease as ammunition for his social-policy battles. In 1991, he won Senate approval for two amendments: one requiring patients undergoing "invasive" medical procedures to be tested for AIDS except in "emergency situations," and another calling for prison terms and fines for health-care workers infected with the AIDS virus who fail to notify their patients.

"I am the father of a nurse," he said during floor debate on the latter amendment. "I want my daughter protected. That is why I have for the last six years attempted to bring attention to the callous disregard for public safety and common sense which has been exhibited by the AIDS lobby and its allies in the Senate." The Senate adopted it 81-18.

Both amendments were later removed in conference.

During the 102nd Congress, Helms fought to bar funding for two proposed surveys of Americans' sexual behavior. He charged that "the sexual liberation crowd" was backing the studies — which were approved by the scientific peer-review process but which the Department of Health and Human Services declined to fund — in an effort "to cook the scientific facts to legitimize homosexuality and other sexually promiscuous lifestyles." Backers of the surveys, led by Democrats Paul Simon of Illinois and Edward M. Kennedy of Massachusetts, said they were needed to help combat AIDS and other sexually transmitted diseases.

As so often happens when Helms and Kennedy face off, the debate turned ugly. At one point, after Kennedy refused to read aloud some of the more explicit questions proposed for inclusion in the survey, Helms made a pointed reference to his colleague's well-publicized personal troubles. "These questions may be all right for a nightclub in Miami or Palm Beach at 2 o'clock in the morning on a Saturday night, but they are not fit for young children," he said.

In early 1993, it was Clinton's proposal to lift the ban on gays in the military that triggered Helms' outrage. It "is the No. 1 priority of the homosexual political movement," he said in a floor speech. "They know that the armed forces are the last bastion of traditional morality in this country."

Helms' knack for finding the hottest of the rank-and-file's "hot-button" issues was amply exhibited in his 1990 re-election bid. Threatened by a bid from former Charlotte Mayor Harvey B. Gantt — a black liberal with a mainstream demeanor — Helms turned the election into a referendum on affirmative action programs.

Helms had opposed, and Gantt supported, a 1990 civil rights bill providing enhanced remedies in cases of job discrimination. When President Bush vetoed the act in October 1990 as a "quota bill" — and the Senate sustained his veto by just one vote — Democrats thought they had an opportunity to brand Helms as unsympathetic to minorities.

But Helms boiled the debate down to one issue. At issue, Helms said, was another effort by liberals to expand affirmative action programs that he — and many of those in his white, working-class base — saw as providing unfair preferences to members of racial minorities. In a TV ad that gave his campaign momentum, the hand of a white man, the apparent recipient of a job rejection, crumples a letter while a narrator says: "You needed that job, and you were the best-qualified. But they had to give it to a minority because of a racial quota. Is that really fair?" Gantt denied supporting quotas and tried to brand Helms as running a racist campaign. But Helms went on to win with 53 percent of the vote.

Congress turned again to the civil rights bill in 1991. As supporters worked to craft a compromise with the White House, Helms surprised senators by offering an amendment to a crime bill outlawing any race preferences in hiring. His move held up the crime bill for 24 hours as senators scrambled to line up the votes to kill it — which they did, 71-28. Bush eventually signed a compromise civil rights bill into law in late 1991.

Helms' skill at elevating obscure but emotional issues to the top of the political agenda has been best demonstrated in recent years in the debate over federal funding of the arts. Helms, long an adversary of the National Endowment for the Arts (NEA), repeatedly tied Congress in knots in the 101st and 102nd congresses over his amendments to ban NEA funding for sexually explicit projects.

Arts funding became a wedge issue in 1989 during a furor over NEA funding of two exhibits: one by the late Robert Mapplethorpe, which included photographs of gay sex practices, and another by Andres Serrano, which included a photo showing a crucifix in a vessel of urine.

"Artists have a right, it is said, to express their feelings as they wish; only a philistine would suggest otherwise," Helms said. "Fair enough, but no artist has a pre-emptive claim on the tax dollars of the American people."

The Senate passed Helms' amendments, but House-Senate conferees agreed to milder versions. Helms had his effect, however: The 1990 NEA reauthorization instructed the agency to take into account general standards of decency in making its grants. In 1991, both chambers approved Helms' language, but conferees left it off the bill in exchange for killing language raising grazing fees on public lands — a deal inevitably dubbed "corn for porn."

With his unyieldingly ideological posture, Helms has had relatively little success at winning enactment of the legislation into which he puts so much furious effort. He has always had greater success at blocking legislation than at getting it passed. He is a master of Senate arcanery; together with his mulelike stubbornness, it is a formidable combination. He can often be found on the Senate floor, using his parliamentary skills to tie up legislative action.

But winning is not the point for Helms. "You got to understand how I operate," he once told a reporter. "Somebody said, 'Jesse, why do you so often advance things or take positions that you know you don't have any chance to win?' And my answer to that is, I do it on principle." His propensity to cast the solo "no" led the The News and Observer of Raleigh, N.C., his ardent foe, to dub him "Senator No." Helms relishes the title.

To many members of Congress and to the Bush administration, the Cold War appeared to end with the fall of the Berlin Wall in late 1989. But Helms — who had thrived on Reagan's "evil empire" rhetoric of the early 1980s — warned against a too-rapid rapprochement with the Soviet Union. He steadfastly opposed most arms treaties with the Soviets. "To put it as politely as possible," he said in 1991, "the Soviets are cheats, liars and scoundrels."

Throughout the 1980s, the threat of communism in Central America — in the form of the Sandinista government of Nicaragua and the leftist insurgency against El Salvador's rightist government — fueled Helms' efforts on the Foreign Relations panel. Helms was skeptical throughout the 1990 election process in Nicaragua, fearing that it would leave the Sandinistas in power. Even after opposition candidate Violeta Chamorro defeated Sandinista leader Daniel Ortega, Helms was unenthralled; her coalition included too many leftist groups to earn Helms' trust.

For several months in 1992, Helms single-handedly blocked $104 million in economic aid to Nicaragua. Helms wanted the aid frozen to pressure Chamorro to return property owned by U.S. citizens that the Sandinistas had confiscated. Bush went along with him until after the election, releasing $54 million in December.

Sensing a communist threat in any insurgency against a pro-Western government, Helms has found himself under attack over the years for supporting right-wing regimes accused of human rights abuses. He opposed U.S. sanctions against South Africa and supported the governments of Augusto Pinochet of Chile and Ferdinand Marcos of the Philippines.

Helms had an opportunity to take over as Foreign Relations chairman in 1985 (when Republicans held the Senate majority); however, he had made a promise during his 1984 campaign to stay as Agriculture chairman and oversee the interests of North Carolina's tobacco growers in the 1985 farm bill.

With that pledge met, Helms in 1987 stepped over Indiana Republican Richard G. Lugar, who had been serving as chairman, to claim the post of ranking Republican. Citing his seniority and contrasting his hard-line approach to Lugar's pragmatism, Helms won the post on a 24-17 vote.

But Helms' efforts, here as elsewhere, have been geared more toward obstruction than production. His invariable opposition to provisions in committee legislation contributed to the committee's failure to pass foreign aid authorization bills in most recent years.

Foreign Relations' poor record at moving its major annual legislative responsibility has taken its toll on its image and that of the unassertive Democratic chairman, Claiborne Pell of Rhode Island. In early 1991, Foreign Relations Democrats gave new powers to its subcommittees at the expense of Pell and Helms. The arrangement functioned well, to an extent: In 1991, the Senate passed a foreign aid authorization bill for the first time in six years. But the bill died in the House.

Helms did achieve a long-sought goal in the 102nd Congress with the enactment of legislation aimed at halting the spread of chemical and biological weapons. He and Pell had repeatedly cosponsored bills to impose sanctions on countries and companies that contribute to the weapons' proliferation.

Whatever his legislative legacy on Foreign Relations, Helms is surely more visible there than in his past position as Agriculture chairman in the 1980s. He virtually abdicated control of the committee during his first four years as chairman, allowing a coalition of Republicans, led by then-Majority Leader Bob Dole of Kansas, to take the lead on farm legislation.

One of the little-noticed aspects of Helms' highly public career was his long tenure on the Senate Ethics Committee. A member since 1979, Helms gained the most notice in this position just before he stepped down in February 1991.

Helms was one of the six committee members who sat in judgment of the five senators who were accused of ethics violations relating to their association with thrift scandal figure Charles H. Keating Jr. Helms took one of the tougher stands, favoring Senate punishment for at least three of the senators. But when the committee decided to refer only the case of California Democrat Alan Cranston for full Senate action — recommending no punishment for the others — Helms denied that he and his colleagues had gone soft.

However, when the panel's deliberations dragged on through the summer, Helms broke with the Ethics Committee's penchant for secrecy, unleashing a scathing 247-page, 936-footnote report on the case that called for Cranston to be censured by the Senate. Ultimately, the committee "strongly and severely" reprimanded Cranston before the full Senate.

At Home: The smoke from Helms' monumental 1984 re-election battle against Democratic Gov. James B. Hunt Jr. had scarcely lifted before another defense loomed. But the toll on purse and psyche that the bitter 1984 campaign exacted served to dissuade "heavyweight" Democrats from challenging Helms in 1990.

Helms' political future appeared very much in doubt as he prepared for the 1984 balloting. His vaunted political organization, the National Congressional Club, had suffered severe setbacks in 1982, losing every one of the five congressional contests it had targeted in the state. Further, Helms was being plagued by negative publicity over his 1982 vote for raising the cigarette tax as well as his unsuccessful efforts to block creation of a federal holiday for the Rev. Dr. Martin Luther King Jr. Pollsters tracking the battle between Helms and Hunt found Helms significantly behind through most of 1983.

But Helms battled back, drawing on financial support from conservatives across the country to invest $16.5 million in the race, shattering the record for the most money spent by a Senate candidate in U.S. history. His ads assaulting Hunt and the national Democratic Party not only bolstered his own campaign, they created a climate in which other North Carolina Republicans could prosper. When the dust settled on election night, the GOP had captured the governorship and three new House seats.

In many ways, it was an unusually static Senate campaign. The national media dutifully detailed each tortuous twist and turn, from

Hunt's charge that Helms was a supporter of right-wing death squads in El Salvador to the incumbent's complaint that Hunt had misused state airplanes. But most North Carolinians, faced with a choice between a leading apostle of the New Right and an activist Democratic governor, knew relatively early on how they would vote. Only 4 percentage points separated the two in polls taken in May 1984; in late October, it was still considered a dead heat.

Hunt focused his campaign on his record as governor, tirelessly sounding his commitment to improved education and arguing that he was experienced in bringing jobs to the state. He cast Helms as a right-wing radical, too extreme in his views to serve the state's interests effectively.

Helms embraced the support of Reagan wholeheartedly, using taped telephone messages in which Reagan endorsed him. Helms also sought to link Hunt to Democratic presidential candidate Walter F. Mondale and his national party. That charge left Hunt hamstrung, as he sought to distance himself from Mondale's proposal for a tax increase without repudiating his party's presidential nominee.

In the end, Hunt won strong support from the extensive network of teachers, unions, party regulars and other activists he had built up during 10 years in state government. But his margins in the eastern part of the state were not as decisive as he had hoped, and his black support helped produce a conservative white backlash that benefited Helms. Further aided by Reagan's top-of-the-ticket strength and a strong turnout from newly registered fundamentalists, Helms built his victory in the small towns and crossroads communities of the central and western Piedmont. He finished with a 52 percent to 48 percent edge.

Any Helms re-election effort is bound to attract national attention. But Helms' 1990 campaign against Gantt was guaranteed saturation national coverage.

Despite Gantt's obvious vulnerabilities — his liberal positions, his lack of statewide recognition and his race (Gantt was the first black ever to win a major party's statewide nomination in North Carolina) — he also could point to certain advantages that might boost his effort against Helms.

Where Hunt had struggled against Helms' ads to retain his political identity as a moderate, Gantt expended little effort fending off charges that he was liberal. Gantt opposed capital punishment and a capital gains tax cut, supported a woman's right to choose an abortion, and favored increased spending on education, the environment and health care. Anticommunism, the perennial red-meat issue for Helms, had fallen in relevance by 1990. Nor did Gantt have to contend with Republican presidential coattails. A national abortion rights group ran ads attacking Helms for his staunch opposition to abortion.

Gantt also wielded one unpredictable and powerful weapon: enthusiasm. His primary and runoff wins had galvanized a coalition of traditional Helms opponents, students and young professionals.

As always, Helms depended on media ads to get his message out; he refused to debate Gantt and shunned reporters. His campaign's policy required reporters seeking answers from the senator to submit written questions to the campaign fax machine. Helms regularly denounced the state's major newspapers, which he said were biased against him.

On television, Gantt and Helms pounded away at each other in negative ads, each trying to paint the other as extreme. Helms' ads compared his "North Carolina values" with Gantt's "extreme liberal values." Another ad accused Gantt of supporting abortion for sex selection and in the final weeks of pregnancy. One of Helms' radio ads warned that "the gay and lesbian political groups" have come to North Carolina "to elect Harvey Gantt." Helms saved the crusher — the "quotas" ad — for the end.

Gantt's 47 percent showing was only four-tenths of a percentage point off Hunt's 1984 posting. Gantt had secured the Democratic nomination by running up huge margins in the state's most populous county, Mecklenburg (Charlotte), and in the central Piedmont counties. But in November, he carried Mecklenburg by fewer than 30,000 votes. As had Hunt, Gantt won several of the rural northeastern counties. Gantt received 53 percent in the 10 counties with the most registered voters; in those same counties, Hunt received 50 percent. But the margins were not wide enough for Gantt to overcome Helms' strength in the state's less populous counties.

Controversy over the 1990 election continued into 1992. The U.S. Justice Department filed suit alleging that the Helms campaign and the state Republican Party sought to keep blacks from the polls by mailing 125,000 postcards with false or misleading information to black voters in a "ballot security" program days before the election. In February 1992, the state GOP, Helms' campaign and four consulting and marketing groups signed a consent decree prohibiting them from engaging in future such programs. They denied any wrongdoing, however.

For most of his adult life, Helms was a Democrat, even while he delivered conservative editorials for 12 years over WRAL-TV in Raleigh. He left the Democratic Party in 1970 and two years later ran for the Senate.

He was an underdog in that campaign against U.S. Rep. Nick Galifianakis, who had convincingly defeated aging Sen. B. Everett Jordan in the Democratic primary. Media accounts regularly described Helms as a "right-winger," but that label was far less dangerous to him than the liberal McGovern-Shriver presidential ticket was to Galifianakis.

Helms played down his rhetoric and shifted to a pro-Nixon tone. "President Nixon Needs Jesse Helms," the advertisements read, although Helms was far to the right of Nixon on most issues. A year earlier, he had called Nixon's trip to China "appeasement" of the communists.

In a Republican sweep, Nixon won nearly 70 percent of the state's presidential vote. Helms defeated Galifianakis with 54 percent of the vote, and the GOP won the governorship for the first time since 1896.

Six years later, a host of Democrats sought to prove that Helms' win was a coattail fluke. State Insurance Commissioner John Ingram was underfinanced and disorganized, but he forced the early favorite, moderate banker Luther H. Hodges Jr., into a runoff and won.

Ingram's populist themes had some appeal for rural and working-class conservatives who had supported Helms in 1972. But Helms had a reputation and an organization. Many of his constituents were proud that in a single Senate term he had become an articulate and nationally known defender of the right, one who had been promoted as a vice presidential choice by more than 800 national convention delegates in 1976. Helms' Congressional Club had been powerful enough to engineer Reagan's victory in the 1976 North Carolina primary. Helms eventually collected about $7.5 million, more than any Senate candidate in U.S. history up to that time, and won with 55 percent.

Committees

Foreign Relations (Ranking)
International Economic Policy, Trade, Oceans & Environment; Terrorism, Narcotics & International Operations; Western Hemisphere & Peace Corps Affairs

Agriculture, Nutrition & Forestry (3rd of 8 Republicans)
Agricultural Production & Stabilization of Prices (ranking); Domestic & Foreign Marketing & Product Promotion; Nutrition & Investigations

Rules & Administration (3rd of 7 Republicans)

Elections

1990 General		
Jesse Helms (R)	1,088,331	(53%)
Harvey B. Gantt (D)	981,573	(47%)
1990 Primary		
Jesse Helms (R)	157,345	(84%)
L.C. Nixon (R)	15,355	(8%)
George Wimbish (R)	13,895	(7%)

Previous Winning Percentages: **1984** (52%) **1978** (55%) **1972** (54%)

Campaign Finance

	Receipts	Receipts from PACs		Expend-itures
1990				
Helms (R)	$13,306,640	$835,104	(6%)	$13,355,336
Gantt (D)	$7,859,877	$695,852	(9%)	$7,811,520

Key Votes

1993	
Require unpaid family and medical leave	N
Approve national "motor voter" registration bill	N
Approve budget increasing taxes and reducing deficit	N
Support president's right to lift military gay ban	N
1992	
Approve school-choice pilot program	Y
Allow shifting funds from defense to domestic programs	N
Oppose deeper cuts in spending for SDI	+
1991	
Approve waiting period for handgun purchases	N
Raise senators' pay and ban honoraria	N
Authorize use of force in Persian Gulf	Y
Confirm Clarence Thomas to Supreme Court	Y

Voting Studies

	Presidential Support		Party Unity		Conservative Coalition	
Year	**S**	**O**	**S**	**O**	**S**	**O**
1992	62	15	71	3	71	3
1991	84	11	78	5	90	5
1990	68	32	88	11	84	14
1989	71	28	86	11	87	11
1988	60	26	72	12	81	5
1987	77	22	94	5	94	3
1986	90	10	95	5	95	5
1985	79	21	94	6	97	3
1984	86	10	90	8	100	0
1983	56	41	77	20	95	2
1982	75	25	87	13	99	1
1981	84	16	88	11	94	6

Interest Group Ratings

Year	ADA	AFL-CIO	CCUS	ACU
1992	5	13	100	100
1991	5	20	88	100
1990	6	22	92	100
1989	5	20	75	100
1988	5	23	75	100
1987	10	20	89	100
1986	0	0	95	100
1985	0	5	93	100
1984	0	0	89	100
1983	0	0	89	100
1982	0	8	95	100
1981	0	5	100	100

Lauch Faircloth (R)

Of Clinton — Elected 1992; 1st Term

Born: Jan. 14, 1928, Concord, N.C.
Education: Graduated from Roseboro H.S., 1945.
Military Service: Army, 1954-55.
Occupation: Farm owner.
Family: Divorced; one child.
Religion: Presbyterian.
Political Career: N.C. Highway Commission, 1961-73, chairman, 1969-73; N.C. secretary of commerce, 1977-83; sought Democratic nomination for governor, 1984.
Capitol Office: 708 Hart Bldg. 20510; 224-3154.

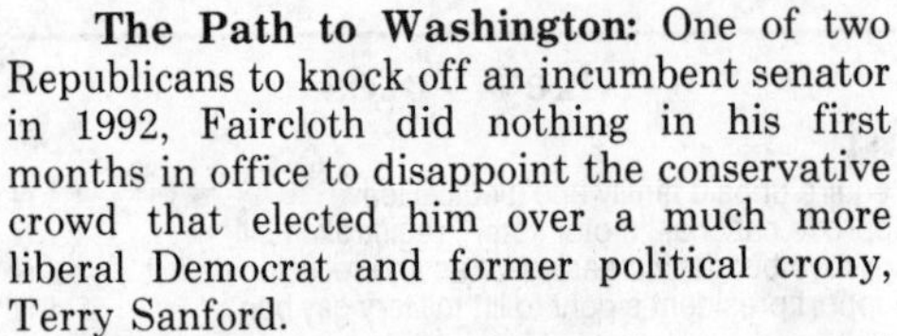

The Path to Washington: One of two Republicans to knock off an incumbent senator in 1992, Faircloth did nothing in his first months in office to disappoint the conservative crowd that elected him over a much more liberal Democrat and former political crony, Terry Sanford.

Faircloth (whose first name is pronounced "lock") campaigned using themes and strategies honed by Jesse Helms' National Congressional Club, whose operatives helped run his race. If North Carolina voters thought they were electing anything other than a mind-mate of Helms, Faircloth's early actions should have disabused them of the notion.

During the campaign, Faircloth bristled at suggestions that he and Helms would march in lockstep. But during his first four months in the Senate, Faircloth was indistinguishable from his senior home-state colleague. Out of 105 recorded votes, the two parted company on just one substantive issue — when Helms was one of only two senators opposing a committee funding resolution.

They even traveled in tandem on the issue that gained Faircloth the most early visibility in the Senate: opposition to Roberta Achtenberg, a lesbian nominated as assistant secretary of Housing and Urban Development.

Achtenberg, a San Francisco supervisor, was apparently the first openly gay person ever nominated for a senior administration job. In April, conservative Christian groups launched a last-minute campaign to block her appointment as assistant secretary for fair housing and equal opportunity. At her confirmation hearing, Faircloth questioned her about various state gay-rights initiatives.

A supporter of the military ban on homosexuals, Faircloth then objected to Achtenberg's role in trying to block United Way grants to Bay Area Boy Scout organizations, because of the scouts' refusal to admit gays. "Do the Boy Scouts have the right to say they don't want homosexual scoutmasters teaching children?" Faircloth asked. "If we are going to be a tolerant society, isn't there room for the Boy Scouts to make that decision?"

He was then one of four committee members to vote against her, but Faircloth, Helms and others failed to block her confirmation on the floor.

Faircloth did not make waves in his first months on his other two committees: Armed Services and Environment and Public Works. But he was hardly invisible on Banking, where he weighed in not only on the Achtenberg nomination, but also on housing, trade and monetary affairs.

In January, when Henry G. Cisneros appeared for his confirmation hearing as secretary of HUD, Faircloth suggested that the department spends too much on homeless programs. "It's only my fifth day in the Senate, but I haven't seen one agency volunteering to cut anything yet," Faircloth said.

Faircloth warned U.S. Trade Representative Mickey Kantor that he was opposed to the North American Free Trade Agreement because it would result in an exodus of jobs to Mexico. He called attention to similar job losses that have already occurred in New York's apparel industry.

And he raised an objection to proposals by some senior committee Democrats to put political constraints on monetary policy decisions by the Federal Reserve. "Congress needs to get its own act together before taking on further banking responsibilities," he said.

Faircloth got to the Senate after a campaign against Sanford that was billed from the beginning as a grudge match.

A multimillionaire farmer and business owner without a college degree, Faircloth was a lifelong Democrat who had enjoyed a symbiotic political alliance with Sanford. They met in the early 1950s and worked together on Democrat Kerr Scott's successful Senate bid. Faircloth backed Sanford's successful bid for governor in 1960 and was named to the highway commission.

In 1984, after serving as commerce secretary under Democratic Gov. James B. Hunt Jr., Faircloth ran for governor — with the help of Sanford, who reportedly helped secure a loan for the campaign and whose daughter was his student coordinator. Faircloth placed third in the Democratic primary.

The political bedfellows parted ways in 1986. Both were eying the Senate seat vacated by Republican John P. East, and apparently gave each other mixed signals about their plans. Sanford's decision to enter the race stunned Faircloth. The two hardly spoke to each other again. After supporting GOP Sen. Jesse Helms' 1990 re-election bid, Faircloth switched parties on Valentine's Day 1991, saying he was too conservative to remain a Democrat.

He immediately began plotting for a race between what the media called two "former friends."

In the primary, Faircloth outspent his three opponents and had support from key allies of moderate GOP Gov. James G. Martin as well as from Helms' legendary campaign organization.

For the general election, Faircloth personally kept a low profile, barring reporters from many of his events and prompting critics to dub him the "stealth candidate." His campaign was based on hard-hitting TV ads against Sanford, which were financed in part by $752,000 in loans from his own pocket. He wound up spending nearly $3 million, about $500,000 more than Sanford.

Faircloth lambasted Sanford as too liberal for North Carolina, highlighting his votes against the Persian Gulf War and for federal spending. Campaign ads accused Sanford of supporting welfare, while Faircloth said he supported "workfare." Capitalizing on anti-incumbent sentiment, he called Sanford "just another Washington politician." He played up broad conservative themes, telling one gathering, "I am for less taxes, less spending and less control of our lives by a bureaucracy."

Sanford, 75, was sidelined by heart surgery for two crucial weeks in October, which followed another hospital stay in the summer. He renewed campaigning after leaving the hospital Oct. 22, but reportedly looked pale and weak.

Faircloth, 65, initially skirted the health issue, announcing that he would pull his attack ads when Sanford entered the hospital in favor of a spot asking viewers to pray for the ailing Sanford. But Faircloth later directly questioned Sanford's fitness after the incumbent abandoned his tactic of ignoring his opponent and ran an ad accusing Faircloth of flip-flopping from past positions to become an anti-abortion, anti-tax candidate in the 1992 race.

On most big issues, Faircloth aligned himself with the conservative wing of the national GOP, supporting school choice, a capital gains tax cut, a "flexible freeze" on spending, a line-item veto and tougher criminal penalties. He opposed national health care but favored tax credits to help families cover health costs. He opposed gun control, the family leave bill, new environmental protection laws and abortion in all cases except rape, incest and to save the woman's life.

Unlike some Republicans, Faircloth did not shy from the top of the ticket, catching a ride on George Bush's state train tour and appearing with Dan Quayle. As Bush carried North Carolina by just over 20,000 votes, Faircloth ran nearly 104,000 votes ahead of Sanford, posting a 4 percentage-point victory.

Committees

Armed Services (9th of 9 Republicans)
Defense Technology, Acquisition & Industrial Base; Force Requirements & Personnel; Military Readiness & Defense Infrastructure

Banking, Housing & Urban Affairs (5th of 8 Republicans)
Economic Stabilization & Rural Development (ranking); Housing & Urban Affairs; Securities

Environment & Public Works (6th of 7 Republicans)
Clean Air & Nuclear Regulation; Clean Water, Fisheries & Wildlife; Toxic Substances, Research & Development

Campaign Finance

	Receipts	Receipts from PACs		Expend-itures
1992				
Faircloth (R)	$2,961,865	$365,783	(12%)	$2,952,102
Sanford (D)	$2,410,525	$838,515	(35%)	$2,486,380

Key Votes

1993

Require unpaid family and medical leave	N
Approve national "motor voter" registration bill	N
Approve budget increasing taxes and reducing deficit	N
Support president's right to lift military gay ban	N

Elections

1992 General		
Lauch Faircloth (R)	1,297,892	(50%)
Terry Sanford (D)	1,194,015	(46%)
Bobby Yates Emory (LIBERT)	85,948	(3%)
1992 Primary		
Lauch Faircloth (R)	129,159	(48%)
Sue Myrick (R)	81,801	(30%)
Eugene Johnston (R)	46,112	(17%)
Larry E. Harrington (R)	13,496	(5%)

1 Eva Clayton (D)

Of Littleton — Elected 1992; 1st Term

Born: Sept. 16, 1934, Savannah, Ga.
Education: Johnson C. Smith U., B.S. 1955; North Carolina Central U., M.S. 1962; U. of North Carolina, 1967.
Occupation: Consulting firm owner; non-profit executive; state official; university official.
Family: Husband, Theaoseus Clayton; four children.
Religion: Presbyterian.
Political Career: Sought Democratic nomination for U.S. House, 1968; N.C. assistant secretary of natural resources, 1977-81; Warren County Commission, 1982-92, chairman 1982-90.
Capitol Office: 222 Cannon Bldg. 20515; 225-3101.

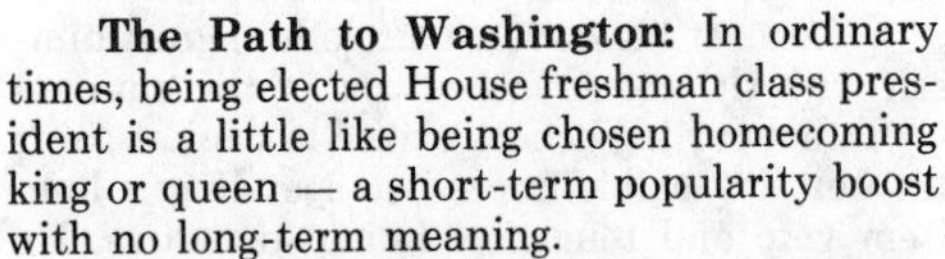

The Path to Washington: In ordinary times, being elected House freshman class president is a little like being chosen homecoming king or queen — a short-term popularity boost with no long-term meaning.

But this is no ordinary class, and Clayton is no ordinary politician. On her second day as a class officer, she participated in an exclusive leadership meeting with Bill Clinton, the House Speaker, the Senate majority leader and a few other congressional leaders.

As a black woman, she helps those powerful white men achieve a picture of balance and equity, and in turn, she gets access that is most unusual for a first-termer.

As Clayton made her way through the maze of House orientation and organizing meetings in December, she displayed a combination of ambition and discretion that is likely to serve her well as she continues to try to parlay her ceremonial office into influence.

Just hours after the newly elected Democratic women met during the class orientation, several emerged to say they had decided to rally around Clayton for president. They said her leadership and political savvy made her perfect for the job.

Typically, Clayton made no public comment on her campaign, though few found it coincidental that the newcomers to the Black Caucus also recommended her for the job. The combination was powerful: She was elected president for the first session; a male colleague will take over the second.

Clayton passed her first big test of loyalty to the leadership in April 1993 over whether to grant the president modified line-item veto authority. Though opposed to the concept and going against the firmly stated position of the Congressional Black Caucus, Clayton supported the leadership on a close procedural vote that allowed the bill to come to the floor. She ultimately voted with most of the Black Caucus against final passage, though the bill passed easily.

Clayton arrived in Washington with the help of organized labor, women's groups, ministers and minority activists across her rural 28-county district.

Although she won in a district designed to elect a black, her victory over six other contenders reflected her canny campaign style.

The 1st was drawn with a 57 percent black-voter base with the intent of electing an African-American to the House, but when five black candidates and two whites entered the contest, it was far from clear who would come out on top.

Clayton, a Warren County commissioner during the 1980s, was less well-known in the regional news media than several of the other candidates, but wooing the media never became a priority. Instead, she looked to grass-roots supporters who were familiar with her work in the community as far back as 1968, when she first ran for Congress.

As a graduate student that year, she went door to door in the black community in an effort to unseat Democratic Rep. L. H. Fountain, whom black leaders felt was unresponsive to their concerns. She got 30 percent of the vote, though Clayton says she knew she had embarked on a long shot when none of the men who had criticized Fountain decided to challenge him.

Contacts from her community experiences coupled with financial backing from national women's organizations helped Clayton make the runoff against state Sen. Walter B. Jones Jr., whose father represented much of the 1st District for 26 years until his death in 1992.

Even then, there was no lock on the seat. And at that point, Clayton made history her theme. She and former state Sen. Melvin Watt in the new 12th District held the promise to be the first blacks elected to Congress from North Carolina in this century, and Clayton aimed to become the first woman elected to the House from the state.

North Carolina 1

East — Parts of Rocky Mount, Fayetteville and Greenville

When the Justice Department finally approved the radical redrawing of North Carolina's congressional districts in 1992, black voting power was concentrated in two districts, one rural and one urban.

The 1st is primarily rural and agricultural, stretching from the Virginia border almost to South Carolina, winding through 28 counties to patch together the black communities of northeastern North Carolina down to Wilmington and Fayetteville.

Covering 2,039 miles around its perimeter, the 1st takes in nine whole counties and parts of 19 more. The main body is located on the Virginia border; from there, it snakes south in widely varying directions.

The northern part includes the mostly poor blacks of Bertie, Hertford and Northampton counties. Roanoke Rapids (Halifax County), a textile and wood products center, and populous Rocky Mount (Nash County) are shared with the 2nd District.

Pitt County (Greenville), which is divided between the 1st and the 3rd, has some pharmaceutical and paper products manufacturing, but its main employer is government.

On the western edge of Lenoir County, the district narrows into a thin corridor along the Lenoir and Wayne County borders. From there, it expands into Duplin County, skirting Sampson County without crossing in, and breaks north through Bladen County into Cumberland County.

Once in Cumberland — which is also parceled into the 7th and 8th districts — the 1st takes in some of Fayetteville, which is dominated by the Fort Bragg and Pope Air Force Base. The Cumberland County segment is the second-biggest population source. Black neighborhoods from Wilmington (New Hanover County) are also a source of votes in the southern extremity.

The 1st is staunchly Democratic — nearly 90 percent of the district's voters are registered Democrats. It was fertile ground for Senate nominee Terry Sanford in 1986, unsuccessful Democratic Senate nominee Harvey B. Gantt in 1990 and Bill Clinton in 1992.

Blacks make up 57 percent of the district's population, but that figure is somewhat deceiving. When it comes to voter registration numbers — a better voting pattern indicator — whites make up about 49 percent of the electorate.

The white voters of the 1st claim the Democratic roots of their forefathers, but often support GOP candidates at the state and national level. A fair number are "Jessecrats," conservative Democratic supporters of GOP Sen. Jesse Helms. Republicans can also find quarter in some of the increasingly affluent coastal turf of Beaufort and Craven counties.

1990 Population: 552,394. White 229,853 (42%), Black 316,273 (57%), Other 6,268 (1%). Hispanic origin 4,101 (1%). 18 and over 399,878 (72%), 62 and over 92,837 (17%). Median age: 33.

Committees

Agriculture (15th of 28 Democrats)
Department Operations; Environment, Credit & Rural Development; Specialty Crops & Natural Resources

Small Business (13th of 27 Democrats)
Procurement, Taxation & Tourism; Rural Enterprises, Exports & the Environment

Campaign Finance

	Receipts	Receipts from PACs		Expend-itures
1992				
Clayton (D)	$551,491	$281,665	(51%)	$551,028
Tyler (R)	$7,055	0		$6,131

Key Votes

1993

Require parental notification of minors' abortions	N
Require unpaid family and medical leave	Y
Approve national "motor voter" registration bill	Y
Approve budget increasing taxes and reducing deficit	Y
Approve economic stimulus plan	Y

Elections

1992 General		
Eva Clayton (D)	116,078	(67%)
Ted Tyler (R)	54,457	(31%)
C. Barry Williams (LIBERT)	2,727	(2%)
1992 Special †		
Eva Clayton (D)	118,324	(57%)
Ted Tyler (R)	86,273	(41%)
C. Barry Williams (LIBERT)	4,121	(2%)
1992 Primary Runoff		
Eva Clayton (D)	43,210	(55%)
Walter B. Jones Jr. (D)	35,729	(45%)
1992 Primary		
Walter B. Jones Jr. (D)	33,634	(38%)
Eva Clayton (D)	27,477	(31%)
Willie D. Riddick (D)	9,112	(10%)
Staccato Powell (D)	5,893	(7%)
Thomas C. Hardaway (D)	5,771	(7%)
Thomas B. Brandon III (D)	5,085	(6%)
Don Smith (D)	1,227	(1%)

† On Election Day, Clayton was elected to a full term and to fill out the remainder of the term of Walter B. Jones, D-N.C., who died Sept. 15, 1992.

District Vote for President

	1992	
D	109,767	(61%)
R	51,881	(29%)
I	17,765	(10%)

2 Tim Valentine (D)

Of Nashville — Elected 1982; 6th Term

Born: March 15, 1926, Nash County, N.C.
Education: The Citadel, A.B. 1948; U. of North Carolina, LL.B. 1952.
Military Service: Army Air Corps, 1944-46.
Occupation: Lawyer.
Family: Wife, Barbara Reynolds; four children, three stepchildren.
Religion: Baptist.
Political Career: N.C. House, 1955-61; N.C. Democratic Party chairman, 1966-68.
Capitol Office: 2229 Rayburn Bldg. 20515; 225-4531.

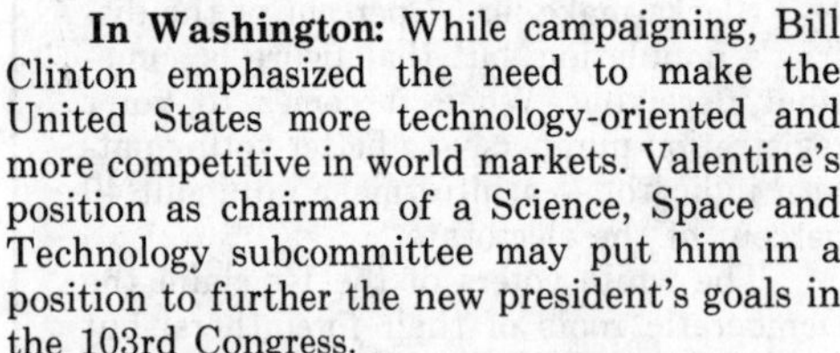

In Washington: While campaigning, Bill Clinton emphasized the need to make the United States more technology-oriented and more competitive in world markets. Valentine's position as chairman of a Science, Space and Technology subcommittee may put him in a position to further the new president's goals in the 103rd Congress.

Valentine, a folksy yet eloquent politician, is the embodiment of the Southern gentleman. His name has been closely linked to the National Competitiveness Act that died in the last Congress. It was taken up again in the 103rd. The bill, designed to boost U.S. competitiveness, seeks to coordinate and expand federal efforts to improve the international competitiveness of U.S. enterprises. It would authorize $2 billion for fiscal 1994-95 for grants to promote advanced technologies, create a network of outreach centers to help manufacturers adopt modern production techniques and expand the capital available to develop critical technologies.

Valentine has been very active on technology issues since he was first elected in 1982. He speaks for the scientific community in the Research Triangle (Durham County, one corner of the Triangle, is in the 2nd). In 1988, he introduced a bill to create a national board to coordinate semiconductor research and development.

In the 102nd Congress, Valentine saw his efforts to promote energy efficiency pay off. The 1992 energy bill included some provisions that Valentine and his North Carolina Democratic colleague, Rep. David Price, devised. The measures called for establishing a nationwide system of regional centers to promote energy-efficient lighting, heating and cooling, and building design.

At home, he and Price got $5 million in federal funds in 1991 to build a new Environmental Protection Agency facility in the Research Triangle Park.

On the Public Works and Transportation Committee, Valentine in 1991 led the fight for fairer formulas for highway funding in the surface transportation bill. He was representing the so-called donor states that pay more into the Highway Trust Fund in gasoline taxes than they receive in federal highway dollars. The fight was successful: Donor states won a change in the formula that guarantees them a higher return.

Amending the Constitution twice became an issue for Valentine in 1990. An original signer of the proposed amendment to ban flag desecration, Valentine at the last minute "heard the voice of his own conscience" and voted against the measure.

Valentine, however, had no qualms about constitutional tinkering to require the exclusion of illegal aliens for purposes of determining population for reapportionment. The issue was important for North Carolina's bid to gain a 13th congressional seat.

A defender of rural interests in his district, Valentine gravitated to the bloc of Southerners who swap old-time stories in the back of the House chamber. Although Valentine often sides with the conservative coalition of Republicans and Southern Democrats, he is no party turncoat. In 1992, he voted with a majority of House Democrats 60 percent of the time; he sided with the president 34 percent of the time in House votes.

Valentine handled a difficult assignment in the 101st Congress by waging the tobacco industry's fight against a smoking ban on airline flights. Fearful of a renewed assault by anti-smoking advocates, Valentine opted to accept a two-year extension of a ban on flights of two hours or less. The strategy failed, however, as a permanent ban on most domestic flights eventually became law.

At Home: Early in his House career, black voters coalesced to threaten Valentine's election efforts. A decade later, it was a lack of black voters that almost dragged him to defeat.

To win nomination in the 2nd in 1982,

North Carolina 2

North Central — Parts of Durham and Rocky Mount

The half-moon shaped 2nd is home to features of North Carolina's past, present and future economies. The northern edge of the crescent holds the high-tech industry of Research Triangle Park; the southern edge contains resorts and retirement communities. They are connected by a rich tobacco-producing region.

In the 1950s, an unusual coalition of academic, political and business leaders decided North Carolina needed to diversify its economic base beyond the traditional furniture, tobacco and textile industries. They came up with the idea of Research Triangle Park, a new industrial area where America's emerging high-tech industries could draw on the brainpower of nearby Duke University, the University of North Carolina and North Carolina State University.

Today, in the 2nd District's portion of southern Durham County, that vision is the source of thousands of jobs in biotechnology, supercomputers, microelectronics and pharmaceuticals.

Outside the Triangle, tobacco, the state's traditional cash crop, is a crucial component of the local economy. The tobacco fields of Nash, Edgecombe, Harnett and Wilson counties make it the district's chief agricultural commodity. Tobacco is the major agricultural crop of Johnston County, with sweet potatoes coming in second.

The golfing resorts of Pinehurst and Southern Pines (Moore County) attract vacationers and affluent retirees to the Sandhills area of the district's southwestern fringe.

Unlike the white-collar executives and engineers attracted to Durham County — many of whom hew to Durham's progressive political traditions — the newcomers to Moore County are more reliably Republican.

With only four counties wholly contained in the 2nd — along with parts of nine others — the district includes partial sections of a number of smaller-sized cities.

Rocky Mount, shared with the 1st, is a food processing and textile center. Also shared with the 1st is tobacco-oriented Wilson and a sliver of Halifax County reaching into Roanoke Rapids.

The politics of the 2nd is as varied as its economic interests. Party registration figures give Democrats an almost 3-to-1 advantage, but many of those small-town voters are Democratic in name only: In the 1990 Senate race, conservative GOP Sen. Jesse Helms won 60 percent in the areas that make up the 2nd.

In 1992, Johnston County, the second most-populous jurisdiction after Durham County, gave 51 percent to conservative GOP House challenger Don Davis. Moore County backed him with 56 percent.

Black voters help boost Democratic fortunes, particularly in Franklin and Granville counties, where blacks make up more than a third of the population. Rep. Valentine was able to stay close in Harnett and Johnston counties in 1992 in part due to the backing of black voters. Districtwide, about 22 percent of the population is black.

1990 Population: 552,378. White 421,058 (76%), Black 121,229 (22%), Other 10,091 (2%). Hispanic origin 6,478 (1%). 18 and over 420,128 (76%), 62 and over 87,205 (16%). Median age: 34.

Valentine had to overcome H. M. "Mickey" Michaux Jr., a black former U.S. attorney and state legislator from Durham County. Valentine finished second to Michaux in the primary, but won the runoff by casting himself as a conservative and Michaux as a labor lackey who would raise taxes and cut defense. Lingering black dissatisfaction was evident in a general election write-in campaign waged for Michaux, but Valentine won comfortably.

Two years later, black state Rep. Kenneth B. Spaulding challenged Valentine in the Democratic primary. Determined to avoid being labeled a liberal, Spaulding portrayed himself as a fiscal conservative. That helped him cut his losses among white voters, and Jesse Jackson helped Spaulding stoke black voters' passions. But Jackson's activity also sparked a backlash among rural whites, which helped Valentine. The incumbent's rural strength helped him clinch renomination with 52 percent.

By mending relations with black voters after 1984, Valentine held a tight grip on the 2nd. But redistricting excised a large chunk of Democratic-voting blacks and replaced them with "Jessecrats" — conservative white Democrats who tend to support GOP Sen. Jesse Helms.

Aiming to tap into that conservative sentiment in 1992, Republicans nominated retired Army officer Don Davis. Davis, who noted that in some respects he was further to the right than Helms, had won 41 percent against Democrat H. Martin Lancaster in the 3rd District in 1990.

The challenger attempted to portray Valentine as a tax-and-spend liberal incumbent, but constituents did not see the veteran of small-town politicking that way. Valentine won 54 percent.

The son of a state Supreme Court justice, Valentine was elected to the state legislature in 1954 at age 28. He served three terms, then left to spend more time practicing law. In 1965 he became the legislative liaison for Democratic Gov. Dan K. Moore. Valentine returned to his Nash County home when Moore's term ended, devoting his time to the Chamber of Commerce and the Baptist church. After an auto accident killed his wife in August 1981, a desire to put that tragedy behind him persuaded Valentine to run for Congress.

Committees

Public Works & Transportation (7th of 39 Democrats)
Surface Transportation (vice chairman); Aviation; Water Resources & the Environment

Science, Space & Technology (7th of 33 Democrats)
Technology, Environment & Aviation (chairman); Science

Elections

1992 General		
Tim Valentine (D)	113,693	(54%)
Don Davis (R)	93,893	(44%)
Dennis Bryant Lubahn (LIBERT)	3,983	(2%)
1990 General		
Tim Valentine (D)	130,979	(75%)
Hal Sharpe (R)	44,263	(25%)

Previous Winning Percentages: **1988** (100%) **1986** (75%) **1984** (68%) **1982** (54%)

District Vote for President

1992

D 85,542 (40%)
R 98,516 (46%)
I 30,643 (14%)

Campaign Finance

	Receipts	Receipts from PACs		Expend-itures
1992				
Valentine (D)	$443,499	$237,040	(53%)	$457,958
Davis (R)	$180,889	$19,110	(11%)	$180,484
1990				
Valentine (D)	$261,712	$159,202	(61%)	$286,351
Sharpe (R)	$58,015	$1,400	(2%)	$56,842

Key Votes

1993	
Require parental notification of minors' abortions	N
Require unpaid family and medical leave	N
Approve national "motor voter" registration bill	N
Approve budget increasing taxes and reducing deficit	Y
Approve economic stimulus plan	N
1992	
Approve balanced-budget constitutional amendment	Y
Close down space station program	-
Approve U.S. aid for former Soviet Union	N
Allow shifting funds from defense to domestic programs	N
1991	
Extend unemployment benefits using deficit financing	N
Approve waiting period for handgun purchases	Y
Authorize use of force in Persian Gulf	Y

Voting Studies

	Presidential Support		Party Unity		Conservative Coalition	
Year	S	O	S	O	S	O
1992	34	54	60	29	63	31
1991	45	51	59	35	89	8
1990	42	58	66	30	89	11
1989	52	47	69	29	73	27
1988	40	58	70	25	95	5
1987	40	55	67	30	88	9
1986	41	57	67	31	90	8
1985	46	52	71	25	84	13
1984	43	44	51	38	86	7
1983	44	56	54	42	90	8

Interest Group Ratings

Year	ADA	AFL-CIO	CCUS	ACU
1992	45	42	29	48
1991	25	58	70	55
1990	33	42	43	42
1989	30	33	70	39
1988	45	71	62	48
1987	44	50	60	29
1986	30	43	65	55
1985	35	35	59	48
1984	20	46	38	55
1983	40	35	60	57

3 H. Martin Lancaster (D)

Of Goldsboro — Elected 1986; 4th Term

Born: March 24, 1943, Wayne County, N.C.
Education: U. of North Carolina, A.B. 1965, J.D. 1967.
Military Service: Navy, 1967-70; Naval Reserve, 1970-present.
Occupation: Lawyer.
Family: Wife, Alice Matheny; two children.
Religion: Presbyterian.
Political Career: N.C. House, 1979-87.
Capitol Office: 2436 Rayburn Bldg. 20515; 225-3415.

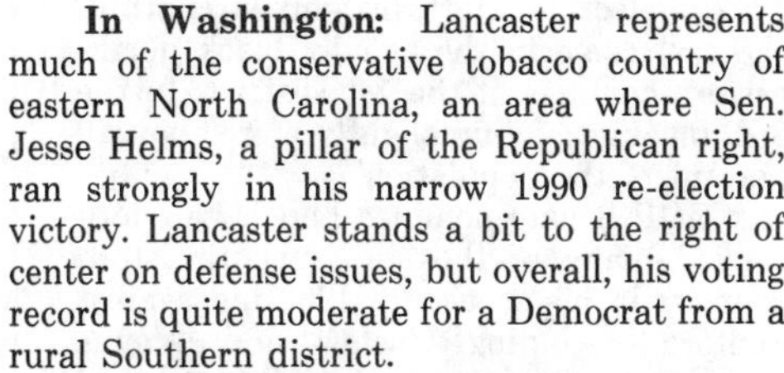

In Washington: Lancaster represents much of the conservative tobacco country of eastern North Carolina, an area where Sen. Jesse Helms, a pillar of the Republican right, ran strongly in his narrow 1990 re-election victory. Lancaster stands a bit to the right of center on defense issues, but overall, his voting record is quite moderate for a Democrat from a rural Southern district.

An at-large whip in the Democratic leadership structure, Lancaster has voted with his party's House majority on some controversial social issues: During the 102nd Congress, he voted in favor of a seven-day waiting period for the purchase of a handgun (the "Brady bill"), he backed a civil rights bill that President George Bush initially vetoed, and he supported a measure to lift the Bush administration's executive order prohibiting federally funded family planning clinics from providing abortion counseling (this "gag rule" was revoked in 1993 in one of President Clinton's first acts in office).

If any of those stands give qualms to the 3rd's conservative voters, Lancaster eases their minds with his record on the Armed Services Committee. His House district is economically reliant on U.S. military facilities, including the Marines' Camp Lejeune training base (which has 22 percent of all Marine personnel) in Jacksonville and the Seymour Johnson Air Force Base in Lancaster's hometown of Goldsboro.

During the 102nd Congress, Lancaster opposed efforts led by more liberal Democrats to slash deeply into funding for the Strategic Defense Initiative anti-ballistic missile program. Earlier, he had opposed efforts to terminate production of the B-2 stealth bomber.

Lancaster was thus a rather reliable vote for the Bush administration's attempts to maintain high defense-spending levels in the post-Cold War era. But his stance also made him a valuable ally to Wisconsin Democratic Rep. Les Aspin, who sought to steer Armed Services on a centrist course during his tenure as committee chairman from 1985 to 1993.

Lancaster was one of the quiet, studious Southern Democrats who made up the junior portion of Aspin's controlling coalition on the committee (others included Owen B. Pickett of Virginia, John Tanner of Tennessee, Glen Browder of Alabama and Gene Taylor of Mississippi). They provided a conservative counterweight to efforts by more-liberal Democrats to make deep and rapid cuts in the defense budget.

Aspin, now Clinton's secretary of Defense, will count on members such as Lancaster to parry the budget-slashing tendencies of his much more liberal successor as chairman, Ronald V. Dellums of California.

Lancaster showed early in the 103rd that he would not hesitate to distance himself from some of Clinton's ideas about social reforms for military personnel that may not sit well with traditionally minded residents of the 3rd.

In January 1993, Lancaster criticized Clinton for making a priority of removing the ban on homosexual personnel in the armed forces. "I think the president has made a real mistake in making this the first significant issue that Congress will face," Lancaster said. "He is expending an awful lot of capital on this issue that he ought to be expending on the economy." Clinton deferred a decision on the gay ban until July 1993.

In January 1991, Lancaster voted to give Bush the authority to use military force to end Iraq's occupation of Kuwait. And from his seat on the Small Business Committee, he sponsored with Missouri Democratic Rep. Ike Skelton a measure that would have provided federal disaster assistance to small-business owners who suffered economic hardship during the Persian Gulf War, either because of their own or employees' service in that conflict or their location near military facilities from which numerous personnel (and crucial customers) were deployed.

Along with his district-related defense agenda on Armed Services, Lancaster looks after his coastal constituency on the Merchant Marine and Fisheries Committee. In May 1991, he made a floor speech supporting a measure that would have enforced economic sanctions against foreign shipyards that receive govern-

North Carolina 3

East — Goldsboro; part of Greenville; Outer Banks

In a state full of horribly disfigured congressional districts, the 3rd ranks as one of the worst. It includes the Tidewater region as far south as Onslow County then juts west before sweeping into the tobacco-producing areas of the Coastal Plain.

The fragile barrier islands of the Outer Banks bring tourism dollars into the 3rd, particularly during the summer. Development is a serious concern of the year-round residents of the northern islands, around Nags Head, but is a less vexing issue farther south where the islands are less accessible and much of the land is designated as a protected seashore.

On the mainland, tourism is also a prominent economic feature of Albemarle and Pamlico sounds, as is fishing and the seafood canning industry.

Onslow County (Jacksonville), the southern edge of the 3rd's coastline, is economically dependent on the "few good men" of the Camp Lejeune Marine Corps training base. The 1991 deployment of troops to the Persian Gulf War so drained Onslow's economic lifeblood that GOP then-Gov. James G. Martin declared the county an "economic emergency area."

Farther inland, the business of the 3rd is agriculture. A finger reaches into Pitt County (Greenville); turkey-producing Duplin County is the gateway to the tobacco country of Sampson and Wayne counties.

All of rural and agricultural Sampson is included in the 3rd along with most of Wayne County, where the landscape is dominated by huge tobacco warehouses and fields.

Goldsboro, the Wayne County seat, was another "economic emergency area" after the pilots of Seymour Johnson Air Force Base left for the Persian Gulf. Almost one-fifth of the district's people live in Wayne County, making it the most populous jurisdiction in the 3rd.

Eastern Carolina has long been a Democratic stronghold, but in recent years dissatisfaction with state and national Democratic candidates has translated into Republican gains.

In his 1986 Senate race, Terry Sanford won every county east of Raleigh, but in his 1992 re-election effort, his only strength in the east came in the heavily black northeastern counties of the 1st District. In the 3rd, blacks make up slightly more than 20 percent of the population.

GOP Senate nominee Lauch Faircloth carried many of the state's southeastern counties in his successful 1992 bid against Sanford, including Onslow and Wayne counties, where voters remembered Sanford's vote against authorizing force in the Persian Gulf. And despite the heavy Democratic registration advantage, conservative GOP Sen. Jesse Helms won 59 percent in the district in 1990.

Rep. Lancaster, who voted in favor of using force, carried all but two counties in 1992. Holdouts for Lancaster's Republican challenger were Onslow and Craven counties, where GOP strength has increased with the influx of affluent, conservative-minded retirees.

1990 Population: 552,387. White 423,398 (77%), Black 118,640 (21%), Other 10,349 (2%). Hispanic origin 8,659 (2%). 18 and over 413,263 (75%), 62 and over 79,197 (14%). Median age: 32.

ment subsidies, thereby gaining a competitive advantage over non-subsidized U.S. shipyards.

"A decade of massive foreign subsidies ... has severely handicapped our shipyards," Lancaster said. "American industries should not have to battle alone against foreign governments, but that is exactly what the U.S. shipbuilding industry has been forced to do."

Lancaster also keeps an eye out for his district's large agricultural sector, which includes tobacco, peanut and corn growers. He has introduced legislation in past Congresses to mandate degradable plastics for consumer products — to help the environment, he says, and also for growers of corn, which is used to make degradable plastics.

At Home: It's not often that a convicted felon poses a stiff challenge to an incumbent, but that was Lancaster's fate in 1992 after redistricting radically reshaped the 3rd District.

The new lines dealt Lancaster one of the nation's most contorted districts. It left him some of his old turf in the tobacco-producing southeast, but also added unfamiliar coastal areas that stretched to the Virginia border.

Republican state Sen. Tommy Pollard aimed to attract the mainly white and conservative voters who populate these areas by claiming that Lancaster was too liberal to represent them. Lancaster's five overdrafts at the House bank were also ammunition for Pollard.

Echoing themes heard in the presidential race, Lancaster emphasized trust as an issue. He pointed to Pollard's assault conviction for shooting a man in 1975 (the governor commuted his sentence).

Though Pollard was able to convince the man he shot to endorse him, it was not quite enough for voters. Lancaster got 54 percent, finishing 11 points ahead of Pollard and carrying 17 of the 19 counties that are partly or wholly included in the 3rd.

When Lancaster announced in 1985 that he was leaving the state legislature to devote more time to his family and law practice, he did not expect to be back campaigning within six months. But Rep. Charles Whitley's surprise retirement announcement caused him to reassess.

As soon as he announced his candidacy for Whitley's seat in Congress, Lancaster became the Democratic primary favorite. He had left his mark in the state House on a range of issues, from licensing for medical practitioners to the creation of grass-roots arts programs. The high point of his legislative career occurred when Democratic Gov. James B. Hunt Jr. asked him to shepherd through the House a controversial measure to toughen the state's drunken-driving laws.

He moved quickly to shore up his one potential weakness — a perception by some that he had associated with the more liberal bloc of Democrats in the state House. Lancaster devoted much of his campaign to courting business leaders and establishing conservative credentials.

The only one of his opponents who could hope to match Lancaster's support was Lewis Renn, Whitley's top aide in Washington.

Lancaster was able to take most of the black vote, which then made up a significant proportion of the total in the Democratic primary. While each of the candidates won his home county, Lancaster finished either first or second in the remaining seven counties. Renn was eligible for a runoff but finished so far behind Lancaster in the primary that he chose to pass up the opportunity.

The well-financed Lancaster then had little trouble defeating GOP state Rep. Gerald Hurst. Lancaster had no opposition in 1988. In 1990, the third-place finisher in the Republican primary, a 100-year-old ophthalmologist, drew more attention than the nominee. Even with GOP Sen. Helms winning the 3rd comfortably, Lancaster still captured 59 percent of the vote.

Committees

Armed Services (14th of 34 Democrats)
Military Forces & Personnel; Readiness; Research & Technology

Merchant Marine & Fisheries (15th of 29 Democrats)
Coast Guard & Navigation; Fisheries Management

Small Business (24th of 27 Democrats)

Elections

1992 General		
H. Martin Lancaster (D)	101,739	(54%)
Tommy Pollard (R)	80,759	(43%)
Mark Jackson (LIBERT)	4,552	(2%)
1990 General		
H. Martin Lancaster (D)	83,930	(59%)
Don Davis (R)	57,605	(41%)

Previous Winning Percentages: 1988 (100%) **1986** (64%)

District Vote for President

1992

D	74,639 (39%)
R	89,038 (46%)
I	28,223 (15%)

Campaign Finance

	Receipts	Receipts from PACs		Expend-itures
1992				
Lancaster (D)	$588,664	$300,165	(51%)	$548,584
Pollard (R)	$238,256	0		$236,233
1990				
Lancaster (D)	$421,283	$204,450	(49%)	$499,436
Davis (R)	$88,138	$500	(1%)	$84,160

Key Votes

1993	
Require parental notification of minors' abortions	N
Require unpaid family and medical leave	N
Approve national "motor voter" registration bill	Y
Approve budget increasing taxes and reducing deficit	Y
Approve economic stimulus plan	Y
1992	
Approve balanced-budget constitutional amendment	Y
Close down space station program	Y
Approve U.S. aid for former Soviet Union	Y
Allow shifting funds from defense to domestic programs	N
1991	
Extend unemployment benefits using deficit financing	Y
Approve waiting period for handgun purchases	Y
Authorize use of force in Persian Gulf	Y

Voting Studies

	Presidential Support		Party Unity		Conservative Coalition	
Year	**S**	**O**	**S**	**O**	**S**	**O**
1992	46	52	73	24	75	25
1991	40	60	74	23	78	22
1990	38	61	76	22	83	17
1989	45	52	73	23	78	22
1988	38	62	78	19	84	16
1987	37	62	71	25	86	12

Interest Group Ratings

Year	ADA	AFL-CIO	CCUS	ACU
1992	45	50	75	58
1991	40	58	60	40
1990	39	50	43	50
1989	40	42	80	30
1988	60	71	64	40
1987	60	75	40	17

4 David Price (D)

Of Chapel Hill — Elected 1986; 4th Term

Born: Aug. 17, 1940, Johnson City, Tenn.
Education: Mars Hill College, 1958-59; U. of North Carolina, B.A. 1961; Yale U., B.D. 1964, Ph.D. 1969.
Occupation: Professor.
Family: Wife, Lisa Kanwit; two children.
Religion: American Baptist.
Political Career: N.C. Democratic Party chairman, 1983-84.
Capitol Office: 2458 Rayburn Bldg. 20515; 225-1784.

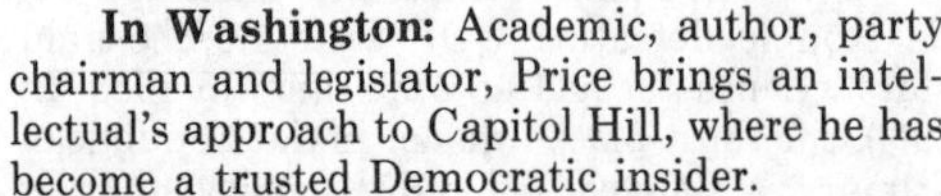

In Washington: Academic, author, party chairman and legislator, Price brings an intellectual's approach to Capitol Hill, where he has become a trusted Democratic insider.

Now that redistricting has given him solid footing in his district, Price can finally devote more of his attention to his role in the House. He is on the Appropriations Committee and has a seat on Budget, where he will work in the 103rd Congress to help craft and pass the Clinton administration's economic program.

After a cautious first term in which he toiled to establish himself in a district previously held by a conservative Republican, Price has emerged as a leadership loyalist from the border South.

A political science professor and former state party chairman who was staff director of the Democratic Party's post-1980 presidential rules commission, Price quickly caught the eye of the House leadership. His first term was somewhat shaky, as he reversed positions on a gun-control amendment he had cosponsored shortly before the 1988 election and broke party ranks to support a daily recitation of the Pledge of Allegiance in the House (becoming one of just seven Democrats to do so).

But in the 101st Congress, Price's voting record reflected the confidence he placed in his political organization following a comfortable re-election win. He voted against a constitutional amendment banning physical desecration of the flag and opposed cutting the tax on capital gains. He also backed federal funding for abortion, mandatory family and medical leave, the 1990 budget summit agreement and the 1989 congressional pay raise package that revised Congress' ethics rules.

Price joined Appropriations at the start of the 102nd Congress. On the Agriculture Subcommittee, he defended spending for agriculture research. The fiscal 1993 agriculture appropriations conference report contained language, added at Price's request, to consider funding a new project at North Carolina State University researching the many uses of wood.

He also helped win funds for construction of a new laboratory at the National Institute of Environmental Health Sciences and to upgrade instrument landing systems and study air traffic at Raleigh-Durham International Airport. The fiscal 1992 transportation appropriations bill included $2.6 million to make U.S. 64 a four-lane highway in his own district and that of Democratic colleague Tim Valentine.

Price acknowledges that he engages in the venerable Appropriations ritual of steering funds homeward and that he returns home to tell his constituents about the newly won projects. But, he says, "I'm somewhat more self-conscious" about it. He seeks to convey to his constituents that his work is "not merely the dispensing of pork."

Price made an impressive legislative debut on the Banking Committee with his bill requiring banks to disclose fully the terms of home-equity loans. He touted the bill, which was signed into law in 1988, in his re-election campaign, appealing to the sizable white-collar suburbanite population in his district.

In the 101st Congress, Price pursued his goal of making housing more affordable as the committee worked on the first major overhaul of federal housing programs since 1974. Price added language expanding a federally backed "reverse mortgage" program that allows senior citizens to draw cash equity from their homes. He also won inclusion of a program allowing state and local governments to help lower-income families buying their first homes by providing low-interest "soft-second mortgages." Repayment on the government-guaranteed loans would be deferred for five years.

On the Science, Space and Technology Committee, Price introduced legislation to establish a grant program improving science and mathematics teaching in schools. Portions of his bill became law at the end of the 101st Congress as part of a mathematics-science scholarship bill. Price also introduced legislation in the 101st and 102nd Congresses to restore income tax deductibility for student loans and scholarships.

In the 102nd Congress, President Bush

North Carolina 4

Central — Raleigh; Chapel Hill

Of the state's 10 majority-white congressional districts, the 4th is the most progressive. Located on the eastern edge of the Piedmont plateau, it was the only white-majority district to back black 1990 Democratic Senate nominee Harvey B. Gantt against GOP Sen. Jesse Helms; Democrats make up about two-thirds of all the voters here.

The Democratic base draws deeply from a well of votes in the Research Triangle area, two corners of which are in the 4th. The University of North Carolina (23,800 students) is in Chapel Hill (Orange County); Raleigh (Wake County) has North Carolina State University (27,200 students).

The large numbers of white-collar and professional jobs in the region make it one of the most affluent districts in the state.

Orange County has a more liberal bent than the rest of the 4th, due primarily to the university community of Chapel Hill. In 1992, Rep. Price won Orange by nearly 3-to-1; Bill Clinton won more than 60 percent.

But the bulk of 4th District residents live outside Orange County. Wake County is the population nexus, casting about three-fourths of the vote. Much of that vote comes from the state government complex in Raleigh, North Carolina's capital. The pool of state employees gives the county a Democratic tilt, but the high-growth suburbs outside Raleigh are gradually redefining local politics.

One town, Cary, grew so fast in the 1980s that it surpassed Chapel Hill in population. Before the opening of Research Triangle Park in the early 1960s, Cary was a sleepy hamlet, surrounded by undeveloped fields and farmland. But its proximity to the Triangle and its location along the Interstate 40 corridor spurred a population boom from 7,600 people to 43,400 between 1970 and 1990 — a 471 percent increase.

Like other emerging northern and western Wake County towns, Cary fits the classic suburban demographic profile: Large numbers of double-income, young, mostly white families who are independent or GOP voters. A high percentage of residents are white-collar executives who work at the biotechnology, pharmaceutical, supercomputer and electronics industries of Research Triangle Park (outside the 4th in southern Durham County) or in the office parks of Wake County.

The towns outlying Raleigh exhibited a tendency for split-ticket voting in 1992. Clinton carried the county — though he ran below his districtwide average — and Price cruised with 62 percent. But in the Senate race, Republican nominee Lauch Faircloth edged out Democratic incumbent Terry Sanford.

On the western edge of the 4th, largely rural Chatham County is the least populous county in the 4th, but is reliably Democratic: Democratic candidates swept the presidential, Senate and House races in 1992. Its agrarian landscape includes some textile industry, along with Chapel Hill spillover growth along its northern border with Orange County.

1990 Population: 552,387. White 426,361 (77%), Black 111,162 (20%), Other 14,864 (3%). Hispanic origin 7,217 (1%). 18 and over 428,984 (78%), 62 and over 57,298 (10%). Median age: 31.

signed into law Price's bill authorizing National Science Foundation grants to two-year or community colleges as a means of promoting technical education and training, especially for "non-traditional" students and high-school dropouts.

At Home: Price laid the groundwork for his move from academia to electioneering with a long career as a party activist at the state and national level. In 1986, he beat GOP Rep. Bill Cobey by 12 percentage points — the largest victory margin achieved by a House challenger that year.

While teaching political science at Duke, Price spent nearly two years as state party chairman, winning generally high marks for his performance. He also made invaluable contacts with local party leaders in the district and used them to build an early financial and organizational edge over three primary rivals in 1986.

In that primary, Price proved to be a somewhat stiff and awkward campaigner. He fell short of the 50 percent needed to avoid a runoff, but drew a reprieve when the second finisher from the primary demurred.

Cobey, who had won the traditionally Democratic 4th in 1984, was considered vulnerable from the outset. His affable nature and constituent-service operation had helped him win over some voters who disagreed with his conservative ideology, but he was operating with little margin for error. And he committed a serious one in mid-September. He mailed out a campaign letter (addressed to "Dear Christian Friend") in which he said he was "an ambassador for Christ" who needed the support of fundamentalists.

Injecting religion in the campaign might have been a questionable tactic against any candidate, but it seemed particularly inappropriate against Price, an active Baptist and Sunday school teacher with a divinity degree.

In 1988, Price faced Republican Tom Fetzer, a former operative for GOP Sen. Jesse Helms' political organization, the National Congressional Club. The club's past campaign tactics and attention to social issues had put off many Democrats and even some Republicans, but its resources helped make Fetzer a threat. Price, however, was ready for accusations that he was too liberal for the 4th; his work on the home-equity legislation aimed straight at affluent suburbanites inclined to vote Republican. In the end, Price improved on his 1986 showing.

In 1990, Price stared down another well-financed Republican challenge. Raleigh businessman John H. Carrington had run two close statewide campaigns in the 1980s, financing them largely out of his own pocket. A political loner, he depended on television commercials and shunned public appearances in those races.

Carrington ran radio ads throughout the spring and summer attacking Congress; in September he began his TV campaign with ads criticizing Price for accepting money from banking and savings and loan interests while he sat on the Banking Committee. "Should Congress Have a Price?" his ads asked. But voters were not swayed: Price posted a 58 percent win.

While all of the focus during North Carolina redistricting in 1991 and 1992 was on the creation of two majority-black districts, Price's 4th was quietly getting more Democratic. Its population increased by nearly one-third in the 1980s, the fastest growth of any district in the state.

Redistricting relieved Price of heavily Republican Randolph County, which he had never carried. In November, he notched his best victory margin yet, defeating Republican Vicky Goudie, a state employee from Raleigh, by nearly 2-to-1.

Committees

Appropriations (23rd of 37 Democrats)
Commerce, Justice, State & Judiciary; Transportation

Budget (18th of 26 Democrats)

Elections

1992 General		
David Price (D)	171,299	(65%)
LaVinia "Vicky" Rothrock Goudie (R)	89,345	(34%)
Eugene Paczelt (LIBERT)	4,416	(2%)
1990 General		
David Price (D)	139,396	(58%)
John Carrington (R)	100,661	(42%)

Previous Winning Percentages: **1988** (58%) **1986** (56%)

District Vote for President

	1992
D	125,723 (47%)
R	105,020 (39%)
I	38,699 (14%)

Campaign Finance

	Receipts	Receipts from PACs		Expend-itures
1992				
Price (D)	$480,758	$275,211	(57%)	$444,259
Goudie (R)	$12,330	$1,486	(12%)	$12,270
1990				
Price (D)	$771,624	$385,210	(50%)	$793,291
Carrington (R)	$893,349	0		$890,838

Key Votes

1993	
Require parental notification of minors' abortions	N
Require unpaid family and medical leave	Y
Approve national "motor voter" registration bill	Y
Approve budget increasing taxes and reducing deficit	Y
Approve economic stimulus plan	Y
1992	
Approve balanced-budget constitutional amendment	Y
Close down space station program	Y
Approve U.S. aid for former Soviet Union	Y
Allow shifting funds from defense to domestic programs	Y
1991	
Extend unemployment benefits using deficit financing	Y
Approve waiting period for handgun purchases	Y
Authorize use of force in Persian Gulf	N

Voting Studies

	Presidential Support		Party Unity		Conservative Coalition	
Year	**S**	**O**	**S**	**O**	**S**	**O**
1992	25	74	91	8	52	48
1991	40	60	86	12	59	41
1990	24	75	92	8	48	52
1989	34	66	90	9	56	44
1988	28	68	83	14	71	24
1987	29	69	84	13	72	28

Interest Group Ratings

Year	ADA	AFL-CIO	CCUS	ACU
1992	85	67	25	13
1991	60	83	50	10
1990	61	75	29	21
1989	75	83	60	14
1988	75	93	62	24
1987	80	81	33	9

5 Stephen L. Neal (D)

Of Winston-Salem — Elected 1974; 10th Term

Born: Nov. 7, 1934, Winston-Salem, N.C.
Education: U. of California, Santa Barbara, 1954-56; U. of Hawaii, A.B. 1963.
Occupation: Publisher.
Family: Wife, Rachel Landis Miller; two children.
Religion: Presbyterian.
Political Career: No previous office.
Capitol Office: 2469 Rayburn Bldg. 20515; 225-2071.

In Washington: Neal's ascension in the 103rd Congress to chair the Banking subcommittee principally responsible for regulation of the financial services industry would ordinarily be of great moment to his powerhouse home-state banking interests.

But turnover on the committee swept out several key allies and replaced them with a huge contingent of freshmen unlikely to be receptive to a dramatic overhaul of banking laws. For the near term at least, any legislative effort intended to benefit banks will likely face an arduous road no less difficult to traverse than Neal's ordinary path to re-election.

His chairmanship also got off to a rocky start when he hired as his top subcommittee aide Paul Nelson, formerly full committee staff director under discredited former Chairman Fernand J. St Germain of Rhode Island. When Nelson's continued close ties to some banking interests were disclosed at the start of the 103rd Congress, he resigned.

Neal has a politically cautious style that, combined with his rank as the No. 2 Democrat on the Banking Committee, helps him survive repeated Republican challenges in a district that leans toward more clear-cut conservatism. He has fostered ties to the state's business community to the extent that local business leaders have shied from opposing him. Reserved yet personable, Neal fits in well politically with other North Carolina Democrats, a group of moderates who are the most reliable supporters of House Democratic leaders among Southerners. Meanwhile, he keeps enough distance from the national party's more controversial stands to survive at home.

Still, the full-time effort at electoral survival — he has garnered more than 54 percent only twice in 10 elections — seems to have detracted from Neal's profile on Banking, and in the House in general. Though Neal has perhaps the best technical knowledge of banking issues on the committee, he is a low-key subcommittee chairman more given to compromise than confrontation. Only occasionally does he take the lead on a significant issue.

In 1991, Neal enjoyed a high profile as the prime backer of a plan to permit banks to open branch offices across state lines. Many larger banking companies across the country own banks in multiple states and would like to consolidate those independent banks into single networks of branches. Smaller banks, however, generally oppose interstate branching.

No company is more aggressive in pursuing the goal of interstate branching than NationsBank (formerly North Carolina National Bank), now the fourth-largest banking company in the country. Neal sponsored the Bank Efficiency Act in 1991 to permit immediate consolidation of interstate branching systems, and a version of the measure was included in a sweeping banking overhaul bill that died on the House floor. After the House passed a much more restrictive banking bill, the branching idea was declared dead for the 102nd Congress. Neal reintroduced his bill at the start of the 103rd.

Also in 1991, Neal served notice that he wanted to bar one increasingly common practice by banks — the payment of interest on only a portion of bank deposits, called the "investible balance" because it was the portion available for banks to lend after setting aside mandatory reserves. "That would seem to be a deceptive practice," Neal said during deliberations on the Truth in Savings Act. "I was just outraged when I discovered that." The 1991 banking bill, as enacted, contained an explicit ban on the practice.

In 1989, when Congress debated spending $50 billion to salvage the savings and loan industry, Neal backed the notion of imposing strict standards for the amount of capital thrifts must maintain as a cushion against losses. On a key House vote on whether to allow thrifts with "supervisory good will" — a type of "phantom" capital — to count it in meeting the new standards, Neal bucked the industry and voted against the amendment.

That was a shift from two years earlier, when Neal sponsored a thrift industry-backed proposal to pump $5 billion into the insolvent Federal Savings and Loan Insurance Corpora-

North Carolina 5

Northwest — Part of Winston-Salem

Beginning in the 1970s, voters in the 5th started a march toward the Republican side, creating a quadrennial panic among local Democratic officeholders, who feared being dragged down by their party's national ticket. A recession-induced interruption in 1992 marked the first time Democrats saw a break in that procession.

The heart of the district is Winston-Salem, an old-time tobacco town dominated by the leaf since Richard Joshua Reynolds built his first plug chewing tobacco factory in the 1870s. The city remains a tobacco-producing center, where the R. J. Reynolds conglomerate still keeps its tobacco and Planters Lifesavers headquarters, but it has strayed from its industrial origins.

Textiles are also an important component of the local economy, but nowadays, tobacco and textiles take a back seat to service industries, now the largest employment sector. Health-care services is the largest single industry in Forsyth County.

In the 1980s, downsizing in the tobacco industry and the gradual erosion of the manufacturing base translated into slower growth for Winston-Salem than in North Carolina's other major cities.

The 1992 presidential election was a prime indicator of local economic unrest, as the Democratic presidential ticket remained competitive in Forsyth County and across the district for the first time since 1976.

It was not enough, though, for Democratic Sen. Terry Sanford, who lost populous Forsyth and virtually every other county in the 5th. Two years earlier, GOP Sen. Jesse Helms won 56 percent of the district vote.

One exception in the 1990 and 1992 Senate races was rural Caswell County, a Democratic stronghold in the eastern reaches of the 5th, where blacks make up about 40 percent of the electorate.

The city of Winston-Salem is about 40 percent black also, but most of the black neighborhoods were excised from the 5th during 1992 redistricting and added to the majority-minority 12th District.

Republicans have traditionally run well in the GOP hill country in the western reaches of the 5th, between the Blue Ridge and Appalachian mountains. Early settlers of the area set up small farms with dairy cows, poultry, apple trees and tobacco, and developed strong antagonism toward the flatland tobacco planters who were wealthier, politically powerful and Democratic.

From mountainous Watauga County, the 5th shoots east and south to take in parts of Republican Wilkes County, and parts of furniture and textile-producing Burke and Caldwell counties.

The mostly rural counties of the northern tier, along the Virginia border, are typified by small, textile towns such as Mount Airy. The fictional town of Mayberry, the setting for the long-running "Andy Griffith Show," was loosely based on Griffith's memories of growing up in this Surry County town. Surry and neighboring Stokes County backed George Bush and successful GOP Senate challenger Lauch Faircloth in 1992.

1990 Population: 552,386. White 463,183 (84%), Black 83,824 (15%), Other 5,379 (1%). Hispanic origin 4,259 (1%). 18 and over 428,782 (78%), 62 and over 91,914 (17%). Median age: 35.

tion. The Reagan administration wanted $15 billion. But the industry — which would have had to foot the entire bill through higher insurance premiums — argued that the problem was not so large.

Neal carved a niche for himself as chairman of the Subcommittee on Domestic Monetary Policy for six years, a perch from which he could oversee the Federal Reserve Board and its regulation of the money supply. It was a good place for Neal to preach his essentially monetarist view that national economic health depends on a modest and steady growth in the money supply, rather than any combination of federal tax and spending policies.

Beginning with the 101st Congress, Neal introduced legislation to require the Fed to set a five-year goal of reducing inflation to zero or to a level where it no longer affects economic decision-making. Fed Chairman Alan Greenspan endorsed the plan; and to reciprocate, Neal praised Greenspan for his watchfulness to prevent a surge in inflation. The Bush administration and others opposed the idea, however, criticizing it as an effort by Congress to "micromanage" the Fed. The bill did not make it out of subcommittee in that Congress or the next.

Although it has caused him some problems at home, Neal votes with the Democratic leadership more often than not. In the 101st Congress, he voted against a proposed constitutional amendment to ban physical desecration of the flag. In the 102nd, he voted against giving President Bush authority to use force against Iraq, instead backing continued economic sanctions. And he backed a seven-day waiting period for handgun purchases, though he is generally opposed to gun control.

During House floor consideration in 1990 of a comprehensive civil rights bill, Neal and Texas Democrat Michael A. Andrews offered a compromise amendment designed to answer the administration's objection that the legislation would impose racial hiring quotas. The amendment was adopted by a vote of 397-24, but the bill died after the Senate failed by a single vote to override Bush's veto.

Other of Neal's efforts are more closely linked to the interests of his district, perched geographically and politically between the Republican-leaning Appalachian foothills and the traditionally Democratic Piedmont. Besides banking, Neal promotes two more-troubled industries, tobacco and textiles.

He opposes the increasing number of measures to raise cigarette taxes and limit smoking; in 1986, he dubbed bills to restrict smoking in federal buildings the "Smokers Segregation and Persecution Acts." In the 102nd and 103rd Congresses, he introduced bills to allow tobacco growers to deduct for income tax purposes the payments they make to support the price-support system for producers. He has regularly joined fellow Southerners in an unsuccessful fight to set quotas on textile imports.

At Home: A Watergate-spawned Democrat in a district with a demonstrated affection for the GOP, Neal always expects tough elections and is always prepared for them. But the wave of Republicanism that has swept through the state in recent presidential elections has tested even his best-laid plans.

Even in 1992, with fellow Southerner Arkansas Gov. Bill Clinton heading the Democratic ticket, Neal had a nail-biter. His GOP opponent, sales manager Richard M. Burr, did not have the high profile of some of Neal's previous opponents but redistricting changes made up for it.

Neal lost some of the black neighborhoods that provided his margins of victory in other races; they were replaced with rural, white Democratic voters.

Burr's attempts to graft those voters on to the district's considerable GOP base met with some success. Sensing an upset opportunity, national GOP operatives provided additional resources to Burr's effort in the final weeks of the campaign. But without the usual heavy drag at the top of the ticket, Neal posted 53 percent and won every county.

His opponent in 1980 was state Sen. Anne Bagnal, an energetic Republican who stressed her strong opposition to abortion and the Equal Rights Amendment and criticized Neal's support for President Jimmy Carter. Although Neal voted with Carter no more often than the average House Democrat, he enthusiastically touted the president and invited him to appear in the district during the campaign.

Ronald Reagan carried the 5th over Carter by nearly 15,000 votes, laying down coattails for Bagnal that helped her hold Neal to 51 percent, the worst showing he had made to that date since his initial election to the House in 1974.

Neal rebounded in 1982, winning handily over Bagnal in a good Democratic year in North Carolina. But by 1984, he was in trouble again. Reagan's position at the top of the ticket helped spark an outbreak of straight-ticket GOP voting in North Carolina.

The GOP nominee was broadcast executive Stuart Epperson, a political neophyte who entered the race only shortly before the filing deadline. A graduate of fundamentalist Bob Jones University, Epperson began by stressing his conservative stance on school prayer. But local GOP leaders convinced him that an economic emphasis would give him broader appeal. He spent the later stages of the campaign criticizing Neal's support for U.S. involvement in the International Monetary Fund (IMF), arguing that such a stance would encourage foreign competition and thus hurt local textile markets.

Neal defended his record and dismissed Epperson as an amateur dependent for support upon Reagan's coattails. Still, he needed all his political strength to hold on to his seat. Bolstered by the campaigns of Reagan, GOP gubernatorial candidate James G. Martin and Sen. Jesse Helms, Epperson took five of the district's eight counties and came within 3,232 votes of an upset.

Epperson returned for a rematch in 1986, and proved more polished than in his first outing. He also offered a more focused message. Hoping to capitalize on discontent over the slumping textile industry, Epperson spent most of the campaign railing against Neal for supporting IMF loans that the Republican claimed were used to help build textile plants in foreign countries — and thus cost the 5th District jobs. Neal sought to discredit his opposition by arguing that the only people who saw sinister implications in the IMF were Epperson and fringe political figure Lyndon H. LaRouche Jr. But he also was careful to address Epperson's charges, denying that IMF money had been used to finance any foreign textile plants.

In the end, Epperson could not match the momentum of his 1984 campaign. Without the benefit of the top-of-the-ticket presence of a Reagan or a Helms, the Republican managed to carry only two counties as Neal posted a 54 percent tally.

Neal again had cause for concern in 1988. Michael S. Dukakis was not expected to run well in North Carolina, and the GOP offered a different style of candidate in Lyons Gray, a wealthy and well-known business-oriented establishment Republican.

Gray, owner of an industrial roofing company, was a member of a very prominent family in Winston-Salem, and he had had some political exposure as well. Gray lost to Epperson in the 1986 Republican House primary.

Unlike previous GOP nominees, Gray did not try to paint Neal as a dangerous liberal. In fact, his ads said Neal was not a bad representative. But the ads continued, "Not bad isn't good enough." He criticized Neal as an ineffective member overly attentive to big banks.

But Neal, experienced at tough campaigns, quickly put Gray on the defensive. He got an opening in late summer when Gray returned a questionnaire to the AFL-CIO stating his opposition to legislation limiting textile imports. That position is not palatable to most in North Carolina, and Gray quickly insisted it was a staff error. But the incident and a few other missteps shifted the focus from Neal.

In the end, Neal did almost as well as he had in 1986, taking 53 percent of the vote. Gray carried three counties, leaving five, including sizable Forsyth (Winston-Salem), to Neal.

Neal had been one of the nation's most surprising winners in 1974, defeating four-term Rep. Wilmer D. Mizell, one of the most popular Republicans in the state. Mizell, a former National League pitcher, flirted with the idea of running for the Senate in 1974, finally deciding to keep what he and everyone else considered a safe House seat.

But it was not a good year to be a Republican in North Carolina. Neal, a publisher of several suburban newspapers, linked Mizell to the Nixon administration and the state's economic troubles and took 52 percent.

Two years later, Mizell came back for a rematch but Neal's cautious legislative record helped belie that attempt, and a strong Democratic ticket helped him win with 54 percent of the vote.

Committees

Banking, Finance & Urban Affairs (2nd of 30 Democrats)
Financial Institutions Supervision, Regulation & Deposit Insurance (chairman); Economic Growth; General Oversight, Investigations & the Resolution of Failed Financial Institutions; International Development, Finance, Trade & Monetary Policy

Government Operations (6th of 25 Democrats)
Legislation & National Security

Elections

1992 General		
Stephen L. Neal (D)	117,835	(53%)
Richard M. Burr (R)	102,086	(46%)
Gary Albrecht (LIBERT)	3,758	(2%)
1990 General		
Stephen L. Neal (D)	113,814	(59%)
Ken Bell (R)	78,747	(41%)

Previous Winning Percentages: **1988** (53%) **1986** (54%) **1984** (51%) **1982** (60%) **1980** (51%) **1978** (54%) **1976** (54%) **1974** (52%)

District Vote for President

1992
D 97,607 (43%)
R 98,853 (44%)
I 30,460 (13%)

Campaign Finance

	Receipts	Receipts from PACs		Expend-itures
1992				
Neal (D)	$493,627	$339,570	(69%)	$517,594
Burr (R)	$188,189	$18,134	(10%)	$188,130
1990				
Neal (D)	$671,884	$398,879	(59%)	$647,331
Bell (R)	$178,200	$2,550	(1%)	$174,574

Key Votes

1993	
Require parental notification of minors' abortions	N
Require unpaid family and medical leave	Y
Approve national "motor voter" registration bill	Y
Approve budget increasing taxes and reducing deficit	Y
Approve economic stimulus plan	N
1992	
Approve balanced-budget constitutional amendment	Y
Close down space station program	Y
Approve U.S. aid for former Soviet Union	N
Allow shifting funds from defense to domestic programs	?
1991	
Extend unemployment benefits using deficit financing	Y
Approve waiting period for handgun purchases	Y
Authorize use of force in Persian Gulf	N

Voting Studies

	Presidential Support		Party Unity		Conservative Coalition	
Year	**S**	**O**	**S**	**O**	**S**	**O**
1992	26	70	75	18	63	35
1991	38	58	68	23	62	24
1990	36	59	66	25	74	24
1989	29	65	74	16	59	41
1988	24	68	76	12	55	24
1987	32	67	73	21	74	26
1986	28	71	75	18	54	40
1985	36	64	72	17	60	33
1984	39	51	65	22	51	36
1983	38	50	64	20	55	33
1982	42	44	48	32	59	25
1981	42	55	66	27	64	29

Interest Group Ratings

Year	ADA	AFL-CIO	CCUS	ACU
1992	65	50	29	27
1991	55	64	50	30
1990	50	55	43	32
1989	65	67	60	19
1988	70	92	50	21
1987	68	60	60	5
1986	65	71	50	29
1985	50	53	48	33
1984	65	42	31	32
1983	60	73	59	32
1982	25	60	50	50
1981	55	73	17	20

6 Howard Coble (R)

Of Greensboro — Elected 1984; 5th Term

Born: March 18, 1931, Greensboro, N.C.
Education: Appalachian State U., 1949-50; Guilford College, A.B. 1958; U. of North Carolina, J.D. 1962.
Military Service: Coast Guard, 1952-56; Coast Guard Reserve, 1960-81.
Occupation: Lawyer; insurance claims supervisor.
Family: Single.
Religion: Presbyterian.
Political Career: N.C. House, 1969; secretary, N.C. Department of Revenue, 1973-77; GOP nominee for N.C. treasurer, 1976; N.C. House, 1979-83.
Capitol Office: 403 Cannon Bldg. 20515; 225-3065.

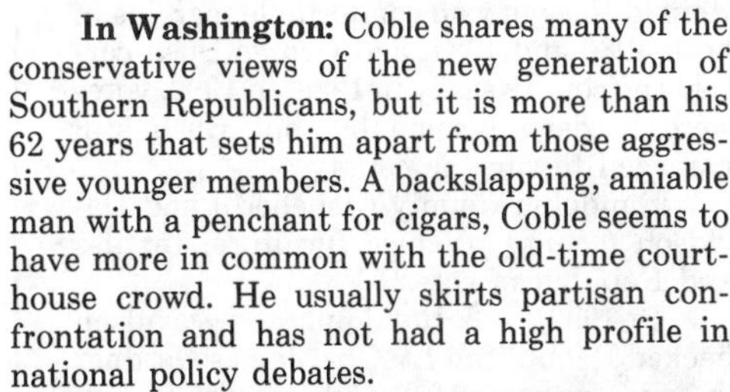

In Washington: Coble shares many of the conservative views of the new generation of Southern Republicans, but it is more than his 62 years that sets him apart from those aggressive younger members. A backslapping, amiable man with a penchant for cigars, Coble seems to have more in common with the old-time courthouse crowd. He usually skirts partisan confrontation and has not had a high profile in national policy debates.

When Coble's views do get wider notice, it is for his occasional nipping at the ankles of the House for its pay, pensions and perks.

He was part of the chorus of criticism against the congressional pay raise in 1989 and was among the first to call for term limits. In February 1989, Coble introduced legislation to limit House members to three four-year terms. He points out that his plan would also keep a lid on congressional pensions. "A lot of [House members] are fat, a lot are soft, and a lot are sitting around waiting for their pensions," he said.

Coble's objections to the pension program date to his first term. In 1985, he introduced legislation to reduce retirement pay for House members, a move that some colleagues regarded as rank demagoguery. It is a theme he has pursued. In a February 1993 letter to White House budget director Leon E. Panetta, he suggested eliminating the federal contribution to the congressional pension plan as a further spending cut for the Clinton economic team to consider. He is one of the few members of Congress who refuses to participate in the pension program, calling it "a taxpayer rip-off."

In another swipe at congressional practices, in 1990 he cosponsored a bill to put strict limits on congressional travel, after the airing of a critical TV news report about a Ways and Means Committee trip to Barbados.

Coble's anti-institutional bent puts him on common ground with some of the younger Republicans, and he was an early supporter of Georgian Newt Gingrich's bid for minority whip early in the 101st Congress. Once elected, Gingrich named Coble an assistant regional whip.

Coble also is vocal when the subject is textiles. More than 30,000 of his constituents work in the textile industry, and he has consistently demanded protectionist relief for the industry. "The only place free trade exists is in an economics textbook," he says.

Searching for ways to boost local industry, Coble is an ardent foe of the growth of the Federal Prison Industries program, which gives prisons an advantage in winning furniture contracts over the many companies in his district.

Coble prides himself on being a fiscal conservative, but he is ready enough to play the federal spending game when the 6th District benefits. Federal sewer and construction grants he announced in 1988 did not hurt his reelection bid, nor did the nearly $500,000 grant to upgrade the security system at the Piedmont Triad International Airport in 1990.

In 1990, Coble cast an uncharacteristic vote on the Judiciary Committee in favor of the Brady bill, which sought to impose a seven-day waiting period on handgun purchases. He had never supported gun control before and has not done so since. Coble was apparently swayed by the pressure exerted by activists Sarah and James S. Brady, Ronald Reagan's former press secretary who was wounded in the 1981 assassination attempt against Reagan. "I fell off the wagon because of an emotional spin," Coble said shortly afterward. "I probably will revert to my old ways."

At Home: Coble started 1984 thinking about running for governor. He had gained some statewide name recognition among Republicans, not only in the legislature but also as an assistant U.S. attorney, and as secretary of the Department of Revenue under GOP Gov. James E. Holshouser Jr. in the mid-1970s. But he bypassed a statewide bid to challenge freshman Democrat Robin Britt in the 6th.

North Carolina 6

Central — Part of Greensboro

The 6th is a monument to the folly of North Carolina's 1992 redistricting process. Many of the districts are cartographically imaginative, but the 6th is exceptional. It is split in half by a thin reed that is the 12th District; the point where the two halves of the 6th District connect cannot be seen by the naked eye.

Almost 40 percent of the district's population lives in middle-class Guilford County (Greensboro), home to two corners of the Piedmont Triad. The third-largest city in North Carolina, Greensboro's economy is a blend of manufacturing and service industry.

Textile giants such as Burlington Industries and Cone Mills employ thousands, as does AT&T Technologies. There is an American Express regional credit card service center, tobacco-processing, insurance services, and six colleges and universities.

Furniture-making High Point is located in the southwestern part of Guilford County. The third corner of the Triad, Winston-Salem, is outside 6th District confines, in the neighboring 5th District.

Guilford County's relatively large managerial class produces a Republican vote, though it is far from monolithic. In 1992, Bill Clinton carried the county, while Rep. Coble racked up 73 percent. Democratic Sen. Terry Sanford squeaked by successful Republican challenger Lauch Faircloth in 1992.

Prior to 1992 redistricting, all of Greensboro and surrounding Guilford County was included in the 6th; now the 6th lacks the black neighborhoods of the city, which were added to the majority-minority 12th District. The 12th divides the 6th along the I-85 population corridor.

Textile-oriented Alamance County produces hosiery, upholstery and drapery fabrics, textured yarn and other finished fabrics.

North of the interstate, the Alamance turf belongs to the 12th. Some of the factory outlet town of Burlington is in the 6th, but most of its black residents are in the 12th. Less-developed southern Alamance is in the 6th.

With a union-resistant textile industry, Alamance usually stays in the Republican fold, despite a Democratic registration edge. Ronald Reagan won comfortable margins in both 1980 and 1984, and George Bush carried the county easily in 1988. In 1992, votes were harder to come by, but Bush still managed to win the county.

Randolph County (Asheboro) and Davidson County produce furniture, textiles and Republican votes.

In 1992, both Randolph and Davidson backed Republican Lt. Gov. James Gardner in his unsuccessful gubernatorial bid; George Bush scored better than 50 percent in each.

Parts of Davie and Rowan counties — mostly outside the population centers — are also included in the 6th. Both backed Bush in 1992; Davie gave GOP Sen. Jesse Helms 70 percent in his 1990 re-election against Democrat Harvey B. Gantt.

1990 Population: 552,385. White 504,464 (91%), Black 41,329 (7%), Other 6,592 (1%). Hispanic origin 3,784 (1%). 18 and over 428,096 (77%), 62 and over 84,176 (15%). Median age: 35.

Despite his reputation, it took all of Coble's efforts just to make himself the GOP nominee. Former state Sen. Walter C. Cockerham, a millionaire construction company owner, had been stumping the district and courting Republican votes for several months before Coble entered the race.

The primary caused a split between local GOP moderates and the party's conservative faction.

Coble's roots were on the moderate side, as evidenced by his close ties to Holshouser, arch-enemy of the conservative wing. Cockerham devoted much of his time to branding Coble a "liberal lawyer" and casting himself in the mold of North Carolina GOP Sen. Jesse Helms. And Cockerham had the support of the Helms-affiliated National Congressional Club, a group Coble had publicly criticized.

But Coble played up his reputation for fiscal stinginess in monitoring the state budget, earned after his return to the North Carolina House in 1979. Armed with the support of most local GOP leaders, Coble pulled through by a scant 164 votes.

Coble continued to stress his fiscal conservatism against Britt, whom he sought to paint as an extravagant liberal. Coble criticized Britt for having gone against Reagan on two of every three votes cast in 1983, and accused Britt of voting to pay people to operate automatic elevators on Capitol Hill.

Britt was unable to overcome the liberal label. Although Britt's careful cultivation of the Greensboro business community helped him carry Guilford County, he failed to run up sufficient margins to compensate for Coble's strength in the 6th's outlying territory. Tapping into the flow of conservative Democrats who crossed party lines for Reagan, Coble finished with a 2,662-vote edge.

But Coble could not rest long on his laurels. Britt immediately began plotting a comeback. The 1986 results would be even closer than those of 1984; only 79 votes separated the winner and the loser on Election Day. Britt spent the early months of 1987 appealing the election results, but his challenge proved unsuccessful.

When Britt opted not to run again in 1988, Democrats turned to Tom Gilmore, a well-known and well-funded former state legislator. But while Gilmore had a zest for campaigning, his campaign had little zest. He continued with some of Britt's attacks on the textile issue; Britt had contended that the textile industry was suffering from Coble's inability to persuade his House GOP colleagues to override Reagan's veto of a 1985 textile bill. And he criticized Coble's record on the environment, calling attention to the incumbent's presence on Environmental Action's "Dirty Dozen" list.

But Coble had endeared himself to many in the 6th, and he could point to his success at delivering for the district after two terms. With national trends going his way, Coble won 62 percent of the vote and 67 percent in 1990. In 1992, he increased his winning percentage to 71 percent.

Committees

Judiciary (7th of 14 Republicans)
Civil & Constitutional Rights; Intellectual Property & Judicial Administration

Merchant Marine & Fisheries (5th of 18 Republicans)
Coast Guard & Navigation (ranking); Fisheries Management

Elections

1992 General		
Howard Coble (R)	162,822	(71%)
Robin Hood (D)	67,200	(29%)
1990 General		
Howard Coble (R)	125,392	(67%)
Helen R. Allegrone (D)	62,913	(33%)

Previous Winning Percentages: 1988 (62%) **1986** (50%) **1984** (51%)

District Vote for President

1992

D 75,747 (32%)
R 120,200 (51%)
I 38,331 (16%)

Campaign Finance

	Receipts	Receipts from PACs		Expend-itures
1992				
Coble (R)	$504,213	$207,135	(41%)	$435,093
Hood (D)	$28,026	$8,300	(30%)	$27,822
1990				
Coble (R)	$572,043	$223,860	(39%)	$572,846
Allegrone (D)	$35,188	$9,500	(27%)	$33,135

Key Votes

1993	
Require parental notification of minors' abortions	Y
Require unpaid family and medical leave	N
Approve national "motor voter" registration bill	N
Approve budget increasing taxes and reducing deficit	N
Approve economic stimulus plan	N
1992	
Approve balanced-budget constitutional amendment	Y
Close down space station program	Y
Approve U.S. aid for former Soviet Union	N
Allow shifting funds from defense to domestic programs	N
1991	
Extend unemployment benefits using deficit financing	N
Approve waiting period for handgun purchases	N
Authorize use of force in Persian Gulf	Y

Voting Studies

	Presidential Support		Party Unity		Conservative Coalition	
Year	**S**	**O**	**S**	**O**	**S**	**O**
1992	75	25	92	8	75	25
1991	70	30	89	8	86	11
1990	68	32	92	7	93	7
1989	81	17	94	6	98	2
1988	61	39	90	10	92	8
1987	70	30	92	7	95	5
1986	68	31	84	14	92	8
1985	69	30	87	9	91	9

Interest Group Ratings

Year	ADA	AFL-CIO	CCUS	ACU
1992	10	25	75	92
1991	15	25	80	90
1990	6	8	93	83
1989	10	8	100	82
1988	10	21	93	92
1987	4	6	100	87
1986	10	36	89	81
1985	0	12	91	81

7 Charlie Rose (D)

Of Fayetteville — Elected 1972; 11th Term

Born: Aug. 10, 1939, Fayetteville, N.C.
Education: Davidson College, B.A. 1961; U. of North Carolina, LL.B. 1964.
Occupation: Lawyer.
Family: Wife, Joan Teague; three children.
Religion: Presbyterian.
Political Career: 12th Judicial District chief prosecutor, 1967-71; sought Democratic nomination for U.S. House, 1970.
Capitol Office: 2230 Rayburn Bldg. 20515; 225-2731.

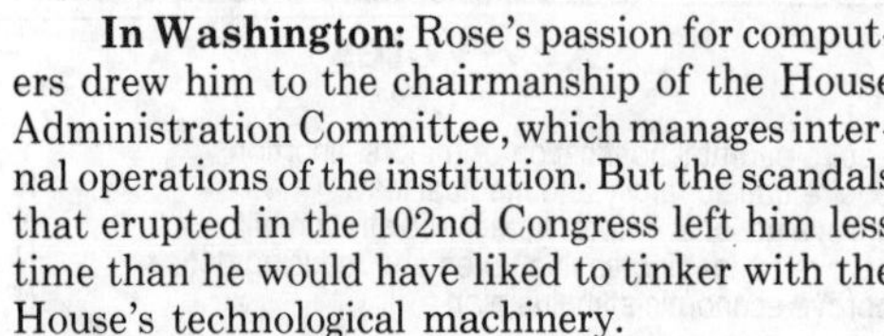

In Washington: Rose's passion for computers drew him to the chairmanship of the House Administration Committee, which manages internal operations of the institution. But the scandals that erupted in the 102nd Congress left him less time than he would have liked to tinker with the House's technological machinery.

The atmosphere is not likely to improve quickly in the 103rd Congress, as House Administration finds itself awash in a tide of budget-cutting sentiment. Members are looking for cuts in federal spending, be they symbolic or real.

Rose's penchant for the behind-the-scenes politics of old also landed him in hot water with members of both parties on his committee, who criticized him for unilaterally hiring outside consultants. Rose has the authority to act on routine administrative matters when Congress is in recess, but some members say he has abused the authority.

The North Carolina Democrat's interest in House Administration seems unusual on the face of it. Once regarded as a comer for statewide office (or for party leadership in the House), he has been seen as biding his time — waiting for seniority to confer the chairmanship of the Agriculture Committee. In the meantime, he stands third in the Democratic batting order on that committee and uses his clout to defend tobacco and peanut interests.

But in 1991, Rose gave up his chairmanship of the Tobacco and Peanuts Subcommittee, which he had held for a decade, and took the helm at House Administration (the preceding chairman, aging Frank Annunzio of Illinois, had been ousted by vote of the Democratic Caucus). The move offered Rose the chance to spend more time nudging Congress into the technological age. Rose is considered the resident expert on computers and Congress' technological capacity.

When he arrived on Capitol Hill in 1973, Rose quickly joined House Administration and persuaded its leaders to update the existing limited and primitive computer system. The new technology has given members better legislative data and communications. And it has brought them the computerized mailing lists that facilitate the courting of constituents and contributions.

But the internal scandals of the 102nd — and the resultant outcries for congressional reform, both within and outside the institution — may mean Rose will have to wait before initiating further advances in technology.

House Administration was not caught up in the most far-reaching scandal of the 102nd: the House bank scandal. The office of the House Sergeant at Arms had overseen the bank operations, and its chief eventually took the fall for the overdrafts. Rose had no personal association with the controversy, either, having written no overdrafts himself.

But Rose did find his committee enmeshed in other controversies. The bank story brought fresh attention to members' unpaid bills at the House restaurant, mass mailings beyond their district lines and allegations of mismanagement, embezzlement and other wrongdoings at the House Post Office by both Post Office employees and lawmakers.

The House Post Office scandal was first reported on Capitol Hill in August 1991. Less than two months later, the restaurant scandal was added to Rose's woes, when Rep. Pat Roberts of Kansas, the ranking Republican of House Administration's Subcommittee on Personnel and Police, released a letter detailing more than $300,000 owed to the House restaurant by about 250 members.

Rose downplayed both incidents, sticking to the old-fashioned manner of dealing with such controversies. Rose had actually known about problems at the restaurant and Post Office well before they became common knowledge; he had tried to handle both problems quietly — out of public sight. When the backstage efforts failed, Rose took the lead in a House probe of the post office that found "no credible evidence" of violations of House rules or federal law.

Rose came to these controversies having

North Carolina 7

Southeast — Part of Fayetteville

It is no coincidence that Rep. Rose slipped to a career-low 57 percent after his 1991 vote against authorizing force in the Persian Gulf. For in the military-dependent southeastern region of North Carolina, that stand was extremely controversial.

Cumberland County is the 7th's most-populous county, and it has a heavy military cast. It is home to more than 40,000 troops stationed at Fort Bragg and Pope Air Force Base, and thousands of military retirees.

When 75 percent of the troops stationed here were deployed in the gulf war, the county took the equivalent of an economic Scud missile. Local business suffered: Unemployment claims and food stamp applications soared, sales tax revenues plummeted, and mobile home sales were cut in half. GOP Gov. James Martin declared Cumberland and three other counties economic emergency areas.

One of the other economic emergency areas was coastal Onslow County (Jacksonville), site of Camp Lejeune Marine Corps training base. Like Cumberland, the Onslow economy is heavily dependent on the troops who spend their paychecks on the local service industries.

The 7th shares Cumberland County with the 1st and the 8th — and Onslow County with the 3rd — and many voters in these counties showed their dissatisfaction with Rose's gulf vote at the ballot box in 1992. Rose won in Cumberland County, but not as easily as he had in past elections. Onslow County, which was added to the 7th in redistricting, backed Rose's GOP challenger.

As a whole, the district has a Democratic tilt — Democrats make up 70 percent of registered voters — that is usually reflected at the local and statewide levels. But in recent years, the vote has drifted toward the GOP at the national level.

New Hanover County, in the Cape Fear region, is the district's second most-populous. Population is centered in Wilmington, a 250-year-old port city nestled between the Cape Fear River and the Atlantic Ocean. The restoration of its waterfront area has brought tourism and some white-collar prosperity into this old fishing center, and the completion of I-40, which connects Wilmington to the Raleigh-Durham area, is expected to further boost the economy.

GOP strength is more pronounced in New Hanover County than in the rest of the 7th; it voted Republican in the 1988 presidential and gubernatorial elections. In 1992, Republicans carried the House, Senate and presidential elections, though former Democratic Gov. James B. Hunt Jr. did win New Hanover in the open gubernatorial race.

Blacks make up a sizable chunk of the region's population, but most are taken in by the fingers of the majority-minority 1st District, which reaches in all directions through the 7th.

American Indians are the 7th's other significant minority. Of the 80,000 Indians who live in North Carolina, half of them reside in Robeson County. The county is shared with the 8th District, but most of the Democratic-voting Indians live in the 7th.

1990 Population: 552,386. White 394,855 (71%), Black 103,428 (19%), Other 54,103 (10%). Hispanic origin 16,241 (3%). 18 and over 414,413 (75%), 62 and over 60,924 (11%). Median age: 29.

had some experience of his own with the rules of the House. In 1987, he was forced to defend himself against a complaint that he had improperly converted nearly $64,000 in campaign contributions for his own use and used campaign funds as collateral for a $75,000 personal loan.

Rose maintained that the $64,000 was repayment for loans he and his father had made to his first campaign, but in early 1988, the House ethics committee issued a formal "letter of reproval" to Rose for breaking House rules. No further action was taken, and Rose apologized for "inadvertent human errors."

Rose's relationship with the status quo was also called into question in 1992, when House Republicans, led by California Rep. Bill Thomas, ranking Republican of House Administration, pushed legislation that would bar mailings outside members' districts. Incumbents use such mailings in redistricting years to introduce themselves to voters they might represent after the next election.

Rose, who had updated House computers to improve members' ability to send mass mailings, made a statement in support of Thomas' bill. But he did not hold hearings on it in the House Administration Committee, indicating that he thought the bill fell more appropriately within the jurisdiction of the Post Office and Civil Service Committee.

Later, after a federal court had outlawed out-of-district mailings in July 1992, Rose gave a floor speech saying such mailings should be banned. And when Thomas' proposal came to the floor attached to other legislation, Rose voted for it.

At the outset of the 103rd, House Administration weathered the budget-cutting storm by approving an overall freeze in funding for congressional committees (and rejecting calls for cuts as deep as 25 percent). Rose had to spend some of his early-session energy defending administrative decisions he had made between sessions — in particular his decision to hire, without committee approval, former Rep. Larry Smith, D-Fla., as a consultant to the House Restaurant System.

At the same time, however, new circumstances on Agriculture were improving Rose's position. He was able to once again assert his authority over tobacco by assuming the chair of a newly created subcommittee on Specialty Crops and Natural Resources. The subcommittee's jurisdiction happened to include tobacco, peanuts and honey.

Tobacco has been a North Carolina way of life since early Colonial times, and Rose has spent much of his career close to the smoking controversy. He was besieged by anti-smoking forces in the 1980s, when he chaired the old Tobacco and Peanuts Subcommittee.

Rose had his biggest successes in that role in 1981, the first year he held the job. Tobacco subsidies were being attacked by a coalition of consumer advocates and urban fiscal conservatives when Rose came up with an ingenious argument. He told fellow Democrats that the entire North Carolina Democratic delegation might be wiped out at the polls in 1982 if the tobacco subsidy program died on the House floor. He sold his argument so well that, by the time of the vote, Speaker Thomas P. "Tip" O'Neill of Massachusetts sounded as loyal to tobacco as any Tarheel, and Rose prevailed by nearly 50 votes on the floor. The only compromise Rose was forced to accept required growers to pay the costs of storing surplus tobacco purchased by the government.

In the 101st Congress, Rose locked horns with North Carolina's senior senator, Republican Jesse Helms, over Rose's effort to require cigarette companies to track their use of foreign-grown tobacco. Rose and Helms have battled in the past in the internecine war between tobacco growers and cigarette manufacturers: Rose champions the growers' interest, while Helms has been allied with the manufacturers. Rose's language on the subject was eventually retained in the 1990 farm bill.

In 1987, Rose and other tobacco legislators were powerless to prevent a ban on smoking for short domestic air flights. The proposal arose on the House floor as an amendment to an appropriation bill and sailed to enactment. In 1989, Congress extended the ban to cover most domestic flights.

Tobacco was also under attack early in the 103rd. The biggest threat appears to be an increase in the federal tax on cigarettes. One idea being considered within the Clinton administration would raise the tax from 24 cents a pack to $2 a pack. Seemingly convinced that a tax increase is inevitable, Rose and other tobacco-state lawmakers are considering a plan that would put the greatest tax burden on tobacco manufacturers that rely heavily on tobacco imports for use in their products.

At Home: Unwilling to wait for Rep. Alton Lennon's long-promised retirement, Rose went after him in a 1970 primary and came so close that Lennon finally did retire two years later.

To run in 1970, Rose had to take a leave from his work as chief prosecutor in the 12th Judicial District (Cumberland and Hoke counties). Running a well-financed, well-organized campaign that called attention to Lennon's 64 years, Rose received a respectable 43 percent of the vote.

Early in 1971, Rose began producing a monthly television program outlining the history of each county in the district. He said the shows were not political, but made it clear he would try again for Congress in 1972. In December, Lennon announced his retirement.

State Sen. Hector McGeachy and Fayetteville lawyer Doran Berry joined Rose in the 1972 Democratic primary. Few issues separated them; Rose was better known because of his earlier campaign and because his father and grandfather had served in the Legislature.

Rose polled 49 percent in the initial primary, far ahead of McGeachy's 26 percent. Still, McGeachy demanded a runoff, and Rose won it with 56 percent.

In 1974, McGeachy was back again, challenging Rose in the primary with a campaign that courted the black vote. But Rose had used a mobile office during his first term to keep in touch with rural constituents, and he developed close ties with the district's business community. Rose won renomination with 61 percent, and that was his last significant primary challenge. Rose was unopposed in November 1974.

Some Republicans thought Rose's personal life might hamper him in the 1982 election. Shortly after receiving an uncontested divorce from his wife, Rose was married in September 1982 to an aide on his Tobacco and Peanuts Subcommittee. Voters, however, were apparently not bothered by the divorce and quick remarriage — Rose got 71 percent of the vote.

Rose was mentioned as a possible candidate for governor in 1984, when incumbent Democrat James B. Hunt Jr. left office. But he decided to stay in the House. Battling a Republican tide that diminished the Democrats' ranks in the congressional delegation from nine members to six, he was re-elected with 59 percent.

Rose also suffered a scare in 1986. He appeared headed for routine re-election when a political bomb dropped on him in mid-September. Media reports that Rose had borrowed money from his campaign committee raised questions about the propriety of his actions —

and gave a much-needed burst of momentum to GOP challenger Thomas J. Harrelson.

But if voters were concerned about Rose's propriety, they did not show it. Although Harrelson, a Southport businessman, former state House member and former state Environmental Management official, amassed more money than any Rose challenger in memory, he managed only 36 percent of the vote districtwide. In 1988 and 1990, Republicans ran poorly funded campaigns against Rose that failed to reach Harrelson's share level. The GOP nominees in those two years received almost identical numbers of votes.

The campaign contribution issue keeps Republicans talking about Rose in every cycle, usually to no avail. Rose's southeastern district remained basically intact with redistricting, and he escaped direct linkage with the scandals in the House bank and Post Office in 1992. But some constituents seemed to be holding him accountable for what happened on his watch and for his vote against authorizing the use of force in the Persian Gulf because Rose faced another weak challenger and managed just 57 percent: a career low.

Committees

House Administration (Chairman)
Administrative Oversight (chairman)

Agriculture (3rd of 28 Democrats)
Specialty Crops & Natural Resources (chairman); Department Operations; Foreign Agriculture & Hunger; General Farm Commodities; Livestock

Joint Library (Chairman)

Joint Printing (Vice Chairman)

Elections

1992 General		
Charlie Rose (D)	92,414	(57%)
Robert C. Anderson (R)	66,536	(41%)
Marc Kelley (LIBERT)	4,151	(3%)
1990 General		
Charlie Rose (D)	94,946	(66%)
Robert C. Anderson (R)	49,681	(34%)

Previous Winning Percentages: **1988** (67%) **1986** (64%) **1984** (59%) **1982** (71%) **1980** (69%) **1978** (70%) **1976** (81%) **1974** (100%) **1972** (60%)

District Vote for President

1992
D 70,664 (43%)
R 70,136 (43%)
I 22,216 (14%)

Campaign Finance

	Receipts	Receipts from PACs		Expend-itures
1992				
Rose (D)	$395,280	$251,535	(64%)	$254,579
Anderson (R)	$14,280	0		$17,374
1990				
Rose (D)	$328,232	$196,654	(60%)	$153,315
Anderson (R)	$24,449	0		$21,131

Key Votes

1993	
Require parental notification of minors' abortions	N
Require unpaid family and medical leave	Y
Approve national "motor voter" registration bill	Y
Approve budget increasing taxes and reducing deficit	Y
Approve economic stimulus plan	Y
1992	
Approve balanced-budget constitutional amendment	N
Close down space station program	N
Approve U.S. aid for former Soviet Union	Y
Allow shifting funds from defense to domestic programs	Y
1991	
Extend unemployment benefits using deficit financing	Y
Approve waiting period for handgun purchases	Y
Authorize use of force in Persian Gulf	N

Voting Studies

	Presidential Support		Party Unity		Conservative Coalition	
Year	S	O	S	O	S	O
1992	25	73	88	9	50	50
1991	29	63	84	8	38	57
1990	19	75	88	7	48	44
1989	36	58	85	10	37	61
1988	19	65	77	7	47	26
1987	30	61	79	10	72	19
1986	29	64	78	12	54	42
1985	28	70	84	10	53	42
1984	35	50	77	13	47	39
1983	26	61	74	12	42	42
1982	32	49	63	19	60	32
1981	49	43	54	22	63	25

Interest Group Ratings

Year	ADA	AFL-CIO	CCUS	ACU
1992	95	83	38	4
1991	70	92	40	0
1990	61	75	23	21
1989	80	83	50	15
1988	60	100	25	11
1987	76	75	43	5
1986	55	67	44	37
1985	60	56	25	17
1984	60	67	42	14
1983	75	75	31	10
1982	40	58	47	35
1981	50	85	29	23

North Carolina - 8th District

8 W.G. "Bill" Hefner (D)

Of Concord — Elected 1974; 10th Term

Born: April 11, 1930, Elora, Tenn.
Education: Graduated from Sardis H.S., 1948.
Occupation: Broadcasting executive.
Family: Wife, Nancy Hill; two children.
Religion: Baptist.
Political Career: No previous office.
Capitol Office: 2470 Rayburn Bldg. 20515; 225-3715.

In Washington: Hefner's experiences as a gospel singer and a radio executive would have served him well had he sought the congressional spotlight. However, the chairman of the Appropriations Subcommittee on Military Construction employs his down-to-earth style not on center stage, but in the back rooms where spending decisions are made.

The collapse of the Soviet military threat and growing concern over federal spending have put pressure on the U.S. defense budget. The drive to find savings has led to fierce debates over the need for certain expensive bombers, warships and other weapons systems.

But so far, the budget cutting has largely bypassed the pool of military construction money Hefner oversees as chairman. A fraction of the more than $275 billion appropriated for defense during George Bush's final year as president, the "mil-con" budget (about $8.5 billion) pays for such locally popular, noncontroversial projects as roads, buildings and housing at the nation's military facilities.

Still, the military construction budget is no longer growing, as it did during President Ronald Reagan's buildup in the early 1980s. And a substantial amount of Hefner's money pot is now dedicated to closing military bases deemed obsolete by a series of federal commissions.

From his position as chairman, Hefner does what he can to implant his priorities for military construction.

A spokesman for improved living and working conditions at domestic military bases, Hefner frequently favored efforts to divert money that the Reagan and Bush administrations requested for military construction overseas. He was an early advocate of demanding that U.S. allies pick up more of the cost for their own defense, a principle known as burden-sharing. (Hefner plays a low-key role in the overall defense debate as a member of the Appropriations Subcommittee on Defense.)

Hefner also derailed attempts to reduce the mil-con budget. In late 1991, he blasted a proposal by then-Defense Secretary Dick Cheney for a pause in construction spending. The members of the armed forces operate "the most sophisticated weapons in the world, and then you go and see . . . some of the conditions they live in — they're just atrocious," Hefner said.

He also has used his weight to keep controversial issues off his subcommittee's agenda. When the base-closing process began in 1989, some members with affected districts hinted that they might try use the military construction bill to bar funds to implement the shutdowns. Hefner pledged to block any rear-guard action. "The [full] committee can do whatever it wants, but I don't see it in this subcommittee," he said in March 1989.

The annual military construction bill is usually enacted with little public notice. Hefner gives audience to the House members who have requests for military construction projects in their districts; most requests are granted. Hefner does not leave his own constituents wanting. For example, recent bills have provided money to replace a hospital at Fort Bragg, which employs many residents of the 8th District.

A moderate Southern Democrat, Hefner acted during the early Reagan years as a liaison between the liberal Democratic leadership and the party's conservative members. But Hefner takes his cues from a more "progressive" strain of Southern Democratic politics: In 1986, 1988 and 1990, he opposed Reagan and Bush on more than 60 percent of House votes.

Hefner's uncharacteristic explosion of temper in August 1992 left no doubt about his party loyalties. Flamboyant GOP Rep. Robert K. Dornan of California denounced Democratic presidential candidate Bill Clinton on the House floor as a "womanizer/adulterer" and a "draft dodger." After his speech, Hefner — who had had heart bypass surgery two months before — confronted and almost came to blows with Dornan.

Yet Hefner's views on social issues show that he is a more conservative Democrat than Clinton. First elected in 1974 on a promise to restore "Christian morality" to government, Hefner opposes abortion except in cases of rape, incest or when the woman's life is in danger. In

North Carolina 8

South Central — Kannapolis; part of Fayetteville

Geography and jobs determine politics in the 8th. Along the I-77 and I-85 corridors, the textile-producing counties are wealthier and vote Republican. The poorer, rural counties that make up the district's eastern portion are Democratic.

The Republican voters of the 8th can be divided into two groups. The textile workers of Rowan and Cabarrus counties are centered in the towns of Concord, Kannapolis and Salisbury. They make textiles and textile machinery, and there is some tobacco processing.

Only part of Salisbury (Rowan County) is in the 8th, but all of Kannapolis is included. All of Cabarrus County (Concord), on the southern border of Rowan, is within 8th District confines.

Farther south, the Republican vote is of a suburban variety, in the Charlotte orbit (Mecklenburg County). Only a tiny part of Mecklenburg itself is in the 8th; the real lode of GOP votes is found in the bedroom communities of Union County, which is the district's second most-populous county after Cabarrus.

The vote here has become increasingly Republican over the past two decades, as Union County experienced a quadrupling of GOP registration. Many of these voters live in Charlotte satellites such as Indian Trail, Stallings, and Monroe, the Union County seat. Concord has also seen some Charlotte spillover.

In 1990, these Republican areas helped boost GOP Sen. Jesse Helms to a 55 percent showing in the 8th District against former Charlotte mayor Harvey B. Gantt. In 1992 presidential voting, George Bush carried the district's western section.

Anson County and the counties east of the Pee Dee River are more rural and agriculture-oriented; they also have a higher-percentage of black voters than the rest of the 8th. Of North Carolina's 10 white-majority congressional districts, the 8th has the highest percentage of blacks — 23 percent.

Blacks and American Indians make up a majority in the Democratic stronghold of Hoke County.

A small portion of Robeson County — home to a significant number of Lumbee Indians — is grafted onto the district's far southeastern fringe. Most of the county's Democratic-voting Indians are in the 7th District.

Gantt carried Anson, Hoke, Richmond and Robeson handily in 1990. In 1992, Bill Clinton easily won all four counties.

Neighboring Cumberland County is home to Fort Bragg and a chunk of black voters. The county is parceled among the 1st, 7th and 8th districts, all of which delve into the city of Fayetteville.

Moore County, in the Sandhills region, was once Democratic, but it is now an anomaly in the Democratic east. A steady stream of retirees to resorts and golfing communities has made it a Republican bastion. Most of the county — including the resorts of Pinehurst and Southern Pines — is in the 4th.

1990 Population: 552,387. White 402,406 (73%), Black 128,417 (23%), Other 21,564 (4%). Hispanic origin 7,771 (1%). 18 and over 403,678 (73%), 62 and over 79,038 (14%). Median age: 33.

January 1993, he proposed a constitutional amendment to guarantee the right of Americans to pray in public places, including school graduations and athletic events.

The long-tenured Hefner made one bid for a House leadership position, when he ran for majority whip at the start of the 100th Congress. But he seemed uncomfortable asking colleagues for support and received just 15 of 260 votes in a contest won by then-California Rep. Tony Coelho.

At Home: Even quintuple heart bypass surgery could not quench Hefner's fighting spirit in 1992. He took exception to some of Dornan's comments about Bill Clinton for good reason. In 1984 and 1988, Hefner was almost dragged under by a wave of GOP presidential votes.

But, as expected, Clinton provided relative cover for Hefner in 1992. Not only did he knock off the strong challenge of state Rep. Coy C. Privette, but he did so by winning 58 percent of the vote in a three-way race.

In 1984, Hefner's GOP opponent was Harris D. Blake, a hardware store owner and former member of the Moore County Board of Education who had challenged him in 1982.

Blake benefited from Ronald Reagan's presence at the top of the ticket, and from the financial support of Helms' National Congressional Club; he carried a five-county area in the northern and central parts of the district. Hefner clung to his base among the traditionally Democratic counties at the district's southern end, eking out 51 percent.

Two years later, Hefner climbed back up to 58 percent, but 1988 brought more trouble. The

GOP touted its challenger, lawyer Ted Blanton, but most Democrats did not take his effort too seriously.

But Blanton put himself in a position to ride a wave of GOP presidential votes, and that wave came crashing in on Election Day. He took 49 percent overall; Hefner again survived because of his strong base in the Democratic counties in the south.

With great fanfare from national Republicans, Blanton was back in 1990. However, Blanton did not excel at fundraising. Nor did his campaign's prestige soar when media reports noted that he had spent $11,660 for living expenses, using campaign funds for such personal expenses as his home mortgage and babysitting.

Blanton counted on a torrent of anti-incumbent sentiment to wash Hefner out of office. But a more attentive Hefner, armed with a superior campaign operation, rebuffed the Republican, winning 55 percent of the vote.

Running in 1974, Hefner pledged to revive "Christian morality" in government and laced his political speeches with renditions of his favorite hymns. That might have been seen as an incautious church-state mixture in some places, but not in the Bible Belt 8th. As a promoter and singer of gospel music in the Carolinas and Virginia, he had made many local and statewide TV appearances. With his excellent name recognition, he gradually won back thousands of conservative Democrats who had drifted toward GOP Rep. Earl B. Ruth. Hefner's blend of inspiration, entertainment and politicking helped him soundly defeat Ruth.

Committee

Appropriations (14th of 37 Democrats)
Military Construction (chairman); Defense

Elections

1992 General		
W. G. "Bill" Hefner (D)	113,162	(58%)
Coy C. Privette (R)	71,842	(37%)
J. Wendell Drye (LIBERT)	10,447	(5%)
1992 Primary		
W. G. "Bill" Hefner (D)	32,790	(67%)
Don Dawkins (D)	16,373	(33%)
1990 General		
W. G. "Bill" Hefner (D)	98,700	(55%)
Ted Blanton (R)	80,852	(45%)

Previous Winning Percentages: **1988** (51%) **1986** (58%) **1984** (51%) **1982** (57%) **1980** (59%) **1978** (59%) **1976** (66%) **1974** (57%)

District Vote for President

1992
D 81,769 (42%)
R 85,753 (44%)
I 27,018 (14%)

Campaign Finance

	Receipts	Receipts from PACs		Expend-itures
1992				
Hefner (D)	$566,530	$356,179	(63%)	$594,617
Privette (R)	$108,333	$8,505	(8%)	$108,332
1990				
Hefner (D)	$660,311	$445,293	(67%)	$656,383
Blanton (R)	$306,813	$34,074	(11%)	$300,893

Key Votes

1993	
Require parental notification of minors' abortions	N
Require unpaid family and medical leave	Y
Approve national "motor voter" registration bill	Y
Approve budget increasing taxes and reducing deficit	Y
Approve economic stimulus plan	Y
1992	
Approve balanced-budget constitutional amendment	?
Close down space station program	Y
Approve U.S. aid for former Soviet Union	N
Allow shifting funds from defense to domestic programs	Y
1991	
Extend unemployment benefits using deficit financing	Y
Approve waiting period for handgun purchases	Y
Authorize use of force in Persian Gulf	N

Voting Studies

	Presidential Support		Party Unity		Conservative Coalition	
Year	**S**	**O**	**S**	**O**	**S**	**O**
1992	13	53	61	8	38	21
1991	34	59	79	16	78	19
1990	33	67	79	19	89	11
1989	41	55	75	19	78	10
1988	29	61	76	15	68	16
1987	33	65	81	15	84	16
1986	30	67	80	13	64	26
1985	35	49	63	12	60	7
1984	48	45	64	25	80	17
1983	40	54	66	21	72	22
1982	47	48	57 †	39 †	87 †	10 †
1981	53	41	57	33	76	23

† Not eligible for all recorded votes.

Interest Group Ratings

Year	ADA	AFL-CIO	CCUS	ACU
1992	40	88	17	6
1991	55	91	40	10
1990	44	58	50	38
1989	65	75	50	26
1988	65	92	50	25
1987	64	75	40	4
1986	50	57	40	36
1985	25	53	37	46
1984	40	54	47	33
1983	45	75	56	27
1982	20	50	64	67
1981	35	79	31	33

9 Alex McMillan (R)

Of Charlotte — Elected 1984; 5th Term

Born: May 9, 1932, Charlotte, N.C.
Education: U. of North Carolina, B.A. 1954; U. of Virginia, M.B.A. 1958.
Military Service: Army, 1954-56.
Occupation: Food store executive.
Family: Wife, Caroline Houston; two children.
Religion: Presbyterian.
Political Career: Mecklenburg County Commission, 1972-74.
Capitol Office: 401 Cannon Bldg. 20515; 225-1976.

In Washington: McMillan has come of age in the House at perhaps both the right and the wrong times. He is a quintessential Charlottean, conservative but not overly ideological — pragmatic to a fault from a city whose power base of affluent bankers and insurance executives happily wears its reputation for progressive politics.

But McMillan is the protégé of Minority Leader Robert H. Michel of Illinois, just when Michel's influence in the Republican Conference has been eclipsed by more adversarial leaders, such as Newt Gingrich of Georgia and Dick Armey of Texas.

Michel, who made McMillan his designee to the Budget Committee in the 102nd Congress, was unable to engineer McMillan's selection as the committee's ranking member in the 103rd. McMillan would have seemed the logical heir to the mantle worn by like-minded Ohio moderate Bill Gradison, who was giving up the ranking spot. Instead, the GOP tapped John R. Kasich, a more aggressive member of the Ohio delegation, who in recent years has championed (with minimal success) alternative budgets to those fashioned by the Democrats.

If McMillan does not fit the mold of opposition naysayer, however, he might turn out to be just the sort of Republican who can work with Democrats in the House and in the White House — who know there will come times when they will need Republican votes.

In the 101st and 102nd Congresses, McMillan showed himself to be a good soldier for the Bush administration under adverse conditions. He supported the 1990 bipartisan budget agreement crafted by congressional leaders and the president, when many House Republicans ran for cover from its tax increases. Then in 1992, when an impasse among Republicans was preventing the House from voting to put more money into the depleted coffers of the thrift bailout, McMillan worked the cloakroom trying to line up votes for the administration. (Democrats refused to vote for more money unless a majority of Republicans went along.)

Also in 1992, he and Gradison tried to negotiate a long-term deficit-reduction plan with Budget Committee Chairman Leon E. Panetta, D-Calif. McMillan's unwillingness to take a no-tax pledge in the negotiations may have cost him the ranking spot on Budget. But the experience might prove fruitful in the 103rd, with Panetta running President Clinton's Office of Management and Budget.

Beyond Budget, McMillan has begun building a base on the Energy and Commerce Committee, where North Carolina once had an influential voice in ranking Republican James T. Broyhill. After Broyhill was appointed to the Senate in 1986, McMillan worked to replace him, winning the committee seat on his second try, at the start of the 101st Congress. (He lobbied unsuccessfully for Ways and Means.) Charlotte is home to financial institutions that play an ever-widening role in regional and national banking. And thanks to its wide jurisdictional responsibilities, Energy and Commerce is arguably more important to the district's commerce than is Banking, where McMillan was a less visible member during his first two terms.

Though committee Democrats believe McMillan is someone with whom they can work, he can be a willing adversary. In the 102nd he led GOP efforts to thwart an expansion of the so-called Exon-Florio amendment to permit the president to block foreign takeovers of U.S. businesses. And he worked to scale back the Consumer Product Safety Commission, ultimately forcing a compromise on a reduced authorization level for the agency.

In keeping with his business background, McMillan is loath to impose mandates on employers. In 1989 he supported President Bush's veto of a bill raising the minimum wage to $4.55. In the 101st and 102nd Congresses, McMillan voted against family leave and civil rights legislation that employers contended would unduly burden them. But he is not a complete devotee of free enterprise, supporting quotas on imported textiles — a necessity, given his region's economic interest — even in

North Carolina 9

West Central — Part of Charlotte

The boom times of the 1970s and 1980s have transformed Charlotte into the economic colossus of North Carolina and a rival to Atlanta in regional economic clout.

With a highly diversified economy, Charlotte serves as a supply, service and distribution center for the Piedmont region of North and South Carolina. The city's big banking concerns have expanded their influence beyond the Southeast, becoming prominent players in financial affairs all along the Eastern seaboard. And if having a professional basketball team is a prerequisite for a city to claim national prominence, then the recent arrival of the Hornets franchise meets that condition.

The Uptown central business district has the headquarters of the Duke Power Co., NationsBank and First Union Bank as well as numerous other banking and insurance operations. Many of the white-collar executives who work in the downtown office towers commute from the affluent southeastern part of the city, where the old-line GOP establishment is based.

The city's Republican leanings are leavened by working-class Democratic allegiances and a black community that accounts for one-third of the population. The city weathered racial tensions over busing in the early 1970s, and in 1983 Charlotte elected its first black mayor, Harvey B. Gantt. He won virtually all the black vote, but also drew significant white support.

Attending Charlotte's economic prosperity has been rampant growth in the city and surrounding Mecklenburg County, leading to problems with traffic congestion and scraps between established neighborhoods and developers. The county once had substantial rural areas, particularly in the north, but the pastoral lands are giving way to suburban sprawl.

Politically, Mecklenburg is a mixed bag. Blacks and working-class whites keep the county competitive for Democrats at the state and local levels. In 1990, Gantt, the Democratic nominee against GOP Sen. Jesse Helms, carried 58 percent of the county's vote. Former Democratic Gov. James B. Hunt Jr. won Mecklenburg with 53 percent in his 1992 bid to recapture the office.

Presidential elections are a different story. The county has gone Republican in the past four White House contests, albeit narrowly for George Bush in 1992.

The 9th used to contain the county in its entirety, but 1992 redistricting divided it between the 9th and 12th districts (with a small part in the 8th). Most of the county's blacks, who live north and west of the central city, are included in the black-majority 12th.

Mecklenburg County has roughly two-thirds of the 9th's population, and, without Charlotte's black votes, the district is a GOP stronghold.

The 12th cuts a thin line west through the 9th, into Gastonia (Gaston County) to siphon out more black votes. Most of the Republican, textile-oriented county is in the 9th, though, accounting for nearly a third of the district's population.

1990 Population: 552,387. White 492,424 (89%), Black 49,308 (9%), Other 10,655 (2%). Hispanic origin 5,820 (1%). 18 and over 421,616 (76%), 62 and over 69,897 (13%). Median age: 33.

the face of presidential vetoes.

McMillan revealed his moderate streak during 1988 debate on the omnibus drug bill, when he was one of five Southern Republicans voting to retain a seven-day waiting period for handgun purchases. Though he had received more than $10,000 in campaign contributions from the National Rifle Association since first running for Congress, he voted against the NRA position. McMillan did so again in May 1991, when the House approved the waiting period. And in 1991 he voted in committee to end an administration-imposed "gag rule" against abortion counseling in federally supported family planning clinics. Despite his strong anti-abortion voting record, McMillan said the issue was freedom of speech.

At Home: McMillan may have a more patrician demeanor than James G. Martin and Charles Raper Jonas, the previous two GOP incumbents in his district, but his fiscal conservatism and his emphasis on economics over social issues put him in the Martin-Jonas mold.

In securing his 1984 victory, McMillan drew heavily on a local GOP network established a generation ago by Jonas and cultivated by Martin, whose bid for governor opened the 9th. That network, anchored in wealthy southeastern Charlotte, helped McMillan get past a strong Democratic foe by a scant 321 votes.

Although he had last served in public office in 1974, McMillan was widely regarded as a top GOP prospect. A Democrat-turned-Republican, he won his one previous election in 1972, capturing the Mecklenburg County (Charlotte) Commission seat left vacant by Martin, who ran successfully that year for the House. McMillan retired from his post after one term, citing a desire to focus on his business career, eventually moving up in the ranks in the retail food industry to become president of Harris-Teeter Super Markets Inc., a local chain.

When Martin announced his gubernatorial bid in 1983, McMillan began actively seeking the seat. Although a favorite, he encountered a formidable primary obstacle in Carl "Buddy" Horn, who served for two years in the Civil Rights Division of the Reagan Justice Department and who had the endorsement of Sen. Jesse Helms' National Congressional Club. Horn's support for school prayer and a constitutional amendment to ban abortion rallied fundamentalist Christians and contrasted markedly with McMillan's moderate politics.

With early spring polls showing Horn ahead, McMillan went on the offensive, running television ads branding Horn a "rookie" and reminding Republicans that Horn had voted for Democrat George McGovern for president in 1972. McMillan won the primary with 58 percent.

McMillan had a tougher time in the fall. His opponent was D. G. Martin, a lawyer and political neophyte who proved capable of attracting support in Democratic areas and in southeastern Charlotte's wealthy white communities.

McMillan invoked his experience as a retailer to legitimize his call for a freeze on federal spending. He criticized Martin for his willingness to raise taxes to deal with the deficit and for supporting homosexual rights.

Martin won Mecklenburg County, which dominates the district, but thanks to a financial advantage and top-of-the-ticket GOP strength, McMillan took enough margins in three outlying counties to overcome his Mecklenburg loss.

Martin tried again in 1986. He kept up his visibility by writing a column in a free weekly newspaper and by making regular appearances on a local cable television show. But Martin had trouble finding issues to use against McMillan, who left little to chance. He used his position on Banking to court some of the businessmen who had backed Martin in 1984. Martin again got a narrow lead in Mecklenburg. But McMillan's well-funded advertising blitz helped him stay close in Charlotte, and he overcame the deficit in the outlying counties to win with 51 percent.

With those first two tough campaigns under his belt, McMillan moved on to easy victories in 1988, 1990 and 1992.

Committees

Budget (2nd of 17 Republicans)

Energy & Commerce (8th of 17 Republicans)
Commerce, Consumer Protection & Competitiveness; Health & the Environment; Telecommunications & Finance

Elections

1992 General

Alex McMillan (R)	153,650	(67%)
Rory Blake (D)	74,583	(33%)

1990 General

Alex McMillan (R)	131,936	(62%)
David P. McKnight (D)	80,802	(38%)

Previous Winning Percentages: **1988** (66%) **1986** (51%) **1984** (50%)

District Vote for President

1992

D 80,953 (33%)
R 131,335 (53%)
I 36,706 (15%)

Campaign Finance

	Receipts	Receipts from PACs		Expend-itures
1992				
McMillan (R)	$345,961	$268,000	(77%)	$236,315
Blake (D)	$31,720	$2,350	(7%)	$30,914
1990				
McMillan (R)	$399,007	$278,085	(70%)	$385,183

Key Votes

1993

Require parental notification of minors' abortions	Y
Require unpaid family and medical leave	N
Approve national "motor voter" registration bill	N
Approve budget increasing taxes and reducing deficit	N
Approve economic stimulus plan	N

1992

Approve balanced-budget constitutional amendment	Y
Close down space station program	N
Approve U.S. aid for former Soviet Union	?
Allow shifting funds from defense to domestic programs	N

1991

Extend unemployment benefits using deficit financing	N
Approve waiting period for handgun purchases	Y
Authorize use of force in Persian Gulf	Y

Voting Studies

	Presidential Support		Party Unity		Conservative Coalition	
Year	**S**	**O**	**S**	**O**	**S**	**O**
1992	78	17	83	14	94	6
1991	78	22	85	14	92	8
1990	66	33	79	19	85	13
1989	80	17	78	20	98	0
1988	61	38	79	19	89	11
1987	64	36	83	16	98	2
1986	66	32	69	28	94	6
1985	79	20	81	15	98	2

Interest Group Ratings

Year	ADA	AFL-CIO	CCUS	ACU
1992	15	33	88	84
1991	15	25	100	85
1990	11	17	79	67
1989	0	8	100	74
1988	15	21	100	88
1987	4	6	100	83
1986	10	36	100	82
1985	5	6	91	81

10 Cass Ballenger (R)

Of Hickory — Elected 1986; 4th Term

Born: Dec. 6, 1926, Hickory, N.C.

Education: U. of North Carolina, 1944-45; Amherst College, B.A. 1948.

Military Service: Navy Air Corps, 1944-45.

Occupation: Plastics company executive.

Family: Wife, Donna Davis; three children.

Religion: Episcopalian.

Political Career: Catawba County Board of Commissioners, 1966-74, chairman, 1970-74; N.C. House, 1975-77; N.C. Senate, 1977-86.

Capitol Office: 2238 Rayburn Bldg. 20515; 225-2576.

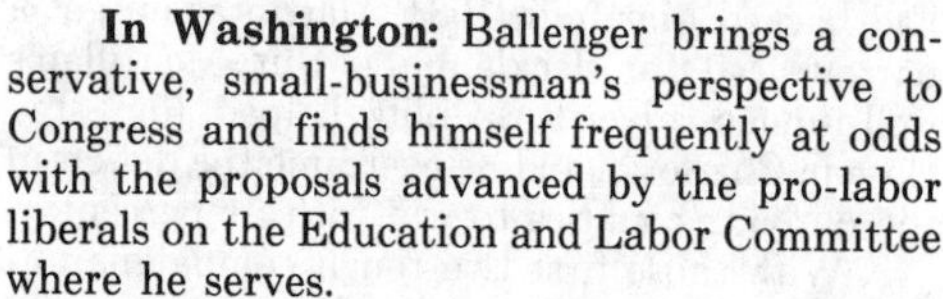

In Washington: Ballenger brings a conservative, small-businessman's perspective to Congress and finds himself frequently at odds with the proposals advanced by the pro-labor liberals on the Education and Labor Committee where he serves.

The prompt enactment in early 1993 of a long-fought bill requiring businesses to provide unpaid family leave bodes ill for Ballenger. But as an early backer and close ally of Dick Armey of Texas, Ballenger is not of the mettle to back down from the partisan fight that has defined the committee — especially on labor issues — in recent years.

While the combative Armey, the Republican Conference chairman, frequently defines the opposite stance from Democratic Chairman William D. Ford of Michigan (with whom Armey has a somewhat rancorous relationship), Ballenger can sometimes offer an alternative, based on his business experience, that can appeal to Democrats.

Ballenger has fought efforts to raise the minimum wage, arguing that it would hurt small businesses by increasing labor costs and ultimately costing jobs. He has opposed committee bills strengthening existing worker safety and health rules and one requiring employers to notify employees before they close a plant, again on grounds that they were too costly. And he opposed a relatively minor bill in 1991 requiring businesses to warn their employees of any electronic monitoring, saying that it was just another measure in a long list of misguided government regulations.

Acknowledging a deep interest in foreign policy, especially in Central America, Ballenger traded a coveted seat on the Public Works and Transportation Committee for a position on the Foreign Affairs Committee. He also picked up an assignment on the District of Columbia panel.

In the global arena as in domestic policy, Ballenger emerges as a tightfisted manager. In 1992, he voted against giving aid to the new democratic regime in Russia. His fiscal conservatism also swayed him from supporting a spending bill for fiscal 1993 that contained loan guarantees to Israel.

In the years when Congress hotly debated U.S. support for the Nicaraguan contras, Ballenger took a personal interest in the region; he and his wife had performed volunteer work in Guatemala in the 1970s. In October 1987, they went to Nicaragua to help restart Radio Católica, the voice of the Catholic Church. Shortly after Radio Católica resumed broadcasting, the Sandinista government renewed its censorship of the station. Incensed, Ballenger took the House floor to denounce the government, and called those sympathetic to it "witless peaceniks."

Ballenger is capable of loosening his firm grasp on the purse strings if the recipient falls into one of his areas of special concern, such as measures originating in the Select Education Subcommittee, where he is ranking Republican. He complained during panel consideration of a bill in 1992 that sought to extend the authority of the Department of Education's research and development arm that the funding level was only enough to continue existing research.

The health of the textile industry also is a special concern. His district leads the nation in textile workers, and as a member of the House Textile Caucus, in 1990 he helped gain a three-year extension of a suspension of duties on some imported textile machines.

Ballenger is a loyal party man, but he can stray from the conservative fold. Although he supported President Ronald Reagan's anti-abortion stance, he was one of 27 House members who changed position in 1989 by voting with the abortion rights side on an appropriations bill. Ballenger said his wife and three daughters persuaded him to change his mind.

In 1991 he voted with anti-abortion members on another appropriations measure but said it was because of funding questions, not abortion. The following year he joined the abortion rights supporters, this time backing a free-

North Carolina 10

West — Hickory; Lincolnton

Splashed across the western Piedmont Plateau and the Appalachian and Blue Ridge mountains is the most rock-ribbed Republican district in North Carolina — the 10th.

In 1990, GOP Sen. Jesse Helms posted his best showing in any North Carolina district in what was then the 10th. Against Democratic challenger Harvey B. Gantt, Helms captured 66 percent of the vote. In 1992 presidential voting, George Bush won the 10th with more than 50 percent, one of his better showings in the country.

The 10th is composed of six whole counties and parts of 11 more. It is small-town North Carolina: No city has more than 30,000 residents. Textiles, furniture and agriculture form the backbone of the economy.

From the main body of the district, three heads sprout forth: one in the north, one reaching northwest to the Tennessee border and one stretching west toward Asheville, but stopping short.

Catawba County, in the main cluster of counties, is the population center. The furniture-making industry — particularly upholstered furniture — employs a large segment of the work force in Hickory (the largest city entirely in the 10th). There is also production of cotton and synthetic yarns.

Neighboring Iredell County — split among the 8th, 10th and 12th districts — is mostly rural and agricultural, with some manufacturing. It is the second-most populous jurisdiction in the 10th.

Northeast of Catawba County, the district takes in parts of Davie and Forsyth counties and all of Yadkin County. The Forsyth portion is west of Winston-Salem.

Textile- and furniture-oriented Davie and textile- and tobacco-producing Yadkin are die-hard Republican bastions. Yadkin was one of just 13 North Carolina counties to back Barry Goldwater in 1964. In 1980, when the Republican gubernatorial nominee pulled in an anemic 37 percent, Yadkin and Davie counties were in his corner. Sen. Helms is especially popular in these counties: In 1990, he won 70 percent in Davie.

West of Yadkin County, the district line makes a loop through Republican Wilkes County. A section of the 5th District slices down into the 10th; beyond it are more Republican votes in mountainous Avery and Mitchell counties, on the Tennessee border.

In 1992, both counties voted a straight Republican ticket: presidential, Senate, gubernatorial and House. Both backed successful GOP Senate challenger Lauch Faircloth over Democratic Sen. Terry Sanford by better than 2-to-1.

A segment of the 10th reaches into the woodlands of Western North Carolina, taking in parts of Buncombe, Henderson, McDowell, Polk and Rutherford counties. Forestry, tourism and recreation are staples of the local economies here. Buncombe is competitive for both parties but does not provide enough votes to make a dent in the 10th. The other counties lean Republican.

1990 Population: 552,386. White 517,542 (94%), Black 30,155 (5%), Other 4,689 (1%). Hispanic origin 3,991 (1%). 18 and over 421,456 (76%), 62 and over 83,185 (15%). Median age: 35.

standing bill to release federally funded family planning clinics from an administration ban on discussing abortion.

Ballenger readily stepped forward early in 1993 when the "Nannygate" scandal rattled the new administration and led to the demise of two prospective U.S. attorneys general. He was one of 11 lawmakers who admitted to The Washington Times that they had been delinquent in paying taxes on domestic employees. In his case it was a part-time housekeeper, and he said he would rectify the situation "on Friday, when she comes in."

At Home: The 10th was open in 1986 because its veteran incumbent, Republican James T. Broyhill, had been appointed to the Senate. Both Ballenger and George S. Robinson, his chief GOP rival, promised to emulate Broyhill.

Ballenger was a state senator who had founded a plastics company and built it into a 250-employee business. He reminded audiences that he had been on the state advisory budget commission under two GOP governors and once served on a White House panel on economic affairs. Robinson, a pro-business state representative from Broyhill's hometown of Lenoir, was president of a lumber company.

Robinson's backers pointed out that their candidate, who at age 40 was roughly 20 years younger than Ballenger, would be able to build seniority in the way Broyhill had. But Ballenger enhanced his link with Broyhill by endorsing him in his Senate primary fight, then chastising Robinson for not doing the same. (Robinson subsequently did.)

Ballenger also accused Robinson of having ties to the National Congressional Club, GOP Sen. Jesse Helms' political organization that was backing Broyhill's primary foe. The claim irked some Robinson supporters all the way through November. Robinson had no official links to the club and did have ties to Broyhill: He started his political career as his campaign driver.

Ballenger, a former Catawba County commissioner, had a strong base in what was then the district's second-largest county, and he ran harder than Robinson in populous Gastonia. In November, Ballenger won a comfortable 57 percent against Democrat Lester D. Roark, the former mayor of Shelby.

In subsequent elections, Ballenger has won easily, never falling below 61 percent.

Committees

District of Columbia (4th of 4 Republicans)
Fiscal Affairs & Health (ranking); Judiciary & Education

Education & Labor (8th of 15 Republicans)
Select Education (ranking); Labor-Management Relations; Labor Standards, Occupational Health & Safety

Foreign Affairs (13th of 18 Republicans)
Economic Policy, Trade & the Environment; Western Hemisphere Affairs

Elections

1992 General		
Cass Ballenger (R)	149,033	(63%)
Ben Neill (D)	79,206	(34%)
Jeffrey Clayton Brown (LIBERT)	6,888	(3%)
1990 General		
Cass Ballenger (R)	106,400	(62%)
Daniel R. Green Jr. (D)	65,710	(38%)

Previous Winning Percentages: 1988 (61%) 1986 * (57%)

** Elected to a full term and to fill a vacancy at the same time.*

District Vote for President

1992
D 76,021 (32%)
R 127,067 (53%)
I 35,546 (15%)

Campaign Finance

	Receipts	Receipts from PACs		Expend-itures
1992				
Ballenger (R)	$277,122	$167,925	(61%)	$278,963
Neill (D)	$25,660	$6,500	(25%)	$23,101
1990				
Ballenger (R)	$297,417	$183,749	(62%)	$302,006
Green (D)	$39,178	$11,800	(30%)	$37,846

Key Votes

1993	
Require parental notification of minors' abortions	Y
Require unpaid family and medical leave	N
Approve national "motor voter" registration bill	N
Approve budget increasing taxes and reducing deficit	N
Approve economic stimulus plan	N
1992	
Approve balanced-budget constitutional amendment	Y
Close down space station program	Y
Approve U.S. aid for former Soviet Union	N
Allow shifting funds from defense to domestic programs	N
1991	
Extend unemployment benefits using deficit financing	N
Approve waiting period for handgun purchases	N
Authorize use of force in Persian Gulf	Y

Voting Studies

	Presidential Support		Party Unity		Conservative Coalition	
Year	S	O	S	O	S	O
1992	69	27	90	6	83	10
1991	79	17	93	3	100	0
1990	73	26	90	6	91	6
1989	79	20	93	5	95	5
1988	63	35	94	5	95	5
1987	71	27	91	7	98	2

Interest Group Ratings

Year	ADA	AFL-CIO	CCUS	ACU
1992	10	27	75	92
1991	10	17	90	95
1990	6	8	86	83
1989	10	9	100	96
1988	10	14	100	92
1987	8	19	93	82

11 Charles H. Taylor (R)

Of Brevard — Elected 1990; 2nd Term

Born: Jan. 23, 1941, Brevard, N.C.
Education: Wake Forest U., B.A. 1963, J.D. 1966.
Occupation: Tree farmer; banker.
Family: Wife, Elizabeth Owen; three children.
Religion: Baptist.
Political Career: N.C. House, 1967-73, minority leader, 1969-71; N.C. Senate, 1973-75, minority leader, 1973-75; GOP nominee for U.S. House, 1988.
Capitol Office: 516 Cannon Bldg. 20515; 225-6401.

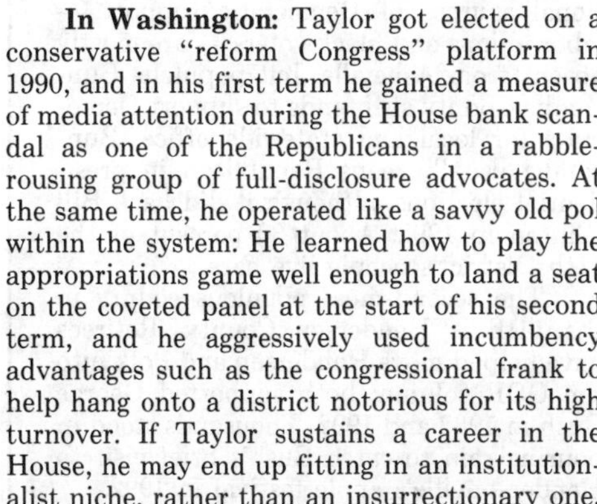

In Washington: Taylor got elected on a conservative "reform Congress" platform in 1990, and in his first term he gained a measure of media attention during the House bank scandal as one of the Republicans in a rabble-rousing group of full-disclosure advocates. At the same time, he operated like a savvy old pol within the system: He learned how to play the appropriations game well enough to land a seat on the coveted panel at the start of his second term, and he aggressively used incumbency advantages such as the congressional frank to help hang onto a district notorious for its high turnover. If Taylor sustains a career in the House, he may end up fitting in an institutionalist niche, rather than an insurrectionary one.

A millionaire tree farmer and banker, Taylor capitalized on anti-Congress sentiment to win the 11th on his second try in 1990. Arriving in Washington with an agenda for change, he stressed his support for a balanced-budget constitutional amendment, a presidential line-item veto and 12-year term limits. He favored repeal of the raise that took House pay from $89,500 in 1989 to $125,100 in 1991, and he donated his net proceeds from that increase to district charities.

In a piece of reform soldiering on behalf of the GOP, Taylor in July 1992 proposed a constitutional amendment to make party ratios on committees and subcommittees directly proportional to overall party representation in the House.

"Even though Republicans constitute 38 percent of the House and Democrats 62 percent, some committees and subcommittees give only 30 percent of their seats to the Republicans," he said in a statement introducing the measure. "As the majority dilutes the political power of minority representatives, they disenfranchise the electorate the minority represents."

The amendment proposal and the four other measures Taylor sponsored in the 102nd Congress died in committee. None of those or his other first-term efforts brought him nearly as much public notice as did his membership in the "Gang of Seven." Taylor and six other class of '90 Republican freshmen confronted Democrats and tweaked protocol with full-disclosure demands during the House bank overdraft scandal that first arose in September 1991 and steamed well into 1992. The leadership closed the bank, and full disclosure of overdrafters came despite an ethics committee recommendation to the contrary.

Though he was the lowest-profile member of the gang, Taylor was involved enough to get political mileage out of the perk-bashing effort in his 1992 re-election campaign.

Taylor made full use of another incumbent's perk, the franking privilege. In September 1991, the Gannett News Service reported that Taylor had spent in excess of $207,000 on taxpayer-financed mailings, more than all but eight other members. In 1992, the House downsized its franking allocations, but Taylor still mailed generously, spending 98 percent of the allocation, according to The Associated Press. In explaining the mailings, Taylor's office noted that it is difficult to reach constituents in all corners of the sprawling 11th with media advertising.

Also, in his 1992 campaign Taylor heard criticism from his Democratic challenger for his 1991 congressional office budget of $850,000, "the highest of any North Carolina Congress member," according to The Charlotte Observer.

Taylor curried favor with the home folk by bringing home federal pork. In 1991, he persuaded the Bush administration and fellow members to approve a $29.8 million appropriation for a new federal building in Asheville. Though money had been provided in 1990 to buy the building site, President Bush had left construction funds out of his fiscal 1992 budget, and Taylor successfully lobbied in a pinchpenny atmosphere to make sure building money was allocated from General Services Administration funds.

In 1992, he got $12.6 million of Department of Veterans Affairs money set aside for a new nursing home at the Asheville VA medical center.

The health-care industry is growing in the 11th, as is the number of retirees, who are drawn to the area by the relatively low cost of living and temperate climate.

North Carolina 11

West — Asheville

In the 1980s, the mountains of Western North Carolina were the stage for arguably the most competitive congressional district in the nation. In 1980, 1982, 1984, 1986 and 1990, voters tossed out their incumbent. Every contest between 1982 and 1990 was decided by fewer than 5,000 votes.

The current 11th District is slightly more Democratic than the 1980s version, but as voters proved in the 1992 House race, party affiliation counts for little.

Most of the mountainous district is covered by the Cherokee, Nantahala and Pisgah national forests or the Great Smoky Mountains National Park. Accordingly, the local political and economic agenda often revolves around development and natural resource issues.

Tourism and recreation revenues also have a disproportionate impact on local economies, especially in the poorer, far western tip of the state.

The heart of Western North Carolina is Asheville (Buncombe County). Known as "The Land of the Sky" for its location high in the Blue Ridge Mountains, the city is the biggest in the 11th.

An expanding health-care industry and some light industry anchor Asheville's economy, and the city is also a hub for the southern Appalachian and Cherokee arts and crafts produced in the region.

Asheville and surrounding communities have found recent years especially prosperous, due to a wave of newcomers who have discovered the region's low property taxes and temperate climate.

Retirees and business executives seeking a second home have fueled a building boom in towns such as Flat Rock and Hendersonville in Henderson County, and in Tryon (Polk County), where upscale condominiums are popping up on mountainsides and in the piney woods. The University of North Carolina-Asheville responded to the influx by setting up the North Carolina Center for Creative Retirement.

The combination of retirees and traditional mountain Republicans keeps the 11th competitive, despite a wide Democratic registration advantage. Two traditional sources of Democratic support — labor unions and black voters — are mostly absent from Asheville, but populous Buncombe County still tends to support Democrats for local and statewide office. Buncombe usually leans Republican in presidential elections, although it did back Bill Clinton in 1992. About 30 percent of the 11th District's people live here.

The second-most populous county in the 11th is Henderson County. Retirees have helped move Henderson and Polk into the GOP column; both supported George Bush in 1988 and 1992. Thousands stood in pouring rain to catch Bush's brief visit to Hendersonville's apple festival in 1992.

Outside Buncombe County, there is some labor strength in the paper and pulp mill towns. The poorer Tennessee-border counties have experienced trying times as several sawmills have shut down; this translated into support for Clinton in 1992.

1990 Population: 552,387. White 502,058 (91%), Black 39,767 (7%), Other 10,562 (2%). Hispanic origin 3,633 (1%). 18 and over 430,457 (78%), 62 and over 116,213 (21%). Median age: 38.

Taylor focused on these GOP-leaning constituents in his National Triad Program Act, a bill to establish programs that would help state and local agencies to prevent crimes against the elderly. He reintroduced the measure early in the 103rd.

Environment vs. jobs issues also regularly arise in the 11th, a heavily wooded region that includes several national forests and part of the Great Smoky Mountains National Park. Running in 1990 as a challenger who was pegged as pro-development, Taylor took issue with Democratic Rep. James McClure Clarke's bill designating 90 percent of the park a wilderness area. A member of the Interior and Insular Affairs Committee in his first term, Taylor showed his support for local lumber interests in opposing a bill sponsored by then-Democratic Rep. Ed Jenkins of Georgia that set 7,800 acres of Chattahoochee National Forest off-limits to loggers. Taylor said the bill would cost thousands of jobs in North Carolina lumber mills dependent on Georgia timber. But the bill became law.

At the beginning of the 103rd, media reports said North Carolina GOP Sen. Jesse Helms was proposing a land deal that would set aside 13,000 forested acres as wilderness in exchange for opening 13,000 acres for general use. Some of the affected land lay in the 11th.

At Home: Taylor set a new standard for the politically volatile 11th District by winning in 1992 with 55 percent. In most districts, that would not seem like much, but the Asheville-based 11th is arguably the most competitive district in the nation.

This constituency changed between Democratic and Republican hands five times in the six elections from 1980 through 1992, with Democratic Rep. Clarke and Republican Rep. Bill Hendon each getting knocked out on two separate occasions (Clarke in 1984 and 1990, Hendon in 1982 and 1986). Every one of those races was decided by fewer than 5,000 votes.

Taylor managed his impressive 1992 feat by assiduously courting the residents of the small cities and mountain hamlets that dot Western Carolina. Redistricting before the election made this district even tougher for him by excising a chunk of Republican voters, but by Taylor's count he held more than 70 town meetings in his first term.

He touted his role as a freshman renegade in the Gang of Seven. He also cultivated a folksy image, contrasting himself against his patrician Democratic challenger, Asheville lawyer and former state Rep. John S. Stevens. Taylor ended up winning 13 of the district's 16 counties and a 22,000-vote margin.

When he toppled Clarke in 1990, he won 11 of 17 counties and prevailed by 2,673 votes. Taylor's victory was notable in that it came in a non-presidential year. His best opportunity to get to Congress had appeared to be in 1988, as George Bush polled 59 percent in the 11th; despite the coattails, Taylor fell 1,500 votes short in that first try against Clarke. But Taylor softened some of his rough edges for the rematch, toning down his attacks on the low-key and grandfatherly Clarke and presenting himself as a folksy family man in shirt sleeves.

Some media reports said Taylor's 1992 re-election came with a million-dollar price tag that put him among the country's top 50 spenders in 1992 House races. But Taylor's camp called that an incorrect reading of Federal Election Commission reports stemming from the fact that Taylor's campaign had refinanced 1988 and 1990 debts. According to Taylor, spending on the 1992 campaign was under $500,000.

Committee

Appropriations (20th of 23 Republicans)
Commerce, Justice, State & Judiciary; Legislative Branch

Elections

1992 General

Charles H. Taylor (R)	130,158	(55%)
John S. Stevens (D)	108,003	(45%)

1990 General

Charles H. Taylor (R)	101,991	(51%)
James McClure Clarke (D)	99,318	(49%)

District Vote for President

1992

D 105,064 (43%)
R 104,383 (43%)
I 34,646 (14%)

Campaign Finance

	Receipts	Receipts from PACs		Expend-itures
1992				
Taylor (R)	$1,216,256	$298,425	(25%)	$1,212,765
Stevens (D)	$431,367	$113,595	(9%)	$431,722
1990				
Taylor (R)	$523,580	$111,689	(21%)	$523,867
Clarke (D)	$486,131	$278,941	(57%)	$499,869

Key Votes

1993	
Require parental notification of minors' abortions	Y
Require unpaid family and medical leave	N
Approve national "motor voter" registration bill	N
Approve budget increasing taxes and reducing deficit	N
Approve economic stimulus plan	N
1992	
Approve balanced-budget constitutional amendment	Y
Close down space station program	N
Approve U.S. aid for former Soviet Union	Y
Allow shifting funds from defense to domestic programs	—
1991	
Extend unemployment benefits using deficit financing	N
Approve waiting period for handgun purchases	N
Authorize use of force in Persian Gulf	Y

Voting Studies

Year	Presidential Support S	Presidential Support O	Party Unity S	Party Unity O	Conservative Coalition S	Conservative Coalition O
1992	76	19	89	8	88	10
1991	84	16	91	7	95	5

Interest Group Ratings

Year	ADA	AFL-CIO	CCUS	ACU
1992	15	25	86	87
1991	10	17	90	90

12 Melvin Watt (D)

Of Charlotte — Elected 1992; 1st Term

Born: Aug. 26, 1945, Steele Creek, N.C.
Education: U. of North Carolina, B.S. 1967; Yale U., J.D. 1970.
Occupation: Lawyer.
Family: Wife, Eulada Paysour; two children.
Religion: Presbyterian.
Political Career: N.C. Senate, 1985-87.
Capitol Office: 1232 Longworth Bldg. 20515; 225-1510.

The Path to Washington: Watt hails from what may be the most maligned newly drawn district — a snake-like ink-blot splashed across the center of North Carolina along Interstates 85 and 77 to create a majority bloc of black voters. He earned the right to represent the 12th by praising its virtues as the state's premier urban district, dismissing criticism that it does not encompass a single community.

"It depends on how you define community," Watt said. "It makes a lot more sense to define congressional districts in terms of communities of interests than in geographic terms."

Still, Watt could find himself running in a new district as a result of a court challenge to the North Carolina congressional district map. In a case that made it all the way to the Supreme Court, five white plaintiffs from Durham argued that the obvious race-conscious cartography of the map violated their constitutional right to equal protection.

Watt and the 1st District's Eva Clayton are the first black North Carolinians in Congress since 1901, when Republican George Henry White resigned to protest state lawmakers' decision to strip blacks of their voting rights.

It seems likely that Watt will be one of the comers of the freshman class.

The product of a fatherless household, Watt was brought up in rural Mecklenburg County in a tin-roofed shack without running water or electricity. He attended a segregated high school and then moved on to the University of North Carolina at Chapel Hill, where he graduated Phi Beta Kappa, and Yale University, where he received a law degree and a coveted spot on the Yale Law Review.

He was dubbed "the most effective freshman legislator" during his only other stint in elective office, the 1985-87 term in the North Carolina Senate, a job to which he was appointed by local Democrats after their candidate died at the end of the campaign. He quit to spend more time with his two sons, but later reemerged to run the 1990 U.S. Senate campaign of former Charlotte Mayor Harvey B. Gantt, who nearly upset GOP incumbent Jesse Helms.

With his sons grown and following his footsteps through Yale, Watt entered the crowded primary once the district took shape in 1992.

He overcame three strong challengers in the primary, outspending each by far and winning 47 percent of the vote — far more than the 40 percent needed to avoid a runoff. His victory was aided by white voters, who make up more than 40 percent of the district and likely were drawn to Watt's comparatively less confrontational approach to race issues. Watt skated to victory in the general election, winning with 70 percent against black Republican Barbara Gore Washington in an overwhelmingly Democratic district.

In organizational meetings, freshman Democrats gave him one of their three seats on the prestigious Steering and Policy Committee, which controls committee assignments.

He also landed seats on two committees he wanted — Banking, Finance and Urban Affairs, for its sway over big-city issues and the banking industry, and Judiciary, for its jurisdiction over affairs of interest to Watt, a civil rights lawyer.

Though he said he would watch out for banking interests in his state, home to three of the nation's biggest banks, Watt said he would keep his eye on consumers: "Where there's a direct conflict between the bank's interest and the consumer's, I'll be on the consumer's side."

On Judiciary matters, Watt opposes the death penalty and is leery of attempts to speed executions. He favors abortion rights and federal funding of abortions for poor women and opposes waiting periods and parental notification. And he is a strong gun-control advocate: "I think we ought to take all of them and ship them somewhere else — throw them in the ocean," he says. "That's probably an exaggeration, but not far from it."

Given his district's liberal leanings, Watt predicts he will not have to vote against his political predilections. "I can represent this district and be Mel Watt rather than have to think about making political decisions," he told a North Carolina newspaper, adding later, "I don't have to equivocate on where I stand."

North Carolina 12

The I-85 Corridor — Parts of Charlotte, Greensboro and Durham

The 12th is best described as the mother of all gerrymanders, a congressional district so notorious in its design that it sparked an editorial in The Wall Street Journal and drew criticism from 1992 GOP presidential candidate Patrick J. Buchanan during a campaign stop in North Carolina.

The scandal was in the shape. Known as the "I-85 District," the serpentine 12th winds across the Piedmont Plateau mostly along the Interstate 85 corridor, linking small parts of 10 counties and including all of none.

The district was the Democratic-controlled legislature's response to the 1992 Justice Department mandate that North Carolina have two majority-minority districts. Rather than significantly weaken white Democratic incumbents, the 12th was stretched to extremes.

Through the marvels of computer technology, mapmakers were able to pick and choose precincts to give the 12th a 57 percent black population and an overwhelming 4-to-1 Democratic registration advantage.

The predominantly black neighborhoods of Durham, Greensboro, Winston-Salem, Charlotte and Gastonia provide much of the vote. The district closely parallels the old Southern Railroad system route, which had a hand in dictating black settlement patterns in a bygone era of the state's history.

Durham is the 12th's eastern frontier. Tobacco processing was once the big game in town here, but nowadays, Duke University is Durham County's largest single employer.

Durham has long been home to a black political and economic elite, whose rise was nurtured by an organization that used to be known as the Durham Committee for Negro Affairs. Now referred to simply as the Durham Committee, the group has been a locus of power in black politics since pre-World War II days.

Besides Duke, the district also takes in several of the state's historically black colleges and universities.

From Durham, the lines travel west, cutting into Burlington (Alamance County) and into the cities of the Piedmont Triad: Greensboro (Guilford County), Winston-Salem (Forsyth County) and High Point (Guilford County).

More than half the district lives in either Guilford (Greensboro) or Mecklenburg (Charlotte) counties. The 12th only covers part of Charlotte, but it is the population anchor of the district; it contains more black voters than any city in the 12th.

Any candidate for the 12th must be careful, though, not to couch his message in Charlotte-oriented terms, for voters in other cities along I-85 have expressed concern about a Charlotte-dominated district that will be less attuned to their local interests.

Economically, the 12th is widely diverse. Since it courses through six of the state's 10 largest cities, it relies on the fortunes of the state's traditional industries — tobacco, textiles and furniture. In Charlotte, banking and financial concerns dominate the local economy.

1990 Population: 552,387. White 230,889 (42%), Black 312,791 (57%), Other 8,707 (2%). Hispanic origin 4,772 (1%). 18 and over 411,687 (75%), 62 and over 77,540 (14%). Median age: 32.

Committees

Banking, Finance & Urban Affairs (26th of 30 Democrats)
Consumer Credit & Insurance; Housing & Community Development; International Development, Finance, Trade & Monetary Policy

Judiciary (20th of 21 Democrats)
Administrative Law & Governmental Relations; Economic & Commercial Law

Post Office & Civil Service (10th of 15 Democrats)
Postal Operations & Services

Campaign Finance

	Receipts	Receipts from PACs		Expend-itures
1992				
Watt (D)	$483,601	$208,732	(43%)	$480,713
Washington (R)	$25,388	$506	(2%)	$22,761

Key Votes

1993	
Require parental notification of minors' abortions	N
Require unpaid family and medical leave	Y
Approve national "motor voter" registration bill	Y
Approve budget increasing taxes and reducing deficit	Y
Approve economic stimulus plan	Y

Elections

1992 General		
Melvin Watt (D)	127,262	(70%)
Barbara Gore Washington (R)	49,402	(27%)
Curtis Wade Krumel (LIBERT)	4,160	(2%)
1992 Primary		
Melvin Watt (D)	26,495	(47%)
Mickey Michaux (D)	16,187	(29%)
Larry D. Little (D)	8,298	(15%)
Earl Jones (D)	5,338	(9%)

District Vote for President

	1992	
D	128,952	(66%)
R	50,357	(26%)
I	17,308	(9%)

North Dakota

STATE DATA

Governor:
Edward T. Schafer (R)
First elected: 1992
Length of term: 4 years
Term expires: 1/97
Salary: $68,284
Term limit: No
Phone: (701) 224-2200
Born: Aug. 8, 1946; Bismarck, N.D.
Education: U. of North Dakota, B.S., B.A. 1969; U. of Denver, M.B.A. 1970
Occupation: Distributing company owner; real estate developer
Family: Wife, Nancy Jones; two children; two stepchildren
Religion: Episcopalian

Political Career: Republican nominee for U.S. House, 1990

Lt. Gov.: Rosemarie Myrdal (R)
First elected: 1992
Length of term: 4 years
Term expires: 1/97
Salary: $56,116
Phone: (701) 224-2200

State election official: (701) 224-2905
Democratic headquarters: (701) 255-0460
Republican headquarters: (701) 255-0030

STATE LEGISLATURE

Legislative Assembly meets January-April in odd-numbered years.

Senate: 49 members, 4-year terms.
1992 breakdown: 25D, 24R; 41 men, 8 women; 49 whites
Salary: $90/day in session + $180/month year-round; $62.50/day not in session
Phone: (701) 224-2916

House of Representatives: 98 members, 2-year terms.
1992 breakdown: 65R, 33D; 82 men, 16 women; 98 whites
Salary: $90/day in session + $180/month year-round; $62.50/day not in session
Phone: (701) 224-2916

URBAN STATISTICS

City	Pop.
Fargo	74,084
Mayor John Lindgren, D	
Grand Forks	49,425
Mayor Michael Polovitz, D	
Bismarck	49,256
Mayor Bill Sorensen, N-P	
Minot	34,544
Mayor George Christensen, N-P	

U.S. CONGRESS

Senate: 2 D, 0 R
House: 1 D, 0 R

TERM LIMITS

For Congress: Yes
Senate & House: 12 years
For state offices: Yes
Senate & House: 12 years

ELECTIONS

1992 Presidential Vote

Bill Clinton	32.2%
George Bush	44.2%
Ross Perot	23.1%

1988 Presidential Vote

George Bush	56%
Michael S. Dukakis	43%

1984 Presidential Vote

Ronald Reagan	65%
Walter F. Mondale	34%

POPULATION

1990 population		638,800
1980 population		652,717
Percent change		−2%
Rank among states:		47
White		95%
Black		1%
Hispanic		1%
Asian or Pacific islander		1%
Urban		53%
Rural		47%
Born in state		73%
Foreign-born		1%
Under age 18	175,385	27%
Ages 18-64	372,360	58%
65 and older	91,055	14%
Median age		32.4

MISCELLANEOUS

Capital: Bismarck
Number of counties: 53
Per capita income: $16,088 (1991)
Rank among states: 38
Total area: 70,702 sq. miles
Rank among states: 17

DIVIDE
BURKE
RENVILLE
BOTTINEAU
ROLETTE
TOWNER
CAVALIER
PEMBINA
WILLIAMS
Williston
MOUNTRAIL
WARD
Minot
MCHENRY
PIERCE
BENSON
RAMSEY
WALSH
GRAND FORKS
Grand Forks
NELSON
MCKENZIE
MCLEAN
SHERIDAN
WELLS
EDDY
AT LARGE
FOSTER
GRIGGS
STEELE
TRAILL
DUNN
MERCER
OLIVER
BURLEIGH
KIDDER
STUTSMAN
BARNES
CASS
West Fargo
Fargo
GOLDEN VALLEY
BILLINGS
Dickinson
STARK
Mandan
Bismarck
MORTON
Jamestown
SLOPE
HETTINGER
GRANT
EMMONS
LOGAN
LA MOURE
RANSOM
RICHLAND
BOWMAN
ADAMS
SIOUX
MCINTOSH
DICKEY
SARGENT

Kent Conrad (D)

Of Bismarck — Elected 1986; 2nd Term

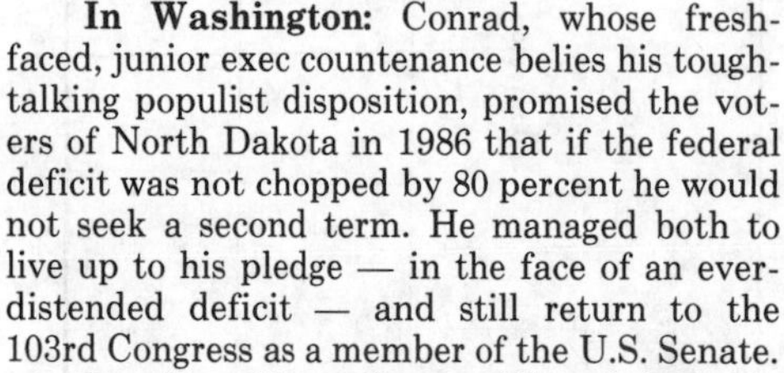

Born: March 12, 1948, Bismarck, N.D.
Education: U. of Missouri, 1967; Stanford U., B.A. 1971; George Washington U., M.B.A. 1975.
Occupation: Management and personnel director.
Family: Wife, Lucy Calautti; two children.
Religion: Unitarian.
Political Career: Candidate for N.D. auditor, 1976; N.D. tax commissioner, 1981-87.
Capitol Office: 724 Hart Bldg. 20510; 224-2043.

In Washington: Conrad, whose fresh-faced, junior exec countenance belies his tough-talking populist disposition, promised the voters of North Dakota in 1986 that if the federal deficit was not chopped by 80 percent he would not seek a second term. He managed both to live up to his pledge — in the face of an ever-distended deficit — and still return to the 103rd Congress as a member of the U.S. Senate.

Despite evidence from public opinion polls that Conrad could have reneged and still won re-election, he announced in April 1992 that he would not run again. Through a quirk of fate — the death of North Dakota senior Sen. Quentin N. Burdick five months later — the state's voters were able to hold Conrad in office while he technically kept his vow.

North Dakota has long been fertile soil for populists willing to till its natural distrust of powerful outsiders — Eastern bankers, railroad magnates and flour mill barons. When hard times sweep across the prairie, these attitudes harden, to the benefit of politicians like Conrad. He built his reputation as a tax commissioner taking on big business. He spent his first term carrying water for his farmers.

No mere windmill tilter, Conrad earned the sobriquet "Chainsaw" back home because, he once said, "when you are going after big timber you have to use strong tactics."

Whether or not Conrad looks his part, he has certainly played it, holding fast by his causes. From the 1990 farm bill to "emergency" supplemental appropriations bills to President Clinton's first proposals to cut spending and raise taxes, he has agitated to get the best deal for his farmers.

In his first term, Conrad found that his seats on the Agriculture and Budget committees were strategically vital for defending farm programs pressured by calls for deficit reduction. In the 103rd Congress, he also took a seat on the Finance Committee, where he could fight for his constituents' rural health needs, protect the Farm Belt's special tax interests and further pursue his goal of reducing the deficit by spreading the pain. To make the move, he gave up a seat on the Energy Committee.

On Agriculture, he is part of a clique of junior populist Democrats who advocate greater government subsidies for their farmers. Led by Conrad and Nebraskan Bob Kerrey, the prairie populists sought a more partisan slant to the 1990 farm bill.

Having been elected with the help of farmers disgruntled about policies included in the 1985 farm bill, Conrad was hardly receptive to suggestions that the 1990 farm bill continue the 1985 bill's trend of reducing federal support levels. "The agriculture sector has been pushed to the limit," he said. Continuing the decline in target prices for commodities "is not a policy that is going to do anything but threaten the health of rural America."

When Clinton sent his first budget request to Capitol Hill in the early days of the 103rd Congress, Conrad's voice was heard in a chorus of complaints that Clinton's proposed farm program cuts were too deep.

When Republicans Hank Brown of Colorado and John H. Chafee of Rhode Island tried in 1992 to kill off the honey program at a savings of $23 million the first year, Conrad teamed with South Dakota Democrat Tom Daschle to save it. "This is a brave assault on the federal deficit here tonight," Conrad said sarcastically. "Let's get serious. This isn't even worth talking about." The honey program survived on a 56-41 vote.

As the least experienced of the 11 Democrats in the Senate class of 1986 — all of the others were former governors or House members — Conrad took traditional steps to close this gap, developing expertise in a limited number of areas by doing his homework.

Conrad's unflagging persistence in pursuit of his causes — and his preference for long, impassioned speeches — can wear on his colleagues. While his hard work and thorough preparation are readily acknowledged, he is also criticized for a tendency toward stridency. Unlike Kerrey, who voted for the farm bill when it first passed the Senate, Conrad voted against Senate passage as well as the House-Senate conference agreement.

At one especially contentious back-room session, supporters of a compromise on the farm bill's section revamping federal wetlands protections virtually dared Conrad to break the deal. Conrad favored extensive loosening of a federal law, known as "swampbuster," that bars draining swamps and marshes for farming.

Conrad has attempted to board a number of money bills in his search for vehicles to aid drought-stricken farmers in North Dakota. In 1990, he offered an amendment to a midyear aid bill (ostensibly for Panama and Nicaragua) that would have allowed farmers in drought areas to avoid repaying crop subsidies that were paid but later reduced when the droughts of 1988 and 1989 raised market prices. Senators voted 52-43 to kill it, but Conrad waged a last-ditch effort to add it to the bill. As the Senate was preparing to clear the bill late in the evening, Conrad offered his amendment again. Frustrated colleagues, however, convinced him that most senators were in bed and in no mood to vote on it again, and he conceded defeat.

His other passion is the budget deficit, which he would attack with measures as harsh as a spending freeze, Social Security excepted. He voted against President Bush's Treasury secretary nominee, Nicholas F. Brady, after Brady expressed the belief that the nation's economy could simply grow out of the deficit.

Conrad offered a plan in 1990 to reduce the budget deficit by $56.5 billion, in part through $19.5 billion in new revenues and an $11.1 billion "tax compliance program." The Budget Committee rejected his proposal by a 7-16 vote, but Chairman Jim Sasser of Tennessee, in order to win the vote of Virginia Democrat Charles S. Robb, included the tax compliance program in the committee's budget resolution.

In 1991, Conrad lost, on a 10-11 vote, his bid to freeze most domestic spending, while protecting agriculture, education, health care and veterans programs. And in 1992, his alternative deficit-reduction plan, incorporating a spending freeze, restraints on entitlements and a tax increase for millionaires, was rejected 3-18.

One way Conrad has sought to entwine his desires to shift money to domestic programs and to bring the budget into shape is through cutting U.S. troops stationed overseas, requiring allies to assume a greater burden for their defense. During consideration of the 1989 defense appropriations bill, he offered an amendment to return 30,000 troops stationed in Europe and transfer from the Pentagon's budget to education programs the $1 billion that he said would be saved. "We are paying for their defense umbrella even though we have to borrow the money from them to do it," he said. His amendment was rejected 23-76. In 1990, the Senate accepted Conrad's amendment to cut by 10,000 the number of U.S. military personnel stationed in Japan.

Conrad has shown himself to be a party loyalist, though he is less so than most Democrats from the prairie — including the late Burdick and Byron L. Dorgan, who joined Conrad in the Senate for the 103rd, after spending 12 years as North Dakota's at-large House member. Conrad is given more to discussion of policy than politics, however, and his populism, though no passing fancy, is tempered with pragmatism. "Hard ideological positions carry a danger," he says. "Hiding behind rhetorical barriers doesn't get things done."

At Home: Conrad spent 1992 pioneering a way for members who have taken the term limit pledge to stay in Congress even after their time's up: Just switch seats.

Back in 1986, during his race against Republican Sen. Mark Andrews, Conrad promised not to seek re-election unless the trade and budget deficits were dramatically reduced during his term in office. By early 1992, Conrad appeared to be backing off that pledge, joking that he had written it under the influence of a 104-degree fever and collecting funds for a possible re-election run.

But Conrad ended up keeping his word, announcing his retirement in April 1992 with the explanation: "There is a tremendous air of cynicism in the country, and I do not want to contribute to it." While his decision met with approval in North Dakota, political cynics suggested that he simply may have been biding his time until another office — the governorship, for instance — came open. Sidelined, Conrad endorsed Dorgan for his seat.

Few expected Conrad back so soon, but on Sept. 8, 1992, Burdick died, leaving two years in his Senate term and an election in December. Conrad wasted little time in making a Perot-like bid for the people to call him to serve.

They did call, and by Oct. 4, he was again a Democratic candidate for senator. His opponent was GOP state Rep. Jack Dalrymple, who immediately made his position on Conrad's political comeback clear. After trying to haunt Conrad with his 1986 promise, Dalrymple accused him of reneging on a pledge to return campaign contributions he had collected before deciding to run for Burdick's seat.

North Dakotans sided with Conrad, .who won with 63 percent of the vote.

Conrad's showy 1992 win followed an unexpected victory in 1986. The troubles besetting North Dakota's farms and small towns gave Conrad an opening against Andrews, and his skillful use of the issue propelled him into contention against the favored incumbent. On Election Day, Conrad carried only one of the state's four major population centers; his victory was built in the countryside.

Conrad's chief Senate campaign issue was the Reagan administration's farm policy, which was wildly unpopular in a state where farms and small-town banks were failing and where rural families were breaking apart as their members headed to the cities to find work. The election, Conrad insisted, was a referendum on Republican farm and economic policies; if voters wanted to send a message to Washington, he told them, he would be the messenger.

He went on the attack early, trying to tie Andrews to the administration's programs. Though the Republican by and large had opposed Reagan agricultural policies, he had voted for the 1985 farm bill, which many farmers believed hurt them. Storming around the state with then-Rep. Dorgan, Conrad relentlessly pressed the point, bringing up Andrews' vote whenever the opportunity arose.

He also set out to undermine Andrews' credibility. When the senator aired a commercial claiming that the price of wheat had risen after the Senate passed an export amendment he had sponsored, Conrad pointed out that the price rise was only a brief interruption in a long-term decline.

Andrews responded in kind. He challenged Conrad's claim to have cut his departmental budget as tax commissioner and pointed out that Conrad had been endorsed in a Village Voice article — a sure sign that he was too liberal for North Dakota.

But the debate between the two may have been secondary to the deeper factors working in Conrad's favor. In addition to the farm situation, there was a growing perception that Andrews had lost touch with his base.

Part of the way into the campaign, Andrews was stung by press stories revealing that a close friend of his had hired private detectives to investigate first Dorgan and then Conrad. Andrews denied any involvement, but the publicity hurt him all the same.

Possibly as troubling to voters was a multimillion-dollar lawsuit that Andrews and his wife, Mary, had pursued against family physicians after Mary Andrews was crippled by meningitis. Though early in the case there had been widespread sympathy for the incumbent and his wife, by the time of the election there was evidence that voters had grown uncomfortable with the sight of a wealthy senator demanding large sums of money from family doctors.

Andrews was further hurt by the delay in ending Congress' 1986 session. As Conrad's attacks found their mark, Republicans worried that Andrews' continued presence in Washington would only underline the Democrats' contention that he had grown distant from the state's concerns. By the time Andrews did return home, Conrad had taken a slight lead in the polls, and Andrews had to try to make up lost ground. He never succeeded.

Committees

Agriculture, Nutrition & Forestry (6th of 10 Democrats)
Agricultural Credit (chairman); Domestic & Foreign Marketing & Product Promotion; Rural Development & Rural Electrification

Budget (8th of 12 Democrats)

Finance (11th of 11 Democrats)
International Trade; Medicare & Long Term Care; Taxation

Indian Affairs (4th of 10 Democrats)

Elections

1992 Special

Kent Conrad (D)	103,246	(63%)
Jack Dalrymple (R)	55,194	(34%)
Darold Larson (I)	4,871	(3%)

Previous Winning Percentage: 1986 (50%)

Campaign Finance

	Receipts	Receipts from PACs		Expend-itures
1992				
Conrad (D)	$1,732,692	$1,184,509	(68%)	$2,110,684
Dalrymple (R)	$300,843	$28,400	(9%)	$282,104
Larson (I)	$22,527	$250	(1%)	$22,237

Key Votes

1993	
Require unpaid family and medical leave	Y
Approve national "motor voter" registration bill	Y
Approve budget increasing taxes and reducing deficit	Y
Support president's right to lift military gay ban	Y
1992	
Approve school-choice pilot program	N
Allow shifting funds from defense to domestic programs	Y
Oppose deeper cuts in spending for SDI	N
1991	
Approve waiting period for handgun purchases	Y
Raise senators' pay and ban honoraria	N
Authorize use of force in Persian Gulf	N
Confirm Clarence Thomas to Supreme Court	N

Voting Studies

	Presidential Support		Party Unity		Conservative Coalition	
Year	**S**	**O**	**S**	**O**	**S**	**O**
1992	32	67	69	29	61	37
1991	36	63	72	26	43	58
1990	34	66	75	24	38	62
1989	55	45	70	30	42	58
1988	48	50	78	20	35	65
1987	37	63	82	17	47	53

Interest Group Ratings

Year	ADA	AFL-CIO	CCUS	ACU
1992	90	75	20	12
1991	75	75	20	43
1990	67	56	42	30
1989	70	90	50	29
1988	80	93	29	24
1987	85	90	39	8

Byron L. Dorgan (D)

Of Bismarck — Elected 1992; 1st Term

Born: May 14, 1942, Regent, N.D.

Education: U. of North Dakota, B.S. 1965; U. of Denver, M.B.A. 1966.

Occupation: Public official.

Family: Wife, Kimberly Olson; four children.

Religion: Lutheran.

Political Career: N.D. tax commissioner, 1969-80; Democratic nominee for U.S. House, 1974; U.S. House, 1981-93.

Capitol Office: 713 Hart Bldg. 20510; 224-2551.

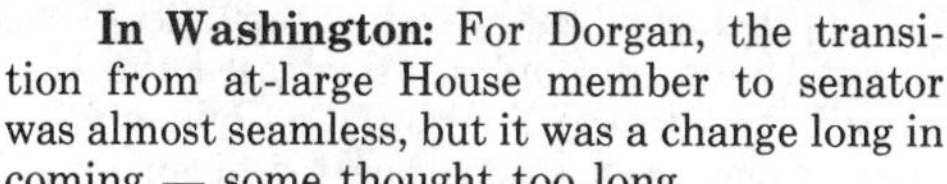

In Washington: For Dorgan, the transition from at-large House member to senator was almost seamless, but it was a change long in coming — some thought too long.

For most of the 1980s, Dorgan was widely regarded as a senator-in-waiting, waiting for North Dakota's very senior and not very effective senator, Quentin N. Burdick, to retire. But Dorgan bypassed challenging Burdick for renomination in 1988, when at age 80 he sought and won a fifth full term. When Dorgan did finally move up to the Senate in 1992, it was not to replace Burdick, but to take the seat vacated by one-termer Kent Conrad.

Conrad announced in April 1992 that he was retiring to fulfill an earlier pledge that he would not seek re-election unless the federal deficit was reduced. But in the end, Conrad managed to stay in the Senate, while technically keeping his vow: Following Burdick's September 1992 death, he won a special election to serve the last two years of Burdick's term.

Dorgan's populist voice on economic policy will undoubtedly be heard more often in the more airy Senate chamber; in the structured debates of the House, his chances to speak were limited, but he took them.

Aggressively partisan on taxes and trade, Dorgan bitterly opposed the Republican administrations of Presidents Reagan and Bush. In the 101st Congress, when much of the rhetorical exchange had to do with big financial institutions and taxes on the wealthy, Dorgan was in his glory. "Those who make millions can well afford to pay more in taxes than two-wage-earner families with four children struggling to make ends meet on $25,000 a year," he said.

Early in the 103rd Congress, with a Democrat in the White House, Dorgan was broadly supportive of administration economic proposals that espoused many of his own views. Nonetheless, he did not forget his constituents and complained that some suggested farm spending cuts were too deep and that a proposed new tax on energy use was onerous for coal producers and farmers. "I think the president's plan has some elements in it that are tough for the northern Great Plains," he said. But in floor votes on a budget blueprint implementing President Clinton's plan, Dorgan remained loyal.

Though he supported "sense of the Senate" language that the energy tax and other provisions not disproportionately affect agricultural or mining interests, he sided with Clinton and nearly every Senate Democrat on the votes that mattered.

The only bump in the road that Dorgan hit traveling from one side of the Capitol to the other was in his committee assignments. He was a longtime member of Ways and Means in the House, where he turned his populist rhetoric on big banks and corporations, and it was assumed by many that he would have a seat on the Senate Finance Committee. Instead, Conrad captured that prize at the start of the 103rd.

Dorgan instead will have to use his seat on the Commerce Committee to pursue concerns about trade policy. In the 102nd Congress, as part of a broad trade bill that went no further than the House floor, Dorgan won inclusion of language that was aimed at preventing Canadian wheat from being imported into the United States and then re-exported through government programs intended to benefit domestic producers.

Dorgan can work through the Governmental Affairs Committee to continue a crusade he began in the House to reduce administrative waste in the federal government and cut down on overhead expenses. In 1992, he pursued administrative cuts for several government departments, winning, on a 257-162 vote, an amendment to cut Interior Department overhead. In 1991, he lost by 84-339 in a similar battle on the Transportation Department's budget.

Dorgan is a contemporary echo of the prairie populism that swept North Dakota in the early 1900s. His talk dwells on the struggles of common folk against distant forces over which they have no control. "People feel powerless," he has said, "and they feel powerless because they're preyed upon by bigger interests."

But Dorgan's legislative style has little in common with the crude bluster of predecessors such as William L. Langer, the North Dakotan who once pounded on a Senate lectern so hard that it broke. Dorgan is not immune from bluster when he denounces a David Rockefeller or a Paul Volcker, but he also knows how to work in the legislative process.

Dorgan's populism smacks at times of old-fashioned isolationism when he turns his attention to trade. He has promoted efforts to match U.S. food surpluses with need around the world. And he certainly understands the need for foreign markets for his state's vast production of wheat. Yet he can get quite exercised in his defense of farm and business interests against international competition.

In 1988, he was the only Ways and Means member to vote in committee against the free trade pact with Canada, arguing that it failed to guarantee access for U.S. wheat. In 1991 he carried a resolution to the House floor to block special "fast track" consideration of the North American Free Trade Agreement, which would extend the free trade zone with Canada south to Mexico. The resolution failed, 192-231.

In the 101st Congress he joined with other members questioning the tax payments of foreign, primarily Japanese, corporations. "A nation up to its neck in debts should look to [taxing] deadbeats before it starts raising taxes on honest folks," he said. On another occasion, explaining the U.S. trade deficit with Japan, he said: "While they open their arms to our sailors and soldiers they close their markets to our telephones and TVs."

Dorgan's 11 years as state tax commissioner provided him with expertise and credibility that helped make him a force on Ways and Means. He spent much time working on schemes to guarantee that the earnings of large corporations were taxed. In the 99th Congress, he was a strong supporter of efforts to overhaul the tax code, which he called "a feedlot for the rich and a straitjacket for the rest."

Dorgan argued that reforming the code was more important than protecting parochial interests. He opposed some agriculture tax subsidies, such as accelerated write-offs for new hog barns, though some North Dakotans wanted them. "Doing tax reform is like administering medicine," Dorgan said. "They don't like the taste, but they will like the result."

Dorgan also generated some national attention in 1990 by opposing the MX missile program, which would have brought $70 million and 350 jobs to Grand Forks, N.D.

Overall, however, Dorgan has put home-state interests first. He astutely voted against the 1985 farm bill; while criticized for not revealing his position until passage was assured, Dorgan avoided the fate that befell GOP Sen. Mark A. Andrews — whose vote for the bill helped cost him his job in the next election.

On a smaller scale, Dorgan bore the brunt of ridicule early in 1991 for defending a $500,000 appropriation for a German-Russian interpretive center at the North Dakota birthplace of bandleader Lawrence Welk. Derided as pork-barreling, the project was lauded by Dorgan as a boost to a part of North Dakota devastated by drought.

Dorgan's populism has made him a skeptic about foreign aid, as well. When the Reagan administration proposed an $8.4 billion increase in the U.S. payment to the International Monetary Fund in 1983, Dorgan joined with colleagues on both the right and the left to delay its passage. He said the money went to help large banks that had made bad loans to the Third World. In August 1992 he voted against a bill to provide aid to the former republics of the Soviet Union; the bill also increased the U.S. contribution to the IMF by $12.3 billion.

He has been a longtime foe of an unfettered Federal Reserve Board and the high interest rates he says it has often promoted. In 1981 he introduced a bill he called "The Paul Volcker Retirement Act," which would have let Congress remove the Fed chairman with a 60 percent vote of both chambers. "With a central bank like the Federal Reserve Board," he wrote in a 1983 article on farm problems, "who needs soil erosion, grasshoppers or drought?" The second bill he sponsored in the Senate was a reprise of a House measure to remove some of the secrecy of Fed deliberations.

At Home: Following Conrad's unexpected declaration in the spring of 1992 that he would give up his Senate seat, Dorgan jumped into the race and went on to win with the ease one would expect of a veteran politician. He defeated the Republican nominee, Fargo City Commissioner Steve Sydness, by 20 points.

Sydness cited Dorgan's 98 overdrafts at the House bank as evidence that he had lost touch with the voters. Dorgan initially claimed that he had no overdrafts, but he later admitted his mistake, and the blunder did not seriously erode the good will he had built up with voters during six House terms.

Dorgan, long a popular figure in the state, had been pushed to run for Senate before, but had declined. Heading into the 1986 election, some polls suggested that he could easily defeat GOP Sen. Andrews. When Dorgan demurred, Conrad, his one-time protégé and successor as state tax commissioner, ran and won.

Heading into the 1988 election, Dorgan got plenty of encouragement from polls and fellow Democrats to run for Burdick's Senate seat. Dorgan backers hoped to pressure Burdick into retiring, but there was no budging him. Dorgan sought another House term and Burdick won re-election easily.

Dorgan's stands are rooted partly in the populism of the state's old Non-Partisan

League and partly in the small-town values with which he was raised. His father was active in the Democratic-leaning Farmers' Union in Regent, N.D., where Dorgan grew up and where, he likes to say, he graduated in the top five in his high school class — of nine.

Dorgan was working in the state tax department in 1969 when he caught the eye of Democratic Gov. William Guy; when the incumbent tax commissioner died in 1969, Dorgan, then 27, got the post.

As tax commissioner, Dorgan spoke out on local issues such as property tax revision and on global ones such as military spending. He sued out-of-state corporations to force them to pay taxes, sending auditors to ensure that the firms were accurately reporting financial information. The voters loved it.

Dorgan made it clear he had political ambitions by taking on then-Rep. Andrews in 1974. It was an uphill battle, but Dorgan held Andrews to 56 percent, the only time the Republican had fallen below 60 percent since 1964.

In 1980, GOP Sen. Milton R. Young retired and Andrews was nominated to succeed him. Dorgan ran for Andrews' House seat. Although he was the favorite from the start, Dorgan still sought to temper his liberal reputation by supporting an anti-abortion constitutional amendment and decrying government waste. That was a successful combination; the state went overwhelmingly for Ronald Reagan, but Dorgan won with a comfortable 57 percent.

Considered by many observers to be the state's most popular politician, Dorgan won in 1990 by a margin most politicians would envy. Despite a sluggish farm economy, he carried all 53 counties and garnered 65 percent of the vote.

Committees

Commerce, Science & Transportation (10th of 11 Democrats)
Consumer; Foreign Commerce & Tourism; Surface Transportation

Governmental Affairs (8th of 8 Democrats)
Regulation & Government Information; Oversight of Government Management; Permanent Subcommittee on Investigations

Indian Affairs (9th of 10 Democrats)

Joint Economic

Elections

1992 General		
Byron L. Dorgan (D)	179,347	(59%)
Steve Sydness (R)	118,162	(39%)
Tom Asbridge (I)	6,448	(2%)

Previous Winning Percentages: **1990 *** (65%) **1988 *** (71%) **1986 *** (76%) **1984 *** (79%) **1982 *** (72%) **1980 *** (57%)

** House elections.*

Campaign Finance

	Receipts	Receipts from PACs		Expend-itures
1992				
Dorgan (D)	$1,054,618	$785,943	(75%)	$1,124,512
Sydness (R)	$507,163	$154,553	(30%)	$498,107

Key Votes

1993	
Require unpaid family and medical leave	Y
Approve national "motor voter" registration bill	Y
Approve budget increasing taxes and reducing deficit	Y
Support president's right to lift military gay ban	Y
House Service:	
1992	
Approve balanced-budget constitutional amendment	Y
Close down space station program	Y
Approve U.S. aid for former Soviet Union	N
Allow shifting funds from defense to domestic programs	N
1991	
Extend unemployment benefits using deficit financing	Y
Approve waiting period for handgun purchases	N
Authorize use of force in Persian Gulf	N

Voting Studies

	Presidential Support		Party Unity		Conservative Coalition	
Year	**S**	**O**	**S**	**O**	**S**	**O**
House Service:						
1992	25	75	78	20	44	56
1991	30	69	75	23	51	49
1990	17	82	82	16	35	61
1989	24	74	83	14	37	61
1988	28	70	81	16	47	53
1987	13	83	83	12	30	70
1986	26	73	82	15	44	56
1985	23	78	83	15	22	78
1984	33	61	75	22	31	68
1983	18	77	77	18	33	60
1982	36	62	81	17	33	64
1981	37	55	80	18	37	53

Interest Group Ratings

Year	**ADA**	**AFL-CIO**	**CCUS**	**ACU**
House Service:				
1992	70	83	38	28
1991	75	75	40	25
1990	72	73	43	21
1989	85	75	30	21
1988	75	93	38	17
1987	92	81	14	0
1986	70	71	29	27
1985	65	76	27	10
1984	75	46	33	22
1983	80	67	45	32
1982	85	90	32	5
1981	65	73	16	20

AL Earl Pomeroy (D)

Of Valley City — Elected 1992; 1st Term

Born: Sept. 2, 1952, Valley City, N.D.
Education: U. of North Dakota, B.A. 1974; U. of Durham (England), 1975; U. of North Dakota, J.D. 1979.
Occupation: Lawyer.
Family: Wife, Laurie Kirby.
Religion: Presbyterian.
Political Career: N.D. House, 1981-85; N.D. insurance commissioner, 1985-93.
Capitol Office: 318 Cannon Bldg. 20515; 225-2611.

The Path to Washington: Pomeroy came to Capitol Hill with experience in agriculture, the state legislature and insurance, including an eight-year stint as North Dakota's insurance commissioner and a national profile among insurance regulators.

The son of a Valley City farm retailer who sold feed, seed and fertilizer, Pomeroy is both a lawyer and a former grain-bin builder. As president of the National Association of Insurance Commissioners, he pushed for a solvency program to strengthen state insurance regulation and reduce company failures.

Pomeroy's cost-containing health agenda focused on the elimination of wasteful spending. Favoring a standard-setting, supervisory role for the federal government, he backed proposals that would limit how much states can pay in Medicaid costs; allow small companies, including agribusinesses, to purchase health insurance cooperatively; and require health-care facilities to operate within state-approved budgets.

Pomeroy also supported the development of an electronic-based claims payment system, greater implementation of managed health-care delivery systems and managed-competition proposals being advanced by the Conservative Democratic Forum.

Pomeroy focused heavily on farm issues during the campaign that took him through barns and farmyards.

It was no surprise that he landed a slot on the Agriculture Committee. Agriculture, particularly the production of durum — which is used to make pasta — accounts for approximately half of North Dakota's economy.

He opposed the North American Free Trade Agreement in its initial form. Though he held out the slim possibility that side agreements could persuade him to support the pact, Pomeroy joined the congressional anti-NAFTA caucus at its inception in May 1993.

Pomeroy's move to the U.S. House came as a surprise. At age 39, with his second term as state insurance commissioner ending, Pomeroy decided to leave politics and announced that he and his wife were joining the Peace Corps, with a likely billet to Russia. But on the day of the state Democratic convention, the couple set aside dreams of cultural exploration abroad.

Two days earlier a political scramble had been touched off when Democratic Sen. Kent Conrad announced that he was retiring rather than renege on a 1986 campaign promise not to seek re-election unless the deficit was reduced. Democratic Rep. Byron L. Dorgan jumped into the race to succeed him rather than seek a seventh House term. Hours before the nominations were to begin, Pomeroy, a well-recognized 12-year veteran office holder, accepted party entreaties to run for Dorgan's seat.

Pomeroy had four successful elections under his belt as well as a couple of years' experience in Washington as the national spokesman for insurance regulators. At age 28, he had bucked the 1980 Reagan landslide and won election to North Dakota's House of Representatives.

In his second state House term, he became chairman of the Judiciary Committee and rose to the insurance commissioner's post in 1984. Commissioners frequently have had rapid ascents in North Dakota: Conrad and Dorgan were both state tax commissioners.

Unopposed in the primary and the overwhelming favorite afterward, Pomeroy dispatched Fargo businessman John T. Korsmo, a newcomer in the general election, winning 57 percent. Described by one Bismarck columnist as a "loose cannon with a bad haircut," the conservative Korsmo had trouble painting clean-cut Pomeroy as an insidious career politician.

Pomeroy's win continued Democrats' monopoly of North Dakota's congressional delegation. It includes Conrad, who ended up winning a special election to succeed the late Sen. Quentin N. Burdick, and Dorgan.

This was not the first year the three have worked or campaigned together. In 1974, when Dorgan challenged GOP Rep. Mark Andrews' reelection bid, Conrad was Dorgan's campaign manager. The 21-year-old Pomeroy acted as driver.

North Dakota

At large

The decade of the 1980s is one that North Dakotans — and especially the North Dakota Republican Party — probably are glad to have behind them.

With weakness in the agricultural economy and a drop in farmland values causing many small farms to disappear from the map, North Dakota became one of only four states in the nation to lose population during the 1980s, dropping 2 percent to just under 639,000. Today it has the unwelcome distinction of being the only state with fewer people now than it had in 1930.

The GOP too saw its fortunes decline during the 1980s. At the start of the decade, Republicans were riding high; Jimmy Carter had flopped spectacularly in the state's 1980 presidential voting, taking only 26 percent, the lowest for any Democratic nominee since the 1920s. Republicans captured the governorship, and they vastly outnumbered Democrats in the state Legislature.

But Democrats retook the governorship in 1984, and two years later — with economic hard times settling in — they won control of the state Senate for the first time in history. Many struggling farmers had come to view the state Democratic Party as the modern vehicle for an old force in North Dakota politics, the agrarian populist movement. The original organized expression of that populism was the Non-Partisan League, which early in this century spoke for the "little man" and his suspicions of concentrated business interests — railroads, banks and grain companies.

The legacy of the NPL is visible today in the state-owned bank and grain mill, and in a weak executive-strong Legislature governmental system that provides for maximum citizen influence.

As the calendar turned to the 1990s, there were signs that agriculture in North Dakota was getting back on an even keel, albeit with large-scale, highly mechanized operations playing a more dominant role. In the 1992 election, Republican Edward T. Schafer won the governorship, and the state voted Republican for president, as it has in every postwar election except one (1964).

But George Bush won with only 44 percent of the vote, barely better than Barry Goldwater's losing 1964 tally. Bill Clinton bombed, taking only 32 percent. The surging force was Ross Perot, who captured 23 percent and ran second (ahead of Clinton) in 18 counties in the southern and western parts of the state, where agrarian populist discontent with "the establishment" always has been most palpable.

Much of North Dakota's population exodus has occurred from the western portion of the state. Too dry for a good wheat crop, the dry buttes and rolling grasslands attracted cattle ranches. There is also some energy development, although the area oil industry was hard hit by the 1980s slide in oil prices.

The coal industry in the southwestern part of the state also has been through some rough times, although it got a boost from the Great Plains coal gasification plant in Beulah (Mercer County). The plant is the only such facility in North America. Constructed with grand expectations of transforming huge amounts of coal to natural gas, the plant's financial competitiveness suffered with the downtown in energy prices, but private interests bought it from the federal government in 1988 and turned a profit one year later.

Still, within the state, population migration in recent years has been from west to east. The biggest population centers are both on the Red River, which defines North Dakota's eastern border with Minnesota. Fargo (Cass County) grew 21 percent in the 1980s to a population of 74,000. To the north are the 49,000 residents of Grand Forks (Grand Forks County). With major medical facilities and the two major state universities (the University of North Dakota in Grand Forks and North Dakota State University in Fargo), eastern North Dakota offers most of the white-collar jobs that are available in the state.

The east is also the state's most prosperous agricultural area — the moisture in the soil allowed it to weather even the great dust storms of the 1930s. The Red River flows through a region that produces wheat, sugar beets and potatoes.

The two other population centers are in the central part of the state: Bismarck (Burleigh County) and Minot (Ward County). Bismarck is the state capital, and every fall representatives of the United Tribes (from all over the Americas) gather here for the International Powwow.

One of North Dakota's two major Air Force bases, Grand Forks, was added to the list in May 1993 of military facilities that may close.

1990 Population: 638,800. White 604,142 (95%), Black 3,524 (1%), Other 31,134 (5%). Hispanic origin 4,665 (1%). 18 and over 463,415 (73%), 62 and over 107,200 (17%). Median age: 32.

Committees

Agriculture (20th of 28 Democrats)
Environment, Credit & Rural Development; Foreign Agriculture & Hunger; General Farm Commodities; Specialty Crops & Natural Resources

Budget (24th of 26 Democrats)

Campaign Finance

	Receipts	Receipts from PACs		Expend-itures
1992				
Pomeroy (D)	$431,979	$296,260	(69%)	$430,228
Korsmo (R)	$143,817	$58,532	(41%)	$150,639

Key Votes

1993

Require parental notification of minors' abortions	N
Require unpaid family and medical leave	Y
Approve national "motor voter" registration bill	Y
Approve budget increasing taxes and reducing deficit	Y
Approve economic stimulus plan	Y

Election

1992 General

Earl Pomeroy (D)	169,273	(57%)
John T. Korsmo (R)	117,442	(39%)
Anna Belle Bourgois (I)	7,394	(2%)
Grady Blount (I)	3,789	(1%)

District Vote for President

	1992
D	99,168 (32%)
R	136,244 (44%)
I	71,084 (23%)

Ohio

STATE DATA

Governor:
George V. Voinovich (R)
First elected: 1990
Length of term: 4 years
Term expires: 1/95
Salary: $109,998
Term limit: 2 terms
Phone: (614) 644-0813
Born: July 15, 1936; Collinwood, Ohio
Education: Ohio U., B.A., 1958; Ohio State U., J.D., 1961
Occupation: Lawyer
Family: Wife, Janet Allan; three children
Religion: Roman Catholic
Political Career: Ohio assistant attorney general, 1963-64; Ohio House, 1967-71; Cuyahoga County auditor, 1971-76; Cuyahoga County Commission, 1977-78; lieutenant governor, 1979; mayor of Cleveland, 1979-90; Republican nominee for U.S. Senate, 1988

Lt. Gov.: Mike DeWine (R)
First elected: 1990
Length of term: 4 years
Term expires: 1/95
Salary: $57,011
Phone: (614) 466-3396

State election official: (614) 466-2585
Democratic headquarters: (614) 221-6563
Republican headquarters: (614) 228-2481

REDISTRICTING

Ohio lost two House seats in reapportionment, dropping from 21 districts to 19. The legislature passed the map March 26, 1992; the governor signed it March 27.

STATE LEGISLATURE

General Assembly. Meets January-July in odd years, January-June in even years.

Senate: 33 members, 4-year terms
1992 breakdown: 20R, 13D; 28 men, 5 women; 30 whites, 3 blacks
Salary: $42,427
Phone: (614) 466-4900

House of Representatives: 99 members, 2-year terms
1992 breakdown: 53D, 46R; 76 men, 23 women; 87 whites, 12 blacks
Salary: $42,427
Phone: (614) 466-3357

URBAN STATISTICS

City	Pop.
Columbus	632,910
Mayor Gregory S. Lashutka, R	
Cleveland	505,616
Mayor Michael R. White, D	
Cincinnati	364,114
Mayor Dwight Tillery, D	
Toledo	332,943
Mayor John McHugh, D	

U.S. CONGRESS

Senate: 2 D, 0 R
House: 10 D, 9 R

TERM LIMITS

For Congress: Yes
Senate: 2 terms
House: 4 terms
For state offices: Yes
Senate: 2 terms
House: 4 terms

ELECTIONS

1992 Presidential Vote

Bill Clinton	40.2%
George Bush	38.3%
Ross Perot	21.0%

1988 Presidential Vote

George Bush	55%
Michael S. Dukakis	44%

1984 Presidential Vote

Ronald Reagan	59%
Walter F. Mondale	40%

POPULATION

1990 population		10,847,115
1980 population		10,797,630
Percent change		+<1%
Rank among states:		7
White		88%
Black		11%
Hispanic		1%
Asian or Pacific islander		1%
Urban		74%
Rural		26%
Born in state		74%
Foreign-born		2%
Under age 18	2,799,744	26%
Ages 18-64	6,640,410	61%
65 and older	1,406,961	13%
Median age		33.3

MISCELLANEOUS

Capital: Columbus
Number of counties: 88
Per capita income: $17,916 (1991)
Rank among states: 23
Total area: 41,330 sq. miles
Rank among states: 35

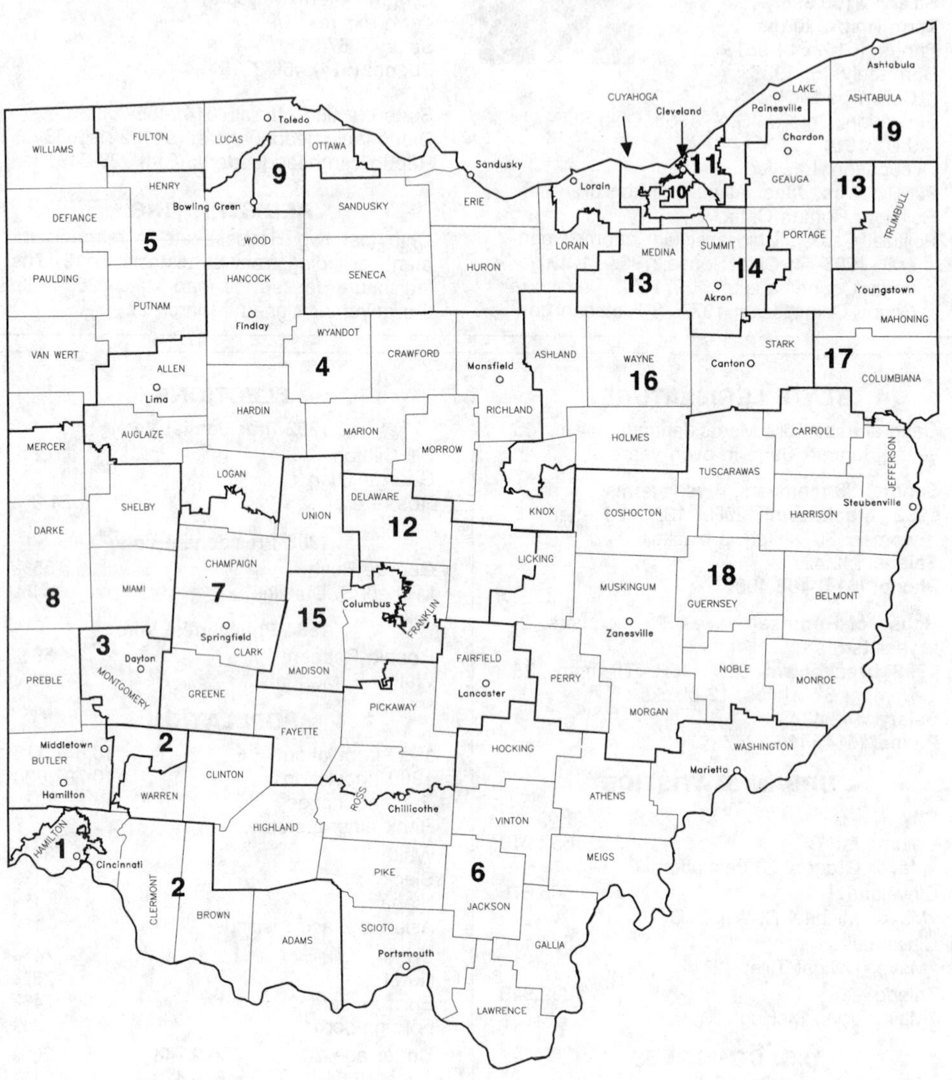

WILLIAMS
FULTON
LUCAS
Toledo
OTTAWA
9
Sandusky
HENRY
Bowling Green
SANDUSKY
ERIE
DEFIANCE
5
WOOD
PAULDING
HANCOCK
SENECA
HURON
PUTNAM
Findlay
VAN WERT
WYANDOT
CRAWFORD
4
ALLEN
Lima
HARDIN
MARION
Mansfield
RICHLAND
ASHLAND
MERCER
AUGLAIZE
MORROW
LOGAN
SHELBY
DARKE
UNION
DELAWARE
12
CHAMPAIGN
MIAMI
7
8
Springfield
CLARK
15
Columbus
FRANKLIN
3
Dayton
MONTGOMERY
PREBLE
GREENE
MADISON
PICKAWAY
FAYETTE
2
Middletown
BUTLER
Hamilton
WARREN
CLINTON
HAMILTON
1
Cincinnati
CLERMONT
2
BROWN
HIGHLAND
ROSS
Chillicothe
ADAMS
PIKE
SCIOTO
Portsmouth
CUYAHOGA
Cleveland
11
10
Lorain
LORAIN
MEDINA
13
SUMMIT
Akron
14
PORTAGE
Ashtabula
LAKE
Painesville
ASHTABULA
Chardon
GEAUGA
19
13
TRUMBULL
Youngstown
MAHONING
STARK
Canton
17
COLUMBIANA
WAYNE
16
HOLMES
CARROLL
TUSCARAWAS
JEFFERSON
Steubenville
HARRISON
KNOX
COSHOCTON
LICKING
MUSKINGUM
Zanesville
18
GUERNSEY
BELMONT
FAIRFIELD
Lancaster
PERRY
NOBLE
MONROE
MORGAN
HOCKING
WASHINGTON
Marietta
ATHENS
VINTON
MEIGS
6
JACKSON
GALLIA
LAWRENCE

John Glenn (D)

Of Columbus — Elected 1974; 4th Term

Born: July 18, 1921, Cambridge, Ohio.
Education: Muskingum College, B.S. 1962.
Military Service: Marine Corps, 1942-65.
Occupation: Astronaut; soft drink company executive.
Family: Wife, Anna Margaret Castor; two children.
Religion: Presbyterian.
Political Career: Sought Democratic nomination for U.S. Senate, 1970; sought Democratic nomination for president, 1984.
Capitol Office: 503 Hart Bldg. 20510; 224-3353.

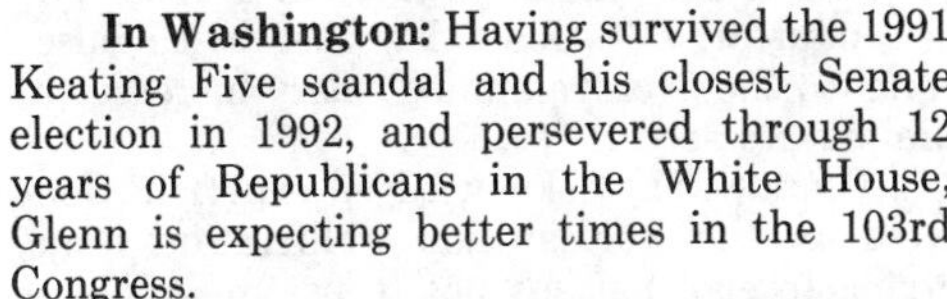

In Washington: Having survived the 1991 Keating Five scandal and his closest Senate election in 1992, and persevered through 12 years of Republicans in the White House, Glenn is expecting better times in the 103rd Congress.

President Clinton shares many of the views Glenn has championed for years as chairman of the Governmental Affairs Committee. Clinton campaigned on a promise to reinvent government and eliminate wasteful spending. He supports legislation to give the Environmental Protection Agency Cabinet status. And he favors an overhaul of the Hatch Act.

Glenn began the 103rd Congress with a flurry of action designed to take advantage of Clinton's inclinations. The day after Clinton's inaugural address, Glenn introduced far-reaching legislation aimed at restructuring government. A few weeks later, Clinton announced a major review aimed at many of the same goals.

Glenn also pushed the EPA Cabinet bill through the Senate in early May, and his committee approved an overhaul of the Hatch Act later that month.

A centrist Democrat with a technocrat's temperament, Glenn remains well suited to the nuts-and-bolts matters on the docket of the Governmental Affairs Committee. His passion for detail mixes well with the committee's mission to study the government's entrails.

Glenn is the polar opposite of the typically ambitious legislator; he has spent most of his career focusing on a handful of issues. Indeed, colleagues who admire the former astronaut's character and dedication wonder if he might have accomplished more had he not always been so narrowly focused. To a great extent, Glenn's career has been restricted because that is how his mind works. He does not take readily to new concepts or easily shift his tactics. Once he gets an idea into his head, he sticks to it tenaciously.

Respected as an American icon throughout his prominent public life, Glenn has tried to live by the words he issued even after his dismal 1984 bid for the presidency: "You keep climbing." But Glenn's entanglement in the Keating Five scandal made his climb a steeper one. The Senate Ethics Committee's investigation into his dealings with savings and loan operator Charles H. Keating Jr. concluded that Glenn had not done anything improper or illegal, but the episode took some luster off Glenn's public image.

Glenn was caught up early in the investigation of possible wrongdoing by five lawmakers suspected of doing favors for a wealthy campaign contributor. Of the five senators (the others were Democrats Alan Cranston of California, Donald W. Riegle Jr. of Michigan and Dennis DeConcini of Arizona, and Republican John McCain of Arizona), Glenn may have been Keating's oldest friend in the Senate. They had both personal and political connections. The two met in 1970, when Glenn first ran for the Senate.

Glenn emphasized that he ended virtually all contacts with Keating after federal regulators informed senators that criminal charges might be filed in the case. His only action after that time was to set up a lunch meeting in January 1988 between Keating and then-House Speaker Jim Wright of Texas. In the summer of 1987, Glenn testified, he turned down Keating's offer to raise campaign contributions because of Keating's battles with the regulators.

The Ethics Committee concluded that Glenn had "exercised poor judgment" in arranging the luncheon meeting some eight months after Glenn learned of the possible criminal referral. But, the committee added, the evidence indicated that Glenn's participation did not go beyond serving as host and his actions "did not reach the level requiring institutional action against him."

Glenn, the master of General Accounting Office detail, does not transfer well into macro politics. This was evident in his 1984 presidential campaign. Advertised for months as the main competitor to Walter F. Mondale for the Democratic nomination, he proved poor at public speaking, made weak showings in a succession of primaries and caucuses and quickly dropped out of the race.

Just when Glenn seemed resigned to finishing out his political career in the Senate, Massachusetts Democratic Gov. Michael S. Dukakis began to hint strongly in 1988 that he might make Glenn his running mate. Instead, Dukakis chose Texas Sen. Lloyd Bentsen, who he hoped could put the state in the Democratic column for president. Ever the good sport, Glenn introduced Bentsen at the convention in what, ironically, was perhaps his best-ever national speech — one that generated more audience response than Bentsen's.

On Governmental Affairs, Glenn has been an active chairman. He played a key role in the passage of legislation to create the Cabinet-level Department of Veterans Affairs. But he unsuccessfully advocated new agencies — created from components of the Commerce Department and the Office of the U.S. Trade Representative — to enhance U.S. competitiveness in trade and industrial policy. Beginning in 1990, he has consistently sponsored legislation to elevate the Environmental Protection Agency to Cabinet-level status, but differences with the Bush White House kept it from becoming law. With Clinton in office, Glenn moved quickly in 1993 and the Senate passed an EPA-Cabinet bill. The House seemed likely to follow suit.

But Glenn and Clinton certainly have some differences. During the 102nd Congress, when many in Congress were calling for a repeal of military policies that exclude women pilots from combat, Glenn and McCain led the majority of the members of the Senate Armed Services Committee in opposing an immediate repeal. They preferred to wait for the outcome of additional studies before a decision was made. No repeal was enacted in the 102nd, but Clinton overturned the exclusion rule himself early in 1993.

As U.S. troops began to fight in the Persian Gulf in January 1991, Senate Majority Leader George J. Mitchell appointed Glenn chairman of a Democratic task force to review legislative proposals for aiding military families. In March, Congress cleared a package of new benefits — including a broad range of tax, health, pay and other benefits for returning troops — for veterans and military personnel.

Glenn led the effort in the 101st and 102nd Congresses to amend the Hatch Act, which prohibits the nation's 3 million federal employees from taking part in partisan politics. Glenn's committee approved the measure in July 1989, and Congress cleared the bill in 1990, only to see President Bush veto it. The bill never made it to the floor in the 102nd because the Senate lacked the 67 votes needed to override a veto.

Glenn said that the Hatch Act was outdated and that its hundreds of unclear rules intimidated federal workers from any political participation. "We must balance the need to protect the integrity of the civil servants with our duty to protect the constitutional right of all citizens who participate in the nation's political processes," Glenn said. The Senate fell two votes short of overriding Bush's veto.

Glenn continued to push Hatch Act repeal legislation in the 103rd.

Glenn has also promoted legislation in the 102nd and the 103rd Congress to repeal the honoraria ban on federal employees, which prohibits them from accepting writing or speaking fees.

Aiming to close the gap between federal and private-sector salaries, Glenn sponsored an overhaul of the federal pay system in 1990. The new plan provides federal workers with raises equal to the average annual salary increases in the private sector.

Glenn is the acknowledged expert in Congress on the nuclear non-proliferation issue, urging foreign nations not to use materials or technology to build nuclear weapons.

Glenn's anti-proliferation efforts brought him into frequent conflict with the Reagan administration. Throughout the 1980s, Glenn fought President Ronald Reagan over efforts to send military aid to India and Pakistan, to sell nuclear-power materials to China and to offer U.S. nuclear fuels to the Japanese. He continued that stance under President Bush.

Since the start of the 99th Congress, Glenn has served on Armed Services. Over most of his career, Glenn has tilted to the hawkish side on national security matters. But his overall record is that of a centrist who, despite his background as a test pilot, has not hesitated to oppose weapons systems if he deems them too expensive.

Glenn also has reservations about the use of force abroad when it becomes, in his mind, overly adventurist — as in U.S. efforts to protect Kuwaiti tankers in 1987 or to liberate Kuwait from Iraqi occupation in 1991.

Glenn also has used his position on Armed Services to defend abortion rights. He coauthored a controversial 1990 amendment to permit overseas military hospitals to perform abortions. The proposal was supported by most senators but did not have enough support to end a filibuster or overturn a veto, and it was eventually withdrawn.

At Home: Glenn drew no punishment in the Keating Five investigation, but the whiff of scandal weakened his popularity in Ohio, and gave Lt. Gov. (and former Rep.) Mike DeWine a fighting chance against Glenn in 1992. National Republicans even began to promote DeWine as their best opportunity to defeat a Democratic incumbent.

DeWine sounded 1992's most common candidate klaxon, running as the candidate of "change." His strategy from the start was to focus attention on what his campaign considered Glenn's twin albatrosses: the Keating affair and the seemingly irreducible $3 million debt remaining from his 1984 presidential bid. And Glenn, seeking his fourth six-year term at age 71, appeared vulnerable in what seemed like a year of "change."

But selling DeWine as a credible outsider proved to be difficult. The Republican had served four terms in the House before being elected to his statewide post; before that, he was a county prosecutor and state senator. He also had overdrafts at the House bank (although he voluntarily disclosed them and even revealed overdrafts outside the period investigated by the House ethics committee). And DeWine, although he held statewide office, was not well-known to most Ohio residents, having been elected in tandem with gubernatorial candidate George V. Voinovich.

As DeWine sought to tar Glenn with the Keating and debt questions, he also questioned the incumbent's accomplishments during his tenure. "After 18 years in the Senate, what on Earth has John Glenn done?" DeWine demanded at a campaign rally, implying that Glenn's terrestrial achievements did not measure up to his pioneering in space. DeWine's most attention-getting ad was a takeoff on a well-known battery commercial: A toy astronaut rolled across the screen beating a drum with the message that Glenn "keeps owing and owing," referring to the $3 million debt.

Although Glenn had not faced a strenuous challenge in years, the Keating scandal had forced him to gird for one. He made a tactical decision to engage DeWine early, criticizing him for his opposition to abortion rights and his overdrafts and accusing him of having an undistinguished congressional record.

On Election Day, DeWine carried 48 of the state's 88 counties. But Glenn won nearly every county in a swath across industrial northern and eastern Ohio, and did well in rural, usually Republican southern Ohio as well. He won by more than 400,000 votes, but it was his narrowest Senate victory.

The decision to take the campaign to DeWine may have spelled the difference, enabling Glenn to put DeWine on the defensive from the outset. But it was clear that Glenn did not enjoy the negative tone of the campaign. On election night, he blamed DeWine for employing "the politics of sleaze, smear and character assassination."

Until recently, political vulnerability had been a stranger to Glenn. After he won his Senate seat in 1974 with 65 percent of the vote, he twice won re-election easily.

However, Glenn did have difficulty getting to the Senate in the first place. His career in Congress was delayed for a decade, first by an injury and then by an unexpected defeat.

Glenn had achieved national hero status in 1962, when he became the first American to orbit the Earth. Still basking in the glow of his space exploits — which had brought him into close contact with the Kennedys — Glenn decided to run for office in 1964 as a Democrat.

Glenn returned to Ohio to challenge 74-year-old Sen. Stephen M. Young in the 1964 Democratic primary. But he did not get very far: A bathroom fall injured his inner ear, and he had to drop out of the primary.

Glenn's political ambitions then temporarily subsided. Instead of attending party functions, he plunged into business. Glenn served on the boards of Royal Crown Cola and the Questor Corp., oversaw four Holiday Inn franchises he partly owned, lectured and filmed television documentaries.

In 1970, with Young retiring, Glenn decided to run for the seat, competing for the Democratic nomination against Howard M. Metzenbaum, then a millionaire businessman and labor lawyer. Initially a strong favorite, Glenn found that his frequent absences from Ohio over the preceding six years had hurt him politically, giving him the image of an outsider among state Democrats. Although not well-known then to the public, Metzenbaum had the support of the party establishment and a superb, well-financed campaign organization.

Glenn, whose celebrity status was bringing out large crowds, was overconfident. Meanwhile, Metzenbaum erased his anonymity through saturation television advertising. On primary day, Glenn carried 75 of the state's 88 counties but was badly beaten in the urban areas. He lost the nomination by 13,442 votes.

Metzenbaum was beaten in the general election by Republican Robert A. Taft Jr. Three years later, however, he made it to the Senate as an appointee, chosen by Democratic Gov. John J. Gilligan to fill a vacancy. Metzenbaum immediately began campaigning for a full term in his own right, and Glenn — who made up for his previous mistake by becoming a regular on the political circuit — decided to challenge him for the nomination.

The Metzenbaum appointment outraged Glenn and gave him an issue during their rematch in the 1974 primary. Glenn rejected Gilligan's offer to be his running mate as lieutenant governor and denounced the governor as a "boss" who practiced "machine politics."

The underdog Glenn of 1974 proved to be much tougher than the favored Glenn of 1970. This time, he did much better in Metzenbaum's base of Cuyahoga County (Cleveland) and maintained his customary strength in rural areas. Glenn was thus able to even the score with Metzenbaum, winning the primary by 91,000 votes. In the fall, Glenn crushed a weak Republican opponent, Cleveland Mayor Ralph J. Perk, whose campaign was disorganized and underfinanced.

Six years later, Glenn had only nominal

opposition for a second term. His win, with 69 percent of the vote, marked him as a 1984 presidential contender. His bid for the Democratic nomination fell flat, though. Despite his image as a hero and as a moderate alternative to Mondale, Glenn was never able to spark widespread interest in his campaign.

Glenn bounced back with another strong Senate campaign in 1986. He had worked hard to mend fences with Ohio voters in the wake of his failed White House bid, making dozens of appearances across the state to boost other Democrats and his own political stock.

His GOP foe, Rep. Thomas Kindness, was aggressive and relatively well-financed. He pounded away at what he saw as Glenn's main weakness — the lingering multimillion-dollar debt from his presidential campaign.

Kindness maintained that Glenn received preferential treatment from the banks that the average Ohioan would not get, but he was unable to wound Glenn. Not well-known outside his conservative southwest Ohio district, he lacked the money to mount a statewide media blitz that might have shaken the incumbent's image. He lost in a landslide.

Since their battles in the 1970s, Glenn has come to terms with Metzenbaum, who in 1976 was elected to the Senate and is now in his third full term. While much has been made of the long rivalry between the two, Glenn helped ensure Metzenbaum's re-election during a heated 1988 contest with then-Cleveland Mayor Voinovich.

Many expected Glenn to give his Senate colleague just token support, but Glenn piloted Metzenbaum around the state the day he formally announced he was seeking re-election. And late in the campaign, after Voinovich accused Metzenbaum of being soft on child pornography, Glenn appeared in a hard-hitting TV ad and accused the Republican of "the lowest gutter politics." While Metzenbaum was already on his way to victory, the Glenn ad was credited with boosting him to a comfortable 57 percent of the vote.

Committees

Governmental Affairs (Chairman)
Permanent Subcommittee on Investigations (vice chairman)

Armed Services (6th of 11 Democrats)
Military Readiness & Defense Infrastructure (chairman); Coalition Defense & Reinforcing Forces; Nuclear Deterrence, Arms Control & Defense Intelligence

Select Intelligence (3rd of 9 Democrats)

Special Aging (2nd of 11 Democrats)

Elections

1992 General		
John Glenn (D)	2,444,419	(51%)
Mike DeWine (R)	2,028,300	(42%)
Martha Kathryn Grevatt (I)	321,234	(7%)

Previous Winning Percentages: **1986** (62%) **1980** (69%) **1974** (65%)

Campaign Finance

	Receipts	Receipts from PACs	Expend-itures
1992			
Glenn (D)	$3,946,713	$1,190,451 (30%)	$3,999,271
DeWine (R)	$3,048,971	$588,975 (19%)	$3,053,156

Key Votes

1993	
Require unpaid family and medical leave	Y
Approve national "motor voter" registration bill	Y
Approve budget increasing taxes and reducing deficit	Y
Support president's right to lift military gay ban	Y
1992	
Approve school-choice pilot program	N
Allow shifting funds from defense to domestic programs	Y
Oppose deeper cuts in spending for SDI	N
1991	
Approve waiting period for handgun purchases	Y
Raise senators' pay and ban honoraria	N
Authorize use of force in Persian Gulf	N
Confirm Clarence Thomas to Supreme Court	N

Voting Studies

	Presidential Support		Party Unity		Conservative Coalition	
Year	**S**	**O**	**S**	**O**	**S**	**O**
1992	30	68	83	17	37	58
1991	41	56	83	14	38	63
1990	39	61	79	21	41	59
1989	59	38	82	16	50	47
1988	53	45	86	11	27	73
1987	38	60	82	12	28	66
1986	42	52	74	23	29	70
1985	42	56	79	18	42	57
1984	39	43	55	25	28	51
1983	39	35	57	12	20	52
1982	35	45	67	17	26	51
1981	53	42	74	21	34	66

Interest Group Ratings

Year	ADA	AFL-CIO	CCUS	ACU
1992	80	75	10	11
1991	90	75	0	10
1990	89	67	25	9
1989	65	100	38	26
1988	80	79	31	9
1987	80	100	18	12
1986	65	87	44	30
1985	75	86	34	27
1984	65	67	38	5
1983	65	93	31	16
1982	70	87	55	28
1981	80	68	44	7

Howard M. Metzenbaum (D)

Of Lyndhurst — Elected 1976; 3rd Full Term

Also served January-December 1974 (appointed).

Born: June 4, 1917, Lyndhurst, Ohio.

Education: Ohio State U., B.A. 1939, LL.B. 1941.

Occupation: Lawyer; newspaper publisher; parking company executive.

Family: Wife, Shirley Turoff; four children.

Religion: Jewish.

Political Career: Ohio House, 1943-47; Ohio Senate, 1947-51; Democratic nominee for U.S. Senate, 1970; sought Democratic nomination for U.S. Senate, 1974.

Capitol Office: 140 Russell Bldg. 20510; 224-2315.

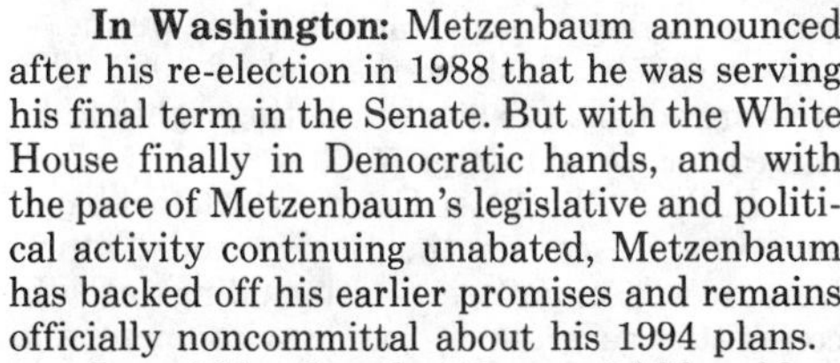

In Washington: Metzenbaum announced after his re-election in 1988 that he was serving his final term in the Senate. But with the White House finally in Democratic hands, and with the pace of Metzenbaum's legislative and political activity continuing unabated, Metzenbaum has backed off his earlier promises and remains officially noncommittal about his 1994 plans.

It could be that the 76-year-old liberal has had second thoughts. Or he may simply prefer not to be seen as a lame duck in his final years in office. In any event, he has made it clear that lawyer-entrepreneur Joel Hyatt, his son-in-law, will be his choice to succeed him when he steps down.

With a Democrat in the White House, Metzenbaum is clearly going to be happier than he was in the Reagan and Bush years, but he is anything but supportive of the New Democrat centrism that President Clinton is associated with. In 1990, upset by what he saw as a large number of fellow Democrats becoming "shadow Republicans," Metzenbaum used $50,000 in leftover 1988 campaign funds to found the Center for Democratic Values (CDV), a left-of-center organization aimed at promoting traditional liberalism. In a slap at the more centrist Democratic Leadership Council, to which Clinton belonged, the CDV's manifesto declared that the country "does not need two Republican parties."

During the early 1980s, Metzenbaum won a reputation as the Senate's leading liberal obstructionist and bill-killer. Though his role changed when seniority gave him official leadership positions, he did not abandon the confrontational, independent style that had previously forced his influence upon the Senate. He remains the self-appointed scourge of "special-interest" legislation on behalf of consumers and the Treasury.

He often defies Senate traditions of quiet, mutual back-scratching, publicly exposing the tax breaks and special provisions that colleagues bury deep within big bills, and opposing federal spending for some members' local projects that typically would get a rubber stamp of approval. He is a master of Senate rules, and most effective at employing them at the end of each congressional session, when time is short and members are eager to leave town. Just his threat of a filibuster has killed many bills.

But he also knows how to move legislation. On Judiciary, where he leads the Antitrust Subcommittee, Metzenbaum helped enact antitrust bills, a measure protecting workers' insurance benefits at bankrupt companies, a ban on plastic guns and the first penalties aimed at fraud by major contractors. A strong proponent of gun control, Metzenbaum was the chamber's point man on the Brady bill, which aimed to establish a seven-day waiting period for people wanting to buy handguns. He continued in that vein in the 102nd Congress, including the waiting period provisions in a larger anti-crime bill, which was killed by a filibuster. Metzenbaum immediately reintroduced the Brady bill at the start of the 103rd Congress.

Metzenbaum used his Judiciary subcommittee in the 102nd Congress to probe alleged price fixing among three major infant-formula companies, helping prompt a Federal Trade Commission investigation into the matter. Financial settlements with two of the companies required them to provide 54 million servings of infant formula to a federal feeding program. Charges were brought against the third company.

Metzenbaum also conducted oversight hearings on how the government is restructuring the savings and loan industry. He is a stern critic of the Resolution Trust Corporation (RTC), which manages and disposes of assets from thrifts that have failed since January 1989.

Republicans have accused Metzenbaum of using his hearings for political purposes. His response: "I am trying to get the government to do what it should be doing. A senator has to jump up and down and make enough noise to get the bureaucrats to work."

A February 1991 hearing implicating a GOP gubernatorial candidate in Arizona led Minority Leader Bob Dole of Kansas to charge that Metzenbaum had abused his Senate power. The flap arose from a hearing on losses stemming from the insolvency of Southwest Savings and Loan Association in Phoenix. The subcommittee had investigated a tip that the RTC failed to investigate the possible liability of Southwest's directors and officers for the losses.

The subcommittee also looked at the business dealings of a former director, J. Fife Symington, who at the time of the hearing was in a tight race for governor of Arizona. In a Senate floor speech, Dole accused Metzenbaum of trying to tilt the Arizona race with a sneak attack on Symington. Despite the hearing and the controversy, Symington won his election. Republicans, however, continued to criticize Metzenbaum, demanding that he investigate failed thrifts with ties to Democrats as well.

Metzenbaum has also used the subcommittee to push legislation to ensure that retailers could take legal action against vertical price fixing, which occurs when a manufacturer conspires with a retailer to force a rival dealer to charge at least a certain price for the manufacturer's goods.

Demonstrating his legislative horse-trading skills, Metzenbaum got the bill through committee in 1990 when he persuaded Arizona Democrat Dennis DeConcini, who opposed the measure, to vote for it if it meant the difference between committee approval and rejection. Earlier, Metzenbaum had dropped efforts to block committee consideration of a DeConcini bill overhauling RICO, the federal anti-racketeering law.

In an effort to get a floor vote on his bill in the 101st Congress, Metzenbaum held up a major judgeships bill until the last day of Congress. He finally relented after winning a promise from Senate Judiciary leaders that the vertical price-fixing measure would be sent to the floor early in 1991. The Senate finally passed the bill in May 1991. The House passed a similar measure but later rejected a conference report on the bill.

Active on a wide range of Judiciary issues, Metzenbaum worked with Massachusetts Democrat Edward M. Kennedy on a major civil rights bill in 1990 and 1991. Metzenbaum sparked a controversy when he criticized opponents of the measure by saying, "We do not agree and are not going to yield to the David Dukes of America" — a reference to the controversial former Louisiana state representative and former Ku Klux Klan leader. The remark upset Republicans, who repudiated Metzenbaum's charge of racism.

As Labor Subcommittee chairman, Metzenbaum helped enact legislation in the 102nd Congress to broaden the Job Training Partnership Act to encourage a wider range of opportunities for women in non-traditional jobs.

In 1988, he used his chairmanship to play a lead role in battling for a law mandating advance notice to workers of plant closings, a top Democratic priority. He also used his place on Labor in 1990 to help produce compromise legislation reversing a 1989 Supreme Court ruling that allowed age-based discrimination in employee benefits.

Metzenbaum helped enact measures improving the system of nutrition labeling of food products, increasing certain penalties for child labor law violations, and restricting employers' ability to terminate pension plans. His bill to amend the Orphan Drug Act — which granted marketing monopolies and other incentives to companies that developed drugs to treat diseases afflicting a small fraction of the public — was vetoed by Bush at the end of 1990. The measure sought to allow marketing rights to be shared for certain drugs.

Early in the 101st Congress, Metzenbaum gave up his seat on the Energy and Natural Resources Committee — including a subcommittee gavel — to join Environment and Public Works. A consistent critic of the oil and gas industry, Metzenbaum had little success with his crusades on the Energy Committee, where he was one of a very few members oriented toward consumer and environmental issues. In 1989, he lost his vigorous battle against the decontrol of natural gas prices — a defeat that may have helped lead to his leaving the panel.

During the Reagan and Bush administrations, Metzenbaum was the Democrats' point man in the Senate on controversial nominations. In September 1991, he had to engage in some shuttle opposition, racing between simultaneous hearings in the Judiciary and Intelligence committees to grill Clarence Thomas about his Supreme Court nomination and then to interrogate Robert M. Gates, Bush's nominee to head the CIA. Metzenbaum opposed them both, but each was confirmed. Metzenbaum led the unsuccessful charge against Edwin Meese III, President Ronald Reagan's nominee to be attorney general, and was in the forefront when the Senate rejected Supreme Court nominee Robert H. Bork.

Metzenbaum received some negative publicity from a trip he took to the Middle East in April 1990, when he and four other senators met with Iraqi President Saddam Hussein — less than four months before Iraq's Aug. 2 invasion of Kuwait. A transcript of the meeting released by the Iraqis after their invasion quoted Metzenbaum as telling Saddam: "I am now aware that you are a strong and intelligent man and that you want peace."

The transcript made all five senators seem

clueless about the destructive intentions of the Iraqi dictator. But at a news conference after the session, Metzenbaum called the meeting with Saddam "the least gratifying or satisfying" of the trip and criticized the Iraqi strongman for having "somewhat of a war psychosis."

At Home: An early and overwhelming success in business, Metzenbaum had to struggle through years of trial and failure in Ohio politics before reaching the Senate. But the experience made him a wily, independent politician, adept at gut-level tactics, fundraising and quasi-populist oratory. These traits may not lend much to Senate comity, but they enabled the veteran Democrat to dismiss a well-funded Republican challenger in 1988.

That year, national GOP officials were high on Cleveland Mayor George V. Voinovich, who was popular in the state's most Democratic territory and had solid business backing. Voinovich would vindicate himself by winning the governorship two years later, but against Metzenbaum he proved a disappointment.

Even as the GOP ballyhooed its 1988 strategy — saying Voinovich could win in Republican-dominated southern and western Ohio and cut into the Democratic base in Cleveland's Cuyahoga County — Metzenbaum was taking control of the debate.

When a national GOP document labeling him a communist sympathizer was leaked to the press in July 1987, Democrats (and some Republicans) took to the Senate floor within hours to defend Metzenbaum and condemn such campaign tactics. Voinovich's repudiation of the document was lost in the well-orchestrated fury.

In late September, Voinovich ran tough TV ads portraying Metzenbaum as soft on child pornography. The Democrat countered with a testimonial TV ad by fellow Ohio Sen. John Glenn condemning Voinovich's "gutter politics." Coming from Glenn — who had twice clashed with Metzenbaum in bitter Senate primaries — the ad hit home. Editorialists characterized Voinovich's ad as a desperation tactic. Metzenbaum won Cuyahoga County by 2-to-1 and showed surprising strength downstate. He won a decisive 57 percent overall.

(Despite his failure against Metzenbaum, Voinovich's potential as a statewide candidate was not necessarily overstated; he came back to easily defeat Democrat Anthony J. Celebrezze Jr. for Ohio's governorship in 1990.)

Even before Metzenbaum suggested he might not seek a fourth term, he was promoting his son-in-law, Hyatt, as a future Democratic leader. The founder of Hyatt Legal Services, the younger man frequently appeared at campaign events with Metzenbaum. By 1992, he had already raised several hundred thousand dollars in preparation for a long-anticipated 1994 bid to succeed his father-in-law.

Glenn's role in Metzenbaum's win seemed to put an end to years of talk of a cool relationship between the two. They first clashed in the 1970 primary to succeed Democratic Sen. Stephen M. Young, who was retiring. At the time, Glenn was a national hero and a household name, and Metzenbaum was an obscure figure even in much of Cleveland.

Metzenbaum had worked his way through college selling magazines and Fuller brushes, but soon struck it rich in business, winning franchises for the operation of parking lots at airports.

For a while, Metzenbaum pursued business and politics simultaneously. In 1942, the year after he graduated from law school, he bucked the Cuyahoga County Democratic organization and won a race for the state House. Later, he moved up to the state Senate. His major achievement in the Legislature came in 1949, when he won passage of a bill regulating consumer credit.

Metzenbaum left public office in 1951 to run his parking lots and practice law. His record as a labor lawyer was to help him build a political base in the 1970s.

Over the years, Metzenbaum served as a board member and financial angel for such groups as Karamu, a black cultural institution in Cleveland, and the National Council on Hunger and Malnutrition. He fought to integrate a number of exclusive Cleveland clubs.

In the 1970 primary, the aggressive millionaire put Glenn on the defensive by arguing that money should be diverted from the space program to domestic concerns. Glenn had to play down his astronaut days. To counter Glenn's celebrity status, Metzenbaum aired TV ads presenting himself as an independent-minded businessman driven to run for office by the declining state of government.

Metzenbaum, with years of party work behind him, had the endorsement of most party leaders. He built a superior campaign organization and won the nomination by 13,442 votes.

That fall, Metzenbaum faced another famous name, Robert A. Taft Jr., son of Ohio's most dominant political figure of modern times. Taft won narrowly, taking a hard line against campus protesters (it was the year of the fatal shootings at Kent State) and labeling the Democrat "an ultraliberal."

But three years later, Metzenbaum found himself occupying the office he could not win in 1970. GOP Sen. William B. Saxbe resigned to become President Richard M. Nixon's attorney general. Democratic Gov. John J. Gilligan, looking for support from organized labor, named Metzenbaum to the vacancy, giving him a full year in the Senate before Saxbe's term was to expire.

Incumbency, however, proved no advantage in 1974, when Metzenbaum fought a rematch with Glenn and lost. Metzenbaum's wealth backfired on him in ways he had managed to avoid in 1970. Under pressure from Glenn, he made public his tax returns — revealing that he had paid no federal taxes in 1969. Glenn got the nomination and was elected to the Senate that fall.

So Metzenbaum had to run as a challenger again in 1976 in pursuit of a full Senate term. This time in the Democratic primary he had advantages in money, name recognition and party support, and the wealth and tax issues were behind him. He easily took the nomination from Rep. James V. Stanton and, in the fall, launched a new attack on Taft's effectiveness.

He claimed he had accomplished more in one year in the Senate than Taft had in six, and focused on the energy issue, blaming much of America's economic problem on the oil companies. He campaigned in alliance with Jimmy Carter, taking advantage of Carter's spring and summer popularity in Ohio. By November, his winning margin was 117,000 votes — more than 10 times as great as Carter's margin in Ohio.

Metzenbaum's 1982 re-election was never close. The decline in the auto and steel industries severely affected Ohio, creating a favorable forum for Metzenbaum's feisty brand of economic populism. After the sudden death in April of the front-running GOP challenger, Rep. John M. Ashbrook, Republican leaders backed state Sen. Paul E. Pfeifer, who lacked both name identification and money. Metzenbaum coasted to victory with 57 percent of the vote.

Committees

Environment & Public Works (8th of 10 Democrats)
Clean Air & Nuclear Regulation; Superfund, Recycling & Solid Waste Management; Water Resources, Transportation, Public Buildings & Economic Development

Judiciary (3rd of 10 Democrats)
Antitrust, Monopolies & Business Rights (chairman); Constitution; Courts & Administrative Practice

Labor & Human Resources (3rd of 10 Democrats)
Labor (chairman); Aging; Disability Policy; Education, Arts & Humanities

Select Intelligence (2nd of 9 Democrats)

Elections

1988 General		
Howard M. Metzenbaum (D)	2,480,038	(57%)
George V. Voinovich (R)	1,872,716	(43%)
1988 Primary		
Howard M. Metzenbaum (D)	1,070,934	(84%)
Ralph A. Applegate (D)	210,508	(16%)

Previous Winning Percentages: **1982** (57%) **1976** (50%)

Campaign Finance

	Receipts	Receipts from PACs		Expend-itures
1988				
Metzenbaum (D)	$7,312,533	$1,028,183	(14%)	$8,547,545
Voinovich (R)	$7,828,764	$1,326,627	(17%)	$8,236,432

Key Votes

1993	
Require unpaid family and medical leave	Y
Approve national "motor voter" registration bill	Y
Approve budget increasing taxes and reducing deficit	Y
Support president's right to lift military gay ban	Y
1992	
Approve school-choice pilot program	N
Allow shifting funds from defense to domestic programs	Y
Oppose deeper cuts in spending for SDI	N
1991	
Approve waiting period for handgun purchases	Y
Raise senators' pay and ban honoraria	Y
Authorize use of force in Persian Gulf	N
Confirm Clarence Thomas to Supreme Court	N

Voting Studies

	Presidential Support		Party Unity		Conservative Coalition	
Year	**S**	**O**	**S**	**O**	**S**	**O**
1992	25	72	91	6	5	95
1991	27	69	93	6	10	90
1990	27	68	85	10	8	89
1989	39	59	92	7	8	89
1988	36	55	87	6	24	68
1987	32	65	88	9	3	91
1986	24	76	86	13	5	93
1985	26	72	87	10	17	83
1984	26	69	79	16	4	91
1983	36	60	80	19	11	86
1982	32	64	88	5	4	85
1981	30	59	82	5	7	81

Interest Group Ratings

Year	ADA	AFL-CIO	CCUS	ACU
1992	90	100	11	0
1991	100	83	10	0
1990	78	89	8	10
1989	95	100	25	7
1988	80	100	15	4
1987	100	100	22	4
1986	100	93	21	4
1985	100	100	29	0
1984	100	91	22	5
1983	100	100	11	12
1982	100	92	11	28
1981	85	94	7	0

1 David Mann (D)

Of Cincinnati — Elected 1992; 1st Term

Born: Sept. 25, 1939, Cincinnati, Ohio.
Education: Harvard U., A.B. 1961, LL.B. 1968.
Military Service: Navy, 1961-65.
Occupation: Lawyer.
Family: Wife, Elizabeth Taliaferro; three children.
Religion: Methodist.
Political Career: Cincinnati City Council, 1974-93, mayor, 1980-82, 1991.
Capitol Office: 503 Cannon Bldg. 20515; 225-2216.

The Path to Washington: Mann comes to the House with the somewhat vexing problem of being an urban Democrat — with liberal credentials and an avowed desire to funnel federal money into urban areas — who won election as a converted fiscal conservative who favors a constitutional amendment requiring a balanced federal budget.

His predicament is complicated by a closer-than-expected election and the worry that had he faced more organized opposition, he might have lost.

Mann hews to a traditional Democratic view — forged in 18 years on the city council, three as mayor — that government should do more for people who are without jobs and housing. He wants to attack crime and promote inner-city education with federal money.

From the Judiciary Committee, Mann can pursue his interest in crime. His Armed Services slot, however, may give him few opportunities to serve the 1st directly. Mann, with a background in tax law, had hoped that there might be room for freshmen on the Ways and Means Committee and that he might fill the seat held by retiring Ohio Democrat Don J. Pease. That opportunity did not arise.

But he concluded that voters wanted something different in 1992. He added a twist to his call for activism — that government somehow should do more for less. Campaigning as an outsider, he charged that Washington was out of touch. And after fighting against a 1991 voter initiative that put term limits on council members, Mann in 1992 embraced a statewide initiative to limit the House members' terms.

His newfound fiscal conservatism won out over his activism in March 1993 when he became one of only three Democratic freshmen to vote against President Clinton's proposed $16.3 billion economic stimulus package, a measure supported by many big-city mayors.

Mann did not even have his eye on the House race when the campaign began. Faced with the city council term limit, he had filed for an elected judgeship on the state appeals court. But that was before one-term House incumbent Rep. Charles Luken announced at the end of June — after he had been nominated in an uncontested primary — that he would not seek re-election.

After a three-week campaign, Mann squeaked by longtime state Sen. William F. Bowen in a crowded special primary election.

Mann, who is white, has always won black voters' support. But Bowen, who is black, picked up most of the black vote. Mann's margin of victory was supplied by suburban Hamilton County whites, some of whom were registered Republicans who voted in the special primary.

Mann used targeted campaign mailings to pitch his message to different constituencies, and Bowen attacked him for appealing to white sympathies by saying he wanted to protect "West Side values." Hoping to reverse his 418-vote loss, Bowen contested the GOP crossover vote as unconstitutional. He dropped that complaint but did not endorse Mann in the general election.

Once past the special primary, Mann expected only token opposition in November because there was no formally identified Republican candidate on the ballot. That hope turned out to be a bit premature.

Luken had appeared to have a clear shot at re-election because the district was reconfigured during redistricting to his advantage. As a result, J. Kenneth Blackwell, a former Cincinnati mayor who lost narrowly to Luken in 1990, chose not to run.

That left Steve Grote, a local baker and Green Township trustee, as the only interested Republican. But he submitted flawed nominating petitions and was disqualified. At the last minute, however, he got on the ballot as an independent.

Grote gained the backing — and most of the votes — of local Republicans, however. And with Libertarian James A. Berns pulling 5 percent, he held Mann to a slim 51 percent majority.

In all the fuss over Luken, Blackwell considered a late entry. He and the local GOP argued that because the Democrats had to replace Luken on the November ballot, the Republicans should have another chance to field a candidate. The state Supreme Court denied the request.

Ohio 1

Hamilton County — Western Cincinnati and suburbs

Nestled snugly in the southwestern corner of the state, the 1st reaches out to take in almost every Democrat in the Cincinnati area, leaving the surrounding 2nd District solidly Republican and this district more Democratic.

Cincinnati's black population helped former Democratic Rep. Thomas A. Luken build a majority here in the 1980s, and 1992's round of redistricting has made that majority even more solid.

The latest redistricting was aimed at aiding Luken's successor, his son Charles, who took over the seat in 1990 after his father retired. But in 1992, the younger Luken halted his re-election run just after winning the Democratic primary, leaving this custom-built district open for the taking.

Mann was able to sweep into the seat in 1992 after the Republican Party was unable to replace its nominee, who had been disqualified from the ballot.

The new 1st includes about 85 percent of Cincinnati's 364,000 residents. Democrats count on heavy support from the city's black community — blacks make up 44 percent of this part of Cincinnati and only 14 percent of the rest of the district. Only 5 percent of the residents of the 2nd District's eastern slice of the city are black.

Forming another dominant political bloc are the German Catholics who have defined the city's cautious, conservative personality for more than 100 years. Once clustered in the West Side section of the city known as "Over-the-Rhine," the German-Americans gradually moved out to suburbs such as Cheviot and Green Township.

As a fairly conservative Catholic Democrat, Charles Luken was able to retain the support of this crucial bloc in 1990. But in state and national contests, the German Catholics often vote Republican.

At the bottom of Walnut Hill, in the flat Ohio River basin, is downtown Cincinnati, with the Taft Museum and wharves for old stern-wheelers such as the Delta Queen. Construction of Riverfront Stadium and Coliseum (home of baseball's Reds and football's Bengals) in the early 1970s symbolized a downtown renewal project designed to lure suburban dollars back to the city.

A major Ohio River port and a regional center of commerce, the city is headquarters for the giant Procter & Gamble Co. and Milacron, a world leader in the production of machine tools.

Cincinnati's diverse economy prevented it from suffering the degree of hardship that hit other industrial cities in the state in the early 1980s recession.

The 1980s defense buildup boosted the revenues of numerous area defense contractors, the largest being General Electric Co., which provides jobs for blue-collar workers in the western section of the city.

In 1992 presidential voting, both Bill Clinton and George Bush took 43 percent of the vote in the 1st. Clinton was the raw-vote winner, collecting 155 more ballots than Bush.

1990 Population: 570,900. White 391,483 (69%), Black 171,871 (30%), Other 7,546 (1%). Hispanic origin 3,421 (1%). 18 and over 420,468 (74%), 62 and over 91,686 (16%). Median age: 32.

Committees

Armed Services (25th of 34 Democrats)
Military Acquisition; Oversight & Investigations

Judiciary (19th of 21 Democrats)
Administrative Law & Governmental Relations; Crime & Criminal Justice; Economic & Commercial Law

Campaign Finance

	Receipts	Receipts from PACs		Expend-itures
1992				
Mann (D)	$281,158	$107,550	(38%)	$278,294
Grote (I)	$83,526	$8,752	(10%)	$83,038
Berns (I)	$1,245	0		$1,817

Key Votes

1993	
Require parental notification of minors' abortions	N
Require unpaid family and medical leave	Y
Approve national "motor voter" registration bill	Y
Approve budget increasing taxes and reducing deficit	Y
Approve economic stimulus plan	N

Elections

1992 General		
David Mann (D)	120,190	(51%)
Steve Grote (I)	101,498	(43%)
James A. Berns (I)	12,734	(5%)
1992 Primary Special †		
David Mann (D)	14,861	(34%)
William F. Bowen (D)	14,443	(33%)
Virginia Rhodes (D)	6,423	(15%)
Mary Ann Boyd (D)	3,656	(8%)
Steven Reece (D)	1,932	(4%)
Earladeen Badger (D)	1,014	(2%)
Raymond Ellis (D)	654	(2%)

† Charles Luken, D, withdrew his name after winning the June 2, 1992 primary. A primary special was held on Aug. 4, 1992 to replace him.

District Vote for President

	1992
D	104,494 (43%)
R	104,339 (43%)
I	34,531 (14%)

2 Rob Portman (R)

Of Hyde Park — Elected 1993; 1st Term

Born: Dec. 19, 1955, Cincinnati, Ohio.
Education: Dartmouth College, B.A. 1979; U. of Michigan, J.D. 1984.
Occupation: Lawyer; White House aide; congressional aide.
Family: Wife, Jane Dudley; two children.
Religion: Methodist.
Political Career: No previous office.
Capitol Office: 238 Cannon Bldg. 20515; 225-3164.

The Path to Washington: The March 16 special primary election was the main obstacle for Republican Rob Portman, who defeated both a former representative and a wealthy home builder that day to advance to the May 4 general election in Ohio's most Republican district. Once that hurdle was cleared, Portman had a clear path to Capitol Hill.

Portman won 36 percent of the GOP primary vote to beat former Ohio 6th District Rep. Bob McEwen's 30 percent and builder Jay Buchert's 25 percent. He replaced Republican Rep. Bill Gradison, who resigned in January 1993 to become president of the Health Insurance Association of America, an industry group.

On May 4, Portman overwhelmed Democrat Lee Hornberger, who, like Portman, is a lawyer from Cincinnati. Portman used the name recognition he had built during a tough primary battle earlier this year to pile up 70 percent of the vote to Hornberger's 30 percent.

Just 18 hours after the polls closed at 7:30 p.m. on May 4, Portman was sworn in, and two hours later, he hit the House floor and cast his first vote, opposing the proposed rule for floor debate on the "motor voter" bill.

Portman's staff denied that he had bought airline tickets for Washington before the polls closed, but a campaign spokesman conceded: "I knew what the flight schedule was."

Portman goes back a long way with Gradison: He worked on Gradison's 1976 campaign while in college and later was an intern in his office. Portman announced his candidacy for Gradison's seat the morning after Gradison announced his retirement, and Gradison endorsed Portman in the primary campaign's waning hours.

The new 2nd District, which takes in suburban eastern Cincinnati and suburban and rural areas to the east and north, had been designed with Gradison in mind; virtually every Democrat in the immediate vicinity had been drawn into Cincinnati's downtown-based 1st District.

Gradison won 70 percent in the 2nd in 1992, and Portman matched that exactly in his first victory — a feat that bodes well for his longevity in the House.

Portman carried each of the five counties that make up the 2nd District. His vote share was biggest (74 percent) where it mattered most, in Hamilton County.

Slightly more than half the May 4 ballots were cast in the 2nd District portion of Hamilton County, which includes some of Cincinnati and most of its suburbs.

Portman's vote share was least (53 percent) where it mattered least, in Brown County, source of just 6 percent of the overall tally.

Fresh from law school in 1984, Portman arrived in Washington to practice international trade law for Patton, Boggs & Blow, a prominent and politically well-connected firm. He stayed just two years, but the stint was long enough for Portman to catch flak for it when he ran for Congress. In the GOP primary, he was criticized over some of the firm's clients — who have included Haiti's autocratic Duvalier family — and over some of its partners, including Commerce Secretary Ronald H. Brown, a former chairman of the Democratic National Committee.

In 1987, Portman went home to Cincinnati to practice law, returning to Washington two years later to work in the Bush White House, first as an associate counsel and later as a deputy assistant to the president and director of the White House's Office of Legislative Affairs. After leaving the White House, he returned to the Cincinnati law firm.

Portman lined up early support from Cincinnati's business community and won the backing of the Hamilton County GOP for the primary.

During the campaign, Portman spoke in favor of lower taxes, more spending cuts, welfare reform, campaign-finance reform, a line-item veto and a balanced-budget amendment.

Once in Washington, Portman picked up assignments to two of the House's less desirable panels, Government Operations and Small Business — not unusual for a member elected in a special election.

Ohio 2

Southwest and Eastern Cincinnati and suburbs

Redistricting in 1992 gave the formerly politically mixed 2nd and 1st districts clearer partisan personalities — the second solidly Republican and the 1st more Democratic.

The map shifted most of the Democratic eastern part of Cincinnati out of the 2nd; in exchange, the 2nd added rural western Hamilton County, a reliably Republican area.

The 2nd also picked up all of Adams County and the northern and western parts of Warren County, two more rural Republican counties, from the old 6th District.

The net effect of these changes has been to create a district that is the most solidly Republican in the state, and one with a distinct split between its suburban and rural elements.

Only 53,000 of the 364,000 residents in the city of Cincinnati remain in the 2nd. Only 5 percent of those 53,000 are black; overall, the city is 38 percent black.

Not quite 60 percent of the district's vote is cast in the Hamilton County areas.

Cincinnati's wealthy Republican establishment — including the Taft family — has exercised a great deal of political influence over the years. But that influence is now concentrated more in the suburbs than in the city. Unlike suburban Cleveland, suburban Cincinnati is solidly in Republican hands.

The Cincinnati area has less heavy industry than the urban centers of northeastern Ohio. But manufacturing plants dot the Mill Creek Valley, which extends north from downtown into the suburbs.

More than 150,000 of the 2nd's residents and 23 percent of its voters are in fast-growing Clermont County just east of Hamilton County. It grew 34 percent in the 1970s and 9 percent in the 1980s. As Clermont has moved closer to the Cincinnati metropolitan orbit, it has become more Republican.

The outlying counties of the 2nd — Brown, Adams and Warren — have considerably less political pull than Hamilton and Clermont, casting under one-fifth of the district vote. The suburbanization of Clermont County is moving it more into sync with Hamilton, dropping further the influence of the rural counties.

Almost 60 percent of Warren County's residents are in the 2nd, living along the county's western and northern sides. Northern Warren is in Dayton's media market, making it the only portion of the district to be outside Cincinnati's gravitational pull.

Ironically, while remappers designed both Cincinnati-area districts with their incumbents' comfort in mind (Charles Luken in the 1st and Bill Gradison here), both of them left the House before they could fully enjoy the benefits of the new lines. Gradison had good luck with the district in his limited experience with it: He walked away with 70 percent of the vote in 1992 (he resigned early in 1993).

George Bush ran very strongly here in 1992, pulling down 53 percent of the vote to Bill Clinton's 28 percent and Ross Perot's 19 percent.

1990 Population: 570,902. White 551,917 (97%), Black 12,889 (2%), Other 6,096(1%). Hispanic origin 2,931 (1%). 18 and over 417,784 (73%), 62 and over 79,924 (14%). Median age: 33.

Committees

Government Operations (17th of 17 Republicans)

Small Business (18th of 18 Republicans)

Campaign Finance †

	Receipts	Receipts from PACs		Expend-itures
1993				
Portman (R)	$688,398	0		$656,725
Hornberger (D)	$31,546	$100	(0%)	$18,645

† Figures are through May 25, 1993

Elections

1993 Special		
Rob Portman (R)	53,020	(70%)
Lee Hornberger (D)	22,652	(30%)
1993 Special Primary		
Rob Portman (R)	17,531	(35%)
Bob McEwen (R)	14,542	(29%)
Jay Buchert (R)	12,488	(25%)
Robert W. Dorsey (R)	2,937	(6%)
Ken Callis (R)	1,179	(2%)

District Vote for President

1992

D 78,957 (28%)
R 146,098 (53%)
I 52,006 (19%)

3 Tony P. Hall (D)

Of Dayton — Elected 1978; 8th Term

Born: Jan. 16, 1942, Dayton, Ohio.
Education: Denison U., A.B. 1964.
Occupation: Real estate broker.
Family: Wife, Janet Dick; two children.
Religion: Presbyterian.
Political Career: Ohio House, 1969-73; Ohio Senate, 1973-79; Democratic nominee for Ohio secretary of state, 1974.
Capitol Office: 2264 Rayburn Bldg. 20515; 225-6465.

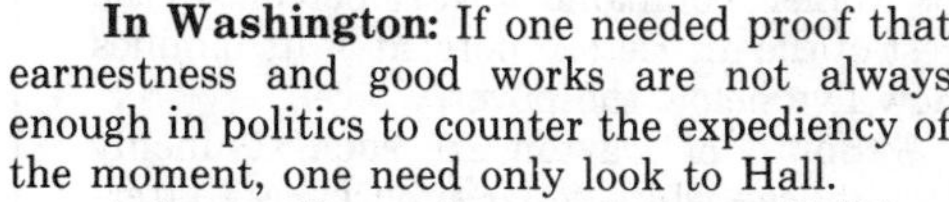

In Washington: If one needed proof that earnestness and good works are not always enough in politics to counter the expediency of the moment, one need only look to Hall.

A former Peace Corps volunteer, Hall is a dedicated legislator and activist on hunger and human rights issues, whose agenda flows from his own deeply held religious beliefs.

But at the start of the 103rd Congress, Hall was stripped of his platform to pursue that agenda when the Select Committee on Hunger was abolished. It was no personal slight to Hall; he is held in high regard by his colleagues. Minnesota Democrat Timothy J. Penny said of Hall: "He knows more about Zaire, Ethiopia and Somalia than most of us know about our home districts." Instead, a wave of frugality — and reaction to voters who wanted Congress to change the way it does business — led members to drop four select committees.

Hall pleaded with his colleagues to retain the Hunger panel he chaired since 1989. He complained bitterly that the Democratic leadership would not even hold a floor vote. The slightly built Hall even embarked on a 22-day water-only fast that raised his profile but did not win back his committee.

Despite the fact that the Hunger panel had no direct legislative responsibilities, Hall used it to advantage. Domestically, Hall's efforts have been most visible in congressional deliberations over the federal government's nutrition program for women, infants and children, known as WIC. In 1990, rising food prices had forced many states to overspend their budgets for the program, potentially forcing them to cut out thousands of eligible people. After conducting a survey on the extent of the problem, Hall sponsored legislation to let states borrow against their 1991 WIC budgets to avoid kicking people out of the program. The emergency authorization sped through Congress.

Early in the 102nd Congress, Hall introduced anti-hunger legislation that included a large funding increase for the WIC program. Provisions of that bill to create a grant program to help welfare recipients start small were enacted in 1992 as part of a job training bill. Other provisions to allow beneficiaries to start a small business without immediately losing their government assistance were incorporated into a sweeping urban aid tax bill in late 1992. President George Bush vetoed that measure the day after he was defeated for reelection.

Even before assuming the chairmanship, Hall had shown a knack for drawing attention to hunger issues. He and other House members once organized a media-savvy gourmet luncheon serving only food that had been culled from Capitol Hill trash cans. Consistent with this effort is Hall's promotion of gleaning programs, which gather the produce left behind after commercial harvests.

Hall has turned a similar determination toward hunger abroad, be it on high-profile causes or more technical ones, such as satellite programs that will gather information about threats to the ecosystem and world agriculture. During the 102nd Congress, Hall argued that U.S. food aid had become politicized; he was among a group of legislators who fought to redirect food assistance toward the neediest countries.

Hall has earned respect for his pursuit of issues that otherwise might get lost in the legislative shuffle, but he is a very unlikely member of the Rules Committee. He won a seat there in his second term, though he has never been inclined toward the stratagems and backroom maneuvering that characterize most of the committee's work. If he is a less active member of Rules, however, he is generally regarded as a team player by his fellow Democrats.

Hall comes alive on Rules primarily on issues affecting his district. During the 101st and 102nd Congresses, he used his leverage on Rules to protect the nuclear weapons plant at Miamisburg. In the 100th Congress, Hall was also an active participant in committee deliberations on "dial-a-porn." The Senate attached language to the 1988 omnibus education bill to ban the sexually explicit services, but conferees, citing constitutional questions, scaled back the

Ohio 3

Southwest — Dayton

With a large blue-collar work force and a population that is 40 percent black, Dayton is a Democratic island in a sea of rural western Ohio Republicanism. Most of Dayton's suburbs yield GOP majorities, but the urban vote has managed to keep the 3rd Democratic in most elections.

The Dayton area, lifelong home of the Wright Brothers, claims to be the birthplace of aviation, the refrigerator, the cash register and the electrical automobile starter. Much of the high-skill industry in the region is a legacy of these local inventions. General Motors is a major employer, with many plants here. The city is the headquarters of the NCR Corp. (formerly National Cash Register Co.)

In the early 1970s, the Dayton area was one of the most affluent parts of Ohio outside the Cleveland suburbs. But since then, there have been severe economic problems. GM's large Frigidaire division, Firestone Tire and Rubber, and the McCall Publishing Co. have all left. NCR remains, but has slashed its work force.

The city boasts a large, thriving military industry, increasingly rare in this era of base closings. Wright-Patterson Air Force Base, northeast of the 3rd in the 7th's Greene County, is the nation's largest military installation in terms of number of people who work here — 17,300 civilians and 9,600 military personnel.

The number of aerospace and advanced technology companies in the 3rd has exploded in the past 10 years, from fewer than 100 in 1982 to more than 800 in 1993. These companies now employ about 25,000 people.

But the other job losses have forced many people out of the area. Dayton's population declined 16 percent in the 1970s and 6 percent more in the 1980s, to 182,000, its lowest level in more than 60 years.

The 3rd encompasses all of Montgomery County except for a chip off the southwest corner ceded to the 8th District. Surrounding the city are much-better-off suburbs. Dayton's per capita income is only 60 percent of the rest of the district's; 34 percent of its family households are headed by women, compared with 13 percent in the rest of the district; 22 percent of its families now live below the poverty level.

South of Dayton are such staunchly Republican white-collar suburbs as Kettering, which is about one-third of Dayton's size with 61,000 residents. Its residents are as white as their collars; 97 percent are white non-Hispanics and less than 1 percent are black. Less than 3 percent of its families live in poverty.

The fast-growing townships north of Dayton, a scattering of cities with 10,000 to 14,000 residents, are largely blue-collar suburban. This is a swing-voting area.

Ronald Reagan and George Bush had little trouble taking the old 3rd District with 56 percent of the vote in 1984 and 54 percent in 1988, but Bill Clinton managed to score a narrow victory in the redrawn 3rd in 1992, receiving 41 percent of the vote to Bush's 40 percent.

1990 Population: 570,901. White 460,661 (81%), Black 101,809 (18%), Other 8,431 (1%). Hispanic origin 4,533 (1%). 18 and over 429,073 (75%), 62 and over 87,630 (15%). Median age: 33.

ban and restricted access instead. When the bill arrived at the House Rules Committee, however, Hall was one of two Democrats to buck the leadership and block consideration until a floor vote on an outright ban was secured.

While Hall's international principles often link him to House liberals, he splits company with them on certain social issues. He advocates teaching ethics in schools and routinely introduces bills to establish a commission to identify what values should be taught and how.

On one such values issue — abortion — Hall stands on the anti-abortion side. In 1988, he was one of 90 Democrats who joined with 126 Republicans in a 216-166 House vote to allow federal funding of abortions only when the pregnancy endangered the woman's life.

At Home: Hall was the clear choice of organized labor and the Montgomery County Democratic Party when liberal GOP Rep. Charles W. Whalen decided to retire in 1978. Once a small-college football all-star at Denison University, Hall had represented Dayton in the Ohio legislature for nearly a decade. He had access to ample campaign funds through his father, who ran a lucrative real estate business and served as the city's mayor for five years.

Four years before his congressional bid, Hall had gained attention as the Democratic nominee for secretary of state against Republican stalwart Ted W. Brown, who had held that post for 24 years. Hall chastised Brown for not reporting campaign contributions from a chicken dinner fundraising event, brandishing a rubber chicken during one appearance. He lost but came closer to defeating Brown than anyone had in 16 years; the campaign placed him in a good position to run for Congress.

To reach Washington, Hall had to defeat Republican Dudley P. Kircher, a former Chamber of Commerce official who was considerably more conservative than Whalen. Hall emphasized his legislative experience and attacked Kircher as the "voice of big business." Strong support from organized labor helped Hall offset Kircher's $130,000 spending edge. The Democrat took 70 percent of the vote in Dayton, allowing him to win narrowly districtwide.

Redistricting gave Hall a safer seat in 1982. Republicans did not field a candidate that year or in 1984. In the two ensuing elections, Hall faced Ron Crutcher, a black Republican. Crutcher received some attention from the national media, but Hall trounced him both times, taking 74 percent in 1986 and 77 percent in 1988. This experience again deterred the district GOP, which in 1990 gave Hall a free ride for the third time in a decade.

Another round of redistricting left Hall's district largely unchanged in 1992. But national Republicans thought they glimpsed a vulnerable incumbent in Hall, who had voted in 1991 against authorizing the use of force against Iraq. They recruited Peter Davis, a political newcomer and a Persian Gulf War veteran.

Davis ran TV ads criticizing Hall for not living in the district and complained that Hall was more interested in fighting famine than in tending the district's needs. Although he was better funded than Hall's past opponents, Davis was unable to overcome Hall's popularity. And Hall outspent him by more than 3-to-1. Still, Davis held him to 60 percent, Hall's lowest tally since 1980.

Committee

Rules (6th of 9 Democrats)
Rules of the House

Elections

1992 General		
Tony P. Hall (D)	146,072	(60%)
Peter W. Davis (R)	98,733	(40%)
1990 General		
Tony P. Hall (D)	116,797	(100%)

Previous Winning Percentages: **1988** (77%) **1986** (74%) **1984** (100%) **1982** (88%) **1980** (57%) **1978** (54%)

District Vote for President

1992

D 107,798 (41%)
R 104,414 (40%)
I 47,612 (18%)

Campaign Finance

	Receipts	Receipts from PACs		Expend-itures
1992				
Hall (D)	$342,116	$235,200	(69%)	$596,272
Davis (R)	$174,717	0		$174,058
1990				
Hall (D)	$173,805	$130,592	(75%)	$133,861

Key Votes

1993	
Require parental notification of minors' abortions	Y
Require unpaid family and medical leave	Y
Approve national "motor voter" registration bill	Y
Approve budget increasing taxes and reducing deficit	Y
Approve economic stimulus plan	Y
1992	
Approve balanced-budget constitutional amendment	Y
Close down space station program	N
Approve U.S. aid for former Soviet Union	Y
Allow shifting funds from defense to domestic programs	Y
1991	
Extend unemployment benefits using deficit financing	Y
Approve waiting period for handgun purchases	Y
Authorize use of force in Persian Gulf	N

Voting Studies

	Presidential Support		Party Unity		Conservative Coalition	
Year	**S**	**O**	**S**	**O**	**S**	**O**
1992	28	69	80	11	40	56
1991	35	61	86	11	38	62
1990	22	72	78	12	28	63
1989	31	62	77	13	34	56
1988	24	66	79	8	37	50
1987	23	68	72	11	40	49
1986	14	83	78	13	20	74
1985	29	68	81	12	33	56
1984	27	63	72	15	25	63
1983	21	74	75	17	26	72
1982	36	57	73	14	30	60
1981	47	46	69	24	51	44

Interest Group Ratings

Year	**ADA**	**AFL-CIO**	**CCUS**	**ACU**
1992	60	67	25	25
1991	75	75	30	10
1990	72	100	8	8
1989	80	83	56	7
1988	75	93	23	17
1987	72	73	29	9
1986	65	64	44	9
1985	65	88	41	11
1984	70	77	38	22
1983	85	94	10	13
1982	70	76	30	17
1981	45	62	44	33

4 Michael G. Oxley (R)

Of Findlay — Elected 1981; 6th Full Term

Born: Feb. 11, 1944, Findlay, Ohio.
Education: Miami U. (Oxford, Ohio), B.A. 1966; Ohio State U., J.D. 1969.
Occupation: FBI agent; lawyer.
Family: Wife, Patricia Pluguez; one child.
Religion: Lutheran.
Political Career: Ohio House, 1973-81.
Capitol Office: 2233 Rayburn Bldg. 20515; 225-2676.

In Washington: Oxley's outgoing, genial nature makes him one of the higher-profile Republicans on the Energy and Commerce Committee, where he ranks fourth in the GOP lineup.

A former FBI agent, he is energetic and competitive both on and off the House floor, whether sparring on policy questions, playing on the golf course or working out in the House gym.

Cut from the Reagan anti-regulatory mold, Oxley is a frequent critic of government involvement in the television and telephone industries. He opposed the cable television reregulation bill, which became law when Congress overrode a presidential veto on Oct. 5, 1992. As the 102nd Congress drew to a close, Oxley fumed that the law, which requires the Federal Communications Commission to oversee cable prices and service, was costing taxpayers more money and would not increase competition.

"The ink is barely dry on the cable bill, and its supporters have already begun charging the taxpayer for this special-interest law," he complained weeks after the override when Democratic Energy Chairman John D. Dingell of Michigan proposed giving the FCC a bigger budget to enforce the new law.

Oxley made two failed attempts to revise the cable bill. He urged shifting the regulatory burden to the states, instead of the FCC, and he offered legislation that would have allowed telephone companies to compete in the cable business. The bill, cosponsored by then-Tennessee Sen. Al Gore, was not acted upon in the 102nd. Oxley reintroduced the measure in the 103rd.

The bill not only emphasized Oxley's interest in emerging technologies but highlighted his dedication to free trade.

He has opposed Democratic efforts to reinstate the "fairness doctrine" regulation on the broadcasting industry; it was repealed administratively in 1987. President Ronald Reagan vetoed a reinstatement bill passed in the 100th Congress, but Democratic leaders revived the issue in 1989, when many members felt the media was giving them an unfair rap over a proposed pay raise.

Oxley lost a House floor vote to strip the fairness doctrine provision from the 1989 budget-reconciliation bill, but the measure was eventually dropped from the budget package.

Oxley is usually loyal to Republican leaders, even when confronted with positions not all to his liking. He supported the 1990 budget summit, despite his preference for a no-new-taxes, spending-freeze budget. "Trying to sell this agreement is like putting earrings on a pig," he admitted.

In 1992, he supported President Bush 86 percent of the time on House floor votes on which Bush took a position.

On Energy and Commerce, Oxley's usually easygoing nature allows him to cooperate with the majority — especially with Chairman Dingell, who shares his aversion to strict acid rain controls and concerns for protecting the auto industry.

In the 103rd Congress, Oxley replaced defeated GOP Rep. Don Ritter of Pennsylvania as the ranking member on the Subcommittee on Transportation and Hazardous Materials. The post enables Oxley to keep a close eye on rail and waste disposal issues of particular interest to Ohio constituents.

During the 101st and 102nd, Oxley lobbied Congress and the Bush administration to protect the Lima tank factory in his district. First he won defense dollars to upgrade older M-1 and M-1A1 tanks. Then in October 1992 the Kuwaiti Defense Ministry chose the M-1A2 Abrams, manufactured in Lima, as its main battle tank.

A member of the Select Committee on Narcotics Abuse and Control, Oxley urged in the 100th Congress that the national drug director be in the Cabinet, saying, "I want a stud in there fighting the war on drugs, someone with real clout." He successfully offered a measure making it easier to set up "sting" operations against money-launderers.

At Home: After a tough special election contest in 1981, Oxley has faced no difficulty holding his House seat. But the general voter

Ohio 4

West Central — Mansfield; Lima; Findlay

The 4th is a solid block of Ohio Corn Belt counties dominated by farms and small towns. The land supports corn, soybeans and livestock. And Republicans.

Not one of the 11 counties in the 4th has supported a Democratic presidential candidate since 1964; two of the three largest — Allen and Hancock — have backed the GOP national ticket since the Roosevelt-Landon contest of 1936.

Democrats have oases of support in the 4th, but they are few and far between. They can normally count on votes in Richland County, especially in Mansfield, the district's largest city.

And Lima (population 46,000), sometimes votes Democratic, but it is a small enough part of Allen County that the rest of the county's solidly Republican outlying areas overwhelm Lima's sentiments.

Auglaize County in the 4th's southwestern corner is Democratic in the west and Republican in the east. The west is populated by descendants of Germans who settled in the 19th century; they never caught the conservatism that swept through much of the rest of the area.

Economically, corn and soybeans are king in this district, which sprawls across three of Ohio's area codes. The bulk of this district's industry is in its past.

Marion (population 34,000) — named after Revolutionary War Gen. Francis Marion, the "Swamp Fox" — used to make steam shovels and steam rollers, but now instead grows popping corn.

Lima and Findlay both emerged as small manufacturing centers at the end of the 19th century when oil and gas were found nearby.

Lima was one of the original refinery centers for John D. Rockefeller's Standard Oil. Although the petroleum boom passed long ago, Findlay (population 36,000), as headquarters of Marathon Oil, is still the 4th's most prosperous part — and the most Republican part of this Republican district.

Close ties to the automobile industry caused economic hardships in Mansfield and Lima during the 1982 recession. They made a partial recovery in the latter 1980s and have not suffered tremendously in the latest recession, though the Mansfield auto plant's employment has slipped somewhat. Smaller auto-related companies have taken up some of the slack.

One of the bright spots in the district's industrial base is its General Dynamics plant, which opened in Lima in 1982 and became its second-largest employer behind a Ford plant. The General Dynamics facility builds the Army's M-1 Abrams tank. British Petroleum still operates an oil refinery here that it opened in the 1920s. Many of Logan County's jobs depend on the Honda plant in Marysville in the neighboring 7th District.

Knox County in the 4th's southeast corner is within Columbus' range, making Knox less culturally isolated than many of its neighbors.

George Bush did well all across the 4th in 1992, taking 46 percent of the vote to Bill Clinton's 31 percent.

1990 Population: 570,901. White 539,111 (94%), Black 26,333 (5%), Other 5,457 (1%). Hispanic origin 5,262 (1%). 18 and over 417,141 (73%), 62 and over 91,326 (16%). Median age: 34.

dissatisfaction with Congress in 1990 cost several Ohio House members a few points off their usual victory margins. Oxley was one of them; after running unopposed in 1988, Oxley defeated Democrat Thomas E. Burkhart, a bus factory worker, with 62 percent. In 1992, with voter dissatisfaction no less acute, he won with 61 percent against Raymond M. Ball, a steel company administrator.

When GOP Rep. Tennyson Guyer died in April 1981, Oxley, a four-term state House member, was an early favorite in the special election to succeed him. But Oxley faced stiff primary competition. Running in the early days of Reagan's presidency, the Republican candidates tried to out-Reagan one another. Robert J. Huffman, a Reagan backer in the 1976 presidential race, branded Oxley a latecomer because he had supported Bush for president in 1980. Oxley won narrowly.

Winning the Republican nomination traditionally had been tantamount to election in this Republican Corn Belt district. But in state Rep. Dale Locker, the Democrats fielded their best possible candidate.

Locker was a farmer and chairman of the state House Agriculture and Natural Resources Committee, ideal credentials for the 4th District.

Oxley outgunned Locker financially, spending $275,000 and flooding the media with advertisements in the closing days of the campaign. But his efforts nearly failed because he was unable to develop the personal rapport with voters that had made the 4th District safe for Guyer. Carrying only six of the district's 12 counties, Oxley struggled to a 341-vote victory. A recount delayed his swearing-in for nearly a month.

Locker weighed a rematch in 1982 but backed off when the state legislature fashioned new district boundaries to Oxley's advantage. Redistricting in 1992 brought offsetting changes and had little impact on Oxley's chances.

Committee

Energy & Commerce (4th of 17 Republicans)
Transportation & Hazardous Materials (ranking); Telecommunications & Finance

Elections

1992 General		
Michael G. Oxley (R)	147,346	(61%)
Raymond M. Ball (D)	92,608	(39%)
1990 General		
Michael G. Oxley (R)	103,897	(62%)
Thomas E. Burkhart (D)	64,467	(38%)

Previous Winning Percentages: **1988** (100%) **1986** (75%) **1984** (78%) **1982** (65%) **1981 †** (50%)

† Special election.

District Vote for President

1992	
D	77,918 (31%)
R	118,088 (46%)
I	58,957 (23%)

Campaign Finance

	Receipts	Receipts from PACs		Expend-itures
1992				
Oxley (R)	$491,631	$281,775	(57%)	$648,337
Ball (D)	$68,810	$46,125	(67%)	$68,324
1990				
Oxley (R)	$298,581	$200,233	(67%)	$330,272
Burkhart (D)	$19,103	$12,000	(63%)	$19,102

Key Votes

1993	
Require parental notification of minors' abortions	Y
Require unpaid family and medical leave	N
Approve national "motor voter" registration bill	N
Approve budget increasing taxes and reducing deficit	N
Approve economic stimulus plan	N
1992	
Approve balanced-budget constitutional amendment	Y
Close down space station program	N
Approve U.S. aid for former Soviet Union	Y
Allow shifting funds from defense to domestic programs	N
1991	
Extend unemployment benefits using deficit financing	N
Approve waiting period for handgun purchases	Y
Authorize use of force in Persian Gulf	Y

Voting Studies

	Presidential Support		Party Unity		Conservative Coalition	
Year	S	O	S	O	S	O
1992	86	11	86	10	96	2
1991	79	20	83	16	95	5
1990	73	27	82	14	94	2
1989	80	19	86	11	93	7
1988	68	31	81	9	92	5
1987	67	26	80	12	98	2
1986	80	16	85	8	86	14
1985	75	24	88	6	96	4
1984	67	26	86	8	93	5
1983	85	12	87	10	83	16
1982	77	17	81	13	90	10
1981	67 †	29 †	85 †	13 †	88 †	12 †

† Not eligible for all recorded votes.

Interest Group Ratings

Year	ADA	AFL-CIO	CCUS	ACU
1992	5	17	86	96
1991	5	8	100	80
1990	0	17	93	79
1989	5	8	100	93
1988	20	14	100	88
1987	4	0	100	95
1986	0	7	100	95
1985	10	0	91	86
1984	5	0	64	75
1983	10	0	95	91
1982	10	15	82	90
1981	0	20	92	83

5 Paul E. Gillmor (R)

Of Old Fort — Elected 1988; 3rd Term

Born: Feb. 1, 1939, Tiffin, Ohio.
Education: Ohio Wesleyan U., B.A. 1961; U. of Michigan, J.D. 1964.
Military Service: Air Force, 1965-66.
Occupation: Lawyer.
Family: Wife, Karen Lako; three children.
Religion: Protestant.
Political Career: Ohio Senate, 1967-89, minority leader, 1978-80, 1983-84, president, 1981-82, 1985-88; sought GOP nomination for governor, 1986.
Capitol Office: 1203 Longworth Bldg. 20515; 225-6405.

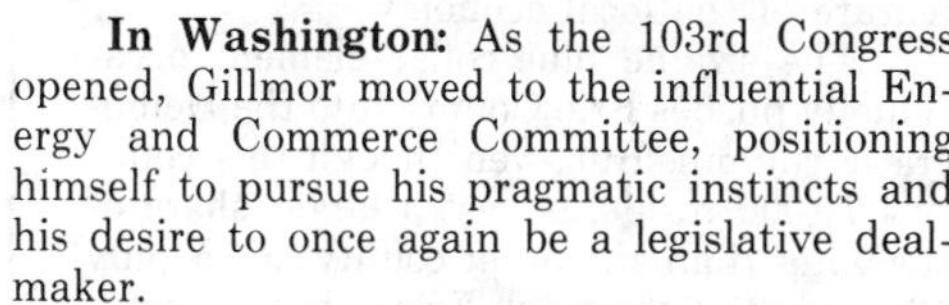

In Washington: As the 103rd Congress opened, Gillmor moved to the influential Energy and Commerce Committee, positioning himself to pursue his pragmatic instincts and his desire to once again be a legislative deal-maker.

He reached that point via an unusual route.

In December 1992, Gillmor was pushed as a candidate to replace Bill Thomas of California as the ranking Republican on the House Administration Committee. Thomas was viewed as too conciliatory with Democrats, and Minority Whip Newt Gingrich in particular saw the Thomas replacement as a part of the leadership overhaul that brought in Texas conservatives Dick Armey and Tom DeLay.

But Gillmor, who was surprised by his nomination, made no secret of his distaste for the job on a panel that deals with the internal business of the House.

"It's not a plum, it's something you do for the good of the institution and the caucus," he said at the time. "I don't look at it as a committee where you make a lot of friends."

Despite his lack of interest, Gillmor almost was elected to the spot. Thomas hung on to it by a vote of 87-72. Then Gillmor got the slot on Energy and Commerce, which for Republicans is an exclusive committee assignment. That meant he had to quit House Administration altogether. It also meant giving up his seat on the Banking, Finance and Urban Affairs Committee.

Gillmor was happy about the switch. The Energy and Commerce Committee is "involved in more substantive issues than any other House committee," he explained. "It is one of the most influential or powerful committees in the House."

As a member of the Telecommunications Subcommittee, Gillmor will be involved in shaping the debate on a range of emerging technologies, including cable television and the future of the so-called Baby Bells.

The move to a broader, higher-profile role in the House also will allow him to keep an eye out for his constituents. Gillmor has said he will use his spot on Energy to watch over waste disposal issues, which are of particular interest to Ohio.

Gillmor came to Capitol Hill in 1988 with a reputation as a seasoned inside operator — a reputation earned during his 22-year tenure in the Ohio General Assembly.

During his first two terms, he was a loyal Republican conservative but on occasion took more moderate positions. In October 1990, he supported the bipartisan budget-summit agreement, reviled by GOP conservatives for its tax increase provisions. Of the 15 GOP House members first elected in 1988, Gillmor was one of just three to vote for the package.

Recognizing Gillmor's institutional bent, House Republican leaders made him the only freshman named to a bipartisan task force set up at the start of the 101st Congress to review ethics standards and members' pay. Gillmor ended up opposing the ethics reform/pay raise legislation approved by Congress in November 1989, citing his opposition to the large salary increase.

On Banking, Gillmor supported funding for the S&L bailout. While serving on House Administration he supported a measure requiring each representative to disclose the amount spent on franked mailings and giving each member an individual mailing budget. He also was involved in negotiations to freeze 1992 House committee accounts at 1991 levels.

In 1992 he spoke on the House floor in favor of repealing Coast Guard user fees that he described as "taxation of relaxation." The repeal, supported overwhelmingly by Democrats and Republicans alike, was passed.

During the three-way presidential contest in 1992 Gillmor filed legislation that would have prevented the House from choosing a president in the event no candidate received a majority of the Electoral College. His at-

Ohio 5

Northwest — Bowling Green; Sandusky

This solidly Republican district is a mixture of fertile, flat farmland and small towns. It spread its wings a bit in 1992 redistricting, tacking a county and a half onto its eastern and western ends, though it shed a bit of land up north.

Added to the 5th were Van Wert County and half of Mercer County — agricultural areas that run along the western Indiana border — and, to the east, the rest of Huron County and most of Lorain County (near Cleveland). The district lost its section of Fulton County and part of Wood and Ottawa counties (near Toledo) to the 9th District.

The nature of the 5th's population concentrations changed slightly in remapping. The Lake Erie port of Sandusky (population 30,000) is still the district's largest community.

But about half of Bowling Green in Wood County (population 28,000) has moved to the 9th District, along with Bowling Green State University and its 18,000 students. Tiffin, a city of 19,000 in Seneca County, is now the district's second most-populous city.

An additional 95,000 people live in seven other cities throughout the district, with populations ranging from 11,000 to 18,000. The other residents of the 5th live in smaller towns and rural areas.

The district's western counties are almost exclusively devoted to agriculture. Packing plants operated by Heinz and Campbell attest to the quality of the region's tomatoes. The district's population is 96 percent white, but the Mexican-American farmworkers who live in migrant camps during harvest season have added an ethnic element to this otherwise homogeneous region. The 5th is 3 percent Hispanic — a large number considering that Hispanics make up just about 1 percent of Ohio's total population.

Erie County, midway between Cleveland and Toledo on Lake Erie, has long been a major recreation area. Sandusky, the county seat, is a fishing market and coal port. In the surrounding countryside, fruit orchards and vineyards abound. German immigrants established wineries in Sandusky a century ago, and they remain a key feature of the local economy.

The sizable blue-collar element occasionally pushes Erie County into the Democratic column. But even though this county's 77,000 residents cast a larger share of the votes than any other county's, it is only 12 percent of the total; Erie is but a Democratic ripple in the large Republican pond.

Wood County, which sprawls from the outskirts of Toledo deep into the Ohio Corn Belt, accounts for a tenth of the district's voters. The county is consistently Republican; the loss of the Bowling Green university community deprives the district of what base for moderate-to-liberal contenders there was. Independent John B. Anderson drew 10 percent of the Wood County vote for president in 1980, his best county showing in Ohio. In 1992, Ross Perot received 22 percent.

1990 Population: 570,901. White 547,282 (96%), Black 11,957 (2%), Other 11,662 (2%). Hispanic origin 17,643 (3%). 18 and over 411,006 (72%), 62 and over 88,928 (16%). Median age: 33.

tempted repeal of the 12th Amendment to the Constitution failed.

At Home: A state legislator who comes to Congress is uniformly regarded as having received a promotion. Gillmor, however, had to sacrifice a good bit of power when he left Columbus for Washington. As president of the Ohio Senate for six of his last eight years there, Gillmor was the highest-ranking Republican in state government.

When he decided to seek the House seat of retiring GOP Rep. Delbert L. Latta, Gillmor knew well that his biggest challenge would be in the primary: As Senate president in the early 1980s, Gillmor had a say over the redistricting plan that made the 5th a GOP stronghold.

The 1988 GOP primary was indeed a bruising one. The 30-year incumbent wanted to hand the seat to his son, 32-year-old lawyer Robert E. Latta. The resulting face-off turned bitter and personal; Gillmor won narrowly.

During Gillmor's 22 years in the state Senate, he represented more than two-thirds of Latta's House territory, and the two men competed for dominance of the local political scene. When Gillmor announced he would run for the House, Rep. Latta briefly threatened to drop his retirement plans and seek re-election.

The younger Latta campaigned aggressively, aided by his father's ready-made organization. However, Gillmor towered over the newcomer in personal recognition. Gillmor not only had his own solid political base in most of the 5th, but also was known throughout the district from his 1986 bid for the GOP gubernatorial nomination. (Although he lost statewide, he carried the 5th in that primary.)

Gillmor ran a media-oriented campaign, highlighting his legislative experience. He stressed his fiscal conservatism and cited his successes as the Senate Republican leader. He was known as an accessible, consensus-oriented leader able to move legislation despite the GOP's narrow Senate majority.

Those credentials boosted Gillmor to victory, but just barely. He won by 27 votes — the smallest margin in any 1988 House contest.

In the general election, though, the district's Republican tendencies kicked in for Gillmor. His foe was wealthy Democratic attorney Thomas Murray, who had gotten just 35 percent against Del Latta in 1986.

Although Murray spent $850,000, mainly on TV ads, Gillmor topped 60 percent. By 1990, Gillmor was solidly established in the 5th. He ran unopposed in 1992.

Committee

Energy & Commerce (13th of 17 Republicans)
Oversight & Investigations; Telecommunications & Finance; Transportation & Hazardous Materials

Elections

1992 General		
Paul E. Gillmor (R)	187,860	(100%)
1990 General		
Paul E. Gillmor (R)	113,615	(68%)
P. Scott Mange (D)	41,693	(25%)
John E. Jackson (I)	10,612	(6%)

Previous Winning Percentage: 1988 (61%)

District Vote for President

1992
D 87,883 (33%)
R 109,020 (41%)
I 66,648 (25%)

Campaign Finance

	Receipts	Receipts from PACs		Expend-itures
1992				
Gillmor (R)	$244,817	$160,137	(65%)	$254,988
1990				
Gillmor (R)	$325,743	$230,425	(71%)	$254,688
Mange (D)	$250	0		$248

Key Votes

1993	
Require parental notification of minors' abortions	Y
Require unpaid family and medical leave	Y
Approve national "motor voter" registration bill	?
Approve budget increasing taxes and reducing deficit	N
Approve economic stimulus plan	N
1992	
Approve balanced-budget constitutional amendment	Y
Close down space station program	N
Approve U.S. aid for former Soviet Union	Y
Allow shifting funds from defense to domestic programs	N
1991	
Extend unemployment benefits using deficit financing	Y
Approve waiting period for handgun purchases	N
Authorize use of force in Persian Gulf	Y

Voting Studies

	Presidential Support		Party Unity		Conservative Coalition	
Year	**S**	**O**	**S**	**O**	**S**	**O**
1992	73	26	75	21	90	6
1991	73 †	26 †	67 †	30 †	95	5
1990	69	29	66	32	91	9
1989	77	22	65	32	90	10

† Not eligible for all recorded votes.

Interest Group Ratings

Year	ADA	AFL-CIO	CCUS	ACU
1992	20	50	75	80
1991	10	25	70	65
1990	11	17	57	74
1989	0	0	100	93

6 Ted Strickland (D)

Of Lucasville — Elected 1992; 1st Term

Born: Aug. 4, 1941, Portsmouth, Ohio.
Education: Asbury College, B.A. 1963; U. of Kentucky, M.A. 1966; Asbury Theological Seminary, M.A. 1967; U. of Kentucky, Ph.D. 1980.
Occupation: Professor.
Family: Wife, Frances Smith.
Religion: Methodist.
Political Career: Democratic nominee for U.S. House, 1976, 1978, 1980.
Capitol Office: 1429 Longworth Bldg. 20515; 225-5705.

The Path to Washington: The outcome of this bitterly fought campaign, written in two acts, was not so much a win by Strickland as a loss by two fatally wounded GOP incumbents — Reps. Clarence E. Miller and Bob McEwen.

When the 1992 campaign began, the Republican Party put this seat securely in its column. And Strickland — a moderately liberal Democrat who lost three times before as a House challenger (once against McEwen) — may have trouble holding onto it given the region's conservative leanings.

A psychologist who has worked with inmates at the state's penitentiaries and who taught at Shawnee State University, Strickland has an abiding interest in education. His seat on the Education and Labor Committee will give him a platform to pursue his concerns about children's issues. And it will help him with organized labor, which provided needed campaign support.

Strickland's seat on the Small Business Committee could prove useful in seeking economic development opportunities for the 6th, which embraces a large slice of Appalachia and is the poorest corner of the state.

Strickland campaigned on a "jobs for Appalachia" theme, supporting capital gains tax breaks in rural enterprise zones and proposing creation of an unofficial economic development director for the district. He also supported comprehensive health-care reform but did not propose specific solutions.

This contest was one of only two primaries in the country pitting two GOP incumbents against each other. State mapmakers obliterated Miller's district, putting five of the 12 counties he represented in McEwen's 6th. But any advantage McEwen might have gained paled next to his 166 overdrafts at the House bank. (Miller had no overdrafts.)

Miller (elected in 1966) and McEwen (elected in 1980 over Strickland) attacked each other's integrity, tactics and records in a campaign that went far beyond violating the GOP's "11th Commandment" not to speak ill of a fellow Republican.

McEwen emerged the victor after a recount by 286 votes, but he was mortally wounded. Miller refused to concede, pursuing a court challenge until late August. The primary sapped McEwen's cash, and by September, national GOP leaders were pleading for political action committees to pump cash into McEwen's coffers.

Strickland advanced to the general election after he upended Chillicothe Mayor Joseph P. Sulzer by a 2-to-1 margin and streaked past a third candidate in an uneventful primary that was eclipsed by the Republican donnybrook.

Sulzer, a lawyer and Vietnam veteran, took a more conservative tack than Strickland, supporting restrictions on abortion and opposing gun control. Strickland, who concedes that he has changed his mind on abortion over the years, now supports abortion rights and favors the Freedom of Choice Act.

And though he said in the campaign that he supports "reasonable" limits on gun ownership, he opposes the Brady bill and has said that he has not seen any gun control measures that he could support.

In the general-election campaign, McEwen accused Strickland of flip-flopping on abortion and gun control. But Strickland countered that McEwen was too conservative for the district — making an issue of the fact that erstwhile GOP presidential candidate Patrick J. Buchanan had campaigned for McEwen and that Strickland had been targeted by the National Rifle Association and anti-abortion groups.

Strickland hit McEwen hardest on his abuse of congressional perquisites. He repeatedly raised the overdraft issue and accused the incumbent of misusing the congressional frank by mailing thousands of pieces into portions of Miller's 10th District — which he did not at the time represent — but that would be in the 6th in the 103rd Congress. And Strickland turned up evidence of McEwen being paid for speaking engagements on days when he missed House floor votes.

For his part, Strickland promised to serve no more than 10 years, and he refused coverage under the health-care plan for House members.

Ohio 6

South — Portsmouth; Chillicothe; Athens

The 6th is the largest district in the state, taking in all of Ohio's southeast corner and reaching across to Warren County in Ohio's southwest. What suburbs it had near Dayton and Cincinnati were stripped away in the 1992 redistricting, leaving behind a collection of some of Ohio's poorest rural areas.

Scioto County is the 6th's most populous, with 80,000 residents and 14 percent of the total. It contains Portsmouth, the district's largest city (population 23,000).

While steel and bricks have been linchpins of Portsmouth's economy throughout the century, the largest employer in the district is the nearby uranium-enrichment facility owned by the Department of Energy and operated by Martin Marietta. In Chillicothe (20,000 of whose 22,000 residents are in the 6th), 44 miles due north of Portsmouth in Ross County, nearby forests support a large paper plant.

Athens County has a number of government employers, including Ohio University, with 17,500 students, that cushions it somewhat from adverse economic conditions. Athens was one of just two Ohio counties to support George McGovern for president in 1972; Michael S. Dukakis and Bill Clinton each carried it with more than 50 percent of the vote in 1988 and 1992, respectively.

The Democratic influence is counterbalanced by neighboring Meigs County, where the GOP has a better than 2-to-1 advantage.

Many of the poorer voters in other counties along the Ohio River still call themselves Democrats — a remnant of Civil War days when Confederate sympathies were strong in this area — but nowadays their conservative outlook leads them toward GOP candidates in most elections.

The counties immediately east of the Cincinnati area are rural Republican country. Clinton and Highland counties lie on the outer fringe of the Corn Belt.

Farther east the land is poorer, the Appalachian Mountains rise and GOP strength begins to ebb. Seven of the eight poorest counties in the state (in terms of proportion of families in poverty) are here in the 6th: Pike, Scioto, Jackson, Meigs, Lawrence, Vinton and Gallia. Only Adams County to the immediate west in the 2nd District is poorer. Clinton carried five of those seven counties in 1992, losing only Jackson and Gallia.

One-fifth of the 6th's land area is contained within the three regions of the Wayne National Forest in the district's eastern Appalachian section, including almost all of Lawrence County on Ohio's southern edge.

In 1992, George Bush and Clinton ran almost evenly in this district, with Bush taking 40.3 percent of the vote to Clinton's 39.7 percent. Clinton won eight of the 14 counties that are all or partly in the 6th; several of these victories were by less than 350 votes. Despite the name affinity, Bush did prevail decisively in Clinton County, taking 48 percent of the vote to the Democrat's 30 percent.

1990 Population: 570,901. White 554,194 (97%), Black 12,086 (2%), Other 4,621(1%). Hispanic origin 2,180 (<1%). 18 and over 421,059 (74%), 62 and over 90,625 (16%). Median age: 33.

Committees

Education & Labor (24th of 28 Democrats)
Elementary, Secondary & Vocational Education; Labor Standards, Occupational Health & Safety; Postsecondary Education

Small Business (16th of 27 Democrats)
Regulation, Business Opportunities & Technology; Rural Enterprises, Exports & the Environment

Campaign Finance

1992	Receipts	Receipts from PACs		Expend-itures
Strickland (D)	$240,391	$112,457	(47%)	$237,082
McEwen (R)	$598,006	$273,355	(46%)	$716,672

Key Votes

1993

Require parental notification of minors' abortions	N
Require unpaid family and medical leave	Y
Approve national "motor voter" registration bill	Y
Approve budget increasing taxes and reducing deficit	Y
Approve economic stimulus plan	Y

Elections

1992 General		
Ted Strickland (D)	122,720	(51%)
Bob McEwen (R)	119,252	(49%)
1992 Primary		
Ted Strickland (D)	23,339	(55%)
Joseph P. Sulzer (D)	11,015	(26%)
Bob Smith (D)	8,427	(20%)

District Vote for President

	1992	
D	98,768	(40%)
R	100,162	(40%)
I	49,796	(20%)

7 David L. Hobson (R)

Of Springfield — Elected 1990; 2nd Term

Born: Oct. 17, 1936, Cincinnati, Ohio.
Education: Ohio Wesleyan U., B.A. 1958; Ohio State U., J.D. 1963.
Military Service: Air National Guard, 1958-63.
Occupation: Financial executive.
Family: Wife, Carolyn Alexander; three children.
Religion: Methodist.
Political Career: Candidate for Ohio House, 1982; Ohio Senate, 1982-91, majority whip, 1986-88, president pro tempore, 1988-90.
Capitol Office: 1507 Longworth Bldg. 20515; 225-4324.

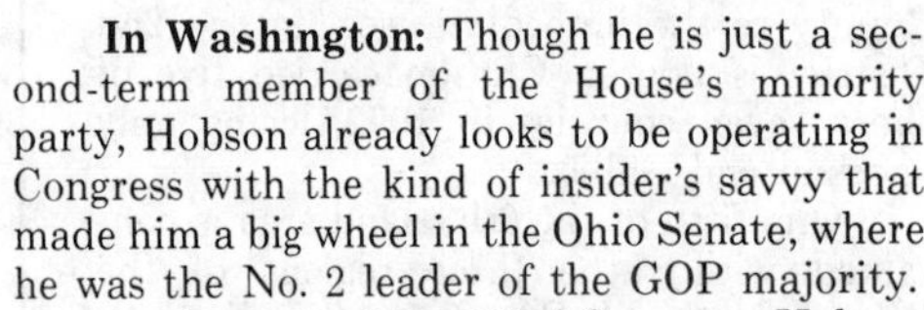

In Washington: Though he is just a second-term member of the House's minority party, Hobson already looks to be operating in Congress with the kind of insider's savvy that made him a big wheel in the Ohio Senate, where he was the No. 2 leader of the GOP majority.

At the start of the 103rd Congress, Hobson picked up prized seats on both the Appropriations and Budget committees.

As a freshman, Hobson got assignments on the low-profile Public Works and Government Operations panels. But the GOP leadership also named him as the only freshman on the ethics committee, a sign that Hobson made a good first impression as a person of integrity and sound judgment.

Health-care issues were one of Hobson's specialties in the state legislature, and during his first House term, he worked with other members of the Ohio congressional delegation to get a waiver from the federal government for the state's health-care program for indigents (which Hobson had sponsored as a state senator).

Hobson also made some headway in Congress with legislation to require state agencies to register people convicted of child abuse with the Justice Department, so they can more readily be identified by potential employers. Under the plan, if a job applicant gives written consent, a potential employer may do a background check through local law enforcement agencies.

The measure received bipartisan support in the 102nd Congress and was incorporated into the crime bill that passed the House, but that bill ultimately was sidetracked by partisan feuding between President Bush and congressional Democrats. Hobson reintroduced the legislation in 1993.

Hobson supports a balanced-budget constitutional amendment and is a critic of excessive government spending, and as a freshman he was part of a group of Republicans agitating for the Democratic leadership to release the names of all members who had overdrafts at the House bank, rather than just the top overdrafters.

But Hobson is older (56) and has a less confrontational manner than many of the GOP conservatives elected to the House in the past couple of election cycles. He should be a good fit for the Appropriations Committee, because he is not bashful about going after federal funds for his district; on Public Works he worked to secure $15.8 million for a bypass on Route 68 near Springfield and $3 million for a bicycle path from Xenia to Dayton.

Hobson is generally supportive of party positions — he voted with a majority of Republicans 85 percent of the time in 1992, and supported President Bush's positions on 67 percent of floor votes.

But he does break ranks on some high-profile issues. He supported the Civil Rights Act in its early stages, despite lobbying from the Bush administration, and he voted to overturn the ban on abortion counseling at federally funded clinics.

At Home: When Republican Rep. Mike DeWine embarked on what would be a successful 1990 bid for lieutenant governor, Hobson ran for the House and upheld his reputation as DeWine's heir apparent.

Hobson's election marked the second time he had followed in DeWine's footsteps. He was appointed in December 1982 to the state Senate seat DeWine gave up to run for the House.

Elected in 1984, Hobson was chosen by his GOP colleagues as Senate majority whip two years later. In November 1988, the same month he won re-election, Hobson moved up to president pro tem, the Senate's second-ranking position.

Hobson also had a lengthy list of legislative successes. Many of the bills he sponsored were in the area of health care, including measures dealing with AIDS, aging and mental health that earned him widespread praise in the state and district media.

This interest in health issues did not stem

Ohio 7

West central — Springfield; Lancaster

This district resembles a gaping mouth that is set to swallow Columbus whole. Its nine counties surround Columbus' district (the 15th) on three sides.

The 7th is bisected by U.S. Route 40; the northern section contains a third of the district's land, but casts only 15 percent of its vote. Champaign, Logan and Union to the north are rural counties that combine agriculture and small industry and have been GOP strongholds for generations; they backed Alfred M. Landon for president in 1936.

South of Route 40, the people are concentrated in Clark County (Springfield) and in Greene County, which extends into Dayton's eastern suburbs.

Springfield's site along Route 40 (the old National Road) enabled it to develop into the area's leading population center with 70,000 residents. The city's economy suffered substantially in the early 1980s, but got a boost in 1983 when International Harvester consolidated its truck-making operations here.

Greene County has a working-class mix of blacks and Southern whites. Wright-Patterson Air Force Base, in the county's far southwest corner, is responsible for a substantial amount of military-related employment. The base is the nation's largest military installation in terms of number employed — 17,300 civilians and 9,600 military personnel work here.

The Air Force has recently bolstered Wright-Patterson's security by consolidating several "commands" into a new one based here: the Air Force Materiel Command, which controls one-fifth of the Air Force's budget. The base is the largest single-site employer in the state.

Up north, the economic picture is rosier in Union County than in many of Ohio's other rural areas. Lying just northwest of Columbus, this is an attractive site for industries seeking open land, low taxes and — despite the county's name — no history of unions.

Much of the area's economic stimulus has come from an unusual source: Japan. Honda opened a motorcycle plant in Marysville in the western part of Union County in 1979, and three years later the company opened its first American auto plant there. Honda employs 5,700 people between the two facilities, making it the largest private employer in the region. (Other Honda plants in adjoining districts employ 3,800 more people.) The Marysville auto plant built 342,000 Honda Accords in 1992; it is the only plant that builds the Accord coupe and station wagon. Honda of America exported more than 55,000 cars in 1992 — with 20,000 of them going to Japan.

Fairfield County, in the 7th's far southeast corner, has experienced high growth (for this region) in recent years, as bedroom communities blossomed along Route 33, a four-lane highway connecting Lancaster with the thriving city of Columbus, 30 miles northwest.

George Bush did well in the 7th in 1992, taking 45 percent of the vote to Bill Clinton's 34 percent. Bush was especially strong in Union County, taking 53 percent.

1990 Population: 570,902. White 534,087 (94%), Black 30,347 (5%), Other 11,089 (2%). Hispanic origin 3,745 (1%). 18 and over 421,456 (74%), 62 and over 82,366 (14%). Median age: 34.

from Hobson's personal experience. He entered politics as a businessman who served as chairman of financial corporations and on the boards of a bank, an oil company and a restaurant company.

Appointed early in his career to the Senate Health Committee, Hobson led an investigation into the scandal-plagued state Department of Mental Retardation that brought the ouster of the agency's director. He also drew up a measure to provide respite care for sufferers of Alzheimer's disease and wrote a comprehensive bill for the detection and treatment of AIDS.

The AIDS bill encouraged testing for the disease by ensuring confidentiality, instituted state regulation of long-term facilities for AIDS patients and provided protection from discrimination for victims of the disease. Staving off conservative critics who portrayed the proposal as a gay rights bill, Hobson pushed it through the Republican-controlled Senate by a 22-8 vote.

Hobson was generally supportive of abortion rights, a position that contrasted with DeWine's strong anti-abortion stance.

Hobson's record on health issues and his sizable voter base — he already represented more than half of the 7th District in the state Senate — made him the strong favorite in the House contest.

The Democratic nominee was Jack Schira, a retired Air Force colonel who took 26 percent in a 1988 challenge to DeWine. Schira was a determined but poorly funded candidate who borrowed against his home and credit cards to finance his campaign. Hobson carried all of the district's counties, winning with 62 percent of the vote.

Two years later, Hobson pushed his vote share up to 71 percent.

Committees

Appropriations (21st of 23 Republicans)
Military Construction

Budget (11th of 17 Republicans)

Standards of Official Conduct (6th of 7 Republicans)

Elections

1992 General		
David L. Hobson (R)	164,195	(71%)
Clifford S. Heskett (D)	66,237	(29%)
1990 General		
David L. Hobson (R)	97,123	(62%)
Jack Schira (D)	59,349	(38%)

District Vote for President

1992

D	84,111	(34%)
R	112,517	(45%)
I	54,050	(22%)

Campaign Finance

	Receipts	Receipts from PACs		Expend-itures
1992				
Hobson (R)	$380,267	$196,975	(52%)	$298,896
1990				
Hobson (R)	$389,738	$202,427	(52%)	$389,136
Schira (D)	$89,592	$32,200	(36%)	$89,019

Key Votes

1993	
Require parental notification of minors' abortions	N
Require unpaid family and medical leave	N
Approve national "motor voter" registration bill	N
Approve budget increasing taxes and reducing deficit	N
Approve economic stimulus plan	N
1992	
Approve balanced-budget constitutional amendment	Y
Close down space station program	N
Approve U.S. aid for former Soviet Union	Y
Allow shifting funds from defense to domestic programs	N
1991	
Extend unemployment benefits using deficit financing	N
Approve waiting period for handgun purchases	N
Authorize use of force in Persian Gulf	Y

Voting Studies

	Presidential Support		Party Unity		Conservative Coalition	
Year	S	O	S	O	S	O
1992	67	33	85	15	88	13
1991	77	23	85	15	95	5

Interest Group Ratings

Year	ADA	AFL-CIO	CCUS	ACU
1992	15	33	88	80
1991	10	25	80	80

8 John A. Boehner (R)

Of West Chester — Elected 1990; 2nd Term

Born: Nov. 17, 1949, Cincinnati, Ohio.
Education: Xavier U., B.S. 1977.
Military Service: Navy, 1969.
Occupation: Plastics and packaging executive.
Family: Wife, Debbie Gunlack; two children.
Religion: Roman Catholic.
Political Career: Ohio House, 1985-91.
Capitol Office: 1020 Longworth Bldg. 20515; 225-6205.

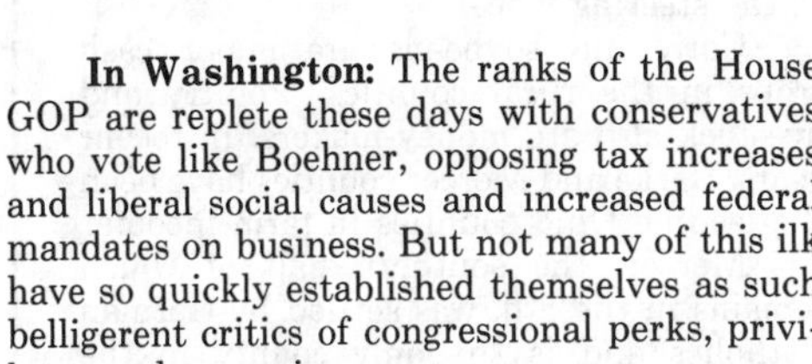

In Washington: The ranks of the House GOP are replete these days with conservatives who vote like Boehner, opposing tax increases and liberal social causes and increased federal mandates on business. But not many of this ilk have so quickly established themselves as such belligerent critics of congressional perks, privileges and pay raises.

In his first House term, Boehner received national media attention for his reformist efforts, most notably as a member of the GOP's "Gang of Seven" (which castigated the Democratic leadership over the House bank scandal) and as an advocate of a constitutional amendment prohibiting a congressional pay raise from taking effect without an intervening election.

Boehner's efforts helped earn him a spot at the beginning of the 103rd Congress on the House Administration Committee, giving him a formal post to pursue his aggressive oversight of the chamber's internal affairs. He also was named chairman of the Conservative Opportunity Society — the group that first made the House GOP a more confrontational force in the 1980s — and selected as an assistant deputy whip.

In the fall of 1991, when problems with the House bank surfaced, Boehner and several other young Republicans became concerned that Democratic leaders would let abusers of the bank get off with a mere scolding. A late-night strategy meeting gave rise to the Gang of Seven; its members aggressively sought media attention for their complaints about the handling of the bank's problems. The public got so stirred up about the matter that in October 1991, the House voted to close the bank. Continued GOP pressure played a role in the ethics committee's April 1992 decision to release the names of all members who had overdrafts at the bank, instead of just the abusers, as first planned.

In his effort to hold the line on congressional pay, Boehner found an unusual weapon: a constitutional amendment on the subject that had languished for years. The amendment, originally proposed by James Madison and first approved by Maryland in 1789, prevents any congressional pay raise from taking effect until an election has intervened.

At the start of the 102nd Congress, the amendment was a few states short of the two-thirds majority required for ratification. Reform-minded GOP House freshmen dubbed it their "class project," and Boehner rode herd on the effort, sponsoring two House resolutions related to the amendment and acting as a spokesman, strategist and cheerleader for the cause.

In May 1992, with approval of the measure in Michigan, it became the 27th Amendment to the Constitution.

Armed with the amendment, Boehner quickly tried to employ it to block the automatic cost of living adjustments (COLAs) in congressional pay that were approved in 1989. Joining the Denver-based American Constitutional Law Foundation, Boehner initiated a lawsuit to challenge the COLA's constitutionality. A district court upheld the pay raise (a ruling now under appeal), prompting Boehner and his colleagues to look for other avenues of attack. Early in the 103rd, Congress voted to put the 1994 COLA on hold.

Also during the 102nd, Boehner attempted to persuade Congress to cancel a government loan to a company developing a computerized voter registration list that members could use for mass mailings. He complained that such lists might exclude the non-voting from district mailings: "If you vote, you count; if you don't vote, you don't count," he observed.

This concern for the non-voting did not persuade Boehner to support the Democratic-led drive to pass "motor voter" legislation broadening opportunities for registration. Among Boehner's beefs with the bill was that it was designed to register more residents of inner cities and thus would help the Democratic Party.

Boehner also turned his reformist tendencies inward, pushing successfully in December 1992 for House Republicans to prohibit most GOP members from serving as the ranking member on more than one committee or subcommittee. The rule, set to take effect in 1995,

Ohio 8

Southwest — Hamilton; Middletown

Butler County is the anchor of this southwestern Ohio district, which has changed shape several times in recent redistrictings but always remained solidly Republican.

Butler contains more than half the district's population and two medium-sized manufacturing centers along the Great Miami River — Hamilton (population 61,000) and Middletown (population 46,000). Steel, paper, automobile bodies, machine tools and a variety of other metal products are made in the two cities.

Most of what few minorities there are in this district live in the two cities; Hamilton is 7 percent black and Middletown is 11 percent black. The rest of the district is about 1 percent black. All other minorities make up about 1 percent of the district.

But both Hamilton and Middletown have lost population in recent years. Most of Butler County's 291,000 residents live not in the two cities but in suburban communities and small towns such as Oxford, the home of Miami University's 16,000 students.

Population expansion in Butler County's suburban territory, just north of the Cincinnati beltway, has made the county one of the state's fastest-growing, and the new arrivals have escalated a rightward trend in the local Republican Party.

Ronald Reagan carried Butler in 1980 with 62 percent of the vote, and increased that to 73 percent in 1984. In 1988, George Bush carried Butler with 69 percent of the vote, well above his statewide average of 55 percent. He beat Bill Clinton here by 19 points in 1992, winning 49 percent of the vote. In recent years the county has elected some of the state's most conservative Republican legislators.

The other half of the 8th's residents live outside Butler County in a string of fertile Corn Belt counties running north along the Indiana border and east toward Springfield. The land is flat and the roads are straight. Once leaving the Miami Valley in northern Butler, a motorist can drive north through the 8th along Route 127 without more than an occasional slight turn of the steering wheel.

Corn and soybeans are major cash crops in the rural counties. Poultry and livestock also are money-makers. In recent years, Darke and Mercer counties have been the leading Ohio counties in farm income.

Mercer, the southern half of which remains in the 8th, was settled by German Catholics and is the only county in the district with much of a Democratic heritage; Democrats have a slight advantage lead in Darke County.

But Mercer likes its Democrats conservative. It has not backed the party's presidential candidate since 1968.

Shelby County and a bit of southwestern Auglaize County were added to the 8th in the last redistricting. Shelby voted heavily for Bush and Ross Perot in 1992, giving them 44 percent and 29 percent of the vote, respectively, to Clinton's 26 percent — Perot's best whole-county total in the district.

1990 Population: 570,901. White 549,313 (96%), Black 15,892 (3%), Other 5,696 (1%). Hispanic origin 2,763 (<1%). 18 and over 415,676 (73%), 62 and over 80,274 (14%). Median age: 32.

drew grumbles from some senior members.

Occupied mostly with institutional affairs, Boehner has not delved deeply into legislative issues. On the Education and Labor Committee, he is part of the conservative faction that opposed family leave legislation, citing the costs to business. He has voted for big-ticket items such as the superconducting super collider, the space station and the Strategic Defense Initiative. But he opposed the 1991 highway bill and as a freshman tended to avoid pork-barrel politics, unless you take pork literally: He is using his seat on the Agriculture Committee to press for allowing more of Ohio's pork products into the former Soviet Union.

At Home: In the reliably Republican 8th, the GOP primary surprise in 1990 was not that embattled Rep. Donald E. "Buz" Lukens was ousted but that Boehner emerged victorious. A state representative and local businessman, Boehner was barely a blip on the radar screen at the beginning of the campaign, but he steadily climbed until upsetting former six-term Republican Rep. Thomas N. Kindness in the May primary.

Lukens was doomed after his May 1989 conviction on a misdemeanor charge stemming from a sexual liaison with a 16-year-old girl. All seven county Republican leaders demanded that Lukens either resign or at least not seek reelection, but he held on through the primary. He finally resigned the seat after a second allegation of sexual misconduct in October.

Kindness started out as the heavy favorite, with polls showing him leading Boehner by more than 60 percentage points. Boehner made up for his lack of name recognition by running a smart and aggressive primary campaign.

While Kindness focused his sights on the wounded incumbent, Boehner ignored Lukens and chipped away at Kindness' lead by questioning his ethics, framing Kindness as a shady lobbyist who abandoned the district after losing a 1986 challenge to Democratic Sen. John Glenn. Drawing on his contacts in the business community, Boehner used his financial resources to keep the heat on Kindness. He outspent Kindness more than 5 to 1, pummeling him with extensive media coverage.

Kindness responded to the barrage of negative ads by describing Boehner as "an immature yuppie." But Boehner stuck to his theme and suggested that Kindness might have conflicts of interest on issues involving his former clients. Boehner won with 49 percent; Kindness trailed with 32 percent. Lukens finished third with 17 percent.

The general election was not as close or nasty, with Boehner sweeping every county against the Democratic nominee, former Hamilton Mayor Gregory V. Jolivette.

Though Lukens had ceased to be an issue, he threw a monkey wrench into the race late in the fall campaign. His resignation triggered a series of cumbersome electoral problems, forcing the governor to rescind his order for a special election. The seat remained vacant for the remainder of the 101st Congress.

In 1992, Boehner easily dispatched Fred Sennet, a college instructor from Fairfield.

Committees

Agriculture (10th of 18 Republicans)
General Farm Commodities; Livestock

Education & Labor (11th of 15 Republicans)
Elementary, Secondary & Vocational Education; Labor-Management Relations

House Administration (6th of 7 Republicans)
Office Systems (ranking); Accounts

Elections

1992 General		
John A. Boehner (R)	176,362	(74%)
Fred Sennet (D)	62,033	(26%)
1990 General		
John A. Boehner (R)	99,955	(61%)
Gregory V. Jolivette (D)	63,584	(39%)

District Vote for President

1992

D 75,189 (29%)
R 120,847 (47%)
I 59,937 (23%)

Campaign Finance

	Receipts	Receipts from PACs		Expend-itures
1992				
Boehner (R)	$557,539	$238,854	(43%)	$527,474
Sennet (D)	$6,730	$4,500	(67%)	$6,730
1990				
Boehner (R)	$737,441	$219,526	(30%)	$732,765
Jolivette (D)	$115,495	$48,825	(42%)	$114,852

Key Votes

1993	
Require parental notification of minors' abortions	Y
Require unpaid family and medical leave	N
Approve national "motor voter" registration bill	N
Approve budget increasing taxes and reducing deficit	N
Approve economic stimulus plan	N
1992	
Approve balanced-budget constitutional amendment	Y
Close down space station program	N
Approve U.S. aid for former Soviet Union	Y
Allow shifting funds from defense to domestic programs	N
1991	
Extend unemployment benefits using deficit financing	N
Approve waiting period for handgun purchases	N
Authorize use of force in Persian Gulf	Y

Voting Studies

	Presidential Support		Party Unity		Conservative Coalition	
Year	**S**	**O**	**S**	**O**	**S**	**O**
1992	87	11	94	3	94	6
1991	84	14	96	4	97	0

Interest Group Ratings

Year	ADA	AFL-CIO	CCUS	ACU
1992	5	17	88	96
1991	0	0	100	95

9 Marcy Kaptur (D)

Of Toledo — Elected 1982; 6th Term

Born: June 17, 1946, Toledo, Ohio.
Education: U. of Wisconsin, B.A. 1968; U. of Michigan, M.U.P. 1974; Massachusetts Institute of Technology, 1981.
Occupation: Urban planner; White House aide.
Family: Single.
Religion: Roman Catholic.
Political Career: No previous office.
Capitol Office: 2104 Rayburn Bldg. 20515; 225-4146.

In Washington: A voice of moral outrage over issues of concern to her Rust Belt constituency, Kaptur took a leading role in opposition to the North American Free Trade Agreement (NAFTA), which would eliminate trade and investment barriers between the United States and Mexico. Her role as a defender of U.S. manufacturing jobs and her new status as a target of the Mexican media is a political plus in the 9th District. She was even mentioned in 1993 as one of several Democrats with 1994 Senate aspirations.

After several years of striving, Kaptur won a seat on the coveted Appropriations Committee late in the 101st Congress. While she has yet to develop a reputation as a deal-broker and legislative heavy lifter, hers is a vote on which the Democratic leadership can generally depend.

As a member of the Appropriations subcommittee that funds space programs as well as housing and veterans programs, Kaptur took a stand in the 102nd Congress against one of the panel's big-ticket science projects, the controversial $30 billion-plus space station *Freedom.* Calling it an "orbiting tin can," she said the country could not afford a $120 billion, 30-year mortgage on the future.

First swept into office by voter anger over the 1982 recession, Kaptur remains an ardent spokesman for industrial Toledo, which is heavily dependent on the automobile industry. Republican free-traders set her blood to boiling — "appeasement," she once called it. Kaptur backed the Democratic trade bill that was three years in the making, and, in 1987, strongly supported the Gephardt "fair trade" amendment. She added her own amendment, calling on U.S. trade negotiators to oppose most-favored-nation status for countries not maintaining open markets.

In October 1992, Kaptur was among 97 members, including Democratic Majority Whip David E. Bonior of Michigan and Chief Deputy Whip Barbara B. Kennelly of Connecticut, who signed a letter to Bill Clinton urging him to reject NAFTA and commit himself to reopen negotiations once in office. The lawmakers cited controversial estimates that the United States might lose as many as 500,000 jobs to Mexico if the agreement goes through. But Clinton gave NAFTA a qualified endorsement the next day.

In the 103rd Congress, an increasing number of members began voicing concern over the effect of the agreement on U.S. jobs, clouding its prospects for congressional approval. "Certain powerful interests are going to benefit from this agreement," Kaptur said in a House speech in February 1993. "But you can bet it is not going to be the glass factory worker in Toledo or the Mexican who toils 12 hours a day for $1 an hour."

Kaptur and seven other female members of Congress visited Mexico City in May 1993. During the trip, she repeated the prediction of Clinton's budget director, Leon E. Panetta, that NAFTA would be defeated if Congress voted on it at that time. The Washington Post reported that a columnist in a Mexico City newspaper wrote that Panetta's and Kaptur's comments were part of an organized "Anti-Mexico Week." He referred to Kaptur as "Marcy Kaput."

Balancing Kaptur's trade stance is her concern for Toledo's port, which has some import traffic. In 1985, she opposed a bill to impose a 25 percent surcharge on certain countries' imports. In 1984, she successfully advocated a three-year suspension of the duty on metal umbrella frames; Toledo has one of the few U.S. umbrella-making companies. She introduced a bill in the 103rd Congress to extend through 1994 the existing temporary suspension of the umbrella-frame duty.

Kaptur's most notable divergence from the majority of the Democratic Caucus — and most Democratic women in the House — is on certain abortion-related questions. Kaptur opposes the use of federal funds for abortions. In 1989, she voted against federal funding for poor women's abortions in cases of rape and incest, and she voted to prohibit the District of Columbia from using any funds — federal or city — to perform abortions. In 1992, she was one of only two Democratic women (out of 17) to oppose

Ohio 9

Northwest — Toledo

Toledo is an old port city, one whose more recent fortunes have risen and fallen, and fallen further, with the health of the automobile industry. But by the beginning of the 1990s, it was Wall Street, not Detroit, that had undermined Toledo's economy.

The city had climbed back from the depths of the early 1980s recession by mid-decade, and there was some cause for optimism. A Jeep plant and a General Motors transmission factory were operating at full capacity; unemployment in Toledo slipped below 10 percent in 1986.

The optimism ceased as a wave of corporate takeovers and restructurings by out-of-town interests weakened such major Toledo glass producers as Libbey-Owens-Ford, Owens-Illinois and Owens-Corning, causing thousands of job losses.

Undergirding Toledo's economy are the several crude oil and gas pipelines that terminate there, and the refineries they feed.

And millions have been spent to improve the city's Toledo Express Airport. The Burlington Air Express delivery company opened a $50 million terminal and sorting center there in 1991, creating more than 800 jobs.

Almost three-fifths — 333,000 — of the district's residents live in Toledo, an important port city that sits at the mouth of the largest river that flows into the Great Lakes, the Maumee.

The city, built on the site of a remote 18th-century fort, is now a lonely Democratic outpost in rural Republican northwestern Ohio. Democrats outnumber Republicans in surrounding Lucas County (which holds an additional 129,000 residents) by more than 2-to-1.

But a smaller black population keeps Democratic majorities in Toledo lower than those in Dayton or Cleveland. Jimmy Carter carried the city in 1980, but with only 49 percent of the vote. Democrats Walter F. Mondale and Michael S. Dukakis carried on the tradition in 1984 and 1988. And Bill Clinton won it handily in 1992.

Toledo is an ethnic city. There are major concentrations of Germans, Irish, Poles and Hungarians. While traditionally Democratic, most blue-collar ethnics here vote Republican at least occasionally.

To the east of the city are blue-collar, traditionally Democratic suburbs. Republicans are concentrated in the more affluent suburbs on Toledo's west side, where Ottawa Hills has one of the highest per capita incomes of any community in Ohio.

The whole of Fulton County was included in the 9th in 1992 redistricting. Fulton is one of the most Republican counties in Ohio, but part of it is in Toledo's orbit and contains some solid Democratic precincts.

The 9th now has about a third of Wood County's land mass and 55,000 of its residents — about half its people. The part of Wood County in the district includes 15,000 of Bowling Green's 28,000 residents, along with Bowling Green State University and its 18,000 students.

1990 Population: 570,901. White 484,770 (85%), Black 69,444 (12%), Other 16,687 (3%). Hispanic origin 19,347 (3%). 18 and over 421,341 (74%), 62 and over 86,721 (15%). Median age: 32.

allowing private abortions to be conducted in overseas military bases. She did, however, vote to overturn the Bush administration's ban on abortion counseling at federally funded family planning clinics — the so-called "gag rule."

Kaptur arrived in Congress without elective-office experience, and she sought to compensate for that by hitching her fortunes to those of Texan Jim Wright, then the majority leader. Soon after he became Speaker in 1987, Wright rewarded Kaptur's loyalty with an appointment to the panel that makes Democrats' committee assignments. In 1989, he backed her successful bid for the Budget Committee. He also named her vice chairman of the leadership task force on trade. But when Wright resigned in June 1989, Kaptur failed in her first solo try for a leadership spot: She ran third in a bid for Democratic Caucus vice chairman.

Her next reach for a higher rung came in May 1990, when there was a vacancy on the Appropriations Committee. Kaptur had tried for the prestigious panel before, but this time, playing the gender and geography cards, she succeeded.

Kaptur noted that the committee had just one Democratic woman, Lindy (Mrs. Hale) Boggs of Louisiana, who was retiring at the end of the 101st Congress; she also stirred up other Rust Belt members to quash a move by Californians for a sixth Appropriations seat.

The 1989 ethics legislation included language Kaptur backed to restrict former government officials from working on behalf of foreign interests for one year. Kaptur is now pushing to extend the prohibition to five years.

At Home: Kaptur's victory over GOP Rep. Ed Weber was one of the Democrats' surprise 1982 successes. Although a poised and aggressive candidate, she had to overcome a late start and a poorly financed, under-organized campaign with little help from the national party.

Kaptur took the Democratic nomination essentially by default in February 1982 when the local party gave up on trying to find a proven vote-getter to challenge the personally popular Republican incumbent. At that point in the election year, national Republican Party strategists were pointing to Weber as a symbol of the way their first-term House members were entrenching themselves in Democratic territory.

But Kaptur began hammering away at Weber's voting record, using his support for President Ronald Reagan's economic policies during a recession as evidence of insensitivity to Toledo's economic plight. Weber never shifted in his public backing for Reagan's program; that was his undoing in a region with double-digit unemployment.

Overconfident, he failed to exploit one vulnerability in Kaptur's record. Although she was a Toledo native, Kaptur had spent many years away, most recently as the assistant director of urban affairs for President Jimmy Carter. But with Weber ignoring the issue, neither Kaptur's absence nor her Carter connection proved to be any problem.

In 1984, Republicans nominated Frank Venner, a longtime TV newscaster. Although he had no previous political experience, Venner was a familiar figure to a generation of Toledo voters. But he had trouble translating his avuncular, non-ideological TV image into a partisan campaign. He had plenty of campaign money, but neither a strong grass-roots organization nor a potent local issue to use against Kaptur. Fortified by support from labor and the district's large ethnic population, Kaptur won 55 percent. That was her last close race. In 1992, she won with 74 percent of the vote.

Committee

Appropriations (21st of 37 Democrats)
Agriculture, Rural Development, FDA & Related Agencies; District of Columbia; Veterans Affairs, Housing & Urban Development & Independent Agencies

Elections

1992 General		
Marcy Kaptur (D)	178,879	(74%)
Ken D. Brown (R)	53,011	(22%)
Ed Howard (I)	11,162	(5%)
1990 General		
Marcy Kaptur (D)	117,681	(78%)
Jerry D. Lammers (R)	33,791	(22%)

Previous Winning Percentages: **1988** (81%) **1986** (78%) **1984** (55%) **1982** (58%)

District Vote for President

1992
D 118,818 (47%)
R 81,881 (33%)
I 50,155 (20%)

Campaign Finance

	Receipts	Receipts from PACs	Expend-itures
1992			
Kaptur (D)	$290,940	$208,305 (72%)	$335,095
Brown (R)	$44,782	$8,650 (19%)	$43,930
1990			
Kaptur (D)	$227,820	$114,830 (50%)	$211,524
Lammers (R)	$200	0	$200

Key Votes

1993	
Require parental notification of minors' abortions	N
Require unpaid family and medical leave	Y
Approve national "motor voter" registration bill	Y
Approve budget increasing taxes and reducing deficit	Y
Approve economic stimulus plan	Y
1992	
Approve balanced-budget constitutional amendment	N
Close down space station program	Y
Approve U.S. aid for former Soviet Union	N
Allow shifting funds from defense to domestic programs	Y
1991	
Extend unemployment benefits using deficit financing	Y
Approve waiting period for handgun purchases	Y
Authorize use of force in Persian Gulf	N

Voting Studies

	Presidential Support		Party Unity		Conservative Coalition	
Year	**S**	**O**	**S**	**O**	**S**	**O**
1992	23	75	86	10	50	48
1991	29	67	85	8	41	54
1990	23	76	86	8	41	56
1989	33	64	86	9	29	71
1988	21	70	86	8	45	50
1987	19	75	82	6	30	60
1986	17	77	84	4	24	68
1985	26	70	84	9	27	69
1984	26	63	79	12	20	73
1983	12	85	85	10	15	82

Interest Group Ratings

Year	ADA	AFL-CIO	CCUS	ACU
1992	75	100	14	8
1991	85	82	30	5
1990	72	100	15	8
1989	75	82	44	11
1988	75	100	43	13
1987	80	94	21	0
1986	75	93	33	5
1985	60	88	41	14
1984	75	83	33	22
1983	90	94	20	4

10 Martin R. Hoke (R)

Of Cleveland — Elected 1992; 1st Term

Born: May 18, 1952, Lakewood, Ohio.
Education: Amherst College, B.A. 1973; Case Western Reserve U., J.D. 1980.
Occupation: Cellular phone company president; lawyer.
Family: Divorced; three children.
Religion: Protestant.
Political Career: No previous office.
Capitol Office: 212 Cannon Bldg. 20515; 225-5871.

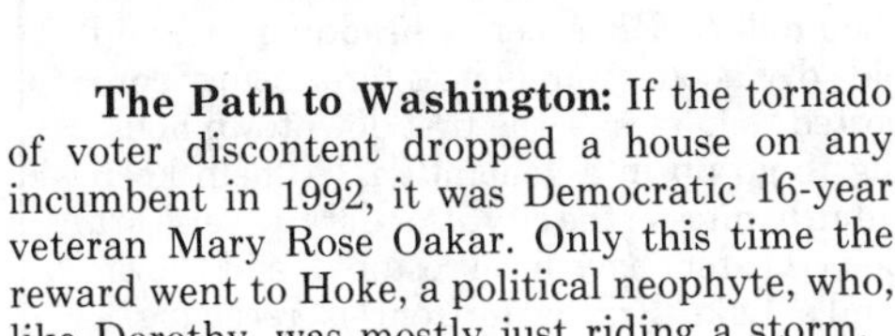

The Path to Washington: If the tornado of voter discontent dropped a house on any incumbent in 1992, it was Democratic 16-year veteran Mary Rose Oakar. Only this time the reward went to Hoke, a political neophyte, who, like Dorothy, was mostly just riding a storm.

At his victory celebration, as if to complete the life-imitating-art parallel, Hoke had the band play, "Ding, Dong, the Witch Is Dead."

Hoke, a lawyer and millionaire founder of a successful cellular telephone company, may find that he is not in Cleveland anymore when he gets to Capitol Hill. He pushes standard Republican fare about less government and lower taxes — particularly on capital gains. And he hews to his anti-government line by opposing interference in private decisions. That leads him to a qualified endorsement of abortion rights.

Hoke does not shy from speaking his mind. In an interview with The New York Times on the social lives of single representatives, he said: "I could date [fellow representatives] Maria Cantwell or Blanche Lambert — they're hot."

Hoke's campaign was marred by missteps, particularly on substance and policy. He called for a $200 billion cut in defense spending. Yet, when he realized that would be a 70 percent cut, he revised his estimate downward twice. He raised the possibility of decriminalizing drug use to cut down on crime, then disavowed the idea. His campaign literature called for reforming the Federal Savings and Loan Insurance Corporation (FSLIC), which reminded voters of Oakar's senior position on the Banking Committee and of the cost of the thrift bailout. It overlooked the fact that the FSLIC was abolished in 1989.

When Hoke got down to attacking the incumbent, however, he was as polished as any experienced politician. He proved much more articulate on the stump than Oakar. And, most important, he made her the issue. To Hoke, Oakar was the "poster child for what is wrong with Congress." Named as one of the 22 abusers of the House bank — with 213 overdrafts — Oakar was an early target of congressional critics.

The (Cleveland) Plain Dealer, which had endorsed her in every prior election, wrote lengthy editorials castigating her for failing to keep watch over the bank and the House Post Office — which was embroiled in multiple scandals from cocaine sales to fraud — from her position as a subcommittee chairman on the House Administration Committee. In its news columns, the Plain Dealer reported allegations that she had placed ghost employees on the Post Office staff. That charge was later disproved, and Oakar sued the newspaper for libel (the case is pending). But the damage was done.

Nevertheless, Oakar had survived previous ethical and legal lapses and had been overwhelmingly re-elected on the strength of her white ethnic appeal and success at bringing home federal aid for her struggling city. It appeared that she would prevail again in 1992, after six other Democrats jumped into the primary and split the anti-Oakar vote. She won easily over her strongest challenger, Cuyahoga County Commissioner Timothy F. Hagen, who declined to confront her through most of the campaign and waited for her to fire the first negative shot before responding in kind.

But Oakar's vulnerability showed when she pulled in less than 40 percent. The newly drawn 10th contains a large slice of suburban Cleveland not used to voting for her. Those voters provided Hoke with his 57 percent victory.

Hoke was not gentle.

Attacking Oakar from the start, he won his primary in a bit of an upset over Rocky River Mayor Earl Martin and three others. He then pursued Oakar relentlessly through TV ads that dredged up old and new dirt on her ethical scrapes. And he executed a well-rehearsed attack during a nationally televised Sunday morning news show in the campaign's final weeks.

Hoke survived a baptism of fire that may have tempered him for the certain assault he will face in 1994. In the final days of the campaign, an Oakar aide was linked to anonymous charges aired by a Cleveland TV station that Hoke was a cocaine user. Oakar said he had failed to pay child support and ridiculed his having adopted the name and lifestyle of a Sikh in the late 1970s. Hoke successfully parried the attacks.

Ohio 10

Cleveland — West Side and suburbs

This was a district designed with the safety of its former occupant, Democrat Mary Rose Oakar, firmly in mind. Many Democrats see Hoke's win in 1992 solely as a referendum on Oakar, and they expect to win the seat back.

"The joke around here the day after the election was that Martin Hoke had just been elected to his last term in Congress," says a local observer.

The line between the 10th and 11th districts generally divides Cleveland's white and black populations. The 10th is the white district, containing the state's largest concentration of ethnic voters. Poles, Czechs, Italians, Irish and Germans are the largest groups, but there are dozens of other ethnic communities represented by at least a restaurant or two on the West Side.

The city's steel industry fueled the ethnic influx around the turn of the century, with immigrants settling near the West Side mills. Steel, automobile and aluminum plants combine with smaller businesses to make up the employment base today.

But many of the younger people who work there have bought homes in the suburbs. Cleveland suffered a 12 percent population loss in the 1980s. As a result of this — and the addition of more western Cleveland suburbs — more than half the electorate now lies outside the city's limits.

The downtown area was gerrymandered in order to divvy up sources of campaign contributions, not votes. Its businesses are split between the 10th and Louis Stokes' 11th District. The city's economic problems of the 1970s, notably its near-bankruptcy under then-Mayor Dennis Kucinich, made it a national symbol of urban decay. But Cleveland today is stronger than many industrial cities of the Frost Belt, mainly because it is making the successful transition to a service economy.

To offset auto and steel slumps, a consortium made up of the city's largest companies mapped out a long-term, diversified plan for growth — a number of small, high-tech companies have already been attracted. Condominiums are being constructed near the $200 million BP America headquarters, and old dry-goods warehouses are being converted to homes — the first downtown housing to go up in a generation. To help keep suburbanites in the city after dark, several art deco theaters have been restored, and Cleveland's Lake Erie waterfront is receiving a facelift. Even the Cuyahoga River — which was once so polluted that it caught fire — has been cleaned up.

Children and grandchildren of European immigrants have moved out of Cleveland to inner suburbs such as Parma, due south of the city. In recent years they have moved again. Parma's population declined in the 1970s and '80s, as residents left their ranch homes of the 1950s for the open spaces of outer suburbs such as Strongsville. But even with the population loss, Parma (population 88,000) is still the eighth-largest city in Ohio. Nearby steel mills and automobile plants give this section of the district a strong union presence.

1990 Population: 570,903. White 537,301 (94%), Black 11,982 (2%), Other 21,620 (4%). Hispanic origin 22,966 (4%). 18 and over 435,467 (76%), 62 and over 104,152 (18%). Median age: 35.

Committees

Budget (17th of 17 Republicans)

Science, Space & Technology (14th of 22 Republicans)
Space; Technology, Environment & Aviation

Campaign Finance

1992	Receipts	Receipts from PACs		Expend-itures
Hoke (R)	$684,560	0		$682,166
Oakar (D)	$1,237,668	$529,853	(43%)	$1,292,286

Key Votes

1993

Require parental notification of minors' abortions	N
Require unpaid family and medical leave	Y
Approve national "motor voter" registration bill	N
Approve budget increasing taxes and reducing deficit	N
Approve economic stimulus plan	N

Elections

1992 General		
Martin R. Hoke (R)	136,433	(57%)
Mary Rose Oakar (D)	103,788	(43%)
1992 Primary		
Martin R. Hoke (R)	13,119	(33%)
Earl Martin (R)	11,016	(28%)
Sally Conway Kilbane (R)	9,744	(25%)
Carol Fedor (R)	3,621	(9%)
Bill Smith (R)	1,704	(4%)

District Vote for President

1992

D 107,460 (42%)
R 92,849 (36%)
I 58,095 (22%)

11 Louis Stokes (D)

Of Shaker Heights — Elected 1968; 13th Term

Born: Feb. 23, 1925, Cleveland, Ohio.
Education: Case Western Reserve U., 1946-48; Cleveland-Marshall College of Law, J.D. 1953.
Military Service: Army, 1943-46.
Occupation: Lawyer.
Family: Wife, Jeannette Francis; four children.
Religion: African Methodist Episcopal Zion.
Political Career: No previous office.
Capitol Office: 2365 Rayburn Bldg. 20515; 225-7032.

In Washington: For two decades in the House, Stokes had something of a two-track career. He is a senior Democrat on the Appropriations Committee and the man to whom the Democratic leadership had turned when it had a touchy ethics assignment.

The 102nd Congress marked a fork in Stokes' career. His 551 overdrafts at the House bank probably ended his reputation as the go-to guy for handling ethics messes. That leaves the Appropriations track, where, as the new chairman of the Subcommittee on VA, HUD and Independent Agencies beginning in the 103rd Congress, Stokes is likely to focus his energies. Unless, that is, Stokes decides to leave the House for a 1994 Senate bid. In the spring of 1993, he looked at running for the seat of Democratic Sen. Howard M. Metzenbaum, who was expected to retire after the 103rd Congress.

Stokes is the first black to chair a major Appropriations subcommittee. As a member of the VA-HUD panel, Stokes consistently has spoken for minority concerns, supporting funds for black colleges and housing programs and backing affirmative action in the workplace.

In 1991, with Congress searching to define its ethical standards in the wake of several financial and personal scandals, Stokes was asked for the second time in a decade to chair the ethics committee.

But as the House bank scandal began to unfold that fall, Stokes recused himself. In a letter to Speaker Thomas S. Foley of Washington, Stokes wrote, "I have admitted that on occasions . . . my account was overdrawn." Not until the ethics panel released its report in April 1992 was it revealed that there had been 551 such occasions. The task of leading the ethics committee's investigation fell to New York Democrat Matthew F. McHugh.

Stokes' first turn in the ethics chair was from 1981 to 1985. He took the job at the request of then-Speaker Thomas P. "Tip" O'Neill Jr. of Massachusetts. In calling on Stokes, O'Neill took the chair from Florida's Charles E. Bennett, a man with a rigid code of personal ethics that O'Neill found too unyielding.

With the case of the last figure in the Abscam bribery scandal, valued leadership lieutenant John P. Murtha of Pennsylvania, pending before the committee, O'Neill replaced Bennett with Stokes, a committee member who had been a voice for the accused. The committee ultimately recommended no action against Murtha, provoking its counsel to resign.

Like his predecessor in the VA-HUD chair, Bob Traxler of Michigan, Stokes has expressed doubt about expensive space projects such as the $30 billion-plus space station, which the panel funds as part of the NASA budget. He backed Traxler's amendment to kill the station in 1992, saying it was a vote of conscience because the VA-HUD bill lacked money for urban aid, as well as a vote against an agency run "as though it were a white male, old boys' country club."

But Stokes has a home-state interest in the project: Cleveland is home to the Lewis Research Center, which does the space station's electrical work. It is next door to his district.

Stokes served in the late 1960s on the House Committee on Un-American Activities, a panel he worked to abolish. He was tapped during the late 1970s to chair the committee investigating the assassinations of President John F. Kennedy and the Rev. Dr. Martin Luther King Jr.

The Kennedy assassination returned to public prominence with the 1991 release of Oliver Stone's controversial movie "JFK," which suggested a conspiracy and ongoing cover-up of the murder. Stokes responded early in 1992 with a bill to open an array of sealed Kennedy files. "I think it's important for the American people to know that their government did not assassinate their president," he said. Under the bill signed into law, a commission will review and release to the public all documents except those that greatly compromise national security or a person's privacy.

Between 1983 and 1989, Stokes served on the Intelligence Committee, rising to the chairmanship of that panel during the 100th Congress. A strong critic of the administration's actions in the Iran-contra affair, Stokes gained the spotlight with his dogged questioning of witnesses before

Ohio 11

Cleveland — East Side and suburbs

One of the axioms of Ohio politics is that to win statewide, a Democratic candidate must build a 100,000-vote edge in Cuyahoga County. Most of that lead has to be built in the 11th, which is anchored in Cleveland's heavily black East Side. Bill Clinton picked up a spare 132,000 votes here in 1992 over George Bush, which allowed him to walk away with Ohio's 21 electoral votes with nearly a 91,000-vote margin.

This compact district — the smallest and most densely populated in the state — includes poor inner-city areas as well as middle-class territory farther from the downtown area.

Nineteen percent of the 11th's families — and almost a third of those in its section of Cleveland — live below the poverty line. Conditions improve out toward the city's eastern suburbs, where blue and white collars are worn by their diverse black population.

Devastated by the riots of the 1960s, inner-city neighborhoods of Hough and Glenville can claim some new residential and commercial development, but they still bear the scars of poverty.

Out toward the lake, this area includes the middle-class, white ethnic neighborhoods of Collinwood and St. Clare, inhabited by Italians, and Poles, Yugoslavs and other Eastern Europeans.

Overall, the 11th is 59 percent black and heavily Democratic. During the past decade, it has been the most Democratic district in the state.

Any hopes that Stokes would be made vulnerable when his district was extended east to take in some white working-class areas — his old 21st District was 62 percent black — were dashed in 1992 when he pulled down 69 percent of the vote in a field of four, compared with 80 percent against a single opponent in 1990.

New to Stokes' territory is Euclid, a white, ethnic, working-class city of 55,000 east of Cleveland. Euclid "is Democratic, but hardly comfortable with the black part of this district," says a local observer. A Democrat from Euclid running against Stokes as an independent in 1992 hoped — in vain — to capitalize on this sentiment.

Some of the 11th's other major suburbs are Cleveland Heights, Shaker Heights and University Heights (populations, 54,000, 31,000 and 15,000).

With a large proportion of Jews and young professionals, these are among Ohio's most liberal communities. North of Shaker Heights is Cleveland Heights, many of whose integrated neighborhoods are a short walk from University Circle, home of Case Western Reserve University and Cleveland's cultural hub.

From the circle area, commuters drive along historic Euclid Avenue to their jobs downtown. While the avenue now bears the marks of poverty, it was known as "Millionaires' Row" at the turn of the century. Few of the old mansions remain. The one belonging to John D. Rockefeller, founder of Standard Oil, was razed after his death in 1937.

1990 Population: 570,901. White 226,986 (40%), Black 334,348 (59%), Other 9,567 (2%). Hispanic origin 6,402 (1%). 18 and over 424,718 (74%), 62 and over 102,401 (18%). Median age: 34.

the special committee investigating the scandal, including the central figures, White House aides John M. Poindexter and Oliver L. North.

Much of Stokes' legislative activity is influenced by his race. In making a point to North about respecting even those laws he opposed, Stokes reminisced about being a black soldier in World War II. "I wore [the uniform] as proudly as you do, even though our government required black and white soldiers in the same Army to live, sleep, eat and travel separate and apart, while fighting and dying for our country," Stokes said.

At Home: While the House bank uproar swirled about his colleagues, Stokes had remained mum about his overdrafts. By the time the ethics committee report revealed that he had had 551, the filing deadline for candidates had passed, leaving him unopposed in the primary in his heavily Democratic district.

Stokes faced three other opponents in November, including Republican Beryl E. Rothschild, the mayor of University Heights, and Edmund Gudenas, a Euclid City Council member. They combined to hold Stokes to a career-low 69 percent in his redrawn district.

Stokes is feeling some pressure from a new generation of black leaders emerging in Cleveland, symbolized by the 1989 election of Michael White as mayor. But the Stokes family is still a dominant force in city politics, as it has been for more than two decades. Stokes' younger brother, Carl, grabbed the spotlight in the mid-1960s when he first ran for mayor of Cleveland. Carl Stokes temporarily left politics after two terms as mayor (1967-71), but he re-emerged in 1983 to be elected to the Cleveland Municipal Court and was re-elected in 1987 and again in 1991.

Louis Stokes' first victory was won as much in court as on Cleveland's East Side. Representing a black Republican, he charged in a 1967 suit that the Ohio legislature had gerrymandered the state's congressional districts, dividing the minority vote and preventing the election of a black candidate. Stokes won an appeal before the U.S. Supreme Court, forcing the lines to be redrawn.

In remapping, Rep. Charles A. Vanik, a white Democrat, wound up with a 21st District that was about 60 percent black. Vanik then decided to run in an adjacent district that contained much of his former, heavily ethnic European constituency.

Stokes had plenty of company in the 1968 contest for the open 21st: 13 other candidates filed to run in the Democratic primary. The outcome was little in doubt, though. Aided by his brother in City Hall and by his reputation as a civil rights lawyer, Stokes won with 41 percent of the primary vote. That November, he became the first black congressman from Ohio by defeating Charles P. Lucas — the Republican he had represented in court the previous year.

Stokes weighed a return to the courtroom to contest the design of his district — now the 11th — after the 1992 remapping. Although he threatened to challenge the map because the percentage of black population decreased, he had sought to add some affluent white suburbs in Cuyahoga County.

Committee

Appropriations (6th of 37 Democrats)
Veterans Affairs, Housing & Urban Development & Independent Agencies (chairman); District of Columbia; Labor, Health & Human Services, Education & Related Agencies

Elections

1992 General

Louis Stokes (D)	154,718	(69%)
Beryl E. Rothschild (R)	43,866	(20%)
Edmund Gudenas (I)	19,773	(9%)
Gerald C. Henley (I)	5,267	(2%)

1990 General

Louis Stokes (D)	103,338	(80%)
Franklin H. Roski (R)	25,906	(20%)

Previous Winning Percentages: **1988** (86%) **1986** (82%) **1984** (82%) **1982** (86%) **1980** (88%) **1978** (86%) **1976** (84%) **1974** (82%) **1972** (81%) **1970** (78%) **1968** (75%)

District Vote for President

1992
D 169,877 (73%)
R 37,880 (16%)
I 23,423 (10%)

Campaign Finance

	Receipts	Receipts from PACs		Expend-itures
1992				
Stokes (D)	$391,172	$149,293	(38%)	$449,248
Rothschild (R)	$79,879	$2,260	(3%)	$79,232
1990				
Stokes (D)	$250,022	$137,575	(55%)	$198,984

Key Votes

1993	
Require parental notification of minors' abortions	N
Require unpaid family and medical leave	Y
Approve national "motor voter" registration bill	Y
Approve budget increasing taxes and reducing deficit	Y
Approve economic stimulus plan	Y
1992	
Approve balanced-budget constitutional amendment	N
Close down space station program	Y
Approve U.S. aid for former Soviet Union	N
Allow shifting funds from defense to domestic programs	Y
1991	
Extend unemployment benefits using deficit financing	Y
Approve waiting period for handgun purchases	Y
Authorize use of force in Persian Gulf	N

Voting Studies

	Presidential Support		Party Unity		Conservative Coalition	
Year	**S**	**O**	**S**	**O**	**S**	**O**
1992	10	87	92	2	6	92
1991	24	74	90	4	0	100
1990	14	81	88	5	7	89
1989	28	70	90	1	7	80
1988	16	59	81	1	0	66
1987	13	77	91	1	9	77
1986	11	82	87	2	2	80
1985	15	83	93	1	5	93
1984	22	68	88	3	0	93
1983	11	80	86	3	6	85
1982	27	65	91	4	10	86
1981	29	66	93	4	5	91

Interest Group Ratings

Year	ADA	AFL-CIO	CCUS	ACU
1992	95	92	14	0
1991	100	100	22	0
1990	100	100	29	4
1989	95	91	33	0
1988	70	100	25	0
1987	88	100	7	0
1986	100	93	12	0
1985	95	100	24	0
1984	95	85	33	0
1983	80	94	18	0
1982	85	100	24	10
1981	90	93	11	0

12 John R. Kasich (R)

Of Westerville — Elected 1982; 6th Term

Born: May 13, 1952, McKees Rocks, Pa.
Education: Ohio State U., B.S. 1974.
Occupation: Legislative aide.
Family: Divorced.
Religion: Christian.
Political Career: Ohio Senate, 1979-83.
Capitol Office: 1131 Longworth Bldg. 20515; 225-5355.

In Washington: Perpetually in motion, Kasich is a whirlwind of restless energy, who is sometimes criticized for having a cocky manner and a lack of focus. But Kasich now has a position that will allow him to narrow his aim. As ranking Republican on the House Budget Committee, Kasich has the opportunity to use his talent, conservative fiscal principles and in-your-face style to criticize Democratic economic policy while highlighting GOP alternatives. He will have to make the most of it quickly, however. He must rotate off the Budget Committee at the end of the 103rd Congress.

Kasich ascended to the ranking position in 1993 when the party bypassed the more senior and more moderate Alex McMillan of North Carolina as part of a broader GOP move toward a more combative, less compromising role in dealing with a Democratic president and the large Democratic majority in the House.

Embracing the assignment with his usual enthusiasm, Kasich quickly launched a counter-offensive against President Clinton's economic plan. Appearing on the floor, at news conferences, on television interview shows and whatever other forums he could find, he criticized Clinton's budget as low on spending cuts, high on taxes and too reliant on defense cuts.

When, in response to entreaties by conservative Democrats to cut more spending, Budget Committee Democrats added an additional $63 billion in spending cuts, Kasich criticized the additional cuts as lacking in specifics.

Facing the cameras covering the markup, Kasich referred to Clinton's previous call that any GOP plan name specific cuts by saying, "Mr. President, if you are watching, will you please give us your specifics? We are tired of generalities. . . . Shame on you, Mr. President."

During the same markup, Kasich's relentless criticisms so annoyed Budget Chairman Martin Olav Sabo of Minnesota that the usually reserved Sabo snapped, "If you would just listen for a second."

Kasich felt strongly that any GOP criticisms would lack resonance unless Republicans had a credible plan of their own, so he offered an alternative that ultimately drew more votes than any GOP budget in the previous seven years, including two Kasich had offered in 1989 and 1990.

Kasich's plan, according to supporters, would have reduced the deficit by over $425 billion over five years, as much as Clinton's budget, without raising taxes or touching Social Security as much as Clinton's plan.

The plan included provisions such as limiting benefits to high-income Medicare recipients, eliminating campus-based student aid and the Legal Services Corporation, and eliminating 50,000 additional federal jobs,

While praised by such unlikely sources as The New York Times, Kasich's proposal was ultimately defeated 135-295 with 41 Republicans voting against it and three Democrats voting for it.

Kasich has warned against drastic cuts in defense spending, but from his post on the Armed Services Committee, he has taken aim at some major weapons programs. In the 101st Congress, Kasich launched his most audacious budget-cutting effort: the elimination of the high-cost B-2 stealth bomber.

Expressing concern that the B-2 would soak up too much of the defense budget, Kasich stepped out front with a small group of GOP conservatives who called themselves "cheap hawks." He also struck an unusual alliance with California Rep. Ronald V. Dellums, an arms control advocate and one of the most liberal House Democrats, in an effort to scrap the B-2.

Though providing a strategic justification for the cutback, Kasich's main case against the B-2 was budgetary. "We don't have the money to pay for this," he said. The campaign to kill the B-2 fell short in 1989.

But the fall of communism in Eastern Europe and the warming of U.S.-Soviet relations boosted Kasich's cause. Working with Dellums and other allies, Kasich lobbied to line up commitments, including one from then-Armed Services Chairman Les Aspin of Wisconsin, who helped insert provisions killing the B-2 in the fiscal 1991 House defense authorization bill. Ultimately, however, a House-Senate conference

Ohio 12

Central — Eastern Columbus and suburbs

Columbus has not suffered from the kind of economic collapse that has afflicted most of Ohio's industrial cities in recent years. It is primarily a white-collar town, one whose diverse industrial base is bolstered by the state government complex, a major banking center and numerous scientific research companies.

No longer is Columbus recognized only as the home of the Ohio State University football team; an economic renaissance in the early 1990s led a slew of national publications to list the city as one of the most progressive and prosperous.

According to marketers, Columbus is a mirror for the nation, so average that it serves as a favored test bed for all sorts of fast-food menu items and other consumer products.

More than three-quarters of the 12th District's residents live in Columbus and its Franklin County suburbs. Democrats must do very well in the city to have a chance districtwide.

Forty-five percent of Columbus is in the 12th; the rest is to the west in the 15th District. The 12th's section of Columbus is more heavily black, poorer and less well-educated than the other. Forty-three percent of the 12th's 284,000 Columbus residents are black, compared with just 6 percent in the 15th's western half of the city. Nearly 18 percent of its families live below the poverty level, compared with 8 percent of the 15th's section. Nineteen percent of its adult residents have a college degree, compared with 29 percent on the west side.

As one moves east from the state Capitol building along Broad Street, the black Democratic vote goes down and the Republican vote goes up. Only 4 percent of the 12th's Franklin County suburbs of Columbus are black.

About three miles east of the Capitol is affluent Bexley, an independent community of 13,000 surrounded by the city.

While usually Republican, Bexley has a large Jewish population and sometimes votes for strong Democratic candidates. Two miles farther east is Whitehall, another independent town, with 21,500 largely blue-collar residents who frequently split their tickets.

Whitehall is the site of the Defense Logistic Agency's Defense Construction Supply Center, which employs 4,700. The center will pick up 2,000 to 3,000 more jobs when a similar facility in Dayton closes.

Farther out from Whitehall are newer suburbs. Some of these, such as Reynoldsburg and Gahanna, are predominantly blue collar. Residents are employed at such large plants as McDonnell Douglas and AT&T.

The rest of the 12th is rural and Republican, with a smattering of light industry. The remaining 23 percent of the district's residents are split between Licking and Delaware counties. The half of Licking County in the district often gives Rep. Kasich a 3-to-1 margin, and Delaware County is equally favorable to Republican candidates — it gave Kasich a 5-to-1 margin in 1992.

1990 Population: 570,902. White 427,286 (75%), Black 132,718 (23%), Other 10,898 (2%). Hispanic origin 4,834 (1%). 18 and over 416,053 (73%), 62 and over 66,229 (12%). Median age: 31.

settled on $2.35 billion for the B-2 program.

The saga of the B-2 appeared to end in the 102nd Congress when a compromise was reached capping B-2 production at 20 planes, a far cry from the 132 that the Bush administration originally had proposed.

Kasich has also taken on the Pentagon's "black budget" of secret weapons programs whose classified nature makes them difficult for Congress to monitor. His efforts gained credibility in January 1991, when Defense Secretary Dick Cheney canceled the A-12, an advanced, carrier-based "black budget" bomber plagued by hidden cost overruns.

However, Kasich's defense belt-tightening efforts do not indicate any shifting from his ideological moorings. On most defense issues, he is on the right flank of Armed Services.

A staunch advocate of the Strategic Defense Initiative (SDI), Kasich often has objected when members tried to shift funds from that program to their own pet defense projects.

Along with his sweeping attempts to realign the budget, Kasich often takes a "micro" approach. For instance, Kasich's language halting a planned 500,000-square-foot expansion of the Pentagon building that would have cost $110 million was included in the 1993 defense authorization bill.

At the very end of the 102nd Congress, Kasich teamed up with Republicans Jon Kyl of Arizona and Duncan Hunter of California to block a vote on a bill to ease Cold War controls on the export of many high-technology goods. A staunch opponent of arms proliferation, Kasich objected to provisions in the bill that would have lessened the authority of the secretary of Defense to block the export of high-tech goods with potential military value.

Kasich's almost childlike exuberance can be simultaneously annoying and endearing. The 41-year-old congressman was caught trying to savor some of his youth when he was prevented from joining famed rock band the Grateful Dead on stage at a Washington concert in June 1991.

At Home: When Kasich won a House seat in 1982, his district stood out as a political oddity. In 1980, a Republican year nationally, district voters turned out a GOP incumbent for Democrat Bob Shamansky. In 1982, a recession year marked by Democratic House gains, Kasich unseated Shamansky.

However, Kasich moved with ease to re-establish a Republican pattern in the 12th. He won his first re-election with 70 percent, and has not fallen below that mark since.

Republican officials had targeted the 12th in 1982. They considered Shamansky's 1980 victory a fluke, due more to the complacency of GOP Rep. Samuel Devine than to any change in the district's traditional Republican leanings.

Although Shamansky had the advantage of incumbency, Kasich was well-positioned for his challenge. A redistricting plan, passed by the legislature in which Kasich served, added a rural, predominantly Republican area to the 12th while removing some heavily black wards on the east side of Columbus.

Although Shamansky carried Franklin County (Columbus), his margin was not enough to overcome Kasich's lead in the rural counties. Kasich won with 51 percent of the vote.

An energetic grass-roots campaigner, Kasich entered electoral politics by upsetting a veteran Democratic state senator in 1978. He visited every household in his district several times during that campaign.

Redistricting in 1992 united the black wards of Columbus that had been split between the 12th and 15th districts, placing them in Kasich's district. But while the 12th became less Republican, Kasich sailed to a sixth term with a 71 percent victory over Democrat Bob Fitrakis, a professor from Columbus.

Committees

Budget (Ranking)

Armed Services (4th of 22 Republicans)
Readiness (ranking); Research & Technology

Elections

1992 General

John R. Kasich (R)	170,297	(71%)
Bob Fitrakis (D)	68,761	(29%)

1990 General

John R. Kasich (R)	130,495	(72%)
Mike Gelpi (D)	50,784	(28%)

Previous Winning Percentages: **1988** (79%) **1986** (73%) **1984** (70%) **1982** (51%)

District Vote for President

1992

D 98,158 (40%)
R 101,946 (42%)
I 45,536 (19%)

Campaign Finance

	Receipts	Receipts from PACs		Expend-itures
1992				
Kasich (R)	$279,301	$116,470	(42%)	$242,096
Fitrakis (D)	$44,702	$17,200	(38%)	$44,659
1990				
Kasich (R)	$328,624	$128,715	(39%)	$278,977
Gelpi (D)	$42,854	$5,463	(13%)	$47,815

Key Votes

1993	
Require parental notification of minors' abortions	Y
Require unpaid family and medical leave	N
Approve national "motor voter" registration bill	N
Approve budget increasing taxes and reducing deficit	N
Approve economic stimulus plan	N
1992	
Approve balanced-budget constitutional amendment	Y
Close down space station program	Y
Approve U.S. aid for former Soviet Union	N
Allow shifting funds from defense to domestic programs	N
1991	
Extend unemployment benefits using deficit financing	N
Approve waiting period for handgun purchases	N
Authorize use of force in Persian Gulf	Y

Voting Studies

	Presidential Support		Party Unity		Conservative Coalition	
Year	S	O	S	O	S	O
1992	71	26	71	25	79	19
1991	77	23	81	17	97	3
1990	69	30	78	19	94	6
1989	70	29	68	30	90	10
1988	61	38	76	20	100	0
1987	68	31	74	21	93	5
1986	70	29	75	22	88	12
1985	74	26	90	7	98	2
1984	61	38	82	17	92	8
1983	77	23	90	10	87	13

Interest Group Ratings

Year	ADA	AFL-CIO	CCUS	ACU
1992	15	42	86	84
1991	15	8	100	85
1990	11	17	86	92
1989	20	9	90	100
1988	15	29	93	92
1987	8	0	93	78
1986	10	29	89	82
1985	5	12	86	90
1984	5	23	75	67
1983	10	6	85	91

13 Sherrod Brown (D)

Of Lorain — Elected 1992; 1st Term

Born: Nov. 9, 1952, Mansfield, Ohio.

Education: Yale U., B.A. 1974; Ohio State U., M.A. 1979, M.A. 1981.

Occupation: Teacher.

Family: Divorced; two children.

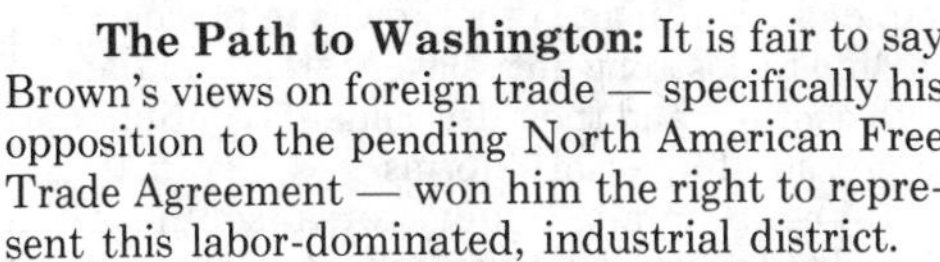

Religion: Presbyterian.

Political Career: Ohio House, 1975-83; Ohio secretary of state, 1983-91; defeated for re-election as Ohio secretary of state, 1990.

Capitol Office: 1407 Longworth Bldg. 20515; 225-3401.

The Path to Washington: It is fair to say Brown's views on foreign trade — specifically his opposition to the pending North American Free Trade Agreement — won him the right to represent this labor-dominated, industrial district.

Throughout the campaign, he maintained a strident stance against eliminating trade barriers between the United States and Mexico, proving his mastery of the details of the two countries' trade relationship and offering specific conditions under which he might find a free-trade zone acceptable.

Those conditions — chief among them the formation of free-trade unions in Mexico and a uniform North American minimum wage — are not likely to be met. And that puts Brown in the position of promising to vote "no" whenever the trade pact reaches the House floor. But that clearly sat well with the foundry and assembly-line workers from Lorain and the Cleveland and Akron outskirts that make up the 13th.

The move from candidate to legislator has not tempered Brown's views on the agreement. He is a vocal member of the anti-NAFTA caucus, has tried to organize district opposition to the agreement and wrote an opinion piece that appeared in the Christian Science Monitor on NAFTA's costs.

Brown also differs with President Clinton on campaign finance reform. Unlike Clinton, he opposes public funding of congressional elections, preferring instead to limit the amount of contributions a candidate who does not agree to voluntary spending limits can accept.

Having won a coveted seat on the Energy and Commerce Committee, he also can pursue his other chief interest, universal health insurance coverage. Brown campaigned vigorously for his committee seat. At one point he parted with a favored baseball card — that of 1950s Boston Red Sox outfielder Jimmy Piersall, who suffered from a mental illness. Brown gave the card to California Rep. Vic Fazio, chairman of the Democratic Congressional Campaign Committee, with the note: "Don't be crazy. Vote for Sherrod Brown for Energy and Commerce."

Brown's election marked a successful return for the one-time "boy wonder" of Ohio politics. In 1974, a week before his 22nd birthday, Brown was elected to the state House, where he served four terms. In 1982, he was elected secretary of state, a post to which he was re-elected in 1986 and from which he was expected to vault to higher office.

But Brown suffered an embarrassing defeat in 1990 at the hands of Republican Robert A. Taft II, the latest in a long line of politically successful Ohio Tafts. Brown had proposed a two-month, unpaid leave of absence from his secretary of state job to take an educational trip to Japan, and Taft hammered him with ads that proclaimed "Sayonara, Sherrod."

Brown's House race victory came at the expense of Margaret R. Mueller, a millionaire social worker, who had run unsuccessfully three times against Democratic Rep. Dennis E. Eckart.

Mueller spent freely in those four campaigns, but not once has she reached 40 percent. She differed with Brown on nearly every significant issue raised in the campaign, except for term limits, which both supported.

But Mueller's strong support for the free-trade agreement easily provided the most visible contrast and probably was the deciding issue in the race. Brown won 53 percent to 35 percent.

To reach the general election, both Brown and Mueller had to survive crowded primaries; eight Democrats and six Republicans vied for this open seat, created when reapportionment forced state mapmakers to eliminate two seats.

Among Democrats, Brown was the clear front-runner from the outset, although he had moved into the district to run and his opponents tried to tag him as a carpetbagger. He carried all seven counties in the district, winning 45 percent of the primary vote. Mueller had a more difficult time in the GOP primary, but her doggedness helped her best former state Rep. Jeffrey P. Jacobs by 5,000 votes. Jacobs, whose family owns the Cleveland Indians baseball team and who also is a millionaire, was the early favorite in the race.

Ohio 13

Northeast — Suburbs of Cleveland, Akron and Youngstown

Lying squarely in the midst of industrial northern Ohio, the 13th has all the problems of a declining Frost Belt economy. Heavily dependent on the automobile and steel industries, populous Lorain County approached Depression-era conditions in the early 1980s.

The district centers around two distinct sets of communities: the Cleveland suburbs in Lorain and Lorain County, and a band of suburbs in northern Summit and southern Cuyahoga counties, which also revolve around Cleveland but are beginning to look south to Akron as well. The Ohio Turnpike is all that connects the two; they are completely separate communities.

The 13th also includes sparsely populated land off to the east in Portage, Geauga and Trumbull counties. To the southwest is Medina County.

The geography makes it tough for a House challenger to build the name recognition needed to topple an incumbent. Speaking of Rep. Brown, one local observer said, "The chances of any challenger taking him on in such a fragmented community are next to nil."

Economically, the most serious trouble spot in the district is the once-booming port city of Lorain. But while the local economy there has been battered, the old New Deal political coalition is alive and well. Blue-collar ethnics, blacks and Hispanics in Lorain combine with those in nearby Elyria and academics in the college town of Oberlin to produce Democratic majorities.

As one of the traditional immigration centers on the Great Lakes, the city of Lorain has an ethnic diversity that matches the West Side of Cleveland. Fifty-six different ethnic groups have been counted within its borders. Today, Hispanics make up 17 percent of Lorain's population, a far higher share than any other city in Ohio.

About 10 miles south of Lorain is Oberlin, which roughly divides the district's urban, Catholic Democrats in the north and its rural, Protestant Republicans in the south. Founded in 1833, Oberlin College was the first coeducational institution of higher learning in the country, and among the first to admit black students. The Yankees who founded Oberlin and other towns in this part of Ohio took strong anti-slavery stands in the 19th century, and their descendants continue to crusade for social reforms.

The Summit County area south of Cleveland is a checkerboard of industrial and residential suburbs upon which much of the city's industry has scattered.

That Cleveland's economy is beginning to recover can be seen in its increasing creep out to surrounding counties. Medina County identifies more with rural central Ohio than with the rest of the 13th. But on the northern edge of Medina, Brunswick (population 28,000) has new suburban Cleveland development. To the east, Cleveland's growth is beginning to seep into the northern part of Portage County, but the rest of Portage remains quite rural. Trumbull County, farther east, orients itself south toward the 17th District cities of Youngstown and Warren.

1990 Population: 570,894. White 534,340 (94%), Black 25,954 (5%), Other 10,600 (2%). Hispanic origin 16,567 (3%). 18 and over 413,086 (72%), 62 and over 76,067 (13%). Median age: 33.

Committees

Energy & Commerce (24th of 27 Democrats)
Health & the Environment; Oversight & Investigations

Foreign Affairs (17th of 27 Democrats)
Asia & the Pacific; Europe & the Middle East

Post Office & Civil Service (14th of 15 Democrats)

Campaign Finance

1992	Receipts	Receipts from PACs		Expend-itures
Brown (D)	$495,275	$263,816	(53%)	$486,354
Mueller (R)	$866,740	$43,721	(5%)	$864,338

Key Votes

1993

Require parental notification of minors' abortions	N
Require unpaid family and medical leave	Y
Approve national "motor voter" registration bill	Y
Approve budget increasing taxes and reducing deficit	Y
Approve economic stimulus plan	Y

Elections

1992 General		
Sherrod Brown (D)	134,486	(53%)
Margaret R. Mueller (R)	88,889	(35%)
Mark Miller (I)	20,320	(8%)
Tom Lawson (I)	4,719	(2%)
Werner J. Lange (I)	3,844	(2%)
1992 Primary		
Sherrod Brown (D)	30,820	(45%)
Margaret Rose Mathna (D)	15,234	(22%)
Christopher Rothgery (D)	4,825	(7%)
Tom Muzilla (D)	4,237	(6%)
Ed Boyle (D)	3,968	(6%)
Bernice G. Kammiller (D)	3,347	(5%)
William VanderWyden III (D)	3,064	(5%)
F. James Hammar (D)	2,317	(3%)

District Vote for President

	1992	
D	101,104	(38%)
R	94,651	(36%)
I	70,624	(27%)

14 Tom Sawyer (D)

Of Akron — Elected 1986; 4th Term

Born: Aug. 15, 1945, Akron, Ohio.
Education: U. of Akron, B.A. 1968, M.A. 1970.
Occupation: Teacher.
Family: Wife, Joyce Handler; one child.
Religion: Presbyterian.
Political Career: Ohio House, 1977-83; mayor of Akron, 1984-86.
Capitol Office: 1414 Longworth Bldg. 20515; 225-5231.

In Washington: In the 102nd Congress, Sawyer worked hard at policing the accuracy of the 1990 census and the calculations that followed, a task that fell to him as chairman of the Post Office Subcommittee on Census and Population. When evidence pointed to an undercount with a bias against minorities, Sawyer pressed for an adjustment of the head count but was rebuffed by the Bush administration.

The original census count was used for the 1990 reapportionment of House seats and for redrawing electoral districts at all levels. But the issue of adjustment remains alive in the courts, and changes may yet be made affecting the formulas by which some federal dollars are distributed. Moreover, the groundwork laid by Sawyer's subcommittee may well lead to a more sophisticated and accurate census in 2000.

The fight over the 1990 census was protracted, and Sawyer kept on fighting even after Commerce Secretary Robert A. Mosbacher, the Bush Cabinet member with authority over the Census Bureau, overruled that agency's recommendation on July 15, 1991. Although Mosbacher acknowledged the disproportionate undercount of racial minorities, he said it was better to rely on the traditional head count than to risk the vagaries of adjustment by statistical projection.

The census always preoccupies House members because it dictates how many seats each state will have for the next decade and determines the allocation of about $40 billion in federal aid annually. The high stakes put Sawyer in a tough position to forge any consensus within Congress on how to deal with the undercount. Republicans opposed any deviation from the head count mandated in the Constitution, and some Democrats saw themselves disadvantaged by adjustment as well.

The accuracy of the 1990 census was at issue even before the counting officially began, in large measure because minorities had been undercounted in the past. Throughout 1989 and early 1990, Sawyer did not take a position, but by May 1990, he was sounding more like an advocate for adjustment, and in March 1991 he pointed out that the undercount of blacks in the 1990 census was likely to be higher than in 1980.

At the insistence of Sawyer, Congress did mandate a study on ways to improve the nation's future decennial census. The $1.4 million study was to examine methods used in the 1990 census and recommend how they could be made more timely and accurate.

Sawyer's ascent to the chairmanship of the subcommittee was equal parts skillful politicking and good timing. At the start of the 101st Congress, there were two Post Office subcommittee chairs open, and every other Democratic committee member already headed a panel at Post Office or elsewhere. Sawyer gathered enough support to make it onto the full committee and then competed with another new member, Pennsylvania Democrat Paul E. Kanjorski, for the Census chairmanship.

One key to Sawyer's winning the subcommittee chair was his stand on the counting procedure for the 1990 census. He, along with most House Democratic leaders, wanted to continue the policy of counting undocumented aliens. Kanjorski opposed counting illegal aliens. Sawyer had also proved himself loyal to the leadership on a range of issues.

On the often-partisan Education and Labor Committee, Sawyer has distinguished himself not only as a serious-minded debater but as one of the few who does not polarize the issue. Sawyer is a former teacher and once chaired the Education Committee in the Ohio House.

"You've got to be patient," Sawyer once said with reference to his committee work. "You get into a position where you're trusted by sufficient numbers of others in those areas where you hope to make a difference."

By the 101st Congress, Sawyer had gained enough confidence and influence to attempt to make his mark. He pushed a measure aimed at eliminating adult illiteracy by providing $1.25 million to set up a national center, state resource centers and work force literacy demonstration programs. The measure was eventually incorporated into an omnibus education measure that stalled shortly before Congress

Ohio 14

Northeast — Akron

The 14th is in a part of Ohio that was built on rubber — tires in particular. At one time, nearly 90 percent of America's tires were manufactured here.

Within the district's confines in Akron — once referred to as the "premier factory town in America" — are the corporate headquarters of the Goodyear, Goodrich, Firestone and General Tire companies.

The 14th became one of the most Democratic districts in the state on the strength of votes from the blue-collar workers who kept the rubber factories humming.

But the district's economy is changing. While the major rubber companies are still important employers, the jobs with a future are white-collar. The last quarter-century has seen a steady transfer of manufacturing from the old, high-wage factories in Akron to new plants in lower-wage areas of the Sun Belt. Many Akron residents have left: The city's 1990 population of 223,000 was less than it was more than a half-century ago. Many downtown storefronts are vacant, and the streets can be eerily quiet, especially at night.

Sawyer and other Akron leaders have fought to forge a high-tech future for the city, and they have had enough success that Akron's unemployment rate in recent years has been lower than that of some other industrial centers in northern Ohio.

What has kept the city alive through these tough years is this: While the tire companies have quit manufacturing here, their headquarters and labs have remained, employing engineers, scientists and executives who work more with polymers these days than with rubber.

The resiliency of Akron's smaller businesses has helped as well. "Much to everyone's surprise, much of the supporting industry didn't vanish; they found other things to do," says a local observer. "It could have been a lot worse."

An unintended benefit of the population flight out of Akron has been that the city is now smaller than its britches. It is an area with public facilities and a housing stock built to handle far more people than live here. The city is doing better than others, such as Youngstown, in the area.

In the boom years of the rubber industry, before World War II, Akron was a mecca for job-seeking Appalachians. The annual West Virginia Day was one of the city's most popular events, and it was said that more West Virginians lived in Akron than in Charleston.

These days, the Appalachian descendants combine with blacks, ethnics and the academic community at the University of Akron to keep the city reliably Democratic. North of Akron, suburbs and farmland in northern Summit County provide Republican votes. Usually, they are too few to overcome the Democratic advantage in Akron and swing the 14th to the GOP. Both Jimmy Carter in 1980 and Michael S. Dukakis in 1988 won Akron by a wide enough margin to carry Summit County narrowly. Bill Clinton in 1992 won by a comfortable margin.

1990 Population: 570,900. White 500,576 (88%), Black 62,400 (11%), Other 7,924 (1%). Hispanic origin 3,419 (1%). 18 and over 433,423 (76%), 62 and over 93,084 (16%). Median age: 34.

adjourned in October 1990.

Congress returned to the issue in early 1991 and cleared an adult literacy bill July 15. Sponsored by Sawyer, the measure authorized $197.5 million in new spending in fiscal 1992 and $1.1 billion in adult education and literacy programs through fiscal 1995.

In July 1990, the House overwhelmingly passed a Sawyer-sponsored measure to authorize $250 million for programs aimed at improving the quality of science and mathematics education in the United States. Congress cleared the measure in October, but only after reducing the spending levels in the bill significantly.

Sawyer's soft-spoken and thoughtful demeanor, combined with the respect of members from both parties, made him a logical choice in 1993 to fill a Democratic vacancy on the politically sensitive House ethics committee.

At Home: Like most of Ohio's House delegation, Sawyer saw his victory margin in 1990 sliced by a general anti-Washington mood among voters. Although he defeated Republican Jean E. Bender, a state Board of Education member, with relative ease, his tally was 15 points lower than in 1988. He rebounded in 1992, however, with a solid win over Robert Morgan, a retired school principal.

Sawyer first won the seat in 1986 after surviving a primary battle between the new Akron and the old Akron. On one side was Sawyer, the young mayor of Akron and an apostle of high technology; on the other was state Sen. Oliver Ocasek — a 60-year-old, Humphrey-style, pro-labor warhorse.

Ocasek might have been an ideal House

candidate in the days when Akron was the "rubber capital of the world." But as the rubber industry and many of its blue-collar jobs fled to the Sun Belt, the influence of organized labor in Akron diminished.

Sawyer, on the other hand, came from a white-collar background. The son of a prominent Akron businessman, he was a high school teacher before he won a seat in the Ohio House. His election to the Akron mayoralty in 1983 ended nearly 20 years of GOP rule.

When Sawyer announced his House bid, some Akron residents were upset. He had promised to serve at least one full four-year term as mayor but was running for higher office after only three years. However, Sawyer received a key boost when retiring Democratic Rep. John F. Seiberling endorsed his candidacy.

Sawyer proved to be the consummate media-age politician. While Ocasek was garrulous and emotional and boasted ties to old-time labor leaders, Sawyer was reserved, methodical and adept at the task of nuts-and-bolts organization. He emerged from the primary with a comfortable 49-39 percent victory.

Sawyer then had to get past the Republicans' most prominent local officeholder, Summit County Prosecutor Lynn Slaby. Although he ran a well-funded campaign in which he emphasized his blue-collar roots, Slaby could not get an angle on Sawyer. When Slaby called his foe a tax-and-spend liberal, Sawyer noted that Akron had not raised taxes during his mayoralty. He won with 54 percent, then soared to 75 percent against a lesser-known candidate in 1988.

Sawyer had a tougher time in 1990. First, Slaby jumped on Sawyer's vote for a House pay raise issue and threatened to seek a rematch. He backed off but threw his support to William Fink, an insurance man with local GOP backing.

However, Fink never made it to the main event, losing narrowly to the low-key Bender in the primary. Yet Sawyer — who saw 27 percent of the Democratic primary vote go to a little-known opponent — remained shadowed by the pay raise issue and the simple fact that he was the incumbent. Although Bender never achieved much visibility, Sawyer won with a comfortable but not overwhelming 60 percent.

In 1992, running in a redrawn district that added new territory in Portage County, Sawyer won three-quarters of the vote against two primary challengers. He went on to capture more than two-thirds in November against Morgan.

Committees

Education & Labor (9th of 28 Democrats)
Elementary, Secondary & Vocational Education; Postsecondary Education; Select Education

Foreign Affairs (26th of 27 Democrats)
International Security, International Organizations & Human Rights

Post Office & Civil Service (5th of 15 Democrats)
Census, Statistics & Postal Personnel (chairman)

Standards of Official Conduct (7th of 7 Democrats)

Elections

1992 General		
Tom Sawyer (D)	165,335	(68%)
Robert Morgan (R)	78,659	(32%)
1992 Primary		
Tom Sawyer (D)	54,933	(75%)
Jack Resnick (D)	13,109	(18%)
Dennis S. Chrobak (D)	4,786	(7%)
1990 General		
Tom Sawyer (D)	97,875	(60%)
Jean E. Bender (R)	66,460	(40%)

Previous Winning Percentages: **1988** (75%) **1986** (54%)

District Vote for President

1992
D 119,144 (46%)
R 81,603 (31%)
I 60,338 (23%)

Campaign Finance

	Receipts	Receipts from PACs	Expend-itures
1992			
Sawyer (D)	$195,200	$148,625 (76%)	$209,155
1990			
Sawyer (D)	$262,812	$187,195 (71%)	$264,793
Bender (R)	$2,003	0	$3,021

Key Votes

1993	
Require parental notification of minors' abortions	N
Require unpaid family and medical leave	Y
Approve national "motor voter" registration bill	Y
Approve budget increasing taxes and reducing deficit	Y
Approve economic stimulus plan	Y
1992	
Approve balanced-budget constitutional amendment	N
Close down space station program	Y
Approve U.S. aid for former Soviet Union	Y
Allow shifting funds from defense to domestic programs	Y
1991	
Extend unemployment benefits using deficit financing	Y
Approve waiting period for handgun purchases	Y
Authorize use of force in Persian Gulf	N

Voting Studies

	Presidential Support		Party Unity		Conservative Coalition	
Year	S	O	S	O	S	O
1992	17	83	95	3	15	85
1991	31	69	91	6	14	86
1990	21	79	92	8	30	70
1989	33	67	97	2	22	78
1988	24	75	94	5	18	82
1987	21	79	93	4	30	70

Interest Group Ratings

Year	ADA	AFL-CIO	CCUS	ACU
1992	95	83	38	4
1991	90	92	30	0
1990	89	92	14	0
1989	95	100	40	0
1988	95	93	36	4
1987	88	88	20	0

15 Deborah Pryce (R)

Of Dublin — Elected 1992; 1st Term

Born: July 29, 1951, Warren, Ohio.

Education: Ohio State U., B.A. 1973; Capital U., J.D. 1976.

Occupation: Judge; lawyer.

Family: Husband, Randy Walker; two children, one stepchild.

Religion: Presbyterian.

Political Career: Franklin County Municipal Court judge, 1985-92.

Capitol Office: 128 Cannon Bldg. 20515; 225-2015.

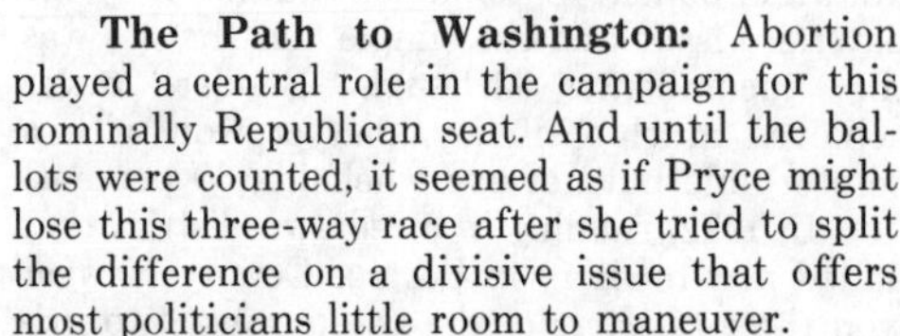

The Path to Washington: Abortion played a central role in the campaign for this nominally Republican seat. And until the ballots were counted, it seemed as if Pryce might lose this three-way race after she tried to split the difference on a divisive issue that offers most politicians little room to maneuver.

Early in the 103rd Congress, she sided with abortion rights forces as one of 51 Republicans to vote for a bill codifying the Clinton administration's lifting of the "gag rule" that prohibited staff at federally funded family planning clinics from discussing abortion.

Pryce, a self-described reformer, also was elected as interim president of the GOP freshman class. Party moderates recruited her at the last minute as a consensus candidate in lieu of the two men who were vying for the job — John L. Mica of Florida and Nick Smith of Michigan.

She landed a seat on the Government Operations Committee, from which she can pursue a portion of her reform agenda — particularly on budget rules and government organization. And she will fill a slot on Banking, Finance and Urban Affairs, where her predecessor from the 15th District, Republican Chalmers P. Wylie, was ranking member for 10 years.

The 15th opened up when Wylie decided to retire after 26 years. Wylie was high on the list of House bank offenders, with 515 overdrafts. And while he said that the bank scandal did not precipitate his decision, it came after the district had been redrawn with him in mind.

Pryce jumped into the race along with more than a half-dozen other Republicans. Her troubles began when she sought her party's nomination at the Franklin County GOP Convention, where she allowed several anti-abortion members of the central committee to believe she had joined their camp. (Pryce's main adversaries for the party endorsement all supported abortion rights in at least a limited form.)

With the aid of the anti-abortion faction, Pryce eked out the endorsement — and ran unopposed in the GOP primary. Soon after the central committee gave her its blessing, however, Pryce clarified her views. Though personally opposed to abortion, Pryce said she supported abortion rights generally, yet at the same time supported the rights of states to impose "reasonable restrictions" on the availability of abortions. When anti-abortion activists accused her of having lied to win their approval, Pryce countered they had relied on rumors and misunderstandings.

Meanwhile, the expected Democratic nominee, state Rep. Richard Cordray, was firmly in the abortion rights camp and won endorsements from the National Abortion Rights Action League and its Ohio chapter.

That left abortion opponents without a candidate for November. The result was the entry into the race of independent Linda S. Reidelbach, a GOP political novice and staunch abortion opponent, who had the backing of the Ohio Right to Life Society.

Pryce campaigned on a combined theme of reform and deep spending cuts to reduce the federal budget deficit. In particular, she wanted to limit franked mail to constituent questionnaires and to cut in half Congress' budget. On the broad fiscal front, Pryce not only favored constitutional amendments requiring a balanced budget and granting the president a line-item veto, she also favored a 10 percent cut in federal spending in fiscal 1993 — roughly $150 billion — exempting only Social Security and interest on the federal debt.

On issues other than abortion, Pryce and Cordray often were closely aligned. Pryce won the endorsement of the Columbus Dispatch, chiefly on the expectation that she would be a more reliable agent to reduce government's overall presence.

Once the ballots were counted, it was not clear that Reidelbach had harmed Pryce in any serious way. Cordray's hope that the two would split the conservative vote and give him an edge evaporated when he managed only 38 percent. Pryce won with less than a majority but with a margin in excess of 15,000 votes. Reidelbach was a distant third.

Ohio 15

Central — Western Columbus and suburbs

Of the two districts that divide Ohio's capital, Columbus, the 15th — on Columbus' western side — traditionally has been the more Republican.

Although this district includes most of the academic community at Ohio State University, the Democratic vote there is offset by the solid Republican areas in northern Columbus and the rock-ribbed Republican suburbs west of the Olentangy and Scioto rivers. In Upper Arlington and similar affluent suburbs, it is not unusual for Republican presidential candidates to draw more than two-thirds of the vote.

Apart from the large university vote — Ohio State has 54,000 students — the major pocket of Democratic strength in the district is on the near West Side of Columbus. Sandwiched between the Scioto River and the Ohio State Hospital for the Insane are neighborhoods of lower-income whites of Appalachian heritage.

The 15th includes far less of the heavily black East Side of Columbus than it did in the 1980s. Only 6 percent of the 15th's portion of Columbus is black, compared with 43 percent of the 12th District's section.

The 15th includes the blue-collar communities in the southeast portion of Franklin County, which enhance the Democratic vote, but just slightly.

The 15th does not include the heart of downtown Columbus, with the state Capitol and the offices of Ohio's major banking and commercial institutions. But with nearly two-thirds of Franklin County's land area, the district contains most of the region's expanding service base, which includes several large high-technology research centers.

Columbus is no tourist attraction. Swarms of visitors descend on the city only at Ohio State Fair time in August and on the half-dozen Saturdays in the fall when the Ohio State Buckeyes are playing football at home.

But the area has gained a reputation as a good place to raise a family. During the 1970s, it was the only major urban center in Ohio to gain population: It now boasts 633,000 residents overall, with 348,000 of them in the 15th.

In the 1980s recession years, the service-industry-oriented economy of Columbus suffered, but its suffering paled in comparison to that of many other Ohio cities.

In the latest round of redistricting, the 15th picked up what parts of Madison County it did not already have and also bit the northwestern corner from Pickaway County. While Madison compares with Franklin in size, it is far less densely populated: It has only 80 residents for each of its 465 square miles; Franklin County has 1,780 people for each of its 540 square miles.

Consequently, Franklin County holds 92 percent of the district's residents and Madison County contains only 6 percent. The other 2 percent are in Pickaway County to the south.

1990 Population: 570,902. White 527,361 (92%), Black 27,884 (5%), Other 15,657 (3%). Hispanic origin 5,459 (1%). 18 and over 443,164 (78%), 62 and over 70,267 (12%). Median age: 31.

Committees

Banking, Finance & Urban Affairs (12th of 20 Republicans)
Consumer Credit & Insurance; Financial Institutions Supervision, Regulation & Deposit Insurance; Housing & Community Development

Government Operations (15th of 16 Republicans)
Environment, Energy & Natural Resources

Campaign Finance

1992	Receipts	Receipts from PACs		Expenditures
Pryce (R)	$573,534	$219,027	(38%)	$590,480
Cordray (D)	$312,488	$129,810	(42%)	$312,366
Reidelbach (I)	$42,953	$1,750	(4%)	$41,841

Key Votes

1993

Require parental notification of minors' abortions	N
Require unpaid family and medical leave	N
Approve national "motor voter" registration bill	N
Approve budget increasing taxes and reducing deficit	N
Approve economic stimulus plan	N

Elections

1992 General

Deborah Pryce (R)	110,390	(44%)
Richard Cordray (D)	94,907	(38%)
Linda S. Reidelbach (I)	44,906	(18%)

District Vote for President

1992

D 89,180 (36%)
R 109,371 (44%)
I 50,135 (20%)

16 Ralph Regula (R)

Of Navarre — Elected 1972; 11th Term

Born: Dec. 3, 1924, Beach City, Ohio.
Education: Mount Union College, B.A. 1948; William McKinley School of Law, LL.B. 1952.
Military Service: Navy, 1944-46.
Occupation: Lawyer; businessman.
Family: Wife, Mary Rogusky; three children.
Religion: Episcopalian.
Political Career: Ohio Board of Education, 1960-64; Ohio House, 1965-67; Ohio Senate, 1967-73.
Capitol Office: 2309 Rayburn Bldg. 20515; 225-3876.

In Washington: Regula is ideally suited for the Appropriations Committee, a panel where deals are crafted with a minimum of partisan posturing. But with a more confrontational House Republican leadership pushing members to take on Democrats, Regula may find himself operating in an atmosphere less and less to his liking.

A serious man, Regula is an entrenched establishment Republican who generally works well with Democrats. That has made him a key player on the committee — he is the ranking GOP member of the Interior Subcommittee. It has also made him somewhat conspicuous in Republican ranks, where his moderate politics and conciliatory disposition discord with the harsher partisan tone set by the new breed of Republican leaders. As a member of the GOP's oldest generation — he is tied for 10th in seniority among Republicans in the House — he could be a prominent target for those who say that the party needs a younger and more aggressive countenance.

Regula tends to stray from the party line more often than the average Republican. In the 102nd Congress, he backed a move to rescind the ban, backed by President Bush, on allowing abortion counseling at federally funded family planning clinics. His amendment to a 1992 bill reauthorizing family planning programs would have allowed abortion counseling only if the patient requested it. It won House approval, but Bush vetoed the bill. Regula voted to override Bush's veto, but the attempt fell 10 votes short.

In the 101st Congress, conservatives, responding to protests that the National Endowment for the Arts had supported blasphemous and pornographic projects, sought to restrict the NEA's funding discretion. Regula blocked an attempt by California Republican Dana Rohrabacher that would have instructed conferees on the Interior appropriations bill to support North Carolina GOP Sen. Jesse Helms' amendment to restrict art funding.

The 102nd Congress featured the unlikely bonding of NEA funding and increased fees for livestock grazing on public lands. Regula tried to forge a compromise between environmentalists, led by Oklahoma Democrat Mike Synar, who sought to increase grazing fees nearer to market value, and ranchers, who wanted no increases. He offered an amendment to the Bureau of Land Management's reauthorization in 1991 capping increases at 33 percent a year. The House adopted it, 254-165, but that bill died in the Senate.

But during consideration of the fiscal 1992 Interior appropriations bill, Synar won House approval for his more ambitious increase. The Senate approved no grazing fee increase, but it included Helms-backed NEA language, setting up a standoff in conference. Finally, Oregon Democratic Rep. Les AuCoin, a grazing fee opponent, suggested a trade-off: House negotiators would drop the grazing fee boost in exchange for Senate abandonment of the Helms language. House conferees agreed to the "corn for porn" swap, despite Regula's objections (he called it an "unholy deal"). But the deal stuck.

Although they differed on the "corn for porn" deal, the grazing fee debate put Regula and Interior Subcommittee Chairman Sidney R. Yates on the same side. Regula generally gets along well with Yates, although they clash regularly over the question of permitting oil drilling on the outer continental shelf. Regula fervently supports drilling, but Yates usually prevails.

On environmental concerns, Regula is viewed as more sympathetic than many Republicans. But when it comes to energy development, Regula sharply disagrees with many Appropriations Democrats. He ardently believes that the United States should aggressively tap its domestic energy resources.

As a member of the District of Columbia Subcommittee, Regula intervened in 1990 in the continuing debate over voting rights for District residents. He introduced a bill to annex the District back into Maryland, an idea also espoused by Maryland Democratic Gov. William Donald Schaefer. Jesse Jackson denounced the proposal, saying it was akin to creating a South African-style segregated black "home-

Ohio 16

Northeast — Canton

Although it has undergone a variety of changes over the years, the 16th is still centered on Stark County and the city of Canton, just as it was when William McKinley represented it more than a century ago, before he moved on to the Ohio governorship and then the presidency.

While it is a working-class city like nearby Akron and Youngstown and often votes Democratic in local elections, Canton does not share in the solidly Democratic tradition of the rest of northeastern Ohio. That is partly a result of the conservative mentality brought to the community by the family-run Timken Co. — a large steel and roller-bearing company that is the district's largest employer.

With sizable black and ethnic populations, Canton proper (population 84,000) goes Democratic on occasion. But the suburbs in surrounding Stark County are solidly Republican. Since 1920, only three Democratic presidential candidates have carried the county — which accounts for nearly two-thirds of the district's population: Franklin D. Roosevelt, Lyndon B. Johnson and Bill Clinton. In 1992, Clinton took 40 percent in Stark County to George Bush's 35 percent and Ross Perot's 24 percent.

Besides Timken, Canton is the national headquarters of the Hoover Co., the vacuum cleaner manufacturer, and Diebold Inc., a producer of bank safes and commercial security equipment. But it is more famous as the home of the Professional Football Hall of Fame and for the front porch from which McKinley ran his 1896 presidential campaign. McKinley, who was assassinated in 1901, is buried in a park on the west end of Canton in a large memorial that roughly resembles the Taj Mahal. The Hall of Fame is at the other end of the park.

The portion of the 16th outside Stark County is mostly rural and Republican. Wooster (population 22,000), the Wayne County seat, is the site of Rubbermaid's corporate headquarters. Nearby Orrville (population 8,000) is the home of the Smucker family, which markets jams and peanut butter.

The 16th was extended south in 1982 by redistricting to annex Holmes County, and west in 1992 to pick up Ashland County.

Many of Holmes' 33,000 residents are Amish, and motorists driving through the county have to be careful not to plow into the back of a horse-drawn buggy. Houses without electricity are common in the county, and the income level is less than 70 percent of the state's average — just $9,191 per capita. Although tourism and leather and noodle factories have brought new employment to the agricultural area, much business is still conducted in small Amish family-owned shops that sell buggies and other necessities.

Ashland County is a very rural, very Republican area that usually rewards statewide GOP candidates with 60 percent or more of the vote. Rep. Regula took 66 percent of the vote here in 1992, compared with his districtwide tally of 64 percent.

1990 Population: 570,902. White 538,938 (94%), Black 27,419 (5%), Other 4,545 (1%). Hispanic origin 3,612 (1%). 18 and over 419,742 (74%), 62 and over 94,741 (17%). Median age: 34

land." The bill went nowhere. Regula left the D.C. panel after the 102nd Congress.

Representing an industrial district, Regula has taken a number of stands to please union organizers. In the 100th Congress, he was one of just 17 Republicans to support the Gephardt amendment to the trade bill. The measure would have mandated retaliatory tariffs against countries with unfair trade practices, but it was so controversial that most of its provisions were eventually dropped from the bill.

In the 102nd Congress, he split with the Bush White House on a bill to extend permanently jobless benefits to long-term unemployed workers. But he opposed a labor-backed resolution to discontinue so-called fast-track procedures that bar lawmakers from amending trade pacts submitted for congressional approval.

One of Regula's minor but consistent crusades is for federal recognition of President William McKinley, his hometown's most famous native. A graduate of the McKinley School of Law, Regula observes McKinley's January birthday by giving red carnations to his colleagues; he once got the Interior Subcommittee to adopt an amendment prohibiting the renaming of Mount McKinley in Alaska. In the 102nd Congress, he helped block an effort by Alaska GOP Sen. Ted Stevens to rename the peak Mount Denali.

At Home: Regula has been a political force in northeast Ohio since winning a House seat in 1972. Between 1978 and 1988 — a period of economic difficulty for the industrial areas of his district — Regula dipped below 70 percent of the vote only once.

But in 1990, Regula could not avoid a general anti-incumbent mood that affected most House incumbents in Ohio; nor could he totally escape voter wrath over his vote for a congressional pay raise. Running against Democrat Warner D. Mendenhall, an underfinanced college professor, Regula won with 59 percent, still his lowest re-election tally in 10 campaigns.

In 1992, with anti-incumbent sentiment still prevalent, Mendenhall returned, raising nearly half his money from political action committees (Regula does not take PAC money). But Regula worked hard to avoid an upset. He skipped the Republican National Convention to campaign, and spent more than $200,000 — more than he has ever spent in any of his 11 House elections. His efforts paid off, as his tally rose to 64 percent of the vote.

Regula came to the House after eight years in the state legislature, where he specialized in writing conservation bills. His state Senate constituency included a large part of Stark County, the heart of the 16th, and when GOP Rep. Frank T. Bow retired in 1972 after 22 years in Congress, Regula won Bow's endorsement.

Redistricting that year removed part of Democratic Mahoning County from the 16th, making it more Republican. Regula defeated Democrat Virgil Musser with 57 percent.

By 1974 — a poor Republican year nationally — Regula was up to 66 percent. Democrats then quit making serious efforts against Regula. He hit 79 percent in 1980, a peak he matched in 1988 before his unusual 1990 dropoff.

Committee

Appropriations (4th of 23 Republicans)
Interior (ranking); Transportation

Elections

1992 General		
Ralph Regula (R)	158,489	(64%)
Warner D. Mendenhall (D)	90,224	(36%)
1990 General		
Ralph Regula (R)	101,097	(59%)
Warner D. Mendenhall (D)	70,516	(41%)

Previous Winning Percentages: **1988** (79%) **1986** (76%) **1984** (72%) **1982** (66%) **1980** (79%) **1978** (78%) **1976** (67%) **1974** (66%) **1972** (57%)

District Vote for President

	1992
D	95,193 (37%)
R	98,953 (39%)
I	60,824 (24%)

Campaign Finance

	Receipts	Receipts from PACs	Expend-itures
1992			
Regula (R)	$168,665	0	$209,305
Mendenhall (D)	$109,794	$50,975 (46%)	$105,293
1990			
Regula (R)	$110,331	0	$156,205
Mendenhall (D)	$68,042	$10,750 (16%)	$68,021

Key Votes

1993	
Require parental notification of minors' abortions	N
Require unpaid family and medical leave	Y
Approve national "motor voter" registration bill	N
Approve budget increasing taxes and reducing deficit	N
Approve economic stimulus plan	N
1992	
Approve balanced-budget constitutional amendment	Y
Close down space station program	N
Approve U.S. aid for former Soviet Union	Y
Allow shifting funds from defense to domestic programs	N
1991	
Extend unemployment benefits using deficit financing	Y
Approve waiting period for handgun purchases	Y
Authorize use of force in Persian Gulf	Y

Voting Studies

	Presidential Support		Party Unity		Conservative Coalition	
Year	S	O	S	O	S	O
1992	55	44	73	27	81	19
1991	69	30	70	29	86	14
1990	56	44	75	24	81	19
1989	70	30	60	40	93	7
1988	56	43	67	30	87	13
1987	52	48	56	43	81	19
1986	56	44	56	43	80	20
1985	60	40	57	42	82	18
1984	58	41	63	35	78	19
1983	66	32	68	31	80	20
1982	64	35	65	34	75	23
1981	72	28	75	25	79	21

Interest Group Ratings

Year	ADA	AFL-CIO	CCUS	ACU
1992	35	67	100	72
1991	20	58	60	55
1990	17	42	71	63
1989	20	25	100	54
1988	30	64	93	76
1987	28	38	67	52
1986	15	71	61	45
1985	25	35	59	52
1984	35	46	75	33
1983	25	35	75	61
1982	25	35	59	59
1981	15	27	89	87

17 James A. Traficant Jr. (D)

Of Poland — Elected 1984; 5th Term

Born: May 8, 1941, Youngstown, Ohio.
Education: U. of Pittsburgh, B.S. 1963; Youngstown State U., M.S. 1973, 1976.
Occupation: County drug program director; sheriff.
Family: Wife, Patricia Choppa; two children.
Religion: Roman Catholic.
Political Career: Mahoning County sheriff, 1981-85.
Capitol Office: 2446 Rayburn Bldg. 20515; 225-5261.

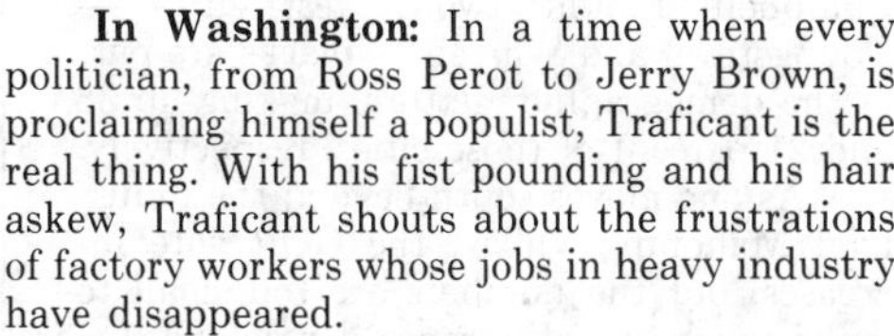

In Washington: In a time when every politician, from Ross Perot to Jerry Brown, is proclaiming himself a populist, Traficant is the real thing. With his fist pounding and his hair askew, Traficant shouts about the frustrations of factory workers whose jobs in heavy industry have disappeared.

His approach is usually bombastic and often vulgar: He is probably the only House member for whom the phrase "shit or get off the pot" is common coin in public discourse. Even he admits on rare occasions that he goes too far. In 1990, he apologized and tried to strike from the record a floor attack against members, whom he called "wimps, prostitutes and sellouts" after they declined to adopt several of his amendments to cut defense spending.

Traficant's forceful and often crude approach sets him far apart from most other House members. "If you're not entertaining, you'll never get a chance to influence anybody," he told the (Cleveland) Plain Dealer in 1991. Though his act plays well to the home crowd, it does not receive favorable notices from his colleagues.

When Traficant requested in 1991 that Ohio Democrats support his bid for a seat on the Ways and Means Committee in the 103rd Congress, his colleagues refused. Retiring Rep. Dennis E. Eckart told the Plain Dealer, "I would get laughed out of the room if our state tried to nominate Jim Traficant for Ways and Means." After the delegation's choice, Edward F. Feighan, also decided to retire, Traficant again sought support from the delegation.

While that endeavor proved unsuccessful, Traficant may have begun to give more thought toward his advancement in the House. In 1992, he reversed his position on the balanced-budget constitutional amendment, which he had cosponsored, aligning himself with Democratic leaders, who were lobbying strenuously against it. Traficant denied that committee considerations affected his vote.

At the start of the 103rd Congress he got a partial reward and some added institutional responsibility. He became chairman of the Public Works Subcommittee on Public Buildings and Grounds.

Traficant's one-man-wrecking-crew approach to two appropriations bills in 1991 hardly endeared him to senior Democrats. After amendments he sought were barred on procedural grounds, he shredded the defense and the Treasury-Postal Service bills, raising one point of order after another to strike language that violated rules against including legislative provisions on appropriations bills.

In a sense, though, Traficant was giving voice to another group of dispossessed: members frustrated with appropriators' unchallenged authority. Kansas Democrat Dan Glickman commented: "I wouldn't be surprised if there weren't a lot of members sitting quietly in their offices saying, 'Go to it, Jim.' Appropriators think they can write all the laws they want."

If there is a madness to Traficant's manner, it certainly is not without its method. His tough talk about industrial decline and foreign competition resonates in the working-class wards of Youngstown and the other aging mill towns of his district. His "raging populist" image has made him a local folk hero, enabling him to thrive even in the face of questions about his personal ethics.

Nor is Traficant's rage unfocused. He has channeled his desire to bolster U.S. industry into a series of amendments and has had some success in getting them enacted. The core of his effort is "Buy American" legislation aimed at gaining preference for U.S.-made products in federal contracting. The idea is not new, but early versions of it were often "buy only American" that Congress rejected as extreme. Traficant hit on a formula he has attached to a number of spending bills requiring an agency to give preference to a bid from a U.S. company if its finished product is made domestically, the "domestic content" is at least half American parts, and the bid is within 6 percent of the lowest foreign bid.

In 1987, Traficant won approval of a $30 million program to provide counseling for persons faced with mortgage foreclosure because of circumstances beyond their control, such as job layoffs. The measure harked back to the inci-

Ohio 17

Northeast — Youngstown, Warren

Once called America's "Little Ruhr" after Germany's Ruhr Valley in recognition of its industrial productivity, the Youngstown-Warren area now is a symbol of the nation's industrial decline. Many of the giant steel furnaces that once lighted the eastern Ohio sky are dark. Most of the workers who have not retired or left the area are looking for other jobs.

Located on the state's eastern border with Pennsylvania, the region was long a steel center serving Cleveland and Pittsburgh. Only a decade ago the steel plants in the Mahoning River Valley employed more than 50,000 workers. Now the work force is a fraction of that.

The 17th has begun to diversify its economy, but many of the gains made in the late 1980s have been lost. Youngstown (population 96,000) lost 17 percent of its population in the 1980s, and for those who stayed, an unemployment rate approaching 20 percent has not been uncommon. In the 1980s, the city was one of only five in the nation to drop from the ranks of those with 100,000 or more people.

Troubles have plagued one of Youngstown's few corporate bright spots. Phar-Mor, a rapidly expanding national chain of discount drug stores with headquarters in Youngstown, declared bankruptcy in August 1992 after its president was accused of misappropriating funds and overstating the company's worth by nearly $500 million. The chain has closed 86 of its 310 stores, and employment in its Youngstown operations has dropped 600 jobs to 1,900. More layoffs are expected.

With its remaining blue-collar base, the 17th is one of Ohio's solidly Democratic areas in most elections.

Mahoning and Trumbull were among the 10 Ohio counties that voted for Jimmy Carter in 1980, and both have been in the Democratic column since.

Most Democratic candidates build comfortable majorities in the string of declining ethnic communities along the Mahoning River. Italians dominate in Niles and Lowellville. Eastern Europeans and Greeks are the most important groups in Campbell. In the two largest cities — Youngstown and Warren — blacks are part of the demographic mixture, making up 38 and 21 percent of those cities, respectively.

As one moves south beyond the industrial Mahoning Valley, the GOP vote increases, but the numbers are too small to make much of a difference districtwide.

Rural Columbiana County is a swing region, one influenced by Pennsylvania and West Virginia. But it is enough smaller than Mahoning and Trumbull counties that it is not expected to have great political pull in the new 17th.

A fight is raging over a hazardous waste incinerator in East Liverpool along the West Virginia border. The opening of the plant — built to burn up to 60,000 tons of toxic waste a year — has been delayed by concerns voiced by the community and echoed by Vice President Al Gore, who has called for a General Accounting Office study.

1990 Population: 570,900. White 509,008 (89%), Black 55,796 (10%), Other 6,096 (1%). Hispanic origin 7,693 (1%). 18 and over 428,405 (75%), 62 and over 110,092 (19%). Median age: 36.

dent that first made him a local legend: In 1982, during his tenure as Mahoning County (Youngstown) sheriff, Traficant went to jail for three days rather than serve several laid-off factory workers with foreclosure orders.

That act helped give Traficant such a loyal following that he has survived legal problems to which other politicians would have succumbed. In 1987, a federal tax court ruled that Traficant had accepted $108,000 in bribes from organized-crime figures while serving as sheriff, and held him liable for back taxes, interest and civil penalties. But Traficant — who was acquitted in 1983 on federal criminal charges involving the same allegations — brushed off questions of corruption and portrayed himself as a victim of the Internal Revenue Service (IRS). Traficant appealed the ruling all the way to the U.S. Supreme Court, adding that he would go over to the IRS and "punch their lights out."

Traficant has drawn criticism from Jewish groups for championing the causes of two individuals — Arthur Rudolph and John Demjanjuk — accused of being former Nazi war criminals and deported to Israel for trial. Jewish groups accused Traficant of making anti-Semitic remarks during public appearances in behalf of the men. They also questioned his column for a newsletter that had originally been called "Zionist Watch." His repeated efforts to slice U.S. aid to Israel have not quelled their concerns.

Even with his mercurial nature and his sense for the dramatic, Traficant startled colleagues by announcing plans to run in the 1988 Democratic presidential primaries (while seeking House reelection) to promote the Rust Belt's interests.

Traficant made the ballot only in a handful of House districts in Ohio and Pennsylvania. Still, he topped 30,000 votes in the Ohio primary (just over 2 percent of the total) and earned a delegate to the Democratic National Convention.

At Home: Traficant has always been most comfortable operating outside political convention. A former football star at the University of Pittsburgh, Traficant ran an anti-drug program in Mahoning County before being elected sheriff in 1980. He quickly became a hero to the district's hard-hit factory workers. But within two years, he had alienated virtually every government official in the area, claiming that most were controlled by organized crime.

Those allegations took on an ironic cast when Traficant himself was indicted for bribery. It seemed certain that he would be convicted: The FBI had tape recordings of Traficant accepting $163,000 from underworld figures.

Yet Traficant, despite a lack of legal training, elected to defend himself in court, and put on a tour de force against some of the federal government's best lawyers. Traficant said he took the money only to get evidence against the mobsters and managed to convince the jury. After a seven-week trial, he was acquitted, touching off an ecstatic celebration by his fans in Youngstown and generating national media attention, including a front-page profile in The Wall Street Journal.

In 1984, Traficant's soaring popularity spurred him to challenge GOP Rep. Lyle Williams, a genial ex-barber with a knack for reaching the working-class majority. Although he was underfinanced and had to overcome the hostility of Democratic leaders with whom he had previously butted heads — one official sought to get him committed to a mental institution — he had broad popular support. Traficant drew large crowds with his attacks on banks, big business and the IRS.

Williams warned that Traficant would embarrass the district. But the 17th's continuing high unemployment became an insurmountable problem for an incumbent who had promised to bring more jobs: Traficant won with 53 percent.

Traficant's unexpected victory hardly mollified district Democratic leaders, who threw their support in the 1986 primary to Austintown Township Trustee Michael R. Antonoff. Largely ignoring his challenger, Traficant relied on his personal popularity and support from organized labor to win renomination by nearly 4-to-1.

That win established Traficant as an indomitable local figure. He has not faced a serious challenge since.

Committees

Public Works & Transportation (10th of 39 Democrats)
Public Buildings & Grounds (chairman); Economic Development; Surface Transportation

Science, Space & Technology (10th of 33 Democrats)
Space

Elections

1992 General		
James A. Traficant Jr. (D)	216,503	(84%)
Salvatore Pansino (R)	40,743	(16%)
1992 Primary		
James A. Traficant Jr. (D)	108,658	(92%)
M. Ross Norris (D)	10,054	(8%)
1990 General		
James A. Traficant Jr. (D)	133,207	(78%)
Robert R. DeJulio Jr. (R)	38,199	(22%)

Previous Winning Percentages: **1988** (77%) **1986** (72%) **1984** (53%)

District Vote for President

	1992	
D	133,213	(50%)
R	68,417	(26%)
I	64,936	(24%)

Campaign Finance

	Receipts	Receipts from PACs		Expend-itures
1992				
Traficant (D)	$155,474	$85,120	(55%)	$98,740
Pansino (R)	$3,488	0		$3,488
1990				
Traficant (D)	$99,644	$54,930	(55%)	$79,064
DeJulio (R)	$1,125	0		$1,700

Key Votes

1993	
Require parental notification of minors' abortions	N
Require unpaid family and medical leave	Y
Approve national "motor voter" registration bill	Y
Approve budget increasing taxes and reducing deficit	N
Approve economic stimulus plan	Y
1992	
Approve balanced-budget constitutional amendment	N
Close down space station program	N
Approve U.S. aid for former Soviet Union	N
Allow shifting funds from defense to domestic programs	Y
1991	
Extend unemployment benefits using deficit financing	Y
Approve waiting period for handgun purchases	Y
Authorize use of force in Persian Gulf	N

Voting Studies

	Presidential Support		Party Unity		Conservative Coalition	
Year	**S**	**O**	**S**	**O**	**S**	**O**
1992	21	78	89	9	42	58
1991	26	74	82	17	46	54
1990	19	81	86	14	37	63
1989	29	71	83	17	37	63
1988	17	83	89	10	37	63
1987	17	82	89	7	28	72
1986	10	90	87	13	24	76
1985	13	85	87	7	11	89

Interest Group Ratings

Year	ADA	AFL-CIO	CCUS	ACU
1992	85	90	50	8
1991	85	100	20	15
1990	72	92	29	13
1989	90	100	40	25
1988	95	100	21	8
1987	88	100	0	5
1986	95	100	28	9
1985	95	100	27	0

18 Douglas Applegate (D)

Of Steubenville — Elected 1976; 9th Term

Born: March 27, 1928, Steubenville, Ohio.
Education: Graduated from Steubenville H.S., 1947.
Occupation: Real estate broker.
Family: Wife, Betty Engstrom; two children.
Religion: Presbyterian.
Political Career: Ohio House, 1961-69; Ohio Senate, 1969-77.
Capitol Office: 2183 Rayburn Bldg. 20515; 225-6265.

In Washington: Although Applegate is well into his second decade in the House, he has not attained anywhere near the public profile of some of his colleagues in the Democratic class of 1976, a group that includes leadership figures such as Majority Leader Richard A. Gephardt of Missouri and Majority Whip David E. Bonior of Michigan, and activist legislators such as Dan Glickman of Kansas and Norm Dicks of Washington. Instead, Applegate has focused most of his energies working quietly on matters of direct interest to his southeastern Ohio constituents, and on veterans' concerns.

But Applegate's years of service have lifted him to the fourth-ranking Democratic spot on the Public Works and Transportation Committee, and at the beginning of the 103rd Congress he took the chair of its Subcommittee on Water Resources and Environment. This assignment will put Applegate in the spotlight as Congress moves to reauthorize the clean water act. From his new post, he will also be drawn into debates over other divisive environmental matters, such as striking a balance between protecting wetlands and permitting economic development.

Applegate's chief legislative priority in past Congresses has been on veterans' compensation. In taking the Water Resources Subcommittee, he relinquished the chairmanship of the Veterans' Affairs Subcommittee on Compensation, Pension and Insurance, a post he had held since 1983. A strong supporter of efforts during the 100th Congress to establish the Veterans Administration as a Cabinet post, Applegate generally manned the barricades against efforts to reduce veterans' benefits. In the 102nd Congress, he pushed through a measure that increased the benefits for survivors of veterans who died of combat-related injuries. It increased the benefits to spouses from $636 a month to $750 a month and the amount for dependents from $71 to $100 a month per child in fiscal 1993, $150 a month in fiscal 1994 and $200 a month in fiscal 1995 and after.

Despite his past emphasis on veterans' issues, Applegate is no stranger to environmental topics, which will occupy much of his time on his new subcommittee. He has been active in the effort to give states the right to restrict the interstate transportation of both hazardous and solid waste. Applegate's rural, hilly district is attractive to big cities in densely populated states that are looking for places to unload their solid waste, and the Constitution limits state governments' ability to restrict interstate transportation of waste products.

In the 101st Congress, Applegate advocated a centralized computer data bank to track hazardous waste shipments across the country. The proposal is a priority for firefighters, who in responding to highway accidents involving vehicles carrying chemicals often have inadequate information about the chemicals involved. Although the issue does not fall under the jurisdiction of Applegate's Public Works subcommittee, he continues to push legislation that would give states more authority over interstate transportation of solid waste.

Another issue that drives Applegate is economic hardship in his district, where manufacturers have been wounded by foreign competition. He has emblazoned his House stationery with the slogan "Buy American! Save American Jobs!" In early 1989, he called on the Customs Service to investigate a "blatantly outrageous" solicitation by a Taiwanese flag-maker, who enticed American companies to save on labor costs by having their U.S. flags made by his company, then switching the labels from "Made in Taiwan" to "Made in the U.S.A." after delivery.

Applegate votes a moderate Democratic line that is consistent with the thinking of his constituents. On economic issues, he typically sides with the Democratic leadership; he voted in 1993 to approve Clinton's economic stimulus package and the budget resolution outlining Clinton's fiscal 1994 tax, spending and deficit-reduction proposals.

But Applegate sometimes parts ways with the leadership on social policy issues. An opponent of abortion, he supported a bill early in the 103rd that would require parental notification when minors seek abortions at federally funded clinics. And in 1991, Applegate voted against a

Ohio 18

East — Steubenville; Zanesville

Coal and steel gave the 18th its polluted air, its dirty rivers, its economic livelihood and its Democratic vote. Redistricting in 1992 gave it more farmers and more Republicans.

Cramped along the steep banks of the Ohio River, Steubenville (population 22,000) long had some of the nation's foulest air pollution. But jobs in the smoke-belching plants along a 50-mile stretch of the Ohio River take priority over clean air, a fact that successful politicians quickly learn.

Locals boast that there was not an air pollution alert in Steubenville in the 1980s. But the clearing skies are a gloomy sign for the local economy. For years the unemployment rate in Steubenville and surrounding Jefferson County has been in or near double digits, a situation expected to get worse later this decade as new Clean Air Act regulations make the high-sulfur coal that the area mines less desirable to buyers.

West of Jefferson is economically depressed Harrison County. The closing in 1985 of a pottery plant that employed about 1,000 people pushed up the already high unemployment rate.

In Jefferson, Belmont and Monroe counties, the steelworking and coal-mining Democrats of the district show strong party allegiance, though they tend to shy away from supporting liberals. This part of Ohio resembles West Virginia and eastern Kentucky. Some cattle are raised, but the hilly terrain makes farming generally unprofitable. Under the hills, however, there are extensive coal deposits.

As one moves west, the district becomes less Democratic, and the tractors of Republican farmers replace the giant shovels of Democratic coal miners.

A sweep of counties added to the 18th's southwest end in the 1992 redistricting — Muskingum, Perry, Morgan and half of Licking — are birds of a feather with the nearby farming counties that were already part of the district.

Licking County is a pocket of prosperity; the areas around Newark — two-thirds of whose 44,000 residents are in the 18th — are a growing center for manufacturing and research, with Owens-Corning and Diebold as major employers. Dow Chemical also has a large research facility here. But the city is bracing for the closure of Newark Air Force Base, announced in March 1993.

The addition of Muskingum County has added the city of Zanesville to the 18th. With 27,000 residents, Zanesville is now the largest city completely in the district. The city was the state capital in the early 1800s and was once the country's pottery capital.

Rep. Applegate did well across the district in 1992, winning every county — some by more than 60 percentage points, one (conservative Morgan County) by only four votes.

In the 1992 presidential race, Bill Clinton lost all of the 18th's southwest counties except the traditionally more Democratic Perry; he won elsewhere in the district. He finished with 43 percent of the vote to George Bush's 34 percent.

1990 Population: 570,900. White 554,522 (97%), Black 13,483 (2%), Other 2,895 (1%). Hispanic origin 1,937 (<1%). 18 and over 421,743 (74%), 62 and over 104,287 (18%). Median age: 35.

waiting period for handgun purchases.

At Home: When he first ran for the House in 1976, Applegate's bland manner helped distance him from the scandal that felled his predecessor, Democrat Wayne Hays. Chairman of the House Administration Committee, Hays quit his campaign for a 15th term that year following allegations that he had kept a woman, Elizabeth Ray, on his payroll solely to provide him with sex.

Though Hays' downfall was unexpected, Applegate was prepared to step in. During his career in the state legislature, Applegate had quietly planned for a campaign when Hays retired. When Hays renounced his nomination just three months before the election, party leaders turned to Applegate, who represented about half the district in the state Senate.

He had little trouble defeating the GOP candidate and William Crabbe, the Democratic mayor of Steubenville who earlier had launched an independent campaign for Hays' seat.

By the time other Democrats could get a shot at Applegate, he had a firm hold. He took 82 percent of the primary vote in 1978.

With his generally low profile in Washington, Applegate seems an unlikely presidential candidate. Yet he briefly was one in 1988. Democratic Rep. James A. Traficant Jr. from the neighboring 17th District entered the Ohio presidential primary as a favorite-son candidate. Applegate followed suit, and wound up winning a delegate to the Democratic National Convention.

Like Traficant, Applegate said his main goal was to draw attention to the plight of the region's Rust Belt cities. But he was also trying to blunt the publicity edge held by Traficant: There was talk that the two could get thrown into a single district in 1990s redistricting.

That did not happen: Instead, legislators splintered the southern Ohio 10th District of Republican Clarence E. Miller. Applegate's 18th was one of the districts picking up some of the pieces of Miller's Republican-friendly seat in 1992.

Applegate still carried every county in the redrawn district, but in the new areas, his Republican challenger, former state Sen. Bill Ress, ran close. Applegate won Morgan County by only four votes, and ran well below his districtwide average in Muskingum, Perry and Licking counties. He saw his re-election tally drop to 68 percent — a hale performance by most incumbents' standards, but for Applegate, a 14-year low.

Committees

Public Works & Transportation (4th of 39 Democrats)
Water Resources & the Environment (chairman); Public Buildings & Grounds; Surface Transportation

Veterans' Affairs (3rd of 21 Democrats)
Compensation, Pension & Insurance; Hospitals & Health Care

Elections

1992 General		
Douglas Applegate (D)	166,189	(68%)
Bill Ress (R)	77,229	(32%)
1990 General		
Douglas Applegate (D)	120,782	(74%)
John A. Hales (R)	41,823	(26%)

Previous Winning Percentages: **1988** (77%) **1986** (100%) **1984** (76%) **1982** (100%) **1980** (76%) **1978** (60%) **1976** (63%)

District Vote for President

1992
D 110,494 (43%)
R 87,429 (34%)
I 58,578 (23%)

Campaign Finance

	Receipts	Receipts from PACs		Expend-itures
1992				
Applegate (D)	$117,262	$88,170	(75%)	$102,335
Ress (R)	$27,288	$250	(1%)	$26,810
1990				
Applegate (D)	$125,772	$78,205	(62%)	$94,754

Key Votes

1993

Require parental notification of minors' abortions	Y
Require unpaid family and medical leave	Y
Approve national "motor voter" registration bill	Y
Approve budget increasing taxes and reducing deficit	Y
Approve economic stimulus plan	Y

1992

Approve balanced-budget constitutional amendment	N
Close down space station program	N
Approve U.S. aid for former Soviet Union	N
Allow shifting funds from defense to domestic programs	Y

1991

Extend unemployment benefits using deficit financing	Y
Approve waiting period for handgun purchases	N
Authorize use of force in Persian Gulf	N

Voting Studies

	Presidential Support		Party Unity		Conservative Coalition	
Year	S	O	S	O	S	O
1992	28	70	79	20	38	60
1991	41	59	66	31	65	30
1990	30	69	73	24	52	46
1989	45	52	67	29	63	34
1988	28	65	71	24	63	29
1987	31	68	73	23	60	40
1986	24	74	75	20	50	50
1985	29	69	63	23	45	51
1984	39	60	65	32	54	44
1983	27	72	69	27	48	49
1982	39	57	64	31	56	41
1981	45	53	45	50	72	25

Interest Group Ratings

Year	ADA	AFL-CIO	CCUS	ACU
1992	70	92	38	12
1991	45	92	20	45
1990	50	92	36	33
1989	70	83	50	33
1988	70	100	29	24
1987	64	75	27	13
1986	65	93	35	23
1985	55	59	50	19
1984	50	69	44	33
1983	70	88	35	30
1982	45	84	41	46
1981	35	60	21	27

19 Eric D. Fingerhut (D)

Of Cleveland — Elected 1992; 1st Term

Born: May 6, 1959, Cleveland, Ohio.
Education: Northwestern U., B.S. 1981; Stanford U., J.D. 1984.
Occupation: Lawyer.
Family: Single.
Religion: Jewish.
Political Career: Ohio Senate, 1991-93.
Capitol Office: 431 Cannon Bldg. 20515; 225-5731.

The Path to Washington: Fingerhut comes to Washington with the sort of absolute conviction that often imbues aspiring government reformers — and that often gets disparaged as youthful arrogance.

Drawing on his "good-government" background (he headed Ohio's chapter of Common Cause for two years in the late 1980s), Fingerhut ran a primary campaign focused almost entirely on changing the way Congress does business.

Although he concentrated more on substantive matters in the months leading up to the general election, he remained committed to his goal of reform, supporting term limits and keying on campaign finance.

In guileless fashion, he announced even before he had been elected that he would seek to lead the Class of '92. And during the opening days of their orientation in December, the 63 Democratic freshmen chose him as their unofficial chief.

But Fingerhut quickly came to realize the dilemmas a reform Democrat faces. His aggressive efforts in behalf of the freshmen may have hurt him in the eyes of the leadership. Though seen from the beginning as a potential star in the class, he was passed over for his first-choice committee assignment, Public Works and Transportation.

He also drew criticism at home from organized labor for inviting Ross Perot to a town forum. "I think Eric has a short memory of how he got elected," said the executive director of the AFL-CIO, which contributed to Fingerhut's campaign.

Fingerhut also co-chaired the Democratic freshmen's Task Force on Reform. Heeding advice from Speaker Thomas S. Foley of Washington to "be realistic" in what they tried to accomplish, the freshmen produced a limited package. Its core issue — campaign financing and lobbying — closely resembled the leadership's plans.

Fingerhut is full of ideas. He produced a 16-page outline for economic revitalization of northern Ohio titled: "A New Deal for the 19th." He carries a moderate liberal agenda for universal health care, gun control and abortion rights that would be acceptable to a broad majority of the Democratic Caucus.

To season the mix, he favors spending cuts before tax increases to cover the cost of needed new spending and deficit reduction, and a universal health-care plan that relies largely on private sector involvement.

Fingerhut landed two of his other choices for committees — Science, Space and Technology, and Foreign Affairs. The former will be critical to his vision for a national industrial policy — not to mention the job-producing NASA/Lewis Research Center near Cleveland-Hopkins International Airport, a key location for work on the space station *Freedom*.

The 19th became an opportunity that the ambitious Fingerhut could not pass up when Democratic Rep. Edward F. Feighan chose to retire after being named as one of the 22 abusers of the House bank.

Fingerhut was joined in the primary by eight rival Democrats and five Republicans. In a campaign truncated by delays in finishing the state's redistricting plan, there was no clear front-runner on the Democratic ballot and no defining issues.

Fingerhut won with less than 25 percent of the vote, relying on money (he spent more than $200,000 on the primary), name recognition in Cuyahoga County (Cleveland) and the endorsement of the state Senate minority leader.

Little more than 5,000 votes separated the top three finishers — Fingerhut, Cuyahoga County Auditor Tim McCormack and former Cleveland Mayor Dennis Kucinich.

Robert A. Gardner, a Lake County commissioner, had a somewhat easier time winning the GOP primary. He sounded a moderate conservative line, not too different from Fingerhut's on many substantive issues.

Though the campaign was polite through most of the fall, it turned nasty in the final weeks with both candidates running attack television ads. Fingerhut capitalized on help from retiring Ohio Democratic Rep. Dennis E. Eckart and House Majority Leader Richard A. Gephardt of Missouri to win 53 percent of the vote.

Ohio 19

Cleveland suburbs — Ashtabula and Lake counties

The 19th is one of the most politically competitive districts in the Cleveland area, and one of the most strangely shaped in Ohio. Its western fingers reach around and up into Cleveland's western suburbs, squeeze east and then north to Lake County along Lake Erie's shore. The district ends up in Ashtabula County in Ohio's far northeastern corner.

The combination of the competition and geography makes the 19th a difficult district to campaign in: It is full of Republicans and Democrats, autoworkers and farmers.

Brook Park, the 19th's westernmost city, is an autoworkers' community just west of Parma. The city is blue-collar, Democratic, overwhelmingly white and very sensitive to the ups and downs of the automobile industry. Many of its 23,000 residents settled here to work at the city's large Ford plant. Starting with Brook Park, the 19th forms a small bowl around three sides (west, south and east) of Parma, in the 10th District.

Heading east, a ribbon of the tiny village of Oakwood connects to the band of Republican eastern Cleveland suburbs that head straight north into Lake County. These suburbs are substantially better off economically than those on the western side; median household income in such areas as Pepper Pike and Gates Mills hovers around $100,000, compared with just $37,000 in Brook Park and $18,000 in Cleveland proper.

Cuyahoga County tends to vote narrowly Democratic. Bill Clinton took 40 percent of the vote in 1992 to George Bush's 37 percent.

The far northeastern communities of the 19th, reliant on the steel, chemical and automobile industries for jobs, are among the most depressed parts of the state.

But there is growth: As migration from Cleveland moved eastward between 1950 and 1970, the population of Lake County more than doubled. The rapid growth has slowed, but the suburbs continue to creep farther east, obliterating the truck gardens and vineyards along Lake Erie.

Mentor (population 47,000), one of the area's fastest-growing cities, has traditionally been an industrial Democratic area, but its growth is coming from Republicans moving in. The county's Republican farmers and suburbanites are no longer canceled out politically by ethnic Democrats in the western part of the county. Bush won Lake County in 1992 — his only win among the 19th's three counties — taking 39 percent of the vote to Clinton's 36 percent.

Lake County casts 36 percent of the 19th's ballots; Cuyahoga County casts 47 percent. The remaining votes are in Ashtabula County. Employment here has recovered only modestly since the early 1980s, when the jobless rate hit 20 percent.

The steel and chemical plants situated along Lake Erie have been severely hurt by foreign competition, and it is hard to find signs of revival. Ashtabula is reliably Democratic in most elections; only a strong GOP county organization keeps the party's candidates close. Clinton won 44 percent of the vote here in 1992.

1990 Population: 570,901. White 552,620 (97%), Black 10,214 (2%), Other 8,067 (1%). Hispanic origin 4,982 (1%). 18 and over 436,566 (76%), 62 and over 106,606 (19%). Median age: 36.

Committees

Banking, Finance & Urban Affairs (30th of 30 Democrats)
Economic Growth; International Development, Finance, Trade & Monetary Policy

Foreign Affairs (21st of 27 Democrats)
Asia & the Pacific; Economic Policy, Trade & the Environment

Science, Space & Technology (20th of 33 Democrats)
Space

Campaign Finance

1992	Receipts	Receipts from PACs		Expend-itures
Fingerhut (D)	$617,946	$210,017	(34%)	$611,478
Gardner (R)	$460,938	$63,815	(14%)	$450,117

Key Votes

1993

Require parental notification of minors' abortions	N
Require unpaid family and medical leave	Y
Approve national "motor voter" registration bill	Y
Approve budget increasing taxes and reducing deficit	Y
Approve economic stimulus plan	Y

Elections

1992 General

Eric D. Fingerhut (D)	138,465	(53%)
Robert A. Gardner (R)	124,606	(47%)

1992 Primary

Eric D. Fingerhut (D)	20,929	(24%)
Tim McCormack (D)	16,053	(19%)
Dennis Kucinich (D)	15,453	(18%)
Frank J. Valenta (D)	14,254	(17%)
Thomas J. Coyne Jr. (D)	11,258	(13%)
Kathleen M. Cotter (D)	4,407	(5%)
Tom Milkovich (D)	1,974	(2%)
Jackie Hrnyak (D)	1,011	(1%)
Joan C. Durbak (D)	957	(1%)

District Vote for President

1992

D	114,357	(40%)
R	106,950	(37%)
I	66,429	(23%)

Oklahoma

STATE DATA

Governor:
David L. Walters (D)
First elected: 1990
Length of term: 4 years
Term expires: 1/95
Salary: $70,000
Term limit: 2 terms
Phone: (405) 521-2342
Born: Nov. 20, 1951; Canute, Okla.
Education: U. of Oklahoma, B.S. 1973; Harvard U., M.B.A. 1977
Occupation: Real estate executive
Family: Wife, Rhonda Smith; three children
Religion: Roman Catholic
Political Career: Okla. Commission for Human Services, 1983-86; Democratic nominee for governor, 1986

Lt. Gov.: Jack Mildren (D)
First elected: 1990
Length of term: 4 years
Term expires: 1/95
Salary: $40,000
Phone: (405) 521-2161

State election official: (405) 521-2391
Democratic headquarters: (405) 239-2700
Republican headquarters: (405) 528-3501

REDISTRICTING

Oklahoma retained its six House seats in reapportionment. The legislature passed the map May 24, 1991; the governor signed it May 27.

STATE LEGISLATURE

Legislature. Meets February-May yearly.

Senate: 48 members, 4-year terms
1992 breakdown: 37D, 11R; 42 men, 6 women; 45 whites, 2 blacks, 1 other
Salary: $32,000
Phone: (405) 524-0126

House of Representatives: 101 members, 2-year terms
1992 breakdown: 68D, 33R; 93 men, 8 women; 98 whites, 3 blacks
Salary: $32,000
Phone: (405) 521-2711

URBAN STATISTICS

City	Pop.
Oklahoma City Mayor Ronald J. Norick, N-P	444,719
Tulsa Mayor M. Susan Savage, D	367,302
Lawton Mayor John T. Marley, N-P	80,561
Norman Mayor Bill Nations, N-P	80,071

U.S. CONGRESS

Senate: 1 D, 1 R
House: 4 D, 2 R

TERM LIMITS

For Congress: No
For state offices: Yes
No more than 12 years combined (Senate and/or House) service

ELECTIONS

1992 Presidential Vote

George Bush	42.6%
Bill Clinton	34.0%
Ross Perot	23.0%

1988 Presidential Vote

George Bush	58%
Michael S. Dukakis	41%

1984 Presidential Vote

Ronald Reagan	69%
Walter F. Mondale	31%

POPULATION

1990 population		3,145,585
1980 population		3,025,290
Percent change		+4%
Rank among states:		28
White		82%
Black		7%
Hispanic		3%
Asian or Pacific islander		1%
Urban		68%
Rural		32%
Born in state		63%
Foreign-born		2%
Under age 18	837,007	27%
Ages 18-64	1,884,365	60%
65 and older	424,213	13%
Median age		33.2

MISCELLANEOUS

Capital: Oklahoma City
Number of counties: 77
Per capita income: $15,827 (1991)
Rank among states: 40
Total area: 69,919 sq. miles
Rank among states: 18

Oklahoma - Congressional Districts

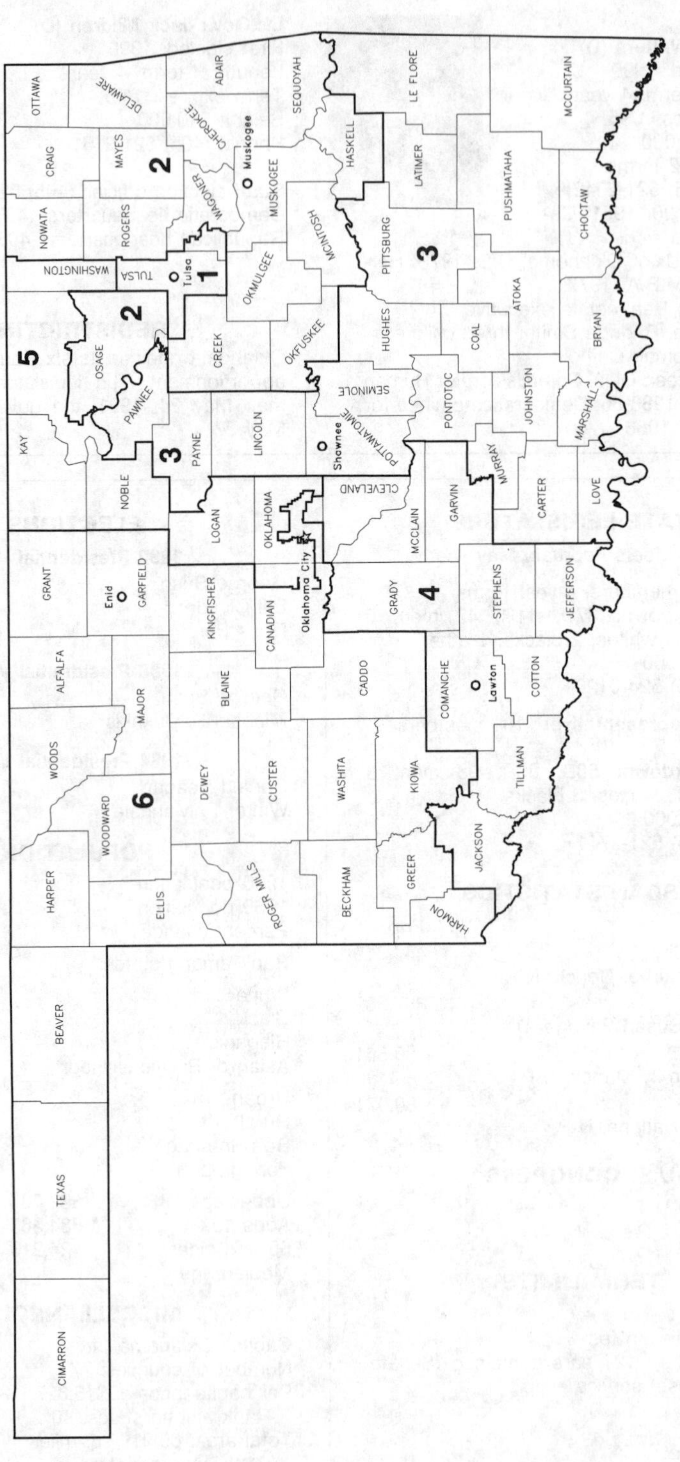

David L. Boren (D)

Of Seminole — Elected 1978; 3rd Term

Born: April 21, 1941, Washington, D.C.
Education: Yale U., B.A. 1963; Oxford U., M.A. 1965; U. of Oklahoma, J.D. 1968.
Military Service: National Guard, 1968-75.
Occupation: Lawyer.
Family: Wife, Molly Wanda Shi; two children.
Religion: Methodist.
Political Career: Okla. House, 1967-75; governor, 1975-79.
Capitol Office: 453 Russell Bldg. 20510; 224-4721.

In Washington: Someone watching Boren in the last year of the Bush administration might have thought he was undergoing a transformation from determined bipartisan to lockstep Democrat. But his actions in the first few months of the Clinton presidency were enough to bury that notion.

A centrist who has eschewed partisanship during his Senate tenure, Boren may find himself playing an increasingly uncomfortable role in the next few years. No longer able to traffic between a Republican president and the Senate's Democratic leadership, Boren has been placed in the position of conservative objector to proposals from a president of his own party. The last time he was in that spot — during his first two years in the Senate and Jimmy Carter's last two in the White House — Boren found himself siding more often with Republicans.

Blessed with a sharp mind and a keen sense of timing, Boren has a knack for staying close to the shifting tides of public opinion without appearing captive to them. Like Bill Clinton — and George Bush before him — Boren wants to be liked. Yet Boren is not about to be taken for granted — by his Republican friends or his fellow Democrats.

In the first half of 1993, Boren was increasingly emboldened in confrontations with Clinton over the president's plans for reducing the budget deficit and reorienting federal fiscal policy.

At first Boren was enthusiastic. "This is the best, most promising budget I've seen since I've been in Congress," he said in late February. When his remarks were interpreted as unconditional support, Boren immediately came under fire at home for not defending the oil and gas industry against a broad-based energy tax that was a centerpiece of Clinton's revenue-raising efforts.

Within days Boren had written to Clinton urging a change that was also sought by other Oil Patch members to force consumers and not producers to pay the tax. Boren also was one of three Democrats who voted on the floor with a united bloc of Republicans to strip the energy tax out of the budget blueprint; that amendment failed 46-53.

The administration agreed soon after the floor vote that pipelines would collect the tax, but that local distribution companies would pay it and that consumers would see a line on their monthly gas bills indicating the amount of the tax passed on to them. However, the change did not appear to satisfy Boren completely.

In May, when Congress began actually drafting a deficit-reduction bill to enact the tax increases and spending cuts in Clinton's plan, Boren again called for the energy tax to be dropped and for additional spending cuts to be substituted for the tax. From his position as the No. 3 Democrat on the closely divided Finance Committee, he was in a position to get his demands met or help defeat the bill before it reached the floor. "I'm prepared, if I have to, to keep it from coming out of the Finance Committee," he told The Los Angeles Times late in the month.

But days later, both Boren and the White House were sounding conciliatory themes, and Finance Chairman Daniel Patrick Moynihan of New York indicated that the energy tax might have to be revised somewhat — a clear signal that compromise was in the works.

"I think, you know, people misunderstood. I've never been opposed to energy taxes per se," Boren said on CBS' "Face the Nation." "We still must make sure we get this plan better balanced so that we have more spending cuts than we have tax increases. And we have to make sure that the kind of energy tax we have is levied in a way that it won't raise the price of all of our products in the world marketplace."

The energy tax was not the only part of Clinton's economic plan that Boren weighed in against. Boren's early objections to a $16.3 billion spending bill that Clinton said was needed to stimulate job creation in the short run gave comfort to Republicans who were in disarray over how best to respond to the president's proposals.

Boren and Louisiana Democrat John B. Breaux teamed up to ask that about half of the spending be delayed until after the broader deficit-reduction bill was enacted. "We're ready to sacrifice ... to get the deficit reduced," Boren said. "But if you slide back into your old ways of spending first and cutting later, you're going to lose our support." When Appropriations Chairman Robert C. Byrd of West Virginia constructed the floor debate to make it next to impossible to offer a simple amendment to the plan, an angry Boren took the floor and refused to yield for more than four hours.

Before long, the Republicans were united in opposition and even though Boren was eventually mollified through negotiations with the administration — and though he supported Clinton on key votes to move the stimulus bill forward — the GOP blocked its progress with a filibuster that the Democrats were powerless to thwart.

Despite his dancing right up to the edge of the cliff, Boren did not appear to earn the undying enmity of the White House in the first few months of 1993. Part of the reason could have been Boren's disarming personality; it also could have been Boren's long friendship with Clinton's chief of staff, Thomas F. "Mack" McLarty III, a former Arkansas gas executive. But the chief explanation may lie in Boren's willingness to run with the occasional Democratic issue, in this case a key Clinton initiative that has long been on Boren's own agenda, campaign finance reform.

Republicans greet Boren's continuing efforts to overhaul the campaign finance system with deep partisan suspicion. But "good government" issues have always worked well for Boren, who as a candidate for governor in 1974 campaigned with a broom close to hand, promising to sweep Oklahoma City clean. On Capitol Hill, he has been at it since the mid-1980s, working and reworking his campaign reform plan but never quite finding the right formula to hold onto Democratic support while pulling aboard more than a small handful of Republicans.

After acrimonious debates that spanned several Congresses, the 102nd finally managed to send a bill to the White House. The Democratic measure would have created voluntary spending limits on a state-by-state basis, with participating candidates receiving taxpayer-financed incentives, such as vouchers for reduced broadcast and postage costs. It would also have tightened limits on contributions from political action committees, and curtailed the use of "soft-money" spending by political parties.

When the bill reached his desk, Bush promptly vetoed it, objecting to the public financing provisions and saying it would not go far enough to get rid of PAC contributions. The Senate's effort to override the veto fell nine votes short, 57-42. Boren reintroduced his bill in the 103rd Congress, and Clinton followed with his own, somewhat stiffer version that further restricted "soft money" and also sought a ban on contributions from lobbyists. "We'll be back again and again until we get it passed into law," Boren vowed in 1992.

Boren's crusade for limits on PACs and on campaign spending has attracted widespread attention and made him something of a hero for those who worry about the effects of the current campaign finance system on American politics. He refuses contributions from PACs, but he does accept a substantial share of his own campaign funding from wealthy individual oil producers; he has consistently sought to protect federal support for the oil and gas industry.

Cynics see Boren's commitment to campaign finance reform as a reflection of his own campaign fundraising situation. Boren can afford to reject PAC money because the independent oil producers and royalty holders so important to Oklahoma's economy generally do not operate through PACs, preferring to give money to candidates on their own.

Given Boren's record in the Senate, his sponsorship of the campaign finance bill ought to remove some of the partisan taint that attaches to it. He hates partisanship and says that following the Democrats' lead does not come easily. "I have to make myself be a team player," he says. "It's not a natural inclination."

Nevertheless, his voting record took on a far more partisan cast in 1992, when Congress' Democratic leadership was in open war with Bush. Boren opposed Bush on a host of key issues — among them a vote to tear down budgetary walls that prevented the use of the "peace dividend" to pay for increased spending on domestic programs, and votes to override vetoes of a family leave bill and a measure reversing an administration ban on abortion counseling at federally funded clinics. Boren voted with Bush on issues where the president took a position only 33 percent of the time in 1992, his lowest-ever presidential support score.

But Boren largely views partisanship as yet another symptom of congressional inefficiency. And he has become increasingly outspoken in his criticism of the Senate's procedures, which he sees as leading the institution into paralysis and decline. He believes individual senators have too much power to frustrate the majority.

To solve those problems, Boren helped persuade Congress in 1992 to set up a special Joint Committee on the Organization of Congress; he was then named co-chairman, along with Indiana Democratic Rep. Lee H. Hamilton. The 28-member group was given until late 1993 to look into committee structures, the relationship between the chambers and the use of congressional resources and make suggestions to improve legislative effectiveness. "If we don't pass a reform measure this year, we'll have term limits imposed on us by the American public," Boren said in February 1993. "We'll be blown out of here like a stick of dynamite."

Boren took over the congressional reform committee just as he was giving up his chair of the panel where he had been most intensely active in recent years, the Select Intelligence Committee. For six years, until Senate rules required him to rotate off, Boren chaired the panel, gaining respect for his knowledge of intelligence matters and his even-handedness.

When Bush nominated Robert M. Gates to head the CIA in 1991, it was Boren's prompt support for Gates that helped ensure his confirmation six months later. Gates was a controversial pick because of his service as chief deputy to CIA Director William J. Casey and his possible involvement in the Iran-contra scandal. Gates had been rejected for the CIA post in 1987, just as a congressional investigation into the Iran-contra affair was heating up.

But Boren was pleased by Gates' promise to be more open with Congress about the CIA's activities. And he favored Gates, with his long inside knowledge of the agency, at a time when it was undergoing a radical restructuring in response to the collapse of the Soviet Union.

Boren had served on the select committee named to investigate the Iran-contra affair during the 100th Congress, but his work left no clear impression. Although the Iran-contra affair had deepened the legislative branch's mistrust of executive branch covert activities, Boren did not use the occasion to probe the affair; he was given more to speechmaking than asking detailed questions.

Despite Boren's support for Bush's CIA nominee, Bush unexpectedly vetoed a fiscal 1991 intelligence authorization bill requiring that Congress be notified of requests by agencies to a foreign government or private citizen to conduct covert actions on behalf of the United States. The veto was a slap at Boren, who had led Senate efforts to excise legislative language requiring the president to notify Congress within 48 hours of initiating a covert operation; Bush objected that the bill still required notification in "timely fashion."

And in 1992, Bush refused to go along with Boren's sweeping plan to reorganize the government's intelligence-gathering agencies.

Boren himself was not always on board with the Bush administration on intelligence and defense matters. He joined Senate Armed Services Chairman Sam Nunn of Georgia in opposing the 1991 resolution authorizing Bush to use force against Iraq. And in 1992, he objected strenuously when then-Attorney General William P. Barr refused to request appointment of a special prosecutor to look into the administration's failure to pursue evidence of fraud and corruption in a series of U.S.-backed loans to Iraq from the Atlanta branch of an Italian bank.

Boren does not look on first glance to be a power broker or even a politician. Oklahoma political cartoonists used to draw him as the Pillsbury Doughboy. But he knows the system and how to operate within it. "The appearance of having influence develops rapidly," Boren once said, "and so can the appearance of not having influence."

From his first days in the Senate, when he got Finance Committee Chairman Russell B. Long to find him a seat on the tax-writing panel, he has developed that influence to become one of the chamber's most effective supporters of the oil and gas industries, working on matters such as the 1988 repeal of the windfall-profits tax on oil.

Throughout the 1986 debate that produced major tax reform, Boren had little to say about the general philosophy of overhauling the tax code, or about most of the issues contained in the legislation. But he played a key role in developing a coalition for it on Finance, providing oil-state support for the bill's attacks on many business tax breaks in exchange for preserving the depletion allowance and other tax support for the oil and gas industries.

Boren stood out after the 1980 elections as a leading Democratic proponent of cooperation with the new Reagan administration and the GOP leadership in the Senate.

By 1985, a new, more militant Boren had emerged, most visibly as a spokesman for farmers suffering from the devastated agricultural economy. In tandem with Nebraska Democrat Jim Exon, Boren led Farm Belt Democrats into a confrontation with the Reagan administration and the Senate leadership over emergency help for debt-ridden farmers.

Then chairman of the Agriculture Committee's Farm Credit Subcommittee, Boren played a major role in the $4 billion bailout and overhaul of the Farm Credit System. In early 1987, he announced his intention to move quickly. "We're not going to play 'Ring around the Rosy' around here," he said, adding, "This train is going to move." But it took most of the year for the subcommittee and then the full committee to produce a bill. A major reason was that Boren pushed hard to produce a consensus, requiring dozens and dozens of hours of markups.

At Home: Boren advanced very quickly in politics by knowing how to promote the right issue at the right time.

Few Oklahoma Democrats took him seriously in 1974, when, as a four-term state legislator, he decided to run for governor. A Rhodes scholar and political science professor, he had been neither influential nor popular among insiders in the Oklahoma House. But he had a reputation as a reformer, which he exploited at a time of scandal not only in Washington but in Oklahoma City, where Democratic Gov. David Hall was under investigation on corruption charges that later sent him to prison.

Boren campaigned with a broom, promising to sweep out corruption in the state capital, supporting financial disclosure and open government. He took the nomination and won big in November.

As governor, Boren changed focus, drawing national attention as a spokesman for his state's oil producers. When he chose to run for the Senate in 1978, he was in a perfect position to seek votes and campaign support as an oil industry loyalist, and he was the favorite throughout the year. He led a seven-man primary field and went on to defeat former U.S. Rep. Ed Edmondson in a runoff.

The primary took a bizarre turn when, after a minor candidate accused the governor of being a homosexual, Boren swore on a Bible that it was not true. The accuser was discredited, and Boren suffered no lasting damage.

Boren's gubernatorial record brought him far more business support than most Democrats can expect in Oklahoma, and he had no trouble against his 1978 Republican opponent.

By 1984, Boren's stock had soared so high that state Republican leaders seemed reluctant even to talk about their chances against him. When no Republicans of stature challenged him for re-election, they shifted attention toward their 1986 chances of capturing the governorship.

Will E. Crozier, a former state Transportation Department worker who became the eventual Republican nominee, voiced concern that Boren had moved too far left on some issues. Boren blew him away, carrying every county in the state in amassing 76 percent of the vote.

In 1990, Republicans so feared Boren's political organization could damage their shot at the open governor's seat that they tried to persuade their only candidate, Stephen Jones, a lawyer and former party official, to withdraw. But Jones remained in the race, unable to stomach his party's giving Boren a free ride.

Boren demolished Jones, carrying every county in the state and posting the highest re-election mark — 83 percent — of any Senate candidate in 1990 who had an opponent on the ballot. Democrat David Walters was elected governor by a wide margin.

Lately, Boren's attention has been drifting toward the national arena. He told state party officials before the 1992 Democratic National Convention that if Clinton did not win, then he would seek the presidency in 1996.

Committees

Agriculture, Nutrition & Forestry (3rd of 10 Democrats)
Domestic & Foreign Marketing & Product Promotion (chairman); Agricultural Credit; Agricultural Production & Stabilization of Prices

Finance (3rd of 11 Democrats)
Taxation (chairman); Energy & Agricultural Taxation; International Trade

Joint Organization of Congress (Co-Chairman)

Joint Taxation

Elections

1990 General		
David L. Boren (D)	735,684	(83%)
Stephen Jones (R)	148,814	(17%)
1990 Primary		
David L. Boren (D)	445,969	(84%)
Virginia Jenner (D)	47,909	(9%)
Manuel Ybarra (D)	25,169	(5%)

Previous Winning Percentages: **1984** (76%) **1978** (66%)

Campaign Finance

	Receipts	Receipts from PACs	Expend-itures
1990			
Boren (D)	$1,253,344	0	$1,372,014
Jones (R)	$140,911	0	$140,912

Key Votes

1993	
Require unpaid family and medical leave	Y
Approve national "motor voter" registration bill	Y
Approve budget increasing taxes and reducing deficit	Y
Support president's right to lift military gay ban	Y
1992	
Approve school-choice pilot program	N
Allow shifting funds from defense to domestic programs	Y
Oppose deeper cuts in spending for SDI	N
1991	
Approve waiting period for handgun purchases	Y
Raise senators' pay and ban honoraria	Y
Authorize use of force in Persian Gulf	N
Confirm Clarence Thomas to Supreme Court	Y

Voting Studies

	Presidential Support		Party Unity		Conservative Coalition	
Year	**S**	**O**	**S**	**O**	**S**	**O**
1992	33	55	58	34	71	21
1991	60	40	65	33	75	20
1990	58	39	58	34	76	22
1989	77	20	51	46	71	24
1988	63	31	59	30	81	11
1987	46	46	60	32	91	3
1986	67	30	42	54	92	4
1985	47	45	52	39	75	18
1984	62	29	41	53	91	0
1983	41	56	60	35	73	25
1982	60	38	52	42	87	10
1981	60	35	54	40	86	10

Interest Group Ratings

Year	ADA	AFL-CIO	CCUS	ACU
1992	60	50	50	35
1991	45	42	56	45
1990	56	63	55	23
1989	30	50	100	63
1988	25	62	58	48
1987	35	56	50	63
1986	40	27	65	65
1985	45	47	54	55
1984	35	30	79	71
1983	55	53	56	54
1982	45	50	65	84
1981	30	32	71	60

Don Nickles (R)

Of Ponca City — Elected 1980; 3rd Term

Born: Dec. 6, 1948, Ponca City, Okla.
Education: Oklahoma State U., B.B.A. 1971.
Military Service: National Guard, 1970-76.
Occupation: Machine company executive.
Family: Wife, Linda Lou Morrison; four children.
Religion: Roman Catholic.
Political Career: Okla. Senate, 1979-81.
Capitol Office: 713 Hart Bldg. 20510; 224-5754.

In Washington: With his youthful vigor and staunchly conservative views, Nickles has been touted by the Republican right as a rising star ever since his long-shot victory in 1980. Now in his third term in the Senate, Nickles has visibly begun to fulfill those expectations.

At the start of the 102nd Congress, Nickles was elected to the Senate GOP leadership as chairman of the Republican Policy Committee. His election was part of a move by younger Senate conservatives to increase their role in setting the party's legislative agenda: He defeated the more senior, and on some issues more moderate, Sen. Pete V. Domenici of New Mexico by a 23-20 vote in the Republican Conference.

Nickles had previously served as chairman of the National Republican Senatorial Committee (NRSC) during the 1990 election cycle. Although the Republicans suffered a net loss of one seat in that cycle — a disappointment given earlier hopes — his election to leadership indicated that Nickles was not held personally responsible — at least by his fellow conservatives.

Early in that cycle, Nickles was credited by many of his partisan allies for helping recruit an attractive and savvy group of GOP House veterans — Lynn Martin of Illinois, Patricia Saiki of Hawaii, Claudine Schneider of Rhode Island, Tom Tauke of Iowa, Bill Schuette of Michigan and former Rep. Hal Daub of Nebraska — to run against targeted Democratic incumbents. The luster dimmed when this crop of challengers was mowed down in November without exception, but their disappointing performance was deemed to have been beyond Nickles' control.

A wave of anti-Washington sentiment among the electorate made 1990 the wrong year for a slate of "insider" challengers. Moreover, the efforts of these candidates to uphold anti-tax positions against their more liberal opponents were undercut by President Bush's decision to renege on his "no new taxes" pledge.

With his move to the Republican policy post, Nickles escapes the vagaries of electoral politics for a more certain role as an ideological spokesman. This enables him to give fuller attention to the two prestige committee assignments — Appropriations and Budget — that he obtained at the start of the 101st Congress.

Nickles leaves little doubt about his placement on the political spectrum. He is a solidly conservative Republican, an advocate of cutting the federal budget and barring tax increases while maintaining substantial funding for the military. Part of the "New Right" movement when he was first elected, Nickles remains a leading Senate opponent of abortion. He chaired the platform committee for the 1992 Republican convention, where he staved off efforts to soften the party's anti-abortion stance.

Early in the Clinton administration, he bucked the president, successfully pushing an amendment to keep in place the ban on allowing foreigners with the HIV infection to immigrate to the United States. Clinton had promised during the campaign to rescind the ban.

A former business executive, Nickles stands out as a supporter of business interests.

One of Nickles' causes is the revision of the Davis-Bacon Act, which requires contractors on federal construction projects to pay "prevailing wage" rates. In September 1989, he proposed to allow builders of federally subsidized homes or shelters to hire poor tenants and homeless people at lower wage rates; his amendment was tabled, 58-42.

Nickles came closer when he tried to ease environmental enforcement provisions of the Clean Air Act in 1990. An amendment by Nickles and Democrat Howell Heflin of Alabama to that effect was defeated on a 47-50 vote.

Nickles has joined with the senators from Michigan to battle sharp increases in automobile fuel efficiency standards. During debate on the Clean Air Act, he and Michigan Democrat Carl Levin led the fight against strict limits on carbon dioxide emissions, which they said would result in a "backdoor" increase in fuel efficiency requirements.

In the 102nd Congress, Nickles successfully

— and with some wit — argued against a proposal that by 2001 would have ensured that 10 percent of the motor fuel sold by refiners would be so-called alternative fuels — ethanol, methanol, natural gas and electricity. Oklahoma's oil refineries were in no position to produce such fuels, Nickles said, adding, "That is like trying to mandate to the apple tree that you produce 10 percent oranges."

When Iraq's invasion of Kuwait in August 1990 set off concerns about U.S. dependency on Middle East oil, advocates of higher fuel efficiency standards resumed their efforts; a bill proposed that September by Nevada Democrat Richard H. Bryan and Washington Republican Slade Gorton appeared to have majority support. Extended debate followed, and Nickles helped block a cloture vote to cut it off.

Like most members from the "energy belt," Nickles backs most priorities of the oil, gas and nuclear power industries. In 1989, Nickles, the ranking Republican on the Senate Energy and Natural Resources subcommittee on regulation and conservation, co-wrote a bill to abolish price controls on natural gas. That bill was subsumed in legislation that went out under the name of Energy Committee Chairman J. Bennett Johnston of Louisiana.

Nickles favors boosting the economies of oil-reliant states like Oklahoma by providing incentives for domestic oil exploration and placing a fee on imported oil. At the beginning of the 102nd Congress, he gained the position of ranking Republican on the Appropriations Interior Subcommittee, augmenting his influence on such issues.

During his time as ranking Republican on the Appropriations Legislative Branch Subcommittee, Nickles tried without much success to strictly limit taxpayer-funded mailings by members of Congress. He did work to push through certain reforms of Senate "franking" practices in 1990, including bans on the use of campaign and personal funds for mass mailings and the transfer of mail funds between senators. He also proposed a 5 percent across-the-board cut in legislative branch funding; House-Senate conferees accepted a 2 percent cut.

When the Senate passed a measure in the fall of 1991 putting new constraints on members' behavior, Nickles wanted to go even further. He offered an amendment to subject the Senate and the House to about a dozen major laws covering job bias, unionizing rights, equal pay, occupational safety and privacy, but his proposal was tabled 61-38. Then he proposed that Senate employers be subject to punitive damages and to allow workers a jury trial in federal court, but this, too, was tabled 54-42.

In his budget-cutting zeal, Nickles sometimes steps on some big toes. During the 1990 budget debate, Nickles proposed an amendment to limit fiscal 1991 spending to the previous year's levels. The amendment failed, and Nickles incurred the wrath of Appropriations Committee Chairman Robert C. Byrd.

The wily West Virginian allowed a $975,000 earmark for a levee in Tulsa, requested by Nickles, but not without a lecture on how the money might not have been available if Nickles' amendment had passed. Byrd later eliminated funding favored by Nickles to resume Amtrak service to Oklahoma.

At Home: Nickles began his 1992 re-election campaign as a prohibitive favorite, even though he faced an estimable opponent, former state House Speaker Steve Lewis. Lewis won statewide notice for steering through the Legislature a landmark education and tax reform bill. In 1990, he had run a close third in the Democratic gubernatorial primary.

But Lewis failed to dent Nickles' popularity, despite waging an aggressive campaign. Although Nickles raised more than twice as much money as his opponent, Lewis was not uncompetitive financially: He raised about $1.5 million.

Lewis aired TV ads attacking Nickles' opposition to abortion, saying that Nickles "would make women criminals" if his position were law. Nickles fired back with an ad stating that Lewis "believes in abortion on demand." He also blasted him as "Steve 'the Taxman' Lewis" for his support for tax increases in the Legislature.

Nickles was never in serious jeopardy and the final result was not close: Nickles won by more than a quarter-million votes. He is the only Republican in Oklahoma history ever elected to a third Senate term. And his 58 percent-plus showing had been topped by a Republican Senate candidate only once before, in 1924, by William B. Pine.

Nickles had shown similar strength in winning his second term in 1986. When that campaign began, Nickles was regarded as one of the most vulnerable Republicans facing re-election. He had been aided in 1980 by President Ronald Reagan's coattails. And unlike his first contest, in which he defeated former Oklahoma City District Attorney Andy Coats, this one presented him with a formidable Democratic opponent: 1st District Rep. James R. Jones.

Jones assailed Nickles for lacking leadership skills needed in a state hard-hit by the energy and farm recessions.

Some of Nickles' media efforts were aimed at reinforcing his conservative, clean-cut image; but the core of his campaign was a series of ads portraying Jones as a liberal and accusing him of persistently voting for congressional pay raises. Jones did not respond immediately to Nickles. But with polls indicating that the liberal label was sticking, Jones attempted to refute Nickles' claims. He cited House vote studies that placed him as a Democratic moderate and quoted Washington sources who said Nickles was distorting Jones' record. But Jones' delayed reaction to Nickles' attacks placed him on the defensive during the crucial late weeks of the campaign and Nickles won handily, with 55 percent of the vote.

When Nickles rose from the state Legislature in 1980 to become the youngest member of the Senate, his journey took place almost overnight. He had been active in Republican politics for several years, but he waited until 1978 to run for his first public office, a seat in the state Senate. But his first-term status there did not deter him from entering the 1980 Republican primary to replace retiring GOP Sen. Henry Bellmon.

Nickles' calls for a return to traditional family values drew a favorable response from Oklahoma's large evangelical community. Boosted by organizational support from fundamentalist Christian groups, Nickles startled political observers by topping a five-man field in the GOP primary and then winning the runoff in a walk.

The general election pitted Nickles against Coats, whose role in the prosecution of a famous Oklahoma City murder case made his name a household word in central Oklahoma. But Coats was on the defensive much of the time, seeking to convince voters that he was not a closet liberal, as Nickles alleged.

Nickles' organization mounted successful voter registration drives to shore up Republican strength and helped spread his conservative themes to sympathetic Democrats. Aided by Reagan's strong showing in the state, Nickles won with 54 percent of the vote.

Committees

Appropriations (7th of 13 Republicans)
Interior (ranking); Defense; Energy & Water Development; Foreign Operations; VA, HUD & Independent Agencies

Budget (3rd of 9 Republicans)

Energy & Natural Resources (5th of 9 Republicans)
Renewable Energy (ranking); Energy Research & Development; Mineral Resources Development & Production

Indian Affairs (7th of 8 Republicans)

Elections

1992 General

Don Nickles (R)	757,876	(59%)
Steve Lewis (D)	494,350	(38%)
Roy V. Edwards (I)	21,225	(2%)
Thomas D. Ledgerwood II (I)	20,972	(2%)

Previous Winning Percentages: **1986** (55%) **1980** (54%)

Campaign Finance

	Receipts	Receipts from PACs		Expend-itures
1992				
Nickles (R)	$3,235,075	$1,148,233	(35%)	$3,316,336
Lewis (D)	$1,456,533	$274,668	(19%)	$1,455,848

Key Votes

1993	
Require unpaid family and medical leave	N
Approve national "motor voter" registration bill	N
Approve budget increasing taxes and reducing deficit	N
Support president's right to lift military gay ban	N
1992	
Approve school-choice pilot program	Y
Allow shifting funds from defense to domestic programs	N
Oppose deeper cuts in spending for SDI	Y
1991	
Approve waiting period for handgun purchases	N
Raise senators' pay and ban honoraria	N
Authorize use of force in Persian Gulf	Y
Confirm Clarence Thomas to Supreme Court	Y

Voting Studies

	Presidential Support		Party Unity		Conservative Coalition	
Year	**S**	**O**	**S**	**O**	**S**	**O**
1992	77	20	90	5	87	11
1991	89	9	88	9	93	8
1990	83	16	91	7	89	11
1989	86	11	96	4	97	3
1988	80	20	92	6	100	0
1987	73	22	91	6	91	9
1986	86	14	82	18	99	1
1985	82	18	79	20	87	12
1984	83	14	85	13	96	2
1983	66	34	83	16	91	5
1982	81	19	85	15	95	5
1981	85	13	87	11	89	10

Interest Group Ratings

Year	ADA	AFL-CIO	CCUS	ACU
1992	0	8	89	96
1991	0	25	100	95
1990	0	11	100	96
1989	0	0	88	96
1988	0	7	86	92
1987	5	10	94	100
1986	0	0	79	91
1985	0	0	90	87
1984	0	0	95	91
1983	10	7	78	96
1982	10	4	75	100
1981	5	5	94	100

1 James M. Inhofe (R)

Of Tulsa — Elected 1986; 4th Term

Born: Nov. 17, 1934, Des Moines, Iowa.
Education: U. of Tulsa, B.A. 1959.
Military Service: Army, 1954-56.
Occupation: Real estate developer; insurance executive.
Family: Wife, Kay Kirkpatrick; four children.
Religion: Presbyterian.
Political Career: Okla. House, 1967-69; Okla. Senate, 1969-77; GOP nominee for governor, 1974; GOP nominee for U.S. House, 1976; mayor of Tulsa, 1978-84; defeated for re-election as mayor of Tulsa, 1984.
Capitol Office: 442 Cannon Bldg. 20515; 225-2211.

In Washington: A stalwart of the Republican Party's right wing, Inhofe has kept faith with Tulsa conservatives — including important energy interests and religious fundamentalists — who have helped him fend off significant Democratic challenges in all four of his House elections.

Now serving for the first time with a Democrat in the White House, Inhofe can be expected to spend a lot of time just saying no. In early 1993, he consistently cast "nay" votes on Clinton administration priorities — against the family and medical leave act, against the "motor voter" bill making it easier to register to vote and against the president's budget plan and economic stimulus package.

A firm believer in the free market and a harsh critic of Congress and the federal bureaucracy, Inhofe has voted against abortion rights, gun control, economic aid to the former Soviet Union and reductions in defense spending. He supports term limits and a balanced-budget constitutional amendment.

Inhofe's fiery brand of conservatism, coupled with highly public financial disputes with members of his family, have made him a controversial figure in the 1st, as evidenced by his election percentages: 55, 53, 56 and 53.

As a freshman, Inhofe won no points for collegiality when he told hometown crowds that Congress is home to "a bunch" of communists and communist sympathizers. He named Michigan Democrat George W. Crockett Jr. and California Democrat George Miller. Crockett, who retired in 1991, denied being a communist. Miller declined to respond at all.

Inhofe also said that Massachusetts Democrat Barney Frank tells his constituents "the reason to keep him in office is that he is a practicing homosexual."

When the Reagan administration, under pressure from Congress, agreed to new notification procedures for covert intelligence operations, Inhofe was disappointed. "I'm not sure I want to know" about covert activities, Inhofe said. "If I know, the rest of Congress is going to know, and if the rest of Congress knows, the enemy is going to know."

Of late, Inhofe's castigations of Congress have been less pointed, but his rhetoric continues to incorporate sharp attacks on targets such as Jane Fonda, Angela Davis, lawyers, criminals and liberals.

Contending that government overregulation is destroying businesses, Inhofe in 1992 referred to the Occupational Safety and Health Administration and the Environmental Protection Agency as "Gestapo bureaucracies."

An enthusiastic supporter of Operation Desert Storm, Inhofe visited Kuwait after the conflict with a group of fellow congressmen. The group ran afoul of the U.S. Department of Agriculture for bringing back souvenir bags of sand, in violation of a federal law that forbids bringing foreign soil into the country.

In the 103rd, Inhofe joined the Armed Services Committee, where he can be expected to wage a fierce rear-guard action against efforts to wring a "peace dividend" from the defense budget. A strong military is consistent with his ideology and with the economic well-being of his district's aeronautics industry.

A licensed commercial pilot, Inhofe serves on the Aviation Subcommittee of the Public Works and Transportation Committee. In the 102nd, a measure he sponsored to help general aviation pilots safely navigate the airways near crowded airports passed the House.

In the summer of 1991, Inhofe and three other pilots made an around-the-world flight retracing Oklahoma aviator Wiley Post's 1931 flight, including stops in the Soviet Union.

At Home: Two years after being unseated as Tulsa's mayor, Inhofe in 1986 won election to Congress in a district that Tulsa dominates. That is the sort of up-and-down career Inhofe has had during a quarter-century in politics.

Inhofe won a state House seat in 1966 and after one term moved up to the state Senate, where he opposed the Equal Rights Amend-

Oklahoma 1

Tulsa; part of Wagoner County

The precipitous fall of oil prices from the early to mid-1980s had a resounding impact on the city that not long ago was calling itself "The Oil Capital of the World." But by diversifying its economy, Tulsa has rebounded, propelled by its thriving aerospace and aviation industries.

American Airlines is the city's largest employer, providing about 10,000 jobs. American has moved its national headquarters for flight reservations to Tulsa, and the company's maintenance depot is at Tulsa International Airport. Tulsa also is a deepwater port accessible to the Gulf of Mexico, a status it gained in 1971 with the opening of the Arkansas River Navigation System.

McDonnell Douglas Corp. and Rockwell International are leading companies in Tulsa, although the receding defense budget has curtailed their expansion. Together, they now employ about 3,500.

Tulsa has become a manufacturing hub of flight simulators for military and civilian use. With several technical schools and aviation academies, it also has developed a worldwide reputation as an aviation training center.

Once a post office on the Pony Express trail, Tulsa was transformed by the discovery of oil nearby in 1901 and 1905. Oil drove Tulsa's economic development until the last decade. The repercussions of the 1980s price drop can be seen in the grand estates in southeast Tulsa, whose values plummeted with the oil fortunes that built them.

But with the local economy on the mend, real estate prices are beginning to rise. Young professionals are moving into some of the older, established neighborhoods in the central section of the city and renovating single-family homes, making the area near the University of Tulsa one of the city's hottest housing markets. This area is also home to a number of blue-collar families.

Tulsa was a forerunner in the trend of Sun Belt cities evolving into Republican-voting bastions. Tulsa County has gone Republican in all but two presidential elections since 1920. North Tulsa's predominantly black neighborhoods provide Democrats with their best turf.

But Tulsa's conservatism differs from Oklahoma City's more viscerally anti-government brand. Tulsa, for example, strongly backed a landmark 1990 education and tax reform law. That year, Democratic gubernatorial nominee David Walters crushed his conservative GOP opponent, who sought the law's repeal. In 1991, a ballot measure to repeal the law lost in Tulsa County by more than 2-to-1.

Tulsa's fundamentalist community is in the east, anchored by Oral Roberts University (4,100 students), a prominent tourist attraction. The 200-foot glass and steel prayer tower and the 60-foot bronze "Praying Hands" sculpture are big draws.

Southeast of Tulsa, the 1st takes in the city of Broken Arrow, home to many Tulsa workers who commute via the Broken Arrow Expressway. Broken Arrow also has a sizable fundamentalist community. In 1970, Broken Arrow had fewer than 12,000 people; its population now tops 58,000.

1990 Population: 524,264. White 436,341 (83%), Black 50,149 (10%), Other 37,774 (7%). Hispanic origin 12,288 (2%). 18 and over 386,158 (74%), 62 and over 72,438 (14%). Median age: 33.

ment and sponsored a resolution calling for a constitutional amendment to balance the federal budget. He was an early supporter of Ronald Reagan for president in 1968.

Inhofe also established a reputation for being outspoken. In 1972, he said Sen. George S. McGovern should be "hanged with Jane Fonda" after the Democratic presidential nominee implied U.S. soldiers were guilty of atrocities in Vietnam.

Democratic success at portraying Inhofe as an extremist contributed to his first defeats. As the GOP nominee for governor in 1974, he got barely one-third of the vote, losing to then-state Rep. David L. Boren. In 1976, Inhofe left the state Senate to challenge Democratic U.S. Rep. James R. Jones; he lost by almost 9 percentage points.

But Tulsa's sizable bloc of staunch conservatives remained supportive of Inhofe. He built on this base for his first comeback, becoming Tulsa mayor in 1978. Having served three terms, he was a strong re-election favorite in 1984. But a heavy black turnout in north Tulsa helped Democrat Terry Young score an upset.

Two years later, the 1st came open with Jones' decision to run for the Senate. Inhofe hesitated but finally announced his candidacy in May. He quickly activated his grass-roots network, and with a significant name-recognition advantage over energy company executive D. W. "Bill" Calvert, he easily won nomination.

Democrats failed to recruit a well-known candidate to succeed Jones. Their nominee, law professor Gary Allison, ran vigorously, but Inhofe blasted him for supporting abortion and opposing aid to the Nicaraguan contras. Allison accused Inhofe of playing on religion when he brought in religious broadcaster Pat Robertson for a fundraiser. Outspent more than 3-to-1, Allison kept Inhofe to 55 percent.

Inhofe weathered a turbulent 1988. He stirred considerable local publicity by suing his brother over the sale of stock in the family insurance business; his brother countersued.

Fortunately for Inhofe, Democrats offered a candidate with no name recognition and little political experience — Kurt Glassco, who was an assistant district attorney in Tulsa before becoming legal counsel to Democratic Gov. George Nigh. Inhofe again had a substantial financial advantage; he outspent Glassco nearly 2-to-1. But as George Bush won the 1st handily, Inhofe took only 53 percent.

Glassco was back in 1990, with greater name recognition and more fundraising success. He hoped to benefit by running in a non-presidential year on a ticket with popular Democrats Boren and gubernatorial nominee David Walters. As expected, Boren and Walters carried Tulsa by large margins. But Glassco did not run as well in Tulsa County as he had in 1988. His switched position on abortion rights — in 1988 he opposed abortion, but in 1990, challenged by an abortion rights supporter in the primary, he renounced his opposition — may have cost him votes in the city that is home to Oral Roberts University. His lawsuits behind him, Inhofe bumped up to 56 percent.

But another brush with litigation and a strong challenger combined to pull Inhofe back down in 1992. During the year, Inhofe lost a lawsuit filed by the Federal Deposit Insurance Corporation, which sought to recover proceeds of a loan default stemming from the failure of his Quaker Life Insurance Co. The judge ordered him to pay the FDIC $588,238 plus attorneys' fees and costs.

The Democratic nominee, Tulsa County Commissioner John Selph, had resisted entreaties in 1988 and 1990 to take on Inhofe. With his ties to the business community and countywide profile, Selph had been considered the Democrats' best bet to defeat Inhofe.

The contest turned nasty. Selph aired a TV ad that said that Inhofe had won a $3 million lawsuit against his brother but was refusing to pay "your" dollars back by his failure to pay the $588,000 court judgment to the FDIC; Inhofe had appealed the decision. Inhofe said Selph favored raising taxes.

But Selph may have waited too long to plunge in. By 1992, redistricting had made the 1st more Republican by adding the rest of Tulsa County. And Bush and GOP Sen. Don Nickles carried Tulsa County by wide margins. Inhofe won his fourth term with 53 percent of the vote.

Committees

Armed Services (15th of 22 Republicans)
Military Acquisition; Readiness

Merchant Marine & Fisheries (7th of 18 Republicans)
Coast Guard & Navigation; Merchant Marine

Public Works & Transportation (5th of 24 Republicans)
Investigations & Oversight (ranking); Aviation; Water Resources & the Environment

Elections

1992 General		
James M. Inhofe (R)	119,211	(53%)
John Selph (D)	106,619	(47%)
1992 Primary		
James M. Inhofe (R)	36,354	(68%)
Richard L. Bunn (R)	17,339	(32%)
1990 General		
James M. Inhofe (R)	75,618	(56%)
Kurt Glassco (D)	59,521	(44%)

Previous Winning Percentages: 1988 (53%) **1986** (55%)

District Vote for President

	1992	
D	73,495	(30%)
R	122,189	(49%)
I	52,088	(21%)

Campaign Finance

	Receipts	Receipts from PACs		Expend-itures
1992				
Inhofe (R)	$425,361	$227,931	(54%)	$418,928
Selph (D)	$331,132	$56,775	(17%)	$328,960
1990				
Inhofe (R)	$609,786	$306,071	(50%)	$612,116
Glassco (D)	$411,069	$194,950	(47%)	$406,280

Key Votes

1993	
Require parental notification of minors' abortions	Y
Require unpaid family and medical leave	N
Approve national "motor voter" registration bill	N
Approve budget increasing taxes and reducing deficit	N
Approve economic stimulus plan	N
1992	
Approve balanced-budget constitutional amendment	Y
Close down space station program	N
Approve U.S. aid for former Soviet Union	N
Allow shifting funds from defense to domestic programs	N
1991	
Extend unemployment benefits using deficit financing	N
Approve waiting period for handgun purchases	N
Authorize use of force in Persian Gulf	Y

Voting Studies

	Presidential Support		Party Unity		Conservative Coalition	
Year	**S**	**O**	**S**	**O**	**S**	**O**
1992	81	17	92	4	92	4
1991	68	27	90	6	97	3
1990	69	31	92	6	96	4
1989	72	24	93	5	95	5
1988	64	34	88	6	95	3
1987	73	23	91	2	95	5

Interest Group Ratings

Year	ADA	AFL-CIO	CCUS	ACU
1992	10	36	75	96
1991	5	9	90	100
1990	11	0	77	88
1989	5	17	100	96
1988	10	38	92	92
1987	4	0	100	100

2 Mike Synar (D)

Of Muskogee — Elected 1978; 8th Term

Born: Oct. 17, 1950, Vinita, Okla.
Education: U. of Oklahoma, B.B.A. 1972; Northwestern U., M.S. 1973; U. of Edinburgh (Scotland), 1974; U. of Oklahoma, LL.B. 1977.
Occupation: Rancher; real estate broker; lawyer.
Family: Single.
Religion: Episcopalian.
Political Career: No previous office.
Capitol Office: 2329 Rayburn Bldg. 20515; 225-2701.

In Washington: Synar takes on the special interests and beats them, and he does it from a rural district not naturally fertile for spawning national political forays. As exuberant and impetuous in his eighth term as in his first, he careens through a far-reaching legislative agenda with political abandon and is not bashful about prodding less adventurous colleagues to climb aboard.

In the 103rd Congress, Synar crosses a threshold in his career, gaining a position of influence within the Democratic Caucus: He takes over the chairmanship of the Democratic Study Group, the party's liberal think tank. On Energy and Commerce, a committee with a range of interests as broad as his own, he is on the verge of chairing a subcommittee.

His occasional brashness, coupled with the sheer wattage of his personality, probably would alienate more of his colleagues if it were not for one thing: He seems genuinely concerned about making what he sees as good public policy, and he has a knack for doing it. For some members, his intense style and his quick, ever-present wit come off as arrogance. But it is not vanity that drives Synar. Rather, it is his supreme confidence in the justice of his causes. "I have probably been *the* maverick, *the* reformer, *the* outsider, probably more than any other person in the United States Congress," he said in a 1992 interview.

The passion with which Synar approaches his job, and his longstanding crusade against special interests — in 1992, tobacco, oil and insurance companies, ranchers and the gun lobby poured money into Synar's district in an expensive but unsuccessful effort to defeat him in the primary — make him sound less a veteran incumbent than an idealistic character out of a Frank Capra movie.

"I really believe this stuff. I really believe in what I'm doing.... And I take high-risk propositions. Do I make people mad? Absolutely. Has it caused me a tremendous amount of problems? Absolutely. And am I on the edge all the time, being in political danger? Absolutely. But that's what you have to do to make a difference."

Aside from his affection for winning attention, at the core, he pursues issues seriously. And he pursues a far broader range of issues than most.

While it is sometimes difficult to find a member's fingerprints on legislation, Synar leaves the trail of a child who has dipped his hands in an inkwell. He is among the most active members on Energy and Commerce, and also contributes to Judiciary and Government Operations, where he chairs the Environment, Energy and Natural Resources Subcommittee.

Synar has used this matrix of committee posts to project himself into an array of disputes. In the 102nd Congress alone, he was embroiled in some of the largest questions before Congress, such as campaign finance reform, grazing rights and national energy policy. He freely involves himself in politically difficult issues, and freely reminds others that he does so. "If you don't like fighting fires, don't be a fireman . . . and if you don't like voting, don't be a congressman," he said while working on a particularly sensitive piece of legislation.

Synar is the House's leading advocate of raising fees for ranchers who graze their herds on public lands, mostly in the West. He cites the fee, which is only a fraction of the private market rate, as a federal giveaway that must be ended: "We're not Uncle Sam, we're Uncle Sucker. We're giving away our children's and grandchildren's assets." He managed to attach an increase onto the Interior Department's appropriations bill in 1990, but the provision was erased in the House-Senate conference.

In the 102nd Congress, Synar sought to attach grazing fee increases in both the fiscal 1993 Interior spending bill and in a reauthorization of the Bureau of Land Management. But the latter bill died in the Senate after passing the House. And a smaller grazing fee increase inserted into the House version of the Interior bill was stripped out in conference.

President Clinton's first budget proposal called for increases in grazing fees and other plans to overhaul federal land-use policy. But in

Oklahoma 2

Northeast — Muskogee

The 2nd is Oklahoma's most imaginatively shaped district. It starts in the "Green Country" of northeast Oklahoma, but after curling underneath Tulsa County, it squirms through a gap between the 1st and 3rd districts to collect a large portion of rural, Democratic Osage County.

Democrats can do quite well here. Rep. Synar's only troubles are in primaries. The 2nd was one of two districts carried by Bill Clinton in 1992. In 1988, Democrat Michael S. Dukakis carried more than half the counties in the 2nd.

In recent years, tourism and recreation have joined the traditional engines of the 2nd's economy, agriculture and energy. The 2nd has part of the state's largest lake (Eufaula) and takes in several others, including Grand Lake O' the Cherokees, Fort Gibson, Tenkiller and Keystone. Accompanying the growth in the tourism industry has been a wave of retirees moving to the resort areas, where real estate prices are low. The population of Delaware County, which contains most of Grand Lake, grew by 17 percent during the 1980s.

But recreation has not supplanted the more time-honored enterprises. Soybeans, wheat and beef cattle are the district's main agricultural products. Many farmers raise both crops and livestock, helping them weather fluctuations in the farm economy. Eastern counties such as Adair, Delaware and Ottawa feature poultry production; several poultry and meat companies are close by, just over the Arkansas border.

The farm crisis of the 1980s did not spare rural areas in the 2nd. Small towns such as Stigler (Haskell County) suffered the same fate as many other Midwestern communities, with farm-implement dealers and other agriculture-related businesses struggling and sometimes failing.

Muskogee — with 37,700 people, the 2nd's largest city — dredges silica sand from the Arkansas River beds for use in its glass industry. The Department of Veterans Affairs serves several states from its regional office in Muskogee.

Two of the 2nd's fastest-growing counties during the 1980s were Wagoner (15 percent) and Rogers (19 percent), which border Tulsa County and are absorbing Tulsa's exurbanization. They are the 2nd's only GOP strongholds. Along the 2nd's southern tier, voters resemble their "Little Dixie" neighbors, lending Democrats generous margins.

For many Indians, northeast Oklahoma was the end of the Trail of Tears — the U.S. Army's forced march in 1838 of Cherokees away from their homes in the Southeast. The largest Indian population in Oklahoma is concentrated within the 2nd's boundaries; the Cherokee Nation has its headquarters in Tahlequah (Cherokee County), and members of other tribes are scattered through surrounding counties.

Humorist Will Rogers, who was part Cherokee, was born near Claremore (Rogers County). His life and works are commemorated at the Will Rogers Memorial and celebrated each November during Will Rogers Days.

1990 Population: 524,264. White 404,216 (77%), Black 26,568 (5%), Other 93,480 (18%). Hispanic origin 5,946 (1%). 18 and over 382,426 (73%), 62 and over 94,676 (18%). Median age: 35.

April 1993, Clinton abruptly dropped the plans under pressure from Western Democratic senators whose votes were considered crucial to the success of his economic package. Synar initially responded to the White House's move by hinting that he might hold up legislation to elevate the Environmental Protection Agency to Cabinet-level status.

Synar has long had a keen interest in reforming the way campaigns are funded. He joined with Wisconsin Democrat David R. Obey in the 101st Congress to propose severe restrictions on political action committees and greater reliance on public financing of campaigns. Their efforts were unsuccessful, but Synar was back on the issue in the 102nd, this time working with Kansas Democrat Dan Glickman on a bill restricting both PAC money and individual contributions. Their bill would allow public financing for those who agreed to spending limits. Congress passed a bill overhauling campaign finance laws in 1992 but could not override President Bush's veto.

Also in the 102nd, Synar helped write the House version of the bill that overhauled the nation's energy policy for the first time in more than a decade. He worked with Tennessee Democrat Jim Cooper on developing a strategy to cut carbon dioxide emissions.

The best evidence that Synar means what he says about legislating in the national interest is the tenuous connection between many of his crusades and his political interests in Oklahoma. One of his goals is to pass legislation that would ban all tobacco company advertising and promotions. His bill has prompted attacks from advertisers and tobacco companies, and from the American Civil Liberties Union, which says it would violate free speech guarantees.

In the 102nd Congress, Synar worked out a compromise with Energy and Commerce Republican Thomas J. Bliley Jr., whose Virginia district contains one of the country's largest cigarette processing plants, to put some teeth into laws on the sale of tobacco products to minors.

Synar's belief that members should have the courage of their convictions has led him to take some risks and win some glory. He took a heavily publicized gamble in the 99th Congress. While most members embraced the Gramm-Rudman deficit-reduction plan, which was portrayed as a test of congressional will to cut the budget, Synar led the charge against it, splitting with the rest of the Oklahoma delegation on final passage and launching the legal challenge that succeeded in having the pivotal section of the new law declared unconstitutional.

At Home: Synar's relish for confronting and flouting some of the country's most powerful and moneyed special interests has long earned him a place atop many interest groups' "most wanted" lists. In 1992, several of them made him a top target. The convergence of those forces and the nationwide anti-incumbent choler nearly succeeded in unseating him in the battle for the Democratic nomination.

The vessel for those forces was Muskogee County District Attorney Drew Edmondson. The Edmondson name matched the Synar name for district prominence. Edmondson's father, Ed, represented the 2nd from 1953 to 1973, and his uncle had served as governor and interim senator. Drew Edmondson had sought the 2nd District seat in 1976; he lost to Democratic Rep. Ted Risenhoover in the primary. With his familiar name and ability to amass a large campaign treasury, Edmondson promised to be Synar's most formidable challenger.

Edmondson's charge — that Synar had become too much a part of the Washington scene that he said he wanted to change — found some listeners among Democrats. More than a few voters agreed with Edmondson that Synar's pursuits demonstrated that the incumbent's interests lay far from northeast Oklahoma.

Synar had to convey the somewhat paradoxical message that he, a 14-year incumbent, was better equipped to reform Washington than his challenger.

But if some had decided that it was time to send a message to Synar, it was equally clear that they had a hard time envisioning Edmondson as a conduit for congressional reform. Synar, who does not accept PAC contributions, assailed his opponent as a captive of the special interests he has angered during his career — tobacco companies, the insurance industry, ranchers and big oil companies, to name a few. The National Rifle Association invested heavily in an "independent expenditure" campaign to oust Synar, paying for TV, radio and newspaper ads that attacked him as too liberal for the 2nd.

Edmondson retorted that Synar accepted funds from individuals who represented special interests, such as employees of the motion picture industry and trial lawyers, and that most of his funds came from beyond the 2nd District.

Neither candidate's ads dwelled too long on the positive. Even though Synar had a relatively paltry 11 overdrafts at the House bank, an Edmondson TV ad focused on that as evidence that the incumbent had broken faith with his constituents. Synar ran ads criticizing Edmondson's record as a prosecutor.

Voters complained about the campaign's vituperative tone. By the time the primary arrived, they displayed their displeasure by giving 19 percent of the primary vote to two other, little-known candidates on the ballot. Synar ran nearly 5,500 votes ahead of Edmondson, but he was forced into a runoff.

Synar deployed an all-fronts populist appeal to his constituents to win the runoff. He ran ads portraying the election as a battle against "special interests," contending that powerful lobbies wanted to end his career and that Edmondson was already controlled by them. Synar widened his margin over Edmondson by about 1,100 votes, winning renomination with 53 percent.

In the heavily Democratic 2nd, winning the nomination all but ensured Synar an eighth term, giving him time to spare for other activities, such as helping Bill Clinton prepare for the presidential debates. Synar played the role of Ross Perot in mock debates.

As expected, Synar did not have difficulty against his two opponents in November. Still, he was held to 56 percent. It was the first time in 12 years that he had received less than 60 percent in a general election.

Edmondson's challenge represented the culmination of three elections' efforts by conservative Democrats to oust Synar. Their first attempt came in the 1988 Democratic primary, in which state Sen. Frank Shurden challenged Synar from the right. But Synar got 70 percent in the primary and won easily in November.

In 1990, conservative Democrats lined up behind Jack Ross, a businessman, lawyer and rancher who criticized Synar for what he described as the incumbent's antipathy toward business. He accused Synar of voting with the "Eastern liberal establishment." Synar, in turn, labeled Ross "the special-interest candidate" for accepting PAC contributions.

Ross hammered at Synar in TV ads and appearances for voting against an anti-flag-desecration amendment. One of his last ads, however, brought down the wrath of the state party. In mock surveillance film footage, a man dressed in shirt sleeves and suspenders — Synar's characteristic garb — was depicted stepping out of a car and accepting a briefcase in a surreptitious manner as the announcer criticized him for accepting a contribution from the owner of a troubled thrift. The Democratic chairman scolded Ross for crossing the line. Synar held on for a 56 percent to 44 percent victory and won easily again in November.

A clean-cut son of a prominent ranching family, Synar jumped into a House campaign in 1978, challenging Risenhoover in the Democratic primary just one year after returning home from school to practice law.

Although he was inexperienced, he was the right sort of challenger to Risenhoover, who had become controversial because of a divorce and a reputation as a playboy. The incumbent spent much of the primary trying to refute charges that he slept in a heart-shaped water bed in his Washington apartment. Compared with Risenhoover, Synar appeared fresh, polished and seemly, and he won an 8,000-vote upset.

Synar was helped by his name. His father and five uncles have long been prominent in the Muskogee area. In 1971, they were selected the "Outstanding Family" in the United States by the All-American Family Institute.

After his 1978 election, Synar set up an intensive constituent-service operation. He announced that a majority of his staff members would remain in Oklahoma. Those steps helped protect him in 1980 when GOP nominee Gary Richardson attacked him for having a liberal record; Synar held on with 54 percent.

Committees

Energy & Commerce (7th of 27 Democrats)
Energy & Power; Health & the Environment; Telecommunications & Finance

Government Operations (5th of 25 Democrats)
Environment, Energy & Natural Resources (chairman)

Judiciary (6th of 21 Democrats)
Economic & Commercial Law; Intellectual Property & Judicial Administration

Elections

1992 General		
Mike Synar (D)	118,542	(56%)
Jerry Hill (R)	87,657	(41%)
William S. Vardeman (I)	7,314	(3%)
1992 Primary Runoff		
Mike Synar (D)	56,662	(53%)
Drew Edmondson (D)	50,084	(47%)
1992 Primary		
Mike Synar (D)	47,562	(43%)
Drew Edmondson (D)	42,080	(38%)
Robert W. Blackstock (D)	15,446	(14%)
Charles Lee Kilgore (D)	5,059	(5%)
1990 General		
Mike Synar (D)	90,820	(61%)
Terry M. Gorham (R)	57,331	(39%)

Previous Winning Percentages: **1988** (65%) **1986** (73%) **1984** (74%) **1982** (73%) **1980** (54%) **1978** (55%)

District Vote for President

1992
D 96,510 (43%)
R 81,375 (36%)
I 49,107 (22%)

Campaign Finance

	Receipts	Receipts from PACs	Expend-itures
1992			
Synar (D)	$1,191,392	0	$1,190,197
Hill (R)	$32,044	0	$30,312
Vardeman (I)	$120	0	$1,777
1990			
Synar (D)	$622,454	0	$631,839
Gorham (R)	$63,271	$6,625 (10%)	$62,793

Key Votes

1993	
Require parental notification of minors' abortions	N
Require unpaid family and medical leave	Y
Approve national "motor voter" registration bill	Y
Approve budget increasing taxes and reducing deficit	Y
Approve economic stimulus plan	Y
1992	
Approve balanced-budget constitutional amendment	N
Close down space station program	Y
Approve U.S. aid for former Soviet Union	Y
Allow shifting funds from defense to domestic programs	Y
1991	
Extend unemployment benefits using deficit financing	Y
Approve waiting period for handgun purchases	Y
Authorize use of force in Persian Gulf	N

Voting Studies

	Presidential Support		Party Unity		Conservative Coalition	
Year	**S**	**O**	**S**	**O**	**S**	**O**
1992	18	78	91	7	21	77
1991	28	70	93	5	19	78
1990	17	82	93	4	13	85
1989	28	71	92	6	24	76
1988	26	73	93	5	13	87
1987	21	76	90	7	23	74
1986	24	71	83	11	24	70
1985	25	75	88	10	33	65
1984	44	51	80	13	36	53
1983	33	66	85	12	43	55
1982	43	55	79	17	44	52
1981	37	61	90	10	27	72

Interest Group Ratings

Year	ADA	AFL-CIO	CCUS	ACU
1992	95	83	25	0
1991	90	75	30	0
1990	94	91	21	8
1989	85	67	40	4
1988	100	86	38	0
1987	84	75	13	13
1986	70	57	22	15
1985	75	53	36	14
1984	80	38	31	17
1983	75	71	50	17
1982	55	70	50	26
1981	80	73	16	13

3 Bill Brewster (D)

Of Marietta — Elected 1990; 2nd Term

Born: Nov. 8, 1941, Ardmore, Okla.
Education: Southwestern Oklahoma State U., B.S. 1964.
Military Service: Army Reserve, 1966-71.
Occupation: Pharmacist; rancher; real estate executive.
Family: Wife, Suzie Nelson; one child.
Religion: Baptist.
Political Career: Okla. House, 1983-91.
Capitol Office: 1727 Longworth Bldg. 20515; 225-4565.

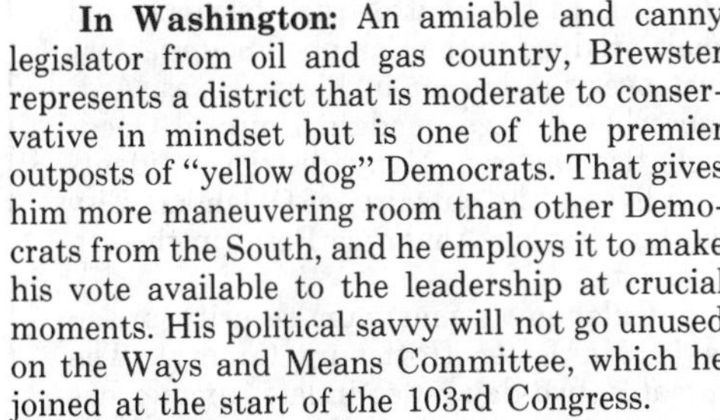

In Washington: An amiable and canny legislator from oil and gas country, Brewster represents a district that is moderate to conservative in mindset but is one of the premier outposts of "yellow dog" Democrats. That gives him more maneuvering room than other Democrats from the South, and he employs it to make his vote available to the leadership at crucial moments. His political savvy will not go unused on the Ways and Means Committee, which he joined at the start of the 103rd Congress.

In his first term, on issues such as civil rights legislation and abortion rights, Brewster developed a reputation as one whose vote was worth courting — and could be won over. In 1991, he signaled his initial skepticism with a civil rights bill reversing six Supreme Court decisions concerning discrimination and harassment in the workplace. "I come from a business background," he said, "and if it hurts business, I'm against it." But Brewster's concerns were sufficiently addressed to enable him to vote for the bill by the time it reached the floor.

He made an immediate splash on his new committee when Ways and Means was negotiating with the Clinton administration on the final details of its tax package in the spring of 1993. Brewster and other lawmakers from energy-producing states wanted changes in President Clinton's proposed energy tax to ensure that producers would not have to absorb the tax. Brewster helped broker a deal with the administration to revise the tax to allow utilities to pass it on to consumers without first getting approval from state regulators.

As a member of Public Works' Surface Transportation Subcommittee, Brewster was conveniently situated in 1991 as the panel worked on the massive five-year highway authorization bill. The final bill contained some projects in the 3rd, including a provision that would designate as part of the Interstate system a 140-mile section of U.S. 69 from Checotah to the Texas border.

As the only pharmacist in Congress, Brewster brings a specialized perspective to the issue of skyrocketing drug prices. In the 102nd Congress, the Veterans' Affairs Subcommittee on Hospitals and Health Care approved a bill that would have required drug manufacturers to roll prices charged to the Department of Veterans Affairs back to their Sept. 1, 1990, levels, adjusted only for inflation. Brewster called the industry's profits "at least exorbitant and maybe even obscene." But he cast the sole subcommittee vote against the bill, explaining that he did not support it because it would result in price shifting. "Anytime you artificially impose price limits, you raise prices somewhere else," he said. The final bill did not require companies to roll back prices.

Brewster broke from Democratic leaders in 1992 with his support for a constitutional amendment to require a balanced budget. He joined with five other moderate-to-conservative Democrats to urge Speaker Thomas S. Foley of Washington to permit a balanced-budget amendment to reach the House floor.

Early in the 103rd Congress, Brewster joined New York Democrat Charles E. Schumer in proposing to ensure that proposed spending cuts and revenue increases were directed toward reducing the federal budget deficit. Their proposal, to create a deficit-reduction "guaranty trust fund," would steer to the trust fund all net tax increases, savings in Social Security, entitlement cuts and debt service, to be used exclusively to cut the deficit. It also would prevent tax increases from being used for new spending. Clinton embraced their legislation in a speech in May 1993; Republicans derided it as a meaningless gimmick.

At Home: Voters in "Little Dixie" — the poor, southeastern region of the state — are accustomed to having their House members around for a while: Brewster is only the third person to represent the 3rd in the past 46 years. Carl Albert held the 3rd from 1947 to 1977, the last six as Speaker of the House. Wes Watkins was in the House for 14 years before leaving to run for governor in 1990.

First elected to the state House in 1982, Brewster, from Marietta (Love County), represented two counties and part of a third in the

Oklahoma 3

Southeast — 'Little Dixie'

The only district in the state that lacks a major urban area, the 3rd sprawls across southeastern Oklahoma, with a three-county appendage on its northern end. The largest city in the 3rd, Stillwater (Payne County) has 36,700 people. Only two other cities in the district, Shawnee (Pottawatomie) and Ardmore (Carter), have more than 20,000 people.

Oklahoma's southeastern district historically has been its most reliably Democratic. Since becoming a state in 1907, the "Little Dixie" region has never elected a Republican to the House. The area was settled largely by migrants from Texas and Arkansas, and its voters are conservative Democrats of the "yellow dog" variety. The 3rd was one of two Oklahoma districts Bill Clinton won in 1992.

In elections for offices below the presidency, most voters in the 3rd harbor little sympathy for the GOP. The most reliable territory for a Republican is along the district's northern corridor, which has more in common with more-Republican northern Oklahoma than with Little Dixie. In the three southern counties George Bush carried in 1988 — Pontotoc, Carter and Le Flore — Democratic nominees for Senate and governor easily won in competitive 1986 contests, as well as in the more lopsided 1990 races. Bush won only three 3rd District counties in 1992, all in the northern corridor.

Although the 3rd has a significant energy industry, with several counties producing oil and natural gas, Little Dixie largely missed out on the oil discoveries that brought wealth — and Republicanism — to central and western Oklahoma. Wracked by rural depression in the 1920s and again in the 1980s, this region is the least prosperous area of Oklahoma today. Primarily rural, the 3rd relies on farming and livestock to fuel its economy. Beef cattle, chickens and hogs are raised throughout the 3rd. Tyson Foods, with headquarters in nearby Springdale, Ark., is building a $50 million hog-breeding complex in Holdenville (Hughes County). Bryan, Hughes and Love are among the nation's leading peanut-growing counties.

Timber is harvested in the Ouachita National Forest, in the southeastern part of the 3rd. In the south, truck farmers send their produce to the Campbell Soup factory just over the border in Paris, Texas. Ardmore has a large, modern Uniroyal Goodrich tire factory. Many district residents who live on the outskirts of Oklahoma City work at Tinker Air Force Base (in the 4th District).

Oklahoma's maximum-security prison is in McAlester (Pittsburg County). The inmates' two-day rodeo in late summer has become a popular annual attraction. Lake Texoma in the southwest is a popular summer vacation destination.

The names of Coal and Pittsburg counties are reminders that coal was once mined in abundance in eastern Oklahoma; Latimer and Le Flore counties also have significant coal reserves. Coal mining now accounts for a fraction of its previous share of the area's economy, but high-sulfur bituminous coal is still mined in those counties.

1990 Population: 524,264. White 437,177 (83%), Black 21,186 (4%), Other 65,901 (13%). Hispanic origin 7,291 (1%). 18 and over 388,310 (74%), 62 and over 99,042 (19%). Median age: 34.

southwestern corner of the 3rd. In the Legislature, he specialized in business and energy issues.

Brewster's House campaign began tragically, but by the time the Democratic primary balloting was over, he had bested the scion of a political legend to secure his party's nomination, making his election a virtual lock.

Anticipating Watkins' long-rumored departure to run for governor, Brewster began assembling a campaign organization in the summer of 1989. In six months, he had a preliminary organization in all 20 counties of the district.

But the day Brewster officially launched his campaign, two of his children died in a plane crash on their way home from the districtwide campaign swing. Three weeks later, on the floor of the state House, he affirmed his intention to continue his run for Congress.

Following Brewster into the House contest was the namesake of an Oklahoma political legend — Lt. Gov. Robert S. Kerr III, the grandson of the late Robert S. Kerr, the powerful Democratic senator (1949-63) and governor responsible for bringing many federal irrigation projects to Oklahoma.

Kerr began with near-universal name recognition. His grandfather is revered in the area; the Kerr home, in the 3rd District town of Poteau, is a museum.

But the lieutenant governor's own ties to the district were more tenuous. Born and raised in Oklahoma City, Kerr bought a home in the district only after he switched his sights from the governor's race to the House bid.

Brewster worked hard to compete with the

Kerr name. He had assembled a formidable organization and was able to keep pace with Kerr in fundraising. Brewster chided Kerr for his recent move to the district.

The 3rd District is not conducive to electronic media campaigns: The largest city has fewer than 40,000 people. Brewster and Kerr attacked the daunting geography of the sprawling district by waging an old-fashioned, town-by-town canvass for votes. TV ads helped Brewster bolster his message that Kerr was a carpetbagger, but the rudiments of his successful effort lay in his ground-level campaign. Brewster managed to win a majority — 51 percent — of the vote in the four-candidate primary, averting a runoff with Kerr, who received 41 percent.

In November, Brewster crushed his GOP opponent, who had lost to Watkins three times. He easily won a second term in 1992.

Committee

Ways & Means (23rd of 24 Democrats)
Oversight; Social Security

Elections

1992 General		
Bill K. Brewster (D)	155,934	(75%)
Robert W. Stokes (R)	51,725	(25%)
1990 General		
Bill K. Brewster (D)	107,641	(80%)
Patrick K. Miller (R)	26,261	(20%)

District Vote for President

1992

D 94,763 (42%)
R 77,054 (34%)
I 55,974 (25%)

Campaign Finance

	Receipts	Receipts from PACs		Expend-itures
1992				
Brewster (D)	$423,953	$266,973	(63%)	$386,144
Stokes (R)	$6,338	$88	(1%)	$6,338
1990				
Brewster (D)	$448,824	$179,466	(40%)	$446,766

Key Votes

1993	
Require parental notification of minors' abortions	N
Require unpaid family and medical leave	N
Approve national "motor voter" registration bill	N
Approve budget increasing taxes and reducing deficit	Y
Approve economic stimulus plan	N
1992	
Approve balanced-budget constitutional amendment	Y
Close down space station program	N
Approve U.S. aid for former Soviet Union	Y
Allow shifting funds from defense to domestic programs	N
1991	
Extend unemployment benefits using deficit financing	N
Approve waiting period for handgun purchases	N
Authorize use of force in Persian Gulf	Y

Voting Studies

	Presidential Support		Party Unity		Conservative Coalition	
Year	S	O	S	O	S	O
1992	43	57	75	22	85	15
1991	45	54	71	26	84	14

Interest Group Ratings

Year	ADA	AFL-CIO	CCUS	ACU
1992	60	50	75	48
1991	20	67	60	45

4 Dave McCurdy (D)

Of Norman — Elected 1980; 7th Term

Born: March 30, 1950, Canadian, Texas.

Education: U. of Oklahoma, B.A. 1972, J.D. 1975; U. of Edinburgh (Scotland), 1977-78.

Military Service: Air Force Reserve, 1969-72, 1985-present.

Occupation: Lawyer.

Family: Wife, Pamela Plumb; three children.

Religion: Lutheran.

Political Career: Okla. assistant attorney general, 1975-77.

Capitol Office: 2344 Rayburn Bldg. 20515; 225-6165.

In Washington: In 1991, when he was chairman of the Select Intelligence Committee, McCurdy made a comment about his plans for the panel that summed up his personal style. "I've got a vision of where I want to go and an agenda," McCurdy told The Associated Press. "And I don't want to wait around to get there."

Two years later, McCurdy may still have such a vision, but by now he surely knows he will have to wait around to get there.

Not long ago, the Oklahoman was a golden boy whose future seemed unlimited. Elected to Congress at age 30, he was a moderate who stood to the right of his party on defense and intelligence issues. He made a perfect bridge to Republicans in the White House, and he was not shy about engineering deals.

But McCurdy's assertive manner may be his political curse as well as his blessing. He clearly has the qualities of a political rising star: He is intelligent, articulate and handsome. But many colleagues view him as too overtly ambitious, lacking the necessary admixture of humility.

In the 102nd Congress, McCurdy was chairman of the Select Intelligence Committee, a post perfectly suited to his interests. He was also an influential member of the Armed Services Committee. And, in the fall of 1991, he contemplated a bid for the Democratic nomination for president.

McCurdy soon gave up the White House idea and got behind the candidacy of Arkansas Gov. Bill Clinton. The two had served together as the No. 1 and No. 2 officers of the Democratic Leadership Council (DLC), a group of Democrats interested in moderating the party's image.

Although some would question McCurdy's devotion to Clinton — particularly when stories of marital infidelity and draft avoidance rocked Clinton's campaign — McCurdy denies ever reconsidering his own decision not to run. He seconded the Arkansan's nomination at the Democratic National Convention.

McCurdy chose instead to fight on other fronts. When the House bank scandal was ravaging the 102nd Congress, he criticized the way Speaker Thomas S. Foley of Washington handled it. McCurdy was mentioned as a potential challenger to Foley. He could have started with a built-in base within a House coalition he had founded — the Mainstream Forum.

McCurdy's reform efforts often had a rhetorical bite that irritated party elders. "The agenda of the people's body should not be arbitrarily governed by a few power brokers who answer to no one," he said in early 1992, as he pushed to limit members' tenures as committee chairmen to eight years.

All this seemed to fade into the background, however, as the 1992 election elevated Clinton to the presidency and the Democrats preserved all but 10 seats of their majority in the House. In the heady weeks that followed, McCurdy was regarded as a leading candidate for a Cabinet position. But he was also widely portrayed as campaigning for one, an allegation he strongly and consistently denied. In the end, the prize post of Defense secretary went to Armed Services Committee Chairman Les Aspin of Wisconsin, with whom McCurdy had often been allied.

Foley, meanwhile, had solidified his position in the Democratic Caucus and was unopposed for re-election as Speaker. Foley was also being urged to demonstrate a tougher attitude toward caucus dissidents, specifically by making an example of McCurdy. When the 103rd Congress began, Foley did not reappoint McCurdy to Select Intelligence. He noted that the committee had a six-year rotation policy and McCurdy had been there nine years.

The eviction closed the circle on McCurdy's own maneuvering to claim the chairmanship, an undertaking that had angered some colleagues. In 1987, with his six-year rotation on Intelligence likely to leave him short of the chairmanship, McCurdy had dropped off the committee.

But in 1989, he had persuaded then-Speaker Jim Wright of Texas to reappoint him to the committee as second in seniority. Two years later Wright was gone (forced by ethics problems to quit the House), but his successor, Foley, was willing to waive the six-year limit on membership

Oklahoma 4

Southwest; part of Oklahoma City

The military is a ubiquitous force in the 4th, and Rep. McCurdy, with a senior position on the Armed Services Committee, has worked to keep it that way. Altus Air Force Base, in Jackson County, is one of the Air Force's principal pilot training bases. The Army's Fort Sill is on the northwest side of Lawton (Comanche County). The district stretches north and east into Oklahoma County (Oklahoma City) to snare within its confines Tinker Air Force Base. With a combined civilian and military staff of more than 23,000, Tinker is the largest single-site employer in the state.

Agriculture and energy are the other dominant industries. Tillman and Jackson counties are among the nation's leaders in cotton harvesting. Jackson, Comanche, Stephens and Grady counties also grow wheat.

Despite price fluctuations, the energy industry has become important to the 4th's economy over the past 20 years. The gas- and oil-producing Anadarko Basin extends down from the 6th District into Comanche and Stephens counties. Halliburton employs about 2,500 people in Duncan (Stephens County) for oil-drilling research, development and manufacturing for its worldwide drilling enterprise.

The 1980s plummet in oil prices had a dramatic impact on much of the 4th, which had previously thrived on oil. As in many energy-dependent communities in the Southwest, banks and savings and loans failed during the decade. Oil prices bottomed out in 1986, but they have not approached the 1981 level of about $32 per barrel.

With a population of about 81,000, Lawton is the third-largest city in Oklahoma (although it trails No. 2 Tulsa by more than 280,000). Connected by an interstate turnpike to Oklahoma City and Wichita Falls, Texas, Lawton is the commercial center of southwest Oklahoma. Goodyear's tire and rubber plant — one of the largest factories in the state — employs more than 2,300.

The city of Norman has slightly more than 80,000 people and is home to the University of Oklahoma (19,250 students). The university's new energy center conducts research into oil-drilling techniques and alternative fuels. The university and such government-sponsored research programs as the National Severe Storm Laboratory are attracting high-tech industries.

On the southern border, the Red River, which marks the frontier between Texas and Oklahoma, has spawned considerable aggravation and acrimony over the years because of its capricious disregard for the states' boundaries. The river changes course whenever it floods, which results in hundreds of acres of farmers' land ending up in the other state. Some disputes have led to gunfire.

Bedroom communities have sprouted along I-44 from Chickasha into Oklahoma County. Suburban Moore, outside the Oklahoma City limits in Cleveland County, grew by 15 percent in the 1980s; it is strongly Republican. Elsewhere, though, lies conservative Democratic terrain. Democratic statewide candidates usually carry the 4th.

1990 Population: 524,265. White 441,223 (84%), Black 37,708 (7%), Other 45,334 (9%). Hispanic origin 21,023 (4%). 18 and over 381,702 (73%), 62 and over 68,635 (13%). Median age: 31.

and appoint McCurdy chairman of the panel.

Despite the lack of a full committee chairmanship, the legislatively active McCurdy has hardly withdrawn from the scene. In early 1993, he was among the leading budget dissidents urging Clinton to cut more spending and rely less on tax increases (including an energy tax highly unpopular in Oklahoma).

McCurdy will also reconcentrate his defense policy efforts on Armed Services and the Military Installations and Facilities Subcommittee that he chairs. But here, too, he must adjust to a new order under new Chairman Ronald V. Dellums of California.

Although recent setbacks have slowed McCurdy's ascent, they hardly appear career-threatening. Still in his early 40s, McCurdy has plenty of time, although the inauguration of Clinton as the first "baby boomer" president makes McCurdy look less precocious than he once did.

In 1985, McCurdy and other junior members led the movement that replaced an aged Armed Services chairman with the far more activist Aspin. McCurdy remained a member of Aspin's coterie of centrists who steered House defense policy between the big defense-spending policies of the Reagan and Bush administrations and the defense-cutting zeal of more liberal Democrats.

In 1985, he gained attention for the "McCurdy compromise," which maintained U.S. funding for Nicaragua's anti-communist contras. During the 1990-91 Persian Gulf crisis, McCurdy supported President Bush's hard-line approach to ending Iraq's occupation of Kuwait.

In late 1990, McCurdy visited with U.S. troops deployed in the Persian Gulf region — not with a House delegation, but as a member of the Air Force Reserve, which enabled him to get a more inside view of the military operations there.

McCurdy is a powerful advocate for the U.S. military (Fort Sill and Tinker Air Force Base are in his district). But he also recognizes the need for post-Cold War defense reductions. As head of an Armed Services panel on the defense industrial base during the 102nd Congress, McCurdy introduced an "economic conversion" package to aid communities and people affected by cutbacks.

On Intelligence, McCurdy presided over the first round of post-Cold War reforms of the nation's intelligence-gathering bureaucracies. Although he warned of too rapid a budget cut, McCurdy played a key role in trimming the intelligence budget by 6 percent in 1992.

At Home: A former assistant attorney general with a law practice in Norman, McCurdy had not been active in politics when he began his 1980 campaign. But what McCurdy lacked in political experience he made up for in hustle.

With help from several key backers of retiring Democratic Rep. Tom Steed, he built his own organization. That network and his appeal as a "fresh face" enabled McCurdy to get within 5,000 votes of veteran state Rep. James B. Townsend in the primary, and overtake him in the runoff.

The general election was just as tight. The GOP nominated Howard Rutledge, a retired Navy captain and former prisoner of war in Vietnam whose calls for strengthening defense capability endeared him to the district's sizable military community. But McCurdy found enough support for his economic themes to win by 2,906 votes.

Rutledge returned in 1982, asking conservative Democrats to cross party lines. Rutledge commercials painted McCurdy as a profligate liberal, but McCurdy carried all 12 counties in the 4th, amassing 65 percent of the vote. He won just as easily in 1984, a good GOP year.

Though urged to make a 1986 Senate bid, McCurdy deferred to 1st District Rep. James R. Jones, the state's senior House Democrat. Jones lost to GOP Sen. Don Nickles while McCurdy enjoyed a routine, overwhelming victory. He has not had a real test since. Even after redistricting revised the Oklahoma political landscape in 1992, McCurdy won with 71 percent of the vote.

Committees

Armed Services (6th of 34 Democrats)
Military Installations & Facilities (chairman); Readiness; Research & Technology

Science, Space & Technology (6th of 33 Democrats)
Energy; Space

Elections

1992 General		
Dave McCurdy (D)	140,841	(71%)
Howard Bell (R)	58,235	(29%)
1990 General		
Dave McCurdy (D)	100,879	(74%)
Howard Bell (R)	36,232	(26%)

Previous Winning Percentages: **1988** (100%) **1986** (76%) **1984** (64%) **1982** (65%) **1980** (51%)

District Vote for President

	1992
D	72,613 (33%)
R	90,467 (42%)
I	53,921 (25%)

Campaign Finance

	Receipts	Receipts from PACs	Expenditures
1992			
McCurdy (D)	$541,804	$267,250 (49%)	$539,284
1990			
McCurdy (D)	$342,376	$149,775 (44%)	$357,531
Bell (R)	$3,905	0	$2,923

Key Votes

1993	
Require parental notification of minors' abortions	N
Require unpaid family and medical leave	Y
Approve national "motor voter" registration bill	Y
Approve budget increasing taxes and reducing deficit	Y
Approve economic stimulus plan	Y
1992	
Approve balanced-budget constitutional amendment	Y
Close down space station program	N
Approve U.S. aid for former Soviet Union	Y
Allow shifting funds from defense to domestic programs	N
1991	
Extend unemployment benefits using deficit financing	Y
Approve waiting period for handgun purchases	Y
Authorize use of force in Persian Gulf	Y

Voting Studies

Year	Presidential Support S	Presidential Support O	Party Unity S	Party Unity O	Conservative Coalition S	Conservative Coalition O
1992	42	51	67	24	77	21
1991	41	55	75	20	84	14
1990	44	56	73	25	78	17
1989	55	44	69	25	73	24
1988	33	58	73	22	79	13
1987	36	57	74	20	70	21
1986	31	62	70	21	72	24
1985	44	56	68	27	85	15
1984	46	45	56	29	71	12
1983	41	51	55	37	79	13
1982	58	36	48	43	79	19
1981	57	42	55	43	88	12

Interest Group Ratings

Year	ADA	AFL-CIO	CCUS	ACU
1992	70	64	75	32
1991	30	64	60	26
1990	56	58	14	33
1989	35	50	89	40
1988	60	71	64	30
1987	44	36	40	27
1986	35	42	80	38
1985	30	35	64	52
1984	35	33	33	30
1983	50	53	47	50
1982	25	28	62	67
1981	35	60	37	40

5 Ernest Jim Istook Jr. (R)

Of Oklahoma City — Elected 1992; 1st Term

Born: Feb. 11, 1950, Fort Worth, Texas.
Education: Baylor U., B.A. 1971; Oklahoma City U., J.D. 1977.
Occupation: Lawyer.
Family: Wife, Judy Bills; five children.
Religion: Mormon.
Political Career: Warr Acres City Council, 1983-87; Okla. House, 1987-93.
Capitol Office: 1116 Longworth Bldg. 20515; 225-2132.

The Path to Washington: It is safe to say that if the House bank scandal had never erupted, Istook would not be a member of Congress today. In early 1992, eight-term Rep. Mickey Edwards was counting on another easy re-election campaign in his heavily Republican district.

But when the House ethics committee named Edwards, with 386 overdrafts, as one of the 22 abusers of the House bank, his seemingly unshakable standing began to crumble.

In three terms in the Oklahoma House, Istook compiled a record as a conservative who opposed taxes and abortion rights. He opposed Oklahoma's landmark 1990 education and tax reform bill.

At the same time, he actively supported government ethics reform efforts. He also sponsored a parental school-choice bill, and one tying athletic participation to academic performance.

"I'm a principled conservative," Istook said during the campaign. "I'm not a knee-jerk-reaction conservative. And I think in the Legislature I still have a good relationship with the [Democratic] members not because I played ball with them, but because I have tried to take constructive approaches. . . .

"But I'm not a pork barreler; I have never traded a vote in the Legislature. I've never played pork barrel games. And I don't intend to be a pork barreler. Things for Oklahoma will be things that are deserved for Oklahoma."

He was one of 12 freshman Republicans to vote against a Democratic line-item veto proposal early in the 103rd Congress, charging that the proposal would do nothing in the end to reduce pork-barrel spending. "You can preserve pork with a refrigerator," Istook was quoted as saying, "or you can preserve pork by curing it with salt, or you can do it with smoke — smoke and mirrors."

He voted for a stronger substitute version of the bill that failed.

Istook's almost ascetic approach toward targeted public works spending — he said at a debate during the primary that he would not support a project for his district unless it was in the nation's interest as well — contrasts markedly with the philosophy of his equally conservative predecessor.

Edwards measured his effectiveness in part by his ability to channel federal funds to projects in his district and state.

Istook's stance could be tested by his new position on the Appropriations Committee.

He was one of only two Republican freshmen — along with Henry Bonilla of Texas — to gain a slot on the much-desired panel.

Istook was neither the best-known nor the best-financed of the three leading candidates seeking the Republican nomination in the primary. Edwards had represented the Oklahoma City-based district since 1977. And former U.S. Attorney Bill Price had run statewide in 1990 as the Republican nominee for governor.

The primary was billed as a match between two heavyweights, Edwards and Price. Both spent lavishly on TV advertising. Meanwhile, Istook ran a ground-level campaign that relied less on paid media ads and more on targeting likely GOP voters through direct mail and phone banks. He also refrained from attacking Edwards in his campaign ads. Price's campaign ads assailed the incumbent for his lengthy tenure as well as his problems with the bank.

Price took first place in the primary, but it was Istook, not Edwards, who made the runoff. Edwards came in third with 26 percent of the vote.

Istook's reluctance to attack Edwards left him well-positioned to claim the votes of Edwards' supporters, who bore considerably more animus toward Price than Istook. In the runoff, Istook carried all seven counties wholly or partly contained in the 5th, defeating Price by 12 percentage points.

The Democratic nominee was Laurie Williams, an oil and gas lawyer from Oklahoma City making her first bid for political office.

Williams, who ran as a conservative Democrat, labeled Istook an "extremist," taking issue in particular with his anti-abortion position. Williams received a higher percentage of the vote than any Democrat since 1976, the last time the 5th was open.

Oklahoma 5

North Central — Part of Oklahoma City

As it sweeps from Oklahoma City north to the Kansas border, the 5th collects Republican-minded voters all along the way. Democrats may still have a registration edge in the 5th, but this is unmistakably GOP terrain. It was George Bush's best district in 1992; most of the counties in the 5th gave him more than 60 percent of the vote in 1988. Only the portion of Osage County in the district can be described as Democratic territory.

Oklahoma City enjoyed modest population growth of about 10 percent in the 1980s; much of this increase came in the city's more affluent northwest section, which remains in the new 5th. The district takes in such well-to-do suburbs as Nichols Hills, as well as medium-income suburbs such as Bethany. Remappers shifted the poorer black neighborhoods that had been in the 5th over to the 6th District. Bush carried the Oklahoma City portion of the 5th by more than 2-to-1 over Bill Clinton in 1992.

Oklahoma City's growth did not stop at the city limits. It spread north to Edmond and west — along the Northwest Expressway — into Canadian County. Edmond's population expanded by more than 50 percent in the 1980s; with slightly more than 52,300 people, it is now the sixth-largest city in Oklahoma. Canadian County experienced similarly rapid growth. Its population rose by 32 percent in the last decade, faster than any other county's.

Since the discovery of a large oil pool underneath Oklahoma City in the 1930s, much of the city's economy has revolved around the oil industry. But the sharp drop in oil prices from the early to the mid-1980s forced "O.K. City" (as locals call it) to diversify. The aviation industry is now a significant area employer, with the Federal Aviation Administration's training facility at the airport (in the 6th). The military has a prominent presence as well, with Tinker Air Force Base on the outskirts of the city (in the 4th). Others work in state government, trucking and meatpacking.

The 5th's northeastern anchor is Bartlesville (Washington County), the home of Phillips Petroleum. Oil has been of paramount importance to the local economy since 1897. Now, Bartlesville is a genteel community of 34,000, boasting modern architecture — including an office and apartment building designed by Frank Lloyd Wright — a symphony orchestra, ballet and an annual Mozart festival.

Energy and agriculture are key components of the 5th's economy. Farmers grow wheat and soybeans and raise beef cattle. Phillips, Kerr-McGee and Conoco have refineries in the district. Conoco has a large refinery in Ponca City (Kay County).

Guthrie (Logan County) was Oklahoma's first capital. The town, which is renovating its Victorian-era buildings, is being restored to the early 20th century. To the north in Noble County, Perry's annual Cherokee Strip Celebration commemorates the 1893 land run that led to its founding. The Cherokee Strip is a 12,000-square-mile area that makes up much of what is now north-central Oklahoma.

1990 Population: 524,264. White 453,965 (87%), Black 29,186 (6%), Other 41,113 (8%). Hispanic origin 16,718 (3%). 18 and over 388,030 (74%), 62 and over 80,604 (15%). Median age: 33.

Committee

Appropriations (22nd of 23 Republicans)
District of Columbia; Treasury, Postal Service & General Government

Campaign Finance

	Receipts	Receipts from PACs		Expend-itures
1992				
Istook (R)	$365,630	$72,277	(20%)	$364,915
Williams (D)	$349,220	$19,060	(5%)	$336,418

Key Votes

1993

Require parental notification of minors' abortions	Y
Require unpaid family and medical leave	N
Approve national "motor voter" registration bill	N
Approve budget increasing taxes and reducing deficit	N
Approve economic stimulus plan	N

Elections

1992 General		
Ernest Jim Istook Jr. (R)	123,237	(53%)
Laurie Williams (D)	107,579	(47%)
1992 Primary Runoff		
Ernest Jim Istook Jr. (R)	26,659	(56%)
Bill Price (R)	20,679	(44%)
1992 Primary		
Bill Price (R)	20,485	(37%)
Ernest Jim Istook Jr. (R)	17,975	(32%)
Mickey Edwards (R)	14,519	(26%)
John David Hershberger (R)	2,294	(4%)
Robert W. Schafer (R)	659	(1%)

District Vote for President

1992

D 61,842 (25%)
R 129,465 (52%)
I 59,681 (24%)

6 Glenn English (D)

Of Cordell — Elected 1974; 10th Term

Born: Nov. 30, 1940, Cordell, Okla.
Education: Southwestern State College, B.A. 1964.
Military Service: Army Reserve, 1965-71.
Occupation: Petroleum landman.
Family: Wife, Jan Pangle; two children.
Religion: Methodist.
Political Career: No previous office.
Capitol Office: 2206 Rayburn Bldg. 20515; 225-5565.

In Washington: Now completing his second decade in Congress, English, who is in his early 50s, is nearing the top spot on two committees — Agriculture (where he ranks fourth) and Government Operations (where he ranks third). In the meantime, he keeps busy as chairman of the Agriculture Subcommittee on Environment, Credit and Rural Development, showing a tenacious and sometimes combative leadership style.

The subcommittee oversees commodity futures, and English has played a central role in efforts to strengthen federal regulation of the commodity futures trading markets. In the 101st Congress, his subcommittee produced a bill to force futures exchanges to become more aggressive in rooting out illegal and unfair trading practices. The measure, added to a bill reauthorizing the Commodity Futures Trading Commission, sailed through the House but died in the Senate, snagged on a dispute over what regulatory agency would have jurisdiction over certain stock-index future contracts.

In the 102nd Congress, English returned to the CFTC bill. Both chambers passed bills in 1991, and after a lengthy conference, English and other conferees reached a compromise. Congress cleared legislation in 1992 reauthorizing the CFTC and giving it new powers to crack down on trader misconduct.

Also in 1992, English won enactment of a measure making it easier for young people to get loans to start farms. The legislation eases loan requirements of the Farmers Home Administration and provides support for new farmers for 10 years, as long as the farmer draws up a detailed 10-year farming plan. It was part of a five-bill package that included another English bill designed to improve rural telecommunications systems to enable rural health-care providers to consult more easily with specialists at large urban hospitals. The program would be administered by the Rural Electrification Administration (REA).

English's subcommittee was responsible for the conservation title of the 1990 farm bill, which necessitated negotiating an accord between environmentalists and farm groups. The two factions ultimately agreed to support three areas of the controversial section of the bill: a "swampbuster" program, which denies government subsidies to farmers who drain and plant wetlands; an incentive program to pay farmers to reduce water pollution; and a program to pay farmers to retire 2.5 million acres of wetlands from production.

"Many felt that the gap could not be bridged," English said after the agreement. "It took a lot of meetings ... table-pounding and hand-wringing."

Through the years, English has been an unceasing advocate of high price-support levels for wheat and other Oklahoma commodities. During work on the 1990 farm bill, he failed in his attempts to raise or maintain the existing price supports for wheat. He favored a plan to allow farmers to vote for mandatory production controls as a way to raise prices. Frustrated in those efforts, English voted against the entire farm bill, saying it would drive down market prices and increase surpluses.

In the 100th Congress, English came to the aid of disaster-affected wheat growers. His 1987 bill authorized payments to certain winter wheat producers — mainly in Oklahoma, Kansas and Missouri — who could not plant their 1987 crop because of floods.

But instead of giving outright disaster-relief payments, the bill created a program that essentially paid farmers not to plant. English's bill gave 92 percent of expected income subsidies to wheat farmers who were unable to plant their crops — and who agreed not to plant another crop in 1987. The so-called "0/92" plan was endorsed by the Reagan administration, which wanted to eliminate overproduction by encouraging farmers to plant only as much of a crop as they believed would sell on the open market. The 0/92 plan was reauthorized as part of the 1990 farm bill.

In 1993, however, President Clinton's initial economic plan proposed eliminating the 0/92 program starting in 1996, and to scale back dramatically the activities of the REA.

That idea drew immediate and strong opposition from rural electric cooperatives, who

Oklahoma 6

West and Panhandle; part of Oklahoma City

In terms of economy, occupation, personality and politics, the 6th spans a wider range than any other Oklahoma district. From inner-city black neighborhoods and booming suburbs in and around Oklahoma City to the wild frontier of the Panhandle, the 6th encompasses all aspects of Oklahoma. It is massive: Covering more than 25,000 square miles, the 6th District is larger than 10 states.

Western Oklahoma is traditionally the state's most conservative region. Residents share an aversion to most government activity other than military expenditures and agricultural subsidies. Part of the Dust Bowl, western Oklahoma was devastated in the 1930s and 1940s. It made great strides in the two postwar decades, becoming a region of massive wheat farms and cattle ranches. But the double shock in the 1980s of falling energy prices and the farm credit crisis dealt the district another economic setback. Most counties in the 6th lost population then, many by more than 10 percent.

The historical origins of Oklahoma's settlers indicate the state's voting patterns. Northern Oklahoma's settlers came from Kansas and Nebraska, importing their Republican voting habits. The northern tier of the 6th is the most solid GOP territory in the state. Many of these counties gave George Bush more than 70 percent of the vote in 1988. He won many of them in 1992 by more than 2-to-1. Two Panhandle counties, Texas and Beaver, were the only ones in the state carried by 1990 Republican gubernatorial nominee Bill Price.

Texans settled the southwestern part of Oklahoma. Like the area they left, the southern part of the district is dominated by conservative, "yellow dog" Democrats. Bill Clinton carried the six southernmost counties in 1992.

Agriculture and energy are the mainstays of the 6th's economy. Hard red winter wheat is grown across the district, especially in the north and northwest. Beef cattle are also raised in the 6th. In the south, cotton and peanuts are key commodities. Caddo County ranks second in the nation in peanuts harvested. Much of the energy production in the district is in the Panhandle, where there are huge gas fields.

About 40 percent of the district's population lives in Oklahoma County (Oklahoma City). While the rest of the district lost population during the 1980s, Oklahoma and adjacent Canadian County grew; Canadian boomed by 32 percent, the most in the state. Clinton carried the 6th's share of Oklahoma County.

Oklahoma City is split among three districts. The 6th's portion includes the most famous symbols of the state's oil wealth: working wells on the grounds of the state Capitol. Also included in the 6th are most of the city's 71,000 blacks. Many district residents work at Tinker Air Force Base, General Motors, the Federal Aviation Administration's training center at Will Rogers World Airport and at an AT&T plant on I-40 in the neighboring 5th District.

1990 Population: 524,264. White 410,590 (78%), Black 69,004 (13%), Other 44,670 (9%). Hispanic origin 22,894 (4%). 18 and over 381,952 (73%), 62 and over 91,759 (18%). Median age: 34.

launched a grass-roots lobbying campaign that brought rural folk to Washington to plead with Congress to protect the REA. In the spring of 1993, English brokered a deal between the Agriculture Committee and the administration that would actually enhance its standing and influence in rural America rather than end it. Under the arrangement, the REA would be renamed and folded into the Agriculture Department.

On Government Operations, English chaired the Government Information, Justice and Agriculture Subcommittee through the 101st Congress. There he crusaded for personal privacy and against Reagan administration attempts to soften the Freedom of Information Act.

In the 99th and 100th Congresses, he made drug enforcement a top priority of his subcommittee, using his chairmanship to help write sweeping antidrug bills. He pushed successfully to get the military to lend aircraft and radar to the Customs Service to intercept smugglers. When drugs suddenly became a prominent national issue shortly before the 1986 elections, members racing to familiarize themselves with the subject looked to English. Five of the 12 committees reporting legislation for an omnibus anti-drug package based their recommendations at least in part on proposals by English.

At Home: English started his career as a petroleum landman — someone who arranges oil and gas leases. But politics soon attracted him. In the 1960s he went to California to be chief assistant to the Democrats in the California Legislature, at a time when dictatorial Assembly Speaker Jesse Unruh held sway. English then returned to Oklahoma and served as executive director of the Oklahoma Democratic Party from 1969 to 1973.

In 1974 English entered the Democratic primary in the 6th District, held for the previous three terms by Republican John Newbold Happy Camp, a genial and innocuous small-town banker. English prevailed in a runoff against insurance agent David Hutchens, then launched a town-to-town November campaign, contrasting his youth and energy with Camp's barely visible effort. He beat Camp by 9 percentage points.

After eight mostly uneventful re-elections, Republicans put up a higher-profile challenger in 1992: Bob Anthony, a state corporation commissioner whose name was known across Oklahoma for his family's chain of Anthony's clothing stores. Anthony was the first Republican in nearly 60 years to win the statewide post when he was elected in 1988.

Anthony, while outspent, competed financially with English. They attacked each other in TV ads, with English accusing Anthony of driving his family's company into bankruptcy by trying to finance the company using junk bonds, and Anthony charging that English was beholden to out-of-state special interests.

Anthony talked about free trade, fiscal conservatism and term limits, but voters seemed to value English's seniority and his potential to reach the chair of the Agriculture Committee. Redistricting also had made the 6th more Democratic. English won two-thirds of the vote.

Committees

Agriculture (4th of 28 Democrats)
Environment, Credit & Rural Development (chairman); Department Operations; General Farm Commodities; Specialty Crops & Natural Resources

Government Operations (3rd of 25 Democrats)

Elections

1992 General

Glenn English (D)	134,734	(68%)
Bob Anthony (R)	64,068	(32%)

1990 General

Glenn English (D)	110,100	(80%)
Robert Burns (R)	27,540	(20%)

Previous Winning Percentages: **1988** (73%) **1986** (100%) **1984** (59%) **1982** (75%) **1980** (65%) **1978** (74%) **1976** (71%) **1974** (53%)

District Vote for President

1992
D 73,843 (34%)
R 92,379 (43%)
I 49,106 (23%)

Campaign Finance

	Receipts	Receipts from PACs		Expend-itures
1992				
English (D)	$379,380	$203,400	(54%)	$553,316
Anthony (R)	$378,197	0		$375,794
1990				
English (D)	$238,141	$146,050	(61%)	$157,414

Key Votes

1993

Require parental notification of minors' abortions	Y
Require unpaid family and medical leave	Y
Approve national "motor voter" registration bill	Y
Approve budget increasing taxes and reducing deficit	Y
Approve economic stimulus plan	N

1992

Approve balanced-budget constitutional amendment	Y
Close down space station program	N
Approve U.S. aid for former Soviet Union	N
Allow shifting funds from defense to domestic programs	N

1991

Extend unemployment benefits using deficit financing	Y
Approve waiting period for handgun purchases	N
Authorize use of force in Persian Gulf	N

Voting Studies

	Presidential Support		Party Unity		Conservative Coalition	
Year	**S**	**O**	**S**	**O**	**S**	**O**
1992	52	48	64	35	85	15
1991	43	56	62	36	86	14
1990	47	53	60	38	93	7
1989	64	35	60	39	95	5
1988	47	52	65	33	95	5
1987	52	48	62	35	81	16
1986	43	51	63	34	82	18
1985	58	43	53	44	95	4
1984	52	44	43	50	75	12
1983	46	51	53	46	85	15
1982	65	35	43	57	82	16
1981	55	43	54	46	80	20

Interest Group Ratings

Year	ADA	AFL-CIO	CCUS	ACU
1992	55	67	75	56
1991	35	67	40	50
1990	50	58	64	54
1989	25	33	100	68
1988	40	64	71	60
1987	44	38	73	39
1986	35	50	61	48
1985	15	24	82	76
1984	15	23	63	78
1983	45	47	60	61
1982	20	30	77	64
1981	25	47	53	47

Oregon

STATE DATA

Governor: Barbara Roberts (D)
First elected: 1990
Length of term: 4 years
Term expires: 1/95
Salary: $80,000
Term limit: 2 terms
Phone: (503) 378-3111
Born: Dec. 21, 1936; Corvallis, Ore.
Education: Portland State U., 1961-64; Harvard U., 1989; Marylhurst College, 1989-present
Occupation: Accountant
Family: Husband, Frank Roberts; two children; two stepchildren
Religion: Unspecified
Political Career: Parkrose School Board, 1973-83; Multnomah County Commission, 1978-79; Ore. House, 1981-85; Ore. secretary of state, 1985-91

No lieutenant governor

State election official: (503) 378-4144
Democratic headquarters: (503) 224-8200
Republican headquarters: (503) 620-4330

REDISTRICTING

Oregon retained its five House seats in reapportionment. Federal court approved the map Dec. 2, 1991; that map became law Dec. 16, after the legislature failed to act.

STATE LEGISLATURE

Legislative Assembly. Meets January-June or January-July.

Senate: 30 members, 4-year terms
1992 breakdown: 16D, 14R; 23 men, 7 women; 27 whites, 1 black, 2 others
Salary: $998/month + $75/day (7 days a week) in session; $400-$550/month in expenses not in session
Phone: (503) 378-8168

House of Representatives: 60 members, 2-year terms
1992 breakdown: 32R, 28D; 43 men, 17 women; 58 whites, 2 blacks
Salary: same as Senate
Phone: (503) 378-8551

URBAN STATISTICS

City	Pop.
Portland	437,319
Mayor Vera Katz, D	
Eugene	112,669
Mayor Ruth Bascom, D	
Salem	107,786
Mayor R. G. Andersen-Wyckoff, N-P	

U.S. CONGRESS

Senate: 0 D, 2 R
House: 4 D, 1 R

TERM LIMITS

For Congress: Yes
  Senate: 12 years in lifetime
  House: 6 years in lifetime
For state offices: Yes
  Senate: 2 terms
  House: 3 terms
  No more than 12 years combined

ELECTIONS

1992 Presidential Vote

Bill Clinton	42.5%
George Bush	32.5%
Ross Perot	24.2%

1988 Presidential Vote

Michael S. Dukakis	51%
George Bush	47%

1984 Presidential Vote

Ronald Reagan	56%
Walter F. Mondale	44%

POPULATION

1990 population		2,842,321
1980 population		2,633,105
Percent change		+8%
Rank among states:		29
White		93%
Black		2%
Hispanic		4%
Asian or Pacific islander		2%
Urban		70%
Rural		30%
Born in state		47%
Foreign-born		5%
Under age 18	724,130	25%
Ages 18-64	1,726,867	61%
65 and older	391,324	14%
Median age		34.5

MISCELLANEOUS

Capital: Salem
Number of counties: 36
Per capita income: $17,592 (1991)
  Rank among states: 27
Total area: 97,073 sq. miles
  Rank among states: 10

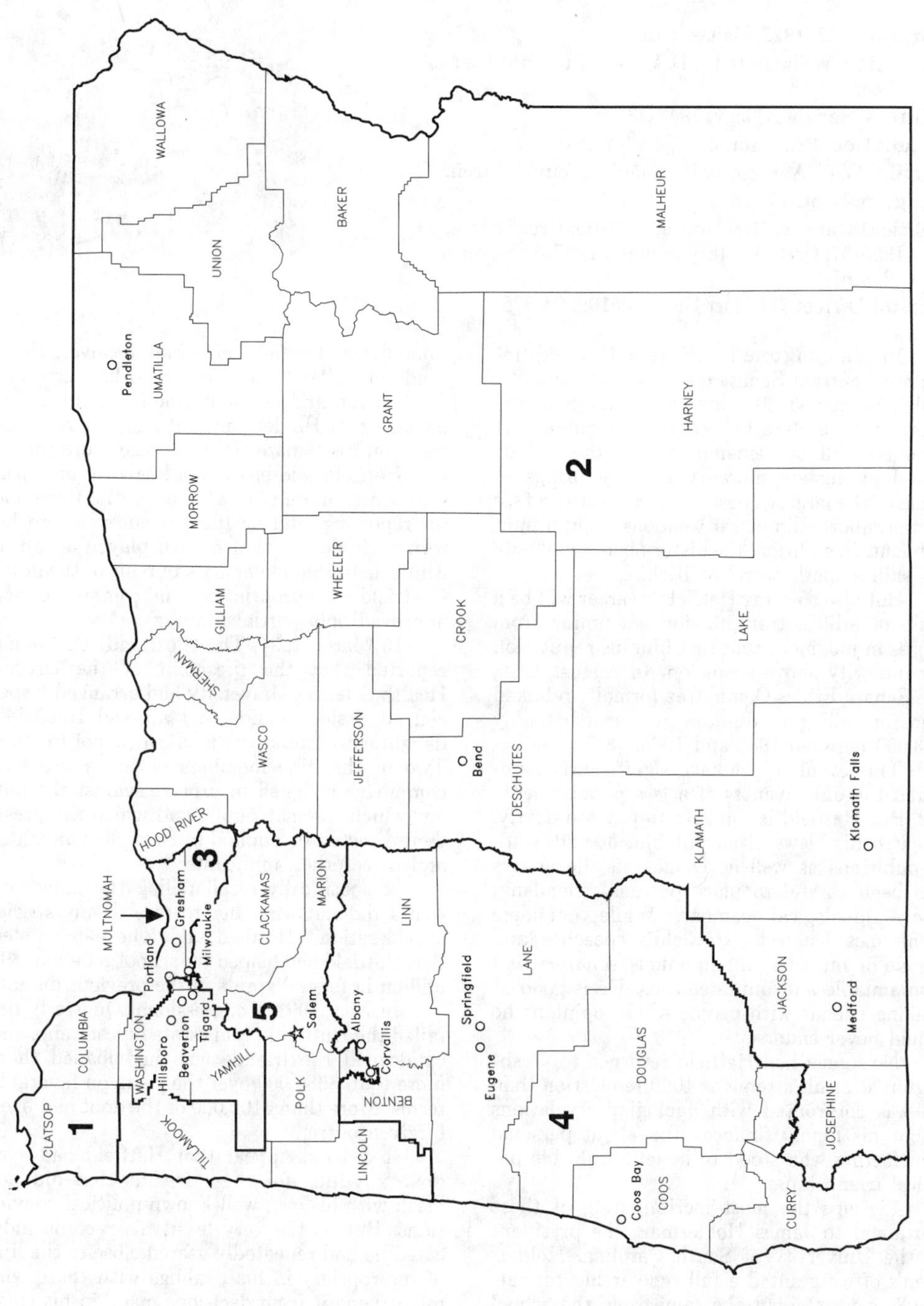
WALLOWA
BAKER
MALHEUR
UNION
UMATILLA
Pendleton
GRANT
HARNEY
2
MORROW
GILLIAM
WHEELER
CROOK
LAKE
SHERMAN
WASCO
JEFFERSON
Bend
DESCHUTES
KLAMATH
Klamath Falls
HOOD RIVER
3
MULTNOMAH
Gresham
Milwaukie
Portland
CLACKAMAS
MARION
LINN
Springfield
LANE
JACKSON
Medford
COLUMBIA
WASHINGTON
Hillsboro
Beaverton
Tigard
5
Salem
Albany
Corvallis
Eugene
DOUGLAS
YAMHILL
POLK
BENTON
CLATSOP
1
TILLAMOOK
LINCOLN
4
JOSEPHINE
Coos Bay
COOS
CURRY

Mark O. Hatfield (R)

Of Portland — Elected 1966; 5th Term

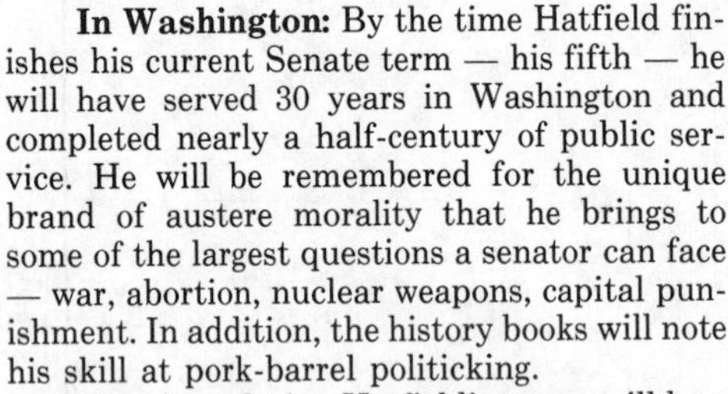

Born: July 12, 1922, Dallas, Ore.
Education: Willamette U., B.A. 1943; Stanford U., M.A. 1948.
Military Service: Navy, 1943-46.
Occupation: Professor; college administrator.
Family: Wife, Antoinette Kuzmanich; four children.
Religion: Baptist.
Political Career: Ore. House, 1951-55; Ore. Senate, 1955-57; Ore. secretary of state, 1957-59; governor, 1959-67.
Capitol Office: 711 Hart Bldg. 20510; 224-3753.

In Washington: By the time Hatfield finishes his current Senate term — his fifth — he will have served 30 years in Washington and completed nearly a half-century of public service. He will be remembered for the unique brand of austere morality that he brings to some of the largest questions a senator can face — war, abortion, nuclear weapons, capital punishment. In addition, the history books will note his skill at pork-barrel politicking.

But also coloring Hatfield's career will be a stain of ethical transgression, stemming from lapses in judgment that cost him his reputation for integrity above suspicion. In August 1992, the Senate Ethics Committee formally rebuked him for failing to disclose gifts worth nearly $43,000 between 1983 and 1988.

This event might have significantly hampered the effectiveness of a less popular senator. But Hatfield is unlikely to pay too dearly. Though his views often put him at odds with Republicans as well as Democrats, he always has been careful to place personal friendship above ideological combat. While outsiders sometimes listen to Hatfield's speeches and decide he must be sanctimonious, senators find him amiable and unpretentious. He is good at making friends with people whose opinions he would never endorse.

No sooner had Hatfield returned to Washington after his strenuous 1990 re-election than he was confronted with damaging revelations about his family finances and about personal benefactors who stood to benefit from his political friendship.

Perhaps the most incriminating of these pertained to James Holderman, the president of the University of South Carolina. Holderman's office granted a full scholarship to Hatfield's son at about the same time the school was winning a $16.3 million federal grant. Holderman at the time was lobbying Congress for grants; Congress earmarked the grant for the university in a bill that Hatfield helped oversee as chairman of the Appropriations Committee. Hatfield also had received thousands of dollars' worth of artwork, a compact disc player and reimbursement of travel expenses from Holderman and had not reported them on his Senate financial disclosure forms.

Hatfield said he did not know the artworks were worth more than $100 each, the threshold for reporting, and he filed amendments to his forms. He denied that he had played a significant role in the university's pursuit of the grant (Hatfield's Appropriations subcommittee had approved only partial funding).

In March 1991, The (Portland) Oregonian reported that the president of the Oregon Health Sciences University had arranged a special admissions policy that allowed Hatfield's daughter to attend the medical school in 1989. Two of the nine members of the admissions committee resigned in protest against the policy, which was not public and which the president directed be applied to Hatfield's daughter and three other applicants.

"I specifically recall telling the university that I did not want her to receive any special consideration," Hatfield said. The paper noted that Hatfield had helped the school get about $91 million in federal grants in the previous decade.

In May 1991, Congressional Quarterly detailed the Hatfields' real estate investments and catalogued the friends who had loaned them more than $680,000 over the years on favorable terms. More than $100,000 of the debt had been forgiven outright.

It did not appear that Hatfield had ever done anything for these friends that did not mesh with his own well-known political convictions. But at the very least, his records indicated he had repeatedly veered close to the line of impropriety in his dealings with those who might benefit from decisions made in his committee.

In the midst of the Ethics Committee investigation, Hatfield announced in September 1991 that he had failed to disclose more than $55,000 in gifts as required by government ethics laws. Most came from a friend and former House member who once lobbied Hatfield (Oregon Republican John R. Dellenback, 1967-75), and another large chunk came from the wife of a prominent California banker.

In its 15-month investigation, the Ethics Committee found no evidence of criminal violations or willful wrongdoing by Hatfield. And it found no connection between his official actions and acceptance of gifts, though it said his repeated acceptance and non-disclosure of gifts from Holderman while his school was vying for congressional grants was "inappropriate" conduct that "cannot be condoned." The committee attributed Hatfield's shortcomings to "a serious lack of concern for, and negligence in connection with, his legal obligation to disclose such gifts." The panel did find, however, that he had violated the 1978 Ethics in Government Act and Senate rules. While declaring his actions "improper conduct reflecting upon the Senate," it did not recommend discipline by the full chamber. Hatfield issued a contrite statement accepting the committee's judgment.

Hatfield occasionally has acknowledged lapses over the years, but the Holderman scrape jarred him, friends said. He announced new ethics rules for his office in 1991: no more speaking fees and no more gifts from anyone except family and close friends with no stake in the business of his office. And he appointed an aide to be his office's ethical watchdog.

Since coming to the Senate in 1967, Hatfield and his wife, Antoinette, have been subjected to several investigations by the news media and three by the Ethics Committee. But none had evoked the uneasiness that surrounded the most recent episodes.

In the best-known case, the senator and his wife were criticized for $55,000 in real estate and interior decorating fees she received from a Greek businessman who solicited — and got — help from the senator in a major business venture. Hatfield tried to advance a $15 billion trans-Africa oil pipeline project being promoted by the entrepreneur, Basil Tsakos. Hatfield and his wife said that she had earned the $55,000.

In 1984 the Ethics Committee decided it lacked enough evidence for a full-scale investigation; the next year it issued a report clearing the Hatfields. A month before the committee's vote, Hatfield admitted "an error in judgment" and an "insensitivity to the appearance of impropriety." He donated $55,000 to charity, and Oregonians accepted his version of events implicitly by re-electing him easily that fall.

Hatfield's straight-laced moralism would seem to make him an unlikely candidate to be ensnared in dubious ethical activity. But his case demonstrates that if someone is surrounded by wealth and privilege for so many years, even a member with devout religious beliefs such as Hatfield can be drawn into behavior outside the bounds of reasonableness.

The ethics trouble was the latest in a series of difficulties Hatfield has had to endure, including his tougher-than-expected re-election in 1990 and his 1987 relinquishment of the Appropriations Committee gavel when Democrats regained control of the Senate.

Over the years, his Appropriations assignment has brought him not only political benefits at home (jurisdiction over public forests and range lands, hydroelectric power and harbors) but also leverage in Congress. As a member of Appropriations, he quickly became adept at the senatorial art of quid pro quo.

Hatfield held the chairmanship of Appropriations when the GOP controlled the Senate from 1981 to 1987, and the job forced upon him responsibility for a rightward march he himself did not wholly support.

President Ronald Reagan's military buildup violated Hatfield's personal philosophy, which is deeply averse to weaponry and war. Reagan's tax cuts, he believed, were regressive. Reagan's spending cuts, he often said, went too far.

While some other liberal Republicans were stripped of party influence for straying from the dominant conservative ideology, Hatfield avoided a great deal of criticism despite holding views that even many Democrats would find too radical.

It seldom happens, for example, that a chairman castigates members of the opposition party for failing to provide strong enough criticism of his own party's president. But it happened in 1986, when Hatfield essentially wrote off the GOP as a source of resistance to the Strategic Defense Initiative (SDI) and other aspects of Reagan's defense buildup. "Face up to the facts," he told the Democrats during debate on that year's continuing resolution. "There are only a handful of Republicans ... who will challenge this madness. You are the loyal opposition. Take a stand."

With the return of the Democratic majority in 1987, Hatfield was in some respects liberated. As ranking minority member on Appropriations, he could practice his unorthodox combination of moral indignation and pork-barrel politics without the burdens or restraints of the chairmanship.

Few senators have achieved Hatfield's popularity while clinging so tenaciously to views outside the mainstream. He is a near-pacifist on defense issues and nearly always a vote against any military spending bill. When war loomed in the Persian Gulf in 1991, Hatfield was the only senator to oppose not only the authorization of military action (a course chosen by only one other GOP senator) but also the extension of sanctions offered as an alternative by the Democratic leadership. Both options were too bellicose for Hatfield, whose floor statement said, "They do not offer us the alternative of peace."

"If we want to avoid war we ought to say

so, right here and now. Instead of playing this dangerous game ... we ought to bring our troops home once and for all." In March, he even cast the lone opposing vote when the Senate approved a package of benefits for Persian Gulf veterans by a tally of 97-1. In August 1991, on the anniversary of Iraq's invasion of Kuwait, he cast one of two dissenting votes on a non-binding amendment backing a future attack against Iraqi leader Saddam Hussein if he refused to comply with United Nations orders to turn over all materials for nuclear, chemical and biological weapons.

Hatfield is nearly as lonely in his outspoken contention that U.S. policy in the Middle East tilts too far toward Israel. He has spoken for Palestinian refugees and advocated limits on military aid to Israel. He moralizes about the importance of human rights as an emphasis in U.S. foreign policy.

He has led the opposition to the MX missile and SDI, pressed for human rights concessions from authoritarian foreign regimes, and filibustered against reinstatement of the draft. He was equally unyielding in opposition to Reagan's policies in Central America. In the 102nd Congress he and Massachusetts Democrat Edward M. Kennedy sponsored a bill to stop U.S. officials from summarily turning back refugees from Haiti.

In the early 1980s, Hatfield signed on as co-leader of the nuclear weapons freeze campaign, and over the years he has backed numerous failed attempts to restrict nuclear weapons testing. Not until after the end of the Cold War would Congress finally approve a ban on nuclear testing.

In the 102nd Congress, he and Majority Leader George J. Mitchell of Maine introduced a bill to impose a one-year moratorium on U.S. nuclear weapons tests as long as the former Soviet republics do not test. With the support of Nebraska Democrat Jim Exon, he later modified it to a nine-month ban, after which the administration could conduct limited testing for safety issues before a permanent ban would take effect in 1996. It became law as part of the fiscal 1993 energy and water appropriations bill.

Hatfield's politics are shaped by a born-again religious conviction. Not to be confused with the fundamentalism of the evangelical right, Hatfield's religious views emphasize help for the poor and separation of church and state.

An ardent abortion foe, Hatfield also opposes a constitutional amendment to permit prayer in the public schools. But he does believe that student religious organizations should have access to public educational facilities.

Hatfield parted from some anti-abortion activists in the 102nd Congress with his support for efforts to overturn a 1988 ban on federally funded research using tissue from aborted fetuses. Scientists say that such tissue might alleviate or cure Parkinson's disease, diabetes and other diseases. Some abortion opponents contended that such research would, if successful, encourage abortions. But Hatfield was among several abortion opponents — including South Carolina Republican Strom Thurmond — who rejected those contentions. "I strongly believe that allowing fetal tissue research is a pro-life position," Hatfield said.

The provision overturning the ban was added to the bill reauthorizing part of the National Institutes of Health. President Bush vetoed the bill because it lifted the ban, and the House sustained the veto. But in one of his first actions in office, President Clinton rescinded the ban. Hatfield backed efforts in the 103rd Congress to codify Clinton's action.

Hatfield's "pro-life" stance is also reflected in his opposition to capital punishment. He was willing to stand against anti-drug legislation at the end of the 1988 session because it contained a death penalty. "It is not responsible for this body to have an eye-for-eye mentality," he said. Hatfield introduced multiple amendments before casting one of just three votes in the Senate against the politically popular bill.

Hatfield renewed his efforts against the death penalty in June 1990, proposing to amend the Senate's anti-crime package by changing every death sentence in the bill to life in prison without possibility of release. His amendment received only 25 votes. He offered his life-imprisonment alternative again in February 1991, this time to a proposal that would allow federal prosecutors to seek the death penalty for terrorists who murder U.S. citizens in this country or abroad. Once again, it got 25 votes.

Despite all this, Hatfield has functioned well in the world of Appropriations, which carries a long tradition of collegiality and accommodation.

The assignment has allowed Hatfield to practice the lessons of constituent service he learned at the knee of Warren G. Magnuson of Washington, a Pacific Northwest cohort and longtime Appropriations powerhouse. The ports along the Oregon coast and the funding for federal lands have profited handsomely.

Hatfield once explained that he would like to cut the federal budget substantially, but since that was impossible he was determined to steer as much of it as possible to his home state. He has never been bashful about doing that.

Hatfield has bent his effort to such thorny Northwestern perennials as the balancing of nature and livelihood. That has brought him into the long-running debate over saving the threatened northern spotted owl. While he has attempted to mediate the jobs vs. owl question, in the 102nd Congress he joined his Oregon colleague, Republican Bob Packwood, on a bill much more to the timber industry's liking than a stringent House bill. Their bill would have guaranteed timber sales and worker retraining programs and restricted citizen appeals. The

Energy and Natural Resources Committee never acted on it.

Hatfield is the only member of Congress who has been able to get a bill to the floor instituting a national policy of nickel deposits on bottles and cans. All other suggestions of this kind since 1970 have died in committee (Hatfield's died on the floor in 1976, 26-60). He and Vermont Republican James M. Jeffords have sponsored a 10-cent deposit bottle bill; it died in the 102nd Congress, but they reintroduced it in the 103rd.

Hatfield teamed with Kentucky Democrat Wendell H. Ford in the 102nd Congress on a bill that would require states to register people to vote when they apply for a driver's license. Bush vetoed the bill in June 1992, but "motor voter" legislation became law early in the Clinton administration.

While serving on Appropriations, Hatfield has remained on the Energy and Natural Resources Committee. He was one of the most active Senate opponents of the nuclear breeder reactor. His feeling was partially explained by the fact that, as a young naval officer, he was a member of the first American military team to enter Hiroshima, one month after the atom bomb demolished the city.

Though he does not flaunt his faith during Senate debate, Hatfield courts a religious constituency with speeches and newsletters. He participates regularly in Capitol prayer meetings and has written three books for religious publishing houses describing the tribulations of a Christian in politics.

At Home: In 42 years in Oregon politics, Hatfield has never lost an election. But in 1990, his broad-based coalition built largely on peace and pork suffered widespread defections.

Hatfield did not look like he had serious political problems when he launched his bid for a fifth Senate term. With well-known Democrats such as Reps. Ron Wyden and Les AuCoin staying out of the race, the nomination went virtually by default to a political newcomer, Harry Lonsdale.

But as the wealthy founder of a high-tech research firm, Lonsdale was able to pump nearly $1.5 million into his campaign. And he benefited from an array of issues on which Hatfield was at odds with vocal and well-organized interest groups.

Since the Vietnam War, Hatfield's pacifism had helped him draw widespread support from the left. But other parts of his voting record were in the spotlight in 1990. His anti-abortion stance drew opposition from the National Abortion Rights Action League and the National Organization for Women. His sympathy for the timber industry in its battle with environmentalists over the future of old-growth forests and the spotted owl drew opposition from such "green" groups as the League of Conservation Voters.

Hatfield also found his integrity sharply questioned by Lonsdale, who voiced concern about the incumbent's ready acceptance of honoraria and political action committee (PAC) money. Lonsdale boasted that he was accepting no PAC contributions.

By late September, it was clear that Hatfield was vulnerable to what the media began to describe as an "Oregon surprise." A summertime lead of 36 percentage points in The Oregonian's poll was sliced to just 6 percentage points.

But to Hatfield's advantage, he had time to respond. And faced with the prospect of defeat, he responded aggressively, dropping his traditional low-budget, "speak no evil" style of campaigning in favor of an attack strategy. His ads trumpeted allegations that Lonsdale's company had engaged in improper toxic-waste disposal and chided the challenger for defending in writing during the mid-1980s the activities of religious cult leader Bhagwan Shree Rajneesh, who had set up a commune in Oregon.

Lonsdale's momentum stalled, and Hatfield won re-election with 54 percent of the vote. The Democrat narrowly carried Multnomah County (Portland) but Hatfield more than offset that with a strong showing in the Portland suburbs and the populous Willamette Valley. He carried 31 of Oregon's 36 counties.

A major factor in Hatfield's victory was the reservoir of good will that he had built up over four decades in Oregon politics. It has enabled him to attract support across partisan and ideological lines.

Earlier in his career, Hatfield won the gratitude of liberals with his opposition to loyalty oaths for teachers; their support was reinforced by his opposition to the Vietnam War.

Organized labor, when it has not been able to back him against a Democratic competitor, usually has remained neutral. Hatfield sometimes likes to play up his labor connections; his father, a blacksmith, belonged to the railroad brotherhood.

A political science professor and university dean, Hatfield acquired Republicanism from his mother, who had been raised in the staunchly GOP territory of East Tennessee. In 1958, as secretary of state in Oregon, he blended an effective campaign style with youthful good looks to unseat Democratic Gov. Robert D. Holmes.

As governor, Hatfield ran an administration that kept state spending down and did not raise taxes. He launched an aggressive "Sell Oregon" drive that helped spur exports. And in 1962, he withstood a strong re-election challenge from Democrat Robert Y. Thornton, the state attorney general, who lacked the labor support he needed to defeat a popular governor.

Constitutionally forbidden to run for a third term as governor in 1966, Hatfield took aim at the Senate seat being vacated by Democrat Maurine Neuberger.

In that race, the central issue was the Vietnam War, which Hatfield opposed and his Democratic rival, Rep. Robert B. Duncan, favored. As Duncan saw it, the conflict concerned whether "Americans will die in the buffalo grass of Vietnam or the rye grass of Oregon."

Hatfield had been the lone dissenting vote on a National Governors' Conference resolution supporting the war. Afterward, in his Senate campaign, he put up billboards with the word "Courage" in large letters. He blamed the war for the state's lagging lumber industry, reasoning that the conflict had brought a downturn in home construction. Fearful of being painted as unpatriotic, however, Hatfield criticized the "inexcusable excesses of some anti-war demonstrations." Hatfield defeated Duncan, but with a slim 52 percent majority.

Running for re-election in 1972, he did better against an even more militant Vietnam dove, former Sen. Wayne Morse, who was seeking a comeback as the Democratic nominee. Despite Hatfield's anti-war activities, the Nixon White House cooperated with his re-election that year, and this helped defuse conservative resentment that had built up toward him in Oregon. Morse had difficulty finding an issue to use against Hatfield; in 1966, Morse had announced that he would vote for Hatfield over Duncan because of the war issue.

Hatfield won re-election with 54 percent; more comfortable victories followed in 1978 and 1984.

Committees

Appropriations (Ranking)
Energy & Water Development (ranking); Commerce, Justice, State & Judiciary; Interior; Labor, Health & Human Services & Education; Transportation

Energy & Natural Resources (2nd of 9 Republicans)
Public Lands, National Parks & Forests; Renewable Energy; Water & Power

Indian Affairs (8th of 8 Republicans)

Rules & Administration (2nd of 7 Republicans)

Joint Library

Joint Printing

Elections

1990 General		
Mark O. Hatfield (R)	590,095	(54%)
Harry Lonsdale (D)	507,743	(46%)
1990 Primary		
Mark O. Hatfield (R)	220,449	(78%)
Randy Prince (R)	59,970	(21%)

Previous Winning Percentages: **1984** (67%) **1978** (62%) **1972** (54%) **1966** (52%)

Campaign Finance

	Receipts	Receipts from PACs		Expend-itures
1990				
Hatfield (R)	$2,200,139	$969,720	(44%)	$2,357,058
Lonsdale (D)	$1,496,111	0		$1,479,099

Key Votes

1993	
Require unpaid family and medical leave	Y
Approve national "motor voter" registration bill	Y
Approve budget increasing taxes and reducing deficit	N
Support president's right to lift military gay ban	Y
1992	
Approve school-choice pilot program	N
Allow shifting funds from defense to domestic programs	Y
Oppose deeper cuts in spending for SDI	N
1991	
Approve waiting period for handgun purchases	Y
Raise senators' pay and ban honoraria	Y
Authorize use of force in Persian Gulf	N
Confirm Clarence Thomas to Supreme Court	Y

Voting Studies

	Presidential Support		Party Unity		Conservative Coalition	
Year	**S**	**O**	**S**	**O**	**S**	**O**
1992	53	47	45	53	47	53
1991	59	40	51	49	48	52
1990	38	51	31	58	32	59
1989	69	30	39	58	34	66
1988	55	38	39	51	30	70
1987	41	46	47	48	41	56
1986	42	57	54	43	50	47
1985	45	40	49	35	32	42
1984	43	45	48	48	45	51
1983	64	29	56	33	45	45
1982	61	29	57	27	45	45
1981	76	19	71	26	58	39

Interest Group Ratings

Year	ADA	AFL-CIO	CCUS	ACU
1992	7	75	56	23
1991	60	58	50	24
1990	78	67	22	35
1989	80	50	63	21
1988	70	62	57	30
1987	65	60	61	28
1986	75	47	39	30
1985	45	39	70	18
1984	75	40	72	24
1983	60	29	50	13
1982	60	47	50	30
1981	55	22	88	29

Bob Packwood (R)

Of Portland — Elected 1968; 5th Term

Born: Sept. 11, 1932, Portland, Ore.
Education: Willamette U., B.A. 1954; New York U., LL.B. 1957.
Occupation: Lawyer.
Family: Divorced; two children.
Religion: Unitarian.
Political Career: Ore. House, 1963-69.
Capitol Office: 259 Russell Bldg. 20510; 224-5244.

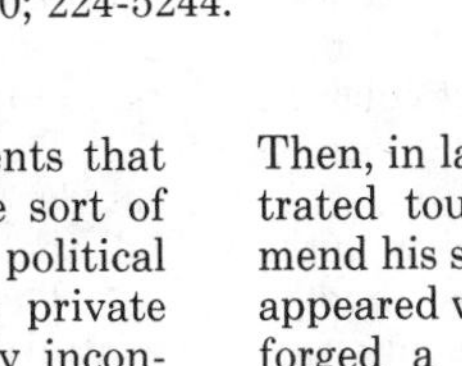

In Washington: The turn of events that befell Packwood in late 1992 had the sort of surreal quality that often attaches to political figures when revelations about their private lives emerge that appear to be wholly incongruous with their public actions.

Six months after winning his toughest campaign in 24 years, Packwood was faced with an unprecedented challenge: to keep from being thrown out of office over a charge of lying during the final days before the election. He got past that immediate problem, but there remained an underlying threat to his career: allegations from more than a score of women, some of them former employees, that they had been the targets of his unwelcome and sometimes aggressive sexual advances.

For a man known as one of the staunchest advocates of women's causes on Capitol Hill — from his vigorous defense of abortion rights to his sponsorship of resolutions recognizing the strides made by women and girls in sports — it was a stunning accusation.

Packwood was, after all, one of only two Republicans to oppose the confirmation of Clarence Thomas as a justice of the Supreme Court. And it was the unpracticed way that the Senate handled Anita F. Hill's allegations that she had been sexually harassed by Thomas that forever altered the Senate's approach to the subject. The spotlight that shone on the Judiciary Committee in 1991 would only burn hotter when the Ethics Committee took up Packwood's case in 1993.

In late November 1992, The Washington Post first published the charges of sexual harassment; in the months that followed, Packwood became an active recluse. As the Senate prepared to do battle over the tax code by addressing the tax plans of President Clinton, he was still a pivotal figure as ranking Republican on the Finance Committee. But he was far less visible in Washington and at home.

For two months after the storm hit, he did not show his face in Oregon. Acknowledging a problem with alcohol abuse, he spent a brief time in an alcohol rehabilitation program. Then, in late January 1993, he made an orchestrated tour of his home state to attempt to mend his shattered reputation. In particular, he appeared with timber groups, with whom he has forged a strong association in the past few years, angering environmentalists who used to consider Packwood their ally.

But Packwood was hounded by editorials and demonstrators calling for his resignation. A group of Oregon citizens petitioned the Senate Rules Committee to throw out his election on the charge that he had lied to the Post. Packwood had told the newspaper before the election that the harassment allegations made against him were false. Yet just over two weeks after the story appeared, Packwood apologized at a Capitol Hill press conference: "The important point is that my actions were unwelcome and insensitive, and these women were offended, appropriately so, and I am truly sorry."

The petitioners charged that Packwood's denials to the Post (and to Oregon reporters who knew the Post was pursuing the story) amounted to defrauding Oregon voters. But in May 1993, the Rules Committee declined to accept the petitioners' argument, feeling it would be bad precedent to reject a duly elected senator on a charge of lying. "I see your request as one that really opens a Pandora's box for this body," California Democrat Dianne Feinstein told a lawyer for the petitioners.

Meanwhile, the Ethics Committee had opened an investigation into whether Packwood had violated rules or otherwise brought disrepute to the chamber. If faced with disciplinary proceedings, Packwood promised to mount a vigorous defense.

Despite his earlier apology, he promised to raise questions about the stories of the women accusing him. And he insisted he would not resign, suggesting that whatever he did, it could not deserve more serious punishment than the censure handed to Democrat Alan Cranston in 1992 in the Keating Five case. "On the scale of values, is it worse to have caused the public to lose billions of dollars, or is what I did worse?" he asked rhetorically during a January interview with the Eugene, Ore., Register-Guard.

The turmoil seemed to do little to change Packwood's behavior as a lawmaker. One of the Senate's most enigmatic yet conspicuous members, he has frequently been labeled a moderate. At best, the term describes the mean of his extremes: one minute he can be a hard-line conservative, pressing for a deep cut in the tax on capital gains, and the next he looks like a liberal, voting to override a Republican president's veto of a family leave bill.

In the early months of the 103rd Congress, he continued his independent ways. He supported the Democratic-sponsored "motor voter" registration bill and backed Democrats in votes on some amendments to President Clinton's budget blueprint — in particular on programs such as Head Start that he has favored in the past.

At the same time, Packwood stuck with the GOP and opposed Clinton on most budget votes, on an economic stimulus plan and on an unemployment benefits bill.

Packwood has always been prone to buck the party line; historically, he has voted with a majority of Republicans just a little more than half the time. Nonetheless, Packwood has proved willing to serve in harness on the Finance Committee. In the 101st Congress he carried the White House water on the issue President Bush called his top tax priority: a lower tax rate on capital gains.

Many found this an ironic, if not cynical, reversal for Packwood. The elimination of the differential rate for capital gains, paired with a lower tax rate for income overall, was a centerpiece of the tax code overhaul of 1986 — the single most memorable achievement of Packwood's career.

But one of the industries most sensitive to capital gains taxes is timber, one of Oregon's economic roots. Moreover, Packwood's turnabout on the issue was as much a continuation of his earlier performance as a contradiction of it. Packwood's role in the tax overhaul legislation of the 99th Congress was one of the great riddles of recent congressional history. It may never be possible to unravel its tangle of sincere conversion and opportunism, of tactical weakness and strategic insight.

When Packwood took the Finance chair in 1985, he embraced the status quo in which the tax code was used not only to produce revenue, but also to enable government to enact a social and economic agenda. "I kind of like the present tax code," he said at the time.

So Packwood found himself in an uneasy position in 1985 when President Ronald Reagan proposed eliminating most tax subsidies in order to reduce rates for individual taxpayers.

Packwood opened committee work with a "reform" proposal that reflected his longtime interests, retaining many existing tax breaks for business. The Finance markup quickly threatened to become a fiasco. Senators kept voting to add new breaks, rejecting efforts to cut back. Within a few weeks, the resulting bill was estimated to add $30 billion to the federal deficit. "There are some things that make us look foolish," Packwood said plaintively of an amendment, "and there are some things that *really* make us look foolish."

Packwood faced genuine embarrassment, if not ridicule; one national magazine was calling him "Senator Hackwood." Desperate, he canceled further markups. It was then, over a long liquid lunch with an aide at a Capitol Hill bar, that Packwood had his key insight. Concluding that his approach was hopeless, he settled on a drastic tack: Set the top individual tax rate at 25 percent and eliminate virtually all deductions to pay for it.

The plan proved too radical, but it broke the deadlock. And its premise undergirded the bill that finally was enacted.

The 1986 Senate elections cost the GOP control of the Senate and deprived Packwood of the Finance chair. As ranking member, trade has been a major concern. With industries that export natural resources and import components, Oregon is especially sensitive to trade matters. So it is not surprising that Packwood is an active free-trader. He played a major role in opposing quotas to restrict textile and shoe imports, and he worked on the Canada free-trade accord. He is a booster of a free-trade pact to bind all of North America.

Packwood's most publicized moment in the 100th Congress stemmed from his opposition to campaign finance legislation pushed by Democrats. Republicans were using quorum calls as a tactic for stalling debate. Packwood had retreated into his office, where he had bolted one door and blocked another with a heavy chair. On orders from the majority leader, the sergeant at arms of the Senate arrested Packwood to force his attendance at a quorum call, a tactic not used in the Senate since 1942. Packwood forced the sergeant's deputies to carry him into the chamber. During the fracas, he reinjured a broken finger, which he proudly displayed at a news conference the next day.

Packwood seems to pride himself in a sore-thumb sort of prominence. In 1982, he startled the capital by publicly accusing Reagan of alienating blacks, Jews, women and blue-collar workers. He was not only a senior GOP senator; he was chairman of the National Republican Senatorial Committee.

But Packwood's reputation as a maverick arrived with him in 1969, when at 36 he was the youngest senator. He was fresh from a stunning upset of veteran Democrat Wayne Morse, and was heralded by Newsweek as one of the "bright new stars" of the Senate. He promptly demonstrated his independent-mindedness by helping Democrats defeat two of President Richard M. Nixon's Supreme Court nominees and by a series of speeches chiding the Senate as irresponsible, especially in its practice of awarding chairmanships purely by seniority.

At Home: Packwood began 1992 as one of the most vulnerable senators facing re-election. But by catching some lucky breaks — and making some for himself through hard-nosed politics — Packwood prevailed with 53 percent of the vote.

At the outset, though, Packwood's prospects did not look promising. In 18-year Democratic Rep. Les AuCoin, he faced his most formidable opponent since winning the seat. A rift between the state GOP establishment and the right-wing Oregon Citizens Alliance threatened to split the party and spawn an independent, conservative challenge to Packwood. With anti-incumbent sentiment flourishing in Oregon, Packwood's approval ratings in statewide polls were in the danger level. In October 1991, fearing he could not generate enough campaign cash, he dropped his pledge not to accept political action committee funds — a vow that had been in effect only since his last election. Finally, 1992 was shaping up as a strong year for the Democratic ticket, as Oregon appeared set to vote for the Democratic presidential nominee for the second consecutive election.

But things began breaking Packwood's way. AuCoin proved to be an unexciting, occasionally tongue-tied speaker. He was caught in the House bank scandal and was barely able to squeeze by his Democratic primary challenger, millionaire businessman Harry Lonsdale.

In the meantime, Packwood amassed a mammoth campaign treasury and helped bandage temporarily the intraparty rift, averting a conservative challenge. Though his four little-known primary challengers held him below 60 percent, he was never in danger of losing the nomination. And although AuCoin was one of the leading House advocates for abortion rights, the National Abortion Rights Action League endorsed Packwood, another longstanding ally.

AuCoin's lengthy tenure coupled with his 83 overdrafts at the House bank enabled Lonsdale to keep AuCoin off balance. Packwood chimed in during the primary with an ad taking aim at AuCoin. AuCoin won the nomination by 330 votes, but only after a lengthy recount procedure and a threat by Lonsdale to run an active write-in campaign.

When AuCoin staggered out of his primary having spent most of his campaign treasury, Packwood was poised with the second-largest amount of cash on hand of any Senate candidate in the country: At midyear, AuCoin had $222,000; Packwood had $3 million.

Packwood maintained his huge financial edge throughout. He waged a scorching media campaign that raised voters' negative opinion of AuCoin, peppering him over his "bounced" checks and calling him "a study in hypocrisy."

Through his masterful demonstration of political hardball, Packwood set the agenda of the campaign. AuCoin never managed to right himself and fire effective counteroffensives. Packwood carried all but seven of the state's 36 counties; Democrats won every other statewide contest.

Campaigning, organizing and fundraising are in Packwood's blood. His great-grandfather was a member of the 1857 Oregon constitutional convention and held a variety of political appointments; his father was a business lobbyist before the state Legislature.

As an undergraduate at Willamette University, Packwood studied political science under Mark O. Hatfield, his Senate colleague since 1969. That experience may have colored their future relationship, which was for a long time the cordial but cool cooperation of an established senior statesman and an ambitious rival for public recognition.

As a young politician, Packwood had a reputation for outspokenness and boat-rocking. In 1962, he startled the party establishment by announcing that Sig Unander, that year's GOP Senate nominee against Morse, stood no chance.

The Morse whom Packwood encountered in 1968 was a weaker political figure than the one who beat Unander. Morse had narrowly survived a rough primary with former Rep. Robert Duncan. Packwood was to the right of Morse on several issues, including the most salient issue of the day, the Vietnam War. While Packwood was critical of the South Vietnamese government, he castigated Morse for voting to cut off funds for the war.

But ideology was not the focal point of the campaign. The main issue was Morse himself. Packwood labeled Morse as ineffective, saying that the state had been harmed by the Democrat's contentious style. Other senators were reluctant to help Morse get federal projects for Oregon, he charged. Morse was 68 years old in 1968; he was still vigorous, but Packwood managed nonetheless to win support on the issue of youth vs. age. Starting out far behind but building a splendid campaign organization, Packwood edged Morse by 3,293 votes out of nearly 815,000 cast.

The 1974 contest began as a rematch between Packwood and Morse. But Morse died suddenly in midsummer, and the Democrats replaced him with state Sen. Betty Roberts, who had just lost the 1974 gubernatorial primary. Roberts benefited from statewide name recognition and a good campaign organization, but she also had a large debt from her bid for governor. Packwood worked hard to insulate himself from Watergate in the year of Nixon's resignation. He was sharply critical of the departed president and objected to the pardon he got from President Gerald R. Ford. It was enough to earn him 55 percent in a terrible Republican year.

In 1980, Packwood found himself targeted by anti-abortion groups. There was talk of a $200,000 "right to life" drive to unseat him in the primary. The immediate effect of this rumor was to help Packwood mobilize abortion rights supporters. In the primary, two conservative GOP opponents spent most of their time fighting each other, and Packwood won handily.

In the general election, Packwood's campaign finances became a central issue. Democrat Ted Kulongoski, a state senator, charged that Packwood was trying to buy the election and was also profiting handsomely from speaking engagement fees. Labor had trouble making up its mind, with the state AFL-CIO backing Kulongoski against the wishes of its executive council, which recommended no endorsement. Packwood drew the support of the building trade unions in Portland.

With a nearly 8-to-1 financial advantage and a strong national Republican tide, Packwood won, though Kulongoski and one minor candidate held him to 52 percent of the vote.

Packwood responded to his mediocre 1980 finish by embarking on a nationwide fundraising effort for 1986. His direct-mail strategy targeted feminists, pro-Israel voters and other activists who supported his policy stands. Adding in a healthy dose of business-related PAC money, Packwood raised more than $6 million before the campaign year began.

Packwood returned to Oregon and blitzed the airwaves with a media campaign that his primary opponent, Joe Lutz, a Portland preacher and anti-abortion activist, could not match. Packwood prevailed, but his below-60 percent tally again suggested vulnerability.

The Democratic primary winner, 4th District Rep. James Weaver, was an aggressive populist and a caustic critic of Packwood's support of Reagan defense policies and his alleged ties to special interests. But a House ethics investigation into campaign finances from earlier House campaigns cut Weaver's effort short. In August, he unexpectedly announced on the eve of his testimony that he was withdrawing from the Senate race.

Scrambling to choose a replacement for Weaver, state Democrats settled on state Rep. Rick Bauman, who earlier in the year had finished last in the three-man Senate primary. Though Bauman, a personable liberal, was respected by his state House colleagues, he lacked name recognition and money. The last obstacle to Packwood's re-election disappeared when Lutz decided not to run as a write-in candidate.

Committees

Finance (Ranking)
International Trade; Medicare & Long Term Care; Taxation

Commerce, Science & Transportation (2nd of 9 Republicans)
Communications (ranking); Foreign Commerce & Tourism; National Ocean Policy Study; Surface Transportation

Joint Taxation

Elections

1992 General		
Bob Packwood (R)	717,455	(53%)
Les AuCoin (D)	639,851	(47%)
1992 Primary		
Bob Packwood (R)	176,939	(59%)
John DeZell (R)	61,128	(20%)
Stephanie Jones Salvey (R)	27,088	(9%)
Randy Prince (R)	20,358	(7%)
Valentine Christian (R)	10,501	(4%)

Previous Winning Percentages: **1986** (63%) **1980** (52%) **1974** (55%) **1968** (50%)

Campaign Finance

	Receipts	Receipts from PACs		Expend-itures
1992				
Packwood (R)	$5,804,130	$1,275,128	(22%)	$6,078,359
AuCoin (D)	$2,293,658	$775,502	(34%)	$2,629,397

Key Votes

1993	
Require unpaid family and medical leave	Y
Approve national "motor voter" registration bill	Y
Approve budget increasing taxes and reducing deficit	N
Support president's right to lift military gay ban	Y
1992	
Approve school-choice pilot program	Y
Allow shifting funds from defense to domestic programs	Y
Oppose deeper cuts in spending for SDI	Y
1991	
Approve waiting period for handgun purchases	Y
Raise senators' pay and ban honoraria	N
Authorize use of force in Persian Gulf	Y
Confirm Clarence Thomas to Supreme Court	N

Voting Studies

	Presidential Support		Party Unity		Conservative Coalition	
Year	**S**	**O**	**S**	**O**	**S**	**O**
1992	60	37	50	49	50	47
1991	68	31	59	40	75	23
1990	56	41	45	53	51	46
1989	79	18	55	43	79	18
1988	58	40	41	56	54	46
1987	53	45	56	40	38	50
1986	49	45	58	36	63	30
1985	72	25	67	26	63	28
1984	65	27	58	36	62	32
1983	66	24	56	35	50	41
1982	75	24	67	32	59	40
1981	86	13	80	16	71	25

Interest Group Ratings

Year	ADA	AFL-CIO	CCUS	ACU
1992	60	50	30	33
1991	50	67	60	43
1990	72	44	42	35
1989	30	60	57	61
1988	55	64	57	40
1987	60	80	61	31
1986	60	40	58	33
1985	35	43	66	40
1984	60	40	56	33
1983	30	31	47	30
1982	55	58	52	30
1981	35	21	94	47

1 Elizabeth Furse (D)

Of Hillsboro — Elected 1992; 1st Term

Born: Oct. 13, 1936, Nairobi, Kenya.
Education: Evergreen State College, B.A. 1974.
Occupation: Community activist.
Family: Husband, John C. Platt; two children.
Religion: Protestant.
Political Career: No previous office.
Capitol Office: 316 Cannon Bldg. 20515; 225-0855.

The Path to Washington: Running in a political year alternately dubbed the "Year of the Outsider" and the "Year of the Woman," Furse, a liberal community activist waging her first bid for political office, could claim proprietorship over both themes in her primary and general-election races against politically connected men. She is the first Oregon woman in the House since Democrat Edith Green, who served from 1955 to 1974.

Furse's win retained Democratic control of the 1st, which had been held for 18 years by Les AuCoin. AuCoin lost a ferocious Senate battle to Republican Sen. Bob Packwood. Redistricting made the already marginal 1st more Republican.

Born in Kenya, Furse grew up in South Africa, working with her mother, the founder of a women's anti-apartheid group in the 1950s. In the United States, Furse worked as a community organizer in Watts during the 1960s and on behalf of the northwestern Indians during the 1970s. (She became a U.S. citizen in 1972.) In 1986, she founded the Oregon Peace Institute, a group that tries to resolve conflict through non-violence.

Furse demonstrated political abilities that belied her neophyte status, enabling her to outflank her primary opponent, lobbyist and former congressional aide Gary Conkling, in fundraising and organization. And she proved herself capable of competing with a 24-year veteran of state government with her victory in November over Tony Meeker, the state treasurer.

Although she had never sought office, Furse had developed skills that would serve her well in the political realm. Years of activism and organizing gave her numerous opportunities to hone her speaking style and to cultivate allies.

And Furse thrived in an area of conventional politicking — fundraising — thanks in part to a February endorsement from the women's political group EMILY's List.

Democrats privately criticized Conkling's effort as disorganized and listless. In the final weeks of the campaign, however, he went on the attack, releasing Furse's voting record since 1984. It showed that she had voted in only six of 34 elections. Furse challenged the accuracy of some of the records. But the controversy failed to slow Furse, who took a 60 percent to 40 percent win.

The contest between Furse and Meeker presented one of the nation's most interesting political matchups. Few districts in the country hosted a highly competitive House race with opponents so ideologically distinct and with such disparate backgrounds.

Meeker, a longstanding opponent of abortion, in no way sought to obscure his lengthy service in government: His campaign résumé was titled, "Tony Meeker: A Profile of Experience."

Meeker had sought the 1st District seat in 1986, when, as minority leader of the state Senate, he challenged AuCoin. A well-regarded state legislator, Meeker sought to appeal to moderate Republicans and independents by stressing his work on such issues as protecting women from employment discrimination and banning no-return bottles.

But his sponsorship of an anti-abortion initiative caused many independents and Republicans to slam the door on his House bid. AuCoin rolled up a surprisingly one-sided victory, winning by 23 percentage points.

In the 1992 contest, Furse contrasted her support for abortion rights with Meeker's position; in moderate-to-liberal Portland and vicinity, past results on ballot questions showed that voters were more likely to side with Furse on abortion rights. And Meeker had to contend with unfavorable publicity surrounding his office: A former Treasury real estate manager had pleaded guilty to racketeering.

The district's widely diverse constituency includes loggers, environmentalists and high-tech entrepreneurs who have settled in a region around Portland known as the "Silicon Forest."

Once in Washington, Furse was placed on three committees: Armed Services; Banking, Finance and Urban Affairs; and Merchant Marine and Fisheries. Early in the 103rd Congress, she initiated an effort to change the name of the last to the "Committee on Marine Affairs and Environmental Policy." Roll Call reported her saying that the old name did not adequately convey what the committee does.

Oregon 1

Western Portland and suburbs

The Portland-based 1st starts on the western bank of the Willamette River, which splits Oregon's largest city. The district's urban component is downtown Portland and nearby city neighborhoods that tend to be liberal and affluent; to the west are fast-growing Republican suburbs.

Metropolitan Portland has drawn California exiles and other out-of-staters searching for "livability" — less congestion, a moderate cost of living, a big city that still has a sense of community. Portlanders flock downtown to Saturday Market beneath the Burnside Bridge and attend events in Pioneer Courthouse Square and Waterfront Park. Each June the "City of Roses" hosts its popular Rose Festival.

In the past two decades, businesses and people have streamed into the suburbs west of Portland. The 1st is dominated by suburban Washington County; with 312,000 people, it is the state's second-most-populous county. Washington was the state's fastest-growing county in the 1980s; its population increased almost 27 percent. Suburban growth and 1991 redistricting have amplified the 1st's GOP element. During remapping, Republicans lobbied hard to include in the 1st the GOP-heavy Clackamas County city of Lake Oswego.

The high-tech businesses that sprouted along U.S. 26 in Washington County during the 1980s suffered a decline, leaving empty office space; the high-tech industry now appears to be on the rebound. Still, bedroom communities of Portland such as Beaverton, Tigard and Hillsboro, once modest in size, have become satellite cities with their own economies. Electronics and computer companies such as Textronix, Intel and Mentor Graphics provide thousands of jobs. Nike, the sports-shoe manufacturer, has its futuristic headquarters in Beaverton. Portland's light-rail line is slated to connect the downtown with Hillsboro, 18 miles to the west, by the mid-1990s.

Republicans outnumber Democrats in suburban Washington County. But the Republicans here are some of the most liberal in the country, and they are more than willing to cast split ballots.

Outside the Portland metropolitan area, the 1st becomes rural and more Democratic. The fishing and logging counties of Columbia and Clatsop are the strongest Democratic areas of the 1st outside Portland, although many of those Democrats are more conservative than Portland's affluent liberals. Columbia County has voted for every Democratic presidential nominee since 1932; Clatsop County went for Adlai E. Stevenson in 1956 and has remained in the Democratic column for president.

Both the logging and salmon industries are threatened by court action enforcing the Endangered Species Act. The last of the big canneries closed in Astoria in the mid-1980s. Tourism buoys the local economy of some coastal communities, such as Seaside and Cannon Beach. Oregon's modest wine industry is centered in the Tualatin and northern Willamette valleys of Yamhill County, which tends to vote Republican.

1990 Population: 568,461. White 529,999 (93%), Black 4,498 (1%), Other 33,964 (6%). Hispanic origin 22,569 (4%). 18 and over 425,695 (75%), 62 and over 78,899 (14%). Median age: 34.

Committees

Armed Services (33rd of 34 Democrats)
Research & Technology

Banking, Finance & Urban Affairs (22nd of 30 Democrats)
Consumer Credit & Insurance; Housing & Community Development

Merchant Marine & Fisheries (17th of 29 Democrats)
Environment & Natural Resources; Merchant Marine

Campaign Finance

	Receipts	Receipts from PACs		Expenditures
1992				
Furse (D)	$785,545	$186,049	(24%)	$778,290
Meeker (R)	$723,936	$320,585	(44%)	$719,611

Key Votes

1993

Require parental notification of minors' abortions	N
Require unpaid family and medical leave	Y
Approve national "motor voter" registration bill	Y
Approve budget increasing taxes and reducing deficit	Y
Approve economic stimulus plan	Y

Elections

1992 General		
Elizabeth Furse (D)	152,917	(52%)
Tony Meeker (R)	140,986	(48%)
1992 Primary		
Elizabeth Furse (D)	38,600	(60%)
Gary Conkling (D)	25,684	(40%)

District Vote for President

1992

D 103,190 (41%)
R 86,699 (34%)
I 64,043 (25%)

2 Bob Smith (R)

Of Burns — Elected 1982; 6th Term

Born: June 16, 1931, Portland, Ore.
Education: Willamette U., B.A. 1953.
Occupation: Cattle rancher; businessman.
Family: Wife, Kaye Tomlinson; three children.
Religion: Presbyterian.
Political Career: Ore. House, 1961-73, speaker, 1969-73; Ore. Senate, 1973-83, minority leader, 1977-83.
Capitol Office: 108 Cannon Bldg. 20515; 225-6730.

In Washington: After a decade in Congress, Smith has demonstrated that he is first and foremost a creature of Oregon, not of Capitol Hill. His focus is firmly on his district and state; he fiercely defends the interests of Oregon's cattle ranchers and is one of the House's leading timber industry advocates.

In fact, speculation in early 1993 had Smith taking his homestate emphasis home in the form of a campaign for governor in 1994. Some thought he might have grown tired of being a minority-party backbencher, especially one who arrived too old to climb the GOP leadership ladder.

Smith's Oregon credentials are many. He served more than 20 years in Oregon's legislature, including stints as House Speaker and Senate minority leader. Now, as the lone Republican remaining in Oregon's House delegation, Smith is apt to make even more friends as a champion for the needs of industries throughout the state.

Having shown he can make a mark on policy on the Agriculture Committee, Smith broadened his interests by joining Interior (now Natural Resources) in 1989 — after first winning party permission to serve on both panels.

Smith believes government should give free enterprise wide latitude. His antipathy toward federal regulation and involvement defines his role on Natural Resources, where Smith tempers his concern for the outdoors with his attention to Oregon's vital timber industry.

The biggest recent threat to timber jobs in the Northwest has been the movement to restrict logging in ancient "old growth" forests to protect the threatened northern spotted owl.

In that debate and others, Smith fits right in on the GOP side of the Natural Resources Committee, where most of his party colleagues share his "Sagebrush Rebellion" antagonism toward federal government encroachment. When he joined the committee, all but two of its 14 Republicans were from states west of the Missouri River.

Shortly into his first year on the panel, Smith triggered a GOP walkout during committee consideration of a bill to set up a $1 billion-a-year trust fund to buy land for parks, wildlife preserves, forests and historic sites. A Smith amendment forbade using the money from the trust fund to buy land unless the seller was willing. He said the intent was to protect private lands from federal condemnation.

Tempers rose as Democrats rejected Republican arguments for the amendment. Smith warned that Western members were "very sensitive" on the question of condemnation. "I guarantee you," he said, "if you want an East-West fight ... this is an East-West fight." The amendment was rejected 14-24, and the Republicans got up and left. Though the bill never advanced beyond the committee, the issue of "fair takings" has remained important to Smith.

On another matter, Smith worked with Minnesota Democrat Bruce F. Vento to win passage of Smith's bill to create a 56,000-acre national volcanic monument at Newberry Crater in the Deschutes National Forest. A local committee that included environmentalists, hunters, geothermal energy interests, timber interests and the federal government helped Smith forge an agreement on the designation. The bill, which included an exchange of geothermal leases with an energy company, was signed into law in 1990.

In 1988, Smith was the only Oregon member to oppose a landmark river-protection bill for his state. His objections were not eased until the House tacked on a section authorizing construction of Oregon's Umatilla Basin water project. In the 101st Congress, he steadfastly opposed a move by Oregon Democrat Peter A. DeFazio to add a portion of the upper Klamath River to the federal Wild and Scenic Rivers system. The measure would have blocked construction of a hydroelectric plant in Smith's district. Smith lobbied House members, showering them with "Dear Colleague" letters. He succeeded: The bill did not even make it to the floor.

For years, Smith has fought efforts to impose higher fees on ranchers who graze their

Oregon 2

East and Southwest — Medford; Bend

The 2nd is enormous, covering more than two-thirds of Oregon and bordering Washington, Idaho, Nevada and California. It is the state's most reliably Republican district, and the only one George Bush carried in 1992.

For the most part, people in the 2nd work the land, whether that means timber, livestock, crops or fruit. In a district where the federal government owns three-quarters of the land, loggers' jobs ride on court action restricting timber harvesting in national forests. Fishermen who make their living catching salmon on the Columbia River have also been snagged by endangered-species action.

Jack rabbits outnumber voters in the 2nd; any House candidate has to focus on a few widely scattered population centers. Although the district's two most-populous counties, Jackson and Deschutes, both registered double-digit growth in the 1980s, most of the counties in the 2nd lost population during the last decade.

With about 47,000 people, Medford (Jackson County) is the largest city in the 2nd. Medford is surrounded by pear, cherry and apple orchards of the fruit-growing Rogue River Valley. Less than 20 miles southeast of Medford is Ashland, which has hosted the Oregon Shakespeare Festival since 1935, drawing more than 400,000 visitors annually from February through October.

Population in Deschutes County has soared since 1970, as nearby skiing areas lured people to build summer homes and vacation condominiums. In 1986, Democratic gubernatorial candidate Neil Goldschmidt referred to Bend, the county's population center, as "the middle of nowhere"; in the ensuing four years, Deschutes grew faster than any other county in the state. Its 21 percent growth during the 1980s was behind only the 27 percent of Washington County, in Portland's suburbs in the 1st District.

Bend has attracted high-tech and light industry, emblematic of central Oregon's effort to diversify its economy and reduce its dependence on timber. Deschutes County also grows potatoes, mint and hay.

Jackson and Deschutes both tend to prefer Republican candidates. Although Bush lost both in 1992, GOP Sen. Bob Packwood carried both comfortably in his tough re-election battle.

Beef cattle graze on public land throughout eastern Oregon. Alfalfa and hay grow on the dry, thinly settled plateau. In the north, most people live along or near the irrigated Columbia River Valley, where wheat ripens on steep golden hillsides. Umatilla is the No. 2 wheat-harvesting county in the nation. Pears, cherries and apples grow near Hood River, a popular wind-surfing destination. Potatoes are grown and processed for export around Hermiston. Near Hermiston is the Umatilla Ordnance Depot, where the Army stores an estimated 5,200 tons of World War I- and II-era nerve and mustard gas weapons, destined for incineration.

1990 Population: 568,464. White 532,857 (94%), Black 1,658 (<1%), Other 33,949 (6%). Hispanic origin 30,470 (5%). 18 and over 418,063 (74%), 62 and over 106,398 (19%). Median age: 36.

cattle on public lands. A rancher himself, Smith characterized one amendment, sponsored by Oklahoma Democrat Mike Synar, as an attack by environmentalists who wanted to drive livestock operators out of business.

"Eliminate the livestock," Smith said. "Eliminate the timber industry with the spotted owl. Eliminate the sheep industry in this country. Let us vote for the Synar amendment and eliminate all of us." Despite Western members' entreaties, the House adopted the amendment by a wide margin as part of the fiscal 1991 Interior appropriations bill. Conferees, however, stripped it from the final bill.

Already past 50 when he came to Congress, Smith started his House career knowing he would never be the power in Washington that he was in Salem. But he soon began looking to escape the status of middle-aged minority backbencher.

The route he found was his relationship with Edward Madigan of Illinois, the shrewd senior Republican on Agriculture who became secretary of Agriculture in 1991. As the panel began writing the 1985 farm bill, Smith offered Madigan strategy ideas — and Madigan realized there was a good deal to be learned from a man with 25 years of legislative experience. Eventually, Smith joined Madigan at agriculture conferences with Republican Bob Dole of Kansas, the Senate's key farm-policy voice.

Smith has earned respect from his committee colleagues for his grasp of the cost of programs as well as for his political skills. He tends to the wheat growers and cattlemen of his sprawling district, advocating ways to reduce foreign barriers to U.S. exports. Early in the 102nd Congress, Smith took over the ranking position on Agriculture's Subcommittee on Conservation, Credit and Rural Development.

Founder and co-chairman of the House beef caucus, Smith often serves as a liaison with Western cattle producers — which can put him at cross-purposes with dairy interests. During work on the 1985 farm bill, he was upset with a proposal to reduce dairy surpluses by slaughtering dairy cows (thus adding to the supply of beef). Fearing the plan would drive down meat prices, Smith pushed for language requiring the government to buy surplus meat for schools and for the military.

At Home: Redistricting in 1981 gave Smith an opening to move to Congress. When GOP Rep. Denny Smith chose to run in the newly created 5th, eastern Oregon's rural, sprawling, conservative 2nd was left without an incumbent.

Stressing his legislative experience as Republican leader of the state Senate and Speaker of the Oregon House, Smith easily won his primary. The surprise Democratic primary winner was Larryann Willis, a rancher and Democratic National Committee member.

Trusting in opinion polls that showed him leading, Smith stayed clear of Willis. She tried to provoke Smith; when he refused to debate, she challenged him to a steer-roping contest, but he refused that, too.

Accustomed to easy campaigns in his safe legislative district, Smith had some difficulty adjusting to a hotly contested election. His organization was embarrassed when a poorly planned fundraiser featuring Bob Hope drew a sparse crowd and actually lost money.

But Smith reassured rural voters with his opposition to designating more wilderness in Oregon, and he convinced others that Willis was a liberal because she advocated deferring the third phase of the Reagan income-tax cut. Smith took 56 percent, beat Willis in a 1984 rematch and has won in each election year since.

Committees

Agriculture (5th of 18 Republicans)
Department Operations (ranking); General Farm Commodities; Livestock

Natural Resources (5th of 15 Republicans)
Oversight & Investigations (ranking); National Parks, Forests & Public Lands

Elections

1992 General		
Bob Smith (R)	184,163	(67%)
Denzel Ferguson (D)	90,036	(33%)
1990 General		
Bob Smith (R)	127,998	(68%)
Jim Smiley (D)	60,131	(32%)

Previous Winning Percentages: **1988** (63%) **1986** (60%) **1984** (57%) **1982** (56%)

District Vote for President

1992
D 97,672 (35%)
R 106,839 (38%)
I 74,539 (27%)

Campaign Finance

	Receipts	Receipts from PACs		Expend-itures
1992				
Smith (R)	$462,680	$165,725	(36%)	$401,670
Ferguson (D)	$87,850	$8,550	(10%)	$87,361
1990				
Smith (R)	$374,114	$148,953	(40%)	$284,700

Key Votes

1993	
Require parental notification of minors' abortions	Y
Require unpaid family and medical leave	N
Approve national "motor voter" registration bill	N
Approve budget increasing taxes and reducing deficit	N
Approve economic stimulus plan	N
1992	
Approve balanced-budget constitutional amendment	Y
Close down space station program	N
Approve U.S. aid for former Soviet Union	N
Allow shifting funds from defense to domestic programs	N
1991	
Extend unemployment benefits using deficit financing	Y
Approve waiting period for handgun purchases	N
Authorize use of force in Persian Gulf	Y

Voting Studies

	Presidential Support		Party Unity		Conservative Coalition	
Year	S	O	S	O	S	O
1992	84	14	93	5	90	8
1991	78	19	88	10	95	5
1990	66	34	91	9	96	4
1989	79	21	89	9	88	12
1988	66	33	91	8	92	8
1987	57	40	77	15	84	14
1986	66	31	82	13	86	12
1985	63	33	82	14	84	11
1984	53	38	70	20	83	14
1983	71	21	74	8	90	7

Interest Group Ratings

Year	ADA	AFL-CIO	CCUS	ACU
1992	5	25	75	92
1991	5	17	90	85
1990	6	8	93	88
1989	10	17	100	79
1988	5	21	86	92
1987	24	19	86	64
1986	5	14	100	82
1985	20	12	90	75
1984	10	8	75	71
1983	0	12	82	85

3 Ron Wyden (D)

Of Portland — Elected 1980; 7th Term

Born: May 3, 1949, Wichita, Kan.
Education: Stanford U., A.B. 1971; U. of Oregon, J.D. 1974.
Occupation: Lawyer; professor.
Family: Wife, Laurie Oseran; two children.
Religion: Jewish.
Political Career: No previous office.
Capitol Office: 1111 Longworth Bldg. 20515; 225-4811.

In Washington: Wyden has a knack for seizing topics that dominate coffee shop talk and beauty parlor chatter across the nation. Issues such as faulty liposuction and success rates at fertility clinics have put him on the talk-show circuit more than once, prompting critics inside the Beltway to say he prefers grabbing headlines to tackling tough issues.

But if more senior members look askance at Wyden's television-age approach to policy-making, his ability to generate attention for sometimes obscure crusades has enabled him to build a hefty résumé of legislative accomplishments.

During the years of Presidents Ronald Reagan and George Bush, the unabashedly liberal Wyden worked the margins, content to chip away where his nature would have preferred to overhaul. Now, operating in the friendlier climate of a Democratic administration, Wyden is well-armed for an all-out assault on what he considers the evils of the day. And he is well-placed to work alongside Chairman John D. Dingell of Michigan on the powerful Oversight and Investigations Subcommittee of the Energy and Commerce Committee.

Given the dwindling supply of federal dollars, the regulatory arena may give liberals such as Wyden their best opportunities.

To date, Wyden's ability to use the media tools at hand in a persistent and imaginative way has produced a string of new laws in areas a more conventional legislator might not tackle. In the 102nd Congress alone, he helped pass laws setting standards for fertility clinics, protecting Department of Energy workers who report safety violations, and devising a strategy to conserve the Pacific yew, a tree that produces the cancer-fighting drug taxol.

Early in the 103rd Congress, Wyden was tapped to draft environmental protections for the North American Free Trade Agreement. While the request from Democratic leaders acknowledged Wyden's ability to pursue a single issue, it also hinted that Wyden might be left out of broader decision-making on the agreement.

Like NAFTA, the ongoing health-care debate will challenge Wyden to extend himself. After trying unsuccessfully with the Bush administration, Wyden and other prominent Oregon politicians persuaded the Clinton administration to provide necessary waivers for the so-called Oregon Plan, a Medicaid rationing program that eliminates some services in order to provide basic coverage to more people. The plan is sometimes characterized as "health-care rationing."

On other medical issues, Wyden advocates managed competition, access to the controversial French abortion pill RU-486 and stricter price controls on prescription drugs.

Perhaps his most significant legislative accomplishment in the 102nd was passage of a bill that provides malpractice insurance to federally funded health clinics. The centers in turn will have the money to care for an additional 500,000 patients each year.

In the 101st, working with Sen. Tom Daschle of South Dakota, Wyden pushed through stringent federal controls on so-called Medigap insurance, private policies designed to cover services not included by Medicare. The Medigap bill passed as part of the omnibus budget bill of 1990, as did another Wyden initiative on drug purchasing for state Medicaid programs. That law requires drug companies to sell to Medicaid at the same discounts they offer their best private customers.

Working under two of the most proficient legislators in the House, Dingell and Democrat Henry A. Waxman of California, chairman of the Health Subcommittee, Wyden has honed his own skills while cultivating invaluable friendships.

In 1987, as chairman of the Small Business Subcommittee on Regulation, Business Opportunity and Energy, Wyden applied Dingell's technique of holding high-profile hearings to investigate the cosmetics industry, plastic surgeons and diet companies.

The subcommittee has also found occasion to probe the issues of medical waste, child care and computer crime, and has given Wyden a forum for airing the Northwest's concerns. In

Oregon 3

East and North Portland and eastern suburbs

Socially and politically, Portland is two cities. East of the Willamette River, in the 3rd, Portland is a working-class town. Blue-collar neighborhoods abut middle-class suburbs. The section west of the river is generally more affluent and elegant.

In an area with little cultural diversity — the Portland metropolitan area is more than 90 percent white — northeast and southeast Portland are veritable melting pots. The Albina section is home to many of Portland's blacks; it is the poorest area in the city. There are also Asian and Hispanic communities east of the river. Some young white professionals live in the Irvington, Alameda and Laurelhurst sections of East Portland.

Democratic candidates take comfortable margins in the 3rd, thanks to blacks in the Albina section, blue-collar whites in North Portland and the many elderly residents of the east side.

But many voters in the 3rd are conservative, white working-class "Reagan Democrats," particularly in such areas as the St. Johns section of North Portland, East County, the Clackamas County suburb of Milwaukie, and the cities of Gresham and Troutdale east of Portland.

New to the 3rd for the 1990s is a section west of the Willamette River in southwest Portland that includes the large homes and winding streets of Dunthorpe, one of Portland's most expensive neighborhoods. Democrats are few and far between here, but the small number of Republican voters in this area does not alter the 3rd's overall Democratic cast.

While Portland's commercial center remains west of the Willamette, the city has been investing of late in some east side projects. The Lloyd Center, one of the country's oldest urban malls, has had significant renovation. The Oregon Museum of Science and Industry has moved from southwest Portland to a new, larger east side home under the Marquam Bridge. Pro basketball's Portland Trail Blazers are expected to move into a larger east side arena at the new Oregon Convention Center in the mid-1990s.

Over the last decade there was growth in the east side suburbs of Multnomah County, a few of which are as sumptuous as the in-town residential areas west of the Willamette. Gresham, the eastern terminus of Portland's light-rail line, is the largest of the 3rd's suburban cities.

Gresham tripled in size during the 1970s and grew in the 1980s to a population of 68,200; it is now Oregon's fourth-largest city. Gresham's annual Mount Hood Festival of Jazz draws national and international artists each August.

Once outside the suburbs, Multnomah and Clackamas counties quickly turn rural. There are a few farms along the Columbia River, the 3rd's northern boundary. Visitors to the underwater viewing room at the Bonneville Lock and Dam can observe migrating fish ascending a fish ladder.

Mount Hood National Forest occupies most of the district's eastern part.

1990 Population: 568,465. White 496,062 (87%), Black 33,709 (6%), Other 38,694 (7%). Hispanic origin 17,946 (3%). 18 and over 428,542 (75%), 62 and over 90,244 (16%). Median age: 34.

1988, his hearings on Canadian plywood tariffs led to a written assurance from the Reagan administration that the federal government would fight this trade barrier. In the 103rd, he set the subcommittee's sights on revamping the Small Business Administration and promoting self-employment programs for the unemployed.

As legislators wrestled with the AIDS problem in the 100th Congress, Wyden's subcommittee held hearings exposing quality control problems in labs testing for the deadly disease. As the debate expanded to problems at unregulated physician-run labs conducting Pap tests for cervical cancer — recommended annually for all women — the hearings gained widespread publicity and became a springboard for successful legislation offered by Dingell and Wyden to crack down on the labs.

The two do not always agree like this, but Wyden gives the chairman as many votes as he can. As Wyden tells it, when he first joined Energy and Commerce in 1981, he went straight to Dingell to tell him he could not support his efforts to weaken the Clean Air Act — but that he would try to help whenever he could. This candor formed the basis of what has been a productive relationship.

His ties to Waxman date back to the 1982 Clean Air debate, when Wyden became a key figure in an alliance of liberals opposed to a Dingell-backed effort to relax pollution controls. The environmentalist faction scored a major victory with Wyden's amendment to keep tight controls in areas that met air quality standards.

At Home: The main imponderable about

Wyden is if and when he will mount a bid for higher office. He has passed three times on a chance at the Senate, declining to challenge Republican incumbents Bob Packwood in 1986 or 1992 or Mark O. Hatfield in 1990.

Instead, Wyden seems content to bide his time. "What's wrong with being a senator at 50?" his father and informal adviser, Peter Wyden, has been quoted as saying. With the departure of 1st District Democrat Les AuCoin, who ran unsuccessfully against Packwood in 1992, Wyden is now the senior member of Oregon's House delegation.

Electorally secure in his staunchly Democratic district, Wyden has not had a tough race since he first won the seat in 1980. In that year, he began with a high Portland profile as executive director of the state's Gray Panthers, an organization promoting senior citizens' interests.

In taking on incumbent Democrat Robert Duncan, Wyden relied on a sizable volunteer force made up of senior citizens, environmentalists and other young urban liberals like himself. He charged that Duncan's record on mass transit, housing and heating cost issues was not sensitive enough to urban needs in the 1980s.

Duncan, a more traditional labor Democrat, had loyal supporters in the district's working-class neighborhoods. But Wyden cut into that base by winning some union endorsements that had routinely gone to Duncan in earlier elections.

While Wyden campaigned full time for several months, Duncan tended to his work in Washington and mostly ignored his opponent. Wyden took 60 percent of the vote to win the primary comfortably. He won an even larger vote share in November.

Committees

Energy & Commerce (9th of 27 Democrats)
Health & the Environment; Oversight & Investigations; Telecommunications & Finance

Small Business (5th of 27 Democrats)
Regulation, Business Opportunities & Technology (chairman)

Joint Economic

Elections

1992 General		
Ron Wyden (D)	208,028	(77%)
Al Ritter (R)	50,235	(19%)
Blair Bobier (LIBERT)	11,413	(4%)
1990 General		
Ron Wyden (D)	169,731	(81%)
Philip E. Mooney (R)	40,216	(19%)

Previous Winning Percentages: **1988** (99%) **1986** (86%) **1984** (72%) **1982** (78%) **1980** (72%)

District Vote for President

1992
D 146,835 (53%)
R 72,338 (26%)
I 58,900 (21%)

Campaign Finance

	Receipts	Receipts from PACs		Expenditures
1992				
Wyden (D)	$229,749	$123,675	(54%)	$357,402
Ritter (R)	$6,660	$521	(8%)	$3,036
1990				
Wyden (D)	$708,598	$341,242	(48%)	$693,855
Mooney (R)	$5,739	0		$4,436

Key Votes

1993	
Require parental notification of minors' abortions	N
Require unpaid family and medical leave	Y
Approve national "motor voter" registration bill	Y
Approve budget increasing taxes and reducing deficit	Y
Approve economic stimulus plan	Y
1992	
Approve balanced-budget constitutional amendment	N
Close down space station program	Y
Approve U.S. aid for former Soviet Union	Y
Allow shifting funds from defense to domestic programs	Y
1991	
Extend unemployment benefits using deficit financing	Y
Approve waiting period for handgun purchases	Y
Authorize use of force in Persian Gulf	N

Voting Studies

	Presidential Support		Party Unity		Conservative Coalition	
Year	**S**	**O**	**S**	**O**	**S**	**O**
1992	17	81	90	8	19	79
1991	31	68	94	5	24	73
1990	24	76	94	6	22	78
1989	27	69	91	7	20	80
1988	29	70	87	13	34	66
1987	18	79	89	8	23	77
1986	23	76	89	11	38	62
1985	26	74	84	14	36	64
1984	25	75	88	12	20	80
1983	13	85	91	8	15	84
1982	30	69	92	7	8	90
1981	26	68	83	10	12	85

Interest Group Ratings

Year	ADA	AFL-CIO	CCUS	ACU
1992	95	73	25	0
1991	85	83	30	5
1990	89	92	29	4
1989	80	82	50	18
1988	90	86	43	16
1987	84	81	14	9
1986	80	79	28	14
1985	60	71	59	29
1984	95	62	31	8
1983	90	82	35	9
1982	95	95	18	18
1981	100	87	6	13

4 Peter A. DeFazio (D)

Of Springfield — Elected 1986; 4th Term

Born: May 27, 1947, Needham, Mass.
Education: Tufts U., B.A. 1969; U. of Oregon, 1969-71, M.S. 1977.
Military Service: Air Force, 1967-71.
Occupation: Congressional aide.
Family: Wife, Myrnie L. Daut.
Religion: Roman Catholic.
Political Career: Lane County Commission, 1982-86.
Capitol Office: 1233 Longworth Bldg. 20515; 225-6416.

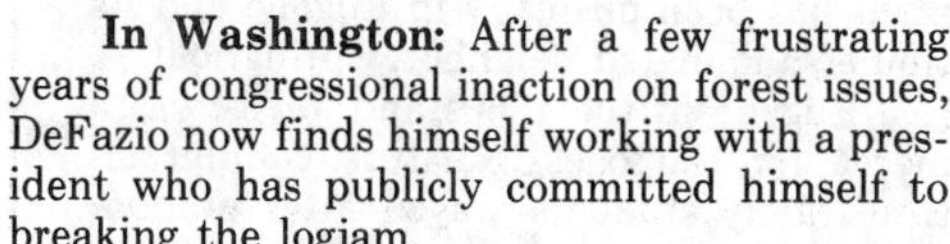

In Washington: After a few frustrating years of congressional inaction on forest issues, DeFazio now finds himself working with a president who has publicly committed himself to breaking the logjam.

The new attention from the White House is good news for DeFazio. His populist, activist approach has landed him some significant roles on issues of vital concern to the Northwest, such as banning the export of unprocessed logs and protecting "old growth" forests that are the habitat of the threatened northern spotted owl. It has led him to broaden his political outlook; he took a long look at running for the Senate in 1992 — and he is likely to do so again.

But his approach also has alienated some of his colleagues; they say DeFazio's independence has angered the Democratic leadership on occasion, including in his first term when he took the House floor and denounced the administration of the Ways and Means Committee.

DeFazio's self-guided tendencies may help explain why his ambitions to win a seat on the Budget Committee have been thwarted. Although he votes a large majority of the time with his party, he is prone to go his own way on the votes that matter most to leadership.

In the 101st Congress, he opposed the 1989 pay raise and ethics rules revision as well as the 1990 budget summit plan.

In the 100th Congress, he was one of 48 Democrats to vote against a deficit-reduction package calling for a $12 billion tax increase. "I think the bill's a turkey," he said. "It was presented as a test of faith in leadership. I am a strong supporter of leadership in the House, but they made a mistake on this bill."

Like fellow Oregon Democrat Ron Wyden (and former member Les AuCoin), DeFazio is a legislative activist, and he has found opportunity to act serving on the Public Works and Interior (now Natural Resources) committees. Thanks in part to his background as a congressional staffer, he is one of the more knowledgeable members on timber and energy issues.

In the 102nd Congress, DeFazio wrote a substitute to House Interior Chairman George Miller's forest bill. It called for a "managed old growth" compromise between unlimited logging and undisturbed wilderness. For his efforts, DeFazio was excoriated by both loggers and environmentalists, both of whom tagged the bill as extreme. The substitute went nowhere, as did all other efforts at a forest bill.

DeFazio also was active in a successful effort to expand the Wild and Scenic Rivers Act, extending protection to 1,400 miles of Oregon's rivers.

In the spotted owl debate, the most bedeviling Northwest issue of recent years, DeFazio has emphasized caution. His district has more old-growth forest than any other; the listing of the owl as a threatened species by the Fish and Wildlife Service has curtailed logging in its habitat. DeFazio introduced a compromise bill calling for alternatives to mitigate the listing's impact. The bill had five Northwestern cosponsors but did not advance beyond subcommittee level.

The Public Works Committee, which is used to bipartisan logrolling, served DeFazio as a forum for verbal assaults on the Bush administration. He greeted the administration's 1990 transportation policy initiative with derision. "This is a Twinkie transportation policy. Airy and light with nothing but fluff at the core. I sincerely hope it will have a shorter shelf life."

DeFazio took an active interest in the airline industry's financial woes. He introduced a bill to limit the leveraged-buyout acquisitions of airlines. The House, reacting to takeovers by Frank Lorenzo and Donald J. Trump, overwhelmingly approved a similar bill, but it languished in the Senate, threatened with a veto.

He also pushed for a bill to force the Bush administration to intervene in the management dispute between Eastern Airlines and its unions. President Bush, he said, "did nothing" to avert Eastern's bankruptcy.

In the 102nd Congress, DeFazio teamed up with Massachusetts Democratic Rep. Barney Frank and delayed consideration of the urban aid bill for two days to press the case for "notch

Oregon 4

Southwest — Eugene

Loggers, fishermen and environmentalists combine to give the 4th a potentially combustible political mix.

Many of the district's communities are dependent on the wood-products industry; others make their living in salmon fishing. But more than half the district vote is cast in Lane County (Eugene), home to the University of Oregon (16,900 students) and a sizable environmentalist faction. A politician running districtwide has the precarious task of balancing the economic needs of loggers and fishermen against others' concerns for protection of the environment.

Most of the ancient, old-growth forest that is the habitat of the threatened northern spotted owl is in the Cascade Range in the eastern part of the 4th. Court orders enforcing the Endangered Species Act have blocked logging in national forestland, affecting many area residents who make their living cutting timber on public lands.

Roseburg (Douglas County), which calls itself the Timber Capital of the Nation, is perhaps the most timber-dependent community in the district. Mill closures and other timber-related cutbacks have boosted its unemployment rate. An influx of retirees from California has helped keep Roseburg's population from dropping precipitously. In January 1993, Douglas' 14 percent unemployment rate was the second-highest in the state. Unemployment linked to the timber industry also has been high in Linn County (Albany).

Along the Pacific Coast, Coos County (Coos Bay) has also seen once-thriving timber mills close. Coos and Linn both suffer from double-digit unemployment. Coastal towns such as Charleston, Bandon and Port Orford rely on the salmon fishing industry, which faces cutbacks because of declining runs.

With a university and some light industry, Eugene has weathered the timber decline better through economic diversity. But a large segment of Eugene's economy is still linked to timber processing. For the workers and their families whose lives are tethered to the lumber industry, jobs and growth are more important than environmental preservation. Industrial employment has been unsteady in Eugene and its timber-dominated neighbor, Springfield.

Eugene in the 1960s and 1970s was a mecca for the back-to-nature counterculture. Many students stayed after graduation. As they moved into workaday society, they learned how to influence local politics; they usually elect liberal Democrats. But the electoral history of Lane County is mixed. Lane voted for Republican presidential candidates in 1968, 1972 and 1980, and for Democrats in 1976, 1984, 1988 and 1992. In 1990, it voted for Democrat Barbara Roberts for governor and Republican Mark O. Hatfield for Senate. Democrat Les AuCoin beat GOP Sen. Bob Packwood in Lane in 1992.

Agriculture also contributes to the 4th's economy. There are some dairy farms on the south coast (Bandon prides itself on its cheddar cheese). In the north, ryegrass is grown in the fertile Willamette Valley.

1990 Population: 568,465. White 545,768 (96%), Black 2,659 (<1%), Other 20,038 (4%). Hispanic origin 13,409 (2%). 18 and over 424,702 (75%), 62 and over 98,733 (17%). Median age: 35.

babies" — Social Security recipients who fell between the cracks in rules changes and whose benefits are not as high as those for others of nearly the same age.

Their proposal to raise benefits was an expensive one: It was estimated to cost at least $46 billion over 10 years, and it put their House colleagues in the uncomfortable position of either voting against Social Security benefits or voting to increase the deficit. And DeFazio and Frank paid for it. "We were pretty well beat about the head and shoulders," DeFazio said.

During House floor consideration of the five-year farm programs reauthorization in 1990, DeFazio added one of the few significant amendments to the bill. It replaced a hodgepodge of state laws with a national standard governing which foods may be labeled "organic." Agriculture Committee Democrat Charles W. Stenholm of Texas offered an alternative amendment giving the Agriculture Department authority for setting standards. But DeFazio said that approach was a ploy to kill the organic standard by lawmakers who saw it as a threat to traditional, chemical-intensive agriculture. DeFazio's amendment was adopted, 234-187.

DeFazio shares with many of his Northwestern constituents a skepticism toward international adventurism, voting against foreign aid and questioning U.S. military missions. As a freshman, he opposed President Ronald Reagan's efforts to provide naval escorts to Kuwaiti oil tankers in the Persian Gulf.

At Home: DeFazio's strength and his weakness as a House candidate were the same: He was identified with Jim Weaver, his predecessor in the 4th. In the end, the Weaver connection was more help than hindrance. DeFazio portrayed himself as heir to Weaver's populist appeal, but kept apart from Weaver's personal quarrels and financial entanglements.

DeFazio first went to work for Weaver in 1977, fresh from a graduate program in gerontology at the University of Oregon. He handled senior citizens' issues in Weaver's Eugene office, spent two years in Washington as his legislative aide, then returned to Eugene as Weaver's constituent services director. After that, DeFazio won election to the Lane County (Eugene) Commission in 1982.

As an elected official, DeFazio proved to be less abrasive than Weaver but equally aggressive. He sued to nullify contracts between Oregon utilities and the Washington Public Power Supply System, whose failed nuclear projects had resulted in utility rate increases. He also led the fight against a 1983 proposal for a Eugene city income tax.

When Weaver announced he would not seek re-election in 1986, DeFazio stepped in. He had ties to environmentalists and liberals in Eugene's university community, a residence in the timber-oriented suburb of Springfield, and name familiarity throughout Lane County. DeFazio had primary opposition from state Sen. Bill Bradbury, popular in the coastal areas, and state Sen. Margie Hendriksen, who had labor and feminist support. But DeFazio edged Bradbury by just under 1,000 votes with Hendriksen a close third.

Republicans nominated Bruce Long, who had taken 42 percent against Weaver in 1984. Long sought to cultivate the many voters Weaver had alienated over the years; time and again, he described DeFazio as "Jim Weaver Jr." Allegations that Weaver had used campaign funds to play the commodities market made DeFazio's ties to the incumbent seem all the more undesirable.

But DeFazio had no connection with Weaver's financial troubles, and he deflected the "clone" critique by insisting that he was an independent thinker who had picked up valuable experience in Weaver's office. DeFazio called Long a dogmatic conservative lacking in sympathy for district voters.

Long was better financed than in 1984, but his media efforts could not overshadow DeFazio's Lane County base and strong organization. DeFazio carried Lane by almost 18,000 votes, won with similar strength in Coos County and held down Long's margin in Douglas County. Since then, DeFazio has won re-election with ease.

Committees

Natural Resources (12th of 28 Democrats)
Energy & Mineral Resources; National Parks, Forests & Public Lands; Oversight & Investigations

Public Works & Transportation (11th of 39 Democrats)
Aviation; Surface Transportation

Elections

1992 General		
Peter A. DeFazio (D)	199,372	(71%)
Richard L. Schulz (R)	79,733	(29%)
1990 General		
Peter A. DeFazio (D)	162,494	(86%)
Tonie Nathan (LIBERT)	26,432	(14%)

Previous Winning Percentages: 1988 (72%) **1986** (54%)

District Vote for President

1992

D 123,387 (42%)
R 93,889 (32%)
I 74,447 (26%)

Campaign Finance

	Receipts	Receipts from PACs		Expend-itures
1992				
DeFazio (D)	$248,887	$173,500	(70%)	$301,116
Schulz (R)	$6,348	$500	(8%)	$6,348
1990				
DeFazio (D)	$257,547	$172,635	(67%)	$217,527
Nathan (LIBERT)	$3,341	0		$3,343

Key Votes

1993	
Require parental notification of minors' abortions	N
Require unpaid family and medical leave	Y
Approve national "motor voter" registration bill	Y
Approve budget increasing taxes and reducing deficit	Y
Approve economic stimulus plan	Y
1992	
Approve balanced-budget constitutional amendment	Y
Close down space station program	Y
Approve U.S. aid for former Soviet Union	N
Allow shifting funds from defense to domestic programs	Y
1991	
Extend unemployment benefits using deficit financing	Y
Approve waiting period for handgun purchases	N
Authorize use of force in Persian Gulf	N

Voting Studies

	Presidential Support		Party Unity		Conservative Coalition	
Year	**S**	**O**	**S**	**O**	**S**	**O**
1992	12	84	85	7	21	75
1991	26	70	88	8	27	68
1990	19	75	86	8	19	80
1989	23	73	89	6	2	98
1988	20	71	86	10	24	61
1987	12	87	87	10	19	81

Interest Group Ratings

Year	ADA	AFL-CIO	CCUS	ACU
1992	90	82	25	9
1991	80	100	20	11
1990	83	83	36	14
1989	95	92	40	7
1988	80	86	25	13
1987	100	93	20	4

5 Mike Kopetski (D)

Of Keizer — Elected 1990; 2nd Term

Born: Oct. 27, 1949, Pendleton, Ore.
Education: American U., B.A. 1971; Lewis and Clark College, J.D. 1978.
Occupation: Advertising executive.
Family: Separated; one child.
Religion: Unspecified.
Political Career: Sought Democratic nomination for U.S. House, 1982; Ore. House, 1985-89; Democratic nominee for U.S. House, 1988.
Capitol Office: 218 Cannon Bldg. 20515; 225-5711.

In Washington: Kopetski's legislative activity in his first term, in particular his strong push to enact a moratorium on nuclear testing, brought him into contact with several senior Democrats. His performance impressed them enough to win him a seat on the Ways and Means Committee at the start of the 103rd Congress.

But a drunken-driving conviction has slowed his momentum. Kopetski was arrested late at night in a Northern Virginia housing project in March 1993 after a police officer observed him approaching pedestrians in his car. Immediately after his June conviction, Kopetski said he was unsure he would run for re-election.

In Congress, Kopetski mostly votes down the line with the Democratic leadership. Soon after he arrived, he cast a vote against authorizing the use of force against Iraq. He participated in Democratic whip efforts on such issues as civil rights and abortion rights. But he veers well away from the liberal wing on the issue of gun control, to which he is unalterably opposed.

With the Soviet Union disintegrating, Kopetski, backed by Majority Leader Richard A. Gephardt of Missouri and 36 other Democrats, called in 1991 for a moratorium on U.S. nuclear weapons tests. Pentagon officials insisted that continued testing was essential to ensure the safety and effectiveness of the U.S. stockpile.

Kopetski offered an amendment to the defense authorization bill to ban test explosions during fiscal 1993 unless the president certified to Congress that a former Soviet republic had conducted a nuclear test. "The Soviet Union no longer exists," he said on the House floor. "Let us discuss nuclear disarmament in the context of the new world configuration." The House approved Kopetski's amendment, 237-167.

The Senate, however, outdid the House, adding an even stronger amendment to the fiscal 1993 energy and water appropriations bill. The amendment called for an immediate test moratorium for nine months, followed by a three-year period of limited testing to check safety improvements, after which tests would be banned permanently.

The House had yet to vote for a permanent ban, and Energy and Water Appropriations Subcommittee Chairman Tom Bevill of Alabama was loath to incorporate an amendment on his bill that might trigger a veto. But Speaker Thomas S. Foley of Washington met with Bevill, Gephardt, key Armed Services Committee members Les Aspin of Wisconsin (the chairman), John M. Spratt Jr. of South Carolina and Kopetski. The group decided to press ahead with the Senate-passed restrictions on the energy bill, gambling — correctly — that President Bush would not veto the bill because it included funding for the superconducting super collider. The House approved the test ban, 224-151.

In the spring of 1993, however, the Clinton administration proposed to continue test detonations of less than 1 kiloton after 1996. The proposal called for the tests to continue until 2001, followed by a five-year moratorium.

Kopetski joined his Senate cosponsors in writing to President Clinton to protest. In a House floor speech, he denounced the White House proposal. "The president must disavow this dangerous policy as quickly as possible," he said.

Dozens of members weighed in to protest the proposal. By late May, a divided Clinton administration all but ruled out the proposal to continue testing after 1996.

Kopetski, whose district includes some of the ancient forestland that is the habitat of the threatened northern spotted owl, could not avoid the ferocious debate over protecting owls and preserving the jobs of timber workers. As a member of the Agriculture Subcommittee on Forests, Family Farms and Energy, he and Washington Republican Sid Morrison stepped forward in May 1992 with a bipartisan compromise that stemmed from a widely respected report by four scientists. Their amendment, adopted on an 8-5 vote, incorporated an option that the report said would hurt the region's economy the least while still offering "a moderate possibility" of preserving the forests and its inhabitants.

Oregon 5

Willamette Valley, Pacific Coast — Salem; Corvallis

Oregon's four major industries — timber, agriculture, fishing and tourism — are all represented in the 5th, whose shape bears a passing resemblance to that of the state fish, the chinook salmon. While hardly solid Democratic territory, the 5th has enough traditional Democrats in coastal Tillamook and Lincoln counties and enough independent voters in some of Clackamas County's Portland suburbs to offset generally big Republican margins in Marion County.

Some old-growth forests are in Mount Hood National Forest in the eastern part of the district. Logging families and owners of small, family-run mills in places such as Mill City, Detroit and Molalla have no use for the environmental protections aimed at preserving the northern spotted owl — or for politicians sympathetic to the owl.

Forty percent of the 5th's population is in Marion County (Salem), usually a dependable Republican base. GOP Sens. Bob Packwood and Mark O. Hatfield scored well above their statewide percentages in Marion in their re-elections in 1992 and 1990. In 1988, GOP Rep. Denny Smith's paltry 1,500-vote margin here set the tone for his near-loss districtwide to Kopetski. In their rematch two years later, Kopetski won Marion by more than 3,500 votes. George Bush barely carried Marion in 1992.

Clackamas, Marion and Polk counties are at the heart of the Willamette Valley, Oregon's most productive agricultural area. It is the center of Oregon's greenhouse and nursery crop industry, the state's second-largest agricultural commodity group. Trees and shrubs are grown, primarily for export. The area is renowned for its fruits and berries, as well as its grass seeds. Willamette hops from Marion and Clackamas go into some of the country's finest beers. Polk County grows cherries and wine grapes; wineries dot Polk and Marion counties. Marion is among the top counties in the nation for snap beans.

Along the coast, tourism and fishing fuel the economy. The resort town of Newport (Lincoln County) is also a vibrant fishing community known for its Dungeness crabs. Sport fishing is popular in such coastal towns as Lincoln City, Waldport and Yachats. To the north in Tillamook County, dairy and timber predominate. The Tillamook County Creamery Association employs more than 300 people to produce its famous cheddar cheese.

The district reaches into Portland's Clackamas County suburbs; West Linn is one of Oregon's wealthiest communities. Along the Clackamas River is Oregon City, the western terminus of the Oregon Trail, 2,000 miles from Independence, Mo. Incorporated in 1844, Oregon City is the oldest city west of the Missouri River.

The 5th contains only a corner of Benton County, but that includes the city of Corvallis, the district's only major city outside of Salem. It is the home of Oregon State University's 14,900 students and numerous political activists who make Corvallis the most liberal area in the 5th.

1990 Population: 568,466. White 532,101 (94%), Black 3,654 (1%), Other 32,711 (6%). Hispanic origin 28,313 (5%). 18 and over 421,189 (74%), 62 and over 90,921 (16%). Median age: 34

"If we don't do something, we will continue as we have in the past two years, which is gridlock," he said. "It would save us a lot of time, anguish and court costs if we were to adopt this." The Agriculture Committee approved the measure, but the bill did not advance.

Kopetski has not compromised on his opposition to gun control. In the 102nd Congress, he voted against requiring a seven-day waiting period before purchasing a handgun. During debate in 1991 on the crime bill, he voted for an amendment by Missouri Democrat Harold L. Volkmer to remove a provision that would have banned 13 assault-type semiautomatic weapons and limited gun clips to seven rounds of ammunition. The 247-177 vote came a day after a man wielding an automatic pistol murdered 22 people at a Texas cafeteria.

In addition to Agriculture, in his first term Kopetski served on the Judiciary and Science committees. On Ways and Means, he sits on the Human Resources and the Select Revenue Measures subcommittees. Kopetski has demonstrated considerable interest in the issue of mental health, introducing sense-of-the-Congress resolutions in the 102nd and 103rd Congresses to seek assurance that any health-care reform include mental health-care benefits. He is one of the founders of the House Working Group on Mental Illness and Health Issues.

Kopetski attracted attention in Washington even before he was sworn in. According to The (Portland) Oregonian, at a White House reception for newly elected members, Kopetski met Vice President Dan Quayle, who, upon learning that Kopetski was from Oregon, informed the Democrat that he had campaigned there in 1990. "I've been wanting to thank you for that," Kopetski replied, startling the vice president, who, Kopetski said, "was definitely shocked" by his rejoinder.

At Home: Two years after holding Republican Rep. Denny Smith to the smallest margin of victory of any incumbent, Kopetski returned in 1990 to oust the vulnerable Republican, who was saddled with well-publicized questions over his involvement in the savings and loan scandal.

Kopetski's 707-vote loss to the heavily favored Smith had been one of the surprises of Election Day 1988. With limited resources, Kopetski built a crack organization and effectively disseminated his message with free media. Smith spent much of his time outside the 5th promoting his "anti-crime" ballot initiative. Although he lacked the money for a TV ad campaign, Kopetski was aided by an independent cable TV ad campaign financed by a wealthy Oregon family unhappy with Smith's conservatism.

Smith started to worry late in the campaign and began running TV ads criticizing Kopetski as a tax-and-spend liberal. That last-minute offensive may have made the difference. The anti-crime initiative passed overwhelmingly, but Smith did not pull ahead of Kopetski until absentee ballots were counted. After the voting, Smith was one of the few Republican candidates anywhere to blame his showing on Michael S. Dukakis' coattails. The Democrat narrowly lost the 5th's presidential vote.

Kopetski returned in 1990 with another strong organizational effort. In his campaign literature, Kopetski detailed "five ways Denny Smith personally contributed to the $500 billion savings and loan crisis." Smith was the director of a Salem S&L for 10 years, had business dealings with another Oregon thrift and lobbied in behalf of a third. All three failed. A former investigator for the Senate Watergate Committee, Kopetski was able to cast himself as an upright alternative to Smith.

As in 1988, Smith tried to convince 5th District voters that Kopetski was too liberal. He portrayed the Democrat as sympathetic to radical environmentalists who oppose logging.

But Kopetski, adopting a moderate position on the contentious timber question and criticizing Smith's voting record on issues relating to the environment, women, education and senior citizens, argued that it was the incumbent who was outside the district's mainstream.

One of Smith's most controversial attacks was a hard-hitting radio ad late in the campaign. The ad, featuring the sounds of Adolf Hitler speaking to a frenzied crowd, accused Kopetski of insufficiently supporting President Bush's Persian Gulf policy. An announcer intoned, "Mike, appeasement is wrong."

The attack backfired, as local media lambasted Smith for running the "Hitler ad." With the endless budget negotiations handcuffing members to Washington, Smith could not match the pace of his challenger. The result was not close: Kopetski won with 55 percent of the vote.

Redistricting in 1991 gave Kopetski a reshaped but more Democratic district. Republicans decided against fielding a strong challenger in the 5th, and Kopetski won a second term with 64 percent of the vote.

Committee

Ways & Means (21st of 24 Democrats)
Human Resources; Select Revenue Measures

Elections

1992 General		
Mike Kopetski (D)	174,443	(64%)
Jim Seagraves (R)	97,984	(36%)
1990 General		
Mike Kopetski (D)	124,610	(55%)
Denny Smith (R)	101,650	(45%)

District Vote for President

1992
D 116,790 (40%)
R 103,387 (35%)
I 73,071 (25%)

Campaign Finance

	Receipts	Receipts from PACs		Expend-itures
1992				
Kopetski (D)	$338,338	$241,832	(71%)	$325,620
Seagraves (R)	$39,613	0		$39,612
1990				
Kopetski (D)	$851,729	$399,283	(47%)	$843,297
Smith (R)	$841,077	$386,986	(46%)	$884,828

Key Votes

1993	
Require parental notification of minors' abortions	N
Require unpaid family and medical leave	Y
Approve national "motor voter" registration bill	Y
Approve budget increasing taxes and reducing deficit	Y
Approve economic stimulus plan	Y
1992	
Approve balanced-budget constitutional amendment	N
Close down space station program	N
Approve U.S. aid for former Soviet Union	Y
Allow shifting funds from defense to domestic programs	Y
1991	
Extend unemployment benefits using deficit financing	Y
Approve waiting period for handgun purchases	N
Authorize use of force in Persian Gulf	N

Voting Studies

	Presidential Support		Party Unity		Conservative Coalition	
Year	S	O	S	O	S	O
1992	25	72	90	7	21	73
1991	37	63	86	11	27	70

Interest Group Ratings

Year	ADA	AFL-CIO	CCUS	ACU
1992	85	67	38	4
1991	75	83	20	5

Pennsylvania

STATE DATA

Governor:
Robert P. Casey (D)

First elected: 1986
Length of term: 4 years
Term expires: 1/95
Salary: $105,000
Term limit: 2 terms
Phone: (717) 787-2500
Born: Jan. 9, 1932; Jackson Heights, N.Y.
Education: College of the Holy Cross, B.A. 1953; George Washington U., J.D. 1956
Occupation: Lawyer
Family: Wife, Ellen Theresa Harding; eight children
Religion: Roman Catholic
Political Career: Pa. Senate, 1963-67; sought Democratic nomination for governor, 1966; Pa. auditor general, 1969-77; sought Democratic nomination for governor, 1970, 1978

Lt. Gov.: Mark S. Singel (D)
First elected: 1986
Length of term: 4 years
Term expires: 1/95
Salary: $83,000
Phone: (717) 787-3300

State election official: (717) 787-5280
Democratic headquarters: (717) 238-9381
Republican headquarters: (717) 234-4901

REDISTRICTING

Pennsylvania lost two House seats in reapportionment, dropping from 23 districts to 21. Commonwealth court judge issued map Feb. 24, 1992; state Supreme court approved March 10.

STATE LEGISLATURE

General Assembly. Biennial session; meets year-round.

Senate: 50 members, 4-year terms
1992 breakdown: 25D, 24R; 45 men, 4 women; 46 whites, 3 blacks
Salary: $47,000 + expenses
Phone: (717) 787-5920

House of Representatives: 203 members, 2-year terms
1992 breakdown: 105D, 98R; 182 men, 21 women; 188 whites, 14 blacks, 1 Hispanic
Salary: $47,000 + expenses
Phone: (717) 787-2372

URBAN STATISTICS

City	Pop.
Philadelphia Mayor Edward Rendell, D	1,585,577
Pittsburgh Mayor Sophie Masloff, D	369,879
Erie Mayor Joyce Savocchio, D	108,718
Allentown Mayor Joseph S. Daddona, D	105,301
Scranton Mayor James P. Connors, R	81,805

U.S. CONGRESS

Senate: 1 D, 1 R
House: 11 D, 10 R

TERM LIMITS

For Congress: No
For state offices: No

ELECTIONS

1992 Presidential Vote

Bill Clinton	45.1%
George Bush	36.1%
Ross Perot	18.2%

1988 Presidential Vote

George Bush	51%
Michael S. Dukakis	48%

1984 Presidential Vote

Ronald Reagan	53%
Walter F. Mondale	46%

POPULATION

1990 population		11,881,643
1980 population		11,863,895
Percent change		+<1%
Rank among states:		5
White		89%
Black		9%
Hispanic		2%
Asian or Pacific islander		1%
Urban		69%
Rural		31%
Born in state		80%
Foreign-born		3%
Under age 18	2,794,810	24%
Ages 18-64	7,257,727	61%
65 and older	1,829,106	15%
Median age		35

MISCELLANEOUS

Capital: Harrisburg
Number of counties: 67
Per capita income: $19,128 (1991)
Rank among states: 16
Total area: 45,308 sq. miles
Rank among states: 33

Pennsylvania - Congressional Districts

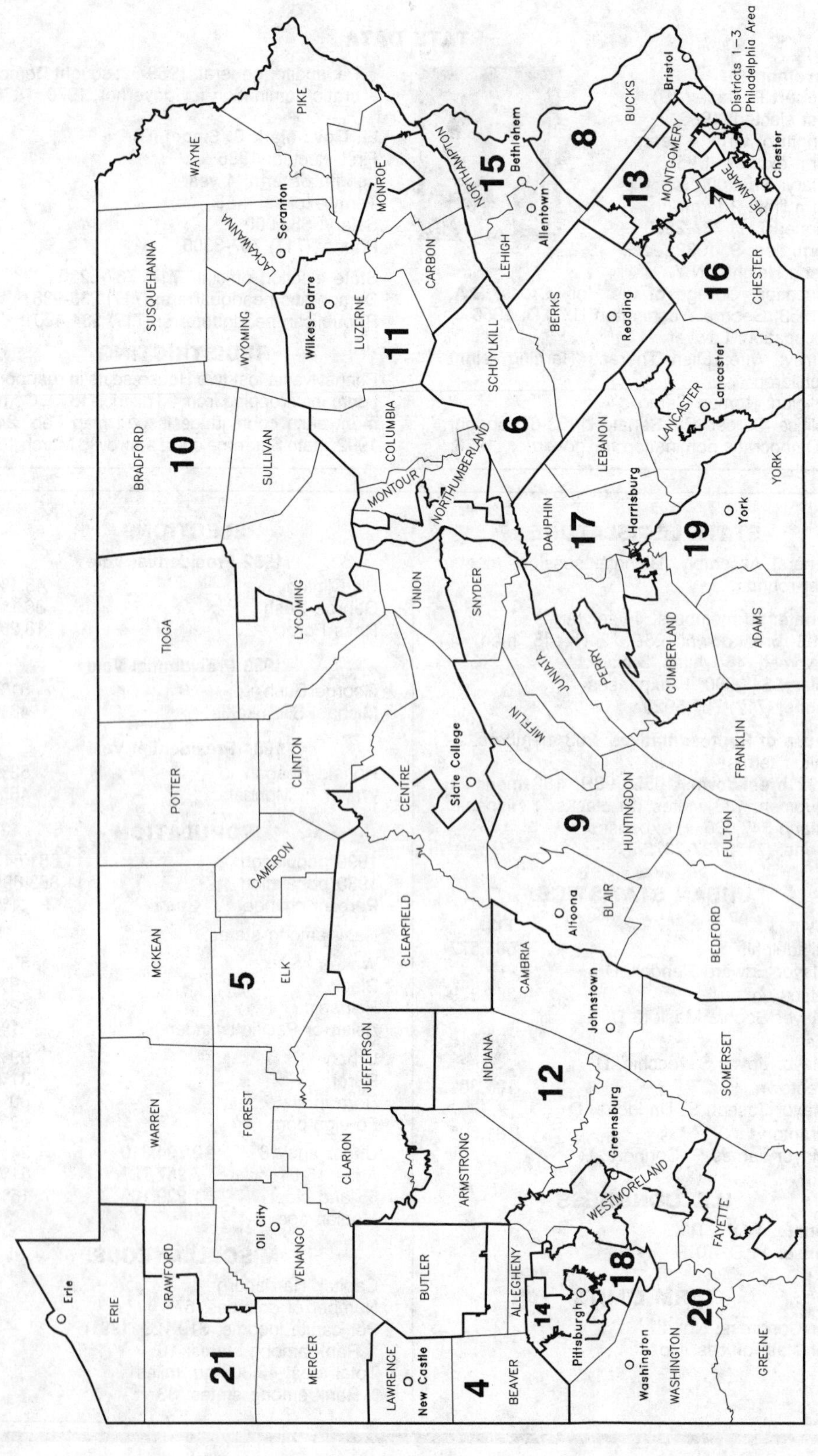

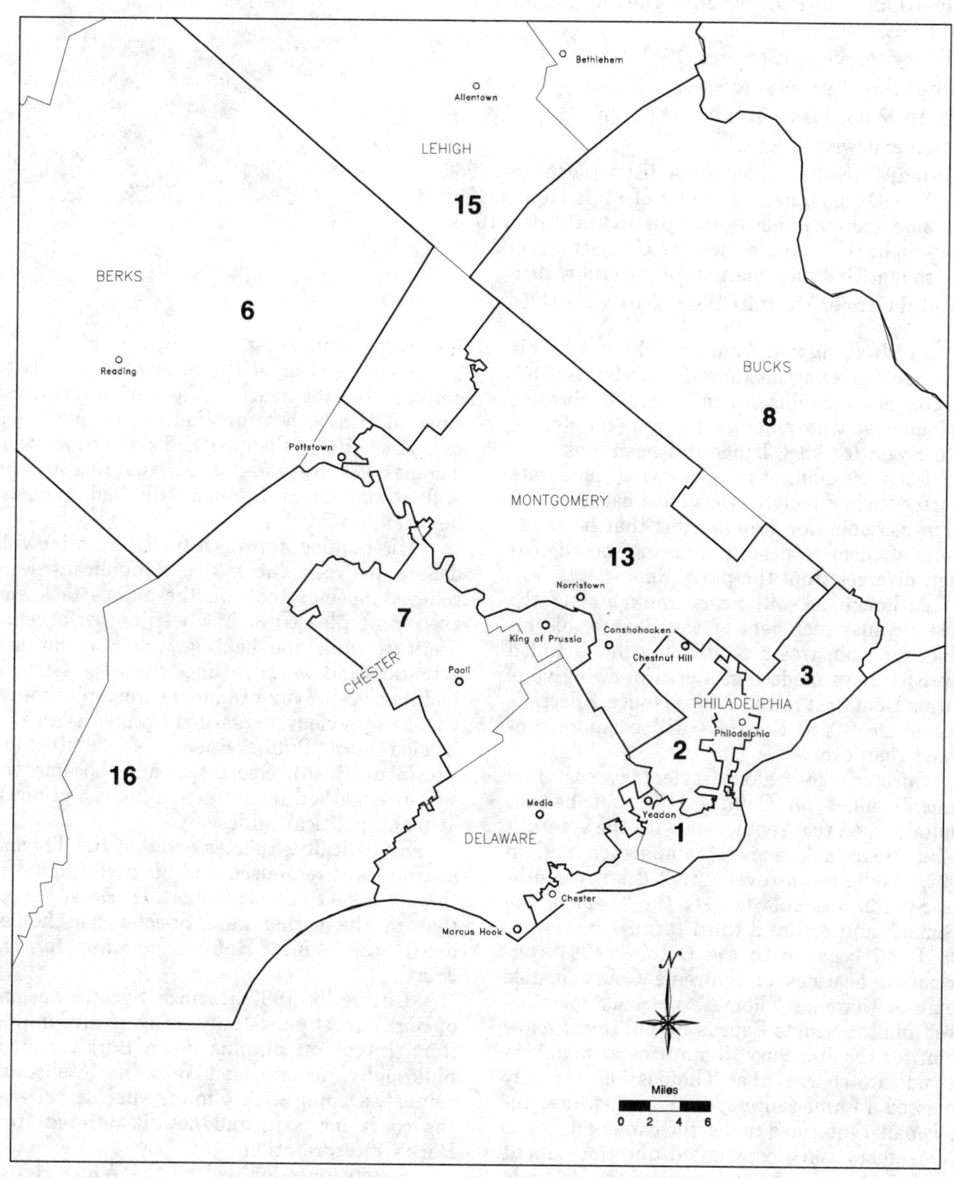
Bethlehem
Allentown
LEHIGH
15
BERKS
6
Reading
BUCKS
8
Pottstown
MONTGOMERY
13
Norristown
7
King of Prussia
Conshohocken
Chestnut Hill
CHESTER
Paoli
3
PHILADELPHIA
Philadelphia
2
16
Media
Yeadon
1
DELAWARE
Chester
Marcus Hook
Miles
0 2 4 6

Arlen Specter (R)

Of Philadelphia — Elected 1980; 3rd Term

Born: Feb. 12, 1930, Wichita, Kan.
Education: U. of Pennsylvania, B.A. 1951; Yale U., LL.B. 1956.
Military Service: Air Force, 1951-53.
Occupation: Lawyer; professor.
Family: Wife, Joan Levy; two children.
Religion: Jewish.
Political Career: Philadelphia district attorney, 1966-74; GOP nominee for mayor of Philadelphia, 1967; defeated for re-election as district attorney, 1973; sought GOP nomination for U.S. Senate, 1976; sought GOP nomination for governor, 1978.
Capitol Office: 530 Hart Bldg. 20510; 224-4254.

In Washington: Sometimes known by his less-than-flattering nickname "Snarlin' Arlen," Specter is an intelligent, intense and abrasive individualist who matches his zeal for debate with a zest for klieg lights and headlines.

Each session, the otherwise moderate Specter finds a truly conservative cause to call his own, reminding Republicans that he really is one of them — despite a voting record that often diverges from the party line.

Although he will never rank among the most popular members of the Senate, his instinct for mainstream politics and his detailed approach have made him a critical swing vote. With a Democrat in the White House, Specter's vote in the 103rd Congress will be more contested than ever.

Specter's go-it-alone style may cost him valuable allies on Capitol Hill, but he has capitalized on that reputation with the voters at home. He is a legendary campaigner, and in 1992, despite a controversy that destroyed others, Specter was able to defy the "Year of the Woman" and secure a third term.

It all began with the October 1991 confirmation hearings of Supreme Court Justice nominee Clarence Thomas, a drama televised live from the Senate Caucus Room. It was a low point for the Judiciary Committee as members delved into charges that Thomas had sexually harassed a former employee. The all-white, all-male panel squirmed under the camera lights as its members asked convoluted questions about pornographic movies and pubic hairs on soda cans.

Initially, Specter backed Thomas. But when Professor Anita F. Hill's charges became public, Specter turned to one of his favorite fence-sitting techniques: calling for another hearing. For the new hearing, the GOP recruited Specter, a former prosecutor with a quick mind and dogged persistence, as its lead interrogator. The nation would see Specter at his best — and worst.

Steering clear of the most lurid details to emerge from the hearings, Specter nevertheless came at Hill with a forcefulness unequaled on the panel. He challenged Hill's assertions that Thomas was interested in a sexual relationship and at one point implied Hill had perjured herself.

His bulldog approach fueled a nationwide debate between the sexes; Republicans were relieved Specter took on the odious task and even more pleased at how well he performed.

But while the hearing won him national attention and warm feelings from the GOP, it had its price. Many prominent women's groups, who had previously regarded Specter as an ally, labeled him "Public Enemy No. 2" (behind President Bush). Specter's name became the sure-fire method for triggering hoots and howls at many political rallies.

Stylistically, Specter's role in the Thomas hearings was reminiscent of his performance in the 1987 hearings on Robert H. Bork, except that in the earlier case Specter had helped defeat the White House's nominee for the court.

During the 1987 hearings, Specter was one of Bork's most persistent and aggressive inquisitors. Intent on pinning down Bork's judicial philosophy, he engaged Bork in intellectual combat, arguing with him on what he believed the court has said and how it differed from Bork's interpretation.

Specter was lobbied by the White House, deluged with mail and prominently featured in news stories. But as the contentious and partisan debate dragged on through the summer and fall, Specter drew criticism for his indecision. Finally, just days before the committee vote, he announced "with great reluctance" that he would vote against Bork.

Sometimes the outcome appears less important to Specter than the process; ever the lawyer, he seems equally comfortable defending either side of a case. While many tire of the tedious review of court decisions, lengthy background checks and meticulous questioning to grasp a nominee's philosophy, the process seems to suit those who master it — and Specter is such a master.

He makes no apologies for his manner. But he does seem to value balance in that he attacks his targets with equal vigor. During the 1992 investigation into sexual harassment at the Navy's Tailhook convention, for example, Specter went after the accused Navy men with great gusto. Some saw in this an effort to refurbish his image with women's groups; others just saw Specter being himself.

The Thomas hearings aside, Specter remains one of the more liberal Republicans in the Senate, particularly on social issues.

In the 102nd, he voted to override Bush's veto of the family leave bill (later signed into law by President Clinton.) He also broke with Bush in supporting an extension of unemployment benefits and sought far more liberal civil rights legislation than the president eventually agreed to.

After the 1992 elections, Specter co-founded the Republican Majority Coalition, a group he described as "moderate" and intended to expand the party's base. Observers generally characterized it as a counterbalance to the Christian Right on social issues, especially abortion (all the new group's members were supporters of abortion rights).

As the 103rd Congress opened, Specter solidified his reputation for going his own way and frustrating both parties in turn. He was among a group of four Republicans who switched their votes to support Senate approval of the so-called motor voter bill. He also supported Clinton's early attempts to reverse the military's ban on gays.

At the same time, he filed several bills more closely associated with conservatives, including legislation to create a presidential line-item veto and balance the federal budget. He also submitted a barrage of tough crime-related bills. They include legislation to restrict the number of appeals in capital cases (known as habeas corpus), and impose the death penalty for terrorists and criminals who kill someone in a drive-by shooting.

Opposition to gun control and a tough-on-crime stance are tailor-made for Specter's rural Republican constituents as well as for white ethnic Democratic voters in the cities. Together with Strom Thurmond of South Carolina, Specter authored a successful habeas corpus amendment to the 1990 crime bill that restricted appeals by death row inmates.

The one constant is Specter's love of legal discourse. Whenever there's a debate involving the Constitution, Specter hustles to the floor. When questions were raised about the constitutionality of certain provisions of the 1989 contra accord, Specter was soon on the scene. "I heard the comments . . . and thought it appropriate to come to the floor to raise for general consideration some issues which I brought up yesterday in the hearings before the Foreign Operations Subcommittee on Appropriations," he said.

Even the rare whiff of Specter humor can involve the Constitution. In mid-1989, Specter's wife, a member of the Philadelphia City Council, asked whether it was all right to complain about the miserable conditions on a trip to the Amazon. "That's guaranteed under the Constitution," he quipped.

In the low-key confirmation hearing of David H. Souter to the Supreme Court, Specter again displayed his interest in constitutional matters, pursuing Souter's view of a Pennsylvania case that had recently come before the court that dealt with the Establishment Clause — a constitutional provision prohibiting state sponsorship of religion.

Specter saw his image shift from thoughtful toward tentative as a result of a series of votes on an amendment to ban certain assault weapons in 1989. First, when the Constitution Subcommittee was deadlocked on the weapons ban, Specter cast the lone vote against reporting it without recommendation; he wanted another hearing.

Months later, when the full Judiciary Committee took up the issue, Specter did not participate. He "took a walk," in insiders' parlance. Specter's failure to vote allowed the ban to pass by a one-vote margin; a tie would have killed it. When the amendment to the crime bill was brought before the full Senate, Specter voted with a majority of Republicans to kill it.

Specter's approach to all issues is detailed and analytical. After he voted in 1989 against impeaching then-federal Judge Alcee L. Hastings, Specter released a 76-page statement explaining his decision.

His argumentative style makes him difficult to work for, and some on the Appropriations Committee consider him difficult to work with.

His weak rapport with colleagues contributed to an embarrassing snub in 1990 when Democratic Sen. Frank R. Lautenberg of New Jersey bluntly denied a request by Specter to address transportation appropriations conferees. Specter had wanted to talk about a House provision that would have cut Pennsylvania's highway budget by 25 percent if the state failed to dedicate funding to mass transit.

Not being a conferee, Specter had no right to speak, according to Lautenberg. "I know of no precedent for a senator objecting to a unanimous consent request to speak before a committee," Specter fumed outside the meeting. Finally, teaming up with fellow Pennsylvanian John Heinz (who was killed in a 1991 plane crash), Specter blocked consideration of the bill, and hours before Congress adjourned, the amendment was effectively nullified.

The spat continued into the following year when Lautenberg promised Pennsylvania Democratic Sen. Harris Wofford (Heinz's successor) $15 million for a Pittsburgh transit project. Wofford announced the money even before the Appropriations Committee approved it, cutting Specter out of any credit for the money.

Representing a state with more registered Democrats than Republicans, Specter routinely calls attention to the plight of struggling Rust Belt cities. For a Republican, he earns good marks from labor unions. Specter has pressed for legislation aimed at giving U.S. firms more protection from subsidized imports and goods "dumped" below cost in this country by foreign producers.

Early in the 103rd, however, construction and transportation workers were unable to persuade Specter to support the Clinton administration's $16.3 billion stimulus package in the face of a Republican filibuster.

The Foreign Operations Subcommittee gives Specter a platform for his ardent support for Israel. In late 1990, Specter criticized a Bush administration proposal to sell advanced weapons to Saudi Arabia. He also condemned the administration's "rush to judgment" when it backed a U.N. resolution criticizing Israel for the killing of 21 Palestinians at Temple Mount.

At Home: Not long after Wofford's special Senate election upset win in 1991, giddy Democrats began eyeing Specter's seat. Even at Wofford's victory bash, potential aspirants were posturing unabashedly. It came at the close of a rough year for Specter. Even before he was criticized for grilling Hill, he was mocked in the major motion picture "JFK" as the chief author of the "single-bullet theory" in the Warren Commission report on President John F. Kennedy's assassination. Making matters worse was a brewing primary challenge from the right.

But as the 1992 campaign opened, Democrats were unable to find a top-tier challenger to Specter. Less-than-inspiring Lt. Gov. Mark S. Singel led the field, which also included a little known district attorney from Allegheny County, and an even lesser known candidate named Lynn Yeakel, president of a Philadelphia-based women's fundraising organization.

Specter was more concerned about fending off the state's best-known abortion opponent, GOP state Rep. Stephen F. Freind. The author of the state's restrictive abortion law, Freind launched an all-out assault on Specter.

Specter and the state's right wing have never had an easy co-existence. His vote against confirming Bork prompted some to tag him "Benedict Arlen." But conservatives never jelled behind Freind, who was considered by many as a single-issue candidate. Despite all the rancor, Specter won 65 percent in the primary.

On the Democratic side, Yeakel rode a wave of publicity for female candidates that began with the Senate primary victory of Carol Moseley-Braun in Illinois. Weak in early polls, Yeakel rocketed from nowhere to the top of the five-candidate field in the final month of the primary. Polls taken soon after the primary showed her in striking distance of Specter.

But Yeakel squandered her momentum over the summer. Her campaign was beset with internal problems. She did not help matters with several campaign-trail gaffes such as botching the name of one central Pennsylvania county when she visited.

Specter, meanwhile, reached out to various women's groups by stressing his longtime support for women's issues and attempting to explain his role in the Thomas confirmation hearings. And Specter campaigned extensively; his office noted that since his election in 1980, he had made over 1,600 trips home.

By the fall, Yeakel attempted to dispel the notion that she was a single-issue candidate and drew closer, but by then, Specter's nearly flawless campaign effort was in high gear. He squeaked by with slightly less than a majority of the vote.

In 1986 also, Democrats had begun the campaign hopeful that they could defeat Specter and end what was then a 24-year drought in Pennsylvania Senate elections. They ended the year buried under the third-largest Senate election landslide in the state in the last half-century.

Specter won with money, high name recognition and the type of moderate Republican image that has enabled GOP candidates to monopolize recent Keystone State Senate elections. A weak campaign by his Democratic rival, Rep. Bob Edgar, boosted Specter. Specter easily outspent Edgar and blunted him virtually everywhere. He won 61 counties, including all of rural central Pennsylvania and in Delaware County, Edgar's base in the Philadelphia suburbs.

For Specter, the impressive victory added luster to a political career that had sputtered in the previous decade. Once the bright young star of Pennsylvania GOP politics, he had lost his momentum in defeats for mayor of Philadelphia in 1967 and for re-election as the city's district attorney in 1973. When he lost two statewide primaries, in 1976 and 1978, it appeared that his triumphs were behind him.

But he decided to make one more try when Republican Richard S. Schweiker announced he would not seek re-election in 1980. This time, Specter had the good fortune of running against a Democrat, former Pittsburgh Mayor Pete Flaherty, who was also a two-time statewide loser.

Heinz and GOP Gov. Dick Thornburgh agreed to support Specter after the primary, helping Specter make inroads on Flaherty's western Pennsylvania base. At the same time, Flaherty could not overcome the longstanding suspicion of him in the Philadelphia area. Specter carried Philadelphia itself by 12,000 votes and won by immense margins in its suburbs, enough to offset Flaherty's showing in the west.

Specter's roots in Philadelphia politics reach back to the early 1960s, when he was an assistant district attorney and a hard-working young reformer.

In 1967, Specter took on Mayor James Tate. The Democrats were split by feuds between machine regulars and reformers; Specter and his "clean government" campaign were expected to romp. They did not. Tate, rejected by the organization, nonetheless won the Democratic nomination easily. Then, as riots were breaking out in other cities, he and his new police chief, Frank Rizzo, clamped a "limited emergency" on the city to prevent disturbances. Specter could not stop Tate from riding voters' gratitude to a narrow victory.

When he completed his second term as district attorney in 1973, Specter looked like a contender for governor in 1974. But that talk ended abruptly when voters denied him a third term as district attorney that fall.

Specter went into private law practice briefly and in 1976 entered the GOP primary to replace retiring Sen. Hugh Scott. The front-runner was Heinz, then a congressman, whose personal fortune gave him a clear edge. Specter made it close in a bitter contest that kept relations between the two delicate for years.

In 1978, Specter ran for governor and rounded up strong financial and organizational backing in Philadelphia and its suburbs. But he had to split the area's vote with two other candidates, including Thornburgh, the eventual winner.

Committees

Appropriations (5th of 13 Republicans)
Labor, Health & Human Services & Education (ranking); Agriculture, Rural Development & Related Agencies; Defense; Foreign Operations; Transportation

Energy & Natural Resources (8th of 9 Republicans)
Energy Research & Development; Public Lands, National Parks & Forests; Renewable Energy

Judiciary (5th of 8 Republicans)
Technology & the Law (ranking); Antitrust, Monopolies & Business Rights

Special Aging (10th of 10 Republicans)

Veterans' Affairs (4th of 5 Republicans)

Elections

1992 General		
Arlen Specter (R)	2,358,125	(49%)
Lynn Yeakel (D)	2,224,966	(46%)
John F. Perry III (LIBERT)	219,319	(5%)
1992 Primary		
Arlen Specter (R)	683,118	(65%)
Stephen F. Freind (R)	366,608	(35%)

Previous Winning Percentages: 1986 (56%) **1980** (51%)

Campaign Finance

	Receipts	Receipts from PACs		Expend-itures
1992				
Specter (R)	$6,869,894	$1,409,209	(21%)	$8,854,815
Yeakel (D)	$5,021,067	$371,721	(7%)	$5,028,669

Key Votes

1993	
Require unpaid family and medical leave	Y
Approve national "motor voter" registration bill	Y
Approve budget increasing taxes and reducing deficit	N
Support president's right to lift military gay ban	Y
1992	
Approve school-choice pilot program	N
Allow shifting funds from defense to domestic programs	Y
Oppose deeper cuts in spending for SDI	Y
1991	
Approve waiting period for handgun purchases	N
Raise senators' pay and ban honoraria	N
Authorize use of force in Persian Gulf	Y
Confirm Clarence Thomas to Supreme Court	Y

Voting Studies

	Presidential Support		Party Unity		Conservative Coalition	
Year	**S**	**O**	**S**	**O**	**S**	**O**
1992	45	55	41	57	37	58
1991	68	32	67	33	75	25
1990	58	42	53	46	59	41
1989	66	34	55	45	71	29
1988	63	35	48	49	59	35
1987	40	60	46	53	41	59
1986	31	65	27	68	29	64
1985	61	34	51	43	58	37
1984	65	35	67	32	55	45
1983	59	41	46	54	45	55
1982	55	44	50	49	40	59
1981	77	22	64	34	51	47

Interest Group Ratings

Year	ADA	AFL-CIO	CCUS	ACU
1992	65	83	60	30
1991	40	58	50	71
1990	39	89	50	48
1989	40	50	75	57
1988	60	83	62	33
1987	80	90	47	15
1986	75	87	44	33
1985	55	71	55	36
1984	50	45	68	36
1983	80	76	37	16
1982	70	56	35	26
1981	50	58	72	40

Harris Wofford (D)

Of Bryn Mawr — Elected 1991; 1st Term

Appointed to the Senate May 1991.

Born: April 9, 1926, New York City, N.Y.

Education: U. of Chicago, B.A. 1948; Yale U., LL.B. 1954; Howard U., J.D. 1954.

Military Service: Army Air Corps, 1944-45.

Occupation: Lawyer; college president; Peace Corps official; White House official.

Family: Wife, Clare Lindgren; three children.

Religion: Roman Catholic.

Political Career: Pa. Democratic Party chairman, 1986; Pa. secretary of labor and industry, 1987-91.

Capitol Office: 530 Dirksen Bldg. 20510; 224-6324.

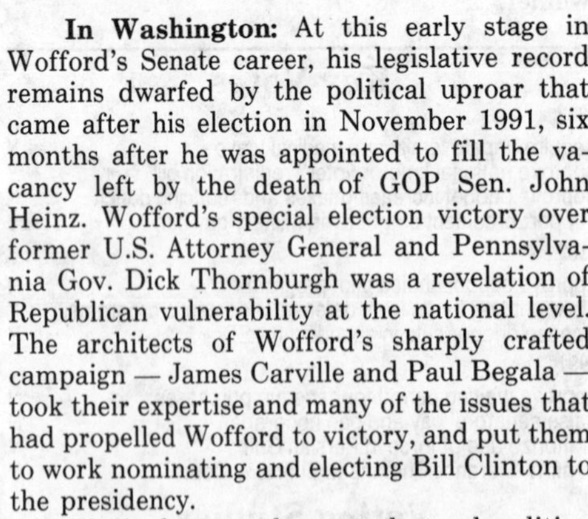

In Washington: At this early stage in Wofford's Senate career, his legislative record remains dwarfed by the political uproar that came after his election in November 1991, six months after he was appointed to fill the vacancy left by the death of GOP Sen. John Heinz. Wofford's special election victory over former U.S. Attorney General and Pennsylvania Gov. Dick Thornburgh was a revelation of Republican vulnerability at the national level. The architects of Wofford's sharply crafted campaign — James Carville and Paul Begala — took their expertise and many of the issues that had propelled Wofford to victory, and put them to work nominating and electing Bill Clinton to the presidency.

Wofford, a neophyte at electoral politics, defeated veteran pol Thornburgh by articulating middle-class concerns about health care and a declining U.S. economy, while calling for a middle-class tax cut. He effectively painted his opponent as a Washington insider too accustomed to strolling the corridors of power to understand the concerns of everyday folk.

Those knowledgeable about Pennsylvania politics were not greatly surprised by Thornburgh's defeat — he had struggled to win his second term as governor in 1982, and he ran a lackluster Senate campaign that seemed early on to take victory for granted. But national Democrats made Wofford out to be a giant-killer. The next year, he received serious consideration as a potential vice presidential running mate for Clinton.

Assuming he wants to stay in the Senate, Wofford will face another electoral test in 1994, when Heinz's unfinished term expires. Because of the Clinton-Wofford link, the senator may again draw national media attention, with his re-election fate seen as one indicator of how Clinton's presidency is faring at mid-term.

So far in the Senate, Wofford has not made a deep mark on the legislative debate over health care reform, which was the defining issue of his 1991 bid. By the start of the 103rd Congress, he had not yet translated his campaign slogan — "If criminals have a right to a lawyer, I think working Americans should have the right to a doctor" — into original legislation. Instead, Wofford has cosponsored a health care proposal with Democratic Sen. Tom Daschle of South Dakota.

Nonetheless, Wofford played host in 1993 when Hillary Rodham Clinton traveled to Harrisburg, Pa., for the first of her public forums on health-care reform. And in 1992, he led a group of Democratic senators in writing to Majority Leader George J. Mitchell of Maine to ask him to bring a health-care reform bill to the floor for debate.

During the portion of his term before the November 1991 election, Wofford showed a knack for political symbolism. In August 1991, having promised on the campaign trail to refrain from bombarding constituents with mass mailings at taxpayer expense, he successfully pushed an amendment to the legislative appropriations bill that permitted him to return $150,000 from his mass mailing account to the Treasury. In October, he filed legislation to require members of Congress to pay for health care received at the Office of the Attending Physician. He termed the bill a "wake-up call" for Congress. It also made a great campaign ad. The free services ended in 1992.

The first bill filed by Wofford was aimed at the hearts and pocketbooks of middle-class voters. It would change the formula for determining a family's financial ability to pay for a child's college expenses, limiting consideration of home or farm equity. He announced the legislation standing on the lawn of a home recently sold by a family that was burdened with college loan debts for three children.

Given his identification with the cause of health-care reform, Wofford had a tougher time putting a positive spin on media reports that he had accepted campaign contributions from a number of political action committees in the health-care field, including groups representing medical specialties, druggists, hospitals, nursing home operators and insurance companies. According to one report, Wofford received $74,000 from such sources in 1991 and 1992.

Consistent with his campaign focus on middle-class concerns about the eroding job base, Wofford voted against the Bush administration's request for fast-track consideration of the North American Free Trade Agreement, arguing that environmental and occupational standards in Mexico are so lax that U.S. firms cannot compete. He also opposed continuation of most-favored-nation trade status for China, saying workers in this country should not compete with forced labor in China's prisons. But he is no hard-line protectionist. On the Small Business Committee, he is chairman of the Export Expansion and Agricultural Development Subcommittee.

Wofford's other committee assignments are Labor and Human Resources, Environment and Public Works, and Foreign Relations. On the latter panel in March 1992, he joined with Democrats in pledging to support aid to the former Soviet Union, provided that the Bush administration would actively lobby Republicans to do the same.

On the issue of abortion, Wofford makes neither advocates or opponents of the procedure fully happy, but his stand may reflect the Pennsylvania mainstream. He has said he supports the Supreme Court's *Roe v. Wade* decision legalizing abortion, and he also has expressed support for Pennsylvania's abortion law, which imposes some restrictions on access to abortion. That law was signed by Democratic Gov. Robert P. Casey, who appointed Wofford to the Senate.

In the 103rd Congress, Wofford joined with Democratic Sen. David L. Boren of Oklahoma in proposing legislation to put welfare recipients to work in a "community WPA" styled after Franklin D. Roosevelt's Works Progress Administration. The bill won early support from Clinton.

While Wofford's 1991 campaign was his first bid for elective office, he is no stranger to Washington. Former President John F. Kennedy first brought Wofford onto the national scene as a liaison to the black community in the 1960 presidential campaign and as special assistant for civil rights during his administration. Wofford had gained the ear and trust of the Rev. Dr. Martin Luther King Jr. in the early 1950s, while traveling and speaking about the work of Mohandas K. Gandhi and his method of non-violent protest.

In the final days of Kennedy's 1960 campaign, Wofford urged the candidate to call Coretta Scott King and express his concern for her husband's safety. Rev. King was being held in a Georgia jail. The phone call is credited with solidifying crucial support for Kennedy in the black community. After serving as Kennedy's point man on civil rights in the new administration, Wofford left to help R. Sargent Shriver establish the Peace Corps.

At Home: Wofford's stunningly clear-cut victory in his 1991 special Senate election proved to be the reliable harbinger of the 1992 presidential campaign that Democrats hoped it would be.

Like Clinton, Wofford was a relatively unknown quantity at the beginning of the campaign. But he was able to chop into Thornburgh's huge early lead with an aggressive "anti-Washington" message that the much better-known Republican actually encouraged by portraying himself as a well-connected Washington insider.

By the final days of the campaign, polls showed that Wofford had pulled even. On Election Day, he zoomed past Thornburgh to win by 10 percentage points. He became Pennsylvania's first Democratic senator since Joseph S. Clark was driven from office in 1968.

With a message of economic protest, Wofford built a constituency that featured, but was not limited to, the old New Deal coalition of white ethnics, minorities and liberals. He easily carried Pennsylvania's Democratic keystones — liberal Philadelphia and the more socially conservative blue-collar coal and steel country of western Pennsylvania.

But most ominous for Republicans nationally was the resonance of Wofford's message in the relatively affluent suburban bedroom communities near Philadelphia, where, to the astonishment of many Republicans, Wofford ran even with Thornburgh.

The Senate race was billed in many quarters as a referendum on President Bush and his domestic policies. Besides serving as Bush's attorney general for three years, Thornburgh had headed the White House Domestic Policy Council and was the beneficiary of several presidential campaign visits on his behalf.

Yet even before the votes were in, the Pennsylvania race had jolted the Bush administration into thinking domestic. On the eve of the election, Bush postponed a two-week trip to Asia. On the morning after the balloting he acknowledged: "There's a message here.... When the economy is slow, people are concerned. They're hurting out there. They're concerned about their livelihood."

In victory, Wofford described himself as "the messenger of a message that came through loud and clear."

Republicans said Wofford won because of Thornburgh's relatively passive, front-running campaign, which gave the Democrat a vacuum in which to operate much of the fall. Thornburgh was laid-back and self-assured, emphasizing his integrity and effectiveness as governor from 1979 to 1987. He left the impression that he, rather than Wofford, was the Senate incumbent.

While Wofford seized on the pocketbook concerns of middle-class voters, Thornburgh stressed the need for fiscal responsibility. He tried to link Wofford with Casey and the massive package of tax increases that the governor had gotten enacted in 1991.

But Thornburgh's line of argument fell flat. Wofford was able to embrace the role of feisty underdog, even though the calls of "Give 'em hell, Harris" that occasionally rang out at union halls seemed a bit odd for a candidate with such a professorial air.

It was as a child during the New Deal that Wofford began to identify with the Democrats. He recounts that as a 10-year-old during the 1936 presidential campaign, he walked to school for months rather than ride in the family car, which bore a bumper sticker supporting the GOP candidate, Alfred M. Landon.

Wofford also showed an early interest in civil liberties. He and his wife visited India and then wrote a book titled "India Afire" (1951), about the work of Mohandas K. Gandhi.

In 1954, Wofford was one of the first white students to earn a law degree at predominantly black Howard University in Washington. He subsequently taught law at Howard and the University of Notre Dame and served on the staff of the U.S. Commission on Civil Rights before being hired by Kennedy to be an adviser in his 1960 presidential campaign.

With the passing of the New Frontier, Wofford opened a new phase of his life in academia that brought him to Pennsylvania. He was a university president, first at a small college in New York, then starting in 1970, at Bryn Mawr College. In 1978, Wofford left Bryn Mawr to join a Philadelphia law firm.

He soon reconnected with Casey, whom he had met in the 1950s when both were young lawyers at a Washington law firm. When Casey was mounting his first successful gubernatorial campaign in 1986, he tapped Wofford to head the Democratic state committee. The following year, he brought Wofford into his Cabinet as secretary of Labor and Industry.

Wofford was considering a 1992 challenge to GOP Sen. Arlen Specter when in April 1991 Heinz died in a midair collision of his private plane with a helicopter.

But Wofford was not Casey's first choice for the vacancy. Chrysler Corp. Chairman Lee A. Iacocca was offered the appointment but turned it down, and several other Democrats Casey was reportedly considering withdrew before Wofford was finally tapped in May.

Yet Wofford did not seem to mind that he was not Casey's top pick. He labeled the governor's overture to Iacocca "a bold move that had my support and, luckily, he said no."

In a state where major statewide races are nearly always close, Wofford probably will have to fight hard to hold his seat in 1994. But he could get a break from the political calendar. The Pennsylvania governorship is also up in 1994, and since Casey is prevented by law from seeking re-election, the gubernatorial race has been an early focus of GOP attention.

Committees

Environment & Public Works (9th of 10 Democrats)
Clean Water, Fisheries & Wildlife; Superfund, Recycling & Solid Waste Management; Toxic Substances, Research & Development

Foreign Relations (9th of 11 Democrats)
International Economic Policy, Trade, Oceans & Environment; Near Eastern & South Asian Affairs; Western Hemisphere & Peace Corps Affairs

Labor & Human Resources (10th of 10 Democrats)
Aging; Children, Families, Drugs & Alcoholism; Education, Arts & Humanities; Employment & Productivity

Small Business (8th of 12 Democrats)
Export Expansion & Agricultural Development (chairman); Urban & Minority-Owned Business Development

Elections

1991 Special		
Harris Wofford (D)	1,860,760	(55%)
Dick Thornburgh (R)	1,521,986	(45%)

Campaign Finance

1991	Receipts	Receipts from PACs		Expend-itures
Wofford (D)	$3,334,767	$956,415	(29%)	$3,241,555
Thornburg (R)	$3,818,378	$854,367	(22%)	$3,840,994

Key Votes

1993	
Require unpaid family and medical leave	Y
Approve national "motor voter" registration bill	Y
Approve budget increasing taxes and reducing deficit	Y
Support president's right to lift military gay ban	Y
1992	
Approve school-choice pilot program	N
Allow shifting funds from defense to domestic programs	Y
Oppose deeper cuts in spending for SDI	N
1991	
Approve waiting period for handgun purchases	Y
Raise senators' pay and ban honoraria	N
Confirm Clarence Thomas to Supreme Court	N

Voting Studies

Year	Presidential Support S	Presidential Support O	Party Unity S	Party Unity O	Conservative Coalition S	Conservative Coalition O
1992	28	70	90	8	21	76
1991	27 †	67 †	87 †	9 †	22 †	72 †

† Not eligible for all recorded votes.

Interest Group Ratings

Year	ADA	AFL-CIO	CCUS	ACU
1992	100	92	20	0
1991	79	89	0	27

1 Thomas M. Foglietta (D)

Of Philadelphia — Elected 1980; 7th Term

Born: Dec. 3, 1928, Philadelphia, Pa.
Education: St. Joseph's College, B.A. 1949; Temple U., J.D. 1952.
Occupation: Lawyer.
Family: Single.
Religion: Roman Catholic.
Political Career: Philadelphia City Council, 1955-75; GOP nominee for mayor of Philadelphia, 1975.
Capitol Office: 341 Cannon Bldg. 20515; 225-4731.

In Washington: Foglietta has proved adept at blending the demands of two constituencies: the white, affluent liberals of Center City and the poor, mostly black residents who make up the majority of his district. The founder and chairman of the Congressional Urban Caucus, he is outspoken on issues that affect minorities.

At the start of the 103rd Congress, he gained a position of prominence, winning a seat on the Appropriations Committee. In addition to a spot on the Transportation Subcommittee, he got the No. 2 slot on the Military Construction Subcommittee.

A white Republican-turned-Democrat who now represents a majority-minority district, Foglietta has been sensitive to racial politics. He challenged the suburb of Tinicum, just outside Philadelphia, when its police appeared to be stopping only black motorists in their anti-drug efforts. In the 102nd Congress, he formed the 77-member Congressional Urban Caucus, of which he is still chairman. The group has lobbied for more money for summer jobs and against funding for the $30 billion-plus space station *Freedom*, which competes for funds with subsidized housing programs in its appropriations bill.

Foglietta's highest-profile pursuit in recent years has been his vigorous work in behalf of the Philadelphia Naval Shipyard (PNSY), an aging facility where battleships and aircraft carriers are maintained.

During the 100th Congress, he lobbied hard to keep PNSY off the 1988 version of the "hit list." He released a long report intended "to demonstrate ... that the Philadelphia Navy Yard is the Navy's most efficient and most productive shipyard." The report noted that PNSY is the only facility fully equipped to refit conventional carriers.

The commission spared the shipyard from cutbacks when it reported to President Ronald Reagan in 1988. However, the commission did recommend the shutdown of the Philadelphia Naval Hospital in the southern part of the 1st District; Foglietta responded by calling for a replacement hospital to be built nearby.

Then, in February 1990, President George Bush's defense secretary, Dick Cheney, included PNSY among bases still subject to review. Foglietta howled, noting that most of the closures would affect bases in Democratic-held House districts. But in early 1991, another presidentially appointed commission also recommended closing PNSY. Foglietta sponsored a joint resolution to stop the closure of 25 major military installations targeted for closing. But the measure received only 60 votes on the House floor.

In 1993, Foglietta found himself with another fight — this time to save the Defense Personnel Support Center, which employs about 4,000 civilians in South Philadelphia. The center was included on an early list of military facilities recommended for closure.

While the future of the shipyard was in question, Foglietta worked during the 101st Congress to ensure that it would have a productive present. He lobbied for funding to refit the carrier *USS Kennedy* at PNSY. The project — aided by Pennsylvanians John P. Murtha and Joseph M. McDade, the chairman and ranking Republican on the Appropriations Defense Subcommittee — got $405 million in funding.

In the 102nd Congress, Foglietta joined with 7th District Republican Curt Weldon in fighting off Florida Democrat Earl Hutto, who wanted the Navy to move a ship it was decommissioning at Philadelphia to Pensacola, Fla. Foglietta also has worked to funnel economic conversion dollars to the shipyard.

Foglietta also exhibits a wider worldview. He is one of the leading House advocates of international human rights, with a particular interest in the government of South Korea. He and several other Americans attracted international publicity in 1985 when they were roughed up by government police at the Seoul airport while accompanying exiled opposition leader Kim Dae Jung on his re-entry into South Korea.

At Home: Foglietta shed his lifelong GOP label and fought his way through a complicated political situation to secure his first term in

Pennsylvania 1

South and central Philadelphia; part of Chester

Many of the personalities and places commonly associated with Philadelphia can be traced to the 1st District.

Broad Street courses the 1st, beginning at the Montgomery County border. It cuts through the Oak Lane and Olney sections and the Democratic-voting poor and working-class African-American neighborhoods of North Philly. Temple University is situated by Cecil B. Moore Avenue.

Broad Street also marks the Center City border with the 2nd District. Center City, west of Broad Street — including City Hall — is in the 2nd. The 1st District portion of Center City is east of City Hall, in the 5th Ward. However, the waterfront area of the 5th Ward belongs to the 3rd District.

Besides the historical presence of the Liberty Bell and Independence Hall, the 1st boasts the pop cultural landmarks of South Philly. At 9th and Passyunk Avenues, tourists, locals and political candidates find it difficult to pass up a cheesesteak at Pat's or across the street at Geno's. Right down the street is the famous Italian Market where vendors hawk fresh vegetables, meats, cheeses and fish.

Italian culture permeates much of South Philly. There are Catholic churches that still say Mass in Italian; bocce courts can be found at Marconi Plaza park.

These are the neighborhoods of Hollywood's "Rocky Balboa" and former mayor Frank Rizzo, where Rizzo's tough law-and-order stance had great appeal. When Irish-Americans controlled the Democratic Party decades ago, Italian-Americans mostly sided with the GOP. Now they vote Democratic in local and congressional elections.

Veterans Stadium and the Spectrum, homes to the city's professional sports teams, are situated at Broad and Pattison. Past the stadiums, the row houses end and the Philadelphia Naval Shipyard begins. (The embattled shipyard is scheduled for closure under the 1991 base-closing plan.) Oil refineries line the Schuylkill River just before it empties into the Delaware River.

The one ward west of the Schuylkill is in southwest Philadelphia. In the late 19th century, the large factories located here attracted Irish, Italian and black immigrants. But as the General Electric, Fels Naptha and American Tobacco Company factories shut down, the adjoining areas such as Elmwood and Kingsessing went into decline. The bleak economic landscape for those who did not move away manifested itself in racial turmoil. Today, the whites, blacks, and the recently arrived Vietnamese and Cambodians eye each other with suspicion.

Outside city limits, south of the Philadelphia International Airport, the 1st takes in bits of Delaware County along Interstate 95. Working-class whites in Glenolden and Tinicum retain the GOP loyalties taught to them by the Republican county machine.

Black voters in the blighted city of Chester, almost all of which is in the district, boost the district's minority population to just over half.

1990 Population: 565,842. White 213,114 (38%), Black 296,314 (52%), Other 56,414 (10%). Hispanic origin 55,891 (10%). 18 and over 412,588 (73%), 62 and over 86,364 (15%). Median age: 31.

Congress in 1980. He ran in November as an independent, a status that usually guarantees failure. But the circumstances of that autumn were far from usual. Democratic incumbent Michael "Ozzie" Myers, indicted in the Abscam bribery scandal, had been renominated nonetheless. Anti-Myers Democrats were looking for a candidate, and Foglietta was available. When Myers was convicted on bribery charges and expelled from the House a month before the election, Foglietta was positioned to win. Once elected, he acknowledged his political debt by voting with Democrats to organize the 97th Congress.

To gain a second term as a Democrat in 1982, Foglietta survived a tough primary that pitted him against not only U.S. Rep. Joseph F. Smith but also against the organization of former Mayor Frank Rizzo, still a powerful figure in the 1st. As a Republican, Foglietta had unsuccessfully challenged Rizzo for mayor in 1975.

Rizzo's support helped make Smith competitive in South Philadelphia. But it also brought out a large vote for Foglietta from blacks and from Center City liberals antagonistic toward Rizzo.

Foglietta was challenged in the 1984 and 1986 primaries by Jimmy Tayoun, who, in the state House and then the Philadelphia City Council, became famous for tending to the personal needs of his constituents. One Tayoun campaign leaflet noted that he "keeps faith with the Bill Barrett tradition of personal evening service." Barrett, who represented the 1st for 29 years following World War II, was a bit player in Washington but was very popular in Philadelphia because he returned there every night to hold evening office hours.

Foglietta prevailed on the backing of black voters and young, liberal Center City professionals. Tayoun's most faithful backers were old-line, working-class whites, including many Irish and Poles in the "river wards" along the Delaware River.

The crucial votes were in the Italian community of South Philadelphia. Tayoun voiced more conservative views on social issues, but Foglietta's roots in the Italian community are deep. His father was a Republican city councilman, and Foglietta followed in those footsteps, serving on the City Council for two decades. Against Tayoun, he won renomination in the primary with 52 percent.

Two years later, Tayoun sought to make his primary rematch with the incumbent at least partly a referendum on Philadelphia's controversial Mayor W. Wilson Goode. But his effort to link the two politicians failed. Foglietta raised his vote share to 60 percent and expanded his base from liberals, blacks and Italians to include some non-Italian ethnics as well.

Redistricting changes posed no problem for Foglietta in 1992, but it may cause him some worry in the future. With its majority of minority voters, the district may well see challengers arise in the Democratic primary. One such prospect, a popular black state legislator, geared up for a run at Foglietta in 1992 before deciding against it.

Committee

Appropriations (26th of 37 Democrats)
Military Construction; Transportation

Elections

1992 General		
Thomas M. Foglietta (D)	150,172	(81%)
Craig Snyder (R)	35,419	(19%)
1990 General		
Thomas M. Foglietta (D)	73,423	(79%)
James Love Jackson (R)	19,018	(21%)

Previous Winning Percentages: **1988** (76%) **1986** (75%) **1984** (75%) **1982** (72%) **1980** (38%)

District Vote for President

1992
D 149,699 (73%)
R 39,042 (19%)
I 17,021 (8%)

Campaign Finance

	Receipts	Receipts from PACs		Expend-itures
1992				
Foglietta (D)	$387,584	$168,450	(43%)	$366,203
Snyder (R)	$43,647	$3,000	(7%)	$41,210
1990				
Foglietta (D)	$465,317	$226,918	(49%)	$234,057
Jackson (R)	$9,230	$1,000	(11%)	$5,969

Key Votes

1993	
Require parental notification of minors' abortions	N
Require unpaid family and medical leave	Y
Approve national "motor voter" registration bill	Y
Approve budget increasing taxes and reducing deficit	Y
Approve economic stimulus plan	Y
1992	
Approve balanced-budget constitutional amendment	N
Close down space station program	Y
Approve U.S. aid for former Soviet Union	N
Allow shifting funds from defense to domestic programs	Y
1991	
Extend unemployment benefits using deficit financing	Y
Approve waiting period for handgun purchases	Y
Authorize use of force in Persian Gulf	N

Voting Studies

	Presidential Support		Party Unity		Conservative Coalition	
Year	S	O	S	O	S	O
1992	16	76	83	3	13	77
1991	23	72	92	3	5	89
1990	24	76	92	5	17	80
1989	28	63	91	2	15	83
1988	16	70	83	4	8	79
1987	16	77	81	2	21	72
1986	16	68	79	5	10	82
1985	20	75	90	4	13	80
1984	22	57	80	2	7	83
1983	24	68	87	4	11	85
1982	32	56	81	5	18	77
1981	25	58	80	8	13	73

Interest Group Ratings

Year	ADA	AFL-CIO	CCUS	ACU
1992	80	91	33	0
1991	95	100	11	0
1990	78	100	14	0
1989	95	100	40	0
1988	90	92	42	4
1987	84	93	8	0
1986	90	100	14	5
1985	90	94	14	5
1984	95	100	50	0
1983	90	100	20	4
1982	85	100	20	5
1981	90	87	11	0

2 Lucien E. Blackwell (D)

Of Philadelphia — Elected 1991; 1st Full Term

Born: Aug. 1, 1931, Whiset, Pa.
Education: West Philadelphia H.S., 1945-47.
Military Service: Army, 1953-54.
Occupation: Labor official.
Family: Wife, Jannie Brooks; six children.
Religion: Baptist.
Political Career: Pa. House, 1973-75; Philadelphia City Council, 1975-91; Consumer Party candidate for mayor of Philadelphia, 1979; sought Democratic nomination for mayor of Philadelphia, 1991.
Capitol Office: 410 Cannon Bldg. 20515; 225-4001.

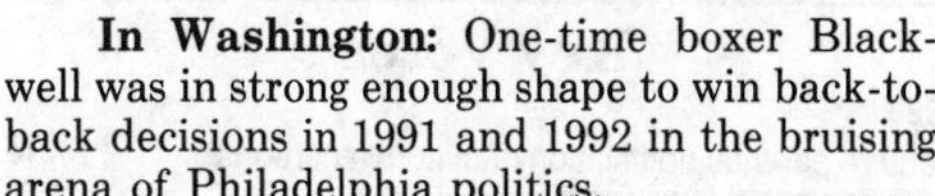

In Washington: One-time boxer Blackwell was in strong enough shape to win back-to-back decisions in 1991 and 1992 in the bruising arena of Philadelphia politics.

Blackwell first captured the 2nd in November 1991, when a special election was held to fill the seat of the Rev. William H. Gray III. Although Gray was majority whip at the time, the No. 3 Democrat in the House, he resigned to become president of the United Negro College Fund.

In electing Blackwell, voters in the black-majority 2nd opted for a man markedly different from Gray, the impressive cleric whose ambition and ability moved him quickly onto the national stage. A decade older, Blackwell was part of a different generation in Philadelphia politics, one that saw little chance of crossing racial lines.

Blackwell has more of a "common man" approach and appeal. His formal education concluded with high school, and he has lived in the same West Philadelphia row house for more than 30 years. A longtime president of the local longshoremen's union, he has been deep in the roiling world of Philadelphia city politics throughout his adult life, earning a reputation as "Lucien the Solution" — a combative city council member and two-time candidate for mayor (he finished second in the May 1991 Democratic primary).

That was good training for the challenge Blackwell took on as Gray's successor. For immediately after his first House campaign, Blackwell found himself in the midst of a second. With little time between campaigns to zero in on legislation, the new man from Philadelphia carefully backed away from the spotlight.

Quickly dispelling any notion that he had been elected to take the House by storm, Blackwell pledged at his initial swearing-in, "I come here not in a braggadocio way." And he kept his own focus on the people whose votes he would need again in less than one year's time.

According to The Philadelphia Inquirer, Blackwell told supporters that if he ever failed to respond to their needs, "I hope God will rip out my eyes and pull out my tongue and throw it to the four winds."

Blackwell has sought to broaden the reputation for aggressive constituent service he earned as a city council member. Although he antagonized his council colleagues at times, these exertions helped him achieve what he describes as "96 percent name recognition" — and they helped him build a base of support among the working class and poor of West and North Philadelphia.

Blackwell soon learned the many uses of the Congressional Record.

Although any one member's actual time on the floor is strictly limited, "extensions of remarks" can be added to each day's record. And Blackwell has added such remarks saluting retirees or commending the pillars of Philadelphia. He also enjoys recapping news articles he has perused during his morning commute from Philadelphia to Washington. "Mr. Speaker, as I read last Thursday's Washington Post on the train from Philadelphia, I was ecstatic to read. . . ."

Blackwell has a seat on the Public Works Committee and has moved into a seat on the Budget Committee, where Gray was chairman in the 99th and 100th. On both panels, he serves as an activist advocate for labor. Championing the cause of disenfranchised employees, Blackwell introduced a bill in the 102nd Congress to protect the credit rating of consumers who lose their jobs when employers relocate or cut their work force. He also sponsored legislation preventing an employer from discriminating against a prospective employee based on any of the applicant's genetic traits — including predisposition to certain diseases.

At Home: Despite his long and storied political career — and in some measure because of it — Blackwell was hard pressed to succeed Gray. Blackwell had the Democratic Party's endorsement, which in this heavily partisan

Pennsylvania 2

West Philadelphia; Chestnut Hill; Yeadon

William Penn's statue atop City Hall stands like a sentinel over Philadelphia. From his vantage point, he views a variety of neighborhoods across the 2nd, all with one thing in common: an affinity for Democrats.

Republicans need not apply in the 2nd; Democrats enjoy an overwhelming districtwide edge in voter registration. Here, the Democratic primary is the only forum for political redress.

Stretching west from City Hall, the 2nd begins under the skyscrapers of Center City's 8th Ward. Many of the white-collar professionals who labor here by day live outside the district, but some prefer to live nearby in ritzy Rittenhouse Square. The whites of this area are not a large part of the district vote, but their wealth allows them to weigh in disproportionately in any political campaign.

From there, the 2nd crosses the Schuylkill River, and immediately encounters two massive edifices, the U.S. Postal Service building and the 30th Street train station. Traveling westbound on Walnut Street, past the campuses of Drexel University and the University of Pennsylvania, a sea of row houses seems to continue indefinitely. These are the neighborhoods of West Philly.

Two generations ago, Irish, Greeks, and Jews lived under de facto ethnic segregation in these areas. Today, West Philly is nearly all black. Some of these working-class and lower-middle-class neighborhoods are gripped by urban blight; others are well-maintained.

It was the western edge of West Philadelphia that drew notoriety in May 1985, when an ill-conceived police battle against the cult group MOVE led to a fire that burned down two square blocks of row houses.

Farther north, City Line Avenue forms a border with Montgomery County. The middle-class and affluent sections of Overbrook are on the city side, while the posh Main Line begins across the street.

Cutting a wide swath through the northern part of the 2nd is vast and verdant Fairmount Park, which flanks the Schuylkill River and contains the city's art museum, zoo and "Boathouse Row."

Adjoining the park to the northwest is Germantown. Once home to Philadelphia's upper crust, it and nearby Mount Airy now are racially diverse and mostly middle-class. The park runs as far north as the Montgomery County border, where it ends in affluent Chestnut Hill.

Farther north along the Schuylkill River, Roxborough and Manayunk are older neighborhoods experiencing a wave of gentrification. Although longtime residents complain about the upscale restaurants and shops that now occupy Manayunk's Main Street, the businesses have revitalized what was a dying area.

The 2nd abruptly halts at the city's Montgomery County border, but it reaches a finger into Darby, Lansdowne and Yeadon, which are black, Democratic sections of Delaware County.

1990 Population: 565,650. White 196,070 (35%), Black 352,111 (62%), Other 17,469 (3%). Hispanic origin 8,872 (2%). 18 and over 439,005 (78%), 62 and over 99,760 (18%). Median age: 33.

district is usually enough. But he had to hold off two younger rivals with less political baggage: state Sen. Chaka Fattah, a Democrat who got on the ballot as the Consumer Party candidate, and John F. White Jr., the former head of the state welfare department, who ran as an independent.

Blackwell's task was complicated by the scheduling of the special election. When Gray first spoke of retiring, in June 1991, it was assumed the special could be held on the regular Election Day of Nov. 5 (when a new mayor and U.S. senator would also be elected).

But Gray postponed his actual resignation until September. Gray said he did this to help the new whip, Rep. David E. Bonior of Michigan, settle into the job. But back home, the move was seen as an attempt to thwart Blackwell, who had been a bitter rival in the past. (State law stipulates that a special House election may not be held sooner than 60 days after a resignation.) Critics said Gray pushed back his resignation so that his successor could not be chosen in November. That would push the vote into 1992 and give Blackwell's rivals a chance to get organized.

But Blackwell went to court and won an order setting the special election on Nov. 5. Within days, Democratic ward leaders named Blackwell their choice as the party nominee. That meant that voters in the 2nd who pulled the straight-ticket lever for Democratic senatorial and mayoral candidates would automatically be voting for Blackwell too.

Neither Fattah nor White had nearly the assets needed to overcome the party imprimatur and the bonds Blackwell had forged with poor and working class voters he had represented over 17 years on the council.

Both Fattah and White worked the district's white neighborhoods in search of votes, reached out to more affluent African Americans and tried to pick off smaller numbers of votes within Blackwell's West and North Philadelphia base. But neither managed to break 30 percent. Blackwell won with 39 percent.

For the winner, the campaign never stopped. The Democratic primary came just five months later in April, and Blackwell had to defend himself against C. Delores Tucker, the former secretary of the Commonwealth. Redistricting dropped the district's black population from 82 percent to 62 percent, and while Tucker, too, is an African American, she was seen as being stronger than Blackwell among whites and among voters of both races in the more affluent northwestern wards.

Tucker had considered running in the 1991 special election, but declined after Blackwell secured the party nod. For the primary, she came well-armed with financial backing from national women's groups and the support of some national civil rights leaders. Tucker ran against the "party bosses" and called Blackwell a "puppet" of the Democratic City Committee.

Blackwell did not return fire but concentrated on his organization and party and union support. Tucker ran well in the small slice of Delaware County that was grafted onto the district in redistricting, and in the more affluent wards. But in the end she fell short with 46 percent.

Committees

Budget (23rd of 26 Democrats)

Public Works & Transportation (24th of 39 Democrats)
Economic Development (vice chairman); Aviation; Investigations & Oversight

Elections

1992 General		
Lucien E. Blackwell (D)	164,355	(77%)
Larry Hollin (R)	47,906	(22%)
1992 Primary		
Lucien E. Blackwell (D)	48,299	(54%)
C. Delores Tucker (D)	41,528	(46%)
1991 Special		
Lucien E. Blackwell (D)	51,820	(39%)
Chaka Fattah (Consumer)	37,068	(28%)
John F. White Jr. (I)	36,469	(28%)
Nadine G. Smith-Bulford (R)	6,928	(5%)

District Vote for President

1992
D 184,284 (80%)
R 31,836 (14%)
I 14,510 (6%)

Campaign Finance

	Receipts	Receipts from PACs		Expenditures
1992				
Blackwell (D)	$236,129	$133,010	(56%)	$228,229
Hollin (R)	$170,009	$4,400	(3%)	$170,007

Key Votes

1993	
Require parental notification of minors' abortions	N
Require unpaid family and medical leave	Y
Approve national "motor voter" registration bill	Y
Approve budget increasing taxes and reducing deficit	Y
Approve economic stimulus plan	Y
1992	
Approve balanced-budget constitutional amendment	N
Close down space station program	Y
Approve U.S. aid for former Soviet Union	N
Allow shifting funds from defense to domestic programs	Y

Voting Studies

Year	Presidential Support S	Presidential Support O	Party Unity S	Party Unity O	Conservative Coalition S	Conservative Coalition O
1992	12	85	90	4	6	94
1991	31 †	69 †	94 †	6 †	0 †	100 †

† Not eligible for all recorded votes.

Interest Group Ratings

Year	ADA	AFL-CIO	CCUS	ACU
1992	90	100	29	0
1991	--	100	--	0

3 Robert A. Borski (D)

Of Philadelphia — Elected 1982; 6th Term

Born: Oct. 20, 1948, Philadelphia, Pa.
Education: U. of Baltimore, B.A. 1972.
Occupation: Stockbroker.
Family: Wife, Karen Lloyd; four children.
Religion: Roman Catholic.
Political Career: Pa. House, 1977-83.
Capitol Office: 2161 Rayburn Bldg. 20515; 225-8251.

In Washington: Borski enters his second decade in Congress as a man who has received both rewards and brickbats for his quiet, district-centered approach to politics. In 1992, Borski defeated a strong Republican challenger with relative ease. But The Philadelphia Inquirer's endorsement of his opponent, dismissing Borski as one of "the munchkins on Capitol Hill," had to sting. In Washington, Borski remains little-known among many of his colleagues, though well-liked by those who do know him.

In the 103rd Congress, Borski will have a chance to break out of the munchkin mold from his new seat on the Foreign Affairs Committee, where he succeeds fellow Philadelphia Democrat Thomas M. Foglietta. Borski's choice of the Foreign Affairs panel is the first sign he has given of wanting to play on a wider stage, after devoting himself singlemindedly to the concerns of his constituents for years.

Despite a brush with the tar of the House bank scandal (he had 33 overdrafts), Borski was appointed to the House ethics committee in February 1993, a sign that he has the trust of Democratic leaders.

Borski is known as a reliable vote on most key issues. In the early months of the 103rd, he remained true to that reputation, supporting President Clinton with votes in favor of the Family and Medical Leave Act, the "motor voter" registration law, the fiscal 1994 budget resolution and the economic stimulus package. More surprisingly, Borski also voted against requiring federally funded clinics to notify the parents of minors seeking abortions. In the past, Borski has supported restrictions on access to abortion, in line with the culturally conservative ethnic Catholics who make up much of his district.

As a member of the Public Works and Transportation Committee and chairman of the panel's Investigations and Oversight Subcommittee, Borski is well-placed to protect district interests when and if Congress follows up on Clinton's promise to invest in the nation's infrastructure.

However, he will be operating without the assistance of former Rep. William H. Gray, a Philadelphian who used to sit on the Appropriations Transportation Subcommittee. The two worked together to obtain mass transit money for the city until Gray resigned in 1991.

Borski has said he will push the Public Works panel to move beyond its traditional focus on roads and bridges, and to pay more attention to the transportation needs of urban areas, particularly mass transit.

On the Public Works panel, Borski has also concentrated on safety issues. During the 102nd, he wrote language in the highway bill to bar the use of triple trailers on state highways that do not already allow them.

Borski's Oversight Subcommittee prodded the Federal Aviation Administration to force foreign airlines operating in this country to come closer to compliance with U.S. safety standards. Prompted by hearings Borski held on the issue, the FAA began spot inspections of foreign airliners, turning up problems such as cracks and corrosion, malfunctioning or missing navigational equipment and poorly trained flight crews. Since the program began, the FAA has denied a number of airlines the right to fly into the United States.

The subcommittee also held hearings on the Environmental Protection Agency's troubled "superfund" program for cleaning up toxic waste sites. Borski has said the subcommittee will continue its oversight of superfund and will hold a comprehensive review of transportation safety issues in the 103rd Congress.

As a member of the Foreign Affairs Subcommittee on Europe and the Middle East, Borski will be dealing with issues of concern to his numerous Jewish, Irish and Italian constituents. He will have to be more diplomatic than he was as a freshman, when on a trip to Northern Ireland he irritated British officials by meeting with leaders of Sinn Fein, the political wing of the Irish Republican Army.

At Home: Borski may not cut a high profile in Washington, but his concentration on local issues and his assiduous courtship of constituents so far has given him a firm grip on a

Pennsylvania 3

Northeast Philadelphia

In a Democratic and racially diverse city, the 3rd stands alone in its racial homogeneity and its status as the only Philadelphia district where Republicans usually fare well.

The body of the 3rd is known as the Great Northeast, named for its geographic expanse. This part of Philadelphia borders suburban Montgomery and Bucks counties, and many of its communities have taken on quasi-suburban traits of their own. Yet this is the only congressional district wholly contained in the city of Philadelphia.

The mostly white residents who migrated to Northeast neighborhoods established themselves in the past two generations as the black population grew in other parts of the city. And as many residents began to equate the national Democratic Party with policies that provide preferential treatment for minorities, Republican voter registration swelled.

Democrats outnumber Republicans in the 3rd, but in 1980, 1984 and 1988, the Republican presidential ticket carried Northeast. Bill Clinton broke the losing streak in 1992, carrying the district easily over an unpopular President Bush.

This strength was not limited to federal elections: Philadelphia's handful of Republican state legislators and GOP City Council members usually hail from this area.

Conservative social attitudes and concern about crime inspire loyalty to tough law-and-order candidates — such as former Mayor Frank Rizzo. Also welcome is the presence of city police officers and firefighters, many of whom live in the Northeast. Holmesburg Prison is here, as is the Philadelphia Police Academy.

With scores of hospitals, the Northeast Philadelphia Airport and three bridges that connect to New Jersey, infrastructure issues are also of particular concern to 3rd District residents.

Besides large numbers of Catholics, the Great Northeast boasts a large Jewish population, many of whom live west of Roosevelt Boulevard in Bustleton and Somerton.

South of Cottman Avenue, the district begins to lose its suburban feel. The Irish and Polish residents of the Democratic wards by the Delaware River are crowded in row houses under Interstate 95. Union ties bind voters here to the Democratic Party, but they often part company on social issues.

Huge losses of industrial jobs in Kensington, Bridesburg and Port Richmond have left these white ethnic communities reeling.

In such lower-income neighborhoods as Kensington, this economic uncertainty has translated into racial tensions among whites, blacks and Hispanics.

The southern border of the 3rd reaches as far south as Washington Street in South Philadelphia. It snakes close to the river while taking in Penn's Landing, Philadelphia's revitalized waterfront area. Some of the boutiques, shops and restaurants of funky South Street are also within 3rd District confines.

1990 Population: 565,866. White 505,152 (89%), Black 27,493 (5%), Other 33,221 (6%). Hispanic origin 26,543 (5%). 18 and over 437,241 (77%), 62 and over 118,551 (21%). Median age: 35.

once-Republican seat.

Redistricting and a challenge from an old nemesis gave a scare to Borski in 1992, but in the end he was re-elected with 59 percent of the vote.

His 1992 opponent, former GOP Rep. Charles F. Dougherty, was the man Borski beat for the seat 10 years earlier. It was Dougherty's second attempt to win back the seat since losing it. After Borski won re-election easily in 1984, Dougherty tried a comeback in 1986, only to lose the GOP primary to former state Sen. Robert A. Rovner.

In 1992, Dougherty returned to run in a district made slightly less Democratic by redistricting. He criticized Borski for his 33 overdrafts at the House Bank and mocked the incumbent's low-key demeanor and party fealty. Even The Philadelphia Inquirer piled on, when, in an endorsement of Dougherty, the paper said the challenger "simply has more backbone than most of the munchkins on Capitol Hill — and that includes Borski."

Dougherty kept the pressure on to the end, but Borski showed an unexpected strength in winning by 20 percentage points.

Borski launched himself toward Congress by managing another candidate's campaign — the losing 1981 special election effort of Democratic City Chairman David Glancey in the old 3rd District. Borski emerged from the effort with greater visibility and a determination to run for Congress himself. In 1982, when redistricting grafted his state legislative base in the blue-collar "river ward" of Bridesburg onto Dougherty's territory in Philadelphia's semi-suburban Northeast, Borski made his move.

More experienced Democrats stayed out, convinced Dougherty was too strong. Despite the recession, several unions sided with the more dynamic and articulate Dougherty. But concerns about reductions in Social Security helped Borski, and Dougherty's disdain for the Irish Republican Army hurt him. With economic discontent strong in blue-collar Philadelphia, the clean-cut Borski seemed a good vehicle for protesting hard times. He won by 2,664 votes.

Committees

Foreign Affairs (13th of 27 Democrats)
Europe & the Middle East

Public Works & Transportation (6th of 39 Democrats)
Investigations & Oversight (chairman); Aviation; Water Resources & the Environment

Standards of Official Conduct (6th of 7 Democrats)

Elections

1992 General

Robert A. Borski (D)	130,828	(59%)
Charles F. Dougherty (R)	86,787	(39%)
John J. Hughes (I)	4,356	(2%)

1990 General

Robert A. Borski (D)	89,908	(60%)
Joseph Marc McColgan (R)	59,901	(40%)

Previous Winning Percentages: 1988 (63%) **1986** (62%) **1984** (64%) **1982** (50%)

District Vote for President

1992

D 124,944 (52%)
R 75,474 (31%)
I 39,617 (17%)

Campaign Finance

	Receipts	Receipts from PACs		Expend-itures
1992				
Borski (D)	$512,477	$275,319	(54%)	$664,231
Dougherty (R)	$215,322	$46,154	(21%)	$215,321
1990				
Borski (D)	$325,222	$152,800	(47%)	$277,011
McColgan (R)	$74,723	$1,000	(1%)	$74,417

Key Votes

1993	
Require parental notification of minors' abortions	N
Require unpaid family and medical leave	Y
Approve national "motor voter" registration bill	Y
Approve budget increasing taxes and reducing deficit	Y
Approve economic stimulus plan	Y
1992	
Approve balanced-budget constitutional amendment	N
Close down space station program	N
Approve U.S. aid for former Soviet Union	Y
Allow shifting funds from defense to domestic programs	Y
1991	
Extend unemployment benefits using deficit financing	Y
Approve waiting period for handgun purchases	Y
Authorize use of force in Persian Gulf	Y

Voting Studies

	Presidential Support		Party Unity		Conservative Coalition	
Year	**S**	**O**	**S**	**O**	**S**	**O**
1992	28	70	91	8	40	60
1991	36	59	89	9	38	54
1990	27	71	90	7	33	67
1989	41	59	87	10	41	59
1988	26	73	92	6	24	74
1987	19	81	91	3	26	72
1986	20	77	93	6	24	76
1985	24	74	94	4	20	78
1984	30	68	93	6	17	81
1983	21	73	91	6	16	83

Interest Group Ratings

Year	ADA	AFL-CIO	CCUS	ACU
1992	80	83	29	16
1991	60	91	10	30
1990	83	100	21	8
1989	75	92	50	7
1988	80	100	23	12
1987	80	100	13	5
1986	75	100	33	10
1985	80	88	23	5
1984	75	100	38	8
1983	85	100	20	4

4 Ron Klink (D)

Of Jeannette — Elected 1992; 1st Term

Born: Sept. 23, 1951, Canton, Ohio.
Education: Graduated from Meyersdale H.S., 1969.
Occupation: Television journalist.
Family: Wife, Linda Hogan; two children.
Religion: United Church of Christ.
Political Career: No previous office.
Capitol Office: 1130 Longworth Bldg. 20515; 225-2565.

The Path to Washington: Klink was perfectly positioned for his ascension to Congress. He was that exalted species, the outsider, but one with high name recognition as a local television journalist. He also got a boost from redistricting: The already heavily Democratic 4th District had been redrawn to bring in more Democratic voters.

Now, Klink, who defeated five-term incumbent Democrat Joe Kolter in the primary, must turn to the task of somehow revitalizing his economically ravaged district.

Economic issues concern Klink for good reason. The 4th District, which at one time was known for its steel-producing capacity and strong union influence, was disproportionately affected by the crumbling of heavy industry in the early 1980s and has never rebounded from the loss of its industrial base. Steel towns such as Aliquippa and Jeannette have become shadows of their former selves as the huge factories owned by companies such as U.S. Steel shut down in the face of overseas competition.

Klink's new slot on the Small Business Committee could put him in the position of giving the voters what he said they wanted: a representative who could rebuild the economy and produce jobs.

Klink's general-election victory was all but assured in April 1992, when he won a four-way primary battle that resulted in the ouster of the little-regarded Kolter.

Kolter's reputation had been marred by two widely read, unflattering profiles. A 1990 story in The Wall Street Journal painted Kolter as a prototypical incumbent interested in little more than highway and airport construction projects. The other article, in the Pittsburgh Press, printed transcripts from portions of a leaked audio tape in which Kolter planned to manipulate the electorate — at one point on the tape Kolter called himself "a political whore."

Klink's chances got even better when organized labor withdrew its support for Kolter after the congressman missed a key vote on extending unemployment benefits.

However, Klink's efforts were not without criticism. Although he had covered the region for 14 years as a reporter for KDKA-TV, a network affiliate, he had never held elective office.

His lack of political experience attracted some criticism of Klink as a "talking head" with little substantive policy knowledge.

But while Kolter was unsuccessfully trying to shore up his labor base, Klink was able to concentrate on specifics. He published a booklet on how he would turn the district's economy around. Though Klink said he began working on the proposal long before he became a candidate, there are many similarities between it and the plans laid forth by the new Democratic administration.

"They parallel in so many ways a lot of the things in my plan," he said. "We are far apart on some issues — I'm pro-life, for example — but in most economic issues I'm very close."

Early in the 103rd Congress, Klink voted for a modified line-item veto supported by the president and also backed the president's budget and $16.3 billion economic stimulus package.

But in keeping with his anti-abortion rights position, he was one of 28 Democrats to vote against a bill codifying the overturning of the "gag rule" that prohibited staff at federally funded family planning clinics from discussing abortion.

Klink went to work after the primary, meeting with the House leadership in May to lobby for spots on such influential committees as Energy and Commerce and Appropriations.

Like many other freshmen, Klink did not get either of those prize assignments, but he was given spots on Banking, Finance and Urban Affairs; Education and Labor; and Small Business.

In the general election, Klink rolled to a victory over his Republican opponent with 78 percent of the vote. College professor Gordon R. Johnston had run twice before — in 1988, he had gotten 29 percent of the vote; in 1990, he jumped to 44 percent, but it was attributed by local observers to disenchantment with Kolter.

Pennsylvania 4

West — Beaver County; part of Westmoreland County

The mostly abandoned steel mills that line the Beaver and Ohio rivers in western Pennsylvania haunt the 4th District towns that once lived and breathed by them.

In Aliquippa, a seven-mile-long steelworks employed 15,000 at its peak. Today, it is operated by a skeleton crew. So, too, is the town, which has about one-third of the population it did in the 1950s. Across the river in Ambridge, there is a similar story of economic struggle.

The hard-luck Beaver Valley and the district's largest city, New Castle (Lawrence County), also have experienced the decline of heavy manufacturing in the past generation. Union strength remains unbroken, though, providing the district with a solid Democratic majority. Beaver and Lawrence counties turned in two of the state's strongest showings for unsuccessful Democratic Senate nominee Lynn Yeakel in 1992. In presidential voting, Bill Clinton handily won both counties, topping George Bush by more than 2-to-1 in Beaver and by about 8,000 votes in Lawrence.

Beaver County, dotted by boroughs and townships with evocative (if not imaginative) names such as Big Beaver, Little Beaver, Beaver Falls, South Beaver and Raccoon, is the district's most populous county. A little more than one-third of the Democratic primary vote is cast here.

In 4th District congressional politics, Beaver and Lawrence counties are suspicious of candidates who do not hail from the region. Observers say that voters here would be more inclined to support a candidate from over the border in Youngstown, Ohio, than a candidate from rival Westmoreland County, which is miles to the east, on the other side of Pittsburgh. Westmoreland is connected to the rest of the 4th by only a thin corridor of land in northern Allegheny County.

Traditionally, the representative of the 4th has hailed from the district's western region. Beaver County has been accustomed to throwing around its weight in elections ever since the late 19th century, when local product Matthew Quay was a U.S. senator and head of a powerful local political machine. But in the 1992 House contest, voters in the western region set aside their geographic bias and supported Klink, who is from Westmoreland County.

The Allegheny River divides Westmoreland County from Allegheny County. On the Allegheny County side are Natrona Heights and Tarentum; on the eastern side of the river in Westmoreland are Lower Burrell and Arnold. Farther south, the 4th takes in Jeannette, but the district stops short of one of southwestern Pennsylvania's population centers, the city of Greensburg. Roughly one-fourth of the district's registered Democrats hail from Westmoreland.

A thorough search will turn up some Republicans, located mostly in farming communities or in Butler County, whose southern tier is in the 4th. (The rest of Butler is in the 21st.) In 1980, 1984 and 1988, Butler County voted Republican for president.

1990 Population: 565,792. White 544,659 (96%), Black 17,973 (3%), Other 3,160 (1%). Hispanic origin 2,633 (<1%). 18 and over 431,903 (76%), 62 and over 112,761 (20%). Median age: 37.

Committees

Banking, Finance & Urban Affairs (29th of 30 Democrats)
Economic Growth

Education & Labor (22nd of 28 Democrats)
Labor-Management Relations; Postsecondary Education

Small Business (21st of 27 Democrats)
Procurement, Taxation & Tourism; SBA Legislation & the General Economy

Campaign Finance

	Receipts	Receipts from PACs		Expenditures
1992				
Klink (D)	$264,293	$18,150	(7%)	$240,419
Johnston (R)	$14,238	0		$13,993

Key Votes

1993

Require parental notification of minors' abortions	Y
Require unpaid family and medical leave	Y
Approve national "motor voter" registration bill	Y
Approve budget increasing taxes and reducing deficit	Y
Approve economic stimulus plan	Y

Elections

1992 General		
Ron Klink (D)	186,684	(78%)
Gordon R. Johnston (R)	48,484	(20%)
Drew Ley (I)	2,754	(1%)
1992 Primary		
Ron Klink (D)	45,884	(45%)
Mike Veon (D)	22,379	(22%)
Joe Kolter (D)	19,683	(19%)
Frank LaGrotta (D)	13,153	(13%)

District Vote for President

	1992	
D	118,644	(48%)
R	76,124	(31%)
I	50,611	(21%)

5 William F. Clinger (R)

Of Warren — Elected 1978; 8th Term

Born: April 4, 1929, Warren, Pa.
Education: Johns Hopkins U., B.A. 1951; U. of Virginia, LL.B. 1965.
Military Service: Navy, 1951-55.
Occupation: Lawyer.
Family: Wife, Julia Whitla; four children.
Religion: Presbyterian.
Political Career: No previous office.
Capitol Office: 2160 Rayburn Bldg. 20515; 225-5121.

In Washington: A moderate Republican not known for generating waves, Clinger has another side to his persona that occasionally produces political gems that his more flamboyant colleagues might envy.

In the 102nd, Clinger gained national attention (if little congressional support) with his bill directing the architect of the Capitol to design and build a "National Debt Clock" as a constant reminder of the expanding federal debt. The cost would have been underwritten by private contributions. "Every time we leave our offices to vote," Clinger said, "we'll see the exact consequences of our actions."

This was not the first time it appeared that Clinger had stepped out of character. However, despite his easygoing style, he is also an astute politician who knows the game and can play when he deems it necessary.

That quality may appear more often in the 103rd, as he moves into his new role as ranking Republican on the Government Operations Committee. Although the committee rarely puts forth major legislation — its role is oversight — it can sometimes be an attention-getter.

Early in 1993, Clinger made news by asking the General Accounting Office to review Hillary Rodham Clinton's role as head of the President's Task Force on Health Care Reform. Clinger questioned whether she should be allowed to head the task force and conduct private meetings.

Although White House officials and Senate Democrats disputed Clinger's contention, he argued that the practice could be a violation of the Federal Advisory Committee Act, which says that task force meetings must be conducted in public if any members are not federal employees.

Clinger's activism contributed to a court challenge. The judge found that the first lady's role violated current law but that parts of the relevant law were unconstitutional. Mrs. Clinton continued to head the task force and perform her duties, but Clinger felt he had scored a hit. In addition, the White House released the names of task force members in response to a GAO request. Major task force meetings were subsequently opened to the public.

On Government Operations, Clinger will serve opposite Chairman John Conyers Jr. of Michigan, who shared a friendship and close working relationship with former ranking member Frank Horton of New York. Horton, a largely nonpartisan liberal Republican, shared Conyers' views on many issues. His retirement at the end of the 102nd, and Clinger's move to the ranking slot, will introduce a more partisan note and likely will make Conyers' life more difficult on the committee.

Clinger was one of the Republican moderates who set aside their trepidation and voted to elect conservative firebrand Newt Gingrich of Georgia as GOP minority whip in March 1989. A low-key establishment type on Public Works, Clinger seemed to be just the sort of "Old Bull" Republican who would have backed GOP regular Edward Madigan of Illinois for the whip's job.

But in supporting Gingrich, Clinger showed an eye for insider politics. Clinger stood to gain legislative influence with a Gingrich victory: The Georgian promised to take a leave from Public Works if he won, opening his ranking position on the high-profile Aviation Subcommittee for Clinger, who was next in seniority. The position quickly afforded Clinger opportunities on hot topics from air terrorism to airline deregulation.

Clinger, an attorney, came to Congress with a public works background — he was general counsel to the federal Economic Development Administration (EDA) under President Gerald R. Ford — and he has dedicated his House career to the field.

Clinger balances concern for the national debt with an appetite for public projects important to his district. He supports his colleagues' attempts to do the same. Though some critics deride the Public Works Committee as a chute for pork barrel spending, Clinger is a steadfast supporter of public works projects and a critic of "shortsighted" people who scorn them as wasteful. "Congressional efforts to cut back on spending have the unfortunate effect of discouraging public and private investment in our infrastructure," Clinger said in 1988.

Early in the 100th Congress, public works

Pennsylvania 5

Northwest, Central — State College

To get a rough idea of the size of the 5th, take a ride on meandering Route 6, which runs along the northern tier of the district. It is not as quick as I-80, which crosses east-west through Pennsylvania's midsection, but the old road affords more time to notice the hundreds of small hamlets that dot the rural landscape.

The road also cuts through the heartland of the Allegheny National Forest Region, an area covering about one-half million acres of woodland. It runs by Pine Creek Gorge in Tioga County — the attraction known as "Pennsylvania's Grand Canyon" — and continues on all the way past Warren, on the western outskirts of the district.

With hundreds of thousands of acres of state game land, hunting and fishing are sacred pursuits for many of the people here. In some areas, schools close for the first day of hunting season.

Tourism and recreation are the district's economic mainstays, but beyond those industries, there is not much else.

Geographically, the 5th is the state's largest congressional district. It includes all of 11 counties and parts of six others.

Population is fairly lightly sprinkled through the rural counties. The only sizable concentration of people is in Centre County, where the borough of State College is home to Pennsylvania State University, which has 39,000 students and 2,200 faculty members.

A sleepy college town three decades ago, State College has grown to form the nucleus of an emerging metropolitan area. The university has spawned a small high-tech industrial complex outside town that attracts Republican-voting engineers.

Centre County as a whole tends to vote Republican, but the university community keeps it competitive for Democrats. In 1992, Bill Clinton and Democratic Senate nominee Lynn Yeakel both carried Centre County.

Neighboring Clinton County is nominally Democratic; in 1992, it supported Clinton and Yeakel. West of Clinton County, paper mill workers help give Elk County a strong Democratic tilt.

The counties of the northern tier, on the New York border, are less receptive to Democrats. They form the top segment of the GOP voting bloc known as the Republican "T." The "T" is rooted in the strongly Republican counties that begin on the Maryland border and rise north, before fanning out east and west on the northern tier. McKean, Potter and Tioga counties stuck with George Bush in his losing 1992 effort, and they also backed GOP Sen. Arlen Specter.

Another Republican loyalist in 1992 was Jefferson County. But the county's politics take a back seat to its most famous resident, Punxsutawney Phil, the groundhog who becomes a national media star every Feb. 2; Phil was featured in the movie "Groundhog Day," which was released in 1993. Another 5th District icon is Edwin Drake, the 19th century Jed Clampett who drilled America's first crude oil well near what is now Oil City (Venango County).

1990 Population: 565,813. White 553,157 (98%), Black 5,600 (1%), Other 7,056 (1%). Hispanic origin 3,456 (1%). 18 and over 431,688 (76%), 62 and over 95,173 (17%). Median age: 33.

funding caused Clinger to cross swords with a Pennsylvania Republican colleague, conservative activist and Gingrich ally Robert S. Walker. Clinger took the House floor to defend an $88 billion highway bill — which included a road improvement project in his district — stating, "Every project that is funded under this demonstration area is a vitally needed project." Walker disagreed, saying the bill contained "page after page after page after page after page after page of pork."

Clinger's most visible effort in the 101st Congress concerned not aviation but a more earthbound subject: trash.

A reporter in Clinger's Pennsylvania district alerted him to the practice of "backhauling," whereby truckers use the same vehicle to haul garbage in one direction and food in another. Clinger sponsored two hearings to investigate the matter, and in October 1989 introduced a bill to ban backhauling that poses a health threat. The House adopted most of Clinger's provisions as part of a compromise package on the issue, and a backhauling bill became law in late 1990. "We don't eat food out of garbage cans, and we shouldn't be expected to eat food out of garbage trucks," Clinger said.

At Home: After winning two bruising re-elections in 1984 and 1986, Clinger has restored his secure position in this mountainous Pennsylvania district. In 1992, he picked up both parties' nominations and went unopposed.

Clinger contributed to his own woes in the mid-1980s by getting a bit too comfortable. After he returned the old 23rd District to GOP control in 1978, he won two easy re-elections.

Then in 1984, he seemed to relax against Democrat Bill Wachob, who controlled the campaign debate. Wachob pounded away at the wealthy incumbent, contending that the district needed a more active congressman who would fight for programs to create more jobs. Without Reagan's coattails, Clinger might have been defeated. As it was, he lost five of the district's 12 counties, including the most populous, Centre County (State College).

In their 1986 rematch, Clinger was far more aggressive with Wachob, pointing to his record as a state legislator and calling him a "very liberal Democrat" with views "out of sync" with the traditionally Republican district. And Clinger maintained he was much more effective than Wachob painted him, pointing to a number of projects he had won for the 23rd.

Wachob was supported by an array of teachers, environmentalists and consumer activists. But Clinger effectively portrayed himself as a hard-working, moderate Republican, and he had the money to make his case. He swept 10 counties, including Centre, and pushed his share of the vote up to 55 percent.

After an easy re-election in 1988, Clinger slipped a bit to 59 percent in 1990 against a little-known Democrat whose campaign was designed to tap anti-Congress sentiment.

The son of a businessman in Warren County, at the district's northwest corner, Clinger worked in advertising for a mail-order house, then became a lawyer. Following his work in the Economic Development Administration, he came home to challenge Democratic Rep. Joseph Ammerman, who had ousted the district's aging GOP incumbent, Albert Johnson, in 1976.

Ammerman had compiled a liberal voting record as a freshman, which might have been enough of a liability for a Democrat in a traditionally Republican district. But in late August 1978, Ammerman broke his hip in an automobile accident and was hospitalized for six weeks, losing valuable campaign time.

Clinger cited his Washington experience to illustrate his campaign theme that many federal programs did not work and needed revamping. While his win over Ammerman was not spectacular, it discouraged any strong opposition until 1984.

Committees

Government Operations (Ranking)
Legislation & National Security

Public Works & Transportation (2nd of 24 Republicans)
Aviation (ranking); Surface Transportation; Water Resources & the Environment

Elections

1992 General		
William F. Clinger (R, D)	188,911	(100%)
1990 General		
William F. Clinger (R)	78,189	(59%)
Daniel J. Shannon (D)	53,465	(41%)

Previous Winning Percentages: **1988** (62%) **1986** (55%) **1984** (52%) **1982** (65%) **1980** (74%) **1978** (54%)

District Vote for President

	1992	
D	78,049	(36%)
R	89,373	(41%)
I	48,093	(22%)

Campaign Finance

	Receipts	Receipts from PACs		Expend-itures
1992				
Clinger (R)	$286,477	$142,894	(50%)	$266,090
1990				
Clinger (R)	$349,208	$190,302	(54%)	$338,431
Shannon (D)	$6,764	0		$6,765

Key Votes

1993	
Require parental notification of minors' abortions	Y
Require unpaid family and medical leave	N
Approve national "motor voter" registration bill	N
Approve budget increasing taxes and reducing deficit	N
Approve economic stimulus plan	N
1992	
Approve balanced-budget constitutional amendment	Y
Close down space station program	N
Approve U.S. aid for former Soviet Union	Y
Allow shifting funds from defense to domestic programs	N
1991	
Extend unemployment benefits using deficit financing	Y
Approve waiting period for handgun purchases	N
Authorize use of force in Persian Gulf	Y

Voting Studies

	Presidential Support		Party Unity		Conservative Coalition	
Year	**S**	**O**	**S**	**O**	**S**	**O**
1992	75	19	71	24	83	8
1991	76	23	66	32	81	16
1990	66	32	65	29	89	9
1989	78	22	66	32	90	10
1988	47	47	67	28	76	24
1987	54	42	59	38	74	23
1986	52	47	48	49	84	14
1985	50	48	54	38	65	31
1984	56	42	54	42	64	34
1983	61	39	62 †	37 †	66	34
1982	65	35	61	38	77	23
1981	63	37	69	31	72	28

† Not eligible for all recorded votes.

Interest Group Ratings

Year	ADA	AFL-CIO	CCUS	ACU
1992	10	8	88	90
1991	15	42	90	70
1990	28	18	77	55
1989	20	17	100	64
1988	25	62	86	63
1987	24	50	73	43
1986	50	86	44	45
1985	35	59	57	48
1984	40	38	67	54
1983	15	18	95	52
1982	25	20	64	36
1981	30	20	89	73

6 Tim Holden (D)

Of St. Clair — Elected 1992; 1st Term

Born: March 5, 1957, St. Clair, Pa.
Education: Bloomsburg U., B.A. 1980.
Occupation: Sheriff.
Family: Separated.
Religion: Roman Catholic.
Political Career: Schuylkill County sheriff, 1985-93.
Capitol Office: 1421 Longworth Bldg. 20515; 225-5546.

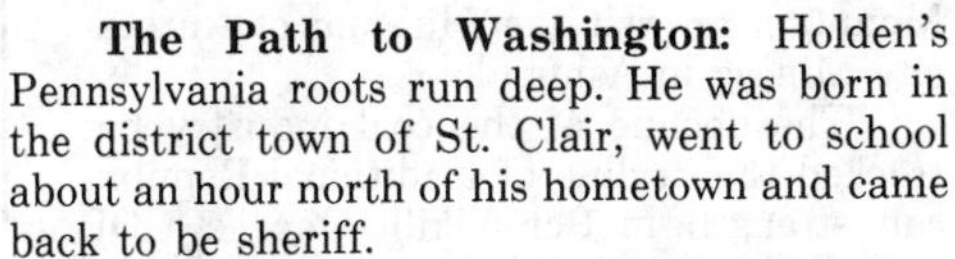

The Path to Washington: Holden's Pennsylvania roots run deep. He was born in the district town of St. Clair, went to school about an hour north of his hometown and came back to be sheriff.

When Holden shows up at a fire hall barbecue or a high school football game, he moves with the easy affability of someone who has spent most of his life at such events.

His family has a tradition of public service: His father, Joseph "Socks" Holden, served as a Schuylkill County commissioner for almost two decades beginning in 1959. And his great-grandfather, John Siney, founded the Miner's Benevolent Association, the forerunner of the United Mine Workers Union.

Although redistricting made the 6th more appealing for a Republican challenger, Holden was able to retain the seat for the Democrats, despite the fact that he hails from the less-populated Schuylkill County portion of the district. That side of the district is dominated by farming businesses.

In the more Republican east side of the district, residents are struggling to redefine the local economy in the face of the decline of heavy industry and the railroad center in Reading.

In the primary, Holden benefited from the fact that two candidates from the more-populous eastern half split the vote in that section, allowing Holden a plurality of 39 percent.

Then during the general election, Holden emphasized his "man of the people" roots — in an effort to contrast himself with his opponent, John E. Jones, a lawyer and judge from Schuylkill County.

"I'm not an elitist. I'm not personally wealthy, and I don't just come around when I'm running for office," Holden said.

Jones had a big financial advantage over Holden. He outspent Holden by more than $150,000 — but much of that money went to acquainting the district with the new Republican challenger.

Holden, meanwhile, had to introduce himself to neighboring Berks County, the eastern end of the district.

He was somewhat hampered by the fact the fact that retiring incumbent Gus Yatron, though from Berks County, had seen his popularity in the area decline.

Jones tried to paint Holden as a lightweight liberal who would bring little in intellect or leadership to the job of U.S. representative.

Holden characterized himself as a "conservative Democrat." He used his name recognition in Schuylkill County to run a campaign stressing his commitment to keeping high-paying jobs in the district.

Holden opposes the recently concluded North American Free Trade Agreement because he contends that it would export U.S. jobs to Mexico, where wages are significantly lower.

He favors the establishment of a national board of health-care professionals to set rates for medical care and pharmaceuticals. But he opposes the creation of a national health-care system, which he calls "socialized medicine."

In the environmental arena, Holden campaigned on a platform stressing the need to reduce the amount of untreated sewage that is dumped into regional streams and the Susquehanna River.

Holden defeated Jones 52 percent to 48 percent in the general election.

Holden said he was heartened by the election of Bill Clinton and said he agreed with Clinton's calls for change in health care, job creation and environmental protection.

"I agree with a lot of the things Clinton said during the campaign, like the line-item veto," Holden said. "I think I'll have a voting record that will be close to his proposals."

In addition to supporting a Democratic version of the line-item veto that the House passed in April 1993, Holden was also one of only 33 Democrats to support the more potent GOP substitute.

Farming is a major industry in the district, and Holden lobbied hard for — and got — a seat on the Agriculture Committee.

He was turned down, however, in his bid for a seat on the prestigious Energy and Commerce Committee.

Pennsylvania 6

Southeast — Reading

The story of the 6th is a tale of two counties, both hit hard by deindustrialization. Berks County, the more populous of the two, learned to diversify its economy. Schuylkill County, the poorer cousin to the north, never truly weaned itself from King Coal.

Reading, the largest city in Berks and the district, is no longer recognized as a major railroad or manufacturing center. It remains more industrialized than most of the state but now features a large and diverse economic base where no single employer accounts for more than 8 percent of the work force. Where there once were steel and textile mills, now there are factory outlet stores. Bargain hunters often board buses to make the pilgrimage to the city that bills itself "the outlet capital of the world."

The city has seen an influx of Hispanics looking for work, which in turn sparked a migration of whites to the surrounding suburbs. Because of this migration, the outlying areas — once mainly agricultural and always supportive of Republicans — now turn in even bigger numbers for GOP candidates. In 1992, Berks County voted for George Bush and GOP Sen. Arlen Specter.

In southern Berks, residential developments have sprouted because the completion of Route 422 made it feasible to commute from this area to jobs in the Philadelphia area.

Schuylkill County is divided by the physical presence of Broad Mountain. To locals, "north of the mountain" means the coal belt that begins north of Pottsville, or what remains of the belt.

The domes of Eastern Orthodox churches built by the Eastern European miners in the late 19th century still dominate the roof lines of small, church-filled towns such as St. Clair. The "Molly McGuires," a secret organization that battled mine companies and their agents to provide better working and living conditions in the coal fields, were drawn from the ranks of Irish and Welsh immigrant miners.

Today, the county's coal tradition is a vein for tourism. Visitors can take a ride in an open mine car deep into Mahanoy Mountain or visit the Museum of Anthracite Mining in Ashland.

The decline of the coal industry has tracked the decline of traditional Republican strength in Schuylkill. Once a GOP stronghold, Schuylkill has become more receptive to Democrats in recent years, though Bush and Specter still managed to win here in 1992.

Pottsville, the largest city in the county, is where the county's remaining coal operations do business. It is home to the family-owned Yuengling brewery, America's oldest. Schuylkill County residents refer to it as "Vitamin Y."

Along the Susquehanna River, the 6th also takes in a strip of Northumberland County that includes Sunbury, another former manufacturing and railroad city that has fallen on hard times. The southeastern tip of the district dips into Montgomery County, to take in part of Pottstown.

1990 Population: 565,760. White 538,487 (95%), Black 13,870 (2%), Other 13,403 (2%). Hispanic origin 18,862 (3%). 18 and over 435,116 (77%), 62 and over 114,327 (20%). Median age: 36.

Committees

Agriculture (21st of 28 Democrats)
Department Operations; Environment, Credit & Rural Development; Livestock

Armed Services (31st of 34 Democrats)
Military Acquisition; Oversight & Investigations

Campaign Finance

	Receipts	Receipts from PACs	Expend-itures
1992			
Holden (D)	$293,468	$99,400 (34%)	$284,349
Jones (R)	$447,913	$92,604 (21%)	$442,058

Key Votes

1993

Require parental notification of minors' abortions	Y
Require unpaid family and medical leave	Y
Approve national "motor voter" registration bill	Y
Approve budget increasing taxes and reducing deficit	Y
Approve economic stimulus plan	Y

Elections

1992 General		
Tim Holden (D)	108,312	(52%)
John E. Jones (R)	99,694	(48%)
1992 Primary		
Tim Holden (D)	20,057	(39%)
Warren H. Haggerty Jr. (D)	16,647	(33%)
John A. Reusing (D)	14,193	(28%)

District Vote for President

	1992
D	78,326 (36%)
R	89,791 (41%)
I	50,207 (23%)

7 Curt Weldon (R)

Of Aston — Elected 1986; 4th Term

Born: July 22, 1947, Marcus Hook, Pa.
Education: West Chester State College, B.A. 1969.
Occupation: Teacher; consultant.
Family: Wife, Mary Gallagher; five children.
Religion: Protestant.
Political Career: Mayor of Marcus Hook, 1977-82; Delaware County Council, 1981-86; GOP nominee for U.S. House, 1984.
Capitol Office: 2452 Rayburn Bldg. 20515; 225-2011.

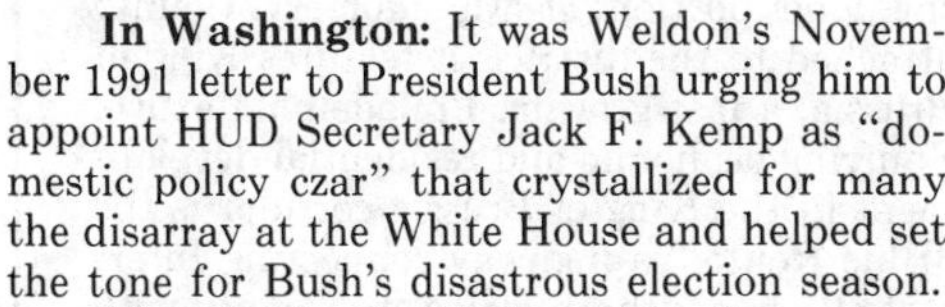

In Washington: It was Weldon's November 1991 letter to President Bush urging him to appoint HUD Secretary Jack F. Kemp as "domestic policy czar" that crystallized for many the disarray at the White House and helped set the tone for Bush's disastrous election season.

"We need one leader with the energy, enthusiasm and national clout to tackle our domestic agenda," said the letter, co-written by Weldon and Dan Burton of Indiana, and signed by 79 other House Republicans. "We must declare war on our domestic ills. Jack Kemp is the man to lead that war."

Weldon's choice of Kemp over Bush to cure the nation's problems illustrated his affinity for a conservative but activist federal role — an affinity that has been evident throughout Weldon's House tenure, whether it be pushing for fire safety regulations or fighting for military weaponry. It also illustrates his willingness to buck leaders of his own party, especially when his district is at stake.

For several years, Weldon has used his position on the Armed Services Committee to preserve the V-22 Osprey tilt-rotor helicopter, despite Bush administration efforts to kill it. He piloted the aircraft — whose production employs many in his district — past opposition from Bush Defense Secretary Dick Cheney and gave it enough momentum to survive repercussions from the crashes of two prototypes in 1991 and 1992.

In one high-profile 1989 episode, Weldon helped lead the successful fight against Cheney's proposal to cancel the Osprey. Weldon was one of only three committee Republicans to oppose the Defense secretary.

On other defense issues, Weldon has staked out a markedly conservative stance. He has repeatedly voted for more spending on the Strategic Defense Initiative, for supporting the contras in Nicaragua and for continued nuclear testing. In 1987, he was named the "most effective freshman" by the conservative American Security Council. But Weldon's single-minded efforts in behalf of the Osprey have kept him from becoming a Republican spokesman on broader defense issues.

Weldon's independence shows in his voting record. During President Ronald Reagan's last two years in office, Weldon sided with him less than half the time on those issues on which Reagan staked out a position. He backed Bush only slightly more often and voted against the two presidents on 14 of 21 override attempts.

Before Democratic Rep. Mike Espy of Mississippi became President Clinton's Agriculture secretary, he teamed up with Weldon to create The Empowerment Network, a nonprofit group seeking to take a middle ground by downplaying the role of government and emphasizing the authority of the individual and the individual's responsibility for his or her actions. The group draws heavily on the rhetoric espoused by Clinton in "Putting People First," his 1992 campaign manifesto.

While plenty of members aim to set the world on fire when they come to Congress, Weldon makes a splash by trying to stamp out fires. A founder of the Fire Services Caucus — the largest in Congress — he aggressively promotes fire safety. If there is smoke, count on Weldon to be there.

During the 1990 debate over a constitutional amendment to ban flag burning, Weldon led a squad of GOP House members who cased Capitol Hill brandishing fire extinguishers in search of demonstrators who might set Old Glory afire. In 1988, the former volunteer fire chief fought a blaze in the office of then-Speaker Jim Wright of Texas.

In a more conventional legislative pursuit in the 102nd Congress, Weldon sponsored and saw passed the "Fire Service Bill of Rights," a group of symbolic provisions that included a call for assuring fire and rescue personnel of proper notification when hazardous materials or infectious diseases are encountered on the job.

During the 101st Congress, Weldon helped exempt firefighting equipment from the Clean Air Act's phaseout of chlorofluorocarbons and worked on the 1990 Hotel-Motel Fire Safety Act.

At Home: Weldon's first victory in the

Pennsylvania 7

Suburban Philadelphia — Part of Delaware County

The anchor of the 7th District, Delaware County, provides a textbook example of a suburban Republican machine. There are more than a few working-class towns in the district, but in elections from the township level to the presidency, most voters pull the GOP lever.

From the 1920s to the mid-1970s, local politics were ruled by the "war board," a secretive group officially called the Delaware County Republican Board of Supervisors. The current GOP organization is a looser confederation, but party discipline and patronage still keep most of the 7th's voters in line.

That is what made George Bush's countywide defeat in 1992 so hard for local GOP officials to swallow. Bush visited Delaware County several times; its national prominence as a middle-class bastion makes it a must-stop for GOP statewide or presidential candidates.

Normally, one of the few places in the county where Democrats find sanctuary is Swarthmore, where Swarthmore College is located. The academic community at the respected liberal arts institution provides an island in a sea of Republicanism.

Closer to Philadelphia, older suburbs such as Norwood, Ridley Park and Upper Darby are mostly white and working class. Marcus Hook, an old oil refinery town along the Delaware River, also fits that description. The only concentrations of blacks in the county — in Yeadon, Darby and the city of Chester — are sliced out of the 7th and pieced onto the Philadelphia-based congressional districts.

Surrounding these areas, farther out on West Chester Pike, are more comfortably middle-class places such as Springfield and Newtown Square. In the district's southwest corner, Birmingham and Thornbury townships are less developed. The white-collar professionals in wealthy Radnor Township and on Philadelphia's affluent Main Line are less attuned to the GOP organization, but remain staunchly Republican. (Most of the Main Line is in the neighboring 13th, in Montgomery County.)

Upper Merion Township stands out as the lone portion of Montgomery County attached to the district; it features King of Prussia, a fast-growing Philadelphia exurb. Spurring economic and residential development in the King of Prussia corridor is the "Blue Route," a highway connecting Interstate 95 in southern Delaware County with the Schuylkill Expressway near King of Prussia. After decades of suburban discord over whether to build the route, its recent completion reduced traffic congestion in Delaware County and facilitated north-south commuting.

The 7th also contains a portion of Chester County. Tredyffrin Township holds the majority of its population, and includes the old-money mansions in Paoli and the newer residential developments of Chesterbrook. Farther west are less populous but emerging exurban townships such as East Whiteland, West Pikeland and West Vincent.

1990 Population: 565,746. White 530,827 (94%), Black 21,685 (4%), Other 13,234 (2%). Hispanic origin 5,305 (1%). 18 and over 440,851(78%), 62 and over 104,385 (18%). Median age: 36.

Republican 7th ended 12 years of Democratic control. The man frustrating the GOP was Bob Edgar, who lost a Senate bid in 1986. Weldon was the unanimous choice of local Republicans to succeed Edgar. The son of a factory worker and the youngest of nine children, Weldon is a former volunteer fireman, teacher and mayor of his hometown, Marcus Hook — a good fit for the 7th's conservative mix of blue- and white-collar workers.

Weldon rose to prominence as the architect of Marcus Hook's revival. A small working-class city at the 7th's southern end, it was gripped by economic decline and gang warfare when Weldon became GOP mayor in 1977. Ordering a series of tough police raids, he broke up the Pagan motorcycle gang and ended its illicit drug trafficking.

Weldon's accomplishments caught the eye of the powerful Delaware County GOP, and in 1981, with machine backing, Weldon won a County Council seat. He was elected chairman by popular ballot in early 1984.

In 1984, Weldon ran against Edgar, taking on a task that had thwarted five Republicans before him. Weldon lost by only 412 votes, and his near-miss made him the favorite when Edgar's Senate race opened up the 7th.

Weldon has won easy victories since then, although in 1990 he was criticized by his Democratic foe for his role in a Delaware County economic development agency he founded and chaired. According to a June 1989 audit by the Department of Housing and Urban Development, the agency misspent at least $1.6 million in federal funds. Weldon said that he had a largely absentee role in the agency's management and that a disgruntled former agency employee was trying to make him appear guilty of a cover-up. Voters seemed to accept Weldon's explanation; he won by nearly 2 to 1.

Those same charges were recycled in 1992 by Democrat Frank Daly. Helped by subtle changes through redistricting — and Weldon's nine overdrafts at the House bank — Democrats hoped to make a dent in Weldon's formidable base of support. But even in a year when the unthinkable happened — Bush lost in the GOP stronghold of Delaware County — Weldon crushed Daly with 66 percent.

Committees

Armed Services (7th of 22 Republicans)
Military Acquisition; Readiness

Merchant Marine & Fisheries (6th of 18 Republicans)
Oceanography, Gulf of Mexico & the Outer Continental Shelf (ranking); Environment & Natural Resources

Elections

1992 General		
Curt Weldon (R)	180,648	(66%)
Frank Daly (D)	91,623	(33%)
1992 Primary		
Curt Weldon (R)	73,304	(77%)
Fiorindo Vagnozzi (R)	21,413	(23%)
1990 General		
Curt Weldon (R)	105,868	(65%)
John Innelli (D)	56,292	(35%)

Previous Winning Percentages: 1988 (68%) **1986** (61%)

District Vote for President

1992
D 111,518 (39%)
R 123,954 (43%)
I 49,802 (17%)

Campaign Finance

	Receipts	Receipts from PACs		Expend-itures
1992				
Weldon (R)	$465,223	$185,187	(40%)	$565,974
Daly (D)	$177,826	$14,862	(8%)	$173,865
1990				
Weldon (R)	$504,744	$207,805	(41%)	$480,165
Innelli (D)	$109,966	$6,400	(6%)	$109,618

Key Votes

1993	
Require parental notification of minors' abortions	Y
Require unpaid family and medical leave	Y
Approve national "motor voter" registration bill	N
Approve budget increasing taxes and reducing deficit	N
Approve economic stimulus plan	N
1992	
Approve balanced-budget constitutional amendment	Y
Close down space station program	N
Approve U.S. aid for former Soviet Union	Y
Allow shifting funds from defense to domestic programs	N
1991	
Extend unemployment benefits using deficit financing	Y
Approve waiting period for handgun purchases	Y
Authorize use of force in Persian Gulf	Y

Voting Studies

	Presidential Support		Party Unity		Conservative Coalition	
Year	S	O	S	O	S	O
1992	68	31	82	16	83	17
1991	54	41	71	24	76	22
1990	50	44	67	29	80	15
1989	65	33	56	39	85	12
1988	45	49	66	25	84	16
1987	52	41	69	27	79	16

Interest Group Ratings

Year	ADA	AFL-CIO	CCUS	ACU
1992	25	83	88	80
1991	30	55	60	65
1990	33	42	69	54
1989	35	60	89	62
1988	30	77	71	59
1987	40	40	73	55

8 James C. Greenwood (R)

Of Erwinna — Elected 1992; 1st Term

Born: May 4, 1951, Philadelphia, Pa.
Education: Dickinson College, B.A. 1973.
Occupation: State official.
Family: Wife, Christina Paugh; four children.
Religion: Presbyterian.
Political Career: Pa. House, 1981-87; Pa. Senate, 1987-93.
Capitol Office: 515 Cannon Bldg. 20515; 225-4276.

The Path to Washington: Careful research told Greenwood that he could run successfully on a platform of change against a 14-year incumbent, despite his own 12-year political career.

Greenwood's pre-campaign survey showed that while voters in his district were annoyed with Congress and its members, "they didn't want to draw names at random from the phone book." They wanted to find someone who understood the system and would work for them, he said.

Incumbent Rep. Peter H. Kostmayer tried to tag Greenwood as "just another politician," but Greenwood shot back that he was different. His favorite line was that he has been "fired in the oven of the political process, but I haven't shattered."

The same could not be said of members of Congress, according to Greenwood, who called their attitude "me first" and cited "bounced checks, international junkets [and] deluxe perks" as evidence that Congress was no longer working. His campaign was helped by revelations of Kostmayer's 50 overdrafts at the House bank.

Greenwood faced an ethical dilemma of his own early in the 103rd Congress. Media reports in February 1993 disclosed that a House GOP conference that Greenwood (and more than 100 other GOP representatives) attended had been financed by lobbyists, some of whom had attended the conference. Greenwood subsequently announced that he intended to pay for the trip personally and that he would no longer accept PAC contributions.

Greenwood was also helped by the fact that in 1992 Republican registration in the district was at an all-time high, with 42,000 more GOP voters than Democrats, according to the National Republican Congressional Committee.

Greenwood served six years in the state House and then six in the Senate, where he made a name for himself on several issues.

He said his most significant accomplishment was crafting a change in the collective bargaining rights of teachers. Pennsylvania was the "teacher strike capital of the country," he said; the bill he helped pass into law changed the process to require final best offer arbitration. Greenwood noted that in 1991 there were 28 teacher strikes in the state and only three in 1992.

He also played a large role in passing a solid waste act that mandated recycling in Pennsylvania and set up a state "superfund" for environmental compensation, and in getting a housing bill through the Senate.

Greenwood sought and secured a seat on the much-sought-after Energy and Commerce Committee, which handles a wide range of issues.

"It's a legislating committee," he said, "and I'm a legislator. I want to be in a place where I can most effect legislation."

Greenwood called deficit reduction "the single most urgent crisis" for the country. He strongly supports a constitutional balanced-budget amendment, noting that Pennsylvania must have a balanced budget and that the requirement works.

To those who try to draw distinctions between a state's budget and the much more massive federal budget, with its responsibilities for defense, Greenwood said that while the federal government has duties "50 times larger than the states, it also has 50 times the income."

On taxes, Greenwood pledged not to vote for raising the marginal tax rate. (He noted during his campaign that as a state senator he had voted against every effort to raise taxes and supported every tax cut.) He has also pledged not to serve more than six terms in the House.

Within the Republican Party, Greenwood considers himself a centrist and a fiscal conservative, but he supports abortion rights. "I believe the federal government should be involved in fewer things rather than more," he said.

It was a high school romance that brought Greenwood into politics initially — his girlfriend's father was a state legislator — and while the romance ultimately ended, the professional marriage of Greenwood and politics is lasting.

After working for his girlfriend's father as a legislative assistant and campaign manager, he later decided to run for office, winning his state House seat in 1980 and then moving to the Senate in 1986.

Pennsylvania 8

Northern Philadelphia suburbs — Bucks County

Population growth and development have changed some of the character of the 8th, but not its politics. Bucks County is still Republican turf, as evidenced in 1992.

Former Democratic Rep. Peter H. Kostmayer had held the seat for all but two years since 1977 with tenacious constituent service and the votes of independents and Democrats from lower Bucks County. His environmentalist credentials also had some appeal among moderate Republicans. But even as Bill Clinton narrowly won the county in 1992 — with less than 40 percent — voters threw out their Democratic incumbent. In the Senate contest, the county backed GOP Sen. Arlen Specter for reelection.

Part of the reason for Kostmayer's upset was the selection of a strong GOP nominee, one whose moderate brand of Republicanism had countywide appeal from the landed gentry and farmers of Upper Bucks to the newly arrived independent voters. These newcomers — who include business executives from New Jersey and Manhattan — have fueled a two-decade population boom that has altered some of the area's rural charm.

Places such as Newtown Township experienced exponential growth in the 1980s; New Hope, a quaint artists' colony along the Delaware River, has turned into a tourist mecca.

The lure was Bucks County's rich history and rolling countryside. Established in 1682 as one of Pennsylvania's three original counties, Bucks contains mansions such as Pennsbury Manor, the Georgian-style mansion and plantation William Penn built for himself and his second wife. Washington Crossing was the site from which, on Christmas Day 1776, George Washington crossed the Delaware River to attack Hessian mercenaries in Trenton. In the early 20th century, New York intellectuals and prominent writers such as Dorothy Parker and Pearl S. Buck found refuge in Bucks County.

Much of the countryside in upper Bucks remains largely undeveloped and heavily Republican. Democrats can stay competitive in the county's midsection in communities such as Warminster and Doylestown.

Lower Bucks is more fertile ground for Democrats, with its grittier ambiance and closer association with Philadelphia. Levittown's tightly spaced homes, built after World War II, attracted thousands of ethnic Democrats moving from the big city.

Democratic strength surged in the 1980s as lower Bucks struggled with industrial problems typified by the massive layoffs in the remaining work force at the USX (formerly U.S. Steel) Fairless Works. But Republicans still hold a clear countywide voter registration advantage.

As a whole, the 8th contains all of Bucks County and about 25,000 voters in Montgomery County. One of five districts that take in some slice of Montgomery, the 8th has a portion of the county that includes Horsham and part of Lower Moreland Township.

1990 Population: 565,787. White 537,517 (95%), Black 15,995 (3%), Other 11,679 (2%). Hispanic origin 9,162 (2%). 18 and over 421,078 (74%), 62 and over 76,344 (13%). Median age: 34.

Committee

Energy & Commerce (16th of 17 Republicans)
Commerce, Consumer Protection & Competitiveness; Health & the Environment

Campaign Finance

	Receipts	Receipts from PACs		Expend-itures
1992				
Greenwood (R)	$721,654	$179,742	(25%)	$717,249
Kostmayer (D)	$1,239,616	$530,921	(43%)	$1,242,355

Key Votes

1993

Require parental notification of minors' abortions	N
Require unpaid family and medical leave	N
Approve national "motor voter" registration bill	N
Approve budget increasing taxes and reducing deficit	N
Approve economic stimulus plan	N

Elections

1992 General		
James C. Greenwood (R)	129,593	(52%)
Peter H. Kostmayer (D)	114,095	(46%)
William H. Magerman (MFC)	5,850	(2%)
1992 Primary		
James C. Greenwood (R)	36,394	(79%)
Joseph P. Schiaffino (R)	9,472	(21%)

District Vote for President

1992

D 101,630 (40%)
R 99,269 (39%)
I 56,261 (22%)

9 Bud Shuster (R)

Of Everett — Elected 1972; 11th Term

Born: Jan. 23, 1932, Glassport, Pa.
Education: U. of Pittsburgh, B.S. 1954; Duquesne U., M.B.A. 1960; American U., Ph.D. 1967.
Military Service: Army, 1954-56.
Occupation: Computer industry executive.
Family: Wife, Patricia Rommel; five children.
Religion: United Church of Christ.
Political Career: No previous office.
Capitol Office: 2188 Rayburn Bldg. 20515; 225-2431.

In Washington: Those who do great works usually are not memorialized until after they die. But House members who help create public works often have things named after them while they are still very much alive.

Take, for example, the Bud Shuster By-Way. Funding for this brief stretch of four-lane highway, running parallel to the Pennsylvania Turnpike through Shuster's home town of Everett, was obtained by Shuster, a veteran of the House Public Works and Transportation Committee and now (as of 1993) its ranking Republican.

Shuster typifies the "Public Works Republican," a breed characterized by overall fiscal conservatism but a soft spot for asphalt, especially when it is laid close to home. During the reign of conservative Presidents Reagan and Bush, Shuster typically supported their positions better than two-thirds of the time on House floor votes. He supported not only their conservative defense and foreign policies, but also in many cases their effort to cut or limit the growth of federal spending.

However, public works funding, or "infrastructure investment" as it has come to be known, is the one area inviolate to Shuster and like-minded committee members. Critics of Congress may decry its "pork barrel" spending on a range of projects, but public works advocates are like as not to deem the projects worthy — indeed, critical — investments in the nation's future economic viability.

"There's no such thing as a Republican or a Democratic bridge," said Shuster in early 1993, "or a Republican or a Democratic airport."

Such devotion to the cause brought Shuster and other leaders of the Public Works Committee into conflict in 1991 with the Bush administration over the shape of the highway bill. After their first version — which included a 5-cents-per-gallon increase in the gasoline tax — met with White House disapproval and went down to defeat, Shuster helped fashion a new bill that was sold more as a job-creation measure.

Shuster's jousting with Bush, though, was no worse than with his predecessor. When the Reagan administration attacked congressional proposals for highway "demonstration projects" as wasteful, Shuster was enraged. "It's a congressional prerogative," he said. "We find it absolutely repugnant that an administration can say that it's all right for a faceless bureaucrat to decide where money should be spent, but it's wrong for a congressman to identify crucial, needed projects."

It was on a measure loaded with such demonstration projects — the $88 billion highway bill enacted in the 100th Congress — that Shuster had one of his most notable breaks with Reagan. Working closely, as he had on previous road-funding bills, with then-Public Works Chairman James J. Howard of New Jersey, Shuster helped craft the legislation; when Reagan vetoed the bill, Shuster strongly supported its override. He played a similar role on the clean water act amendments enacted in 1987 over Reagan's veto.

Each of these pieces of legislation contained projects that Shuster had promoted as necessary to the economic development and recovery of Pennsylvania's 9th District, a rugged, rural stretch dotted with struggling blue-collar towns such as Altoona.

Projects Shuster has pushed include a $90 million upgrade for Route 220 from Altoona to Tyrone; a Franklin County exit off Interstate 81; a $5.5 million Route 36 bypass around the town of Loysburg; and $3.2 million for a bus-testing facility in Altoona.

Sometimes his projects have generated flak. A column by humorist Dave Barry in early 1992 lampooned an automated pedestrian sidewalk that Shuster sought for Altoona.

That May, the Altoona Mirror ran a story intimating that Shuster had money inserted in the 1991 transportation bill for an experimental monorail project that was likely to be developed by a company employing Shuster's daughter and a former aide. Shuster denied any ethical wrongdoing.

Shuster, whose district's ailing industrial areas have an interest in trade protection, also

Pennsylvania 9

South Central — Altoona

This south-central Pennsylvania region long has been a passageway from the East to Pittsburgh and beyond. Transportation was its primary focus, in particular the railroad industry.

The district's largest city, Altoona (Blair County), once prospered as a rail center despite its relatively inaccessible location in the Allegheny Mountains. Johnstown was but 40 miles to the west, but between them loomed the Alleghenies.

Crossing the southern Alleghenies was a significant undertaking in the mid-19th century, but the old Pennsylvania Railroad overcame the harsh landscape by devising engineering marvels such as Horseshoe Curve, just west of Altoona.

The Pennsylvania Railroad also nurtured the city of Altoona, but as the rail industry declined, population withered. When the railroad workers left, they took their Democratic loyalties with them. In 1992, George Bush and GOP Sen. Arlen Specter both carried Blair County.

Today, the remnants of the railroad industry serve as a tourism draw. Besides Horseshoe Curve, railroad buffs can visit the Railroaders Memorial Museum in Altoona or the Allegheny Portage Railroad National Historic Site. The Allegheny Portage was part of an early attempt to link Philadelphia with Pittsburgh and the West.

The Pennsylvania Turnpike, the nation's first superhighway, crosses the southern section of the 9th District's tortured topography. Its epitome is Breezewood, best known as the "Town of Motels." Though Bedford County features 14 historic covered bridges, travelers recognize it better for the garish display of neon signs adorning the hotels and fast-food restaurants of the turnpike's Interchange 12, at Breezewood.

Before the turnpike's opening in 1940, Bedford County was a destination point, rather than a stopover. The pure and soothing waters of Bedford Springs attracted not only the afflicted, but the elite. President James Buchanan — who was born in the 9th — made the resort his summer White House.

For the most part, the 9th is a series of small villages scattered among the mountains. It has little industry; its farmers raise cattle for beef and milk.

The isolation and agricultural character of the region breeds a strong sense of conservatism. The eight counties wholly contained in the 9th backed both Bush and Specter; Snyder County, the 9th's easternmost, on the Susquehanna River, voted more than 2-to-1 for Bush.

Clearfield County's industrial tradition gives Democrats an edge, but its voting habits are as anomalous to the district as its location in the extreme northwest. The district includes all of Clearfield, save for one township that is in the 5th.

The 5th and the 9th districts also share Centre County, home to Pennsylvania State University in State College. State College is not in the 9th, but outlying towns such as Port Matilda and Philipsburg in the western portion of Centre County are included.

1990 Population: 565,803. White 556,077 (98%), Black 6,654 (1%), Other 3,072 (1%). Hispanic origin 2,470 (<1%). 18 and over 425,600 (75%), 62 and over 104,203 (18%). Median age: 35.

uses his position to promote "Buy American" provisions in public works bills. In another manifestation of Shuster's concerns about hard economic times in his district, he cast one of his infrequent votes against Bush in September 1991 when he supported extended unemployment benefits.

Shuster's interests are not confined to public works and jobs. Indeed, during the 102nd Congress he had something of a profile in the media as the ranking Republican on the Intelligence Committee.

There, one of his causes was requiring members and staff of the committee to take an oath of secrecy in dealing with U.S. intelligence information. "This city leaks like a sieve," he said, "and we need to set an example."

The effort by Shuster, initially opposed by Democrats, signaled that the committee's Republicans would be more confrontational toward its liberal majority. Shuster's three-term tenure on Intelligence ended with the 102nd.

Shuster's willingness to take on committee Democrats called to mind his early years in Congress. Angling then for a GOP leadership position, he tried to earn his stripes by blasting the Democrats from the House floor.

Shuster was president of his 1972 Republican House class; six years later, he out-campaigned front-runner Bill Frenzel of Minnesota for the chairmanship of the Republican Policy Committee. In that post, he gained a reputation as a partisan "hatchet man," firing a verbal barrage at the Democratic majority nearly every day on the floor, launching a brief filibuster to protest changes in the schedule, and bringing a toy duck on the floor to complain about a "lame-duck" session.

However, Shuster's one big thrust at a top leadership position, minority whip, was thwarted by Trent Lott of Mississippi in 1981. Starting as a distinct underdog, Shuster campaigned with his typical intensity and closed the gap. But Lott held on to win by a 96-90 vote of the House Republican Conference.

At Home: While Shuster has some detractors in local political circles, even in the GOP organization of the 9th's most populous county, Blair (Altoona), he remains untouchable at the polls. Not since 1984 has he had primary or general election opposition.

In 1984, he did draw an interesting Democratic challenger in 62-year-old Nancy Kulp, who played Miss Jane Hathaway on "The Beverly Hillbillies" television comedy. Retired from show business and living on a Pennsylvania farm, she accused Shuster of voting down the line with Reagan and ignoring the needs of farmers, veterans and elderly constituents.

Shuster counterattacked vigorously. Among his salvos was a radio commercial featuring the leading actor from the series, Buddy Ebsen. In the ad Ebsen said that he had "dropped her a note to say, 'Hey, Nancy, I love you dearly but you're too liberal for me' — I've got to go with Bud Shuster." Voters agreed; Shuster won re-election with two-thirds of the vote.

Before entering politics, Shuster had a successful business career with the Radio Corporation of America and as an independent electronics entrepreneur. When GOP Rep. J. Irving Whalley announced his retirement in 1972, Shuster embarked on a self-generated campaign and won the Republican primary over a state senator with significant party backing.

Committee

Public Works & Transportation (Ranking)

Elections

1992 General		
Bud Shuster (R)	182,406	(100%)
1990 General		
Bud Shuster (R)	106,632	(100%)

Previous Winning Percentages: **1988** (100%) **1986** (100%) **1984** (67%) **1982** (65%) **1980** (100%) **1978** (75%) **1976** (100%) **1974** (57%) **1972** (62%)

District Vote for President

1992

D	66,929 (33%)
R	97,772 (48%)
I	40,204 (20%)

Campaign Finance

	Receipts	Receipts from PACs	Expend-itures
1992			
Shuster (R)	$557,315	$187,250 (34%)	$556,385
1990			
Shuster (R)	$417,658	$181,469 (43%)	$429,942

Key Votes

1993	
Require parental notification of minors' abortions	Y
Require unpaid family and medical leave	N
Approve national "motor voter" registration bill	N
Approve budget increasing taxes and reducing deficit	N
Approve economic stimulus plan	N
1992	
Approve balanced-budget constitutional amendment	Y
Close down space station program	Y
Approve U.S. aid for former Soviet Union	N
Allow shifting funds from defense to domestic programs	N
1991	
Extend unemployment benefits using deficit financing	Y
Approve waiting period for handgun purchases	N
Authorize use of force in Persian Gulf	Y

Voting Studies

	Presidential Support		Party Unity		Conservative Coalition	
Year	**S**	**O**	**S**	**O**	**S**	**O**
1992	74	26	86	10	92	8
1991	68	28	75	20	92	3
1990	63	36	78	19	85	9
1989	76	23	74	26	100	0
1988	68	27	75	21	89	5
1987	66	31	74	23	88	12
1986	77	22	85	11	90	8
1985	66	34	86	10	87	11
1984	63	37	83	15	90	8
1983	71	21	85	5	90	8
1982	56	23	60	13	60	18
1981	76	22	89	11	99	1

Interest Group Ratings

Year	ADA	AFL-CIO	CCUS	ACU
1992	5	17	88	100
1991	15	42	90	95
1990	11	9	92	96
1989	10	17	100	89
1988	5	14	100	100
1987	20	47	80	70
1986	5	29	94	90
1985	10	24	86	81
1984	0	31	56	83
1983	0	0	85	91
1982	20	29	93	80
1981	0	20	89	100

10 Joseph M. McDade (R)

Of Scranton — Elected 1962; 16th Term

Born: Sept. 29, 1931, Scranton, Pa.
Education: U. of Notre Dame, B.A. 1953; U. of Pennsylvania, LL.B. 1956.
Occupation: Lawyer.
Family: Wife, Sarah Scripture; five children.
Religion: Roman Catholic.
Political Career: No previous office.
Capitol Office: 2370 Rayburn Bldg. 20515; 225-3731.

In Washington: Shadowed by a bribery investigation back home in Pennsylvania that led to a federal indictment, McDade has endured a tough initiation period since ascending early in 1991 to the post of ranking Republican on the Appropriations Committee — one of the pivotal positions in Congress.

But McDade's broad popularity among his colleagues and his invincibility at home have enabled him to remain effective at what he does best: steering millions of federal dollars back to his economically embattled industrial hometown, Scranton. His legal problems, however, have made some other Republicans uneasy. In 1992, after an editorial in The New York Times suggested he should relinquish his posts as ranking Republican on the full committee and the Defense Subcommittee, McDade wrote a letter asking House Minority Leader Robert H. Michel of Illinois to decide if he should step aside; party leaders decided to allow him to continue. At the beginning of the 103rd Congress, he was chosen again to serve in these posts.

In May 1992, a federal grand jury issued a five-count indictment against McDade, charging him with enriching himself over five years with more than $100,000 worth of favors, bribes and illegal gratuities extorted from several defense firms seeking government contracts. The indictment connected the allegedly illicit gains — mostly subsidized trips, campaign contributions, speaking fees, scholarship money for his son and gifts — to official favors McDade provided to the contractors both when he was ranking Republican on the Small Business Committee and as ranking Republican on the Defense Subcommittee.

The indictment was the culmination of a four-year investigation. Reports of the matter first surfaced in The Wall Street Journal, which reported in December 1988 that a now-bankrupt defense firm, United Chem-Con Corp. of Lancaster, Pa., won $54 million in defense contracts with McDade's help. At that time, McDade said he helped the minority-owned business obtain Navy contracts to help bring jobs to his economically troubled district.

McDade promised to fight the indictment. The day before it was issued, his office released a statement charging a conflict of interest on the part of the U.S. attorney prosecuting the case. It said the prosecutor had accepted campaign contributions from United Chem-Con when he was campaign treasurer for GOP Sen. Arlen Specter.

The federal court rejected that charge in July 1992 in dismissing an earlier motion to dismiss the indictment on grounds of government misconduct. In May 1993, the court refused another motion to dismiss, this time rejecting arguments by McDade and leaders of both parties that the charges violated constitutional limits on prosecuting lawmakers.

For Republicans who regularly pepper congressional Democrats with charges of ethical impropriety, McDade poses a problem. Indeed, if McDade were a Democrat, he would have had to relinquish his committee post at least temporarily under rules adopted by that party's caucus. The Republican Conference has no such rule, and an attempt to implement one failed during organization for the 103rd Congress. McDade hailed that decision as a victory for the presumption of innocence. "I certainly would step down as ranking member if I was convicted," he told reporters.

McDade was already in his fourth term as the ranking member of the Defense Subcommittee when the 102nd began. In channeling the immense sums within that jurisdiction, he had enjoyed special inside leverage thanks to his pairing with that subcommittee's chairman: McDade's Pennsylvania colleague John P. Murtha.

They worked together to bring Pennsylvania a $963 million modernization contract for an aircraft carrier in 1990. The fiscal 1992 defense bill included $60 million for 80 armored ammunition carriers built in York, as well as a provision continuing the longstanding congressional campaign to ensure the purchase of U.S.-mined coal to heat U.S. bases in Europe. McDade points to his ability to secure appropriations for the Tobyhanna Army Depot, the largest employer in the region with more than 4,000 employees.

His most visible — and controversial — achievement in recent years has been the secur-

Pennsylvania 10

Northeast — Scranton

The city of Scranton dominated the politics of northeastern Pennsylvania in the early part of this century, but as the coal-and-railroad town declined in population, the political influence of Scranton and Lackawanna County has slipped.

No longer does the rest of the region take its cue from Scranton, the most populous city in the 10th. While Lackawanna retains its traditional Democratic loyalties, Republicans have solidified their position in the outlying counties. In 1992, Lackawanna was the lone county in the 10th to support either Democrats Bill Clinton for president or Lynn Yeakel for the Senate.

The county's Democratic majority casts its vote in Scranton and in some of the outlying blue-collar towns such as Moosic. Republicans can be found in more affluent suburbs such as Clarks Summit and Dalton.

At one time, Scranton was known as the "Anthracite Capital of the World." The city entered the Industrial Age by manufacturing iron. From an outpost of 650 people in 1840, Scranton grew to 260,000 in 1950. But the coal industry was already beginning to peter out in the 1940s, and the city's fortunes have declined through most of the postwar era.

Scranton has attempted to diversify its economic base, but the turnaround has been slow. There are some signs of improvement, though: The city has begun to appear on some lists of the "most livable places," thanks mostly to its affordable housing and relatively low crime rate. Business publications have also taken note of Scranton, touting the city as a good place to relocate or start a new business.

Among many local civic boosters, hopes for restoring the city's economic vitality hinge on the development of Steamtown National Historic Site, a railroad park-and-retail complex aimed at attracting tourists. This controversial national historic site and its adjacent $100 million mall have been pilloried as an example of federal pork barrel politics run amok. But what outsiders see as pork looks like a potential godsend to Scrantonians.

The population growth that the 10th saw during the 1980s came to the east of Lackawanna County. There, on the New Jersey border, Pike County has experienced spectacular growth as business executives who commute to New York have moved to the area. Pike's population boomed by 55 percent in the 1970s and 53 percent in the 1980s. Population has increased in Wayne and Monroe counties also, but to a lesser degree.

Pocono Mountain resorts and ski areas boost Monroe County's economy. Only part of Monroe County is in the 10th, but it is an especially scenic portion that includes the Delaware Water Gap National Recreation Area.

North and west of Scranton are reliably Republican and agricultural Bradford and Susquehanna counties. Democrats can be found on the far western edge of the district in Williamsport, the 10th's second-largest city and home to the annual Little League World Series.

1990 Population: 565,681. White 554,920 (98%), Black 6,215 (1%), Other 4,546 (1%). Hispanic origin 4,337 (1%). 18 and over 428,771 (76%), 62 and over 113,630 (20%). Median age: 36.

ing of funds for the Steamtown National Historic Site, a 40-acre park and steam railroad museum. The project has deen derided as a prime example of pork-barrel spending and criticized for its high cost and dubious historical value. In the 102nd Congress, funding for the project was capped at $66 million.

Spurring economic development at home has been at the heart of McDade's career, and his committee assignments have positioned him well to pursue his goal. Before 1991, he augmented his standing on the Defense Subcommittee with ranking status on the Small Business Committee (until he took over as ranking member on Appropriations). McDade's savvy in using his positions on behalf of his constituents made him secure in a marginally Republican district.

McDade has not been quite so impervious to political consequences on Capitol Hill. Shortly after the Wall Street Journal story appeared, McDade was dealt a setback in the House: He lost a bid to become Republican Conference secretary.

For such a senior member to seek such a modest leadership post was unusual, but McDade said he decided to run after Northeastern Republicans concluded that they needed a regional representative in the leadership.

McDade's strategy for the leadership contest was to call in chits he had collected in years of service on Appropriations. But many restive House Republicans wanted a break from the "Old Bull" politics-as-usual wing of the House GOP. Conservative activist Vin Weber of Minnesota was elected instead.

In another sense, his rejection was not

surprising: He had, over the course of his career, voted against his party's majority as often as he had voted with it. He had, however, managed to do so without personally alienating party colleagues. He tends to break from the GOP line on labor votes, rather than on the more ideologically divisive social policy issues.

When he first took over the ranking spot on Appropriations' Defense Subcommittee in 1985, many GOP conservatives feared McDade would not be as reliable a party loyalist as his predecessor. But he proved to be a dependable foot soldier for Republican views on the panel.

McDade's previous role on Appropriations — ranking member on the Interior Subcommittee — did not require such partisan diligence on his part. For nearly a decade, he and Chairman Sidney R. Yates of Illinois were one of the more successful legislative teams in the House.

At Home: McDade has endeared himself to constituents of both parties with his efforts to promote economic development — vital in his depressed coal-producing region.

And McDade's legal problems have had little effect on his political standing back home. Even as allegations swirled around him, local Democrats could not muster a candidate to face him in 1992. He rolled up 90 percent of the vote against a Libertarian challenger.

McDade's GOP label appeals to voters in the district's outlying, rural parts, and his pro-labor voting record pleases the blue-collar Democrats in Lackawanna County (Scranton), the district's focal point. Unions regularly back him, and local Democratic organizations stopped endorsing candidates against him long ago. As an Irish Catholic, he has unusual appeal for a Republican among the county's large ethnic population.

A lawyer and former municipal solicitor in his home city, McDade succeeded Republican William W. Scranton, after whose ancestors the city is named.

Handpicked by Scranton for the 1962 House nomination, McDade won an unspectacular election victory. In the face of Lyndon B. Johnson's presidential landslide in 1964, his winning margin was narrower yet. By 1966, however, he had enlisted the support of organized labor, and his vote tally has not dipped below 60 percent since.

Committee

Appropriations (Ranking)
Defense (ranking); Interior

Elections

1992 General

Joseph M. McDade (R)	189,414	(90%)
Albert A. Smith (LIBERT)	20,134	(10%)

1990 General

Joseph M. McDade (R)	113,490	(100%)

Previous Winning Percentages: **1988** (73%) **1986** (75%) **1984** (77%) **1982** (68%) **1980** (77%) **1978** (77%) **1976** (63%) **1974** (65%) **1972** (74%) **1970** (65%) **1968** (67%) **1966** (67%) **1964** (51%) **1962** (52%)

District Vote for President

	1992	
D	88,150	(38%)
R	95,820	(42%)
I	46,878	(20%)

Campaign Finance

	Receipts	Receipts from PACs		Expend-itures
1992				
McDade (R)	$375,429	$242,172	(65%)	$343,892
1990				
McDade (R)	$383,030	$236,778	(62%)	$373,388

Key Votes

1993

Require parental notification of minors' abortions	Y
Require unpaid family and medical leave	Y
Approve national "motor voter" registration bill	N
Approve budget increasing taxes and reducing deficit	N
Approve economic stimulus plan	N

1992

Approve balanced-budget constitutional amendment	Y
Close down space station program	N
Approve U.S. aid for former Soviet Union	Y
Allow shifting funds from defense to domestic programs	N

1991

Extend unemployment benefits using deficit financing	Y
Approve waiting period for handgun purchases	Y
Authorize use of force in Persian Gulf	Y

Voting Studies

	Presidential Support		Party Unity		Conservative Coalition	
Year	**S**	**O**	**S**	**O**	**S**	**O**
1992	57	22	51	27	65	13
1991	68	25	56	36	70	19
1990	47	41	43	40	65	20
1989	66	29	47	44	80	12
1988	44	51	61	33	71	24
1987	45	47	34	53	72	19
1986	49	42	31	58	66	24
1985	59	38	44	47	67	29
1984	57	35	41	48	63	25
1983	57	30	44	43	60	31
1982	40	45	36	55	53	41
1981	62	30	55	34	63	25

Interest Group Ratings

Year	ADA	AFL-CIO	CCUS	ACU
1992	15	75	86	76
1991	30	56	44	65
1990	33	58	46	57
1989	35	67	80	46
1988	40	86	50	54
1987	40	71	36	37
1986	45	93	35	63
1985	20	75	38	57
1984	30	77	56	41
1983	30	60	60	52
1982	60	75	32	33
1981	25	47	78	93

11 Paul E. Kanjorski (D)

Of Nanticoke — Elected 1984; 5th Term

Born: April 2, 1937, Nanticoke, Pa.
Education: Temple U., 1957-62; Dickinson School of Law, 1962-65.
Military Service: Army, 1960-61.
Occupation: Lawyer.
Family: Wife, Nancy Hickerson; one child.
Religion: Roman Catholic.
Political Career: Sought Democratic nomination for U.S. House special election, 1980; sought Democratic nomination for U.S. House, 1980.
Capitol Office: 2429 Rayburn Bldg. 20515; 225-6511.

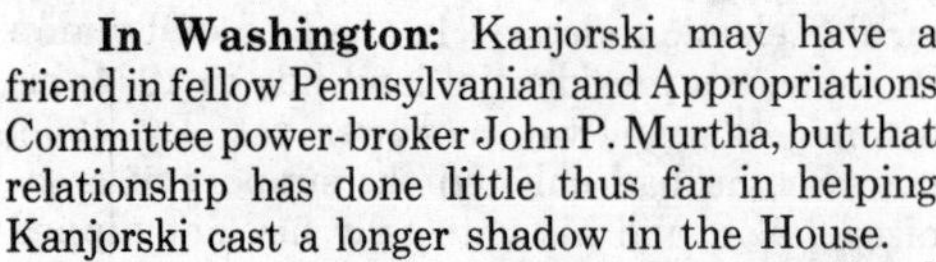

In Washington: Kanjorski may have a friend in fellow Pennsylvanian and Appropriations Committee power-broker John P. Murtha, but that relationship has done little thus far in helping Kanjorski cast a longer shadow in the House.

Nor have Kanjorski's own forays earned him much regard as a legislative operator, though the causes and projects he has pushed have played well in his Rust Belt district.

Most recently, Kanjorski has charged White House officials with excessive and underdocumented travel expenses; he has excoriated Texas financiers and officials for their disproportionately high number of failed savings and loan institutions, and for the resulting cost to the U.S. taxpayer; and he has blasted the oil companies for profiteering.

None of these endeavors has borne legislative fruit, though in the 102nd Congress, he managed to get a bill out of the Post Office and Civil Service Committee that would have given the White House a specific travel budget — $180 million a year — and required documentation for trips. But the bill went no further, and Kanjorski lost one lever to press the issue anew when his Human Resources Subcommittee was eliminated as part of congressional cutbacks at the start of the 103rd Congress.

That loss was offset, however, when he landed a subcommittee chairmanship on the Banking Committee, where Kanjorski has increasingly concentrated his attention. The Economic Growth Subcommittee will give him a platform to launch missiles at practices that he believes restrict the availability of credit and to pursue his district's needs.

It will also give him a chance to push a pet issue: the rollback of rules intended to prevent banks from "redlining" poor and minority neighborhoods where they do not want to lend. Kanjorski thinks the 1977 Community Reinvestment Act imposes too many burdens on smaller banks and would like to exempt most of them from the anti-redlining law. In the early stages of committee consideration of a bank overhaul bill in 1991, Kanjorski seemed to have the votes to curtail the law's scope. But the law's supporters succeeded in blocking any changes as part of the overhaul bill.

Kanjorski has also been a constant voice in calling for states (such as Texas) with large numbers of failed savings and loans to pay part of the thrift bailout cost if they want their state-chartered institutions to remain eligible for federal deposit insurance. Opponents, who believe that the cost should be spread equally among taxpayers in all states, succeeded in thwarting Kanjorski in early 1991, when his amendment threatened to derail a bill to keep the bailout operating. His similar efforts had been repeatedly blocked during consideration of the original thrift salvage bill in 1989.

Another ill-fated Kanjorski initiative is reimposing the windfall profits tax whenever the price of oil rises above a certain level. He proposed directing the windfall revenue to help finance the thrift bailout. His tax proposal, floated at a September 1989 hearing of the House Ways and Means Committee, raised the hackles of Texas members on that panel. In response to Iraq's invasion of Kuwait in 1990 and attendant concerns about a runup in oil prices, Kanjorski again championed the tax.

At the start of the 102nd Congress, Kanjorski sought a higher-profile platform for espousing his ideas — a seat on the Budget Committee. But he fell short by one vote. His appearance on an ABC-TV news show in 1990, where he served as a congressional scold of junketing Ways and Means Committee members, came only a few months before the Budget Committee selections.

Kanjorski's election to the Post Office and Civil Service Committee — and his bid for the Census Subcommittee chairmanship — demonstrated both the extent and the limit of the influence of his Pennsylvania colleague, Murtha. At the start of the 101st Congress, Murtha successfully backed Kanjorski for an opening on Post Office. But when Kanjorski sought the

Pennsylvania 11

Northeast — Wilkes-Barre

The Democratic legacy of the 11th District's industrial heritage is showing signs of fraying. In the 1992 presidential election, Bill Clinton won Luzerne and Carbon counties, but lost in the other areas that complete the district.

This region had long been Democratic territory, primarily because of Luzerne County's Democratic influence. In the 11th's largest city, Wilkes-Barre, and in other Wyoming Valley towns, the Democratic tradition dates back to the days when the anthracite coal-mining industry dominated the local economy.

But as the costs of mining anthracite coal rose and the use of oil and natural gas for home heating increased, the local industry began a steep decline. So did the region's population, and along with it, Democratic hegemony.

Voter registration figures reveal a district with a distinct Democratic advantage, but in 1980 and 1984, Ronald Reagan won in the region, as did George Bush in 1988. In 1992, Democratic Senate nominee Lynn Yeakel managed victory only in Carbon County.

Luzerne County, with its rich ethnic stew of Eastern Europeans, Italians, Irish and Welsh, still casts more than half the district's vote. Much of the county vote comes from Wilkes-Barre's outlying towns such as Pittston and Kingston, but Hazleton, in southern Luzerne County, is also of some size.

Politics takes a back seat to football in neighboring Columbia County. Berwick is a hard-core gridiron town, where residents shoehorn into Crispin Field to forget about the demise of the coal industry and watch the Berwick Bulldogs, annually one of the nation's finest high school teams.

Another vestige of the coal industry in Columbia County is the decades-old mine fire that still burns beneath the borough of Centralia. The threat of cave-ins and explosions scared most residents away over the years, and the rest were bought out by the federal government.

Jim Thorpe, a Carbon County coal region town on the eastern side of the 11th, has fared much better. Once a haven for the wealthy — locals boast that 13 of America's 70 millionaires lived here in the late 19th century — this picturesque Lehigh River town fell on hard times when the demand for anthracite coal waned in the 1930s and 1940s.

In hopes of reviving the town, officials in 1954 changed the town's name from Mauch Chunk to that of the famed Olympic athlete Jim Thorpe, who died in 1953 and is buried here. Today, tourism is thriving after the town became a demonstration preservation project for the Department of Interior.

Elsewhere in the county, in Panther Valley coal towns such as Lansford and Nesquehoning, the economic outlook is not as promising.

Northeast of Carbon County, the Monroe County portion of the district includes some of the southern Pocono Mountain resort areas.

1990 Population: 565,913. White 556,762 (98%), Black 5,283 (1%), Other 3,868 (1%). Hispanic origin 4,119 (1%). 18 and over 441,306 (78%), 62 and over 126,417 (22%). Median age: 37.

Census Subcommittee chair, where he would be utile to Murtha in his fight to keep illegal aliens from being counted in the 1990 census, the Democratic leadership supported Ohioan Tom Sawyer. Sawyer won easily.

At Home: Kanjorski owes his presence in the House largely to an intestinal parasite and a sunny beach. Those are peculiar agents of change, but the 11th is a district with peculiar politics. In one five-year span (1980-85), five different people represented it.

The outcome of Kanjorski's 1984 primary challenge to incumbent Democrat Frank Harrison might have been different but for the discovery that water supplies in parts of the 11th were contaminated with the giardiasis parasite. As people boiled their water to make it drinkable, Harrison flew off for his second congressional excursion to Central America.

Kanjorski pounced on Harrison with a largely self-financed blitz of clever ads portraying him as an aloof globe-trotter. One ad showed a picture of a sunny Costa Rican beach and noted Harrison's visit there, then switched to a shot of a teakettle on a stove and concluded, "It's enough to make you boil."

Harrison tried to ignore Kanjorski and stressed his experience in Washington. That pitch failed to excite voters, and Kanjorski leaped from long shot to victor.

Kanjorski was rated the favorite over Republican Robert P. Hudock. But Hudock livened things up by accusing Kanjorski of charging excessive fees for his private legal work in behalf of local communities seeking federal grants. Hudock also accused Kanjorski of taking payment from citizens and businesses seeking relief money from Washington after Hurricane Agnes hit the area in 1972.

Kanjorski responded that his firm charged competitive fees, and he said he had helped bring more than $50 million in federal aid to the 11th. He noted that he had often provided free legal services, including working without pay as Nanticoke's assistant city solicitor for 14 years.

An opponent of abortion and gun control and an advocate of prayer in schools and tuition tax credits, Kanjorski was viewed by most voters as reflecting their values, not those of the national Democratic Party. So even though Walter F. Mondale lost the district to Ronald Reagan, Kanjorski won with 59 percent.

In 1986, Kanjorski was not as much the focus as was his GOP challenger, Marc L. Holtzman. In a district that is aging, heavily Catholic and struggling economically, Holtzman was 26 years old, Jewish and wealthy. He counted on White House connections and a treasury well in excess of $1 million to make him competitive.

Kanjorski pointed to things he had already done and noted his ties to the House leadership.

Holtzman boasted of what he could do if given a chance. He had parlayed his role as executive director of Reagan's 1980 Pennsylvania campaign into contacts with conservative leaders. He said his contacts would help him bring in new industry. In the end, he drew a lower share of the vote than any GOP House candidate in the 11th District in a decade — spending approximately $29 per vote in the process.

That victory and Kanjorski's re-election without opposition in 1988 and 1990, and his easy 1992 victory over a GOP challenger, have brought stability to a district that was once a turnstile.

The door began revolving in 1980, after 31-year veteran Daniel J. Flood was forced to resign for soliciting illegal campaign contributions. The Democrat who replaced Flood in an April 1980 special election, Raphael E. Musto, lost to Republican James L. Nelligan that November. Because of the recession, Nelligan lost to Harrison in 1982. In the 1984 Democratic primary, Harrison lost to Kanjorski.

Committees

Banking, Finance & Urban Affairs (7th of 30 Democrats)
Economic Growth (chairman); Consumer Credit & Insurance; Financial Institutions Supervision, Regulation & Deposit Insurance; International Development, Finance, Trade & Monetary Policy

Post Office & Civil Service (6th of 15 Democrats)
Civil Service

Elections

1992 General		
Paul E. Kanjorski (D)	138,875	(67%)
Michael A. Fescina (R)	68,112	(33%)
1990 General		
Paul E. Kanjorski (D)	88,219	(100%)

Previous Winning Percentages: **1988** (100%) **1986** (71%) **1984** (59%)

District Vote for President

1992

D	91,671 (42%)
R	84,203 (38%)
I	42,960 (20%)

Campaign Finance

	Receipts	Receipts from PACs		Expend-itures
1992				
Kanjorski (D)	$311,016	$235,360	(76%)	$342,314
Fescina (R)	$55,029	$10	(0%)	$54,724
1990				
Kanjorski (D)	$308,351	$224,185	(73%)	$405,637

Key Votes

1993	
Require parental notification of minors' abortions	Y
Require unpaid family and medical leave	Y
Approve national "motor voter" registration bill	Y
Approve budget increasing taxes and reducing deficit	Y
Approve economic stimulus plan	Y
1992	
Approve balanced-budget constitutional amendment	N
Close down space station program	Y
Approve U.S. aid for former Soviet Union	N
Allow shifting funds from defense to domestic programs	Y
1991	
Extend unemployment benefits using deficit financing	Y
Approve waiting period for handgun purchases	N
Authorize use of force in Persian Gulf	N

Voting Studies

	Presidential Support		Party Unity		Conservative Coalition	
Year	**S**	**O**	**S**	**O**	**S**	**O**
1992	31	69	85	15	46	54
1991	37	63	85	14	59	41
1990	25	74	87	13	44	54
1989	36	63	85	14	44	56
1988	32	68	88	12	50	50
1987	26	74	88	11	56	44
1986	22	78	83	14	54	46
1985	33	63	80	17	47	53

Interest Group Ratings

Year	ADA	AFL-CIO	CCUS	ACU
1992	80	83	25	16
1991	50	92	10	25
1990	67	92	21	21
1989	80	92	40	14
1988	70	100	36	20
1987	80	94	13	4
1986	65	93	28	32
1985	55	76	32	19

12 John P. Murtha (D)

Of Johnstown — Elected 1974; 10th Full Term

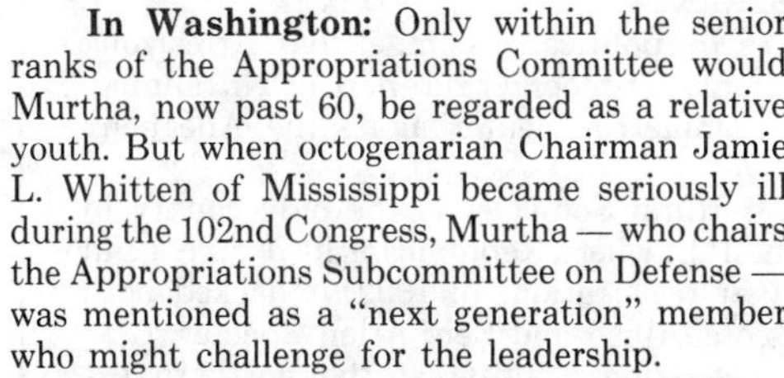

Born: June 17, 1932, New Martinsville, W.Va.
Education: U. of Pittsburgh, B.A. 1962.
Military Service: Marine Corps, 1952-55, 1966-67; Marine Corps Reserve, 1967-90.
Occupation: Car wash operator and owner.
Family: Wife, Joyce Bell; three children.
Religion: Roman Catholic.
Political Career: Democratic nominee for U.S. House, 1968; Pa. House, 1969-74.
Capitol Office: 2423 Rayburn Bldg. 20515; 225-2065.

In Washington: Only within the senior ranks of the Appropriations Committee would Murtha, now past 60, be regarded as a relative youth. But when octogenarian Chairman Jamie L. Whitten of Mississippi became seriously ill during the 102nd Congress, Murtha — who chairs the Appropriations Subcommittee on Defense — was mentioned as a "next generation" member who might challenge for the leadership.

In June 1992, Kentucky Democrat William H. Natcher — a year older than Whitten — filled in for the increasingly infirm chairman. Before the start of the 103rd Congress, the Democratic Caucus voted Whitten out, and Natcher had dibs on the job.

Murtha, an ally of Natcher's, said he would not stage a challenge. But Democrat David R. Obey of Wisconsin, one of the younger of the 13 Appropriations subcommittee chairmen, suggested he might run for chairman; Murtha, who sees his own hand on the gavel, hinted he would jump in if Obey did.

Both demurred, and 20-term member Natcher claimed the chairmanship without opposition. Although Natcher, 83 when he took the reins, appeared hale, it is likely that Murtha — now in his 10th House term — will not have to wait as long before making his bid.

A Murtha-Obey contest would have been a contrast in styles. Murtha, a blue-collar Democrat, is liberal on economic and labor issues but conservative on defense and social policy; Obey is more consistently liberal. Murtha built his political reputation in the back rooms of Congress; Obey is more given to public crusading.

Murtha's political situation at home allows him confidence that he will be around to stake his claim on the chairmanship if the opportunity arises during the 1990s: After getting a good break in Pennsylvania redistricting, he was unopposed for re-election in 1992.

Yet as recently as 1990, Murtha did not appear so secure. Blindsided by an aggressive primary challenger, Murtha received just 51 percent of the vote. That scare was a harbinger of the broad public dissatisfaction with Congress that produced so much anti-Washington rhetoric during the 1992 campaign cycle. Murtha's trouble highlighted the voters' paradoxical attitude about the legislative process: They love the deal, but loathe the deal-makers.

Murtha over the years had channeled millions of federal dollars into roads, bridges, research facilities and economic development programs back home. But 1990 challenger Kenneth B. Burkley nearly scored an upset by portraying Murtha as a sleazy pol.

The close call was a blow to a member who once campaigned as "John P. Murtha — The 'P' Is for Power." Murtha moved quickly to reinforce his local position. Though congenial to his colleagues, Murtha had been rather inaccessible to the media; after his narrow escape, Murtha hired a press secretary and embarked on a series of "community days" in his district.

Murtha also accepted the higher profile that his Defense Subcommittee chairmanship (which he obtained in 1989) provides. Once camera shy, Murtha now may be seen on TV news shows when a big defense issue arises.

In recent years, House defense policy was largely shaped by the Armed Services Committee and its chairman, Les Aspin of Wisconsin; the Appropriations Committee generally signed off on its program. Even so, Murtha was able to have an impact on issues of particular interest to him, including those pertaining to the Marine Corps (in which he served as an officer), the National Guard and reserves (which he strongly supports) and Pennsylvania (he joins ranking Appropriations Committee Republican Joseph M. McDade of Pennsylvania in securing a steady flow of funds for home-state projects).

With Aspin now serving as President Clinton's secretary of Defense, Murtha might find himself with a somewhat greater policy-making role in the House. Aspin's successor as Armed Services chairman is Ronald V. Dellums of California, an eloquent but strongly liberal member whose zeal for slashing the defense budget far exceeds that of his committee or Congress as a whole. Although the Clinton administration itself

Pennsylvania 12

Southwest — Johnstown

Pennsylvania's Laurel Highlands are the setting for the 12th, a region once noted for its coal, iron and steel industries but nowadays better-known for its chronic hard luck.

Johnstown, the biggest city in the 12th, is famous for the floods that have devastated the town three times over the past century. The Great Flood of 1889 was the worst, when an earthen dam outside town collapsed, sending 20 million tons of water surging through the Conemaugh Valley. The town was virtually destroyed and 2,200 people were killed. In 1936, another flood struck, killing 25. The most recent flood, in 1977, took the lives of 85 residents.

The early 1980s recession took a similarly heavy toll on Johnstown's economy, flattening what remained of the city's coal and steel industries and sending unemployment rates over 27 percent, the nation's highest at the time.

Johnstown has attempted to bounce back, partly by capitalizing on its flood history. In 1989, the city stressed the centennial anniversary of the Great Flood; tourists can visit the Johnstown Flood Museum.

Besides the hard times, another constant has been the Johnstown and Cambria County Democratic tradition. There were defections to Ronald Reagan in 1980, but Jimmy Carter still managed to carry Cambria County. Four years later, voters registered their unhappiness with Reagan's unwillingness to impose mandatory steel quotas by backing Walter F. Mondale.

In 1988 and 1992, Michael S. Dukakis and Bill Clinton won comfortably in Cambria. Even Democratic Senate nominee Lynn Yeakel won here in 1992, though she ran poorly across the rest of the district.

The western portions of Westmoreland and Fayette counties in the 12th are also fonts of Democratic votes. Fayette is a rural, Democratic stronghold where unions are king and Republicans need not apply. Westmoreland is less reliably Democratic, though Republicans are outregistered here 2-to-1. For beer connoisseurs, most notable in the Westmoreland County part of the 12th is Latrobe, home to the Rolling Rock brewery.

In politically competitive Armstrong County, Democrats run best in Kittanning, a commercial center along the Allegheny River.

Rural Somerset is the only county in the 12th where Republicans have an edge in voter registration. In 1992, it backed both George Bush and Sen. Arlen Specter.

Clarion County, at the northern extreme of the 12th, votes Republican, but virtually all of the county (except New Bethlehem) belongs to the 5th District.

Indiana County is a mixture of farms and mines, which bills itself as the "Christmas tree capital of the world" for its abundance of blue spruces, and Scotch, Norway, and white pines. But St. Nick is not the real hero; it is the hometown boy whose statue stands in front of the county courthouse — actor Jimmy Stewart.

1990 Population: 565,794. White 556,028 (98%), Black 7,302 (1%), Other 2,464 (<1%). Hispanic origin 2,175 (<1%). 18 and over 431,900 (76%), 62 and over 115,464 (20%). Median age: 36.

has proposed some substantial reductions, it may have to rely on members such as the pro-defense Murtha to speak out against the deeper cuts Dellums advocates.

Yet Murtha showed early on that he was not in lockstep with Clinton. Their differences can be seen as symbolic of how much the world has changed in the past few years.

During the Cold War, Murtha was a hawk. A Vietnam War veteran and staunch anti-communist, he supported the defense buildup under the Reagan administration and backed such incursions as the U.S. invasion of Grenada. He also strongly backed President Bush's forceful action to end Iraq's occupation of Kuwait in early 1991. Clinton, on the other hand, avoided service during Vietnam and was dubious about the big Reagan-Bush defense budgets.

However, in the post-Cold War era, Murtha has become more cautious about the financial and human costs of U.S. military actions, while Clinton, with his humanitarian instincts, seems more willing to intervene in bloody civil wars that have arisen in a more chaotic world.

During the 1992 campaign, Clinton criticized Bush for a slow reaction to the ethnic strife in the former Yugoslavia. But Murtha warned, "This could be a quagmire and then some."

Murtha also came out against Bush's December 1992 deployment of troops to a humanitarian mission in Somalia, which Clinton supported. Noting that "everybody's moved by the fact that people are starving," he said the United States should not get involved militarily when national security is not clearly at stake.

In March 1993, Murtha warned that Clinton's planned budget cuts could result in a return to the "hollow" military of the late 1970s. "You can't keep reducing defense if you're going to try to be all over the world and be all things to all people," he told reporters.

Although he has been more outspoken on defense policy of late, Murtha's main thing on Appropriations is still dealing out the dollars. He makes sure his favored constituencies get their share.

Murtha is a leading advocate of some Marine Corps programs, including the V-22 Osprey tilt-rotor airplane, that remained in the budget despite efforts by the Bush administration to eliminate them.

He stands out as a guardian of the Guard and reserves. When Bush took the first post-Cold War whack at the military personnel payroll, Murtha blocked him from cutting the reserves at a faster rate than active-duty forces.

But woe to those in the military who get on Murtha's wrong side. A critic of the Navy's bureaucracy, Murtha was furious at its leadership's slow reaction to allegations of sexual assault by Navy aviators during the 1991 Tailhook incident. In 1992 he pushed through the House a cut of 10,000 Navy personnel positions, although the reduction was later dropped.

Murtha never forgets Pennsylvania in his Appropriations role. The dean of a coalition of Rust Belt House Democrats, Murtha holds court in the "Pennsylvania corner" of the House floor.

During the 102nd Congress, he helped get $60 million to build armored ammunition carriers in York, Pa. During the 101st Congress, he and McDade obtained $401 million to overhaul an aircraft carrier at the Philadelphia Naval Shipyard, which is targeted for closure under the 1991 military base-closing law.

Murtha's pro-Pennsylvania activities extend to his assignment on the Appropriations Interior Subcommittee. In 1992, he worked with McDade to preserve $13 million in funding for Steamtown, a railroad museum in McDade's district.

Murtha is the sort of deal-making insider that "good government" watchdog groups criticize, but in his only brush with ethics trouble, he emerged unscathed. In 1980, Murtha was reported to be one of the targets of the FBI's "Abscam" investigation, in which undercover agents posed as Arab sheiks and offered members of Congress $50,000 to help them get into the United States. Videotapes clearly showed that Murtha turned down the money, though he did name two other members who, he said, "expect to be taken care of."

Murtha said he participated in the meeting only to seek investments by the Arabs in coal mining operations, banks and other businesses in his district. The ethics committee in July 1981 cleared Murtha of wrongdoing.

However, the incident did have a negative effect on Murtha's leadership ambitions. A favorite of then-Speaker Thomas P. "Tip" O'Neill Jr. of Massachusetts, Murtha seemed likely to become majority whip in 1981. Those plans were scratched after Murtha was touched by the Abscam controversy.

At Home: Murtha's smooth sailing in 1992 — he drew neither primary nor general-election opposition — was a stark contrast with his experience two years earlier, when his Democratic primary foe, Greensburg lawyer Burkley, made the contest a referendum on Murtha's use of congressional power. Murtha, Burkley argued, might be an influential member of Congress, but he was using his clout to secure his own financial well-being rather than to help his economically struggling constituency.

Burkley's campaign was both feisty and irreverent. He mocked the value of Murtha's incumbency by appearing at abandoned factories and vacant storefronts in the 12th with a cardboard likeness of the incumbent. He offered a $1,000 reward to anyone who could get Murtha to debate him.

And Burkley capped his low-budget campaign with a mailing to 40,000 Democratic households in the district titled "John P. Murtha's Wheel of Fortune." A takeoff on the TV game show, the mailing portrayed Murtha as a junketeer and congressional pay-raiser. The thrust of the mailing was summed up in bold letters under a gaudy drawing of a gaming wheel: "With every spin ... Murtha continues to line his pockets — and you pay for the fabulous prizes."

Had Murtha ignored the attacks, he probably would have lost. But tapping defense contractors and lobbyists, heavy industry and unions, Murtha financed a massive blitz that accused Burkley of lies and distortion, while pointing to a variety of economic development projects within the district that Murtha had helped make possible.

Prominent political figures, businessmen and celebrities — including Gov. Robert P. Casey, former House Speaker O'Neill, Chrysler Corp. Chairman Lee A. Iacocca and actor E. G. Marshall — made ads attesting to Murtha's honesty, integrity and effectiveness. And Murtha billboards dotted roadsides across the district reading: "Experience ... Makes It Happen."

Some Murtha advisers feared that his saturation advertising ran the risk of overkill, but it probably staved off an upset. Burkley carried his home base, populous Westmoreland County on the outskirts of Pittsburgh, but Murtha won elsewhere to attain a 4,775-vote victory. Against a less aggressive GOP opponent, Murtha's reelection that fall was anticlimactic.

In 1992 redistricting, Burkley's hometown of Greensburg was removed from the 12th and put in the 20th District, held by Democratic Rep. Austin J. Murphy. Burkley ran there in the primary, finishing third as Murphy won.

Murtha has not been involved in many

close races. When longtime GOP Rep. John P. Saylor died in 1973, the Cambria County (Johnstown) Democratic organization seized its chance to recapture a nominally Democratic district. They found an attractive candidate in Murtha, a personable state legislator who had won a Bronze Star and two Purple Hearts as a Marine in Vietnam.

Murtha won narrowly over Harry M. Fox, a former Saylor aide, in a 1974 special election focused on the Republican Party's Watergate problems. He handily dispatched Fox the following November and won easily for the next decade and a half.

That included 1980, when Abscam had become public. Murtha's opponent tried to make the bribery scandal an issue; Murtha slipped a little, but still drew 59 percent of the vote.

In 1982, Pennsylvania's Republican-controlled Legislature combined Murtha's district with that of fellow Democrat Don Bailey. The primary paired two excellent campaigners and close friends with similar pro-labor views.

The merged district contained about the same number of former constituents of each candidate, making it a battle between two organizations: Murtha had one in his home base, Cambria County, and Bailey had one in his native Westmoreland County. Bailey refused suggestions that he bring up Abscam or a second Murtha liability — his sponsorship of House members' tax breaks and pay increases.

While both Democrats worked hard, Murtha fielded a superior get-out-the-vote operation. In addition, Murtha convinced voters that he could better help the economically depressed steel district through his greater seniority and influence with the House leadership. Murtha won by a comfortable 52-38 percent margin.

Committee

Appropriations (8th of 37 Democrats)
Defense (chairman); Interior; Legislative Branch

Elections

1992 General

John P. Murtha (D)	166,916	(100%)

1990 General

John P. Murtha (D)	80,686	(62%)
Willeam Choby (R)	50,007	(38%)

Previous Winning Percentages: **1988** (100%) **1986** (67%) **1984** (69%) **1982** (61%) **1980** (59%) **1978** (69%) **1976** (68%) **1974** (58%) **1974 *** (50%)

* *Special election.*

District Vote for President

1992

D 102,777 (46%)
R 72,671 (34%)
I 44,852 (21%)

Campaign Finance

	Receipts	Receipts from PACs		Expend-itures
1992				
Murtha (D)	$935,459	$540,060	(58%)	$794,097
1990				
Murtha (D)	$878,887	$496,920	(57%)	$1,097,107
Choby (R)	$6,454	0		$5,951

Key Votes

1993

Require parental notification of minors' abortions	N
Require unpaid family and medical leave	Y
Approve national "motor voter" registration bill	Y
Approve budget increasing taxes and reducing deficit	Y
Approve economic stimulus plan	Y

1992

Approve balanced-budget constitutional amendment	N
Close down space station program	Y
Approve U.S. aid for former Soviet Union	Y
Allow shifting funds from defense to domestic programs	N

1991

Extend unemployment benefits using deficit financing	Y
Approve waiting period for handgun purchases	N
Authorize use of force in Persian Gulf	Y

Voting Studies

	Presidential Support		Party Unity		Conservative Coalition	
Year	**S**	**O**	**S**	**O**	**S**	**O**
1992	39	54	81	13	67	27
1991	44	52	82	15	62	35
1990	33	64	85	13	61	39
1989	51	47	77	17	61	37
1988	35	60	79	16	58	39
1987	43	55	82	12	70	30
1986	42	56	76	15	68	28
1985	52	46	77	20	75	22
1984	52	43	77	18	63	34
1983	54	40	74	22	58	38
1982	53	39	68	21	64	30
1981	45	50	70	27	64	33

Interest Group Ratings

Year	ADA	AFL-CIO	CCUS	ACU
1992	65	92	63	28
1991	40	92	30	26
1990	56	100	21	22
1989	45	100	30	27
1988	55	100	29	46
1987	60	100	13	26
1986	40	93	25	52
1985	45	82	14	50
1984	40	69	38	27
1983	55	88	16	35
1982	45	90	33	37
1981	45	80	22	13

13 Marjorie Margolies-Mezvinsky (D)

Of Narberth — Elected 1992; 1st Term

Born: June 21, 1942, Philadelphia, Pa.
Education: Skidmore College, 1959-61; U. of Pennsylvania, B.A. 1963; Columbia U., 1969-70.
Occupation: Television journalist.
Family: Husband, Edward Mezvinsky; four children, four stepchildren, three legal guardianships.
Religion: Jewish.
Political Career: No previous office.
Capitol Office: 1516 Longworth Bldg. 20515; 225-6111.

The Path to Washington: Within weeks of her election, Margolies-Mezvinsky already had begun building consensus among women in Congress.

After she unexpectedly broke a 76-year Republican reign over the district, Margolies-Mezvinsky led several bipartisan meetings of the House's 24 new women. Their goals: full funding of Head Start for preschoolers, family and medical leave, and initiatives that codify *Roe v. Wade* and address sexual harassment in Congress.

Margolies-Mezvinsky's concern for families did not begin in Congress. She has been sponsoring and mothering children since 1970 when she became the first unmarried American citizen to adopt a foreign child. Now married to former Iowa congressman Edward Mezvinsky, she has housed nearly 20 foreign-born youngsters and helped raise six American children.

Margolies-Mezvinsky's professional life began in the late 1960s when she started reporting for local TV. A best-selling author, she has also won five Emmys.

She distinguished herself early in the 103rd Congress as the only Democratic freshman to vote against both President Clinton's budget and $16.3 billion economic stimulus package. They are votes the leadership will probably forgive, however, because they know they are lucky to have a Democrat in the 13th at all.

In December 1991 a local group of Democratic women approached Margolies-Mezvinsky about considering a long-shot run for Congress. A year after her husband lost a bid for lieutenant governor, she thought it would be a chance to get her own political feet wet.

The odds were against her winning the 13th District, which had not given a Democratic challenger more than 44 percent of the vote since Lawrence Coughlin first won in 1968.

But in February 1992, Coughlin announced his retirement after 12 terms, and two months later Margolies-Mezvinsky won the nomination to face Republican nominee Jon D. Fox, a popular Montgomery County commissioner.

Fox started with an advantage. But Margolies-Mezvinsky enjoyed the powerful combination of outsider status in a year favoring anti-incumbency and being female in the "Year of the Woman."

The candidates had similar positions on many issues: reducing the deficit, creating jobs, controlling taxes, improving health care, reforming Congress and aiding Israel. But their differences became evident as they began receiving endorsements.

The National Abortion Rights Action League endorsed Margolies-Mezvinsky because Fox supported some restrictions on abortion. The AFL-CIO endorsed Margolies-Mezvinsky for advocating more sensitivity to families in the workplace, while the National Federation of Independent Business and the National Rifle Association backed Fox.

But issues did not dominate the race. Margolies-Mezvinsky repeatedly charged that Fox had spent most of his political career running for whatever office was higher than the one he held. Fox argued that Margolies-Mezvinsky, who regularly commuted to New York and Washington, had too few roots in Montgomery County and too many out-of-state supporters to properly represent the district.

In July he announced that 60 percent of her campaign contributions had come from outside the 13th and that more than a third came from people living in New York and Washington, while nearly three-fourths of his money came from within the district.

On Election Day, Margolies-Mezvinsky edged Fox by less than 1,500 votes. A write-in effort for anti-abortion candidate Ann Miller, who picked up a few thousand votes, may have made the difference.

In Washington, Margolies-Mezvinsky secured a seat on the Energy and Commerce Comittee.

Pennsylvania 13

Northwest Philadelphia suburbs — The Main Line

The 13th is the unlikeliest of venues to be represented by a Democrat in the House. It is the wealthiest district in Pennsylvania, and one of the most Republican.

Anchored solely in Montgomery County, the 13th includes Lower Merion Township, home to Philadelphia's aristocracy. The area is known as the Main Line, for the Pennsylvania Railroad's Main Line of Public Works, along which doctors, lawyers and old-money families built their posh estates. The white-collar professionals of Bryn Mawr, Narberth and Ardmore still ride into the city on the commuter trains that run along this line. A smaller portion of the Main Line is contained in the 7th District.

Though some Democratic-voting blacks have moved out of Philadelphia into areas such as Abington and Cheltenham, the county is overwhelmingly white and Republican. In 1990, Montgomery was the only county in the state to cling to GOP state Auditor General Barbara Hafer, as her unsuccessful gubernatorial campaign went down to spectacular defeat.

Two years later, the county experienced a bout of ballot topsy-turvy as it deserted George Bush, backed GOP Sen. Arlen Specter and elected Margolies-Mezvinsky. Without the recent infighting that has gripped the local GOP, a Democratic congressional candidate would have an extremely difficult time winning in the county.

As a wealthy, suburban county that borders a troubled big city, Montgomery follows developments in Philadelphia with interest and concern. When redistricting plans surfaced in the state legislature that would have grafted part of the county into a city-based district, county legislators fought hard to kill the proposals.

Norristown, the county seat, has the largest concentration of minorities in the county. At the end of each workday when the white-collar legal community departs, Norristown reverts to a small borough with some big city urban problems. North of Norristown, Hatfield and Lansdale are other population centers.

The western portion of the county, especially along the Route 422 corridor, is coming to grips with problems associated with rapid growth. New residential developments are sprouting to house employees of the pharmaceutical companies that have relocated to Upper Providence Township. Local infrastructure improvements have made the surrounding region accessible and attractive to commuters and businesses. Even in the former farmland communities of Lower Salford, Worcester and Franconia, the loosely organized lobby of Pennsylvania Dutch farmers jokingly referred to as the "Mennonite-Industrial Complex" is seeing its influence diminish.

Central Montgomery County already experienced that growth, particularly around the Fort Washington area. There the Northeast extension of the Pennsylvania Turnpike toll road begins its way north to Allentown, Wilkes-Barre and Scranton.

1990 Population: 565,793. White 514,755 (91%), Black 34,507 (6%), Other 16,531 (3%). Hispanic origin 6,825 (1%). 18 and over 439,132 (78%), 62 and over 104,795 (19%). Median age: 36.

Committees

Energy & Commerce (26th of 27 Democrats)
Oversight & Investigations; Telecommunications & Finance

Government Operations (23rd of 25 Democrats)
Commerce, Consumer & Monetary Affairs

Small Business (19th of 27 Democrats)
SBA Legislation & the General Economy

Campaign Finance

	Receipts	Receipts from PACs		Expend-itures
1992				
Margolies-Mezvinsky (D)	$568,961	$172,273	(30%)	$559,060
Fox (R)	$714,397	$168,711	(24%)	$719,618

Key Votes

1993

Require parental notification of minors' abortions	N
Require unpaid family and medical leave	Y
Approve national "motor voter" registration bill	Y
Approve budget increasing taxes and reducing deficit	N
Approve economic stimulus plan	N

Elections

1992 General		
Marjorie Margolies-Mezvinsky (D)	127,685	(50%)
Jon D. Fox (R)	126,312	(50%)
1992 Primary		
Marjorie Margolies-Mezvinsky (D)	28,095	(79%)
Bernard Tomkin (D)	7,318	(21%)

District Vote for President

1992

D 119,042 (44%)
R 107,811 (40%)
I 44,280 (16%)

14 William J. Coyne (D)

Of Pittsburgh — Elected 1980; 7th Term

Born: Aug. 24, 1936, Pittsburgh.
Education: Robert Morris College, B.S. 1965.
Military Service: Army, 1955-57.
Occupation: Accountant.
Family: Single.
Religion: Roman Catholic.
Political Career: Pa. House, 1971-73; sought Democratic nomination for Pa. Senate, 1972; Pittsburgh City Council, 1974-81.
Capitol Office: 2455 Rayburn Bldg. 20515; 225-2301.

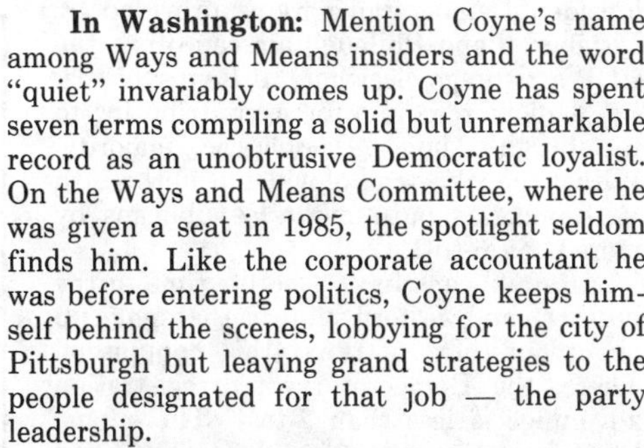

In Washington: Mention Coyne's name among Ways and Means insiders and the word "quiet" invariably comes up. Coyne has spent seven terms compiling a solid but unremarkable record as an unobtrusive Democratic loyalist. On the Ways and Means Committee, where he was given a seat in 1985, the spotlight seldom finds him. Like the corporate accountant he was before entering politics, Coyne keeps himself behind the scenes, lobbying for the city of Pittsburgh but leaving grand strategies to the people designated for that job — the party leadership.

At the start of the 103rd, Coyne received his reward for over a decade of loyal service, filling one of the Budget Committee seats reserved for Ways and Means members.

From that perch, Coyne can keep an eye on his favorite subject: cities, especially those with "Pittsburgh" in the name. In the 102nd, Coyne landed an additional $17 million for a transportation project linking the city to its new airport, Midfield Terminal, secured funding for the Software Engineering Institute and for a pediatric clinic research center and financed a study of the environmental status of a defunct ammunition plant.

When not looking out for his hometown, Coyne is advocating changes in the tax code. Priorities in the 103rd include a number of invest-in-America type revisions, including permanently extending the research and experimentation tax credit, extending the tax exclusion for employer-provided education assistance, and reforming the federal tax treatment of passive foreign investment companies to improve the United States' international competitiveness.

One of Coyne's major activities in the last several Congresses has been overseeing the extensions of tax breaks for small-issue industrial development bonds (IDBs). Provisions allowing such tax treatment for the bonds, which permit state and local governments to offer low-cost financing to small manufacturers, have been one of roughly a dozen special breaks to be renewed periodically by Congress.

Gridlock in the 102nd Congress put an end to easy extension of these IDB provisions, and although Coyne's industrial development bond exemption rode along on two tax bills, both died with vetoes from President Bush. Meanwhile, the exemption expired in June 1992.

And in the 102nd, Coyne had a unique opportunity to combine his love of both Pittsburgh and tax policy. Pittsburgh is now the world headquarters for MagLev Inc., the company developing a high-speed rail prototype system. Not coincidentally, Coyne had for some time been the chief proponent of making tax-exempt bonds issued for high-speed intercity rail projects as attractive as similar issues for student loans and airport renovations.

Coyne proposed a bill that would exempt all (instead of 75 percent) of these bonds from the cap on private-purpose issues that can be sold in a state. He would have paid for the exemptions by requiring state and local governments to better inform taxpayers about user fees not deductible from federal taxes.

Ways and Means sent the proposal to the House floor, where the bill met strong opposition from members who faulted the method by which Coyne proposed to replace revenue lost due to the tax break. Coyne's bill failed, 48-369; because he was on a plane back from Pittsburgh during its consideration, he did not speak in its behalf.

Coyne may get a second chance in the 103rd on both IDBs and high-speed rail bonds; both were included in President Clinton's tax plan.

Powerful Pennsylvania Democrat John P. Murtha is chiefly responsible for Coyne having a place on Ways and Means. Coyne did little campaigning on his own, but Murtha made it clear that Coyne was his choice to give the Pennsylvania steel industry some representation on the influential tax-writing panel. Coyne had four competitors for one remaining seat, including Michael A. Andrews, a Texan favored by then-Majority Leader Jim Wright. But after

Pennsylvania 14

Pittsburgh and suburbs

The place once referred to as "hell with the lid off" is now a gleaming city of water, glass and steel. Since the 1950s, Pittsburgh has undergone an economic transformation that has made the hub of western Pennsylvania into a world-class city — albeit one with far fewer high-wage, working-class jobs than existed in days past.

No one calls it "the smoky city" anymore. Gone is the pollution and griminess created by the steel mills and heavy industry that hugged the Allegheny, Monongahela and Ohio rivers. In their places are medical centers and universities, parks and skyscrapers. There are more than 150 research and development facilities.

With a relatively high quality of life, Pittsburgh ranks high on lists of the "most livable places"; its amenities make it a preferred location for Hollywood filmmakers.

The "Golden Triangle" area, where the Allegheny and Monongahela meet to form the Ohio River, is a thriving downtown with a large corporate community. Companies such as Alcoa, Westinghouse, USX and H. J. Heinz have headquarters here in the city where such industrial giants as Andrew Carnegie, Andrew Mellon and H. J. Heinz made their fortunes. The USX Tower, a 64-story edifice, is one of the largest buildings between New York and Chicago.

The Fort Duquesne Bridge — one of hundreds of bridges and tunnels that connect the city's valleys and ridges — is a gateway to Three Rivers Stadium and Pittsburgh's North Side.

The economic and cultural renaissance has made for a more sophisticated city, yet at the same time Pittsburgh has retained its traditional ethnic character. About 80 distinct neighborhoods dot the city, including the Oakland academic-medical complex — the site of Carnegie-Mellon University, the University of Pittsburgh and Children's Hospital — and the Eastern European working-class enclaves on the South Side. Italians live in Bloomfield, Poles and Germans in Lawrenceville, and Jews in Squirrel Hill. There are black neighborhoods in Homewood and East Liberty.

Pittsburgh's Democratic tradition is another constant. In statewide elections, lopsided Democratic margins provided by Pittsburgh and Philadelphia can offset the GOP advantage elsewhere in Pennsylvania.

Unions remain a force, contributing to Pittsburgh's huge Democratic majority. Within the city — all of which is in the 14th — Democrats outnumber Republicans by more than 6-to-1.

Republicans have a better time in the northern and western suburbs that make up about one-third of the 14th's population. There, the Democratic voter registration advantage is less than 2-to-1. The suburbanites are generally younger, more affluent and less bound by traditional party loyalties than residents in the city.

In many of these areas, Republicans control local offices. The fast-growing North Hills area, partly in the 14th, is filled with executives from Pittsburgh's burgeoning high-tech industry.

1990 Population: 565,787. White 455,246 (80%), Black 100,771 (18%), Other 9,770 (2%). Hispanic origin 4,385 (1%). 18 and over 449,638 (79%), 62 and over 117,747 (21%). Median age: 36.

some complicated horse-trading that produced an alliance between Murtha and Ways and Means Chairman Dan Rostenkowski of Illinois, Coyne won by one vote. (Andrews later joined the committee when another seat came open.)

Asked to cite accomplishments, Coyne will likely mention his work in the 101st Congress that helped establish demonstration projects for home dialysis, or a change he fostered in Medicare reimbursement rates.

As a member of the Banking Committee in his first two terms, Coyne argued for Pittsburgh's business and financial interests, supported extending Clean Air Act compliance dates for the steel industry, backed the Export-Import Bank and supported money to keep the International Monetary Fund solvent.

One of Coyne's chief concerns has been the plight of urban areas in economic decline. In 1988, he introduced a bill to revive the federal revenue-sharing program and target money to local governments whose communities are suffering high unemployment.

In the 100th and 101st Congresses, he sponsored legislation to require the Bureau of Labor Statistics to collect and report data on so-called discouraged workers. Coyne says that the unemployment rate "understates the problem of joblessness in the United States" because it does not include workers who stop looking for work because they no longer believe they can find a job. Neither of Coyne's proposals has emerged from committee.

Coyne also proposed his own version of the "enterprise zone" concept. He felt the plan advanced during the Reagan administration, offering tax incentives to promote development, would be useful only to big businesses. To help cash-starved small and medium-sized businesses get started, Coyne suggested giving them direct aid through existing programs such as community development block grants.

At Home: Coyne's political career has never forced him to stray very far from his inner-city Pittsburgh roots. He still lives in the house where he was born. Before coming to Congress, he was active in Pittsburgh politics for a decade, working loyally with the city Democratic organization.

Coyne was elected to the state House in 1970 but lost a state Senate bid in 1972. In 1973, he was elected to the City Council, where he served as city chairman of the Pittsburgh Democratic Party.

When the 14th opened up in 1980 with the retirement of longtime Democratic Rep. William S. Moorhead, Coyne had the connections to claim it. The city Democratic organization helped him easily defeat Rep. Moorhead's son in the primary. He went on to an easy victory over the GOP nominee that fall.

Coyne has gotten very good at winning elections, typically pulling in over 70 percent of the district vote. Despite redistricting, which slightly changed the 14th, and a primary challenger who demanded that the district elect a Congress member who would "do something," he had no trouble in 1992.

Committees

Budget (13th of 26 Democrats)

Ways & Means (10th of 24 Democrats)
Trade

Elections

1992 General		
William J. Coyne (D)	165,633	(72%)
Byron W. King (R)	61,311	(27%)
1992 Primary		
William J. Coyne (D)	70,162	(76%)
Al Guttman (D)	21,607	(24%)
1990 General		
William J. Coyne (D)	77,636	(72%)
Richard Edward Caligiuri (R)	30,497	(28%)

Previous Winning Percentages: **1988** (79%) **1986** (90%) **1984** (77%) **1982** (75%) **1980** (69%)

District Vote for President

1992
D 145,419 (58%)
R 66,016 (26%)
I 38,460 (15%)

Campaign Finance

	Receipts	Receipts from PACs	Expend-itures
1992			
Coyne (D)	$264,042	$172,007 (65%)	$323,937
King (R)	$72,141	$8,000 (11%)	$73,936
1990			
Coyne (D)	$156,692	$141,600 (90%)	$130,904

Key Votes

1993	
Require parental notification of minors' abortions	N
Require unpaid family and medical leave	Y
Approve national "motor voter" registration bill	Y
Approve budget increasing taxes and reducing deficit	Y
Approve economic stimulus plan	Y
1992	
Approve balanced-budget constitutional amendment	N
Close down space station program	Y
Approve U.S. aid for former Soviet Union	Y
Allow shifting funds from defense to domestic programs	Y
1991	
Extend unemployment benefits using deficit financing	Y
Approve waiting period for handgun purchases	Y
Authorize use of force in Persian Gulf	N

Voting Studies

	Presidential Support		Party Unity		Conservative Coalition	
Year	S	O	S	O	S	O
1992	19	81	96	3	19	81
1991	28	70	93	4	16	81
1990	17	81	93	2	7	91
1989	30	70	96	0	15	83
1988	19	76	92	3	11	79
1987	14	86	93	3	19	81
1986	17	81	95	3	6	94
1985	19	79	94	2	9	89
1984	30	68	91	6	17	78
1983	26	67	91	4	12	85
1982	42	57	91	7	26	74
1981	38	62	89	10	16	84

Interest Group Ratings

Year	ADA	AFL-CIO	CCUS	ACU
1992	95	92	50	4
1991	80	83	20	0
1990	100	100	29	4
1989	100	100	10	4
1988	95	100	31	0
1987	96	100	7	0
1986	100	100	22	0
1985	95	100	19	0
1984	85	85	33	5
1983	90	100	20	4
1982	90	95	27	5
1981	95	87	16	0

15 Paul McHale (D)

Of Bethlehem — Elected 1992; 1st Term

Born: July 26, 1950, Bethlehem, Pa.

Education: Lehigh U., B.A. 1972; Georgetown U., J.D. 1977.

Military Service: Marine Corps, 1972-74; Marine Corps Reserve, 1974-present.

Occupation: Lawyer; adjunct professor.

Family: Wife, Katherine Pecka; three children.

Religion: Roman Catholic.

Political Career: Sought Democratic nomination for U.S. House, 1980; Pa. House, 1983-91; sought Democratic nomination for Pa. Commonwealth Court, 1989.

Capitol Office: 511 Cannon Bldg. 20515; 225-6411.

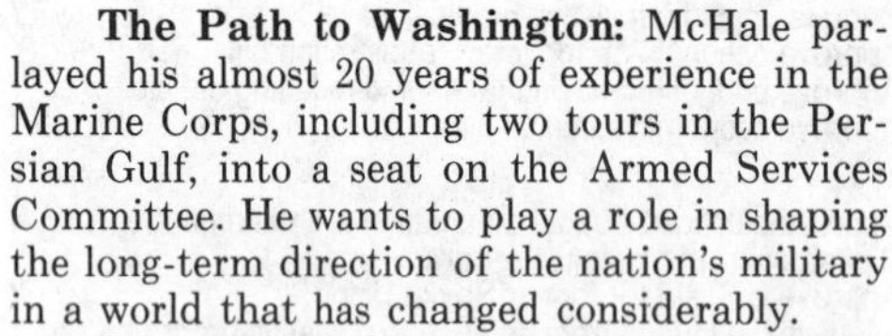

The Path to Washington: McHale parlayed his almost 20 years of experience in the Marine Corps, including two tours in the Persian Gulf, into a seat on the Armed Services Committee. He wants to play a role in shaping the long-term direction of the nation's military in a world that has changed considerably.

For nearly half a century, he observed, there was the possibility of confrontation with the communist bloc. Now that has dissipated.

"The world is more fragmented; the threat is less likely to be severe but wider-ranging," McHale said, adding that as a result of the change, the country "has to take a look at our weapons to see if they match the contemporary threat."

Before coming to Congress, McHale served in the Pennsylvania state House, and although he did not deal with national defense issues in that role, he believes that his military experience as an active duty Marine and a longtime reservist gives him the qualifications to serve on the panel.

McHale resigned from the Pennsylvania House in February 1991 to fight in the Persian Gulf. (He had done previous duty in 1990 while still a state legislator.)

In the state legislature, McHale prided himself on being a consensus builder, backing measures to promote child-passenger safety and family and medical leave.

Describing himself as a mainstream Democrat, he plans to adopt the same look-for-compromise posture in the House. "I prefer to work with others," he said, but added that "there are times in politics when you have to act aggressively. My response to members on the other side of the aisle is directly related to their approach to politics."

McHale got his first taste of politics as an observer, when he spent a semester of college in Washington and was able to watch Congress operate. What he saw impressed and invigorated him, he said, and his first bid for office was an unsuccessful attempt in 1980 to win a U.S. House seat.

He won his state seat two years later, keeping the position until his resignation.

McHale sees his first term in Congress as one to earn credibility with his colleagues.

But he has an eye on a leadership role and noted that he has a good relationship with Democrat John P. Murtha, the veteran Pennsylvania power broker, and Majority Leader Richard A. Gephardt of Missouri.

During the campaign, McHale had criticized seven-term incumbent Republican Don Ritter as ineffective, asserting that the district needed "someone who is a leader in Congress, not someone on the sidelines."

Although McHale said a balanced-budget amendment to the Constitution "is certainly not a panacea," he supports one that would be phased in over time.

McHale also supported a line-item veto and took pains to say that he supported it even when it looked like George Bush might be re-elected.

McHale's views on abortion have brought him criticism from both sides of the issue.

He opposes any "gag rule" that would limit advice to women about abortion, supports fetal tissue research and supports abortion rights in the first trimester.

Anti-abortion groups consider his stand too liberal, but abortion rights groups do not consider him a staunch ally because he favors some restrictions on abortion after the first trimester.

Early in the 103rd Congress, he expressed trepidation about the Freedom of Choice Act, which would make abortions legal nationwide, because of its limited restrictions on abortions late in pregnancy.

Unlike many freshmen, McHale opposes term limits; he said voters can end an incumbent's tenure when they want.

Pennsylvania 15

East — Allentown; Bethlehem

With its backing of Bill Clinton in 1992, the Lehigh Valley returned to the Democratic fold. In doing so, residents shucked the Republican congressman who had represented them since 1978 and voted for a Democratic presidential nominee for the first time since 1976.

The Valley had strayed to the GOP in recent years despite having all the makings of a Democratic stronghold. The heavy industrial tradition, strong unions and sizable ethnic population could not overcome disaffection with the liberal image of the national Democratic Party.

The Republican trend was partly because the district's largest city, Allentown (Lehigh County), had fared better than most of Pennsylvania's other older, industrial cities. Although singer Billy Joel chose Allentown in 1982 to represent the plight of the newly unemployed, the recession did not hit the city quite as hard as some other places because of its diversified economy. Even after Mack Trucks moved one of its main plants to South Carolina in 1987 — in search of lower, non-union wages — the city's then-thriving small companies helped brace the economy.

Two hundred and fifty years ago, Germans settled this region, and their work ethic still exists. Many of the newer businesses depend on the high-quality craftsmanship of the Pennsylvania Dutch, who are conservative and union-resistant. But the German influence has been diluted in recent years by a steady, westward migration from New Jersey and New York into the region.

On the New Jersey border, industrial Northampton County eagerly returned to its Democratic roots in 1992. Voters backed Democrats for president, the Senate and the House, unlike Lehigh County, which stuck with Republican Sen. Arlen Specter while voting for Democrats Clinton and McHale. Northampton boasts a slightly stronger industrial heritage, mainly in Bethlehem and Easton. Bethlehem Steel's smokestacks dominate the Bethlehem city landscape. Though employment at the steel mills is a fraction of what it was in World War II, the company is still a pillar of the local economy. Easton, home to former heavyweight boxing champion Larry Holmes, produces chemicals and paper products.

At Christmastime, Bethlehem sheds its gritty, steel town veneer and transforms into a shining city of glittering trees and candlelit windows. The scene is completed with a Star of Bethlehem that sparkles from atop South Mountain. The Christmas spirit dates back to the mid-1700s, when Moravian Protestants first established a communal church-village. Moravian College, one of the oldest in America, traces its roots to the 18th century.

Lehigh and Northampton counties provide the bulk of the district vote, but a small nub of northwestern Montgomery County is awkwardly grafted on to the southern portion of the district. This Republican section voted for then-Republican Rep. Don Ritter in 1992.

1990 Population: 565,810. White 531,721 (94%), Black 12,175 (2%), Other 21,914 (4%). Hispanic origin 26,766 (5%). 18 and over 434,888 (77%), 62 and over 102,494 (18%). Median age: 35.

Committees

Armed Services (30th of 34 Democrats)
Military Acquisition; Readiness

Science, Space & Technology (21st of 33 Democrats)
Energy; Technology, Environment & Aviation

Campaign Finance

	Receipts	Receipts from PACs		Expend-itures
1992				
McHale (D)	$223,578	$109,450	(49%)	$220,995
Ritter (R)	$890,459	$500,652	(56%)	$865,974

Key Votes

1993

Require parental notification of minors' abortions	N
Require unpaid family and medical leave	Y
Approve national "motor voter" registration bill	Y
Approve budget increasing taxes and reducing deficit	Y
Approve economic stimulus plan	Y

Elections

1992 General		
Paul McHale (D)	111,419	(52%)
Don Ritter (R)	99,520	(47%)
Eugene A. Nau (NL)	2,385	(1%)
1992 Primary		
Paul McHale (D)	30,818	(74%)
Dave Clark (D)	10,891	(26%)

District Vote for President

	1992	
D	92,363	(42%)
R	81,349	(37%)
I	47,740	(22%)

16 Robert S. Walker (R)

Of East Petersburg — Elected 1976; 9th Term

Born: Dec. 23, 1942, Bradford, Pa.
Education: Millersville U., B.S. 1964; U. of Delaware, M.A. 1968.
Military Service: National Guard, 1967-73.
Occupation: High school teacher; congressional aide.
Family: Wife, Sue Albertson.
Religion: Presbyterian.
Political Career: No previous office.
Capitol Office: 2369 Rayburn Bldg. 20515; 225-2411.

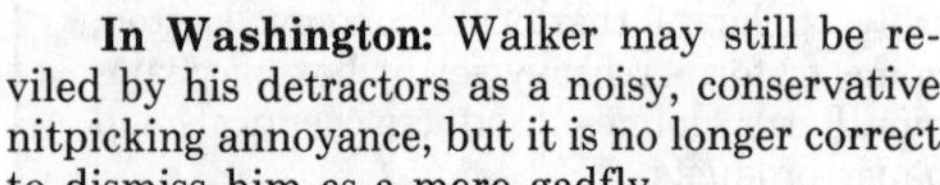

In Washington: Walker may still be reviled by his detractors as a noisy, conservative nitpicking annoyance, but it is no longer correct to dismiss him as a mere gadfly.

Brought into the House Republican leadership by Minority Whip Newt Gingrich of Georgia in 1989, Walker became the sole chief deputy whip in early 1993, when the other chief deputy, Wisconsin's Steve Gunderson, quit. What frustrated Gunderson — the House GOP's increasingly conservative and confrontational posture — defines Walker. He has emerged as one of the minority's most persistent parliamentary bulldogs.

A fiscal and social conservative, Walker cut his teeth in the House as a member of the Conservative Opportunity Society (COS). When the group emerged as a force in the mid-1980s, Gingrich got most of the credit as the spinner of ideas. Walker was seen as a blunt instrument — strident, repetitious and obstructionist, the quintessential legislative outsider.

Walker gave no quarter when he joined the leadership. "I don't see much evidence that Republicans won great victories when they were not confrontational but passive instead," he said. "In 34 years, we were not able to get a majority; there's no victory there."

When it comes to feuding with the Democratic majority, Walker becomes most incensed when internal rules and procedures are at issue — a fact that paradoxically casts him as something of an institutionalist.

Nothing angers Walker more than the closed rules that Democrats use to bring legislation to the floor without risk of amendments they oppose. He has referred to the Democratic tactic as "Bolshevik" and compared the plight of the GOP in the House to Jews in Nazi Germany and slaves in the pre-Civil War South.

While the rules deny Walker many substantive victories, he often succeeds at making the process of winning as unpleasant as possible for Democrats. During consideration of the 1993 legislative appropriations bill, for instance, he brought House business to a crawl. He repeatedly objected to routine requests to make one-minute speeches and demanded vote after vote on pro forma matters, insisting at one point on a rare teller vote, a time-consuming procedure requiring members to file down the aisles to record their yeas and nays.

Walker used House rules to his advantage in 1992 in forcing the Democratic leadership to disclose information about the House bank and Post Office scandals. Threatening to go to the floor with privileged motions that would allow Walker to expound on his theories of wrongdoing, he and other Republicans forced the Democrats to disclose the names of those who had written overdrafts at the bank.

Walker, Gingrich and others first gained prominence by using C-SPAN — the cable TV system that carries live broadcasts of House proceedings — to sell their conservative message nationwide. In 1984, Walker was giving a "special order" speech (at the end of the legislative day) two days after he and Gingrich used a special order to excoriate Democrats for past foreign policy statements. Speaker Thomas P. O'Neill Jr. secretly ordered the TV cameras to pull back and pan the House. For the first time, viewers saw that the chamber was virtually empty. The next day, as Gingrich grilled O'Neill for his unannounced move, the Speaker got so angry at the Georgian that his language overstepped the bounds of House custom. He was officially rebuked.

While the COS members were often referred to as the Republicans' "bomb throwers," their weapons actually were more like flash grenades, causing a lot of heat and smoke, but little injury to their targets. The firebrands crafted and passed few substantive pieces of legislation, and the Democrats expanded their House majority in the 1986 and 1988 elections. The heyday of the COS seemed over.

In fact, the COS leadership had spent less time on the House floor railing to an empty chamber than consolidating its support among younger conservative members and reaching out to a cadre of mainly young, moderate Republican colleagues who also were frustrated with their party's "permanent" minority

Pennsylvania 16

Southeast — Lancaster

Rapid growth and development are redefining the character of the two formerly rural counties that make up the 16th. But development has not altered the historical partisan preference of either Chester or Lancaster counties.

In these two counties — especially Chester — over the past two decades, rural Republicanism has been superseded by a new brand: suburban Republicanism. In Chester County, the mushroom farmers of Kennett Square cast their GOP ballots along with the managers, scientists and executives who moved to such places as Birmingham Township in the 1980s. West Goshen Township, by West Chester University, has also experienced recent growth.

Scenic farm country and a favorable business climate made Lancaster County one of the state's fastest-growing areas in the 1980s. The strong work ethic of the local labor force makes the county a preferred location for companies looking to start new plants in proximity to the East Coast's major markets.

This is the heart of Pennsylvania Dutch Country, which was etched into popular consciousness by the movie "Witness." The Amish "plain people" featured in the movie still farm the area, though increasing property values and suburban encroachment have driven many away.

Some of the sects cling closer to the old ways than others. They range from the Old Order Amish, who in effect live in the mid-19th century, to the "black bumper Mennonites" who allow electricity in their homes and drive cars, but paint any chrome bumpers black.

Besides setting the county's conservative political tone, they affect the county's economy, for tourists flock to Dutch Country to gawk at the horse and buggies, eat at the family-style restaurants and browse at the quilt shops.

Slightly less than half the district's vote is cast in Lancaster County. Not all of the county is in the 16th — the northwestern part is in the 17th — but the city of Lancaster and affluent suburbs such as Manheim Township and Warwick Township are in the 16th.

The Amish and Mennonites are joined in their support of Republican candidates by the affluent communities outside the city of Lancaster. Household incomes for the business executives of Manheim and Warwick townships far outpace the rest of the county.

Anti-abortion strength also bolsters Republican candidates, especially in Chester County, where an organization of conservative Christian activists is taking root.

Even as George Bush lost statewide in 1992, he won Lancaster County by almost 2-to-1. Lancaster and Chester were also kind to GOP Sen. Arlen Specter in his 1992 re-election bid.

Democratic strength in the district is limited to municipalities such as Coatesville and Phoenixville in Chester County. There are also pockets of Democratic support in the city of Lancaster.

1990 Population: 565,835. White 517,422 (91%), Black 29,578 (5%), Other 18,835 (3%). Hispanic origin 21,706 (4%). 18 and over 416,976 (74%), 62 and over 81,737 (14%). Median age: 33.

status. In 1989, that coalition clinched Gingrich's victory for whip over a traditional GOP insider, Edward Madigan of Illinois.

The GOP winners in the 1990 and 1992 elections tilted the House Republican Conference more and more toward the confrontational mode. Now members of this ilk control nearly all the GOP leadership spots except the top one, still held by veteran Rep. Robert H. Michel of Illinois. But following the lead of his troops, even he has become more forward about taking on Democrats. Walker, when asked about the GOP leadership's role under a Democratic administration, predicted that Republicans would strike an even more aggressive posture and give junior members of the party a chance to make a name for themselves.

At times, Walker and his allies have revealed a capacity to hone their legislative efforts, and even to compromise, to bring a sweeping proposal to fruition. After much wrangling, Walker's "drug-free workplace" measure was enacted as part of an omnibus anti-drug-abuse bill in the 100th Congress; it allows the government to end funding to contractors who fail to make a "good-faith" effort to keep illegal drug use out of their work sites.

Walker attached his proposal to several science authorization bills, then used his skill at House floor tactics to attach it to a series of appropriations bills. Democrats drew up an alternative that softened the edges of the drug-free workplace concept. Walker at first dismissed the compromise as a "drugs-in-the-workplace amendment." But by the time the Government Operations Committee attached the revised plan to the omnibus drug bill — virtually guaranteeing its adoption — Walker was on board.

The ranking Republican on the Science, Space and Technology Committee, Walker breaks from his usually tightfisted fiscal approach when it comes to the space station and the superconducting super collider. While critics call the projects federal boondoggles, Walker can sound positively visionary discussing them. "The destiny of man will be in the stars," he said of the space station in 1992.

At Home: Walker's confrontational Republican politics have played well not only among the new arrivals in burgeoning Lancaster County but also among his Pennsylvania Dutch constituents. Conservatism sells well here, and Walker is a born salesman. To publicize his campaign against food stamp abuse, he went to work in a grocery store. When he wanted to go after the Department of Energy, he made a list of questionable-sounding grants — for such things as a solar hot dog cooker — that was then cited on Johnny Carson's "Tonight" show.

After a short stint working as a teacher, Walker signed on as an aide to his representative, Republican Edwin D. Eshleman, and eventually became his administrative assistant. When Eshleman decided to step down in 1976, he backed his young protégé in an 11-way primary fight for the seat.

Walker stressed his Washington experience and, with the help of Eshleman's endorsement and the top ballot position, eked out a primary victory with 20 percent of the vote. That turned out to be his only big hurdle. He has won every general election with ease.

Committees

Chief Deputy Whip

Science, Space & Technology (Ranking)

Joint Organization of Congress

Elections

1992 General		
Robert S. Walker (R)	137,823	(65%)
Robert Peters (D)	74,741	(35%)
1990 General		
Robert S. Walker (R)	85,596	(66%)
Ernest Eric Guyll (D)	43,849	(34%)

Previous Winning Percentages: **1988** (74%) **1986** (75%) **1984** (78%) **1982** (71%) **1980** (77%) **1978** (77%) **1976** (62%)

District Vote for President

1992

D 72,719 (32%)
R 109,037 (49%)
I 43,279 (19%)

Campaign Finance

	Receipts	Receipts from PACs		Expenditures
1992				
Walker (R)	$134,434	$58,350	(43%)	$158,564
Peters (D)	$10,509	$5,305	(50%)	$10,507
1990				
Walker (R)	$96,737	$43,810	(45%)	$98,284

Key Votes

1993	
Require parental notification of minors' abortions	Y
Require unpaid family and medical leave	N
Approve national "motor voter" registration bill	N
Approve budget increasing taxes and reducing deficit	N
Approve economic stimulus plan	N
1992	
Approve balanced-budget constitutional amendment	Y
Close down space station program	N
Approve U.S. aid for former Soviet Union	Y
Allow shifting funds from defense to domestic programs	N
1991	
Extend unemployment benefits using deficit financing	N
Approve waiting period for handgun purchases	N
Authorize use of force in Persian Gulf	Y

Voting Studies

	Presidential Support		Party Unity		Conservative Coalition	
Year	**S**	**O**	**S**	**O**	**S**	**O**
1992	81	15	93	4	92	4
1991	81	19	96	3	97	3
1990	85	15	95	4	85	15
1989	79	21	98	2	93	7
1988	78	22	95	3	95	5
1987	83	17	97	3	91	9
1986	82	17	96	4	94	6
1985	80	20	93	5	85	15
1984	66	30	92	6	88	12
1983	80	20	94	6	81	19
1982	68	32	92	8	84	16
1981	72	18	84	12	80	15

Interest Group Ratings

Year	ADA	AFL-CIO	CCUS	ACU
1992	10	25	88	96
1991	5	8	90	100
1990	11	8	71	96
1989	10	0	100	93
1988	5	7	93	100
1987	4	0	87	96
1986	0	14	94	86
1985	15	12	91	86
1984	10	8	60	83
1983	20	6	80	96
1982	15	20	82	96
1981	10	27	89	100

17 George W. Gekas (R)

Of Harrisburg — Elected 1982; 6th Term

Born: April 14, 1930, Harrisburg, Pa.
Education: Dickinson College, B.A. 1952, Dickinson School of Law, LL.B., J.D. 1958.
Military Service: Army, 1953-55.
Occupation: Lawyer.
Family: Wife, Evangeline Charas.
Religion: Greek Orthodox.
Political Career: Pa. House, 1967-75; defeated for reelection to Pa. House, 1974; Pa. Senate, 1977-83.
Capitol Office: 2410 Rayburn Bldg. 20515; 225-4315.

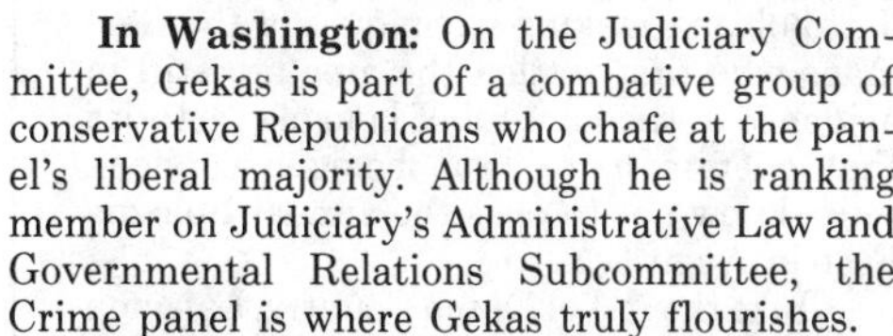

In Washington: On the Judiciary Committee, Gekas is part of a combative group of conservative Republicans who chafe at the panel's liberal majority. Although he is ranking member on Judiciary's Administrative Law and Governmental Relations Subcommittee, the Crime panel is where Gekas truly flourishes.

The man who once vowed to use "every parliamentary maneuver known to mankind" to ensure enactment of a death penalty bill has made capital punishment a personal crusade. At every twist and turn of the legislative process, Gekas is there with a fistful of amendments adding the death penalty as punishment for an array of crimes.

Unlike panel members who view violent crime as an argument in favor of stricter gun controls, Gekas sees such incidents as reinforcement of his stance supporting capital punishment.

A floor debate in 1991 illustrated the differing views. As the House took up a major anticrime bill, a man wielding an automatic pistol stormed a cafeteria in Killeen, Texas, killing 22 people before killing himself. Gekas seized upon the slayings as proof that the House should adopt his amendment to expand the list of capital crimes. Crime Subcommittee Chairman Charles E. Schumer of New York told his colleagues that the incident bolstered the case for his proposed ban on assault-style semiautomatic weapons.

The House agreed with Gekas, however, voting to strip the weapons ban and adopt his amendment, which lowered the threshold of eligibility for capital punishment to include defendants who show a "reckless disregard" for human life, rather than the more stringent "intent to kill."

His seat on the Intelligence Committee in the 102nd Congress simply broadened Gekas' death-penalty perspective.

At the start of the 103rd Congress, he reintroduced legislation that would expand the list of capital crimes to include such actions as terrorist murders committed in the United States or against U.S. citizens abroad. "One of President Clinton's biggest applause lines during his recent address to Congress was his call for passage of a comprehensive crime bill," Gekas said. "He would do well in following up that claim by supporting my legislation, which we have been trying to enact for 12 years."

Election years have usually provided greater opportunities for Gekas and his hardline positions. His first death penalty victory came in 1988 when concerns about the drug crisis persuaded 299 House members to support capital punishment for drug-related murders.

Two years later, Gekas came close to a second victory. After winning approval in both chambers for legislation that ordered the death penalty for a host of crimes, Gekas watched the proposal fall apart as conferees disagreed on language for appeals by death row inmates. He was so annoyed that he alone voted against the final package, which was adopted 313-1.

Gekas takes a hard line against other criminals as well. Warning that the threat by "animal rights terrorists" still exists, he frequently tries to toughen the penalties for protesters who destroy animal research facilities.

A high scorer when it came to supporting the Republican leadership and President Bush on the House floor, Gekas rarely strays from the far right.

In the debate over whether to reauthorize the independent counsel statute, he has been a vocal proponent of allowing the attorney general to call for outside investigations of members of Congress. Gekas says his approach would "establish with the public once and for all that Congress is not in the business of protecting itself."

Throughout the 102nd, Gekas fought to restrict the services of the federally funded Legal Services Corporation, which provides money for civil legal aid for the poor. He failed in efforts to prohibit the LSC from becoming involved in any cases or any lobbying dealing with abortion. But the 188-216 vote signaled that Gekas might be able to round up more

Pennsylvania 17

South Central — Harrisburg

One of the few places where Democrats can be found in the 17th is in Harrisburg, or more precisely, on the 65-acre state Capitol complex in Harrisburg. For outside the legislative chambers and the state government buildings, Democrats are few and far between.

Harrisburg, the district's largest city with just over 52,000 people, is about 100 miles west of Philadelphia and 150 miles east of Pittsburgh in Republican-minded central Pennsylvania.

Its modest skyline is dominated by a magnificent Capitol building topped with a dome inspired by the design of St. Peter's Basilica in Rome. Inside, ornate tiles and murals decorate the corridors and chambers. A grand stairway of Italian marble — modeled after the Opera House of Paris — is the centerpiece of the Rotunda.

Operating within these walls are many state government workers and legislative staffers who help make Harrisburg a Democratic oasis; the city's large black community — which accounts for more than half of Harrisburg's population — enhances the Democratic tilt.

As a whole, though, Dauphin County turns in Republican margins. The Harrisburg suburbs and outlying conservative small towns provide about 80 percent of the county vote; they helped George Bush carry Dauphin in 1988 and 1992. GOP Sen. Arlen Specter won 56 percent in Dauphin County in 1992 while squeaking by to victory statewide.

To get the real flavor of Dauphin County, most visitors skip Harrisburg and go to Hershey, otherwise known as "Chocolatetown, U.S.A." The massive chocolate factory stands at the center of town, emanating the most pleasing of industrial odors. The neat and well-tended company town even has street lights shaped like the bite-size Hershey's Kisses.

Another well-known site in Dauphin County is Three Mile Island, site of a 1979 nuclear accident that had a profound impact on many Americans' attitudes toward nuclear energy.

Besides Dauphin, the only other county wholly within the 17th is Lebanon County, in Pennsylvania Dutch Country. The bologna-making techniques of the Germans who first settled the area are still in evidence in the handful of bologna factories that operate here. True bologna connoisseurs know not to miss the annual Bologna Fest in August.

Like the rest of Dutch Country, Lebanon County evinces a strong strain of conservatism. With a 2-to-1 GOP voter registration advantage, the county stayed in the Republican column for president even in 1992, albeit with just 50 percent for Bush; Bill Clinton failed to crack 30 percent.

Across the scenic and shallow Susquehanna River on the western side of the 17th, the district takes in parts of Republican Perry and Cumberland counties. At its southeastern extreme, the district includes part of Republican Lancaster County, which has some of the suburbs of the city of Lancaster.

1990 Population: 565,742. White 516,393 (91%), Black 37,793 (7%), Other 11,556 (2%). Hispanic origin 10,619 (2%). 18 and over 427,245 (76%), 62 and over 92,724 (16%). Median age: 34.

support in the future.

Late in the 102nd Gekas found a new interest: campaign finance. He won few friends in the summer of 1992 when he suggested that his retiring colleagues not be permitted to convert campaign funds to personal use. Despite the defeat on the legislation, he remained undaunted: "This is my first foray into this thing; I'm not going to give up."

Gekas can display a softer side, particularly when it comes to people he considers victims. As part of the Older Americans Act, reauthorized in the 102nd Congress, Gekas won a provision that helps prevent elderly homeowners from being evicted. The amendment stemmed from the case of a 92-year-old Harrisburg woman evicted for failure to pay back taxes. "Many elderly citizens who own property on which they live are unaware of the legal consequences" of failure to pay taxes, he said.

At least partially influenced by the fact that the Three Mile Island nuclear plant is in his district, Gekas cosponsored legislation with Schumer in the 101st to make those responsible for environmental disasters face criminal penalties. The subcommittee approved the bill, but Schumer and Gekas could not agree about how much leeway to give investigators.

At Home: A member of Harrisburg's small but influential Greek community, Gekas took the traditional path to political success in central Pennsylvania. He went to a local college and law school, became an assistant district attorney, then moved on to the state Capitol.

Gekas fashioned his state legislative career around the same hard-line stand against crime.

He managed capital punishment legislation, chaired the state Senate Judiciary Committee and wrote a tough mandatory sentencing bill.

Gekas encountered remarkably few obstacles on his path to Congress in 1982. He launched his campaign after Democratic Rep. Allen Ertel announced for governor and after the GOP-controlled General Assembly approved new district lines favoring the election of a Republican.

In the primary, Gekas was endorsed by the GOP in Dauphin County (Harrisburg) and won nomination handily over a candidate backed by the Lycoming County GOP. Gekas rolled over his November opponent, Dauphin County Commissioner Larry J. Hochendoner, who had lost to Gekas in a 1976 state Senate contest. With a 3-1 spending advantage, Gekas ran media ads almost daily showing him at an eatery waiting on tables and serving pizza. In 1988 and 1990, Democrats did not field a candidate against him. In 1992, Gekas took nearly 70 percent of the vote against Democrat Bill Sturges.

Committees

Judiciary (6th of 14 Republicans)
Administrative Law & Governmental Relations (ranking); Crime & Criminal Justice

Select Intelligence (5th of 7 Republicans)
Legislation (ranking)

Elections

1992 General		
George W. Gekas (R)	150,158	(70%)
Bill Sturges (D)	65,881	(30%)
1990 General		
George W. Gekas (R)	110,317	(100%)

Previous Winning Percentages: **1988** (100%) **1986** (74%) **1984** (73%) **1982** (58%)

District Vote for President

1992
D 73,654 (32%)
R 115,598 (50%)
I 41,103 (18%)

Campaign Finance

	Receipts	Receipts from PACs		Expend-itures
1992				
Gekas (R)	$112,141	$68,435	(61%)	$190,885
Sturges (D)	$47,235	$21,300	(45%)	$47,217
1990				
Gekas (R)	$128,438	$53,410	(42%)	$93,331

Key Votes

1993	
Require parental notification of minors' abortions	N
Require unpaid family and medical leave	N
Approve national "motor voter" registration bill	N
Approve budget increasing taxes and reducing deficit	N
Approve economic stimulus plan	N
1992	
Approve balanced-budget constitutional amendment	Y
Close down space station program	N
Approve U.S. aid for former Soviet Union	Y
Allow shifting funds from defense to domestic programs	N
1991	
Extend unemployment benefits using deficit financing	Y
Approve waiting period for handgun purchases	N
Authorize use of force in Persian Gulf	Y

Voting Studies

	Presidential Support		Party Unity		Conservative Coalition	
Year	**S**	**O**	**S**	**O**	**S**	**O**
1992	74	20	90	6	83	13
1991	74	25	84	14	97	3
1990	81	19	92	7	94	6
1989	69	29	92	6	88	12
1988	72	27	93	5	97	3
1987	70	29	90	10	84	16
1986	76	23	83	16	92	8
1985	73	28	85	15	87	13
1984	62	35	81	17	88	12
1983	79	20	82	17	76	22

Interest Group Ratings

Year	ADA	AFL-CIO	CCUS	ACU
1992	15	18	88	88
1991	5	25	100	90
1990	0	17	86	91
1989	15	0	100	96
1988	10	21	93	92
1987	8	13	87	83
1986	10	36	83	73
1985	15	29	73	76
1984	20	15	75	67
1983	20	6	95	70

18 Rick Santorum (R)

Of Mount Lebanon — Elected 1990; 2nd Term

Born: May 10, 1958, Winchester, Va.

Education: Pennsylvania State U., B.A. 1980; U. of Pittsburgh, M.B.A. 1981; Dickinson School of Law, J.D. 1986.

Occupation: Lawyer; legislative aide.

Family: Wife, Karen Garver; two children.

Religion: Roman Catholic.

Political Career: No previous office.

Capitol Office: 1222 Longworth Bldg. 20515; 225-2135.

In Washington: When second-termer Santorum asked a colleague how he should conduct himself as a newly named member of the Ways and Means Committee (and ranking member of its Human Resources Subcommittee), the colleague said: "Not like you did last year."

That exchange embodies Santorum's dilemma. Thus far, he has succeeded, in his campaigns and in Congress, largely as an intense young reformer. He scored a high-profile upset in winning election and became one of the "Gang of Seven" freshmen who defied their institutional elders and helped force disclosure of all overdrafts at the House bank.

To accomplish anything legislatively on a committee where bomb-throwing goes worse than unrewarded, however, he must tone down his act. Yet, at the same time, as vice-chair of the National Republican Congressional Committee (NRCC), he will be advising challengers on the fine points of winning as an outsider.

Santorum's balancing act was on view early in the 103rd Congress. First, the gang testified as a group before the Joint Committee on the Organization of Congress and offered its own package of reforms, a few of which were recycled from bills Santorum had introduced in the 102nd Congress.

And in early May, when the Ways and Means Committee took up President Clinton's tax proposals, the meeting was closed to the public, as such markups had been throughout the administrations of Ronald Reagan and George Bush. But Republicans decided to vote against closing the meeting on Clinton's tax increases, and Santorum went further yet. He left the session to participate in a protest organized by junior GOP members in the hallway. He later returned to the meeting, missing no votes.

Despite the activist image of the gang, Santorum himself is not particularly ideological. In his first Congress he supported the legislative position of the Republican White House with average frequency, and he was a little above average in his party unity score.

Such scores could represent a potential burden in a district that is predominantly blue-collar and 70 percent Democratic by registration. But Santorum's young career was made by beating the odds. He took out seven-term incumbent Doug Walgren in 1990 and won his first race in his new district with more than 60 percent of the vote in 1992. In his first term, along with the rest of the gang, he took on a reluctant bipartisan leadership and won over the issue of the bank.

In a September 1991 floor speech, Speaker Thomas S. Foley chastised members for their exorbitant numbers of overdrafts. The leadership tooks steps to close the bank and tried to close the book on the issue.

Santorum and other freshmen held a late-night meeting that spawned the gang, the members of which spent the rest of the week giving floor speeches and calling news conferences demanding an investigation into the bank scandal. Their efforts received little or no press coverage until a William Safire column in The New York Times credited them with "banging their spoons against their high chairs" and calling attention to the matter.

The next week, Santorum and other gang members began pressing for full disclosure of all overdrafts, raising hackles all over the chamber. Ultimately, full disclosure revealed that more than 250 members had overdrawn their accounts. The scandal fed the country's anti-incumbent mood and contributed to the defeat, retirement or near-defeat of dozens of members.

Santorum's had an even greater impact on the 1992 elections. Having won his first race with virtually no help from the national party, Santorum wanted to ensure that similarly dedicated candidates were not ignored in the future. As a freshman, he co-chaired the NRCC buddy system, which assigns incumbents to advise challengers. In 1992, Santorum personally helped Republicans Rick A. Lazio of New Jersey and fellow Pennsylvanian Jim Greenwood unseat incumbents who were hobbled by overdrafts at the bank.

Santorum insists that to be successful,

Pennsylvania 18

Pittsburgh suburbs; Clairton; McKeesport

The story of the Mon Valley is surely one of America's grandest boom-and-bust tales. The denizens of the Monongahela Valley were at the forefront of establishing America as the world's industrial giant in the years leading up to and through World War II, but in the post-industrial decades since, this once-proud region has withered.

It all began in 1851, when the first steel mill opened. Production expanded so rapidly that the local labor pool was quickly exhausted, forcing U.S. Steel to place advertisements in European newspapers seeking workers.

Thousands of Hungarians, Irish, Italians, Poles, Russians, Serbs and Ukrainians were among those who heeded the call; by the late 1940s, U.S. Steel employed 80,000 here.

The company controlled all facets of life. Transportation systems were designed to move workers efficiently at shift changes. Local government and politics were dictated by U.S. Steel policies, particularly so before the United Steelworkers union came into existence in 1942.

But after World War II expansion, the steel industry began its downward spiral. And as the steel works began closing, the towns that lived and breathed with the industry drew their last gasps.

By the mid-1980s, declining population and loss of industry slashed the tax bases of such Allegheny County towns as Homestead, Duquesne and McKeesport. Clairton — the setting for the movie "The Deer Hunter" — was forced to furlough its entire police force and to turn off the street lights. Perhaps more telling was the closing of the McKeesport McDonald's restaurant.

These desperate conditions were reflected in the Valley's voting patterns. Angry and unemployed workers voted in favor of Democrat Walter F. Mondale in 1984; one local steelworkers official said, "In this area, if Ronald Reagan bought a cemetery, people would quit dying." In 1988, Michael S. Dukakis posted even bigger victory margins in areas that now make up the 18th.

Today, despite the massive job losses, the steelworkers union, building trades council and the United Mine Workers still hold sway; Democrats make up 70 percent of the 18th's registration.

The steelworkers who were able to find new employment — mostly in lower-paying service jobs — proved steadfast in their support of Democratic candidates in 1991, when Harris Wofford won 57 percent here in the special Senate election against Allegheny County native Dick Thornburgh, the former governor and U.S. attorney general. Bill Clinton easily bested George Bush in 1992.

Outside the Mon Valley, the 18th contains the northern, eastern and southern Pittsburgh suburbs.

Located entirely within the bounds of Allegheny County, the 18th also includes the middle-class areas of Penn Hills, Shaler and Monroeville, along with the old-money GOP communities of Fox Chapel and Mount Lebanon.

1990 Population: 565,781. White 516,212 (91%), Black 43,969 (8%), Other 5,600 (1%). Hispanic origin 3,299 (1%). 18 and over 447,927 (79%), 62 and over 126,757 (22%). Median age: 38.

Republican campaign strategists must go beyond the standard candidate profile to find people "who will work their tails off." Adds Santorum: "I'm not going to ask people how much money they have, I'm going to ask them how many doors they will knock on."

He also decries the past myopia of GOP congressional campaign strategists. "One of our new ideas has to be: Don't run campaigns out of Washington ... we can't be sending out 22-year-old naysayers telling us why we can't win races."

Santorum has found less success in the legislative arena, where his crusading and cocky manner may have held him back. Like most GOP freshmen, he was unable to move any of the more than 30 bills he sponsored in the 102nd past the committee stage.

Some of his bills would have limited franking privileges and mileage allowances for House members. He also sponsored legislation that would have eliminated the tobacco price-support program.

In both 1991 and 1992, Santorum played a role in the considerations of the budget for the House chamber. In 1991, he introduced an amendment to the legislative appropriations bill that would have limited the Appropriations Committee's right to shift unspent money between accounts. He said such funds should go to reduce the deficit. The amendment failed on a near party-line vote.

In 1992, after Democrats had introduced a rule that would have sharply reduced opportunity for GOP amendments, Santorum tried to paint the rules vote as one of substance and not of process. "This is a put-up vote; this is one that counts," said Santorum.

The rule passed, and it allowed points of order that were later used to kill two of Santorum's amendments calling for "space audits" of House-controlled rooms in the Capitol complex — an effort to prevent Democrats from hogging all the prime space.

At Home: Santorum offers a lesson in how the Republican Party could take over the House in spite of itself. Although his campaign was virtually ignored by the NRCC, Santorum combined shoe leather, an extensive volunteer network, an aggressive style and good luck (the incumbent Democrat was overconfident) to fashion one of the biggest upsets of 1990.

When he launched his challenge in early 1990, no one gave the energetic young man much of a chance against the entrenched, seven-term Democratic Rep. Walgren.

But Santorum made up for the lack of outside help and money — he raised barely $250,000 — by running textbook grass-roots campaign. He took a leave of absence from his law firm in March to visit thousands of households (he puts the number at 25,000) and piece together a volunteer organization. Heavy on anti-abortion activists and Young Republicans, his volunteers reportedly numbered 2,000.

Walgren responded slowly and without much heat. In their first debate in late October, Santorum crisply depicted Walgren as a career Washington insider who had lost touch with his district. Walgren gave long rebuttals that frequently had to be cut off by the moderator.

Walgren did mount a media offensive near the end of the campaign that criticized Santorum as a carpetbagger, new to the Pittsburgh area. But the ads, which featured a photo of Santorum, largely served to underscore the surprising competitiveness of his challenge.

But for all his success in getting elected and getting noticed, Santorum was given up for dead by most political observers after the 1992 redistricting map came out. Democratic lawmakers had been careful to banish Santorum to a heavily Democratic, working-class district bearing little resemblance to the ground he had seized from Walgren.

Twelve Democrats lined up for a shot at Santorum. The winner was a Republican state senator, Frank A. Pecora, who had switched parties to make the race. Pecora drew scathing criticism from his primary opponents (after his party switch he continued to sit with the Republican Caucus in the legislature). Local Democratic officials never embraced his candidacy, and Santorum was suddenly back in business.

Pecora had represented almost one-third of the new 18th's communities in the state Senate. But Santorum duplicated his grass-roots effort of 1990. He also greatly outspent his challenger, highlighting his gang activities in his TV commercials. Remarkably, Santorum not only won in the new 18th, he did so with better than three-fifths of the vote.

Committee

Ways & Means (13th of 14 Republicans)
Human Resources (ranking); Oversight

Elections

1992 General		
Rick Santorum (R)	154,024	(61%)
Frank A. Pecora (D)	96,655	(38%)
Denise Winebrenner Edwards (NEW I)	3,650	(1%)
1990 General		
Rick Santorum (R)	85,697	(51%)
Doug Walgren (D)	80,880	(49%)

District Vote for President

1992

D 137,507 (52%)
R 80,795 (30%)
I 46,754 (18%)

Campaign Finance

	Receipts	Receipts from PACs		Expend-itures
1992				
Santorum (R)	$654,854	$267,454	(41%)	$626,793
Pecora (D)	$288,862	$118,300	(41%)	$284,757
1990				
Santorum (R)	$257,786	$27,660	(11%)	$251,496
Walgren (D)	$601,897	$423,415	(70%)	$717,124

Key Votes

1993	
Require parental notification of minors' abortions	Y
Require unpaid family and medical leave	N
Approve national "motor voter" registration bill	Y
Approve budget increasing taxes and reducing deficit	N
Approve economic stimulus plan	N
1992	
Approve balanced-budget constitutional amendment	Y
Close down space station program	N
Approve U.S. aid for former Soviet Union	N
Allow shifting funds from defense to domestic programs	N
1991	
Extend unemployment benefits using deficit financing	N
Approve waiting period for handgun purchases	N
Authorize use of force in Persian Gulf	Y

Voting Studies

	Presidential Support		Party Unity		Conservative Coalition	
Year	**S**	**O**	**S**	**O**	**S**	**O**
1992	70	28	80	16	79	21
1991	72	28	88	12	97	3

Interest Group Ratings

Year	ADA	AFL-CIO	CCUS	ACU
1992	20	58	88	83
1991	15	42	80	80

19 Bill Goodling (R)

Of Jacobus — Elected 1974; 10th Term

Born: Dec. 5, 1927, Loganville, Pa.
Education: U. of Maryland, B.S. 1953; Western Maryland College, M.Ed. 1956; Pennsylvania State U., 1960-62.
Military Service: Army, 1946-48.
Occupation: Public school superintendent.
Family: Wife, Hilda Wright; two children.
Religion: Methodist.
Political Career: Dallastown School Board president, 1964-67.
Capitol Office: 2263 Rayburn Bldg. 20515; 225-5836.

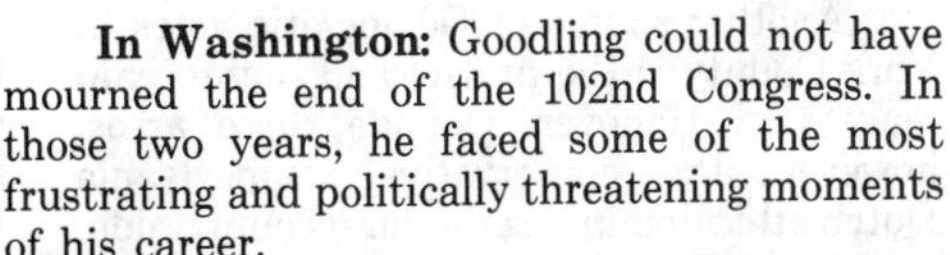

In Washington: Goodling could not have mourned the end of the 102nd Congress. In those two years, he faced some of the most frustrating and politically threatening moments of his career.

With 430 overdrafts at the House bank, Goodling, a mild-mannered, well-liked former teacher, was vulnerable at home after more than 15 years of relative stability. Called a liar by a local minister and challenged by an independent as well as a Democrat, Goodling managed to hang on and win re-election. But with President George Bush's defeat, Goodling lost much of his clout on the Education and Labor Committee, where as ranking Republican he was able to serve as a deal-maker between the Republican White House and the Democratic Congress. Now he must go head-on with the more aggressive, brash and politically crafty chairman, William D. Ford of Michigan, without the White House to back him up.

The 102nd Congress was a stormy one for the Education and Labor Committee. Although the panel has always been prone to partisan battles over labor issues, education was a topic members could often agree on. But in 1992 election year politics turned education issues into a battleground. Goodling was sorely undercut on some legislation by Ford, and even Goodling's allies acknowledge that he had a tough time holding his own in the legislative gamesmanship.

With Bush calling himself the "education president," Goodling was charged with carrying the administration banner on education programs. However, that job was made virtually impossible by the committee's Democrats, who were ideologically opposed and politically hostile to programs that were most important to Bush.

One program that was particularly important to Bush and hence to Goodling was private school choice, which would have provided federal vouchers to parents, allowing poor families to send their children to private schools.

Democrats argued that the plan would take needed federal dollars from already suffering public schools, but Ford worked out a deal with then-White House Chief of Staff John H. Sununu to allow a limited amount of private school choice with federal dollars. After the Senate voted down a school choice plan, however, Ford discarded his bill and introduced a new one that did not include choice provisions. Republicans were livid and accused Ford of going back on his word, but Ford was unmoved, insisting that his deal was with Sununu, who no longer worked at the White House.

Goodling offered a substitute amendment including the choice provisions during committee consideration, but the measure was voted down on a party-line vote.

During consideration of a reauthorization of the Higher Education Act, which provides loans and grants to college students, relations between Ford and Republicans grew even worse.

Republican Rep. Tom Coleman of Missouri thought he had a commitment from Ford to put a cap on spending on one provision, but when the bill was printed, the cap was gone. Coleman and Goodling confronted Ford, who denied that the agreement ever existed.

A former teacher and school administrator, Goodling is a devoted supporter of an array of federal education programs — the school lunch program, Head Start and Even Start among them.

That education agenda and Goodling's willingness to seek compromise give him an image as a political moderate eager to accommodate.

But that is not a complete picture. School aid aside, Goodling is a chamber of commerce Republican who sticks with his conservative colleagues on nearly every labor issue that comes before the committee. And when his hackles are up, he is a ready partisan combatant. When Democrats tried to roll a child-care bill through the committee in 1989, he led a

Pennsylvania 19

South Central — York

Republicans running statewide in Pennsylvania are boosted by a T-shaped voting bloc that begins on the Maryland border and rises north, where it fans out along the New York border. The 19th is at the base of that bloc.

This placid farm country rests on the western fringe of Pennsylvania Dutch Country, taking in all of sparsely populated Adams and populous York counties, and most of Cumberland County to the north. The Susquehanna River forms the eastern border with the 16th and 17th districts.

Democrats are limited to what passes for urbanized areas in the reliably Republican 19th. More than half the population lives a rural existence.

With its solidly Republican character, about the only skirmishing that occurs here is when hundreds of Civil War enthusiasts stage re-enactments at Gettysburg National Military Park, site of one of the war's bloodiest battles.

Even as Pennsylvania deserted George Bush in 1992, the counties of the 19th stayed true to him. In York and Adams counties, Bush won about 45 percent. GOP Sen. Arlen Specter also fared far better in the 19th than across the rest of the state, pulling in about 53 percent in York County.

Specter's victory margin dipped a little against Democratic nominee Lynn Yeakel in Adams County, where the heavy Republican vote is leavened somewhat by Gettysburg College. With 7,000 residents, Gettysburg is the largest town in Adams County. The others are rural farming villages.

Democrats are mostly concentrated in York, the district's largest city and the nation's capital for a brief period in 1777-78 when the British occupied Philadelphia. Then, nearby forges turned out munitions for patriot troops. Now the area's industry makes barbells and assembles Harley-Davidson motorcycles.

A relatively short ride from Baltimore along Interstate 83, York — and its suburbs such as Springettsbury Township — experienced moderate growth in the 1980s as newcomers in search of lower taxes and affordable real estate moved in. One sure sign of York's status in the Baltimore orbit is an Orioles baseball ticket outpost.

Another source of Democratic votes in York County is the pretzel and potato chip makers of Hanover. Outside these areas, however, the conservative Pennsylvania Dutch ethic dominates the rural countryside.

Among Cumberland County's population centers is Carlisle, a supply center for expeditions against the French during the French and Indian War, and later an active station along the Underground Railroad.

The West Shore suburbs — across the Susquehanna from Harrisburg — are home to state employees and blue-collar workers who live in Lemoyne and New Cumberland. The 17th District creeps across the river to grab East Pennsboro Township, Mechanicsburg and Shiremanstown, but affluent Camp Hill, home to the Book of the Month Club, is in the 19th. Outside the suburbs, the Cumberland County terrain becomes more Republican.

1990 Population: 565,831. White 542,646 (96%), Black 14,769 (3%), Other 8,416 (1%). Hispanic origin 7,489 (1%). 18 and over 432,100 (76%), 62 and over 91,193 (16%). Median age: 34.

Republican boycott; when they ignored Bush's education proposals in 1990, he helped stage a GOP walkout.

Conservatives had hoped Goodling would bring those combative partisan traits with him when he rejoined the Foreign Affairs Committee after a six-year stint on the Budget Committee. However, he has not taken an active role. He even passed up a ranking member position on the panel.

Despite Goodling's status as ranking member on Education and Labor and consistent supporter of Bush's agenda, he had some disappointing dealings with the administration in the 101st Congress. After taking the lead as the administration's spokesman on education funding and increasing the minimum wage, he wound up fighting the president from the left on the former and from the right on the latter.

The 1989 debate on the minimum wage revealed Goodling's most conservative, probusiness instincts. With Democrats pushing a $4.65 minimum and Bush backing a $4.25 minimum with a six-month subminimum training wage, moderate Pennsylvania Republican Tom Ridge, working with a pair of Democrats, stepped in with a compromise plan to raise the wage to $4.55, with a two-month subminimum. While the Ridge plan passed the House, Goodling criticized it as subverting Bush's hard-line stand. When asked if Ridge had any Republican friends left, he fired back, "On our side of the aisle, he would have none."

At Home: Before being named an abuser of the House bank by the ethics committee, Goodling had worked hard to make the 19th securely Republican. But his 430 overdrafts turned the district into a battleground in 1992.

A poll taken by the Harrisburg News-Patriot in March 1992, shortly after the check scandal broke, showed that only 26 percent of respondents would vote to re-elect Goodling. In April, Thomas Humbert, a credible third-party candidate, jumped into the race.

Humbert picked up some support from local business and GOP leaders, leading to speculation that he would siphon off votes from Goodling to Democrat Paul Kilker's advantage. But Kilker was ill-prepared to take advantage of Goodling's problems. He was slow to mount an effective challenge, and Goodling went on to win in all three counties with 45 percent, enough to come out on top in the three-way race.

Until his first run for Congress in 1974, Goodling was a high school principal and had held just one elective office — on the Dallastown School Board. He was the surprise winner in a seven-way congressional primary, outdistancing the favored John W. Eden, who once had challenged Goodling's father. Waging his first general election campaign in the Watergate year of 1974, the younger Goodling won by barely 5,000 votes.

Committees

Education & Labor (Ranking)
Elementary, Secondary & Vocational Education (ranking)

Foreign Affairs (2nd of 18 Republicans)
Europe & the Middle East

Elections

1992 General

Bill Goodling (R)	98,599	(45%)
Paul V. Kilker (D)	74,798	(34%)
Thomas M. Humbert (I)	44,190	(20%)

1990 General

Bill Goodling (R)	96,336	(100%)

Previous Winning Percentages: **1988** (77%) **1986** (73%) **1984** (76%) **1982** (71%) **1980** (76%) **1978** (79%) **1976** (71%) **1974** (51%)

District Vote for President

1992

D 74,445 (33%)
R 104,258 (47%)
I 43,759 (20%)

Campaign Finance

	Receipts	Receipts from PACs		Expend-itures
1992				
Goodling (R)	$200,014	$12,950	(6%)	$201,951
Kilker (D)	$238,418	$58,142	(24%)	$238,346
Humbert (I)	$123,830	$6,088	(5%)	$122,486
1990				
Goodling (R)	$41,011	0		$40,698

Key Votes

1993

Require parental notification of minors' abortions	Y
Require unpaid family and medical leave	N
Approve national "motor voter" registration bill	N
Approve budget increasing taxes and reducing deficit	N
Approve economic stimulus plan	N
1992	
Approve balanced-budget constitutional amendment	Y
Close down space station program	Y
Approve U.S. aid for former Soviet Union	N
Allow shifting funds from defense to domestic programs	N
1991	
Extend unemployment benefits using deficit financing	N
Approve waiting period for handgun purchases	Y
Authorize use of force in Persian Gulf	Y

Voting Studies

	Presidential Support		Party Unity		Conservative Coalition	
Year	S	O	S	O	S	O
1992	72	28	83	14	81	19
1991	68	23	70	20	78	8
1990	54	39	71	20	72	17
1989	65	29	76	17	83	7
1988	50	47	77	19	84	13
1987	57	39	72	24	79	21
1986	60	37	69	28	76	24
1985	61	38	74	19	69	24
1984	50	44	66	28	71	29
1983	54	40	71	26	61	38
1982	61	36	74	24	66	30
1981	59	36	74	17	65	21

Interest Group Ratings

Year	ADA	AFL-CIO	CCUS	ACU
1992	10	33	75	83
1991	20	25	70	73
1990	22	27	64	68
1989	25	17	90	68
1988	30	50	93	63
1987	28	19	80	48
1986	25	43	88	55
1985	25	18	77	57
1984	35	31	63	48
1983	35	24	65	61
1982	25	25	64	62
1981	30	20	74	93

20 Austin J. Murphy (D)

Of Monongahela — Elected 1976; 9th Term

Born: June 17, 1927, Speers, Pa.

Education: Duquesne U., B.A. 1949; U. of Pittsburgh, LL.B. 1952, J.D. 1972.

Military Service: Marine Corps, 1944-46; Marine Corps Reserve, 1948-50.

Occupation: Lawyer.

Family: Wife, Eileen Ramona McNamara; six children.

Religion: Roman Catholic.

Political Career: Pa. House, 1959-71; Pa. Senate, 1971-77.

Capitol Office: 2210 Rayburn Bldg. 20515; 225-4665.

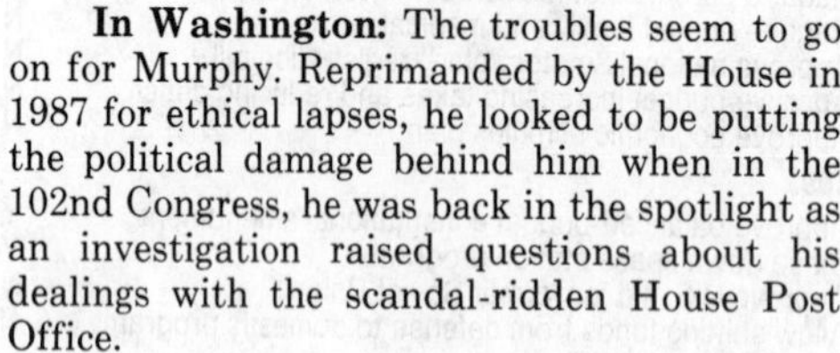

In Washington: The troubles seem to go on for Murphy. Reprimanded by the House in 1987 for ethical lapses, he looked to be putting the political damage behind him when in the 102nd Congress, he was back in the spotlight as an investigation raised questions about his dealings with the scandal-ridden House Post Office.

In mid-1991, a federal probe of embezzlement and drug dealing by employees of the House Post Office expanded to look into the possibility that members may have been connected with the wrongdoing. A postal supervisor testified before a federal grand jury about a scheme in which members converted official expense vouchers or campaign checks to cash through transactions that were disguised as stamp purchases.

The grand jury subpoenaed office expense account records from Murphy and two other Democrats — Ways and Means Chairman Dan Rostenkowski of Illinois and Joe Kolter of Pennsylvania. (Kolter later lost his 1992 bid for renomination.)

When subsequent subpoenas sought information only from Rostenkowski and Kolter, it appeared that those two were the main targets of the probe. However, as of spring 1993, Murphy had not been officially cleared. The Justice Department still was actively investigating the Post Office matter, and the House ethics committee was waiting for the department to complete its work before addressing the allegations.

Whatever the final disposition of the matter, merely being mentioned in connection with it brought a round of media retellings of Murphy's December 1987 reprimand by the full House. The House ethics committee had voted 11-0 to assess Murphy its mildest punishment — a reprimand — for diverting government resources to his former law firm, for allowing another member to vote for him on the House floor and for keeping a "ghost employee" on his payroll.

Until he was thrust into the limelight by publicity about his ethics, Murphy had spent his House career working largely behind the scenes.

Like most Rust Belt Democrats, Murphy typically toils rather quietly on behalf of coal miners, steelmakers and other blue-collar types, speaking up publicly only when the interests of working men and women — and the labor unions that represent them — are threatened.

Murphy looks out for miners and other blue-collar workers from his position on the Education and Labor Committee, where he is the fourth-ranking Democrat and chairman of the subcommittee on Labor Standards, Occupational Health and Safety. In the 102nd Congress, he pushed a bill aimed at increasing benefits for miners suffering from black lung disease; it won voice vote approval in the House but was never taken up by the Senate.

Murphy speaks up for coal interests from his seat on the Natural Resources Committee, where he is also the No. 4 Democrat in seniority. He regularly sides with pro-development forces against environmentalists and generally is a pro-industry vote on nuclear power issues.

Despite Murphy's senior position on two committees, the stigma of the reprimand probably disqualifies him from being a leadership point man on high-profile legislation. In two Congresses during the 1980s, he was a leading proponent of Democratic efforts to increase the minimum wage, but he was not part of the final negotiating team on the bill that increased the wage in 1989.

At Home: The life of a politician in coal country can be a little like the life of a miner — rough. Murphy, proud of his Marine Corps past, displays a relish for combat that suits his district. In 1973 he got into a fight with motorcycle gang members who were harassing him. In 1979, after Iranians seized American hostages, Murphy declared his willingness to rejoin the Marines and attack Tehran.

His toughest-ever re-election challenge

Pennsylvania 20

Southwest — The Mon Valley; Washington

With West Virginia on its southern and western borders, the 20th is Pennsylvania's own version of Appalachia. Much of the district is rural, poor and, like its neighbor, rock-ribbed Democratic territory.

Politics in the 20th is not for the weak of heart. From the industrial areas along the Monongahela River to the coal fields of Fayette and Greene counties, hardball politics is the rule. Then-United Mine Workers President W. A. "Tony" Boyle was convicted here in the 1969 murder of union rival Joseph A. "Jock" Yablonski.

Part of the reason is the sense of economic desperation that often grips the region. Coal mining has always been subject to boom-and-bust cycles, and with mining's increasing mechanization and the shift of production from Eastern mines to those out West, unemployment is high in Fayette and Greene coal country. The UMW's clout has diminished, but the union remains an important political force.

Along the Monongahela, the slow demise of the steel industry has led to massive job losses from Donora to Brownsville, the borough that marks the unofficial end to the industrialized Mon Valley.

Outside of Pittsburgh and Philadelphia, this is the most reliably Democratic region in the state. Democratic Gov. Robert P. Casey racked up about 80 percent in Fayette and in less-populous Greene County in 1990; even Democratic presidential nominee Michael S. Dukakis ran strong in these counties in 1988. In 1992, Washington, Fayette and Greene counties voted for Bill Clinton by ratios of more than 2-to-1. In Fayette and Greene counties, Democrats outnumber Republicans more than 3-to-1.

The population centers of the 20th are the city of Washington (Washington County) and Greensburg (Westmoreland County). The city of Washington is home to the county's old factory-owning families and occasionally supports Republicans. Peters Township, a white-collar bedroom community for Pittsburgh commuters on the Allegheny County line, also is receptive to GOP candidates.

Greensburg, Westmoreland's county seat, has no major military installation, but it was perhaps the U.S. town most tragically touched by the Persian Gulf War. Eleven reservists of the 14th Quartermaster Detachment, based in Greensburg, were killed by an Iraqi Scud missile attack one week after arriving in Saudi Arabia.

Westmoreland's economy took a hit in 1988 when Volkswagen closed its assembly plant in New Stanton just over the line in the 12th District, but shortly afterward the Sony Corporation of America moved in to build large-screen color televisions.

The 20th is one of three House districts that take in a part of Westmoreland. Allegheny County is also shared by three districts. The only counties wholly contained in the 20th are Washington — where about one-third of the people in the 20th live — and Greene County in the district's southwestern corner.

1990 Population: 565,815. White 544,113 (96%), Black 17,889 (3%), Other 3,813 (1%). Hispanic origin 2,877 (1%). 18 and over 436,822 (77%), 62 and over 114,810 (20%). Median age: 37.

came in 1992. First, rumors that he would retire attracted four primary challengers. Then it was reported that he had six overdrafts at the House bank. Though that was not a big number, opponents coupled the checks with the earlier reprimand to try to paint a picture of Murphy as lacking ethical standards.

Murphy barely squeaked by Washington County Commissioner Frank R. Mascara to win renomination. Then came the news that Murphy was part of the federal investigation of misdeeds in the House Post Office.

Winning the Democratic primary in this heavily Democratic district is normally tantamount to election, but Murphy was no normal incumbent. His GOP challenger, Bill Townsend, a 27-year-old advertising agency owner, waged an aggressive campaign, complete with "Scandal of the Week" news releases aimed at embarrassing the incumbent. Townsend distanced himself from his party label to cope with the massive Democratic registration edge in the district. But in a year when the national Democratic ticket ran well in the district, Murphy managed to hold on with 51 percent of the vote.

Though Murphy had never struggled so to hold his seat, he had faced some pesky foes over the years. In 1984, for instance, it seemed that Murphy might come to blows with his GOP challenger, Nancy Pryor. Her campaign rhetoric was unusually inflammatory; at one point she said Murphy and the national Democratic Party "endorsed and approved of humans having sex with dogs, sex with sheep, sex with chickens, to name only a few."

But the election itself was nowhere near as

interesting as the campaign; Murphy won by a 4-to-1 margin.

In 1990, three years after his reprimand by the House, Murphy drew a determined primary challenge from William A. Nicolella, a candy company owner. He accused Murphy of leading a double life — with a wife and family back in the district and a woman friend and teenage son born out of wedlock in the Washington, D.C., suburbs.

The story had appeared in print before, but several days prior to the primary, Nicolella supplied Pittsburgh TV stations and The Associated Press with footage purportedly taken around Murphy's Northern Virginia home that Nicolella said proved his accusation.

Murphy responded in two statements, accusing Nicolella of making "venomous" and "slanderous" attacks. "I have never abandoned my responsibility to any of my children," Murphy said. He won renomination with 70 percent and took a comfortable 63 percent in November.

To win the seat vacated by Democrat Thomas E. Morgan in 1976, Murphy had to navigate his way through a 12-candidate primary field. Morgan had his own candidate, but with almost two decades as a state legislator under his belt, Murphy prevailed with 29 percent of the vote.

Committees

Education & Labor (4th of 28 Democrats)
Labor Standards, Occupational Health & Safety (chairman); Labor-Management Relations

Natural Resources (4th of 28 Democrats)
Energy & Mineral Resources; Insular & International Affairs; National Parks, Forests & Public Lands

Elections

1992 General		
Austin J. Murphy (D)	114,898	(51%)
Bill Townsend (R)	111,591	(49%)
1992 Primary		
Austin J. Murphy (D)	36,585	(36%)
Frank R. Mascara (D)	33,942	(34%)
Kenneth B. Burkley (D)	14,422	(14%)
William A. Nicolella (D)	8,520	(8%)
Eugene G. Saloom (D)	7,755	(8%)
1990 General		
Austin J. Murphy (D)	78,375	(63%)
Suzanne Hayden (R)	45,509	(37%)

Previous Winning Percentages: **1988** (72%) **1986** (100%) **1984** (79%) **1982** (79%) **1980** (70%) **1978** (72%) **1976** (55%)

District Vote for President

1992
D 121,815 (51%)
R 69,802 (29%)
I 48,249 (20%)

Campaign Finance

	Receipts	Receipts from PACs		Expend-itures
1992				
Murphy (D)	$235,296	$174,750	(74%)	$309,425
Townsend (R)	$53,209	$7,010	(13%)	$51,775
1990				
Murphy (D)	$199,802	$139,310	(70%)	$191,739
Hayden (R)	$3,260	$50	(2%)	$3,258

Key Votes

1993	
Require parental notification of minors' abortions	Y
Require unpaid family and medical leave	Y
Approve national "motor voter" registration bill	Y
Approve budget increasing taxes and reducing deficit	Y
Approve economic stimulus plan	Y
1992	
Approve balanced-budget constitutional amendment	N
Close down space station program	Y
Approve U.S. aid for former Soviet Union	X
Allow shifting funds from defense to domestic programs	Y
1991	
Extend unemployment benefits using deficit financing	Y
Approve waiting period for handgun purchases	N
Authorize use of force in Persian Gulf	N

Voting Studies

	Presidential Support		Party Unity		Conservative Coalition	
Year	**S**	**O**	**S**	**O**	**S**	**O**
1992	23	70	64	32	29	60
1991	34	53	63	28	51	38
1990	29	69	61	33	44	54
1989	34	62	49	45	41	56
1988	28	59	50	36	47	42
1987	21	69	68	20	56	40
1986	21	77	75	19	50	42
1985	36	63	78	20	49	49
1984	35	63	65	28	46	51
1983	22	77	78	18	38	57
1982	35	57	71	19	41	49
1981	38	53	58	30	52	40

Interest Group Ratings

Year	ADA	AFL-CIO	CCUS	ACU
1992	65	83	38	29
1991	50	82	33	39
1990	50	83	69	33
1989	75	92	50	30
1988	60	100	33	24
1987	60	81	15	5
1986	70	93	33	19
1985	60	76	36	19
1984	55	77	47	42
1983	80	94	25	17
1982	55	89	25	33
1981	55	85	29	20

21 Tom Ridge (R)

Of Erie — Elected 1982; 6th Term

Born: Aug. 26, 1945, Munhall, Pa.
Education: Harvard U., B.A. 1967; Dickinson School of Law, J.D. 1972.
Military Service: Army, 1968-70.
Occupation: Lawyer.
Family: Wife, Michele Moore; two children.
Religion: Roman Catholic.
Political Career: Erie assistant district attorney, 1979-82.
Capitol Office: 1714 Longworth Bldg. 20515; 225-5406.

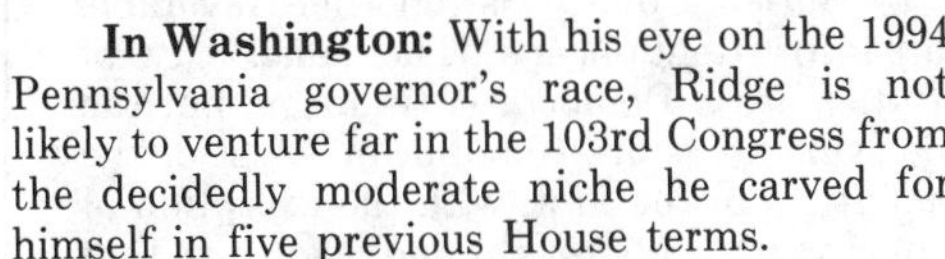

In Washington: With his eye on the 1994 Pennsylvania governor's race, Ridge is not likely to venture far in the 103rd Congress from the decidedly moderate niche he carved for himself in five previous House terms.

His cultivated Jaycee image is fitting for a Republican who aspires to statewide office in Pennsylvania. (Before announcing his bid for the statehouse in early 1993, Ridge turned down a chance to run statewide in 1990.)

But Ridge has proved particularly adept at fashioning a record that can appeal to all sides: He regularly earns better than 50 percent ratings from both business and labor. This ambidextrous approach to issues has made him popular in his district: a mainly blue-collar corner of northwest Pennsylvania, centered on the industrial city of Erie. Like many Erie men of working-class backgrounds, Ridge enlisted in the Army and served in Vietnam (although, in Ridge's case, he did it after first earning a college degree from Harvard).

Ridge has also shown a willingness to buck a Republican president from time to time on both economic and social issues. In 1992, he voted against President George Bush's stated position more often than all but a handful of House Republicans. Thus he is likely to be among the Republicans most closely courted by the Clinton administration. Ridge is proficient at forging interparty alliances on issues ranging from banking to defense to labor. And he seems genuinely troubled by increasing partisanship in the House. Following the Persian Gulf War, he lamented to The Washington Post that because of President Bush's success, "there may be a tendency not to be bipartisan but to polarize in an election cycle.... I loathe, but anticipate, that possibility."

When Ridge breaks with the GOP leadership, he often does so publicly — leaving his more conservative colleagues exasperated. In both 1991 and 1992, Ridge voted to overturn the Bush administration's so-called "gag rule" barring federally financed family planning clinics from providing abortion counseling.

In February 1992, he voted against the Democrats' tax bill and then voted against a competing package crafted by the Bush administration, as well. Prior to those floor votes, Ridge wrote an article for the opinion pages of The Philadelphia Inquirer urging Bush to drop his "obsession" with cutting the tax rate on capital gains income. Such a tax cut would do little, Ridge wrote, except "to churn the stock market and increase the profits of stock brokers and traders. The President would do better to embrace more meaningful economic initiatives."

Ridge also took on Bush in early 1989 over the minimum wage. Democrats on the Education and Labor Committee wanted a minimum well above the existing rate of $3.35 an hour, aiming for $4.65 with no subminimum "training wage" for new employees. Bush proposed a minimum of $4.25 with a six-month training wage. Ridge and two Democrats suggested raising the wage to $4.55 an hour, with a two-month training wage for new hires with minimal work experience. The compromise passed the House. Bush vetoed the bill, and Ridge was one of just 20 Republicans to vote for an override, which failed.

Ridge's interest in unconventional solutions was evident during the banking overhaul debate of 1991. He worked to forge a compromise on "redlining" — the bank practice of denying loans to poor and minority neighborhoods. Ridge was among those Banking Committee members who found existing anti-redlining rules onerous, particularly for smaller banks. But lacking the votes to roll back those rules, Ridge approached consumer advocates with a carrot instead of a stick. He proposed to reduce the deposit insurance premiums paid by banks willing to "greenline" marginal neighborhoods. The idea appealed to some Democrats and made it into the final bill when other rules changes did not.

Ridge has been on the Banking Subcommittee on Housing since his freshman term. In the 101st Congress, the panel produced the first major revamp of federal housing programs

Pennsylvania 21

Northwest — Erie

The state's third-largest after Philadelphia and Pittsburgh, Erie is Pennsylvania's forgotten big city. Even among Great Lakes neighbors Cleveland and Buffalo, Erie is a lesser light. But it is the population center of the 21st District.

Local politics are Democratic, with two ethnic groups — Italians and Poles — vying for power. Actually, the first considerable immigration to the city was that of the Pennsylvania Dutch, followed by Italians, Poles and Russians.

Italians settled on the West Side and Poles on the East Side. Together, the blue-collar communities worked on East Side assembly-line jobs at General Electric and other heavy industries.

More recently, though, younger Italians have begun a move out of the 6th Ward, toward such suburbs as Summit and Millcreek townships, where their traditional Democratic loyalties have weakened.

That mobility has largely been absent in the Polish community. The Polish East Side is now larger than the city's Italian community, and more Democratic. Organized labor is a force here.

Local politics sometimes reflects the divisions between the two communities. In 1982, when a Pole defeated an Italian for the Democratic House nomination, many disappointed Italians supported Rep. Ridge in November, helping him win. His cordial relations with labor helped him stay there.

The independent and GOP voters outside the city make Erie County politically competitive. Ronald Reagan carried it in 1980 and 1984, but Michael S. Dukakis in 1988 and Bill Clinton in 1992 won it back. But as voters backed Clinton and Democratic Senate challenger Lynn Yeakel in 1992, Ridge won with 71 percent.

Outside of Erie County (where Democrats have a healthy voter registration advantage), Republicans fare better. South of Erie, Crawford County toes the Republican line. The dairy farmers and retirees in the Conneaut Lake area backed George Bush and GOP Sen. Arlen Specter in 1992. The county is divided between the 21st and 5th districts, but the 21st District portion includes what passes for the county's largest city, Meadville.

Butler County is another favorable area for Republicans. The small city of Butler has a Democratic tradition, but the outlying areas are Republican. Most of the county is in the 21st, with the exception of some southern boroughs and townships that belong to the 4th.

The tone is more Democratic in industrial Mercer County. The Shenango Valley steel towns such as Farrell, Hermitage, Sharon, Sharpsville and Wheatland vote Democratic like the rest of western Pennsylvania, and have been equally hard-hit by steel industry decline. The less-populous and industrial eastern section of the county is Republican.

Mercer was one of just two Pennsylvania counties to support Reagan in 1980 and then switch to Walter F. Mondale in 1984, mostly because people felt Reagan had done little to save the steel industry.

1990 Population: 565,802. White 538,923 (95%), Black 21,849 (4%), Other 5,030 (1%). Hispanic origin 4,471 (1%). 18 and over 425,058 (75%), 62 and over 100,741 (18%). Median age: 34.

since 1974. Ridge organized the GOP opposition to a Democratic-sponsored program to spur production of rental housing. But Democrats pitted the rental-housing program against the administration's Homeownership and Opportunity for People Everywhere (HOPE) program, which was being pushed by Housing Secretary Jack F. Kemp and was designed to help public housing tenants buy their buildings. Ridge agreed not to put up a fight on rental housing, and the Democrats promised to keep HOPE.

Another Ridge compromise was enacted in the final bill to stem losses in the Federal Housing Administration's mortgage insurance program. Initially, Ridge joined with Minnesota Democrat Bruce F. Vento to devise a plan without increasing up-front costs. But when that plan had passed the House, Ridge persuaded the House-Senate conferees to adopt another compromise that would cost buyers $833 up front in cash.

Ridge has made some ventures into defense policy. Skeptical of the Strategic Defense Initiative (SDI), he teamed with Charles E. Bennett, a Florida Democrat and arms control liberal, in yearly attempts to cut it.

In 1989, by 248-175, the House adopted their amendment to spend $3.1 billion on SDI's research program instead of the $4.9 billion Bush requested. In 1990, their amendment to slice SDI to $2.3 billion was adopted 225-189. And in 1992, Ridge was among 11 Republicans to back an amendment by Illinois Democrat Richard J. Durbin to pare almost $1 billion from the program. The amendment, opposed by Armed Services Committee Chairman Les Aspin, failed.

In the 101st Congress, Ridge joined the Post Office and Civil Service Committee and got the ranking GOP slot on its Census and Population Subcommittee. Previously, he and others had filed suit in federal court to block the inclusion of illegal aliens in the U.S. census. Ridge said such an inclusion, which he described as inherently inaccurate, penalized areas (such as Erie) that attract few immigrants. The suit was thrown out on procedural grounds.

After the 1990 census, Ridge argued against mathematical adjustments in the count to correct for presumed undercounts and other inaccuracies, pitting him against Subcommittee Chairman Tom Sawyer of Ohio. Ridge defended Commerce Secretary Robert A. Mosbacher's decision to let the original count stand against Sawyer's attacks.

At Home: Blue-collar voters in many parts of the country returned to their Democratic roots in 1982, but not the ones in northwestern Pennsylvania. They elected Ridge over a labor-oriented Democrat in a district that had been expected to return to Democratic control with GOP Rep. Marc L. Marks' retirement.

Ridge capitalized on a good organization and exhaustive personal effort to defeat Democratic state Sen. Buzz Andrezeski by 729 votes. He was aided by Democratic disunity and by his departure from the Reagan line of cutting social programs and boosting military spending.

Ridge's start in local politics came as chief of George Bush's Erie County 1980 presidential campaign. He won the GOP House nomination after other prominent Republicans decided that Democrats would handily recapture the 21st, which they had held before Marks' 1976 victory.

At first, Ridge had trouble raising money from local business interests, which had written off the race. But Ridge impressed national GOP leaders and key Washington business groups, who sent him the money he needed.

Andrezeski, banking on his labor support, campaigned less vigorously than Ridge, who worked the Italian-dominated West Side of Erie, where the Polish-American Andrezeski was unpopular because he had defeated an Italian in the primary. Ridge lost Erie by 8,000 votes; suburban and rural support elected him. Since then, Ridge has worked hard to entrench himself. In 1990 he had no opposition.

Committees

Banking, Finance & Urban Affairs (5th of 20 Republicans)
Economic Growth (ranking); General Oversight, Investigations & the Resolution of Failed Financial Institutions; Housing & Community Development

Post Office & Civil Service (6th of 9 Republicans)
Census, Statistics & Postal Personnel

Veterans' Affairs (5th of 14 Republicans)
Oversight & Investigations (ranking); Education, Training & Employment

Elections

1992 General		
Tom Ridge (R)	150,729	(68%)
John C. Harkins (D)	70,802	(32%)
1990 General		
Tom Ridge (R)	92,732	(100%)

Previous Winning Percentages: **1988** (79%) **1986** (81%) **1984** (65%) **1982** (50%)

District Vote for President

	1992
D	105,538 (45%)
R	81,003 (35%)
I	47,923 (20%)

Campaign Finance

	Receipts	Receipts from PACs	Expend-itures
1992			
Ridge (R)	$530,372	$299,785 (57%)	$705,861
Harkins (D)	$15,801	$700 (4%)	$15,800
1990			
Ridge (R)	$454,349	$246,265 (54%)	$361,712

Key Votes

1993	
Require parental notification of minors' abortions	N
Require unpaid family and medical leave	N
Approve national "motor voter" registration bill	N
Approve budget increasing taxes and reducing deficit	N
Approve economic stimulus plan	N
1992	
Approve balanced-budget constitutional amendment	Y
Close down space station program	N
Approve U.S. aid for former Soviet Union	N
Allow shifting funds from defense to domestic programs	N
1991	
Extend unemployment benefits using deficit financing	Y
Approve waiting period for handgun purchases	N
Authorize use of force in Persian Gulf	Y

Voting Studies

	Presidential Support		Party Unity		Conservative Coalition	
Year	**S**	**O**	**S**	**O**	**S**	**O**
1992	50	47	72	21	69	25
1991	58	41	66	27	89	8
1990	49	51	68	27	70	28
1989	56	43	69	27	76	24
1988	40	56	66	28	74	26
1987	40	56	59	34	56	42
1986	47	53	59	37	68	32
1985	44	54	60	35	58	36
1984	42	50	45	49	53	44
1983	51	46	56	40	66	31

Interest Group Ratings

Year	ADA	AFL-CIO	CCUS	ACU
1992	30	50	63	68
1991	15	58	90	70
1990	22	33	57	58
1989	45	67	80	57
1988	50	86	71	36
1987	48	60	64	19
1986	35	64	61	41
1985	30	47	73	48
1984	50	38	60	36
1983	35	47	80	39

Rhode Island

STATE DATA

Governor: Bruce Sundlun (D)
First elected: 11/90
Length of term: 2 years *
Term expires: 1/95
Salary: $69,000
Term limit: No *
Phone: (401) 277-2080
Born: Jan. 19, 1920; Providence, R.I.
Education: Williams College, B.A. 1946; Harvard U., LL.B. 1949
Military Service: Army Air Force, 1942-45; Air Force Reserve, 1945-80
Occupation: Lawyer; businessman
Family: Wife, Marjorie Lee; five children.
Religion: Jewish
Political Career: Assistant U.S. attorney, 1949-51; special assistant to U.S. attorney general, 1951-54; nominee for governor, 1986, 1988

Lt. Gov.: Robert A. Weygand (D)
First elected: 11/92
Length of term: 2 years *
Term expires: 1/95
Salary: $52,000
Phone: (401) 277-2371

State election official: (401) 277-2345
Democratic headquarters: (401) 231-1992
Republican headquarters: (401) 453-4100

REDISTRICTING

Rhode Island retained its two House seats in reapportionment. The legislature passed the map May 14, 1992. The governor took no action on it, and the map became law May 22.

** After 1994, each office will be limited to two 4-year terms.*

STATE LEGISLATURE

Legislature. Meets January-May.

Senate: 50 members, 2-year terms
1992 breakdown: 39D, 11R; 39 men, 11 women; 49 whites, 1 black
Salary: $5/day
Phone: (401) 277-6655

House of Representatives: 100 members, 2-year terms
1992 breakdown: 85D, 15R; 74 men, 26 women; 91 whites, 8 blacks, 1 Hispanic
Salary: $5/day
Phone: (401) 277-2466

URBAN STATISTICS

City	Pop.
Providence	160,728
Mayor Vincent A. Cianci Jr., N-P	
Warwick	85,427
Mayor Kathryn O'Hare, D	
Cranston	76,060
Mayor Michael A. Traficante, R	
Pawtucket	72,644
Mayor Robert Metivier, D	
East Providence	50,380
Mayor Rolland Grant, D	

U.S. CONGRESS

Senate: 1 D, 1 R
House: 1 D, 1 R

TERM LIMITS

For Congress: No.
For state offices: No

ELECTIONS

1992 Presidential Vote

Bill Clinton	47.0%
George Bush	29.0%
Ross Perot	23.2%

1988 Presidential Vote

Michael S. Dukakis	56%
George Bush	44%

1984 Presidential Vote

Ronald Reagan	52%
Walter F. Mondale	48%

POPULATION

1990 population		1,003,464
1980 population		947,154
Percent change		+6%
Rank among states:		43
White		91%
Black		4%
Hispanic		5%
Asian or Pacific islander		2%
Urban		86%
Rural		14%
Born in state		91%
Foreign-born		9%
Under age 18	225,690	22%
Ages 18-64	627,227	63%
65 and older	150,547	15%
Median age		34.0

MISCELLANEOUS

Capital: Providence
Number of counties: 5
Per capita income: $18,840 (1991)
Rank among states: 19
Total area: 1,212 sq. miles
Rank among states: 50

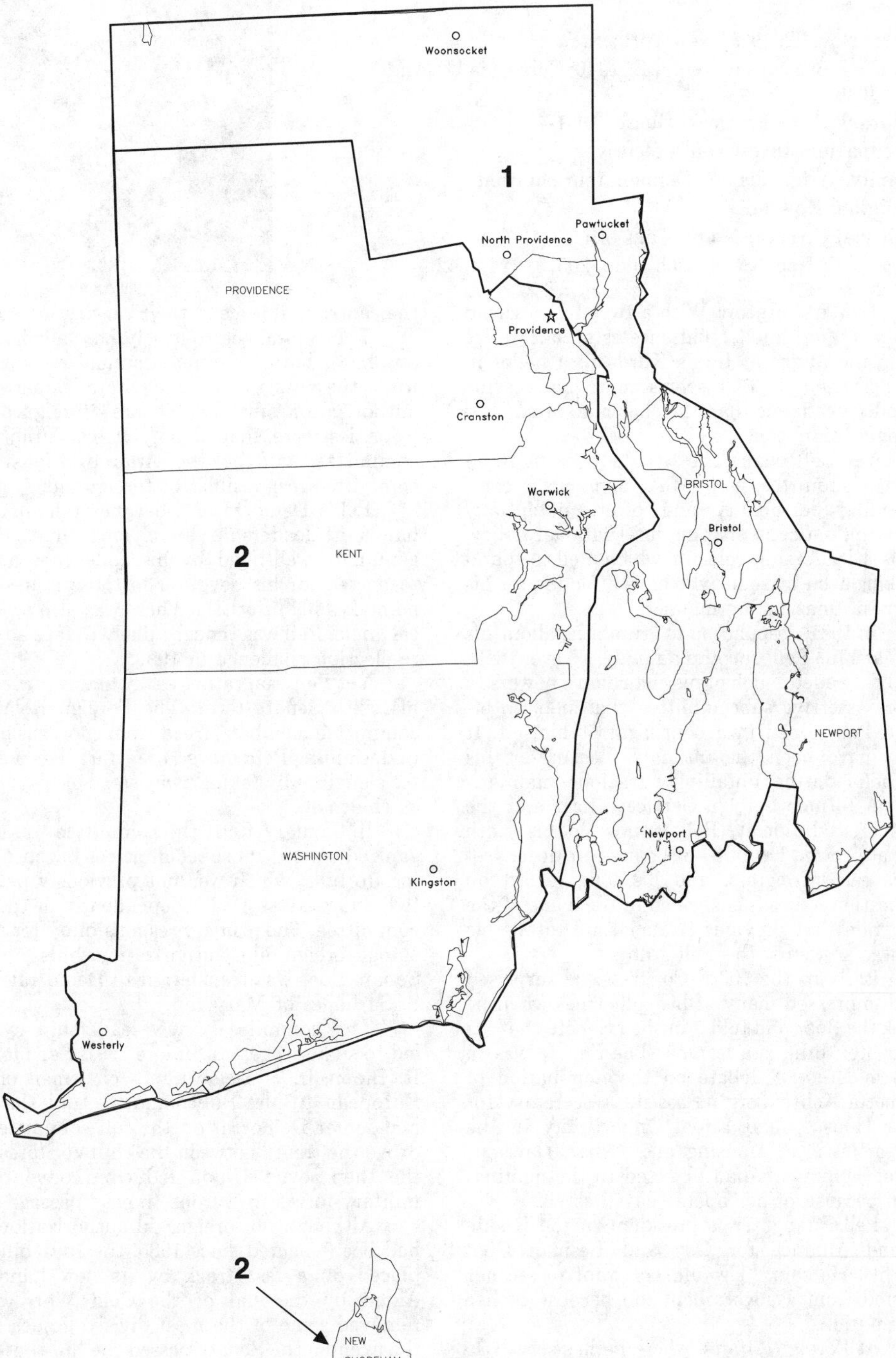
Woonsocket
1
Pawtucket
North Providence
PROVIDENCE
Providence
Cranston
BRISTOL
Warwick
Bristol
2
KENT
NEWPORT
Newport
WASHINGTON
Kingston
Westerly
2
NEW
SHOREHAM

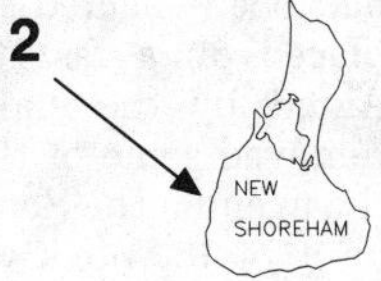

Claiborne Pell (D)

Of Newport — Elected 1960; 6th Term

Born: Nov. 22, 1918, New York, N.Y.
Education: Princeton U., A.B. 1940; Columbia U., A.M. 1946.
Military Service: Coast Guard, 1941-45.
Occupation: Investment executive.
Family: Wife, Nuala O'Donnell; four children.
Religion: Episcopalian.
Political Career: No previous office.
Capitol Office: 335 Russell Bldg. 20510; 224-4642.

In Washington: With a tweedy, patrician manner and intellectual interests that range from the plight of Iraq's Kurds to a belief in parapsychology, Pell seems more an absent-minded academic than the chairman of a major Senate committee.

Yet Pell chairs the Senate Foreign Relations Committee, a role that demands a commanding personality and offers potentially great influence in shaping international policy. It is a leadership role for which Pell is found lacking even by some who have affection for his earnest, unassuming manner.

In 1991, responding to grumbling about his leadership, Pell uncomplainingly — even willingly — ceded much of his chairman's powers to more assertive subcommittee chairmen. In effect, Pell joined in a coup against himself. It may have been the ultimate measure of his accommodating, unfailingly gracious, manner.

A former Foreign Service officer and the son of a diplomat, Pell is now in his sixth Senate term. He puts his name on dozens of bills each Congress, and his long record on education issues is enshrined in the name of the program that provides financial aid to eligible college students: the Pell grants.

Early in the 103rd Congress, he surprised and impressed many of his colleagues when he took the floor and told a hushed Senate that his daughter Julia is a lesbian. The Senate was in the midst of a debate on the nomination of Roberta Achtenberg as assistant secretary for Fair Housing and Equal Opportunity in the Department of Housing and Urban Development. Opponents had objected to the nomination because of her openly gay lifestyle.

Pell's daughter is president of the Rhode Island Alliance for Gay and Lesbian Civil Rights. He said: "I would not want to see her barred from a government job because of her orientation."

At Foreign Affairs, where he has served as chairman since 1987, Pell has watched with seeming detachment as the committee has lost much of its traditional prestige and as its members have been pulled in different directions by the centrifugal force of their varying ideologies.

The committee routinely has failed to act on one or both of its main annual responsibilities: the foreign aid and State Department authorization bills. The Senate's foreign policy priorities were shaped not by his authorizing committee, but by the Appropriations subcommittee responsible for foreign aid.

Pell's Democratic colleagues tolerated his hands-off leadership for a long time. He is genuinely well-liked by his colleagues and is respected for his devotion to those issues that he makes his priorities. There was also a political angle: Pell was thought likely to face a tough re-election challenge in 1990.

Yet Pell won rather easily and returned for his sixth Senate term. The Foreign Relations committee members, freed from concerns about undermining Pell, moved to restart the committee's engines by taking away some of his powers as chairman.

In January 1991, the committee was reorganized so that its subcommittees began marking up bills, which was not previously permitted, and were staffed independently of the full committee. The primary responsibility for managing foreign aid authorization bills on the Senate floor was transferred to Democrat Paul S. Sarbanes of Maryland.

The committee's new leadership system led to some successes. In late 1991, Sen. Joseph R. Biden Jr. of Delaware — chairman of the European Affairs Subcommittee and the second-senior Democrat on the full committee — drove the treaty between the United States and the then-Soviet Union reducing conventional military forces in Europe to easy passage.

Although no foreign aid authorization bill had been enacted since 1985, the 1991 bill was placed on a fast track by its new handlers. Aided by the end of the Cold War, which removed some of the most divisive issues from the agenda, the Senate passed the bill that July on a 74-18 vote.

While Sarbanes acted as the Democratic floor leader on the bill, Pell sat mainly in the background. A Foreign Relations Committee aide described him as "a friendly uncle" taking pride in his nephews' successes.

But the Senate panel, so often blamed for the failure of the bill in the past, was frustrated this time by the House. By the end of the 1991 session, recession-weary voters were demanding a greater effort on domestic issues, and Democrats were hammering President Bush for focusing too much on foreign affairs. The conference report on the foreign aid authorization bill was rejected by the House.

Even with stronger leadership skills, Pell would have had difficulty moving legislation through the ideological minefield that existed during the Reagan and early Bush administrations. His efforts were frequently parried by Foreign Relations' ranking Republican, Jesse Helms of North Carolina, a conservative ideologue who has frequently used his parliamentary skills to scuttle foreign policy legislation that did not fit his worldview.

"Claiborne has not had strong views as to what ought to occur, and Jesse has been very adept at stymieing even those views that [Pell] has," veteran committee member and former Chairman Richard G. Lugar, R-Ind. said in 1991.

Despite sharp ideological differences, Pell and Helms worked together through the 101st and 102nd Congresses to gain enactment of a bill placing sanctions against nations and businesses that trade in chemical weapons.

The Pell-Helms effort was spurred by the 1988 incident in which Iraq's government forces used poison gas against that nation's Kurdish minority.

The sanction provisions passed Congress in 1990 as part of a bill reauthorizing the Export Administration Act. However, Bush pocket-vetoed the bill that November, stating that the sanctions "unduly interfere with the president's responsibility for carrying out foreign policy."

The onset of the Persian Gulf War in early 1991 — and threats by Saddam Hussein to use chemical weapons against Israel and the U.S.-led military coalition — gave momentum to Pell's efforts. When Bush made the executive prerogative argument, Pell accused him of countenancing chemical weapons trade by nations, including prewar Iraq, in which the administration had a geopolitical interest. "It means that the most disgusting regime on earth could gas thousands of people, could even commit genocide, and the act would be excused if ... sanctions might have a bad effect on relations," Pell said.

The final measure contained a provision demanded by Bush that granted the president authority to waive the sanctions against a particular country if he determined it to be in the national interest. In order to skirt the stalled authorization bill, the chemical weapons sanctions were attached to a bill extending unemployment benefits and signed by Bush in December 1991.

The poison gas issue highlighted three aspects of Pell's foreign policy activities: an abhorrence of war and weapons of mass destruction (he opposed U.S. involvement in the Vietnam War and is a leading advocate of nuclear arms control); a long-running commitment to universal human rights; and a more recent adoption of the cause of the Near East's autonomy-seeking Kurds.

Although Pell voted against the January 1991 resolution authorizing Bush to use force against Iraq, he was among the senators who raised an alarm about the president's slow response to the plight of the Kurds, who revolted after the war and were suppressed by Saddam's troops.

In the 102nd Congress, Pell proposed a bill to expand U.S. aid to the democratizing Soviet republics; many of its provisions were later combined with proposals — submitted by Lugar and Democratic Sen. Sam Nunn of Georgia, the chairman of the Armed Services Committee — to provide U.S. funding for demilitarization efforts in those republics.

The final measure, titled the Freedom Support Act, was enacted in 1992. Pell managed the bill on the floor with Republican Lugar.

Pell was one of the first members to call for the United States to impose strong sanctions against Serbia, widely regarded as the aggressor in the bloody civil war between ethnic groups in the former Yugoslavia. He was also one of the first to call for war crime tribunals. His father, Rep. Herbert C. Pell, was one of those calling for the post-World War II Nuremberg tribunals a generation earlier.

Pell sharply criticized Bush for what he viewed as complacency in the face of atrocities committed by ethnic Serbs against Muslims and Croats in Bosnia. Referring to Bush's rapid response to Iraq's invasion of Kuwait, Pell said, "If we are only prepared to defend victims of aggression when they are rich in natural resources, we are setting a poor example for a new world order."

As long as he remains in the Senate, Pell can be expected to continue his commitment to federal aid to education. Compared to his much-criticized role on Foreign Relations, Pell's leadership shortcomings are much less in evidence in his position as chairman of the more consensus-minded Labor and Human Resources Subcommittee on Education, Arts and Humanities.

In 1972, Pell pushed through legislation establishing Basic Educational Opportunity Grants (BEOGs) for low- and middle-income college students. The program marked a basic shift in policy, because it provided aid directly to students, instead of channeling it through the institutions, as earlier programs had done. The BEOG program was renamed "Pell grants" in 1980.

In April 1991, Bush proposed an education

bill that would have held the line on overall Pell grant spending while raising the maximum grant from $2,400 to $3,700 — thus potentially cutting 400,000 students from the program. Pell argued that Bush "is moving in precisely the wrong direction," adding, "We need larger Pell grants for more students, not larger grants for fewer students."

The number of income-eligible students served by Pell grants is limited by the amount of money that congressional appropriators devote to it. Pell tried during the 102nd Congress to push a plan to make the grant program an entitlement for all eligible students. But the annual cost would have greatly increased spending on the grants, and the increasing priority on restraining the federal budget deficit made the entitlement plan unpassable. Pell eventually pulled his proposal from consideration.

Pell opposes proposals to make civilian or military "national service" a condition for receiving federal aid for postsecondary education. However, Pell, like President Clinton, supports legislation to provide aid in exchange for voluntary national service.

The long-tenured Pell also serves on the Senate Rules Committee and is vice chairman of the Joint Library Committee, which oversees the activities of the Library of Congress.

At Home: Pell's predecessor in the Senate was Theodore Green, who first arrived in the chamber well past retirement age and served into his 90s. Incredible as that seems, Pell the Newport blueblood is well on his way toward matching Green's record for Senate longevity. Far from resenting his privileged background, Pell's blue-collar constituents have handed him landslide victories five out of six times. Only Republican John H. Chafee, now his Senate colleague, was able to hold him under 60 percent of the vote in 1972.

Pell's pro-labor record has kept him in the good graces of the unions, always a potent force in Rhode Island. And while he does not have much personal rapport with the state's ethnic voters, he can talk to them: He speaks Portuguese, Italian and French.

Pell's career not only survived in the generally Republican election years of 1972, 1978 and 1984, but it prospered. So it should not have surprised anyone when he flourished in the more favorable climate of 1990, when Rhode Island Democrats were recapturing both the governorship and the 2nd District House seat. Some had thought Pell, at 71, a better candidate for retirement than re-election — especially after the GOP recruited five-term House veteran Claudine Schneider to challenge him.

Doubts about Pell's fitness multiplied when, in an August debate, he could not remember any bills he had sponsored strictly for Rhode Island. His memory, he said pleasantly, "is not as good as it should be."

The senator gave pause once again in the autumn when an aide asserted there were secret messages in Persian Gulf speeches by U.S. officials. The aide said a code word ("Simone") was audible when tapes of the speeches were played backwards. "It sounds wacky [but] there may be some merit to it," said Pell, who reported this research in a letter to the secretary of Defense.

But Rhode Islanders had long since grown accustomed to Pell's eccentricities. Despite his begoggled and half-doddering manner, Pell once again managed not only to rise to electoral challenge but to crush it.

Campaigning actively and emphasizing local economic concerns, he dispelled doubts about his age, health and sensitivity to the homefolk.

Criticism of his performance as Senate Foreign Relations chairman, so common in Washington, did little damage in Rhode Island. It may even have allowed Pell, the consummate inside player, some insulation against the anti-insider mood of the day.

Schneider, meanwhile, never found a suitable key for her anti-incumbent pitch. Loath to assail Pell personally, she often sounded as though she thought the only thing wrong with him was his party label (scarcely a disqualification in a Democratic state). When she shifted to more ideological grounds of attack, the similarities between her voting record and Pell's undercut her effectiveness. While voters continued to show high regard for her personally, she was unable to sell her "time for a change" theme and Pell rang up more than 61 percent of the vote.

Pell's father, Herbert, briefly represented Manhattan's Silk Stocking District in the House and served as a foreign envoy for Franklin D. Roosevelt. Claiborne Pell was born in New York and spent summers in the exclusive Rhode Island resort of Newport, where the Pells had been going for five generations. The family moved there permanently when he was 9.

After graduating from Princeton in 1940, Pell went to Europe to try to help concentration camp inmates. The Nazis arrested him several times. He was a Coast Guard officer during World War II and spent several years in the foreign service. He later became an investment banker and publisher and served as registration chairman for the Democratic National Committee.

Pell decided to run in 1960 and stunned the political community by overwhelming two former governors to win the Democratic nomination for the Senate. In the fall, Pell was helped to victory by his close ties to Democratic presidential nominee John F. Kennedy, a fellow New Englander highly popular in Rhode Island.

Running for a second term in 1966, Pell had an equally easy time with his GOP opponent — a retired Women's Army Corps officer named Ruth M. Briggs, who insisted upon being called "Colonel." She sought to make an issue of Pell's dovish line on the Vietnam War and to portray him as a wealthy dilettante ("the prize entertainer of the Kennedys"). She failed to draw even a third of the vote.

Chafee, in 1972, gave Pell his toughest race. He tried to weigh down Pell with his fellow anti-war Democrat Sen. George McGovern of South Dakota, the Democrats' presidential nominee.

But Pell deflected the tactic by repudiating McGovern's call for cutting the defense budget. Ultimately, the moderate Chafee had the same trouble Schneider would have 18 years later defining a compelling reason to retire Pell.

Things were back to normal for Pell in 1978, when he buried Republican James G. Reynolds, a little-known bakery executive who complained that Pell was more interested in the arts than in saving jobs for Rhode Island. In 1984, the GOP tried to recruit Schneider but had to settle for Barbara Leonard, the president of a screw manufacturing company. The widow of a longtime GOP fundraiser, Leonard herself was a political novice; Pell was re-elected with 73 percent of the vote.

Committees

Foreign Relations (Chairman)
Terrorism, Narcotics & International Operations

Labor & Human Resources (2nd of 10 Democrats)
Education, Arts & Humanities (chairman); Aging; Children, Families, Drugs & Alcoholism

Rules & Administration (2nd of 9 Democrats)

Joint Library

Elections

1990 General

Claiborne Pell (D)	225,105	(62%)
Claudine Schneider (R)	138,947	(38%)

Previous Winning Percentages: **1984** (73%) **1978** (75%) **1972** (54%) **1966** (68%) **1960** (69%)

Campaign Finance

	Receipts	Receipts from PACs		Expenditures
1990				
Pell (D)	$2,138,199	$885,678	(41%)	$2,350,128
Schneider (R)	$1,989,616	$688,865	(35%)	$2,056,923

Key Votes

1993	
Require unpaid family and medical leave	Y
Approve national "motor voter" registration bill	Y
Approve budget increasing taxes and reducing deficit	Y
Support president's right to lift military gay ban	Y
1992	
Approve school-choice pilot program	N
Allow shifting funds from defense to domestic programs	Y
Oppose deeper cuts in spending for SDI	N
1991	
Approve waiting period for handgun purchases	Y
Raise senators' pay and ban honoraria	Y
Authorize use of force in Persian Gulf	N
Confirm Clarence Thomas to Supreme Court	N

Voting Studies

	Presidential Support		Party Unity		Conservative Coalition	
Year	S	O	S	O	S	O
1992	28	68	83	9	11	82
1991	32	68	89	10	20	78
1990	25	72	86	9	11	81
1989	49	48	85	11	18	76
1988	43	51	89	6	8	92
1987	32	67	92	7	19	81
1986	30	67	75	20	16	80
1985	29	67	82	14	7	92
1984	31	66	82	14	15	81
1983	41	48	81	15	14	82
1982	36	59	75	19	17	78
1981	42	52	82	14	10	82

Interest Group Ratings

Year	ADA	AFL-CIO	CCUS	ACU
1992	80	82	30	8
1991	90	83	22	0
1990	94	78	18	19
1989	85	80	43	4
1988	100	100	36	0
1987	90	90	28	0
1986	80	67	42	17
1985	95	95	29	9
1984	100	100	22	5
1983	90	94	26	0
1982	95	92	37	0
1981	95	95	17	0

John H. Chafee (R)

Of Warwick — Elected 1976; 3rd Term

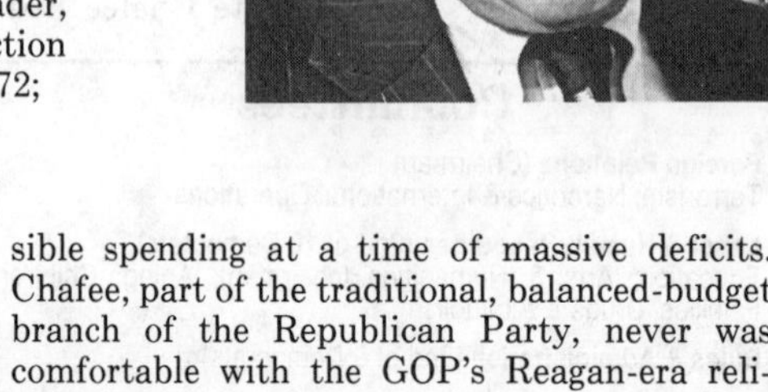

Born: Oct. 22, 1922, Providence, R.I.
Education: Yale U., B.A. 1947; Harvard U., LL.B. 1950.
Military Service: Marine Corps, 1942-45, 1951-52.
Occupation: Lawyer.
Family: Wife, Virginia Coates; five children.
Religion: Episcopalian.
Political Career: R.I. House, 1957-63, minority leader, 1959-63; governor, 1963-69; defeated for re-election as governor, 1968; secretary of the Navy, 1969-72; GOP nominee for U.S. Senate, 1972.
Capitol Office: 567 Dirksen Bldg. 20510; 224-2921.

In Washington: Although their party lost the White House in 1992, it may turn out that Chafee and the Senate's other GOP moderates have more leverage to shape policy in Bill Clinton's Washington than they did in the twilight of George Bush's presidency.

One reason is that the Senate's "magic number" has changed from 34 to 41. With the 1992 election approaching, Bush and congressional Democrats often seemed more interested in scoring partisan points than in passing laws. In that climate, Bush needed just 34 votes in the Senate; that number put teeth in his veto threats, since it was enough to deny Democrats the two-thirds majority required for a veto override. And Bush almost always could line up 34 votes from the GOP right; moderates such as Chafee were superfluous.

Now, however, with Democrats holding both Congress and the presidency, the math is different. The only way Senate Republicans can guarantee themselves influence in shaping policy is by demonstrating that they can muster 41 votes — enough to sustain filibusters. Democrats need 60 votes to invoke cloture, which closes off debate and permits legislative action. Because there are only 44 Senate Republicans, Chafee's advice, counsel — and vote — are avidly sought by the GOP leadership.

The "new math" may especially work to enhance Chafee's clout when moderate Democrats defect from Clinton to fashion policies less liberal than those supported by the White House. In those situations, Chafee likely will be courted to join a bipartisan centrist bloc.

The early months of the 103rd Congress saw both scenarios develop. In April, Chafee joined in the unanimous Senate Republican opposition to Clinton's $16.3 billion economic stimulus package; GOP filibuster threats stalled and finally doomed the measure. Although conservatives led the effort, Chafee was a prominent moderate critic, appearing on such programs as the "MacNeil/Lehrer NewsHour" to make his case that the package was irresponsible spending at a time of massive deficits. Chafee, part of the traditional, balanced-budget branch of the Republican Party, never was comfortable with the GOP's Reagan-era reliance on supply-side economics and the deficits that strategy tolerated.

And in May, when a bipartisan group of four Senate moderates produced a deficit reduction package to compete with Clinton's, Chafee, though not in the group, was close by, and offering words of encouragement: "This is a group that gathered because of a sincere feeling that the president's package was lopsided on taxes and didn't have enough spending cuts," he told The New York Times.

Even though Chafee and Bush are both New England-bred Episcopalians and studied at Yale at the same time, much of the senator's political agenda is more in play with Clinton in the Oval Office. One of Chafee's major efforts in the 102nd Congress was aimed at lifting the so-called "gag rule," which prevented employees in clinics that receive federal funding from discussing abortion with a patient. The bill passed both the House and Senate in 1991 but was vetoed by Bush; the Senate overrode, but not the House. One of Clinton's first actions as president was to reverse the gag rule.

So as Chafee points toward a 1994 re-election campaign, he will likely not look back with any special fondness on the Reagan-Bush years. Because of his frequent departures from the party line, Chafee at the end of 1990 was ousted from his post as chairman of the Senate Republican Conference, the No. 3 position in the GOP leadership.

Chafee had managed to fend off two prior challenges from the right, relying on his personal popularity to sway the conservative-dominated GOP Conference. But at the end of the 101st Congress, he met his equal in popularity, Thad Cochran of Mississippi, who benefited from conservatives exasperated by such Chafee actions as his votes against school prayer and the flag-desecration and balanced-budget amendments, and his support for overriding Bush's veto of civil rights legislation. Even so, Cochran won by a single vote, 22-21.

Chafee chairs the Senate Republican Health Care Task Force, which spent a year and a half mulling options before presenting its plan in November 1991. Although Bill and Hillary Rodham Clinton now get the first crack at shaping the health-care debate, Chafee expects to use the task force as a bully pulpit as Congress digs into the complex business of legislating changes in the current system.

As ranking Republican on the Environment and Public Works Committee, Chafee played a vital role in the 101st Congress on the reauthorization of the Clean Air Act.

Chafee approached the clean air rewrite with a position on acid rain tough enough that he joined with environmental groups, and a few other senators, to condemn Maine Sen. George J. Mitchell's proposed compromise on Clean Air Act amendments at the end of the 1988 session. Chafee was a key participant in drafting the bill's smog-reduction program, the largest title in the bill. In the Environmental Protection Subcommittee, where he was also ranking Republican, Chafee split with Democrats on how to reduce automobile tailpipe emissions. Democrats, led by Environmental Protection Chairman Max Baucus of Montana, leaned toward tough restrictions on emissions through two rounds of reductions. Chafee and the Republicans favored easing up on tailpipes and putting more emphasis on a program mandating the production and sale of alternative fuels and clean-fueled cars in the nation's nine smoggiest cities.

When Baucus refused to slow the accelerated markup process to consider the GOP proposal, Chafee led a rare partisan rebellion on the panel. He and the five other subcommittee Republicans voted against the bill's motor vehicle provisions. They were approved on a 7-6 vote. But Chafee's proposal became part of the Senate-White House compromise on the bill.

Chafee also added a controversial amendment that would end by 2000 the use of chlorofluorocarbons (CFCs) and other chemicals blamed for destroying the ozone layer in the upper atmosphere. Under the bill, the chemicals are required to be phased out sooner than called for in an international agreement on CFCs signed by the United States.

Chafee worked with New York Democrat Daniel Patrick Moynihan on the 1991 highway bill, which gives states unprecedented control over how they spend federal surface transportation dollars. But a provision from Chafee that would have made it easier for states to ban or remove existing billboards from highways was overturned by the Senate after fierce protest from the outdoor advertising industry.

At Home: Chafee's affability and moderate record have carried him through more than 35 years of politics in Rhode Island, winning most of the time and recovering from defeat.

His toughness showed in 1988, when he faced a telegenic and talented campaigner, Lt. Gov. Richard A. Licht. The 40-year-old nephew of the man who had ousted Chafee from the governorship in 1968, Licht got an early start organizing and fundraising; he had raised more than Chafee by the start of 1988. Before winning statewide, Licht had built a solid record as a legislator on issues of wide voter appeal, such as child care and protection of open spaces.

But Chafee turned some of Licht's assets against him. He seized on Licht's campaign treasury to portray himself as the fiscal underdog in the race. And when Licht returned a controversial $250 contribution from Tom Hayden, a leftish California legislator (married at that time to actress Jane Fonda), Chafee said the Democrat must lack "backbone" if he caved in to pressure "over a measly $250."

As expected, Democrat Michael S. Dukakis easily carried Rhode Island for president. But Chafee won a comfortable 55 percent.

Chafee's survival was a closer question in 1982, when Democratic former state Attorney General Julius C. Michaelson came within 8,200 votes of victory simply by emphasizing that Chafee belonged to the party of Ronald Reagan and that Reagan was no friend of Rhode Island.

Chafee fought off Michaelson by reasserting his value to Rhode Island. He boasted of his role in negotiations that persuaded General Dynamics' Electric Boat division to keep its large shipyard in the state.

Chafee's position on the Finance Committee and his efforts to ease the burden on American businesses abroad helped him build a campaign treasury twice the size of Michaelson's. The challenger, general counsel to the state AFL-CIO, depended heavily on union support.

Michaelson carried Democratic Providence and the industrial Blackstone Valley by nearly 20,000 votes, a margin that Chafee barely offset by sweeping the rest of the state.

The close result was not unusual for Chafee. When he ran for governor in 1962, after serving as state House minority leader, he won by 398 votes over Democratic incumbent John A. Notte Jr., who had damaged himself by advocating a state income tax. That issue was to cause Chafee trouble six years later.

As a three-term governor in the 1960s, Chafee pushed for an increase in Rhode Island's social and welfare spending, calling it "a state version of the Great Society." He won reelection easily in 1964 and in 1966.

In 1968, however, running against Democrat Frank Licht, he got caught on the wrong side of a dispute over state taxes. Chafee insisted an income tax was necessary to prevent a boost in the sales tax. Licht disagreed, and upset Chafee by 7,808 votes.

After his defeat, Chafee was appointed

Navy secretary in the Nixon administration. That seemed likely to help the 1972 Senate campaign he was planning against Democratic Sen. Claiborne Pell. When he left the Pentagon to begin the campaign, he looked strong.

But it did not turn out that way. Though Pell has always been accused of aloofness, he knew what to do that year, running superb TV advertising and speaking a collection of European languages to voters in the ethnic neighborhoods of Providence and the mill towns. And the old tax issue was still a partial liability for Chafee. Even the rare Republican presidential victory in the state that fall did not help him. Pell won 54 percent of the vote.

That might have been the end of Chafee's political career, had Democrats not done everything but throw the state's other Senate seat at him in 1976 by fighting with each other all year.

Gov. Philip W. Noel was the front-runner for the 1976 Democratic nomination, but he crippled himself by making comments in a wire service interview that sounded like racial slurs. He had to resign as the party's national platform chairman, and he went on to lose the Senate primary by 100 votes to Cadillac dealer Richard P. Lorber, who spent lavishly of his own money and accused Noel not only of racial insensitivity but of bossism.

Noel then refused to back Lorber in the general election, allowing Chafee to resurrect his old coalition of the early 1960s — Republicans, independents and dissident Democrats. Lorber tried to paint the well-to-do Chafee as an elitist, but the charge did not stick. Chafee won every town in the state except one.

Committees

Environment & Public Works (Ranking)
Clean Water, Fisheries & Wildlife (ranking)

Finance (5th of 9 Republicans)
Health for Families & the Uninsured (ranking); International Trade; Medicare & Long Term Care

Select Intelligence (5th of 8 Republicans)

Small Business (9th of 9 Republicans)
Urban & Minority-Owned Business Development (ranking); Export Expansion & Agricultural Development

Elections

1988 General

John H. Chafee (R)	217,273	(55%)
Richard A. Licht (D)	180,717	(45%)

Previous Winning Percentages: **1982** (51%) **1976** (58%)

Campaign Finance

	Receipts	Receipts from PACs		Expend-itures
1988				
Chafee (R)	$2,455,215	$1,045,319	(43%)	$2,841,985
Licht (D)	$2,838,216	$655,752	(23%)	$2,735,917

Key Votes

1993	
Require unpaid family and medical leave	Y
Approve national "motor voter" registration bill	N
Approve budget increasing taxes and reducing deficit	N
Support president's right to lift military gay ban	Y
1992	
Approve school-choice pilot program	N
Allow shifting funds from defense to domestic programs	N
Oppose deeper cuts in spending for SDI	N
1991	
Approve waiting period for handgun purchases	Y
Raise senators' pay and ban honoraria	Y
Authorize use of force in Persian Gulf	Y
Confirm Clarence Thomas to Supreme Court	Y

Voting Studies

	Presidential Support		Party Unity		Conservative Coalition	
Year	**S**	**O**	**S**	**O**	**S**	**O**
1992	62	38	59	40	55	45
1991	62	35	52	45	45	52
1990	58	41	58	36	65	30
1989	81	19	57	43	71	29
1988	45	49	34	63	22	76
1987	50	47	46	54	31	69
1986	67	31	64	34	62	37
1985	72	26	68	30	52	47
1984	71	26	66	28	60	36
1983	80	18	67	33	45	50
1982	54	45	47	50	30	69
1981	75	23	68	29	50	47

Interest Group Ratings

Year	ADA	AFL-CIO	CCUS	ACU
1992	40	17	80	44
1991	60	45	40	24
1990	50	11	55	43
1989	35	30	75	39
1988	90	86	36	4
1987	80	60	56	16
1986	60	33	63	35
1985	35	24	76	39
1984	60	18	56	58
1983	60	29	42	35
1982	80	50	43	14
1981	45	47	61	38

1 Ronald K. Machtley (R)

Of Portsmouth — Elected 1988; 3rd Term

Born: July 13, 1948, Johnstown, Pa.
Education: U.S. Naval Academy, B.S. 1970; Suffolk U., J.D. 1978.
Military Service: Navy, 1970-75; Naval Reserve, 1975-present.
Occupation: Lawyer.
Family: Wife, Kati Croft; two children.
Religion: Presbyterian.
Political Career: No previous office.
Capitol Office: 326 Cannon Bldg. 20515; 225-4911.

In Washington: Machtley is one of the more liberal House Republicans — a political necessity in his very Democratic district. His political leanings have allowed him to shore up his political base at home, quieting speculation that his 1988 victory over veteran incumbent Fernand J. St Germain was a fluke.

On social issues, he has emerged as an advocate of abortion rights, and he was an early supporter of the Family and Medical Leave Act, even voting in 1990 to override President Bush's veto of the bill.

In 1992, he opposed Bush 51 percent of the time on issues on which Bush took a position.

As a member of the Armed Services Committee, Machtley has shown he is not averse to trimming the Pentagon budget. He favors closing out the B-2 stealth bomber program and has voted for cuts in spending on the Strategic Defense Initiative.

Machtley is quick to object, however, when cutting defense will hurt Rhode Island. A U.S. Naval Academy graduate and Navy veteran, Machtley is a strong supporter of that branch of the military, which has a major economic impact on his state. He fought hard to keep funding for the *Seawolf* submarine — despite criticism of its value in the military — because its manufacturer, Electric Boat, is one of the largest private employers of Rhode Island residents. It makes submarine frames at its factory in Quonset Point, and many Rhode Islanders work at Electric Boat's facility over the border in Groton, Conn.

He was also quick to criticize President Clinton's proposals to reduce the Pentagon budget because of its effect on the Navy.

Machtley has used his Armed Services seat to push for abortion rights. He wrote a provision of a military appropriation bill that allows U.S. servicewomen stationed overseas access to an abortion in military hospitals. The provision prompted Bush to veto the bill, but Machtley stood firm.

Machtley voiced support for the January 1991 resolution authorizing Bush to use military force to end Iraq's occupation of Kuwait. Earlier, though, he joined more than two dozen House members in signing a letter telling Bush that he needed such a congressional authorization before committing U.S. troops to war.

Machtley's ability to work with Democrats was exhibited by his work with Rep. Edward J. Markey of Massachusetts to re-establish the New England Energy Caucus, which aims to reduce that region's dependence on foreign oil. He and Markey also joined up to pass an amendment to the fiscal 1991 defense authorization bill that requires stronger energy conservation measures at U.S. military facilities.

At Home: After taking the seat from Democratic hands in 1988 and winning by a comfortable margin in 1990, Machtley put his stamp on this overwhelmingly Democratic district in 1992. He won with 70 percent of the vote, easily dispatching a weak Democratic candidate.

Machtley's initial victory was probably the most surprising and most important upset of the 1988 federal elections. It was surprising because Machtley had begun the year as a slightly buffoonish also-ran in a primary many saw as a choice between sacrificial lambs. It was important because Machtley's eventual victim was 28-year veteran Democrat St Germain, the autocratic Banking Committee chairman and a symbol of dubious ethics in Congress.

In a year when the GOP was unable to field challengers to many key Democrats in the House, taking St Germain's scalp was significant consolation. When Machtley was introduced to the other Republican House freshmen after the election, he reportedly received a round of applause.

In 1988, it seemed the worst of St Germain's legal entanglements might be over. Readers of The Wall Street Journal were well-versed in St Germain's dealings with lobbyists for the savings and loan industry, for which his committee wrote regulatory legislation. But the Justice Department had declined to indict him, and the House ethics committee seemed unlikely to deal harshly with him.

John A. Holmes Jr., a former GOP state

Rhode Island 1

East — Part of Providence; Pawtucket; Newport

The 1st binds the genteel Newport communities in southern Rhode Island with ethnic Providence neighborhoods and the blue-collar industrial towns of the Blackstone Valley in the north.

The Rhode Island portion of the Blackstone Valley, a highly industrialized, 15-mile region, is anchored on the south by Pawtucket and on the north by Woonsocket, a heavily French-Canadian wool- and textile-manufacturing city along the Massachusetts border. Pawtucket was the site of the first factory in America and is now home to about 250 manufacturing plants. The valley's economy includes metalworking and jewelry companies among much light manufacturing.

The valley is the backbone of the state's Democratic majorities. Although Woonsocket broke with Pawtucket and Central Falls by voting Republican for president in 1984, all three went Democratic in 1988 and in 1992. There are pockets of GOP strength in Lincoln, an affluent bedroom community, and Burrillville, a town of 16,000 that was added to the 1st in 1992 redistricting.

Moving south, the 1st takes in part of Providence, along with its smaller suburbs. Within the capital city, the 1st includes all of the heavily Italian Fourth Ward and most of the Italian Fifth Ward; both generally vote Democratic. On the generally more affluent East Side of Providence, the votes of upper-income conservatives are partially offset by liberals around Brown University; this section also has communities of immigrants from Portugal and the Cape Verde Islands.

South of Providence, the pristine coastal preserves along the scenic Narragansett Bay and Atlantic Ocean dominate. Fishing, shipping and naval operations are vital to the coastal economy. In Portsmouth, defense contractor Raytheon has become an important employer with its work in sonar technology for Navy submarines. The company gained notice in 1991 because its Patriot missiles, which were made at other New England facilities, were used in the gulf war. But because of defense cuts, Raytheon has eliminated more than 1,100 jobs in Rhode Island since 1989.

Some of the smaller seacoast villages around the bay are wealthy residential areas that tend to favor the GOP, but the neighboring larger towns, such as Newport and Tiverton, vote Democratic. Newport and Tiverton have backed the Democratic nominee in four of the past five presidential elections, voting Republican only in 1984.

Newport, renowned for the ostentatious wealth of its 19th century social elite, lures tourists with its restored palatial mansions. It is home to the Newport Navy Base, which maintains and houses several ships and contains the Naval Education and Training Center and the Naval Undersea Warfare Center, a large research and development complex. The naval operations employ about 10,000 civilian and military employees.

The center has been designated as one of four "superlab" sites nationwide. The Navy will consolidate the facility with its sister center in New London, Conn., which means more than 1,000 new jobs for Newport.

1990 Population: 501,677. White 465,599 (93%), Black 16,361 (3%), Other 19,717 (4%). Hispanic origin 18,967 (4%). 18 and over 392,873 (78%), 62 and over 92,969 (19%). Median age: 34.

chairman, challenged St Germain in 1986. He was back in 1988 to try again but few gave him much chance. The district seemed already to have passed its own judgment. And the larger presidential turnout was expected to help St Germain.

Machtley, meanwhile, had burst on the local political scene with a gimmick that seemed sure to overshadow his message — a piglet he named "Lester T. Pork." What we need in Congress, the candidate said, is Ron Machtley and Les Pork. Machtley also organized such conventional stunts as a jog across the district. But he seemed destined to retire from politics remembered only as "the guy with the pig."

Then a series of unforeseen events changed the situation. First, Holmes vacated the primary field by inexplicably failing to file his nomination papers on time. Blame fell on a campaign aide, but some muttered that Holmes had simply lost his stomach for another beating. In any event, the nomination was Machtley's by default.

Second, St Germain received a scare in the Democratic primary in September. Scott Wolf, a young but seasoned campaign worker and pollster, collected 45 percent of the primary vote. It was St Germain's worst showing in a primary since he was elected. Suddenly, it became respectable to say St Germain was beatable. And as the fall wore on, quite a few political observers began saying it.

Machtley knew how to communicate the seriousness of his intentions. He dropped the pig and produced campaign literature emphasizing his acceptability as an alternative to St Germain, touting his commitment to such nonpartisan subjects as health care, housing, education and clean water.

Machtley had been trained as an engineer at the Naval Academy and served five years on active duty. He had then put himself through law school in Boston while working full-time. He had built up a law practice in Newport and performed community service for such causes as the YMCA and the local hospital. He was an elder in his Presbyterian church.

True, he lacked the roots of most local politicians and had never run for office. And when his campaign took hold he was still strapped for cash. But he received considerable free media coverage, thanks in part to the novelty of a close November race. He hounded St Germain into a debate that Machtley later called the turning point. He was able to establish that investigations of St Germain that had yet to yield an indictment or censure did not constitute total exoneration. And he highlighted the fresh news that the Justice Department had passed along its collection of evidence to the House ethics panel for further review. As the campaign became a true contest, St Germain fought back with the hardy perennial issue of Social Security. But this did not stem the tide.

In reaching 56 percent, Machtley ran well in his strongholds (60 percent in Newport, for example) while holding St Germain even in his. He also managed 57 percent in normally Democratic North Providence.

In 1990, Machtley had to defend his newly won territory against Wolf, the Democrat who had softened up St Germain for him in 1988. For a time, it appeared again that Wolf would have the magic. Rhode Island's economy has been among the most severely damaged in the downturn that struck the region in the late 1980s. And Wolf thought he had found just the right issue in attacking Machtley as an anachronism from the Reagan era — conservative in economics and obsessed with the military.

But Wolf was not able to climb into the big leagues financially. So he found it difficult to force his way into the voters' consciousness in a year with hotly contested campaigns for senator, governor and mayor. Machtley, by contrast, had established himself with his heroics of 1988 and needed relatively little further introduction. He won with slightly more than 55 percent, nearly equaling his percentage showing from two years earlier.

In 1992, Machtley again drew no primary opposition, but in this heavily Democratic state, the primary tends not to be his toughest race. Fearing the generalized anti-incumbent sentiment, Machtley launched an aggressive general election campaign. Machtley's Democratic opponent, state Sen. David R. Carlin Jr., had trouble overcoming an ultra-conservative image born in a bitter primary fight. Machtley was able to capitalize on that, noting that as one of the most liberal Republicans in the House he matches the district's personality better. Machtley easily dispatched Carlin in the general election.

Committees

Armed Services (12th of 22 Republicans)
Military Acquisition; Military Installations & Facilities

Government Operations (10th of 16 Republicans)
Employment, Housing & Aviation (ranking)

Small Business (5th of 18 Republicans)
Minority Enterprise, Finance & Urban Development (ranking)

Elections

1992 General		
Ronald K. Machtley (R)	135,982	(70%)
David R. Carlin Jr. (D)	48,092	(25%)
Frederick E. Dick (RPI)	6,012	(3%)
Norman J. Jacques (I)	4,003	(2%)
1990 General		
Ronald K. Machtley (R)	89,963	(55%)
Scott Wolf (D)	73,131	(45%)

Previous Winning Percentage: **1988** (56%)

District Vote for President

	1992	
D	107,702	(50%)
R	61,011	(28%)
I	47,733	(22%)

Campaign Finance

	Receipts	Receipts from PACs	Expend-itures
1992			
Machtley (R)	$608,563	$223,144 (37%)	$564,588
Carlin (D)	$92,189	$43,750 (47%)	$90,459
1990			
Machtley (R)	$857,775	$333,189 (39%)	$879,464
Wolf (D)	$369,300	$104,646 (28%)	$370,118

Key Votes

1993	
Require parental notification of minors' abortions	N
Require unpaid family and medical leave	Y
Approve national "motor voter" registration bill	Y
Approve budget increasing taxes and reducing deficit	N
Approve economic stimulus plan	N
1992	
Approve balanced-budget constitutional amendment	Y
Close down space station program	Y
Approve U.S. aid for former Soviet Union	N
Allow shifting funds from defense to domestic programs	N
1991	
Extend unemployment benefits using deficit financing	Y
Approve waiting period for handgun purchases	Y
Authorize use of force in Persian Gulf	Y

Voting Studies

	Presidential Support		Party Unity		Conservative Coalition	
Year	**S**	**O**	**S**	**O**	**S**	**O**
1992	47	51	58	38	71	27
1991	52	47	58	39	59	38
1990	38	62	50	48	50	48
1989	49	50	60	38	61	39

Interest Group Ratings

Year	ADA	AFL-CIO	CCUS	ACU
1992	55	50	38	44
1991	45	58	50	47
1990	61	50	64	25
1989	55	50	70	46

2 Jack Reed (D)

Of Cranston — Elected 1990; 2nd Term

Born: Nov. 12, 1949, Providence, R.I.
Education: U.S. Military Academy, B.S. 1971; Harvard U., M.P.P. 1973, J.D. 1982.
Military Service: Army, 1967-79.
Occupation: Lawyer.
Family: Single.
Religion: Roman Catholic.
Political Career: R.I. Senate, 1985-91.
Capitol Office: 1510 Longworth Bldg. 20515; 225-2735.

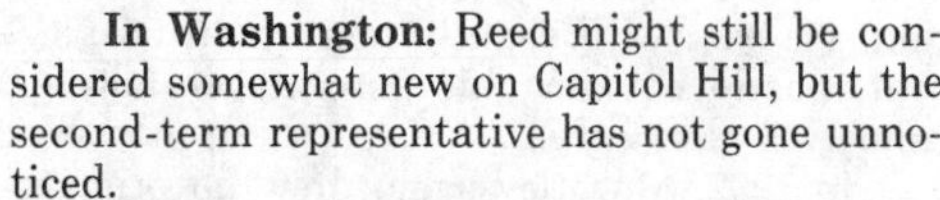

In Washington: Reed might still be considered somewhat new on Capitol Hill, but the second-term representative has not gone unnoticed.

As a freshman, the smart, hard-working Reed caught the eye of several important chairmen and kept his constituents happy with his attention to Rhode Island interests. As a result, he finds himself with a promising array of political options — from a likely seat on the powerful Appropriations Committee to running for statewide office.

Working-class roots, military service, a cordial personality and friends in high places have been the building blocks of Reed's success.

At the start of the 103rd Congress, Reed was rewarded with the regional whip slot for the influential New England Democratic delegation. He was also considered for the region's seat on Appropriations, and although it went to Massachusetts Rep. John W. Olver, Reed is considered the leading contender for any opening. An Appropriations slot would enable Reed to broaden his reach beyond the more parochial interests he has focused on.

But his dedication to local issues served him well in the 102nd.

Reed, along with Rhode Island GOP Sen. John H. Chafee, was instrumental in securing a $180 million loan guarantee to help repay depositors hurt during a state banking crisis. It was Reed who convinced House Banking Chairman Henry B. Gonzalez of Texas to travel to Rhode Island to listen to people whose livelihoods were threatened in the shutdown of nearly four dozen banks and credit unions.

He lobbied members of the Banking Committee so hard on the issue that many panel members joked that they thought Reed was on the committee. When the bill reached the House floor, Reed was poised at the doors, asking for votes. It was hardly necessary; the bill passed under suspension of rules with no debate.

He resumed the effort in the 103rd by filing legislation to extend the deadline for people affected by the bank crisis to reinvest their money instead of having to pay capital gains taxes on money they did not have access to.

As the Clinton administration continues previous efforts to downsize the military, Reed's work to secure money for defense-reliant states such as Rhode Island will become even more valuable. In the 102nd, Reed served on a task force that developed a $1 billion diversification package that grew to $1.7 billion during conference on the defense authorization bill.

And his post on the Merchant Marine and Fisheries Committee enables Reed to keep his hand in ocean issues, which are of particular interest to his state.

A graduate of West Point and the John F. Kennedy School of Government at Harvard, Reed has developed an interest in education issues. Popular with Education and Labor Chairman William D. Ford of Michigan, Reed was active in the reauthorization of the Higher Education Act, which opens the federal loan program to more middle-class college students. "The middle class in this country is being squeezed out of the educational pipeline," he said.

He was involved in the successful effort to raise Pell grants from $2,600 to $4,500 and devoted his congressional pay raise to form the Reed Student Grant Program for youths in his district.

In February 1993, Reed filed a bill to establish a federal library division and give $200 million to school library programs.

Reed has the ability to take his work seriously without taking himself too seriously. (For instance, he told a TV interviewer who asked about David H. Souter's nomination for the Supreme Court that any short bachelor from Harvard should be on the Supreme Court.) But more often, he is given to military precision in his words and deeds.

On most issues he is a loyal Democrat, voting with his party 94 percent of the time in House votes in 1992 and opposing President Bush's position 86 percent of the time. He supports national health care and in early 1993

Rhode Island 2

West — Western Providence; Warwick

Stretching from the rolling hillsides of upstate Rhode Island through the Providence metropolitan area and on to quiet fishing villages in the south, the 2nd is reliably Democratic. In the past five presidential elections, the district has gone Republican only once, in 1984 for Ronald Reagan.

The largest concentration of voters in the 2nd is in Providence, the state capital and a Democratic stronghold. The city's population has slid from a high of 268,000 in 1925 to about 161,000 in 1990. As blue-collar ethnics have departed, the minority population has increased; blacks and Hispanics made up one-third of the city's population in 1990.

The 2nd takes in about two-thirds of Providence, including the business district, where pedestrian shopping areas have had some success at reviving downtown. Also included is South Providence, once a mixed Irish and Jewish middle-class neighborhood that is increasingly black and Hispanic; Federal Hill and Silver Lake, where Italian-Americans predominate; and Elmhurst, a middle-class, ethnic community near Providence College.

Outside Providence, there are small GOP pockets. Scituate, to the east of Providence, and East Greenwich, to the south, were the only communities in the state to favor George Bush over Bill Clinton in 1992.

Just south of Providence along Interstates 95 and 295 are the district's next two largest cities, Warwick and Cranston. With significant white-collar populations — especially in Warwick — both cities are swing areas on the few occasions when statewide races are closely contested.

Nearby Quonset Point, in the town of North Kingstown, is home to one of the district's largest private employers, General Dynamics' Electric Boat Division (3,700 employees). Workers here assemble the hulls for the *Seawolf* nuclear submarines that are completed in Electric Boat's Groton, Conn., facility. Many residents in the southwestern Rhode Island town of Westerly commute to the Groton facility to complete the submarine work.

Westerly, an old shipping center that now blends light manufacturing with its fishing trade, is more frequently found in the Democratic column than most of the other towns on Rhode Island's western border; many of them are old Yankee enclaves that vote Republican. Westerly, which is home to a large Italian-American population, gave Clinton a comfortable win in 1992.

Westerly, a 40-minute drive from Providence, is located in Washington County, the fastest-growing county in the state in the 1980s. Washington County, with coastal cities and maritime commerce as well as the inland marshes known as the "Great Swamp," grew 18 percent during the 1980s. Much of the growth stems from residential development along the shore line, which has lured city dwellers seeking more pleasant surroundings.

In the Washington County town of Kingston is the University of Rhode Island, the largest in the state (15,600 students) and one of the district's top employers.

1990 Population: 501,787. White 451,776 (90%), Black 22,500 (4%), Other 27,511 (5%). Hispanic origin 26,785 (5%). 18 and over 384,901 (77%), 62 and over 86,417 (17%). Median age: 34.

supported a short-term stimulus package to revive the economy. He is a proponent of greater tax equity and works to protect blue-collar concerns.

In 1991 and 1992 he voted to overturn the so-called gag rule that prohibited workers at federally funded clinics from discussing abortion options. He also opposed sending troops into the Persian Gulf.

At Home: Reed began the 1990 election season a minor player in a drama of state politics featuring hot races for governor and senator.

But before the year was out, his was the star to watch in his party's statewide future.

By reclaiming one of the state's two House seats for his party, Reed not only broke into the big time but positioned himself to succeed one of Rhode Island's senators or its Democratic governor (the three's average age is 72).

Reed's life has been a mix of common man and elite opportunity. His father was a school custodian and his mother a factory worker in South Providence. At his Catholic prep school he was an overachieving, 124-pound defensive back who graduated second in his class. He won his West Point appointment from Democratic Sen. John O. Pastore in 1967 and, when commissioned, volunteered for duty in Vietnam. The Army sent him to Harvard to learn administration instead. He later commanded a company of the 82nd Airborne, which did not see combat during his service, and taught at West Point.

At 29, Reed decided to leave the Army and was admitted to Harvard Law School. He studied corporate law, spent a year with a firm in Washington, and then returned home with an eye on politics. He took a job with Rhode Island's biggest corporate law firm and a year later was elected to the state Senate.

The road up from there was not clearly marked. In 1990, when GOP Rep. Claudine Schneider ran for the Senate, Reed joined an active field of Democratic hopefuls. In the primary, he easily outdistanced both a businessman with deep pockets and the district's former congressman, Edward P. Beard, who served from 1975 to 1981.

Still, Reed entered the fall campaign an underdog to Republican Gertrude M. "Trudy" Coxe, who had run the state's best-known environmental organization. He attacked her for owning stocks in oil companies while promoting pristine waterways. He ripped her for supporting a capital gains tax cut as a sequel to tax cuts for the rich in the 1980s. He leavened his message by stressing his own work on issues such as tax credits for day care and children's mental health programs.

In the end, his message of roots and upward mobility found listeners in traditional Democratic neighborhoods and enabled him to win a surprisingly comfortable victory.

With Reed's star ascendant at home and on the Hill, the state GOP was unable to field significant opposition for the 1992 election. He sailed to victory with 71 percent of the vote.

Committees

Education & Labor (14th of 28 Democrats)
Elementary, Secondary & Vocational Education; Postsecondary Education & Training

Judiciary (16th of 21 Democrats)
Intellectual Property & Judicial Administration

Merchant Marine & Fisheries (14th of 29 Democrats)
Environment & Natural Resources; Merchant Marine

Select Intelligence (12th of 12 Democrats)
Oversight & Evaluation

Elections

1992 General		
Jack Reed (D)	144,450	(71%)
James W. Bell (R)	49,998	(24%)
Thomas J. Ricci (I)	6,715	(3%)
John Turnbull (IT)	3,250	(2%)
1992 Primary		
Jack Reed (D)	50,518	(76%)
Spencer E. Dickinson (D)	15,592	(24%)
1990 General		
Jack Reed (D)	108,818	(59%)
Gertrude M. "Trudy" Coxe (R)	74,953	(41%)

District Vote for President

1992
D 105,597 (45%)
R 70,590 (30%)
I 57,312 (25%)

Campaign Finance

	Receipts	Receipts from PACs		Expend-itures
1992				
Reed (D)	$816,308	$416,190	(51%)	$815,622
Bell (R)	$39,695	0		$39,260
1990				
Reed (D)	$902,877	$302,216	(33%)	$897,224
Coxe (R)	$577,919	$121,238	(21%)	$571,643

Key Votes

1993	
Require parental notification of minors' abortions	N
Require unpaid family and medical leave	Y
Approve national "motor voter" registration bill	Y
Approve budget increasing taxes and reducing deficit	Y
Approve economic stimulus plan	Y
1992	
Approve balanced-budget constitutional amendment	N
Close down space station program	Y
Approve U.S. aid for former Soviet Union	N
Allow shifting funds from defense to domestic programs	Y
1991	
Extend unemployment benefits using deficit financing	Y
Approve waiting period for handgun purchases	Y
Authorize use of force in Persian Gulf	N

Voting Studies

	Presidential Support		Party Unity		Conservative Coalition	
Year	S	O	S	O	S	O
1992	14	86	94	5	17	83
1991	29	71	92	7	27	70

Interest Group Ratings

Year	ADA	AFL-CIO	CCUS	ACU
1992	90	92	13	4
1991	95	92	20	0

South Carolina

STATE DATA

Governor:
Carroll A. Campbell Jr. (R)
First elected: 1986
Length of term: 4 years
Term expires: 1/95
Salary: $101,959
Term limit: 2 consecutive terms
Phone: (803) 734-9818
Born: July 24, 1940; Greenville, S.C.
Education: American U., M.A. 1985
Occupation: Real estate broker; businessman; farmer
Family: Wife, Iris Rhodes; two children
Religion: Episcopalian
Political Career: S.C. House, 1971-75; Republican nominee for lieutenant governor, 1974; executive assistant to Gov. James B. Edwards, 1975-76; S.C. Senate, 1977-79; U.S. House, 1979-87

Lt. Gov.: Nick A. Theodore (D)
First elected: 1986
Length of term: 4 years
Term expires: 1/95
Salary: $43,860
Phone: (803) 734-2080

State election official: (803) 734-9060
Democratic headquarters: (803) 799-7798
Republican headquarters: (803) 798-8999

REDISTRICTING

South Carolina retained its six House seats in reapportionment. Federal court issued a map May 1, 1992.

STATE LEGISLATURE

General Assembly. Meets January-June.

Senate: 46 members, 4-year terms
1992 breakdown: 30D, 16R; 43 men, 3 women; 39 whites, 7 blacks
Salary: $10,400
Phone: (803) 734-2806

House of Representatives: 124 members, 2-year terms
1992 breakdown: 73D, 50R, 1I; 105 men, 19 women; 106 whites, 18 blacks
Salary: $10,400
Phone: (803) 734-2010

URBAN STATISTICS

City	Pop.
Columbia Mayor Robert D. Coble, D	98,052
Charleston Mayor Joseph P. Riley Jr., D	80,414
North Charleston Mayor W. Robert Kinard, R	70,218
Greenville Mayor William D. Workman III, R	58,282
Spartanburg Mayor James E. Talley, N-P	43,467

U.S. CONGRESS

Senate: 1 D, 1 R
House: 3 D, 3 R

TERM LIMITS

For Congress: No
For state offices: No

ELECTIONS

1992 Presidential Vote

George Bush	48.0%
Bill Clinton	39.9%
Ross Perot	11.5%

1988 Presidential Vote

George Bush	62%
Michael S. Dukakis	38%

1984 Presidential Vote

Ronald Reagan	64%
Walter F. Mondale	36%

POPULATION

1990 population		3,486,703
1980 population		3,120,820
Percent change		+12%
Rank among states:		25
White		69%
Black		30%
Hispanic		1%
Asian or Pacific islander		1%
Urban		55%
Rural		45%
Born in state		68%
Foreign-born		1%
Under age 18	920,207	26%
Ages 18-64	2,169,561	62%
65 and older	396,935	11%
Median age		32

MISCELLANEOUS

Capital: Columbia
Number of counties: 46
Per capita income: $15,420 (1991)
Rank among states: 43
Total area: 31,113 sq. miles
Rank among states: 40

GREENVILLE
SPARTANBURG
CHEROKEE
YORK
Spartanburg
Rock Hill
PICKENS
Greenville
OCONEE
4
UNION
CHESTER
LANCASTER
CHESTERFIELD
ANDERSON
MARLBORO
Anderson
LAURENS
5
FAIRFIELD
DARLINGTON
DILLON
3
NEWBERRY
KERSHAW
LEE
RICHLAND
ABBEVILLE
Florence
MARION
GREENWOOD
Columbia
FLORENCE
SALUDA
Sumter
HORRY
MCCORMICK
LEXINGTON
SUMTER
RICHLAND
EDGEFIELD
CALHOUN
CLARENDON
Myrtle Beach
WILLIAMSBURG
AIKEN
6
1
ORANGEBURG
GEORGETOWN
BARNWELL
BERKELEY
2
BAMBERG
DORCHESTER
ALLENDALE
CHARLESTON
COLLETON
HAMPTON
Charleston
CHARLESTON
BEAUFORT
JASPER
BEAUFORT

Strom Thurmond (R)

Of Aiken — Elected 1954; 6th Full Term

Did not serve April-November 1956.

Born: Dec. 5, 1902, Edgefield, S.C.
Education: Clemson College, B.S. 1923.
Military Service: Army, 1942-46; Army Reserve, 1924-60.
Occupation: Lawyer; teacher; coach; education administrator.
Family: Separated; three children.
Religion: Baptist.
Political Career: Edgefield superintendent of education, 1929-33; S.C. Senate, 1933-38; U.S. Circuit Court of Appeals, 1938-46; governor, 1947-51; States' Rights nominee for president, 1948; sought Democratic nomination for U.S. Senate, 1950.
Capitol Office: 217 Russell Bldg. 20510; 224-5972.

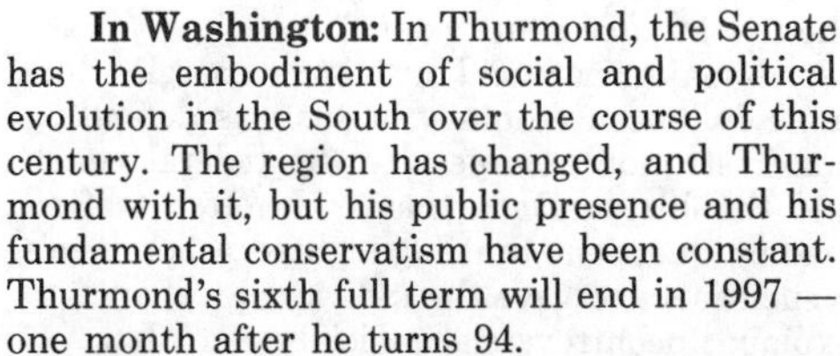

In Washington: In Thurmond, the Senate has the embodiment of social and political evolution in the South over the course of this century. The region has changed, and Thurmond with it, but his public presence and his fundamental conservatism have been constant. Thurmond's sixth full term will end in 1997 — one month after he turns 94.

Thurmond is the only man in modern Senate history to have seen life in the chamber from each of the partisan perspectives: He has served in the minority and the majority as a Republican, in the majority as a Democrat, and, for a few days in late 1954, in the minority as a Democrat. Thurmond served as chairman of the Judiciary Committee from 1981 through 1987, then settled comfortably back into the ranking spot there as Democrats retook the Senate.

Thurmond's fame and notoriety come from civil rights, and for decades this overshadowed his longstanding interest in the military. But at the start of the 103rd Congress, Thurmond gave up his ranking position on Judiciary to take that position on Armed Services, a position that would allow him to look after military installations in South Carolina.

Immediately he was one of the loud voices of dissent on President Clinton's plan to lift the ban on gays in the military, adding resonance to the argument of those who claim this opposition mirrors the opposition that surfaced when the armed services were integrated in 1948.

But neither the shifting national power structure nor Thurmond's own changing roles have altered his ideological conservatism. Thurmond's brand of conservatism, once dismissed as strident, is echoed today by the brash new generation of Republicans ascendant in both the House and the Senate.

Time has also failed to alter his perfected blend of Southern cordiality and hard-nosed political deal-making. These personal qualities enable Thurmond to work well with liberal committee chairmen Edward M. Kennedy of Massachusetts, on Labor and Human Resources, and Joseph R. Biden Jr. of Delaware, who, though he took the Judiciary gavel from Thurmond in 1987, still refers to him as "Mr. Chairman."

This respect, rooted in Thurmond's experience, is a key to his success. He was long out of college and well into his political career before most of his Senate colleagues were born. And none questions whether Thurmond's grasp of political nuance remains firm, though he has slowed a bit in recent years and his hearing is failing. His 1991 separation from his wife, who is half his age, may deny him some of his extraordinary image of vigor, but when he threatens a filibuster, colleagues know that Thurmond, a physical fitness enthusiast, still has the stamina to make good.

In recent years, Thurmond has been conspicuously passive on civil rights legislation. While he has opposed nearly every civil rights bill to pass through the Judiciary Committee, he has allowed others to take the lead in doing so. The new, somewhat mellowed Thurmond seems to believe that dignity and courtesy are more important than winning at any cost.

Even when he chaired Judiciary in 1982, he made no move to block the Voting Rights Act extension. And on rare occasion Thurmond has even lent his support to such bills. In 1983, he helped produce the compromise that preserved the U.S. Civil Rights Commission, and he voted to create a public holiday honoring the Rev. Dr. Martin Luther King Jr.

In 1991, after months of bruising negotiations, he supported another civil rights bill that rolled back several Supreme Court decisions that detractors said made employment discrimination almost impossible to prove. After the lopsided Senate vote, Thurmond ran into a group of civil rights lobbyists and told them it was "a good vote ... 93-5 ... and I wasn't one of the five."

It was a not-so-subtle recognition on Thurmond's part of the reputation he built in the Senate as one of the most vocal obstructionists on civil rights in the 1950s and 1960s — an era when even some Southerners were irritated with his intransigence. In 1957, segregationist senators led by Georgia's Richard Russell were willing to let a weak civil rights measure pass, largely to boost the national standing of their Southern colleague and presidential aspirant, Majority Leader Lyndon B. Johnson of Texas. Thurmond alone insisted on protesting. His 24-hour-and-18-minute filibuster set a record for one man holding the floor.

In a legendary episode in 1964, the year Thurmond switched parties, he wrestled Democrat Ralph Yarborough of Texas to the floor outside the committee room to prevent a quorum for action on civil rights legislation (the chairman stepped in and Yarborough was able to complete the quorum).

But if blocking civil rights bills is no longer his mission, Thurmond has a new emphasis that liberals say is tinged with racial overtones: He is a leading Senate proponent of the death penalty. In 1984, Thurmond sparked the first Senate debate on the issue in a decade when he offered legislation to re-establish the federal death penalty. Thurmond asserted that convicted murderers were not people but "more like animals," and "when you have individuals in society more like animals than humans, they have to be dealt with in the most severe manner."

The Senate, then GOP-controlled, passed the bill, which died in the House. A similar measure got no further than committee approval in 1986. Finally, in 1988, a narrower measure became law as part of an anti-drug package; it applies to drug traffickers who murder and to those who kill police officers during a drug crime.

In the 101st Congress, he introduced sweeping anti-crime legislation that would have permitted the death penalty for 30 federal crimes, allowed the sentence for those as young as 16 and for mentally retarded people, except those unable to tell right from wrong. His legislation also sought to limit the appeals process for those on death row.

As part of a unanimous-consent agreement to stop Republican members from offering death penalty amendments to unrelated legislation, Biden, who also supports the death penalty, agreed to hold a committee vote on Thurmond's bill.

When the panel took up the bill, Thurmond could not stop Democrats, led by Kennedy, from adding a "racial justice" provision that Thurmond called a "killer amendment." The amendment would have required prosecutors to prove by "clear and convincing" evidence that racial disparities in sentencing are not the result of discrimination. "Race should play no role whatsoever," Thurmond said. "But this would allow vicious killers to get off by talking about the race of a defendant."

When the matter got to the full Senate in mid-1990, however, Thurmond prevailed. The Kennedy language was struck by a 58-38 margin. But little agreement could be reached with the House, and the final bill was stripped of its most controversial provisions, including the death penalty. Controversy over a crime bill in the 102nd Congress ensured the same fate.

Supporters of gun control were encouraged in the 100th Congress, when Thurmond teamed up with Ohio Democrat Howard M. Metzenbaum to cosponsor a successful bill that banned the manufacture, import and sale of "plastic" guns that evade security detectors. He said then, "I think the time has come to stand with the law enforcement people."

A major share of Thurmond's energies during Republican administrations was defending administration nominees to the federal bench and the Justice Department. He often crafted leading questions that highlighted a nominee's credentials and gave the individual a chance to explain uncontroversial judicial principles.

Thurmond was a vigorous supporter of Clarence Thomas, President Bush's nominee to the Supreme Court, standing by Thomas despite charges of sexual harassment leveled by Anita F. Hill and criticism from civil rights activists who thought Thomas, an African American, too conservative. As a concession both to the nature of politics in the television age and the issues at hand, Thurmond played a minor public role in the hearings on the harassment charges, delegating the bulk of the inquiry to younger colleagues. But privately he remained a constant Thomas booster, even going to Thomas' suburban Virginia home to congratulate him after the confirmation vote.

In 1989, Thurmond was a leading defender of William Lucas to head the Civil Rights Division of the Justice Department. As it became apparent that Democrats who questioned Lucas' credentials were going to reject his nomination, Thurmond said: "He's a minority yes. Minorities are entitled to a chance. Years ago they didn't have a chance. I know down South they didn't, and up North either. I say let's confirm this man and show the world that we are fair."

In 1987, Thurmond was equally powerless to save Ronald Reagan from the embarrassing defeat of Supreme Court nominee Robert H. Bork, whom a majority of Democrats rejected as too ideologically conservative.

Almost always a team player, Thurmond

bucked the Bush administration over the issue of fetal tissue research. His youngest daughter has diabetes, and Thurmond said he was convinced such research could lead to medical advances in the area. Bush vetoed legislation that would have accomplished this and despite Thurmond's vote, the Senate was unable to override. President Clinton ended the ban by executive action in 1993.

On another health issue, Thurmond argued for nearly 20 years to get warnings on alcohol product labels, finally winning passage of legislation in 1988. The law requires warnings that consumption of alcohol during pregnancy may cause birth defects and that consumption impairs the ability to drive a car, operate machinery and may cause health problems.

At the beginning of the 103rd Congress, Thurmond introduced legislation to require similar warnings on alcohol advertisements. Two weeks after he introduced the measure, his oldest daughter was killed by a drunk driver while crossing a street in Columbia, S.C.

On his committees and off, Thurmond looks out for South Carolina; constituent service is one reason he has survived changing times. He makes sure his state receives a flow of federal largess — even if he votes against the programs themselves and the bills that provide the money. And as the Voting Rights Act has made blacks an important political force, they have been conspicuous among the beneficiaries of Thurmond's work. "I'm not a racist," he insists, "and I've done everything I could to help the people of both races throughout my lifetime." In 1971 he became the first Southern senator to hire a black professional staffer; he later sponsored the South's first black federal judge.

Thurmond has been active in seeking to protect the textile industry against growing foreign competition, even when it meant defying Republican presidents' free-trade philosophy. "Free trade will destroy America," Thurmond once said.

Now in his 10th decade, Thurmond often seems like an envoy from another era, from the turn-of-the-century rural South. During one committee hearing, he graciously greeted a panel of women who had come to testify. "These are the prettiest witnesses we have had in a long time," Thurmond said. "I imagine you are all married. If not, you could be if you wanted to be."

Thurmond also has a fondness for ceremony not found in many younger politicians. He relished his role as president pro tempore, which he forfeited to Mississippi's John C. Stennis when Democrats regained control of the Senate, and greatly regretted losing the honor of presiding over the Senate's opening each day.

An episode illustrating Thurmond's love of ritual, as well as his relative vigor, occurred during a 1987 ceremony in Philadelphia to commemorate the bicentennial of the compromise that created the bicameral Congress. An aged and befuddled Stennis was presiding over the Senate's program and mistakenly called on Thurmond to speak. Thurmond, just a year younger than the Stennis, responded with senatorial savoir-faire. Though he had not expected to be called on, he arose and said, "I do not know of any senator who is not ready to respond at any time with any sentiment," then delivered a lucid extemporaneous address on the Constitution — with a characteristic emphasis on states' rights.

At Home: Thurmond has punctuated his long political career with turns and reversals, and always he has managed to carry his constituents with him.

They supported him in 1948 when, as governor, he bolted the Democratic Party to run as the States' Rights candidate for president. In 1964 he announced that he was joining the GOP because the Democrats were "leading the evolution of our nation to a socialistic dictatorship." And despite the state's historic partisan leanings, he easily won re-election two years later.

Since the mid-1960s, black voting strength has grown in South Carolina, and Thurmond has adjusted again, although his efforts to help black communities have never brought much of the black vote; his long record of opposing civil rights bills is not that easily forgotten.

For most white South Carolinians, Thurmond's feistiness and physical vigor remain appealing. As a 75-year-old in 1978 competing with a man barely half his age, Thurmond traveled the state with his wife and four young children in a camper called "Strom Trek," passing out family recipes, riding parade elephants and sliding down firehouse poles.

Thurmond learned politics from one of his father's friends, Democratic Sen. Benjamin "Pitchfork Ben" Tillman. Early in his career Thurmond was a populist, representing poor white farmers from the upcountry against the Tidewater establishment. In 1946, after returning from World War II service in Europe, Thurmond was elected governor. He was in his second year in office when the Democratic National Convention decided to adopt a strong civil rights plank, and Thurmond offered himself as a regional candidate for president on the States' Rights Democratic ticket. He carried South Carolina, Alabama, Mississippi and Louisiana.

Thurmond made a first try for the Senate in 1950, but lost the Democratic primary to incumbent Olin D. Johnston. Four years later, however, he won — the first and so far the only senator to be elected as a write-in candidate. Sen. Burnet R. Maybank had died and the 31-member State Democratic Committee froze Thurmond out by choosing state Sen. Edgar A. Brown. Thurmond focused his campaign on whether "31 men" or the voters should make the decision. His write-in campaign defeated Brown by nearly 60,000 votes.

True to a 1954 promise, Thurmond resigned in 1956 and ran for re-election without the benefit of incumbency. No one filed against him — a happy circumstance that repeated itself in 1960, when it was time to run for a full six-year term. In 1966 and 1972 he decimated Democrats Bradley Morrah and Eugene N. Zeigler, respectively.

In 1978 Thurmond encountered a stiff re-election challenge from Charles "Pug" Ravenel, who had won the Democratic primary for governor four years before, but was ruled ineligible for failure to meet residency requirements.

A media-oriented "New South" politician, Ravenel tried to remind blacks of the senator's segregationist past. But Ravenel suffered from a carpetbagger's image. He had left the state to be an investment banker in New York, returning only shortly before his 1974 gubernatorial bid. Thurmond won 56 percent.

The 1984 campaign was no problem for Thurmond. No Democrat of any consequence wanted to challenge him; one of those mentioned as a contender, former U.S. Rep. Kenneth Holland, ended up leading a Democrats-for-Thurmond organization. For a few days in the summer, it appeared that Jesse Jackson might try an independent campaign, but Jackson quickly reconsidered, and the obscure Democratic nominee, minister Melvin Purvis, failed to reach even a third of the vote. Thurmond's 1990 re-election was another runaway.

Committees

Armed Services (Ranking)

Judiciary (2nd of 8 Republicans)
Antitrust, Monopolies & Business Rights (ranking); Courts & Administrative Practice

Labor & Human Resources (5th of 7 Republicans)
Employment & Productivity (ranking); Children, Families, Drugs & Alcoholism; Education, Arts & Humanities; Labor

Veterans' Affairs (2nd of 5 Republicans)

Elections

1990 General

Strom Thurmond (R)	482,032	(64%)
Bob Cunningham (D)	244,112	(33%)
William H. Griffin (LIBERT)	13,805	(2%)
Marion C. Metts (AM)	10,317	(1%)

Previous Winning Percentages: **1984** (67%) **1978** (56%) **1972** (63%) **1966** (62%) **1960** † (100%) **1956** † (100%) **1954** †* (63%)

** Thurmond was elected as a write-in candidate in 1954. He resigned April 4, 1956, and was elected to fill the vacancy caused by his own resignation in a 1956 special election.*

† Thurmond was elected as a Democrat in 1954-60.

Campaign Finance

	Receipts	Receipts from PACs		Expend-itures
1990				
Thurmond (R)	$2,077,112	$562,695	(27%)	$1,916,702
Cunningham (D)	$6,379	0		$6,232

Key Votes

1993

Require unpaid family and medical leave	?
Approve national "motor voter" registration bill	N
Approve budget increasing taxes and reducing deficit	N
Support president's right to lift military gay ban	—

1992

Approve school-choice pilot program	Y
Allow shifting funds from defense to domestic programs	N
Oppose deeper cuts in spending for SDI	Y

1991

Approve waiting period for handgun purchases	Y
Raise senators' pay and ban honoraria	Y
Authorize use of force in Persian Gulf	Y
Confirm Clarence Thomas to Supreme Court	Y

Voting Studies

	Presidential Support		Party Unity		Conservative Coalition	
Year	**S**	**O**	**S**	**O**	**S**	**O**
1992	78	22	94	6	95	5
1991	88	10	92	7	98	3
1990	78	22	89	10	100	0
1989	90	10	98	2	100	0
1988	82	15	80	15	89	0
1987	69	28	88	9	84	16
1986	89	10	91	8	97	0
1985	87	13	92	7	97	3
1984	87	10	95	5	98	0
1983	86	12	92	6	93	7
1982	89	9	92	5	86	4
1981	90	7	91	6	100	0

Interest Group Ratings

Year	ADA	AFL-CIO	CCUS	ACU
1992	10	25	100	89
1991	10	25	70	90
1990	6	33	75	83
1989	5	0	88	96
1988	0	21	93	92
1987	15	30	71	96
1986	5	0	78	91
1985	0	14	97	91
1984	0	9	84	100
1983	5	6	79	70
1982	5	12	86	75
1981	0	5	100	93

Ernest F. Hollings (D)

Of Charleston — Elected 1966; 5th Full Term

Born: Jan. 1, 1922, Charleston, S.C.
Education: The Citadel, B.A. 1942; U. of South Carolina, LL.B. 1947.
Military Service: Army, 1942-45.
Occupation: Lawyer.
Family: Wife, Rita "Peatsy" Liddy; four children.
Religion: Lutheran.
Political Career: S.C. House, 1949-55; lieutenant governor, 1955-59; governor, 1959-63; sought Democratic nomination for U.S. Senate, 1962; sought Democratic nomination for president, 1984.
Capitol Office: 125 Russell Bldg. 20510; 224-6121.

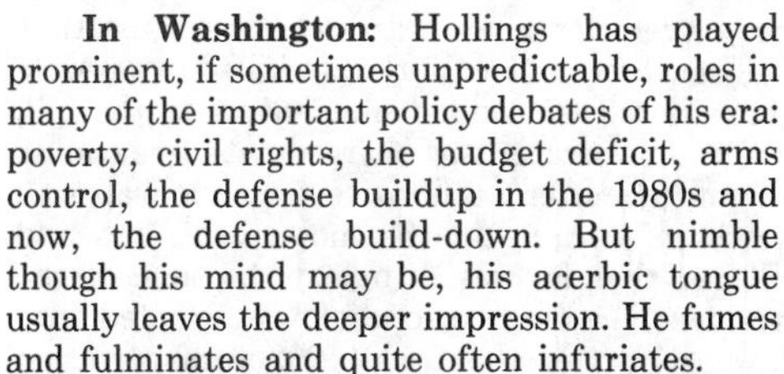

In Washington: Hollings has played prominent, if sometimes unpredictable, roles in many of the important policy debates of his era: poverty, civil rights, the budget deficit, arms control, the defense buildup in the 1980s and now, the defense build-down. But nimble though his mind may be, his acerbic tongue usually leaves the deeper impression. He fumes and fulminates and quite often infuriates.

A stubborn, independent cuss, Hollings often leaps mouth first into controversies. Some of his GOP colleagues still hold a grudge dating to the 1989 fight over John Tower's nomination to become secretary of Defense, when he described the former Senate Armed Services chairman as "Mr. Alcohol Abuser." And in 1992, when responding to media reports of a Japanese lawmaker's criticism of U.S. workers, Hollings reminded a group of workers in South Carolina that the atomic bombs dropped on Japan at the end of World War II were made in the United States. He told the workers they "should draw a mushroom cloud and put underneath it: 'Made in America by lazy and illiterate Americans and tested in Japan.' "

It is this image of Hollings as impolitic, even mean-spirited, that can isolate him from his colleagues and divert attention from the work he does as Commerce Committee chairman, and from a legislative record lengthy with triumph. Yet his style has played well enough at home to win him five Senate re-elections.

Handsome, graceful and impeccably tailored, Hollings (who is now past 70) remains an impressive presence in committee and on the Senate floor. He speaks in a rich, booming Low Country patois and has a colorful command of the language. He dismissed the 1983 invasion of Grenada as an "an attack on a golf course." He once pronounced U.S. aid to El Salvador's then-ruling regime as "delivery of lettuce by way of a rabbit."

But his loquaciousness knows no boundaries, and he tends toward bombast; some wonder whether his mind and his mouth simply move too quickly for discretion to keep pace, or whether he just does not care that his judgments fall harshly.

Hollings, long known as a defense hawk, took on the Navy early in 1993 after the Pentagon targeted the naval facilities in Charleston, S.C., for closure. He accused the Navy of "using deceptive arguments" to justify the inclusion of NAVALEX — the Naval Electronic Systems Engineering Center in Charleston — on the base-closing list. "We've caught them red-handed with their own documents in a ploy to close down NAVALEX," Hollings said. "This is another nail in the Navy's credibility coffin."

Hollings' mordant defense of his home-state base seems not totally in keeping with his reputation as a leader in deficit reduction. He has been associated with some major legislative endeavors aimed at balancing the budget, chief among them the 1985 Gramm-Rudman-Hollings law (usually labeled just Gramm-Rudman), which set up a mechanism for automatic spending cuts if deficit targets were not met.

Hollings continues to father legislation to pare the deficit. In April 1989, he offered a plan — defeated in committee — to combine program cuts and tax increases to cut the deficit significantly. He sought to eliminate the income tax "bubble" that favored the very wealthy, delay tax-bracket indexing and add a $10-per-barrel fee on oil imports. In the 103rd Congress, he renewed his support of a value-added tax, a consumption levy on each stage of a product's manufacture and distribution.

In his campaign to get federal spending under control, Hollings also has set his sights on smaller, symbolic pieces of the budget pie. He angered officials of the Federal Bureau of Investigation and Drug Enforcement Agency in 1992 by eliminating $47 million and $16 million respectively from their overtime budgets. The law enforcement agencies had used the money to pay their officers three hours of overtime a week for time spent on physical exercise. Hollings said it was an unnecessary perk.

Despite all this, Hollings responded angrily in 1993 when the budget ax threatened to fall close to home. He began to fight the decision to close the Charleston naval complex even before it was officially targeted. Days before the Pentagon released its list of recommended base closings in March, Hollings called a news conference to say Charleston would be on the list. He then took up the charge to save the base, rallying the community to seek a reprieve from the Defense Base Closure and Realignment Commission.

Questions about Hollings' constancy for the deficit-reduction cause have been raised before. As chairman of the Appropriations Subcommittee on Commerce, Justice, State and Judiciary, he consistently has worked to steer federal money to South Carolina. In 1991, he won a budget increase of 31 percent for five manufacturing technology centers — known as "Hollings Centers" — around the country, including one in Columbia. That same year, he won approval of a $1 million grant toward the purchase of land in Beaufort County, S.C., for a nature park and potential fish hatchery.

Hollings bristles when questioned about the federal money he has funneled to his home state. "I'm not going for the West Virginia pork barrel," he said in 1991, referring to Senate Appropriations Committee Chairman Robert C. Byrd's legendary and unapologetic effort to direct more than a billion dollars to his home state. But like Byrd, Hollings has engineered the transfer of government jobs and agencies to his home state. At Hollings' behest, the Justice Department spent $10 million in fiscal 1992 to transfer its prosecutor-training program from Washington, D.C., to the law center at the University of South Carolina, where Hollings got his law degree.

Hollings gave up his ranking spot on Budget in 1983 to take the same position on Commerce, Science and Transportation, and he assumed the chairmanship of that panel when Democrats took control of the Senate at the start of the 100th Congress in 1987. Because he also chairs the Appropriations Subcommittee on Commerce, he can control both authorization and spending legislation for programs.

In the 100th and 101st Congresses, home-state concerns prompted Hollings to join with his South Carolina colleague, Republican Strom Thurmond, in an attempt to curb textile imports pinching the state's textile industry. The two managed to steer the quota legislation to passage in 1985, 1988 and 1990, three times overcoming entrenched opposition and three times watching it later die by veto.

From his Commerce perch, Hollings has also put himself in the middle of some of the most divisive policy debates of the past decade. He was involved in the drive to re-regulate the cable industry, which succeeded in 1992, and he has been a key player in the debate over product liability. A former trial lawyer who retains close ties to the profession, Hollings takes a harsh view of measures that would impose federal limits on a manufacturer's responsibility for harm caused by its products.

Hoping to capitalize on fears that the United States is losing its competitive hold abroad, Hollings has tried to get the Senate to loosen court restrictions on the seven regional telephone companies formed after the breakup of the American Telephone and Telegraph Co. in 1984. In June 1991, Hollings won Senate approval of a bill to accomplish that goal, but it got no further in the 102nd.

Hollings has helped shape anti-drug legislation, too. In the 102nd, he won approval of a measure that requires drug and alcohol testing of operators of aircraft, trains and commercial motor vehicles, such as trucks. An August 1991 rail accident in New York that killed five people and injured 171 added momentum to the bill; the train operator was charged with five counts of murder after authorities found a vial with traces of cocaine in the motorman's cab and alleged that he was drunk at the time of the accident. Hollings' proposal was enacted into law as part of the fiscal 1992 transportation appropriations bill.

Hollings has taken the lead on some less controversial issues, too. He was the sponsor of a bill, enacted in 1991, that prohibits computer-voiced telephone solicitations and junk faxes, and the same year he persuaded colleagues to increase research funds for cancer and Alzheimer's disease by a combined total of $175 million.

Hollings has long had a reputation as a hawk, despite his attempts to freeze military spending as part of a deficit-reduction package. Although he opposed the MX missile and the B-1 bomber, he has generally backed spending increases for weapons. In the post-Cold War era, he has argued against steep cuts in the defense budget. In 1992, Hollings joined Jim Exon of Nebraska and Christopher J. Dodd of Connecticut, fellow Democrats on the Budget Committee, in successfully fighting off Budget Chairman Jim Sasser's attempt to cut defense spending by $10 billion in fiscal 1993. Instead, the committee approved Hollings' request for a $5 billion cut in line with President Bush's defense budget proposal.

Hollings is not afraid, though, to cross swords with the Senate's leading Democrat on defense issues, Sam Nunn of Georgia. He trod boldly onto the Armed Services chairman's turf in 1987 by challenging Nunn's reinterpretation of the anti-ballistic missile treaty, perhaps the key issue underlying testing of Strategic Defense Initiative weapons.

Joining Nunn, however, Hollings opposed the resolution in January 1991 authorizing the president to use force in the Persian Gulf. Hollings was the only member of the South Carolina delegation to oppose the resolution.

At Home: Hollings started building his political career in South Carolina at a time of emotional argument about racial issues. He succeeded in combining old-time rhetoric with a tangible record of moderation. Modern times have brought new issues to the fore, but Hollings has kept up a balancing act, appealing to traditionally Democratic-voting rural and small-town whites, as well as rural and urban blacks, while clinging to enough of the business- and defense-minded GOP vote to survive in a state that has evolved into one of the national Republican Party's premier bastions.

As a candidate in the late 1950s, Hollings firmly espoused states' rights and condemned school integration. In his inaugural speech as governor in 1959, Hollings criticized President Dwight D. Eisenhower for commanding a "marching army, this time not against Berlin, but against Little Rock." But as chief executive of the state, he quietly integrated the public schools.

In fact, despite grumblings about his rhetoric, blacks provided Hollings' margin of victory in 1966, when he won his Senate seat against a more conservative GOP opponent. Since then, he never has faced a credible candidate to his left, and blacks have generally supported him.

During the Depression, the Hollings family's paper business went bankrupt, and an uncle borrowed money to send him to The Citadel, where he received an Army commission. After World War II, Hollings returned for law school, a legal career and eventually politics.

As a young state legislator, he attracted notice with his plan to solve the problem of inferior black schools without integration. He said a special sales tax should be imposed to upgrade the black schools.

Hollings twice won unanimous election to the state House speakership and in 1954 moved up to lieutenant governor. In 1958, Democratic Gov. George B. Timmerman was ineligible to succeed himself. Hollings won a heated three-way race for the nomination, defeating Donald S. Russell, former University of South Carolina president and a protégé of ex-Gov. James F. Byrnes. The primary turned on political alliances and geography. Hollings' base lay in Tidewater and Russell's in Piedmont.

As governor, Hollings worked hard to strengthen his state's educational system, establishing a commission on higher education. In 1960 his campaigning for John F. Kennedy helped him carry South Carolina for president.

Barred from seeking a second gubernatorial term in 1962, he challenged Democratic Sen. Olin D. Johnston. Portraying himself as "a young man on the go," Hollings attacked Johnston's endorsement by the state AFL-CIO and charged that "foreign labor bosses" were seeking to control the state. Hollings failed to draw much more than one-third of the vote.

The senator died in 1965, however, and Donald Russell — by then governor — had himself appointed to the seat. That provided the issue for Hollings' comeback in 1966. He ousted Russell in the special primary to finish Johnston's term.

The 1966 election year was not an ordinary one in South Carolina. The national Democratic Party was unpopular, and GOP state Sen. Marshall Parker seized on Hollings' connections to it in an effort to defeat him. He nearly made it, but Hollings matched his conservative rhetoric and survived with 51 percent of the vote.

Running for a full term two years later, Hollings had little trouble turning back Parker. He rolled over weak opponents in 1974 and 1980. In 1985, Republicans tried to stir up talk that Hollings was bored with the Senate and dispirited by the failure of his 1984 bid for the Democratic presidential nomination. But Hollings discredited the rumor early on by stumping all over the state and raising a hefty campaign treasury. Well-known Republicans ducked, leaving the nomination to a little-known former U.S. attorney. He was crushed in the race.

One of the most striking endorsements of the 1988 presidential campaign came from Hollings: In June, he declared he would support the Rev. Jesse Jackson at the Atlanta convention. In 1984, when Hollings' White House bid collapsed early and Jackson went on to dominate the state's Democratic caucuses, Hollings had more than a few unkind words for Jackson, at one point calling his "rainbow coalition" a "blackbow" coalition.

But in 1988, Jackson ran even better in the state's Democratic caucuses. Perhaps with an eye on maintaining a line of communication to black voters, Hollings went along with a majority of the convention delegation in supporting Jackson, a native of Greenville, S.C.

Support from black voters did indeed prove vital for Hollings when he sought a fifth full term in 1992. It was a roller-coaster of an election cycle for Hollings, in which he first looked vulnerable, then secure, then vulnerable again. In the heady days after the 1991 Persian Gulf War, Republicans thought that Hollings' vote against use of force would seriously undermine his prospects for re-election in strongly pro-defense South Carolina. But voters' focus seemed to drift from the war in early 1992, and the campaign of the presumed GOP nominee, former Rep. Thomas F. Hartnett, did not draw rave reviews for its vigor and fund-raising.

Money remained a weak spot for Hartnett to the end — Hollings poured more than $3.6 million into the campaign, outspending his challenger by 4-1 — but the Republican did find his voice in the fall and put a real scare into Hollings.

Hartnett's portrayal of Hollings as an arrogant, entrenched incumbent resonated with many voters already in an anti-incumbent mood. And ironically, Hartnett benefited from the travails of his party's presidential ticket, because it needed to shore up its Southern base. Bush, who could take South Carolina for granted in 1988, paid close attention to the state in 1992, helping mobilize the GOP faithful.

And these days there are many more Republican faithful in South Carolina than Hollings ever faced early in his career, even in his close 1966 race. Where the population and level of affluence have increased in South Carolina in recent years, the GOP has grown — in suburbs of Columbia, Greenville and Charleston, in resort and retirement communities all along the Atlantic Coast from Myrtle Beach south to Hilton Head, and in the Augusta, Ga., to Aiken corridor on the western side of the state.

With Bush winning 48 percent overall in South Carolina — his second-best showing in the country — Hartnett prevailed in two-thirds of the state's 15 most-populous counties. Hollings' pro-business image and his efforts to boost military spending in the state helped him hold down his losses in white-collar, retirement and military-dependent areas, but it was strong support from traditionally Democratic rural and small-town South Carolina that re-elected him. Of the 29 counties casting fewer than 20,000 votes, Hollings carried every one. And he ran particularly well in black-majority areas such as Orangeburg County, where he took two-thirds of the vote. In the end, Hollings won with 50 percent, three points ahead of Hartnett.

Committees

Commerce, Science & Transportation (Chairman)
National Ocean Policy Study (chairman); Communications; Foreign Commerce & Tourism; Science

Appropriations (3rd of 16 Democrats)
Commerce, Justice, State & Judiciary (chairman); Defense; Energy & Water Development; Interior; Labor, Health & Human Services & Education

Budget (2nd of 12 Democrats)

Elections

1992 General

Ernest F. Hollings (D)	591,030	(50%)
Thomas F. Hartnett (R)	554,175	(47%)
Mark Johnson (LIBERT)	22,962	(2%)

Previous Winning Percentages: **1986** (63%) **1980** (70%) **1974** (70%) **1968** (62%) **1966 *** (51%)

* *Special election.*

Campaign Finance

	Receipts	Receipts from PACs		Expend-itures
1992				
Hollings (D)	$2,736,893	$1,052,164	(38%)	$3,642,045
Hartnett (R)	$907,376	$153,311	(17%)	$886,816

Key Votes

1993	
Require unpaid family and medical leave	N
Approve national "motor voter" registration bill	Y
Approve budget increasing taxes and reducing deficit	Y
Support president's right to lift military gay ban	Y
1992	
Approve school-choice pilot program	N
Allow shifting funds from defense to domestic programs	N
Oppose deeper cuts in spending for SDI	Y
1991	
Approve waiting period for handgun purchases	N
Raise senators' pay and ban honoraria	N
Authorize use of force in Persian Gulf	N
Confirm Clarence Thomas to Supreme Court	Y

Voting Studies

	Presidential Support		Party Unity		Conservative Coalition	
Year	**S**	**O**	**S**	**O**	**S**	**O**
1992	38	62	58	42	55	45
1991	56	44	63	37	65	35
1990	52	48	73	27	57	43
1989	67	33	61	39	71	29
1988	49	49	71	25	81	14
1987	47	53	58	42	88	13
1986	70	30	54	46	74	26
1985	52	48	59	41	75	25
1984	32	44	59	22	49	26
1983	8	35	49	8	23	20
1982	44	45	73	20	55	36
1981	54	38	58	35	67	30

Interest Group Ratings

Year	ADA	AFL-CIO	CCUS	ACU
1992	35	50	60	63
1991	55	75	40	62
1990	50	67	42	48
1989	45	80	63	50
1988	55	86	29	48
1987	40	80	17	62
1986	35	73	32	52
1985	45	62	55	52
1984	60	89	40	38
1983	70	90	36	12
1982	55	74	53	50
1981	55	58	35	14

1 Arthur Ravenel Jr. (R)

Of Mount Pleasant — Elected 1986; 4th Term

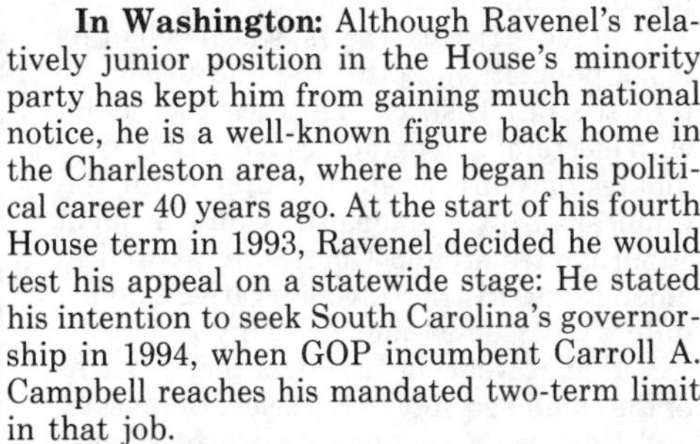

Born: March 29, 1927, St. Andrews Parish, S.C.
Education: College of Charleston, B.A. 1950.
Military Service: Marine Corps, 1945-46.
Occupation: Businessman.
Family: Wife, Jean Rickenbaker; six children, four stepchildren.
Religion: French Huguenot.
Political Career: S.C. House, 1953-59; S.C. Senate, 1981-87.
Capitol Office: 231 Cannon Bldg. 20515; 225-3176.

In Washington: Although Ravenel's relatively junior position in the House's minority party has kept him from gaining much national notice, he is a well-known figure back home in the Charleston area, where he began his political career 40 years ago. At the start of his fourth House term in 1993, Ravenel decided he would test his appeal on a statewide stage: He stated his intention to seek South Carolina's governorship in 1994, when GOP incumbent Carroll A. Campbell reaches his mandated two-term limit in that job.

In the House, Ravenel has been an idiosyncratic figure. His overall voting record is rather moderate for a Southern Republican. But on occasion he has shown a penchant for the sort of rough rhetoric that usually comes from hard-line conservatives in the House GOP.

Ravenel made a mark soon after arriving in Washington with a proposal that the U.S. military intercept, shoot down and kill smugglers using airplanes to bring illegal drugs into the country. At the conclusion of the Persian Gulf War in 1991, Ravenel, a member of the Armed Services Committee, was among a small group of House Republicans who called for the assassination of Iraqi President Saddam Hussein.

Yet Ravenel is by no means a sure conservative vote. During the 102nd Congress, he opposed President Bush roughly 40 percent of the time on House votes on which Bush took a position. In 1989, Ravenel's moderate views on environmental issues spurred a senior Republican member to try to block his bid for a seat on the Merchant Marine and Fisheries Committee. But Ravenel, a founder of the modern Republican Party in South Carolina, got his seat — by threatening to jump to the Democratic Party.

In the early months of the 103rd Congress, Ravenel was focused on responding to a threat to a vital pillar of the 1st District economy. The military base realignment plan submitted by an independent commission in March 1993 slated the Charleston naval complex for closure. Ravenel came out strongly against a shutdown, which he said would eliminate some 20,000 military and civilian jobs, and he opposed further cutbacks in the many military programs that benefit the economy of South Carolina as a whole.

Ravenel acknowledged the nation's changing post-Cold War defense needs. "We understand that a peacetime economy requires significant adjustments," he said just after the commission's report was released. But Ravenel argued to preserve the Charleston naval facilities on their merits. "We're asking why the Navy is closing the shipyard with the lowest operating cost per 'manday,' outstanding safety and environmental records and with an 18 percent minority workforce," he said. He also noted that the Charleston complex had been targeted in earlier budget reductions. "We've already taken 'our fair share' of the downsizing," he said.

Among members affected by the base-closing process, Ravenel was relatively well-positioned to make a case for exempting his home turf: He took over in the 103rd Congress as ranking Republican on the Armed Services Subcommittee on Military Acquisition. Also, the cause of defending the Charleston complex was embraced by South Carolina's two veteran senators: Republican Strom Thurmond and Democrat Ernest F. Hollings.

But entering the fight, Ravenel had to know that the odds were against him. The House by overwhelming margins had ratified two previous base-closing proposals. And Ravenel was unlikely to get much sympathy from members whose districts endured the earlier cutbacks; he voted in both 1989 and 1991 to uphold the base-closing lists.

Ravenel, in fact, has a reputation on Armed Services as a "cheap hawk" whose backing for a strong defense is tempered by his conservative fiscal philosophy. Though mainly supportive of the defense programs of the Reagan and Bush administrations, he was among a small group of Republicans who argued against certain big-ticket weapons systems. For example, Ravenel voted to limit production of the

South Carolina 1

East — Part of Charleston; Myrtle Beach

The 1st encompasses two of South Carolina's growth hot spots: Charleston and its suburbs, which were part of the district in the 1980s, and, up the Atlantic Coast, newly added Myrtle Beach (Horry County). Remapping in 1992 shifted the 1st north and east to make way for the black-majority 6th.

A 1980s boom in tourism and federal spending at Charleston's many military installations and industries produced a vibrant economy and fueled population growth of more than 40 percent in some parts of the 1st.

But where defense dollars supported a strong economy in the past decade, there is potential now for economic trouble; military downsizing may hit Charleston with a vengeance. Two major military installations — the Charleston Naval Station and Hospital, and the Charleston Naval Shipyard — appeared on the Pentagon's 1993 base-closure list. If they do close, some estimates say that military, defense-contractor and civilian job losses could reach 60,000. In 1992, the military directly or indirectly supplied one-third of the payroll and one-fourth of the jobs in the southern counties of Berkeley, Charleston and Dorchester — an estimated annual impact on the area's economy of $4.2 billion.

The proposed closure comes on top of substantial job losses during the early 1990s. Between 1989 and 1992, the naval base shed 10,000 jobs. Myrtle Beach got a taste of the same medicine when its Air Force base closed, eliminating 4,000 military and civilian jobs.

So far at both ends of the district, layoffs have been absorbed by growth in the non-military sector. Charleston's historic district and nearby beaches are a cash cow; five million tourists visit the area annually, leaving an estimated $850 million a year behind. A growing health-care industry, anchored by the Medical University of South Carolina, employs about 15,000.

Myrtle Beach thrives on tourism as well, drawing visitors to its surf, myriad golf courses and honky-tonk amusements. Beaches of the "Grand Strand" — 60 miles of shoreline from the North Carolina border down into Georgetown County — feature waters warmed by the Gulf Stream, just a few miles offshore.

In redistricting, the 1st saw much of its black population, both rural and urban, go into the 6th District. That leaves the 1st with electoral demographics most GOP candidates only dream about. Support for Republicans is high among the white, affluent suburbanites around Charleston as well as among the district's conservative-minded military personnel and its many retirees.

Rep. Ravenel in 1992 took three-fourths of the combined vote in Berkeley, Dorchester and Charleston counties. In Horry County (which was in a Democratic-held district in the 1980s), he got 55 percent.

Despite the district's overall right-of-center tilt, there is a moderate shading on some issues. Widespread support for protecting the area's waterways, marshes, beaches and wildlife has spawned a strong environmental movement.

1990 Population: 581,125. White 453,075 (78%), Black 117,022 (20%), Other 11,028 (2%). Hispanic origin 8,027 (1%). 18 and over 427,603 (74%), 62 and over 67,603 (12%). Median age: 31.

expensive radar-evading B-2 stealth bomber.

But if Ravenel can be cheap, he is fairly consistently a hawk. In February 1991, he supported a House resolution to suspend an executive order that bars assassination of foreign leaders; the proposal would have applied only to Iraqi leaders. Ravenel called himself "an Old Testament Christian: an eye for an eye and a tooth for a tooth" and said he would applaud the killing of Saddam Hussein.

Ravenel voices a similarly harsh prescription for drug crimes. When the military identifies a plane or ship as unquestionably smuggling drugs, he said in his 1988 campaign, "I think those drug planes should be shot down and I think the ships bringing the drugs in should be sunk ... [and] any survivors machine-gunned in the water."

Ravenel's willingness to cut his own path spurred the biggest confrontration of his House career. In 1989, Republican Rep. Don Young of Alaska, a senior member of the Merchant Marine Committee, blocked Ravenel's bid for membership; Young was miffed that Ravenel had not pledged support for one of his priorities, a plan to open Alaska's Arctic National Wildlife Refuge to oil drilling.

Ravenel responded by threatening to jump parties. But then-Republican National Committee Chairman Lee Atwater, a fellow South Carolinian, interceded. Persuading Young to drop his objection, Atwater got Ravenel his seat in November 1989 and kept him in the party.

At Home: Old hands on the South Carolina political scene know Ravenel as "Daddy Rabbit," a nickname that reflects both his colorful personal style and his pioneering role in establishing the Republican Party in the Charleston area.

Entering politics in the 1950s as a Democrat, he represented Charleston in the state House for three terms. He switched to the GOP in 1960 and for the next two decades worked to expand the local party, all the while making a fortune in home-building, real estate and cattle-raising. In 1980, he unseated a Democratic state senator. Four years later, when reapportionment placed him in another district, he again ousted an incumbent Democrat.

Throughout his career in public office, Ravenel's personality and his somewhat moderate political proclivities have enabled him to establish a rapport with blacks and blue-collar workers who are rarely supportive of conservative GOP businessmen. In the legislature, his interests included protection of the coastal environment and programs for the mentally retarded.

In 1986, when GOP Rep. Thomas F. Hartnett left the 1st to run for lieutenant governor, Ravenel easily secured the Republican nomination, while Democrats endured a bruising contest eventually won by Jimmy Stuckey, former chairman of the Charleston County Council.

The nominees agreed on most national issues: They supported the Reagan military buildup and opposed any tax increase. Both promised to bring federal funds to the district's military facilities. Their most substantive clashes were on aid to the Nicaraguan contras, which Ravenel favored, and increased federal support for education, which Ravenel opposed.

Ravenel put Stuckey on the defensive by reviving a charge that first surfaced in the Democratic primary — that Stuckey as a private attorney had defended drug traffickers.

On Election Day, Ravenel won 52 percent, trailing Stuckey in three rural counties, but carrying the city of Charleston, the GOP suburbs in Dorchester and lower Berkeley counties, and the Hilton Head resort area in Beaufort County. In 1988 and 1990 he won re-election with ease, and after 1992 redistricting made the 1st an even safer Republican redoubt, Ravenel posted a best-ever winning tally of 66 percent.

Committees

Armed Services (9th of 22 Republicans)
Military Acquisition (ranking); Military Forces & Personnel

Merchant Marine & Fisheries (8th of 18 Republicans)
Environment & Natural Resources; Fisheries Management

Elections

1992 General		
Arthur Ravenel Jr. (R)	121,938	(66%)
Bill Oberst Jr. (D)	59,908	(32%)
John R. Peeples (AM)	2,608	(1%)
1990 General		
Arthur Ravenel Jr. (R)	80,839	(65%)
Eugene Platt (D)	42,555	(34%)

Previous Winning Percentages: **1988** (64%) **1986** (52%)

District Vote for President

1992	
D	62,513 (33%)
R	103,700 (53%)
I	49,103 (14%)

Campaign Finance

	Receipts	Receipts from PACs		Expend-itures
1992				
Ravenel (R)	$282,816	$127,076	(45%)	$561,793
Oberst (D)	$56,972	0		$56,902
1990				
Ravenel (R)	$221,611	$113,350	(51%)	$99,261
Platt (D)	$13,924	0		$14,040

Key Votes

1993	
Require parental notification of minors' abortions	N
Require unpaid family and medical leave	Y
Approve national "motor voter" registration bill	N
Approve budget increasing taxes and reducing deficit	N
Approve economic stimulus plan	N
1992	
Approve balanced-budget constitutional amendment	Y
Close down space station program	Y
Approve U.S. aid for former Soviet Union	Y
Allow shifting funds from defense to domestic programs	N
1991	
Extend unemployment benefits using deficit financing	Y
Approve waiting period for handgun purchases	N
Authorize use of force in Persian Gulf	Y

Voting Studies

	Presidential Support		Party Unity		Conservative Coalition	
Year	**S**	**O**	**S**	**O**	**S**	**O**
1992	58	40	63	35	83	15
1991	57	43	55	43	84	16
1990	54	46	59	39	83	17
1989	64	33	50	45	80	15
1988	49	48	55	44	95	5
1987	58	42	61	35	88	12

Interest Group Ratings

Year	ADA	AFL-CIO	CCUS	ACU
1992	40	42	75	80
1991	25	58	70	75
1990	28	25	57	63
1989	25	25	100	70
1988	25	64	86	76
1987	20	31	87	61

2 Floyd D. Spence (R)

Of Lexington — Elected 1970; 12th Term

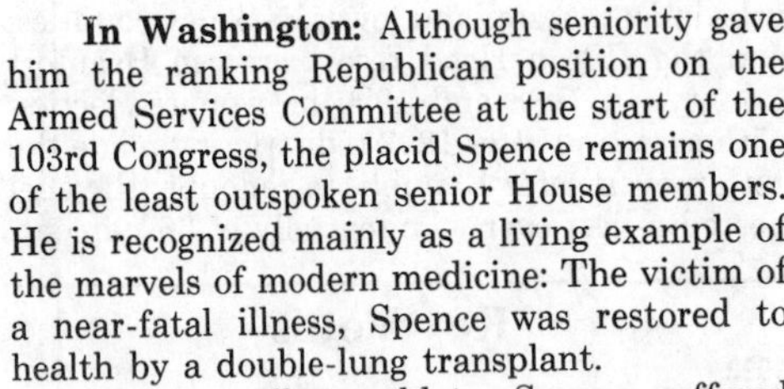

Born: April 9, 1928, Columbia, S.C.
Education: U. of South Carolina, A.B. 1952, J.D. 1956.
Military Service: Navy, 1952-54; Naval Reserve, 1947-85.
Occupation: Lawyer.
Family: Wife, Deborah Williams; four children.
Religion: Lutheran.
Political Career: S.C. House, 1957-63; GOP nominee for U.S. House, 1962; S.C. Senate, 1967-71, minority leader, 1967-71.
Capitol Office: 2405 Rayburn Bldg. 20515; 225-2452.

In Washington: Although seniority gave him the ranking Republican position on the Armed Services Committee at the start of the 103rd Congress, the placid Spence remains one of the least outspoken senior House members. He is recognized mainly as a living example of the marvels of modern medicine: The victim of a near-fatal illness, Spence was restored to health by a double-lung transplant.

Once a college athlete, Spence suffered from an obstructive lung disease that left him so breathless he could barely speak; he required a wheelchair and portable oxygen supply. But in May 1988, doctors in Jackson, Miss., replaced Spence's damaged lungs with those of a man who had been killed in a traffic accident.

"It's just like a new life," Spence told The (Columbia, S.C.) State newspaper in 1989. One of the few new federal initiatives to which the conservative Spence has signed his name is a proposal to include information with each income tax refund check encouraging Americans to sign organ donor cards.

The transplant operation restored Spence's health, but it did not change his view of his role as a congressman: He remains the antithesis of an activist member. And that is not likely to be altered by his rise to the ranking Republican spot on Armed Services (he is also ranking Republican on the Military Acquisition Subcommittee).

House Republicans can have confidence that Spence will maintain a pro-defense party line, as he has throughout his House career. But Spence will be overshadowed by committee Chairman Ronald V. Dellums, D-Calif., an eloquent liberal Democratic activist.

Spence and Dellums come from opposite ends of the country and the ideological spectrum. The ranking Republican opposed the defense spending cuts proposed in President Clinton's first budget plan; Dellums called for deeper cuts, with the money diverted to domestic programs.

A supporter of the military buildup inspired by President Ronald Reagan during the 1980s, Spence had warned even during the Bush administration against a post-Cold War rush to cut defense spending. In a March 1993 letter to Budget Committee Chairman Martin Olav Sabo of Minnesota, Spence said he was "shocked" at Clinton's projected cuts of $127 billion in defense budget authority and $112 billion in outlays over five years. "I am concerned about the level of military capability U.S. forces will be left" with under the proposal, Spence wrote.

But Spence also warned the military leadership against absenting itself from the debate on defense restructuring. At a February 1993 Armed Services hearing, Spence told Chairman of the Joint Chiefs of Staff Colin L. Powell Jr. that he feared the initiative on military reform could slip to those who favor drastic changes in military organization.

"We need a bold vision from our military leaders," Spence said. "Without one, efforts to further reduce defense spending may lead to a politically driven outcome that neither the military nor the nation can afford."

Spence's views dovetail with the priority that got him on the committee as a freshman in 1971: preserving the numerous military facilities in his home state, a cause joined by South Carolina's Strom Thurmond, the ranking Republican on Senate Armed Services.

Yet the two may be powerless to prevent a big hit on South Carolina's defense-reliant economy: A preliminary base realignment report released in March 1993 called for closing Charleston's huge Navy complex, which had nearly 20,000 military and civilian employees.

The military is one of the few parts of the government that Spence would like to stay big. "There are already too many regulations, too many laws, too much government, too many interferences in the personal lives of people," he told the Columbia newspaper in 1990. In 1973, he proposed the first House resolution for a constitutional amendment mandating a balanced federal budget.

Spence's only other committee assignment

South Carolina 2

Central and South — Columbia suburbs; Hilton Head

Winding downward from the state capital of Columbia to the Atlantic Ocean, the 2nd illustrates the contrasts that growth has brought to South Carolina. Anchored at either end by the first- and third-richest counties in the state — Lexington and Beaufort, respectively — the 2nd also contains the poorest county, Allendale, in its midsection. The population of Atlantic Coast towns skyrocketed during the 1980s, while inland counties such as Hampton and Allendale struggled to retain population.

More than three-fourths of the votes cast in the 2nd come from the thriving ends of the district.

To the north, Columbia (Richland County) and its bedroom communities in nearby Lexington County enjoyed a boom during the 1980s, as service businesses and midsize companies that produce everything from software to nuclear casings kept the area's economy vibrant. However, the main source of jobs here continues to be state, federal and local government agencies, as well as the University of South Carolina (26,000 students); together these employ nearly 60,000 and provide a fairly stable base of white-collar jobs.

At the southern end of the 2nd, Beaufort County is another bastion of affluence. The swank resorts of Hilton Head Island abound with retirees and vacationers sweating in the sun; only five miles away, recruits sweat at the Parris Island Marine Corps camp. The enormous popularity of Hilton Head caused its population to boom by 111 percent during the 1980s.

Growth and wealth at both ends of the 2nd — as well as a 1992 redistricting map that shifted most of the district's black residents into the majority-black 6th District — have put it firmly in the GOP column. Lexington County, with its mix of white-collar professionals and blue-collar social conservatives, gave George Bush 61 percent of its presidential vote in 1992 — a tally that qualifies Lexington as the strongest GOP county in the state. Beaufort County, which a generation ago was rural and Democratic, is now reliably Republican as well.

Between the poles of the 2nd, however, lie some of the poorest areas of South Carolina, places that were passed over by the boom of the 1980s and remain mired in rural poverty. In Allendale County, one in three people lives below the poverty line; in Hampton and Jasper counties, one in four falls below the line. Tenant farming and sharecropping are long-lived traditions in these black-majority, thinly settled counties.

Although South Carolina's GOP has made considerable progress in recent years luring white voters who once called themselves Democrats, there are still a number of die-hard white Democrats in the middle part of the 2nd. Their votes, in combination with the district's 25 percent black population, enabled Bill Clinton to carry Jasper, Hampton, Allendale and Calhoun counties in 1992. However, those Democrats' voices were drowned out by the Republicans to their north and south. Bush won the 2nd with 52 percent.

1990 Population: 581,111. White 423,509 (73%), Black 147,626 (25%), Other 9,976 (2%). Hispanic origin 8,268 (1%). 18 and over 431,032 (74%), 62 and over 72,407 (12%). Median age: 31.

---

is as a member of the Veterans' Affairs Committee. Earlier, he served 15 years on the House ethics committee. But his health problems forced him to give up that seat in 1988, just as the committee embarked on its investigation of House Speaker Jim Wright, which resulted in Wright's resignation in 1989.

At Home: A series of Democratic challengers have described Spence as a do-nothing congressman, citing the exceptionally low number of bills he has produced in his career. But Spence has a ready response. "I don't know that my people necessarily like hot dogs, and you see a lot of hot dogs" around the House, Spence said in a 1990 interview with the State. "They'll introduce a bill at the drop of a hat; that's not my style." So far, Spence's perception of his constituency has proved right.

It is usually to a challenger's advantage to campaign against an incumbent of infirm health. But in 1988, Democrats never could get a handle on the health issue against Spence, even though his illness, transplant surgery and recovery limited his campaigning.

Democrats got off to a bad start in the spring, when a national party operative working in South Carolina was quoted as saying of Spence, "If he's out there [campaigning] in a wheelchair, maybe the voters will decide we have to do something else." In the fall, Democratic challenger Jim Leventis had to campaign in the context of flattering media attention of the recovering Spence as a medical marvel who had won a reprieve from death.

Leventis was a strong, well-financed contender. A 50-year-old attorney and banker, he boasted personal or professional contacts with many in the business and political elite of Columbia, the 2nd's largest city. He vigorously campaigned door-to-door and tried to draw Spence into face-to-face exchanges.

But the incumbent refused to oblige, campaigning in his usual low-key manner, turning up the heat just a little at the end by telling voters, "If you like Dukakis, you'll love Leventis." Democratic presidential nominee Michael S. Dukakis lost the 2nd by 20 percentage points; in crucial Lexington County, suburban home of Columbia's professional class, Spence amassed 68 percent of the vote, overcoming Leventis' modest margins in Richland County (Columbia) and majority-black Orangeburg County. Overall, Spence took 53 percent.

Dispirited by the loss, Democrats did not offer a candidate against Spence in either 1990 or 1992.

After his days as a star athlete at the University of South Carolina and then practice as a lawyer, Spence won a state House seat as a Democrat. But he quit the party in 1962, complaining it was too liberal, and began campaigning for Congress as a Republican.

Stressing his opposition to the "socialistic" Kennedy administration, Spence was a consensus choice for the 1962 GOP nomination in the open 2nd. But he narrowly lost to a conservative Democrat, state Sen. Albert W. Watson.

Watson himself switched parties in 1965, and in 1970 ran for governor as a Republican. Spence tried again for Congress, stressing his opposition to the busing decisions of the U.S. Supreme Court. He defeated Democrat Heyward McDonald by 6,088 votes.

Committees

Armed Services (Ranking)
Military Acquisition (ranking)

Veterans' Affairs (6th of 14 Republicans)
Housing & Memorial Affairs

Elections

1992 General		
Floyd D. Spence (R)	148,667	(88%)
Gebhard Sommer (LIBERT)	20,816	(12%)
1990 General		
Floyd D. Spence (R)	90,054	(89%)
Gebhard Sommer (LIBERT)	11,101	(11%)

Previous Winning Percentages: **1988** (53%) **1986** (54%) **1984** (62%) **1982** (59%) **1980** (56%) **1978** (57%) **1976** (58%) **1974** (56%) **1972** (100%) **1970** (53%)

District Vote for President

1992

D 82,964 (36%)
R 119,122 (52%)
I 25,592 (11%)

Campaign Finance

	Receipts	Receipts from PACs		Expend-itures
1992				
Spence (R)	$169,036	$108,900	(64%)	$179,539
1990				
Spence (R)	$188,988	$106,533	(56%)	$130,173

Key Votes

1993	
Require parental notification of minors' abortions	Y
Require unpaid family and medical leave	N
Approve national "motor voter" registration bill	N
Approve budget increasing taxes and reducing deficit	N
Approve economic stimulus plan	N
1992	
Approve balanced-budget constitutional amendment	Y
Close down space station program	N
Approve U.S. aid for former Soviet Union	N
Allow shifting funds from defense to domestic programs	N
1991	
Extend unemployment benefits using deficit financing	N
Approve waiting period for handgun purchases	N
Authorize use of force in Persian Gulf	Y

Voting Studies

	Presidential Support		Party Unity		Conservative Coalition	
Year	**S**	**O**	**S**	**O**	**S**	**O**
1992	76	24	82	17	98	2
1991	74	19	75	18	86	8
1990	62	36	75	24	94	4
1989	72	24	69	29	98	0
1988	37	21	37	14	47	3
1987	61	32	68	20	91	7
1986	69	30	75	23	94	2
1985	61	39	84	13	93	7
1984	59	36	84	13	88	8
1983	74	26	87	10	97	2
1982	74	26	84	15	93	5
1981	74	26	92	8	96	4

Interest Group Ratings

Year	ADA	AFL-CIO	CCUS	ACU
1992	15	42	75	92
1991	10	25	80	95
1990	17	17	71	79
1989	10	25	100	93
1988	10	50	71	85
1987	4	20	93	73
1986	10	43	76	77
1985	0	12	95	81
1984	5	8	63	83
1983	0	6	80	100
1982	0	5	86	91
1981	0	13	89	100

3 Butler Derrick (D)

Of Edgefield — Elected 1974; 10th Term

Born: Sept. 30, 1936, Springfield, Mass.
Education: U. of South Carolina, 1954-58; U. of Georgia, LL.B. 1965.
Occupation: Lawyer.
Family: Wife, Beverly Grantham; two children, two stepchildren.
Religion: Episcopalian.
Political Career: S.C. House, 1969-75.
Capitol Office: 221 Cannon Bldg. 20515; 225-5301.

In Washington: Derrick is one of the most influential Southern legislators in the House, a product of the Democratic class of 1974 who now sits just one place down from the chairmanship of the Rules Committee.

His formal ascendancy to the inner circle of the House leadership came in mid-1991, when he was selected to be one of the party's chief deputy whips. The choice of Derrick was a transparent attempt to appeal to the Southern wing of the party. Always one of the more moderate Democrats from his region, Derrick has become an effective inside player and part of his party's liberal-oriented leadership while keeping his political footing in a state that is increasingly enamored of the GOP. In 1992, Derrick's district went solidly for George Bush for president, giving Bill Clinton barely better than one-third of the vote.

Derrick also is gaining wider recognition for his legislative talents. When Joe Moakley of Massachusetts became Rules chairman in 1989, Derrick became its No. 2 Democrat. He is nearly a decade younger than Moakley and on track to chair the panel one day.

For a man of the media age, Derrick has a quiet operating style, more prone to hammer out a compromise in a corner of the House chamber than to give a speech center stage. His behind-the-scenes pursuits enable him to get much more done in a given Congress than he gets, or takes, credit for. But that is not to say that Derrick shuns high-profile issues.

In 1991, during work on an omnibus anticrime bill, Derrick led a Democratic effort to overhaul the law of habeas corpus, which conservative critics have complained is abused by death row inmates seeking to delay their executions. In the process, Derrick and others had to hold off a Republican assault led by Henry J. Hyde of Illinois, who wanted vastly to curtail habeas corpus appeals.

Derrick accused the Republicans of "tampering with the rights guaranteed in English Common Law for 700 to 800 years," and the Democrats' approach prevailed in the bill, which ultimately died in the Senate.

As chairman of Rules' Subcommittee on the Legislative Process, Derrick engaged President Bush over the issue of the pocket veto. Bush contended that he could exercise a pocket veto — that is, disapprove a bill by merely withholding his signature — whenever Congress adjourned for more than three days. Derrick insisted, with the backing of a federal appeals court, that a president could pocket-veto a bill only after the final adjournment.

Rules and Judiciary approved legislation to codify this position in 1990, but it stalled before reaching the House floor or the Senate.

In the 100th Congress, Derrick chaired the Congressional Textile Caucus and took the lead in pushing a major bill to aid the domestic industry, much of which is located in the South, by imposing quotas on imports. A similar bill had passed in the previous Congress, but died in 1985, when supporters failed to muster a majority to override a veto. The same fate befell the bill in 1988 and 1990.

During the 1980s, Derrick faced some GOP rumblings at home (three times he was held to 60 percent of the vote or less), and he could occasionally be found voting with the conservative coalition of Republicans and Southern Democrats. But even then, Derrick usually came through when his party needed him, and since 1991, he has voted steadily with the majority of Democrats — 87 percent of the time in 1992.

He was the only South Carolina House member supporting a $600 million cut in funding for the Strategic Defense Initiative in 1990, and he also voted against administration requests for military aid to the Nicaraguan contras in 1988 and non-military aid in 1989. In April 1991, Derrick disregarded his long-standing opposition to gun control and voted for the Brady bill — imposing a seven-day waiting period for handgun purchases.

But Derrick keeps on good terms with his district's business establishment.

In 1992, he voted for a balanced-budget constitutional amendment, while the rest of the Democratic leadership was pushing vigorously — and successfully — to defeat it. And when

South Carolina 3

West — Anderson; Aiken

As South Carolina has grown in recent years, it has grown steadily more Republican. That trend is clear in the 3rd, a one-time "yellow dog" Democratic district where GOP candidates now typically win up-ballot contests. Still, Rep. Derrick keeps his hold, buoyed by the district's black residents (21 percent of the population), by rural whites who retain their traditional Democratic ties, and by business-minded conservatives who value Derrick's senior position on the Rules Committee and his spot in the House Democratic leadership.

Nearly half the district vote is cast in three counties — Anderson, Pickens and Oconee — that are part of South Carolina's "Upcountry" and have a diverse economic base. The biggest, Anderson, benefits from its proximity to the Greenville-Spartanburg area, just a few miles up Interstate 85 in the 4th District. Northern and foreign industries find wages, taxes and living costs in the Upcountry hospitable. The plants and businesses have brought in an increasingly skilled and white-collar work force.

Now, towns once dependent upon cotton mills churn out a variety of products, including tires, auto parts and refrigerators. At the same time, many textile mills have converted to high-tech fiber manufacturers; in the city of Anderson, Clarks Schwabel makes the skin for stealth fighters.

Clemson University and its 17,000 students provide economic insurance for Pickens County, and a conservative pull comes from its agriculture and engineering-oriented faculty.

Growth, prosperity and a large business community in the northern part of the 3rd have boosted GOP fortunes, though Democrats still dominate local political offices. In 1992, George Bush won better than 50 percent in all three northern counties, reaching 58 percent in Pickens County.

Traditional Democratic voting habits still hold sway in the rural midsection of the district, where a sizable black population and less prosperity have kept the GOP from building momentum. Abbeville, McCormick and Edgefield were the only counties in the district not to support Bush in 1992. McCormick even refused to back GOP Sen. Strom Thurmond when he easily won re-election in 1990, perhaps to spite state officials for changing the name of their local lake — Clark's Hill — to Thurmond Lake.

At its southern end, the 3rd includes most of the people in Aiken County, although 1992 redistricting put the eastern half of the county in the 2nd. Known as the polo center of the South — matches are every Sunday at Whitney Field — the town of Aiken is a picture of gentility preserved, with more than 70 historic homes and gardens, six golf courses and three racetracks.

Aiken is Thurmond's home base, and the white-collar commuters to Augusta, Ga., and Ph.Ds working at the Savannah River Nuclear Complex give it a solid GOP base; Bush won 56 percent here in 1992. The fate of the Savannah River plutonium plant is in doubt, though, as the Energy Department has indefinitely suspended operations there.

1990 Population: 581,104. White 456,723 (79%), Black 120,579 (21%), Other 3,802 (1%). Hispanic origin 3,126 (1%). 18 and over 435,406 (75%), 62 and over 91,115 (16%). Median age: 34.

Democrats were trying to make a major issue of Republican opposition to plant-closing notification legislation in 1988, Derrick was one of 16 House Democrats to vote against the measure. Derrick voted in 1989 to sustain two Bush vetoes: one of a Democratic plan to boost the minimum wage; another of a measure requiring businesses to provide unpaid family and medical leave to their employees. In early 1993, however, when the family leave bill was finally enacted, Derrick was a supporter.

At Home: Derrick's increasing influence in the House has helped him hold the support of his district's business community, which may regard him as a bit too liberal on some issues but overall sees him as a valuable contact in the House's majority party. Derrick has combined this normally Republican bloc with the traditional Democrats in the 3rd — black voters and rural, working-class whites — to win reasonably comfortable re-elections even when his party's presidential ticket has lost the district badly.

Derrick's most competitive election was in 1988, when the Dukakis-Bentsen ticket got just one-third of the vote in the 3rd. At the start of 1988, Derrick looked solid. He was an easy winner in 1986, and in 1984 had taken 58 percent despite a Ronald Reagan landslide in the 3rd and opposition from an aggressive young Republican real estate developer.

Establishment Republicans, pessimistic about 1988, let a newer wing of the local GOP — evangelical conservatives — take on the incumbent. Surgeon Henry S. Jordan, an activist in Pat Robertson's presidential campaign, had built some name recognition in a 1986 try for the GOP Senate nomination. But he had to spend much of 1988 just trying to prove he had a broader agenda than the social-issues activism associated with Robertson's movement.

Still, on Election Day, Jordan ran well in the fastest-growing areas of the 3rd. He carried Aiken County and stayed close in Anderson and Pickens counties; Derrick ran strongest in the district's more rural areas and finished with 54 percent of the vote.

That enticed the national GOP to look more closely at the 3rd, but Derrick responded with a vengeance. Over the next four years, he spent nearly $1.6 million to secure his hold, raising about two-thirds of that from political action committees. Altogether, his GOP challengers in 1990 and 1992 spent less than $93,000. Real estate broker Ray Haskett managed 42 percent in 1990, but two years later, Aiken County Council member Jim Bland slipped to 39 percent.

Derrick's recent electoral experience has been more like his uneventful early campaigns. The 3rd was up for grabs in 1974 when veteran Democrat W. J. Bryan Dorn retired, and Derrick won it like an incumbent breezing to reelection. He had been a state representative since 1969 and was a member of the influential state House Ways and Means Committee. He professed fiscal conservatism, right-to-work views and hard-line support for national defense. He also identified himself publicly as a racial moderate, nominating the first black to a South Carolina school board.

Derrick won the Democratic primary with 65 percent of the vote. In November, he carried all but one county in defeating former state Sen. Marshall J. Parker, twice an unsuccessful GOP Senate candidate, with 62 percent. He won 60 percent in a 1980 rematch with Parker.

Committees

Chief Deputy Whip

House Administration (10th of 12 Democrats)
Libraries & Memorials; Personnel & Police

Rules (2nd of 9 Democrats)
Legislative Process (chairman)

Elections

1992 General		
Butler Derrick (D)	119,119	(61%)
Jim Bland (R)	75,660	(39%)
1990 General		
Butler Derrick (D)	72,561	(58%)
Ray Haskett (R)	52,419	(42%)

Previous Winning Percentages: **1988** (54%) **1986** (68%) **1984** (58%) **1982** (90%) **1980** (60%) **1978** (82%) **1976** (100%) **1974** (62%)

District Vote for President

1992
D 69,365 (35%)
R 102,458 (52%)
I 26,609 (13%)

Campaign Finance

	Receipts	Receipts from PACs		Expend-itures
1992				
Derrick (D)	$681,632	$469,870	(69%)	$673,677
Bland (R)	$17,536	$347	(2%)	$17,339
1990				
Derrick (D)	$848,063	$542,789	(64%)	$907,904
Haskett (R)	$74,939	0		$74,264

Key Votes

1993	
Require parental notification of minors' abortions	N
Require unpaid family and medical leave	Y
Approve national "motor voter" registration bill	Y
Approve budget increasing taxes and reducing deficit	Y
Approve economic stimulus plan	Y
1992	
Approve balanced-budget constitutional amendment	Y
Close down space station program	Y
Approve U.S. aid for former Soviet Union	Y
Allow shifting funds from defense to domestic programs	N
1991	
Extend unemployment benefits using deficit financing	Y
Approve waiting period for handgun purchases	Y
Authorize use of force in Persian Gulf	Y

Voting Studies

	Presidential Support		Party Unity		Conservative Coalition	
Year	S	O	S	O	S	O
1992	30	69	87	12	67	33
1991	41	58	82	14	46	51
1990	31	68	81	17	70	28
1989	43	55	79	19	73	24
1988	33	60	76	18	66	21
1987	28	68	83	15	56	42
1986	28	68	81	13	52	48
1985	29	69	74	17	60	35
1984	39	54	73	25	61	39
1983	35	57	72	16	42	49
1982	36	52	70	22	56	41
1981	50	45	62	30	55	35

Interest Group Ratings

Year	ADA	AFL-CIO	CCUS	ACU
1992	80	58	63	28
1991	70	75	70	37
1990	44	58	62	33
1989	35	50	80	43
1988	70	71	54	36
1987	72	75	40	17
1986	55	57	44	26
1985	60	53	36	10
1984	50	15	47	35
1983	75	69	53	23
1982	50	55	52	46
1981	60	53	37	40

4 Bob Inglis (R)

Of Greenville — Elected 1992; 1st Term

Born: Oct. 11, 1959, Savannah, Ga.
Education: Duke U., A.B. 1981; U. of Virginia, J.D. 1984.
Occupation: Lawyer.
Family: Wife, Mary Anne Williams; three children.
Religion: Presbyterian.
Political Career: No previous office.
Capitol Office: 1237 Longworth Bldg. 20515; 225-6030.

The Path to Washington: Inglis is one of the few true outsiders in the 1992 class — his race for the 4th District seat was his first stab at electoral politics.

And he is one of the few winners who can attribute part of his success to presidential coattails: George Bush took 48 percent of the vote in the state and helped propel Inglis to an upset over three-term incumbent Liz J. Patterson.

Though a seat in the House is Inglis' first political office, he is a man on the move in state political circles. One of many new members who has called for term limits, Inglis promises to serve no more than six years in the House. But that does not mean he intends to give up politics.

He is already looking to 1998, when Democratic Sen. Ernest F. Hollings, who narrowly won in 1992, will be up for re-election. Inglis is not shy about saying that by then, he will be ready to make a move to the Senate, challenging Hollings or any other comers.

Inglis' soft-spoken, aw-shucks manner belies a steely intellect, quiet self-confidence and determination. A summa cum laude graduate of Duke University and a graduate of the University of Virginia law school, at 31 he became the youngest partner in one of Greenville's most prestigious law firms. Not immodestly, he says his partners were sorry to see him go because of the income he generated for the firm with his substantial commercial practice.

Though he had stayed clear of electoral politics, Inglis knew that he would one day seek public office. He began plotting his quest for the 4th District seat after the 1990 elections, betting that an anti-incumbent sentiment would continue to build. He also committed himself to an intensive door-to-door effort — helped by a huge cadre of volunteers — to help counter the strong ties Patterson had built up in the district, long a GOP bastion.

Inglis was thought to be a long shot, in part because of Patterson's success with a moderate voting record and conscientious contact with her constituents. She was one of the Democratic Party's success stories in the South, and there was beginning to be talk of a run at statewide office.

After the election, Patterson blamed her stunning loss on negative campaigning by Inglis and by the Christian Coalition, which distributed thousands of leaflets opposing her. Inglis, who says he is not part of the coalition and did not ask for its help, says Patterson simply underestimated him.

Inglis makes the careful distinction that he campaigned hard against Congress but not directly against Patterson. He believes one flier, hung on 75,000 doors, was particularly effective. The front detailed congressional problems, from alleged cocaine sales by House workers to bounced checks, and then inside said that Patterson had done little or nothing to change the status quo. "It was nothing personal," Inglis maintains.

Inglis now hopes to shake things up. He intends to press for reforms, starting with term limits and the abolition of political action committees. He accepted no PAC money; more than half of Patterson's campaign contributions came from PACs. He advertised himself as "unbought and not for sale" and presented himself as "a citizen statesman, not a professional politician." These professionals, he contended, were "driving the country straight into the ditch."

In the 103rd Congress, his efforts to stop departing members from purchasing furniture from their district offices at discount rates won him an appearance on ABC's "Prime Time Live."

His general philosophy for government is to see more focus on citizen responsibility. And his slot on the Judiciary Committee may allow him to press for an "opportunity society" that encourages hard work and self-reliance. Too many in government, he says, have spent too much time listening to those "whining about their rights" and not enough time "telling them to shoulder their responsibilities."

And from his position on the Budget Committee, Inglis may be able to work for a constitutional amendment requiring a balanced federal budget. On other issues, he favors a presidential line-item veto and opposes abortion except in cases of rape or incest or when the woman's life is endangered.

South Carolina 4

Northwest — Greenville; Spartanburg

The nucleus of the 4th is Greenville County, one of the most-populous and most-industrialized counties in the state and a showpiece of the New South.

The city of Greenville developed as a textile center after the Civil War, and although employment in the mills and clothing manufacturers declined as that industry moved farther south, the city has not suffered the same depressing fate as other textile-dependent areas. Instead, civic leaders lured Frost Belt and overseas investment to the area, ensuring a robust economy and driving the steady population growth of Greenville and Spartanburg counties.

The city relied on private employers, including Michelin, General Electric and 3M, to sustain high employment and help blunt the effects of the early 1990s recession. The world supply of Pepto-Bismol is also manufactured here.

Greenville County has a history of conservatism dating to its Tory leanings during the American Revolution, and it was one of the first areas in the state to take to Republicanism after World War II.

Growth in such white-collar occupations as engineering and management have made the area increasingly affluent, and has intensified its GOP leanings. George Bush won 57 percent of the Greenville County vote in 1992.

Beneath an apparently unified conservative voting population, however, lie fault lines that can cleave GOP supporters. Winning candidates must convince two rather disparate groups to become political bedfellows: mainstream, business-oriented conservatives often find themselves at odds with intensely conservative Christians and fundamentalists focused around the Greenville-based Bob Jones University. Former Democratic Rep. Liz J. Patterson held onto her seat for six years by splitting these two factions. When the conservatives' rift healed in 1992, the united GOP elected Inglis to office.

Democrats in the county tend to be conservative and often vote for GOP candidates. A small band of liberal Democrats in the city of Greenville does not offer much of a launching pad for left-leaning candidates.

Spartanburg County scored a coup over rival Greenville with the 1992 announcement that BMW will build its U.S. assembly line there; it expects to employ upwards of 2,000 by the end of the decade. Agriculture also plays a role in the county's economy; Spartanburg's sprawling orchards hold bragging rights to the second biggest peach crop in the South.

Rank-and-file textile workers and farm laborers give Spartanburg firmer Democratic loyalties than Greenville. In 1992, Patterson won the county.

But when it comes to statewide and national races, voters here typically opt for the GOP, although not by the margins that Greenville provides. Rounding out this compact district, rural Union County usually delivers its votes to Democratic candidates.

1990 Population: 581,113. White 460,805 (79%), Black 114,332 (20%), Other 5,976 (1%). Hispanic origin 4,655 (1%). 18 and over 437,837 (75%), 62 and over 86,874 (15%). Median age: 34.

Committees

Budget (16th of 17 Republicans)

Judiciary (13th of 14 Republicans)
Administrative Law & Governmental Relations; Economic & Commercial Law

Campaign Finance

	Receipts	Receipts from PACs		Expend-itures
1992				
Inglis (R)	$226,577	0		$215,364
Patterson (D)	$351,850	$207,910	(59%)	$348,528

Key Votes

1993

Require parental notification of minors' abortions	Y
Require unpaid family and medical leave	N
Approve national "motor voter" registration bill	N
Approve budget increasing taxes and reducing deficit	N
Approve economic stimulus plan	N

Elections

1992 General		
Bob Inglis (R)	99,879	(50%)
Liz J. Patterson (D)	94,182	(48%)
Jo Jorgensen (LIBERT)	4,286	(2%)
1992 Primary		
Bob Inglis (R)	21,301	(71%)
Bill McCuen (R)	4,760	(16%)
Jerry L. Fowler (R)	4,029	(13%)

District Vote for President

1992

D 65,092 (33%)
R 107,983 (55%)
I 24,136 (12%)

5 John M. Spratt Jr. (D)

Of York — Elected 1982; 6th Term

Born: Nov. 1, 1942, Charlotte, N.C.
Education: Davidson College, A.B. 1964; Oxford U., M.A. 1966; Yale U., LL.B. 1969.
Military Service: Army, 1969-71.
Occupation: Lawyer.
Family: Wife, Jane Stacy; three children.
Religion: Presbyterian.
Political Career: No previous office.
Capitol Office: 1536 Longworth Bldg. 20515; 225-5501.

In Washington: A brainy lawyer and former bank president, Spratt made a quiet, steady rise to influence during his first decade in the House. Along with several other centrist Democrats on the Armed Services Committee, he was part of the inner circle of advisers to the panel's chairman, Rep. Les Aspin of Wisconsin.

Around his 10th anniversary in the House, though, Spratt stumbled twice. In 1992, the investigation of the House bank showed that he had 45 overdrafts — not an egregiously high number, but embarrassing for a banker with degrees from Davidson, Oxford and Yale Law.

Then as the 103rd Congress was getting organized, Spratt unsuccessfully sought the Budget Committee chairmanship, running as the candidate of moderate and right-leaning House Democrats against liberal Rep. Martin Olav Sabo of Minnesota. Within the liberal-tilted Democratic Caucus, Sabo had a clear edge. He defeated Spratt by a vote of 149-112, taking the chair vacated when President Clinton chose Rep. Leon E. Panetta of California to direct the Office of Management and Budget.

It seems unlikely that these events will have a long-term negative impact on Spratt's career. Weathering publicity over the checks, he won re-election in November 1992 with 61 percent of the vote. The chairmanship contest with Sabo was genteel, and after it was over Spratt returned to a busy legislative schedule. He took over the chairmanship of the Government Operations Subcommittee on Commerce, Consumer and Monetary Affairs (giving up his seat on Budget). He was appointed by Speaker Thomas S. Foley to the Joint Committee on the Organization of Congress, created to study institutional reforms.

And he settled back in as a key player on Armed Services, where he will be an important contact for old ally Aspin, who was confirmed in January 1993 as Clinton's secretary of Defense.

Spratt tends to be more "pro-defense" than many of his Democratic House colleagues. However, Spratt and others in Aspin's controlling group of Democratic centrists kept a skeptical eye on the Defense Department's policies under the Reagan and Bush administrations. "Our role is to be defense advocates, but not Department of Defense advocates," Spratt said.

Spratt proved his independence during the late 1980s debates on the Strategic Defense Initiative (SDI). Spratt opposed the Reagan and Bush administrations' vision of the anti-ballistic missile (ABM) system as a network of space-based weapons: Spratt viewed this as a violation of the 1972 U.S.-Soviet ABM treaty. In 1988, it was a measure of Aspin's regard for then third-termer Spratt that he picked him to lead the SDI fight in the House; the brief was carried in the Senate by Armed Services Committee Chairman Sam Nunn of Georgia.

Spratt also chairs a special Armed Services panel on defense nuclear facilities that are under Department of Energy supervision. (South Carolina is host to the Savannah River nuclear materials production plant, which has been plagued by safety problems.)

With Aspin now in charge at the Pentagon, he will count on Spratt to make the case in Congress for military spending cuts and streamlining sought by Clinton. But Spratt also can be expected to oppose deeper cuts that will be advocated by Aspin's much more liberal successor as Armed Services chairman, Ronald V. Dellums of California.

Spratt's centrist position is seen in other areas. His views on social policy are somewhat more liberal than those of many of his rural Southern constituents: He favors abortion rights and supported the civil rights bill enacted in 1991. But he leans conservative on fiscal issues: In June 1992, he backed Texas Democratic Rep. Charles W. Stenholm's failed effort to pass a balanced-budget constitutional amendment.

When he ran for Budget chairman, Spratt hoped his colleagues would see him as more in line than Sabo with the newly elected Clinton — a fellow Oxford and Yale man who ran as a centrist in his 1992 presidential campaign.

But Spratt was up against the numbers: Most Democrats in the House have mainly liberal records. The outcome was also not

South Carolina 5

North Central — Rock Hill

Touching on four distinct regions of South Carolina, the 5th extends from the hills of Cherokee County south to the low country around Sumter. To command a districtwide media presence, a candidate has to buy time in four cities outside the district — Greenville, Columbia, Florence and Charlotte, N.C.

This geographic diversity makes it difficult to pigeonhole the district's personality. In the west, rural counties such as Newberry, Chester, Lancaster and Kershaw produce cotton for the textile mills that have historically dominated this region's economy. The small but growing cities of Rock Hill and Sumter add urbane, progressive immigrants from the North to the population mix. In the east, residents of Chesterfield, Dillon and Marlboro counties depend heavily on tobacco farming.

Linking the two rural parts of the district is their common struggle with declining economies. About 20 percent of the tobacco-producing counties live in poverty, and modernization has stripped many mills in the west of their plentiful, low-skill jobs.

To the north, the city of Rock Hill provides population and suburban affluence to the district. Once heavily textile-dependent, county residents now gravitate north toward white-collar jobs in Charlotte. In fact, the area's biggest challenge may be to avoid surrendering its identity to Charlotte's yuppie hordes, who stream down I-77 searching for bedroom communities. Native industry here still includes textile mills; many have converted from weaving cotton to producing high-tech fibers for industrial uses.

Rock Hill grew modestly during the 1980s, but is anticipating faster growth in the 1990s. A pending settlement in the Catawba Indians' claim to 144,000 acres in two counties — which stymied investment as buyers worried about a proposed lawsuit against 62,000 individual landowners — is expected to unleash a pent-up drive for development.

By and large, the district remains true to its Democratic roots, with most mill and agricultural workers inheriting ideological proclivities from their parents and grandparents. These "yellow dog" Democrats helped Rep. Spratt win all the district's counties in 1992, although his 61 percent was his lowest tally ever.

In national elections, increasing affluence has persuaded some areas to abandon their Democratic heritage.

Bush reaped 49 percent of the vote in York County, down from his 65 percent showing in 1988 but still a respectable draw in a three-way race.

York County's days as a hotbed of religious conservatism have been fading, however, since television evangelist Jim Bakker's downfall and incarceration forced him to abandon his PTL headquarters in Fort Mill; some of Bakker's supporters have moved elsewhere.

Other conservative votes in the district come from the counties of Sumter (home of Shaw Air Force Base) and Kershaw.

1990 Population: 581,131. White 396,287 (68%), Black 179,155 (31%), Other 5,689 (1%). Hispanic origin 3,233 (1%). 18 and over 422,575 (73%), 62 and over 83,253 (14%). Median age: 32.

wholly based on philosophy. Sabo, a taciturn but well-liked and more senior member, had lined up support even when Panetta's appointment was still a rumor.

In his new role as a Government Operations subcommittee chairman in 1993, Spratt held hearings on the "credit crunch" that some financial experts believed was hindering business and consumer lending. He also serves as chairman of the House Textile Caucus, a reflection of his district's large textile industry.

Spratt applied himself during the 102nd Congress to resolving a local land claim by a group of Catawba Indians. To satisfy the ancient claim on 144,000 acres of land in South Carolina's York, Lancaster and Chester counties, the Catawbas threatened to sue all property owners in those areas, effectively freezing real estate transactions.

Spratt helped negotiate a deal under which the Catawbas would get $50 million in public and private funds; rights to about 4,000 acres; tribal recognition (which would allow for limited self-government and eligibility for payments under federal Indian programs); and other benefits. He continued to work during the 103rd to pass legislation to implement the plan.

At Home: With his lofty academic credentials and background in law and banking, Spratt is not the obvious choice for a district where many of the Democratic voters come from poor textile towns and dusty farms.

But after emerging from a field of four Democratic candidates in 1982, Spratt has won six general elections with ease. Even in 1992, when Spratt was coping with the check overdrafts, a general anti-incumbent mood, new turf given him in redistricting and a Bush presidential victory in the 5th, GOP businessman Bill Horne managed just 39 percent.

In his first campaign, Spratt worked hard to turn his elitist credentials into an asset. "People are glad to see a candidate with these qualifications," he said. "That's my come-on." If his style on the stump remained a bit scholarly, no one seemed to mind.

When Democratic Rep. Ken Holland announced his retirement just before the filing deadline, Spratt jumped for the Democratic nomination, as did former Holland aide John Winburn and state Rep. Ernie Nunnery.

Winburn had Holland's contacts and Nunnery had a base in Chester County, but Spratt's banking interests and his law practice gave him strong connections in political and business circles. Many Democratic leaders quietly backed him.

And when Winburn called Spratt "a millionaire banker, lawyer and hobby farmer" who could not relate to ordinary people, Spratt persuasively argued that his work with small-town clients and depositors had given him an understanding of their circumstances. "I wouldn't have kept my job if I couldn't relate to those people," he said. Spratt finished first in the primary with 38 percent of the vote, then took 55 percent in a runoff against Winburn.

In November, Republican John Wilkerson, a longtime friend and legal client of Spratt, accused the Democrat of being too liberal for the district. But Spratt appealed to the district's partisan loyalties and had a clear organizational edge. When he visited county courthouses, rural areas and factories, he often had a locally popular political figure close at hand. One source described Wilkerson's core supporters as "the country club boys — the fellows who put ice in their whiskey." Spratt won two-thirds of the vote.

Committees

Armed Services (9th of 34 Democrats)
Military Acquisition; Oversight & Investigations

Government Operations (10th of 25 Democrats)
Commerce, Consumer & Monetary Affairs (chairman)

Joint Organization of Congress

Elections

1992 General		
John M. Spratt Jr. (D)	112,031	(61%)
Bill Horne (R)	70,866	(39%)
1990 General		
John M. Spratt Jr. (D)	91,775	(100%)

Previous Winning Percentages: **1988** (70%) **1986** (100%) **1984** (92%) **1982** (68%)

District Vote for President

1992

D 81,197 (43%)
R 85,971 (45%)
I 23,437 (12%)

Campaign Finance

	Receipts	Receipts from PACs		Expend-itures
1992				
Spratt (D)	$281,855	$146,775	(52%)	$381,942
Horne (R)	$102,751	$350	(0%)	$102,728
1990				
Spratt (D)	$110,158	$84,950	(77%)	$173,157

Key Votes

1993	
Require parental notification of minors' abortions	N
Require unpaid family and medical leave	Y
Approve national "motor voter" registration bill	Y
Approve budget increasing taxes and reducing deficit	Y
Approve economic stimulus plan	Y
1992	
Approve balanced-budget constitutional amendment	Y
Close down space station program	Y
Approve U.S. aid for former Soviet Union	Y
Allow shifting funds from defense to domestic programs	N
1991	
Extend unemployment benefits using deficit financing	Y
Approve waiting period for handgun purchases	Y
Authorize use of force in Persian Gulf	Y

Voting Studies

	Presidential Support		Party Unity		Conservative Coalition	
Year	**S**	**O**	**S**	**O**	**S**	**O**
1992	34	66	83	15	79	21
1991	40	59	82	15	73	27
1990	29	69	86	14	72	28
1989	49	51	83	16	68	32
1988	33	63	78	19	82	18
1987	31	66	80	16	81	12
1986	28	71	84	13	54	46
1985	41	58	79	17	73	27
1984	41	58	77	22	56	44
1983	37	61	74	20	60	40

Interest Group Ratings

Year	ADA	AFL-CIO	CCUS	ACU
1992	75	67	50	28
1991	50	83	30	21
1990	56	67	36	33
1989	65	67	80	29
1988	55	79	57	29
1987	72	69	47	9
1986	60	64	59	33
1985	35	38	57	38
1984	70	38	31	21
1983	65	75	50	14

6 James E. Clyburn (D)

Of Columbia — Elected 1992; 1st Term

Born: July 21, 1940, Sumter, S.C.
Education: South Carolina State College, B.S. 1962.
Occupation: State official.
Family: Wife, Emily England; three children.
Religion: African Methodist Episcopal.
Political Career: S.C. Human Affairs commissioner, 1974-92; sought Democratic nomination for S.C. secretary of state, 1978, 1986.
Capitol Office: 319 Cannon Bldg. 20515; 225-3315.

The Path to Washington: Clyburn is used to firsts in his professional life. With his election to Congress, he becomes South Carolina's first black representative in nearly a century.

When he was named by then-Gov. John West as a special assistant for human resources in 1971, Clyburn was one of five blacks who were the first to serve in state government in more than 70 years. Three years later, he became South Carolina Human Affairs commissioner, a position he held until his election to the House.

Though not a legislator in South Carolina, Clyburn, by virtue of his long state service, is well-connected to the political power structure, state and federal, and should have little trouble forging alliances with other delegation members, including the Republican members.

Clyburn was active in the civil rights movement in the '60s, and although he was often on the opposite side of the state's senior U.S. senator, Strom Thurmond, the two have enjoyed a warm working relationship for several years. Similarly, prominent members of Clyburn's campaign team were the Who's Who of the white Democratic Party establishment.

Though Clyburn has had an important state job for nearly 20 years, he always has wanted to move on. (He lost two previous races for secretary of state.)

Running for Congress was a lifelong dream, he says, and the only question was when he would give it a try. "If conditions were different, I would have done it at 32," he explains, "rather than 52," a not-so-oblique reference to the hard realities of race in South Carolina.

Twenty years ago, in the aftermath of the landmark 1965 Voting Rights Act, blacks were just beginning to be a political force in the state, and the prospects for winning a federal office were minimal.

Clyburn does not, however, limit his civil rights agenda to blacks. He supported President Clinton's call to end the ban on homosexuals in the military and favors raising the limit on damages in sexual harassment cases.

During redistricting, the 6th was reconfigured to be majority black. Clyburn, with wide name recognition in the district, easily outpolled four opponents in the primary and then trounced his GOP challenger.

One of Clyburn's main missions at the human affairs office was to defuse tensions, racial and otherwise. He believes his bent for accommodation and his ability to negotiate with different factions will serve him well in congressional work. Indeed, his colleagues already have selected him to be president of the freshman class in 1994.

Clyburn's interests in Congress will reflect his district: There are plenty of low-income areas in need of assistance, particularly in Columbia, the state capital. Clyburn supports enterprise zones, which would give tax breaks to businesses if they set up shop in designated economically deprived areas. There are also numerous crops grown in the district's rural areas, including tobacco, tomatoes and peanuts.

Clyburn will not be able to pursue his interests in farming from a seat on the Agriculture Committee — instead he won a slot on Public Works and Transportation. He also was assigned to the Veterans' Affairs Committee, which handles several issues that are important to him because of the number of military retirees in his district and in neighboring areas.

Clyburn, an abortion rights supporter, also has spoken favorably of parental consent requirements for minors seeking abortion. "I tend to believe that any 13-year-old who makes a mistake ought to bring the family into the process," he once said.

But in March 1993, Clyburn voted with the Democratic leadership and President Clinton in opposing a GOP effort to require federally funded clinics to give parents 48-hour notification before performing an abortion on a minor. More than 40 Democrats bucked the party line to support notification, but Clyburn, an assistant whip, stuck with the leadership.

Clyburn also voted for family leave, and he favors tax credits and other economic incentives for businesses offering child-care facilities.

South Carolina 6

Central and South — Florence; parts of Columbia and Charleston

After drawing a 6th District with more nooks and crannies than an English muffin, mapmakers sat back and watched it perform as expected in 1992, electing South Carolina's first black representative this century. Creating the majority-minority 6th required radical surgery during redistricting, with planners shearing off white and increasingly Republican Horry County and moving the bulk of the district south and inland to increase its black population.

The redrawn district is a fearsome piece of political real estate: Sprawling over all or part of 16 counties in eastern South Carolina, it encompasses land from the North Carolina border down to the beaches south of Charleston.

Along the way, district lines reach out to slice black precincts from Columbia and Charleston, cutting through the downtowns of both. Overall, the black population exceeds 60 percent, although blacks make up 58 percent of registered voters.

South Carolina's first black-majority district is also its most poverty-ridden. Of the six poorest counties in the state, five are within Clyburn's jurisdiction. The counties of Lee, Bamberg, Marion and Williamsburg are losing population as residents leave farms or abandoned textile mills. For those who stay in these rural areas, agriculture remains an important part of life.

Urban poverty brings its own problems in parts of Columbia and Charleston; nearly one in three families earned less than $13,000 in 1989. And in both urban and rural areas, blacks bear the brunt of the poverty. The average white in most counties earns more than $7,000 more annually than the average black.

Many residents of the 6th work outside the district.

Richland County residents commute to state government occupations in Columbia, which provides more than 30,000 jobs. Neighboring military installations also breathe life into the district economy, including Charleston Naval Base in the 1st, Shaw Air Force Base in the 5th and Fort Jackson in the 2nd. Shaw and Fort Jackson seem safe from military downsizing, but the naval base is slated to lose about 16,000 jobs in the next round of military downsizing.

The city of Florence, with 30,000 residents, provides the largest complete population center within the district, and has become a magnet for Northern investment in recent years. Hoffman-LaRoche, a major pharmaceutical company, recently relocated its research and development facility here, and area textile mills turn out high-tech synthetic fibers.

Not surprising given its demographics, the 6th supports Democrats on every level; Bill Clinton won here in 1992, and six of the 12 South Carolina counties that voted for Michael S. Dukakis in 1988 are in the district. Clyburn won his seat by an almost 2-1 margin in the general election. Republican strength in the 6th lies in suburban areas surrounding the cities of Columbia and Charleston, as well as in Florence, the one county Clyburn did not win.

1990 Population: 581,119. White 216,575 (37%), Black 361,170 (62%), Other 3,374 (1%). Hispanic origin 3,242 (1%). 18 and over 412,043 (71%), 62 and over 82,900 (14%). Median age: 31.

Committees

Public Works & Transportation (32nd of 39 Democrats)
Economic Development; Public Buildings & Grounds; Surface Transportation

Veterans' Affairs (19th of 21 Democrats)
Education, Training & Employment; Oversight & Investigations

Campaign Finance

	Receipts	Receipts from PACs		Expend-itures
1992				
Clyburn (D)	$321,121	$101,210	(32%)	$324,379
Chase (R)	$115,338	$900	(1%)	$114,289

Key Votes

1993

Require parental notification of minors' abortions	N
Require unpaid family and medical leave	Y
Approve national "motor voter" registration bill	Y
Approve budget increasing taxes and reducing deficit	Y
Approve economic stimulus plan	Y

Elections

1992 General		
James E. Clyburn (D)	120,647	(65%)
John Chase (R)	64,149	(35%)
1992 Primary		
James E. Clyburn (D)	41,415	(56%)
Frank Gilbert (D)	11,089	(15%)
Ken Mosely (D)	9,494	(13%)
Herbert U. Fielding (D)	9,130	(12%)
John Roy Harper II (D)	2,680	(4%)

District Vote for President

1992

D	118,394 (62%)
R	59,799 (31%)
I	12,322 (7%)

South Dakota

STATE DATA

Governor:
Walter D. Miller (R)
(appointed after death of George S. Mickelson, R)
Length of term: 4 years
Term expires: 1/95
Salary: $65,174 (3% increase effective 7/93)
Term limit: 2 consecutive terms
Phone: (605) 773-3212
Born: Oct. 5, 1925
Education: S.D. School of Mines, 1943-44
Occupation: Rancher; insurance executive
Family: Widowed; 4 children
Religion: Protestant
Political Career: S.D. House, 1967-87; lieutenant governor, 1987-93

Lt. Gov: Steve T. Kirby (R)
(appointed after Miller took over after Mickelson's death)
Length of term: 4 years
Term expires: 1/95
Salary: $224 per day (part-time office)
Phone: (605) 773-3212

State election official: (605) 773-3537
Democratic headquarters: (605) 335-7337
Republican headquarters: (605) 224-7347

STATE LEGISLATURE

Legislature. Meets January-February in even years, January-March in odd years.

Senate: 35 members, 2-year terms
1992 breakdown: 20D, 15R; 28 men, 7 women; 32 whites, 1 black, 2 others
Salary: $4,267 for first session; $3,730 for second.
Phone: (605) 773-3251

House of Representatives: 70 members, 2-year terms
1992 breakdown: 41R, 29D; 56 men, 14 women; 69 whites, 1 other
Salary: Same as upper chamber
Phone: (605) 773-3251

URBAN STATISTICS

City	Pop.
Sioux Falls	100,836
Mayor Jack White, R	
Rapid City	54,523
Mayor Edward McLaughlin, R	
Aberdeen	24,927
Mayor Timothy G. Rich, N-P	

U.S. CONGRESS

Senate: 1 D, 1 R
House: 1 D, 0 R

TERM LIMITS

For Congress: Yes
Senate: 2 six-year terms
House: 6 two-year terms
For state offices: Yes
4 consecutive terms in both houses

ELECTIONS

1992 Presidential Vote

George Bush	40.7%
Bill Clinton	37.1%
Ross Perot	21.9%

1988 Presidential Vote

George Bush	53%
Michael S. Dukakis	47%

1984 Presidential Vote

Ronald Reagan	63%
Walter F. Mondale	37%

POPULATION

1990 population		696,004
1980 population		690,768
Percent change		+1%
Rank among states:		45
White		92%
Black		<1%
Hispanic		1%
Asian or Pacific islander		<1%
Urban		50%
Rural		50%
Born in state		70%
Foreign-born		1%
Under age 18	198,462	29%
Ages 18-64	395,211	57%
65 and older	102,331	15%
Median age		32.5

MISCELLANEOUS

Capital: Pierre
Number of counties: 67
Per capita income: $16,392 (1991)
Rank among states: 36
Total area: 77,116 sq. miles
Rank among states: 16

South Dakota - Congressional District

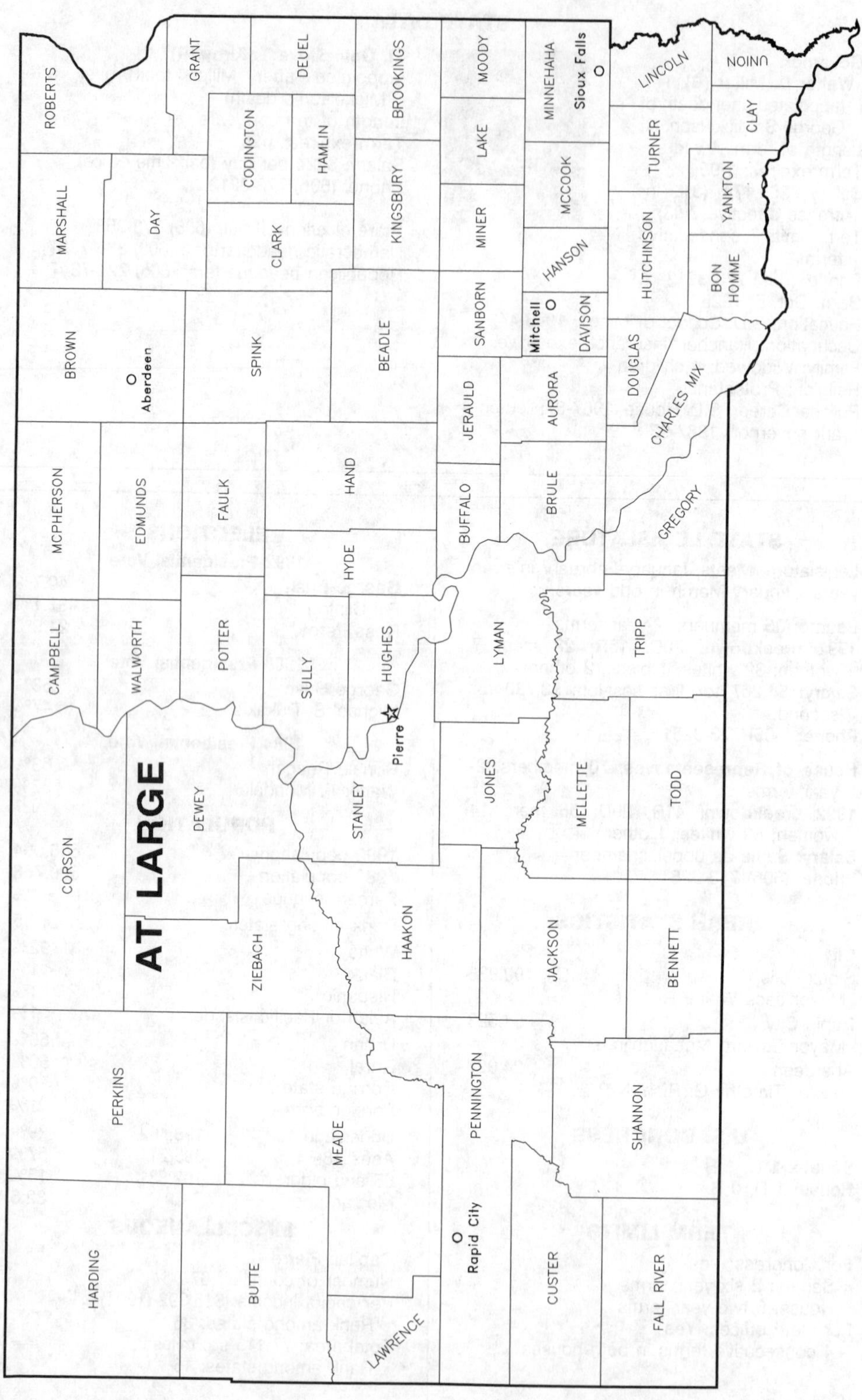

Larry Pressler (R)

Of Humboldt — Elected 1978; 3rd Term

Born: March 29, 1942, Humboldt, S.D.
Education: U. of South Dakota, B.A. 1964; Oxford U., M.A. 1965; Harvard U., M.A., J.D. 1971.
Military Service: Army, 1966-68.
Occupation: Lawyer.
Family: Wife, Harriet Dent; one stepchild.
Religion: Roman Catholic.
Political Career: U.S. House, 1975-79.
Capitol Office: 283 Russell Bldg. 20510; 224-5842.

In Washington: Pressler's assiduous attention to the concerns of his home state have made him unbeatable back in South Dakota but have sometimes frayed his relations with Senate colleagues and hindered his efforts to be considered a legislator of the first rank.

Take the events of Aug. 11, 1992, as a case in point. As the Senate rushed to recess, Pressler placed a hold on dozens of pending nominations by the Bush administration because a new federal judge had not been named to fill a vacancy that involved South Dakota.

By evening, senators had begun to complain about the delay — and most were Pressler's GOP colleagues. When Pressler refused to relent, Senate Minority Whip Alan K. Simpson of Wyoming lashed back, saying that he had intervened on Pressler's behalf with the Bush administration many times in the past.

"Each and every time, whatever is accomplished is never enough," said Simpson. "It is an insatiable maw of requests that I can no longer meet. Therefore, I honestly say . . . whatever you wish to do, I will be here in a friendly adversary position to prevent you from doing it."

Pressler subsequently lifted his hold on the nominations, but he went on to claim victory, saying that the White House began the process to fill the vacancy the following day.

It is not unusual for Pressler to find himself torn between his independent agenda and the role of loyal Republican team player. He goes back and forth between the two in a manner that can make him appear unpredictable even to many fellow Republicans.

In 1989, on those issues on which President Bush staked out a position, Pressler voted against him more often than any other GOP senator. Yet in the 102nd Congress, his presidential support scores rose dramatically and his party unity scores were at their highest level ever (hovering around 90 percent).

While Senate critics complain that Pressler's support can come at a high price, Pressler has indicated that his party loyalty during the Bush years had come at some personal cost. "I've supported a lot of things that were marginal," he said in late 1992.

As the 103rd Congress began, Pressler seemed to relish being a part of the GOP Senate minority. He was the first member of the Judiciary Committee to publicly oppose President Clinton's choice of Zoë Baird to be attorney general.

And he was an eager opponent of Clinton's economic stimulus package, which Senate Republicans killed. "The people of the country are behind us," said Pressler in April 1993. "They're excited about cutting spending. We've got an issue and we shouldn't let go of it."

First impressions die hard, and Pressler has spent much of his Senate career trying to recast an image of himself as an overly eager young man in a hurry. Within months of entering the Senate in 1979, Pressler was running for president in a Republican field that would also include Ronald Reagan, George Bush, former Treasury Secretary John B. Connally and veteran Sens. Bob Dole and Howard H. Baker Jr.

Pressler argued the advantage of his youth (he was 37) and talked about the need to promote rural America. But he withdrew after 105 days during which he raised little money and failed to carry on long enough to reach the voting in Iowa or New Hampshire. When he returned to the chamber early in 1980, he had acquired a reputation for being a little flaky.

But the presidential campaign did lead to his most priceless national attention. Late in 1979, FBI agents posing as Arab sheiks invited him to a Georgetown house to offer him a bribe, knowing that he badly needed money for his presidential effort. Pressler refused to have anything to do with the offer and stormed out of the meeting. It briefly made him a minor hero. "I turned down an illegal contribution," he said afterward. "Where have we come to if that's considered heroic?"

Pressler looked less heroic when he thrust himself into the national limelight a decade later, casting himself as Hamlet for the nightly news during the drama of John Tower's nomination to be secretary of Defense.

Pressler's was one of the few uncertain

Republican votes on Tower in early 1989. In the days just before the vote, he was a favorite subject of media interviewers, and he seemed unable or unwilling to avoid sharing each step in his soul-searching.

Pressler said he had serious questions about Tower's ability to reform procurement practices and mismanagement at the Pentagon. Of particular concern to Pressler were the faulty electronics in the 34 B-1 bombers at Ellsworth Air Force Base, located near Rapid City, S.D. Before the vote, Pressler received specific assurances from the White House that the B-1s would be fixed. In the end, he voted for Tower.

As a rule, Pressler is sensitive to the ripple effect that legislation may have on what he sees as the oft-forgotten rural voter. For example, he sought a probe of whether prescription drug pricing is weighted against less-populated areas. He also opposed loosening restrictions on regional Bell telephone companies until one — U.S. West Inc. — revealed whether a $10 million settlement with the Justice Department for violating terms of the American Telephone & Telegraph Co. breakup would be passed on to ratepayers.

One of his legislative high points was a 1980 amendment to bar the use of federal funds to enforce the Carter administration's grain embargo against the Soviet Union. The amendment, opposed by President Jimmy Carter, passed the Senate but was dropped in conference.

Nonetheless, it was a signal of growing farm discontent with the embargo, and it contributed to the change of attitude that led the Reagan administration to cancel the embargo early the next year. This greatly enhanced Pressler's standing with South Dakota farmers.

Pressler's home-state focus often earns him scorn in the state's largest newspaper, the Argus Leader in Sioux Falls. Nonetheless, it plays well in towns such as Yankton, where after the local college shut down, Pressler combed the federal bureaucracy until he could find an agency willing to use its campus. The Bureau of Prisons complied, making plans for a minimum-security prison on the site.

Pressler has not been shy over the years to use his committee assignments to route federal largess to South Dakota. As the 100th Congress opened, he took a seat on the Environment and Public Works Committee, just in time to tuck several million dollars' worth of South Dakota projects into highway and water pollution measures later vetoed by Reagan. Pressler's override vote helped ensure roadwork at the Mount Rushmore National Memorial and erosion control along the Missouri River, which cuts through South Dakota.

As the 101st Congress began, he traded Environment for the Banking Committee. That panel has jurisdiction over coinage, and Pressler helped gain passage of a law to mint a coin commemorating the 50th anniversary of Mount Rushmore, with proceeds going for park improvements and to reduce the federal deficit. At the end of the 101st, Pressler left Banking.

Over the years, though, Pressler has dug his teeth into some significant national issues. From his seats on both the Senate Commerce, Science and Transportation and Judiciary committees, he has taken an interest in consumer protection, from proposals to curb phone telemarketing to legislation that would make "carjacking" a federal crime.

And from his seat on the Senate Foreign Relations Committee, he has taken an active interest in international relations. Sometimes, the subjects he has focused on have seemed a bit arcane, such as his resolution urging U.S. recognition of the Republic of Kosovo.

But Pressler has taken an interest in global hot spots, urging a linkage in aid to Russia with Russian troop withdrawal from the Baltic republics.

Pressler also has an amendment bearing his name, enacted in 1985, that calls for a cutoff in U.S. aid to Pakistan if the president cannot certify that Pakistan does not possess a nuclear device. In 1990 the Pressler amendment was employed, as Bush was unable to certify that Pakistan did not have a nuclear device.

At Home: For years, Democrats regarded Pressler as though he were a boxer with a glass jaw. In spite of his unbeaten record in congressional races, they were confident that an aggressive, well-financed opponent could beat him.

Democrats felt they had such a candidate in 1990 in Ted Muenster, a veteran political insider who had been a business executive, college vice president and chief of staff to Democratic Gov. Richard F. Kneip. Muenster boasted close ties to the state's business community and was on good terms with elements of the state GOP establishment unhappy with Pressler's frequent flights of independence.

Muenster pounded away at the theme that Pressler was no longer the fresh-faced "farm boy from Humboldt" whom South Dakota voters had first elected more than a decade earlier, but a professional politician who had lost touch with his home state in the pursuit of an upscale lifestyle in Washington. Yet in a year when anti-Congress sentiment ran high, Pressler's reputation for parochialism and independence worked to his advantage. His nearly yearlong media campaign reminded voters that he voted "South Dakota first."

To win, Muenster needed to carry his home base of Minnehaha County (Sioux Falls) and carve deeply into Pressler's rural base. But Muenster did neither. Pressler narrowly won populous Minnehaha, and his years of carefully cultivating the farm vote paid off with a sweep of 52 of South Dakota's 66 counties. Still, Pressler's tally against Muenster and a minor independent candidate was 52 percent, a lower percentage than in any of his previous House or Senate elections.

From the beginning of his political career, Pressler has offered South Dakota a political persona hard to resist: the good-natured, unassuming farm boy who succeeded early in life on sheer talent. His Rhodes scholarship and his Harvard master's degree combined perfectly with his roots on the Humboldt farm, still his official residence.

Those attributes were more than enough to give Pressler his 1974 victory over Democratic Rep. Frank Denholm. Pressler campaigned as a moderate Republican, noting his membership in Common Cause and criticizing South Dakota's Oahe irrigation project on environmental grounds. He took 55 percent. In 1976, he easily won a second term.

Democratic Sen. James Abourezk chose to retire in 1978, and Pressler began the campaign year as the odds-on favorite to succeed him. That never changed, even though Democrats had a competent challenger in former Rapid City Mayor Don Barnett. Pressler had built enormous good will through his faithful attendance at events across the state (he still drives his 1928 John Deere "D" tractor in small-town parades) and through gestures such as donating a House pay increase to charity.

In 1984, Democrats offered George Cunningham, a longtime aide to former South Dakota Sen. George McGovern. Probably the nation's most colorful Senate loser that year, Cunningham denounced Pressler as a "flash-dancing, Fred Astaire type ... who deals more with public relations than with public policy." But Cunningham admitted early in the year that his polling numbers were "in the toilet," and that is where they stayed. Pressler won 74 percent of the vote.

Committees

Small Business (Ranking)
Rural Economy & Family Farming (ranking); Export Expansion & Agricultural Development; Urban & Minority-Owned Business Development

Commerce, Science & Transportation (3rd of 9 Republicans)
Aviation (ranking); Communications; Foreign Commerce & Tourism; National Ocean Policy Study; Science

Foreign Relations (4th of 8 Republicans)
Terrorism, Narcotics & International Operations (ranking); East Asian & Pacific Affairs; Near Eastern & South Asian Affairs

Judiciary (8th of 8 Republicans)
Juvenile Justice; Technology & the Law

Special Aging (2nd of 10 Republicans)

Elections

1990 General

Larry Pressler (R)	135,682	(52%)
Ted Muenster (D)	116,727	(45%)
Dean Sinclair (I)	6,567	(3%)

Previous Winning Percentages: **1984** (74%) **1978** (67%) **1976 *** (80%) **1974 *** (55%)

** House elections.*

Campaign Finance

	Receipts	Receipts from PACs		Expenditures
1990				
Pressler (R)	$1,982,702	$861,339	(43%)	$1,664,341
Muenster (D)	$1,335,356	$492,661	(37%)	$1,323,770

Key Votes

1993	
Require unpaid family and medical leave	N
Approve national "motor voter" registration bill	?
Approve budget increasing taxes and reducing deficit	N
Support president's right to lift military gay ban	N
1992	
Approve school-choice pilot program	Y
Allow shifting funds from defense to domestic programs	N
Oppose deeper cuts in spending for SDI	Y
1991	
Approve waiting period for handgun purchases	N
Raise senators' pay and ban honoraria	N
Authorize use of force in Persian Gulf	Y
Confirm Clarence Thomas to Supreme Court	Y

Voting Studies

	Presidential Support		Party Unity		Conservative Coalition	
Year	**S**	**O**	**S**	**O**	**S**	**O**
1992	73	27	91	9	84	16
1991	88	12	89	10	85	15
1990	58	39	74	22	49	46
1989	59	41	75	25	61	39
1988	73	25	88	10	97	3
1987	63	37	75	20	81	13
1986	77	20	72	25	82	16
1985	74	25	72	24	78	15
1984	61	39	50	44	72	23
1983	59	31	64	31	80	16
1982	70	24	67	20	77	13
1981	61	24	58	32	63	27

Interest Group Ratings

Year	ADA	AFL-CIO	CCUS	ACU
1992	20	17	90	85
1991	5	8	80	86
1990	22	0	83	83
1989	35	40	63	75
1988	0	29	79	96
1987	25	50	82	81
1986	10	33	68	86
1985	10	20	71	74
1984	45	55	71	45
1983	20	33	50	57
1982	10	35	70	67
1981	30	41	67	43

Tom Daschle (D)

Of Aberdeen — Elected 1986; 2nd Term

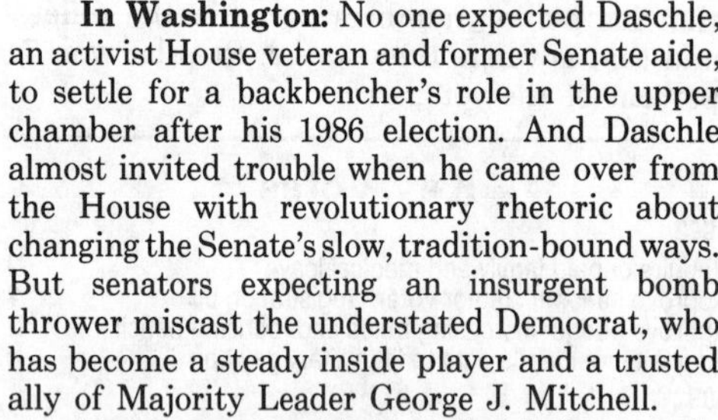

Born: Dec. 9, 1947, Aberdeen, S.D.
Education: South Dakota State U., B.A. 1969.
Military Service: Air Force, 1969-72.
Occupation: Congressional aide.
Family: Wife, Linda Hall; three children.
Religion: Roman Catholic.
Political Career: U.S. House, 1979-87.
Capitol Office: 317 Hart Bldg. 20510; 224-2321.

In Washington: No one expected Daschle, an activist House veteran and former Senate aide, to settle for a backbencher's role in the upper chamber after his 1986 election. And Daschle almost invited trouble when he came over from the House with revolutionary rhetoric about changing the Senate's slow, tradition-bound ways. But senators expecting an insurgent bomb thrower miscast the understated Democrat, who has become a steady inside player and a trusted ally of Majority Leader George J. Mitchell.

To be sure, Daschle has a legislative agenda he aggressively pursues as one of the so-called "prairie populists," a group of Midwestern Democrats who press relentlessly for increased aid and price supports for farmers. But throughout his years in Congress he has cultivated the confidence of the Democratic leadership, working to earn a position of influence within the party hierarchy. In the House, he was on the panel charged with making committee assignments. In the Senate, Mitchell made him co-chairman of the Democratic Policy Committee just two years into his freshman term.

Daschle seeks to build the relationships that grease legislative wheels — frequenting a senators-only lunchroom, for example, to pick up intelligence. He resists the go-it-alone style typical of the Senate, even objecting that it, unlike the House, assigns floor seating: "Camaraderie develops when you can move around," he has said. "The chemistry of intermixing — the collegiality — is very important to the way the House gets its work done." His engaging, almost deferential personality, his recognized ability to work within the system and his readiness to seek the counsel of senior members make him a favorite of senators above and below him on the seniority ladder.

He has shown a genius for choosing the right mentors. Months before his election, he became the first Democrat in what would be the large and savvy 1986 class to endorse Robert C. Byrd's re-election as majority leader. (Byrd later supported Daschle's bid for a seat on the Finance Committee.) When Byrd stepped aside in 1988, Daschle quickly emerged as point man for Mitchell, who ultimately won a three-way war of succession. Mitchell immediately named Daschle as policy committee co-chairman, sharing a post previously held exclusively by the party leader.

Thus far, Daschle has been content to pursue his relatively limited legislative agenda while taking on responsibilities geared toward propelling his rise within the Democratic leadership.

During the 102nd Congress, for example, when the massive energy bill ran into a filibuster effort organized primarily by Democrats, Daschle was deployed to try to negotiate an agreement to move ahead. The gap between the bill's lead sponsor, Louisiana Democrat J. Bennett Johnston, and environmentalist senators, led by Colorado Democrat Tim Wirth, proved too vast to bridge in 1991. But a bill was enacted the following year.

For the 103rd, Daschle accepted a seat on the Ethics Committee, one of the least-liked chores in the Senate, but one given to members who have earned the trust of party leaders.

(In a break from the leadership, Daschle voted against the 1991 bill raising senators' pay and banning honoraria, but Byrd had given a pass to senators seeking re-election in 1992.)

If Daschle has few qualms about fulfilling the tasks Mitchell assigns him, it is in part because he and Mitchell are philosophically in concert. At his core, Daschle is an old-fashioned liberal Democrat not unlike Iowan Tom Harkin, another "prairie populist" who came over from the House. But unlike Harkin, Daschle has adopted a far less confrontational method of operating.

It also helps that as a senator from a largely rural Midwestern state, he does not have to contend with the spectrum of demands that assail senators from more populous states.

So far in the Senate, Daschle has concentrated on the causes that dominated his House work — agriculture and veterans. On both the Finance and Agriculture committees, he has been able to help South Dakota's farmers.

During consideration of the 1990 farm bill, the "prairie populists" wanted to raise federal price support levels over those in the 1985 bill. This put them at odds not only with Republicans demanding further cuts, but also with many Democrats, including Agriculture Chairman Patrick J. Leahy, whose objective in the bill was to hold support levels steady.

While Daschle was at times passionate in his pleas for family farmers, he also revealed a pragmatic streak not evident in some of the fervent populists. "I think we have to assume that if we go to [higher price supports], we are going to face major opposition in the Congress," he said as Democrats fought among themselves over funding levels.

Daschle, along with Harkin, Nebraska's Bob Kerrey and the other populists, wanted to drive a wedge between farmers and President Bush, as Democrats had done with the Reagan administration, enabling many of the party's 1986 candidates to run against the 1985 farm bill. But senior Democrats feared that increased spending would derail the bill, and on vote after vote the prairie populists lost to a coalition of senior Democrats, led by Leahy, and a united GOP. Daschle was among those voting against the final package.

Daschle uses his seat on Finance to help farmers. As chairman of the Energy and Agricultural Taxation Subcommittee, he has promoted tax breaks for corn-based ethanol fuels. In 1992, the Finance Committee voted 15-5 for his amendment to broaden the existing tax breaks for ethanol; parts of his amendment became law as part of the energy bill. (He also watches out for the ethanol industry as chairman of Agriculture's Subcommittee on Research.)

Co-chairman of Vietnam-era Veterans in Congress, Daschle got a slot on the Veterans' Affairs Committee at the start of the 102nd Congress. As a senator, he persisted in a campaign he had begun in the House to compensate Vietnam veterans for illnesses believed caused by exposure to the defoliant Agent Orange.

Agent Orange legislation died in the 100th and 101st Congresses, but in the 102nd, Daschle and other supporters succeeded in linking the legislation to the swell of public support for the military brought on by the Persian Gulf conflict. Congress finally approved Agent Orange compensation legislation in early 1991.

Daschle was a controversial figure in his earlier years at the House Agriculture Committee. His proposals tended to put members of both parties in a spot, skeptical of the sums he wanted for farm subsidies but reluctant to oppose them. Daschle figured the more ambitious the plan, the better farmers would fare in the final compromise. But some Republicans condemned his projects, such as a 1981 farm crisis bill, as political demagoguery.

Generally, however, Daschle was a leadership favorite. He was close to Ways and Means Chairman Dan Rostenkowski and was an effective insider on Steering and Policy, which makes Democratic committee assignments.

Daschle's shrewd moves in early 1985 formed the foundation for his successful Senate bid the next year. He won national attention as chief sponsor of a multibillion-dollar effort to advance credit to struggling farmers. President Ronald Reagan vetoed the bill, but Daschle had reinforced his image as a defender of agriculture while his rival, GOP Sen. James Abdnor, had to struggle against being linked to administration stinginess.

A few months later, Daschle voted against the comprehensive farm bill, criticizing its price-support levels. Abdnor voted for the bill, giving Daschle a campaign issue.

At Home: When Daschle first began planning his Senate campaign, he was considered one of the Democrats' surest bets in 1986. The farm economy was on the ropes, and Abdnor had a reputation as bumbling and ineffective.

But Abdnor exceeded expectations, and Daschle needed all the organization and persistence he could muster to eke out a victory.

Abdnor faced a primary challenge from bombastic GOP Gov. William J. Janklow, who hammered at his support for Reagan farm policies and his inability to get things done. But Abdnor's consultants moved aggressively to inoculate the senator against charges of ineffectiveness, starting an extensive TV ad campaign in late 1985. Abdnor, whose amiable and low-key nature had endeared him to voters for nearly three decades, scored a strong primary victory.

Daschle then faced the challenge of framing the general election as a referendum on Abdnor's politics, not his personality. Abdnor handed him an issue shortly after the primary, when he stumbled at a forum by suggesting that farmers might have to "sell below cost" to compete.

In a long-running TV ad, Daschle showed Abdnor giving his faltering "below cost" explanation, and then he made his own forceful argument for a fair price for farmers. Abdnor said his remarks were misinterpreted, but his explanation did not erase the original flub.

The contest tightened considerably in the fall, however, with two visits by Reagan and a bevy of personal attacks on Daschle. In his ads, Abdnor linked Daschle with actress and former anti-war activist Jane Fonda, who had been pictured with Daschle at a fundraiser. Abdnor also hoped to tie Daschle to Fonda's efforts, in her health books, to discourage the consumption of red meat. Promoting vegetarianism in meat-producing South Dakota is a political felony.

Despite the Fonda connection and a concerted effort by media consultant Roger Ailes to convince the electorate that Abdnor was quietly effective, Daschle prevailed with his contention that Abdnor was instead effectively quiet. Daschle's massive effort to turn out the farm vote, along with his late October charge that Abdnor had voted to cut Social Security, gave him a narrow victory.

His re-election in 1992 was much easier. He beat teacher Charlene Haar by 2-to-1.

Daschle won his House seat originally on sheer energy. In a year, he and his first wife rang more than 40,000 doorbells as they campaigned to win the 1978 Democratic primary over Frank Denholm, the former representative favored to win, and then defeat Republican nominee Leo Thorsness.

The 1st District was open in 1978 with incumbent Larry Pressler running for the Senate. Early on, it seemed likely to go for Thorsness, a former prisoner of war in Vietnam who had drawn 47 percent of the vote in a 1974 challenge to Democratic Sen. George McGovern.

But Daschle's nonstop campaign brought him even with Thorsness, and a few weeks before the election, Daschle looked like a winner. Then Republicans began hitting Daschle on his opposition to an anti-abortion amendment and his promise to vote against right-to-work laws. The contest got close again; only a final canvass a week after Election Day gave Daschle a 139-vote win.

Daschle had become familiar with politics and legislation while working for Sen. James Abourezk as a legislative assistant. He moved back to South Dakota in late 1976 to become field director for Abourezk and to prepare his 1978 House campaign.

In 1982, reapportionment had merged South Dakota's two districts, and he met the state's other House incumbent, Republican Clint Roberts. The contest matched not only the state's two parties, but also its two regions. Daschle represented the Corn Belt territory of eastern South Dakota; Roberts spoke for the western ranching counties. The Republican's homespun conservative style reflected western South Dakota's traditional resentment against a liberal Washington establishment.

Roberts tried to pin the Eastern label on Daschle, noting that while he had been running a ranch, Daschle had been on a government payroll. But Daschle told voters that what the state needed in Congress was not a farmer, but someone who knew how to write farm bills. Roberts took virtually every county in his old district, but Daschle got 59 percent in his eastern territory, for 52 percent overall.

Committees

Agriculture, Nutrition & Forestry (7th of 10 Democrats)
Agricultural Research, Conservation, Forestry & General Legislation (chairman); Agricultural Credit; Rural Development & Rural Electrification

Finance (9th of 11 Democrats)
Energy & Agricultural Taxation (chairman); International Trade; Medicare & Long Term Care

Indian Affairs (3rd of 10 Democrats)

Select Ethics (3rd of 3 Democrats)

Veterans' Affairs (6th of 7 Democrats)

Elections

1992 General

Tom Daschle (D)	217,095	(65%)
Charlene Haar (R)	108,733	(33%)
Gus Hercules (LIBERT)	4,353	(1%)
Kent Hyde (I)	4,314	(1%)

Previous Winning Percentages: **1986** (52%) **1984 *** (57%) **1982 *** (52%) **1980 *** (66%) **1978 *** (50%)

** House elections.*

Campaign Finance

	Receipts	Receipts from PACs	Expend-itures
1992			
Daschle (D)	$2,838,866	$1,350,572 (48%)	$2,878,375
Haar (R)	$479,045	$71,491 (15%)	$478,421

Key Votes

1993	
Require unpaid family and medical leave	Y
Approve national "motor voter" registration bill	Y
Approve budget increasing taxes and reducing deficit	Y
Support president's right to lift military gay ban	Y
1992	
Approve school-choice pilot program	N
Allow shifting funds from defense to domestic programs	Y
Oppose deeper cuts in spending for SDI	N
1991	
Approve waiting period for handgun purchases	Y
Raise senators' pay and ban honoraria	N
Authorize use of force in Persian Gulf	N
Confirm Clarence Thomas to Supreme Court	N

Voting Studies

	Presidential Support		Party Unity		Conservative Coalition	
Year	**S**	**O**	**S**	**O**	**S**	**O**
1992	25	75	82	18	37	63
1991	27	73	90	9	38	63
1990	31	66	87	12	41	59
1989	49	51	90	9	24	76
1988	44	52	91	6	30	70
1987	37	62	88	12	44	53
House Service:						
1986	20	80	84	15	44	56
1985	16	71	83	9	33	55
1984	32	60	67	17	41	53
1983	16	76	75	12	42	51
1982	31	62	80	14	34	56
1981	42	57	77	17	37	60

Interest Group Ratings

Year	ADA	AFL-CIO	CCUS	ACU
1992	95	75	20	22
1991	85	83	10	24
1990	83	56	33	9
1989	80	90	50	7
1988	85	93	36	13
1987	85	89	33	8
House Service:				
1986	80	64	22	18
1985	70	60	38	16
1984	70	46	50	17
1983	75	71	42	17
1982	80	89	35	40
1981	70	71	22	20

AL Tim Johnson (D)

Of Vermillion — Elected 1986; 4th Term

Born: Dec. 28, 1946, Canton, S.D.

Education: U. of South Dakota, B.A. 1969, M.A. 1970; Michigan State U., 1970-71; U. of South Dakota, J.D. 1975.

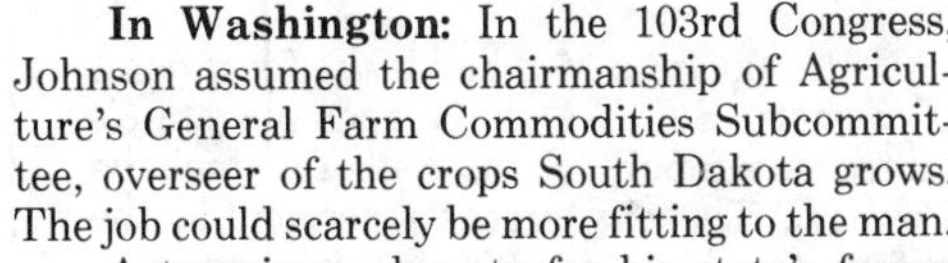

Occupation: Lawyer.

Family: Wife, Barbara Brooks; three children.

Religion: Lutheran.

Political Career: S.D. House, 1979-83; S.D. Senate, 1983-87.

Capitol Office: 2438 Rayburn Bldg. 20515; 225-2801.

In Washington: In the 103rd Congress, Johnson assumed the chairmanship of Agriculture's General Farm Commodities Subcommittee, overseer of the crops South Dakota grows. The job could scarcely be more fitting to the man.

A tenacious advocate for his state's farms, water projects, bridges and roads, Johnson leaves little doubt about what he seeks when he addresses his colleagues: He wants more. But his quiet, thoughtful style has allowed him to pursue his interests without generating undue contention.

Johnson's other panel is Natural Resources, where he won a spot in 1989, after the resignation of Majority Whip Tony Coelho. He has used his post to seek authority for water projects.

Johnson worked with South Dakota's senators, Democrat Tom Daschle and Republican Larry Pressler, in 1988 to pass a bill authorizing a $100 million drinking water project for south-central South Dakota. The Mni Wiconi project was needed, Johnson said, because the water in the area contained unsafe levels of chemicals, minerals and other impurities. The fiscal 1990 energy and water appropriations bill contained the first installment of funding for the project.

In the 102nd Congress, Johnson, Pressler and Daschle teamed to win authorization of the Mid-Dakota Project. The omnibus water bill authorized $100 million for a central South Dakota municipal and rural pipeline system to provide drinking water to about 30,000 South Dakotans. The Bush administration opposed the project, but it was part of the final package.

Johnson also won money in the 102nd Congress for some of the highway projects he sought. The fiscal 1992 transportation appropriations bill included $3.2 million for a bridge between Niobrara, Neb., in Republican Doug Bereuter's district, and Springfield, S.D. And the fiscal 1993 bill approved $3.3 million for a bridge between Newcastle, Neb., and Vermillion, Johnson's hometown.

Part of the secret to Johnson's effectiveness is his avoidance of flamboyance when securing funds for his home projects. Unlike such public-works paradigms as West Virginia Democratic Sen. Robert C. Byrd, Johnson quietly acquires and eschews the boasting. Perhaps because of this, fewer members detected the irony when Johnson proposed strengthening the president's power to rescind individual spending items — a measure Johnson promotes as "legislation to cut out pork barrel spending."

"I think that there is unjustified spending that goes on in the House," he said in 1992, "and we need a mechanism that allows more accountability [than a line-item veto], that automatically requires a vote from members of Congress, and that is what our rescission legislation would do." A version of enhanced-rescission authority passed the House near the end of the 102nd Congress; it had to be pulled from the floor when its coalition came apart in April 1993.

Johnson spent a considerable amount of time in the 101st Congress working on the 1990 farm bill, a five-year reauthorization of farm programs. Johnson suggested a program to set a loan level for oilseeds, such as sunflower, canola and safflower seeds, that would make growing them as financially attractive as growing wheat, the most common crop in oilseed regions. The Wheat, Soybeans and Feed Grains Subcommittee adopted his amendment to support the price of sunflower and other oilseeds at 10.5 cents per pound. The price dropped to 8.5 cents by the time the bill was passed, however.

Johnson also pressed for higher price-support levels for dairy products. Lawmakers decided to place a floor under the previously sliding scale of subsidies, assuring dairy farmers a base rate of $10.10 per 100 pounds of milk product. But others sought a higher level. An amendment to raise the rate to $10.60 fell on a 14-24 vote. Johnson proposed raising the rate by $3 to $13.10; his amendment lost 13-28.

Johnson is also concerned about oats, a crop South Dakota leads the nation in harvesting. In 1987, he added his Oats Promotion Act to the budget-reconciliation bill. The measure allowed more oats to be planted in 1988-90, exempting the crop from acreage limits.

In the 101st Congress, Johnson won enactment of a bill to mint gold, silver and ordinary

South Dakota

At large

The contrasts of beauty and poverty in South Dakota are striking. Its varied and breathtaking landscape, with stark mountains, desert canyons and sweeping farmland and grassland, has helped make tourism the second-largest industry.

But the violent battles that raged a century ago between white settlers and American Indians have left a terrible legacy. On South Dakota's numerous Indian reservations, unemployment and poverty are rife: More than half the people live below the poverty level; nearly one-quarter of the work force is jobless. Shannon County, home to the Pine Ridge Indian Reservation, has a poverty rate of 63 percent, the highest in the nation.

Wounded Knee is located in Shannon County; there in 1890, 250 Sioux were massacred in one day, after their chief, Sitting Bull, had been killed.

State lawmakers declared 1990 a Year of Reconciliation, and Gov. George Mickelson invited tribal representatives to sit cross-legged in the Capitol rotunda and smoke the peace pipe. The state has renamed Columbus Day, calling it Native American Day, and state officials drafted an elementary and high school curriculum to include Indian studies. South Dakota ranks 45th in terms of population among the 50 states, but it has the fourth-highest percentage of Indians in its population.

Republican Mickelson was elected to a second term in 1990 on a pledge to try to boost the state's economy, but returning from an out-of-state economic development trip in April 1993, he and several others died in a plane crash. He was succeeded by Lt. Gov. Walter Miller, also a Republican, who will complete the term, which runs through 1994.

The Missouri River, running north to south through the center of South Dakota, divides not only the geography and economy of the state, but also its political predilections.

The flat, rich farmland east of the river holds two-thirds of the state's population and nourishes an agricultural economy based on corn and soybeans. Voters in the east tend to support Democrats. "West River" is rolling, arid grassland suited for grazing and ranching. Mining, including gold mining, is also a feature of the western mountains. Most western voters are Republicans.

Ronald Reagan carried South Dakota for president in 1980 with 61 percent of the vote, and he improved to 63 percent in 1984, but disenchantment with GOP farm policy began to set in mid-decade, and when George Bush sought the White House in 1988, he managed just 53 percent against Michael S. Dukakis. In 1992, support for indpendent presidential candidate Ross Perot cut into both major-party nominees: Bush dropped to 41 percent, but he beat Bill Clinton, who got 37 percent. Perot won 22 percent.

Corn's primacy in South Dakota's economy is symbolized by the Corn Palace in Mitchell, an auditorium whose exterior is festooned with mosaics made from colored cobs.

Not far from Mitchell is the focal point of eastern South Dakota and the state's largest metropolis, Sioux Falls (Minnehaha County). The city grew 24 percent in the 1980s, to about 101,000, as it made the transition from meatpacking town to regional commerce hub. Though meatpacker John Morrell & Co. is still a major employer, the city has become a service center whose banks, insurance companies, medical facilities and retailers are affected by the health of the agricultural economy, if not entirely dependent on it. In 1992, Clinton won Minnehaha County with 42 percent.

On the western side of the Missouri, the towns are fewer, and there is still something of the old Wild West feel. Much of the majestic, high plains scenery in the 1990 Academy Award-winning film "Dances With Wolves" was shot here.

Near the western border of the state is South Dakota's second-largest city, Rapid City (Pennington County), with a population of more than 55,000. Originally a market for surrounding ranchers and farmers, it has prospered in recent years partly thanks to tourism: The Badlands, the Black Hills and Mount Rushmore are nearby.

In neighboring Lawrence County, legalized gambling has helped rejuvenate the town of Deadwood, once a gold-mining boom town. Calamity Jane and Wild Bill Hickok are buried at Mount Moriah Cemetery in Deadwood.

Bush won Pennington County with 48 percent of the vote in 1992, and he carried every other county west of the Missouri except three — all of them dominated by votes from Indian reservations.

1990 Population: 696,004. White 637,515 (92%), Black 3,258 (<1%), Other 55,231 (8%). Hispanic origin 5,252 (1%). 18 and over 497,542 (71%), 62 and over 120,737 (17%). Median age: 33.

coins to commemorate the 50th anniversary of the Mount Rushmore National Memorial. President Bush also signed his bill to exchange 12,000 acres of Black Hills forest land in South Dakota owned by a California mining company with U.S. Forest Service land in Colorado.

At Home: Johnson won his first term in 1986 with a knack for organization and an instinct for dealing with an opponent who was his own worst enemy.

It was a year dominated by militant farm protest on the Dakota plains, yet Johnson won without being a farmer or sounding militant. A little-known state senator from the extreme southeast corner of the state, he had not even been the early favorite in his own party when Daschle decided to run for the Senate.

Johnson had to beat a folksy state senator with longstanding farm credentials: Jim Burg, who had received national publicity when he led a delegation of state legislators on a farm protest mission to Washington in 1985.

The cerebral Johnson, who was one of only two lawyers in the state Senate, sometimes seemed to be arguing a case when he was socializing with voters. But a strong organization and a sophisticated direct-mail effort lifted him to a narrow primary victory.

The Republican nominee, Dale Bell, had run statewide twice before. But Bell's belligerent ideological conservatism and the contentious nature of his earlier campaigns hobbled him. The state also was rife with resentment of Reagan administration farm policies. Johnson's strategy was to avoid controversy and make himself the vehicle for Bell's critics in both parties; he presented himself simply as a moderate and an experienced alternative to Bell. In the Legislature, Johnson had maintained friendly relations with both sides and worked well with GOP Gov. William J. Janklow. His approach won him backing from the state's major banking interests and the Realtors' association.

Bell tried labeling Johnson a George McGovern liberal and a captive of special interests. At the same time, Bell, whose strength had always been among "movement conservatives," tried to distance himself from Reagan farm policies, developing an opposition-style theme of "send them a message." The voters sent Bell a message instead: Johnson won 53 of the state's 66 counties and nearly 60 percent of the overall vote.

In 1988, the state's leading Republicans assessed their chances of unseating Johnson and chose to skip the race. State Treasurer David Volk, who had been winning elections since 1972, was the challenger, and he enjoyed a united front of GOP support. But Johnson nonetheless carried every county en route to 72 percent of the vote.

His win kept alive a streak: the state has not turned out a first-term House member since 1898. It also spurred talk of Johnson's challenging Pressler in 1990 — a race Johnson declined to make. Instead, he garnered two-thirds of the vote in winning re-election against a Republican opponent who proposed reducing House membership to 300 as a budget-cutting move. In 1992, Johnson sailed to another term with 69 percent of the vote.

Committees

Agriculture (9th of 28 Democrats)
General Farm Commodities (chairman); Environment, Credit & Rural Development

Natural Resources (14th of 28 Democrats)
National Parks, Forests & Public Lands; Native American Affairs

Elections

1992 General		
Tim Johnson (D)	230,070	(69%)
John Timmer (R)	89,375	(27%)
Ronald Wieczorek (I)	6,746	(2%)
Robert J. Newland (LIBERT)	3,931	(1%)
1990 General		
Tim Johnson (D)	173,814	(68%)
Don Frankenfeld (R)	83,484	(32%)

Previous Winning Percentages: **1988** (72%) **1986** (59%)

District Vote for President

	1992	
D	124,888	(37%)
R	136,718	(41%)
I	73,295	(22%)

Campaign Finance

	Receipts	Receipts from PACs		Expend-itures
1992				
Johnson (D)	$452,528	$221,653	(49%)	$376,741
Timmer (R)	$171,489	$16,330	(10%)	$170,143
Newland (LIBERT)	$1,000	0		$1,000
1990				
Johnson (D)	$516,816	$251,800	(49%)	$463,625
Frankenfeld (R)	$215,087	$6,608	(3%)	$211,617

Key Votes

1993	
Require parental notification of minors' abortions	N
Require unpaid family and medical leave	Y
Approve national "motor voter" registration bill	Y
Approve budget increasing taxes and reducing deficit	Y
Approve economic stimulus plan	Y
1992	
Approve balanced-budget constitutional amendment	Y
Close down space station program	Y
Approve U.S. aid for former Soviet Union	Y
Allow shifting funds from defense to domestic programs	Y
1991	
Extend unemployment benefits using deficit financing	Y
Approve waiting period for handgun purchases	N
Authorize use of force in Persian Gulf	N

Voting Studies

	Presidential Support		Party Unity		Conservative Coalition	
Year	**S**	**O**	**S**	**O**	**S**	**O**
1992	29	71	81	17	40	60
1991	34	66	80	19	54	46
1990	25	75	82	17	54	46
1989	34	66	83	17	41	59
1988	25	75	77	22	66	34
1987	26	74	84	14	56	44

Interest Group Ratings

Year	ADA	AFL-CIO	CCUS	ACU
1992	70	67	50	32
1991	65	83	40	20
1990	67	83	36	25
1989	85	83	40	21
1988	70	93	36	28
1987	80	81	27	13

Tennessee

STATE DATA

Governor:
Ned McWherter (D)
First elected: 1986
Length of term: 4 years
Term expires: 1/95
Salary: $85,000
Term limit: 2 consecutive terms
Phone: (615) 741-2001
Born: Oct. 15, 1930; Palmersville, Tenn.
Education: Graduated from Dresden H.S., 1948
Military Service: National Guard, 1948-69
Occupation: Farmer; businessman
Family: Widowed; two children
Religion: Methodist
Political Career: Tenn. House, 1969-87

Lt. Gov.: John S. Wilder (D)
First elected: 1971
Length of term: 2 years (elected by the State Senate)
Term expires: 1/95
Salary: $49,500
Phone: (615) 741-2368

State election official: (615) 741-7956
Democratic headquarters: (615) 327-9779
Republican headquarters: (615) 292-9497

REDISTRICTING

Tennessee retained its nine House seats in reapportionment. The legislature passed the map May 6, 1992; the governor signed it May 7.

STATE LEGISLATURE

General Assembly. Meets for 90 days over 2 years, beginning in January.

Senate: 33 members, 4-year terms
1992 breakdown: 19D, 14R; 30 men, 3 women; 30 whites, 3 blacks
Salary: $16,500
Phone: (615) 741-2730

House of Representatives: 99 members, 2-year terms
1992 breakdown: 63D, 36R; 86 men, 13 women; 87 whites, 12 blacks
Salary: $16,500
Phone: (615) 741-2901

URBAN STATISTICS

City	Pop.
Memphis	610,337
Mayor W. W. Herenton, N-P	
Nashville-Davidson	488,374
Mayor Philip N. Bredesen, D	
Knoxville	165,121
Mayor Victor Ashe, R	
Chattanooga	152,466
Mayor Gene Roberts, R	
Clarksville	75,494
Mayor Donald W. Trotter, N-P	

U.S. CONGRESS

Senate: 2 D, 0 R
House: 6 D, 3 R

TERM LIMITS

For Congress: No
For state offices: No

ELECTIONS

1992 Presidential Vote

Bill Clinton	47.1%
George Bush	42.4%
Ross Perot	10.1%

1988 Presidential Vote

George Bush	58%
Michael S. Dukakis	42%

1984 Presidential Vote

Ronald Reagan	58%
Walter F. Mondale	42%

POPULATION

1990 population		4,877,185
1980 population		4,591,120
Percent change		+6%
Rank among states:		17
White		83%
Black		16%
Hispanic		1%
Asian or Pacific islander		1%
Urban		61%
Rural		39%
Born in state		69%
Foreign-born		1%
Under age 18	1,216,604	25%
Ages 18-64	3,041,763	62%
65 and older	618,818	13%
Median age		34

MISCELLANEOUS

Capital: Nashville
Number of counties: 95
Per capita income: $16,325 (1991)
Rank among states: 37
Total area: 42,144 sq. miles
Rank among states: 34

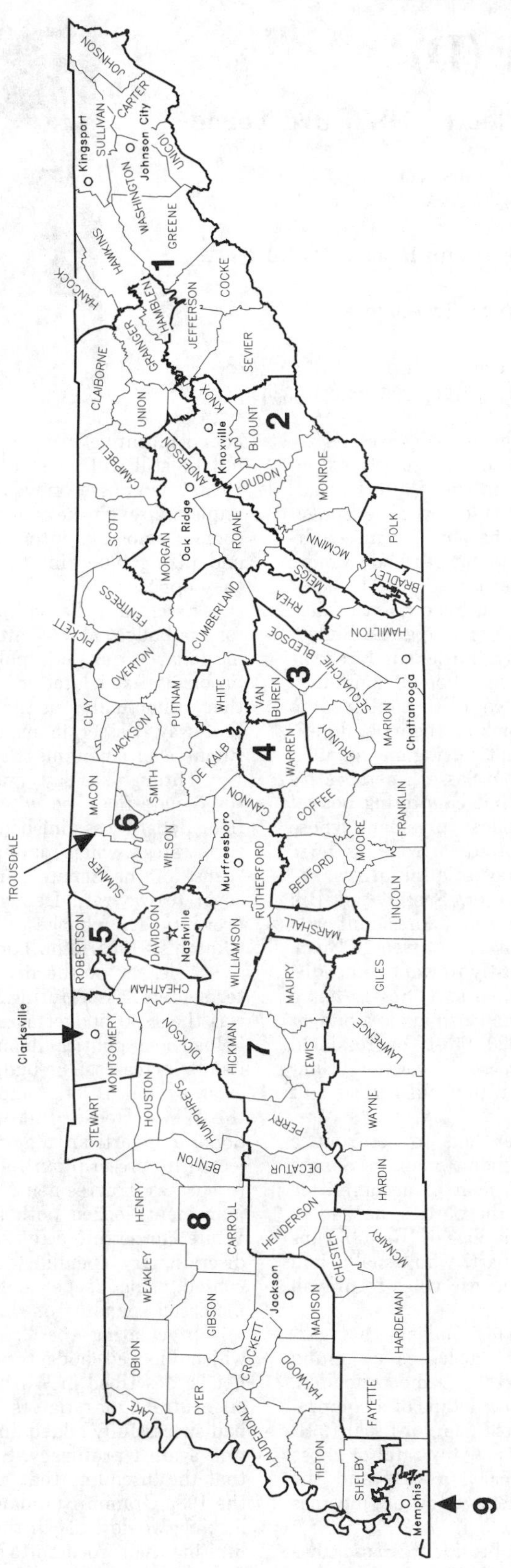

JOHNSON
SULLIVAN
CARTER
Kingsport
Johnson City
UNICOI
WASHINGTON
HAWKINS
GREENE
1
HANCOCK
HAMBLEN
COCKE
JEFFERSON
GRAINGER
CLAIBORNE
SEVIER
UNION
KNOX
Knoxville
BLOUNT
2
CAMPBELL
ANDERSON
Oak Ridge
LOUDON
MONROE
SCOTT
MORGAN
ROANE
MCMINN
POLK
MEIGS
BRADLEY
FENTRESS
CUMBERLAND
RHEA
PICKETT
HAMILTON
BLEDSOE
OVERTON
SEQUATCHIE
Chattanooga
3
CLAY
PUTNAM
WHITE
VAN BUREN
JACKSON
MARION
GRUNDY
WARREN
4
DE KALB
SMITH
MACON
CANNON
COFFEE
FRANKLIN
6
TROUSDALE
WILSON
Murfreesboro
MOORE
SUMNER
RUTHERFORD
BEDFORD
LINCOLN
ROBERTSON
5
DAVIDSON
Nashville
WILLIAMSON
MARSHALL
CHEATHAM
MAURY
GILES
Clarksville
MONTGOMERY
DICKSON
HICKMAN
7
LEWIS
LAWRENCE
STEWART
HOUSTON
HUMPHREYS
PERRY
WAYNE
BENTON
DECATUR
HARDIN
HENRY
CARROLL
8
HENDERSON
CHESTER
MCNAIRY
WEAKLEY
GIBSON
Jackson
MADISON
HARDEMAN
OBION
CROCKETT
HAYWOOD
LAKE
DYER
FAYETTE
LAUDERDALE
TIPTON
SHELBY
Memphis
9

Jim Sasser (D)

Of Nashville — Elected 1976; 3rd Term

Born: Sept. 30, 1936, Memphis, Tenn.
Education: U. of Tennessee, 1954-55; Vanderbilt U., B.A. 1958, J.D. 1961.
Military Service: Marine Corps Reserve, 1957-63.
Occupation: Lawyer.
Family: Wife, Mary Gorman; two children.
Religion: Protestant.
Political Career: No previous office.
Capitol Office: 363 Russell Bldg. 20510; 224-3344.

In Washington: The stars in Sasser's zodiac finally aligned after the 1992 elections put a like-minded Democrat in the White House.

Sasser joked when he took over the Budget Committee in 1989 that he had become chairman only because he could not persuade a more senior committee member to take the job. But he soon stopped laughing at his own wisecrack.

For four years after occupying the Budget chair, Sasser was doubly burdened: First, he had to deal with grueling "budget summits" and cope with convoluted rules contrived to prevent Congress from making the federal deficit bigger, even if it wasn't getting any smaller. Second — and worse, from Sasser's perspective — he had to spend his time countering budget proposals from a Republican president whose priorities were vastly different from his own, instead of pursuing Democratic initiatives.

In early 1993, however, Sasser had Bill Clinton in the White House, a president who needed his help and who was not George Bush, a man Sasser seemed mostly to want to needle. Although generally a genial sort, Sasser has a sharp political edge. When Bush made a budget offer in the spring of 1990, most congressional leaders were conciliatory. Sasser was not. "Simply putting a new suit on that old corpse isn't going to revive it," he said.

Under Bush, Sasser had to confront a paradox in his role as point man in Senate budget debates. As chairman of a committee closely divided between the parties, he had to be far more accommodating of Republicans than his House counterpart, who usually had more than enough Democratic votes to prevail in committee.

But even in producing budgets that garnered support across the aisle, Sasser found ways to present them with a Democratic spin. Thus, when recounting the details of a comprehensive, summit-negotiated deal for fiscal 1991, Sasser readily stressed a new tax rate for those earning more than $175,000 a year and the tightening of allowed deductions on incomes greater than $125,000.

With a Democratic president, Sasser has added incentive to cater less to conservatives, but he still will have to step nimbly. In early 1993, when Sasser moved Clinton's first budget request through the committee, he had to cajole some Democrats into supporting a spending and taxing blueprint that contained elements they opposed.

Essentially, he told panel Democrats: Vote for the budget now — after all, its specifics are in dollar terms, not policy — and get your problems fixed later in a "reconciliation" bill that will actually put the budget into effect. In that way, Sasser managed to stave off every Republican amendment in committee.

Through six days and 45 roll-call votes on the Senate floor, he prevailed again. After the floor debate was finished, Sasser boasted that the strategy, when combined with a blizzard of "sense of the Senate" amendments that gave cover to wayward Democrats, enabled him to prevent GOP changes to a single number in Clinton's $1.5 trillion budget.

A legacy of the divided government that tormented Sasser during Bush's four-year term was the 1990 budget agreement that ironically helped spell political doom for Bush, because of its tax increases. The budget deal was produced after a months-long summit negotiation with the White House. But when the talking was done, a bipartisan majority of the House rejected its prescription for reducing the deficit. A successor agreement, approved before adjournment, locked both the Congress and the White House into a five-year deal that capped discretionary spending, and for a time prevented using deeper defense cuts to finance increased spending on domestic programs.

In creating the "pay-as-you-go" system, which blocked budgetary changes that could not be described in Washington lingo as "deficit-neutral," negotiators contended that they had successfully added another layer of protection against profligacy. Sasser and others said that the discipline that had been promised by the 1985 Gramm-Rudman law, but found to be lacking, would exist in the new process. But in limiting their freedom to set priorities, the deal also further drained meaning from the yearly deliberations of the Budget committees — which had been declining in perceived firepower anyway.

Sasser, whose other Senate roles include chairing the Appropriations Subcommittee on Military Construction, chafed under the new constraints. Though hardly a spendthrift by congressional standards, Sasser is no deficit hawk, either. It was Sasser who led the 1992 fight in the Senate to tear down the "walls" erected in the late 1990 budget agreement, which were intended to prevent domestic-side appropriators from tapping into the defense budget. Sasser and the Senate Democratic leadership could not get past a filibuster on the floor over a bill to breach the walls. A motion to cut off debate failed to gain the necessary 60 votes, falling short 50-48. Eight Democrats jumped ship on the vote.

In early 1993, Sasser was a booster of Clinton's proposal to spend an extra $16.3 billion to stimulate job growth after the 1990-91 recession, which had left unemployment at about 7 percent. Earlier, in January 1992, he had joined with Maryland Democrat Paul S. Sarbanes to propose a stimulus bill in excess of $50 billion to aid cities struggling to recover from the recession.

When Clinton produced his first budget in early 1993, Sasser defended it against critics who carped that it would not result even years later in putting an end to the red ink. "The Congress and the administration have gone about as far as we can in deficit reduction without endangering the economy," Sasser said.

From his seat on the Banking Committee, Sasser has often cast a critical eye at the Federal Reserve's monetary policy, worrying that the Fed's tendency toward tight credit harms growth. In the 103rd Congress, Sasser took over the Subcommittee on International Finance and Monetary Policy. And he signed onto a Sarbanes bill that would strip the presidents of the regional Federal Reserve banks — who are not accountable to Congress or the president — of their power to help control credit.

Sasser is quite willing to invest taxpayers' money in federal projects he favors, but he casts a decidedly jaundiced eye at some big defense and big science projects. By razor-thin margins, the Senate defeated his 1991 amendments to terminate the B-2 Stealth bomber program (which had already been curtailed), and to cut back the Strategic Defense Initiative. And in 1992, the Budget Committee refused to support Sasser's proposal to cut defense spending generally by $5 billion more than Bush had requested; three Democrats abandoned him. He had better luck on the floor in 1992, winning his amendment to pare back SDI.

Arguing on the Senate floor in 1992 against the multibillion-dollar superconducting super collider, Sasser urged termination of the Texas-based atom-smasher: "Allowing the super collider to continue to suck up billions of research dollars that might otherwise have gone to countless smaller-scale projects may be the greatest threat of all to our leadership role in basic scientific research." The amendment he backed failed by a wide margin.

Sasser had spent more than a decade in the Senate without a major focus before taking the Budget job. Where he is now responsible for the broad outlines of government fiscal policy, previously he had picked at its million-dollar footnotes and line items to ferret out waste and fraud. He once boasted of saving $2 million a year by deleting federal money for watering indoor plants.

In his first dozen years on Budget, Sasser had rarely been a major participant in its deliberations, and in the mid-1980s, he told a reporter he wanted off. Sasser remained, but even so, he did not seem eager to claim the top seat when Chairman Lawton Chiles announced his impending retirement in 1988. Sasser was third in line, but the more senior Democrats — Ernest F. Hollings and J. Bennett Johnston — already were committee chairmen.

Sasser did not distinguish himself in his debut, helping to draft the fiscal 1990 budget in 1989. But neither did anyone else. Bush was intent on setting a more conciliatory tone than existed throughout President Ronald Reagan's tenure, and Congress proved willing to accept bipartisanship over serious deficit reduction.

White House and congressional leaders talked for nine weeks; Sasser moved cautiously, reflecting both his nature and relative inexperience. By April, the negotiators had a compromise budget that met the law's $100 billion deficit target, thanks mainly to accounting gimmicks, rosy economic assumptions and unspecified taxes. Though the pact drew many scoffs, lawmakers were in no mood to fight. "This is the best we can do at this particular time in our history," Sasser told the Senate.

Before taking the Budget chair, Sasser had begun assuming a broader role in foreign policy debates. He spoke against Reagan's policies toward Nicaragua, and tried to develop a consensus Democratic stand on contra aid that would put the party on record in support of a diplomatic solution without seeming to overlook Nicaragua's anti-democratic actions.

But even in this area, Sasser's involvement sprang from his line-by-line approach to policymaking. In the 98th Congress, while others debated overall U.S. strategy in Central America, Sasser was studying federal spending for construction of military facilities in Honduras, Nicaragua's neighbor. As ranking Democrat — and chairman since 1987 — of Appropriations' Military Construction Subcommittee, he concluded the Reagan administration was preparing for potential armed intervention in the region. Landing strips and facilities for temporary use in training exercises actually were intended to be permanent, Sasser argued. But he had mixed success in attacking the spending in Honduras.

When Reagan made a televised pitch for contra aid in 1986, Democratic leaders picked Sasser to give the party's response. That year, Sasser offered his own proposal tying aid to renewed negotiations; if Nicaragua's rulers refused to negotiate, military aid would be released to the rebels. But that satisfied neither those who favored immediate aid nor those who wanted none at all. Sasser's amendment was rejected by a 2-to-1 margin.

He later adopted a more critical approach. "We're going precisely down the path that this country traveled in Vietnam," he said in August. He did better with a proposal to kill the entire aid program, losing 54-46.

In the 100th Congress, Sasser had a high-profile role on another issue, after a 1987 Iraqi attack on a U.S. frigate in the Persian Gulf drew critical attention to the Reagan policy of providing Navy escorts for Kuwaiti tankers there. Sasser was part of a Democratic leadership team that reviewed military plans for the escort policy. Also, then-Majority Leader Robert C. Byrd, D-W.V., named Sasser one of three senators to go to the Middle East to investigate. Upon his return from the region, Sasser said Reagan should either get Kuwait to withdraw its request for protection or enlist allies' help. "We should not sail in the gulf's troubled waters alone," he said.

Sasser came to the Senate as a loyal supporter of Jimmy Carter. He cooled, however, when the administration opposed some Tennessee federal projects, such as the Tellico Dam that was held up on environmental grounds. Pressed to vote with Carter to transfer the Panama Canal, Sasser did, but not without complaint.

Sasser has maintained a liberal-to-moderate record, but he sometimes shows the strain of coming from a basically conservative Southern state. Voting with his party on such issues as the Persian Gulf, the Panama Canal and social controversies does not come easy to him. One issue with potentially serious political consequences came up in 1982, a Sasser re-election year: He cast the tie-breaking procedural vote to kill Jesse Helms' amendment aimed at restricting abortions. But he consistently supported Helms' bid to restore voluntary prayer in public schools by stripping federal courts of jurisdiction over the issue.

Much later, in May 1993, when the Senate considered the nomination of Roberta Achtenberg, a lesbian, for an assistant secretary's post in the Department of Housing and Urban Development, Sasser voted no.

At Home: Sasser's 1976 Senate campaign in behalf of "a government that reflects our decency" bore a pronounced and deliberate similarity to Carter's call for "a government as good as its people." When Carter won the Tennessee presidential primary that year with 78 percent of the vote, Sasser joked that he wanted not only to cling to Carter's coattails, but to get inside the coat.

It was a successful strategy. In November, Carter won Tennessee by nearly 200,000 votes, helping Sasser to a comfortable victory over GOP Sen. William E. Brock III, who a year earlier was considered safe for re-election.

Sasser had used his three-year chairmanship of the state Democratic Party to lay a base of support. His chief Democratic rival was liberal Nashville businessman John J. Hooker, whose unsuccessful tries for the governorship in 1966 and 1970 had given him wide name recognition but a loser's image. Sasser was endorsed by several minority and labor groups who saw him as a fresh face and a possible winner. With support from most of the party leadership, he defeated Hooker convincingly.

Brock displayed the same organizing skill that later was to make him a successful national GOP chairman. But his background as a candy heir, his upper-crust image and his quiet personal style contrasted unfavorably with Sasser's down-to-earth manner and ready humor.

Sasser portrayed Brock as a country-club Republican, a special-interest senator representing banks and insurance companies. It was a perfect issue in a state always susceptible to populist rhetoric, and doubly so with Carter reinforcing Sasser's themes.

Because Sasser compiled a generally noncontroversial record and avoided political blunders during his first term, he was well-positioned for re-election in 1982. Some conservative Republicans thought Sasser's support was soft, and on that supposition GOP Rep. Robin L. Beard gave up a safe House district to try for the Senate.

Beard failed utterly in searching for a theme that would induce voters to desert Sasser. At first, Beard called Sasser a free-spending "Kennedy liberal." Then, in his ads, he unveiled a small plastic mouse, dubbed "flipping Jimmy," meant to convince voters that Sasser had shifted from left to center as his re-election neared. In the end, Beard was stressing the abortion and school prayer issues in an attempt to mobilize religious fundamentalists and others with strong feelings on social matters.

Sasser occasionally sparred with Beard, but mostly he stressed his work to improve government accounting practices and reduce bureaucratic costs. He was able to stay on the offensive by blaming economic hard times on Reaganomics. Beard had to contend with Tennesseans' lukewarm feelings for Reagan — Carter nearly carried the state in 1980 — and with an unemployment rate that was above the national average throughout 1982.

Sasser buried Beard in Middle and West Tennessee, and even carried traditionally Republican East Tennessee; no Democrat had done that since the GOP began seriously contesting statewide elections in the mid-1960s.

Sasser's 1982 showing was still on many minds six years later. GOP leaders again insisted Sasser's support was soft, but they failed to recruit a proven vote-getter, such as former GOP Gov. Lamar Alexander.

Their nominee was little-known Kingsport attorney Bill Andersen, a candidate who spent much of his considerable energy introducing himself to members of his own party.

Andersen criticized Sasser as a man lacking the stature of the state's other leading politicians, including junior Democratic Sen. Al Gore and Alexander. But Andersen had trouble raising money and was not really in a position to talk about stature. Again Sasser romped, taking all but one county in Republican East Tennessee.

Committees

Budget (Chairman)

Appropriations (6th of 16 Democrats)
Military Construction (chairman); Commerce, Justice, State & Judiciary; Defense; Energy & Water Development; Transportation

Banking, Housing & Urban Affairs (4th of 11 Democrats)
International Finance & Monetary Policy (chairman); Securities

Governmental Affairs (4th of 8 Democrats)
General Services, Federalism & the District of Columbia (chairman); Federal Services, Post Office & Civil Service; Permanent Subcommittee on Investigations

Joint Organization of Congress

Elections

1988 General		
Jim Sasser (D)	1,020,061	(65%)
Bill Andersen (R)	541,033	(35%)

Previous Winning Percentages: **1982** (62%) **1976** (53%)

Campaign Finance

	Receipts	Receipts from PACs		Expend-itures
1988				
Sasser (D)	$3,218,986	$1,379,817	(43%)	$3,069,615
Andersen (R)	$612,421	$26,925	(4%)	$613,704

Key Votes

1993	
Require unpaid family and medical leave	Y
Approve national "motor voter" registration bill	Y
Approve budget increasing taxes and reducing deficit	Y
Support president's right to lift military gay ban	Y
1992	
Approve school-choice pilot program	N
Allow shifting funds from defense to domestic programs	Y
Oppose deeper cuts in spending for SDI	N
1991	
Approve waiting period for handgun purchases	Y
Raise senators' pay and ban honoraria	N
Authorize use of force in Persian Gulf	N
Confirm Clarence Thomas to Supreme Court	N

Voting Studies

	Presidential Support		Party Unity		Conservative Coalition	
Year	**S**	**O**	**S**	**O**	**S**	**O**
1992	35	65	85	14	58	39
1991	36	64	91	9	40	60
1990	33	67	90	9	41	59
1989	55	43	89	7	29	68
1988	41	56	87	11	38	59
1987	35	65	94	6	38	63
1986	24	76	87	13	37	63
1985	33	67	87	13	52	48
1984	34	58	88	8	30	62
1983	39	58	85	11	35 †	65 †
1982	42	55	72	25	62	36
1981	57	40	72	17	57	29

† Not eligible for all recorded votes.

Interest Group Ratings

Year	ADA	AFL-CIO	CCUS	ACU
1992	95	83	10	7
1991	90	83	0	5
1990	72	78	17	9
1989	85	100	57	8
1988	75	86	43	9
1987	80	90	28	12
1986	70	87	32	17
1985	60	86	38	26
1984	90	91	37	18
1983	75	93	32	16
1982	55	84	50	47
1981	45	59	67	31

Harlan Mathews (D)

Of Nashville — Appointed 1993; 1st Term

Appointed to the Senate Jan. 1993.

Born: Jan. 17, 1927, Sumiton, Ala.

Education: Jacksonville State College, B.A. 1949; Vanderbilt U., M.A. 1958; Nashville School of Law, J.D. 1962.

Military Service: Navy, 1944-46.

Occupation: Public official.

Family: Wife, Patsy Jones; two children.

Religion: Protestant.

Political Career: Tenn. commissioner of finance and administration, 1961-71; Tenn. treasurer, 1974-87.

Capitol Office: 506 Dirksen Bldg. 20510; 224-4944.

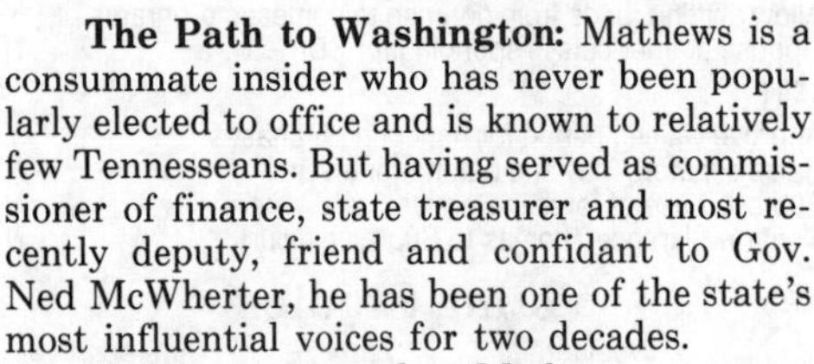

The Path to Washington: Mathews is a consummate insider who has never been popularly elected to office and is known to relatively few Tennesseans. But having served as commissioner of finance, state treasurer and most recently deputy, friend and confidant to Gov. Ned McWherter, he has been one of the state's most influential voices for two decades.

McWherter turned to Mathews as a caretaker after dismissing the idea of choosing a fellow Democrat who would try to hold on to the seat vacated by Al Gore when a special election is held in 1994.

Mathews' first act as senator-designate was to make it clear he is taking the job for only two years. "I promise the people of Tennessee. . . . I will not spend a single hour worrying about reelection, because I do not plan to seek reelection," he said at a news conference after his appointment.

But just a few months later, he announced that he was reconsidering. In April, Mathews filed a statement of candidacy with the Federal Election Commission, a move that allows him to spend more money canvassing the state.

Mathews promised a decision by the end of 1993 and said he was reconsidering not because he had a "burning desire to be a senator for the rest of my life" but because supporters had urged him to. At the same time, he added, "There's no question about the Senate work being challenging. It offers a level of service, coupled with responsibility, above any that I've had an opportunity to do before."

At his first news conference as an appointed senator, Mathews described himself as a fiscal conservative and said he would concentrate on the deficit and health issues.

In 1969, when he was Tennessee's commissioner of finance, Mathews helped put the state's first Medicaid program in place at a yearly cost of $38 million. The price tag has risen since then, he said, to $2.8 billion.

"It's just symptomatic of what's happening," Mathews said. "I have two granddaughters. They'll never be able to afford a home . . . unless we find some way" to solve the government's financial problems.

Mathews said his priority would be to help break the deadlock in Washington, and he predicted that his voting record would not be substantially different from Gore's.

An early backer of Bill Clinton's presidential candidacy, Mathews had at first insisted that he was not interested in the Senate appointment and instead publicly declared his interest in getting Clinton to put him on the board of directors of the Tennessee Valley Authority (TVA).

Mathews, who has had two brushes with corruption probes but has never been charged, dismissed suggestions that he could not have survived the FBI background check for the TVA post.

Mathews was called before a federal grand jury in 1989 investigating alleged ties between illegal bingo gambling and state officials.

Reports at the time said he was asked about alleged contributions from the gambling interests to McWherter's campaign and a political action committee that Mathews controlled. Also questioned was Tennessee Secretary of State Gentry Crowell, who committed suicide soon thereafter.

During Mathews' term as state treasurer in the 1980s, he came under scrutiny for depositing about $100 million of state funds in financial institutions controlled by two friends, brothers Jake and C. H. Butcher, who were subsequently imprisoned for bank fraud. Mathews insisted at the time that the state deposits were properly protected and no state funds were lost.

Mathews was born in Alabama but settled in Tennessee. He began government service in 1950 and was named to the budget staff of Gov. Frank Clement in 1954, rising to be commissioner of the Department of Finance and Administration in 1961.

Mathews served 10 years as commissioner, then left the government when Republicans took over the Statehouse.

Mathews returned to Nashville in 1973 to become a legislative aide to the state comptroller and was elected state treasurer by the General Assembly in 1974.

In 1986, Mathews managed McWherter's gubernatorial campaign. After that, he was McWherter's deputy, or Cabinet secretary, working mostly on budget and financial matters.

Upon his arrival in Congress, Mathews was assigned to the Energy and Foreign Relations committees. He picked up a seat on the Rules Committee as well. The seat on Energy will allow him to keep a close eye on the Oak Ridge nuclear facilities in Tennessee.

Committees

Energy & Natural Resources (10th of 11 Democrats)
Mineral Resources Development & Production (vice chairman); Energy Research & Development; Renewable Energy

Foreign Relations (11th of 11 Democrats)
East Asian & Pacific Affairs; Near Eastern & South Asian Affairs; Western Hemisphere & Peace Corps Affairs

Rules & Administration (9th of 9 Democrats)

Joint Printing

Key Votes

1993

Require unpaid family and medical leave	Y
Approve national "motor voter" registration bill	Y
Approve budget increasing taxes and reducing deficit	Y
Support president's right to lift military gay ban	Y

1 James H. Quillen (R)

Of Kingsport — Elected 1962; 16th Term

Born: Jan. 11, 1916, near Gate City, Va.
Education: Graduated from Dobyns-Bennett High School, 1934.
Military Service: Navy, 1942-46.
Occupation: Newspaper publisher; real estate and insurance broker; banker.
Family: Wife, Cecile Cox.
Religion: Methodist.
Political Career: Tenn. House, 1955-63.
Capitol Office: 102 Cannon Bldg. 20515; 225-6356.

In Washington: Always an obscure member of Congress, Quillen has receded even further into the shadows of Capitol Hill after 30 years in the House.

The onetime ranking Republican on the Rules Committee faded quickly from the national scene when he relinquished that post in 1990 to make way for a new generation of more combative Republicans.

Quillen did not seem to mind losing what limited time in the spotlight he had. Never concerned with increasing his clout in Congress, giving up the ranking spot gave him the freedom to focus more attention on serving the constituents of his upper East Tennessee district — an effort that has paid off handsomely, bringing him the kind of popularity and influence on his home turf that few members achieve.

Tennessee's statewide GOP candidates have learned that they must get along with Quillen to succeed in his territory, despite the fact that the numbers favor Republicans. Former GOP Gov. Winfield Dunn was unsuccessful in his bid to return to the governorship in 1986 — Democrat Ned McWherter defeated him — in part because Quillen's network in the usually heavily Republican 1st did not rally around him. Quillen and Dunn parted ways in a feud several years earlier.

And in 1988, Quillen's public praise for the state's senior senator, Democrat Jim Sasser, helped doom GOP candidate Bill Andersen's long-shot bid. Andersen originally had shown some interest in taking Quillen's spot in the House, and Quillen had been miffed by that apparent attempt to nudge him out.

Quillen will be nearly 80 when the 103rd Congress ends, and he has often been rumored to be considering retirement. In March 1993, he had quintuple bypass heart surgery. But given Andersen's experience in 1988, it seems unlikely any Republican will start jockeying to succeed Quillen until it is clear he is ready to go.

If Quillen is careful about lending his support to candidates in Tennessee, he is even more careful about sharing his massive campaign treasury with GOP candidates around the country. That has frustrated a number of House Republicans, who expect such a senior member to play a party-building role.

But Quillen is a self-made man with a dim view of handouts, and he has learned to work with the Democratic majority to get what he wants for his district. It is not in Quillen's interest to give money to conservative candidates who aim to topple the Democratic power structure with which Quillen has reached accommodation.

Rules can be a place for partisan strategizing and legislative intrigue, but Quillen is not the person for it. He would rather look after his constituents.

Though Quillen relinquished the ranking spot voluntarily (he cited his wife's ill health), there was no groundswell in the GOP Conference for him to reconsider his decision. His willingness to work with the Democrats from his senior perch often irked the more-partisan younger generation of House Republicans, who favor the more aggressive and confrontational style epitomized by Minority Whip Newt Gingrich of Georgia — and invoked by Rep. Gerald B. H. Solomon of New York, Quillen's replacement as ranking Republican.

Quillen, who still holds a seat on Rules, did speak out at times, challenging Democratic procedures or policies. In 1987, when the House was voting for $725 million in new aid for the homeless, Quillen was concerned that the money would promote the problem, not redress it. "I don't want the Congress to create more homelessness on our streets," he said. "Instead of solving the problem, we would make it entirely more complicated."

When Congress considered legislation in 1989 to bail out and restructure the savings and loan industry, Quillen allied himself with S&L interests, pressing to allow thrifts that carry on their books "supervisory good will" — a form of intangible capital — to count it toward their capital requirements.

The treatment of good will became the

Tennessee 1

Northeast — Tri-cities

The Tennessee Valley Authority freed this district and much of East Tennessee from the pervasive rural poverty of an earlier era. Isolated highland towns, tobacco patches and livestock clearings were once the norm in the 1st, but small cities have grown up around industries drawn to the area by the availability of TVA power.

However, industry has not changed the 1st's GOP voting habits. For most of the past 70 years, only two people have represented the 1st, both Republicans. In 1992, it did Bill Clinton little good here to put Tennessee Sen. Al Gore on his ticket; George Bush still won by 15 points. Voters are not blindly Republican, though. A majority did vote Democratic in the non-competitive Senate elections of 1988 and 1990, backing Jim Sasser and Gore.

There are pockets of genuine Democrats, primarily in the Tri-cities area of Kingsport, Bristol and Johnson City. About 45 percent of the district's people live in this extreme northeastern corner of Tennessee, and the area's industrial work force occasionally helps Democrats win local offices. Sporadic support for Democrats, though, should not be construed as liberalism; the union influence remains small, and no Democrat campaigns to the left of moderate.

Whatever Democratic votes can be squeezed out of the Tri-cities, the rural counties in the district usually drown them. Routinely at election time the rural areas deliver the highest GOP tallies in the state: Voters have a deep-seated suspicion of big government and an antipathy toward the Democratic Party dating to their ancestors' Union loyalties during the Civil War.

Economic diversity helped the 1st weather the recent recession without much trouble. The Tri-cities' industrial base includes manufacturers of paper, glass, medical equipment and electronics; employment at major companies such as Eastman Kodak's chemical division in Kingsport has held steady. The Tri-cities have each spent the past few years annexing the land inside the triangle they form, and their borders now abut one other. Regional cooperation is marred by squabbles over which city is responsible for utilities and taxes in borderline industrial parks.

Economic success in the population centers, however, has not brought better times to the entire area. Three counties in the 1st rank among the state's poorest: more than 40 percent of Hancock County's residents live below the poverty line. Farmers raise tobacco, poultry and livestock; there is zinc and limestone mining.

To the south, in Sevier County, a tourism boom pushed the population up 23 percent in the 1980s. Millions every year visit the Great Smoky Mountains National Park, some stopping along the way to take in attractions such as Dollywood, a theme park launched by country music star Dolly Parton. On the edge of the national park, Gatlinburg is chock-full of motels and amusements, but tourists lost their chance to see the world's largest hairball when the original Ripley's Believe it or Not museum burned in 1992.

1990 Population: 541,875. White 528,585 (98%), Black 10,272 (2%), Other 3,018 (<1%). Hispanic origin 2,132 (<1%). 18 and over 418,894 (77%), 62 and over 92,276 (17%). Median age: 36.

most charged issue during the thrift debate, cast largely as a question of treating thrifts in keeping with past practices vs. protecting taxpayers already being asked to bail out the ailing industry. For those such as Quillen who wanted to be lenient toward thrifts carrying large amounts of good will, the issue was one of fairness and survival for a number of S&Ls. "A Deal Is a Deal," read a button often sported by Quillen. Their efforts, however, ultimately proved unsuccessful.

But over the years, Quillen has been most conspicuous when Tennessee is directly involved in an issue. An emergency appropriations bill came to Rules in 1985 packed with controversial water projects — including one worth $5 million in Quillen's district. The committee sent the bill to the floor with a rule that left a number of water projects vulnerable to procedural objections — but the projects backed by Quillen and some other Rules members were protected.

At times, the Tennessean's questions to committee witnesses are notable for comic relief. He once broke up a hearing at Rules by putting a goldfish in his water pitcher. The hearing was on a bill to soften the Endangered Species Act, which was threatening to block construction of the $119 million Tellico Dam in Tennessee because it would destroy the habitat of a small fish, the snail darter. Quillen was a booster of the dam. He said he wanted to see how long it would take people to notice the fish in his pitcher, hoping to demonstrate the insignificance of the even-smaller darter.

At Home: To make it to Congress in 1962,

Quillen had to weather the quarrels of a Republican Party cast into disarray by the passing of a political dynasty. GOP Rep. B. Carroll Reece, a former party national chairman, dominated 1st District politics for 40 years until his death in 1961. Reece's widow served out his term, then gave her blessing to Quillen, a four-term state representative.

Quillen called himself a staunch conservative who opposed "wasteful spending overseas to buy friendship when friendship cannot be bought." Though he got only 29 percent of the vote, that topped the five-candidate GOP primary field and gave him the nomination.

The 1st had not elected a Democrat since 1878, yet Quillen was held to 54 percent in the general election. His low total was blamed partly on GOP disunity after the hard-fought primary and partly on a higher-than-usual Democratic turnout. A longstanding patronage arrangement between Reece and local Democrats had collapsed when Reece died.

Once in office, Quillen quickly learned the skills of entrenchment. A prodigious letter-writer, he sent notes of congratulations and condolence and numerous franked mailings to his constituents. And he made the rounds to county courthouses during his frequent trips home.

By 1964, GOP factional fights had dissipated and Quillen easily won re-election. Since then, Quillen occasionally has encountered Democratic foes who complain he is little more than a "pen pal" who opposes education, health and welfare measures his rural constituents need. But none of the foes has made significant headway. In 1990, he was unopposed. In 1992, he had a Democratic challenger but still walked away with 67 percent of the vote.

The most tangible monument to Quillen's work is the Quillen-Dishner College of Medicine at East Tennessee State University in Johnson City. The congressman spent years promoting it, and it is named for him and a generous donor. Former Gov. Dunn's opposition to this school led to the feud between him and Quillen.

Committee

Rules (2nd of 4 Republicans)
Legislative Process (ranking)

Elections

1992 General

James H. Quillen (R)	114,797	(67%)
J. Carr "Jack" Christian (D)	47,809	(28%)
Don Fox (I)	4,126	(2%)
Fred A. Hartley (I)	3,416	(2%)

1990 General

James H. Quillen (R)	47,796	(100%)

Previous Winning Percentages: **1988** (80%) **1986** (69%) **1984** (100%) **1982** (74%) **1980** (86%) **1978** (65%) **1976** (58%) **1974** (64%) **1972** (79%) **1970** (68%) **1968** (85%) **1966** (87%) **1964** (72%) **1962** (54%)

District Vote for President

1992

D	75,681	(37%)
R	106,939	(52%)
I	24,230	(12%)

Campaign Finance

	Receipts	Receipts from PACs	Expend-itures
1992			
Quillen (R)	$455,846	$267,050 (59%)	$325,383
1990			
Quillen (R)	$596,536	$360,350 (60%)	$263,291

Key Votes

1993	
Require parental notification of minors' abortions	#
Require unpaid family and medical leave	N
Approve national "motor voter" registration bill	?
Approve budget increasing taxes and reducing deficit	?
Approve economic stimulus plan	?
1992	
Approve balanced-budget constitutional amendment	Y
Close down space station program	N
Approve U.S. aid for former Soviet Union	N
Allow shifting funds from defense to domestic programs	N
1991	
Extend unemployment benefits using deficit financing	N
Approve waiting period for handgun purchases	N
Authorize use of force in Persian Gulf	Y

Voting Studies

Year	Presidential Support S	Presidential Support O	Party Unity S	Party Unity O	Conservative Coalition S	Conservative Coalition O
1992	69	21	69	23	77	15
1991	68	25	64	27	92	3
1990	65	29	60	31	85	7
1989	71	21	60	35	85	5
1988	48	41	59	31	82	5
1987	55	38	55	33	86	5
1986	62	33	49	40	82	8
1985	68	29	56	35	80	11
1984	69	20	60	27	81	12
1983	79	16	70	21	85	10
1982	69	29	68	26	88	11
1981	63	17	70	14	67	3

Interest Group Ratings

Year	ADA	AFL-CIO	CCUS	ACU
1992	5	33	75	92
1991	5	33	80	90
1990	6	25	92	83
1989	15	25	100	85
1988	15	36	100	91
1987	12	31	64	76
1986	20	38	60	77
1985	15	18	67	81
1984	20	42	82	67
1983	0	6	95	83
1982	10	15	76	76
1981	5	21	100	92

2 John J. "Jimmy" Duncan Jr. (R)

Of Knoxville — Elected 1988; 3rd Term

Born: July 21, 1947, Lebanon, Tenn.
Education: U. of Tennessee, B.S. 1969; George Washington U., J.D. 1973.
Military Service: National Guard, 1970-87.
Occupation: Judge; lawyer.
Family: Wife, Lynn Hawkins; four children.
Religion: Presbyterian.
Political Career: Knox County Criminal Court judge, 1981-88.
Capitol Office: 115 Cannon Bldg. 20515; 225-5435.

In Washington: Duncan spent his first two terms in Congress tending largely to local matters, avoiding the limelight and performing as a reliable party backbencher.

Duncan has said that he plans to emulate his father, who made himself a popular congressman in East Tennessee for more than two decades by tending to local concerns and eschewing the national spotlight.

Duncan has a safe seat in the most Republican part of the state and he seems content with those horizons for now. In January 1993 he rejected requests from several GOP leaders to run for one of the two U.S. Senate seats that will be up for grabs in Tennessee in 1994.

National Republican Senatorial Committee Chairman Phil Gramm of Texas even visited Knoxville to meet with some of Duncan's supporters there before the congressman had officially demurred.

Duncan willingly characterizes himself as being more conservative than his father in political philosophy. His ratings from the American Conservative Union have tended to be a shade higher than those compiled by his father.

In the 102nd Congress, Duncan's fiscal stringency led him to oppose some of President Bush's priorities. In 1991 and again in 1992, he voted to eliminate funding for two big-ticket science projects backed by President Bush: the $8 billion-plus superconducting super collider and the $30 billion-plus space station *Freedom.*

He carried his pinchpenny philosophy over into the debate on funding the Strategic Defense Initiative. He was one of 11 Republicans voting in 1992 to reduce SDI funding from $4.4 billion to $3.3 billion.

Still, on many of the high-profile issues of the 102nd Congress, father and son probably would have cast identical votes. Duncan cast votes against requiring a seven-day waiting period for the purchase of handguns and for a constitutional amendment to required a balanced federal budget. The elder Duncan voted in 1986 to weaken gun control laws, and in 1982 backed a balanced-budget constitutional amendment.

Duncan the son is also close to his father in keeping his office's focus local. On the Natural Resources and Public Works committees, tending to local matters in the 101st Congress meant bringing home $2.5 million for a courthouse in Knoxville and adding a few projects for his district to authorization bills as they went through his committees.

He was able to get $1 million into the fiscal 1990 Interior appropriations bill for the first resurfacing in 25 years of the Foothills Parkway in the Great Smoky Mountains National Park. He is one of only three non-Western Republicans on the panel.

At the same time, Duncan wants to make good on his promises with regard to federal spending overall. On the Public Works Subcommittee on Public Buildings, he persuaded the Secret Service to revise its plans for a new building, saving at least $28 million. He sponsored a successful amendment to cut $30 million from NASA's research into the existence of life elsewhere in the universe.

In the 102nd Congress, he joined the Banking Committee, where he offered an unsuccessful amendment to eliminate a $12.2 million increase in the authorization for the International Monetary Fund. Duncan and likeminded colleagues argued that any increase would be irresponsible in light of the swelling federal budget deficit. The amendment, however, was rejected on a vote of 16-35. He did not rejoin the panel at the start of the 103rd.

The Persian Gulf War gave Duncan a couple of moments of national attention in 1990. President Bush signed into law his resolution to declare a national day of prayer for U.S. troops and citizens in the Middle East and their families. And Duncan scored a publicity coup with his effort to send videotapes of college football games to U.S. troops.

At Home: Duncan entered politics with

Tennessee 2

East — Knoxville

With a winning tradition dating to the Civil War, the 2nd's GOP defines the word "entrenched." Since the days when parts of this area tried to secede from Tennessee to rejoin the Union, the majority of voters here have remained fixed in their partisan preference. No Democrat has held this House seat since then, and only rarely does one even put up a good fight for it.

The GOP's standard playbook does well in the 2nd: support for a strong defense and frugality in federal spending (especially on welfare programs). Most also endorse the party's current social-issue posture, opposing abortion and objecting to gays in the military.

Residents' conservatism translates into solid margins for GOP presidential candidates, and even bigger wins for Rep. Duncan. Voters will, however, support popular Democrats in statewide races when the GOP fails to put forward a top-drawer challenger.

Knox County dominates the district, casting nearly 60 percent of its ballots. The city of Knoxville itself (population 165,000) has a sizable Democratic vote: Labor unions have some strength, blacks are a substantial presence in the eastern part of the city and there are some liberal elements in the University of Tennessee community. However, the suburbs of Knox County — predominantly white-collar professionals in the west, with middle-income workers in the south and north — easily deliver the votes to keep Republicans in charge.

Though the typical resident of the 2nd is a critic of "big government," state and federal jobs are a big component of the economy. In addition to hosting the university, Knoxville is headquarters for the Tennessee Valley Authority, and a number of Knox Countians commute to neighboring Anderson County (in the 3rd District) to work at the Oak Ridge National Laboratories and related companies. Manufacturers turn out a range of goods, including boats, mobile homes, electronics and apparel, and Knoxville is headquarters for Whittle Communications, parent company of the Channel One classroom TV station.

The economy of the 2nd also feeds on outsiders' dollars: I-75 and I-40 meet at Knoxville, and visitors passing through "the gateway to the Smokies" put about $377 million into the area economy in 1991. Knoxville is a regional retail and entertainment center: The hordes that throng to UT football and basketball games enrich merchants, innkeepers and restaurateurs for miles around.

South of Knox is Blount County, second-largest in the 2nd. Its economy has long revolved around the Alcoa Aluminum plant. Nippondenzo, which started production in March 1990, eventually brought slightly more than 1,000 jobs to Blount with the opening of an automotive parts plant, echoing a trend of foreign investment across Tennessee.

At the southern end of the district, 1992 remapping moved Democratic Polk County from the 2nd to the 3rd and gave Duncan some strongly conservative Chattanooga suburbs in Bradley County.

1990 Population: 541,864. White 500,016 (92%), Black 35,785 (7%), Other 6,063 (1%). Hispanic origin 2,983 (<1%). 18 and over 416,775 (77%), 62 and over 85,247 (16%). Median age: 34.

one of the best known names in East Tennessee's public life. His father had been mayor of Knoxville in the late 1950s and then served a generation in Congress. His uncle was a judge. And the younger Duncan, too, took the courtroom route into politics. He served eight years as a criminal court judge in Knox County, the main population center in the 2nd District.

The years on the bench were helpful, allowing Duncan to build up enough of a reputation and a résumé to be a strong candidate in his own right when his father, in failing health, decided that the 100th Congress would be his last (the elder Duncan died shortly after making his retirement announcement).

But in his initial congressional campaign in 1988, there was little doubt that Duncan campaigned primarily as his father's son, both in style and substance. Although he is generally known as "Jimmy," he capped off his heir-apparent campaign by appearing on the ballot as John J. Duncan.

His heir-to-the-job strategy proved successful in the end, but it gave Democrats an opening to make a race of it in this traditional bastion of mountain Republicanism. Duncan campaigned in the old-style, door-to-door and barbecue-to-barbecue manner for which his father had been known. His Democratic opponent, Dudley Taylor, waged a hard-hitting media campaign the likes of which had not been seen in this district.

As Duncan put together a loose-knit organization run mainly by family and friends, Taylor, who stepped down from his post as state revenue commissioner to run, began putting together a strong effort. He had the assistance of influential state Democrats, including his former boss, Democratic Gov. Ned McWherter. Little known to most voters at the outset, Taylor quickly raised his profile by aggressively courting news coverage and making equally aggressive use of paid media.

Taylor hammered away at Duncan for running a Rose Garden strategy and relying on the senior Duncan's reputation. And the charges got some attention. Duncan's refusal to debate Taylor even once gave the Democrat an opportunity to score debating points throughout the campaign, as did the Republican's decision to hold only infrequent news conferences.

Duncan also chose to ignore a wave of more negative attacks that came at him. One of Taylor's advertisements played up links between Duncan and financier C. H. Butcher Jr. and a major banking scandal that had erupted in the state. Federal regulators had sued Duncan and other principals of a failed savings and loan, saying they engaged in a conspiracy in which control of the thrift was given to Butcher in exchange for elimination of debts Duncan's brother owed to Butcher's banks. Taylor also tried to portray Duncan as being soft on crime.

Local Republicans prodded Duncan into taking out ads rebutting Taylor's "vicious and false allegations." He easily won the general election (and a same-day special election for the right to fill out the remainder of his father's term in the 100th Congress until the swearing-in of the 101st).

Taylor toyed with running again in 1990, but chose not to, leaving Duncan with no Democratic opposition. Things did not get much tougher for the incumbent in 1992: Duncan had a Democratic opponent but dismissed him, collecting 72 percent of the vote.

Committees

Natural Resources (7th of 15 Republicans)
National Parks, Forests & Public Lands; Oversight & Investigations

Public Works & Transportation (7th of 24 Republicans)
Public Buildings & Grounds (ranking); Aviation; Investigations & Oversight

Elections

1992 General		
John J. "Jimmy" Duncan Jr. (R)	148,377	(72%)
Troy Goodale (D)	52,887	(26%)
Randon J. Krieg (I)	4,134	(2%)
1990 General		
John J. "Jimmy" Duncan Jr. (R)	62,797	(81%)
Peter Hebert (I)	15,127	(19%)

Previous Winning Percentage: **1988** * (56%)

** Elected to a full term and to fill a vacancy at the same time.*

District Vote for President

1992

D 92,889 (41%)
R 108,109 (48%)
I 25,196 (11%)

Campaign Finance

	Receipts	Receipts from PACs		Expend-itures
1992				
Duncan (R)	$258,496	$162,509	(63%)	$170,836
Goodale (D)	$6,471	0		$6,471
1990				
Duncan (R)	$325,691	$165,501	(51%)	$200,935

Key Votes

1993	
Require parental notification of minors' abortions	Y
Require unpaid family and medical leave	N
Approve national "motor voter" registration bill	N
Approve budget increasing taxes and reducing deficit	N
Approve economic stimulus plan	N
1992	
Approve balanced-budget constitutional amendment	Y
Close down space station program	Y
Approve U.S. aid for former Soviet Union	N
Allow shifting funds from defense to domestic programs	N
1991	
Extend unemployment benefits using deficit financing	N
Approve waiting period for handgun purchases	N
Authorize use of force in Persian Gulf	Y

Voting Studies

	Presidential Support		Party Unity		Conservative Coalition	
Year	**S**	**O**	**S**	**O**	**S**	**O**
1992	63	37	87	12	71	29
1991	65	34	84	14	86	11
1990	74	26	87	13	87	13
1989	64	35	73	27	95	5

Interest Group Ratings

Year	ADA	AFL-CIO	CCUS	ACU
1992	25	42	63	84
1991	20	33	80	100
1990	11	25	79	88
1989	20	33	90	75

3 Marilyn Lloyd (D)

Of Chattanooga — Elected 1974; 10th Term

Born: Jan. 3, 1929, Fort Smith, Ark.
Education: Shorter College, 1959-63.
Occupation: Radio station executive.
Family: Husband, Bob Fowler; four children.
Religion: Church of Christ.
Political Career: No previous office.
Capitol Office: 2406 Rayburn Bldg. 20515; 225-3271.

In Washington: Though she is one of the more senior Democrats and chairs a subcommittee, Lloyd has failed either to have a major impact in any policy area or to secure her House seat — she got no more than 57 percent in her past five elections.

Lloyd has spent much of her time in Congress tending to local concerns, especially the nuclear facilities at Oak Ridge, using her senior positions on the Armed Services and Science, Space and Technology committees to watch over the site.

Lloyd chairs the Science Subcommittee on Energy, which puts her in a good position to watch out for Oak Ridge. She is also involved in oversight of the environmental cleanup effort at Oak Ridge and other nuclear facilities.

Lloyd backs research that could lead to "energy independence through a balanced national energy policy." While she supports efforts on solar energy and conservation, nuclear power plays a big part in her formula. For years, she fought to preserve the Clinch River nuclear breeder reactor in her district; however, the expensive project was scrapped in 1983.

In 1990, Lloyd made a bold bid to take over the Science Committee. Lloyd was fourth in seniority on the panel when Democrat Robert A. Roe of New Jersey left the committee chairmanship to claim the top spot at Public Works. Lloyd bid against second-ranking Democrat George E. Brown Jr. of California, saying, "I would be honored by the opportunity to serve as the first woman committee chair."

But Lloyd never really had a chance, and Brown won by a 166-33 vote.

On Armed Services, Lloyd is in the dwindling group of the committee's "Old Guard" conservative Democrats. She has generally supported big-ticket military items and has taken little interest in broader reform issues.

In the early 1990s, Lloyd began taking a more outspoken role on women's issues. In 1992, she joined fellow Armed Services Democrats Beverly B. Byron of Maryland and Patricia Schroeder of Colorado in harshly criticizing the Navy for its handling of the Tailhook convention scandal, in which dozens of women were sexually assaulted. "Men must accept women as human beings and not sex objects. That is the issue," she said.

In the 102nd Congress Lloyd also announced a major switch on her abortion position. After years of opposition, she announced she was pro-abortion rights and cited her bout with breast cancer as helping to change her mind: "I value the right to make my own decision about my health care and treatment options," she said. "I have become convinced that all women should have access to the best reproductive health-care services when faced with their own difficult and trying decisions."

But Lloyd stopped short of fully supporting the agenda of women's rights groups; she was one of only 42 Democrats who voted against family leave legislation in 1992. (She supported the 1993 version of the bill that President Clinton signed into law but said she still had reservations.)

With a constituency that includes a number of textile workers, Lloyd chaired the Congressional Textile Caucus during the 101st Congress. During that period, she was the chief House sponsor of a bill limiting textile imports; although a version of the bill passed both chambers in 1990, President Bush vetoed it.

She served on the Select Committee on Aging from its 1975 inception and was active in the unsuccessful fight to preserve it in 1993.

At Home: Despite redistricting, which added Democrats to the 3rd District, and despite the fact that Al Gore was on the national ticket, Lloyd struggled to a narrow victory.

Lloyd took 49 percent of the vote to defeat Republican Zach Wamp, a real estate broker and a recovering cocaine addict, who had 47 percent.

Close races have become the norm for Lloyd, but she has always managed to pull through.

In 1984, Lloyd had failed to pay attention to an aggressive but little-known foe and nearly lost; two years later, she had a tough campaign against a political neophyte who was initially not considered a serious threat.

In 1987, Lloyd announced she would not run again. But after several months, she surprised those vying to succeed her by announc-

Tennessee 3

Southeast — Chattanooga; Oak Ridge

The 3rd is a mixture of agricultural counties and two main commercial hubs: Chattanooga (Hamilton County) in the south and Oak Ridge (Anderson County) in the north. The district starts above Oak Ridge, pinches through narrow Meigs County on its way south to Chattanooga and then broadens out along the Georgia border.

In elections, the 3rd shows a moderate-to-conservative personality. The district went solidly Republican in presidential elections of the 1980s, but in 1992, the Clinton-Gore ticket nearly won here, something Democrats have not managed in the 3rd since Jimmy Carter led their ticket in 1976. In the end, George Bush prevailed districtwide by just 65 votes out of more than 220,000 cast.

In House voting over the past decade, Rep. Lloyd has found the 3rd a tough sell. She has scored below 60 percent in her last five elections; in 1992 she prevailed by only 2,930 votes, despite Bill Clinton's good showing in the 3rd and a 1992 remap that aimed to bolster her. Democratic cartographers excised from the 3rd a sizable portion of conservative Bradley County (just above Chattanooga), and they gave Lloyd several solidly Democratic rural counties — Sequatchie, Van Buren, Bledsoe and Polk.

She won all the new counties except Bledsoe, and strongly Democratic Anderson County gave her a big victory (60 percent). But Hamilton County, where nearly 55 percent of the district's vote is cast, went against her. Hamilton and the part of Bradley County still in the 3rd were the only parts of the district to support Bush over Clinton. (Hamilton has voted Republican in all but one presidential election since 1952.)

Much economic activity in the 3rd centers around the district's nuclear facilities: the Oak Ridge National Laboratories and the Tennessee Valley Authority's Sequoia and Watts Bar nuclear power plants near Chattanooga. Lloyd has been a strong supporter of the nuclear industry. But with decreased federal money going to nuclear energy and research, officials looking for new sources of economic activity are promoting a plan that would transform the route connecting Oak Ridge and neighboring Knoxville into a Technology Corridor for high-technology research and development. A highway that will link Knoxville's airport to the Technology Corridor is scheduled for completion in 1994.

The 3rd is known for several other white- and blue-collar industries. In Chattanooga, insurance, chemical and service companies have joined the older metal, textile and candy industries. (Former GOP Sen. Bill Brock calls the city home, and his family owns the Brock Candy Co.) The TVA's Office of Power has headquarters in the city as well.

The Chattanooga Choo Choo and Terminal, made famous by Glenn Miller's song, and the new Chattanooga Aquarium help generate revenue from tourism, as do Rock City, Ruby Falls and historic sites connected with the Civil War's "Battle Above the Clouds" on Lookout Mountain.

1990 Population: 541,866. White 473,405 (87%), Black 62,781 (12%), Other 5,680 (1%). Hispanic origin 3,359 (<1%). 18 and over 410,195 (76%), 62 and over 89,781 (17%). Median age: 35.

ing that she would run. Two top GOP contenders dropped out once Lloyd got back in. But one, Harold Coker, stayed and made Lloyd work to win another term.

Coker, unlike Lloyd's earlier foes, began with a political base and name recognition stemming from his service on the Hamilton County Commission. Coker launched a variety of attacks, saying that Lloyd had not paid enough attention to the Tennessee Valley Authority, which had recently laid off workers, and that her 1982 move from the Public Works Committee to Armed Services had boosted her campaign treasury and honoraria totals more than it boosted the district.

But Lloyd, who had learned the dangers of complacency, was quick to defend herself and strike back. She was first to issue the challenge for a debate, and she criticized Coker for refusing to release his business tax returns. Her conservative voting record, scrupulous attention to constituents and vigorous campaigning sank Coker. She posted her best showing since 1982, 57 percent.

Lloyd's strong performance led many to believe she would have an easier time in 1990, when two popular Democrats, Gov. Ned McWherter and then-Sen. Gore, were running.

But McWherter and Gore were so popular that neither drew a credible foe, and Tennessee ended up with the lowest voter turnout rate in the nation. In the 3rd, fewer than half as many people voted in the 1990 House election as had voted in 1988. That was a prime reason why Lloyd managed only 53 percent against her little-known challenger, Republican Grady L. Rhoden.

Lloyd's initial victory in 1974 was a surprise. The Democratic nomination had gone to her husband Mort, a well-known Chattanooga newsman. But when he died in a plane crash, the 3rd's county chairmen met and chose his widow as the nominee. She had owned and operated a radio station with her husband but was a political novice and seemed to have little chance against two-term GOP Rep. Lamar Baker.

But Lloyd was aggressive and she found a winning combination of issues in the Watergate year: opposition to busing, more rights for women and criticism of President Gerald R. Ford's pardon of former President Richard M. Nixon. She unseated Baker with 51 percent.

In her first term, Lloyd built a following with question-and-answer town hall meetings and covered-dish suppers. Baker tried a comeback in 1976, but lost by more than 2-to-1. After the 1978 election, Lloyd appeared on voters' ballots as Marilyn Lloyd Bouquard, a result of her marriage to Chattanooga engineer Joseph P. Bouquard. But they divorced in 1983, and she became Marilyn Lloyd once again.

In 1984 she faced John Davis, a political consultant. Davis got off to a slow start financially, but as the campaign wore on, he proved adept at winning media coverage. Combining a pro-business message with a moderate background more appealing to middle-of-the-road voters who had been turned off by Lloyd's earlier, more conservative opponents, Davis won 48 percent of the vote.

Davis was expected back for a rematch in 1986, but he was upset in the primary by Chattanooga attorney Jim Golden, a political outsider with a strong base in the 3rd's evangelical community. But establishment Republicans remained wary of Golden's background. Their resistance, combined with Lloyd's renewed attention to her campaign machinery, brought her 54 percent.

Committees

Armed Services (7th of 34 Democrats)
Military Acquisition

Science, Space & Technology (2nd of 33 Democrats)
Energy (chairman); Investigations & Oversight

Elections

1992 General		
Marilyn Lloyd (D)	105,693	(49%)
Zach Wamp (R)	102,763	(47%)
Carol Hagan (I)	4,433	(2%)
1990 General		
Marilyn Lloyd (D)	49,662	(53%)
Grady L. Rhoden (R)	36,855	(39%)
Pete Melcher (I)	5,598	(6%)
George E. Googe (I)	1,546	(2%)

Previous Winning Percentages: **1988** (57%) **1986** (54%) **1984** (52%) **1982** (62%) **1980** (61%) **1978** (89%) **1976** (68%) **1974** (51%)

District Vote for President

1992
D 97,296 (44%)
R 97,361 (44%)
I 25,789 (12%)

Campaign Finance

	Receipts	Receipts from PACs		Expend-itures
1992				
Lloyd (D)	$463,643	$272,250	(59%)	$637,790
Wamp (R)	$275,655	$125	(0%)	$267,844
1990				
Lloyd (D)	$415,056	$233,750	(56%)	$234,107
Rhoden (R)	$1,415	0		$1,414

Key Votes

1993	
Require parental notification of minors' abortions	N
Require unpaid family and medical leave	Y
Approve national "motor voter" registration bill	Y
Approve budget increasing taxes and reducing deficit	Y
Approve economic stimulus plan	Y
1992	
Approve balanced-budget constitutional amendment	Y
Close down space station program	N
Approve U.S. aid for former Soviet Union	N
Allow shifting funds from defense to domestic programs	N
1991	
Extend unemployment benefits using deficit financing	?
Approve waiting period for handgun purchases	Y
Authorize use of force in Persian Gulf	Y

Voting Studies

	Presidential Support		Party Unity		Conservative Coalition	
Year	**S**	**O**	**S**	**O**	**S**	**O**
1992	46	51	65	29	90	10
1991	37	44	52	28	78	8
1990	43	56	71	25	94	6
1989	56	38	61	34	90	5
1988	47	51	59	37	89	3
1987	40	49	54	27	81	9
1986	53	44	39	55	92	6
1985	52	45	56	39	82	16
1984	52	42	48	47	90	10
1983	54	41	41	50	90	7
1982	47	47	56	38	73	22
1981	57	36	55	41	83	12

Interest Group Ratings

Year	ADA	AFL-CIO	CCUS	ACU
1992	45	64	63	50
1991	30	82	33	50
1990	44	58	50	46
1989	35	73	78	52
1988	50	100	46	54
1987	28	62	42	32
1986	20	50	53	62
1985	35	75	45	48
1984	35	50	50	67
1983	25	47	55	78
1982	25	60	52	55
1981	30	67	37	53

4 Jim Cooper (D)

Of Shelbyville — Elected 1982; 6th Term

Born: June 19, 1954, Shelbyville, Tenn.
Education: U. of North Carolina, B.A. 1975; Oxford U., B.A., M.A. 1977; Harvard U., J.D. 1980.
Occupation: Lawyer.
Family: Wife, Martha Hays; two children.
Religion: Episcopalian.
Political Career: No previous office.
Capitol Office: 125 Cannon Bldg. 20515; 225-6831.

In Washington: Cooper is an accomplished legislator who announced in early 1993 that he is giving up his safe House seat to seek a Senate seat in 1994. Almost immediately, he was endorsed by Gov. Ned McWherter, who had refused to appoint Cooper to the seat in the first place.

Cooper had earned high marks in his 10 years in Washington, and several major newspapers in the state suggested that Cooper be nominated to fill out the term of Vice President Al Gore. But McWherter said Cooper should earn the seat and not be given it. Instead he chose Harlan Mathews, who said at the time he would not be a candidate in 1994.

A moderate who supported his party 75 percent of the time on partisan votes in 1992, Cooper is urbane and soft-spoken, and seems the antithesis of the backslapping Southern pol. Yet he has proved adept at building social relationships in the House. For a number of younger members, sweaty games of basketball in the House gym are a primary networking tool. But Cooper decided that the way to get to know some of his more senior colleagues was to meet them on their own ground, so he took up playing golf.

From his seat on Energy and Commerce he has become a key player in a wide range of issues from health care to telecommunications policy to clean air. Though he got on the panel with the help of Democratic Chairman John D. Dingell of Michigan, Cooper has not been afraid to go his own way on the panel, especially on environmental issues.

Cooper is perhaps the leading proponent of the "managed competition" approach to health care under which doctors, hospitals and insurance companies would form networks that would compete with one another to offer low cost services.

Cooper has questioned suggestions from some moderate and conservative Democrats that people with higher incomes pay more for Medicare coverage. "You would be undercutting the national consensus that has built and preserved these programs," he said.

He also plays a role on telecommunications issues and is sponsor of legislation that would limit the ability of regional telephone companies to offer information services. Cooper's bill would enable these companies to provide services only where 50 percent of local phone customers have access to competing services and 10 percent subscribe to them. The issue was not resolved in the 102nd Congress but could resurface in the 103rd.

In his first term on Energy and Commerce, Cooper threw himself into one of the toughest issues before the committee — the effort to write clean air legislation to deal with urban smog and acid rain. Renewal of the Clean Air Act had been a political migraine for several years before Cooper got to the committee, because of a standoff between an environmentalist faction, led by California Democrat Henry A. Waxman, and a more industry-oriented faction, led by Dingell.

In an effort to break the deadlock, Cooper teamed with the so-called group of nine, a caucus of moderate-to-conservative committee Democrats determined to find the acceptable middle ground that had eluded Dingell and Waxman.

Cooper was a diligent player in all aspects of the group's behind-closed-doors effort. The group's efforts helped lay the groundwork for much of the clean air debate in the 101st Congress. And Cooper's contributions earned him credibility with other members, perhaps making them more receptive to his views in the coal/acid rain debate, where he has a more direct interest.

On that issue, Cooper tried to sell a compromise plan that set timetables and standards for reduction of emissions from utilities that are the primary cause of acid rain. To pay for that reduction, Cooper proposed a tax on utilities based on how cleanly they burned coal. His plan also allowed utilities to choose the means of meeting the reduction requirements.

Cooper eventually saw elements of his proposal — such as the provision giving utilities flexibility in meeting the standards — written into the 1990 Clean Air Act. And during the intense negotiations leading up to the bill's passage, Cooper helped defeat an effort to require that all utilities share in the cost of cleaning up

Tennessee 4

Northeast and south central

Like the state itself, the 4th is a long, sprawling district, extending nearly 300 miles. Beginning in the rural flatlands in the southwest and not too far from Memphis, it snakes up through the rolling terrain in Middle Tennessee, stretches north onto the Cumberland Plateau and encompasses a sliver of Knox County in East Tennessee.

The 4th is so large that from east to west it touches four states — Mississippi, Alabama, Kentucky and Virginia. And it spans the time zone dividing line, giving it both Central and Eastern times.

Politically, the 4th is a moderate-to-conservative Democratic district. It supported Bill Clinton in his quest for the presidency, giving him 48 percent of the vote. The 4th had not voted Democratic for president since 1976. It consistently supports moderate Rep. Cooper without much problem. Cooper's home of Bedford County — one of the most Democratic parts of the district — continues to be a stronghold for him.

Redistricting in 1992 did not change the 4th much. In the southwest, it added Hardin and Wayne counties, near the Tennessee River, and Pickett County in the north. The new lines also added a part of east Knox County. Van Buren, Bledsoe, Sequatchie and Morgan counties in the southwest joined the 3rd. Hancock County merged with the 1st.

With no large urban center in the 4th, people form their political opinions by talking with neighbors in feed stores, roadside cafes and small-town shops that surround the courthouse squares. And despite the district's usual Democratic leanings, some of the northern mountainous counties have supported the GOP because of Union sentiment from the Civil War.

The 4th is home to some unique legal history: In 1925, the "Scopes monkey trial" was held in Dayton in Rhea County. In that case, the state court upheld a law making it illegal to teach the theory of evolution in public schools. The ruling was later overturned, but religion and social conservatism still play a role in the district's politics.

Agriculture and light industry make up the bulk of the 4th's economy. Soybeans and cotton are harvested in the western counties. In the northern counties, tobacco grows in the valleys, and beef and dairy cattle graze on hillsides too steep for plowing.

Coal has long been an economic staple, but underground activity has mostly given way to surface mining.

In addition, many plants specializing in automotive parts assist the Saturn and Nissan plants in the state. Warren County raises trees and shrubs for the nursery industry. And the Jack Daniels Distillery in Moore County produces the famous sour mash whiskey. But its product cannot be purchased there; Moore is a "dry" county.

The 4th is also known for the Tennessee Walking Horse National Celebration, which is held every August and September in Shelbyville.

1990 Population: 541,868. White 518,991 (96%), Black 19,669 (4%), Other 3,208 (<1%). Hispanic origin 2,376 (<1%). 18 and over 405,759 (75%), 62 and over 93,601 (17%). Median age: 35.

the worst polluters, many of them in the Midwest.

But for all of Cooper's hard work and expertise on clean air, he was conspicuously absent from the list of conferees chosen by Dingell to work out differences with the Senate. Once perceived as perhaps too closely allied to Dingell, Cooper during the clean air deliberations apparently had shown too much independence for the chairman's taste.

Earlier, Cooper also had clashed with Dingell over legislation affecting the banking industry. Cooper is one of the committee's strongest supporters of legislation granting powers to banks to engage in new lines of business.

In 1988, when Dingell offered a bill with sharper limits on some activities by banks than were included in a Banking Committee bill, Cooper complained that it was "a giant step backward."

During the 101st and 102nd Congresses, he successfully pushed several safety and consumer-oriented bills.

He succeeded in adding provisions to the 1991 highway bill to give grants to states to pass laws mandating the use of motorcycle helmets and automobile safety belts. Cooper argued that it could save at least 11,000 lives annually and prevent injuries, thus saving as much as $5 billion in annual medical costs.

Maintaining that consumers often are unwittingly trapped into paying exorbitant long-distance rates from phones in airports, hotel lobbies and other public facilities, Cooper wrote legislation mandating that long-distance carriers identify themselves at the outset of a call and requiring that carriers disclose their rates and in some cases justify them to the Federal Communications Commission.

Cooper also has some parochial interests. The walking-horse industry brings in a reported $37 million annually to Cooper's district, so he was agitated when the Agriculture Department, in response to a lawsuit, banned use of the padded horseshoes and braceletlike chains that enhance the horses' famous high step.

The American Horse Protection Association, which brought the suit, argued that the devices hurt the horses. But Cooper and other members of the Tennessee delegation worked to find a compromise with Agriculture Department officials that would keep the walking-horse industry in business.

Cooper can look beyond the parochial position, however, even on issues involving his district. There are a number of tobacco farmers in the 4th, and Cooper has surprised colleagues in Washington with his criticism of cigarette smoking. During the 101st Congress, he backed continuing a smoking ban on domestic airline flights.

Cooper says, "I'm not anti-tobacco; I'm anti-cancer," and points out that he is "anxious to keep [his constituents] alive as long as possible."

At Home: Though he is a Rhodes scholar who spent his formative years at prestigious schools far from Tennessee, Cooper has an easy rapport with his rural constituency.

Most voters in the 4th are as comfortable with Cooper's background as one front-porch philosopher, who, told in 1982 that Cooper was a Rhodes scholar, said, "That's good to hear. It's about time somebody did something about the roads around here."

Several prominent Democrats considered running in the newly created 4th in 1982, but none entered; they were dissuaded by Cooper's full-time campaigning and his family's financial resources. His father, Prentice Cooper, was Tennessee's governor from 1939 to 1945, and many older people in the 4th remember voting for or hearing about Prentice.

After an easy primary he faced Republican Cissy Baker, the daughter of then-Senate Majority Leader Howard H. Baker Jr.

Cooper was rated the front-runner because of the district's Democratic leanings and because Baker had struggled in the primary, winning 55 percent against two weak opponents. But few expected Cooper to win as lopsidedly as he did, carrying all but one of 23 counties.

Committees

Budget (10th of 26 Democrats)

Energy & Commerce (15th of 27 Democrats)
Energy & Power; Health & the Environment; Telecommunications & Finance

Elections

1992 General		
Jim Cooper (D)	98,984	(64%)
Dale Johnson (R)	50,340	(33%)
Ginnia C. Fox (I)	3,970	(3%)
1992 Primary		
Jim Cooper (D)	52,281	(85%)
John Dooley (D)	6,370	(10%)
J. Patrick Lyons (D)	3,025	(5%)
1990 General		
Jim Cooper (D)	52,101	(67%)
Claiborne "Clay" Sanders (R)	22,890	(30%)
Gene M. Bullington (I)	2,281	(3%)

Previous Winning Percentages: **1988** (100%) **1986** (100%) **1984** (75%) **1982** (66%)

District Vote for President

1992

D	100,292	(48%)
R	83,922	(40%)
I	23,838	(11%)

Campaign Finance

	Receipts	Receipts from PACs	Expend-itures
1992			
Cooper (D)	$158,744	$16,750 (11%)	$179,510
1990			
Cooper (D)	$183,494	$107,400 (59%)	$56,922
Sanders (R)	$16,497	0	$12,588

Key Votes

1993	
Require parental notification of minors' abortions	N
Require unpaid family and medical leave	Y
Approve national "motor voter" registration bill	Y
Approve budget increasing taxes and reducing deficit	Y
Approve economic stimulus plan	Y
1992	
Approve balanced-budget constitutional amendment	Y
Close down space station program	N
Approve U.S. aid for former Soviet Union	Y
Allow shifting funds from defense to domestic programs	N
1991	
Extend unemployment benefits using deficit financing	N
Approve waiting period for handgun purchases	Y
Authorize use of force in Persian Gulf	Y

Voting Studies

	Presidential Support		Party Unity		Conservative Coalition	
Year	S	O	S	O	S	O
1992	42	56	75 †	22 †	74 †	23 †
1991	49 †	51 †	72 †	26 †	78 †	22 †
1990	37 †	62 †	74	25	62 †	34 †
1989	48	50	78	18	66	32
1988	34	65	84	15	66	32
1987	25	66	77	14	53	35
1986	31	68	80	14	52	40
1985	43	55	85	13	40	60
1984	42	52	74	20	49	51
1983	32	59	69	24	56	35

† Not eligible for all recorded votes.

Interest Group Ratings

Year	ADA	AFL-CIO	CCUS	ACU
1992	70	67	63	32
1991	35	42	70	40
1990	56	67	64	29
1989	60	58	60	21
1988	70	79	69	28
1987	68	73	43	9
1986	70	64	53	14
1985	55	71	45	24
1984	80	67	53	26
1983	45	59	50	43

5 Bob Clement (D)

Of Nashville — Elected 1988; 3rd Full Term

Born: Sept. 23, 1943, Nashville, Tenn.

Education: U. of Tennessee, B.S. 1967; Memphis State U., M.B.A. 1968.

Military Service: Army, 1969-71; National Guard, 1971-present.

Occupation: College president; marketing, management and real estate executive.

Family: Wife, Mary Carson; two children, two stepchildren.

Religion: Methodist.

Political Career: Tenn. Public Service Commission, 1973-79; sought Democratic nomination for governor, 1978; Democratic nominee for U.S. House, 1982.

Capitol Office: 1230 Longworth Bldg. 20515; 225-4311.

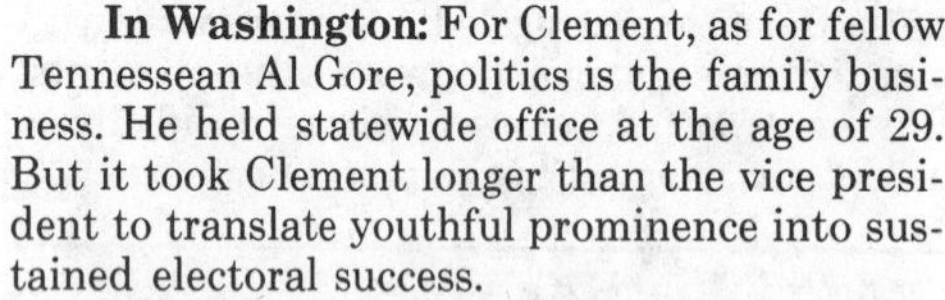

In Washington: For Clement, as for fellow Tennessean Al Gore, politics is the family business. He held statewide office at the age of 29. But it took Clement longer than the vice president to translate youthful prominence into sustained electoral success.

Clement is four years older than Gore, but it took him until 1988 to reach Congress (more than a decade after Gore's first election to the House). But the extra years of seasoning helped transform Clement, once seen as a fiery populist, into a quiet and loyal party man whose eyes stay firmly fixed on the interests of his district.

In early 1993, Clement was weighing whether to attempt the leap from Capitol Hill to the governor's mansion in Nashville. With a dozen or more Democrats weighing their odds of succeeding Gov. Ned McWherter, Clement could rely on the statewide name recognition he enjoys as the son of a three-term governor. Clement is not mentioned as often as a potential contestant in the 1994 race for Gore's old Senate seat (now held by appointed Democrat Harlan Mathews), not having made McWherter's short list of potential appointees.

The senior member of the class of 1988 — he won a January 1988 special election — Clement became class representative on the Democratic Steering and Policy Committee, which makes committee assignments. He has tried for more, but his 1990 bid for a seat on Appropriations was not successful.

Clement's main committee addresses continue to be Public Works and Veterans' Affairs, but he has yet to accumulate enough legislative victories on either panel to define his record. Colleagues and staff regard him as primarily oriented toward constituent service rather than issues or ideology.

A consistent supporter of nuclear power, Clement did win an important victory for that industry in 1992 — if only in the symbolic sense.

Over the opposition of Interior Committee Chairman George Miller of California, Clement won a floor vote on an amendment to the national energy bill, streamlining a licensing process that the nuclear industry said was cumbersome and fraught with unreasonable delay. The House adopted Clement's amendment by a margin of nearly 100 votes. While no utilities are currently contemplating construction of new nuclear plants, the easing of regulatory hurdles is seen by the industry as key to eventually allowing such construction to take place.

Clement also has proposed legislation to restore rail service between Chicago and Jacksonville, Fla., and through Nashville; to increase penalties for drug dealing at truck stops; and to increase Social Security benefits for the "notch babies," people who turned or will turn 65 in or after 1982, and are affected by changes in benefit computation rules enacted in 1977.

During the Reagan and Bush years, Clement sided with his party more often than many Southern Democrats. He opposed President Ronald Reagan on aid to the Nicaraguan contras and supported a seven-day waiting period for handgun purchases.

With two fellow Southerners heading up the new Democratic administration, Clement can be expected to find the party line even more congenial. Already in the 103rd, he has sponsored a proposed constitutional amendment to give the president a line-item veto on appropriations bills (a power Bill Clinton had sought during the 1992 campaign).

At Home: With his resounding triumph in the 1988 House special election, Clement resurrected a moribund political career.

By winning the race to succeed Democratic Rep. Bill Boner, who became Nashville's mayor,

Tennessee 5

Nashville

Nashville is "Music City USA" and the capital of Tennessee, and country music and government paychecks propel the economy. More than 90 percent of the 5th's vote comes out of Nashville and Davidson County, and in most years Democrats win here. Ronald Reagan in 1984 and George Bush in 1988 carried the 5th, but not by much. In 1992 the district returned to form, giving the Clinton-Gore ticket 53 percent.

There is no question that country music is Nashville's most famous industry, but with almost 17,000 jobs, state government is the district's leading employer. Davidson County is also home to 17 colleges and universities, the best-known of which is Vanderbilt University. Several publishers of religious material have headquarters here, and there is a sizable manufacturing sector.

Government workers, the academic communities and labor unions uphold Nashville's traditional position as the focal point of Middle Tennessee Democratic populism. That brand of politics is a legacy of Andrew Jackson, who built his political career in the area and returned to The Hermitage, his home east of Nashville, after serving two terms as president.

Nashville's population is less than one-quarter black — a relatively low figure for a large Southern city — and white voters have not been so prone to drift from their traditional Democratic loyalties.

Though the state capitol complex is a permanent anchor, downtown Nashville has struggled, a victim of retail flight to the suburbs and the success of Opryland, the sprawling theme park east of the city where the Grand Ole Opry moved from its original downtown site at Ryman Auditorium.

But signs of life are springing up downtown, with a revival of the live-entertainment scene and the restaurant business, and remodeling of old buildings. There is talk of resurrecting a Department of Transportation feasibility study to determine the viability of restoring Amtrak service to Nashville. One proposed route would run from Chicago through Nashville to Jacksonville, Fla.

To keep pace in the area of air transportation, Nashville replaced its aged airport with a new facility. The 1991 highway bill included funding aimed at enhancing mass transit in the city.

Economically, the 5th benefits not only from the industries within its borders but also from some big manufacturing facilities nearby. Since the early 1980s, Tennessee has made a vigorous effort to market the state's work force and business climate to foreign investors, especially the Japanese. Nissan built a huge plant south of Nashville, and other Japanese companies have followed. General Motors chose a site near Nashville for its massive Saturn facility; Saturn sales have been so brisk that the company cannot meet demand and is looking to expand.

Redistricting in 1992 just slightly altered the look of the 5th, moving a small slice of Davidson County and about half of Robertson County to the 7th. Robertson accounts for only about 6 percent of the total district vote.

1990 Population: 541,910. White 408,535 (75%), Black 123,525 (23%), Other 9,850 (2%). Hispanic origin 4,905 (<1%). 18 and over 416,547 (77%), 62 and over 76,165 (14%). Median age: 33.

Clement set aside bitter memories from two previous defeats — including a 1982 House bid he was favored to win — and stepped out of the shadow cast by his father, the late Frank G. Clement, who was Tennessee's governor for three terms in the 1950s and 1960s.

In 1972, Bob Clement became a political "boy wonder" by winning East Tennessee's seat on the state Public Service Commission (PSC). Then 29, he was the youngest candidate ever elected statewide in Tennessee.

In six years on the PSC, Clement built up the already formidable visibility of the Clement name. But when he sought the nomination for governor in 1978, he lost to wealthy businessman Jake Butcher.

In 1979, President Jimmy Carter appointed Clement to the Tennessee Valley Authority board, where, as he had on the PSC, he drew headlines for trying to hold down utility rates.

In 1982, Clement sought the open 7th District, a Democratic-leaning constituency running from his family's traditional base west of Nashville all the way to Memphis. But the lesser-known GOP nominee, Memphis businessman Don Sundquist, won thanks to a huge Republican vote from Memphis' suburbs.

Clement recused himself from politics and became president of Cumberland College. Its location — in Lebanon, east of Nashville — helped Clement remain visible in the capital.

After Boner won the 1987 mayor's race, the special Democratic primary for the 5th boiled down to Clement, relying on a heavy vote from the working-class whites who were Boner's base, and wealthy businessman Phil Bredesen, who had narrowly lost the mayoralty to Boner and ran a media-heavy House campaign aimed at more affluent Democrats and GOP-leaning voters. Clement won with 40 percent to Bredesen's 36 percent.

In the Democratic 5th, home of such House members as Andrew Jackson and Sam Houston, Clement had not even had to face a GOP opponent in November 1988 or 1990. In 1992, Tom Stone managed 26 percent running as a Republican; it was 8 percentage points more than he had received when he ran as an independent two years earlier.

Committees

Public Works & Transportation (13th of 39 Democrats)
Aviation; Economic Development; Surface Transportation

Veterans' Affairs (13th of 21 Democrats)
Education, Training & Employment; Hospitals & Health Care

Elections

1992 General		
Bob Clement (D)	125,233	(67%)
Tom Stone (R)	49,417	(26%)
Steven L. Edmondson (I)	6,724	(4%)
Richard H. Wyatt (I)	3,507	(2%)
1992 Primary		
Bob Clement (D)	42,794	(66%)
Chip Forrester (D)	15,724	(24%)
David Mills (D)	6,043	(9%)
1990 General		
Bob Clement (D)	55,607	(72%)
Tom Stone (I)	13,577	(18%)
Al Borgman (I)	5,383	(7%)
Maurice C. Kuttab (I)	2,192	(3%)

Previous Winning Percentages: 1988 (100%) 1988* (62%)

* *Special election.*

District Vote for President

1992

D 112,795 (53%)
R 79,398 (37%)
I 21,531 (10%)

Campaign Finance

	Receipts	Receipts from PACs		Expend-itures
1992				
Clement (D)	$557,480	$288,762	(52%)	$600,244
Stone (R)	$11,372	0		$10,590
1990				
Clement (D)	$424,581	$272,825	(64%)	$298,005

Key Votes

1993	
Require parental notification of minors' abortions	N
Require unpaid family and medical leave	Y
Approve national "motor voter" registration bill	Y
Approve budget increasing taxes and reducing deficit	Y
Approve economic stimulus plan	Y
1992	
Approve balanced-budget constitutional amendment	Y
Close down space station program	Y
Approve U.S. aid for former Soviet Union	?
Allow shifting funds from defense to domestic programs	N
1991	
Extend unemployment benefits using deficit financing	Y
Approve waiting period for handgun purchases	Y
Authorize use of force in Persian Gulf	Y

Voting Studies

	Presidential Support		Party Unity		Conservative Coalition	
Year	S	O	S	O	S	O
1992	25	67	75	15	58	40
1991	43	56	80	19	78	22
1990	25	74	85	14	59	41
1989	42	52	74	22	66	32
1988	31	66	79	14	63	32

Interest Group Ratings

Year	ADA	AFL-CIO	CCUS	ACU
1992	65	75	63	39
1991	50	75	40	20
1990	44	83	29	29
1989	60	64	50	19
1988	75	93	36	20

6 Bart Gordon (D)

Of Murfreesboro — Elected 1984; 5th Term

Born: Jan. 24, 1949, Murfreesboro, Tenn.
Education: Middle Tennessee State U., B.S. 1971; U. of Tennessee, J.D. 1973.
Occupation: Lawyer.
Family: Single.
Religion: Methodist.
Political Career: Tenn. Democratic Party chairman, 1981-83.
Capitol Office: 103 Cannon Bldg. 20515; 225-4231.

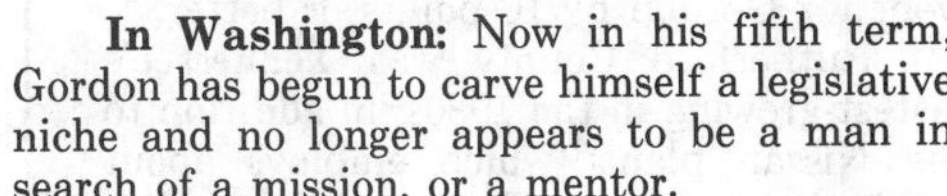

In Washington: Now in his fifth term, Gordon has begun to carve himself a legislative niche and no longer appears to be a man in search of a mission, or a mentor.

Gordon has served on the Rules Committee since the 100th Congress, where he provides a solid Democratic vote. He is not someone Republicans appeal to when seeking to mitigate the panel's tendency toward majoritarian control.

Gordon's amiable personality and rapport with party leaders in Tennessee are enough to cause his name to be mentioned for statewide office. But his relatively liberal voting record could be a liability at home.

Once the protégé of Speaker Jim Wright, Gordon has not moved quite as much in leadership circles since Wright left the scene in 1989. But he remains a member of the far-flung Democratic whip organization, and his fealty to the leadership is unquestioned.

Capitalizing on publicity he gained in an undercover sting of questionable trade school practices, Gordon worked diligently in the 102nd Congress to preserve the integrity of federal student aid programs.

In March 1991, he went undercover for NBC News posing as a prospective vocational education student. He was encouraged at a school in Memphis to sign up for a truck-driving course, using student loans to pay his way. "They were more interested in getting me to sign up for the school," Gordon said on "Exposé," the television show, "than they were in seeing that I would be placed in a good job later or got good training."

In 1992, Gordon persuaded the House to include provisions in a reauthorization bill for federal higher education programs targeting shoddy trade schools. It would have denied Pell grants to students at schools that already had lost their eligibility for guaranteed student loans because of a high rate of defaults.

By a vote of 351-39, the House adopted a second Gordon amendment, denying Pell grants to inmates in federal or state prisons.

Neither provision survived intact in the face of strong opposition from the trade school lobby and its patron, House Education and Labor Chairman William D. Ford of Michigan, and concern that Gordon's amendments could have a disproportionate impact on black students. The language barring Pell grants to schools with a large number of defaults was dropped entirely; the other amendment was limited to denying Pell grants to inmates on death row or those serving life sentences with no possibility of parole.

Gordon also played a role over three Congresses in the fight over the Family and Medical Leave Act.

During 1990 debate on the bill, Gordon joined with Pennsylvania Republican Curt Weldon to offer a compromise — a watered-down version of the original committee measure — that gave enough protection to small businesses to win the support of some centrist Democrats and Republicans. Congress approved the bill, but President Bush vetoed it.

Much the same thing happened in 1991, when Gordon joined with Illinois Republican Henry J. Hyde as House sponsors of a compromise first worked out in the Senate by Connecticut Democrat Christopher J. Dodd and Missouri Republican Christopher S. Bond. That version, too, cleared Congress but died under Bush's veto.

Early in the 103rd Congress, the bill was finally enacted, and Gordon was still a visible proponent, managing the rule that governed floor debate.

Gordon let his interests look abroad in 1990. He initiated an effort early in the year to arrange donations of $40,000 worth of computer equipment to help Czechoslovakia prepare for its elections and was later appointed to a task force to help the new Eastern Europe democracies with technological assistance.

And in June 1992 he helped Maine Democrat Thomas H. Andrews lead an unsuccessful floor fight to halt production of more B-2 bombers. Citing members' support for a balanced-budget constitutional amendment, Gordon said, "The budget is balanced by tough

Tennessee 6

North Central — Murfreesboro

This slice of Middle Tennessee embodies qualities of both the Old and New South.

In most of the 6th's counties, the pace of life is still relatively unhurried, people work in small factories or on farms, and old courthouse networks call the political shots — nearly always calling them Democratic.

But on the western edge of the 6th, in the four counties that border Davidson County (Nashville), there are clear signs of change, brought on in large part by the expansion of suburbia and the influence of two gargantuan vehicle-assembly plants — one run by Japan's Nissan in Smyrna, and the other by General Motors' Saturn subsidiary, in Spring Hill, just outside the Williamson County line.

The political impact of the suburbanizing and industrializing is most obvious in Williamson County. Many residents there are white-collar commuters to jobs in and around Nashville, just to the north. In most elections, Williamson delivers a stronger GOP vote than any other Middle Tennessee county. In 1992, George Bush won 55 percent of the vote in Williamson, and 60 percent in a small slice of Davidson County that is included in the 6th. Every other county in the 6th backed the Clinton-Gore ticket.

Similarly, in the 1992 House contest between Democratic Rep. Gordon and Marsha Blackburn, she won nearly 60 percent in Williamson and the slice of Davidson. Her strong showing in Williamson, which casts just under one-fifth of the district's vote, was the main reason Gordon tallied under 60 percent for the first time ever.

Though 1992 redistricting moved Maury County out of the 6th, and with it the Saturn facility, almost 30 percent of the plant's workers live in Williamson County. Demand for Saturn's cars has been so strong that the company has strained to keep up; employment is approaching 7,000, and expansion is on the horizon.

In the other three counties adjoining Davidson County — Rutherford, Sumner and Wilson — liberalism in the national Democratic Party provokes some wariness, but traditional party ties still bind: Clinton won each by 5 to 6 points over Bush, and all went for Gordon by 10 points or better.

Rutherford County was Tennessee's fastest-growing in the 1980s; in addition to the Nissan plant (which employs about 5,500), it has Middle Tennessee State University in Murfreesboro, the Stones River National Battlefield and a large outlet shopping mall.

In the areas of the 6th that are part of the Nashville orbit, economic conditions have been fairly favorable in recent years. The same cannot be said for many of the rural and small-town areas on the eastern side of the 6th. Textile producers and other small-scale manufacturers there offer primarily lower-wage jobs, and remoteness from urban areas means the service-sector economy is not large.

The Democratic advantage in the eastern counties is enormous. In 1992, nearly all of them voted by at least 2-to-1 for Clinton-Gore and for Gordon.

1990 Population: 541,977. White 505,849 (93%), Black 31,010 (6%), Other 5,118 (1%). Hispanic origin 3,159 (<1%). 18 and over 399,124 (74%), 62 and over 71,309 (13%). Median age: 33.

choices.... I urge my colleagues to put their votes where their mouth is." The amendment failed 162-212, though it won support from a majority of Democrats.

Late in 1992, Congress cleared a bill designed to clamp down on abuses in the 900-number pay-per-call industry. The final version was a compromise adapted from a bill first introduced by Gordon almost two years earlier.

Gordon's willingness to support the party well exceeds that of most Southern Democrats. On partisan votes in 1989 and 1990, he voted with the majority of his party more than 90 percent of the time on the floor; in 1991 and 1992, he voted with the party more than 85 percent of the time, leaving him still the most loyal Tennessee Democrat.

He is distinguished by his votes on high-profile social issues. He has supported abortion rights and the Brady bill's seven-day waiting period for handgun purchases.

Gordon departs from party orthodoxy most often on fiscal matters. In 1992, he voted for a constitutional amendment to require a balanced federal budget, when the leadership was working vigorously to prevent passage. And he also opposed voiding the terms of the 1990 budget agreement to allow money to be shifted from defense spending to domestic needs for fiscal 1993, another leadership priority.

But in early 1993, he voted with the party to approve President Clinton's budget resolution and his ill-fated economic stimulus proposal.

When the House debated the conflict in the Persian Gulf in early 1991, Gordon joined just two other colleagues in the chamber in voting for the continued use of sanctions and then, after the resolution failed, voting to "close ranks" with the president and support the authorization of force.

At Home: Gordon was still in college when he worked on the unsuccessful 1968 House campaign of a state representative from his hometown. Sixteen years later, the Senate candidacy of Democratic Rep. Al Gore enabled Gordon to wage his own successful campaign.

Gordon built his political credentials within the state party structure. Fresh out of law school, he won a seat on the state Democratic Executive Committee, and in 1979 he parlayed his contacts into a position as the party's executive director. Two years later, he won the party chairmanship. In that position he computerized the party mailing list and set up a direct-mail program — experience that proved crucial to his House campaign.

Gordon's chief rivals in his initial 1984 House contest were state Rep. Lincoln Davis, who represented a cluster of counties in the Upper Cumberland region of the 6th, and Bryant Millsaps, the state House chief clerk, who shared Gordon's home base of Murfreesboro.

Gordon set himself apart in the primary with a sophisticated phone bank and direct-mail operation. In the final weeks, while Millsaps focused on TV advertising and Davis on pulling out his Upper Cumberland vote, Gordon's forces repeatedly wrote and telephoned undecided voters. Gordon won the six-way contest with 28 percent.

During the campaign, Gordon had to deal with the potentially explosive issue of a paternity suit that had been brought against him and was later dismissed. Gordon denied fathering the child, and none of his primary opponents raised the issue. But his GOP opponent, Williamson County construction executive Joe Simkins, accused him of a "cover-up," after the Nashville Banner alleged that Gordon had paid the woman to drop the suit.

Simkins, whose brother was publisher of the Banner, set a "countdown deadline" for Gordon to explain the settlement. Gordon simply ignored the challenge, as did most voters. He won all but two counties on Election Day.

Gorton easily won re-election in 1986, 1988 and 1990, but in 1992, GOP leaders had hoped their candidate, Marsha Blackburn, might give Gordon an unpleasant surprise. Blackburn, a fashion consultant and GOP activist, waged an energetic campaign and ultimately held Gordon to 57 percent, his lowest-ever margin of victory.

Committees

Budget (17th of 26 Democrats)

Rules (8th of 9 Democrats)
Legislative Process

Elections

1992 General		
Bart Gordon (D)	120,177	(57%)
Marsha Blackburn (R)	86,289	(41%)
H. Scott Benson (I)	5,952	(3%)
1992 Primary		
Bart Gordon (D)	45,576	(83%)
Bob Ries (D)	4,912	(9%)
Don Schneller (D)	4,371	(8%)
1990 General		
Bart Gordon (D)	60,538	(67%)
Gregory Cochran (R)	26,424	(29%)
Ken Brown (I)	3,793	(4%)

Previous Winning Percentages: **1988** (76%) **1986** (77%) **1984** (63%)

District Vote for President

1992
D 109,895 (48%)
R 93,036 (40%)
I 28,151 (12%)

Campaign Finance

	Receipts	Receipts from PACs		Expend-itures
1992				
Gordon (D)	$662,234	$388,590	(59%)	$988,920
Blackburn (R)	$184,657	$18,226	(10%)	$181,515
1990				
Gordon (D)	$620,052	$355,275	(57%)	$367,090
Cochran (R)	$11,400	0		$8,996

Key Votes

1993	
Require parental notification of minors' abortions	N
Require unpaid family and medical leave	Y
Approve national "motor voter" registration bill	Y
Approve budget increasing taxes and reducing deficit	Y
Approve economic stimulus plan	Y
1992	
Approve balanced-budget constitutional amendment	Y
Close down space station program	Y
Approve U.S. aid for former Soviet Union	?
Allow shifting funds from defense to domestic programs	N
1991	
Extend unemployment benefits using deficit financing	Y
Approve waiting period for handgun purchases	Y
Authorize use of force in Persian Gulf	Y

Voting Studies

	Presidential Support		Party Unity		Conservative Coalition	
Year	**S**	**O**	**S**	**O**	**S**	**O**
1992	24	69	86	10	67	31
1991	37	62	89	11	68	32
1990	25	73	93	6	46	52
1989	35	64	91	7	59	39
1988	23	73	84	8	53	45
1987	27	69	82	10	63	37
1986	27	72	83	12	56	40
1985	33	66	79	13	42	56

Interest Group Ratings

Year	ADA	AFL-CIO	CCUS	ACU
1992	70	67	50	25
1991	60	92	40	15
1990	67	92	21	13
1989	75	92	50	11
1988	80	93	36	12
1987	64	87	29	0
1986	75	86	39	9
1985	55	63	45	20

7 Don Sundquist (R)

Of Memphis — Elected 1982; 6th Term

Born: March 15, 1936, Moline, Ill.
Education: Augustana College (Rock Island, Ill.), B.A. 1957.
Military Service: Navy, 1957-59.
Occupation: Printing, advertising and marketing executive.
Family: Wife, Martha Swanson; three children.
Religion: Lutheran.
Political Career: No previous office.
Capitol Office: 339 Cannon Bldg. 20515; 225-2811.

In Washington: After a 10-year career in the House made up of tending to his constituents, burnishing his image and building his party, Sundquist seems likely to pack up in 1994 and head back to Tennessee for a run at the governor's mansion. He will bring with him a list of accomplishments directly benefiting Tennessee.

During his time in Washington, Sundquist has shown his political acumen by quietly working his way into the hearts and minds of his colleagues and party leaders. The payoff in the 101st Congress was a coveted seat on the Ways and Means Committee.

That seat has allowed Sundquist to take care of his constituents: "Somehow when a bill gets out of committee, it always has a lot in it for West Tennessee," says a colleague. "You don't quite know how he did it."

Though Sundquist has been involved in issues strategizing for the GOP, the Ways and Means assignment came to him mostly because of his political sensibilities, not any particular legislative achievement.

He is thought of as being more interested in the politics of various issues than in the issues themselves, and he sticks to the broad scope. He wants Republicans to do more to see that the federal government does less. He is the archetypal New South conservative businessman — a man who bemoans bureaucratic inefficiencies and believes that many things the federal government does can be done better by local government or the private sector.

He has worked hard to get to know his colleagues, and more than a few of them seek his political advice before a difficult vote.

Sundquist is perhaps best known for the major step out of character he took at the end of the 101st Congress, when he overreached and sought a party leadership post still occupied by a senior member unwilling to give it up. The post was the chairmanship of the House GOP campaign committee, held since the 1970s by Guy Vander Jagt of Michigan, the No. 2 Republican on the Ways and Means Committee.

Sundquist is usually known as a first-rate vote-counter. But when the votes for the campaign chair were counted Dec. 3, 1990, Vander Jagt had won, 98-66.

Although the party had lost seats in four of the past five elections and many House Republicans were grumbling about the committee's contribution, Sundquist may have gone too far in aggressively criticizing the committee's operations, especially the financial end involving its chief financial officer and staff fundraiser. Sundquist's airing of such issues in public made some of his colleagues more than a little uncomfortable.

Sundquist's bid also suffered from circumstances beyond his control. When he announced in the fall of 1990, many conservative House Republicans were in a boil about the budget deal cut by President Bush and the congressional leadership — especially Bush's abandoning his "no new taxes" pledge. Sundquist, an ally of Bush's since the early 1970s, was perceived as the president's man. Vander Jagt was seen as the defender of the campaign committee's co-chairman, Edward J. Rollins, who had offended the White House in 1990 by telling GOP candidates to distance themselves from the president's tax and budget positions.

When he was national chairman of the Young Republicans in the 1970s, Sundquist became acquainted with Bush, then the chairman of the Republican National Committee. Sundquist supported Bush's first presidential bid, in the 1980 cycle. And in the 1988 presidential contest, he was a chief House organizer for Bush's primary and general-election campaigns.

Though he failed to win the post, Sundquist did succeed in shaking up the campaign committee's leadership. The party and Vander Jagt were scarred by the experience, and while the incident may have helped Vander Jagt lose his August 1992 primary, many believe the committee itself is stronger for having had the fight.

In the 102nd, Sundquist went to bat for the Brother International typewriter factory in the Memphis suburb of Bartlett. At issue was

Tennessee 7

West Central — Clarksville; part of Shelby County

Though Sundquist has held the 7th comfortably since a tight election in 1982, the district's political balance would make any open-seat race highly competitive. The 7th combines Republican suburbanites, West Tennessee Dixiecrats, Middle Tennessee populists and a significant number of blue-collar workers. In 1992 redistricting, the 7th became more Democratic.

Despite losing 100,000 of its GOP-leaning residents to other districts in the remap, the Shelby County part of the 7th remains the district's GOP bastion. The 7th still has the most upscale and Republican Memphis suburbs, including Bartlett, Collierville and Germantown.

Many of the better-paid employees at such Memphis-based companies as Federal Express and International Paper Co. live in the east Shelby suburbs. Much of the area has a nouveau riche feel, with showy homes, malls and office parks that draw commerce away from center-city Memphis. The area grew rapidly in the 1980s (Germantown's population, for example, expanded 50 percent), while the city of Memphis saw a 9 percent population loss.

In 1992, the portion of Shelby in the 7th gave George Bush 67 percent of its presidential votes. That was enough to deliver the district comfortably to Bush; Shelby casts more than 40 percent of the vote in the 7th. Of the 14 other counties in the district, Bush won just two.

The 7th runs the gamut of Tennessee agriculture. In Shelby's eastern neighbor, Fayette County, the flat land is ideal for cotton growing. Moving east, the more rolling terrain becomes less suitable for row crops; tobacco and cattle are more prevalent. Corn, soybeans, hay and hogs are also important in the district. Maury County, added to the 7th in remapping, is the state's largest producer of beef cattle, but it is best known for its GM Saturn plant, in the tiny two-stoplight town of Spring Hill. Positive consumer response to the initial Saturn models has kept the plant humming; its work force grew from 5,000 in 1991 to an anticipated 7,000 by the end of 1993. Saturn is now considering where to expand production to meet demand.

Also in Maury is the Tennessee Farm Bureau, which provides services for farmers across the state. The largest insurer of rural property in Tennessee, it is a political force despite its policy of not endorsing candidates. Every aspirant for statewide office must take into account its significant, though tacit, influence.

A potential swing county in an open House race could be Montgomery, which has the district's largest city, Clarksville (population 75,000). Clarksville is home to Fort Campbell and the 101st Airborne Division, and the county's active duty and retired military personnel help give it a conservative tinge. But conservative has not always meant Republican: Bill Clinton won Montgomery by almost 1,500 votes in 1992. The fort and its 5,200 civilian employees likely will be safe from military downsizing, considering the Pentagon's emphasis on "rapid deployment" units such as the 101st.

1990 Population: 541,937. White 467,034 (86%), Black 67,145 (12%), Other 7,758 (1%). Hispanic origin 6,182 (1%). 18 and over 396,773 (73%), 62 and over 66,807 (12%). Median age: 32.

whether tariffs should be slapped on Brother's products because it is owned by a foreign company. Pushing for the tariffs was Smith Corona, the well-known New York typewriter firm, which had GOP Sen. Alfonse M. D'Amato in its corner.

Sundquist managed to get the tariff provisions removed from the pending urban aid bill, much to the amazement of D'Amato. "I find it hard to believe how the minority member, and not one with great seniority, would have had the ability" to have the provision struck, he said.

Sundquist was usually found in Bush's corner, even when the political price looked steep. When the Ways and Means Subcommittee on Human Resources approved an ambitious increase in spending for children's programs in June 1990, Sundquist expressed the administration's disapproval and, calling himself the "skunk at a garden party," cast the lone nay vote.

When Ways and Means marked up a tax package in July 1989 and the Bush administration registered just one objection to it (excise tax increases on pipe tobacco and snuff), Sundquist was the man offering another source of revenue so the offending provision could be struck.

At Home: A winner of five easy re-elections in a district that stretches from Memphis to Nashville, Sundquist is being mentioned as a possible solution to the Tennessee GOP's dearth of appealing talent eligible to succeed Democratic Gov. Ned McWherter in 1994.

That is remarkable progress for a man who had little public profile just 12 years ago, when he launched his first bid for Congress. That race was an impressive debut: He parlayed expertise gained in 12 years of GOP trenchwork into an upset over the scion of a well-known Tennessee political family.

Sundquist began his campaign in late 1981, when GOP Rep. Robin Beard was preparing his Senate bid. Many of the Republican activists Sundquist contacted knew him from his stints as Shelby County (Memphis) party chairman and his work for Beard, former Gov. Winfield Dunn and former Sens. William E. Brock III and Howard H. Baker Jr.

The district's GOP establishment and crucial business leaders supported Sundquist, keeping other Republicans out of the primary. That sent Sundquist into a tough November contest with Bob Clement, a rural populist and son of the late Gov. Frank G. Clement (Bob Clement was later elected to the House from the 5th District).

The outcome hinged on the "Shelby factor." About 40 percent of the 7th's voters live in eastern Shelby County, a heavily Republican area containing affluent residential sections of Memphis and its suburbs. The 7th's other 15 counties are predominantly rural, and most of the voters there are conservative Democrats. In 1982, unemployment was high in all the rural counties, making them even less receptive to entreaties from a well-off suburban GOP businessman.

To compensate for his problems outside the Memphis area, Sundquist concentrated on mobilizing Shelby County's GOP suburbanites, who found little to like in Clement's political message, an arm-waving populism he inherited from his father.

Sundquist took three-fourths of the Shelby vote, exceeding his most optimistic projections. The combined vote in the district's other 15 counties went 65 percent to 35 percent for Clement, but that was not enough to offset the Democrat's dismal showing in Shelby.

For a while, it looked as if Sundquist might face a 1984 battle with former state Rep. Harold Byrd, who had lost to Clement in the 1982 Democratic primary, but that challenge never materialized, nor has any other of significance. The general anti-incumbent mood of 1990 touched Sundquist; re-elected with 80 percent of the vote in 1988, he mustered 62 percent against the same Democratic nominee in 1990.

Committee

Ways & Means (5th of 14 Republicans)
Select Revenue Measures; Trade

Elections

1992 General		
Don Sundquist (R)	125,101	(62%)
David R. Davis (D)	72,062	(36%)
Rickey Boyette (I)	2,290	(1%)
1990 General		
Don Sundquist (R)	66,141	(62%)
Ken Bloodworth (D)	40,516	(38%)

Previous Winning Percentages: **1988** (80%) **1986** (72%) **1984** (100%) **1982** (51%)

District Vote for President

1992
D 91,644 (40%)
R 114,544 (50%)
I 22,486 (10%)

Campaign Finance

	Receipts	Receipts from PACs		Expend-itures
1992				
Sundquist (R)	$819,006	$359,884	(44%)	$1,001,217
Davis (D)	$106,633	$35,900	(34%)	$106,774
1990				
Sundquist (R)	$648,472	$351,985	(54%)	$451,944

Key Votes

1993	
Require parental notification of minors' abortions	Y
Require unpaid family and medical leave	N
Approve national "motor voter" registration bill	N
Approve budget increasing taxes and reducing deficit	N
Approve economic stimulus plan	N
1992	
Approve balanced-budget constitutional amendment	Y
Close down space station program	N
Approve U.S. aid for former Soviet Union	N
Allow shifting funds from defense to domestic programs	N
1991	
Extend unemployment benefits using deficit financing	N
Approve waiting period for handgun purchases	N
Authorize use of force in Persian Gulf	Y

Voting Studies

	Presidential Support		Party Unity		Conservative Coalition	
Year	**S**	**O**	**S**	**O**	**S**	**O**
1992	77	20	83	11	92	8
1991	74	19	84	9	95	0
1990	74	25	90	9	94	2
1989	80	17	86	10	98	0
1988	64	28	86	5	89	5
1987	60	34	86	10	91	9
1986	74	24	86	13	92	6
1985	75	23	87	10	91	7
1984	73	26	76	20	90	7
1983	70	29	83	14	91	6

Interest Group Ratings

Year	ADA	AFL-CIO	CCUS	ACU
1992	5	18	75	96
1991	0	17	100	90
1990	6	8	86	79
1989	5	17	90	78
1988	10	17	100	96
1987	8	25	80	82
1986	5	14	72	82
1985	15	18	91	81
1984	5	17	69	79
1983	0	18	74	87

8 John Tanner (D)

Of Union City — Elected 1988; 3rd Term

Born: Sept. 22, 1944, Halls, Tenn.
Education: U. of Tennessee, B.S. 1966, J.D. 1968.
Military Service: Navy, 1968-72; National Guard, 1974-present.
Occupation: Lawyer; businessman.
Family: Wife, Betty Ann Portis; two children.
Religion: Disciples of Christ.
Political Career: Tenn. House, 1977-89.
Capitol Office: 1427 Longworth Bldg. 20515; 225-4714.

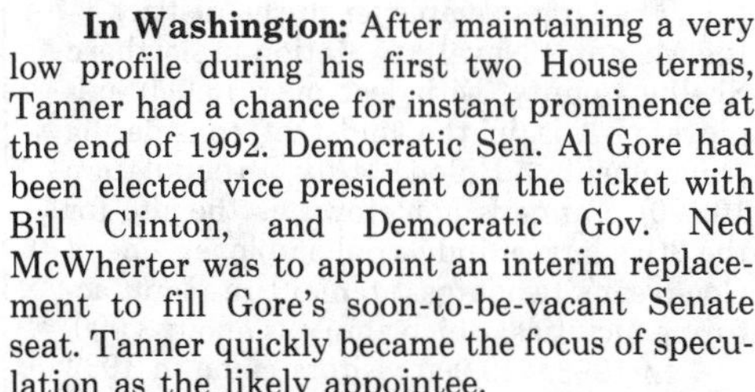

In Washington: After maintaining a very low profile during his first two House terms, Tanner had a chance for instant prominence at the end of 1992. Democratic Sen. Al Gore had been elected vice president on the ticket with Bill Clinton, and Democratic Gov. Ned McWherter was to appoint an interim replacement to fill Gore's soon-to-be-vacant Senate seat. Tanner quickly became the focus of speculation as the likely appointee.

Tanner, during his 12 years as a state legislator, had been a protégé of McWherter (then the state House Speaker). Tanner's West Tennessee district, where he has run without major-party opposition in his last two House contests, is also McWherter's political base. So the job of holding down the Senate seat — at least until the 1994 special election to fill out the last two years of Gore's unexpired term — was said to be Tanner's for the asking.

Remarkably, he did not ask. Instead, he told McWherter that he preferred to serve the third House term to which he was easily elected in 1992. The matter was handled in Tanner's typical style, with no fanfare and little self-generated publicity.

Tanner's pass on the appointment does not preclude his going for the seat in 1994. (McWherter's choice was state official Harlan Mathews, who, though appointed as a "caretaker" has hinted that he might run for the seat.) Nor is it out of the question, given his long prior experience in the state capital of Nashville, that Tanner could run in the 1994 open race for governor. (Under the state's "two terms and out" law, McWherter cannot seek a third term.)

But two of Tanner's more senior Democratic colleagues in Tennessee's House delegation, Jim Cooper and Bart Gordon, are also viewed as possible contenders for those statewide offices in 1994. Moreover, Tanner has shown no indication of being driven by ambition for higher office.

Tanner has been attentive to national issues as a member of the Armed Services and Science, Space and Technology committees, and he has been diligent about issues affecting West Tennessee. But he has gone about his business while remaining well out of the spotlight. This is not a member who will be found fulminating to the C-SPAN cameras during the special orders period. He is no legislative activist, having proposed just a handful of bills during his first four years in the House.

Tanner would have been comfortable in the House of old, where junior members were seldom seen and were heard even less. While Tanner as a freshman took a seat on the Armed Services Committee and was regarded by senior colleagues as having serious potential, he has kept mainly to himself.

The Armed Services post has enabled Tanner to oversee funding for several military facilities that are in the 8th District. He has also found areas in which his defense policy and home district interests overlap. A member from a mainly rural district, Tanner in 1992 proposed a pilot program under which National Guard medical units would provide medical care in underserved rural and urban areas; the measure was included in the fiscal 1993 defense authorization bill.

Generally viewed as a "pro-defense" Democrat, he voted in January 1991 for the resolution authorizing President George Bush to use military force against Iraq. He has also shown himself to be concerned with establishing U.S. military priorities that fit both post-Cold War strategic needs and the country's straitened fiscal circumstances. "The strategic weapons systems, such as the Strategic Defense Initiative (SDI) [and] the B-2 stealth bomber . . . may not be necessary in this changing environment. Funding for these weapons programs may have to be reduced," Tanner said in a 1991 report to his constituents.

But Tanner also urges against deep and rapid defense budget cuts, given the uncertain future of the democratic movement in the former Soviet Union.

"The success of the reform movement in Russia is a far, far cry from a certainty; they face terrific obstacles," Tanner said in February 1992 upon his return from a trip to Moscow. "We need to be cautious on a bidding war to see

Tennessee 8

West — Jackson; part of Shelby County

The 1992 round of redistricting did little to alter the essentially rural and Democratic makeup of the 8th. The inclusion of more Republican areas of suburban Shelby County only slightly outweighed the addition of rural Houston and Humphreys counties.

The result was a district little different from the one that GOP House candidates have failed to capture since the end of Reconstruction.

The 8th is slightly more favorable to GOP presidential candidates. Though Bill Clinton won the 8th with 48 percent of the vote (just slightly more than his 47 percent statewide) and took 14 of the 17 counties in the district, Shelby and Madison counties — the two counties with the largest populations with a combined 36 percent of the district's vote — went solidly for Bush 51 percent to 41 percent.

Soybeans, corn, wheat and cotton remain the 8th's staple crops, but industrial activity has diversified in recent years, particularly in Jackson, the district's largest city.

The surrounding farm counties look to Jackson as a source of retail goods and such services as specialty health care. The city's diversified industrial base allowed it to weather the recent recession better than the 8th's small towns and farms. Since 1989, Jackson (population 49,000) has attracted plants such as a Maytag appliance manufacturing plant and a company that manufactures air compressors. Still, the largest industrial employer in Jackson is the Procter & Gamble facility that makes Pringle's potato chips and employs more than 1,750.

Republicans have in recent years gained some ground in Madison County (Jackson), thanks in part to an influx of managerial personnel to Jackson's increasingly diversified industries.

Madison County's economic success contrasts with the slower economic growth of the rest of the 8th. In 1991, 13 of the 15 rural counties in the district had unemployment percentages higher than the state average of 6.7 percent, while Madison's fell slightly below average.

The largest employer in the district — the Memphis Naval Air Station in northern Shelby County, with just over 13,000 employees — is in the midst of considering realignment. Union City (population 10,500), Tanner's hometown, is the site for the 8th's largest industrial employer, one of Goodyear's two largest radial tire-manufacturing facilities, which employs about 3,000.

In 1992, 219,000 visitors came in 1992 to see the Civil War-era Fort Donelson in Dover, the site of an early victory the Union sorely needed. The 1862 capture of the Confederate fort gave the Union control of the Cumberland River, which cuts through the northeast edge of the district, running northwest from Nashville. The site also helped to immortalize the victorious general, Ulysses S. Grant, who in response to a Confederate request for terms of surrender, responded, "No terms. Unconditional surrender."

1990 Population: 541,907. White 430,674 (79%), Black 106,761 (20%), Other 4,472 (1%). Hispanic origin 3,812 (1%). 18 and over 402,139 (74%), 62 and over 90,884 (17%). Median age: 34.

who can cut defense the most." That year, Tanner voted against House proposals to cut the SDI anti-ballistic missile program by $1 billion and to knock down the budget "walls" then in effect that barred the shifting of defense funds to domestic programs.

Tanner's low-key style is well suited for the Science Committee, which typically receives less attention than most House panels. But he may benefit from an increased focus on the committee that is likely to result from President Clinton's emphasis on promoting high-tech growth industries. Tanner is a longtime political associate of Gore, who has the job of reviewing the federal government's technology-related programs.

In 1990, Tanner was a member of the Science subcommittee dealing with environmental research and earned a place on the conference committee that crafted the final version of the Clean Air Act.

In the wake of the October 1989 earthquake that hit San Francisco, Tanner advocated more funding for seismological research and enhanced availability of earthquake insurance for homeowners. His district is in the potential earthquake zone near the New Madrid Fault.

In 1989, he was elected an officer of the House Sportsman's Caucus, which was formed, he said, "to educate our colleagues" about the commitment of sportsmen to conservation, wildlife management and other issues related to the outdoors.

At Home: The retirement of longtime Democratic Rep. Ed Jones after nearly two decades brought the rare prospect of a competitive election in the 8th. But Tanner came out of the blocks practically before the contest had begun. A longtime ally of the incumbent — who had been friends with Tanner's grandfather — Tanner had already laid the groundwork. He quickly assembled an enviable organization and financial base, boosted by his connections to Jones and McWherter.

Tanner also had some natural appeal to business interests: In Union City he was a member of a local law firm and senior vice president of a local savings and loan association; in the state House he served as chairman of the Commerce Committee.

But Tanner, who went to the University of Tennessee on a basketball scholarship, appeals to more than just the buttoned-down set. His relaxed, "good ol' boy" style helped him win over rural voters, who hold considerable sway in the 8th.

During the primary season, Tanner traveled the district on a 230-stop listening tour, mixing easily with voters at country stores and other local gathering spots. He made a similar tour for the general election.

The five-way Democratic primary included Jackson Mayor Bob Conger and former Democratic Gov. Ray Blanton, whose gubernatorial term was so scandal-ridden that it eventually landed him in prison. But none of the Democrats made a dent in Tanner's armor. On primary day, he garnered 66 percent of the vote.

The GOP nominee, Jackson lawyer Ed Bryant, had organized the district for Pat Robertson's 1988 presidential campaign. Bryant tried to convince voters that Tanner would be controlled by a liberal national Democratic Party leadership in Washington.

"Bull," said Tanner. "Ed Jones has been his own man and John Tanner will be his own man." Tanner's support for the death penalty and the presidential line-item veto, together with his opposition to national health insurance proposals, made it difficult for anyone to portray him as a liberal. He won with more than 60 percent of the vote.

In 1990, he faced no general-election opposition. In 1992, challenged only by four minor candidates, he racked up 84 percent of the vote.

Committees

Armed Services (17th of 34 Democrats)
Oversight & Investigations; Military Acquisition

Science, Space & Technology (12th of 33 Democrats)
Investigations & Oversight; Space

Elections

1992 General		
John Tanner (D)	136,852	(84%)
Lawrence J. Barnes (I)	9,605	(6%)
David L. Ward (I)	6,930	(4%)
John E. Vinson (I)	5,435	(3%)
Millard J. McKissack II (I)	4,600	(3%)
1990 General		
John Tanner (D)	62,241	(100%)

Previous Winning Percentage: **1988** (62%)

District Vote for President

	1992
D	101,328 (48%)
R	89,533 (43%)
I	19,328 (9%)

Campaign Finance

	Receipts	Receipts from PACs	Expenditures
1992			
Tanner (D)	$258,798	$164,739 (64%)	$167,669
Vinson (I)	$10,910	0	$10,734
1990			
Tanner (D)	$314,094	$135,500 (43%)	$153,941

Key Votes

1993	
Require parental notification of minors' abortions	N
Require unpaid family and medical leave	Y
Approve national "motor voter" registration bill	Y
Approve budget increasing taxes and reducing deficit	Y
Approve economic stimulus plan	Y
1992	
Approve balanced-budget constitutional amendment	Y
Close down space station program	N
Approve U.S. aid for former Soviet Union	N
Allow shifting funds from defense to domestic programs	N
1991	
Extend unemployment benefits using deficit financing	N
Approve waiting period for handgun purchases	N
Authorize use of force in Persian Gulf	Y

Voting Studies

	Presidential Support		Party Unity		Conservative Coalition	
Year	S	O	S	O	S	O
1992	38	56	71	26	77	21
1991	41	53	64	26	81	5
1990	31	67	73	21	85	9
1989	47 †	51 †	75 †	21 †	90	10

† Not eligible for all recorded votes.

Interest Group Ratings

Year	ADA	AFL-CIO	CCUS	ACU
1992	65	58	38	50
1991	30	42	67	50
1990	44	58	54	29
1989	40	67	70	44

9 Harold E. Ford (D)

Of Memphis — Elected 1974; 10th Term

Born: May 20, 1945, Memphis, Tenn.
Education: Tennessee State U., B.S. 1967; John Gupton Mortuary, L.E.D., L.F.D. 1969; Howard U., M.B.A. 1982.
Occupation: Funeral director.
Family: Wife, Dorothy Bowles; three children.
Religion: Baptist.
Political Career: Tenn. House, 1971-75.
Capitol Office: 2211 Rayburn Bldg. 20515; 225-3265.

In Washington: After a six-year absence, Ford is back at the helm of the Ways and Means Subcommittee on Human Resources.

Ford was acquitted in April 1993 of the bank, mail and tax-fraud charges on which he had been indicted in April 1987. He quickly reassumed his position as chairman of the panel, which Democratic Caucus rules had forced him to relinquish. Ford had been reelected as the subcommittee's head in each Congress since his indictment, but had to turn the gavel over to a series of acting chairmen.

Ford is now clear to take control of the welfare reform and family support issues under the subcommittee's jurisdiction. Within weeks of his acquittal, he was deep in talks with the Clinton administration on how best to draft legislation.

He is also now clear to demonstrate that his legal troubles were all that blocked him from being an effective member of Congress; for the past six years his profile has been next to invisible in the House.

In its indictment, a federal grand jury in Knoxville charged that Ford had traded his influence for more than $1 million in bank loans arranged by Tennessee financiers Jake and C. H. Butcher Jr. Prosecutors charged that these loans were never to be repaid and were, in fact, bribes.

The charges followed a three-year investigation in Memphis but were filed in Knoxville, where the Butchers were based and where federal prosecutors may have thought they could more easily obtain a conviction. But Ford's attorneys won a change of venue back to Memphis, where he continues to enjoy tremendous political popularity and influence.

Ford was tried in federal court in Memphis in 1990, but the jury, dividing largely along racial lines, could not reach a verdict and was dismissed on April 27. Undeterred, federal prosecutors refused to drop the charges.

The judge who conducted the first trial — himself black — concluded that black jurors had been subjected to direct and indirect pressure to acquit Ford, including Ford's charges of government racism. Seeking a panel that was untainted by the years of publicity about the case, the judge ordered that the jury for the retrial be selected from the mostly white Jackson area and bused 90 miles to Memphis.

Ford fought that decision on all fronts, charging it was unfair and would stack the case against him. The Congressional Black Caucus lobbied the Clinton Justice Department to ask the judge to dismiss the jury, which it did. The judge refused, and the jury ended up acquitting Ford on all charges anyway. But the episode led Republican lawmakers to claim that the Clinton administration had interfered improperly in the case.

Ford's legal problems began just as he had attained a position of real influence as leader of the panel rewriting national welfare policy. When discussions of overhauling the welfare system picked up steam in early 1987, Ford, as chairman of the relevant subcommittee (it was then called Public Assistance and Unemployment Compensation), had the support of the House Democratic leadership for his bill. Although he soon had to cut the measure's cost in half, he moved it through his subcommittee in March 1987. He was indicted the following month.

Ford brings a minority-rights perspective to discussions of welfare policy, complementing the viewpoint of his one-time Senate counterpart, New York's Daniel Patrick Moynihan, who chaired the Finance Subcommittee on Social Security and Family Policy before taking the helm of the full committee in the 103rd Congress. Ford did not wait for Moynihan to act before launching his own welfare-overhaul bill, which expanded benefits but required states to make work, education or training mandatory for welfare recipients.

In the opening rounds of the welfare debate, Ford insisted that any bill would have to focus on expanding benefits as well as moving recipients off the welfare rolls whenever possible. The centerpiece of his bill was a program aimed at training welfare recipients so they can move into the work force. Under the plan, welfare mothers with children older than age 3 could be required to participate in work or

Tennessee 9

Memphis

On the bluffs above the Mississippi River is Memphis, a city of 610,000 and historically the crossroads for eastern Arkansas, northern Mississippi and West Tennessee. Named after the city in Egypt because of the Nile-like appearance of the twisting Mississippi, Memphis underscored that link in 1991 by opening the Great American Pyramid. The 32-story structure, which houses a 22,000-seat arena, is part of a larger plan to revitalize the city's economy — and especially its flagging downtown — by bringing in more special events and visitors. Memphis is already well-known to millions of Elvis Presley fans as the site of Graceland; since "the King's" 1977 death, a ceaseless stream of admirers has visited his grave on the mansion grounds.

Now, another famous Southerner is memorialized by a museum in Memphis: the Rev. Dr. Martin Luther King Jr. The National Civil Rights Museum opened in 1991 on the site of the former Lorraine Motel, where King was assassinated in 1968.

Other downtown attractions include Mud Island — a 52-acre island park that celebrates the city's river history — and Beale Street, where W. C. Handy developed the blues in the early 1900s. Restoration along Beale Street aims to revive its onetime role as the center of city nightlife.

But the task of reviving downtown is complicated by the city's racial relationships. Memphis' population is 55 percent black, and nearly all the blacks live around and near downtown. The bulk of the white population is segregated in the eastern part of the city and is prone to head further east into the overwhelmingly white suburbs for entertainment.

Ford's House election in 1974 marked the assertion of black political power in the 9th, which was then more compact and much more black than Memphis as a whole. The city itself did not elect a black mayor until 1991, when Ford and other leaders in the black community united behind longtime school superintendent Willie Herenton.

Because of inner-city population decline in Memphis over the years, mapmakers have had to expand the 9th. In 1992, for the first time, the district moved outside the city limits; its black population has held almost steady at 59 percent. The 9th reached east and south to pick up about 80,000 new residents, including some in conservative white areas that had been in the 7th. Still, the 9th remains strongly Democratic: Bill Clinton won two-thirds of its presidential vote in 1992, and Ford took 58 percent, the same as in 1990.

The growth of tourism-related business has helped compensate for the decline since the 1970s of Memphis' industrial base, although the new service-sector jobs are comparatively low-paying. The city also has become a leading distribution center (Federal Express is Memphis-based), and medical services are a big business (St. Jude's Hospital, one of the nation's top pediatric-care facilities, is here). Also, roughly one-third of the nation's cotton crop passes through the Memphis Cotton Exchange.

1990 Population: 541,981. White 214,979 (40%), Black 321,087 (59%), Other 5,915 (1%). Hispanic origin 3,833 (1%). 18 and over 394,375 (73%), 62 and over 80,918 (15%). Median age: 31.

training activities. Major portions of Ford's program were incorporated into the final welfare package that became law in 1988.

One of Ford's more controversial goals was to require states to make two-parent households eligible for support if the principal wage earner is unemployed; under existing law, about half the states help only if one parent is gone.

At Home: Politicians slapped with indictments often fall prey to electoral trouble, but Ford had a strong base to support him. His is the dominant political family in the Memphis black community. His brother John, a former City Council member, serves in the state Senate; his brother James is on the City Council. Shortly after Rep. Ford was indicted, he arrived to a cheering crowd at the Memphis airport and claimed that the federal prosecutor "wants to destroy the black political power in Tennessee." Ford's faithful supporters helped him win another House term easily in 1988.

They also helped him quash his most serious primary challenger in 1990. State Rep. Pam Gaia, a 16-year legislator, waged a campaign offering "honesty and integrity." But with a huge funding advantage and continued support in Memphis' black community, Ford collected 69 percent; Gaia, who is white, managed only 27 percent. In November against typically weak GOP opposition, though, Ford was held to 58 percent, his lowest-ever re-election tally. He won by the same percentage in 1992.

The Ford organization is extensive, reaching down to the block level in many neighborhoods. In addition to mobilizing that network on their own behalf, the Ford brothers often endorse candidates in Democratic primaries for local and statewide offices.

Harold Ford began his political career in 1970, winning election to the Tennessee House at age 25. In his first term, he was majority whip and chaired a committee that investigated the rates and practices of utilities in the state.

Redistricting in 1972 increased the black population in the Memphis congressional district to 48 percent. That caused trouble for Republican Rep. Dan H. Kuykendall.

Kuykendall had won three House elections with increasing ease by taking virtually all the votes of the district's whites. But in 1972, running within the new borders for the first time, he was held to 55 percent by a black Democrat who made little attempt to attract white support.

Ford challenged Kuykendall in 1974. After winning a six-way Democratic primary, Ford ran a broader and more active campaign than did the 1972 Democratic nominee. Ford reached out to white voters, stressing economic issues and promising to listen to whites as well as blacks if he were elected.

Reaping political benefit from Kuykendall's longstanding association with Richard M. Nixon, who resigned the presidency that year, Ford edged past the incumbent by 744 votes, becoming Tennessee's first black congressman.

Before the 1976 election, a court-ordered readjustment of district lines removed 12,000 white suburban voters from Ford's district and put them in the adjoining 6th. The readjustment gave Ford a black majority, and in the next three elections he won handily.

Although 1981 redistricting reduced the share of blacks in the district's voting population to just above 50 percent, Ford won easily in the 1982 primary and general election.

Committees

Ways & Means (7th of 24 Democrats)
Human Resources (chairman); Oversight

Elections

1992 General		
Harold E. Ford (D)	123,276	(58%)
Charles L. Black (R)	60,606	(28%)
Richard Liptock (I)	14,075	(7%)
James Vandergriff (I)	12,265	(6%)
William Rolen (I)	2,517	(1%)
1992 Primary		
Harold E. Ford (D)	74,145	(65%)
Larry S. Patterson (D)	36,321	(32%)
Mark Flanagan (D)	2,716	(2%)
Terrance H. Endsley (D)	1,555	(1%)
1990 General		
Harold E. Ford (D)	48,629	(58%)
Aaron C. Davis (R)	25,730	(31%)
Thomas M. Davidson (I)	7,249	(9%)
Isaac Richmond (I)	2,032	(2%)

Previous Winning Percentages: **1988** (82%) **1986** (83%) **1984** (72%) **1982** (72%) **1980** (100%) **1978** (70%) **1976** (61%) **1974** (50%)

District Vote for President

1992
D 151,590 (66%)
R 68,358 (30%)
I 9,400 (4%)

Campaign Finance

	Receipts	Receipts from PACs	Expend-itures
1992			
Ford (D)	$202,187	$118,450 (59%)	$194,631
1990			
Ford (D)	$283,087	$169,925 (60%)	$284,282

Key Votes

1993	
Require parental notification of minors' abortions	?
Require unpaid family and medical leave	?
Approve national "motor voter" registration bill	?
Approve budget increasing taxes and reducing deficit	?
Approve economic stimulus plan	?
1992	
Approve balanced-budget constitutional amendment	N
Close down space station program	Y
Approve U.S. aid for former Soviet Union	?
Allow shifting funds from defense to domestic programs	Y
1991	
Extend unemployment benefits using deficit financing	Y
Approve waiting period for handgun purchases	Y
Authorize use of force in Persian Gulf	N

Voting Studies

	Presidential Support		Party Unity		Conservative Coalition	
Year	S	O	S	O	S	O
1992	10	69	69	7	13	67
1991	20	62	74	5	5	84
1990	8	53	62	3	6	67
1989	21	64	85	0	2	80
1988	12	57	61	2	5	66
1987	9	48	63	1	9	40
1986	16	73	71	4	12	70
1985	18	78	87	2	7	85
1984	29	57	81	4	15	76
1983	20	65	78	3	10	74
1982	27	56	81	6	19	64
1981	34	59	89	4	9	85

Interest Group Ratings

Year	ADA	AFL-CIO	CCUS	ACU
1992	85	86	29	5
1991	80	100	14	0
1990	89	100	27	5
1989	80	100	10	0
1988	85	100	36	0
1987	68	93	0	0
1986	100	91	8	0
1985	90	94	14	0
1984	80	83	31	0
1983	75	93	35	0
1982	80	100	30	0
1981	85	100	11	0

STATE DATA

Governor:
Ann W. Richards (D)
First elected: 1990
Length of term: 4 years
Term expires: 1/95
Salary: $99,122.04
Term limit: No
Phone: (512) 463-2000
Born: Sept. 1, 1933; Lakeview, Texas
Education: Baylor U., B.A. 1954; U. of Texas, Austin, 1955
Occupation: Teacher; legislative aide
Family: Divorced; four children
Religion: Methodist
Political Career: Travis County Commission, 1977-82; Texas treasurer, 1983-91

Lt. Gov.: Bob Bullock (D)
First elected: 1990
Length of term: 4 years
Term expires: 1/95
Salary: $7,200 + per diem during legislative session
Phone: (512) 463-0001

State election official: (512) 463-5650
Democratic headquarters: (512) 478-8746
Republican headquarters: (512) 477-9821

REDISTRICTING

Texas gained three House seats in reapportionment, increasing from 27 districts to 30. The legislature passed the map Aug. 25, 1991; the governor signed it Aug. 29; federal court upheld it Dec. 24.

STATE LEGISLATURE

Legislature. Meets January-May in odd-numbered years.

Senate: 31 members, 4-year terms
1992 breakdown: 18D, 13R; 27 men, 4 women; 23 whites, 2 blacks, 6 Hispanics
Salary: $7,200 + per diem during session
Phone: (512) 463-0100

House of Representatives: 150 members, 2-year terms
1992 breakdown: 92D, 58R; 124 men, 26 women; 110 whites, 14 blacks, 26 Hispanics
Salary: $7,200 + per diem during session
Phone: (512) 463-0845

URBAN STATISTICS

City	Pop.
Houston Mayor Bob Lanier, R	1,630,864
Dallas Mayor Steve Bartlett, N-P	1,007,617
San Antonio Mayor Nelson Wolff, N-P	935,933
El Paso Mayor William S. Tilney, D	515,342
Austin Mayor Bruce Todd, D	465,622

U.S. CONGRESS

Senate: 0 D, 2 R
House: 21 D, 9 R

TERM LIMITS

For Congress: No
For state offices: No

ELECTIONS

1992 Presidential Vote

Bill Clinton	37.1%
George Bush	40.6%
Ross Perot	22.0%

1988 Presidential Vote

George Bush	56%
Michael S. Dukakis	43%

1984 Presidential Vote

Ronald Reagan	64%
Walter F. Mondale	36%

POPULATION

1990 population		16,986,510
1980 population		14,229,191
Percent change		+19%
Rank among states:		3
White		75%
Black		12%
Hispanic		26%
Asian or Pacific islander		2%
Urban		91%
Rural		9%
Born in state		65%
Foreign-born		9%
Under age 18	4,835,839	28%
Ages 18-64	10,434,095	61%
65 and older	1,716,576	10%
Median age		30.8

MISCELLANEOUS

Capital: Austin
Number of counties: 254
Per capita income: $17,305 (1991)
Rank among states: 31
Total area: 266,807 sq. miles
Rank among states: 2

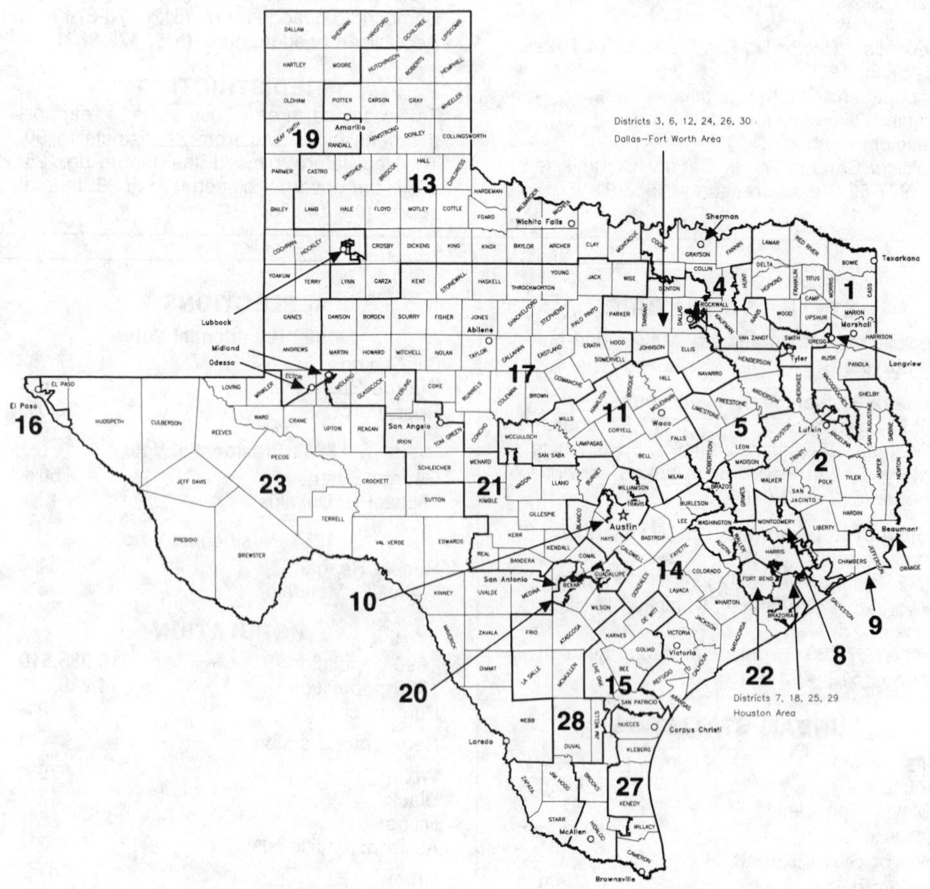
Districts 3, 6, 12, 24, 26, 30
Dallas—Fort Worth Area
Districts 7, 18, 25, 29
Houston Area
Amarillo
Lubbock
Midland
Odessa
El Paso
Wichita Falls
Abilene
San Angelo
Sherman
Texarkana
Marshall
Longview
Tyler
Lufkin
Waco
Austin
San Antonio
Beaumont
Victoria
Corpus Christi
Laredo
McAllen
Brownsville
1
2
4
5
8
9
10
11
13
14
15
16
17
19
20
21
22
23
27
28

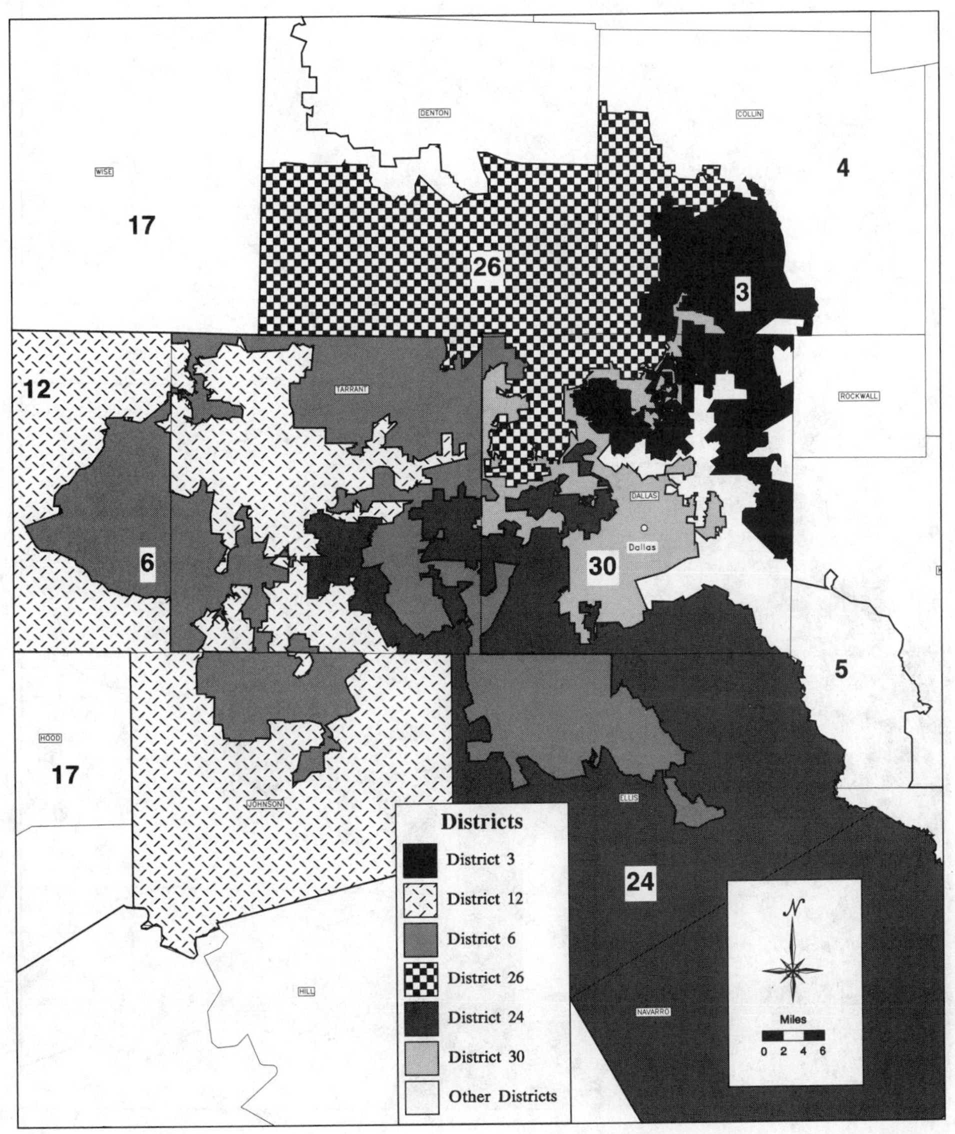
DENTON
COLLIN
WISE
4
17
26
3
12
TARRANT
ROCKWALL
DALLAS
Dallas
6
30
5
HOOD
17
ELLIS
JOHNSON
Districts
District 3
District 12
District 6
District 26
District 24
District 30
Other Districts
24
HILL
NAVARRO
Miles
0 2 4 6

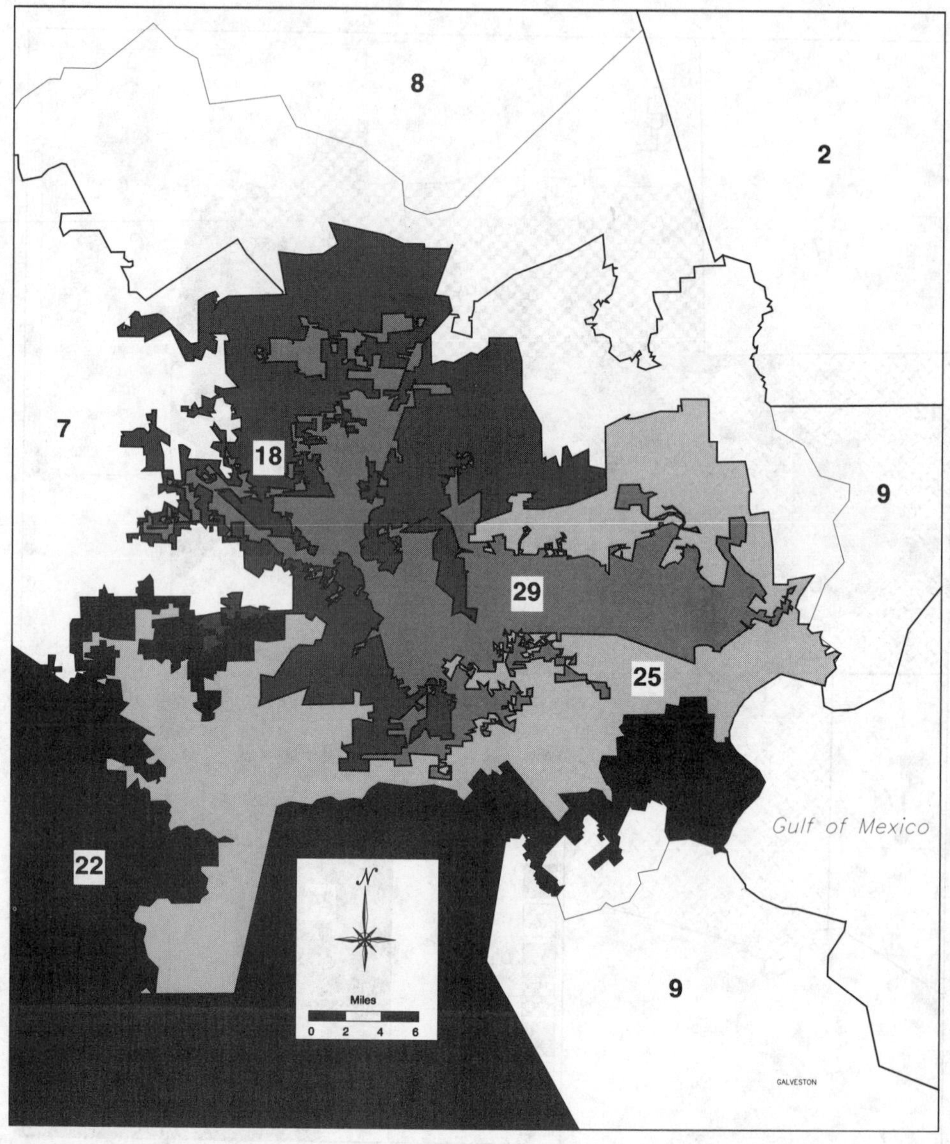
8
2
7
18
9
29
25
Gulf of Mexico
22
N
Miles
0 2 4 6
9
GALVESTON

Phil Gramm (R)

Of College Station — Elected 1984; 2nd Term

Born: July 8, 1942, Fort Benning, Ga.
Education: U. of Georgia, B.B.A. 1964, Ph.D. 1967.
Occupation: Professor.
Family: Wife, Wendy Lee; two children.
Religion: Episcopalian.
Political Career: Sought Democratic nomination for U.S. Senate, 1976; U.S. House, 1979-85.
Capitol Office: 370 Russell Bldg. 20510; 224-2934.

In Washington: Rather than helping him secure a place on the national political stage — something he clearly covets — Gramm's keynote address to the Republican National Convention in August 1992 left him a ways to go to establish his credentials as an appealing spokesman with a vision for the Republican Party.

Everyone knew Gramm's step up into the spotlight on the podium of Houston's Astrodome would be a defining moment. But as Bill Clinton can attest, one dud speech does not necessarily doom one's chances to grasp the brass ring. And Gramm's ambitions were, if anything, heightened, not diminished, by his failure to wow the crowd.

Now in the midst of his second Senate term, Gramm is an established operator in the institution and is recognized as a party leader on budget issues. At the same time, it is easy to find people in Washington — his fellow Republicans as well as members of his former party — whose views of Gramm range from disdain to loathing. His critics call him arrogant, transparently ambitious, demagogic and deceitful.

But however one feels about Gramm, there is no disputing that he has accomplished a great deal, and in a remarkably short time.

An ardent champion of free-market economics, Gramm wants to do more than tinker around the edges of the welfare state. He is out to shrink the whole concept of American government on behalf of the middle class: in Gramm's words, the "people who do the work, pay the taxes and pull the wagon." For a man given to homespun, self-deprecating humor, Gramm is not modest about his own role in that revolution. "I want to make sure we've changed government forever," he says. "If I don't do it, it may not get done."

In the 103rd Congress, Gramm placed himself squarely in the path of President Clinton, whose economic policies he found without merit.

Gramm joined with other Republicans to offer a calculated series of unsuccessful amendments to the budget resolution for fiscal 1994 that discomfited Democrats. One, a sweeping effort by Gramm to eliminate most of the new taxes and spending increases in Clinton's budget, was tabled on a 55-44 vote. Democrat Richard C. Shelby of Alabama was the only defector in this otherwise party-line vote. Gramm promised to keep up the heat as the year progressed.

It was only weeks later that the GOP, with Gramm playing a leading role, derailed a $16.3 billion supplemental appropriations bill that Clinton and the Democrats touted as a needed, job-creating stimulus for a weak economy. The Democrats dubbed the measure an "emergency" in order to skirt budget constraints enacted in the wake of Gramm's earlier efforts. "This is a payoff for the political campaign," Gramm scoffed. "It has nothing to do with economic growth."

Playing the role of spoiler is one of Gramm's strengths. But his name became a household word as a result of the budget laws he helped enact. In less than a decade, Gramm combined politically powerful ideas, shrewd timing and boundless tenacity to enact two landmark laws that shaped budget debates for the 1980s and beyond. No recent member has had so great an impact in so short a time.

In 1981, as a second-term Democratic House member, he devised the Gramm-Latta package embodying President Ronald Reagan's priority-reordering program of social spending cuts, defense buildup and tax reductions. In 1985, as a first-year GOP senator who had been kept off the Budget Committee, he was the driving force behind the Gramm-Rudman anti-deficit law. By 1990, he had made his way onto the Budget and Appropriations panels and onto the GOP budget summit team — signs that he and his party elders finally had come to terms.

Beginning with the 102nd Congress, he appeared to stake his reputation on winning enactment of a constitutional amendment requiring a balanced federal budget. In 1992, even after the House had narrowly defeated a balanced-budget amendment and others had given up the fight for the year, Gramm threatened to attach it to a Bush administration bill to shore up regulation of several government-created corporations that engaged in the buying and selling of home mortgages. But he ran up against one of his own favorite ploys — a filibuster, this one by Senate Appropriations

Committee Chairman and President Pro Tem Robert C. Byrd of West Virginia. Gramm and his supporters fell one vote short of cutting off Byrd's talkathon and abandoned the constitutional amendment effort for the year.

At the start of the 103rd Congress, he announced an all-out, grass-roots drive in support of the amendment. Only a procedural move by the Democratic leadership prevented Gramm from offering the balanced-budget amendment to a must-pass measure that was enacted in April to increase the ceiling on the federal debt. Gramm promised that it would not be the last time the issue was raised in 1993.

Not surprisingly, Gramm the budget-cutter has another side to his congressional persona. His state hardly lacks for influential patrons on Capitol Hill, and Gramm willingly wears that hat, unabashedly helping to secure federal financial support for things deep in the heart of Texas.

He consistently promotes funding the multibillion-dollar, superconducting super collider being built in Texas, and he opposes drastic redesign of the multibillion-dollar space station *Freedom*, a large piece of which is to be built in Houston. Gramm, adamant about cutting Pentagon waste, was instrumental in the mid-1980s in securing a new naval base near Corpus Christi as home to a battleship group. And he does not ignore the small stuff: The fiscal 1993 military construction appropriations bill included $248 million for new base construction and family housing, $125 million above President Bush's request.

While the legislative Gramm has been achieving standing, the political Gramm also has been busy. Fresh off a landslide re-election, Gramm in late 1990 earned a new perch from which to gain attention, as his Senate colleagues elected him chairman of the National Republican Senatorial Committee (NRSC).

At the outset of campaigning for the 1992 elections, some believed the Republicans might seize control of the Senate, especially in the afterglow of the Persian Gulf War. "They are going to pay for that vote," Gramm said of Democrats who had voted against using force to oust Iraqi troops from Kuwait. But the economic slump proved a much heavier burden for Bush and GOP candidates than anyone could have imagined at the time.

After all the votes were counted, the makeup of the Senate was unchanged. Yet, given Bush's defeat, that outcome could be seen as a vindication of sorts for Gramm's hard work. When Gramm tried for a second stint as NRSC chief, he drew a challenge from Mitch McConnell of Kentucky, who harbored no apparent aspirations for higher office, and thus was less suspect than Gramm. Gramm edged McConnell by one vote to win another term.

In early 1993, Gramm was a central player in Texas' special Senate election to choose a successor to Lloyd Bentsen, who resigned to become Clinton's Treasury secretary. Democratic Gov. Ann W. Richards appointed former Rep. Bob Krueger as Bentsen's interim replacement, but in May 1 all-party voting that included two dozen candidates, Krueger turned in a lackluster finish, running just behind Republican Kay Bailey Hutchison, the state treasurer. Krueger and Hutchison advanced to a June runoff, but Hutchison was elected.

Gramm's national standing could be affected by the disclosure in late 1992 that a Texas builder, who owned three failed savings and loan associations, had picked up half the cost of completing a vacation house that Gramm owned in Maryland. Common Cause, the citizen's watchdog group, called for an Ethics Committee investigation, and then-committee Chairman Terry Sanford of North Carolina said the staff would look into the matter. There was no resolution in early 1993.

Gramm occasionally looks beyond fiscal matters to pursue his cause on social issues such as abortion, drugs and crime. In 1990, he pushed for mandatory minimum sentencing on anti-drug legislation and unsuccessfully fought to remove language from an anti-crime measure that banned a number of semiautomatic assault-style weapons.

But Gramm's best love seems to be pursuing free-market theories and advocating less government regulation, and he often does both from his Banking Committee post. During the 100th Congress, amid trouble in the stock and commodity markets, Gramm counseled against government intervention (his wife, Wendy Lee, was chairman of the Commodity Futures Trading Commission until January 1993). In the 101st Congress, Gramm successfully opposed efforts that would have significantly weakened the CFTC's authority over futures trading.

Gramm was a strong advocate of dramatically overhauling banking laws in 1991 — if somewhat more restrained in his views than some of his Republican colleagues. When Banking Committee Chairman Donald W. Riegle Jr. of Michigan proposed to hamstring the Federal Reserve's lending to weakened banks, Gramm threatened to kill the entire banking bill with a filibuster. Riegle and Gramm eventually compromised over the Fed.

And Gramm found himself in the middle of debate in 1989 over financing the bailout of the bankrupt insurance fund that protected savings and loan depositors. Riegle and House Democrats wanted the first $50 billion borrowed for the bailout to count as part of the federal budget, with an exemption from Gramm-Rudman. Gramm vowed to block an on-budget scheme, arguing that an exemption from the anti-deficit law would open the door to future exemptions. A compromise was finally approved that put two-fifths of the spending "on budget" in fiscal 1989 — a move that did not require a Gramm-Rudman exemption because the budget year was nearly over — and put the remainder "off budget."

It was Gramm's lightning campaign to enact Gramm-Rudman that clearly illustrated the keys to his success. He pressed the issue with energy and a single-minded intensity. "You don't have to worry about stepping on people's toes," he observes. "They're going to step out of your way." Even more important, perhaps, was Gramm's sense of timing: He is an opportunist and an effective one.

In 1981, Gramm had capitalized on Reagan's honeymoon; by 1985, Gramm saw that lawmakers and the public were ready for radical steps, despairing over spiraling deficits and Congress' inability to control them through conventional means. The only way to force Congress to eliminate the deficit was to install a process that threatened a worse alternative — indiscriminate, across-the-board spending cuts.

Gramm-Rudman's goal of a balanced budget by 1991, later pushed back to 1993, has since been largely forgotten. With the deficit persisting, Gramm has seen his handiwork come under increasing criticism. In 1989, South Carolina Democrat Ernest F. Hollings divorced himself from the law that bore his name, and others faulted the law for leading to accounting gimmickry rather than true deficit reduction.

In 1990, Congress passed a five-year package of tax increases and spending cuts that included new mechanisms aimed at producing a balanced budget. Gramm voted against that plan, although Bush said it "extended" and "strengthened" the Gramm-Rudman law and its enforcement mechanisms.

In landing a seat on the Budget Committee for the 101st Congress, Gramm fulfilled a goal he had had since winning election to the Senate in 1984. The fact that it took him four years to achieve it is a measure of the institutional response to his brash independence.

Initially at least, some top Senate Republicans were cool toward Gramm because of his stormy career in the House as a Democrat. Almost as soon as he got to the House in 1979, he had begun fighting with top Democrats. When he campaigned for a seat on the Budget Committee at the start of his second term in 1981, Democratic House leaders sought and received Gramm's written assurance that he would loyally support the party's budget.

Just months later, he did the opposite — and in a spectacular way, secretly collaborating with Republicans on Reagan's budget, while sitting in on Budget Democrats' caucuses and reporting back to the White House. The alleged spy was barred from Democrats' meetings. He then helped engineer Reagan's budget victory on the House floor by lining up conservative Democrats to vote with the GOP.

Democrats felt betrayed, and at the start of the next Congress, Gramm was evicted from Budget. But he was prepared for that, and he had even hired a GOP pollster for some soundings about a party switch. Charging that he had been punished "for practicing in Washington what I preach at home," Gramm left the party, resigned his House seat and won re-election to it as a Republican in 1983. He rejoined Budget, adapting easily to the role of GOP partisan.

At Home: Whatever the effects of Gramm's 1983 party switch in Washington, the move bolstered his political career at home. His comfortable victory in the 1983 special House election set the stage for his stunning 1984 Senate triumph. In 1990, his first Senate re-election bid was never a worry. And in early 1993 Gramm became the senior senator with Bentsen's resignation.

The Democrats' hopes in 1983 rested on forcing Gramm into a runoff. But Gramm won the special election outright, tapping a massive treasury and a superior organization to take 55 percent. His victory gave the 6th District to the GOP for the first time in Texas history.

In building that victory, Gramm invested heavily in media markets encompassing Dallas, Houston and Fort Worth — giving him exposure that proved invaluable in his subsequent Senate campaign. When GOP Sen. John Tower announced he would retire at the end of the 98th Congress, Gramm was already a familiar figure in the state's populous parts.

Bolstered by his superior name recognition, Gramm took a commanding lead for the Republican Senate nomination; he spent the spring of 1984 canvassing areas not normally hospitable to the GOP.

The Democrats, meanwhile, had a tortuous nominating campaign. State Sen. Lloyd Doggett, a hard-charging liberal, struggled to finish a close second in the grueling primary, then squeezed past conservative U.S. Rep. Kent Hance in a runoff that further polarized the party and drained Doggett's resources.

With Doggett nominated, Gramm launched a statewide media campaign questioning Doggett's commitment to traditional family values. One ad observed that Doggett had accepted a contribution from a gay group that raised part of the money at an all-male striptease show.

Doggett tried to cast Gramm as a right-wing extremist. He accused Gramm of attempting to cut Social Security and of calling for the eventual elimination of federal education aid. But Gramm made impressive inroads into conservative, rural East and West Texas — territory that would ordinarily go Democratic. Aided by a 3-to-1 spending advantage and Reagan's strong campaign, Gramm took 59 percent of the vote.

Gramm's high profile in Washington discouraged Democrats with statewide stature from challenging him in 1990. The nomination went to state Sen. Hugh Parmer, who assailed the incumbent for "Gramm-standing" — claiming credit for federal largess in Texas that he had nothing to do with, or had even opposed at one point. Parmer also tried to link Gramm to anger over the savings and loan crisis, citing Gramm's campaign contributions from thrift-related sources. But Parmer never shook his underdog image, and Gramm spent much of his time campaigning for GOP House candidates. He took 60 percent of the vote.

Before he ran for Congress in 1976, Gramm's life was centered on the academic community at Texas A&M University, where he taught economics.

Gramm was barely known statewide when he challenged Bentsen in the 1976 Democratic Senate primary. Claiming that Bentsen had moved to the left to mount his ill-fated 1976 presidential campaign, Gramm presented himself as a conservative alternative. Under-financed, he drew only 29 percent of the vote.

Two years later, with better name recognition and financial support, Gramm sought the Democratic nomination to succeed Rep. Olin E. Teague, challenging a Fort Worth TV weatherman. Gramm survived an expensive primary and runoff by building a campaign treasury of nearly a half-million dollars. In the general election, his national New Right support preempted a successful Republican challenge.

In 1982, Gramm faced a spirited primary challenge from a candidate cheered on by the national Democratic establishment — Jack Teague, son of Gramm's House predecessor. Teague called Gramm a turncoat who had abandoned his party's traditional concern for the disadvantaged and average-income people.

But Gramm cast the election as a referendum on whether he was fulfilling his promises to carry the district's fiscal conservatism to Washington, and he won the primary with 62 percent of the vote. Republicans made no effort to oppose him.

Committees

Appropriations (8th of 13 Republicans)
VA, HUD & Independent Agencies (ranking); Agriculture, Rural Development & Related Agencies; Commerce, Justice, State & Judiciary; Defense; Foreign Operations

Banking, Housing & Urban Affairs (2nd of 8 Republicans)
Securities (ranking); Economic Stabilization & Rural Development; International Finance & Monetary Policy

Budget (4th of 9 Republicans)

Elections

1990 General

Phil Gramm (R)	2,302,357	(60%)
Hugh Parmer (D)	1,429,986	(37%)
Gary Johnson (LIBERT)	89,089	(2%)

Previous Winning Percentages: **1984** (59%) **1983 †** (55%) **1982 *** (95%) **1980 *** (71%) **1978 *** (65%)

** House elections. Gramm was elected as a Democrat in 1978-82.*

† Special House election.

Campaign Finance

	Receipts	Receipts from PACs		Expend-itures
1990				
Gramm (R)	$11,626,377	$1,426,839	(12%)	$9,799,104
Parmer (D)	$1,674,600	$263,762	(16%)	$1,677,087

Interest Group Ratings

Year	ADA	AFL-CIO	CCUS	ACU
1992	0	8	100	93
1991	0	17	89	95
1990	0	22	92	91
1989	0	0	88	96
1988	0	0	92	95
1987	5	10	89	100
1986	0	89	0	100
1985	0	0	86	95
House Service:				
1984	10	22	78	64
1983	0	0	88	100
1982	10	10	73	91
1981	0	13	89	93

Key Votes

1993	
Require unpaid family and medical leave	N
Approve national "motor voter" registration bill	N
Approve budget increasing taxes and reducing deficit	N
Support president's right to lift military gay ban	N
1992	
Approve school-choice pilot program	Y
Allow shifting funds from defense to domestic programs	N
Oppose deeper cuts in spending for SDI	Y
1991	
Approve waiting period for handgun purchases	N
Raise senators' pay and ban honoraria	N
Authorize use of force in Persian Gulf	Y
Confirm Clarence Thomas to Supreme Court	Y

Voting Studies

	Presidential Support		Party Unity		Conservative Coalition	
Year	**S**	**O**	**S**	**O**	**S**	**O**
1992	90	10	91	1	89	5
1991	93	4	92	5	90	3
1990	78	14	88	8	100	0
1989	86	12	91	6	82	16
1988	78	15	85	4	92	3
1987	87	9	92	5	84	13
1986	99	1	95	4	97	1
1985	87	13	95	5	88	12
House Service:						
1984	37	27	58	5	69	8
1983	73	16	79 †	1 †	93	0
1982	84	14	10	87	89	10
1981	75	22	20	77	99	0

† Not eligible for all recorded votes. Gramm resigned from the House Jan. 5, 1983. He had been elected as a Democrat and cast his first three votes of 1983 as a member of that party. His party unity support score as a Democrat was 33 percent; opposition was 67 percent. Gramm was re-elected Feb. 12, 1983, as a Republican and sworn in Feb. 22. The scores for party unity reflect his votes as a Republican.

Kay Bailey Hutchison (R)

Of Dallas — Elected 1993; 1st Term

Born: July 22, 1943, Galveston, Texas.
Education: U. of Texas, J.D. 1967, B.A. 1992.
Occupation: Broadcast journalist; banking executive; candy manufacturer.
Family: Husband, Ray Hutchison.
Religion: Episcopalian.
Political Career: Texas House, 1973-77; Texas state treasurer, 1991-93.
Capitol Office: 703 Hart Bldg. 20510; 224-5922.

The Path to Washington: Hutchison's special-election victory in June 1993 was a breakthrough both for her sex and for her party. Like many of the women beginning their Washington careers in the 103rd Congress, Hutchison was the first woman from her state to occupy her office. And her triumph was a significant boost for Republicans, giving the GOP control of both Texas Senate seats for the first time since Reconstruction.

Hutchison also helped her party counteract the Democratic dominance of the "Year of the Woman" phenomenon in 1992, when all the women elected to the Senate and most of those elected to the House were Democrats.

But while Hutchison may share in some of the "Year of the Woman" afterglow, she is likely to part company with her first-term sisters in the Senate more often than she votes with them.

Even before she was sworn in, Hutchison was highlighting the differences between herself and the four Democratic women who won new seats in the Senate in 1992. For starters, Hutchison's candidacy had little relation to the contentious 1991 Supreme Court nomination hearings of Clarence Thomas. Only when pressed on the matter does Hutchison concede the Judiciary Committee hearings "showed the panel was out of touch."

Her feminist pitch on the campaign trail was hardly radical, telling voters she hoped to create a society that is "better for our sons and open for our daughters."

Her own assessment of her place in the Senate was on point: "I am not philosophically in touch with the women that won in '92. But on some issues we will come together."

The most visible test for Hutchison may come on the question of abortion. Like the only other Republican woman in the Senate, Nancy Landon Kassebaum of Kansas, Hutchison supports abortion rights.

But with a raft of abortion-related matters slated to come before the 103rd Congress, the issue could become increasingly complex for her. She said during the spring campaign that she opposed using government funds for abortion and supported some restrictions on abortion — such as requiring parental consent for minors. Her mixed positions prompted her Democratic opponent, interim Sen. Bob Krueger, to label her not "pro-choice" but "multiple choice."

Hutchison expects to team up with other women in Congress on legislation benefiting children and on crime bills dealing with female victims. While serving in the state House in 1975, Hutchison cosponsored legislation with then-state Rep. Sarah Weddington that gave added protections to victims of sexual offenses, including a ban on the publication of the names of rape victims. Weddington, a Democrat, was the lawyer for the plaintiff in the landmark Supreme Court case legalizing abortion, *Roe v. Wade.*

Hutchison also advocates establishing gender equity in Individual Retirement Accounts. She hopes to eliminate discrepancies that limit non-working spouses to setting aside $250 annually for their retirement, while working people can set aside up to $2,000.

Hutchison proved her political mettle — and Texas voters confirmed their trend toward the GOP — in the 1993 special election to replace Lloyd Bentsen, who retired to become President Clinton's Treasury secretary. Democratic Gov. Ann W. Richards appointed Krueger to the seat in January, after a handful of better-known Democrats declined the opportunity.

Krueger, a state railroad commissioner at the time of his appointment, had served in the House from 1975 to 1979 and had run unsuccessfully for the Senate twice before (in 1978 and 1984). Political analysts expected him to enter the runoff as the front-runner because Hutchison had been busy fending off several Republican rivals, including GOP Reps. Joe L. Barton and Jack Fields. But instead, it was Hutchison, then-state treasurer, who headed into the final weeks with momentum, money and the all-important conservative mantle.

She topped the 24-person field in the all-party May 1 primary and then went on to defeat Krueger in the head-to-head contest June 5, 67 percent to 33 percent.

Hutchison's winning percentage was the largest vote share any challenger has ever achieved against an incumbent senator. She carried 239 counties, Krueger just 15. She won every county in every metropolitan area, rolling up a margin of more than 100,000 votes in Harris County (Houston) alone.

Krueger's counties, by contrast, lay mostly in the state's impoverished southern extreme, along the Mexican border. And even where he won, Krueger did not pile up many votes. His combined margin in all the counties he carried was fewer than 7,600 votes.

The only tarnish on all this triumph came a few days after the votes were counted, when a grand jury in Travis County (Austin) issued subpoenas for 14 members of Bailey's state Treasury staff and two of her campaign aides. The state prosecutor involved, a Democrat, said he wanted to know whether state records had been tampered with following earlier inquiries into the use of state office staff and equipment for campaign purposes.

Hutchison and her aides depicted the investigation as a political assault. They said it had been orchestrated by high-level state Democrats interested in challenging Hutchison's reelection in 1994, when Bentsen's term expires and Hutchison must face the voters again to win a full term of her own.

With the exception of the abortion issue, Hutchison is a solid conservative rooted in the anti-regulatory, pro-entrepreneurial beliefs that represent the core philosophies of the Texas GOP.

"I see three enemies of small business," she said frequently on the campaign trail, "taxation, regulation and litigation."

She supports the presidential line-item veto, a balanced-budget constitutional amendment and pay freezes for members of Congress. Although she advocates slashing government spending and reducing the federal deficit, Hutchison defends two expensive, Texas-based projects — the superconducting super collider and the space station *Freedom* — as good science that will benefit the entire nation. She predicts the projects (which together have price tags approaching $40 billion) will provide a host of innovations, similar to the developments in the computer and medical industries that emanated from earlier space exploration.

"The space station is not a Texas project; eight states are involved," she said. "One-third of the jobs are in Texas and two-thirds are elsewhere."

But Hutchison is a pragmatic politician who realizes she will be in the minority party on Capitol Hill as she fights for the two programs. Because of that, Hutchison has said she will cross party lines and accept program reductions if that is what it takes to preserve the projects.

"I'll work with the other Democratic leaders that have the same interest" in the projects, she said, mentioning Bentsen, Richards and Democratic Rep. Jack Brooks, chairman of the House Judiciary Committee.

If Hutchison's ideology is tried and true Texas conservative, her style is anything but. In a state where male and female politicians win by strutting their stuff in ten-gallon hats and cowboy boots, Hutchison worked her way up in the system quietly — and in a pair of high heels. She is a petite, soft-spoken woman who has trouble rousing a large crowd but charms people one-on-one.

That style may well prove a successful one in the Senate. But Hutchison will need some time to matter as much in that chamber as Bentsen. A silver-haired Tory Democrat who held the seat for 22 years, Bentsen became something of an elder statesman after running a respectable campaign as the party's vice presidential nominee in 1988. She will also have to contend with the presence of the state's senior senator, high-powered, high-energy Republican Phil Gramm.

And most importantly, she must repeat her performance in an astonishingly short period of time. She must defend the seat in 1994, when the field of potential challengers could include the nationally known and politically powerful Richards.

Committees

New member -- assignments to be determined

Campaign Finance †

	Receipts	Receipts from PACs		Expend-itures
1993				
Hutchison (R)	$4,061,882	$587,965	(14%)	$3,648,559
Krueger (D)	$3,609,476	$698,109	(19%)	$3,194,086

† Figures are through May 28, 1993.

Elections

1993 Special Runoff *		
Kay Bailey Hutchison (R)	1,183,766	(67%)
Bob Krueger (D)	574,089	(33%)
1993 Special		
Kay Bailey Hutchison (R)	593,338	(29%)
Bob Krueger (D)	593,239	(29%)
Joe L. Barton (R)	284,135	(14%)
Jack Fields (R)	277,560	(14%)
Richard Fisher (D)	165,564	(8%)
Jose Angel Gutierrez (D)	52,103	(3%)

** Nearly complete, unofficial returns.*

1 Jim Chapman (D)

Of Sulphur Springs — Elected 1985; 4th Full Term

Born: March 8, 1945, Washington, D.C.
Education: U. of Texas, B.B.A. 1968; Southern Methodist U., J.D. 1970.
Occupation: Lawyer.
Family: Wife, Betty Brice; two children.
Religion: Methodist.
Political Career: District attorney, 8th Judicial District of Texas, 1977-85; sought Democratic nomination for Texas Senate, 1984.
Capitol Office: 2417 Rayburn Bldg. 20515; 225-3035.

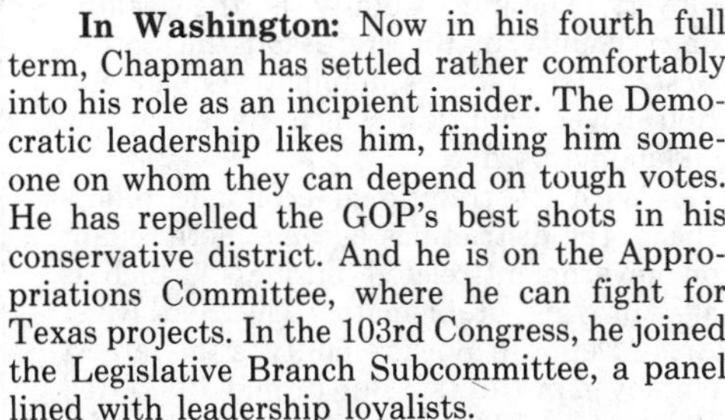

In Washington: Now in his fourth full term, Chapman has settled rather comfortably into his role as an incipient insider. The Democratic leadership likes him, finding him someone on whom they can depend on tough votes. He has repelled the GOP's best shots in his conservative district. And he is on the Appropriations Committee, where he can fight for Texas projects. In the 103rd Congress, he joined the Legislative Branch Subcommittee, a panel lined with leadership loyalists.

Chapman's primary mission is to protect a huge government project dear to the heart of Texas: the superconducting super collider (SSC), a massive atom smasher with a price tag in excess of $8 billion being built south of Dallas. Chapman's efforts for the collider in the 101st Congress, when Congress appropriated nearly $500 million for it, led Texas Republican Rep. Joe L. Barton to compare him to Sam Houston and other Texas heroes. "I'd vote for him," Barton said of Chapman.

The project has become a target for members who have questioned its scientific merits — and who see it as absorbing funds that otherwise could be spent on their priorities. Its support has also eroded as its identity has been increasingly tied to one state. Chapman promotes it from his seat on the subcommittee that funds it, Energy and Water Development.

Congress approved $484 million for the SSC in 1991, $50 million below the Bush administration's request but $50 million more than the amount the House approved. But in 1992, SSC supporters were stunned when critics led a charge on the House floor and won a 232-181 vote to kill the project. A counteroffensive by the administration and other supporters in the Senate saved the project. In conference, appropriators approved $517 million for the SSC in fiscal 1993.

Chapman also sits on the VA-HUD subcommittee which, in addition to funding programs for housing and veterans, provides money for the nation's space programs. There, he defends another large-ticket science project that has been targeted for extinction by critics, the $30 billion-plus space station *Freedom*. Opponents tried unsuccessfully in 1991 and 1992 to kill the space station, the government's largest big-science project. Although his district receives no direct funding from NASA or the space station, Chapman has taken a stand in behalf of his state, which will receive at least $3.1 billion in contracts for the space station.

In 1991, the Appropriations Committee eliminated funding for the space station to stay within the strict limits on domestic spending imposed by the 1990 budget agreement. On the House floor, Chapman and California Republican Bill Lowery offered an amendment, drafted by the Office of Management and Budget, to restore nearly $2 billion in space station funding. The amendment, which also cut the funds used to maintain public housing by $217 million, was adopted 240-173. In 1993, President Clinton ordered NASA to reduce the station's size and cost.

In the 101st Congress, Chapman wrote the controversial "food handlers" amendment to the Americans with Disabilities Act. The amendment would have allowed the transfer of workers with diseases such as AIDS that are not transmissible through food but that nonetheless may be wrongly perceived to be so by much of the public. The House approved the language, and the Senate instructed its conferees to adopt it. But the conferees refused. When the bill came up for final passage, support for the amendment grew tepid, and Chapman could not muster the votes to restore it.

Chapman is evidence that while Jim Wright may be gone from the House, the former Speaker's handiwork is still evident. Wright helped Chapman win a 1985 special election and saw to it that he got an Appropriations seat at the start of the 101st Congress.

Chapman's 1989 appointment to Appropriations added fuel to resentment of Texans' profiteering under Wright, but he earned the Speaker's gratitude in late 1987, when he saved him from defeat on a controversial budget bill

Texas 1

Northeast — Texarkana; Marshall

Texas' personality has both Southern and Western elements, and the former is dominant in the 20 counties that make up the 1st. Life in northeastern Texas has a distinctly Southern feel; many people's livelihoods are linked to the land — in timber, dairying and other agricultural pursuits.

The closest thing to a big city in the district is Texarkana (Bowie County), a community divided by the Arkansas-Texas line. More than half of its 53,000 residents live on the Texas side. The city is a peculiar blend of togetherness and separation: There is a joint Chamber of Commerce and some utility services are shared, but there are separate mayors, police departments and school systems.

Texarkana's most famous native is billionaire businessman and White House aspirant Ross Perot. The 1992 presidential vote in Bowie County almost exactly mirrored that of the district as a whole. Perot got 22 percent of the county's vote, while Bill Clinton and George Bush each took 39 percent. Clinton carried the county by a mere 49 votes; districtwide, he won by 1,229 votes.

Economically, the 1st has been through some tough times of late. An important area employer, Lone Star Steel, filed for bankruptcy protection in 1989. As is the case with many businesses in Texas, the fortunes of Lone Star rise and fall with the price of crude oil. When the oil industry crashed in 1984, there was little demand for the pipeline Lone Star produced; foreign competition further hampered the company. Once the largest employer in the district (7,000 jobs in 1981), Lone Star now has fewer than 2,000 workers.

Also in recent years, Canadian imports have posed a threat to local timber sales, and Mexican cattle ranchers have put a dent in the East Texas market. Nevertheless, those two industries remain staples of the region. Wood is in abundance and sold to furniture makers, paper mills and lumber companies.

In many of the small towns of rural East Texas, cows, chickens and trees outnumber people. Food processors Tyson Foods and Pilgrim Industries are big employers. Hopkins County is the leading dairy county in the state and the Southwest. Cattle ranches dominate Lamar and Red River counties, which lie along the Oklahoma border.

With its traditional economic pillars shaky, the district has become more reliant on government-related business, which is also proving problematic. The Red River Army Depot in Bowie County is the largest employer in the 1st. But in mid-1993, Red River was on a list of facilities proposed for closing as the Pentagon cuts costs.

The 1st has been dubbed the buckle on the Southern Bible Belt; most voters are churchgoing conservatives. Clinton ran strongest in the counties along the Arkansas, Louisiana and Oklahoma borders; Bush fared best in the counties on the district's western border, topping out with a 49 percent tally in Nacogdoches County.

1990 Population: 566,217. White 449,976 (79%), Black 102,480 (18%), Other 13,761 (2%). Hispanic origin 18,058 (3%). 18 and over 416,554 (74%), 62 and over 106,626 (19%). Median age: 34.

that contained new taxes. Chapman's post-last-minute vote change gave Wright a 206-205 victory.

Chapman has demonstrated his loyalty to the post-Wright leaders as well. Although he votes with his party less than three-quarters of the time, he has sided with the Democrats on some major party-line showdowns. In 1990, for example, he voted for the budget summit agreement that raised taxes. He backed the 1991 civil rights bill, and in 1992 he voted for a Democratic substitute to a tax bill that would have cut taxes for the middle class while imposing a 10 percent surtax on millionaires.

But Chapman's record is too conservative for some Democrats back home. In January 1993, Chapman was reported to be at the top of Gov. Ann W. Richards' list of candidates to appoint to the Senate seat being vacated by Lloyd Bentsen, who was leaving to become Treasury secretary. Opposition from homosexual activists and environmentalists helped torpedo his chances. Homosexual activists were particularly upset over Chapman's food handlers' legislation.

At Home: In his 1985 special election, Chapman was at the center of a battle the parties saw as crucial to their future in the South.

Republican Sen. Phil Gramm had helped engineer a federal judgeship for Democratic Rep. Sam B. Hall Jr., then helped recruit rancher and engineer Edd Hargett, a former Texas A&M football star, as the Republican candidate to replace Hall. The national GOP threw its weight behind Hargett, seeing a chance for the party to make inroads in traditionally Democratic territory.

Chapman was one of six Democrats competing on the same ballot with Hargett. He managed 30 percent of the vote and forced a runoff with Hargett, who took 42 percent.

In the runoff, Chapman presented himself as a traditional conservative Democrat and questioned Hargett's credentials to serve in Congress. He got his biggest boost, however, when local newspapers reported the Republican saying, "I don't know what trade policies have to do with bringing jobs to East Texas." Chapman pounced, pointing to layoffs at a local steel plant. Hargett could not overcome the trade issue. With support from courthouse Democrats, labor and trial lawyers, Chapman narrowly won the runoff.

National GOP leaders claimed that the party had shown real strength in the South by coming so close, but they dropped the issue in 1986, and Chapman won a full term unopposed. The 1988 GOP nominee, farmer-broadcaster Horace McQueen, drew 38 percent, but Republicans had higher hopes for their 1990 pick, Hamp Hodges. Hodges, a businessman and decorated Vietnam veteran, fared no better, though.

Republicans were optimistic again in 1992, with a congressional redistricting that added some more conservative territory in Gregg County and a prominent Texarkanan on the ballot. Nearly a year before the election, the GOP was touting Robert E. "Swede" Lee, the president of the local Chamber of Commerce who helped secure federal support for extending Interstate 49 northward into the city.

But Chapman quickly countered that argument by noting that he had invited Lee to Washington to meet with congressional leaders about the highway. And Chapman devoted more time to visiting Nacogdoches County, an academic community added to the 1st.

Soon after winning his primary, Lee dropped out, citing financial worries. It was too late for the GOP to name a replacement, and Chapman coasted to re-election.

Committee

Appropriations (20th of 37 Democrats)
Energy & Water Development; Legislative Branch; Veterans Affairs, Housing & Urban Development & Independent Agencies

Elections

1992 General		
Jim Chapman (D)	152,209	(100%)
1990 General		
Jim Chapman (D)	89,241	(61%)
Hamp Hodges (R)	56,954	(39%)

Previous Winning Percentages: 1988 (62%) 1986 (100%) 1985 † (51%)

† Special election runoff.

District Vote for President

	1992
D	85,745 (39%)
R	84,516 (38%)
I	50,499 (23%)

Campaign Finance

	Receipts	Receipts from PACs	Expend-itures
1992			
Chapman (D)	$342,246	$212,577 (62%)	$208,815
1990			
Chapman (D)	$533,989	$296,839 (56%)	$463,377
Hodges (R)	$420,961	$2,328 (1%)	$408,677

Key Votes

1993	
Require parental notification of minors' abortions	N
Require unpaid family and medical leave	Y
Approve national "motor voter" registration bill	Y
Approve budget increasing taxes and reducing deficit	Y
Approve economic stimulus plan	Y
1992	
Approve balanced-budget constitutional amendment	Y
Close down space station program	N
Approve U.S. aid for former Soviet Union	N
Allow shifting funds from defense to domestic programs	Y
1991	
Extend unemployment benefits using deficit financing	Y
Approve waiting period for handgun purchases	Y
Authorize use of force in Persian Gulf	Y

Voting Studies

	Presidential Support		Party Unity		Conservative Coalition	
Year	S	O	S	O	S	O
1992	31	64	74	17	73	19
1991	40 †	49 †	68 †	21 †	84	8
1990	34	62	71	19	78	19
1989	49	47	70	22	85	12
1988	36	61	70	23	87	3
1987	39	60	71	22	88	9
1986	37	61	69	24	86	10
1985	42 †	56 †	59 †	32 †	94 †	0 †

† Not eligible for all recorded votes.

Interest Group Ratings

Year	ADA	AFL-CIO	CCUS	ACU
1992	75	75	25	24
1991	30	67	44	26
1990	33	83	43	27
1989	50	50	60	39
1988	50	71	64	52
1987	48	63	47	9
1986	40	69	50	38
1985	--	20	92	71

2 Charles Wilson (D)

Of Lufkin — Elected 1972; 11th Term

Born: June 1, 1933, Trinity, Texas.
Education: Sam Houston State U., 1950-51; U. of Texas, 1951-52; U.S. Naval Academy, B.S. 1956.
Military Service: Navy, 1956-60.
Occupation: Lumberyard manager.
Family: Divorced.
Religion: Methodist.
Political Career: Texas House, 1961-67; Texas Senate, 1967-73.
Capitol Office: 2256 Rayburn Bldg. 20515; 225-2401.

In Washington: Wilson revels in his reputation as a swashbuckler, cavalierly dancing on the political precipice. On the surface, the smooth-talking, backslapping Texan seems a throwback to an era when men were men and ladies were not seen on Capitol Hill.

Even as analysts dubbed 1992 the "Year of the Woman" and House and Senate leaders installed women in positions of influence, Wilson remained the quintessential bachelor on the lookout for a prospective date.

As the 103rd Congress got under way, Wilson was asked by The New York Times what he thought of the growing female presence in Congress. He replied: "I love it. A couple of 'em are pretty cute."

But if Wilson's verbal shockers and fast-lane lifestyle seem to fly in the face of modern trends, they have done little to impede his aggressive and effective work on behalf of East Texas and causes he passionately cares about. His friendly, independent ways often earn him respect from unlikely quarters. And for all his machismo, Wilson does seem to take some women seriously.

An ardent supporter of abortion rights, he is close to Texas Gov. Ann W. Richards and columnist Molly Ivins. He has several women on his staff and has formed working relationships with a handful of prominent female lawmakers, among them Deputy Whip Barbara B. Kennelly of Connecticut.

This respect for some women — he still calls Colorado Democrat Patricia Schroeder "babycakes" — was not entirely voluntary. He is keenly aware of the new political climate.

Nowhere was that more evident than in back-to-back re-election campaigns against Republican Donna Peterson, a sharp West Point graduate who appealed to the Bible Belt district with her opposition to abortion rights. After underestimating Peterson's electoral appeal in 1990, Wilson hunkered down in 1992 for his toughest fight ever.

Changing realities forced Wilson to shift his priorities as well, replacing his true love, foreign affairs, with a more East Texas-oriented agenda.

With his seat on the Appropriations Committee, Wilson has been able to obtain money for the types of projects that earn constituent gratitude. For years, he has been steadily expanding the budget and land holdings in the Big Thicket National Preserve, securing $2.5 million for a visitors center. Strongly supported by the many veterans in the 2nd, Wilson was instrumental in having a Department of Veterans Affairs clinic built in his hometown of Lufkin in 1991. In February 1993, he announced the clinic would receive $260,000 more for six new employees.

At the start of the 103rd he filed a bill prohibiting the export of wood chips unless American manufacturers had reciprocal access to markets for finished products. The legislation was aimed at concerns during the 1992 election that East Texas timberland owners were selling the low-value wood chips to Japanese firms, which were making the higher-priced goods such as finished wood products, paper and building lumber.

Wilson has been known throughout his career as the most persistent House defender of independent oil interests. He found a chance to mix his interest in foreign affairs and home-state business in 1989, when he traveled to Iraq to push the Arab state to buy oil drilling equipment from Lufkin Industries. And in 1992 he voted in favor of a sweeping energy bill that included tax relief for independent oil and gas drillers.

A graduate of the U.S. Naval Academy, Wilson has also lived up to his reputation as a pro-defense conservative. From his seat on Appropriations' Defense Subcommittee, he has supported weapons systems that have been controversial within the Democratic Caucus.

In 1985, Wilson issued a prescient warning on defense issues to his party's liberal wing. "If the perception persists in this country that the Democratic Party is the party of isolation and . . . weakness on defense," he said, "we are flat

Texas 2

East — Lufkin; Orange

Stretching along Texas' eastern border, from Louisiana in the north to Port Orange in the south, the 2nd is another world from the dusty, barren landscape of West Texas, far removed from the barrios on the Mexican border and light years away from the glitz of metropolitan Dallas and Houston.

Instead, the thick forests of East Texas' Piney Woods call to mind stretches of Oregon, Washington state or New England. And the "Golden Triangle" of Orange, Port Arthur and Beaumont, with its shipyards, refineries and fishing docks, more resembles East Coast cities such as Philadelphia and Norfolk, Va.

But the image of the typical Texan as a rough-and-ready character fits the people here just as well as it does any in the Lone Star State. Rep. Wilson has always fashioned himself in that mold, and his fun-loving, take-no-guff style — along with a depressed local economy that increasingly relies on government dollars — helped him win his come-from-behind re-election bid in 1992.

Located 36 miles from the Gulf of Mexico on the Sabine River, Orange once drew its revenue from timber, cattle, rice and oil.

Today, the city is better known for "Chemical Row," an industrial corridor that saw massive layoffs in the late 1980s.

The ports of Orange and Arthur rely heavily on federal dollars; in late 1992 the Orange Shipbuilding Co. won a Navy contract to build refueling barges, including one of the type used in the Persian Gulf. In late 1992 Lamar University (2,000 students) received $5 million to open a Navy ship design center and $2 million for an Air Force project aimed at computerizing and standardizing bidding and manufacturing guidelines.

Although Jefferson County (Beaumont and Port Arthur) is just over the district line in the 9th, it plays an integral role in the economy of the 2nd. Shipyards, petrochemical refineries and a steel mill are prevalent in the county.

In the northern and western counties of the 2nd, timber remains the primary industry, despite slowdowns in the construction trades and increased competition from abroad. In the 1992 campaign, Wilson appealed to voters in this area by opposing plans to sell wood chips to the Japanese; such raw-material sales enable foreign competitors to do the more lucrative work of producing finished products.

Angelina County, with 70 percent of its land in commercial forests, is the leading timber-producing county in Texas. Wilson's hometown of Lufkin has 60 manufacturing companies that employ more than 8,000 people.

At election time, populist Democrats fare better than outright liberals in East Texas. Democratic presidential hopefuls Walter F. Mondale and Michael S. Dukakis failed to carry the 2nd, but Bill Clinton, a Southerner with a more moderate image than those of his predecessors, narrowly won the district in 1992.

1990 Population: 566,217. White 449,827 (79%), Black 94,345 (17%), Other 22,045 (4%). Hispanic origin 31,976 (6%). 18 and over 414,273 (73%), 62 and over 97,719 (17%). Median age: 34.

through in the South and West, and we can forget about winning presidential elections."

The subcommittee post also enabled Wilson to steer nearly $8 million in military contracts and subcontracts back to a variety of businesses and schools in his district in late 1992 and early 1993.

Although Wilson brags about how proud he is to hail from the party that brought America Social Security and the GI Bill of Rights, he keeps his liberal social views in check. His conservative positions on gun control, lifting the ban on gays in the military and a balanced-budget amendment sell well at home.

For much of the 1980s, Wilson's most serious purpose was the maintenance of U.S. support for the Mujahedeen rebels in Afghanistan. His congressional efforts and trips to the front — where he purchased Red Army belt buckles that had been plucked off corpses — prompted CBS' "60 Minutes" to profile him as a savior of the rebel cause.

In promoting the "Muj," as he called the rebels, Wilson's rhetoric about the Soviet occupiers was pure Cold War, observing in private that he wanted to help the rebels in Afghanistan because "it's the only place in the world where we are killing Russians."

After the Soviets completed the withdrawal of their 100,000-plus troops from Afghanistan and conceded the invasion had been a mistake, Wilson took to the House floor to commend the Soviet leadership.

As President Bush prepared to battle Iraq in late 1990, Wilson was a ready ally, providing a key vote for a debt relief package for Egypt.

"Egypt is the glue that holds the Arabs together," he said.

With Desert Storm and the Cold War over, many wondered where Wilson would direct his foreign affairs interests in the 103rd. By March 1993, they found their answer: Wilson told Secretary of State Warren M. Christopher he expected that the United States and NATO would need up to 50,000 troops "to end the ethnic horrors" in Bosnia.

When Wilson was appointed to the Intelligence panel in 1987, his conservatism prompted complaints from liberal Democrats who feared Wilson, the party's self-appointed "head hawk," would too often side with Republicans. But his conservatism helped the leadership quell GOP complaints that the panel was being unfairly stacked with liberals. He completed his last term on the committee in 1992.

Even with his conservative record on foreign policy and defense issues, Wilson still has managed to vote with a majority of fellow Democrats more than 60 percent of time on partisan chamber votes since the mid-1980s.

Wilson has had his share of personal controversy in recent years, although he has emerged relatively unscathed.

In 1983, the Justice Department investigated but did not charge Wilson during a probe into Capitol Hill drug use. That same year, Wilson was fined for colliding with a car on a Washington bridge, then leaving the scene of the accident; the car he was driving carried his official House license plates.

Wilson saw one of his Afghanistan adventures tarnished when it was revealed that he had exacted revenge on the Defense Intelligence Agency (DIA) for denying his then-girlfriend a seat on a U.S. government plane in Pakistan in February 1986. The story came to light nearly two years later, when Wilson slipped a provision into a 1987 year-end omnibus spending bill that cut six planes from the DIA fleet.

In 1992, Wilson was hit with a scandal that dealt fatal blows to many other respected careers. He had 81 overdrafts at the House bank, including a $10,000 loan to his campaign.

At Home: Like the two cats that prowl the halls of his Capitol Hill office, Wilson seems to have at least nine lives.

After a serious challenge in 1990, Wilson won re-election in 1992 with 56 percent — a close call by Texas standards, but considering his problems, the victory was a testament to his hard-driving ambition, hefty campaign treasury and uncanny ability to read the voters of the 2nd better than anybody else.

Wilson's on-the-edge lifestyle of beautiful women, dis otheques and world travel is legendary. But even he himself worried that he had crossed the line in 1992. In comparison with his private peccadilloes, his 81 overdrafts at the House bank smacked of abuse of his public power. Although he made no apologies — "I bounced checks," he said, "but I wasn't guilty of child molestation" — he did head home to the Piney Woods to focus on his toughest re-election bid ever.

With the end of the Cold War, Wilson, who collects an array of weapons in his home in the Lufkin woods, lost his favorite saber-rattling campaign theme.

And he was pitted against Peterson, who earned her political stripes in 1990 when she made headlines by castrating a bull and taking 44 percent of the vote. She also touted her conservative credentials, highlighting her opposition to abortion rights. (Wilson, who supported John F. Kennedy in 1960 while most Texas Democrats were backing Lyndon B. Johnson, has grown more conservative over the years.)

By 1992, some of Peterson's welcome had worn thin, and serious questions arose over inflated claims in her military record.

Wilson, meanwhile, hired his first campaign manager and cruised the 2nd in a giant RV handing out maps, potholders and other goodies with the slogan "Takin' Care of the Home Folks."

The relatively close scrape in 1992 was reminiscent of his tough race in 1984, a year after his car accident and the federal drug probe in which his name was mentioned. The controversy prompted four Democrats to challenge him in the primary. The candidate best positioned to take advantage of Wilson's troubles was Nacogdoches bank executive Jerry K. Johnson. A farm-bred Baptist deacon and Sunday school teacher, Johnson projected a clean-cut image in contrast to Wilson's flamboyance.

Johnson avoided overt mention of the drug issue. But he was not shy about painting the incumbent as a man whose taste for glamour had superseded his interest in the concerns of the district. "Unlike the incumbent, I won't go into the Washington real estate and nightclub business and forget where I come from or who I'm working for," Johnson said.

But Wilson was well-prepared for the fight. Tapping his close ties to defense contractors and the independent oil industry, he amassed a substantial treasury, using the money to run TV ads that showed him talking with laid-off blue-collar workers and trumpeting his support for "domestic content" legislation.

Wilson sought to defuse controversy over the Justice Department investigation by attacking the department. He told constituents that he was "set up" by an embittered former business partner.

Squelching speculation that he might be forced into a runoff, Wilson captured 55 percent of the districtwide primary vote and won handily in November.

The next two elections were easy for Wilson, but then Peterson caught him off-guard in

1990. Given Wilson's reputation as a ladies' man, there were some chuckles that "Charlie would rather date his opponent than beat her."

But Wilson continues to be one of the rare politicians who successfully combines his active legislative career with the pursuit of pleasure.

In the late 1970s, Wilson was a partner in a downtown Washington discotheque. With his monogrammed cowboy boots and wide-brimmed Western hat, he was a recognized man about town, and he always seemed to be escorting a beautiful actress, model or socialite. The divorced Wilson's steady dates included a woman whose picture had appeared on the cover of *Playboy*. His 1986 traveling companion, Annelise Ilschenko, was a lobbyist and the 1975 winner of the Miss World USA contest. "Sure, I like pretty girls," he says. "I'm single."

He has never seemed embarrassed about being labeled a playboy or a smiling Texas rogue; he clearly revels in it.

"I am something of a bon vivant who lives on the edge," he told a reporter in 1992.

If there is one thing Wilson does not advertise about his unusually public private life, it is this: His proud-as-a-peacock strut is not simply the reflection of his cocky nature. He has a bad back.

Committee

Appropriations (9th of 37 Democrats)
Defense; Foreign Operations, Export Financing & Related Programs

Elections

1992 General		
Charles Wilson (D)	118,625	(56%)
Donna Peterson (R)	92,176	(44%)
1992 Primary		
Charles Wilson (D)	74,674	(71%)
Stuart F. Williamson (D)	16,938	(16%)
Edgar J. Groce (D)	13,912	(13%)
1990 General		
Charles Wilson (D)	76,974	(56%)
Donna Peterson (R)	61,555	(44%)

Previous Winning Percentages: **1988** (88%) **1986** (66%) **1984** (59%) **1982** (94%) **1980** (69%) **1978** (70%) **1976** (95%) **1974** (100%) **1972** (74%)

District Vote for President

1992
D 91,698 (43%)
R 76,372 (35%)
I 47,167 (22%)

Campaign Finance

	Receipts	Receipts from PACs		Expend-itures
1992				
Wilson (D)	$1,217,912	$638,825	(52%)	$1,193,599
Peterson (R)	$344,053	$118,550	(34%)	$344,065
1990				
Wilson (D)	$663,504	$439,517	(66%)	$740,342
Peterson (R)	$125,013	$8,000	(6%)	$124,884

Key Votes

1993	
Require parental notification of minors' abortions	N
Require unpaid family and medical leave	Y
Approve national "motor voter" registration bill	Y
Approve budget increasing taxes and reducing deficit	Y
Approve economic stimulus plan	Y
1992	
Approve balanced-budget constitutional amendment	Y
Close down space station program	N
Approve U.S. aid for former Soviet Union	?
Allow shifting funds from defense to domestic programs	N
1991	
Extend unemployment benefits using deficit financing	Y
Approve waiting period for handgun purchases	N
Authorize use of force in Persian Gulf	Y

Voting Studies

	Presidential Support		Party Unity		Conservative Coalition	
Year	**S**	**O**	**S**	**O**	**S**	**O**
1992	37	54	66	19	77	19
1991	32	52	61	23	86	5
1990	35	50	64	18	61	26
1989	47	38	61	20	51	39
1988	36	43	61	20	53	34
1987	39	54	66	17	65	26
1986	38	50	61	18	72	12
1985	40	43	63	15	60	22
1984	36	32	44	21	59	15
1983	45	37	53	28	66	13
1982	47	30	51	30	63	15
1981	57	34	54	36	68	24

Interest Group Ratings

Year	ADA	AFL-CIO	CCUS	ACU
1992	65	82	71	45
1991	25	82	50	30
1990	44	83	17	40
1989	45	82	40	50
1988	35	82	46	55
1987	56	93	8	43
1986	35	92	27	50
1985	40	75	44	55
1984	35	73	38	26
1983	45	75	50	48
1982	25	47	56	47
1981	20	50	58	50

3 Sam Johnson (R)

Of Dallas — Elected 1991; 1st Full Term

Born: Oct. 11, 1930, San Antonio, Texas.
Education: Southern Methodist U., B.B.A. 1951; George Washington U., M.S.I.A. 1974.
Military Service: Air Force, 1951-79.
Occupation: Home builder.
Family: Wife, Shirley Melton; three children.
Religion: Methodist.
Political Career: Texas House, 1985-91.
Capitol Office: 1030 Longworth Bldg. 20515; 225-4201.

In Washington: For most of his three years in Congress, Johnson has served quietly, occupying the back benches of the House chamber and his lower-tier seats on the Banking and Science committees, establishing a conservative voting record and enduring the trials of serving in a body dominated by liberal Democrats.

Johnson is by nature an unassuming man who has lived through infinitely tougher times and whose patience was developed as a prisoner of war in Vietnam.

When his conservative spirit has been pricked, however, he has shed his shell and allowed his more partisan side take center stage.

In March 1993, it was Johnson who took to the House floor to bar further federal spending on a telephone counseling service for gay and bisexual men, known as Project Aries. The previously little-known program at the University of Washington was designed to develop techniques for reducing the risk of the spread of AIDS; its 800-number service targeted men in rural areas who did not have access to counseling commonly available in cities.

Project Aries became a conservative cause célèbre, and during floor debate on Johnson's amendment, some — Republican Robert K. Dornan of California, foremost among them — derided it as nothing more than "some sort of homosexual 800 number . . . that just talks dirty on the phone to you."

Johnson, however, was more restrained and he confined his comments chiefly to objections that the service was an unnecessary and redundant federal expense. "There is even a 24-hour toll-free AIDS counseling program in my hometown of Dallas, which surprised the heck out of me," he said.

His amendment to halt the $2 million, two-year-old project (after most of the money had already been spent) was adopted 278-139.

Johnson does not talk much of his POW experiences — though he described the serious injuries he received from beatings that went untreated in his 1992 book, "Captive Warriors." Nevertheless, he retains strong feelings about that time, which surface on occasion.

During the 1992 presidential campaign, Johnson was one of several Republicans (among them Dornan) who used after-hours "special orders" speeches to deride Bill Clinton's post-college trip to Moscow and his avoidance of military service. In characterizing Clinton as anti-American for those actions, he compared him with North Vietnamese leader Ho Chi Minh.

In early 1993, he dismissed his attacks on Clinton as election-year rhetoric. "I think we need to work with him to try to make things better for America," he told The Dallas Morning News.

Johnson's background as a home builder in Texas — a career he assumed after leaving the Air Force in 1979 — gives him an insider's perspective on the Banking, Finance and Urban Affairs Committee.

In 1992, he offered an amendment in the Housing Subcommittee to increase by $1 billion — almost 400 percent — the authorized spending level for the HOPE program, a favorite of the Bush administration and especially HUD Secretary Jack F. Kemp, that was started to sell public housing units to tenants. His amendment was rejected on an 11-24 vote.

He has also been a leading critic of the savings and loan bailout and the management of the Resolution Trust Corporation, which is the lead salvage agency for failed thrifts. In early 1993, Johnson objected to suggestions that a change in administrations would alleviate his management concerns. "How is anything going to change . . . when the same guys are running the RTC," he said.

In April 1992, Johnson was among a group of conservative Republicans who led a fight to kill an additional appropriation for the RTC. Johnson tried to kill the bill, which would have provided about $17 billion more for the bailout, by referring it back to committee. His motion failed, 173-247. But on a subsequent vote, by a wider 125-298 margin the House rejected the bill outright.

Johnson also has a seat on the Science, Space and Technology Committee, where he is, not surprisingly, a strong supporter of projects that benefit Texas, notably the superconducting super collider and the space station.

Texas 3

North Dallas; northern suburbs

If you have never been to the 3rd, close your eyes and picture the TV show "Dallas," which celebrated the lifestyle and material trappings of the city's high-income oil barons and other business elite. The 3rd, which includes upscale sections of northern and eastern Dallas County and part of Collin County, is one of the most affluent districts in the country, and normally one of the most Republican in presidential voting. Median family income in the 3rd exceeds $50,000, which helps explain why this has been dubbed the "Golden District."

George Bush won here in 1992 with 48 percent of the vote, well below the typical GOP tally because 30 percent of those casting ballots went for billionaire businessman Ross Perot, who makes his home here. Bill Clinton was a non-factor, running third with barely a fifth of the vote.

The Park Cities, University Park and Highland Park, with their corporate chieftains and wealthy heirs, epitomize the prosperity of much of the district. Located in University Park is Southern Methodist University, an 8,500-student campus affiliated with the Methodist church. SMU has always had an upper-crust air about it — at football games, students have been known to hold up signs that say, "Our maids went to UT" (the University of Texas). The university, with its heavy business orientation, has helped stock Dallas' myriad financial firms and other corporations with MBAs.

Three-fourths of the vote in the 3rd comes out of Dallas County; the balance is cast in Collin County (Plano). Collin has has seen tremendous residential growth in recent years, due in part to the arrival in the area of a number of corporate headquarters, including those of the J. C. Penney Co. and Electronic Data Systems Corp., the computer firm that Perot founded and later sold to General Motors. Executives for these companies help sustain a market for half-million-dollar mansions in developments such as West Plano's Deerfield.

The Collin County part of the 3rd, filled with young, upwardly mobile professionals, is only slightly less Republican than the district's Dallas County sections. Conservative attitudes and old Texas traditions prevail: High school football games in Plano draw capacity crowds of 10,000 on Friday nights in the fall.

Although downtown Dallas is not in the 3rd, its presence is felt in the district. The city's white-collar companies draw heavily from the 3rd for their work force. And Dallas' museums, orchestra and other cultural amenities rely on patronage from the residents of the 3rd.

Not all the 3rd is glitz and glamour. Communities such as Garland and Mesquite are popular middle-class suburbs. Mesquite, a city of 101,500 east of Dallas, hosts the world-renowned Mesquite Rodeo every Friday and Saturday night from April through September. It was here that Joe Kool, reputedly one of the toughest bulls in the world to ride, appeared regularly for a decade.

1990 Population: 566,217. White 505,389 (89%), Black 24,823 (4%), Other 36,005 (6%). Hispanic origin 34,062 (6%). 18 and over 419,575 (74%), 62 and over 58,784 (10%). Median age: 33.

At 62, Johnson is older than most of the young conservatives who dominate the House GOP leadership. He is well-liked by fellow Republicans. And Johnson's solid conservative voting record suits his suburban district — one of the most Republican in the state (and home to Ross Perot) — enabling him to win reelection in 1992 with 86 percent of the vote.

Johnson was part of the group — and the only member of Congress — who went to Andrews Air Force Base on Inauguration Day 1993 to see off outgoing-President Bush and his wife, Barbara, as they returned to Houston. Johnson said he wanted to give the Bushes a warm Texas send-off, similar to one Bush gave to Lyndon B. Johnson, when he left office in January 1969.

At Home: It is not unusual for members of Congress to have crossed paths somewhere before coming to the Capitol. But Johnson met the first of his future colleagues in a North Vietnamese prison camp, where a fellow prisoner was John McCain, later to become a Republican senator from Arizona.

Johnson was shot down over North Vietnam in 1966 and held prisoner for six years and 10 months, half that time in solitary confinement. While a POW, he lost partial use of his right arm.

Johnson's career as a highly decorated Air Force officer spanned nearly 30 years. Besides tours as a fighter pilot over both Korea and Vietnam, he flew with the Thunderbirds — the Air Force's precision demonstration team — and directed the Air Force's "Top Gun" fighter pilot school.

But it was during his imprisonment in North Vietnam that he began planning a future in politics. In a radio ad run during his first campaign, Johnson told of vowing that when he was free he would never be content just to gripe about government again.

Johnson's political debut came in 1984, when, at age 54, he won a seat in the Texas House representing the GOP suburbs of Collin County. His military heroics had provided him an entree, but it was his skill at coalition-building that helped him advance. He fashioned a reputation as a law-and-order conservative, promoting criminal justice legislation that included expanding the rights of crime victims and increasing the number of prison beds.

While making friends in Austin, he was broadening his contacts in the Dallas area by serving as co-chairman of Bush's North Texas campaign in 1988 and as chairman of former Rep. Steve Bartlett's re-election campaigns in 1988 and 1990.

His career path was altered in March 1991 when Bartlett resigned to run for mayor of Dallas.

Though only one of a dozen candidates who entered the race, Johnson was nevertheless well-positioned to succeed Bartlett. Not only did he have a strong base in the Collin County portion of the district (he lives in a part of Dallas that reaches into the county), but he had the backing of three-fourths of his GOP colleagues in the Texas House, the GOP chairmen in both counties in the district, businessman T. Boone Pickens and former Dallas Cowboys quarterback Roger Staubach.

In the initial balloting, Johnson finished with 20 percent, second to Tom Pauken, a former head of ACTION (the federal volunteer agency) in the Reagan administration who had twice lost close races in another congressional district; he garnered 27 percent.

But Johnson roared past Pauken in the runoff, buoyed by endorsements from several defeated primary candidates.

Johnson swept Collin County and did just well enough in populous Dallas County. Democrats had all but conceded the seat to the GOP from the start. By 1992 they did not put up a candidate, enabling Johnson to coast to a second term over a Libertarian candidate.

Committees

Banking, Finance & Urban Affairs (11th of 20 Republicans)
Financial Institutions Supervision, Regulation & Deposit Insurance; Housing & Community Development; International Development, Finance, Trade & Monetary Policy

Science, Space & Technology (12th of 22 Republicans)
Science; Space

Small Business (7th of 18 Republicans)
Procurement, Taxation & Tourism; Regulation, Business Opportunities & Technology

Elections

1992 General		
Sam Johnson (R)	201,569	(86%)
Noel Kopala (LIBERT)	32,570	(14%)
1992 Primary		
Sam Johnson (R)	44,920	(83%)
David Corley (R)	9,107	(17%)
1991 Special Runoff		
Sam Johnson (R)	24,004	(53%)
Tom Pauken (R)	21,647	(47%)
1991 Special Primary		
Tom Pauken (R)	15,018	(27%)
Sam Johnson (R)	10,855	(20%)
Bill Hammond (R)	6,756	(12%)
Paul Zane Pilzer (R)	5,909	(11%)
Dan Branch (R)	5,484	(10%)
Pete Sessions (R)	5,156	(9%)
Wayne E. Putnam (D)	2,324	(4%)
Farrell Ray (R)	1,139	(2%)
Robert E. Lyle (R)	806	(1%)
Mel Richardson (I)	802	(1%)

District Vote for President

	1992	
D	58,352	(21%)
R	133,807	(48%)
I	84,088	(30%)

Campaign Finance

	Receipts	Receipts from PACs		Expend-itures
1992				
Johnson (R)	$466,977	$213,475	(46%)	$481,802

Key Votes

1993	
Require parental notification of minors' abortions	Y
Require unpaid family and medical leave	N
Approve national "motor voter" registration bill	N
Approve budget increasing taxes and reducing deficit	N
Approve economic stimulus plan	N
1992	
Approve balanced-budget constitutional amendment	Y
Close down space station program	N
Approve U.S. aid for former Soviet Union	Y
Allow shifting funds from defense to domestic programs	N
1991	
Extend unemployment benefits using deficit financing	N

Voting Studies

	Presidential Support		Party Unity		Conservative Coalition	
Year	**S**	**O**	**S**	**O**	**S**	**O**
1992	84	12	85	9	94	0
1991	84 †	16 †	86 †	10 †	93 †	4 †

† Not eligible for all recorded votes.

Interest Group Ratings

Year	ADA	AFL-CIO	CCUS	ACU
1992	10	25	88	100
1991	0	0	100	100

4 Ralph M. Hall (D)

Of Rockwall — Elected 1980; 7th Term

Born: May 3, 1923, Fate, Texas.

Education: Texas Christian U., 1943; U. of Texas, 1946-47; Southern Methodist U., LL.B. 1951.

Military Service: Navy, 1942-45.

Occupation: Lawyer; businessman.

Family: Wife, Mary Ellen Murphy; three children.

Religion: Methodist.

Political Career: Rockwall County judge, 1951-63; Texas Senate, 1963-73; sought Democratic nomination for lieutenant governor, 1972.

Capitol Office: 2236 Rayburn Bldg. 20515; 225-6673.

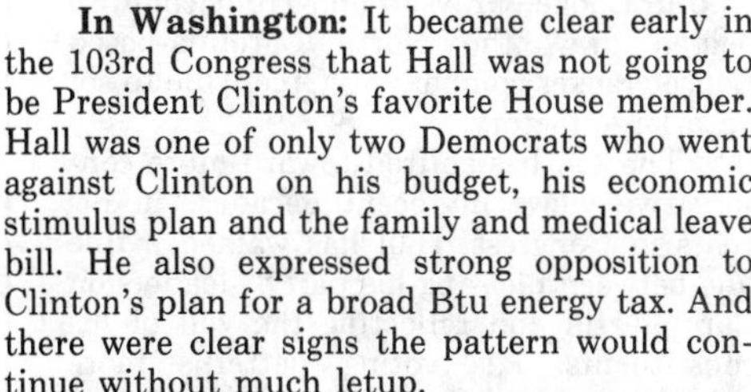

In Washington: It became clear early in the 103rd Congress that Hall was not going to be President Clinton's favorite House member. Hall was one of only two Democrats who went against Clinton on his budget, his economic stimulus plan and the family and medical leave bill. He also expressed strong opposition to Clinton's plan for a broad Btu energy tax. And there were clear signs the pattern would continue without much letup.

In fact, little else should be expected of Hall. His conservative East Texas district was one of a handful in which Clinton finished behind both President Bush and Ross Perot. And Hall's record shows a strong inclination to put his district's views ahead of party needs. On largely party-line votes in 1992, he voted with Democrats only 49 percent of the time. But that was a career high. In the 102nd Congress he supported Bush almost two-thirds of the time on issues on which Bush staked out a position.

Hall also finds himself at odds with Clinton's calls for a sharply scaled-back space station program. As chairman of the Space Subcommittee of the Science, Space and Technology Committee, Hall has worked hard to preserve the space station *Freedom* and to promote medical and other kinds of research in space. As NASA worked on a new space station design early in 1993, Hall was busy trying to preserve as much of the old one as he could, while keeping the Johnson Space Center in Houston as its focal point.

That is not to say, however, that he has been totally accepting of NASA policies. He has not been afraid to admonish NASA officials for excessive spending, and in 1991, for the first time in history, his subcommittee cut $485 million from NASA's budget request.

"You can't just pitch your briefcases on the table and tell Congress what you want anymore," Hall said.

Hall has also used his committee position — he is the fifth-ranking Democrat — to support and lobby for the superconducting super collider, which is being built in Texas.

Hall also serves on the Energy and Commerce Committee, where he is a favorite of Chairman John D. Dingell of Michigan, even if the two do not always see eye-to-eye. Hall's folksy humor and encyclopedic supply of rural Texas stories can defuse tension, and his political acumen gives him considerable influence when he decides to weigh in.

Hall is not particularly active on Energy and Commerce, except when the Texas oil and gas industries are affected.

In the 102nd Congress, he worked hard against an amendment by Massachusetts Democrat Edward J. Markey to the energy bill that would have placed additional regulations on state natural gas laws.

During the intense deliberations over the 1990 Clean Air Act, Hall and fellow Texan Jack Fields, a Republican, at one stage weakened proposed mandates for auto companies to build vehicles that run on alternative fuels. Their amendment increased the percentage of gasoline that could be included in a "clean fuel" mix of gasoline and methanol, and it put reformulated gasoline on the list of "clean alternative fuels." It also stripped a proposed requirement that automakers sell 1 million clean-fuel vehicles a year by 1997.

Hall and other supporters said the amendment would create a level playing field for alternative fuels other than methanol, but critics saw it as a major victory for the auto and oil industries.

On communications issues, Hall was a strong supporter and player on legislation to reregulate the cable industry. He is reluctant to give regional Bell companies entry into new businesses such as information services and manufacturing because he fears the so-called Baby Bells will use their monopolies to freeze out other competitors.

Hall is often at odds with his party. In August 1990, he was one of only two Democrats

Texas 4

Northeast — Sherman; part of Tyler

Although the core of Sam Rayburn's home district remains intact, the 4th of the 1990s is dramatically different in its economic and political makeup.

For 48 years Rayburn represented the compact square in a northeast corner of Texas; from 1934 until his death in 1961 the lines were not touched. During his congressional tenure the 4th was a sparsely populated, agricultural district. The region missed out on the insurance fortunes of Dallas and the oil wealth of West Texas and the Gulf Coast. With no large industry, the people relied on the land. The rich, dark soil, known as blacklands, is conducive to cotton, hay, oats and sorghum. (At one time, Greenville had the largest inland cotton compressor in the nation.)

Since then, state mapmakers have expanded the boundaries, the land has been "cottoned out" and the urban sprawl of Dallas has reached the 4th. Most of the small, family farms have been replaced by large corporate entities.

From Rep. Hall's home in Rockwall, the glittering Dallas skyline is easily visible. Residents throughout Rockwall County commute to Dallas, many working at banks, insurance firms or telecommunications companies; AT&T is a major employer. Population in Collin and Rockwall counties doubled in the 1970s, and nearly again in Rockwall in the 1980s.

The E-Systems plant in Greenville is another example of the changes evident in the 4th. The company, which develops and modifies aircraft, receives contracts from the U.S. military, foreign countries and private companies.

At the eastern end of the 4th, where cotton once flourished, oil boomed in the 1970s and early 1980s. When the industry crashed in 1984, the region was hurt. There remains a good deal of oil in the ground, particularly in Longview (Gregg County) and Tyler (Smith County), but little pumping is taking place. Tyler's economy is bolstered by its abundant rose industry. The self-proclaimed "Rose Capital of the World" is responsible for a large share of the world's roses.

Agriculture has not disappeared entirely from the 4th. The substantial peanut crop in Cooke, Grayson and Hunt counties helped draw the North Carolina-based Lance cracker company to Greenville to set up a large factory.

The 4th has shifted toward more conservative views in recent decades. In his years in Congress, Hall has walked a fine line between pleasing his party's leaders on Capitol Hill and reflecting the will of his constituents. His voting patterns more closely resembled George Bush's views than the Democratic Party line. Hall's opposition to abortion rights and gay rights fits the district well. In the 1992 presidential contest Bush won the 4th with 41 percent.

And the GOP down-ballot candidates have been making gains in the 4th as well. In the 1980s all local officials in Rockwall County were Democrats; by 1993 all but one were Republican.

1990 Population: 566,217. White 500,239 (88%), Black 47,413 (8%), Other 18,565 (3%). Hispanic origin 24,592 (4%). 18 and over 413,296 (73%), 62 and over 92,359 (16%). Median age: 34.

voting to expel Massachusetts Rep. Barney Frank on ethics charges, and in 1985 he voted "present" rather than support Thomas P. O'Neill Jr. for Speaker. After the latter, he seemed untroubled that the leadership might retaliate by removing him from Energy and Commerce. "I wouldn't blame them if they did," he said cheerfully. "I do what I have to do, and they do what they have to do."

At Home: An early starter in politics, Hall was elected judge in his home county while still in law school. After 12 years, he moved up to the state Senate and spent a decade there, rising to become president pro tem.

In 1972 Hall entered statewide politics, running for lieutenant governor on a conservative platform. But he finished fourth in the Democratic primary, retired from politics and concentrated on business.

When 4th District Democrat Ray Roberts announced his retirement in 1980, Hall re-entered politics. His primary foe was Jerdy Gary, son of a former Oklahoma governor. Hall contrasted his Texas upbringing with Gary's Oklahoma roots and won nomination with 57 percent. Because of Ronald Reagan's popularity among the 4th's voters, Hall's contest with Republican John H. Wright was closer than expected. Reagan's showing helped the Tyler business manager pull 48 percent. But Republicans have not mounted a comparable challenge since.

In 1992 Hall had his first primary fight since winning his seat in 1980. But redistricting preserved the most conservative parts of the 4th for Hall and eliminated liberal-leaning areas that might have been more inclined to support his opponent, Roger Sanders. The primary might have slowed Hall a bit, but by November he had secured a comfortable margin against his Republican opponent, David L. Bridges. Hall won with 58 percent of the vote to Bridges' 38 percent.

Committees

Energy & Commerce (10th of 27 Democrats)
Energy & Power; Health & the Environment; Telecommunications & Finance

Science, Space & Technology (5th of 33 Democrats)
Space (chairman); Science

Elections

1992 General		
Ralph M. Hall (D)	128,008	(58%)
David L. Bridges (R)	83,875	(38%)
Steven Rothacker (LIBERT)	8,450	(4%)
1992 Primary		
Ralph M. Hall (D)	36,837	(66%)
Roger Sanders (D)	18,833	(34%)
1990 General		
Ralph M. Hall (D)	108,300	(100%)

Previous Winning Percentages: **1988** (66%) **1986** (72%)
1984 (58%) **1982** (74%) **1980** (52%)

District Vote for President

1992
D 65,617 (28%)
R 95,181 (41%)
I 69,626 (30%)

Campaign Finance

	Receipts	Receipts from PACs		Expend-itures
1992				
Hall (D)	$520,216	$349,840	(67%)	$739,979
Bridges (R)	$35,797	$1,825	(5%)	$34,412
1990				
Hall (D)	$261,431	$202,850	(78%)	$209,902

Key Votes

1993	
Require parental notification of minors' abortions	Y
Require unpaid family and medical leave	N
Approve national "motor voter" registration bill	Y
Approve budget increasing taxes and reducing deficit	N
Approve economic stimulus plan	N
1992	
Approve balanced-budget constitutional amendment	Y
Close down space station program	N
Approve U.S. aid for former Soviet Union	N
Allow shifting funds from defense to domestic programs	N
1991	
Extend unemployment benefits using deficit financing	N
Approve waiting period for handgun purchases	N
Authorize use of force in Persian Gulf	Y

Voting Studies

	Presidential Support		Party Unity		Conservative Coalition	
Year	**S**	**O**	**S**	**O**	**S**	**O**
1992	63	37	49	50	92	8
1991	66	32	46	51	95	3
1990	51	38	39	41	78	7
1989	69	29	39	58	93	5
1988	58	41	47	53	92	8
1987	52	45	44	52	88	9
1986	56	40	38	59	88	10
1985	58	39	45	46	84	5
1984	49	50	44	54	81	17
1983	48	49	38	57	83	11
1982	58	42	40	60	81	19
1981	61	34	40	54	80	15

Interest Group Ratings

Year	ADA	AFL-CIO	CCUS	ACU
1992	40	50	63	76
1991	5	17	80	90
1990	6	20	77	71
1989	5	8	80	89
1988	15	43	86	92
1987	24	44	73	70
1986	10	33	80	80
1985	15	31	67	70
1984	15	46	44	67
1983	35	56	61	62
1982	5	30	64	73
1981	5	27	74	79

5 John Bryant (D)

Of Dallas — Elected 1982; 6th Term

Born: Feb. 22, 1947, Lake Jackson, Texas.
Education: Southern Methodist U., B.A. 1969, J.D. 1972.
Occupation: Lawyer.
Family: Wife, Janet Elizabeth Watts; three children.
Religion: Methodist.
Political Career: Texas House, 1974-83.
Capitol Office: 205 Cannon Bldg. 20515; 225-2231.

In Washington: With his hound-dog eyes and generally low-key manner, Bryant doesn't look the type to stir controversy. But appearances notwithstanding, he is a strong-willed populist with driving political ambition and no qualms about speaking his mind.

In the spring of 1992, Bryant raised eyebrows with blunt criticism of his party's leader, Speaker Thomas S. Foley. With Republicans making political hay of the unfolding House bank scandal and several major pieces of legislation stalled, Bryant took to the floor April 2 to call for Foley to leave the speakership.

"It is time for new leadership in this institution," Bryant said. "For Tom Foley, political leadership is not a responsibility which he relishes.... And, regrettably, for Speaker Foley, even management of the daily institutional operation of the House is an annoyance."

A year later, at an April 1993 Judiciary Committee hearing, Bryant gave a piece of his mind to Stephen E. Higgins, director of the Bureau of Alcohol, Tobacco and Firearms, when he felt Higgins was dodging his questions about the fiery deaths of Branch Davidians at their Waco compound. "Stop repeating my question," Bryant snapped.

Such episodes help create an impression that Bryant chafes at the pace of progress in the House and might be happier seeking statewide office. Bryant, in fact, announced in 1989 that he would leave the House to run for state attorney general. But he changed his mind and opted to continue his congressional career. In early 1993, he was among those mentioned as a possible replacement for Democratic Sen. Lloyd Bentsen, who became Treasury secretary.

Personality and ambitions aside, Bryant continues to be a productive legislator on a range of issues. And while it seems unlikely he will ever be pals with Foley, Bryant should be on good terms with the new occupants of the White House. He campaigned actively for the Clinton-Gore ticket, and early in the 103rd Congress he sponsored a key piece of the administration's "reform" agenda: a bill to define the term "lobbyist" in a way that would require thousands more people in the nation's capital to register as lobbyists and disclose details of their work.

Bryant's views put him closer to the national Democratic Party line than many other Texas Democrats; in the 102nd, for instance, he backed legislation on family leave, civil rights and broadening voter registration opportunities. On gun control, Bryant — a hunter himself — is one of the few Texans in the House opposing the wishes of the National Rifle Association and backing a waiting period for handgun purchases.

During the 102nd, Bryant worked the floor in support of an omnibus crime bill, and when Republicans said the measure was soft on crime, he criticized them for their "gross misrepresentation of the bill."

"I can't imagine how you can sleep at night," chastised Bryant, drawing hisses from the GOP side of the aisle.

But Bryant is generally more of a populist than a liberal. With unemployment and the federal budget deficit becoming sources of greater public worry, he has joined a growing congressional chorus in favor of spending more money at home and less abroad.

In May 1991 he won House support for an amendment to cut by 75 percent the force of 76,500 foreign nationals working at U.S. military bases overseas. The move was intended to pressure host governments to pay the salaries.

One of Bryant's most publicized crusades in the 100th and 101st Congresses was for a measure requiring new disclosures of foreign ownership of U.S. companies' assets. Although Bryant won House approval for the measure during the 100th, it died in the Senate.

In the next Congress, legislators and Bush administration officials coalesced behind an alternative backed by Sen. Jim Exon of Nebraska and Rep. Philip R. Sharp of Indiana, both Democrats. That bill, which eventually became law, seeks to refine and better analyze existing data on foreign investment rather than collect and disclose new information, as Bryant advocated.

On the Judiciary Committee, Bryant has

Texas 5

Downtown Dallas; eastern and southern suburbs

When Wal-Mart came to the Robertson County town of Hearne in 1980, local merchants were dismayed. Virtually every clothier, appliance store and mom-and-pop shop soon shut down. Ten years later, Wal-Mart closed its store, citing unprofitability. The 5,100 people of Hearne were even more upset by Wal-Mart's departure.

The tale of Hearne and the Wal-Mart that came and went is a familiar story in the rural and small-town areas in the 5th, a district that stretches from Dallas County 200 miles south.

Athens (Henderson County) lost the Harvey Industries television manufacturing plant, Four Winns boat company and the bra maker Hollywood Vassarette in the late 1980s. Teague's economy in Freestone County has sputtered since the railroads declined in the 1970s.

For these towns south of Dallas, the future seems to lie in one word: prisons. The prison system is the largest employer in Anderson County, where three large units of the Texas Department of Corrections are situated. Seagoville and other locales in the 5th are bidding for more.

About 60 percent of the district's residents live in Dallas County. Downtown Dallas was removed from the 5th in 1992 redistricting, but some suburban neighborhoods to the east and northwest of the city remain in the 5th.

Oaklawn is a fashionable section where young professionals and a sizable gay community reside. East Dallas is a mix of upscale professionals, longtime residents, pockets of middle-class neighborhoods revived by gentrification, and Hispanic and blue-collar workers. The Swiss Avenue Historic District boasts 200 Georgian, Spanish and Prairie style houses, built at the turn of the century by the Dallas elite.

Although North Dallas is no longer a part of the 5th, major telecommunications companies there employ many of the district's residents.

Just outside the city are several towns that have grown popular because of their proximity to Dallas. Factory workers and office clerks live in some of the more modest communities, such as Seagoville and Balch Springs. Mesquite, once predominantly farmland, is now a collection of spacious, well-kept, single-family homes for Dallas' lawyers and upper-level managers.

People in the more rural, poorer Robertson County on the southwestern edge of the 5th raise cattle and poultry.

The 5th has a sizable minority population — about 35 percent non-white. Although there are more Hispanic residents, blacks have moved more quickly into local politics. In 1993, the 5th had at least one black mayor and several African-American county commissioners.

Drawn to suit Rep. Bryant, the reconfigured 5th responds well to moderate or conservative Democrats.

Bill Clinton won the district in the 1992 presidential contest and independent Ross Perot, who lives in Dallas, exceeded his national average in the 5th.

1990 Population: 566,217. White 404,282 (71%), Black 92,564 (16%), Other 69,371 (12%). Hispanic origin 101,099 (18%). 18 and over 414,181 (73%), 62 and over 80,321 (14%). Median age: 31.

been active on immigration issues of concern to Texas. During the immigration reform debates of the 101st, Bryant was one of only a few Democrats to oppose raising immigration ceilings, arguing that the nation's resources were inadequate to accommodate more newcomers. But he did back measures to allow the family members of illegal aliens legalized under previous "amnesty" provisions to remain in this country. At the start of the 103rd, he became chairman of Judiciary's Administrative Law and Governmental Relations Subcommittee.

Bryant's wide-ranging concerns have included sports betting and children's television. In the 102nd, he authored a bill prohibiting sports betting in most states. The legislation, which became law, halted a nascent trend toward governments' handling betting on sports as a revenue-raising measure.

After bluntly telling a convention of broadcasters in Texas that he considered children's TV to be in sorry shape, Bryant during the 100th Congress worked on a bill to protect children from exploitation by commercial broadcasters. He wanted to limit advertising on children's TV and require educational programming. Congress passed a compromise that included advertising limits, but it was later vetoed. In the 101st, however, Bryant saw the bill become law, without the president's signature.

At Home: Redistricting helped create an opportunity for Bryant to run for Congress in 1982; a decade later, it seemed for a time that remapping might threaten his electoral viability. But the scare was only temporary, and he won a sixth term by a comfortable margin.

In 1981, the Legislature initially altered the Dallas-based 5th to tilt it Republican, and that persuaded incumbent Democrat Jim Mattox to run for attorney general. A three-judge federal panel restored the 5th's Democratic boundaries early in 1982, but by then Mattox was committed to his statewide campaign. Bryant was left as the front-runner in a constituency considerably better for Democrats.

The real test for Bryant was the primary, in which his chief foe was former Dallas Mayor Pro Tem Bill Blackburn. Although Blackburn had good funding and name recognition, his political ties were to downtown Dallas and its business community, and these were no assets in the blue-collar 5th. Bryant took a decisive 66 percent, had no trouble in November and drew no Republican opposition in 1984.

In 1986, the GOP ended up fielding an energetic, if inexperienced, candidate. Oil and gas lobbyist Tom Carter branded Bryant a menace to entrepreneurs. But Bryant had established allies in the Dallas business community, including some usually Republican captains of the energy industry. Although Carter managed a strong showing in suburban communities such as Garland and Mesquite, he faltered in the 5th's more politically competitive territory. Bryant won with almost 60 percent and in the next two elections held at about that level.

With priority in Texas' 1992 redistricting being given to minority empowerment, there was speculation that Bryant's Democratic base might be undermined. The new map did cost him several minority and working-class white precincts in Dallas County; they went into a new majority-minority 30th District. But other subtractions and additions made the entire process basically a wash for Bryant. Against an underfunded challenger, he took 59 percent.

Committees

Budget (7th of 26 Democrats)

Energy & Commerce (13th of 27 Democrats)
Health & the Environment; Oversight & Investigations; Telecommunications & Finance

Judiciary (13th of 21 Democrats)
Administrative Law & Governmental Relations (chairman); International Law, Immigration & Refugees

Elections

1992 General		
John Bryant (D)	98,567	(59%)
Richard Stokley (R)	62,419	(37%)
William H. Walker (LIBERT)	6,344	(4%)
1990 General		
John Bryant (D)	65,228	(59%)
Jerry Rucker (R)	41,307	(38%)
Kenneth Ashby (LIBERT)	2,939	(3%)

Previous Winning Percentages: **1988** (61%) **1986** (59%) **1984** (100%) **1982** (65%)

District Vote for President

1992

D 70,766 (40%)
R 59,237 (34%)
I 45,033 (26%)

Campaign Finance

	Receipts	Receipts from PACs		Expend-itures
1992				
Bryant (D)	$632,643	$355,133	(56%)	$818,987
Stokley (R)	$44,585	$10,850	(24%)	$44,542
1990				
Bryant (D)	$936,755	$458,721	(49%)	$1,034,446
Rucker (R)	$453,796	$45,875	(10%)	$453,165

Key Votes

1993	
Require parental notification of minors' abortions	N
Require unpaid family and medical leave	Y
Approve national "motor voter" registration bill	Y
Approve budget increasing taxes and reducing deficit	Y
Approve economic stimulus plan	Y
1992	
Approve balanced-budget constitutional amendment	Y
Close down space station program	N
Approve U.S. aid for former Soviet Union	N
Allow shifting funds from defense to domestic programs	Y
1991	
Extend unemployment benefits using deficit financing	Y
Approve waiting period for handgun purchases	Y
Authorize use of force in Persian Gulf	N

Voting Studies

	Presidential Support		Party Unity		Conservative Coalition	
Year	**S**	**O**	**S**	**O**	**S**	**O**
1992	18	70	82	10	60	35
1991	21	73	88	6	38	57
1990	13	84	89	9	33	67
1989	24	43	70	5	24	44
1988	19	74	87	7	42	55
1987	25	71	88	5	49	44
1986	18	80	84	12	54	46
1985	23	78	89	8	31	67
1984	22	62	74	6	17	64
1983	24	76	84	10	36	60

Interest Group Ratings

Year	ADA	AFL-CIO	CCUS	ACU
1992	80	82	38	14
1991	80	92	33	11
1990	83	92	29	17
1989	75	91	30	12
1988	85	100	27	9
1987	80	100	14	4
1986	65	93	44	23
1985	55	88	41	10
1984	75	92	38	0
1983	80	94	20	13

6 Joe L. Barton (R)

Of Ennis — Elected 1984; 5th Term

Born: Sept. 15, 1949, Waco, Texas.
Education: Texas A&M U., B.S. 1972; Purdue U., M.S. 1973.
Occupation: Engineering consultant.
Family: Wife, Janet Sue Winslow; three children.
Religion: Methodist.
Political Career: Candidate for U.S. Senate (special election), 1993.
Capitol Office: 1514 Longworth Bldg. 20515; 225-2002.

In Washington: During his first eight years in the House, such media attention as Barton generated usually came when he was doggedly defending a federal project in Texas, such as the superconducting super collider. But in 1993, Barton marketed himself to the statewide and even national audience as the leading advocate of "family values."

Running in the April all-party Senate contest to pick a permanent replacement for Lloyd Bentsen, Barton sought to portray himself as the squeaky-cleanest candidate in the race. Among other things, he emphasized that he wrote no overdrafts at the House bank, married his high school sweetheart, attends church regularly and opposes abortion. Barton closed one debate by noting that while other candidates in the race had more money, "none have more personal values."

But the overriding issue in the contest, he said, was President Clinton's plan to abolish the ban on homosexuals in the military. With a military base bathroom as his backdrop, Barton spoke to reporters of the potential dangers of forcing heterosexual soldiers to sleep and bathe with homosexual soldiers.

Barton mobilized his loyal backers and energized some conservative religious activists, but he could not attract a broad enough audience. He got about 14 percent of the vote, good for third place in the 24-person field, but well short of the top finishers, Democrat Bob Krueger (who was appointed to fill Bentsen's seat) and Republican Kay Bailey Hutchison, the eventual winner.

Early in the 103rd Congress, the issues Barton stressed in his Senate race became part of his legislative program, joining several home-state concerns to which he has long been dedicated. He filed legislation codifying the military gay ban and refiled a bill requiring mandatory drug testing of House members. Barton, who routinely submits to random drug tests, urged Clinton and the White House staff to follow the practice.

Not long after coming to Congress in 1985, Barton established himself as one of the leading voices supporting passage of a balanced-budget constitutional amendment.

At the same time, Barton has come to be known as a backer of two of the most expensive projects funded by the federal government — the superconducting super collider (SSC) and the space station *Freedom*. Both projects are Texas-based; Barton is particularly keen on the super collider, an atom smasher being built in his district.

In one House debate over funding for the $8 billion-plus super collider, Florida Democrat Lawrence J. Smith complained: "The gentleman from Texas is obviously a contortionist, being on two sides of fiscal policy at the same time."

After lobbying hard for the project, Barton and other delegation members were rewarded by the government's 1988 decision to build the SSC in Texas. But since then, advocates of the project have had to fight to protect it from critics who characterize it as an unaffordable luxury in times of extreme federal fiscal distress.

Beginning in January 1989, Barton worked closely with fellow Texas Rep. Jim Chapman, a Democrat on the Appropriations Committee, to steer the super collider project through the appropriations process.

With foes continuing to rail against the super collider at the outset of the 102nd, Barton, an engineer, positioned himself to keep an even closer eye on its progress by joining the Science, Space and Technology Committee.

Barton's slot on the Energy and Commerce Committee enables him to tend to various district interests, particularly the oil and gas industries. Although he was not a pivotal figure in debate over the 1990 Clean Air Act, Barton was an active voice for Texas interests, and he successfully pushed an amendment requiring some cities to use portable pollution detection devices.

During the 21-month odyssey to approve a comprehensive energy bill in the 102nd Congress, Barton joined with Democrat Bob Clement of Tennessee and other allies in successfully

Texas 6

Suburban Dallas — Part of Fort Worth; part of Arlington

When the 6th was redrawn in the mid-1960s to suit the needs of Democratic Rep. Olin E. "Tiger" Teague, cries went out that it was the most gerrymandered district in Texas. In 1992 redistricting, the shape of the 6th became even more illogical. Compressed from 14 counties into five, the 6th is now in two separate pieces that are connected only by Eagle Mountain Lake, in northwestern Tarrant County.

While the district's boundary lines are contorted, its people have a good deal in common. About 85 percent of them live in Tarrant County, which includes Fort Worth and Arlington; parts of both cities are in the 6th. Overall, Fort Worth is larger, but Arlington is the district's biggest population center; about 134,000 of its 261,700 people are in the district.

The Fort Worth area has experienced several economic evolutions. Initially the city's commerce was centered around oil and cattle (the old "Cowtown" nickname still sticks). Then the emphasis shifted to military work: Huge defense contractors such as General Dynamics (now owned by Lockheed) and Bell Helicopter Textron, maker of the experimental V-22 Osprey tiltrotor aircraft, became the largest employers in the region. Carswell Air Force Base housed 6,500 military personnel.

Now, with the cutbacks in defense spending, the city and surrounding region are heading for another economic shift. Carswell has been downsizing since 1991, and the fate of projects at both Lockheed and Bell are in doubt.

With its mild climate, affordable housing and the nation's second-busiest airport (Dallas-Fort Worth), the "Metroplex" (as local boosters dub the area) began attracting a variety of corporate headquarters in the 1980s. Today, the 6th has numerous white-collar employees from companies such as IBM, J.C. Penney, American Airlines, Exxon and GTE. Part of Alliance Airport, a private cargo-shipping business formed by Ross Perot Jr., is in the 6th.

Until the 1980s, Arlington was a blue-collar, low-income community centered around a General Motors plant. GM remains an important employer, but abetted by the city's location between Dallas and Fort Worth, Arlington has emerged as a major entertainment center, with amusement parks, hotels and the Texas Rangers baseball team (the stadium is just across the district line, in the 24th).

Southeast of Tarrant County is Ellis County, focal point of the multibillion-dollar superconducting super collider project. Rep. Barton is a native of Ellis County, and he worked to draw the atom-smasher to the area, but budget constraints continue to cast doubts on the future of the project.

In most elections the 6th is good territory for Republican candidates; Barton's tallies since 1984 have ranged from comfortable to overwhelming. But in 1992 presidential voting, independent candidate Ross Perot far exceeded his 1992 national average in the 6th, placing second behind George Bush with 30 percent of the vote.

1990 Population: 566,217. White 514,448 (91%), Black 25,030 (4%), Other 26,739 (5%). Hispanic origin 30,856 (5%). 18 and over 411,725 (73%), 62 and over 43,402 (8%). Median age: 31.

streamlining licensing procedures for nuclear power plants.

While Barton's interest in energy is predictable, he surprised some during his first term on the Energy and Commerce Committee with his methodical work on consumer-protection legislation. More than many conservatives, Barton has shown an interest in a strong Consumer Product Safety Commission, and in the 100th Congress he pushed new safety regulations for three-wheel all-terrain vehicles, known as ATVs.

Rarely does Barton stray from the GOP line. Though he opposed President Bush in supporting a civil rights bill in 1990, a year later he voted against the bill. In the opening months of the 103rd, he voted against family leave and paired against the "motor voter" bill, as well as legislation to extend unemployment benefits. His loyalty and willingness to work hard for the party was rewarded in the 101st Congress with a deputy whip's slot, which he still holds.

At Home: Following an easy November 1992 re-election in a 6th District dramatically reshaped by redistricting, Barton entered the 1993 special Senate election despite the presence of better-funded and better-known candidates.

He staked his claim to Bentsen's seat on his credentials as the most conservative candidate in the race. In one highly publicized advertisement that was shown to reporters, Barton warned that Sen. Krueger wanted to "force soldiers to sleep in bunks with homosexuals."

After failing to make the runoff, Barton moved quickly to endorse Hutchison, a show of unity that should keep him in good standing with party regulars.

The skinny, bespectacled Barton may not fit the image of the successful politician, but he has a knack for capturing votes.

An engineering consultant for Atlantic Richfield Co., Barton had never run for office before he sought the 6th in 1984.

A recount of the GOP primary votes made Barton the nominee, pitting him against Democrat Dan Kubiak, a former state representative and rancher with a folksy Texas twang and easygoing style.

Barton managed to counter those assets by sticking close to coattails provided by Ronald Reagan and Phil Gramm, who had left the 6th District seat to run for the Senate. Barton called himself a "committed conservative," while portraying Kubiak as a "convenient conservative." Barton accused Kubiak of supporting Democratic presidential nominee Walter F. Mondale's proposals to raise taxes, and he hammered away at his sizable contributions from the AFL-CIO.

Barton also made shrewd use of his ties to his alma mater, Texas A&M University in College Station. That base of support, coupled with the Reagan-Gramm electoral tide and the solid GOP vote in the suburbs of Houston and Fort Worth, were too much for Kubiak to overcome.

Area Democrats were not prepared to concede the 6th, however. They mounted an aggressive challenge to Barton in 1986 behind Fort Worth lawyer Pete Geren.

Geren, who subsequently was elected to fill the vacancy in the 12th created by House Speaker Jim Wright's 1989 resignation, had an ample personal fortune, the enthusiastic support of party leaders and close ties to Bentsen, having spent two years as director of his Texas offices. Geren claimed Barton had taken conservatism to extremes, placing ideology over the needs of his constituency.

Barton pointed to meetings he convened to coach local entrepreneurs on how to secure federal contracts, and he claimed credit for helping free offshore oil and gas royalties that had been entangled in bureaucracy.

Geren performed well for a first-time candidate but could not overcome Barton's support in the GOP-minded urban and suburban neighborhoods of Tarrant and Montgomery counties. In the next three elections, Barton took two-thirds or more of the November vote.

Committees

Energy & Commerce (7th of 17 Republicans)
Energy & Power; Telecommunications & Finance

Science, Space & Technology (10th of 22 Republicans)
Investigations & Oversight; Science

Elections

1992 General		
Joe L. Barton (R)	189,140	(72%)
John Dietrich (D)	73,933	(28%)
1992 Primary		
Joe L. Barton (R)	34,366	(79%)
Mike McGinn (R)	9,089	(21%)
1990 General		
Joe L. Barton (R)	125,049	(66%)
John E. Welch (D)	62,344	(33%)

Previous Winning Percentages: **1988** (68%) **1986** (56%) **1984** (57%)

District Vote for President

1992

D 67,131 (24%)
R 125,693 (46%)
I 82,671 (30%)

Campaign Finance

	Receipts	Receipts from PACs		Expend-itures
1992				
Barton (R)	$1,366,250	$374,046	(27%)	$1,026,628
Dietrich (D)	$13,803	0		$13,751
1990				
Barton (R)	$770,957	$253,403	(33%)	$458,346
Welch (D)	$6,285	0		$6,568

Key Votes

1993	
Require parental notification of minors' abortions	Y
Require unpaid family and medical leave	N
Approve national "motor voter" registration bill	X
Approve budget increasing taxes and reducing deficit	N
Approve economic stimulus plan	?
1992	
Approve balanced-budget constitutional amendment	Y
Close down space station program	N
Approve U.S. aid for former Soviet Union	N
Allow shifting funds from defense to domestic programs	N
1991	
Extend unemployment benefits using deficit financing	N
Approve waiting period for handgun purchases	N
Authorize use of force in Persian Gulf	Y

Voting Studies

	Presidential Support		Party Unity		Conservative Coalition	
Year	S	O	S	O	S	O
1992	77	13	84	5	85	4
1991	70	23	81	13	89	5
1990	68	29	86	7	94	2
1989	67	27	88	8	95	5
1988	70	18	89	4	82	0
1987	77	21	90	5	88	7
1986	76	22	93	4	92	4
1985	85	15	94	3	91	5

Interest Group Ratings

Year	ADA	AFL-CIO	CCUS	ACU
1992	5	27	75	100
1991	10	8	90	90
1990	6	0	77	87
1989	10	8	90	89
1988	5	0	100	96
1987	4	6	93	100
1986	0	7	94	95
1985	5	0	95	100

7 Bill Archer (R)

Of Houston — Elected 1970; 12th Term

Born: March 22, 1928, Houston, Texas.

Education: Rice U., 1945-46; U. of Texas, B.B.A. 1949, LL.B. 1951.

Military Service: Air Force, 1951-53.

Occupation: Lawyer; feed company executive.

Family: Wife, Sharon Sawyer; five children, two stepchildren.

Religion: Roman Catholic.

Political Career: Hunters Creek Village Council, 1955-62; Texas House, 1967-71.

Capitol Office: 1236 Longworth Bldg. 20515; 225-2571.

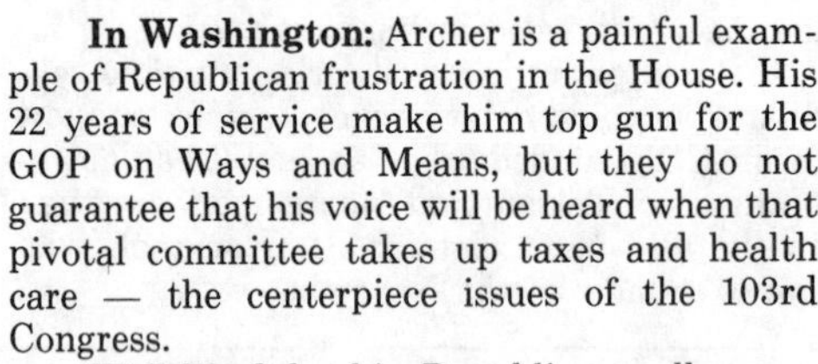

In Washington: Archer is a painful example of Republican frustration in the House. His 22 years of service make him top gun for the GOP on Ways and Means, but they do not guarantee that his voice will be heard when that pivotal committee takes up taxes and health care — the centerpiece issues of the 103rd Congress.

Well-liked by his Republican colleagues, and occasionally mentioned as a possible successor to Minority Leader Robert H. Michel of Illinois, Archer has proved himself adept at listening to the interests and concerns of junior members in weekly meetings of the committee's minority.

But this is not enough when the full committee meets. Archer has not established a partnership with Democratic Ways and Means Chairman Dan Rostenkowski of Illinois, largely because he is not inclined to engage in the one-on-one deal-making that has enabled some GOP members of the panel to do business with the tightfisted chairman. On occasion, Archer has also crossed the chairman, a step rarely taken without consequences.

In the 101st Congress, for example, Archer helped lead a crusade that led to repeal of one of the chairman's proudest achievements of the previous year: the program to protect the elderly against catastrophic health costs. Archer and his allies had heard the outcry from those senior citizens who were having to pay up to $800 for the first year of the program. When Rostenkowski sent a "fix-it" bill to the floor in September 1989, Archer and Democratic Rep. Brian Donnelly of Massachusetts persuaded the House Rules Committee to permit a vote on near-total repeal, which eventually prevailed by a ratio of more than 5-to-1.

But rather than feel frustrated by his position, Archer radiates a sort of peace. As leader of the loyal opposition, he keeps to the anti-tax, free-market agenda that he and most of the Republican Conference prefer. With no Republican administration to defend — or White House program to sell — Archer is free to return to the no-compromise stance that had characterized his earlier House career.

Archer will work to guard the committee's jurisdiction; in this much, at least, he is Rostenkowski's ally. But this does not obligate him to defend his committee's products or its chairman, when Archer is under as much pressure as he is within his own party.

At a closed Ways and Means session in early January 1993, Archer argued for a freeze in the committee's budget, with no increase for inflation. Customarily, such motions from the minority are made and then allowed to die on a voice vote. But in this instance, several junior Republicans demanded a roll call vote so as to put the Democrats on record against the freeze. In the language of internal committee politics, this gesture achieved two ends: hardening the lines of partisan conflict and signaling Archer not to accommodate the Democrats at any turn.

With a Democrat in the White House, Archer's role has changed markedly from when he first inherited the ranking spot in mid-1988, following the death of John J. Duncan of Tennessee. Archer had been known for preferring conservative principle over compromise, but in this new role he surprised observers with his flexibility and potential for effective leadership.

In that first summer, Archer showed a commitment to leading while getting along. He checked staff shifts with other members and set to work on the committee's major product, a "technical corrections" tax bill. While designed chiefly to fix glitches in the 1986 tax overhaul law, the bill also extended important tax credits and included plums for individual companies.

Rostenkowski had let it be known that grandstanding opponents would be cut out of the important off-the-field bargaining on issues important to their districts. Archer seemed to take the sincerity of this threat on faith. He voted for the bill on the floor and in conference, while working to hone some features he deplored.

Texas 7

Western Houston; northwestern suburbs

The urban sprawl of Houston takes up only a portion of the 7th geographically, but it dominates the district in most other respects. The 7th is a collection of white, affluent, reliably Republican neighborhoods. Residents of the old 7th gave George Bush one of his two largest margins in 1988, and four years later the district gave him a solid 57 percent.

About half the district's residents live within the city limits, and many work downtown. All of the 7th — and parts of six other districts — are in Harris County, a region that covers 34 incorporated areas and has 2.8 million people. With a population that is 6 percent black and 12 percent Hispanic, the 7th is somewhat less racially integrated than the city as a whole.

Although none of downtown Houston is included in the 7th, there is plenty of commercial enterprise in the district. Thousands of bankers, real estate brokers, developers, insurance executives and retail employees live in the west and northwest parts of the city. Compaq Computer Corp., with its headquarters and a manufacturing plant on the district boundary line, is a major employer. Founded in 1982 by three former Texas Instruments workers, Compaq felt the squeeze of competition in 1991 and responded with a restructuring and about 2,000 layoffs. The belt-tightening and several new products helped the company rebound; 1992 worldwide sales reached $4.1 billion. Like Compaq, Continental Airlines is a major source of jobs for residents of the 7th, although it is in the neighboring 18th.

Office parks and small factories sprouted up along Route 290 in the 1970s when land was particularly affordable. Toshiba opened a turbine-engine plant in the area then and remains a major employer. Cameron Forged Products, a tool manufacturer, is another of the longtime residents. Cameron, which previously relied heavily on defense contracts, retrained its work force in the late 1980s and early 1990s to produce engine parts for commercial clients.

The River Oaks, Memorial and Tanglewood neighborhoods are home to some of Houston's wealthiest families. And they soon will have a new neighbor — the Bushes moved to Tanglewood in 1993 to build a home on a lot they had owned for years.

Houstonians also boast of their ballet, symphony, opera company, museums and theaters. Many of the area's dedicated arts patrons live in the imitation Tudor mansions, imitation French chateaux and imitation Spanish villas of River Oaks.

Memorial includes a number of small, self-incorporated villages near Interstate 10 that have their own mayors and some discrete municipal services. Residents of Hedwig, Bunker Hill and Piney Point moved into the villages decades ago and never left, prompting the creation of the phrase "the graying of Memorial."

The 7th is a religious and politically active area. The 10,000-member Second Baptist Church is located here, as well as several sizable Presbyterian churches.

1990 Population: 566,217. White 471,894 (83%), Black 33,514 (6%), Other 60,809 (11%). Hispanic origin 67,616 (12%). 18 and over 412,822 (73%), 62 and over 42,189 (7%). Median age: 32.

When George Bush moved into the White House, Archer was put in the position of carrying the administration's water. Archer shared a great deal with the new president, from whom he had inherited his Houston district in 1970 and his seat on Ways and Means a few years later. Both men had spent much of their legislative careers defending the interests of the oil industry, and both had been less than enthusiastic about President Ronald Reagan's second-term tax overhaul.

Bush, as Reagan's vice president, kept his opposition private. But Archer helped lead House Republican opposition to the Reagan plan in 1985 and 1986, having some success in the first year and going down fighting (arrayed against the leaders of his own party) in 1986. Archer argued that the overhaul's lower personal tax rates carried too high a price in terms of business, investment and the economy.

Once Bush became president, he and Archer were able to reopen one of the issues from the 1986 overhaul — the capital gains tax. In the spring of 1989, Archer worked with a handful of Ways and Means Democrats in introducing a capital-gains tax cut that eventually passed the committee over Rostenkowski's opposition and triumphed on the House floor. Only a procedural maneuver in the Senate kept that tax cut from enactment.

The confluence of Archer's Bush connection and his committee role made him a surprise convert to the budget deal the White House negotiated with House and Senate leaders in 1990. That deal included tax increases, but Archer stood with his president and with Rostenkowski in voting for the doomed package on Oct. 4.

In 1992, Archer gained a measure of revenge on the 1986 bill by adding several tax breaks for independent oil producers to a broad energy bill enacted by Congress.

Beyond protecting the oil industry and espousing a general aversion to taxes, Archer has a limited personal agenda: He still wants to dramatically reduce taxes on capital gains; he wants to return to the system of accelerated depreciation instituted by the first Reagan administration tax bill in 1981 (another casualty of the 1986 tax bill); and he wants to protect Social Security, an area in which he has acquired and displayed considerable expertise. Archer was an early objector to raising the rates of payroll taxes to finance ever-greater increases in Social Security benefits.

At Home: Archer occupies a "silk-stocking" district initially drawn in the mid-1960s with Bush, a New England-born WASP, in mind. But Archer himself is a native Houstonian, raised a Catholic and a Democrat. After law school and the Air Force, Archer launched his political career in 1955 as a member of the Hunters Creek Village Council.

Archer made his mark as a conservative Democrat, winning a seat in the Texas Legislature in 1966. But in 1968 he switched parties and won re-election as a Republican. Since the territory of his state Legislative district closely coincided with that of Bush's House district, Archer was the early favorite in 1970 when Bush ran for the U.S. Senate.

Archer easily won the GOP primary and went on to defeat a young law partner of John B. Connally in November. He has had no electoral problems since then.

Committees

Ways & Means (Ranking)
Joint Taxation

Elections

1992 General		
Bill Archer (R)	169,407	(100%)
1990 General		
Bill Archer (R)	114,254	(100%)

Previous Winning Percentages:		**1988**	(79%)	**1986**	(87%)		
1984	(87%)	**1982**	(85%)	**1980**	(82%)	**1978**	(85%)
1976	(100%)	**1974**	(79%)	**1972**	(82%)	**1970**	(65%)

District Vote for President

1992	
D	52,501 (22%)
R	137,541 (57%)
I	49,201 (21%)

Campaign Finance

	Receipts	Receipts from PACs	Expend-itures
1992			
Archer (R)	$121,947	0	$121,751
1990			
Archer (R)	$241,863	0	$200,871

Key Votes

1993	
Require parental notification of minors' abortions	Y
Require unpaid family and medical leave	N
Approve national "motor voter" registration bill	X
Approve budget increasing taxes and reducing deficit	N
Approve economic stimulus plan	N
1992	
Approve balanced-budget constitutional amendment	Y
Close down space station program	N
Approve U.S. aid for former Soviet Union	N
Allow shifting funds from defense to domestic programs	N
1991	
Extend unemployment benefits using deficit financing	N
Approve waiting period for handgun purchases	N
Authorize use of force in Persian Gulf	Y

Voting Studies

	Presidential Support		Party Unity		Conservative Coalition	
Year	S	O	S	O	S	O
1992	80	13	85	10	85	4
1991	84	14	85	11	100	0
1990	84	15	86	13	98	2
1989	81	16	75	22	98	2
1988	79	18	80	19	92	3
1987	82	18	84	13	91	7
1986	82	17	81	15	98	2
1985	88	11	80	15	87	7
1984	70	30	94	6	88	12
1983	77	22	92 †	5 †	96	4
1982	82	18	90	8	89	10
1981	67	30	93	5	92	7

† Not eligible for all recorded votes.

Interest Group Ratings

Year	ADA	AFL-CIO	CCUS	ACU
1992	0	17	75	100
1991	0	0	100	95
1990	0	8	86	88
1989	0	0	90	88
1988	0	0	100	100
1987	0	0	100	95
1986	0	0	94	95
1985	5	0	100	100
1984	0	15	94	100
1983	5	0	85	100
1982	0	0	86	100
1981	5	0	89	100

8 Jack Fields (R)

Of Humble — Elected 1980; 7th Term

Born: Feb. 3, 1952, Humble, Texas.
Education: Baylor U., B.A. 1974, J.D. 1977.
Occupation: Lawyer; cemetery executive.
Family: Wife, Lynn Hughes; one child, one stepchild.
Religion: Baptist.
Political Career: Candidate for U.S. Senate (special election), 1993.
Capitol Office: 2228 Rayburn Bldg. 20515; 225-4901.

In Washington: After a dozen years in the House, Fields finds himself elevated to some positions of real power in the 103rd Congress: He is now ranking Republican on the Merchant Marine and Fisheries Committee and on Energy and Commerce's Telecommunications and Finance Subcommittee.

But the news in early 1993 was Fields' attempt to elevate himself out of the House altogether, running for the Senate seat vacated by Treasury Secretary Lloyd Bentsen.

The May 1 special election did not require Fields to give up his House seat, so it was a rare free shot at the Senate. And despite his fourth-place finish, the race boosted Fields' statewide name recognition.

With the campaign over, Fields was back in the House, free to concentrate on his legislative duties. Among these, he apparently counted opposition to every major initiative of the Clinton administration. Early in the 103rd, he voted against Clinton's budget, the family leave bill, an extension of unemployment benefits, the "motor voter" bill and the resumption of fetal tissue research. He was also expected to vote against reconciliation, gays in the military and the kind of health-care reform ideas that were taking shape in the administration in late spring.

Fields is known for looking out for Texas' interests and has yet to make a name for himself as a legislative strategist whose breadth matches the broad scope of Energy and Commerce's jurisdiction.

Fields was elected in 1980 at age 28, with no political experience but much conservative zeal. In his early House years he was known as one of the "Reagan robots."

But his new posts give him visibility and the opportunity to do more. Observers will be watching how he works with Democrat Gerry E. Studds of Massachusetts, Merchant Marine's new chairman. Fields is a deeply religious Baptist who spoke out against gays in the military during his Senate campaign; Studds is himself openly gay.

Fields' decision to take Energy and Commerce's ranking Telecommunications post was puzzling to some. Throughout his career, one of Fields' main activities has been speaking up for Texas interests, particularly Houston's oil and gas industries.

In the 101st Congress, Fields was most visibly working the Texas angle during deliberations over the 1990 Clean Air Act reauthorization.

Fields assisted in maneuvering to gain subcommittee approval of a controversial amendment in October 1989, full committee approval the following March, and final conference agreement in October 1990 of a slightly modified version.

Fields joined fellow Texan Ralph M. Hall, a Democrat, to weaken President Bush's proposed mandates for auto companies to build "clean cars" — vehicles that run on alternative fuels. Their amendment increased the percentage of gasoline that could be included in a "clean fuel" mix of gasoline and methanol, and it put reformulated gasoline on the list of "clean alternative fuels." It also stripped a proposed requirement that automakers sell 1 million clean-fuel vehicles a year by 1997.

Fields said the amendment would "level the playing field" for alternative fuels other than methanol, but critics portrayed it as gutting a key portion of the administration's clean air legislation and saw it as a major victory for the auto and oil industries.

Joining other oil-state members and the business interests they represented, Fields led the criticism of Bush for his June 1990 decision to ban offshore oil drilling for huge areas around the country. "He made a terrible mistake for all the wrong reasons," said Fields. "As a former oilman, President Bush should have known better."

On the Merchant Marine Committee in the 101st Congress, Fields pushed legislation to provide new veterans benefits to about 2,000 elderly merchant mariners. His measure went through subcommittee and shortly before Congress adjourned late in 1990, Fields attached the bill to must-pass deficit-reduction legislation.

Texas 8

Northern Houston suburbs; College Station

Texas is known for oil barons, vast open expanses and former President George Bush. The 8th has all that, plus dairy farms, a robust medical industry and the Texas A&M Aggies.

Reconfigured in 1992 redistricting, the 8th resembles a lopsided barbell; it has distinct eastern and western sections and a narrow corridor connecting them. Most of the population lives on the barbell's eastern end. Suburban Houston turf in Harris County accounts for nearly 45 percent of the total vote; the next county north, Montgomery, casts another 30 percent. In 1992, the 8th District sections of both those counties backed Bush's re-election. (He got 58 percent in Harris.) Those showings helped Bush win 55 percent districtwide; Ross Perot and Bill Clinton were well back, with 23 percent and 22 percent, respectively.

Houston's largest employer is the Texas Medical Center, a conglomeration of 41 nonprofit health-related institutions that employs more than 51,000 people and treats 3.5 million patients annually. Many of the doctors, nurses, lab technicians, researchers and managers at the Medical Center live in the tidy suburbs of the 8th.

The oil and gas industry obviously plays a major role in the region's economy. Although the Port of Houston is no longer in the 8th, many of the refinery managers commute to the port from their homes in the district.

Similarly, the corporate headquarters of Exxon, Shell and Pennzoil are all in Houston. The city accounts for 23 percent of all U.S. jobs in crude petroleum and natural gas extraction, 14 percent of all U.S. jobs in oil and gas services, and 38 percent of the nation's jobs in oil and gas field machinery manufacturing.

Executives at the Houston Advanced Research Center, Exxon and the Lifecell medical research company live in Woodlands or Kingwood, two planned communities that offer office space, housing and shops all in the same neighborhood.

Although the residential areas that dominate the Harris County part of the 8th are described as suburban, traffic congestion here rivals that of some East Coast cities.

In the western half of the district, the joke goes that there are more cows than people. Washington County is best known for Brenham's Blue Bell Creameries, which produces ice cream using milk from local dairies. Ten miles east of Brenham is Chappell Hill, the first town in Texas planned by a woman. The entire county is renowned for its fine German and Polish bakeries and sausage shops, a legacy of the Eastern European immigrants who flocked to this area in the 1800s and put down roots.

Farther north is Brazos County, home of College Station and Texas A&M University, the state's oldest public institution of higher education. The university, which has 41,000 students, will be the site of Bush's presidential library. Brazos County, where Bush won 50 percent in 1992, casts just under one-fifth of the district's total vote.

1990 Population: 566,217. White 506,747 (89%), Black 29,707 (5%), Other 29,763 (5%). Hispanic origin 40,728 (7%). 18 and over 408,226 (72%), 62 and over 49,207 (9%). Median age: 30.

When a number of similarly extraneous measures were removed from the bill as non-deficit-reducing, Fields added to his proposal a $100 application fee to be imposed on mariners seeking benefits. But the Budget Committee said it ultimately would cost the government $3 million over five years, so it was stripped out.

Field reintroduced that bill in the 102nd Congress to no avail, and again early in the 103rd.

At Home: Given Fields' ambition and his impressive fundraising ability, it was not surprising he entered the special Senate race in 1993. Despite the presence of another House member, Republican Joe L. Barton, and state Treasurer Kay Bailey Hutchison (the eventual winner), Fields held his own and may have paved the way for possible future statewide contests, if he loosens his style.

Fields portrayed himself as the candidate of working people in the all-party Senate election, even though his 1992 financial disclosure forms indicated that his cemetery business holdings were worth between $1.25 million and $2.5 million.

The one smirch in his Senate campaign came when allegations that Hutchison had slapped a former employee were traced to Fields supporters: former Gov. John B. Connally and his daughter, Sharon Ammann.

Whatever Fields' statewide prospects prove to be, he has had no trouble in hanging on to his House seat. A fifth-generation Houstonian, Fields won two terms as president of the student body at Baylor University. After law school, he joined the family cemetery business as a vice president.

A novice at public office when he announced his 1980 candidacy against Democratic Rep. Bob Eckhardt, Fields showed unusual aptitude for a newcomer. He drew the interest of New Right activists, national Republicans and corporate contributors, all eager to defeat Eckhardt, the most liberal member of the Texas delegation and a staunch anti-corporate populist. Potentially strong GOP primary opponents were scared off by Fields' prodigious organizing.

Eckhardt had been losing ground in his changing constituency; in 1978 and 1980, he had been pressed in the primary by conservative Democrats who won more than 40 percent. Labor and consumer groups worked hard for him in 1980, but many blue-collar workers abandoned their Democratic voting habits to support Fields and Ronald Reagan. The challenger unseated Eckhardt by under 5,000 votes.

Redistricting strengthened Fields' position for 1982, and he did not draw top-drawer Democratic opposition. But he won less than 60 percent, and Democrats waged a more vigorous campaign two years later. Their 1984 nominee, former congressional aide Don Buford, argued that a Fields mailing to the district announcing town hall meetings had violated rules governing use of the congressional frank.

But early in October, the House ethics committee cleared Fields of any abuse of the frank. Fields cast Buford as a "suitcase politician" — referring to the Democrat's relatively recent arrival in the district. Bolstered by the district's big Reagan vote, he took 65 percent, and has coasted since.

Committee

Merchant Marine & Fisheries (Ranking)

Energy & Commerce (3rd of 17 Republicans)
Telecommunications & Finance (ranking); Transportation & Hazardous Materials

Elections

1992 General		
Jack Fields (R)	179,349	(77%)
Chas. Robinson (D)	53,473	(23%)
1990 General		
Jack Fields (R)	60,603	(100%)

Previous Winning Percentages: **1988** (100%) **1986** (68%) **1984** (65%) **1982** (57%) **1980** (52%)

District Vote for President

1992

D 55,330 (22%)
R 134,583 (55%)
I 55,343 (23%)

Campaign Finance

	Receipts	Receipts from PACs		Expend-itures
1992				
Fields (R)	$757,980	$453,076	(60%)	$746,361
1990				
Fields (R)	$385,273	$269,275	(70%)	$420,288

Key Votes

1993	
Require parental notification of minors' abortions	Y
Require unpaid family and medical leave	N
Approve national "motor voter" registration bill	?
Approve budget increasing taxes and reducing deficit	N
Approve economic stimulus plan	N
1992	
Approve balanced-budget constitutional amendment	Y
Close down space station program	N
Approve U.S. aid for former Soviet Union	N
Allow shifting funds from defense to domestic programs	N
1991	
Extend unemployment benefits using deficit financing	N
Approve waiting period for handgun purchases	N
Authorize use of force in Persian Gulf	Y

Voting Studies

	Presidential Support		Party Unity		Conservative Coalition	
Year	**S**	**O**	**S**	**O**	**S**	**O**
1992	77	15	89	4	88	4
1991	79	18	92	5	97	0
1990	79	19	92	3	100	0
1989	78	20	88	6	95	5
1988	70	23	92	1	84	3
1987	73	25	94	2	95	5
1986	79	20	95	4	98	2
1985	74	21	89	4	91	9
1984	58	37	84	12	80	15
1983	83	17	91	6	92	4
1982	84	14	89	9	92	8
1981	76	18	88	8	96	1

Interest Group Ratings

Year	ADA	AFL-CIO	CCUS	ACU
1992	5	25	75	96
1991	0	8	100	100
1990	6	8	93	88
1989	0	8	100	96
1988	0	0	100	100
1987	4	13	93	86
1986	0	0	94	95
1985	10	6	91	90
1984	5	23	81	88
1983	5	6	80	96
1982	5	0	86	100
1981	0	7	95	100

9 Jack Brooks (D)

Of Beaumont — Elected 1952; 21st Term

Born: Dec. 18, 1922, Crowley, La.
Education: Lamar Community College, 1939-41; U. of Texas, B.J. 1943, J.D. 1949.
Military Service: Marine Corps, 1942-45; Marine Corps Reserve, 1945-72.
Occupation: Lawyer.
Family: Wife, Charlotte Collins; three children.
Religion: Methodist.
Political Career: Texas House, 1947-51.
Capitol Office: 2449 Rayburn Bldg. 20515; 225-6565.

In Washington: Brooks is nearly the last of an era: Of Congress' 535 members, only one has served longer than he — the infirm Jamie L. Whitten of Mississippi. In 1993, Brooks celebrated his 40th anniversary as a member of the House, and the years are starting to show.

A bout in 1989 with acute idiopathic pancreatitis left Brooks clearly less vigorous, and close associates have learned to speak into Brooks' good ear. Also, Brooks dates himself with sometimes indelicate behavior and remarks regarding women and minorities — behavior that seems especially out of step with all the new blacks, Hispanics and women joining the House in 1993.

Brooks' demeanor confounds liberals, who generally find him to be a legislative ally, but at times an unseemly partner. Some women who deal with Brooks blanch when he addresses them as "dear" and puts his arm around them, seeing such actions not as gestures of grandfatherly warmth but as inappropriately overfamiliar behavior from a powerful politician. And liberals wonder whether the sort of man who tactlessly will boast of hiring a black staffer is the best person to carry the civil rights torch.

Despite his personality, the cigar-chomping, sour-pussed Brooks remains a powerful chairman whose Judiciary Committee is certain to be at the center of several major policy debates during the 103rd Congress.

In those debates, Brooks can be expected to behave first and foremost as a partisan. As he sought his first House term in 1952, he worked hard against the Democrats for Eisenhower movement sweeping Texas; when he arrived in Washington, his party loyalty impressed the equally partisan House Democratic leader from Texas, Sam Rayburn, who had to surrender the Speaker's chair that year to Republican Joseph W. Martin Jr. of Massachusetts.

Bill Clinton's election as president in 1992 gives Brooks the chance to follow the lead of a Democratic president, something unusual for him. In only 12 of Brooks' 40 years as a congressman has his party held the White House.

In early 1993, Brooks sponsored and began moving out of his Judiciary Committee a piece of the Clinton administration's technology agenda. The bill, dealing with antitrust restrictions, would encourage more U.S. firms to enter into joint ventures.

Also in the 103rd Congress, Brooks renewed work on what has been one of Judiciary's major recent endeavors: legislation affecting the Baby Bell regional telephone companies.

The crusty Texan played the first hand well, winning a jurisdictional dispute with Energy and Commerce Committee Chairman John D. Dingell of Michigan and scoring a victory for newspaper publishers and long distance telephone companies, which oppose allowing the regional phone companies to enter new markets.

Beyond its work in the 102nd Congress on a civil rights bill, on the Baby Bells matter and on cable reregulation, Judiciary was not especially active. To critics who had hoped for more from the committee, Brooks said some issues did not move because no consensus was evident on them, or because they faced a certain veto by President Bush. But with a Democrat in the White House, the pressure is on to produce.

The numerous activist liberal Democrats on Judiciary — many from the East or West Coast — might seem an unlikely posse for Brooks, given his stands on issues such as gun control (opposed). But Brooks is savvy enough to look for areas of agreement with younger liberals and to pitch important legislation in a way that stokes their partisanship.

After Bush killed a civil rights bill in 1990, arguing that it imposed hiring quotas, Brooks and supporters found a new line of attack. In unveiling a revised version in the spring of 1991, he touted the bill's benefits for working women. It would allow victims of intentional discrimination based on gender to sue for monetary damages — a big improvement, Brooks said, on the existing situation, in which: "If they flagrantly harass you and mistreat you in your job, a white woman, there is no compensation." (Victims of racial discrimination already could

Texas 9

Southeast — Beaumont; Galveston

Tucked in the southeast corner of Texas, the 9th runs from Houston's outlying suburbs to Port Arthur, near the Gulf Coast. Geographically small by Texas standards, the 9th is jampacked with refineries and petrochemical plants on land, and with commercial cargo ships and fishing boats on its waters. Also here is NASA's enormous Johnson Space Center.

The 9th's past and present are inextricably tied to petroleum.

The largest city in the 9th is Beaumont, in Jefferson County. The city was chartered in 1838, but it came of age in 1901 when the great gusher, Spindletop, erupted. Texas oil production soared from 836,000 barrels in 1900 to 4.4 million in 1901. Spindletop triggered Beaumont's industrial development; within a month of its discovery the city's population tripled.

Just as Spindletop and other Gulf Coast wells catapulted the region's economy, the oil market plunge of the mid-1980s devastated the area. With a worldwide glut, oil dropped to $9 a barrel, refineries closed and unemployment in some communities hit 22 percent by 1986. Port Arthur, Beaumont and Galveston all lost population in the 1980s.

There was a silver lining to the bust: Petrochemical plants were able to buy their raw materials for a song. From the cheap petroleum, the plants refine a host of chemicals that eventually go into making a variety of products, including plastics, foam and carpeting.

The increase in petrochemical production boosted the entire "Golden Triangle" region of Beaumont, Port Arthur and Orange. As that business picked up in the early 1990s, the construction or modernizing of refineries created thousands of jobs.

But the construction work will be short-lived, and the worldwide economic slump has hindered the petrochemical companies. Some communities in the 9th have turned to an industry they believe is more recession-proof and a good job provider: prisons. By the end of 1994, Beaumont expects to have five prisons with 5,100 beds and 2,570 employees.

The 9th remains heavily dependent on coastal industries such as ship repairing and commercial fishing. It is said to be the largest maritime district in the nation; other large coastal cities are split between districts. The Intracoastal Waterway runs the entire length of the 9th, carrying cargo ships from the Houston Ship Channel as far as New York City. About 1,800 boats fish out of the district's ports. And the beaches of Galveston County are a big tourist lure.

At the edge of the 9th, 23 miles south of Houston, sits the Johnson Space Center, a complex that employs 19,000 people. Although President Clinton has recommended spending $2.3 billion on NASA's space station *Freedom*, almost half is to be spent scaling back the project, throwing into jeopardy the station's future and the jobs of thousands at the center.

Clinton won the 9th in 1992 by collecting large margins in Jefferson and Galveston counties.

1990 Population: 566,217. White 410,234 (72%), Black 122,712 (22%), Other 33,271 (6%). Hispanic origin 53,487 (9%). 18 and over 410,971 (73%), 62 and over 78,571 (14%). Median age: 33.

win unlimited damages under a Reconstruction-era law.)

He and a handful of other Democratic leaders moved the new bill through the House with relative ease. But most of the real negotiating ensued between the White House and the Senate. A deal was finally struck in the wake of the contentious Clarence Thomas Supreme Court nomination hearings, which focused attention on the issue of sexual harassment.

Distracted in 1989 by the fall of friend, fellow Texan and House Speaker Jim Wright, and by his own struggle with pancreatitis, Brooks got off to a slow start at the Judiciary helm in the 101st. But he did manage to win over committee liberals who had been wary about how he would perform as chairman. A key test for them was his handling of a proposed constitutional amendment to ban flag desecration. Brooks was a lead sponsor of a 1989 statute to ban such behavior, and after the Supreme Court struck down the statute, he supported a constitutional amendment.

But Brooks helped liberals who opposed the amendment by quickly sending it to the House floor over protests from Republicans, who said they needed more time to lobby for support.

The GOP has accused Brooks of stalling a number of bills, including anti-crime legislation, of which Brooks is no big fan. "We have got almost as many crime bills passed as they have crimes committed," he once griped.

He relented, however, and helped move through an election-year crime bill in 1990. While it included new death penalty language that Brooks supported over liberals' objections, the bill also carried tough new standards for convicting capital case defendants.

In the 102nd, Brooks reconfigured the Judiciary subcommittees, making Charles E. Schumer of New York chairman of a revamped Crime and Criminal Justice Subcommittee. The pair brought a compromise anti-crime bill to the floor in November 1991, and Brooks, dean of the Texas delegation, helped turn around four Texans. Their support was critical; the bill passed 205-203. But the measure died in the Senate amidst Republican filibuster threats.

Brooks, who chaired the Government Operations Committee before taking over Judiciary, has a reputation as an unrelenting inquisitor. He has received considerable national exposure during investigations of scandals involving Republican administrations.

An early critic of what he perceived as President Richard M. Nixon's abuses of office, Brooks' Government Operations subcommittee investigated federal spending on Nixon's vacation White Houses. When Watergate broke, Brooks was a ready prosecutor during the impeachment proceedings. "He didn't even need to hear the evidence," an aide said later. "He was ready to impeach."

Thirteen years later, Wright named Brooks to the Iran-contra investigation committee, and, to no one's surprise, Brooks was the most vocally partisan critic of the Reagan administration. Talking to reporters, Brooks called both former national security adviser John M. Poindexter and former State Department official Elliott Abrams "a lying son of a bitch."

From Judiciary in the 102nd, Brooks issued subpoenas to Attorney General Dick Thornburgh and aides as part of an investigation into charges that the Justice Department stole a computer program from Inslaw Inc., a federal contractor. When Thornburgh was slow to respond, Brooks held a hearing with empty chairs, blasting Thornburgh for not cooperating. Brooks' committee later found that the "evidence raises serious concerns about the possibility of a high-level conspiracy."

In his early House years, Brooks voted like most other Texas congressmen — in favor of the oil industry and against many of the early civil rights bills. He did refuse to sign the segregationist Southern Manifesto in 1956. But when his friend and fellow Texan Lyndon B. Johnson became president, Brooks moved significantly to the left. In 1964, he was one of only 11 Southern Democrats to support that year's Civil Rights Act. He voted for every subsequent civil rights bill and for all of LBJ's Great Society legislation.

Brooks, who as a junior House member was riding in the motorcade when President John F. Kennedy was killed in Dallas in 1963, was instrumental three decades later in opening to public scrutiny documents relating to the assassination. He helped negotiate a bill in the 102nd Congress that established the means for making those government reports public.

His image as an irascible, foul-mouthed Texan, a man of strong loyalties and fierce independence, is one Brooks has carefully nurtured; once when The Washington Post ran a photograph of Brooks with a snarling expression, he proudly showed it all around.

Early in the 103rd Congress, during a break in hearings investigating the federal siege of the Branch Davidian cult compound near Waco, an open microphone caught Brooks in a typical moment of blunt-spokenness.

He was telling the head of the Bureau of Alcohol, Tobacco and Firearms how he would have handled the standoff: "The first night, I'd have run everybody off, quietly put a bomb in that damned water tank, put tear gas in there. If they wanted to shoot, kill them when they came out. If they didn't want to shoot, put them in a paddy wagon."

At Home: "I'm just like old man Rayburn," Brooks likes to say. "Just a Democrat, no prefix or suffix." That label has kept Brooks in office for more than 40 years, although critics have had some success in recent years portraying him as too liberal for his Gulf Coast district.

Brooks' strong support from the 9th's sizable union and minority populations has carried him past several conservative challenges.

After years of easy victories, Brooks had unexpected trouble in the 1980 primary with Wilbur L. "Bubba" Pate, a bus terminal manager. He challenged Brooks from the right and nearly forced him into a runoff. In addition to faulting Brooks as philosophically out of step with the 9th, Pate said the incumbent had amassed a personal fortune while serving most of his adult life in Congress, and he noted that Brooks had earned more than $50,000 in salary and director fees from Texas banks.

Brooks won just over 50 percent in the primary (to 43 percent for Pate), avoiding a runoff only because heavily unionized Galveston gave him a hefty majority.

Pate and three other right-of-Brooks Democrats tried their luck in 1982, believing the incumbent's 1980 stumble portended a fall. But Brooks' fighting instincts had been stirred. He reminded voters of the federal plums he had brought to the 9th, such as money for improvement of local port facilities and for research at area colleges.

Most important, the conservative mood that swept over Texas' blue-collar workers in 1980 had evaporated by 1982; Brooks was on the offensive, criticizing Reaganomics as dangerous to working-class citizens. He won renomination with 53 percent.

Republicans finally put up a fight in 1984, with Galveston attorney Jim Mahan. Reagan carried the 9th for president, but Brooks prevailed with 59 percent.

Brooks had no trouble in the next two elections, but his hospitalization in 1989 piqued GOP interest in the 9th for 1990. Republicans nominated Maury Meyers, a popular former mayor of Beaumont. Meyers portrayed Brooks as an entrenched Washingtonian, and he advocated congressional term limits. But Brooks rebounded from his illness and reminded voters again that his seniority brought clout in Congress and federal money to the district. He won his 20th term with 58 percent of the vote.

Republican Steve Stockman, who had lost in the 1990 GOP primary, tried again in 1992. Stockman portrayed Brooks as an insider and part of a gridlocked Capitol Hill. Relying on themes developed by party leaders, Stockman ran TV ads noting Brooks had been in Congress longer than Fidel Castro of Cuba and Saddam Hussein of Iraq had held power. Brooks pledged to keep fighting for federal dollars for Texas programs such as the Johnson Space Center.

Stockman carried the Harris County (Houston) portion of the district, but Jefferson County (Beaumont-Port Arthur) went very heavily for both Brooks and Clinton. Overall, Brooks finished more than 22,000 votes ahead, although his 54 percent tally was his career-low general-election tally.

A child of the Depression, Brooks worked his way through the University of Texas, served in the Marine Corps in World War II and won a seat in the state House in 1946. Promoting himself as a lawyer and small farmer, he ran for Congress in 1952, when Democratic Rep. Jesse M. Combs retired. Brooks won, surviving a 12-way primary and a runoff.

Committee

Judiciary (Chairman)
Economic & Commercial Law (chairman)

Elections

1992 General		
Jack Brooks (D)	118,690	(54%)
Steve Stockman (R)	96,270	(43%)
Billy Joe Crawford (LIBERT)	6,401	(3%)
1990 General		
Jack Brooks (D)	79,786	(58%)
Maury Meyers (R)	58,399	(42%)

Previous Winning Percentages: **1988** (100%) **1986** (62%) **1984** (59%) **1982** (68%) **1980** (100%) **1978** (63%) **1976** (100%) **1974** (62%) **1972** (66%) **1970** (65%) **1968** (61%) **1966** (100%) **1964** (63%) **1962** (69%) **1960** (70%) **1958** (100%) **1956** (100%) **1954** (100%) **1952** (79%)

District Vote for President

1992
D 98,959 (44%)
R 80,813 (36%)
I 47,418 (21%)

Campaign Finance

	Receipts	Receipts from PACs	Expend-itures
1992			
Brooks (D)	$606,190	$456,357 (75%)	$471,285
Stockman (R)	$99,616	$17,535 (18%)	$98,622
1990			
Brooks (D)	$775,167	$459,444 (59%)	$885,090
Meyers (R)	$462,656	$21,900 (5%)	$447,974

Key Votes

1993	
Require parental notification of minors' abortions	N
Require unpaid family and medical leave	Y
Approve national "motor voter" registration bill	Y
Approve budget increasing taxes and reducing deficit	Y
Approve economic stimulus plan	Y
1992	
Approve balanced-budget constitutional amendment	N
Close down space station program	N
Approve U.S. aid for former Soviet Union	Y
Allow shifting funds from defense to domestic programs	?
1991	
Extend unemployment benefits using deficit financing	Y
Approve waiting period for handgun purchases	N
Authorize use of force in Persian Gulf	Y

Voting Studies

	Presidential Support		Party Unity		Conservative Coalition	
Year	**S**	**O**	**S**	**O**	**S**	**O**
1992	30	62	85	10	52	35
1991	31 †	61 †	82 †	10 †	62	30
1990	18	71	87	5	39	52
1989	16 †	49 †	69 †	3 †	25 †	52 †
1988	24	70	82	5	26	61
1987	20	75	87	5	40	60
1986	21	69	76	7	50	34
1985	24	74	87	5	35	56
1984	30	58	77	14	46	46
1983	32	63	81	14	47	51
1982	44	44	70	16	55	38
1981	42	33	55	23	57	35

† Not eligible for all recorded votes.

Interest Group Ratings

Year	ADA	AFL-CIO	CCUS	ACU
1992	75	83	33	23
1991	55	92	30	17
1990	61	100	23	17
1989	65	73	40	17
1988	75	100	23	9
1987	88	94	13	0
1986	70	100	33	9
1985	70	94	28	11
1984	55	77	43	11
1983	75	76	32	17
1982	50	74	40	20
1981	45	64	33	21

10 J.J. Pickle (D)

Of Austin — Elected 1963; 15th Full Term

Born: Oct. 11, 1913, Roscoe, Texas.
Education: U. of Texas, B.A. 1938.
Military Service: Navy, 1942-45.
Occupation: Public relations and advertising executive.
Family: Wife, Beryl Bolton McCarroll; three children.
Religion: Methodist.
Political Career: No previous office.
Capitol Office: 242 Cannon Bldg. 20515; 225-4865.

In Washington: Pickle will pass two milestones in the 103rd Congress — his 80th birthday and his 30th anniversary as a member of the House. But in the grand Texas tradition, he shows no desire to take off his boots anytime soon.

And while Pickle finds himself still two rungs removed from the chairmanship of Ways and Means, waiting for two younger men to retire or step aside, he has the wherewithal to be a key player on the committee. And he remains a legend in Austin, enjoying big reelection margins.

Pickle's Texas Hill Country drawl is an instant reminder of Lyndon B. Johnson, who represented the same congressional district for a decade. And Pickle's legislative career suggests its own echoes of Johnson, for whom he campaigned as a young man and whose name he nearly always pronounces in reverent tones.

More recently, Pickle has been associated with another Texas power, former Speaker Jim Wright. A week before Wright's resignation in the late spring of 1989, Pickle was appearing in debates on national television to defend the Speaker against ethics charges and to say he should not resign.

Like both Wright and LBJ, Pickle is a man of rural populist roots who also has been able to hobnob with the haves and accommodate the corporate pillars of Texas politics. But he seems more comfortable with his role of small-business protector and specialist in the problems of the Social Security system. Lately, his concern has run more to the myriad ways that poorly managed, open-ended government programs can put the taxpayer on the hook for billions of dollars.

Whatever the issue, he is dogged and often successful in getting what he wants.

Over the years, Pickle has managed to involve himself in just about every major issue that confronts Ways and Means, from Social Security to trade to the complete revision of the tax code. During the 101st Congress he defended Chairman Dan Rostenkowski's position on pension anti-discrimination rules unpopular with business, and he did what he could to rescue the ill-fated catastrophic-illness extension of Medicare. Given the sometimes rocky relations between Rostenkowski and No. 2 Democrat Sam Gibbons of Florida, Pickle at times functions as the chairman's senior ally.

But he also displayed his independence from both Rostenkowski and the House Democratic leadership by joining an effort to cut the tax on capital gains — profits from the sale of assets that appreciate in value.

While never viewed as beholden to the chairman, Pickle has shown deference to Rostenkowski. In the 99th Congress, despite deep reservations about the sweeping tax overhaul bill, Pickle went along with it. He objected to the big shift of tax burden to business and to the shaving of tax breaks for the oil and gas industry. But in the end he voted for Rostenkowski's bill and was rewarded with a seat on the House-Senate conference committee.

Nevertheless, Pickle set his own course in the capital gains episode of 1989. In the spring, six Democrats organized by Ed Jenkins of Georgia declared themselves for the cut before Rostenkowski had established his opposition to it. When all 13 Ways and Means Republicans joined in, Jenkins could wield a working majority of the committee.

Pickle's presence among the rebels surprised many, not only because of his presumed fealty but because his constituency is among the most liberal in Texas. But Pickle's district, based in the state capital, has come to rely increasingly on high-tech firms attracted by the University of Texas, also in Austin. He has become a leading advocate of the tax credit for businesses with big research and development costs; extending that credit in 1989 meant finding the dollars to pay for it. A capital gains cut offered at least a short-term shot of revenue as long-frozen assets were unloaded to take advantage of the tax cut, with the added potential of helping smaller, high-risk enterprises attract capital.

The capital gains cut won committee approval that fall and was passed by the full House, marking the nadir of the 101st Congress

Texas 10

Central — Austin

The vast rural district that Lyndon B. Johnson represented in the House in the 1950s has been shrinking in size and growing in population ever since he left the 10th.

In the 1980s, the district took in five counties and most of a sixth. But for the 1990s, the 10th is limited just to Austin and Travis County, where population grew by 35 percent in the 1980s, on top of 42 percent growth in the 1970s. Austin, the state capital, has become an urban mecca for students, computer engineers, music lovers and tourists.

The economic troubles of the oil industry grazed Austin in the mid-1980s; real estate speculation fizzled and local banks suffered. But the underpinnings of Austin's economy are unique in Texas, and they helped the city's economy remain stable.

The state of Texas, with 57,000 workers, is the 10th's largest employer. Another economic anchor is the University of Texas at Austin; with nearly 50,000 students and 20,000 employees, the school gives the city a youthful feeling (T-shirts and jeans are ubiquitous) and its liberal political bent. In a state that George Bush carried for president in 1992, Travis County was one of the few counties to hand Bill Clinton a solid majority.

The university also has been a catalyst for Austin's emergence as a center for high-tech industry. One local success story is Dell Computer: Begun in a dorm room in the early 1980s by UT student Michael Dell, the computer-maker now employs 2,800 people.

Two public-private research consortiums add to the synergy. In 1983, Austin won the right to host the headquarters of Microelectronics & Computer Technology Corp. Five years later, the city welcomed Sematech, a joint venture using federal and private money to develop new applications for semiconductors. Two major semiconductor makers, Motorola (7,000 employees) and Advanced Microdevices (2,400 workers), are in Austin.

Another boost to Austin's economic vitality is a thriving cultural and entertainment life. The city's country music scene gets national exposure on the public television show "Austin City Limits," and connoisseurs of blues, rock and new wave music flock to clubs on East Sixth Street. Austin also draws visitors to its many lakes and parks: One big annual event is the Austin Aqua Festival, with water shows, a homemade-raft contest and music.

As Austin's growth surged over the past 20 years, some residents who had been drawn by the city's college-town feel began to fret that Austin would become huge, sprawling and impersonal — "Houstonized," in local parlance. Though Texas has a strong frontier spirit that tends to regard growth-management measures as un-American, the prevailing mood in Austin is different: Developers are required to contribute to infrastructure projects in return for zoning permits. In the fall of 1992 the city approved the Balcones Canyonlands Conservation Plan, a proposal that allows the government and the Nature Conservancy to purchase 30,000 acres to protect endangered wildlife.

1990 Population: 566,217. White 412,897 (73%), Black 63,145 (11%), Other 90,175 (16%). Hispanic origin 121,271 (21%). 18 and over 430,148 (76%), 62 and over 48,790 (9%). Median age: 29.

for the Democratic leadership, which opposed the cut as a giveaway for the rich. The cut was dropped from a deficit-reduction bill, however, when it failed to win approval in the Senate.

In the 100th Congress, Pickle had some of the same priorities as the committee worked on technical corrections to the tax bill. He had more than 270 members sign on to his plan to extend the life of the research and development tax credit for business and a basic research credit for universities.

"Vigorous research and development is the key to achieving the technological advances that will create and improve on products we can sell here and abroad," he argued. The expiring provisions were all modified to some degree because of revenue concerns, but Pickle took some satisfaction from seeing them extended. Additional extensions were granted in 1990 and 1991, but the provisions expired in June 1992. Further extensions were contained in a pair of Democratic tax bills that died in 1992 under President Bush's veto.

As chairman of Ways and Means' Oversight Subcommittee, Pickle exercises a broad mandate. He scored a success of sorts in the 102nd Congress with the imposition of capital standards and additional regulation on several "government-sponsored enterprises." These private corporations are chartered by Congress, and their bonds and other securities are treated in the marketplace as if they have an implicit government guarantee. Thanks in large part to Pickle's efforts through his subcommittee, Congress in 1989 mandated that the administration act to limit the potential that these businesses could fail and leave Uncle Sam holding the bag. The fruit of those labors was a series of bills enacted in 1992.

During the debate, Pickle clashed with fellow Texan Henry B. Gonzalez, chairman of the Banking Committee and a strong supporter of two of these businesses — the Federal National Mortgage Association (Fannie Mae) and the Federal Home Loan Mortgage Corporation (Freddie Mac), which together generate a huge amount of capital for home mortgages. Gonzalez thought Pickle had no business trying to regulate them; Pickle thought Gonzalez's regulatory bills were too weak.

Pickle also has been very concerned about the potential collapse of the government agency that backs up private pension plans. And his subcommittee's investigations led to a 1992 bill targeting waste and fraud in the Medicare system, in particular benefits paid to dead people and unscrupulous sellers of medical equipment. The provisions of that bill were included in one of the vetoed 1992 tax bills, so Pickle reintroduced it at the start of the 103rd Congress.

In the 101st Congress, he went after investors who had reaped big profits by moving money to Puerto Rico in the wake of the 1986 tax bill but who had not lived up to the bill's quid pro quo of local investment in the island's development. And he made a big splash with hearings regarding tax avoidance by the U.S. subsidiaries of huge foreign corporations, most of them Japanese.

In the 100th Congress, the subcommittee investigated tax breaks for televangelists and lobbying and election-related activity by tax-exempt public charities.

Whatever work he does on Oversight, Pickle will have difficulty matching an earlier achievement as head of the Social Security Subcommittee in the 98th Congress.

As chairman of that subcommittee, he was convinced that the way to save the Social Security system from a long-term collapse was to raise the retirement age. Democratic leaders, including Speaker Thomas P. O'Neill Jr. of Massachusetts and senior citizens spokesman Claude Pepper of Florida, wanted to solve long-term financing problems with eventual increases in the payroll tax. Few expected Pickle would prevail on the floor, but he did, in what was the most impressive and significant victory of his career.

Through months of argument over what to do about Social Security, Pickle and Pepper were the spokesmen for two diametrically opposite points of view. When the Florida Democrat said he could not support an increase in the retirement age or any other benefit change, Pickle replied, "There are other possibilities we have to consider. I can take just as intractable a position as you."

In March 1983, Ways and Means approved a compromise package of tax increases and modest benefit cuts, with the understanding that Pickle and Pepper would offer their respective alternatives on the floor. In the end, the House voted 228-202 for Pickle's plan, with support from most Republicans and a majority of Ways and Means.

Pickle's approach later became law, and his victory represented the culmination of a long personal struggle to put the system on a sound financial footing. Afterward, he gave up his Social Security chairmanship, explaining that his main task had been accomplished.

Much of Pickle's earlier House career consisted of balancing his own New Deal instincts and LBJ's national goals against his constituents' increasing ambivalence toward liberal programs. He arrived in the House in December 1963 — less than a month after Johnson's assumption of the presidency — and in his first two years backed both the Civil Rights Act of 1964 and the Voting Rights Act of 1965. "I caught hell in my district," he noted later. He then opposed civil rights legislation in 1966 and 1968, both times on grounds that its open housing provisions were too strong. In the years since the Johnson administration, he, like most Texas Democrats, has gradually moved closer to the voting patterns of Democrats from other Southern states.

At Home: Pickle belongs to a dwindling generation of Texas politicians who were political protégés of LBJ. He solidified his grip on his central Texas district during the Johnson White House years, and it looks safe for him as long as he lasts.

Pickle was a campaign manager and a congressional aide to Johnson before World War II and an adviser in LBJ's 1948 Senate campaign. But he didn't seek office himself until 1963, when he resigned from the Texas Employment Commission to run in a special election. A vacancy had been created when Democratic Rep. Homer Thornberry retired to accept a judgeship.

Long before Pickle made his political debut, however, he had become controversial in Texas politics. He had gained the disfavor of liberal Democrats in 1954, when he worked for the re-election of Gov. Allan Shivers against the liberal favorite, Ralph Yarborough.

Liberals supported their own candidate in the 1963 House race. But Pickle's ties to political and business interests, and the pickle-shaped campaign pins and recipe books he handed out, helped him run narrowly ahead of the three-man field in the first round of voting in early November. He was expected to have problems winning the December runoff election against a conservative Republican opponent.

That changed with the Nov. 22 assassination of President John F. Kennedy. Pickle's House race became the first test of voter support for the district's most famous citizen, President Johnson. In a surge of party harmony,

Pickle won easily.

During the height of the Johnson presidency, Pickle had no primary or GOP opposition. In 1968 he had an aggressive Republican challenger, Ray Gabler, who accused him of profiting from land condemnation for a federally aided reservoir project. Pickle denied any breach of ethics but was held to 62 percent.

Pickle had no other serious challenge until 1980, when the Reagan tide in Texas and voter dissatisfaction with a court-ordered busing plan in Austin held him to 59 percent.

As in earlier races, Pickle ran better in the rural areas than in populous Austin. But he was still able to carry every county and did not face another Republican opponent until 1986. In that year, Carole Rylander, a former Austin mayor and lifelong Democrat, switched parties to challenge Pickle. Though she was well-known and campaigned energetically, Pickle rose to the challenge.

Aided by early fundraising, laser-printed direct-mail technology and the first professional campaign manager he had hired in a half-dozen years, Pickle amassed a stunning 72 percent.

That showing deterred a GOP challenge two years later. However, in 1990 Republican nominee David Beilharz waged an aggressive campaign against the incumbent. Beilharz tried to stir up anti-incumbent fervor against Pickle, but Pickle largely ignored his opponent, and to good effect; Pickle took almost two-thirds of the vote.

The anti-incumbent mood that swept the country gave Pickle a Democratic opponent in 1992. But with his clout in Washington and long years of service to voters in the 10th, Pickle easily disposed of the primary challenge by John Longsworth. He defeated four others in the general election, including a retired Republican professor.

Committees

Ways & Means (3rd of 24 Democrats)
Oversight (chairman); Social Security

Joint Taxation

Elections

1992 General		
J.J. Pickle (D)	177,233	(68%)
Herbert Spiro (R)	68,646	(26%)
Terry Blum (LIBERT)	6,353	(2%)
Jeff Davis (I)	6,056	(2%)
Stephen Hopkins (write-in)	3,510	(1%)
1992 Primary		
J.J. Pickle (D)	55,703	(82%)
John Longsworth (D)	12,034	(18%)
1990 General		
J.J. Pickle (D)	152,784	(65%)
David Beilharz (R)	73,766	(31%)
Jeff Davis (LIBERT)	8,905	(4%)

Previous Winning Percentages: **1988** (93%) **1986** (72%) **1984** (100%) **1982** (90%) **1980** (59%) **1978** (76%) **1976** (77%) **1974** (80%) **1972** (91%) **1970** (100%) **1968** (62%) **1966** (74%) **1964** (76%) **1963** * (63%)

** Special election*

District Vote for President

1992

D 128,813 (48%)
R 84,560 (32%)
I 54,304 (20%)

Campaign Finance

	Receipts	Receipts from PACs		Expend-itures
1992				
Pickle (D)	$421,708	$263,432	(62%)	$363,561
Spiro (R)	$119,690	$350	(0%)	$117,934
1990				
Pickle (D)	$491,649	$247,900	(50%)	$562,967
Beilharz (R)	$261,543	0		$261,528

Key Votes

1993	
Require parental notification of minors' abortions	X
Require unpaid family and medical leave	Y
Approve national "motor voter" registration bill	Y
Approve budget increasing taxes and reducing deficit	Y
Approve economic stimulus plan	Y
1992	
Approve balanced-budget constitutional amendment	Y
Close down space station program	N
Approve U.S. aid for former Soviet Union	Y
Allow shifting funds from defense to domestic programs	N
1991	
Extend unemployment benefits using deficit financing	?
Approve waiting period for handgun purchases	Y
Authorize use of force in Persian Gulf	N

Voting Studies

	Presidential Support		Party Unity		Conservative Coalition	
Year	**S**	**O**	**S**	**O**	**S**	**O**
1992	40	56	75	20	73	27
1991	41	56	78	17	54	43
1990	33	66	81	17	67	33
1989	47	52	82	15	66	32
1988	32	60	80	12	53	42
1987	34	62	82	16	77	23
1986	39	57	63	25	80	18
1985	40	59	82	15	64	29
1984	47	47	70	22	69	27
1983	44	49	68	25	72	21
1982	53	43	57	36	74	19
1981	61	36	58	39	75	24

Interest Group Ratings

Year	ADA	AFL-CIO	CCUS	ACU
1992	65	64	63	33
1991	45	55	56	16
1990	61	33	50	25
1989	50	67	30	33
1988	80	100	38	16
1987	60	63	43	22
1986	40	43	44	38
1985	50	65	43	38
1984	65	62	40	25
1983	60	56	40	30
1982	30	42	58	43
1981	40	60	58	20

11 Chet Edwards (D)

Of Waco — Elected 1990; 2nd Term

Born: Nov. 24, 1951, Corpus Christi, Texas.
Education: Texas A&M U., B.A. 1974; Harvard U., M.B.A. 1981.
Occupation: Radio station executive.
Family: Wife, Lea Ann Wood.
Religion: Methodist.
Political Career: Sought Democratic nomination for U.S. House, 1978; Texas Senate, 1983-91.
Capitol Office: 328 Cannon Bldg. 20515; 225-6105.

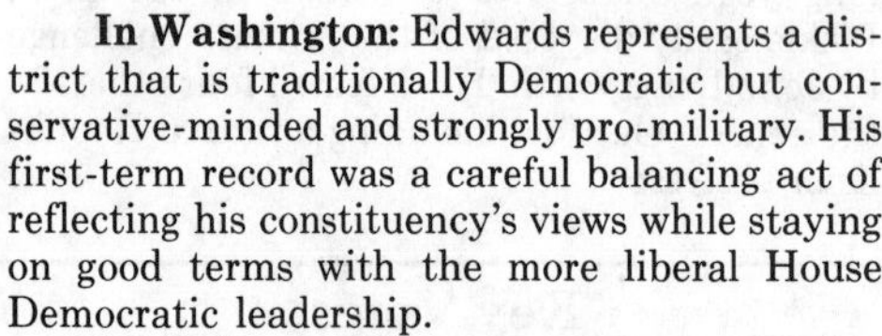

In Washington: Edwards represents a district that is traditionally Democratic but conservative-minded and strongly pro-military. His first-term record was a careful balancing act of reflecting his constituency's views while staying on good terms with the more liberal House Democratic leadership.

Edwards won the most attention for his involvement with the Gang of Six — a group of freshman Democrats who in 1992 agitated for party leaders to schedule a vote on a balanced-budget constitutional amendment.

The activities of the group helped generate considerable public pressure for the House to act on the amendment. At a time when the institution already was suffering from negative publicity over scandals in the House bank and House Post Office, voting against the amendment began to look politically risky. House Speaker Thomas S. Foley, an opponent of the amendment, predicted it would win, and a decisive majority of members did support it. But in the end, the vote was 280-153 — just a few votes shy of the two-thirds majority needed for passage.

Edwards' advocacy of the amendment won him generally favorable reviews at home, and he further sought to earn an image for frugality by returning more than $200,000 in congressional office-allowance money in his first year and by using barely a third of his budget for franked mailings.

But if Edwards sometimes takes a stroll to the right of center, he is certainly closer to being a national Democrat than his predecessor in the 11th, Marvin Leath, who was a leading House "Boll Weevil" in the 1980s.

For the most part, Edwards has stayed in step with the goals of the Democratic leadership and sided with President Clinton on several key issues early in his administration. Edwards voted for legislation mandating that businesses provide unpaid family and medical leave; he voted for Clinton's budget plan as well as his $16 billion economic stimulus package, which included $9.6 million for highway and hospital construction in the 11th District.

Edwards' brief tenure in Washington has been marked by two tragic events — both involving firearms — that made international news. Those events have focused special attention on Edwards during House consideration of gun-control legislation.

In October 1991, several hours into the debate on a crime bill that included a ban on assault weapons, news broke that a man wielding an automatic pistol had opened fire in a cafeteria in the 11th District city of Killeen. The gunman killed 22 people and wounded at least 20 more before killing himself.

Edwards had planned to vote against the assault-weapon ban, backing up his stand with statistics suggesting that state gun bans do little to deter crime. But after the cafeteria calamity, he changed his mind.

"I'll never see this issue quite the same again," Edwards said. "Statistics don't mean much to me now."

Later, though, Edwards showed he would not stray too far from the majority view in the 11th that gun-control measures are suspect: He voted against a bill calling for a waiting period for handgun purchases to allow law enforcement officials to conduct background checks of buyers.

In the early months of 1993, Edwards' district was again the focus of national attention when the Branch Davidian religious sect and its leader, David Koresh, clashed with government agents trying to serve arrest warrants on the group for possession of illegal firearms. After four agents were killed in a botched raid on the sect's compound outside Waco, there was a 51-day standoff between Koresh's followers and law enforcement officials. It ended with the incineration of the compound and the death of Koresh and nearly all his followers.

Given the huge arsenal that the Koresh sect allegedly had stockpiled, the events near Waco were sure to be much-cited when the 103rd Congress addressed the matter of a waiting period for handgun purchases. Clinton had pledged to sign such a measure if Congress were

Texas 11

Central — Waco

At the height of the Persian Gulf War, 26,000 soldiers were deployed from Fort Hood, the largest installation of armored forces in the free world. The deployment crushed the little town of Killeen; about 150 local businesses folded and others hung on by a thread. So when the troops returned in mid-1991 and immediately went on a buying spree, the townsfolk were thrilled.

But the roller coaster experience of the gulf war was a troubling sign of times to come for the people of Killeen. Although the base was spared in the 1993 round of proposed closings, post-Cold War defense cuts are expected to eventually reach the 40,000 military personnel stationed at Hood.

And though Killeen stands to lose and gain the most from any changes at Fort Hood, the base's economic impact is felt throughout most of the 11th. Retired veterans — from Fort Hood and elsewhere — stay in Central Texas, drawn to its mild climate and full line of services. The district has three Veterans Affairs medical centers, more than any other in the country.

One of the major employers in the district is Chrysler Technologies Airborne Systems, a Waco-based company that updates and modifies military aircraft.

In many respects, the city of Waco (population 103,600) is the core of the 11th. In the district's geographic center, Waco is also the educational, cultural and economic lifeblood of Central Texas. Split by the Brazos River, Waco is the largest marketing center between Dallas and Austin.

As the home of the world's largest Baptist-affiliated university, Baylor University (11,800 students), Waco is also known as the "Baptist Rome." A former military base has been converted into Texas State Technical Institute.

One-third of the district's residents live in Bell and McLennan counties. These two counties also provide the bulk of Democratic votes. Residents tend to vote ideology more than party and they don't like change; in 50 years the 11th has had just three congressmen.

The remainder of the sprawling 11th, shaped like an animal's head with a large snout pointing west, is agricultural and sparsely populated. Unlike the Piney Woods of East Texas, the rolling hills of this region have few trees.

The 11th has had an unfortunate share of attention-getting tragedies. In spring 1993, a complex outside Waco known as Ranch Apocalypse was the scene of a deadly standoff between federal agents and members of the Branch Davidians, a religious sect organized by David Koresh. Four agents were killed as they attempted to serve an arrest warrant on Koresh in February. The FBI took over, and in mid-April injected non-lethal tear gas into the buildings. But rather than fleeing, the residents remained and, according to authorities, set fire to their compound. Dozens of people died inside the compound.

And in 1991, an armed gunman drove his truck through the window of a Luby's Cafeteria in nearby Killeen and killed 22 people.

1990 Population: 566,217. White 430,594 (76%), Black 90,248 (16%), Other 45,375 (8%). Hispanic origin 69,887 (12%). 18 and over 413,528 (73%), 62 and over 84,363 (15%). Median age: 30.

to pass it.

With seats on both the Armed Services and the Veterans' Affairs committees, Edwards is well-positioned to look out for the military interests of his district, which includes Fort Hood and several large veterans facilities. In the 102nd, Edwards successfully pushed for more than $100 million in construction projects for Fort Hood, including $28 million for family housing that was part of the fiscal 1993 defense authorization bill.

In addition, as Armed Services was getting organized for the 103rd Congress, Edwards showed himself to be a crafty inside operator. According to The Dallas Morning News, Edwards "masterminded" a complex set of trades among all four Texas Democrats on Armed Services that enabled each to end up with the subcommittee assignment most beneficial to his district.

On Veterans' Affairs, Edwards has supported increases in veterans benefits. He also succeeded in pushing through the House a bill that would authorize grants to establish research centers at certain medical schools. But the Senate did not take up the matter.

At Home: Edwards' first campaign for the 11th, in 1990, was a tough one. Outspent by his GOP foe, Edwards prevailed with 53 percent of the vote. But two years later, Republican firefighter James W. Broyles failed to make his anti-Congress attacks stick to Edwards, who had laid careful groundwork for re-election. He won a second term with two-thirds of the vote.

Edwards' political career dates to the mid-1970s. After graduating from Texas A & M University in 1974, he spent three years as an aide to Texas Democratic Rep. Olin E. "Tiger" Teague.

When Teague decided to retire, he encouraged Edwards to try for his seat. But Edwards narrowly missed making the Democratic primary runoff, closely trailing the eventual winner, Phil Gramm, who later switched to the GOP and was elected to the Senate.

Edwards took a break from politics to enter the business world. But he soon returned and became, at 31, the state's youngest senator. Youth did not cow Edwards in the state Senate, where he sponsored dozens of bills, including measures to make Texas part of the Super Tuesday primary and to attract the superconducting super collider project.

Edwards' energy and ambition did not go unnoticed, and it was no large surprise when he began campaigning for lieutenant governor in 1989. But once Rep. Leath announced he was stepping down, Edwards moved his residence into the 11th and set his sights on the House race.

Democrats gave him the nomination without a primary fight, but Republicans went all-out for the district. State Rep. Hugh D. Shine, the GOP nominee, labeled Edwards an out-of-touch carpetbagger. He also claimed Edwards pandered for gay support when running for lieutenant governor but wanted to distance them from his campaign in the conservative 11th.

Edwards countered with a radio ad in which a Baptist minister assured voters that Edwards did not support homosexuality.

At times, it was as though Edwards was campaigning against two men: Shine and Edwards' old rival, Gramm. Gramm had been Edwards' teacher at Texas A&M, but the student and teacher fell out during their fierce 1978 competition for Teague's seat. Gramm poured it on in 1990, campaigning for Shine repeatedly in the district and appearing in one of his campaign commercials.

But Edwards battled back with powerful endorsements and political pledges. Voters took notice of Edwards' chit, secured from House Speaker Thomas S. Foley, for Leath's seat on the Armed Services Committee.

Committees

Armed Services (22nd of 34 Democrats)
Military Installations & Facilities; Oversight & Investigations; Research & Technology

Veterans' Affairs (11th of 21 Democrats)
Compensation, Pension & Insurance; Hospitals & Health Care

Elections

1992 General		
Chet Edwards (D)	119,999	(67%)
James W. Broyles (R)	58,033	(33%)
1990 General		
Chet Edwards (D)	73,810	(53%)
Hugh D. Shine (R)	64,269	(47%)

District Vote for President

1992
D 66,521 (36%)
R 75,651 (41%)
I 42,365 (23%)

Campaign Finance

	Receipts	Receipts from PACs		Expend-itures
1992				
Edwards (D)	$465,342	$321,575	(69%)	$420,880
Broyles (R)	$16,045	$400	(2%)	$17,150
1990				
Edwards (D)	$672,399	$345,480	(51%)	$668,936
Shine (R)	$878,663	$133,667	(15%)	$842,226

Key Votes

1993	
Require parental notification of minors' abortions	N
Require unpaid family and medical leave	Y
Approve national "motor voter" registration bill	Y
Approve budget increasing taxes and reducing deficit	Y
Approve economic stimulus plan	Y
1992	
Approve balanced-budget constitutional amendment	Y
Close down space station program	N
Approve U.S. aid for former Soviet Union	Y
Allow shifting funds from defense to domestic programs	N
1991	
Extend unemployment benefits using deficit financing	Y
Approve waiting period for handgun purchases	N
Authorize use of force in Persian Gulf	Y

Voting Studies

	Presidential Support		Party Unity		Conservative Coalition	
Year	**S**	**O**	**S**	**O**	**S**	**O**
1992	43	56	75	23	85	15
1991	41	56	78	20	95	5

Interest Group Ratings

Year	ADA	AFL-CIO	CCUS	ACU
1992	55	75	63	40
1991	40	75	50	35

12 Pete Geren (D)

Of Fort Worth — Elected 1989; 2nd Full Term

Born: Jan. 29, 1952, Fort Worth, Texas.
Education: Georgia Institute of Technology, 1970-73; U. of Texas, B.A. 1974, J.D. 1978.
Occupation: Lawyer.
Family: Wife, Rebecca Ray; two children.
Religion: Baptist.
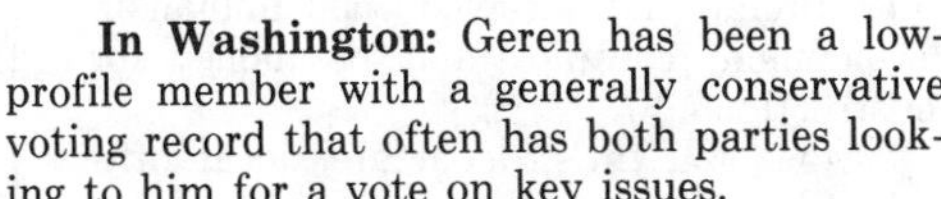
Political Career: Democratic nominee for U.S. House, 6th District, 1986.
Capitol Office: 1730 Longworth Bldg. 20515; 225-5071.

In Washington: Geren has been a low-profile member with a generally conservative voting record that often has both parties looking to him for a vote on key issues.

Early in the Clinton administration, Geren voted against the family leave bill favored by the White House and most Democrats. He also opposed the president's budget, arguing that it would not make a dent in the deficit. Geren's idea of a solution runs more to passing a constitutional amendment that requires a balanced budget.

Geren's quiet style and middle-of-the-road philosophy could not stand in greater contrast to his predecessor, former House Speaker Jim Wright. Geren replaced Wright in a 1989 special election after Wright resigned in the wake of allegations that he violated House gift and income rules.

Regardless of the circumstances of departure, Wright was a tough act to follow in a district long accustomed to having its needs seen to by a powerful congressional insider. Eager to hit the ground running, Geren showed up at his swearing-in ceremony carrying two bills ready for the hopper.

The soft-spoken Geren has none of Wright's theatrical manner and biting oratory that so grated on Republicans such as Georgia's Newt Gingrich, who filed the formal complaint against Wright with the ethics committee.

And while Geren says he still calls Wright occasionally for advice, he has shown little of the former Speaker's populist streak or partisan edge. During Geren's short tenure, he has often voted against the Democratic leadership, reflecting his concern about securing a constituency that supported Wright because of his influence, not his ideology.

He has used his position on the Public Works Committee — where Wright spent the majority of his congressional career — to tend to local matters.

In the 1991 highway bill, he obtained $33.5 million to expand the road from Fort Worth to Springtown. Outside the committee, he and Republican Rep. Curt Weldon of Pennsylvania worked together to save the V-22 Osprey aircraft, part of which is built in Fort Worth and part in Weldon's district. The Pentagon and the White House of President George Bush opposed the V-22, but it received congressional funding. At the start of the 103rd Congress, Geren joined the Armed Services Committee where he can keep a closer eye on such matters.

In the 102nd Congress, Geren was unsuccessful in his effort to prevent the closing of Carswell Air Force Base, which appeared on the 1991 "hit list" produced by the Bush administration. The base has been downsizing ever since.

Geren's voting record is decidedly mixed. While opposing his party's leadership on the balanced budget and other economic issues, he provided a key vote in 1991 for passage of the crime bill, which failed to clear Congress.

Geren's fiscal conservatism does not always extend to local matters: He is a strong supporter of both the superconducting super collider, which would be built not far from his district line, and the space station *Freedom*.

Geren was also one of the conservative Democrats who, during the debate over civil rights legislation, looked for middle ground between the Republican White House and the more liberal members of the Democratic Caucus.

In his first term, Geren took the conservative side on a variety of issues: He supported amending the Constitution to ban flag desecration, he favored cutting the capital gains tax, he opposed family and medical leave and also the pay raise/ethics reform package. According to The Dallas Morning News, Geren's staff submitted a petition asking him to change his position on the flag amendment. He declined.

At Home: Clouded as Wright's departure was, he remained popular in Fort Worth and retained considerable influence in choosing his successor. Geren, who had worked as a staff member for Treasury Secretary Lloyd Bentsen when he was in the Senate and for other Democrats, quickly got the nod. GOP heavyweights, meanwhile, lined up behind first-time candidate Bob Lanier, a physician and television

Texas 12

Northwest Tarrant County; part of Fort Worth

The 12th has an unusual hour-glass shape, but there is a unifying theme: transportation. Within this Fort Worth-based district are three major airports, an Air Force base, three railroad lines, several interstate highways and a myriad of businesses that depend on one or more of these conveyances.

The focus on transportation stems from Fort Worth's past importance as a rail center. The earliest settlers of Fort Worth extended the rail line themselves in 1873 when financial problems halted construction 26 miles to the east. Once the trains came through, Fort Worth emerged as a major cattle trading post; stockyards ringed the city and meatpacking plants flourished.

Today, bits of that history remain. On the city's north side, a handful of stockyards survive, and one of the largest cattle trading posts has been converted into a complex of shops, offices and kiddie rides called the Stockyard Station.

Although the Santa Fe Railroad is still active — shipping automobiles, chemicals, farm products and other commodities — the air industry has far surpassed rail.

One of the district's largest employers is American Airlines, which has both its headquarters and a maintenance facility just over the district line. The maintenance shop provided a critical boost to the local economy at just the right time. In 1991, General Dynamics in Fort Worth laid off 3,500 after the Pentagon canceled the A-12 stealth attack plane program. But opportunities at the American facility helped ease the impact of the loss.

Still, uncertainty remains for many of the blue-collar aviation workers. When Speaker Jim Wright represented this district, his clout helped protect the federal contracts that kept them at work. But Wright is gone and the General Dynamics air division has been bought by Lockheed; there are concerns that future construction of the F-22 fighter plane will take place in Georgia instead of Fort Worth.

Another aircraft that has been a local economic staple — the V-22 Osprey — has had a checkered test period. Built by Bell Helicopter Textron, the experimental tilt-rotor aircraft has received $500 million in development contracts but no money for construction.

Since Wright's departure, local officials are redoubling their efforts to stimulate private enterprise. Boosters say the closure of Carswell Air Force Base creates an opportunity to attract manufacturers and other private development at the site. Before downsizing began in 1991, 6,500 military personnel were stationed at the base.

Alliance Airport, a commercial shipping operation initiated by Ross Perot Jr., started off slow, but the pace of business has been picking up.

The bulk of the 12th's voters are moderate-to-conservative Democrats, as Rep. Geren's 63 percent tally in 1992 suggests. But the presidential race was extremely competitive here, with Bill Clinton narrowly edging out George Bush and Ross Perot running a very strong third.

1990 Population: 566,217. White 453,695 (80%), Black 45,426 (8%), Other 67,096 (12%). Hispanic origin 92,253 (16%). 18 and over 412,814 (73%), 62 and over 79,053 (14%). Median age: 31.

personality.

Lanier finished first in the August special election, but he fell shy of the absolute majority needed to avoid a runoff. Geren finished second ahead of Jim Lane, a Fort Worth lawyer with ties to local labor groups and liberal activists.

Because of the district's long history of sending a Democrat to Congress, Geren began the runoff race as the favorite. But his conservatism made it hard to bring some of Lane's backers into the fold, and Geren himself had a stiff campaign style that conveyed an impression of upper-crust wealth. Some of his views gave party regulars pause: He criticized, for example, the way Senate Democrats had treated Supreme Court nominee Robert H. Bork, whose nomination was rejected by the Senate in 1987.

At times, candidate Geren seemed indecisive on crucial issues. He said he supported the landmark *Roe v. Wade* abortion rights ruling that legalized abortion nationwide, but he also said he personally opposed abortion and advocated "reasonable restrictions" on abortion in the latter stages of pregnancy.

Lanier, for his part, tried to tar Geren as a carpetbagger, reminding voters that Geren in 1986 had run unsuccessfully in the neighboring 6th District against GOP Rep. Joe L. Barton.

It took campaign appearances by Wright, Bentsen and others in the Texas Democratic delegation to spur Geren down the homestretch, but he won the September runoff with 51 percent.

Since then, Geren has come into his own electoral right. He needed no help from any

Texas Democratic heavyweights in two successful re-election campaigns. Redistricting in 1992 changed the district slightly but left the party registration essentially unchanged. Geren had little trouble surviving the changes. David Hobbs, a former legislative director for Rep. Dick Armey, thought he saw prospects in the revamped 12th and in Geren's marginal involvement in the House bank scandal (he wrote three overdrafts). But even with the financial and emotional backing of Armey, Hobbs was not able to break 40 percent.

Committees

Armed Services (32nd of 34 Democrats)
Military Acquisition

Public Works & Transportation (17th of 39 Democrats)
Aviation; Water Resources & the Environment

Science, Space & Technology (13th of 33 Democrats)
Space; Technology, Environment & Aviation

Elections

1992 General		
Pete Geren (D)	125,492	(63%)
David Hobbs (R)	74,432	(37%)
1990 General		
Pete Geren (D)	98,026	(71%)
Mike McGinn (R)	39,438	(29%)

Previous Winning Percentages: **1989** * (51%)

** Special runoff election.*

District Vote for President

1992	
D	75,792 (37%)
R	71,212 (35%)
I	56,564 (28%)

Campaign Finance

	Receipts	Receipts from PACs		Expend-itures
1992				
Geren (D)	$809,664	$356,168	(44%)	$812,234
Hobbs (R)	$386,959	$36,318	(9%)	$384,635
1990				
Geren (D)	$497,798	$257,509	(52%)	$495,937
McGinn (R)	$23,255	0		$22,695

Key Votes

1993	
Require parental notification of minors' abortions	Y
Require unpaid family and medical leave	N
Approve national "motor voter" registration bill	Y
Approve budget increasing taxes and reducing deficit	N
Approve economic stimulus plan	N
1992	
Approve balanced-budget constitutional amendment	Y
Close down space station program	N
Approve U.S. aid for former Soviet Union	N
Allow shifting funds from defense to domestic programs	N
1991	
Extend unemployment benefits using deficit financing	Y
Approve waiting period for handgun purchases	N
Authorize use of force in Persian Gulf	Y

Voting Studies

	Presidential Support		Party Unity		Conservative Coalition	
Year	**S**	**O**	**S**	**O**	**S**	**O**
1992	57	42	59	38	90	8
1991	49	48	58	38	100	0
1990	44	56	69	30	91	9
1989	51 †	49 †	74 †	24 †	94 †	6 †

† Not eligible for all recorded votes.

Interest Group Ratings

Year	ADA	AFL-CIO	CCUS	ACU
1992	45	55	88	60
1991	15	50	70	60
1990	39	50	79	46
1989	--	60	83	78

13 Bill Sarpalius (D)

Of Amarillo — Elected 1988; 3rd Term

Born: Jan. 10, 1948, Los Angeles, Calif.

Education: Clarendon College, A.S. 1970; Texas Tech U., B.A. 1972; West Texas State U., M.A. 1978.

Occupation: Agriculture consultant; public school teacher.

Family: Divorced; one child.

Religion: Methodist.

Political Career: Texas Senate, 1981-89.

Capitol Office: 126 Cannon Bldg. 20515; 225-3706.

In Washington: Sarpalius is a conservative Democrat who in his first two terms rarely looked beyond the interests of his own district. And when he did, he was more likely to vote with President George Bush than with his fellow Democrats. On issues on which Bush took a position in 1992, Sarpalius supported the president 56 percent of the time.

But with a fellow Southern Democrat in the White House, Sarpalius may feel more comfortable. Early in 1993 he sided with President Clinton on two key votes. He supported the budget resolution that outlined Clinton's economic plan, and he voted for passage of the president's stimulus plan.

Sarpalius has kept a generally low profile. But his profile may get a boost in the 103rd Congress because he has assumed the chairmanship of the Small Business Subcommittee on Rural Enterprises, Exports and the Environment. One of his goals, he says, is to coordinate and consolidate the small-business export programs scattered among different federal agencies.

The post suits Sarpalius and his district well. Sarpalius, who has a master's degree in agriculture and represents a largely agricultural district, will be able to keep an eye out for the cotton, wheat and corn industries — key staples of the 13th.

Sarpalius also sits on the Agriculture Committee, but there he usually takes a back seat to other Texas Democrats who are in a better position to look out for the state, including Chairman E. "Kika" de la Garza and Charles W. Stenholm.

Sarpalius has long been known for focusing on his district's and state's interests. In 1992, he supported funding of NASA's space station *Freedom*, and the superconducting super collider. Parts of *Freedom* are to be built in Texas, and the super collider could funnel $200 million to the Lone Star State.

He also voted for legislation that would have provided public financing for the Texas bullet train.

During an Agricultural Committee debate to reauthorize agricultural credit programs for the former Soviet Union, he expressed reservations about helping foreign farmers while those in his district suffered.

In the end, however, Sarpalius still supported the legislation.

There have been times when being a conservative Democrat has led Sarpalius into apparently conflicting positions. In 1990 he opposed the civil rights bill, but he switched to support the 1991 version of the measure, which was very similar. He was the only House member who made such a switch.

On some other high-profile controversies, Sarpalius has been more consistently conservative. He opposes abortion and was one of only two House Democrats — the other was fellow Texan Ralph M. Hall — voting in 1990 to expel Massachusetts Rep. Barney Frank from the House for misusing his official position to help a male prostitute — a penalty much harsher than the ethics committee's recommendation of a reprimand.

At Home: Former GOP Rep. Beau Boulter decided to try to snatch his old seat back in 1992, and Republicans felt they had their strongest candidate in years.

But some resentment still lingered from Boulter's 1988 decision to sacrifice the seat in his quixotic bid to unseat then-Sen. Lloyd Bentsen. Sarpalius, on the other hand, benefited from a redistricting plan that added Democratic territory in Lubbock and Denton to the district.

Even with a boost at the polls from Bush, Boulter did not come close, capturing 40 percent of the vote to Sarpalius' 60 percent.

Betting against Sarpalius' political fortunes has proved a losing proposition. He was a long shot when he first ran for public office in 1980 but upset a Republican state senator in a conservative district. Because his election to Congress swung the 13th from Republican to Democratic hands, he was a top GOP target for 1990. But Sarpalius turned a supposedly close race into a strong win.

Even one term in Congress may have seemed

Texas 13

Eastern Panhandle — Wichita Falls; part of Amarillo

Since Sarpalius took the 13th from the GOP in 1988, he has made voters increasingly comfortable with Democratic representation in the House. He hit 60 percent in 1992, thwarting the comeback try of the Republican who had held the 13th in the mid-1980s.

But this district remains politically competitive. In 1992 presidential voting, George Bush carried the 13th with 43 percent of the vote. Both he and Sarpalius won for the same reason: the region's conservative bent. Even the district's most conservative elements — politically active religious groups — have trouble finding fault with Sarpalius, an opponent of abortion.

The massive 13th comprises three distinct regions: the Panhandle, the South Plains and the Red River Valley. It takes more than eight hours to traverse the sparsely settled district, which includes all or part of 38 counties. It is not uncommon for residents to travel 60 miles for health care.

Thanks to the addition of several counties along its southern border in 1992 redistricting, the 13th became the largest cotton-producing district in the nation. More than 1.8 million acres of cotton grow in the fertile land above the Ogallala aquifer. Heavy agribusiness use of the aquifer has prompted concerns about depletion, and interest in conservation measures is increasing. Other leading crops include wheat, sorghum, sugar beets, corn and hay.

The biggest single chunk of votes in the 13th comes out of Wichita County, where the blue-collar-oriented city of Wichita Falls gives Democratic candidates a warm reception. Sarpalius got 62 percent in Wichita County in 1992, and Bill Clinton ran just 935 votes behind Bush in rural areas. Once heavily reliant on the oil industry, the area has weathered the oil slump with the assistance of income from Sheppard Air Force Base, just north of the city. Among the Air Force's largest training bases, Sheppard is headquarters of the NATO Jet Training Center.

At the northwestern corner of the 13th is the district's second-biggest concentration of people, in Potter County (Amarillo). The city of 158,000 is divided between the 13th and 19th districts. The downtown business district, in the 13th, has been suffering since the oil crash of the mid-1980s; vacant office buildings and closed shops are much in evidence. Government-related business helps keep Amarillo going: The federal Bureau of Mines and a state prison are major local employers, and the Pantex nuclear plant is in contention to expand its existing operation dismantling nuclear weapons.

Potter County (with almost 15 percent of the district's vote) was good to Bush in 1992, giving him nearly a majority. Sarpalius took Potter with 57 percent.

Though the bulk of the 13th has a rural and small-town feel, on its far eastern edge the district pokes in to take a part of Denton County, which is in the orbit of the Dallas-Fort Worth metropolitan area. The voters here tend to be more liberal than the district norm: Clinton got 42 percent here, well above his district average.

1990 Population: 566,217. White 446,833 (79%), Black 45,342 (8%), Other 74,042 (13%). Hispanic origin 109,959 (19%). 18 and over 409,490 (72%), 62 and over 96,431 (17%). Median age: 32.

a fantasy to Sarpalius, who was afflicted with polio and abandoned by his father at age 10. Two years later, his alcoholic mother put Sarpalius and his two younger brothers in Cal Farley's Boys Ranch, a home for wayward boys.

Sarpalius went on to college, taught agriculture technology at Boys Ranch and earned a master's degree in agriculture. He joined a private agribusiness concern and then won state Senate elections in 1980 and 1984.

Though Sarpalius was not considered a legislative heavyweight in Austin, he was popular at home and was a logical contender for Congress when Boulter left.

But shortly after announcing his candidacy, Sarpalius saw his image tarnished by a late-night incident at an Amarillo club in January 1988. Recently divorced, Sarpalius had gone to celebrate his birthday at the club, but he wound up with his jaw broken as a result of a fight that he said was a setup. A blood-alcohol test Sarpalius requested revealed that he had not been drinking; subsequent investigations indicated that his assailant was paid by the bar owner to attack him.

Sarpalius' sophisticated campaign enabled him to win a majority in a three-way primary and go on to defeat Republican nominee Larry Milner.

In 1990, Republican Dick Waterfield's challenge began to founder when GOP Gov. William P. Clements Jr. claimed Sarpalius had told him he lived at the Boys Ranch only because his parents worked there. Ranch staff dismissed Clements' version, and the incident helped resurrect sympathy for Sarpalius' past hardships. He won 56 percent.

Committees

Agriculture (10th of 28 Democrats)
Department Operations; Environment, Credit & Rural Development; General Farm Commodities

Small Business (11th of 27 Democrats)
Rural Enterprises, Exports & the Environment (chairman)

Elections

1992 General		
Bill Sarpalius (D)	117,892	(60%)
Beau Boulter (R)	77,514	(40%)
1990 General		
Bill Sarpalius (D)	81,815	(56%)
Dick Waterfield (R)	63,045	(44%)

Previous Winning Percentage: **1988** (52%)

District Vote for President

	1992
D	73,454 (36%)
R	87,492 (43%)
I	41,189 (20%)

Campaign Finance

	Receipts	Receipts from PACs		Expend-itures
1992				
Sarpalius (D)	$521,447	$320,769	(62%)	$521,328
Boulter (R)	$370,708	$17,158	(5%)	$370,582
1990				
Sarpalius (D)	$685,539	$387,684	(57%)	$667,930
Waterfield (R)	$684,141	$68,725	(10%)	$679,117

Key Votes

1993	
Require parental notification of minors' abortions	Y
Require unpaid family and medical leave	N
Approve national "motor voter" registration bill	Y
Approve budget increasing taxes and reducing deficit	Y
Approve economic stimulus plan	Y
1992	
Approve balanced-budget constitutional amendment	Y
Close down space station program	N
Approve U.S. aid for former Soviet Union	N
Allow shifting funds from defense to domestic programs	N
1991	
Extend unemployment benefits using deficit financing	N
Approve waiting period for handgun purchases	N
Authorize use of force in Persian Gulf	Y

Voting Studies

	Presidential Support		Party Unity		Conservative Coalition	
Year	**S**	**O**	**S**	**O**	**S**	**O**
1992	56	43	66	34	85	15
1991	58	41	60	38	97	3
1990	48	48	58	38	94	4
1989	60	38	60	38	85	12

Interest Group Ratings

Year	ADA	AFL-CIO	CCUS	ACU
1992	40	50	75	64
1991	25	42	60	70
1990	28	45	92	74
1989	40	42	80	64

14 Greg Laughlin (D)

Of West Columbia — Elected 1988; 3rd Term

Born: Jan. 21, 1942, Bay City, Texas.

Education: Texas A&M U., B.A. 1964; U. of Texas, LL.B. 1967.

Military Service: Army Reserve, 1964-67; Army, 1967-70; Army Reserve, 1970-present.

Occupation: Lawyer.

Family: Wife, Ginger Jones; two children.

Religion: Methodist.

Political Career: Democratic nominee for U.S. House, 1986.

Capitol Office: 236 Cannon Bldg. 20515; 225-2831.

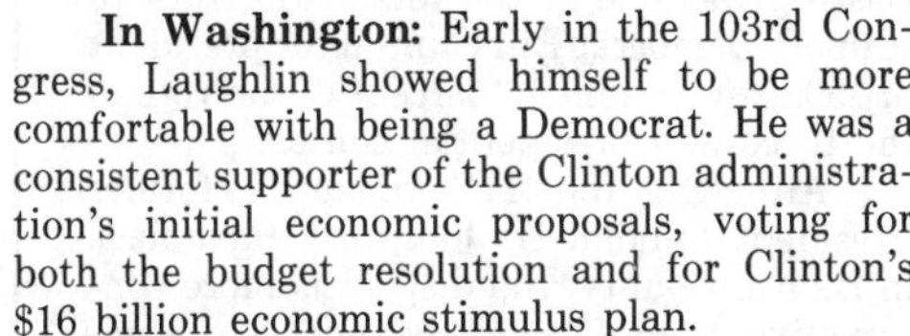

In Washington: Early in the 103rd Congress, Laughlin showed himself to be more comfortable with being a Democrat. He was a consistent supporter of the Clinton administration's initial economic proposals, voting for both the budget resolution and for Clinton's $16 billion economic stimulus plan.

But the energy provisions in Clinton's tax bill proved too much for Laughlin — and a half-dozen other Texas Democrats — who voted against it in May 1993.

In the past, Laughlin has had qualms about being identified with the national Democratic Party and its liberal leaders. He sided with his fellow Texan, GOP President Bush, on several policy confrontations in the 102nd Congress.

One was the 1991 extension of unemployment benefits, an article of the Democratic catechism, because it would have increased the federal budget deficit. Another was his 1992 vote against shifting funds from defense to domestic programs. And yet another was his support for the use of force in the Persian Gulf in 1991.

Laughlin's position on social issues in the 103rd has been less predictable than his views on the economy. He opposed the family and medical leave measure — signed by Clinton a little more than two weeks after he took office — yet joined Democrats in rejecting a GOP proposal that would have required parental notification for minors seeking abortions at federally funded clinics.

Laughlin has not suffered politically by bucking the House leadership, however. Although he sometimes wanders from the Democratic fold, he seldom wanders far and has never done so in a rebellious manner.

He has maintained a cordial working relationship with House leaders, occasionally proving himself a key ally. In late 1991, it was Laughlin, a former assistant district attorney, and fellow Texas Democrat Jim Chapman, a former district attorney, who persuaded four other conservative Texas Democrats to vote for a broad crime bill. Among other things, the measure included a waiting period for handgun purchases.

Laughlin had voted against a waiting period for handgun purchases earlier in the year, but he supported the crime bill and its expansion of the federal death penalty. So, arguing that the bill would not interfere with prosecutors, he helped persuade Reps. Chet Edwards, Pete Geren, Ralph M. Hall and Charles W. Stenholm to switch their votes at the last minute. The House approved the measure by a 205-203 vote Nov. 27; it died in the Senate at the end of the 102nd.

Laughlin has been recognized by House leaders for his willingness to work with them. He was named to the Select Intelligence Committee in the 103rd Congress. He was among the members of the committee who made a trip to Russia during Congress' 1993 spring recess.

Laughlin's role in House passage of the crime bill and his appointment to the Intelligence panel indicate that he has broadened his interests since first being elected in 1988. In his first two terms, Laughlin made constituent service his top priority.

He still touts his constituent service and proudly points out that, consistent with his fiscal conservatism, his office is listed in the bottom quarter of congressional office expenditures among the Texas delegation. Such achievements may not seem lofty, but they are critical for Laughlin, who in 1988 ousted a GOP incumbent dogged by reports of office mismanagement and constituent neglect. Laughlin combines his scrupulous attention to the 14th with a typical Tory conservatism that fits the district's majority.

While Laughlin has voted a conservative line, he did face criticism back home for his votes to fund the National Endowment for the Arts (NEA). Laughlin defended his record, noting that he voted to cut $45,000 from the NEA budget — the amount it gave to the most controversial exhibits. But Laughlin said he was upset that the NEA went on to fund other

Texas 14

Southeast; Gulf Coast

Larger than the state of Massachusetts, the 14th stretches from the western outskirts of Austin to the Gulf Coast. Residents are dispersed widely across this huge land mass; the district's personality is rural and small-town Texas.

Two industries — agriculture and petrochemicals — dominate the 14th. Almost every major farm commodity is grown somewhere in the district. Grain, sorghum and rice are the most notable crops, grown primarily in the southern counties of Matagorda, Wharton, Jackson, Victoria, Refugio and Colorado. Hay is a major crop in Fayette County and Austin County, just over the 14th's boundary line in the 8th. Altogether, agriculture generates between $1.5 billion and $2 billion a year for the district.

Closer to the coastline, petrochemical plants dot the landscape. Dow, Du Pont, British Petroleum and Oxychem all have refineries in the 14th. When oil prices dropped in the mid-1980s because of a worldwide glut, petrochemical companies flourished. The companies use oil as a base product to produce chemicals that are combined with other chemicals to make such items as antifreeze, foam and plastics.

Victoria, population 55,100, is the district's only sizable city. Originally settled by the French explorer La Salle in 1685, the city was named in 1824 for a Mexican president, Guadalupe Victoria. After centuries as a leading cattle and cotton capital, Victoria today is a major oil and chemical center.

Intermingled with the chemical plants are lively fishing ports that haul in shrimp for tourists and locals. Port Lavaca in Calhoun County successfully combines commercial fishing, tourism and offshore drilling businesses. In adjacent Aransas County, nature lovers flock to Goose Island State Park, Aransas National Wildlife Refuge and several bird sanctuaries.

Bastrop County, in the northwestern corner of the huge district, is being pulled into the suburban orbit of growing Austin, in the 10th District. Less than 25 miles from the state capital, the city of Bastrop also boasts the University of Texas cancer research center. Austin's liberal views have begun to rub off on its neighboring county; Bastrop was one of the few in the 14th to support Democrat Bill Clinton for president in 1992, giving him 43 percent of the vote in the three-way presidential contest.

Although the 14th includes former President Lyndon B. Johnson's birthplace in Blanco County, the district is more conservative than its famous native. Democratic Rep. Laughlin has retained his hold on the seat with fiscally cautious views and a dedication to home-state concerns. Republican George Bush won the district in 1992.

Minorities make up more than one-third of the 14th. Victoria, Matagorda and Lavaca counties all have sizable black and Hispanic communities, and Waller County's Prairie View A&M University, founded in 1878, is a predominantly black college with 5,600 students.

1990 Population: 566,217. White 440,178 (78%), Black 60,290 (11%), Other 65,749 (12%). Hispanic origin 133,703 (24%). 18 and over 407,375 (72%), 62 and over 91,303 (16%). Median age: 32.

projects he considered improper and said he would oppose future funding for the agency.

At Home: Laughlin's solid understanding of his diverse district — and his willingness to traverse it regularly — have stood him in good stead with the voters of Victoria, Hays and Bastrop counties.

Laughlin grew up in a small town in Brazoria County, between Houston and the Gulf of Mexico. After college and law school, he served as an intelligence officer in the Army and then returned to his native area of Texas to practice law.

He made his first bid for public office at the congressional level, challenging an incumbent in 1986. The incumbent was Mac Sweeney, a young former White House aide who had beaten a Democratic incumbent in the district two years earlier on the strength of Ronald Reagan's enormous re-election victory. Outspent and little-known, Laughlin nevertheless drew 48 percent of the vote.

He was back in 1988, first turning aside a Democratic rival in the March primary, then raising more than $600,000 — enough to put him on competitive footing financially.

Equally important, Laughlin presented himself as a conservative Democrat of the old Texas school, a man who had prosecuted criminals and who still served as a lieutenant colonel in the Army Reserve.

Sweeney distributed campaign literature portraying Laughlin, who had handled personal injury cases, as an ambulance chaser. But the ad, which included a heavy-handed appeal to Hispanics, drew charges of racism and complaints from lawyers' groups.

Sweeney also suffered from having the second-worst voting attendance record among Texas' 27 House members in 1988, and from reports of inattentiveness to constituents. Laughlin captured the seat with 53 percent of the vote.

In 1990, a cattleman named Joe Dial challenged Laughlin. Dial played his rancher's hat against Laughlin's trial lawyer background and kept Laughlin on the defensive over votes to fund the NEA, characterizing them as support for obscene art.

But the incumbent pointed to plenty of conservative votes to offset the liberal label. And with the onset of problems in the Persian Gulf, Laughlin benefited from his military background. He improved on his 1988 showing.

In 1992, pitted against a chemical plant worker and a firefighter, Laughlin coasted to his largest margin yet and collected more than two-thirds of the vote.

Committees

Merchant Marine & Fisheries (11th of 29 Democrats)
Coast Guard & Navigation; Environment & Natural Resources; Oceanography, Gulf of Mexico & the Outer Continental Shelf

Post Office & Civil Service (12th of 15 Democrats)
Oversight & Investigations

Public Works & Transportation (16th of 39 Democrats)
Aviation; Investigations & Oversight; Surface Transportation

Select Intelligence (10th of 12 Democrats)
Legislation; Program & Budget Authorization

Elections

1992 General		
Greg Laughlin (D)	135,930	(68%)
Humberto J. Garza (R)	54,412	(27%)
Vic Vreeland (I)	9,329	(5%)
1990 General		
Greg Laughlin (D)	89,251	(54%)
Joe Dial (R)	75,098	(46%)

Previous Winning Percentage: 1988 (53%)

District Vote for President

1992
D 78,776 (37%)
R 86,178 (41%)
I 47,097 (22%)

Campaign Finance

	Receipts	Receipts from PACs		Expend-itures
1992				
Laughlin (D)	$618,011	$353,940	(57%)	$540,139
Garza (R)	$13,589	$974	(7%)	$13,550
1990				
Laughlin (D)	$829,150	$433,314	(52%)	$851,294
Dial (R)	$479,218	$41,621	(9%)	$450,095

Key Votes

1993	
Require parental notification of minors' abortions	N
Require unpaid family and medical leave	N
Approve national "motor voter" registration bill	#
Approve budget increasing taxes and reducing deficit	Y
Approve economic stimulus plan	Y
1992	
Approve balanced-budget constitutional amendment	Y
Close down space station program	N
Approve U.S. aid for former Soviet Union	Y
Allow shifting funds from defense to domestic programs	N
1991	
Extend unemployment benefits using deficit financing	N
Approve waiting period for handgun purchases	N
Authorize use of force in Persian Gulf	Y

Voting Studies

	Presidential Support		Party Unity		Conservative Coalition	
Year	**S**	**O**	**S**	**O**	**S**	**O**
1992	41	48	65	23	69	19
1991	49	50	61	34	95	5
1990	47	48	58	33	85	7
1989	63	30	59	36	95	5

Interest Group Ratings

Year	ADA	AFL-CIO	CCUS	ACU
1992	45	50	63	52
1991	10	67	60	55
1990	28	36	83	59
1989	20	44	67	56

15 E. "Kika" de la Garza (D)

Of Mission — Elected 1964; 15th Term

Born: Sept. 22, 1927, Mercedes, Texas.
Education: St. Mary's U. of San Antonio, LL.B. 1952.
Military Service: Navy, 1945-46; Army, 1950-52.
Occupation: Lawyer.
Family: Wife, Lucille Alamia; three children.
Religion: Roman Catholic.
Political Career: Texas House, 1953-65.
Capitol Office: 1401 Longworth Bldg. 20515; 225-2531.

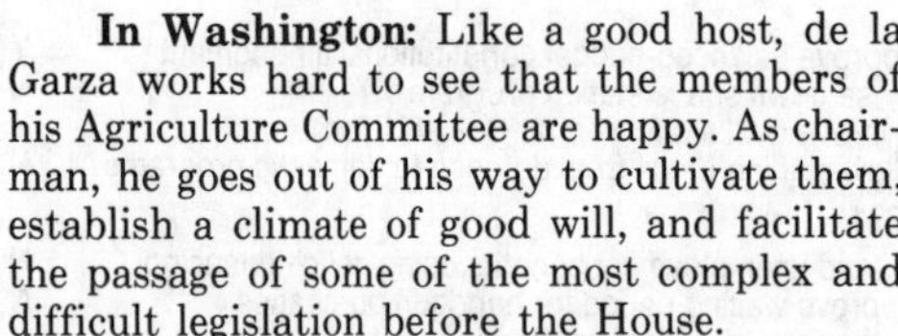

In Washington: Like a good host, de la Garza works hard to see that the members of his Agriculture Committee are happy. As chairman, he goes out of his way to cultivate them, establish a climate of good will, and facilitate the passage of some of the most complex and difficult legislation before the House.

De la Garza frequently travels to the districts of junior colleagues to help with their campaigns and steers political action funds their way. When the time comes to pick members of a conference committee, he tries to include at least one freshman. His news releases routinely credit the accomplishments of other panel members, including Republicans, many of whom play a major role on what is one of the least partisan committees in the institution.

After spending most of the 1980s perfecting his role as chairman, de la Garza has a good sense of how to pass cumbersome legislation. When Congress began work on the 1985 and 1990 farm reauthorizations, he made it clear that he opposed the Republican administration's calls for drastic cuts in agricultural spending. But he sees himself as the coordinator of the massive farm bill, rather than the craftsman of its individual parts. Stressing his role as facilitator, he gives his Agriculture subcommittees considerable freedom to draw up the various sections of the legislation. That style also prevails on the legislation that moves through Agriculture in the "off years" — when the committee's work is not monopolized by a farm bill.

In the deficit-conscious climate that has prevailed since the 1980s, de la Garza must worry about attacks on farm spending from urban and suburban members. De la Garza, a master strategist, is acutely aware of the tenuous support for farm programs and is keenly sensitive to charges that they are wasteful giveaways. In overseeing the drafting of the 1990 farm bill, he succeeded in striking a balance between populists who sought to increase farm benefits and others seeking to cut subsidies.

During House action on the 1990 farm bill, a bipartisan urban-suburban coalition led a concerted effort to bar subsidies to farmers who earn more than $100,000. The assault was led by Texas Republican Dick Armey and New York Democrat Charles E. Schumer.

The means-test concept had appeal in a year marked by tortuous budget negotiations, but de la Garza and the farm bloc defeated the Armey-Schumer amendment, helped in part by the perception that Armey and Schumer were "anti-farmer" and that their plan, backed by the Bush administration, aimed merely to cut the budget rather than help smaller farmers. "This amendment is a meat-ax approach," de la Garza said. "Can members imagine a shoeshine boy from Mission, Texas, being accused of protecting the rich and the greedy? Ridiculous." The amendment was rejected 159-263, but the means-testing concept resurfaced in President Bush's fiscal 1992 budget.

De la Garza, who represents sugar cane growers in his South Texas district, and Louisiana Democrat Jerry Huckaby, chairman of the sugar subcommittee, worked hard to round up Democratic votes to defeat an amendment sponsored by New York Democrat Thomas J. Downey and Ohio Republican Bill Gradison. The amendment would have made a 2-cents-per-pound cut in the 18-cents-per-pound sugar price support. De la Garza forged a coalition of pro-labor, pro-environmental and pro-farm Democrats to repel the cut.

His summation was uniquely de la Garza: "So the bottom line is, it is jobs in the United States of America, farmers in the United States of America. Vote 'no' on the Downey amendment. It is jobs U.S.A., jobs U.S.A., jobs U.S.A.! [You] cannot cut it anymore. You cannot hide it anymore. It is jobs, jobs, jobs in the U.S.A.! Vote 'no' on the amendment." It was rejected 150-271.

Unlike his Senate counterpart, Vermont Democrat Patrick J. Leahy, de la Garza has little interest in enacting restrictions on farm-

Texas 15

South — Bee, Brooks, Hidalgo and San Patricio counties; McAllen

The 15th remains the most heavily Hispanic district in Texas (nearly 75 percent of the population) and a reliable vote-getting region for any Democrat.

Despite losing the state, Bill Clinton won the 15th in the 1992 presidential contest with more than 53 percent of the vote, his highest non-urban district tally in Texas.

The 1992 redistricting compressed the boundaries of the 15th, shifting two of the fastest-growing counties in the state — Starr and Zapata — into the newly formed 28th. Despite the removal of two heavily Hispanic border counties, the 15th retains its Spanish flavor.

Goliad County, created in 1836 from a Spanish municipality, is among the state's most historic areas. Bisected by the San Antonio River, the region has several missions, historic churches and a statue of Gen. Ignacio Zaragoza, the Mexican leader who fought back French troops in 1862, leading to the celebration of Cinco de Mayo.

Hidalgo County, named for the leader of Mexico's independence movement, Miguel Hidalgo y Costillo, is 85 percent Hispanic. Anchored by McAllen, a major port of entry into Mexico, the county is noteworthy for its foreign trade and popularity with travelers. Many Midwesterners and Canadians spend the winter season in McAllen, drawn by its subtropical climate and tourist activities.

Home to nearly 384,000 people, Hidalgo is the most populous county in the 15th. It is also the seventh-poorest county in Texas, with more than 40 percent of its residents living below the poverty level. Hidalgo County's economy is heavily dependent on agriculture; cotton, grain, vegetables and sugar cane are among the most common crops. (Districtwide, the median household income is between $17,500 and $20,000, about $10,000 less than the statewide average.)

And like most of the counties along the Rio Grande, Hidalgo is reliant upon *maquiladora* plants for much of its income. The system of "twin" plants enables the bulk of production work to be done at one facility on the Mexican side of the border, while some finishing and distribution is handled by its American counterpart.

Although manufacturing along the border has picked up, the region's agribusiness was hurt by a freeze in the winter of 1989 and previous drought problems. More farmers have been forced to invest in irrigation, a costly investment but one that is paying off.

Outside Hidalgo, the most populous county is San Patricio, with just under 59,000 people. San Patricio is closely linked economically with the port city of Corpus Christi, which lies just across the bay in the 27th District.

In the northern, sparsely populated counties of the 15th, cattle, agriculture and some oil production account for most revenue. Timber and furniture-making are important industries in De Witt County.

Panna Maria, in Karnes County, is the oldest Polish settlement in the state.

1990 Population: 566,217. White 427,363 (75%), Black 6,273 (1%), Other 132,581 (23%). Hispanic origin 422,066 (75%). 18 and over 369,299 (65%), 62 and over 74,994 (13%). Median age: 28.

ers' use of chemicals and promoting organic farming — a position shared by most Agriculture Committee members. "Somehow it has gotten out of hand, [the idea] that organic is good for you," he said. "All this organics is going to be very, very expensive." Although he accepted a House amendment that would have greatly restricted the export of chemicals considered too dangerous for use in the United States (and which can return to this country on imported food), he opposed it in the House-Senate conference. The restrictions on the so-called "circle of poison" were Leahy's pet program, and he battled doggedly with de la Garza to keep them in the bill. In the end, Leahy withdrew them, resolving to reintroduce them.

As was the case in 1985, de la Garza's efforts in 1990 did not produce a farm bill that clearly bore his imprint, but they did produce a bill the House passed, and by a lopsided vote, in contrast to the two-vote margin by which the farm bill had cleared Congress in 1981.

De la Garza's approach has enabled him to keep the unwieldy farm bill together. In 1985, it also helped him maintain an effective working arrangement with his predecessor as chairman, Thomas S. Foley of Washington, despite tensions that had existed between the two in previous Congresses. When he first took the chairmanship, de la Garza had been reluctant to consult Foley on much of the committee's business. But in the 99th Congress he deferred willingly to Foley on wheat and feed grains, a major portion of the bill.

That is not to say that everything goes

smoothly in committee. During work on a bill to save the financially ailing Farm Credit System in 1987, there was an unusual amount of partisan bickering, and Republicans employed obstructionist tactics. But from that point, a measure began to take shape as de la Garza pursued his accustomed democratic approach to legislating. He tends to control his committee by not controlling it too much; to put the wrangling to rest on the farm credit bill, de la Garza set up committee task forces to hammer out compromises. Under de la Garza's watch, the panel produced a sweeping reorganization of the Farm Credit System, which passed 41-2.

"No one is entirely happy," he said. "But then no one's saying it's a no-good communist bill. It's somewhere in the middle, which is what good legislation should be."

De la Garza's cooperative style is a benefit within his committee, but he is forced into a more confrontational role when waging turf fights with other panels. During work on a supplemental appropriations bill in 1987, Appropriations Chairman Jamie L. Whitten of Mississippi included $10 million for Agriculture Department studies on mandatory production controls. De la Garza complained that the policy was unrealistic and the maneuver an encroachment on his jurisdiction.

"How many days of hearings did you have?" he demanded. Whitten shot back, "I've been doing this for 39 years!" After some discussion, de la Garza agreed not to move against the studies, and an effort by a third party to do so failed by a wide margin.

De la Garza is a man capable of considerable personal charm, an amateur linguist and gourmet cook who converses with foreign dignitaries in their own languages. But he is a proud man, a descendant of Spanish land grantees who came to South Texas in the 18th century, and he has sometimes displayed an arrogance that made personal relations difficult.

In his earlier years on the Agriculture Committee, de la Garza was known to ridicule the idiosyncrasies of colleagues in a manner that was meant to be funny but was often taken as an insult. Outside the committee, his voting record sometimes frustrated liberal Democrats who found him reluctant to identify with liberal Hispanics of less impressive background. Both these tendencies were factors in his unexpectedly narrow 110-92 election to the Agriculture chairmanship in 1981.

"The thing about all this Chicano and Mexican-American and so forth," he once told a reporter, "is that the Spanish-speaking are members of the white race. Period. Finis."

On Agriculture, he has always paid close attention to the crops of South Texas — sugar and cotton — and to the area's water problems. During his first decade in the House, he worked hardest to obtain a federal sugar allotment for his growers and a project to control the level of salt in the Rio Grande on the Mexican border. Salt in the river's water was making it difficult to irrigate the district's farms.

As he moved toward a senior position on Agriculture, de la Garza continued to be a spokesman for sugar growers. In 1977, when major farm legislation became law, he successfully amended it to set up a sugar price support program similar to the ones for other crops. The next year, arguing that the newly enacted price supports had not been sufficient to keep the industry prosperous, he sponsored a bill to return to a system of strict quotas and fees that would limit the amount of foreign sugar entering the United States. A similar plan was later implemented.

De la Garza supports his South Texas growers in their demand for an ample supply of farm workers to help harvest perishable crops. When the House debated immigration policy in 1984, he argued for an Agriculture Committee amendment that established a new "guest worker" program for foreign labor. Agribusiness interests from all over the country backed that effort; Hispanics opposed it. De la Garza was the only member of the Congressional Hispanic Caucus who voted for the amendment, which passed the House. But de la Garza disagreed with other parts of the immigration package and voted against it in 1984 and in 1986. It finally became law in the 99th Congress.

Outside his panel, de la Garza votes a moderate Democratic line, supporting labor-backed initiatives such as requiring employers to give workers unpaid family leave and increasing the minimum wage. But he also opposes abortion and backed a constitutional amendment to ban flag desecration. In 1990 and 1992, he voted for a constitutional amendment to require a balanced federal budget.

In early 1991, de la Garza — whose son, a Navy doctor, was working in the Persian Gulf — voted to continue economic sanctions and diplomatic efforts to pressure Iraq to withdraw from Kuwait. But when that resolution was rejected, he voted to authorize Bush to use military force against Iraq.

At Home: The election of de la Garza in 1964 was a milestone of sorts for South Texas Hispanics, who had always been the dominant population group in the 15th District but had never elected one of their own.

It was not, however, a political revolution. The new congressman was backed by the same Anglo business interests that had sent Democrats Lloyd Bentsen and Joe Kilgore to Congress in the 1950s. In six terms in the Texas Legislature, de la Garza had maintained a conservative voting record and had opposed passage of a state civil rights bill.

With Kilgore's retirement in 1964, the Democratic primary ended in a runoff between de la Garza and state Rep. Lindsey Rodriguez, an ardent supporter of the Johnson administration and the liberal 1964 Democratic platform. De la Garza featured a photograph of Johnson in his campaign literature, but hedged in his commitment to the platform or the Democratic administration.

Rodriguez had the support of PASO (Political Association of Spanish-speaking Organizations), which had succeeded in electing Hispanic slates in several Texas localities. He accused de la Garza, as a descendant of Spanish land grantees, of being aloof from the problems that faced the large mass of poor Hispanics in the district. De la Garza, he complained, was no more than a puppet for the wealthy Anglo business establishment.

While de la Garza's business supporters were controversial, they did provide him a campaign budget that dwarfed Rodriguez's, and they gave him the courthouse machine backing that traditionally has won elections here. De la Garza coasted to victory by a margin of nearly 2-to-1. That fall he won the seat over nominal GOP opposition by an even wider margin.

Since the 15th is one of Texas' Democratic strongholds, de la Garza has had no trouble in general elections. In his 14 re-elections since 1964, the GOP has offered opposition only five times.

In 1992 the GOP did not even bother to recruit a candidate, although political newcomer Tom Haughey decided to run on his own. He drew the baseline Republican vote, and de la Garza coasted to yet another victory, unimpeded by his 284 overdrafts at the House bank.

Committee

Agriculture (Chairman)

Elections

1992 General		
E. "Kika" de la Garza (D)	86,351	(60%)
Tom Haughey (R)	56,549	(40%)
1990 General		
E. "Kika" de la Garza (D)	72,461	(100%)

Previous Winning Percentages: **1988** (94%) **1986** (100%) **1984** (100%) **1982** (96%) **1980** (70%) **1978** (66%) **1976** (74%) **1974** (100%) **1972** (100%) **1970** (76%) **1968** (100%) **1966** (100%) **1964** (69%)

District Vote for President

	1992
D	80,085 (53%)
R	52,080 (34%)
I	20,072 (13%)

Campaign Finance

	Receipts	Receipts from PACs		Expend-itures
1992				
de la Garza (D)	$248,430	$184,825	(74%)	$267,600
Haughey (R)	$13,695	$221	(2%)	$13,452
1990				
de la Garza (D)	$86,524	$58,675	(68%)	$121,145

Key Votes

1993	
Require parental notification of minors' abortions	Y
Require unpaid family and medical leave	Y
Approve national "motor voter" registration bill	Y
Approve budget increasing taxes and reducing deficit	Y
Approve economic stimulus plan	Y
1992	
Approve balanced-budget constitutional amendment	Y
Close down space station program	N
Approve U.S. aid for former Soviet Union	Y
Allow shifting funds from defense to domestic programs	Y
1991	
Extend unemployment benefits using deficit financing	Y
Approve waiting period for handgun purchases	N
Authorize use of force in Persian Gulf	Y

Voting Studies

	Presidential Support		Party Unity		Conservative Coalition	
Year	S	O	S	O	S	O
1992	33	54	80	13	60	31
1991	38	54	78	14	51	38
1990	24	73	84	10	56	43
1989	43	50	74	15	49	44
1988	21	57	73	6	32	37
1987	33	59	76	14	65	21
1986	27	64	72	16	64	32
1985	34	59	75	14	60	36
1984	44	46	66	21	59	25
1983	41	50	70	17	61	27
1982	49	32	67	25	67	19
1981	57	39	62	31	68	27

Interest Group Ratings

Year	ADA	AFL-CIO	CCUS	ACU
1992	70	75	43	19
1991	45	58	40	32
1990	61	83	15	23
1989	50	73	56	21
1988	50	73	50	20
1987	60	73	27	5
1986	55	85	39	27
1985	60	76	20	24
1984	40	85	53	43
1983	50	75	42	24
1982	25	61	42	60
1981	45	80	32	40

16 Ronald D. Coleman (D)

Of El Paso — Elected 1982; 6th Term

Born: Nov. 29, 1941, El Paso, Texas.
Education: U. of Texas, El Paso, B.A. 1963; U. of Texas, Austin, J.D. 1967; U. of Kent (England), 1981.
Military Service: Army, 1967-69.
Occupation: Lawyer.
Family: Wife, Amy Crandus; three children.
Religion: Presbyterian.
Political Career: Texas House, 1973-83.
Capitol Office: 440 Cannon Bldg. 20515; 225-4831.

In Washington: Coleman received considerable national publicity during the 102nd Congress, but it was the type of exposure that anyone would hope to avoid.

Coleman's 673 overdrafts at the House bank placed him among the top 10 offenders in Congress; he led the Texas delegation in overdrafts. Also, in a book written by a former aide, Coleman was unflatteringly portrayed as more concerned with making headlines than making policy.

Despite his problems, Coleman used his increasing seniority on the Appropriations Committee, where he has served since his second term, to help bring additional federal funds and projects to his El Paso district, including $6 million for 100 additional U.S. Customs Service employees and $42 million for construction at Fort Bliss.

Before the list of overdrafters was released, Coleman said he had floated only four checks. Later, Coleman said, "I was obviously negligent with my personal financial recordkeeping." But his explanation did not go over well in the district. The El Paso Herald-Post editorialized that Coleman is "either grossly stupid or a liar ... Coleman's behavior — his deceit and the unbelievable arrogance of that deceit — cannot be countenanced."

The overdraft controversy was the chief reason that Coleman's 1992 re-election tally fell to 52 percent, his career low.

Coleman's probity also was called into question when a June 1991 Wall Street Journal article said that he had permitted a businessman with an interest in legislation to pay off a $65,000 bank loan Coleman owed. Coleman's lawyer said the relationship was proper and "fully commercial."

Adding to these problems for Coleman was the book "Hill Rat," in which his former press aide, John Jackley, described Coleman as uninterested in the mechanics of governing except when he could get media attention or federal money for the district, or both.

Coleman's close attention to district concerns is easy to understand. In his early congressional years, he had to work to nail down the West Texas 16th, whose voters had a more conservative orientation than the national Democratic Party line. He did well enough entrenching himself that he ran unopposed in 1988 and 1990. But in 1992, redistricting shrank the 16th down just to El Paso and boosted its Hispanic population from 60 to 70 percent. Even if Coleman can put behind him the problems he encountered in the 102nd Congress, it seems likely that Hispanics soon will begin to contend for election to the 16th.

In the meantime, though, Coleman remains valued by the leadership as a loyal vote. When he first came to Congress, he benefited from his relationships with then-Majority Leader Jim Wright of Texas and Texas veteran Jack Brooks. But Coleman — who can be good-humored and collegial, if also at times a swaggering partisan — established himself in his own right. At the start of the 103rd, the leadership gave him a seat on the Intelligence Committee to add to duties on Appropriations, where he sits on the Interior, Military Construction and Transportation panels.

As chairman of the Congressional Border Caucus, Coleman promised to be a key person to watch as the Clinton administration grappled with the North American Free Trade Agreement. Coleman seeks improved U.S. relations with Mexico, but he also is an advocate of organized labor and has expressed concerns about the wage disparity between the United States and Mexico.

Coleman has been a forceful spokesman for U.S. efforts to reduce the debt burden of Mexico as a means of averting economic and political upheaval there. He also has sought to improve conditions in the *"colonias"* — squalid border communities lacking basic utilities.

At Home: Seeking a sixth term and facing unfavorable odds, Coleman benefited from a good showing in the 16th by Democratic presidential candidate Bill Clinton. The win was also testimony to Coleman's capacity for getting down and dirty.

As an outgrowth of redistricting, which

Texas 16

West — El Paso and suburbs

When the mosquito control unit hits the streets of El Paso, it doesn't stop at the border. When the El Paso Ballet was looking for new sources of revenue, it changed its name, ditching El Paso in favor of the more international Ballet of the Americas. And when Mexicans want jobs and Texans want inexpensive goods, they can cross the Bridge of the Americas.

This is life in the 16th, a compact, multicultural district on the Mexican border where jobs, entertainment, health and government blend and blur between El Paso and its sister city, Ciudad Juarez. Both English and Spanish are spoken fluently, native holiday celebrations are shared and families are split between the two cities. Nowhere is the interdependency more evident than in the *maquiladoras,* or twin plants, in which Mexican workers do the bulk of labor — making everything from cars to clothing — and Americans complete the products with finishing details. By one estimate, there are about 300 such plants in the El Paso-Juarez area alone.

Despite their commercial and cultural affinity, the two cities do not always get along. Shortly before Christmas 1992 the Mexican government lowered duty-free limits from $300 a person to $50 a person. That means Mexicans, who often shop at cleaner El Paso stores, can now bring just $50 worth of goods home duty-free.

Textile manufacturing is the biggest industry in El Paso; a large Levi Strauss plant is a major employer. The region is one of the few in the nation where long-staple Egyptian cotton, one of the finest cotton fibers, is grown.

El Paso's Fort Bliss is also a major employer, credited in 1992 with pumping nearly $1 billion into the region's economy. Fort Bliss is home of the Patriot missile systems, the famed Scud-intercepter of the Persian Gulf War. Patriot crew members are trained at the U.S. Army Air Defense Center here.

The University of Texas at El Paso adds 16,500 students to the city; many other El Paso residents travel west to New Mexico State University, which is nearby.

El Paso's population is 80 percent Hispanic; the district's is 70 percent. Although a Hispanic candidate failed to get past the 1992 Democratic House primary, Hispanics occupy several prominent elected offices and essentially control all elections. Despite losing the Anglo vote in the 16th, Rep. Coleman won a tough re-election campaign in 1992 by taking 80 percent of the Hispanic vote.

In the 1992 presidential contest, Democrat Bill Clinton defeated Texans George Bush and Ross Perot in El Paso County. The Democratic performance index, a scale developed by the state Democratic Party that uses previous election data to predict polling trends, is 62 percent for the 16th.

As El Paso's population has grown, the city has struggled with problems such as pollution and poverty. Nearly 27 percent of the people in the county fall below the poverty level.

1990 Population: 566,217. White 432,989 (76%), Black 20,272 (4%), Other 112,596 (20%). Hispanic origin 398,384 (70%). 18 and over 382,985 (68%), 62 and over 59,389 (10%). Median age: 28.

increased the share of Hispanics in the 16th, Coleman faced a Democratic primary challenge from Charles Ponzio, a past president of the El Paso Hispanic Chamber of Commerce. Ponzio garnered publicity by dogging Coleman to debate him, but his candidacy was weakened by the entry of two other Democrats. Coleman retained the loyalty of many old-time Hispanic political operatives, and he won the primary easily.

On the GOP side, former TV sportscaster Chip Taberski had to go through a runoff before winning nomination. The locally well-known personality hungrily attacked Coleman for the 673 overdrafts. Taberski ran one ad in which an actor resembling Coleman entered a bank to cash a check. As the Coleman impersonator stood at the window, the clerk admonished him, saying there was no money in his account.

Feeling the heat, Coleman fired his own stink bombs, reminding voters that Taberski supported "English first" programs and once referred to a football game between two border towns as a matchup of "illegal aliens." He also stressed how much the district had benefited from his membership on the Appropriations Committee.

Left to choose between two Anglo candidates, most Hispanics stuck with the one they knew better. Still, Coleman's 52 percent invited speculation about his future vulnerability.

Though Coleman had enjoyed the luxury of no GOP opposition in 1988 and 1990, it was not a new posture for him to be on the defense against aggressive attack.

After proving his viability in a crowded Democratic primary in 1982, Coleman faced a popular El Paso judge in a runoff. The match against Judge T. Udell Moore Jr. was a test of strength between business and labor. A few years earlier, when Mexican-American clothing workers struck El Paso's Farah Manufacturing Co., Coleman was their attorney. Moore made it clear at the time that he would vote to deny the strikers food stamps. The Hispanic vote decided the runoff; with support from the barrios of South El Paso, Coleman won with nearly 55 percent.

For November, the National Republican Congressional Committee designed a candidacy from scratch for El Paso Councilman Pat Haggerty, an ex-seminarian and former Democrat. Despite a relatively liberal background, Haggerty campaigned as a Ronald Reagan Republican, denouncing Coleman as a "labor liberal" and charging that the city had become too dependent on federal help.

But those pages from the GOP's 1980 playbook did not address fears about the economy, then in recession in many places. Coleman, with the help of the Hispanic community, scored a 10-point victory.

Republicans had good reason to suspect they might be able to topple Coleman in 1984. Reagan was leading the ticket, and GOP leaders felt they had a savvy nominee in former banker Jack Hammond.

Hammond stressed his business credentials and voiced a pro-Reagan, anti-tax line, but he also pointed to his past work with the League of United Latin American Citizens. But Coleman survived it all, taking 57 percent even as Reagan swept all eight counties in the 16th.

The GOP threw Coleman a curve in 1986, challenging him with retired Mexican-American accountant Roy Gillia. Party leaders figured that Gillia and Roy R. Barrera Jr., the GOP nominee for state attorney general, together could produce a Hispanic Republican turnout capable of toppling Coleman. It was not to be. The 16th's Hispanic community showed almost no interest in voting Republican, and Coleman walked away with two thirds of the vote.

Committees

Appropriations (18th of 37 Democrats)
Interior; Military Construction; Transportation

Select Intelligence (6th of 12 Democrats)
Legislation (chairman); Oversight & Evaluation

Elections

1992 General		
Ronald D. Coleman (D)	66,731	(52%)
Chip Taberski (R)	61,870	(48%)
1992 Primary		
Ronald D. Coleman (D)	27,562	(64%)
Charles Ponzio Jr. (D)	11,104	(26%)
Robert Kenneth Jones (D)	2,704	(6%)
Jorge Artalejo (D)	1,856	(4%)
1990 General		
Ronald D. Coleman (D)	62,455	(96%)
William Burgett (write-in)	2,854	(4%)

Previous Winning Percentages: **1988** (100%) **1986** (66%) **1984** (57%) **1982** (54%)

District Vote for President

1992
D 65,614 (51%)
R 45,367 (35%)
I 18,779 (14%)

Campaign Finance

	Receipts	Receipts from PACs		Expend-itures
1992				
Coleman (D)	$777,219	$486,544	(63%)	$780,038
Taberski (R)	$212,848	$16,355	(8%)	$209,271
1990				
Coleman (D)	$279,452	$162,285	(58%)	$286,407

Key Votes

1993	
Require parental notification of minors' abortions	N
Require unpaid family and medical leave	Y
Approve national "motor voter" registration bill	Y
Approve budget increasing taxes and reducing deficit	Y
Approve economic stimulus plan	Y
1992	
Approve balanced-budget constitutional amendment	N
Close down space station program	N
Approve U.S. aid for former Soviet Union	Y
Allow shifting funds from defense to domestic programs	Y
1991	
Extend unemployment benefits using deficit financing	Y
Approve waiting period for handgun purchases	N
Authorize use of force in Persian Gulf	N

Voting Studies

	Presidential Support		Party Unity		Conservative Coalition	
Year	**S**	**O**	**S**	**O**	**S**	**O**
1992	28	66	82	10	58	40
1991	34	65	88	11	54	43
1990	20	76	90	7	44	52
1989	35	62	90	6	34	63
1988	27	69	89	6	37	58
1987	30	68	92	6	51	49
1986	29	69	81	16	64	36
1985	31	68	89	9	51	47
1984	42	55	76	21	61	37
1983	37	61	81	16	48	49

Interest Group Ratings

Year	ADA	AFL-CIO	CCUS	ACU
1992	85	83	29	13
1991	60	92	40	10
1990	67	83	23	17
1989	75	91	22	18
1988	80	93	29	17
1987	84	100	13	4
1986	70	86	56	35
1985	60	71	33	19
1984	65	92	38	35
1983	75	88	40	4

17 Charles W. Stenholm (D)

Of Stamford — Elected 1978; 8th Term

Born: Oct. 26, 1938, Stamford, Texas.
Education: Tarleton State Junior College, 1957-59; Texas Tech U., B.S. 1961, M.S. 1962.
Occupation: Cotton farmer.
Family: Wife, Cynthia Ann Watson; three children.
Religion: Lutheran.
Political Career: No previous office.
Capitol Office: 1211 Longworth Bldg. 20515; 225-6605.

In Washington: Stenholm, the spiritual godfather of fiscal austerity among House Democrats, began the 103rd Congress with an opportunity finally to achieve some of his long-sought goals. Bill Clinton had moved his party's rhetoric toward Stenholm's during 1992; Stenholm's challenge was to persuade the twenty-somethings running the Clinton White House not to forget the lessons of that campaign.

From his position on the Budget Committee, Stenholm scored an early success when he and other conservatives forced $63 billion more in spending cuts into Clinton's budget request.

Simultaneously, Stenholm gave Clinton an early warning that his $16.3 billion stimulus bill was in trouble because it was laden with pork and would add to the deficit, all the while doing little to aid the economy.

Neither Clinton nor House leaders would listen to Stenholm. They steamrollered him, denying him the chance to offer a mitigating floor amendment and winning passage of the stimulus bill by a vote of 235-190. In the Senate, however, sounds of discontent immediately were heard from some conservative Democrats, and soon the Republicans were united in opposition. The White House proved unable to break a GOP filibuster and ultimately had to admit defeat, pulling the bill from consideration with the hope of trying later with a more focused package.

Weeks later, Stenholm had another feather in his cap, after the House passed a bill granting a modified line-item veto to the president. Working with Democrat John M. Spratt Jr. of South Carolina, Stenholm refined the measure from a version that had overwhelmingly passed the House in the 102nd Congress but died in the Senate. This time, House Democrats — Stenholm and the leadership, at least — were in lock step.

Then, in May, Stenholm was able to prove his loyalty to president and party by endorsing the budget-reconciliation bill that would enact into law much of Clinton's plan for tax increases and spending cuts. Allied with fellow Democratic deficit-hawk Timothy J. Penny of Minnesota, Stenholm held out for administration assent to a cap of sorts designed to limit the growth in spending on entitlements, such as Medicare and Medicaid. Stenholm's eleventh-hour support for the bill was crucial; he brought aboard as many as 30 reluctant Democrats and the bill passed 219-213.

In 1992, Stenholm was the strategic mastermind behind the defeat of a Democratic leadership plan to shift defense savings into increased domestic spending. And he came close to winning passage of a constitutional amendment requiring a balanced federal budget. He appeared to have the votes locked up until last-minute pressure from the leadership caused 12 cosponsors to switch and vote against the measure; he came up nine votes short.

Stenholm may consistently depart from liberal orthodoxy. But he commands respect as a man of principle and substance, and his relationship with Democratic leaders remains cordial because he will sometimes help them on sticky votes. Since 1989 he has participated in strategy sessions as a deputy whip.

When some conservative Democrats got behind President George Bush's proposed cut in the capital gains tax in 1989, Stenholm lobbied Southern Democrats for Speaker Thomas S. Foley of Washington. In 1989, Stenholm undercut Texas Republican Dick Armey, who wanted to reduce the appropriation for the National Endowment for the Arts by 10 percent, in response to publicity over two NEA financed projects that had been denounced as blasphemous and obscene. Stenholm proposed cutting NEA's budget by only the amount of the two controversial grants — $45,000. The House agreed, and Armey said admiringly that it was "very good strategy to come in and 'Boll Weevil' me."

Stenholm reserves much of his energy for the Agriculture Committee, where he is respected for his mastery of highly technical legislative matters. "There is nothing that comes out of the ground that Charlie Stenholm doesn't know about," remarked one colleague.

As chairman of the Livestock, Dairy and Poultry Subcommittee, Stenholm was responsible for the dairy title in the 1990 farm bill. He and ranking subcommittee Republican Steve

Texas 17

West Central — Abilene

In the oil industry's heyday, 100 rigs dotted the rolling prairie of the 17th. Today, there are only about a dozen in the enormous district, which lies west of Fort Worth. As was the case elsewhere in oil-dependent Texas, entire towns in the 17th virtually collapsed with the industry; businesses closed and banks foreclosed on mortgages. For a time, a popular local bumper sticker warned off job-seeking newcomers with this message: "Welcome to Texas. Now Go Home."

To survive, many of the people who held on in West Texas returned to the land or looked to the government. In the 1990s, agriculture, prisons and the defense industry are the 17th's three top sources of jobs.

The only large city in the district is Abilene (Taylor County), with almost 107,000 people. In 1991 it became a member of the Texas Main Street Project, a private-public effort to revitalize the downtown by renovating and reusing historic buildings. Three church-sponsored colleges in Abilene help nurture the 17th's large and powerful evangelical community. Taylor County showed its conservatism clearly in 1992, giving George Bush nearly half its presidential vote; Bill Clinton was a distant second, not very far ahead of Ross Perot. Bush carried the 17th overall with 40 percent of the vote.

Dyess and Goodfellow Air Force bases are reliable employers. More than 5,500 people are stationed at Dyess, in Abilene. It is the only training base in the country for the B-1B bomber, and personnel here also train on refueling planes and maintain a fleet of several dozen aircraft.

Goodfellow is in Tom Green County (San Angelo), which is split between the 17th and 21st districts. Though the base itself is just over the 17th boundary line, it still has a major economic impact here. Goodfellow has appeared on proposed base-closing lists, but a new firefighting training unit has been added to its intelligence-training operation.

The 17th is also home to a number of defense-related private companies. A Lockheed plant in Abilene (purchased from General Dynamics in early 1993) builds components for the F-16 aircraft. The future of the facility is cloudy, given the uncertainty over whether the Air Force will end procurements of the F-16 by the late 1990s.

The area around San Angelo is a major producer of wool and mohair; Tom Green County, with its rocky terrain, is ideally suited to sheep and goats. Counties in the northeastern corner of the 17th rely heavily on beef sales, while the counties at the opposite end of the district, more than 200 miles away, are major cotton producers.

The prison business is booming in the 17th. On the western side of the district, the Big Spring federal correctional facility has given an economic boost to Howard County. It has 285 employees tending 1,270 inmates. Other prisons in the 17th include Abilene's 2,250-bed maximum-security unit, employing 900, and the Price Daniel unit in Snyder (Scurry County), with 420 workers.

1990 Population: 566,217. White 485,216 (86%), Black 20,038 (4%), Other 60,963 (11%). Hispanic origin 97,116 (17%). 18 and over 412,570 (73%), 62 and over 106,238 (19%). Median age: 34.

Gunderson of Wisconsin produced a plan that set a floor, at $10.10 per 100 pounds of milk products, below the previously sliding scale of government price supports for milk. Stenholm and Gunderson fended off attempts to raise the support floor and rejected administration calls to cut subsidy levels further.

In the 103rd, Stenholm took the chair of the Department Operations and Nutrition Subcommittee, where he can prepare for the next farm bill fracas in 1995 and fight for nutrition programs, which he defends at all cost.

Stenholm generally has preferred to help farmers cut back production rather than to increase their direct subsidies. The 1990 farm bill contained a concept Stenholm and Kansas Republican Pat Roberts had long favored to reduce government subsidies. Known as "triple base," the plan reduced by 15 percent the amount of cropland eligible for government income-support payments. Farmers participating could grow anything but fruits and vegetables on that 15 percent of land normally used for subsidized crops.

Prior to 1981, Stenholm had no record of leadership experience, but he emerged as the head of a "Boll Weevils" group that used its leverage to get conservative Democrats prime committee assignments and to help shape and pass the 1981 Reagan economic program.

The group, which evolved into the Conservative Democratic Forum (CDF), became less strategically crucial after the 1982 elections, when Democrats added significantly to their majority. But the CDF still meets weekly and has about 50 regular members.

Despite his criticisms of the Democratic

Party, Stenholm has made it clear he does not plan to leave it. "I'm a Democrat, period," he said in 1986. "Philosophically, I am what I am, and that's a conservative Democrat. I believe that philosophy, tempered with the liberal and moderate viewpoints, is best for the country."

But Stenholm was not prepared to accept a socialist into his party's fold. When Vermont independent Bernard Sanders, a self-described socialist, sought admission into the Democratic Caucus after he was elected to the House in 1990, Stenholm circulated among CDF members a letter opposing Sanders' admission. Sanders subsequently agreed not to apply.

At Home: Stenholm is a third-generation West Texan, descended from Swedish immigrants who settled near Stamford, where he was born. Agriculture has been the focus of his life and the basis of his political career.

He moved into politics in 1966, when the U.S. Agriculture Department made a ruling unfavorable to the cotton-growing plains section of Texas. As executive vice president of the Rolling Plains Cotton Growers Association, he visited Washington to lobby against the ruling and had partial success in changing it.

In 1977, President Jimmy Carter appointed Stenholm to a panel advising the U.S. Agricultural and Conservation Service. He resigned that post to run for the House in 1978, when veteran Democrat Omar Burleson retired.

Stenholm had a much smaller campaign treasury than his major rival for the Democratic nomination, wealthy Abilene lawyer and businessman A. L. "Dusty" Rhodes. But as a farmer and former member of the state Democratic executive committee, Stenholm had extensive agricultural and party ties. Although Rhodes spent more than $600,000, Stenholm outran the crowded primary field and defeated Rhodes by 2-to-1 in a runoff. An easy winner in the fall, he did not face a Republican again until 1992.

Stenholm had 86 overdrafts at the House bank, but his GOP opponent, Eastland business owner Jeannie Sadowski, did not pose a serious threat. Nevertheless, despite outspending Sadowski by more than 20-to-1, Stenholm was held to 66 percent, his all-time low.

Committees

Agriculture (6th of 28 Democrats)
Department Operations (chairman); Foreign Agriculture & Hunger; General Farm Commodities; Livestock; Specialty Crops & Natural Resources

Budget (8th of 26 Democrats)

Elections

1992 General		
Charles W. Stenholm (D)	136,213	(66%)
Jeannie Sadowski (R)	69,958	(34%)
1990 General		
Charles W. Stenholm (D)	104,100	(100%)

Previous Winning Percentages: **1988** (100%) **1986** (100%) **1984** (100%) **1982** (97%) **1980** (100%) **1978** (68%)

District Vote for President

	1992
D	73,388 (34%)
R	86,490 (40%)
I	55,834 (26%)

Campaign Finance

	Receipts	Receipts from PACs	Expend-itures
1992			
Stenholm (D)	$412,834	$274,726 (67%)	$377,949
Sadowski (R)	$17,222	0	$17,791
1990			
Stenholm (D)	$254,175	$98,075 (39%)	$311,378

Key Votes

1993	
Require parental notification of minors' abortions	Y
Require unpaid family and medical leave	N
Approve national "motor voter" registration bill	N
Approve budget increasing taxes and reducing deficit	Y
Approve economic stimulus plan	N
1992	
Approve balanced-budget constitutional amendment	Y
Close down space station program	N
Approve U.S. aid for former Soviet Union	Y
Allow shifting funds from defense to domestic programs	N
1991	
Extend unemployment benefits using deficit financing	N
Approve waiting period for handgun purchases	Y
Authorize use of force in Persian Gulf	Y

Voting Studies

	Presidential Support		Party Unity		Conservative Coalition	
Year	**S**	**O**	**S**	**O**	**S**	**O**
1992	68	29	52	47	88	10
1991	66	33	48	49	95	5
1990	56	44	52	47	91	9
1989	71	28	54	45	85	10
1988	57	39	45	50	87	8
1987	64	34	39	57	93	2
1986	66	34	32	67	88	12
1985	66	31	35	64	96	2
1984	58	37	23	70	85	8
1983	63	35	21	77	92	7
1982	74	26	17	78	93	4
1981	75	24	28	67	91	5

Interest Group Ratings

Year	ADA	AFL-CIO	CCUS	ACU
1992	30	25	57	72
1991	5	17	90	70
1990	22	25	71	67
1989	25	17	80	61
1988	20	46	77	78
1987	12	25	80	74
1986	5	21	78	81
1985	20	24	86	90
1984	10	15	56	79
1983	15	13	85	91
1982	5	5	86	91
1981	0	20	84	93

18 Craig Washington (D)

Of Houston — Elected 1989; 2nd Full Term

Born: Oct. 12, 1941, Longview, Texas.
Education: Prairie View A&M U., B.S. 1966; Texas Southern U., J.D. 1969.
Occupation: Lawyer.
Family: Separated; five children.
Religion: Baptist.
Political Career: Texas House, 1973-83; Texas Senate, 1983-89.
Capitol Office: 1711 Longworth Bldg. 20515; 225-3816.

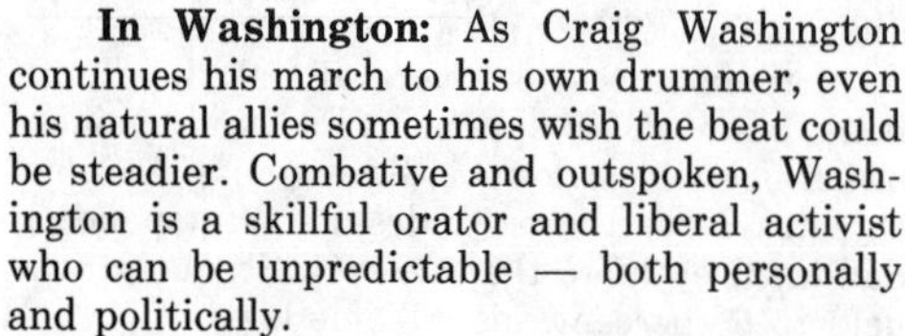

In Washington: As Craig Washington continues his march to his own drummer, even his natural allies sometimes wish the beat could be steadier. Combative and outspoken, Washington is a skillful orator and liberal activist who can be unpredictable — both personally and politically.

Washington surprised many with his December 1992 run for the chair of the Congressional Black Caucus against the reserved but popular Maryland Democrat Kweisi Mfume. Though Washington said he would have been a more combative chairman, Mfume won easily, 27-9.

With the start of the 103rd Congress, Washington brought his idiosyncratic brand of politics to the Energy and Commerce Committee — having won a seat on that panel just ahead of five arriving Democrats from the class of 1992.

In some ways, Washington exemplifies the most liberal faction of the House. After the Persian Gulf War started in January 1991, he was one of just six members to oppose a resolution backing the president and supporting U.S. troops. But his mercurial tendencies occasionally set him apart from his natural allies. "I am opposed to raising taxes of any kind," he said in mid-1990.

As a member of the Judiciary Committee, Washington tried to have his say on many of the prominent issues of the 1990s, including crime, flag burning and discrimination against the disabled. But it was on the civil rights bill (vetoed once, altered and ultimately signed by President George Bush) that Washington gained the most attention.

When House negotiators compromised on some amendments in pursuit of administration support, Washington balked. Calling the amended version a "hollow shell of a civil rights bill," Washington was the only Democratic conferee who voted against the changes.

After the compromise bill received overwhelming House support, Washington mocked late converts who had opposed the bill earlier on the basis of anti-quota arguments. "Where did the quotas go?" Washington asked. "They swam upstream, as red herrings often do."

Possessed of a fiery personality and temperament — he once got into a fight in the Texas Legislature — Washington was involved in another contretemps on the floor in October 1990. Illinois Republican Henry J. Hyde, angry over a sarcastic floor statement by Democrat Barney Frank of Massachusetts, made a sardonic quip about Frank's homosexuality. Washington jumped to Frank's defense, nearly engaging in fisticuffs with several Republicans present.

Washington took on Hyde again during debate over the 1991 crime bill. One provision would have allowed prisoners under sentence of death to challenge their sentences using statistics that show the death penalty is applied disproportionately by race. Hyde wanted to strike the provision, an action that Washington claimed "amounted to nothing more than an attempt to legally lynch."

Washington voted with the Bush administration less than 10 percent of the time when the White House expressed a clear position. But there is a flexibility to his ideology that follows neither the party line nor any other easily discernible alliance.

He voted with a minority of Democrats and Congressional Black Caucus members to increase funding for Housing Secretary Jack F. Kemp's HOPE project to help public housing tenants purchase units. He also broke with Democrats on the Civil and Constitutional Rights Subcommittee to support an amendment (sponsored by Hyde) allowing states to ban ads for doctors stating their willingness to perform sex-selection abortions. Generally an abortion rights advocate, Washington explained the vote by saying, "I certainly wouldn't want to see an ad like that in the Yellow Pages."

Washington also can eschew traditional minority alliances if the issue conflicts with his overarching commitment to civil liberties. Early in the 103rd Congress, he opposed hate-crimes legislation introduced by New York Democrat Charles E. Schumer that would require longer sentences for crimes motivated by racism or other bias. Washington said the bill could violate free speech and other individual rights.

In addition, he has demonstrated a long-

Texas 18

Downtown Houston

Once a compact, urban district centered around Houston's downtown, the 18th for the 1990s is an X-shaped contortion with tentacles that stretch to two outlying airports, scooping up a handful of cozy suburbs along the way.

After reapportionment in 1990 gave Texas three new House districts, mapmakers set out to increase minority representation. In Houston, they took large parts of the old 18th — primarily its Hispanic sections — and shifted them into a new 29th District with a majority of Hispanics. The population remaining in the 18th is 51 percent black and 15 percent Hispanic.

Now the district has well-to-do suburbs in northwest Harris County, such as Hedwig Village. They add Republican votes to the 18th and lift the district up a notch on the income scale. The median household income for the district is between $22,500 and $25,000. Many of the suburbanites shop at the upscale Galleria Mall, which remapping also included in the 18th.

While the district now has some pockets of economic comfort, life in the 18th continues to be a struggle for most. The North Forest School District is one of the most financially strapped in the state. There is virtually no commercial property to tax in the area, and the mostly low-income black residents cannot afford to pay higher property taxes on their homes.

One of the burning questions locally is the future of Allen Parkway Village, a post-World War II subsidized housing complex on the west side. Initially built by the federal government to house whites, the 1,000 units were integrated in the 1960s and became predominantly black in the 1970s. By the early 1990s, fewer than 40 families lived in the dilapidated complex, which has been plagued with asbestos and lead paint problems.

Many area residents are concerned that developers want to revamp the 37-acre property into an extension of the adjacent downtown business district.

With an estimated 10,000 families on Houston's waiting list for affordable housing, some leaders contend that the whole complex should be repaired and reopened.

Others are skeptical of this plan, feeling the complex may have gone too far downhill to be rescued. The fate of the complex will have a dramatic impact on the entire west side and its residents.

Few live in downtown Houston, although its businesses provide jobs at all levels for the district's residents. The effects of the mid-1980s oil bust are still evident in Houston. Downtown buildings once named for and primarily occupied by companies such as Exxon share quarters with banks and law firms. Lower-income residents of the 18th work as clerks in the offices, bellhops in the hotels and custodians at the nearby Texas Medical Center.

Previously represented by Barbara C. Jordan and Mickey Leland, the 18th has always been one of the most Democratic districts in the state. Bill Clinton coasted in this district in 1992.

1990 Population: 566,217. White 213,315 (38%), Black 288,382 (51%), Other 64,520 (11%). Hispanic origin 86,840 (15%). 18 and over 414,418 (73%), 62 and over 62,041 (11%). Median age: 30.

standing opposition to concentrating minority voters in districts designed to elect minority members. In concert with several other black members of the House, Washington contends such concentrations minimize minority voting power. He opposed the creation of such districts during a 1980 redistricting fight in the Texas Legislature, even though the stand seemingly ran counter to his political interests.

Yet it is in the translation from words and principle to action that Washington occasionally falls short, frustrating colleagues who otherwise see star potential in the Houston congressman.

Because of his ambivalence toward the 1991 crime bill, Washington failed to vote at all. He explained his action by saying that he "panicked" on the floor — adding that if the leadership had needed his vote, he would have voted yes. The missed vote was not an isolated incident. During the 102nd Congress, Washington missed enough votes — mostly on procedural motions — to have one of the lowest voting participation records in the House.

Indicating an impatience with the dilatory nature of the institution, he says, "When it comes to a choice between form and substance, I choose substance." He keeps a log of votes that he missed with an explanation of what he was doing instead.

Early in the 103rd Congress, however, Washington missed an important vote on which the Black Caucus had taken a vocal position in opposition to the Democratic leadership. The vote involved granting the president modified line-item veto authority.

Washington did much the same in the Texas Legislature. Colleagues in the Texas

House and Senate recall him as a spellbinding orator who insisted on playing by his own rules.

Washington was named one of the Texas Legislature's 10 best legislators by Texas Monthly magazine three times and one of its worst once. In one profile, the liberal publication said he "had done more than any man in history to end racism on the floor of the Texas House."

Yet the same magazine in 1977 dubbed him "missing in action" for spending more time practicing law in Houston than on the floor of the Texas House. When he returned to the House after an extended absence, the magazine reported, he was introduced on the floor of the House as "a distinguished former member."

Washington began his congressional service under an unusual cloud. Days before being sworn in, he was sentenced by two Texas judges to brief prison terms for contempt of court for failing to appear in court in behalf of two clients. He managed to settle the issue without serving any jail time.

At Home: Washington is the third in a succession of outspoken, liberal black Democrats who have represented the 18th.

Barbara C. Jordan held the seat for three terms in the 1970s. Civil rights and anti-hunger activist Mickey Leland succeeded her in 1978 and held the seat until his August 1989 death in a plane crash in Ethiopia.

Washington had been a close ally of Leland since 1972, when they were running for the Texas Legislature. Many Leland supporters rallied behind Washington in the 11-way race to fill the vacant seat.

Washington had his own credentials and contacts to bolster his campaign. A Houston lawyer and state senator, he was known to tackle tough battles and serve as a "conscience" in the chamber. He took first place in the November special election, but his 41 percent tally was not enough to avoid a runoff with City Council member and fellow Democrat Anthony Hall.

In the runoff, Hall was backed by members of the Houston business community who wanted a more conservative representative. Hall said Washington took on losing causes.

But Washington effectively presented some of his "losing causes" in a positive light, saying he was not afraid to champion individual rights on controversial issues such as flag burning (Washington had filibustered against a measure to amend the Texas Constitution to ban flag burning). During the campaign, he refused Hall's challenge to take a drug test. Washington got a boost when Leland's widow endorsed him. He beat Hall with almost 57 percent of the vote and ran unchallenged to win his first full term in 1990.

Redistricting altered his district dramatically in 1992, shifting much of the Hispanic community into the new 29th District. But Washington had no trouble, winning re-election with nearly two-thirds of the vote.

Committees

Energy & Commerce (22nd of 27 Democrats)
Energy & Power; Health & the Environment

Government Operations (20th of 25 Democrats)
Environment, Energy & Natural Resources; Human Resources & Intergovernmental Relations

Judiciary (15th of 21 Democrats)
Civil & Constitutional Rights; Crime & Criminal Justice

Elections

1992 General		
Craig Washington (D)	111,422	(65%)
Edward Blum (R)	56,080	(33%)
Gregg Lassen (LIBERT)	4,706	(3%)
1990 General		
Craig Washington (D)	54,477	(100%)

Previous Winning Percentage: **1989 *** (57%)

** Special runoff election.*

District Vote for President

	1992	
D	118,349	(66%)
R	40,150	(22%)
I	20,382	(11%)

Campaign Finance

	Receipts	Receipts from PACs		Expend-itures
1992				
Washington (D)	$185,635	$121,250	(65%)	$184,742
Blum (R)	$211,586	$8,400	(4%)	$209,453
1990				
Washington (D)	$144,647	$87,250	(60%)	$157,053

Key Votes

1993	
Require parental notification of minors' abortions	N
Require unpaid family and medical leave	Y
Approve national "motor voter" registration bill	Y
Approve budget increasing taxes and reducing deficit	Y
Approve economic stimulus plan	Y
1992	
Approve balanced-budget constitutional amendment	N
Close down space station program	Y
Approve U.S. aid for former Soviet Union	N
Allow shifting funds from defense to domestic programs	Y
1991	
Extend unemployment benefits using deficit financing	Y
Approve waiting period for handgun purchases	Y
Authorize use of force in Persian Gulf	N

Voting Studies

	Presidential Support		Party Unity		Conservative Coalition	
Year	**S**	**O**	**S**	**O**	**S**	**O**
1992	6	90	80	4	6	85
1991	23	70	80	4	3	92
1990	12	81	73	4	7	80

Interest Group Ratings

Year	ADA	AFL-CIO	CCUS	ACU
1992	90	83	13	0
1991	95	100	11	0
1990	94	100	31	5

19 Larry Combest (R)

Of Lubbock — Elected 1984; 5th Term

Born: March 20, 1945, Memphis, Texas.
Education: West Texas State U., B.B.A. 1969.
Occupation: Farmer; congressional aide; electronics wholesaler.
Family: Wife, Sharon McCurry; two children.
Religion: Methodist.
Political Career: No previous office.
Capitol Office: 1511 Longworth Bldg. 20515; 225-4005.

In Washington: Combest took on a new persona in the 102nd Congress. For most of his first three terms, Combest was known as an effective — if quiet — behind-the-scenes negotiator on legislation of importance to his rural district.

But he stepped into the spotlight in late 1992 when he charged the chairman of the House Banking Committee, fellow Texan Henry B. Gonzalez — with intentionally releasing classified information.

In September 1992, Gonzalez kept a lonely, late-night vigil on the floor of the House, criticizing at length the Bush administration's policy toward Iraq prior to the Persian Gulf War.

Combest took on Gonzalez, arguing that in those long speeches the Banking chairman had deliberately revealed classified information.

The battle culminated on Sept. 18, when the House on a largely party-line vote decided not to refer Gonzalez to the ethics committee for investigation. Members voted 216-150 to table, thus killing, a resolution that Combest introduced that would have begun an investigation into the alleged leaks.

Though he lost the vote, his fight helped shore up his shaky relationship with the House Republican leadership, and in early 1993 he was appointed ranking Republican on the Select Intelligence Committee, a position he very much wanted.

Combest sees his new role as a check against a Democratic Congress and administration making deep cuts in the nation's intelligence budget. He warns that "the cost of cutting too deeply into intelligence resources is measured in lives."

Combest's experience as a congressional staff member helped him move quickly into the inside politics of the Agriculture Committee, to which he was appointed in 1985. There he worked with influential Republican Edward Madigan of Illinois, and when Madigan tried for House GOP whip in 1989, Combest was a key backer among younger Republicans. But Madigan lost to Newt Gingrich, leaving Combest to quietly make his peace with the new minority leadership.

Combest refocused on Agriculture, tending to the interests of West Texas' cotton and feed grain producers. He has the knowledge, desire and electoral security to become a legislator with impact. Though Gingrich and his combative allies draw more attention, there will be plenty of opportunities for legislative deal-making, and that still is Combest's forte.

In 1985 and 1990, Combest was quietly attentive as the Agriculture Committee wrote the five-year farm bill. On farm subsidies, he generally supported the frugal views of the Republican administrations — and many conservative West Texas producers — but his fiscal austerity slackened when it came to cotton, the 19th's key crop.

Combest worked well with Charles W. Stenholm, the influential Agriculture Democrat who represents the adjoining 17th District. During committee work on the 1988 drought-relief bill, Combest got an amendment passed to compensate cotton producers who had hail-damaged crops.

Many other Republican insiders share Combest's pragmatic attitude toward legislative bargaining. Their influence helped him get on the Intelligence Committee in 1989. In the 101st Congress, Combest argued against large cuts in the intelligence budget, warning that Soviet intelligence activities had not subsided.

As that stand suggests, Combest furrows a steady conservative line outside Agriculture. In 1990, he was one of four House members to vote 100 percent of the time with the "conservative coalition" of Republicans and Southern Democrats when it was called into play. During the year, Combest was one of two Texas Republicans to vote consistently to cut funding for the superconducting super collider, an $8 billion atom smasher being built in Texas.

Combest has been outspoken in his crusade against the Legal Services Corporation, the federal program of legal services to the poor. The business establishment in Combest's district has attacked the Texas Rural Legal Aid office for organizing unions, promoting strikes

Texas 19

Western Panhandle — Parts of Lubbock and Amarillo

For the visitor in search of the authentic Wild West complete with cowboys, oil rigs, barbecues and vast stretches of parched, barren countryside, the 19th delivers. But the romanticized images of Western life belie the tough times that have plagued the region's residents.

Enormously dependent on oil and gas, the northwestern reaches of Texas were devastated in the mid-1980s when an oil glut and foreign competition sent prices plummeting from a high of $37 a barrel to less than $10 in 1986. Banks began calling notes on small independents, prompting oil company bankruptcies and massive bank failures. Since 1986, only one bank in the Midland-Odessa region has kept its same name and ownership; most of the others were bought by out-of-state conglomerates. Idled rigs collected rust, while petroleum engineers and geologists took huge pay cuts to work at local wholesale shops as clerks and cashiers. Many others left the area entirely.

Ector County, the center for Permian Basin oil field operations, is one of the state's leading oil-producing counties, generating more than 2 billion barrels since 1926. To the north, Amarillo is the hub for the Panhandle oil industry. Pipelines in the area extend as far as the Gulf Coast. Other counties in the 19th heavily dependent on the energy business include Midland, a major oil center, and Yoakum, which produces minerals, oil and natural gas.

Agriculture too has been a somewhat reliable, albeit challenging, line of work in the hot, dry region.

The 19th's agricultural emphasis shifted slightly from cotton to cattle with the addition of several northern Panhandle counties in the 1992 redistricting. Nevertheless, cotton remains a staple, particularly in Lubbock County. A top agricultural county in the state, Lubbock has more than 230,000 irrigated acres. The city of Lubbock, which is split between the 19th and 13th districts, calls itself the world's largest cottonseed processing center. Reese Air Force Base is another important employer in the city.

Cattle ranching is dominant in Oldham, Hansford and Randall counties.

The Amarillo Livestock Auction is one of the nation's largest, beginning on Wednesdays and often lasting several days. The city (population 157,600) is split between districts and counties; Randall County residents are in the 19th, Potter County in the 13th.

The cowboy feel of the 19th is genuine. Amarillo sponsors Cowboy Mornings, chuckwagon breakfasts served after a ride across the plains. The Odessa-based Chuck Wagon Gang is a group of 250 local businessmen (women are discouraged from joining) who travel the globe serving up barbecue and promoting West Texas. And the city, named in 1891 by Russian railroad laborers after their hometown, boasts the world's largest barbecue pit, big enough to grill 16,500 pounds of beef, some say.

The F-shaped 19th is good GOP territory. Rep. Combest topped 77 percent in 1992 and George Bush far exceeded his state margin, with 60 percent of the vote.

1990 Population: 566,217. White 487,509 (86%), Black 14,410 (3%), Other 64,298 (11%). Hispanic origin 110,776 (20%). 18 and over 403,001 (71%), 62 and over 70,986 (13%). Median age: 31.

and representing illegal aliens.

As a protégé and longtime employee of the late Texas Sen. John Tower, Combest probably was horrified to see his account of Tower's past drinking featured in a 1989 front-page story in The Washington Post.

The story said Combest told Armed Services Committee Sens. Sam Nunn, D-Ga., and John W. Warner, R-Va., that Tower, President George Bush's nominee for Defense secretary, drank as much as a full bottle of Scotch two to three times a week in the 1970s. Combest later said it was Tower and a group of friends who drank a full bottle in an evening. Tower's nomination was rejected.

At Home: After a stint with the U.S. Agricultural Stabilization Service, Combest went to work for Tower in 1971 as a specialist in agricultural affairs. He later became director of Tower's Texas offices and served as treasurer for his 1978 re-election campaign. Combest then returned to West Texas to sell electronic equipment, remaining active in GOP affairs.

When former Democratic Rep. Kent Hance — now a Republican — announced for the Senate in 1984, Combest quickly jumped for the 19th. It had not elected a Republican in its 50-year history but voted regularly for GOP state and national candidates and was ripe to switch.

Combest was forced into a runoff by a hard-right conservative, but with support from many old-line GOP leaders, he won the runoff easily.

In November, Combest met Don Richards, a former Hance aide. Both stressed their farm roots and conservatism. Combest portrayed Richards as part of a too-liberal party. Richards spurned the national Democratic line on tax increases and gay rights, and he cast himself as a conservative in Hance's mold. Combest carried the most populous counties — Ector and Lubbock — to overcome Richards' rural strength. He has won easily since.

In 1992 he took 77 percent of the vote against Democrat Terry Lee Moser.

Committees

Select Intelligence (Ranking)
Program & Budget Authorization (ranking)

Agriculture (6th of 18 Republicans)
Environment, Credit & Rural Development (ranking); General Farm Commodities

Small Business (2nd of 18 Republicans)
Regulation, Business Opportunities & Technology (ranking)

Elections

1992 General		
Larry Combest (R)	162,057	(77%)
Terry Lee Moser (D)	47,325	(23%)
1990 General		
Larry Combest (R)	83,795	(100%)

Previous Winning Percentages: **1988** (68%) **1986** (62%) **1984** (58%)

District Vote for President

1992

D 50,815 (23%)
R 130,639 (60%)
I 36,068 (17%)

Campaign Finance

	Receipts	Receipts from PACs		Expend-itures
1992				
Combest (R)	$241,559	$125,675	(52%)	$197,657
Moser (D)	$4,389	0		$5,198
1990				
Combest (R)	$197,121	$85,976	(44%)	$111,838

Key Votes

1993	
Require parental notification of minors' abortions	Y
Require unpaid family and medical leave	N
Approve national "motor voter" registration bill	N
Approve budget increasing taxes and reducing deficit	N
Approve economic stimulus plan	N
1992	
Approve balanced-budget constitutional amendment	Y
Close down space station program	N
Approve U.S. aid for former Soviet Union	N
Allow shifting funds from defense to domestic programs	N
1991	
Extend unemployment benefits using deficit financing	N
Approve waiting period for handgun purchases	N
Authorize use of force in Persian Gulf	Y

Voting Studies

	Presidential Support		Party Unity		Conservative Coalition	
Year	**S**	**O**	**S**	**O**	**S**	**O**
1992	79	21	82	17	94	6
1991	77	23	82	17	100	0
1990	78	22	82	16	100	0
1989	85	15	73	27	95	5
1988	68	29	75	23	97	0
1987	64	25	75	19	86	7
1986	78	22	82	18	100	0
1985	75	25	89	11	96	4

Interest Group Ratings

Year	ADA	AFL-CIO	CCUS	ACU
1992	10	33	88	100
1991	0	8	90	95
1990	0	8	79	96
1989	0	0	90	96
1988	0	21	93	92
1987	0	13	93	89
1986	5	21	94	91
1985	5	0	91	100

20 Henry B. Gonzalez (D)

Of San Antonio — Elected 1961; 16th Full Term

Born: May 3, 1916, San Antonio, Texas.

Education: San Antonio College, 1937; U. of Texas, Austin, 1937-39; St. Mary's U. of San Antonio, LL.B. 1943.

Occupation: Teacher; public relations consultant; translator.

Family: Wife, Bertha Cuellar; eight children.

Religion: Roman Catholic.

Political Career: Candidate for Texas House, 1950; San Antonio City Council, 1953-57, mayor pro tem, 1955-57; Texas Senate, 1957-61; sought Democratic nomination for governor, 1958; candidate for U.S. Senate, special election, 1961.

Capitol Office: 2413 Rayburn Bldg. 20515; 225-3236.

In Washington: As a committee chairman, Gonzalez may never be counted in the ranks of such commanding gavel-wielders as Dan Rostenkowski or John D. Dingell. His small 'd' democratic style does not instill enough fear, and his sometimes quirky manner can leave his colleagues scratching their heads.

But in two terms leading the Banking, Finance and Urban Affairs Committee, Gonzalez has helped fend off one of the biggest financial debacles in the nation's history — the near-collapse of the savings and loan industry. He also helped avert a lesser crisis affecting banks by shepherding an overhaul of the deposit insurance system in 1991. In addition, he has enacted a pair of bills that overhauled government-assisted housing programs and, important to Gonzalez, preserved the stock of public housing.

He has taken on powerful people without regard to partisan considerations — from S&L kingpin Charles H. Keating Jr. and the five U.S. senators he tried to enlist in his service; to longtime Democratic wise man Clark M. Clifford; and to President George Bush (about his administration's financial dealings with Iraq).

Overall, it is a record that would do credit to any chairman, but in Gonzalez's case it has rehabilitated his image beyond expectation. For years, few members of Congress had a reputation on Capitol Hill so contrary to their image back home as Gonzalez, who was revered in San Antonio while being dismissed by most House colleagues as a flake.

When autocratic Banking Committee Chairman Fernand J. St Germain of Rhode Island was upset in the 1988 elections, Gonzalez was not the automatic choice of committee members to succeed him, but he did move up to the chair. Then, Chairman Gonzalez developed a close working relationship with ranking Republican Chalmers P. Wylie of Ohio — a relationship so close that some committee Democrats felt Gonzalez was concocting strategy less with them than with Wylie.

That, combined with sentiment among many Democrats that Gonzalez had caved into last-minute White House pressure on a key issue involving financing the thrift bailout in 1989, led to a challenge to his chairmanship at the start of the 102nd Congress. A senior committee Democrat, Bruce F. Vento of Minnesota, launched a late-starting bid to unseat Gonzalez, but he fell well short. Still, more than a third of the entire House Democratic Caucus voted against Gonzalez, who prevailed by a vote of 163-89.

Now, having adjusted better to the demands of being chairman and having shown a willingness to assert himself more, Gonzalez has shored up his position. His hold on the chair was not challenged at the start of the 103rd.

Gonzalez gained national publicity during the 102nd by exposing the Bush administration's role in a scandal involving as much as $5 billion in loans to Iraq from the Atlanta branch of an Italian government-run bank, the Banca Nazionale del Lavoro. Gonzalez alleged that the Bush administration — in cozying up to Iraqi President Saddam Hussein before the Persian Gulf War — had ignored evidence of fraud and corruption involving the loans, a large portion of which the federal government guaranteed.

Gonzalez helped agitate for appointment of an independent prosecutor to investigate the allegations, a request denied by Bush's attorney general, William P. Barr. Republicans, meanwhile, sought an ethics committee investigation of whether Gonzalez had violated House rules by disclosing confidential documents during a series of House floor speeches. On a 215-150 party-line vote, Democrats blocked the GOP move against Gonzalez.

In an ironic twist, Gonzalez was potentially a victim of a rules change proposed by the Democratic leadership at the start of the 103rd to limit

Texas 20

Downtown San Antonio

Population growth split the city of San Antonio into four congressional districts in 1992. Today, San Antonio and its 940,000 residents make up the third-largest city in Texas and the 10th-largest in the nation. The 20th, which once consisted of all of Bexar County, now takes in central San Antonio and a handful of more rural communities to the west and southwest.

The 20th, which is 61 percent Hispanic, has a history of minority accomplishments. In 1981, San Antonio became the first major U.S. city to elect a Mexican-American mayor, Henry G. Cisneros (now secretary of Housing and Urban Development). Texas Attorney General Dan Morales is from San Antonio, and Hispanics dominate local and state legislative seats.

San Antonio's popular tourist spots are tied to its ethnic culture and history. The Alamo, the city's oldest mission and the site of the 1836 battle with Mexico, is in the heart of downtown.

Despite the city's Hispanic majority and background — it was founded in the early 18th century by the Spanish — Anglos have controlled its economy since its early days as a cattle center. Today, government payrolls are the region's lifeblood; San Antonio is the state's largest military center. And the city and school district rank among the largest employers. Three military facilities are within the 20th: Fort Sam Houston, a major health services command; Kelly Air Force Base, the district's largest employer with 16,600 people; and Lackland Air Force Base, which includes the Wilford Hall military hospital. Two other San Antonio installations (Randolph Air Force Base and Brooks Air Force Base) are just outside the 20th's boundaries, but play a major role in the district.

Tourism is the region's second-highest revenue producer. Besides the Alamo and other historic sites, the city's scenic Paseo del Rio, or Riverwalk, is a popular draw with its shops, restaurants and hotels winding along the San Antonio River.

Despite its popularity with visitors and mentions in national magazines that San Antonio is one of the most "livable" cities in the country, it is also one of the poorest. Nearly 15 percent of its residents are without private or public health coverage; almost one-fifth of the people fall below the poverty line. Even the tourism industry, despite the dollars it brings to the 20th, is responsible for predominantly low-wage, service jobs. Local officials hope a new division of Southwestern Bell will bring better management positions to the city.

In the 1992 redistricting, Rep. Gonzalez picked up some outlying communities in Bexar County he had represented before the 1980s' remapping. Most of the region's growth has been to the north, but in the 20th the new rural and suburban towns to the west and southwest are sparsely populated with retired veterans, small farmers and a handful of mid-level managers who commute into San Antonio.

Although George Bush carried Texas, Democrat Bill Clinton won the 20th comfortably.

1990 Population: 566,217. White 406,322 (72%), Black 32,629 (6%), Other 127,266 (22%). Hispanic origin 343,870 (61%). 18 and over 398,984 (12%), 62 and over 65,519 (12%). Median age: 29.

"special orders" — after-hours House floor speeches of the kind that Gonzalez used repeatedly to discuss the Iraqi loans. He has long been famous for holding the floor for hours on all manner of subjects, and he delivered 31 special orders in 1992 alone, more than any other member. Republicans also make extensive use of special orders to level partisan attacks, and they viewed the proposal as an effort to muzzle them. GOP protests forced the Democratic leadership to rescind the rules change.

On the Banking Committee, Gonzalez's egalitarian leadership style is a radical departure from that of St Germain. Committee members of both parties are free to pursue matters at length, which has, at times, led to interminable bill-drafting sessions with hundreds of amendments. On occasion, the process has produced bills so laden with extraneous matter that they were rejected by the committee at the end of the day. But the more open process has virtually eliminated complaints by junior members that their ideas are ignored.

Gonzalez also has won points with his panel's rank and file for standing up to attempts by Energy and Commerce Committee Chairman Dingell to poach on Banking's territory. In 1992, Dingell tried to rewrite laws governing trading in federal government securities in the wake of a bid-rigging scandal involving the Salomon Brothers investment house. Dingell's bill would have for the first time subjected banks — the biggest dealers in Treasury bonds — to scrutiny by the Securities and Exchange Commission. Gonzalez, who is no deregulatory fanatic, was appalled at what he considered both unnecessary regulation by the SEC and a grab by Energy and Commerce for jurisdiction over banks.

When House leaders tried to bring up Dingell's version of the bill under a special procedure barring amendments, Gonzalez took his complaint to the floor and beat Dingell. The bill died.

Gonzalez's influence on Banking was extended in the 103rd by a huge turnover on the committee; nearly half the panel's membership was new in 1993, and dominant among the newcomers were a batch of urban, Democratic freshmen who will be closely aligned with Gonzalez's pro-consumer, pro-housing emphasis.

Wylie's retirement, however, presents Gonzalez a new challenge in dealing with committee Republicans. In past years, he and the new ranking Republican, Jim Leach of Iowa, were not always on the best of terms. In 1989, after Leach succeeded in stripping special-interest provisions from the thrift bailout bill — including one sponsored by Gonzalez — the chairman called Leach a demagogue. For his part, Leach was angered by Gonzalez's attacks on his friend George Bush over the Iraqi loan scandal.

Shortly after taking over the committee in the 101st Congress, Gonzalez showed signs he could be formidable in the chair. He formed a ready alliance with the Bush administration over its bill to salvage the thrift industry and bail out its bankrupt deposit insurance fund with $50 billion. That became crucial when GOP lawmakers defected under industry pressure.

When a Banking subcommittee first began working on the bill, Gonzalez objected that industry-backed amendments were weakening it. "This is back to the old way of doing things," he said. "I won't be a party to it." When he got the bill in full committee, Gonzalez formed a working majority to restore stiffer capital requirements for thrifts and otherwise turn up the regulatory heat.

Gonzalez was presented with his first real test as chairman when a last-minute veto threat from Bush over the bill's on-budget financing forced a second conference. Conferees produced a compromise that put $20 billion on budget and $30 billion off. House Democrats fumed at Gonzalez for accepting the compromise; he argued that Democrats should be pleased with housing and consumer provisions in the bill. The conference report was adopted, but only 82 of the 217 Democrats who voted supported it.

After enactment of the bailout, Congress had difficulty keeping it financed and operating, a problem hardly of Gonzalez's making or within his power to overcome. Likewise, the defeat on the House floor of the first two of three banking overhaul bills in 1991 was due more to institutional aversion to banking bills than to a weakness in Gonzalez's leadership.

When he became full committee chairman, Gonzalez kept the Housing Subcommittee he has chaired since 1981 because that panel reflects his top priority. Gonzalez is the House's most ardent advocate of increased federal housing aid. As Housing Subcommittee chairman, he was a harsh critic of Reagan administration efforts to dismantle many housing programs. And at times Gonzalez displayed an impracticality that exacerbated a housing stalemate that lasted through most of Reagan's presidency. But with Bush in the White House, an improved climate for negotiation led to enactment of housing bills in 1990 and 1992.

Hearings in 1990 about the collapse of Keating's Lincoln Savings and Loan Association displayed the essential Gonzalez, a bulldog tenaciously pursuing his agenda regardless of whose flower bed he uproots. In this case, it was largely the Democrats' bed being uprooted: Members of his party were concerned about the bad light cast on the four Democratic senators among the "Keating Five."

The Keating show was repeated after a fashion in 1991, when Gonzalez brought Clark Clifford and his partner, Robert A. Altman, before the committee to explore their involvement in the world's biggest-ever bank scandal, involving the failed Luxembourg-based Bank of Credit and Commerce International.

Gonzalez has been a fighter since the beginning of his career, whether pressing lonely crusades of principle or personal quarrels. He is a passionate populist, and a sincere if long-winded one. He twice called for Reagan's impeachment — after the 1983 Grenada invasion and in 1987 amid the Iran-contra scandal — and in the 102nd Congress he introduced resolutions to impeach Bush for conducting the Persian Gulf War.

He can also be stubborn and short-tempered and prone to eruptions of anger, traits that in bygone years helped earn him a reputation in Washington as a high-strung eccentric.

Gonzalez engaged in one of several well-publicized feuds in 1977 during his brief chairmanship of the House Assassinations Committee — a panel he had proposed to investigate the murders of President John F. Kennedy and the Rev. Martin Luther King Jr. Within weeks, Gonzalez fired the panel's top lawyer for allegedly misusing committee funds. With the committee in an uproar, Gonzalez quit a week later, saying the investigation could never succeed because "vast and powerful forces, including the country's most sophisticated crime element, won't stand for it."

Gonzalez's reputation also suffered from his quarrels that have not been merely verbal. In 1963, he threatened to "pistol whip" and then struck a House Republican who claimed Gonzalez's "left-wing voting record" served the socialist-communist cause. In a San Antonio restaurant 23 years later, Gonzalez struck a man who had called him a communist; prosecutors later dropped misdemeanor charges.

At Home: Gonzalez does not campaign in

San Antonio as a voice for Hispanics. "I have never sought public office on an ethnic basis," he says, "and I never will.... I have never palmed myself off as some sort of ethnic leader." But he is a hero to many in his city's Mexican-American neighborhoods, and their votes have helped make him politically unassailable.

Since his original victory in a 1961 special election, Gonzalez has had no electoral problems. But it was different in the beginning for Gonzalez, the son of Mexican immigrants, who began climbing the local political ladder after World War II. He sought office while helping his father, the managing editor of a Spanish-language newspaper, run a translation service.

Gonzalez made it to the state Senate in 1957 and quickly drew attention by filibustering against Democratic Gov. Price Daniel's bill to allow the state to close schools threatened by disturbances surrounding integration.

In 1958 Gonzalez ran as the liberal alternative to Daniel in the Democratic gubernatorial primary. He was beaten by a margin of more than 3-to-1, but the defeat only encouraged his ambition. Three years later, he sought the Senate seat vacated by Lyndon B. Johnson. While Gonzalez carried his home base, Bexar County, his statewide appeal as a candidate with a Hispanic name was limited. He ran sixth out of 73 candidates, gaining 9 percent of the vote.

But he soon had another chance. Later in 1961, Democrat Paul Kilday resigned from the House to accept a judgeship, and Gonzalez became the consensus Democratic candidate for the seat.

The special election was a clear liberal-conservative choice. Gonzalez was warmly endorsed by the Kennedy administration. John Goode, a former GOP county chairman, had the active assistance of Arizona Sen. Barry Goldwater and Texas' newly elected GOP senator, John Tower. With strong support in Hispanic areas, Gonzalez won with 55 percent. He became the first person of Mexican-American extraction to be elected to the House from Texas.

Committee

Banking, Finance & Urban Affairs (Chairman)
Housing & Community Development (chairman); Consumer Credit & Insurance; International Development, Finance, Trade & Monetary Policy

Elections

1992 General

Henry B. Gonzalez (D)	103,755	(100%)

1990 General

Henry B. Gonzalez (D)	56,318	(100%)

Previous Winning Percentages: **1988** (71%) **1986** (100%) **1984** (100%) **1982** (92%) **1980** (82%) **1978** (100%) **1976** (100%) **1974** (100%) **1972** (97%) **1970** (100%) **1968** (82%) **1966** (87%) **1964** (65%) **1962** (100%) **1961 *** (55%)

** Special election.*

District Vote for President

1992

D 81,380 (48%)
R 57,974 (34%)
I 28,966 (17%)

Campaign Finance

	Receipts	Receipts from PACs	Expend-itures
1992			
Gonzalez (D)	$45,040	$11,525 (26%)	$43,147
1990			
Gonzalez (D)	$141,688	$80,800 (57%)	$112,901

Key Votes

1993	
Require parental notification of minors' abortions	N
Require unpaid family and medical leave	Y
Approve national "motor voter" registration bill	Y
Approve budget increasing taxes and reducing deficit	Y
Approve economic stimulus plan	Y
1992	
Approve balanced-budget constitutional amendment	N
Close down space station program	Y
Approve U.S. aid for former Soviet Union	N
Allow shifting funds from defense to domestic programs	Y
1991	
Extend unemployment benefits using deficit financing	Y
Approve waiting period for handgun purchases	Y
Authorize use of force in Persian Gulf	N

Voting Studies

	Presidential Support		Party Unity		Conservative Coalition	
Year	S	O	S	O	S	O
1992	23	77	94	6	38	63
1991	32	67	93	7	16	84
1990	15	85	93	7	22	78
1989	38	62	93	6	20	80
1988	16	82	96	3	13	84
1987	15	85	93	6	21	77
1986	17	82	90	7	10	88
1985	21	74	94	3	15	78
1984	26	72	89	10	20	75
1983	11	88	88	10	31	63
1982	45	53	84	14	34	60
1981	34	64	81	15	31	63

Interest Group Ratings

Year	ADA	AFL-CIO	CCUS	ACU
1992	80	92	38	4
1991	75	100	10	0
1990	100	100	21	4
1989	80	92	30	0
1988	100	100	15	0
1987	96	88	7	9
1986	100	93	17	0
1985	85	88	14	0
1984	95	100	38	13
1983	90	88	10	17
1982	60	80	27	27
1981	70	93	0	7

21 Lamar Smith (R)

Of San Antonio — Elected 1986; 4th Term

Born: Nov. 19, 1947, San Antonio, Texas.
Education: Yale U., B.A. 1969; Southern Methodist U., J.D. 1975.
Occupation: Lawyer; rancher.
Family: Wife, Elizabeth Lynn Schaefer; two children.
Religion: Christian Scientist.
Political Career: Texas House, 1981-82; Bexar County Commissioners Court, 1983-85.
Capitol Office: 2443 Rayburn Bldg. 20515; 225-4236.

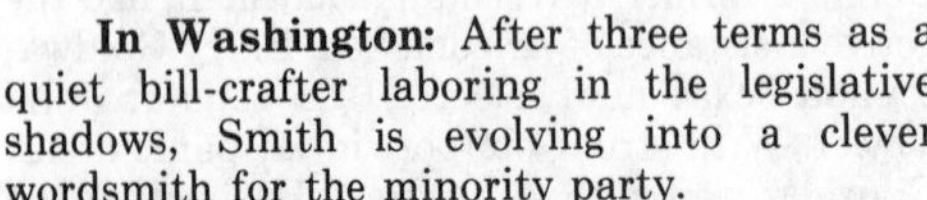

In Washington: After three terms as a quiet bill-crafter laboring in the legislative shadows, Smith is evolving into a clever wordsmith for the minority party.

While Smith's remarks have lacked the nastier, more aggressive edge taken by better-known debaters in both parties, he is recognized for his agility as well as his willingness in sparring with Democrats. At the start of the 103rd Congress, he was given a slot on the Budget Committee and named chairman of the "Theme Team," party leader Robert H. Michel's new 17-member group coordinating the House GOP response to the Clinton administration.

Smith has adroitly merged his interests in budget and immigration issues with his new rhetorical duties, dispensing his own brand of verbal tweaks on a range of conservative topics.

"Mr. Speaker, trial balloons for new taxes proposed by the Clinton administration are hardening into balls and chains around the ankles of American taxpayers," he said in January 1993.

On the subject of legislation allowing people to register to vote when they receive a driver's license, he said: "I am convinced that the bill was named motor-voter with Zoë Baird's chauffeur in mind." (Baird withdrew her nomination for attorney general after acknowledging she had hired illegal aliens to handle domestic chores, including driving.)

"This bill . . . will provide illegal aliens with just one more means to cover their illegal status and thus act as an encouragement for illegal aliens to register [to vote]."

His quips aside, Smith has long sought to have a substantive impact on both fiscal issues and immigration.

As the second-ranking Republican on Judiciary's Immigration subcommittee, Smith is in the right place to monitor immigration developments that may have a dramatic impact on his state. Early in the 103rd, he filed a bill that would require convicted illegal aliens who are subject to deportation to register with government authorities so they can be deported once they are paroled and released.

Smith is concerned that higher immigration would increase joblessness, reduce wages and increase crime. "If you favor increasing immigration," he once said, "you have to take responsibility for the consequences."

When the House passed its immigration measure in 1990, it rejected a number of Smith amendments. Smith sought to limit total immigration to 630,000 a year, the limit set in the Senate bill and favored by the White House. Another Smith amendment that was rejected would have ordered increased federal funds to states to pay for the education and health costs for newly legalized aliens.

Smith did support a number of provisions ultimately included in the legislation, such as streamlining the deportation process for criminal aliens; granting immigration officials greater arrest authority; and adding 20 new judges to speed deportation hearings.

During debate in the 102nd Congress over reauthorizing the Legal Services Corporation, Smith won approval of an amendment prohibiting the LSC from providing assistance to undocumented aliens on matters that did not relate to wages or other employment rights. Smith also wants to tie the rate of immigration to the rate of unemployment in the United States.

On budgetary issues, Smith has pressed for trimming government spending and reducing the federal deficit. He led an effort to cut $142 million from six agencies in the fiscal 1992 budget.

A reliable Republican member on most conservative issues, Smith nevertheless can vote unpredictably, particularly on the complicated issue of abortion. He supports such restrictions on abortion as parental notification and a 24-hour waiting period, and he opposes federal financing for abortions. But Smith opposed President Bush's so-called "gag rule" prohibiting abortion counseling at family-planning clinics that receive federal money.

Smith explains his gag rule vote by saying the question of counseling is a free speech issue, and patients have a right to know all their options. But Smith has opposed lifting the ban

Texas 21

South Central — Western Bexar County; Austin Suburbs

The 21st typifies the lengths to which Texas mapmakers went to divide Democratic and Republican neighborhoods in the 1992 redistricting.

For 350 miles the boundaries of the 21st run in simple, straight blocks, often paralleling county lines. But as the 21st approaches Bexar County, the lines go berserk. Four congressional districts lay claim to portions of the San Antonio-based county, and the 1992 redistricting carved out separate slices for each party. The result: two Democratic House members and two Republicans.

Because of the spaghetti-like lines, several institutions in one district have dramatic influence over the neighboring districts.

Four Air Force bases and the Army's Fort Sam Houston are located in San Antonio. Although none of the bases are in the 21st, the military is believed to be the district's largest employer. The five San Antonio installations generate an estimated $3.4 billion annually and employ more than 70,000 people.

San Antonio's military history goes back centuries; its greatest moment was in 1836 when 183 soldiers fought to defend the Alamo against an attack by the 6,000-man army led by Gen. Antonio Lopez de Santa Anna.

Tourism is the second-largest employer in San Antonio, frequently overlapping with military interests. The Alamo, in the heart of downtown around the corner from a bustling new shopping mall, is a popular attraction. Fort Sam Houston has more than 900 historic buildings and two museums on its 3,300 acres.

Almost a quarter of the people in the 21st live in Bexar County, most in the affluent neighborhoods of San Antonio and its suburbs. The predominantly white residents are well-paid, well-educated professionals — doctors, lawyers, engineers and insurance executives.

As the 21st moves west, the counties become less populous and the economic emphasis shifts to agriculture. Gillespie County is the largest peach-producing county in the state. Peach orchards are also prevalent in Menard County.

The central parts of the district produce a combination of crops and cattle. Pecans, peanuts and hay grow in abundance. The 21st is home to the state's largest goat market, in Kimble County, and the self-proclaimed "sheep and wool capital" of the nation is in Tom Green County.

More than 300 miles west of San Antonio lies San Angelo. The city's Goodfellow Air Force Base is just over the district line but employs many 21st District residents. The 21st takes in the wealthier northwest neighborhoods of the city.

Before redistricting, Rep. Smith represented all of Midland, the West Texas oil center. Today, the 21st shares the city with two other districts.

Midland, Comal, Kerr and Williamson counties, combined with the portions of San Antonio in the 21st, deliver wide margins for Republican candidates.

1990 Population: 566,217. White 517,100 (91%), Black 13,972 (2%), Other 35,145 (6%). Hispanic origin 79,655 (14%). 18 and over 420,498 (74%), 62 and over 91,310 (16%). Median age: 34.

on gays in the military, indicating that he fears it would hurt morale in the services and grant legitimacy to alternative lifestyles.

From the time Smith came to Washington in 1987, he has been voicing concerns about ethical standards in Congress. In particular, he wanted to restrict the lobbying activities of former members of Congress. He cosponsored legislation with Democratic Rep. Barney Frank of Massachusetts to restrict such activities, and the bill cleared Congress only to die at the desk of President Ronald Reagan. A similar bill was ultimately enacted as part of the pay-and-ethics package cleared at the end of 1989.

Smith takes pride in having passed a bill of his own in his first term, and while it was not a major act, it did signal his desire to move legislation. The bill authorized the National Park Service to accept the donation of a 67,000-acre ranch next to Texas' Big Bend National Park.

When he joined the Budget Committee in 1993, Smith temporarily suspended his work on the Science, Space and Technology Committee.

At Home: Though Smith's Yale University background and polished manner are not the first things you might expect from a Texas pol, he has made them work for him. When the 21st was open in 1986, he aggressively courted rural voters and won them over, it would seem, for good. His three subsequent re-elections have been non-events.

Smith spent a year in the Texas House and two years on the Bexar county commission, representing San Antonio suburbs. In 1985, when GOP Rep. Tom Loeffler announced plans to leave the 21st for a gubernatorial campaign,

Smith wasted no time in announcing his own candidacy.

Smith was the moderate in the GOP House runoff against Van Archer, a San Antonio city councilman. Smith finished first by a modest margin in the initial GOP primary and took 53 percent of the runoff vote against Archer.

In the primary and runoff, Smith had to overcome questions about his support of legal abortion (Archer opposed it) and his affiliation with Christian Science. Critics said his religion would prevent him from voting for medical care appropriations — a problem in a district where a medical equipment company was the largest private employer.

But Smith dealt successfully with these problems and benefited from contacts he made in three years as Bexar County Republican chairman. He had the active support of Sen. Phil Gramm, for whom he had organized Bexar County during Gramm's successful 1984 campaign.

Smith's Democratic opponent was former state Sen. Pete Snelson, whose political base in Midland, at the western end of the district, positioned him to play to lingering rural perceptions of Smith as an elitist, big-city lawyer.

But Snelson was plagued by debt from previous campaigns. Smith cast himself as fiscally more conservative and signed a no-tax-increase pledge. He won San Antonio and Midland, overcoming Snelson's rural support.

The 1992 redistricting altered the district's lines but had little impact on its conservative tilt. The wealthy sections of San Antonio, combined with the sprawling counties to the west, helped Smith to a 72 percent share of the vote.

Committees

Budget (8th of 17 Republicans)

Judiciary (8th of 14 Republicans)
Crime & Criminal Justice; International Law, Immigration & Refugees

Elections

1992 General		
Lamar Smith (R)	190,979	(72%)
James M. Gaddy (D)	62,827	(24%)
William E. Grisham (LIBERT)	10,847	(4%)
1990 General		
Lamar Smith (R)	144,570	(75%)
Kirby J. Roberts (D)	48,585	(25%)

Previous Winning Percentages: 1988 (93%) **1986** (61%)

District Vote for President

1992

D 70,402 (25%)
R 143,720 (52%)
I 63,276 (23%)

Campaign Finance

	Receipts	Receipts from PACs		Expend-itures
1992				
Smith (R)	$544,187	$134,839	(25%)	$476,501
Gaddy (D)	$6,916	0		$5,694
1990				
Smith (R)	$679,487	$130,230	(19%)	$399,059
Roberts (D)	$15,763	$43	(0%)	$15,732

Key Votes

1993	
Require parental notification of minors' abortions	Y
Require unpaid family and medical leave	Y
Approve national "motor voter" registration bill	N
Approve budget increasing taxes and reducing deficit	N
Approve economic stimulus plan	N
1992	
Approve balanced-budget constitutional amendment	Y
Close down space station program	N
Approve U.S. aid for former Soviet Union	Y
Allow shifting funds from defense to domestic programs	N
1991	
Extend unemployment benefits using deficit financing	N
Approve waiting period for handgun purchases	N
Authorize use of force in Persian Gulf	Y

Voting Studies

	Presidential Support		Party Unity		Conservative Coalition	
Year	S	O	S	O	S	O
1992	77	21	85	9	96	2
1991	75	23	84	11	95	5
1990	68	31	82	13	91	6
1989	80	14	85	8	95	2
1988	66	32	91	7	97	0
1987	74	25	81	14	95	2

Interest Group Ratings

Year	ADA	AFL-CIO	CCUS	ACU
1992	20	36	88	88
1991	5	25	70	84
1990	11	25	86	83
1989	0	0	100	93
1988	5	23	92	100
1987	0	6	93	96

22 Tom DeLay (R)

Of Sugar Land — Elected 1984; 5th Term

Born: April 8, 1947, Laredo, Texas.
Education: Baylor U., 1965-67; U. of Houston, B.S. 1970.
Occupation: Pest control executive.
Family: Wife, Christine Ann Furrh; one child.
Religion: Baptist.
Political Career: Texas House, 1979-85.
Capitol Office: 407 Cannon Bldg. 20515; 225-5951.

In Washington: Almost from the day he arrived in Congress, DeLay had his sights trained on a leadership post. A lengthy journey that was not without detours finally led him to his goal at the start of the 103rd Congress with his election as Republican Conference secretary, the fifth-ranking position in the House Republican hierarchy.

DeLay's 95-71 victory over Ohioan Bill Gradison establishes him as one of the rising stars in the activist conservative faction that now dominates the GOP conference. It came at the same organizational meeting that elected his Texas ally, Dick Armey, to the No. 3 leadership post of conference chairman.

The Texans complement each other in style: While both are anti-tax, anti-government conservatives, DeLay, a member of the Appropriations Committee, toils more from the inside than Armey, who is more partial to verbal cannonades. A classic Texas wheeler-dealer, DeLay possesses enough pragmatism to allow him to converse with members of the party's more moderate bloc, who have had to fend off charges of apostasy from their more uncompromising conservative brethren.

DeLay's rise is all the more remarkable for his initial foray into GOP internal politics, in which he was dealt a significant setback after backing the losing candidate for minority whip.

Trying to tone down the anti-government fervor he brought to Congress, DeLay positioned himself for advancement in a more establishment-minded House GOP leadership. But when a new generation of conservative Republicans began muscling into power by electing Newt Gingrich as GOP whip in 1989, DeLay, who supported Gingrich's opponent in the whip's race, found himself on the outs.

DeLay went to work bridging the gap, and by the start of the 102nd Congress, it was clear he had succeeded. He won the chairmanship of the House Republican Study Committee, a conservative policy group.

In his first term, DeLay lined up the votes he needed to win a seat on the GOP panel that determines committee assignments and passed the word to a competing colleague that the contest was over. In his second term, he was named an assistant regional whip, and he impressed many Republicans with his instincts and vote-counting skills. He earned a deputy whip slot at the start of the 101st Congress. But DeLay then decided to become chief lieutenant for Illinois' Edward Madigan in his 1989 campaign against Gingrich for the vacant whip post.

DeLay's conservatism, age and Southerner status might have made him a natural Gingrich ally. But Madigan was the favorite of the leaders DeLay had courted since his first term, and the chances were good that if Madigan moved up, so would DeLay. When Madigan lost, Gingrich put his allies at the top of the whip structure, costing DeLay his deputy whip's job. (DeLay still had a plum committee assignment, Appropriations, which he won in 1987.)

DeLay's return to the more confrontational wing of the House GOP became plain during debate on the 1990 budget. He joined the uprising led by Gingrich and voted against the budget summit agreement worked out between top congressional leaders and President Bush.

Throughout his House tenure, DeLay has been known for his impassioned opposition to government regulation, a conviction he developed when he was in the pest control business in Texas. His pro-business predilection was on display during the debate on family leave legislation, which became law in 1993. In the 99th Congress, he was among those who blocked full House consideration of a parental leave bill.

"[T]his bill demonstrates the mind-numbing illogic of setting social norms through paternalistic federal mandates," he said during the 1993 debate. "This bill is unfair, anti-business, anti-growth, invasive, deathly expensive and paid for through a hidden tax. Yep, sounds like Democrats are back in town."

When it comes to bringing money home to Texas, however, DeLay often will set aside his limited-government views. His philosophy on the ultimate deal-cutting committee was captured when he protested a Democratic move to eliminate funding for Vice President Dan

Texas 22

Southwest Houston and suburbs; Fort Bend and Brazoria counties

The 22nd is a testament to Houston's phenomenal growth of the past two decades. During the 1970s, the district was focused within the city. In the 1980s, the 22nd shifted south and west to include newly sprouted suburbs. In the 1992 redistricting, the 22nd was pulled even farther away from Houston, swallowing up the Clear Lake neighborhood in the east. Once a city-based district, the 22nd of the 1990s has more voters outside Harris County (Houston) than in it.

The influx of Houston professionals boosted Harris County's population by 38 percent in the 1970s and by 17 percent in the 1980s.

Yet the most astronomical growth has occurred just outside Harris County, in neighboring Fort Bend. The county population jumped 150 percent in the 1970s and 72 percent the following decade. Sugar Land, formed in the 1820s around the sugar industry, has become one of the most popular new suburbs. Signs of Sugar Land's new appeal are evident everywhere: new retail shops, new homes and new banks. First Colony is a planned community in Sugar Land that offers some houses for less than $100,000 and others that cost millions.

The common theme running through the contorted 22nd is the district's universally conservative outlook.

GOP Rep. DeLay took an impressive 69 percent in his new district in 1992 and Republican George Bush ran well ahead of his statewide total in the 22nd. If anything, the 1992 redistricting made the 22nd even more Republican. In Brazoria and Fort Bend counties, Republicans performed well at every level, from Bush to railroad commissioners to judges; the rare exception was an occasional county post.

The residents tend to be more involved in religion, better paid (the median household income is between $37,500 and $40,000) and better educated (25 percent of the district's residents have at least an associate degree) than the state as a whole.

Houston executives who tired of long commutes have bought property in Bellaire and West University Place, tearing down the older, smaller homes and replacing them with expensive, modern versions.

NASA's Johnson Space Center, in the adjacent 9th District, is a major employer for the 22nd and probably the single reason why the Clear Lake Area has grown. The massive complex southeast of Houston is designing and building components of the space station *Freedom*, a project that is undergoing revisions that could mean a loss of jobs at the space center.

Once past the Houston suburb of Pearland, Brazoria County rapidly turns rural. Rice, sorghum and cattle are major revenue producers in this sparsely populated region. Beyond the district boundaries down to the Gulf Coast, Brazoria County also includes oil and gas wells and 20 miles of natural beaches. Commercial fishing and tourism provide revenue in this part of the county, which is in the adjacent 14th District.

1990 Population: 566,217. White 435,660 (77%), Black 44,266 (8%), Other 86,291 (15%). Hispanic origin 90,920 (16%). 18 and over 406,687 (72%), 62 and over 47,645 (8%). Median age: 32.

Quayle's Council on Competitiveness. "Partisanship is unworthy of this committee," he said.

Like most of the state delegation, DeLay supports funding for the $8 billion-plus superconducting super collider, which is being built in Texas. In 1990 he opposed two of three attempts to cut its funding, voting only for a 2 percent funding cut for the giant atom smasher. He opposed efforts in the 102nd Congress to kill the project.

He is also an enthusiastic booster of another big-ticket project with a Texas connection, the $30 billion-plus space station *Freedom.* During a 1992 debate on an amendment to scuttle project funding, he asked: "Can you deprive your state and your constituents of this important source of jobs and revenue?" DeLay is now better-situated to push for space station funds: In the 103rd Congress, he joined the Appropriations panel that funds space programs, the Subcommittee on VA, HUD and Independent Agencies.

On Appropriations' Transportation Subcommittee, DeLay generally advocates allowing the private sector to supply mass transit services, but he also works to bring Houston what he considers its "fair return" on tax payments. Yet he fought for two years to block his hometown from getting money to build a controversial new monorail system. Though he says he is not anti-transit, many voters oppose the system, which would link downtown Houston with DeLay's outlying suburban district.

In 1990, he won his request to lower the amount of transit funding for Houston from $38 million to $30 million because the city was not spending previous funds fast enough. In 1991, he battled Texas' two senators, Democrat Lloyd Bentsen and Republican Phil Gramm, to keep Houston from getting monorail funds. The House accepted DeLay's request for zero funding, but during conference, DeLay cut a deal with the senators: Houston would get the $30 million included in the Senate's version, but the bill would specify that the money could not be used on the monorail absent a "strong consensus."

That put DeLay in the awkward position of convincing conferees that Houston should get the $30 million he had previously opposed. It angered some of his House colleagues, but they still grudgingly accepted the $30 million.

At Home: When Republican Rep. Ron Paul announced his candidacy for the Senate in 1984, DeLay quickly became the front-runner to fill the 22nd District seat. A six-year veteran of the Texas House, DeLay already had represented parts of the 22nd's constituency, and his efforts to scale back government during his days in the Legislature stood him in good stead in a district whose residents demand an adherence to conservative orthodoxy.

But DeLay did not capture the GOP nomination easily. The eleventh-hour entrance of J. C. Helms, a wealthy real estate developer from Bellaire, gave DeLay a scare. Helms had had some success in the neighboring 25th District two years earlier, finishing first in the GOP primary but failing to convert on his momentum in the runoff. His alliance with hard-right conservatives in the Harris County (Houston) GOP further heightened the impression that he might manage to force a runoff with DeLay.

Helms sought to outflank DeLay on the right, casting himself as the natural philosophical heir to the libertarian Paul. DeLay offered a more mainstream conservative approach. He cited his experience as owner of a pest control company to demonstrate knowledge of small business and called for a balanced budget.

Helms created a stir late in the campaign by running radio ads accusing DeLay of being late in paying payroll taxes from his business — a charge DeLay acknowledged while reminding Helms that the taxes were eventually paid. Visiting up to 60 homes a day, DeLay held his own in Harris County and won easily in his home base of Fort Bend. He clinched the GOP nomination with 54 percent. Since then, his elections have been a breeze.

The political makeup of the 22nd changed little in the 1992 redistricting, and DeLay had no problem thwarting a challenge from a little-known teacher who had difficulty making the case that the fiscal conservative had lost touch with his constituents.

Committee

Conference Secretary

Appropriations (11th of 23 Republicans)
Transportation; Veterans Affairs, Housing & Urban Development & Independent Agencies

Elections

1992 General		
Tom DeLay (R)	150,221	(69%)
Richard Konrad (D)	67,812	(31%)
1990 General		
Tom DeLay (R)	93,425	(71%)
Bruce Director (D)	37,721	(29%)

Previous Winning Percentages: **1988** (67%) **1986** (72%) **1984** (65%)

District Vote for President

1992
D 63,175 (27%)
R 116,614 (51%)
I 50,732 (22%)

Campaign Finance

	Receipts	Receipts from PACs		Expend-itures
1992				
DeLay (R)	$338,826	$225,613	(67%)	$360,136
Konrad (D)	$40,621	$630	(2%)	$39,836
1990				
DeLay (R)	$324,134	$168,475	(52%)	$297,153

Key Votes

1993	
Require parental notification of minors' abortions	Y
Require unpaid family and medical leave	N
Approve national "motor voter" registration bill	N
Approve budget increasing taxes and reducing deficit	N
Approve economic stimulus plan	N
1992	
Approve balanced-budget constitutional amendment	Y
Close down space station program	N
Approve U.S. aid for former Soviet Union	N
Allow shifting funds from defense to domestic programs	N
1991	
Extend unemployment benefits using deficit financing	N
Approve waiting period for handgun purchases	N
Authorize use of force in Persian Gulf	Y

Voting Studies

	Presidential Support		Party Unity		Conservative Coalition	
Year	**S**	**O**	**S**	**O**	**S**	**O**
1992	82	16	90	7	92	6
1991	75	20	89	5	92	0
1990	83	16	91	5	98	2
1989	79	19	87	8	90	5
1988	78	18	88	7	97	0
1987	78	19	91	5	100	0
1986	83	14	91	4	100	0
1985	85	13	87	7	96	4

Interest Group Ratings

Year	ADA	AFL-CIO	CCUS	ACU
1992	5	8	71	100
1991	5	9	90	100
1990	6	8	93	92
1989	0	0	80	96
1988	0	0	92	100
1987	0	0	93	100
1986	0	7	94	100
1985	5	0	95	100

23 Henry Bonilla (R)

Of San Antonio — Elected 1992; 1st Term

Born: Jan. 2, 1954, San Antonio, Texas.
Education: U. of Texas, Austin, B.A. 1976.
Occupation: Television executive.
Family: Wife, Deborah Knapp; two children.
Religion: Baptist.
Political Career: No previous office.
Capitol Office: 1529 Longworth Bldg. 20515; 225-4511.

The Path to Washington: Border-community Hispanics who supported Democrat Bill Clinton helped Bonilla become the first Hispanic Republican to represent Texas in Congress. His election also symbolized the increased clout of Hispanic Republicans in the state.

To reward him, fellow Texas Republican Bill Archer of Texas helped Bonilla win a seat on the Appropriations Committee. The job of "controlling the purse strings of America," as Bonilla put it, should help him retain the seat in the heavily Democratic 23rd.

On two projects important to Texas, Bonilla said early in the 103rd Congress that he supports the superconducting super collider, but has questions about the space station.

Bonilla worked at several television stations across the country before returning to his native San Antonio to work as a public affairs executive for a local station.

Although a political neophyte, Bonilla made great hay out of Rep. Albert G. Bustamante's many liabilities. It is difficult to say whether Bonilla deserves the credit, or Bustamante the blame, for the election outcome.

Bonilla's recipe for success relied on many of the same ingredients Bustamante used to oust Rep. Abraham Kazen Jr. in 1984. Then, it was Bustamante, the son of migrant farmers, who argued that the incumbent was inaccessible and ineffective.

By 1992, Bustamante was the one viewed as out of touch with his constituents, considered to be some of the poorest people in the country.

The House bank scandal also wounded the incumbent. Bustamante's 30 "cheques calientes" offended voters who said they struggled to balance their checkbooks each month. Bonilla found the Spanish phrase for "hot checks" to be one of his most effective campaign lines.

While some were willing to forgive the overdrafts as shoddy bookkeeping, few could swallow Bustamante's purchase of a $500,000 home in the ritzy Dominion neighborhood of San Antonio.

While Bustamante worked on Capitol Hill, Bonilla took a leave of absence to drive across the lower half of the state shaking hands in general stores and coffee shops. Everywhere he went, Bonilla introduced himself as an agent of change, chatting in Spanish with many residents. The technique paid off in the district, which is 63 percent Hispanic.

Bonilla was temporarily tripped up in the fall by accusations that his anchorwoman wife, Deborah Knapp, used a telephone and computer at her news station for campaign work. But the popular TV couple turned the controversy into an asset. Knapp took a leave of absence, hit the trail introducing herself as Deborah Bonilla and immediately became a star attraction for the candidate.

Bonilla supports balanced-budget legislation, a line-item veto and term limits of two four-year terms for House members. The term-limit proposal is a bit of a twist from many of the plans being touted. He supports a four-year term because he says too much time is devoted to fundraising in a two-year cycle.

Bonilla arrived in Washington promising to watch out for small-business interests. He was endorsed by the U.S. Chamber of Commerce, and he advocates cutting paperwork and taxes for new and small businesses.

Bonilla opposes raising the minimum wage and is eager to move forward with the North American Free Trade Agreement, predicting that it will bring much-needed revenue to his poverty-stricken district.

A press secretary to former Pennsylvania Gov. Richard Thornburgh, Bonilla is an ardent supporter of the death penalty and wants to restrict appeals for convicted criminals.

Despite his conservative views, Bonilla attracted independents and Democrats to his first bid for office. During the campaign, supporters in the Democratic border town of Del Rio sported Clinton buttons with their Bonilla stickers.

One of the country's few prominent Hispanic Republicans, Bonilla was touted by the national GOP and was given the high-profile task of delivering the GOP response to an important Clinton radio address in February 1993.

Texas 23

Southwest — Laredo; San Antonio suburbs

Tough times have beset many in the 23rd, Texas' largest House district. In its far western reaches, defunct oil wells dot the landscape. Along the hundreds of miles of Mexican border that mark the southern limit of the district are impoverished immigrants, many of them living in some of Texas' most destitute villages and towns.

Eight of the 20 poorest counties in the state are in the 23rd. Half of the people in Zavala and Maverick counties fall below the poverty level. The median household income for the entire district is under $22,500, well below the median for the state. And some local officials say those figures are high, claiming that minorities along the Mexican border were undercounted in the 1990 census.

The border communities often seem to have more in common with their Mexican neighbors than with the rest of Texas. Laredo (Webb County) celebrates Mexican Independence Day and is connected to its Mexican sister city, Nuevo Laredo, by three bridges. Nine of 10 people in Webb County are Hispanic. A private 1993 study of census data concluded that Laredo has one of the highest poverty rates in the nation.

All along the border, people find work in *maquiladoras* — twin-plant manufacturing operations in which the bulk of production work is done by lower-cost labor in a Mexican facility and then finishing work is handled at a U.S. plant. Clothing and heavy machinery are common products. Other immigrants work the land, earning their keep from vegetables, cotton, sheep and goats.

Residents on both sides of the Rio Grande get together for work, entertainment and sometimes to cooperate on regional political issues. In 1992, officials from Del Rio (U.S.) and Coahuila (Mexico) jointly opposed construction of two hazardous waste facilities along the border.

About 70 percent of the district's residents are minority-group members; 63 percent are Hispanic. Typically the minority vote goes Democratic, but that tradition was upset in 1992 as Bonilla became Texas' first Hispanic Republican in Congress.

Bonilla benefited from 1992 redistricting, which added 21 counties to the 23rd, and from voter antipathy toward Democratic Rep. Albert G. Bustamante. Also, Bonilla's conservative, less-government pitch played well with the district's independent-minded ranchers and oilmen and with affluent voters in the Bexar County suburbs of San Antonio. The biggest single bloc of votes in the 23rd — nearly 30 percent — comes from Bexar County, and George Bush won the area with a decisive 58 percent in 1992. But in other parts of the 23rd, many who backed Bonilla supported Bill Clinton for president. Districtwide, Clinton edged Bush by one point, 42-41.

Because of redistricting in 1992, several of San Antonio's military installations are out of the 23rd. But their presence is still felt. Brooks and Randolph Air Force bases, located just outside the 23rd, continue to be major employers. The flight training center at Laughlin Air Force Base and part of Fort Bliss are in the district.

1990 Population: 566,217. White 418,282 (74%), Black 16,484 (3%), Other 131,451 (23%). Hispanic origin 354,149 (63%). 18 and over 374,947 (66%), 62 and over 63,204 (11%). Median age: 29.

Committee

Appropriations (23rd of 23 Republicans)
District of Columbia; Labor, Health & Human Services, Education & Related Agencies

Campaign Finance

1992	Receipts	Receipts from PACs		Expenditures
Bonilla (R)	$588,673	$109,888	(19%)	$594,032
Bustamante (D)	$466,029	$263,986	(57%)	$758,453

Key Votes

1993

Require parental notification of minors' abortions	Y
Require unpaid family and medical leave	N
Approve national "motor voter" registration bill	N
Approve budget increasing taxes and reducing deficit	N
Approve economic stimulus plan	N

Elections

1992 General		
Henry Bonilla (R)	98,259	(59%)
Albert G. Bustamante (D)	63,797	(38%)
David Alter (LIBERT)	4,291	(3%)
1992 Primary		
Henry Bonilla (R)	9,013	(63%)
Dick Bowen (R)	5,216	(37%)

District Vote for President

1992

D	72,452 (42%)
R	70,577 (41%)
I	28,846 (17%)

24 Martin Frost (D)

Of Dallas — Elected 1978; 8th Term

Born: Jan. 1, 1942, Glendale, Calif.
Education: U. of Missouri, B.A., B.J. 1964; Georgetown U., J.D. 1970.
Military Service: Army Reserve, 1966-72.
Occupation: Lawyer.
Family: Wife, Valerie Hall; three children.
Religion: Jewish.
Political Career: Sought Democratic nomination for U.S. House, 1974.
Capitol Office: 2459 Rayburn Bldg. 20515; 225-3605.

In Washington: Though job security is an underlying goal of the activities of many members of Congress, Frost spent much of the 1980s and the 102nd Congress planning and implementing his party's redistricting strategy and fending off potential challenges to his own political career.

He chaired IMPAC 2000, the Democrats' organization that sought to prepare grass-roots Democrats to make the most of their opportunities following the reapportionment of the House after the 1990 census. His efforts were rewarded at the start of the 103rd Congress when he was named a floor whip, one of the top jobs in the Democratic whip organization.

Frost had a special interest in the issue because population shifts made it likely that a new majority-minority district would be created in Dallas, with much of it being taken from Frost's political base.

However, after extensive lobbying and contributing $42,200 to state legislators from a newly created PAC, Frost got a district that should see him safely through the 1990s. Dallas also got a new majority-minority district, which promptly elected former Democratic state Sen. Eddie Bernice Johnson, who had chaired the state Senate's redistricting committee.

Johnson had long been critical of court orders in the early 1980s that failed to create a majority-minority district in Dallas. Frost had been a beneficiary of those orders, as they left plenty of Democratic minority voters in his district. But Johnson and Frost cooperated in the 1992 round of redistricting.

Frost took a hand in protesting the Commerce Department's refusal to adjust the 1990 census to redress an apparent undercount of minorities. He said the guidelines set by the department stacked the deck against an adjustment. Explaining why the administration proposed the guidelines, Frost said, "Clearly, an adjustment would benefit Democrats, and it would be harmful to Republicans." The Census Bureau recommended adjustment, but the Commerce Department rejected the recommendation.

As part of his efforts to help the Democrats in redistricting, Frost managed to go a bit too far. He heads a Democratic Caucus panel that offered a proposal in December 1990 that would have allowed members of Congress to accept unlimited contributions to pay legal costs of redistricting. But House Democrats ditched the idea after it met with harsh criticism that it looked like a slush fund for incumbents.

Frost's efforts on redistricting were consonant with his role as a House insider. One of his mentors had been former House Speaker Jim Wright of Fort Worth, who helped him to his seats on the Budget Committee and, later, on Rules.

A shrewd institutional player, Frost still holds seats on both the Rules and the House Administration committees, where he can have an impact in his own right. And party leaders still can count on Frost despite Wright's absence; Frost voted with the Democratic majority more than 80 percent of the time in 1992.

Partly in recognition of his party service and loyalty, Frost was named in April 1990 to head a task force to help the new Eastern Europe democracies. The task force visited Czechoslovakia, Poland and Hungary and set up a program of technological assistance for the newly formed parliaments of those countries.

Frost remains actively involved in the ongoing fight for funding the superconducting super collider (SSC), most of which will be located in his new district. But in 1992, SSC supporters were stunned when the House voted to kill it. A counteroffensive by the Bush administration and Senate supporters saved the project.

He also went to Japan in early 1993 to encourage a $1 billion Japanese investment in the project. And when the General Accounting Office issued a report critical of the SSC, Frost called it a "flawed analysis" offered as part of an effort to derail the project.

In 1993, he had to fight for another local cause when Defense Secretary Les Aspin included the Dallas Naval Air Station on a list of military facilities recommended for closure. The station's closing would cost the Dallas area

Texas 24

Parts of Dallas and Tarrant counties

The blue-collar laborers living in the 24th have borne the brunt of the economic woes in the Dallas-Fort Worth metroplex. A military base is closing, a semiconductor company went through bankruptcy reorganization and defense contractors have laid off thousands. Highly trained engineers find themselves doing manual labor; factory workers are jobless.

Carswell Air Force Base, once home to 6,500 military personnel, has been reducing staff since 1991 and will shut down by the end of 1993.

When the government canceled the A-12 stealth attack plane in early 1991, more than 3,500 workers at the Fort Worth General Dynamics plant lost their jobs. Bought in 1993 by Lockheed, the contractor is struggling to rebuild.

Bell Helicopter Textron is largely reliant on the experimental V-22 Osprey helicopter, a project that has continued to receive research funds — but no construction money as of mid-1993.

Former aerospace giant LTV Corp. filed for Chapter 11 protection in 1986 and has since sold its aerospace division to two companies. The new companies, which still make components of the B-2 bomber and C-17 cargo planes, are laying off workers and taking other belt-tightening measures.

Most of the contractors are trying to lessen their dependence on military dollars by targeting foreign governments and private businesses, but diversification efforts are slow. One company, however, is taking a different tack. Turbomeca recently entered a joint venture to build engines for the T-45 Goshawk, a Navy training plane.

The General Motors plant in Arlington and the Dallas-Fort Worth International Airport are major employers for the residents of the 24th.

Although the 24th is dominated geographically by Navarro and Ellis counties in the south, its population base is in Tarrant and Dallas counties. The two northern counties account for 80 percent of the votes in the 24th, making it a predominantly urban district. Many of the factory workers and GM retirees live in the North Oak Cliff section of Dallas and the portions of Arlington in the 24th.

The 1992 redistricting shifted most of the minority voters from the old 24th into the 30th, a new majority-black district. The few remaining black neighborhoods in the 24th are in Southeast Fort Worth. Blacks living in Forest Hill, Poly and Stop 6 often work in area hospitals or at the airport.

To the south, Navarro County boasts the longest continuous oil flow in the state; more than 200 million barrels since 1895. The rest of the county's economy is split between livestock and crops.

The multibillion-dollar superconducting super collider is being built in Ellis County, split between the 24th and the 6th.

The 24th is favorable territory for Democratic candidates. Bill Clinton's 1992 finish exceeded his statewide tally. Ann W. Richards won the 24th in her successful 1990 gubernatorial race.

1990 Population: 566,217. White 364,542 (64%), Black 108,340 (19%), Other 93,335 (16%). Hispanic origin 123,540 (22%). 18 and over 396,176 (70%), 62 and over 59,560 (11%). Median age: 29.

1,374 military and 268 civilian jobs.

Frost was a member of the Democratic task force on campaign finance reform whose final product was passed by the House in the 102nd Congress. But he opposed the subsequent agreement forged in conference with the Senate because it would have limited the amount of money that state parties contribute to campaigns.

The Texas Democratic Party developed a coordinated campaign with congressional candidates that helped Gov. Ann W. Richards win her race against a Republican millionaire who spent his own money liberally.

Frost's soft voice and shy smile suggest a self-effacing personality. But he is a man of calculating ambition and no small amount of self-esteem. Even some who admire his political instincts consider him at times too strong-willed, and wanting in finesse.

As ingratiating as he was with Wright, Frost has crossed swords with some other powerful members. Frost's efforts to defend industrial development bonds held up progress on tax bills in the early 1980s; the moves did not do much to endear him to Ways and Means Committee Chairman Dan Rostenkowski of Illinois.

At Home: Frost demonstrated his resilience in 1992 when he overcame a difficult redistricting and his first Republican challenger in six years. The redrawn 24th was about 60 percent new for him, and Republicans saw opportunity in the new lines. Dallas trust administrator Steve Masterson waged an aggressive campaign that took aim at Frost on political and personal issues.

Masterson filed complaints with the House

Commission on Congressional Mailing Standards and filed lawsuits in federal court, accusing Frost of abusing the free mailing privilege. He also accused Frost of voting to force the Boy Scouts to accept homosexual Scoutmasters. The former charges were all dismissed and the latter related to a procedural vote. In the end, they availed Masterson little.

Frost got to Congress in 1978 by defeating incumbent Dale Milford in a primary, something he had failed to do four years earlier. In 1974, Frost complained that Milford was too supportive of the Nixon administration. But the incumbent withstood the challenge to win the Democratic primary with 58 percent of the vote. On his second try, Frost revived his complaints that Milford was too conservative. He also built an effective precinct organization and was endorsed by the state AFL-CIO and two of the largest newspapers in the area. He beat Milford, drawing 55 percent.

Frost's Republican rival that November tried to turn the tables, claiming that Frost was a tool of organized labor and too liberal for the district. But Frost won with 54 percent.

For a moment in 1982, it seemed Frost might be in trouble. The Legislature had redrawn his district to be 64 percent black and Hispanic, and professor Lucy Patterson, the first black woman elected to the Dallas City Council, planned a primary challenge, hoping minority voters would unite behind her.

But Frost gathered early endorsements from many minority leaders. And then, the district's boundaries were changed again before the Democratic primary. A three-judge federal panel undid the Legislature's work, making the 24th a white-majority district with a combined black and Hispanic population just under 50 percent. With the court-drawn lines, there were not enough minority voters in the 24th to sustain Patterson's primary challenge. She switched parties, and Frost swamped her, taking more than 70 percent.

That experience bolstered Frost's confidence for 1984. He spent much of his time early in the year organizing the Texas presidential primary campaign of Colorado Democratic Sen. Gary Hart, then signed on as a state coordinator for Walter F. Mondale after Hart was beaten. Frost won re-election with 59 percent while the district went to President Ronald Reagan. In 1986, Frost reached 67 percent; in the next two elections, the GOP left him alone entirely.

Committees

House Administration (5th of 12 Democrats)
Accounts (chairman); Elections; Libraries & Memorials; Office Systems

Rules (4th of 9 Democrats)
Legislative Process

Joint Library

Elections

1992 General		
Martin Frost (D)	104,174	(60%)
Steve Masterson (R)	70,042	(40%)
1990 General		
Martin Frost (D)	86,297	(100%)

Previous Winning Percentages: **1988** (93%) **1986** (67%) **1984** (59%) **1982** (73%) **1980** (61%) **1978** (54%)

District Vote for President

1992

D	73,019	(41%)
R	60,020	(33%)
I	46,811	(26%)

Campaign Finance

	Receipts	Receipts from PACs		Expend-itures
1992				
Frost (D)	$1,241,725	$667,804	(54%)	$1,549,556
Masterson (R)	$109,317	$15,370	(14%)	$109,306
1990				
Frost (D)	$679,688	$411,405	(61%)	$597,310

Key Votes

1993	
Require parental notification of minors' abortions	N
Require unpaid family and medical leave	Y
Approve national "motor voter" registration bill	Y
Approve budget increasing taxes and reducing deficit	Y
Approve economic stimulus plan	Y
1992	
Approve balanced-budget constitutional amendment	Y
Close down space station program	N
Approve U.S. aid for former Soviet Union	Y
Allow shifting funds from defense to domestic programs	Y
1991	
Extend unemployment benefits using deficit financing	Y
Approve waiting period for handgun purchases	Y
Authorize use of force in Persian Gulf	Y

Voting Studies

	Presidential Support		Party Unity		Conservative Coalition	
Year	**S**	**O**	**S**	**O**	**S**	**O**
1992	30	66	82	11	71	29
1991	35	61	80	10	54	43
1990	22	77	91	5	43	57
1989	38	58	86	8	39	61
1988	21	66	84	5	37	42
1987	31	67	83	9	60	30
1986	23	66	74	11	52	38
1985	26	69	83	9	47	47
1984	33	48	63	14	42	47
1983	34	59	79	13	48	47
1982	34	58	82	12	40	59
1981	34	38	70	17	52	41

Interest Group Ratings

Year	ADA	AFL-CIO	CCUS	ACU
1992	75	73	57	25
1991	65	100	20	20
1990	67	100	14	8
1989	75	82	40	4
1988	70	92	23	9
1987	88	93	29	0
1986	55	73	43	26
1985	55	82	35	24
1984	65	100	36	25
1983	75	82	20	22
1982	70	85	23	10
1981	50	77	24	14

25 Michael A. Andrews (D)

Of Houston — Elected 1982; 6th Term

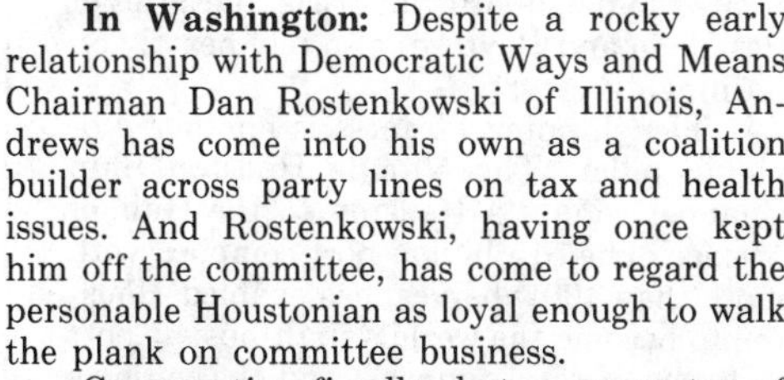

Born: Feb. 7, 1944, Houston, Texas.
Education: U. of Texas, B.A. 1967; Southern Methodist U., J.D. 1970.
Occupation: Lawyer.
Family: Wife, Ann Bowman; two children.
Religion: Episcopalian.
Political Career: Democratic nominee for U.S. House, 1980.
Capitol Office: 303 Cannon Bldg. 20515; 225-7508.

In Washington: Despite a rocky early relationship with Democratic Ways and Means Chairman Dan Rostenkowski of Illinois, Andrews has come into his own as a coalition builder across party lines on tax and health issues. And Rostenkowski, having once kept him off the committee, has come to regard the personable Houstonian as loyal enough to walk the plank on committee business.

Conservative fiscally, but a supporter of abortion rights (including abortions paid for by Medicaid), Andrews long has been regarded as a man with the looks and the yen to run for statewide office. But his ambition has not been matched by good opportunities.

He might have run for the Senate had Texas Democrat Lloyd Bentsen been elected vice president in 1988. He might have seen a new path had Democrat Ann W. Richards not been elected governor in 1990. His closest brush came in 1993, when Bentsen resigned his Senate seat to become Treasury secretary. Andrews was mentioned as a likely replacement but was handicapped by close ties to Houston business interests and spotty support from organized labor. His 121 overdrafts at the House bank were perhaps the final straw, and Richards appointed former Rep. Bob Krueger.

Despite all that, Andrews has seemed content to focus on the task at hand and has proved himself at ease working the levers of legislative compromise in the House.

In the 102nd Congress Andrews was the chief House engineer of a plan to partially reverse a central element of the 1986 tax code rewrite. In an effort to put an end to commercial real estate construction projects that were driven by tax benefits and not by their economic value, Congress in 1986 barred the use of losses on rental property from offsetting non-rental income. Andrews concluded that the change went too far. He devised a compromise to allow real estate development professionals (not the lawyers and dentists who used to invest in limited real estate partnerships) to offset development income with rental losses. The change was incorporated into two separate tax bills that cleared Congress in 1992, but which died under President George Bush's veto.

Andrews was more successful with a comprehensive energy bill enacted in 1992, winning inclusion of tax credits for vehicles that use alternative fuels. And he further aided his Houston constituency by leading the fight in committee to delete a requirement that would have required petroleum producers and importers to give 1 percent of their oil to the government's Strategic Petroleum Reserve or pay an equivalent cash tax. His amendment to strike the provision was adopted 23-12.

During floor consideration in 1990 of a civil rights bill, Andrews teamed with North Carolina Democrat Stephen L. Neal to offer a compromise to deflect objections that the bill would require racial quotas. Their amendment was adopted 397-24, but the bill died when the Senate failed to override Bush's veto.

In 1992 Andrews weighed into the middle of the health-care debate by cosponsoring a "managed competition" bill. The proposal included a controversial plan to limit tax deductions for employer-paid health insurance to encourage competition and cut costs.

Andrews showed further evidence of his desire to have a say in the most contentious issues by joining both the Budget and Joint Economic committees in the 103rd Congress.

When Andrews first attempted to land a seat on Ways and Means in 1985, Rostenkowski objected, believing that Andrews was not enough of a party loyalist. But Andrews faced no opposition when a new vacancy on the panel opened in mid-1986, and he set immediately to prove his worth to the chairman.

In 1987, Andrews devised a compromise floor amendment for a welfare overhaul bill that drew enough support to stave off a conservative proposal that sponsors feared would have gutted the committee's bill.

The next year, Rostenkowski appointed Andrews head of a task force to defeat Florida Democrat Claude Pepper's initiative to provide long-term care at home to disabled and elderly people. Rostenkowski was furious that Pepper

Texas 25

South Houston and suburbs

Downtown Houston is an array of glittering towers, but the city has several skylines instead of just the traditional one. With no current zoning regulations, clusters of skyscrapers are scattered across Houston.

The most-populous city in Texas and the fourth-largest in the nation, Houston and Harris County have the headquarters or major corporate offices of more than 200 firms. Eighteen companies on the 1992 Fortune 500 list and 21 on the 1992 Forbes 500 list call Houston home. The city hosts a thriving arts community, diverse and innovative restaurants and prestigious Rice University and its 4,100 students.

The lines of the 25th were given numerous new contortions in 1992 redistricting to accommodate establishment of the neighboring 29th District, which is majority-Hispanic.

But the 25th, based in southern and eastern Harris County, remains an ethnically diverse, urbanized district with growing populations of blacks (27 percent of the district's population), Hispanics (17 percent) and Asians (4 percent).

Minority-group voters and blue-collar residents in Pasadena and Deer Park help give Democrats a solid base in the 25th.

In 1992, Rep. Andrews won re-election with a solid 56 percent, despite the new lines and a vigorous Republican challenger. In presidential voting, Bill Clinton outdistanced Houstonian George Bush by 11 points in the 25th.

In 1990, Democrats Ann W. Richards, Bob Bullock and Dan Morales all topped 56 percent in the 25th in their successful campaigns for governor, lieutenant governor and attorney general, respectively.

For many in the 25th, life revolves around petroleum-based products, although the Houston-area economy has diversified since the oil industry took a sharp turn down in the mid-1980s. Employment in the oil and gas industries accounted for 68 percent of Houston's economic base in 1981; by 1993 it was down to 42 percent. Harris County has the nation's largest concentration of petrochemical plants and related businesses. Although more refineries are located in neighboring districts, the cities of Pasadena and Baytown also rely heavily on refining.

The shipping business is another economic pillar. The 50-mile Houston Ship Channel connects Houston to the Gulf of Mexico. The $15 billion port complex, with more than 100 wharves, has enabled Houston to become the world's sixth-busiest port in terms of total tonnage, and the nation's largest in foreign tonnage.

The Texas Medical Center is the largest private employer in the 25th. The 650-acre complex has 41 member institutions, including 14 hospitals, two medical schools and four nursing schools. The center is credited with directly contributing $4 billion to the Houston economy each year.

Although the Johnson Space Center is now in the 9th District, it continues to draw a substantial share of its work force from the 25th.

1990 Population: 566,217. White 343,593 (61%), Black 152,574 (27%), Other 70,050 (12%). Hispanic origin 94,525 (17%). 18 and over 405,030 (72%), 62 and over 50,180 (9%). Median age: 30.

had used his Rules Committee chairmanship to bypass Ways and Means over the proposal to pay for the program by raising the Medicare tax. When senior citizens deluged the Capitol with bags of green peppers to show support for Pepper, Andrews said he felt "like cannon fodder" mobilizing opposition. In the end, however, enough members gulped at the cost to keep the bill off the floor by a vote of 169-243.

Andrews' relations with the chairman hit a sour note in 1989, when Andrews was part of the "Gang of Six" committee Democrats who allied with Republicans to send a steep cut in the tax on income from capital gains to the floor over Rostenkowski's objections. The measure passed the House but later died in the Senate. Andrews' subsequent success on the panel would indicate that the wound has healed.

Though he long since has left his previous assignment on the Science, Space and Technology Committee, Andrews remains a protector of the Johnson Space Center and particularly of work there on the space station *Freedom*, which puts $385 million a year into Houston's economy.

At Home: On paper, the odds were stacked against Andrews in his 1992 re-election bid, his slimmest victory ever. His overdrafts at the House bank, support for a congressional pay raise, changes in the district's makeup and a female GOP opponent who supported abortion rights all signaled a grueling fall for Andrews.

But what the inside-the-Beltway analyses failed to account for was the strength of his constituent service and his dedication to one-on-one campaigning.

Dolly Madison McKenna was a well-financed, well-connected, moderate GOP businesswoman in search of a district. But instead of the heavily Republican district McKenna was hoping for, the 1992 redistricting created a new Hispanic district. That left McKenna the 25th, where Andrews' ties to downtown cut into McKenna's likely base.

McKenna made headway in the anti-Washington, "Year of the Woman" climate, criticizing Andrews as the typical insider. But he responded using every resource he had. He hired political scientists to analyze the new district and traveled home constantly. He collected $528,000 from political action committees and spent $1.4 million (ranking him the 17th-biggest spender). He also sent a check to the Treasury for $2,420, representing $20 for each overdraft. And voters were slow to criticize Andrews for the overdrafts, in light of his previous good service and his warm personality.

McKenna finished with a respectable 70,000 votes in Harris County, but Andrews prevailed with 56 percent.

Andrews' quest for Congress began in the 1980 Democratic primary in the old 22nd District, held by GOP Rep. Ron Paul. Former Democratic Rep. Bob Gammage, seeking to reclaim the seat he had lost to Paul in 1978, was viewed as stale by Democratic financiers. That helped Andrews, who ran a close second in the primary and beat Gammage in the runoff.

If there had been no presidential contest, Andrews probably would have won in 1980. But Ronald Reagan's strong showing in the 22nd gave Paul a narrow 51 percent victory.

In 1981, however, redistricting created a new, heavily Democratic 25th District. Andrews, the front-runner from the start, found himself in a runoff with state District Judge John Ray Harrison.

Harrison, whose base was among blue-collar whites in Pasadena, argued that Andrews had shifted to the left to appeal to the district's sizable minority population. Andrews did make an appeal for black votes, appearing arm in arm in ads with Democratic Rep. Mickey Leland, the black liberal from central Houston. Harrison passed out copies of the ad in white areas.

But Andrews took 58 percent in the runoff and won the general election with surprising ease over Republican Mike Faubion. Andrews won his next four elections without a difficult test. In 1988, he crushed his GOP challenger by better than 2-to-1, and two years later faced no Republican opposition.

Committees

Budget (15th of 26 Democrats)

Ways & Means (11th of 24 Democrats)
Health

Joint Economic

Elections

1992 General		
Michael A. Andrews (D)	98,975	(56%)
Dolly Madison McKenna (R)	73,192	(41%)
Richard Mauk (LIBERT)	4,710	(3%)
1992 Primary		
Michael A. Andrews (D)	25,291	(82%)
Mary R. Whipple (D)	5,371	(18%)
1990 General		
Michael A. Andrews (D)	67,427	(100%)

Previous Winning Percentages: **1988** (71%) **1986** (100%) **1984** (64%) **1982** (60%)

District Vote for President

	1992	
D	85,325	(47%)
R	64,896	(36%)
I	32,489	(18%)

Campaign Finance

	Receipts	Receipts from PACs		Expend-itures
1992				
Andrews (D)	$974,838	$527,931	(54%)	$1,397,469
McKenna (R)	$587,399	0		$585,616
1990				
Andrews (D)	$539,864	$344,883	(64%)	$294,340

Key Votes

1993	
Require parental notification of minors' abortions	N
Require unpaid family and medical leave	Y
Approve national "motor voter" registration bill	Y
Approve budget increasing taxes and reducing deficit	Y
Approve economic stimulus plan	Y
1992	
Approve balanced-budget constitutional amendment	Y
Close down space station program	N
Approve U.S. aid for former Soviet Union	Y
Allow shifting funds from defense to domestic programs	N
1991	
Extend unemployment benefits using deficit financing	Y
Approve waiting period for handgun purchases	Y
Authorize use of force in Persian Gulf	Y

Voting Studies

	Presidential Support		Party Unity		Conservative Coalition	
Year	**S**	**O**	**S**	**O**	**S**	**O**
1992	39	60	73	24	83	17
1991	47	50	75	24	81	16
1990	32	68	79	20	69	31
1989	45	51	78	21	83	17
1988	37	62	75	21	87	11
1987	39	60	75	23	81	19
1986	37	61	72	24	96	4
1985	39	59	77	21	84	16
1984	48	50	64	33	81	17
1983	45	54	61	37	78	21

Interest Group Ratings

Year	ADA	AFL-CIO	CCUS	ACU
1992	70	55	63	38
1991	30	58	50	35
1990	56	75	29	25
1989	35	45	50	48
1988	75	86	62	29
1987	68	69	47	0
1986	50	64	61	45
1985	30	50	71	57
1984	45	69	38	29
1983	60	59	65	36

26 Dick Armey (R)

Of Lewisville — Elected 1984; 5th Term

Born: July 7, 1940, Cando, N.D.
Education: Jamestown College, B.A. 1963; U. of North Dakota, M.A. 1964; U. of Oklahoma, Ph.D. 1969.
Occupation: Economist.
Family: Wife, Susan Byrd; five children.
Religion: Presbyterian.
Political Career: No previous office.
Capitol Office: 301 Cannon Bldg. 20515; 225-7772.

In Washington: Armey's December 1992 election to the No. 3 post in the GOP leadership provided emphatic affirmation that the House's minority party is moving further to define itself as an aggressive conservative force confronting the Democratic majority. As chairman of the Republican Conference, Armey is one rung on the leadership ladder below Minority Whip Newt Gingrich, the originator and mastermind of the confrontationalist strategy.

In winning the post, Armey unseated easygoing Californian Jerry Lewis, an old-style mainstream conservative whom Armey portrayed as too willing to accommodate Democrats.

"The politics of confrontation works and the politics of appeasement fails," he said in November. "What are we going to do — bargain with them? . . . What do we say — 'We'll accept your principle if you'll do just a little bit less of it'? I think it's more productive for the party to say, 'Look, you're fundamentally incorrect.' "

More and more, that attitude characterizes the posture of the House GOP in its day-to-day dealings with the Democratic majority and in its response to the legislative agenda of the Clinton administration. Along with Armey, two other like-minded conservatives were elevated into Republican leadership positions for the 103rd: Bill McCollum of Florida as conference vice chairman and Texan Tom DeLay as conference secretary. Like Armey, both of them defeated less contrarian party colleagues. The lone certifiable "Old Bull" in the GOP leadership is Minority Leader Robert H. Michel of Illinois, now past 70, and he is expected to retire before long.

Armey, while unquestionably conservative, does embody some conflicting strains in his party. His anti-federal spending, anti-welfare-state philosophy looks almost libertarian, but he has the political smarts to realize that electoral realities force some necessary exceptions. He is, after all, from Texas, which is home to one of the government's biggest-ticket science projects, the superconducting super collider (SSC), an $8 billion-plus atom smasher under construction in Waxahachie. He backs the SSC, and he also defends the $30 billion-plus space station *Freedom*, which has a sizable Texas component as well.

If it were being built in any other state, the SSC, which has been buffeted by rising costs, vague scientific promise and alleged mismanagement, would be just the kind of venture that Armey loves to skewer as an ill-conceived boondoggle. But it is a Texas project, and Armey joins his state delegation's almost unbroken line of defense against attempts to cancel the controversial endeavor.

Armey voted against a 1992 amendment that would have cut virtually all of the collider's fiscal 1993 funding. But in expressing concern that the SSC has not won a more ringing endorsement from scientists, he offered this glimpse into his own self-consciousness: "You always want objective scientific information to validate your politically mandatory position."

Armey's energy and hard work attracted support in his leadership contest even from some moderate Republicans, who were lured by the promise of action implicit in his candidacy. He began his campaign six months out and cultivated votes one by one.

If Lewis' natural constituency was the established senior members, Armey's was the large class of activist freshmen who would join Congress in 1993. Each retirement of a veteran GOP member in 1992 had the potential to cost Lewis two votes: a Lewis vote from the veteran and an Armey vote from his replacement. Freshmen took credit for giving confrontationalists a clean sweep of the three contested leadership posts, and in particular for spelling the difference in Armey's narrow 88-84 victory.

While even some of Armey's most liberal Democratic colleagues can find him engaging, his personal style is not to everyone's taste. His rhetoric can strike moderate Republicans as uncompromising and polarizing. Following the leadership elections, Steve Gunderson of Wisconsin, a chief deputy whip, and Fred Upton of Michigan, a deputy whip, resigned their party posts, citing the new lineup's rightward tilt.

And Armey's partisan commentary can tend toward the inflammatory, especially when old-style liberal Democrats such as Education

Texas 26

Suburban Dallas; parts of Irving and Denton

In the 1980s, the 26th was the third-fastest-growing district in the United States.

Denton County, the biggest chunk of land in the district, grew 89 percent in the 1970s and 91 percent in the 1980s. Southern Denton County, home to once-rural communities that are now Dallas suburbs, has continued to grow into the 1990s.

The region's astonishing growth was attributed primarily to the appeal of the "Golden Triangle," an area bordered by the Dallas-Fort Worth International Airport and two major highways, I-35 East and I-35 West.

The airport is the world's largest in acreage, as well as one of the busiest. The Dallas-Fort Worth metroplex spans 100 miles in north-central Texas. Although the region was hurt by defense cutbacks and the resignation of hometown favorite Speaker Jim Wright in 1989, its diversified economy and mild weather have kept it from more serious economic demise in the late 1980s.

With the rapid population growth, the boundaries of the 26th were compressed and shifted in the 1992 redistricting, making room for a new minority-influence district in Dallas.

About 55 percent of the district's voters live in Dallas County. Although the city is not in the 26th, many district residents look to Dallas for employment and entertainment. The downtown financial district is a significant source of jobs for the people of the 26th.

Arts patrons head to the second-largest city in Texas for its fine symphony and museums. For different types of recreation, the 26th has the Dallas Cowboys' home field, Texas Stadium, and Lake Lewisville State Park.

The district's largest employer is high-tech giant Texas Instruments; its Lewisville plant manufactures the Army's HARM missile, which gained praise in Desert Shield/Desert Storm. Other major employers include Xerox, Exxon, GTE and American Airlines, which has headquarters just over the district boundary line.

Most of the residents of the 26th are white and fairly well off. The median household income for the district, between $37,500 and $40,000, well exceeded state and national averages. Denton County's booming growth helped make it solidly Republican by the early 1990s. And the county has made the entire 26th fertile vote-getting turf for any Republican candidate. George Bush won every county in the district in compiling a 47 percent win here in the 1992 presidential contest. Rep. Armey continues to win large margins.

Low taxes, a strong military and less government regulation top the agenda of many voters in the 26th. These sentiments were borne out in the presidential election results of 1992. Although Bush won the district, independent Dallas billionaire Ross Perot placed second in the three-way race with more than 32 percent of the vote, far surpassing his national average.

1990 Population: 566,217. White 493,309 (87%), Black 23,679 (4%), Other 49,229 (9%). Hispanic origin 51,827 (9%). 18 and over 422,747 (75%), 62 and over 36,726 (6%). Median age: 31.

and Labor Committee Chairman William D. Ford of Michigan are the targets. "I see confrontation as a tool," Armey said after his election as conference chairman. "If it becomes necessary, I am capable of using it."

Armey has not been shy about criticizing the new Democratic president. At a White House meeting in February 1993 between President Clinton and the bipartisan congressional leadership, Armey bluntly told Clinton that his economic package would fail because it was based on faulty economic assumptions and that it would torpedo his presidency. Democratic Sen. Robert C. Byrd of West Virginia then dressed Armey down for his discourtesy. According to the Capitol Hill newspaper Roll Call, Senate Minority Leader Bob Dole of Kansas eased some of the tension at the end of the meeting when he cracked to Clinton, "Next time we're going to bring our hard-liners."

Before setting his designs on the leadership, Armey had made a name for himself in Congress as a butcher of sacred cows. He championed a landmark bill to close military bases in the 100th Congress and then took aim at the fiefdom of farm programs in the 101st Congress. He lost that foray but ended up with a central role in defining the debate over the direction of government programs for farmers.

Passage of the base-closing measure altered his reputation as a legislator. As a freshman in the 99th Congress, he sometimes seemed more interested in lecturing on free-market economics than in building consensus. But by channeling his energies into the base-closing bill and lobbying colleagues one by one to support it, Armey proved he could listen and persuade, not just lecture.

Seeking support from both Democrats and Republicans was a departure from the confrontational approach Armey used as a freshman, when he was a self-described "budget commando" arguing — mostly unsuccessfully — for federal spending reductions. But a June 1988 comment to The Wall Street Journal illustrated the evolution in his legislative style. Armey said he had "risked being labeled a bomb-thrower, a loose cannon," and added, "You can be so ideologically hidebound you can cut yourself out of the process."

While Armey clearly valued being a part of the process, he little tempered his free-market conservatism. When President Bush retracted his "no new taxes" pledge to help forge an agreement on the fiscal 1991 budget, Armey sponsored a resolution at a July 1990 Republican Conference meeting opposing new taxes. It carried by a 2-to-1 margin in a secret vote and presaged the later mutiny of House Republicans led by Gingrich against the 1990 budget summit agreement.

As in the base-closing debate, Armey was peculiarly situated to launch his assault on farm programs. He was a junior member of the minority party crusading on the turf of a powerful committee — in this case, Agriculture — to which he did not belong. He entered the debate only after immersing himself in the arcane jargon and labyrinthine network of government farm programs.

His opening strike was an article in the winter 1990 issue of the Heritage Foundation's publication *Policy Review*, titled "Moscow on the Mississippi: America's Soviet-Style Farm Policy." "Even as *perestroika* comes to the communist world," Armey began, "our own federal farm programs remain as American monuments to the folly of central planning."

Armey joined with New York Democrat Charles E. Schumer to form the Coalition for a Common Sense Farm Policy, an amalgam of free-market conservative Republicans and liberal and mostly urban Democrats.

Armey's message was conservative: "The free market works and central planning does not," he wrote. But the appeal was also populist. Armey and Schumer's prime vehicle was a floor amendment to the farm bill to bar farmers earning more than $100,000 a year from collecting subsidies. The coalition's tactics put farm-state lawmakers on the defensive, but in the end, the Armey-Schumer amendment was rejected 159-263.

In his fight to close obsolete military bases, Armey also lost his first battle. To insulate base-closing decisions from politics, he proposed giving all base-closing responsibility to an independent commission that would review military needs and develop a list of unnecessary bases. His bill also waived many restrictions that had tied up base closings for more than a decade.

In 1987, Armey sought to attach his proposal to the fiscal 1988 defense authorization bill. Though he had lobbied only briefly, the measure fell just short, 192-199. In 1988, Armey tried again; after parliamentary wrangling, he offered a proposal with this concession: Congress would be allowed to kill the base-closing plan, but only if both chambers passed a resolution disapproving the entire list. The amendment passed 223-186 and became law.

At year's end, the blue-ribbon panel released a list of targeted bases that was somewhat more modest than expected. Estimated savings were less than $700 million a year, rather than the originally touted $2 billion-plus. But that modesty ensured the plan's success: Only a few dozen members' districts were affected. The disapproval resolution went down 43-381, ratifying the base-closure list.

Armey has clearly made an impact during his relatively short tenure in Congress, but his brashness has had its costs. Perhaps in part because of his high-profile opposition to the administration's budget proposals in 1990 — conservatives outside the July GOP Conference meeting reportedly gave out buttons that said "Read Armey's Lips" — Armey failed to get a seat on the Rules Committee at the start of the 102nd Congress, when the panel had two vacancies. At the same time, his colleagues also denied him the top Republican spot on the Budget Committee.

Armey got a seat on Budget at the start of his second term in 1987, and he showed a willingness to work with ideological opposites. In 1988, he joined liberal California Democrat Barbara Boxer on an amendment to that year's budget resolution, adding $220 million for Coast Guard drug-interdiction efforts; then-committee Chairman William H. Gray III of Pennsylvania kidded that their alliance was "historic."

On the Education and Labor Committee, where the Democratic majority has a very strong liberal bent, Armey finds it harder to eschew partisanship. He is a staunch opponent of labor-oriented measures that would increase costs or regulatory mandates for business. He is also a nemesis of its chairman, Ford.

Armey has vowed to make Ford's life as miserable as possible, not because of his politics but because of his personality. He calls Ford "autocratic and heavy-handed." For his part, Ford calls Armey "just a kind of pain in the ass."

With his new leadership post, Armey left the Banking and Budget committees, but he stayed on the Education and Labor panel. "If Bill Ford were not the chairman of Ed and Labor, I'd probably get off," he said in November 1992. "I like to think of him as being stuck with me." Armey also has kept his spot as the senior House Republican on the Joint Economic Committee.

Armey aggressively opposed legislation requiring businesses to provide unpaid family leave to workers caring for a newborn child or ill family member, maintaining that because only affluent workers could afford unpaid leave, more work would fall to lower-paid employees. Armey called the family leave idea "yuppie welfare . . . a perverse redistribution of income."

In 1989, Armey revisited one of his earliest issue battles when he sought to cut funds for the National Endowment for the Arts. As a freshman in 1985, Armey circulated "dirty" poetry by NEA grant recipients to garner support for freezing NEA funding. In the 101st Congress, he tried to cut NEA's appropriation by 10 percent after an uproar over photographs many members found sacrilegious or obscene.

But Interior Appropriations Subcommittee Chairman Sidney R. Yates of Illinois outmaneuvered Armey, enlisting conservative Texas Democrat Charles W. Stenholm, who offered an amendment to cut NEA funding by only the amount of two highly controversial grants. The House adopted Stenholm's language, 361-65. Armey complimented Yates for his tactics. "It was very good strategy to come in and 'Boll Weevil' me."

At Home: Armey cites a belief in the free enterprise system as the genesis of his political career. He was popular on the Dallas area conservative lecture circuit, praising the philosophy of economist George Gilder and extolling "the miracle of the market." But beyond volunteering for Jim Bradshaw, the GOP nominee in the 26th in 1982, Armey had no previous political experience when he challenged freshman Democratic Rep. Tom Vandergriff in 1984.

Although the district had been voting routinely Republican for most major offices, Vandergriff began with a solid base in Arlington, the Tarrant County city where he had been mayor for a quarter-century before narrowly winning the 1982 House election.

Armey drew some negative publicity. Following a meeting with editors of the Fort Worth Star-Telegram, he was quoted as saying he favored a gradual phaseout of the Social Security system. Then Armey said he was "embarrassed" to have been a professor, calling some college classes "pure junk," citing black studies courses as an example.

But Armey prevailed by stressing his conservative economic notions, allying himself firmly with President Ronald Reagan and branding Vandergriff a lackey for House Speaker Thomas P. O'Neill Jr. Taking advantage of an unusual outbreak of straight-ticket GOP voting, Armey won with 51 percent. In his four re-elections, Armey has always topped two-thirds of the vote.

Committees

Conference Chairman

Education & Labor (5th of 15 Republicans)
Labor-Management Relations; Postsecondary Education

Joint Economic

Elections

1992 General		
Dick Armey (R)	150,209	(73%)
John Wayne Caton (D)	55,237	(27%)
1990 General		
Dick Armey (R)	147,856	(70%)
John Wayne Caton (D)	62,158	(30%)

Previous Winning Percentages: **1988** (69%) **1986** (68%) **1984** (51%)

District Vote for President

	1992	
D	52,771	(21%)
R	118,610	(47%)
I	81,502	(32%)

Campaign Finance

	Receipts	Receipts from PACs		Expenditures
1992				
Armey (R)	$482,973	$195,110	(40%)	$475,756
Caton (D)	$10,091	$9,000	(89%)	$9,589
1990				
Armey (R)	$441,625	$162,306	(37%)	$198,305
Caton (D)	$15,135	$13,600	(90%)	$14,303

Key Votes

1993	
Require parental notification of minors' abortions	Y
Require unpaid family and medical leave	N
Approve national "motor voter" registration bill	N
Approve budget increasing taxes and reducing deficit	N
Approve economic stimulus plan	N
1992	
Approve balanced-budget constitutional amendment	Y
Close down space station program	N
Approve U.S. aid for former Soviet Union	N
Allow shifting funds from defense to domestic programs	N
1991	
Extend unemployment benefits using deficit financing	N
Approve waiting period for handgun purchases	N
Authorize use of force in Persian Gulf	Y

Voting Studies

	Presidential Support		Party Unity		Conservative Coalition	
Year	**S**	**O**	**S**	**O**	**S**	**O**
1992	85	13	95	1	96	4
1991	86	14	97	1	100	0
1990	81	18	95	4	94	6
1989	76	24	94	2	90	5
1988	82	15	94	3	92	8
1987	81	17	95	2	98	2
1986	82	17	97	2	100	0
1985	88	11	94	4	93	5

Interest Group Ratings

Year	ADA	AFL-CIO	CCUS	ACU
1992	0	8	75	100
1991	0	0	100	100
1990	6	8	93	96
1989	0	0	90	96
1988	0	0	100	100
1987	0	0	100	96
1986	0	7	100	100
1985	15	0	95	95

27 Solomon P. Ortiz (D)

Of Corpus Christi — Elected 1982; 6th Term

Born: June 3, 1937, Robstown, Texas.
Education: Institute of Applied Science, 1962; Del Mar College, 1965-67.
Military Service: Army, 1960-62.
Occupation: Law enforcement official.
Family: Divorced; two children.
Religion: Methodist.
Political Career: Nueces County constable, 1965-69; Nueces County Commission, 1969-77; Nueces County sheriff, 1977-83.
Capitol Office: 2445 Rayburn Bldg. 20515; 225-7742.

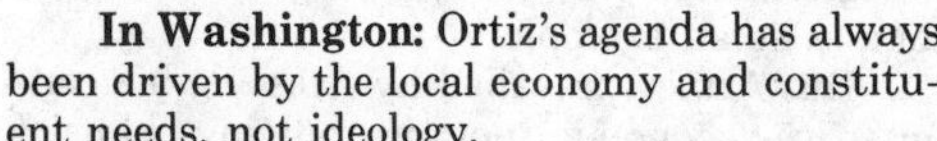

In Washington: Ortiz's agenda has always been driven by the local economy and constituent needs, not ideology.

While other members of the Armed Services Committee debate the "big picture" defense strategy issues, Ortiz has his work cut out for him in defending South Texas' military facilities. In May 1993, the Defense Base Closure and Realignment Commission added the Corpus Christi Naval Hospital and Air Station and the Ingleside Naval Station to the list of facilities that it will consider closing.

Ortiz's main focus in the 102nd Congress was the Congressional Hispanic Caucus. He served as chairman and helped push through legislation to increase access to voting materials in languages other than English.

The bill, the Voting Rights Language Assistance Act of 1992, lowered the threshold for determining which states and other jurisdictions are required to provide second-language voting materials. Rep. Jose E. Serrano, D-N.Y., sponsored the bill; President George Bush signed it into law in August 1992.

Ortiz's local focus also keeps him close to issues relating to the immigration of people from Mexico and elsewhere in Latin America. In early 1989, he was a leader in efforts to make the federal government manage an influx of Central American immigrants.

Mainly from Nicaragua and El Salvador, thousands of newcomers had crossed the Rio Grande into South Texas seeking political asylum. A federal court order restricted the refugees to the Brownsville area, and encampments of immigrants sprouted up, overtaxing local governments.

Ortiz's initial reaction to the newcomers was sympathetic. But when local officials warned that they could not cope with the influx, Ortiz said the federal government should slow the flow. Noting that most of the newcomers had come for economic reasons, Ortiz said, "That doesn't mean they qualify for political asylum.... We have to draw the line somewhere." His concern about maintaining order reflects his background as a former county sheriff.

Ortiz was a leading advocate of rolling back regulations ordering gulf shrimp fishermen to install "turtle excluder devices."

Ortiz sided with shrimpers in his district who said the cumbersome devices, which keep sea turtles from getting entangled in fishing nets, could sharply reduce their shrimp yields.

"The dedicated and hard-working men and women who own and operate shrimp fishing vessels are being threatened by federal regulations, which may cause many of these people to lose their businesses," Ortiz said in April 1989.

In general, Ortiz follows a less liberal line than other Hispanic House members. In March 1993, he joined most Republicans and a minority of Democrats in voting to require that federally funded abortion clinics give parents 48 hours' notice before performing an abortion on a minor.

Otherwise, he was a consistent Clinton administration supporter in the early days of the 103rd Congress. He voted for the Family and Medical Leave Act, for the "motor voter" registration bill and for Clinton's budget — all of which cleared Congress early in 1993. Ortiz also voted for Clinton's $16.3 billion stimulus plan, which died at the hands of a Republican filibuster in the Senate.

Ortiz picked up a Merchant Marine subcommittee chair at the beginning of the 103rd; the former Oceanography, Great Lakes and Outer Continental Shelf Subcommittee, chaired by former Rep. and Great Lakes area resident Dennis M. Hertel of Michigan, was transformed into the Oceanography, Gulf of Mexico and Outer Continental Shelf Subcommittee and handed over to Ortiz, who was not even a member of the old panel in the 102nd Congress.

At Home: Since his 1964 election as constable, Ortiz has been a groundbreaker for Hispanics in South Texas politics, holding a succession of offices previously closed to Mexi-

Texas 27

Gulf Coast — Corpus Christi; Brownsville

Tucked in the southeastern corner of Texas, the compact 27th is anchored by two dramatically different cities that have become something of rivals ever since the 1982 redistricting threw them together.

In the northern county of Nueces is Corpus Christi. This cosmopolitan city of 257,500, with its mild climate, beaches and museums, is a tourist mecca. Hispanics hold a slight majority in Corpus Christi but are often outvoted by Anglos.

Nueces County has a heavy military influence that could suffer greatly if several proposed base closures occur. The Corpus Christi Army Depot, the largest employer in the city, builds and repairs helicopters. In May 1993, the Corpus Christi Naval Air Station and Naval Hospital were included in a list of proposed base closures. Just across Corpus Christi Bay in Ingleside is a naval station proponents had hoped would become the headquarters for the Navy's mine warfare command operations. But it too was included on the closure list. Although the base is not in the 27th, Rep. Ortiz keeps a watchful eye on the base, whose docks are in Ortiz's district.

Brownsville, by comparison, is almost entirely Hispanic. Located in southernmost Cameron County, the smaller, grittier city has a distinctly south-of-the-border flavor; breakfast tacos are common fare and many of the residents are bilingual. A private study of census data concluded in 1993 that Brownsville has the worst poverty rate in the nation.

There is no military presence in the southern part of the district. The export-import trade of fruits and vegetables with Brownsville's sister city of Matamoros, Mexico, is an important local industry. Brownsville has trouble competing with the better-known Corpus Christi for tourists and has problems, such as drug trafficking, that are related to illegal border crossings.

Despite the competition between the two cities, they have much in common and offer a unifying thread for the 27th. Both are port cities reliant on the energy and fishing industries.

Both cities watched the local shrimping catch decline in the mid-1980s, partly as a result of new laws requiring the use of nets with devices that enable turtles — and, fishermen say, some shrimp — to escape.

Although Ortiz sometimes describes himself and his district as conservative, recent elections and surveys show a more liberal bent to the 27th.

Nueces County provides a reliable base for any Democrat. Ann Richards won the county comfortably in her 1990 gubernatorial campaign. In 1992, Democrat Bill Clinton exceeded his national average in Nueces, going on to win every county in the 27th. Nueces County also routinely sends Democrats, often Hispanics, to the state Legislature.

Surveys conducted in 1992 by the University of Corpus Christi showed a majority of district residents supported some abortion rights and gay rights, and more than half identified themselves as Democrats.

1990 Population: 566,217. White 445,735 (79%), Black 13,760 (2%), Other 106,722 (19%). Hispanic origin 374,783 (66%). 18 and over 380,622 (67%), 62 and over 71,319 (13%). Median age: 29.

can-Americans. He was chosen Nueces County's first Hispanic commissioner in 1968, its first Hispanic sheriff in 1976.

Redistricting in 1982 gave Ortiz the opening he needed to get to Congress. As adjusted by a three-judge federal panel, the 27th was good territory for a Mexican-American Democrat; its Hispanic population exceeded 60 percent.

Four of the five candidates who filed for the Democratic nomination in 1982 were Hispanic. Although attorney Jorge Rangel was the favorite in the Washington business-money community, Ortiz had the loyal backing of the poorer Hispanics in Corpus Christi. That gave him a first-place primary finish and a spot in the June runoff.

Ortiz's runoff foe was the one non-Hispanic, Joseph Salem, a Corpus Christi jeweler and former state representative. Salem had strong labor ties, but many of the oil and other business interests who had backed Rangel turned to Ortiz, leery that Salem was too liberal.

The decisive runoff votes were cast in Brownsville. Although Salem had some initial appeal to the Hispanic majority there, Ortiz scored a coup by gaining the support of state Pardons and Paroles Board Chairman Ruben M. Torres. With Torres' support, Ortiz won about 60 percent of the Cameron County (Brownsville) runoff vote, allowing him to draw 64 percent districtwide. That was Ortiz's last competitive contest. In 1986, 1988 and 1990, the GOP did not even challenge him.

In 1992, Republican Jay Kimbrough challenged Ortiz but not seriously. The loss of

Hispanic voters in the south (due to redistricting) and the overall anti-Congress mood probably did more to shave votes from Ortiz than Kimbrough.

Committees

Armed Services (11th of 34 Democrats)
Military Installations & Facilities; Readiness

Merchant Marine & Fisheries (6th of 29 Democrats)
Oceanography, Gulf of Mexico & the Outer Continental Shelf (chairman); Environment & Natural Resources

Elections

1992 General		
Solomon P. Ortiz (D)	87,022	(55%)
Jay Kimbrough (R)	66,853	(43%)
Charles Henry Schoonover (LIBERT)	2,969	(2%)
1990 General		
Solomon P. Ortiz (D)	62,822	(100%)

Previous Winning Percentages: **1988** (100%) **1986** (100%) **1984** (64%) **1982** (64%)

District Vote for President

	1992
D	78,491 (48%)
R	58,802 (36%)
I	27,391 (17%)

Campaign Finance

	Receipts	Receipts from PACs	Expend-itures
1992			
Ortiz (D)	$274,610	$99,518 (36%)	$343,904
Kimbrough (R)	$64,628	$1,950 (3%)	$57,832
1990			
Ortiz (D)	$235,873	$100,790 (43%)	$140,756

Key Votes

1993	
Require parental notification of minors' abortions	Y
Require unpaid family and medical leave	Y
Approve national "motor voter" registration bill	Y
Approve budget increasing taxes and reducing deficit	Y
Approve economic stimulus plan	Y
1992	
Approve balanced-budget constitutional amendment	Y
Close down space station program	N
Approve U.S. aid for former Soviet Union	N
Allow shifting funds from defense to domestic programs	N
1991	
Extend unemployment benefits using deficit financing	Y
Approve waiting period for handgun purchases	N
Authorize use of force in Persian Gulf	Y

Voting Studies

	Presidential Support		Party Unity		Conservative Coalition	
Year	**S**	**O**	**S**	**O**	**S**	**O**
1992	37	55	81	16	71	29
1991	41	53	76	19	73	24
1990	30	69	86	13	52	46
1989	50	47	77	18	61	34
1988	29	61	78	10	53	34
1987	37	55	79	12	81	16
1986	36	59	78	14	70	22
1985	36	61	76	14	64	33
1984	41	51	77	17	53	41
1983	44	52	75	21	66	29

Interest Group Ratings

Year	ADA	AFL-CIO	CCUS	ACU
1992	60	83	38	40
1991	30	67	56	26
1990	56	83	43	21
1989	60	73	50	29
1988	55	100	29	26
1987	56	80	33	17
1986	45	85	29	40
1985	60	88	16	33
1984	60	92	44	29
1983	65	82	32	32

28 Frank Tejeda (D)

Of San Antonio — Elected 1992; 1st Term

Born: Oct. 2, 1945, San Antonio, Texas.
Education: St. Mary's U. of San Antonio, B.A. 1970; U. of California, Berkeley, J.D. 1974; Harvard U., M.P.A. 1980; Yale U., LL.M. 1989.
Military Service: Marine Corps, 1963-67; Marine Corps Reserve, 1967-present.
Occupation: Lawyer.
Family: Divorced; three children.
Religion: Roman Catholic.
Political Career: Texas House, 1977-87; Texas Senate, 1987-93.
Capitol Office: 323 Cannon Bldg. 20515; 225-1640.

The Path to Washington: If ease of election provides any measure of success in Congress, Tejeda should have no trouble making his mark early.

During 16 years in the Legislature, Tejeda assiduously built strong ties to the Hispanic and business communities around San Antonio. His low-key manner was a contrast to typically flamboyant Texas politics, and his devotion to his constituents guaranteed his popularity.

He waltzed to victory in 1992 with a broad base of support and virtually no opposition.

An ex-Marine, decorated Vietnam veteran and conservative, pro-business Democrat, Tejeda nonetheless exhibits a streak of social activism. He puts education, health care and job training at the top of his list of concerns.

Given his Hispanic heritage and his district's proximity to Mexico, he supported negotiations leading to the North American Free Trade Agreement. But he also expressed the caveat that the U.S. government must help retrain workers displaced by any movement of jobs.

Tejeda is, however, perhaps most concerned about veterans issues and the damage that steep cuts in defense spending might do to the numerous military installations in and around his district — some of which faced possible closure in 1993. He sought and received seats on the Armed Services and Veterans' Affairs committees.

In the Texas Legislature, he championed bills to build housing for veterans and to protect crime victims. He fought to support minority rights, working to assist minority and woman-owned businesses and promoting voting rights.

Tejeda promoted measures to ensure voting rights for minorities, and he attacked the practice of dismissing jurors on the basis of race or ethnicity. In April 1993, Tejeda called for the removal of a federal judge accused of uttering racial slurs against Hispanics in open court.

If Tejeda made any enemies while in Austin, it was the state's trial lawyers, with whom he often clashed. He managed an investigation into questionable activities by two state Supreme Court justices who had won their seats on the bench with significant financial aid from personal injury lawyers. And he helped push to enactment a bill revising the state's worker compensation law.

That change in the law was expected to reduce the business share of the cost of injuries, while not dramatically changing benefits paid to workers. The revision required arbitration in disputes and prevented civil damage suits — effectively taking trial lawyers out of the loop.

The bar struck back in 1990, organizing a vigorous, well-financed primary challenge to his re-election to the state Senate. Tejeda proved his mettle, winning easily, despite a nasty campaign that raised questions about his divorce.

The outcome of that race cemented his ties to the state's business lobby and apparently squelched any idea that opponents might have had to question his claim on the 28th.

Tejeda was the only freshman elected in 1992 to a new district who did not face major-party opposition either in a primary or the general election.

The Hispanic-majority 28th was tailor-made for Tejeda — with his help at the drafting table. Though it encompasses nine whole counties and parts of four more, the bulk of its population comes from Bexar County, which he represented in Austin.

Alone on the ballot in the primary, Tejeda faced Libertarian David C. Slatter in November, but he hardly had to campaign.

Tejeda spent time getting to know his new territory, which reaches from San Antonio and its suburbs to the Rio Grande, and includes two of the nation's poorest counties — Starr and Zapata.

Not having to promote his own candidacy gave Tejeda time to tend to other political bridge-building. He leaped to the defense of the Democratic presidential contender when President Bush attacked Bill Clinton for avoiding serving in Vietnam. And Tejeda helped organize and lead a National Veterans Task Force for Clinton.

Texas 28

South San Antonio; Zapata

Mapmakers looking to create a new Hispanic-majority district in south-central Texas found two population bases — San Antonio and the Mexican border — and connected them with a winding trail of South Texas counties. The result was the 28th, one of three new districts acquired in reapportionment for the 1990s.

The 28th is heavily influenced by its proximity to Mexico and its abundance of military bases.

San Antonio has five military installations, two of which are in the 28th. Brooks Air Force Base, southeast of downtown, is primarily an aerospace research center. A new Air Force Center for Environmental Excellence at Brooks is expected to bring more than 200 new people to the base and help solidify its future. Randolph Air Force Base is a major training and recruitment center. A navigator training program is scheduled to move from Mather Air Force Base in California to Randolph; about 500 military personnel and 250 students would transfer with the program.

San Antonio is also home to Lackland Air Force Base, Fort Sam Houston and Kelly Air Force Base — the area's largest job-producer and employer of half the Hispanics in the Air Force. Units at Kelly were targeted in early 1993 for possible closure.

The military presence has been a significant factor in keeping the region's economy afloat during the oil crash of the mid-1980s and the nationwide recession of the early 1990s. The five installations generate about $3.4 billion annually and employ about 69,000 people. With the five bases and a pleasant climate, San Antonio is a popular spot with retirees. Almost two-thirds of the district's population is in Bexar County, the northernmost county in the 28th, which includes San Antonio, the third-largest city in Texas, and its suburbs. Harlandale, an old German town that has become an increasingly Hispanic San Antonio neighborhood, is Rep. Tejeda's vote-getting base.

As the district moves south toward the Rio Grande, it becomes more rural and poorer. Starr is the second-poorest county in the nation, with more than 63 percent of its residents living below the poverty level. About 41 percent of the people in neighboring Zapata County fall below the poverty line.

These two overwhelmingly Hispanic counties, taken from the 15th District to help create the 28th in the 1992 redistricting, were two of the fastest-growing in the state.

Truckers who ship food and other products to the border communities complain that there is little worth bringing back north, a situation that makes shipping far less lucrative. The bulk of the region's jobs are low-paying field jobs.

The 28th is overwhelmingly Democratic; Bill Clinton received 55 percent of the vote in the district in 1992. One often overlooked Republican enclave in the district is the northeast section of San Antonio, a predominantly white, middle-class suburb.

1990 Population: 566,217. White 388,123 (69%), Black 48,295 (9%), Other 129,799 (23%). Hispanic origin 341,843 (60%). 18 and over 382,636 (68%), 62 and over 72,937 (13%). Median age: 29.

Committees

Armed Services (24th of 34 Democrats)
Military Installations & Facilities; Oversight & Investigations; Research & Technology

Veterans' Affairs (15th of 21 Democrats)
Compensation, Pension & Insurance; Hospitals & Health Care

Campaign Finance

	Receipts	Receipts from PACs		Expend-itures
1992				
Tejeda (D)	$305,673	$131,725	(43%)	$304,286
Slatter (LIBERT)	$1,567	0		$1,401

Key Votes

1993

Require parental notification of minors' abortions	Y
Require unpaid family and medical leave	Y
Approve national "motor voter" registration bill	Y
Approve budget increasing taxes and reducing deficit	Y
Approve economic stimulus plan	Y

Elections

1992 General

Frank Tejeda (D)	122,457	(87%)
David C. Slatter (LIBERT)	18,128	(13%)

District Vote for President

1992

D 94,112 (55%)
R 51,293 (30%)
I 27,200 (16%)

29 Gene Green (D)

Of Houston — Elected 1992; 1st Term

Born: Oct. 17, 1947, Houston, Texas.
Education: U. of Houston, B.B.A. 1971.
Occupation: Lawyer.
Family: Wife, Helen Lois Albers; two children.
Religion: Methodist.
Political Career: Texas House, 1973-85; Texas Senate, 1985-93.
Capitol Office: 1004 Longworth Bldg. 20515; 225-1688.

The Path to Washington: The 29th is a marvel of census-based, computer-assisted draftsmanship, intended to comply with the Voting Rights Act and enhance the political power of Houston's growing Hispanic population.

That Green, an Anglo, won this seat is mostly a testament to the bitter rivalries among Houston's Hispanic leaders — and the lack of a unifying force to make a community out of the disconnected neighborhoods of the 29th.

Green's ability to retain this seat will depend on his political savvy and whether the district's Hispanics are able to unite behind a candidate. Though 55 percent of the district's voting-age population is Hispanic, nearly 60 percent of its voters are Anglo. Many of the latter are working-class whites from "Redneck Alley," where Green grew up and which he had represented in the Texas Legislature since 1973.

With knowledge garnered from his tenure on the education committee in the state Senate and his wife's experience as a public school teacher, Green showed an impressive command of education issues early in the 103rd Congress.

To win election in this overwhelmingly Democratic district, Green easily defeated Republican Clark Kent Ervin, a black Houston lawyer who had strong financial backing from the city establishment.

To win the Democratic nomination, Green struggled through a primary, where he finished second to Houston City Council member Ben Reyes, and through two runoffs. Turnout in all three elections was remarkably light — and improbably increased from the primary to the first runoff to the second.

Reyes bested Green by almost 2,000 votes in the five-way primary but managed to net only 34 percent of the vote. Without a majority, Reyes was forced into a runoff with Green, who edged to the front, winning the first runoff by 180 votes. When it was discovered that some Republicans who had voted in the primary had crossed over and illegally cast ballots in the runoff, the results were thrown out and a second runoff held. Green won the court-ordered rematch by about 1,100 votes.

In winning the nomination, Green was able to make the controversial Reyes the focus of voter disenchantment. Reyes pleaded no contest in 1991 to a misdemeanor theft charge: He had a magnolia tree removed from the site of a condemned house the city was bulldozing and planted in his own yard.

Reyes also was accused of, but never charged with, steering city business to relatives, and he filed for personal bankruptcy in 1990.

Because of Reyes' problems, a variety of Hispanic organizations backed other candidates, including former state Rep. Albert Luna and Municipal Judge Sylvia R. Garcia, in the primary. Likewise, some turned to Green in the runoff.

With the spotlight on Reyes, Green's low-key demeanor in the Legislature proved to be an asset. Viewed as a reliable Democratic vote, Green has been an advocate on consumer issues, repeatedly sponsoring bills to force automobile insurers to base their rates on drivers' records, not demographic profiles.

But Green, too, had liabilities.

In February, a month before the primary, he dropped his longstanding opposition to abortion when he came under attack for having sponsored anti-abortion bills in the Legislature. Green said he had gradually come to alter his views, but he was widely seen as having enjoyed a timely conversion on the road to Washington.

Green also had the dubious distinction of being labeled one of the state's 10 worst legislators by Texas Monthly magazine, chiefly on the strength of his having sponsored a bill to permit citizens to carry concealed handguns. Green said he acted in response to several women in his district who complained that they needed to protect themselves from street crime.

The measure passed the state Senate in 1991, days after the U.S. House passed the so-called Brady bill requiring a waiting period for gun purchases. Green's bill died in the Texas House.

And while it did not become law, it earned Green a strong endorsement from the National Rifle Association and a hefty independent expenditure campaign in his behalf from the group.

Texas 29

East Houston; Baytown

On a map, the 29th seems to hover over Houston like a giant bird, wings outstretched; its shape has been compared to the form of the Aztec god Quetzalcoatl.

The district is the handiwork of mapmakers operating under Voting Rights Act mandates to maximize minority-group representation. In this case, the cartographers' goal was to pull together a Hispanic-majority district in the city, no matter how far-flung the Hispanic neighborhoods might be. Texas gained three House seats in 1990 reapportionment; the 28th and 29th districts were drawn for Hispanics, the 30th to elect a black.

The 29th ended up with such contorted, confusing boundaries that residents in seven precincts of the 29th initially voted in other districts in 1992. But numerically, the mapmakers did their job: Hispanics make up 61 percent of the total population and 55 percent of the voting-age population. Blacks account for 10 percent of the total as well as voting-age population.

While two-thirds of the people in the 29th have the common bond of being in a minority group, there is no broader sense of community in the district. The Hispanic populations in San Antonio and other cities closer to the Mexican border are more cohesive than Houston's disparate Hispanic population. Most of the city's 700,000 Hispanics have arrived in the past two decades, emigrating not just from Mexico, but from all over Central America. They have few connections to each other and no generational ties to Houston. Voter registration among Hispanics is dismally low.

All this helps explain why in 1992 the 29th elected an Anglo to the House.

The entire district is contained within Harris County. The boundary lines wrap around Houston's downtown and stretch north toward the Intercontinental Airport along I-45 and I-59. To the south, the lines almost reach Hobby Airport. The 29th includes Houston's east side, home to Mexican-American barrios; the inexpensive apartment complexes of the Spring Branch section; the Houston Ship Channel and the Hispanic neighborhoods of Baytown, an otherwise Anglo-dominated, working-class city near oil refineries.

Most of the people in the 29th are blue-collar. They work at the nearby refineries, at two coffee factories and on oil rigs in the gulf. There are carpenters and plumbers, and also school teachers and middle managers for Shell Oil. The Lyondell refinery and petrochemical plant, spun off from ARCO in 1989, employs about 2,300.

Pockets of economic comfort are found in the Heights section of Houston and in Aldine, a suburb to the north. The Heights, just north of downtown, languished into the early 1980s, but as young professionals began restoring historic homes in the neighborhood, its image improved. Antique shops now line 19th Street.

Though voter turnout in the 29th is very low, the bulk who do cast ballots side with Democrats. Bill Clinton won more than half the district's vote in 1992.

1990 Population: 566,217. White 305,990 (54%), Black 57,994 (10%), Other 202,233 (36%). Hispanic origin 343,332 (61%). 18 and over 377,455 (67%), 62 and over 52,987 (9%). Median age: 27.

Committees

Education & Labor (19th of 28 Democrats)
Elementary, Secondary & Vocational Education; Labor-Management Relations; Postsecondary Education

Merchant Marine & Fisheries (19th of 29 Democrats)
Merchant Marine; Oceanography, Gulf of Mexico & the Outer Continental Shelf

Campaign Finance

	Receipts	Receipts from PACs		Expenditures
1992				
Green (D)	$710,945	$409,700	(58%)	$700,791
Ervin (R)	$514,229	$59,252	(12%)	$509,818

Key Votes

1993

Require parental notification of minors' abortions	N
Require unpaid family and medical leave	Y
Approve national "motor voter" registration bill	Y
Approve budget increasing taxes and reducing deficit	Y
Approve economic stimulus plan	Y

Elections

1992 General		
Gene Green (D)	64,064	(65%)
Clark Kent Ervin (R)	34,609	(35%)
1992 Primary Runoff		
Gene Green (D)	18,927	(52%)
Ben Reyes (D)	17,795	(48%)
1992 Primary		
Ben Reyes (D)	10,504	(34%)
Gene Green (D)	8,533	(28%)
Sylvia R. Garcia (D)	6,487	(21%)
Albert Luna (D)	4,661	(15%)
Andrew C. Burks Jr. (D)	804	(3%)

District Vote for President

	1992
D	54,424 (52%)
R	31,864 (30%)
I	18,440 (18%)

30 Eddie Bernice Johnson (D)

Of Dallas — Elected 1992; 1st Term

Born: Dec. 3, 1935, Waco, Texas.
Education: Texas Christian U., B.S. 1967; Southern Methodist U., M.P.A. 1976.

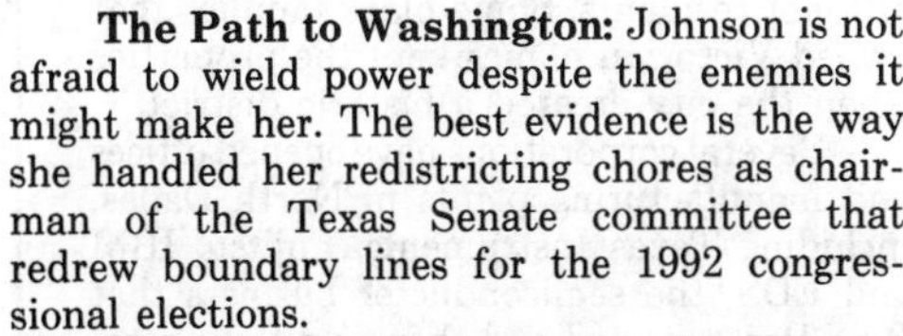

Occupation: Airport shop owner; businesswoman.
Family: Divorced; one child.
Religion: Baptist.
Political Career: Texas House, 1973-77; Texas Senate, 1987-93.
Capitol Office: 1721 Longworth Bldg. 20515; 225-8885.

The Path to Washington: Johnson is not afraid to wield power despite the enemies it might make her. The best evidence is the way she handled her redistricting chores as chairman of the Texas Senate committee that redrew boundary lines for the 1992 congressional elections.

Johnson drew the 30th to her liking despite loud complaints from incumbents in her party — who feared for their political lives — and from other blacks who complained that she was drawing a district tailor-made for herself. Her maneuvering led Texas Monthly magazine to put her on its 10 worst legislators list and to compare her to "a two-year-old child on a white silk sofa with a new set of Magic Markers."

Johnson tossed off the barbs and held her ground, even threatening to file a lawsuit over the matter. She declared after she had easily won election to Congress that she stood "on principle. I did what I knew was right."

Her Democratic primary opponent, Adolph A. Hauntz Jr., contended that Johnson would have trouble working with the Texas delegation in Washington because she alienated many of the members by the way she handled redistricting. But Johnson retorted that Hauntz had no experience in public life and that she was much better qualified for the seat.

Johnson was hardly a novice when she went into the state Senate in 1987 — the first black since Reconstruction and the first woman to represent Dallas in that chamber. She had been elected to the state House in 1972, where she likewise had broken ground as the first black woman elected to public office from Dallas.

She resigned her seat in 1977 to accept an appointment in the Carter administration as regional director for what was the Department of Health, Education and Welfare. It was a good fit, given that she had worked as a nurse before her legislative stint and also has a master's degree in public administration. She has said she wants to use her HEW experience to help improve health care and protect the environment.

In between her state House and state Senate terms, Johnson turned to private business, setting up Eddie Bernice Johnson and Associates, which helped businesses expand or relocate in the Dallas-Fort Worth area. She continued to operate the business after her election to the Senate and expanded it in 1988 to include operations in airport concession management.

Given the breadth of her past experience and the force of personality she has shown in public life, Johnson could be expected to emerge as a leader in her class. Yet she demurred: "I have never sought a leadership position."

Although Johnson resumed her political career by serving in the state Senate, coming to Congress had always been in the back of her mind. "People in my district were telling me to think about it back in 1974," she has said.

In Washington, Johnson intends to make job creation a priority because her district sorely needs more employment.

Her assignment to the Public Works and Transportation Committee should help her play a role in designing programs that can help the Dallas area. She also won a slot on the Science, Space and Technology Committee.

Like several states, Texas has a keen interest in the defense industry, but Johnson says that there have to be different ways to create employment "without always building up defense."

Johnson parts company with many of her first-year colleagues by opposing a constitutional amendment to balance the budget. "It is a false issue and would cause severe tax increases." Likewise, she does not support term limits: "Voters limit terms."

She did, however, vote early in the 103rd Congress to give the president modified line-item veto authority, in opposition to the stated position of the Congressional Black Caucus.

She supports abortion rights, liberal family leave policies and changes in the welfare system that would give parents incentive to work.

Texas 30

Downtown Dallas; part of Grand Prairie

This is the district Eddie Bernice Johnson drew.

It circles the inner city of Dallas, juts out toward Arlington, climbs north along the Dallas-Fort Worth airport, approaches North Lake and backtracks toward Dallas before making a final sharp jog out to Plano. It is 50 percent black, more than two-thirds minority. It is overwhelmingly Democratic — Bill Clinton took 63 percent in the district, far surpassing his 37 percent statewide.

In the words of a federal panel of judges, the 30th resembles a "microscopic view of a new strain of a disease." The judges concluded the district "received well-deserved ridicule as the most gerrymandered district in the United States."

The 30th was the result of a complicated chain of events triggered by rapid population gains in Texas in the 1980s. The state acquired three new congressional seats in the 1990 reapportionment. As chairwoman of the Texas Senate Subcommittee on Congressional Districts, Johnson designed this one to suit her political strengths.

The contorted lines of the 30th produced an outcry from other candidates who felt the lines unfairly benefited Johnson. But the federal judges let the boundaries stand for one simple reason: They give minorities a majority vote.

All of downtown Dallas is included in the 30th. The eighth-largest city in the nation and second to Houston in the state, Dallas is a major banking and insurance center, as well as a popular draw for tourists and conventioneers. More than 100 companies relocated to Dallas in the 1980s and more than 500 foreign companies have offices here.

A generation of Americans recall Dallas as the scene of President John F. Kennedy's assassination in 1963. The site and nearby memorial are in the historic west end of downtown. Known also for its museums and symphony, Dallas nevertheless has experienced a decline in tourism since 1990. In 1993 city officials and the Chamber of Commerce began a major promotional effort.

The State-Thomas neighborhood, adjacent to downtown, included some of the city's first homes owned by blacks. Most were razed by speculators in the 1960s, and the area today has predominantly white, affluent residents. Some black families that owned Victorian homes kept the properties when the city created a historic district.

Several corporations have opened offices and manufacturing plants in North Dallas, including Texas Instruments, Fujitsu, IBM and EDS, the semiconductor business that Ross Perot started and then sold to General Motors.

Although the city of Arlington is not in this district, many residents of the 30th work at the General Motors plant there. Other district residents commute to the superconducting super collider complex south of Dallas.

There are no military bases in the 30th, but a number of residents work at the Naval Air Station in Arlington, which is on the 1993 base-closure list.

1990 Population: 566,217. White 212,481 (38%), Black 283,225 (50%), Other 70,511 (12%). Hispanic origin 96,732 (17%). 18 and over 407,638 (72%), 62 and over 54,834 (10%). Median age: 29.

Committees

Public Works & Transportation (39th of 39 Democrats)
Investigations & Oversight; Public Buildings & Grounds; Surface Transportation

Science, Space & Technology (27th of 33 Democrats)
Science; Technology, Environment & Aviation

Campaign Finance

	Receipts	Receipts from PACs		Expend-itures
1992				
Johnson (D)	$283,350	$114,176	(40%)	$282,734
Cain (R)	$2,100	$1,000	(48%)	$1,754

Key Votes

1993

Require parental notification of minors' abortions	N
Require unpaid family and medical leave	Y
Approve national "motor voter" registration bill	Y
Approve budget increasing taxes and reducing deficit	Y
Approve economic stimulus plan	Y

Elections

1992 General		
Eddie Bernice Johnson (D)	107,831	(72%)
Lucy Cain (R)	37,853	(25%)
Ken Ashby (LIBERT)	5,063	(3%)
1992 Primary		
Eddie Bernice Johnson (D)	41,587	(92%)
Adolph A. Hauntz Jr. (D)	3,794	(8%)

District Vote for President

	1992	
D	98,031	(63%)
R	33,514	(21%)
I	25,078	(16%)

Utah

STATE DATA

Governor:
Michael O. Leavitt (R)
First elected: 1992
Length of term: 4 years
Term expires: 1/97
Salary: $75,000
Term limit: No
Phone: (801) 538-1000
Born: Feb. 11, 1951; Cedar City, Utah
Education: Southern Utah U., B.A. 1978
Military Service: National Guard, 1969-75
Occupation: Insurance executive
Family: Wife, Jacalyn Smith; five children
Religion: Mormon
Political Career: Utah Board of Regents, 1989-92

Lt. Gov.: Olene Walker (R)
First elected: 1992
Length of term: 4 years
Term expires: 1/97
Salary: $60,000
Phone: (801) 538-1040

State election official: (801) 538-1041
Democratic headquarters: (801) 484-1200
Republican headquarters: (801) 533-9777

REDISTRICTING

Utah retained its three House seats in reapportionment. The legislature passed the map Oct. 31, 1991; the governor signed it Nov. 8.

STATE LEGISLATURE

Legislature. Meets 45 days yearly, January-March.

Senate: 29 members, 4-year terms
1992 breakdown: 18R, 11D; 27 men, 2 women; 29 whites
Salary: In session $85 a day, $35 a day expenses, $0.27 a mile, $50 a night lodging
Phone: (801) 538-1035

House of Representatives: 75 members, 2-year terms
1992 breakdown: 49R, 26D; 63 men, 12 women; 74 whites, 1 Hispanic
Salary: Same as Senate
Phone: (801) 538-1029

URBAN STATISTICS

City	Pop.
Salt Lake City	159,936
Mayor Deedee Corradini, N-P	
West Valley City	86,976
Mayor Brent F. Anderson, N-P	
Provo	86,835
Mayor Joseph Jenkins, R	
Sandy City	75,058
Mayor Larry Smith, R	
Orem	67,561
Mayor Stella Welsh, N-P	

U.S. CONGRESS

Senate: 0 D, 2 R
House: 2 D, 1 R

TERM LIMITS

For Congress: No
For state offices: No

ELECTIONS

1992 Presidential Vote

George Bush	43.4%
Bill Clinton	24.7%
Ross Perot	27.3%

1988 Presidential Vote

George Bush	66%
Michael S. Dukakis	32%

1984 Presidential Vote

Ronald Reagan	75%
Walter F. Mondale	25%

POPULATION

1990 population		1,722,850
1980 population		1,461,037
Percent change		+18%
Rank among states:		35
White		94%
Black		1%
Hispanic		5%
Asian or Pacific islander		2%
Urban		87%
Rural		13%
Born in state		67%
Foreign-born		3%
Under age 18	627,444	36%
Ages 18-64	945,448	55%
65 and older	149,958	9%
Median age		26.2

MISCELLANEOUS

Capital: Salt Lake City
Number of counties: 29
Per capita income: $14,529 (1991)
Rank among states: 48
Total area: 84,899 sq. miles
Rank among states: 11

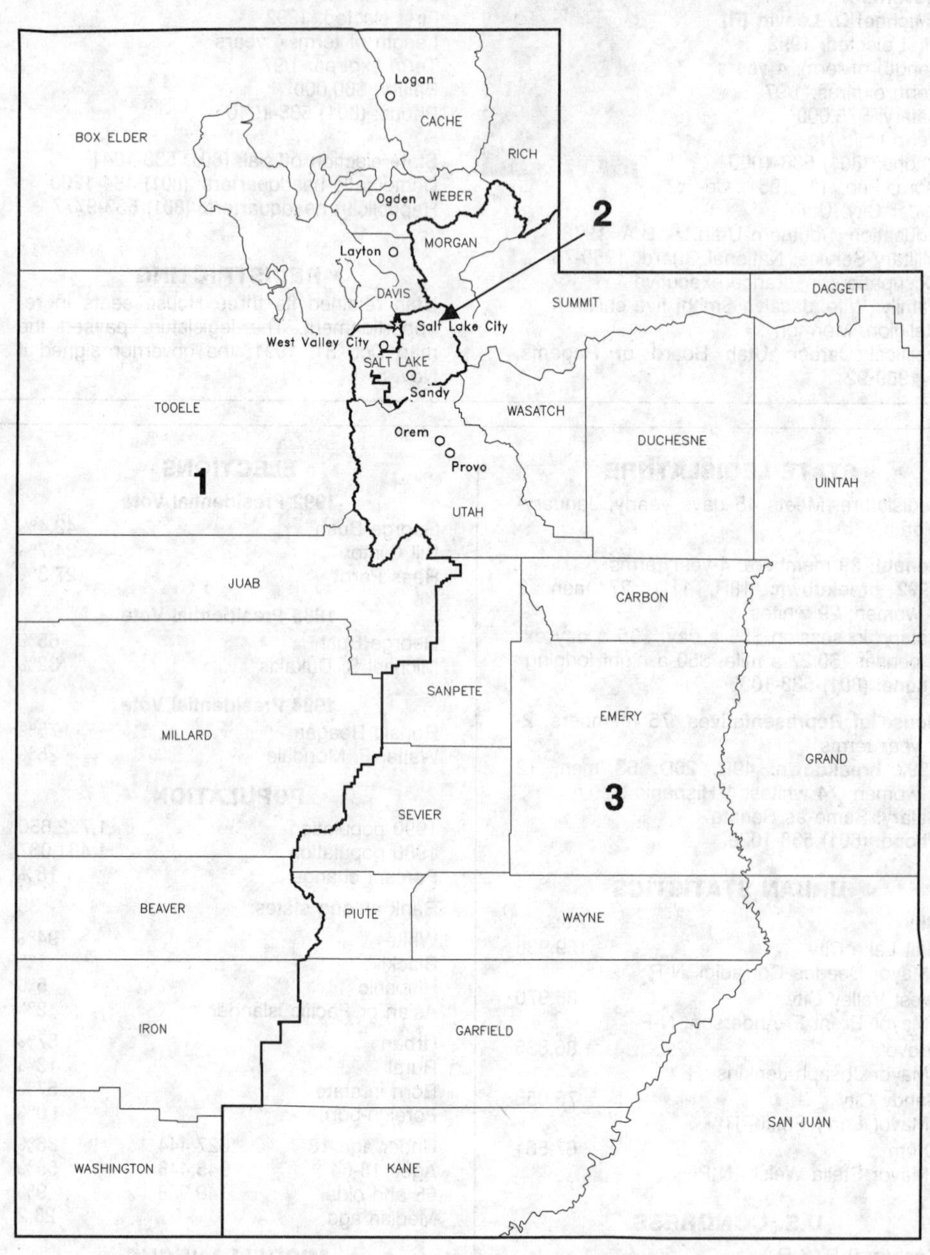
BOX ELDER
Logan
CACHE
RICH
Ogden
WEBER
2
Layton
MORGAN
DAVIS
DAGGETT
SUMMIT
Salt Lake City
West Valley City
SALT LAKE
Sandy
TOOELE
WASATCH
DUCHESNE
Orem
Provo
1
UINTAH
UTAH
JUAB
CARBON
SANPETE
EMERY
MILLARD
GRAND
3
SEVIER
BEAVER
PIUTE
WAYNE
IRON
GARFIELD
SAN JUAN
WASHINGTON
KANE

Orrin G. Hatch (R)

Of Salt Lake City — Elected 1976; 3rd Term

Born: March 22, 1934, Pittsburgh, Pa.
Education: Brigham Young U., B.S. 1959; U. of Pittsburgh, J.D. 1962.
Occupation: Lawyer.
Family: Wife, Elaine Hansen; six children.
Religion: Mormon.
Political Career: No previous office.
Capitol Office: 135 Russell Bldg. 20510; 224-5251.

In Washington: As one of a handful of conservative Senate Republicans who has demonstrated a willingness over the years to negotiate frequently with Democrats, Hatch may be an interesting barometer of the Clinton administration's fortunes on Capitol Hill.

In the past, Hatch has been known to shift from confrontational conservative to accommodating moderate. When the GOP controlled the White House, that trait put him at center stage during debates on a range of social policies, earning him considerable positive publicity and a hefty list of legislative accomplishments.

But from time to time, there are flashes of the conservative militant Hatch, the one who came to the Senate in 1977 with a virtual declaration of war on the liberal Washington establishment and its "soft-headed inheritors of wealth."

Now, with a Democrat in the White House and Hatch shifting to the ranking Republican seat on the Judiciary Committee, the question is: Will he seek out a middle-man role between the two parties, or adopt a more uncomplicated adversarial position?

Hatch in the 103rd Congress will be contending with more than just the new dynamics of Washington. Government investigators and the media are scrutinizing his financial affairs, and he also is preparing for his 1994 re-election campaign; the staunchly conservative nature of Utah could influence Hatch to tack to the right.

As the ranking Republican on the Labor and Human Resources Committee for six years, Hatch reached out to his ideological opposites, finding common ground with a man many conservatives love to hate, Massachusetts Democrat Edward M. Kennedy. Over the years, the two have worked on a wide range of issues; in the 102nd alone the pair were instrumental in passing a summer jobs program, enacting penalties for drug manufacturers that defraud the Food and Drug Administration, and winning approval of legislation requiring drug makers to offer discounts to public health programs.

The "odd couple" developed enough of a friendship that in early 1993 Hatch rejected GOP entreaties to campaign against Kennedy in his 1994 re-election bid.

But Hatch left the top Republican spot on Labor after the 102nd Congress to become the ranking member on Judiciary, where the Democratic chairman is Joseph Biden Jr. of Delaware.

Hatch tends to strike a more aggressively partisan posture on legal matters, as he demonstrated during the 1991 confirmation hearings of Supreme Court nominee Clarence Thomas.

A strong Thomas supporter, Hatch argued against the need for additional Judiciary hearings when it became public that professor Anita F. Hill had accused Thomas of sexually harassing her when she worked with him at the Equal Employment Opportunity Commission. "If any of the Democrats had wanted to pursue Hill's charges further they could have put off the committee vote. . . . They all knew about it."

Once Hill arrived in the ornate Senate Caucus Room, Hatch and Arlen Specter of Pennsylvania led the Republican assault as TV cameras relayed the spectacle to millions of Americans. Hatch disputed Hill's allegations as fantasy or fabrication, and he expressed sympathy with the accused.

"How do you feel right now, Judge, after what you've been through?" Hatch asked of Thomas.

In the aftermath, Biden complained that Hatch and other Republicans, in their desire to back the Bush administration's nominee, did not consider Hill's charges with an open mind.

It was not the first time Hatch had loyally stood by an administration nominee.

He fought to the bitter end for the unsuccessful 1987 Supreme Court nominations of Robert H. Bork and Douglas H. Ginsburg. And as Bush's nomination of William Lucas to head the Civil Rights Division of the Justice Department headed toward defeat, Hatch defended the credentials of Lucas, a black officeholder in Michigan, and waded into an awkward debate over racism. "As county executive, he headed a county that was larger in population than 20 states," Hatch said. "What more does a black man or a white man or anyone else have to do?

We have to give these people an opportunity, after what they've been through."

But when President Clinton's first attorney general nominee struggled under the admission she had hired illegal aliens to serve as domestic help, there was no sign of Hatch the partisan bulldog; he was one of the first and few to rally around Zoë Baird.

"Sometimes these laws are very difficult to comply with," he said shortly before Baird withdrew from contention.

Hatch's own compliance with ethical standards has come into question as a result of actions involving the scandal-ridden Bank of Credit and Commerce International (BCCI).

In the spring of 1993, apparently at Hatch's request, the Senate Ethics Committee began investigating his connections to the bank, which was closed in 1991 after investigators linked it to widespread fraud, bribes, arms trafficking and tax evasion. In 1990 Hatch defended a lenient plea bargain with BCCI in a speech on the Senate floor. News reports indicate he also asked BCCI for a loan for a friend and had a number of telephone calls and meetings with BCCI managers.

Before 1980, Hatch wore just one hat in the Senate: that of conservative ideologue. In 1979, when he ran for the chairmanship of the Senate GOP campaign committee, Hatch thought he had rounded up the support to win. But some senators said afterward that Hatch's reputation as a strident conservative had cost him votes.

That perception began to change as Hatch took over the Labor Committee in 1981. Even under GOP rule, the committee had a moderate-to-liberal majority. The course pursued by Hatch was a relatively successful one — at least in terms of the volume of legislation, particularly in the area of health policy, that became law. But his eagerness to compromise left some of his fellow Republicans wondering whether he had abandoned his principles in an unseemly rush to get something enacted.

The promise and pitfalls inherent in Hatch's split persona have been evident in his approach to civil rights legislation.

Though Hatch likes to say he is "second to none" in his support for civil rights, he was a leading foe of civil rights forces throughout the 1980s. In their first head-on clash, Hatch won a 1980 victory on Judiciary in blocking legislation to strengthen federal enforcement of open-housing laws.

A decade later, he played a shifting role in the effort to enact a new civil rights bill. He started 1990 as a critic of the legislation, well before it was clear where the White House would stand. When the administration made moves toward negotiating, Hatch was sharply critical, but then he crafted his own compromise language. Legislation cleared Congress, but Bush vetoed it, and Hatch shifted again, leading the successful fight to sustain the president's veto by arguing that the bill imposed hiring quotas.

In 1991, the bill's authors agreed to modify the affirmative action sections and put caps on punitive damages. In the wake of the Thomas-Hill hearings, the bill passed with Hatch's support, and Bush signed it.

When it came to the 101st Congress' child-care bill, however, Hatch brokered a deal and stuck by it. With support from a Utah women's advisory group, Hatch was one of the earliest Senate supporters of a federal role in child care. "Let us get with the real world and let us try to solve these problems," he said.

Like most Republicans, Hatch opposed the original Act for Better Child Care (ABC) bill proposed in the 100th. But he worked with the lead Senate sponsor, Connecticut Democrat Christopher J. Dodd, to strike a compromise. At Hatch's insistence, the 1989 version gave states a larger role in setting federal health and safety standards and more flexibility in implementing them.

"I have been personally likened to Karl Marx, Benedict Arnold and even Brutus," Hatch said.

As Republicans drafted their alternative bill, they jokingly refused to let Hatch see it, and he wound up being one of three Republicans to oppose it. And as the GOP criticized the ABC bill, Hatch became incensed. "I have never seen an issue where the conservative side of the equation has distorted a bill more than this bill," he said. "I am personally offended by it."

On the Americans with Disabilities Act, Hatch authored an unsuccessful amendment to create a refundable tax credit for small businesses to offset the costs of the bill. Despite the failure of that plan, Hatch, the GOP floor manager, was emotional in support for the final bill. He broke down briefly as he spoke of the courage of his late brother-in-law who had battled polio.

During that debate, Hatch also revealed a longstanding sensitivity to AIDS patients. Conservatives advocated language that would have permitted workers with a communicable disease to be transferred out of food-handling jobs even if the disease could not be transmitted through food. "Let us not use somebody's feelings, fears or misconceptions," he said. "Let us use science."

He offered a successful amendment that called for the development of a list of diseases that can be transferred by food handling. Similarly, Hatch has been a key supporter of AIDS research and education legislation, and in 1990, he played a role in keeping groups helping children with AIDS from splitting their lobbying efforts from less-popular groups representing other AIDS victims.

In 1987 and again in 1990, Hatch chastised Sen. Jesse Helms for his opposition to AIDS legislation. "Should we just let the disease run rampant because we do not agree with the morals of certain people?" Hatch said in 1990. "I do not condone homosexual activity, but that does not have a thing to do with this bill."

Whatever inclinations Hatch has to seek a middle ground, he not infrequently can be found anchoring the right side of the GOP spectrum.

When President Bush issued Christmas Eve pardons of former Defense Secretary Caspar W. Weinberger and five other Republicans involved in the Iran-contra scandal, Hatch said he would have preferred even broader pardons. (In the 100th Congress, serving on the select Senate committee investigating the Iran-contra affair, Hatch implored members to understand its "really worthy foreign policy objectives.")

In July 1991, Hatch signed a letter urging Bush to look more critically at China's human rights abuses, economic policies and role in arms proliferation.

When Hatch feels strongly about an issue he will go to great lengths to fight for his position. Such was the case in the October 1992 debate over charging drug manufacturers "user fees." Hatch used the bill to fight for an unrelated cause, but one of personal interest to him — vitamins. He threatened to block the user fee bill, which he supported, until the FDA agreed to back off plans to limit health claims made by vitamin producers. Hatch, who frequently offers visitors to his Capitol office a glass of "green goop," won a one-year delay in implementation of the FDA proposal.

Hatch is an ardent abortion-rights foe; he voted against requiring businesses to provide unpaid family and medical leave; and he says that imposing a waiting period on handgun purchases (the "Brady bill") would lead to the "persecution of decent law-abiding sportspeople."

As chairman of the Constitution Subcommittee at Judiciary while the GOP controlled the Senate, Hatch became enmeshed in controversies over conservative-backed constitutional amendments, many of which he proposed. He made only intermittent progress however, and on occasion found himself at odds with his allies over strategy.

On abortion, for instance, Hatch argued that only a constitutional amendment would be sufficient to overturn the Supreme Court's decision permitting abortion — a crucial difference with groups wanting simply to ban abortion by statute. Moreover, his amendment in effect turned the issue over to the states, while some anti-abortion groups sought a national prohibition. Despite his efforts, the amendment was defeated in 1983.

At Home: While Hatch has grown wise in the ways of Washington, he was a political neophyte when he launched his first Senate campaign in 1976. It was a textbook example of anti-Washington politics.

Hatch's lack of government experience at any level almost certainly helped him. In his private legal practice, he had represented clients fighting federal regulations.

Hatch was recruited for a Senate race against incumbent Democrat Frank E. Moss by conservative leader Ernest Wilkinson, who had challenged Moss in 1964. Hatch's competitor for the GOP nomination was Jack W. Carlson, who had a long résumé in the federal government punctuated by service as assistant secretary of the Interior. Carlson, the front-runner, underscored his Washington experience.

That was the wrong record for Utah in 1976. Hatch, sensing the state was fed up with federal rules, took the opposite approach. The party convention gave him nearly half the vote, and the day before the primary balloting, Hatch reinforced his conservative credentials by running newspaper ads trumpeting an endorsement from Ronald Reagan. He won by almost 2-to-1.

The primary gave Hatch a publicity bonus that helped him catch up to Moss, who faced no party competitors. Moss, seen as a liberal by Utah standards, had helped himself at home by investigating Medicaid abuses and fighting to ban cigarette ads from television. He stressed his seniority and the tangible benefits it had brought the state. But Hatch argued successfully that the real issue was limiting government and taxes, and that he would be more likely to do that than Moss.

Bidding for a second term in 1982, Hatch came under strong challenge for being rigid both in his conservative views and his personal style. Ted Wilson, his affable opponent, was a well-known figure throughout the state, having served two terms as mayor of Salt Lake City.

Wilson was not the only one with designs on the incumbent. After Hatch blocked the labor law revision in 1978, AFL-CIO President George Meany had vowed, "We'll defeat you no matter what it takes." But unions are not the most useful allies in conservative Utah. Being a labor target almost certainly did Hatch more good than harm.

Meanwhile, he worked hard to meet complaints about his demeanor. Funding a TV ad campaign with a treasury nearly three times the size of his opponent's, Hatch ran spots that showed him playing with children and dogs.

Wilson branded Hatch's politics as extremist, indicted his style as "strident and contentious," accused him of caring more about national conservative causes than about Utah, and, finally, criticized the Reagan economic philosophy that Hatch vowed he would continue to fight for if re-elected.

The latter approach probably did not help Wilson. Utah gave Reagan 73 percent in 1980 — his best showing in the country — and the president's popularity remained high there in late 1982. Buoyed by two Reagan visits to the state during the campaign, Hatch won a solid 58 percent of the vote.

In 1988, Democrats had trouble finding an opponent for Hatch. When former Gov. Scott M. Matheson announced in 1987 that he would not run, Brian Moss won the Democratic nomination almost by default.

Moss, son of the former senator Hatch had ousted, boasted of his family's roots in Utah and took up the complaint that the Pittsburgh-born Hatch was pursuing a national conservative agenda rather than focusing on ways to retool Utah's struggling economy. But Moss had little going for him besides his famous name; he was outspent by more than 25-to-1.

As in 1982, Hatch spent much of his money on advertising that highlighted his caring side.

As it turned out, the only campaign problem Hatch encountered was self-inflicted. Speaking in Republican southern Utah in early September, he launched into an assault on the Democratic Party, labeling it "the party of homosexuals ... the party of abortion ... the party that has basically, I think, denigrated a lot of the values that have made this country the greatest country in the world." Hatch's remarks drew national attention. But the underfunded Moss was not in a position to take advantage, and Hatch coasted to victory with 67 percent of the vote.

Committees

Judiciary (Ranking)
Patents, Copyrights & Trademarks (ranking); Antitrust, Monopolies & Business Rights; Constitution

Finance (8th of 9 Republicans)
Energy & Agricultural Taxation (ranking); International Trade; Medicare & Long Term Care

Labor & Human Resources (6th of 7 Republicans)
Labor (ranking); Education, Arts & Humanities; Employment & Productivity; Disability Policy

Elections

1988 General

Orrin G. Hatch (R)	430,089	(67%)
Brian H. Moss (D)	203,364	(32%)

Previous Winning Percentages: 1982 (58%) 1976 (54%)

Campaign Finance

	Receipts	Receipts from PACs		Expend-itures
1988				
Hatch (R)	$4,138,756	$1,173,764	(28%)	$4,005,182
Moss (D)	$153,159	$71,800	(47%)	$153,475

Key Votes

1993	
Require unpaid family and medical leave	N
Approve national "motor voter" registration bill	N
Approve budget increasing taxes and reducing deficit	N
Support president's right to lift military gay ban	N
1992	
Approve school-choice pilot program	Y
Allow shifting funds from defense to domestic programs	N
Oppose deeper cuts in spending for SDI	+
1991	
Approve waiting period for handgun purchases	N
Raise senators' pay and ban honoraria	N
Authorize use of force in Persian Gulf	Y
Confirm Clarence Thomas to Supreme Court	Y

Voting Studies

Year	Presidential Support S	Presidential Support O	Party Unity S	Party Unity O	Conservative Coalition S	Conservative Coalition O
1992	82	12	88	4	95	5
1991	86	7	90	7	88	10
1990	77	22	89	11	97	3
1989	81	18	85	15	97	3
1988	78	17	82	16	100	0
1987	71	24	88	8	91	6
1986	92	8	92	8	95	5
1985	82	16	85	12	85	15
1984	78	19	91	9	98	2
1983	72	28	90	9	93	7
1982	79	13	80	12	90	6
1981	87	11	89	8	91	7

Interest Group Ratings

Year	ADA	AFL-CIO	CCUS	ACU
1992	5	17	100	96
1991	10	25	90	86
1990	11	33	92	87
1989	5	10	88	93
1988	5	36	86	96
1987	5	11	100	92
1986	5	13	95	96
1985	10	19	86	91
1984	10	18	83	95
1983	0	6	100	80
1982	5	5	70	79
1981	0	11	100	93

Robert F. Bennett (R)

Of Salt Lake City — Elected 1992; 1st Term

Born: Sept. 18, 1933, Salt Lake City, Utah.
Education: U. of Utah, B.S. 1957.
Military Service: National Guard, 1957-61.
Occupation: Management consultant.
Family: Wife, Joyce McKay; six children.
Religion: Mormon.
Political Career: No previous office.
Capitol Office: 241 Dirksen Bldg. 20510; 224-5444.

The Path to Washington: Although he had never held elective office before winning a Senate seat in 1992, Bennett came to Congress with political experience, family connections and a successful business career that exposed him to many of the issues and people he will deal with as Utah's junior senator.

During the first months of the 103rd Congress, Bennett kept a generally low profile, but he did earn the spotlight for challenging Ross Perot's views on trade policy when the Texas billionaire testified before the Senate Banking Committee in April 1993.

During the hearing, the former and possibly future presidential candidate reiterated his assertion that ratifying the North American Free Trade Agreement (NAFTA) would cause a massive job loss in the United States because companies would be encouraged to move to Mexico to take advantage of its lower wages.

Bennett accused Perot of ignoring what he said is the economic reality that business owners place a higher premium on factors such as worker productivity and access to markets than on labor costs.

"The horse has left the barn and you are securing and hammering on the door," Bennett said. "In my opinion, the factories are in Mexico now. . . . NAFTA is about markets, not factories. NAFTA is about opening markets in Mexico for American goods."

Bennett's road to the Senate followed a familiar path in Utah, where the biggest hurdle for a Republican seeking statewide office generally is the GOP primary. The outnumbered Democratic Party has an uphill fight in general elections.

Bennett's most serious competition was in the primary against Joe Cannon, a steel company executive. Bennett won nomination by about 3 percentage points, then went on to a 15-point November victory over the Democratic nominee, Rep. Wayne Owens (1973-75; 1987-93) for the right to replace retiring Republican Sen. Jake Garn.

Though Bennett was making his first try for elective office, his family name is familiar to many people in Utah: He is the son of four-term U.S. Sen. Wallace F. Bennett, who served from 1951 to 1974. Robert Bennett is a millionaire businessman who made his fortune with the Franklin Day Planner, a schedule-organizer.

During the general election campaign, Owens and the media devoted attention to Bennett's connection to the 1972 Watergate break-in. He bought a public relations firm that employed E. Howard Hunt, who was indicted in the Watergate burglary. Bennett said he fired Hunt after the scandal. And at one point, Bennett had to contend with allegations that he was "Deep Throat," the informant who guided reporters to the heart of the Watergate issue. Bennett denied he was the source, as did journalists who covered the story.

In his campaign, Bennett said he would bring a businesslike approach to Washington and would not stay longer than two terms. He supported a line-item veto for the president, called for federal spending cuts and said the private sector could handle many of the tasks now performed by government. He opposed a broader federal role in areas such as education, saying the central government should limit its involvement in education to measuring performance at the local level.

His economic proposals include cutting the capital gains tax rate to 15 percent — it is now 28 percent — and reverting to the tax structure that existed before the 1990 budget agreement.

Generally, Bennett opposes abortion, but he would make exceptions if the woman was the victim of rape or incest, the pregnancy endangered her life or the fetus was severely deformed. He opposes most gun-control measures and was endorsed by the National Rifle Association.

One of the big issues in the general election contest was Owens' support for designating 5.4 million acres of federally owned land in Utah as wilderness. Bennett said doing so would throw rural Utah into a depression "of 1934 standards." He favored multiple use of land and more regional and local clean air and water standards.

Once in the Senate, Bennett got a seat on the Energy and Natural Resources Committee, where he can participate in debates on wilderness designation and on the Endangered Species Act and try to check the moves of a Clinton administration that he fears is too cozy with environmentalists. Also from Energy, Bennett will watch over Utah's effort to negotiate to sell the federal government some parcels of state land that sit inside national parks, national forests and Indian reservations.

Bennett's seat on the Banking Committee continues a political tradition in Utah, where banks are a growth industry. Garn served as chairman and ranking Republican on the panel and Bennett's father served on it before Garn.

Committees

Banking, Housing & Urban Affairs (6th of 8 Republicans)
Economic Stabilization & Rural Development; International Finance & Monetary Policy

Energy & Natural Resources (7th of 9 Republicans)
Water & Power (ranking); Mineral Resources Development & Production; Public Lands, National Parks & Forests

Small Business (8th of 9 Republicans)
Export Expansion & Agricultural Development; Innovation, Manufacturing & Technology

Joint Economic

Campaign Finance

1992	Receipts	Receipts from PACs		Expend-itures
Bennett (R)	$4,532,966	$343,210	(8%)	$4,439,376
Owens (D)	$1,934,683	$601,937	(31%)	$1,904,750

Key Votes

1993

Require unpaid family and medical leave	N
Approve national "motor voter" registration bill	N
Approve budget increasing taxes and reducing deficit	N
Support president's right to lift military gay ban	N

Elections

1992 General		
Robert F. Bennett (R)	420,069	(55%)
Wayne Owens (D)	301,228	(40%)
Anita R. Morrow (POP)	17,549	(2%)
Maury Modine (LIBERT)	14,341	(2%)
1992 Primary		
Robert F. Bennett (R)	135,514	(51%)
Joe Cannon (R)	128,125	(49%)

1 James V. Hansen (R)

Of Farmington — Elected 1980; 7th Term

Born: Aug. 14, 1932, Salt Lake City, Utah.
Education: U. of Utah, B.S. 1960.
Military Service: Navy, 1952-54.
Occupation: Insurance executive; developer.
Family: Wife, Ann Burgoyne; five children.
Religion: Mormon.
Political Career: Farmington City Council, 1968-72; Utah House, 1973-81, Speaker, 1979-81.
Capitol Office: 2466 Rayburn Bldg. 20515; 225-0453.

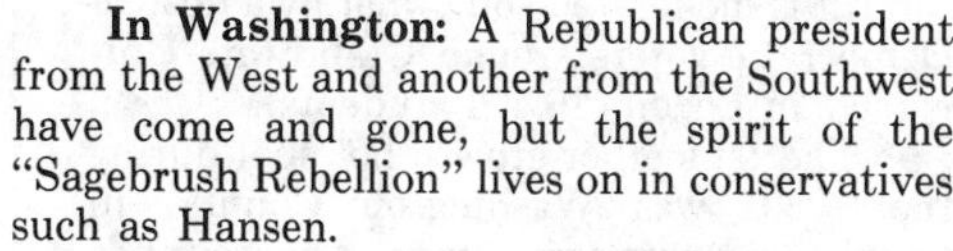

In Washington: A Republican president from the West and another from the Southwest have come and gone, but the spirit of the "Sagebrush Rebellion" lives on in conservatives such as Hansen.

Even as President Clinton and his Interior secretary, Bruce Babbitt, revisit the regulatory controversies of the 1980s, Hansen and his colleagues are looking for ways to loosen a previous generation of federal regulations on Western lands and resources.

"We simply don't believe," he has said, "that the bureaucrats on the Potomac know best when it comes to creating a park, expanding a town, drilling for oil or grazing a cow."

Hansen will have plenty of opportunity to voice his views in the 103rd Congress as the No. 2 Republican on the Natural Resources (formerly Interior) Committee, and as the new ranking member of the National Parks, Forests and Public Lands Subcommittee.

In the 102nd Congress, Hansen signed on early to help with the omnibus Western water bill, working with Chairman George Miller of California to authorize completion of the Central Utah Project.

Hansen began the 102nd Congress as the new ranking Republican of the House ethics committee, just in time for the House bank scandal to reverberate through the House.

Hansen was generally sympathetic to members ensnared in the controversy, especially those who had only a few overdrafts — but he did not shrink from demanding full disclosure when the time came.

Two things are likely to allow Hansen an easier time of it in the 103rd Congress: He will no longer be on ethics (having moved to Select Intelligence) and he will no longer have to deal with Wayne Owens, the Utah Democrat from Salt Lake City who had been his nemesis. Owens gave up his seat in an unsuccessful bid for the Senate in 1992. Owens served on the majority side of the Interior Committee and repeatedly clashed with Hansen on issues such as wilderness designation. Utah, like other Western states, has been embroiled in a lengthy debate over how much of its land should be set aside as wilderness. Landholders, developers and agricultural interests in the mountain states often regard wilderness bills with deep suspicion.

In essence, Hansen felt that Owens was forever trying to turn Hansen's entire district into a park.

In 1989, Hansen tried something bold to rid the delegation of Owens: He offered a plan to draw Owens' core constituency in Salt Lake City out of his district, and suggested that the Utah Legislature redistrict immediately rather than wait for the 1990 census figures. The plot never hatched. Owens was re-elected in 1990 and his district passed in 1992 into the hands of a new Democrat, Karen Shepherd, who won a seat on Natural Resources.

At Home: Although Hansen makes no secret of his desire to be governor someday, he took a pass on the opportunity to run for the office when it was open in 1992. His decision to stand pat was doubly surprising because one of Utah's Senate seats was also left vacant in 1992 by the retirement of three-term Republican Jake Garn.

Hansen's 12 years in the House have been marked by bumpy elections, but he now appears to have a grip on the 1st. He won his current, seventh term with more than 65 percent of the vote, one of his best tallies.

Redistricting changed the district little. Instead, Hansen's firmer standing appears attributable to his enhanced visibility both at home and in Washington. He may also have benefited from his ethics committee work, cleaning house at the House bank.

Hansen's early political fortunes were closely linked to those of two others: Ronald Reagan and former Democratic Rep. Gunn McKay. When Reagan marched to his first national victory in 1980, the Utah 1st was one of his best districts anywhere. That helped Hansen oust McKay to win his seat for the first time. Hansen did not have Reagan at the top of the ticket when McKay attempted comebacks in 1986 and 1988, but by then he was strong

Utah 1

West — Salt Lake City suburbs; Ogden; Logan; rural Utah

The 1st takes in the entire western side of Utah, but most of that land is sparsely settled. More than 70 percent of the voters live in the district's northeastern corner, where population boomed during the 1980s in Cache County (Logan), Weber County (Ogden) and Davis County (just above Salt Lake City).

Republicans dominate the 1st, and Democrats are a distinct minority. George Bush took 49 percent of the district's presidential vote in 1992, and Ross Perot finished second with 29 percent. Bill Clinton ran a poor third, with 22 percent. Rep. Hansen took almost two-thirds of the House vote, his second-best career tally.

The federal government puts groceries on many tables in the 1st. Important employers in the Ogden area are the Internal Revenue Service, Hill Air Force Base and Defense Depot Ogden. To the south in Tooele County are the Dugway Proving Ground and Tooele Army Depot.

In addition, federal contracts are important to some of the district's larger private employers, such as Hercules (which does aerospace work) and Thiokol (known for building solid rocket motors). With defense cutbacks looming, some of these contractors are moving to diversify into other lines of work such as satellite manufacturing and communications. One company makes a product that looks to have a bright future in the 1990s: Morton Automotive, in Box Elder County. It has been dubbed the "airbag capital" thanks to brisk sales of its automotive safety device.

Davis County is the district's most populous. Salt Lake City bedroom communities such as Bountiful and others in the southern part of Davis County are solidly Republican.

Moving north into Weber County, the Democratic and independent vote picks up, partly a legacy of the area's past as a center of rail-related blue-collar employment. The nation's first transcontinental rail link (in 1869) was at Promontory, just north of Ogden.

There is dairy farming country farther north, in Cache County. Cache's Republican tilt is moderated somewhat by a dose of Democratic voters around Utah State University in Logan (16,400 students).

The 1st's other growth hot spot during the 1980s was Washington County, in Utah's southwestern corner. The county's population went up 86 percent in the past decade (to nearly 20,000), as retirees and wintering wealthy were drawn to the temperate climate and verdant golf courses of Washington and neighboring Iron County. In electoral terms, this influx reinforced the area's conservative bent. Bush won 59 percent of the vote in Washington County in 1992.

Cedar City, in mineral-rich Iron County, suffered from a collapse in the mining industry in the early 1980s, but it is now beginning to see its economic base improve. It has become home to a number of high-tech companies that left expensive locations in California.

1990 Population: 574,286. White 541,913 (94%), Black 5,419 (1%), Other 26,954 (5%). Hispanic origin 26,771 (5%). 18 and over 360,394 (63%), 62 and over 64,962 (11%). Median age: 26.

enough to hold the territory on his own.

Hansen needed the element of surprise to beat McKay the first time. Accustomed to being vulnerable but still winning, McKay was slow to prepare for the campaign.

It was a costly mistake. Hansen was Speaker of the Utah House and had already logged nearly two decades in state and local politics. In the Utah Legislature, he had developed a reputation as a pragmatic conservative adept at conciliation.

But Hansen probably would not have won without Reagan's coattails. Drawing out GOP voters, Reagan polled more than three-quarters of the vote in the 1st, helping Hansen offset McKay's strength in the Ogden area and enabling the GOP challenger to register a narrow 52 percent to 48 percent victory. Against less formidable opposition, Hansen pushed his tally to 63 percent in 1982 and to 71 percent in 1984.

In 1986, McKay was ready for a rematch. But he was hampered by a late start and a district nap that was substantially different from when he last ran in 1980.

Despite Reagan's absence from the ballot, Hansen still sought to tap the president's popularity; citing the economic successes and conservative tenor of the Reagan years, he asked voters if they wanted to change the direction in which the country was headed.

In a district where only one out of every six voters was a Democrat, McKay did not dare take on Reagan. But he had no qualms about criticizing Hansen, whom he dismissed as a rubber stamp for the national GOP and an inadequate spokesman for the district's troubled mining, manufacturing and agricultural interests. McKay pointed to his earlier congressional career as a model of effectiveness and claimed that as a member of the House majority, he could get more done than Hansen could. But his comeback bid fell just short, as Hansen again won with 52 percent.

The result encouraged McKay to try again in 1988. Certain that he had lost narrowly because he had started late, McKay began early to organize and raise money. Hansen, certain that his skimpy margin of victory in 1986 was due to his own passive campaign, also staged a more aggressive effort. And with George Bush running almost as well as Reagan had in Utah, Hansen finally beat his old rival easily: He swept 15 of the district's 16 counties, taking 60 percent of the vote.

Hansen was expected to have an even easier time in 1990, when political neophyte Kenley Brunsdale, an aide to Owens, waged a low-budget bid against him.

Republicans tried to laugh Brunsdale off as "an absolute clone" of Owens. But the challenger ran a persistent campaign, tweaking the incumbent by listing the bills he would propose if elected to address specific legislative interests in the district, such as his proposal to block construction of a controversial gas pipeline.

Brunsdale's 44 percent against Hansen raised eyebrows. In tandem with a third-party candidate, the Democrat held Hansen to 52 percent. In 1992, however, Hansen easily dispatched a little-known, underfinanced Democrat, Ron Holt, a Weber State University professor.

Committees

Armed Services (6th of 22 Republicans)
Oversight & Investigations (ranking); Research & Technology

Natural Resources (2nd of 15 Republicans)
National Parks, Forests & Public Lands (ranking); Oversight & Investigations

Select Intelligence (6th of 7 Republicans)
Legislation; Oversight & Evaluation

Elections

1992 General		
James V. Hansen (R)	160,037	(65%)
Ron Holt (D)	68,712	(28%)
William J. "Dub" Lawrence (IP)	16,505	(7%)
1990 General		
James V. Hansen (R)	82,746	(52%)
Kenley Brunsdale (D)	69,491	(44%)
Reva Marx Wadsworth (AM)	6,429	(4%)

Previous Winning Percentages: **1988** (60%) **1986** (52%)
1984 (71%) **1982** (63%) **1980** (52%)

District Vote for President

1992
D 50,622 (22%)
R 115,627 (49%)
I 68,884 (29%)

Campaign Finance

	Receipts	Receipts from PACs		Expend-itures
1992				
Hansen (R)	$221,781	$147,351	(66%)	$240,969
Holt (D)	$64,884	$30,550	(47%)	$64,451
1990				
Hansen (R)	$271,159	$180,750	(67%)	$237,357
Brunsdale (D)	$133,729	$66,850	(50%)	$133,084

Key Votes

1993	
Require parental notification of minors' abortions	Y
Require unpaid family and medical leave	N
Approve national "motor voter" registration bill	N
Approve budget increasing taxes and reducing deficit	N
Approve economic stimulus plan	N
1992	
Approve balanced-budget constitutional amendment	Y
Close down space station program	N
Approve U.S. aid for former Soviet Union	Y
Allow shifting funds from defense to domestic programs	N
1991	
Extend unemployment benefits using deficit financing	N
Approve waiting period for handgun purchases	N
Authorize use of force in Persian Gulf	Y

Voting Studies

	Presidential Support		Party Unity		Conservative Coalition	
Year	**S**	**O**	**S**	**O**	**S**	**O**
1992	89	8	81	9	85	8
1991	82	15	89	7	95	3
1990	83	15	85	10	93	4
1989	80	17	89	7	95	2
1988	66	22	78	8	84	0
1987	73	23	86	8	91	9
1986	79	16	80	8	84	8
1985	81	15	85	9	96	2
1984	74	16	88	5	85	5
1983	77	13	83	3	89	2
1982	77	12	77	8	85	5
1981	71	16	80	4	83	4

Interest Group Ratings

Year	ADA	AFL-CIO	CCUS	ACU
1992	5	18	88	100
1991	0	0	100	100
1990	0	0	79	92
1989	0	8	100	100
1988	0	0	100	100
1987	4	0	100	95
1986	0	0	93	91
1985	5	0	86	95
1984	0	15	81	88
1983	0	0	89	100
1982	0	6	81	100
1981	0	8	94	100

2 Karen Shepherd (D)

Of Salt Lake City — Elected 1992; 1st Term

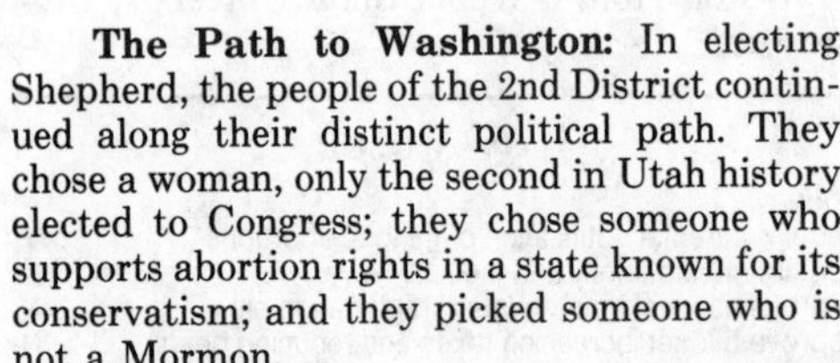

Born: July 5, 1940, Silver City, N.M.
Education: U. of Utah, B.A. 1962; Brigham Young U., M.A. 1963.
Occupation: University official.
Family: Husband, Vincent Shepherd; two children.
Religion: Protestant.
Political Career: Utah Senate, 1991-93.
Capitol Office: 414 Cannon Bldg. 20515; 225-3011.

The Path to Washington: In electing Shepherd, the people of the 2nd District continued along their distinct political path. They chose a woman, only the second in Utah history elected to Congress; they chose someone who supports abortion rights in a state known for its conservatism; and they picked someone who is not a Mormon.

An unusual choice for Utah, perhaps, but not for the 2nd, which had been represented for the past six years by another Democrat, Wayne Owens, who regularly cast votes that seemed risky in the conservative state. Owens gave up the seat to run unsuccessfully for the Senate.

But Shepherd is unlikely to hew to the party line quite as closely as Owens. She backs at least two causes unpopular with the Democratic leadership: a balanced-budget constitutional amendment and term limits.

The leadership, happy to have held on to a marginal district, is not likely to punish Shepherd for straying from the fold. In fact, her committee seats — Natural Resources (formerly Interior), and Public Works and Transportation — are designed to help her back home.

The Public Works slot, especially with a new administration coming to town armed with blueprints, is rich in possibilities because it authorizes federally funded state highway and bridge-building projects. Shepherd sought and received a seat on the Economic Development Subcommittee, which she says will look into ways to convert the nation's defense-based economy to a post-Cold War economy.

Shepherd, a former English teacher who campaigned on a platform that stressed children's issues, opened a children's play area at her campaign headquarters. Her 10-point plan for children included such things as cracking down on parents who fail to pay child support and fully funding the popular Head Start preschool program for disadvantaged children.

Shepherd's child-oriented campaign helped her overcome her one big disadvantage: She is the only member of the Utah delegation who is not Mormon.

Shepherd also tried her hand at making changes early in the 103rd Congress, co-chairing the Democratic freshmen's Task Force on Reform.

While the package produced by the Democratic freshmen included such ideas as requiring that no member chair more than one committee or subcommittee simultaneously, issues such as public financing of congressional elections exposed rifts in the class.

Salt Lake City makes up less than one-quarter of the district's population. Outside the city, Republican strength is more pronounced, with a distinct Republican edge in the outlying suburbs, especially in south Salt Lake County.

Republican Enid Greene, a Mormon, had been favored to beat Shepherd in the general election. And Shepherd, who faced no primary opposition, was one of the few freshman Democrats who had no help from the top of the ticket. Bill Clinton lost to George Bush by nearly 20,000 votes in the 2nd.

Ideologically, Shepherd and Greene could not have been much more different. They both enjoyed noting that the only thing they had in common was gender.

Greene emphasized her strong opposition to abortion rights and the need for fiscal conservatism. She called for a spending freeze and favored a presidential line-item veto.

However, in a state so closely tied to family values, Greene, 34 and single, found it hard to compete with Shepherd, 52, a married woman with grown children. Shepherd won by 4 percentage points.

Shepherd got a boost from having represented a chunk of the 2nd District in the state Senate. It was those neighborhoods — some of the city's poorest and wealthiest — that gave Shepherd her first taste of politics. She was elected to the state Senate in 1990 and opted to run for Congress because state redistricting would have forced her to run against a fellow Democrat to hold the seat.

She also was known statewide for her work as publisher and editor of Network magazine, a publication geared toward working women.

Utah 2

Central — Parts of Salt Lake City

Nowhere in Utah is the physical presence of the Mormon Church more evident than in the state capital, Salt Lake City. Downtown is dominated by Temple Square's massive Tabernacle, world headquarters of a church that is closely identified with abstemious lifestyles and conservative politics.

The irreverent used to joke that newcomers needed to set their watches back 20 years when they arrived in Salt Lake City. But the city has long been more culturally cosmopolitan than Utah as a whole, and its politics more dimensional. Non-Mormon Democratic candidates have won the past two mayoral elections, and in 1992, Shepherd kept up the Democrats' 2nd District winning streak that Wayne Owens began in 1986. (Owens left the House for an unsuccessful Senate bid.) Salt Lake boosters aiming to broaden the city's image are bidding for sponsorship of the 2002 Winter Olympics.

Since it was founded in 1847, Salt Lake City has been a focal point of Utah's economy. Employment in industries such as financial services, transportation, tourism and manufacturing — and lately in high-technology fields such as computers — have made the city one of the West's premier business centers.

Companies have been attracted to Utah because of its low cost of living and doing business, its right-to-work laws, its high birth rate — which maintains a steady labor supply — and its well-educated workers, many of whom know a language in addition to English because the Mormon tradition is to send its young men and women around the world to serve as missionaries.

When energy prices dropped in the 1980s, jobs provided by Salt Lake City's "new age" employers helped rescue the state from recession, and they were a magnet for newcomers: During the past decade, more than 100,000 people moved into Salt Lake County, many of them settling in the city's southwestern suburbs.

While most of the rest of Utah votes Republican, Salt Lake City and some of its suburbs tend to show a more Democratic bent, as is evident from the success of Democrats in Salt Lake's mayoral contests and in 2nd District House voting. The city has a large population of Democratic-voting blue-collar workers and liberal young professionals.

But even in the 2nd, the political worldview looks fairly conservative to most outsiders. In the 1992 presidential race, George Bush and Ross Perot received more than two-thirds of the vote. Bill Clinton's 32 percent was easily his best showing in Utah's three districts.

Salt Lake City's central section and the communities surrounding the University of Utah in the northern hills lean Democratic. But in the wealthy Wasatch foothills section called the East Bench, Republicans hold sway. Voters in such suburban communities as Cottonwood, Sandy City and Draper usually opt for the GOP.

Population: 574,241. White 541,889 (94%), Black 3,497 (1%), Other 28,855 (5%). Hispanic origin 28,310 (5%). 18 and over 379,147 (66%), 62 and over 62,226 (11%). Median age: 26.

Committees

Natural Resources (20th of 28 Democrats)
National Parks, Forests & Public Lands; Oversight & Investigations

Public Works & Transportation (30th of 39 Democrats)
Aviation; Economic Development; Water Resources and the Environment

Campaign Finance

1992	Receipts	Receipts from PACs		Expenditures
Shepherd (D)	$640,031	$201,601	(31%)	$617,594
Greene (R)	$471,058	$123,150	(26%)	$446,334

Key Votes

1993

Require parental notification of minors' abortions	N
Require unpaid family and medical leave	Y
Approve national "motor voter" registration bill	Y
Approve budget increasing taxes and reducing deficit	Y
Approve economic stimulus plan	Y

Elections

1992 General

Karen Shepherd (D)	127,738	(51%)
Enid Greene (R)	118,307	(47%)
A. Peter Crane (IP)	6,274	(2%)

District Vote for President

	1992
D	81,233 (32%)
R	101,169 (39%)
I	75,921 (29%)

3 Bill Orton (D)

Of Provo — Elected 1990; 2nd Term

Born: Sept. 22, 1948, North Ogden, Utah.
Education: Brigham Young U., B.S. 1973, J.D. 1979.
Occupation: Lawyer.
Family: Single.
Religion: Mormon.
Political Career: No previous office.
Capitol Office: 1122 Longworth Bldg. 20515; 225-7751.

In Washington: Through two elections, Orton has acquired more than a tenuous hold on his mostly Republican district by promoting himself as a party maverick beholden only to his conservative Provo constituents.

Orton has taken advantage of the wide berth he is given by the Democratic leadership, voting often against his party colleagues but frequently enough on crucial matters to keep from being branded a disloyal renegade.

He found himself opposite the Democratic majority more often in 1992 than all but five of his fellow Democrats. And Orton regularly bucks party orthodoxy on high-profile issues. For instance, he backed a Bush administration "gag rule" barring abortion counseling at federally funded family planning clinics, and he opposed rewriting the rules from the 1990 budget agreement to allow deeper cuts in defense, with the savings diverted to increase spending for domestic programs. But given his conservative Mormon credentials and constituency, Orton's positions against abortion (in most cases) and in favor of fiscal restraint are not a surprise. Nor is his opposition to gun control out of character.

Where his vote may count more with party leaders is on those issues that don't cut close to home, but are tests of party fealty in Washington. Orton has hewed to the party line on campaign finance reform and a bill to increase voter registration by requiring states to make registration forms available at motor vehicle and other government offices. He stuck with the Democrats on one of two partisan tax bills in 1992, a measure that was aimed at boosting investment in urban areas; it died under a presidential veto.

Sometimes Orton seems to take his individualist tendencies too far, and himself too seriously. Such was the case in early 1992 when he cast the single "aye" in a meaningless floor vote intended to show how little support there was for President Bush's own tax proposals. The amendment failed 1-427, and Orton said he opposed the measure. But he voted yes "to get the process moving."

He brought that same first-among-equals hubris with him in 1990 when, as a freshman, he sought assignment to the Ways and Means Committee, even though the Democratic leadership had indicated that such requests would not be honored. As a tax lawyer with 10 years of IRS experience, Orton felt singularly well-qualified for the tax-writing committee — and he has not been reluctant to share that self-evaluation with colleagues.

So when he tried again for one of a handful of Ways and Means vacancies before the start of the 103rd Congress, Orton was disappointed again. Party leaders chose instead a more loyal classmate of Orton's, Mike Kopetski of Oregon, who had spent his two years working to impress the leadership with his legislative acumen and a willingness to learn.

It surely did not help Orton's cause that he took the opposite side of a fight with Ways and Means Chairman Dan Rostenkowski of Illinois, who wanted to allow businesses to depreciate the value of their "good will" as part of a broader tax simplification package. Orton complained about the proposed deduction not only because of its potential to lose revenue, but also because he said it would benefit corporate raiders.

Orton's aspirations extend beyond prestigious House committees. He continues to explore a Senate bid, possibly against Republican Orrin G. Hatch in 1994. Orton had considered running in 1992 for the seat vacated by Republican Jake Garn, but deferred to fellow Democrat Wayne Owens, who lost a not very close election to Republican Robert F. Bennett.

Though failing to grab the brass ring at Ways and Means, Orton has a chance to raise his profile with a seat on the Budget Committee in the 103rd Congress. There he joins a small cadre of fiscal hawks led by Charles W. Stenholm of Texas, all of whom share Orton's support for a constitutional amendment to balance the budget, a presidential line-item veto, and the predicted consequences of both, a downsized federal government.

Orton has been active in several informal budget working groups, and joined Stenholm's Conservative Democratic Forum, where he chairs a task force on tax policy in the 103rd. He supported President Clinton's budget blue-

Utah 3

East — Provo; Orem; rural Utah

Some of the rural eastern counties of the 3rd saw sharp population declines during the 1980s. In Grand County, for instance — reeling from the collapse of the uranium mining industry — population dropped nearly 20 percent, to 6,620 people.

But outmigration from the rural areas was more than offset by huge growth in the district's urbanized areas: Provo, Orem and the Salt Lake City suburbs. The population in Utah County (Provo and Orem) grew 21 percent during the past decade, topping 263,000. Utah County is the biggest source of votes in the 3rd, casting more than 45 percent of the district's total.

In 1992, George Bush won 61 percent of the vote in Utah County. Provo, the most intense Mormon community in the state, is home to Brigham Young University, which was founded in 1875 to prepare Mormon youth for teaching and religious proselytizing. Today BYU has 6,900 students and offers degrees in a range of fields, but it remains devoutly Mormon.

Democrat Orton's initial House victory in 1990 was earthshaking for the 3rd, which had been considered an impregnable Republican stronghold. His success proved that voters here are not unwilling to consider a Democrat, as long as he stands on the right side of the political spectrum.

Redistricting in 1992 gave Orton a slight boost, transferring from the 2nd into the 3rd a working-class, heavily Democratic section of Salt Lake City. In his re-election bid, that area helped Orton amass 71 percent of the vote in the Salt Lake County portion of the 3rd. Bill Clinton managed to win the Salt Lake County part of the 3rd, and Ross Perot nearly beat Bush for second place there.

The Provo-Orem area has seen a steady influx of new businesses: Wordperfect Inc., Novell Inc. and SoftCopy are among the software companies that have come here in recent years, helping make that industry a leading district employer. Geneva Steel's blue-collar workers in the northern section of Utah County give the area a bloc of Democratic voters.

The rest of the district is rural and sparsely populated. Much of it is mountains and desert, and the GOP is dominant. Cattle ranching, oil drilling and mining have been the traditional industries in the 3rd, but with oil prices flat and the mining industry in the doldrums, tourism — especially as related to skiing — is becoming an important income source. In the northeastern corner of the district, the life-size dinosaurs of Dinosaurland in Vernal (Uintah County) have become a popular tourist attraction. To the south, thousands of visitors tour the 3rd's national parks: Arches, Canyonlands, Capitol Reef and Bryce Canyon.

Other communities in the district are trying to diversify their economies to spare themselves the financial pains they felt in the 1980s. Carbon County, for instance, has opened its doors to a new power plant and a locally owned and operated landfill. Carbon County was Clinton's best in Utah in 1992, giving him 53 percent of the vote.

1990 Population: 574,323. White 532,043 (93%), Black 2,660 (<1%), Other 39,620 (7%). Hispanic origin 29,516 (5%). 18 and over 355,865 (62%), 62 and over 54,027 (9%). Median age: 24.

print in early 1993, but he was also one of only 20 members (and the only Democrat) to support a substitute that would have eliminated most of the tax increases in Clinton's plan and would have added spending cuts.

He backed the House Democratic leadership's modified line-item veto, sponsored by Stenholm. And with Stenholm he was one of 22 Democrats to oppose Clinton's $16.3 billion economic stimulus bill, saying it was more courageous for him to vote no. "I cannot defend playing hide the pea under the shell," he said.

In taking the seat on Budget, Orton gave up an assignment to Foreign Affairs. But he retained his seat on Banking, where attrition after the 102nd Congress puts him in the middle ranks, potentially in a position to wield influence in the 103rd.

Orton did attempt to steer debate on a 1991 bill overhauling banking rules. He offered an amendment to restrict state-chartered banks to the same investment activities as those chartered by the federal government.

Embraced by consumer groups as a bold move to limit state-inspired risks to the deposit insurance system, the amendment was attacked by the Bush administration as an encroachment on states' rights and an attempt to do away with the so-called dual banking system. Orton's more prosaic colleagues viewed it as an overreaching ploy by the real estate industry to prevent state banks from acquiring brokerage affiliates. Orton eventually withdrew the amendment.

Orton, whose own district is home to rangeland and mining activities, has adopted the typical Western lawmaker's opposition to large increases in grazing fees and mining royalties. Orton has teamed with Republican Barbara F. Vucanovich of Nevada to offer alternative legislation to blunt persistent efforts to impose mining royalties on federal lands. He says other proposals would devastate the domestic mining industry and drive mining jobs overseas.

Early in the 103rd, Orton took umbrage at the efforts of freshman New York Democrat Maurice D. Hinchey to designate an additional 10 percent of Utah's land area — all of it already in the federal government's hands — as protected wilderness. Orton, who says he is not opposed to setting aside some additional wilderness areas, nevertheless accused Hinchey of interfering in Utah politics for the purpose of raising campaign funds.

At Home: Of all the districts to change party hands in 1990, Utah's 3rd was the most stunning. Home to some of the nation's most impregnable Republican territory, the 3rd had never given a Democratic House nominee more than one-third of the vote in its four-election existence.

Orton achieved the seemingly impossible, carrying the 3rd and winning resoundingly over his GOP foe, former state Sen. Karl Snow.

The little-known Orton was given no chance of success when he entered the contest to succeed retiring GOP Rep. Howard C. Nielson. But an ideological holy war tore the GOP asunder, leaving Snow a bloodied nominee who was unable to rely on united support in his party ranks.

Two other clouds gloomed Snow's horizon. He was dogged by negative publicity concerning his ownership of certain stocks and his business association with a convicted felon.

Snow, a moderate by Utah standards, was also damaged by an advertisement placed by his own campaign in a Provo newspaper on the Sunday before Election Day.

The ad, which asserted that "values do matter" in urging readers to "vote Republican," featured a photograph of Snow with his wife and children. The caption read: "Snow and his family." To its right was a photograph of Orton's face and the caption: "Orton and his family." Orton is not married.

Republicans and Democrats agreed that the ad largely backfired on Snow.

But Orton did not manage victory through disaffected voters alone. Throughout the campaign, he promoted himself as a conservative Democrat acceptable to his fellow Mormons, who usually prefer the GOP.

In the 1992 election, a change in the district map helped Orton prevail against Republican lawyer Richard R. Harrington. Redistricting slightly boosted the Democratic strength in the 3rd, although some of the Democratic voters have more liberal views than Orton. Still, that coupled with the GOP's inability to field a stronger candidate gave Orton his comfortable victory.

Committees

Banking, Finance & Urban Affairs (13th of 30 Democrats)
Economic Growth; Financial Institutions Supervision, Regulation & Insurance; International Development, Finance, Trade & Monetary Policy

Budget (22nd of 26 Democrats)

Elections

1992 General		
Bill Orton (D)	135,029	(59%)
Richard R. Harrington (R)	84,019	(37%)
Wayne L. Hill (IP)	5,764	(3%)
1990 General		
Bill Orton (D)	79,163	(58%)
Karl Snow (R)	49,452	(36%)
Robert Smith (AM)	6,542	(5%)

District Vote for President

	1992
D	51,574 (24%)
R	105,836 (49%)
I	58,595 (27%)

Campaign Finance

	Receipts	Receipts from PACs		Expend-itures
1992				
Orton (D)	$257,559	$190,995	(74%)	$241,403
Harrington (R)	$71,306	$24,800	(35%)	$71,074
1990				
Orton (D)	$86,601	$32,000	(37%)	$88,234
Snow (R)	$291,945	$108,090	(37%)	$290,439

Key Votes

1993	
Require parental notification of minors' abortions	Y
Require unpaid family and medical leave	N
Approve national "motor voter" registration bill	Y
Approve budget increasing taxes and reducing deficit	Y
Approve economic stimulus plan	N
1992	
Approve balanced-budget constitutional amendment	Y
Close down space station program	Y
Approve U.S. aid for former Soviet Union	Y
Allow shifting funds from defense to domestic programs	N
1991	
Extend unemployment benefits using deficit financing	N
Approve waiting period for handgun purchases	N
Authorize use of force in Persian Gulf	Y

Voting Studies

	Presidential Support		Party Unity		Conservative Coalition	
Year	S	O	S	O	S	O
1992	55	42	56	41	67	31
1991	58	39	57	37	68	27

Interest Group Ratings

Year	ADA	AFL-CIO	CCUS	ACU
1992	55	42	63	56
1991	25	33	60	63

Vermont

STATE DATA

Governor:
Howard Dean (D)
First elected: 1992 (Succeeded gov. 8/91)
Length of term: 2 years
Term expires: 1/95
Salary: $80,724
Term limit: No
Phone: (802) 828-3333
Born: Nov. 17, 1948; East Hampton, N.Y.
Education: Yale U., B.A. 1971; Albert Einstein College of Medicine, M.D. 1978
Occupation: Physician; professor
Family: Wife, Judith Steinberg-Dean; two children
Religion: Congregationalist
Political Career: Vt. House, 1983-87; lieutenant governor, 1987-91

Lt. Gov.: Barbara W. Snelling (R)
First elected: 1992
Length of term: 2 years
Term expires: 1/95
Salary: $33,654
Phone: (802) 828-2226

State election official: (802) 828-2304
Democratic headquarters: (802) 229-5986
Republican headquarters: (802) 223-3411

STATE LEGISLATURE

General Assembly. Meets biennially, January-April (session often extended).

Senate: 30 members, 2-year terms
1992 breakdown: 16R, 14D; 19 men, 11 women; 30 whites
Salary: $480/week
Phone: (802) 828-2241

House of Representatives: 150 members, 2-year terms
1992 breakdown: 87D, 57R, 4I, 2 Progressives; 100 men, 50 women; 148 whites, 2 blacks
Salary: $480/week
Phone: (802) 828-2247

URBAN STATISTICS

City	Pop.
Burlington Mayor Peter Clavelle, N-P	39,127
Rutland Mayor Jeffrey Wennberg, N-P	18,230
Town of Essex Town Manager Patrick C. Scheidel	16,498
Bennington Town Manager Stuart A. Hurd	16,451
Colchester Town Manager David G. Timmons	14,731

U.S. CONGRESS

Senate: 1 D, 1 R
House: 1 I, 0 D, 0 R

TERM LIMITS

For Congress: No
For state offices: No

ELECTIONS

1992 Presidential Vote

Bill Clinton	46.1%
George Bush	30.4%
Ross Perot	22.8%

1988 Presidential Vote

George Bush	51%
Michael S. Dukakis	48%

1984 Presidential Vote

Ronald Reagan	58%
Walter F. Mondale	41%

POPULATION

1990 population		562,758
1980 population		511,456
Percent change		+10%
Rank among states:		48
White		99%
Black		<1%
Hispanic		1%
Asian or Pacific islander		1%
Urban		32%
Rural		68%
Born in state		57%
Foreign-born		3%
Under age 18	143,083	25%
Ages 18-64	353,512	63%
65 and older	66,163	12%
Median age		33

MISCELLANEOUS

Capital: Montpelier
Number of counties: 14
Per capita income: $17,747 (1991)
Rank among states: 26
Total area: 9,614 sq. miles
Rank among states: 43

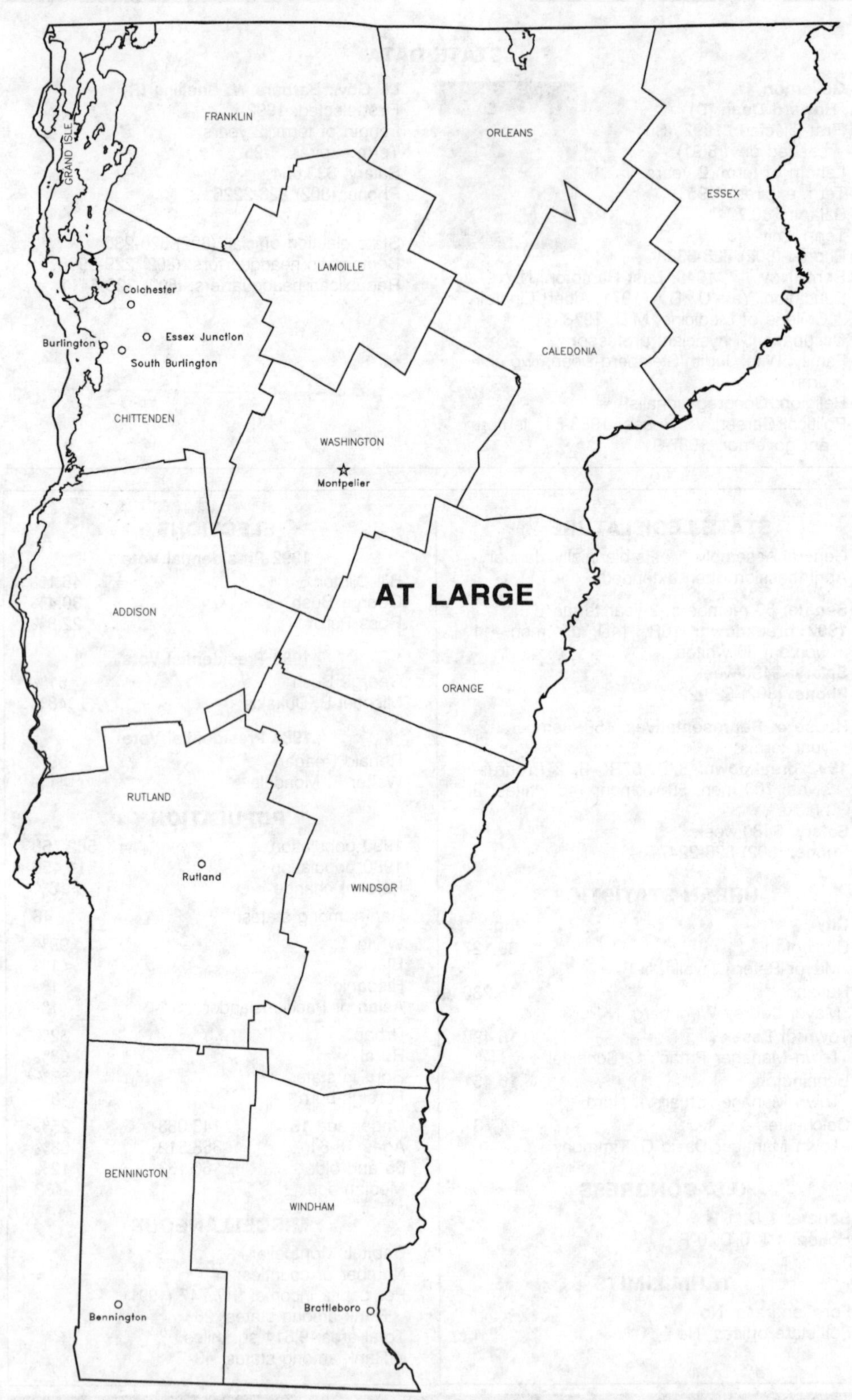
FRANKLIN
ORLEANS
ESSEX
GRAND ISLE
LAMOILLE
Colchester
Essex Junction
Burlington
South Burlington
CALEDONIA
CHITTENDEN
WASHINGTON
Montpelier
AT LARGE
ADDISON
ORANGE
RUTLAND
Rutland
WINDSOR
BENNINGTON
WINDHAM
Bennington
Brattleboro

Patrick J. Leahy (D)

Of Middlesex — Elected 1974; 4th Term

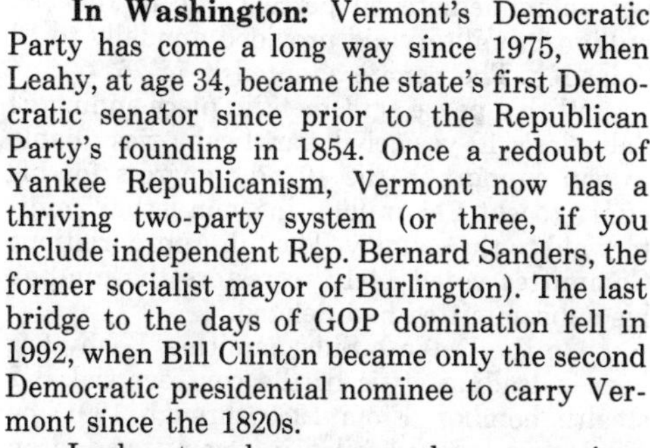

Born: March 31, 1940, Montpelier, Vt.
Education: St. Michael's College, B.A. 1961; Georgetown U., J.D. 1964.
Occupation: Lawyer.
Family: Wife, Marcelle Pomerleau; three children.
Religion: Roman Catholic.
Political Career: Chittenden County state's attorney, 1967-75.
Capitol Office: 433 Russell Bldg. 20510; 224-4242.

In Washington: Vermont's Democratic Party has come a long way since 1975, when Leahy, at age 34, became the state's first Democratic senator since prior to the Republican Party's founding in 1854. Once a redoubt of Yankee Republicanism, Vermont now has a thriving two-party system (or three, if you include independent Rep. Bernard Sanders, the former socialist mayor of Burlington). The last bridge to the days of GOP domination fell in 1992, when Bill Clinton became only the second Democratic presidential nominee to carry Vermont since the 1820s.

Leahy, too, has come a long way since blazing a trail for his state party in 1974. In recent years, the liberal positions he has staked out on a variety of fronts — including foreign policy, defense spending and judicial nominations — have defined the posture of the national Democratic Party.

In the 102nd Congress, largely from his posts on the Foreign Operations and Defense subcommittees on Appropriations (he chairs the former) and on the Judiciary Committee, Leahy played central — though not necessarily victorious — roles in high-profile fights over U.S. policy in El Salvador, American aid to Israel, spending for the B-2 bomber and the nomination of Clarence Thomas to the Supreme Court.

Leahy also is chairman of the Agriculture Committee, but his interests there are specialized. In contrast with past chairmen and most current committee members, Leahy has not dwelt on the multibillion-dollar programs subsidizing America's major farm commodities. Beyond passionately defending dairy programs, a major concern in Vermont, he has focused on the environment, rural development and nutrition programs — issues that most past chairmen treated as secondary interests, or not at all. He also has taken a keen interest in streamlining the Department of Agriculture — to the consternation of several Democratic senators.

It was Leahy's role as liberal inquisitor during the Thomas hearings in the fall of 1991 that has had the most wide-reaching political impact. The rhetoric he employed in opposing Thomas — before and after the nominee was confronted by Anita F. Hill's accusation of sexual harassment — helped introduce a theme that Democrats used to good effect in the 1992 presidential campaign: namely, that the Bush administration had become captive to an extremist conservative element.

Leahy signaled his discomfort with Thomas before the hearings began, telling The New York Times that Thomas' past statements on government enforcement of minority rights "strike me as the views of a combative, hard-line ideologue."

During the Judiciary Committee hearings, Leahy basically ignored the tradition that holds that it is bad senatorial form to press a nominee directly for his views on an issue that would come before the Supreme Court. Leahy pressed the elusive nominee for his views on several issues, most notably abortion. He elicited Thomas' assertions that he had never debated or discussed the landmark *Roe v. Wade* decision — statements that Thomas' opponents exhibited as proof that the nominee was being deliberately evasive.

Leahy defined the Thomas nomination as a partisan Bush administration move that deserved a partisan Democratic response. "When the president makes the political decision to tip the balance of the court and pack it with people having a right-wing ideology, then the Senate has the right to do the people's business and reject those nominees," Leahy said after Thomas narrowly won Senate confirmation.

Though Democrats lost that battle, the efforts of Leahy and others during the Thomas hearings helped raise the profile of abortion rights as a voting issue in the 1992 elections. In winning the presidency, Bill Clinton campaigned on a promise to nominate only abortion rights advocates to the Supreme Court.

Although he chairs the Agriculture Committee, Leahy does not hide his greater interest in Appropriations. "If I could do anything I wanted on the Senate," he told the Burlington Free Press in 1991, "it would be to become chair of Appropriations. I'm not all that far from it." Leahy, the fifth-ranking Democrat on the committee, is at least seven years younger than each senator above him in seniority.

As chairman of Appropriations' Foreign Operations Subcommittee, Leahy helps shape U.S. policy on foreign aid. Early in the 103rd Congress, with Russian President Boris N. Yeltsin's government under pressure from Russian lawmakers, he urged President Clinton to shift money from other parts of the foreign aid budget to provide the former Soviet republics with increased assistance.

During the 102nd Congress, Leahy was at the center of the debate over approving $10 billion in new housing loan guarantees to Israel. The deal had wide backing in Congress, but President Bush refused to back the program because of Israel's policy of aggressively expanding Jewish settlements in Israel's occupied territories. Leahy proposed reducing the guarantees by the amount Israel spent building settlements. He and Bob Kasten of Wisconsin, Foreign Operations' ranking Republican and a prominent supporter of Israel, offered the linkage proposal in March 1992, but the administration rejected it. Only after a new, more conciliatory government was elected in Israel did Bush relent. The final package included elements of Leahy and Kasten's plan.

Leahy in 1987 had to make a premature exit from a post he had parlayed into prominence on foreign affairs — vice chairman of the Intelligence Committee — after he admitted leaking information to a reporter.

Leahy's early departure from Intelligence, months before his eight-year stint was to expire, was a public embarrassment, and it also reinforced some colleagues' private view of him as a spotlight seeker. That view partly explains Leahy's late 1988 loss when he tried to become secretary of the Senate Democratic Conference; also important was the fact that the winner, moderate David Pryor of Arkansas, offered regional and ideological balance to a liberal leadership circle lacking a Southerner.

The object of Leahy's leak was not classified information, but a draft Intelligence Committee report about the just-revealed Iran-contra affair. It was compiled in the last days of GOP control of the panel, and Democrats voted not to release the report when they took over for the 100th Congress. The Reagan administration, meanwhile, claimed the report cleared the president. Leahy, in a statement, said he let a reporter see the document "to show that it was being held up because there were major gaps and other problems with it, and not because of a desire to embarrass the president."

Leahy served on the committee at a time of intense controversy over intelligence issues, including a string of spy scandals and covert actions in Central America, all of which made the articulate, witty and outspoken administration critic highly sought after by the media.

In the 101st Congress, Leahy focused on El Salvador. He was far less sympathetic to administration requests for aid to that country than his predecessor in the Foreign Operations chair, Daniel K. Inouye of Hawaii. In committee, Leahy in 1989 won approval of an amendment placing detailed restrictions on military aid to El Salvador. But on the floor, the Senate voted to remove the language.

The November 1989 murder of six priests at a Roman Catholic university in San Salvador — by Salvadoran military personnel, ruled a U.N. commission that later investigated the incident — altered Congress' mood on aid. In 1990, Leahy and Connecticut Democrat Christopher J. Dodd offered an amendment requiring an immediate 50 percent cut in the $85 million in military aid provided annually to El Salvador. The Senate adopted it 74-25.

With a peace agreement in place ending El Salvador's 12-year civil war, Leahy was unable to win support in the 102nd Congress for his effort to cut $11 million in "non-lethal" military aid to the country. The full Appropriations Committee voted 14-12 to restore the funding his subcommittee had deleted.

On the Defense Subcommittee, Leahy has been a leading critic of the controversial B-2 stealth bomber. From 1989 through 1991, he regularly tried and failed in committee and on the floor to cap funding for the bomber.

The late 1991 collapse of the Soviet Union and doubts over the plane's "stealthiness" called the B-2's basic mission into question. In 1992, the Senate rejected, 45-53, Leahy's amendment to drop $2.7 billion for four additional B-2s. But the authorization provides that no new planes may be completed unless Congress passes go-ahead legislation in 1993.

Until he became Agriculture Committee chairman in 1987, Leahy did not devote much attention to farm policy. And even up to the point where work on the 1990 farm bill was about to start, no one was certain where exactly he wanted to move the insular committee — or whether his members would follow. Leahy's non-traditional interests on Agriculture can sometimes be frustrating to senators — particularly a group of Midwestern Democrats — who essentially want the panel to advocate higher government price supports for their farmers.

When Leahy took over Agriculture, farm-state members were wary of the New England liberal who had been known to poke fun at farm programs and who vowed when he became chairman to put a stop to "business as usual" on the panel, where logrolling is a tradition. More than anything else, farm-state members and commodity group lobbyists worried about Leahy's environmental agenda.

Leahy did press for strict new pesticide regulations, and farm programs did take a $13.6 billion cut in the final 1990 farm bill. Nevertheless, even some who had been wary of Leahy gave him generally good grades for his performance in negotiating the legislation. He was able to keep Republicans on board and produce a farm bill with less of the partisan recrimination that accompanied the 1985 bill.

He is a congenial chairman; no one complains that Leahy fails to give him a fair hearing. He has forged a close working relationship with ranking Republican Richard G. Lugar of Indiana, who, like Leahy, has more interest in environmental protection than many committee members. Together, Leahy and Lugar brokered a compromise on a section of the 1990 farm bill that bars draining swamps and marshes for farming.

But Leahy was well out in front of the committee's consensus with his amendment to bar the export of pesticides that cannot be used domestically and may not be present as residue on food sold in the United States. His proposal aimed to curtail what was dubbed the "circle of poison," in which domestically banned pesticides re-enter the United States on imported fruit and vegetables. But opposition from committee Republicans, the Bush administration and House conferees forced him to withdraw it.

When it comes to dairy, however, Leahy is as protective of his state's farmers as any committee member. He helped draft the part of the 1985 farm bill that created the "whole herd buyout" program, which paid milk producers to send their entire herds to slaughter so milk production would be cut — and with it the government's purchases of dairy surpluses.

In 1991, he waged a yearlong campaign to raise the price paid to milk producers and place limits on the amount of milk farmers could produce. He convinced his colleagues that beleaguered dairy farmers needed relief from deteriorating milk prices and won a 60-40 vote to add it to a fast-track bill paying for the Persian Gulf War. But he was forced to abandon it two days later in the face of adamant White House opposition. He continued the rest of the year to try to work out a deal with the administration. His final effort was rejected 47-51.

At the Judiciary Committee, Leahy is chairman of the Technology Subcommittee. He sponsored a bill in the 102nd Congress to loosen antitrust restrictions on companies conducting joint manufacturing ventures. The bill, expected to be most useful to high-technology firms, passed the Senate but not the House. Action on the measure is expected in the 103rd Congress.

In the 101st Congress, Leahy, a longtime opponent of gun control measures, supported a bill outlawing certain semiautomatic assault weapons. He was castigated by the National Rifle Association, but he defended his action. "I'm as anti-gun control as anyone, but there are areas where the legitimate rights of gun owners have to step back." The Judiciary Committee approved the measure by a vote of 7-6, but ultimately it was stripped from the 1990 anti-crime bill.

At Home: When he first won office a quarter-century ago, Leahy was in the vanguard of Democratic gains in Vermont. At 26, he was elected Chittenden County state's attorney in 1967. He revamped the office and headed a national task force of district attorneys probing the 1973-74 energy crisis.

In 1974, Leahy ran for the Senate seat being vacated by Republican George D. Aiken. Leahy was just 34, presenting a contrast with the 82-year-old political institution he hoped to replace. But he was already balding and graying, and he looked older than he was.

Leahy was an underdog against GOP Rep. Richard W. Mallary. But Mallary proved a rather awkward campaigner, and Watergate made Vermont more receptive to a Democrat, enabling Leahy to score his breakthrough victory.

Leahy survived in 1980 by emphasizing his roots in the state rather than his ties to the Democratic Party. Campaigning against the national GOP tide, he fought off New York-born challenger Stewart Ledbetter with the slogan: "Pat Leahy: Of Vermont, For Vermont."

It took all of Leahy's ingenuity to overcome Ledbetter, a former state banking and insurance commissioner. Using money from national GOP groups, Ledbetter argued that Leahy was a free-spending liberal who was weak on defense. Ronald Reagan's coattails almost elected him.

Although polls throughout Leahy's second term showed his popularity rising in Vermont, GOP officials looked forward to taking him on in 1986. His narrow re-election had pegged him as the most vulnerable Democratic incumbent up that year — a status that was reinforced when Republican Richard A. Snelling, who had retired in 1985 after four terms as governor, agreed to tackle Leahy.

Leahy, however, was well prepared and well financed, and the "battle of the titans" never developed. As Leahy had been building his organization, Snelling had spent much of 1985 on an Atlantic sailing excursion. Early polls showed Leahy with a large lead, and that hurt Snelling's fundraising. The moderate Snelling also had trouble defining a distinction between himself and Leahy; on many issues, the two agreed. Snelling tried out running as a Reaganite, but that rang false; as governor, he had been a sharp critic of Reagan's budget priorities. In the end, Snelling resorted to attacking Leahy's attendance record and labeling him one of the Senate's "biggest spenders." Leahy won with a landslide 63 percent tally.

That overwhelming victory put Republicans in a sour mood about their prospects for denying Leahy a fourth term in 1992. Two months into the year, his only GOP challenger of any note was a little-known businessman. But with the tide of anti-Washington sentiment rising, a "name" Republican, Secretary of State James H. Douglas, jumped into the race, hoping that Leahy's long tenure in office would be a turnoff to voters who regarded Congress as an aristocracy of incumbency.

As the year wore on, the angry voter mood helped make Douglas' campaign competitive. But Leahy, who had not taken re-election for granted even when he looked safe in 1991, kicked his already humming campaign into high gear.

Vermont's anti-status quo vote was evident in Ross Perot's surprisingly strong 23 percent showing in the state's presidential balloting, but Douglas got up only to 43 percent — 11 points behind Leahy.

Committees

Agriculture, Nutrition & Forestry (Chairman)

Appropriations (5th of 16 Democrats)
Foreign Operations (chairman); Defense; Interior; VA, HUD & Independent Agencies

Judiciary (5th of 10 Democrats)
Technology & the Law (chairman); Patents, Copyrights & Trademarks

Elections

1992 General		
Patrick J. Leahy (D)	154,762	(54%)
James H. Douglas (R)	123,854	(43%)
Jerry Levy (LU)	5,121	(2%)

Previous Winning Percentages: **1986** (63%) **1980** (50%) **1974** (50%)

Campaign Finance

	Receipts	Receipts from PACs		Expend-itures
1992				
Leahy (D)	$932,940	$308,052	(33%)	$950,331
Douglas (R)	$196,635	0		$195,737

Key Votes

1993	
Require unpaid family and medical leave	Y
Approve national "motor voter" registration bill	Y
Approve budget increasing taxes and reducing deficit	Y
Support president's right to lift military gay ban	Y
1992	
Approve school-choice pilot program	N
Allow shifting funds from defense to domestic programs	Y
Oppose deeper cuts in spending for SDI	N
1991	
Approve waiting period for handgun purchases	N
Raise senators' pay and ban honoraria	Y
Authorize use of force in Persian Gulf	N
Confirm Clarence Thomas to Supreme Court	N

Voting Studies

	Presidential Support		Party Unity		Conservative Coalition	
Year	S	O	S	O	S	O
1992	23	75	90	4	5	92
1991	28	72	90	10	18	80
1990	32	68	93	7	22	78
1989	47	53	96	4	8	92
1988	34	58	93	5	8	92
1987	33	62	85	9	9	84
1986	24	70	83	11	21	75
1985	29	68	83	16	27	73
1984	30	62	85	11	15	77
1983	41	58	89	10	18	82
1982	37	62	91	9	12	88
1981	34	60	76	8	4	84

Interest Group Ratings

Year	ADA	AFL-CIO	CCUS	ACU
1992	100	100	10	0
1991	95	92	20	5
1990	94	56	17	4
1989	100	100	38	0
1988	100	86	36	0
1987	90	89	31	4
1986	85	87	29	9
1985	70	86	41	13
1984	95	91	35	10
1983	85	88	32	4
1982	90	92	45	20
1981	95	89	6	0

James M. Jeffords (R)

Of Shrewsbury — Elected 1988; 1st Term

Born: May 11, 1934, Rutland, Vt.
Education: Yale U., B.S.I.A. 1956; Harvard U., LL.B. 1962.
Military Service: Navy, 1956-59; Naval Reserve, 1959-present.
Occupation: Lawyer.
Family: Wife, Elizabeth Daley; two children.
Religion: Congregationalist.
Political Career: Vt. Senate, 1967-69; Vt. attorney general, 1969-73; sought Republican nomination for governor, 1972; U.S. House, 1975-89.
Capitol Office: 513 Hart Bldg. 20510; 224-5141.

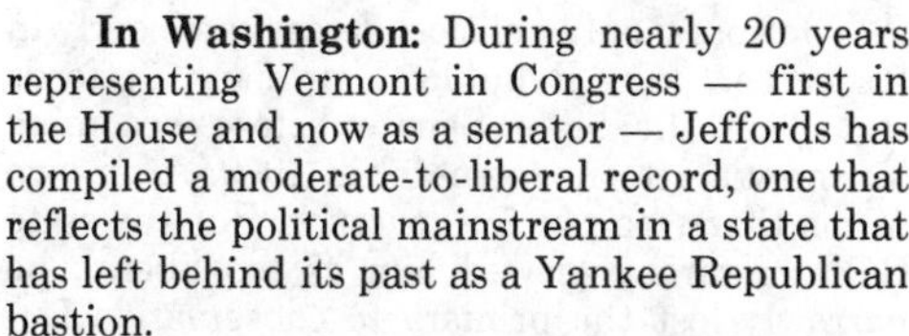

In Washington: During nearly 20 years representing Vermont in Congress — first in the House and now as a senator — Jeffords has compiled a moderate-to-liberal record, one that reflects the political mainstream in a state that has left behind its past as a Yankee Republican bastion.

When he was in the House, Jefford's independence from the GOP line stood out; the consensus of opinion in the House Republican Conference was shifting decidedly to the right.

In the Senate, Jeffords usually does not stand out so clearly. This is not because he has changed his philosophy or style, but because individualism is better accepted in the Senate. Often his views are shared by other influential Republican moderates, particularly on domestic issues such as education, child care and workers' benefits that are his fortes.

Early in the 103rd Congress, Jeffords' independent streak was evident as he joined five other Republicans and Democrats to break a filibuster on the "motor voter" bill designed to make voter registration easier. But on an issue of utmost importance to the GOP Senate leadership — opposition to President Clinton's $16.3 billion economic stimulus plan — Jeffords stuck firmly with the Republican line.

Jeffords never liked the looks of Ronald Reagan's song sheet for the GOP. In only one year of Reagan's tenure did Jeffords support the president's positions on legislation more often than he opposed them. When George Bush became president, he had less of an ideological mission than Reagan, and initially that helped Jeffords appear as more of a GOP loyalist: He backed Bush on 68 percent of Senate votes in 1989.

On the most dramatic vote of his Senate tenure, in January 1991, Jeffords supported the resolution authorizing Bush to use force to end Iraq's occupation of Kuwait. In doing so, Jeffords crossed a peace constituency that is a potent force in Vermont politics.

But as the 102nd Congress wore on, Jeffords often found himself at odds with Bush on key issues. He opposed Supreme Court nominee Clarence Thomas, who was ultimately confirmed. He voted to override Bush's vetoes of a bill extending unemployment benefits and of legislation changing campaign finance laws. And just before the 1992 Republican convention, Jeffords publicly suggested that Bush drop Vice President Dan Quayle from the ticket.

Jeffords was most outspoken in disagreeing with Bush on issues that came before him as a member of the Senate Labor and Human Resources Committee. In April 1991, he questioned the intentions of Bush administration officials after they pressured business executives to break off negotiations with civil rights activists on a job-discrimination bill. "The president has assured me very sincerely that he wants a civil rights bill," Jeffords said. "But it's getting harder and harder for me to live with that" assertion.

A similar bill — aimed at reversing several Supreme Court decisions limiting affirmative action and providing substantial monetary relief in some cases of job discrimination — was the subject of heated debate in 1990. Jeffords joined with moderate Republicans John C. Danforth of Missouri and Arlen Specter of Pennsylvania to broker a compromise between Democrats who described the bill as a successor to the landmark civil rights acts of the 1960s and Republicans (including Bush) who portrayed it as a "jobs quota" bill.

However, with the 1990 elections looming, Jeffords conceded that the issue had taken on a partisan dimension that went beyond the debate over the legislation's provisions. "No matter what we do to modify the language of the bill to address their specific concerns, it will never be enough for some of my [Republican] colleagues and the administration," said Jeffords, who voted in October 1990 for the narrowly defeated effort to override Bush's veto of the bill. He was instrumental in crafting the eventual compromise that was enacted in the wake of the bruising Thomas confirmation hearings.

During the past two Congresses, Jeffords voted with committee Democrats and against the position taken by Bush and the majority of his Republican colleagues on a number of contentious issues. These included a Democratic-backed minimum wage increase, federal aid for child care, assistance to family-planning organizations that provide abortion counseling, lifting the ban on fetal tissue research and mandated unpaid family and medical leave.

A supporter of family leave since his House days, Jeffords crossed back over to that chamber in June 1990 to participate in a news conference by bill supporters, calling the measure "a declaration of independence for the American family." Family leave legislation ultimately was enacted in the 103rd Congress, signed into law by President Clinton.

Jeffords also had a seat on the Environment and Public Works Committee through the last Congress, and he pushed several environmentally related proposals during the 102nd. He sought to amend the Resource Conservation and Recovery Act to force states to recycle bottles, but his proposal was rejected in committee. In the full Senate, Jeffords tried to amend a massive energy bill to promote non-gasoline motor fuels, but the amendment was tabled 57-39. During consideration of the fiscal 1992 and 1993 Interior appropriations bills, he pushed an amendment to increase grazing fees on federal lands, but the amendment was rejected both times.

Jeffords was successful at winning approval for a study of hazardous chemicals and substances that workers may bring into the home from their workplace.

Jeffords was supportive during the 101st Congress of efforts to rewrite the Clean Air Act. He was unhappy, however, about a provision to set up regional, semi-autonomous commissions to oversee smog-reduction efforts. Expressing concern that Vermont, which had no areas exceeding federal air pollution standards, would be forced to pay for the cleanup of heavily polluted areas in its region, Jeffords attached an amendment subjecting regional commission decisions to approval by the federal Environmental Protection Agency.

At the start of the 103rd Congress, Jeffords took a seat on the Foreign Relations Committee, leaving Environment and Public Works.

Although proud of his image as an independent thinker, Jeffords is sensitive to being labeled a gadfly. Rejecting the implication that he had simply been a nuisance to fellow Republicans, Jeffords in 1988 produced a legislative résumé of his House years that ran over 100 pages. Among his highlighted achievements was his role in crafting legislation that in 1982 replaced the expiring Comprehensive Employment and Training Act (CETA) with the Job Training Partnership Act.

At Home: Jeffords is well-suited to politics in modern-day Vermont. The electorate has tilted to the left over the last two decades, with the arrival of thousands of liberal urbanites seeking the state's greener pastures. With Democrats gaining an upper hand, only moderate Republicans like Jeffords have had a chance to win statewide.

Jeffords has in fact faced stronger opposition from conservatives in his own party than he has in general elections. In the 1988 Senate primary, Jeffords received 61 percent of the vote against a conservative neophyte, Michael Griffes. Jeffords then breezed to victory over a Democrat, former U.S. Attorney William Gray, with 68 percent of the vote.

Jeffords' only political defeat came early in his career, in a Republican primary. Jeffords served in the state Senate before becoming Vermont's attorney general in 1969. After two terms there, he ran for governor. But the state GOP hierarchy viewed him as too liberal; he narrowly lost the primary to conservative Luther Hackett.

Jeffords bounced back in 1974, winning a three-way primary for Vermont's open House seat. He went on to defeat Burlington's Democratic Mayor Francis Cain with 53 percent of the vote. Jeffords quickly became indomitable in his House seat. In six re-election contests, he never received less than 65 percent of the vote. In 1986, his last House election, he ran without Democratic opposition.

During his House tenure, Jeffords was often mentioned as a possible candidate for higher office. In 1982, he was regarded as a likely Republican successor to GOP Gov. Richard A. Snelling, who was thought to be retiring; conservatives who distrusted Jeffords persuaded Snelling to seek another two-year term.

But as 1988 approached and GOP Sen. Robert T. Stafford's retirement became imminent, Jeffords gained regard as his heir apparent. No Democratic officeholder came forward to contest him, and the honor fell without opposition to Gray, who had never before run for office.

Before getting to Gray, Jeffords had to contend with Griffes, a 35-year-old Navy veteran who returned to Vermont from a job with the Washington office of Grumman Corp., a defense contractor. Griffes ran an ideological campaign, describing Jeffords as "not a Republican."

But Jeffords responded by pointing out Griffes' lack of Vermont roots: His family moved to the state when he was 17, and he had spent most years since out of state. Citing Griffes' residence in the Arlington suburbs of Washington, Jeffords said the contest was between a "Vermont Republican" and a "Virginia Republican." He won easily.

Jeffords entered the general election contest an overwhelming favorite and was never threatened. Gray's main thrust was to make a connection between a contribution Jeffords received from the Teamsters union's political action committee and his opposition to federal efforts to take over the corruption-plagued union. But Jeffords quashed the issue, denying any connection between his fundraising and his House voting behavior; he said his position on the Teamsters' takeover was based solely on his opposition to federal intervention in union operations. The Election Day result showed that the issue did Jeffords no serious harm.

Committees

Foreign Relations (7th of 8 Republicans)
African Affairs (ranking); International Economic Policy, Trade, Oceans & Environment; Near Eastern & South Asian Affairs

Labor & Human Resources (2nd of 7 Republicans)
Education, Arts & Humanities (ranking); Children, Families, Drugs & Alcoholism; Disability Policy; Labor

Special Aging (5th of 10 Republicans)

Veterans' Affairs (5th of 5 Republicans)

Elections

1988 General		
James M. Jeffords (R)	163,183	(68%)
William Gray (D)	71,460	(30%)
1988 Primary		
James M. Jeffords (R)	30,555	(61%)
Mike Griffes (R)	19,593	(39%)

Previous Winning Percentages: **1986** * (89%) **1984** * (65%) **1982** * (69%) **1980** * (79%) **1978** * (75%) **1976** * (67%) **1974** * (53%)

** House elections.*

Campaign Finance

	Receipts	Receipts from PACs		Expend-itures
1988				
Jeffords (R)	$976,451	$650,393	(67%)	$876,877
Gray (D)	$551,423	$109,950	(20%)	$549,908

Key Votes

1993	
Require unpaid family and medical leave	Y
Approve national "motor voter" registration bill	Y
Approve budget increasing taxes and reducing deficit	N
Support president's right to lift military gay ban	Y
1992	
Approve school-choice pilot program	N
Allow shifting funds from defense to domestic programs	N
Oppose deeper cuts in spending for SDI	N
1991	
Approve waiting period for handgun purchases	Y
Raise senators' pay and ban honoraria	Y
Authorize use of force in Persian Gulf	Y
Confirm Clarence Thomas to Supreme Court	N

Voting Studies

	Presidential Support		Party Unity		Conservative Coalition	
Year	**S**	**O**	**S**	**O**	**S**	**O**
1992	45	52	36	58	37	55
1991	54	43	36	58	35	55
1990	51	46	36	61	49	46
1989	68	26	40	53	58	34
House Service:						
1988	26	64	29	61	45	47
1987	25	71	32	60	47	51
1986	41	58	29	69	44	56
1985	30	56	37	53	33	55
1984	47	42	31	52	32	49
1983	41	51	31	60	27	67
1982	44	47	35	58	38	55
1981	41	55	35 †	55 †	24	68

† Not eligible for all recorded votes.

Interest Group Ratings

Year	ADA	AFL-CIO	CCUS	ACU
1992	65	56	60	27
1991	65	50	22	10
1990	72	44	25	26
1989	40	40	71	44
House Service:				
1988	70	92	54	21
1987	68	50	67	26
1986	60	71	56	14
1985	55	65	59	16
1984	60	18	50	29
1983	65	50	55	27
1982	65	45	53	10
1981	60	40	53	57

AL Bernard Sanders (I)

Of Burlington — Elected 1990; 2nd Term

Born: Sept. 8, 1941, Brooklyn, N.Y.

Education: U. of Chicago, B.A. 1964.

Occupation: College lecturer; free-lance writer.

Family: Wife, Jane O'Meara Driscoll; one child, three stepchildren.

Religion: Jewish.

Political Career: Mayor of Burlington, 1981-89; independent candidate for U.S. Senate, 1972, 1974; independent candidate for governor, 1972, 1976, 1986; independent candidate for U.S. House, 1988.

Capitol Office: 213 Cannon Bldg. 20515; 225-4115.

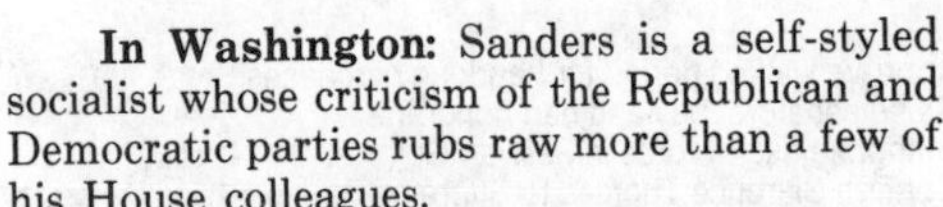

In Washington: Sanders is a self-styled socialist whose criticism of the Republican and Democratic parties rubs raw more than a few of his House colleagues.

But if any of them hoped he would be a one-term wonder, the 1992 election should have disabused them of the notion. Sanders' solid re-election victory demonstrated his appeal to a large bloc of liberal Vermonters.

Sanders is the first identifiable socialist in the House since Victor L. Berger of Wisconsin (1911-13, 1923-29), and he is the first truly independent member since Henry F. Reams of Ohio (1951-55). The Brooklyn-raised son of Jewish immigrants from Poland, Sanders joined in radical politics in college and became a supporter of democratic socialist systems such as that of Sweden.

He denies affiliation with Marxism and has tried to dispel the perception that his chief goal is to create a third political party. But in early 1991 he traveled to Montreal to speak to Canada's democratic-socialist New Democratic Party, underscoring his desire for a closer relationship between it and Vermont's independent political movement, the Progressive Coalition.

In his 1990 House campaign, Sanders battled the claims of incumbent Republican Peter Smith that he would be ineffective as an independent. He promised to enlist in the Democratic Caucus. But when Sanders got to Washington, conservative Democrats opposed his admission, and even some liberals thought a socialist member would harm the party's image. Sanders reached a compromise with Speaker Thomas S. Foley, under which he would not apply to the Democratic Caucus but would get committee assignments.

After Sanders' re-election in 1992, the Democratic Steering and Policy Committee recommended that he be treated on the Banking and Government Operations committees as if he was the most junior second-term Democrat. The concession meant Sanders would rank ahead of the freshmen on his committees. But it skirted the question of whether he might one day be eligible to chair a subcommittee.

Sanders votes like a liberal Democrat — though he sometimes expresses distaste at choosing the lesser of two evils. He voted against the Democrats' budget resolution in 1991 because he felt it was too much like President Bush's proposal. But in early 1993, he voted for President Clinton's budget and taxing plans and his economic stimulus proposal.

On the Banking Committee, Sanders is most interested in consumer and housing issues. When smaller financial institutions are the focus of a fight, he often sides with them against larger competitors, reflecting his vision of a neighborhood-based network of small businesses and lenders.

Sanders, though, sometimes confounds left-leaning Democrats in Washington, as he did in the 102nd with his vote against imposing a waiting period for handgun purchases. That stance was not so surprising to Vermonters, who who knew that Smith had lost in part because of his stated 1989 support for a ban on certain automatic weapons.

So far in the House, Sanders' primary role has been to raise issues that others tend to avoid or to challenge mainstream thinking. He formed the House Progressive Forum with Democrats Peter DeFazio of Oregon, Ronald V. Dellums of California, Lane Evans of Illinois, Maxine Waters of California and others as a foil for the influence of the Conservative Democratic Forum.

Sanders' independence constrains legislative influence, but he is not without accomplishments. He got an amendment into a 1991 banking overhaul bill that preserved banks' abilities to invest in affordable housing. He was also prime sponsor of a House bill to provide federal support to state cancer registries; it became law in the 102nd Congress. The bill's provisions were included in an authorization bill for the National Institutes of Health that died when it was vetoed over unrelated provisions regarding fetal tissue research. But the

Vermont

At large

Some things about Vermont remain immutable. The least-populous state in the Northeast and third-smallest in the nation, it has a scenic beauty that remains largely unsullied. However, a growth spurt of more than 44 percent since 1960 has driven Vermont's population to nearly 563,000. This growth has had outsized impacts on the demographics and politics of the state.

Much of the population increase stemmed from young urbanites who resettled here and brought with them their liberal politics. These upscale emigres joined remnants of the 1960s counterculture who had settled in the state in the early '70s, and a state that had been drifting to the political left became firmly planted there.

Shattered by these developments was Vermont's reputation as the sturdiest bastion of Yankee Republicanism. Democrat Patrick J. Leahy, first elected to the Senate in 1974, earned a fourth term in 1992, and Democrat Howard Dean won the governorship with 75 percent of the vote, the largest Democratic gubernatorial victory in state history.

Dean, as lieutenant governor, inherited the top job upon the 1991 death of GOP Gov. Richard A. Snelling. Dean has a consensus-oriented style and enough of an image as a moderate that his 1992 winning coalition included many centrist Republicans.

Though the new politics of Vermont has seen the Democratic Party grow in strength, moderate Republicans can still gain and hold statewide office.

In 1988, moderate Republican James M. Jeffords — then the state's at-large House member — won the Senate campaign to succeed like-minded Republican Robert T. Stafford. In 1990, Snelling — who was governor from 1977 to 1985 — regained the office by pledging fiscal responsibility in the midst of a state budget crisis. Although Snelling's death put the governorship in Democratic hands, Snelling's widow, Barbara, ran for lieutenant governor in 1992 as a Republican and won easily.

There is a vocal conservative element within the state GOP — the Vermont Republican Assembly — but it is widely perceived as too far to the right to thrive in general elections. The conservatives, however, sometimes can turn out enough loyalists to take primary nominations away from moderates, who are not always as effective at grass-roots organizing.

Although Vermont has moved away from its historical voting patterns, its modern political persona retains an element of the state's stubborn independence. In 1992, nearly a quarter of the Vermonters voting for president picked independent Ross Perot. And in the House, the state is represented by self-described socialist Sanders.

In his 1990 House campaign, Sanders succeeded in portraying GOP Rep. Peter Smith — himself a liberal Republican — as a big-business shill and tool of the Establishment. Sanders' populist message fueled his rise, but his credibility was enhanced by his tenure as mayor of Burlington, where during the 1980s he shepherded the state's largest city through a period of prosperity.

Although its manufacturing heritage has faded, Burlington (population 39,000) enjoyed good times in the last decade, thanks in large part to a boom in its electronics industry. However, that industry was hit hard by the 1990-91 recession, and Burlington has been through the same economic slump that all of New England has endured. The Burlington area has been jarred by large-scale layoffs at companies such as Digital Electronics Corp.

Statewide, both the construction and manufacturing industries have seen a total loss of about 12,000 jobs over the past four years. To help fill the vacuum, state officials are trying to make tourism more of a year-round source of income by marketing Vermont as more than just an appealing ski-season destination for visitors.

Burlington and Chittenden County cast about one-fourth of the state's vote; Democratic candidates for statewide office can usually count on strong support here. Bill Clinton won a majority in Chittenden County in 1992.

Clinton's best 1992 showing — 54 percent — came in southern Vermont's Windham County, which borders Massachusetts. Other small urban centers such as Montpelier and Rutland, reliably Republican in bygone times, now have more Democrats.

At the village level and in most rural areas, Yankee Vermonters still tend to vote Republican, particularly in the northeastern part of the state, which has been less affected by development.

1990 Population: 562,758. White 555,088 (99%), Black 1,951 (<1%), Other 5,719 (1%). Hispanic origin 3,661 (<1%). 18 and over 419,675 (75%), 62 and over 79,608 (14%). Median age: 33.

bill's Senate sponsor, Vermont Democrat Patrick J. Leahy, pushed it through the Senate and it was cleared on the last day of the session.

At Home: Sanders' 1990 win culminated a 20-year effort that moved him from the fringe to the vortex of Vermont politics. His comfortable 1992 re-election spawned speculation of a Senate bid in Sanders' future.

In 1968, Sanders joined a wave of liberals abandoning urban life for bucolic Vermont. Many of the transplants joined the then-small state Democratic Party and helped convert it into a force capable of winning statewide elections. However, Sanders considered both major parties to be dominated by corporate interests and accused them of ignoring the needs of the poor, the elderly and working Americans. He helped found Vermont's Liberty Union Party.

Sanders' confrontational style brought him attention, but also a reputation as a gadfly. In four bids for state office in the 1970s, Sanders never topped 6 percent of the vote.

Yet Sanders was building a grass-roots base in Burlington. In 1981, he ran for mayor and unseated the Democratic incumbent by 10 votes. First written off as a fluke, Sanders won three more terms by increasing margins. He pursued populist goals but also presided over the revitalization of Burlington's downtown.

In 1986, Sanders took 15 percent of the vote for governor as an independent, and he was seen as a spoiler when he ran in 1988 for the open House seat. But Sanders lost to Smith by only 4 points and nearly doubled the vote of Democrat Paul N. Poirier. Retiring as mayor in 1989, Sanders considered running for governor before tackling Smith again. No prominent Democrat was willing to risk Poirier's fate.

Sanders stayed even in the polls with Smith, a moderate Republican, and his economic message was reinforced by the federal budget debate, in which leading Democrats called for taxing the wealthy. With Sanders gaining momentum in the final weeks of the campaign, Smith ran "attack" TV ads, one of which used an old quote out of context to imply that Sanders admired Fidel Castro. Vermont media blasted Smith's negativism, and Sanders surged past him to win with 56 percent.

In 1992, Democrats went out of their way not to field a strong House candidate, and the Republican nominee was Tim Philbin, a favorite of the state GOP's conservative wing. Sanders was the only acceptable candidate to leftists, Democrats and even some liberal Republicans, and he won 58 percent.

Committees

Banking, Finance & Urban Affairs
Consumer Credit & Insurance; Housing & Community Development; International Development, Finance, Trade & Monetary Policy

Government Operations
Environment, Energy & Natural Resources; Human Resources & Intergovernmental Relations

Elections

1992 General		
Bernard Sanders (I)	162,724	(58%)
Tim Philbin (R)	86,901	(31%)
Lewis E. Young (D)	22,279	(8%)
Pete Diamondstone (LU)	3,660	(1%)
John Dewey (NL, NA)	3,549	(1%)
1990 General		
Bernard Sanders (I)	117,522	(56%)
Peter Smith (R)	82,938	(40%)
Dolores Sandoval (D)	6,315	(3%)
Peter Diamondstone (LU)	1,965	(1%)

District Vote for President

	1992
D	133,592 (46%)
R	88,122 (31%)
I	65,991 (23%)

Campaign Finance

	Receipts	Receipts from PACs		Expend-itures
1992				
Sanders (I)	$591,543	$147,057	(25%)	$575,791
Philbin (R)	$78,382	0		$72,958
1990				
Sanders (I)	$571,556	$72,250	(13%)	$569,772
Smith (R)	$682,870	$299,954	(44%)	$688,907
Sandoval (D)	$13,830	$300	(2%)	$12,850

Key Votes

1993	
Require parental notification of minors' abortions	N
Require unpaid family and medical leave	Y
Approve national "motor voter" registration bill	Y
Approve budget increasing taxes and reducing deficit	Y
Approve economic stimulus plan	Y
1992	
Approve balanced-budget constitutional amendment	N
Close down space station program	Y
Approve U.S. aid for former Soviet Union	N
Allow shifting funds from defense to domestic programs	Y
1991	
Extend unemployment benefits using deficit financing	Y
Approve waiting period for handgun purchases	N
Authorize use of force in Persian Gulf	N

Voting Studies

	Presidential Support		Party* Unity		Conservative Coalition	
Year	S	O	S	O	S	O
1992	11	88	86	7	8	92
1991	22	77	84	8	14	86

* These scores computed as if Sanders voted as a Democrat.

Interest Group Ratings

Year	ADA	AFL-CIO	CCUS	ACU
1992	95	100	13	0
1991	95	100	10	15

Virginia

STATE DATA

Governor:
L. Douglas Wilder (D)
First elected: 1989
Length of term: 4 years
Term expires: 1/94
Salary: $108,000
Term limit: Cannot serve 2 consecutive terms.
Phone: (804) 786-2211
Born: Jan. 17, 1931; Richmond, Va.
Education: Virginia Union U., B.S. 1951; Howard U., J.D. 1959
Military Service: Army, 1952-53
Occupation: Lawyer
Family: Divorced; three children
Religion: First African Baptist
Political Career: Va. Senate, 1969-85; lieutenant governor, 1986-90; sought Democratic nomination for U.S. president, 1992

Lt. Gov.: Donald S. Beyer Jr. (D)
First elected: 1989
Length of term: 4 years
Term expires: 1/94
Salary: $29,550 + $10,200 in per diem
Phone: (804) 786-2078

State election official: (804) 786-6551
Democratic headquarters: (804) 644-1966
Republican headquarters: (804) 780-0111

REDISTRICTING

Virginia gained one House seat in reapportionment, increasing from 10 districts to 11. The legislature passed the map Dec. 9, 1991; the governor signed it Dec. 11. The Justice Department approved the map Feb. 18, 1992.

STATE LEGISLATURE

General Assembly. Meets January-February in odd years, January-March in even years.

Senate: 40 members, 4-year terms
1992 breakdown: 22D, 18R; 36 men, 4 women; 36 whites, 4 blacks
Salary: $18,000
Phone: (804) 786-2366

House of Delegates: 100 members, 2-year terms
1992 breakdown: 58D, 41R, 1I; 88 men, 12 women; 93 whites, 7 blacks
Salary: $17,640
Phone: (804) 786-6530

URBAN STATISTICS

City	Pop.
Virginia Beach	393,089
Mayor Meyera E. Oberndorf, N-P	
Norfolk	261,250
Mayor Mason C. Andrews, N-P	
Richmond	202,798
Mayor Walter T. Kenney, N-P	
Newport News	171,439
Mayor Barry E. DuVal, N-P	

U.S. CONGRESS

Senate: 1 D, 1 R
House: 7 D, 4 R

TERM LIMITS

For Congress: No
For state offices: No

ELECTIONS

1992 Presidential Vote

Bill Clinton	40.6%
George Bush	45.0%
Ross Perot	13.6%

1988 Presidential Vote

George Bush	60%
Michael S. Dukakis	39%

1984 Presidential Vote

Ronald Reagan	62%
Walter F. Mondale	37%

POPULATION

1990 population		6,187,358
1980 population		5,346,818
Percent change		+16%
Rank among states:		12
White		77%
Black		19%
Hispanic		3%
Asian or Pacific islander		3%
Urban		69%
Rural		31%
Born in state		54%
Foreign-born		5%
Under age 18	1,504,738	24%
Ages 18-64	4,018,150	65%
65 and older	664,470	11%
Median age		32.6

MISCELLANEOUS

Capital: Richmond
Number of counties: 95
Per capita income: $19,976 (1991)
Rank among states: 12
Total area: 40,767 sq. miles
Rank among states: 36

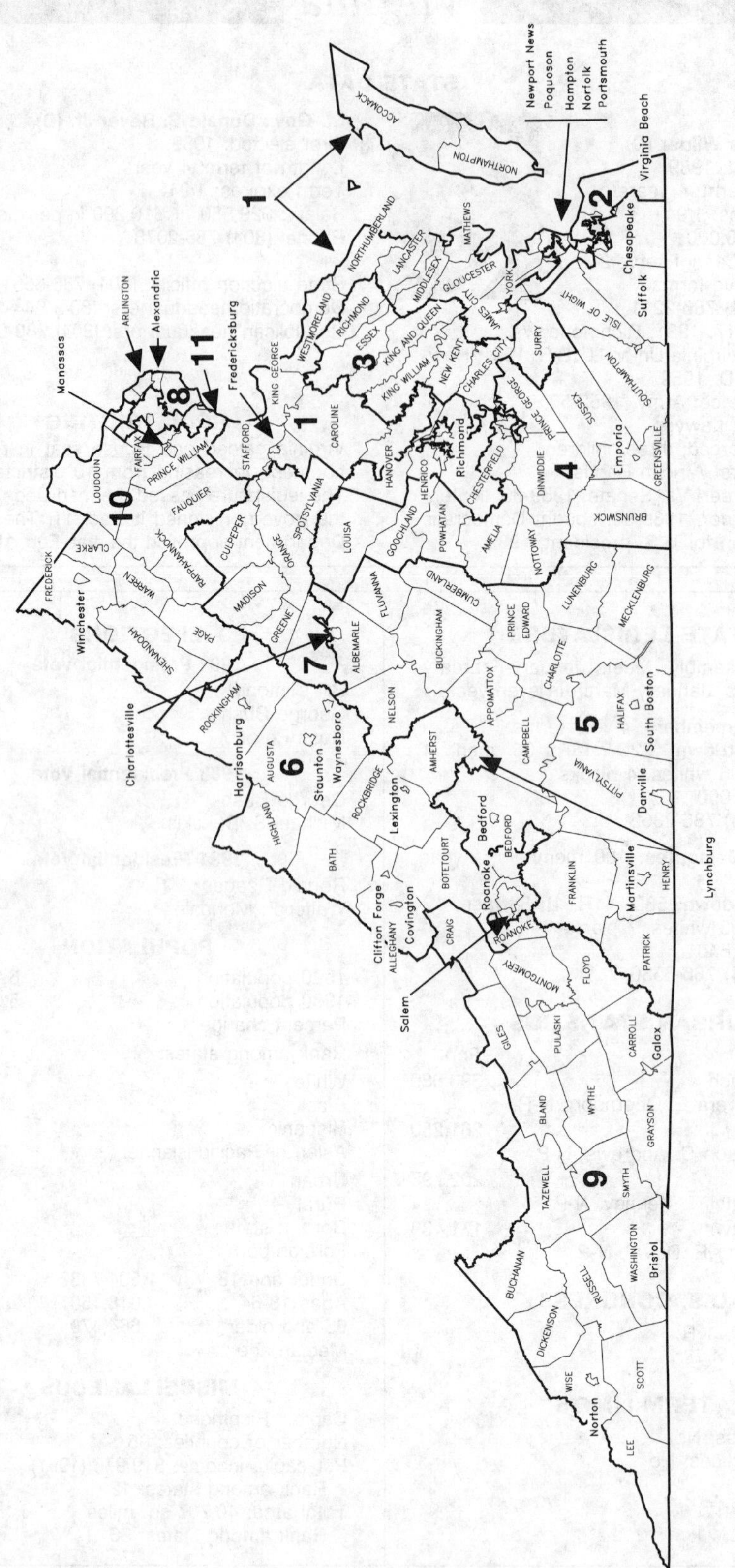
1
2
3
4
5
6
7
8
9
10
11
FREDERICK
Winchester
CLARKE
LOUDOUN
FAIRFAX
ARLINGTON
Alexandria
Manassas
PRINCE WILLIAM
FAUQUIER
WARREN
SHENANDOAH
PAGE
RAPPAHANNOCK
CULPEPER
MADISON
GREENE
ORANGE
STAFFORD
Fredericksburg
KING GEORGE
SPOTSYLVANIA
CAROLINE
WESTMORELAND
NORTHUMBERLAND
RICHMOND
ESSEX
LANCASTER
MIDDLESEX
MATHEWS
GLOUCESTER
KING AND QUEEN
KING WILLIAM
NEW KENT
JAMES CITY
CHARLES CITY
YORK
ACCOMACK
NORTHAMPTON
Newport News
Poquoson
Hampton
Norfolk
Portsmouth
Virginia Beach
Chesapeake
Suffolk
ISLE OF WIGHT
SURRY
SOUTHAMPTON
SUSSEX
PRINCE GEORGE
Emporia
GREENSVILLE
BRUNSWICK
DINWIDDIE
Richmond
HENRICO
HANOVER
CHESTERFIELD
POWHATAN
GOOCHLAND
LOUISA
FLUVANNA
ALBEMARLE
Charlottesville
AMELIA
NOTTOWAY
LUNENBURG
MECKLENBURG
CUMBERLAND
BUCKINGHAM
PRINCE EDWARD
CHARLOTTE
APPOMATTOX
HALIFAX
South Boston
CAMPBELL
PITTSYLVANIA
Danville
Lynchburg
NELSON
AMHERST
ROCKINGHAM
Harrisonburg
AUGUSTA
Staunton
Waynesboro
HIGHLAND
BATH
ROCKBRIDGE
Lexington
ALLEGHANY
Clifton Forge
Covington
BOTETOURT
Bedford
BEDFORD
Roanoke
ROANOKE
CRAIG
Salem
FRANKLIN
HENRY
Martinsville
PATRICK
FLOYD
MONTGOMERY
GILES
PULASKI
CARROLL
Galax
BLAND
WYTHE
GRAYSON
TAZEWELL
SMYTH
BUCHANAN
RUSSELL
WASHINGTON
Bristol
DICKENSON
WISE
Norton
SCOTT
LEE

John W. Warner (R)

Of Middleburg — Elected 1978; 3rd Term

Born: Feb. 18, 1927, Washington, D.C.
Education: Washington and Lee U., B.S. 1949; U. of Virginia, LL.B. 1953.
Military Service: Navy, 1944-46; Marine Corps, 1950-52.
Occupation: Lawyer; farmer.
Family: Divorced; three children.
Religion: Episcopalian.
Political Career: Assistant U.S. attorney, 1956-60; under secretary of the Navy, 1969-72; secretary of the Navy, 1972-74.
Capitol Office: 225 Russell Bldg. 20510; 224-2023.

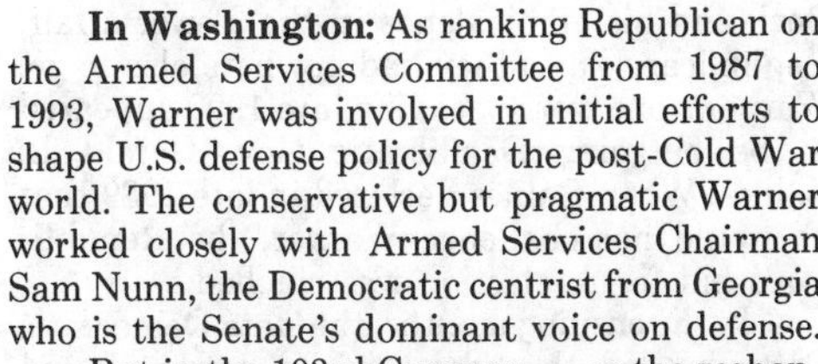

In Washington: As ranking Republican on the Armed Services Committee from 1987 to 1993, Warner was involved in initial efforts to shape U.S. defense policy for the post-Cold War world. The conservative but pragmatic Warner worked closely with Armed Services Chairman Sam Nunn, the Democratic centrist from Georgia who is the Senate's dominant voice on defense.

But in the 103rd Congress — as the reshaping of the military takes form under the Democratic Clinton administration — Warner has been relegated to a secondary role. Sen. Strom Thurmond of South Carolina claimed the ranking position on Armed Services, bumping Warner.

Thurmond, who gave up his ranking position on the Judiciary Committee, said he made the switch to protect South Carolina's defense-related facilities from budget cuts. But the move by the harder-edged Thurmond was hailed by the activist conservative wing of the Senate Republicans, who took umbrage at Warner's genial partnership with Nunn.

Warner can take solace in the experience of GOP colleague Richard G. Lugar of Indiana, who was superseded in 1987 by hard-line conservative Jesse Helms of North Carolina for the ranking Republican position on the Foreign Relations Committee. By working aggressively to shape enactable legislation, Lugar has maintained an effective foreign policy role.

Warner's downgrading on Armed Services hardly leaves him without a portfolio on national security issues. With the 103rd Congress he became the vice chairman of the Select Intelligence Committee, which deals with issues of parochial as well as policy interest: The Pentagon and the CIA's headquarters are in the Northern Virginia suburbs of Washington.

Warner also maintains a range of legislative interests. He is the ranking Republican on the Environment and Public Works Subcommittee on Water Resources, Transportation, Public Buildings and Economic Development. A list provided by Warner's office of his achievements in the 102nd Congress indicates that he quickly reoriented to his new lead role: It referred mainly to issues involved with transportation and the environment and none that pertained directly to defense. He is also a member of the Rules and Administration Committee.

Some critics viewed Warner's top rank on Armed Services with skepticism from the start. Though well-educated (with a law degree from the University of Virginia) and grounded in defense issues (he is a former secretary of the Navy), Warner came to the Senate with a reputation as more socialite than erudite: He was married for a time to actress Elizabeth Taylor.

Republican partisans feared that Nunn, with his intellectual approach and his ability as chairman to sway crucial Democratic votes, would constantly roll Warner. They complained that Warner's policy markers were often too close to the centrist positions laid down by Nunn, undercutting efforts by Republicans to hold out for a more conservative line.

The turning point for Warner's relationship with the conservative camp came in early 1989, when the Senate's Democratic majority defeated former Sen. John Tower's nomination as President Bush's secretary of Defense. Although Warner was a friend and supporter of Tower — a Texas Republican and former Armed Services chairman — several Republican senators blamed him for allowing Nunn to drag out the investigation of Tower's personal life that resulted in the defeat of the nomination.

At the start of the 102nd Congress, Minority Leader Bob Dole of Kansas sent a shot across the Navy man's bow: He gave Republican seats on Armed Services to such hard-line conservative members as Trent Lott of Mississippi, Daniel R. Coats of Indiana and Robert C. Smith of New Hampshire. Warner initially appeared to take the message to heart. In March 1991, he led an aggressive challenge to the congressional position on the Strategic Defense Initiative anti-ballistic missile system, which Nunn had helped develop. But Warner's foray only served to reinforce Nunn's overwhelming clout on defense issues.

Warner backed the Reagan and Bush administrations' vision of a space-based network of rockets designed to destroy enemy missiles shortly after launch. But Nunn — arguing that this plan was flawed and in violation of the U.S.-Soviet anti-ballistic missile (ABM) treaty of 1972 — steered the program toward a system of ground-based missile interceptors.

Playing off the well-publicized use of Patriot missiles to destroy Iraqi Scud rockets during the Persian Gulf War, Warner tried but failed to push through a provision that would have increased spending on a space-based system. But Nunn threatened to counter with his own proposal oriented to his ground-based approach. Warner then withdrew his amendment.

That July, Warner returned to the path of compromise. He and Republican Sen. William S. Cohen of Maine wrote to Bush recommending that he emphasize the ground-based approach preferred by Nunn; at the same time, they proposed renegotiation of the ABM treaty, a priority of conservatives, to allow for a more expansive anti-missile system.

The proposal antagonized conservatives who avidly favored space-based weapons and who saw Warner as again giving ground on one of their deeply held positions. But as was often the case during his tenure as ranking Republican, Warner's effort produced legislative results: With Nunn's backing, a version of the Warner-Cohen plan was enacted as part of the defense authorization bill in 1991.

In March 1992, Warner was a member of a delegation to Moscow headed by Nunn and Lugar, leading advocates of assistance to the republics of the former Soviet Union. Warner lobbied Bush — who had been weakened by criticism that he favored foreign over domestic policy — to throw his weight behind the first major aid package for the ex-Soviet republics.

The senior senator from a state laden with military facilities and defense contractors, Warner has plenty of parochial interests on Armed Services. In September 1992, he pushed through an amendment providing military hardware for the National Guard and reserves: Among the items was $60 million for night-vision goggles produced in Roanoke, Va. Although Warner had criticized "pork-barrel" spending in the defense budget, he told the Atlanta Constitution, "Any lawmaker thinks in terms of his state and the defense industrial base. Obviously that influenced my thinking."

In 1993, Warner surprised Northern Virginia residents and their House members by leading forces trying to drop funding for the space station project, which provides jobs in the suburb of Reston. "Are we going to do things the same old way, protect our states and stick it to the other guy's ribs?" Warner said. "Or are we going to stand up and try to make further cuts at home even if it hurts us politically?"

But behind this self-sacrificing stand was a strategy: According to news reports, Warner figured that taking the lead on cutting some big-ticket items would provide leverage in saving the rest of the state's defense-related economy.

During 1991 deliberations on the bill that overhauled the national highway system, Warner focused his efforts on getting a better funding deal for his home state: Virginia was one of the "donor states" that provided more money in federal gasoline taxes than it got back in highway and transit funds. The final legislation guaranteed each state at least a 90 percent return on its gas tax contribution.

At Home: After two terms, some senators will be secure, some will be in trouble and some will look shaky only in the presence of a specific challenger. Warner fell into the third category. His party standing was sure. Despite his 1987 vote against Supreme Court nominee Robert H. Bork and his ambivalence in the Tower affair, Republicans knew they had nowhere else to go. Warner's one worry heading into 1990 appeared to be outgoing Democratic Gov. Gerald L. Baliles. When Baliles declared in late 1989 that he would not challenge Warner, the Republican's bid for re-election was cinched.

In the ensuing months, the state Democratic Party heeded the advice of its newly elected governor, L. Douglas Wilder, that offering no candidate was preferable to fielding a poor one. Democrats' remaining efforts were devoted to ensuring that Nancy B. Spannaus, a supporter of fringe political figure Lyndon H. LaRouche Jr., did not appear on the ballot as a Democrat. They succeeded: Spannaus appeared as an independent. She was Warner's only opposition; he won a third term with a career-high 81 percent.

Such longevity seemed improbable in 1978, when Warner's political career looked to be stalled. His campaign for the Senate had impressed Virginia Republicans at the state GOP convention in June, but the nomination went to Richard Obenshain.

Then the state's politics and Warner's future were reordered by an airplane accident. Obenshain's light plane crashed Aug. 2 and he was killed instantly. Virginia Republicans needed a nominee, and Warner, the runner-up in June, was the obvious choice. He had courted the convention delegates with a lavish campaign costing nearly $500,000, and attracted enough votes to force six ballots before being defeated. He had also been a good loser and backed Obenshain afterward.

Warner brought to the fall campaign the same assets he had in June: personal wealth and a statewide reputation, achieved not only as Navy secretary under Richard M. Nixon and chief bicentennial planner under President Gerald R. Ford, but as Taylor's husband.

He also had liabilities. Despite his Virginia education, he was looked upon as an outsider who arrived late on the state's political scene. Some voters also saw him as a socialite and fortune hunter. Before he married Taylor, he was married to heiress Catherine Mellon and received a reported $7 million from her in their divorce settlement.

But Warner's celebrity wife turned out to be a help to him. Taylor's presence on the campaign trail guaranteed large crowds, and when she proved willing to voice her enthusiasm for conservative causes, Virginia Republicans cheered her on.

The Democratic nominee, former state Attorney General Andrew Miller, was seeking to recover from a defeat in the 1977 gubernatorial primary by the state's best-known liberal Democrat, Henry E. Howell. In 1978 Miller campaigned for the Senate as a fiscal conservative, but Warner tied him to the Democratic Party of Howell, and Miller never managed to extricate himself. Warner won by fewer than 5,000 votes in the closest Senate election in Virginia history.

Six years later, Warner was in a totally different type of contest, winning re-election by more than 805,000 votes in a race that was a mismatch from the beginning.

Then-Gov. Charles S. Robb led the search for a suitable Democratic challenger, but Warner helped to discourage the effort by raising more than $1 million by the end of 1983. After a host of better-known Democrats turned down the nomination, it went by default to former state Rep. Edythe C. Harrison, who had lost her previous race for the state legislature.

Harrison peppered Warner with a variety of charges, including conflict of interest for investing in defense stocks while serving on the Armed Services Committee. She also made barbed personal attacks. Referring to Warner's celebrated marriages, she declared: "Women took him up, and a woman is going to bring him down."

But even leading Democrats doubted that the woman would be Harrison. A longtime ally of the liberal Howell, she was given lukewarm support by much of her own party.

With money, incumbency, strong ticket mates and a grip on the conservative political mainstream, Warner swept all but two of the state's 95 counties and all 41 independent cities. According to exit polls, he also captured nearly one-quarter of the black vote, more than twice the share won in Virginia by Ronald Reagan.

Committees

Select Intelligence (Vice Chairman)

Armed Services (2nd of 9 Republicans)
Coalition Defense & Reinforcing Forces (ranking); Nuclear Deterrence, Arms Control & Defense Intelligence; Regional Defense & Contingency Forces

Environment & Public Works (4th of 7 Republicans)
Water Resources, Transportation, Public Buildings & Economic Development (ranking); Superfund, Recycling & Solid Waste Management; Toxic Substances, Environmental Oversight, Research & Development

Rules & Administration (4th of 7 Republicans)

Elections

1990 General

John W. Warner (R)	876,782	(81%)
Nancy B. Spannaus (I)	196,755	(18%)

Previous Winning Percentages: **1984** (70%) **1978** (50%)

Campaign Finance

	Receipts	Receipts from PACs		Expend-itures
1990				
Warner (R)	$1,750,032	$621,899	(36%)	$1,151,605

Key Votes

1993

Require unpaid family and medical leave	N
Approve national "motor voter" registration bill	N
Approve budget increasing taxes and reducing deficit	N
Support president's right to lift military gay ban	N
1992	
Approve school-choice pilot program	Y
Allow shifting funds from defense to domestic programs	N
Oppose deeper cuts in spending for SDI	Y
1991	
Approve waiting period for handgun purchases	Y
Raise senators' pay and ban honoraria	Y
Authorize use of force in Persian Gulf	Y
Confirm Clarence Thomas to Supreme Court	Y

Voting Studies

	Presidential Support		Party Unity		Conservative Coalition	
Year	**S**	**O**	**S**	**O**	**S**	**O**
1992	67	25	86	13	79	21
1991	89	11	82	18	95	5
1990	78	22	69	31	97	3
1989	86	13	81	19	89	11
1988	74	23	71	26	95	3
1987	60	36	75	16	88	9
1986	87	13	86	13	87	12
1985	82	18	82	18	92	8
1984	86	13	87	12	91	6
1983	82	16	84	14	89	11
1982	83	17	87	13	96	2
1981	87	13	88	8	97	2

Interest Group Ratings

Year	ADA	AFL-CIO	CCUS	ACU
1992	20	17	100	74
1991	20	25	80	76
1990	28	56	75	70
1989	5	10	88	89
1988	5	36	86	87
1987	25	50	94	60
1986	5	7	79	73
1985	5	19	79	74
1984	10	0	89	90
1983	20	18	53	56
1982	5	19	81	86
1981	5	5	100	74

Charles S. Robb (D)

Of McLean — Elected 1988; 1st Term

Born: June 26, 1939, Phoenix, Ariz.

Education: Cornell U., 1957-58; U. of Wisconsin, B.B.A. 1961; U. of Virginia, J.D. 1973.

Military Service: Marine Corps, 1961-70; Marine Corps Reserve, 1970-91.

Occupation: Lawyer.

Family: Wife, Lynda Johnson; three children.

Religion: Episcopalian.

Political Career: Lieutenant governor, 1978-82; governor, 1982-86.

Capitol Office: 493 Russell Bldg. 20510; 224-4024.

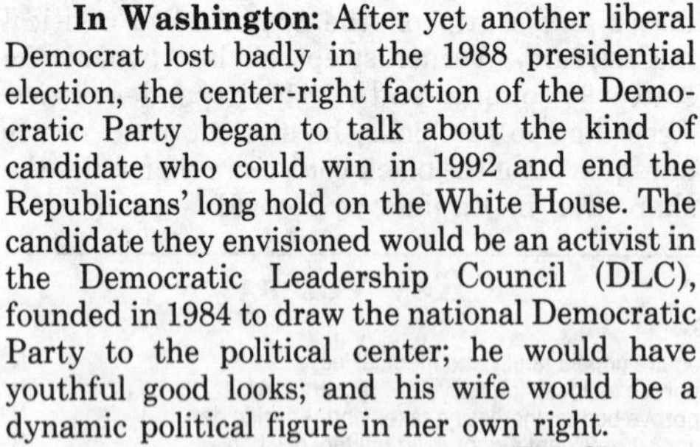

In Washington: After yet another liberal Democrat lost badly in the 1988 presidential election, the center-right faction of the Democratic Party began to talk about the kind of candidate who could win in 1992 and end the Republicans' long hold on the White House. The candidate they envisioned would be an activist in the Democratic Leadership Council (DLC), founded in 1984 to draw the national Democratic Party to the political center; he would have youthful good looks; and his wife would be a dynamic political figure in her own right.

But they were not thinking of Bill Clinton, at least not initially. The centrist leader that many had foreseen as the Democrats' potential giant-killer was Virginia Sen. Charles S. Robb, a founding member of the DLC, a square-jawed ex-Marine and the husband of politically outgoing Lynda Johnson Robb, the daughter of President Lyndon B. Johnson.

Well before Clinton's emergence, Robb had staked out an image as a different kind of Democrat. Though he is a thorough partisan — he served during the 1991-92 election cycle as chairman of the Democratic Senatorial Campaign Committee (DSCC) — and is rather liberal for a Southern Democrat on such social issues as minority rights and abortion, Robb developed a record as a hawk on defense issues and as a conservative on fiscal matters.

But a presidential race was not to be. Robb, who had built his career in conservative Virginia on a straight-arrow image, endured a two-year rash of embarrassing publicity that raised serious questions about his personal and political ethics, and ended speculation about his prospects as a centrist Democratic presidential contender.

The period covered by the 102nd Congress could not have gone much worse for Robb. In March 1991, Tai Collins, a former Virginia beauty queen, went public with claims that she had been romantically involved with Robb (she later posed nude for Playboy magazine).

The NBC-TV program that broadcast Collins' charges also rekindled rumors — which first surfaced during his 1988 Senate campaign and were denied by Robb — that then-Gov. Robb had attended beachfront parties during the mid-1980s with friends who were under investigation on suspicion of cocaine trafficking.

But his worst and longest lasting problems ensued after newspapers in June 1991 published transcripts — leaked by Robb's Senate aides — of an illegally taped telephone call between Virginia Democratic Gov. L. Douglas Wilder and an associate. Over the next year and a half, three top Robb aides were convicted under wiretapping laws for their possession of the tape; Robb, who claimed just a tangential connection to the tape, was accused in one aide's guilty plea of having knowledge of the tape and its illegal origin, and Robb endured an 18-month federal investigation during which he twice testified before a grand jury.

Robb did not regain his footing until January 1993 (at the start of the 103rd Congress), when the grand jury in Norfolk decided not to indict him on conspiracy and obstruction of justice charges relating to the Wilder tape.

Even so, Robb will have to overcome the skepticism of many Virginians over his explanations of these events: that he had wine and a massage with Tai Collins in a New York hotel room, but no sexual relations; that he was aware for some time about the Wilder tape, but its possible illegality occurred to him much later; that he saw no evidence that any of his companions on the Virginia Beach party scene were unsavory characters.

Clearly, with a re-election bid around the corner in 1994, Robb cannot afford many more stumbles. As of mid-1993, it appeared that Robb might face a primary challenge from Wilder. The illegal tape incident brought to a boil a long-simmering feud between Virginia's two most prominent Democrats. The bitterness of the rivalry, extraordinary for an incumbent senator and governor of the same party, has at times been matched by its pettiness.

During the notorious 1988 car phone conversation coincidentally intercepted by an electronics buff and Robb ally, then-Lt. Gov. Wilder was heard stating with apparent satisfaction that Robb's career would be ruined by the rumors of his partying with drug users; Robb's office leaked the tape in a backfired scheme to show that those rumors were spread by Robb's political enemies, including Wilder.

With Robb looking vulnerable, Virginia Republicans — who have had trouble recruiting candidates for statewide office in recent years — may have a doozy in 1994: former Marine Lt. Col. Oliver L. North, a hard-line conservative crusader who, as a National Security Council aide during the Reagan administration, was a central figure in the Iran-contra scheme.

Yet even at the depths of his problems during the 102nd Congress, Robb showed his resilience and unwillingness to be consumed by controversy. "I'm going to have one of the thickest skins in the business before this is over," he said in June 1991.

Any hopes Robb may have had of developing a national constituency in his role as the Democrats' chief Senate campaign fundraiser were dashed by the series of scandals. He accepted a low profile after local news coverage of his visit on behalf of one Democratic candidate was dominated by Robb's own problems. Yet Robb worked doggedly behind the scenes as the DSCC raised a record amount of campaign cash; his efforts helped Democrats stay steady with a 57-43 seat advantage, despite the unpredictability of the 1992 election year.

Needing to step up his legislative agenda to counteract any loss of personal prestige, Robb gained a seat on the Armed Services Committee at the start of the 103rd Congress, to go with his existing assignments on Foreign Relations and Commerce. It was a timely appointment, given the importance of military bases and defense industries to Virginia's economy and the corresponding threat of the ongoing post-Cold War defense spending reductions. (Robb joined Virginia Republican Sen. John W. Warner, who is the second-most senior GOP member on the Armed Services Committee.)

Robb, who has tended to cut his own path on policy issues, also has shown that he may not stick to the safest route. Although Virginia has a large conservative constituency, Robb in January 1993 came out strongly in support of President Clinton's proposal to end the ban on homosexuals serving in the military. (Even before Clinton took a position, Robb had written to Gen. Colin L. Powell Jr., chairman of the Joint Chiefs of Staff, urging that the ban be lifted.)

Robb, a Vietnam War hero who served during the 102nd Congress on a special committee that investigated the fate of Americans still listed as missing in action, drew upon his own long service in the military. He said opponents of lifting the gay ban had legitimate reasons for concern. "The specter of drill sergeants dancing together is unsettling to say the least," Robb said. But he added, "We cannot let fear prevent patriotic Americans from serving in the armed forces."

Just after becoming DSCC chairman in 1991, Robb broke with the Democratic leadership and took a strong stand in favor of the resolution that authorized President Bush to use force to end Iraq's occupation of Kuwait.

Robb then appeared on NBC-TV's "Meet the Press" in March 1991 and called the impact of Democrats' votes against the war resolution "catastrophic or devastating" (while underlining that he had supported the resolution). With Republicans then threatening to use the issue politically, such an action by any Democratic senator would have been regarded as tactless; it was especially so for Robb, who had been chosen by his colleagues to help ensure their re-elections in 1992.

Robb enraged the party's liberal wing when he voted for the controversial nomination of conservative Clarence Thomas to the Supreme Court in September 1991. A group of feminists picketed a DSCC meeting the next month.

The loss of his seat on the Budget Committee at the start of the 102nd Congress may have been the price Robb paid for staking out positions on deficit reduction that differed with those of the Democratic leadership.

The official story was that leaders from both parties wanted to shrink the panel. Robb was the lowest-ranking Democrat and thus had to go. But Robb said that the committee chairman, Tennessee Democrat Jim Sasser, told him, "If you had voted with me and provided the support I needed, I would've been more willing to go to bat for you."

However, Majority Leader George J. Mitchell denied that was the case and backed it up as he stood by Robb, even as his barrage of bad publicity led some to call for his ouster as DSCC chairman. At the start of the 103rd Congress, Robb was given a seat on the Joint Economic Committee.

At Home: Few politicians have found the road to the Senate as smoothly paved as Robb did. That may make the road ahead seem that much more rocky as he seeks a second term in 1994.

His feud with Gov. Wilder, who is barred from seeking re-election in 1993, may culminate in open political warfare, as Wilder has done little to quell speculation that he may challenge Robb in the Democratic primary. Meanwhile, Republicans' hopes are riding on the celebrity status and fundraising prowess of North. What's more, Robb ended 1992 with a negative balance in his campaign treasury.

So popular was Robb after his governorship that he was all but conceded the Senate seat even before he announced for it. The mere belief that he would run was widely believed to have influenced Republican Paul S. Trible Jr.'s decision not to seek re-election in 1988.

It is difficult to overstate the importance of Robb's political career to Democrats in Virginia. The collapse of the old Harry Byrd organization in the 1960s brought an era of Republican dominance at the statewide level. Party-switching was common. Before Robb, the state had elected three GOP governors in succession.

But then came Robb, a decorated Vietnam War hero and former White House guard whose wife was the daughter of President Johnson. Robb had left the Marines and gone to law school. After practicing law for four years, he was elected lieutenant governor. Four years later, Robb won the governorship.

In Richmond, Robb carefully built a reputation for fiscal conservatism with a human face. He appointed minorities and women to judgeships and other state posts. But such moves were made with a kind of square-jawed respectability. Robb seemed immune to the taint of liberalism.

State law barred a successive term, but Robb's popularity was talismanic enough in 1985 to help elect a slate of other Democrats — including the first black (Wilder) and also the first woman elected statewide in Virginia history (then-Attorney General Mary Sue Terry, a 1993 gubernatorial candidate).

Although Virginia had not elected a Democrat to the Senate since 1966, polls in 1987 showed Robb running ahead of Trible. When Trible stepped aside, the Virginia GOP had no clear replacement — and the prospect of facing Robb attracted no one of note.

Robb raised $3 million almost effortlessly while the Republicans scrambled through a long list of celebrity prospects. In the end, they chose a candidate who seemed more of a political novelty than a serious contender: Maurice A. Dawkins.

A black Baptist minister, Dawkins had been a civil rights activist and a Washington lobbyist, and he was also a spellbinding speaker. But his bid was erratic from the start, running into controversy over details of his personal business. The state party took over management of the campaign, and soon Dawkins was adapting the stories about Robb's Virginia Beach friends for use on the stump.

Robb tried to ignore the matter, then dismissed it out of hand. Although the issue was not affecting the polls, Robb's campaign clearly wanted to bury it. The candidate volunteered for a drug test, which proved negative, and, before joint appearances, Robb confronted Dawkins about GOP use of the issue. Dawkins publicly accepted Robb's account of the facts, but the issue was clearly his only weapon. The final result was unmercifully lopsided.

Committees

Armed Services (10th of 11 Democrats)
Defense Technology, Acquisition & Industrial Base; Military Readiness & Defense Infrastructure; Regional Defense & Contingency Forces

Commerce, Science & Transportation (9th of 11 Democrats)
Communications; National Ocean Policy Study; Science; Surface Transportation

Foreign Relations (8th of 11 Democrats)
East Asian & Pacific Affairs (chairman); Near Eastern & South Asian Affairs; Western Hemisphere & Peace Corps Affairs

Joint Economic

Elections

1988 General		
Charles S. Robb (D)	1,474,086	(71%)
Maurice A. Dawkins (R)	593,652	(29%)

Campaign Finance

	Receipts	Receipts from PACs		Expend-itures
1988				
Robb (D)	$3,198,630	$914,763	(29%)	$2,881,666
Dawkins (R)	$283,095	$23,148	(8%)	$282,229

Key Votes

1993	
Require unpaid family and medical leave	Y
Approve national "motor voter" registration bill	Y
Approve budget increasing taxes and reducing deficit	Y
Support president's right to lift military gay ban	Y
1992	
Approve school-choice pilot program	N
Allow shifting funds from defense to domestic programs	N
Oppose deeper cuts in spending for SDI	N
1991	
Approve waiting period for handgun purchases	Y
Raise senators' pay and ban honoraria	Y
Authorize use of force in Persian Gulf	Y
Confirm Clarence Thomas to Supreme Court	Y

Voting Studies

	Presidential Support		Party Unity		Conservative Coalition	
Year	**S**	**O**	**S**	**O**	**S**	**O**
1992	42	58	74	26	50	50
1991	59	41	74	26	70	30
1990	55	45	73	27	76	24
1989	73	27	69	31	82	18

Interest Group Ratings

Year	ADA	AFL-CIO	CCUS	ACU
1992	60	75	30	30
1991	60	67	10	43
1990	61	56	33	22
1989	45	80	63	36

1 Herbert H. Bateman (R)

Of Newport News — Elected 1982; 6th Term

Born: Aug. 7, 1928, Elizabeth City, N.C.
Education: College of William and Mary, B.A. 1949; Georgetown U., J.D. 1956.
Military Service: Air Force, 1951-53.
Occupation: Lawyer.
Family: Wife, Laura Yacobi; two children.
Religion: Protestant.
Political Career: Va. Senate, 1968-82; sought GOP nomination for U.S. House, 1976; sought GOP nomination for lieutenant governor, 1981.
Capitol Office: 2350 Rayburn Bldg. 20515; 225-4261.

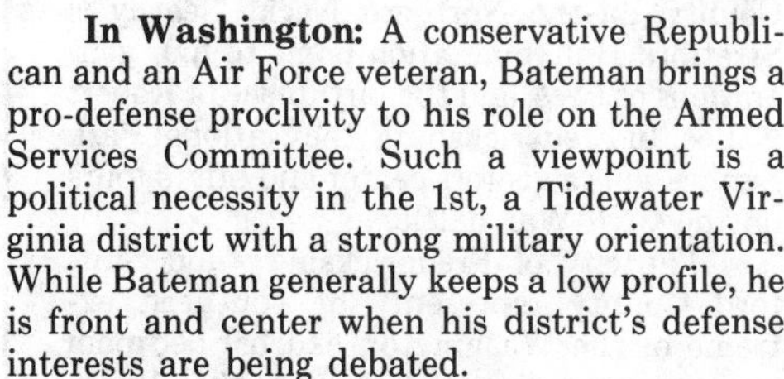

In Washington: A conservative Republican and an Air Force veteran, Bateman brings a pro-defense proclivity to his role on the Armed Services Committee. Such a viewpoint is a political necessity in the 1st, a Tidewater Virginia district with a strong military orientation. While Bateman generally keeps a low profile, he is front and center when his district's defense interests are being debated.

Bateman, whose district includes the huge Newport News Shipbuilding and Drydock Co., backed Reagan administration plans for a 600-ship Navy. Although that goal has been downsized given new fiscal and strategic realities, Bateman works for a stream of defense projects for his district's contractors.

In the Clinton era of continued defense cuts, Bateman will be busy trying to protect the military facilities in his district from some of the cuts that are expected in the post-Cold War period. His district was largely spared from the base-closure list in March 1993, although one of the targeted facilities is the nearby Norfolk Naval Aviation Depot.

During the 102nd Congress, Bateman obtained $832 million to buy nuclear components for an aircraft carrier that is expected to be built at Newport News Shipbuilding starting in 1995. The program, authorized during the Bush administration, likely will keep Newport News Shipbuilding the nation's only carrier manufacturer operating at least through 2004. The company is already at work on two new carriers.

Bateman has a broader agenda than sheer parochialism on Armed Services, serving as the No. 2 Republican on the Military Acquisition Subcommittee and on the Readiness Subcommittee.

After the Navy's 1992 Tailhook scandal, he urged his colleagues to resist the temptation to use the incident as a catalyst to allow women into combat positions. "There are conscientious people who believe there are reasons women should not be assigned to combat," he said during an Armed Services Committee meeting.

Still, Bateman does have a notable knack for finding the local angle. In June 1987, he questioned President Ronald Reagan's decision to safeguard Kuwaiti oil tankers caught up in the Iran-Iraq War by reflagging them and providing them with U.S. Navy escorts. However, Bateman was more concerned by the action's effect on the domestic merchant marine industry than with foreign policy issues.

Though not known as an environmental crusader, Bateman is protective of the Chesapeake Bay, which separates the two parts of his district. During the 102nd Congress, he succeeded in getting $19.8 million for bay cleanup and preservation. He also got $1.4 million for a study to determine what has been destroying oyster beds in Chesapeake Bay and other coastal areas.

At Home: Redistricting for the 1990s may have ended for good Bateman's pattern of having a close race every other election year. Once a a safe haven for Democrats, the 1st is now considerably more Republican; it lost much of its black population to the majority-black 3rd District. While Bateman will not know for certain until 1994, his impressive showing in 1992 was an encouraging way to start the decade.

In 1990, protracted budget negotiations, a late congressional adjournment and President Bush's broken "no new taxes" pledge all contributed to an anti-incumbent mood. Bateman struggled to defeat a political newcomer, Andrew H. Fox, a former TV reporter for Norfolk's NBC affiliate.

Fox did not raise much money, but he attracted an enthusiastic squad of volunteer workers. In the final days, polls showed Bateman in a dangerously close race. Bush's late-campaign strategy of denouncing Iraqi leader Saddam Hussein may have shifted the voters' attention and helped save Bateman, who won by just 2,806 votes.

The 1990 loss did not slow Fox, who simply began his 1992 campaign. This time, however, he was no longer running on a shoestring. He

Virginia 1

East — Parts of Newport News and Hampton; Fredericksburg

The vulture-shaped 1st swoops from its perch in the Hampton Roads area in southeastern Virginia to the Middle Peninsula and Northern Neck, wings north into the Washington exurbs in Stafford County, and pokes a beak into Richmond's northern suburbs. It also soars across the Chesapeake Bay to include Accomack and Northampton counties on Virginia's Eastern Shore, which adjoins Maryland.

Republicans perform well in the 1st. George Bush held Michael S. Dukakis to less than one-third of the vote here in 1988; Bill Clinton did only slightly better in 1992. The area within the 1st voted for the unsuccessful GOP nominees for governor in 1985 and 1989.

About 40 percent of the 1st's population is in the Peninsula area between Williamsburg and Hampton. The Newport News Shipbuilding and Drydock Co., the state's largest private employer, is not in the 1st — redistricting in 1991 moved it into the 3rd — but many of its 24,500 employees live in the 1st, entwining the econonic vitality of many district residents with the shipyard's. The shipyard lost the *Seawolf* submarine to Connecticut, but it has a backlog of contracts for aircraft carriers and submarines to last through the end of the decade; work on a new carrier, CVN 76, has been authorized to begin by 1995.

Colonial Virginia and its plantation economy were centered in the rural inland counties of the Middle Peninsula (bracketed by the York and Rappahannock rivers), the Northern Neck (between the Rappahannock and the Potomac) and along the bay. For generations, fishing, oystering and crabbing have sustained the economy of the counties along the bay. Corn, soybeans and wheat are important to the inland areas. Accomack County farmers raise chickens for processing in the many plants along the Delmarva (Delaware-Maryland-Virginia) Peninsula. Virginia's wine country reaches into the Northern Neck and Eastern Shore.

Tourism is also important in "America's First District," as Rep. Bateman calls it. Several sites recall Virginia's Colonial past, including Williamsburg, Jamestown and Yorktown. The plantation where George Washington was born is a national monument along the Potomac River in Westmoreland County, on the Northern Neck. Nearby is Stratford Hall, plantation home to four generations of Lees, and the birthplace of Robert E. Lee. In Fredericksburg, the National Park Service runs a visitors center and offers tours on the Civil War battle.

The city of Fredericksburg and Stafford County represent the southern extreme of the Washington exurbs; bedroom communities sprouted during the 1980s, when Stafford's population grew by more than 50 percent. The Virginia Railway Express began its Fredericksburg-to-Washington commuter rail link in July 1992. While Fredericksburg frequently supports Democrats, Stafford usually votes Republican. Independent Ross Perot's fiscal conservatism may have appealed to the new suburbanites in Stafford, where he received 18 percent, well above his statewide mark.

1990 Population: 562,677. White 450,051 (80%), Black 100,824 (18%), Other 11,802 (2%). Hispanic origin 8,930 (2%). 18 and over 418,734 (74%), 62 and over 77,393 (14%). Median age: 33.

became one of the leading congressional challengers in receiving political action committee contributions. The National Rifle Association also aided with an "independent expenditure" campaign targeted at Bateman, as well as campaign contributions. (Bateman was the only Republican the NRA targeted for defeat.)

Fox attacked Bateman for voting for the 1989 congressional pay raise and ethics reform package. Bateman countered that voters would not elect a Democrat backed by labor PACs. Fox's claim to the "outsider's" title may have been devalued as attention was trained on his heavy PAC funding.

Bateman did not try to maintain Fox's furious campaign pace, choosing instead to remind voters of his experience winning projects for the 1st. Voters may have found Bateman's avuncular style more appealing than Fox's frenetic ubiquity. While Fox certainly contacted more people across the 1st, familiarity apparently did not breed affection: Bateman crushed Fox by 19 percentage points.

Bateman has been near the center of Newport News' civic and political life since he set up his legal practice three decades ago. He ran for the state Senate in 1967 as a Democrat and won. He was re-elected three times, twice as a Democrat and once as a Republican.

But until 1982, Bateman was blunted in his tries for higher office; his strong support from Virginia's conservative political establishment was neutralized by a poor sense of timing.

In early 1976, he switched parties with an eye on the Tidewater House seat of retiring Democratic Rep. Thomas N. Downing. But

Paul S. Trible Jr., a hard-working young county prosecutor, locked up the GOP nomination. In 1981, GOP leaders encouraged Bateman to run for lieutenant governor. But he was challenged by a religious fundamentalist and a young state legislator; he finished second at the GOP state convention.

The two rebuffs, coupled with his narrow state Senate re-election in 1979, seemed to make Bateman cautious on competing strenuously for higher office. When GOP officials sought a House successor for Trible, who was running for the Senate in 1982, Bateman bluntly told them: "I'm a candidate if I'm the nominee." Bateman easily won the district convention.

His Democratic opponent was John McGlennon, a political science professor who stepped in after the original nominee withdrew. The switch probably doomed Democratic hopes, but it also seemed to make Bateman somewhat overconfident. He waged a haphazard campaign and won with a tepid 54 percent.

That result encouraged McGlennon to try again in 1984. But with Reagan and GOP Sen. John W. Warner both carrying the 1st by more than 50,000 votes, Bateman took nearly 60 percent.

Democrats figured they still had a good chance to beat Bateman in 1986, when he would not have popular top-of-the-ticket help. But a challenger was slow to emerge. State Sen. Robert C. Scott finally entered, bidding to become the state's first black member of Congress since the late 19th century.

The incumbent gave Scott few openings. Bateman stressed his success at bringing jobs to the district, highlighted by Defense Secretary Caspar W. Weinberger's election-eve appearance with Bateman to help dedicate a nuclear-powered aircraft carrier.

Scott ran virtually even with Bateman in the urban Tidewater, even carrying the city of Hampton. But Bateman rolled up 60 percent in the rural portion of the 1st to win a third term. Now they are colleagues: Scott was elected in 1992 in the new 3rd District.

Committees

Armed Services (5th of 22 Republicans)
Military Acquisition; Readiness

Merchant Marine & Fisheries (3rd of 18 Republicans)
Merchant Marine (ranking); Coast Guard & Navigation

Elections

1992 General		
Herbert H. Bateman (R)	133,537	(58%)
Andrew H. Fox (D)	89,814	(39%)
Donald L. Macleay Jr. (I)	8,677	(4%)
1990 General		
Herbert H. Bateman (R)	72,000	(51%)
Andrew H. Fox (D)	69,194	(49%)

Previous Winning Percentages: **1988** (73%) **1986** (56%) **1984** (59%) **1982** (54%)

District Vote for President

1992
D 81,826 (34%)
R 120,131 (50%)
I 39,307 (16%)

Campaign Finance

	Receipts	Receipts from PACs		Expend-itures
1992				
Bateman (R)	$766,895	$294,121	(38%)	$764,820
Fox (D)	$419,287	$241,283	(58%)	$419,878
1990				
Bateman (R)	$526,099	$218,750	(42%)	$549,818
Fox (D)	$106,176	$33,474	(32%)	$102,092

Key Votes

1993	
Require parental notification of minors' abortions	Y
Require unpaid family and medical leave	N
Approve national "motor voter" registration bill	N
Approve budget increasing taxes and reducing deficit	N
Approve economic stimulus plan	N
1992	
Approve balanced-budget constitutional amendment	Y
Close down space station program	N
Approve U.S. aid for former Soviet Union	Y
Allow shifting funds from defense to domestic programs	N
1991	
Extend unemployment benefits using deficit financing	N
Approve waiting period for handgun purchases	Y
Authorize use of force in Persian Gulf	Y

Voting Studies

Year	Presidential Support S	Presidential Support O	Party Unity S	Party Unity O	Conservative Coalition S	Conservative Coalition O
1992	81	17	70	28	83	17
1991	82	17	69	26	86	11
1990	69	31	63	33	96	4
1989	74	21	61	31	90	2
1988	64	35	68	29	92	5
1987	64 †	34 †	63 †	34 †	91 †	9 †
1986	69	29	64	35	88	12
1985	69	31	67	30	89	11
1984	71	27	71	26	90	3
1983	87	10	81	17	85	13

† Not eligible for all recorded votes.

Interest Group Ratings

Year	ADA	AFL-CIO	CCUS	ACU
1992	10	17	88	84
1991	10	17	100	80
1990	6	0	79	83
1989	0	17	100	81
1988	20	14	85	84
1987	12	25	79	74
1986	0	7	78	68
1985	10	6	77	71
1984	0	8	64	76
1983	0	0	100	91

2 Owen B. Pickett (D)

Of Virginia Beach — Elected 1986; 4th Term

Born: Aug. 31, 1930, Richmond, Va.

Education: Virginia Polytechnic Institute and State U., B.S. 1952; U. of Richmond, LL.B. 1955.

Occupation: Lawyer; accountant.

Family: Wife, Sybil Catherine Kelly; three children.

Religion: Baptist.

Political Career: Va. House, 1972-86; Va. Democratic Party chairman, 1980-82; Democratic National Committee, 1980-82; withdrew from campaign for U.S. Senate, 1982.

Capitol Office: 2430 Rayburn Bldg. 20515; 225-4215.

In Washington: From the inception of his House career, Pickett tallied a middle-of-the-road record. This was a reflection of the diverse constituency in his Tidewater Virginia district: The largest voting groups were mainly conservative whites — including huge numbers of military personnel and retirees associated with Norfolk's defense establishment — and a more liberal segment of blacks who made up nearly a quarter of the population.

However, a redistricting plan enacted before the 1992 election created a new black-majority district that touched on Norfolk and removed thousands of black voters from Pickett's base. Pickett's district thus leaned further to the conservative side, making him potentially more vulnerable to a Republican challenge.

The shift in Pickett's voting record likely was a reflection of that change. In 1991, he supported President George Bush on 52 percent of House votes on which Bush took a position. But in 1992, Pickett's support for Bush jumped to 65 percent.

Pickett ended up winning in 1992 with 56 percent of the vote, but he is likely to continue reaching for security by following a right-of-center course.

In March 1993, Pickett was one of 22 Democratic House members to vote against Democratic President Clinton's $16 billion "economic stimulus" program, and was one of just 11 Democrats to vote against Clinton's first full budget proposal.

A low-key member who is no political rebel, Pickett was careful to praise the efforts of the Democrats' first White House occupant in more than a decade. "The president's proposal contains many positive and worthwhile programs, and I applaud him for beginning the difficult and unpopular process of moving our nation away from the ruinous fiscal policies of the past 12 years," Pickett said.

But he said he was compelled to vote against the budget because it contained "precipitous cuts" in defense that placed "an unfair burden on our federal workers and military personnel." These interests provide the focus of Pickett's major legislative efforts as a member of the Armed Services Committee.

When Pickett gained a hard-won appointment to Armed Services during his freshman term, he was regarded as a member with bigger ambitions. (A veteran of the Virginia House and state Democratic Party chairman from 1980 to 1982, Pickett had made a brief bid for his party's Senate nomination in 1982.)

But Pickett has maintained a very low profile with little public visibility, although his diligent style and pro-defense stance made him a junior member of then-Armed Services Chairman Les Aspin's dominant centrist coalition.

Although Pickett is critical of Clinton and now-Defense Secretary Aspin's defense-cutting strategy, he remains useful to Aspin as one of the committee's counterweights to more liberal members — including new Chairman Ronald V. Dellums of California — who want to cut the defense budget even more deeply than the administration.

On major defense issues during the Bush years, Pickett generally supported Pentagon priorities. He voted against slashing funds for the Strategic Defense Initiative and opposed early efforts to sharply limit production of the B-2 bomber.

Pickett also guarded his parochial interests. Like other House members with established naval facilities in their districts, Pickett opposed the plan, promoted during the Reagan and Bush administrations, to disperse the U.S. Navy fleet to several "strategic homeports."

Pickett's home base is not immune to defense budget pressures. A proposed list of military base closings released in early 1993 called for the closure of the Norfolk Naval Aviation Depot, eliminating more than 4,000 area jobs.

Pickett's concerns about national security and his district's maritime employment base also drive his efforts on the Merchant Marine and Fisheries Committee. In February 1993, he

Virginia 2

Parts of Norfolk and Virginia Beach

Venerable Norfolk and upstart Virginia Beach share billing in the Tidewater-area 2nd, but it is Virginia Beach that overshadows its neighbor. With 50 percent growth during the 1980s, Virginia Beach blazed past Norfolk to become the most populous city in the commonwealth.

An influx of military families, business people and retirees has changed Virginia Beach's earlier identity as a summer tourist center. The sprawling city's retail and service trade has boomed, and some light industry has moved in as well. Only one congressional district in the country has more military retirees.

The port city of Norfolk's roots date to its settlement in 1682, and its strategic location has been valued ever since. The British destroyed most of the city in the Revolutionary War; it served as the Confederacy's main naval station in the Civil War; and it was a major naval training station in the two world wars. Lately, the unionized port city has been striving to polish its image. The builder of Baltimore's Inner Harbor renovated Norfolk's waterfront, creating a modestly successful area of offices and shops called "Waterside."

Defense is the main industry in the Hampton Roads area, and all four districts that touch the region that includes Hampton, Norfolk, Newport News and Virginia Beach depend on the massive concentration of naval installations, shipbuilders and shipping companies for economic stability. The Norfolk Naval Base is the largest in the world. Many residents of the 2nd work in the 3rd making ships and submarines at the Newport News Shipbuilding and Drydock Co., the largest private employer in Virginia. Norfolk's ship repair industry employs 30,000 people. The Hampton Roads harbor area ranks first in export tonnage among the nation's Atlantic ports; it is the biggest coal shipper in the world.

Redistricting moved more than 60 percent of Norfolk's black population to the new, majority-black 3rd. Still, the 2nd retains some Democratic leanings. Democrats running for Virginia statewide office can carry the 2nd, if sometimes narrowly. Democrat L. Douglas Wilder won 50 percent here in his 1989 gubernatorial race; the rest of the ticket fared better. But in presidential contests, the GOP nominee is secure. George Bush had no trouble carrying the 2nd in 1988 and 1992.

Virginia Beach is one of the state's prime strongholds of conservatism. It is home to the religious broadcasting empire of Pat Robertson, who sought the GOP nomination for president in 1988. But Robertson does not enjoy universal support among the 2nd's Republicans. In Virginia's 1988 GOP presidential primary, he placed a distant third in Virginia Beach behind Bush and Kansas Sen. Bob Dole.

There is no question that the current 2nd is more Republican than the district in which Rep. Pickett was first elected in 1986. Within the boundaries in place for the 1990s, Pickett was outpolled in his 1986 contest, 46 percent to 44 percent.

1990 Population: 562,276. White 439,282 (78%), Black 93,454 (17%), Other 29,540 (5%). Hispanic origin 18,383 (3%). 18 and over 419,231 (75%), 62 and over 50,178 (9%). Median age: 28.

called on Clinton to include revitalization of the nation's declining merchant marine industry in his economic plans.

"With a strong maritime policy, grounded in trade policies that eliminate the unfair shipbuilding subsidies of our competitors, the United States can put thousands of Americans back to work and re-establish itself as the world's undisputed maritime leader," Pickett said. He also said the merchant marine was vital to the nation's defense, noting that "a strong sealift capability is essential to meeting the heavy force deployment requirements of a major contingency."

At Home: Given its demographic makeup, it is a fair bet that the 2nd District will someday have a Republican representative. But that day probably will not come until Pickett decides he no longer wishes to serve.

When Virginia legislators redrew the state's congressional map for the 1990s, they created a new, majority-black 3rd District in southeastern Virginia. But to do so, they had to remove blacks from adjacent districts, which made the 1st, 2nd and 4th districts more white and more Republican.

Pickett had been able to rely on Democratic votes from the 2nd's 23 percent black population in Norfolk and Virginia Beach. But as redrawn, blacks make up less than 17 percent of the district.

Republicans sought unsuccessfully to recruit a well-known candidate to challenge Pickett in 1992 in his new, more suburban confines. Instead, the nomination went to a political newcomer, Jim Chapman, a 35-year-old lawyer from Norfolk.

Chapman proved to be an attractive candidate, impressing observers with his smooth speaking style. His neophyte status offered voters a contrast to Pickett's two decades of political service.

But 2nd District voters were not prepared to cast out their incumbent. Although Chapman raised nearly $200,000, he spent only half of what Pickett was able to spend. Even as Bush was carrying the 2nd with 48 percent, Pickett won a fourth term with 56 percent.

By the time he won the congressional seat vacated by retiring Republican G. William Whitehurst in 1986, Pickett already had served as chairman of the state party, launched, then abandoned a Senate bid, headed a Democratic presidential campaign in Virginia and served long enough in the state House of Delegates to be a senior member of the Appropriations Committee.

Neither an orator nor a gregarious backslapper, the wealthy Virginia Beach lawyer-accountant prefers to work studiously behind the scenes. But when state Democrats had important decisions to make, Pickett was nearly always in on them. He played a major role, for example, in fashioning the state's budget and retirement system. In 1980, he was chosen Democratic state chairman.

Pickett chaired the party through Charles S. Robb's successful gubernatorial campaign in 1981 and tried the waters as a Senate candidate in 1982, dropping out before the primary.

Two years later, Pickett chaired Walter F. Mondale's presidential campaign in Virginia. That placed him at odds with some of his old allies among party moderates but built bridges to Norfolk, which is one-third black and heavily unionized — the Democratic core of the 2nd. Pickett's personal roots in more Republican Virginia Beach helped him cut his losses there.

Pickett's Republican opponent in 1986, state Sen. A. J. "Joe" Canada, was generally regarded as the more appealing campaigner. But Canada was jolted early in the campaign by newspaper stories detailing his involvement with a bankrupt Virginia Beach mortgage company and business deals he had made with a Richmond stockbroker who had been accused of embezzlement. While no one linked Canada to criminal wrongdoing, Pickett said Canada's poor judgment was a legitimate issue.

Canada narrowly carried Virginia Beach, but Pickett won by nearly 2-to-1 in Norfolk. In 1988, Pickett surpassed 60 percent, and in 1990 the Republicans did not even field a candidate.

Committees

Armed Services (13th of 34 Democrats)
Military Forces & Personnel; Readiness; Research & Technology

Merchant Marine & Fisheries (8th of 29 Democrats)
Coast Guard & Navigation; Merchant Marine

Elections

1992 General		
Owen B. Pickett (D)	99,253	(56%)
J.L. "Jim" Chapman IV (R)	77,797	(44%)
1990 General		
Owen B. Pickett (D)	55,179	(75%)
Harry G. Broskie (I)	15,915	(22%)

Previous Winning Percentages: **1988** (61%) **1986** (49%)

District Vote for President

	1992
D	62,946 (35%)
R	85,773 (48%)
I	30,587 (17%)

Campaign Finance

	Receipts	Receipts from PACs		Expend-itures
1992				
Pickett (D)	$281,279	$128,450	(46%)	$373,047
Chapman (R)	$192,337	$11,185	(6%)	$190,447
1990				
Pickett (D)	$240,133	$135,500	(56%)	$82,828

Key Votes

1993	
Require parental notification of minors' abortions	N
Require unpaid family and medical leave	N
Approve national "motor voter" registration bill	N
Approve budget increasing taxes and reducing deficit	N
Approve economic stimulus plan	N
1992	
Approve balanced-budget constitutional amendment	N
Close down space station program	N
Approve U.S. aid for former Soviet Union	Y
Allow shifting funds from defense to domestic programs	N
1991	
Extend unemployment benefits using deficit financing	Y
Approve waiting period for handgun purchases	N
Authorize use of force in Persian Gulf	Y

Voting Studies

	Presidential Support		Party Unity		Conservative Coalition	
Year	**S**	**O**	**S**	**O**	**S**	**O**
1992	65	35	68	30	73	23
1991	52	46	70	26	89	8
1990	47	52	72	27	78	22
1989	52 †	47 †	72 †	26 †	83	15
1988	34	65	80	16	82	16
1987	39	61	78	19	70	30

† Not eligible for all recorded votes.

Interest Group Ratings

Year	ADA	AFL-CIO	CCUS	ACU
1992	35	25	88	52
1991	25	58	60	35
1990	50	75	64	42
1989	45	42	80	37
1988	50	86	50	40
1987	72	81	40	22

3 Robert C. Scott (D)

Of Newport News — Elected 1992; 1st Term

Born: April 30, 1947, Washington, D.C.
Education: Harvard U., A.B. 1969; Boston College, J.D. 1973.
Military Service: Army Reserve, 1970-76; National Guard, 1974-76.
Occupation: Lawyer.
Family: Divorced.
Religion: Episcopalian.
Political Career: Va. House, 1979-83; Va. Senate, 1983-93; Democratic nominee for U.S. House, 1986.
Capitol Office: 501 Cannon Bldg. 20515; 225-8351.

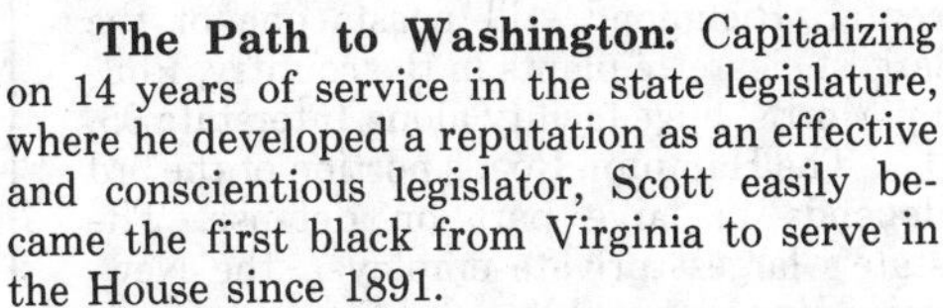

The Path to Washington: Capitalizing on 14 years of service in the state legislature, where he developed a reputation as an effective and conscientious legislator, Scott easily became the first black from Virginia to serve in the House since 1891.

Scott should have a long tenure, given his overwhelming showing in both the primary and general elections. He will also have ample opportunity to secure a lock on the seat by pursuing what he sees as the biggest needs of his economically distressed district from seats on the Judiciary and Education and Labor committees. Jobs, education, crime and civil rights are at the top of his agenda, along with access to health care.

Scott passed his first big test of loyalty to the Democratic leadership in late April 1993 over whether to grant the president limited line-item veto authority. Though opposed to the concept and going against the firmly stated position of the Congressional Black Caucus, Scott supported the leadership on a close procedural vote that allowed the bill to come to the floor. He ultimately voted with most of the caucus against final passage, though the bill passed easily.

In his second venture at a House seat, Scott had everything in his favor — demographics, name recognition and a record to run on. He also outspent his opponents. But all lacked the money to spread their messages and — especially in the primary — to attract the attention of voters, many of whom were unaware of the campaign, uninterested in the race or confused about redistricting.

Scott overcame three other black candidates — two politically connected Democrats and an unknown Republican — in the newly created 3rd, with its 64 percent black population and decidedly Democratic tilt.

After he won the primary, Scott's victory in the general election was mostly an afterthought. Republican Daniel Jenkins, a technician with Philip Morris U.S.A. in Richmond, was nominated by a sparsely attended district GOP convention. He was never much of a factor. Scott cruised to victory, 79 percent to 21 percent.

But even the primary, which might have been hotly contested, failed to generate much excitement. Turnout amounted to only 15 percent, with two-thirds of the vote going to Scott.

Scott gained a huge advantage by having represented the Hampton Roads area around Norfolk in the state House and Senate since 1978, after he ousted a white incumbent. A 1986 run in the old 1st against incumbent Republican Herbert H. Bateman greatly boosted Scott's name recognition among voters in the rural Tidewater counties that were moved into the 3rd, though they provided far fewer votes.

Scott's two primary opponents, Jean W. Cunningham and Jacqueline G. Epps, were Richmond lawyers. Both Epps, the chairman of the Virginia State Retirement System, and Cunningham, with six years as a member of the state House, had support among party activists. But that did little to help them overcome Scott's huge advantage away from Richmond. They split the vote from their end of the district. The cities in the Hampton Roads area — Hampton, Norfolk, Newport News and Portsmouth — provided 62 percent of the vote, and Scott captured 82 percent of that.

Scott's middle-class background could have hurt him with some of the district's voters. He is the son of a teacher and a physician and he attended Harvard University and Boston College Law School. But Scott deflected charges that he was not attuned to the needs of the poorer and rural constituents of the 3rd, pointing to his service in the legislature. And he shored up his base by winning early endorsements from the Rainbow Coalition and the Virginia AFL-CIO.

Issues did not clearly separate the three Democrats. Scott campaigned as an unconditional supporter of abortion rights and an opponent of capital punishment, as did Cunningham. Though Epps tried to distinguish herself with more moderate views on those and other issues, the voters did not respond.

Virginia 3

Southeast — Parts of Richmond and Tidewater area

The capital city of Richmond, long the center of Virginia's government and commerce, is probably best known outside the Old Dominion as the capital of the Confederacy. But in the 1990s, Richmond is the largest component of the majority-black 3rd, which is the commonwealth's first district to elect a black representative in more than 100 years. More than one-fourth of the 3rd's population lives in Richmond.

Most of the area that was represented by John Mercer Langston, the only other black representative in Virginia's history, now lies in the 4th. A dispute over Langston's election in 1888 delayed his seating; his victory was not ratified by the full House until September 1890, and less than two months later he was defeated for re-election.

The 3rd takes in the eastern side of Richmond, including the state Capitol, and stretches southeast along the James River to west Norfolk, and northeast to the Rappahannock River and Richmond County, in the Northern Neck. In addition to Richmond and Norfolk, it includes predominantly black sections of the cities of Newport News, Portsmouth, Petersburg and Hopewell, plus part of the city of Suffolk.

Nearly half of the 3rd's population is in the southernmost part extending from James City County to Norfolk. But almost as many people live in the westernmost portion that makes up Richmond, Henrico and Charles City counties and the cities of Petersburg and Hopewell. With his Newport News base, Scott easily defeated two Richmond-based opponents in the 1992 Democratic primary, winning the southwestern sector with more than 82 percent of the vote.

This is by far the most heavily Democratic district in Virginia. Bill Clinton won 66 percent of the vote here in the 1992 presidential race. Four years earlier, the areas that make up the 3rd backed Democratic nominee Michael S. Dukakis, who lost badly in most other parts of Virginia. Democratic gubernatorial nominees Gerald L. Baliles in 1985 and L. Douglas Wilder in 1989 each received 75 percent of the vote in the areas within the 3rd.

State government is a major component driving the economy of Richmond and vicinity, but the city is also a manufacturing center; Richmond still boasts one of the largest cigarette plants in the country, Phillip Morris' huge facility along Interstate 95.

The Hampton Roads portion of the 3rd depends in large part on defense. The state's largest private employer, the Newport News Shipbuilding and Drydock Co., is in the 3rd, with 24,500 employees building Navy carriers and submarines. The Hampton Roads area has a heavy concentration of naval installations as well as shipbuilding and ship repair companies.

The eastern counties — New Kent, King William, King and Queen, Essex and Richmond — are mainly rural and sparsely populated. Those counties and Charles City County were in the 1st District in the 1980s, when Scott made his first bid for Congress — a 1986 challenge to 1st District Republican Rep. Herbert H. Bateman.

1990 Population: 562,431. White 190,557 (34%), Black 360,378 (64%), Other 11,496 (2%). Hispanic origin 7,622 (1%). 18 and over 414,401 (74%), 62 and over 80,826 (14%). Median age: 31.

Committees

Education & Labor (18th of 28 Democrats)
Human Resources; Postsecondary Education; Select Education

Judiciary (18th of 21 Democrats)
Economic & Commercial Law

Science, Space & Technology (30th of 33 Democrats)
Energy

Campaign Finance

	Receipts	Receipts from PACs	Expend-itures
1992			
Scott (D)	$519,276	$185,250 (36%)	$500,359
Jenkins (R)	$16,834	0	$16,318

Key Votes

1993

Require parental notification of minors' abortions	N
Require unpaid family and medical leave	Y
Approve national "motor voter" registration bill	Y
Approve budget increasing taxes and reducing deficit	Y
Approve economic stimulus plan	Y

Elections

1992 General		
Robert C. Scott (D)	132,432	(79%)
Daniel Jenkins (R)	35,780	(21%)
1992 Primary		
Robert C. Scott (D)	23,381	(67%)
Jean Wooden Cunningham (D)	7,520	(22%)
Jacqueline G. Epps (D)	4,003	(11%)

District Vote for President

1992

D	124,857	(66%)
R	48,843	(26%)
I	16,779	(9%)

4 Norman Sisisky (D)

Of Petersburg — Elected 1982; 6th Term

Born: June 9, 1927, Baltimore, Md.
Education: Virginia Commonwealth U., B.S. 1949.
Military Service: Navy, 1945-46.
Occupation: Beer and soft drink distributor.
Family: Wife, Rhoda Brown; four children.
Religion: Jewish.
Political Career: Va. House, 1974-82.
Capitol Office: 2352 Rayburn Bldg. 20515; 225-6365.

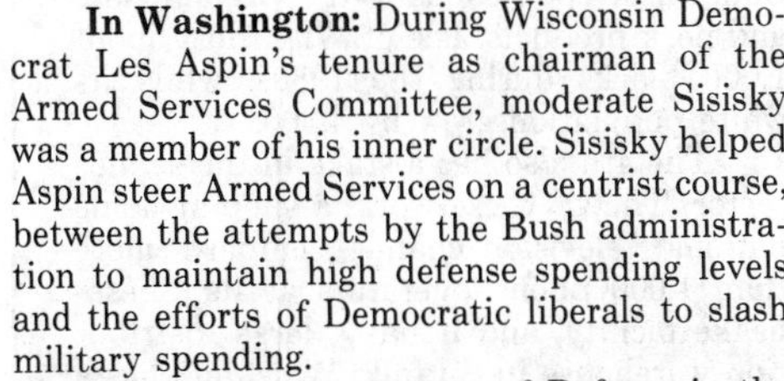

In Washington: During Wisconsin Democrat Les Aspin's tenure as chairman of the Armed Services Committee, moderate Sisisky was a member of his inner circle. Sisisky helped Aspin steer Armed Services on a centrist course, between the attempts by the Bush administration to maintain high defense spending levels and the efforts of Democratic liberals to slash military spending.

Now, Aspin is secretary of Defense in the Democratic Clinton administration; and Sisisky is the chairman of the Armed Services Subcommittee on Oversight and Investigations, which, among other duties, oversees the military's peacekeeping and domestic relief operations. Aspin will again count on Sisisky as one of the pro-defense counterweights to the liberal, defense-cutting agenda of Aspin's successor as chairman, Democrat Ronald V. Dellums of California.

But Sisisky — who represents a Tidewater Virginia district with a large military constituency — showed early on that he will not be uncritical if he thinks President Clinton himself is making defense carry too much of the burden of reducing the federal budget deficit.

In March 1993, Sisisky was one of just 11 House Democrats who opposed Clinton's first budget proposal, which was billed as a serious deficit-reduction measure. "I strongly believe that drastic action is needed to reduce our spiraling deficit," Sisisky said. "But the House budget resolution simply goes too far in cutting defense."

Sisisky was also one of 22 Democrats who voted against Clinton's $16.3 billion "economic stimulus" proposal that month. But these actions probably do not mark a sea change in the moderate course Sisisky has followed for more than 10 years in the House.

Sisisky tries to strike a balance between the mainly conservative views of his Southern white constituents and the more liberal leanings of his sizable black constituency. During his first decade in Congress, blacks made up 40 percent of his district's population; even a 1992 redistricting plan that took part of Sisisky's territory to create a new, black-majority district left him with a constituency that is nearly a third black.

Sisisky has voted mainly with his party on domestic issues. He favors abortion rights; in 1990 and 1991, he supported a civil rights bill strongly opposed by President Bush.

But the millionaire beverage distributor opposed business mandates supported by most Democrats, such as the Family and Medical Leave Act enacted in February 1993. And his pro-military views led Sisisky to support most of the Reagan and Bush administrations' defense-spending policies. In 1992, he supported Bush on 49 percent of the votes on which the president took a position.

Sisisky is part of Armed Services' "Tidewater Trio." With Sisisky, fellow Democrat Owen B. Pickett and Republican Herbert H. Bateman to look out for the interests of the Norfolk-area naval bases and other local military facilities, few regions are as well-defended on Armed Services.

Sisisky has won victories for local defense-related interests in the course of his Armed Services work. Even as Congress got serious about post-Cold War defense reductions during the 102nd Congress, Sisisky played a key role in securing funding for construction of a new aircraft carrier at a Newport News shipyard.

But Sisisky has shown an interest in reforming some of the Pentagon's bureaucratic practices, which could come into play in his role as oversight subcommittee chairman.

It was on a defense purchasing issue that Sisisky made a mark as a freshman. Upon learning of a Pentagon request to build schools for military dependents in Western Europe at a price of $8,500 per pupil, Sisisky headed for a telephone and called a contact in Virginia's Department of Education to find out how much schools cost. The figure he came back with was roughly half the requested amount. Sisisky later claimed credit for saving taxpayers about $143 million.

As a member of the Military Acquisition Subcommittee as well as the Investigations Subcommittee, which has looked into purchasing problems, Sisisky employs his business back-

Virginia 4

Southeast — Chesapeake; part of Portsmouth

Like the neighboring 1st, 2nd and 3rd districts, the 4th has a piece of the Hampton Roads area in southeastern Virginia, and thus its economy is powered in great measure by the vast industry linked to the region's huge military presence. Almost half the district's population is in Chesapeake, Portsmouth, Suffolk and Virginia Beach.

The industrial city of Chesapeake anchors the southeastern end of the 4th. Home to thousands of Hampton Roads shipyard and factory workers, Chesapeake has been booming; its population grew by 33 percent in the 1980s. Chesapeake is a district headquarters for the Coast Guard, whose finance center is in Chesapeake. The Norfolk Naval Shipyard, in the portion of Portsmouth in the 4th, employs 10,500 people.

The district's military component goes beyond Hampton Roads. Fort Lee, in Petersburg, and Fort Pickett, near Blackstone, are primarily used for training troops. Although it is home to the Defense Commissary Agency headquarters, Fort Lee in mid-1993 was on a list of 78 facilities facing possible closure.

The 4th is typical of many conservative Democratic districts in the South, supporting certain Democrats for state and some federal offices — such as Rep. Sisisky, former Gov. Gerald L. Baliles and former Attorney General Mary Sue Terry — but demonstrating a strong preference for Republican presidential nominees. George Bush held Democrats Michael S. Dukakis and Bill Clinton to scores of 44 percent of the vote in 1988 and 40 percent in 1992, respectively.

Agriculture is also important to the district's economy. Peanuts and tobacco are the important crops in the rural Southside counties along the North Carolina border. Democratic ties are still strong here, particularly in a swath that stretches from Suffolk to Brunswick County. Southampton is the No. 4 peanut-harvesting county in the nation.

There is some industry in the smaller cities of the 4th. Hopewell calls itself the chemical capital of the South. Suffolk processes peanuts. Petersburg makes tobacco products. Smithfield, in Isle of Wight County, is eponymous with Virginia ham and pork products. Isle of Wight lost about 1,000 blacks during the 1980s, while its white population grew by 4,300.

The 4th also has a stake in the service sector. The QVC Network, a shop-at-home national television channel, employs more than 1,000 phone operators at its Chesapeake facility, and it has a large distribution warehouse in Suffolk. Wal-Mart has a regional distribution center in Dinwiddie County.

The northern part of the district has also been experiencing population expansion. Louisa, Goochland and Powhatan counties all had double-digit growth in the 1980s, owing to the westward expansion of Richmond's suburbs. Louisa County also has been drawing retirees and second-home buyers from Charlottesville and the Washington area. The district's only nuclear power plant, North Anna, is in Louisa.

1990 Population: 562,466. White 372,263 (66%), Black 180,479 (32%), Other 9,724 (2%). Hispanic origin 6,442 (1%). 18 and over 415,002 (74%), 62 and over 79,000 (14%). Median age: 33.

ground. He once opposed an inflation allowance for military contracts, citing his experiences in supplying Pepsi-Cola to military bases.

There are some who doubt the applicability of Sisisky's private-sector experience to the contracting practices of a huge government bureaucracy. With his bluff personality and booming voice, he can also come off as a bit of a "Senator Claghorn," the archetype of the blustery Southern politician.

But Sisisky is known to his colleagues as a diligent member who has taken on a wide variety of assignments. During the 102nd Congress, he served on four Armed Services subcommittees and three of the special panels that Aspin set up to deal with specific issues.

Sisisky also applies his entrepreneurial background on the Small Business Committee, where he formerly chaired a subcommittee dealing with exports, tax policy and special problems. Sisisky — who supported the House resolution in January 1991 that authorized the use of force to end Iraq's occupation of Kuwait — led a delegation to Kuwait at the end of the Persian Gulf War. "Clearly, American business will be playing a key role in rebuilding Kuwait," Sisisky said.

At Home: After a decade of intraparty friction and underfinanced campaigns, Democrats united behind the wealthy Sisisky in 1982. He combined a large campaign treasury and an affable campaign style to oust veteran GOP Rep. Robert W. Daniel Jr. He was subsequently re-elected four times without a Republican opponent.

In 1992, he did face a GOP foe, but it did not change the outcome. Redistricting removed black voters from the 4th to help create a new, majority-black 3rd District in southeastern Virginia, leaving Sisisky with a more white and more Republican district.

But Republicans privately acknowledged that no GOP challenger was likely to unseat the popular Democrat. Hopewell City Council member A. J. "Tony" Zevgolis tested that assumption. But unknown across most of the district and vastly outspent, Zevgolis fell well short; Sisisky prevailed by more than 2-to-1.

The son of Lithuanian immigrants, Sisisky was born in Baltimore. His family moved during the Depression to Richmond, where his father worked in a delicatessen. Sisisky was raised there and attended a local college.

During the 1982 campaign, Sisisky described himself as a self-made businessman. Critics said he married into a wealthy Petersburg family and took over its soft-drink company. But regardless of how he got his start, Sisisky is a natural salesman who turned the operation into one of the most successful Pepsi-Cola distributorships in the country.

After years as a pillar of the business community, Sisisky won a seat in the state House in 1973. With Virginia politics then in a state of flux, he ran as an independent, but caucused with the Democrats and in 1975 sought re-election as a Democrat. In the legislature he was known as a master compromiser; he was often an intermediary between conservative Southside legislators and their more liberal Northern Virginia counterparts.

Sisisky was widely recognized as his party's strongest potential challenger against Daniel in 1982. But when a black activist announced in early 1982 that he might run as an independent, Sisisky threatened to pull out of the race. Only when the threat of the independent candidacy subsided did Sisisky resume his campaign.

Sisisky charged that Daniel's pro-Reagan record did not represent blacks (who made up 40 percent of the population), farmers or the blue-collar workers of industrial Tidewater. Daniel countered by branding Sisisky a liberal and claiming he was trying to buy the election. In the end, Sisisky carried 15 out of 20 jurisdictions, winning overwhelmingly in Petersburg and in blue-collar Portsmouth.

Committees

Armed Services (8th of 34 Democrats)
Oversight & Investigations (chairman); Military Acquisition

Small Business (6th of 27 Democrats)
Procurement, Taxation & Tourism; Regulation, Business Opportunities & Technology

Elections

1992 General		
Norman Sisisky (D)	147,649	(68%)
A.J. "Tony" Zevgolis (R)	68,286	(32%)
1990 General		
Norman Sisisky (D)	71,051	(78%)
Don L. McReynolds (I)	12,295	(14%)
Loretta F. Chandler (I)	7,102	(8%)

Previous Winning Percentages: 1988 (100%) **1986** (100%) **1984** (100%) **1982** (54%)

District Vote for President

1992
D 90,641 (40%)
R 106,392 (47%)
I 31,467 (14%)

Campaign Finance

	Receipts	Receipts from PACs		Expend-itures
1992				
Sisisky (D)	$257,047	$160,750	(63%)	$466,010
Zevgolis (R)	$82,161	$3,413	(4%)	$82,068
1990				
Sisisky (D)	$240,553	$158,200	(66%)	$275,502
McReynolds (I)	$19,854	0		$19,883

Key Votes

1993	
Require parental notification of minors' abortions	N
Require unpaid family and medical leave	N
Approve national "motor voter" registration bill	Y
Approve budget increasing taxes and reducing deficit	N
Approve economic stimulus plan	N
1992	
Approve balanced-budget constitutional amendment	Y
Close down space station program	N
Approve U.S. aid for former Soviet Union	Y
Allow shifting funds from defense to domestic programs	N
1991	
Extend unemployment benefits using deficit financing	Y
Approve waiting period for handgun purchases	N
Authorize use of force in Persian Gulf	Y

Voting Studies

	Presidential Support		Party Unity		Conservative Coalition	
Year	**S**	**O**	**S**	**O**	**S**	**O**
1992	49	50	71	28	92	6
1991	45	49	68	25	76	14
1990	43 †	57 †	77	22	91	9
1989	51 †	47 †	73 †	25 †	78	20
1988	38	61	77	20	76	21
1987	45	54	74	24	86	9
1986	39	60	75	21	70	30
1985	39 †	58 †	76	22	78	20
1984	54	42	66	32	73	24
1983	43	56	61	32	75	21

† Not eligible for all recorded votes.

Interest Group Ratings

Year	ADA	AFL-CIO	CCUS	ACU
1992	55	55	88	48
1991	30	73	67	39
1990	39	50	50	42
1989	55	67	60	21
1988	55	86	50	40
1987	52	63	60	39
1986	45	57	56	48
1985	40	47	36	38
1984	40	46	33	38
1983	65	88	30	43

5 Lewis F. Payne Jr. (D)

Of Nellysford — Elected 1988; 3rd Full Term

Born: July 9, 1945, Amherst, Va.

Education: Virginia Military Institute, B.S. 1967; U. of Virginia, M.B.A. 1973.

Military Service: Army, 1968-70.

Occupation: Real estate developer; businessman.

Family: Wife, Susan King; four children.

Religion: Presbyterian.

Political Career: No previous office.

Capitol Office: 1119 Longworth Bldg. 20515; 225-4711.

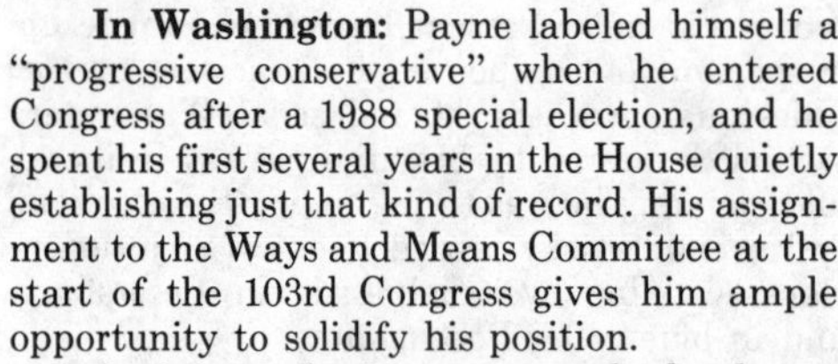

In Washington: Payne labeled himself a "progressive conservative" when he entered Congress after a 1988 special election, and he spent his first several years in the House quietly establishing just that kind of record. His assignment to the Ways and Means Committee at the start of the 103rd Congress gives him ample opportunity to solidify his position.

A former businessman and developer, Payne sits on the Trade Subcommittee, where he is a sentinel for foreign practices that hurt his district's textile industry.

Payne introduced legislation in the 102nd and 103rd Congresses that would deny duty-free status to goods from the U.S. protectorate of Saipan, one of the Northern Mariana Islands in the west Pacific Ocean. Payne complained that Saipan "has been exploiting its status as a United States territory by exporting goods duty-free and tagged with the 'made in USA' label while [its] ... industries circumvent federal labor standards."

Payne effectively balances a conservative stance on defense and fiscal matters with a more liberal approach on certain high-profile social issues.

He has bolstered his conservative image with votes to support using force against Iraq and by backing a constitutional ban on flag desecration.

And his support of President Bush's vetoes of a minimum wage increase and the family and medical leave bill endeared him to the business community.

But Payne complemented those stands with his consistent support of abortion rights and with his backing of Democratic efforts to pass a civil rights bill, important to the minorities in his district.

Payne's balancing act is evident in the ratings he earned in 1991 from the Chamber of Commerce (70 percent favorable) and the AFL-CIO (58 percent).

Payne also voted for the controversial 1990 budget-summit agreement that raised taxes and cut spending, following the Democratic leadership line. Perhaps not coincidentally, he got a seat on the Budget Committee at the start of the 102nd Congress.

Payne has consistently championed a constitutional amendment to require a balanced federal budget. In 1992, he joined with five other moderate-to-conservative Democrats to urge Speaker Thomas S. Foley of Washington to permit a balanced-budget amendment to reach the House floor.

On Public Works in the 102nd Congress, Payne and North Carolina Democrat Tim Valentine fought for more funds for so-called donor states (those that get back less in highway funds than they pay in highway taxes) during consideration of the 1991 highway authorization bill. The massive bill included several projects in the 5th District.

Payne was an engineer and businessman who spent 15 years building the Wintergreen resort in Nelson County and never ran for office before 1988. He first won the 5th in a June special election to fill the unexpired term of 19-year veteran Dan Daniel, who had died in January.

Payne was around for only a few months of the 100th Congress. He did little to attract attention in Washington, concentrating instead on getting better acquainted with his district. He was assigned to the Public Works Committee and to the Veterans' Affairs Committee, both solid opportunities to help constituents and both panels on which Virginia had not been represented.

At Home: Republicans targeted the 5th when Daniel in January 1988 announced plans to retire. (He died four days later.)

Daniel was a product of the old Harry Byrd machine and a one-time advocate of "massive resistance" to desegregation. Although Daniel stayed in the Democratic Party, he usually voted with Republicans in the House.

The leading Republican candidate was Linda Arey, an attorney who had been a public liaison aide in the Reagan White House. She successfully organized local and county caucuses leading to the district convention, where she defeated a GOP state senator from Danville.

Virginia 5

South — Danville; Charlottesville

Virginia's leading cash crop is tobacco, and the 5th is in the heart of tobacco country. Agriculture and textiles are the main industries in the 5th, which is in Virginia's rural "Southside," a region of farms, small towns and isolated factory cities along the state's southern tier that resembles the Deep South more closely than any other part of the state does. It is relatively poor and has a substantial black population. Tobacco and soybeans are major crops, but this region lacks the rich soil of the Tidewater region.

Charlottesville, home to the University of Virginia and its 17,600 students, is new to the 5th for the 1990s. It is an incongruity: an upscale, liberal enclave in an otherwise conservative, rural district. Charlottesville was the only jurisdiction in the 5th to vote Democratic in the 1988 presidential race, giving Michael S. Dukakis 56 percent of the vote. Bill Clinton did even better in 1992, despite competing against two major candidates; he captured 58 percent in Charlottesville.

Rep. Payne has quickly established a grip on the 5th, but the district has long refused to swallow more liberal Democratic candidates at the state and national levels. Barry Goldwater won many of the 5th's counties in 1964, as did George C. Wallace in 1968. George Bush carried the 5th by more than 20 percentage points in 1988.

But certain Democrats can make inroads in the 5th. Districtwide in 1992, Bush beat Clinton by only 6 percentage points. Former Attorney General Mary Sue Terry, a politically centrist Democrat, received 64 percent of the vote in her 1989 re-election campaign.

The district's two most famous landmarks are Thomas Jefferson's home, Monticello, just south of Charlottesville, and Appomattox Court House, where Robert E. Lee surrendered to Ulysses S. Grant to end the Civil War.

About 60 miles south of Appomattox is the district's largest city, Danville, a tobacco and textile center on the North Carolina border. Alone among counties and independent cities along the southern tier, Danville saw its population rise during the 1980s. The textile industry employs an estimated 45,000 people in the district. The largest company, Dan River, employs about 4,700 at its Danville plant.

Just to the west is Henry County, which surrounds the textile and furniture town of Martinsville. Henry is the most populous county in the district, and outside of Charlottesville, it is the best area in the 5th for Democrats. Clinton carried Henry and Martinsville.

The rest of the people are scattered through farming areas and a few factory towns.

Campbell and Bedford counties originally were Lynchburg bedroom communities, but both engaged in aggressive economic recruitment in the 1980s and succeeded in attracting numerous small businesses. Bedford's population grew by more than 30 percent in the 1980s.

1990 Population: 562,268. White 418,171 (74%), Black 139,344 (25%), Other 4,753 (1%). Hispanic origin 3,226 (1%). 18 and over 433,192 (77%), 62 and over 97,446 (17%). Median age: 35.

Payne, meanwhile, got a late start but quietly organized key Democrats. The son of a state trooper and a teacher, he had become wealthy enough in his development business to finance 40 percent of his special-election campaign's $500,000 cost out of his own deep pockets.

At the Democrats' district meeting in March, he was declared the nominee by acclamation. He was not an accomplished public speaker, but as a self-made success, Army veteran and family man, he seemed to embody many of the virtues Southside Virginians value. He campaigned as a fiscal conservative and managed to alienate neither the blacks who constitute a quarter of the district nor the bedrock Dixiecrats whose votes decide elections in the 5th.

The national GOP had hopes of prevailing in the district for the first time in a century. In June, Arey broadcast a radio endorsement from President Ronald Reagan, and she got a campaign visit from Vice President George Bush. But her advertising reach was shortened by dwindling campaign funds. Payne prevailed with a solid 59 percent of the vote, and Arey decided against making another bid that November.

In her place, Republicans nominated state Rep. Charles Hawkins. He did not become the party's official nominee until September and could not raise much money. Yet he benefited from the 5th's strong preference for GOP presidential nominee Bush and held Payne to 54 percent of the vote.

But by 1990, Republican interest in the 5th had dissipated. Payne was unopposed for re-election.

In 1992, redistricting did nothing to improve GOP chances in the 5th; the Republican challenger was a little-known health-care administrator. Payne breezed to a 69 percent victory.

Committee

Ways & Means (17th of 24 Democrats)
Select Revenue Measures; Trade

Elections

1992 General		
Lewis F. Payne Jr. (D)	133,031	(69%)
W.A. "Bill" Hurlburt (R)	60,030	(31%)
1990 General		
Lewis F. Payne Jr. (D)	66,532	(100%)

Previous Winning Percentages: **1988** (54%) **1988 *** (59%)

** Special election.*

District Vote for President

1992

D	90,769 (41%)
R	104,236 (47%)
I	26,978 (12%)

Campaign Finance

	Receipts	Receipts from PACs		Expend-itures
1992				
Payne (D)	$418,643	$219,044	(52%)	$414,696
Hurlburt (R)	$56,215	$2,971	(5%)	$54,705
1990				
Payne (D)	$317,828	$187,650	(59%)	$317,271

Key Votes

1993	
Require parental notification of minors' abortions	N
Require unpaid family and medical leave	N
Approve national "motor voter" registration bill	Y
Approve budget increasing taxes and reducing deficit	Y
Approve economic stimulus plan	Y
1992	
Approve balanced-budget constitutional amendment	Y
Close down space station program	Y
Approve U.S. aid for former Soviet Union	Y
Allow shifting funds from defense to domestic programs	N
1991	
Extend unemployment benefits using deficit financing	Y
Approve waiting period for handgun purchases	N
Authorize use of force in Persian Gulf	Y

Voting Studies

Year	Presidential Support S	Presidential Support O	Party Unity S	Party Unity O	Conservative Coalition S	Conservative Coalition O
1992	44	56	76	23	75	23
1991	47	50	66	30	84	14
1990	42	58	75	25	83	17
1989	56	43	67	29	88	10
1988	41 †	59 †	77 †	21 †	93 †	7 †

† Not eligible for all recorded votes.

Interest Group Ratings

Year	ADA	AFL-CIO	CCUS	ACU
1992	65	50	63	32
1991	35	58	70	50
1990	33	50	64	33
1989	35	36	90	50
1988	--	83	56	50

6 Robert W. Goodlatte (R)

Of Roanoke — Elected 1992; 1st Term

Born: Sept. 22, 1952, Holyoke, Mass.

Education: Bates College, B.A. 1974; Washington and Lee U., J.D. 1977.

Occupation: Lawyer; congressional aide.

Family: Wife, Maryellen Flaherty; two children.

Religion: Christian Scientist.

Political Career: Roanoke City GOP Committee chairman, 1980-83.

Capitol Office: 214 Cannon Bldg. 20515; 225-5431.

The Path to Washington: Although this is Goodlatte's first elected office, he is a long-time GOP activist, going back to his days as president of the student Republicans at Bates College in Maine. Many years later, Goodlatte was still involved in party politics as a top aide to GOP Rep. M. Caldwell Butler, and then as chairman of the 6th District Republican Party. He also headed the local Bush-for-President effort in 1988 and the local committee to re-elect Republican Sen. John W. Warner in 1990.

Goodlatte had thought about running for Congress in 1986, but the arrival of his second child at the start of the campaign season kept him from entering the race. When incumbent Democrat Jim Olin chose not to seek re-election in 1992, Goodlatte decided the time was right, and he campaigned on the promise to exert "Republican leadership ... for a change."

In previous years in the district, the GOP has fought internally over its congressional nominee because of clashes between more traditional Republicans and conservative religious activists. But within weeks of his decision to run, Goodlatte had united these antagonistic elements behind him, leaving the rancor to the Democrats.

Stephen Alan Musselwhite, an insurance executive and a moderate, emerged with the Democratic nomination, but he was never able to unite the party behind him.

Although Goodlatte went out of his way during the campaign to stress his opposition to organized labor's legislative agenda, labor leaders refused to back Musselwhite, in large part because he did not back legislation to ban employers from permanently replacing striking workers.

Musselwhite also had to contend with bad publicity over letters he wrote to a judge asking for leniency for two white-collar criminals.

The 6th, which had been held by the GOP for 30 years before Olin's 1982 election, is generally described as a moderate-to-conservative district. Goodlatte believes he fits that description philosophically, and says that in his mind this means a "limited government, decentralized, not trying to solve every problem with more spending programs and with regulation."

Like so many first-year members, Goodlatte supports a balanced-budget amendment and a presidential line-item veto. Yet unlike most freshmen, Goodlatte opposed all budget plans offered on the House floor in March 1993, including a Republican substitute by John R. Kasich of Ohio that received the support of all but 41 Republicans but which Goodlatte believed did not go far enough in reducing the deficit.

Goodlatte backs term limits and was among a group of GOP members who pushed through a rule prohibiting anyone in the Republican caucus from holding any top committee post for more than six consecutive years.

Goodlatte's district is the most heavily agricultural in Virginia. It is a district in which poultry and dairy farming predominate. As a result, Goodlatte sought and received a spot on the House Agriculture Committee. He also took a seat on the Judiciary Committee.

Goodlatte says he is also interested in building up his district's economy by helping to expand the high-technology businesses in the district.

Though Goodlatte has not previously held office, he believes that his experience working for the popular Butler — who warmly endorsed him — will be a help.

Goodlatte ran Butler's district offices and gained a firsthand appreciation for the importance of constituent service. His campaign brochures noted that he "made a name for himself serving people of the 6th District" by helping citizens with a host of problems, from cutting through red tape to "finding out why a Social Security check for a senior citizen was late."

Goodlatte opposes abortion except in cases of rape, incest or when the woman's life is in danger. He has said he supports allowing research with fetal tissue, but in March 1993 he voted on the House floor against a Democratic-sponsored measure to streamline the guidelines for donating tissue for such research.

On the issue of illegal drugs, Goodlatte says, "The message to criminals must be clear: If you sell drugs to our children, threaten our neighborhoods or injure innocent citizens, you'll be put behind bars for a long time. Guaranteed."

Virginia 6

West — Roanoke; Lynchburg

The 6th is home to mountains and caverns, dairy farmers and cattle ranchers, isolated towns and large cities — and quite a few Republicans.

The Shenandoah Valley, which runs most of the length of the 6th, cultivated Republicanism long before it was acceptable in other parts of Virginia. The descendants of the area's 18th-century English, German and Scots-Irish settlers feuded with the Tidewater plantation aristocracy and became GOP mavericks in state politics.

The brand of Republicanism in the rural Valley traditionally has been a moderate one; when Virginia's conservative Democrats were identified with resistance to integration in the 1960s, Valley Republicans were progressive on racial issues. The GOP lost its grip on the 6th in the 1980s partly because the state party came to be dominated by staunchly conservative suburbanites outside Washington and Richmond, and by party-switching conservative Democrats. In 1985, when there was no moderate on the Republican ticket, the Democrats running for the three top state offices all carried the 6th. In 1989, the 6th did vote Republican for governor (against black Democrat L. Douglas Wilder), but the Democratic nominees for lieutenant governor and attorney general won the 6th. Goodlatte's 1992 victory ended Democrats' decadelong control of the 6th District House seat.

Roanoke, the major population center in the 6th, has an array of industries producing furniture and electrical products. Its sizable black and union elements make it the base of Democratic strength in the 6th. Bill Clinton won Roanoke by 12 points in 1992. In 1989, Wilder won the city with 59 percent. Democrats also can succeed in towns to the north, such as Covington and Clifton Forge, and in the counties around them, Bath and Alleghany. In his 1985 bid for lieutenant governor, Wilder won these cities but lost the counties. Clinton carried all but Bath. There are chemical plants and pulpwood and paper mills in this area, but the job picture is cloudy. Unemployment in December 1992 was 22 percent in Bath County.

Democratic support in the city of Roanoke is usually surpassed by the Republican vote in Roanoke's suburbs, in Lynchburg and in most of the district's rural areas. The nuclear energy company Babcock & Wilcox is one of Lynchburg's major employers, but the city is best known as the home of evangelist Jerry Falwell, his huge Thomas Road Baptist Church and Falwell-founded Liberty University (10,500 students). Goodlatte won 59 percent in Lynchburg in 1992.

Outside metropolitan Roanoke and Lynchburg, the district depends mainly on dairy farming, livestock and poultry. Rockingham County ranks third in the country in turkeys sold. Tourism enhances the local economy, with visitors traveling to Shenandoah National Park, George Washington National Forest and numerous caverns that dot the valley. Staunton boasts two museums of local notables: One is the house where Woodrow Wilson was born; the other celebrates The Statler Brothers, a country music group.

1990 Population: 562,572. White 492,594 (88%), Black 64,643 (11%), Other 5,335 (1%). Hispanic origin 3,855 (1%). 18 and over 437,920 (78%), 62 and over 98,709 (18%). Median age: 35.

Committees

Agriculture (14th of 18 Republicans)
Livestock; Specialty Crops & Natural Resources

Judiciary (14th of 14 Republicans)
Administrative Law & Governmental Relations; Economic & Commercial Law

Campaign Finance

	Receipts	Receipts from PACs		Expend-itures
1992				
Goodlatte (R)	$464,535	$120,492	(26%)	$452,048
Musselwhite (D)	$597,405	$97,890	(16%)	$597,020

Key Votes

1993

Require parental notification of minors' abortions	Y
Require unpaid family and medical leave	N
Approve national "motor voter" registration bill	N
Approve budget increasing taxes and reducing deficit	N
Approve economic stimulus plan	N

Elections

1992 General

Robert W. Goodlatte (R)	127,309	(60%)
Stephen Alan Musselwhite (D)	84,618	(40%)

District Vote for President

1992

D 84,037 (37%)
R 111,405 (50%)
I 29,207 (13%)

7 Thomas J. Bliley Jr. (R)

Of Richmond — Elected 1980; 7th Term

Born: Jan. 28, 1932, Chesterfield County, Va.
Education: Georgetown U., B.A. 1952.
Military Service: Navy, 1952-55.
Occupation: Funeral director.
Family: Wife, Mary Virginia Kelley; two children.
Religion: Roman Catholic.
Political Career: Richmond City Council, 1968-77; mayor of Richmond, 1970-77.
Capitol Office: 2241 Rayburn Bldg. 20515; 225-2815.

In Washington: A cordial former mayor, Bliley has built relationships with members of the Energy and Commerce Committee that have helped make him one of the more involved Republicans on a panel dominated by activist Democrats.

Ushered into Congress the same year Ronald Reagan arrived in Washington, Bliley is a forceful conservative spokesman, particularly on abortion. But with the start of the 103rd Congress, Bliley lost his White House allies and now finds himself increasingly at odds with the new administration.

And as he moves up the ladder and takes on positions of influence within his own party, the parochial necessity of tending to Virginia's tobacco interests becomes a handicap to Bliley's ability to horse trade.

As the new ranking Republican on the Energy Committee's Health Subcommittee, Bliley is pitted against a savvy Democratic liberal, Chairman Henry A. Waxman of California. If early indications are correct, their relationship could be testy.

In March 1993, Bliley publicly challenged Waxman's plan to channel breast cancer study money to two counties on Long Island, N.Y. In opposing Waxman's amendment to an authorization bill for the National Institutes of Health, Bliley noted that Waxman's administrative assistant, Philip Schiliro, had run unsuccessfully for a House seat on Long Island.

In the markup, Bliley and Waxman argued for nearly 20 minutes over what counties had the highest cancer rates, until full committee Chairman John D. Dingell of Michigan stepped in and asked the two to resolve their differences.

Bliley's friendship with Dingell dated to when Bliley was ranking Republican on the Subcommittee on Oversight and Investigations. After holding widely publicized hearings on testing and approval of generic drugs, the pair crafted legislation that set up harsh penalties for drug companies that defraud the Food and Drug Administration. He also negotiated a compromise that guaranteed drug purchases made by the Department of Veterans Affairs would receive a 24 percent discount.

In the 101st Congress, Bliley was a pivotal player in resolving legal conflicts over so-called orphan drugs, which treat diseases so rare that there may not be enough of a market to support their development. The government has granted special exclusivity rights to developers of such drugs, leading to hard feelings when successful "orphans" reap huge profits for their makers. Bliley's compromise was to allow a fairer share of the new market for competitors that develop the same drug simultaneously.

As a former mayor of Richmond, Bliley has had a long association with his district's conservative business interests. Prominent among them is the cigarette manufacturing company, Philip Morris. Although he often seems resigned to the job, Bliley is identified as the tobacco industry's sentry on the Health Subcommittee.

In the 102nd, he persuaded fellow subcommittee member Mike Synar, an Oklahoma Democrat, to adopt a less stringent law regarding selling tobacco products to minors. In 1990, Bliley managed to beat back an amendment barring the sale of any tobacco products to people "who appeared" to be under 25. But he was not able to stop the subcommittee from approving a ban on the marketing of look-alike products such as bubble-gum cigarettes and chewing tobacco.

In 1985, Bliley tried to block an initiative by Waxman aimed at snuff and chewing tobacco. Waxman wanted to require health warnings on labels and in advertisements, and he sought to mandate a label design that drew attention to the warning. Bliley temporarily blocked it, but the producers, facing the prospect of conflicting labeling requirements in several states, soon consented to federal regulation.

In the 100th Congress, the tobacco industry's biggest loss came when Congress banned smoking on certain domestic airline flights. "The bottom line," Bliley said in floor debate, "is that there is no significant scientific evidence to support the assertion that environmental tobacco smoke is harmful to non-smokers." The ban was broadened to include nearly

Virginia 7

Central — Part of Richmond and suburbs

Some of the fastest-growing areas in Virginia are in the scythe-shaped 7th, which cuts a path from the Blue Ridge Mountains through Virginia's Piedmont region to Richmond and its rapidly expanding suburbs, collecting all or part of nine counties.

The 7th is the state's most Republican district. In redistricting before the 1992 election, most of the blacks in Richmond and Henrico County were placed in the new, majority-black 3rd District, leaving whiter, more Republican areas in the 7th. The district's share of the majority-black city of Richmond, for example, has an 88 percent white population. In the 1988 presidential race, George Bush won 73 percent of the vote in the areas that make up the 7th; in 1992, he got 55 percent in the district. The 7th as now constituted was the only district in Virginia that in 1985 backed the GOP nominees for governor, lieutenant governor and attorney general, all of whom lost statewide.

More than 70 percent of the people in the 7th live in Richmond and adjacent Henrico and Chesterfield counties. The capital city is the third-largest in Virginia and the longtime center of state government and commerce, although nowadays, Northern Virginia and the Hampton Roads area are almost as economically important. Richmond was one of the South's early manufacturing centers, concentrating on tobacco processing. The Phillip Morris cigarette plant — one of the largest in the country — is in the 3rd, but many of its roughly 5,000 employees live in the 7th. The company employs 6,000 more people in the Richmond area.

While Richmond's population dropped during the 1980s, Chesterfield's population rose by nearly 50 percent and Henrico's by more than 20 percent. Hanover County, to the north of Henrico, grew by more than 25 percent. Hanover and Chesterfield are among the most heavily Republican counties in the state. Bush won the 7th District portions of both by better than 2-to-1 in 1992.

As the district pushes north, the exurbs of Richmond and Washington converge. Longtime farming areas such as Spotsylvania County are being taken over by people who drive or ride long-distance commuter buses to jobs in metropolitan Washington; nearby Fredericksburg is the terminus for a new commuter train to Washington. Spotsylvania's population jumped by 67 percent in the 1980s.

The Piedmont in the northern part of the district includes part of Virginia's wine country. Orange, Madison and Culpeper counties have several wineries. The area also contains the Civil War battlefields of Chancellorsville, Spotsylvania and Wilderness. Shenandoah National Park forms the 7th's western frontier.

A glimmer of Democratic viability can be found in Albemarle County, stemming from the campus of the University of Virginia, just over the district's boundary in Charlottesville. In 1992, Bill Clinton lost the 7th's portion of Albemarle by only 696 votes; his 42 percent showing was his best in the district.

1990 Population: 562,643. White 494,047 (88%), Black 56,283 (10%), Other 12,313 (2%). Hispanic origin 5,797 (1%). 18 and over 424,882 (76%), 62 and over 75,367 (13%). Median age: 34.

all domestic flights.

Bliley consistently supported President Bush and the GOP in House floor votes more often than his Republican colleagues. In 1992 and 1993, he led the fight to add parental notification requirements for any federally funded clinics that also perform abortions with private funds. The parental notification amendment failed in part because it did not include a "bypass clause" that would allow minors to appeal to a court and limited incest exemptions to girls raped by their fathers or parental guardians.

Bliley has lobbied for increased federal spending for maternity and pediatric care and, in his capacity as ranking GOP member of the District of Columbia Committee, has supported Mayor Sharon Pratt Kelly's efforts to make Washington, D.C., more self-sufficient. Bliley cosponsored legislation in the 102nd establishing a formula for determining the federal government's annual payment to the District. But while he is willing to give D.C. leaders more control, Bliley is not willing to make the leap to statehood. If people are unhappy at not having congressional representation, "they can move to Maryland," he said.

At Home: A pleasant, soft-spoken mortician, Bliley was coaxed into politics in 1968 by civic leaders who sought him out to run for City Council. He left city government in 1977 after nearly a decade of service to devote more time to his funeral home. But he enthusiastically reentered politics shortly after Democrat David E. Satterfield announced his retirement from Congress in 1980.

A Democrat when in Richmond government, Bliley announced his conversion to the GOP only when he launched his House campaign in 1980. Critics said the switch was motivated by the district's GOP voting pattern; Bliley said it was prompted by a leftward swing in the state Democratic leadership.

Bliley's support from the Richmond business community virtually assured his election. With a well-funded campaign, he overwhelmed his little-known Democratic opponent and two independent candidates. In 1982, Bliley faced a more aggressive challenger in Henrico County Supervisor John Waldrop. The Democrat criticized Bliley for backing deep cuts in social and educational programs, a charge that played well in mostly black Richmond. Bliley lost the city but won easily in the white suburbs where most of the votes were.

Redistricting inconvenienced the previous occupant of what had been labeled the 7th, but not Bliley. Republican George F. Allen had won a special election in November 1991 to succeed ailing 7th District Rep. D. French Slaughter Jr. But weeks later, the Virginia General Assembly passed a plan that combined Bliley's 3rd and Allen's 7th districts. Allen deferred to Bliley, saying he would not challenge him. While much of Bliley's district is new to him, it is also very much Republican. Democrats did not even offer a candidate in 1992.

Committees

District of Columbia (Ranking)

Energy & Commerce (2nd of 17 Republicans)
Health & the Environment (ranking); Telecommunications & Finance

Elections

1992 General		
Thomas J. Bliley Jr. (R)	211,618	(83%)
Gerald E. Berg (I)	43,267	(17%)
1990 General		
Thomas J. Bliley Jr. (R)	77,125	(65%)
Jay Starke (D)	36,253	(31%)
Rose L. Simpson (I)	4,317	(4%)

Previous Winning Percentages: **1988** (100%) **1986** (67%) **1984** (86%) **1982** (59%) **1980** (52%)

District Vote for President

1992

D 85,357 (30%)
R 154,575 (55%)
I 42,724 (15%)

Campaign Finance

	Receipts	Receipts from PACs		Expend-itures
1992				
Bliley (R)	$721,526	$441,292	(61%)	$698,964
1990				
Bliley (R)	$632,395	$398,462	(63%)	$710,739
Starke (D)	$57,857	$28,925	(50%)	$57,909

Key Votes

1993	
Require parental notification of minors' abortions	Y
Require unpaid family and medical leave	N
Approve national "motor voter" registration bill	N
Approve budget increasing taxes and reducing deficit	N
Approve economic stimulus plan	N
1992	
Approve balanced-budget constitutional amendment	Y
Close down space station program	N
Approve U.S. aid for former Soviet Union	Y
Allow shifting funds from defense to domestic programs	N
1991	
Extend unemployment benefits using deficit financing	N
Approve waiting period for handgun purchases	N
Authorize use of force in Persian Gulf	Y

Voting Studies

Year	Presidential Support S	Presidential Support O	Party Unity S	Party Unity O	Conservative Coalition S	Conservative Coalition O
1992	86	13	89	8	94	4
1991	81	19	88	9	97	0
1990	66	34	84	13	91	7
1989	80	17	88	9	100	0
1988	61	38	86	11	89	8
1987	70	29	86	12	91	7
1986	69	30	82	16	94	6
1985	74	26	83	15	87	13
1984	74	25	82	14	88	8
1983	85	12	87	10	96	3
1982	86	13	92	5	97	3
1981	75	25	88	11	89	9

Interest Group Ratings

Year	ADA	AFL-CIO	CCUS	ACU
1992	15	25	86	96
1991	0	17	100	95
1990	17	17	93	83
1989	0	8	100	96
1988	10	21	93	96
1987	4	6	100	96
1986	5	14	88	73
1985	5	24	82	81
1984	5	15	94	83
1983	5	0	84	96
1982	0	5	91	96
1981	0	13	100	93

8 James P. Moran Jr.(D)

Of Alexandria — Elected 1990; 2nd Term

Born: May 16, 1945, Buffalo, N.Y.
Education: College of the Holy Cross, B.A. 1967; City U. of New York, Graduate School, 1967-68; U. of Pittsburgh, M.A. 1970.
Occupation: Investment banker.
Family: Wife, Mary Howard; four children, one stepchild.
Religion: Roman Catholic.
Political Career: Alexandria City Council, 1979-84, vice mayor, 1982-84; mayor of Alexandria, 1985-91.
Capitol Office: 430 Cannon Bldg. 20515; 225-4376.

In Washington: A brash and boisterous liberal, Moran secured an assignment to the Appropriations Committee at the start of his second term, a suitable posting for someone with Moran's boundless energy and ambition. He will be the No. 2 Democrat on the Legislative Branch Subcommittee, the panel that handles the politically thankless task of funding Congress' operations.

As with most of his colleagues from the Washington, D.C., metropolitan area, Moran is an advocate for the thousands of government employees who live and work in the region. He backed an effort in the 103rd Congress to ease restrictions on federal employees' political participation. Early in the 103rd Congress, Moran sought to stave off a planned transfer of about 11,000 Navy jobs out of Crystal City in Arlington. The shift was included as part of the latest military base-closing plan.

Moran began his congressional career with an embarrassing public reversal on the question of authorizing the use of force against Iraq. In a passionate floor speech, he said he would back President Bush's request for that authority. But the next day, Moran changed his mind and voted instead with the majority of Democrats against the use of force. He said that after military and CIA briefings, he had become convinced that it would not be "a clean and quick war."

Moran has voiced philosophical differences with some establishment Democratic tenets, particularly on the subject of welfare. In the past 25 years, he said in a 1990 interview, Democrats have become identified as "ideological elitists who are against people being responsible for their own actions and against family values." He has argued that blue-collar white ethnic voters have left the party because they feel threatened by some of the Democrats' policies. "The Founding Fathers never suggested we could make people happy, just enable them to pursue happiness."

Moran's accent betrays his suburban Boston upbringing. He attended Holy Cross on a football scholarship. He spent a decade in Washington specializing in budget analysis for the federal government and serving on the Senate Appropriations Committee staff.

At Home: Moran ousted GOP Rep. Stan Parris, long one of the scrappiest street fighters in Washington-area politics, to win his seat in 1990. In one of the noisiest House races on the East Coast, Moran, the flamboyant mayor of Alexandria, exchanged blows high and low with Parris in their raucous brawl.

Parris, a twice-failed candidate for the GOP gubernatorial nomination, had garnered regionwide notice for his scorching denunciations of the District of Columbia government of Mayor Marion S. Barry Jr. and for his confrontational conservative rhetoric.

Moran also had a reputation for pugnacity. His service in Alexandria was stormy. First elected to the City Council in 1979, Moran became vice mayor in 1982 as the leading vote-getter in the council election. But his career derailed in 1984 when, after pleading no contest to a misdemeanor conflict of interest charge, he resigned as vice mayor as part of his plea agreement.

A year later, however, Moran resurrected his career. He ran as an independent against the incumbent mayor and defeated him. His continued sensitivity to ethical questions was evident during the 1990 House campaign, when he returned a $10,000 check from an Alexandria developer after reporters asked him about it.

As mayor, Moran stirred some controversy for his forceful approach to drug enforcement. Civil libertarians complained when he ordered eviction of families of suspected drug users from public housing units. He was not averse to the occasional publicity stunt: In December 1989, he challenged Barry to a boxing match to raise funds for anti-drug programs.

Moran and Parris clearly did not like each other. Parris compared Moran to Iraqi leader Saddam Hussein, and Moran called Parris "a racist" and "a fatuous jerk" and professed a

Virginia 8

D.C. suburbs — Part of Fairfax County; Arlington; Alexandria

When critics deride the insular perspective afflicting those who live "inside the Beltway," they may be referring to the suburban residents of the Northern Virginia 8th, most of whose territory is within the confines of the Capital Beltway, Interstate 495, which rings Washington.

The area's growth, originally spurred by the rapid expansion of the federal government, now stems from an array of white-collar and service-industry employers. The military presence in the district starts with the Pentagon, in Arlington, and includes Fort Myer and Fort Belvoir.

Three of the most-affluent counties or independent cities in the nation are in the 8th: the cities of Falls Church and Alexandria, and Arlington County. Each had a per capita income above $22,000 by the late 1980s.

The 8th hugs the Potomac River bank from affluent, predominantly white McLean in the north, through the ethnically, racially and economically diverse neighborhoods of Arlington and the city of Alexandria to the Route 1 corridor of southern Fairfax County. It is hospitable to most Democrats. Bill Clinton carried the 8th with 51 percent of the vote in 1992. He received 58 percent in both Arlington and Alexandria, which ranked among his best showings in the state; he also carried Falls Church. George Bush, who carried the territory within the 8th in 1988 with 52 percent, won the Fairfax portion of the 8th in 1992 by 32 votes. In 1989, Democrat L. Douglas Wilder's 62 percent showing in the 8th was crucial to his successful gubernatorial bid.

Fairfax County, with a population over 800,000, is the most populous jurisdiction in Virginia. Even though it is split among three districts — the 8th, 10th and 11th — it is the most populous portion in each of them. One-third of the county is in the 8th, accounting for almost half the population in the district.

Arlington is home to three of every 10 district residents. While there are relatively few blacks in Arlington, it has become a melting pot for other minorities. Asians, Hispanics and other minority groups make up roughly one-quarter of the population. Arlington has one of the largest concentrations of Vietnamese in the country, and it has numerous Vietnamese-owned businesses.

The old Colonial seaport of Alexandria casts about one-fifth of the district vote; it is reliable Democratic territory. The restaurants and shops of its revitalized Old Town section compete with the Georgetown area of Washington, and thousands of Democratic-voting young professionals live there. On the fringe of Old Town is a black community that enhances Democratic strength. Blacks make up 22 percent of Alexandria's population.

The southern portion of Fairfax County includes George Washington's 500-acre estate at Mount Vernon and Gunston Hall, home of George Mason, one of the framers of the Constitution. It also houses the District of Columbia's Lorton Reformatory.

1990 Population: 562,484. White 427,308 (76%), Black 75,128 (13%), Other 60,048 (11%). Hispanic origin 48,994 (9%). 18 and over 453,533 (81%), 62 and over 64,690 (12%). Median age: 34.

desire to "break his nose."

"I have good reason to punch Stan Parris in the nose, that jerk," Moran said on a local TV station.

Using the results of the 1989 gubernatorial race as a guidepost, Moran banked on voters in the 8th rejecting Parris' conservative social-issue positions. In 1989, Democrat L. Douglas Wilder carried the 8th over Republican J. Marshall Coleman by more than 20,000 votes. One of Wilder's most powerful issues in Northern Virginia was his support for abortion rights; Coleman opposed abortion.

From the day he announced his candidacy, Moran castigated Parris for his longstanding opposition to abortion. Planned Parenthood helped by taking out newspaper ads criticizing Parris' abortion position, and Moran ran TV ads accusing Parris of depriving women of their freedom. One of his ads depicted women locked in jail cells, warning that Parris wanted to make abortion illegal. The ad ended with an image of the Statue of Liberty behind bars.

With no presidential race on the ballot, Moran was unhindered by a top-of-the-ticket draw for Republicans; GOP Sen. John W. Warner had no major-party opposition. Boosted by the abortion issue, Moran ended up on top by a surprisingly wide margin, 52 percent to 45 percent.

When Democrats in the Virginia General Assembly turned to redistricting in late 1991, they transformed the 8th District from a Republican stronghold to a Democratic one, removing GOP suburbs in Fairfax County and adding Democratic Arlington County.

But even within his new friendly confines, Moran found himself with a fight on his hands. Republicans were unable to field a known heavyweight contender, but their nominee, Arlington lawyer Kyle E. McSlarrow, was one of the year's unexpected delights for the Virginia GOP. The 32-year-old political newcomer ran a nettlesome campaign against Moran that succeeded in getting under the Democrat's skin. With mounds of free media attention, McSlarrow launched daily assaults on the liberal freshman.

McSlarrow accused Moran of illegally using public money when he sent franked mail to homes outside his existing district (but in the new one). Some McSlarrow supporters filed a lawsuit, but a federal judge dismissed it.

Some incumbents, granted such a secure district, would have ignored such gibes. But Moran is not one to back down from a fight.

Name-calling marked most meetings between McSlarrow and Moran. McSlarrow called Moran a crook; Moran slammed him as a right-wing extremist. After hinting that McSlarrow's use of illegal drugs was more extensive than the Republican had admitted (McSlarrow said he used marijuana and cocaine as a teenager), Moran acknowledged that he had tried marijuana while in college.

Moran outspent McSlarrow by 2-to-1. He dusted off his ad with the women behind bars to remind voters that he supports abortion rights while McSlarrow opposed abortion.

Moran carried the Fairfax County portion of the 8th, the most populous section of the district, by only 765 votes. But he racked up big margins in Arlington and Alexandria, spurring him to a 56 percent to 42 percent win.

Committee

Appropriations (33rd of 37 Democrats)
Commerce, Justice, State & Judiciary; Legislative Branch

Elections

1992 General		
James P. Moran Jr. (D)	138,542	(56%)
Kyle E. McSlarrow (R)	102,717	(42%)
Alvin O. West (I)	5,601	(2%)
1990 General		
James P. Moran Jr. (D)	88,475	(52%)
Stan Parris (R)	76,367	(45%)
Robert T. Murphy (I)	5,958	(3%)

District Vote for President

1992	
D	133,183 (51%)
R	96,799 (37%)
I	28,967 (11%)

Campaign Finance

	Receipts	Receipts from PACs		Expend-itures
1992				
Moran (D)	$925,436	$436,121	(47%)	$923,999
McSlarrow (R)	$426,951	$86,389	(20%)	$424,895
1990				
Moran (D)	$883,236	$257,821	(29%)	$883,216
Parris (R)	$864,864	$313,852	(36%)	$982,157

Key Votes

1993	
Require parental notification of minors' abortions	N
Require unpaid family and medical leave	Y
Approve national "motor voter" registration bill	Y
Approve budget increasing taxes and reducing deficit	Y
Approve economic stimulus plan	Y
1992	
Approve balanced-budget constitutional amendment	Y
Close down space station program	N
Approve U.S. aid for former Soviet Union	Y
Allow shifting funds from defense to domestic programs	Y
1991	
Extend unemployment benefits using deficit financing	Y
Approve waiting period for handgun purchases	Y
Authorize use of force in Persian Gulf	N

Voting Studies

	Presidential Support		Party Unity		Conservative Coalition	
Year	S	O	S	O	S	O
1992	30	66	83	10	48	50
1991	40	58	79	16	30	68

Interest Group Ratings

Year	ADA	AFL-CIO	CCUS	ACU
1992	80	73	50	13
1991	70	83	40	10

9 Rick Boucher (D)

Of Abingdon — Elected 1982; 6th Term

Born: Aug. 1, 1946, Abingdon, Va.
Education: Roanoke College, B.A. 1968; U. of Virginia, J.D. 1971.
Occupation: Lawyer.
Family: Single.
Religion: Methodist.
Political Career: Va. Senate, 1974-82.
Capitol Office: 2245 Rayburn Bldg. 20515; 225-3861.

In Washington: A quiet man with a professorial air, Boucher enters his second decade in Congress as a respected but somewhat ill-defined figure. While seen as a potential aspirant to statewide office, Boucher has not gone out of his way to pursue the high-profile issues that would raise his visibility outside his southwest Virginia district. Boucher's colleagues universally note his intelligence and drive, while also noting his tendency to apply those qualities to only a handful of issues that interest him.

Boucher carries a fairly heavy load of committee assignments, which may be one reason for his pick-and-choose approach. He sits on the powerful Energy and Commerce Committee as well as Judiciary, and he chairs the Science Subcommittee on Science, Space and Technology.

Boucher is scrupulous about putting the interests of his district first. While considered one of the most liberal members of the Virginia delegation, he nonetheless is a staunch supporter of the coal interests so important to his district. Since the departure of Illinois' Terry Bruce, who was defeated in a a primary in 1992, Boucher is the main voice for coal on Energy and Commerce. Boucher is also a reliable vote against gun control measures.

One of Boucher's legislative initiatives with the potential to raise his profile is his bill to increase oversight and regulation in the financial planning industry. The measure would require disclosure of fees and commissions received by financial advisers and restrict the sale of high-risk investment products to protect unsophisticated investors. The bill passed the House in the 102nd Congress, and Boucher has refiled it for the 103rd, with the strong support of Energy and Commerce Chairman John D. Dingell of Michigan.

Recently, Boucher has devoted much of his energy to two issues that are complex, important to certain constituencies, yet always a few degrees short of the boiling point: reform of the 1970 Racketeer Influenced, Corrupt Organizations Act and increasing competition in the cable television market.

Beginning with the 99th Congress, the former Wall Street lawyer has championed a bill to limit liability under the act. Originally designed to allow prosecutors to use punishingly high monetary damages as a weapon against organized crime, the racketeering act now is often used in civil suits against corporations, in part because it allows such high damages. Business groups see it as an intrusion on free enterprise, and Boucher's bill would limit the act's use in civil matters.

While the legislation made it out of committee in the 101st and 102nd Congresses, it did not reach the floor either time. The bill is opposed by law enforcement and consumer groups, which fear its effect on the battle against white-collar crime.

In the 103rd Congress, Boucher is continuing to push a bill that would allow telephone companies to get into the business of providing cable television in their service areas. Boucher says his bill would improve service and reduce rates by breaking the effective monopoly local cable companies enjoy, while speeding the introduction of cable service to rural areas and encouraging phone companies to extend their fiber-optic cable networks.

In a rare dramatic break with the Democratic leadership, Boucher was the only Democrat on the Judiciary Committee to refuse to sign a request that an independent counsel be appointed to investigate possible criminal misconduct associated with the Bush administration's policy toward Iraq before the Persian Gulf War. The charges arose from House investigations into agricultural loan guarantees and other assistance to Iraq. Many of the loans were made by the Banca Nazionale del Lavoro (BNL), which was the subject of a criminal investigation by the Justice Department.

Boucher said he believed a "traditional criminal investigation" would be sufficient. Attorney General William P. Barr refused the Democratic request for an independent counsel.

In 1992, Boucher was one of 14 lawmakers found to have taken action on legislation directly affecting their personal financial interests, in a study for Gannett News Service. While such actions are allowed under congres-

Virginia 9

Southwest — Blacksburg; Bristol

Bordering four states, the 9th contains some of the most beautiful and most depressed areas in Virginia.

The Appalachians, which form a diagonal spine down the district, and Mount Rogers National Recreation Area, on the southern tier near the North Carolina and Tennessee borders, provide stunning scenery.

But the coal-dependent western portion of the 9th lags behind the state in economic health. Four of the five jurisdictions with the highest poverty rates in the state are in the 9th; three are in the coal fields region, an area comprising Buchanan, Dickenson, Lee, Russell, Scott, Tazewell and Wise counties and the independent city of Norton. Unemployment in Buchanan, Lee and Wise hovered near 10 percent in March 1993; Dickenson's unemployment rate was 14 percent.

The "Fighting Ninth" earned that name not only because of its tradition of fiercely competitive two-party politics but also because of its ornery isolation from the political establishment in Richmond.

Southwestern Virginia was settled by Scots-Irish and German immigrants who felt little in common with the English settlers in the Tidewater and Piedmont regions. The Civil War divided the anti-secession mountaineers from the state's slaveholding Confederates. In the postwar era, when Democrats routinely dominated Virginia politics, the 9th was the only district in which Republicans were consistently strong.

But in recent years, as the state GOP moved into alliance with Richmond's business establishment and Northern Virginia's affluent suburbanites, the party has lost ground in the 9th. A number of the region's burley tobacco growers and other small-scale farmers now are teaming up with the traditionally Democratic coal miners.

Democrats are strongest in the coal-mining counties along the Kentucky and West Virginia borders. Bill Clinton carried the five coal counties bordering those states in 1992, as had Michael S. Dukakis four years earlier. Democrat L. Douglas Wilder carried four of them in his 1989 gubernatorial race.

The coal fields region has little in common with the rest of Virginia — as many as seven other state capitals are closer than Richmond. Virginia may be a right-to-work state, but the United Mine Workers still wield influence here; in a 1989 write-in campaign, a UMW-backed independent crushed a 21-year incumbent for a local state House seat.

Republicans normally have an edge in the corridor of counties roughly traced by Interstate 81 as it runs north from Bristol to Radford. Carroll County, on the North Carolina border, is also solidly Republican.

Montgomery County, which contains the district's largest city, Blacksburg, is economically atypical of the 9th. Home to Virginia Tech, the state's largest university with nearly 24,000 students, Blacksburg is a far more tidy and prosperous-looking place than most of the factory and coal towns in the district.

1990 Population: 562,380. White 543,103 (97%), Black 13,948 (2%), Other 5,329 (1%). Hispanic origin 2,839 (1%). 18 and over 433,970 (77%), 62 and over 91,220 (16%). Median age: 34.

sional conflict-of-interest rules adopted in 1977, similar actions would violate stiffer rules governing other federal employees.

In Boucher's case, his membership on the Energy Subcommittee on Telecommunications and Finance and his votes on banking legislation were seen as conflicting with his ownership of $5,000 in First Virginia Bank stock and with his position as a member of the bank's board. Boucher said his bank interests would never influence his vote.

At Home: The hard work and careful organization that have helped Boucher in the House have also been the secret of his success in the 9th, where voters no longer seem to mind that he lacks a rough-and-tumble air.

Boucher needed all his assets to weather bruising elections in 1982 and 1984. But in 1986, he became the district's first House candidate since 1853 to run unopposed, and again in 1990 he drew no opposition.

In 1992, Republicans tried to recruit the man whom Boucher defeated in 1982 to win the 9th, former Republican Rep. William C. Wampler. But despite heavy pressure, Wampler declined. Boucher went on to a 26 percentage point win over the GOP nominee, Radford City Council member L. Garrett Weddle, as Bill Clinton became the first Democrat in 16 years to win the 9th.

Despite his scholarly look, Boucher came naturally to politics. Both his grandfather and great-grandfather served in the Virginia House. His father was commonwealth's attorney in Washington County (Abingdon).

After graduating from the University of Virginia Law School, Boucher joined a Wall

Street firm. He took time out to work as an advance man for George McGovern's 1972 presidential campaign. The following year he returned to Abingdon to practice law, ultimately joining his family's firm in 1978.

He also began laying the groundwork for his political debut, which he made in a 1975 bid for state Senate. Energetically buttonholing district convention delegates, Boucher defeated a veteran incumbent for the Democratic nomination, then coasted to election.

Democratic Gov. Charles S. Robb and other state party leaders urged Boucher to challenge Wampler in 1982, when high unemployment was plaguing the district's coal fields. Boucher raised enough money to finance billboards and media advertising on the three TV stations that together cover the district.

Wampler dismissed Boucher as "a Henry Howell with an Ivy League look," a reference to the controversial Tidewater populist who lost decisively in his last gubernatorial race in 1977. But Boucher jabbed back, describing the affable Wampler — known to constituents as the "bald eagle of the Cumberland" — as a nice man but ineffective legislator. Boucher termed himself the true fiscal conservative, citing Wampler's support for Reaganomics and its ensuing budget deficits.

The economy was a powerful issue. In some of the coal counties, unemployment neared 20 percent in fall 1982. Boucher, drawing on the active support of the United Mine Workers of America, ran exceptionally well. Boucher also neutralized Wampler in his home base, the Bristol area just north of Tennessee. Bristol was also part of Boucher's state Senate district; Wampler won it only narrowly. Boucher won by just 1,123 votes out of more than 150,000 cast.

When Wampler decided against a rematch in 1984, Boucher became a clear favorite. But he did not have an easy race against his well-financed GOP challenger, state Rep. Jefferson Stafford. One of the legislature's most conservative members, Stafford charged that Boucher was too liberal, tying him to Walter F. Mondale, whose presidential campaign Boucher helped to lead in Virginia. Although Stafford carried most of the 17 counties in the 9th, Boucher survived by taking large majorities in the coal-producing areas.

Committees

Energy & Commerce (14th of 27 Democrats)
Energy & Power; Telecommunications & Finance; Transportation & Hazardous Materials

Judiciary (12th of 21 Democrats)
Economic & Commercial Law

Science, Space & Technology (9th of 33 Democrats)
Science (chairman)

Elections

1992 General		
Rick Boucher (D)	133,284	(63%)
L. Garrett Weddle (R)	77,985	(37%)
1990 General		
Rick Boucher (D)	67,215	(97%)

Previous Winning Percentages: **1988** (63%) **1986** (99%) **1984** (52%) **1982** (50%)

District Vote for President

	1992	
D	99,099	(45%)
R	93,673	(43%)
I	26,676	(12%)

Campaign Finance

	Receipts	Receipts from PACs		Expend-itures
1992				
Boucher (D)	$639,537	$404,579	(63%)	$660,452
Weddle (R)	$99,174	$5,016	(5%)	$100,089
1990				
Boucher (D)	$524,268	$366,584	(70%)	$252,685

Key Votes

1993	
Require parental notification of minors' abortions	N
Require unpaid family and medical leave	Y
Approve national "motor voter" registration bill	Y
Approve budget increasing taxes and reducing deficit	Y
Approve economic stimulus plan	Y
1992	
Approve balanced-budget constitutional amendment	N
Close down space station program	N
Approve U.S. aid for former Soviet Union	Y
Allow shifting funds from defense to domestic programs	Y
1991	
Extend unemployment benefits using deficit financing	Y
Approve waiting period for handgun purchases	N
Authorize use of force in Persian Gulf	N

Voting Studies

	Presidential Support		Party Unity		Conservative Coalition	
Year	**S**	**O**	**S**	**O**	**S**	**O**
1992	21	78	86	9	44	56
1991	34	62	84	10	43	49
1990	20	79	90	5	35	57
1989	27 †	67 †	88	6	27	68
1988	19	74	87	5	29	66
1987	22	68	86	7	42	51
1986	23	72	83	6	36	50
1985	29	68	87	7	35	64
1984	35	56	78	12	44	47
1983	22	74	88	7	29	64

† Not eligible for all recorded votes.

Interest Group Ratings

Year	ADA	AFL-CIO	CCUS	ACU
1992	90	82	38	8
1991	65	75	40	10
1990	72	100	23	13
1989	80	73	30	8
1988	75	100	29	9
1987	76	94	7	0
1986	65	86	20	6
1985	60	65	48	19
1984	70	62	33	29
1983	80	88	35	13

10 Frank R. Wolf (R)

Of Vienna — Elected 1980; 7th Term

Born: Jan. 30, 1939, Philadelphia, Pa.

Education: Pennsylvania State U., B.A. 1961; Georgetown U., LL.B. 1965.

Military Service: Army, 1962-63; Army Reserve, 1963-67.

Occupation: Lawyer.

Family: Wife, Carolyn Stover; five children.

Religion: Presbyterian.

Political Career: Sought GOP nomination for U.S. House, 1976; GOP nominee for U.S. House, 1978.

Capitol Office: 104 Cannon Bldg. 20515; 225-5136.

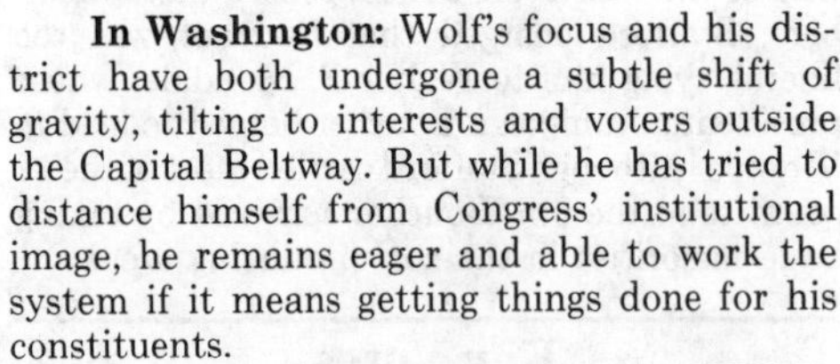

In Washington: Wolf's focus and his district have both undergone a subtle shift of gravity, tilting to interests and voters outside the Capital Beltway. But while he has tried to distance himself from Congress' institutional image, he remains eager and able to work the system if it means getting things done for his constituents.

He is in a good position to do so. Wolf is best known for his machinations on the Appropriations Committee to keep federal jobs in his district and to ease the daily grind for the thousands who fight their way across the Potomac's crowded bridges to work in Washington. At the beginning of the 103rd Congress, he chose to lead his party's contingent on the spending panel's Transportation Subcommittee, giving him even more direct influence than he had when he was the top Republican on the Treasury-Postal Subcommittee.

Every member seeks highway funding for his district, but none plays a more personal role in trying to unravel traffic tie-ups than Wolf. An ombudsman for commuters, he fires off letters to D.C., state and federal transportation officials aimed at easing backups on bridges and at tollgates. And he knows how to add provisions to appropriations bills that put teeth in his requests.

In the 102nd Congress, Wolf was able to use his position to force state officials to reopen carpool lanes on a main commuter artery that had angered local commuters. He helped thwart the designs of Sen. Robert C. Byrd upon several thousand CIA jobs, which the Senate's Democratic lion had almost succeeded in moving from Northern Virginia to his own West Virginia.

Another attempted raid — by Colorado Democrat David E. Skaggs, who tried to get a planned expansion of the Smithsonian's Air and Space Museum moved from Virginia's Dulles Airport to Denver — was fought off by Wolf. He succeeded in pressuring the National Science Foundation to move its headquarters to Arlington from its pricey location near the White House. And he got money for an experimental telecommuting center to allow some federal workers who live in Virginia to do their work without crossing the Potomac at all.

At the same time he has broadened his horizons. His bill to suspend trade breaks given to the Federal Republic of Yugoslavia in view of its support for the Bosnian Serbs was enacted in 1992. He is one of 14 House members of the Helsinki human rights commission, and has sponsored amendments designed to punish Romania (before it overthrew dictator Nicolae Ceausescu in 1989) and China for human rights violations.

As Wolf has gained seniority and baby boom suburbanites have gained political clout, some of his parochial concerns have taken on national import. Child care, for instance, has priority for Wolf, because of the many working parents in the 10th.

He keeps his conservative ideals intact, however, favoring bigger tax breaks for families over more direct government action. In the 102nd Congress, some of the most liberal Democrats were among the 262 cosponsors of his bill to increase the personal exemption for children under 18 by 52 percent. In the 103rd, he voted against a bill requiring businesses to give unpaid leave to workers to take care of a family member.

Wolf works well with Democrats, particularly on suburban transportation and jobs issues with Maryland's Steny H. Hoyer, who is chairman of the Treasury-Postal Appropriations Subcommittee (as well as the Democratic Caucus). Lest Wolf be cast as a collaborationist, however, he has taken to decrying the strong-arm tactics Democrats have used to run the House. And after boasting in newsletters to constituents about the usefulness of his post as senior Republican on the Select Committee on Children, Youth and Families, he denounced the panel as "basically a fig leaf" in the floor debate that led to its extinction in early 1993.

Unlike most members who represent large

Virginia 10

North — Part of Fairfax County; Manassas

From small-town apple country to people-packed Washington suburbs, the 10th bridges a dizzying range of economies and lifestyles. Draping the northern portion of the state, it links the Blue Ridge Mountains and booming Fairfax County. About the only thing the localities have in common is their strong preference for Republicans.

About 60 percent of the 10th's population is in the Northern Virginia suburbs of Washington: Fairfax, Prince William and Loudoun counties and the cities of Manassas and Manassas Park. Fairfax, the most populous jurisdiction in Virginia, has the largest share of the district's population. Only one-sixth of Fairfax County is in the 10th, but it still accounts for one-fourth of the district's population. Some of the county's fastest-growing parts are in the 10th, including Centreville, whose population more than tripled during the 1980s to top 26,000, and Chantilly, which more than doubled to exceed 29,000.

The westward expansion of the D.C. suburbs was reflected in Manassas, which posted the largest percentage increase in the state of any county or independent city: 81 percent. Commuting from Manassas became easier in 1992 with the opening of the Virginia Railway Express, whose western branch connects Manassas and D.C.

Loudoun County's population rose by 50 percent; the population of the county seat of Leesburg nearly doubled during the 1980s. Prince William County's population rose nearly 50 percent, making it the third most-populous county in Virginia.

Beyond suburbia, agriculture and manufacturing fuel the economy. Winchester is the center of the state's apple-growing industry. Virginia ranks sixth in the nation in apples harvested, and Frederick and Clarke counties lead the state. Winchester is also the home of Virginia's political dynasty, the Byrd family. But like former Sen. Harry F. Byrd Jr., who took over his father's Senate seat in 1965 and later became an independent, the district has abandoned its Democratic roots. George Bush won the 10th by a 3-to-2 margin in 1992, carrying every county and independent city; in 1988, he got more than two-thirds of the votes cast by the areas within the 10th. In the 1989 gubernatorial race, Republican J. Marshall Coleman won the area with more than 54 percent.

The district's ample natural beauty draws visitors year-round. At the eastern end of the district, the Potomac River cascades at Great Falls Park in Fairfax County. Loudoun and Fauquier counties are part of Northern Virginia's "hunt" country, a rolling landscape dotted with sprawling country houses, horse farms and an occasional vineyard. Skyline Drive, a 105-mile scenic highway through Shenandoah National Park across the ridge of the Blue Ridge Mountains, begins in Front Royal (Warren County). George Washington National Forest straddles the West Virginia border. The 10th also has some important Civil War battle sites, including Manassas and New Market.

1990 Population: 562,664. White 510,926 (91%), Black 32,476 (6%), Other 19,892 (4%). Hispanic origin 12,606 (2%). 18 and over 411,822 (73%), 62 and over 52,782 (9%). Median age: 32.

numbers of federal employees, Wolf opposed legislation rolling back the limits on the workers' political activities. While agreeing that the 1939 Hatch Act needed revision, he led the opposition to the Democratic bill because it did not exempt workers in sensitive positions such as U.S. attorneys and Internal Revenue Service agents. In early 1993, he rounded up enough votes to defeat an attempt to approve the bill without amendments, and it passed only after modifications — not enough to satisfy Wolf — were made.

At Home: Democrats have derisively referred to Wolf as a "pothole" politician. But during the 1980s, he built an increasingly smooth and secure political base.

Redistricting in late 1991 splayed Wolf's district, previously focused in the Washington suburbs of Northern Virginia, across the northern portion of the state, relinquishing part of suburban Fairfax County and all of Arlington County in favor of rural counties unfamiliar with Wolf and uninterested in Washington traffic problems.

The Democratic nominee, Raymond E. Vickery, sought to test Wolf's vote-getting ability in the new territory. Vickery, a lawyer from Vienna, served in the state House in the 1970s. But the 10th remains very much Republican, and Wolf beat Vickery 64 percent to 33 percent.

Democratic hopes of ousting Wolf were highest in 1986, when the party ran John G. Milliken, a past chairman of the Arlington County Board of Supervisors. Unlike previous challengers, who had to fend off either a liberal reputation or a carpetbagger stigma, Milliken had long experience in local government and a reputation as a moderate Democrat.

As chairman of the Washington Metropolitan Area Transit Authority and the Northern Virginia Transportation Commission, Milliken had dealt with many of the same transportation questions that Wolf had. Milliken said he could match Wolf's expertise on suburban issues yet be more forceful on national ones.

But while Milliken had the image, the roots and the money — nearly $750,000 — needed to challenge Wolf, he had trouble making a case for replacing the hard-working, if undynamic, incumbent. Wolf swamped Milliken in the populous outer suburbs of Fairfax and Loudoun counties, while running virtually even with his challenger in Democratic Arlington.

Wolf's impressive victory chilled Democrats' spirits. The most prominent opponent against the Republican since then has been fringe political figure Lyndon H. LaRouche Jr., who ran as an independent in 1990. LaRouche's personal campaigning was hampered by his incarceration in a federal prison in Minnesota.

Wolf's career has been a testament to persistence. Barely a year after Democrat Joseph L. Fisher first won his House seat in 1974, Wolf began campaigning to defeat him. His 1976 effort had the backing of local Reagan activists, but did not survive the primary.

In 1978, with more name recognition and better financing, he won the GOP nomination, but lost to Fisher by almost 9,000 votes. His reward came in 1980. Backed by a huge budget, Wolf emerged with a narrow win.

In the early campaigns, Fisher chided Wolf for a lack of government experience. But having been a lobbyist, an aide to GOP Rep. Edward G. Biester of Pennsylvania, and deputy assistant secretary of the Interior, Wolf could claim he knew his way around the Capitol.

Committee

Appropriations (10th of 23 Republicans)
Transportation (ranking); Treasury, Postal Service & General Government

Elections

1992 General		
Frank R. Wolf (R)	144,471	(64%)
Raymond E. Vickery (D)	75,775	(33%)
Alan R. Ogden (I)	6,874	(3%)
1990 General		
Frank R. Wolf (R)	103,761	(61%)
N. MacKenzie Canter III (D)	57,249	(34%)
Barbara S. Minnich (I)	5,273	(3%)
Lyndon H. LaRouche Jr. (I)	2,293	(1%)

Previous Winning Percentages: **1988** (68%) **1986** (60%) **1984** (63%) **1982** (53%) **1980** (51%)

District Vote for President

1992
D 83,214 (33%)
R 124,783 (50%)
I 41,228 (17%)

Campaign Finance

	Receipts	Receipts from PACs		Expend-itures
1992				
Wolf (R)	$452,307	$180,401	(40%)	$431,829
Vickery (D)	$202,243	$13,116	(6%)	$191,260
1990				
Wolf (R)	$514,240	$192,395	(37%)	$511,853
Canter (D)	$97,467	$7,150	(7%)	$93,659
LaRouche (I)	$648,572	0		$647,836

Key Votes

1993	
Require parental notification of minors' abortions	Y
Require unpaid family and medical leave	N
Approve national "motor voter" registration bill	N
Approve budget increasing taxes and reducing deficit	N
Approve economic stimulus plan	N
1992	
Approve balanced-budget constitutional amendment	Y
Close down space station program	N
Approve U.S. aid for former Soviet Union	Y
Allow shifting funds from defense to domestic programs	N
1991	
Extend unemployment benefits using deficit financing	N
Approve waiting period for handgun purchases	Y
Authorize use of force in Persian Gulf	Y

Voting Studies

	Presidential Support		Party Unity		Conservative Coalition	
Year	**S**	**O**	**S**	**O**	**S**	**O**
1992	78	22	86	13	96	4
1991	81	18	81	17	92	8
1990	71	29	78	21	83	15
1989	81	19	83	16	93	7
1988	59	40	82	17	87	13
1987	65	35	76	23	79	21
1986	67	33	74	25	78	22
1985	70	30	72	25	75	24
1984	64	33	71	27	86	12
1983	77	23	79	19	87	13
1982	56	39	69	28	78	15
1981	76 †	24 †	83	17	88 †	12 †

† Not eligible for all recorded votes.

Interest Group Ratings

Year	ADA	AFL-CIO	CCUS	ACU
1992	20	42	88	84
1991	15	17	80	80
1990	6	0	71	83
1989	10	17	90	89
1988	25	43	86	88
1987	16	13	73	87
1986	5	21	67	86
1985	15	24	73	71
1984	10	25	63	63
1983	5	6	75	96
1982	10	20	82	67
1981	10	0	100	93

11 Leslie L. Byrne (D)

Of Falls Church — Elected 1992; 1st Term

Born: Oct. 27, 1946, Salt Lake City, Utah.
Education: U. of Utah, 1964-65.
Occupation: Human resources consultant.
Family: Husband, Larry Byrne; two children.
Religion: Roman Catholic.
Political Career: Va. House, 1986-92.
Capitol Office: 1609 Longworth Bldg. 20515; 225-1492.

The Path to Washington: The newly drawn 11th District is a jumble of affluent and middle-class suburbs with a mixed political personality. It went for George Bush in the 1992 presidential election, as did the state, but it elected Democrat Byrne over her GOP opponent by a comfortable 50 percent to 45 percent.

Byrne says polls show she did particularly well with two-income households, a sign, she says, that economic and family issues are important to her constituents and key to solidifying her role in a district with highly transient residents who have no strict party allegiances.

Byrne plans to concentrate on issues of concern to families, better transportation for the traffic-clogged district so people can get to work more easily and ensuring job growth.

Byrne started her career in the House with a boost from party elders, winning an appointment as at-large whip, the first rung on the House leadership ladder.

Before coming to Congress, Byrne served in the Virginia House of Delegates, winning election in 1985 from a district that had long been dominated by Republicans.

Although that was her first elective office, she was already known in the district as the president of a local business consulting firm, an active participant in community affairs and president of the local League of Women Voters.

She was re-elected to her state House seat with handsome margins in 1987, 1989 and 1991 and held a key position on the Finance Committee.

Byrne won the U.S. House seat in an acrimonious, closely contested race against Henry N. Butler, a law professor whose father, Republican M. Caldwell Butler, held a southwest Virginia House seat from 1972 to 1983.

Butler took a strongly conservative line on fiscal issues, calling for a range of tax cuts and incentives to recharge the economy. He attacked Byrne for what he said were 34 votes to raise taxes and described her positions as "economic death."

Byrne responded by accusing Butler of distorting her record, and she issued a point-by-point rebuttal of many of his assertions. She also called Butler "an economic arsonist" and "a shill for big business."

Byrne came out for stepped-up federal efforts on education, infrastructure and job creation. But she also took more moderate positions, supporting a constitutional amendment to balance the budget and a line-item veto.

Though concerned that a pay freeze for federal employees in President Clinton's budget would disproportionately hit the significant number of federal workers living in her Northern Virginia district, she supported both the budget and the stimulus package in early 1993.

In the 103rd, Byrne made good on a campaign promise to support family leave legislation. She also promised in the campaign to work to encourage job growth with targeted tax incentives to industries that create jobs and eliminating tax breaks for those that do not.

Byrne says a balanced-budget amendment will do nothing to address the deficit unless something is done to tackle the high costs of health care, particularly in the entitlement programs Medicare and Medicaid.

In the health area generally, Byrne believes costs can be contained by standardizing insurance forms and eliminating duplication of new technologies.

As she did in the state legislature (where she worked to double Northern Virginia's share of state transportation money), Byrne intends to focus on transportation issues in Congress. She secured a seat on the Public Works and Transportation panel, which should help her shape legislation in this area.

She is strongly in favor of abortion rights and says she has no qualms being vocal about the issue in her largely suburban district, where she believes constituents share her views. During the campaign, Butler also supported a woman's right to have an abortion, but he opposed federal funding of abortions for poor women.

Byrne also supports a waiting period for handgun purchases and used the well-publicized endorsement of Handgun Control Inc. to make that point clear to constituents. Butler opposed the waiting period.

Virginia 11

D.C. suburbs — Parts of Fairfax and Prince William counties

Growth in the Northern Virginia suburbs of Washington during the 1980s helped earn Virginia an additional congressional district. Fairfax County, the most populous jurisdiction in Virginia with a population of more than 800,000, grew by 220,000 during the 1980s — a rate of 37 percent and more than one-fourth of the commonwealth's overall population expansion of 840,000.

The 11th, with a shape that vaguely recalls the human digestive tract, was drawn by Democratic legislators and signed by a Democratic governor with the intent of electing a Democrat, but it is more competitive than the neighboring 8th. George Bush won the areas within the 11th in both 1988 and 1992, although his 60 percent showing in his first election was trimmed to 43 percent four years later. Democrat L. Douglas Wilder received just under 57 percent of the vote within the 11th in his 1989 gubernatorial race. Bush lost the Fairfax County portion of the 11th to Bill Clinton, but recouped by winning in Prince William and in Fairfax City.

The 11th is primarily middle- to upper-middle-class suburbia. Many residents work in downtown Washington, either for the federal government or for companies whose business is linked to the government. But as the suburbs have expanded, they have developed their own employment base: Rush hour in Northern Virginia no longer follows a single, to-and-from Washington pattern; much traffic moves from one suburb to another. Dozens of companies have put down roots in office-park developments in Fairfax; one is Mobil Corp., whose headquarters are in Merrifield. Mobil's operations in Fairfax County employ 3,800. The area's business roster includes many high-tech companies, some of them defense-related, including computer engineering, manufacturing and consulting firms.

Fairfax County accounted for nearly eight of every 10 votes cast in the 11th in 1992. Growth and all its effects on property tax rates, school quality, traffic and crime are the primary concerns of Fairfax residents. Recently they have been buffeted by a weak real estate market and threatened defense cutbacks.

The planned community of Reston, founded in 1961 in the northern part of the county, grew by 33 percent during the 1980s to nearly 49,000. Adjacent to Reston, the town of Herndon saw its population rise by more than 40 percent to about 16,000. Unincorporated places in the county such as Burke (split between the 11th and 8th districts), Bailey's Crossroads, Lincolnia and Seven Corners all grew by more than 20 percent.

Suburban expansion spread into Prince William County, which grew by 71,000 in the 1980s, a nearly 50 percent rise. About three-fifths of the county's population is in the 11th. Woodbridge has the Washington area's closest professional baseball team, the minor league Prince William Cannons. A few miles south on I-95 is Potomac Mills, an immense mall of about 200 factory outlet stores that has become Virginia's No. 1 draw for visitors.

1990 Population: 562,497. White 454,067 (81%), Black 46,037 (8%), Other 62,393 (12%). Hispanic origin 41,594 (7%). 18 and over 419,933 (75%), 62 and over 43,129 (8%). Median age: 32.

Committees

Post Office & Civil Service (9th of 15 Democrats)
Compensation & Employee Benefits

Public Works & Transportation (27th of 39 Democrats)
Investigations & Oversight; Surface Transportation; Water Resources & the Environment

Campaign Finance

1992	Receipts	Receipts from PACs		Expenditures
Byrne (D)	$793,566	$309,330	(39%)	$773,128
Butler (R)	$861,761	$279,327	(32%)	$844,695

Key Votes

1993

Require parental notification of minors' abortions	N
Require unpaid family and medical leave	Y
Approve national "motor voter" registration bill	Y
Approve budget increasing taxes and reducing deficit	Y
Approve economic stimulus plan	Y

Elections

1992 General

Leslie L. Byrne (D)	114,172	(50%)
Henry N. Butler (R)	103,119	(45%)
A.T. "Art" Narro (I)	6,681	(3%)
Perry J. Mitchell (I)	4,155	(2%)

District Vote for President

1992

D 102,721 (43%)
R 103,907 (43%)
I 34,719 (14%)

Washington

STATE DATA

Governor: Mike Lowry (D)
First elected: 1992
Length of term: 4 years
Term expires: 1/97
Salary: $121,000 (Will accept only $90,000)
Term limit: 2 terms
Phone: (206) 753-6780
Born: March 8, 1939; St. John, Wash.
Education: Washington State U., B.A. 1962
Occupation: Real estate investor; rancher; college instructor; lobbyist; legislative aide
Family: Wife, Mary Carlson; one child
Religion: Baptist
Political Career: Candidate for King County executive, 1973; King County Council, 1975-78; U.S. House, 1979-89; Democratic nominee for U.S. Senate special election, 1983; Democratic nominee for U.S. Senate, 1988

Lt. Gov.: Joel Pritchard (R)
First elected: 1988
Length of term: 4 years
Term expires: 1/97
Salary: $62,700
Phone: (206) 786-7700

State election official: (206) 753-7121
Democratic headquarters: (206) 583-0664
Republican headquarters: (206) 451-1988

REDISTRICTING

Washington gained one House seat in reapportionment, increasing from eight districts to nine. Redistricting commission map became law Feb. 12, 1992.

STATE LEGISLATURE

Legislature. Meets January-March in odd years, January-April in even years.

Senate: 49 members, 4-year terms
1992 breakdown: 28D, 21R; 32 men, 17 women; 46 whites, 1 black, 2 Hispanics
Salary: $25,900
Phone: (206) 786-7550

House of Representatives: 98 members, 2-year terms
1992 breakdown: 65D, 33R; 57 men, 41 women; 92 whites, 1 black, 2 Hispanics, 3 others
Salary: $25,900
Phone: 206-786-7750

URBAN STATISTICS

City	Pop.
Seattle Mayor Norman Rice, D	516,259
Spokane Mayor Sheri S. Barnard, N-P	177,165
Tacoma Mayor Karen L. R. Vialle, N-P	176,664

U.S. CONGRESS

Senate: 1 D, 1 R
House: 8 D, 1 R

TERM LIMITS

For Congress: Yes
Senate: 2 terms
House: 3 terms
For state offices:
Senate: 2 consecutive terms
House: 3 consecutive terms

ELECTIONS

1992 Presidential Vote

Bill Clinton	43.4%
George Bush	32.0%
Ross Perot	23.7%

1988 Presidential Vote

Michael S. Dukakis	50%
George Bush	49%

1984 Presidential Vote

Ronald Reagan	56%
Walter F. Mondale	43%

POPULATION

1990 population		4,866,692
1980 population		4,132,156
Percent change		+18%
Rank among states:		18
White		89%
Black		3%
Hispanic		4%
Asian or Pacific islander		4%
Urban		76%
Rural		24%
Born in state		48%
Foreign-born		7%
Under age 18	1,261,38726%	
Ages 18-65	3,030,017	62%
65 and older	575,288	12%
Median age		33.1

MISCELLANEOUS

Capital: Olympia
Number of counties: 39
Per capita income: $19,442 (1991)
Rank among states: 13
Total area: 68,139 sq. miles
Rank among states: 20

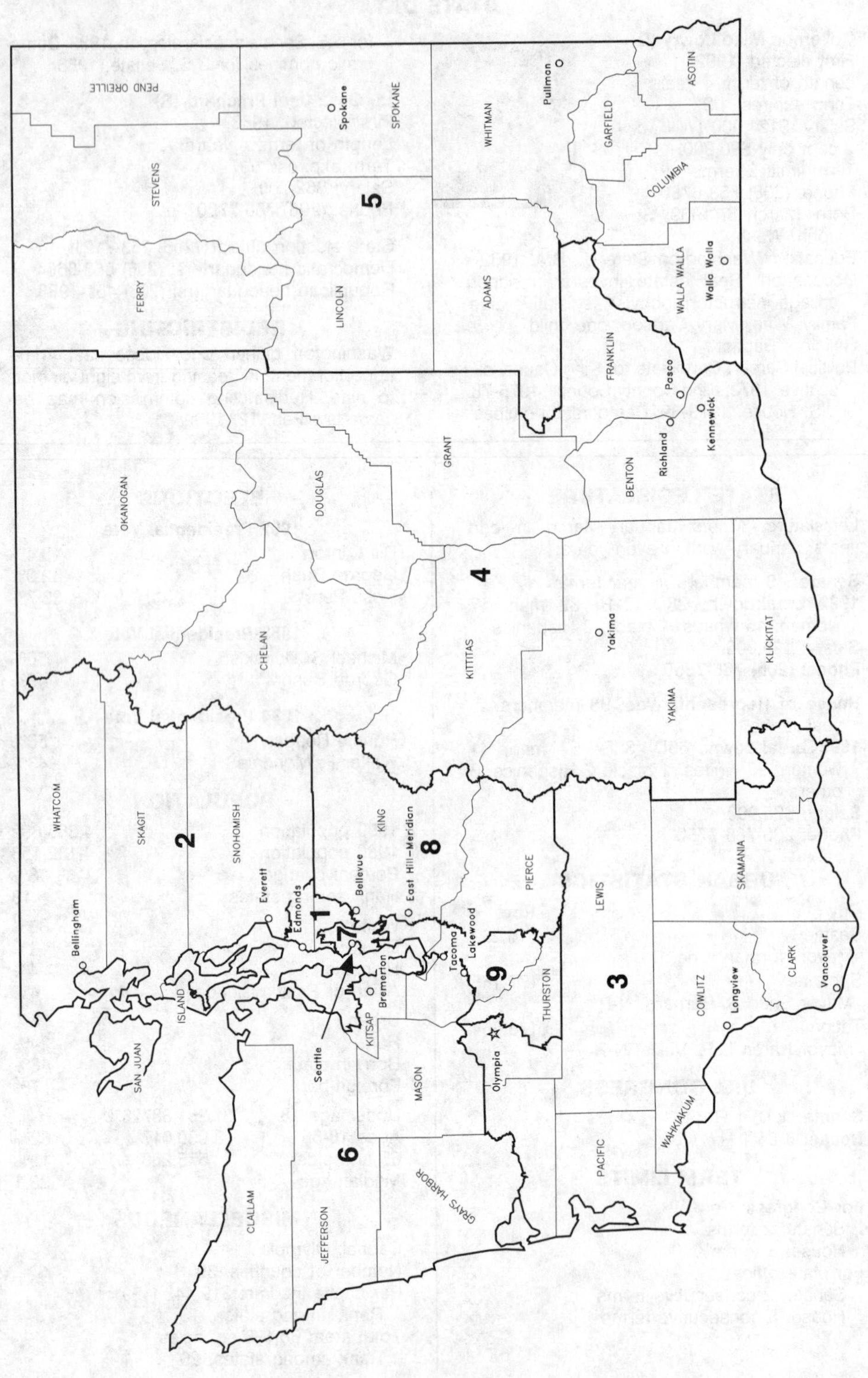
PEND OREILLE
STEVENS
FERRY
OKANOGAN
SPOKANE
Spokane
LINCOLN
WHITMAN
Pullman
GARFIELD
ASOTIN
COLUMBIA
WALLA WALLA
Walla Walla
ADAMS
FRANKLIN
Pasco
Kennewick
Richland
BENTON
GRANT
DOUGLAS
CHELAN
KITTIAS
YAKIMA
Yakima
KLICKITAT
WHATCOM
Bellingham
SKAGIT
SNOHOMISH
Everett
Edmonds
ISLAND
SAN JUAN
KING
Bellevue
East Hill-Meridian
Seattle
KITSAP
Bremerton
Tacoma
Lakewood
PIERCE
LEWIS
SKAMANIA
THURSTON
Olympia
MASON
CLALLAM
JEFFERSON
GRAYS HARBOR
PACIFIC
WAHKIAKUM
COWLITZ
Longview
CLARK
Vancouver
1
2
3
4
5
6
7
8
9

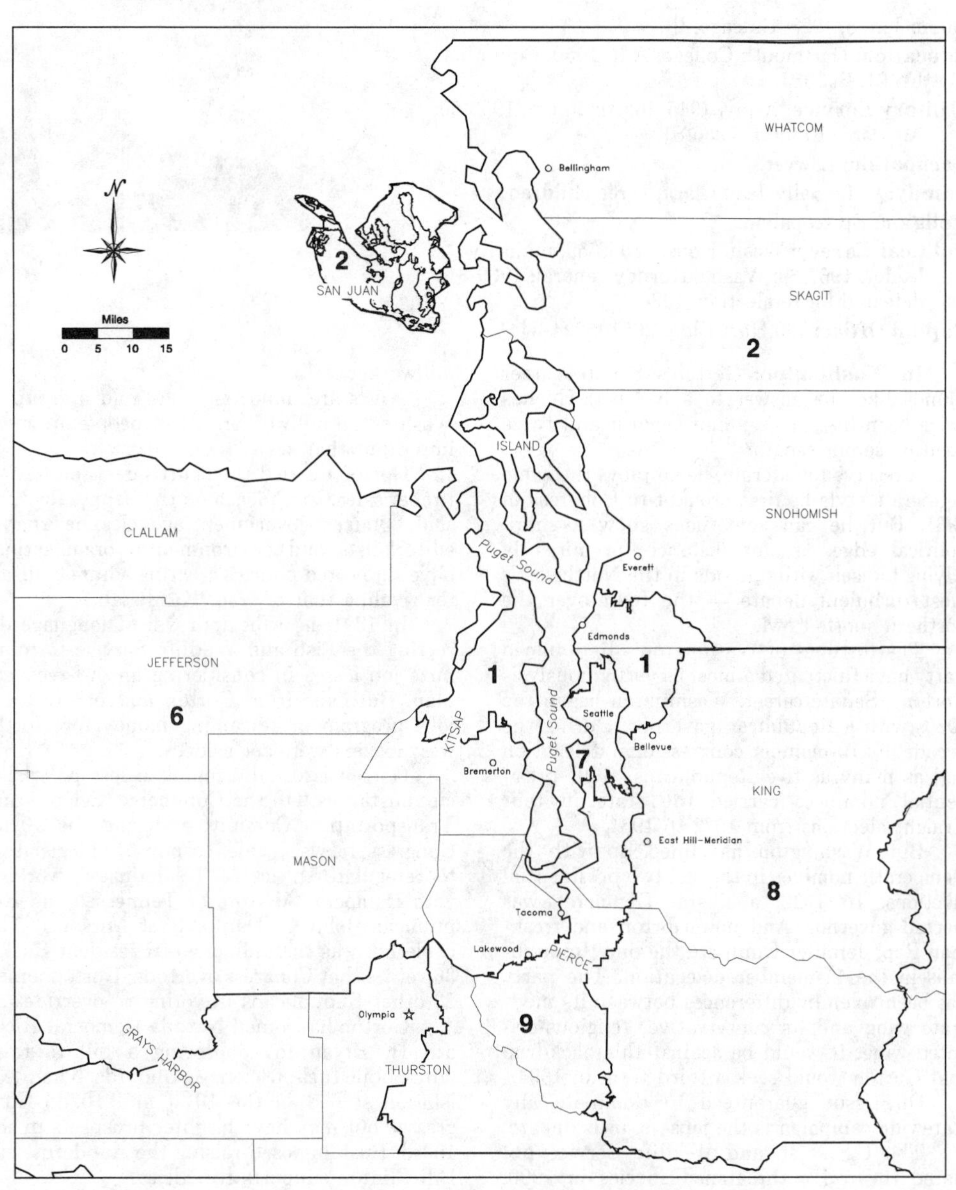
WHATCOM
Bellingham
2
SAN JUAN
Miles
0 5 10 15
SKAGIT
2
ISLAND
SNOHOMISH
CLALLAM
Puget Sound
Everett
Edmonds
JEFFERSON
1
1
6
KITSAP
Puget Sound
Seattle
Bellevue
Bremerton
7
KING
MASON
East Hill-Meridian
8
Tacoma
Lakewood
PIERCE
GRAYS HARBOR
Olympia
9
THURSTON

Slade Gorton (R)

Of Seattle — Elected 1980; 2nd Term

Did not serve 1987-89.

Born: Jan. 8, 1928, Chicago, Ill.

Education: Dartmouth College, A.B. 1950; Columbia U., LL.B. 1953.

Military Service: Army, 1945-46; Air Force, 1953-56; Air Force Reserve, 1956-81.

Occupation: Lawyer.

Family: Wife, Sally Jean Clark; three children.

Religion: Episcopalian.

Political Career: Wash. House, 1959-69, majority leader, 1967-69; Wash. attorney general, 1969-81; defeated for re-election, 1986.

Capitol Office: 730 Hart Bldg. 20510; 224-3441.

In Washington: Gorton's Senate career sounds like the answer to a bar bet: He has twice been his state's junior senator and twice been its senior senator.

A reserved moderate, he employs the same deliberate style he first brought to Congress in 1981. But he can sometimes show a sharp political edge, as, for instance, prominently allying himself with one side in the Northwest's most turbulent debate — the fight over the northern spotted owl.

The fortunes of Washington's Republican Party have fluctuated almost as vertiginously as Gorton's Senate career. Washington began the 1980s with a Republican governor. During the decade, its 10-member congressional delegation had as many as five Republicans. GOP presidential nominees carried the state in four straight elections from 1972 to 1984.

But Washington has lined up with the Democratic nominee in the last two presidential elections. In 1992, a liberal Democrat was elected governor. And now Gorton and freshman Rep. Jennifer Dunn are the only Republicans in the 11-member delegation. The party has been riven by differences between its moderate wing and its conservative, religious-oriented wing. It would be against this backdrop that Gorton would seek a third term in 1994.

One issue guaranteed to dominate any statewide campaign is the jobs-vs.-owls debate.

The U.S. Fish and Wildlife Service declared the owl a threatened species in 1990, requiring a plan to curtail logging in the ancient old-growth forests where the owl lives. In 1991, a federal judge ordered a stop to most timber sales in old-growth forests until the U.S. Forest Service produces an environmental statement and a plan to protect the owl.

Gorton staked out a position adamantly against curbs on logging in old-growth forests. In visits to timber-dependent communities, Gorton proclaimed solidarity with loggers and millworkers.

"Owls are important," he told a group of Washington millworkers. "But people are more important than owls."

Gorton decried the court's decision to halt timber sales. In a speech on the Senate floor, he said, "Judges, government agencies, newspaper editorialists and environmental organizations have supported policies creating a human disaster rivaling that of Iraqi Kurdistan."

In 1991, he won approval of language directing the Fish and Wildlife Service to minimize job losses in considering an owl-recovery plan. But calls from Gorton and others for a jobs program or retraining money for Northwest loggers were set aside.

Gorton is usually found in less polarizing circumstances. On the Commerce, Science and Transportation Committee during the 102nd Congress, he was a chief cosponsor of legislation to reregulate the cable TV industry, working with Democrat Al Gore of Tennessee and Republican John C. Danforth of Missouri. The cable bill was the only one of President Bush's 36 vetoes that Congress overrode; Gorton joined 23 other Republicans in voting to override.

Gorton has joined Nevada Democrat Richard H. Bryan in sponsoring a bill to raise automobile fuel-efficiency standards. Their legislation stalled in the 101st and 102nd Congresses but may have brighter prospects in the 103rd. Bush opposed raising the standards, but Bill Clinton supports the idea.

During consideration of the 1991 highway bill, the Senate approved Gorton's amendment requiring that all new cars and light trucks be equipped with air bags. The final bill required driver and passenger air bags on cars manufactured after September 1996 and on trucks and buses made after 1998.

Gorton found himself at odds with Bush over U.S.-China policy. During Senate consideration of a legal-immigration bill in 1989, Gorton added an amendment to allow Chinese students to stay in the United States for up to four years and to qualify for legal residency without returning to China, where they faced possible government reprisals. Later that year, Bush vetoed a bill to allow all Chinese nationals in the country on student visas to remain and work as long as the U.S. government was deferring deportments. Gorton was one of eight Republicans who voted to override the veto.

In the 102nd Congress, he sought to attach human rights conditions to the annual renewal of China's most-favored-nation trading status. Although he faced heavy pressure from the White House to back an unconditional renewal, he introduced a measure setting conditions on renewing the MFN status for 1992; his version was slightly weaker than a bill by Senate Majority Leader George J. Mitchell of Maine. Gorton voted to override Bush's veto of conditional MFN status in March 1992. However, when the Senate tried in October to override Bush's veto of an MFN bill for 1993, Gorton voted to sustain the veto, contending that Democrats were trying to embarrass Bush a month before Election Day.

As a member of the Ethics Committee in the 102nd Congress, Gorton asked to remove himself from consideration of charges of sexual misconduct lodged against his Washington colleague, Democrat Brock Adams, because he believed the charges. The committee declined to investigate the charges against Adams, who had given up his 1992 re-election bid.

Gorton left Ethics in the 103rd Congress, taking a seat on the Budget Committee. At the start of the 103rd, Gorton challenged Alan K. Simpson for minority whip. He lost 25-14.

During his early years in the Senate, Gorton was generally supportive of President Ronald Reagan's policies, backing his first-term attempts at cutting federal programs and taxes and increasing defense spending. But Gorton maintained a consumerist orientation from his days as state attorney general, and he was a staunch supporter of federal programs for community development and the homeless. In early 1985, Gorton was a leader among Republicans on the Budget Committee who, under the guidance of then-Majority Leader Bob Dole of Kansas, drafted a plan for a budget freeze that included a controversial provision eliminating cost of living allowances (COLAs) for Social Security recipients.

A high-profile wrangle in the 99th Congress over federal judgeships ended up having a high political cost back home for Gorton. Reagan had tapped Daniel A. Manion, a conservative Indiana lawyer, to be a federal judge. At the same time, the White House held up the judicial nomination of Seattle lawyer and Gorton ally William L. Dwyer, whose liberal views alienated key GOP conservatives.

Gorton let it be known he might line up with Senate Democrats opposing Manion; the Democrats, in fact, thought they had Gorton's crucial vote in the bag and forced a floor vote in June 1986. But in the midst of the roll call, a White House official called Gorton to tell him that Reagan would proceed with the Dwyer nomination. Gorton then voted for Manion, who was narrowly confirmed.

Ironically, it was Dwyer who issued the 1991 order halting timber harvests in old-growth forests. On the Senate floor, Gorton denounced Dwyer's "anti-human" decision.

At Home: The 1988 victory that returned Gorton to the Senate capped a most unusual political journey. First elected in 1980, he was defeated for re-election in 1986, but won two years later. Now he is again Washington's senior senator, a status he held from 1983 to 1987.

The 1988 retirement of GOP Sen. Daniel J. Evans gave Gorton an opening to resurrect his career. Gorton made the most of it, edging Democratic Rep. Mike Lowry (now governor) to become the 11th senator to be popularly elected, defeated, then returned to the Senate.

Born to a wealthy Chicago family (whose ancestors included the founders of the Gorton's of Gloucester fish-processing company), Gorton says the state's progressive politics led him to settle there. As attorney general, he crafted a pro-consumer record that placed him in the moderate mold of the state's most popular Republicans.

This profile aided Gorton in his 1980 bid against Democratic Sen. Warren G. Magnuson, whose legendary efforts to obtain public works projects had earned him six Senate terms. Gorton ousted Magnuson with 54 percent of the vote.

Many of Gorton's constituents, however, were never personally comfortable with him. Averse to the hail-fellow world of personal politics, the brusque, cerebral Gorton was known to cut off political associates and inquisitive constituents in mid-sentence. It was thus easy for state Democrats to convince voters in 1986 that Gorton was "aloof" and "arrogant."

Then came the Manion affair. Gorton defended his actions by saying that he dealt with the White House to protect a home-state interest. But Democrats angrily portrayed him as "Slippery Slade," a craven vote-trader.

In his re-election bid, Gorton was hurt by this image, by his support for freezing Social Security COLAs and by the uncertain fate of the Hanford nuclear reservation.

Adams argued that Gorton had not done enough to ensure that Hanford did not get a permanent high-level nuclear waste dump. He also blasted Gorton for supporting continued plutonium production at Hanford's aging "N Reactor" as well as a plan to produce tritium there.

An overconfident Gorton was slow to respond. Then, in the final week of the campaign, what was expected to be a triumphant moment turned sour for him. Reagan flew to Spokane to appear at a Gorton rally. But when pressed on the Hanford issue by reporters, Reagan showed a lack of familiarity, creating an impression that Gorton had little access to the president.

Adams won with 51 percent, and Gorton returned to legal practice in Seattle. In 1987, he worked as a Department of Energy consultant on options for the Hanford facility.

But late that year, Evans announced that he would retire. Unable to persuade GOP Reps. Sid Morrison or Rod Chandler to run, the party leadership turned to Gorton. Hard-line conservatives were uneasy with the choice but could produce only two weak primary challengers, and Gorton breezed into the general election.

He then faced Lowry, who held off House colleague Don Bonker in a more grueling primary. Lowry had developed a liberal activist following with his outspoken support of federal social programs and his opposition to Reagan's defense buildup. But with his scraggly beard, rumpled clothes and penchant for arm-waving harangues, Lowry was vulnerable to GOP charges that he was an extremist. This image was part of the reason he lost to Evans in the 1983 Senate special election to fill the seat of Democrat Henry M. Jackson, who died in 1983.

The 1988 contest thus matched the losers of the last two Washington Senate races and both set out to soften the negatives that had defeated them. Gorton spent more than $1 million on ads in which he apologized for being arrogant. Lowry shaved, adopted a neat appearance and restrained his rhetoric and temper.

Still, the home-stretch themes were negative. Gorton, pointing to the state's "strong defense" tradition, portrayed Lowry as far out of the mainstream, attacking his House votes against the 1986 and 1988 omnibus drug bills. In turn, Lowry tried to revive the Social Security and Hanford issues Adams had used.

This already unusual campaign was overshadowed by two strange events. In late September, the state media turned its attentions to the sexual misconduct allegations against Adams. Then, in early October, Lowry collapsed in Chicago while en route to Seattle, and was hospitalized briefly for a bleeding ulcer.

Gorton got a late break when Nevada, not Hanford, was designated as the site for the nuclear waste dump and the N Reactor was closed for safety reasons. But Lowry still lashed out at Gorton in a TV ad for supporting a tritium "bomb factory" and for receiving $60,000 in consulting fees from the Department of Energy. Gorton quickly responded with a big gun: Evans. In a last-minute ad, Evans described Lowry's charges as "lies, distortion and garbage."

Gorton won with 51 percent.

Committees

Appropriations (10th of 13 Republicans)
Military Construction (ranking); Agriculture, Rural Development & Related Agencies; Energy & Water Development; Interior; Labor, Health & Human Services & Education

Budget (8th of 9 Republicans)

Commerce, Science & Transportation (7th of 9 Republicans)
Consumer (ranking); Aviation; Communications; National Ocean Policy Study

Indian Affairs (4th of 8 Republicans)

Select Intelligence (4th of 8 Republicans)

Elections

1988 General		
Slade Gorton (R)	944,359	(51%)
Mike Lowry (D)	904,183	(49%)
1988 Primary †		
Slade Gorton (R)	335,846	(36%)
Mike Lowry (D)	297,399	(32%)
Don Bonker (D)	241,170	(26%)
Doug Smith (R)	31,512	(3%)
William Goodloe (R)	26,224	(3%)

† In Washington's "jungle primary," candidates of all parties are listed on one ballot.

Previous Winning Percentage: **1980** (54%)

Campaign Finance

1988	Receipts	Receipts from PACs		Expend-itures
Gorton (R)	$2,736,101	$939,406	(34%)	$2,851,591
Lowry (D)	$2,202,177	$618,074	(28%)	$2,191,187

Key Votes

1993	
Require unpaid family and medical leave	N
Approve national "motor voter" registration bill	N
Approve budget increasing taxes and reducing deficit	N
Support president's right to lift military gay ban	N
1992	
Approve school-choice pilot program	+
Allow shifting funds from defense to domestic programs	N
Oppose deeper cuts in spending for SDI	Y
1991	
Approve waiting period for handgun purchases	Y
Raise senators' pay and ban honoraria	Y
Authorize use of force in Persian Gulf	Y
Confirm Clarence Thomas to Supreme Court	Y

Voting Studies

	Presidential Support		Party Unity		Conservative Coalition	
Year	S	O	S	O	S	O
1992	68	28	80	18	68	26
1991	86	14	82	18	80	20
1990	76	24	81	19	86	14
1989	89	11	80	20	87	13
1986	73	25	74	25	72	26
1985	77	19	79	17	70	27
1984	83	17	83	16	81	19
1983	85	15	76	23	70	30
1982	76	24	78	22	76	24
1981	87	13	86	13	77	21

Interest Group Ratings

Year	ADA	AFL-CIO	CCUS	ACU
1992	25	36	90	72
1991	30	17	80	67
1990	17	0	92	78
1989	15	20	88	75
1986	25	69	65	19
1985	35	50	41	47
1984	35	18	78	83
1983	35	24	58	65
1982	45	35	62	43
1981	10	6	94	67

Patty Murray (D)

Of Seattle — Elected 1992; 1st Term

Born: Oct. 11, 1950, Seattle, Wash.
Education: Washington State U., B.A. 1972.
Occupation: Educator.
Family: Husband, Rob Murray; two children.
Religion: Roman Catholic.
Political Career: Shoreline School Board, 1983-89; Wash. Senate, 1989-93.
Capitol Office: 302 Hart Bldg. 20510; 224-2621.

The Path to Washington: Murray came to the Senate as one of those political "outsiders" who had the inside track in the 1992 election. The self-styled "mom in tennis shoes," Murray seemed to embody just about every national campaign trend: She was a woman who sought to enter the predominantly male Senate, an outsider who vowed to oust the incumbent and a relative newcomer seeking a voice among the pros.

One of her main attractions, she said, was that voters believed a working mother with two children would better understand and represent their interests in Washington than those men in blue suits and red ties.

Two early breaks gave Murray a decisive boost in her Senate race. First, the disgraced incumbent, Democrat Brock Adams, dropped out in March, leaving Murray as the only Democrat in the race at the time. Then popular retiring Democratic Gov. Booth Gardner opted against the contest.

Still, to win the primary and the general election, she had to get past two better-known, popular moderates with years of congressional experience, Democratic former Rep. Don Bonker and GOP Rep. Rod Chandler. Their political qualifications, however, provided Murray with the exact contrast she sought: She was able to portray both as Washington insiders (with the accompanying neckware to boot).

In truth, Murray is far more the politician than she let on in her campaign, leading The Seattle Times to say at one point that she was "neatly packaged as unpackaged."

Murray had her first taste of politics in 1979 when she petitioned the state Legislature not to cut funding for a co-op preschool program in which she was involved. One legislator gave Murray the mom-in-tennis-shoes label — implying she could have little influence — that she used to such advantage in 1992. She went on to organize 12,000 families statewide and preserve the preschool program.

That just whetted Murray's appetite. She went on to serve six years on the Shoreline School Board just outside Seattle before winning election to the state Senate in 1988. She became the Democratic whip two years later.

During her first year in the state Senate, she went against her party leadership and successfully pushed for expansion of a family leave bill to cover parents of terminally ill children. She did so by threatening to launch a statewide initiative on the issue. In subsequent years, Murray continued to devote her attention to issues related to families, children and education. In 1992, she helped secure passage of legislation to protect individuals from accidental exposure to pesticides near their homes.

Still in her first state Senate term, Murray decided in late 1991 to challenge Adams for the U.S. Senate. The incumbent had been trying to overcome an image of electoral vulnerability that arose in 1988, when news broke that in 1987 a woman had accused him of having drugged and sexually molested her. Adams denied the allegations, but the questions continued to dog him.

Murray was the first Democrat in the race, but she did not focus on Adams' ethical woes. Rather, she said she entered because of her outrage over the Senate's handling of the Clarence Thomas Supreme Court confirmation hearings. "It's not just Brock," she told the Times. "It's the whole U.S. Senate."

On March 1, 1992, the Times presented detailed and similar accounts by eight unidentified women who said Adams had made unwanted and inappropriate sexual advances toward them. Some accused him of drugging them; one woman said that in the early 1970s, Adams drugged and raped her. That day, Adams announced that he was ending his re-election campaign.

As soon as Gardner declared that he would not run, former Rep. Bonker entered the race. Bonker, who lost in the 1988 Democratic primary for the Senate, touted his Washington experience, saying that he, unlike Murray, would not need to trained to be a senator if elected. Murray portrayed him as a Washington insider who had not left the nation's capital even after leaving Congress. (Bonker worked as a consultant in Washington.) They also clashed over timber and environmental issues.

On primary day, Murray was the big winner. Not only did she surpass Bonker by more than 100,000 votes, but she also outpolled Chandler, who was on the same ballot in Washington's all-candidate "jungle primary." She was the 11th woman nominated for the Senate in 1992, setting a new record and capturing national headlines and network TV time.

In the House, Chandler was known as a party moderate with a former PR man's gift for a quote. Although he faced opposition for the GOP Senate nomination, he was endorsed before the primary by the National Republican Senatorial Committee. He cruised past his two rivals — one on his left and one on his right — to win the nomination.

In the weeks following the primary, Murray maintained a daunting lead. Her suburban populism, level gaze and tone of empathy resonated far beyond expectations.

Chandler counterattacked, portraying Murray as dangerously naive. His first TV ad of October suggested that her views on defense and the environment would cost the state 130,000 jobs. The figures were dubious and debatable, but Murray's lead in polls shrank from 24 percentage points to 11.

The heavy-handed approach proved to have its limits. When Murray answered a doctor's question at a health-care forum with a recitation of her parents' illnesses, Chandler said: "I'm about to burst into tears, but I don't think she answered the question." (Many in the audience of 200 gasped.) The following day, Chandler concluded an hourlong debate between the two by reciting the chorus from Roger Miller's song "Dang Me." The last line — "Woman would you weep for me?" — prompted Murray to say: "That's just the attitude that got me into this race, Rod."

For much of October, Chandler's poll numbers would not budge. Murray, whose chances had been summarily and repeatedly dismissed, sailed into Election Day without ever relinquishing her lead, winning 54 percent to 46 percent.

With the election behind her, Murray bristled at suggestions that she ever ran as a political outsider. She raised the objection, despite the clear anti-establishment tenor of her campaign against Chandler. "He is a very polished politician. I am who I am," Murray said of her opponent at one point.

Instead, Murray said her message was meant to show that she would be a voice for those she did not believe were represented in the 102nd Congress — average two-worker families with children, just trying to get by.

For the most part, Murray's positions meshed with the congressional Democratic leadership's agenda: She is a proponent of family leave legislation, health-care reform, tax relief for the middle class, abortion rights and reinvestment in infrastructure.

In the wake of sexual harassment allegations against Oregon GOP Sen. Bob Packwood, Murray called for the establishment of a clear sexual harassment policy for the U.S. Senate, similar to one she authored while in the state Senate.

Murray landed a coveted seat on the Appropriations Committee, as did another female newcomer, California Democrat Dianne Feinstein. Although Feinstein, having won a special election, was sworn in before Murray, Appropriations Chairman Robert C. Byrd requested and got seniority for Murray over Feinstein because Feinstein supports the line-item veto, which Byrd adamantly opposes.

Murray also serves on the Banking Committee, where she and yet another Democratic woman freshman, Barbara Boxer of California, rebelled against efforts by committee Chairman Donald W. Riegle Jr. of Michigan to push through a no-strings-attached 1993 funding bill for the highly unpopular savings and loan bailout agency, the Resolution Trust Corporation. They forced Riegle to accept amendments that required the Treasury Department to prove it had instituted administrative reforms at RTC.

Committees

Appropriations (15th of 16 Democrats)
District of Columbia; Interior; Labor, Health & Human Services & Education; Legislative Branch

Banking, Housing & Urban Affairs (11th of 11 Democrats)
International Finance & Monetary Policy; Securities

Budget (12th of 12 Democrats)

Campaign Finance

	Receipts	Receipts from PACs	Expend-itures
1992			
Murray (D)	$1,496,204	$439,766 (29%)	$1,342,038
Chandler (R)	$2,592,759	$1,143,695 (44%)	$2,504,777

Key Votes

1993

Require unpaid family and medical leave	Y
Approve national "motor voter" registration bill	Y
Approve budget increasing taxes and reducing deficit	Y
Support president's right to lift military gay ban	Y

Elections

1992 General		
Patty Murray (D)	1,197,973	(54%)
Rod Chandler (R)	1,020,829	(46%)
1992 Primary †		
Patty Murray (D)	318,455	(28%)
Rod Chandler (R)	228,083	(20%)
Don Bonker (D)	208,321	(19%)
Leo K. Thorsness (R)	185,498	(16%)
Tim Hill (R)	128,232	(11%)
Gene David Hart (D)	15,894	(1%)
Marshall (D)	11,659	(1%)

† In Washington's "jungle primary," candidates of all parties are listed on one ballot.

1 Maria Cantwell (D)

Of Mountlake Terrace — Elected 1992; 1st Term

Born: Oct. 13, 1958, Indianapolis, Ind.
Education: Miami U. (Oxford, Ohio), B.A. 1981.
Occupation: Public relations consultant.
Family: Single.
Religion: Roman Catholic.
Political Career: Wash. House, 1987-93.
Capitol Office: 1520 Longworth Bldg. 20515; 225-6311.

The Path to Washington: Of all the districts that exchanged a Republican member for a Democratic one in 1992, the case of Washington's 1st may have been the most strikingly ironic. Not only has the 1st been in the GOP column for 40 years, but the 1992 redistricting plan also increased its Republican tilt.

Nonetheless, Cantwell led her race wire to wire and won with a 13-point margin. Portraying herself as a pro-business, pro-abortion rights moderate, Cantwell dominated the September primary, in which candidates of all parties appear on one ballot, and swept past state Sen. Gary Nelson in November.

Cantwell's message played well with the nonpartisan moderates in her district. But she also got a boost by starting her campaign early, when most Democrats still thought incumbent GOP Rep. John Miller would run again. The fast start helped her build a strong coalition of women's groups, business leaders, environmentalists and labor organizations.

Cantwell's fast break was typical of the career she has rapidly built since arriving in the suburbs north of Seattle as a political organizer for a Democratic presidential candidate in the early 1980s. A native of Indiana, Cantwell elected to stay in the Northwest, start her own public relations firm and run for office. She was first elected to the state House in 1986 at the age of 28.

While articulate and energetic, Cantwell is also renowned for her calm. She quickly rose in the state Legislature to become chairman of the Committee on Trade and Economic Development. She also served on the transportation and health-care panels, but she is best known for managing passage of state growth-management laws in the state Legislature.

In an interview, Cantwell said that many of her constituents had been hostile to booming growth in the 1980s but that recession had raised awareness of the need for balance between jobs and quality-of-life issues.

By the same token, she said, there needed to be a balance between stimulating the national economy and reducing the budget deficit and between health-care access and costs.

And if striking such delicate balances makes public life a slippery slope, she says, so be it. "Real leaders make decisions and stick to them, even if they don't get re-elected," she says.

The 1st District is sometimes referred to as "Technology Corridor" because its four major business parks are home to Microsoft and a host of other computer software, biotechnology and high-tech companies. Cantwell identified herself with such growth industries, even while espousing ideas that business generally opposes — such as family leave and plant-closing notification.

While she supported the Democratic ticket ardently in the fall, she says her views on targeting growth sectors for economic assistance are "closer to [Democratic presidential candidate Paul E.] Tsongas or even [independent candidate Ross] Perot."

The 1st is also home to many long-distance commuters who warmed to Cantwell's calls for better mass transit and her promise to serve on the Public Works and Transportation Committee. Speaker Thomas S. Foley, a fellow Washingtonian, took an interest in Cantwell's candidacy and helped her make good on the Public Works promise when she arrived in the capital. She also will be on the Merchant Marine and Fisheries and Foreign Affairs committees.

She was also one of only three first-year representatives to receive a coveted slot on the Democratic Steering and Policy Committee that makes Democratic committee assignments.

Cantwell speaks of organizing the growing ranks of suburban-based legislators in Congress. She saw the same kind of group increase its power in the Washington Legislature.

"We became a force," she said. "Our concerns are different from urban and rural legislators' concerns."

Cantwell will need to show results soon to hold her electoral ground. The new map did not have the presumed effect, in part because Nelson never seemed to regain his footing after a divisive three-way battle for the GOP nomination. His sharply conservative image also may have hurt him in a suburban district long represented by Republican moderates.

Washington 1

Puget Sound (west and east) — North Seattle suburbs; Kitsap Peninsula

The 1st traditionally has connected residential neighborhoods in the northern part of Seattle with the first tier of suburbs beyond the city limits. This is a prosperous and, on balance, a politically moderate area. The GOP held the seat through the 1980s, but never won it decisively, partly because most of the voters here are well to the left of national Republican doctrine on social issues.

Analysts of Washington's 1992 redistricting plan said it boosted Republican strength in the 1st, but when GOP Rep. John Miller decided to retire, Democrat Cantwell won the open-seat contest to succeed him. Meanwhile, in presidential voting, Bill Clinton carried the 1st with 41 percent of the vote; independent Ross Perot, who ran well throughout the suburbs and exurbs of Seattle, got 27 percent in the 1st.

The huge majority of people in the district live north of Seattle in western Snohomish and King counties, in communities such as Mill Creek and Bothell that are along or just inland from Puget Sound. At its southern end, the 1st slices a bit off the top of Seattle, takes in some "Gold Coast" suburbs such as Medina on the eastern shore of Lake Washington and includes part of Bellevue, which has blossomed into a full-fledged satellite city of Seattle.

Much of the land in the 1st — but only about 15 percent of its population — is west across Puget Sound, in Kitsap County. Tony Bainbridge Island is here, as are several military facilities, including a base that services the Navy's Trident submarines. Home to many with defense-related jobs, Kitsap County is also a popular retirement location for military personnel. The eastern and western lobes of the district are connected by ferries that cross the sound.

In 1992, the King County portions of the 1st were the best turf for Democrats. Cantwell won 56 percent in King, and Clinton ran ahead of his districtwide average here. Snohomish was strong Perot country: His 32 percent tally was enough to drop George Bush down into third place in the county. The GOP fared somewhat better in Kitsap, but both Clinton and Cantwell won there, too.

The 18 percent population boom that Washington state enjoyed during the 1980s was greatly felt in the communities of the 1st, as newcomers drawn by high-technology jobs and scenic suburban surroundings settled here. Biotechnology and electronics firms are major employers, and there are a swarm of small computer-related companies around the headquarters of software giant Microsoft.

So robust was the growth in the 1980s that overcrowding and traffic became hot political issues. But the 1990s have brought a new set of concerns, ones related not to growth but to economic retrenchment.

As is the case everywhere in greater Seattle, much business and commerce in the 1st is related to Boeing, the mammoth aircraft maker that has plants in Everett to the north and an array of facilities south of the district. Hit by downturns in both the military and civilian sectors of aviation, Boeing in 1993 announced major job cutbacks.

1990 Population: 540,745. White 495,515 (92%), Black 7,103 (1%), Other 38,127 (7%). Hispanic origin 12,648 (2%). 18 and over 401,047 (74%), 62 and over 62,756 (12%). Median age: 33.

Committees

Foreign Affairs (19th of 27 Democrats)
Economic Policy, Trade & the Environment

Merchant Marine & Fisheries (27th of 29 Democrats)
Fisheries Management

Public Works & Transportation (28th of 39 Democrats)
Aviation; Surface Transportation

Campaign Finance

	Receipts	Receipts from PACs		Expend-itures
1992				
Cantwell (D)	$625,170	$287,103	(46%)	$621,961
Nelson (R)	$138,864	$56,727	(41%)	$114,546

Key Votes

1993

Require parental notification of minors' abortions	N
Require unpaid family and medical leave	Y
Approve national "motor voter" registration bill	Y
Approve budget increasing taxes and reducing deficit	Y
Approve economic stimulus plan	Y

Elections

1992 General		
Maria Cantwell (D)	148,844	(55%)
Gary Nelson (R)	113,897	(42%)
Patrick L. Ruckert (I)	4,322	(2%)
Anne Fleming (NL)	4,211	(2%)
1992 Primary †		
Maria Cantwell (D)	67,727	(52%)
Gary Nelson (R)	32,384	(25%)
Mark Gardner (R)	17,698	(14%)
John K. Dahl (R)	6,885	(5%)
Anne Fleming (NL)	2,366	(2%)
Patrick L. Ruckert (I)	1,967	(2%)

† In Washington's "jungle primary," candidates of all parties are listed on one ballot.

District Vote for President

	1992	
D	112,353	(41%)
R	88,456	(32%)
I	73,259	(27%)

2 Al Swift (D)

Of Bellingham — Elected 1978; 8th Term

Born: Sept. 12, 1935, Tacoma, Wash.
Education: Whitman College, 1953-55; Central Washington U., B.A. 1957.
Occupation: Broadcaster; congressional aide.
Family: Wife, Paula Jean Jackson; two children.
Religion: Unitarian.
Political Career: No previous office.
Capitol Office: 1502 Longworth Bldg. 20515; 225-2605.

In Washington: The 103rd is Swift's last Congress; he announced in October 1991 that his 1992 campaign would be the end of his political road.

This gives him one more shot at getting a raft of initiatives enacted after a frustrating 102nd Congress, during which Republicans blocked many of them — such as the "motor voter" bill and the solid waste reauthorization law.

In the 103rd, Swift got off to a fast start: motor-voter passed both houses early in the Congress and a bill he sponsored combating fraudulent telemarketing practices moved quickly through the House.

But the focus of Swift's Energy and Commerce Committee work, the solid waste law, the Resource Conservation and Recovery Act (RCRA), was put on a back burner by the Clinton administration.

On Capitol Hill, Swift's resonant voice is an instant reminder of his days delivering the 11 o'clock news in Bellingham, but it is hard to imagine anyone doing more than Swift to dispel the stereotype of the local TV anchorman as a prisoner of style over substance.

A patient and diligent legislator who often toils outside the spotlight, Swift has thrown himself into some of the more challenging and thankless issues before Congress, such as campaign finance reform and clean air legislation.

At the start of the 102nd Congress, Swift became one of the few House members to wield two gavels. He continued as chair of the House Administration Subcommittee on Elections and he gained the helm of the Transportation and Hazardous Materials Subcommittee on Energy and Commerce. The assignment positioned him to address issues important to his refinery-rich district, such as RCRA and the re-establishment of Amtrak service between Seattle and Vancouver, British Columbia.

Swift came to his new post well-trained in dealing with hazardous material; in the 101st Congress, he was the key Democratic player in the House on another issue fraught with danger and avoided by colleagues: campaign finance reform. As chairman of a bipartisan House task force, Swift authored a bill passed by the House that attempted to restructure political action committees and create voluntary spending limits with incentives such as discounted broadcast and postage rates.

The bill died in conference, and in the 102nd Congress Swift relinquished the lead role on the issue to a new committee task force headed by Democratic Rep. Sam Gejdenson of Connecticut.

Swift has also been at the center of efforts to prevent the TV networks from projecting presidential election outcomes while polling places are still open. He won pledges from the three major networks in 1985 that they would not forecast results for any state while its polls were open. Since then, he has lobbied persistently for a bill that would close all polls in the continental United States simultaneously at 9 p.m. EST in presidential election years.

Although Swift did not have enough seniority to chair an Energy and Commerce subcommittee until 1991, he earned respect for his legislative activity on the panel. That respect, as well as the personal relationships he has forged, helped him become de facto chairman of a caucus of nine moderate-to-conservative committee Democrats, who organized in the 100th Congress to try to break a long deadlock between environmentalists and an industry-oriented faction who disagreed on reauthorizing the Clean Air Act. Their work on the intractable issue helped create momentum for passage of clean-air legislation in the 101st Congress.

One of Swift's favorite legislative subjects is broadcast deregulation, which emerged as an issue in 1984 after the Federal Communications Commission (FCC) repealed federal guidelines for TV commercials and public-affairs programming. The battle lines on broadcast deregulation divide mainly between "public interest" forces and those more sympathetic to the broadcast industry. The public-interest side wants strict requirements for news and public-affairs programs, plus a competitive broadcast license-renewal process — resisted by the in-

Washington 2

Puget Sound — Everett; Bellingham

Washington's 2nd is a swing district that usually is highly competitive, but in 1992 it went big for the Democratic ticket — Rep. Swift, Senate winner Patty Murray and presidential contender Bill Clinton — emblematic of the statewide sweep by Democrats.

The 2nd's geographic and political focal point is Everett, a rapidly growing blue-collar city whose history is linked to the timber and shipping industries. Labor conflicts plagued those industries between the two world wars, and unions became the basis of the local Democratic strength.

But the tendency to vote Democratic is tempered by the district's reliance on defense-related industry, which prospered in the 1980s.

Everett is the site of a new Navy homeport, which is expected to add about 7,000 military and civilian jobs to the area. But the not-yet-completed facility was added in May 1993 to a list of facilities that face possible closure as the Pentagon seeks to cut costs. In another blow, Boeing announced in January 1993 that it would lay off thousands of workers in the next few years because of defense industry cuts and decreased demand for commercial aircraft.

Everett may be in better shape than many communities that depend on the defense industry because its diversified economic base is rounded out with a number of high-tech companies, including Alliant Tech, a marine systems manufacturer, and Advanced Technologies Lab, a medical equipment manufacturer.

Everett and surrounding Snohomish County cast nearly one-half of the district's vote. Throughout the 1980s, the county tended to lean Republican in presidential contests and Democratic in statewide contests.

But in the 1992 three-way presidential contest, Snohomish County gave 40 percent of its vote to Clinton. The county also supported Murray and Democratic gubernatorial nominee Mike Lowry.

The second-largest group of votes in the 2nd comes from Whatcom County, a Democratic-leaning portion of the district's northern edge along the Canadian border. Bellingham, Swift's home base, is a port town and home to Western Washington University (10,000 students), one of the largest employers in the area. Still, many of Whatcom's residents are dependent on trade along the Canadian border and on the dairy, shipping, canning and timber industries.

Between Snohomish and Whatcom is Skagit County, a more rural and usually Republican-leaning area, though it too backed Clinton for president in 1992. Skagit is best known for its tulips; its annual Tulip Festival attracts thousands of visitors.

Island County lies between Juan de Fuca Strait and Puget Sound. Its proximity to Seattle has lured tourists and an influx of retirees, who tend to vote Republican as do the civilian and military employees of Whidbey Naval Air Station, home to A-6 bombers and Island County's largest employer.

1990 Population: 540,739. White 506,507 (94%), Black 4,822 (1%), Other 29,410 (5%). Hispanic origin 16,214 (3%). 18 and over 396,004 (73%), 62 and over 79,071 (15%). Median age: 33.

dustry. Swift has favored a middle-ground approach that would require the FCC to set broad categories of public-interest standards but drop competitive license renewals.

In the 101st Congress, Swift helped gain a permanent ban on the export of raw logs from federal lands and a restriction on the export of logs from state lands in the Northwest.

At Home: Swift surprised more than a few of his Democratic colleagues by announcing that 1992 would be his last campaign. He said he wanted to be able to campaign against term limits (defeated in 1991 but passed in 1992) without seeming self-interested. Others saw the decision against the backdrop of his close 1990 race and redistricting. Population growth in the 2nd ran ahead of the state as a whole, meaning the Redistricting Commission had to constrict its borders. The Olympic Peninsula was lost to the 6th, along with its largely Democratic constituencies. But Swift's real base on the eastern shore of Puget Sound remained intact.

Some thought Swift's announcement was designed to discourage serious opposition in 1992, a year that was shaping up as shaky for incumbents.

If so, it worked: Swift pushed his share of the vote to 52 percent against a longtime warrior of the right, Republican state Sen. Jack Metcalf, whose arch-conservative image did not play in this moderate district.

While Swift's 1992 election certainly was not his best, it looked more like the easy races he had had until his 1990 re-election campaign, where he took just over 50 percent of the vote. His GOP opponent, Doug Smith, took 41 percent of the vote and an active Libertarian got roughly 8 percent.

Starting out as a disc jockey after graduating from college, Swift spent more than a decade learning the broadcast trade at KVOS-TV in Bellingham, interspersing his progress there with two separate stints as administrative assistant to the local Democratic congressman, Lloyd Meeds.

By the time he decided to try for Congress in 1978, upon Meeds' retirement, Swift had a decade as a TV news director to his credit and was familiar to viewers along Puget Sound.

But he was considered a long shot because the Democratic field also included Brian Corcoran, longtime press secretary to Sen. Henry M. Jackson. Corcoran had Jackson's good will and tapped the senator's contributors. He had a weakness, though, in his tepid personal manner and inarticulate speaking style.

Swift, armed with the self-confidence generated by years in front of the camera, was poised to exploit Corcoran's vulnerability. He came from far behind to claim the nomination by 3,881 votes.

Swift's next hurdle was Republican John Nance Garner, a namesake and distant relative of Franklin D. Roosevelt's vice president. Garner, who had nearly ousted Meeds in 1976, spent lavishly against Swift in 1978, but Swift attacked Garner's heavy spending, turning that advantage into a liability. The outcome was a 51 percent victory for Swift. In the five succeeding elections, Swift took 59 percent of the vote or better.

Committees

Energy & Commerce (5th of 27 Democrats)
Transportation & Hazardous Materials (chairman); Energy & Power

House Administration (2nd of 12 Democrats)
Elections (chairman); Accounts

Joint Organization of Congress

Elections

1992 General		
Al Swift (D)	133,207	(52%)
Jack Metcalf (R)	107,365	(42%)
R.M. "Robin" Dexter (I)	8,702	(3%)
Karen Leibrant (NL)	6,646	(3%)
1992 Primary †		
Al Swift (D)	56,290	(43%)
Jack Metcalf (R)	31,661	(24%)
Tim Erwin (R)	13,114	(10%)
Doug Smith (R)	9,856	(8%)
Frank D. "Don" Sadowski (D)	6,344	(5%)
David Montgomery (R)	5,123	(4%)
Karen Leibrant (NL)	3,814	(3%)
R.M. "Robin" Dexter (I)	2,076	(2%)
1990 General		
Al Swift (D)	92,837	(51%)
Doug Smith (R)	75,669	(41%)
William L. McCord (LIBERT)	15,165	(8%)

† In Washington's "jungle primary," candidates of all parties are listed on one ballot.

Previous Winning Percentages: **1988** (100%) **1986** (72%) **1984** (59%) **1982** (60%) **1980** (64%) **1978** (51%)

District Vote for President

1992
D 109,438 (41%)
R 87,957 (33%)
I 68,875 (26%)

Campaign Finance

	Receipts	Receipts from PACs		Expend-itures
1992				
Swift (D)	$914,905	$649,844	(71%)	$1,060,650
Metcalf (R)	$200,700	$7,797	(4%)	$201,029
1990				
Swift (D)	$503,123	$272,542	(54%)	$465,249
Smith (R)	$11,408	0		$11,373

Key Votes

1993	
Require parental notification of minors' abortions	N
Require unpaid family and medical leave	Y
Approve national "motor voter" registration bill	Y
Approve budget increasing taxes and reducing deficit	Y
Approve economic stimulus plan	Y
1992	
Approve balanced-budget constitutional amendment	N
Close down space station program	N
Approve U.S. aid for former Soviet Union	Y
Allow shifting funds from defense to domestic programs	Y
1991	
Extend unemployment benefits using deficit financing	Y
Approve waiting period for handgun purchases	Y
Authorize use of force in Persian Gulf	N

Voting Studies

	Presidential Support		Party Unity		Conservative Coalition	
Year	S	O	S	O	S	O
1992	24	76	91	7	35	65
1991	31	68	89	8	16	81
1990	19	80	92	6	15	85
1989	31	65	93	4	27	73
1988	23	72	92	4	16	76
1987	21	78	92	4	21	77
1986	19	78	93	4	22	76
1985	26	73	93	5	29	69
1984	33	65	91 †	7 †	22	78
1983	18	80	91	4	11	89
1982	42	56	90	7	26	73
1981	43	55	86	14	31	69

† Not eligible for all recorded votes.

Interest Group Ratings

Year	ADA	AFL-CIO	CCUS	ACU
1992	90	75	25	4
1991	90	83	30	0
1990	89	92	21	4
1989	85	92	40	0
1988	90	85	36	0
1987	92	88	23	9
1986	90	79	18	9
1985	75	76	27	14
1984	80	77	33	4
1983	90	100	25	0
1982	85	100	23	14
1981	85	80	21	13

3 Jolene Unsoeld (D)

Of Olympia — Elected 1988; 3rd Term

Born: Dec. 3, 1931, Corvallis, Ore.
Education: Oregon State U., 1949-51.
Occupation: Public official.
Family: Widowed; three children.
Religion: Theist.
Political Career: Democratic National Committee, 1980-88; Wash. House, 1985-89.
Capitol Office: 1527 Longworth Bldg. 20515; 225-3536.

In Washington: Unsoeld's steady concentration on her coastal district's interests is beginning to pay off in electoral security. And her continuing position under Speaker Thomas S. Foley's wing has been a boost to her efforts to shore up her support back home.

In the 102nd Congress, eight Unsoeld bills became law, including a bill to impose sanctions against drift net fishing, and a ban on oil and gas drilling within the Olympic Coast National Marine Sanctuary's boundaries. She was one of seven female House members who marched to the Senate in October 1991 to urge a full hearing of Anita F. Hill's sexual harassment charges against Supreme Court nominee Clarence Thomas.

The 103rd Congress promised to offer Unsoeld more opportunities to focus on her district. From her position on the Merchant Marine and Fisheries Committee, she should have input on discussions about the renewal of the Magnuson Act, which regulates the nation's fisheries and sets limits on foreign fishing.

Unsoeld has a bit of an image problem. Colleagues are quick to point out her dedication and her seemingly limitless energy, but they also note that on some issues, she sometimes seems out of her league. "She always looks lost on the floor," says an observer.

Now in her third term, she has relied heavily on the good will of fellow Washington Democrat Foley.

In the 101st Congress — his first term as Speaker — Foley was not about to lose a seat in his own back yard, and he made re-electing Unsoeld a pet cause. Democratic House members contributed more than $42,000 to her campaign treasury, and Unsoeld was the rare freshman to see more than a dozen bills or amendments with her name on them become law.

Known as a staunch liberal in the state Legislature, Unsoeld has repaid Foley with a solidly Democratic voting record, casting fewer votes in support of President Bush than anyone else in the delegation in 1991 and 1992.

But to try to solidify further her shaky base at home, she has taken a few positions that have stunned her liberal backers. Her supporters were dismayed in the 101st Congress when she set aside her past support for gun control to champion the National Rifle Association's views on semiautomatic assault weapons. "I don't think we should punish law-abiding citizens just because some lawbreakers have abused [the right to bear arms]," she said. "For me, it's a civil rights issue."

She authored an amendment to the 1990 crime bill that essentially gutted a prohibition on semiautomatic weapons by banning only firearms assembled with foreign parts. The amendment passed 257-172. In early 1991, she voted against requiring a seven-day waiting period for handgun purchases.

Unsoeld also offered successful legislation in the 101st Congress to increase funding for Drug Abuse Resistance Education (DARE) and to authorize the restoration of the Chehalis River.

At Home: Unsoeld has had to struggle to win her three elections with barely a majority of the vote, but her victory margins show an upward progression with each election. In 1992, 3rd District voters sent her back to Washington with 56 percent, up slightly from her 1990 tally and far more than the scant 627-vote majority she received in 1988.

Unsoeld was not expected to have such difficulty in her first House campaign, to succeed Democratic Rep. Don Bonker in the reliably Democratic district. But while Bonker had been regarded as a moderate, Unsoeld was seen mainly as a liberal activist.

Unsoeld entered politics as an independent lobbyist in Olympia on "good government" issues such as campaign finance reform. She won her first elective office, a state House seat, in 1984 and was best known in the Legislature for her work on the environment.

In 1988, Unsoeld won the Democratic nomination for the 3rd despite her opponent's claims that she was confrontational and anti-business.

However, Republican nominee Bill Wight used the same charge to greater effect. While

Washington 3

Southwest — Olympia; Vancouver

The 3rd, stretching from Puget Sound west to the Pacific and south to the Columbia River border with Oregon, is heavy with maritime and timber interests. With its large number of blue-collar voters, it contains some of the most Democratic territory in the state.

Democratic presidential candidates have fared well here. In the three-way 1992 presidential contest, Democrat Bill Clinton carried the 3rd as had Democrat Michael S. Dukakis in 1988. Rep. Unsoeld raised her victory margin here to 56 percent of the vote in 1992. About 70 percent of the district vote comes from two counties: Thurston (Olympia) in the northern end, and Clark (Vancouver) in the south. Clinton won both easily.

Olympia, the state capital, and its surroundings was one of the fastest-growing metropolitan areas in the country in the 1980s; the Olympia metropolitan area's population soared nearly 30 percent to just over 161,000. Olympia's communities of environmental and "good government" activists — from which Unsoeld emerged — give Democrats a leg up in the county. Neighboring Lacey is a burgeoning twin city to Olympia that adds to the Democratic vote on this end of the district.

Clark County has also seen its population surge with the growth of its Portland, Ore., suburbs. Because Washington does not have an income tax and Oregon does not have a sales tax, many retirees have flocked to live on the Washington side and do their shopping in Oregon.

Vancouver (Clark County) is an industrial and high-tech center. Among the employers here are the James River Pulp and Paper Co. and the computer companies Hewlett Packard, SEH America and Kyocera. The city has renovated a historic section of the district known as Officers Row, a string of 21 homes dating back to the Civil War era, including one in which Ulysses S. Grant lived.

The 3rd has vast stretches of woodlands, including the scenic Coastal Range and much of the Cascade Mountains, with Mount Rainier just outside the eastern border. Timber dominates the economy and, in recent years, there have been more downs than ups. The area's mills produce paper, timber and cardboard under the state's strict water-pollution standards. Logging is a major activity of Cowlitz County, which includes the cities of Longview and Kelso. Along the coast, fishing and dockwork predominate, and there is a strong labor presence among the longshoremen.

East of Cowlitz are the newest additions to the district, Skamania and part of Klickitat counties, which rely heavily on the timber industry for their economic base, and the Columbia River Gorge National Scenic Area, a popular tourist attraction.

Rural Lewis County in the northern end of the district provides the only dependable GOP majorities in the 3rd. Republican George Bush won the county in both the 1992 and 1988 presidential elections.

1990 Population: 540,745. White 512,446 (95%), Black 4,855 (1%), Other 23,444 (4%). Hispanic origin 13,467 (3%). 18 and over 392,267 (73%), 62 and over 82,435 (15%). Median age: 34.

portraying Unsoeld as an extremist, Wight came off as thoughtful and more moderate than previous GOP nominees in the 3rd. Wight was a retired Army lieutenant colonel who had worked as a Pentagon and Senate aide before returning to his native area in 1988. His determination earned him media attention and national GOP money.

But on Election Day, Unsoeld won by 627 votes. That margin — the slimmest of any House victor nationwide — would have been enticement enough for the GOP. But Republicans got further encouragement from controversy over federal efforts to protect the northern spotted owl, which would threaten some logging jobs in districts such as the 3rd.

While Unsoeld tried to stake out a middle ground on the issue, 1990 Republican nominee Bob Williams, a former state representative and Weyerhaeuser Co. accountant, took her to task for countenancing job-threatening owl protections. National GOP leaders, bent on making the race a national partisan slugfest, helped out with plenty of money and campaign appearances from administration officials.

But Unsoeld had prepared well for such an onslaught. While bringing in federal flood aid and port-dredging projects for the district, she also had secured the money needed for a high-power campaign, reaching the half-million-dollar mark in contributions by early summer.

Unsoeld outpolled Williams in the September primary, in which all candidates ran on the same ballot. But she fell under attack from the left in October after sponsoring the amendment that aided domestic gun manufacturers and subsequently accepting a $5,000 campaign contribution from the National Rifle Association. Liberals had no place to go in the conservative Williams, however, and Unsoeld thwarted his challenge with a healthy, if not massive, margin of 54 percent to 46 percent.

In 1992, redistricting made the 3rd marginally more Republican with the loss of territory in Thurston and Grays Harbor counties in exchange for rural Republican ground in Skamania and Klickitat counties. But Unsoeld retained her Vancouver base and Olympia, and the September primary showed her stronger than ever. She received more than 2½ times the total vote of her leading rival and November GOP opponent, former state Rep. Pat Fiske.

Fiske was unable to build enough momentum, money or name recognition needed to overtake the incumbent, and Unsoeld got her best general-election tally to date.

Committees

Education & Labor (11th of 28 Democrats)
Elementary, Secondary & Vocational Education; Labor-Management Relations; Postsecondary Education

Merchant Marine & Fisheries (12th of 29 Democrats)
Environment & Natural Resources; Fisheries Management

Elections

1992 General		
Jolene Unsoeld (D)	138,043	(56%)
Pat Fiske (R)	108,583	(44%)
1992 Primary †		
Jolene Unsoeld (D)	59,510	(52%)
Pat Fiske (R)	22,848	(20%)
Bill Hughes (R)	16,737	(15%)
Chuck O'Reilly (D)	10,495	(9%)
Gary Snell (R)	5,575	(5%)
1990 General		
Jolene Unsoeld (D)	95,645	(54%)
Bob Williams (R)	82,269	(46%)

† In Washington's "jungle primary," candidates of all parties are listed on one ballot.

Previous Winning Percentage: 1988 (50%)

District Vote for President

1992
D 104,748 (42%)
R 82,647 (33%)
I 61,613 (25%)

Campaign Finance

	Receipts	Receipts from PACs	Expend-itures
1992			
Unsoeld (D)	$664,434	$365,370 (55%)	$619,941
Fiske (R)	$218,204	$86,822 (40%)	$212,192
1990			
Unsoeld (D)	$1,297,700	$624,498 (48%)	$1,298,593
Williams (R)	$829,603	$204,768 (25%)	$817,944

Key Votes

1993	
Require parental notification of minors' abortions	N
Require unpaid family and medical leave	Y
Approve national "motor voter" registration bill	Y
Approve budget increasing taxes and reducing deficit	Y
Approve economic stimulus plan	Y
1992	
Approve balanced-budget constitutional amendment	N
Close down space station program	Y
Approve U.S. aid for former Soviet Union	Y
Allow shifting funds from defense to domestic programs	Y
1991	
Extend unemployment benefits using deficit financing	Y
Approve waiting period for handgun purchases	N
Authorize use of force in Persian Gulf	N

Voting Studies

	Presidential Support		Party Unity		Conservative Coalition	
Year	S	O	S	O	S	O
1992	12	81	93	4	10	79
1991	25	72	93	5	19	78
1990	15	76	90	4	13	80
1989	27	73	95	3	2	98

Interest Group Ratings

Year	ADA	AFL-CIO	CCUS	ACU
1992	90	100	38	0
1991	90	100	10	5
1990	83	92	36	9
1989	100	100	40	4

4 Jay Inslee (D)

Of Selah — Elected 1992; 1st Term

Born: Feb. 9, 1951, Seattle, Wash.
Education: Stanford U., 1969-70; U. of Washington, B.A. 1973; Willamette U., J.D. 1976.
Occupation: Lawyer.
Family: Wife, Trudi Tindall; three children.
Religion: Protestant.
Political Career: Wash. House, 1989-93.
Capitol Office: 1431 Longworth Bldg. 20515; 225-5816.

The Path to Washington: Inslee pulled off perhaps the biggest surprise in Washington's nine House races Nov. 3 when he beat Republican Richard "Doc" Hastings by 51 percent to 49 percent for the seat of GOP Rep. Sid Morrison, who lost a gubernatorial primary in September.

Inslee began the 1992 election season as a long shot in a strongly contested race for the open seat, but before the year was out, his was the star to watch in the state party's future.

Inslee, a litigator with the Selah law firm of Peters, Fowler & Inslee since his 1976 graduation from the Williamette University College of Law, started his campaign much later than the other candidates and was not well-known.

He is a relative newcomer to politics, first winning his state House seat in 1988. There, he served as vice chairman of the Appropriations Committee and of the panel that helped negotiate a budget deal that reduced the state's deficit.

Though many of his colleagues consider him an affable and able legislator, several tried to dissuade him from running for the open seat, noting that redistricting had done little to change the rural Republican and conservative flavor of the 4th.

Inslee toyed with the idea for several months, announcing in November that he was considering a run for the seat, declaring in January that he would not seek the seat and finally telling voters in April that he would.

Inslee said that he decided to run because "we had our House in order in Washington state" and that it was time for him to try to straighten out the House in the other Washington.

The state Democratic Party eagerly welcomed his decision. Although Democratic state Sen. Jim Jesernig already had launched a full-scale campaign and was considered the favorite, party officials were heartened to have two strong candidates seeking to reclaim the seat, which Democrat Mike McCormack held throughout the 1970s (before losing to Morrison in 1980).

Inslee made up for lost campaign time and a bare-bones campaign budget by regularly standing on different street corners and waving at motorists. Jesernig painted the district with his signs; Inslee noted that while his signs could not be found all over, he could be. Inslee also promised to give constituents his home telephone number so that they could call anytime.

Inslee's calls to halve the deficit within five years, overhaul the nation's health care and reform Congress in a number of ways, including cutting salaries of House members, seemed to resonate among voters.

But in the Sept. 15 "jungle primary" (all candidates for the seat appear on the same ballot, with each party's top vote-getter advancing to the November general election), it was Inslee's folksy style and his tireless campaigning throughout the 4th that lifted him past his main Democratic opponent, Jesernig, by just 1,100 votes.

Inslee and his low-budget campaign were expected to have a tough fight in November against his better-financed Republican opponent, a former state representative and president of the Columbia Basin Paper & Supply.

Hastings had easily outpolled three Republican challengers in the primary, due largely to strong support from evangelical groups who backed his anti-abortion rights stand and to his better name recognition from his business ties and years in the state Legislature.

But Inslee used the same formula he used to beat Jesernig in the primary, canvassing the district with his presence and cultivating an image of being fiscally conservative and socially progressive.

Meantime, Hastings, who said his political career was inspired by former President Ronald Reagan, found himself struggling to garner support outside of his conservative base. In editorials, much of the local news media called him too conservative for the district.

On Election Day, Inslee's attention to voters in the northern part of the district helped turn the race in his favor again. He won all but two of the district's nine counties.

Early in the 103rd Congress, Inslee was one of an informal group of Democratic freshmen who worked with the leadership in successfully bringing to the floor a bill granting the president modified line-item veto authority.

Washington 4

Central — Yakima and Tri-Cities

The 4th, lying just east of the Cascade Mountains, is a big chunk of central Washington, bordering Canada on the north and Oregon on the south. The voters here consistently support Republican presidential candidates, but in elections for other offices, Democrats often fare well.

The 4th was the only Washington districts that George Bush carried in the 1992 presidential contest. At the same time, Inslee's victory switched the House seat into the Democratic column. He carried seven of the district's 10 counties, losing only in the southeastern corner of the 4th, where voters in the Tri-Cities area of Pasco, Kennewick and Richland are staunchly Republican.

Democrats got a shot at the 4th as six-term GOP Rep. Sid Morrison left the House to run for governor. (He lost in the primary.) Before Morrison, the district had been in Democratic hands for a decade.

Balancing GOP strength in the Tri-Cities are several areas with Democratic proclivities. Kittitas County, in the center of the 4th, voted a straight Democratic ticket in 1992. Clinton also won Klickitat County (on the Columbia River border with Oregon) and Okanogan County (which borders Canada).

The 4th's economy revolves around agriculture — primarily fruits and wheat, winemaking and cattle — and the Hanford Nuclear Reservation, formerly the site of much of the nation's nuclear weapons-materials production. The reservation is mostly in Benton County, just north of the Tri-Cities. In 1988, the federal government shut down Hanford's N reactor, a plutonium plant, because of safety problems and the decreased need for plutonium given the warming in U.S.-Soviet relations. The shutdown resulted in the initial loss of 1,000 jobs in the two-county (Benton and Franklin) area of about 150,000.

The Department of Energy then estimated that it would cost up to $50 billion to clean up the hazardous waste that had accumulated at Hanford. In early 1989, the state and federal governments agreed on a cleanup plan; the project, which will bring about 2,000 jobs to the Hanford area, is expected to take at least 30 years.

Nearby, construction is under way for a $220 million Molecular Science Research Lab, scheduled for completion in 1996. Researchers there will develop technologies for the cleanup of hazardous waste around the country.

Northwest of the Tri-Cities is the district's other urban concentration, Yakima (Yakima County). Voters here lean Republican, although Inslee, whose hometown of Selah is in Yakima County, carried the county in 1992. George Bush won Yakima County with 45 percent.

Yakima County was largely desert before a huge irrigation project helped make it one of the nation's premier apple-growing areas; more than 50 percent of the nation's apples come from the district. Also in the 4th is the immense Grand Coulee Dam, on the Columbia River in Grant County.

1990 Population: 540,744. White 449,913 (83%), Black 5,276 (1%), Other 5,555 (16%). Hispanic origin 85,804 (16%). 18 and over 380,303 (70%), 62 and over 80,621 (15%). Median age: 32.

Committees

Agriculture (18th of 28 Democrats)
Department Operations; Environment, Credit & Rural Development; Specialty Crops & Natural Resources

Science, Space & Technology (26th of 33 Democrats)
Energy; Technology, Environment & Aviation

Campaign Finance

	Receipts	Receipts from PACs		Expend-itures
1992				
Inslee (D)	$257,153	$98,886	(38%)	$255,159
Hastings (R)	$360,445	$129,581	(36%)	$355,859

Key Votes

1993

Require parental notification of minors' abortions	N
Require unpaid family and medical leave	Y
Approve national "motor voter" registration bill	Y
Approve budget increasing taxes and reducing deficit	Y
Approve economic stimulus plan	Y

Elections

1992 General		
Jay Inslee (D)	106,556	(51%)
Richard "Doc" Hastings (R)	103,028	(49%)
1992 Primary †		
Richard "Doc" Hastings (R)	28,952	(24%)
Jay Inslee (D)	27,429	(23%)
Jim Jesernig (D)	26,320	(22%)
Alex McLean (R)	13,605	(11%)
Jeffrey C. Sullivan (R)	12,074	(10%)
Bill Almon (R)	9,168	(8%)
Joe Walkenhauer (D)	3,774	(3%)

† In Washington's "jungle primary," candidates of all parties are listed on one ballot.

District Vote for President

	1992
D	71,848 (35%)
R	87,996 (43%)
I	45,252 (22%)

5 Thomas S. Foley (D)

Of Spokane — Elected 1964; 15th Term

Born: March 6, 1929, Spokane, Wash.

Education: U. of Washington, B.A. 1951, LL.B. 1957.

Occupation: Lawyer.

Family: Wife, Heather Strachan.

Religion: Roman Catholic.

Political Career: Spokane County deputy prosecuting attorney, 1958-60; Wash. assistant attorney general, 1960-61.

Capitol Office: 1201 Longworth Bldg. 20515; 225-2006.

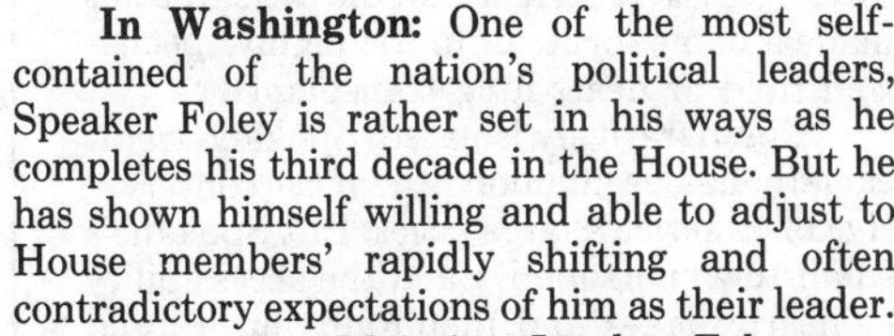

In Washington: One of the most self-contained of the nation's political leaders, Speaker Foley is rather set in his ways as he completes his third decade in the House. But he has shown himself willing and able to adjust to House members' rapidly shifting and often contradictory expectations of him as their leader.

When then-Majority Leader Foley was chosen as Speaker in June 1989 (during the 101st Congress), his cool style was seen as an antidote to the roughshod manner of his predecessor, Jim Wright of Texas.

But when the scandal involving members' overdrafts at the House bank unraveled during the 102nd Congress, Foley's measured quality was seen as a failing. He was attacked for being indecisive. His insular personality and institutionalist instincts were blamed for his failure to anticipate the outrage of a recession-worried electorate that was already expressing dissatisfaction with Congress. That led to enough dissent within the House that, for a time, Foley's leadership seemed threatened.

But Foley survived the storm. He reacted to the public relations nightmare by pushing reforms of House procedures — including the closing of the House bank and the hiring of an independent administrator. And thereafter, he asserted himself more directly to project a Democratic legislative agenda.

Moreover, he proceeded to politic for his own job, lining up the support of key chairmen and campaigning in behalf of members senior and junior alike. Within days of the election, Foley was on a tour of the nation, meeting virtually every freshly elected Democrat. He was re-elected Speaker for the 103rd Congress without opposition in the Democratic Caucus.

When the caucus met a month after the November election, it also gave Foley more power to control the House agenda. The caucus created a working group to set the party's legislative program, with Foley appointing all 20 members.

The 1992 election of Democrat Bill Clinton as president further invigorated Foley, who pledged to see the new administration's program through to enactment.

As the torchbearer for a program shaped in the Democratic White House, Foley is more in his element than he was as an adversary of the Reagan and Bush administrations. Foley believes strongly in the legislative axiom that "the president proposes and Congress disposes."

Moreover, Foley recognizes that his future political standing — and that of his colleagues who make up the Democratic majority — is dependent on Clinton's success. "Nobody's going to have divided government to blame anymore. We will have the first opportunity we've had in a long time to prove government can work — and the people will be watching," he said as the 103rd Congress opened.

But even as he accepted his colleagues' demand for more aggressive action, Foley was reminded of why he was averse to riding herd over the House in the first place.

Foley succeeded famously in pushing Clinton's initial, politically hazardous economic program to passage in the House. But in the process, he found himself in the cross-fire.

Many Democrats, including some who previously had chastised him as unwilling to lead, chafed at being pushed and shoved. Meanwhile, Republicans — with whom Foley had enjoyed a cooperative relationship through most of his career — accused him of crushing their rights as the House minority.

Despite all of this and the pressure to change his manner of leading, Foley remains personally unchanged. At 6 feet 3 inches, he is physically imposing, even after an ascetic diet-and-exercise regimen, begun in 1990, turned him from portly to svelte (a difference of some 80 pounds). Though a Westerner by birth and bidding (the first Speaker from west of the Rocky Mountains), Foley is a notably formal man who prefers to campaign in a suit and wingtip shoes, even in the rural stretches of his expansive district.

Foley, who once sought a career in the judiciary, is widely admired for an intellectual bent that is rare in the House. He has an interest in ideas and a taste for the arts. His conversation is rich with select words and his-

Washington 5

East — Spokane

In most election years, Foley's success is rather an anomaly for Democrats in this heavily rural eastern Washington district. Though Democrats seeking higher office can be competitive here, the 5th usually has a Republican tilt.

But the three-way White House race of 1992 gave Democrat Bill Clinton a chance to break his party's presidential losing streak in the 5th.

Aided by the popularity of Ross Perot, who got 23 percent of the vote in the 5th and weakened George Bush, Clinton ran first, taking 40 percent overall. In 1988, Michael S. Dukakis won almost as many votes in the district as Clinton did four years later, but Dukakis lost narrowly to Bush.

Clinton's success did not transfer to the Democratic nominees for governor and senator, Mike Lowry and Patty Murray. Both lost every county in the district, though they won statewide.

And Foley himself had an unaccustomed brush with serious GOP competition. Four lightly populated counties went for his Republican challenger, who kept Foley's winning tally down to 55 percent, his poorest showing in a dozen years.

Though the 5th covers 11 counties and a lot of ground, in electoral terms one place counts: Spokane. With 177,000 people, the city is Washington's second-largest. Spokane County casts about two-thirds of the district's vote.

Spokane is the banking and marketing center of the "Inland Empire," which encompasses wheat- and vegetable-farming counties in eastern Washington, eastern Oregon, northern Idaho and western Montana. The city developed a sizable aluminum industry thanks to the availability of low-cost hydroelectric power from New Deal-era dams along the Columbia River. Boeing also is a presence here. Though the company plans to lay off thousands in the Seattle area, its Spokane facility, which makes airplane floor panels and environmental ducts, could hold its ground as Boeing retrenches.

Spokane also is becoming known as a major medical center for the Inland Empire. The Sacred Heart Medical Center has made a name for itself in the highly specialized field of heart-lung transplants.

Comparatively isolated, Spokane traditionally has been among the most conservative of America's large cities. But Spokane's small-town personality and the accessibility of nearby lakes and mountains have lured many newcomers to the Spokane area in recent years — particularly California emigrants. This influx has served to moderate Spokane's conservatism. Clinton won Spokane County with 41 percent in 1992, and Foley took it with 57 percent.

There are two other small population centers of note. Pullman (Whitman County) is the site of Washington State University (18,000 students). Though the county has tended to support Republicans for president, it went for Clinton in 1992. Holding fast for the GOP was traditionally Republican Walla Walla County.

1990 Population: 540,744. White 504,014 (93%), Black 6,496 (1%), Other 30,234 (6%). Hispanic origin 18,304 (3%). 18 and over 398,869 (74%), 62 and over 85,387 (16%). Median age: 33.

torical allusions. An audiophile, his expensive equipment is primarily devoted to classical fare.

Although it sometimes seems hard to remember now, Foley's succession to the Speakership was greeted with praise and some sighs of relief from both sides of the aisle. Wright (whose ethics problems forced him to quit the House) was a strong-armed partisan warrior who often plunged into issues debates without consulting other Democratic members.

Foley, who served under Wright, was always cast as the contrasting, conciliatory figure. Shaping policy by cultivating consensus among the party's many factions, he often reached out to Republicans. It was even said at times that Foley would be the House Republicans' consensus choice among Democrats to serve as Speaker.

But as he rose to the highest position in the House (and second in line to the presidency, behind the vice president), the bipartisan comity Foley had fostered and enjoyed quickly evaporated. A memo circulated by the Republican National Committee's press office referred to Foley as "coming out of the liberal closet." It also compared him to Barney Frank of Massachusetts, a liberal who has publicly declared himself a homosexual.

President Bush, who in his first two years as president often took an accommodating approach toward the Democratic-controlled Congress, pronounced the memo "disgusting," and its author promptly resigned. Foley, in a characteristic response, calmly denied the memo's implication and accepted the apologies of embarrassed Republicans. "A very cheap smear," he said. "I think the issue is closed."

Yet even within the Democratic ranks, it was not long before Foley's ways were criticized. Within months of becoming Speaker, he saw his majority scattered and defeated on the issue of a capital gains tax cut proposed by Bush.

In mid-1990, Foley was a lead player in the four-month-long "budget summit" between congressional and Bush administration officials. When an initial budget deal was presented to the House that October, Foley found his troops unhappy about the tilt of the tax package and the depth of cuts in safety-net programs.

With Republicans rankling at the deal's tax increases (it was the measure on which Bush broke his "no new taxes" pledge), it was roundly rejected by majorities in both parties.

Qualms about Foley's style grew during the 1991 debate on a massive bill authorizing highway and mass transit funding. Foley had pushed for the bill to be passed before an August House recess. But the bill stalled over members' objections to a 5-cent-per-gallon increase in the federal gasoline tax (strongly favored by Foley) and a dispute between two powerful committee chairmen over how the proceeds of any gas tax revenues should be dedicated.

This incident spurred a line of criticism that would be oft-heard over the next year. "I am loath to criticize Foley, but this is an example of where his style doesn't serve us well," said Rep. Timothy J. Penny of Minnesota, an independent-minded Democrat. "He's too laid-back, too deferential to committee chairmen and frankly, too unwilling to set deadlines."

Foley did try to keep the Democrats' political agenda on track. Bush — whose popularity ratings had plummeted because of the economy — was blaming a "gridlocked Congress" for the nation's problems; Foley pushed for approval of a hotly disputed crime bill (which passed the House on a 205-203 vote) and campaign finance reform bill, strongly opposed by Bush, in an attempt to show that any miasma in Washington was the fault of the White House.

In the 102nd Congress, Foley also made a major issue of Bush's initial refusal to extend unemployment benefits. He prodded Ways and Means Chairman Dan Rostenkowski of Illinois, who was reluctant to reopen the tax debate so soon after the 1990 budget summit, to produce legislation providing a middle-class tax cut to be financed with increased taxes on the wealthy.

But whatever Foley achieved in the 102nd Congress was largely eclipsed by scandals involving the House bank and other congressional institutions. In September 1991, the General Accounting Office reported that the bank — into which many members had their salaries directly deposited — had allowed members to write checks on their accounts even when there were insufficient funds to cover the checks. The issue was fodder not only for editorialists and talk-show rabble-rousers, but also for Republican activists who blamed the Democrats' long-term control of the House for its inefficient and possibly corrupt bureaucracy.

Foley tried at first to tamp the issue, joining with Minority Leader Robert H. Michel of Illinois (another institutionalist long known for his hail-fellow manner) in banning the overdraft policy and scolding House members in a statement on the House floor. "This is a matter that's over and done with," Foley stated hopefully. But that was not to be. As Republicans cried "cover-up," Foley ordered the bank closed outright and announced an ethics committee investigation.

The furor grew during early 1992, as evidence appeared of serious mismanagement and possible misuse of the House Post Office and restaurant by members. The bank problem reemerged with a roar in March 1992, when Foley backed an ethics committee recommendation to release only the names of those who had abused their privileges at the bank most often. This time, Michel — under pressure from Republicans who oppose his conciliatory style — abandoned Foley and backed "full disclosure" of all overdrafters' names. Many Democrats, panicky over the political impact of the scandal, joined in.

In early April, as the full disclosure date approached, Foley came under heavy fire from within the Democratic Caucus. In private meetings, members excoriated Foley for not acting earlier and more decisively to clean up the matter. There were reports that some younger, activist members, such as George Miller of California and Dave McCurdy of Oklahoma, might be testing the waters for a possible challenge. Rep. John Bryant of Texas took the matter public, calling in a House floor speech for Foley to step down as Speaker.

But Foley rode out the bad weather and awaited his moment. After the long list of overdrafters' names was released, Foley argued that the scandal had been blown out of proportion by media coverage and by Republicans who, he suggested, were trying to gain control of the institution by destroying its reputation.

He engaged in a modest reform campaign, eliminating several long-cherished perks for members and endorsing a proposal for an ad hoc committee (later named the Joint Committee on the Organization of Congress and empaneled at the start of the 103rd Congress) to conduct a more sweeping review of congressional organization and legislative procedure.

Early in the 103rd Congress, Foley also unsheathed what had been a well-gloved iron hand. He decided not to reapppoint McCurdy as chairman of the House Select Committee on Intelligence, where all members serve by the Speaker's appointment. Foley said McCurdy's nine-year tenure on Intelligence, which nor mally has a six-year rotation, was enough. The move was nonetheless widely read as retaliation for McCurdy's criticism of Foley during the House bank crisis.

But even the energized and assertive Foley found that he was no more immune to criticism than he had been before. Throughout the early months of 1993, Republicans railed against the leadership's use of "closed" rules to limit floor debate and amendments on legislation. Just one year after the bank scandal, when they derided Foley as a hopelessly weak leader, conservative Republican activists were denouncing him as a martinet — even as Foley himself was promising an end to the parade of closed rules.

Nonetheless, under Foley, the House moved quickly to enact major pieces of Clinton's legislative program, including his budget proposal (which contained controversial tax increases and spending cuts) and "economic stimulus" package. These bills passed the House with few Democratic defections.

But in the process, Foley learned again how difficult it is to satisfy everyone in his fractious caucus. During consideration of the budget resolution, Foley accepted the arguments of deficit-minded Democrats that more program cuts were needed; liberal members of the party protested loudly.

But on the economic stimulus package, Foley backed the Rules Committee in barring an amendment by conservative Democrat Charles W. Stenholm of Texas that would have required offsetting cuts in spending. "I think our leadership has to understand you can't do that but a few times," said Stenholm, who joined an outcry that Democratic conservatives were "steamrollered."

Foley has risen high without having once displayed the kind of vaunting ambition usually associated with such success. Even his first candidacy for Congress in 1964 was reluctantly undertaken at the urging of others.

In 1974 Foley chaired the Democratic Study Group, the strategy and research arm of liberal and moderate Democrats. The next year, he became Agriculture Committee chairman in unusual circumstances. His predecessor, the elderly and conservative W. R. Poage of Texas, was targeted for removal by the huge bloc of reform-minded "Watergate baby" Democrats. Ever the institutionalist, Foley backed Poage; but when he was unseated anyway, the insurgents turned to Foley and promoted him over several more senior members of the panel.

Foley continued to rise within Democratic ranks, becoming chairman of the caucus in 1977. After the 1980 election, the position of Democratic whip opened up. Then-Speaker Thomas P. "Tip" O'Neill Jr., facing an adversarial relationship with newly elected President Ronald Reagan, was looking for a successor with parliamentary skills. Rostenkowski was then the chief deputy whip, first in line for promotion, but he decided to take over Ways and Means instead. Foley stepped in.

When O'Neill announced his plan to retire at the end of the 99th Congress, Foley did not seem to be guaranteed the majority leader's spot. Some members wanted a more partisan figure; yet in the end no challenger to Foley emerged. The same dynamic was apparent when, in 1989, Foley rose without opposition to the Speakership.

At Home: In its recent travails, the House as a whole has benefited from Foley's image of rectitude, and over the years his personal abilities have been enough to secure his standing in a district naturally suited to another kind of politics. While most of his wins have been comfortable ones, he has had to scramble on occasion. The 1992 election cycle served as a reminder that the 5th is no Democratic bastion, and that Foley is not impervious to anti-Congress sentiment or to the recycled attacks of an old foe.

Foley wanted to be a judge, as was his father. He spent two years as deputy prosecutor in Spokane County and a year as assistant state attorney general. In 1961 he moved to Washington, D.C., to work for Sen. Henry M. Jackson as counsel to the Senate Interior Committee.

Three years later he was a reluctant congressional candidate, persuaded to run by the favorable political climate for Democrats, by Jackson's encouragement and by a Spokane politico who taunted him about the race on the day before the filing deadline. Foley managed to file with minutes to spare.

The young candidate had no primary competition because no other Democrats wanted to challenge Republican Walt Horan, who had held the seat since 1942. But Horan was ailing at 66, and Foley had fundraising help from Jackson and Sen. Warren Magnuson (not to mention the boost of a Democratic presidential landslide). He upset the incumbent in November by 12,000 votes.

After 1964, Foley worked hard to keep his district, and by 1970 Republicans had stopped running strong candidates against him.

But in 1976 he made a political mistake. Republican nominee Charles Kimball was killed in an airplane crash the month before the election, and Foley essentially stopped campaigning and allowed a political unknown to hold him under 60 percent of the vote.

The 1976 result convinced Republicans that Foley was vulnerable in 1978. As Agriculture chairman, Foley had become a target for resentment over farm issues among his wheat-growing constituents. Even worse for the incumbent, Indian tribal official Mel Tonasket ran as an independent and took away Democratic votes. Foley scraped by with just 48 percent in the three-way contest.

Again in 1980, Republicans had high hopes. Foley's opponent this time was John Sonneland, a Spokane surgeon who had once served as state co-chairman of Common Cause. The incumbent campaigned hard, stressing his more conservative ideas, such as a tax cut and congressional veto of federal regulations produced by the executive branch. The GOP tide that year left Foley with a career-low margin of scarcely 7,000 votes.

Sonneland was back in 1982, replacing the strident personal attacks he had used in 1980 with attempts to convince voters that Foley had placed national interests above local concerns. But Foley, chastened by the pair of close calls, had paid renewed attention to the district. He not only trounced Sonneland by nearly 2-to-1 in their mutual home base of Spokane County, but also carried most of the 5th District's rural counties for the first time in several elections.

Thereafter, in each re-election campaign through 1990, Foley won with two-thirds of the vote or better. But, in 1992, Sonneland returned riding a wave of anti-incumbent, anti-House sentiment. He and three other Republicans on the all-party primary ballot managed to hold Foley to 53 percent of the overall primary vote in September, a tally that gave the GOP hope that Foley was wounded. But Sonneland in November was unable to improve on the general anti-Foley feeling expressed by voters in September. Despite an enormous outpouring of TV advertising (especially by Eastern Washington standards), the Speaker dispatched Sonneland with 55 percent of the vote.

Speaker of the House

Elections

1992 General		
Thomas S. Foley (D)	135,965	(55%)
John Sonneland (R)	110,443	(45%)
1992 Primary †		
Thomas S. Foley (D)	68,536	(53%)
John Sonneland (R)	27,384	(21%)
Duane Sommers (R)	20,110	(15%)
Marlyn A. Derby (R)	10,833	(8%)
William Johns (R)	3,077	(2%)
1990 General		
Thomas S. Foley (D)	110,234	(69%)
Marlyn A. Derby (R)	49,965	(31%)

† In Washington's "jungle primary," candidates of all parties are listed on one ballot.

Previous Winning Percentages: **1988** (76%) **1986** (75%) **1984** (70%) **1982** (64%) **1980** (52%) **1978** (48%) **1976** (58%) **1974** (64%) **1972** (81%) **1970** (67%) **1968** (57%) **1966** (57%) **1964** (54%)

District Vote for President

1992

D 99,676 (40%)
R 90,294 (37%)
I 56,472 (23%)

Campaign Finance

	Receipts	Receipts from PACs		Expend-itures
1992				
Foley (D)	$561,826	$406,490	(72%)	$913,647
Sonneland (R)	$478,555	0		$477,806
1990				
Foley (D)	$467,084	$326,337	(70%)	$457,754
Derby (R)	$7,154	$375	(5%)	$5,006

Key Votes

1992

Approve balanced-budget constitutional amendment	N
Approve U.S. aid for former Soviet Union	Y

1991

Authorize use of force in Persian Gulf	N

Voting Studies

	Presidential Support		Party Unity		Conservative Coalition	
Year	**S**	**O**	**S**	**O**	**S**	**O**
1992	10 ‡	90 ‡	100 ‡	0 ‡	0 ‡	100 ‡
1991	13 ‡	88 ‡	78 ‡	11 ‡	0 ‡	100 ‡
1990	40 ‡	60 ‡	100 ‡	0 ‡	0 ‡	100 ‡
1989	27 ‡	73 ‡	97 ‡	0 ‡	17 ‡	83 ‡
1988	23	67	91	4	21	76
1987	25	71	90	4	30	58
1986	23	73	91	4	40	54
1985	29	71	90	3	29	69
1984	38	57	81	12	32	56
1983	29	59	83	8	25	55
1982	39	51	83	12	40	55
1981	54	45	80	17	51	45

‡ As Speaker of the House, Foley voted at his discretion.

Interest Group Ratings

Year	ADA	AFL-CIO	CCUS	ACU
1992	--	50	--	0
1991	--	100	--	0
1990	--	--	--	0
1989	--	100	--	0
1988	85	86	38	4
1987	80	87	27	9
1986	75	86	33	14
1985	75	76	27	10
1984	80	54	56	26
1983	85	81	32	13
1982	65	79	33	27
1981	55	73	32	13

6 Norm Dicks (D)

Of Bremerton — Elected 1976; 9th Term

Born: Dec. 16, 1940, Bremerton, Wash.
Education: U. of Washington, B.A. 1963, J.D. 1968.
Occupation: Congressional aide.
Family: Wife, Suzanne Callison; two children.
Religion: Lutheran.
Political Career: No previous office.
Capitol Office: 2467 Rayburn Bldg. 20515; 225-5916.

In Washington: Apprenticeships to powerful home-state Democrats have served Dicks well. During the 1970s, Dicks was chief aide to Sen. Warren G. Magnuson and had ties to Sen. Henry M. Jackson, two legends for their abilities to deliver federal funds to Washington state. Dicks used this background to get on the House Appropriations Committee as a freshman in 1977; Dicks now is one of the youngest senior members of the spending committee.

Dicks also has benefited from his alliance with Rep. Thomas S. Foley, who in 1989 became House Speaker. Dicks is regarded as the Speaker's "point man" on Appropriations and the Select Intelligence Committee.

Placed on Intelligence by Foley in 1991, Dicks was a candidate for the committee chairmanship at the start of the 103rd Congress. Although Foley opted for Kansas Rep. Dan Glickman, Dicks did get the chairmanship of the Oversight and Evaluation Subcommittee.

On Appropriations, Dicks has seats on the Defense and Military Construction subcommittees that enable him to oversee programs crucial to the military facilities in his Puget Sound region and Seattle-based Boeing Co., a defense aviation contractor. On the Interior Subcommittee, Dicks is able to play a role in the debate over logging in forests inhabited by the endangered northern spotted owl.

Dicks has an aggressive style that stands out on the mannerly Appropriations Committee. The late Magnuson kidded him about his bullish manner: He said Dicks, as a linebacker for a Rose Bowl-bound University of Washington football team, was always five yards offside.

Dicks applies this intensity to defense issues. His generally pro-defense leanings have philosophical roots: He was a protégé of the late Jackson, a leading Democratic hawk. But they also have much to do with his constituency's reliance on the jobs provided by the U.S. military and by defense industries.

Dicks has been a leading supporter of the B-2 bomber, a high-tech, high-cost stealth aircraft program on which Boeing is a major subcontractor. He is a strong advocate of a Navy homeport project in Everett, Wash.

Yet his overall record on defense is that of a centrist: He has favored cuts in the Strategic Defense Initiative anti-missile system and took a lead on arms control policy during the mid-1980s.

Dicks' moderate approach was evident following Iraq's 1990 invasion of Kuwait. When the Democratic Caucus called that December on President Bush to seek congressional authorization for military action in the Persian Gulf, Dicks was one of those who added language that said the president could move immediately if American lives were in danger. But like most Democrats, Dicks opposed the January 1991 resolution that authorized the use of force.

Dicks' strong defense views provided him with political cover. He won re-election easily in 1992, and had time to campaign for the election of Bill Clinton as president; Dicks was one of Clinton's early House endorsers.

In early 1993, Dicks supported Clinton's efforts to mediate the spotted owl controversy, which had practically halted timber harvesting in such woodlands as the Olympic National Forest, largely located in Dicks' district.

On the Appropriations Interior Subcommittee, Dicks in 1991 tried to overcome legal restrictions on timber harvesting, but his amendment to allow more cutting on federal lands was defeated. Dicks, who chastised Bush for failing to resolve conflicts within his administration on the issue, has praised Clinton for his hands-on approach, which included a "forest summit" held in Portland, Ore., in April 1993.

Like all Appropriations members, Dicks brings to his district the kind of goodies that congressional watchdogs deride as pork barrel. In 1992, he obtained funding for a covered walkway in Tacoma that would provide a view of Mount Rainier on clear days.

This is in the tradition of Magnuson and Jackson, who in their day received near-universal praise from back home. But the public's temper has changed, and Dicks has taken some flak from those who see his actions as typical of

Washington 6

West — Bremerton

The 6th continues to be anchored in Bremerton, Tacoma and the southern Puget Sound region, but its shape changed considerably in 1992 redistricting. In the 1980s, the 6th was a fairly narrow district that ran well to the south of Tacoma. For the 1990s, though, the 6th has a squarish shape because it expands west and north from Bremerton and Tacoma all the way to the Pacific, taking in the mountainous and forested Olympic Peninsula. (The peninsula had been in the 2nd District.)

With this addition, the 6th becomes one of the key districts in the Northwest to watch as logging interests and environmentalists haggle over how to balance use of the forest with preservation of habitat for such endangered species as the northern spotted owl.

The unemployment rate in the 6th has been running above the state average, partly because demand for timber is slack and partly because some areas are off-limits to development while federal officials try to decide how to classify them.

Weyerhaeuser Co. still operates a mill in the peninsula community of Grays Harbor, but another timber giant, ITT Rainier, recently announced that it was closing its Grays Harbor plant.

On the peninsula, communities are trying to diversify to get beyond dependence on timber. The shipping of logs once was the only bill of fare in the port of Grays Harbor, but locals hope that a channel-deepening project now under way will help the port get into exporting many other commodities. Also in Grays Harbor County, a regional airport is being renovated to attract new business.

Other maritime pursuits boost the economy: The fishing industry is a large employer in Port Angeles on the Strait of Juan de Fuca and in Grays Harbor. The district is also home to the Puget Sound Naval Shipyard in Bremerton.

Tourism is a possible source of increased income for the peninsula. Located here are the Olympic National Park (in Clallam and Jefferson counties) and the Olympic National Forest. They attract thousands of sightseers annually to northwest Washington.

The inclusion of the lightly settled peninsula into the 6th gives the district new concerns, but still, the bulk of the district's residents live in urbanized areas. The combined clout of Pierce County (Tacoma) and Kitsap County (Bremerton) accounts for about two-thirds of the district's vote.

The 6th takes in downtown and northern Tacoma. This industrial city's blue-collar, heavily unionized electorate generally tilts Pierce County to Democrats. In the 6th District part of Pierce, Bill Clinton won 46 percent in 1992.

Low housing prices and a high quality of life helped Bremerton make the No. 1 ranking on Money magazine's 1990 list of "Best Places to live." The city, on the Kitsap Peninsula, has a strong labor vote, but surrounding Kitsap County (much of which is in the 1st District) leans Republican. Clinton won the 6th District's part of Kitsap with 38 percent in 1992.

1990 Population: 540,742. White 472,221 (87%), Black 28,997 (5%), Other 39,524 (7%). Hispanic origin 16,735 (3%). 18 and over 403,037 (75%), 62 and over 92,217 (17%). Median age: 34.

wasteful congressional spending. "How dare Norm Dicks be proud of being an Appropriations member?" said local critic Sherry Bockwinkel in 1991. "Most of these people are making outrageous spending decisions."

Bockwinkel had been campaign manager for Democrat Mike Collier, who ran against Dicks in the 1990 primary. After Dicks won easily, Bockwinkel led a 1991 referendum campaign to place term limits on elected officials, including members of Congress. A retroactive limit in the referendum would have barred senior members, including Dicks and Foley, from seeking re-election after 1992. It required a vigorous campaign by Washington's congressional delegation, warning of a disastrous loss of clout for the state, to defeat the measure by a 54 percent to 46 percent vote.

Bockwinkel and her supporters then dropped the retroactive clause from the term-limit proposal and offered it in November 1992. It was approved, 52 percent to 48 percent. Its six-year limit on House members and 12-year limit on U.S. senators is likely to face court challenge.

At Home: After three years as administrative assistant to Magnuson, Dicks decided to go home in 1976 and run for Congress. He had been planning a campaign in the 6th District whenever incumbent Democrat Floyd Hicks chose to retire, and when Hicks was named to the state Supreme Court in 1976, Dicks began running with his usual intensity.

He had to compete with three major candidates for the nomination: a young activist state representative, a former president of Pacific

Lutheran University and the mayor of Tacoma. But Dicks' ability to tap the resources of labor and other interest groups helped him put together a winning coalition. He won the primary with 36 percent of the vote.

Dicks had no trouble against a weak Republican that fall, but he went on a slide in the next two elections, pestered by Republican James Beaver, a conservative law professor from Tacoma. Dicks managed to clear 60 percent in 1978, but in 1980, Beaver was buoyed by financial support from the New Right, and held Dicks to 54 percent.

After that narrow escape, Dicks took steps to ensure that his 1982 race would not be so close. He took out full-page newspaper ads to tell voters that "Stormin' Norman" was as effective in the House as he had been on the college gridiron.

While Beaver had attacked the incumbent from the right, Dicks' 1982 challenger, GOP state Sen. Ted Haley, was more liberal. Haley painted the incumbent as a profligate spender too friendly with military contractors. But that charge just gave Dicks an excuse to talk about the projects he had brought home. He claimed credit for the completion of the Tacoma Spur Highway and numerous Navy ship overhauls at Bremerton. Dicks' 63 percent tally indicated he was moving toward security, and he has since won decisive re-election victories.

Republican Sen. Daniel J. Evans' decision to retire in 1988 at first piqued Dicks' interest. But two of his Democratic House colleagues, Mike Lowry and Don Bonker, jumped into the Senate contest, and Dicks recognized he faced an uncertain future as the most conservative candidate in a primary dominated by liberal voters. He stayed put in the 6th, and sailed to victory that year and in his next two elections.

Committees

Appropriations (10th of 37 Democrats)
Defense; Interior; Military Construction

Select Intelligence (3rd of 12 Democrats)
Oversight & Evaluation (chairman); Legislation

Elections

1992 General		
Norm Dicks (D)	152,933	(64%)
Lauri J. Phillips (R)	66,664	(28%)
Tom Donnelly (I)	14,490	(6%)
Jim Horrigan (LIBERT)	4,075	(2%)
1992 Primary †		
Norm Dicks (D)	73,832	(58%)
Lauri J. Phillips (R)	34,325	(27%)
Dennis Christiani (D)	10,306	(8%)
Tom Donnelly (I)	6,968	(5%)
Jim Horrigan (LIBERT)	1,882	(1%)
1990 General		
Norm Dicks (D)	79,079	(61%)
Norbert Mueller (R)	49,786	(39%)

† In Washington's "jungle primary," candidates of all parties are listed on one ballot.

Previous Winning Percentages: **1988** (68%) **1986** (71%) **1984** (66%) **1982** (63%) **1980** (54%) **1978** (61%) **1976** (74%)

District Vote for President

1992
D 106,373 (44%)
R 77,538 (32%)
I 60,578 (25%)

Campaign Finance

	Receipts	Receipts from PACs		Expend-itures
1992				
Dicks (D)	$546,865	$310,818	(57%)	$617,460
Phillips (R)	$6,266	0		$6,438
1990				
Dicks (D)	$392,043	$240,055	(61%)	$565,257
Mueller (R)	$8,048	0		$7,598

Key Votes

1993	
Require parental notification of minors' abortions	N
Require unpaid family and medical leave	Y
Approve national "motor voter" registration bill	Y
Approve budget increasing taxes and reducing deficit	Y
Approve economic stimulus plan	Y
1992	
Approve balanced-budget constitutional amendment	N
Close down space station program	N
Approve U.S. aid for former Soviet Union	Y
Allow shifting funds from defense to domestic programs	Y
1991	
Extend unemployment benefits using deficit financing	Y
Approve waiting period for handgun purchases	Y
Authorize use of force in Persian Gulf	N

Voting Studies

	Presidential Support		Party Unity		Conservative Coalition	
Year	**S**	**O**	**S**	**O**	**S**	**O**
1992	36	61	85	11	56	44
1991	36	59	85	9	43	54
1990	28	70	91	8	37	63
1989	38	57	91	7	41	59
1988	29	68	90	7	53	47
1987	28	71	87	5	42	51
1986	27	73	90	7	46	54
1985	35	61	85	9	44	53
1984	43	49	79	15	54	42
1983	38	61	83	11	34	60
1982	40	53	89	8	36	63
1981	50	42	68	24	60	35

Interest Group Ratings

Year	ADA	AFL-CIO	CCUS	ACU
1992	80	73	25	8
1991	70	82	38	5
1990	83	92	21	4
1989	75	91	40	7
1988	85	86	36	9
1987	76	88	13	9
1986	70	79	28	23
1985	70	88	38	24
1984	70	62	38	13
1983	75	94	32	13
1982	65	90	23	10
1981	50	80	42	27

7 Jim McDermott (D)

Of Seattle — Elected 1988; 3rd Term

Born: Dec. 28, 1936, Chicago, Ill.
Education: Wheaton College, B.S. 1958; U. of Illinois, M.D. 1963.
Military Service: Navy Medical Corps, 1968-70.
Occupation: Psychiatrist.
Family: Divorced; two children.
Religion: Episcopalian.
Political Career: Wash. House, 1971-73; sought Democratic nomination for governor, 1972; Wash. Senate, 1975-87; Democratic nominee for governor, 1980; sought Democratic nomination for governor, 1984.
Capitol Office: 1707 Longworth Bldg. 20515; 225-3106.

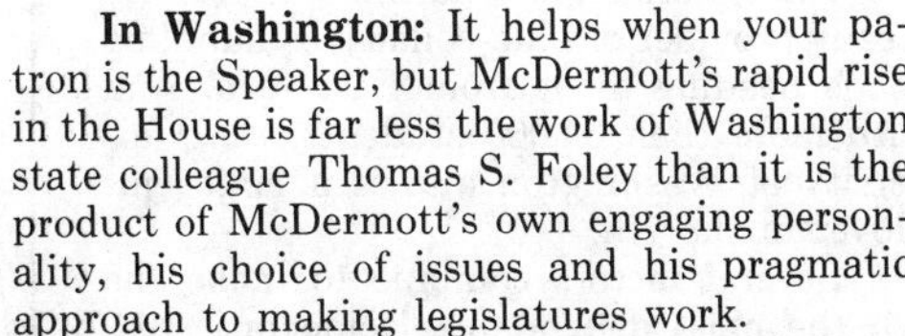

In Washington: It helps when your patron is the Speaker, but McDermott's rapid rise in the House is far less the work of Washington state colleague Thomas S. Foley than it is the product of McDermott's own engaging personality, his choice of issues and his pragmatic approach to making legislatures work.

After only one term, he managed to win a seat on the refined Ways and Means Committee, where even as the lowliest Democrat he was able to make an impact. An uncharacteristically large turnover prior to the 103rd Congress moved McDermott to the middle ranks of the committee.

But where much is given, much may be required: McDermott in 1991 was handed the unwelcome task of serving on the House ethics committee, where he sat on the task force investigating abuses of the House bank. His hard work and even disposition were noticed, and he ascended to the chairmanship of the ethics panel in the 103rd.

McDermott's politics are about as liberal as can be found in Congress. But his intellect and reserved manner have made him a player in policy debates, not a gadfly confined to the left fringe. A veteran of his state Legislature, he has also spent time presiding over the House, learning its rules and mores. And though he takes positions that are sometimes well outside his party's mainstream, McDermott — with his full silver beard and ready sense of humor — is well-liked by colleagues.

As early as the fall of 1989, McDermott was talked up for a vacancy on Ways and Means by virtue of his expertise on health issues (a psychiatrist by profession) and ties to Foley. Passed over that time, McDermott made it aboard in the 102nd Congress. One of just two physicians in the House, McDermott wanted Ways and Means less for the tax debate than for his goal of national health insurance.

While a state legislator, he wrote legislation creating state-sponsored health coverage for the unemployed and uninsured working poor. As a House freshman, he sponsored a bill to help states plan health-care initiatives that could later serve as models for a national program. At the start of the 103rd Congress, McDermott staked out the most liberal position in the House, introducing a bill to create a single-payer system of health insurance with the government as the conduit for claims and payments.

During his first two years on Ways and Means, McDermott had a leading role in the tax component of a sweeping energy policy bill. McDermott pushed for an increase in employer-provided, tax-free mass transit subsidies, and he helped form a coalition on Ways and Means to finance this and other conservation and alternative-energy provisions. Among the tax changes used to offset the new tax benefits was a cap on employer-provided, tax-free parking, and an increase in the excise tax on chemicals that destroy upper-atmosphere ozone.

In the 102nd Congress, McDermott founded a congressional task force on the international AIDS crisis, one of his primary concerns. He continues to chair that task force in the 103rd. When he was still a freshman on the Banking Committee he had pushed a federal role in housing AIDS victims. Despite strong opposition from Republicans, McDermott was instrumental in winning a $156 million authorization for housing assistance for people with AIDS. He also spoke for AIDS patients during debate on the Americans with Disabilities Act, opposing an amendment to allow restaurants to transfer workers with contagious diseases out of food-handling jobs. Alluding to medical evidence that AIDS cannot be spread through food, McDermott said, "This amendment asks us to make policy in spite of the facts we know, in deliberate deference to the fears and preju-

Washington 7

Seattle and suburbs

Ferryboats plying the clear-blue waters of Puget Sound, snow-capped Mount Rainier looming to the southeast — these images identify Seattle to most people. Thousands of newcomers settled in the Seattle area during the 1980s, drawn by the city's pleasant aura and an economy prospering on aerospace manufacturing and trade with the Pacific Rim.

But there was a down side to that growth: traffic-choked highways and streets, downtown towers blocking the sun and suburban developments devouring open space. Concern that Seattle was becoming a less livable place spawned a slow-growth movement that in May 1989 managed the passage of an initiative placing limits on downtown development.

Downtown remains an architecturally diverse blend of the Northwest's tallest skyscrapers and turn-of-the-century buildings erected when the city was in its infancy.

Tourists take in the Space Needle at the old World's Fair site; its observation level offers a commanding view. Visitors and locals alike gather at Pike Place Market, a reconditioned old outdoor market in the pier district that offers a variety of foods and shopping wares. Seattle is becoming known for its active music scene, and the Kingdome hosts a variety of sporting events.

Seattle, with a population of 516,000, has a number of ethnic enclaves; its varied blue-collar population includes well-defined Scandinavian, Italian, Asian and Hispanic communities.

In economic terms, the fortunes of the 7th — and the entire Seattle area — are tied closely to the vitality of the Boeing aircraft company. Interstate 5 heading north into Seattle parallels the runway of Boeing Field. Boeing thrived during the defense boom of the 1980s; now though, defense spending is on a slide, as is the commercial airline industry.

In an announcement sure to have profound repercussions on the economy of Seattle and the entire state of Washington, Boeing said in early 1993 that it would be laying off thousands of workers. Both white-collar and blue-collar workers will be affected.

The other big economic pillar in the 7th, the export-import business, is a fairly steady provider of blue-collar jobs handling goods heading to or from East Asia. And with more than 34,000 students, the University of Washington also is a large employer in the 7th.

Several factors combine to make the 7th the most dependable Democratic district in the state: the strength of organized labor in this industrial area, a minority population that is the largest among Washington House districts (10 percent black, 12 percent Asian) and a substantial bloc of liberal urbanites.

In 1992 presidential voting, Bill Clinton won 65 percent in the 7th. That was over 20 points better than his showing in any other district in the state.

1990 Population: 540,747. White 408,480 (76%), Black 53,926 (10%), Other 78,341 (14%). Hispanic origin 19,148 (4%). 18 and over 447,790 (83%), 62 and over 92,223 (17%). Median age: 35.

dices of others." Nonetheless, the amendment passed, but was later dropped in conference.

As a freshman, McDermott proved his abilities to operate as an insider, when he sought and got a seat on Banking's International Development Subcommittee, and then preserved the panel's jurisdiction.

He wanted to be in a position to look out for the Export-Import Bank, a major source of money for foreign airlines that purchased planes from his district's most important employer, the Boeing Co. But Ohio Democrat Mary Rose Oakar, the new chairman of the Economic Stabilization Subcommittee, threw a wrench in McDermott's plans when she tried to grab oversight of the Ex-Im Bank for herself. McDermott moved quickly to counter Oakar, and prevailed at the committee's organizing caucus meeting.

In the 102nd Congress and at the start of the 103rd, McDermott took the lead in trying to amend a sweeping civil rights bill that, when enacted in 1991, overturned the effects of several Supreme Court decisions. One of the court decisions involved charges of discrimination affecting an Alaska cannery, the Wards Cove Packing Co. Just before the 1991 law was passed by the Senate, a last-minute amendment exempted workers at that plant from the benefits of the new law. McDermott's bill would repeal the Senate amendment.

In his first two terms, McDermott also could be found organizing liberal opposition to foreign policy decisions of the Bush administration. In the early stages of the Persian Gulf War, for example, McDermott was among 42 legislators who wrote to President Bush urging against further military escalation, such as a ground offensive.

And before a cease-fire in El Salvador's civil war, McDermott was a leading House opponent of continued U.S. military assistance to El Salvador. He proposed essentially a complete reversal of U.S. policy and the provision of foreign aid only for basic human needs.

At Home: Even from a continent away, the 1988 open-seat race for the 7th caught McDermott's eye. The former state senator left his job in Africa to stage a political comeback.

McDermott's earlier political career included more than 14 years in the state Legislature, and three unsuccessful campaigns for governor. But in 1987 McDermott quit the state Senate to take a three-year job in Zaire as a Foreign Service psychiatrist.

When 7th District Democrat Mike Lowry tried for the Senate in 1988, replacement talk centered on Democrats closer to home, such as Seattle City Councilman (and later mayor) Norm Rice and King County Assessor Ruthe Ridder. Then, in February, McDermott sent word from Zaire that he had been released from his Foreign Service commitment and would seek Lowry's seat.

With his record as a legislative leader and visibility from statewide campaigns, he soon became the front-runner. He won endorsements from the state labor council and most local party organizations. He had more money and won the primary after a late media blitz. In the strongly Democratic 7th, his November win was a given, as were his 1990 and 1992 re-elections. Redistricting in 1992 left the 7th clearly the most Democratic district in the state.

Born in Chicago, McDermott moved to Seattle in 1966 to set up a practice, then left for a stint as a Navy psychiatrist in Long Beach, Calif. In 1970 he came back and won a state House race. In 1972 he ran third in the Democratic gubernatorial primary. After winning state Senate elections in 1974 and 1978, he challenged Democratic Gov. Dixy Lee Ray in the 1980 primary. He beat the conservative Ray, but then lost to Republican John Spellman. His third try for governor flopped, as he lost by nearly 2-to-1 in a 1984 primary against Booth Gardner (who unseated Spellman and served two terms as governor).

Committees

Standards of Official Conduct (Chairman)

District of Columbia (4th of 8 Democrats)
Fiscal Affairs & Health (chairman); Judiciary & Education

Ways & Means (14th of 24 Democrats)
Health; Human Resources

Elections

1992 General		
Jim McDermott (D)	222,604	(78%)
Glenn C. Hampson (R)	54,149	(19%)
Paul Glumaz (I)	7,197	(3%)
1992 Primary †		
Jim McDermott (D)	102,818	(73%)
Glenn C. Hampson (R)	26,042	(18%)
Ken Yeager (D)	8,741	(6%)
Paul Glumaz (I)	3,288	(2%)
1990 General		
Jim McDermott (D)	106,761	(72%)
Larry Penberthy (R)	35,511	(24%)
Robbie Scherr (SW)	5,370	(4%)

† In Washington's "jungle primary," candidates of all parties are listed on one ballot.

Previous Winning Percentage: **1988** (76%)

District Vote for President

1992
D 191,781 (66%)
R 54,478 (19%)
I 45,167 (15%)

Campaign Finance

	Receipts	Receipts from PACs		Expend-itures
1992				
McDermott (D)	$222,346	$169,015	(76%)	$191,472
Hampson (R)	$39,520	0		$30,317
1990				
McDermott (D)	$230,973	$196,253	(85%)	$204,296

Key Votes

1993	
Require parental notification of minors' abortions	N
Require unpaid family and medical leave	Y
Approve national "motor voter" registration bill	Y
Approve budget increasing taxes and reducing deficit	Y
Approve economic stimulus plan	Y
1992	
Approve balanced-budget constitutional amendment	N
Close down space station program	Y
Approve U.S. aid for former Soviet Union	Y
Allow shifting funds from defense to domestic programs	Y
1991	
Extend unemployment benefits using deficit financing	Y
Approve waiting period for handgun purchases	Y
Authorize use of force in Persian Gulf	N

Voting Studies

	Presidential Support		Party Unity		Conservative Coalition	
Year	**S**	**O**	**S**	**O**	**S**	**O**
1992	18	82	94	4	13	88
1991	27	70	95	5	8	92
1990	20	79	92	5	7	93
1989	29	67	94	2	10	85

Interest Group Ratings

Year	ADA	AFL-CIO	CCUS	ACU
1992	95	83	25	0
1991	95	83	20	0
1990	94	92	21	0
1989	95	100	20	4

8 Jennifer Dunn (R)

Of Bellevue — Elected 1992; 1st Term

Born: July 29, 1941, Seattle, Wash.
Education: Stanford U., 1959; U. of Washington, 1960-62; Stanford U., A.B. 1963.
Occupation: State party official.
Family: Divorced; two children.
Religion: Episcopalian.
Political Career: Wash. Republican Party chairman, 1980-92.
Capitol Office: 1641 Longworth Bldg. 20515; 225-7761.

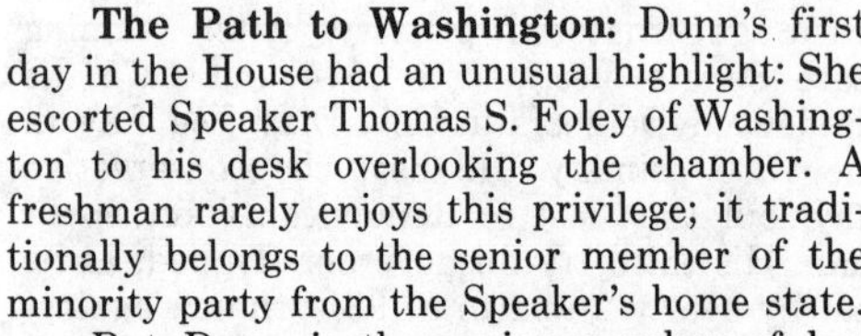

The Path to Washington: Dunn's first day in the House had an unusual highlight: She escorted Speaker Thomas S. Foley of Washington to his desk overlooking the chamber. A freshman rarely enjoys this privilege; it traditionally belongs to the senior member of the minority party from the Speaker's home state.

But Dunn is the senior member of her state's GOP delegation by virtue of being the only House Republican from Washington. On her bittersweet Election Day, she won a congressional seat in her first try for public office and watched her party lose every other major race in her state: president, senator, governor and all of the other eight House seats.

That mattered more to Dunn than it might to some candidates, because she served as chairman of the state GOP for 11 years, resigning in 1992 to run for the 8th District seat being vacated by GOP Rep. Rod Chandler (who ran unsuccessfully for the Senate).

At one time in Dunn's tenure, Republicans had held the governorship, both Senate seats and near-parity in House and legislative seats. But a slumping economy, coupled with intraparty squabbles over social policy issues such as abortion and homosexuality, have taken their toll.

Upon arriving on Capitol Hill, Dunn was picked for the GOP's Committee on Committees, the body that makes Republican committee assignments. While an honor, this selection had its price. Dunn said that as a member of the selection committee, she sacrificed her chance for a seat on the Energy and Commerce panel, which had been her first choice.

Dunn has also shown an early interest in shaking things up. During a closed-door markup of the 1993 tax bill, Dunn was one of a group of GOP freshmen, led by Richard W. Pombo of California, that held a news conference outside the Ways and Means hearing room to protest the committee's practice of closing markups to the public. To make the point, the group unveiled a sign that read "DO NOT DISTURB!!! DEMOCRATS RAISING TAXES!!!"

The next week, Dunn and Pombo introduced a resolution to amend the rules of the House to require that all committees or subcommittees hold open meetings except in matters of national security or where a person's reputation could be damaged.

Dunn fits a more traditional than contemporary pattern for women officeholders. Instead of entering politics from academia, the law or issue activism, she graduated from college, married and had two children before becoming involved as a campaign volunteer. As her two sons grew up, Dunn got involved in politics full time.

When Ronald Reagan was swept into the White House in 1980 and Republicans won the Washington governorship, Dunn was elected state party chair. She later served as vice chairman of the executive committee of the Republican National Committee and as chairman of the national organization of GOP state chairmen. Reagan also appointed her to his advisory councils on volunteer service and historic preservation.

Although she supports abortion rights, she was respected by both sides for her handling of that issue. Nevertheless, when she became a candidate, Dunn had to deal with a sharp challenge from Pam Roach, a first-term GOP state senator and an ardent opponent of abortion. Roach cast Dunn as the epitome of the older and more affluent suburbs of King County, where Republicans are often more focused on economics than on social issues. Roach, a Mormon, had the backing of many religious conservatives and anti-abortion activists.

Roach's strategy very nearly worked. The all-party primary field included two other Republicans. In the end, Dunn's 32 percent share of the primary vote was barely enough to eclipse Roach's 29 percent.

Things got easier in the general election. Abortion was no longer an issue, and Dunn's Democratic opponent, Mercer Island businessman George O. Tamblyn, had switched parties in the course of the 1992 election cycle. Tamblyn was unable to make a case against Dunn's conservative economics and moderate social views. She collected 60 percent of the November vote.

Washington 8

Puget Sound (East) — King County suburbs; Bellevue

The 8th includes some of Seattle's most prosperous suburbs as well as the landmark that affords the city unique allure — snow-capped, 14,410 foot Mount Rainier.

Encompassing the mainly affluent suburbs and exurbs east of Seattle, the 8th has long been considered the state's most Republican district west of the Cascade Mountains.

In the 1980s, 35 percent population growth in the 8th also made it the state's fastest-growing district.

In redistricting, large chunks of land that had been in the 8th were put into the newly created 9th District (the extra seat that Washington gained in reapportionment for the 1990s).

The 8th District retains a GOP tilt, although independents are influential. The 1992 House election was a lopsided 60 percent victory by Republican Dunn. However, at the same time, Bill Clinton narrowly carried the 8th over George Bush, 38 percent to 34 percent, with independent Ross Perot pulling in 27 percent.

For the past 20 years, the suburban area covered by the 8th enjoyed its position as a beneficiary of Seattle's economic boom. But while the boom brought benefits, it also brought the traffic jams and rising housing costs that are the downside of growth. While not as obvious as the "no-growth" movement in Seattle — where an initiative to restrict downtown development won approval in 1989 — there is a "slow-down" constituency in the 8th.

With almost 87,000 residents (some of whom live in the 1st), Bellevue is the population center of the 8th and of the King County suburbs that make up the bulk of the district.

Separating Seattle and Bellevue is Lake Washington, and in the middle of the lake is the exclusive community of Mercer Island.

While Bellevue's white-collar constituency offers strong GOP votes, Mercer Island shows an independent streak, often offering up a split ticket.

Part of the reason for the difference is that Mercer Island has a sizable contingent of Jewish residents who tend to be more liberal on social issues.

In the southern half of the district is Pierce County, a rural, sparsely populated section of the 8th dotted with small towns that have attracted a substantial number of retirees and families eager to flee the hassles of urban living.

Residents of the 8th work at a variety of white- and blue-collar businesses, but Boeing, located in Renton, is a key employer here as it is throughout the metropolitan area.

Boeing announced in January 1993 that it would lay off thousands of workers in the next few years because of decreased demand for its commercial and military aircraft.

Other large local employers are Paccar, which manufactures trucks, and the computer companies of Microsoft and Nintendo.

1990 Population: 540,742. White 497,553 (92%), Black 8,876 (2%), Other 34,313 (6%). Hispanic origin 12,434 (2%). 18 and over 388,671 (72%), 62 and over 53,320 (10%). Median age: 33.

Committees

Housc Administration (7th of 7 Republicans)
Personnel & Police (ranking); Accounts; Elections

Public Works & Transportation (12th of 24 Republicans)
Aviation; Economic Development; Surface Transportation

Science, Space & Technology (20th of 22 Republicans)
Space

Joint Organization of Congress

Campaign Finance

	Receipts	Receipts from PACs		Expend-itures
1992				
Dunn (R)	$709,207	$168,373	(24%)	$704,674
Tamblyn (D)	$410,842	$31,150	(8%)	$410,465
Adams (I)	$14,104	0		$14,104

Key Votes

1993	
Require parental notification of minors' abortions	Y
Require unpaid family and medical leave	N
Approve national "motor voter" registration bill	?
Approve budget increasing taxes and reducing deficit	N
Approve economic stimulus plan	N

Elections

1992 General		
Jennifer Dunn (R)	155,874	(60%)
George O. Tamblyn (D)	87,611	(34%)
Bob Adams (I)	14,686	(6%)
1992 Primary †		
Jennifer Dunn (R)	39,405	(32%)
George O. Tamblyn (D)	28,213	(23%)
Pam Roach (R)	35,387	(29%)
Roy A. Ferguson (R)	8,832	(7%)
Michael Campbell (R)	8,166	(7%)
Bob Adams (I)	3,671	(3%)

† In Washington's "jungle primary," candidates of all parties are listed on one ballot.

District Vote for President

	1992	
D	102,857	(38%)
R	92,276	(34%)
I	72,526	(27%)

9 Mike Kreidler (D)

Of Olympia — Elected 1992; 1st Term

Born: Sept. 28, 1943, Tacoma, Wash.

Education: Pacific U., B.S. 1967, D.Optom. 1969; U. of California, Los Angeles, M.P.H. 1972.

Military Service: Army Medical Corps, 1969-71; Army Reserve, 1971-present.

Occupation: Optometrist.

Family: Wife, Lela Lopez; three children.

Religion: Church of Christ.

Political Career: North Thurston School Board, 1973-77; Wash. House, 1977-85; Wash. Senate, 1985-93.

Capitol Office: 1535 Longworth Bldg. 20515; 225-8901.

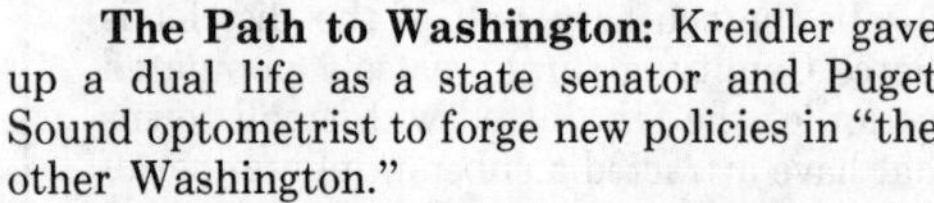

The Path to Washington: Kreidler gave up a dual life as a state senator and Puget Sound optometrist to forge new policies in "the other Washington."

A 20-year practitioner in a nonprofit, managed-care cooperative and key architect of a new Washington state health strategy, Kreidler entered the House with a seat on the Energy and Commerce Committee. He successfully won an assignment to the Health Subcommittee so he can pursue his goal of changing the way health care is distributed and financed.

Kreidler's health-care model is the Washington state proposal that he helped write. The plan calls for universal access to comprehensive health services and outlines both cost containment standards and incentives for choosing care programs. It also calls for doubling state resources devoted to public health care by 2000.

In May 1993, Kreidler supported an amendment offered by Republican Alex McMillan of North Carolina. To try to reduce spiraling Medicare costs, the amendment would force couples earning between $125,000 and $200,000 to pay 75 percent of the premium that goes to pay doctor's bills, three times what they currently pay. The amendment failed on voice vote.

Kreidler, a lieutenant colonel in the Army Reserves, also will sit on the Veterans' Affairs Committee. The 9th has more veterans than 90 percent of the nation's 434 other districts, as well as two big bases — the Army's Fort Lewis and the Air Force's McChord — and a large system of military hospitals.

Kreidler entered the race for Congress in February, when other potential candidates were leery of declaring their candidacy in the newly created 9th District. Not only did an evenly divided party registration make it a gamble for both major parties, but its very existence was threatened by a Massachusetts reapportionment lawsuit until late June.

In September, Kreidler captured the Democratic nomination by outdistancing two primary challengers. That victory, coupled with a rise in Democratic momentum nationwide, brought him a substantial campaign treasury to raise his profile in the northern counties, where his Republican opponent, state Sen. Pete von Reichbauer, resides.

Von Reichbauer, vice president of a food services company, won the Republican nomination in a bitter race against King County Councilman Paul Barden with 26 percent of the primary vote.

Both general-election candidates had been leaders in the Legislature — Kreidler on health care and cleaning up Puget Sound, and von Reichbauer on business and insurance issues; both put improving the economy at the top of their congressional agendas.

Kreidler supported gun control and advocated universal health care overseen by the federal government, and the fiscally conservative von Reichbauer opposed both. But the campaign included more than policy issues. Kreidler was criticized for living in Olympia; von Reichbauer was branded "a consummate political animal."

Von Reichbauer was criticized for getting free rent for his campaign headquarters and using his position as state Senate Financial Institutions and Insurance Committee chairman to collect campaign contributions from insurance companies and other businesses.

In the final days of the campaign, von Reichbauer launched an attack that boomeranged. He attacked Kreidler for voting against the Eli Creekmore child-protection legislation, named for the Everett toddler who was abused and then murdered in the mid-1980s.

However, the Democratic candidate and three newspapers pointed out that Kreidler had been among the sponsors of a legislative package that aimed to tighten child-protection standards, improve the training of social workers and strengthen penalties for abusers. Kreidler said the one bill he voted against would have limited the role of Child Protective Services.

That was the last straw for von Reichbauer. Kreidler won 52 percent of the vote.

Washington 9

Puget Sound — Tacoma; parts of King, Pierce and Thurston counties

Population growth during the 1980s earned Washington a ninth House seat in reapportionment, and the state's redistricting commission drew the new 9th right where the growth had been greatest: in the suburbs and exurbs east and south of Seattle.

The new 9th strings together an array of communities without much sense of commonality, starting at the south end of Seattle, going on down past Tacoma and then heading west to Olympia, the state capital. The district's "Main Street" is a 60-mile stretch of Interstate 5, where the crush of commuter and commercial traffic sometimes keeps the road jammed nearly all day.

Most of the residents of the 9th rely on their autos to get them to work — in office towers in Seattle and Bellevue, in factories and workshops of Boeing or at the shipyards and docks of Tacoma (where mammoth cargoes of logs are loaded for shipment).

Other sources of income and jobs in the 9th include the office and industrial complexes around Sea-Tac International Airport, McChord Air Force Base and the Army's Fort Lewis (Pierce County). The military presence that has long shaped the Puget Sound region is inescapable in the 9th. Veterans, active military personnel and their families constitute about one-fifth of the district population.

Some residents of the 9th make their living off the land: At the southern reaches of the district, along the Thurston County border, forests and farms predominate.

Just over half the 9th's vote is cast in the district's northeastern end, a slice of King County that includes the headquarters of the timber giant Weyerhaeuser Co., in Federal Way. The district's largest city (68,000 people), Federal Way recently incorporated to get a handle on its growth.

But if King contributes the majority of votes in the 9th, most of the district's land area lies in Pierce and Thurston counties. Here, many residents live in scattered subdivisions and unincorporated areas where open space is plentiful and farm animals are not uncommon. Some of these communities surround older, established towns such as Puyallup (home of the Western Washington State Fairgrounds), while for others, "downtown" consists of commercial strip developments and suburban malls. One local political consultant called the 9th "an entire district with nothing at its heart but Chuck E. Cheeses."

The political character of the 9th is just beginning to emerge. While Washington does not register voters by party, a 1992 poll found Democrats and Republicans within one percentage point of each other in the 9th (with a 41 percent plurality calling themselves independents). In the September 1992 open primary, candidates calling themselves Democrats got nearly as many votes (47,456) as those with the GOP label (48,773).

In his two presidential bids, Ronald Reagan ran well in the areas that make up the 9th. But George Bush struggled here in 1988 and stumbled badly four years later, losing by 11 percentage points to Bill Clinton as Ross Perot polled 26 percent in the district.

1990 Population: 540,744. White 462,288 (85%), Black 29,450 (5%), Other 49,006 (9%). Hispanic origin 19,816 (4%). 18 and over 397,317 (73%), 62 and over 60,893 (11%). Median age: 31.

Committees

Energy & Commerce (25th of 27 Democrats)
Energy & Power; Health & the Environment

Veterans' Affairs (20th of 21 Democrats)
Hospitals & Health Care; Housing & Memorial Affairs; Oversight & Investigations

Campaign Finance

1992	Receipts	Receipts from PACs		Expenditures
Kreidler (D)	$430,480	$165,387	(38%)	$430,476
von Reichbauer (R)	$420,106	$138,600	(33%)	$414,594
Wilson (I)	$2,128	0		$2,130

Key Votes

1993

Require parental notification of minors' abortions	N
Require unpaid family and medical leave	Y
Approve national "motor voter" registration bill	Y
Approve budget increasing taxes and reducing deficit	Y
Approve economic stimulus plan	Y

Elections

1992 General		
Mike Kreidler (D)	110,902	(52%)
Pete von Reichbauer (R)	91,910	(43%)
Brian Wilson (I)	6,585	(3%)
Timothy J. Brill (I)	3,522	(2%)
1992 Primary †		
Pete von Reichbauer (R)	25,917	(26%)
Mike Kreidler (D)	23,687	(23%)
Paul Barden (R)	22,856	(23%)
Tim McDonnell (D)	14,387	(14%)
Dick Hill (D)	9,382	(9%)
Brian Wilson (I)	3,263	(3%)
Timothy J. Brill (I)	1,606	(2%)

† In Washington's "jungle primary," candidates of all parties are listed on one ballot.

District Vote for President

	1992	
D	93,963	(42%)
R	69,562	(31%)
I	58,039	(26%)

West Virginia

STATE DATA

Governor:
Gaston Caperton (D)
First elected: 1988
Length of term: 4 years
Term expires: 1/97
Salary: $72,000
Term limit: 2 consecutive terms
Phone: (304) 558-2000
Born: Feb. 21, 1940; Charleston, W.Va.
Education: U. of North Carolina, B.A. 1963
Occupation: Insurance executive
Family: Wife, Rachel Worby; two children
Religion: Episcopalian
Political Career: No previous office

No lieutenant governor

State election official: (304) 345-4000
Democratic headquarters: (304) 342-8121
Republican headquarters: (304) 344-3446

REDISTRICTING

West Virginia lost one House seat in reapportionment, dropping from four districts to three. The legislature passed the map Oct. 11, 1991; the governor signed it Oct. 12. Federal court upheld the map Jan. 7, 1992.

STATE LEGISLATURE

Legislature. Meets January-March yearly, except during gubernatorial election years, when it meets February-April.

Senate: 34 members, 4-year terms
1992 breakdown: 32D, 2R; 29 men, 5 women; 34 whites
Salary: $6,500
Phone: (304) 357-7800

House of Delegates: 100 members, 2-year terms
1992 breakdown: 79D, 21R; 83 men, 17 women; 98 whites, 1 black
Salary: $6,500
Phone: (304) 340-3200

URBAN STATISTICS

City	Pop.
Charleston Mayor Kent S. Hall, R	57,287
Huntington Mayor Robert Nelson, D	54,844
Wheeling Mayor John W. Lipphardt, N-P	34,882
Parkersburg Mayor Helen Albright, R	33,862
Morgantown Mayor Charlene Marshall, N-P	25,879

U.S. CONGRESS

Senate: 2 D, 0 R
House: 3 D, 0 R

TERM LIMITS

For Congress: No
For state offices: No

ELECTIONS

1992 Presidential Vote

Bill Clinton	48.4%
George Bush	35.4%
Ross Perot	15.9%

1988 Presidential Vote

Michael S. Dukakis	52%
George Bush	48%

1984 Presidential Vote

Ronald Reagan	55%
Walter F. Mondale	45%

POPULATION

1990 population		1,793,477
1980 population		1,949,644
Percent change		−8%
Rank among states:		34
White		96%
Black		3%
Hispanic		<1%
Asian or Pacific islander		<1%
Urban		36%
Rural		64%
Born in state		99%
Foreign-born		1%
Under age 18	443,577	25%
Ages 18-64	1,081,003	60%
65 and older	268,897	15%
Median age		35.4

MISCELLANEOUS

Capital: Charleston
Number of counties: 55
Per capita income: $14,174 (1991)
Rank among states: 49
Total area: 24,232 sq. miles
Rank among states: 41

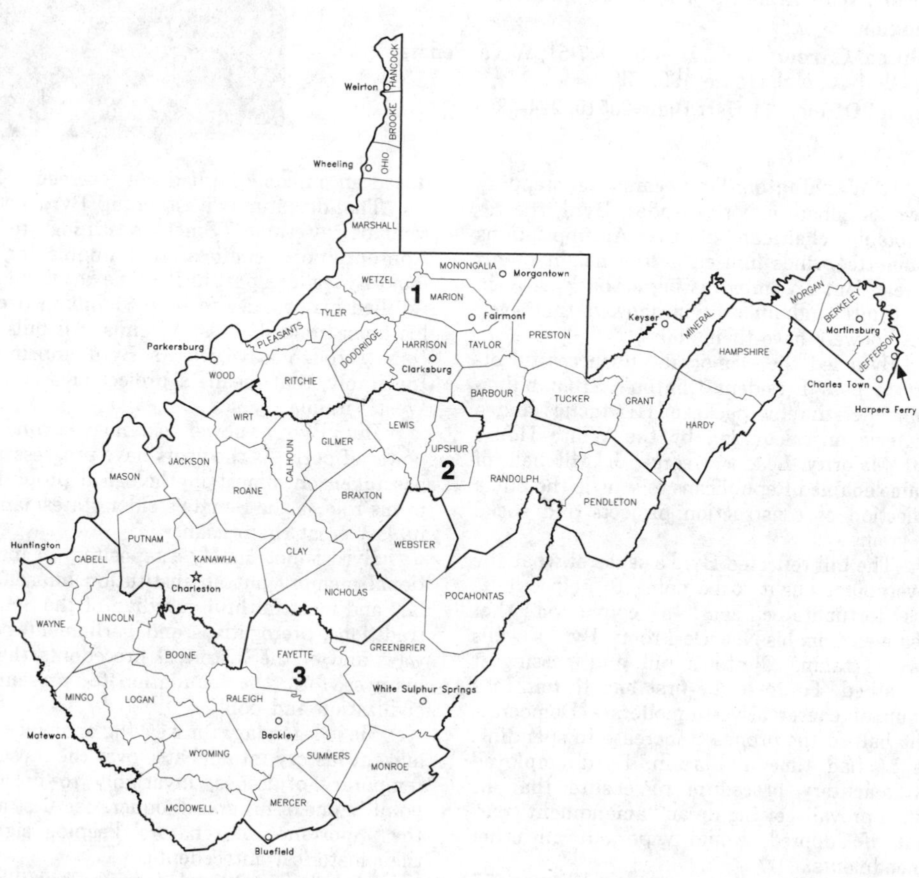
HANCOCK
Weirton
BROOKE
Wheeling
OHIO
MARSHALL
MONONGALIA
Morgantown
WETZEL
1
MARION
Fairmont
TYLER
PLEASANTS
Parkersburg
DODDRIDGE
HARRISON
Clarksburg
TAYLOR
PRESTON
WOOD
RITCHIE
BARBOUR
TUCKER
Keyser
MINERAL
MORGAN
BERKELEY
Martinsburg
HAMPSHIRE
JEFFERSON
Charles Town
Harpers Ferry
GRANT
HARDY
WIRT
LEWIS
UPSHUR
2
GILMER
CALHOUN
JACKSON
MASON
ROANE
BRAXTON
RANDOLPH
PENDLETON
PUTNAM
Huntington
CABELL
KANAWHA
Charleston
CLAY
WEBSTER
NICHOLAS
POCAHONTAS
WAYNE
LINCOLN
BOONE
FAYETTE
3
GREENBRIER
White Sulphur Springs
MINGO
LOGAN
RALEIGH
Beckley
Matewan
WYOMING
SUMMERS
MONROE
MCDOWELL
MERCER
Bluefield

Robert C. Byrd (D)

Of Sophia — Elected 1958; 6th Term

Born: Nov. 20, 1917, North Wilkesboro, N.C.
Education: American U., J.D. 1963.
Occupation: Lawyer.
Family: Wife, Erma Ora James; two children.
Religion: Baptist.
Political Career: W.Va. House, 1947-51; W.Va. Senate, 1951-53; U.S. House, 1953-59.
Capitol Office: 311 Hart Bldg. 20510; 224-3954.

In Washington: Four years after stepping down as Senate majority leader, Byrd, the redoubtable chairman of the Appropriations Committee, finds himself at the height of his powers. But an embarrassing setback early in the Clinton administration showed that even those powers have their limits.

Byrd led the Democrats' unsuccessful effort to pass President Clinton's $16.3 billion economic stimulus package. His tactics and a strategic miscalculation by the White House and Majority Leader George J. Mitchell of Maine enabled Republicans to scuttle the bill, a collection of construction projects and social programs.

The bill reflected Byrd's sense of what the government ought to be doing to help out its less fortunate citizens, a conviction that stemmed from his New Deal roots. Byrd saw his task as taking Clinton's bill and passing it unscathed. To do so, he first had to rein in a group of conservative-to-moderate Democrats who balked the proposed increase in spending. As he had time and again, Byrd employed parliamentary procedure to ensure that he would prevail, setting up an "amendment tree" that, if adopted, would wipe out all other amendments.

The strategy (which Mitchell and White House officials had endorsed) kept dissident Democrats from joining with Republicans to whittle down the proposal. Its principal effect, however, was to anger and galvanize Senate Republicans, who howled that Byrd was abusing powers that should only be wielded by the majority leader. All 43 Republicans voted repeatedly against allowing floor consideration of the bill, even after Byrd withdrew his amendment tree; their filibuster, stiffened by the White House's reluctance to cut the bill's cost, ultimately killed the package.

The episode constituted an early turning point in the new president's administration. It forced Clinton to acknowledge that winning approval for his programs would require some deal-cutting with the Senate. For Byrd, it was an uncommon instance when his actions produced an outcome he had not foreseen.

That defeat notwithstanding, Byrd's power remains awesome. Since returning to the Appropriations chair after relinquishing the majority leader's post in 1989, he has more than fulfilled his promise to send $1 billion back to his home state of West Virginia. All bills that come through leave with a Byrd imprimatur. Inevitably, that means a project or a study in West Virginia.

But Byrd's power extends beyond the power of pork. As the years have progressed, he has taken on almost mythological proportions in his role as the Senate's elder statesman and its last great rhetorician.

Byrd is not merely a repository of institutional memory but an institution himself, the last and most faithful guardian of the Senate's traditions, prerogatives and parliamentary byways and of the historical precedents that, in his eyes, form the foundation for present-day civilization and politics.

He is legendary for weaving analogies from ancient history into debates over the most contemporary of issues, invariably to bolster a point in one of his grandiloquent lectures about the importance of senators' keeping sight of their historical antecedents.

In 1991, he defended Anita F. Hill's belated accusation of sexual harassment by Supreme Court nominee Clarence Thomas by citing the 6th century A.D. historian Procopius' reluctance to publish a scandalous history.

His mastery of parliamentary arcana and his love for the institution are unparalleled, as is his seemingly limitless vocabulary. What other member could conceivably have described detractors of pork barrel spending as "ultracrepidarian critics," as he did in 1993? (Ultracrepidarian: going beyond one's sphere; presumptuous.) "I have a reverence for this institution," he said in 1993. "I have a reverence for the legislative branch under the Constitution. I have a reverence for the separation of powers and checks and balances of the Constitution. I have a reverence for American history. I have a reverence for the history of England. I have a reverence for the history of the Romans. I have a reverence for history."

"'Whatsoever thy hand findeth to do, do it with thy might,'" he said in 1989, quoting Ecclesiastes. "I have that sense of duty. I follow it meticulously."

Byrd's didactic fascination with the Bible and ancient history suggests that he wants to leave as enduring a mark on the mores of his beloved Senate as he is leaving on the hills of West Virginia. But the changing times that ushered him out as Democratic leader may make that task impossible; with his quirky ways and focus on carrying home federal largess, Byrd seems more a symbol of a bygone Senate than a force that will shape the chamber's future.

"I am chagrined at what appears to be a rank thoughtlessness on the part of some members in both houses and an absolutely uncaring attitude about this institution, an absence entirely of institutional memory, an almost intended, it seems to be, lack of knowledge of history," he said in 1993.

Emblematic of Byrd's love of tradition is the seriousness with which he approaches his role as Senate president pro tempore, a job he inherited in 1989 as the most senior member of the Senate majority. The ritualistic position entitles Byrd to preside over the Senate whenever he chooses, and he has done so more than any predecessor in memory. He has also put more money into the office; in his first four years, its annual budget rose from $156,000 to $432,000.

An intensely private man, Byrd was often criticized during his 12-year tenure as Democratic leader for being too stilted and old-fashioned to represent his party in the television age. He has a strong drive for self-improvement; it propelled him from the coal patch to the top levels of U.S. politics, and it motivates him to study and absorb the words of history's great men. But when he muses on the Senate floor about the thoughts of Shakespeare and Socrates, of Machiavelli and Thucydides, Byrd can come across as oddly formal and rhetorically overblown.

However, the insiders' world of Appropriations is ideal for Byrd. Here, he is judged by his devotion to institutional and legislative detail, a realm in which he has no equal. He presides as a sort of benevolent dictator, calling to mind some of the 1950s-era chairmen Byrd watched when he first came to Congress.

As majority leader, Byrd controlled the chamber with his legendary parliamentary skill. As chairman, with the sharp crack of his gavel, he starts hearings on time and tolerates no digression. The Appropriations subcommittees that were once the fiefdoms of their chairmen are now beholden to Byrd.

Byrd is not an omnipotent force, as his successor as leader, Mitchell, proved in 1990 when he narrowly won a pivotal battle against Byrd on the clean air bill. But as a man with a vest pocket full of IOUs and the power to grant future funding favors, Byrd must be reckoned with. "A lot of people are deathly afraid of Byrd," said Utah Republican Orrin G. Hatch, after Byrd gutted an agreement Hatch had spent months negotiating.

Many have suggested that senators follow Byrd not because they like him but because they fear him. He has been known to admonish colleagues in public session, or summarily gavel their requests out of order. He has a long memory and does not hesitate to punish those who cross him. In 1990, after Oklahoma Republican Don Nickles tried in the Budget Committee to cap spending limits, Byrd deleted funds to help restart Amtrak service in Oklahoma.

In July 1991, Byrd, after lining up votes for a month with the help of party leaders, presented without notice an amendment to give senators a 23 percent raise and to ban members from pocketing honoraria. After little debate, Byrd's amendment was approved, 53-35.

Byrd's mere pronouncement in the spring of 1992 that he would oppose a balanced-budget amendment to the Constitution helped turn the tide against that proposal, which up to that point had been steadily building momentum.

Byrd was a linchpin to crafting an agreement between the White House and congressional leaders in 1990 during months of budget-summit negotiations. Because no budget plan would pass without Byrd's support, Richard G. Darman, director of the Office of Management and Budget (OMB), often dealt directly with Byrd.

Byrd steadfastly demanded that the package include an increase in funding for domestic programs. Darman eventually agreed to let domestic funding rise with inflation, and he allowed for an extra $20.7 billion in domestic spending over the first three years covered by the budget agreement. In exchange, Byrd agreed to let OMB determine which pieces of supplemental spending bills constitute emergency spending exempt from caps, and he allowed OMB to determine whether expenditures meet budget guidelines or trigger an automatic cut in a related program.

When Byrd returned to the helm of Appropriations in 1989, he said his goal was to bring $1 billion to the state in five years; he did it in less than two. The fiscal 1992 appropriations bills, for example, contained about half a billion dollars in projects and earmarked funds for his rural home state.

Among the plums he has picked off is a $185 million FBI fingerprint lab that is being transferred from Washington, D.C., to West Virginia. The fiscal 1992 transportation appropriations bill contained $162.7 million in road projects for West Virginia, including the biggest single earmark: $148.5 million for a project called Corridor G, an Appalachian highway that traverses the western part of the state.

"Oh, they say he is trying to get everything he can for West Virginia," Byrd said during debate on the 1991 highway authorization bill. "I would not be worth my salt if I did not attempt to represent the people of West Virginia, but I am also thinking of the nation.... They may call me provincial if they wish. I do not care."

Byrd's emphasis on procedure and prerogatives over policy helps explain the ease with which he has moved from his party's right toward its left. Few would have forecast a leadership role for Byrd when he arrived in the Senate in 1959. He was parochial and far to the right of most Democrats. He filibustered the 1964 Civil Rights Act, at one point holding the floor with a 14-hour speech that is among the longest on Senate record — something he now says he deeply regrets.

But by 1967, he had a toehold on the Senate leadership ladder, after defeating veteran liberal Joseph Clark of Pennsylvania to become secretary of the Democratic Caucus. Byrd catered to his colleagues, scheduling routine business for their convenience. Four years later he ousted a stunned Edward M. Kennedy from the No. 2 leadership job, majority whip. Shaken by the 1969 Chappaquiddick tragedy, Kennedy had been neither an active nor effective whip.

For six years Byrd was a loyal lieutenant to Majority Leader Mike Mansfield of Montana, sitting through long days of floor work while deferring to Mansfield as party spokesman. When Mansfield retired, some liberals wanted Hubert H. Humphrey of Minnesota to succeed him, believing he would be a more eloquent spokesman. But Byrd once again had a long column of accounts receivable. Humphrey, already seriously ill, withdrew. Byrd was elected by acclamation.

Byrd became majority leader as Jimmy Carter became president, and the two had an uneasy relationship. Byrd seemed to regard Carter as an amateur at the exercise of power and made sure the president knew where the credit belonged when Byrd rescued the administration's legislation. He was instrumental in saving the Panama Canal treaties through nonstop negotiations with wavering senators and Panamanian officials in 1978.

Many Democrats' lingering unease about Byrd crystallized after the 1980 elections cost the party the White House and plunged Senate Democrats into the minority. Byrd's style seemed less appropriate for a party out of power, and his resistance to the Reagan administration was not a sure thing at the start. He voted for President Ronald Reagan's 1981 tax- and budget-cut bills. But he became a strong foe after the administration proposed cuts in Social Security.

The feeling that the party needed a more aggressive, telegenic public symbol, however, never went away, and led to an open campaign against Byrd after the 1984 elections. By the time challenger Lawton Chiles of Florida began his campaign, Byrd already had commitments from more than half his colleagues, but the final vote, 36-11 for Byrd, indicated that he had some vulnerabilities.

He moved to shore up his strength in the 99th Congress, working to put more verve into his formal oratory and giving the Democratic response to some of Reagan's televised speeches. The unexpectedly large Democratic gains in the 1986 Senate elections ensured that Byrd would remain secure for at least another two years. J. Bennett Johnston of Louisiana had prepared for a face-off with Byrd, but dropped his bid when it became clear the new Democratic majority was in no mood to dump its leader in the midst of triumph.

The 100th Congress was perhaps Byrd's most successful term as Senate leader. Republicans met Byrd's return with some dread, complaining that he had used his parliamentary skills to override their legitimate minority rights during his first stint as majority leader in the 1970s. Some Democrats, too, were a bit apprehensive, but Byrd rallied them behind an ambitious agenda and helped make the 100th Congress one of the most productive in more than 20 years.

When it was over, he stepped down on his own.

At Home: Since Byrd was elected to the Senate in 1958, he has held the seat with ease — a tribute both to the respect he has engendered at home and the long-running impotence of the state's Republican Party. In five reelections, Byrd's lowest vote share has been 65 percent.

That came in 1988, against freshman GOP state Sen. M. Jay Wolfe. Wolfe campaigned gamely on a conservative platform that combined right-to-work with right-to-life, and enlisted religious broadcaster Pat Robertson to visit West Virginia in his behalf. But he was outspent nearly 10-to-1, and he could not refute Byrd's argument that as Appropriations chairman, he could steer federal money West Virginia's way.

Wolfe had no trouble getting the GOP nomination to meet Byrd, largely because the memory of the incumbent's decisive 1982 victory was vivid in Republicans' minds. Taking advantage of a beleaguered economy and a badly mismanaged GOP effort that year, Byrd had taken nearly 70 percent of the vote, humiliating Republican Cleve Benedict, an heir to the Procter & Gamble fortune, who gave up a House seat to run.

The senator was born Cornelius Calvin Sale Jr. When he was 1, his mother died and his father gave him to an aunt and uncle, Vlurma and Titus Byrd; they raised him in the hardscrabble coal country of southern West Virginia.

Byrd graduated first in his high school class, but it took him 12 more years before he could afford to start college. He worked as a gas station attendant, grocery store clerk, shipyard welder and butcher before his talents as a fiddle player helped win him a seat in the state Legislature in 1946.

Friends drove Byrd around the hills and hollows, where he brought the voters out by playing "Cripple Creek" and "Rye Whiskey." From then on, he never lost an election. As he himself once put it, "There are four things people believe in in West Virginia — God Almighty; Sears, Roebuck; Carters Little Liver Pills; and Robert C. Byrd."

When Democrat Erland Hedrick retired from the old 6th District in 1952, Byrd was an obvious contender. But he had to surmount his past membership in the Ku Klux Klan. He had joined the Klan at age 24 and as late as 1946 wrote a letter to the imperial grand wizard urging a Klan rebirth "in every state of the Union."

When this came up publicly in 1952, his opponents and Democratic Gov. Okey L. Patteson called on him to drop out. He refused, explaining his Klan membership as a youthful indiscretion committed because of his alarm over communism. He won the election.

After three House terms, he ran for the Senate in 1958 with AFL-CIO and United Mine Workers support. He crushed his primary opposition and unseated Republican Chapman Revercomb, a veteran who had been in and out of the Senate in the 1940s and won a two-year term in a 1956 comeback. Revercomb was a weak incumbent before the campaign even began, and the 1958 recession hurt the state badly, driving many voters closer to their New Deal Democratic roots.

For the next two decades, West Virginians returned Byrd to the Senate without fuss. In 1964, he trounced Cooper Benedict, a former deputy assistant secretary of Defense and the father of Cleve Benedict. In 1970, the GOP victim was Charleston Mayor Elmer H. Dodson. In 1976, no one at all filed against Byrd.

Committees

President Pro Tempore

Appropriations (Chairman)
Interior (chairman); Defense; Energy & Water Development; Labor, Health & Human Services & Education; Transportation

Armed Services (8th of 11 Democrats)
Coalition Defense & Reinforcing Forces; Defense Technology, Acquisition & Industrial Base; Force Requirements & Personnel

Rules & Administration (3rd of 9 Democrats)

Elections

1988 General		
Robert C. Byrd (D)	410,983	(65%)
M. Jay Wolfe (R)	223,564	(35%)
1988 Primary		
Robert C. Byrd (D)	252,767	(81%)
Bobbie E. Myers (D)	60,186	(19%)

Previous Winning Percentages: **1982** (69%) **1976** (100%) **1970** (78%) **1964** (68%) **1958** (59%) **1956 *** (57%) **1954 *** (63%) **1952 *** (56%)

** House elections.*

Campaign Finance

	Receipts	Receipts from PACs		Expend-itures
1988				
Byrd (D)	$1,407,167	$938,720	(67%)	$1,099,709
Wolfe (R)	$115,314	$23,103	(20%)	$115,284

Key Votes

1993	
Require unpaid family and medical leave	Y
Approve national "motor voter" registration bill	Y
Approve budget increasing taxes and reducing deficit	Y
Support president's right to lift military gay ban	Y
1992	
Approve school-choice pilot program	N
Allow shifting funds from defense to domestic programs	Y
Oppose deeper cuts in spending for SDI	N
1991	
Approve waiting period for handgun purchases	Y
Raise senators' pay and ban honoraria	Y
Authorize use of force in Persian Gulf	N
Confirm Clarence Thomas to Supreme Court	N

Voting Studies

	Presidential Support		Party Unity		Conservative Coalition	
Year	**S**	**O**	**S**	**O**	**S**	**O**
1992	27	73	74	25	61	39
1991	49	51	76	24	68	33
1990	42	58	74	26	62	38
1989	54	46	83	17	50	50
1988	56	44	81	19	49	51
1987	40	60	85	15	44	56
1986	36	64	84	16	30	70
1985	37	63	81	19	55	45
1984	53	45	77	22	45	55
1983	48	51	81	19	36	61
1982	40	60	81	19	56	44
1981	47	48	78	14	43	53

Interest Group Ratings

Year	ADA	AFL-CIO	CCUS	ACU
1992	100	92	20	19
1991	65	83	10	33
1990	56	89	25	26
1989	60	100	38	14
1988	55	86	29	36
1987	70	100	28	23
1986	75	93	16	26
1985	65	90	21	43
1984	75	73	37	50
1983	65	94	37	16
1982	60	92	48	55
1981	70	89	39	86

John D. Rockefeller IV (D)

Of Charleston — Elected 1984; 2nd Term

Born: June 18, 1937, New York, N.Y.
Education: International Christian U. (Tokyo, Japan), 1957-60; Harvard U., A.B. 1961.
Occupation: Public official.
Family: Wife, Sharon Percy; four children.
Religion: Presbyterian.
Political Career: W.Va. House, 1967-69; W.Va. secretary of state, 1969-73; Democratic nominee for governor, 1972; governor, 1977-85.
Capitol Office: 109 Hart Bldg. 20510; 224-6472.

In Washington: If all goes as he confidently expects it to, Rockefeller will cap his first decade in the Senate with the enactment of a sweeping overhaul of the nation's health-care system. Acting as President Clinton's surrogate on health policy — much as he did in the 1992 campaign — Rockefeller has the opportunity to erect Clinton's most lasting monument — and to advance his own latent White House ambitions in the process.

Years of tending the Senate's back benches, studying the issues and minding the chamber's folkways have paid off for the towering but bookish Rockefeller. He has become a Senate power, a protégé of Majority Leader George J. Mitchell of Maine and an influential voice on his committees.

Rockefeller's increasing importance in the Senate only augments the political assets he always enjoyed as an heir to America's most legendary fortune and a scion of one its best-known political families.

Rockefeller coyly denied interest in the presidency until mid-1991, when he said he was thinking of seeking the Democratic nomination in 1992. Such talk had first begun nearly a generation ago in 1968, when he was nominated to be West Virginia's secretary of state. It was revived periodically during his less-than-awe-inspiring tenure as governor. And although such talk was finally being taken seriously, Rockefeller eventually concluded that he was not prepared to face a national campaign in 1992.

"Jay" Rockefeller is an old hand at winning over those who think a man born into wealth and power must be spoiled and aloof. More than 20 years ago, he impressed the people of Emmons, W.Va., as a sincere, idealistic VISTA volunteer. During his first term in Washington, he reassured the Senate. He often impresses observers as personable and unpretentious, according courteous treatment to staff and witnesses at hearings. In his first years in the Senate, he was often found writing in the chamber, his 6-foot-6-inch frame folded into one of the spartan desks. His behavior is the perfect antidote to the expectation of arrogance.

Early on, he made health the centerpiece of his legislative agenda. Now, as chairman of the Finance subcommittee that oversees Medicare and chairman of the Veterans' Affairs Committee (with jurisdiction over the mammoth Veterans Affairs health network), he is uniquely placed to demonstrate his virtuosity on the issue.

Rockefeller is also a devoted advocate of children and family issues. He heads the National Commission on Children and uses his Finance seat to push for expanded tax benefits for children.

If Rockefeller has a liability, it is his constant striving toward a middle ground, an attribute some find too accommodating. "Jay doesn't want to offend anybody," said Democratic Rep. Pete Stark of California, another major congressional player in the health-care arena. "But at some point you've got to decide where the winners and losers are."

Generally expected to address international issues, his one-time academic specialty, Rockefeller initially focused on West Virginia concerns — the cost of shipping coal by rail, the job prospects of miners, steelmakers and other workers in Rust Belt industries.

In the 101st Congress, events thrust him to the forefront on health care, another likely topic of interest given his state's large population of elderly residents and of black-lung disease victims. He capitalized on that opening in the 102nd Congress, brokering deals to aid key constituencies and to prove his ability to navigate the shoals of the health-care system.

With the decline of the coal industry, the financial underpinning of health-care trust funds that serve retired miners and their survivors was jeopardized. Rockefeller negotiated a deal between the coal industry and mine workers to bail out the trust funds, in part by tracking down negligent former employers of retired miners and making them pay into the funds. The deal was incorporated into a broad energy bill, enacted in 1992.

The same year, Rockefeller managed to salvage a prescription-drug price discount for VA medical centers. The discount had been threatened by a requirement that drug companies sell to state Medicaid programs at the lowest price given other bulk purchasers. Manufacturers seemed intent on raising prices across the board rather than selling to a huge Medicaid clientele at the VA's deep discount. Rockefeller found a way to preserve the Medicaid price limit and the VA discount, without upsetting manufacturers. He got it included in a broad veterans health bill.

In many ways, political necessity shaped Rockefeller's parochial agenda. A senator elected with a disappointing 52 percent of the vote after two terms as governor and a $12 million campaign could not afford to range too far afield. But Rockefeller also seems to delight in disappointing those who expected him to grab headlines in preparation for a leap onto the national stage. "I've done my homework," Rockefeller told a West Virginia newspaper in 1989. "I've started out in a low-profile way but I've gained the respect of my colleagues." He also won over more home-state voters, as he won re-election in 1990 with 68 percent.

Rockefeller gained the chairmanship of the new Finance Subcommittee on Medicare and Long-Term Care at the start of the 101st Congress. Six months later, after the death of Rep. Claude Pepper, Rockefeller was chosen to chair the bipartisan Pepper Commission on health policy. It was Rockefeller's work in that forum that established his prominence. A politically and philosophically divided commission in March 1990 proposed the creation of two programs: one to provide basic health insurance to those lacking it and a second to underwrite long-term care. The estimated price tag for the two programs was $66.2 billion annually over five years, though the commission did not specify where the revenues should come from. In April 1991, Rockefeller warned that efforts to institute government-sponsored, universal health care would be "neither fiscally sound nor politically pragmatic."

Rockefeller is credited with pushing to fruition in 1989 a far-reaching overhaul of Medicare's physician-payment system. He set out with Republican Dave Durenberger of Minnesota to forge a compromise between the two chambers' bills even after Senate leaders told him that the issue was dead. Rockefeller persevered; over the course of a few days he hammered out a compromise. "He wouldn't take 'no' for an answer," Durenberger said.

In 1990, Rockefeller was one of the leaders on Finance who successfully pushed for enactment of new Medigap rules to regulate more directly private insurance plans that supplement Medicare.

A member of both the Finance and Commerce committees, Rockefeller weighs in routinely in trade debates. He spent several years living in Japan and speaks the language, which gives him an understanding of the country that few of his colleagues possess. Yet his state has been badly hurt by competition from Japanese manufacturing. He has supported the aggressive pursuit of reciprocity in trade, on one occasion urging the Bush administration to cite Japan for unfair trade practices. But, although Rockefeller chairs the Senate Steel Caucus, he worries that erecting barriers to protect West Virginia steelmakers could provoke foreign competitors to stop buying coal from West Virginia mines.

At Home: Given his background, Rockefeller seems an odd leader for one of the poorest states. But in a state where money often talks and Democrats nearly always win, he has been a successful politician. He is well-known — newspapers need only refer to him as Jay in the headlines — though his wealth and celebrity engender no small amount of resentment in a state beset with the nation's second-lowest per capita personal income: Past polls have shown him with negative ratings as high as 40 percent.

But Rockefeller has won many friends by patiently working his way up the political ladder over two decades, serving in low-visibility offices before twice winning the governorship and capturing the Senate seat of retiring Democrat Jennings Randolph in 1984.

Rockefeller moved to West Virginia in 1964 as a VISTA volunteer in the Action for Appalachia Youth program, then decided to stay and enter politics, starting near the bottom; he ran for a seat in the state's lower house in 1966. After winning that, he captured the statewide office of secretary of state in 1968.

His political ascent was interrupted in 1972 when he lost the governor's race to Republican Arch A. Moore Jr. Rockefeller was hurt by carpetbagger charges and an environmental platform that opposed strip mining. After the election, he recanted some of his environmental positions and strengthened his ties to the state by serving as president of West Virginia Wesleyan College. Running for governor again in 1976, he won by nearly 2-to-1 over former GOP Gov. Cecil H. Underwood (1957-61). Moore was ineligible to seek re-election.

Despite their differing backgrounds, Rockefeller and the Legislature generally got along well in his first term. Rockefeller, the amateur classical pianist with the Harvard degree, and the pols from West Virginia's grimy courthouses reached an understanding, affording Rockefeller some major legislative successes.

Still, Rockefeller left nothing to chance in 1980, winning re-election after a campaign that bombarded households with direct-mail appeals and TV commercials, even on Pittsburgh and Washington, D.C., stations.

When it was reported he was spending almost $12 million in his re-election campaign against Moore, who was seeking a comeback, bumper stickers appeared with the slogan, "Make Him Spend It All, Arch." But Moore was unable either to drive Rockefeller broke or out of office. Rockefeller won by 9 points.

Rockefeller's second term was stymied by the state's economic problems. Heavily dependent on the battered coal industry, West Virginia was staggered by high unemployment and sinking revenues. He was the prime target of criticism when taxes were raised, salaries frozen and state spending cut.

With West Virginia's governors restricted to two consecutive terms, it was long apparent that Rockefeller would run for the Senate in 1984, but not who would run against him. Democratic Sen. Randolph helped him by announcing his retirement plans in early 1983. About a year later, Moore, his strongest potential GOP rival, decided to pass this time, and joined the governor's race.

But Rockefeller was not home free. He was near the nadir of his popularity when he entered the Senate race. Even many supporters admitted that he had not met the high expectations he had raised as governor; West Virginia struggled toward the end of his second term with the country's highest unemployment rate.

Rockefeller blamed the economic problems on ties to fading industries — steel and glass as well as coal — a global oil glut and Reagan administration policies. He touted the integrity of his administration and its scattered successes, such as efforts to bolster tourism. "Tough Leadership for Tough Times" became the tag line for his campaign.

Republicans nominated a wealthy young political neophyte, John Raese, who promised to match Rockefeller's spending dollar for dollar. But with Rockefeller mounting another $12 million campaign, that was a pipe dream.

Raese's campaign was further stalled by a series of gaffes. But Rockefeller made Raese the target of his late media barrage — a tactic widely considered to be a mistake — and the attacks gave Raese publicity he could not afford himself. Aided by Reagan's surge atop the ticket, Raese pulled nearly even with Rockefeller in election-eve polls. But Rockefeller survived, with large majorities in the industrial northern Panhandle and in the southern coal fields.

In his 1990 re-election, Rockefeller spent more than $300,000 in a primary against two challengers who spent less than $1,000 between them, and refused to agree to a $2 million spending limit for the general election. Burned by past charges of attempting to buy public office with his personal fortune, Rockefeller shied away from using his own funds, and instead amassed a campaign treasury from PACs.

Republicans nominated John Yoder, a lawyer from Harpers Ferry. Yoder threw Rockefeller off balance briefly by charging that he was "bought" by special interests. But a lack of funds crippled Yoder's campaign as fall approached. The Rockefeller effort kicked into full gear just as Yoder was being deserted by his national party; Rockefeller won all but three counties.

Committees

Veterans' Affairs (Chairman)

Commerce, Science & Transportation (5th of 11 Democrats)
Science (chairman); Communications; Foreign Commerce & Tourism; Surface Transportation

Finance (8th of 11 Democrats)
Medicare & Long Term Care (chairman); Health for Families & the Uninsured; International Trade

Elections

1990 General		
John D. Rockefeller IV (D)	276,234	(68%)
John Yoder (R)	128,071	(32%)
1990 Primary		
John D. Rockefeller IV (D)	200,161	(85%)
Ken B. Thompson (D)	21,669	(9%)
Paul Nuchims (D)	14,467	(6%)

Previous Winning Percentage: **1984** (52%)

Campaign Finance

	Receipts	Receipts from PACs	Expend-itures
1990			
Rockefeller (D)	$3,479,161	$1,425,405 (41%)	$2,650,320
Yoder (R)	$22,541	0	$22,904

Key Votes

1993	
Require unpaid family and medical leave	Y
Approve national "motor voter" registration bill	Y
Approve budget increasing taxes and reducing deficit	Y
Support president's right to lift military gay ban	Y
1992	
Approve school-choice pilot program	N
Allow shifting funds from defense to domestic programs	Y
Oppose deeper cuts in spending for SDI	N
1991	
Approve waiting period for handgun purchases	Y
Raise senators' pay and ban honoraria	Y
Authorize use of force in Persian Gulf	N
Confirm Clarence Thomas to Supreme Court	N

Voting Studies

	Presidential Support		Party Unity		Conservative Coalition	
Year	S	O	S	O	S	O
1992	28	72	88	10	26	68
1991	36	64	91	8	28	73
1990	26	73	86	13	41	59
1989	51	49	78	20	50	50
1988	49	50	88	9	30	68
1987	36	60	92	6	28	72
1986	31	69	79	19	18	80
1985	31	61	83	12	47	47

Interest Group Ratings

Year	ADA	AFL-CIO	CCUS	ACU
1992	100	91	20	7
1991	90	75	10	5
1990	83	78	25	13
1989	80	90	38	14
1988	70	86	36	16
1987	90	100	24	8
1986	75	93	32	13
1985	60	90	36	14

1 Alan B. Mollohan (D)

Of Fairmont — Elected 1982; 6th Term

Born: May 14, 1943, Fairmont, W.Va.
Education: College of William and Mary, A.B. 1966; West Virginia U., J.D. 1970.
Military Service: Army Reserve, 1970-83.
Occupation: Lawyer.
Family: Wife, Barbara Whiting; five children.
Religion: Baptist.
Political Career: No previous office.
Capitol Office: 2242 Rayburn Bldg. 20515; 225-4172.

In Washington: Given his focus on obtaining federal programs for West Virginia's economically troubled 1st District, Mollohan benefits from his ties to a pair of senior Democrats: Senate Appropriations Committee Chairman Robert C. Byrd and House Appropriations Defense Subcommittee Chairman John P. Murtha. While his alliances with them have helped him push through a number of projects, he toils hard in his own right to secure funding for his hard-pressed Appalachian district, performing the task work on the Appropriations Committee necessary to win the projects.

Mollohan is a sure vote for the Democratic leadership on labor and trade issues. However, he takes a more conservative line on defense than most House Democrats, and he breaks with party orthodoxy on abortion.

His strong feelings on such an emotional and divisive issue, however, have not noticeably hampered his efficacy on Appropriations. His warm relationships with his colleagues help allay resistance that his staunch opposition to abortion might otherwise produce among Democrats.

Mollohan has taken to the floor on several occasions to speak on such abortion-related amendments as supporting restrictions on the District of Columbia to pay for abortions for poor women, opposing abortion funding in cases of rape or incest, and resisting moves to fund the U.N. family planning fund over its support for China's abortion program. "[O]ur duty as lawmakers," he said in 1990 during debate on the D.C. spending bill, "[is] to protect the youngest members of our human family, America's next generation of artists and dancers and teachers and shop owners and yes, even congressmen and women. . . ."

Mollohan remains loyal to his district's bedrock industries, coal and steel. He supports "Buy American" legislation that gives preference to domestic materials in U.S. construction projects. His opposition to what he calls "unsound" acid rain legislation that penalizes coal-burning plants and factories made Mollohan one of only 21 House members in May 1990 to vote against reauthorizing the Clean Air Act.

Yet he works hard to diminish the district's dependence on these declining industries. He has lobbied the Appalachian Regional Commission and the Economic Development Administration for funds to expand the Mid-Atlantic Aerospace Complex at Benedum Airport, which is outside Clarksburg in Harrison County.

Mollohan and Byrd have been instrumental in cultivating a fledgling aircraft industry near Clarksburg. After Mollohan and local business owners helped persuade a Clarksburg oil and gas company to launch a business refurbishing midsize aircraft, Mollohan found some business for the new company, the West Virginia Air Center.

The Air Force, as part of general restructuring of U.S. defenses, was looking to unload 18 C-23 light transport planes. Mollohan persuaded the planes' manufacturer to consider Benedum Airport as a place to refurbish and service the C-23s, which the Pentagon transferred to the Army National Guard. Now the Air Center does the work in its 145,000-square-foot hangar.

Byrd and Mollohan led both Pratt & Whitney and Grumman to Benedum, too. And Lockheed Corp. manufactures parts for its C-130 transport plane nearby. "When Grumman [officials were] looking around to locate their facility, I simply referred them to Lockheed and Pratt & Whitney and walked away," Mollohan said. "The West Virginia worker is the easiest thing in the world to sell."

Mollohan is on the Appropriations subcommittee that oversees the Federal Bureau of Investigation, and he acted as a House sponsor for one of Byrd's pet projects: locating an FBI fingerprinting center at Clarksburg. The center is slated to open in 1994.

While Byrd has more of a direct interest in West Virginia projects, it was Murtha's personal patronage that helped Mollohan advance in the House. A western Pennsylvania power broker whose sphere includes West Virginia, Murtha sponsored Mollohan's bid for an

West Virginia 1

North — Wheeling; Parkersburg; Morgantown

Its economy dependent on coal and heavy industries such as steel, chemicals and glass, northern West Virginia was crushed by economic depression during the 1980s. Factories closed or slashed payrolls; coal mines mechanized and got by with thousands fewer workers. The 1st contains six of West Virginia's 10 largest cities. All lost population during the 1980s; Wheeling fell 19 percent to under 35,000.

However, a nascent technology sector brightens economic prospects for the 1st. Morgantown, which has a population of nearly 26,000, is the site of West Virginia University (22,000 students) and the hub of the area's high-tech growth. Located amid the coal fields of Monongalia County (the state's third-leading coal-producing county), Morgantown is home to Software Valley, an organization that promotes regional computer-oriented business and research activity.

Other areas are working to diversify. Clarksburg and Bridgeport (Harrison County) will benefit from West Virginia Democratic Sen. Robert C. Byrd's biggest federal plum, a $185 million relocation of the FBI's fingerprinting center. Wheeling (Ohio County) is also making some progress with aid from Byrd's funding pipeline. A computer software industry is growing around Wheeling Jesuit College, site of the federal government's National Technology Transfer Center and the Classroom of the Future, both NASA programs.

Since the mid-1980s, Wheeling has benefited from tourists' interest in the "Festival of Lights," a fall/winter display of Christmas lights at Oglebay Park just outside the city. Wheeling itself has become known as the "City of Lights."

Though trimmed down, traditional industries still play an important economic role. Weirton Steel Co. in Hancock and Boone counties is the one of the nation's largest employee-owned companies. Blue-collar voters have given a strong edge in the industrial and coal-mining areas to Rep. Mollohan and to Democratic presidential candidates: Bill Clinton won Marion County in 1992 with 56 percent of the vote.

However, there are Republican pockets in the 1st that make it competitive in presidential contests. Although George Bush lost nearly 2-to-1 in many of the 1st's central counties, he won in the far east and far west ends of the district.

Although Wheeling is known as an industrial town, it has long doubled as the commercial center for the Northern Panhandle. It has a sizable white-collar constituency that leans Republican.

Farther down the Ohio River is Parkersburg, which has nearly 34,000 residents. The region has a large chemical industry and is also a regional trade center. Farmland adds to GOP strength in Wood County; Bush won 60 percent there in 1988.

In the Eastern Panhandle, coal mines again give way to farms. This is West Virginia's strongest Republican area, with a GOP tradition dating back to the Civil War: Bush won the eastern counties of Mineral, Preston, and Grant in 1992.

1990 Population: 598,056. White 583,753 (98%), Black 9,662 (2%), Other 4,641 (1%). Hispanic origin 3,147 (1%). 18 and over 456,552 (76%), 62 and over 112,314 (19%). Median age: 36.

Appropriations seat.

Mollohan's image as a loyalist got him a seat on the ethics committee, which he held from 1985 to 1991. It also won him a spot on the Budget Committee at the start of the 103rd Congress.

The ethics assignment forced him to pass judgment in 1989 on House Speaker Jim Wright of Texas. He and Pennsylvania Democrat Joseph M. Gaydos, another Murtha ally, voted "no" on most charges against Wright, but Mollohan said his ties to Murtha did not influence him. "I vote 'em the way I see 'em," he said.

At Home: In 1992, Mollohan faced what most state observers considered his toughest challenge in a decade: a re-election battle against Rep. Harley O. Staggers Jr., a matchup necessary because of congressional redistricting that cost the state one of its four House seats.

Both men had followed their fathers, Robert H. Mollohan and Harley O. Staggers Sr., to Congress and had solid political bases in the new 1st District.

Staggers tried to paint himself as the "outsider" in the matchup, unceasingly criticizing Mollohan for writing bad checks at the House bank, while Mollohan highlighted the importance of his seat on the Appropriations Committee to the 1st District.

Mollohan prevailed easily in the end with more than 60 percent of the vote.

Mollohan's 1982 campaign to succeed his father, who had retired, was his most difficult. Though Alan Mollohan was born in Fairmont, for a decade he had been a Washington, D.C., lawyer who counted Pittsburgh-based Consolidation Coal Co. as a major client. Rank-and-file miners were leery about a corporate lawyer representing them; many lined up behind Mollohan's pro-labor primary opponent, state Sen. Dan Tonkovich.

The elder Mollohan, however, had close ties to party officials, business and labor leaders. Their support proved crucial to his son, who won the primary by 3,137 votes. In the fall, Mollohan won 53 percent of the vote against GOP state Rep. John F. McCuskey.

In 1984, Mollohan bucked a Republican tide and fended off a GOP challenge from state Rep. Jim Altmeyer with a late media barrage focusing on Altmeyer's spotty attendance record in the state House. Republicans have had a hard time mustering opposition since then; Mollohan was unopposed in 1986 and faced a self-employed historian and filling station owner in 1988 and 1990. He had no Republican opposition in 1992.

Committees

Appropriations (19th of 37 Democrats)
Commerce, Justice, State & Judiciary; Veterans Affairs, Housing & Urban Development & Independent Agencies

Budget (16th of 26 Democrats)

Elections

1992 General		
Alan B. Mollohan (D)	172,924	(100%)
1992 Primary		
Alan B. Mollohan (D)	57,568	(62%)
Harley O. Staggers Jr. (D)	36,038	(38%)
1990 General		
Alan B. Mollohan (D)	72,849	(67%)
Howard K. Tuck (R)	35,657	(33%)

Previous Winning Percentages: **1988** (75%) **1986** (100%) **1984** (54%) **1982** (53%)

District Vote for President

1992
D 113,756 (46%)
R 86,131 (35%)
I 45,856 (19%)

Campaign Finance

	Receipts	Receipts from PACs		Expend-itures
1992				
Mollohan (D)	$494,159	$242,669	(49%)	$629,436
1990				
Mollohan (D)	$197,997	$131,498	(66%)	$206,688
Tuck (R)	$34,020	0		$34,077

Key Votes

1993	
Require parental notification of minors' abortions	Y
Require unpaid family and medical leave	Y
Approve national "motor voter" registration bill	Y
Approve budget increasing taxes and reducing deficit	Y
Approve economic stimulus plan	Y
1992	
Approve balanced-budget constitutional amendment	N
Close down space station program	N
Approve U.S. aid for former Soviet Union	Y
Allow shifting funds from defense to domestic programs	Y
1991	
Extend unemployment benefits using deficit financing	Y
Approve waiting period for handgun purchases	N
Authorize use of force in Persian Gulf	Y

Voting Studies

	Presidential Support		Party Unity		Conservative Coalition	
Year	**S**	**O**	**S**	**O**	**S**	**O**
1992	35	60	81	14	58	40
1991	41	59	79	17	62	38
1990	31	66	84	11	50	50
1989	55	43	74	25	76	24
1988	36	59	74	19	61	24
1987	40	56	83	12	67	33
1986	36	61	79	15	70	28
1985	40	60	82	17	69	31
1984	49	50	76	22	63	36
1983	34	66	78	21	54	46

Interest Group Ratings

Year	ADA	AFL-CIO	CCUS	ACU
1992	70	100	43	21
1991	50	92	20	30
1990	61	100	21	21
1989	55	92	40	36
1988	50	100	23	48
1987	68	100	13	17
1986	50	100	24	35
1985	55	82	23	38
1984	55	85	44	33
1983	65	94	20	30

2 Bob Wise (D)

Of Clendenin — Elected 1982; 6th Term

Born: Jan. 6, 1948, Washington, D.C.
Education: Duke U., A.B. 1970; Tulane U., J.D. 1975.
Occupation: Lawyer.
Family: Wife, Sandra Casber; two children.
Religion: Episcopalian.
Political Career: W.Va. Senate, 1981-83.
Capitol Office: 2434 Rayburn Bldg. 20515; 225-2711.

In Washington: With his role as administration watchdog made less relevant by the election of Bill Clinton, Wise headed for the Public Works Committee, where he assumed the chair on the Economic Development panel.

The move from the Government Operations Committee, where he chaired the Government Information Subcommittee, put Wise in the middle of the debate over the need for a short-term boost in federal spending to create jobs. It is an appropriate place for a six-term representative whose state's senior senator, Appropriations Chairman Robert C. Byrd, has an affinity for spending federal dollars on the types of infrastructure programs that are authorized by the subcommittee Wise now chairs.

The Public Works post also gives Wise the opportunity to protect West Virginia's interests: His subcommittee has jurisdiction over the Appalachian Regional Commission and the Economic Development Administration, agencies that fund some state programs.

Wise came to Washington as a self-described populist with a penchant for challenging established power, and he lived up to that reputation early in his first term. He had been in office only a few months when he took on his state's congressional delegation by opposing the Stonewall Jackson Dam, a long-planned flood-control project in his district.

Wise had campaigned on a promise to fight the dam, and when the 1983 water development appropriations bill came up, he attached an amendment eliminating funding for it, calling the dam a waste of money. His move angered the state's other Democratic congressmen, including then-Senate Democratic leader Byrd. Still, Wise managed to persuade a majority of the House to go his way. Only Senate support for the dam saved it; the House-Senate conference preserved funding.

Despite his iconoclastic start, Wise fairly soon began working within the system, applying himself to slicing off pieces of the federal pie for his constituency. The reason was simple: economic necessity. There are so many bad roads, decrepit bridges, unemployed workers and black-lung disease victims in his district that Wise decided he had to get along with the appropriators who can provide relief. Learning from Byrd's example, Wise has had some success in securing funds for such district projects as lock and dam renovation.

Wise has been an outspoken advocate for wider use of alternative transportation fuels — in particular the use of compressed natural gas, an abundant natural resource in West Virginia. In 1990, Wise decided to practice what he preaches: He converted his personal car to dual-fuel; it can now use either compressed natural gas or gasoline. Since then, Wise has purchased another natural-gas-powered car, and he uses it to commute to and from work.

In 1991, Wise began leasing a new mobile office van, dubbed the "Wise fleet," that can operate on natural gas or gasoline. He has encouraged federal agencies to convert their vehicles to dual-fuel use. Wise got one step closer to his goal of converting all government vehicles to alternative-fuel use with an amendment to the 1992 energy bill requiring the federal government to increase its purchases of alternative-fuel vehicles.

While Wise is now more loyal to his party and to "the system" than when first elected, he has not shied from challenging those in power when he thinks change is necessary to make the House operate more efficiently.

Wise's latest challenge to the status quo came as Democrats met to organize the House for the 103rd Congress. In his role as chairman of the Democratic Study Group (DSG), Wise proposed changes that would have weakened committee chairmen's influence on the legislative agenda by establishing a new policy council to help the party define its goals. The proposal caused a rift between committee chairmen and their allies and younger members of the DSG.

In the end, both sides agreed to let the Speaker appoint a 20-member panel — half from the Steering and Policy Committee, dominated by older members, and half from the rank and file. Committee chairmen will work with the group to set the agenda.

West Virginia 2

Center — Charleston; Eastern Panhandle

The "bicoastal" 2nd spans the state, starting on the west at the Ohio River, moving east to take in the state capital of Charleston (in Kanawha County) and ending in the historic Eastern Panhandle town of Harpers Ferry, at the confluence of the Shenandoah and Potomac rivers.

The 2nd's mountainous middle — which includes Kanawha, the state's largest county with about 208,000 residents — retains its industrial character and Democratic orientation. Rep. Wise, who has regularly won by wide margins, is from Clendenin in Kanawha County.

Charleston, with just over 57,000 people, is the district's dominant city. Chemical plants that provide jobs in "Chemical Valley" along the Kanawha River also spark environmental concerns. Charleston's economy is bolstered by the state payroll and by the Charleston Town Center, a regional mall that draws shoppers from across West Virginia, Kentucky and Ohio.

There is a conservative streak in Kanawha County, evidenced by school-busing and textbook-banning controversies of the recent past. However, the economic dropoff in Kanawha's industrial sector has helped Democrats maintain their edge in the county, which lost 10 percent of its population in the 1980s; Bill Clinton won the county in 1992 with 47 percent. The mainly Democratic mountain regions north and east of Kanawha remain heavily dependent on coal.

Republican strength in the 2nd is concentrated in two fast-growing exurban areas at the district's edges.

In the Eastern Panhandle, the populations of Berkeley (just over 59,000) and Jefferson (nearly 36,000) counties — within commuting distance of Washington — grew by 27 percent and 19 percent, respectively.

The commuter class in the Panhandle is being joined by white-collar workers brought in by the federal government. Efforts to consolidate Central Intelligence Agency functions at a Jefferson County site, supported by Sen. Robert C. Byrd, have caused a stir among D.C.-area legislators.

The white-collar growth has supplemented a local GOP tradition that began in the Civil War era, when the eastern counties were at the front lines of some Civil War incidents. (Abolitionist John Brown staged his 1859 raid on the U.S. arsenal at Harpers Ferry and was hanged in nearby Charles Town.) In 1988 and 1992, George Bush carried all the Eastern Panhandle.

The other area where Republicans dominate for president and compete for lower offices is Putnam County, just west of Charleston. Putnam's population increased 12 percent during the 1980s to nearly 43,000. Bush won the county with 55 percent in 1988 and carried it with 44 percent in 1992.

The more level terrain at the ends of the district also supports much of West Virginia's agricultural activity. Jefferson County leads the state in corn and dairy cattle; Berkeley is tops in hogs. In the far west, Mason County grows corn and tobacco and raises livestock.

1990 Population: 597,921. White 574,038 (96%), Black 19,982 (3%), Other 3,901 (1%). Hispanic origin 2,725 (<1%). 18 and over 448,825 (75%), 62 and over 104,298 (17%). Median age: 35.

Just as Wise lives by example in his advocacy of alternative fuels, he has made a case for internal reform by rejecting most of the accoutrements of congressional service. He does not mass-mail newsletters to constituents, and he supports a ban on honoraria. Wise accepts the same salary he received when he first came to Congress; the balance from subsequent raises is donated to scholarship funds at four West Virginia colleges. Members who are irritated by such gestures are often quick to point out that Wise's wife is a high-level Ways and Means staff aide, but she was there before they met.

At Home: While Wise launched his political career as a maverick, he has nurtured it with unabashed displays of state boosterism. He regularly gives district voters what one newspaper described as "an upbeat, feel-good-about-ourselves pitch that sounds like a cross between Norman Vincent Peale ... and President Reagan." And he has gained wide visibility with projects such as "West Virginia First," a TV program designed to encourage high school students to stay in the state.

Critics complain that Wise's real forte is public relations, but there is no doubt that he is a rising star in West Virginia politics.

Rather than join an established firm after law school, Wise set up his own practice oriented to low- and moderate-income clients. He then directed a statewide tax reform group that repeatedly took coal companies to court to force them to pay more property tax on their large landholdings.

But legal action had its limits, Wise decided. "Where people lose the battle is when they have to actually go to court," he once said. "It's much better if they win their case in the legislative process."

So in 1980 he capitalized on the resentment of teachers against the small size of a pay raise to upset the conservative state Senate president in the Democratic primary. With a reputation as a giant-killer, he ran for Congress in 1982, benefiting from labor support to swamp a Democratic primary field that included the state House majority leader.

GOP Rep. David Michael Staton had won the seat in 1980 with an extensive grass-roots campaign of his own, but his re-election effort was more aloof. If Staton was worried about Wise, he did not show it. "I don't think it will even be close," he said at one point.

It was not close. Wise's small campaign budget and feuds with party leaders masked an effective volunteer network and a knack for drawing enough free media attention to neutralize Staton's ads. He won a decisive 58 percent of the vote.

Each election since then, Wise has won more easily. His most spirited re-election contest was in 1986, when Charleston newscaster Tim Sharp left his job in early September to fill the vacancy on the GOP ticket.

Sharp enjoyed instant name identification as a TV news anchorman. But Sharp drew more ink than votes. Wise swept every county in the district, taking 65 percent overall. After Wise thrashed 1988 GOP nominee Paul W. Hart with 74 percent, Republicans did not field a challenger in 1990.

Wise continued his string of easy re-election victories in 1992 by crushing Republican Samuel A. Cravotta, who began his campaign late in the year after the Republican nominee dropped out of the race.

Republicans had hoped that the addition of the Eastern Panhandle, the GOP's strongest base in the state, to Wise's district would increase their chances at defeating the popular Democrat, but Wise coasted with nearly three-fourths of the vote.

Committees

Budget (6th of 26 Democrats)

Public Works & Transportation (9th of 39 Democrats)
Economic Development (chairman); Investigations & Oversight; Water Resources & the Environment

Elections

1992 General		
Bob Wise (D)	143,988	(71%)
Samuel A. Cravotta (R)	59,102	(29%)
1990 General		
Bob Wise (D)	75,327	(100%)

Previous Winning Percentages: 1988 (74%) **1986** (65%) **1984** (68%) **1982** (58%)

District Vote for President

1992	
D	104,257 (45%)
R	90,375 (39%)
I	36,813 (16%)

Campaign Finance

	Receipts	Receipts from PACs		Expend-itures
1992				
Wise (D)	$295,894	$170,755	(58%)	$330,052
1990				
Wise (D)	$182,913	$126,118	(69%)	$53,137

Key Votes

1993	
Require parental notification of minors' abortions	N
Require unpaid family and medical leave	Y
Approve national "motor voter" registration bill	Y
Approve budget increasing taxes and reducing deficit	Y
Approve economic stimulus plan	Y
1992	
Approve balanced-budget constitutional amendment	Y
Close down space station program	N
Approve U.S. aid for former Soviet Union	Y
Allow shifting funds from defense to domestic programs	Y
1991	
Extend unemployment benefits using deficit financing	Y
Approve waiting period for handgun purchases	N
Authorize use of force in Persian Gulf	N

Voting Studies

	Presidential Support		Party Unity		Conservative Coalition	
Year	S	O	S	O	S	O
1992	18	76	84	8	50	48
1991	26	70	90	6	41	54
1990	19	81	92	6	28	72
1989	31	60	85	7	44	46
1988	21	73	87	9	58	39
1987	17	80	86	5	40	60
1986	23	72	88	8	40	60
1985	26	74	84	9	27	71
1984	33	61	76	17	37	61
1983	13	85	84	13	30	67

Interest Group Ratings

Year	ADA	AFL-CIO	CCUS	ACU
1992	80	92	38	17
1991	70	100	30	5
1990	72	100	21	13
1989	75	100	30	14
1988	75	100	36	12
1987	84	100	7	0
1986	75	93	22	5
1985	70	82	32	10
1984	70	92	27	18
1983	90	88	10	13

3 Nick J. Rahall II (D)

Of Beckley — Elected 1976; 9th Term

Born: May 20, 1949, Beckley, W.Va.
Education: Duke U., A.B. 1971; George Washington U., 1972.
Occupation: Broadcasting executive; travel agent.
Family: Divorced; three children.
Religion: Presbyterian.
Political Career: No previous office.
Capitol Office: 2269 Rayburn Bldg. 20515; 225-3452.

In Washington: Rahall's ascension to the chairmanship of the Interior Committee's Subcommittee on Mining and Natural Resources in the 99th Congress came as no surprise. He represents one of the nation's leading coal-producing states and has avidly defended the interests of the industry and the miners in his district.

But Rahall has a new priority in the 103rd Congress: getting additional federal money for two national highway corridors that are to be routed through West Virginia's 3rd District. To try to achieve that goal, he relinquished the top spot on the Mining Subcommittee and took the chairmanship of the Public Works Committee's Subcommittee on Surface Transportation.

Coal-related issues will remain high on Rahall's legislative agenda, however. He has led the effort in the House to amend the 1872 mining law and is pursuing the changes again in the 103rd. He is also seeking changes in the way benefits are awarded to coal miners suffering from black lung disease.

Rahall is still in a position to influence the debate over coal. The Surface Transportation Subcommittee deals with coal-shipping issues, and Rahall is also a member of Natural Resources' new Subcommittee on Energy and Mineral Resources, which assumed the jurisdiction of the former Mining Subcommittee.

Rahall sometimes surprises those who write him off as resolutely pro-industry. On the then-Interior Committee in the 102nd Congress, he advocated a bill to study extending national park status to part of the New River in West Virginia. And on many wilderness or historic preservation bills that go through the committee, Rahall votes with conservationists. He has fought strip mining on U.S. forest land, and in 1990 sought to curtail timbering on some federal land in West Virginia.

In the 101st Congress, deliberations on reauthorizing the Clean Air Act caused anxiety in many parts of West Virginia. The bill set up an ambitious program to reduce pollutants that cause acid rain, and high-sulfur coal, mined in West Virginia, has been tagged as a chief source of those pollutants.

Rahall told the Virginia Coal Council in 1989 that the bill could pit low-sulfur coal producers against high-sulfur producers. He exemplified the split: His district produces low-sulfur coal, and, assured that the clean air bill did not hurt southern West Virginia, Rahall voted for it.

Though Rahall's coal boosterism benefits mine owners, he also tries to protect the miners and votes a pro-labor line. In early 1987, Rahall pledged to use his subcommittee chairmanship to block proposed Reagan administration cutbacks in federal mining health and safety research. And he has long supported making it easier for miners with black lung disease to claim benefits.

Rahall calls for a national revival in coal use, but his enthusiasm fades somewhat when his region's interests are at stake. He has consistently fought plans to build a coal slurry pipeline in the West, which would make Western coal cheaper to transport and more competitive with Eastern coal.

Of Lebanese heritage, Rahall has been a vigorous critic of Israel and backs ties to Arab states. As part of a congressional delegation that toured Beirut in 1982, he met with Palestine Liberation Organization leader Yasir Arafat. In the 100th Congress, Rahall fought efforts to close the PLO's office at the United Nations, and sponsored resolutions supporting Palestinians' efforts toward self-determination and statehood. At the outset of the 1991 Persian Gulf War, Rahall denounced FBI interviews of Arab-American business and community leaders aimed at gathering information about possible terrorist activity in the United States.

Rahall opposed plans in the 102nd to approve $10 billion in U.S. loan guarantees to Israel; he suggested instead that Congress approve $10 billion in loan guarantees to state, city and county governments in the United States to be spent on domestic needs.

At Home: In 1990, Rahall came as close to defeat as he ever has, winning only 52 percent of the vote in a rematch against Marianne R.

West Virginia 3

South — Huntington; Beckley

The 3rd — which takes in the state's southern counties — is known as the "coal district." Six of the state's 10 leading coal-producing counties — including the top two (Boone and Mingo) — are in the 3rd.

Dependence on coal produces a common economic trait: hardship. While coal has been produced at near-record tonnages in recent years, technological advances have sharply reduced the need for labor. One glaring example of distress is McDowell County in southern West Virginia. Its population slipped 29 percent — from almost 50,000 to just over 35,000 — during the past decade.

Soaring unemployment added misery to a region that has always had pockets of Appalachian poverty. Democrats remain the dominant political force here; Bill Clinton won the 3rd with 55 percent in 1992.

Every county in the 3rd lost residents during the 1980s. Although emigration has reduced the work force by thousands, unemployment remains stubbornly high in many areas. Insufficient highways and other infrastructural deficiencies hinder growth in mountain country.

The population of Huntington (Cabell County), the second-largest city in the state, fell 14 percent in the 1980s to just under 55,000 but is cushioned by an Ohio River location that provides for a diversified economy. CSX railroad, Inco Alloys, Ashland Coal and an Owens-Illinois glass company — along with ARMCO Steel Co. and Ashland Oil Inc. in the Ashland, Ky., area — provide jobs. And Huntington is home to Marshall University (12,700 students), whose football team won its first NCAA Division I-AA championship in 1992. Huntington's white-collar sector and tobacco growers help make Cabell the most Republican part of the 3rd. George Bush won Cabell with 53 percent in 1988. But GOP success does not run deep: Only one of Cabell's six state House members is a Republican, and Clinton carried the county in 1992.

Yet this is a hardy success rate for the GOP compared with the rest of the district. Just to the east is the heart of coal country, Democratic turf where some residents still idolize John F. Kennedy, whose 1960 primary win in West Virginia was pivotal to his presidential nomination.

Near the eastern edge of the coal fields is Beckley (population 18,000), which promotes as economic assets its location near Interstates 77 and 64 and the surrounding area's tourist potential: Local rivers are popular with white-water rafters. (Dan Quayle, a white-water enthusiast, occasionally rafted in the area while he was vice president.) The eastern part of the 3rd also has the state's most venerable tourist establishment: the Greenbrier resort in White Sulphur Springs.

Some communities are crafting aspects of their industrial heritage into tourist attractions. These aspects include the sometimes ugly events in Mingo County, site of the "West Virginia Mine Wars" between labor activists and union-busting mine owners during the 1920s (the subject of the movie "Matewan"). "Bloody Mingo" was also the site of part of the fighting between the Hatfields and McCoys.

1990 Population: 597,500. White 567,732 (95%), Black 26,651 (4%), Other 3,117 (1%). Hispanic origin 2,617 (<1%). 18 and over 444,523 (74%), 62 and over 108,210 (18%). Median age: 35.

Brewster, a former Mercer County GOP chairman.

But redistricting strengthened Rahall's base in the state's most southern and most Democratic district, and Brewster decided against a third challenge in 1992 in part because of financial problems. Rahall trounced former White House aide Ben Waldman.

Once the strongest vote-getter in the state delegation, Rahall's re-election percentage dropped into the 60s for the first time in 1984, after a Las Vegas casino filed suit against him to collect more than $60,000 in gambling debts. The suit, which drew headlines a month before the election, was eventually dropped. But coming on the heels of Rahall's separation from his wife, the episode gave his little-known GOP challenger unexpected fodder.

In 1986, a strong Democratic year, Rahall won 71 percent; but in 1988, he dropped to a surprising 61 percent against the woefully underfunded Brewster.

That anemic showing set the stage for tough primary and general-election campaigns in 1990. In the primary, Rahall faced a comeback attempt from his predecessor in the 4th, Democrat Ken Hechler. Pledging a return to "high moral standards again," Hechler implied that Rahall lacked them, and he criticized the incumbent as too dependent on out-of-state special-interest money. The local media rehashed Rahall's past troubles, including a 1988 guilty plea to alcohol-related reckless driving charges. But Rahall, anticipating a tough fight, worked hard to shore up his base in the party, and prevailed with 57 percent of the vote.

The GOP again nominated Brewster. Economic development themes, lingering voter concerns about Rahall's personal problems and the general anti-incumbent sentiment of 1990 benefited her. Though again heavily outspent, Brewster took 48 percent of the vote.

Rahall was a little-known travel agent and radio sales manager when he entered politics in 1976. His opportunity grew out of then-Rep. Hechler's campaign for governor. Rahall was far from the best-known contender in the Democratic field, but he had family money, and he spent it on a media campaign none of his foes could match, evoking the images of Hechler, President Franklin D. Roosevelt and Sen. Robert C. Byrd. Rahall won the nomination with 37 percent.

After the primary, Hechler (who did not get the gubernatorial nomination) mounted a write-in drive to keep his House seat. Rahall could never have beaten Hechler in a primary, but the write-in effort was too difficult even for a popular incumbent, especially after Rahall received Democratic organization support. Hechler got nearly 60,000 write-ins, but Rahall won with a 46 percent tally. Hechler immediately announced that he would run again in 1978, but he found that incumbency gave Rahall the advantages he once enjoyed. Rahall won renomination with 56 percent of the vote.

Committees

Natural Resources (5th of 28 Democrats)
Energy & Mineral Resources; National Parks, Forests & Public Lands

Public Works & Transportation (3rd of 39 Democrats)
Surface Transportation (chairman); Economic Development; Water Resources & Environment

Elections

1992 General		
Nick J. Rahall II (D)	122,279	(66%)
Ben Waldman (R)	64,012	(34%)
1990 General		
Nick J. Rahall II (D)	39,948	(52%)
Marianne R. Brewster (R)	36,946	(48%)

Previous Winning Percentages: **1988** (61%) **1986** (71%) **1984** (67%) **1982** (81%) **1980** (77%) **1978** (100%) **1976** (46%)

District Vote for President

1992
D 112,988 (55%)
R 65,468 (32%)
I 26,160 (13%)

Campaign Finance

	Receipts	Receipts from PACs		Expend-itures
1992				
Rahall (D)	$444,624	$247,758	(56%)	$309,313
Waldman (R)	$151,594	$18,849	(12%)	$150,822
1990				
Rahall (D)	$536,855	$287,250	(54%)	$566,348
Brewster (R)	$66,671	$750	(1%)	$61,471

Key Votes

1993	
Require parental notification of minors' abortions	Y
Require unpaid family and medical leave	Y
Approve national "motor voter" registration bill	Y
Approve budget increasing taxes and reducing deficit	Y
Approve economic stimulus plan	Y
1992	
Approve balanced-budget constitutional amendment	N
Close down space station program	N
Approve U.S. aid for former Soviet Union	N
Allow shifting funds from defense to domestic programs	Y
1991	
Extend unemployment benefits using deficit financing	#
Approve waiting period for handgun purchases	N
Authorize use of force in Persian Gulf	Y

Voting Studies

	Presidential Support		Party Unity		Conservative Coalition	
Year	S	O	S	O	S	O
1992	25	69	79	17	35	60
1991	36	59	85	11	49	46
1990	14	81	79	16	37	63
1989	40	58	80	15	34	63
1988	25	64	85	11	39	50
1987	24 †	71 †	87 †	10 †	35 †	65 †
1986	21	76	90	6	34	66
1985	20	79	88	6	25	75
1984	32	58	83	9	22	64
1983	15	78	76	16	29	62
1982	29	58	77	10	23	55
1981	37	53	77	17	37	53

† Not eligible for all recorded votes.

Interest Group Ratings

Year	ADA	AFL-CIO	CCUS	ACU
1992	70	100	38	20
1991	65	100	11	21
1990	78	100	36	13
1989	85	91	40	19
1988	70	100	29	22
1987	76	100	7	4
1986	90	93	17	9
1985	80	88	18	5
1984	70	83	29	4
1983	85	100	25	9
1982	70	89	25	5
1981	75	93	11	14

Wisconsin

STATE DATA

Governor:
Tommy G. Thompson (R)
First elected: 1986
Length of term: 4 years
Term expires: 1/95
Salary: $92,277
Term limit: None.
Phone: (608) 266-1212
Born: Nov. 19, 1941; Elroy, Wis.
Education: U. of Wisconsin, B.S. 1963, J.D. 1966
Military Service: Army Reserve, 1966-76
Occupation: Lawyer; real estate broker
Family: Wife, Sue Ann Mashak; three children
Religion: Roman Catholic
Political Career: Wis. Assembly, 1967-87; sought Republican nomination for U.S. House special election, 1979

Lt. Gov.: Scott McCallum (R)
First elected: 1986
Length of term: 4 years
Term expires: 1/95
Salary: $49,673
Phone: (608) 266-3516

State election official: (608) 266-8005
Democratic headquarters: (608) 255-5172
Republican headquarters: (608) 257-4765

REDISTRICTING

Wisconsin retained its nine House seats in reapportionment. The legislature passed the map April 14, 1992; the governor signed it April 28.

STATE LEGISLATURE

Legislature. Meets for 5 floor periods of varying length over 2-year session.

Senate: 33 members, 4-year terms
1992 breakdown: 17R, 16D; 25 men, 8 women; 31 whites, 2 blacks
Salary: $35,070
Phone: (608) 266-2517

State Assembly: 99 members, 2-year terms
1992 breakdown: 50D, 45R, 4 vacancies; 67 men, 28 women; 90 whites, 5 blacks
Salary: $35,070
Phone: (608) 266-1501

URBAN STATISTICS

City	Pop.
Milwaukee	628,088
Mayor John O. Norquist, D	
Madison	190,766
Mayor Paul Soglin, R	
Green Bay	96,466
Mayor Samuel Halloin, N-P	
Racine	84,298
Mayor N. Owen Davies, N-P	
Kenosha	80,352
Mayor John Antaramian, D	

U.S. CONGRESS

Senate: 2 D, 0 R
House: 4 D, 5 R

TERM LIMITS

For Congress: No
For state offices: No

ELECTIONS

1992 Presidential Vote

Bill Clinton	41.1%
George Bush	36.8%
Ross Perot	21.5%

1988 Presidential Vote

Michael S. Dukakis	51%
George Bush	48%

1984 Presidential Vote

Ronald Reagan	54%
Walter F. Mondale	45%

POPULATION

1990 population		4,891,769
1980 population		4,705,767
Percent change		+4%
Rank among states:		16
White		92%
Black		5%
Hispanic		2%
Asian or Pacific islander		1%
Urban		66%
Rural		34%
Born in state		76%
Foreign-born		2%
Under age 18	1,288,982	26%
Ages 18-64	2,951,566	60%
65 and older	651,221	13%
Median age		32.9

MISCELLANEOUS

Capital: Madison
Number of counties: 72
Per capita income: $18,046 (1991)
Rank among states: 22
Total area: 56,153 sq. miles
Rank among states: 26

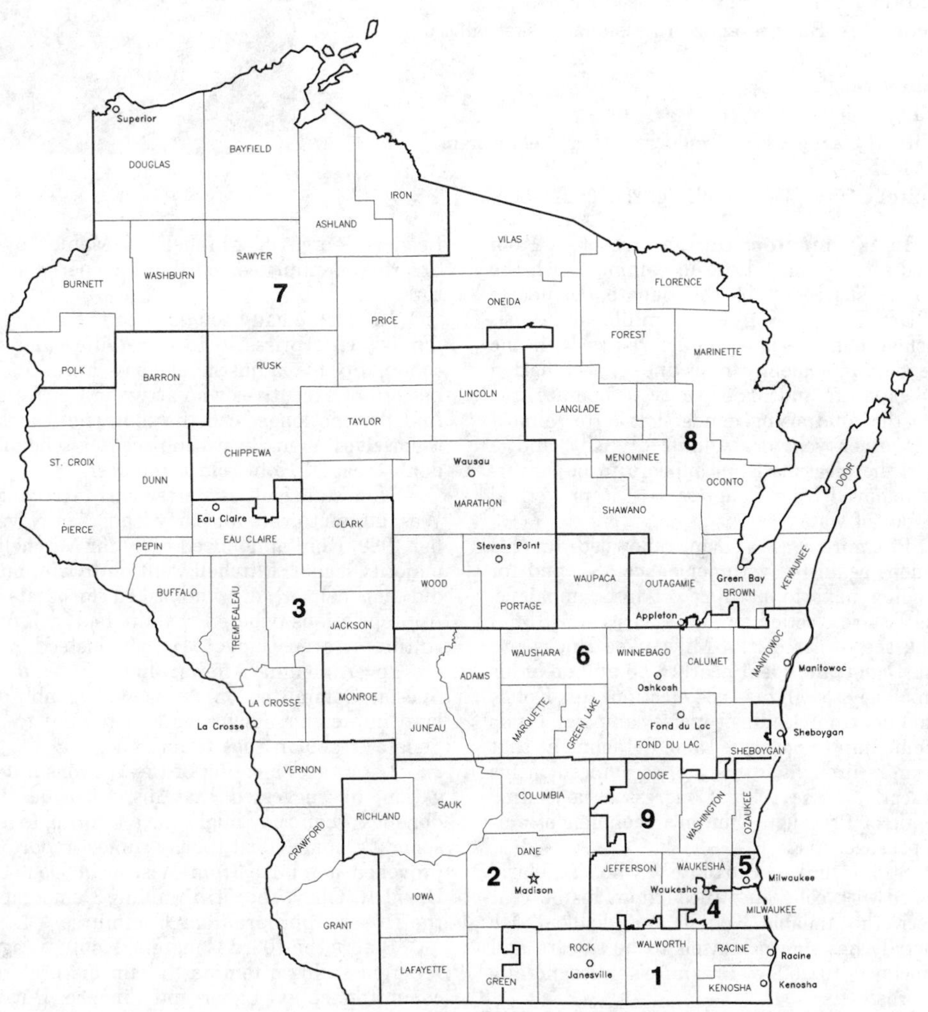
Superior
DOUGLAS
BAYFIELD
IRON
ASHLAND
VILAS
SAWYER
BURNETT
WASHBURN
7
FLORENCE
ONEIDA
PRICE
FOREST
MARINETTE
POLK
BARRON
RUSK
LINCOLN
LANGLADE
TAYLOR
8
ST. CROIX
CHIPPEWA
MENOMINEE
DUNN
Wausau
OCONTO
DOOR
MARATHON
Eau Claire
CLARK
SHAWANO
PIERCE
PEPIN
EAU CLAIRE
KEWAUNEE
Stevens Point
Green Bay
BUFFALO
WOOD
WAUPACA
OUTAGAMIE
BROWN
3
TREMPEALEAU
PORTAGE
JACKSON
Appleton
WAUSHARA
6
WINNEBAGO
CALUMET
MANITOWOC
Manitowoc
ADAMS
Oshkosh
LA CROSSE
MONROE
MARQUETTE
GREEN LAKE
Fond du Lac
La Crosse
JUNEAU
Sheboygan
FOND DU LAC
SHEBOYGAN
VERNON
DODGE
COLUMBIA
RICHLAND
SAUK
9
WASHINGTON
OZAUKEE
CRAWFORD
DANE
5
JEFFERSON
WAUKESHA
2
Milwaukee
Madison
IOWA
Waukesha
4
MILWAUKEE
GRANT
ROCK
WALWORTH
RACINE
Racine
LAFAYETTE
Janesville
GREEN
1
KENOSHA
Kenosha

Herb Kohl (D)

Of Milwaukee — Elected 1988; 1st Term

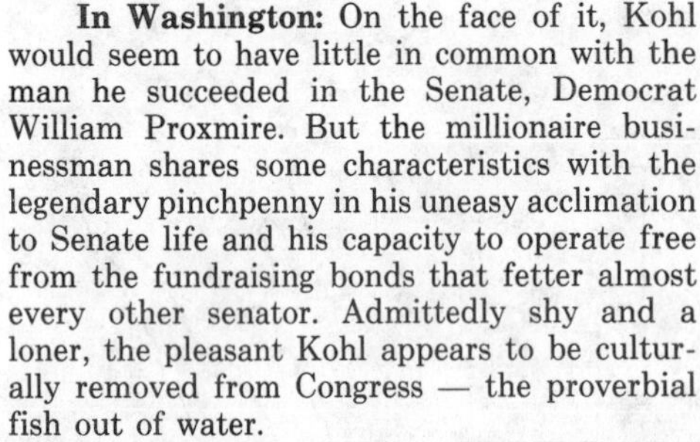

Born: Feb. 7, 1935, Milwaukee, Wis.

Education: U. of Wisconsin, B.A. 1956; Harvard U., M.B.A. 1958.

Military Service: Army Reserve, 1958-64.

Occupation: Businessman; professional basketball team owner.

Family: Single.

Religion: Jewish.

Political Career: Wis. Democratic Party chairman, 1975-77.

Capitol Office: 330 Hart Bldg. 20510; 224-5653.

In Washington: On the face of it, Kohl would seem to have little in common with the man he succeeded in the Senate, Democrat William Proxmire. But the millionaire businessman shares some characteristics with the legendary pinchpenny in his uneasy acclimation to Senate life and his capacity to operate free from the fundraising bonds that fetter almost every other senator. Admittedly shy and a loner, the pleasant Kohl appears to be culturally removed from Congress — the proverbial fish out of water.

Proxmire was a man renowned for his sermons against government excess — and for spending next to nothing on his campaigns. (His last re-election, in 1982, cost him $145.) Kohl, the owner of the Milwaukee Bucks pro basketball team, spent nearly $7.5 million of his own money to win his 1988 election. But Kohl's immunity from needing to raise campaign funds permits him to have the same detachment that Proxmire brought to his job, as evinced in his role early in the 103rd Congress as a leading skeptic of President Clinton's economic stimulus package.

Still, unlike Proxmire, who regularly clashed with colleagues throughout his 32-year career, the amiable Kohl is not disliked. He generally has shown himself to be sincere and disinclined to follow Proxmire's idiosyncratic patterns.

Kohl endured a rough beginning — it took him several months to choose his top aide — and he has had difficulty getting on track. His record suggests that he was much more adept at amassing a fortune in the business world than accumulating a legislative portfolio. But in the 102nd Congress, he began to emerge, becoming a notable participant in some areas.

The Judiciary Committee added a new panel on Juvenile Justice and made Kohl its chairman. He also chaired a subcommittee on Governmental Affairs. And for the 103rd Congress, he received a spot on the Appropriations Committee. He was also named by Majority Leader George J. Mitchell of Maine to the Steering Committee, part of the party structure.

Kohl's life had been devoted to running his family's enterprises in food, retailing and real estate. So his adjustment may have fit the pattern of executives who arrive in Congress to find they no longer call the shots, not even for themselves. "I'm always subject to a schedule I don't create," Kohl told a reporter.

Kohl's difficulties started early. Arriving in Washington to vote for party leaders in November 1988, Kohl announced early for Mitchell as majority leader. Mitchell went on to win, but it did not help Kohl, who asked for seats on Appropriations (where Proxmire had sat), Agriculture or even Budget. He got, instead, seats on Governmental Affairs, Judiciary and the Special Committee on Aging — arguably the least impressive assignments meted out to any Senate freshman that term.

Later, at a meeting of the Wisconsin delegation, he suggested that his colleagues had done less than they might have to bring federal spending home. That touchy subject reportedly provoked a rebuke from Wisconsin Democrat David R. Obey, the fifth-ranking Democrat on the House Appropriations Committee.

Before the 103rd Congress, Kohl was again rebuffed in his attempts to gain his preferred committee spots, Labor and Finance. But the seat on Appropriations is as coveted as consolation prizes go. He was, however, given the chairmanship of the District of Columbia Subcommittee, a duty without political allure that most senators shun.

On foreign policy and defense, his positions are predictably liberal. A consistent vote to cut weapons systems, Kohl was an early and loud voice opposing President George Bush's buildup of U.S. forces in the Persian Gulf. He called the administration's escalating talk of war in December 1990 "deplorable" and criticized Bush for turning the sensitive, multifaceted Middle East situation into "a game of chicken."

But though Kohl has proved less of an iconoclast than Proxmire, he has inherited his predecessor's preoccupation with the budget deficit. Kohl's maiden speech was a jeremiad against the deficit, which he said would bring "the economic collapse we all fear."

Early in the 103rd, Kohl was out front in challenging Clinton's $16.3 billion stimulus plan. He touched off the administration's ire by championing an amendment to require spending cuts to offset roughly $11 billion of the stimulus package. His amendment attracted nine Democratic votes but fell on a point of order, 52-48. Kohl was one of five Democratic senators who voted with a unified GOP against cutting off a Republican filibuster on the bill. In preventing a vote on Clinton's full proposal, the opponents handed Clinton his first big legislative setback.

On Judiciary, Kohl lacks the star quality other Democratic committee members have obtained; three of his nine colleagues on the panel have already run for president. He goes off in a number of directions, but with the exception of chemical warfare, has not become closely identified with any major theme or issue.

Kohl had a moment in the national spotlight during the 102nd Congress, when the Judiciary Committee considered the nomination of Judge Clarence Thomas for the Supreme Court. Kohl voted with most committee Democrats against favorably recommending Thomas, before Anita F. Hill's charges of sexual harassment were publicized. He found it difficult to decide on Thomas with his "very skimpy judicial record and conflicting answers to our questions."

Kohl expressed dismay at the unrelenting partisanship displayed during the hearings. "The partisanship never stops here," he told The Milwaukee Journal. "It's a fact of life, and that's a sad thing.... [The people] see it in the hearings, for example. What was the bottom line? Winning. Winning. And if winning meant destroying Anita Hill, well that's the bottom line....

"It's kill, kill, kill," he said, "and it's very bad for the country."

On the Juvenile Justice Subcommittee, Kohl worked to reauthorize a 1974 act that provides federal grants to states to combat juvenile crime and delinquency. He also helped draft a bill authorizing funding for states to enforce criminal laws on interstate child support.

Kohl has been interested in a privacy measure aimed at regulating telephone Caller ID service — by requiring phone companies to give customers the option of blocking the display of their numbers free of charge. During the 102nd Congress, he offered a bill to give consumers the option of preventing their number from appearing on Caller ID services, saying the blocking was needed to protect callers' privacy. The bill bogged down, however, when Republicans attempted to attach their version of the crime bill.

As chairman of the Government Information and Regulation panel at Governmental Affairs (which he dropped in the 103rd), Kohl presided over a debate that had serious home-state implications: whether the Census Bureau should adjust its figures to reflect an admitted undercount in the 1990 census. An adjustment would have cost Wisconsin one of its House seats. Kohl, while denying that his interest was parochial, pronounced himself "unequivocally opposed to any adjustment." The Bush administration chose not to adjust.

At Home: Kohl will have to compile a substantial record of achievement in the Senate before people stop talking about how he got there. Making his first try for public office, Kohl announced about six months before the election yet spent just under $7.5 million, nearly all of it his own. He blew away the best competition in his own party and beat an attractive Republican moderate in November.

Kohl showed some rough edges in the campaign, on one occasion naming Jimmy Carter's secretary of Defense when asked who was then holding the job. Kohl also made a remark about the employment his basketball team had provided for blacks that some found in poor taste.

But Kohl's errors were swept away in a sea of positive images. Mostly, these were communicated by Kohl's saturation TV advertising, which emphasized his private-sector success and commitment to service — beginning with his immigrant parents.

It was a campaign on a scale unlike any the state had seen. Kohl's total outlay doubled the previous state record (he even bought time on Minnesota stations to reach border counties). A Milwaukee columnist suggested that one channel on everyone's TV set simply be rented to Kohl for the duration.

Although his political involvement had been as financier and, briefly, state party chairman, Kohl showed some flair for debate. In the primary, facing former Gov. Anthony S. Earl and 1986 Senate nominee Ed Garvey, Kohl deflected their jibes and jabs with personal affability and a simple thematic message: "Nobody's senator but yours."

Kohl's emphasis on his independence played well, especially against efforts to vilify him as a plutocrat. He found the one positive he could in being one of the state's richest men and used it to strike an improbable, but apparently effective, parallel with Proxmire. Proxmire had served three decades without spending much (and sometimes virtually nothing) on his re-election campaigns. He got away with it because he was popular enough to discourage challengers in his weight class. Kohl claimed similar independence based on his ability to self-finance his campaigns.

Some Wisconsin Democrats had been eager to unleash Kohl's assets in the 1986 election against GOP Sen. Bob Kasten. That was the year after Kohl had spent $18.5 million to keep the Milwaukee Bucks franchise in town. But Kohl turned down the overtures then.

When Kohl entered the Democratic primary in late spring 1988, Earl was the front-runner and Rep. Jim Moody of Milwaukee was an apparent second. Moody dropped out, but Earl and Garvey made a bitter fight of it. Earl spent money on negative ads satirizing Kohl's miscues and lack of political sophistication.

Kohl, staying on the high road, posted an easy plurality in the September primary. His November foe was Susan Engeleiter, GOP leader in the state Senate.

In the GOP primary, Engeleiter defeated a much more conservative opponent, former state party Chairman Steve King, who challenged her for the nomination when popular Republican Gov. Tommy G. Thompson demurred. King openly questioned whether Engeleiter, with young children at home, should be in public office at all.

Engeleiter was never in danger of losing the nomination, but her winning margin was smaller than expected, and King's attacks highlighted issues on which she differed from much of her party — including her support for limited abortion rights and for the Equal Rights Amendment.

By forcing Engeleiter rightward, albeit briefly, King may have given the liberal Kohl running room in the center he otherwise would not have had. Engeleiter tried to compete with the continuing deluge of Kohl ads on TV by portraying herself as more in tune with ordinary people's problems. She downplayed ideology by labeling herself "A Wisconsin Original."

But her financing had never been in a league with Kohl's, so she tried to break out with a dramatic tactic in a debate between the two candidates. She accused a company Kohl's family had owned of selling coffeecakes to the military at inflated prices. Kohl seemed unperturbed. Newspaper reporters subsequently found the difference in price attributable to a difference in size. The issue fizzled.

In the campaign's closing weeks, polls found Engeleiter gaining on Kohl. But time ran out before she could find an issue or other means of closing the last few percentage points of deficit. Shortly after the election, President Bush named her to head the Small Business Administration, a job she held for two years.

Committees

Appropriations (14th of 16 Democrats)
District of Columbia (chairman); Agriculture, Rural Development & Related Agencies; Labor, Health & Human Services & Education; Military Construction

Judiciary (8th of 10 Democrats)
Juvenile Justice (chairman); Courts & Administrative Practice; Technology & the Law

Small Business (11th of 12 Democrats)
Government Contracting & Paperwork Reduction; Rural Economy & Family Farming

Special Aging (9th of 11 Democrats)

Elections

1988 General		
Herb Kohl (D)	1,128,625	(52%)
Susan Engeleiter (R)	1,030,440	(48%)
1988 Primary		
Herb Kohl (D)	249,226	(47%)
Anthony S. Earl (D)	203,479	(38%)
Ed Garvey (D)	55,225	(10%)
Douglas LaFollette (D)	19,819	(4%)
Edmond Hou-Seye (D)	5,040	(1%)

Campaign Finance

	Receipts	Receipts from PACs	Expend-itures
1988			
Kohl (D)	$7,576,540	0	$7,491,600
Engeleiter (R)	$2,945,328	$993,692 (34%)	$2,908,101

Key Votes

1993	
Require unpaid family and medical leave	Y
Approve national "motor voter" registration bill	Y
Approve budget increasing taxes and reducing deficit	Y
Support president's right to lift military gay ban	Y
1992	
Approve school-choice pilot program	N
Allow shifting funds from defense to domestic programs	Y
Oppose deeper cuts in spending for SDI	N
1991	
Approve waiting period for handgun purchases	Y
Raise senators' pay and ban honoraria	N
Authorize use of force in Persian Gulf	N
Confirm Clarence Thomas to Supreme Court	N

Voting Studies

	Presidential Support		Party Unity		Conservative Coalition	
Year	**S**	**O**	**S**	**O**	**S**	**O**
1992	30	70	79	21	26	74
1991	41	59	83	17	40	58
1990	25	75	86	12	19	81
1989	47	53	87	13	18	82

Interest Group Ratings

Year	ADA	AFL-CIO	CCUS	ACU
1992	95	83	30	11
1991	90	58	20	24
1990	94	67	8	9
1989	95	90	25	11

Russell D. Feingold (D)

Of Middleton — Elected 1992; 1st Term

Born: March 2, 1953, Janesville, Wis.

Education: U. of Wisconsin, B.A. 1975; Oxford U., B.A. 1977; Harvard U., J.D. 1979.

Occupation: Lawyer.

Family: Wife, Mary Erpenbach; two children, two stepchildren.

Religion: Jewish.

Political Career: Wis. Senate, 1983-93.

Capitol Office: 502 Hart Bldg. 20510; 224-5323.

The Path to Washington: Although negative campaigning is an accepted and widely used component of modern politicking, Feingold's 1992 Senate victory dramatically illustrated that the tactic has its limitations.

During Wisconsin's lengthy Democratic primary campaign (voters picked Senate nominees in September), Feingold, a little-known longshot, held his fire while his two better-known and better-financed opponents, Rep. Jim Moody and millionaire Milwaukee businessman Joseph W. Checota, vigorously hurled accusations and criticisms at each other. Feingold darted through the mud past them to score a stunning primary victory, and then proceeded to knock off Republican Sen. Bob Kasten in November.

A 10-year veteran of the state Legislature, Feingold pitched himself as an unconventional candidate with a series of amusing advertisements, emulating techniques that Minnesota Democrat Paul Wellstone had used to upset GOP Sen. Rudy Boschwitz in 1990. In one ad Feingold led a tour of his Middleton home, remarking in front of an open closet, "Look, no skeletons." Another featured a mock tabloid newspaper headline touting his endorsement from Elvis Presley.

Moody and Checota battered each other first in a war of words, then with negative campaign ads. The attacks worked so well that voters soured on both leading contenders. Meanwhile, Feingold stressed that his lifestyle and values were more typical of Wisconsin. The primary result was nothing short of astounding: Feingold won the nomination with nearly 70 percent of the vote.

Although twice elected to the Senate, Kasten never enjoyed wide personal popularity; his previous winning margins were 50 percent in 1980, when he defeated incumbent Gaylord Nelson, and 51 percent in 1986, a year after he was arrested for drunken driving.

In 1986, Kasten had the good fortune to draw as his challenger Ed Garvey, a combative personality who did not have united Democratic support. But in Feingold, Kasten had a foe with no such baggage. Feingold's being Jewish did not hurt, either. Kasten, a strong supporter of aid to Israel, had in previous campaigns raised considerable out-of-state funds from Jewish groups.

After the primary, polls showed Kasten trailing Feingold by more than 20 percentage points. But once Kasten focused on portraying his foe as an extreme liberal, he began closing ground. Kasten sought to paint Feingold as a tax-and-spend liberal who was soft on crime. Feingold's pitch was based less on ideology than on his image of being a straightforward, maverick politician.

In an analysis of Feingold's voting record in the state Legislature, the Milwaukee Journal described him as a "liberal-populist," noting his strong support for abortion rights, environmental regulations and higher taxes for corporations and wealthy individuals.

One typical Feingold stand was his backing of consumers at the expense of the state's powerful dairy industry in a fight over whether farmers should be allowed to use synthetic hormones to increase cows' milk production. Feingold's own position papers highlighted a standard liberal wish list, including urban aid, universal health care and environmental protection.

Kasten, always aware of his electoral vulnerability, had been known for assembling efficient congressional and campaign staffs, and he was practiced at the art of waging aggressive, negative campaigns. But Wisconsin's political climate in 1992 was much less hospitable toward candidates taking an attack posture. Though Kasten made headway cutting into Feingold's lead, at the same time he had to contend with criticism that he was running an unfair negative campaign.

On Election Day, Feingold compiled large margins in Milwaukee County and in his home base, Dane County (Madison), while minimizing Kasten's margin in the strongly Republican Milwaukee suburbs of Waukesha County. Despite being outspent by well over 2-to-1, Feingold prevailed, 53 percent to 46 percent.

Feingold's Senate triumph recalled his earliest political bid. In his first run for the state Senate in 1982 at the age of 29, he similarly took on an entrenched incumbent, refused advice to go negative, worked door-to-door and won narrowly — by 31 votes out of a total of 47,000 cast.

In the Senate, Feingold took seats on the Agriculture, Foreign Relations and Special Aging committees. Despite his admission to the nation's most exclusive club, Feingold vowed to retain his outsider status, going so far as to paint on his garage door his "contract" with his constituents. Among his promises were to continue to live in Wisconsin and send his children to public schools there, to eschew campaign contributions from outside the state, to accept no pay raises during his six-year term and to visit each of the state's 72 counties each year.

Committees

Agriculture, Nutrition & Forestry (10th of 10 Democrats)
Agricultural Production & Stabilization of Prices; Domestic & Foreign Marketing & Product Promotion; Nutrition & Investigations

Foreign Relations (10th of 11 Democrats)
African Affairs; European Affairs; International Economic Policy, Trade, Oceans & Environment

Special Aging (10th of 11 Democrats)

Campaign Finance

	Receipts	Receipts from PACs		Expenditures
1992				
Feingold (D)	$1,995,732	$459,613	(23%)	$1,979,454
Kasten (R)	$5,107,974	$1,294,783	(25%)	$5,427,163

Key Votes

1993

Require unpaid family and medical leave	Y
Approve national "motor voter" registration bill	Y
Approve budget increasing taxes and reducing deficit	Y
Support president's right to lift military gay ban	Y

Elections

1992 General		
Russell D. Feingold (D)	1,290,662	(53%)
Bob Kasten (R)	1,129,599	(46%)
1992 Primary		
Russell D. Feingold (D)	367,746	(70%)
Jim Moody (D)	74,472	(14%)
Joseph W. Checota (D)	71,570	(14%)
Thomas Keller (D)	8,678	(2%)

1 Peter W. Barca (D)

Of Kenosha — Elected 1993; 1st Term

Born: Aug. 7, 1955, Kenosha, Wis.
Education: U. of Wisconsin, Milwaukee, B.S. 1977; U. of Wisconsin, Madison, M.A., 1982.
Occupation: Educator; employment specialist.
Family: Wife, Kathy Hau; two children.
Religion: Roman Catholic.
Political Career: Wis. Assembly, 1985-93, majority caucus chairman, 1991-93.
Capitol Office: 1719 Longworth Bldg. 20515; 225-3031.

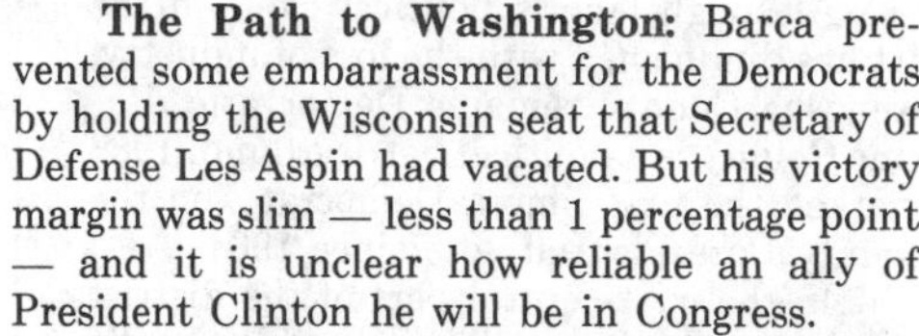

The Path to Washington: Barca prevented some embarrassment for the Democrats by holding the Wisconsin seat that Secretary of Defense Les Aspin had vacated. But his victory margin was slim — less than 1 percentage point — and it is unclear how reliable an ally of President Clinton he will be in Congress.

Barca made a point of keeping his distance from the president during his special election campaign and had to repeatedly fight off Republican efforts to frame the contest as a referendum on the early months of the Clinton administration.

While saying he supported the "spirit" of Clinton's economic program, Barca ticked off a number of specific points he disagreed with. He opposed Clinton's energy tax proposal. He opposed raising the tax on Social Security benefits unless the earnings threshold was raised. And he criticized the North American Free Trade Agreement.

Yet in a career in the Wisconsin Assembly that spanned nearly a decade, Barca quietly advanced by being a team player. He chaired the Employment and Training Committee and co-chaired the Joint Committee on Audit before becoming majority caucus chairman, the third-ranking position in the Assembly's Democratic leadership, in 1991.

Words such as sincere, hard-working and low-key are often used to describe him, but the word colorful is not. Says one Wisconsin newsman: "He's not the first guy to come to mind if you're having a party."

He was not the first candidate to come to mind when Aspin's House seat suddenly came open, either. The seat initially attracted a wide field of potential candidates, including several legislators and former state party Chairman Jeffrey Neubauer, the early favorite for the Democratic nomination.

But Barca quickly emerged as a major competitor by lining up endorsements from a number of prominent legislators as well as powerful labor elements, including the state AFL-CIO and the United Auto Workers.

In the end, though, it was Barca's strong base in his hometown of Kenosha and his ability to turn out the home folks on Election Day that made the difference. Running up big margins in Kenosha County, the district's third largest, enabled him to win the Democratic primary easily and go on to narrowly defeat Republican Mark W. Neumann in the May 4 special election.

Barca, though, could not claim his seat until several weeks later. Neumann, a wealthy home builder, had run a hard-hitting campaign against Aspin the previous fall and was slow to admit a second congressional defeat. Trailing Barca by fewer than 1,000 votes out of 110,000 cast, Neumann requested a recount before finally conceding when it confirmed the original result.

As a politician, Barca defies easy labeling. The product of a middle-class Italian-American family and a Catholic upbringing, he has indicated that he would support the Freedom of Choice Act pending in Congress. Still, he proudly depicts himself as a reflection of his hometown, and his political concerns in the state Legislature were often unmistakably local.

Although not as dependent as it once was on automobile manufacturing, Kenosha remains a blue-collar union town. It has had its share of economic hardship. American Motors once had a large plant in Kenosha, which was subsequently taken over by the Chrysler Corp. But Chrysler shut down the Kenosha assembly plant in the late 1980s, laying off thousands of workers. Subsequently, Barca spent much of his time on job retraining programs and legislation that enabled the city to build a new industrial park.

Before he was elected to the Legislature in 1984, Barca was a teacher of emotionally disturbed children, the director of a camp for disabled children and a job training specialist for people with disabilities. He is a member of the AFL-CIO.

While Neumann chided him for building a career in the public sector, Barca claimed a greater understanding of the problems of the working class.

Wisconsin 1

Southeast — Racine; Kenosha

Although it is dominated by four industrialized cities, the 1st is far from a Democratic stronghold.

Until Les Aspin's election in 1970, Democrats had won this district only twice in the 20th century — in 1958 and 1964. Both incumbents were defeated after serving single terms. The party also endured a long dry spell in presidential voting here. After Lyndon B. Johnson carried the district in 1964, not until 1988 did it return to the Democratic column, with a 51 percent victory for Michael S. Dukakis. In 1992, Bill Clinton won the 1st by 6 percentage points.

The district's two largest cities are sandwiched between Milwaukee and Chicago along Lake Michigan: Racine, originally settled by Danish immigrants, and Kenosha, with a sizable Italian community.

Located in Racine are the district's largest employers: J. I. Case, makers of farm equipment, and S. C. Johnson and Son, which makes home-care products. The Racine lakefront is in the process of being revitalized with a marina and condominiums. Racine is also known for its thin, buttery Danish pastries known as kringles. Kenosha has a branch of the University of Wisconsin and a Chrysler plant where about 1,100 people make Jeep engines. The city was dealt a sharp blow by the December 1988 closure of the main Chrysler-AMC plant, a cornerstone of Kenosha's economy for almost nine decades. Chrysler spent millions of dollars in severance pay, economic development aid and contributions to local civic groups, and the state helped retrain workers.

Kenosha's economic base is diversifying, and the area's affordable real estate prices are attracting some Chicago commuters. Within weeks of the big Chrysler plant closing, a waterfront development project was planned. A corporate park opened in Pleasant Prairie, just east of Interstate 94. Kenosha is still the headquarters for Jockey International Inc. and the Snap-On Tools Corp. The city has two factory outlet shopping centers popular with bargain-hunters; another lure for visitors is Dairyland, the nation's largest greyhound dog racing track.

Although labor's political clout in the 1st has diminished with the loss of industry, Kenosha County remains Democratic. Racine County is a political battleground; 1988 marked the first time a Democrat won the county's presidential vote since 1964.

In the west-central part of the district are the smaller industrial cities of Janesville and Beloit, in politically marginal Rock County. Beloit was settled by a group of immigrants from New Hampshire that founded Beloit College in 1846. Janesville's employers include a General Motors plant.

The strongest GOP vote in the 1st comes from Walworth County in the middle of the district. Resort complexes around Lake Geneva and Lake Delavan cater to wealthy vacationers from Milwaukee and Chicago. Soybeans grow so well in rural Walworth County that the Japanese Kikkoman soy sauce company built a plant in Walworth to brew and bottle its product.

1990 Population: 543,530. White 500,231 (92%), Black 29,539 (5%), Other 13,760 (3%). Hispanic origin 18,652 (3%). 18 and over 397,289 (73%), 62 and over 81,464 (15%). Median age: 33.

Committees

New member — assignments to be determined

Elections

1993 Special		
Peter W. Barca (D)	55,605	(50%)
Mark W. Neumann (R)	54,930	(49%)
1993 Special Primary		
Peter W. Barca (D)	31,073	(49%)
Jeffrey Neubauer (D)	21,610	(34%)
Wayne W. Wood (D)	8,254	(13%)
Jeffrey C. Thomas (D)	1,814	(3%)
Samuel Platts (D)	1,094	(2%)

District Vote for President

1992
D 109,790 (41%)
R 94,712 (35%)
I 62,465 (23%)

Campaign Finance †

	Receipts	Receipts from PACs		Expend-itures
1993				
Barca (D)	$348,183	$144,250	(41%)	$279,039
Neumann (R)	$353,189	$47,305	(13%)	$266,294

† Figures are through May 25, 1993.

2 Scott L. Klug (R)

Of Madison — Elected 1990; 2nd Term

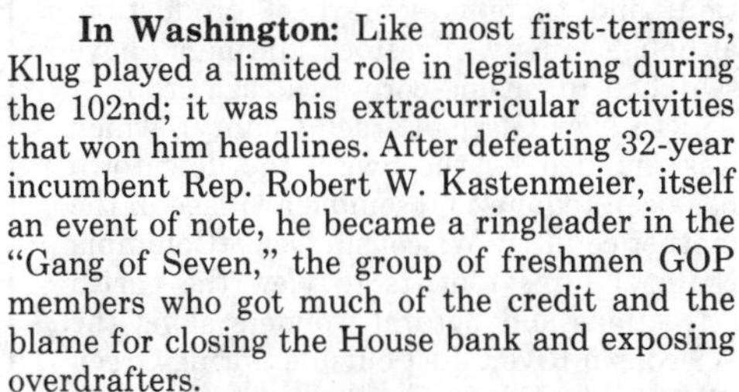

Born: Jan. 16, 1953, Milwaukee.

Education: Lawrence U., B.S. 1975; Northwestern U., M.S.J. 1976; U. of Wisconsin, M.B.A. 1990.

Occupation: Television journalist; business development and investment executive.

Family: Wife, Tess Summers; three children.

Religion: Roman Catholic.

Political Career: No previous office.

Capitol Office: 1224 Longworth Bldg. 20515; 225-2906.

In Washington: Like most first-termers, Klug played a limited role in legislating during the 102nd; it was his extracurricular activities that won him headlines. After defeating 32-year incumbent Rep. Robert W. Kastenmeier, itself an event of note, he became a ringleader in the "Gang of Seven," the group of freshmen GOP members who got much of the credit and the blame for closing the House bank and exposing overdrafters.

And although Klug will never pass any GOP purity test — he favors abortion rights, for starters — he has already been rewarded for his bomb-throwing technique and fiscal conservatism with a position on the Energy and Commerce Committee in the 103rd.

Beyond his dogged Jack-and-the-Beanstalk approach to entrenched incumbents and check-kiters, Klug did have interests in the 102nd other than agitating for reform. In his first two years, he managed to leave fingerprints on several pieces of legislation and to paint himself as a moderate Republican on several controversies of the day.

But it was the House bank controversy that brought national attention to Klug and the six others who became the gang. As junior members of the minority party, they might have had anonymity and plenty of time on their hands. But in September 1991, as Speaker Thomas S. Foley of Washington admonished House members for abusing their banking privileges, Klug and Republican Rick Santorum of Pennsylvania saw an opportunity. Angry at the thought that bank abusers would be given only a light scolding, Klug and Santorum gathered a few other like-minded colleagues for a late-night strategy meeting.

The result was a frontal assault. They began with daily floor speeches decrying the "whitewash behind the House bank scandal" and carried on into a media blitz that included all seven but often featured Klug — perhaps the most telegenic of the gang after years as a local TV journalist. The heightened attention helped bring about the closing of the bank by year's end. Four months after that, in April 1992, the gang saw its early calls for full disclosure answered with the publication of the full list of overdrafters.

Ironically, Klug's name was among them. In his few months in Congress, he had managed to write three overdrafts. And while that number was minuscule compared with the hundreds written by some members, it was enough for some colleagues to tag him a hypocrite.

"Sure, it's embarrassing," said Klug, adding that he had only wanted to target the worst abusers.

When the House bank no longer provided fodder, the Gang of Seven moved on to other aspects of congressional reform. In 1992, Klug sponsored an amendment forcing the Speaker to return his $6.8 million "slush fund" of leftover members' money to the Treasury, an effort which passed 426-0. He even strayed outside Congress' halls in his search for waste, preventing the IRS from using tax dollars to buy private health club memberships for its employees.

Gang-related events gave Klug something to brag about to the folks back home. In a traditionally liberal district — the 2nd is home to the state capital and the main campus of the University of Wisconsin — Klug has had to work hard to retain his seat. His office tallied tours of 138 local businesses and 90 schools, speaking engagements at 170 organizations, and 20 town meetings during his first term. A key part of Klug's continuing campaign has been his identity as a district-based outsider, and working as part of the gang has lent credence to that claim.

As one might expect from a Republican elected by a liberal district, Klug has little in common with conservative ideologues. He supported President George Bush's announced position on only 54 percent of the floor votes in 1992. And on many of the high-profile, high-controversy social issues of the day, Klug showed up in the enemy's camp. He was among a handful of Republicans to support the Family and Medical Leave Act during the 102nd, even working to draft the bill as a member of the Education and Labor Committee.

Wisconsin 2

South — Madison

Once described by former GOP Gov. Lee Dreyfus as "23 square miles surrounded by reality," Madison has long been Wisconsin's liberal centerpiece — Progressive magazine is published here — and it is one of the few cities with a foreign policy. Since 1924, when Robert M. La Follette carried Dane County as the Progressive Party's presidential candidate, Democrats have nearly always won here.

But times have changed, and politics have moderated considerably in the 2nd District. This was graphically demonstrated by Republican Klug's 1990 upset of Democratic Rep. Robert W. Kastenmeier, a 32-year veteran, and Klug's 1992 re-election with more than 60 percent of the vote.

As the state's capital and home to its main university campus, Madison is dominated by its white-collar sector. About one-third of the area's work force is employed in government, primarily for the state or the University of Wisconsin, which helps keep employment stable. White-collar jobs are also supplied by several locally based insurance companies, such as American Family and CUNA Mutual. In addition, meat processor Oscar Mayer employs about 2,800 in Madison, and Rayovac batteries has headquarters here.

Beyond the city limits, rapidly growing Dane County suburbs such as Verona, Fitchburg and Middleton strike a more conservative tone than the city itself, as do outlying communities such as Stoughton and Mount Horeb. But Democrats usually have carried Dane. Michael S. Dukakis won the county with 60 percent in 1988, and Democratic Senate candidate Herb Kohl polled 58 percent. In 1992, Bill Clinton won the district with 50 percent of the vote to George Bush's 32 percent. At the same time, Klug won the county by more than 40,000 votes.

The 2nd also covers a sizable portion of southern Wisconsin's Republican-voting rural areas, where farmers and small-town folks have long chafed at Madison's dominance of district politics. Outside the Madison area, agriculture and tourism sustain the district's economy. Dairying is important, and there is some beef production, although many livestock farmers have switched to raising corn as a cash crop.

In New Glarus (Green County), which was founded by the Swiss, the downtown has been redone to resemble a village in the mother country. Wisconsin Dells (Columbia County) lures tourists to view the garish attractions and natural wonders along the Wisconsin River. Just outside Spring Green (Sauk County) is Frank Lloyd Wright's Taliesin, a studio complex frequently used by the legendary architect that is now a thriving artist colony.

About 50 miles west of Madison is Dodgeville (Iowa County), headquarters to mail-order clothier Lands' End. Since the company moved here in 1978, property values have increased, the local economy has blossomed and additional facilities were opened in Cross Plains (Dane County) and Reedsburg (Sauk County.)

1990 Population: 543,532. White 519,172 (96%), Black 11,147 (2%), Other 13,213 (2%). Hispanic origin 6,743 (1%). 18 and over 412,393 (76%), 62 and over 73,613 (14%). Median age: 32.

In 1991, Klug also declared his preference for the Democrats' civil rights bill over the GOP alternative, as well as for the Democratic version of campaign finance reform, their motor-voter registration bill and their attempts to enact a seven-day waiting period before handgun purchases.

Lest he lose his GOP credentials entirely, Klug cultivates fiscal conservatism, favoring such GOP standbys as the balanced-budget amendment and presidential line-item veto. He bills himself as a member of the congressional "pork busters" coalition, and he has voted to stanch the flow of spending on projects such as the superconducting super collider and extended unemployment benefits. He also voted against lowering the budget walls that prevent the transfer of funds from defense to domestic spending or from foreign aid to transportation spending.

Klug's assignment on Education and Labor allowed him to work on the reauthorization of the Higher Education Act, where he fought for the exclusion of a family's home or farm when computing assets on a student loan application. In effect, this would raise the income level at which families could qualify for such loans.

Klug also opposed attempts to make Pell grants an entitlement program (funded at the level of demand) and authored a measure to broaden loan forgiveness to include students who focus their careers in special education for youngsters with disabilities.

Moving up to the Energy and Commerce Committee in the 103rd will give Klug a chance to work on health-care reform. His own approach to saving the nation's health-care system entails promoting managed competition through changes in the tax code — changes he says would encourage the formation of "Accountable Health Partnerships" similar to health maintenance organizations (HMOs).

At Home. When Klug, a former TV journalist who had never held office, began a 1990 campaign to unseat 32-year House incumbent Kastenmeier, hardly anyone — from the national GOP to Kastenmeier's local supporters — took his challenge seriously.

So tenuous was his party affiliation before his jump into politics that he did not even join the GOP until a few days before announcing his candidacy in 1990.

But Klug had high name familiarity from two years as an investigative reporter and news anchor on WKOW-TV in Madison, and he campaigned effectively against the liberal Kastenmeier, a local institution still revered for his early opposition to the Vietnam War, as an anachronism typical of an ineffective Congress.

Klug attacked Kastenmeier's seniority, making congressional term limits a centerpiece of his campaign. "The reason I got into this [race], the ideology that really drives me, is the sense that Congress itself is a very troubled institution," Klug said. "We need legislation to limit terms in office to 12 years."

While Madison itself has a reputation for doctrinaire liberalism, Klug sought to identify himself with the pocketbook concerns of young families in the growing suburbs of surrounding Dane County and the rural counties beyond that. Kastenmeier depicted his opponent as a carpetbagger, but Klug was far from foreign, having grown up in the Milwaukee area and gotten a business degree at the University of Wisconsin.

In the end, the incumbent carried Dane County, but by fewer than 4,000 votes. Klug prevailed by more than 15,000 votes in the surrounding counties.

As a freshman, Klug solidified his support with frequent visits home and a voting record that appealed to the mainstream. Those who initially assumed Klug would attract a big field of prospective challengers in 1992 were proved wrong. In the end, the main contenders were Democrats David Clarenbach, a youthful leader from the state Legislature, and Ada E. Deer, a party activist and lecturer at the University of Wisconsin. Campaigning to become the first American Indian woman in Congress, Deer upset Clarenbach in the September primary and gained some attention in media accounts of women candidates.

But Deer proved disappointing as a campaigner, and her reform message did not sell well against Klug. Eschewing campaign contributions from special interests, she raised only about 60 percent as much money as Klug, who was re-elected easily with more than 60 percent of the vote.

Committee

Energy & Commerce (14th of 17 Republicans)
Energy & Power; Health & the Environment

Elections

1992 General		
Scott L. Klug (R)	183,366	(63%)
Ada E. Deer (D)	108,291	(37%)
1990 General		
Scott L. Klug (R)	96,938	(53%)
Robert W. Kastenmeier (D)	85,156	(47%)

District Vote for President

1992
D 149,340 (50%)
R 94,368 (32%)
I 52,552 (18%)

Campaign Finance

	Receipts	Receipts from PACs		Expend- itures
1992				
Klug (R)	$879,091	$226,266	(26%)	$829,378
Deer (D)	$525,120	$674	(0%)	$522,956
1990				
Klug (R)	$183,789	$32,800	(18%)	$178,129
Kastenmeier (D)	$358,609	$184,314	(51%)	$371,928

Key Votes

1993	
Require parental notification of minors' abortions	N
Require unpaid family and medical leave	Y
Approve national "motor voter" registration bill	Y
Approve budget increasing taxes and reducing deficit	N
Approve economic stimulus plan	N
1992	
Approve balanced-budget constitutional amendment	Y
Close down space station program	N
Approve U.S. aid for former Soviet Union	N
Allow shifting funds from defense to domestic programs	N
1991	
Extend unemployment benefits using deficit financing	N
Approve waiting period for handgun purchases	Y
Authorize use of force in Persian Gulf	Y

Voting Studies

Year	Presidential Support S	Presidential Support O	Party Unity S	Party Unity O	Conservative Coalition S	Conservative Coalition O
1992	54	45	73	24	67	33
1991	68	32	67	31	76	22

Interest Group Ratings

Year	ADA	AFL-CIO	CCUS	ACU
1992	40	33	63	56
1991	35	33	80	55

3 Steve Gunderson (R)

Of Osseo — Elected 1980; 7th Term

Born: May 10, 1951, Eau Claire, Wis.
Education: U. of Wisconsin, B.A. 1973; Brown School of Broadcasting, 1974.
Occupation: Public official.
Family: Single.
Religion: Lutheran.
Political Career: Wis. Assembly, 1975-79.
Capitol Office: 2235 Rayburn Bldg. 20515; 225-5506.

In Washington: A collegial moderate in a party with a seemingly decided lack of interest in collegiality or moderation, Gunderson took the highly unusual step of pulling himself off the leadership ladder at the start of the 103rd Congress. He resigned as one of two chief deputy GOP whips, calling the House Republican leadership "hard right." But although he turned his back on the party for its more conservative and confrontational direction, the House Republican Conference had just as clearly left him behind.

"It was clear to me that the [1992 GOP national] convention was going to be a disaster," he said. "We are continuing to send the same message of intolerance." He told the Atlanta Journal-Constitution: "The only tension or force driving what this party says about social issues tends to be the right."

The move by Gunderson, who four years earlier had helped partisan firebrand Newt Gingrich of Georgia win a narrow race for GOP whip, reflected the changing sentiment among the majority of House Republicans about how they will operate in the party's full-opposition status. Had George Bush been re-elected, someone with Gunderson's ability to lubricate legislative gears by easing differences between Democrats and Republicans would have had a place in the leadership structure. "We need a governing conservatism that responds to real-life problems, but does so in ways that empower people — not bureaucracies — and maximizes choice rather than federal regulation," Gunderson has said.

But with a Democrat in the White House and Democrats controlling both houses of Congress, the guiding philosophy of the House GOP need no longer be even partly geared toward making government work. Gunderson's penchant for achieving a middle ground and blurring partisan differences thus has little role these days in the Republican Conference, where partisanship and confrontation are valued more highly.

Gunderson's decision to side with Gingrich over moderate Illinois Republican Edward Madigan in the 1989 whip contest reflected his longstanding desire to reach out to his party's aggressive conservative wing while pursuing an ambitious political agenda. Gunderson worked hard for Gingrich in his contest against Madigan, whose reputation as a low-key insider might have seemed a better fit for the Wisconsin Republican. "Newt adds an element to the leadership team that doesn't exist today," Gunderson said at the time. "He's a ball of energy. He's a visionary and a strategist."

But while Gunderson participated in Gingrich-led assaults such as the revolt of House Republicans against congressional leaders and President Bush to scuttle the fiscal 1991 budget resolution, it was less evident what role Gingrich envisioned for Gunderson. When Gunderson quit, Gingrich said he would leave the position unfilled; adversarial conservative Robert S. Walker is the remaining chief deputy whip.

Gunderson's two committee assignments lend him opportunities to operate effectively beyond partisan differences. On Education and Labor, whose ranks are lined with highly partisan liberal Democrats and conservative Republicans, he is a team player among the panel's moderate Republicans who try to work with the Democratic majority when the subject is education. But he can dig in his heels when the issue is labor legislation. He opposed legislation in the 102nd and 103rd Congresses to require employers to provide up to 12 weeks' unpaid leave to care for a new baby or sick relative.

In the 102nd Congress, Gunderson worked on the five-year reauthorization of the Higher Education Act and on unsuccessful legislation to provide grants to states and schools to improve public schools. After Chairman William D. Ford of Michigan twice reneged on deals he had cut with Republicans on education bills, Gunderson was one of the few remaining members trying to steer a middle course on the issue of school choice. Gunderson and ranking Republican Bill Goodling of Pennsylvania are among the few Republicans on the committee who like Ford. "As partisan as he is," Gunderson said, "it never comes between us as friends.... Bill Ford has never lied to me and never betrayed me."

Wisconsin 3

West — Eau Claire; La Crosse

In a state that bills itself as "America's Dairyland," the 3rd stands at the head of the herd. It has more cows than people and is one of the leading milk-producing districts in the nation.

But some dramatic economic and demographic changes are taking place in the 3rd, which hugs Wisconsin's western border with Minnesota and Iowa. Traditionally, the rural areas have relied mainly on small dairy farms, and its two biggest cities — Eau Claire and La Crosse — have been strongly influenced by heavy manufacturing.

Now, the cities are finding alternatives to heavy industry, and the communities closest to the Twin Cities are becoming thriving suburbs. The more successful dairy farms have evolved into multifamily operations, and tourism in some rural areas has taken hold. But downsizing of the dairy industry has taken its toll, particularly in rural communities without easy access to Interstate 94.

As a result, while the district's population growth in the 1980s mirrored the 4 percent increase in the state as a whole, there were wide differences within the 3rd. All of the counties along the district's northern edge (east and northeast of Minneapolis-St. Paul) grew during the decade. The pacesetter was St. Croix County, immediately east of the Twin Cities, which grew by 16 percent. But all of the counties in the southern two-thirds of the district lost population, except for La Crosse County, which grew by 8 percent.

There are only two cities of size in the district. Eau Claire, once a wild lumber outpost, has a paper mill producing disposable diapers and napkins. A Uniroyal plant that was once the city's largest employer is no more. However, blue-collar jobs have been replaced by white-collar opportunities in a burgeoning computer industry.

La Crosse, Wisconsin's only major Mississippi River city, once featured two locally owned Fortune 500 companies as its mainstays — the Trane Co., manufacturers of heating and air conditioning equipment, and G. Heileman Brewing Inc. But both were subject to hostile takeovers in the 1980s and have scaled down operations.

Democrats traditionally have held sway in the northern part of the district, around Eau Claire, and Republicans have had an edge in the south and in La Crosse. Some of those identifications are changing along with the economy, making the area quite competitive in state elections. Democrats have been gaining of late: In 1988, Michael S. Dukakis won the 3rd with 52 percent, and in 1992 Bill Clinton carried the district with 43 percent of the vote.

The 3rd remains heavily Scandinavian and German — dairy farmers in Osseo (Trempealeau County) still trade gossip over coffee and pie at the Norske Nook — though there are signs of growing ethnic diversity. The district also boasts five branches of the state university, which has helped attract three National Football League teams to set up summer training camps there.

1990 Population: 543,533. White 532,723 (98%), Black 1,329 (<1%), Other 9,481 (2%). Hispanic origin 2,632 (<1%). 18 and over 398,432 (73%), 62 and over 89,022 (16%). Median age: 32.

Gunderson's other assignment is the Agriculture Committee, where partisanship is the exception rather than the norm. He has been demonstrating his legislative acumen for some time on Agriculture, where he is ranking Republican on the subcommittee dealing with the dairy programs crucial to Wisconsin. While Gunderson also has branched out into other legislative areas, he is primarily known as "Mr. Dairy," and is second to none in his understanding of dairy-related matters.

When the dairy subcommittee worked on its portion of the 1990 farm bill, Gunderson and Chairman Charles W. Stenholm of Texas produced a plan that set a floor under the previously sliding scale of government price supports for milk. In the 102nd Congress, he backed an effort to put caps on milk production and boost price supports. The bill died as a coalition of dairy groups from different regions collapsed.

At Home: For a man who insists his real ambition was to become a radio hockey announcer, Gunderson rose in politics quickly. He won his broadcasting license at age 23 and a seat in the Legislature the same year.

As a close associate of GOP Gov. Lee Sherman Dreyfus, Gunderson could have obtained a leadership job in the Legislature. But he quit in mid-1979 to work in Washington as Rep. Toby Roth's legislative director.

In six months, Gunderson was back in Wisconsin, this time to challenge Democratic Rep. Alvin Baldus. Gunderson's job-hopping stirred some complaints that his ambition exceeded his commitment to public service, but 1980 was an excellent Republican year in Wisconsin, and he beat Baldus by demonstrating the same energy that marked his service in the Legislature. Gunderson personally visited thousands of homes in the rural counties of the district, leaving behind his grandmother's recipe for lefse, a Norwegian potato bread.

Gunderson's 1982 Democratic challenger, state Sen. Paul Offner, hoped to unseat him using the Reagan connection. An economist with a Ph.D. from Princeton, Offner presented a detailed plan for economic recovery, including his own federal budget. But Gunderson's tireless campaigning and artful dairy maneuvers won him 57 percent of the vote.

In 1986, Democrats claimed to have a strong candidate in Leland Mulder, a farmer who aimed to tap into rural resentment toward the Reagan administration. Gunderson, however, had no trouble deflecting that strategy. He won 64 percent and stayed above 60 percent even in 1988 — when his district went for Democrat Michael S. Dukakis for president — and in 1990. In 1992, he fell slightly below 60 percent in a race against Paul Sacia, a former lobbyist with the Wisconsin Farm Bureau and National Farmers Union. It had appeared early on that Gunderson might be in trouble, because the dairy industry had hit hard times. However, Sacia's campaign never completely got off the ground. Gunderson had stored up good will and more than enough cash. He outspent his opponent by at least $400,000. In addition, key campaign staffers for Sacia quit the month before the election.

Committees

Agriculture (3rd of 18 Republicans)
Livestock (ranking); Environment, Credit & Rural Development; Department Operations

Education & Labor (4th of 15 Republicans)
Elementary, Secondary & Vocational Education; Labor-Management Relations; Postsecondary Education

Elections

1992 General		
Steve Gunderson (R)	146,903	(56%)
Paul Sacia (D)	108,664	(42%)
Jay B. Evenson (I)	4,736	(2%)
1990 General		
Steve Gunderson (R)	94,509	(61%)
James L. Ziegeweid (D)	60,409	(39%)

Previous Winning Percentages: **1988** (68%) **1986** (64%) **1984** (68%) **1982** (57%) **1980** (51%)

District Vote for President

1992

D 120,261 (43%)
R 90,731 (33%)
I 67,134 (24%)

Campaign Finance

	Receipts	Receipts from PACs		Expend-itures
1992				
Gunderson (R)	$427,112	$222,462	(52%)	$458,846
Sacia (D)	$33,559	$7,100	(21%)	$33,109
1990				
Gunderson (R)	$388,310	$196,595	(51%)	$341,458
Ziegeweid (D)	$57,161	$31,860	(56%)	$57,576

Key Votes

1993	
Require parental notification of minors' abortions	Y
Require unpaid family and medical leave	N
Approve national "motor voter" registration bill	Y
Approve budget increasing taxes and reducing deficit	N
Approve economic stimulus plan	N
1992	
Approve balanced-budget constitutional amendment	Y
Close down space station program	N
Approve U.S. aid for former Soviet Union	Y
Allow shifting funds from defense to domestic programs	N
1991	
Extend unemployment benefits using deficit financing	Y
Approve waiting period for handgun purchases	N
Authorize use of force in Persian Gulf	Y

Voting Studies

	Presidential Support		Party Unity		Conservative Coalition	
Year	**S**	**O**	**S**	**O**	**S**	**O**
1992	62	37	67	32	77	23
1991	68	31	68	31	92	8
1990	60	40	67	31	80	19
1989	77	23	66	32	85	15
1988	46	52	58	40	84	13
1987	61	38	68	29	84	12
1986	52	44	66	29	78	20
1985	50	50	74	22	73	25
1984	61	39	74	26	75	25
1983	61	39	70	30	65	35
1982	56	44	74	26	68	32
1981	70	30	75	25	75	25

Interest Group Ratings

Year	ADA	AFL-CIO	CCUS	ACU
1992	40	50	88	64
1991	20	33	100	80
1990	33	8	77	63
1989	20	17	100	81
1988	45	79	71	54
1987	20	19	86	65
1986	40	67	72	45
1985	35	29	77	43
1984	20	15	75	50
1983	20	12	85	57
1982	45	21	64	50
1981	30	20	84	100

4 Gerald D. Kleczka (D)

Of Milwaukee — Elected 1984; 5th Full Term

Born: Nov. 26, 1943, Milwaukee, Wis.
Education: U. of Wisconsin, 1961-62, 1967, 1970.
Military Service: Air National Guard, 1963-69.
Occupation: Accountant.
Family: Wife, Bonnie L. Scott.
Religion: Roman Catholic.
Political Career: Wis. Assembly, 1969-73; Wis. Senate, 1975-84.
Capitol Office: 2301 Rayburn Bldg. 20515; 225-4572.

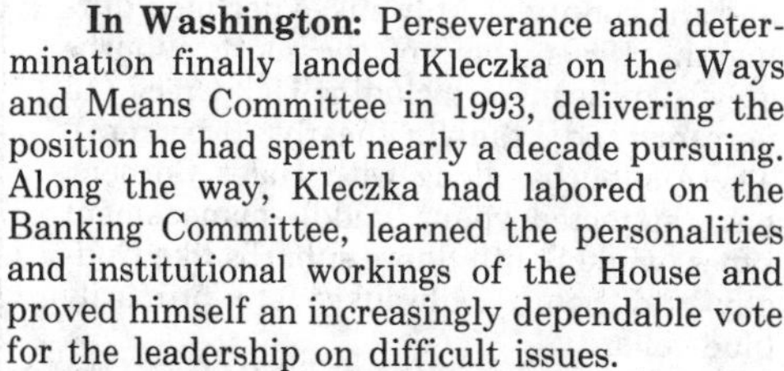

In Washington: Perseverance and determination finally landed Kleczka on the Ways and Means Committee in 1993, delivering the position he had spent nearly a decade pursuing. Along the way, Kleczka had labored on the Banking Committee, learned the personalities and institutional workings of the House and proved himself an increasingly dependable vote for the leadership on difficult issues.

Perhaps most of all, Kleczka in the 1980s displayed patience, an attribute not often associated with street-smart, combative urban populists. Kleczka had long believed himself more than qualified for the tax-writing job, having been chairman of the powerful Joint Finance Committee during his years in the state Legislature. But forbearance was forced on him by the presence on Ways and Means of another Milwaukee Democrat, Jim Moody, who had preceded Kleczka in Congress by less than one full term.

Kleczka compared his wait to the gestation period of an elephant. But if he had to bide his time, he resolved to use the time well. He was a familiar face on the House floor, where he made friends, internalized the chamber's customs and learned about how issues affected votes.

His patience was sorely tried when, in 1988, Moody announced that he would vacate his seat to run for the Senate and then changed his mind. Kleczka had to wait another four years for Moody to retire.

It was also in 1992 that Kleczka demonstrated his greatest party solidarity to date. He was, for example, a cosponsor in 1992 of a joint resolution to amend the Constitution to require a balanced federal budget. Yet when that measure reached the House floor and the Democratic leadership needed every vote it could muster to deny the measure the two-thirds majority it needed, Kleczka provided one. He denies that the vote was related in any way to his bid for Ways and Means, but his vote in that pressure-packed situation is remembered by those who idealize a place on that committee in the future.

Kleczka had already been given a token of approval in the 102nd Congress when he was given a seat on House Administration, an insider panel where Kleczka could engender even greater good will by taking an assignment on a task force developing proposals for overhauling campaign finance laws. In early 1993 he was paying even more dues by serving as chairman of the panel's task force on contested elections.

Kleckza (pronounced Kletch-kuh), has a quick and sharp tongue to rival those of Charles E. Schumer and Barney Frank, two fellow activist liberals with whom he often allied during eight years on the Banking Committee. When former Banking subcommittee Chairman Frank Annunzio butchered Kleckza's name once too often (calling him "Congressman Klee-zak"), he fired back, "Thank you, Chairman Annunciation."

He has an independent streak that allows him to challenge authority publicly and privately, and he sometimes has to work to keep his temper under control: Early in his state legislative career, Kleczka actually came to blows with a lobbyist for a brewery. Some of that pugnaciousness followed him to Washington. In 1988, the American Bankers Association said that Kleczka, Schumer and others would "pay a heavy price" for introducing a bill to broaden bank powers that did not meet the industry's demands. Kleczka immediately took to the floor, labeling the broadside "legislative terrorism" and calling for an investigation into the ABA's lobbying tactics.

Like many Banking Committee Democrats, Kleczka chafed under the leadership of Chairman Henry B. Gonzalez of Texas. Along with Georgia Democrat Doug Barnard Jr., Kleczka led an abortive move early in the 102nd to reallocate some of the committee staff to members who do not have subcommittee chairs. And he showed his annoyance when Gonzalez allied with then-ranking Republican Chalmers P. Wylie of Ohio to block amendments to a bill in early 1991 that would have added $30 billion to the thrift bailout. When Wylie suggested — only partly in jest — that the committee approve the bill on a voice vote, Kleczka retorted: "Turn out the lights, too."

But Kleczka's more lasting legacy on Banking will probably highlight his mastery of finance issues and his populist's disinclination

Wisconsin 4

Southern Milwaukee and Milwaukee County suburbs; southeast Waukesha County

The heart of Milwaukee has long been its South Side bungalow belt. The plain but sturdy houses evoke a feeling from the 1950s. Television viewers still associate the city as the setting for "Laverne and Shirley." Milwaukee has worked hard to promote itself as cosmopolitan, but many residents still value bowling, bratwurst and beer. This is home to conservative Democrats.

Since the turn of the century, the city's huge Polish community has been based on its South Side, and the area remains predominately Polish and German. Neighborhoods are conspicuously tidy; residents regularly sweep the gutters and scrub the sidewalks. The mix of ethnics has made Serb Hall a traditional meeting place for Friday fish fries as well as for candidates seeking working-class votes. The city's strong ethnic heritage is celebrated nearly every summer weekend during a series of lakefront festivals, immediately southeast of downtown.

The migration of some white ethnics to nearby southern suburbs has made room for a wider mix on the South Side. A Hispanic community is growing on the Near South Side, populated mainly by Mexicans and Puerto Ricans. A large population of Vietnamese and Laotians is also located here.

For years, manufacturing was the dominant occupation on the South Side. Although service-industry jobs have increased, many in the 4th still make machinery for mining and construction, and electronic equipment. Johnson Controls Inc., Delco Electronics and Harnischfeger Corp. all have a strong presence in the district. Allen-Bradley Co. is known both for its increasingly automated plant and for displaying the world's largest four-sided analog clock, which stands tall among the South Side church steeples.

West Allis-based Allis-Chalmers is a shadow of its former self now that it has gone through bankruptcy and parts of the company have been purchased by a German firm. West Allis still hosts the annual state fair, where longtime Sen. William Proxmire made a ritual of shaking the hands of thousands of visitors.

While the population of both the city and the county of Milwaukee declined during the 1980s, some of the south suburbs grew significantly, including Oak Creek (15 percent) and Franklin (nearly 30 percent). These suburbs, along with Hales Corners, have attracted young middle-management types, while South Shore suburbs like Cudahy and South Milwaukee are primarily blue-collar.

Just west of Milwaukee County, the 4th includes the Waukesha County suburbs of New Berlin and Muskego, which grew by 10 percent in the 80s, as well as the city of Waukesha, which grew by 13 percent.

Some of the migrants who left the city for the suburbs also left the Democratic Party, boosting the Republican vote in contests for state and national office. The district includes only a part of Waukesha County — which is a Republican stronghold — though the city of Waukesha itself leans Democratic.

1990 Population: 543,527. White 510,138 (94%), Black 4,778 (1%), Other 28,611 (5%). Hispanic origin 34,354 (6%). 18 and over 410,090 (75%), 62 and over 87,474 (16%). Median age: 34.

to trust big money. He consistently favored consumers and was circumspect about proposals to relax regulatory reins on banks and savings and loans.

When issues pitted big banks against smaller ones, Kleczka was a ready ally of the smaller institutions that dominate the Wisconsin financial landscape. During 1991 debate on a bill to overhaul the federal deposit-insurance system, he fought vigorously against protecting some "too big to fail" banks with 100 percent deposit insurance while depositors in lesser institutions did not benefit from full coverage. Kleczka repeatedly sought to force big banks to pay deposit-insurance premiums on deposits made in their overseas branches. Such deposits were not supposed to be insured, but often received de facto coverage when large banks failed. But his amendments offered in committee and subcommittee were routinely rejected by 2-to-1 margins.

He prevailed on a key big-bank issue in 1991, winning approval of an amendment in committee that would have applied the Community Reinvestment Act (the basic federal anti-redlining law) on a state-by-state or city-by-city basis to banks that open branch offices across state lines. (The entire section permitting interstate branching was eventually dropped from the bill.)

As a member of the Banking Subcommittee on Housing, Kleczka succeeded in 1992 in attaching an amendment to a housing bill aimed at protecting elderly residents of high-rise public housing from physical harm by encouraging housing projects to set aside separate floors for the elderly.

Kleczka had been a consistent vote against

abortion until the Supreme Court's *Webster* decision. But shortly after the July 1989 ruling, he voted with the majority as the House narrowly agreed with Senate language allowing federal funding of abortions in cases of rape and incest. His vote was part of the 50-vote swing from 1988. And in 1991 and 1992 he voted with most Democrats to overturn the Bush administration's rule forbidding federally financed family planning clinics from offering abortion counseling.

At Home: Kleczka represents a secure Democratic district that kept his predecessor in office for 35 years with little challenge.

Before coming to Washington, Kleczka spent virtually his entire adult life in the Wisconsin Legislature. First elected at age 24, he was able to improve both his role and reputation over the 15 years that followed. At first, Kleczka was viewed as one more neighborhood-minded ethnic Democrat from Milwaukee's South Side. He was seen as being focused more on local politics (including his feud with the city's long-tenured mayor, Henry Maier) than on abstract issues. He had a reputation for hard-nosed campaigning and occasional quarrels on the Assembly floor. Nonetheless, as he rose gradually to the chairmanship of Joint Finance, he also became known as an effective budget specialist.

When Democratic Rep. Clement J. Zablocki, the House Foreign Affairs chairman, died in late 1983, Kleczka was the front-runner to succeed him. Kleczka had no difficulty picking up support from state Senate colleagues and from economic interests over which Joint Finance held power. He claimed much of Zablocki's backing and was also the choice of the state's Democratic U.S. House delegation. His advertising stressed a different theme: his roots. One TV ad showed an infant in a crib and a grandfather, while a voice described Kleczka as "a leader and a neighbor."

The combination of money, endorsements and roots yielded 32 percent of the vote — enough to win in a five-way primary.

By winning big with 44 percent in the city portion of the district, Kleczka overcame his poor showing in affluent suburban precincts and took the nomination decisively over runner-up E. Michael McCann, the Milwaukee County district attorney who ran respectably everywhere but had no specific base to help him.

Kleczka has had few worries on the home front since then. In 1990 he overwhelmed his Republican foe by a margin of more than 2-to-1; it was his first GOP challenge since 1984. In 1992, the story was much the same, with Kleczka winning 66 percent of the vote.

Committees

House Administration (8th of 12 Democrats)
Contested Elections (chairman); Elections; Office Systems; Personnel & Police

Ways & Means (15th of 24 Democrats)
Health; Oversight

Joint Printing

Elections

1992 General		
Gerald D. Kleczka (D)	173,482	(66%)
Joseph L. Cook (R)	84,872	(32%)
Daniel Slak (I)	2,803	(1%)
1990 General		
Gerald D. Kleczka (D)	96,981	(69%)
Joseph L. Cook (R)	43,001	(31%)

Previous Winning Percentages: **1988** (100%) **1986** (100%) **1984** (67%) **1984 *** (65%)

* *Special election.*

District Vote for President

1992

D	116,048	(40%)
R	108,463	(38%)
I	59,263	(21%)

Campaign Finance

	Receipts	Receipts from PACs		Expend-itures
1992				
Kleczka (D)	$260,726	$156,407	(60%)	$309,036
Cook (R)	$67,268	$2,000	(3%)	$67,267
1990				
Kleczka (D)	$304,440	$186,048	(61%)	$393,562
Cook (R)	$31,850	$2,800	(9%)	$27,986

Key Votes

1993	
Require parental notification of minors' abortions	N
Require unpaid family and medical leave	Y
Approve national "motor voter" registration bill	Y
Approve budget increasing taxes and reducing deficit	Y
Approve economic stimulus plan	Y
1992	
Approve balanced-budget constitutional amendment	N
Close down space station program	Y
Approve U.S. aid for former Soviet Union	N
Allow shifting funds from defense to domestic programs	Y
1991	
Extend unemployment benefits using deficit financing	Y
Approve waiting period for handgun purchases	Y
Authorize use of force in Persian Gulf	N

Voting Studies

	Presidential Support		Party Unity		Conservative Coalition	
Year	**S**	**O**	**S**	**O**	**S**	**O**
1992	20	78	93	4	33	63
1991	23	75	89	4	22	73
1990	21	78	91	6	17	78
1989	28	66	88	5	17	78
1988	19	73	90	5	16	79
1987	17	81	89	4	28	70
1986	24	76	85	9	28	70
1985	28	71	87	6	24	75
1984	42 †	56 †	84 †	15 †	28 †	72 †

† Not eligible for all recorded votes.

Interest Group Ratings

Year	ADA	AFL-CIO	CCUS	ACU
1992	80	82	25	4
1991	85	91	11	0
1990	89	83	23	17
1989	95	83	40	0
1988	95	93	36	4
1987	84	88	13	5
1986	75	86	25	9
1985	75	82	23	14
1984	76	67	38	9

5 Thomas M. Barrett (D)

Of Milwaukee — Elected 1992; 1st Term

Born: Dec. 8, 1953, Milwaukee, Wis.
Education: U. of Wisconsin, B.A. 1976, J.D. 1980.
Occupation: Lawyer.
Family: Wife, Kristine Mansfield; one child.
Religion: Roman Catholic.
Political Career: Candidate for Wis. Assembly, 1982; Wis. Assembly, 1984-89; Wis. Senate, 1989-93.
Capitol Office: 313 Cannon Bldg. 20515; 225-3571.

The Path to Washington: Campaigning door-to-door may be a lost art in this media-intensive age, but Barrett remains one of its leading practitioners. In that sense, he is like his predecessor, Democrat Jim Moody.

Like Moody, Barrett represented much of Milwaukee in the state Assembly and then in the state Senate by making a science of greeting residents at their homes. The soft-spoken Barrett claims to have knocked on nearly 70,000 doors during his legislative tenure.

Even the most energetic politicians might find this activity to be a grind, but the at-home approach seems to fit Barrett's down-home manner. "I find it relaxing, and it's something I'm very comfortable doing," he says. "And when you talk to someone at their home, they're relaxed."

The 5th is Wisconsin's most Democratic district. So when Moody prepared to make his unsuccessful run for the Senate, interest in his replacement was focused mainly on several candidates in the Democratic primary.

Milwaukee County Supervisor Terrance L. Pitts sought and received support as the only black candidate in the race and had a political base on the city's North Side. Frederick P. Kessler, a former state representative from the East Side, had twice resigned as a circuit court judge to run for the House, barely losing to Moody in 1982. Finally, Marc Marotta, a lawyer and former college basketball player, aggressively courted lawyers, Marquette University alumni and the city's Italian community.

Barrett, typically, did not go out of his way to seek media coverage or use his legislative position to raise huge campaign funds. His favorite venues were the one-on-one meetings and public forums, where he promoted himself as a pragmatic legislator who stayed in touch with constituents.

The grass-roots effort served Barrett well. He upended predictions that the outcome would be close by running strongly throughout the city and eight suburbs.

He piled up particularly impressive totals in his state Senate district, which usually turns out at the polls in large numbers.

Barrett kept up the pace in the general election, and the results were never in doubt. He won by more than 2-to-1 over Republican Donalda Ann Hammersmith, a small-business owner from Shorewood who stressed her business experience, gender and anti-abortion views.

Barrett's legislative record was well-suited to the congressional campaign he ran. He had earned a reputation as a conscientious lawmaker who worked doggedly on health-care reform, child abuse prevention, 911 emergency phone service, handgun limits, more funding for juvenile justice and a variety of consumer-oriented matters.

At the start of the 103rd Congress, Barrett assumed a seat on the Banking Committee and its Financial Institutions Subcommittee, where he was one of several freshmen to play a role in the drafting of the 1993 thrift bailout bill. He successfully pressed for a bill provision with Republican Spencer Bachus of Alabama, adopted in subcommittee, to restrict the bonuses of Resolution Trust Corporation (RTC) executives.

A lifelong resident of the district, Barrett says he was inspired to go into politics by his late father, who sold ditch-digging equipment and frequently discussed political issues at home.

It did not take long for the younger Barrett to begin his political career once he obtained his economics and law degrees.

He failed in his first campaign in 1982, losing the Democratic primary for a state Legislature seat to Tom Meaux by 39 votes.

But Meaux soon resigned to run for the Milwaukee County Board of Supervisors, and Barrett seized the opportunity. He won the state Legislature seat in a special election in April 1984 and has not had a close election since then.

He was re-elected three times before winning a 1989 special election for an open state Senate seat, easily defeating state Rep. Shirley Krug in what was expected to be a close primary contest. He ran unopposed for re-election to the state Senate in 1990.

Wisconsin 5

Northern Milwaukee, Milwaukee County suburbs; southeast Waukesha County

The Menomonee River Valley marks the boundary between Milwaukee's North and South sides. The 5th is the North Side district and reliably Democratic. The old district gave Michael S. Dukakis 63 percent of its vote in 1988, and the similarly drawn 5th handed 57 percent to Bill Clinton in 1992, the best showings that each nominee posted in Wisconsin. The city's portion of the district encompasses most of the city's traditional German neighborhoods as well as its black neighborhoods and its affluent East Side.

Milwaukee remains one of the nation's most segregated cities, and the great majority of the metro area's black population lives on or near the city's North Side. Although parts of Milwaukee are impoverished, its ghetto is not as stark as those in other cities. This reflects in part the city's old but sturdy housing stock and the lack of high-rise public housing. But all this does not hide the inner-city despair; the gulf between races in terms of jobs, income and home ownership has been as wide here as in any city in the country.

The city's black population continues to increase and to spread, generally moving out to the west and northwest in search of newer housing and a better quality of life. One area around Sherman Park shifted in 20 years from 98 percent white to 82 percent black. Attempts are being made to keep other parts of Sherman Park integrated.

Milwaukee's manufacturing base, hit hard in the early 1980s recession, is doing better. Major employers in the 5th include Briggs & Stratton, makers of gasoline engines, and A. O. Smith, which makes automobile parts and supplies. Motorcyclists revere the Harley-Davidson Motor Co. here.

The 5th is the focal point of what remains of Milwaukee's best-known industry — brewing. Schlitz, Pabst and Miller were once the locally owned giants, but much has changed. Pabst and Miller are no longer locally owned, and Schlitz closed its Milwaukee brewery in 1981.

North and west of the black neighborhoods are modest, middle-class areas.

The East Side, between the Milwaukee River and Lake Michigan, features comfortable homes, academics who work at Milwaukee's branch of the University of Wisconsin, and middle and upper managers.

The houses get bigger and more expensive in the North Shore suburbs. Just north of the city line, Shorewood's inclusion of young professionals and multifamily housing gives it a Democratic leaning. But farther north, the 5th also includes the more exclusive villages of Whitefish Bay, Fox Point and Bayside. In the city's boom days, brewers and other industrial barons built mansions along the North Shore; today the property values are still stunning by Wisconsin standards, as are the Republican turnouts. In some of these affluent communities, such as River Hills, George Bush won by margins of close to 2-to-1.

West of the city is Wauwatosa, a residential area with older housing stock that is shedding some of its Republicanism as it attracts young professionals.

1990 Population: 543,530. White 333,040 (61%), Black 191,141 (35%), Other 19,349 (4%). Hispanic origin 14,377 (3%). 18 and over 395,942 (73%), 62 and over 82,137 (15%). Median age: 31.

Committees

Banking, Finance & Urban Affairs (21st of 30 Democrats)
Consumer Credit & Insurance; Financial Institutions Supervision, Regulation & Deposit Insurance; Housing & Community Development

Government Operations (16th of 25 Democrats)
Human Resources & Intergovernmental Relations

Natural Resources (28th of 28 Democrats)
Oversight & Investigations

Campaign Finance

1992	Receipts	Receipts from PACs		Expend-itures
Barrett (D)	$356,052	$154,526	(43%)	$387,469
Hammersmith (R)	$100,092	$2,350	(2%)	$98,338

Key Votes

1993

Require parental notification of minors' abortions	N
Require unpaid family and medical leave	Y
Approve national "motor voter" registration bill	Y
Approve budget increasing taxes and reducing deficit	Y
Approve economic stimulus plan	Y

Elections

1992 General

Thomas M. Barrett (D)	162,344	(69%)
Donalda Ann Hammersmith (R)	71,885	(30%)

1992 Primary

Thomas M. Barrett (D)	34,301	(41%)
Terrance L. Pitts (D)	18,928	(23%)
Frederick P. Kessler (D)	15,729	(19%)
Marc Marotta (D)	13,411	(16%)

District Vote for President

	1992	
D	142,047	(57%)
R	76,935	(31%)
I	32,138	(13%)

6 Tom Petri (R)

Of Fond du Lac — Elected 1979; 7th Full Term

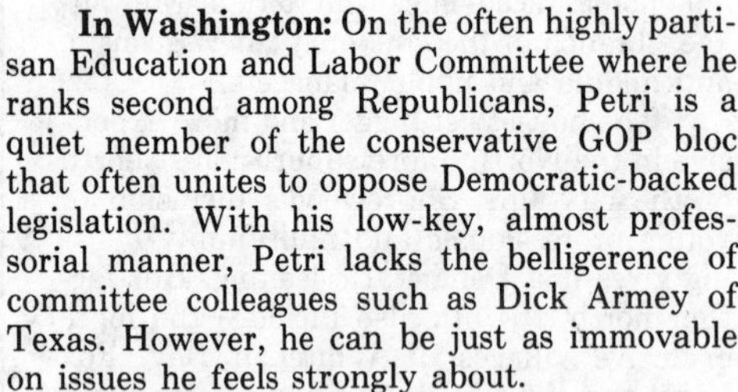

Born: May 28, 1940, Marinette, Wis.
Education: Harvard U., A.B. 1962, J.D. 1965.
Occupation: Lawyer.
Family: Wife, Anne Neal; one child.
Religion: Lutheran.
Political Career: White House aide, 1969-70; Wis. Senate, 1973-79; GOP nominee for U.S. Senate, 1974.
Capitol Office: 2262 Rayburn Bldg. 20515; 225-2476.

In Washington: On the often highly partisan Education and Labor Committee where he ranks second among Republicans, Petri is a quiet member of the conservative GOP bloc that often unites to oppose Democratic-backed legislation. With his low-key, almost professorial manner, Petri lacks the belligerence of committee colleagues such as Dick Armey of Texas. However, he can be just as immovable on issues he feels strongly about.

Although he began his career as a moderate, Petri has moved further to the right, especially on fiscal matters and on social issues such as abortion. On environmental issues, however, he is more of a centrist.

Over the years, Petri has become closely associated with one issue that turns out to be a favorite of President Clinton's, and this could mean a high profile role for Petri in the 103rd Congress.

Clinton wants to expand the earned income tax credit (EITC), a tax break for the working poor, that Petri has been trying to expand for a long time. He has sponsored a bill that would increase the current EITC for low-income families and expand it to middle-income families. The bill would also target larger families for tax credits.

Petri began promoting EITC during the 1988-89 debate on raising the minimum wage. He argued that such a break would target aid to those who needed it, while an across-the-board increase in the minimum wage amounted to "trying to achieve a goal with random bombing when a rapier will do."

House Democrats repeatedly blocked Petri's efforts to offer the idea as an amendment to minimum wage legislation, and he ran into the same resistance that meets any revenue-losing idea in the current deficit-conscious climate. Still, House Democrats showed increasing interest in the idea as a way to help the working poor, and even the chairman of the tax-writing Ways and Means Committee, Dan Rostenkowski of Illinois, came to express the view that an expanded EITC would make more sense than raising the minimum wage.

Later, during 1989 debate on child-care legislation, Petri's colleagues on Education and Labor vigorously fought the idea of expanding the EITC to allow parents to pay for day care. Instead, it was Rostenkowski and other Ways and Means Democrats who successfully pushed the plan, which helped win White House backing for the bill. Petri complained that the Democratic plan was structured to make "welfare more attractive.... One of the reasons we're pushing the EITC is to help make work more attractive than welfare."

Petri is also a longtime proponent of student loan reform. In the 102nd Congress, the Education and Labor Committee took up the Higher Education Act and adopted a Petri proposal under which student loans in danger of default would be repaid at a rate based on one's income. In the 99th Congress, he won funding for a similar demonstration program in which those with high incomes after graduation paid higher interest rates to subsidize lower rates for other borrowers.

Petri has spent much of his congressional career nitpicking pork-barrel projects. Over the years, he has riled even the most powerful House members in his crusade against federal largess. In the closing days of the 102nd, Petri successfully took on Democratic Rep. Vic Fazio of California in an effort to kill a $1 billion dam project near Auburn, Calif.

On the Public Works Committee, Petri may find himself breaking with his quiet image more often in the 103rd Congress. At the start of the session, Petri became ranking Republican on the Public Works Surface Transportation Subcommittee, where new Chairman Nick J. Rahall II of West Virginia, is known for his effort to steer federal dollars home.

Despite his budget-cutting zeal and his opposition to pork, Petri looks out for his home state. He takes credit for winning passage of provisions to change the funding formula for allocating federal highway funds. As a result, Wisconsin will receive more than $1 billion in additional highway money through 1997.

Petri's accomplishments and manner have

Wisconsin 6

Central — Oshkosh; Fond du Lac; Manitowoc

The 6th encompasses almost the entire width of central Wisconsin, stretching from Lake Michigan west to within about 30 miles of the Minnesota border. The district has been closely contested in many state and national elections, but it has sent only one Democrat to Congress since 1938.

The farms and market towns are generally Republican, while Democratic strength is in several small industrialized cities in the eastern part of the 6th — Manitowoc and Two Rivers in Manitowoc County and Neenah-Menasha in Winnebago County, and Fond du Lac in Fond du Lac County.

The most Democratic of the bunch is Manitowoc, a prominent Lake Michigan shipbuilding center in the days when wooden vessels plied the seas. More than half the jobs in Manitowoc now are involved in manufacturing and processing, and unions are an important force. Goods produced include Mirro-Foley's aluminum pots and pans, and the Manitowoc Co.'s ice-making machine for motels. Tourism got a boost with the recent launching of a car ferry service across Lake Michigan to Ludington, Mich. Manitowoc County went solidly for Jimmy Carter in 1976, voted narrowly for Ronald Reagan in 1980 and 1984, swung back to the Democratic side in 1988 and stayed there in 1992.

Republicans have an easier time in Winnebago and Fond du Lac counties. Both counties went Republican in the 1986 and 1988 Senate races, and George Bush carried them in the 1988 and 1992 presidential elections. Winnebago's population increased 7 percent in the 1980s.

Oshkosh is on the western shore of Lake Winnebago, the state's largest lake. Tourism and a state university branch boost the economy, and factories in Winnebago County turn out auto parts, wood and paper products, and Oshkosh B'Gosh clothing. Oshkosh Truck is the largest defense contractor in a state that has traditionally ranked low in defense spending. So many airplane buffs travel to Oshkosh for the annual Experimental Aircraft Association convention that it briefly becomes the busiest airport in the world in terms of takeoffs and landings.

Toward the northern end of the lake is Neenah-Menasha, where paper goods company Kimberly-Clark is one of the 6th's major employers.

At the southern tip of the lake is Fond du Lac County, home of Mercury outboard motors, Speed Queen laundry equipment, and a large Giddings & Lewis tool manufacturing plant. The city of Fond du Lac has strong historical justification for its GOP inclinations. About 20 miles west of the city is Ripon, which lays claim to being the birthplace of the Republican Party, in 1854.

Besides the industry in the district, farming has a strong presence. After all-important dairying, output from the district's farms is diverse, including corn, peas, beans and cranberries. Republican strength in the rural part of the 6th is most concentrated in Green Lake County, a resort area with large summer homes. Republicans are also strong in Waupaca and Waushara counties.

1990 Population: 543,652. White 533,561 (98%), Black 1,944 (<1%), Other 8,147 (2%). Hispanic origin 4,753 (1%). 18 and over 400,512 (74%), 62 and over 95,741 (18%). Median age: 34.

made him popular with voters over the years. In 1992 he faced his first serious challenge in a decade, but despite having to defend 77 overdrafts at the House bank, he came out on top.

At Home: Petri built his Wisconsin career out of the moderate Republican politics that worked for his predecessor, William A. Steiger, who died of a heart attack at age 40, one month after winning his seventh House term in 1978.

In the 1979 special election held to choose Steiger's successor, Petri campaigned on the same reformist issues Steiger had used. His campaign literature boasted of the high ratings he had received in the state Senate from the self-styled citizens' lobby, Common Cause. He noted that he had been a Peace Corps volunteer in Somalia and served as executive director of the Ripon Society, a moderate GOP group.

His opponent Gary Goyke, a fellow state senator with a more forceful campaign style, made an issue of Petri's generous campaign financing. Goyke implied that the Republican had come out against national health insurance because of a $5,000 contribution he had received from the political action committee of the American Medical Association, a charge Petri denied. For his part, Petri said Goyke had his own source of political funding in organized labor.

Petri won the special election on his strength in rural areas and his ability to cut into Goyke's vote in blue-collar cities, especially Sheboygan, which Petri narrowly carried. His overall margin of victory was barely 1,200 votes.

Eighteen months later there was a rematch. But the 1980 election was a pale shadow of the first contest. Petri had enhanced his Steiger-like image by hiring some of Steiger's aides and taking his predecessor's place on Education and Labor. With a strong Republican tide at the statewide level, Petri carried every county in the district against Goyke the second time around. In 1982, despite a strong Democratic trend in statewide politics, Petri romped to another term with 65 percent. From 1984 to 1990, Petri never received less than three-fourths of the vote.

Then in 1992, a year of anti-incumbent fervor, he was challenged by state Rep. Peggy A. Lautenschlager.

Lautenschlager started with a big disadvantage. She had little name recognition in the western part of the district, little money for mass advertising and she declined to launch a heavy door-to-door campaign.

Petri, though criticized for his 77 overdrafts at the House bank, still had solid support, and he had the money to advertise early and often (he outspent Lautenschlager by $350,000). Petri apologized to voters for the overdrafts and used the advertisements to switch attention to his efforts to cut wasteful spending and boost the EITC for the working poor.

Rather than striking out at Petri on the check scandal in the beginning of the year, when the issue was hottest, she waited until the final days of the campaign.

In the end, she lacked the popularity and momentum needed to defeat an incumbent with a good record overall for aiding his district. Petri won with more the 53 percent of the vote.

Committees

Education & Labor (2nd of 15 Republicans)
Postsecondary Education (ranking); Elementary, Secondary & Vocational Education

Post Office & Civil Service (7th of 9 Republicans)
Census, Statistics & Postal Personnel (ranking)

Public Works & Transportation (3rd of 24 Republicans)
Surface Transportation (ranking); Public Buildings & Grounds; Water Resources & the Environment

Elections

1992 General		
Tom Petri (R)	143,875	(53%)
Peggy A. Lautenschlager (D)	128,232	(47%)
1990 General		
Tom Petri (R)	111,036	(100%)

Previous Winning Percentages: **1988** (74%) **1986** (97%) **1984** (76%) **1982** (65%) **1980** (59%) **1979** * (50%)

** Special election.*

District Vote for President

1992
D 101,123 (35%)
R 118,177 (41%)
I 71,065 (24%)

Campaign Finance

	Receipts	Receipts from PACs		Expend-itures
1992				
Petri (R)	$433,702	$204,000	(47%)	$775,594
Lautenschlager (D)	$333,541	$114,711	(34%)	$319,363
1990				
Petri (R)	$240,501	$98,455	(41%)	$131,156

Key Votes

1993	
Require parental notification of minors' abortions	Y
Require unpaid family and medical leave	Y
Approve national "motor voter" registration bill	N
Approve budget increasing taxes and reducing deficit	N
Approve economic stimulus plan	N
1992	
Approve balanced-budget constitutional amendment	Y
Close down space station program	N
Approve U.S. aid for former Soviet Union	N
Allow shifting funds from defense to domestic programs	N
1991	
Extend unemployment benefits using deficit financing	N
Approve waiting period for handgun purchases	N
Authorize use of force in Persian Gulf	Y

Voting Studies

	Presidential Support		Party Unity		Conservative Coalition	
Year	**S**	**O**	**S**	**O**	**S**	**O**
1992	67	33	73	27	73	25
1991	68	32	69	30	89	11
1990	69	31	78	20	80	19
1989	66	34	67	33	76	24
1988	62	36	66	32	84	13
1987	55	43	70	28	67	30
1986	73	27	74	25	76	24
1985	61	39	60	35	60	40
1984	54	46	76	24	75	25
1983	60	39	76	23	72	28
1982	53	40	71	28	70	30
1981	57	41	71	23	67	32

Interest Group Ratings

Year	ADA	AFL-CIO	CCUS	ACU
1992	25	25	63	76
1991	10	8	90	85
1990	22	8	86	75
1989	20	17	90	75
1988	35	50	79	75
1987	16	13	80	61
1986	5	0	94	73
1985	30	35	59	62
1984	20	8	63	83
1983	20	24	80	52
1982	35	30	64	64
1981	40	7	83	100

7 David R. Obey (D)

Of Wausau — Elected 1969; 12th Full Term

Born: Oct. 3, 1938, Okmulgee, Okla.
Education: U. of Wisconsin, B.S. 1960, M.A. 1962.
Occupation: Real estate broker.
Family: Wife, Joan Lepinski; two children.
Religion: Roman Catholic.
Political Career: Wis. Assembly, 1963-69.
Capitol Office: 2462 Rayburn Bldg. 20515; 225-3365.

In Washington: Since he arrived in the House, Obey has been described as temperamental, impulsive and bullheaded. He has shown, however, that his energy, expertise, determination and obstinacy can all come together to form a complex brand of effective leadership as chairman of the Appropriations Subcommittee on Foreign Operations. Still, when the time comes for his next step — a bid for the chairmanship of the full Appropriations Committee — his personal traits may yet prove to be impediments.

That day was postponed when Democrats at the start of the 103rd Congress gave the gavel to acting Chairman William H. Natcher of Kentucky. Natcher had taken over from the ailing Jamie L. Whitten of Mississippi in mid-1992 and creditably steered the panel for the rest of the session. After sounding out support for Natcher in the Democratic Caucus, Obey chose not to wage a challenge. But with Whitten out of the picture and the committee chaired by Natcher — who is, at age 83, a transitional figure — Obey is viewed as a contender for the committee chair sometime this decade.

Should he run, he is virtually assured of meeting some opposition. John P. Murtha, the hawkish Pennsylvanian who chairs the Defense Subcommittee, is one of the old-school Democrats who took exception to Obey's reformist zeal in the 1970s. He was rumored to be gearing up to take on Obey if he challenged Natcher in 1992. Iowan Neal Smith, the No. 3 Democrat on Appropriations, has said that under that scenario, he would assert seniority and run as well.

Obey tends to provoke strong reactions from his colleagues. He has referred to his antagonists at times as "banshees," "monkeys" and "Little Leaguers." A liberal reformer with a deep loyalty to the institution, he is the forerunner of the generation that is replacing the old guard on Appropriations. He has been around for nearly a quarter-century and has seen all manner of battle in Congress — and provoked his share of them. He is a loner and a liberal partisan, a complex man of undisputed intelligence, principled independence and a zeal for political combat.

In October 1990, Obey helped organize the rebellion that scuttled the budget summit agreement between Bush administration officials and the congressional leadership. In part, Obey's objections were institutional: The closed-door summit had disrupted the normal budget process and encroached on Appropriations' role and control.

But Obey also objected to the summit on substance. He helped shape the Democratic theme that President George Bush was protecting the wealthy and putting the burden of deficit reduction on the less affluent. He even put some heat on his own party, stating that "after 10 years of wimpy conduct, the Democratic Party finally is back where it ought to be — fighting hard for tax fairness for middle-class working families."

Obey continued the call for tax fairness in the 102nd and 103rd Congresses. He led liberals' opposition to a proposed cut in the corporate tax rate included in the Democrats' 1992 tax bill, arguing, "This is not what we think the Democratic Party ought to stand for."

Although Obey's irascibility wears on his colleagues, he has also exhibited a capacity for cultivating allies when it comes to moving his annual foreign aid bill, arguably the least popular spending measure on which members must vote. A self-described "low-dollar man on foreign aid," he worked with the Bush administration and ranking Republican Mickey Edwards of Oklahoma to produce tight annual bills. He denounces waste in foreign aid and frequently takes a scalpel to foreign operations spending levels. That has enabled him to pass his bills by wide, bipartisan margins in recent years.

In other areas, however, Obey had few kind words for the Republican administration's spending priorities. During negotiations over a 1991 supplemental spending bill for defense and disaster relief, Obey grumbled at the Bush administration's unwillingness to agree to some of the domestic spending on the bill. "The administration salivates for every damn dollar that can be spent for international affairs," he

Wisconsin 7

Northwest — Wausau; Superior; Stevens Point

The 7th reaches from the center of Wisconsin all the way north to Lake Superior. The southern part of the district is devoted largely to dairy farming; in the north, a booming recreation industry has brought new life to old mining and lumbering areas that were exploited and abandoned earlier in this century.

The southern end of the 7th is anchored by Marathon and Wood counties, politically marginal territory that supported Ronald Reagan in 1984 but has since been of divided mind. In 1988, Michael S. Dukakis won Marathon County by 176 votes, and George Bush carried Wood County by 475 votes. In 1992, Bill Clinton carried Marathon County by 534 votes, while Bush took Wood County by 635 votes.

Marathon County's major city is Wausau, with paper mills, prefabricated-home manufacturers and white-collar employment in the insurance industry.

In Wood County, Wisconsin Rapids is a paper mill town — Consolidated Papers and Georgia Pacific's Nekoosa-Edwards are the biggest — and Marshfield has a large medical clinic and research facility. The cities are processing centers for the surrounding dairylands. Southern Wood County is notable for its cranberry crops, while Marathon County is a leading ginseng exporter. In 1992 redistricting, the district got all of Wood County.

The heaviest Democratic vote in the southern part of the 7th comes out of Portage County. The city of Stevens Point there has a large Polish population, a branch of the state university and the headquarters of the Sentry Insurance Co. Potatoes are an important crop in rural Portage and Wood counties.

A scattering of streams, rivers, lakes, national forests and state parks covers the northern reaches of the 7th, luring tourists and retirees from urban centers.

Along the Mississippi River, commuters to Minneapolis-St. Paul have begun settling in the western Polk County communities of St. Croix Falls and Balsam Lake. To the east, Chippewa Falls has Cray Research, makers of supercomputers.

The northern sections of the 7th share the same solid Democratic traditions found in Minnesota's Iron Range and in the nearby western end of Michigan's Upper Peninsula. The major Democratic bastion is the region's only sizable city, Superior, a working-class town. Its economy is fueled by production of dairy products, port operations and education. A branch of the University of Wisconsin is in Superior. The city is also home to one of the nation's largest municipal forests, with 4,500 acres.

The huge port facilities of Superior and its larger neighbor, Duluth, Minn., are a funnel for soybeans, wheat and a wide range of other commodities raised on the farms of the Midwest. But a slump in ship repairing and the general hardscrabble nature of the land have taking their toll. Three of the four Wisconsin counties that adjoin Lake Superior — Douglas, Ashland and Iron — lost population in the 1980s.

1990 Population: 543,529. White 528,450 (97%), Black 822 (<1%), Other 14,257 (3%). Hispanic origin 2,592 (<1%). 18 and over 395,676 (73%), 62 and over 97,007 (18%). Median age: 34.

said. "There is simply unhappiness [among committee members] because the president wants to play Winston Churchill abroad and Scrooge at home."

During the course of the successful U.S.-led military effort to end Iraq's occupation of Kuwait in early 1991, most members were effusively praising Israel and the Arab nations that backed the campaign. But Obey — who had opposed the January 1991 resolution authorizing Bush to use military force — took another stance: He called for a postwar cutoff of U.S. aid to the Middle East until serious moves were made toward permanent peace in the region. After the war, Obey rejected Bush administration suggestions of renewed military aid to such allies as Egypt, Israel and Turkey. "Reloading everyone's guns is exactly what we should not be doing," he said.

These comments reflected Obey's longstanding effort to change the orientation of U.S. foreign aid. He advocates using American dollars more to advance economic development in the nascent democracies of Eastern Europe and the struggling nations of the Third World, and less to reward and provide military assistance to geopolitical allies.

His skepticism of many of the programs under his jurisdiction is rather unusual for an Appropriations subcommittee chairman. At least before the 1990 budget agreement placed caps on the various spending categories, many Appropriations subcommittees would come in with "high ball" proposals in the hope of meeting the Republican administrations somewhere in the middle. But Obey's budget proposal for foreign aid frequently fell far below the administration requests.

Also unusual is Obey's plain-spoken bluntness on the subject of Israel, one of Congress' most sacred cows but one that Obey has shown no fear of challenging. He is not, however, a reflexive critic of the Jewish state. Obey told a Council on Foreign Relations dinner in February 1991, "The Arab world must recognize Israel and its legitimate security requirements." He added, "We also have a right to demand of Israel one very big thing — a recognition of the right and necessity of the Palestinian people to have their own homeland. . . ."

In the spring of 1992, as Congress prepared to clear a must-pass stopgap spending bill that contained about half of Israel's annual aid package, Obey fumed over the possibility that Senate supporters of Israel would try to place controversial loan guarantees sought by Israel on the measure. In an interview, he could not contain his anger at senators he described as "so damned greedy" that they would risk Israel's aid program by pressing for the guarantees. "When are people going to realize that enough is enough, even for Israel?" he raged.

Obey's perspective reflects his recognition that foreign aid is highly unpopular among the majority of Americans, who view it as taking money away from domestic programs. Also a member of the Appropriations Labor, Health and Human Services Subcommittee (which oversees most social programs), Obey says foreign aid cannot be exempted from the stringency of these lean economic times.

In 1992, he and Majority Leader Richard A. Gephardt sponsored an amendment to the transportation appropriations bill that would have shifted $400 million in outlays, or actual fiscal 1993 spending, from foreign aid coffers to highway, mass transit and aviation accounts. The amendment was adopted by a 213-190 vote, despite protests that it violated the spirit of the 1990 budget agreement. However, it also put the transportation bill's price tag over Bush's budget request. Under threat of a veto, the amendment was dropped in conference.

Outside of his foreign aid bailiwick, Obey shows an aversion to big-ticket projects that he views as draining dollars from other needed programs. In 1989, he tried without success to block the passage of a bill providing the first construction funds for the superconducting super collider (SSC), a giant $8 billion-plus atom-smasher being built in Texas. "It's one of the largest public works projects in the history of this country," Obey said. "Absent new revenues, the SSC will destroy the rest of the science budget in this country." He backed efforts in the 102nd Congress to kill the SSC as well as the $30 billion-plus space station *Freedom*.

Obey was an enthusiastic supporter of Bill Clinton's presidential candidacy; he was considered one of Clinton's best surrogate campaigners in 1992. He proved an ally in Clinton's early legislative initiatives, including the ill-fated economic stimulus package, which he supported as a measure to alleviate unemployment.

Though Obey is not widely popular, respect for his integrity is widespread. In the 1970s, he wrote a strict ethics code for the House that limited lawmakers' outside income.

Obey's name repeatedly was invoked in 1989 by Speaker Jim Wright of Texas as he sought unsuccessfully to stave off the ethics committee's investigation. As the author of the ethics code, Obey had a stake in its correct interpretation. This provoked him to argue, publicly and in an affidavit, that a rule covering gifts from associates with a legislative interest had been applied too broadly in Wright's case and one dealing with book royalties not broadly enough.

But Obey's influence cut both ways. In early May 1989, it was reported that Obey told some Democrats that Wright deserved a chance to defend himself but was finished politically. The news was one of the clearest signals Wright's fight was lost; he resigned from the speakership and the House soon thereafter.

Obey also took on the issue of congressional campaign finance reform, sponsoring a proposal with Democrat Mike Synar of Oklahoma that included public financing and restrictions on political action committee contributions.

Obey's interest in ethics has persisted. In 1992, with public antipathy toward Congress peaking, the House approved the appointment of a House administrator for internal operations — an idea Obey had been advocating since the 1970s. Later that year, Obey was named to the bipartisan joint committee on congressional reform.

Obey's reform efforts have had a cost in career terms. Late in 1980, Obey was a logical choice to chair the Budget Committee, but he lost out to a more conservative candidate, Oklahoma Democrat James R. Jones. While Jones may have more closely fit the prevailing national political sentiment, Obey also was hurt by some Democrats' lingering resentment over his role in writing the ethics code.

As a sort of consolation prize, Obey chaired the Joint Economic Committee in the 99th Congress, which gave him a one-term platform to denounce President Ronald Reagan's economic policies. In mid-1987, Obey briefly scouted for support to run for Budget chairman again, but he soon dropped out of the race. In the 103rd, he is again chair of the Joint Economic Committee.

At Home: More than 20 years ago, when The Wall Street Journal wanted to write about the advantages of incumbency, it sent a reporter to Obey's district, confident of witnessing an expert. The young Democrat had been in office only a few months at the time, but his techniques already were bearing fruit. He was sending out free government publications, writing columns for local newspapers and flooding the district with newsletters, even though he admitted in one that "there hasn't been that much to talk about yet."

Obey knew that unless he made a strong personal impression with the voters, they would return him to his Wausau real estate business. Chosen in a 1969 special election to succeed Melvin R. Laird, who had been named secretary of Defense, Obey was the first Democrat ever to represent the 7th District.

When Laird's seat had opened up, Obey was beginning his fourth term in the state Assembly, where he had been since age 24. The GOP House candidate, state Sen. Walter Chilsen, was a well-known former newscaster who called himself a "Laird Republican." He tried to make student violence a campaign theme. But Obey deflected that issue. He focused on discontent with the Nixon administration's low milk-support prices and on the unpopular fiscal policies of GOP Gov. Warren Knowles. The changed mood in farming areas turned what was a 44,000-vote Laird win in November 1968 into a 4,055-vote margin for Obey five months later. In 1970, he breezed to re-election.

In 1972, redistricting put Obey in the same district with Alvin E. O'Konski, a 30-year House veteran who was twice his age. The new district was marginally Democratic and had more of Obey's old constituents than O'Konski's. After agonizing for months, the Republican finally decided to retire, but it was too late to have his name removed from the ballot. Obey won with 63 percent of the vote.

Since then, Obey has met little opposition. In early 1990, though, Obey found himself the target of an unusual recall effort by constituents opposed to spearfishing rights for the Chippewa Indians. They accused Obey of not working to rewrite the 19th century treaties that gave the Indians special fishing and hunting rights off their reservation. Doubts about the recall effort's constitutionality were never resolved as the recall proponents failed to file the required 43,401 signatures. Obey was easily re-elected.

Committees

Joint Economic (Chairman)

Appropriations (5th of 37 Democrats)
Foreign Operations, Export Financing & Related Programs (chairman); Labor, Health & Human Services, Education & Related Agencies; Legislative Branch

Joint Organization of Congress

Elections

1992 General

David R. Obey (D)	166,200	(64%)
Dale R. Vannes (R)	91,772	(36%)

1990 General

David R. Obey (D)	100,069	(62%)
John L. McEwen (R)	60,961	(38%)

Previous Winning Percentages: **1988** (62%) **1986** (62%) **1984** (61%) **1982** (68%) **1980** (65%) **1978** (62%) **1976** (73%) **1974** (71%) **1972** (63%) **1970** (68%) **1969** * (52%)

* *Special election.*

District Vote for President

1992

D 117,203 (42%)
R 93,238 (34%)
I 67,558 (24%)

Campaign Finance

	Receipts	Receipts from PACs	Expend-itures
1992			
Obey (D)	$497,123	$267,575 (54%)	$524,574
Vannes (R)	$20,879	0	$20,327
1990			
Obey (D)	$620,219	$311,550 (50%)	$467,346
McEwen (R)	$10,886	0	$10,683

Key Votes

1993

Require parental notification of minors' abortions	N
Require unpaid family and medical leave	Y
Approve national "motor voter" registration bill	Y
Approve budget increasing taxes and reducing deficit	Y
Approve economic stimulus plan	Y
1992	
Approve balanced-budget constitutional amendment	N
Close down space station program	Y
Approve U.S. aid for former Soviet Union	Y
Allow shifting funds from defense to domestic programs	Y
1991	
Extend unemployment benefits using deficit financing	Y
Approve waiting period for handgun purchases	N
Authorize use of force in Persian Gulf	N

Voting Studies

Year	Presidential Support S	Presidential Support O	Party Unity S	Party Unity O	Conservative Coalition S	Conservative Coalition O
1992	14	84	93	5	15	85
1991	29	71	92	6	24	73
1990	15	83	92	6	15	83
1989	31	67	88	8	17	76
1988	20	76	93	4	8	87
1987	13	87	93	3	7	93
1986	19	79	92	5	20	76
1985	15	84	93	4	7	91
1984	31	68	89	9	17	81
1983	22	77	94	5	11	88
1982	38	57	86	11	18	79
1981	29	70	83	11	13	81

Interest Group Ratings

Year	ADA	AFL-CIO	CCUS	ACU
1992	100	92	38	0
1991	85	92	20	15
1990	83	91	21	9
1989	95	83	20	0
1988	90	100	9	4
1987	100	94	0	0
1986	85	93	12	10
1985	90	94	18	5
1984	85	69	25	13
1983	100	94	20	0
1982	100	100	9	5
1981	85	87	11	7

8 Toby Roth (R)

Of Appleton — Elected 1978; 8th Term

Born: Oct. 10, 1938, Strasburg, N.D.
Education: Marquette U., B.A. 1961.
Military Service: Army Reserve, 1962-69.
Occupation: Real estate broker.
Family: Wife, Barbara Fischer; three children.
Religion: Roman Catholic.
Political Career: Wis. Assembly, 1973-79.
Capitol Office: 2234 Rayburn Bldg. 20515; 225-5665.

In Washington: Increasingly the most visible opponent of foreign aid in the House, Roth is among the leading congressional foes of U.S. overseas involvement in general. Late in 1992, he was an articulate spokesman against an open-ended commitment of troops to famine-stricken Somalia.

One of Roth's press conferences attacking Democrats on the subject in 1991 drew an unannounced appearance by 1992 presidential candidate Patrick J. Buchanan — who called for an end to foreign assistance and put Roth in the uncomfortable position of demurring when reporters asked if he was supporting Buchanan's primary challenge to President Bush.

Roth has his boosters in the chamber, chiefly those who follow his Midwestern isolationist tack. And he occasionally scores points on the floor. But his opposition to the military intervention in Somalia was typical of his experiences. For a variety of reasons, his efforts have more impact as statements of principle than as legislative endeavors. In 1991 the House adopted Roth's amendment to a foreign aid authorization bill that would have blocked the Agency for International Development from spending more than $2 billion appropriated in prior years. But the bill never became law.

In the eyes of many colleagues, Roth's behavior runs from colorful to ill-tempered. He favors using troops to patrol the U.S.-Mexican border. He often asserts that one in five Haitian refugees seeking to enter the United States has AIDS (U.S. health officials set the figure far lower). He has advocated making English the nation's official language and eliminating some bilingual government services. And he has been among the most steadfast opponents of spending taxpayer money to salvage the savings and loan industry, repeatedly voting against the bailout of the federal deposit insurance fund.

Roth speaks often with a certitude that goes beyond confidence. "I'm not like all these other politicians," he told The Milwaukee Journal in 1992. "I have strong feelings about these things." He suggested in the early 1980s that he might have run for the White House if Republican Ronald Reagan had not gotten there first.

Roth has a stubborn streak that borders on obstinacy, and even some Republicans say he is difficult to work with. In 1989 his refusal to compromise caused his own amendment to be dropped from the savings and loan bailout bill. The House had adopted Roth's language requiring all banks to have annual independent audits of their books — a practice not then required — as a "first line of defense" against a banking crisis similar to the thrift industry collapse. Bankers objected that such a requirement would be costly overkill and singled out Roth's condition that such audits include review of a "manager's statement" of compliance with federal banking rules.

House-Senate conferees were plainly unwilling to preserve the amendment intact, and Roth's allies in the House urged him to drop the manager's statement review. Roth refused, and the conference committee dropped the entire audit requirement. Democratic Rep. Gerald D. Kleczka, a fellow Wisconsinite who had tried to mediate the issue, expressed exasperation at Roth's unwillingness to yield. "He had it right in his hand and it just blew away," Kleczka said.

During the 1980s, Roth supported limits on imports from Marxist-controlled Ethiopia. However, his overall record on economic sanctions is mixed. He has opposed U.S. sanctions against South Africa as an ineffective way to end apartheid. When South African President F. W. de Klerk took some steps to ease apartheid in 1990, Roth called for "flexibility" in U.S. policy, including an end to the ban on air flights between the United States and South Africa instituted by a 1986 sanctions bill.

Roth is most wary of sanctions that might disadvantage U.S. exporters — including 8th District farmers — against foreign competitors. This stance provoked Roth in 1988 to oppose a bill to invoke sanctions against Iraq in response to the Iraqi government's use of poison gas against its Kurdish minority.

Roth called the use of chemical weapons

Wisconsin 8

Northeast — Green Bay; Appleton

More than half the 8th District vote is cast in the Fox River Valley counties of Outagamie (Appleton) and Brown (Green Bay). Germans are the most noticeable ethnic group in the industrialized valley. Most of them are Catholic and, even if Democratic, tend to be conservative.

The economy of the valley and the vast wooded area to the north depends on trees and paper. The district is a worldwide exporter of paper, grain and dairy products. Green Bay, best known for its football Packers, is the smallest city to have a National Football League club.

Thirty miles southwest of Green Bay, on the north shore of Lake Winnebago, lies Appleton. Here, too, paper manufacturers and papermaking equipment industries are important employers. Appleton also has white-collar jobs in insurance, finance and health care.

The paper industry, and its reliance on consumer necessities, has enabled the Fox Cities generally to survive recent recessionary times without major dislocations in employment. This follows a decade in which population increased by 11 percent in Brown County and by 9 percent in Outagamie County, enhancing Green Bay's standing as the state's second-largest media market.

Politically, Brown traditionally prefers Republican presidential candidates, though it made an exception in 1960 for John F. Kennedy, a Catholic. Ronald Reagan won Brown County easily in his two White House campaigns, and George Bush edged Michael S. Dukakis here in 1988.

Outagamie County gave Bush a more comfortable margin in 1988, helping him to a 53 percent tally in the similarly drawn old district. In 1992, both Brown and Outagamie counties went comfortably for Bush. Appleton's Republican heritage includes being the hometown of the late Sen. Joseph R. McCarthy, infamous for his communist witch hunts in the 1950s.

The rural counties in the north-central part of the district also are mostly Republican, although there are pockets of Democratic strength.

The small city of Kaukauna inspired the only real skirmish in the state's 1992 redistricting efforts, when Green Bay Democrats successfully fought a proposal to move Kaukauna into the 6th District. Kaukauna's Democratic inclinations derive from the strong union presence at the Thilmany division of International Paper.

Resorts and vacation homes are the focal point for tourists in Door and Vilas counties. Door County's peninsula, which separates Green Bay from Lake Michigan, is dotted with picturesque small towns. Vilas County is in a lakes region on the Michigan border. Both counties are solidly Republican, influenced by the prosperity attained by serving nature-seekers from all over the Midwest.

The district also contains several different tribes of Chippewa Indians, including the Lac du Flambeau, whose exercise of their spearfishing rights has occasionally sparked violent protests by whites.

1990 Population: 543,404. White 521,764 (96%), Black 1,526 (<1%), Other 20,114 (4%). Hispanic origin 3,391 (1%). 18 and over 396,279 (73%), 62 and over 89,420 (16%). Median age: 33.

"despicable," but said that by applying unilateral sanctions, "we're not doing anything to Iraq; we're shooting our own exporters in the foot." His was a lonesome position: He was the only member of Foreign Affairs, and one of just 16 House members, to vote against the bill.

At Home: In the course of four years, Roth went from being relatively secure to being relatively vulnerable — and back again. His 70 percent share of the vote in 1988 was his highest in a House race to that point; his 54 percent share in 1990 was his lowest. In 1992, Roth was back up to 70 percent, defeating an inexperienced challenger.

Roth's rocky 1990 could have been due in part to anti-Congress feelings afoot in the land that year. But it was also attributable to an aggressive Democratic challenge from state Sen. Jerome Van Sistine, who had a base in the district's one big city (Green Bay) and friends in organized labor.

Van Sistine maintained that the conservative Roth was no friend of the working class and that as a member of the House Banking Subcommittee on Financial Institutions he bore some responsibility for the savings and loan crisis. Roth disputed both charges. As evidence of his hands-on concern for job creation in the district, Roth pointed to the annual trade export conference he holds in Green Bay or Appleton. But Van Sistine had the money to get out his message. He carried Brown County (Green Bay) by 8,000 votes, more than matching Roth's 6,000-vote edge in Outagamie County (Appleton). But Roth also carried nine of the other 11 counties partially or entirely within the 8th to hold on to the seat.

Roth initially got to the House the same way he has worked to stay there — by assembling a large and efficient volunteer organization and shaking thousands of hands.

In 1978, Roth challenged vulnerable Democratic Rep. Robert J. Cornell. GOP leaders were wary because Roth was not from Green Bay, the political center of the district. And while Roth's eager-beaver campaign style had worked well in Appleton during his campaigns for the Wisconsin Assembly, party veterans thought he might seem overbearing in a broader campaign against Cornell. They were wrong. Cornell, a Roman Catholic priest, never relished running for office the way Roth does. The incumbent spent his time giving wooden speeches while Roth was out at shopping centers shaking hands. In the last two weeks of the campaign, Roth (by his count) shook 63,000 hands. His volunteer organization and nearly 3-to-1 spending advantage were just as important. Roth won both Brown and Outagamie counties and carried all but four other counties to take 58 percent overall.

Two years later Roth faced former Green Bay Mayor Michael Monfils, used the same approach and won by an even larger margin. His percentage was down significantly in 1982 against Ruth Clusen, former national president of the League of Women Voters, but his 57 percent tally was still comfortable in a year when Democrats were sweeping to victory in statewide contests.

Committees

Banking, Finance & Urban Affairs (6th of 20 Republicans)
General Oversight, Investigations & the Resolution of Failed Financial Institutions (ranking); Economic Growth

Foreign Affairs (4th of 18 Republicans)
Economic Policy, Trade & the Environment (ranking); Asia & the Pacific

Elections

1992 General		
Toby Roth (R)	191,704	(70%)
Catherine L. Helms (D)	81,792	(30%)
1990 General		
Toby Roth (R)	95,902	(54%)
Jerome Van Sistine (D)	83,199	(46%)

Previous Winning Percentages: **1988** (70%) **1986** (67%) **1984** (68%) **1982** (57%) **1980** (68%) **1978** (58%)

District Vote for President

1992
D 101,493 (35%)
R 115,128 (40%)
I 69,373 (24%)

Campaign Finance

	Receipts	Receipts from PACs		Expend-itures
1992				
Roth (R)	$589,778	$292,200	(50%)	$444,548
Helms (D)	$41,727	$17,300	(41%)	$42,827
1990				
Roth (R)	$390,432	$203,083	(52%)	$499,968
Van Sistine (D)	$284,761	$214,895	(75%)	$274,112

Key Votes

1993	
Require parental notification of minors' abortions	Y
Require unpaid family and medical leave	N
Approve national "motor voter" registration bill	N
Approve budget increasing taxes and reducing deficit	N
Approve economic stimulus plan	N
1992	
Approve balanced-budget constitutional amendment	Y
Close down space station program	N
Approve U.S. aid for former Soviet Union	N
Allow shifting funds from defense to domestic programs	N
1991	
Extend unemployment benefits using deficit financing	N
Approve waiting period for handgun purchases	N
Authorize use of force in Persian Gulf	Y

Voting Studies

	Presidential Support		Party Unity		Conservative Coalition	
Year	**S**	**O**	**S**	**O**	**S**	**O**
1992	67	28	83	15	69	19
1991	69	29	81	17	84	16
1990	63	35	77	20	89	7
1989	72	27	81	16	90	10
1988	51	39	78	14	87	0
1987	61	37	79	18	84	14
1986	68	27	79	17	88	8
1985	55	36	76	13	73	24
1984	51	44	61	28	83	14
1983	71	27	84	14	82	18
1982	57	38	73	22	78	18
1981	64	33	77	14	80	12

Interest Group Ratings

Year	ADA	AFL-CIO	CCUS	ACU
1992	15	8	75	83
1991	20	8	80	100
1990	6	8	93	83
1989	10	9	100	86
1988	10	36	92	83
1987	4	0	100	91
1986	0	8	81	82
1985	10	13	95	80
1984	15	38	63	65
1983	5	7	72	81
1982	10	16	68	86
1981	10	0	88	100

9 F. James Sensenbrenner Jr. (R)

Of Menomonee Falls — Elected 1978; 8th Term

Born: June 14, 1943, Chicago, Ill.
Education: Stanford U., A.B. 1965; U. of Wisconsin, J.D. 1968.
Occupation: Lawyer.
Family: Wife, Cheryl Warren; two children.
Religion: Episcopalian.
Political Career: Wis. Assembly, 1969-75; Wis. Senate, 1975-79.
Capitol Office: 2332 Rayburn Bldg. 20515; 225-5101.

In Washington: Sensenbrenner will never win any popularity contests. The adjectives used to describe him range from officious and pompous to rude and nitpicking. He does little to quell the criticism with his blatant rustling of newspapers during hearings he finds tiresome.

Complaints about Sensenbrenner's demeanor come from partisans ranging the political spectrum. Democrats bristle at his harsh, conservative rhetoric, and even Republicans appreciative of his diligence on the liberal-dominated Judiciary Committee find him tough to take on a personal level.

But the icy regard in which Sensenbrenner is held does not deter him. As ranking Republican on the Civil and Constitutional Rights Subcommittee — a post he held until 1991, he consistently criticized civil rights legislation. He furiously waved the GOP banner with amendments to the 1990 and 1991 civil rights bills, the 1988 *Grove City* bill and the 1988 Fair Housing Act. He called the 1991 bill a "lawyers' bonanza" and tried unsuccessfully to eliminate a provision allowing women and religious minorities who face intentional bias to win unlimited money damages. He also objected because the provisions of the measure did not apply to Congress.

Sensenbrenner often railed against the subcommittee for its reputation as a "graveyard" for conservative legislation. He called the 1990 debate on a constitutional amendment to ban flag desecration a test "to determine whether we will obfuscate the issues with legal mumble jumble or show leadership in responding to the will of the people."

Sensenbrenner was bumped from that subcommittee's ranking spot in 1991, when Henry J. Hyde's term on the Intelligence Committee expired and seniority allowed him to supersede Sensenbrenner. In turn, Sensenbrenner snagged the ranking seat on the Crime Subcommittee.

That assignment gives him plenty of opportunity to air his conservative views. But it also highlighted his independence from other conservatives on at least one issue: the seven-day waiting period for handgun purchases, the so-called Brady bill. Sensenbrenner supported that bill, noting that Wisconsin's 48-hour waiting period has been effective "in cooling off crimes of passion. If it can work at the state level, it can work at the federal level."

Although not otherwise a gun control advocate, Sensenbrenner has promoted the waiting period idea since 1988, when he offered it as an amendment to the omnibus drug bill.

Although he supports the waiting period, Sensenbrenner opposed a ban on assault weapons that was in the 1991 crime bill. During debate on the measure, he supported an amendment removing the ban, saying it was a "feel-good measure" that was "not going to affect criminals in any way, shape or form."

Sensenbrenner, a strong abortion opponent, used the 1992 debate on the Freedom of Choice Act to propose a "conscience clause" amendment that would have allowed states to shield institutions such as religious hospitals from performing abortions. The amendment was defeated, but the committee passed an amendment shielding individuals with moral objections from having to perform abortions.

Sensenbrenner revealed an ability to temper his conservative dogma with compromise during consideration of the Americans With Disabilities Act. Serving as a lead conservative negotiator, he helped work out a compromise that included three amendments important to small businesses. When Democrats accepted those measures, Sensenbrenner in turn fought efforts to dilute the compromise.

Despite his support for the final package, Sensenbrenner persistently pushed an unsuccessful and contentious amendment backed by the Bush administration. It sought to bar punitive-damage awards for victims of intentional discrimination.

At the start of the 101st Congress, Sensenbrenner took over as ranking Republican on the

Wisconsin 9

Milwaukee suburbs; part of Waukesha County; Sheboygan

The 9th is the closest thing Wisconsin has to a suburban district, encompassing much of the counties immediately west and north of Milwaukee. Consequently, the 9th is also Wisconsin's most staunchly Republican district. In the 1980s, Jimmy Carter, Walter F. Mondale and Michael S. Dukakis all failed to surpass 40 percent of the vote in the old 9th, and Bill Clinton did not even break 30 percent in 1992 in the similarly redrawn 9th.

Waukesha County, just west of Milwaukee County, is the centerpiece of state Republicanism, regularly running up the biggest GOP numbers in the state. County Republicans have an even more pronounced influence on the 9th District because the areas where Democrats are most numerous — the city of Waukesha and Muskego and New Berlin on the county's southeastern side — are part of the 4th District.

In earlier generations, the lakes of Waukesha County drew Milwaukee's leading families to buy real estate in the county for summer retreats. Republicans still compile huge margins in small Oconomowoc Lake and Chenequa. But suburbanization has taken hold elsewhere. Affluent Elm Grove is rock-ribbed Republican territory. Middle-managers are attracted to adjacent Brookfield, which has also sprouted the metropolitan area's second-largest office market.

Not everything is booming in Waukesha; the county's population growth slowed from 21 percent in the 1970s to just under 9 percent in the 1980s. Menomonee Falls, which attracted working-class Germans from Milwaukee's northwest side, saw a 3 percent population drop in the past decade.

Among the county's manufacturers are the General Electric Medical Systems Group, QuadGraphics printing and companies that build electrical transformers and internal combustion engines.

Ozaukee and Washington counties routinely cast 60 percent of their votes for GOP presidential candidates. Washington County is a combination of fast-growing bedroom communities and agricultural lands being encroached on by development, with a smattering of industry. The county seat, West Bend, is home to the West Bend Co., maker of small kitchen appliances. Port Washington, the Ozaukee County seat, is home to Allen-Edmonds shoes as well as a picturesque lakefront and marina.

Farther north, Sheboygan County is marginally Republican in presidential elections. The city of Sheboygan contains medium-size industries, such as Vollrath stainless steel and Bemis manufacturing. Kohler is headquarters for the Kohler Co., the nation's largest producer of plumbing equipment, as well as the American Club, the state's premier resort hotel.

The district also includes most of Dodge and Jefferson counties, which are largely rural. Dairying is important here. In Dodge County, Waupun is well-known as a major state prison site, Beaver Dam is a resort community, and the Horicon Marsh is a federal and state preserve for geese and ducks.

1990 Population: 543,532. White 533,444 (98%), Black 2,313 (<1%), Other 7,775 (1%). Hispanic origin 5,700 (1%). 18 and over 396,174 (73%), 62 and over 80,726 (15%). Median age: 34.

Science, Space and Technology Subcommittee on Space. There, he is part of the panel's bipartisan consensus in favor of U.S. space programs. "Even in times of budget constraints," he says, "the American people want a vibrant space program."

Like others on the panel, Sensenbrenner says he is frustrated by its declining influence in the budgetary process. But he says the fault lies with committee members' unrealistic authorizations and failure to establish priorities. "If we take this bill as it is now written to the floor," he complained in late 1990, "we will be deliberately contributing to our declining relevance."

He was highly critical of NASA's management practices and worked with subcommittee Chairman Ralph M. Hall of Texas to help Congress flex its budgetary muscle to make the agency more accountable.

Sensenbrenner is among those interested in capping funding for the superconducting super collider. He wrote a successful 1990 amendment axing a provision that would have guaranteed Texas a refund of its $1 billion investment if the project is scrapped before the end of 1995.

At Home: Sensenbrenner has held public office practically since his graduation from law school. Despite his reputation for pomposity, his personal resources and conservative views have earned him an undefeated record at the polls.

Sensenbrenner is heir to a paper and cellulose manufacturing fortune, much of which stems from his great-grandfather's invention of the sanitary napkin shortly after World War I.

Marketing it under the brand name Kotex, Sensenbrenner's ancestor went on to become chairman of the board of Kimberly-Clark.

To reach Congress in 1978, Sensenbrenner had to dip into family wealth to overcome an unexpectedly strong GOP primary challenge. With Republican Bob Kasten leaving the 9th District to run for governor, Sensenbrenner was viewed as the obvious successor. He had been elected to four terms in the state Assembly before moving in 1975 to the state Senate, where he quickly rose to be assistant minority leader. He had a solid political base in the older, more affluent lakeside suburbs, and his conservative stance reminded voters of the popular Kasten.

But his opponent was Susan Engeleiter, a state legislator who would later become state Senate GOP leader, the party nominee for the U.S. Senate in 1988 and then director of the Small Business Administration.

Just 26 when she challenged Sensenbrenner, Engeleiter put on a strong campaign in the western, more middle-class part of the district, which she represented in the state Assembly. More gregarious than Sensenbrenner, she outpolled him by 5,600 votes in the 9th's four western counties. Only Sensenbrenner's familiarity in the most Republican of Milwaukee's suburbs allowed him to win the primary by 589 votes.

The 1978 Democratic nominee, Milwaukee lawyer Matthew J. Flynn, was also on his way to higher visibility in statewide politics as party chairman and a candidate for the U.S. Senate. But he could not raise enough money to compete with Sensenbrenner, who campaigned on his support for cutting taxes and defeated Flynn by a solid margin. Re-election has come easily since then. In 1982 and 1990 he had no Democratic opposition. In 1992, he beat Democrat Ingrid K. Buxton, capturing 70 percent of the vote.

Committees

Judiciary (4th of 14 Republicans)
Crime & Criminal Justice (ranking); Intellectual Property & Judicial Administration

Science, Space & Technology (2nd of 22 Republicans)
Space (ranking)

Elections

1992 General		
F. James Sensenbrenner Jr. (R)	192,898	(70%)
Ingrid K. Buxton (D)	77,362	(28%)
David E. Marlow (I)	4,619	(2%)
1990 General		
F. James Sensenbrenner Jr. (R)	117,967	(100%)

Previous Winning Percentages: **1988** (75%) **1986** (78%) **1984** (73%) **1982** (100%) **1980** (78%) **1978** (61%)

District Vote for President

1992

D 84,301 (29%)
R 139,103 (48%)
I 62,931 (22%)

Campaign Finance

	Receipts	Receipts from PACs		Expend-itures
1992				
Sensenbrenner (R)	$283,602	$75,709	(27%)	$457,292
Buxton (D)	$29,344	$10,507	(36%)	$27,125
1990				
Sensenbrenner (R)	$266,285	$98,635	(37%)	$98,609

Key Votes

1993	
Require parental notification of minors' abortions	Y
Require unpaid family and medical leave	N
Approve national "motor voter" registration bill	N
Approve budget increasing taxes and reducing deficit	N
Approve economic stimulus plan	N
1992	
Approve balanced-budget constitutional amendment	Y
Close down space station program	N
Approve U.S. aid for former Soviet Union	N
Allow shifting funds from defense to domestic programs	N
1991	
Extend unemployment benefits using deficit financing	N
Approve waiting period for handgun purchases	Y
Authorize use of force in Persian Gulf	Y

Voting Studies

	Presidential Support		Party Unity		Conservative Coalition	
Year	S	O	S	O	S	O
1992	69	30	90	9	65	35
1991	66	33	87	11	86	14
1990	75	25	93	6	80	20
1989	66	34	88	12	78	22
1988	68	30	92	8	87	13
1987	68	31	92	6	77	21
1986	73	27	89	11	80	20
1985	68	33	87	11	69	31
1984	45	20	56	9	44	12
1983	70	30	85	14	74	25
1982	60	36	84	16	70	30
1981	59	41	77	21	75	24

Interest Group Ratings

Year	ADA	AFL-CIO	CCUS	ACU
1992	15	17	88	92
1991	20	17	100	90
1990	6	0	86	83
1989	20	0	89	71
1988	15	21	100	88
1987	8	0	93	91
1986	10	7	89	77
1985	20	6	86	71
1984	5	11	69	80
1983	10	6	75	83
1982	25	15	73	86
1981	20	13	84	100

Wyoming

STATE DATA

Governor:
Michael J. Sullivan (D)
First elected: 1986
Length of term: 4 years
Term expires: 1/95
Salary: $70,000
Term limit: 2 terms in a 16-year period *
Phone: (307) 777-7434
Born: Sept. 22, 1939; Omaha, Neb.
Education: U. of Wyoming, B.S. 1961, J.D. 1964
Occupation: Lawyer; banker; nursing home director
Family: Wife, Jane Metzler; three children
Religion: Roman Catholic
Political Career: No previous office

No lieutenant governor

Secretary of State: Kathy Karpan (D)
First elected: 1986
Length of term: 4 years
Term expires: 1/95
Salary: $52,500
Phone: (307) 777-7378

State election official: (307) 777-7186
Democratic headquarters: (307) 637-8940
Republican headquarters: (307) 234-9166

** Does not apply to Sullivan*

STATE LEGISLATURE

Legislature. General session meets for 40 days, January-March, in odd years; budget session meets 20 days, February-March, in even years.

Senate: 30 members, 4-year terms
1992 breakdown: 20R, 10D; 25 men, 5 women; 29 whites, 1 Hispanic
Salary: $75 a day
Phone: (307) 777-7711

House of Representatives: 60 members, 2-year terms
1992 breakdown: 41R, 19D; 43 men, 17 women; 60 whites
Salary: $75 a day
Phone: (307) 777-7852

URBAN STATISTICS

City	Pop.
Cheyenne	50,008
Mayor Leo Pando, R	
Casper	46,801
Mayor George Parks, N-P	
Laramie	26,687
Mayor Amber Travsky, N-P	

U.S. CONGRESS

Senate: 0 D, 2 R
House: 0 D, 1 R

TERM LIMITS

For Congress: Yes
Senate: 12 years in any 24-year period
House: 6 years in any 12-year period
For state offices: Yes
Senate: 12 years in any 24-year period
House: 6 years in any 12-year period

ELECTIONS

1992 Presidential Vote

George Bush	39.6%
Bill Clinton	34.0%
Ross Perot	25.6%

1988 Presidential Vote

George Bush	61%
Michael S. Dukakis	38%

1984 Presidential Vote

Ronald Reagan	71%
Walter F. Mondale	28%

POPULATION

1990 population		453,588
1980 population		469,557
Percent change		−3%
Rank among states:		50
White		94%
Black		1%
Hispanic		6%
Asian or Pacific islander		1%
Urban		65%
Rural		35%
Born in state		43%
Foreign-born		2%
Under age 18	135,525	30%
Ages 18-64	270,868	60%
65 and older	47,195	10%
Median age		32

MISCELLANEOUS

Capital: Cheyenne
Number of counties: 23
Per capita income: $17,188 (1991)
Rank among states: 33
Total area: 97,809 sq. miles
Rank among states: 9

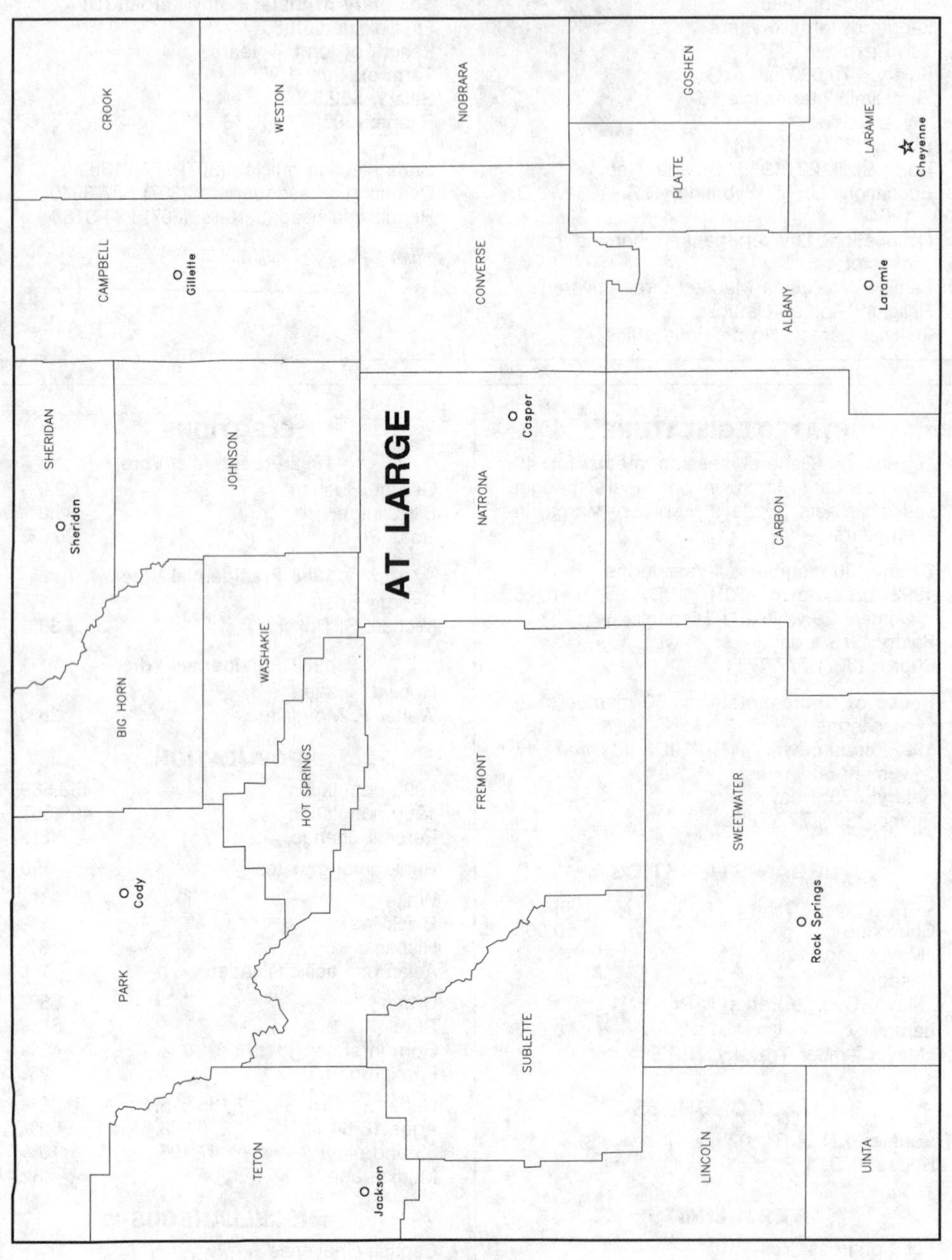
AT LARGE
CROOK
WESTON
NIOBRARA
GOSHEN
LARAMIE
Cheyenne
PLATTE
CAMPBELL
Gillette
CONVERSE
ALBANY
Laramie
SHERIDAN
Sheridan
JOHNSON
NATRONA
Casper
CARBON
WASHAKIE
BIG HORN
HOT SPRINGS
FREMONT
SWEETWATER
Rock Springs
PARK
Cody
SUBLETTE
TETON
Jackson
LINCOLN
UINTA

Malcolm Wallop (R)

Of Big Horn — Elected 1976; 3rd Term

Born: Feb. 27, 1933, New York, N.Y.
Education: Yale U., B.A. 1954.
Military Service: Army, 1955-57.
Occupation: Rancher; meatpacking executive.
Family: Wife, French Carter; five children.
Religion: Episcopalian.
Political Career: Wyo. House, 1969-73; Wyo. Senate, 1973-77; sought GOP nomination for governor, 1974.
Capitol Office: 237 Russell Bldg. 20510; 224-6441.

In Washington: Regarded as one of the Senate's premier conservative ideologues, Wallop nevertheless demonstrated in the 102nd Congress that he is willing to work with Democrats on substantive legislation.

Promoted to the ranking Republican seat on the Energy Committee at the start of the 102nd, Wallop found an acceptable partner in Chairman J. Bennett Johnston of Louisiana, one of the more conservative Senate Democrats.

With Johnston orchestrating the behind-the-scenes negotiations and Wallop lobbying GOP senators and the Bush administration, the two successfully ushered a comprehensive energy plan through the Senate. Although significantly altered from their original proposal, the bill was signed into law Oct. 24, 1992. Introduced during the Persian Gulf War, the sweeping legislation offered incentives for conservation, opened electric utility markets and provided tax relief for oil and gas drillers.

Joining Johnston was not that difficult for Wallop. Both are from states whose economies are heavily reliant on resource development (Louisiana has oil and natural gas; Wyoming has those, and coal and uranium as well).

Clearly overshadowed by Johnston, Wallop remained in the background until West Virginia Democrat John D. Rockefeller IV added a controversial tax on coal companies to bail out a troubled health fund for retired workers. So outraged was Wallop that non-union firms in the West might be forced to pay for benefits they never negotiated, he blocked the bill from reaching the Senate floor until negotiators found another source of money for the benefits.

Although Johnston and Wallop gave up on their desire to permit drilling in the Arctic National Wildlife Refuge and sacrificed higher gas mileage standards, they declared passage of the energy bill a victory. As Wallop put it: "It is nothing short of miraculous, the number of interests that have come together in this."

At the start of the 103rd Congress, Wallop was quick to raise a warning to the new Clinton administration.

First, he put former Arizona Gov. Bruce Babbitt on notice that he was highly suspicious of an Interior secretary who served as president of the League of Conservation Voters, the self-described political arm of the environmental movement.

Then Wallop and other Western lawmakers won a round with the Clinton administration in a battle over federal grazing fees. President Clinton, lobbying for votes on his economic package, agreed not to raise the fees on Western ranchers who use federal rangelands. But Clinton and other Democrats who believe the ranchers get too sweet a deal vowed to return to the issue.

Wallop beat back similar attempts in the 102nd during debate on the 1992 Interior appropriations bill. "All those provisions were like poisonous snakes that kept rising up to bite us in the buns," he said afterward.

As strong as Wallop's words on environmental issues can be, they do not approach his rhetoric on defense and foreign policy matters. Wallop was a staunch supporter of U.S. aid to the contras fighting the then-Marxist government of Nicaragua. In 1987, he told the Senate that the debate on continued aid for the contras offered a stark choice. A vote to cut off aid, he said, "is a vote for communism in Central America."

While he is interested in a wide range of national security issues, Wallop is preoccupied with the Strategic Defense Initiative (SDI). Since 1979, he has campaigned for rapid deployment of a nationwide defense based on laser-armed satellites. Finally, in 1983, he persuaded President Ronald Reagan to adopt a program of space-based interceptors, dubbed Brilliant Pebbles. That in turn became the core of President George Bush's SDI program.

But efforts to develop such a system have been parried by Armed Services Committee Chairman Sam Nunn of Georgia. Nunn sees any space-based anti-ballistic missile (ABM) system as a violation of the 1972 U.S.-Soviet ABM treaty; he tried to reorient SDI into research on a more limited ground-based missile system and opposed near-term deployment.

Wallop has long contended that if given the choice, the public would much prefer a missile defense to the preservation of an arms control treaty.

Even as the Cold War thawed, Wallop remained dubious of major arms reductions and U.S. aid to the former Soviet Union. "I don't know anybody in Wyoming who would want us to spend $500 million on the Soviet Union, whatever the purpose," he said at the end of 1991.

In the summer of 1992, Wallop threatened to hold hostage the entire defense bill if money was not included for SDI. His reasoning: Ballistic missiles with nuclear or chemical warheads remained available to hard-line communists in the former Soviet Union or some unstable developing nations.

Although Wallop was a reliable defender of the Bush and Reagan administration policies, his views on communism forced him to split with Bush over China's most-favored-nation status. Wallop cosponsored a bill with Majority Leader George J. Mitchell of Maine that would have conditioned China's trade status on a variety of factors, including the release of prisoners arrested in the 1989 Tiananmen Square protests, stopping the export to the United States of products made with prison labor and stopping the supply of arms to the Khmer Rouge guerrillas in Cambodia.

Although he traded his seat on the Finance Committee for Armed Services in the 101st, Wallop has not abandoned an interest in tax issues. In February 1991, he proposed to link a capital gains tax cut, blasted by many Democrats as a break for the rich, with a 2 percent reduction in Social Security taxes. He switched back to Finance in the 103rd, dropping Armed Services.

Wallop's strongly expressed views have made him a spokesman for the Republican right in Congress. However, his often acerbic tone can rub even members of his own party the wrong way. In the fall of 1990, Senate Minority Leader Bob Dole of Kansas was laboring to defend a controversial budget compromise against an onslaught from GOP conservatives. When Wallop persisted, Dole challenged his Wyoming colleague to run against him for leader. "If you feel that way, fine," a senator quoted Dole as saying. "Let's have a ballot right here."

At Home: Although he has won three elections to the Senate, Wallop has never attained the level of statewide popularity enjoyed by GOP colleague Alan K. Simpson and former at-large Rep. Dick Cheney. As a result, even with Republicans' 3-2 edge in voter registration, Wallop's campaigns are always worth watching.

Ironically, in his first statewide campaign, Wallop found himself at odds with the more conservative wing of the Wyoming GOP. Viewed as a moderate in a four-way gubernatorial primary in 1974 — he drew some of his support from voters sympathetic to environmental causes — Wallop came from far behind to finish a close second. When he did not assist the eventual nominee, conservative rancher Dick Jones, many party loyalists were displeased.

But Wallop solved that problem with remarkable ease in 1976, campaigning from the right against three-term Democratic Sen. Gale W. McGee. Although oil companies and other business interests were somewhat leery about backing him, Wallop got valuable help from national conservative organizations.

The challenger's TV ads were especially effective. Wallop saddled up a horse, donned a cowboy hat and urged voters to join the "Wallop Senate drive." He ridiculed occupational health regulations by portraying a cowboy forced to hitch a portable toilet to his horse.

The ads helped Wallop overcome a personal background that might have been a problem. Although he was a third-generation Wyoming resident and an eight-year state legislator, he was born in New York City, educated at Yale and had a grandfather who once sat in Britain's House of Lords.

By the time of his 1982 election, Wallop found himself under fire from environmentalists, who claimed he had forsaken their cause, and from a Democratic opponent who said he was inaccessible to constituents.

The Democrat was former state Sen. Rodger McDaniel, a 10-year state legislator. McDaniel painted the incumbent as a servant of big-oil interests and an uncritical defender of Reagan's economic policies. But like Wallop in 1974, McDaniel had to be careful not to alienate more conservative members of his own party — some of whom were hesitant to back a man who had been state coordinator for Edward M. Kennedy's 1980 presidential campaign.

Wallop played up his support for the president and promised to work to protect Wyoming water. McDaniel, an energetic campaigner, carried several counties along Wyoming's predominantly Democratic southern tier. But Wallop's $1 million treasury enabled him to nail down a 57 percent victory.

In 1988, Wallop again faced an opponent who accused him of being anti-environment and out of touch with voters. And after six years, Wallop showed that he was even more vulnerable to those charges.

The Democratic nominee, state Sen. John P. Vinich, did not have the profile of a winner in conservative Wyoming. A liberal, pro-labor senator with longish hair and sideburns, Vinich sponsored programs to benefit the elderly and to tighten regulations on business in his 14 years in the Legislature.

Vinich, whose iconoclasm often placed him at odds with state Democratic leaders, was not the favorite of party insiders. But he outcampaigned his primary opponents.

Vinich did not try to mask his ideology in the Senate race, but he defied classification as an archetypal liberal. He earned the National Rifle Association's top rating for his record against gun control. And he had been regularly re-elected from a county with a solid GOP registration advantage.

Vinich accused Wallop of concentrating on a national conservative agenda to the detriment of the state's economic interests. He charged Wallop with hypocrisy for criticizing the National Park Service's "let burn" policy, blamed for prolonging the summer's raging fires in Yellowstone National Park. Vinich said Wallop had ample opportunity to alter the policy when he chaired the subcommittee with jurisdiction over the Park Service.

Wallop had a huge fundraising advantage, and he maintained a comfortable lead in polls for most of the fall. But Vinich was boosted by an intensive 11th-hour media blitz bankrolled by the national party and labor organizations. He closed a double-digit poll deficit in the last week but fell 1,322 votes short.

Committees

Energy & Natural Resources (Ranking)

Finance (9th of 9 Republicans)
Deficits, Debt Management & Long-Term Economic Growth (ranking); Energy & Agricultural Taxation; International Trade

Select Intelligence (8th of 8 Republicans)

Small Business (2nd of 9 Republicans)
Government Contracting & Paperwork Reduction; Rural Economy & Family Farming

Elections

1988 General

Malcolm Wallop (R)	91,143	(50%)
John P. Vinich (D)	89,821	(50%)

1988 Primary

Malcolm Wallop (R)	55,752	(83%)
Nora M. Lewis (R)	3,933	(6%)
I.W. Kinney (R)	3,716	(6%)
Michael J. Dee (R)	1,898	(3%)
Russ Hanrahan (R)	1,702	(3%)

Previous Winning Percentages: 1982 (57%) **1976** (55%)

Campaign Finance

	Receipts	Receipts from PACs		Expend-itures
1988				
Wallop (R)	$1,492,048	$872,664	(58%)	$1,344,185
Vinich (D)	$491,599	$248,303	(51%)	$490,230

Key Votes

1993

Require unpaid family and medical leave	—
Approve national "motor voter" registration bill	N
Approve budget increasing taxes and reducing deficit	N
Support president's right to lift military gay ban	N
1992	
Approve school-choice pilot program	Y
Allow shifting funds from defense to domestic programs	N
Oppose deeper cuts in spending for SDI	Y
1991	
Approve waiting period for handgun purchases	N
Raise senators' pay and ban honoraria	Y
Authorize use of force in Persian Gulf	Y
Confirm Clarence Thomas to Supreme Court	Y

Voting Studies

	Presidential Support		Party Unity		Conservative Coalition	
Year	**S**	**O**	**S**	**O**	**S**	**O**
1992	78	18	89	3	92	0
1991	86	10	94	4	83	10
1990	76	17	88	6	89	5
1989	78	13	91	4	92	3
1988	72	16	85	1	89	0
1987	74	15	87	6	88	3
1986	93	5	94	3	95	1
1985	73	14	88	5	83	5
1984	86	4	91	1	94	0
1983	72	22	83	9	82	9
1982	71	18	82	10	86	5
1981	85	9	91	3	93	1

Interest Group Ratings

Year	ADA	AFL-CIO	CCUS	ACU
1992	10	25	100	100
1991	5	25	90	95
1990	6	11	92	95
1989	0	0	100	100
1988	0	11	91	100
1987	0	0	80	96
1986	0	0	95	100
1985	0	5	97	95
1984	5	0	76	91
1983	5	13	83	64
1982	10	8	75	74
1981	10	5	100	71

Alan K. Simpson (R)

Of Cody — Elected 1978; 3rd Term

Born: Sept. 2, 1931, Denver, Colo.
Education: U. of Wyoming, B.S.L. 1954, J.D. 1958.
Military Service: Army, 1954-56.
Occupation: Lawyer.
Family: Wife, Ann Schroll; three children.
Religion: Episcopalian.
Political Career: Cody city attorney, 1959-69; Wyo. House, 1965-77.
Capitol Office: 261 Dirksen Bldg. 20510; 224-3424.

In Washington: In his early days, Simpson charmed the Washington establishment with his earthy wit and folksy wisdom. But his homespun humor took on an edge when used in defense of the Bush administration, and Simpson seemed to be sharpening it further as Bill Clinton arrived in town.

The change seemed to come as the 1990s opened and George Bush, Simpson's close personal friend, seemed to be struggling. In defending Bush, Simpson's Western witticisms became increasingly personal.

From his interrogation of Anita F. Hill during the Supreme Court nomination hearings of Clarence Thomas to his role as the prime critic of Clinton's economic stimulus package at the start of the 103rd Congress, the assistant GOP leader is always there with a biting remark.

Aside from the pure enjoyment the lanky former athlete derives from such jousting, there may be an element of personal ambition underlying Simpson's headline-grabbing outbursts. With renewed talk that Senate Minority Leader Bob Dole of Kansas may again seek the presidency, Simpson — who has been the GOP's assistant leader and whip since 1985 — must remain alert as Dole's potential successors queue up.

The change in tone began in March 1990, when Democratic Rep. Richard A. Gephardt of Missouri criticized Bush as being "without vision" and "without imagination" in his approach to epic political changes in Eastern Europe and the Soviet Union. Simpson responded with a broadside, launched from the Senate floor, in which he described Gephardt — the House majority leader and an unsuccessful candidate for the 1988 Democratic presidential nomination — as a "frustrated font of trivia" with an "obsessive and overweening" ambition to be president.

Although the incident caused a stir, it paled in comparison with the flare-up Simpson provoked with comments during the U.S.-led war against Iraq in early 1991. In a luncheon with the media, Simpson raised questions about TV reporter Peter Arnett, the only Western correspondent left in Baghdad at the time, for televising Iraqi-censored reports on Cable News Network (CNN). Describing Arnett as "what we used to call a sympathizer," Simpson referred to a rumor that Arnett's Vietnamese brother-in-law had been in the Viet Cong when Arnett was winning awards for his coverage of the Vietnam War.

When Simpson had been satisfied that the rumor was untrue, he published an apology in The New York Times. But in the meantime, many in the media had rallied to Arnett's defense. Some pointedly observed that it was Simpson — not Arnett — who once had kind words for Saddam Hussein. (In April 1990, in a meeting with four other senators, Simpson told the dictator: "I believe your problems lie with the Western media and not with the U.S. government.") Simpson's office disputed the accuracy of the transcript of that meeting as released by Saddam, and few jumped on the incident initially. But that forbearance was swiftly canceled when Simpson went after Arnett.

"If Peter Arnett had been anywhere near as bootlicky and obsequious with Saddam Hussein as Alan Simpson . . . we could understand why the CNN correspondent was being assaulted for his interviews and coverage," read a Washington Post editorial.

Another nasty contretemps awaited Simpson before the year was out. When Hill accused Thomas of sexual harassment, Simpson challenged Hill, her motives and her credibility, with vague references to her "proclivities" and warnings from anonymous sources to "watch out for this woman."

"I really am getting stuff over the transom about Professor Hill. I've got letters hanging out of my pocket," he said during the nationally televised hearings.

Soon, Simpson's innuendoes had been compared with those of Joseph R. McCarthy in the red-baiting era. But Simpson, unfazed, stayed on the offensive. He had a heated discussion of the matter on the ABC-TV program "Nightline" with National Public Radio reporter Nina Totenberg, who had a role in bringing Hill's story to national attention. The two went on arguing that night in the street outside the ABC studios in Washington. The following spring, however, Simpson was Totenberg's guest at the White House Correspondents' dinner.

Given that he chides and charms the news media with equal flair, it is hard to tell which of his outbursts, if any, are merely for show. Simpson may shed some light on this point himself: He is working on a book about the media.

But in his worst public moments, Simpson has shown a tendency to speak first, think next and offer a partial mea culpa later.

Back home in Wyoming after the Hill-Thomas hearings, he bemoaned criticism that tarred him with such terms as "McCarthy, sleaze, slime, smarmy . . . evil, ugly, mean-spirited." He went on to tell the crowd that he did not blame anyone but himself for the mess he was in. "The responsibility is mine."

But when asked later about the speech, widely regarded as an apology, he replied: "I wasn't apologizing."

The end of the Bush era was the beginning of a new one for Simpson. Appearing as himself in the 1993 Washington-based movie "Dave," Simpson chats about a fictitious president for whom he has often gone to bat. "We're up here trying to carry the water for him. I've carried more water for him than Gunga Din, for God's sake," Simpson says in his self-scripted scene.

With Clinton in the White House, however, Simpson no longer feels the need to do the administration's bidding. Neither is he prepared to sit still while Democrats dominate the Senate.

"We don't want to be treated like the abused minority," he has said, and he was in the forefront as Senate Republicans united against Clinton's economic stimulus package.

Simpson's increasing duties as Dole's second-in-command have taken him away from some of the legislative functions he once performed with great ease and proficiency. It is ironic, given his current function, that so many of his past legislative accomplishments were the result of closed-door, bipartisan negotiating sessions, particularly with liberal Massachusetts Democrat Edward M. Kennedy.

"We don't vote together an awful lot, but we legislate together a lot," Simpson once said.

On Judiciary, Simpson is the reigning Republican expert on immigration issues. Twice in recent years, he has crossed the partisan divide to craft landmark immigration law with Democratic members.

During the mid-1980s, Simpson and Democratic Rep. Romano L. Mazzoli of Kentucky fought an arduous battle to reform the nation's laws dealing with illegal immigration.

Formidable political obstacles were arrayed against them. Business groups opposed sanctions against employers, and Hispanic leaders warned that the penalties would lead to employment discrimination against Hispanic citizens. Conservatives attacked the notion of amnesty for people who had entered illegally, and state governments worried about the welfare costs of a newly legal population.

In 1982, the Simpson-Mazzoli bill overwhelmingly passed the Senate but died in the House. In the next Congress, the bill passed both chambers, but stalled in conference.

Undaunted, Simpson came back in 1985 with a modified proposal to delay amnesty until employment of illegal aliens had been reduced. Amended in Judiciary to require amnesty within three years, the bill reached the floor in the closing months of 1985 and passed with votes to spare.

However, over Simpson's vehement objections, the Senate had approved a new "guest-worker" program allowing large numbers of seasonal farm workers to enter the country. That provision reflected the most serious unresolved controversy surrounding the issue — Western growers wanted foreign labor for harvest time while labor unions feared exploitation of workers — and it proved to be the bill's major stumbling block in the House.

Simpson staged intensive negotiations with House members, especially the core group of liberals who supported protections for guest workers. "Every one of us gave up something as painful as hell," Simpson said of the talks, "but we stayed at the table."

Although he was unhappy with some of the final provisions, Simpson expressed deep satisfaction over the product of his handiwork. The bill was "the very absolute quintessential immigration reform," Simpson said, adding that final passage "really tickled my butt."

In the 100th Congress, he turned to the other half of the immigration issue — laws governing the visa-allotment system for legal entry, enacted in 1965 and widely considered outdated. Simpson and Kennedy cosponsored legislation to cap annual admissions and replace the system's preferences for uniting families with new preferences favoring foreigners with needed skills.

Their bill won the Senate's overwhelming approval, but the House was uninterested. Congress passed only a stripped-down version increasing allowances for the Irish — Kennedy's priority — and for nurses. However, Simpson and Kennedy revived their efforts in the 101st Congress.

With the bill ready for conference in October 1990, Simpson single-handedly held things up trying to eliminate language that provided an 18-month stay of deportation for illegal El Salvadoran immigrants. He settled for a partial victory. The El Salvador amendment stayed, but Simpson-backed language was added calling for stepped-up border patrols and deportation procedures, as well as civil penalties for document fraud.

The bill won final passage just before adjournment in 1990. The issue was revived in early 1993 when Clinton's first nominee for attorney general, Zoë Baird, withdrew because she had hired two undocumented aliens as domestic help.

On Judiciary issues that create a more clear-cut partisan divide, Simpson can be found among, or in front, of his fellow Republicans. He favors expanding the federal death penalty, opposes gun control and supports administration drug law enforcement efforts. In 1989, he rejected Democrats' complaints that Bush was not seeking enough money to fight drugs. "Money — that's the real drug around this place," Simpson said.

Simpson's partisan fires burn especially hot when the judicial nominations of GOP presidents are questioned. When Ronald Reagan in 1986 picked William H. Rehnquist to be chief justice, Simpson described Rehnquist's critics as a kind of bird: the "bug-eyed zealot." He used the same term for foes of failed Supreme Court nominee Robert H. Bork in 1987.

The one issue on which Simpson deviates greatly from most fellow conservatives is his support for abortion rights. It is this issue above all else that has led many observers to view Simpson, whose overall record is strongly conservative, as a Republican "moderate."

Occasionally, Simpson did try to nudge Bush in a different direction, but in the end he remained loyal. On abortion-related matters he tried to find a middle ground with the White House. When that was impossible, he kept an uncharacteristically low profile so as not to embarrass Bush.

Simpson joined a group of senators who urged Bush to take a tougher stand on trade with China after the Tiananmen Square demonstrations. But on the vote, he sided with Bush. On the question of whether to reregulate the cable television industry, Simpson voted in favor of the Democratic plan but offered to change his vote if it would sustain a presidential veto.

Simpson's pro-business attitude is evident in his work on the Environment and Public Works Committee. When Republicans controlled the Senate in the early 1980s, Simpson gave unenthusiastic support to efforts to revise the Clean Air Act, and remained lukewarm even after Bush made it a priority.

Simpson did play a key role in blocking an effort by Democratic Sen. Robert C. Byrd of West Virginia to provide special benefits to his state's coal miners, who he said could lose their jobs because of the bill. Simpson quipped that he was loath to oppose the Appropriations Committee chairman because of his power over funding for esoteric local projects. Simpson said, "I write him letters all the time, saying, 'How about a little fence around the elk refuge?' " But he warned that Byrd's amendment would cost Republican support, stating, "If you vote for this you're going to lose this bill."

Simpson's other major assignment is the Veterans' Affairs Committee, which he chaired from 1981 to 1985. Here, too, he applies his fiscal conservatism, wagging his head at times at what he calls his colleagues' "veteran-o-mania."

A particular proposal that aggravated Simpson was one to provide disability benefits to Vietnam veterans suffering from cancers allegedly connected to their exposure to the defoliant Agent Orange. Simpson argued that there was no definitive proof that the cancers were service-related.

Late in 1990, supporters of Agent Orange benefits attached provisions to a veterans' cost of living adjustment (COLA) bill in the House and to a health-care bill in the Senate. Simpson stalled them, managing to tie up the Senate bill while his allies in the House tried to extricate the COLA. In the end, they succeeded only in postponing enactment of the COLA and the Agent Orange provisions until early in the 102nd Congress. In August 1992, Simpson helped negotiate an agreement ensuring the Department of Veterans Affairs would receive drug discounts from pharmaceutical companies.

On a more local matter, Simpson and other Western lawmakers won an early round against Clinton when he agreed not to include higher grazing fees in his budget package.

At Home: If Simpson had not come into his 1990 re-election campaign with a solid base of support, his controversial remarks to Saddam Hussein might have caused him political distress. Had the Democrats fielded a first-rank challenger, the flap might even have jeopardized his re-election.

But neither condition pertained in 1990. Polls continued to show Simpson as one of the most popular public officials in Wyoming. He also benefited from the Democrats' recruiting failure: His opponent, college student Kathy Helling, had emerged from a large field of unknown primary candidates.

Although Helling tried gamely to make an issue of Simpson's meeting with Saddam, she had almost no campaign resources. Also, her best-known political stance — a staunch opposition to abortion — hardly warmed the hearts of state and national Democratic officials.

Nonetheless, Simpson, who was expected to win in a landslide, prevailed with 64 percent of the vote, well below the 78 percent he carried in 1984.

Like his father Milward, a former governor and U.S. senator who died in June 1993 at age 95, Simpson is at his best running an old-fashioned personal campaign, trading ranch talk and old jokes. His friendliness was an enormous asset during his 1978 Senate campaign to succeed retiring Republican Sen. Clifford P. Hansen.

During 12 years as a state legislator, Simpson was active in the drafting of a state land-use planning law. His opponent in the 1978 GOP primary, eccentric oilman Hugh "Bigfoot" Binford, invested in a media campaign charging that Simpson had undermined local control of land decisions. He also said Simpson was shaky in his support of state right-to-work laws.

Simpson fought off Binford's assault, calling it full of distortion. But it was his personal acquaintance with thousands of the state's voters that ensured his nomination. He drew 55 percent in the primary, and coasted against liberal Democrat Raymond B. Whitaker.

By 1984, Democrats had a tough time even finding a credible candidate. Their nominee, chemistry professor Victor A. Ryan, had never been active in state party affairs. He criticized Simpson's stand on immigration, called for more trained scientists in the country and for his efforts received 22 percent of the vote.

Committees

Assistant Minority Leader

Environment & Public Works (2nd of 7 Republicans)
Clean Air & Nuclear Regulation (ranking); Superfund, Recycling & Solid Waste Management; Toxic Substances, Research & Development

Judiciary (3rd of 8 Republicans)
Immigration & Refugee Affairs (ranking); Patents, Copyrights & Trademarks

Special Aging (4th of 10 Republicans)

Veterans' Affairs (3rd of 5 Republicans)

Elections

1990 General		
Alan K. Simpson (R)	100,784	(64%)
Kathy Helling (D)	56,848	(36%)
1990 Primary		
Alan K. Simpson (R)	69,142	(84%)
Douglas W. Lewis (R)	6,577	(8%)
Nora Marie Crook (R)	6,201	(8%)

Previous Winning Percentages: 1984 (78%) **1978** (62%)

Campaign Finance

	Receipts	Receipts from PACs		Expend-itures
1990				
Simpson (R)	$1,253,647	$705,773	(56%)	$1,000,462
Helling (D)	$6,431	$2,500	(39%)	$6,243

Key Votes

1993	
Require unpaid family and medical leave	N
Approve national "motor voter" registration bill	N
Approve budget increasing taxes and reducing deficit	N
Support president's right to lift military gay ban	N
1992	
Approve school-choice pilot program	Y
Allow shifting funds from defense to domestic programs	N
Oppose deeper cuts in spending for SDI	Y
1991	
Approve waiting period for handgun purchases	N
Raise senators' pay and ban honoraria	Y
Authorize use of force in Persian Gulf	Y
Confirm Clarence Thomas to Supreme Court	Y

Voting Studies

	Presidential Support		Party Unity		Conservative Coalition	
Year	**S**	**O**	**S**	**O**	**S**	**O**
1992	82	17	90	8	92	8
1991	86	11	88	11	88	10
1990	80	17	86	11	97	0
1989	84	10	81	17	87	8
1988	75	25	80	17	86	5
1987	67	24	81	11	78	13
1986	92	8	90	8	92	4
1985	90	10	91	9	85	15
1984	86	9	90	8	89	2
1983	76	20	78	13	75	18
1982	82	14	83	13	91	6
1981	86	11	90	7	89	8

Interest Group Ratings

Year	ADA	AFL-CIO	CCUS	ACU
1992	15	17	90	89
1991	10	17	80	80
1990	11	11	75	73
1989	10	0	88	70
1988	15	21	86	92
1987	10	11	71	79
1986	10	0	76	86
1985	10	10	90	78
1984	20	0	94	68
1983	25	13	59	61
1982	15	16	76	75
1981	5	0	100	80

AL Craig Thomas (R)

Of Casper — Elected 1989; 2nd Full Term

Born: Feb. 17, 1933, Cody, Wyo.
Education: U. of Wyoming, B.A. 1955; La Salle U., LL.B. 1963.
Military Service: Marine Corps, 1955-59.
Occupation: Power company executive.
Family: Wife, Susan Roberts; four children.
Religion: Methodist.
Political Career: Sought GOP nomination for state treasurer, 1978, 1982; Wyo. House, 1985-89.
Capitol Office: 1019 Longworth Bldg. 20515; 225-2311.

In Washington: It is doubtful Thomas will ever rival his predecessor Dick Cheney, who rose to minority whip before leaving the House in 1989 to become secretary of Defense. But he does not aspire to. Thomas' focus is on the parochial concerns of his Wyoming constituents.

A self-described conservative pragmatist, Thomas seems interested in making government work — especially for his home state — whether by expanding medical insurance to cover rural Wyoming citizens or by pushing for more funds for completion of the Buffalo Bill Dam near his hometown of Cody. "I'm not one who thinks efficiency in government is an oxymoron," he once said.

On Government Operations, Thomas helped agitate for a subcommittee hearing in 1990 on alleged monopolistic practices in the meatpacking industry; Wyoming producers had complained when the Justice Department found no antitrust violations.

On Natural Resources, Thomas has sought to protect his state's economy by pushing tax incentives for domestic oil exploration and acid rain legislation that would make Wyoming's cleaner-burning, low-sulfur coal more attractive.

Sometimes on Natural Resources, Thomas has had to play defense. In 1992, he opposed efforts by Democrat Nick J. Rahall II of West Virginia, then the Mining Subcommittee chairman, to protect Eastern coal-mining companies from Western competition by prohibiting the Interior Department's Bureau of Land Management from leasing any of its public land to coal mining operations that would compete with privately owned companies.

Thomas decried Rahall's initiative as a thinly veiled attempt at "regional protectionism."

On most issues Thomas tends to follow the credo of other mountain state Republicans: The government that governs least, governs best.

In 1991, he joined several other congressional colleagues in urging President Bush to issue an executive order freezing the number of civilian federal employees at 2.9 million. And he introduced legislation that would limit the federal government's ability to acquire land in states where over one-fourth of the land is already in federal hands; the federal government owns half of Wyoming's land.

Throughout his political career, Thomas has shown an interest in finding ways to promote government efficiency. As a member of the Wyoming Legislature, Thomas promoted consolidation of dozens of state agencies into a Cabinet-style government.

In Congress, he lines up with most of his Republican House colleagues in supporting a presidential line-item veto, a balanced-budget constitutional amendment and a 12-year term limit for members of Congress, saying the last-named would cure the institutional inertia he blames for government overspending.

Upon beginning his House career, Thomas indicated that he would not be another Cheney. "Where Dick would have accomplished something but would have done it through more the insider route, I will probably fuss more," he said.

But in a House with such outspoken members as Californian Robert K. Dornan and Ohioan James A. Traficant Jr., "fussing" is performance art, and Thomas, with a Western proclivity for a few choice words, has not broken into that chorus line.

At Home: Thomas appears to have gained a measure of political security since making his way to the House in 1989 with a modest 52 percent of the vote. He has won by wider and wider margins since.

Thomas has taken advantage of Wyoming's natural political contour; it is one of the few states in the country where Republicans hold a voter registration edge.

But Thomas also has given his Democratic opposition few openings to exploit. He is a conservative but no ideologue, possesses an affable personality and returns to the state regularly. "You get an awful lot of time behind a steering wheel," he says of his job.

Thomas has long ties to voters scattered across the state's vast open landscape, having served as an executive with the Farm Bureau and

Wyoming

At Large

Few states have more of a boom-and-bust economy than Wyoming, a fact reflected in its roller-coaster population growth of the past few decades. A population jump of nearly 15 percent in the 1950s was followed by stagnation in the 1960s (1 percent growth). There was a 41 percent growth spurt in the 1970s, but then a 4 percent population decline in the 1980s.

Wyoming's economy has several components: oil and natural gas, extractive industries such as coal and uranium, an agricultural sector focused on ranching, and a steady flow of tourists to attractions such as Devils Tower and Yellowstone National Park.

Wyoming leads the nation in the production of coal and trona, a substance used in the production of glass and baking soda. But many of the state's widely scattered communities tend to depend heavily on a single industry, and they have been vulnerable to any downturn in it.

In the early 1980s the uranium market collapsed. Several years later, Wyoming's lucrative oil industry went bust as oil prices plummeted. By the end of the decade, 14 of Wyoming's 23 counties had lost population; the center of the state's oil industry, Natrona County (Casper), had a 17 percent falloff.

Population growth in the 1980s was largely limited to the four corners of the state. In the northeast, Campbell County (Gillette), the center of the state's coal production, grew 21 percent. In the northwest, Teton County, which includes Grand Teton National Park and the ski resort of Jackson Hole, grew 19 percent.

In the southwest corner, Uinta County (Evanston), a prime producer of natural gas as well as home for some long-range commuters to Salt Lake City, grew 44 percent. And in Wyoming's southeast corner, a cluster of counties anchored by Laramie (Cheyenne) showed some population growth.

The only cities in the state with more than 30,000 people are Cheyenne (just over 50,000) and Casper (almost 47,000). As the capital city, Cheyenne has a more diversfied economy, which enabled it better to weather the economic downturn of the 1980s.

Cheyenne has the state government work force, the Francis E. Warren Air Force Base, where MX missiles are deployed, and an array of new companies that have brought hundreds of jobs to the area. Cheyenne does not have the transportation problems that have hindered the economic development of other parts of the state. It is located only 100 miles north of Denver on Interstate 25.

As Wyoming's economy has undergone gradual change, so has its politics. In 1992, Bill Clinton was the first Democratic presidential candidate since 1964 to carry beleaguered Natrona County, and he was the first Democrat since 1940 to win Teton County.

Yet Wyoming is a conservative state. Democrats have not carried it in a presidential election since 1964 and not won a Senate race since 1970 or a House contest since 1976. Republicans dominate the state Legislature. The Democrats' lone toehold has been the governorship, which the party has held since 1975 due in no small part to GOP infighting.

In most races, Democrats have trouble winning votes beyond the party's historical base in Wyoming's southern tier. Immigrant laborers, many from Italy, were imported to build the Union Pacific rail line through the southern counties, and coal miners followed.

Most of the workers were drawn to the Democratic Party, and although their modern-day descendants are conservative on many issues and gave majorities to Ronald Reagan and George Bush in the 1980s, their Democratic sentiments are still evident. Three of the five Wyoming counties Clinton carried in 1992 were in the southern tier — Albany, Carbon and Sweetwater.

Albany County includes the academic community at the University of Wyoming in Laramie. Carbon and Sweetwater counties have more blue-collar voters, with Sweetwater County the center of the state's trona production. Carbon and Sweetwater were the only two counties in the state to vote against Rep. Thomas in 1992.

The northern part of the state is the Wyoming of ranch, rock and Republicans. Its dry plateaus and basins accommodate the cattle ranches that make Wyoming the "Cowboy State." Ross Perot ran especially well in this part of Wyoming in 1992, finishing second in nine counties. Altogether, Perot captured 26 percent of the statewide vote.

Perot's strength in "Marlboro Country" nearly produced the unthinkable, a Democratic presidential victory in Wyoming. Bush's 40 percent tally statewide was the lowest for a GOP presidential candidate in Wyoming since Alfred M. Landon drew 38 percent in 1936.

1990 Population: 453,588. White 427,061 (94%), Black 3,606 (1%), Other 22,921 (5%). Hispanic origin 25,751 (6%). 18 and over 318,063 (70%), 62 and over 57,538 (13%). Median age: 32.

as general manager of the Wyoming Rural Electric Association. And he has been in the forefront of Wyoming politicians on the issue of health care, touring in the summer of 1991 with a special legislative committee holding hearings.

Thomas' Democratic opponent in 1992, eye surgeon Jon Herschler, tried to make the healthcare issue his own. But despite his famous name — the late Ed Herschler, who was at most distantly related, served three terms as governor in the 1970s and 1980s — the Democrat was a newcomer and lacked Thomas' deep roots in the state. The incumbent swept all but two of Wyoming's 23 counties, taking 58 percent of the vote.

Thomas grew up in Cody, where he was a high school classmate of GOP Sen. Alan K. Simpson. But his political career was slow to develop. He lost two GOP primaries for state treasurer before winning a state House seat in 1984 at age 51.

When Cheney left Congress to join George Bush's Cabinet, the GOP nominated Thomas to replace Cheney, as much for his work as a party insider as for his legislative résumé. The selection was made by the Republican state central committee, and Thomas knew many of the members through his work as state party secretary and Natrona County GOP chairman.

Thomas was pitted in the special election against Democratic state Sen. John P. Vinich, who had built high name recognition in a narrow 1988 Senate loss to GOP Sen. Malcolm Wallop.

Both campaigns had gaffes. The National Republican Congressional Committee (NRCC) helped Thomas raise considerable sums of campaign money. But its intervention was a mixed blessing. Embarrassed by special-election defeats in Indiana and Alabama earlier in 1989, NRCC Co-Chairman Edward J. Rollins was quoted as saying he would send two top aides to Wyoming to "take charge" of Thomas' campaign. His remarks played poorly in Wyoming, where people are easily piqued by out-of-state influence.

But Thomas survived his overbearing allies with help from a major misstep by Vinich. Attempting to portray Thomas as soft on crime, he denounced Thomas' vote in the Legislature on a sentencing bill. However, Vinich, who was one of only three state senators taking the opposite view on the bill, was widely condemned for distorting the issue.

In the end, Thomas was able to portray himself as an acceptable conservative in the Cheney mold while pounding away at Vinich as a labor-backed liberal. Thomas won by a solid 9 percentage points.

In 1990, Thomas fended off a vigorous effort by Democrat Pete Maxfield. Accusing Thomas of failing to boost Wyoming's lagging energy-based economy, Maxfield called for an oil import fee. Thomas won with 55 percent of the vote.

Committees

Banking, Finance & Urban Affairs (10th of 20 Republicans)
Consumer Credit & Insurance; Financial Institutions Supervision, Regulation & Deposit Insurance; Housing & Community Development

Government Operations (8th of 16 Republicans)
Information, Justice, Transportation & Agriculture (ranking)

Natural Resources (6th of 15 Republicans)
Native American Affairs (ranking); Energy & Mineral Resources; National Parks, Forests & Public Lands

Elections

1992 General		
Craig Thomas (R)	113,882	(58%)
Jon Herschler (D)	77,418	(39%)
Craig Alan McCune (LIBERT)	5,677	(3%)
1990 General		
Craig Thomas (R)	87,078	(55%)
Pete Maxfield (D)	70,977	(45%)

Previous Winning Percentage: **1989 *** (52%)

* *Special election.*

District Vote for President

	1992	
D	68,160	(34%)
R	79,347	(40%)
I	51,263	(26%)

Campaign Finance

	Receipts	Receipts from PACs		Expend-itures
1992				
Thomas (R)	$479,523	$222,403	(46%)	$459,523
Herschler (D)	$344,240	$78,200	(23%)	$348,361
1990				
Thomas (R)	$404,308	$174,996	(43%)	$437,772
Maxfield (D)	$239,474	$33,950	(14%)	$239,116

Key Votes

1993	
Require parental notification of minors' abortions	Y
Require unpaid family and medical leave	Y
Approve national "motor voter" registration bill	N
Approve budget increasing taxes and reducing deficit	N
Approve economic stimulus plan	N
1992	
Approve balanced-budget constitutional amendment	Y
Close down space station program	N
Approve U.S. aid for former Soviet Union	Y
Allow shifting funds from defense to domestic programs	N
1991	
Extend unemployment benefits using deficit financing	N
Approve waiting period for handgun purchases	N
Authorize use of force in Persian Gulf	Y

Voting Studies

	Presidential Support		Party Unity		Conservative Coalition	
Year	S	O	S	O	S	O
1992	77	22	83	12	81	17
1991	77	16	93	6	92	3
1990	70	28	86	13	89	9
1989	72 †	25 †	85 †	12 †	95 †	3 †

† *Not eligible for all recorded votes.*

Interest Group Ratings

Year	ADA	AFL-CIO	CCUS	ACU
1992	20	45	88	79
1991	0	0	100	95
1990	11	0	100	79
1989	5	0	89	88

Non-Voting Representatives in the House

Puerto Rico sends a "resident commissioner" to the House for a four-year term, while the District of Columbia, the Virgin Islands, Guam and American Samoa elect delegates who serve two-year terms.

While not exactly members of the House, they are getting closer. At the urging of D.C.'s delegate, Eleanor Holmes Norton, the House Democratic Caucus gave the five "non-voting representatives" floor-voting privileges for the first time in their history.

Adopted by the House over Republican objections on Jan. 5, 1993, the rule change allows the five to vote when the House is acting as the Committee of the Whole. The chamber works on bills as a Committee of the Whole so as to expedite amendments. The five may not vote, however, if their participation would determine the outcome. If it does, an automatic re-vote must be taken on which the delegates may not vote. As before, the five are allowed to give floor speeches, serve on committees and even hold chairmanships.

Because the Natural Resources Committee (formerly Interior) has jurisdiction over U.S. territorial affairs, the representatives from Puerto Rico, American Samoa, Guam and the Virgin Islands all serve there. Ron de Lugo of the Virgin Islands chairs the Insular and International Affairs Subcommittee.

There are two newcomers in the 103rd: Robert A. Underwood of Guam (who replaced Ben Blaz) and Carlos Romero-Barceló of Puerto Rico (who replaced Jaime B. Fuster).

Following are the capsule profiles of those who serve in the House on a non-voting basis.

Ron de Lugo (D)

Of St. Thomas — Elected 1972; 10th Term

Did not serve 1979-81.

Born: Aug. 2, 1930, Englewood, N.J.
Education: Attended Colegio San Jose.
Military Service: Army, 1948-50.
Occupation: Broadcast journalist.
Family: Wife, Sheila Paiewonsky; two children, two stepchildren.
Religion: Roman Catholic.
Political Career: Virgin Islands Senate, 1956-66; Democratic National Committee, 1959-61; St. Croix administrator, 1961; candidate for governor, 1978.
Capitol Office: 2427 Rayburn Bldg. 20515; 225-1790.

Eni F.H. Faleomavaega (D)

Of Pago Pago — Elected 1988; 3rd Term

Born: Aug. 15, 1943, Vailoatai, Am. Samoa.
Education: Brigham Young U., A.A. 1964, B.A. 1966; Texas Southern U., 1969; U. of Houston, J.D. 1972; U. of California, Berkeley, LL.M. 1973.
Military Service: Army, 1966-69; Army Reserve, 1983-present.
Occupation: Lawyer; congressional aide.
Family: Wife, Hinanui Bambridge Cave; five children.
Religion: Mormon.
Political Career: Am. Samoa deputy attorney general, 1981-84; Democratic candidate for U.S. House, 1984; lieutenant governor, 1985-89.
Capitol Office: 109 Cannon Bldg. 20515; 225-8577.

Eleanor Holmes Norton (D)

Of Washington — Elected 1990; 2nd Term

Born: June 13, 1937, Washington, D.C.
Education: Antioch College, B.A. 1960; Yale U., M.A. 1963, LL.B. 1964.
Occupation: Professor; lawyer.
Family: Divorced; two children.
Religion: Episcopalian.
Political Career: New York City Human Rights Commission, 1971-77; Equal Employment Opportunity Commission chairman, 1977-81.
Capitol Office: 1415 Longworth Bldg. 20515; 225-8050.

Carlos Romero-Barceló (D/NPP)

Of San Juan — Elected 1992; 1st Term

Born: Sept. 4, 1932, San Juan, Puerto Rico.
Education: Yale U., B.A. 1953; U. of Puerto Rico, LL.B. 1956.
Occupation: Lawyer; real estate broker.
Family: Wife, Kathleen Donnelly; four children.
Religion: Roman Catholic.
Political Career: Mayor of San Juan, 1967-77; governor, 1977-85; Puerto Rico Senate, 1986-88.
Capitol Office: 1517 Longworth Bldg. 20515; 225-2615.

Robert Anacletus Underwood (D)

Of Baza Gardens — Elected 1992; 1st Term

Born: July 13, 1948, Tamuning, Guam.
Education: California State U., Los Angeles, B.A. 1969, M.A. 1971; U. of Southern California, Ph.D. 1987.
Occupation: Professor; college administrator.
Family: Wife, Lorraine Aguilar; five children.
Religion: Roman Catholic.
Political Career: No previous office.
Capitol Office: 507 Cannon Bldg. 20515; 225-1188.

Senate Committees and Subcommittees

The standing and select committees of the U.S. Senate are listed below in alphabetical order. The listing includes telephone number, room number, and party ratio for each full committee. Membership is given in order of seniority on the committee.

Subcommittees are listed alphabetically under each committee. Membership is listed in order of seniority on the subcommittee.

Members of the majority party, Democrats, are shown in Roman type; members of the minority party, Republicans, are shown in italic type.

The word "vacancy" indicates that a committee or subcommittee seat had not been filled at press time. Subcommittee vacancies do not necessarily indicate vacancies on full committees, or vice versa.

Asterisks (*) indicate that chairmen and/or ranking minority members are *ex officio* members of all subcommittees of which they are not regular members.

The partisan committees of the Senate are listed on p. 1711. Members of these committees are listed in alphabetical order, not by seniority.

The telephone area code for Washington, D.C., is 202. Abbreviations for Senate office buildings are: SD — Dirksen Bldg., SH — Hart Bldg., SR — Russell Bldg, and Capitol. The ZIP code for all Senate offices is 20510.

Agriculture, Nutrition and Forestry

224-2035 SR-328A

Party Ratio: D 10 - R 8

Patrick J. Leahy, D-Vt., chairman

David Pryor, Ark.	*Richard G. Lugar, Ind.*
David L. Boren, Okla.	*Bob Dole, Kan.*
Howell Heflin, Ala.	*Jesse Helms, N.C.*
Tom Harkin, Iowa	*Thad Cochran, Miss.*
Kent Conrad, N.D.	*Mitch McConnell, Ky.*
Tom Daschle, S.D.	*Larry E. Craig, Idaho*
Max Baucus, Mont.	*Paul Coverdell, Ga.*
Bob Kerrey, Neb.	*Charles E. Grassley, Iowa*
Russell D. Feingold, Wis.	

Agricultural Credit

224-2035 SR-328A

Conrad — chairman

Daschle	*Grassley*
Boren	*Craig*
Baucus	*Coverdell*

Agricultural Production and Stabilization of Prices

224-2035 SR-328A

Pryor — chairman

Baucus	*Helms*
Kerrey	*Dole*
Feingold	*Cochran*
Boren	*McConnell*
Heflin	*Craig*
Harkin	*Grassley*

Agricultural Research, Conservation, Forestry and General Legislation

224-2035 SR-328A

Daschle — chairman

Kerrey	*Craig*
Harkin	*Cochran*

Domestic and Foreign Marketing and Product Promotion

224-2035 SR-328A

Boren — chairman

Pryor	*Cochran*
Conrad	*Helms*
Baucus	*Coverdell*
Feingold	*McConnell*
Heflin	*Grassley*

Nutrition and Investigations

224-2035 SR-328A

Harkin — chairman

Pryor	*McConnell*
Kerrey	*Dole*
Feingold	*Helms*

Rural Development and Rural Electrification

224-2035 SR-328A

Heflin — chairman

Conrad	*Coverdell*
Daschle	*Dole*

Appropriations

224-3471 S-128 Capitol

Party Ratio: D 16 - R 13

Robert C. Byrd, D-W.Va., chairman

Daniel K. Inouye, Hawaii	*Mark O. Hatfield, Ore.*
Ernest F. Hollings, S.C.	*Ted Stevens, Alaska*
J. Bennett Johnston, La.	*Thad Cochran, Miss.*
Patrick J. Leahy, Vt.	*Alfonse M. D'Amato, N.Y.*
Jim Sasser, Tenn.	*Arlen Specter, Pa.*
Dennis DeConcini, Ariz.	*Pete V. Domenici, N.M.*
Dale Bumpers, Ark.	*Don Nickles, Okla.*
Frank R. Lautenberg, N.J.	*Phil Gramm, Texas*
Tom Harkin, Iowa	*Christopher S. Bond, Mo.*
Barbara A. Mikulski, Md.	*Slade Gorton, Wash.*
Harry Reid, Nev.	*Mitch McConnell, Ky.*
Bob Kerrey, Neb.	*Connie Mack, Fla.*
Herb Kohl, Wis.	*Conrad Burns, Mont.*
Patty Murray, Wash.	
Dianne Feinstein, Calif.	

Agriculture, Rural Development and Related Agencies

224-7240 SD-140

Bumpers – chairman

Harkin	*Cochran*
Kerrey	*Specter*
Johnston	*Bond*
Kohl	*Gramm*
Feinstein	*Gorton*

Commerce, Justice, State and Judiciary

224-7277 S-146A Capitol

Hollings – chairman

Inouye	*Domenici*
Bumpers	*Stevens*
Lautenberg	*Hatfield*
Sasser	*Gramm*
Kerrey	*McConnell*

Defense

224-7255 SD-119

Inouye – chairman

Hollings	*Stevens*
Johnston	*D'Amato*
Byrd	*Cochran*
Leahy	*Specter*
Sasser	*Domenici*
DeConcini	*Nickles*
Bumpers	*Gramm*
Lautenberg	*Bond*
Harkin	

District of Columbia

224-731 S-205 Capitol

Kohl – chairman

Murray	*Burns*
Feinstein	*Mack*

Energy and Water Development

224-7260 SD-132

Johnston – chairman

Byrd	*Hatfield*
Hollings	*Cochran*
Sasser	*Domenici*
DeConcini	*Nickles*
Reid	*Gorton*
Kerrey	*McConnell*

Foreign Operations

224-7209 SD-136

Leahy – chairman

Inouye	*McConnell*
DeConcini	*D'Amato*
Lautenberg	*Specter*
Harkin	*Nickles*
Mikulski	*Mack*
Feinstein	*Gramm*

Interior

224-7233 SD-127

Byrd – chairman

Johnston	*Nickles*
Leahy	*Stevens*
DeConcini	*Cochran*
Bumpers	*Domenici*
Hollings	*Gorton*
Reid	*Hatfield*
Murray	*Burns*

Labor, Health and Human Services, Education

224-7283 SD-186

Harkin – chairman

Byrd	*Specter*
Hollings	*Hatfield*
Inouye	*Stevens*
Bumpers	*Cochran*
Reid	*Gorton*
Kohl	*Mack*
Murray	*Bond*

Legislative Branch

224-7338 SD-132

Reid – chairman

Mikulski	*Mack*
Murray	*Burns*

Military Construction

224-7276 SD-131

Sasser – chairman

Inouye	*Gorton*
Reid	*Stevens*
Kohl	*McConnell*

Transportation

224-7281 SD-156

Lautenberg – chairman

Byrd	*D'Amato*
Harkin	*Domenici*
Sasser	*Hatfield*
Mikulski	*Specter*

Treasury, Postal Service and General Government

224-6280 SD-190

DeConcini — chairman

Mikulski	*Bond*
Kerrey	*D'Amato*

VA, HUD and Independent Agencies

224-7211 SD-142

Mikulski — chairman

Leahy	*Gramm*
Johnston	*D'Amato*
Lautenberg	*Nickles*
Kerrey	*Bond*
Feinstein	*Burns*

Armed Services

224-3871 SR-228

Party Ratio: D 11 - R 9

Sam Nunn, D-Ga., chairman

Jim Exon, Neb.	*Strom Thurmond, S.C.*
Carl Levin, Mich.	*John W. Warner, Va.*
Edward M. Kennedy, Mass.	*William S. Cohen, Maine*
Jeff Bingaman, N.M.	*John McCain, Ariz.*
John Glenn, Ohio	*Trent Lott, Miss.*
Richard C. Shelby, Ala.	*Daniel R. Coats, Ind.*
Robert C. Byrd, W.Va.	*Robert C. Smith, N.H.*
Bob Graham, Fla.	*Dirk Kempthorne, Idaho*
Charles S. Robb, Va.	*Lauch Faircloth, N.C.*
Joseph I. Lieberman, Conn.	

Coalition Defense and Reinforcing Forces

224-3871 SR-228

Levin — chairman

Exon	*Warner*
Glenn	*Cohen*
Shelby	*Coats*
Byrd	*Smith*
Graham	*Kempthorne*

Defense Technology, Acquisition and Industrial Base

224-3871 SR-228

Bingaman — chairman

Levin	*Smith*
Kennedy	*Cohen*
Byrd	*Lott*
Graham	*Coats*
Robb	*Kempthorne*
Lieberman	*Faircloth*

Force Requirements and Personnel

224-3871 SR-228

Shelby — chairman

Kennedy	*Coats*
Byrd	*McCain*
Lieberman	*Faircloth*

Military Readiness and Defense Infrastructure

224-3871 SR-228

Glenn — chairman

Bingaman	*McCain*
Shelby	*Smith*
Robb	*Faircloth*

Nuclear Deterrence, Arms Control and Defense Intelligence

224-3871 SR-228

Exon — chairman

Levin	*Lott*
Bingaman	*Warner*
Glenn	*Kempthorne*

Regional Defense and Contingency Forces

224-3871 SR-228

Kennedy — chairman

Exon	*Cohen*
Graham	*Warner*
Robb	*McCain*
Lieberman	*Lott*

Banking, Housing and Urban Affairs

224-7391 SD-534

Party Ratio: D 11 - R 8

Donald W. Riegle Jr., D-Mich., chairman

Paul S. Sarbanes, Md.	*Alfonse M. D'Amato, N.Y.*
Christopher J. Dodd, Conn.	*Phil Gramm, Texas*
Jim Sasser, Tenn.	*Christopher S. Bond, Mo.*
Richard C. Shelby, Ala.	*Connie Mack, Fla.*
John Kerry, Mass.	*Lauch Faircloth, N.C.*
Richard H. Bryan, Nev.	*Robert F. Bennett, Utah*
Barbara Boxer, Calif.	*William V. Roth Jr., Del.*
Ben Nighthorse Campbell, Colo.	*Pete V. Domenici, N.M.*
Carol Moseley-Braun, Ill.	
Patty Murray, Wash.	

Economic Stabilization and Rural Development

224-7391 SD-534

Shelby — chairman

Campbell	*Faircloth*
Dodd	*Bennett*
Kerry	*Gramm*
Bryan	*Mack*

Housing and Urban Affairs

224-6348 SD-535

Sarbanes — chairman

Kerry	*Bond*
Bryan	*Domenici*
Boxer	*Mack*
Moseley-Braun	*Faircloth*
Dodd	*Roth*

International Finance and Monetary Policy

224-1564 SD-534

Sasser – chairman

Murray	*Mack*
Sarbanes	*Gramm*
Kerry	*Bennett*
Boxer	*Roth*
Campbell	*Bond*

Securities

224-9213 SD-534

Dodd – chairman

Sasser	*Gramm*
Shelby	*Roth*
Bryan	*Bond*
Moseley-Braun	*Faircloth*
Murray	*Domenici*

Budget

224-0642 SD-621

Party Ratio: D 12 - R 9

Jim Sasser, D-Tenn., chairman

Ernest F. Hollings, S.C.	*Pete V. Domenici, N.M.*
J. Bennett Johnston, La.	*Charles E. Grassley, Iowa*
Donald W. Riegle Jr., Mich.	*Don Nickles, Okla.*
	Phil Gramm, Texas
Jim Exon, Neb.	*Christopher S. Bond, Mo.*
Frank R. Lautenberg, N.J.	*Trent Lott, Miss.*
Paul Simon, Ill.	*Hank Brown, Colo.*
Kent Conrad, N.D.	*Slade Gorton, Wash.*
Christopher J. Dodd, Conn.	*Judd Gregg, N.H.*
Paul S. Sarbanes, Md.	
Barbara Boxer, Calif.	
Patty Murray, Wash.	

Commerce, Science and Transportation

224-5115 SD-508

Party Ratio: D 11 - R 9

Ernest F. Hollings, D-S.C., chairman

Daniel K. Inouye, Hawaii	*John C. Danforth, Mo.*
Wendell H. Ford, Ky.	*Bob Packwood, Ore.*
Jim Exon, Neb.	*Larry Pressler, S.D.*
John D. Rockefeller IV, W.Va.	*Ted Stevens, Alaska*
	John McCain, Ariz.
John Kerry, Mass.	*Conrad Burns, Mont.*
John B. Breaux, La.	*Slade Gorton, Wash.*
Richard H. Bryan, Nev.	*Trent Lott, Miss.*
Charles S. Robb, Va.	*Judd Gregg, N.H.*
Byron L. Dorgan, N.D.	
1 vacancy	

Aviation

224-9350 SH-428

Ford – chairman

Exon	*Pressler*
Inouye	*McCain*
Kerry	*Stevens*
Bryan	*Gorton*

Communications

224-9340 SH-227

Inouye – chairman

Hollings	*Packwood*
Ford	*Pressler*
Exon	*Stevens*
Kerry	*McCain*
Breaux	*Burns*
Rockefeller	*Gorton*
Robb	

Consumer

224-0415 SH-227

Bryan – chairman

Ford	*Gorton*
Dorgan	*McCain*
1 vacancy	*Burns*

Foreign Commerce and Tourism

224-9325 SH-428

Kerry – chairman

Hollings	*Gregg*
Rockefeller	*Packwood*
Bryan	*Pressler*
Dorgan	

Merchant Marine

224-4914 SH-425

Breaux – chairman

Inouye	*Lott*
1 vacancy	*Stevens*

National Ocean Policy Study

224-4912 SH-425

Hollings – chairman

Kerry – vice chairman

Inouye	*Stevens*
Ford	*Danforth*
Breaux	*Packwood*
Robb	*Pressler*
1 vacancy	*Gorton*
	Lott
	Gregg

Science, Technology and Space

224-9360 SH-427

Rockefeller – chairman

Hollings	*Burns*
Kerry	*Pressler*
Bryan	*Lott*
Robb	*Gregg*
1 vacancy	

Surface Transportation

224-9350 SH-428

Exon – chairman

Rockefeller	*McCain*
Inouye	*Packwood*
Breaux	*Burns*
Robb	*Lott*
Dorgan	*Gregg*
1 vacancy	

Energy and Natural Resources

224-4971 SD-304

Party Ratio: D 11 - R 9

J. Bennett Johnston, D-La., chairman

Dale Bumpers, Ark.	*Malcolm Wallop, Wyo.*
Wendell H. Ford, Ky.	*Mark O. Hatfield, Ore.*
Bill Bradley, N.J.	*Pete V. Domenici, N.M.*
Jeff Bingaman, N.M.	*Frank H. Murkowski, Alaska*
Daniel K. Akaka, Hawaii	*Don Nickles, Okla.*
Richard C. Shelby, Ala.	*Larry E. Craig, Idaho*
Paul Wellstone, Minn.	*Robert F. Bennett, Utah*
Ben Nighthorse Campbell, Colo.	*Arlen Specter, Pa.*
Harlan Mathews, Tenn.	*Trent Lott, Miss.*
1 vacancy	

Energy Research and Development

224-7569 SH-312

Ford — chairman
Shelby — vice chairman

Bumpers	*Domenici*
Bingaman	*Specter*
Wellstone	*Nickles*
Mathews	*Craig*
1 vacancy	*Lott*

Mineral Resources Development and Production

224-7568 SD-362

Akaka — chairman
Mathews — vice chairman

Bumpers	*Craig*
Ford	*Murkowski*
Campbell	*Nickles*
	Bennett

Public Lands, National Parks and Forests

224-7934 SD-308

Bumpers — chairman
Campbell — vice chairman

Bradley	*Murkowski*
Bingaman	*Hatfield*
Akaka	*Lott*
Shelby	*Domenici*
Wellstone	*Bennett*
1 vacancy	*Craig*
	Specter

Renewable Energy, Energy Efficiency and Competitiveness

224-4756 SH-212

Bingaman — chairman
Wellstone — vice chairman

Bradley	*Nickles*
Akaka	*Specter*
Shelby	*Lott*
Mathews	*Hatfield*
1 vacancy	*Domenici*
	Murkowski

Water and Power

224-6836 SD-306

Bradley — chairman

Ford	*Bennett*
Campbell	*Hatfield*

Environment and Public Works

224-6176 SD-456

Party Ratio: D 10 - R 7

Max Baucus, D-Mont., chairman

Daniel Patrick Moynihan, N.Y.	*John H. Chafee, R.I.*
George J. Mitchell, Maine	*Alan K. Simpson, Wyo.*
Frank R. Lautenberg, N.J.	*Dave Durenberger, Minn.*
Harry Reid, Nev.	*John W. Warner, Va.*
Bob Graham, Fla.	*Robert C. Smith, N.H.*
Joseph I. Lieberman, Conn.	*Lauch Faircloth, N.C.*
Howard M. Metzenbaum, Ohio	*Dirk Kempthorne, Idaho*
Harris Wofford, Pa.	
Barbara Boxer, Calif.	

Clean Air and Nuclear Regulation

224-3597 SH-505

Lieberman — chairman

Moynihan	*Simpson*
Graham	*Faircloth*
Metzenbaum	*Kempthorne*

Clean Water, Fisheries and Wildlife

224-5031 SH-415

Graham — chairman

Mitchell	*Chafee*
Lautenberg	*Durenberger*
Reid	*Faircloth*
Lieberman	*Kempthorne*
Wofford	

Superfund, Recycling and Solid Waste Management

224-3597 SH-505

Lautenberg — chairman

Moynihan	*Durenberger*
Graham	*Simpson*
Metzenbaum	*Smith*
Wofford	*Warner*
Boxer	

Toxic Substances, Research and Development

224-3597 SH-505

Reid — chairman

Lautenberg	*Smith*
Lieberman	*Warner*
Wofford	*Simpson*
Boxer	*Faircloth*

Water Resources, Transportation, Public Buildings and Economic Development

224-3597 SH-505

Moynihan — chairman

Mitchell	*Warner*
Reid	*Durenberger*
Metzenbaum	*Smith*
Boxer	*Kempthorne*

Finance

224-4515 SD-205

Party Ratio: D 11 - R 9

Daniel Patrick Moynihan, D-N.Y., Chairman

Max Baucus, Mont.	*Bob Packwood, Ore.*
David L. Boren, Okla.	*Bob Dole, Kan.*
Bill Bradley, N.J.	*William V. Roth Jr., Del.*
George J. Mitchell, Maine	*John C. Danforth, Mo.*
David Pryor, Ark.	*John H. Chafee, R.I.*
Donald W. Riegle Jr., Mich.	*Dave Durenberger, Minn.*
	Charles E. Grassley, Iowa
John D. Rockefeller IV, W.Va.	*Orrin G. Hatch, Utah*
	Malcolm Wallop, Wyo.
Tom Daschle, S.D.	
John B. Breaux, La.	
Kent Conrad, N.D.	

Deficits, Debt Management and Long-Term Economic Growth

224-4515 SD-205

Bradley — chairman

Riegle	*Wallop*

Energy and Agricultural Taxation

224-4515 SD-205

Daschle — chairman

Boren	*Hatch*
Breaux	*Dole*
	Wallop

Health for Families and the Uninsured

224-4515 SD-205

Riegle — chairman

Bradley	*Chafee*
Mitchell	*Roth*
Rockefeller	*Durenberger*
	Danforth

International Trade

224-4515 SD-205

Baucus — chairman

Moynihan	*Danforth*
Boren	*Packwood*
Bradley	*Roth*
Mitchell	*Chafee*
Riegle	*Grassley*
Rockefeller	*Hatch*
Daschle	*Wallop*
Breaux	
Conrad	

Medicare and Long Term Care

224-4515 SD-205

Rockefeller — chairman

Baucus	*Durenberger*
Mitchell	*Packwood*
Pryor	*Dole*
Daschle	*Chafee*
Conrad	*Grassley*
	Hatch

Private Retirement Plans and Oversight of the Internal Revenue Service

224-4515 SD-205

Pryor — chairman

Moynihan	*Grassley*

Social Security and Family Policy

224-4515 SD-205

Breaux — chairman

Moynihan	*Dole*
	Durenberger

Taxation

224-4515 SD-205

Boren — chairman

Baucus	*Roth*
Pryor	*Packwood*
Conrad	*Danforth*

Foreign Relations

224-4651 SD-446

Party Ratio: D 11 - R 8

Claiborne Pell, D-R.I., Chairman

Joseph R. Biden Jr., Del.	*Jesse Helms, N.C.*
Paul S. Sarbanes, Md.	*Richard G. Lugar, Ind.*
Christopher J. Dodd, Conn.	*Nancy Landon Kassebaum, Kan.*
John Kerry, Mass.	*Larry Pressler, S.D.*
Paul Simon, Ill.	*Frank H. Murkowski, Alaska*
Daniel Patrick Moynihan, N.Y.	*Hank Brown, Colo.*
Charles S. Robb, Va.	*James M. Jeffords, Vt.*
Harris Wofford, Pa.	*Paul Coverdell, Ga.*
Russell D. Feingold, Wis.	
Harlan Mathews, Tenn.	

African Affairs

224-4651 SD-446

Simon — chairman

Moynihan	*Jeffords*
Feingold	*Kassebaum*

East Asian and Pacific Affairs

224-4651 SD-446

Robb — chairman

Biden	*Murkowski*
Kerry	*Lugar*
Mathews	*Pressler*

European Affairs

224-4651 SD-446

Biden — chairman

Sarbanes	*Lugar*
Simon	*Kassebaum*
Feingold	*Brown*

International Economic Policy, Trade, Oceans and Environment

224-4651 SD-446

Sarbanes — chairman

Biden	*Kassebaum*
Dodd	*Helms*
Kerry	*Murkowski*
Wofford	*Brown*
Feingold	*Jeffords*

Near Eastern and South Asian Affairs

224-4651 SD-446

Moynihan — chairman

Sarbanes	*Brown*
Robb	*Pressler*
Wofford	*Jeffords*
Mathews	*Coverdell*

Terrorism, Narcotics and International Operations

224-4651 SD-446

Kerry — chairman

Pell	*Pressler*
Dodd	*Helms*
Simon	*Murkowski*
Moynihan	*Coverdell*

Western Hemisphere and Peace Corps Affairs

224-4651 SD-446

Dodd — chairman

Robb	*Coverdell*
Wofford	*Helms*
Mathews	*Lugar*

Governmental Affairs

224-4751 SD-340

Party Ratio: D 8 - R 5

John Glenn, D-Ohio, Chairman

Sam Nunn, Ga.	*William V. Roth Jr., Del.*
Carl Levin, Mich.	*Ted Stevens, Alaska*
Jim Sasser, Tenn.	*William S. Cohen, Maine*
David Pryor, Ark.	*Thad Cochran, Miss.*
Joseph I. Lieberman, Conn.	*John McCain, Ariz.*
Daniel K. Akaka, Hawaii	
Byron L. Dorgan, N.D.	

Federal Services, Post Office and Civil Service

224-2254 SH-601

Pryor — chairman

Sasser	*Stevens*
Akaka	*Cochran*

General Services, Federalism and the District of Columbia

224-4718 SH-432

Sasser — chairman

Lieberman	*McCain*
Akaka	*Stevens*

Oversight of Government Management

224-3682 SH-442

Levin — chairman

Pryor	*Cohen*
Lieberman	*Stevens*
Akaka	*Cochran*
Nunn	*McCain*
Dorgan	

Permanent Investigations

224-3721 SR-100

Nunn — chairman
Glenn — vice chairman

Levin	*Roth*
Sasser	*Stevens*
Pryor	*Cohen*
Lieberman	*Cochran*
Dorgan	*McCain*

Regulation and Government Information

224-9000 SH-605

Lieberman — chairman

Nunn	*Cochran*
Levin	*Cohen*
Dorgan	*McCain*

Indian Affairs

224-2251 SH-838

Party Ratio: D 10 - R 8

Daniel K. Inouye, D-Hawaii, Chairman

Dennis DeConcini, Ariz.	*John McCain, Ariz.*
Tom Daschle, S.D.	*Frank H. Murkowski, Alaska*
Kent Conrad, N.D.	*Thad Cochran, Miss.*
Harry Reid, Nev.	*Slade Gorton, Wash.*
Paul Simon, Ill.	*Pete V. Domenici, N.M.*
Daniel K. Akaka, Hawaii	*Nancy Landon Kassebaum, Kan.*
Paul Wellstone, Minn.	*Don Nickles, Okla.*
Byron L. Dorgan, N.D.	*Mark O. Hatfield, Ore.*
Ben Nighthorse Campbell, Colo.	

Judiciary

224-5225 SD-224

Party Ratio: D 10 - R 8

Joseph R. Biden Jr., D-Del., chairman

Edward M. Kennedy, Mass.	*Orrin G. Hatch, Utah*
Howard M. Metzenbaum, Ohio	*Strom Thurmond, S.C.*
Dennis DeConcini, Ariz.	*Alan K. Simpson, Wyo.*
Patrick J. Leahy, Vt.	*Charles E. Grassley, Iowa*
Howell Heflin, Ala.	*Arlen Specter, Pa.*
Paul Simon, Ill.	*Hank Brown, Colo.*
Herb Kohl, Wis.	*William S. Cohen, Maine*
Dianne Feinstein, Calif.	*Larry Pressler, S.D.*
Carol Moseley-Braun, Ill.	

Antitrust, Monopolies and Business Rights

224-5701 SH-308

Metzenbaum — chairman

DeConcini	*Thurmond*
Heflin	*Specter*
Simon	*Hatch*

Constitution

224-5573 SD-524

Simon — chairman

Metzenbaum	*Brown*
DeConcini	*Hatch*
Kennedy	

Courts and Administrative Practice

224-4022 SH-223

Heflin — chairman

Metzenbaum	*Grassley*
Kohl	*Thurmond*
Moseley-Braun	*Cohen*

Immigration and Refugee Affairs

224-7878 SD-520

Kennedy — chairman

Simon	*Simpson*

Juvenile Justice

224-4933 SH-305

Kohl — chairman

Biden	*Cohen*
Moseley-Braun	*Pressler*

Patents, Copyrights and Trademarks

224-8178 SH-327

DeConcini — chairman

Kennedy	*Hatch*
Leahy	*Simpson*
Heflin	*Grassley*
Feinstein	*Brown*

Technology and the Law

224-3406 SH-815

Leahy — chairman

Kohl	*Specter*
Feinstein	*Pressler*

Labor and Human Resources

224-5375 SD-428

Party Ratio: D 10 - R 7

Edward M. Kennedy, D-Mass., chairman

Claiborne Pell, R.I.	*Nancy Landon Kassebaum, Kan.*
Howard M. Metzenbaum, Ohio	*James M. Jeffords, Vt.*
Christopher J. Dodd, Conn.	*Daniel R. Coats, Ind.*
Paul Simon, Ill.	*Judd Gregg, N.H.*
Tom Harkin, Iowa	*Strom Thurmond, S.C.*
Barbara A. Mikulski, Md.	*Orrin G. Hatch, Utah*
Jeff Bingaman, N.M.	*Dave Durenberger, Minn.*
Paul Wellstone, Minn.	
Harris Wofford, Pa.	

Aging

224-3239 SH-615

Mikulski — chairman

Pell	*Gregg*
Metzenbaum	*Coats*
Dodd	*Durenberger*
Wofford	

Children, Family, Drugs and Alcoholism

224-5630 SH-639

Dodd — chairman

Pell	*Coats*
Mikulski	*Kassebaum*
Bingaman	*Jeffords*
Kennedy	*Gregg*
Wellstone	*Thurmond*
Wofford	*Durenberger*

Disability Policy

224-6265 SH-113

Harkin — chairman

Metzenbaum	*Durenberger*
Simon	*Jeffords*
Bingaman	*Hatch*

Education, Arts and Humanities

224-7666 SD-648

Pell — chairman

Metzenbaum	*Jeffords*
Dodd	*Kassebaum*
Simon	*Coats*
Mikulski	*Gregg*
Bingaman	*Thurmond*
Kennedy	*Hatch*
Wellstone	*Durenberger*
Wofford	
Harkin	

Employment and Productivity

224-5575 SD-644

Simon — chairman

Harkin	*Thurmond*
Mikulski	*Coats*
Bingaman	*Gregg*
Wofford	*Hatch*

Labor

224-5546 SH-608

Metzenbaum — chairman

Harkin	*Hatch*
Dodd	*Kassebaum*
Kennedy	*Jeffords*
Wellstone	*Thurmond*

Rules and Administration

224-6352 SR-305

Party Ratio: D 9 - R 7

Wendell H. Ford, D-Ky., chairman

Claiborne Pell, R.I.	*Ted Stevens, Alaska*
Robert C. Byrd, W.Va.	*Mark O. Hatfield, Ore.*
Daniel K. Inouye, Hawaii	*Jesse Helms, N.C.*
Dennis DeConcini, Ariz.	*John W. Warner, Va.*
Daniel Patrick Moynihan, N.Y.	*Bob Dole, Kan.*
Christopher J. Dodd, Conn.	*Mitch McConnell, Ky.*
Dianne Feinstein, Calif.	*Thad Cochran, Miss.*
Harlan Mathews, Tenn.	

Select Ethics

224-2981 SH-220

Party Ratio: D 3 - R 3

Richard H. Bryan, D-Nev., chairman

Mitch McConnell, Ky., vice chairman

Barbara A. Mikulski, Md.	*Robert C. Smith, N.H.*
Tom Daschle, S.D.	*Larry Craig, Idaho*

Select Intelligence

224-1700 SH-211

Party Ratio: D 9 - R 8

Dennis DeConcini, D-Ariz., chairman

Howard M. Metzenbaum, Ohio	*John W. Warner, Va.*
John Glenn, Ohio	*Alfonse M. D'Amato, N.Y.*
Bob Kerrey, Neb.	*John C. Danforth, Mo.*
Richard H. Bryan, Nev.	*Slade Gorton, Wash.*
Bob Graham, Fla.	*John H. Chafee, R.I.*
John Kerry, Mass.	*Ted Stevens, Alaska*
Max Baucus, Mont.	*Richard G. Lugar, Ind.*
J. Bennett Johnston, La.	*Malcolm Wallop, Wyo.*

Small Business

224-5175 SR-428A

Party Ratio: D 12 - R 9

Dale Bumpers, D-Ark., chairman

Sam Nunn, Ga.	*Larry Pressler, S.D.*
Carl Levin, Mich.	*Malcolm Wallop, Wyo.*
Tom Harkin, Iowa	*Christopher S. Bond, Mo.*
John Kerry, Mass.	*Conrad Burns, Mont.*
Joseph I. Lieberman, Conn.	*Connie Mack, Fla.*
Paul Wellstone, Minn.	*Paul Coverdell, Ga.*
Harris Wofford, Pa.	*Dirk Kempthorne, Idaho*
Howell Heflin, Ala.	*Robert F. Bennett, Utah*
Frank R. Lautenberg, N.J.	*John H. Chafee, R.I.*
Herb Kohl, Wis.	
Carol Moseley-Braun, Ill.	

Competitiveness, Capital Formation and Economic Opportunity

224-5175 SR-428A

Lieberman — chairman

Harkin	*Mack*
Lautenberg	*Bond*

Export Expansion and Agricultural Development

224-5175 SR-428A

Wofford — chairman

Harkin	*Coverdell*
Bumpers	*Pressler*
Lautenberg	*Bennett*
Moseley-Braun	*Chafee*

Government Contracting and Paperwork Reduction

224-5175 SR-428A

Nunn — chairman

Lieberman	*Bond*
Harkin	*Wallop*
Kohl	

Innovation, Manufacturing and Technology

224-5175 SR-428A

Levin — chairman

Kerry	*Burns*
Bumpers	*Kempthorne*
Heflin	*Bennett*

Rural Economy and Family Farming

224-5175 SR-428A

Wellstone — chairman

Nunn	*Pressler*
Levin	*Wallop*
Bumpers	*Burns*
Heflin	*Coverdell*
Kohl	*Kempthorne*

Urban and Minority-Owned Business Development

224-5175 SR-428A

Kerry — chairman

Nunn	*Chafee*
Wellstone	*Mack*
Wofford	*Pressler*
Moseley-Braun	

Special Aging

224-5364 SD-G31

Party Ratio: D 11 - R 10

David Pryor, D-Ark., chairman

John Glenn, Ohio	*William S. Cohen, Maine*
Bill Bradley, N.J.	*Larry Pressler, S.D.*
J. Bennett Johnston, La.	*Charles E. Grassley, Iowa*
John B. Breaux, La.	*Alan K. Simpson, Wyo.*
Richard C. Shelby, Ala.	*James M. Jeffords, Vt.*
Harry Reid, Nev.	*John McCain, Ariz.*
Bob Graham, Fla.	*Dave Durenberger, Minn.*
Herb Kohl, Wis.	*Larry E. Craig, Idaho*
Russell D. Feingold, Wis.	*Conrad Burns, Mont.*
1 vacancy	*Arlen Specter, Pa.*

Veterans' Affairs

224-9126 SR-414

Party Ratio: D 7 - R 5

John D. Rockefeller IV, D-W.Va., chairman

Dennis DeConcini, Ariz.	*Frank H. Murkowski, Alaska*
George J. Mitchell, Maine	*Strom Thurmond, S.C.*
Bob Graham, Fla.	*Alan K. Simpson, Wyo.*
Daniel K. Akaka, Hawaii	*Arlen Specter, Pa.*
Tom Daschle, S.D.	*James M. Jeffords, Vt.*
Ben Nighthorse Campbell, Colo.	

Senate Partisan Committees

Democratic Leaders

President .... Al Gore, Tenn.
President Pro Tempore .... Robert C. Byrd, W.Va.
Majority Leader .... George J. Mitchell, Maine
Majority Whip .... Wendell H. Ford, Ky.
Conference Chairman ...... George J. Mitchell, Maine
Conference Secretary .... David Pryor, Ark.
Assistant Floor Leader ..... Barbara A. Mikulski, Md.
Chief Deputy Whip .... John B. Breaux, La.

Deputy Whips (by region, each listed with an assistant deputy whip):

East .... Patrick J. Leahy, Vt.
John Kerry, Mass. (asst.)
South .... Bob Graham, Fla.
Charles S. Robb, Va. (asst.)
Midwest .... Tom Harkin, Iowa
Byron L. Dorgan, N.D. (asst.)
West .... Barbara Boxer, Calif.
Patty Murray, Wash. (asst.)

Policy Committee

224-5551 S-118 Capitol

George J. Mitchell, Maine, chairman
Tom Daschle, S.D., co-chairman
Vice chairmen: Jeff Bingaman, N.M.; John Glenn, Ohio; Charles S. Robb, Va.; Paul S. Sarbanes, Md.

Daniel K. Akaka, Hawaii
Dale Bumpers, Ark.
Carol Moseley-Braun, Ill.
Ben Nighthorse Campbell, Colo.
Byron L. Dorgan, N.D.
Russell D. Feingold, Wis.
Wendell H. Ford, Ky. (ex officio)
Howell Heflin, Ala.
Ernest F. Hollings, S.C.
Frank R. Lautenberg, N.J.
Daniel Patrick Moynihan, N.Y.
Claiborne Pell, R.I.
David Pryor, Ark. (ex officio)
Donald W. Riegle Jr., Mich.
John D. Rockefeller IV, W.Va.

Steering Committee

224-3735 S-309 Capitol

Daniel K. Inouye, Hawaii, chairman

Max Baucus, Mont.
Joseph R. Biden Jr., Del.
David L. Boren, Okla.
Barbara Boxer, Calif.
John B. Breaux, La.
Richard H. Bryan, Nev.
Robert C. Byrd, W.Va.
Kent Conrad, N.D.
Dennis DeConcini, Ariz.
Christopher J. Dodd, Conn.
Jim Exon, Neb.
Wendell H. Ford, Ky.
Bob Graham, Fla.
Tom Harkin, Iowa
Edward M. Kennedy, Mass.
John Kerry, Mass.
Herb Kohl, Wis.
Patrick J. Leahy, Vt.
Carl Levin, Mich.
Howard M. Metzenbaum, Ohio
George J. Mitchell, Maine
Sam Nunn, Ga.
David Pryor, Ark.
Jim Sasser, Tenn.

Democratic Senatorial Campaign Committee

224-2447 430 S. Capitol St. S.E. 20003

Bob Graham, Fla., chairman

Republican Leaders

Minority Leader .... *Bob Dole, Kan.*
Assistant Minority Leader ..... *Alan K. Simpson, Wyo.*
Conference Chairman............ *Thad Cochran, Miss.*
Conference Secretary .... *Trent Lott, Miss.*

Deputy Whips:

Christopher S. Bond, Mo.
Hank Brown, Colo.
Thad Cochran, Miss.
Paul Coverdell, Ga.
Dave Durenberger, Minn.
Charles E. Grassley, Iowa
Judd Gregg, N.H.
Nancy Landon Kassebaum, Kan.
John McCain, Ariz.
Frank H. Murkowski, Alaska
Larry Pressler, S.D.
Robert C. Smith, N.H.
Arlen Specter, Pa.
Malcolm Wallop, Wyo.
John W. Warner, Va.

Policy Committee

224-2946 SR-347

Don Nickles, Okla., chairman

John H. Chafee, R.I.
Thad Cochran, Miss.
Alfonse M. D'Amato, N.Y.
John C. Danforth, Mo.
Bob Dole, Kan.
Pete V. Domenici, N.M.
Phil Gramm, Texas
Orrin G. Hatch, Utah
Mark O. Hatfield, Ore.
Jesse Helms, N.C.
Nancy Landon Kassebaum, Kan.
Trent Lott, Miss.
Richard G. Lugar, Ind.
Frank H. Murkowski, Alaska
Bob Packwood, Ore.
Larry Pressler, S.D.
William V. Roth Jr., Del.
Alan K. Simpson, Wyo.
Ted Stevens, Alaska
Strom Thurmond, S.C.
Malcolm Wallop, Wyo.
John W. Warner, Va.

Committee on Committees

224-2644 SD-183

Conrad Burns, Mont., chairman

Robert F. Bennett, Utah
Paul Coverdell, Ga.
Lauch Faircloth, N.C.
Judd Gregg, N.H.
Dirk Kempthorne, Idaho
Frank H. Murkowski, Alaska

National Republican Senatorial Committee

675-6000 425 Second St. N.E. 20002

Phil Gramm, Texas, chairman

Robert F. Bennett, Utah
Hank Brown, Colo.
Conrad Burns, Mont.
Daniel R. Coats, Ind.
Paul Coverdell, Ga.
Alfonse M. D'Amato, N.Y.
Lauch Faircloth, N.C.
Slade Gorton, Wash.
Dirk Kempthorne, Idaho
Richard G. Lugar, Ind.
Connie Mack, Fla.
John McCain, Ariz.
Bob Packwood, Ore.
Ted Stevens, Alaska
John W. Warner, Va.

House Committees and Subcommittees

The standing and select committees of the U.S. House are listed below in alphabetical order (except Select Intelligence, which follows Ways and Means on p. 1729). The listing includes the telephone number, room number and party ratio for each full committee. Membership is given in order of seniority on the committee.

If a non-voting delegate or the resident commissioner is a committee member, the party ratio reflects that membership. Non-voting representatives, who have limited voting privileges on the floor, have equal status on committees.

Subcommittees are listed alphabetically under each committee. Membership is listed in order of seniority on subcommittees.

Members of the majority party, Democrats, are shown in Roman type; members of the minority party, Republicans, are shown in italic type.

The word "vacancy" indicates that a committee or subcommittee seat had not been filled at press time. Subcommittee vacancies do not necessarily indicate vacancies on full committees, or vice versa.

Asterisks (*) indicate that chairmen and/or ranking minority members are also *ex officio* members of all subcommittees of which they are not regular members.

The House partisan committees begin on p. 1730. Their members are listed alphabetically.

The telephone area code for Washington, D.C., is 202. Abbreviations for House office buildings are: CHOB — Cannon House Office Bldg., LHOB — Longworth House Office Bldg., RHOB — Rayburn House Office Bldg., HOB Annex #1 and #2 — House Office Bldg. Annex #1 and #2, and Capitol. The ZIP code for all House offices is 20515.

Agriculture

225-2171 1301 LHOB

Party Ratio: D 28 - R 19

E. "Kika" de la Garza, D-Texas, chairman

George E. Brown Jr., Calif.	*Pat Roberts, Kan.*
Charlie Rose, N.C.	*Bill Emerson, Mo.*
Glenn English, Okla.	*Steve Gunderson, Wis.*
Dan Glickman, Kan.	*Tom Lewis, Fla.*
Charles W. Stenholm, Texas	*Bob Smith, Ore.*
Harold L. Volkmer, Mo.	*Larry Combest, Texas*
Timothy J. Penny, Minn.	*Wayne Allard, Colo.*
Tim Johnson, S.D.	*Bill Barrett, Neb.*
Bill Sarpalius, Texas	*Jim Nussle, Iowa*
Jill L. Long, Ind.	*John A. Boehner, Ohio*
Gary A. Condit, Calif.	*Thomas W. Ewing, Ill.*
Collin C. Peterson, Minn.	*John T. Doolittle, Calif.*
Cal Dooley, Calif.	*Jack Kingston, Ga.*
Eva Clayton, N.C.	*Robert W. Goodlatte, Va.*
David Minge, Minn.	*Jay Dickey, Ark.*
Earl F. Hilliard, Ala.	*Richard W. Pombo, Calif.*
Jay Inslee, Wash.	*Charles T. Canady, Fla.*
Tom Barlow, Ky.	*Terry Everett, Ala.*
Earl Pomeroy, N.D.	*Nick Smith, Mich.*
Tim Holden, Pa.	
Cynthia A. McKinney, Ga.	
Scotty Baesler, Ky.	
Karen L. Thurman, Fla.	
Sanford D. Bishop Jr., Ga.	
Bennie Thompson, Miss.	
Pat Williams, Mont.	
Blanche Lambert, Ark.	

Department Operations and Nutrition

225-1496 1301-A LHOB

Stenholm – chairman

Brown (Calif.)	*Smith (Ore.)*
Sarpalius	*Emerson*
Dooley	*Gunderson*
Inslee	*Allard*
English (Okla.)	*Barrett (Neb.)*
Glickman	*Ewing*
McKinney	*Kingston*
Bishop	*Canady*
Volkmer	
Clayton	
Holden	
Rose	
Lambert	

Environment, Credit and Rural Development

225-0301 1430 LHOB

English (Okla.) – chairman

Johnson (S.D.)	*Combest*
Long	*Gunderson*
Clayton	*Allard*
Minge	*Barrett (Neb.)*
Barlow	*Nussle*
Pomeroy	*Ewing*
Holden	*Dickey*
McKinney	*Pombo*
Thurman	*1 vacancy*
Penny	
Sarpalius	
Peterson (Minn.)	
Hilliard	
Inslee	
Baesler	

Foreign Agriculture and Hunger

225-1867 1336 LHOB

Penny — chairman

Rose	*Allard*
Barlow	*Lewis (Fla.)*
McKinney	*Doolittle*
Baesler	*Canady*
Thurman	*1 vacancy*
Pomeroy	
Stenholm	

General Farm Commodities

225-0301 1430 LHOB

Johnson — chairman

Glickman	*Emerson*
Peterson (Minn.)	*Smith (Ore.)*
Volkmer	*Combest*
Long	*Barrett (Neb.)*
Dooley	*Nussle*
Minge	*Boehner*
Pomeroy	*Ewing*
Rose	*Doolittle*
English (Okla.)	*Dickey*
Stenholm	
Sarpalius	
Condit	
Barlow	
Bishop	
Williams	

Livestock

225-1867 1336 LHOB

Volkmer — chairman

Condit	*Gunderson*
Hilliard	*Lewis (Fla.)*
Stenholm	*Smith (Ore.)*
Holden	*Boehner*
Long	*Goodlatte*
Peterson (Minn.)	*Pombo*
Rose	
Dooley	
Thurman	

Specialty Crops and Natural Resources

225-8906 1336 LHOB

Rose — chairman

Baesler	*Lewis (Fla.)*
Bishop	*Emerson*
Brown (Calif.)	*Doolittle*
Condit	*Kingston*
Clayton	*Goodlatte*
Thurman	*Dickey*
Minge	*Pombo*
Inslee	
Pomeroy	
English (Okla.)	
Stenholm	
Peterson (Minn.)	

Appropriations

225-2771 H-218 Capitol

Party Ratio: D 37 - R 23

William H. Natcher, D-Ky., chairman

Jamie L. Whitten, Miss.	*Joseph M. McDade, Pa.*
Neal Smith, Iowa	*John T. Myers, Ind.*
Sidney R. Yates, Ill.	*C. W. Bill Young, Fla.*
David R. Obey, Wis.	*Ralph Regula, Ohio*
Louis Stokes, Ohio	*Robert L. Livingston, La.*
Tom Bevill, Ala.	*Jerry Lewis, Calif.*
John P. Murtha, Pa.	*John Edward Porter, Ill.*
Charles Wilson, Texas	*Harold Rogers, Ky.*
Norm Dicks, Wash.	*Joe Skeen, N.M.*
Martin Olav Sabo, Minn.	*Frank R. Wolf, Va.*
Julian C. Dixon, Calif.	*Tom DeLay, Texas*
Vic Fazio, Calif.	*Jim Kolbe, Ariz.*
W. G. "Bill" Hefner, N.C.	*Dean A. Gallo, N.J.*
Steny H. Hoyer, Md.	*Barbara F. Vucanovich, Nev.*
Bob Carr, Mich.	*Jim Ross Lightfoot, Iowa*
Richard J. Durbin, Ill.	*Ron Packard, Calif.*
Ronald D. Coleman, Texas	*Sonny Callahan, Ala.*
Alan B. Mollohan, W.Va.	*Helen Delich Bentley, Md.*
Jim Chapman, Texas	*James T. Walsh, N.Y.*
Marcy Kaptur, Ohio	*Charles H. Taylor, N.C.*
David E. Skaggs, Colo.	*David L. Hobson, Ohio*
David Price, N.C.	*Ernest Jim Istook Jr., Okla.*
Nancy Pelosi, Calif.	*Henry Bonilla, Texas*
Peter J. Visclosky, Ind.	
Thomas M. Foglietta, Pa.	
Esteban E. Torres, Calif.	
George "Buddy" Darden, Ga.	
Nita M. Lowey, N.Y.	
Ray Thornton, Ark.	
Jose E. Serrano, N.Y.	
Rosa DeLauro, Conn.	
James P. Moran, Va.	
Pete Peterson, Fla.	
John W. Olver, Mass.	
Ed Pastor, Ariz.	
Carrie Meek, Fla.	

Agriculture, Rural Development, FDA and Related Agencies

225-2638 2362 RHOB

Durbin — chairman

Whitten	*Skeen*
Kaptur	*Myers*
Thornton	*Vucanovich*
DeLauro	*Walsh*
Peterson (Fla.)	
Pastor	
Smith (Iowa)	

Commerce, Justice, State and Judiciary

225-3351 H-309 Capitol

Smith (Iowa) — chairman

Carr	*Rogers*
Mollohan	*Kolbe*
Moran	*Taylor (N.C.)*
Skaggs	
Price	

Defense

225-2847 H-144 Capitol

Murtha – chairman

Dicks	*McDade*
Wilson	*Young (Fla.)*
Hefner	*Livingston*
Sabo	*Lewis (Calif.)*
Dixon	*Skeen*
Visclosky	
Darden	

District of Columbia

225-5338 H-302 Capitol

Dixon – chairman

Stokes	*Walsh*
Durbin	*Istook*
Kaptur	*Bonilla*
Skaggs	
Pelosi	

Energy and Water Development

225-3421 2362 RHOB

Bevill – chairman

Fazio	*Myers*
Chapman	*Gallo*
Peterson (Fla.)	*Rogers*
Pastor	
Meek	

Foreign Operations, Export Financing and Related Programs

225-2041 H-307 Capitol

Obey – chairman

Yates	*Livingston*
Wilson	*Porter*
Olver	*Lightfoot*
Pelosi	*Callahan*
Torres	
Lowey	
Serrano	

Interior

225-3081 B-308 RHOB

Yates – chairman

Murtha	*Regula*
Dicks	*McDade*
Bevill	*Kolbe*
Skaggs	*Packard*
Coleman	

Labor, Health and Human Services, and Education

225-3508 2358 RHOB

Natcher – chairman

Smith (Iowa)	*Porter*
Obey	*Young (Fla.)*
Stokes	*Bentley*
Hoyer	*Bonilla*
Pelosi	
Lowey	
Serrano	
DeLauro	

Legislative Branch

225-5338 H-302 Capitol

Fazio – chairman

Moran	*Young (Fla.)*
Obey	*Packard*
Murtha	*Taylor (N.C.)*
Carr	
Chapman	

Military Construction

225-3047 B-300 RHOB

Hefner – chairman

Foglietta	*Vucanovich*
Meek	*Callahan*
Dicks	*Bentley*
Dixon	*Hobson*
Fazio	
Hoyer	
Coleman	

Transportation

225-2141 2358 RHOB

Carr – chairman

Durbin	*Wolf*
Sabo	*DeLay*
Price	*Regula*
Coleman	
Foglietta	

Treasury, Postal Service and General Government

225-5834 H-164 Capitol

Hoyer – chairman

Visclosky	*Lightfoot*
Darden	*Wolf*
Olver	*Istook*
Bevill	
Sabo	

Veterans Affairs, HUD and Independent Agencies

225-3241 H-143 Capitol

Stokes – chairman

Mollohan	*Lewis (Calif.)*
Chapman	*DeLay*
Kaptur	*Gallo*
Torres	
Thornton	

Armed Services

225-4151 2120 RHOB

Party Ratio: D 34 - R 22

Ronald V. Dellums, D-Calif., chairman

G.V. "Sonny" Montgomery, Miss.	*Floyd D. Spence, S.C.*
Patricia Schroeder, Colo.	*Bob Stump, Ariz.*
Earl Hutto, Fla.	*Duncan Hunter, Calif.*
Ike Skelton, Mo.	*John R. Kasich, Ohio*
Dave McCurdy, Okla.	*Herbert H. Bateman, Va.*
Marilyn Lloyd, Tenn.	*James V. Hansen, Utah*
Norman Sisisky, Va.	*Curt Weldon, Pa.*
John M. Spratt Jr., S.C.	*Jon Kyl, Ariz.*
Frank McCloskey, Ind.	*Arthur Ravenel Jr., S.C.*
Solomon P. Ortiz, Texas	*Robert K. Dornan, Calif.*
George J. Hochbrueckner, N.Y.	*Joel Hefley, Colo.*
Owen B. Pickett, Va.	*Ronald K. Machtley, R.I.*
H. Martin Lancaster, N.C.	*H. James Saxton, N.J.*
Lane Evans, Ill.	*Randy "Duke" Cunningham, Calif.*
James Bilbray, Nev.	*James M. Inhofe, Okla.*
John Tanner, Tenn.	*Steve Buyer, Ind.*
Glen Browder, Ala.	*Peter G. Torkildsen, Mass.*
Gene Taylor, Miss.	*Tillie Fowler, Fla.*
Neil Abercrombie, Hawaii	*John M. McHugh, N.Y.*
Thomas H. Andrews, Maine	*James M. Talent, Mo.*
Chet Edwards, Texas	*Terry Everett, Ala.*
Don Johnson, Ga.	*Roscoe G. Bartlett, Md.*
Frank Tejeda, Texas	
David Mann, Ohio	
Bart Stupak, Mich.	
Martin T. Meehan, Mass.	
Robert A. Underwood, Guam	
Jane Harman, Calif.	
Paul McHale, Pa.	
Tim Holden, Pa.	
Pete Geren, Texas	
Elizabeth Furse, Ore.	
1 vacancy	

Military Acquisition

225-6999 2343 RHOB

Dellums — chairman

Lloyd	*Spence*
Spratt	*Bateman*
McCloskey	*Weldon*
Evans	*Ravenel*
Tanner	*Dornan*
Taylor (Miss.)	*Hefley*
Abercrombie	*Machtley*
Andrews (Maine)	*Saxton*
Mann	*Cunningham*
Stupak	*Inhofe*
McHale	
Holden	
Geren	
Sisisky	

Military Forces and Personnel

225-7560 2343 RHOB

Skelton — chairman

Montgomery	*Kyl*
Pickett	*Ravenel*
Lancaster	*Buyer*
Bilbray	*Fowler*
Stupak	*Talent*
Meehan	*Bartlett*
Underwood	
Harman	
2 vacancies	

Military Installations and Facilities

225-7120 2119 RHOB

McCurdy — chairman

Montgomery	*Hunter*
McCloskey	*Fowler*
Ortiz	*McHugh*
Hochbrueckner	*Everett*
Bilbray	*Stump*
Browder	*Machtley*
Taylor (Miss.)	*Saxton*
Abercrombie	*Torkildsen*
Edwards (Texas)	
Johnson (Ga.)	
Tejeda	
Underwood	

Oversight and Investigations

225-2086 2343 RHOB

Sisisky — chairman

Spratt	*Hansen*
Tanner	*Kyl*
Browder	*Hefley*
Edwards (Texas)	*McHugh*
Johnson (Ga.)	*Everett*
Tejeda	*Dornan*
Mann	
Harman	
Holden	

Readiness

225-9644 2343 RHOB

Hutto — chairman

Ortiz	*Kasich*
Pickett	*Bateman*
Lancaster	*Weldon*
Evans	*Dornan*
Browder	*Cunningham*
Meehan	*Inhofe*
Underwood	
McHale	
McCurdy	

Research and Technology

225-5627 2117A RHOB

Schroeder — chairman

Hochbrueckner	*Stump*
Pickett	*Buyer*
Lancaster	*Torkildsen*
Bilbray	*Talent*
Edwards (Texas)	*Bartlett*
Johnson (Ga.)	*Hunter*
Tejeda	*Kasich*
Meehan	*Hansen*
Harman	
Furse	
Hutto	
McCurdy	

Banking, Finance and Urban Affairs

225-4247 2129 RHOB

Party Ratio: D 30 - R 20 - I 1

Henry B. Gonzalez, D-Texas, Chairman

Stephen L. Neal, N.C.	*Jim Leach, Iowa*
John J. LaFalce, N.Y.	*Bill McCollum, Fla.*
Bruce F. Vento, Minn.	*Marge Roukema, N.J.*
Charles E. Schumer, N.Y.	*Doug Bereuter, Neb.*
Barney Frank, Mass.	*Tom Ridge, Pa.*
Paul E. Kanjorski, Pa.	*Toby Roth, Wis.*
Joseph P. Kennedy II, Mass.	*Al McCandless, Calif.*
	Richard H. Baker, La.
Floyd H. Flake, N.Y.	*Jim Nussle, Iowa*
Kweisi Mfume, Md.	*Craig Thomas, Wyo.*
Maxine Waters, Calif.	*Sam Johnson, Texas*
Larry LaRocco, Idaho	*Deborah Pryce, Ohio*
Bill Orton, Utah	*John Linder, Ga.*
Jim Bacchus, Fla.	*Joe Knollenberg, Mich.*
Herb Klein, N.J.	*Rick A. Lazio, N.Y.*
Carolyn B. Maloney, N.Y.	*Rod Grams, Minn.*
Peter Deutsch, Fla.	*Spencer Bachus, Ala.*
Luis V. Gutierrez, Ill.	*Michael Huffington, Calif.*
Bobby L. Rush, Ill.	*Michael N. Castle, Del.*
Lucille Roybal-Allard, Calif.	*Peter T. King, N.Y.*
Thomas M. Barrett, Wis.	
Elizabeth Furse, Ore.	**Independent**
Nydia M. Velazquez, N.Y.	**Bernard Sanders, Vt.**
Albert R. Wynn, Md.	
Cleo Fields, La.	
Melvin Watt, N.C.	
Maurice D. Hinchey, N.Y.	
Cal Dooley, Calif.	
Ron Klink, Pa.	
Eric D. Fingerhut, Ohio	

Consumer Credit and Insurance

225-8872 604 OHOB

Kennedy — chairman

Gonzalez	*McCandless*
LaRocco	*Castle*
Gutierrez	*King*
Rush	*Pryce*
Roybal-Allard	*Linder*
Barrett (Wis.)	*Knollenberg*
Furse	*Bereuter*
Velazquez	*Thomas (Wyo.)*
Wynn	*Lazio*
Fields (La.)	*Grams*
Watt	*Bachus*
Hinchey	*Baker (La.)*
Kanjorski	
Flake	
Waters	**Sanders (I)**
Maloney	
Deutsch	

Economic Growth and Credit Formation

226-7315 109 FHOB

Kanjorski — chairman

Neal (N.C.)	*Ridge*
LaFalce	*McCollum*
Orton	*Roth*
Klein	*Nussle*
Velazquez	*Roukema*
Dooley	*King*
Klink	
Fingerhut	

Financial Institutions Supervision, Regulation and Deposit Insurance

226-3280 212 OHOB

Neal — chairman

LaFalce	*McCollum*
Vento	*Leach*
Schumer	*Baker (La.)*
Frank	*Nussle*
Kanjorski	*Thomas (Wyo.)*
Kennedy	*Johnson*
Flake	*Pryce*
Mfume	*Linder*
LaRocco	*Lazio*
Orton	*Grams*
Bacchus	*Bachus*
Waters	*Huffington*
Klein	
Maloney	
Deutsch	
Barrett (Wis.)	
Hinchey	

General Oversight, Investigations and the Resolution of Failed Financial Institutions

225-2828 139 FHOB

Flake — chairman

Neal (N.C.)	*Roth*
Velazquez	*Ridge*
Hinchey	

Housing and Community Development

225-7054 B-303 RHOB

Gonzalez — chairman

Vento	*Roukema*
Schumer	*Bereuter*
Mfume	*Ridge*
LaFalce	*Baker (La.)*
Waters	*Thomas (Wyo.)*
Klein	*Johnson*
Maloney	*Knollenberg*
Deutsch	*Lazio*
Gutierrez	*Grams*
Rush	*Bachus*
Roybal-Allard	*Castle*
Barrett (Wis.)	*Pryce*
Furse	
Velazquez	
Wynn	**Sanders (I)**
Fields (La.)	
Watt	

International Development, Finance, Trade and Monetary Policy

226-7515 B-304 RHOB

Frank — chairman

Neal (N.C.)	*Bereuter*
LaFalce	*McCandless*
Kennedy	*McCollum*
Waters	*Roukema*
LaRocco	*Johnson*
Orton	*Huffington*
Bacchus	*King*
Gonzalez	*Baker (La.)*
Kanjorski	*Nussle*
Rush	*Castle*
Fields (La.)	
Watt	
Fingerhut	**Sanders (I)**
1 vacancy	

Budget

226-7200 214 OHOB

Party Ratio: D 26 - R 17

Martin Olav Sabo, D-Minn., chairman

Richard A. Gephardt, Mo.	*John R. Kasich, Ohio*
Dale E. Kildee, Mich.	*Alex McMillan, N.C.*
Anthony C. Beilenson, Calif.	*Jim Kolbe, Ariz.*
Howard L. Berman, Calif.	*Christopher Shays, Conn.*
Bob Wise, W.Va.	*Olympia J. Snowe, Maine*
John Bryant, Texas	*Wally Herger, Calif.*
Charles W. Stenholm, Texas	*Jim Bunning, Ky.*
Barney Frank, Mass.	*Lamar Smith, Texas*
Jim Cooper, Tenn.	*C. Christopher Cox, Calif.*
Louise M. Slaughter, N.Y.	*Wayne Allard, Colo.*
Mike Parker, Miss.	*David L. Hobson, Ohio*
William J. Coyne, Pa.	*Dan Miller, Fla.*
Barbara B. Kennelly, Conn.	*Rick A. Lazio, N.Y.*
Michael A. Andrews, Texas	*Bob Franks, N.J.*
Alan B. Mollohan, W.Va.	*Nick Smith, Mich.*
Bart Gordon, Tenn.	*Bob Inglis, S.C.*
David Price, N.C.	*Martin R. Hoke, Ohio*
Jerry F. Costello, Ill.	
Harry A. Johnston, Fla.	
Patsy T. Mink, Hawaii	
Bill Orton, Utah	
Lucien E. Blackwell, Pa.	
Earl Pomeroy, N.D.	
Glen Browder, Ala.	
Lynn Woolsey, Calif.	

District of Columbia

225-4457 1310 LHOB

Party Ratio: D 8 † - R 4

Pete Stark, D-Calif., chairman

Ronald V. Dellums, Calif.	*Thomas J. Bliley Jr., Va.*
Alan Wheat, Mo.	*Dana Rohrabacher, Calif.*
Jim McDermott, Wash.	*H. James Saxton, N.J.*
Eleanor Holmes Norton, D.C. †	*Cass Ballenger, N.C.*
John Lewis, Ga.	
William J. Jefferson, La.	
1 vacancy	

† Delegate not counted in official ratio of 7-4

Fiscal Affairs and Health

225-4457 1310 LHOB

McDermott — chairman

Jefferson	*Ballenger*
Wheat	*Saxton*
Norton	
1 vacancy	

Government Operations and Metropolitan Affairs

225-4457 1310 LHOB

Wheat — chairman

Stark	*Saxton*
Lewis (Ga.)	*Rohrabacher*
Jefferson	
1 vacancy	

Judiciary and Education

225-4457 1310 LHOB

Norton — chairman

Lewis (Ga.)	*Rohrabacher*
Stark	*Ballenger*
McDermott	
1 vacancy	

Education and Labor

225-4527 2181 RHOB

Party Ratio: D 28 † - R 15

William D. Ford, D-Mich., chairman

William L. Clay, Mo.	*Bill Goodling, Pa.*
George Miller, Calif.	*Tom Petri, Wis.*
Austin J. Murphy, Pa.	*Marge Roukema, N.J.*
Dale E. Kildee, Mich.	*Steve Gunderson, Wis.*
Pat Williams, Mont.	*Dick Armey, Texas*
Matthew G. Martinez, Calif.	*Harris W. Fawell, Ill.*
Major R. Owens, N.Y.	*Paul B. Henry, Mich.*
Tom Sawyer, Ohio	*Cass Ballenger, N.C.*
Donald M. Payne, N.J.	*Susan Molinari, N.Y.*
Jolene Unsoeld, Wash.	*Bill Barrett, Neb.*
Patsy T. Mink, Hawaii	*John A. Boehner, Ohio*
Robert E. Andrews, N.J.	*Randy "Duke" Cunningham, Calif.*
Jack Reed, R.I.	*Peter Hoekstra, Mich.*
Tim Roemer, Ind.	*Howard P. "Buck" McKeon, Calif.*
Eliot L. Engel, N.Y.	*Dan Miller, Fla.*
Xavier Becerra, Calif.	
Robert C. Scott, Va.	
Gene Green, Texas	
Lynn Woolsey, Calif.	
Carlos Romero-Barcelo, P.R. †	
Ron Klink, Pa.	
Karan English, Ariz.	
Ted Strickland, Ohio	
Ron de Lugo, Virgin Islands †	
Eni F. H. Faleomavaega, Am. Samoa †	
Scotty Baesler, Ky.	
Robert A. Underwood, Guam †	

† Delegates and resident commissioner not counted in official ratio of 24-15

Elementary, Secondary and Vocational Education

225-4368 B-346A RHOB

Kildee — chairman

Miller (Calif.)	*Goodling*
Sawyer	*Gunderson*
Owens	*McKeon*
Unsoeld	*Petri*
Reed	*Molinari*
Roemer	*Cunningham*
Mink	*Miller (Fla.)*
Engel	*Roukema*
Becerra	*Boehner*
Green	
Woolsey	
English (Ariz.)	
Strickland	
Payne (N.J.)	
Romero-Barcelo	

Human Resources

225-1850 B-346C RHOB

Martinez — chairman

Kildee	*Henry*
Andrews (N.J.)	*Molinari*
Scott	*Barrett (Neb.)*
Woolsey	*Miller (Fla.)*
Romero-Barcelo	
Owens	
Baesler	

Labor-Management Relations

225-5768 320 CHOB

Williams — chairman

Clay	*Roukema*
Kildee	*Gunderson*
Miller (Calif.)	*Armey*
Owens	*Barrett (Neb.)*
Martinez	*Boehner*
Payne (N.J.)	*Fawell*
Unsoeld	*Ballenger*
Mink	*Hoekstra*
Klink	*McKeon*
Murphy	
Engel	
Becerra	
Green	
Woolsey	
Romero-Barcelo	

Labor Standards, Occupational Health and Safety

225-6876 B-345A RHOB

Murphy — chairman

Clay	*Fawell*
Andrews (N.J.)	*Ballenger*
Miller (Calif.)	*Hoekstra*
Strickland	
Faleomavaega	
1 vacancy	

Postsecondary Education and Training

226-3681 2451 RHOB

Ford (Mich.) — chairman

Williams	*Petri*
Sawyer	*Gunderson*
Unsoeld	*Miller (Fla.)*
Mink	*Roukema*
Andrews (N.J.)	*Henry*
Reed	*Hoekstra*
Roemer	*McKeon*
Kildee	*Armey*
Scott	
Klink	
English (Ariz.)	
Strickland	
Becerra	
Green	

Select Education and Civil Rights

226-7532 518 OHOB

Owens (N.Y.) — chairman

Payne (N.J.)	*Ballenger*
Williams	*Barrett (Neb.)*
Scott	*Fawell*
Sawyer	
1 vacancy	

Energy and Commerce

225-2927 2125 RHOB

Party Ratio: D 27 - R 17

John D. Dingell, D-Mich., chairman

Henry A. Waxman, Calif.	*Carlos J. Moorhead, Calif.*
Philip R. Sharp, Ind.	*Thomas J. Bliley Jr., Va.*
Edward J. Markey, Mass.	*Jack Fields, Texas*
Al Swift, Wash.	*Michael G. Oxley, Ohio*
Cardiss Collins, Ill.	*Michael Bilirakis, Fla.*
Mike Synar, Okla.	*Dan Schaefer, Colo.*
W. J. "Billy" Tauzin, La.	*Joe L. Barton, Texas*
Ron Wyden, Ore.	*Alex McMillan, N.C.*
Ralph M. Hall, Texas	*Dennis Hastert, Ill.*
Bill Richardson, N.M.	*Fred Upton, Mich.*
Jim Slattery, Kan.	*Cliff Stearns, Fla.*
John Bryant, Texas	*Bill Paxon, N.Y.*
Rick Boucher, Va.	*Paul E. Gillmor, Ohio*
Jim Cooper, Tenn.	*Scott L. Klug, Wis.*
J. Roy Rowland, Ga.	*Gary A. Franks, Conn.*
Thomas J. Manton, N.Y.	*James C. Greenwood, Pa.*
Edolphus Towns, N.Y.	*Michael D. Crapo, Idaho*
Gerry E. Studds, Mass.	
Richard H. Lehman, Calif.	
Frank Pallone Jr., N.J.	
Craig Washington, Texas	
Lynn Schenk, Calif.	
Sherrod Brown, Ohio	
Mike Kreidler, Wash.	
Marjorie Margolies-Mezvinsky, Pa.	
Blanche Lambert, Ark.	

Commerce, Consumer Protection and Competitiveness

226-3160 151 FHOB

Collins (Ill.) — chairman

Towns	*Stearns*
Slattery	*McMillan*
Rowland	*Paxon*
Manton	*Greenwood*
Lehman	
Pallone	

Energy and Power

226-2500 331 FHOB

Sharp — chairman

Markey	*Bilirakis*
Lehman	*Barton*
Washington	*Hastert*
Kreidler	*Stearns*
Lambert	*Klug*
Swift	*Franks (Conn.)*
Synar	*Crapo*
Tauzin	
Hall (Texas)	
Boucher	
Cooper	

Health and the Environment

225-4952 2415 RHOB

Waxman — chairman

Synar	*Bliley*
Wyden	*Bilirakis*
Hall (Texas)	*McMillan*
Richardson	*Hastert*
Bryant	*Upton*
Rowland	*Paxon*
Towns	*Klug*
Studds	*Franks (Conn.)*
Slattery	*Greenwood*
Cooper	
Pallone	
Washington	
Brown (Ohio)	
Kreidler	

Oversight and Investigations

225-4441 2323 RHOB

Dingell — chairman

Brown (Ohio)	*Schaefer*
Margolies-Mezvinsky	*Moorhead*
Waxman	*Upton*
Collins (Ill.)	*Gillmor*
Wyden	
Bryant	

Telecommunications and Finance

226-2424 316 FHOB

Markey — chairman

Tauzin	*Fields (Texas)*
Boucher	*Bliley*
Manton	*Oxley*
Lehman	*Schaefer*
Schenk	*Barton*
Margolies-Mezvinsky	*McMillan*
Synar	*Hastert*
Wyden	*Gillmor*
Hall (Texas)	
Richardson	
Slattery	
Bryant	
Cooper	

Transportation and Hazardous Materials

225-9304 324 FHOB

Swift — chairman

Lambert	*Oxley*
Tauzin	*Fields (Texas)*
Boucher	*Schaefer*
Rowland	*Upton*
Manton	*Paxon*
Studds	*Gillmor*
Pallone	*Crapo*
Schenk	
Sharp	
Markey	
Richardson	

Foreign Affairs

225-5021 2170 RHOB

Party Ratio: D 27 † - R 18

Lee H. Hamilton, D-Ind., chairman

Sam Gejdenson, Conn.	*Benjamin A. Gilman, N.Y.*
Tom Lantos, Calif.	*Bill Goodling, Pa.*
Robert G. Torricelli, N.J.	*Jim Leach, Iowa*
Howard L. Berman, Calif.	*Toby Roth, Wis.*
Gary L. Ackerman, N.Y.	*Olympia J. Snowe, Maine*
Harry Johnston, Fla.	*Henry J. Hyde, Ill.*
Eliot L. Engel, N.Y.	*Doug Bereuter, Neb.*
Eni F.H. Faleomavaega, Am. Samoa †	*Christopher H. Smith, N.J.*
	Dan Burton, Ind.
James L. Oberstar, Minn.	*Jan Meyers, Kan.*
Charles E. Schumer, N.Y.	*Elton Gallegly, Calif.*
Matthew G. Martinez, Calif.	*Ileana Ros-Lehtinen, Fla.*
	Cass Ballenger, N.C.
Robert A. Borski, Pa.	*Dana Rohrabacher, Calif.*
Donald M. Payne, N.J.	*David A. Levy, N.Y.*
Robert E. Andrews, N.J.	*Donald Manzullo, Ill.*
Robert Menendez, N.J.	*Lincoln Diaz-Balart, Fla.*
Sherrod Brown, Ohio	*Ed Royce, Calif.*
Cynthia McKinney, Ga.	
Maria Cantwell, Wash.	
Alcee L. Hastings, Fla.	
Eric D. Fingerhut, Ohio	
Peter Deutsch, Fla.	
Albert R. Wynn, Md.	
Don Edwards, Calif. ‡	
Frank McCloskey, Ind. ‡	
Tom Sawyer, Ohio ‡	
1 vacancy	

† Delegate not included in official ratio of 26-18
‡ Temporary member as of press date

Africa

226-7807 709 OHOB

Johnston — chairman

Payne (N.J.)	*Burton*
Hastings	*Diaz-Balart*
Torricelli	*Royce*
Edwards (Calif.)	*1 vacancy*
Engel	

Asia and the Pacific

226-7801 707 OHOB

Ackerman — chairman

Faleomavaega	*Leach*
Martinez	*Rohrabacher*
Torricelli	*Royce*
Brown (Ohio)	*Roth*
Fingerhut	

Economic Policy, Trade and the Environment

226-7820 702 OHOB

Gejdenson — chairman

Oberstar	*Roth*
McKinney	*Manzullo*
Cantwell	*Bereuter*
Fingerhut	*Meyers*
Wynn	*Ballenger*
Johnston	*Rohrabacher*
Engel	
Schumer	

Europe and the Middle East

225-3345 B359 RHOB

Hamilton — chairman

Engel	*Gilman*
Schumer	*Goodling*
Borski	*Meyers*
Andrews (N.J.)	*Gallegly*
Brown (Ohio)	*Levy*
Hastings	*Leach*
Deutsch	
Lantos	

International Operations

225-3424 2103 RHOB

Berman — chairman

Faleomavaega	*Snowe*
Martinez	*Hyde*
Andrews (N.J.)	*Diaz-Balart*
Menendez	*Levy*
Lantos	*Manzullo*
Johnston	
Edwards (Calif.)	

International Security, International Organizations and Human Rights

226-7825 B-358 RHOB

Lantos — chairman

Berman	*Bereuter*
Ackerman	*Snowe*
Martinez	*Smith (N.J.)*
McCloskey	*Burton*
Sawyer	

Western Hemisphere Affairs

226-7812 705 OHOB

Torricelli — chairman

Menendez	*Smith (N.J.)*
Oberstar	*Ros-Lehtinen*
McKinney	*Ballenger*
Deutsch	*Gallegly*
Wynn	

Government Operations

225-5051 2157 RHOB

Party Ratio: D 25 - R 17 - I 1

John Conyers Jr., D-Mich., chairman

Cardiss Collins, Ill.	*William F. Clinger, Pa.*
Glenn English, Okla.	*Al McCandless, Calif.*
Henry A. Waxman, Calif.	*Dennis Hastert, Ill.*
Mike Synar, Okla.	*Jon Kyl, Ariz.*
Stephen L. Neal, N.C.	*Christopher Shays, Conn.*
Tom Lantos, Calif.	*Steven H. Schiff, N.M.*
Major R. Owens, N.Y.	*C. Christopher Cox, Calif.*
Edolphus Towns, N.Y.	*Craig Thomas, Wyo.*
John M. Spratt Jr., S.C.	*Ileana Ros-Lehtinen, Fla.*
Gary A. Condit, Calif.	*Ronald K. Machtley, R.I.*
Collin C. Peterson, Minn.	*Dick Zimmer, N.J.*
Karen L. Thurman, Fla.	*Bill Zeliff, N.H.*
Bobby L. Rush, Ill.	*John M. McHugh, N.Y.*
Carolyn B. Maloney, N.Y.	*Steve Horn, Calif.*
Thomas M. Barrett, Wis.	*Deborah Pryce, Ohio*
Donald M. Payne, N.J.	*John L. Mica, Fla.*
Floyd H. Flake, N.Y.	*Rob Portman, Ohio*
Jimmy Hayes, La.	
Craig Washington, Texas	
Barbara-Rose Collins, Mich.	**Independent**
Corrine Brown, Fla.	**Bernard Sanders, Vt.**
Marjorie Margolies-Mezvinsky, Pa.	
Lynn Woolsey, Calif.	
1 vacancy	

Commerce, Consumer and Monetary Affairs

225-4407 B377 RHOB

Spratt — chairman

Rush	*Cox*
Margolies-Mezvinsky	*Shays*
Collins (Mich.)	*Zeliff*
1 vacancy	

Employment, Housing and Aviation

225-6751 B349-A RHOB

Peterson — chairman

Lantos	*Machtley*
Rush	*Shays*
Flake	*McHugh*
Thurman	
Collins (Mich.)	

Environment, Energy and Natural Resources

225-6427 B-371C RHOB

Synar — chairman

Thurman	*Hastert*
Maloney	*McHugh*
Hayes	*Pryce*
Washington	*Mica*
Towns	

Sanders (I)

Human Resources and Intergovernmental Relations

225-2548 B-372 RHOB

Towns — chairman

Waxman
Barrett (Wis.)
Payne (N.J.)
Washington

Schiff
Horn
Mica

Sanders

Information, Justice, Transportation and Agriculture

225-3741 B-349C RHOB

Condit — chairman

Owens
Thurman
Woolsey
1 vacancy

Thomas (Wyo.)
Ros-Lehtinen
Horn

Legislation and National Security

225-5147 B-373 RHOB

Conyers — chairman

Collins (Ill.)
English (Ariz.)
Neal (N.C.)
Maloney
Lantos
Brown (Fla.)

McCandless
Clinger
Kyl
Zimmer

House Administration

225-2061 H-326 Capitol

Party Ratio: D 12 - R 7

Charlie Rose, D-N.C., chairman

Al Swift, Wash.
William L. Clay, Mo.
Sam Gejdenson, Conn.
Martin Frost, Texas
Thomas J. Manton, N.Y.
Steny H. Hoyer, Md.
Gerald D. Kleczka, Wis.
Dale E. Kildee, Mich.
Butler Derrick, S.C.
Barbara B. Kennelly, Conn.
Benjamin L. Cardin, Md.

Bill Thomas, Calif.
Newt Gingrich, Ga.
Pat Roberts, Kan.
Robert L. Livingston, La.
Bill Barrett, Neb.
John A. Boehner, Ohio
Jennifer Dunn, Wash.

Accounts

226-7540 611 OHOB

Frost — chairman

Swift
Gejdenson
Hoyer
Kildee
Kennelly
Cardin

Roberts
Gingrich
Boehner
Dunn

Administrative Oversight

225-2061 H-326 Capitol

Rose — chairman

Clay

Thomas (Calif.)
Barrett (Neb.)

Elections

226-7616 802 OHOB

Swift — chairman

Frost
Hoyer
Kleczka
Cardin

Livingston
Roberts
Dunn

Libraries and Memorials

226-2307 612 OHOB

Clay — chairman

Frost
Derrick
Kennelly

Barrett (Neb.)
Roberts

Office Systems

225-1608 722 OHOB

Gejdenson — chairman

Frost
Kleczka
Kennelly

Boehner
Barrett (Neb.)

Personnel and Police

226-7614 722 OHOB

Manton — chairman

Clay
Kleczka
Derrick

Dunn
Livingston

Judiciary

225-3951 2138 RHOB

Party Ratio: D 21 - R 14

Jack Brooks, D-Texas, chairman

Don Edwards, Calif.
John Conyers Jr., Mich.
Romano L. Mazzoli, Ky.
William J. Hughes, N.J.
Mike Synar, Okla.
Patricia Schroeder, Colo.
Dan Glickman, Kan.
Barney Frank, Mass.
Charles E. Schumer, N.Y.
Howard L. Berman, Calif.
Rick Boucher, Va.
John Bryant, Texas
George E. Sangmeister, Ill.
Craig Washington, Texas
Jack Reed, R.I.
Jerrold Nadler, N.Y.
Robert C. Scott, Va.
David Mann, Ohio
Melvin Watt, N.C.
Xavier Becerra, Calif.

Hamilton Fish Jr., N.Y.
Carlos J. Moorhead, Calif.
Henry J. Hyde, Ill.
F. James Sensenbrenner Jr., Wis.
Bill McCollum, Fla.
George W. Gekas, Pa.
Howard Coble, N.C.
Lamar Smith, Texas
Steven H. Schiff, N.M.
Jim Ramstad, Minn.
Elton Gallegly, Calif.
Charles T. Canady, Fla.
Bob Inglis, S.C.
Robert W. Goodlatte, Va.

Administrative Law and Governmental Relations

225-5741 B-351A RHOB

Bryant — chairman

Glickman
Frank
Berman
Mann
Watt

Gekas
Ramstad
Inglis
Goodlatte

Civil and Constitutional Rights

226-7680 806 OHOB

Edwards (Calif.) — chairman

Schroeder	*Hyde*
Frank	*Coble*
Washington	*Canady*
Nadler	

Crime and Criminal Justice

226-2406 362 FHOB

Schumer — chairman

Edwards (Calif.)	*Sensenbrenner*
Conyers	*Smith (Texas)*
Mazzoli	*Schiff*
Glickman	*Ramstad*
Sangmeister	*Gekas*
Washington	
Mann	

Economic and Commercial Law

225-2825 B-353 RHOB

Brooks — chairman

Conyers	*Fish*
Synar	*Gallegly*
Schroeder	*Canady*
Glickman	*Inglis*
Berman	*Goodlatte*
Boucher	*Moorhead*
Scott	
Mann	
Watt	

Intellectual Property and Judicial Administration

225-3926 207 CHOB

Hughes — chairman

Edwards (Calif.)	*Moorhead*
Conyers	*Coble*
Mazzoli	*Fish*
Synar	*Sensenbrenner*
Frank	*McCollum*
Berman	*Schiff*
Reed	
Becerra	

International Law, Immigration and Refugees

225-5727 B-370B RHOB

Mazzoli — chairman

Schumer	*McCollum*
Bryant	*Smith (Texas)*
Sangmeister	*Gallegly*
Nadler	*Canady*
Becerra	

Merchant Marine and Fisheries

225-4047 1334 LHOB

Party Ratio: D 29 - R 19

Gerry E. Studds, D-Mass., chairman

William J. Hughes, N.J.	*Jack Fields, Texas*
Earl Hutto, Fla.	*Don Young, Alaska*
W. J. "Billy" Tauzin, La.	*Herbert H. Bateman, Va.*
William O. Lipinski, Ill.	*H. James Saxton, N.J.*
Solomon P. Ortiz, Texas	*Howard Coble, N.C.*
Thomas J. Manton, N.Y.	*Curt Weldon, Pa.*
Owen B. Pickett, Va.	*James M. Inhofe, Okla.*
George J. Hochbrueckner, N.Y.	*Arthur Ravenel Jr., S.C.*
Frank Pallone Jr., N.J.	*Wayne T. Gilchrest, Md.*
Greg Laughlin, Texas	*Randy "Duke" Cunningham, Calif.*
Jolene Unsoeld, Wash.	*Jack Kingston, Ga.*
Gene Taylor, Miss.	*Tillie Fowler, Fla.*
Jack Reed, R.I.	*Michael N. Castle, Del.*
H. Martin Lancaster, N.C.	*Peter T. King, N.Y.*
Thomas H. Andrews, Maine	*Lincoln Diaz-Balart, Fla.*
Elizabeth Furse, Ore.	*Richard W. Pombo, Calif.*
Lynn Schenk, Calif.	*Helen Delich Bentley, Md.*
Gene Green, Texas	*Charles H. Taylor, N.C.*
Alcee L. Hastings, Fla.	*Peter G. Torkildsen, Mass.*
Dan Hamburg, Calif.	
Blanche Lambert, Ark.	
Anna G. Eshoo, Calif.	
Tom Barlow, Ky.	
Bart Stupak, Mich.	
Bennie Thompson, Miss.	
Maria Cantwell, Wash.	
Peter Deutsch, Fla.	
Gary L. Ackerman, N.Y.	

Coast Guard and Navigation

226-3587 547 FHOB

Tauzin — chairman

Hughes	*Coble*
Hutto	*Bateman*
Lancaster	*Gilchrest*
Barlow	*Fowler*
Stupak	*Castle*
Lipinski	*King*
Pickett	*Diaz-Balart*
Hochbrueckner	*Inhofe*
Pallone	*Pombo*
Laughlin	
Schenk	
Hastings	
Lambert	
Taylor (Miss.)	

Environment and Natural Resources

226-3547 545 FHOB

Studds — chairman

Hochbrueckner	*Saxton*
Pallone	*Young (Alaska)*
Laughlin	*Weldon*
Unsoeld	*Ravenel*
Reed	*Gilchrest*
Furse	*Cunningham*
Hamburg	*Castle*
Lambert	
Eshoo	
Hutto	
Tauzin	
Ortiz	
Thompson	

Fisheries Management

226-3514 579 FHOB

Manton — chairman

Hughes	*Young (Alaska)*
Unsoeld	*Coble*
Taylor (Miss.)	*Ravenel*
Lancaster	*Kingston*
Hamburg	
Cantwell	
Hutto	

Merchant Marine

226-3533 543 FHOB

Lipinski — chairman

Pickett	*Bateman*
Taylor (Miss.)	*Inhofe*
Andrews (Maine)	*Cunningham*
Schenk	*Kingston*
Green	*Fowler*
Hastings	*King*
Reed	*Diaz-Balart*
Furse	*1 vacancy*
Stupak	
Manton	
Ackerman	
Thompson	

Oceanography, Gulf of Mexico and the Outer Continental Shelf

226-2460 575 FHOB

Ortiz - chairman

Green	*Weldon*
Eshoo	*Saxton*
Laughlin	
Schenk	

Natural Resources

225-2761 1324 LHOB

Party Ratio: D 28 † - R 15

George Miller, Calif., chairman

Philip R. Sharp, Ind.	*Don Young, Alaska, ranking member*
Edward J. Markey, Mass.	*James V. Hansen, Utah*
Austin J. Murphy, Pa.	*Barbara F. Vucanovich, Nev.*
Nick J. Rahall II, W.Va.	*Elton Gallegly, Calif.*
Bruce F. Vento, Minn.	*Bob Smith, Ore.*
Pat Williams, Mont.	*Craig Thomas, Wyo.*
Ron de Lugo, Virgin Islands †	*John J. "Jimmy" Duncan Jr., Tenn.*
Sam Gejdenson, Conn.	*Joel Hefley, Colo.*
Richard H. Lehman, Calif.	*John T. Doolittle, Calif.*
Bill Richardson, N.M.	*Wayne Allard, Colo.*
Peter A. DeFazio, Ore.	*Richard H. Baker, La.*
Eni F.H. Faleomavaega, Am. Samoa †	*Ken Calvert, Calif.*
Tim Johnson, S.D.	*Scott McInnis, Colo.*
Larry LaRocco, Idaho	*Richard W. Pombo, Calif.*
Neil Abercrombie, Hawaii	*Jay Dickey, Ark.*
Cal Dooley, Calif.	
Carlos Romero-Barceló, Puerto Rico †	
Karan English, Ariz.	
Karen Shepherd, Utah	
Nathan Deal, Ga.	
Maurice D. Hinchey, N.Y.	
Robert A. Underwood, Guam †	
Patsy T. Mink, Hawaii	
Howard L. Berman, Calif.	
Lane Evans, Ill.	
Tom Barlow, Ky.	
Thomas M. Barrett, Wis.	

† Delegates and resident commissioner not counted in official ratio of 24-15

Energy and Mineral Resources

225-8331 818 OHOB

Lehman - chairman

Sharp	*Vucanovich*
Murphy	*Thomas (Wyo.)*
Markey	*Doolittle*
Rahall	*Allard*
LaRocco	*McInnis*
Deal	*Pombo*
DeFazio	
Barlow	

Insular and International Affairs

225-9297 H2-107 FHOB

de Lugo — chairman

Faleomavaega	*Gallegly*
Romero-Barcelo	*Vucanovich*
Underwood	
Murphy	
Miller (Calif.)	
1 vacancy	

National Parks, Forests and Public Lands

226-7736 812 OHOB

Vento – chairman

Markey	*Hansen*
Rahall	*Smith (Ore.)*
Williams	*Thomas (Wyo.)*
DeFazio	*Duncan*
Johnson (S.D.)	*Hefley*
LaRocco	*Doolittle*
Abercrombie	*Baker (La.)*
Romero-Barcelo	*Calvert*
English (Ariz.)	*Dickey*
Shepherd	
Hinchey	
Underwood	
Murphy	
Richardson	
Mink	

Native American Affairs

226-7393 1522 LHOB

Richardson – chairman

Williams	*Thomas (Wyo.)*
Gejdenson	*Young (Alaska)*
Faleomavaega	*Baker (La.)*
Johnson (S.D.)	*Calvert*
Abercrombie	
English (Ariz.)	

Oversight and Investigations

225-6042 1328 LHOB

Miller – chairman

Gejdenson	*Smith (Ore.)*
Dooley	*Hansen*
Deal	*Vucanovich*
Sharp	*Duncan*
Vento	*Doolittle*
Lehman	*Allard*
DeFazio	*Calvert*
English (Ariz.)	*Pombo*
Shepherd	*Dickey*
Hinchey	
Abercrombie	
Evans	
Barrett (Wis.)	

Post Office and Civil Service

225-4054 309 CHOB

Party Ratio: D 15 † - R 9

William L. Clay, D-Mo., Chairman

Patricia Schroeder, Colo.	*John T. Myers, Ind.*
Frank McCloskey, Ind.	*Benjamin A. Gilman, N.Y.*
Gary L. Ackerman, N.Y.	*Don Young, Alaska*
Tom Sawyer, Ohio	*Dan Burton, Ind.*
Paul E. Kanjorski, Pa.	*Constance A. Morella, Md.*
Eleanor Holmes Norton, D.C. †	*Tom Ridge, Pa.*
	Tom Petri, Wis.
Barbara-Rose Collins, Mich.	*Sherwood Boehlert, N.Y.*
	H. James Saxton, N.J.
Leslie L. Byrne, Va.	
Melvin Watt, N.C.	
Albert R. Wynn, Md.	
Greg Laughlin, Texas	
Sanford D. Bishop Jr., Ga.	
Sherrod Brown, Ohio	
Alcee L. Hastings, Fla.	

† Delegate not counted in official ratio of 14-9

Census, Statistics and Postal Personnel

226-7523 515 OHOB

Sawyer – chairman

McCloskey	*Petri*
Wynn	*Ridge*

Civil Service

225-4025 122 CHOB

McCloskey – chairman

Schroeder	*Burton*
Kanjorski	*Morella*

Compensation and Employee Benefits

226-7546 209 CHOB

Norton – chairman

Ackerman	*Morella*
Byrne	*Young (Alaska)*

Oversight and Investigations

225-6295 219 CHOB

Clay – chairman

Hastings	*Boehlert*
Laughlin	*Saxton*

Postal Operations and Services

225-9124 406 CHOB

Collins – chairman

Watt	*Young (Alaska)*
Bishop	*Gilman*

Public Works and Transportation

225-4472 2165 RHOB

Party Ratio: D 39 †- R 24

Norman Y. Mineta, D-Calif., chairman

James L. Oberstar, Minn.	*Bud Shuster, Pa.*
Nick J. Rahall II, W.Va.	*William F. Clinger, Pa.*
Douglas Applegate, Ohio	*Tom Petri, Wis.*
Ron de Lugo, Virgin Islands †	*Sherwood Boehlert, N.Y.*
Robert A. Borski, Pa.	*James M. Inhofe, Okla.*
Tim Valentine, N.C.	*Bill Emerson, Mo.*
William O. Lipinski, Ill.	*John J. "Jimmy" Duncan Jr., Tenn.*
Bob Wise, W.Va.	*Susan Molinari, N.Y.*
James A. Traficant Jr., Ohio	*Bill Zeliff, N.H.*
Peter A. DeFazio, Ore.	*Thomas W. Ewing, Ill.*
Jimmy Hayes, La.	*Wayne T. Gilchrest, Md.*
Bob Clement, Tenn.	*Jennifer Dunn, Wash.*
Jerry F. Costello, Ill.	*Tim Hutchinson, Ark.*
Mike Parker, Miss.	*Bill Baker, Calif.*
Greg Laughlin, Texas	*Mac Collins, Ga.*
Pete Geren, Texas	*Jay C. Kim, Calif.*
George E. Sangmeister, Ill.	*David A. Levy, N.Y.*
Glenn Poshard, Ill.	*Steve Horn, Calif.*
Dick Swett, N.H.	*Bob Franks, N.J.*
Robert E. "Bud" Cramer, Ala.	*Peter I. Blute, Mass.*
Barbara-Rose Collins, Mich.	*Howard P. "Buck" McKeon, Calif.*
Eleanor Holmes Norton, D.C. †	*John L. Mica, Fla.*
Lucien E. Blackwell, Pa.	*Peter Hoekstra, Mich.*
Jerrold Nadler, N.Y.	*Jack Quinn, N.Y.*
Sam Coppersmith, Ariz.	
Leslie L. Byrne, Va.	
Maria Cantwell, Wash.	
Pat Danner, Mo.	
Karen Shepherd, Utah	
Robert Menendez, N.J.	
James E. Clyburn, S.C.	
Corrine Brown, Fla.	
Nathan Deal, Ga.	
James A. Barcia, Mich.	
Dan Hamburg, Calif.	
Bob Filner, Calif.	
Walter R. Tucker III, Calif.	
Eddie Bernice Johnson, Texas	

† Delegates not counted in official ratio of 37-24

Aviation

225-9161 2251 RHOB

Oberstar — chairman
de Lugo — vice chairman

Lipinski	*Clinger*
Geren	*Boehlert*
Sangmeister	*Inhofe*
Collins (Mich.)	*Duncan*
Coppersmith	*Ewing*
Borski	*Gilchrest*
Valentine	*Dunn*
DeFazio	*Collins (Ga.)*
Hayes	*Kim*
Clement	*Levy*
Costello	*Horn*
Parker	*McKeon*
Laughlin	*Mica*
Swett	
Cramer	
Blackwell	
Cantwell	
Danner	
Shepherd	
Brown (Fla.)	

Economic Development

225-6151 B-376 RHOB

Wise — chairman
Blackwell — vice chairman

Coppersmith	*Molinari*
Clyburn	*Boehlert*
Deal	*Ewing*
Barcia	*Dunn*
Filner	*Hutchinson*
Oberstar	*Baker (Calif.)*
Rahall	*Collins (Ga.)*
Lipinski	*Kim*
Traficant	*Franks (N.J.)*
Clement	*Blute*
Costello	*Mica*
Parker	*Hoekstra*
Swett	*Quinn*
Nadler	
Danner	
Shepherd	
Menendez	
Brown (Fla.)	
Hamburg	

Investigations and Oversight

225-3274 586 FHOB

Borski — chairman
Collins (Mich.) — vice chairman

Wise	*Inhofe*
Laughlin	*Duncan*
Blackwell	*Molinari*
Byrne	*Zeliff*
Barcia	*Gilchrest*
Filner	*Baker (Calif.)*
Johnson	
1 vacancy	

Public Buildings and Grounds

225-9961 B-376 RHOB

Traficant — chairman
Norton — vice chairman

Johnson	*Duncan*
Applegate	*Petri*
Clyburn	*Emerson*
Tucker	

Surface Transportation

225-9989 B-376 RHOB

Rahall — chairman
Valentine — vice chairman

Clement	*Petri*
Costello	*Clinger*
Laughlin	*Emerson*
Poshard	*Zeliff*
Swett	*Dunn*
Cramer	*Hutchinson*
DeFazio	*Baker (Calif.)*
Nadler	*Collins (Ga.)*
Byrne	*Kim*
Cantwell	*Levy*
Danner	*Franks (N.J.)*
Menendez	*Blute*
Clyburn	*McKeon*
Hamburg	
Tucker	
Johnson	
Applegate	
de Lugo	
Lipinski	
Traficant	

Water Resources and the Environment

225-0060 B-370A RHOB

Applegate — chairman
Hayes — vice chairman

Parker	*Boehlert*
Shepherd	*Clinger*
Brown (Fla.)	*Petri*
Deal	*Inhofe*
Barcia	*Emerson*
Filner	*Molinari*
Oberstar	*Zeliff*
Rahall	*Ewing*
Wise	*Gilchrest*
Geren	*Hutchinson*
Sangmeister	*Horn*
Poshard	*Hoekstra*
Norton	*Quinn*
Nadler	
Byrne	
Menendez	
Hamburg	
Tucker	
Borski	
Valentine	

Rules

225-9486 H-312 Capitol

Party Ratio: D 9 - R 4

Joe Moakley, D-Mass., chairman

Butler Derrick, S.C.	*Gerald B.H. Solomon, N.Y.*
Anthony C. Beilenson, Calif.	*James H. Quillen, Tenn.*
	David Dreier, Calif.
Martin Frost, Texas	*Porter J. Goss, Fla.*
David E. Bonior, Mich.	
Tony P. Hall, Ohio	
Alan Wheat, Mo.	
Bart Gordon, Tenn.	
Louise M. Slaughter, N.Y.	

Legislative Process

225-2430 1629 LHOB

Derrick — chairman

Frost	*Quillen*
Wheat	*Goss*
Gordon	
Moakley	

Rules of the House

225-9588 1628 LHOB

Beilenson — chairman

Bonior	*Dreier*
Hall (Ohio)	*Solomon*
Slaughter	
Moakley	

Science, Space and Technology

225-6371 2320 RHOB

Party Ratio: D 33 - R 22

George E. Brown Jr., D-Calif., chairman

Marilyn Lloyd, Tenn.	*Robert S. Walker, Pa.*
Dan Glickman, Kan.	*F. James Sensenbrenner Jr., Wis.*
Harold L. Volkmer, Mo.	
Ralph M. Hall, Texas	*Sherwood Boehlert, N.Y.*
Dave McCurdy, Okla.	*Tom Lewis, Fla.*
Tim Valentine, N.C.	*Paul B. Henry, Mich.*
Robert G. Torricelli, N.J.	*Harris W. Fawell, Ill.*
Rick Boucher, Va.	*Constance A. Morella, Md.*
James A. Traficant Jr., Ohio	*Dana Rohrabacher, Calif.*
	Steven H. Schiff, N.M.
Jimmy Hayes, La.	*Joe L. Barton, Texas*
John Tanner, Tenn.	*Dick Zimmer, N.J.*
Pete Geren, Texas	*Sam Johnson, Texas*
Jim Bacchus, Fla.	*Ken Calvert, Calif.*
Tim Roemer, Ind.	*Martin R. Hoke, Ohio*
Robert E. "Bud" Cramer, Ala.	*Nick Smith, Mich.*
	Ed Royce, Calif.
Dick Swett, N.H.	*Rod Grams, Minn.*
James A. Barcia, Mich.	*John Linder, Ga.*
Herb Klein, N.J.	*Peter I. Blute, Mass.*
Eric D. Fingerhut, Ohio	*Jennifer Dunn, Wash.*
Paul McHale, Pa.	*Bill Baker, Calif.*
Jane Harman, Calif.	*Roscoe G. Bartlett, Md.*
Don Johnson, Ga.	
Sam Coppersmith, Ariz.	
Anna G. Eshoo, Calif.	
Jay Inslee, Wash.	
Eddie Bernice Johnson, Texas	
David Minge, Minn.	
Nathan Deal, Ga.	
Robert C. Scott, Va.	
Xavier Becerra, Calif.	
2 vacancies	

Energy

225-8056 H2-390 FHOB

Lloyd — chairman

Scott	*Fawell*
Cramer	*Schiff*
Swett	*Baker (Calif.)*
Klein	*Grams*
McHale	*Bartlett*
Coppersmith	
Inslee	
Roemer	
McCurdy	

Investigations and Oversight

225-4494 822 OHOB

Hayes — chairman

Tanner	*Henry*
Lloyd	*Morella*
Johnson (Ga.)	*Barton*
Coppersmith	
1 vacancy	

Science

225-8844 2319 RHOB

Boucher — chairman

Hall (Texas)	*Boehlert*
Valentine	*Barton*
Barcia	*Johnson (Texas)*
Johnson (Ga.)	*Smith (Mich.)*
Eshoo	*Blute*
Johnson	
Minge	
1 vacancy	

Space

225-7858 2320 RHOB

Hall (Texas) — chairman

Volkmer	*Sensenbrenner*
Torricelli	*Rohrabacher*
Traficant	*Zimmer*
Bacchus	*Johnson*
Cramer	*Hoke*
Barcia	*Royce*
Fingerhut	*Dunn*
Hayes	*Schiff*
Tanner	*Calvert*
Geren	
Roemer	
Harman	
Eshoo	
McCurdy	
1 vacancy	

Technology, Environment and Aviation

225-9662 B-374 RHOB

Valentine — chairman

Glickman	*Lewis (Fla.)*
Geren	*Morella*
Roemer	*Calvert*
Swett	*Smith (Mich.)*
Klein	*Grams*
McHale	*Linder*
Harman	*Blute*
Johnson (Ga.)	*Bartlett*
Coppersmith	*Rohrabacher*
Eshoo	*Zimmer*
Inslee	*Hoke*
Johnson (Texas)	*Royce*
Minge	
Deal	
Becerra	
Torricelli	
Bacchus	
1 vacancy	

Small Business

225-5821 2361 RHOB

Party Ratio: D 27 - R 18

John J. LaFalce, D-N.Y., chairman

Neal Smith, Iowa	*Jan Meyers, Kan.*
Ike Skelton, Mo.	*Larry Combest, Texas*
Romano L. Mazzoli, Ky.	*Richard H. Baker, La.*
Ron Wyden, Ore.	*Joel Hefley, Colo.*
Norman Sisisky, Va.	*Ronald K. Machtley, R.I.*
John Conyers Jr., Mich.	*Jim Ramstad, Minn.*
James Bilbray, Nev.	*Sam Johnson, Texas*
Kweisi Mfume, Md.	*Bill Zeliff, N.H.*
Floyd H. Flake, N.Y.	*Mac Collins, Ga.*
Bill Sarpalius, Texas	*Scott McInnis, Colo.*
Glenn Poshard, Ill.	*Michael Huffington, Calif.*
Eva Clayton, N.C.	*James M. Talent, Mo.*
Martin T. Meehan, Mass.	*Joe Knollenberg, Mich.*
Pat Danner, Mo.	*Jay Dickey, Ark.*
Ted Strickland, Ohio	*Jay C. Kim, Calif.*
Nydia M. Velázquez, N.Y.	*Donald Manzullo, Ill.*
Cleo Fields, La.	*Peter G. Torkildsen, Mass.*
Marjorie Margolies-Mezvinsky, Pa.	*Rob Portman, Ohio*
Walter R. Tucker III, Calif.	
Ron Klink, Pa.	
Lucille Roybal-Allard, Calif.	
Earl F. Hilliard, Ala.	
H. Martin Lancaster, N.C.	
Thomas H. Andrews, Maine	
Maxine Waters, Calif.	
1 vacancy	

Minority Enterprise, Finance and Urban Development

225-7673 H2-568A FHOB

Mfume — chairman

Conyers	*Machtley*
Flake	*Talent*
Velázquez	*Knollenberg*
Tucker	*Dickey*
Fields (La.)	*Ramstad*
Roybal-Allard	
Hilliard	

Procurement, Taxation and Tourism

225-9368 B-363 RHOB

Bilbray — chairman

Sisisky	*Baker (La.)*
Hilliard	*Knollenberg*
Mfume	*Johnson (Texas)*
Clayton	*1 vacancy*
Klink	

Regulation, Business Opportunities and Technology

225-7797 B-363 RHOB

Wyden — chairman

Skelton	*Combest*
Strickland	*Johnson (Texas)*
Andrews (Maine)	*Dickey*
Sisisky	*Kim*
Bilbray	*Torkildsen*
Meehan	*Huffington*
Tucker	

Rural Enterprises, Exports and the Environment

225-8944 1F CHOB

Sarpalius — chairman

Clayton	*Hefley*
Danner	*Ramstad*
Poshard	*Manzullo*
Strickland	*Collins (Ga.)*
Hilliard	

SBA Legislation and the General Economy

225-5821 2361 RHOB

LaFalce — chairman

Smith (Iowa)	*Hefley*
Mazzoli	*Ramstad*
Poshard	*Manzullo*
Meehan	*Collins (Ga.)*
Fields (La.)	*Meyers*
Margolies-Mezvinsky	*Zeliff*
Klink	*Talent*
Roybal-Allard	*Huffington*

Standards of Official Conduct

225-7103 HT-2 Capitol

Party Ratio: D 7 - R 7

Jim McDermott, D-Wash., chairman

George "Buddy" Darden, Ga.	*Fred Grandy, Iowa*
Benjamin L. Cardin, Md.	*Nancy L. Johnson, Conn.*
Nancy Pelosi, Calif.	*Jim Bunning, Ky.*
Kweisi Mfume, Md.	*Jon Kyl, Ariz.*
Robert A. Borski, Pa.	*Porter J. Goss, Fla.*
Tom Sawyer, Ohio	*David L. Hobson, Ohio*
	Steven H. Schiff, N.M.

Veterans' Affairs

225-3527 335 CHOB

Party Ratio: D 21 - R 14

G.V. "Sonny" Montgomery, D-Miss., chairman

Don Edwards, Calif.	*Bob Stump, Ariz.*
Douglas Applegate, Ohio	*Christopher H. Smith, N.J.*
Lane Evans, Ill.	*Dan Burton, Ind.*
Timothy J. Penny, Minn.	*Michael Bilirakis, Fla.*
J. Roy Rowland, Ga.	*Tom Ridge, Pa.*
Jim Slattery, Kan.	*Floyd D. Spence, S.C.*
Joseph P. Kennedy II, Mass.	*Tim Hutchinson, Ark.*
George E. Sangmeister, Ill.	*Terry Everett, Ala.*
Jill L. Long, Ind.	*Steve Buyer, Ind.*
Chet Edwards, Texas	*Jack Quinn, N.Y.*
Maxine Waters, Calif.	*Spencer Bachus, Ala.*
Bob Clement, Tenn.	*John Linder, Ga.*
Bob Filner, Calif.	*Cliff Stearns, Fla.*
Frank Tejeda, Texas	*Peter T. King, N.Y.*
Luis V. Gutierrez, Ill.	
Scotty Baesler, Ky.	
Sanford D. Bishop Jr., Ga.	
James E. Clyburn, S.C.	
Mike Kreidler, Wash.	
Corrine Brown, Fla.	

Compensation, Pension and Insurance

225-3569 335 CHOB

Slattery — chairman

Applegate	*Bilirakis*
Evans	*Everett*
Sangmeister	*Stearns*
Edwards (Texas)	*King*
Tejeda	

Education, Training and Employment

225-9166 337A CHOB

Montgomery — chairman

Penny	*Hutchinson*
Clyburn	*Stump*
Rowland	*Ridge*
Slattery	*Quinn*
Clement	

Hospitals and Health Care

225-9154 338 CHOB

Rowland — chairman

Applegate	*Smith (N.J.)*
Kennedy	*Stump*
Long	*Burton*
Edwards (Texas)	*Bilirakis*
Clement	*Hutchinson*
Filner	*Everett*
Tejeda	*Buyer*
Gutierrez	*Linder*
Baesler	
Bishop	
Kreidler	
Brown (Fla.)	

Housing and Memorial Affairs

225-9164 337 CHOB

Sangmeister — chairman

Bishop	*Burton*
Brown (Fla.)	*Spence*
Kreidler	*Buyer*

Oversight and Investigations

225-9044 335 CHOB

Evans — chairman

Waters	*Ridge*
Filner	*Bachus*
Gutierrez	*Everett*
Clyburn	*Quinn*
Kreidler	

Ways and Means

225-3625 1102 LHOB

Party Ratio: D 24 - R 14

Dan Rostenkowski, D-Ill., chairman

Sam M. Gibbons, Fla.	*Bill Archer, Texas*
J. J. Pickle, Texas	*Philip M. Crane, Ill.*
Charles B. Rangel, N.Y.	*Bill Thomas, Calif.*
Pete Stark, Calif.	*E. Clay Shaw Jr., Fla.*
Andrew Jacobs Jr., Ind.	*Don Sundquist, Tenn.*
Harold E. Ford, Tenn.	*Nancy L. Johnson, Conn.*
Robert T. Matsui, Calif.	*Jim Bunning, Ky.*
Barbara B. Kennelly, Conn.	*Fred Grandy, Iowa*
William J. Coyne, Pa.	*Amo Houghton, N.Y.*
Michael A. Andrews, Texas	*Wally Herger, Calif.*
Sander M. Levin, Mich.	*Jim McCrery, La.*
Benjamin L. Cardin, Md.	*Mel Hancock, Mo.*
Jim McDermott, Wash.	*Rick Santorum, Pa.*
Gerald D. Kleczka, Wis.	*Dave Camp, Mich.*
John Lewis, Ga.	
Lewis F. Payne Jr., Va.	
Richard E. Neal, Mass.	
Peter Hoagland, Neb.	
Michael R. McNulty, N.Y.	
Mike Kopetski, Ore.	
William J. Jefferson, La.	
Bill Brewster, Okla.	
Mel Reynolds, Ill.	

Health

225-7785 1114 LHOB

Stark – chairman

Levin	*Thomas (Calif.)*
Cardin	*Johnson (Conn.)*
Andrews (Texas)	*Grandy*
McDermott	*McCrery*
Kleczka	
Lewis (Ga.)	

Human Resources

225-1025 B-317 RHOB

Ford (Tenn.) – chairman

Matsui	*Santorum*
McDermott	*Shaw*
Levin	*Grandy*
Kopetski	*Camp*
Reynolds	
Cardin	

Oversight

225-5522 1135 LHOB

Pickle – chairman

Ford (Tenn.)	*Houghton*
Rangel	*Herger*
Jefferson	*Hancock*
Brewster	*Santorum*
Kleczka	
Lewis (Ga.)	

Select Revenue Measures

225-9710 1105 LHOB

Rangel – chairman

Payne (Va.)	*Hancock*
Neal (Mass.)	*Sundquist*
Hoagland	*McCrery*
McNulty	*Camp*
Kopetski	
Jacobs	

Social Security

225-9263 B-316 RHOB

Jacobs – chairman

Pickle	*Bunning*
Jefferson	*Crane*
Brewster	*Houghton*
Reynolds	

Trade

225-3943 1136 LHOB

Gibbons – chairman

Rostenkowski	*Crane*
Matsui	*Thomas (Calif.)*
Kennelly	*Shaw*
Coyne	*Sundquist*
Payne (Va.)	*Johnson (Conn.)*
Neal (Mass.)	
Hoagland	
McNulty	

Select Intelligence

225-4121 H-405 Capitol

Party Ratio: D 12 - R 7

Dan Glickman, D-Kan., chairman

Bill Richardson, N.M.	*Larry Combest, Texas*
Norm Dicks, Wash.	*Doug Bereuter, Neb.*
Julian C. Dixon, Calif.	*Robert K. Dornan, Calif.*
Robert G. Torricelli, N.J.	*C.W. Bill Young, Fla.*
Ronald D. Coleman, Texas	*George W. Gekas, Pa.*
David E. Skaggs, Colo.	*James V. Hansen, Utah*
James Bilbray, Nev.	*Jerry Lewis, Calif.*
Nancy Pelosi, Calif.	
Greg Laughlin, Texas	
Robert E. "Bud" Cramer, Ala.	
Jack Reed, R.I.	

Legislation

225-7311 H-405 Capitol

Coleman – chairman

Dicks	*Gekas*
Bilbray	*Hansen*
Pelosi	*Lewis (Calif.)*
Laughlin	
Cramer	

Oversight and Evaluation

225-5658 H-405 Capitol

Dicks – chairman

Pelosi	*Young (Fla.)*
Reed	*Hansen*
Torricelli	*Bereuter*
Coleman	
Skaggs	

Program and Budget Authorization

225-7690 H-405 Capitol

Glickman – chairman

Richardson	*Combest*
Dixon	*Bereuter*
Torricelli	*Dornan*
Skaggs	*Lewis (Calif.)*
Bilbray	
Laughlin	
Cramer	

House Partisan Committees

Democratic Leaders

Speaker of the House .... Thomas S. Foley, Wash.
Majority Leader .... Richard A. Gephardt, Mo.
Majority Whip .... David E. Bonior, Mich.
Caucus Chairman .... Steny H. Hoyer, Md.
Caucus Vice Chairman .... Vic Fazio, Calif.
Chief Deputy Whips .... Butler Derrick, S.C.
Barbara B. Kennelly, Conn.
John Lewis, Ga.
Bill Richardson, N.M.
Floor Whip .... Martin Frost, Texas
Ex-Officio Whip .... Joe Moakley, Mass.

Deputy Whips .... Tom Bevill, Ala.
W.G. "Bill" Hefner, N.C.
Norman Y. Mineta, Calif.
Charles B. Rangel, N.Y.
Martin Olav Sabo, Minn.
Patricia Schroeder, Colo.
Charles W. Stenholm, Texas
Esteban E. Torres, Calif.
Jolene Unsoeld, Wash.
Alan Wheat, Mo.
Pat Williams, Mont.

Whip Task Force Chairmen ...... Bart Gordon, Tenn.; David R. Obey, Wis.

At-Large Whips:
Thomas H. Andrews, Maine; Xavier Becerra, Calif.; Howard L. Berman, Calif.; Robert A. Borski, Pa.; Rick Boucher, Va.; Leslie L. Byrne, Va.; Benjamin L. Cardin, Md.; Bob Carr, Mich.; Barbara-Rose Collins, Mich.; George "Buddy" Darden, Ga.; Rosa DeLauro, Conn.; Norm Dicks, Wash.; Richard J. Durbin, Ill.; Don Edwards, Calif.; Lane Evans, Ill.; William D. Ford, Mich.; Barney Frank, Mass.; Sam Gejdenson, Conn.; Dan Glickman, Kan.; William J. Jefferson, La.; Eddie Bernice Johnson, Texas; Harry A. Johnston, Fla.; Paul E. Kanjorski, Pa.; Dale E. Kildee, Mich.; H. Martin Lancaster, N.C.; Larry LaRocco, Idaho; Richard H. Lehman, Calif.; Nita M. Lowey, N.Y.; Robert T. Matsui, Calif.; Frank McCloskey, Ind.; Dave McCurdy, Okla.; Robert Menendez, N.J.; George Miller, Calif.; Alan B. Mollohan, W.Va.; Richard E. Neal, Mass.; James L. Oberstar, Minn.; Timothy J. Penny, Minn.; David Price, N.C.; Charlie Rose, N.C.; Dan Rostenkowski, Ill.; Bobby L. Rush, Ill.; Charles E. Schumer, N.Y.; Philip R. Sharp, Ind.; Norman Sisisky, Va.; David E. Skaggs, Colo.; Louise M. Slaughter, N.Y.; John M. Spratt Jr., S.C.; Mike Synar, Okla.; W.J. "Billy" Tauzin, La.; Robert G. Torricelli, N.J.; Bruce F. Vento, Minn.; Peter J. Visclosky, Ind.; Harold L. Volkmer, Mo.; Maxine Waters, Calif.; Bob Wise, W.Va.; Ron Wyden, Ore.

Assistant Whips (by zone number):

1... Anna G. Eshoo, Calif.; Matthew G. Martinez, Calif.
2............................ Jim McDermott, Wash.
3................................ Tim Johnson, S.D.
4.............................. Sidney R. Yates, Ill.
5................................ Jim Slattery, Kan.
6.......... John Bryant, Texas; Jim Chapman, Texas
7.................................... Jack Reed, R.I.
8.. Gary L. Ackerman, N.Y.; Maurice D. Hinchey, N.Y.
9............................ Donald M. Payne, N.J.
10.......... Sander M. Levin, Mich.; Tom Sawyer, Ohio
11.......................... Romano L. Mazzoli, Ky.
12............................ James E. Clyburn, S.C.
13..................... Robert E. "Bud" Cramer, Ala.
14................................ Pete Peterson, Fla.

Steering and Policy Committee

225-8550 H-226 Capitol

Thomas S. Foley, Wash., chairman

Richard A. Gephardt, Mo., vice chairman

Steny H. Hoyer, Md., second vice chairman

David E. Bonior, Mich.
Jack Brooks, Texas
Maria Cantwell, Wash.
Benjamin L. Cardin, Md.
E. "Kika" de la Garza, Texas
Butler Derrick, S.C.
John D. Dingell, Mich.
Julian C. Dixon, Calif.
Richard J. Durbin, Ill.
Vic Fazio, Calif.
Sam Gejdenson, Conn.
Dan Glickman, Kan.
Barbara B. Kennelly, Conn.
Gerald D. Kleczka, Wis.
Ron Klink, Pa.
John Lewis, Ga.
Thomas J. Manton, N.Y.
Patsy T. Mink, Hawaii
Joe Moakley, Mass.
John P. Murtha, Pa.
William H. Natcher, Ky.
David R. Obey, Wis.
Ed Pastor, Ariz.
Bill Richardson, N.M.
Dan Rostenkowski, Ill.
J. Roy Rowland, Ga.
Al Swift, Wash.
Mike Synar, Okla.
W. J. "Billy" Tauzin, La.
Melvin Watt, N.C.
Alan Wheat, Mo.

Personnel Committee

225-4068 B-343-D RHOB

Jack Brooks, Texas, chairman

Democratic Congressional Campaign Committee

863-1500 430 S. Capitol St., S.E. 20003

Vic Fazio, Calif., chairman
Dan Rostenkowski, Ill., vice chairman
Thomas S. Foley, Wash., ex officio
Richard A. Gephardt, Mo., ex officio
David E. Bonior, Mich., ex officio
Steny H. Hoyer, Md., ex officio
Butler Derrick, S.C., ex officio
Barbara B. Kennelly, Conn., ex officio
John Lewis, Ga., ex officio
Bill Richardson, N.M., ex officio

Benjamin L. Cardin, Md., co-chairman
Robert E. "Bud" Cramer, Ala., co-chairman
Barney Frank, Mass., co-chairman
Bart Gordon, Tenn., co-chairman
Greg Laughlin, Texas, co-chairman
Thomas J. Manton, N.Y., co-chairman
John P. Murtha, Pa., co-chairman
Nancy Pelosi, Calif., co-chairman
Jim Slattery, Kan., co-chairman

At-Large Members of Oversight Subcommittee:

Howard L. Berman, Calif.
John D. Dingell, Mich.
Martin Frost, Texas
H. Martin Lancaster, N.C.
Martin Olav Sabo, Minn.
Mike Synar, Okla.

Speaker's Appointments, Full Committee:

Rosa DeLauro, Conn.
Lee H. Hamilton, Ind.
David R. Obey, Wis.
Lynn Schenk, Calif.
Charles W. Stenholm, Texas
W. J. "Billy" Tauzin, La.
Maxine Waters, Calif.
Ron Wyden, Ore.

Republican Leaders

Minority Leader .... *Robert H. Michel, Ill.*
Minority Whip.................. *Newt Gingrich, Ga.*
Conference Chairman............ *Dick Armey, Texas*
Conference Vice Chairman........ *Bill McCollum, Fla.*
Conference Secretary............ *Tom DeLay, Texas*
Chief Deputy Whip............ *Robert S. Walker, Pa.*
Deputy Whips.................. *Joe L. Barton, Texas*
Tom DeLay, Texas
Dennis Hastert, Ill.
Nancy L. Johnson, Conn.
Jon Kyl, Ariz.
Gerald B. H. Solomon, N.Y.

Assistant Deputy Whips: ... *Thomas J. Bliley Jr., Va.*
John A. Boehner, Ohio
Dan Burton, Ind.
Paul B. Henry, Mich.
Robert L. Livingston, La.
Bill Paxon, N.Y.
Pat Roberts, Kan.
Olympia J. Snowe, Maine

Regional Whips:
East .... *Dean A. Gallo, N.J.*
Midwest and Plains .... *Jim Ross Lightfoot, Iowa*
South..................... *Ileana Ros-Lehtinen, Fla.*
West.................... *Barbara F. Vucanovich, Nev.*

Committee on Committees

225-0600 H-230Capitol

Robert H. Michel, Ill., chairman

Wayne Allard, Colo.
Bill Archer, Texas
Bill Baker, Calif.
Cass Ballenger, N.C.
Thomas J. Bliley Jr., Va.
Jim Bunning, Ky.
Jennifer Dunn, Wash.
Dean A. Gallo, N.J.
Newt Gingrich, Ga.
Dennis Hastert, Ill.
James M. Inhofe, Okla.
Scott L. Klug, Wis.
John Linder, Ga.
Joseph M. McDade, Pa.
Ron Packard, Calif.
Ralph Regula, Ohio
Gerald B. H. Solomon, N.Y.
Floyd D. Spence, S.C.
Bob Stump, Ariz.
Fred Upton, Mich.
C. W. Bill Young, Fla.
Don Young, Alaska

Policy Committee

225-6168 1616 LHOB

Henry J. Hyde, Ill., chairman

Bill Archer, Texas
Dick Armey, Texas
Doug Bereuter, Neb.
John A. Boehner, Ohio
Steve Buyer, Ind.
Michael D. Crapo, Idaho
Tom DeLay, Texas
Tillie Fowler, Fla.
Gary A. Franks, Conn.
Dean A. Gallo, N.J.
Newt Gingrich, Ga.
Bill Goodling, Pa.
Steve Gunderson, Wis.
Mel Hancock, Mo.
Dennis Hastert, Ill.
Peter Hoekstra, Mich.
Duncan Hunter, Calif.
Ernest Jim Istook Jr., Okla.
Nancy L. Johnson, Conn.
John R. Kasich, Ohio
Tom Lewis, Fla.
Bill McCollum, Fla.
Joseph M. McDade, Pa.
Jan Meyers, Kan.
Robert H. Michel, Ill.
Michael G. Oxley, Ohio
Bill Paxon, N.Y.
Ileana Ros-Lehtinen, Fla.
Ed Royce, Calif.
Lamar Smith, Texas
Gerald B. H. Solomon, N.Y.
Floyd D. Spence, S.C.
Craig Thomas, Wyo.
Barbara F. Vucanovich, Nev.

Research Committee

225-0871 1622 LHOB

Duncan Hunter, Calif., chairman

Dick Armey, Texas
Doug Bereuter, Neb.
John A. Boehner, Ohio
Dan Burton, Ind.
Charles T. Canady, Fla.
Michael D. Crapo, Idaho
Tom DeLay, Texas
Newt Gingrich, Ga.
Mel Hancock, Mo.
Henry J. Hyde, Ill.
Jim Ross Lightfoot, Iowa
Bill McCollum, Fla.
Robert H. Michel, Ill.
Susan Molinari, N.Y.
Jack Quinn, N.Y.
H. James Saxton, N.J.
Steven H. Schiff, N.M.
Olympia J. Snowe, Maine
Cliff Stearns, Fla.
Barbara F. Vucanovich, Nev.
1 vacancy

National Republican Congressional Committee

479-7000 320 First St., S.E. 20003

Bill Paxon, N.Y., chairman

Susan Molinari, N.Y., chief vice chairman
Rick Santorum, Pa., chief vice chairman
H. James Saxton, N.J., chief vice chairman
John A. Boehner, Ohio, vice chairman
John T. Doolittle, Calif., vice chairman
Nancy L. Johnson, Conn., vice chairman
Robert L. Livingston, La., vice chairman
Jim Nussle, Iowa, vice chairman
Deborah Pryce, Ohio, vice chairman
Robert H. Michel, Ill., ex officio
Newt Gingrich, Ga., ex officio
Dick Armey, Texas, ex officio
Bill McCollum, Fla., ex officio
Tom DeLay, Texas, ex officio
Henry J. Hyde, Ill., ex officio
Duncan Hunter, Calif., ex officio

Spencer Bachus, Ala.
Helen Delich Bentley, Md.
Jim Bunning, Ky.
Dave Camp, Mich.
C. Christopher Cox, Calif.
Jennifer Dunn, Wash.
Bob Franks, N.J.
Dennis Hastert, Ill.
Scott L. Klug, Wis.
Jon Kyl, Ariz.
John Linder, Ga.
Pat Roberts, Kan.
Ileana Ros-Lehtinen, Fla.
Ed Royce, Calif.
Dan Schaefer, Colo.
Steven H. Schiff, N.M.
Olympia J. Snowe, Maine
Gerald B. H. Solomon, N.Y.
James M. Talent, Mo.
Barbara F. Vucanovich, Nev.
Robert S. Walker, Pa.

Joint Committee Assignments 103rd Congress

The joint committees of Congress are listed below. The listing includes the room number, ZIP code and telephone number. The telephone area code for Washington, D.C., is 202.

Membership is drawn from both chambers and both parties. Membership is given in order of seniority on the committees and subcommittees.

In the listing, Democrats are listed on the left in Roman type; Republicans are listed on the right in italics. When a senator serves as chairman, the vice chairman is usually a representative, and vice versa. The chairmanship usually rotates from one chamber to the other at the beginning of each Congress.

Joint Economic Committee

224-5171 SD-G01

David R. Obey (D-Wis.), chairman
Paul S. Sarbanes (Md.), vice chairman

Senate Members

Edward M. Kennedy (Mass.)
Jeff Bingaman (N.M.)
Richard H. Bryan (Nev.)
Charles S. Robb (Va.)
Byron L. Dorgan (N.D.)

William V. Roth Jr. (Del.), ranking member
Connie Mack (Fla.)
Larry E. Craig (Idaho)
Robert F. Bennett (Utah)

House Members

Lee H. Hamilton (Ind.)
Pete Stark (Calif.)
Kweisi Mfume (Md.)
Ron Wyden (Ore.)
Michael A. Andrews (Texas)

Dick Armey (Texas)
H. James Saxton (N.J.)
C. Christopher Cox (Calif.)
Jim Ramstad (Minn.)

Joint Library Committee

226-7633 103 OHOB
Charlie Rose (N.C.), chairman
Claiborne Pell (R.I.), vice chairman

Senate Members

Dennis DeConcini (Ariz.)
Daniel Patrick Moynihan (N.Y.)

Mark O. Hatfield (Ore.)
Ted Stevens (Alaska)

House Members

Martin Frost (Texas) *
Thomas J. Manton (N.Y.) *

Bill Barrett (Neb.) *
Pat Roberts (Kan.) *

** Unofficial as of press date*

Joint Committee on the Organization of Congress

226-0650 175D FHOB

David L. Boren, Okla., co-chairman
Lee H. Hamilton, Ind., co-chairman
Pete V. Domenici, N.M., co-vice chairman
David Dreier, Calif., co-vice chairman

Senate Members

Jim Sasser, Tenn.
Wendell H. Ford, Ky.
Harry Reid, Nev.
Paul S. Sarbanes, Md.
David Pryor, Ark.
George J. Mitchell, Maine, (ex officio)

Nancy Landon Kassebaum, Kan.
Trent Lott, Miss.
Ted Stevens, Alaska
William S. Cohen, Maine
Richard G. Lugar, Ind.
Bob Dole, Kan., (ex officio)

House Members

David R. Obey, Wis.
Al Swift, Wash.
Sam Gejdenson, Conn.
John M. Spratt Jr., S.C.
Eleanor Holmes Norton, D.C.
Richard A. Gephardt, Mo., (ex officio)

Robert S. Walker, Pa.
Gerald B.H. Solomon, N.Y.
Bill Emerson, Mo.
Wayne Allard, Colo.
Jennifer Dunn, Wash.
Robert H. Michel, Ill., (ex officio)

Joint Printing Committee

224-5241 SH-818

Wendell H. Ford (Ky.), chairman
Charlie Rose (N.C.), vice chairman

Senate Members

Dennis DeConcini (Ariz.)	*Ted Stevens (Alaska)*
Harlan Mathews (Tenn.)	*Mark O. Hatfield (Ore.)*

House Members

Sam Gejdenson (Conn.)	*Pat Roberts (Kan.), ranking member*
Gerald D. Kleczka (Wis.)	*Newt Gingrich (Ga.)*

Joint Taxation Committee

225-3621 1015 LHOB

Dan Rostenkowski (Ill.), chairman*
Daniel Patrick Moynihan (N.Y.), vice chairman *

Senate Members

Max Baucus (Mont.)	*Bob Packwood (Ore.)*
David L. Boren (Okla.)	*Bob Dole (Kan.)*

House Members

Sam M. Gibbons (Fla.)	*Bill Archer (Texas)*
J.J. Pickle (Texas)	*Philip M. Crane (Ill.)*

** Chairmanship is for first session of 103rd Congress only; for the second session (beginning January 1994), chairmanship will switch to Senate side*

Seniority in the 103rd Congress

Senate

Senate rank generally is determined according to the official date of the beginning of a member's service, except in the case of new members sworn in at times other than the beginning of a Congress. For those appointed or elected to fill unexpired terms, the date of the appointment, certification or swearing-in determines the senator's rank.

When members are sworn in on the same day, custom decrees that those with prior political experience take precedence. Counted as experience, in order of importance, is senatorial, House and gubernatorial service. Information on prior experience is given where applicable to seniority ranking. The dates following senators' names refer to the beginning of their present service.

Democrats

1. Byrd — Jan. 7, 1959
2. Pell — Jan. 3, 1961
3. Kennedy — Nov. 7, 1962
4. Inouye — Jan. 9, 1963
5. Hollings — Nov. 9, 1966
6. Nunn — Nov. 8, 1972
7. Johnston — Nov. 14, 1972
8. Biden — Jan. 3, 1973
9. Glenn — Dec. 24, 1974
10. Ford — Dec. 28, 1974
11. Bumpers (ex-governor) — Jan. 14, 1975
12. Leahy — Jan. 14, 1975
13. Metzenbaum — Dec. 29, 1976
14. Riegle — Dec. 30, 1976
15. Sarbanes (ex-representative, three House terms) — Jan. 4, 1977
16. DeConcini — Jan. 4, 1977
    Moynihan — Jan. 4, 1977
    Sasser — Jan. 4, 1977
19. Baucus — Dec. 15, 1978
20. Pryor (ex-representative, three House terms) — Jan. 15, 1979
21. Boren (ex-governor) — Jan. 15, 1979
    Exon (ex-governor) — Jan. 15, 1979
23. Bradley — Jan. 15, 1979
    Heflin — Jan. 15, 1979
    Levin — Jan. 15, 1979
26. Mitchell — May 19, 1980
27. Dodd — Jan. 5, 1981
28. Lautenberg — Dec. 27, 1982
29. Bingaman — Jan. 3, 1983
30. Kerry — Jan. 2, 1985
31. Harkin (ex-representative, five House terms) — Jan. 3, 1985
    Simon (ex-representative, five House terms) — Jan. 3, 1985
33. Rockefeller — Jan. 15, 1985
34. Breaux (ex-representative, eight House terms) — Jan. 6, 1987
35. Mikulski (ex-representative, five House terms) — Jan. 6, 1987
36. Daschle (ex-representative, four House terms) — Jan. 6, 1987
    Shelby (ex-representative, four House terms) — Jan. 6, 1987
38. Reid (ex-representative, two House terms) — Jan. 6, 1987
39. Graham (ex-governor) — Jan. 6, 1987
40. Conrad — Jan. 6, 1987
41. Bryan (ex-governor) — Jan. 3, 1989
    Kerrey (ex-governor) — Jan. 3, 1989
    Robb (ex-governor) — Jan. 3, 1989
44. Kohl — Jan. 3, 1989
    Lieberman — Jan. 3, 1989
46. Akaka — May 16, 1990
47. Wellstone — Jan. 3, 1991
48. Wofford — May 9, 1991
49. Feinstein — Nov. 4, 1992
50. Dorgan — Dec. 15, 1992
51. Mathews — Jan. 2, 1993
52. Boxer (ex-representative, five House terms) — Jan. 5, 1993
53. Campbell (ex-representative, three House terms) — Jan. 5, 1993
54. Feingold — Jan. 5, 1993
    Moseley-Braun — Jan. 5, 1993
    Murray — Jan. 5, 1993

Republicans

1. Thurmond — Nov. 7, 1956 *
2. Hatfield — Jan. 10, 1967
3. Stevens — Dec. 24, 1968
4. Dole (ex-representative, four House terms) — Jan. 3, 1969
5. Packwood — Jan. 3, 1969
6. Roth — Jan. 1, 1971
7. Domenici — Jan. 3, 1973
    Helms — Jan. 3, 1973
9. Danforth — Dec. 27, 1976
10. Chafee — Dec. 29, 1976
11. Hatch — Jan. 4, 1977
    Lugar — Jan. 4, 1977
    Wallop — Jan. 4, 1977
14. Durenberger — Nov. 8, 1978
15. Kassebaum — Dec. 23, 1978
16. Cochran — Dec. 27, 1978
17. Simpson — Jan. 1, 1979
18. Warner — Jan. 2, 1979
19. Cohen (ex-representative, three House terms) — Jan. 15, 1979
20. Pressler (ex-representative, two House terms) — Jan. 15, 1979
21. Grassley (ex-representative, three House terms) — Jan. 5, 1981

22. D'Amato — Jan. 5, 1981
   Murkowski — Jan. 5, 1981
   Nickles — Jan. 5, 1981
   Specter — Jan. 5, 1981
26. Gramm (ex-representative, three House terms) — Jan. 3, 1985
27. McConnell — Jan. 3, 1985
28. McCain (ex-representative, two House terms) — Jan. 6, 1987
29. Bond (ex-governor) — Jan. 6, 1987
30. Gorton (ex-senator) — Jan. 3, 1989
31. Lott (ex-representative, eight House terms) — Jan. 3, 1989
32. Jeffords (ex-representative, seven House terms) — Jan. 3, 1989
33. Coats (ex-representative, four House terms) — Jan. 3, 1989
34. Mack (ex-representative, three House terms) — Jan. 3, 1989
35. Burns — Jan. 3, 1989
36. Smith — Dec. 7, 1990
37. Brown (ex-representative, five House terms) — Jan. 3, 1991
   Craig (ex-representative, five House terms) — Jan. 3, 1991
39. Gregg (ex-representative, four House terms) — Jan. 5, 1993
40. Bennett — Jan. 5, 1993
   Coverdell — Jan. 5, 1993
   Faircloth — Jan. 5, 1993
   Kempthorne — Jan. 5, 1993
41. Hutchison — June 14, 1993

** Thurmond began his Senate service Nov. 7, 1956, as a Democrat. He became a Republican on Sept. 16, 1964. The Republican Conference allowed his seniority to count from his 1956 election to the Senate.*

House

House rank generally is determined according to the official date of the beginning of a member's service, except in the case of members elected to fill vacancies, in which instance the date of election determines rank.

When members enter the House on the same day, those with prior House experience take precedence, starting with those with the longest consecutive service. Experience as a senator or governor is disregarded. Prior experience is given where applicable to seniority ranking. The dates after members' names refer to the beginning of their present service.

Democrats

1. Whitten (Miss.) — Nov. 4, 1941
2. Brooks (Texas) — Jan. 3, 1953
3. Natcher (Ky.) — Aug. 1, 1953
4. Dingell (Mich.) — Dec. 13, 1955
5. Rostenkowski (Ill.) — Jan. 7, 1959
   Smith (Iowa) — Jan. 7, 1959
7. Gonzalez (Texas) — Nov. 4, 1961
8. Edwards (Calif.) — Jan. 9, 1963
   Gibbons (Fla.) — Jan. 9, 1963
10. Pickle (Texas) — Dec. 21, 1963
11. Yates (Ill.) (seven terms previously) — Jan. 4, 1965
12. Conyers (Mich.) — Jan. 4, 1965
   de la Garza (Texas) — Jan. 4, 1965
   Foley (Wash.) — Jan. 4, 1965
   Ford (Mich.) — Jan. 4, 1965
   Hamilton (Ind.) — Jan. 4, 1965
17. Bevill (Ala.) — Jan. 10, 1967
   Montgomery (Miss.) — Jan. 10, 1967
19. Clay (Mo.) — Jan. 3, 1969
   Stokes (Ohio) — Jan. 3, 1969
21. Obey (Wis.) — April 1, 1969
22. Dellums (Calif.) — Jan. 21, 1971
   Mazzoli (Ky.) — Jan. 21, 1971
   Rangel (N.Y.) — Jan. 21, 1971
25. Brown (Calif.) (four terms previously) — Jan. 3, 1973
26. Moakley (Mass.) — Jan. 3, 1973
   Rose (N.C.) — Jan. 3, 1973
   Schroeder (Colo.) — Jan. 3, 1973
   Stark (Calif.) — Jan. 3, 1973
   Studds (Mass.) — Jan. 3, 1973
   Wilson (Texas) — Jan. 3, 1973
32. Collins (Ill.) — June 5, 1973
33. Murtha (Pa.) — Feb. 5, 1974
34. Jacobs (Ind.) (four terms previously) — Jan. 14, 1975
35. Derrick (S.C.) — Jan. 14, 1975
   English (Okla.) — Jan. 14, 1975
   Ford (Tenn.) — Jan. 14, 1975
   Hefner (N.C.) — Jan. 14, 1975
   Hughes (N.J.) — Jan. 14, 1975
   LaFalce (N.Y.) — Jan. 14, 1975
   Lloyd (Tenn.) — Jan. 14, 1975
   Miller (Calif.) — Jan. 14, 1975
   Mineta (Calif.) — Jan. 14, 1975
   Neal (N.C.) — Jan. 14, 1975
   Oberstar (Minn.) — Jan. 14, 1975
   Sharp (Ind.) — Jan. 14, 1975
   Waxman (Calif.) — Jan. 14, 1975
48. Markey (Mass.) — Nov. 2, 1976
49. Applegate (Ohio) — Jan. 4, 1977
   Beilenson (Calif.) — Jan. 4, 1977
   Bonior (Mich.) — Jan. 4, 1977
   Dicks (Wash.) — Jan. 4, 1977
   Gephardt (Mo.) — Jan. 4, 1977
   Glickman (Kan.) — Jan. 4, 1977
   Kildee (Mich.) — Jan. 4, 1977
   Murphy (Pa.) — Jan. 4, 1977
   Rahall (W.Va.) — Jan. 4, 1977
   Skelton (Mo.) — Jan. 4, 1977
   Vento (Minn.) — Jan. 4, 1977
   Volkmer (Mo.) — Jan. 4, 1977
61. Dixon (Calif.) — Jan. 15, 1979
   Fazio (Calif.) — Jan. 15, 1979
   Frost (Texas) — Jan. 15, 1979
   Hall (Ohio) — Jan. 15, 1979
   Hutto (Fla.) — Jan. 15, 1979
   Matsui (Calif.) — Jan. 15, 1979
   Sabo (Minn.) — Jan. 15, 1979
   Stenholm (Texas) — Jan. 15, 1979

Swift (Wash.) — Jan. 15, 1979
Synar (Okla.) — Jan. 15, 1979
Williams (Mont.) — Jan. 15, 1979
72. Tauzin (La.) — May 17, 1980
73. Coyne (Pa.) — Jan. 5, 1981
Foglietta (Pa.) — Jan. 5, 1981
Frank (Mass.) — Jan. 5, 1981
Gejdenson (Conn.) — Jan. 5, 1981
Hall (Texas) — Jan. 5, 1981
Lantos (Calif.) — Jan. 5, 1981
McCurdy (Okla.) — Jan. 5, 1981
Schumer (N.Y.) — Jan. 5, 1981
Wyden (Ore.) — Jan. 5, 1981
82. Hoyer (Md.) — May 19, 1981
83. Kennelly (Conn.) — Jan. 12, 1982
84. Martinez (Calif.) — July 13, 1982
85. Carr (Mich.) (three terms previously) — Jan. 3,1983
86. Andrews (Texas) — Jan. 3, 1983
Berman (Calif.) — Jan. 3, 1983
Borski (Pa.) — Jan. 3, 1983
Boucher (Va.) — Jan. 3, 1983
Bryant (Texas)— Jan. 3, 1983
Coleman (Texas) — Jan. 3, 1983
Cooper (Tenn.) — Jan. 3, 1983
Durbin (Ill.) — Jan. 3, 1983
Evans (Ill.) — Jan. 3, 1983
Kaptur (Ohio) — Jan. 3, 1983
Lehman (Calif.) — Jan. 3, 1983
Levin (Mich.) — Jan. 3, 1983
Lipinski (Ill.) — Jan. 3, 1983
McCloskey (Ind.) — Jan. 3, 1983
Mollohan (W.Va.) — Jan. 3, 1983
Ortiz (Texas) — Jan. 3, 1983
Owens (N.Y.) — Jan. 3, 1983
Penny (Minn.) — Jan. 3, 1983
Richardson (N.M.) — Jan. 3, 1983
Rowland (Ga.) — Jan. 3, 1983
Sisisky (Va.) — Jan. 3, 1983
Slattery (Kan.) — Jan. 3, 1983
Spratt (S.C.) — Jan. 3, 1983
Torres (Calif.) — Jan. 3, 1983
Torricelli (N.J.) — Jan. 3, 1983
Towns (N.Y.) — Jan. 3, 1983
Valentine (N.C.) — Jan. 3, 1983
Wheat (Mo.) — Jan. 3, 1983
Wise (W.Va.) — Jan. 3, 1983
115. Ackerman (N.Y.) — March 1, 1983
116. Darden (Ga.) — Nov. 8, 1983
117. Kleczka (Wis.) — April 3, 1984
118. Gordon (Tenn.) — Jan. 3, 1985
Kanjorski (Pa.) — Jan. 3, 1985
Manton (N.Y.) — Jan. 3, 1985
Traficant (Ohio) — Jan. 3, 1985
Visclosky (Ind.) — Jan. 3, 1985
123. Chapman (Texas) — Aug. 3, 1985
124. Bilbray (Nev.) — Jan. 6, 1987
Cardin (Md.) — Jan. 6, 1987
DeFazio (Ore.) — Jan. 6, 1987
Flake (N.Y.) — Jan. 6, 1987
Hayes (La.) — Jan. 6, 1987
Hochbrueckner (N.Y.) — Jan. 6, 1987
Johnson (S.D.) — Jan. 6, 1987
Kennedy (Mass.) — Jan. 6, 1987
Lancaster (N.C.) — Jan. 6, 1987
Lewis (Ga.) — Jan. 6, 1987
Mfume (Md.) — Jan. 6, 1987
Pickett (Va.) — Jan. 6, 1987
Price (N.C.) — Jan. 6, 1987
Sawyer (Ohio) — Jan. 6, 1987
Skaggs (Colo.) — Jan. 6, 1987
Slaughter (N.Y.) — Jan. 6, 1987
140. Pelosi (Calif.) — June 2, 1987
141. Clement (Tenn.) — Jan. 19, 1988
142. Payne (Va.) — June 14, 1988
143. Costello (Ill.) — Aug. 9, 1988
144. Pallone (N.J.) — Nov. 8, 1988
145. Engel (N.Y.)— Jan. 3, 1989
Hoagland (Neb.) — Jan. 3, 1989
Johnston (Fla.) — Jan. 3, 1989
Laughlin (Texas) — Jan. 3, 1989
Lowey (N.Y.) — Jan. 3, 1989
McDermott (Wash.) — Jan. 3, 1989
McNulty (N.Y.) — Jan. 3, 1989
Neal (Mass.) — Jan. 3, 1989
Parker (Miss.) — Jan. 3, 1989
Payne (N.J.) — Jan. 3, 1989
Poshard (Ill.) — Jan. 3, 1989
Sangmeister (Ill.) — Jan. 3, 1989
Sarpalius (Texas) — Jan. 3, 1989
Tanner (Tenn.) — Jan. 3, 1989
Unsoeld (Wash.) — Jan. 3, 1989
160. Long (Ind.) — March 28, 1989
161. Browder (Ala.) — April 4, 1989
162. Condit (Calif.) — Sept. 12, 1989
Geren (Texas) — Sept. 12, 1989
164. Taylor (Miss.) — Oct. 17, 1989
165. Washington (Texas) — Dec. 9, 1989
166. Serrano (N.Y.) — March 20, 1990
167. Mink (Hawaii) — Sept. 22, 1990
168. Andrews (N.J.) — Nov. 6, 1990
169. Thornton (Ark.) (three terms previously) — Jan. 3, 1991
170. Abercrombie (Hawaii) (one term previously) — Jan. 3, 1991
171. Andrews (Maine) — Jan. 3, 1991
Bacchus (Fla.) — Jan. 3, 1991
Brewster (Okla.) — Jan. 3, 1991
Collins (Mich.) — Jan. 3, 1991
Cramer (Ala.) — Jan. 3, 1991
DeLauro (Conn.) — Jan. 3, 1991
Dooley (Calif.) — Jan. 3, 1991
Edwards (Texas) — Jan. 3, 1991
Jefferson (La.) — Jan. 3, 1991
Kopetski (Ore.) — Jan. 3, 1991
LaRocco (Idaho) — Jan. 3, 1991
Moran (Va.) — Jan. 3, 1991
Orton (Utah) — Jan. 3, 1991
Peterson (Minn.) — Jan. 3, 1991
Peterson (Fla.) — Jan. 3, 1991
Reed (R.I.) — Jan. 3, 1991
Roemer (Ind.) — Jan. 3, 1991
Swett (N.H.) — Jan. 3, 1991
Waters (Calif.) — Jan. 3, 1991
190. Olver (Mass.) — June 4, 1991
191. Pastor (Ariz.) — Sept. 24, 1991
192. Blackwell (Pa.) — Nov. 5, 1991
193. Clayton (N.C.) — Nov. 3, 1992

Nadler (N.Y.) — Nov. 3, 1992
195. Baesler (Ky.) — Jan. 5, 1993
Barcia (Mich.) — Jan. 5, 1993
Barlow (Ky.) — Jan. 5, 1993
Barrett (Wis.) — Jan. 5, 1993
Becerra (Calif.) — Jan. 5, 1993
Bishop (Ga.) — Jan. 5, 1993
Brown (Fla.) — Jan. 5, 1993
Brown (Ohio) — Jan. 5, 1993
Byrne (Va.) — Jan. 5, 1993
Cantwell (Wash.) — Jan. 5, 1993
Clyburn (S.C.) — Jan. 5, 1993
Coppersmith (Ariz.) — Jan. 5, 1993
Danner (Mo.) — Jan. 5, 1993
Deal (Ga.) — Jan. 5, 1993
Deutsch (Fla.) — Jan. 5, 1993
English (Ariz.) — Jan. 5, 1993
Eshoo (Calif.) — Jan. 5, 1993
Fields (La.) — Jan. 5, 1993
Filner (Calif.) — Jan. 5, 1993
Fingerhut (Ohio) — Jan. 5, 1993
Furse (Ore.) — Jan. 5, 1993
Green (Texas) — Jan. 5, 1993
Gutierrez (Ill.) — Jan. 5, 1993
Hamburg (Calif.) — Jan. 5, 1993
Harman (Calif.) — Jan. 5, 1993
Hastings (Fla.) — Jan. 5, 1993
Hilliard (Ala.) — Jan. 5, 1993
Hinchey (N.Y.) — Jan. 5, 1993
Holden (Pa.) — Jan. 5, 1993
Inslee (Wash.) — Jan. 5, 1993
Johnson (Ga.) — Jan. 5, 1993
Johnson (Texas) — Jan. 5, 1993
Klein (N.J.) — Jan. 5, 1993
Klink (Pa.) — Jan. 5, 1993
Kreidler (Wash.) — Jan. 5, 1993
Lambert (Ark.) — Jan. 5, 1993
Maloney (N.Y.) — Jan. 5, 1993
Mann (Ohio) — Jan. 5, 1993
Margolies-Mezvinsky (Pa.) — Jan. 5, 1993
McHale (Pa.) — Jan. 5, 1993
McKinney (Ga.) — Jan. 5, 1993
Meehan (Mass.) — Jan. 5, 1993
Meek (Fla.) — Jan. 5, 1993
Menendez (N.J.) — Jan. 5, 1993
Minge (Minn.) — Jan. 5, 1993
Pomeroy (N.D.) — Jan. 5, 1993
Reynolds (Ill.) — Jan. 5, 1993
Roybal-Allard (Calif.) — Jan. 5, 1993
Rush (Ill.) — Jan. 5, 1993
Schenk (Calif.) — Jan. 5, 1993
Scott (Va.) — Jan. 5, 1993
Shepherd (Utah) — Jan. 5, 1993
Strickland (Ohio) — Jan. 5, 1993
Stupak (Mich.) — Jan. 5, 1993
Tejeda (Texas) — Jan. 5, 1993
Thurman (Fla.) — Jan. 5, 1993
Tucker (Calif.) — Jan. 5, 1993
Velázquez (N.Y.) — Jan. 5, 1993
Watt (N.C.) — Jan. 5, 1993
Woolsey (Calif.) — Jan. 5, 1993
Wynn (Md.) — Jan. 5, 1993
256. Thompson (Miss.) — April 14, 1993
257. Barca (Wis.) — May 8, 1993
258. Farr (Calif.) — June 16, 1993

Republicans

1. Michel (Ill.) — Jan. 3, 1957
2. McDade (Pa.) — Jan. 9, 1963
Quillen (Tenn.) — Jan. 9, 1963
4. Myers (Ind.) — Jan. 10, 1967
5. Fish (N.Y.) — Jan. 3, 1969
6. Crane (Ill.) — Nov. 25, 1969
7. Archer (Texas) — Jan. 21, 1971
Spence (S.C.) — Jan. 21, 1971
Young (Fla.) — Jan. 21, 1971
10. Gilman (N.Y.) — Jan. 3, 1973
Moorhead (Calif.) — Jan. 3, 1973
Regula (Ohio) — Jan. 3, 1973
Shuster (Pa.) — Jan. 3, 1973
14. Young (Alaska) — March 6, 1973
15. Goodling (Pa.) — Jan. 14, 1975
Hyde (Ill.) — Jan. 14, 1975
17. Leach (Iowa) — Jan. 4, 1977
Stump (Ariz.) — Jan. 4, 1977 *
Walker (Pa.) — Jan. 4, 1977
20. Livingston (La.) — Aug. 27, 1977
21. Bereuter (Neb.) — Jan. 15, 1979
Clinger (Pa.) — Jan. 15, 1979
Gingrich (Ga.) — Jan. 15, 1979
Lewis (Calif.) — Jan. 15, 1979
Roth (Wis.) — Jan. 15, 1979
Sensenbrenner (Wis.) — Jan. 15, 1979
Snowe (Maine) — Jan. 15, 1979
Solomon (N.Y.) — Jan. 15, 1979
Thomas (Calif.) — Jan. 15, 1979
30. Petri (Wis.) — April 3, 1979
31. Porter (Ill.) — Jan. 22, 1980
32. Bliley (Va.) — Jan. 5, 1981
Dreier (Calif.) — Jan. 5, 1981
Emerson (Mo.) — Jan. 5, 1981
Fields (Texas) — Jan. 5, 1981
Gunderson (Wis.) — Jan. 5, 1981
Hansen (Utah) — Jan. 5, 1981
Hunter (Calif.) — Jan. 5, 1981
McCollum (Fla.) — Jan. 5, 1981
Roberts (Kan.) — Jan. 5, 1981
Rogers (Ky.) — Jan. 5, 1981
Roukema (N.J.) — Jan. 5, 1981
Shaw (Fla.) — Jan. 5, 1981
Skeen (N.M.) — Jan. 5, 1981
Smith (N.J.) — Jan. 5, 1981
Wolf (Va.) — Jan. 5, 1981
47. Oxley (Ohio) — June 25, 1981
48. Bateman (Va.) — Jan. 3, 1983
Bilirakis (Fla.) — Jan. 3, 1983
Boehlert (N.Y.) — Jan. 3, 1983
Burton (Ind.) — Jan. 3, 1983
Gekas (Pa.) — Jan. 3, 1983
Johnson (Conn.) — Jan. 3, 1983
Kasich (Ohio) — Jan. 3, 1983
Lewis (Fla.) — Jan. 3, 1983
McCandless (Calif.) — Jan. 3, 1983
Packard (Calif.) — Jan. 3, 1983
Ridge (Pa.) — Jan. 3, 1983
Smith (Ore.) — Jan. 3, 1983

Sundquist (Tenn.) — Jan. 3, 1983
Vucanovich (Nev.) — Jan. 3, 1983
62. Schaefer (Colo.) — March 29, 1983
63. Saxton (N.J.) — Nov. 6, 1984
64. Dornan (Calif.) (three terms previously) — Jan. 3, 1985
65. Armey (Texas) — Jan. 3, 1985
Barton (Texas) — Jan. 3, 1985
Bentley (Md.) — Jan. 3, 1985
Callahan (Ala.) — Jan. 3, 1985
Coble (N.C.) — Jan. 3, 1985
Combest (Texas) — Jan. 3, 1985
DeLay (Texas) — Jan. 3, 1985
Fawell (Ill.) — Jan. 3, 1985
Gallo (N.J.) — Jan. 3, 1985
Henry (Mich.) — Jan. 3, 1985
Kolbe (Ariz.) — Jan. 3, 1985
Lightfoot (Iowa) — Jan. 3, 1985
McMillan (N.C.) — Jan. 3, 1985
Meyers (Kan.) — Jan. 3, 1985
79. Ballenger (N.C.) — Nov. 4, 1986
80. Baker (La.) — Jan. 6, 1987
Bunning (Ky.) — Jan. 6, 1987
Gallegly (Calif.) — Jan. 6, 1987
Grandy (Iowa) — Jan. 6, 1987
Hastert (Ill.) — Jan. 6, 1987
Hefley (Colo.) — Jan. 6, 1987
Herger (Calif.) — Jan. 6, 1987
Houghton (N.Y.) — Jan. 6, 1987
Inhofe (Okla.) — Jan. 6, 1987
Kyl (Ariz.) — Jan. 6, 1987
Morella (Md.) — Jan. 6, 1987
Ravenel (S.C.) — Jan. 6, 1987
Smith (Texas) — Jan. 6, 1987
Upton (Mich.) — Jan. 6, 1987
Weldon (Pa.) — Jan. 6, 1987
95. Shays (Conn.) — Aug. 18, 1987
96. McCrery (La.) — April 16, 1988
97. Duncan (Tenn.) — Nov. 8, 1988
98. Cox (Calif.) — Jan. 3, 1989
Gillmor (Ohio) — Jan. 3, 1989
Goss (Fla.) — Jan. 3, 1989
Hancock (Mo.) — Jan. 3, 1989
Machtley (R.I.) — Jan. 3, 1989
Paxon (N.Y.) — Jan. 3, 1989
Rohrabacher (Calif.) — Jan. 3, 1989
Schiff (N.M.) — Jan. 3, 1989
Stearns (Fla.) — Jan. 3, 1989
Walsh (N.Y.) — Jan. 3, 1989
108. Thomas (Wyo.) — April 25, 1989
109. Ros-Lehtinen (Fla.) — Aug. 29, 1989
110. Molinari (N.Y.) — March 20, 1990
111. Allard (Colo.) — Jan. 3, 1991
Barrett (Neb.) — Jan. 3, 1991
Boehner (Ohio) — Jan. 3, 1991
Camp (Mich.) — Jan. 3, 1991
Cunningham (Calif.) — Jan. 3, 1991
Doolittle (Calif.) — Jan. 3, 1991
Franks (Conn.) — Jan. 3, 1991
Gilchrest (Md.) — Jan. 3, 1991
Hobson (Ohio) — Jan. 3, 1991
Klug (Wis.) — Jan. 3, 1991
Nussle (Iowa) — Jan. 3, 1991
Ramstad (Minn.) — Jan. 3, 1991
Santorum (Pa.) — Jan. 3, 1991
Taylor (N.C.) — Jan. 3, 1991
Zeliff (N.H.) — Jan. 3, 1991
Zimmer (N.J.) — Jan. 3, 1991
127. Johnson (Texas) — May 18, 1991
128. Ewing (Ill.) — July 2, 1991
129. Bachus (Ala.) — Jan. 5, 1993
Baker (Calif.) — Jan. 5, 1993
Bartlett (Md.) — Jan. 5, 1993
Blute (Mass.) — Jan. 5, 1993
Bonilla (Texas) — Jan. 5, 1993
Buyer (Ind.) — Jan. 5, 1993
Calvert (Calif.) — Jan. 5, 1993
Canady (Fla.) — Jan. 5, 1993
Castle (Del.) — Jan. 5, 1993
Collins (Ga.) — Jan. 5, 1993
Crapo (Idaho) — Jan. 5, 1993
Diaz-Balart (Fla.) — Jan. 5, 1993
Dickey (Ark.) — Jan. 5, 1993
Dunn (Wash.) — Jan. 5, 1993
Everett (Ala.) — Jan. 5, 1993
Fowler (Fla.) — Jan. 5, 1993
Franks (N.J.) — Jan. 5, 1993
Goodlatte (Va.) — Jan. 5, 1993
Grams (Minn.) — Jan. 5, 1993
Greenwood (Pa.) — Jan. 5, 1993
Hoekstra (Mich.) — Jan. 5, 1993
Hoke (Ohio) — Jan. 5, 1993
Horn (Calif.) — Jan. 5, 1993
Huffington (Calif.) — Jan. 5, 1993
Hutchinson (Ark.) — Jan. 5, 1993
Inglis (S.C.) — Jan. 5, 1993
Istook (Okla.) — Jan. 5, 1993
Kim (Calif.) — Jan. 5, 1993
King (N.Y.) — Jan. 5, 1993
Kingston (Ga.) — Jan. 5, 1993
Knollenberg (Mich.) — Jan. 5, 1993
Lazio (N.Y.) — Jan. 5, 1993
Levy (N.Y.) — Jan. 5, 1993
Linder (Ga.) — Jan. 5, 1993
Manzullo (Ill.) — Jan. 5, 1993
McHugh (N.Y.) — Jan. 5, 1993
McInnis (Colo.) — Jan. 5, 1993
McKeon (Calif.) — Jan. 5, 1993
Mica (Fla.) — Jan. 5, 1993
Miller (Fla.) — Jan. 5, 1993
Pombo (Calif.) — Jan. 5, 1993
Pryce (Ohio) — Jan. 5, 1993
Quinn (N.Y.) — Jan. 5, 1993
Royce (Calif.) — Jan. 5, 1993
Smith (Mich.) — Jan. 5, 1993
Talent (Mo.) — Jan. 5, 1993
Torkildsen (Mass.) — Jan. 5, 1993
176. Portman (Ohio) — May 5, 1993

** Stump began House service Jan. 4, 1977, as a Democrat, but later switched parties. The Republican Conference let his seniority count from 1977.*

Pronunciation Guide for Congress

The following is an informal pronunciation guide for some of the most-often-mispronounced names of members of Congress:

SENATE

Alfonse M. D'Amato, R-N.Y. — da-MAH-toe
Dennis DeConcini, D-Ariz. — dee-con-SEE-nee
Pete V. Domenici, R-N.M. — da-MEN-ih-chee
Lauch Faircloth, R-N.C. — LOCK
Dianne Feinstein, D-Calif. — FINE-stine
Daniel K. Inouye, D-Hawaii — in-NO-ay

HOUSE

Jim Bacchus, D-Fla. — BACK-us
Spencer Bachus, R-Ala. — BACK-us
Scotty Baesler, D-Ky. — BAA-zler
James A. Barcia, D-Mich. — BAR-sha
Xavier Becerra, D-Calif. — HAH-vee-air beh-SEH-ra
Anthony C. Beilenson, D-Calif. — BEE-lin-son
Doug Bereuter, R-Neb. — BEE-right-er
Michael Bilirakis, R-Fla. — bil-li-RACK-us
John A. Boehner, R-Ohio — BAY-ner
Henry Bonilla, R-Texas — bo-NEE-uh
David E. Bonior, D-Mich. — BON-yer
Rick Boucher, D-Va. — BOUGH-cher
Steve Buyer, R-Ind. — BOO-yer
Charles T. Canady, R-Fla. — CAN-uh-dee
Michael D. Crapo, R-Idaho — CRAY-poe
Peter A. DeFazio, D-Ore. — da-FAH-zee-o
Peter Deutsch, D-Fla. — DOYCH
Lincoln Diaz-Balart, R-Fla. — DEE-az BAA-lart
Eni F. H. Faleomavaega, D-Am. Samoa — EN-ee FOL-ee-oh-mav-ah-ENG-uh
Harris W. Fawell, R-Ill. — FAY-well
Vic Fazio, D-Calif. — FAY-zee-o
Thomas M. Foglietta, D-Pa. — fo-lee-ET-uh
Elton Gallegly, R-Calif. — GAL-uh-glee
Sam Gejdenson, D-Conn. — GAY-den-son
Robert W. Goodlatte, R-Va. — GOOD-lat
Luis V. Gutierrez, D-Ill. — loo-EES goo-tee-AIR-ez
George J. Hochbrueckner, D-N.Y. — HOCK-brewk-ner
Peter Hoekstra, R-Mich. — HOKE-struh
Amo Houghton, R-N.Y. — HO-tun
James M. Inhofe, R-Okla. — IN-hoff
John R. Kasich, R-Ohio — KAY-sick
Gerald D. Kleczka, D-Wis. — KLETCH-kuh
Scott L. Klug, R-Wis. — KLOOG
Jim Kolbe, R-Ariz. — COLE-bee
Mike Kopetski, D-Ore. — ka-PET-skee
Greg Laughlin, D-Texas — LAWF-lin
Rick A. Lazio, R-N.Y. — LAZZ-ee-o
Richard H. Lehman, D-Calif. — LEE-mun
Nita M. Lowey, D-N.Y. — LOW-e
Ronald K. Machtley, R-R.I. — MAKE-lee
Donald Manzullo, R-Ill. — man-ZOO-low
Marjorie Margolies-Mezvinsky, D-Pa. — mar-GO-lees mez-VIN-skee
Kweisi Mfume, D-Md. — kwy-EE-say mm-FU-may
David Minge, D-Minn. — MIN-gee
David R. Obey, D-Wis. — O-bee
Frank Pallone Jr., D-N.J. — pa-LOAN
Ed Pastor, D-Ariz.— pas-TORE
Nancy Pelosi, D-Calif. — pa-LOH-see
Tom Petri, R-Wis. — PEE-try
Glenn Poshard, D-Ill. — pa-SHARD
Arthur Ravenel Jr., R-S.C. — RAV-nel
Ralph Regula, R-Ohio — REG-you-luh
Dana Rohrabacher, R-Calif. — ROAR-ah-BAH-ker
Ileana Ros-Lehtinen, R-Fla. — il-ee-AH-na ross-LAY-tin-nen
Marge Roukema, R-N.J. — ROCK-ah-muh
Bill Sarpalius, D-Texas — sar-PAUL-us
José E. Serrano, D-N.Y. — ho-ZAY sa-RAH-no (rolled 'R')
Bart Stupak, D-Mich. — STEW-pack
W. J. "Billy" Tauzin, D-La. — TOE-zan
Frank Tejeda, D-Texas — tuh-HAY-duh
Robert G. Torricelli, D-N.J. — tor-uh-SELL-ee
Jolene Unsoeld, D-Wash. — UN-sold
Nydia M. Velázquez, D-N.Y. — NID-ee-uh veh-LASS-kez
Barbara F. Vucanovich, R-Nev. — voo-CAN-oh-vitch
Bill Zeliff, R-N.H. — ZELL-iff

Close Calls in 1992 Election Cycle

There was a marked upsurge in competitive House elections in 1992. 112 members (61 Democrats, 51 Republicans) won seats with no more than 55 percent of the vote. And 56 of the "marginal" victors were incumbents, up from 35 in 1990.

In the chart below, House incumbents are designated by the letter "I," with the year they were first elected in parentheses. Those who won as challengers are designated by the letter "C." Open-seat winners are designated with an "O."

The numbers at right are their percentage shares of the 1992 vote, based on returns from state election agencies. They are based on total votes cast (not just major-party votes.)

DEMOCRATS

Richard H. Lehman (Calif. 19)	I ('82)	46.9
Herb Klein (N.J. 8)	O	47.0
Bob Carr (Mich. 8)	I ('74)	47.6
Dan Hamburg (Calif. 1)	C	47.6
Harold L. Volkmer (Mo. 9)	I ('76)	47.7
David Minge (Minn. 2)	O	47.8
Jane Harman (Calif. 36)	O	48.4
Carlos Romero-Barceló (PR AL)	C	48.4
Marilyn Lloyd (Tenn. 3)	I ('74)	48.8
Karen L. Thurman (Fla. 5)	O	49.2
Leslie L. Byrne (Va. 11)	O	50.0
Marjorie Margolies-Mezvinsky (Pa. 13)	O	50.3
Carolyn B. Maloney (N.Y. 14)	C	50.4
Maurice D. Hinchey (N.Y. 26)	O	50.4
Collin C. Peterson (Minn. 7)	I ('90)	50.4
Pat Williams (Mont. AL)	I ('78)	50.5
Karen Shepherd (Utah 2)	O	50.5
George E. Brown Jr. (Calif. 42)	I ('62)	50.7
Jim Bacchus (Fla. 15)	I ('90)	50.7
Ted Strickland (Ohio 6)	C	50.7
Austin J. Murphy (Pa. 20)	I ('76)	50.7
Sam Gejdenson (Conn. 2)	I ('80)	50.8
Jay Inslee (Wash. 4)	O	50.8
Lynn Schenk (Calif. 49)	O	51.1
Vic Fazio (Calif. 3)	I ('78)	51.2
Peter Hoagland (Neb. 2)	I ('88)	51.2
David Mann (Ohio 1)	O	51.3
Sam Coppersmith (Ariz. 1)	C	51.3
John W. Olver (Mass. 1)	I ('91)	51.5
Dan Glickman (Kan. 4)	I ('76)	51.7
George J. Hochbrueckner (N.Y. 1)	I ('86)	51.7
Ronald D. Coleman (Texas 16)	I ('82)	51.9
William D. Ford (Mich. 13)	I ('64)	51.9
Elizabeth Furse (Ore. 1)	O	52.0
Earl Hutto (Fla. 1)	I ('78)	52.0
Al Swift (Wash. 2)	I ('78)	52.1
Tim Holden (Pa. 6)	O	52.1
Mike Kreidler (Wash. 9)	O	52.1
Martin T. Meehan (Mass. 5)	C	52.2
Paul McHale (Pa. 15)	C	52.2
Frank Pallone Jr. (N.J. 6)	I ('88)	52.3
Gary L. Ackerman (N.Y. 5)	I ('83)	52.4
Frank McCloskey (Ind. 8)	I ('82)	52.5
Sander M. Levin (Mich. 12)	I ('82)	52.6
Eric D. Fingerhut (Ohio 19)	O	52.6
Stephen L. Neal (N.C. 5)	I ('74)	52.7
Romano L. Mazzoli (Ky. 3)	I ('70)	52.7
Sam M. Gibbons (Fla. 11)	I ('62)	52.8
Steny H. Hoyer (Md. 5)	I ('81)	53.0
Karan English (Ariz. 6)	O	53.0
Richard E. Neal (Mass. 2)	I ('88)	53.1
David E. Bonior (Mich. 10)	I ('76)	53.1
Sherrod Brown (Ohio 13)	O	53.3
Jack Brooks (Texas 9)	I ('52)	53.6
Dale E. Kildee (Mich. 9)	I ('76)	53.7
Tim Valentine (N.C. 2)	I ('82)	53.7
Don Johnson (Ga. 10)	O	53.8
Bart Stupak (Mich. 1)	O	53.9
H. Martin Lancaster (N.C. 3)	I ('86)	54.4
John J. LaFalce (N.Y. 29)	I ('74)	54.5
Maria Cantwell (Wash. 1)	O	54.9

REPUBLICANS

Gary A. Franks (Conn. 5)	I ('90)	43.7
Deborah Pryce (Ohio 15)	O	44.1
Rod Grams (Minn. 6)	C	44.4
Bill Goodling (Pa. 19)	I ('74)	45.3
Ken Calvert (Calif. 43)	O	46.7
Don Young (Alaska AL)	I ('73)	46.8
Richard W. Pombo (Calif. 11)	O	47.6
Barbara F. Vucanovich (Nev. 2)	I ('82)	47.9
Steve Horn (Calif. 38)	O	48.6
Jim Ross Lightfoot (Iowa 3)	I ('84)	48.9
Olympia J. Snowe (Maine 2)	I ('78)	49.1
Terry Everett (Ala. 2)	O	49.5
Peter T. King (N.Y. 3)	O	49.6
Carlos J. Moorhead (Calif. 27)	I ('72)	49.7
John T. Doolittle (Calif. 4)	I ('90)	49.8
David A. Levy (N.Y. 4)	O	50.2
Tim Hutchinson (Ark. 3)	O	50.2
Jim Nussle (Iowa 2)	I ('90)	50.2
Robert K. Dornan (Calif. 46)	I ('76)	50.2
Bob Inglis (S.C. 4)	C	50.3
Peter I. Blute (Mass. 3)	C	50.4
James M. Talent (Mo. 2)	C	50.4
John Linder (Ga. 4)	O	50.5
Richard H. Baker (La. 6)	I ('86)	50.6
Steve Buyer (Ind. 5)	C	51.0
Wayne T. Gilchrest (Md. 1)	I ('90)	51.6
Jack Quinn (N.Y. 30)	O	51.7
James C. Greenwood (Pa. 8)	C	51.9
Howard P. "Buck" McKeon (Calif. 25)	O	51.9
Bill Baker (Calif. 10)	O	52.0
E. Clay Shaw Jr. (Fla. 22)	I ('80)	52.0
Charles T. Canady (Fla. 12)	O	52.1
Spencer Bachus (Ala. 6)	C	52.3
Jay Dickey (Ark. 4)	O	52.3
Michael Huffington (Calif. 22)	C	52.5
James M. Inhofe (Okla. 1)	I ('86)	52.8
Duncan Hunter (Calif. 52)	I ('80)	52.9
Tom Petri (Wis. 6)	I ('79)	52.9
Bill Zeliff (N.H. 1)	I ('90)	53.1
Rick A. Lazio (N.Y. 2)	C	53.2
Bob Franks (N.J. 7)	O	53.3
Ernest Jim Istook Jr. (Okla. 5)	C	53.4
Roscoe G. Bartlett (Md. 6)	C	54.2
Al McCandless (Calif. 44)	I ('82)	54.2
Elton Gallegly (Calif. 23)	I ('86)	54.3
Dana Rohrabacher (Calif. 45)	I ('88)	54.5
Harold Rogers (Ky. 5)	I ('80)	54.6
Charles H. Taylor (N.C. 11)	I ('90)	54.7
Scott McInnis (Colo. 03)	O	54.7
Mac Collins (Ga. 3)	C	54.8
Peter G. Torkildsen (Mass. 6)	C	54.8

Index

H

I, J

K

L

M

N

O

P

Q, R

S

T

U, V

W

X, Y, Z

Reapportionment for the 1990s

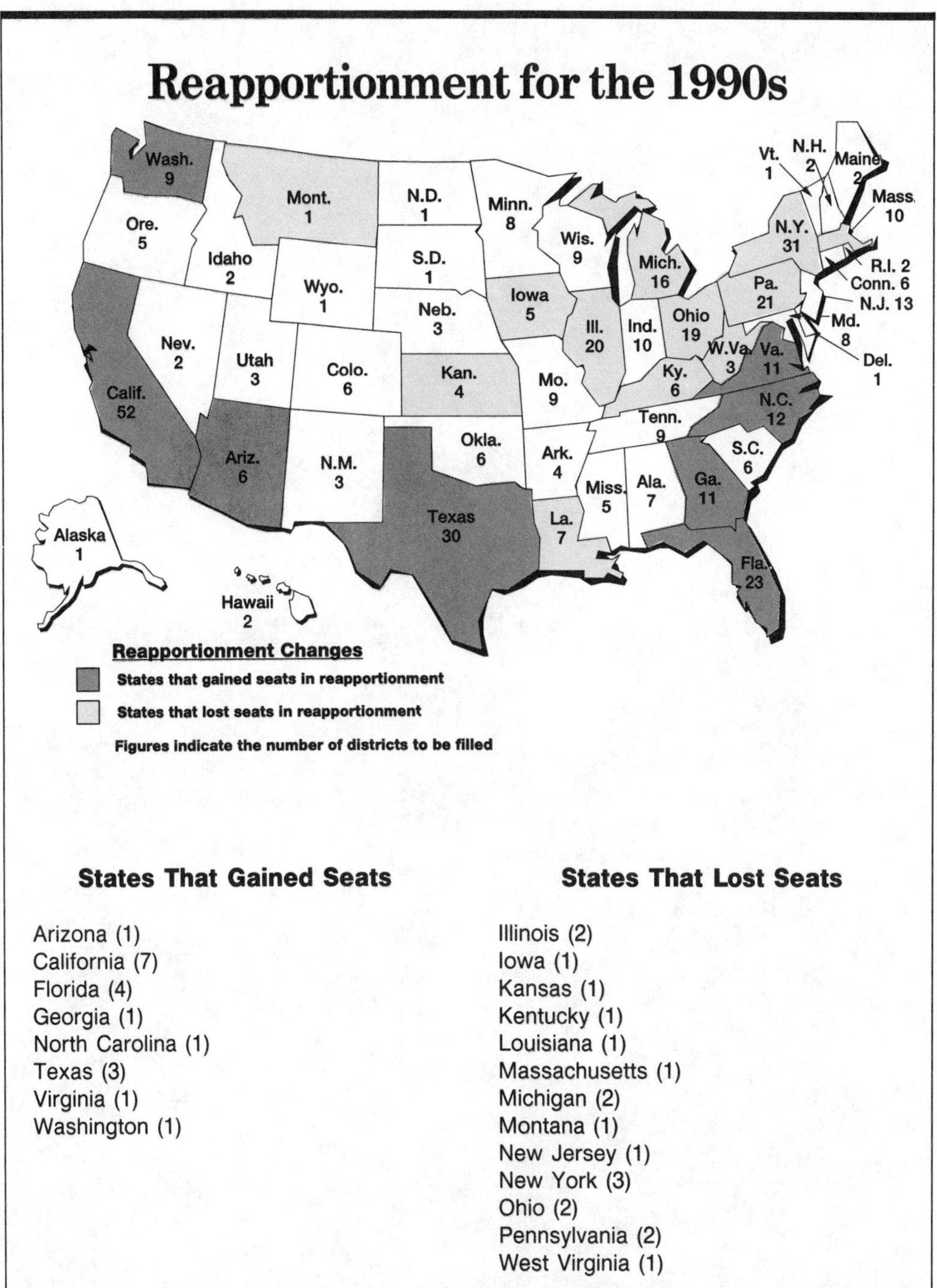

States That Gained Seats

Arizona (1)
California (7)
Florida (4)
Georgia (1)
North Carolina (1)
Texas (3)
Virginia (1)
Washington (1)

States That Lost Seats

Illinois (2)
Iowa (1)
Kansas (1)
Kentucky (1)
Louisiana (1)
Massachusetts (1)
Michigan (2)
Montana (1)
New Jersey (1)
New York (3)
Ohio (2)
Pennsylvania (2)
West Virginia (1)